Literatur(wissenschaft)	*Liter*	literature
Maskulinum	M, *m*	masculine
Mathematik	*Math*	mathematics
Maß(einheit)	*Measure*	
Mechanik	*Mech*	mechanics
Medizin	*Med*	medicine
Meteorologie	*Met*	meteorology
Metallurgie, Hüttenkunde	*Metal*	metallurgy
militärisch	*Mil*	military
Bergbau	*Min*	mining
Mineralogie	*Miner*	mineralogy
Straßenverkehr	*Mot*	motoring and transport
Musik	*Mus*	music
Mythologie	*Myth*	mythology
Substantiv, Hauptwort	N	noun
nautisch	*Naut*	nautical
verneint	*neg*	negative
wird oft als beleidigend empfunden	*neg!*	may be considered offensive
nordenglisch	*N Engl*	Northern English
norddeutsch	*N Ger*	North German
Nationalsozialismus	*NS*	Nazism
Neutrum	NT, *nt*	neuter
Zahlwort	NUM	numeral
Objekt	*obj*	object
obsolet, ausgestorben	*obs*	obsolete
veraltet	*old*	
Optik	*Opt*	optics
Ornithologie, Vogelkunde	*Orn*	ornithology
Parlament	*Parl*	parliament
Passiv	*pass*	passive
pejorativ, abschätzig	*pej*	pejorative
persönlich/Person	*pers*	personal/person
Personalpronomen, persönliches Fürwort	PERS PRON, *pers pron*	personal pronoun
Pharmazie	*Pharm*	pharmacy
Philosophie	*Philos*	philosophy
Phonetik, Phonologie	*Phon*	phonetics
Fotografie	*Phot*	photography
Physik	*Phys*	physics
Physiologie	*Physiol*	physiology
Plural, Mehrzahl	PL, *pl*	plural
poetisch	*poet*	poetic
Dichtung	*Poet*	poetry
Politik	*Pol*	politics
Possessiv-, besitzanzeigend	*poss*	possessive
besitzanzeigendes Adjektiv	POSS ADJ	possessive adjective
Possessivpronomen, besitzanzeigendes Fürwort	POSS PRON, *poss pron*	possessive pronoun
prädikativ	*pred*	predicative
Präfix, Vorsilbe	PREF	prefix
Präposition	PREP, *prep*	preposition
Präpositionsobjekt	PREP OBJ, *prep obj*	prepositional object
Präsens	*pres*	present
Presse	*Press*	
Präteritum, Imperfekt	*pret*	preterite, imperfect
Pronomen, Fürwort	PRON, *pron*	pronoun
sprichwörtlich	*prov*	proverbial
Sprichwort	*Prov*	proverb
Partizip Präsens	PRP, *prp*	present participle
Psychologie	*Psych*	psychology
Partizip Perfekt	PTP, *ptp*	past participle
eingetragene Marke	®	trademark
Rundfunk	*Rad*	radio
Eisenbahn	*Rail*	railways
selten	*rare*	
Reflexivpronomen, rückbezügliches Fürwort	REFL PRON, *refl pron*	reflexive pronoun
regelmäßig	*reg*	regular
Relativ-	*rel*	relative
Religion	*Rel*	religion
Relativpronomen, bezügliches Fürwort	REL PRON, *rel pron*	relative pronoun
jemand(em, -en)	*sb*	somebody
jemand(e)s	*sb's*	somebody's
Schule	*Sch*	school
Naturwissenschaften	*Sci*	science
schottisch	*Scot*	Scottish
Bildhauerei	*Sculpt*	sculpture
trennbar	SEP, *sep*	separable
Handarbeiten	*Sew*	sewing
süddeutsch	*S Ger*	South German
Singular, Einzahl	SING, *sing*	singular
Skisport	*Ski*	skiing
Slang, Jargon	*sl*	slang
Sozialwissenschaften	*Sociol*	social sciences
Raumfahrt	*Space*	space flight
Fachausdruck	*spec*	specialist term
Börse	*St Ex*	Stock Exchange
etwas	*sth*	something
Konjunktiv	*subjunc*	subjunctive
Suffix, Nachsilbe	SUF, *suf*	suffix
Superlativ	*superl*	superlative
Landvermessung	*Surv*	surveying
schweizerisch	*Sw*	Swiss
Technik	*Tech*	technology
Telekommunikation	*Telec*	telecommunications
Textilien	*Tex*	textiles
Theater	*Theat*	theatre, theater
Fernsehen	*TV*	television
Typografie, Buchdruck	*Typ*	typography and printing
Hochschule	*Univ*	university
(nord)amerikanisch	*US*	(North) American
gewöhnlich	*usu*	usually
Verb	VB, *vb*	verb
Tiermedizin	*Vet*	veterinary medicine
intransitives Verb	VI, *vi*	intransitive verb
intransitives und reflexives Verb	VIR, *vir*	intransitive and reflexive verb
reflexives Verb	VR, *vr*	reflexive verb
transitives Verb	VT, *vt*	transitive verb
transitives und intransitives Verb	VTI, *vti*	transitive and intransitive verb
transitives, intransitives und reflexives Verb	VTIR, *vtir*	transitive, intransitive and reflexive verb
transitives und reflexives Verb	VTR, *vtr*	transitive and reflexive verb
vulgär	*vulg*	vulgar
westdeutsch	*W Ger*	West German
Zoologie	*Zool*	zoology

Abkürzungen, Sachbereichs- und Stilangaben

Abbreviations, field labels and style labels

Abkürzung	*abbr*	abbreviation
Akkusativ	*acc*	accusative
Adjektiv	ADJ, *adj*	adjective
attributives Adjektiv, Adjektiv in attributiver Stellung	ADJ ATTR	attributive adjective
prädikatives Adjektiv, Adjektiv in prädikativer Stellung	ADJ PRED	predicative adjective
Verwaltung	*Admin*	administration
Adverb	ADV, *adv*	adverb
Landwirtschaft	*Agr*	agriculture
Anatomie	*Anat*	anatomy
Archäologie	*Archeol*	arch(a)eology
Architektur	*Archit*	architecture
Artikel	*ART, art*	article
Kunst	*Art*	art
Astrologie	*Astrol*	astrology
Astronomie	*Astron*	astronomy
attributiv	ATTR, *attr*	attributive
österreichisch	*Aus*	Austrian
australisch	*Austral*	Australian
Kraftfahrzeuge	*Aut*	automobiles
Hilfsverb	AUX VB, *aux vb*	auxiliary verb
Luftfahrt	*Aviat*	aviation
Kindersprache	*baby-talk*	
biblisch	*Bibl*	biblical
Biologie	*Biol*	biology
Botanik	*Bot*	botany
britisch	*Brit*	British
Hoch- und Tiefbau	*Build*	building
Kartenspiel	*Cards*	
Chemie	*Chem*	chemistry
Schach	*Chess*	
Handel	*Comm*	commerce
Komparativ	*comp*	comparative
Computer	*Comput*	computers
Konjunktion	CONJ, *conj*	conjunction
Zusammenziehung	*contr*	contraction
Kochen	*Cook*	cooking
Kompositum, zusammengesetztes Wort	*cpd*	compound
zusammengesetzte Verben	*cpd vbs*	compound verbs
Dativ	*dat*	dative
altmodisch	*dated*	
Deutsche Demokratische Republik (1949–90)	*DDR*	German Democratic Republic (1949–90)
dekliniert	*decl*	declined
bestimmt	*def*	definite
bestimmter Artikel	DEF ART, *def art*	definite article
demonstrativ, hinweisend	*dem*	demonstrative
demonstratives Adjektiv	DEM ADJ	demonstrative adjective
demonstratives Adverb	DEM ADV	demonstrative adverb
Demonstrativpronomen, hinweisendes Fürwort	DEM PRON, *dem pron*	demonstrative pronoun
Dialekt	*dial*	dialect
Verkleinerung	*dim*	diminutive
Akkusativobjekt	*dir obj*	direct object
kirchlich	*Eccl*	ecclesiastical
Volkswirtschaft	*Econ*	economics
ostdeutsch	*E Ger*	East German
Elektrizität	*Elec*	electricity
betont	*emph*	emphatic
besonders	*esp*	especially
et cetera, und so weiter	*etc*	et cetera
etwas	*etw*	something
Euphemismus, Hüllwort	*euph*	euphemism
Femininum	F, *f*	feminine
Mode	*Fashion*	
figurativ, übertragen	*fig*	figurative
Finanzen	*Fin*	finance
Angeln/Fischen	*Fishing*	
Forstwirtschaft	*Forest*	forestry
förmlich	*form*	formal
Fußball	*Ftbl*	football
gehoben	*geh*	elevated
Genitiv	*gen*	genitive
Geografie	*Geog*	geography
Geologie	*Geol*	geology
Deutschland	*Ger*	Germany
Grammatik	*Gram*	grammar
Heraldik, Wappenkunde	*Her*	heraldry
Geschichte	*Hist*	history
Gartenbau	*Hort*	horticulture
scherzhaft	*hum*	humorous
Jagd	*Hunt*	hunting
Imperativ, Befehlsform	IMPER, *imper*	imperative
unpersönlich	IMPERS, *impers*	impersonal
Industrie	*Ind*	industry
unbestimmt	*indef*	indefinite
unbestimmter Artikel	INDEF ART, *indef art*	indefinite article
Indefinitpronomen, unbestimmtes Fürwort	INDEF PRON, *indef pron*	indefinite pronoun
Dativobjekt	*indir obj*	indirect object
umgangssprachlich	*inf*	informal
Infinitiv	*infin*	infinitive
nicht trennbar(es Verb)	INSEP, *insep*	inseparable
Versicherungen	*Insur*	insurance
Interjektion, Ausruf	*interj*	interjection
interrogativ, fragend	*interrog*	interrogative
interrogatives Adjektiv, Frageadjektiv	INTERROG ADJ	interrogative adjective
interrogatives Adverb, Frageadverb	INTERROG ADV	interrogative adverb
Interrogativpronomen, Fragepronomen	INTERROG PRON, *interrog pron*	interrogative pronoun
unveränderlich	*inv*	invariable
irisch	*Ir*	Irish
ironisch	*iro*	ironical
unregelmäßig	*irreg*	irregular
jemand, jemandes,	*jd, jds*	somebody, somebody's
jemandem, jemanden	*jdm, jdn*	somebody
Rechtspflege, Juristerei	*Jur*	law
Sprachwissenschaft	*Ling*	linguistics
wörtlich	*lit*	literal
literarisch	*liter*	literary

Literatur(wissenschaft)	*Liter*	literature
Maskulinum	M, *m*	masculine
Mathematik	*Math*	mathematics
Maß(einheit)	*Measure*	
Mechanik	*Mech*	mechanics
Medizin	*Med*	medicine
Meteorologie	*Met*	meteorology
Metallurgie, Hüttenkunde	*Metal*	metallurgy
militärisch	*Mil*	military
Bergbau	*Min*	mining
Mineralogie	*Miner*	mineralogy
Straßenverkehr	*Mot*	motoring and transport
Musik	*Mus*	music
Mythologie	*Myth*	mythology
Substantiv, Hauptwort	N	noun
nautisch	*Naut*	nautical
verneint	*neg*	negative
wird oft als beleidigend empfunden	*neg!*	may be considered offensive
nordenglisch	*N Engl*	Northern English
norddeutsch	*N Ger*	North German
Nationalsozialismus	*NS*	Nazism
Neutrum	NT, *nt*	neuter
Zahlwort	NUM	numeral
Objekt	*obj*	object
obsolet, ausgestorben	*obs*	obsolete
veraltet	*old*	
Optik	*Opt*	optics
Ornithologie, Vogelkunde	*Orn*	ornithology
Parlament	*Parl*	parliament
Passiv	*pass*	passive
pejorativ, abschätzig	*pej*	pejorative
persönlich/Person	*pers*	personal/person
Personalpronomen, persönliches Fürwort	PERS PRON, *pers pron*	personal pronoun
Pharmazie	*Pharm*	pharmacy
Philosophie	*Philos*	philosophy
Phonetik, Phonologie	*Phon*	phonetics
Fotografie	*Phot*	photography
Physik	*Phys*	physics
Physiologie	*Physiol*	physiology
Plural, Mehrzahl	PL, *pl*	plural
poetisch	*poet*	poetic
Dichtung	*Poet*	poetry
Politik	*Pol*	politics
Possessiv-, besitzanzeigend	*poss*	possessive
besitzanzeigendes Adjektiv	POSS ADJ	possessive adjective
Possessivpronomen, besitzanzeigendes Fürwort	POSS PRON, *poss pron*	possessive pronoun
prädikativ	*pred*	predicative
Präfix, Vorsilbe	PREF	prefix
Präposition	PREP, *prep*	preposition
Präpositionsobjekt	PREP OBJ, *prep obj*	prepositional object
Präsens	*pres*	present
Presse	*Press*	
Präteritum, Imperfekt	*pret*	preterite, imperfect
Pronomen, Fürwort	PRON, *pron*	pronoun
sprichwörtlich	*prov*	proverbial
Sprichwort	*Prov*	proverb
Partizip Präsens	PRP, *prp*	present participle
Psychologie	*Psych*	psychology
Partizip Perfekt	PTP, *ptp*	past participle
eingetragene Marke	®	trademark
Rundfunk	*Rad*	radio
Eisenbahn	*Rail*	railways
selten	*rare*	
Reflexivpronomen, rückbezügliches Fürwort	REFL PRON, *refl pron*	reflexive pronoun
regelmäßig	*reg*	regular
Relativ-	*rel*	relative
Religion	*Rel*	religion
Relativpronomen, bezügliches Fürwort	REL PRON, *rel pron*	relative pronoun
jemand(em, -en)	*sb*	somebody
jemand(e)s	*sb's*	somebody's
Schule	*Sch*	school
Naturwissenschaften	*Sci*	science
schottisch	*Scot*	Scottish
Bildhauerei	*Sculpt*	sculpture
trennbar	SEP, *sep*	separable
Handarbeiten	*Sew*	sewing
süddeutsch	*S Ger*	South German
Singular, Einzahl	SING, *sing*	singular
Skisport	*Ski*	skiing
Slang, Jargon	*sl*	slang
Sozialwissenschaften	*Sociol*	social sciences
Raumfahrt	*Space*	space flight
Fachausdruck	*spec*	specialist term
Börse	*St Ex*	Stock Exchange
etwas	*sth*	something
Konjunktiv	*subjunc*	subjunctive
Suffix, Nachsilbe	SUF, *suf*	suffix
Superlativ	*superl*	superlative
Landvermessung	*Surv*	surveying
schweizerisch	*Sw*	Swiss
Technik	*Tech*	technology
Telekommunikation	*Telec*	telecommunications
Textilien	*Tex*	textiles
Theater	*Theat*	theatre, theater
Fernsehen	*TV*	television
Typografie, Buchdruck	*Typ*	typography and printing
Hochschule	*Univ*	university
(nord)amerikanisch	*US*	(North) American
gewöhnlich	*usu*	usually
Verb	VB, *vb*	verb
Tiermedizin	*Vet*	veterinary medicine
intransitives Verb	VI, *vi*	intransitive verb
intransitives und reflexives Verb	VIR, *vir*	intransitive and reflexive verb
reflexives Verb	VR, *vr*	reflexive verb
transitives Verb	VT, *vt*	transitive verb
transitives und intransitives Verb	VTI, *vti*	transitive and intransitive verb
transitives, intransitives und reflexives Verb	VTIR, *vtir*	transitive, intransitive and reflexive verb
transitives und reflexives Verb	VTR, *vtr*	transitive and reflexive verb
vulgär	*vulg*	vulgar
westdeutsch	*W Ger*	West German
Zoologie	*Zool*	zoology

Collins German Dictionary

BESTSELLING BILINGUAL DICTIONARIES

HarperCollins Publishers
Westerhill Road
Bishopbriggs
Glasgow
G64 2QT

Eighth Edition 2013

Reprint 10 9 8 7 6 5 4 3 2 1 0

ISBN 978-0-00-751083-2

www.collinslanguage.com

A catalogue record for this book is available from the British Library

HarperCollins Publishers, 10 East 53rd Street, New York, NY 10022

COLLINS GERMAN UNABRIDGED DICTIONARY
Eighth US Edition 2013

Library of Congress cataloging-in-Publication Data has been applied for

ISBN 978-0-06-228882-0

www.harpercollins.com

HarperCollins books may be purchased for educational, business, or sales promotional use. For information, please write to:
Special Markets Department,
HarperCollins Publishers,
10 East 53rd Street,
New York, NY 10022

Typeset by Hagedorn medien (design), Germany, and Aptara in India

Printed in Italy by Lego SpA, Lavis (Trento)

Acknowledgements
We would like to thank those authors and publishers who kindly gave permission for copyright material to be used in the Collins Corpus. We would also like to thank Times Newspapers Ltd for providing valuable data.

EIGHTH EDITION ACHTE AUFLAGE

Senior Editors **Leitende Redakteure**

Maree Airlie Susie Beattie Joyce Littlejohn

Editors **Redakteure**

Persephone Lock Eveline Ohneis-Borzacchiello

Contributions from **Mitarbeit**

Susanne Billes Sonia Brough Susanne Dyka Horst Kopleck Heike Richini

Data Management **Datenverarbeitung**

Oliver Schweiberer Uli Stühlen Thomas Zacher

For the Publisher **Verlagsmitarbeiter**

Lucy Cooper Kerry Ferguson Elaine Higgleton Ruth O'Donovan

SEVENTH EDITION SIEBTE AUFLAGE

Publishing Director **Gesamtleitung**
Lorna Sinclair Knight Vincent Docherty

Project Management **Projektleitung**
Michela Clari Martin Fellermayer Dorothée Ronge

Senior Editors **Leitende Redakteure**
Maree Airlie Joyce Littlejohn

Editors **Redakteure**
Susie Beattie Eveline Ohneis-Borzacchiello

Contributions from **Mitarbeit**
Susanne Billes Sonia Brough Susanne Dyka Horst Kopleck Heike Richini

Data Management **Datenverarbeitung**
Oliver Schweiberer Uli Stühlen Thomas Zacher

FIFTH AND SIXTH EDITIONS FÜNFTE UND SECHSTE AUFLAGE

Publishing Director **Gesamtleitung**
Lorna Sinclair Knight Vincent Docherty

Project Management **Projektleitung**
Michela Clari Dorothée Ronge

Senior Editors **Leitende Redakteure**
Maree Airlie Joyce Littlejohn

Editors **Redakteure**
Susie Beattie Martin Fellermayer Eveline Ohneis-Borzacchiello

Contributions from **Mitarbeit**
Horst Kopleck Sonia Brough

Data Management **Datenverarbeitung**
Oliver Schweiberer Uli Stühlen

FOURTH EDITION VIERTE AUFLAGE

Publishing Director Gesamtleitung
Lorna Sinclair Knight

Project Management Projektleitung
Michela Clari

Senior Editors Leitende Redakteure
Horst Kopleck
Maree Airlie

Editors Redakteure
Veronika Schnorr Christine Bahr
Susie Beattie Stuart Fortey
Phyllis Gautier Sigrid Janssen Barbara Neeb
Robin Sawers Eva Vennebusch
Sabine Citron
Daphne Day Janet Gough

Contributions from Mitarbeit
Elspeth Anderson Alexa Barnes Bob Grossmith
Ulrike Seeberger Claire Singer
Katerina Stein Beate Wengel

Editorial Coordination Koordination
Joyce Littlejohn Caitlin McMahon

Editorial staff Redaktionelle Mitarbeit
Jill Williams Maggie Seaton
Sandra Harper Anne Lindsay
Anne Marie Banks Anne Convery Alice Grandison
Irene Lakhani Cindy Mitchell Helga Panfil

Data Management Datenverarbeitung
Ray Carrick Paul Hassett Sorcha Lenagh

SECOND AND THIRD EDITIONS ZWEITE UND DRITTE AUFLAGE

Senior Editors Leitende Redakteure

Peter Terrell
Horst Kopleck
Helga Holtkamp John Whitlam

Publishing staff Verlagsangestellte

Lorna Sinclair Vivian Marr
Diana Feri Stephen Clarke
Joyce Littlejohn Diane Robinson Christine Bahr

Contributions from Mitarbeit

Veronika Schnorr
Michael Finn Tim Connell
Roland Breitsprecher

FIRST EDITION ERSTE AUSGABE

Senior Editors Leitende Redakteure

Peter Terrell
Veronika Schnorr Wendy V. A. Morris
Roland Breitsprecher

Editors Redakteure

Dr Kathryn Rooney Ingrid Schumacher Dr Lorna A. Sinclair
Dorothee Ziegler Ulrike Seeberger Petra Schlupp

Compilers Mitarbeiter

Dr Christine R. Barker
Alexa H. Barnes
Michael Clark
Francis J. Flaherty
Susanne Flatauer
Ian Graham
Barbara Hellmann
Birgit Kahl
Christian Kay
Angelika Moeller
Günter Ohnemus
Dr John Pheby
Irmgard Rieder
Hanns Schumacher
Olaf Thyen
Karin Wiese
Renate Zenker-Callum

Collins staff Verlagsangestellte

Richard Thomas
Anne Dickinson Irene Lakhani
Susan Dunsmore Valerie McNulty Alice Truten
Elspeth Anderson

CONTENTS

INHALT

INTRODUCTION

Since it was first published in 1980, the COLLINS GERMAN DICTIONARY has become one of the standard reference works of its kind. The scale of its coverage as well as the clarity and accuracy of the information it provides have made it a recognized authority in both English- and German-speaking countries.

The scope and nature of the language treated

The emphasis is firmly placed on contemporary language, and particular attention has been paid to recent coinages and new meanings not found in existing bilingual dictionaries and even absent from some monolingual volumes, but essential if the dictionary is truly to reflect current, living language as it is spoken and written today.

Space has been found, too, for a considerable representation of the vocabulary of literature and science, and especially of those areas which have contributed notably to the modern consciousness – business, computing, education, the environment, medicine, politics, and so on. Brand new to this edition is a Business & Finance Supplement, ideal for those who need to use German for work.

One of our primary concerns has been to make the dictionary equally valid for German-speaking and English-speaking users. Our rigorous policy that every German word in the dictionary has been created and vetted by *German* lexicographers and every English word by *English* lexicographers, with constant discussion between them, means that German-speaking and English-speaking users can approach this dictionary with equal confidence. In addition, we have taken care that each side of the dictionary is equally helpful for translation from and into the foreign language.

The geographical spread of language is not neglected either. A wide coverage of American English is given. Swiss, Austrian and former East German usages are treated. And regionalisms from within the main body of British English and German are covered.

Layout and help

However well-chosen the content of a dictionary may be, much of its value is instantly lost if the user cannot easily and quickly find his or her way to the meaning that meets his or her needs. So we have put considerable effort into devising and implementing a comprehensive system of indicating material.

Not only are all complex entries clearly divided into separate areas of meaning, but the sense of each area is signposted by 'indicators' which immediately highlight the group of meanings in that category. In addition, variations of meaning within each category are precisely pinpointed by further indicating material. The *systematic* and consistent use throughout the dictionary of indicating material, which may take the form of field labels, synonyms, typical subjects or objects of verbs, and so on, is a feature of the dictionary to which we attach the greatest importance. This indicating material is a very effective way of helping the user to pinpoint the exact translation he or she is looking for.

One of the most insidious linguistic traps that besets the student of any foreign language is to use words or expressions inappropriate – occasionally grotesquely so – to the context. The complexities and subtleties of register, especially of social overtones, are impossible to acquire from the printed page, but we have created for this dictionary a range of 'style labels' that accurately characterize the stylistic restrictions that should be placed on any word or expression in the text – both in source language and in target language.

Words and expressions that are unmarked for style or register in source or target language are to be taken as standard language appropriate to any normal context or situation. Wherever this is not the case the nature of the restriction is indicated: formal, literary, school slang, humorous, pejorative, and so on.

A new, user-friendly style of presentation has been chosen for selected longer entries (for example, common verbs and prepositions) to make finding specific meanings or expressions easier.

Another feature of this dictionary is the wealth of phrases provided within many entries. These greatly expand the validity of the information provided by showing how translation and sometimes structure change in different contexts and by giving examples of the idioms and set expressions relating to the headword.

The pages that follow describe these and other features of the dictionary in greater detail.

Cultural Information

The seventh edition of this dictionary contains in-depth entries with information on important aspects of culture and everyday life in German- and English-speaking countries.

German Spelling Reform

This dictionary has fully implemented the latest German spelling reform as of 2006. All headwords on the German-English side of the dictionary which no longer agree with the new spelling regulations are marked with a white triangle.

Up-to-date usage

The aim of any new edition of a dictionary is usually to update the text to incorporate those words and phrases which have only recently come into the language – this dictionary does have several thousand new words and meanings on both sides of the text. However, to create a new edition fit for the 21st century we have moved beyond this and developed several other features which make this book more user-friendly and up-to-date than ever before.

The decisive factor in this was the determination to analyse the meaning and usage of existing entries and to expand or restructure them where appropriate. To achieve this, both traditional lexicographical methods and the latest electronic tools were used. The dictionaries we produce today benefit from use of the huge electronic corpora for English ("Collins Corpus") and German ("Deutsche Textbörse") developed through the groundbreaking research into computational linguistics carried out by COLLINS in partnership with the University of Birmingham since the 1970s. These corpora are collections of texts held on computer, which provide numerous examples of how words are actually used in the widest possible variety of contexts, be it in newspapers, in literature, in official reports or in ordinary spoken language. In much the same way as scientists who analyse objective data to confirm their hypotheses, dictionary editors now have access to vast databases of hard facts and evidence to back up their own linguistic intuition. The result is a degree of accuracy and depth of coverage that would be impossible to achieve using traditional methods alone. Here is an example of how authentic usage, as documented in our corpora, the Collins Corpus and the Deutsche Textbörse, is reflected in our dictionary entries.

turn will heat the air around it. The heated air will then rise, carrying the cloud
quickly and efficiently by circulating heated air through to every corner of your
own unique style. It's been a week of heated argument, stunning performances, and
say that Morgan had been involved in a heated argument with another man shortly
the abolition of the monarchy - and a heated debate on Christianity. And as far as
agency says the congress was marked by heated debates over the new party's rules,
That led to speculation that there were heated debates over whether to accept the
The council spent three hours in heated discussion of the century-old
More drafts were written and discarded. Heated discussions broke out over the wording
over these last 15 years. Those heated discussions with colleagues and
reported to have become involved in a heated dispute with the studio over the length
under the federal plan to end the heated dispute over forests, industry no-go
quickly after we arrived. In rather a heated exchange I told what looked to be a
tape failed to arrive in time. After a heated exchange with organisers, and having
they just went on the open bench in the heated greenhouse, but as the weather was
sown in the early part of the year in a heated greenhouse. The seedlings are grown on
harmonoius relationship. They had a heated meeting on Tuesday night which failed
railwayman to preside over us. I had a heated meeting with the Secretary of State,
proof locks, a rust-proofed body and heated rear window come as standard. Apart
armrest, automatic timer for the heated rear window and an interior light
or sleeping well wrapped up in a heated room. This ties in with the results of
last Christmas. Is it best kept in a heated room or does it prefer cool conditions?
we continue to breed them in cages and heated rooms we will never be able to enjoy
be financially worse off, has caused a heated row. Members of the 7th Armoured
The Tottenham MP became embroiled in a heated row with BR staff after they accused
and enjoy the amenities of a private heated swimming pool, from May to September.
acres of gardens with tennis courts and heated swimming pool screened by trees and
use of the leisure facilities, such as heated swimming pool, sauna, spa bath and
Different special offers every month on heated towel rails and selected suites.
in all type of radiators and heated towel rails, have several traditional
field when he allegedly exchanged heated words before landing his blow. All
irritation of his vice-captain, led to heated words in the dressing room. Other
did not agree, and things quickly grew heated between these two titans of ridicule
Families of deceased and accused grow heated and often irrational. It is common for
ministers became increasingly heated and the supporters of the democratic
star. Without exception each one became heated over the criticism or presumed
users post messages. Debate can become heated, and some messages, known as flames,
Internet debates can easily become heated to the point of mutual vilification.
worse than death. Things got pretty heated before he left them to it, Jeremy went
the tables. Before things got too heated, though, I made my excuses and left my

heated [ˈhiːtɪd] **ADJ** **a** (*lit*) *swimming pool, greenhouse etc* beheizt; *room* geheizt; *rear window, towel rail* heizbar; **~ air** Warmluft *f* **b** (*fig, = angry*) *debate, discussion, dispute, meeting* hitzig, erregt; *argument, exchange, row* heftig; *words* erregt; **to grow** *or* **become ~** (*person*) sich aufregen; (*debate*) hitzig *or* erregt werden; **things got very ~** die Gemüter erhitzten sich

EINLEITUNG

Seit seiner Erstveröffentlichung im Jahre 1980 ist das COLLINS GROSSWÖRTERBUCH zu einem Standardwerk geworden. Durch seine Materialfülle sowie die Klarheit und Genauigkeit der Informationsvermittlung stellt dieses Wörterbuch sowohl in deutsch- als auch englischsprachigen Ländern eine anerkannte Autorität dar.

Inhalt, Umfang und Methodik

Bei diesem Wörterbuch liegt das Schwergewicht eindeutig auf der englischen und deutschen Gegenwartssprache, wobei der Sprache des Alltags besondere Aufmerksamkeit gilt. Die Gesamtzahl der Stichwörter, Zusammensetzungen und Anwendungsbeispiele beträgt fast 350.000. Schon ein kurzer Blick auf eine Auswahl von Stichwörtern und Wendungen zeigt deutlich, dass der Grund für diese Vollständigkeit nicht in der Aufnahme von seltenen Wörtern oder Redewendungen an der Peripherie der Sprache zu suchen ist. Ganz im Gegenteil ist in allen Arbeitsphasen bewusst Wert darauf gelegt worden, Abgelebtes und Ausgestorbenes aus diesem Wörterbuch zu verbannen. Auch ist die Vollständigkeit nicht einfach auf die Aufnahme von Neologismen zurückzuführen, obwohl freilich neue Wörter ebenso wie neu geprägte Redensarten einen breiten Raum in diesem Buch einnehmen.

Die Vollständigkeit beruht ganz einfach auf der Gründlichkeit und Ausführlichkeit, mit der die deutsche und englische Alltagssprache dargelegt werden. Dieses Wörterbuch behandelt ein enormes Spektrum ganz gewöhnlicher Wörter und Redewendungen, die unentbehrlichen – oft recht schwierig zu übersetzenden – Elemente der sprachlichen Kommunikation in aller Gründlichkeit. Damit soll jedoch nicht gesagt sein, dass älteres oder sondersprachliches Wortgut schlechthin in diesem Wörterbuch unberücksichtigt bleibt. Ganz im Gegenteil. Wenn man den Umfang des Wörterverzeichnisses schlagwortartig als den „Wortschatz des gebildeten Laien" beschreibt, heißt das gleichzeitig, dass ältere und sondersprachliche Ausdrücke, die in diesen Wortschatz eingegangen sind, auch in das Wörterbuch aufgenommen wurden. So ist zum Beispiel die Sprache der Computertechnik ebenso wie die der traditionelleren Fachgebiete dokumentiert. Ganz neu in der vorliegenden Ausgabe ist ein Anhang zum Fachwortschatz der Wirtschafts- und Finanzsprache. Dieser ist insbesondere für diejenigen Benutzer von Bedeutung, die Deutsch im Beruf brauchen

Auch die Verbreitung beider Sprachen in geografischer Hinsicht wird nicht vernachlässigt. Amerikanisches Englisch ist weitgehend berücksichtigt worden, und außer dem Sprachgebrauch in Deutschland wird dem in Österreich und der Schweiz gesprochenen Deutsch ausführlich Rechnung getragen. Das Gleiche gilt für den regionalen Sprachgebrauch in Deutschland und Großbritannien.

Für die Verfasser dieses Wörterbuches ist es von Anfang an eine Selbstverständlichkeit gewesen, dass der deutsche Text ausschließlich von Lexikografen mit Deutsch als Muttersprache und der englische Text ausschließlich von Lexikografen mit Englisch als Muttersprache verfasst werden musste. Damit ist die idiomatische Authentizität sowohl in der Ausgangssprache als auch in der Zielsprache gewährleistet.

Deutsche und englische Lexikografen haben im Team gearbeitet, und während der Redaktionsarbeit haben in allen Arbeitsphasen Diskussionen zwischen deutschen und englischen Muttersprachlern stattgefunden. Das heißt, dass der gesamte Text von Redakteuren ausschließlich in ihrer eigenen Sprache verfasst wurde und aus zweisprachiger Sicht geprüft worden ist. Dies ist die sicherste und zuverlässigste Methode, beide Sprachen miteinander zu verzahnen.

Artikelaufbau

Der Artikelaufbau in diesem Wörterbuch zeichnet sich vor allem durch die systematische Verwendung von Indikatoren und Kollokatoren (siehe Seite xiv) aus, die verschiedene Bedeutungs- und Anwendungsbereiche bezeichnen, sodass die angegebenen Übersetzungen sich immer auf den Kontext oder Kontextbereich beziehen, für den sie gelten. Der Benutzer wird nicht mit zwar möglichen, aber dennoch unterschiedlichen beziehungslosen Übersetzungen bombardiert. Stattdessen werden ihm kontextspezifische Übersetzungen geboten. Dies gilt sowohl für Übersetzungen, wo die unterschiedlichen Bedeutungen eines Wortes in der Ausgangssprache zu zeigen sind, als auch für Wörter, deren Gebrauch sich nach dem Kontext richtet, was z. B. bei der Verbindung (Kollokation) von Substantiv und Adjektiv der Fall ist.

Die Phraseologie bildet einen der wichtigsten Teile des Wörterbuchs und lässt sich grob in zwei Bereiche gliedern. Da sind zunächst die festen Wendungen im Deutschen und Englischen: die Sprichwörter, Redensarten und auch die Klischees; dann die Anwendungsbeispiele, mit denen die strukturelle Entsprechung beider Sprachen illustriert werden soll. So wird z. B. gezeigt, wie eine bestimmte allgemeine Übersetzung, sagen wir ein Substantiv, unter Umständen in einem bestimmten Kontext in eine Verbkonstruktion verwandelt werden muss, um die idiomatische Korrektheit – gelegentlich sogar die Verständlichkeit – zu wahren.

Für ausgewählte längere Einträge (z. B. gebräuchliche Verben und Präpositionen) wurde eine neue, benutzerfreundliche Darstellung gewählt, die das Auffinden gesuchter Bedeutungen oder Wendungen erleichtert.

Zur Vervollständigung dieses detaillierten Artikelaufbaus wird ein hoch entwickeltes System von Stilangaben verwendet, damit der Benutzer erkennt, ob eine bestimmte Übersetzung angemessen ist oder welchen Stellenwert ein Stichwort, das er nachschlagen möchte, aus stilistischer Sicht hat. Es wird dem Benutzer mitgeteilt, ja er wird gewarnt, wenn ein Wort umgangssprachlich, dichterisch, förmlich, veraltet, altmodisch, verhüllend o. Ä. ist, und es wird ihm gesagt, ob ein Ausdruck möglicherweise Anstoß erregt, Heiterkeit hervorruft, schwülstig, betulich, professoral oder abstoßend klingt. Weitere Erläuterungen zum Artikelaufbau werden auf den folgenden Seiten gegeben.

Landeskundliche Informationen

Die siebte Auflage dieses Wörterbuchs enthält auch ausführliche Artikel zu Landeskunde und Kultur deutsch- und englischsprachiger Länder.

Deutsche Rechtschreibreform

Dieses Wörterbuch folgt der reformierten deutschen Rechtschreibung nach dem Stand von 2006. Alle nach dem neuesten Stand der Rechtschreibreform inzwischen veralteten Worter, die im deutsch-englischen Teil des Wörterbuchs als Stichwörter erscheinen, sind entsprechend gekennzeichnet.

Aktualität

Jede Neuauflage eines Wörterbuchs zielt normalerweise zunächst auf eine Aktualisierung des Wortschatzes, um solche Wörter und Ausdrücke aufzunehmen, welche erst kürzlich Eingang in die Sprache gefunden haben – in diesem Fall mehrere Tausend neue Wörter und neue Bedeutungen auf beiden Seiten des Wörterbuchs. Für diese, auf das 21. Jahrhundert zielende Neuausgabe wurden jedoch darüber hinaus zahlreiche weitere Anstrengungen unternommen, die dieses Buch benutzerfreundlicher und aktueller machen als jemals zuvor.

Ausschlaggebend hierbei war das Bestreben, bestehende Wörterbuchartikel durch eine Analyse von Wortbedeutung und -gebrauch zu überprüfen und wo angebracht zu erweitern oder neu zu gliedern. Hierbei kamen sowohl traditionelle Methoden der Lexikografie als auch die neueste Computertechnik zur Anwendung. Dank der von COLLINS in Zusammenarbeit mit der Universität Birmingham seit den 70er-Jahren durchgeführten Forschungsarbeiten auf dem Gebiet der Computerlinguistik profitieren unsere Wörterbücher heute von den seither aufgebauten riesigen elektronischen Textkorpora für Englisch („Collins Corpus") und Deutsch („Deutsche Textbörse"). Hierbei handelt es sich um auf Computer gehaltene Textsammlungen, welche Belege dafür enthalten, wie Wörter in den verschiedensten Kontexten gebraucht werden, sei es in der Presse, in der Literatur, in Berichten und Abhandlungen oder in der gesprochenen Sprache. In ähnlicher Weise wie Wissenschaftler Daten heranziehen, um ihre Hypothesen zu überprüfen, so können heute auch unsere Wörterbuchredakteure auf Datenbanken mit einer Fülle von Fakten und Belegen zurückgreifen, um ihr eigenes Sprachgefühl anhand dieser Daten zu verifizieren. Das Resultat ist ein Grad an Genauigkeit und Darstellungsbreite, der mit rein herkömmlichen Methoden unmöglich erreicht werden könnte. Im Folgenden ein Beispiel dafür, wie authentischer Sprachgebrauch, dokumentiert in Korpustexten, sich im entsprechenden Wörterbuchartikel widerspiegelt.

wenig scharlachrote Halsbinde ließ ihn	blühend	aussehen und schenkte ihm, besser
aus'', bedauert ein selbst nicht gerade	blühend	aussehender mittelalterlicher Herr
Lady Campers morgendlich frisches und	blühendes	Aussehen ein. Das kann kaum sichtbar
in ihren Sohn und behielt ihr	blühendes	Aussehen bei, auch das Schwarz der
ohne jede Langeweile unter einem	blühenden	Baum liegen, in Bibliotheken alte
Früher konnte ich mich vor einen	blühenden	Baum hinstellen und eine unglaubliche
laden zum Verweilen ein, die	blühenden	Bäume spenden Schatten, und vom nahen
beharrlich weiterfrisst, ist jede	blühende	Blume, jedes der Natur abgetrotzte
war ein kleiner grüner Fleck mit	blühenden	Blumen und Bäumen. Nach einem Zögern
Sie ist umgeben von Wiesen mit	blühenden	Blumen. Am Brunnen des Innenhofs kann
mehr hinter dieser Geschichte als die	blühende	Fantasie der Autorin. So viel braucht
herauszulesen vermag, hat eine	blühende	Fantasie und schießt über das Ziel hinaus
des Romanhelden, den wegen seiner	blühenden	Fantasie und erfindungsreichen
die unfruchtbares Land und Wüsten in	blühende	Felder und Gärten verwandeln, aus
Ende des Krieges glichen die einst	blühenden	Felder einer trichterübersäten
lebt, aus einer Steinwüste in einen	blühenden	Garten verwandelt. Sein Buch kommt
ist doch das: blühende Felder,	blühende	Gärten, blühende Wiesen, blühende
Dort kontrollieren sie nicht nur das	blühende	Geschäft mit der Prostitution, wofür
autonomer Gruppen, die mit dem Terror	blühende	Geschäfte machen. Und: Von einer
Plattenhersteller durch den weltweit	blühenden	Handel mit Raubkopien Einbußen von
beginnen sich langsam an dem	blühenden	Handel mit Rauschmitteln vor der
erreicht. Der Urlaub hat eine	blühende	Industrie geschaffen, die von einer
begründete damit vor 225 Jahren eine	blühende	Industrie. Die Goldstadt exportiert
zwischen Tang und Shilla hat der	blühenden	Kultur im damaligen China den Weg auf
Und wer nun, ganz undramatisch, der	blühenden	Kultur des Verbrauchs sich zuneigt,
ehemalige DDR in ein wirtschaftlich	blühendes	Land verwandeln, war der zweite
demokratischen und wirtschaftlich	blühenden	Landes zu danken. Österreich habe
Bürgern der DDR schnellen Wohlstand,	blühende	Landschaften zu versprechen und den
erfüllt. Die von ihm versprochenen	blühenden	Landschaften im Osten würden nicht in
festgestellt hatte, dass sie wie das	blühende	Leben aussehe, verfiel auch er in
sie positiv ist. Sie sah aus wie das	blühende	Leben. Valeries Leben hat 1965 in
Die Blumenhalle ist mit 60.000	blühenden	Pflanzen geschmückt. Wolfgang Müller,
Pracht, umgeben von Seerosen und	blühenden	Pflanzen, durch den naturgetreu
worden und hatte sich bald zu einer	blühenden	Stadt entwickelt. Die Gegend war
Assyriens Provinzen sollen mit ihren	blühenden	Städten und großartigen Bauwerken das
Glück, wies die Spekulationen als	blühenden	Unsinn zurück. Angeblich soll Glück
Seite. Dieser Vorwurf ist natürlich	blühender	Unsinn, sagte er mit Nachdruck, denn
der sich wie Raureif auf eine	blühende	Wiese senkte. Das Gelächter
aufwarf. An den Ufern begannen	blühende	Wiesen, die dieses Jahr noch niemand
Weite der Steppen, Berge und Seen,	blühende	Wiesen und weidende Tierherden,
der von Grundwerten faselt, eine	blühende	Zukunft verspricht und dazu noch
für Hongkong eine erfolgreiche und	blühende	Zukunft voraus. Die besondere Lage der

blü|hend **ADJ** *Baum* blossoming; *Blume, Pflanze auch* blooming; *Garten, Wiese, Feld* full of flowers; *(fig) Aussehen* radiant; *Geschäft, Handel, Industrie, Kultur, Stadt* flourishing, thriving; *Fantasie* vivid, lively; *Unsinn* absolute; *Zukunft* glowing; **~e Landschaften** green pastures; **ein wirtschaftlich ~es Land** a country with a thriving economy; **wie das ~e Leben aussehen, ~ aussehen** to look the very picture of health

Using the Dictionary

Layout and order

1.1 Alphabetical order is followed throughout. Where a letter occurs in brackets in a headword, this letter is counted for the alphabetical order, eg **Beamte(r)** will be found in the place of **Beamter, vierte(r, s)** in the place of **vierter.**

1.2 Abbreviations, acronyms and **proper nouns** will be found in their alphabetical place in the word list.

1.3 Superior numbers are used to differentiate between words spelt the same way.

rowing[1], **rowing**[2]; **durchsetzen**[1], **durchsetzen**[2]

1.4 Nouns which are always used in the plural are entered in the plural form.

trousers PL , **Ferien** PL

1.5 Compounds will be found in their alphabetical place in the word list. The term "compound" is taken to cover not only those written in one word or hyphenated (eg **Bettwäsche, large-scale**) but also attributive uses of English nouns (eg **defence mechanism**) and other set word combinations (eg **long jump**) which function in a similar way. Where possible a general translation has been given for the first element.

Mag|net- *in cpds* magnetic

From this the user can derive the translation for compounds not given in the word list.

Where alphabetical order permits, compounds are run on in blocks with the first element printed in a large boldface type at the beginning of each block, and the headwords themselves in a slightly smaller typeface for easy identification. Illustrative phrases appear in a different typeface so that they can easily be distinguished from compounds.

gum: gumtree N Gummibaum *m*; **to be up a ~** (*Brit, inf*) aufgeschmissen sein (*inf*)

1.6 Phrasal verbs (marked ▶) will be found immediately after the main headword entry.

1.7 Idioms and set phrases will normally be found under the first meaningful element or the first word in the phrase which remains constant despite minor variations in the phrase itself. Thus, 'to breast the tape' is included under **breast** whereas 'to lend sb a hand' is treated under **'hand'** because it is equally possible to say 'to give sb a hand'.

Hinweise zur Benutzung des Wörterbuchs

Aufbau und Anordnung der Einträge

1.1 Die alphabetische Anordnung der Einträge ist durchweg gewahrt. In Klammern stehende Buchstaben in einem Stichwort unterliegen ebenfalls der Alphabetisierung, so findet man z.B. **Beamte(r)** an der Stelle von **Beamter, vierte(r, s)** unter **vierter**.

1.2 Abkürzungen, Akronyme und **Eigennamen** sind in alphabetischer Ordnung im Wörterverzeichnis zu finden.

1.3 Hochgestellte Ziffern werden verwendet, um zwischen Wörtern gleicher Schreibung zu unterscheiden.

1.4 Substantive, die stets im Plural verwendet werden, sind in der Pluralform angegeben.

1.5 Zusammengesetzte Wörter stehen an ihrer Stelle im Alphabet. Der Begriff „zusammengesetzte Wörter" bezeichnet nicht nur zusammengeschriebene oder durch Bindestrich verbundene Komposita (z.B. **Bettwäsche, large-scale**) sondern auch die attributive Verwendung englischer Substantive (z. B. **defence mechanism**) und andere feste Verbindungen (z. B. **long jump**), die eine ähnliche Funktion haben. Wo immer möglich, ist für das erste Element eine allgemeine Übersetzung angegeben.

Daraus kann der Benutzer die Übersetzung hier nicht angegebener Zusammensetzungen erschließen.

Wo die alphabetische Ordnung es gestattet, werden die Zusammensetzungen in Blöcken angeordnet, wobei der erste Bestandteil am Anfang jedes Blocks fett und die Stichwörter selbst halbfett erscheinen. Für Wendungen wird eine andere Schrift verwendet, um dem Benutzer die schnelle Identifizierung von Wendungen und zusammengesetzten Wörtern zu erleichtern.

1.6 *Phrasal verbs* (feste Verb-Partikel-Verbindungen im Englischen, durch ▶ bezeichnet) folgen unmittelbar auf das Hauptstichwort.

1.7 Redensarten und feste Wendungen sind im Allgemeinen unter dem ersten bedeutungstragenden Element oder dem ersten Wort der Wendung, das trotz leichter Abwandlungen in der Wendung selbst unverändert bleibt, zu finden. So ist ‚to breast the tape' unter ‚**breast**' aufgenommen, ‚to lend sb a hand' dagegen wird unter ‚**hand**'

Certain very common English and German verbs such as 'be, get, have, make, put, bringen, haben, geben, machen, tun', which form the basis of a great many phrases e.g. 'to make sense', 'to make a mistake', 'etw in Ordnung bringen', 'etw in Gang bringen' have been considered as having a diminished meaning and in such cases the set phrase will be found under the most significant element in the phrase.

abgehandelt, weil es ebenfalls möglich ist, ‚to give sb a hand' zu sagen.

Bei als Funktionsverben gebrauchten Verben wie ‚be, get, have, make, put, bringen, haben, geben, machen, tun' werden die meisten festen Wendungen, wie z. B. ‚to make sense', ‚to make a mistake', ‚etw in Ordnung bringen', ‚etw in Gang bringen', unter dem bedeutungstragenden Bestandteil der Wendung behandelt.

Explanatory material

Erklärende Zusätze

General explanatory notes or 'signposts' in the dictionary are printed *in italics* and take the following forms:

Allgemeine erklärende Zusätze im Wörterbuch sind *kursiv* gedruckt und erscheinen in folgender Form:

2.1 Indicators in brackets ( ):

2.1 Indikatoren, in Klammern stehend ( ):

2.1.1 Explanations and Clarification

2.1.1 Erklärungen und Erläuterungen

lounge N (*in house*) Wohnzimmer *nt*; (*in hotel*) Gesellschaftsraum *m*

2.1.2 synonyms and partial definitions

2.1.2 Synonyme und Teildefinitionen

ge|fühl|voll ADJ **a** (= *empfindsam*) sensitive; (= *ausdrucksvoll*) expressive **b** (= *liebevoll*) loving

2.1.3 within verb entries, typical subjects of the headword

2.1.3 in Verb-Einträgen typische Substantiv-Ergänzungen

peel VI (*wallpaper*) sich lösen; (*paint*) abblättern; (*skin, person*) sich schälen *or* pellen (*inf*)

2.1.4 within noun entries, typical noun complements of the headword

2.1.4 typische Substantiv-Ergänzungen des Stichworts in Substantiv-Einträgen

Schar[1] [ʃaːɐ] **F -, -en** crowd, throng (*liter*); (*von Vögeln*) flock; (*von Insekten, Heuschrecken etc*) swarm

2.2 Collocators or typical complements, not in brackets:

2.2 Kollokatoren oder typische Ergänzungen, ohne Klammern stehend:

2.2.1 in transitive verb entries, typical objects of the headword

2.2.1 typische Objekte des Stichworts bei transitiven Verb-Einträgen

dent VT *hat, car, wing* einbeulen, verbeulen; *wood, table* eine Delle machen in (*+acc*); (*inf*) *pride, confidence* anknacksen (*inf*)

2.2.2 in adjective entries, typical nouns modified by the headword

2.2.2 typische, durch das Stichwort näher bestimmte Substantive in Adjektiv-Einträgen

neu [nɔy] ✪ 50.2 ADJ new; *Seite, Kräfte, Hoffnung, Truppen auch* fresh; (= *kürzlich entstanden auch*) recent; (= *frisch gewaschen*) *Hemd, Socken* clean; *Wein* young

2.2.3 in adverb entries, typical verbs or adjectives modified by the headword

2.2.3 typische, durch das Stichwort näher bestimmte Verben oder Adjektive bei Adverb-Einträgen

vaguely [ˈveɪglɪ] **ADV** vage; *remember also* dunkel; *speak also* unbestimmt; *understand* ungefähr, in etwa

2.3 Field labels are used:

2.3 Sachbereichsangaben werden verwendet:

2.3.1 to differentiate various meanings of the headword

2.3.1 um die verschiedenen Bedeutungen des Stichworts zu unterscheiden

Jung|frau F virgin; (*Astron, Astrol*) Virgo *no art*

2.3.2 when the meaning in the source language is clear but may be ambiguous in the target language

2.3.2 wenn die Bedeutung in der Ausgangssprache klar ist, jedoch in der Zielsprache mehrdeutig sein könnte

Virgo [ˈvɜːgəʊ] **N** (*Astrol*) Jungfrau *f*; **he's (a) ~** er ist Jungfrau

A list of the field labels used in this dictionary is given inside the front and back covers.

Eine Liste dieser Sachbereichsangaben befindet sich auf den Umschlag-Innenseiten.

2.4 Style labels are used to mark all words and phrases which are not neutral in style level or which are no longer current in the language. This labelling is given for both source and target languages and serves primarily as an aid to the non-native speaker.

2.4 Stilangaben werden verwendet zur Kennzeichnung aller Wörter und Wendungen, die keiner neutralen Stilebene oder nicht mehr dem modernen Sprachgebrauch angehören. Die Angaben erfolgen sowohl in der Ausgangs- als auch in der Zielsprache und sollen in erster Linie dem Nichtmuttersprachler helfen.

When a style label is given at the beginning of an entry or category it covers all meanings and phrases in that entry or category.

Stilangaben zu Beginn eines Eintrages oder einer Kategorie beziehen sich auf alle Bedeutungen und Wendungen innerhalb dieses Eintrages oder dieser Kategorie.

(*inf*) denotes colloquial language typically used in an informal conversational context or a chatty letter, but which would be inappropriate in more formal speech or writing.

(*inf*) bezeichnet umgangssprachlichen Gebrauch, wie er für eine formlose Unterhaltung oder einen zwanglosen Brief typisch ist, in förmlicherer Rede oder förmlicherem Schriftverkehr jedoch unangebracht wäre.

(*sl*) indicates that the word or phrase is highly informal and is only appropriate in very restricted contexts, for example among members of a particular age group. When combined with a field label eg (*Mil sl*), (*Sch sl*) it denotes that the expression belongs to the jargon of that group.

(*sl*) soll anzeigen, dass das Wort oder die Wendung äußerst salopp ist und nur unter ganz bestimmten Umständen, z. B. unter Mitgliedern einer besonderen Altersgruppe, verwendet wird. In Verbindung mit einer Sachbereichsangabe, z.B. (*Mil sl*), (*Sch sl*), wird auf die Zugehörigkeit des Ausdrucks zum Jargon dieser Gruppe hingewiesen.

(*vulg*) denotes words generally regarded as taboo which are likely to cause offence.

(*vulg*) bezeichnet Wörter, die allgemein als tabu gelten und an denen vielfach Anstoß genommen wird.

(*neg!*) denotes words that may be considered offensive.

(*neg!*) steht bei zumeist auf Personen bezogenen Bezeichnungen, die von den Betroffenen oft als beleidigend empfunden werden.

(*geh*) denotes an elevated style of spoken or written German such as might be used by an educated speaker choosing his words with care.

(*geh*) bezeichnet einen gehobenen Stil sowohl im gesprochenen wie geschriebenen Deutsch, wie er von gebildeten, sich gewählt ausdrückenden Sprechern verwendet werden kann.

(*form*) denotes formal language such as that used on official forms, for official communications and in formal speeches.

(*form*) bezeichnet förmlichen Sprachgebrauch, wie er uns auf Formularen, im amtlichen Schriftverkehr oder in förmlichen Ansprachen begegnet.

(*spec*) indicates that the expression is a technical term restricted to the vocabulary of specialists.

(*spec*) gibt an, dass es sich um einen Fachausdruck handelt, der ausschließlich dem Wortschatz von Fachleuten angehört.

(*dated*) indicates that the word or phrase, while still occasionally being used especially by older speakers, now sounds somewhat old-fashioned.

(*dated*) weist darauf hin, dass das Wort bzw. die Wendung heute recht altmodisch klingen, obwohl sie besonders von älteren Sprechern noch gelegentlich benutzt werden.

(*old*) denotes language no longer in current use but which the user will find in reading.

(*old*) bezeichnet nicht mehr geläufiges Wortgut, das dem Benutzer jedoch noch beim Lesen begegnet.

(*obs*) denotes obsolete words which the user will normally only find in classical literature.

(*obs*) bezeichnet veraltete Wörter, die der Benutzer im Allgemeinen nur in der klassischen Literatur antreffen wird.

(*liter*) denotes language of a literary style level. It should not be confused with the field label (*Liter*) which indicates that the expression belongs to the field of literary studies, or with the abbreviation (*lit*) which indicates the literal as opposed to the figurative meaning of a word.

(*liter*) bezeichnet literarischen Sprachgebrauch. Es sollte nicht mit der Sachbereichsangabe (*Liter*) verwechselt werden, die angibt, dass der betreffende Ausdruck dem Gebiet der Literaturwissenschaft angehört, und ebenso wenig mit der Abkürzung (*lit*), die die wörtliche im Gegensatz zur übertragenen Bedeutung eines Wortes bezeichnet.

Style labels used in this dictionary are given inside the front and back covers.

In diesem Wörterbuch verwendete Stilangaben und ihre Bedeutungen befinden sich auf den Umschlag-Innenseiten.

2.5 *also, auch* used after explanatory material denotes that the translation(s) following it can be used in addition to the first translation given in the respective entry, category or phrase.

2.5 *also, auch* nach erklärenden Zusätzen gibt an, dass die folgende(n) Übersetzung(en) zusätzlich zu der ersten Übersetzung, die in dem Eintrag oder der Kategorie angegeben ist, benutzt werden kann/können.

Grammatical Information

Grammatische Angaben

Gender

Geschlecht

3.1 All German **nouns** are marked for gender in both sections of the dictionary.

3.1 Alle deutschen **Substantive** sind in beiden Teilen des Wörterbuchs mit der Geschlechtsangabe versehen.

3.2 Where a German translation consists of an adjective plus a noun, the adjective is given in the indefinite form which shows gender and therefore no gender is given for the noun.

3.2 Wenn eine deutsche Übersetzung aus einem Adjektiv und einem Substantiv besteht, wird das Adjektiv in der unbestimmten Form angegeben, die das Geschlecht erkennen lässt. Für das Substantiv erfolgt daher keine Geschlechtsangabe.

große Pause; zweites Frühstück

3.3 Nouns listed in the form **Reisende(r)** MF *decl as adj* can be either masculine or feminine and take the same endings as adjectives.

3.3 Substantive nach dem Muster **Reisende(r)** MF *decl as adj* können sowohl männlich wie weiblich sein und haben die gleichen Deklinationsendungen wie Adjektive.

m **der Reisende, ein Reisender, die Reisenden** *pl*
f **die Reisende, eine Reisende, die Reisenden** *pl*

3.4 Nouns listed in the form **Beamte(r)** M *decl as adj* take the same endings as adjectives.

3.4 Substantive nach dem Muster **Beamte(r)** M *decl as adj* haben die gleichen Deklinationsendungen wie Adjektive.

der Beamte, ein Beamter, die Beamten *pl*

3.5 **Adjectives** listed in the form **letzte(r, s)** do not exist in an undeclined form and are only used attributively.

3.5 **Adjektive** nach dem Muster **letzte(r, s)** haben keine unflektierte Form und werden nur attributiv verwendet.

der letzte Mann, ein letzter Mann
die letzte Frau, eine letzte Frau
das letzte Kind, ein letztes Kind

3.6 The **feminine forms** are shown, where relevant, for all German noun headwords; unless otherwise indicated, the English translation will be the same as for the masculine form.

Where the feminine form is separated alphabetically from the masculine form, it is given as a separate headword.

Where there is no distinction between the translations given for the masculine and feminine forms and yet the context calls for a distinction, the user should prefix the translation with "male/female *or* woman *or* lady ..."

3.6 Für alle deutschen Substantive, die ein natürliches Geschlecht haben, wird die **weibliche** neben der **männlichen Form** angegeben. Wenn nicht anders angegeben, lautet die englische Form für beide gleich.

Wo die weibliche Form in der alphabetischen Reihenfolge nicht unmittelbar auf die männliche folgt, wird sie in jedem Fall als eigenes Stichwort angegeben.

Wo die für die männliche und die für die weibliche Form angegebene Übersetzung dieselbe ist, im entsprechenden Zusammenhang aber betont werden soll, dass es sich um einen Mann bzw. eine Frau handelt, sollte der Benutzer der Übersetzung „male/female *or* woman *or* lady" voranstellen.

Lehrer = male teacher; Lehrerin = female *or* **woman** *or* **lady teacher**

Nouns

4.1 Nouns marked *no pl* are not normally used in the plural or with an indefinite article or with numerals.

no pl is used:

(a) to give warning to the non-native speaker who might otherwise use the word wrongly;
(b) as an indicator to distinguish the uncountable meanings of a headword in the source language.

4.2 Nouns marked *no art* are not normally used with either a definite or an indefinite article except when followed by a relative clause.

4.3 The **genitive and plural endings** are given for all German noun headwords. The genitive and plural endings of German compound nouns are only given where the final element does not exist as a headword in its own right.

4.4 **Irregular plural forms** of English nouns are given on the English-German side.

4.4.1 Most English nouns take *-s* in the plural.

Substantive

4.1 Substantive mit der Angabe *no pl* werden im Allgemeinen nicht im Plural, mit dem unbestimmten Artikel oder mit Zahlwörtern verwendet.

no pl dient:

(a) als Warnung an den Nicht-Muttersprachler, der das Wort sonst falsch benutzen könnte;
(b) zur Unterscheidung der unzählbaren und zählbaren Bedeutungen in der Ausgangssprache.

4.2 Mit *no art* bezeichnete Substantive stehen im Allgemeinen weder mit dem unbestimmten noch mit dem bestimmten Artikel, außer wenn ein Relativsatz von ihnen abhängig ist.

4.3 Bei allen deutschen Substantiv-Stichwörtern sind **Genitivendung und Plural** angegeben, bei zusammengesetzten Substantiven jedoch nur dann, wenn das letzte Element der Zusammensetzung nicht als eigenes Stichwort vorkommt.

4.4 **Unregelmäßige Pluralformen** englischer Substantive sind im englisch-deutschen Teil angegeben.

4.4.1 Die meisten englischen Substantive bilden den Plural durch Anhängen von *-s*.

bed -s, site -s, key -s, roof -s

4.4.2 Nouns ending in *-s, -z, -x, -sh, -ch* take *-es*

4.4.2 Substantive, die auf *-s, -z, -x, -sh, -ch* enden, erhalten die Endung *-es*.

gas -es, box -es, patch -es

4.4.3 Nouns ending in *-y* preceded by a consonant change the *-y* to *ie* and add *-s* in the plural, except in the case of proper nouns.

4.4.3 Substantive, die auf Konsonant + *-y* enden, verwandeln im Plural das auslautende *-y* in *-ie*, auf das die Pluralendung *-s* folgt. Ausnahmen bilden Eigennamen.

lady — ladies, berry — berries
Henry — two Henrys

Nouns ending in *-quy* also change the *-y* to *- ie* and add *-s* in the plural, except in the case of proper nouns.

Auf *-quy* auslautende Substantive verwandeln bei der Pluralbildung ihr *-y* ebenfalls in *-ie*, worauf *-s* folgt.

soliloquy — soliloquies

Adjectives and adverbs

5.1 As a general rule, adjective translations consisting of more than one word should be used postnominally or adverbially, but not before the noun.

Adjektive und Adverbien

5.1 Grundsätzlich sollten Übersetzungen von Adjektiven, die aus mehreren Wörtern bestehen, nur nachgestellt oder adverbial gebraucht und nicht dem Substantiv vorangestellt werden.

ord|nungs|ge|mäß ADJ according to *or* in accordance with the regulations, proper

5.2 On the German-English side of the dictionary adverbs have been treated as separate grammatical entries distinct from adjective entries whenever their use is purely adverbial (*e.g.* **höchst, wohl, sehr**) or when the adverbial use is also common.

5.2 Im deutsch-englischen Teil des Wörterbuchs sind Adverbien immer dann als selbstständige grammatische Einträge von Adjektiven unterschieden worden, wenn es sich um echte Adverbien handelt (*z. B.* **höchst, wohl, sehr**) oder wenn ein adverbialer Gebrauch wahrscheinlich ist.

Where no separate entry is given for the adverbial use of a German adjective, the user should form the English adverb from the translations given according to the rules given on page xxii.

Wo für den adverbialen Gebrauch eines deutschen Adjektivs kein gesonderter Eintrag vorliegt, ist es dem Benutzer selbst überlassen, aus den angegebenen Übersetzungen die englischen Adverbien nach den auf Seite xxii angeführten Regeln zu bilden.

5.3 On the English-German side of the dictionary adverbs have been accorded the status of headwords in their own right.

5.3 Im englisch-deutschen Teil des Wörterbuchs sind die Adverbien als selbstständige Stichwörter aufgeführt.

Verbs

6.1 With all German verbs which form the past participle without *ge-* the past participle form is shown.

Verben

6.1 Bei allen Verben im Deutschen, die das 2. Partizip ohne *ge-* bilden, wird die Partizipform angegeben.

um|ar|men *ptp* **umarmt** VT *insep*
ma|növ|rie|ren *ptp* **manövriert** VTI

6.2 All German verbs beginning with a prefix which can be separable, but which are in this case inseparable verbs, are marked *insep.*

6.2 Alle deutschen Verben, die mit einer trennbaren Vorsilbe beginnen, jedoch untrennbar sind, werden durch *insep* bezeichnet.

ü|ber|rie|seln *ptp* **überrieselt** VT *insep* **ein Schauer überrieselte ihn**

6.3 With all separable German verbs the hyphenation points are shown in the actual headword

6.3 Bei allen trennbaren deutschen Verben erfolgt die Trennungsangabe im Stichwort selbst.

um+schmei|ßen VT *sep irreg* **das schmeißt meine Pläne um**

Verbs beginning with the prefixes *be-, er-, ver-, zer-* are always inseparable.

Verben mit den Vorsilben *be-, er-, ver-, zer-* sind immer untrennbar.

6.4 All German verbs which form their perfect, pluperfect and future perfect tenses with "sein" as the auxiliary are marked *aux sein.*

6.4 Alle deutschen Verben, die die zusammengesetzten Zeiten mit dem Hilfsverb „sein" bilden, sind durch *aux sein* gekennzeichnet.

gehen *pret* **ging**, *ptp* **gegangen** *aux sein* **er ist gegangen** he went

Where the auxiliary is not stated, "haben" is used.

Erfolgt keine Angabe, ist „haben" zu verwenden.

6.5 German **irregular verbs** composed of prefix and verb are marked *irreg*, and the forms can be found under the simple verb. For example, the irregular forms of "eingehen" will be found under "gehen".

6.5 Zusammengesetzte **unregelmäßige** Verben im Deutschen sind durch *irreg* bezeichnet, ihre Stammformen sind beim Simplex angegeben. So sind beispielsweise die Stammformen von „eingehen" unter „gehen" zu finden.

6.6 If the present or past participle of a verb occurs simply as an adjective it is treated as a separate headword in its alphabetical place.

6.6 Wenn 1. oder 2. Partizip eines Verbs den Status eines Adjektivs haben, werden sie als eigenständige Stichwörter in alphabetischer Reihenfolge aufgeführt.

ge|reift ADJ (*fig*) mature
struggling ADJ *artist, musician, actor* am Hungertuch nagend

Phrasal verbs

7.1 Phrasal verbs are covered in separate entries marked ▶ following the main headword.

7.2 Verb + adverb and verb + preposition combinations have been treated as phrasal verbs:

(a) where either the meaning or the translation is not simply derivable from the individual constituents;
(b) for clarity in the case of the longer verb entries.

Where a combination consists simply of a verb plus an adverb or preposition of direction it will frequently be covered under the main headword.

Phrasal verbs

7.1 *Phrasal verbs* (feste Verb-Partikel-Verbindungen) werden in eigenen Einträgen abgehandelt. Sie sind durch ▶ gekennzeichnet und folgen dem Stichworteintrag für das Verb.

7.2 Die Zusammensetzungen Verb + Adverb und Verb + Präposition werden als *phrasal verbs* abgehandelt:

(a) wo entweder die Bedeutung oder die Übersetzung sich nicht aus den Einzelbestandteilen ergibt;
(b) aus Gründen der Übersichtlichkeit bei längeren Verbeinträgen.

Bei einfachen Kombinationen von Verb + Adverb oder Präposition der Richtung ist unter dem Haupteintrag zu suchen.

dash ... VI **a** (= *rush*) ... **to ~ away/back/up** fort-/zurück-/hinaufstürzen

7.3 Irregular preterites and past participles are only given in phrasal verb entries in the rare cases where they differ from those given in the main entry.

7.3 Unregelmäßige Formen des Präteritums und des 2. Partizips werden in Einträgen, die *phrasal verbs* behandeln, nur in den seltenen Fällen angegeben, wo sie von den im Haupteintrag angegebenen abweichen.

7.4 Phrasal verbs are treated in four grammatical categories:

7.4 *Phrasal verbs* werden unter vier grammatischen Kategorien abgehandelt:

7.4.1 VI (intransitive verb)

7.4.1 VI (intransitives Verb)

▶ **grow apart** VI (*fig*) sich auseinander entwickeln

7.4.2 VI *+prep obj*
This indicates that the verbal element is intransitive but that the particle requires an object.

7.4.2 VI *+prep obj*
Hiermit soll gezeigt werden, dass das Verbelement intransitiv ist, dass aber die Partikel ein Objekt erfordert.

▶ **hold with** VI *+prep obj* (*inf*) **I don't hold with that** ich bin gegen so was (*inf*)

7.4.3 VT
This indicates that the verbal element is transitive. In most cases the object can be placed either before or after the particle; these cases are marked *sep*.

7.4.3 VT
Dies gibt an, dass das Verbelement transitiv ist. In den meisten Fällen kann das Objekt vor oder hinter der Partikel stehen; diese Fälle sind mit *sep* bezeichnet.

▶ **hand in** VT *sep* abgeben; *forms, thesis also, resignation* einreichen

In some cases the object must precede the particle; these cases are marked *always separate*.

In einigen Fällen muss das Objekt der Partikel vorangehen; solche Fälle sind durch *always separate* bezeichnet.

▶ **get over with** VT *always separate* hinter sich (*acc*) bringen
let's get it over with bringen wirs hinter uns

Occasionally the object must come after the particle, these cases are marked *insep*.

Gelegentlich muss das Objekt der Partikel nachgestellt werden; solche Fälle sind durch *insep* bezeichnet.

▶ **put forth** VI *+prep obj buds, shoots* hervorbringen

7.4.4 VT *+prep obj*
This indicates that both the verbal element and the particle require an object.

7.4.4 VT *+prep obj*
Hiermit wird gezeigt, dass *sowohl* das Verbelement als auch die Partikel ein Objekt verlangen.

▶ **take upon** VT *+prep obj* **he took that job upon himself** er hat das völlig ungebeten getan

In cases where a prepositional object is optional its translation is covered under VI or VT.

In Fällen, wo ein Präpositionalobjekt möglich, aber nicht nötig ist, findet man die entsprechende Übersetzung unter VI oder VT.

▶ **get off** VI **a** (= *descend, from bus, train etc*) aussteigen (*prep obj* aus); (*from bicycle, horse*) absteigen (*prep obj* von)

▶ **go down** VI hinuntergehen (*prep obj +acc*)

For example:

Zum Beispiel:

he got off er stieg aus/ab
he got off the bus er stieg aus dem Bus aus
he got off his bicycle er stieg von seinem Fahrrad ab
she went down sie ging hinunter
she went down the street sie ging die Straße hinunter

Cross references

8.1 Cross-references are used in the following instances:

8.1.1 to refer the user to the spelling variant treated in depth;

8.1.2 to refer the user to the headword where a particular construction or idiom has been treated;

8.1.3 to draw the user's attention to the full treatment of such words as numerals, languages, days of the week and months of the year under certain key words.

Querverweise

8.1 Querverweise sind gelegentlich verwendet worden:

8.1.1 um den Benutzer auf diejenige Schreibweise zu verweisen, wo die ausführliche Darstellung des Stichworts zu finden ist;

8.1.2 um den Benutzer auf das Stichwort zu verweisen, wo eine bestimmte Konstruktion oder Wendung abgehandelt wird;

8.1.3 um die Aufmerksamkeit des Benutzers auf die ausführliche Behandlung solcher Wortklassen wie Zahlwörter, Sprachbezeichnungen, Wochentage und Monate unter bestimmten Schlüsselwörtern zu lenken.

Punctuation and Symbols / Satzzeichen und Symbole

Punctuation and Symbols		Satzzeichen und Symbole
between translations indicates that the translations are interchangeable; between alternative phrases to be translated indicates that the phrases have the same meaning.	,	zwischen Übersetzungen zeigt an, dass die Übersetzungen gleichwertig sind; zwischen Wendungen in der Ausgangssprache zeigt an, dass die Wendungen die gleiche Bedeutung haben.
between translations indicates a difference in meaning which is clarified by explanatory material unless: (a) the distinction has already been made within the same entry; (b) in the case of some compounds the distinction is made under the simple form; (c) the distinction is self-evident.	;	zwischen Übersetzungen zeigt einen Bedeutungsunterschied an, der durch erklärende Zusätze erläutert ist, außer: (a) wenn die Unterscheidung innerhalb desselben Eintrags schon gemacht worden ist; (b) bei Komposita, wo die Unterscheidung schon unter dem Simplex getroffen wurde (c) wenn die Unterscheidung offensichtlich ist.
between translations indicates parallel structure but different meanings, e.g. **to feel good/bad**. (a) in a source language phrase it will normally be paralleled in the translation; where this is not the case, the translation covers both meanings (b) in a target language phrase where it is not paralleled by an oblique in the source language the distinction will either be made clear earlier in the entry or will be self-evident (c) in compounds it may be used to reflect a distinction made under the simple form.	/	zwischen Übersetzungen zeigt an, dass es sich um analoge Strukturen aber verschiedene Übersetzungen handelt, z. B. **to feel good/bad**. (a) der Schrägstrich in einer ausgangssprachlichen Wendung wird im Allgemeinen seine Entsprechung in der Übersetzung finden; wo das nicht der Fall ist, gilt die Übersetzung für beide Bedeutungen; (b) hat ein Schrägstrich in der Zielsprache kein Äquivalent in der Ausgangssprache, geht die getroffene Unterscheidung entweder aus in dem Eintrag bereits Gesagtem hervor oder sie ist offensichtlich; (c) bei Zusammensetzungen kann der Schrägstrich verwendet werden, um an eine für das Simplex getroffene Unterscheidung anzuknüpfen.
is used within an entry to represent the headword whenever it occurs in an unchanged form. In German headwords of the form **Reisende(r)** MF *decl as adj*, and **höchste(r, s)** ADJ it only replaces the element outside the brackets. In blocks of German compounds it represents the whole compound, not just its first element.	~	wird innerhalb von Einträgen verwendet, um das unveränderte Stichwort zu ersetzen. Bei deutschen Stichwörtern des Typs **Reisende(r)** MF *decl as adj* und **höchste(r, s)** ADJ ersetzt die Tilde den außerhalb der Klammer stehenden Teil des Wortes. In deutschen Komposita-Blöcken ersetzt die Tilde das Stichwort selbst, also nicht nur das erste Element der Zusammensetzung.
separates two speakers.	—	unterscheidet zwischen zwei Sprechern.
indicates that the translation is approximate or the cultural equivalent of the term and may not have exactly the same sense; in the case of institutions, they are those of the country indicated and obviously not the same.	≈	weist darauf hin, dass die Übersetzung eine Entsprechung ist oder aufgrund kultureller Unterschiede nicht genau die gleiche Bedeutung hat. Bei Institutionen werden die des jeweiligen Landes angegeben, die natürlich nicht identisch sind.
is used to separate parts of a word or phrase which are semantically interchangeable.	*or*	wird verwendet, um Bestandteile einer Wendung zu unterscheiden, die semantisch austauschbar sind.

used after indicating material denotes that the translation(s) following it can be used in addition to the first translation(s) given in the respective entry, category or phrase.	*also, auch*	nach erklärenden Zusätzen gibt an, dass die folgende(n) Übersetzung(en) zusätzlich zu der ersten Übersetzung oder Folge von austauschbaren Übersetzungen, die in dem Eintrag oder der Kategorie angegeben sind, benutzt werden kann/können.
in a phrase or translation indicate that the word is stressed.	CAPITALS GROSSBUCHSTABEN	in Wendungen oder Übersetzungen geben an, dass das Wort betont ist.
(in German headwords) shows hyphenation points	|	(in deutschen Stichwörtern) zeigt die Worttrennung an
placed after a headword and its phonetics and followed by a number or numbers, refers to the **Language in Use** section in the middle of this book where, under the same numbers, typical examples of how to express oneself in certain situations are given, as well as the appropriate translations.	✪	hinter einem Stichwort und der zugehörigen Ausspracheangabe wird stets gefolgt von einer bzw. mehreren Ziffern. Diese beziehen sich auf das Kapitel **Sprache Aktiv** in der Mitte dieses Buches, wo unter denselben Ziffern Beispiele mit zugehörigen Übersetzungen dafür zu finden sind, wie man sich in bestimmten Sprachsituationen korrekt ausdrückt.

Adjectives and Adverbs

Declension of German adjectives

Adjectives ending in *-abel, -ibel, -el* drop the *-e-* when declined.

miserabel	**ein miserabler Stil** **eine miserable Handschrift** **ein miserables Leben**
heikel	**ein heikler Fall** **eine heikle Frage** **ein heikles Problem**

Adjectives ending in *-er, -en* usually keep the *-e-* when declined, except:

1 in language of an elevated style level

finster	**seine finstren Züge**

2 in adjectives of foreign origin

makaber	**eine makabre Geschichte**
integer	**ein integrer Beamter**

Adjectives ending in *-auer, -euer* usually drop the *-e-* when declined.

teuer	**ein teures Geschenk**
sauer	**saure Gurken**

German adverbs

German adverbs are in most cases identical in form to the adjective.

Comparison of German adjectives and adverbs

Irregular comparative and superlative forms are given in the text, including those of adjectives and adverbs with the vowels *a, o, u* which take an umlaut:

gut [guːt] ADJ *comp* **besser** [ˈbɛsɐ], *superl* **beste(r, s)** ...
ADV *comp* **besser**, *superl* **am besten**

Where no forms are given in the text, the comparative and superlative are formed according to the following rules:

1 Both adjectives and adverbs add *-er* for the comparative before the declensional endings:

schön — schöner
eine schöne Frau — eine schönere Frau

2 Most adjectives add *-ste(r, s)* for the superlative:

schön — schönste(r, s)
ein schöner Tag — der schönste Tag

3 Most adverbs form the superlative according to the following pattern:

schön — am schönsten
schnell — am schnellsten

4 Adjectives and adverbs of one syllable or with the stress on the final syllable add *-e* before the superlative ending:

(i)	always if they end in *-s, -ß, -st, -tz, -x, -z*
(ii)	usually if they end in *-d, -t, -sch*

spitz	ADJ **spitzeste(r, s)** ADV **am spitzesten**
gerecht	ADJ **gerechteste(r, s)** ADV **am gerechtesten**

The same applies if they are used with a prefix or in compounds, regardless of where the stress falls:

unsanft	ADJ **unsanfteste(r, s)** ADV **am unsanftesten**

Adjektive und Adverbien

Adverbialbildung im Englischen

1 Die meisten Adjektive bilden das Adverb durch Anhängen von *-ly*:

strange -ly, odd -ly, beautiful -ly

2 Adjektive, die auf Konsonant +*y* enden, wandeln das auslautende *-y* in *-i* um und erhalten dann die Endung *-ly*:

happy — happily
merry — merrily

3 Adjektive, die auf *-ic* enden, bilden normalerweise das Adverb durch Anhängen vom *-ally*:

scenic -ally
linguistic -ally

Steigerung der englischen Adjektive und Adverbien

Adjektive und Adverbien, deren Komparativ und Superlativ im Allgemeinen durch Flexionsendungen gebildet werden, sind im Text durch (+*er*) bezeichnet, z. B.

young ADJ (+*er*)

Komparativ und Superlativ aller nicht durch (+*er*) bezeichneten Adjektive und Adverbien sind mit *more* und *most* zu bilden. Das gilt auch für alle auf *-ly* endenden Adverbien, z. B.

grateful — more grateful — most grateful
fully — more fully — most fully

Unregelmäßige Formen des Komparativs und Superlativs sind im Text angegeben, z. B.

bad ADJ *comp* **worse**, *superl* **worst**
well ADV *comp* **better**, *superl* **best**

Die flektierten Formen des Komparativs und Superlativs werden nach folgenden Regeln gebildet:

1 Die meisten Adjektive und Adverbien fügen *-er* zur Bildung des Komparativs und *-est* zur Bildung des Superlativs an:

small — smaller — smallest

2 Bei auf Konsonant +*y* endenden Adjektiven und Adverbien wird das auslautende *-y* in *-i* umgewandelt, bevor die Endung *-er* bzw. *-est* angefügt wird:

happy — happier — happiest

3 Mehrsilbige Adjektive auf *-ey* wandeln diese Endsilbe in *-ier, -iest* um:

homey — homier — homiest

4 Bei Adjektiven und Adverbien, die auf stummes *-e* enden, entfällt dieser Auslaut:

brave — braver — bravest

5 Bei Adjektiven und Adverbien, die auf *-ee* enden, entfällt das zweite *-e*:

free — freer — freest

6 Adjektive und Adverbien, die auf einen Konsonant nach einfachem betontem Vokal enden, verdoppeln den Konsonant im Auslaut:

sad — sadder — saddest

Nach Doppelvokal wird der auslautende Konsonant nicht verdoppelt:

loud — louder — loudest

General rules for forming the genitive

Genitive endings

Genitive endings are formed for masculine and neuter nouns by adding **-s** or **-es**

> **der Mann:** *(gen)* **des Mann(e)s**
> **das Rad:** *(gen)* **des Rad(e)s**

for feminine nouns: no change

> **die Frau:** *(gen)* **der Frau**

Masculine or neuter nouns ending in **-s, -ss, -ß, -x** and **-z** always take the full form of **-es** for the genitive

> **das Glas:** *(gen)* **des Glases**
> **der Fluss:** *(gen)* **des Flusses**
> **das Maß:** *(gen)* **des Maßes**
> **der Komplex:** *(gen)* **des Komplexes**
> **der Geiz:** *(gen)* **des Geizes**

Masculine or neuter nouns ending in **-sch** or **-st** normally take the full form of **-es**, as do those ending in a double consonant

> **der Wunsch:** *(gen)* **des Wunsches**
> **der Gast:** *(gen)* **des Gastes**
> **das Feld:** *(gen)* **des Feldes**
> **der Kampf:** *(gen)* **des Kampfes**

Masculine or neuter nouns ending in **-en, -em, -el, -er** and **-ling** always take the short form of **-s**

> **der Regen:** *(gen)* **des Regens**
> **der Atem:** *(gen)* **des Atems**
> **der Mantel:** *(gen)* **des Mantels**
> **der Sänger:** *(gen)* **des Sängers**
> **der Flüchtling:** *(gen)* **des Flüchtlings**

If the genitive is not formed according to these patterns it will be shown in the entry after the gender and before the plural ending

> **Herz** **-ens, -en** SUBSTANTIV (NT)
> **Klerus** M -, *no pl*

Weak nouns

Weak nouns have the same **-en** ending in the accusative, genitive and dative cases in both singular and plural forms

> **der Mensch:** *(acc)* **den Menschen**
> *(gen)* **des Menschen**
> *(dat)* **dem Menschen**

The Pronunciation of German

A full list of IPA symbols used is given on page xxvi.

Stress and vowel length

1. The stress and the length of the stressed vowel are shown for every German headword, either by providing full or partial phonetics using IPA symbols or by showing stress marks in the headword itself. A full list of IPA symbols used is given on page xxvi.

2. When phonetics are given for the headword a long vowel is indicated in the transcription by the length mark after it:

Chemie [çe'mi:]

3. Where no phonetics are given a short stressed vowel is marked with a dot in the headword:

Muttermal

and a long stressed vowel is marked with a dash:

Vatertag

4. Where phonetics are not given, vowel combinations which represent a stressed diphthong or a stressed long vowel are marked with an unbroken dash in the headword:

beiderlei, Haar, sieben

5. **ie**

Stressed **ie** pronounced [i:] is marked by an unbroken dash:

sieben

When the plural ending **-n** is added, the pronunciation changes to [-i:ən]:

Allegorie, *pl* **Allegorien** [-i:ən]

6. **ee** is pronounced [e:]

When the plural ending **-n** is added the change in pronunciation is shown:

Al|lee [a'le:] **F -, -n** [-'le:ən]

Consonants

Where a consonant is capable of more than one pronunciation the following rules apply:

1. **v**

(i) Note that **v** is often pronounced [f]:

Vater ['fa:tɐ]

(ii) Words ending in **-iv** are pronounced [i:f] when undeclined, but when an ending is added the pronunciation changes to [i:v]:

aktiv [ak'ti:f]

aktive (as in **der aktive Sportler**) [ak'ti:və]

2. **ng**

(i) **ng** is generally pronounced [ŋ]:

Finger ['fɪŋɐ]

(ii) In compound words where the first element ends in **-n** and the second element begins with **g-** the two sounds are pronounced individually:

Eingang ['aingaŋ]

ungeheuer ['ʊngəhɔyɐ]

3. **tion** is always pronounced [-tsio:n] at the end of a word and [-tsion-] in the middle of a word:

Nation [na'tsio:n]

national [natsio'na:l]

4. **st, sp**

(i) Where **st** or **sp** occurs in the middle or at the end of a word the pronunciation is [st], [sp]:

Fest [fɛst], **Wespe** ['vɛspə]

(ii) At the beginning of a word or at the beginning of the second element of a compound word the standard pronunciation is [ʃt], [ʃp]:

Stand [ʃtant], **sperren** ['ʃpɛrən]

Abstand ['ap-ʃtant], **absperren** ['ap-ʃpɛrən]

5. **ch**

(i) **ch** is pronounced [ç] after *ä-, e-, i-, ö-, ü-, y-, ai-, ei-, äu, eu-* and after consonants:

ich [ɪç], **Milch** [mɪlç]

(ii) **ch** is pronounced [x] after *a-, o-, u-, au-*:

doch [dɔx], **Bauch** [baux]

6. **ig** is pronounced [ɪç] at the end of a word:

König ['kø:nɪç]

When an ending beginning with a vowel is added, it is pronounced [ɪg]:

Könige ['kø:nɪgə]

7. **h** is pronounced [h]:

(i) at the beginning of a word

(ii) between vowels in interjections:

oho [o'ho:]

(iii) in words such as **Ahorn** ['a:hɔrn] and **Uhu** ['u:hu].

It is mute in the middle and at the end of non-foreign words:

leihen ['laiən], **weh** [ve:]

8. **th** is pronounced [t].

9. **qu** is pronounced [kv].

10. **z** is pronounced [ts].

Where the pronunciation of a compound or derivative can be deduced from the simplex no phonetics are given.

Glottal Stop

1. A glottal stop *(Knacklaut)* occurs at the beginning of any word starting with a vowel.

2. A glottal stop always occurs in compounds between the first and second elements when the second element begins with a vowel.

Ausspracheangaben zum Englischen

Die Zeichen der im Text verwendeten Lautschrift entsprechen denen der *International Phonetic Association.*

Die Lautschrift gibt die Aussprache für das in Südengland gesprochene britische Englisch (Received Pronunciation) an, das in der gesamten Englisch sprechenden Welt akzeptiert und verstanden wird. Nordamerikanische Formen werden angegeben, wenn die Aussprache des betreffenden Wortes im amerikanischen Englisch erheblich abweicht (z.B. **lever**), nicht aber, wenn die Abweichung nur im „Akzent" besteht, wenn also Verständigungsschwierigkeiten nicht zu befürchten sind.

Jedes Stichwort im englischen Teil ist mit der Lautschrift versehen. Ausnahmen dazu bilden folgende Fälle:

1. zusammengesetzte Stichwörter (*Komposita*), die getrennt geschrieben werden (z.B. **bell pull**, **buffalo grass**). Die Aussprache der einzelnen Teile ist unter dem entsprechenden Stichwort angegeben.

2. *phrasal verbs* (z.B. **bring back**, **bring down**, **bring round**), wo ebenfalls die Einzelbestandteile an anderer Stelle behandelt sind.

3. gleichlautende Stichwörter mit hochgestellten Ziffern (z.B. **bore**[2], **bore**[3], **bore**[4]), wo die Aussprache nur einmal beim ersten Eintrag in der Reihe (d.h. bei **bore**[1]) angeführt ist.

4. wenn bein einem Stichwort auf eine andere Schreibweise verwiesen wird, die Aussprache aber gleichlautet (z.B. **checkered** ... = **chequered**). In diesem Falle wird die Aussprache nur unter dem Wort, auf das verwiesen wird (**chequered**) angegeben.

Sonstiges

1. Die Aussprache von Abkürzungen, die als Kurzwörter (*Akronyme*) gebraucht werden, ist angegeben (z.B. **NATO** ['neɪtəʊ], **ASLEF** ['æzlef]). Wenn jeder Buchstabe einzeln ausgesprochen wird (z.B. **PTA**, **RIP**) erfolgt keine Ausspracheangabe.

2. Endungen in **-less** und **-ness** sind in der Lautschrift als [-lɪs] bzw. [-nɪs] wiedergegeben. Die Aussprache [-ləs] bzw. [nəs] ist ebenso gebräuchlich.

3. Stammformen unregelmäßiger Verben: Präteritum und 1. Partizip sind gesondert an der entsprechenden Stelle in der alphabetischen Reihenfolge angeführt und dort mit der Lautschrift versehen. Die Ausspracheangabe wird bei der Grundform des Verbs nicht wiederholt. So findet man z.B. die phonetische Umschrift für **bought**, **sold** usw. unter diesen Einträgen, nicht aber unter **buy**, **sell** usw.

Phonetic Symbols

Zeichen der Lautschrift

Vowels/Vokale

matt	[a]	
Fahne	[aː]	
Vater	[ɐ]	
	[ɑː]	calm, part
	[æ]	sat
Chanson	[ã]	
Chance	[ɑ̃]	
	[ɑ̃ː]	double entendre
Etage	[e]	egg
Seele, Mehl	[eː]	
Wäsche, Bett	[ɛ]	
zählen	[ɛː]	
Teint	[ɛ̃ː]	
mache	[ə]	above
	[ɜː]	burn, earn
Kiste	[ɪ]	pit, awfully
Vitamin	[i]	
Ziel	[iː]	peat
Oase	[o]	
oben	[oː]	
Fondue	[õ]	
Chanson	[õː]	
Most	[ɔ]	
	[ɒ]	cot
	[ɔː]	born, jaw
ökonomisch	[ø]	
blöd	[øː]	
Götter	[œ]	
Parfum	[œ̃ː]	
	[ʌ]	hut
zuletzt	[u]	
Mut	[uː]	pool
Mutter	[ʊ]	put
Tyrann	[y]	
Kübel	[yː]	
Sünde	[ʏ]	

Diphthongs/Diphthonge

weit	[ai]	
	[aɪ]	buy, die, my
Haus	[au]	
	[aʊ]	house, now
	[eɪ]	pay, mate
	[ɛə]	pair, mare
	[əʊ]	no, boat
	[ɪə]	mere, shear
Heu, Häuser	[ɔy]	
	[ɔɪ]	boy, coin
	[ʊə]	tour, poor

Consonants/Konsonanten

Ball	[b]	ball
mich	[ç]	
	[tʃ]	child
fern	[f]	field
gern	[g]	good
Hand	[h]	hand
ja, Million	[j]	yet, million
	[dʒ]	just
Kind	[k]	kind, catch
links, Pult	[l]	left, little
matt	[m]	mat
Nest	[n]	nest
lang	[ŋ]	long
Paar	[p]	put
rennen	[r]	run
fast, fassen	[s]	sit
Chef, Stein, Schlag	[ʃ]	shall
Tafel	[t]	tab
	[θ]	thing
	[ð]	this
wer	[v]	very
	[w]	wet
Loch	[x]	loch
fix	[ks]	box
singen	[z]	pods, zip
Zahn	[ts]	
genieren	[ʒ]	measure

Other signs/Andere Zeichen

|	glottal stop/Knacklaut
[ʳ]	[r] pronounced before a vowel/vor Vokal ausgesprochenes [r]
[ˈ]	main stress/Hauptton
[ˌ]	secondary stress/Nebenton

NB: Vowels and consonants which are frequently elided (not spoken) are given in *italics:*

Vokale und Konsonanten, die häufig elidiert (nicht ausgesprochen) werden, sind *kursiv* dargestellt:

convention [kənˈvenʃən]
attempt [əˈtempt]

ENGLISH~GERMAN DICTIONARY

WÖRTERBUCH ENGLISCH~DEUTSCH

A, a [eɪ] N A *nt*, a *nt*; (*Sch: as a mark*) Eins *f*, sehr gut; (*Mus*) A *nt*, a *nt*; **from A to Z** von A bis Z; **to get from A to B** von A nach B kommen; **A sharp** (*Mus*) Ais *nt*, ais *nt*; **A flat** (*Mus*) As *nt*, as *nt* → **major**

A **a** *abbr of* **answer** Antw. **b** (*dated Brit Film*) *von der Filmkontrolle als nicht ganz jugendfrei gekennzeichneter Film* **A certificate** *Filmkennzeichnung, die Eltern vor dem nicht ganz jugendfreien Inhalt eines Films warnt*

a [eɪ, ə] INDEF ART *before vowel* **an** **a** ein(e); **so large a school** so eine große *or* eine so große Schule; **a Mr X** ein Herr X; **a certain young man** ein gewisser junger Mann
b (*in negative constructions*) **not a** kein(e); **not a single man** kein einziger *or* nicht ein einziger Mann; **he didn't want a present** er wollte kein Geschenk
c (*with profession, nationality etc*) **he's a doctor/Frenchman** er ist Arzt/Franzose; **he's a famous doctor/Frenchman** er ist ein berühmter Arzt/Franzose; **as a young girl** als junges Mädchen; **a Washington would have …** ein Washington hätte …
d (*= the same*) **to be of an age/a size** gleich alt/groß sein → **kind**
e (*= per*) pro; **50p a kilo** 50 Pence das *or* pro Kilo; **twice a month** zweimal im *or* pro Monat; **50 km an hour** 50 Stundenkilometer, 50 Kilometer pro Stunde
f **in a good/bad mood** gut/schlecht gelaunt; **to come/to have come to an end** zu Ende gehen/sein; **in a loud voice** mit lauter Stimme, laut; **to have a headache/temperature** Kopfschmerzen/erhöhte Temperatur haben

a- PREF **a** (*privative*) **amoral** amoralisch; **atypical** atypisch **b** (*old, dial*) **they came a-running** sie kamen angerannt; **the bells were a-ringing** die Glocken läuteten

A 1 [ˈeɪˈwʌn], **A one** ADJ **a** (*Naut*) erstklassig **b** (*= sound*) kerngesund; (*= fit*) gut in Form **c** (*dated inf*) super (*inf*), spitze (*inf*); **our holidays were ~** unsere Ferien waren super

AA **a** *abbr of* **Automobile Association** Britischer Automobilklub **b** *abbr of* **Alcoholics Anonymous** **c** (*dated Brit Film*) *für Jugendliche ab 14 freigegebener Film*

AAA **a** *abbr of* **American Automobile Association** Amerikanischer Automobilklub **b** *abbr of* **Australian Automobile Association** Australischer Automobilklub

AAIB (*Brit*) *abbr of* **Air Accident Investigation Branch**

A & E *abbr of* **accident and emergency**

aardvark [ˈɑːdvɑːk] N Erdferkel *nt*

Aaron's beard [ˈeərnzˈbɪəd] N Hartheu *nt*

AB *abbr* **a** (*Naut*) *of* **able-bodied seaman** **b** (*US Univ*) = **BA**

ABA *abbr* **a** (*Brit*) *of* **Amateur Boxing Association** **b** (*US*) = **American Bar Association** **c** (*US*) = **American Booksellers' Association**

aback [əˈbæk] ADV **to be taken ~** erstaunt sein; (*= upset*) betroffen sein

abacus [ˈæbəkəs] N *pl* **abaci** [ˈæbəsiː] Abakus *m*

abaft [əˈbɑːft] ADV (*Naut*) achtern

abalone [æbəˈləʊnɪ] N Seeohr *nt*

abandon [əˈbændən] VT **a** (*= leave, forsake*) verlassen; *woman* verlassen, sitzen lassen; *baby* aussetzen; *car* (einfach) stehen lassen; **they ~ed the city to the enemy** sie flohen und überließen dem Feind die Stadt; **to ~ ship** das Schiff verlassen **b** (*= give up*) *project, hope, attempt* aufgeben; **to ~ play** das Spiel abbrechen **c** (*fig*) **to ~ oneself to sth** sich einer Sache (*dat*) hingeben N *no pl* Hingabe *f*, Selbstvergessenheit *f*; **with ~** mit ganzer Seele, mit Leib und Seele

abandoned [əˈbændənd] ADJ **a** (*= dissolute*) verkommen **b** (*= unrestrained*) *dancing* selbstvergessen, hingebungsvoll, hemmungslos (*pej*); *joy* unbändig

abandonment [əˈbændənmənt] N **a** (*= forsaking, desertion*) Verlassen *nt* **b** (*= giving-up*) Aufgabe *f* **c** (*= abandon*) Hingabe *f*, Selbstvergessenheit *f*, Hemmungslosigkeit *f* (*pej*)

abase [əˈbeɪs] VT *person* erniedrigen; *morals* verderben; **to ~ oneself** sich (selbst) erniedrigen

abasement [əˈbeɪsmənt] N Erniedrigung *f*; (*of concept of love etc*) Abwertung *f*; (*= lowering of standards*) Verfall *m*, Niedergang *m*; **~ of morality** Verfall der Moral

abashed [əˈbæʃt] ADJ beschämt; **to feel ~** sich schämen

abate [əˈbeɪt] VI nachlassen; (*storm, eagerness, interest, noise also*) abflauen; (*pain, fever also*) abklingen; (*flood*) zurückgehen VT (*form*) *noise, sb's interest* dämpfen; *fever* senken; *pain* lindern

abatement [əˈbeɪtmənt] N Nachlassen *nt*; (*of storm, eagerness, interest also*) Abflauen *nt*; (*of pain also*) Abklingen *nt*; (*of flood*) Rückgang *m*; (*of rent, tax*) Senkung *f*; **the noise ~ society** die Gesellschaft zur Bekämpfung von Lärm

abattoir [ˈæbətwɑː] N Schlachthof *m*

abbess [ˈæbɪs] N Äbtissin *f*

abbey [ˈæbɪ] N Abtei *f*; (*= church in abbey*) Klosterkirche *f*

abbot [ˈæbət] N Abt *m*

abbr., abbrev. **a** *abbr of* **abbreviation** Abk. **b** *abbr of* **abbreviated** abgek.

abbreviate [əˈbriːvɪeɪt] VT *word, title* abkürzen (*to* mit); *book, speech* verkürzen; **an ~d skirt** (*hum inf*) ein kurzes Röckchen

abbreviation [əˌbriːvɪˈeɪʃən] N (*of word, title*) Abkürzung *f*; (*of book, speech*) Verkürzung *f*

ABC[1] N (*lit, fig*) Abc *nt*; **it's as easy as ~** das ist doch kinderleicht

ABC[2] *abbr of* **American Broadcasting Company** *amerikanische Rundfunkgesellschaft*

ABD (*US Univ*) *abbr of* **all but dissertation** *Status eines Doktoranden, der seine Dissertation noch schreiben muss*; **she was still ~ after four years** nach vier Jahren als Doktorandin hatte sie ihre Dissertation immer noch nicht geschrieben

abdicate [ˈæbdɪkeɪt] VT verzichten auf (*+acc*) VI (*monarch*) abdanken, abdizieren (*dated geh*); (*pope*) zurücktreten

abdication [ˌæbdɪˈkeɪʃən] N (*of monarch*) Abdankung *f*, Abdikation *f* (*dated geh*); (*of pope*) Verzicht *m*; **his ~ of the throne** sein Verzicht auf den Thron

abdomen [ˈæbdəmən] N Abdomen *nt* (*form*); (*of man, mammals also*) Unterleib *m*; (*of insects also*) Hinterleib *m*

abdominal [æbˈdɒmɪnl] ADJ abdominal (*form*); (*in man, mammals also*) Unterleibs-; (*in insects also*) Hinterleibs-; **~ pain** Unterleibsschmerzen *pl*; **~ segments** Abdominalsegmente *pl*; **~ wall** Bauchdecke *f*

abduct [æbˈdʌkt] VT entführen

abduction [æbˈdʌkʃən] N Entführung *f*

abductor [æbˈdʌktəʳ] N Entführer(in) *m(f)*

abeam [əˈbiːm] ADV (*Naut*) querab

abed [əˈbed] ADV (*old*) im Bett; **to be ~** (im Bette) ruhen (*geh*)

Aberdeen Angus [ˌæbədiːnˈæŋgəs] N (*Zool*) Angusrind *nt*

Aberdonian [ˌæbəˈdəʊnjən] N Aberdeener(in) *m(f)* ADJ Aberdeener *inv*

aberrant [əˈberənt] ADJ anomal

aberration [ˌæbəˈreɪʃən] N Anomalie *f*; (*Astron, Opt*) Aberration *f*;; (*in statistics, from course*) Abweichung *f*; (*= mistake*) Irrtum *m*; (*moral*) Verirrung *f*; **in a moment of (mental) ~** (*inf*) in einem Augenblick geistiger Verwirrung; **I must have had an ~** (*inf*) da war ich wohl (geistig) weggetreten (*inf*); **the housing scheme is something of an ~** (*inf*) die Wohnsiedlung ist (ja) eine Geschmacksverirrung (*inf*)

abet [əˈbet] VT *crime, criminal* begünstigen, Vorschub leisten (*+dat*); (*fig*) unterstützen VI → **aid VT**

abetment [əˈbetmənt], **abettal** [əˈbetəl] N **a** (*= support*) Hilfe *f*, Unterstützung *f* **b** (*Jur*) Beihilfe *f*, Vorschub *m*

abetter, abettor [əˈbetəʳ] N Helfershelfer(in) *m(f)*

abeyance [əˈbeɪəns] N *no pl* **to be in ~** (*law, rule, issue*) ruhen; (*custom, office*) nicht mehr ausgeübt werden; **to fall into ~** außer Gebrauch kommen, nicht mehr wirksam sein; **to hold/leave sth in ~** etw ruhen lassen

abhor [əbˈhɔːʳ] VT verabscheuen

abhorrence [əbˈhɒrəns] N Abscheu *f* (*of* vor *+dat*)

abhorrent [əbˈhɒrənt] ADJ abscheulich; **the very idea is ~ to me** schon der Gedanke daran ist mir zuwider; **the notion is ~ to the rational mind** der Verstand widersetzt sich einer solchen Idee

abidance [əˈbaɪdəns] N (*form*) **~ by the rules/laws** die Einhaltung der Regeln/Gesetze

abide [əˈbaɪd] VT **a** (*usu neg, interrog*) (*= tolerate*) ausstehen; (*= endure*) aushalten; **I cannot ~ living here** ich kann es nicht aushalten, hier zu leben **b** (*liter: = wait for*) harren (*+gen*) (*liter*) VI (*old: = remain, live*) weilen (*geh*)

▸ **abide by** VI *+prep obj rule, law, decision, promise, results* sich halten an (*+acc*); *consequences* tragen; **I abide by what I said** ich bleibe bei dem, was ich gesagt habe

abiding [əˈbaɪdɪŋ] ADJ (*liter: = lasting*) unvergänglich; *desire also* bleibend

ability [əˈbɪlɪtɪ] N Fähigkeit *f*; ~ **to pay/hear** Zahlungs-/Hörfähigkeit *f*; **to the best of my** ~ nach (besten) Kräften; *(with mental activities)* so gut ich es kann; **a man of great** ~ ein sehr fähiger Mann; **his** ~ **in German** seine Fähigkeiten im Deutschen; **she has great** ~ sie ist ausgesprochen fähig

abiotic ADJ, **abiotically** ADV [ˌeɪbaɪˈɒtɪk, -lɪ] abiotisch *(spec)*, unbelebt

abject [ˈæbdʒekt] ADJ **a** *(= wretched) state, liar, thief* elend, erbärmlich; *poverty* bitter; *failure* kläglich **b** *(= servile) submission, apology* demütig; *person, gesture* unterwürfig

abjectly [ˈæbdʒektlɪ] ADV *submit, apologize* demütig; *fail* kläglich; *miserable, afraid* erbärmlich

abjectness [ˈæbdʒektnɪs] N **a** *(= wretchedness)* Erbärmlichkeit *f* **b** *(= servility) (of apology)* Demut *f*; *(of person, gesture also)* Unterwürfigkeit *f*

abjuration [ˌæbdʒʊəˈreɪʃn] N Abschwören *nt*

abjure [əbˈdʒʊəˈ] VT abschwören *(+dat)*

Abkhaz [æbˈkɑːz], **Abkhazi** [æbˈkɑːzɪ] ADJ abchasisch N **a** *(person)* Abchase *m*, Abchasin *f* **b** *(Ling)* Abchasisch *nt*

Abkhazia [æbˈkɑːzɪə] N Abchasien *nt*

Abkhazian [æbˈkɑːzɪən] ADJ N = **Abkhaz**

ablative [ˈæblətɪv] N Ablativ *m*; ~ **absolute** Ablativus absolutus ADJ Ablativ-; *noun* im Ablativ; ~ **ending** Ablativendung *f*

ablaut [ˈæblaʊt] N Ablaut *m*

ablaze [əˈbleɪz] ADV ADJ *pred* **a** *(lit)* in Flammen; **to be** ~ in Flammen stehen; **to set sth** ~ etw in Brand stecken; **the paraffin really set the fire** ~ das Paraffin ließ das Feuer wirklich auflodern **b** *(fig: = animated)* **her eyes were** ~ ihre Augen glühten; **his face was** ~ **with joy/anger** sein Gesicht glühte vor Freude/brannte vor Ärger; **to be** ~ **with light** hell erleuchtet sein; **to be** ~ **with colour** *(Brit)* or **color** *(US)* in leuchtenden Farben erstrahlen

able [ˈeɪbl] ADJ **a** *(= skilled, talented) person* fähig, kompetent; *piece of work, exam paper, speech* gekonnt **b** **to be** ~ **to do sth** etw tun können; **if you're not** ~ **to understand that** wenn Sie nicht fähig sind, das zu verstehen; **I'm afraid I am not** ~ **to give you that information** ich bin leider nicht in der Lage, Ihnen diese Informationen zu geben; **you are better** ~ **to do it than he is** Sie sind eher dazu in der Lage als er; **yes, if I'm** ~ ja, wenn es mir möglich ist

-able [-əbl] ADJ *suf* -bar; **washable** waschbar; **to be doable** machbar sein

able-bodied [ˌeɪblˈbɒdɪd] ADJ (gesund und) kräftig; *(Mil)* tauglich

able(-bodied) seaman N Vollmatrose *m*

abled [ˈeɪbld] ADJ nicht behindert

abloom [əˈbluːm] ADJ *pred (poet, liter)* **to be** ~ *(flower)* blühen *(lit, fig)*; *tree* in Blüte stehen *(liter)*

ablution [əˈbluːʃən] N **a** Waschung *f* **b** **ablutions** PL *(= lavatory)* sanitäre Einrichtungen *pl*; **to perform one's ~s** *(esp hum)* seine Waschungen vornehmen; *(= go to lavatory)* seine Notdurft verrichten

ably [ˈeɪblɪ] ADV gekonnt, fähig

ABM *abbr of* **anti-ballistic missile**

abnegate [ˈæbnɪgeɪt] VT entsagen *(+dat)*

abnegation [ˌæbnɪˈgeɪʃən] N Verzicht *m* (of auf *+acc*), Entsagung *f*

abnormal [æbˈnɔːməl] ADJ anormal; *(= deviant, Med)* abnorm; ~ **psychology** Psychologie *f* des Abnormen

abnormality [ˌæbnɔːˈmælɪtɪ] N Anormale(s) *nt*; *(= deviancy, Med)* Abnormität *f*

abnormally [æbˈnɔːməlɪ] ADV *grow, develop* abnormal; *high, low also* abnorm

Abo [ˈæbəʊ] N *(Austral inf)* = **aborigine**

aboard [əˈbɔːd] ADV *(on plane, ship)* an Bord; *(on train)* im Zug; *(on bus)* im Bus; **all ~!** alle an Bord!; *(on train, bus)* alles einsteigen!; **to go** ~ an Bord gehen; **they were no sooner** ~ **than the train/bus moved off** sie waren kaum eingestiegen, als der Zug/Bus auch schon abfuhr PREP ~ **the ship/plane** an Bord des Schiffes/Flugzeugs; ~ **the train/bus** im Zug/Bus

abode [əˈbəʊd] *pret, ptp of* **abide** N *(liter: = dwelling place)* Behausung *f*, Aufenthalt *m (liter)*; *(Jur: also* **place of abode***)* Wohnsitz *m*; **a humble** ~ *(iro)* eine bescheidene Hütte *(iro)*; **of no fixed** ~ ohne festen Wohnsitz

abolish [əˈbɒlɪʃ] VT abschaffen; *law also* aufheben

abolishment [əˈbɒlɪʃmənt], **abolition** [ˌæbəʊˈlɪʃən] N Abschaffung *f*; *(of law also)* Aufhebung *f*

abolitionist [ˌæbəʊˈlɪʃənɪst] N *Befürworter der Abschaffung eines Gesetzes etc*, Abolitionist(in) *m(f) (form)*

A-bomb [ˈeɪbɒm] N Atombombe *f*

abominable [əˈbɒmɪnəbl] ADJ grässlich, abscheulich; *spelling* grässlich, entsetzlich; ~ **snowman** Schneemensch *m*

abominably [əˈbɒmɪnəblɪ] ADV grässlich, abscheulich; ~ **rude** furchtbar unhöflich

abominate [əˈbɒmɪneɪt] VT verabscheuen

abomination [əˌbɒmɪˈneɪʃən] N **a** *no pl* Verabscheuung *f*; **to be held in** ~ **by sb** von jdm verabscheut werden **b** *(= loathsome act)* Abscheulichkeit *f*; *(= loathsome thing)* Scheußlichkeit *f*

aboriginal [ˌæbəˈrɪdʒənl] ADJ der (australischen) Ureinwohner, australid; *tribe also* australisch N = **aborigine**

aborigine [ˌæbəˈrɪdʒɪnɪ] N Ureinwohner(in) *m(f)* (Australiens), Australide *m*, Australidin *f*

aborning [əˈbɔːnɪŋ] *(US)* ADV **to die** ~ *(project, idea)* noch vor seiner/ihrer *etc* Durchführung scheitern ADJ **to be** ~ im Entstehen begriffen sein

abort [əˈbɔːt] VI *(Med) (mother)* eine Fehlgeburt haben, abortieren *(form)*; *(foetus)* abgehen; *(= perform abortion)* die Schwangerschaft abbrechen, einen Abort herbeiführen *(form)*; *(fig: = go wrong)* scheitern; *(Comput)* abbrechen VT *(Med) foetus* (durch Abort) entfernen, abtreiben *(pej)*; *(Space) mission* abbrechen; *(Comput)* abbrechen; **an ~ed coup/attempt** ein abgebrochener Coup/Versuch N *(Space)* Abort *m (form)*

abortion [əˈbɔːʃən] N Schwangerschaftsabbruch *m*, Abtreibung *f (pej)*; *(= miscarriage)* Fehlgeburt *f*, Abort *m (form)*; *(fig: of plan, project etc)* Fehlschlag *m*, Reinfall *m (inf)*; *(pej, = person)* Missgeburt *f (pej)*; **to get** or **have an** ~ abtreiben lassen, eine Abtreibung vornehmen lassen

abortionist [əˈbɔːʃənɪst] N Abtreibungshelfer(in) *m(f)*; *(doctor also)* Abtreibungsarzt *m*/-ärztin *f* → **backstreet abortionist**

abortion pill N Abtreibungspille *f*

abortive [əˈbɔːtɪv] ADJ **a** *(= unsuccessful) attempt, plan* gescheitert, fehlgeschlagen; **to be** ~ scheitern, fehlschlagen **b** *(Med) drug* abortiv *(form)*, abtreibend

abortively [əˈbɔːtɪvlɪ] ADV *end* ergebnislos

abortuary [əˈbɔːtjʊərɪ] N *(US pej)* Abtreibungsklinik *f*

ABO system N *(of blood groups)* ABO System *nt*

abound [əˈbaʊnd] VI *(= exist in great numbers)* im Überfluss vorhanden sein; *(persons)* sehr zahlreich sein; *(= have in great numbers)* reich sein *(in* an *+dat)*; **students/rabbits** ~ **in ...** es wimmelt von Studenten/Kaninchen in ...; **rumours** *(Brit)* or **rumors** *(US)* ~ **in this place** hier kursieren jede Menge Gerüchte

about [əˈbaʊt] ADV **a** *(esp Brit)* herum, umher; *(= present)* in der Nähe; **to run/walk** ~ herum- or umherrennen/-gehen; **I looked (all)** ~ ich sah ringsumher; **to leave things (lying)** ~ Sachen herumliegen lassen; **to be (up and)** ~ **again** wieder auf den Beinen sein; **we were** ~ **early** wir waren früh auf den Beinen; **there's a thief** ~ ein Dieb geht um; **there's plenty of money** ~ es ist Geld in Mengen vorhanden; **there was nobody** ~ **who could help** es war niemand in der Nähe, der hätte helfen können; **at night when there's nobody** ~ nachts, wenn niemand unterwegs ist; **where is he/it? – he's/it's** ~ **somewhere** wo ist er/es? – (er/es ist) irgendwo in der Nähe; **it's the other way** ~ es ist gerade umgekehrt; **day and day** ~ (täglich) abwechselnd → **out, turn, up**

b **to be** ~ **to** im Begriff sein zu; *(esp US inf: = intending)* vorhaben, zu ...; **I was** ~ **to go out** ich wollte gerade ausgehen; **it's** ~ **to rain** es regnet gleich or demnächst; **he's** ~ **to start school** er kommt demnächst in die Schule; **we are** ~ **to run out of coffee** uns geht demnächst der Kaffee aus, wir haben bald keinen Kaffee mehr; **are you** ~ **to tell me ...?** willst du mir etwa erzählen ...?

c *(= approximately)* ungefähr, (so) um ... (herum); **he's** ~ **40** er ist ungefähr 40 or (so) um (die) 40 (herum); ~ **2 o'clock** ungefähr or so um 2 Uhr; **he is** ~ **the same, doctor** sein Zustand hat sich kaum geändert, Herr Doktor; **that's** ~ **it** das ist so ziemlich alles, das wärs (so ziemlich) *(inf)*; **that's** ~ **right** das stimmt (so) ungefähr; **I've had** ~ **enough (of this nonsense)** jetzt reicht es mir aber allmählich (mit diesem Unsinn) *(inf)*; **he was** ~ **dead from exhaustion** er war halb tot vor Erschöpfung → **just, round, time**

PREP **a** *(esp Brit)* um (... herum); *(= in)* in *(+dat)* (... herum); **the fields** ~ **the house** die Felder ums Haus (herum); **scattered** ~ **the room** im ganzen or über das ganze Zimmer verstreut; **somewhere** ~ **here** irgendwo hierherum; **all** ~ **the house** im ganzen Haus (herum); **to sit** ~ **the house** im Haus herumsitzen; **to do jobs** ~ **the house** sich im Haus (herum) nützlich machen; **he looked** ~ **him** er schaute sich um; **there's something** ~ **him/~ the way he speaks** er/seine Art zu reden hat so etwas an sich; **while you're** ~ **it** wenn du gerade or schon dabei bist; **you've been a long time** ~ **it** du hast lange dazu gebraucht; **and be quick** ~ **it!** und beeil dich damit!, aber ein bisschen dalli! *(inf)*

b *(= concerning)* über *(+acc)*; **tell me all** ~ **it** erzähl doch mal; **he knows** ~ **it** er weiß darüber Bescheid, er weiß davon; **what's it all ~?** worum or um was *(inf)* handelt es sich or geht es (eigentlich)?; **he knows what it's all** ~ er weiß Bescheid; **he's promised to do something** ~ **it** er hat versprochen, (in der Sache) etwas zu unternehmen; **they fell out** ~ **money** sie haben sich wegen Geld zerstritten; **how** or **what** ~ **me?** und ich, was ist mit mir? *(inf)*; **how** or **what** ~ **it/going to the cinema?** wie wärs damit/mit (dem) Kino?; **what** ~ **that book? have you brought it back?** was ist mit dem Buch? hast du es zurückgebracht?; **(yes,) what** ~ **it/him?** ja or na und(, was ist damit/mit ihm)?; **he doesn't know what he's** ~ er weiß nicht, was er (eigentlich) tut

about-face [əˌbaʊtˈfeɪs], **about-turn** [əˌbaʊtˈtɜːn] N *(Mil)* Kehrtwendung *f*; *(fig also)* Wendung *f* um hundertachtzig Grad; **to do an** ~ kehrtmachen; *(fig)* sich um hundertachtzig Grad drehen VI *(Mil)* eine Kehrtwendung ausführen or machen INTERJ **about face** or **turn!** (und) kehrt!

above [əˈbʌv] ADV **a** *(= overhead)* oben; *(= in a higher position)* darüber; **from** ~ von oben; **look** ~ schau nach oben; **the apartment** ~ die Wohnung oben or *(above that one)* darüber

b *(in text)* oben

PREP über *(+dat)*; *(with motion)* über *(+acc)*; *(= upstream of)* oberhalb *(+gen)*; ~ **all** vor allem, vor allen Dingen; **I couldn't hear** ~ **the din** ich konnte bei dem Lärm nichts hören; **he valued money** ~ **his family** er schätzte Geld mehr als seine Familie; **to be** ~ **sb/sth** über jdm/etw stehen; **he's** ~ **that sort of thing** er ist über so etwas erhaben; **he's not** ~ **a bit of blackmail** er ist sich *(dat)* nicht zu gut für eine kleine Erpressung; **it's** ~ **my head** or **me** das ist mir zu hoch; **to get** ~ **oneself** *(inf)* größenwahnsinnig werden *(inf)*

ADJ *attr* **the** ~ **persons/figures** die oben genannten or oben erwähnten Personen/Zahlen; **the** ~ **paragraph** der vorangehende or obige Ab-

schnitt
N the ~ *(= statement etc)* Obiges *nt (form)*; *(= person)* der/die Obengenannte *or* oben Genannte; *(several)* die Obengenannten *pl or* oben Genannten *pl*

above: **above board** ADJ PRED, **aboveboard** ADJ ATTR korrekt; **open and ~** offen und ehrlich; **above-mentioned** ADJ oben erwähnt; **above-named** ADJ oben genannt

abracadabra [ˌæbrəkəˈdæbrə] N Abrakadabra *nt*

abrade [əˈbreɪd] VT *(form) skin* aufschürfen, abschürfen; *(Geol)* abtragen

Abraham [ˈeɪbrəhæm] N Abraham *m*; **in ~'s bosom** in Abrahams Schoß

abrasion [əˈbreɪʒən] N *(Med)* (Haut)abschürfung *f*; *(Geol)* Abtragung *f*

abrasive [əˈbreɪsɪv] **ADJ** **a** *cleanser* scharf; *surface* rauh; **~ paper** Schmirgel- *or* Schleifpapier *nt* **b** *(fig) personality, person* aggressiv; *tongue, voice* scharf; *criticism, remarks* harsch **N** *(= cleanser)* Scheuermittel *nt*; *(= abrasive substance)* Schleifmittel *nt*

abrasively [əˈbreɪsɪvlɪ] ADV *say* scharf; *criticize* harsch

abrasiveness [əˈbreɪsɪvnɪs] N **a** *(of cleanser)* Schärfe *f*; *(of surface)* Rauheit *f* **b** *(fig) (of person)* Aggressivität *f*; *(of voice)* Schärfe *f*; *(of criticism)* Harschheit *f*

abreact [ˌæbrɪˈækt] VT *(Psych)* abreagieren

abreaction [ˌæbrɪˈækʃən] N *(Psych)* Abreaktion *f*

abreast [əˈbrest] ADV Seite an Seite; *(Naut also)* Bug an Bug; **to march four ~** im Viererglied *or* zu viert nebeneinander marschieren; **~ of sb/sth** neben jdm/etw, auf gleicher Höhe mit jdm/etw; **to come ~ (of sb/sth)** mit jdm/etw gleichziehen, auf gleiche Höhe mit jdm/etw kommen; **to keep ~ of the times/news** *etc* mit seiner Zeit/den Nachrichten *etc* auf dem Laufenden bleiben

abridge [əˈbrɪdʒ] VT *book* kürzen

abridgement [əˈbrɪdʒmənt] N *(act)* Kürzen *nt*; *(= abridged work)* gekürzte Ausgabe

abroad [əˈbrɔːd] ADV **a** im Ausland; **to go/be sent ~** ins Ausland gehen/geschickt werden; **from ~** aus dem Ausland **b** *(esp liter: = out of doors)* draußen; **to venture ~** sich nach draußen *or* ins Freie wagen; **he was ~ very early** er war schon sehr früh unterwegs **c** **there is a rumour** *(Brit) or* **rumor** *(US)* **~ that ...** ein Gerücht geht um *or* kursiert, dass ...; **to get ~** an die Öffentlichkeit dringen → **publish** **d** *(liter: = far and wide) scatter* weit

abrogate [ˈæbrəʊgeɪt] VT *law, treaty* außer Kraft setzen; *responsibility* ablehnen

abrogation [ˌæbrəʊˈgeɪʃən] N *(of law, treaty)* Außerkraftsetzung *f*, Ungültigkeitserklärung *f*; *(of responsibility)* Ablehnung *f*

abrupt [əˈbrʌpt] ADJ **a** abrupt; *descent, drop* unvermittelt, jäh; *bend* plötzlich; *manner, reply* schroff, brüsk; **to come to an ~ end** ein abruptes Ende nehmen; **to bring sth to an ~ halt** *(lit)* etw abrupt zum Stehen bringen; *(fig)* etw plötzlich stoppen **b** *(= brusque, curt) person* brüsk, schroff

abruptly [əˈbrʌptlɪ] ADV abrupt; *descend, drop* unvermittelt, jäh; *bend* plötzlich; *reply, ask* schroff, brüsk; *(= steeply) rise* steil

abruptness [əˈbrʌptnɪs] N abrupte Art; *(of person)* schroffe *or* brüske Art; *(of descent, drop, bend)* Plötzlichkeit *f*, Jäheit *f*; *(of reply)* Schroffheit *f*

ABS *abbr of* **anti-lock braking system**; **~ brakes** ABS-Bremsen *pl*

abs [æbz] PL *(inf) abbr of* **abductors** Bauchmuskeln *pl*; **~** *pl* **and pecs** *pl* Bauch- und Brustmuskeln *pl*

abscess [ˈæbsɪs] N Abszess *m*

abscond [əbˈskɒnd] VI sich (heimlich) davonmachen, türmen *(inf)*; *(schoolboys also)* durchbrennen

absconder [əbˈskɒndəˈ] N Flüchtige(r) *mf*; *(= child)* Ausreißer(in) *m(f) (inf)*

abseil [ˈæbseɪl] *(Brit)* **VI** *(Mountaineering: also* **abseil down***)* sich abseilen **N** Abstieg *m* (am Seil)

abseil equipment N Abseilgeräte *pl*

abseil ropes PL Abseilgeschirr *nt*

absence [ˈæbsəns] N **a** Abwesenheit *f*; *(esp from school, work etc)* Fehlen *nt*; **in the ~ of the chairman** in Abwesenheit des Vorsitzenden; **sentenced in one's ~** in Abwesenheit verurteilt; **it's not fair to criticize him in his ~** es ist nicht fair, ihn in seiner Abwesenheit zu kritisieren; **her many ~s on business** ihre häufige Abwesenheit aus geschäftlichen Gründen; **~ makes the heart grow fonder** *(Prov)* die Liebe wächst mit der Entfernung *(Prov)*
b *(= lack)* Fehlen *nt*; **~ of enthusiasm** Mangel *m* an Enthusiasmus; **in the ~ of further evidence/qualified staff** in Ermangelung weiterer Beweise/von Fachkräften
c *(= person absent)* **he counted the ~s** er stellte die Zahl der Abwesenden fest; **how many ~s do we have today?** wie viele fehlen heute *or* sind heute nicht da *or* anwesend?
d **~ of mind** Geistesabwesenheit *f*

absent [ˈæbsənt] **ADJ** **a** *(= not present) person* abwesend, nicht da; **to be ~ from school/work** in der Schule/am Arbeitsplatz fehlen; **~!** *(Sch)* fehlt!; **why were you ~ from class?** warum warst du nicht in der Stunde?, warum hast du gefehlt?; **to be** *or* **go ~ without leave** *(Mil)* sich unerlaubt von der Truppe entfernen; **~ parent** nicht betreuender Elternteil; **to ~ friends!** auf unsere abwesenden Freunde!
b *(= absent-minded) expression, look* (geistes)abwesend; **in an ~ moment** in einem Augenblick geistiger Abwesenheit
c *(= lacking)* **to be ~** fehlen [æbˈsent]
VR **to ~ oneself (from)** *(= not go, not appear)* fernbleiben (*+dat*, von); *(= leave temporarily)* sich zurückziehen *or* absentieren *(hum, geh)* (von)

absentee [ˌæbsənˈtiː] N Abwesende(r) *mf*; **there were a lot of ~s** es fehlten viele; *(pej)* es haben viele krankgefeiert

absentee ballot N *(esp US)* ≈ Briefwahl *f*

absenteeism [ˌæbsənˈtiːɪzəm] N häufige Abwesenheit; *(pej)* Krankfeiern *nt*; *(Sch)* Schwänzen *nt*; **the rate of ~ among workers** die Abwesenheitsquote bei Arbeitern

absentee: **absentee landlord** N nicht ortsansässiger Haus-/Grundbesitzer; **absentee voter** N *(esp US)* ≈ Briefwähler(in) *m(f)*

absently [ˈæbsəntlɪ] ADV (geistes)abwesend

absent-minded [ˌæbsəntˈmaɪndɪd] ADJ *(= lost in thought)* geistesabwesend; *(= habitually forgetful)* zerstreut

absent-mindedly [ˌæbsəntˈmaɪndɪdlɪ] ADV *behave* zerstreut; *look* (geistes)abwesend; **he ~ forgot it** in seiner Zerstreutheit hat er es vergessen

absent-mindedness [ˌæbsəntˈmaɪndɪdnɪs] N *(momentary)* Geistesabwesenheit *f*; *(habitual)* Zerstreutheit *f*

absinth(e) [ˈæbsɪnθ] N Absinth *m*

absolute [ˈæbsəluːt] ADJ absolut; *power, monopoly, liberty, support also, command* uneingeschränkt; *monarch also* unumschränkt; *lie, idiot* ausgemacht; **the ~** das Absolute; **the divorce was made ~** die Scheidung wurde ausgesprochen

absolute altitude N *(Aviat)* absolute Höhe, Flughöhe *f* über Grund

absolutely [ˌæbsəˈluːtlɪ] ADV absolut; *agree, trust also, true* vollkommen, völlig; *amazing, fantastic* wirklich; *deny, refuse also* strikt; *forbidden also* streng;; *stupid also* völlig *necessary also* unbedingt; *prove* eindeutig; **~!** durchaus; *(= I agree)* genau!; **do you agree? – ~** sind Sie einverstanden? – vollkommen; **do you ~ insist?** muss das unbedingt *or* durchaus sein?; **he ~ refused to do that** er wollte das absolut *or* durchaus nicht tun; **it's ~ amazing** es ist wirklich erstaunlich; **you look ~ stunning/awful** du siehst wirklich großartig/schrecklich aus; **you're ~ right** Sie haben völlig recht

absolute: **absolute majority** N absolute Mehrheit; **absolute pitch** N absolute Tonhöhe; *(of person)* absolutes Gehör; **absolute zero** N absoluter Nullpunkt

absolution [ˌæbsəˈluːʃən] N *(Eccl)* Absolution *f*, Lossprechung *f*; **to say the ~** die Absolution erteilen

absolutism [ˈæbsəluːˌtɪzəm] N Absolutismus *m*

absolve [əbˈzɒlv] VT *person (from responsibility)* entlassen *(from* aus); *(from sins)* lossprechen *(from* von); *(from blame)* freisprechen *(from* von); *(from vow, oath etc)* entbinden *(from* von, *+gen)*

absorb [əbˈsɔːb] VT absorbieren, aufnehmen; *liquid also* aufsaugen; *knowledge, news also* in sich *(acc)* aufnehmen; *vibration* auffangen, absorbieren; *shock* dämpfen; *light, sound* absorbieren, schlucken; *people, firm* absorbieren, integrieren *(into* in *+acc)*; *costs etc* tragen; *one's time* in Anspruch nehmen; **she ~s things quickly** sie hat eine rasche Auffassungsgabe; **to be ~ed in a book** *etc* in ein Buch *etc* vertieft *or* versunken sein; **to get ~ed in a book** *etc* sich in ein Buch *etc* vertiefen; **she was completely ~ed in her family/job** sie ging völlig in ihrer Familie/Arbeit auf

absorbency [əbˈsɔːbənsɪ] N Saug- *or* Absorptionsfähigkeit *f*

absorbent [əbˈsɔːbənt] ADJ saugfähig, absorbierend

absorbent cotton N *(US)* Watte *f*

absorbing [əbˈsɔːbɪŋ] ADJ fesselnd

absorption [əbˈsɔːpʃən] N Absorption *f*, Aufnahme *f*; *(of liquid also)* Aufsaugung *f*; *(of vibration)* Auffangen *nt*; *(of shock)* Dämpfung *f*; *(of people, firm)* Integration *f*; **her total ~ in her family/studies** ihr vollkommenes Aufgehen in ihrer Familie/ihrem Studium; **to watch with ~** gefesselt *or* gebannt beobachten

abstain [əbˈsteɪn] VI **a** *(from sex, smoking)* sich enthalten *(from +gen)*; **to ~ from alcohol/drinking** sich des Alkohols/Trinkens enthalten *(geh)* **b** *(in voting)* sich der Stimme enthalten

abstainer [əbˈsteɪnəˈ] N **a** *(from alcohol)* Abstinenzler(in) *m(f)* **b** = **abstention b**

abstemious [əbˈstiːmɪəs] ADJ *person, life* enthaltsam; *meal, diet* bescheiden

abstemiousness [əbˈstiːmɪəsnɪs] N *(of person, life)* Enthaltsamkeit *f*; *(of meal, diet)* Bescheidenheit *f*

abstention [əbˈstenʃən] N **a** *no pl (from sex, smoking etc)* Enthaltung *f*; *(from alcohol)* Enthaltung *f*, Abstinenz *f* **b** *(in voting)* (Stimm)enthaltung *f*; **were you one of the ~s?** waren Sie einer von denen, die sich der Stimme enthalten haben?

abstinence [ˈæbstɪnəns] N Abstinenz *f (from* von), Enthaltung *f (from* von); *(= self-restraint)* Enthaltsamkeit *f*; **total ~** völlige Abstinenz; **years of ~** jahrelange Abstinenz

abstinent [ˈæbstɪnənt] ADJ abstinent *(geh)*, enthaltsam

abstract¹ [ˈæbstrækt] **ADJ** *(all senses)* abstrakt; **~ noun** Abstraktum *nt*, abstraktes Substantiv **N** (kurze) Zusammenfassung; **in the ~** abstrakt

abstract² [æbˈstrækt] VT abstrahieren; *information* entnehmen *(from* aus)

abstracted [æbˈstræktɪd] ADJ abwesend, entrückt *(geh)*

abstractedly [æbˈstræktɪdlɪ] ADV abwesend, entrückt *(geh)*; *gaze* wie abwesend

abstraction [æbˈstrækʃən] N Abstraktion *f*; *(= abstract term also)* Abstraktum *nt*; *(= mental separation also)* Abstrahieren *nt*; *(= extraction: of information etc)* Entnahme *f*; *(= absent-mindedness)* Entrücktheit *f (geh)*; **to argue in ~s** in abstrakten Begriffen *or* in Abstraktionen argumentieren

abstractness [ˈæbstræktnɪs] N Abstraktheit *f*

abstruse [æbˈstruːs] ADJ abstrus

abstruseness [æbˈstruːsnɪs] N abstruse Unklarheit

absurd [əbˈsɜːd] ADJ absurd; **don't be ~!** sei nicht albern; **if you think that, you're just being ~** du bist ja nicht recht bei Trost, wenn du das glaubst; **what an ~ waste of time!** so eine blödsinnige Zeitverschwendung!; **the management is being ~ again** das Management spielt mal wieder verrückt *(inf)*; **theatre of the ~** absurdes Theater

absurdist [əbˈsɜːdɪst] ADJ *(Liter, Theat)* absurd

absurdity [əbˈsɜːdɪtɪ] N Absurde(s) *nt no pl* *(of* an *+dat)*; *(thing etc also)* Absurdität *f*

absurdly [əbˈsɜːdlɪ] ADV *behave, react* absurd; *fast, rich, expensive etc* unsinnig; **he suggested very ~ …** er machte absurderweise den Vorschlag, …

abundance [əˈbʌndəns] N (großer) Reichtum *(of* an *+dat)*; *(of hair, vegetation, details, illustrations, information, ideas, colours also, proof)* Fülle *f* *(of* von, *+gen)*; **in ~** in Hülle und Fülle; **to have an ~ of sth** etw im Überfluss haben; **a country with an ~ of oil/raw materials** ein Land mit reichen Ölvorkommen/großem Reichtum an Rohstoffen; **with his ~ of energy** mit seiner ungeheuren Energie; **such an ~ of open space** so unermesslich viel freies Land

abundant [əˈbʌndənt] ADJ reich; *growth, hair* üppig; *time, proof* reichlich; *energy, self-confidence etc* ungeheuer; **to be ~ in sth** reich an etw *(dat)* sein; **apples are in ~ supply** es gibt reichlich Äpfel, es gibt Äpfel in Hülle und Fülle

abundantly [əˈbʌndəntlɪ] ADV reichlich; *grow* in Hülle und Fülle, üppig; **to make it ~ clear that …** mehr als deutlich zu verstehen geben, dass …; **it was ~ clear (to me) that …** es war (mir) mehr als klar, dass …; **that is ~ obvious** das ist mehr als offensichtlich

abuse [əˈbjuːs] **N** **a** *no pl (= insults)* Beschimpfungen *pl*; **a term of ~** ein Schimpfwort *nt*; **to shout ~ at sb** jdm Beschimpfungen an den Kopf werfen; **to heap ~ on sb** jdn mit Beschimpfungen überschütten → **shower, stream**
b *(= misuse)* Missbrauch *m*; *(= unjust practice)* Missstand *m*; **~ of confidence/authority** Vertrauens-/Amtsmissbrauch *m*; **~ of power** Machtmissbrauch *m*; **the system is open to ~** das System lässt sich leicht missbrauchen [əˈbjuːz] **VT** **a** *(= revile)* beschimpfen, schmähen *(geh)* **b** *(= misuse)* missbrauchen; *one's health* Raubbau treiben mit

abuser [əˈbjuːzəˈ] N *(of child, woman, man)* Missbraucher(in) *m(f)*

abusive [əbˈjuːsɪv] ADJ beleidigend; *(Psych) person, relationship* abusiv; **~ language** Beschimpfungen *pl*, Beleidigungen *pl*; **children from an ~ home** Kinder *pl*, die zu Hause missbraucht werden/wurden; **to be/become ~ (towards sb)** (jdm gegenüber) beleidigend *or* ausfallend sein/werden; **he muttered something ~** er murmelte etwas Beleidigendes; **to get ~ (towards sb)** (jdm gegenüber) beleidigend *or* ausfallend werden

abusively [əbˈjuːsɪvlɪ] ADV *refer to* beleidigend; **to shout/scream ~ at sb** jdm Beleidigungen zurufen/entgegenschreien

abusiveness [əbˈjuːsɪvnɪs] N *(of person)* ausfallende Art; **a critic should not descend to mere ~** ein Kritiker sollte sich nicht in reinen Ausfälligkeiten ergehen

abut [əˈbʌt] VI stoßen *(on(to)* an *+acc)*; *(land also)* grenzen *(on(to)* an *+acc)*; *(two houses, fields etc)* aneinanderstoßen/-grenzen

abutment [əˈbʌtmənt] N *(Archit)* Flügel- *or* Wangenmauer *f*

abutter [əˈbʌtəˈ] N *(US)* Anlieger(in) *m(f)*; *(to one's own land)* (Grenz)nachbar(in) *m(f)*

abutting [əˈbʌtɪŋ] ADJ (daran) anstoßend *attr*; *fields also* (daran) angrenzend *attr*

ABV *abbr of* **alcohol by volume** Vol. %

abysmal [əˈbɪzməl] ADJ *(fig)* entsetzlich; *performance, work, taste etc* miserabel

abysmally [əˈbɪzməlɪ] ADV entsetzlich; *perform, work etc also* miserabel; **to fail ~** kläglich versagen; **our team did ~ in the competition** unsere Mannschaft schnitt bei dem Wettkampf miserabel ab

abyss [əˈbɪs] N *(lit, fig)* Abgrund *m*; **the ~ of war** der Abgrund des Krieges

Abyssinia [ˌæbɪˈsɪnɪə] N Abessinien *nt*

Abyssinian [ˌæbɪˈsɪnɪən] **ADJ** *attr* abessinisch **N** Abessinier(in) *m(f)*

AC **a** *abbr of* **alternating current** **b** *abbr of* **aircraftman**

A/C *abbr of* **account** Kto.

acacia [əˈkeɪʃə] N *(also* **acacia tree***)* Akazie *f*

academe [ˈækədiːm] N *(form)* die akademische Welt; **the groves** *pl* **of ~** die akademischen Gefilde *pl (form)*

academic [ˌækəˈdemɪk] **ADJ** **a** akademisch; *publisher, reputation* wissenschaftlich; **~ advisor** *(US)* Studienberater(in) *m(f)*; **~ dean** *(US)* Dekan(in) *m(f)*; **~ officers** *(US)* akademisches Personal; **~ year** akademisches Jahr, Studienjahr *nt*
b *(= intellectual) approach, quality, interest* wissenschaftlich; *interests* geistig; *person, appearance* intellektuell; *style, book* akademisch
c *(= theoretical)* akademisch; **out of ~ interest** aus rein akademischem Interesse; **since the decision has already been made the discussion is purely ~** da die Entscheidung schon getroffen wurde, ist das eine (rein) akademische Diskussion
N Akademiker(in) *m(f)*; *(Univ)* Universitätslehrkraft *f*

academically [ˌækəˈdemɪkəlɪ] ADV **a** wissenschaftlich; **to be ~ inclined** geistige Interessen haben; **to be ~ minded** wissenschaftlich denken; **~ respectable** wissenschaftlich akzeptabel; **~ gifted** intellektuell begabt **b** **she is not doing well ~** *(Sch)* sie ist in der Schule nicht gut; *(Univ)* sie ist nicht mit ihrem Studium nicht sehr erfolgreich; **she's good at handicraft but is not doing so well ~** im Werken ist sie gut, aber in den wissenschaftlichen Fächern hapert es

academicals [ˌækəˈdemɪkəlz] PL akademische Tracht

academician [əˌkædəˈmɪʃən] N Akademiemitglied *nt*

academy [əˈkædəmɪ] N Akademie *f*; **naval/military ~** Marine-/Militärakademie *f*; **~ for young ladies** ≈ höhere Töchterschule

Academy Award N *(Film) Filmpreis der Academy of Motion Picture Arts and Sciences*, Oscar *m (inf)*

Academy Awards ceremony N *(Film)* Oscarverleihung *f (inf)*

acanthus [əˈkænθəs] N *(= plant)* Bärenklau *f*, Akanthus *m (also Archit)*

a cappella [ˌækəˈpelə] *(Mus)* **ADV** *sing* a cappella **ADJ** A-cappella- *attr inv*

ACAS, Acas [ˈeɪkæs] *abbr of* **Advisory Conciliation and Arbitration Service** *Schlichtungsstelle für Arbeitskonflikte*

acc **a** *abbr of* **account** Kto. **b** *abbr of* **accommodation** Übern.

acc. *(Banking) abbr of* **account** Kto.

accede [ækˈsiːd] VI **a** **to ~ to the throne** den Thron besteigen; **to ~ to the Premiership/office of President** die Nachfolge als Premierminister/Präsident antreten **b** *(= agree)* zustimmen *(to +dat)*; *(= yield)* einwilligen *(to* in *+acc)* **c** **to ~ to a treaty** einem Pakt beitreten

accelerate *work-rate, speed, change* [ækˈseləreɪt] **VT** beschleunigen; *speed also* erhöhen **VI** beschleunigen; *(driver also)* Gas geben; *(work-rate, speed, change)* sich beschleunigen, zunehmen; *(growth, inflation etc)* zunehmen; **he ~d away** er gab Gas und fuhr davon; **he ~d out of the bend** er hat in der Kurve beschleunigt *or* Gas gegeben

acceleration [ækˌseləˈreɪʃən] N Beschleunigung *f*; *(of speed also)* Erhöhung *f*; **to have good/poor ~** eine gute/schlechte Beschleunigung haben, gut/schlecht beschleunigen

acceleration ratio N Beschleunigungswert *m*

accelerator [ækˈseləreɪtəˈ] N **a** *(also* **accelerator pedal***)* Gaspedal *nt*, Gas *nt (inf)*; **to step on the ~** aufs Gas treten *or* drücken *(inf)* **b** *(Phys)* Beschleuniger *m*

accent [ˈæksənt] **N** *(all senses)* Akzent *m*; *(= stress also)* Betonung *f*; **~s** *(liter. = tones)* Töne *pl*, Tonfall *m*; **to speak without/with an ~** akzentfrei *or* ohne Akzent/mit Akzent sprechen; **to put the ~ on sth** *(fig)* den Akzent auf etw *(acc)* legen; **the ~ is on bright colours** der Akzent *or* die Betonung liegt auf leuchtenden Farben **VT** [ækˈsent] betonen

accentuate [ækˈsentjʊeɪt] VT betonen; *(in speaking, Mus)* akzentuieren; *(Ling: = give accent to)* mit einem Akzent versehen; **to ~ the need for sth** die Notwendigkeit einer Sache *(gen)* betonen *or* hervorheben

accentuation [ækˌsentjʊˈeɪʃən] N Betonung *f*; *(in speaking, Mus)* Akzentuierung *f*

accept [əkˈsept] ✪ 11.3, 12.1, 12.2, 19.5, 20.6, 25.1, 25.2, 26.3, 27.3 **VT** **a** akzeptieren; *apology, offer, gift, invitation* annehmen; *responsibility* übernehmen; *(= believe) story* glauben; **a photograph of the President ~ing the award** ein Bild von dem Präsidenten, wie er die Auszeichnung entgegennimmt; **we will not ~ anything but the best** wir werden nur das Allerbeste akzeptieren *or* annehmen; **to ~ sb into society** jdn in die Gesellschaft aufnehmen
b *(= recognize) need* einsehen, anerkennen; *person, duty* akzeptieren, anerkennen; **it is generally** *or* **widely ~ed that …** es ist allgemein anerkannt, dass …; **we must ~ the fact that …** wir müssen uns damit abfinden, dass …; **I ~ that it might take a little longer** ich sehe ein, dass es etwas länger dauern könnte; **the government ~ed that the treaty would on occasions have to be infringed** die Regierung akzeptierte, dass der Vertrag gelegentlich verletzt werden würde; **to ~ that sth is one's responsibility/duty** etw als seine Verantwortung/Pflicht akzeptieren
c *(= allow, put up with) behaviour, fate, conditions* hinnehmen; **we'll just have to ~ things as they are** wir müssen die Dinge eben so (hin)nehmen, wie sie sind
d *(Comm) cheque, orders* annehmen; *delivery* annehmen, abnehmen
VI annehmen; *(with offers also)* akzeptieren; *(with invitations also)* zusagen

acceptability [əkˌseptəˈbɪlɪtɪ] N Annehmbarkeit *f*, Akzeptierbarkeit *f*; *(of behaviour)* Zulässigkeit *f*; **social ~** *(of person)* gesellschaftliche Akzeptabilität; *(of behaviour)* gesellschaftliche Zulässigkeit

acceptable [əkˈseptəbl] ADJ annehmbar *(to* für), akzeptabel *(to* für); *behaviour* zulässig; *(= suitable) gift* passend; **that would be most ~** das wäre sehr *or* höchst willkommen; **any job would be ~ to him** ihm wäre jede Stelle recht; **only the best is ~** nur das Beste kann angenommen werden

acceptably [əkˈseptəblɪ] ADV **a** *(= properly) behave, treat* anständig, korrekt **b** *(= sufficiently)* **~ accurate/safe** ausreichend *or* hinlänglich genau/sicher; **noise levels were ~ low** der Lärmpegel war erträglich **c** *(= adequately)* akzeptabel, angemessen

acceptance [əkˈseptəns] ✪ 20.2 N **a** *(of offer, gift, excuse)* Annahme *f*; *(of suggestion, work also, report, findings)* Akzeptierung *f*; *(of responsibility)* Übernahme *f*; *(= believing: of story)* Glauben *nt*; *(= receiving: of award)* Entgegennahme *f*; **his ~ into the family** seine Aufnahme in der *or* die Familie; **to find** *or* **win** *or* **gain ~** *(theories, people)* anerkannt werden, Anerkennung finden; **to meet with general ~** allgemeine Anerkennung finden
b *(= recognition: of need, fact)* Anerkennung *f*
c *(= toleration: of behaviour, fate, conditions)*

Hinnahme *f*
d *(Comm) (of cheque, orders)* Annahme *f*; *(of delivery also)* Abnahme *f*

acceptance: **acceptance house** N *(Fin)* Akzept- *or* Wechselbank *f*; **acceptance trials** PL Abnahmeprüfung *f*

acceptation [ˌæksep'teɪʃən] N *(old, form, of word)* Bedeutung *f*

accepted [ək'septɪd] ADJ *truth, fact* (allgemein) anerkannt; **it's the ~ thing** es ist üblich *or* der Brauch; **to do sth because it is the ~ thing** etw tun, weil es (eben) so üblich ist; **~ text** offizieller Text; **socially ~** gesellschaftsfähig

accepting [ək'septɪŋ] ADJ **to be ~ of sth/sb** für etw/jdn offen *or* zugänglich sein; *(= tolerant)* etw/jdm gegenüber tolerant sein

accepting house N *(Brit Fin)* Akzeptbank *f*

access ['ækses] **N** **a** Zugang *m* *(to* zu); *(esp to room, private grounds etc)* Zutritt *m* *(to* zu); **to be easy of ~** leicht zugänglich sein; **to give sb ~** jdm Zugang gewähren *(to sb/sth* zu jdm/etw), jdm Zutritt gewähren *(to sth* zu etw); **to refuse sb ~** jdm den Zugang verwehren *(to sb/sth* zu jdm/etw), jdm den Zutritt verwehren *(to sth* zu etw); **this door gives ~ to the garden** diese Tür führt in den Garten; **this location offers easy ~ to shops and transport facilities** von hier sind Läden und Verkehrsmittel leicht zu erreichen; **to have ~ to sb/sth** Zugang zu jdm/etw haben; **to gain ~ to sb/sth** sich *(dat)* Zugang zu jdm/etw verschaffen; **the thieves gained ~ through the window** die Diebe gelangten durch das Fenster hinein; **"access only"** „nur für Anlieger", „Anlieger frei"; **right of ~ to one's children** Besuchsrecht für seine Kinder
b *(Comput)* Zugriff *m*; *(= access authorization)* Zugangs- *or* Zugriffsberechtigung *f*
c *(liter: = attack, fit)* Anfall *m*
VT *(Comput) file, data* zugreifen auf *(+acc)*

accessary [æk'sesərɪ] N = **accessory c**

access code N Zugangskode *m*

access course N Brückenkurs *m*

accessibility [ækˌsesɪ'bɪlɪtɪ] N *(of place, information)* Zugänglichkeit *f*

accessible [æk'sesəbl] ADJ *information, person* zugänglich *(to +dat)*; *place also* (leicht) zu erreichen *(to* für)

accession [æk'seʃən] N **a** *(to an office)* Antritt *m* *(to +gen)*; *(also* **accession to the throne**) Thronbesteigung *f*; *(to estate, power)* Übernahme *f* *(to +gen)*; **since his ~ to power** seit seiner Machtübernahme **b** *(= consent: to treaty, demand)* Zustimmung *f* *(to* zu), Annahme *f* *(to +gen)* **c** *(= addition) (to property)* Zukauf *m*; *(to library)* (Neu)anschaffung *f*; **a sudden ~ of strength** *(liter)* eine plötzliche Anwandlung von Kraft

accession criteria PL *(of EU etc)* Beitrittskriterien *pl*

access key N *(Comput)* Zugriffsschlüssel *m*; *(on keyboard)* Zugriffstaste

accessorize [æk'sesəraɪz] VT *dress* mit Accessoires versehen; *room* dekorieren

accessory [æk'sesərɪ] N **a** Extra *nt*; *(in fashion)* Accessoire *nt* **b** **accessories** PL Zubehör *nt*; **toilet accessories** Toilettenartikel *pl* **c** *(Jur)* Helfershelfer(in) *m(f)*; *(actively involved)* Mitschuldige(r) *mf* *(to* an *+dat)*; **to be an ~ after the fact** *(Jur)* sich der Beihilfe schuldig machen; **this made him an ~ to the crime** dadurch wurde er an dem Verbrechen mitschuldig

access: **access path** N *(Comput)* Zugriffspfad *m*; **access permission** N *(Comput)* Zugriffsberechtigung *f*; **access right** N *(Comput)* Zugriffsrecht *m*; **access road** N Zufahrt(sstraße) *f*; **access time** N Zugriffszeit *f*; **access traffic** N Anliegerverkehr *m*; **access violation** N *(Comput)* Zugriffsverletzung *f*

accidence ['æksɪdəns] N *(Gram)* Formenlehre *f*

accident ['æksɪdənt] N *(Mot, in home, at work)* Unfall *m*; *(Rail, Aviat: = disaster)* Unglück *nt*; *(= mishap)* Missgeschick *nt*; *(= chance occurrence)* Zufall *m*; *(inf: = unplanned child)* (Verkehrs)unfall *m (inf)*; **~ and emergency department/unit** Notfallstation *f*, Notaufnahme *f*; **she has had an ~** sie hat einen Unfall gehabt *or (caused it)* gebaut *(inf)*; *(in car, train etc also)* sie ist verunglückt; *(in kitchen etc)* ihr ist etwas *or* ein Missgeschick *or* ein Malheur passiert; **little Jimmy has had an ~** *(euph)* dem kleinen Jimmy ist ein Malheur passiert *(inf)*; **that was an ~ waiting to happen** das musste ja so kommen; **by ~** *(= by chance)* durch Zufall, zufällig; *(= unintentionally)* aus Versehen; **without ~** *(of driver, car)* unfallfrei; **who by an ~ of birth possessed riches** der zufälligerweise reich geboren wurde; **~s will happen** *(prov)* so was kann vorkommen, so was kommt in den besten Familien vor *(inf)*; **it was an ~** es war ein Versehen; **it was pure ~ that ...** es war reiner Zufall, dass ...; **it's no ~ that ...** es ist kein Zufall, dass ...; *(not surprisingly)* es kommt nicht von ungefähr, dass ...

accidental [ˌæksɪ'dentl] **ADJ** **a** *(= unplanned) meeting, benefit* zufällig; *(= unintentional) blow, shooting* versehentlich; **one of the ~ effects of this scheme was ...** eine der Wirkungen, die dieser Plan unbeabsichtigterweise mit sich brachte, war ... **b** *(= resulting from accident) injury, death* durch Unfall; **~ damage** *(Insur)* Unfallschaden *m* **N** *(Mus) (= sign)* Versetzungszeichen *nt*, Akzidentale *f (form)*; *(= note)* erhöhter/erniedrigter Ton

accidentally [ˌæksɪ'dentəlɪ] ADV *(= by chance)* zufällig; *(= unintentionally)* versehentlich; **~ on purpose** *(hum)* versehentlich-absichtlich *(hum)*

accident: **accident insurance** N Unfallversicherung *f*; **accident prevention** N Unfallverhütung *f*; **accident-prone** ADJ vom Pech verfolgt; **she is very ~** sie ist vom Pech verfolgt, sie ist ein richtiger Pechvogel; *(more serious)* ihr passieren ständig Unfälle; **accident report** N Unfallbericht *m*; **accident risk** N Unfallrisiko *nt*

acclaim [ə'kleɪm] **VT** **a** *(= applaud)* feiern *(as* als); *(critics)* anerkennen **b** *(= proclaim)* **to ~ sb king/winner** jdn zum König/als Sieger ausrufen **N** Beifall *m*; *(of critics)* Anerkennung *f*

acclamation [ˌæklə'meɪʃən] N Beifall *m no pl*; *(of audience etc also)* Beifallskundgebung *f*, Beifallsbezeigung *f*; *(of critics also)* Anerkennung *f*; **by ~** durch Akklamation

acclimate [ə'klaɪmeɪt] VT *(US)* = **acclimatize**

acclimatization [əˌklaɪmətaɪ'zeɪʃən], *(US)* **acclimation** [ˌæklaɪ'meɪʃən] N Akklimatisierung *f* *(to* an *+acc)*, Akklimatisation *f* *(to* an *+acc)*; *(to new surroundings etc also)* Gewöhnung *f* *(to* an *+acc)*

acclimatize [ə'klaɪmətaɪz], *(US)* **acclimate** [ə'klaɪmeɪt] **VT** gewöhnen *(to* an *+acc)*; **to become ~d** sich akklimatisieren; *(person also)* sich eingewöhnen **VI** *(also vr:* **acclimatize oneself**) sich akklimatisieren *(to* an *+acc, to a country etc* in einem Land *etc)*

acclivity [ə'klɪvɪtɪ] N *(form)* Hang *m*

accolade ['ækəʊleɪd] N *(= award)* Auszeichnung *f*; *(= praise)* Lob *nt no pl*; *(Hist, Mus)* Akkolade *f*

accommodate [ə'kɒmədeɪt] **VT** **a** *(= provide lodging for)* unterbringen
b *(= hold, have room for)* Platz haben für; *(= contain) machine part etc* enthalten; **the car can ~ five people** das Auto bietet fünf Personen Platz *or* hat Platz für fünf Personen
c *(= be able to cope with: theory, plan, forecasts)* Rechnung *f* tragen *(+dat)*
d *(form: = oblige)* dienen *(+dat)*; *wishes* entgegenkommen *(+dat)*; **I think we might be able to ~ you** ich glaube, wir können Ihnen entgegenkommen
VI *(eye)* sich einstellen *(to* auf *+acc)*
VR **to ~ oneself to sth** sich einer Sache *(dat)* anpassen

accommodating [ə'kɒmədeɪtɪŋ] ADJ entgegenkommend

accommodation [əˌkɒmə'deɪʃən] N **a** *(= lodging: US also* **accommodations**) Unterkunft *f*; *(= room)* Zimmer *nt*; *(= flat)* Wohnung *f*; **"accommodation"** „Fremdenzimmer"; **hotel ~ is scarce** Hotelzimmer sind knapp; **~ wanted** Zimmer/Wohnung gesucht; **they found ~ in a youth hostel** sie fanden in einer Jugendherberge Unterkunft, sie kamen in einer Jugendherberge unter
b *(= space: US also* **accommodations**) Platz *m*; **seating ~** Sitzplätze *pl*; **there is ~ for twenty passengers in the plane** das Flugzeug bietet zwanzig Passagieren Platz *or* hat für zwanzig Passagiere Platz; **sleeping ~ for six** Schlafgelegenheit *f* für sechs Personen; **~ in the hospital is inadequate** die Unterbringungsmöglichkeiten im Krankenhaus sind unzureichend
c *(form: = agreement)* **to reach an ~** eine Übereinkunft *or* ein Übereinkommen *nt* erzielen
d *(of eye)* Einstellung *f* *(to* auf *+acc)*

accommodation: **accommodation address** N Briefkastenadresse *f*; **accommodation agency** N *(Brit) Agentur, die Mietobjekte vermittelt*; **accommodation bill** N Gefälligkeitswechsel *m*; **accommodation bureau** N Wohnungsvermittlung *f*; *(Univ)* Zimmervermittlung *f*; **accommodation ladder** N *(Naut)* Fallreep *nt*; **accommodation office** N *(Univ)* Zimmervermittlung *f*; **accommodation service** N Zimmernachweis *m*; **accommodation train** N *(US)* Personenzug *m*, Bummelzug *m (inf)*

accompaniment [ə'kʌmpənɪmənt] N Begleitung *f (also Mus)*; **with piano ~** mit Klavierbegleitung; **to the ~ of** begleitet von

accompanist [ə'kʌmpənɪst] N Begleiter(in) *m(f)*

accompany [ə'kʌmpənɪ] VT begleiten *(also Mus)*; **pork is often accompanied by apple sauce** Schweinefleisch wird oft mit Apfelmus (als Beilage) serviert; **to ~ oneself** *(Mus)* sich selbst begleiten; **~ing letter** Begleitschreiben *nt*

accomplice [ə'kʌmplɪs] N Komplize *m*, Komplizin *f*, Mittäter(in) *m(f)*; **to be an ~ to a crime** Komplize bei einem Verbrechen sein, Mittäter eines Verbrechens sein

accomplish [ə'kʌmplɪʃ] VT schaffen; **he ~ed a great deal in his short career** er hat in der kurzen Zeit seines Wirkens Großes geleistet; **that didn't ~ anything** damit war nichts erreicht

accomplished [ə'kʌmplɪʃt] ADJ **a** *(= skilled) player, carpenter* fähig; *performance* vollendet; *liar* versiert; *young lady* vielseitig; **to be ~ in the art of ...** die Kunst ... *(gen)* beherrschen **b** *fact* vollendet

accomplishment [ə'kʌmplɪʃmənt] N **a** *no pl* *(= completion)* Bewältigung *f* **b** *(= skill)* Fertigkeit *f*; *(= achievement)* Leistung *f*; **social ~s** gesellschaftliche Gewandtheit

accord [ə'kɔːd] **N** *(= agreement)* Übereinstimmung *f*, Einigkeit *f*; *(Pol)* Abkommen *nt*; **I'm not in ~ with him/his views** ich stimme mit ihm/seinen Ansichten nicht überein; **of one's/its own ~** von selbst; *(of persons also)* aus freien Stücken; **with one ~** geschlossen; *sing, cheer, say etc* wie aus einem Mund(e); **to be in ~ with sth** mit etw in Einklang stehen **VT** *(sb sth* jdm etw) gewähren; *praise* erteilen; *courtesy* erweisen; *honorary title* verleihen; *welcome* bieten **VI** sich *or* einander entsprechen; **to ~ with sth** einer Sache *(dat)* entsprechen

accordance [ə'kɔːdəns] N **in ~ with** entsprechend *(+dat)*, gemäß *(+dat)*

accordingly [ə'kɔːdɪŋlɪ] ADV *(= correspondingly)* (dem)entsprechend; *(= so, therefore)* (dem)entsprechend, folglich

according to [ə'kɔːdɪŋ'tuː] ✪ 26.2 PREP *(= as stated or shown by)* zufolge *(+dat)*, nach; *person, book, letter also* laut; *(= in agreement with, in proportion to)* entsprechend *(+dat)*, nach; **~ the map** der Karte nach *or* zufolge; **~ Peter** laut Peter, Peter zufolge; **we did it ~ the rules** wir haben uns an die Regeln gehalten

accordion [ə'kɔːdɪən] N Akkordeon *nt*, Ziehharmonika *f*

accordion file N *(US)* Ordnungsmappe *f*

accordionist [ə'kɔːdɪənɪst] N Akkordeonspieler(in) *m(f)*, Akkordeonist(in) *m(f)*

accost [ə'kɒst] VT ansprechen, anpöbeln *(pej)*

account [ə'kaʊnt] ✪ 20.7 **N** **a** Darstellung *f*; *(= report)* Bericht *m*; **to keep an ~ of one's expenses/experiences** über seine Ausgaben Buch führen/seine Erlebnisse schriftlich festhalten; **by** *or* **from all ~s** nach allem, was man hört; **by your own ~** nach Ihrer eigenen Darstellung, nach Ihren eigenen Angaben; **to give an ~ of sth** über etw *(acc)* Bericht erstatten; **to give an ~ of oneself** Rede und Antwort stehen; **to give a good ~ of oneself** sich gut schlagen; **to call** *or* **hold sb to ~** jdn zur Rechenschaft ziehen; **to be called** *or* **held to ~ for sth** über etw *(acc)* Rechenschaft ablegen müssen
b *(= consideration)* **to take ~ of sb/sth, to take sb/sth into ~** jdn/etw in Betracht ziehen; **to take no ~ of sb/sth, to leave sb/sth out of ~** jdn/etw außer Betracht lassen; **on no ~, not on any ~** auf (gar) keinen Fall; **on this/that ~** deshalb, deswegen; **on ~ of him** seinetwegen; **on ~ of the weather** wegen *or* aufgrund des Wetters; **on my/his/their ~** meinet-/seinet-/ihretwegen; **on one's own ~** für sich (selbst)
c *(= benefit)* Nutzen *m*; **to turn sth to (good) ~** (guten) Gebrauch von etw machen, etw (gut) nützen
d *(= importance)* **of little ~** von geringer Bedeutung; **of no ~** ohne Bedeutung
e *(Fin, Comm) (at bank, shop)* Konto *nt* *(with* bei); *(= client)* Kunde *m*, Kundin *f*; *(= bill)* Rechnung *f*; **to win sb's ~** jdn als Kunden gewinnen; **to buy sth on ~** etw auf (Kunden)kredit kaufen; **please charge it to my ~** stellen Sie es mir bitte in Rechnung; **£50 on ~** £ 50 als Anzahlung; **~(s) department** *(for customer accounts)* Kreditbüro *nt*; **to settle** *or* **square ~s** *or* **one's ~ with sb** *(fig)* mit jdm abrechnen; **the duel squared all ~s between them** das Duell bereinigte alles zwischen ihnen; **~ payee only** *(Brit)* nur zur Verrechnung
f accounts PL *(of company, club)* (Geschäfts)bücher *pl*; *(of household)* Einnahmen und Ausgaben *pl*; **to keep the ~s** die Bücher führen, die Buchführung machen
VT *(form: = consider)* erachten als; **to ~ oneself lucky** sich glücklich schätzen

▶ **account for** VI +*prep obj* **a** *(= explain)* erklären; *(= give account of) actions, expenditure* Rechenschaft ablegen über *(+acc)*; **how do you account for it?** wie erklären Sie sich *(dat)* das?; **he wasn't able to account for the missing money** er konnte den Verbleib des fehlenden Geldes nicht erklären; **all the children were/all the money was accounted for** der Verbleib aller Kinder/des (ganzen) Geldes war bekannt, man wusste, wo die Kinder alle waren/wo das Geld (geblieben) war; **there's no accounting for taste** über Geschmack lässt sich (nicht) streiten
b *(= be the source of)* der Grund sein für; **this area accounts for most of the country's mineral wealth** aus dieser Gegend stammen die meisten Bodenschätze des Landes; **this area alone accounts for some 25% of the population** diese Gegend allein macht etwa 25% der Bevölkerung aus; **he accounts for most of the accidents** die meisten Unfälle gehen auf sein Konto *(inf)*
c *(= be the cause of defeat, destruction etc of)* zur Strecke bringen; *(illness)* dahinraffen; *chances* zunichtemachen; **Proctor accounted for five Australian batsmen** Proctor hat fünf australische Schlagmänner ausgeschlagen

accountability [ə,kaʊntə'bɪlɪtɪ] N Verantwortlichkeit *f* *(to sb* jdm gegenüber)

accountable [ə'kaʊntəbl] ADJ verantwortlich *(to sb* jdm); **to hold sb ~ (for sth)** jdn (für etw) verantwortlich machen

accountancy [ə'kaʊntənsɪ] N Buchführung *f*, Buchhaltung *f*; *(= tax accountancy)* Steuerberatung *f*

accountant [ə'kaʊntənt] N Buchhalter(in) *m(f)*; *(= external financial adviser)* Wirtschaftsprüfer(in) *m(f)*; *(= auditor)* Rechnungsprüfer(in) *m(f)*; *(= tax accountant)* Steuerberater(in) *m(f)*

account: **account balance** N Kontostand *m*; **account book** N Geschäftsbuch *nt*; **account card** N *(for a shop)* Kundenkreditkarte *f*; **account charge** N Konto(führungs)gebühr *f*; **account day** N *(Brit: St Ex)* Liquidationstag *m*; **account executive** N Kundenbetreuer(in) *m(f)*; **account holder** N *(Banking)* Kontoinhaber(in) *m(f)*

accounting [ə'kaʊntɪŋ] N Buchhaltung *f*, Buchführung *f*; **~ method** Buchhaltungsverfahren *nt*; **~ period** Abrechnungszeitraum *m*; **~ policy** Bilanzierungspolitik *f*

accounting department N *(US: of company)* Buchhaltung *f*

account number N Kontonummer *f*

accounts department N *(Brit: of company)* Buchhaltung *f*

accounts payable N *(Fin)* Verbindlichkeiten *pl*

accounts receivable N *(Fin)* Außenstände *pl*

accoutrements [ə'kuːtrəmənts], *(US also)* **accouterments** [ə'kuːtərmənts] PL Ausrüstung *f*; **the ~ of the trade** das Handwerkszeug

accredit [ə'kredɪt] VT **a** *ambassador, representative* akkreditieren *(form)*, beglaubigen **b** *(= approve officially)* zulassen, genehmigen; *herd* staatlich überwachen; *educational institution* anerkennen; *(= establish) belief, custom* anerkennen; **~ed agent** bevollmächtigter Vertreter **c** *(= ascribe, attribute)* zuschreiben *(to sb* jdm)

accrete [ə'kriːt] **VI** zusammenwachsen; *(= increase)* zunehmen **VT** *(= enlarge)* anwachsen lassen

accretion [ə'kriːʃən] N *(process)* Anlagerung *f*; *(= sth accumulated)* Ablagerung *f*

accrual [ə'kruːəl] N **a** *(= accumulation)* Ansammlung *f*; *(Fin: of interest)* Auflaufen *nt*; *(= addition)* Hinzukommen *nt* **b accruals** PL *(Fin: = liabilities)* Verbindlichkeiten *pl*

accrue [ə'kruː] VI **a** *(= accumulate)* sich ansammeln, zusammenkommen *(to* für); *(Fin: interest)* auflaufen; *(= be added to)* hinzukommen *(to* zu) **b to ~ to sb** *(honour, costs etc)* jdm erwachsen *(geh) (from* aus)

acculturation [ə,kʌltʃə'reɪʃən] N *(Sociol)* Akkulturation *f*

accumulate [ə'kjuːmjʊleɪt] **VT** ansammeln, anhäufen, akkumulieren *(form)*; *evidence* sammeln; *(Fin) interest* akkumulieren *or* zusammenkommen lassen **VI** sich ansammeln *or* akkumulieren *(form)*; *(possessions, wealth also)* sich anhäufen; *(evidence)* sich häufen

accumulation [ə,kjuːmjʊ'leɪʃən] N Ansammlung *f*, Akkumulation *f (form)*; *(of possessions, wealth also)* Anhäufung *f*; *(of evidence)* Häufung *f*

accumulative [ə'kjuːmjʊlətɪv] ADJ = **cumulative**

accumulator [ə'kjuːmjʊleɪtə'] N Akkumulator *m*

accuracy ['ækjʊrəsɪ] N Genauigkeit *f*; *(of missile)* Zielgenauigkeit *f*

accurate ['ækjʊrɪt] ADJ *worker, observation, translation, copy, instrument* genau, akkurat *(rare)*; *missile* zielgenau; **the clock is ~** die Uhr geht genau; **his aim/shot was ~** er hat genau gezielt/getroffen; **the test is 90% ~** der Test ist 90%ig sicher; **her work is slow but ~** sie arbeitet langsam, aber genau; **to be (strictly) ~** um (ganz) genau zu sein

accurately ['ækjʊrɪtlɪ] ADV genau

accursed, **accurst** [ə'kɜːst] ADJ **a** *(inf: = hateful)* verwünscht **b** *(old, liter: = under a curse)* **to be ~** unter einem Fluch *or* bösen Zauber stehen

accusation [,ækjʊ'zeɪʃən] N Beschuldigung *f*, Anschuldigung *f*; *(Jur)* Anklage *f*; *(= reproach)* Vorwurf *m*; **he denied her ~ of dishonesty** er wehrte sich gegen ihren Vorwurf, dass er unehrlich sei; **a look of ~** ein anklagender Blick

accusative [ə'kjuːzətɪv] **N** Akkusativ *m*; **in the ~** im Akkusativ **ADJ** Akkusativ-; **~ case** Akkusativ *m*; **~ ending** Akkusativendung *f*

accusatory [ə'kjuːzətərɪ] ADJ anklagend

accuse [ə'kjuːz] VT **a** *(Jur)* anklagen *(of* wegen, +*gen*); **he is** *or* **stands ~d of murder/theft** er ist des Mordes/Diebstahls angeklagt, er steht unter Anklage des Mordes/Diebstahls *(form)*
b *person* beschuldigen, bezichtigen; **to ~ sb of doing** *or* **having done sth** jdn beschuldigen *or* bezichtigen, etw getan zu haben; **are you accusing me? I didn't take it!** beschuldigen Sie mich? Ich habe es nicht genommen; **are you accusing me of lying/not having checked the brakes?** willst du (damit) vielleicht sagen, dass ich lüge/die Bremsen nicht nachgesehen habe?; **to ~ sb of being untidy** jdm vorwerfen, unordentlich zu sein; **who are you accusing, the police or society?** wen klagen Sie an, die Polizei oder die Gesellschaft?; **I ~ the government of dishonesty** ich werfe der Regierung Unehrlichkeit vor; **a generation stands ~d of hypocrisy** eine Generation wird der Scheinheiligkeit beschuldigt *or* angeklagt *or* geziehen *(geh)*; **we all stand ~d** uns alle trifft eine Schuld

accused [ə'kjuːzd] N **the ~** der/die Angeklagte; *(several)* die Angeklagten *pl*

accuser [ə'kjuːzə'] N Ankläger(in) *m(f)*

accusing [ə'kjuːzɪŋ] ADJ anklagend; **he had an ~ look on his face** sein Blick klagte an

accusingly [ə'kjuːzɪŋlɪ] ADV *say, look* anklagend

accustom [ə'kʌstəm] VT **to ~ sb/oneself to sth** jdn/sich an etw *(acc)* gewöhnen; **to ~ oneself to doing sth** sich daran gewöhnen, etw zu tun; **to be ~ed to sth** an etw *(acc)* gewöhnt sein; **to be ~ed to doing sth** gewöhnt sein, etw zu tun; **it is not what I am ~ed to** ich bin so etwas nicht gewöhnt; **to become** *or* **get ~ed to sth** sich an etw *(acc)* gewöhnen; **to become** *or* **get ~ed to doing sth** sich daran gewöhnen, etw zu tun

accustomed [ə'kʌstəmd] ADJ *attr (= usual)* gewohnt

AC/DC ADJ **a** *abbr of* **alternating current/direct current** Allstrom **b ac/dc** *(inf)* bi *(inf)*

ace[1] [eɪs] **N** **a** *(Cards)* As *nt*; **the ~ of clubs** das Kreuz-As; **to have an ~ up one's sleeve** noch einen Trumpf in der Hand haben; **he was** *or* **came within an ~ of winning** er hätte um ein Haar gesiegt; **to hold all the ~s** *(fig)* alle Trümpfe in der Hand halten; **to be an ~ in the hole** eine Trumpfkarte sein **b** *(inf: = expert)* Ass *nt* *(at* in +*dat)*; **tennis ~** Tennisass *nt* **c** *(Tennis: = serve)* Ass *nt*; **to serve an ~** ein Ass servieren **ADJ** *attr (= excellent)* Star-; **~ photographer** Starfotograf(in) *m(f)*; **he's an ~ striker** *(Ftbl)* er ist ein Stürmer-Ass

ace[2] [eɪs] VT *(US sl: = kill)* umbringen, töten

acerbic [ə'sɜːbɪk] ADJ *person* gerissen; *wit* scharf; *remark, comment, style* bissig

acerbity [ə'sɜːbɪtɪ] N Schärfe *f*

acetate ['æsɪteɪt] N Acetat *nt*, Azetat *nt*

acetic [ə'siːtɪk] ADJ essigsauer

acetic acid N Essigsäure *f*

acetone ['æsɪtəʊn] N Aceton *nt*, Azeton *nt*

acetylene [ə'setɪliːn] N Acetylen *nt*, Azetylen *nt*

ache [eɪk] **N** (dumpfer) Schmerz *m*; **I have an ~ in my side** ich habe Schmerzen in der Seite; **a few little ~s and pains** ein paar Wehwehchen *(inf)*; **with an ~ in one's heart** *(fig)* mit wehem Herzen *(liter)*
VI **a** *(= hurt)* wehtun, schmerzen; **my head/stomach ~s** mir tut der Kopf/Magen weh; **it makes my head/arms ~** davon tut mir der Kopf/tun mir die Arme weh; **I'm aching all over** mir tut alles weh; **it makes my heart ~ to see him** *(fig)* es tut mir in der Seele weh, wenn ich ihn sehe; **my heart ~s for you** mir bricht fast das Herz *(also iro)*
b *(fig: = yearn)* **to ~ for sb/sth** sich nach jdm/etw sehnen; **to ~ to do sth** sich danach seh-

nen, etw zu tun; **I ~d to help him** es drängte mich, ihm zu helfen

achievable [əˈtʃiːvəbl] ADJ erreichbar

achieve [əˈtʃiːv] ✪ 8.1 VT erreichen, schaffen; *success* erzielen; *victory* erringen; *rank also, title* erlangen; **she ~d a great deal** *(= did a lot of work)* sie hat eine Menge geleistet; *(= was quite successful)* sie hat viel erreicht; **he will never ~ anything** er wird es nie zu etwas bringen VI *(Psych, Sociol)* leisten; **the achieving society** die Leistungsgesellschaft

achievement [əˈtʃiːvmənt] N **a** *(act)* Erreichen *nt*; *(of success)* Erzielen *nt*; *(of victory)* Erringen *nt*; *(of rank also, title)* Erlangen *nt*; **~-oriented** leistungsorientiert; **~-oriented society** Leistungsgesellschaft *f* **b** *(= thing achieved) (of individual)* Leistung *f*; *(of society, civilization, technology)* Errungenschaft *f*; **that's quite an ~!** das ist schon eine Leistung! *(also iro)*; **for his many ~s** für seine zahlreichen Verdienste; **~ quotient/test** Leistungsquotient *m*/-test *m*

achiever [əˈtʃiːvəʳ] N Leistungstyp *m (inf)*; **to be an ~** leistungsorientiert sein; **high ~** *(Sch)* leistungsstarkes Kind

Achilles [əˈkɪliːz] N Achill(es) *m*; **~ heel** *(fig)* Achillesferse *f*; **~ tendon** Achillessehne *f*

aching [ˈeɪkɪŋ] ADJ *attr bones, head, muscles, limbs* schmerzend; *(fig) heart* wund, weh *(liter)*

achingly [ˈeɪkɪŋlɪ] ADV schmerzlich; **~ slow** quälend langsam

achy [ˈeɪkɪ] ADJ *(inf)* schmerzend; **I feel ~ all over** mir tut alles weh

acid [ˈæsɪd] ADJ **a** *(= sour, also Chem)* sauer **b** *(fig)* ätzend, beißend N **a** *(Chem)* Säure *f* **b** *(inf: = LSD)* Acid *nt (sl)*; **to drop ~** Acid nehmen *(sl)*

acid drop N saurer *or* saures Drops

acidhead [ˈæsɪdˌhed] N *(inf: = LSD user)* Acidhead *m (sl)*

acidic [əˈsɪdɪk] ADJ sauer

acidity [əˈsɪdɪtɪ] N Säure *f*; *(Chem also)* Säuregehalt *m*; *(of stomach)* Magensäure *f*

acidly [ˈæsɪdlɪ] ADV *(fig)* ätzend, beißend

acid: **acid-proof** [ˈæsɪdpruːf] ADJ säurebeständig; **acid rain** N saurer Regen; **acid rock** N *(Mus)* Acid Rock *m*; **acid test** N Feuerprobe *f*; **acid-tongued** ADJ *person, remark* scharfzüngig

ack-ack [ˈækˈæk] N *(= fire)* Flakfeuer *nt*; *(= gun)* Flak *f*

acknowledge [əkˈnɒlɪdʒ] ✪ 20.5 VT anerkennen; *quotation* angeben; *(= admit) truth, fault, defeat etc* eingestehen, zugeben; *(= note receipt of) letter, present etc* den Empfang bestätigen von; *(= respond to) greetings, cheers etc* erwidern; **to ~ oneself beaten** sich geschlagen geben; **to ~ sb's presence/existence** jds Anwesenheit/Existenz zur Kenntnis nehmen

acknowledged [əkˈnɒlɪdʒd] ADJ *attr* anerkannt

acknowledgement [əkˈnɒlɪdʒmənt] N Anerkennung *f*; *(of quotation)* Angabe *f*; *(= recognition: of truth, fault, defeat etc)* Eingeständnis *nt*; *(of letter, present)* Empfangsbestätigung *f*; *(of greetings, cheers etc)* Erwiderung *f*; **he waved in ~** er winkte zurück; **in ~ of** in Anerkennung *(+gen)*; **to quote without ~** ohne Quellenangabe zitieren; **I received no ~** ich erhielt keine Antwort; **as an ~ of my gratitude** zum Zeichen meiner Dankbarkeit; **~s are due to …** ich habe/wir haben … zu danken; *(in book)* mein/unser Dank gilt …

acme [ˈækmɪ] N Höhepunkt *m*, Gipfel *m*; *(of elegance etc)* Inbegriff *m*; **at the ~ of his powers** auf dem Gipfel seiner (Schaffens)kraft

acne [ˈæknɪ] N Akne *f*

acolyte [ˈækəʊlaɪt] N *(Eccl) (Catholic)* Akoluth *m*; *(Protestant: = server)* Messdiener(in) *m(f)*, Ministrant(in) *m(f)*; *(fig)* Gefolgsmann *m*/-frau *f*

aconite [ˈækənaɪt] N *(Bot)* Eisenhut *m*, Aconitum *nt*; *(= drug)* Aconitin *nt*

acorn [ˈeɪkɔːn] N Eichel *f*

acoustic [əˈkuːstɪk] ADJ akustisch; *(= soundproof) tiles, panel* schalldämpfend; **~ screen** Trennwand *f (zur Schalldämpfung)*

acoustically [əˈkuːstɪkəlɪ] ADV akustisch

acoustic coupler N *(Comput)* Akustikkoppler *m*

acoustic guitar N Akustikgitarre *f*

acoustics [əˈkuːstɪks] N **a** *sing (subject)* Akustik *f* **b** *pl (of room etc)* Akustik *f*

acquaint [əˈkweɪnt] VT **a** *(= make familiar)* bekannt machen; **to be ~ed/thoroughly ~ed with sth** mit etw bekannt/vertraut sein; **to be ~ed with grief** mit Leid vertraut sein; **he's well ~ed with the situation** er ist mit der Situation vertraut; **to become ~ed with sth** etw kennenlernen; *facts, truth* etw erfahren; **to ~ oneself** *or* **to make oneself ~ed with sth** sich mit etw vertraut machen **b** *(with person)* **to be ~ed with sb** mit jdm bekannt sein; **we're not ~ed** wir kennen einander *or* uns nicht; **to become** *or* **get ~ed** sich (näher) kennenlernen

acquaintance [əˈkweɪntəns] N **a** *(= person)* Bekannte(r) *mf*; **we're just ~s** wir kennen uns bloß flüchtig; **a wide circle of ~s** ein großer Bekanntenkreis

b *(with person)* Bekanntschaft *f*; *(with subject etc)* Kenntnis *f (with +gen)*; *(intimate, with sorrow etc)* Vertrautheit *f*; **to make sb's ~, to make the ~ of sb** jds Bekanntschaft machen; **a woman of our ~** eine uns bekannte Dame; **I have some ~ with Italian wines** ich kenne mich mit italienischen Weinen einigermaßen aus; **it improves on ~** man kommt mit der Zeit auf den Geschmack (davon); **perhaps he'll improve on ~** vielleicht gefällt er uns *etc* besser, wenn wir *etc* ihn erst einmal näher kennenlernen → **nodding**

acquaintanceship [əˈkweɪntənsʃɪp] N Bekanntschaft *f (with* mit)

acquiesce [ˌækwɪˈes] VI einwilligen *(in* in *+acc)*; *(submissively)* sich fügen *(in +dat)*

acquiescence [ˌækwɪˈesns] N Einwilligung *f (in* in *+acc)*; *(submissive)* Fügung *f (in* in *+acc)*; **with an air of ~** mit zustimmender Miene

acquiescent [ˌækwɪˈesnt] ADJ fügsam; *smile* ergeben; *attitude* zustimmend

acquire [əˈkwaɪəʳ] VT erwerben; *(by dubious means)* sich *(dat)* aneignen; *habit* annehmen; **I see he has ~d a secretary/wife** wie ich sehe, hat er sich eine Sekretärin/Frau angeschafft *(inf)*; **he ~d a fine tan** er hat eine gute Farbe bekommen; **where did you ~ that?** woher hast du das?; **to ~ a taste/liking for sth** Geschmack/Gefallen an etw *(dat)* finden; **once you've ~d a taste for it** wenn du erst mal auf den Geschmack gekommen bist; **caviar is an ~d taste** Kaviar ist (nur) für Kenner; **~d** *(Psych)* erworben; **~d characteristics** *(Biol)* erworbene Eigenschaften *pl*

acquirement [əˈkwaɪəmənt] N **a** *(act)* = **acquisition a b** *(= skill etc acquired)* Fertigkeit *f*

acquirer [əˈkwaɪərəʳ] N *(Fin)* Erwerber(in) *m(f)*

acquisition [ˌækwɪˈzɪʃən] N **a** *(act)* Erwerb *m*; *(by dubious means)* Aneignung *f*; *(of habit)* Annahme *f*; *(of firm)* Übernahme *f* **b** *(= thing acquired)* Anschaffung *f*; **~ cost(s)** Anschaffungskosten *pl*; **he's a useful ~ to the department** er ist ein Gewinn für die Abteilung

acquisitive [əˈkwɪzɪtɪv] ADJ auf Erwerb aus, habgierig *(pej)*, raffgierig *(pej)*; **the ~ society** die Erwerbsgesellschaft; **magpies are ~ birds** Elstern sind Vögel mit ausgeprägtem Sammeltrieb

acquisitiveness [əˈkwɪzɪtɪvnɪs] N Habgier *f (pej)*

acquit [əˈkwɪt] VT freisprechen; **to be ~ted of a crime/on a charge** von einem Verbrechen/einer Anklage freigesprochen werden VR *(= conduct oneself)* sich verhalten; *(= perform)* seine Sache machen; **he ~ted himself well** er hat seine Sache gut gemacht; *(= stood up well)* er hat sich gut aus der Affäre gezogen

acquittal [əˈkwɪtl] N Freispruch *m (on* von)

acre [ˈeɪkəʳ] N ≈ Morgen *m*; **~s** *(old, liter, = land)* Fluren *pl (old, liter)*; **~s (and ~s) of garden** hektarweise Garten

acreage [ˈeɪkərɪdʒ] N Land *nt*; *(Agr)* Anbaufläche *f*; **what ~ do they have?** wie viel Land *or* wie viele Morgen *(Agr)* haben sie?

acrid [ˈækrɪd] ADJ *taste* bitter; *(of wine)* sauer; *smell* säuerlich; *comment, smoke* beißend

Acrilan® [ˈækrɪlæn] N Acryl *nt*, Akryl *nt*

acrimonious [ˌækrɪˈməʊnɪəs] ADJ *discussion, argument* erbittert; *person, words* bissig; *divorce* verbittert ausgefochten

acrimoniously [ˌækrɪˈməʊnɪəslɪ] ADV *end, split, break up* verbittert

acrimony [ˈækrɪmənɪ] N *(of discussion, argument)* erbitterte Schärfe; *(of person, words)* Bissigkeit *f*

acrobat [ˈækrəbæt] N Akrobat(in) *m(f)*

acrobatic [ˌækrəʊˈbætɪk] ADJ akrobatisch

acrobatics [ˌækrəʊˈbætɪks] PL Akrobatik *f*; **mental ~** *(fig)* Gedankenakrobatik *f*, geistige Klimmzüge *pl (inf)*

acronym [ˈækrənɪm] N Akronym *nt*

acropolis [əˈkrɒpəlɪs] N Akropolis *f*

across [əˈkrɒs] ADV **a** *(direction) (= to the other side)* hinüber; *(= from the other side)* herüber; *(= crosswise)* (quer)durch; **shall I go ~ first?** soll ich zuerst hinüber(gehen/-schwimmen *etc*)?; **to throw sth ~** etw hinüberwerfen; **to row ~** hinüberrudern; **to help sb ~** jdm herüberhelfen; **to cut sth ~** etw (quer) durchschneiden; **he was already ~** er war schon drüben; **~ from your house** gegenüber von eurem Haus, eurem Haus gegenüber; **the stripes go ~** es ist quer gestreift; **draw a line ~** machen Sie einen Strich; *(diagonal)* machen Sie einen Strich querdurch

b *(measurement)* breit; *(of round object)* im Durchmesser

c *(in crosswords)* waagerecht

PREP **a** *(direction)* über *(+acc)*; *(= diagonally across)* quer durch *(+acc)*; **to run ~ the road** über die Straße laufen; **to wade ~ a river** durch einen Fluss waten; **a tree fell ~ the path** ein Baum fiel quer über den Weg; **~ country** querfeldein; *(over long distance)* quer durch das Land; **to draw a line ~ the page** einen Strich durch die Seite machen; **the stripes go ~ the material** der Stoff ist quer gestreift

b *(position)* über *(+dat)*; **a tree lay ~ the path** ein Baum lag quer über dem Weg; **he was sprawled ~ the bed** er lag quer auf dem Bett; **with his arms (folded) ~ his chest** die Arme vor der Brust verschränkt; **from ~ the sea** von jenseits des Meeres *(geh)*, von der anderen Seite des Meeres; **he lives ~ the street from us** er wohnt uns gegenüber; **you could hear him (from) ~ the hall** man konnte ihn von der anderen Seite der Halle hören; **~ the political spectrum** auf allen Seiten des politischen Spektrums

across-the-board [əˈkrɒsðəˈbɔːd] ADJ *attr* allgemein → *also* **board**

acrostic [əˈkrɒstɪk] N Akrostichon *nt*

acrylamide [əˈkrɪləmaɪd] N *(Chem)* Acrylamid *nt*

acrylic [əˈkrɪlɪk] N Acryl *nt*, Akryl *nt* ADJ Acryl-, Akryl-; *dress* aus Acryl *or* Akryl; **~ paint** Acrylfarbe *f*, Akrylfarbe *f*

a/cs pay. *(Fin) abbr of* **accounts payable**

a/cs rec. *(Fin) abbr of* **accounts receivable**

ACT *abbr of* **Australian Capital Territory**

act [ækt] N **a** *(= deed, thing done)* Tat *f*; *(official, ceremonial)* Akt *m*; **my first ~ was to phone him** meine erste Tat *or* mein Erstes war, ihn anzurufen; **an ~ of mercy** ein Gnadenakt *m*; **an ~ of God** eine höhere Gewalt *no pl*; **an ~ of war** kriegerische Aktion *or* Handlung; **an ~ of folly/madness** ein Akt *m* der Dummheit/des Wahnsinns; **a small ~ of kindness** eine Freundlichkeit; **Acts** *(Bibl)* **the Acts of the Apostles** *(Bibl)* die Apostelgeschichte → **faith a**

b *(= process of doing)* **to be in the ~ of doing sth** (gerade) dabei sein, etw zu tun; **to catch sb**

in the ~ jdn auf frischer Tat or (sexually) in flagranti ertappen; to catch/watch sb in the ~ of doing sth jdn dabei ertappen/beobachten, wie er etw tut
c (Parl) Gesetz nt; this was made illegal by an ~ of Parliament passed in 1976 nach einem 1976 vom Parlament verabschiedeten Gesetz ist das verboten
d (Theat) (of play, opera) Akt m; (= turn) Nummer f; a one-~ play ein Einakter m; a one-~ opera eine Oper in einem Akt; to get into or in on the ~ (fig inf) mit von der Partie sein; how did he get in on the ~? (inf) wie kommt es, dass er da mitmischt? (inf); he's really got his ~ together (inf) (= is organized, efficient with sth) er hat die Sache wirklich im Griff; (in lifestyle etc) er hat im Leben erreicht, was er wollte; get your ~ together! reiß dich doch mal zusammen!; to clean up one's ~ (inf) sich zusammenreißen; she'll be a hard or tough ~ to follow man wird es ihr nur schwer gleichmachen; to be a class ~ (inf) Spitze sein (inf)
e (fig: = pretence) Theater nt, Schau f (inf); it's all an ~ das ist alles nur Theater or Schau (inf); to put on an ~ Theater spielen
VT part spielen; play also aufführen; to ~ the innocent die gekränkte Unschuld spielen
VI a (Theat) (= perform) spielen; (= to be an actor) schauspielern, Theater spielen; (fig) Theater spielen, schauspielern, markieren; to ~ on TV im Fernsehen auftreten or spielen; who's ~ing in it? wer spielt darin?; he learned to ~ er nahm Schauspielunterricht; he should learn to ~! er sollte erst mal richtig schauspielern lernen; ... but she can't ~ ... aber sie kann nicht spielen or ist keine Schauspielerin; he's only ~ing er tut (doch) nur so, er markiert or spielt (doch) nur; to ~ stupid/innocent etc sich dumm/unschuldig etc stellen, den Dummen/Unschuldigen etc spielen
b (= function) (brakes etc) funktionieren; (drug) wirken; to ~ as ... wirken als ...; (= have function) fungieren als ...; (person) das Amt des/der ... übernehmen, fungieren als ...; ~ing in my capacity as chairman in meiner Eigenschaft als Vorsitzender; it ~s as a deterrent das wirkt abschreckend; to ~ for or on behalf of sb jdn vertreten
c (= behave) sich verhalten; ~ like a man! sei ein Mann!; she ~ed as if or as though she was hurt/surprised etc sie tat so, als ob sie verletzt/überrascht etc wäre; he ~s like or as though he owns the place (inf) er tut so, als ob der Laden ihm gehört (inf)
d (= take action) handeln; he ~ed to stop it er unternahm etwas or Schritte, um dem ein Ende zu machen; the police couldn't ~ die Polizei konnte nichts unternehmen

▶ **act on** VI +prep obj a (= affect) wirken auf (+acc); the yeast acts on the sugar to produce alcohol die Hefe wirkt auf den Zucker ein und führt zur Alkoholbildung b (= take action on) warning, report, evidence handeln auf (+acc) ... hin; suggestion, advice folgen (+dat); orders handeln aufgrund von; acting on information received, the police ... die Polizei handelte aufgrund der ihr zugegangenen Information und ...; acting on an impulse einer plötzlichen Eingebung gehorchend or folgend; did you act on the letter? haben Sie auf den Brief hin etwas unternommen?

▶ **act out** VT sep fantasies, problems etc durchspielen; the drama/affair was acted out at ... das Drama/die Affäre spielte sich in ... ab

▶ **act up** VI (inf) jdm Ärger machen; (person also) Theater machen (inf); (to attract attention) sich aufspielen; (machine) verrücktspielen (inf); my back is acting up mein Rücken macht mir Ärger

▶ **act upon** VI +prep obj = act on

actable ['æktəbl] ADJ play spielbar; it is very ~ es lässt sich gut spielen or aufführen

acting ['æktɪŋ] ADJ a stellvertretend attr, in Stellvertretung pred b attr (Theat) schauspielerisch N (Theat) (= performance) Darstellung f; (= activity) Spielen nt; (= profession) Schauspielerei f; what was the ~ like? wie waren die Schauspieler?; what was his ~ like? wie hat er gespielt?; I don't like his ~ ich mag seine Art zu spielen nicht; he's done some ~ er hat schon Theater gespielt; (professionally also) er hat schon etwas Schauspielerfahrung

actinic [æk'tɪnɪk] ADJ aktinisch

actinometer [ˌæktɪ'nɒmɪtəʳ] N (Met) Aktinometer nt

action ['ækʃən] N a no pl (= activity) Handeln nt; (of play, novel etc) Handlung f; now is the time for ~ die Zeit zum Handeln ist gekommen; a man of ~ ein Mann der Tat; to take ~ etwas or Schritte unternehmen; have you taken any ~ on his letter? haben Sie auf seinen Brief hin irgendetwas or irgendwelche Schritte unternommen?; course of ~ Vorgehen nt; "action" (on office tray) „zur Bearbeitung"; no further ~ keine weiteren Maßnahmen; (label on file etc) abgeschlossen; the ~ of the play/novel takes place ... das Stück/der Roman spielt ...; ~! (Film) Achtung, Aufnahme!
b (= deed) Tat f; his first ~ was to phone me als Erstes rief er mich an; to suit the ~ to the word dem Wort die Tat folgen lassen, sein Wort in die Tat umsetzen; ~s speak louder than words (Prov) die Tat wirkt mächtiger als das Wort (prov)
c (= motion, operation) in/out of ~ in/nicht in Aktion; machine in/außer Betrieb; (= operational) einsatzfähig/nicht einsatzfähig; to go into ~ in Aktion treten; to put a plan into ~ einen Plan in die Tat umsetzen; to put out of ~ außer Gefecht setzen; he's been out of ~ since he broke his leg er ist nicht mehr in Aktion gewesen or war nicht mehr einsatzfähig, seit er sich das Bein gebrochen hat; he needs prodding into ~ man muss ihm immer erst einen Stoß geben
d (= exciting events) Action f (sl); there's no ~ in this film in dem Film passiert nichts, dem Film fehlt die Action (inf); a novel full of ~ ein handlungsreicher Roman; let's have some ~! (inf) lass uns mal was unternehmen; to go where the ~ is (inf) hingehen, wo was los ist (inf); that's where the ~ is (inf) da ist was los (inf); he was out looking for ~ (inf) er wollte was erleben (inf)
e (Mil) (= fighting) Aktionen pl; (= battle) Kampf m, Gefecht nt; enemy ~ feindliche Handlungen or Aktionen pl; killed in ~ gefallen; he saw ~ in the desert er war in der Wüste im Einsatz; the first time they went into ~ bei ihrem ersten Einsatz; they never once went into ~ sie kamen nie zum Einsatz
f (= way of operating) (of machine) Arbeitsweise f; (of piano etc) Mechanik f; (of watch, gun) Mechanismus m; (= way of moving) (of athlete etc) Bewegung f; (of horse) Aktion f; to hit with a smooth ~ (Sport) ganz weich schlagen
g (esp Chem, Phys: = effect) Wirkung f (on auf +acc)
h (Jur) Klage f; to bring an ~ (against sb) eine Klage (gegen jdn) anstrengen
i (Fin inf) a piece or slice of the ~ ein Stück nt aus dem Kuchen (sl)

actionable ['ækʃnəbl] ADJ verfolgbar; statement klagbar

action: **action committee** N Aktionskomitee nt; **action film** N Actionfilm m; **action group** N Aktionsgruppe f; **action man** N (usu hum) Actionmann m (inf); **action movie** N (esp US) Actionfilm m; **action-packed** ADJ film, book aktions- or handlungsgeladen; **action painting** N Aktion f; **action replay** N Wiederholung f; **action stations** PL Stellung f; ~! Stellung!; (fig) an die Plätze!; **action woman** N (usu hum) Action-Frau f (inf)

activate ['æktɪveɪt] VT mechanism (person) betätigen; (heat) auslösen; (switch, lever) in Gang setzen; alarm auslösen; bomb zünden; (Chem, Phys) aktivieren; (Comput) file aufrufen; (US Mil) mobilisieren

activated sludge ['æktɪveɪtɪd'slʌdʒ] N Belebtschlamm m

activation [ˌæktɪ'veɪʃən] N Aktivierung f

active ['æktɪv] ADJ aktiv (also Gram, Comput); mind, social life rege; volcano aktiv, tätig; dislike offen, unverhohlen; file im Gebrauch; (= radioactive) radioaktiv; to be ~ (terrorists, rebels) operieren; (lawyer, campaigner) aktiv sein; to be physically/politically/sexually ~ körperlich/politisch/sexuell aktiv sein; to be ~ in politics politisch aktiv or tätig sein; they should be more ~ in improving safety standards sie sollten die Verbesserung der Sicherheitsvorschriften etwas tatkräftiger vorantreiben; to be under ~ consideration ernsthaft erwogen werden; on ~ service (Mil) im Einsatz; to see ~ service (Mil) im Einsatz sein; to be on the ~ list (Mil) zur ständigen Verfügung stehen; ~ duty (esp US Mil) aktiver Wehrdienst; to be on ~ duty (esp US Mil) aktiven Wehrdienst leisten; he played an ~ part in it er war aktiv daran beteiligt; ~ assets (Comm) Aktiva pl; ~ partner (Comm) persönlich haftender Gesellschafter; ~ ingredient (Chem) aktiver Bestandteil; ~ suspension (Aut) aktive Aufhängung
N (Gram) Aktiv nt; in the ~ im Aktiv

actively ['æktɪvlɪ] ADV aktiv; dislike offen, unverhohlen

activewear ['æktɪvwɛəʳ], **active wear** N (= sports clothes) Activewear f

activism ['æktɪvɪzm] N Aktivismus m

activist ['æktɪvɪst] N Aktivist(in) m(f)

activity [æk'tɪvɪtɪ] N a no pl Aktivität f; (in market, town, office) Geschäftigkeit f, geschäftiges Treiben; (mental) Betätigung f; a scene of great ~ ein Bild geschäftigen Treibens; a new sphere of ~ ein neues Betätigungsfeld, ein neuer Wirkungskreis
b (= pastime) Betätigung f; classroom activities schulische Tätigkeiten pl; the church organizes many activities die Kirche organisiert viele Veranstaltungen; business/social activities geschäftliche/gesellschaftliche Unternehmungen pl; criminal activities kriminelle Tätigkeiten or Aktivitäten pl; a programme of activities ein Veranstaltungsprogramm nt
c (= radioactivity) Radioaktivität f

activity holiday N (Brit) Aktivurlaub m

actor ['æktəʳ] N (lit, fig) Schauspieler(in) m(f)

actress ['æktrɪs] N (lit, fig) Schauspielerin f

actressy ['æktrɪsɪ] ADJ (pej) theatralisch (pej)

actual ['æktjʊəl] ADJ a eigentlich; reason, price also, result tatsächlich; case, example konkret; in ~ fact eigentlich; what were his ~ words? was genau hat er gesagt?; this is the ~ house das ist hier das Haus; there is no ~ contract es besteht kein eigentlicher Vertrag; your ~ ... (inf) ein echter/eine echte/ein echtes ..., der/die/das echte ...; ~ size wahre Größe b (= precise) genau; I don't remember the ~ figures ich erinnere mich nicht an die genauen Zahlen
c (= existing now) derzeitig; ~ state or situation Ist-Zustand m

actual bodily harm N (Jur) einfache Körperverletzung

actuality [ˌæktjʊ'ælɪtɪ] N (= reality) Wirklichkeit f, Realität f; (= realism) Aktualität f; the actualities of the situation die tatsächlichen Gegebenheiten

actualize ['æktjʊəlaɪz] VT verwirklichen

actually ['æktjʊəlɪ] ADV a (used as a filler) usually not translated; ~ I haven't started yet ich habe noch (gar) nicht damit angefangen; ~ we were just talking about you wir haben eben von Ihnen geredet; ~ his name is Smith er heißt (übrigens) Smith; I'm going too ~ ich gehe (übrigens) auch; ~ what we could do is to ... (wissen Sie,) wir könnten doch ...
b (= to tell the truth, in actual fact) eigentlich; (= by the way) übrigens; as you said before, and ~ you were quite right wie Sie schon sagten, und eigentlich hatten Sie völlig recht; ~ you were quite right, it was a bad idea Sie hatten übrigens völlig recht, es war eine schlechte

Idee; **I don't ~ feel like going there** ich habe eigentlich keine Lust, da hinzugehen; **do you want that/know him? – ~ I do/don't** möchten Sie das/kennen Sie ihn? – ja, durchaus *or* schon/nein, eigentlich nicht; **you don't want that/know him, do you? – ~ I do** Sie möchten das/kennen ihn (doch) nicht, oder? – doch, eigentlich schon; **do you know her? – ~ I'm her husband** kennen Sie sie? – ja, ich bin nämlich ihr Mann; **I thought I could give you a lift but I won't ~ be going** ich dachte, ich könnte Sie mitnehmen, aber ich gehe nun doch nicht; **I bet you haven't done that! – ~ I have** Sie haben das bestimmt nicht gemacht! – doch; **I'm going soon, tomorrow ~** ich gehe bald, nämlich morgen; **it won't be easy, it'll ~ be very difficult** es wird nicht leicht, ja es wird sogar sehr schwierig sein

c (*= truly, in reality: showing surprise*) tatsächlich; **if you ~ own an apartment** wenn Sie tatsächlich eine Wohnung besitzen; **don't tell me you're ~ going now!** sag bloß, du gehst jetzt tatsächlich *or* wirklich!; **oh, you're ~ in/dressed/ready!** oh, du bist sogar da/angezogen/fertig!; **... but ~ I could do it** ... aber ich konnte es doch; **I haven't ~ started/done it/met him yet** ich habe noch nicht angefangen/es noch nicht gemacht/ihn noch nicht kennengelernt; **not ~ ..., but ...** zwar nicht ..., aber ...; **I wasn't ~ there, but ...** ich war zwar selbst nicht dabei, aber ...; **did he ~ say that?** hat er das tatsächlich *or* wirklich gesagt?; **what did he ~ say?** was genau hat er gesagt?, was hat er tatsächlich gesagt?; **what do you ~ want?** was möchten Sie eigentlich?; **does that ~ exist?** gibt es das denn überhaupt *or* tatsächlich?; **as for ~ working ...** was die Arbeit selbst betrifft ...; **as for ~ doing it** wenn es dann darangeht, es auch zu tun; **it's the first time that I've ~ seen him/that I've ~ been home in time for the news** das ist das erste Mal, dass ich ihn mal gesehen habe/dass ich mal rechtzeitig zu den Nachrichten zu Hause bin

d **it's ~ taking place this very moment** das findet genau in diesem Augenblick statt; **it was ~ taking place when he ...** es fand genau zu der Zeit statt, als er ...

actuarial [ˌæktjʊˈeərɪəl] ADJ (*Insur*) versicherungsmathematisch, versicherungsstatistisch

actuary [ˈæktjʊərɪ] N (*Insur*) Aktuar(in) *m(f)*

actuate [ˈæktjʊeɪt] VT (*lit*) auslösen; (*fig*) treiben

acuity [əˈkjuːɪtɪ] N Scharfsinn *m*, Klugheit *f*; (*of mind*) Schärfe *f*

acumassage [ˈækjʊˌmæsɑːʒ] N (*Med*) Akupunktmassage *f*

acumen [ˈækjʊmen] N Scharfsinn *m*; **to show (considerable) ~** (großen) Scharfsinn beweisen; **business ~** Geschäftssinn *m*; **political ~** politische Klugheit

acupressure [ˈækjʊˌpreʃəʳ] N Akupressur *f*

acupuncture [ˈækjʊˌpʌŋktʃəʳ] N Akupunktur *f*

acute [əˈkjuːt] **ADJ** **a** (*= intense, serious*) *pain, shortage, appendicitis* akut; *pleasure* intensiv; **~ beds** (*Med*) Akutbetten *pl* **b** (*= extreme*) *situation, problem, anxiety* akut; *embarrassment* riesig **c** (*= keen*) *eyesight* scharf; *hearing, sense of smell* fein **d** (*= shrewd*) scharf; *person* scharfsinnig; *child* aufgeweckt **e** (*Math*) *angle* spitz **f** (*Ling*) **~ accent** Akut *m*; **e ~** e Akut **N** (*Ling*) Akut *m*

acutely [əˈkjuːtlɪ] ADV **a** (*= intensely*) akut; *feel* intensiv; *embarrassed, sensitive, uncomfortable* äußerst; *ill* akut; **to be ~ aware of sth** sich (*dat*) einer Sache (*gen*) genau *or* sehr bewusst sein; (*= painfully*) sich (*dat*) einer Sache (*gen*) schmerzlich bewusst sein **b** (*= shrewdly*) scharfsinnig; *criticize, observe* scharf

acuteness [əˈkjuːtnɪs] N **a** (*= intensity: of pleasure*) Intensität *f* **b** (*= keenness*) (*of eyesight*) Schärfe *f*; (*of hearing, sense of smell*) Feinheit *f* **c** (*= shrewdness*) Schärfe *f*; (*of person*) Scharfsinn *m*; (*of child*) Aufgewecktheit *f*

acyclic [eɪˈsaɪklɪk] ADJ azyklisch

AD *abbr of* **Anno Domini** n. Chr., A.D.

ad [æd] N *abbr of* **advertisement** Anzeige *f*, Inserat *nt*

adage [ˈædɪdʒ] N Sprichwort *nt*

adagio [əˈdɑːdʒɪəʊ] **ADV** adagio **N** Adagio *nt*

Adam [ˈædəm] N Adam *m*; **~'s apple** Adamsapfel *m*; **I don't know him from ~** (*inf*) ich habe keine Ahnung, wer er ist (*inf*)

adamant [ˈædəmənt] ADJ hart; *refusal also* hartnäckig; **to be ~** unnachgiebig sein, darauf bestehen; **since you're ~** da Sie darauf bestehen; **he was ~ about going** er bestand hartnäckig darauf zu gehen; **he was ~ in his refusal** er weigerte sich hartnäckig

adamantine [ˌædəˈmæntaɪn] ADJ (*liter, lit*) diamanten (*liter*); (*fig*) hartnäckig

adamantly [ˈædəməntlɪ] ADV (*= rigidly*) hartnäckig; **to be ~ opposed to sth** etw scharf ablehnen

adapt [əˈdæpt] **VT** anpassen (*to +dat*); *machine* umstellen (*to, for* auf *+acc*); *vehicle, building* umbauen (*to, for* für); *text, book* adaptieren, bearbeiten (*for* für); **~ed to your requirements** nach Ihren Wünschen abgeändert; **~ed for Arctic conditions** arktischen Verhältnissen angepasst; **~ed for children/television** für Kinder/für das Fernsehen adaptiert *or* bearbeitet; **~ed from the Spanish** aus dem Spanischen übertragen und bearbeitet **VI** sich anpassen (*to +dat*); (*Sci also*) sich adaptieren (*to* an *+acc*)

adaptability [əˌdæptəˈbɪlɪtɪ] N (*of plant, animal, person*) Anpassungsfähigkeit *f*; (*of vehicle, hairstyle*) Vielseitigkeit *f*; (*of schedule*) Flexibilität *f*

adaptable [əˈdæptəbl] ADJ *plant, animal, person* anpassungsfähig; *vehicle, hairstyle* vielseitig; *schedule* flexibel; **to be ~ to sth** (*person, animal, plant*) sich an etw (*acc*) anpassen können; (*vehicle*) sich in etw (*dat*) verwenden lassen

adaptation [ˌædæpˈteɪʃən] N **a** (*of person, plant, animal*) Anpassung *f* (*to* an *+acc*); (*of machine*) Umstellung *f* (*to* an *+acc*); (*of vehicle, building*) Umbau *m*; (*of text*) Bearbeitung *f*; **the ~ of space technology to medical ends** die Nutzung der Raumfahrttechnik für medizinische Zwecke **b** (*of book, play etc*) Adaption *f*, Bearbeitung *f*

adapter [əˈdæptəʳ] N **a** (*of book etc*) Bearbeiter(in) *m(f)* **b** (*for connecting pipes etc*) Verbindungs- *or* Zwischenstück *nt*; (*to convert machine etc*) Adapter *m* **c** (*Elec*) Adapter *m*; (*for several plugs*) Doppel-/Dreifachstecker *m*, Mehrfachstecker *m*; (*on appliance*) Zwischenstecker *m*

adapter card N (*Comput*) Adapterkarte *f*

adaption [əˈdæpʃən] N = **adaptation**

adaptive [əˈdæptɪv] ADJ *ability, capacity* anpassungsfähig; **~ response** Anpassungsreaktion *f*; **~ mechanism** Anpassungsmechanismus *m*

adaptor [əˈdæptəʳ] N = **adapter**

ADC *abbr of* **aide-de-camp**

ADD *abbr of* **attention deficit disorder** ADS

add [æd] **VT** **a** (*Math*) addieren; (*= add on*) hinzu- *or* dazuzählen (*to* zu); (*= add up*) addieren, zusammenzählen; **to ~ 8 and 5** 8 und 5 zusammenzählen *or* addieren; **to ~ 8 to 5** 8 zu 5 hinzuzählen

b *ingredients, money etc* hinzufügen, dazugeben, dazutun (*to* zu); *name* hinzufügen (*to* zu), dazusetzen (*to* an *+acc*); (*= say in addition*) hinzufügen, dazusagen; (*= build on*) anbauen; **~ed to which ...** hinzu kommt, dass ...; **it ~s nothing to our knowledge** unser Wissen wird dadurch nicht erweitert; **transport ~s 10% to the cost** es kommen 10% Transportkosten hinzu; **they ~ 10% for service** sie rechnen *or* schlagen 10% für Bedienung dazu; **to ~ value to sth** den Wert einer Sache (*gen*) erhöhen; **~ed together the books weigh several tons** zusammengenommen wiegen die Bücher mehrere Tonnen; **if we ~ all the money together we can get them a really nice gift** wenn wir das ganze Geld zusammenlegen, können wir ihnen ein wirklich hübsches Geschenk besorgen → **insult N**

VI **a** (*Math*) zusammenzählen, addieren; **she just can't ~** sie kann einfach nicht rechnen

b **to ~ to sth** zu etw beitragen; **to ~ to one's income** sein Einkommen aufbessern; **it will ~ to the time the job takes** es wird die Arbeitszeit verlängern; **the house had been ~ed to** an das Haus war (etwas) angebaut worden

▶ **add on** VT *sep number, amount* dazurechnen; *two weeks* mehr rechnen; *room* anbauen; *storey* aufstocken; (*= append*) *comments etc* anfügen

▶ **add up** **VT** *sep* zusammenzählen *or* -rechnen **VI** **a** (*figures etc*) stimmen; (*fig: = make sense*) sich reimen; **it's beginning to add up** jetzt wird so manches klar; **it all adds up** (*lit*) es summiert sich; (*fig*) es passt alles zusammen **b** **to add up to** (*figures*) ergeben; (*expenses also*) sich belaufen auf (*+acc*); **that all adds up to a rather unusual state of affairs** alles in allem ergibt das eine recht ungewöhnliche Situation; **it doesn't add up to much** (*fig*) das ist nicht berühmt (*inf*)

added [ˈædɪd] ADJ *attr* zusätzlich; **~ value** Mehrwert *m*

addend [ˈædend] N (*US*) Summand *m*

addendum [əˈdendəm] N *pl* **addenda** [əˈdendə] Nachtrag *m*

adder [ˈædəʳ] N Viper *f*, Natter *f*

addict [ˈædɪkt] N (*lit, fig*) Süchtige(r) *mf*, Suchtkranke(r) *mf*; **he's a television/heroin/real ~** er ist fernseh-/heroinsüchtig/richtig süchtig; **to become an ~** süchtig werden

addicted [əˈdɪktɪd] ADJ süchtig; **to be/become ~ to heroin/drugs/drink** heroin-/rauschgift-/ /trunksüchtig sein/werden; **he's ~ to smoking** er ist nikotinsüchtig; **he is ~ to sport/films** Sport ist/Filme sind bei ihm zur Sucht geworden; **you might get ~ to it** das kann zur Sucht werden; (*Med*) davon kann man süchtig werden

addiction [əˈdɪkʃən] N Sucht *f* (*to* nach); (*no pl: = state of dependence*) Sucht *f*, Süchtigkeit *f*; **~ to drugs/alcohol** Rauschgift-/Trunksucht *f*; **~ to sport** übermäßige Sportbegeisterung; **to become an ~** zur Sucht werden

addictive [əˈdɪktɪv] ADJ **to be ~** (*lit*) süchtig machen; (*fig*) zu einer Sucht werden können; **these drugs/watching TV can become ~** diese Drogen können/Fernsehen kann zur Sucht werden; **~ drug** Suchtdroge *f*; **to have an ~ personality** suchtanfällig sein, ein Suchttyp *m* sein (*inf*)

adding machine [ˈædɪŋməˌʃiːn] N Addiermaschine *f*

Addis Ababa [ˌædɪsˈæbəbə] N Addis Abeba *nt*

addition [əˈdɪʃən] ✪ 26.2 N **a** (*Math*) Addition *f*

b (*= adding*) Zusatz *m*; **the ~ of another person would make the team too large** eine zusätzliche *or* weitere Person würde das Team zu groß machen; **the ~ of one more country to the EU** die Erweiterung der EU um ein weiteres Land

c (*= thing added*) Zusatz *m* (*to* zu); (*to list*) Ergänzung *f* (*to* zu); (*to building*) Anbau *m* (*to* an *+acc*); (*to income*) Aufbesserung *f* (*to +gen*); (*to bill*) Zuschlag *m* (*to* zu), Aufschlag *m* (*to* auf *+acc*); **they are expecting an ~ to their family** (*inf*) sie erwarten (Familien)zuwachs (*inf*)

d **in ~** außerdem, obendrein; **in ~ (to this) he said ...** und außerdem sagte er ...; **in ~ to sth** zusätzlich zu etw; **in ~ to her other hobbies** zusätzlich zu ihren anderen Hobbys; **in ~ to being unjustified his demand was also ...** seine Forderung war nicht nur ungerechtfertigt, sondern außerdem noch ...

additional [əˈdɪʃənl] ADJ zusätzlich; **~ charge** Aufpreis *m*; **any ~ expenditure over and above this** alle darüber hinausgehenden Ausgaben; **any ~ suggestions will have to be raised at the next meeting** irgendwelche weiteren Vorschläge müssen bei der nächsten Sitzung vorgebracht werden; **the author has inserted an ~ chapter** der Autor hat ein weiteres Kapitel eingefügt

additionally [əˈdɪʃənlɪ] ADV außerdem; *say* ergänzend; ~ **there is …** außerdem ist da noch …, dazu kommt noch …; ~ **difficult/complicated** (nur) noch schwieriger/komplizierter

additive [ˈædɪtɪv] N Zusatz *m*

additive-free ADJ *food* ohne chemische Zusätze

addle [ˈædl] VT a *brain* benebeln b *egg* faul werden lassen, verderben lassen VI *(egg)* verderben, faul werden

addled [ˈædld] ADJ a *brain, person* benebelt; *(permanently)* verdummt b *egg* verdorben, faul

addle-headed [ˈædlˈhedɪd], **addle-pated** [ˈædlˈpeɪtɪd] ADJ *(inf)* trottelig *(inf)*, dusslig *(inf)*

add-on [ˈædɒn] N *(Comput)* Zusatzgerät *nt*

address [əˈdres] N a *(of person, on letter etc)* Adresse *f*, Anschrift *f*; **home** ~ Privatadresse *f*; *(when travelling)* Heimatanschrift *f*; **what's your ~?** wo wohnen Sie?; **I've come to the wrong ~** ich bin hier falsch *or* an der falschen Adresse; **at this ~** unter dieser Adresse; **who else lives at this ~?** wer wohnt noch in dem Haus?; **"not known at this ~"** „Empfänger unbekannt"
b *(= speech)* Ansprache *f*; **the Address** *(Parl)* die Adresse *(die Erwiderung auf die Thronrede)*
c **form of ~** (Form *f* der) Anrede *f*
d *(Comput)* Adresse *f*
e *(= bearing, way of behaving)* Auftreten *nt*; *(= way of speaking)* Art *f* zu reden
f *(form, = skill, tact)* Gewandtheit *f*
g **to pay one's ~es to a lady** *(liter)* einer Dame die Cour machen *(liter)*
VT a *letter, parcel* adressieren (*to* an *+acc*)
b *(= direct) speech, complaints, remarks* richten (*to* an *+acc*)
c *(= speak to) meeting* sprechen zu; *jury* sich wenden an *(+acc)*; *person* anreden; **don't ~ me as "Colonel"** nennen Sie mich nicht „Colonel"; **how should one ~ an earl?** wie redet man einen Grafen an?
d *problem etc* angehen
VR a **to ~ oneself to sb** *(= speak to)* jdn ansprechen; *(= apply to)* sich an jdn wenden
b *(form)* **to ~ oneself to a task** sich einer Aufgabe *(dat)* widmen

addressable [əˈdresəbl] ADJ *(Comput) network, computer etc* adressierbar

address: **address book** N Adressbuch *nt*; **address bus** N *(Comput)* Adressbus *m*

addressee [ˌædreˈsiː] N Empfänger(in) *m(f)*, Adressat(in) *m(f)*

address label N Adressenaufkleber *m*

Addressograph [əˈdresəʊɡrɑːf] N Adressiermaschine *f*, Adrema® *f*

adduce [əˈdjuːs] VT *(form)* anführen; *evidence* erbringen

adduction [æˈdʌkʃən] N *(form)* Anführung *f*; *(of proof)* Erbringung *f*

adductor [æˈdʌktəˈ] N, **adductor muscle** *(Anat)* Adduktor *m (spec)*, Anziehmuskel *m*

ademption [əˈdempʃən] N *(Jur)* Wegfall *m (eines Vermächtnisses)*

Aden [ˈeɪdn] N Aden *nt*; **Gulf of ~** Golf *m* von Aden

adenoidal [ˌædɪˈnɔɪdl] ADJ adenoid; *voice, adolescent* näselnd; ~ **infection** Infektion *f* der Rachenmandeln

adenoids [ˈædɪnɔɪdz] PL Rachenmandeln *pl*, Polypen *pl (inf)*

adenoma [ˌædɪˈnəʊmə] N *pl* **-s** *or* **adenomata** *(Med)* Adenom *nt*

adept [ˈædept] N *(form)* Meister(in) *m(f)*, Experte *m*, Expertin *f* (*in, at* in *+dat*) ADJ geschickt (*in, at* in *+dat*); **she's quite ~ at that sort of thing** sie hat ein Talent dafür

adequacy [ˈædɪkwəsɪ] N Adäquatheit *f*, Angemessenheit *f*; **we doubt the ~ of his explanation/theory/this heating system** wir bezweifeln, dass seine Erklärung/Theorie/diese Heizung angemessen *or* adäquat *or* ausreichend ist; **he's beginning to doubt his ~ as a father** er zweifelt langsam an seinen Fähigkeiten als Vater

adequate [ˈædɪkwɪt] ADJ adäquat; *(= sufficient also) supply, heating system* ausreichend; *time* genügend *inv*; *excuse* angemessen; **to be ~** *(= sufficient)* (aus)reichen, genug sein; *(= good enough)* zulänglich *or* adäquat sein; **this is just not ~** das ist einfach unzureichend *or (not good enough also)* nicht gut genug; **more than ~** mehr als genug; *heating* mehr als ausreichend; **there are no words ~ to express my gratitude** meine Dankbarkeit läßt sich in Worten gar nicht ausdrücken; **to be ~ to the task** der Aufgabe *(dat)* gewachsen sein

adequately [ˈædɪkwɪtlɪ] ADV a *(= sufficiently) prepared, trained, protected* ausreichend; *insured* angemessen; **to be ~ supplied** genügend Vorräte haben b *(= satisfactorily) function, respond, perform, explain* angemessen; **I speak Turkish ~** ich spreche hinlänglich Türkisch

ADF *(Aviat) abbr of* **automatic direction finder**

adhere [ədˈhɪəˈ] VI (*to* an *+dat*) *(= stick)* haften; *(more firmly)* kleben

▶ **adhere to** VI *+prep obj (= support, be faithful)* bleiben bei; *plan, belief, principle, determination also* festhalten an *(+dat)*; *rule* sich halten an *(+acc)*

adherence [ədˈhɪərəns] N Festhalten *nt* (*to* an *+dat*); *(to rule)* Befolgung *f* (*to +gen*)

adherent [ədˈhɪərənt] N Anhänger(in) *m(f)*

adhesion [ədˈhiːʒən] N a *(of particles etc)* Adhäsion *f*, Haftfähigkeit *f*; *(more firmly: of glue)* Klebefestigkeit *f* b = **adherence**

adhesive [ədˈhiːzɪv] N Klebstoff *m* ADJ haftend; *(more firmly)* klebend; **to be highly/not very ~** sehr/nicht gut haften/kleben; ~ **label** Haftetikett *nt*; ~ **plaster** Heftpflaster *nt*; ~ **strength/powers** Adhäsionskraft *f*; *(of glue)* Klebekraft *f*

adhesive cream N *(for dentures)* Haftcreme *f*

adhesive tape N Klebstreifen *m*

ad hoc [ˌædˈhɒk] ADJ ADV ad hoc *inv*

adhocracy [ˌædˈhɒkrəsɪ] N *no pl* Vertrauen *nt* auf Ad-hoc-Entscheidungen; *(= organization)* Adhokratie *f*

adieu [əˈdjuː] *(old, liter)* N Adieu *nt*, Lebewohl *nt (old)*; **to say one's ~s** Adieu *or* adieu sagen *(old)*, Abschied nehmen INTERJ adieu *(old)*; **to bid sb ~** jdm Adieu *or* adieu *or* Lebewohl sagen *(old)*

ad inf. [ˌædˈɪnf] *abbr of* **ad infinitum**

ad infinitum [ˌædɪnfɪˈnaɪtəm] ADV ad infinitum *(geh)*, für immer

ad interim [ˌædˈɪntərɪm] *(geh)* ADV ad interim *(geh)*, vorläufig ADJ interim *(geh)*, vorläufig

adipose [ˈædɪpəʊs] ADJ *(form)* adipös *(form)*, Fett-; ~ **tissue** Fettgewebe *nt*; *(hum)* Fettpölsterchen *pl*

adiposis [ˌædɪˈpəʊsɪs], **adiposity** [ˌædɪˈpɒsɪtɪ] N *(Med)* Adipositas *f (spec)*, Fettsucht *f*

adjacent [əˈdʒeɪsənt] ADJ angrenzend; **to be ~ to sth** an etw *(acc)* angrenzen, neben etw *(dat)* liegen; **the ~ room** das Nebenzimmer, das Zimmer nebenan

adjectival ADJ, **adjectivally** ADV [ˌædʒekˈtaɪvəl, -ɪ] adjektivisch

adjective [ˈædʒɪktɪv] N Adjektiv *nt*, Eigenschaftswort *nt*

adjoin [əˈdʒɔɪn] VT grenzen an *(+acc)* VI nebeneinanderliegen, aneinandergrenzen

adjoining [əˈdʒɔɪnɪŋ] ADJ benachbart, Nachbar-; *(esp Archit etc)* anstoßend; *field* angrenzend; *(of two things)* nebeneinanderliegend; ~ **province** Nachbarprovinz *f*; **the ~ room** das Nebenzimmer; **in the ~ office** im Büro daneben *or* nebenan

adjourn [əˈdʒɜːn] VT a *(to another day)* vertagen (*until* auf *+acc*); **he ~ed the meeting for three hours** er unterbrach die Konferenz für drei Stunden b *(US: = end)* beenden VI a *(to another day)* sich vertagen (*until* auf *+acc*); **to ~ for lunch/one hour** zur Mittagspause/für eine Stunde unterbrechen b *(= go to another place)* **to ~ to the living room** sich ins Wohnzimmer begeben

adjournment [əˈdʒɜːnmənt] N *(to another day)* Vertagung *f* (*until* auf *+acc*); *(within a day)* Unterbrechung *f*

adjudge [əˈdʒʌdʒ] VT a *(Jur)* **the court ~d that …** das Gericht entschied *or* befand, dass … b *(= award) prize* zuerkennen, zusprechen (*to sb* jdm); **he was ~d the winner** er wurde zum Sieger *or* Gewinner erklärt c *(form, = consider)* erachten für *or* als *(geh)*

adjudicate [əˈdʒuːdɪkeɪt] VT a *(= judge) claim* entscheiden; *competition* Preisrichter(in) sein bei b *(Jur: = declare)* **to ~ sb bankrupt** jdn für bankrott erklären VI entscheiden, urteilen (*on, in* bei); *(in dispute)* Schiedsrichter(in) sein (*on* bei, in *+dat*); *(in competition, dog show etc)* als Preisrichter(in) fungieren

adjudication [əˌdʒuːdɪˈkeɪʃən] N Entscheidung *f*, Beurteilung *f*; *(= result also)* Urteil *nt*; ~ **of bankruptcy** Bankrotterklärung *f*

adjudicator [əˈdʒuːdɪkeɪtəˈ] N *(in competition etc)* Preisrichter(in) *m(f)*; *(in dispute)* Schiedsrichter(in) *m(f)*

adjunct [ˈædʒʌŋkt] N Anhängsel *nt*; **a dictionary is an indispensable ~ to language learning** ein Wörterbuch ist unerlässlich fürs Sprachenlernen

adjuration [ˌædʒʊəˈreɪʃən] N *(liter)* Beschwörung *f*

adjure [əˈdʒʊəˈ] VT *(liter)* beschwören

adjust [əˈdʒʌst] VT a *(= set) machine, engine, carburettor, brakes, height, speed, flow etc* einstellen; *knob, lever* (richtig) stellen; *(= alter) height, speed* verstellen; *length of clothes* ändern; *(= correct, readjust)* nachstellen; *height, speed, flow* regulieren; *figures* korrigieren, anpassen; *formula, plan, production, exchange rates, terms* (entsprechend) ändern; *salaries* angleichen (*to* an *+acc*); *hat, tie* zurechtrücken; **to ~ the lever upwards/downwards** den Hebel nach oben/unten stellen; **you have to ~ this knob to regulate the ventilation** Sie müssen an diesem Knopf drehen, um die Ventilation zu regulieren, die Ventilation lässt sich an diesem Knopf regulieren; **he ~ed the knobs on the TV set** er hat die Knöpfe am Fernsehapparat richtig gestellt; **do not ~ your set** ändern Sie nichts an der Einstellung Ihres Geräts; **to ~ sth to new requirements/conditions** *etc* etw neuen Erfordernissen/Umständen *etc* anpassen; **because of increased demand production will have to be appropriately ~ed** die Produktion muss auf die verstärkte Nachfrage abgestimmt werden *or* muss der verstärkten Nachfrage angepasst werden; **the terms have been ~ed slightly in your favour** *(Brit) or* **favor** *(US)* die Bedingungen sind zu Ihren Gunsten leicht abgeändert worden; **the layout can be ~ed to meet different needs** die Anordnung lässt sich je nach Bedarf ändern; **we ~ed all salaries upwards/downwards** wir haben alle Gehälter nach oben/unten angeglichen; **would you please ~ your dress, sir** *(euph)* ich glaube, Sie haben vergessen, etwas *or* Ihre Hose zuzumachen; **if you could ~ the price slightly** *(hum)* wenn wir uns vielleicht noch über den Preis unterhalten könnten; **to ~ the seasoning (of sth)** (etw) nachwürzen
b **to ~ oneself to sth** *(to new country, circumstances etc)* sich einer Sache *(dat)* anpassen; *(to new requirements, demands etc* sich auf etw *(acc)* einstellen
c *(= settle) differences* beilegen, schlichten; *(Insur) claim* regulieren
VI a *(to new country, circumstances etc)* sich anpassen (*to +dat*); *(to new requirements, demands etc)* sich einstellen (*to* auf *+acc*)
b *(machine etc)* sich einstellen lassen; **the chair ~s to various heights** der Stuhl lässt sich in der Höhe verstellen

adjustability [əˌdʒʌstəˈbɪlɪtɪ] N *(of tool, height, angle)* Verstellbarkeit *f*; *(of height also, speed, temperature)* Regulierbarkeit *f*, Flexibilität *f*

adjustable [əˈdʒʌstəbl] ADJ *tool, angle, strap, shelf, chair* verstellbar; *height* verstellbar, regulierbar; *shape* veränderlich, variabel; *speed, temperature* regulierbar; *tax, deadline, rate of production/repayment* beweglich, flexibel; *person, animal, plant* anpassungsfähig; **partitions make the shape of the office ~** durch Trennwände lässt sich die Form des Büros verändern

adjustable-pitch propeller [əˌdʒʌstəblpɪtʃprəˈpeləʳ] N Verstell-Luftschraube *f*, Verstellluftschraube *f*

adjustable spanner N Engländer *m*

adjuster [əˈdʒʌstəʳ] N *(Insur)* (Schadens)sachverständige(r) *mf*

adjustment [əˈdʒʌstmənt] N **a** *(= setting, of machine, engine, carburettor, brakes, height, speed, flow etc)* Einstellung *f*; *(of knob, lever)* (richtige) Stellung; *(= alteration, of height, speed)* Verstellung *f*; *(of length of clothes)* Änderung *f*; *(= correction, readjustment)* Nachstellung *f*; *(of height, speed, flow)* Regulierung *f*; *(of formula, plan, production, exchange rate, terms)* (entsprechende) Änderung; *(of hat, tie)* Zurechtrücken *nt*; **if you could make a slight ~ to my salary** *(hum inf)* wenn Sie eine leichte Korrektur meines Gehalts vornehmen könnten *(hum)*; **a certain ~ of our traditional outlook** eine gewisse Änderung unserer traditionellen Haltung; **to make ~s** Änderungen vornehmen; **to make ~s to the manuscript/play** Änderungen am Manuskript/Stück vornehmen; **to make ~s to one's plans** seine Pläne ändern; **brakes require regular ~** Bremsen müssen regelmäßig nachgestellt werden
b *(socially etc)* Anpassung *f*
c *(= settlement)* Beilegung *f*, Schlichtung *f*; *(Insur)* Regulierung *f*

adjustment period N Anpassungszeitraum *m*

adjutant [ˈædʒətənt] N **a** *(Mil)* Adjutant(in) *m(f)* **b** *(Orn: also* **adjutant bird***)* Indischer Marabu

adjutant general N Generaladjutant(in) *m(f)*

ad lib¹ [ædˈlɪb] ADV aus dem Stegreif

ad-lib¹ [ædˈlɪb] **ADJ** *attr*, **ad lib²** **ADJ** *pred* improvisiert

ad-lib² **N** Improvisation *f* **VTI** improvisieren

ad libitum ADV *(Mus)* ad libitum, in freiem Tempo

Adm *abbr of* **admiral** Adm

adman [ˈædmæn] N *pl* **-men** [-men] *(inf)* Werbefachmann *m*; **admen** Werbeleute *pl*

admass [ˈædmæs] N *durch Werbung leicht beeinflussbares Publikum*

admin [ˈædmɪn] *abbr of* **administration**; **it involves a lot of ~** damit ist viel Verwaltung verbunden; **~ building** Verwaltungsgebäude *nt*

administer [ədˈmɪnɪstəʳ] **VT** **a** *institution, funds* verwalten; *business, affairs* führen; *(= run) company, department* die Verwaltungsangelegenheiten regeln von; **the civil service ~s the country** die Beamtenschaft verwaltet das Land
b *(= dispense) relief, alms* gewähren; *law* ausführen, vollstrecken, vollziehen; *punishment* verhängen *(to* über *+acc)*; **to ~ justice** Recht sprechen; **to ~ a severe blow to sb** *(fig)* jdm einen schweren Schlag versetzen
c *(= cause to take) (to sb* jdm*) medicine, drugs* verabreichen; *sacraments* spenden; *last rites* geben; **to ~ an oath to sb** jdm einen Eid abnehmen
VI **a** *(= act as administrator)* die Verwaltungsangelegenheiten regeln
b *(form)* **to ~ to the sick** sich der Kranken *(gen)* annehmen *(geh)*; **to ~ to sb's needs** sich jds annehmen *(geh)*

administrate [ædˈmɪnɪstreɪt] = **administer VT, VI a**

administration [ədˌmɪnɪsˈtreɪʃən] N **a** *no pl* Verwaltung *f*; *(of an election, a project etc)* Organisation *f*; **to spend a lot of time on ~** viel Zeit auf Verwaltungsangelegenheiten *or* -sachen verwenden **b** *(= government)* Regierung *f*; **the Schmidt ~** die Regierung Schmidt **c** *no pl (of remedy)* Verabreichung *f*; *(of sacrament)* Spenden *nt*; **the ~ of an oath** die Vereidigung; **the ~ of justice** die Rechtsprechung

administrative [ədˈmɪnɪstrətɪv] ADJ administrativ; **~ body** Verwaltungsbehörde *f*

administrative court N *(US Jur)* Verwaltungsgericht *nt*

administratively [ədˈmɪnɪstrətɪvlɪ] ADV administrativ

administrativia [ədˌmɪnɪstrəˈtɪvɪə] N *(hum)* Verwaltungskram *m (inf)*

administrator [ədˈmɪnɪstreɪtəʳ] N Verwalter(in) *m(f)*; *(Jur)* Verwaltungsbeamte(r) *m*/-beamtin *f*, Administrator(in) *m(f)*

administratrix [ədˈmɪnɪstreɪtrɪks] N *pl* **administratrices** [-trɪsiːz] *(Jur)* Nachlassverwalterin *f*

admirable ADJ, **admirably** ADV [ˈædmərəbl, -ɪ] *(= praiseworthy, laudable)* bewundernswert, erstaunlich; *(= excellent)* vortrefflich, ausgezeichnet

admiral [ˈædmərəl] N Admiral(in) *m(f)*; **Admiral of the Fleet** *(Brit)* Großadmiral(in) *m(f)* → **red admiral**

Admiralty [ˈædmərəltɪ] N *(Brit)* Admiralität *f*; *(= department, building)* britisches Marineministerium; **First Lord of the ~** britischer Marineminister

admiration [ˌædməˈreɪʃən] N **a** Bewunderung *f*; **in ~** bewundernd **b** **to win the ~ of all/of the world** *(person, object)* von allen/von aller Welt bewundert werden

admire [ədˈmaɪəʳ] ✪ 13 VT bewundern

admirer [ədˈmaɪərəʳ] N Bewund(e)rer(in) *m(f)*, Verehrer(in) *m(f)*; *(dated, hum: = suitor)* Verehrer *m (hum)*

admiring ADJ, **admiringly** ADV [ədˈmaɪərɪŋ, -lɪ] bewundernd

admissibility [ədˌmɪsɪˈbɪlɪtɪ] N Zulässigkeit *f*

admissible [ədˈmɪsɪbl] ADJ zulässig; **~ as evidence** als Beweismittel zulässig

admission [ədˈmɪʃən] N **a** *(= entry)* Zutritt *m*; *(to university)* Zulassung *f*; *(to hospital)* Einlieferung *f (to* in *+acc)*; *(= price)* Eintritt *m*; **no ~ to minors** Zutritt für Minderjährige verboten; **to gain ~ to a building** Zutritt zu einem Gebäude erhalten; **he had gained ~ to a whole new world** er hatte Zugang zu einer ganz neuen Welt gefunden; **a visa is necessary for ~ to the country** für die Einreise ist ein Visum nötig; **unrestricted ~ to a country** unbegrenzte Einreiseerlaubnis; **~ fee** Eintrittspreis *m*
b *(Jur, of evidence etc)* Zulassung *f*
c *(= confession)* Eingeständnis *nt*; **on** *or* **by his own ~** nach eigenem Eingeständnis; **that would be an ~ of failure** das hieße, sein Versagen eingestehen

admissions officer [ədˈmɪʃənzˌɒfɪsəʳ] N *(Univ) für die Zulassung verantwortlicher Verwaltungsbeamter*

admit [ədˈmɪt] ✪ 11.1, 18.3, 26.3 VT **a** *(= let in)* hereinlassen; *(= permit to join)* zulassen *(to* zu*)*, aufnehmen *(to* in *+acc)*; **children not ~ted** kein Zutritt für Kinder; **he was not ~ted to the cinema/to college** er wurde nicht ins Kino hineingelassen/zur Universität zugelassen *or* in der Universität aufgenommen; **to be ~ted to hospital** ins Krankenhaus eingeliefert werden; **to be ~ted to the Bar** bei Gericht zugelassen werden; **this ticket ~s two** die Karte ist für zwei (Personen)
b *(= have space for: halls, harbours etc)* Platz bieten für
c *(= acknowledge)* zugeben; **do you ~ (to) stealing his hat?** geben Sie zu, seinen Hut gestohlen zu haben?; **he ~ted himself beaten** er gab sich geschlagen; **it is generally ~ted that ...** es wird allgemein zugegeben, dass ...; **to ~ the truth of sth** zugeben, dass etw wahr ist

▶**admit of** VI *+prep obj (form)* zulassen *(+acc)*

▶**admit to** VI *+prep obj* eingestehen; **I have to admit to a certain feeling of admiration** ich muss gestehen, dass mir das Bewunderung abnötigt

admittance [ədˈmɪtəns] N *(to building)* Zutritt *m (to* zu*)*, Einlass *m (to* in *+acc)*; *(to club)* Zulassung *f (to* zu*)*, Aufnahme *f (to* in *+acc)*; **I gained ~ to the hall** mir wurde der Zutritt zum Saal gestattet; **I was denied ~** mir wurde der Zutritt verwehrt *or* verweigert; **no ~ except on business** Zutritt für Unbefugte verboten

admittedly [ədˈmɪtɪdlɪ] ADV zugegebenermaßen; **~ this is true** zugegeben, das stimmt

admixture [ədˈmɪkstʃəʳ] N *(= thing added)* Zusatz *m*, Beigabe *f*

admonish [ədˈmɒnɪʃ] VT ermahnen *(for* wegen*)*

admonishment [ədˈmɒnɪʃmənt], **admonition** [ˌædməʊˈnɪʃən] N *(form)* **a** *(= rebuke)* Verweis *m*, Tadel *m* **b** *no pl (= reproachfulness)* Vorwurf *m* **c** *(= warning)* Ermahnung *f*

admonitory [ədˈmɒnɪtərɪ] ADJ (er)mahnend

ad nauseam [ˌædˈnɔːzɪæm] ADV bis zum Überdruss, bis zum Geht-nicht-mehr *(inf)*; **and so on ~** und so weiter, und so weiter

ado [əˈduː] N Aufheben *nt*, Trara *nt (inf)*; **much ~ about nothing** viel Lärm um nichts; **without more** *or* **further ~** ohne Weiteres

adobe [əˈdəʊbɪ] N *(= brick)* (ungebrannter) Lehmziegel, Adobe *m*; *(= house) Haus aus Adobeziegeln* **~ wall** *Mauer aus Adobeziegeln*

adolescence [ˌædəʊˈlesns] N Jugend *f*; *(= puberty)* Pubertät *f*, Adoleszenz *f (form)*; **the problems of ~** Pubertätsprobleme *pl*; **in his late ~** in seiner späteren Jugend

adolescent [ˌædəʊˈlesnt] **N** Jugendliche(r) *mf*; **he's still an ~** er ist noch im Heranwachsen/in der Pubertät **ADJ** Jugend-; *(= in puberty)* Pubertäts-, pubertär; *(= immature)* unreif; **his ~ years** seine Jugendjahre; **he is so ~** er steckt noch in der Pubertät; **~ phase** Pubertätsphase *f*; **~ love** jugendliche Liebe

Adonis [əˈdəʊnɪs] N *(Myth, fig)* Adonis *m*

adopt [əˈdɒpt] VT **a** *child* adoptieren, an Kindes statt annehmen *(form)*; *child in a different country, family, city* die Patenschaft übernehmen für; **the orphan was ~ed into the family** das Waisenkind wurde in die Familie aufgenommen; **your cat has ~ed me** *(inf)* deine Katze hat sich mir angeschlossen **b** *idea, suggestion, attitude, method* übernehmen; *mannerisms* annehmen; *career* einschlagen, sich *(dat)* wählen **c** *(Pol) motion* annehmen; *candidate* nehmen

adopted [əˈdɒptɪd] ADJ Adoptiv-, adoptiert; **~ child** Adoptivkind *nt*; **her ~ country/home town** ihre Wahlheimat

adoptee [əˌdɒpˈtiː] N *(esp US)* Adoptivkind *nt*

adoption [əˈdɒpʃən] N **a** *(of child)* Adoption *f*, Annahme *f*, an Kindes Statt *(form)*; *(of city, of child in other country)* Übernahme *f* der Patenschaft; *(into the family)* Aufnahme *f*; **parents by ~** Adoptiveltern *pl*; **Japanese by ~** Japaner(in) *m(f)* durch Adoption **b** *(of method, idea)* Übernahme *f*; *(of mannerisms)* Annahme *f*; *(of career)* Wahl *f*; **his country of ~** seine Wahlheimat; **this custom is Japanese only by ~** dieser Brauch ist von den Japanern nur übernommen worden **c** *(of motion, law, candidate)* Annahme *f*

adoption agency N Adoptionsagentur *f*

adoptive [əˈdɒptɪv] ADJ Adoptiv-; **~ parents** Adoptiveltern *pl*; **~ home/country** Wahlheimat *f*

adorable [əˈdɔːrəbl] ADJ bezaubernd, hinreißend; **she is ~** sie ist ein Schatz

adorably [əˈdɔːrəblɪ] ADV bezaubernd, hinreißend

adoration [ˌædəˈreɪʃən] N **a** *(of God)* Anbetung *f* **b** *(of family, wife)* grenzenlose Liebe *(of* für*)* **c** *(inf, of French, whisky etc)* Liebe *f (of* für*)*

adore [əˈdɔːʳ] VT **a** *God* anbeten **b** *(= love very much) family, wife* über alles lieben **c** *(inf: = like very much) French, whisky etc* (über alles) lieben; **to ~ attention** gern im Mittelpunkt stehen

adorer [əˈdɔːrəʳ] N **a** *(= worshipper)* Anbeter(in) *m(f)* **b** *(= admirer)* Verehrer(in) *m(f)*, Bewunderer *m*, Bewunderin *f*

adoring [əˈdɔːrɪŋ] ADJ bewundernd; **his ~ fans** seine bewundernden *or* ihn anbetenden Fans

adoringly [əˈdɔːrɪŋlɪ] ADV bewundernd, voller Verehrung

adorn [əˈdɔːn] VT schmücken, zieren *(geh)*; **to ~ oneself** sich schmücken

adornment [əˈdɔːnmənt] N Schmuck *m no pl*; *(act)* Schmücken *nt*; *(on dress, cake, design)* Verzierung *f*; *(on manuscript)* Ornament *nt*; *(in prose style)* Ausschmückung *f*

ADP [ˌeɪdiːˈpiː] *abbr of* **automatic data processing** automatische Datenverarbeitung

adrenal [əˈdriːnl] ADJ Nebennieren-; **~ glands** Nebennieren *pl*; **~ hormone** Nebennierenhormon *nt*

adrenalin(e) [əˈdrenəlɪn] N **a** *(Med)* Adrenalin *nt* **b** *(phrases)* **I could feel the ~ rising** ich fühlte, wie mein Blutdruck stieg; **you burn up a lot of ~** Sie verbrauchen eine Menge Energie; **it's impossible to relax now the ~'s going** es ist unmöglich abzuschalten, wenn man so aufgedreht ist; **in a combat situation the ~ just takes over** in einer Kampfsituation leistet man einfach mehr; **working under pressure gets the ~ going** Arbeiten unter Druck weckt ungeahnte Kräfte

adrenalin(e) junkie N *(inf)* Adrenalinjunkie *m (inf)*

Adriatic (Sea) [ˌeɪdrɪˈætɪk(ˈsiː)] N Adria *f*, Adriatisches Meer

adrift [əˈdrɪft] ADV ADJ *pred* **a** *(Naut)* treibend; **to be ~** treiben; **to go ~** *(lit)* sich losmachen *or* loslösen; *(= go awry:) plan, scheme* schiefgehen; **to set** *or* **cut a boat ~** ein Boot losmachen

b *(fig)* **to come ~** *(wire, hair etc)* sich lösen; *(plans, scheme)* fehlschlagen; *(theory)* zusammenbrechen; **we are ~ on the sea of life** wir treiben dahin auf dem Meer des Lebens; **he wandered through the city, lost and ~** (ziellos und) verloren irrte er in der Stadt umher; **you're all ~** *(inf)* da liegst du völlig verkehrt *or* falsch; **after a month's philosophy I felt all ~** nach einem Monat Philosophie war ich vollkommen durcheinander; **to cast** *or* **turn sb ~** jdn auf die Straße setzen

c *(Sport)* **to be 15 points/seconds ~** 15 Punkte/Sekunden zurückliegen

adroit [əˈdrɔɪt] ADJ *lawyer, reply, reasoning* gewandt, geschickt; *mind* scharf; **to be ~ at sth/doing sth** gewandt *or* geschickt in etw *(dat)* sein/darin sein, etw zu tun

adroitly [əˈdrɔɪtlɪ] ADV gewandt, geschickt

adroitness [əˈdrɔɪtnɪs] N *(of lawyer, reply, reasoning)* Gewandtheit *f*, Geschicklichkeit *f*; *(of mind)* Schärfe *f*

adsorb [ædˈsɔːb] VT adsorbieren

adsorption [ædˈsɔːpʃən] N Adsorption *f*

adulate [ˈædjʊleɪt] VT **to ~ sb** jdn beweihräuchern, jdm lobhudeln

adulation [ˌædjʊˈleɪʃən] N Verherrlichung *f*

adulatory [ˌædjʊˈleɪtərɪ, *(US)* ˈædʒələtɔːrɪ] ADJ *(= laudatory) comment* bewundernd; *(stronger)* vergötternd

adult [ˈædʌlt, *(US)* əˈdʌlt] N Erwachsene(r) *mf*; **~s only** nur für Erwachsene ADJ **a** *person* erwachsen; *animal* ausgewachsen; **~ male** *(Zool)* ausgewachsenes Männchen; **he spent his ~ life in New York** er hat sein Leben als Erwachsener in New York verbracht **b** *(= for adults) book, film, classes* für Erwachsene; **~ classes** Kurse *pl* für Erwachsene; **~ education** Erwachsenenbildung *f* **c** *(= mature) decision* reif; **we were very ~ about it** wir waren sehr ruhig und vernünftig

adulterate [əˈdʌltəreɪt] VT **a** *wine, whisky etc* panschen; *food* abwandeln; **some ~d Scottish version of Italian cooking** ein schottischer Abklatsch italienischer Küche **b** *(fig) text, original version* verfälschen, Gewalt antun *(+dat)*; **an ~d version of the original** eine verhunzte Fassung des Originals *(inf)*

adulteration [əˌdʌltəˈreɪʃən] N **a** *(of wine)* Pan(t)schen *nt*; *(of food)* Abwandlung *f* **b** *(fig)* Vergewaltigung *f*, Verhunzung *f (inf)*

adulterer [əˈdʌltərəʳ] N Ehebrecher *m*

adulteress [əˈdʌltərɪs] N Ehebrecherin *f*

adulterous [əˈdʌltərəs] ADJ ehebrecherisch

adultery [əˈdʌltərɪ] N Ehebruch *m*; **to commit ~** Ehebruch begehen; **because of his ~ with three actresses** weil er mit drei Schauspielerinnen Ehebruch begangen hatte

adulthood [ˈædʌlthʊd, *(US)* əˈdʌlthʊd] N Erwachsenenalter *nt*; **to reach ~** erwachsen werden

adumbrate [ˈædʌmbreɪt] VT *(liter)* **a** *(= outline) theory* umreißen **b** *(= foreshadow) coming event* ankündigen

adumbration [ˌædʌmˈbreɪʃən] N *(liter)* **a** *(of theory)* Umriss *m* **b** *(of event)* Ankündigung *f*, Anzeichen *nt*

advance [ədˈvɑːns] N **a** *(= progress)* Fortschritt *m*

b *(= movement forward, of old age)* Voranschreiten *nt*; *(of science)* Weiterentwicklung *f*; *(of sea, ideas)* Vordringen *nt*; **with the ~ of old age** mit fortschreitendem Alter

c *(Mil)* Vormarsch *m*, Vorrücken *nt*

d *(= money)* Vorschuss *m* (on auf *+acc*)

e advances PL *(amorous, fig)* Annäherungsversuche *pl*

f in ~ im Voraus; *(temporal also)* vorher; **to send sb on in ~** jdn vorausschicken; **£10 in ~** £ 10 als Vorschuss; **thanking you in ~** mit bestem Dank im Voraus; **to arrive in ~ of the others** vor den anderen ankommen; **to be (well) in ~ of sb/one's time** jdm/seiner Zeit (weit) voraus sein

VT **a** *(= move forward) date, time* vorverlegen; **the dancer slowly ~s one foot** die Tänzerin setzt langsam einen Fuß vor

b *(Mil) troops* vorrücken lassen

c *(= further) work, project* voran- *or* weiterbringen, förderlich sein für; *cause, interests, career* fördern; *knowledge* vergrößern; *(= accelerate) growth* vorantreiben; *(= promote) employee etc* befördern

d *(= put forward) reason, opinion, plan* vorbringen

e *(= pay beforehand)* (sb jdm) (als) Vorschuss geben, vorschießen *(inf)*; *(= lend)* als Kredit geben

f *(= raise) prices* anheben

VI **a** *(Mil)* vorrücken; **government troops are advancing against the rebels** die Regierungstruppen rücken weiter gegen die Rebellen vor

b *(= move forward)* vorankommen; **to ~ toward(s) sb/sth** auf jdn/etw zugehen; **to ~ upon sb** drohend auf jdn zukommen; **as the sea ~s over the rocks** während die See über die Felsen vordringt; **old age is advancing on all of us** wir alle nähern uns dem Alter

c *(fig: = progress)* Fortschritte *pl* machen; **we've ~d a long way since those days** wir sind seither ein gutes Stück voran- *or* weitergekommen; **the work is advancing well** die Arbeit macht gute Fortschritte; **are we advancing toward(s) some kind of solution?** kommen wir irgend einer Lösung näher?; **as mankind ~s in knowledge** während die Menschheit an Wissen gewinnt

d *(prices)* anziehen; *(costs)* hochgehen, ansteigen

advance: advance booking N Reservierung *f*; *(Theat)* Vorverkauf *m*; **~ opens on …** der Vorverkauf beginnt am …; **advance booking office** N *(Theat)* Vorverkaufsstelle *f*; **advance copy** N Vorausexemplar *nt*, Vorabdruck *m*

advanced [ədˈvɑːnst] ADJ **a** *student, level, age, technology* fortgeschritten; *studies, mathematics etc* höher; *ideas* fortschrittlich; *version, model* anspruchsvoll, weiterentwickelt; *level of civilization* hoch; *position, observation post etc* vorgeschoben; *society, country, economy* hoch entwickelt; **~ work** anspruchsvolle Arbeit; **he is very ~ for his age** er ist für sein Alter sehr weit

b *(= developed) plan, programme* ausgefeilt; **in the ~ stages of the disease** im fortgeschrittenen Stadium der Krankheit

c *(form: = mature)* **~ in years** in fortgeschrittenem Alter; **she is more/less ~ in years than …** sie ist älter/jünger als …

d *(form)* **the summer was well ~** der Sommer war schon weit vorangeschritten

advance: advance guard N Vorhut *f*; **advance man** N *(US Pol)* Wahlhelfer *m*

advancement [ədˈvɑːnsmənt] N **a** *(= furtherance)* Förderung *f* **b** *(= promotion in rank)* Vorwärtskommen *nt*, Aufstieg *m*

advance: advance notice N frühzeitiger Bescheid; *(of sth bad)* Vorwarnung *f*; **to be given ~** frühzeitig Bescheid/eine Vorwarnung erhalten; **advance party** N *(Mil, fig)* Vorhut *f*; **advance payment** N Vorauszahlung *f*; **advance publicity** N Vorabwerbung *f*; **advance warning** N = **advance notice**

advantage [ədˈvɑːntɪdʒ] N **a** Vorteil *m*; **to have an ~ (over sb)** (jdm gegenüber) im Vorteil sein; **that gives you an ~ over me** damit sind Sie mir gegenüber im Vorteil, das verschafft Ihnen mir gegenüber einen Vorteil; **to have the ~ of sb** jdm überlegen sein; **you have the ~ of me** *(form)* ich kenne leider Ihren werten Namen nicht *(form)*; **he had the ~ of youth** er hatte den Vorzug der Jugend; **she had the ~ of greater experience** sie war durch ihre größere Erfahrung im Vorteil; **to get the ~ of sb (by doing sth)** sich *(dat)* (durch etw) jdm gegenüber einen Vorteil verschaffen; **to have the ~ of numbers** zahlenmäßig überlegen sein

b *(= use, profit)* Vorteil *m*; **to take ~ of sb** *(= exploit)* jdn ausnutzen; *(euph: sexually)* jdn missbrauchen; **to take ~ of sth** etw ausnutzen, sich *(dat)* etw zunutze *or* zu Nutze machen; **he took ~ of her while she was drunk** er machte sich *(dat)* ihre Trunkenheit zunutze *or* zu Nutze; **to turn sth to ~** Nutzen aus etw ziehen; **he turned it to his own ~** er machte es sich *(dat)* zunutze *or* zu Nutze; **what ~ is that to us?** welchen Nutzen haben wir davon?; **it is to my ~ to …** es ist vorteilhaft für mich …, es ist für mich von Vorteil …; **to use sth to best ~** das Beste aus etw machen; **to use sth to one's ~** etw für sich nutzen

c *(Tennis)* Vorteil *m*

VT *(old, liter)* zum Vorteil *or* Nutzen gereichen *(+dat) (geh)*

advantageous [ˌædvənˈteɪdʒəs] ADJ von Vorteil, vorteilhaft; **to be ~ to sb** für jdn von Vorteil sein

advantageously [ˌædvənˈteɪdʒəslɪ] ADV vorteilhaft

advent [ˈædvənt] N **a** *(of age, era)* Beginn *m*, Anbruch *m*; *(of jet plane etc)* Aufkommen *nt* **b** *(Eccl)* **Advent** Advent *m*

Advent calendar N Adventskalender *m*

adventitious [ˌædvenˈtɪʃəs] ADJ *(form)* zufällig

adventure [ədˈventʃəʳ] N **a** Abenteuer *nt*, Erlebnis *nt*; **an ~ into the unknown** ein Vorstoß *m* ins Unbekannte **b** *no pl* **love/spirit of ~** Abenteuerlust *f*; **to look for ~** (das) Abenteuer suchen; **a life of ~** ein abenteuerliches Leben *attr* Abenteuer-; **~ holiday** *(Brit)* Abenteuerurlaub *m*

adventure playground N Abenteuerspielplatz *m*

adventurer [ədˈventʃərəʳ] N Abenteurer(in) *m(f)*; *(pej also)* Windhund *m*

adventuresome [ədˈventʃəsəm] ADJ = **adventurous**

adventuress [ədˈventʃərɪs] N *(pej)* Abenteurerin *f*

adventurism [ədˈventʃərɪzəm] N Abenteurertum *nt*

adventurist [ədˈventʃərɪst] N Abenteurer(in) *m(f)* ADJ abenteuerlich

adventurous [ədˈventʃərəs] ADJ **a** *person* abenteuerlustig; *journey* abenteuerlich **b** *(= bold)* gewagt

adventurously [əd'ventʃərəslɪ] ADV *(= boldly)* gewagt; **we should be using the money more ~** wir sollten das Geld etwas riskanter einsetzen

adventurousness [əd'ventʃərəsnɪs] N **a** *(of person)* Abenteuerlust *f*; *(of journey)* Abenteuerlichkeit *f* **b** *(= boldness)* Gewagte(s) *nt*; **the ~ of his style** sein gewagter Stil

adverb ['ædvɜːb] N Adverb *nt*, Umstandswort *nt*

adverbial ADJ, **adverbially** ADV [əd'vɜːbɪəl, -ɪ] adverbial

adversary ['ædvəsərɪ] N Widersacher(in) *m(f)*; *(in contest)* Gegner(in) *m(f)*

adverse ['ædvɜːs] ADJ ungünstig; *criticism, comment also, reaction* negativ, ablehnend; *wind, conditions also* widrig; *effect also* nachteilig

adversely [əd'vɜːslɪ] ADV *comment, criticize, react* negativ; *affect also* nachteilig

adversity [əd'vɜːsɪtɪ] N **a** *no pl* Not *f*; **a time of ~** eine Zeit der Not; **in ~** im Unglück, in der Not **b** *(= misfortune)* Widrigkeit *f (geh)*; **the adversities of war** die Härten des Krieges

advert[1] [əd'vɜːt] VI *(form)* hinweisen, aufmerksam machen *(to* auf *+acc)*

advert[2] ['ædvɜːt] N *(inf) abbr of* **advertisement** Anzeige *f*, Annonce *f*, Inserat *nt*; *(on TV, radio)* Werbespot *m*

advertainment [,ædvə'teɪnmənt] N unterhaltende Werbung, Advertainment *nt*

advertise ['ædvətaɪz] VT **a** *(= publicize)* Werbung *or* Reklame machen für, werben für; **I've seen that soap ~d on television** ich habe die Werbung *or* Reklame für diese Seife im Fernsehen gesehen; **as ~d on television** wie durch das Fernsehen bekannt
b *(in paper etc) flat, table etc* inserieren, annoncieren; *job, post* ausschreiben, inserieren; **to ~ sth in a shop window/on local radio** etw durch eine Schaufensteranzeige/im Regionalsender anbieten; **I saw it ~d in a shop window** ich habe die Anzeige dafür in einem Schaufenster gesehen
c *(= make conspicuous) fact* publik machen; *ignorance* offen zeigen
VI **a** *(Comm)* Werbung *or* Reklame machen, werben
b *(in paper)* inserieren, annoncieren *(for* für*)*; **to ~ for sb/sth** jdn/etw (per Anzeige) suchen; **to ~ for sth on local radio/in a shop window** etw per Regionalsender/durch Anzeige im Schaufenster suchen

advertisement [əd'vɜːtɪsmənt, *(US)* ,ædvə'taɪzmənt] ✪ 19.1, 20.1 N **a** *(Comm)* Werbung *f*, Reklame *f no pl*; *(esp in paper)* Anzeige *f*; **TV ~s** die Werbung *or* Reklame im Fernsehen; **70% of the magazine is made up of ~s** die Zeitschrift besteht zu 70% aus Anzeigen *or* Werbung *or* Reklame; **he is not a good ~ for his school** er ist nicht gerade ein Aushängeschild für seine Schule **b** *(= announcement)* Anzeige *f*; **to put** *or* **place an ~ in the paper (for sb/sth)** eine Anzeige (für jdn/etw) in die Zeitung setzen, (für jdn/etw) in der Zeitung inserieren

advertisement column N Anzeigenspalte *f*

advertiser ['ædvətaɪzə'] N *(in paper)* Inserent(in) *m(f)*; **this company never was a very big ~** diese Firma hat nie viel Werbung *or* Reklame gemacht; **TV ~s** Firmen, die im Fernsehen werben

advertising ['ædvətaɪzɪŋ] N Werbung *f*, Reklame *f*; **he works in ~** er ist in der Werbung (tätig)

advertising *in cpds* Werbe-; **advertising agency** N Werbeagentur *f or* -büro *nt*; **advertising campaign** N Werbekampagne *f or* -feldzug *m*; **advertising media** PL Werbemedien *pl*; **advertising rates** PL Anzeigenpreise *pl*; *(for TV, radio)* Preise *pl* für Werbespots; **advertising space** N Platz *m* für Anzeigen

advertorial [,ædvə'tɔːrɪəl] N Anzeige *f (in Form eines Artikels)*, Advertorial *nt*

advice [əd'vaɪs] ✪ 2.1, 2.2 N **a** *no pl* Rat *m no pl*; **a piece of ~** ein Rat(schlag) *m*; **let me give you a piece of ~** *or* **some ~** ich will Ihnen einen guten Rat geben; **you're a fine one to give ~** du hast gut raten, ausgerechnet du willst hier Ratschläge geben; **his ~ was always useful** er gab immer guten Rat *or* gute Ratschläge; **that's good ~** das ist ein guter Rat; **I didn't ask for your ~** ich habe dich nicht um (deinen) Rat gebeten *or* gefragt; **to take sb's ~** jds Rat (be)folgen; **take my ~** höre auf mich; **to seek (sb's) ~** (jdn) um Rat fragen; *(from doctor, lawyer etc)* Rat (bei jdm) einholen; **to take medical/legal ~** einen Arzt/Rechtsanwalt zu Rate ziehen; **my ~ to him would be ...** ich würde ihm raten ...; **it's not ~ we need** wir brauchen keine guten Ratschläge
b *(Comm: = notification)* Mitteilung *f*, Avis *m or nt*

advice: **advice column** N = **agony column**; **advice columnist** N = **agony columnist**; **advice note** N Benachrichtigung *f*, Avis *m or nt*

advisability [əd,vaɪzə'bɪlɪtɪ] N Ratsamkeit *f*; **he questioned the ~ of going on strike** er bezweifelte, ob es ratsam wäre zu streiken

advisable [əd'vaɪzəbl] ✪ 2.2 ADJ ratsam, empfehlenswert

advisably [əd'vaɪzəblɪ] ADV zu Recht

advise [əd'vaɪz] ✪ 1.1, 2.1, 2.2, 2.3 VT **a** *(= give advice to) person* raten *(+dat)*; *(professionally)* beraten; **to ~ caution** zur Vorsicht raten, Vorsicht empfehlen; **I wouldn't ~ it** ich würde es nicht raten *or* empfehlen; **I would ~ you to do it/not to do it** ich würde dir zuraten/abraten; **to ~ sb against sth** jdm von etw abraten; **to ~ sb against doing sth** jdm abraten, etw zu tun; **what would you ~ me to do?** was *or* wozu würden Sie mir raten?
b *(Comm: = inform)* verständigen, avisieren; **to ~ sb of sth** jdn von etw in Kenntnis setzen; **our agent keeps us ~d of developments** unser Vertreter unterrichtet uns ständig über neue Entwicklungen
VI **a** *(= give advice)* raten; **I shall do as you ~** ich werde tun, was Sie mir raten; **his function is merely to ~** er hat nur beratende Funktion
b *(US)* **to ~ with sb** sich mit jdm beraten

advisedly [əd'vaɪzɪdlɪ] ADV richtig; **and I use the word ~** ich verwende bewusst dieses Wort

advisedness [əd'vaɪzɪdnɪs] N Klugheit *f*, Ratsamkeit *f*

advisement [əd'vaɪzmənt] N *(US)* **to keep sth under ~** etw im Auge behalten; **to take sth under ~** *(= consider more carefully)* sich *(dat)* etw genauer überlegen; *(= consult experts)* Experten zu etw zu Rate ziehen

adviser [əd'vaɪzə'] N Ratgeber(in) *m(f)*; *(professional)* Berater(in) *m(f)*; **legal ~** Rechtsberater(in) *m(f)*; **spiritual ~** geistlicher Berater

advising bank [əd'vaɪzɪŋ,bæŋk] N *(Fin)* avisierende Bank

advisory [əd'vaɪzərɪ] ADJ beratend; **to act in a purely ~ capacity** rein beratende Funktion haben; **~ committee** beratendes Gremium

advocacy ['ædvəkəsɪ] N Eintreten *nt (of* für*)*, Fürsprache *f (of* für*)*; *(of plan)* Befürwortung *f*; **the skills of legal ~** juristische Wortgewandtheit

advocate ['ædvəkɪt] N **a** *(= upholder: of cause etc)* Verfechter(in) *m(f)*, Befürworter(in) *m(f)* **b** *(esp Scot: Jur)* (Rechts)anwalt *m*/-anwältin *f*, Advokat(in) *m(f) (old, dial)* ['ædvəkeɪt] VT eintreten für; *plan etc* befürworten; **those who ~ extending the licensing laws** die, die eine Verlängerung der Öffnungszeiten befürworten; **what course of action would you ~?** welche Maßnahmen würden Sie empfehlen?

advocator ['ædvəkeɪtə'] N = **advocate N**

advowson [əd'vaʊzn] N *(Rel Brit)* Pfründenbesetzungsrecht *nt*

advt *abbr of* **advertisement**

adwoman ['ædwʊmən] N *pl* **-women** [-wɪmɪn] Werbefachfrau *f*

adz(e) [ædz] N Dechsel *f*

AEEU *(Brit) abbr of* **Amalagamated Engineering and Electrical Union** Vereinigte Techniker- und Elektrotechnikergewerkschaft

Aegean [iː'dʒiːən] ADJ ägäisch; *islands* in der Ägäis; **the ~ (Sea)** die Ägäis, das Ägäische Meer

aegis ['iːdʒɪs] N Ägide *f (geh)*; **under the ~ of** unter der Ägide *(geh) or* Schirmherrschaft von

aegrotat ['aɪgrəʊ,tæt] N *Examen, an dem der Prüfling aus Krankheitsgründen nicht teilnimmt und das bei Vorlage eines ärztlichen Attestes für bestanden erklärt wird*

Aeneas [ɪ'niːəs] N Äneas *m*

Aeneid [ɪ'niːɪd] N Äneide *f*

Aeolian [iː'əʊlɪən] ADJ äolisch

Aeolian mode [iː'əʊlɪən-] N *(Mus)* äolische Tonart

aeon ['iːən] N Äon *m (geh)*, Ewigkeit *f*; **through ~s of time** äonenlang *(geh)*

aerate ['ɛəreɪt] VT *liquid* mit Kohlensäure anreichern; *blood* Sauerstoff zuführen *(+dat)*; *soil* auflockern; **~d water** kohlensaures Wasser

aerial ['ɛərɪəl] N *(esp Brit: = antenna)* Antenne *f*
ADJ Luft-; **~ barrage** *(air to ground)* Bombardement *nt*; *(ground to air)* Flakfeuer *nt*; **~ combat** Luftkampf *m*; **~ map** Luftbildkarte *f*; **~ navigation** Luftfahrt *f*; **~ photograph** *or* **shot** Luftbild *nt*, Luftaufnahme *f*; **~ photography** Luftaufnahmen *pl*; **~ reconnaissance** Luftaufklärung *f*; **~ view** Luftbild *nt*, Luftansicht *f*; **in order to obtain an ~ view of the site** um das Gelände von der Luft aus zu betrachten; **~ warfare** Luftkrieg *m*

aerial: **aerial cableway** N Seilbahn *f*; **aerial camera** N Luftbildkamera *f*; **aerial input** N *(TV)* Antennenanschluss *m*

aerialist ['ɛərɪəlɪst] N *(US) (on trapeze)* Trapezkünstler(in) *m(f)*; *(on high wire)* Seiltänzer(in) *m(f)*

aerial: **aerial ladder** N Drehleiter *f*; **aerial mast** N Antennenmast *m*; **aerial railway** N Schwebebahn *f*; **aerial socket** N Antennenanschluss *m*; **aerial tram** N *(US)* Schwebebahn *f*

aero- ['ɛərəʊ] PREF aero- *(form)*, Luft-

aerobatic [,ɛərəʊ'bætɪk] ADJ kunstfliegerisch, Kunstflug-; **~ manoeuvre** *(Brit) or* **maneuver** *(US)* Kunstflugmanöver *nt*

aerobatics [,ɛərəʊ'bætɪks] PL Kunstfliegen *nt*, Aerobatik *f (form)*

aerobic [ɛə'rəʊbɪk] ADJ **a** *(Biol)* aerob; **~ respiration** aerobe Atmung, Sauerstoffatmung *f* **b** *(Sport)* Aerobic-; **~ exercise** Aerobicübung *f*

aerobics [ɛər'əʊbɪks] N *sing* Aerobic *nt*; **to do ~** Aerobic machen

aerodrome ['ɛərədrəʊm] N *(Brit)* Flugplatz *m*, Aerodrom *nt (old)*

aerodynamic [,ɛərəʊdaɪ'næmɪk] ADJ aerodynamisch

aerodynamically [,ɛərəʊdaɪ'næmɪkəlɪ] ADV *efficient, designed, built* aerodynamisch

aerodynamics [,ɛərəʊdaɪ'næmɪks] N **a** *sing (subject)* Aerodynamik *f* **b** *pl (of plane etc)* Aerodynamik *f*

aero engine N Flugzeugmotor *m*

aerofoil ['ɛərəʊfɔɪl] N Tragflügel *m*; *(on racing cars)* Spoiler *m*

aerogramme ['ɛərəʊgræm] N Aerogramm *nt*, Luftpostbrief *m*

aeromodelling [,ɛərəʊ'mɒdəlɪŋ] N Modellflugzeugbau *m*

aeronaut ['ɛərənɔːt] N Aeronaut(in) *m(f)*

aeronautic(al) [,ɛərə'nɔːtɪk(əl)] ADJ aeronautisch

aeronautical engineering N Flugzeugbau *m*

aeronautics [,ɛərə'nɔːtɪks] N *sing* Luftfahrt *f*, Aeronautik *f*

aeroplane ['ɛərəpleɪn] N *(Brit)* Flugzeug *nt*

aeroponics [ˌɛərəʊˈpɒnɪks] N *sing* Aeroponik *f erdlose Kultivierung von Pflanzen in Gewächshäusern*

aerosol [ˈɛərəsɒl] N *(= can)* Spraydose *f*; *(= mixture)* Aerosol *nt*; **~ paint** Spray- *or* Sprühfarbe *f*; **~ spray** Aerosolspray *nt*

aerospace [ˈɛərəʊspeɪs] *in cpds* Raumfahrt-; **aerospace industry** N Raumfahrtindustrie *f*; **aerospace research** N Raumforschung *f*

aerosphere [ˈɛərəʊsfɪəˈ] N Erdatmosphäre *f*

Aertex® [ˈɛəteks] N Aertex® *nt, Baumwolltrikotstoff mit Lochmuster*

Aeschylus [ˈiːskələs] N Aischylos *m*, Äschylus *m*

Aesculapian [ˌiːskjʊˈleɪpɪən] ADJ **a** Äskulap-; **~ staff** Äskulapstab *m* **b** *(Med)* ärztlich

Aesop [ˈiːsɒp] N Äsop *m*; **~'s fables** die äsopischen Fabeln

aesthete, *(US)* **esthete** [ˈiːsθiːt] N Ästhet(in) *m(f)*

aesthetic(al), *(US)* **esthetic(al)** [iːsˈθetɪk,əl] ADJ ästhetisch; **an aesthetical discussion** eine Diskussion über Ästhetik

aesthetically, *(US)* **esthetically** [iːsˈθetɪkəlɪ] ADV in ästhetischer Hinsicht; **~ decorated** ästhetisch schön dekoriert; **~ pleasing** ästhetisch schön

aestheticism, *(US)* **estheticism** [iːsˈθetɪsɪzəm] N Ästhetizismus *m*

aesthetics, *(US)* **esthetics** [iːsˈθetɪks] N *sing* Ästhetik *f*

aestival, *(US)* **estival** [iːˈstaɪvəl] ADJ *(form)* sommerlich

aestivate, *(US)* **estivate** [ˈiːstɪveɪt] VI *(form, animals)* Sommerschlaf halten; *(person)* den Sommer verbringen

aetiological, *(US)* **etiological** [ˌiːtɪəˈlɒdʒɪkəl] ADJ *(Med, fig)* ätiologisch

aetiology, *(US)* **etiology** [ˌiːtɪˈɒlədʒɪ] N *(Med, fig)* Ätiologie *f*

afaik *(in text message etc) abbr of* **as far as I know** soviel ich weiß

afar [əˈfɑːˈ] ADV *(liter)* weit; **from ~** aus der Ferne, von weit her

affability [ˌæfəˈbɪlɪtɪ] N Umgänglichkeit *f*, Freundlichkeit *f*

affable ADJ, **affably** ADV [ˈæfəbl, -ɪ] umgänglich, freundlich

affair [əˈfɛəˈ] N **a** *(= event, concern, matter, business)* Sache *f*, Angelegenheit *f*; **the investigation was an odd ~ altogether** die Untersuchung war schon eine seltsame Sache *or* Angelegenheit; **a scandalous ~** ein Skandal *m*; **the Watergate/Profumo ~** die Watergate-/Profumo-Affäre; **the state of ~s with the economy** die Lage der Wirtschaft; **in the present state of ~s** bei *or* in der gegenwärtigen Lage *or* Situation, beim gegenwärtigen Stand der Dinge; **a state of ~s I don't approve of** ein Zustand, den ich nicht billige; **this is a sorry state of ~s!** das sind ja schöne Zustände!; **your private ~s don't concern me** deine Privatangelegenheiten sind mir egal; **financial ~s have never interested me** Finanzfragen haben mich nie interessiert; **I never interfere with his business ~s** ich mische mich nie in seine geschäftlichen Angelegenheiten ein; **man of ~s** *(liter, form)* Geschäftsmann *m*; **~s of state** Staatsangelegenheiten *pl*; **~s of the heart** Herzensangelegenheiten *pl*; **it's not your ~ what I do in the evenings** was ich abends tue, geht dich nichts an; **that's my/his ~!** das ist meine/seine Sache! → *also* **current ADJ, foreign affairs**
b *(= love affair)* Verhältnis *nt*, Affäre *f* *(dated)*; **to have an ~ with sb** ein Verhältnis mit jdm haben
c *(= duel)* **~ of honour** Ehrenhandel *m*
d *(inf: = object, thing)* Ding *nt*; **what's this funny aerial ~?** was soll dieses komische Antennendings? *(inf)*; **the committee was an odd ~** das Komitee war eine seltsame Sache

affect¹ [əˈfekt] VT **a** *(= have effect on)* sich auswirken auf *(+acc)*; *decision, sb's life* beeinflussen, sich auswirken auf *(+acc)*; *(detrimentally) nerves, material* angreifen; *health, person* schaden *(+dat)* **b** *(= concern)* betreffen **c** *(emotionally: = move)* berühren, treffen; **he was obviously ~ed by the news** die Nachricht hatte ihn sichtlich mitgenommen **d** *(diseases: = attack)* befallen

affect² VT **a** *(= feign) indifference* vortäuschen, vorgeben; *accent* sich befleißigen *(+gen)* *(geh)* **b** *(liter, = like to use etc) clothes, colours* eine Vorliebe *or* Schwäche haben für

affectation [ˌæfekˈteɪʃən] N **a** *(= pretence)* Vortäuschung *f*, Vorgabe *f* **b** *(= artificiality)* Affektiertheit *f no pl*; **her ~s annoy me** ihr affektiertes Benehmen ärgert mich; **an ~** eine affektierte Angewohnheit

affected [əˈfektɪd] ADJ *person, clothes* affektiert; *behaviour, style, accent also* gekünstelt

affectedly [əˈfektɪdlɪ] ADV *dress, speak, behave* affektiert; *simple, ironic* gewollt

affecting [əˈfektɪŋ] ADJ rührend

affection [əˈfekʃən] N **a** *(= fondness)* Zuneigung *f no pl* *(for, towards* zu); **to win sb's ~s** *(dated, hum)* jds Zuneigung gewinnen; **I have** *or* **feel a great ~ for her** ich mag sie sehr gerne; **don't you even feel any ~ for her at all?** fühlst du denn gar nichts für sie?; **you could show a little more ~ toward(s) me** du könntest mir gegenüber etwas mehr Gefühl zeigen; **children who lacked ~** Kinder, denen die Liebe fehlte; **everybody needs a little ~** jeder braucht ein bisschen Liebe; **he has a special place in her ~s** er nimmt einen besonderen Platz in ihrem Herzen ein; **display of ~** Ausdruck *m* von Zärtlichkeit
b *(Med)* Erkrankung *f*, Affektion *f (spec)*

affectionate [əˈfekʃənɪt] ADJ liebevoll, zärtlich; **your ~ daughter** *(letter-ending)* Deine Dich liebende Tochter; **to feel ~ toward(s) sb** jdm sehr zugetan sein, jdn sehr gernhaben

affectionately [əˈfekʃənɪtlɪ] ADV liebevoll, zärtlich; **yours ~, Wendy** *(letter-ending)* in Liebe, deine Wendy

affective [əˈfektɪv] ADJ *(Psych)* affektiv

affective computing N Affective Computing *nt, Forschungsansatz, der menschliches Fühlen und Denken für die Künstliche Intelligenz nutzbar machen möchte*

affidavit [ˌæfɪˈdeɪvɪt] N *(Jur)* eidesstattliche Erklärung; *(to guarantee support of immigrant)* Affidavit *nt*; **to swear an ~ (that)** eine eidesstattliche Erklärung abgeben(, dass)

affiliate [əˈfɪlɪeɪt] VT angliedern *(to +dat)*; **the two banks are ~d** die zwei Banken sind aneinander angeschlossen; **~d** angeschlossen, Schwester-; **~d company** Schwesterfirma *f* VI sich angliedern *(with* an *+acc)* N [əˈfɪlɪət] Schwestergesellschaft *f*; *(= union)* angegliederte Gewerkschaft

affiliation [əˌfɪlɪˈeɪʃən] N **a** Angliederung *f (to, with* an *+acc)*; *(state)* Verbund *m*; **what are his political ~s?** was ist seine politische Zugehörigkeit? **b** *(Brit Jur)* **~ order** Verurteilung *f* zur Leistung des Regelunterhalts; **~ proceedings** gerichtliche Feststellung der Vaterschaft, Vaterschaftsklage *f*

affinity [əˈfɪnɪtɪ] N **a** *(= liking)* Neigung *f (for, to* zu); *(for person)* Verbundenheit *f (for, to* mit) **b** *(= resemblance, connection)* Verwandtschaft *f*, Affinität *f (form)* **c** *(Chem)* Affinität *f*

affinity (credit) card N *Kreditkarte, bei der bei jeder Zahlung ein Betrag an eine wohltätige Organisation abgeführt wird*

affirm [əˈfɜːm] VT **a** *(= assert)* versichern; *(very forcefully)* beteuern; **he ~ed his innocence** er versicherte, dass er unschuldig sei, er beteuerte seine Unschuld **b** *(= ratify)* bestätigen VI *(Jur)* eidesstattlich *or* an Eidesstatt erklären

affirmation [ˌæfəˈmeɪʃən] N **a** *(= assertion)* Versicherung *f*; *(very forceful)* Beteuerung *f* **b** *(Jur)* eidesstattliche Erklärung

affirmative [əˈfɜːmətɪv] N *(Gram)* Bejahung *f*; *(sentence)* bejahender *or* positiver Satz; **to answer in the ~** bejahend *or* mit Ja antworten; **put these sentences into the ~** drücken Sie diese Sätze bejahend aus ADJ bejahend, positiv; *(Gram)* affirmativ *(form)*, bejahend; **the answer is ~** die Antwort ist bejahend *or* ja INTERJ richtig

> **AFFIRMATIVE ACTION**
>
> **Affirmative action** ist der in den USA übliche Ausdruck für die bevorzugte Behandlung ethnischer Minderheiten und Frauen bei der Besetzung von Arbeits- und Ausbildungsplätzen. Diese Politik wurde in den Sechzigerjahren unter Präsident Kennedy begonnen, als erstmals Quoten festgesetzt wurden, um den unterrepräsentierten Bevölkerungsgruppen mehr Arbeits- und Studienplätze zu garantieren. Mit dem Equal Employment Opportunities Act von 1972 wurde eine Kommission geschaffen, die für die Durchsetzung der Garantien sorgen sollte. Allerdings führte **affirmative action** später zu Klagen über Diskriminierung bei Angehörigen der Mehrheiten (z.B. Weißen oder Männern), was als „reverse discrimination" – „Diskriminierung unter umgekehrtem Vorzeichen" – bekannt geworden ist. Daraufhin wurden die strengen Quotenreglementierungen etwas gelockert.

affirmatively [əˈfɜːmətɪvlɪ] ADV bejahend, positiv

affix¹ [əˈfɪks] VT anbringen *(to* auf *+dat)*; *seal* setzen *(to* auf *+acc)*; *signature* setzen *(to* unter *+acc)*

affix² [ˈæfɪks] N *(Gram)* Affix *nt*

afflatus [əˈfleɪtəs] N Inspiration *f*

afflict [əˈflɪkt] VT plagen, zusetzen *(+dat)*; *(emotionally, mentally also)* belasten; *(troubles, inflation, injuries)* heimsuchen; **to be ~ed by a disease** an einer Krankheit leiden; **~ed with gout** von (der) Gicht geplagt; **to be ~ed by doubts** von Zweifeln gequält werden; **the ~ed** die Leidenden *pl*

affliction [əˈflɪkʃən] N **a** *(= distress)* Not *f*, Bedrängnis *f*; *(= pain)* Leiden *pl*, Schmerzen *pl* **b** *(= cause of suffering, blindness etc)* Gebrechen *nt*; *(illness)* Beschwerde *f*; *(worry)* Sorge *f*; **the ~s of old age** Altersbeschwerden *pl*; **the government is itself the nation's greatest ~** die Regierung ist selbst die größte Last für das Volk

affluence [ˈæflʊəns] N Reichtum *m*, Wohlstand *m*; **to live in ~** im Wohlstand leben; **to rise to ~** zu großem Wohlstand kommen

affluent¹ [ˈæflʊənt] ADJ reich, wohlhabend; **the ~ society** die Wohlstandsgesellschaft; **you ~ so-and-so!** du reicher Sack! *(inf)*, du Großkapitalist!

affluent² N *(Geog spec)* Nebenfluss *m*

afford [əˈfɔːd] VT **a** sich *(dat)* leisten; **I can't ~ to buy both of them** ich kann es mir nicht leisten, beide zu kaufen; **he can't ~ to make a mistake** er kann es sich nicht leisten, einen Fehler zu machen; **you can't ~ to miss the chance** Sie können es sich nicht leisten, die Gelegenheit zu verpassen; **I can't ~ the time (to do it)** ich habe einfach nicht die Zeit(, das zu tun); **an offer you can't ~ to miss** ein Angebot, das Sie sich *(dat)* nicht entgehen lassen können; **can you ~ to go? – I can't ~ not to!** können Sie gehen? – ich kann gar nicht anders
b *(liter: = provide)* *(sb sth* jdm etw) gewähren, bieten; *shade* spenden, bieten; *pleasure* bereiten

affordable [əˈfɔːdəbl] ADJ, **affordably** ADV *(= inexpensive) price* erschwinglich; *(= reasonably priced)* finanziell möglich *or* tragbar

afforest [æˈfɒrɪst] VT aufforsten

afforestation [æˌfɒrɪsˈteɪʃən] N Aufforstung *f*

affranchise [æˈfræntʃaɪz] VT befreien

affray [əˈfreɪ] N *(esp Jur)* Schlägerei *f*

affricate [ˈæfrɪkət] N *(Ling)* Affrikata *f (spec)*, Affrikate *f (spec)*

affright [əˈfraɪt] VT *(old, liter)* erschrecken

affront [əˈfrʌnt] VT beleidigen N Beleidigung *f* *(to sb* jds, *to sth* für etw), Affront *m* *(to* gegen);

such poverty is an ~ to our national pride solche Armut verletzt unseren Nationalstolz

Afghan ['æfgæn] **N a** Afghane *m*, Afghanin *f* **b** *(= language)* Afghanisch *nt* **c** *(also* **Afghan hound***)* Afghane *m*, Afghanischer Windhund **d afghan** *(= coat)* Afghan *m* **ADJ** afghanisch

Afghani [æf'gænɪ] **N** *(= person)* Afghane *m*, Afghanin *f* **ADJ** afghanisch

Afghanistan [æf'gænɪstæn] **N** Afghanistan *nt*

aficionado [ə,fɪʃjə'nɑːdəʊ] **N** *pl* **-s** Liebhaber(in) *m(f)*

afield [ə'fiːld] **ADV countries further ~** weiter entfernte Länder; **too/very far ~** zu/sehr weit weg *or* entfernt; **to venture further ~** *(lit, fig)* sich etwas weiter (vor)wagen; **to explore farther ~** die weitere Umgebung erforschen; **to go farther ~ for help** *(fig)* in der weiteren Umgebung Hilfe suchen; **his studies took him farther ~ into new areas of knowledge** seine Forschungen führten ihn immer weiter in neue Wissensbereiche

afire [ə'faɪə'] **ADJ PRED, ADV** in Brand; **to set sth ~** etw in Brand stecken, etw anzünden; *(fig)* etw entzünden; **~ with enthusiasm** hellauf begeistert; **this set his imagination ~** das entzündete seine Fantasie

aflame [ə'fleɪm] **ADJ PRED, ADV** in Flammen; **to set sth ~** etw in Brand stecken, etw anzünden; **to be ~** in Flammen stehen; **to be ~ with colour** *(Brit) or* **color** *(US)* in roter Glut leuchten; **~ with anger/passion** flammend *or* glühend vor Zorn/Leidenschaft

AFL-CIO *abbr of* **American Federation of Labor and Congress of Industrial Organizations** *amerikanischer Gewerkschafts-Dachverband*

afloat [ə'fləʊt] **ADJ PRED, ADV a** *(Naut)* **to be ~** schwimmen; **to stay ~** sich über Wasser halten; *(thing)* schwimmen, nicht untergehen; **to set a ship ~** ein Schiff zu Wasser lassen; **at last we were ~ again** endlich waren wir wieder flott; **cargo ~** schwimmende Ladung; **the largest navy ~** die größte Flotte auf See; **service ~** Dienst *m* auf See; **to serve ~** auf See dienen **b** *(= awash)* überschwemmt, unter Wasser; **to be ~** unter Wasser stehen, überschwemmt sein **c** *(fig)* **to get/keep a business ~** ein Geschäft *nt* auf die Beine stellen/über Wasser halten; **those who stayed ~ during the slump** die, die sich auch während der Krise über Wasser gehalten haben **d** *(fig: rumour etc)* **there is a rumour ~ that ...** es geht das Gerücht um, dass ...

aflutter [ə'flʌtə'] **ADJ PRED ADV** aufgeregt; **her heart was all ~** ihr Herz flatterte

afoot [ə'fʊt] **ADV** im Gange; **there is something ~** da ist etwas im Gange; **what's ~?** was geht hier vor?

afore [ə'fɔː'] *(obs, dial)* **CONJ** bevor **ADV** zuvor

aforementioned [ə,fɔː'menʃənd], **aforesaid** [ə'fɔːsed] **ADJ** *attr (form)* oben genannt, oben erwähnt

aforethought [ə'fɔːθɔːt] **ADJ** → **malice**

a fortiori [eɪ,fɔːtɪ'ɔːraɪ] **ADV** aufgrund des Vorhergehenden

afoul [ə'faʊl] **ADJ PRED ADV** *lines, ropes* verheddert, verwirrt; **to run ~ of the law** mit dem Gesetz in Konflikt geraten

afraid [ə'freɪd] ✪ 6.2, 12.3, 16.2, 21.4, 25.2 **ADJ** *pred* **a** *(= frightened)* **to be ~ (of sb/sth)** (vor jdm/etw) Angst haben, sich (vor jdm/etw) fürchten; **don't be ~!** keine Angst!; **it's quite safe, there's nothing to be ~ of** es ist ganz sicher, Sie brauchen keine Angst zu haben; **go and talk to him then, there's nothing to be ~ of** geh und sprich mit ihm, da ist doch nichts dabei; **I am ~ of hurting him** *or* **that I might hurt him** ich fürchte, ihm wehzutun *or* ich könnte ihm wehtun; **I am ~ he will** *or* **might hurt me, I am ~ lest he (might) hurt me** ich fürchte, er könnte mir wehtun; **to make sb ~** jdm Angst machen *or* einjagen, jdn ängstigen; **I am ~ to leave her alone** ich habe Angst davor, sie allein zu lassen; **I was ~ of not being precise enough** ich fürchtete, dass ich mich nicht genau genug ausdrückte; **I was ~ of waking the children** ich wollte die Kinder nicht wecken; **to be ~ of work** arbeitsscheu sein; **he's not ~ of hard work** er scheut schwere Arbeit nicht, er hat keine Angst vor schwerer Arbeit; **he's not ~ to say what he thinks** er scheut sich nicht zu sagen, was er denkt; **that's what I was ~ of, I was ~ that would happen** das habe ich befürchtet; **go on, do it, what are you ~ of?** tus doch, wovor hast du denn Angst?; **I was ~ you'd ask that** ich habe diese Frage befürchtet; **to be ~ for sb/sth** *(= worried)* Angst um jdn/etw haben; **to be ~ for one's life** Angst um sein Leben haben **b** *(expressing polite regret)* **I'm ~ I can't do it** leider kann ich es nicht machen; **there's nothing I can do, I'm ~** ich kann da leider gar nichts machen; **I'm ~ to say that ...** ich muss Ihnen leider sagen, dass ...; **I'm ~ you'll have to wait** Sie müssen leider warten; **are you going? – I'm ~ not/I'm ~ so** gehst du? – leider nicht/ja, leider; **well, I'm ~ you're wrong** so leid es mir tut, aber Sie haben unrecht; **can I go now? – no, I'm ~ you can't** kann ich jetzt gehen? – nein, tut mir leid, noch nicht

afresh [ə'freʃ] **ADV** noch einmal von vorn *or* Neuem

Africa ['æfrɪkə] **N** Afrika *nt*

African ['æfrɪkən] **N** Afrikaner(in) *m(f)* **ADJ** afrikanisch

African-American [,æfrɪkənə'merɪkən] **ADJ** afroamerikanisch **N** Afroamerikaner(in) *m(f)*

African violet N Usambaraveilchen *nt*

Afrikaans [,æfrɪ'kɑːns] **N** Afrikaans *nt*

Afrikaner [,æfrɪ'kɑːnə'] **N** Afrika(a)nder(in) *m(f)*

Afro ['æfrəʊ] **PREF** afro- **N** *(= hairstyle)* Afrofrisur *f*, Afrolook *m*

Afro-: **Afro-American ADJ** afroamerikanisch **N** Afroamerikaner(in) *m(f)*; **Afro-Asian ADJ** afroasiatisch; **Afro-Caribbean ADJ** afrokaribisch **N** Afrokaribe *m*, Afrokaribin *f*

aft [ɑːft] *(Naut)* **ADV** *sit* achtern; *go* nach achtern **ADJ** Achter-, achter; **~ deck** Achterdeck *nt*

after[1] ['ɑːftə'] **ADJ** *attr (Naut)* Achter-; **the ~ deck** das Achterdeck

after[2] **PREP a** *(time)* nach *(+dat)*; **~ dinner** nach dem Essen; **~ that** danach; **the day ~ tomorrow** übermorgen; **the week ~ next** die übernächste Woche; **I'll be back the week ~ next** ich bin übernächste Woche wieder da; **it was ~ two o'clock** es war nach zwei; **ten ~ eight** *(US)* zehn nach acht **b** *(order)* nach *(+dat)*, hinter *(+dat)*; *(in priorities etc)* nach *(+dat)*; **the noun comes ~ the verb** das Substantiv steht nach *or* hinter dem Verb; **I would put Keats ~ Shelley** für mich rangiert Keats unter Shelley; **~ Germany, Japan is our biggest market** nach Deutschland ist Japan unser größter Markt; **~ you** nach Ihnen!; **I was ~ him** *(in queue etc)* ich war nach ihm dran; **~ you with the salt** kann ich das Salz nach dir haben? **c** *(place)* hinter *(+dat)*; **he shut the door ~ him** er machte die Tür hinter ihm zu; **turn right about a mile ~ the village** biegen Sie etwa eine Meile nach dem Dorf rechts ab; **to shout ~ sb** hinter jdm herrufen *or* -schreien; **to shout sth ~ sb** jdm etw nachrufen **d** *(= as a result of)* nach *(+dat)*; **~ what has happened** nach allem, was geschehen ist; **~ this you might believe me** jetzt wirst du mir vielleicht endlich glauben **e** *(= in spite of)* **to do sth ~ all** etw schließlich doch tun; **~ all our efforts!** und das, nachdem *or* wo *(inf)* wir uns so viel Mühe gegeben haben!; **~ all I've done for you!** und das nach allem, was ich für dich getan habe!; **~ all, he is your brother** er ist immerhin *or* schließlich dein Bruder; **and to do this ~ I had warned him** und das, nachdem ich ihn gewarnt hatte **f** *(succession)* nach *(+dat)*; **you tell me lie ~ lie** du erzählst mir eine Lüge nach der anderen, du belügst mich am laufenden Band; **it's just one thing ~ another** *or* **the other** es kommt eins nach dem anderen *or* eins zum anderen; **one ~ the other** eine(r, s) nach der/dem anderen; **one ~ the other she rejected all the offers** sie schlug ein Angebot nach dem anderen aus; **day ~ day** Tag für *or* um Tag; **we marched on for mile ~ mile** wir marschierten Meile um Meile weiter; **before us lay mile ~ mile of barren desert** vor uns erstreckte sich meilenweit trostlose Wüste **g** *(manner: = according to)* nach *(+dat)*; **~ El Greco** in der Art von El Greco, nach El Greco; **she takes ~ her mother** sie schlägt ihrer Mutter nach **h** *(pursuit, inquiry)* **to be ~ sb/sth** hinter jdm/etw her sein; **she asked** *or* **inquired ~ you** sie hat sich nach dir erkundigt; **what are you ~?** was willst du?; **he's just ~ a free meal/a bit of excitement** er ist nur auf ein kostenloses Essen/ein bisschen Abwechslung aus

ADV *(time, order)* danach; *(place, pursuit)* hinterher; **for years/weeks ~** noch Jahre/Wochen *or* jahrelang/wochenlang danach; **the year/week ~** das Jahr/die Woche danach *or* darauf; **I'll be back some time the year ~** ich komme irgendwann im Jahr danach *or* im darauffolgenden Jahr wieder; **soon ~** kurz danach *or* darauf; **what comes ~?** was kommt danach *or* nachher?; **the car drove off with the dog running ~** das Auto fuhr los und der Hund rannte hinterher

CONJ nachdem; **~ he had closed the door he began to speak** nachdem er die Tür geschlossen hatte, begann er zu sprechen; **what will you do ~ he's gone?** was machst du, wenn er weg ist?; **~ finishing it I will ...** wenn ich das fertig habe, werde ich ...; **~ arriving they went ...** nachdem sie angekommen waren, gingen sie ...

ADJ in ~ years in späteren Jahren

N afters

PL *(Brit inf)* Nachtisch *m*; **what's for ~s?** was gibts hinterher *or* als *or* zum Nachtisch?

after: **afterbirth N** Nachgeburt *f*; **afterburner N** Nachbrenner *m*; **afterburning N** Nachverbrennung *f*; **aftercare N** *(of convalescent)* Nachbehandlung *f*, Nachsorge *f*; *(of ex-prisoner)* Resozialisierungshilfe *f*; **afterdeck N** Achterdeck *nt*; **after-dinner ADJ** *coffee, conversation* nach dem Essen; **~ walk/nap** Verdauungsspaziergang *m*/-schlaf *m*; **~ speech** Tischrede *f*; **aftereffect N** *(of illness) (Psych)* Nachwirkung *f*; *(of events etc also)* Folge *f*; **afterglow N** *(of sun)* Abendrot *nt*, Abendleuchten *nt*; *(fig)* angenehme Erinnerung; **after-hours ADJ** *attr (in shops etc)* nach Geschäftsschluss; *(in pubs)* nach der Polizeistunde; *(in office etc)* nach der Arbeit, nach Dienstschluss; **afterimage N** *(Psych)* Nachempfindung *f*, Nachbild *nt*; **afterlife N** Leben *nt* nach dem Tode; **after-lunch ADJ to have an ~ nap** ein Mittagsschläfchen halten; **aftermath N** Nachwirkungen *pl*; **in the ~ of sth** nach etw; **the country was still suffering the ~ of war** das Land litt immer noch an den Folgen *or* Auswirkungen des Krieges; **aftermost ADJ** *(Naut)* hinterste(r, s)

afternoon [,ɑːftə'nuːn] **N** Nachmittag *m*; **in the ~, ~s** *(esp US)* am Nachmittag, nachmittags; **at three o'clock in the ~** (um) drei Uhr nachmittags; **on Sunday ~** (am) Sonntagnachmittag; **on Sunday ~s** sonntagnachmittags *or* sonntags nachmittags, am Sonntagnachmittag; **on the ~ of December 2nd** am Nachmittag des 2. Dezember, am 2. Dezember nachmittags; **this/tomorrow/yesterday ~** heute/morgen/gestern Nachmittag; **good ~!** Guten Tag!; **~!** Tag! *(inf)* **ADJ** *attr* Nachmittags-; **~ performance** Nachmittagsvorstellung *f*

afternoon tea N *(Brit)* (Nachmittags)tee *m*

after: **afterpains PL** Nachwehen *pl*; **after-sales service N** Kundendienst *m*; **aftershave (lotion) N** Aftershave *nt*, Rasierwasser *nt*; **aftershock N** *(of earthquake)* Nachbeben *nt*; **after-sun ADJ** After-Sun-; **~ lotion/cream** After-Sun-Lotion *f*/-Creme *f* **N** *(= lotion)* After-Sun-Lotion *f*; *(= cream)* After-Sun-Creme *f*; **af-**

tertaste N *(lit, fig)* Nachgeschmack *m*; **to leave an unpleasant ~** einen unangenehmen Nachgeschmack hinterlassen; **after-tax** ADJ *profits etc* nach Steuern, nach Steuerabzug; **afterthought** N nachträgliche *or* zusätzliche Idee; **if you have any ~s about …** wenn Ihnen noch irgendetwas zu … einfällt; **he added as an ~** fügte er hinzu, schickte er nach; **I just mentioned that as an ~** das fiel mir noch dazu *or* nachträglich ein; **the window was added as an ~** das Fenster kam erst später dazu; **after-treatment** N *(Tech, Chem)* Nachbehandlung *f*

afterward ['ɑːftəwəd] ADV *(US)* = **afterwards**

afterwards ['ɑːftəwədz] ADV nachher; *(= after that, after some event etc)* danach; **and ~ we could go to a disco** und anschließend *or* nachher *or* danach gehen wir in eine Disko; **can I have mine now? – no, ~** kann ich meins jetzt haben? – nein, nachher; **this was added ~** das kam nachträglich dazu

afterword ['ɑːftəˌwɜːd] N Nachwort *nt*

afterworld ['ɑːftəˌwɜːld] N Jenseits *nt*

Aga® ['ɑːgə] N *(Brit) eiserner, nach alter Vorlage gebauter Küchenherd*

again [ə'gen] ADV **a** wieder; **~ and ~, time and ~** immer wieder; **to do sth ~** etw noch (ein)mal tun; **I won't do that ~** das mache ich nicht noch einmal, das tue ich nie wieder; **I'll ring ~ tomorrow** ich rufe morgen noch einmal an; **never** *or* **not ever ~** nie wieder; **if that happens ~** wenn das noch einmal passiert; **all over ~** noch (ein)mal von vorn; **what's his name ~?** wie heißt er noch gleich?; **to begin ~** von Neuem *or* noch einmal anfangen; **not ~!** (nicht) schon wieder!; **not mince ~!** (nicht) schon wieder Hackfleisch!; **it's me ~** *(arriving)* da bin ich wieder; *(phoning)* ich bins noch (ein)mal; *(= my fault)* wieder mal ich; **not you ~!** du schon wieder!?; **he was soon well ~** er war bald wieder gesund; **and these are different ~** und diese sind wieder anders; **here we are ~!** da wären wir wieder!; *(finding another example etc)* oh, schon wieder!; **~ we find that …** und wieder einmal *or* wiederum stellen wir fest, dass …
b *(in quantity)* **as much ~** doppelt so viel, noch (ein)mal so viel; **he's as old ~ as Mary** er ist doppelt so alt wie Mary
c *(= on the other hand)* wiederum; *(= besides, moreover)* außerdem; **but then** *or* **there ~, it may not be true** vielleicht ist es auch gar nicht wahr

against [ə'genst] ✪ 26.1 PREP **a** *(opposition, protest)* gegen *(+acc)*; **he's ~ her going** er ist dagegen, dass sie geht; **everybody's ~ me!** alle sind gegen mich!; **to have something/nothing ~ sb/sth** etwas/nichts gegen jdn/etw haben; **~ that you have to consider …** Sie müssen aber auch bedenken …; **~ my will, I decided …** wider Willen habe ich beschlossen …; **~ their wishes** entgegen ihrem Wunsch; **to fight ~ sb** gegen *or* wider *(liter)* jdn kämpfen
b *(indicating impact, support, proximity)* an *(+acc)*, gegen *(+acc)*; **to hit one's head ~ the mantelpiece** mit dem Kopf gegen *or* an das Kaminsims stoßen; **push all the chairs right back ~ the wall** stellen Sie alle Stühle direkt an die Wand
c *(= in the opposite direction to)* gegen *(+acc)*
d *(= in front of, in juxtaposition to)* gegen *(+acc)*; **~ the light** gegen das Licht
e *(= in preparation for) sb's arrival, departure, one's old age* für *(+acc)*; *misfortune, bad weather etc* im Hinblick auf *(+acc)*; **~ the possibility of a bad winter** für den Fall, dass es einen schlechten Winter gibt
f *(= compared with)* **(as) ~** gegenüber *(+dat)*; **she had three prizes (as) ~ his six** sie hatte drei Preise, er hingegen sechs; **the advantages of flying (as) ~ going by boat** die Vorteile von Flugreisen gegenüber Schiffsreisen; **~ the euro** gegenüber dem Euro
g *(Fin: = in return for)* gegen; **the visa will be issued ~ payment of …** das Visum wird gegen Zahlung von … ausgestellt; **to draw money ~ security** gegen Sicherheit(sleistung) *or* Deckung Geld abheben
ADJ PRED *(= not in favour)* dagegen; **how many ~?** wie viele sind dagegen? → **for¹** ADJ

agape [ə'geɪp] ADJ *pred person* mit (vor Staunen) offenem Mund, bass erstaunt *(geh)*

agaric ['ægərɪk] N Blätterpilz *m*

agate ['ægət] N Achat *m*

agave [ə'geɪvɪ] N Agave *f*

age [eɪdʒ] N **a** *(of person, star, building etc)* Alter *nt*; **what is her ~?, what ~ is she?** wie alt ist sie?; **he is ten years of ~** er ist zehn Jahre alt; **trees of great ~** Bäume von hohem Alter; **~ doesn't matter** das Alter spielt keine Rolle; **at the ~ of 15** im Alter von 15 Jahren, mit 15 Jahren; **at your ~** in deinem Alter; **when I was your ~** als ich in deinem Alter war, als ich so alt war wie du; **when you're my ~** wenn du erst in mein Alter kommst, wenn du erst mal so alt bist wie ich; **I have a daughter your ~** ich habe eine Tochter in Ihrem Alter; **but he's twice your ~** aber er ist ja doppelt so alt wie du; **we're of an ~** wir sind gleichaltrig; **he is now of an ~ to understand these things** er ist jetzt alt genug, um das zu verstehen; **over ~** zu alt; **she doesn't look her ~** man sieht ihr ihr Alter nicht an, sie sieht jünger aus, als sie ist; **be** *or* **act your ~!** sei nicht kindisch!
b *(= length of life)* Lebensdauer *f*; *(of human)* Lebenserwartung *f*; **the ~ of a star can be millions of years** ein Stern kann viele Millionen Jahre existieren
c *(Jur)* **to be of ~** volljährig *or* mündig sein; **to come of ~** volljährig *or* mündig werden, die Volljährigkeit erlangen; *(fig)* den Kinderschuhen entwachsen; **under ~** minderjährig, unmündig; **~ of consent** *(for marriage)* Ehemündigkeitsalter *nt*; **intercourse with girls under the ~ of consent** Unzucht *f* mit Minderjährigen
d *(= old age)* Alter *nt*; **bowed with ~** vom Alter gebeugt; **~ before beauty** *(hum)* Alter vor Schönheit
e *(= period, epoch)* Zeit(alter *nt*) *f*; **the atomic ~** das Atomzeitalter; **the ~ of technology** das technologische Zeitalter; **in this ~ of inflation** in dieser inflationären Zeit; **the Stone ~** die Steinzeit; **the Edwardian ~** die Zeit *or* Ära Edwards VII; **the ~ of Socrates** das Zeitalter Sokrates; **down the ~s** durch alle Zeiten; **what will future ~s think of us?** was werden kommende Generationen von uns halten?
f *(inf: = long time)* **~s, an ~** eine Ewigkeit, Ewigkeiten *pl*, ewig (lang) *(all inf)*; **I haven't seen him for ~s** *or* **for an ~** ich habe ihn eine Ewigkeit *or* Ewigkeiten *or* ewig (lang) nicht gesehen *(inf)*; **it's been ~s since we met** wir haben uns ja eine Ewigkeit *etc* nicht mehr gesehen *(inf)*; **to take ~s** eine Ewigkeit dauern *(inf)*; *(person)* ewig brauchen *(inf)*
VI alt werden, altern; *(wine, cheese)* reifen; **you have ~d** du bist alt geworden; **she seems to have ~d ten years** sie scheint um zehn Jahre gealtert zu sein
VT **a** *(dress, hairstyle etc)* alt machen; *(worry etc)* alt werden lassen, altern lassen
b *wine, cheese* lagern, reifen lassen

age bracket N Altersklasse *f*, Altersstufe *f*

aged [eɪdʒd] ADJ **a** im Alter von, … Jahre alt, -jährig; **a boy ~ ten** ein zehnjähriger Junge **b** ['eɪdʒɪd] *person* bejahrt, betagt; *animal, car, building etc* alt, betagt *(hum)* ['eɪdʒɪd] PL **the ~** die alten Menschen, die Alten *pl*

age: **age-defying** [-dɪˌfaɪɪŋ] ADJ *cosmetics* Anti--Aging- *attr*; *behaviour* seinem/ihrem tatsächlichen Alter nicht entsprechend; **age difference, age gap** N Altersunterschied *m*; **age group** N Altersgruppe *f*; **the forty to fifty ~** die (Alters)gruppe der Vierzig- bis Fünfzigjährigen

ag(e)ing ['eɪdʒɪŋ] ADJ *person* alternd *attr*; *animal, thing, population* älter werdend *attr*; **the ~ process** das Altern N Altern *nt*

ageism ['eɪdʒɪzəm] N Altersdiskriminierung *f*, Seniorenfeindlichkeit *f*

ageist ['eɪdʒɪst] ADJ altersdiskriminierend, seniorenfeindlich

age: **ageless** ADJ zeitlos; **she seems to be one of those ~ people** sie scheint zu den Menschen zu gehören, die nie alt werden; **age limit** N Altersgrenze *f*; **age-long** ADJ sehr lange, ewig *(inf)*

agency ['eɪdʒənsɪ] N **a** *(Comm)* Agentur *f*; *(= subsidiary of a company)* Geschäftsstelle *f*; **translation/tourist ~** Übersetzungs-/Reisebüro *nt*; **this garage is** *or* **has the Citroën ~** dies ist eine Citroën-Vertragswerkstätte, diese Werkstatt ist eine *or* hat die Citroën-Vertretung **b** *(= instrumentality)* **through the ~ of friends** durch die Vermittlung von Freunden, durch Freunde; **by the ~ of water** mithilfe *or* mit Hilfe von Wasser, durch Wasser; **to attribute sth to the ~ of Providence** etw der Vorsehung *(dat)* zuschreiben

agenda [ə'dʒendə] N Tagesordnung *f*; **a full ~** *(lit)* eine umfangreiche Tagesordnung; *(fig)* ein volles Programm; **to set the ~** *(lit)* die Tagesordnung festlegen; *(fig)* den Ton angeben; **they have their own ~** sie haben ihre eigenen Vorstellungen; **on the ~** auf dem Programm

agent ['eɪdʒənt] N **a** *(Comm) (= person)* Vertreter(in) *m(f)*; *(= organization)* Vertretung *f*; **who is the ~ for this car in Scotland?** wer hat die schottische Vertretung für dieses Auto?
b *(= literary agent, press agent etc)* Agent(in) *m(f)*; *(Pol)* Wahlkampfleiter(in) *m(f)*; **business ~** Agent(in) *m(f)*
c *(= secret agent, FBI agent etc)* Agent(in) *m(f)*; **~ in charge (of an/the investigation)** Untersuchungsbeamte(r) *m*/-beamtin *f*
d *(= person having power to act)* **man must be regarded as a moral ~** der Mensch muss als moralisch verantwortlich handelndes Wesen angesehen werden; **determinism states that we are not free ~s** der Determinismus behauptet, dass wir nicht frei entscheiden können; **you're a free ~, do what you want** du bist dein eigener Herr, tu was du willst
e *(= means by which sth is achieved)* Mittel *nt*; **she became the unwitting ~ of his wicked plot** unwissentlich wurde sie zum Werkzeug für seinen niederträchtigen Plan
f *(Chem)* **cleansing ~** Reinigungsmittel *nt*; **special protective ~** Spezialschutzmittel *nt*

agent extraordinary N Spezialagent(in) *m(f)*

agent provocateur [ˌæʒɒŋprəvɒkə'tɜː'] N *pl* **-s -s** Agent provocateur *m*, Lockspitzel *m*

age: **age-old** ADJ uralt; **age range** N Altersgruppe *f*; **age-related** ADJ altersspezifisch; **age spot** N Altersfleck *m*

agglomerate [ə'glɒməreɪt] VI agglomerieren [ə'glɒmərɪt] ADJ [ə'glɒmərɪt] agglomeriert N Agglomerat *nt*

agglomeration [əˌglɒmə'reɪʃən] N Anhäufung *f*, Konglomerat *nt*; *(Sci)* Agglomeration *f*

agglutinate [ə'gluːtɪneɪt] VI agglutinieren *(also Ling)*, verklumpen, verkleben [ə'gluːtɪnɪt] ADJ agglutiniert *(also Ling)*, verklumpt, verklebt

agglutinating [ə'gluːtɪneɪtɪŋ] ADJ *(Ling)* agglutinierend

agglutination [əˌgluːtɪ'neɪʃən] N Agglutination *f (also Ling)*, Verklumpung *f*, Verklebung *f*

agglutinative [ə'gluːtɪnətɪv] ADJ agglutinierend

aggrandize [ə'grændaɪz] VT *one's power, empire* vergrößern, erweitern; *person, one's family* befördern; **to ~ oneself** sich befördern; *(= be self-important)* sich wichtigmachen

aggrandizement [ə'grændɪzmənt] N *(of power, empire)* Vergrößerung *f*, Erweiterung *f*; *(of person, one's family)* Beförderung *f*

aggravate ['ægrəveɪt] VT **a** *(= make worse)* verschlimmern **b** *(= annoy)* aufregen; *(deliberately)* reizen; **don't get ~d** regen Sie sich nicht auf

aggravating ['ægrəveɪtɪŋ] ADJ ärgerlich, enervierend *(geh)*; *child* lästig, enervierend *(geh)*; **how ~ for you** wie ärgerlich für Sie!

aggravation [ˌægrə'veɪʃən] N **a** *(= worsening)* Verschlimmerung *f* **b** *(= annoyance)* Ärger *m*;

she was a constant ~ to him sie reizte ihn ständig

aggregate ['ægrɪgɪt] N **a** Gesamtmenge *f*, Summe *f*, Gesamtheit *f*; **considered in (the) ~** insgesamt betrachtet; **on ~** *(Sport)* in der Gesamtwertung **b** *(Build)* Zuschlagstoffe *pl*; *(Geol)* Gemenge *nt* ADJ gesamt, Gesamt-; **~ value** Gesamtwert *m* VT ['ægrɪgeɪt] **a** *(= gather together)* anhäufen, ansammeln **b** *(= amount to)* sich belaufen auf *(+acc)* VI ['ægrɪgeɪt] sich anhäufen, sich ansammeln

aggression [ə'greʃən] N **a** *(= attack)* Aggression *f*, Angriff *m*; **an act of ~** ein Angriff *m*, eine aggressive Handlung **b** *no pl* Aggression *f*; *(= aggressiveness)* Aggressivität *f*; **to get rid of one's ~** seine Aggressionen loswerden

aggressive [ə'gresɪv] ADJ **a** *(= belligerent)* aggressiv; *lover* draufgängerisch, ungestüm **b** *(= forceful) salesman, businessman etc* dynamisch, aufdringlich *(pej)*; *sales technique* aggressiv

aggressively [ə'gresɪvlɪ] ADV *(= belligerently)* aggressiv; *(= forcefully)* energisch; *sell* aggressiv

aggressiveness [ə'gresɪvnɪs] N **a** *(= belligerence)* Aggressivität *f*; *(Sport: of play)* Härte *f*, Aggressivität *f*; *(of lover)* Draufgängertum *nt*, Ungestüm *nt* **b** *(= forcefulness) (of salesman etc)* Dynamik *f*, Aufdringlichkeit *f (pej)*; *(of sales technique)* Aggressivität *f*

aggressivity [,ægre'sɪvɪtɪ] N *(= belligerence)* Aggressivität *f*, Angriffslust *f*; *(= forcefulness)* Dynamik *f*

aggressor [ə'gresə'] N Angreifer(in) *m(f)*, Aggressor(in) *m(f)*

aggrieved [ə'gri:vd] ADJ betrübt *(at, by* über *+acc)*; *(= offended)* verletzt *(at, by* durch*)*; *voice, look* verletzt, gekränkt; **the ~ (party)** *(Jur)* der Beschwerte, die beschwerte Partei

aggro ['ægrəʊ] N *(Brit inf)* **a** *(= aggression, bother)* Aggressionen *pl*; **don't give me any ~** mach keinen Ärger *(inf)* or Stunk *(inf)*; **I get ~ from my mother if …** ich kriege Ärger mit meiner Mutter, wenn … *(inf)*; **she didn't want all the ~ of moving** sie wollte das ganze Theater mit dem Umziehen vermeiden; **motorways are too much ~** Autobahnen sind zu anstrengend **b** *(= fight)* Schlägerei *f*; **football fans looking for ~** Fußballfans, die auf Schlägereien aus sind

aghast [ə'gɑ:st] ADJ *pred* entgeistert *(at* über *+acc)*

agile ['ædʒaɪl] ADJ *person, thinker* beweglich, wendig; *body also, movements* gelenkig, geschmeidig; *animal* flink, behände; **he has an ~ mind** er ist geistig sehr wendig *or* beweglich *or* flexibel

agilely ['ædʒaɪllɪ] ADV *move, jump etc* geschickt, behände; *argue* geschickt, gewandt; *think* flink, beweglich

agility [ə'dʒɪlɪtɪ] N *(of person)* Agilität *f*, Beweglichkeit *f*, Wendigkeit *f*; *(of thinker)* Beweglichkeit *f*, Wendigkeit *f*; *(of body, movements)* Gelenkigkeit *f*, Geschmeidigkeit *f*; *(of animal)* Flinkheit *f*, Behändigkeit *f*

aging ADJ N = **ag(e)ing**

agio ['ædʒɪəʊ] N *(Econ)* Aufgeld *nt*, Agio *nt*

agiotage ['ædʒətɪdʒ] N *(St Ex)* Agiotage *f*

agitate ['ædʒɪteɪt] VT **a** *(lit) liquid* aufrühren; *surface of water* aufwühlen; *washing* hin und her bewegen **b** *(fig: = excite, upset)* aufregen, aus der Fassung bringen; **don't let him ~ you** lass dich von ihm nicht aufregen VI agitieren; **to ~ for sth** sich für etw starkmachen

agitated ADJ, **agitatedly** ADV ['ædʒɪteɪtɪd, -lɪ] aufgeregt, erregt

agitation [,ædʒɪ'teɪʃən] N **a** *(lit, of liquid)* Aufrühren *nt*; *(of surface of water)* Aufwühlen *nt*; *(of clothes in washing machine)* Hin- und Herbewegung *f* **b** *(fig: = anxiety, worry)* Erregung *f*, Aufruhr *m*; *(on stock market)* Bewegung *f* **c** *(Pol: = incitement)* Agitation *f*

agitation documentary N *(US) Film, der auf brisante Missstände aufmerksam macht*

agitator ['ædʒɪteɪtə'] N **a** *(= person)* Agitator(in) *m(f)* **b** *(= device)* Rührwerk *nt*, Rührapparat *m*

agit doc *(US) abbr of* **agitation documentary**

agleam [ə'gli:m] ADJ *pred* erleuchtet; **his eyes were ~ with mischief** seine Augen blitzten *or* funkelten schelmisch

aglitter [ə'glɪtə'] ADJ *pred* **to be ~** funkeln, glitzern

aglow [ə'gləʊ] ADJ *pred* **to be ~** *(sky, fire, face)* glühen; **the sun set the mountains/sky ~** die Sonne ließ die Berge/den Himmel erglühen *or* brachte die Berge/den Himmel zum Glühen; **to be ~ with happiness/health** vor Glück/Gesundheit strahlen

AGM *abbr of* **annual general meeting** JHV *f*

agnail ['ægneɪl] N Niednagel *m*

agnostic [æg'nɒstɪk] ADJ agnostisch N Agnostiker(in) *m(f)*

agnosticism [æg'nɒstɪsɪzəm] N Agnostizismus *m*

ago [ə'gəʊ] ADV vor; **years/a week ~** vor Jahren/einer Woche; **a little while ~** vor kurzem; **that was years/a week ~** das ist schon Jahre/eine Woche her; **he was here a minute ~** er war noch vor einer Minute hier; **how long ~ is it since you last saw him?** wie lange haben Sie ihn schon nicht mehr gesehen?, wann haben Sie ihn das letzte Mal gesehen?; **how long ~ did it happen?** wie lange ist das her?; **he left 10 minutes ~** er ist vor 10 Minuten gegangen; **long, long ~** vor langer, langer Zeit; **how long ~?** wie lange ist das her?; **that was a long time ago** *or* **long ~** das ist schon lange her; **as long ~ as 1950** schon 1950

agog [ə'gɒg] ADJ *pred* gespannt; **the children sat there ~ with excitement** die Kinder sperrten Augen und Ohren auf; **the whole village was ~ (with curiosity)** das ganze Dorf platzte fast vor Neugierde; **~ for news** wild nach Neuigkeiten; **we're all ~ to hear your news** wir warten gespannt auf deine Nachrichten

agonize ['ægənaɪz] VI sich *(dat)* den Kopf zermartern *(over* über *+acc)*; **after weeks of agonizing he finally made a decision** nach wochenlangem Ringen traf er endlich eine Entscheidung

agonized ['ægənaɪzd] ADJ gequält

agonizing ['ægənaɪzɪŋ] ADJ qualvoll, quälend; *cry, experience* qualvoll

agonizingly ['ægənaɪzɪŋlɪ] ADV qualvoll; **~ slow** aufreizend langsam

agony ['ægənɪ] N **a** Qual *f*; **that's ~** das ist eine Qual; **it's ~ doing that** es ist eine Qual, das zu tun; **to be in ~** Schmerzen *or* Qualen leiden; **in an ~ of indecision/suspense** *etc* in qualvoller Unentschlossenheit/Ungewissheit *etc*; **put him out of his ~** *(lit)* mach seiner Qual ein Ende; *(fig)* nun spann ihn doch nicht länger auf die Folter; **to go through** *or* **suffer agonies** Qualen ausstehen **b** *(= death agony)* Todeskampf *m*, Agonie *f*; *(of Christ)* Todesangst *f*

agony *(Brit Press inf)*: **agony aunt** N Briefkastentante *f (inf)*; **agony column** N Kummerkasten *m*; **agony columnist** N Briefkastenonkel *m*/-tante *f (inf)*; **agony uncle** N Briefkastenonkel *m (inf)*

agoraphobia [,ægərə'fəʊbɪə] N *(Med)* Agoraphobie *f (spec)*, Platzangst *f*

agoraphobic [,ægərə'fəʊbɪk] *(Med)* ADJ agoraphobisch *(spec)* N an Agoraphobie *(spec)* or Platzangst Leidende(r) *mf*

agrarian [ə'greərɪən] ADJ Agrar-; **~ reform** Agrarreform *f*; **~ society** Agrargesellschaft *f*

agree [ə'gri:] ✪ 11, 12, 13, 26.1, 26.3 *pret, ptp* **agreed** VT **a** *price, date etc* vereinbaren, abmachen

b *(= consent)* **to ~ to do sth** sich einverstanden *or* bereit erklären, etw zu tun

c *(= admit)* zugeben; **I ~ (that) I was wrong** ich gebe zu, dass ich mich geirrt habe

d *(= come to or be in agreement about)* zustimmen *(+dat)*; **we all ~ that …** wir sind alle der Meinung, dass …; **it was ~d that …** man einigte sich darauf, dass …, es wurde beschlossen, dass …; **we ~d to do it** wir haben beschlossen, das zu tun; **to ~ to differ** *or* **disagree** sich *(dat)* verschiedene Meinungen zugestehen; **we ~ to differ** wir sind uns einig, dass wir uns uneinig sind; **is that ~d then, gentlemen?** sind alle einverstanden? → *also* **agreed**

VI **a** *(= hold same opinion, two or more people)* sich einig sein, übereinstimmen, einer Meinung sein; *(one person)* der gleichen Meinung sein; **to ~ with sb** jdm zustimmen; **I ~!** der Meinung bin ich auch; **we all ~, it's a silly suggestion** wir sind uns alle einig, das ist ein alberner Vorschlag; **I couldn't ~ more/less** ich bin völlig/überhaupt nicht dieser Meinung, ich stimme dem völlig/überhaupt nicht zu; **it's too late now, don't** *or* **wouldn't you ~?** finden *or* meinen Sie nicht auch, dass es jetzt zu spät ist?

b **to ~ with a theory/the figures** *etc (accept)* eine Theorie/die Zahlen *etc* akzeptieren *or* für richtig halten

c *(= come to an agreement)* sich einigen *(about* über *+acc)*

d *(statements, figures etc: = tally)* übereinstimmen

e **to ~ with sth** *(= approve of)* etw befürworten, mit etw einverstanden sein; **I don't ~ with children drinking wine** ich bin dagegen *or* ich bin nicht damit einverstanden, dass Kinder Wein trinken

f *(food, climate etc)* **sth ~s with sb** jdm bekommt etw; **whisky doesn't ~ with me** ich vertrage Whisky nicht, Whisky bekommt mir nicht; **that food didn't ~ with me** das Essen ist mir nicht bekommen

g *(Gram)* übereinstimmen

h *(people: = get on together)* sich vertragen, miteinander auskommen

▸ **agree on** VI *+prep obj solution* sich einigen auf *(+acc)*, Einigkeit erzielen über *(+acc)*; *price, policy also* vereinbaren; **a price/policy/solution has been agreed on** man hat sich auf einen Preis/eine Linie/eine Lösung geeinigt; **we agreed on the need to save** wir waren uns darüber einig, dass gespart werden muss

▸ **agree to** ✪ 12.2 VI *+prep obj* zustimmen *(+dat)*; *marriage also* einwilligen in *(+acc)*, seine Einwilligung geben zu; *conditions, terms also* annehmen, akzeptieren; *increase, payment also* sich einverstanden erklären mit; **I cannot agree to your marrying her** ich kann einer Ehe nicht zustimmen

agreeable [ə'gri:əbl] ADJ **a** *(= pleasant)* angenehm; *decor, behaviour* nett **b** *pred (= willing to agree)* einverstanden; **are you ~ to that?, is that ~ to you?** sind Sie damit einverstanden?

agreeably [ə'gri:əblɪ] ADV angenehm; *decorated* nett; **to be ~ surprised** angenehm überrascht sein; **she behaved ~ for once** sie benahm sich ausnahmsweise nett

agreed [ə'gri:d] ✪ 26.1 ADJ **a** *pred (= in agreement)* einig; **to be ~ on sth** sich über etw einig sein; **to be ~ on doing sth** sich darüber einig sein, etw zu tun; **are we all ~?** sind wir uns da einig?; *(on course of action)* sind alle einverstanden? **b** *(= arranged)* vereinbart; *time* verabredet, vereinbart; **it's all ~** es ist alles abgesprochen; **~?** einverstanden?; **~!** *(regarding price etc)* abgemacht, in Ordnung; *(= I agree)* stimmt, genau

agreement [ə'gri:mənt] ✪ 11.2, 13 N **a** *(= understanding, arrangement)* Abmachung *f*, Übereinkunft *f*; *(= treaty, contract)* Abkommen *nt*, Vertrag *m*; **to break the terms of an ~** die Vertragsbestimmungen verletzen; **to enter into an ~ (with sb)** (mit jdm) einen Vertrag eingehen *or* (ab)schließen; **to reach (an) ~ (with sb)** (mit jdm) zu einer Einigung kommen, (mit jdm) Übereinstimmung erzielen; **there's a tacit ~ in the office that …** im Büro besteht die stillschweigende Übereinkunft, dass …; **we have an ~ whereby if I'm home first …** wir haben abgemacht, dass, wenn ich zuerst nach Hause komme, …

b *(= sharing of opinion)* Einigkeit *f*; **unanimous ~** Einmütigkeit *f*; **by mutual ~** in gegenseitigem Einverständnis *or* Einvernehmen; **to be in ~**

with sb mit jdm einer Meinung sein; **to be in ~ with sth** mit etw übereinstimmen; **to be in ~ about sth** über etw *(acc)* einig sein; **for once we were both in ~ on that point** ausnahmsweise waren wir uns in diesem Punkt einig *or* waren wir in diesem Punkt einer Meinung; **to find oneself in ~ with sb** mit jdm übereinstimmen *or* einiggehen
c *(= consent)* Einwilligung *f (to* zu), Zustimmung *f (to* zu)
d *(between figures, accounts etc)* Übereinstimmung *f*
e *(Gram)* Übereinstimmung *f*

agribusiness [ˈægrɪbɪznɪs] N die Landwirtschaft

agricultural [ˌægrɪˈkʌltʃərəl] ADJ *produce, production, expert, tool etc* landwirtschaftlich; **~ country** Agrarland *nt*; **the ~ country in the north** das landwirtschaftliche Gebiet im Norden; **~ ministry** Landwirtschaftsministerium *nt*; **~ market** *(in EU)* Agrarmarkt; **~ nation** Agrarstaat *m*, Agrarland *nt*; **~ policy** Agrarpolitik *f*; **~ reform** Agrarreform *f*; **~ worker** Landarbeiter(in) *m(f)*

agricultural college N Landwirtschaftsschule *f*

agricultural engineer N Agrartechniker(in) *m(f)*

agricultur(al)ist [ˌægrɪˈkʌltʃər(əl)ɪst] N Landwirtschaftsexperte *m*/-expertin *f*; *(= farmer)* Landwirt(in) *m(f)*

agriculturally [ˌægrɪˈkʌltʃərəlɪ] ADV landwirtschaftlich

agricultural show N Landwirtschaftsausstellung *f*

agriculture [ˈægrɪkʌltʃəˈ] N Landwirtschaft *f*; **Minister of Agriculture** *(Brit)* Landwirtschaftsminister(in) *m(f)*

agrobiotechnology [ˌægrəʊbaɪəʊtekˈnɒlədʒɪ] N Agrobiotechnik *f*

agrochemical [ˌægrəʊˈkemɪkəl] *(Agr)* ADJ agrochemisch N Agrochemikalie *f*

agronomist [əˈgrɒnəmɪst] N Agronom(in) *m(f)*

agronomy [əˈgrɒnəmɪ] N Agronomie *f*

aground [əˈgraʊnd] ADJ *pred ship* gestrandet, aufgelaufen, auf Grund gelaufen ADV **to go** *or* **run ~** auflaufen, auf Grund laufen, stranden

ague [ˈeɪgjuː] N Schüttelfrost *m no art*

ah [ɑː] INTERJ ah; *(pain)* au, autsch; *(pity)* o, ach

aha [ɑːˈhɑː] INTERJ aha

aha effect N Aha-Effekt *m*

ahead [əˈhed] ADV **a there's some thick cloud ~** vor uns *or* da vorne ist eine große Wolke; **the mountains lay ~** vor uns/ihnen *etc* lagen die Berge; **the German runner was/drew ~** der deutsche Läufer lag vorn/zog nach vorne; **he is ~ by about two minutes** er hat etwa zwei Minuten Vorsprung; **to stare straight ~** geradeaus starren; **keep straight ~** immer geradeaus; **full speed ~** *(Naut, fig)* volle Kraft voraus; **we sent him on ~** wir schickten ihn voraus; **in the months ~** in den bevorstehenden Monaten; **I see problems ~** ich sehe Probleme auf mich/uns *etc* zukommen; **we've a busy time ~** vor uns liegt eine Menge Arbeit; **to plan ~** vorausplanen
b ~ of sb/sth vor jdm/etw; **walk ~ of me** geh voran; **the leader is two laps ~ of the others** der Führende hat zwei Runden Vorsprung *or* liegt zwei Runden vor den anderen; **we arrived ten minutes ~ of time** wir kamen zehn Minuten vorher an; **to be/get ~ of schedule** schneller als geplant vorankommen; **the dollar is still ~ of the euro** der Dollar führt immer noch vor dem Euro; **to be ~ of one's time** *(fig)* seiner Zeit voraus sein

ahem [əˈhəm] INTERJ hm

ahold [əˈhəʊld] N *(esp US)* **to get ~ of sb** jdn erreichen; **to get ~ of sth** *(= procure)* sich *(dat)* etw besorgen; **don't let him get ~ of this story** lass ihn diese Geschichte bloß nicht in die Finger kriegen *(inf)*; **to get ~ of oneself** sich zusammenreißen

ahoy [əˈhɔɪ] INTERJ *(Naut)* ahoi; **ship ~!** Schiff ahoi!

AI *abbr of* **artificial intelligence** KI *f*

AIC *abbr of* **agent in charge (of investigation)**

aid [eɪd] N **a** *no pl (= help)* Hilfe *f*; **(foreign) ~** Entwicklungshilfe *f*; **with the ~ of his uncle/a screwdriver** mithilfe *or* mit Hilfe seines Onkels/eines Schraubenziehers; **to come** *or* **go to sb's ~** jdm zu Hilfe kommen; **a sale in ~ of the blind** ein Verkauf zugunsten *or* zu Gunsten der Blinden; **what's all this wiring in ~ of?** *(inf)* wozu sind all diese Drähte da *or* gut?; **what's all this in ~ of?** *(inf)* wozu soll das gut sein?
b *(= useful person, thing)* Hilfe *f (to* für); *(= piece of equipment, audio-visual aid etc)* Hilfsmittel *nt*; *(= hearing aid)* Hörgerät *nt*; *(= teaching aid)* Lehrmittel *nt*
c *(esp US)* = **aide**
VT unterstützen, helfen *(+dat)*; **to ~ sb's recovery** jds Heilung fördern; **~ed by** mit Unterstützung von; **to ~ and abet sb** *(Jur)* jdm Beihilfe leisten; *(after crime)* jdn begünstigen → **aiding and abetting**

aid agency N Hilfsorganisation *f*

aide [eɪd] N Helfer(in) *m(f)*; *(= adviser)* (persönlicher) Berater

aide-de-camp [ˈeɪddəˈkɒŋ] N *pl* **aides-de-camp** **a** *(Mil)* Adjutant(in) *m(f)* **b** = **aide**

aide-memoire [ˈeɪdmemˈwɑːˈ] N Gedächtnisstütze *f*; *(= official memorandum)* Aide-memoire *nt*

aiding and abetting [ˈeɪdɪŋəndəˈbetɪŋ] N *(Jur)* Beihilfe *f*; *(after crime)* Begünstigung *f*; **he was accused of ~** ihm wurde Beihilfe/Begünstigung vorgeworfen

aid programme, *(US)* **aid program** N Hilfsprogramm *nt*

AIDS, Aids [eɪdz] *abbr of* **acquired immune deficiency syndrome** Aids *nt*

AIDS: AIDS orphan N Aidswaise *f*; **AIDS patient** N Aids-Patient(in) *m(f)*; **AIDS-related** ADJ *illness, death* aidsbedingt; **AIDS victim** N Aids-Kranke(r) *mf*

aigrette [ˈeɪgret] N Reiherfeder *f*, Reiherbusch *m (old)*

ail [eɪl] VT *(old)* plagen; **what's ~ing** *or* **what ~s you?** *(inf)* was hast du?, was ist mit dir? VI *(inf)* kränklich sein, kränkeln

aileron [ˈeɪlərɒn] N *(Aviat)* Querruder *nt*

ailing [ˈeɪlɪŋ] ADJ *(lit)* kränklich, kränkelnd; *(fig) industry, economy etc* krankend, krank

ailment [ˈeɪlmənt] N Gebrechen *nt*, Leiden *nt*; **minor ~s** leichte Beschwerden *pl*; **inflation, a national ~** die Inflation, eine nationale Krankheit; **all his little ~s** all seine Wehwehchen

aim [eɪm] N **a** Zielen *nt*; **to take ~** zielen *(at* auf *+acc)*; **to miss one's ~** sein Ziel verfehlen; **his ~ was bad/good** er zielte schlecht/gut
b *(= purpose)* Ziel *nt*, Absicht *f*; **with the ~ of doing sth** mit dem Ziel *or* der Absicht, etw zu tun; **what is your ~ in life?** was ist Ihr Lebensziel?; **to achieve one's ~** sein Ziel erreichen; **what is your ~ in saying that?** warum sagen Sie das?; **what is your ~ in doing that?** was wollen Sie damit bezwecken?
VT **a** *(= direct) guided missile, camera* richten *(at* auf *+acc)*; *stone etc* zielen mit *(at* auf *+acc)*; **he ~ed a kick/punch at my stomach** sein Tritt/Schlag zielte auf meinen Bauch; **to teach sb how to ~ a gun** jdm zeigen, wie man zielt; **to ~ a pistol at sb/sth** mit einer Pistole auf jdn/etw zielen; **he ~ed his pistol at my heart** er zielte auf mein Herz; **the guns were ~ed directly at the city walls** die Kanonen waren direkt auf die Stadtmauer gerichtet; **you didn't ~ the camera properly** du hast die Kamera nicht richtig gehalten
b *(fig) remark, insult, criticism* richten *(at* gegen); **this book/programme** *(Brit) or* **program** *(US)* **is ~ed at the general public** dieses Buch/Programm wendet sich an die Öffentlichkeit; **to be ~ed at sth** *(cuts, measure, new law etc)* auf etw *(acc)* abgezielt sein; **I think that was ~ed at me** ich glaube, das war auf mich gemünzt *or* gegen mich gerichtet
VI **a** *(with gun, punch etc)* zielen *(at, for* auf *+acc)*
b *(= try, strive for)* **to ~ high** sich *(dat)* hohe Ziele setzen *or* stecken; **isn't that ~ing a bit high?** wollen Sie nicht etwas hoch hinaus?; **to ~ at** *or* **for sth** etw anstreben, auf etw *(acc)* abzielen; **with this TV programme** *(Brit) or* **program** *(US)* **we're ~ing at a much wider audience** mit diesem Fernsehprogramm wollen wir einen größeren Teilnehmerkreis ansprechen; **we ~ to please** bei uns ist der Kunde König; **he always ~s for perfection** er strebt immer nach Perfektion; **he ~s at only spending £10 per week** er hat sich zum Ziel gesetzt, mit £ 10 pro Woche auszukommen
c *(inf: = intend)* **to ~ to do sth** vorhaben, etw zu tun, etw tun wollen

aiming point N *(esp Mil)* Zielpunkt *m*

aimless ADJ, **aimlessly** ADV [ˈeɪmlɪs, -lɪ] ziellos; *talk, act* planlos

aimlessness [ˈeɪmlɪsnɪs] N Ziellosigkeit *f*; *(of talk, action)* Planlosigkeit *f*

ain't [eɪnt] *(incorrect)* = **am not, is not, are not, has not, have not**

air [ɛəˈ] N **a** Luft *f*; **a change of ~** eine Luftveränderung; **war in the ~** Luftkrieg *m*; **perfumes drifting in on the ~** vom Windhauch hereingetragene Düfte; **to go out for a breath of (fresh) ~** frische Luft schnappen (gehen); **to take the ~** *(Brit old)* frische Luft schöpfen; **to take to the ~** sich in die Lüfte schwingen *(geh)*; **by ~** per *or* mit dem Flugzeug; **to transport sth by ~** etw auf dem Luftweg transportieren; **to go by ~** *(person)* fliegen, mit dem Flugzeug reisen; *(goods)* per Flugzeug *or* auf dem Luftwege transportiert werden
b *(fig phrases)* **there's something in the ~** es liegt etwas in der Luft; **it's still all up in the ~** *(inf)* es hängt noch alles in der Luft, es ist noch alles offen; **all her plans were up in the ~** *(inf)* all ihre Pläne hingen in der Luft; **to give sb the ~** *(US inf)* jdn abblitzen *or* abfahren lassen *(inf)*; **to clear the ~** die Atmosphäre reinigen; **to be walking** *or* **floating on ~** wie auf Wolken gehen; **to pull** *or* **pluck sth out of the ~** *(fig)* etw auf gut Glück nennen → **castle N a, thin ADJ d**
c *(Rad, TV)* **to be on the ~** *(programme)* gesendet werden; *(station)* senden; **you're on the ~** Sie sind auf Sendung; **he's on the ~ every day** er ist jeden Tag im Radio zu hören; **the programme goes** *or* **is put on the ~ every week** das Programm wird jede Woche gesendet; **we come on the ~ at 6 o'clock** unsere Sendezeit beginnt um 6 Uhr; **to go off the ~** *(broadcaster)* die Sendung beenden; *(station)* das Programm beenden
d *(= demeanour, manner)* Auftreten *nt*; *(= facial expression)* Miene *f*; *(of building, town etc)* Atmosphäre *f*; **with an ~ of bewilderment** mit bestürzter Miene; **an unpleasant ~ of self-satisfaction** ein unangenehm selbstzufriedenes Gehabe; **there was** *or* **she had an ~ of mystery about her** sie hatte etwas Geheimnisvolles an sich; **it gives** *or* **lends her an ~ of affluence** das gibt ihr einen wohlhabenden Anstrich; **she has a certain ~ about her** sie hat so etwas an sich
e airs PL Getue *nt*, Gehabe *nt*; **to put on ~s, to give oneself ~s** sich zieren, vornehm tun; **~s and graces** Allüren *pl*; **to put on ~s and graces** den Vornehmen/die Vornehme herauskehren
f *(Mus)* Weise *f (old)*; *(= tune)* Melodie *f*
g *(liter, Naut: = breeze)* leichte Brise, Lüftchen *nt (liter)*
VT **a** *clothes, bed, room* (aus)lüften
b *anger, grievance* Luft machen *(+dat)*; *opinion* darlegen
c *(esp US Rad, TV) story, series* senden
VI *(clothes etc) (after washing)* nachtrocknen; *(after storage)* (aus)lüften; **to put clothes out to ~** Kleidung *f* zum Lüften raushängen

air *in cpds* Luft-; **air ambulance** N *(= aeroplane)* Rettungsflugzeug *nt*; *(= helicopter)* Rettungshubschrauber *m*; **air bag** N Airbag *m*; **air base** N Luftwaffenstützpunkt *m*; **air bed** N *(Brit)* Luftmatratze *f*; **airborne** ADJ a *(= flying) aircraft* sich in der Luft befindend *attr*; **to be ~** sich in der Luft befinden; **~ freight** Luftfracht *f* b *(Mil)* **~ troops** Luftlandetruppen *pl*; **~ missile** Rakete *f* c *(= floating) bacteria, virus* in der Luft befindlich; **air brake** N *(on truck)* Druckluftbremse *f*; *(Aviat)* Brems- *or* Landeklappe *f*; **airbrick** N Entlüftungsziegel *m*; **air bridge** N Luftbrücke *f*; **airbrush** *(Art)* N Spritzpistole *f*, Airbrush *f* VT mit der Spritzpistole bearbeiten; **air bubble** N Luftblase *f*; **Airbus®** N Airbus® *m*; **air cargo** N Luftfracht *f*; **Air Chief Marshal** N *(Brit)* General *m*; **air commodore** N *(Brit)* Brigadegeneral *m*; **air-conditioned** ADJ klimatisiert; **air conditioning** N *(= process)* Klimatisierung *f*; *(= system)* Klimaanlage *f*; **air-conditioning plant** N Klimaanlage *f*; **air-cooled** ADJ *engine* luftgekühlt; **air corridor** N Luftkorridor *m*; **air cover** N Luftunterstützung *f*; **aircraft** N *pl* **aircraft** Flugzeug *nt*, Maschine *f*; **various types of ~** verschiedene Luftfahrzeuge *pl*; **aircraft carrier** N Flugzeugträger *m*; **aircraft industry** N Flugzeugindustrie *f*; **aircraft(s)man** N Gefreite(r) *m*; **aircrew** N Flugpersonal *nt*; **air current** N Luftströmung *f*; **air cushion** N Luftkissen *nt*; **air display** N Flugschau *f*; **airdrome** N *(US)* Flugplatz *m*, Aerodrom *nt (old)*; **airdrop** N Fallschirmabwurf *m* VT mit Fallschirmen abwerfen; **air-dry** VT lufttrocknen; **air duct** N Luftkanal *m*

Airedale [ˈɛədeɪl] N Airedaleterrier *m*

airer [ˈɛərəʳ] N Trockenständer *m*

air: **airfare** N Flugpreis *m*; **airfield** N Flugplatz *m*; **airflow** N Luftstrom *m*; *(in air conditioning)* Luftzufuhr *f*; **airfoil** N *(US)* Tragflügel *m*; *(on racing cars)* Spoiler *m*; **air force** N Luftwaffe *f*; **Air Force One** N Air Force One *f*, *Dienstflugzeug des US-Präsidenten*; **air force pilot** N Luftwaffenpilot(in) *m(f)*; **airframe** N *(Aviat)* Flugwerk *nt*, Zelle *f*; **air freight** N Luftfracht *f*; *(= charge)* Luftfrachtgebühr *f*; **to send sth by ~** etw als Luftfracht verschicken; **air-freight** VT per Luftfracht senden; **air gun** N Luftgewehr *nt*; **airhead** N *(inf pej)* Hohlkopf *m (inf pej)*; **air hole** N Luftloch *nt*; **air hostess** N Stewardess *f*

airily [ˈɛərɪlɪ] ADV *(= casually) say, reply etc* leichthin, lässig; *(= vaguely)* vage; *(= flippantly)* blasiert, erhaben

airiness [ˈɛərɪnɪs] N a **she liked the ~ of the rooms** ihr gefiel, dass die Zimmer so luftig waren b *(= casualness: of manner, gesture)* Lässigkeit *f*, Nonchalance *f* c *(= vagueness) (of promise)* Vagheit *f*; *(of theory)* Versponnenheit *f* d *(= flippancy)* Blasiertheit *f*, Erhabenheit *f*

airing [ˈɛərɪŋ] N *(of linen, room etc)* (Aus- *or* Durch)lüften *nt*; **to give sth a good ~** etw gut durch- *or* auslüften lassen; **to give an idea an ~** *(fig inf)* eine Idee darlegen

airing cupboard N *(Brit)* (Wäsche)trockenschrank *m*

air: **air-intake** N Luftzufuhr *f*; *(for engine)* Luftansaugstutzen *m*; *(= quantity)* Luftmenge *f*; **airlane** N Flugroute *f*; **airless** ADJ *(lit) space* luftleer; *(= stuffy) room* stickig; *(= with no wind) day* windstill; **air letter** N Luftpostbrief *m*, Aerogramm *nt*; **airlift** N Luftbrücke *f* VT **to ~ sth into a place** etw über eine Luftbrücke herein-/ /hineinbringen; **airline** N a Fluggesellschaft *f*, Luftverkehrsgesellschaft *f*, Fluglinie *f* b *(= diver's tube)* Luftschlauch *m*; **airliner** N Verkehrsflugzeug *nt*; **airlock** N *(in spacecraft etc)* Luftschleuse *f*; *(in pipe)* Luftsack *m*

airmail [ˈɛəmeɪl] N Luftpost *f*; **to send sth (by) ~** etw per *or* mit Luftpost schicken VT mit *or* per Luftpost schicken

airmail: **airmail edition** N *(of newspaper)* Luftpostausgabe *f*; **airmail letter** N Luftpostbrief *m*; **airmail stamp**, **airmail sticker** N Luftpostaufkleber *m*

air: **airman** N *(= flier)* Flieger *m*; *(US: in air force)* Gefreite(r) *m*; **air marshal** N *(Brit)* Generalleutnant *m*; **air mass** N Luftmasse *f*; **air mattress** N Luftmatratze *f*; **air mile** N Flugmeile *f*, ≈ Flugkilometer *m*; **Air Miles** Flugmeilen *pl*; **to collect Air Miles** Flugmeilen sammeln; **air miss** N *(Aviat)* Beinahezusammenstoß *m*; **air passenger** N Fluggast *m*; **airplane** N *(US)* Flugzeug *nt*; **airplay** N *(Rad)* Sendezeit *f*; **the song received extensive ~** das Lied wurde sehr oft im Radio gespielt; **air pocket** N Luftloch *nt*

airport [ˈɛəpɔːt] N Flughafen *m*

airport: **airport bus** N Flughafenbus *m*; **airport tax** N Flughafengebühr *f*

air: **air pressure** N Luftdruck *m*; **airproof** [ˈɛəpruːf] ADJ *(= airtight)* luftdicht; *(= unaffected by air)* luftbeständig; **air pump** N Luftpumpe *f*; **air rage** N aggressives Verhalten von Flugpassagieren, Flugkoller *m (inf)*

air raid N Luftangriff *m*

air-raid: **air-raid shelter** N Luftschutzkeller *m*; **air-raid warden** N Luftschutzwart *m*; **air-raid warning** N Fliegeralarm *m*

air: **air rescue service** N Luftrettungsdienst *m*; **air rifle** N Luftgewehr *nt*; **air route** N Flugroute *f*; **airscrew** N Luftschraube *f*; **air-sea rescue** N Rettung *f* durch Seenotflugzeuge; **air-sea rescue service** N Seenotrettungsdienst *m*; **air security** N Flugsicherheit *f*; **air shaft** N *(Min)* Wetterschacht *m*; **airship** N Luftschiff *nt*; **airshow** N Luftfahrtausstellung *f*; **airsick** ADJ luftkrank; **airsickness** N Luftkrankheit *f*; **airside** [ˈɛəsaɪd] N *Teil des Flughafens nach der Passkontrolle* ADV **to be located ~** *(restaurant, shop)* sich nach *or* hinter der Passkontrolle befinden ADJ **~ restaurant** Restaurant nach *or* hinter der Passkontrolle; **air sleeve**, **air sock** N Windsack *m*; **airspace** N Luftraum *m*; **airspeed** N Eigen- *or* Fluggeschwindigkeit *f*; **airstream** N *(of vehicle)* Luftsog *m*; *(Met)* Luftstrom *m*; **airstrike** N = **air raid**; **airstrip** N Start- und Lande-Bahn *f*; **air supply** N Luftzufuhr *f*; **air supremacy** N Luftüberlegenheit *f*; **air terminal** N (Air) Terminal *m or nt*; **air ticket** N Flugticket *nt*; **airtight** ADJ *(lit)* luftdicht; *(fig) argument, case* hieb- und stichfest; **airtime** N *(Rad, TV)* Sendezeit *f*; **air-to-air** ADJ *(Mil)* Luft-Luft-; **air-to-ground** ADJ *(Mil)* Luft-Boden-; **air-to-sea** ADJ *(Mil)* Luft-See-; **air-to-surface** ADJ *(Mil)* Luft-Boden-; **air traffic** N Flugverkehr *m*, Luftverkehr *m*; **air-traffic control** N Flugleitung *f*; **air-traffic controller** N Fluglotse *m*, Fluglotsin *f*; **air vent** N Ventilator *m*; *(= shaft)* Belüftungsschacht *m*; **Air Vice Marshal** N *(Brit)* Generalmajor *m*; **airwaves** PL Radiowellen *pl*; **airway** N a *(= route)* Flugroute *f*; *(= airline company)* Fluggesellschaft *f*, Luftverkehrsgesellschaft *f* b *(Med)* Atemwege *pl*; **air waybill** N Luftfrachtbrief *m*; **airwoman** N Fliegerin *f*; **airworthiness** N Flugtüchtigkeit *f*; **airworthy** ADJ flugtüchtig

airy [ˈɛərɪ] ADJ *(+er)* a *room* luftig; **to have an ~ feel (to it)** luftig wirken b *(= casual) manner, gesture* lässig, nonchalant; *(= vague) promise* vage; *theory* versponnen; *(= superior, flippant)* blasiert, erhaben c *(liter: = immaterial) phantom* körperlos

airy-fairy [ˈɛərɪˈfɛərɪ] ADJ *(Brit inf)* versponnen; *excuse* windig; *talk* versponnen, larifari *inv (inf)*; **your plans seem rather ~** deine Pläne scheinen ziemlich unausgegoren

aisle [aɪl] N Gang *m*; *(in church)* Seitenschiff *nt*; *(central aisle)* Mittelgang *m*; **~ seat** Sitz *m* am Gang; **to walk down the ~** vor den Altar treten; **to walk down the ~ with sb** jdn zum Altar führen; **he had them rolling in the ~s** *(inf)* er brachte sie so weit, dass sie sich vor Lachen kugelten *(inf) or* wälzten *(inf)*

aitch [eɪtʃ] N h *nt*, H *nt*; **to drop one's ~es** *den Buchstaben „h" nicht aussprechen (= be lower class)* ≈ „mir" und „mich" verwechseln

ajar [əˈdʒɑːʳ] ADJ ADV angelehnt

aka *abbr of* **also known as** alias, anderweitig bekannt als

akela [ɑːˈkeɪlə] N Wölflingsführer *m*

akimbo [əˈkɪmbəʊ] ADV **with arms ~** die Arme in die Hüften gestemmt

akin [əˈkɪn] ADJ *pred* ähnlich *(to +dat)*, verwandt *(to* mit)

à la [ˈɑːlɑː] PREP à la

alabaster [ˈæləbɑːstəʳ] N Alabaster *m* ADJ *(lit)* alabastern, Alabaster-; *(fig liter)* Alabaster-, wie Alabaster; **~ skin** Alabasterhaut *f*

à la carte [ɑːlɑːˈkɑːt] ADV *eat* à la carte, nach der (Speise)karte ADJ *menu* à la carte

alack [əˈlæk] INTERJ *(obs)* wehe; **~ a day** wehe dem Tag

alacrity [əˈlækrɪtɪ] N *(= willingness)* Bereitwilligkeit *f*; *(= eagerness)* Eifer *m*, Eilfertigkeit *f*; **to accept with ~** ohne zu zögern annehmen

Aladdin [əˈlædɪn] N Aladin; **~'s cave** *(fig: = hoard)* Schatzhöhle *f*; **the shop was an ~'s cave of antiques** das Geschäft war eine Fundgrube für Antiquitäten; **~'s lamp** *(lit, fig)* Aladins Wunderlampe *f*

à la mode [ɑːlɑːˈməʊd] ADJ *(US)* mit Eis

alarm [əˈlɑːm] N a *no pl (= fear)* Sorge *f*, Besorgnis *f*, Beunruhigung *f*; **to be in a state of ~** *(= worried)* besorgt *or* beunruhigt sein; *(= frightened)* erschreckt sein; **to cause a good deal of ~** große Unruhe auslösen; **to cause sb ~** jdn beunruhigen b *(= warning)* Alarm *m*; **to raise** *or* **give** *or* **sound the ~** Alarm geben *or (fig)* schlagen c *(= device)* Alarmanlage *f*; **~ (clock)** Wecker *m*; **car/house ~** Auto-/Hausalarmanlage *f* VT a *(= worry)* beunruhigen; *(= frighten)* erschrecken; **don't be ~ed** erschrecken Sie nicht; **the news ~ed the whole country** die Nachricht alarmierte das ganze Land *or* versetzte das ganze Land in Aufregung b *(= warn of danger)* warnen; *fire brigade etc* alarmieren

alarm *in cpds* Alarm-; **alarm bell** N Alarmglocke *f*; **to set ~s ringing** *(fig)* die Alarmglocken klingeln *or* läuten lassen; **alarm call** N *(Telec)* Weckruf *m*; **alarm call service** N Weckdienst *m*; **alarm clock** N Wecker *m*

alarming [əˈlɑːmɪŋ] ADJ *(= worrying)* beunruhigend; *(= frightening)* erschreckend; *news* alarmierend

alarmingly [əˈlɑːmɪŋlɪ] ADV erschreckend

alarmist [əˈlɑːmɪst] N Panikmacher(in) *m(f)*, Kassandra *f (geh)* ADJ *speech* Unheil prophezeiend *attr*; *politician* Panik machend *attr*

alarum [əˈlærəm] N *(old)* = **alarm**

alas [əˈlæs] INTERJ *(old)* leider; **~, he didn't come** leider kam er nicht

Alaska [əˈlæskə] N Alaska *nt*

Alaskan [əˈlæskən] N Einwohner(in) *m(f)* von Alaska ADJ Alaska-; *customs, winter* in Alaska; *fish, produce* aus Alaska

alb [ælb] N *(Eccl)* Alba *f*

Albania [ælˈbeɪnɪə] N Albanien *nt*

Albanian [ælˈbeɪnɪən] ADJ albanisch N a Albaner(in) *m(f)* b *(= language)* Albanisch *nt*

albatross [ˈælbətrɒs] N Albatros *m*; **to be an ~ around sb's neck** ein Mühlstein *m* um jds Hals sein

albeit [ɔːlˈbiːɪt] CONJ *(esp liter)* obgleich, wenn auch

albinism [ˈælbɪnɪzəm] N Albinismus *m*

albino [ælˈbiːnəʊ] N Albino *m* ADJ Albino-; **~ rabbit** Albinokaninchen *nt*

Albion [ˈælbɪən] N *(poet)* Albion *nt*

album [ˈælbəm] N Album *nt*

album cover N Plattenhülle *f*, Cover *nt*

albumen [ˈælbjʊmɪn] N Albumin *nt*

albuminous [ælˈbjuːmɪnəs] ADJ albuminös

alchemical [ælˈkemɪkəl] ADJ alchimistisch

alchemist [ˈælkɪmɪst] N Alchemist(in) *m(f)*

alchemy [ˈælkɪmɪ] N Alchemie *f*, Alchimie *f*

alchie ['ælkɪ] N *(Brit inf)* = **alkie**

alcohol ['ælkəhɒl] N Alkohol *m*; ~ **by volume** Alkoholgehalt *m*

alcohol-free [,ælkəhɒl'fri:] ADJ alkoholfrei

alcoholic [,ælkə'hɒlɪk] ADJ *drink* alkoholisch; *person* alkoholsüchtig, trunksüchtig N *(person)* Alkoholiker(in) *m(f)*, Trinker(in) *m(f)*; **to be an** ~ Alkoholiker(in) *or* Trinker(in) sein; **Alcoholics Anonymous** Anonyme Alkoholiker *pl*

alcoholism ['ælkəhɒlɪzəm] N Alkoholismus *m*, Trunksucht *f*

alcopop ['ælkəpɒp] N *alkoholisches kohlensäurehaltiges Getränk*

alcove ['ælkəʊv] N Alkoven *m*, Nische *f*; *(in wall)* Nische *f*

aldehyde ['ældɪhaɪd] N Aldehyd *m*

al dente [æl'denteɪ, -tɪ] ADJ, ADV *spaghetti* al dente; *rice* körnig

alder ['ɔ:ldə'] N Erle *f*

alder fly N Schlammfliege *f*

alderman ['ɔ:ldəmən] N *pl* **-men** [-mən] Alderman *m (Ratsherr)*

ale [eɪl] N *(old)* Ale *nt* → **real ale**

aleatory [,ælɪ'eɪtərɪ] ADJ *(Jur)* aleatorisch, vom Zufall abhängig; ~ **contract** aleatorischer Vertrag, Spekulationsvertrag *m*

aleck ['ælɪk] N → **smart aleck**

alehouse ['eɪlhaʊs] N *(old)* Wirtshaus *nt*, Schenke *f*, Schänke *f*

alert [ə'lɜ:t] ADJ aufmerksam; *(as character trait)* aufgeweckt; *mind* scharf, hell; *dog* wachsam; **to be** ~ **to sth** vor etw *(dat)* auf der Hut sein VT warnen *(to* vor *+dat)*; *troops* in Gefechtsbereitschaft versetzen; *fire brigade etc* alarmieren N Alarm *m*; **to give the** ~ *(Mil)* Gefechtsbereitschaft befehlen; *(in the fire brigade etc)* den Alarm auslösen; *(fig)* warnen; **to put sb on the** ~ jdn in Alarmbereitschaft versetzen; *(Mil)* jdn in Gefechtsbereitschaft versetzen; **to be on (the)** ~ einsatzbereit sein; *(= be on lookout)* auf der Hut sein *(for* vor *+dat)*

alertly [ə'lɜ:tlɪ] ADV aufmerksam

alertness [ə'lɜ:tnɪs] N Aufmerksamkeit *f*; *(as character trait)* Aufgewecktheit *f*; *(of mind)* Schärfe *f*; *(of dog)* Wachsamkeit *f*

Aleutian Islands [ə'lu:ʃən'aɪləndz] PL Aleuten *pl*

A level ['eɪ,levl] N *(Brit)* Abschluss *m* der Sekundarstufe 2; **to take one's ~s** ≈ das Abitur machen; **3 ~s** ≈ das Abitur in 3 Fächern

> **A LEVELS**
>
> **A levels** sind dem Abitur vergleichbare Hochschulqualifikationen. Zur Beendigung der höheren Schulbildung wählen Schülerinnen und Schüler in England, Wales und Nordirland zwei oder drei Fächer. Die Kurse schließen häufig an GCSE-Kurse der gleichen Fachbereiche an und dauern normalerweise zwei Jahre, die Abschlussprüfungen werden im Alter von 18 Jahren abgelegt. Zu den Universitäten werden Studenten im Allgemeinen nur dann zugelassen, wenn sie von den Universitäten festgelegte Notendurchschnitte in den **A levels** vorweisen können.
> Das entsprechende schottische Pendant ist der **Higher Grade**, der auch oft einfach nur **Higher** genannt wird. Schüler belegen dafür bis zu fünf Fächer und nehmen nach einem Jahr an der Abschlussprüfung teil. → GCSE

Alexander [,ælɪg'zɑ:ndə'] N Alexander *m*; ~ **the Great** Alexander der Große

alexandrine [,ælɪg'zændraɪn] N Alexandriner *m* ADJ alexandrinisch

ALF N *(Brit) abbr of* **Animal Liberation Front** *militante Tierschützerorganisation*

alfalfa [æl'fælfə] N Luzerne *f*, Alfalfa *f*

alfresco [æl'freskəʊ] ADJ im Freien; **an** ~ **lunch** ein Mittagessen im Freien ADV im Freien

algae ['ælgɪ] PL Algen *pl*

algal ['ælgəl] ADJ Algen-; ~ **bloom** Algenblüte *f*

algebra ['ældʒɪbrə] N Algebra *f*

algebraic [,ældʒɪ'breɪɪk] ADJ algebraisch

Algeria [æl'dʒɪərɪə] N Algerien *nt*

Algerian [æl'dʒɪərɪən] N Algerier(in) *m(f)* ADJ algerisch

Algiers [æl'dʒɪəz] N Algier *nt*

algorithm ['ælgə,rɪðəm] N Algorithmus *m*

algorithmic [,ælgə'rɪθmɪk] ADJ algorithmisch

alias ['eɪlɪæs] ADV alias N Deckname *m*

alibi ['ælɪbaɪ] N Alibi *nt* VT ein Alibi liefern für

Alice band ['ælɪs,bænd] N Haarreif *m*

alien ['eɪlɪən] N *(esp Pol)* Ausländer(in) *m(f)*; *(Sci-Fi)* außerirdisches Wesen ADJ **a** *(= foreign)* ausländisch; *(Sci-Fi)* außerirdisch **b** *(= different)* fremd; **to be ~ to sb/sb's nature/sth** jdm/jds Wesen/einer Sache fremd sein **c** *(Comput)* fremd

alienable ['eɪlɪənəbl] ADJ *(Jur)* veräußerlich; *landed property* übertragbar

alienate ['eɪlɪəneɪt] VT **a** *people* befremden; *affections* zerstören, sich *(dat)* verscherzen; *public opinion* gegen sich aufbringen; **to ~ oneself from sb/sth** sich jdm/einer Sache entfremden; **Brecht set out to ~ his audience** Brecht wollte, dass sich die Zuschauer distanzieren **b** *(Jur) property, money* übertragen

alienation [,eɪlɪə'neɪʃən] N **a** Entfremdung *f* *(from* von*)*; *(Theat)* Distanzierung *f*; ~ **effect** Verfremdungseffekt *m*; ~ **of affections** *(Jur)* Entfremdung *f* **b** *(Jur, of property)* Übertragung *f* **c** *(Psych)* Alienation *f*

alight¹ [ə'laɪt] *(form)* VI **a** *(person)* aussteigen *(from* aus*)*; *(from horse)* absitzen *(from* von*)* **b** *(bird)* sich niederlassen *(on* auf *+dat)*; **his eyes ~ed on the ring** sein Blick fiel auf den Ring **c to ~ on a fact/an idea** *etc* auf ein Faktum/eine Idee *etc* stoßen

alight² ADJ *pred* **to be** ~ *(fire)* brennen; *(building also)* in Flammen stehen; **to keep the fire** ~ das Feuer in Gang halten; **to set sth** ~ etw in Brand setzen *or* stecken; **her face was ~ with pleasure** ihr Gesicht *or* sie glühte vor Freude

align [ə'laɪn] VT **a** *wheels of car, gun sights etc* ausrichten; *(= bring into line)* in eine Linie bringen, ausrichten; *(Comput)* bündig ausrichten; ~ **left/right** *(Comput)* links-/rechtsbündig ausrichten
b *(Fin, Pol) currencies, policies* aufeinander ausrichten; **to ~ sth with sth** etw auf etw *(acc)* ausrichten; **to ~ oneself with a party** *(= follow policy of)* sich nach einer Partei ausrichten; *(= join forces with)* sich einer Partei anschließen; **they have ~ed themselves against him/it** sie haben sich gegen ihn/dagegen zusammengeschlossen
VI **a** *(lit)* ausgerichtet sein *(with* nach*)*; *(= come into line)* eine Linie bilden
b *(side, person, country)* sich verbünden *(with* mit*)*

alignment [ə'laɪnmənt] N **a** *(of car wheels, gun sights etc)* Ausrichtung *f*; **to be out of** ~ nicht richtig ausgerichtet sein *(with* nach*)*
b *(of currencies, policies etc)* Ausrichtung *f (with* auf *+acc)*, Orientierung *f (with* nach*)*; **to be out of ~ with one another** nicht übereinstimmen, sich nicht aneinander orientieren; **to bring sb back into ~ with the party** jdn zwingen, wieder auf die Parteilinie einzuschwenken; **his unexpected ~ with the Socialists** seine unerwartete Parteinahme für die Sozialisten; **he argued for a new ~ of the governing parties** er war für eine Neuordnung der Regierungsparteien; **the new ~ of world powers** die Neugruppierung der Weltmächte

alike [ə'laɪk] ✪ 5.4 ADJ PRED, ADV gleich; **they're/they look very** ~ sie sind/sehen sich *(dat)* sehr ähnlich; **they all look ~ to me** für mich sehen sie alle gleich aus; **you men are all ~!** ihr Männer seid doch alle gleich!; **it's all ~ to me** mir ist das gleich *or* einerlei; **they always think** ~ sie sind immer einer Meinung; **winter and summer** ~ Sommer wie Winter

alimentary [,ælɪ'mentərɪ] ADJ *(Anat)* Verdauungs-; ~ **canal** Verdauungskanal *m*

alimony ['ælɪmənɪ] N Unterhaltszahlung *f*; **to pay** ~ Unterhalt zahlen

A list *(inf)* N wichtigste Personen *pl or* Leute *pl (inf)* ADJ **A-list people** A-Promis *pl (inf)*; **A-list star** Superstar *m (inf)*; **to have A-list star potential** das Zeug zum Superstar haben *inf*

aliterate [eɪ'lɪtərət] ADJ **to be** ~ so gut wie nie lesen N *Person, die so gut wie nie liest*

alive [ə'laɪv] ADJ **a** *pred (= living)* lebendig, lebend *attr*; **dead or** ~ tot oder lebendig; **to be** ~ leben; **the greatest musician** ~ der größte lebende Musiker; **the wickedest man** ~ der schlechteste Mensch auf der ganzen Welt; **while ~ he was always ...** zu seinen Lebzeiten war er immer ...; **it's good to be** ~ das Leben ist schön; **no man** ~ niemand auf der ganzen Welt; **to stay** *or* **keep** ~ am Leben bleiben; **to keep sb/sth** ~ *(lit, fig)* jdn/etw am Leben erhalten; **to do sth as well as anyone** ~ etw so gut wie jeder andere können; **to be ~ and kicking** *(hum inf)* gesund und munter sein; **he's been found ~ and well** er ist gesund und munter aufgefunden worden; **he's very much** ~ er ist ausgesprochen lebendig; **to eat sb** ~ *(fig inf)* jdn in der Luft zerreißen; *(Press)* über jdn herfallen; **we were eaten ~ by mosquitos** *(inf)* wir wurden von Moskitos halb tot gestochen *(inf)*
b *(= lively)* lebendig; **to keep one's mind** ~ geistig rege bleiben; **to come** ~ *(= liven up)* lebendig werden; *(= prick up ears etc)* wach werden; **to bring sth** ~ *(story, character)* etw lebendig werden lassen
c *pred (= aware)* **to be ~ to sth** sich *(dat)* einer Sache *(gen)* bewusst sein; **to be ~ to certain possibilities/sb's interests** gewisse Möglichkeiten/jds Interessen im Auge haben
d ~ **with** *(= full of)* erfüllt von; **to be ~ with tourists/fish/insects** *etc* von Touristen/Fischen/Insekten *etc* wimmeln

alkali ['ælkəlaɪ] N *pl* **-(e)s** Base *f*, Lauge *f*; *(metal, Agr)* Alkali *nt*

alkaline ['ælkəlaɪn] ADJ basisch, alkalisch; ~ **solution** Lauge *f*

alkalinity [,ælkə'lɪnɪtɪ] N Alkalität *f*

alkaloid ['ælkəlɔɪd] N Alkaloid *nt*

alkie, (US) alky ['ælkɪ] N *(inf)* Alki *m (sl)*, Säufer(in) *m(f) (inf)*

all [ɔ:l]

✪ 26.1

1 ADJECTIVE	4 NOUN
2 PRONOUN	5 SET STRUCTURES
3 ADVERB	

1 – ADJECTIVE

with nouns *plural* alle; *(singular)* ganze(r, s), alle(r, s)

> When *alle* is used to translate *all the* it is not followed by the German article.

we have considered all the possibilities wir haben alle Möglichkeiten in Betracht gezogen; **she brought all the children** sie brachte alle Kinder mit; **all the problems have been solved** alle *or* sämtliche Probleme wurden gelöst; **all kinds** *or* **sorts of people** alle möglichen Leute; **all the tobacco** der ganze Tabak, aller Tabak; **all the milk** die ganze Milch, alle Milch; **all the fruit** das ganze Obst, alles Obst; **all you boys can come with me** ihr Jungen könnt alle mit mir kommen; **the money was all there** alles Geld *or* das ganze Geld war da; **where's all that water coming from?** wo kommt das ganze *or* all das Wasser her?; **all the time** die ganze Zeit; **all day (long)** den ganzen Tag (lang); **all Spain** ganz Spanien; **to dislike all sport** jeglichen Sport ablehnen; **in all respects** in jeder Hinsicht

♦ **all** + *possessive* **all my strength** meine ganze Kraft; **all my books/friends** alle meine Bücher/Freunde, meine ganzen Bücher/Freunde; **all my life** mein ganzes Leben (lang)

♦ *pronoun* + **all they all came** sie sind alle gekommen; **we all sat down** wir setzten uns alle; **I invited them all** ich habe sie alle eingeladen

Note that *it all* is usually translated by *alles* alone:

he took/spent it all er hat alles genommen/ausgegeben; **it all happened so quickly** alles geschah so schnell, es geschah alles so schnell; **he's seen/done it all** für ihn gibt es nichts Neues mehr, ihn kann nichts mehr erschüttern *(inf)*

♦ **all this/that I don't understand all that** ich verstehe das alles nicht; **what's all this/that about?** was soll das Ganze?; **what's all this/that?** was ist denn das?; *(annoyed)* was soll denn das!; **what's all this I hear about you leaving?** was höre ich da! Sie wollen gehen?

♦ **all possible/due with all possible speed** so schnell wie möglich; **with all due care** mit angemessener Sorgfalt; **with all due speed** in angemessenem Tempo; **they will take all possible precautions** sie werden alle möglichen Sicherheitsvorkehrungen treffen

2 – PRONOUN

a [= everything] alles; **all is well** alles ist gut; **I'm just curious, that's all** ich bin nur neugierig, das ist alles; **that's all that matters** darauf allein kommt es an; **that's all he said** das ist alles, was er gesagt hat, mehr hat er nicht gesagt; **that is all (that) I can tell you** mehr kann ich Ihnen nicht sagen; **it was all I could do not to laugh** ich musste an mich halten, um nicht zu lachen

♦ **all of all of Paris/of the house** ganz Paris/das ganze Haus; **all of it** alles; **I don't need all of it** ich brauche nicht alles; **all of 5 kms/£5** ganze 5 km/£ 5; **it took him all of three hours** er brauchte ganze drei Stunden

♦ **all or nothing** alles oder nichts

b [= everybody] alle *pl*; **all who knew him** alle, die ihn kannten; **all of them** (sie) alle; **the score was two all** es stand zwei zu zwei

3 – ADVERB

(= quite, entirely) ganz; **dressed all in white, all dressed in white** ganz in Weiß (gekleidet); **all woman** ganz Frau; **all dirty/excited** *etc* ganz schmutzig/aufgeregt *etc*; **that's all very fine** *or* **well** das ist alles ganz schön und gut; **all wool** reine Wolle; **an all wool carpet** ein reinwollener Teppich, ein Teppich aus reiner Wolle

♦ **all** + *adverb/preposition* **it was red all over** es war ganz rot; **that's Dave all over** das ist typisch Dave; **all down the front of her dress** überall vorn auf ihrem Kleid; **all along the road** die ganze Straße entlang; **there were chairs all around the room** rundum im Zimmer standen Stühle; **he ordered whiskies/drinks all round** er hat für alle Whisky/Getränke bestellt; **what's the film all about?** wovon handelt der Film überhaupt?; **I'll tell you all about it** ich erzähl dir alles; **it was all about a little girl** es handelte von einem kleinen Mädchen

4 – NOUN

♦ **one's all** alles; **he staked his all on this race/deal** er setzte alles auf dieses Rennen/Unternehmen; **the horses were giving their all** die Pferde gaben ihr Letztes

5 – SET STRUCTURES

♦ **all along** *(= from the start)* von Anfang an, die ganze Zeit (über); **I feared that all along** das habe ich von Anfang an befürchtet, das habe ich schon die ganze Zeit (über) befürchtet

♦ **all but** fast; **he all but died** er wäre fast gestorben; **he all but lost it** er hätte es fast verloren; **the party won all but six of the seats** die Partei hat alle außer sechs Sitzen *or* alle bis auf sechs Sitze gewonnen

♦ **all for** *(= in favour of)* **I'm all for it!** ich bin ganz dafür

♦ **all found** insgesamt, alles in allem

♦ **all in** *(inf: = exhausted)* **to be** *or* **feel all in** total erledigt sein *(inf)*

♦ **all in all** alles in allem

♦ **all one** *(= indifferent)* **it's all one to me** das ist mir (ganz) egal *or* einerlei

♦ **all the** + *comparative* **all the hotter/prettier/happier** *etc* noch heißer/hübscher/glücklicher *etc*; **all the funnier because ...** umso lustiger, weil ...; **I feel all the better for my holiday** *(esp Brit) or* **vacation** *(US)* jetzt, wo ich Urlaub gemacht habe, gehts mir viel besser; **all the more so since ...** besonders weil ...; **all the better to see you with** damit ich dich besser sehen kann

♦ **all the same** trotzdem, trotz allem; **all the same, it's a pity** trotzdem ist es schade; **it's all the same to me** das ist mir (ganz) egal *or* einerlei; **if it's all the same to you** wenn es Ihnen egal ist

♦ **all there/not all there** *(inf: person)* **he's all there/not all there** er ist voll da/nicht ganz da *(inf)*

♦ **all too** + *adjective/adverb* viel zu, allzu; **all too soon/quickly** viel zu *or* allzu früh/schnell

♦ **... and all he ate the orange, peel and all** er hat die ganze Orange gegessen, samt der Schale; **the whole family came, children and all** die Familie kam mit Kind und Kegel; **what with the snow and all** *(inf)* mit dem ganzen Schnee und so *(inf)*

♦ **at all** *(= whatsoever)* überhaupt; **nothing at all** überhaupt *or* gar nichts; **did/didn't you say anything at all?** haben Sie überhaupt etwas gesagt/gar *or* überhaupt nichts gesagt?; *(= in the least)* **I'm not at all sure, I'm not sure at all** ich bin mir ganz und gar nicht sicher, ich bin gar nicht ganz sicher; **I'm not at all angry** *etc*, **I'm not angry** *etc* **at all** ich bin überhaupt nicht wütend *etc*, ich bin ganz und gar nicht wütend *etc*; **it's not bad at all** das ist gar nicht schlecht; **I don't know at all** ich weiß es überhaupt nicht; **if at all possible** wenn irgend möglich

♦ **for all** *(= despite)* trotz; **for all his wealth** trotz (all) seines Reichtums; **for all that** trotz allem, trotzdem

♦ **for all I know for all I know she could be ill** was weiß ich, vielleicht ist sie krank; **is he in Paris? – for all I know he could be** ist er in Paris? – schon möglich, was weiß ich!

♦ **in all** insgesamt; **ten people in all** insgesamt zehn Personen

♦ **all that** *(US inf)* einfach super *(inf)*

♦ **not all that it's not all that bad, it's not as bad as all that** so schlimm ist es nun auch wieder nicht; **it isn't all THAT expensive!** so teuer ist es nun wieder auch nicht

♦ **of all ...! of all the idiots!** so ein Idiot!; **of all the stupid things to do!** so was Dummes!; **why me of all people?** warum ausgerechnet ich?

♦ *superlative* + **of all happiest/earliest/clearest** *etc* **of all** am glücklichsten/frühsten/klarsten *etc*; **that would be best of all** das wäre am besten; **I like him best of all** von allen mag ich ihn am liebsten; **most of all** am meisten; **most of all I'd like to be ...** am liebsten wäre ich ...; **the best car of all** das allerbeste Auto

♦ **to be all things to all men** *(person)* sich mit jedem gutstellen; *(thing, invention, new software etc)* das Ideale sein; **a party which claims to be all things to all men** eine Partei, die behauptet, allen etwas zu bieten

♦ **you all** *(US inf)* ihr (alle); *(to two people)* ihr (beide)

Allah [ˈælə] N Allah *m*

all: **all-American** ADJ *team, player* uramerikanisch; **an ~ boy** ein durch und durch amerikanischer Junge; **all-around** ADJ *(US)* = **all-round**

ALL-AMERICAN

Der Begriff **all-American** wird für Sportlerinnen und Sportler aus College- und Universitätsmannschaften verwendet, die wegen ihrer herausragenden Fähigkeiten und Talente in ihrem Sportbereich in eine Ehrennationalmannschaft berufen wurden. Dabei treten die ausgewählten Spieler nicht als Team an – es ist ein reiner Ehrentitel. Das Football-Team umfasst die bekanntesten Sportler Amerikas, über die auch in den Medien am meisten berichtet wird.

Der Begriff wird außerdem für Menschen verwendet, die die amerikanischen Ansichten und die Ideale der Mittelklasse vortrefflich repräsentieren.

allay [əˈleɪ] VT verringern; *doubt, fears, suspicion* (weitgehend) zerstreuen

all: **all clear** N Entwarnung *f*; **to give/sound the ~** Entwarnung geben, entwarnen; **all-conquering** ADJ *hero, team* alle besiegend; **all-consuming** ADJ *passion, interest* überwältigend; **all-day** ADJ ganztägig; **it was an ~ meeting** die Sitzung dauerte den ganzen Tag; **all-dayer** [ˈɔːl͵deɪəˈ] N *(inf)* ganztägige Veranstaltung

allegation [͵ælɪˈgeɪʃən] N Behauptung *f*

allege [əˈledʒ] VT behaupten; **the remarks ~d to have been made by him** die Bemerkungen, die er gemacht haben soll *or* angeblich gemacht hat; **he is ~d to have said that ...** er soll angeblich gesagt haben, dass ...

alleged [əˈledʒd] ADJ, **allegedly** [əˈledʒɪdlɪ] ADV angeblich

allegiance [əˈliːdʒəns] N Treue *f (to +dat)*; **oath of ~** Fahnen- *or* Treueeid *m*

allegoric(al) [͵ælɪˈgɒrɪk(əl)] ADJ, **allegorically** [͵ælɪˈgɒrɪkəlɪ] ADV allegorisch

allegory [ˈælɪgərɪ] N Allegorie *f*

allegro [əˈlegrəʊ] ADJ ADV allegro **N** Allegro *nt*

all-electric [͵ɔːlɪˈlektrɪk] ADJ **an ~ house** ein Haus, in dem alles elektrisch ist; **we're ~** bei uns ist alles elektrisch

alleluia [͵ælɪˈluːjə] INTERJ (h)alleluja **N** (H)alleluja *nt*

all-embracing [͵ɔːlɪmˈbreɪsɪŋ] ADJ (all)umfassend

Allen® [ˈælən]: **Allen key** N Inbusschlüssel® *m*; **Allen screw** N Inbusschraube® *f*; **Allen wrench** N *(US)* Inbusschlüssel® *m*

allergen [ˈælə͵dʒən] N *(Med)* Allergen *nt*

allergenic [͵æləˈdʒenɪk] ADJ *(Med)* allergen

allergic [əˈlɜːdʒɪk] ADJ *(lit, fig)* allergisch *(to* gegen)

allergist [ˈælədʒɪst] N Allergologe *m*, Allergologin *f*

allergy [ˈælədʒɪ] N Allergie *f (to* gegen); **he seems to have an ~ to work** *(hum)* er scheint gegen Arbeit allergisch zu sein

alleviate [əˈliːvɪeɪt] VT lindern

alleviation [ə͵liːvɪˈeɪʃən] N Linderung *f*

alley [ˈælɪ] N **a** *(between buildings)* (enge) Gasse; *(between gardens)* Weg *m*, Pfad *m*; *(in garden)* Laubengang *m* **b** *(= bowling alley, skittle alley)* Bahn *f*

alley: **alley cat** N streunende Katze; **to fight like ~s** sich in den Haaren liegen; **she's got the morals of an ~** *(inf)* sie treibts mit jedem; **alleyway** N Durchgang *m*

all: **all-fired** ADJ *(US inf)* furchtbar *(inf)*, schrecklich *(inf)*; **All Fools' Day** N *der erste April*; **All Hallows' (Day)** N *(Brit)* = **All Saints' Day**

alliance [əˈlaɪəns] N Verbindung *f*; *(of institutions also, of states)* Bündnis *nt*; *(in historical contexts)* Allianz *f*; **partners in an ~** Bündnispartner *pl*

allied [ˈælaɪd] ADJ **a** *(Mil, Pol: = affiliated)* verbunden; *(for attack, defence etc)* verbündet, aliiert; **~ to** *or* **with/against sb/sth** mit/gegen jdn/etw verbündet; **the Allied forces** die Alliierten; **an Allied attack** eine Offensive der Alliierten **b** *(= like, connected, associated)* **(closely) ~ to** *or* **with sth** (eng) mit etw verbunden **c** *(Biol, fig)* verwandt

Allies [ˈælaɪz] PL *(Hist)* **the ~** die Alliierten *pl*

alligator [ˈælɪgeɪtəˈ] N Alligator *m*; **~(-skin) bag** Alligatorledertasche *f*

all: **all-important** ADJ außerordentlich wichtig; **the ~ question** die Frage, auf die es ankommt; **all-in** ADJ *attr*, **all in** ADJ *pred (= inclusive)* Inklusiv-; ~ **price** Inklusivpreis *m* → *also* **all 5**; **all-inclusive** ADJ Pauschal-; **all-in-one** N Einteiler *m* ADJ *sleepsuit, wetsuit* einteilig; **all-in wrestling** N *(Sport)* Freistilringen *nt*

alliterate [əˈlɪtəreɪt] VI einen Stabreim bilden, alliterieren

alliteration [əˌlɪtəˈreɪʃən] N Alliteration *f*, Stabreim *m*

alliterative [əˈlɪtərətɪv] ADJ alliterierend

all: **all-knowing** ADJ allwissend; **all-male** ADJ *attr* **an ~ household** ein reiner Männerhaushalt; **all-merciful** ADJ *God* allbarmherzig, allgütig; **all-night** ADJ *attr café* (die ganze Nacht) durchgehend geöffnet; *vigil* die ganze Nacht andauernd *attr*; **an ~ party** eine Party, die die ganze Nacht durchgeht; **we had an ~ party** wir haben die ganze Nacht durchgemacht; **it was an ~ journey** wir/sie *etc* sind die ganze Nacht durchgefahren; **we have ~ opening** wir haben (die ganze Nacht) durchgehend geöffnet; **~ opening is common in some countries** in manchen Ländern sind 24-stündige Öffnungszeiten üblich; **we have an ~ service** wir haben einen durchgehenden Nachtdienst; **there is an ~ bus service** die Busse verkehren die ganze Nacht über; **all-nighter** [ɔːlˈnaɪtəˈ] N *(inf) Veranstaltung etc, die die ganze Nacht hindurch andauert*

allocate [ˈæləʊkeɪt] VT *(= allot)* zuteilen, zuweisen *(to sb* jdm); *(= apportion)* verteilen *(to* auf *+acc)*; *tasks* vergeben *(to* an *+acc)*; **to ~ money to** *or* **for a project** Geld für ein Projekt bestimmen; **to ~ costs** Kosten zuweisen *or* umlegen

allocation [ˌæləʊˈkeɪʃən] N *(= allotting)* Zuteilung *f*, Zuweisung *f*; *(= apportioning)* Verteilung *f*; *(= sum allocated)* Zuwendung *f*

allopathy [əˈlɒpəθɪ] N *(Med)* Allopathie *f*

allophone [ˈæləfəʊn] N *(Ling)* Allophon *nt*

allot [əˈlɒt] VT zuteilen, zuweisen *(to sb/sth* jdm/etw); *time* vorsehen *(to* für); *money* bestimmen *(to* für)

allotment [əˈlɒtmənt] N **a** *(= allocation)* Zuteilung *f*, Zuweisung *f*; *(of time)* Vorsehen *nt*; *(of money)* Bestimmung *f*; *(= amount of money allotted)* Zuwendung *f* **b** *(Brit: = plot of ground)* Schrebergarten *m*

all: **all out** ADV mit aller Kraft; **to go ~** sein Letztes *or* Äußerstes geben; **to go ~ to do sth** alles daransetzen, etw zu tun; **to go ~ for victory** alles daransetzen, (um) zu siegen; **all-out** ADJ *strike, war* total; *attack* massiv; *effort, attempt* äußerste(r, s); *support* uneingeschränkt; **all-over** ADJ ganzflächig

allow [əˈlaʊ] ✪ 3.1, 9.2, 10.4 VT **a** *(= permit) sth* erlauben, gestatten; *behaviour etc* gestatten, zulassen; **to ~ sb sth** jdm etw erlauben *or* gestatten; **to ~ sb to do sth** jdm erlauben *or* gestatten, etw zu tun; **to be ~ed to do sth** etw tun dürfen; **smoking is not ~ed** Rauchen ist nicht gestattet; **"no dogs ~ed"** „Hunde müssen draußen bleiben"; **we were ~ed one drink** uns wurde ein Drink erlaubt *or* gestattet; **we're not ~ed much freedom** wir haben nicht viel Freiheit; **will you be ~ed to?** darfst du denn?; **will you ~ him to?** erlauben Sie es ihm?, lassen Sie ihn denn? *(inf)*; **to ~ oneself sth** sich *(dat)* etw erlauben; *(= treat oneself)* sich *(dat)* etw gönnen; **to ~ oneself to be waited on/persuaded** *etc* sich bedienen/überreden *etc* lassen; **~ me!** gestatten Sie *(form)*; **~ me to help you** gestatten Sie, dass ich Ihnen helfe *(form)*; **to ~ sth to happen** etw zulassen, zulassen, dass etw geschieht; **to ~ sb in/out/past** *etc* jdn hinein-/hinaus-/vorbeilassen *etc*; **to be ~ed in/out/past** hinein-/hinaus-/vorbeidürfen

b *(= recognize, accept) claim, appeal, goal* anerkennen

c *(= allocate, grant) discount* geben; *space* lassen; *time* einplanen, einberechnen; *money* geben, zugestehen; *(in tax, Jur)* zugestehen; **~ (yourself) an hour to cross the city** rechnen Sie mit einer Stunde, um durch die Stadt zu kommen; **he ~ed me two hours for that** er gab mir zwei Stunden dafür; **~ 5 cms extra** geben Sie 5 cm zu

d *(= concede)* annehmen; **~ing** *or* **if we ~ that ...** angenommen, (dass) ...

VI **if time ~s** falls es zeitlich möglich ist

▶ **allow for** VI *+prep obj* berücksichtigen; *factor, cost, shrinkage, error also* einrechnen, einkalkulieren; **allowing for the fact that ...** unter Berücksichtigung der Tatsache, dass ...; **after allowing for** nach Berücksichtigung *(+gen)*

▶ **allow of** VI *+prep obj* zulassen

allowable [əˈlaʊəbl] ADJ zulässig; *(Fin, in tax)* absetzbar, abzugsfähig; **~ expenses** *(Fin)* abzugsfähige Kosten

allowance [əˈlaʊəns] N **a** finanzielle Unterstützung; *(paid by state)* Beihilfe *f*; *(parent to child)* Unterhaltsgeld *nt*; *(as compensation, for unsociable hours, overseas allowance etc)* Zulage *f*; *(on business trip)* Spesen *pl*; *(= spending money)* Taschengeld *nt*; **clothing ~** Kleidungsgeld *nt*; **petrol ~** *(Brit)* Benzingeld *nt*; **his father still gives him an ~** sein Vater unterstützt ihn noch immer finanziell; **he gives his wife a dress ~** er gibt seiner Frau einen Zuschuss zu den Kleidungskosten; **he gave her an ~ of £100 a month** er stellte ihr monatlich £ 100 zur Verfügung

b *(Fin: = tax allowance)* Freibetrag *m*

c *(Fin, Comm: = discount)* (Preis)nachlass *m* *(on* für); *(= quantity allowed: for shrinkage etc)* Zugabe *f*

d *(= acceptance: of goal, claim, appeal)* Anerkennung *f*

e Zugeständnisse *pl*; **to make ~(s) for sth** etw berücksichtigen; **to make ~s for sb** bei jdm Zugeständnisse machen; **you have to make ~s** Sie müssen (gewisse) Zugeständnisse machen

allowedly [əˈlaʊɪdlɪ] ADV gewiss, zugegeben

alloy [ˈælɔɪ] N Legierung *f* VT legieren; *(fig liter)* (ver)mischen; **pleasure ~ed with suffering** von Leid getrübte Freude

alloy wheels PL *(Aut)* Alufelgen *pl*

all: **all-party** ADJ *(Pol)* Allparteien-; **~ government** Allparteienregierung *f*; **all-pervading, all-pervasive** ADJ *influence, presence* alles durchdringend; **all-points bulletin** N Rundruf *m* an alle Streifen; **all-powerful** ADJ allmächtig; **all-purpose** ADJ Allzweck-; **~ room** Allzweckraum *m*

all right [ˈɔːlˈraɪt] ADJ *pred* **a** *(= satisfactory)* in Ordnung, okay *(inf)*; **it's ~** *(= not too bad)* es geht; *(= working properly)* es ist in Ordnung; **that's** *or* **it's ~** *(after thanks)* schon gut, gern geschehen; *(after apology)* schon gut, das macht nichts; **it's ~, you don't have to** schon gut, du musst nicht unbedingt; **to taste/look/smell ~** ganz gut schmecken/aussehen/riechen; **is it ~ for me to leave early?** kann ich früher gehen?; **it's ~ by me** ich habe nichts dagegen, von mir aus gern; **it's ~ for you** du hasts gut; **it's ~ for you (to talk)** du hast gut reden; **it's ~ for him to laugh** er hat gut lachen; **I made it ~ with him** ich habe das (mit ihm) wieder eingerenkt; **I saw him ~** *(inf, for petrol, money etc)* ich hab ihn (dafür) entschädigt; **it'll be ~ on the night** es wird schon klappen, wenn es darauf ankommt; **he's ~** *(inf: = is a good guy)* der ist in Ordnung *(inf)*

b *(= safe, unharmed) person, machine* in Ordnung, okay *(inf)*; *object, building, tree etc* heil, ganz, okay *(inf)*; **are you ~?** *(= healthy)* geht es Ihnen gut?; *(= unharmed)* ist Ihnen etwas passiert?; **are you feeling ~?** fehlt Ihnen was?; *(iro)* sag mal, fehlt dir was?; **he's ~ again** es geht ihm wieder gut, er ist wieder in Ordnung *(inf)*; **are you ~ (in there)?** ist alles in Ordnung (da drin)?; **the bomb damaged half the street but our house was ~** die Bombe hat die halbe Straße zerstört, aber unserem Haus ist nichts passiert; **is it ~ for us to come out now?** können wir jetzt rauskommen?; **it's ~ now, Susi's here** jetzt ist alles wieder gut, Susi ist ja da; **it's ~, don't worry** keine Angst, machen Sie sich keine Sorgen; **we're ~ for the rest of our lives** wir haben für den Rest des Lebens ausgesorgt

ADV **a** *(= satisfactorily)* ganz gut, ganz ordentlich; *(= safely)* gut; **did I do it ~?** habe ich es recht gemacht?; **did you get home ~?** bist du gut nach Hause gekommen?; **did you get/find it ~?** haben Sie es denn bekommen/gefunden?

b *(= certainly)* schon; **he'll come ~** er wird schon kommen; **that's the boy ~** das ist der Junge; **he's a clever man ~** er ist schon intelligent; **oh yes, we heard you ~** o ja, und ob wir dich gehört haben

INTERJ gut, schön, okay *(inf)*; *(in agreement)* gut, in Ordnung; **may I leave early? – ~** kann ich früher gehen? – ja; **~ that's enough!** okay *or* komm, jetzt reichts (aber)!; **~, ~! I'm coming** schon gut, schon gut, ich komme ja!

all: **all-round** ADJ *(esp Brit)* Allround-; *student* vielseitig begabt; *improvement* in jeder Beziehung *or* Hinsicht; **~ artist** Allroundkünstler(in) *m(f)*; **a good ~ performance** eine rundum gute Leistung; **all-rounder** N *(Brit)* Allroundmann *m*/-frau *f*; *(Sport)* Allroundsportler(in) *m(f)*; **All Saints' Day** N Allerheiligen *nt*; **all-seater** ADJ *(Brit Sport) stadium, stand* ohne Stehplätze; **all-seater (stadium)** N *(Brit Sport)* (reines) Sitzplatzstadium; **all-singing, all-dancing** ADJ *(Brit inf)* alle Wünsche erfüllend *attr*; **All Souls' Day** N Allerseelen *nt*; **allspice** N Piment *m or nt*; **all-star** ADJ Star-; **~ cast** Starbesetzung *f*; **all-terrain bike** N Mountainbike *nt*; **all-terrain vehicle** N Geländefahrzeug *nt*; **all-ticket** ADJ *sports match* mit Vorverkauf; **all-time** ADJ aller Zeiten; **the ~ record** der Rekord aller Zeiten; **an ~ high/low** der höchste/niedrigste Stand aller Zeiten; **~ great** Unvergessliche(r) *mf*, Unvergessene(r) *mf*; **to be an ~ favourite** *(Brit) or* **favorite** *(US)* seit eh und je beliebt sein ADV **~ best/worst** beste(r, s)/schlechteste(r, s) aller Zeiten

allude [əˈluːd] VI *+prep obj* **to ~ to** anspielen auf *(+acc)*

allure [əˈljʊəˈ] VT locken, anziehen N Reiz *m*

allurement [əˈljʊərmənt] N Anziehungskraft *f*, Reiz *m*

alluring ADJ, **alluringly** ADV [əˈljʊərɪŋ, -lɪ] verführerisch

allusion [əˈluːʒən] N Anspielung *f* *(to* auf *+acc)*

allusive [əˈluːsɪv] ADJ voller Anspielungen

allusively [əˈluːsɪvlɪ] ADV indirekt

alluvial [əˈluːvɪəl] ADJ angeschwemmt

alluvium [əˈluːvɪəm] N Anschwemmung *f*

all: **all-weather** ADJ Allwetter-; **~ jacket** Allwetterjacke *f*; **~ pitch** Allwetterplatz *m*; **~ surface** Allwetterbelag *m*; **all-wheel drive** N Allradantrieb *m*

ally [ˈælaɪ] N Verbündete(r) *mf*, Bundesgenosse *m*/-genossin *f*; *(Hist)* Alliierte(r) *m* [əˈlaɪ] VT verbinden *(with, to* mit); *(for attack, defence etc)* verbünden, alliieren *(with, to* mit); **to ~ oneself with** *or* **to sb** sich mit jdm zusammentun/verbünden *or* alliieren

alma mater [ˈælməˈmeɪtəˈ] N Alma Mater *f*

almanac [ˈɔːlmənæk] N Almanach *m*

almighty [ɔːlˈmaɪtɪ] ADJ **a** *god, person* allmächtig; *power* unumschränkt; **Almighty God** *(Eccl)* **God Almighty** *(Eccl)* der Allmächtige; *(address in prayer)* allmächtiger Gott; **God** *or* **Christ Almighty!** *(inf)* Allmächtiger! *(inf)*, allmächtiger Gott! *(inf)* **b** *(inf) fool, idiot, row* mordsmäßig *(inf)*; *blow* mächtig *(inf)*; **there was an ~ bang and ...** es gab einen Mordsknall und ... *(inf)* N **the Almighty** der Allmächtige

almond [ˈɑːmənd] N Mandel *f*; *(= tree)* Mandelbaum *m*

almond *in cpds* Mandel-; **almond-eyed** ADJ mandeläugig; **almond oil** N Mandelöl *nt*; **almond paste** N Marzipanmasse *f*; **almond-shaped** ADJ mandelförmig

almoner [ˈɑːmənəˈ] N **a** *(dated Brit: in hospital)* Krankenhausfürsorger(in) *m(f)* **b** *(old: = distributor of alms)* Almosenpfleger *m*

almost [ˈɔːlməʊst] ADV fast, beinahe; **he ~ fell** er wäre fast gefallen; **she'll ~ certainly come** sie kommt ziemlich sicher

alms [ɑːmz] PL Almosen *pl*

alms: **alms box** N Almosenstock *m*; **alms-house** ['ɑːmzhaʊs] N Armenhaus *nt*

aloe ['æləʊ] N *(Bot, Med)* Aloe *f*

aloe vera ['æləʊ'vɪərə] N Aloe Vera *f*

aloft [ə'lɒft] ADV *(= into the air)* empor; *(= in the air)* hoch droben; *(Naut)* oben in der Takelung; **to go ~** *(Naut)* in die Takelung hinaufklettern

alone [ə'ləʊn] ADJ *pred* allein(e); **we're not ~ in thinking that** wir stehen mit dieser Meinung nicht allein; **there is one man who, ~ in the world, knows …** es gibt einen, der als Einziger auf der Welt weiß … → **leave, let³**
ADV allein(e); **to live on bread ~** von Brot allein leben; **it's mine ~** das gehört mir (ganz) allein(e); **that charm which is hers ~** der ihr ganz eigene Charme; **the hotel ~ cost £95** das Hotel allein kostete (schon) £ 95, (allein) schon das Hotel kostete £ 95; **Simon ~ knew the truth** nur Simon kannte die Wahrheit; **to stand ~** *(fig)* einzig dastehen; **to go it ~** *(inf: = be independent)* auf eigenen Beinen stehen; **I wanted to go it ~** *(inf)* ich wollte es selbst und ohne fremde Hilfe machen

along [ə'lɒŋ] PREP *(direction)* entlang *(+acc)*, lang *(+acc) (inf)*; *(position)* entlang *(+dat)*; **he walked ~ the river** er ging den *or* an dem Fluss entlang; **somewhere ~ the way** irgendwo unterwegs *or* auf dem Weg; *(fig)* irgendwann einmal; **somewhere ~ here/there** irgendwo hier(herum)/dort(herum); *(= in this/that direction)* irgendwo in dieser Richtung/der Richtung; **the Red Lion? isn't that somewhere ~ your way?** der Rote Löwe? ist der nicht irgendwo in Ihrer Nähe *or* Gegend? → **all 5**
ADV **a** *(= onwards)* weiter-, vorwärts; **to move ~** weitergehen; **he was just strolling ~** er ist bloß so dahingeschlendert; **run ~** nun lauf!; **he'll be ~ soon** er muss gleich da sein; **I'll be ~ about eight** ich komme ungefähr um acht; **are you coming? – yes, I'll be ~ in a minute** kommst du? – ja, (ich komme) gleich
b *(= together)* **~ with** zusammen mit; **to come/sing ~ with sb** mit jdm mitkommen/mitsingen; **take an umbrella ~** nimm einen Schirm mit

alongside [ə'lɒŋ'saɪd] PREP neben *(+dat)*; **he parked ~ the kerb** *(Brit) or* **curb** *(US)* er parkte am Bordstein; **we were moored ~ the pier/the other boats** wir lagen am Pier vor Anker/lagen Bord an Bord mit den anderen Schiffen; **the houses ~ the river** die Häuser am Fluss entlang; **he works ~ me** *(= with me)* er ist ein Kollege von mir; *(= next to me)* er arbeitet neben mir
ADV daneben; **is the launch still ~?** liegt die Barkasse immer noch längsseits?; **a police car drew up ~** ein Polizeiauto fuhr neben mich/ihn *etc* heran; **she was driving ~** sie fuhr nebenher; **they brought their dinghy ~** sie brachten ihr Dingi heran

aloof [ə'luːf] ADV *(lit, fig)* abseits; **to remain ~** sich abseits halten; **to keep** *or* **stand ~ (from sth)** sich (von etw) distanzieren; **buyers held ~** *(Comm)* die Käufer verhielten sich zurückhaltend ADJ unnahbar

aloofness [ə'luːfnɪs] N Unnahbarkeit *f*

aloud [ə'laʊd] ADV laut

alp [ælp] N Berg *m* in den Alpen

alpaca [æl'pækə] N Alpaka *nt attr* Alpaka-; **~ wool** Alpakawolle *f*

alpenhorn ['ælpɪnhɔːn] N Alphorn *nt*

alpenstock ['ælpɪnstɒk] N Bergstock *m*

alpha ['ælfə] N **a** *(= letter)* Alpha *nt* **b** *(Brit Sch, Univ)* Eins *f*; **~ plus** Eins (plus *(hum)*); *(Sch also)* Eins (mit Stern *(hum)*)

alphabet ['ælfəbet] N Alphabet *nt*; **does he know the** *or* **his ~?** kann er schon das Abc?

alphabetic(al) [,ælfə'betɪk(əl)] ADJ alphabetisch; **in alphabetical order** in alphabetischer Reihenfolge

alphabetically [,ælfə'betɪkəlɪ] ADV alphabetisch, nach dem Alphabet

alphabetism ['ælfəbetɪzəm] N *(hum) Benachteiligung einer Person, weil der Anfangsbuchstabe ihres Nachnamens weit hinten im Alphabet steht*

alphabetization [,ælfəbətaɪ'zeɪʃən] N Alphabetisierung *f*

alphabetize ['ælfəbətaɪz] VT alphabetisieren, alphabetisch ordnen

alphanumeric ['ælfənjuː'merɪk] ADJ alphanumerisch

alpha: **alpha particle** N Alphateilchen *nt*; **alpha ray** N Alphastrahl *m*; **alpha rhythm, alpha wave** N *(Physiol)* Alpharhythmus *m*

alpine ['ælpaɪn] ADJ **a** **Alpine** alpin; *dialects* der Alpen **b** *(general)* alpin; *(Geol)* alpinisch; **~ flower** Alpenblume *f*; **~ hut** Berghütte *f*; **~ scenery** Gebirgs- *or* Berglandschaft *f*

Alpine Convention N *(Pol)* Alpenkonvention *f*

alpinism ['ælpɪnɪzəm] N Alpinistik *f*, Alpinismus *m*

alpinist ['ælpɪnɪst] N Alpinist(in) *m(f)*

Alps [ælps] PL Alpen *pl*

al-Qaeda, al-Qaida [,æl'kaɪdə] N al-Qaida *no art*, El Kaida *no art*

already [ɔːl'redɪ] ADV schon; **I've ~ seen it, I've seen it ~** ich habe es schon gesehen

alright [,ɔːl'raɪt] ADJ ADV = **all right**

Alsace ['ælsæs] N das Elsass

Alsace-Lorraine ['ælsæslə'reɪn] N Elsass-Lothringen *nt*

Alsatian [æl'seɪʃən] ADJ elsässisch; **the ~ people** die Elsässer *pl* N *(= dialect)* Elsässisch *nt*

alsatian [æl'seɪʃən] N *(Brit: also* **alsatian dog***)* (Deutscher) Schäferhund

also ['ɔːlsəʊ] ✪ 26 ADV **a** auch; **her cousin ~ came** *or* **came ~** ihre Cousine kam auch; **he has ~ been there** er ist auch (schon) dort gewesen; **not only … but ~** nicht nur … sondern auch; **~ present were …** außerdem waren anwesend … **b** *(= moreover)* außerdem, ferner; **~, I must explain that …** außerdem muss ich erklären, dass …

also-ran [,ɔːlsəʊ'ræn] N **to be among the ~s, to be an ~** *(Sport, fig)* unter „ferner liefen" kommen

Alta *abbr of* **Alberta**

altar ['ɒltə'] N Altar *m*; **to lead sb to the ~** jdn zum Altar führen; **she was left standing at the ~** sie wurde in letzter Minute sitzen gelassen *(inf)*; **to be sacrificed on the ~ of pride** *etc* auf dem Altar des Stolzes *etc* geopfert werden

altar: **altar boy** N Ministrant *m*; **altar cloth** N Altartuch *nt*, Altardecke *f*; **altarpiece** N Altarbild *nt*; **altar rail** N, **altar rails** PL Kommunionbank *f*

alter ['ɒltə'] VT **a** *(= change)* ändern; *(= modify)* (ab)ändern; **to ~ sth completely** etw vollkommen verändern; **that ~s things** das ändert die Sache; **it does not ~ the fact that …** das ändert nichts an der Tatsache, dass … **b** *(US: = castrate, spay)* kastrieren VI sich (ver)ändern; **to ~ for the better/worse** sich zu seinem Vorteil/Nachteil (ver)ändern; *(things, situation)* sich zum Besseren/Schlechteren wenden

alterable ['ɒltərəbl] ADJ veränderbar; **to be ~** sich ändern lassen

alteration [,ɒltə'reɪʃən] N *(= change)* Änderung *f*; *(= modification)* (Ab)änderung *f*; *(of appearance)* Veränderung *f*; **a complete ~** eine vollständige Veränderung; **to make ~s in sth** Änderungen an etw *(dat)* vornehmen; **(this timetable is) subject to ~** Änderungen (im Fahrplan sind) vorbehalten; **closed for ~s** wegen Umbau geschlossen

altercation [,ɒltə'keɪʃən] N Auseinandersetzung *f*

alter ego ['æltər'iːgəʊ] N Alter ego *nt*

alternate [ɒl'tɜːnɪt] ADJ **a** **I go there on ~ days** ich gehe jeden zweiten Tag *or* alle zwei Tage hin; **they do their shopping on ~ days** *(= every other day)* sie machen ihre Einkäufe jeden zweiten Tag; *(= taking turns)* sie wechseln sich täglich mit dem Einkaufen ab; **to go through ~ periods of happiness and despair** abwechselnd Zeiten des Glücks und der Verzweiflung durchmachen; **they put down ~ layers of brick and mortar** sie schichteten (immer) abwechselnd Ziegel und Mörtel aufeinander
b *(= alternative)* alternativ; **~ route** Ausweichstrecke *f* ['ɔːltənɪt]
N *(US)* Vertreter(in) *m(f)*; *(Sport)* Ersatzspieler(in) *m(f)* ['ɔːltəneɪt]
VT abwechseln lassen; *crops* im Wechsel anbauen; **to ~ one thing with another** zwischen einer Sache und einer anderen (ab)wechseln; **the chairs were ~d with benches** Stühle und Bänke waren abwechselnd aufgestellt ['ɔːltəneɪt]
VI (sich) abwechseln; *(Elec)* alternieren; **to ~ between one thing and another** zwischen einer Sache und einer anderen (ab)wechseln; **the two actors ~d in the role** die beiden Schauspieler wechselten sich in der Rolle ab

alternately [ɒl'tɜːnɪtlɪ] ADV **a** *(= in turn)* im Wechsel, wechselweise, (immer) abwechselnd **b** = **alternatively**

alternating ['ɒltɜːneɪtɪŋ] ADJ wechselnd; **a pattern with ~ stripes of red and white** ein Muster mit abwechselnd roten und weißen Streifen; **~ current** Wechselstrom *m*

alternation [,ɒltɜː'neɪʃən] N Wechsel *m*; **the ~ of crops** der Fruchtwechsel

alternative [ɒl'tɜːnətɪv] ADJ Alternativ-; **there is no ~ way** es gibt keine Alternative; **~ route** Ausweichstrecke *f*; **~ society** Alternativgesellschaft *f*; **for him, other than London, the only possible ~ place to live is …** außer London kommt für ihn als Wohnort nur … infrage *or* in Frage, … ist für ihn als Wohnort die einzige Alternative zu London N Alternative *f*; **I had no ~ (but …)** ich hatte keine andere Wahl *or* keine Alternative (als …)

alternatively [ɒl'tɜːnətɪvlɪ] ✪ 26.2 ADV als Alternative, als andere Möglichkeit; **or ~, he could come with us** oder aber, er kommt mit uns mit; **a prison sentence of three months or ~ a fine of £500** eine Gefängnisstrafe von drei Monaten oder wahlweise eine Geldstrafe von £ 500

alternative medicine N Alternativmedizin *f*

alternative theatre, *(US)* **alternative theater** N Alternativtheater *nt*

alternator ['ɒltɜːneɪtə'] N *(Elec)* Wechselstromgenerator *m*; *(Aut)* Lichtmaschine *f*

althorn ['ælthɔːn] N B-Horn *nt*

although [ɔːl'ðəʊ] ✪ 26.2, 26.3 CONJ obwohl, obgleich; **the house, ~ small …** wenn das Haus auch klein ist …, obwohl das Haus klein ist …

altimeter ['æltɪmiːtə'] N Höhenmesser *m*

altitude ['æltɪtjuːd] N Höhe *f*; **what is our ~?** in welcher Höhe befinden wir uns?; **we are flying at an ~ of …** wir fliegen in einer Höhe von …; **at this ~** in dieser Höhe

alt key ['ɒltkiː] N *(Comput)* Alt-Taste *f*; **to hold down the ~** die Alt-Taste gedrückt halten

alto ['æltəʊ] N **a** *(= voice)* Alt *m*, Altstimme *f*; *(= person)* Alt *m* **b** *(also* **alto saxophone***)* Altsaxofon *nt*, Altsaxophon *nt* ADJ Alt-; **an ~ voice** eine Altstimme; **~ part** Altpartie *f* ADV **to sing ~** Alt singen

alto clef N Altschlüssel *m*, C-Schlüssel *m*

altogether [,ɔːltə'geðə'] ADV **a** *(= including everything)* im ganzen, insgesamt; **taken ~, or ~ it was very pleasant** alles in allem war es sehr nett, es war im Ganzen sehr nett **b** *(= wholly)* vollkommen, ganz und gar; **he wasn't ~ wrong** er hatte nicht ganz unrecht; **he wasn't ~ pleased/surprised** er war nicht übermäßig *or* besonders zufrieden/überrascht; **it was ~ a waste of time** es war vollkommene Zeitverschwendung; **that is another matter ~** das ist etwas ganz anderes N **in the ~** *(hum inf)* hüllenlos, im Adams-/Evaskostüm; **the King is in the ~** der König hat ja gar nichts an

alto sax(ophone) N Altsaxofon *nt*, Altsaxophon *nt*

altricial bird [æl,trɪʃəl'bɜːd] N Nesthocker *m*

altruism ['æltrʊɪzəm] N Altruismus *m*

altruist ['æltrʊɪst] N Altruist(in) *m(f)*

altruistic ADJ, **altruistically** ADV [,æltrʊ'ɪstɪk, -əlɪ] altruistisch

alum ['æləm] N Alaun *m*

aluminium [,æljʊ'mɪnɪəm], (*US*) **aluminum** [ə'luːmɪnəm] N Aluminium *nt*; ~ **foil** Alu(minium)folie *f*

alumna [ə'lʌmnə] N *pl* **-e** [ə'lʌmniː] (*US*) ehemalige Schülerin/Studentin, Ehemalige *f*

alumnus [ə'lʌmnəs] N *pl* **alumni** [ə'lʌmnaɪ] (*US*) ehemaliger Schüler/Student, Ehemalige(r) *m*

alveolar [æl'vɪələ'] ADJ alveolar N (*Phon*) Alveolar *m*

always ['ɔːlweɪz] ADV **a** immer; (*= constantly, repeatedly*) ständig, immer; **he is ~ forgetting** er vergisst das immer *or* ständig; **you can't ~ expect to be forgiven** du kannst nicht immer (wieder) erwarten, dass man dir vergibt **b** **we could ~ go by train/sell the house** wir könnten doch auch den Zug nehmen/könnten ja auch das Haus verkaufen; **there's ~ the possibility that ...** es besteht immer noch die Möglichkeit, dass ...; **there's ~ that to fall back on** wir können ja immer noch darauf zurückgreifen; **you can ~ come along later** Sie können ja auch noch später kommen

Alzheimer's (disease) ['æltsˌhaɪməz(dɪˌziːz)] N Alzheimerkrankheit *f*

AM **a** (*Rad*) *abbr of* **amplitude modulation** AM **b** (*Brit Pol*) *abbr of* **Assembly Member** Mitglied *nt* der walisischen Versammlung

am [æm] *1st pers sing present of* **be**

am, a.m. *abbr of* **ante meridiem**; **2 am** 2 Uhr morgens; **10 am** 10 Uhr morgens *or* vormittags; **12 am** 0 Uhr, Mitternacht; **do you mean 7 am or 7 pm?** meinen Sie 7 Uhr morgens oder abends?

amalgam [ə'mælgəm] N Amalgam *nt*; (*fig also*) Gemisch *nt*, Mischung *f*

amalgamate [ə'mælgəmeɪt] VT *companies, unions* fusionieren, verschmelzen; *departments* zusammenlegen; *metals* amalgamieren VI (*companies etc*) fusionieren; (*metals*) amalgamieren

amalgamation [əˌmælgə'meɪʃən] N (*of companies etc*) Fusion *f*; (*of metals*) Amalgamation *f*

amanuensis [əˌmænjʊ'ensɪs] N *pl* **amanuenses** [əˌmænjʊ'ensiːz] Sekretär(in) *m(f)*; (*Hist*) Amanuensis *m*

amaryllis [ˌæmə'rɪlɪs] N Amaryllis *f*

amass [ə'mæs] VT anhäufen; *money also* scheffeln; *fortune, material, evidence also* zusammentragen

amateur ['æmətə'] N **a** Amateur(in) *m(f)* **b** (*pej*) Dilettant(in) *m(f)* ADJ **a** *attr* Amateur-; **~ boxing/competition** Amateurboxen *nt*/-wettkampf *m*; **~ gardener** Hobbygärtner(in) *m(f)*; **~ painter** Hobbymaler(in) *m(f)*; **~ photographer** Hobby- *or* Amateurfotograf(in) *m(f)*; **~ video** Amateurvideo *nt* **b** (*pej*) = **amateurish**

amateur dramatics [ˌæmətədrə'mætɪks] PL Laiendrama *nt*

amateurish ['æmətərɪʃ] ADJ (*pej*) dilettantisch; *performance, work also* laienhaft

amateurishly ['æmətərɪʃlɪ] ADV (*pej*) dilettantisch

amateurishness ['æmətərɪʃnɪs] N (*pej*) Dilettantismus *m*; (*of performance, work*) Laienhaftigkeit *f*

amateurism ['æmətərɪzəm] N **a** Amateursport *m* **b** (*pej*) Dilettantentum *nt*, Dilettantismus *m*

amatory ['æmətərɪ] ADJ Liebes-; *adventure also* amourös; *glance, remark, feelings* verliebt; **~ poem** Liebesgedicht *nt*

amaze [ə'meɪz] VT erstaunen, in Erstaunen (ver)setzen; **I was ~d to learn that ...** ich war erstaunt zu hören, dass ..., mit Erstaunen hörte ich, dass ...; **to be ~d at sth** über etw (*acc*) erstaunt *or* verblüfft sein, sich über etw (*acc*) wundern; **you don't know that, you ~ me!** Sie wissen das nicht, das wundert mich aber; **no, really? you ~ me** (*iro*) nein wirklich? da bin ich aber erstaunt *or* Sie setzen mich in Erstaunen; **it ~s me to think that only two years ago ...** es ist erstaunlich, wenn ich denke, dass erst vor zwei Jahren ...; **it ~s me that he doesn't fall** ich finde es erstaunlich, dass er nicht fällt VI **his generosity never fails** *or* **ceases to ~** seine Großzügigkeit versetzt einen immer wieder in Erstaunen

amazed [ə'meɪzd] ADJ *look, expression* erstaunt

amazement [ə'meɪzmənt] N Erstaunen *nt*, Verwunderung *f*; **much to my ~** zu meinem großen Erstaunen

amazing [ə'meɪzɪŋ] ADJ erstaunlich; (*Brit*) *inf boy, girl* umwerfend (*inf*); **he's the most ~ lawyer I've ever met** er ist der erstaunlichste Rechtsanwalt, den ich je gesehen habe; **darling, you're ~, what a fantastic meal** Schatz, du bist wirklich unschlagbar, so ein tolles Essen!

amazingly [ə'meɪzɪŋlɪ] ADV erstaunlich; *simple, obvious also* verblüffend; **Sara has coped ~ (well)** Sara hat sich erstaunlich gut geschlagen; **~ (enough), he got it right first time** erstaunlicherweise hat er es gleich beim ersten Mal richtig gemacht

Amazon ['æməzən] N Amazonas *m*; (*Myth, fig*) Amazone *f*

ambassador [æm'bæsədə'] N Botschafter(in) *m(f)*; (*fig*) Repräsentant(in) *m(f)*, Vertreter(in) *m(f)*

ambassador extraordinary, (*esp US*) **ambassador-at-large** [æm'bæsədərət,lɑːdʒ] N Sonderbotschafter(in) *m(f)*, Sonderbeauftragte(r) *mf*

ambassadorial [æmˌbæsə'dɔːrɪəl] ADJ Botschafter-; *rank, dignity* eines Botschafters

ambassadress [æm'bæsɪdrɪs] N Botschafterin *f*

amber ['æmbə'] N Bernstein *m*; (*colour*) Bernsteingelb *nt*; (*Brit: in traffic lights*) Gelb *nt* ADJ aus Bernstein; (*= amber-coloured*) bernsteinfarben; (*Brit*) *traffic light* gelb; **the ~ nectar** (*Brit, Austral: inf*) das kühle Nass (*inf*), der Gerstensaft (*hum*)

ambergris ['æmbəgriːs] N Amber *m*, Ambra *f*

ambidextrous [ˌæmbɪ'dekstrəs] ADJ mit beiden Händen gleich geschickt, beidhändig

ambidextrousness [ˌæmbɪ'dekstrəsnɪs] N Beidhändigkeit *f*

ambience ['æmbɪəns] N Atmosphäre *f*, Ambiente *nt* (*geh*)

ambient ['æmbɪənt] ADJ (*liter*) *air* umgebend; **~ temperature** (*Tech*) Umgebungstemperatur *f*; **~ music** Hintergrundmusik *f*

ambiguity [ˌæmbɪ'gjʊɪtɪ] N Zwei- *or* Doppeldeutigkeit *f*; (*of joke, comment etc*) Zweideutigkeit *f*; (*with many possible meanings*) Mehr- *or* Vieldeutigkeit *f*

ambiguous [æm'bɪgjʊəs] ADJ zwei- *or* doppeldeutig; *joke, comment etc* zweideutig; (*= with many possible meanings*) mehr- *or* vieldeutig

ambiguously [æm'bɪgjʊəslɪ] ADV zweideutig; **~ worded** zweideutig formuliert

ambiguousness [æm'bɪgjʊəsnɪs] N Zwei- *or* Doppeldeutigkeit *f*; (*= with many possible meanings*) Mehr- *or* Vieldeutigkeit *f*

ambit ['æmbɪt] N Bereich *m*

ambition [æm'bɪʃən] N **a** (*= desire*) Ambition *f*; **she has ~s in that direction/for her son** sie hat Ambitionen in dieser Richtung/ehrgeizige Pläne für ihren Sohn; **my one** *or* **big ~ in life is ...** meine große Ambition ist es, ...; **my ~ is to become prime minister/to fly to the moon** es ist mein Ehrgeiz *or* Ziel *or* meine Ambition, Premierminister zu werden/zum Mond zu reisen; **it was never my ~ to take over your job** es war nie mein Bestreben *or* meine Absicht, Ihre Stelle zu übernehmen **b** (*= ambitious nature*) Ehrgeiz *m*

ambitious [æm'bɪʃəs] ADJ ehrgeizig, ambitiös (*pej*); *person also* ambitioniert (*geh*); *idea, undertaking* kühn; **he is ~ to ...** er setzt seinen ganzen Ehrgeiz daran, zu ...; **she is ~ for her husband** sie hat ehrgeizige Pläne für ihren Mann; **to be ~ for sth** etw anstreben

ambitiously [æm'bɪʃəslɪ] ADV voll(er) Ehrgeiz, ehrgeizig; **rather ~, we set out to prove the following** wir hatten uns das ehrgeizige Ziel gesteckt, das Folgende zu beweisen

ambitiousness [æm'bɪʃəsnɪs] N (*of person*) Ehrgeiz *m*; (*of idea, undertaking*) Kühnheit *f*

ambivalence [æm'bɪvələns] N Ambivalenz *f*

ambivalent [æm'bɪvələnt] ADJ ambivalent

amble ['æmbl] VI (*person*) schlendern; (*horse*) im Passgang gehen N Schlendern *nt*; (*of horse*) Passgang *m*; **he went for an ~ along the riverside** er machte einen gemütlichen Spaziergang am Fluss entlang

ambrosia [æm'brəʊzɪə] N (*Myth, fig*) Ambrosia *f*

ambulance ['æmbjʊləns] N Krankenwagen *m*, Krankenauto *nt*, Ambulanz *f*; **~ chasing** (*US Jur*) *in den USA verbreitete Praxis von Anwälten, Opfer eines Verbrechens oder Unfalles aufzusuchen und sie zu einer Klage zu veranlassen*

> **AMBULANCE CHASER**
>
> **Ambulance chaser** ist ein abfälliger US-Begriff für einen Rechtsanwalt, der seinen Lebensunterhalt damit verdient, dass er auf Unfallopfer zugeht und sie zu Schadensersatzklagen überredet. In einer etwas allgemeineren Bedeutung wird der Ausdruck für Leute verwendet, die versuchen, vom Unglück anderer zu profitieren.

ambulance: **ambulance driver** N Krankenwagenfahrer(in) *m(f)*; **ambulanceman** N Sanitäter *m*; **ambulance service** N Rettungs- *or* Ambulanzdienst *m*; (*system*) Rettungswesen *nt*

ambulant ['æmbjʊlənt], **ambulatory** ['æmbjʊlətərɪ] (*US*) ADJ *patient* gehfähig

ambush ['æmbʊʃ] N (*= place*) Hinterhalt *m*; (*= troops etc*) im Hinterhalt liegende Truppe/Guerillas *etc*; (*= attack*) Überfall *m* (aus dem Hinterhalt); **to lay an ~ (for sb)** (jdm) einen Hinterhalt legen; **to lie** *or* **wait in ~** (*Mil, fig*) im Hinterhalt liegen; **to lie in ~ for sb** (*Mil, fig*) jdm im Hinterhalt auflauern; **to fall into an ~** in einen Hinterhalt geraten VT (aus dem Hinterhalt) überfallen

ameba N (*US*) = **amoeba**

ameliorate [ə'miːlɪəreɪt] (*form*) VT verbessern VI sich verbessern, besser werden

amelioration [əˌmiːlɪə'reɪʃən] N (*form*) Verbesserung *f*

amen [ˌɑː'men] INTERJ amen; **~ to that!** (*fig inf*) ja, wahrlich *or* fürwahr! (*hum*) N Amen *nt*; **we'll all say ~ to that** (*fig inf*) wir befürworten das alle, wir sind alle dafür

amenability [əˌmiːnə'bɪlɪtɪ] N (*= responsiveness: of people*) Zugänglichkeit *f*; **the ~ of these data to the theory** die Möglichkeit, diese Daten in die Theorie einzuordnen

amenable [ə'miːnəbl] ADJ **a** (*= responsive*) zugänglich (*to +dat*); **he is ~ to reasonable suggestions** er ist vernünftigen Vorschlägen zugänglich; **it is not ~ to this method of classification** es lässt sich in dieses Klassifikationssystem nicht einordnen **b** (*Jur: = answerable*) verantwortlich; **~ to the law** dem Gesetz verantwortlich

amend [ə'mend] VT **a** *law, bill, constitution, text* ändern, amendieren (*form*), ein Amendement einbringen zu (*form*); (*by addition*) ergänzen; **I'd better ~ that to "most people"** ich werde das lieber in „die meisten Leute" (ab)ändern **b** (*= improve*) *habits, behaviour* bessern **c** = **emend**

amendment [ə'mendmənt] N **a** (*to bill, in text*) Änderung *f* (*to +gen*), Amendement *nt* (*form*) (*to +gen*); (*= addition*) Amendement *nt* (*form*) (*to* zu), Zusatz *m* (*to* zu); **the First/Second** *etc* **Amendment** (*US Pol*) das Erste/Zweite *etc* Amendement, Zusatz *m* 1/2 *etc* **b** (*in behaviour*) Besserung *f*

amends [ə'mendz] PL **to make ~ for sth** etw wiedergutmachen; **to make ~ to sb for sth** jdn für etw entschädigen; **I'll try to make ~** ich werde versuchen, das wiedergutzumachen

amenity [ə'mi:nɪtɪ] N **a** *(= aid to pleasant living)* **(public) ~** öffentliche Einrichtung; **the lack of amenities in many parts of the city** der Mangel an Einkaufs-, Unterhaltungs- und Transportmöglichkeiten in vielen Teilen der Stadt; **close to all amenities** in günstiger (Einkaufs- und Verkehrs)lage; **this house has every ~** dieses Haus bietet jeden Komfort; **a high/low ~ district** eine Gegend mit hoher/geringer Wohnqualität **b** *(= pleasantness: of place)* angenehme Lage

amenorrhoea, *(US)* **amenorrhea** [æ,menə'rɪə] N *(Med)* Amenorrhöe *f*

Amerasian [æme'reɪʃn] N *Mensch amerikanisch-asiatischer Herkunft*

America [ə'merɪkə] N Amerika *nt*; **the ~s** Amerika *nt*, der amerikanische Kontinent

American [ə'merɪkən] ADJ amerikanisch; **~ English** amerikanisches Englisch N **a** Amerikaner(in) *m(f)* **b** *(= language)* Amerikanisch *nt*

> **AMERICAN DREAM**
>
> Der **American Dream** ist ein Begriff, in dem all die positiven Werte und Grundsätze zusammengefasst werden, die viele Amerikaner empfinden, wenn sie ihr Leben als Nation beschreiben sollen, und die in der Unabhängigkeitserklärung von 1776 festgeschrieben wurden. Besonders betont werden dabei Individualismus, Fleiß, Aufstiegs- und Verbesserungsmöglichkeiten für alle und die umfassende Gültigkeit von Freiheit und Gerechtigkeit. Viele Einwanderer betrachteten den **American Dream** als eine Möglichkeit, ihr Glück zu versuchen und etwas aus ihrem Leben zu machen. Der Begriff wird auch ironisch verwendet, um auf den Gegensatz zwischen diesen Idealen und den materialistischen Einstellungen hinzuweisen, die nach Meinung Vieler in der gegenwärtigen amerikanischen Gesellschaft vorherrschen.

American Indian N Indianer(in) *m(f)*

Americanism [ə'merɪkənɪzəm] N **a** *(Ling)* Amerikanismus *m* **b** *(= quality)* Amerikanertum *nt*

Americanization [ə,merɪkənaɪ'zeɪʃən] N Amerikanisierung *f*

Americanize [ə'merɪkənaɪz] VT amerikanisieren VI sich amerikanisieren

American plan N Vollpension *f*

Amerindian [æmə'rɪndɪən] N Indianer(in) *m(f)* ADJ indianisch

amethyst ['æmɪθɪst] N Amethyst *m*; *(= colour)* Amethystblau *nt* ADJ *(= amethyst-coloured)* amethystfarben; **~ ring** Amethystring *m*

AmEx® ['æmeks] *(US)* N *abbr of* **American Express** American Express *no art* ADJ **~ card** American Express-Karte *f*

Amex ['æmeks] N *(US) abbr of* **American Stock Exchange** Amex *f*

amiability [,eɪmɪə'bɪlɪtɪ] N Liebenswürdigkeit *f*

amiable ['eɪmɪəbl] ADJ liebenswürdig

amiably ['eɪmɪəblɪ] ADV liebenswürdig; **he very ~ offered to help** er hat sich liebenswürdigerweise angeboten zu helfen

amicable ['æmɪkəbl] ADJ *person* freundlich; *relations* freundschaftlich; *discussion* friedlich; *(Jur) settlement, divorce, agreement* gütlich; **to be on ~ terms** freundschaftlich miteinander verkehren; **to part on ~ terms** sich friedlich trennen

amicably ['æmɪkəblɪ] ADV freundlich; *discuss* friedlich, in aller Freundschaft; *(Jur) settle* gütlich; **they got on quite ~** sie kamen ganz gut miteinander aus

amidships [ə'mɪdʃɪps] ADV *(Naut)* mittschiffs

amid(st) [ə'mɪd(st)] PREP inmitten *(+gen)*

amino acid [ə'mi:nəʊ'æsɪd] N Aminosäure *f*

Amish ['ɑ:mɪʃ] PL **the ~** die Amischen *pl* ADJ amisch; **an ~ man** ein amischer Mann

amiss [ə'mɪs] ADJ *pred* **there's something ~** da stimmt irgendetwas nicht; **what's ~ with you?** *(liter)* was fehlt Ihnen (denn)? ADV **to take sth ~** *(Brit)* (jdm) etw übel nehmen; **to speak ~ of sb** schlecht über jdn sprechen; **to say something ~** etwas Falsches *or* Verkehrtes sagen; **a drink would not come** *or* **go ~** etwas zu trinken wäre gar nicht verkehrt

amity ['æmɪtɪ] N Freundschaftlichkeit *f*

ammeter ['æmɪtə'] N Amperemeter *nt*

ammo ['æməʊ] N *(inf)* Munition *f*

ammonia [ə'məʊnɪə] N Ammoniak *nt*

ammunition [,æmjʊ'nɪʃən] N *(lit, fig)* Munition *f*

ammunition: **ammunition belt** N Patronengurt *m*; **ammunition dump** N Munitionslager *nt*; **ammunition pouch** N Munitionsbeutel *m*

amnesia [æm'ni:zɪə] N Amnesie *f*, Gedächtnisschwund *m*

amnesty ['æmnɪstɪ] N Amnestie *f*; **during** *or* **under the ~** unter der Amnestie; **a general ~** eine Generalamnestie; **Amnesty International** Amnesty International *no art*

amniocentesis [,æmnɪəʊsen'ti:sɪs] N *(Med)* Fruchtwasseruntersuchung *f*, Amniozentese *f (spec)*

amniotic [æmnɪ'ɒtɪk] ADJ *(Anat, Med)* **~ sac** Fruchtblase *f*

amoeba, *(US)* **ameba** [ə'mi:bə] N Amöbe *f*

amoebic, *(US)* **amebic** [ə'mi:bɪk] ADJ amöbisch; **~ dysentery** Amöbenruhr *f*

amok [ə'mɒk] ADV = **amuck**

among(st) [ə'mʌŋ(st)] PREP unter *(+acc or dat)*; **~ other things** unter anderem; **she had sung with Madonna ~ others** sie hatte unter anderem mit Madonna gesungen; **to stand ~ the crowd** (mitten) in der Menge stehen; **they shared it out ~ themselves** sie teilten es unter sich *or* untereinander auf; **talk ~ yourselves** unterhaltet euch; **settle that ~ yourselves** macht das untereinander aus; **he's ~ our best players** er gehört zu unseren besten Spielern; **Manchester is ~ the largest of our cities** Manchester gehört zu unseren größten Städten; **to count sb ~ one's friends** jdn zu seinen Freunden zählen; **this habit is widespread ~ the French** diese Sitte ist bei den Franzosen weitverbreitet; **there were ferns ~ the trees** zwischen den Bäumen wuchs Farnkraut; **to hide ~ the bushes** sich in den Büschen verstecken

amoral [eɪ'mɒrəl] ADJ amoralisch

amorous ['æmərəs] ADJ amourös; *look also* verliebt; **to make ~ advances** Annäherungsversuche *pl* machen

amorously ['æmərəslɪ] ADV verliebt, voller Verliebtheit

amorphous [ə'mɔ:fəs] ADJ amorph, strukturlos, formlos; *style, ideas, play, novel* strukturlos, ungegliedert; *(Geol)* amorph

amorphousness [ə'mɔ:fəsnɪs] N Strukturlosigkeit *f*

amortization [ə,mɔ:taɪ'zeɪʃən] N Amortisation *f*

amortize [ə'mɔ:taɪz] VT *debt* amortisieren, tilgen; *costs* amortisieren

amount [ə'maʊnt] ✪ 20.7 N **a** *(of money)* Betrag *m*; **total ~** Gesamtsumme *f*, Endbetrag *m*; **debts to** *(Brit) or* **in** *(US)* **the ~ of £200** Schulden in Höhe von £ 200; **I was shocked at the ~ of the bill** ich war über die Höhe der Rechnung erschrocken; **in 12 equal ~s** in 12 gleichen Teilen, in 12 gleichen Beträgen; **an unlimited/a large/a small ~ of money** eine unbeschränkte *or* unbegrenzte/große/geringe Summe (Geldes); **a modest ~ of money** ein bescheidener Betrag; **any/quite an ~ of money** beliebig viel/ziemlich viel Geld; **large ~s of money** Unsummen *pl* (Geldes); **it's not the ~ of the donation that counts** nicht die Höhe der Spende ist maßgeblich; **if we increase the ~ of the loan** wenn wir die Darlehenssumme erhöhen

b *(= quantity)* Menge *f*; *(of luck, intelligence, skill etc)* Maß *nt* (of an *+dat*); **an enormous/a modest ~ of work/time** sehr viel/verhältnismäßig wenig Arbeit/Zeit; **any ~ of time/food** beliebig viel Zeit/Essen; **quite an ~ of time/food** ziemlich viel Zeit/Essen; **no ~ of talking would persuade him** kein Reden würde ihn überzeugen; **no ~ of paint can hide the rust** keine noch so dicke Farbschicht kann den Rost verdecken

VI **a** *(= total)* sich belaufen (*to* auf *+acc*)

b *(= be equivalent)* gleichkommen (*to +dat*); **it ~s to the same thing** das läuft *or* kommt (doch) aufs Gleiche hinaus *or* raus *(inf)*; **he will never ~ to much** aus ihm wird nie etwas *or* viel werden, der wird es nie zu etwas *or* zu viel bringen; **their promises don't ~ to very much** ihre Versprechungen sind recht nichtssagend; **so what this ~s to is that ...** worauf es also hinausläuft ist, dass ...

amour [ə'mʊə'] N *(dated, liter)* Liebschaft *f*; *(= person)* Liebe *f*

amour-propre [,æmʊə'prɒprə] N Eigenliebe *f*

amp [æmp] N *(inf) abbr of* **amplifier**

amperage ['æmpərɪdʒ] N elektrische Stromstärke (in Ampere)

amp(ère) ['æmp(εə')] N Ampere *nt*

ampersand ['æmpəsænd] N Et-Zeichen *f*, Und-Zeichen *nt*

amphetamine [æm'fetəmi:n] N Amphetamin *nt*

amphibian [æm'fɪbɪən] N *(= animal, plant)* Amphibie *f*; *(= vehicle)* Amphibienfahrzeug *nt*; *(= aircraft)* Amphibienflugzeug *nt*, Wasser-Land-Flugzeug *nt*; **~ tank** Amphibienpanzer *m*

amphibious [æm'fɪbɪəs] ADJ *animal, plant* amphibisch; *(Mil)* amphibisch; **~ vehicle/aircraft** Amphibienfahrzeug *nt*/-flugzeug *nt*

amphitheatre, *(US)* **amphitheater** ['æmfɪ,θɪətə'] N **a** Amphitheater *nt*; *(= lecture hall)* Hörsaal *m (Halbrund mit ansteigenden Sitzreihen)* **b** *(Geog)* Halbkessel *m*; **a natural ~** ein natürliches Amphitheater

amphora ['æmfərə] N *pl* **-s** *or* **-e** ['æmfəri:] *(form)* Amphora *f*, Amphore *f*

ample ['æmpl] ADJ (+er) **a** *(= plentiful)* reichlich; **that will be ~** das ist reichlich; **more than ~** überreichlich; **to make ~ use of sth** etw reichlich benutzen **b** *(= large) figure, proportions* üppig; *boot of car etc* geräumig; *garden* weitläufig, ausgedehnt

amplification [,æmplɪfɪ'keɪʃən] N weitere Ausführungen *pl*, Erläuterungen *pl*; *(Rad)* Verstärkung *f*; **in ~ of this ...** dies weiter ausführend ...

amplifier ['æmplɪfaɪə'] N *(Rad)* Verstärker *m*

amplify ['æmplɪfaɪ] VT **a** *(Rad)* verstärken **b** *(= expand) statement, idea* näher *or* ausführlicher erläutern, genauer ausführen **c** *(inf: = exaggerate)* übertreiben VI **would you care to ~ a little?** würden Sie das bitte näher *or* ausführlicher erläutern?, würden Sie bitte auf diesen Punkt näher eingehen?; **to ~ on sth** etw näher erläutern *or* ausführen

amplitude ['æmplɪtju:d] N *(of knowledge)* Weite *f*, Breite *f*; *(of bosom)* Üppigkeit *f*, Fülle *f*; *(Phys)* Amplitude *f*

amply ['æmplɪ] ADV reichlich; *proportioned figure* üppig; *proportioned rooms* geräumig, großzügig

ampoule, *(US)* **ampule** ['æmpu:l] N Ampulle *f*

ampulla [æm'pʊlə] N *pl* **-e** [æm'pʊli:] *(Hist, Eccl)* Ampulla *f*

amputate ['æmpjʊteɪt] VTI amputieren

amputation [,æmpjʊ'teɪʃən] N Amputation *f*

amputee [,æmpjʊ'ti:] N Amputierte(r) *mf*

amuck [ə'mʌk] ADV **to run ~** *(lit, fig)* Amok laufen

amulet ['æmjʊlɪt] N Amulett *nt*

amuse [ə'mju:z] VT **a** *(= cause mirth)* amüsieren, belustigen; **you ~ me, how can anyone ...?** dass ich nicht lache *or* da muss ich ja (mal) lachen, wie kann man nur ...?

b *(= entertain)* unterhalten; **let the children do it if it ~s them** lass die Kinder doch, wenn es ihnen Spaß macht

VR **the children can ~ themselves for a while** die Kinder können sich eine Zeit lang selbst beschäftigen; **could you ~ yourself with the magazines in the meantime?** könntest du dir derweil ein bisschen die Zeitschriften ansehen *or* dich derweil mit den Zeitschriften beschäftigen?; **to ~ oneself (by) doing sth** etw zu seinem Vergnügen *or* aus Spaß tun; **how do you ~ yourself now you're retired?** wie vertreiben Sie sich *(dat)* die Zeit, wo Sie jetzt im Ruhestand sind?; **he ~s himself with crossword puzzles** er löst zum Zeitvertreib Kreuzworträtsel; **he's just amusing himself with her** er amüsiert sich nur mit ihr

amused [əˈmjuːzd] **ADJ** *person, look, smile, attitude* amüsiert; **she seemed ~ at my suggestion** sie schien über meinen Vorschlag amüsiert (zu sein); **I was ~ to see/hear that ...** es hat mich amüsiert zu sehen/hören, dass ...; **the teacher shouldn't appear to be ~ by the pupils' mistakes** der Lehrer sollte es sich nicht anmerken lassen, dass ihn die Fehler der Schüler amüsieren; **to keep sb ~** jdn unterhalten, jdm die Zeit vertreiben; **give him his toys, that'll keep him ~** gib ihm sein Spielzeug, dann ist er friedlich; **to keep oneself ~** sich *(dat)* die Zeit vertreiben; **he was anything but ~ to find the door locked** er fand es keineswegs *or* durchaus nicht komisch, dass die Tür verschlossen war; **we are not ~** *(hum)* das ist nicht besonders komisch; **I am not ~** *(hum)* ich finde das nicht lustig

amusedly [əˈmjuːzɪdlɪ] **ADV** amüsiert

amusement [əˈmjuːzmənt] **N** **a** *(= enjoyment, fun)* Vergnügen *nt*; *(= state of being entertained)* Belustigung *f*, Amüsement *nt*; **the toys were a great source of ~** das Spielzeug bereitete großen Spaß; **he gets no ~ out of life** er kann dem Leben kein Vergnügen abgewinnen; **what do you do for ~?** was machst du als Freizeitbeschäftigung?; *(retired people)* was machen Sie zu Ihrer Unterhaltung *or* als Zeitvertreib?; **I see no cause for ~** ich sehe keinen Grund zur Heiterkeit; **to do sth for one's own ~** etw zu seinem Vergnügen *or* Amüsement tun; **to my great ~/to everyone's ~** zu meiner großen/zur allgemeinen Belustigung
b *(= entertainment: of guests)* Belustigung *f*, Unterhaltung *f*
c **amusements** **PL** *(= place of entertainment)* Vergnügungsstätte *f usu pl*; *(at fair)* Attraktionen *pl*; *(= stand, booth)* Buden *pl*; *(at the seaside)* *Spielautomaten und Spiegelkabinett etc* **what sort of ~s do you have around here?** was für Vergnügungs- und Unterhaltungsmöglichkeiten gibt es hier?

amusement: **amusement arcade** **N** *(Brit)* Spielhalle *f*; **amusement park** **N** Vergnügungspark *m*, Lunapark *m (dated)*

amusing [əˈmjuːzɪŋ] **ADJ** **a** amüsant; **how ~** wie lustig *or* witzig!, das ist aber lustig *or* witzig!; **I've just had an ~ thought** mir ist gerade etwas Lustiges *or* Amüsantes eingefallen; **I don't find that very ~** das finde ich nicht gerade *or* gar nicht lustig *or* zum Lachen **b** *(inf) hat, little dress etc* charmant, apart; **an ~ little wine** ein nettes Weinchen *(hum)*

amusingly [əˈmjuːzɪŋlɪ] **ADV** amüsant

an [æn, ən, n] **INDEF ART** → **a** **CONJ** *(obs: = if)* so *(old)*

Anabaptism [ˌænəˈbæptɪzəm] **N** Anabaptismus *m*

Anabaptist [ˌænəˈbæptɪst] **N** Anabaptist(in) *m(f)*, Wiedertäufer(in) *m(f)*

anabolic steroid [ˌænəˈbɒlɪkˈstɪərɔɪd] **N** Anabolikum *nt*

anachronism [əˈnækrənɪzəm] **N** Anachronismus *m*

anachronistic [əˌnækrəˈnɪstɪk] **ADJ** anachronistisch; *(= not fitting modern times)* nicht zeitgemäß, unzeitgemäß

anaconda [ˌænəˈkɒndə] **N** Anakonda *f*

anaemia, *(US)* **anemia** [əˈniːmɪə] **N** Anämie *f*, Blutarmut *f*

anaemic, *(US)* **anemic** [əˈniːmɪk] **ADJ** **a** anämisch, blutarm **b** *(fig)* anämisch, saft- und kraftlos; *colour, appearance* bleichsüchtig, anämisch

anaerobic [ˌænəˈrəʊbɪk] **ADJ** *(Biol, Chem)* anaerob; **~ reaction** anaerobe Reaktion

anaesthesia, *(US)* **anesthesia** [ˌænɪsˈθiːzɪə] **N** Betäubung *f*

anaesthetic, *(US)* **anesthetic** [ˌænɪsˈθetɪk] **N** Narkose *f*, Anästhesie *f (spec)*; *(= substance)* Narkosemittel *nt*, Anästhetikum *nt (spec)*; **general ~** Vollnarkose *f*; **local ~** örtliche Betäubung, Lokalanästhesie *f (spec)*; **the nurse gave him a local ~** die Schwester gab ihm eine Spritze zur örtlichen Betäubung; **the patient is still under the ~** der Patient ist noch in der Narkose; **when he comes out of the ~** wenn er aus der Narkose aufwacht **ADJ** *effect* betäubend, anästhetisch; **~ drug** Betäubungsmittel *nt*

anaesthetist, *(US)* **anesthetist** [æˈniːsθɪtɪst] **N** Anästhesist(in) *m(f)*, Narkose(fach)arzt *m*/ (fach)ärztin *f*

anaesthetize, *(US)* **anesthetize** [æˈniːsθɪtaɪz] **VT** *(Med)* betäuben; *(generally also)* narkotisieren

Anaglypta® [ˌænəˈglɪptə] **N** Prägetapete *f*

anagram [ˈænəgræm] **N** Anagramm *nt*

anal [ˈeɪnəl] **ADJ** anal, Anal-; **~ intercourse** Analverkehr *m*; **you're so ~!** *(inf)* du bist ja so analfixiert!

anal eroticism **N** Analerotik *f*

analgesia [ˌænælˈdʒiːzɪə] **N** Schmerzlosigkeit *f*, Analgesie *f (spec)*

analgesic [ˌænælˈdʒiːsɪk] **N** schmerzstillendes Mittel, Schmerzmittel *nt*, Analgetikum *nt (spec)* **ADJ** schmerzstillend

analog [ˈænəlɒg] **ADJ** *(Tech)* analog

analog computer **N** Analogrechner *m*

analogic(al) [ˌænəˈlɒdʒɪk(əl)] **ADJ**, **analogically** [ˌænəˈlɒdʒɪkəlɪ] **ADV** analog

analogous **ADJ**, **analogously** **ADV** [əˈnæləgəs, -lɪ] analog *(to, with* zu)

analogous computer **N** Analogrechner *m*

analogue [ˈænəlɒg] **N** Gegenstück *nt*, Parallele *f*

analogy [əˈnælədʒɪ] **N** Analogie *f*; **arguing by ~ one could claim that ...** analog könnte man behaupten ...; **to draw an ~** eine Analogie herstellen, einen analogen Vergleich ziehen; **on the ~ of** analog zu, nach dem Muster *(+gen)*; **it's an argument by ~** es ist ein Analogiebeweis, es ist eine analoge Argumentation

anal-retentive [ˌeɪnəlrɪˈtentɪv] **ADJ** analfixiert

analyse, *(esp US)* **analyze** [ˈænəlaɪz] ✪ 26.1 **VT** **a** *(= examine)* analysieren; *(Gram) sentence* (zer)gliedern; **to ~ the situation** *(fig)* die Situation analysieren *or (to others)* erläutern; **to ~ sth into its parts** etw in seine Bestandteile zerlegen **b** *(= psychoanalyse)* psychoanalytisch behandeln, analysieren *(inf)*; **stop analysing me!** hör auf, mich zu analysieren! *(inf)*

analyser, *(US)* **analyzer** [ˈænəlaɪzəʳ] **N** Analysegerät *nt*

analysis [əˈnæləsɪs] **N** *pl* **analyses** [əˈnæləsiːz] **a** *(= examination)* Analyse *f*; *(Gram, of sentence also)* (Zer)gliederung *f*; **what's your ~ of the situation?** wie beurteilen Sie die Situation?; **in the last** *or* **final ~** letzten Endes; **on (closer) ~** bei genauerer Untersuchung **b** *(= psychoanalysis)* Psychoanalyse *f*, Analyse *f (inf)*

analyst [ˈænəlɪst] **N** Analytiker(in) *m(f)*; *(= psychoanalyst also)* Psychoanalytiker(in) *m(f)*; *(Chem)* Chemiker(in) *m(f)*; **food ~** Lebensmittelchemiker(in) *m(f)*; **he gave it to the ~ in the lab** er ließ im Labor eine Analyse davon machen

analytic [ˌænəˈlɪtɪk] **ADJ** analytisch

analytical [ˌænəˈlɪtɪkəl] **ADJ** analytisch; **you should try to be more ~** Sie sollten versuchen, etwas analytischer vorzugehen; **he hasn't got a very ~ mind** er kann nicht analytisch denken

analytically [ˌænəˈlɪtɪkəlɪ] **ADV** analytisch

analyze [ˈænəlaɪz] **VT** *(US)* = **analyse**

analyzer [ˈænəlaɪzəʳ] **N** *(US)* = **analyser**

anapaest, *(US)* **anapest** [ˈænəpiːst] **N** *(Poet)* Anapäst *m*

anaphora [əˈnæfərə] **N** *(Liter, Gram)* Anapher *f*

anaphylactic [ˌænəfɪˈlæktɪk] **ADJ** *(Med)* anaphylaktisch; **~ shock** anaphylaktischer Schock

anarchic(al) [æˈnɑːkɪk(əl)] **ADJ** anarchisch

anarchism [ˈænəkɪzəm] **N** Anarchismus *m*

anarchist [ˈænəkɪst] **N** Anarchist(in) *m(f)*

anarchistic [ˌænəˈkɪstɪk] **ADJ** anarchistisch

anarcho- [æˈnɑːkəʊ] **PREF** anarcho-, Anarcho-; **~syndicalism** Anarcho-Syndikalismus *m*

anarchy [ˈænəkɪ] **N** Anarchie *f*

anathema [əˈnæθɪmə] **N** *(Eccl)* Anathema *(form) nt*, Kirchenbann *m*; *(fig, no art)* ein Gräuel *m*; **voting Labour was ~ to them** der Gedanke, Labour zu wählen, war ihnen ein Gräuel

anathematize [əˈnæθɪmətaɪz] **VT** *(Eccl)* mit dem Bann belegen

anatomical **ADJ**, **anatomically** **ADV** [ˌænəˈtɒmɪkəl, -ɪ] anatomisch

anatomist [əˈnætəmɪst] **N** Anatom(in) *m(f)*

anatomy [əˈnætəmɪ] **N** Anatomie *f*; *(= structure also)* Körperbau *m*; *(fig)* Struktur *f* und Aufbau *m*; **on a certain part of her ~** *(euph)* an einer gewissen Stelle *(euph)*

ANC *abbr of* **African National Congress** ANC *m*, *südafrikanische nationalistische Bewegung*

ancestor [ˈænsɪstəʳ] **N** Vorfahr *m*, Ahne *m*; *(= progenitor)* Stammvater *m*; **~ worship** Ahnenkult *m*

ancestral [ænˈsestrəl] **ADJ** seiner/ihrer Vorfahren; **~ home** Stammsitz *m*

ancestress [ˈænsɪstrɪs] **N** Vorfahrin *f*, Ahne *f*; *(= progenitor)* Ahnfrau *f*, Stammmutter *f*

ancestry [ˈænsɪstrɪ] **N** *(= descent)* Abstammung *f*, Herkunft *f*; *(= ancestors)* Ahnenreihe *f*, Familie *f*; **to trace one's ~** seine Abstammung zurückverfolgen; **of royal ~** königlicher Abstammung *or* Herkunft

anchor [ˈæŋkəʳ] **N** **a** *(Naut)* Anker *m*; *(fig: hope, love, person etc)* Zuflucht *f*, Rettungsanker *m*; **to cast** *or* **drop ~** Anker werfen, vor Anker gehen; **to weigh** *or* **up ~** den Anker lichten; **to be** *or* **lie** *or* **ride at ~** vor Anker liegen; **to come to ~** vor Anker gehen; **the stone served as an ~ for the tent** der Stein diente dazu, das Zelt zu beschweren *or* am Boden festzuhalten
b *(esp US TV: = presenter)* Anchorman *m*, Anchorwoman *f*, Moderator(in) *m(f)*
VT *(Naut, fig)* verankern; **we ~ed the tablecloth (down) with stones** wir beschwerten das Tischtuch mit Steinen; **to be ~ed in sth** *(fig)* in etw *(dat)* (fest) verankert sein
VI *(Naut)* ankern, vor Anker gehen

anchorage [ˈæŋkərɪdʒ] **N** **a** *(Naut)* Ankerplatz *m* **b** *(also* **anchorage dues**) Anker- *or* Liegegebühren *pl*

anchor buoy **N** Ankerboje *f*

anchorite [ˈæŋkəraɪt] **N** Einsiedler *m*, Eremit *m*

anchor: **anchorman** **N** *pl* **-men** *(esp US TV)* Anchorman *m*, Moderator *m*; *(Sport) (in relay race)* Letzte(r) *m*; *(in tug-of-war)* hinterster Mann; *(fig)* eiserne Stütze *f*, Eckpfeiler *m*; **anchor store** **N** *(attractive store)* Magnetbetrieb *m*; **anchorwoman** **N** *pl* **-women** *(esp US TV)* Anchorwoman *f*, Moderatorin *f*; *(Sport: in relay race)* Letzte *f*

anchovy [ˈæntʃəvɪ] **N** Sardelle *f*, An(s)chovis *f*; **~ paste** Sardellen- *or* An(s)chovispaste *f*

ancient [ˈeɪnʃənt] **ADJ** **a** alt; **in ~ times** im Altertum; *(Greek, Roman also)* in der Antike; **~ Rome** das alte Rom; **the ~ Romans** die alten Römer; **~ monument** *(Brit)* historisches Denkmal, historische Stätte **b** *(inf) person, clothes etc* uralt **N** **the ~s** die Völker *or* Menschen des Altertums *or* im Altertum; *(= writers)* die Schriftsteller des Altertums

ancient history N *(lit)* Alte Geschichte; *(fig)* graue Vorzeit; **that's ~** *(fig)* das ist schon längst Geschichte; **he's well-known in the field of ~** er ist ein sehr bekannter Altertumsforscher

anciently ['eɪnʃəntlɪ] ADV in (ur)alten Zeiten; **even as ~ as the times of ...** selbst vor so langer Zeit wie zu Zeiten von ...

ancillary [æn'sɪlərɪ] ADJ *(= subordinate)* Neben-; *(= auxiliary)* Hilfs-; **~ course** *(Univ)* Begleitkurs *m*; **~ industry** Zulieferindustrie *f*; **~ staff/workers** Hilfskräfte *pl*; **~ subject** *(Univ)* Nebenfach *nt*; **~ troops** Hilfstruppen *pl*

and [ænd, ənd, nd, ən] CONJ **a** und; **nice ~ early/warm** schön früh/warm; **when I'm good ~ ready** wenn es mir passt, wenn ich so weit bin; **you ~ you alone** du, nur du allein; **try ~ come** versuch zu kommen; **wait ~ see!** abwarten!, warts ab!; **don't go ~ spoil it!** nun verdirb nicht alles!; **come ~ get it!** komm und hols!; **one more ~ I'm finished** noch eins, dann bin ich fertig; **there are dictionaries ~ dictionaries** es gibt Wörterbücher und Wörterbücher, es gibt sone Wörterbücher und solche *(inf)*; **~/or** und/oder; **~ so on, ~ so forth, ~ so on ~ so forth** und so weiter, und so fort, und so weiter und so fort
b *(in repetition, continuation)* und; **better ~ better** immer besser; **for hours ~ hours/days ~ days/weeks ~ weeks** stundenlang, Stunde um Stunde *(geh)*/tagelang/wochenlang; **for miles ~ miles** meilenweit; **I rang ~ rang** ich klingelte und klingelte, ich klingelte immer wieder; **I tried ~ tried** ich habe es immer wieder versucht; **~ he pulled ~ he pulled** und er zog und zog
c *(with numbers)* **three hundred ~ ten** dreihundert(und)zehn; **one ~ a half** anderthalb, eineinhalb; **two ~ twenty** *(old, form)* zweiundzwanzig

andante [æn'dæntɪ] *(Mus)* ADJ ADV andante N Andante *nt*

Andean ['ændɪən] ADJ Anden-; **~ country** Andenstaat *m*

Andes ['ændi:z] PL Anden *pl*

andiron ['ændaɪrən] N Kaminbock *m*

Andorra [æn'dɔ:rə] N Andorra *nt*

Andorran [æn'dɔrən] N Andorraner(in) *m(f)* ADJ andorranisch

Andrew ['ændru:] N Andreas *m*

androgen ['ændrədʒən] N Androgen *nt*

androgyne ['ændrədʒaɪn] N Hermaphrodit *m*, Zwitter *m*

androgynous [æn'drɒdʒɪnəs] ADJ androgyn, zwitt(e)rig

androgyny [æn'drɒdʒɪnɪ] N Androgynie *f*, Zwittrigkeit *f*

android ['ændrɔɪd] N Androide *m*

anecdotal [,ænɪk'dəʊtəl] ADJ anekdotenhaft, anekdotisch

anecdote ['ænɪkdəʊt] N Anekdote *f*

anemia [ə'ni:mɪə] N *(US)* = **anaemia**

anemic [ə'ni:mɪk] ADJ *(US)* = **anaemic**

anemometer [,ænɪ'mɒmɪtə'] N Windmesser *m*

anemone [ə'nemənɪ] N *(Bot)* Anemone *f*, Buschwindröschen *nt*; *(= sea anemone)* Seeanemone *f*

aneroid barometer ['ænərɔɪdbə'rɒmɪtə'] N Aneroidbarometer *nt*

anesthesia *etc (US)* = **anaesthesia** *etc*

anew [ə'nju:] ADV **a** *(= again)* aufs Neue; **let's start ~** fangen wir wieder von vorn *or* von Neuem an **b** *(= in a new way)* auf eine neue Art und Weise

angel ['eɪndʒəl] N *(lit, fig)* Engel *m*; *(Theat inf: = backer)* finanzkräftiger Hintermann; **on the side of the ~s** *(fig inf)* auf der Seite des Rechts

angel cake N ≈ Biskuitkuchen *m*

Angeleno [,ændʒə'li:nəʊ] N Einwohner(in) *m(f)* von Los Angeles

angel: **angel face** INTERJ *(hum inf)* mein Engel; **angel fish** N *(= shark)* Meerengel *m*, Engelhai *m*; *(= tropical fish)* Großer Segelflosser; **angel food cake** N *(US)* Biskuitkuchen *m*; **angel hair** N *(Christmas decoration)* Engelshaar *nt*

angelic [æn'dʒelɪk] ADJ *(= of an angel)* Engels-; *hosts* himmlisch; *salutation* Englisch; *(= like an angel)* engelhaft, engelgleich *(liter)*; **~ appearance** Engelsgestalt *f*

angelica [æn'dʒelɪkə] N *(Bot)* Angelika *f*, Brustwurz *f*; *(Cook)* kandierte Angelika

angelically [æn'dʒelɪkə lɪ] ADV wie ein Engel, engelgleich

angels-on-horseback [,eɪndʒəlzɒn'hɔ:sbæk] PL *(Brit Cook) in Schinkenscheiben eingewickelte Austern, auf Toast serviert*

angelus ['ændʒɪləs] N Angelusläuten *nt*; *(= prayer)* Angelus *nt*

anger ['æŋgə'] N Ärger *m*; *(= wrath: of gods etc)* Zorn *m*; **a fit of ~** ein Wutanfall *m*, ein Zorn(es)ausbruch *m*; **red with ~** rot vor Wut; **public ~** öffentliche Entrüstung; **to speak/act in ~** im Zorn sprechen/handeln; **words spoken in ~** was man in seiner Wut *or* im Zorn sagt; **to do sth in ~** etw im Zorn tun; **to be filled with ~** zornig *or* wütend sein; **to provoke sb's ~** jdn reizen; **to rouse sb to ~** *(liter)* jdn in Wut *or* Rage bringen; **to make one's ~ clear** seinem Ärger *or* Unmut Luft machen
VT *(stressing action)* ärgern; *(stressing result)* verärgern; *gods* erzürnen *(liter)*; **what ~s me is ...** was mich ärgert, ist ...; **to be easily ~ed** sich schnell *or* leicht ärgern; *(= quick to take offence)* schnell verärgert sein

anger management N Aggressionsbewältigung *f*

angina (pectoris) N Angina pectoris *f*

angiogram ['ændʒɪəʊgræm] N *(Med)* Angiogramm *nt*

angiography ['ændʒɪəʊ,grəfɪ] N *(Med)* Angiographie *f*

angioplasty ['ændʒɪəʊ,plæstɪ] N *(Med)* Angioplastie *f*

angle[1] ['æŋgl] N **a** Winkel *m*; **at an ~ of 40°** in einem Winkel von 40°; **at an ~** schräg; **at an ~ to the street** schräg *or* im Winkel zur Straße; **he was wearing his hat at an ~** er hatte seinen Hut schief aufgesetzt; **~ of climb** *(Aviat)* Steigwinkel *m*; **~ of elevation** *(Math)* Höhenwinkel *m*; **~ of incidence** *(Opt)* Einfallswinkel *m*; **~ parking** Schrägparken *nt*
b *(= projecting corner)* Ecke *f*; *(= angular recess)* Winkel *m*
c *(= position)* Winkel *m*; **if you take the photograph from this ~** wenn du die Aufnahme aus *or* von diesem (Blick)winkel machst
d *(of problem etc: = aspect)* Seite *f*
e *(= point of view)* Standpunkt *m*, Position *f*; **a journalist usually has an ~ on a story** ein Journalist schreibt seine Berichte gewöhnlich von einer gewissen Warte aus; **an inside ~ on the story** die Geschichte vom Standpunkt eines Insiders *or* eines Direktbeteiligten *or* eines direkt Beteiligten; **what's your ~?** *(= what are you getting at?)* worauf wollen Sie hinaus?
VT *lamp etc* (aus)richten, einstellen; *(Sport) shot* im Winkel schießen/schlagen; *(fig) information, report* färben; **the question was ~d at getting one particular answer** es war eine Suggestivfrage

angle[2] VI *(esp Brit Fishing)* angeln

▶ **angle for** VI +*prep obj* **a** *(lit) trout* angeln **b** *(fig) compliments* fischen nach; **to angle for sth** auf etw *(acc)* aus sein; **to angle for sb's sympathy** jds Mitleid erregen wollen

angle: **angle bracket** N **a** *(for shelves)* Winkelband *nt*, Winkelkonsole *f* **b** *(Typ)* spitze Klammer; **angle grinder** N Winkelschleifer *m*, Schleifhexe *f (inf)*; **angle iron** N Winkeleisen *nt*; **Anglepoise (lamp)**® ['æŋglpɔɪz('læmp)] N Architekten- *or* Gelenkleuchte *f*

angler ['æŋglə'] N Angler(in) *m(f)*

Angles ['æŋglz] PL *(Hist)* Angeln *pl*

Anglican ['æŋglɪkən] N Anglikaner(in) *m(f)* ADJ anglikanisch

Anglicanism ['æŋglɪkənɪzəm] N Anglikanismus *m*

anglicism ['æŋglɪsɪzəm] N Anglizismus *m*

anglicist ['æŋglɪsɪst] N Anglist(in) *m(f)*

anglicize ['æŋglɪsaɪz] VT anglisieren

angling ['æŋglɪŋ] N *(esp Brit)* Angeln *nt*

Anglo- ['æŋgləʊ] PREF Anglo-; *(between two countries)* Englisch-; **Anglo-American** N Angloamerikaner(in) *m(f)* ADJ angloamerikanisch; **Anglo-Asian** N Anglo-Inder(in) *m(f)*, Anglo-Asiat(in) *m(f)* ADJ angloindisch, angloasiatisch; **Anglo-Catholic** N Anglokatholik(in) *m(f)* ADJ hochkirchlich, anglokatholisch; **Anglo-German** ADJ englisch-deutsch; **Anglo-Indian** N *(of British origin)* in Indien lebender Engländer *m*/lebende Engländerin *f*; *(= Eurasian)* Angloinder(in) *m(f)* ADJ angloindisch; **Anglo-Irish** PL **the ~** die Angloiren *pl* ADJ angloirisch

Anglomania [,æŋgləʊ'meɪnɪə] N Anglomanie *f*

Anglophile ['æŋgləʊfaɪl] N Anglophile(r) *mf (form)*, Englandfreund(in) *m(f)* ADJ anglophil *(form)*, englandfreundlich

Anglophobe ['æŋgləʊfəʊb] N Anglophobe(r) *mf (form)*, Englandhasser(in) *m(f)*, Englandfeind(in) *m(f)*

Anglophobia [,æŋgləʊ'fəʊbɪə] N Anglophobie *f (form)*, Englandhass *m*

Anglophobic [,æŋgləʊ'fəʊbɪk] ADJ anglophob *(form)*, anti-englisch, englandfeindlich

Anglo-Saxon ['æŋgləʊ'sæksən] N **a** *(Hist: = person)* Angelsachse *m*, Angelsächsin *f* **b** *(= language)* Angelsächsisch *nt* ADJ angelsächsisch

> **ANGLO-SAXON**
>
> **Anglo-Saxon** ist das Englisch, das ab ungefähr 400 n. Chr. bis zur normannischen Eroberung 1066 gesprochen wurde. Wichtige Bestandteile des heute gebräuchlichen, englischen Wortschatzes haben ihren Ursprung in der angelsächsischen Periode, zum Beispiel Wörter wie **man, child, cat, love** und **harvest**.

anglosphere ['æŋgləʊsfɪə'] N Anglosphäre *f*

Angola [æŋ'gəʊlə] N Angola *nt*

Angolan [æŋ'gəʊlən] N Angolaner(in) *m(f)* ADJ angolanisch

angora [æŋ'gɔ:rə] ADJ Angora-; **~ wool** Angorawolle *f* N Angora(wolle *f*) *nt*; *(Tex)* Angoragewebe *nt*; *(= angora rabbit, angora cat, angora goat)* Angorakaninchen *nt*/-katze *f*/-ziege *f*

angostura [æŋgə'stjʊərə] N *(= bark)* Angosturarinde *f*; *(also* **angostura bitters** *)*® Angosturabitter *m*

angrily ['æŋgrɪlɪ] ADV wütend

angry ['æŋgrɪ] ADJ *(+er)* **a** zornig, ungehalten *(geh)*; *letter, look* zornig, wütend; *animal* wütend; **to be ~** wütend *or* böse *or* verärgert sein; **to be ~ with** *or* **at sb** jdm *or* auf jdn *or* mit jdm böse sein, über jdn verärgert sein; **to be ~ at** *or* **about sth** sich über etw *(acc)* ärgern; **to get ~ (with** *or* **at sb/about sth)** (mit jdm/über etw *acc*) böse werden; **you're not ~ (with me), are you?** du bist (mir) doch nicht böse(, oder)?; **to be ~ with oneself** sich über sich *(acc)* selbst ärgern, sich *(dat)* selbst böse sein, über sich *(acc)* selbst verärgert sein; **to make sb ~** *(stressing action)* jdn ärgern; *(stressing result)* jdn verärgern; **it makes me so ~** es ärgert mich furchtbar, es macht mich so wütend *or* böse; **~ young man** Rebell *m*, Angry Young Man *m (geh)*
b *(fig) sea* aufgewühlt; *sky, clouds* bedrohlich, finster; **the sky was an ~ purple** der Himmel war bedrohlich violett
c *(= inflamed) wound* entzündet, böse; **an ~ red** hochrot

angst [æŋst] N (Existenz)angst *f*

anguish ['æŋgwɪʃ] N Qual *f*; **to be in ~** Qualen leiden; **the look of ~ on the faces of the waiting wives** der angsterfüllte Blick in den Gesichtern der wartenden Frauen; **he wrung his hands in ~** er rang die Hände in Verzweiflung; **those**

who suffer the ~ of indecision wer die Qual der Entschlusslosigkeit erleidet; **writhing in ~ on the ground** sich in Qualen auf dem Boden windend; **the news caused her great ~** die Nachricht bereitete ihr großen Schmerz; **the decision caused her great ~** die Entscheidung bereitete ihr große Qual(en)

anguished [ˈæŋgwɪʃt] ADJ qualvoll

angular [ˈæŋgjʊləˈ] ADJ **a** *shape* eckig; *face, features, prose* kantig **b** *(= bony)* knochig **c** *(= awkward)* linkisch, steif

angularity [ˌæŋgjʊˈlærɪtɪ] N **a** *(of shape)* Eckigkeit *f*; *(of face, features)* Kantigkeit *f* **b** *(= boniness)* Knochigkeit *f*

aniline [ˈænɪliːn] N Anilin *nt*; **~ dye** Anilinfarbstoff *m*

anima [ˈænɪmə] N *(Psych)* Anima *f*

animadversion [ˌænɪmædˈvɜːʃən] N *(form)* kritische Äußerung

animal [ˈænɪməl] **N** Tier *nt*; *(as opposed to insects etc)* Vierbeiner *m*; *(= brutal person)* Bestie *f*, Tier *nt*; **man is a social ~** der Mensch ist ein soziales Wesen; **a political ~** ein politisches Wesen, ein Zoon politikon *nt (geh)*; **there's no such ~** *(fig)* so was gibt es nicht! *(inf)*; **the ~ in him** das Tier(ische) *or* Animalische in ihm; **he's little better than an ~** er ist kaum besser als ein Tier

ADJ *attr* Tier-; *fat, products, cruelty, lust* tierisch; **~ behaviour** *(Brit) or* **behavior** *(US) (lit)* das Verhalten der Tiere, tierhaftes Verhalten; *(fig: = brutal)* tierisches Verhalten; **~ experiments/testing** Tierversuche *pl*; **~ magnetism** rein körperliche Anziehungskraft; **~ needs** *(fig)* animalische Bedürfnisse *pl*; **~ spirits** Vitalität *f*; **full of ~ spirits** ausgelassen

animal cracker N *(US)* Keks *m* in Tierform

animalcule [ˌænɪˈmælkjuːl] N mikroskopisch kleines Tierchen

animal husbandry N Viehwirtschaft *f*

animality [ˌænɪˈmælɪtɪ] N Tierhaftigkeit *f*

animal: **animal kingdom** N Tierreich *nt*, Tierwelt *f*; **Animal Liberation Front** N *(Brit) militante Tierschützerorganisation*; **animal liberationist** N militanter Tierschützer, militante Tierschützerin; **animal lover** N Tierfreund(in) *m(f)*; **animal meal** N Tiermehl *f*; **animal park** N *(US)* Wildpark *m*; **animal rights** PL der Tierschutz, Tierrechte *pl*; **~ activist/campaigner** Tierschützer(in) *m(f)*, Tierrechtler(in) *m(f)*; **animal sanctuary** N Tierschutzgebiet *nt*; **animal welfare** N Tierschutz *m*

animate [ˈænɪmɪt] **ADJ** belebt; *creation, creatures* lebend [ˈænɪmeɪt] **VT** *(lit: God)* mit Leben erfüllen; *(fig) (= enliven)* beleben; *(= move to action)* anregen, animieren; *(Film)* animieren; **Disney was the first to ~ cartoons** Disney machte als erster Zeichentrickfilme

animated [ˈænɪmeɪtɪd] ADJ **a** *(= lively)* lebhaft, rege; *discussion, talk* lebhaft, angeregt **b** *(Film)* **~ cartoon/film** Zeichentrickfilm *m*

animatedly [ˈænɪmeɪtɪdlɪ] ADV rege; *talk* angeregt, lebhaft

animation [ˌænɪˈmeɪʃən] N Lebhaftigkeit *f*; *(Film)* Animation *f*; **she loved the ~ of Parisian life** sie liebte das Getriebe des Pariser Lebens

animator [ˈænɪmeɪtəˈ] N Animator(in) *m(f)*

animatronics [ˌænɪməˈtrɒnɪks] N SING *(Film)* Computer-Animation *f*

anime [ˈænɪmeɪ] N Anime *m japanischer Zeichentrickfilm*

animism [ˈænɪmɪzəm] N Animismus *m*

animosity [ˌænɪˈmɒsɪtɪ] N Animosität *f (geh) (towards* gegenüber), Feindseligkeit *f (towards* gegenüber)

animus [ˈænɪməs] N *no pl* **a** Feindseligkeit *f* **b** *(Psych)* Animus *m*

anise [ˈænɪs] N Anis *m*

aniseed [ˈænɪsiːd] N *(= seed)* Anis(samen) *m*; *(= flavouring)* Anis *m*; *(= liqueur)* Anislikör *m*

aniseed ball N Anisbonbon *m or nt*

ankle [ˈæŋkl] N Knöchel *m*

ankle: **ankle biter** N *(Austral hum)* Kind *nt*, Plage *f (hum)*; **anklebone** N Sprungbein *nt*; **ankle boot** N Halbstiefel *m*; **ankle bracelet** N Fußkettchen *nt*; **ankle-deep** **ADJ** knöcheltief **ADV** **he was ~ in water** er stand bis an die Knöchel im Wasser; **the field was ~ in mud** auf dem Feld stand der Schlamm knöcheltief; **ankle joint** N Sprunggelenk *nt*; **ankle sock** N Söckchen *nt*; **ankle strap** N Schuhriemchen *nt*

anklet [ˈæŋklɪt] N **a** Fußring *m*, Fußspange *f* **b** *(US: = sock)* Söckchen *nt*

annalist [ˈænəlɪst] N Chronist(in) *m(f)*, Geschichtsschreiber(in) *m(f)*

annals [ˈænəlz] PL Annalen *pl*; *(of society etc)* Bericht *m*; **in all the ~ of recorded history** in der gesamten bisherigen Geschichte

anneal [əˈniːl] VT *glass* kühlen; *metal* ausglühen; *earthenware* brennen; *(fig)* stählen

annex [əˈneks] **VT** annektieren [ˈæneks] **N** **a** *(to document etc)* Anhang *m*, Nachtrag *m* **b** *(= building)* Nebengebäude *nt*, Annex *m*; *(= extension)* Anbau *m*

annexation [ˌænekˈseɪʃən] N Annexion *f*

annexe [ˈæneks] N *(Brit)* = **annex N b**

annihilate [əˈnaɪəleɪt] VT vernichten; *army also* aufreiben, auslöschen *(geh)*; *(fig) hope* zerschlagen; *theory* vernichten, zerschlagen; *(inf) person, opponent, team* fertigmachen *(inf)*, in die Pfanne hauen *(inf)*; **I felt completely ~d** ich war völlig am Boden zerstört *(inf)*

annihilation [əˌnaɪəˈleɪʃən] N Vernichtung *f*, Auslöschung *f (geh)*; *(fig: of theory)* Vernichtung *f*, Zerschlagung *f*; **our team's ~** die vollständige Niederlage unserer Mannschaft; **her ~ of her opponents** die Art, wie sie ihre Gegner fertigmachte *(inf)*

anniversary [ˌænɪˈvɜːsərɪ] N Jahrestag *m*; *(= wedding anniversary)* Hochzeitstag *m*; **~ celebrations** Feiern *pl* anlässlich eines Jahrestages/Hochzeitstages; **~ dinner/gift** (Fest)essen *nt*/Geschenk *nt* zum Jahrestag/Hochzeitstag; **the ~ of his death** sein Todestag *m*

anno Domini [ˈænəʊˈdɒmɪnaɪ] N **a** *(abbr* **AD***)* nach Christus, Anno Domini; **in 53 ~** im Jahre 53 nach Christus **b** *(inf: = age)* Alter *nt*

annotate [ˈænəʊteɪt] VT mit Anmerkungen versehen, kommentieren; **~d text** kommentierter Text

annotation [ˌænəʊˈteɪʃən] N *(no pl: = commentary, act)* Kommentar *m*; *(= comment)* Anmerkung *f*

annotator [ˈænəʊteɪtəˈ] N Kommentator(in) *m(f)*

announce [əˈnaʊns] ✪ 24 VT *(lit, fig: person)* bekannt geben, verkünden; *arrival, departure, radio programme* ansagen; *(over intercom)* durchsagen; *(= signal)* anzeigen; *(formally) birth, marriage etc* anzeigen; *coming of spring etc* ankündigen; **to ~ sb** jdn melden; **the arrival of flight BA 742 has just been ~d** soeben ist die Ankunft des Fluges BA 742 gemeldet worden

announcement [əˈnaʊnsmənt] N *(= public declaration)* Bekanntgabe *f*, Bekanntmachung *f*; *(of impending event, speaker)* Ankündigung *f*; *(over intercom etc)* Durchsage *f*; *(giving information, on radio etc)* Ansage *f*; *(written: of birth, marriage etc)* Anzeige *f*; **after they had made the ~** nach der Bekanntgabe *etc*

announcer [əˈnaʊnsəˈ] N *(Rad, TV)* Ansager(in) *m(f)*, Radio-/Fernsehsprecher(in) *m(f)*

annoy [əˈnɔɪ] VT *(= make angry, irritate)* ärgern; *(= upset: noise, questions etc)* aufregen; *(= pester)* belästigen; **to be ~ed that …** ärgerlich *or* verärgert sein, weil …; **to be ~ed with sb/about sth** sich über jdn/etw ärgern, (mit) jdm/über etw *(acc)* böse sein; **to get ~ed** sich ärgern, sich aufregen, böse werden; **don't get ~ed** reg dich nicht auf, nur keine Aufregung; **don't let it ~ you** ärgere dich nicht darüber

annoyance [əˈnɔɪəns] N **a** *no pl (= irritation)* Ärger *m*, Verdruss *m (geh)*; **to cause (considerable) ~** (großes) Ärgernis erregen; **smoking can cause ~ to others** Rauchen kann eine Belästigung für andere sein; **to his ~** zu seinem Ärger *or* Verdruss **b** *(= nuisance)* Plage *f*, Belästigung *f*, Ärgernis *nt*

annoying [əˈnɔɪɪŋ] ADJ ärgerlich; *habit* lästig; **the ~ thing (about it) is that …** das Ärgerliche (daran *or* bei der Sache) ist, dass …; **it's so ~!** das kann einen ärgern, das ist derart ärgerlich; **he has an ~ way of speaking slowly** er hat eine Art, langsam zu sprechen, die einen ärgern *or* aufregen kann

annoyingly [əˈnɔɪɪŋlɪ] ADV aufreizend; **~, the bus didn't turn up** ärgerlicherweise kam der Bus nicht

annual [ˈænjʊəl] **N** **a** *(Bot)* einjährige Pflanze **b** *(= book)* Jahresalbum *nt* **ADJ** *(= happening once a year)* jährlich; *(= of or for the year)* Jahres-; **~ accounts** Jahresbilanz *f*; **~ salary** Jahresgehalt *nt*

annual general meeting N Jahreshauptversammlung *f*

annualized [ˈænjʊəlaɪzd] ADJ *figures* auf das Jahr hochgerechnet; **~ percentage** *(Econ)* effektiver Jahreszins

annually [ˈænjʊəlɪ] ADV *(= once a year)* jährlich

annual report N Geschäftsbericht *m*

annual ring N *(of tree)* Jahresring *m*

annuitant [əˈnjuːɪtənt] N *(form)* Rentenempfänger(in) *m(f) (einer Jahresrente)*

annuity [əˈnjuːɪtɪ] N (Leib)rente *f*; **to buy an ~** eine Rentenversicherung abschließen

annuity bond N *(Econ)* Rentenbrief *m*, Rentenpapiere *pl*

annul [əˈnʌl] VT annullieren; *law, decree, judgement also* aufheben; *contract, marriage also* auflösen, für ungültig erklären; *will also* für ungültig erklären

annulment [əˈnʌlmənt] N Annullierung *f*; *(of law, decree, judgement also)* Aufhebung *f*; *(of contract, marriage also)* Auflösung *f*; *(of will also)* Ungültigkeitserklärung *f*

Annunciation [əˌnʌnsɪˈeɪʃən] N *(Bibl)* Mariä Verkündigung *f*; **the feast of the ~** das Fest Maria *or* Mariä Verkündigung

anode [ˈænəʊd] N Anode *f*

anodize [ˈænədaɪz] VT anodisch behandeln, anodisieren

anodyne [ˈænəʊdaɪn] **N** *(Med)* schmerzstillendes Mittel, Schmerzmittel *nt*; *(fig)* Wohltat *f* **ADJ** *(Med)* schmerzstillend; *(fig)* wohltuend, beruhigend

anoint [əˈnɔɪnt] VT salben; **to ~ sb king** jdn zum König salben; **to ~ sb as sth** *(fig)* jdn als etw auserwählen

anointment [əˈnɔɪntmənt] N Salbung *f*

anomalous [əˈnɒmələs] ADJ anomal, ungewöhnlich

anomaly [əˈnɒməlɪ] N Anomalie *f*; *(in law etc)* Besonderheit *f*

anomie, anomy [ˈænəʊmɪ] N Anomie *f*, Gesetzlosigkeit *f*

anon[1] [əˈnɒn] ADV *(old)* alsbald *(dial, old)*, bald; **ever and ~** *(old)* dann und wann; **see you ~** *(hum)* bis demnächst

anon[2] ADJ *abbr of* **anonymous**; **Anon** *(at end of text)* Anonymus *(liter)*, Verfasser unbekannt

anonymity [ˌænəˈnɪmɪtɪ] N Anonymität *f*

anonymous ADJ, **anonymously** ADV [əˈnɒnɪməs, -lɪ] *(lit, fig)* anonym

anopheles [əˈnɒfɪliːz] N *pl* **-les**, **anopheles mosquito** *(Zool)* Anopheles *f*, Malariamücke *f*

anorak [ˈænəræk] N *(Brit)* Anorak *m*; *(pej inf: = nerd)* ungepflegter Fuzzi *(sl)*

anorectic [ˌænəˈrektɪk] ADJ = **anorexic**

anorexia (nervosa) [ænəˈreksɪə(nɜːˈvəʊsə)] N Magersucht *f*, Anorexie *f (spec)*

anorexic [ænəˈreksɪk] ADJ magersüchtig

another [əˈnʌðəˈ] ✪ 19.5, 26.1 **ADJ** **a** *(= additional)* noch eine(r, s); **~ one** noch eine(r, s); **take ~ ten** nehmen Sie noch (weitere) zehn; **I won't give you ~ chance** ich werde dir nicht

noch eine *or* keine weitere Chance geben; **I don't want ~ drink!** ich möchte nichts mehr trinken; **in ~ 20 years he …** noch 20 Jahre, und er …; **without ~ word** ohne ein weiteres Wort; **and (there's) ~ thing** und noch eins, und (da ist) noch (et)was (anderes)
b *(= similar, fig: = second)* ein zweiter, eine zweite, ein zweites; **there is not ~ man like him** so einen Mann gibt es nicht noch einmal *or* gibt es nur einmal; **~ Shakespeare** ein zweiter Shakespeare; **there will never be ~ you** für mich wird es nie jemand geben wie dich *or* du
c *(= different)* ein anderer, eine andere, ein anderes; **that's quite ~ matter** das ist etwas ganz anderes; **~ time** ein andermal; **but maybe there won't be ~ time** aber vielleicht gibt es keine andere Gelegenheit *or* gibt es das nicht noch einmal
PRON ein anderer, eine andere, ein anderes; **have ~!** nehmen Sie (doch) noch einen!; **he has found ~** *(dated, liter)* er hat eine andere gefunden; **many ~** manch anderer; **such ~** noch so einer; **they help one ~** sie helfen einander, sie helfen sich gegenseitig; **tell me ~!** *(inf)* Sie können mir sonst was erzählen *(inf)*, das können Sie mir nicht weismachen; **at one time or ~** irgendwann; **what with one thing and ~** bei all dem Trubel; **I assume this is ~ of your brilliant ideas!** ist das wieder so eine deiner Glanzideen? *(inf)*; **she's ~ of his girlfriends** sie ist (auch) eine seiner Freundinnen; **yes, I'm ~ of his fans** ja, ich bin auch einer seiner Fans

anovulant [æ'nɒvjʊlənt] N *(Med)* Ovulationshemmer *m*

Ansaphone® ['ɑːnsəfəʊn] N Anrufbeantworter *m*

ANSI *abbr of* **American National Standards Institute** *amerikanischer Normenausschuss*

ANSI code N *(Comput)* ANSI-Code *m*

answer ['ɑːnsəʳ] ✪ 19.4 **N a** *(= response)* (*to* auf *+acc*) Antwort *f*, Entgegnung *f (geh)*, Erwiderung *f (geh)*; *(in exam)* Antwort *f*; **to get an/no ~** Antwort/keine Antwort bekommen; **there was no ~** *(to telephone, doorbell)* es hat sich niemand gemeldet; **the ~ to our prayers** ein Geschenk *nt* des Himmels; **the ~ to a maiden's prayer** *(hum)* ein Traummann *m (inf)*, der ideale Mann; **there's no ~ to that** *(inf)* was soll man da groß machen/sagen! *(inf)*; **Germany's ~ to Concorde** Deutschlands Antwort auf die Concorde; **they had no ~ to the new striker** *(Ftbl)* sie hatten dem neuen Stürmer nichts *or* niemanden entgegenzusetzen; **in ~ to your letter/my question** in Beantwortung Ihres Briefes *(form)*/auf meine Frage hin; **she's always got an ~** sie hat immer eine Antwort parat
b *(= solution)* Lösung *f (to +gen)*; **his ~ to any problem is to ignore it** seine Reaktion auf alle Schwierigkeiten ist, sie einfach nicht wahrhaben zu wollen; **there's no easy ~** es gibt dafür keine Patentlösung; **there's only one ~ for depression …** es gibt nur ein Mittel gegen Depression …
c *(Jur)* Einlassung *f (form)*, Stellungnahme *f*; **the defendant's ~ to the charge was …** laut Einlassung des Beklagten … *(form)*; **what is your ~ to the charge?** was haben Sie dazu zu sagen?
VT a antworten auf *(+acc)*; *person* antworten *(+dat)*; *exam questions* beantworten, antworten auf *(+acc)*; *objections, criticism* beantworten; **will you ~ that?** *(phone, door)* gehst du ran/hin?; **to ~ the telephone** das Telefon abnehmen, rangehen *(inf)*; **to ~ the bell** *or* **door** die Tür öffnen *or* aufmachen, hingehen *(inf)*; **who ~ed the phone?** wer war dran *(inf) or* am Apparat?; *(here at this end)* wer hat den Anruf entgegengenommen?; **shall I ~ it?** *(phone)* soll ich rangehen?; *(door)* soll ich hingehen?; **to ~ the call of nature** *(hum)* dem Ruf der Natur folgen; **5,000 men ~ed the call for volunteers** 5.000 Männer meldeten sich auf den Freiwilligenaufruf hin; **the fire brigade ~ed the alarm call** die Feuerwehr rückte auf den Alarm hin aus; **…, he ~ed** …, antwortete er; **~ me this** sagen *or* beantworten Sie mir eins; **~ me!** antworte (mir)!, antworten Sie!; **to anyone who claims … I would ~ this** jemandem, der … behauptet, würde ich Folgendes erwidern *or* entgegen
b *(= fulfil) description* entsprechen *(+dat)*; *hope, expectation* erfüllen; *prayer (God)* erhören; *need* befriedigen; **people who ~ that description** Leute, auf die diese Beschreibung passt *or* zutrifft; **this ~ed our prayers** das war (wie) ein Geschenk des Himmels; **it ~s the/our purpose** es erfüllt seinen Zweck/es erfüllt für uns seinen Zweck
c *(Jur) charge* sich verantworten wegen *(+gen)*
VI a antworten; **if the phone rings, don't ~** wenn das Telefon läutet, geh nicht ran *or* nimm nicht ab
b *(= suffice)* geeignet *or* brauchbar sein, taugen

▶ **answer back** **VI** widersprechen; *(children also)* patzige *or* freche Antworten geben; **don't answer back!** keine Widerrede!; **it's not fair to criticize him because he can't answer back** es ist unfair, ihn zu kritisieren, weil er sich nicht verteidigen kann **VT** *sep* **to answer sb back** jdm widersprechen; *(children also)* jdm patzige *or* freche Antworten geben

▶ **answer for** VI *+prep obj* **a** *(= be responsible for)* verantwortlich sein für; **he has a lot to answer for** er hat eine Menge auf dem Gewissen; **I won't answer for the consequences** ich will für die Folgen nicht verantwortlich gemacht werden **b** *(= guarantee)* sich verbürgen für; *(= speak for also)* sprechen für

▶ **answer to** VI *+prep obj* **a** *(= be accountable to)* **to answer to sb for sth** jdm für etw *or* wegen einer Sache *(gen)* Rechenschaft schuldig sein; **if anything goes wrong you'll have me to answer to** wenn etwas nicht klappt, dann stehen Sie mir dafür ein *or* gerade *or* dann müssen Sie sich vor mir dafür verantworten **b to answer to a description** einer Beschreibung entsprechen **c to answer to the name of …** auf den Namen … hören **d to answer to the wheel/helm/controls** auf das Steuer/das Ruder/die Steuerung ansprechen

answerable ['ɑːnsərəbl] ADJ **a** *question* beantwortbar, zu beantworten *pred*; *charge, argument* widerlegbar **b** *(= responsible)* verantwortlich; **to be ~ to sb (for sth)** jdm gegenüber (für etw) verantwortlich sein; **to be made ~** verantwortlich gemacht werden; **parents are ~ for their children's conduct** Eltern haften für ihre Kinder

answer-back (code) ['ɑːnsəbæk(,kəʊd)] N *(for telex)* Kennung *f*

answerer ['ɑːnsərəʳ] N Antwortende(r) *mf*

answering machine ['ɑːnsərɪŋmə'ʃiːn] N (automatischer) Anrufbeantworter

answerless ['ɑːnsəlɪs] ADJ ohne Antwort; *question (= not answered)* unbeantwortet; *(= not answerable)* unbeantwortbar

answer paper N *(in exam)* Lösung *f*, Antwortbogen *m*

answerphone ['ɑːnsəfəʊn] N *(Brit)* Anrufbeantworter *m*

ant [ænt] N Ameise *f*; **to have ~s in one's pants** *(inf)* Hummeln im Hintern haben *(inf)*, kein Sitzfleisch haben

anta ['æntə] N *pl* **-ae** *(Archit)* Ante *f*, Pilaster *m*

antacid [ænt'æsɪd] N säurebindendes Mittel

antagonism [æn'tægənɪzəm] N *(between people, theories etc)* Antagonismus *m*; *(towards sb, ideas, a suggestion, change etc)* Feindseligkeit *f*, Feindlichkeit *f* (*to(wards)* gegenüber); **to arouse sb's ~** jdn gegen sich aufbringen

antagonist [æn'tægənɪst] N Kontrahent(in) *m(f)*, Gegner(in) *m(f)*, Antagonist(in) *m(f)*; *(esp Pol)* Gegenspieler(in) *m(f)*

antagonistic [æn,tægə'nɪstɪk] ADJ *reaction, attitude* feindselig; *force* gegnerisch, feindlich; *interests* widerstreitend, antagonistisch; **to be ~ to** *or* **toward(s) sb/sth** jdm/gegen etw feindselig gesinnt sein

antagonize [æn'tægənaɪz] VT *person* gegen sich aufbringen *or* stimmen; *(= annoy)* verärgern

Antarctic [ænt'ɑːktɪk] **ADJ** antarktisch, der Antarktis **N the ~** die Antarktis

Antarctica [ænt'ɑːktɪkə] N die Antarktis

Antarctic Circle N südlicher Polarkreis

Antarctic Ocean N Südpolarmeer *nt*

ant: **ant bear** N *(Zool)* Ameisenbär *m*; **ant bird, ant catcher** N *(Zool)* Ameisenvogel *m*; **ant colony** N Ameisenstaat *m*

ante ['æntɪ] **N** *(Cards)* Einsatz *m*; **to raise** *or* **up the ~** *(fig inf)* den Einsatz erhöhen **VT** *(also* **ante up**) einsetzen **VI** setzen, seinen Einsatz machen; **his father ~d up as usual** *(fig inf)* sein Vater blechte wie gewöhnlich *(inf)*

ante- PREF vor-

anteater ['ænt,iːtəʳ] N Ameisenbär *m*, Ameisenfresser *m*

antecedent [,æntɪ'siːdənt] **ADJ** früher; **the crisis and its ~ events** die Krise und die ihr vorangehenden *or* vorausgehenden Ereignisse; **to be ~ to sth** einer Sache *(dat)* voran- *or* vorausgehen **N a ~s** *(of person, = past history)* Vorleben *nt*; *(= ancestry)* Abstammung *f*; *(of event)* Vorgeschichte *f* **b** *(Gram)* Bezugswort *nt*

ante: **antechamber** N Vorzimmer *nt*; **antedate** VT *document, cheque* vordatieren (*to* auf *+acc*); *event* vorausgehen *(+dat)* (*by* um); **antediluvian** [,æntɪdɪ'luːvɪən] ADJ *(lit, fig inf)* vorsintflutlich

antelope ['æntɪləʊp] N Antilope *f*

ante meridiem [,æntɪmə'rɪdɪəm] ADV *(abbr* **am**) vormittags

antenatal ['æntɪ'neɪtl] ADJ vor der Geburt, pränatal *(form)*; **~ care/exercises** Schwangerschaftsfürsorge *f*/-übungen *pl*; **~ clinic** Sprechstunde *f* für Schwangere *or* für werdende Mütter

antenna [æn'tenə] N **a** *pl* **-e** [æn'teniː] *(Zool)* Fühler *m* **b** *pl* **-e** *or* **-s** *(Rad, TV)* Antenne *f*

antepenultimate ['æntɪpɪ'nʌltɪmɪt] ADJ vorvorletzte(r, s)

ante-post ['æntɪ'pəʊst] *(Brit Gambling)* **ADJ ~ bet** Vorwette *f*; **~ favourite** Favorit(in) *m(f)* **ADV to bet ~** eine Vorwette machen

anterior [æn'tɪərɪəʳ] ADJ **a** *(= prior)* früher (*to* als); **to be ~ to** vorangehen *(+dat)*, vorausgehen *(+dat)* **b** *(Anat etc)* vordere(r, s); **~ brain** Vorderhirn *nt*

anteroom ['æntɪruːm] N Vorzimmer *nt*

anthem ['ænθəm] N Hymne *f*; *(by choir)* Chorgesang *m*

anther ['ænθəʳ] N *(Bot)* Staubbeutel *m*, Anthere *f (spec)*

ant hill N Ameisenhaufen *m*

anthologize [æn'θɒlədʒaɪz] **VI** eine Anthologie/Anthologien zusammenstellen **VT** in einer Anthologie zusammenfassen; *(= to include in anthology)* in eine Anthologie aufnehmen

anthology [æn'θɒlədʒɪ] N Anthologie *f*

anthracite ['ænθrəsaɪt] N Anthrazit *m*

anthrax ['ænθræks] N *(Med, Vet)* Anthrax *m (spec)*, Milzbrand *m*; **~ attack** Milzbrandanschlag *m*; **~ letter** Anthrax-Brief *m*, *Brief, der Sporen des Milzbranderregers enthält*

anthropocentric [,ænθrəpəʊ'sentrɪk] ADJ anthropozentrisch

anthropoid ['ænθrəʊpɔɪd] **N** Anthropoid *m (spec)*; *(= ape)* Menschenaffe *m* **ADJ** anthropoid *(spec)*

anthropological [,ænθrəpə'lɒdʒɪkəl] ADJ anthropologisch

anthropologist [,ænθrə'pɒlədʒɪst] N Anthropologe *m*, Anthropologin *f*

anthropology [,ænθrə'pɒlədʒɪ] N Anthropologie *f*

anthropomorphic [,ænθrəʊpə'mɔːfɪk] ADJ anthropomorphisch

anthropomorphism [,ænθrəʊpə'mɔːfɪzəm] N Anthropomorphismus *m*

anthropomorphize [ˌænθrəpəʊˈmɔːfaɪz] VT *god, animal, object etc* anthropomorphisieren

anthroposophical [ˌænθrəpəˈsɒfɪkəl] ADJ anthroposophisch

anthroposophy [ˌænθrəˈpɒsəfɪ] N Anthroposophie *f*

anti [ˈæntɪ] *(inf)* ADJ *pred* in Opposition *(inf)*; **are you in favour** *(Brit) or* **favor** *(US)*? – **no, I'm ~** bist du dafür? – nein, ich bin dagegen PREP gegen *(+acc)*; **~ everything** grundsätzlich gegen alles

anti *in cpds* Anti-, anti-; **anti-abortion** ADJ Antiabtreibungs-; **~ campaign** Antiabtreibungskampagne *f*; **anti-abortionist** N Abtreibungsgegner(in) *m(f)*; **anti-ag(e)ing** ADJ **~ cream** Creme *f* gegen Hautalterung; **anti-aircraft** ADJ Flugabwehr-; **~ defence** *(Brit) or* **defense** *(US)* Luftverteidigung *f*; **~ fire** Flakfeuer *nt*; **~ gun** Flak(geschütz *nt*) *f*; **~ missile** Flugabwehrrakete *f*; **anti-American** ADJ antiamerikanisch; **antiballistic missile** [ˌæntɪbəˈlɪstɪk-] N Antiraketenrakete *f*; **antibiotic** [ˌæntɪbaɪˈɒtɪk] N Antibiotikum *nt* ADJ antibiotisch; **antibody** N Antikörper *m*

antic [ˈæntɪk] N → **antics**

antichoice ADJ abtreibungsfeindlich, gegen Abtreibung

Antichrist [ˈæntɪkraɪst] N Antichrist *m*

anticipate [ænˈtɪsɪpeɪt] VT a *(= expect)* erwarten; **as ~d** wie vorausgesehen *or* erwartet
b *(= see in advance)* vorausberechnen, vorhersehen; *(= see in advance and cater for) objection, need etc* zuvorkommen *(+dat)*; **he always has to ~ what his opponent will do next** er muss immer vorhersehen können *or* vorausahnen, was sein Gegner als Nächstes tun wird; **don't ~ what I'm going to say** nimm nicht vorweg, was ich noch sagen wollte
c *(= do before sb else)* zuvorkommen *(+dat)*; **in his discovery he was ~d by others** bei seiner Entdeckung sind ihm andere zuvorgekommen; **a phrase which ~s a later theme** *(Mus)* eine Melodie, die auf ein späteres Thema vor(aus)greift
d *(= do, use, act on prematurely) income* im Voraus ausgeben; *inheritance* im Voraus in Anspruch nehmen
VI *(manager, driver, chess player etc)* vorauskalkulieren

anticipation [ænˌtɪsɪˈpeɪʃən] N a *(= expectation)* Erwartung *f*; **thanking you in ~** herzlichen Dank im Voraus; **to wait in ~** gespannt warten; **we took our umbrellas in ~ of rain** wir nahmen unsere Schirme mit, weil wir mit Regen rechneten
b *(= seeing in advance)* Vorausberechnung *f*; **we were impressed by the hotel's ~ of our wishes** beeindruckt, wie man im Hotel unseren Wünschen zuvorkam; **his uncanny ~ of every objection** die verblüffende Art, in der *or* wie er jedem Einwand zuvorkam; **the driver showed good ~** der Fahrer zeigte *or* bewies gute Voraussicht
c *(of discovery, discoverer)* Vorwegnahme *f*; *(Mus, of theme etc)* Vorgriff *m (of* auf *+acc)*

anticipatory [ænˈtɪsɪˌpeɪtərɪ] ADJ vorwegnehmend

anti: **anticlerical** ADJ antiklerikal, kirchenfeindlich; **anticlimactic** ADJ enttäuschend; **anticlimax** N Enttäuschung *f*; *(no pl, Liter)* Antiklimax *f*; **anticlockwise** *(esp Brit)* ADJ nach links; **in an ~ direction** entgegen dem Uhrzeigersinn ADV nach links, gegen den Uhrzeigersinn *or* die Uhrzeigerrichtung; **anticoagulant** [ˌæntɪkəʊˈægjʊlənt] N Antikoagulans *nt (spec)* ADJ antikoagulierend *(spec)*, blutgerinnungshemmend; **anticonvulsant** N Antikonvulsivum *nt* ADJ antikonvulsiv; **anticorrosive** ADJ Korrosionsschutz-; **~ paint** Korrosionsschutzfarbe *f*

antics [ˈæntɪks] PL Eskapaden *pl*; *(= tricks)* Possen *pl*, Streiche *pl*; *(= irritating behaviour)* Mätzchen *pl (inf)*; **he's up to his old ~ again** er macht wieder seine Mätzchen *(inf)*; **the photocopier is up to its old ~ again** der Fotokopierer hat wieder seine Mucken *(inf)*

anti: **anticyclical** ADJ antizyklisch; **~ policy** *(Econ)* Konjunkturpolitik *f*; **for ~ reasons** aus konjunkturpolitischen Gründen; **anticyclone** N Antizyklone *f*, Hoch(druckgebiet) *nt*; **anti-dandruff** ADJ *shampoo* gegen Schuppen; **antidazzle** ADJ *(Brit)* blendfrei; **antidepressant** N Antidepressivum *nt* ADJ antidepressiv; **antidote** [ˈæntɪdəʊt] N *(Med, fig)* Gegenmittel *nt (against, to, for* gegen); **antifemale** ADJ frauenfeindlich; **antifreeze** N Frostschutz(mittel *nt*) *m*

antigen [ˈæntɪdʒən] N Antigen *nt*

anti: **antiglare** ADJ *(US)* blendfrei; **anti-globalist** [ˌæntɪˈgləʊbəlɪst] N Globalisierungsgegner(in) *m(f)*; **anti-globalization** [ˌæntɪˌgləʊbəlaɪˈzeɪʃən] ADJ Antiglobalisierungs-; **~ movement** Anti-Globalisierungs-Bewegung *f*; **~ protester** Globalisierungsgegner(in) *m(f)*; **antihero** N Antiheld *m*; **antihistamine** N Antihistamin(ikum) *nt*; **anti-inflammatory** N Entzündungshemmer *m* ADJ *drug* entzündungshemmend; **antiknock agent** [ˌæntɪˈnɒk-] N Antiklopfmittel *nt*; **antilock** ADJ Blockierschutz-; **~ brakes** Blockierschutzbremsen *pl*; **~ braking system** Blockierschutzbremssystem *nt*; **antilog(arithm)** N Antilogarithmus *m*, Numerus *m*; **antimacassar** [ˌæntɪməˈkæsəˈ] N (Sessel-/Sofa)schoner *m*; **antimalarial** ADJ gegen Malaria N Malariamittel *nt*; **anti-marketeer** N EG--Gegner(in) *m(f)*; **antimatter** N Antimaterie *f*; **antimissile** ADJ Raketenabwehr-; **~ system** Raketenabwehrsystem *nt*; **antimist** ADJ **~ cloth** *(Mot)* Antibeschlagtuch *nt*

antimony [ˈæntɪmənɪ] N Antimon *nt*

anti: **antinuclear** ADJ *(= against nuclear energy)* Anti-Atom(kraft)-; *(= against nuclear weapons)* Anti-Atomwaffen-; **the ~ lobby/protesters** die Atomkraftgegner *pl*, die Atomwaffengegner *pl*; **antinuclearist** [ˌæntɪˈnjuːklɪərɪst] N Atomkraftgegner(in) *m(f)*, Kernkraftgegner(in) *m(f)*; **antioxidant** N Antioxidans *nt*; **~s** Antioxidantien *pl*

antipasto [ˌæntɪˈpæstəʊ] N italienische Vorspeise

antipathetic [ˌæntɪpəˈθetɪk] ADJ **to be ~ to sb/sth** eine Antipathie *or* Abneigung gegen jdn/etw haben; **sb/sth is ~ to sb** *(= arouses antipathy in)* jd/etw ist jdm unsympathisch

antipathy [ænˈtɪpəθɪ] N Antipathie *f (towards* gegen), Abneigung *f (towards* gegen)

anti: **antipersonnel** ADJ gegen Menschen gerichtet; **~ bomb** Splitterbombe *f*; **~ mine** Antipersonenmine *f*; **antiperspirant** N Antitranspirant *nt*

antiphony [ænˈtɪfənɪ] N *(Eccl, Mus)* Antifon *f*

antipodean [ænˌtɪpəˈdiːən], *(US)* **antipodal** [ænˈtɪpədəl] ADJ antipodisch; *(Brit)* australisch und neuseeländisch

antipodes [ænˈtɪpədiːz] PL (diametral) entgegengesetzte Teile der Erde; **Antipodes** *(Brit)* Australien und Neuseeland; *(Geog)* Antipodeninseln *pl*

antipope [ˈæntɪˌpəʊp] N Gegenpapst *m*

antiquarian [ˌæntɪˈkweərɪən] ADJ *books* antiquarisch; *coins also* alt; *studies* des Altertums, der Antike; **~ bookshop** Antiquariat *nt* N = **antiquary**

antiquary [ˈæntɪkwərɪ] N *(= collector)* Antiquitätensammler(in) *m(f)*; *(= seller)* Antiquitätenhändler(in) *m(f)*

antiquated [ˈæntɪkweɪtɪd] ADJ antiquiert; *machines, ideas also* überholt; *institutions also* veraltet

antique [ænˈtiːk] ADJ antik; **~ pine** Kiefer *f* antik N Antiquität *f*

antiqued [ænˈtiːkt] ADJ auf antik gemacht

antique: **antique dealer** N Antiquitätenhändler(in) *m(f)*; **antique(s) fair** N Antiquitätenmesse *f*; **antique shop** N Antiquitätengeschäft *nt or* -laden *m*

antiquity [ænˈtɪkwɪtɪ] N a *(= ancient times)* das Altertum; *(= Roman, Greek antiquity)* die Antike; **in ~** im Altertum/in der Antike b *(= great age)* großes Alter; **of great ~** uralt c **antiquities** PL *(= old things)* Altertümer *pl*

anti: **antiriot** ADJ **~ police** Bereitschaftspolizei *f*; **anti-roll bar** N *(Brit Aut)* Stabilisator *m*

antirrhinum [ˌæntɪˈraɪnəm] N Löwenmaul *nt*

anti: **antirust** ADJ Rostschutz-; **~ paint** Rostschutzfarbe *f*; **antiscorbutic** ADJ antiskorbutisch; **anti-Semite** N Antisemit(in) *m(f)*; **anti-Semitic** ADJ antisemitisch; **anti-Semitism** N Antisemitismus *m*; **antiseptic** N Antiseptikum *nt* ADJ *(lit, fig)* antiseptisch; **antiskid** ADJ rutschsicher; **antislavery** ADJ *speech etc* gegen die Sklaverei; **antislip** ADJ *floor* rutschfest, rutschsicher; **antismoking** ADJ *group* Antiraucher-; **~ campaign** Kampagne *nt* gegen das Rauchen; **antisocial** ADJ *person, behaviour etc* unsozial; *(Psych, Sociol)* asozial; **to be in an ~ mood** nicht in Gesellschaftslaune sein; **don't be ~** *(= don't be a spoilsport)* sei kein Spielverderber; *(= don't be aloof etc)* mach doch mit; **may I smoke or would that be ~?** darf ich rauchen oder stört das?; **I work ~ hours** ich arbeite zu Zeiten, wo andere freihaben; **antistatic** ADJ antistatisch; **antitank** ADJ Panzerabwehr-; **~ gun** Panzerabwehrgeschütz *nt*; **~ ditch/obstacle** Panzersperre *f*; **antitechnological** ADJ technologiefeindlich; **antiterrorist** ADJ *squad, measures* zur Terrorismusbekämpfung; **anti-theft device** N Diebstahlsicherung *f*

antithesis [ænˈtɪθɪsɪs] N *pl* **antitheses** [ænˈtɪθɪsiːz] *(= direct opposite)* genaues Gegenteil *(to, of +gen)*; *(of idea, in rhetoric)* Antithese *f (to, of* zu) *(form)*; *(= contrast)* Gegensatz *m*

antithetic(al) [ˌæntɪˈθetɪk(əl)] ADJ *(= contrasting)* gegensätzlich; *phrases* antithetisch *(form)*; *idea* entgegengesetzt, antithetisch *(form)*

anti: **antitoxin** N Gegengift *nt*, Antitoxin *nt*; **antitrade (wind)** N Antipassat(wind) *m*; **antitrust** ADJ *(US)* **~ legislation** Kartellgesetzgebung *f*; **anti-virus software** N *(Comput)* Antivirensoftware *f*; **antivivisectionism** N Ablehnung *f* der Vivisektion; **antivivisectionist** N Gegner(in) *m(f)* der Vivisektion ADJ **his ~ views** seine ablehnende Haltung der Vivisektion gegenüber; **anti-wrinkle** ADJ Antifalten-; **~ cream** Antifaltencreme *f*

antler [ˈæntləˈ] N Geweihstange *f*; **(set** *or* **pair of) ~s** Geweih *nt*

antonym [ˈæntənɪm] N Antonym *nt*, Gegenwort *nt (geh)*

Antwerp [ˈæntwɜːp] N Antwerpen *nt*

anus [ˈeɪnəs] N After *m*, Anus *m (spec)*

anvil [ˈænvɪl] N Amboss *m (also Anat)*

anxiety [æŋˈzaɪətɪ] N a Sorge *f*; **to feel ~** sich *(dat)* Sorgen machen *(about* um, *at* wegen); **no cause for ~** kein Grund zur Sorge *or* Besorgnis; **to cause sb ~** jdm Sorgen machen b *(= keen desire)* Verlangen *nt*; **in his ~ to get away** weil er unbedingt wegkommen wollte

anxiety neurosis N *(Psych)* Angstneurose *f*

anxious [ˈæŋkʃəs] ADJ a *(= worried)* besorgt; *person (as character trait)* ängstlich; *thoughts* ängstlich; **to be ~ about sb/sth** sich *(dat)* um jdn/etw Sorgen machen, um jdn/etw besorgt sein; **to be ~ about doing sth** Angst haben, etw zu tun
b *(= worrying) moment, minutes* der Angst, bang; *wait* bang; **it's been an ~ time for us all** wir alle haben uns (in dieser Zeit) große Sorgen gemacht; **he had an ~ time waiting for ...** es war für ihn eine Zeit voll bangen Wartens auf *(+acc)* ...
c *(= strongly desirous)* **to be ~ for sth** auf etw *(acc)* aus sein; **we are ~ for all the assistance we can get** uns geht es darum, jede nur mögliche Hilfe zu bekommen; **to be ~ to do sth** bestrebt sein *or* darauf aus sein, etw zu tun; **they were ~ to start/for his return** sie warteten sehr darauf abzufahren/auf seine Rückkehr; **I am ~ that he should do it** *or* **for him to do it** mir liegt viel daran, dass er es tut

anxious bench N *(US Rel)* → **anxious seat**

anxiously [ˈæŋkʃəslɪ] ADV a besorgt b *(= keenly)* gespannt

anxiousness [ˈæŋkʃəsnɪs] N *no pl* Sorge *f*; *(= keen desire)* Verlangen *nt*

anxious seat N *(US Rel)* Sünderbank *f*; **to be on the ~** *(fig)* wie auf (glühenden) Kohlen sitzen, Blut und Wasser schwitzen

any [ˈenɪ] ADJ **a** *(in interrog, conditional, neg sentences) not translated (emph: = any at all) (with sing n)* irgendein(e); *(with pl n)* irgendwelche; *(with uncountable n)* etwas; **not ~** kein/keine; **not ANY ... at all** überhaupt kein/keine ...; **if I had ~ plan/ideas/money** wenn ich einen Plan/Ideen/Geld hätte; **if I had ANY plan/ideas/money (at all)** wenn ich irgendeinen Plan/irgendwelche Ideen/(auch nur) etwas Geld hätte; **if you think it'll do ~ good/ANY good (at all)** wenn du glaubst, dass es etwas/irgendetwas nützt; **if it's ~ help (at all)** wenn das (irgendwie) hilft; **it won't do ~ good** es wird nichts nützen; **it wasn't ~ good** *or* **use (at all)** es nützte (überhaupt *or* gar) nichts; **you mustn't do that on ~ account** das darfst du auf gar keinen Fall tun; **without ~ difficulty (at all)** ohne jede Schwierigkeit
b *(= no matter which)* jede(r, s) (beliebige ...); *(with pl or uncountable n)* alle; **~ one will do** es ist jede(r, s) recht; **~ excuse will do** jede Entschuldigung ist recht; **you can have ~ book/books you can find** du kannst jedes Buch/alle Bücher haben, das/die du finden kannst; **take ~ two dresses** nehmen Sie zwei beliebige Kleider; **~ one you like** was du willst; **~ one of us would have done the same** jeder von uns hätte dasselbe getan; **you can't just come at ~ time** du kannst nicht einfach zu jeder beliebigen Zeit kommen; **you can come at ~ time** du kannst jederzeit kommen; **thank you – ~ time** danke! – bitte!; **~ time soon** irgendwann bald; **~ fool could do that** das kann jedes Kind; **~ old ...** *(inf)* jede(r, s) x-beliebige ... *(inf)* → **old**
PRON **a** *(in interrog, conditional, neg sentences) (replacing sing n)* ein(e), welche(r, s); *(replacing pl n)* einige, welche; *(replacing uncountable n)* etwas, welche; **I want to meet psychologists/a psychologist, do you know ~?** ich würde gerne Psychologen/einen Psychologen kennenlernen, kennen Sie welche/einen?; **I need some butter/stamps, do you have ~?** ich brauche Butter/Briefmarken, haben Sie welche?; **have you seen ~ of my ties?** haben Sie eine von meinen Krawatten gesehen?; **don't you have ~ (at all)?** haben Sie (denn) (gar *or* überhaupt) keinen/keine/keines?; **he wasn't having ~ (of it/that)** *(inf)* er wollte nichts davon hören; **the profits, if ~** die eventuellen Gewinne; **few, if ~, will come** wenn überhaupt, werden nur wenige kommen; **I'd like some tea/tomatoes if you have ~** ich hätte gerne Tee, wenn Sie welchen haben/Tomaten, wenn Sie welche haben; **if ~ of you can sing** wenn (irgend)jemand *or* (irgend)einer/-eine von euch singen kann
b *(= no matter which)* alle; **~ who do come ...** alle, die kommen ...; **~ that I have ...** alle, die ich habe ...
ADV **a** *colder, bigger etc* noch; **not ~ colder/bigger** *etc* nicht kälter/größer *etc*; **it won't get ~ colder** es wird nicht mehr kälter; **we can't go ~ further** wir können nicht mehr weiter gehen; **should he grow ~ bigger he'll ...** wenn er noch mehr wächst, wird er ...; **are you feeling ~ better?** geht es dir etwas besser?; **he wasn't ~ too pleased** *(Brit)* er war nicht allzu begeistert; **do you want ~ more soup?** willst du noch etwas Suppe?; **don't you want ~ more tea?** willst du keinen Tee mehr?; **~ more offers?** noch weitere Angebote?; **I don't want ~ more (at all)** ich möchte (überhaupt *or* gar) nichts mehr
b *(esp US inf: = at all)* überhaupt; **you can't improve it ~** du kannst es überhaupt nicht mehr verbessern; **it didn't help them ~** es hat ihnen gar *or* überhaupt nichts genützt

anybody [ˈenɪbɒdɪ] PRON **a** (irgend)jemand, (irgend)eine(r); **not ... ~** niemand, keine(r); **is ~ there?** ist (irgend)jemand da?; **(does) ~ want my book?** will jemand *or* einer mein Buch?; **I can't see ~** ich kann niemand(en) *or* keinen sehen; **don't tell ~** erzähl das niemand(em) *or* keinem
b *(= no matter who)* jede(r); **~ will tell you the same** jeder wird dir dasselbe sagen; **~ with any sense** jeder halbwegs vernünftige Mensch; **it's ~'s game/race** das Spiel/Rennen kann von jedem gewonnen werden; **~ but him, ~ else** jeder außer ihm, jeder andere; **is there ~ else I can talk to?** gibt es sonst jemand(en), mit dem ich sprechen kann?; **I don't want to see ~ else** ich möchte niemand anderen sehen
N *(= person of importance)* jemand, wer *(inf)*; **she'll never be ~** sie wird nie wer sein *(inf)*; **he's not just ~** er ist nicht einfach irgendwer *or* irgendjemand; **everybody who is ~ was there** alles, was Rang und Namen hat, war dort; **he wasn't ~ before she married him** er war niemand, bevor sie ihn geheiratet hat; **Lucy was ~'s last night** *(Brit inf)* Lucy hat gestern Abend mit jedem rumgemacht *(inf)*

anyhow [ˈenɪhaʊ] ADV **a** *(= at any rate)* jedenfalls; *(= regardless)* trotzdem; **~, that's what I think** das ist jedenfalls meine Meinung; **~, I went to see him** (also) jedenfalls, ich habe ihn besucht; **~, you're here now** jetzt bist du jedenfalls da; **I told him not to, but he did it ~** ich habe es ihm verboten, aber er hat es trotzdem gemacht; **he agrees ~, so it doesn't matter** er ist sowieso einverstanden, es spielt also keine Rolle; **it's no trouble, I'm going there ~** es ist keine Mühe, ich gehe sowieso hin; **who cares, ~?** überhaupt, wen kümmert es denn schon?; **~!** gut!, na ja!
b *(= carelessly)* irgendwie; *(= at random)* aufs Geratewohl; **the papers were scattered ~ on his desk** die Papiere lagen bunt durcheinander auf seinem Schreibtisch; **things are all ~** alles ist durcheinander

anymore [ˌenɪˈmɔːʳ] ADV *(+vb)* nicht mehr; **I couldn't trust him ~** ich konnte ihm nicht mehr trauen → **any ADV a**

anyone [ˈenɪwʌn] PRON N = **anybody**

anyplace [ˈenɪpleɪs] ADV *(US inf)* = **anywhere**

anyroad [ˈenɪrəʊd] ADV *(N Engl)* = **anyhow a**

anything [ˈenɪθɪŋ] PRON **a** (irgend)etwas; **not ~** nichts; *(emph)* gar *or* überhaupt nichts; **is it/isn't it worth ~?** ist es etwas/gar nichts wert?; **it's worth ~ between £1,000 and £5,000** es ist irgendwas zwischen £ 1000 und £ 5000 wert; **did/didn't he say ~ else?** hat er (sonst) noch etwas/sonst (gar) nichts gesagt?; **did/didn't they give you ~ at all?** haben sie euch überhaupt etwas/überhaupt nichts gegeben?; **are you doing ~ tonight?** hast du heute Abend schon etwas vor?; **is there ~ more tiring than ...?** gibt es etwas Ermüdenderes als ...?; **hardly ~** kaum etwas; **he's as smart as ~** *(inf)* er ist clever wie noch was *(inf)*
b *(= no matter what)* alles; **~ you like** (alles,) was du willst; **they eat ~** sie essen alles; **not just ~** nicht bloß irgendetwas; **I wouldn't do it for ~** ich würde es um keinen Preis tun; **~ else is impossible** alles andere ist unmöglich; **this is ~ but pleasant** das ist alles andere als angenehm; **~ but that!** alles, nur das nicht!; **~ but!** von wegen! → **if, go, like**[1] **PREP**
ADV *(inf)* **it isn't ~ like him** das sieht ihm überhaupt nicht ähnlich *or* gleich; **if it looked ~ like him ...** wenn es ihm gleichsehen würde ...; **it didn't cost ~ like £100** es kostete bei Weitem keine £ 100; **if it costs ~ like as much as before ...** wenn es auch nur annähernd so viel kostet wie früher ...; **~/not ~ like as wet as ...** auch nur annähernd/nicht annähernd so nass wie ...

anytime [ˈenɪtaɪm] ADV *(esp US)* jederzeit → **any**

anytime minutes PL *(US: for mobile phone)* Freiminuten *pl (die ohne Zeitbindung vertelefoniert werden können)*

anyway [ˈenɪweɪ] ADV = **anyhow a**, → *also* **way**

anyways [ˈenɪweɪz] ADV *(US dial)* = **anyway**

anywhere [ˈenɪweəʳ] ADV **a** *be, stay, live* irgendwo; *go, travel* irgendwohin; **not ~** nirgends/nirgendwohin; **too late to go ~** zu spät, um (noch) irgendwohin zu gehen; **we never go ~** wir gehen nie (irgend)wohin; **he'll never get ~** er wird es zu nichts bringen; **I wasn't getting ~** ich kam (einfach) nicht weiter; **I haven't found ~ to live/to put my books yet** ich habe noch nichts gefunden, wo ich wohnen/meine Bücher unterbringen kann; **the cottage was miles from ~** das Häuschen lag jwd *(inf)*; **they are the oldest caves ~ in the whole of North America** das sind die ältesten Höhlen in ganz Nordamerika; **there could be ~ between 50 and 100 people** es könnten (schätzungsweise) 50 bis 100 Leute sein
b *(= no matter where) be, stay, live* überall; *go, travel* überallhin; **they could be ~** sie könnten überall sein; **~ you like** wo/wohin du willst; **ready to go ~** bereit, überallhin zu gehen

Anzac [ˈænzæk] N *australischer/neuseeländischer Soldat*

AOB *abbr of* **any other business** Sonstiges

AOCB *abbr of* **any other competent business** Sonstiges

A-OK, A-okay ADJ ADV *(esp US inf)* klasse *(inf)*, prima *(inf)*

AONB *abbr of* **Area of Outstanding Natural Beauty**

aorist [ˈeərɪst] N Aorist *m*

aorta [eɪˈɔːtə] N Aorta *f*

apace [əˈpeɪs] ADV geschwind *(geh)*

Apache [əˈpætʃɪ] N **a** Apache *m*, Apachin *f*
b *(= language)* Apache *nt* ADJ Apachen-, der Apachen; **~ leader** Apachenführer *m*

apart [əˈpɑːt] ADV **a** auseinander; **to stand/sit with one's legs ~** mit gespreizten Beinen dastehen/dasitzen; **I can't tell them ~** ich kann sie nicht auseinanderhalten; **to live ~** getrennt leben; **they're still far** *or* **miles ~** *(fig)* ihre Meinungen klaffen *or* gehen immer noch weit auseinander; **to come** *or* **fall ~** entzweigehen, auseinanderfallen; **the company is falling ~** die Firma geht vor die Hunde *(inf)*; **her marriage is falling ~** ihre Ehe geht in die Brüche; **it came ~ in my hands** es fiel mir in der Hand auseinander; **to take sth ~** etw auseinandernehmen
b *(= to one side)* zur Seite, beiseite; *(= on one side)* abseits *(from +gen)*; **he stood ~ from the group** er stand abseits von der Gruppe; **to hold oneself ~** sich abseits halten; **a class/thing ~** eine Klasse/Sache für sich
c *(= excepted)* abgesehen von, bis auf *(+acc)*; **these problems ~** abgesehen von *or* außer diesen Problemen; **~ from that there's nothing else wrong with it** abgesehen davon *or* bis auf das ist alles in Ordnung; **~ from that, the gearbox is also faulty** darüber hinaus *or* außerdem ist (auch) das Getriebe schadhaft

apartheid [əˈpɑːteɪt] N Apartheid *f*

apartment [əˈpɑːtmənt] N **a** *(Brit: = room)* Raum *m* **b apartments** PL *(Brit: = suite of rooms)* Appartement *nt* **c** *(esp US: = flat)* Wohnung *f*; **~ house** *or* **block** *or* **building** Wohnblock *m*

apathetic [ˌæpəˈθetɪk] ADJ apathisch, teilnahmslos; **they are completely ~ about politics** sie sind in politischen Dingen vollkommen apathisch; **they are completely ~ about their future** sie sind vollkommen apathisch, was ihre Zukunft angeht

apathetically [ˌæpəˈθetɪkəlɪ] ADV apathisch, teilnahmslos

apathy [ˈæpəθɪ] N Apathie *f*, Teilnahmslosigkeit *f*

APB *(US) abbr of* **all points bulletin**; **to put out an ~ on sb** nach jdm eine Fahndung einleiten

ape [eɪp] N *(lit, fig)* Affe *m*; **to go ~** *(inf)* ausflippen *(inf)* VT nachäffen *(pej)*, nachmachen

APEC [ˈeɪpek] N *abbr of* **Asia Pacific Economic Co-operation** APEC *f*

Apennines [ˈæpɪnaɪnz] PL Apennin *m*, Apenninen *pl*

aperient [əˈpɪərɪənt] N Abführmittel *nt* ADJ abführend

apéritif [əˌperɪˈtiːf], **aperitive** [əˈperɪtɪv] N Aperitif *m*

aperture [ˈæpətʃjʊəˈ] N Öffnung *f*; *(Phot)* Blende *f*

apeshit [ˈeɪpʃɪt] ADJ **to go ~** *(sl)* ausflippen *(inf)*

apex [ˈeɪpeks] N *pl* **-es** *or* **apices** Spitze *f*; *(fig)* Höhepunkt *m*

aphasia [əˈfeɪzɪə] N Aphasie *f*

aphasic [əˈfeɪzɪk] **ADJ** aphasisch **N** Aphasiker(in) *m(f)*

aphid [ˈeɪfɪd] N Blattlaus *f*

aphorism [ˈæfərɪzəm] N Aphorismus *m*

aphoristic [ˌæfəˈrɪstɪk] ADJ aphoristisch

aphrodisiac [ˌæfrəʊˈdɪzɪæk] **N** Aphrodisiakum *nt* **ADJ** aphrodisisch

apiarist [ˈeɪpɪərɪst] N Bienenzüchter(in) *m(f)*, Imker(in) *m(f)*

apiary [ˈeɪpɪərɪ] N Bienenhaus *nt*

apices [ˈeɪpɪsiːz] *pl of* **apex**

apiculture [ˈeɪpɪˌkʌltʃəˈ] N *(form)* Bienenzucht *f*, Imkerei *f*

apiece [əˈpiːs] ADV pro Stück; *(= per person)* pro Person; **I gave them two ~** ich gab ihnen je zwei; **they had two cakes ~** sie hatten jeder zwei Kuchen

aplastic anaemia, *(US)* **aplastic anemia** [eɪˈplæstɪkəˈniːmɪə] N *(Med)* aplastische Anämie

aplomb [əˈplɒm] N Gelassenheit *f*; **with ~** gelassen

Apocalypse [əˈpɒkəlɪps] N Apokalypse *f*

apocalyptic [əˌpɒkəˈlɪptɪk] ADJ apokalyptisch

Apocrypha [əˈpɒkrɪfə] N **the ~** die Apokryphen *pl*

apocryphal [əˈpɒkrɪfəl] ADJ apokryph; *(= of unknown authorship)* anonym; **this story, which is probably/certainly ~ ...** diese Geschichte, die wahrscheinlich jeder Wahrheit entbehrt …

apogee [ˈæpəʊdʒiː] N *(Astron)* Apogäum *nt*, Erdferne *f*; *(fig: = apex)* Höhepunkt *m*

apolitical [ˌeɪpəˈlɪtɪkəl] ADJ apolitisch

Apollo [əˈpɒləʊ] N *(Myth)* Apollo *m*; *(fig also)* Apoll *m*

apologetic [əˌpɒləˈdʒetɪk] ADJ *(= making an apology)* entschuldigend *attr*; *(= sorry, regretful)* bedauernd *attr*; **a very ~ Mr Smith rang back** Herr Smith rief zurück und entschuldigte sich sehr; **she wrote me an ~ letter** sie schrieb mir und entschuldigte sich vielmals; **I'm afraid you didn't win, he said with an ~ look** es tut mir leid, aber Sie haben nicht gewonnen, sagte er mit bedauernder Miene; **he was most ~ (about it)** er entschuldigte sich vielmals (dafür); **his tone was very ~** sein Ton war sehr bedauernd; **his expression was very ~** seine Miene drückte deutlich sein Bedauern aus

apologetically [əˌpɒləˈdʒetɪkəlɪ] ADV *say, smile* entschuldigend

apologia [ˌæpəˈləʊdʒɪə] N Rechtfertigung *f*, Apologie *f (also Philos)*

apologist [əˈpɒlədʒɪst] N Apologet(in) *m(f)*

apologize [əˈpɒlədʒaɪz] ✪ 18.1 VI sich entschuldigen *(to* bei); **to ~ for sb/sth** sich für jdn/etw entschuldigen

apology [əˈpɒlədʒɪ] N **a** *(= expression of regret)* Entschuldigung *f*; **to make** *or* **offer sb an ~** jdn um Verzeihung bitten; **to make** *or* **offer one's apologies** sich entschuldigen; **Mr Jones sends his apologies** Herr Jones lässt sich entschuldigen; **I owe you an ~** ich muss dich um Verzeihung bitten; **are there any apologies?** lässt sich jemand entschuldigen?; **I make no ~** *or* **apologies for the fact that ...** ich entschuldige mich nicht dafür, dass …
b *(= poor substitute)* trauriges *or* armseliges Exemplar *(for +gen)*; **an ~ for a breakfast** ein armseliges Frühstück
c *(= defence)* Rechtfertigung *f*, Apologie *f*

apoplectic [ˌæpəˈplektɪk] ADJ *(Med)* apoplektisch; *person also* zu Schlaganfällen neigend; *(inf)* cholerisch; **~ fit** *(Med)* Schlaganfall *m*; **he was ~ with rage** *(inf)* er platzte fast vor Wut *(inf)*

apoplexy [ˈæpəpleksɪ] N Apoplexie *f (spec)*, Schlaganfall *m*

apostasy [əˈpɒstəsɪ] N Abfall *m*; *(Rel also)* Apostasie *f (form)*

apostate [əˈpɒstɪt] **N** Renegat(in) *m(f)*, Abtrünnige(r) *mf*; *(Rel also)* Apostat *m*; **he's an ~ from the party** er ist ein Parteirenegat **ADJ** abtrünnig, abgefallen

apostatize [əˈpɒstətaɪz] VI *(from church, faith, party)* abfallen, sich lossagen *(from* von)

a posteriori [ˈeɪpɒsˌterɪˈɔːraɪ] ADV a posteriori

apostle [əˈpɒsl] N *(lit, fig)* Apostel *m*; **the Apostles' Creed** das Apostolische Glaubensbekenntnis

apostolic [ˌæpəsˈtɒlɪk] ADJ apostolisch; **Apostolic succession** apostolische Nachfolge; **the Apostolic See** der Apostolische Stuhl

apostrophe [əˈpɒstrəfɪ] N **a** *(Gram)* Apostroph *m* **b** *(Liter)* Apostrophe *f*

apostrophize [əˈpɒstrəfaɪz] **VT** apostrophieren *(form)* **VI** sich in feierlichen Reden ergehen

apothecary [əˈpɒθɪkərɪ] N *(old)* Apotheker(in) *m(f)*; **apothecaries' weights and measures** Apothekergewichte und -maße

apotheosis [əˌpɒθɪˈəʊsɪs] N Apotheose *f (liter) (into* zu)

app [æp] N *(Comput inf)* App *f (inf)*

appal, *(US also)* **appall** [əˈpɔːl] VT entsetzen; **to be ~led (at** *or* **by sth)** (über etw *acc*) entsetzt sein

Appalachian Mountains [ˌæpəˈleɪtʃɪənˈmaʊntɪnz], **Appalachians** [ˌæpəˈleɪtʃɪənz] PL Appalachen *pl*

appalling ADJ, **appallingly** ADV [əˈpɔːlɪŋ, -lɪ] entsetzlich

apparatus [ˌæpəˈreɪtəs] N *(lit, fig)* Apparat *m*; *(= equipment also)* Ausrüstung *f*; *(in gym)* Geräte *pl*; **a piece of ~** ein Gerät *nt*; **the ~ of government** der Regierungsapparat

apparel [əˈpærəl] **N** *no pl (liter, US Comm)* Gewand *nt (old, liter)*, Kleidung *f* **VT** *usu pass (old)* gewanden *(old)*

apparent [əˈpærənt] ADJ **a** *(= clear, obvious)* offensichtlich, offenbar; **to be ~ to sb** jdm klar sein, für jdn offensichtlich sein; **it must be ~ to everyone** es muss jedem klar sein; **to become ~** sich (deutlich) zeigen; **for no ~ reason** aus keinem ersichtlichen Grund **b** *(= seeming)* scheinbar; **more ~ than real** mehr Schein als Wirklichkeit

apparently [əˈpærəntlɪ] ADV anscheinend

apparition [ˌæpəˈrɪʃən] N **a** *(= ghost, hum: = person)* Erscheinung *f* **b** *(= appearance)* Erscheinen *nt*

appeal [əˈpiːl] **N** **a** *(= request) (for help, money etc)* Aufruf *m*, Appell *m*, (dringende) Bitte *(for* um); *(for mercy)* Gesuch *nt (for* um); **~ for funds** Spendenappell *or* -aufruf *m or* -aktion *f*; **to make an ~ to sb (to do sth)** an jdn appellieren(, etw zu tun); *(charity, organization etc)* einen Appell *or* Aufruf an jdn richten(, etw zu tun); **to make an ~ to sb for sth** jdn um etw bitten; *(charity, organization etc)* jdn zu etw aufrufen; **to make an ~ for mercy** *(officially)* ein Gnadengesuch einreichen
b *(= supplication)* Flehen *nt*
c *(against decision)* Einspruch *m*; *(Jur) (against sentence)* Berufung *f*; *(actual trial)* Revision *f*, Revisionsverfahren *nt*; **he lost his ~** er verlor in der Berufung; **to lodge an ~** Einspruch erheben; *(Jur)* Berufung einlegen *(with* bei); **right of ~** Einspruchsrecht *nt*; *(Jur)* Berufungsrecht *nt*; **she lost the case on ~** sie hat in der Berufung verloren; **Court of Appeal** Berufungsgericht *nt*
d *(for decision, support)* Appell *m*, Aufruf *m*; **the captain made an ~ against the light** der Mannschaftskapitän erhob Einspruch *or* Beschwerde wegen der Lichtverhältnisse
e *(= power of attraction)* Reiz *m (to* für), Anziehungskraft *f (to* auf *+acc)*; **his music has (a) wide ~** seine Musik spricht viele Leute *or* weite Kreise an *or* findet großen Anklang; **skiing has lost its ~ (for me)** Skifahren hat seinen Reiz (für mich) verloren; **I just don't understand the ~ of it** ich verstehe nicht, was daran so reizvoll sein soll
VI **a** *(= make request)* (dringend) bitten, ersuchen *(geh)*; **to ~ to sb for sth** jdn um etw bitten *or* ersuchen *(geh)*; **to ~ to the public to do sth** die Öffentlichkeit (dazu) aufrufen, etw zu tun
b *(against decision: to authority etc)* Einspruch erheben *(to* bei); *(Jur)* Berufung einlegen *(to* bei); **he was given leave to ~** *(Jur)* es wurde ihm anheimgestellt, Berufung einzulegen
c *(= apply: for support, decision)* sich wenden, appellieren *(to* an *+acc)*; *(to sb's feelings etc)* appellieren *(to* an *+acc)*; *(Sport)* Einspruch erheben *(from* bei), Beschwerde einlegen; **to ~ to sb's better nature** an jds besseres Ich appellieren
d *(= be attractive)* reizen *(to sb* jdn), zusagen *(to sb* jdm); *(plan, candidate, idea)* zusagen *(to sb* jdm); *(book, magazine)* ansprechen *(to sb* jdn); **it simply doesn't ~** es findet einfach keinen Anklang; **how does that ~?** wie gefällt Ihnen das?; **the story ~ed to his sense of humour** die Geschichte sprach seinen Sinn für Humor an
VT **to ~ a case/verdict** *(Jur)* mit einem Fall/gegen ein Urteil in die Berufung gehen; **to ~ a decision** Einspruch gegen eine Entscheidung einlegen *or* erheben

appealable [əˈpiːləbl] ADJ *(Jur)* berufungsfähig, revisionsfähig, beschwerdefähig; **the decision is ~** gegen die Entscheidung kann Berufung eingelegt werden

appeal fund N Hilfsfonds *m*, Spendenfonds *m*

appealing [əˈpiːlɪŋ] ADJ **a** *(= attractive)* attraktiv; *person, character* ansprechend, attraktiv; *smile, eyes* attraktiv, reizvoll; *kitten, child* süß, niedlich; *cottage, house* reizvoll, reizend **b** *(= supplicating) look, voice* flehend

appealingly [əˈpiːlɪŋlɪ] ADV **a** *(= in supplication)* bittend; *look, speak* flehentlich, inbrünstig *(geh)* **b** *(= attractively)* reizvoll

appeal judge N Richter(in) *m(f)* am Berufungsgericht

appear [əˈpɪəˈ] VI **a** *(= emerge)* erscheinen, auftauchen; *(sun)* sich zeigen, erscheinen; **to ~ from behind sth** hinter etw *(dat)* hervorkommen *or* auftauchen; **to ~ through sth** sich zwischen *or* durch etw hindurch zeigen; **as will presently ~** *(fig)* wie sich gleich zeigen wird
b *(= arrive)* erscheinen, auftauchen
c *(in public, Jur)* erscheinen; *(personality, ghost also)* sich zeigen; *(Theat)* auftreten; **to ~ in public** sich in der Öffentlichkeit zeigen;; *(Theat)* vor Publikum auftreten **to ~ in court** vor Gericht erscheinen; *(lawyer)* bei einer Gerichtsverhandlung (dabei)sein; **to ~ for sb** jdn vertreten; **to ~ as a witness** als Zeuge/Zeugin auftreten
d *(= be published)* erscheinen; **to ~ in print** gedruckt werden/sein
e *(= seem)* scheinen; **he ~ed (to be) tired/drunk** er wirkte müde/betrunken, er schien müde/betrunken zu sein; **it ~s that ...** es hat den Anschein, dass …, anscheinend …; **so it ~s, so it would ~** so will es scheinen, so hat es den Anschein; **it ~s not** anscheinend nicht, es sieht nicht so aus; **there ~s** *or* **there would ~ to be a mistake** anscheinend liegt (da) ein Irrtum vor, da scheint ein Irrtum vorzuliegen; **how does it ~ to you?** welchen Eindruck haben Sie?, wie wirkt das auf Sie?; **it ~s to me that ...** mir scheint, dass …; **it ~s from his statement that ...** aus seiner Bemerkung geht hervor *or* ergibt sich, dass …

appearance [əˈpɪərəns] ✪ 16.2 N **a** *(= emergence)* Erscheinen *nt*; *(unexpected)* Auftauchen *nt no pl*; *(Theat)* Auftritt *m*; **many court ~s** viele Auftritte vor Gericht; **to put in** *or* **make an ~** sich sehen lassen; **to make one's ~** sich zeigen; *(Theat)* seinen Auftritt haben; **cast in order of ~** Darsteller in der Reihenfolge ihres Auftritts *or* Auftretens
b *(= look, aspect)* Aussehen *nt*; *(esp of person)* Äußere(s) *nt*, äußere Erscheinung; **~s** *(= outward signs)* der äußere (An)schein; **good ~ es-**

sential gepflegtes Äußeres *or* gepflegte Erscheinung wichtig; **in ~** dem Aussehen nach, vom Äußeren her; **at first ~** auf den ersten Blick; **he/it has the ~ of being ...** er/es erweckt den Anschein, ... zu sein; **for ~s' sake, for the sake of ~s** um den Schein zu wahren, um des Schein(e)s willen; *(= as good manners)* der Form halber; **to keep up ~s** den (äußeren) Schein wahren; **to give the ~ of being ...** sich *(dat)* den Anschein geben, ... zu sein; **~s are often deceptive** der Schein trügt oft; **~s were against him** der Schein sprach gegen ihn; **by** *or* **from** *or* **to all ~s** allem Anschein nach → **judge VT c VI b**

appearance money N *(for TV show etc)* Honorar *nt*; *(= attendance fee)* Sitzungsgeld *nt*

appease [əˈpiːz] VT *(= calm) person, anger* beschwichtigen, besänftigen; *(Pol)* (durch Zugeständnisse) beschwichtigen; *(= satisfy) hunger, thirst* stillen; *curiosity* stillen, befriedigen

appeasement [əˈpiːzmənt] N *(of person, anger)* Beschwichtigung *f*, Besänftigung *f*; *(Pol)* Beschwichtigung *f* (durch Zugeständnisse); *(of curiosity)* Befriedigung *f*

appellant [əˈpelənt] N *(Jur)* Berufungskläger(in) *m(f)*

appellate [əˈpelət] ADJ *(Jur)* Berufungs-, Revisions-, Beschwerde-, zweiter Instanz *(nachgestellt)*; **~ court** Berufungsgericht *nt*, Revisionsgericht *nt*; **~ jurisdiction** Zuständigkeit *f* in der Rechtsmittelinstanz

appellation [ˌæpeˈleɪʃən] N Bezeichnung *f*, Benennung *f*

appellee [ˌæpeˈliː] N *(Jur)* Revisionsbeklagte(r) *mf*, Revisionsgegner(in) *m(f)*

append [əˈpend] VT *notes etc* anhängen *(to* an *+acc) (also Comput)*, hinzufügen; *seal* drücken *(to* auf *+acc)*; *signature* setzen *(to* unter *+acc)*; **the seal/signature ~ed to this document** das Siegel, mit dem/die Unterschrift, mit der das Dokument versehen ist

appendage [əˈpendɪdʒ] N *(= limb)* Gliedmaße *f*; *(fig)* Anhängsel *nt*

appendectomy [ˌæpenˈdektəmɪ], **appendicectomy** [əˌpendɪˈsektəmɪ] N Blinddarmoperation *f*, Appendektomie *f (spec)*

appendices [əˈpendɪsiːz] *pl of* **appendix**

appendicitis [əˌpendɪˈsaɪtɪs] N Blinddarmentzündung *f*, Appendizitis *f (spec)*

appendix [əˈpendɪks] N *pl* **appendices** *or* **-es** **a** *(Anat)* Blinddarm *m*, Appendix *m (spec)*; **to have one's ~ out** sich *(dat)* den Blinddarm herausnehmen lassen **b** *(to book etc)* Anhang *m*, Appendix *m*

apperception [ˌæpəˈsepʃən] N *(Philos, Psych)* bewusste Wahrnehmung

appertain [ˌæpəˈteɪn] VI *(form) (= belong)* gehören *(to* zu), eignen *(+dat) (geh)*; *(= relate)* betreffen *(to sb/sth* jdn/etw); **this does not ~ to the argument** das gehört nicht zur Sache

appetite [ˈæpɪtaɪt] N *(for food etc)* Appetit *m*, (Ess)lust *f*; *(fig: = desire)* Verlangen *nt*, Bedürfnis *nt*, Lust *f*; *(= sexual appetite)* Lust *f*, Begierde *f*; **to have an/no ~ for sth** Appetit *or* Lust/keinen Appetit *or* keine Lust auf etw *(acc)* haben; *(fig)* Verlangen *or* Bedürfnis/kein Verlangen *or* Bedürfnis nach etw haben; **to have a good ~** einen guten *or* gesunden Appetit haben; **I hope you've got an ~** ich hoffe, ihr habt Appetit!; **to take away** *or* **spoil one's ~** sich *(dat)* den Appetit verderben

appetizer [ˈæpɪtaɪzəʳ] N *(= food)* Appetitanreger *m*; *(= hors d'oeuvre also)* Vorspeise *f*, Appetithappen *m*; *(= drink)* appetitanregendes Getränk

appetizing [ˈæpɪtaɪzɪŋ] ADJ appetitlich *(also fig)*; *food also* appetitanregend, lecker; *smell* lecker; *description* verlockend

appetizingly [ˈæpɪtaɪzɪŋlɪ] ADV *present* appetitlich, appetitanregend; *describe* verlockend

Appian Way [ˈæpɪənˌweɪ] N Appische Straße

applaud [əˈplɔːd] **VT** *(lit, fig)* applaudieren, Beifall spenden *or* klatschen *(+dat)*; *(fig) efforts, courage* loben; *decision* gutheißen, begrüßen; **the play was vigorously ~ed** das Stück erhielt stürmischen Beifall *or* wurde lebhaft beklatscht **VI** applaudieren, klatschen, Beifall spenden

applaudable [əˈplɔːdəbl] ADJ lobenswert

applause [əˈplɔːz] N *no pl* Applaus *m*, Beifall *m (also fig)*, Klatschen *nt*; **to be greeted with ~** mit Applaus *or* Beifall *(also fig)* begrüßt werden; **to win sb's ~** bei jdm Beifall finden

apple [ˈæpl] N Apfel *m*; **an ~ a day keeps the doctor away** *(Prov)* esst Obst und ihr bleibt gesund; **the ~ doesn't fall far from the tree** *(Prov)* der Apfel fällt nicht weit vom Stamm *(Prov)*; **to be the ~ of sb's eye** jds Liebling sein

apple *in cpds* Apfel-; **apple brandy** N Apfelschnaps *m*; **apple butter** N *(US)* Apfelkonfitüre *f*; **applecart** N *(fig)* **to upset the ~** alles über den Haufen werfen *(inf)*; **apple dumpling** N ≈ Apfel *m* im Schlafrock; **apple fritters** PL in Teig ausgebackene Apfelringe; **apple green** N Apfelgrün *nt*; **apple-green** ADJ apfelgrün; **applejack** N *(US)* Apfelschnaps *m*; **apple juice** N Apfelsaft *m*; **apple pie** N ≈ gedeckter Apfelkuchen, Apfelpastete *f*; **apple-pie bed** *Bett, bei dem Laken und Decken aus Scherz so gefaltet sind, dass man sich nicht ausstrecken kann*; **in apple-pie order** *(inf)* pikobello *(inf)*; **apple sauce** N **a** *(Cook)* Apfelmus *nt* **b** *(dated US inf: = nonsense)* Schmus *m (inf)*; **apple tree** N Apfelbaum *m*; **apple turnover** N Apfeltasche *f*

appliance [əˈplaɪəns] N **a** Vorrichtung *f*; *(= household appliance)* Gerät *nt*; *(= fire engine)* Feuerwehrwagen *m* **b** *(rare, of skill, knowledge)* Anwenden *nt*, Anwendung *f*; **the ~ of science** die Anwendung wissenschaftlicher Methoden → **application b**

applicability [ˌæplɪkəˈbɪlɪtɪ] N Anwendbarkeit *f (to* auf *+acc)*

applicable [əˈplɪkəbl] ADJ anwendbar *(to* auf *+acc)*; *(on forms)* zutreffend *(to* für); **that isn't ~ to you** das trifft auf Sie nicht zu, das gilt nicht für Sie; **not ~** *(on forms)* entfällt, nicht zutreffend

applicant [ˈæplɪkənt] N *(for job)* Bewerber(in) *m(f)* *(for* um, für); *(for grant, loan etc)* Antragsteller(in) *m(f)* *(for* für, auf *+acc)*; *(for patent)* Anmelder(in) *m(f)* *(for +gen)*

application [ˌæplɪˈkeɪʃən] ✪ 19.3 N **a** *(for job etc)* Bewerbung *f* *(for* um, für); *(for grant, loan etc)* Antrag *m* *(for* auf *+acc)*, Gesuch *nt* *(for* für); *(for patent)* Anmeldung *f (for +gen)*; **available on ~** auf Anforderung *or (written)* Antrag erhältlich; **to make ~ to sb for sth** *(form)* bei jdm etw anfordern; *(written)* einen Antrag auf etw *(acc)* an jdn richten

b *(= act of applying, of paint, ointment, lotion)* Auftragen *nt*; *(of dressing, plaster)* Anlegen *nt*; *(of force, pressure, theory, rules)* Anwenden *nt*, Anwendung *f*; *(of skills, knowledge)* Anwendung *f*, Verwendung *f*; *(of funds)* Verwendung *f* *(to* für), Gebrauch *m* *(to* für); *(Comput: = program)* Anwendung *f*, Applikation *f*; *(of embargo, sanctions)* Verhängen *nt*, Verhängung *f*; **the ~ of a dressing to a head wound** das Anlegen eines Kopfverbandes; **"for external ~ only"** *(Med)* „nur zur äußerlichen Anwendung"

c *(= diligence, effort)* Fleiß *m*, Eifer *m*

d *(form: esp Med)* Mittel *nt*; *(= ointment)* Salbe *f*

e = **applicability**

application: **application form** N Antragsformular *nt*, Antrag *m*; *(for job)* Bewerbungsbogen *m*; **application program** N *(Comput)* Anwendungsprogramm *nt*; **application software** N *(Comput)* Anwendersoftware *f*

applicator [ˈæplɪkeɪtəʳ] N Aufträger *m*; *(for tampons, pessaries)* Applikator *m*

applied [əˈplaɪd] ADJ *attr maths, linguistics etc* angewandt; **~ psychology** angewandte Psychologie

appliqué [æˈpliːkeɪ] *(Sew)* **N** Applikationen *pl*; **to do ~** applizieren **VT** applizieren **ADJ** *attr* **~ work** Stickerei *f*

apply [əˈplaɪ] ✪ 19.1 **VT** *paint, ointment, lotion etc* auftragen *(to* auf *+acc)*, applizieren *(spec)*; *dressing, plaster* anlegen, applizieren *(spec)*; *force, pressure, theory, rules* anwenden *(to* auf *+acc)*; *knowledge, skills* verwenden *(to* für), anwenden *(to* auf *+acc)*; *funds* verwenden *(to* für), gebrauchen *(to* für); *brakes* betätigen; *results, findings* verwerten *(to* für); *one's attention, efforts* zuwenden *(to +dat)*, richten *(to* auf *+acc)*; *embargo, sanctions* verhängen *(to* über *+acc)*; **to ~ oneself/one's mind (to sth)** sich/seinen Kopf *(inf)* (bei etw) anstrengen; **that term can be applied to many things** dieser Begriff kann auf viele Dinge angewendet werden *or* trifft auf viele Dinge zu

VI **a** *(= make an application)* sich bewerben *(for* um, für); **to ~ to sb for sth** sich an jdn wegen etw wenden; *(for job, grant also)* sich bei jdm für *or* um etw bewerben; *(for loan, grant also)* bei jdm etw beantragen; **no-one applied for the reward** keiner hat sich für die Belohnung gemeldet; **~ at the office/next door/within** Anfragen im Büro/nebenan/im Laden; **she has applied to college/university** sie hat sich um einen Studienplatz beworben

b *(= be applicable)* gelten *(to* für); *(warning, threat, regulation)* gelten *(to* für), betreffen *(to +acc)*; *(description)* zutreffen (to auf *+acc*, für)

appoint [əˈpɔɪnt] VT **a** *(to a job)* einstellen; *(to a post)* ernennen; **to ~ sb to an office** jdn in ein Amt berufen; **to ~ sb sth** jdn zu etw ernennen *or* bestellen *(geh) or* als etw *(acc)* berufen; **to ~ sb to do sth** jdn dazu bestimmen, etw zu tun; **they ~ed him to the vacant position** sie gaben ihm die (freie) Stelle; *(professorship)* sie haben ihn auf den Lehrstuhl berufen **b** *(= designate, ordain)* bestimmen; *(= agree)* festlegen *or* -setzen, verabreden, ausmachen; **the date ~ed for that meeting** *(form)* der angesetzte Tagungstermin *(form)*

appointed [əˈpɔɪntɪd] ADJ *hour, place* festgesetzt, festgelegt, verabredet; *task* zugewiesen; *representative, agent* ernannt; **at the ~ time** *or* **the time ~** zur festgelegten *or* -gesetzten *or* verabredeten Zeit; **his ~ task** die ihm übertragene Aufgabe; **at the ~ time** zur festgesetzten *or* -gelegten *or* verabredeten Zeit

-appointed [-əˈpɔɪntɪd] ADJ *suf* **well-/poorly-appointed** gut/dürftig ausgestattet

appointee [əpɔɪnˈtiː] N Ernannte(r) *mf*; **he was a Wilson/political ~** er war von Wilson/aus politischen Gründen ernannt worden; **the ~ to the ambassadorship** der neu bestellte Botschafter

appointment [əˈpɔɪntmənt] **N** **a** *(= pre-arranged meeting)* Verabredung *f*; *(= business appointment, appointment with doctor, lawyer etc)* Termin *m* *(with* bei); **to make** *or* **fix an ~ with sb** mit jdm eine Verabredung treffen/einen Termin mit jdm vereinbaren; **I made an ~ to see the doctor** ich habe mich beim Arzt angemeldet *or* mir beim Arzt einen Termin geben lassen; **do you have an ~?** sind Sie angemeldet?; **to keep an ~** einen Termin einhalten; **by ~** auf Verabredung; *(on business, to see doctor, lawyer etc)* mit (Vor)anmeldung, nach Vereinbarung

b *(= act of appointing) (to a job)* Einstellung *f*; *(to a post)* Ernennung *f*; *(to an office)* Berufung *f* *(to* zu); **his ~ to the position of treasurer** seine Bestellung zum Schatzmeister; **this office is not filled by ~ but by election** für dieses Amt wird man nicht bestellt *or* berufen, sondern gewählt; **"by ~ (to Her Majesty)"** *(on goods)* „königlicher Hoflieferant"

c *(= post)* Stelle *f*; **~s (vacant)** Stellenangebote *pl*

d **appointments**

PL *(= furniture etc)* Ausstattung *f*, Einrichtung *f*

appointments: **appointment(s) book** N Terminkalender *m*; **appointments bureau** N Stellenvermittlung *f*; **appointments diary** N Terminkalender *m*

apportion [əˈpɔːʃən] VT *money, food, land* aufteilen; *duties* zuteilen; **to ~ sth to sb** jdm etw zuteilen; **to ~ sth among** *or* **between several peo-**

ple etw zwischen mehreren Leuten aufteilen, etw unter mehrere Leute (gleichmäßig) verteilen; **the blame must be ~ed equally** die Schuld muss allen in gleicher Weise *or* zu gleichen Teilen angelastet werden

apposite [ˈæpəzɪt] ADJ *comment, phrase* treffend, passend; *question* angebracht

apposition [ˌæpəˈzɪʃən] N Apposition *f*, Beifügung *f*; **A is in ~ to B, A and B are in ~** A ist eine Apposition zu B

appraisal [əˈpreɪzəl] N *(of value, damage)* Abschätzung *f*; *(of character, ability)* Beurteilung *f*; **to make an ~ of the situation** die Lage abschätzen; **his careful/accurate ~** seine sorgfältige/genaue Einschätzung

appraise [əˈpreɪz] VT *(= estimate) value, damage* (ab)schätzen; *(= weigh up) person* einschätzen; *character, ability* (richtig) einschätzen, beurteilen; *situation* abschätzen; *poem etc* beurteilen; *performance* bewerten; **an appraising look** ein prüfender Blick; **he ~d the situation accurately/falsely** er hat die Lage genau/falsch eingeschätzt

appreciable [əˈpriːʃəbl] ADJ beträchtlich, deutlich; *difference, change also* nennenswert, merklich

appreciably [əˈpriːʃəblɪ] ADV beträchtlich, deutlich; *differ, change also* nennenswert, merklich

appreciate [əˈpriːʃɪeɪt] ✪ 7.2, 13, 18.4 VT **a** *(= be aware of) dangers, problems, value etc* sich *(dat)* bewusst sein *(+gen)*; *(= understand) sb's wishes, reluctance etc* Verständnis haben für; **I ~ that you cannot come** ich verstehe, dass ihr nicht kommen könnt

b *(= value, be grateful for)* zu schätzen wissen; **nobody ~s me!** niemand weiß mich zu schätzen!; **thank you, I ~ it** vielen Dank, sehr nett von Ihnen; **my liver would ~ a rest** meine Leber könnte eine kleine Erholung gebrauchen; **I would really ~ that** das wäre mir wirklich sehr lieb; **I would ~ it if you could do this by tomorrow** könnten Sie das bitte bis morgen erledigen?; **I would ~ it if you could be a bit quieter** könnten Sie nicht vielleicht etwas leiser sein?; **we would really ~ it if you would pay what you owe** wir wären Ihnen sehr dankbar *or* verbunden, wenn Sie Ihre Schulden bezahlen würden

c *(= enjoy) art, music, poetry* schätzen

VI *(Fin)* **to ~ (in value)** im Wert steigen, an Wert gewinnen

appreciation [əˌpriːʃɪˈeɪʃən] N **a** *(= awareness: of problems, dangers, advantages, value)* Erkennen *nt*

b *(= esteem, respect)* Anerkennung *f*; *(of abilities, efforts)* Anerkennung *f*, Würdigung *f*; *(of person)* Wertschätzung *f*; **in ~ of sth** in Anerkennung einer Sache *(gen)*, zum Dank für etw; **to show one's ~** seine Dankbarkeit (be)zeigen; **to smile one's ~** zum Dank lächeln

c *(= enjoyment, understanding)* Verständnis *nt*; *(of art)* Sinn *m* (of für); **to show (great) ~ of Mozart/art** großes Mozart-/Kunstverständnis zeigen; **to write an ~ of sb/sth** einen Bericht über jdn/etw schreiben

d *(= comprehension)* Verständnis *nt*

e *(= increase)* (Wert)steigerung *f* (*in* bei)

appreciative [əˈpriːʃɪətɪv] ADJ anerkennend; *audience* dankbar; *(= prepared to accept)* bereitwillig; *(= grateful)* dankbar; **to be ~ of sth** etw zu schätzen wissen; *(of music, art etc)* Sinn für etw haben; *(= aware of)* sich *(dat)* einer Sache *(gen)* bewusst sein

appreciatively [əˈpriːʃɪətɪvlɪ] ADV anerkennend; *(= gratefully)* dankbar

apprehend [ˌæprɪˈhend] VT **a** *(= arrest)* festnehmen **b** *(old, form: = understand)* verstehen **c** *(form: = anticipate)* befürchten

apprehension [ˌæprɪˈhenʃən] N **a** *(= fear)* Besorgnis *f*, Befürchtung *f*; **a feeling of ~** eine dunkle Ahnung *or* Befürchtung; **she felt a moment of ~** sie war einen Moment lang beklommen *or* voller Befürchtungen **b** *(= arrest)* Festnahme *f* **c** *(old, form: = understanding)* Erkennen *nt*

apprehensive [ˌæprɪˈhensɪv] ADJ ängstlich; **to be ~ of sth** etw befürchten; **to be ~ that ...** fürchten, dass ...; **he was ~ about the future** er schaute mit ängstlicher Sorge *or* verzagt in die Zukunft; **to be ~ for sb/about sb's safety** sich *(dat)* Sorgen um jdn/jds Sicherheit machen

apprehensively [ˌæprɪˈhensɪvlɪ] ADV ängstlich

apprentice [əˈprentɪs] N Lehrling *m*, Lehrjunge *m (dated)*, Auszubildende(r) *mf (form)*; **to be an ~** Lehrling sein, in der Lehre sein; **~ plumber/electrician** Klempner-/Elektrikerlehrling *m*; **~ jockey** angehender Jockey VT in die Lehre geben *or* schicken (*to* zu, bei); **to be ~d to sb** bei jdm in die Lehre gehen *or* in der Lehre sein

apprenticeship [əˈprentɪʃɪp] N Lehre *f*, Lehrzeit *f*; **to serve one's ~** seine Lehre *or* Lehrzeit absolvieren *or* machen

apprise [əˈpraɪz] VT *(form)* in Kenntnis setzen *(geh)*, Kenntnis geben *(+dat) (geh)*; **I am ~d that ...** man hat mich davon in Kenntnis gesetzt *or* mir davon Kenntnis gegeben, dass ... *(geh)*

appro [ˈæprəʊ] N *abbr of* **approval**; **on ~** *(Comm) (to try out)* zur Probe; *(to look at)* zur Ansicht

approach [əˈprəʊtʃ] VI *(physically)* sich nähern, näher kommen; *(date, summer etc)* nahen

VT **a** *(= come near)* sich nähern *(+dat)*; *(Aviat)* anfliegen; *(in figures, temperature, time)* zugehen auf *(+acc)*, sich nähern *(+dat)*; *(in quality, stature)* herankommen an *(+acc)*; *(fig)* heranreichen an *(+acc)*; **to ~ thirty** auf die dreißig zugehen; **to ~ adolescence/manhood** ins Pubertätsalter/Mannesalter kommen; **the train is now ~ing platform 3** der Zug hat Einfahrt auf Gleis 3; **something ~ing a festive atmosphere** eine annähernd festliche Stimmung

b *(= make an approach to) person, committee, organization* herantreten an *(+acc)* (*about* wegen), angehen (*about* um), ansprechen (*about* wegen, auf *+acc* hin); **I haven't ~ed him yet** ich habe ihn daraufhin noch nicht angesprochen, ich bin damit noch nicht an ihn herangetreten; **he is easy/difficult to ~** er ist leicht/nicht leicht ansprechbar

c *(= tackle) question, problem, task* angehen, herangehen an *(+acc)*, anpacken

N **a** *(= drawing near)* (Heran)nahen *nt*; *(of troops)* Heranrücken *nt*; *(of night)* Einbruch *m*; *(Aviat)* Anflug *m* (*to* an *+acc*); **at the ~ of Easter** als das Osterfest nahte/wenn das Osterfest naht

b *(to person, committee, organization)* Herantreten *nt*; **to make ~es/an ~ to sb** *(with request)* an jdn herantreten; *(man to woman)* Annäherungsversuche machen

c *(= way of tackling, attitude)* Ansatz *m* (*to* zu); **a positive ~ to mathematics/teaching** eine positive Einstellung zu Mathematik/zum Unterrichten; **his ~ to the problem** seine Art *or* Methode, an das Problem heranzugehen, sein Problemansatz *m*; **you've chosen the wrong ~** du gehst die Sache falsch an; **try a different ~** versuchs doch mal anders; **new ~es in psychology** neue Ansätze in der Psychologie

d *(= access)* Zugang *m*, Weg *m*; *(= road)* Zufahrt(sstraße) *f*

e *(= approximation)* Annäherung *f* (*to* an *+acc*)

approachability [əˌprəʊtʃəˈbɪlɪtɪ] N *(of place)* Zugänglichkeit *f*; *(fig: of person)* Umgänglichkeit *f*

approachable [əˈprəʊtʃəbl] ADJ **a** *person* umgänglich, leicht zugänglich; **he's not ~ today** er ist heute nicht ansprechbar **b** *place* zugänglich; **it's ~ from above** man kommt von oben (heran) **c** *text, idea* verständlich

approaching [əˈprəʊtʃɪŋ] ADJ *attr* näher kommend; *date, occasion* herannahend, bevorstehend

approach: **approach lights** PL *(Aviat)* Lichter *pl* der Einflugschneise; **approach path** N *(Aviat)* Einflugschneise *f*; **approach road** N *(to city etc)* Zufahrtsstraße *f*; *(to motorway)* (Autobahn)zubringer *m*; *(= slip road)* Auf- *or* Einfahrt *f*; **approach shot** N *(Golf)* Schlag *m* zwischen Abschlag und Grün

approbation [ˌæprəˈbeɪʃən] N Zustimmung *f*; *(of decision also)* Billigung *f*; *(from critics)* Beifall *m*

appropriate[1] [əˈprəʊprɪɪt] ✪ 1.1, 26.1 ADJ **a** *(= suitable, fitting)* passend, geeignet (*for, to* für), angebracht (*for, to* für); *(to a situation, occasion)* angemessen (*to +dat*); *name, remark* treffend; **it was ~ that he came at that moment** es traf sich gut, dass er da gerade kam; **clothing ~ for** *or* **to the weather conditions** wettergemäße Kleidung; **a style ~ to one's subject** ein dem Thema entsprechender *or* angemessener Stil; **to be ~ for doing sth** geeignet sein, etw zu tun

b *(= relevant)* entsprechend; *body, authority* zuständig; **where ~** wo es angebracht ist/war, an gegebener Stelle; **put a tick where ~** Zutreffendes bitte ankreuzen; **delete as ~** Nichtzutreffendes *or* nicht Zutreffendes streichen; **it may be ~ (for you) to discuss this with your lawyer** sie sollten das vielleicht mit Ihrem Anwalt besprechen

appropriate[2] [əˈprəʊprɪeɪt] VT **a** *(= assume possession or control of)* beschlagnahmen; *(= take for oneself)* sich *(dat)* aneignen, mit Beschlag belegen; *sb's ideas* sich *(dat)* zu eigen machen

b *(= allocate) funds* zuteilen, zuweisen

appropriately [əˈprəʊprɪɪtlɪ] ADV treffend; *dressed* passend (*for, to* für), entsprechend (*for, to +dat*); *(= to fit particular needs) designed, equipped* entsprechend (*for, to +dat*), zweckmäßig (*for, to* für); **~ enough the letter arrived at that very moment** passenderweise kam der Brief genau in dem Augenblick; **rather ~ she was called Goldilocks** der Name Goldköpfchen passte sehr gut zu ihr

appropriateness [əˈprəʊprɪɪtnɪs] N *(= suitability, fittingness)* Eignung *f*; *(of dress, remark, name, for a particular occasion)* Angemessenheit *f*

appropriation [əˌprəʊprɪˈeɪʃən] N **a** *(of land, property)* Beschlagnahme *f*, Beschlagnahmung *f*; *(of sb's ideas)* Aneignung *f* **b** *(= allocation: of funds)* Zuteilung *f*, Zuweisung *f*; **to make an ~ for sth** Mittel für etw zuteilen *or* zuweisen

approval [əˈpruːvəl] N **a** Beifall *m*, Anerkennung *f*; *(= consent)* Zustimmung *f* (*of* zu), Billigung *f* (*of +gen*), Einverständnis *nt* (*of* mit); **to win sb's ~ (for sth)** jds Zustimmung (für etw) gewinnen; **to give one's ~ for sth** seine Zustimmung zu etw geben; **to meet with sb's ~** jds Zustimmung *or* Beifall finden; **to seek sb's ~ for sth** jds Zustimmung zu etw suchen; **to have sb's ~** jds Zustimmung haben; **to show one's ~ of sth** zeigen, dass man einer Sache *(dat)* zustimmt *or* etw billigt; **submitted for the Queen's ~** der Königin zur Genehmigung vorgelegt **b** *(Comm)* **on ~** zur Probe; *(to look at)* zur Ansicht

approval rate N *(Pol)* **his ~ is 52 per cent** 52% der Bevölkerung sind mit seiner Politik einverstanden

approve [əˈpruːv] ✪ 14 VT *(= consent to) decision* billigen, gutheißen; *minutes, motion* annehmen; *project, sale, deal, plan* genehmigen; *(= recommend) hotel, campsite etc* empfehlen; **an ~d campsite** ein empfohlener Campingplatz

VI **to ~ of sb/sth** von jdm/etw etwas halten, etw billigen *or* gutheißen; **I don't ~ of him/it** ich halte nichts von ihm/davon; **do you ~ of him/that?** hältst du etwas von ihm/davon?; **I don't ~ of children smoking** ich billige nicht *or* kann es nicht gutheißen, dass Kinder rauchen; **she doesn't ~** sie missbilligt das; **how's this shirt, do you ~?** gefällt dir dies Hemd?

approved school [əˈpruːvdˈskuːl] N *(Brit dated)* Erziehungsheim *nt*

approving [əˈpruːvɪŋ] ADJ *(= satisfied, pleased)* anerkennend, beifällig; *(= consenting)* zustimmend

approvingly [əˈpruːvɪŋlɪ] ADV anerkennend, beifällig

approx. *abbr of* **approximately** ca.

approximate [ə'prɒksɪmɪt] ADJ ungefähr; **these figures are only ~** dies sind nur ungefähre Werte; **three hours is the ~ time needed** man braucht ungefähr drei Stunden [ə'prɒksəmeɪt] VI **to ~ to sth** einer Sache *(dat)* in etwa entsprechen; **they ~ to one another** sie entsprechen einander in etwa [ə'prɒksəmeɪt] VT **to ~ sth** einer Sache *(dat)* in etwa entsprechen

approximately [ə'prɒksɪmətlɪ] ADV ungefähr, etwa, circa; *correct* in etwa, annähernd

approximation [əˌprɒksɪ'meɪʃən] N Annäherung *f (of, to* an *+acc); (= figure, sum etc)* (An)näherungswert *m;* **his story was an ~ of the truth** seine Geschichte entsprach in etwa *or* ungefähr der Wahrheit

appurtenances [ə'pɜ:tɪnənsɪz] PL *(= equipment)* Zubehör *nt; (= accessories)* Attribute *pl; (Jur: = rights etc)* Rechte *pl;* **with all the ~ of affluence** mit allen Attributen des Wohlstands

APR *abbr of* **annual percentage rate** Jahreszinssatz *m*

après-ski [ˌæpreɪ'ski:] N Après-Ski *nt* ADJ *attr* Après-Ski-; **~ bar** Après-Ski-Lokal *nt*

apricot ['eɪprɪkɒt] N Aprikose *f* ADJ (*also* **apricot-coloured**) aprikosenfarben *attr* Aprikosen-; **~ jam** Aprikosenmarmelade *f*

April ['eɪprəl] N April *m;* **~ shower** Aprilschauer *m* → *also* **September**

April fool N Aprilnarr *m;* **~!** ≈ April, April!; **to play an ~ on sb** jdn in den April schicken

April Fools' Day N der erste April

a priori [eɪpraɪ'ɔ:raɪ] ADV a priori ADJ apriorisch

apron ['eɪprən] N Schürze *f; (Aviat)* Vorfeld *nt; (Theat)* Vorbühne *f*

apron: apron stage N Bühne *f* mit Vorbühne; **apron strings** PL Schürzenbänder *pl;* **to be tied to sb's ~** jdm am Schürzenzipfel hängen *(inf)*

apropos [ˌæprə'pəʊ] PREP (*also* **apropos of**) apropos *(+nom);* **~ of nothing** ganz nebenbei ADJ *pred remark* passend, treffend

apse [æps] N Apsis *f*

APT *abbr of* **advanced passenger train** Hochgeschwindigkeitszug *m*

apt [æpt] ADJ *(+er)* **a** *(= suitable, fitting)* passend; *description, comparison, remark* passend, treffend **b** *(= able, intelligent)* begabt *(at* für) **c** *(= liable, likely)* **to be ~ to do sth** leicht etw tun, dazu neigen, etw zu tun; **he is ~ to be late** er neigt dazu, zu spät zu kommen; **I was ~ to believe him until …** ich war geneigt, ihm zu glauben, bis …; **it is ~ to rain in Glasgow** es regnet oft in Glasgow; **we are ~ to forget that …** wir vergessen leicht *or* gern *(inf)*, dass …

Apt. *abbr of* **apartment** Z, Zi

aptitude ['æptɪtju:d] N Begabung *f;* **she has a great ~ for saying the wrong thing** *(hum)* sie hat ein besonderes Talent dafür, immer das Falsche zu sagen

aptitude test N Eignungsprüfung *f*

aptly ['æptlɪ] ADV passend; **it did not fit ~ into the context** es passte nicht richtig in den Zusammenhang

aptness ['æptnɪs] N **a** *(= suitability)* **the ~ of the name was obvious** der Name war offensichtlich passend **b** *(= aptitude)* Begabung *f* **c** *(= liability, likelihood)* Neigung *f*

aquaculture ['ækwəkʌltʃə'] N Aquakultur *f*

aquajogging ['ækwəˌdʒɒgɪŋ] N Aquajogging *nt*

aqualung ['ækwəlʌŋ] N Tauchgerät *nt*

aquamarine [ˌækwəmə'ri:n] N Aquamarin *m; (= colour)* Aquamarin *nt* ADJ aquamarin

aquanaut ['ækwənɔ:t] N Aquanaut(in) *m(f)*

aquanautics [ˌækwə'nɔ:tɪks] N *sing* Aquanautik *f*

aqua noodle ['ækwə-] N *(= swimming aid)* Aquanudel *f*, Schwimmnudel *f*

aqua park ['ækwə-] N Aquapark *m*

aquaplane ['ækwəpleɪn] N Monoski *m* VI **a** *(Sport)* Wasserski laufen **b** *(car etc)* (auf nasser Straße) ins Rutschen geraten

aquaplaning ['ækwəpleɪnɪŋ] N Aquaplaning *nt;* **in order to prevent the car from ~** um ein Aquaplaning zu verhindern

aquarium [ə'kwɛərɪəm] N Aquarium *nt*

Aquarius [ə'kwɛərɪəs] N Wassermann *m*

aquarobics [ˌækwə'rəʊbɪks] N *sing (Sport)* Aquarobic *nt*

aquatic [ə'kwætɪk] ADJ Wasser-; *plants, animals, organisms etc also* im Wasser lebend, aquatisch *(spec);* **~ sports** Wassersport *m*

aquatint ['ækwətɪnt] N Aquatinta *f*

aqueduct ['ækwɪdʌkt] N Aquädukt *m or nt*

aqueous ['eɪkwɪəs] ADJ *(form) rocks* wasserhaltig; *solution* wässrig

aqueous humour N *(Med)* Kammerwasser *nt*, Humor aquosus *m (spec)*

aquiline ['ækwɪlaɪn] ADJ gebogen; *profile* mit Adlernase, dinarisch *(geh);* **~ nose** Adlernase *f*

Aquinas [ə'kwaɪnəs] N Thomas von Aquin

Arab ['ærəb] N Araber *m (also horse)*, Araberin *f;* **the ~s** die Araber ADJ *attr* arabisch; *policies, ideas also* der Araber; **~ horse** Araber *m*

arabesque [ˌærə'besk] N Arabeske *f*

Arabia [ə'reɪbɪə] N Arabien *nt*

Arabian [ə'reɪbɪən] ADJ arabisch; **tales of the ~ Nights** Märchen aus Tausendundeiner Nacht

Arabic ['ærəbɪk] N Arabisch *nt* ADJ arabisch; **~ numerals** arabische Ziffern *or* Zahlen; **~ studies** Arabistik *f*

arable ['ærəbl] ADJ Acker-; **~ farming** Ackerbau *m;* **~ land** bebaubares Land; *(in use)* Ackerland *nt*

arachnid [ə'ræknɪd] N Spinnentier *nt*

arachnology [ˌæræk'nɒlədʒɪ] N Arachnologie *f*, Spinnenkunde *f*

arachnophobia [əˌræknəʊ'fəʊbɪə] N Arachnophobie *f*, Angst *f* vor Spinnen

Aragon ['ærəgən] N Aragon *nt*, Aragonien *nt*

arbiter ['ɑ:bɪtə'] N **a** *(of fate etc)* Herr(in) *m(f)*, Gebieter(in) *m(f) (of* über *+acc);* **to be the ~ of** Herr(in) sein über *(+acc);* **they were the ~s of good taste/style** sie waren die Päpste des guten Geschmacks/Stils **b** = **arbitrator**

arbitrarily ['ɑ:bɪtrərəlɪ] ADV willkürlich, arbiträr *(geh)*

arbitrariness ['ɑ:bɪtrərɪnɪs] N Willkürlichkeit *f*

arbitrary ['ɑ:bɪtrərɪ] ADJ willkürlich, arbiträr *(geh)*

arbitrate ['ɑ:bɪtreɪt] VT *dispute* schlichten VI **a** *(in dispute)* vermitteln **b** *(= go to arbitration)* vor eine Schlichtungskommission gehen

arbitration [ˌɑ:bɪ'treɪʃən] N Schlichtung *f;* **to submit a dispute to ~** einen Streit vor ein Schiedsgericht *or (esp Ind)* eine Schlichtungskommission bringen; **to go to ~** vor eine Schlichtungskommission gehen; *(dispute)* vor eine Schlichtungskommission gebracht werden

arbitrator ['ɑ:bɪtreɪtə'] N Vermittler(in) *m(f); (esp Ind)* Schlichter(in) *m(f)*

arbor ['ɑ:bə'] N *(US)* = **arbour**

arboreal [ɑ:'bɔ:rɪəl] ADJ *animal, bird* auf Bäumen lebend; *habitat* auf Bäumen

arboretum [ˌɑ:bə'ri:təm] N Arboretum *nt (spec)*, Baumschule *f*

arborist ['ɑ:bərɪst] N Baumzüchter(in) *m(f)*

arbour, *(US)* **arbor** ['ɑ:bə'] N Laube *f*

arbutus [ɑ:'bju:təs] N Arbutus *m*

arc [ɑ:k] N Bogen *m*

arcade [ɑ:'keɪd] N *(Archit)* Arkade *f; (= shopping arcade)* Passage *f*

Arcadia [ɑ:'keɪdɪə] N Arkadien *nt*

Arcadian [ɑ:'keɪdɪən] ADJ *(lit, fig)* arkadisch

arcane [ɑ:'keɪn] ADJ obskur

arch¹ [ɑ:tʃ] N **a** Bogen *m;* **~ of the heavens** Himmelsbogen *m*, Himmelsgewölbe *nt* **b** *(Anat, of foot)* Gewölbe *nt (spec);* **high/fallen ~es** hoher Spann/Senkfuß *m;* **~ support** Senkfußeinlage *f* VI sich wölben; *(arrow etc)* einen Bogen machen VT *back* krümmen; *eyebrows* hochziehen; **the cat ~ed its back** die Katze machte einen Buckel

arch² ADJ *attr* Erz-; **~ enemy** Erzfeind(in) *m(f);* **~ rival** Erzrivale *m*, Erzrivalin *f;* **~ traitor** Hochverräter(in) *m(f)*

arch³ ADJ *(= wicked, mischievous)* neckisch, schelmisch

archaeological, *(US)* **archeological** [ˌɑ:kɪə'lɒdʒɪkəl] ADJ archäologisch

archaeologist, *(US)* **archeologist** [ˌɑ:kɪ'ɒlədʒɪst] N Archäologe *m*, Archäologin *f*

archaeology, *(US)* **archeology** [ˌɑ:kɪ'ɒlədʒɪ] N Archäologie *f*

archaic [ɑ:'keɪɪk] ADJ *word etc* veraltet, archaisch *(spec); (inf: = ancient)* vorsintflutlich; **my car is getting rather ~** mein Auto wird allmählich museumsreif

archaism ['ɑ:keɪɪzəm] N veralteter Ausdruck, Archaismus *m*

arch: archangel ['ɑ:kˌeɪndʒl] N Erzengel *m;* **archbishop** N Erzbischof *m;* **archbishopric** N *(= district)* Erzbistum *nt*, Erzdiözese *f; (= office)* Amt *nt* des Erzbischofs; **archdeacon** N Archidiakon *m*, Erzdiakon *m;* **archdiocese** N Erzdiözese *f*, Erzbistum *nt;* **archducal** ADJ erzherzoglich; **archduchess** N Erzherzogin *f;* **archduchy** N Erzherzogtum *nt;* **archduke** N Erzherzog *m*

arched [ɑ:tʃt] ADJ gewölbt; **~ window** (Rund)bogenfenster *nt;* **the ~ curve of the temple roof** die Wölbung des Tempeldachs

archeological *etc (US)* = **archaeological** *etc*

archer ['ɑ:tʃə'] N Bogenschütze *m*/-schützin *f; (Astron, Astrol)* Schütze *m*

archery ['ɑ:tʃərɪ] N Bogenschießen *nt*

archetypal [ˌɑ:kɪtaɪpəl] ADJ archetypisch *(geh); (= typical)* typisch; **he is the ~ millionaire** er ist ein Millionär, wie er im Buche steht; **an ~ Scot** ein Urschotte *(inf)*

archetypally [ˌɑ:kɪ'taɪpəlɪ] ADV archetypisch

archetype ['ɑ:kɪtaɪp] N Archetyp(us) *m (form); (= original, epitome also)* Urbild *nt*, Urtyp *m*

archetypical [ˌɑ:kɪ'tɪpɪkəl] ADJ = **archetypal**

archfiend [ɑ:tʃ'fi:nd] N **the ~** der Erzfeind

archiepiscopal [ˌɑ:kɪɪ'pɪskəpəl] ADJ erzbischöflich

Archimedes [ˌɑ:kɪ'mi:di:z] N Archimedes *m*

Archimedes' principle [ˌɑ:kɪ'mi:di:z-] N das archimedische Prinzip

archipelago [ˌɑ:kɪ'pelɪgəʊ] N *pl* **-(e)s** Archipel *m;* **the Archipelago** der Archipel(agos); *(= sea)* die Ägäis

architect ['ɑ:kɪtekt] N *(lit, fig)* Architekt(in) *m(f);* **~-designed** von (einem) Architekten entworfen; **he was the ~ of his own downfall** er hat seinen Ruin selbst verursacht

architectural ADJ, **architecturally** ADV [ˌɑ:kɪ'tektʃərəl, -ɪ] architektonisch

architecture ['ɑ:kɪtektʃə'] N Architektur *f (also Comput); (of building also)* Baustil *m*

architrave ['ɑ:kɪtreɪv] N *(Archit)* Architrav *m; (= frame)* architravähnliche Einfassung *(für Tür)*

archival [ɑ:'kaɪvəl] ADJ archivalisch, Archiv-

archive ['ɑ:kaɪv] N Archiv *nt (also Comput);* **~ file** Archivdatei *f;* **~ material/film** Archivmaterial *nt*/-film *m* VT archivieren

archives ['ɑ:kaɪvz] PL Archiv *nt*

archivist ['ɑ:kɪvɪst] N Archivar(in) *m(f)*

archly ['ɑ:tʃlɪ] ADV neckisch, schelmisch

archness ['ɑ:tʃnɪs] N neckische *or* schelmische Art

archpriest ['ɑ:tʃ'pri:st] N *(lit, fig)* Hohepriester *m*

archway ['ɑ:tʃweɪ] N Torbogen *m*

arc lamp, **arc light** N Bogenlampe *f*, Bogenlicht *nt*

arctic [ˈɑːktɪk] ADJ *(lit, fig)* arktisch N a **the Arctic** die Arktis b *(US: = shoe) gefütterter, wasserundurchlässiger Überschuh*

arctic: **Arctic Circle** N nördlicher Polarkreis; **arctic fox** N Polarfuchs *m*; **Arctic Ocean** N Nordpolarmeer *nt*

arc welding N (Licht)bogenschweißung *f*

ardent [ˈɑːdənt] ADJ leidenschaftlich; *supporter, admirer also* begeistert; *love also* glühend; *desire, longing also* brennend, glühend; *request, imprecations* inständig

ardently [ˈɑːdəntlɪ] ADV leidenschaftlich; *love* heiß; *desire, admire* glühend

ardour, *(US)* **ardor** [ˈɑːdəˈ] N *(of person)* Begeisterung *f*, Leidenschaft *f*; *(in voice also)* Überschwang *m*; *(of feelings also)* Heftigkeit *f*; *(of passions)* Glut *f (liter)*, Feuer *nt*; *(of poems, letters)* Leidenschaftlichkeit *f*; **the ~s of youth** die Leidenschaft der Jugend

arduous [ˈɑːdjʊəs] ADJ beschwerlich, mühsam; *course, work* anstrengend; *task* mühselig

arduousness [ˈɑːdjʊəsnɪs] N Beschwerlichkeit *f*; *(of task)* Mühseligkeit *f*; **because of the ~ of the work** weil die Arbeit so anstrengend war/ist

are[1] [ɑːˈ] N Ar *nt*

are[2] *2nd pers sing, 1st, 2nd, 3rd pers pl present of* **be**

area [ˈɛərɪə] N a *(measure)* Fläche *f*; **20 sq metres** *(Brit)* or **meters** *(US)* **in ~** eine Fläche von 20 Quadratmetern

b *(= region, district)* Gebiet *nt*; *(= neighbourhood, vicinity)* Gegend *f*; *(separated off, piece of ground etc)* Areal *nt*, Gelände *nt*; *(on plan, diagram etc)* Bereich *m*; *(= slum area, residential area, commercial area)* Viertel *nt*, Gebiet *nt*; **this is not a very nice ~ to live in** dies ist keine besonders gute Wohngegend; **in the ~** in der Nähe; **do you live in the ~?** wohnen Sie hier (in der Gegend)?; **in the ~ of the station** in der Bahnhofsgegend; **the thief is believed to be still in the ~** man nimmt an, dass sich der Dieb noch in der Umgebung aufhält; **in the London ~** im Raum London, im Londoner Raum; **protected/prohibited/industrial ~** Schutz-/Sperr-/ /Industriegebiet *nt*; **drying/dispatch ~** Trocken-/ /Verteilerzone *f*; **dining/sleeping ~** Ess-/Schlafbereich *or* -platz *m*; **no smoking/recreation ~** Nichtraucher-/Erholungszone *f*; **we use this corner as a discussion ~** wir benutzen diese Ecke für Diskussionen; **the goal ~** *(Ftbl)* der Torraum; **the (penalty) ~** *(esp Brit Ftbl)* der Strafraum; **this ~ is for directors' cars** dieser Platz ist für Direktorenwagen vorgesehen; **you must keep out of this ~** dieses Gebiet darf nicht betreten werden; **this ~ must be kept clear** diesen Platz frei halten; **the public were told to keep well away from the ~** die Öffentlichkeit wurde aufgefordert, das Gebiet unbedingt zu meiden; **a mountainous ~** eine bergige Gegend; **mountainous ~s** Bergland *nt*; **a wooded ~** ein Waldstück *nt*; *(larger)* ein Waldgebiet *nt*; **desert ~s** Wüstengebiete *pl*; **the infected ~s of the lungs** die befallenen Teile *or (smaller)* Stellen der Lunge; **the patchy ~s on the wall** die fleckigen Stellen an der Wand; **the additional message ~ on an air letter** der Raum für zusätzliche Mitteilungen auf einem Luftpostbrief; **the sterling ~** die Sterlingzone

c *(fig)* Bereich *m*; **~s of uncertainty/agreement** Bereiche, in denen Unklarheit/Übereinstimmung besteht; **his ~ of responsibility** sein Verantwortungsbereich *m*; **~ of interest/study** Interessen-/Studiengebiet *nt*; **a sum in the ~ of £100** eine Summe um die £ 100

d *(Brit: = basement courtyard)* Vorplatz *m*

area: **area bombing** N Flächenbombardierungen *pl*; **area code** N *(Telec)* Vorwahl(nummer) *f*, Ortskennzahl *f*; **area command** N Gebiets- *or* Abschnittskommandantur *f*; **area manager** N Bezirks- *or* Gebietsleiter *m*; **area office** N Bezirksbüro *nt*; **areaway** N *(US)* a Vorplatz *m* b *(= passage)* Durchgang *m*, Passage *f*

arena [əˈriːnə] N *(lit, fig)* Arena *f*; **~ of war** Kriegsschauplatz *m*; **to enter the ~** *(fig)* die Arena betreten, auf den Plan treten

aren't [ɑːnt] = **are not, am not**, → **be**

areola [əˈriːələ] N *pl* **areolae** *(Anat: of nipple)* Areola *f (spec)*, Warzenhof *m*; *(Med: of spot) entzündeter Hautring um einen Pickel*

argent [ˈɑːdʒənt] *(obs, poet, Her)* N Silber *nt* ADJ silbern

Argentina [ˌɑːdʒənˈtiːnə] N Argentinien *nt*

Argentine [ˈɑːdʒəntaɪn] N **the ~** Argentinien *nt*

Argentinian [ˌɑːdʒənˈtɪnɪən] N *(= person)* Argentinier(in) *m(f)* ADJ argentinisch

argon [ˈɑːgɒn] N Argon *nt*

Argonaut [ˈɑːgənɔːt] N Argonaut *m*

argot [ˈɑːgəʊ] N Argot *nt or m*; *(criminal also)* Rotwelsch *nt*

arguable [ˈɑːgjʊəbl] ADJ a *(= capable of being maintained)* vertretbar; **it is ~ that ...** es lässt sich der Standpunkt vertreten, dass ..., man kann behaupten, dass ... b *(= open to discussion)* **it is ~ whether ...** es ist (noch) die Frage, ob ...

arguably [ˈɑːgjʊəblɪ] ADV wohl; **this is ~ his best book** dies dürfte (wohl) sein bestes Buch sein

argue [ˈɑːgjuː] ✪ 26.1, 26.3 VI a *(= dispute)* streiten; *(= quarrel)* sich streiten; *(about trivial things)* sich zanken; **he is always arguing** er widerspricht ständig, er muss immer streiten; **there's no arguing with him** mit ihm kann man nicht reden; **don't ~ (with me)!** keine Widerrede!; **don't ~ with your mother!** du sollst deiner Mutter nicht widersprechen!; **I don't want to ~, if you don't want to** ich will mich nicht streiten, wenn Sie nicht wollen; **there is no point in arguing** da erübrigt sich jede (weitere) Diskussion; **you can't ~ with a line of tanks** mit Panzern kann man nicht diskutieren; **a 25% increase, you can't ~ with that** *(inf)* eine 25%ige Erhöhung, da kann man nichts sagen *(inf)* or nicht meckern *(inf)*; **he wasn't used to employees arguing** Angestellte, die ihre Meinung sagten, war er nicht gewöhnt

b *(= present reasons)* **to ~ for** *or* **in favour** *(Brit)* or **favor** *(US)* **of sth** für etw sprechen; *(in book)* sich für etw aussprechen; **to ~ against sth** gegen etw sprechen; *(in book)* sich gegen etw aussprechen; **to ~ from a position of ...** von einem *or* dem Standpunkt ... *(gen)* aus argumentieren; **this ~s in his favour** *(Brit)* or **favor** *(US)* das spricht zu seinen Gunsten; **just one thing ~s against him/it** nur eins spricht gegen ihn/dagegen

VT a *(= debate) case, matter* diskutieren, erörtern; *(Jur)* vertreten; **a well ~d case** ein gut begründeter *or* dargelegter Fall; **to ~ a case for reform** die Sache der Reform vertreten; **to ~ one's way out of sth** sich aus etw herausreden

b *(= maintain)* behaupten; **he ~s that ...** er vertritt den Standpunkt, dass ..., er behauptet, dass ...; **I'm not arguing that ...** ich will nicht behaupten, dass ...

c *(= persuade)* **to ~ sb out of/into sth** jdm etw aus-/einreden

d *(= indicate)* erkennen lassen, verraten

▶ **argue away** VI diskutieren VT *sep facts* wegdiskutieren

▶ **argue out** VT *sep problem, issue* ausdiskutieren; **to argue sth out with sb** etw mit jdm durchsprechen

arguer [ˈɑːgjuːəˈ] N a *(= quarreller)* streitsüchtiger Mensch, Streithammel *m (inf)* b *(= reasoner)* logisch argumentierender Mensch; **to be a logical ~** logisch argumentieren (können)

argufy [ˈɑːgjuːfaɪ] VI *(esp hum)* wegen jeder Kleinigkeit streiten

argument [ˈɑːgjʊmənt] ✪ 26.1 N a *(= discussion)* Diskussion *f*; **to spend hours in ~ about how to do sth** stundenlang darüber diskutieren, wie man etw macht; **for the sake of ~** rein theoretisch; **he just said that for the sake of ~** das hat er nur gesagt, um etwas (dagegen) zu sagen; **it is beyond ~** das ist unbestreitbar; **he is open to ~** er lässt mit sich reden; **this is open to ~** darüber lässt sich streiten

b *(= quarrel)* Auseinandersetzung *f*; **to have an ~** sich streiten; *(over sth trivial)* sich zanken; **without ~** widerspruchslos

c *(= reason)* Beweis(grund) *m*, Argument *nt*; *(= line of reasoning)* Argumentation *f*, Beweisführung *f*; **first state your theory, then list the ~s for and against** stellen Sie erst Ihre These auf und nennen Sie dann die Gründe und Gegengründe; **one of the best ~s I have heard in favour** *(Brit)* or **favor** *(US)* **of private education** eines der besten Argumente zugunsten *or* zu Gunsten der Privatschule, die ich gehört habe; **there's an even stronger ~ than that** es gibt ein noch stärkeres Argument; **that's not a rational ~, it's just a dogmatic assertion** das ist kein rationales Argument, das ist bloß eine dogmatische Behauptung

d *(= theme: of play, book etc)* Aussage *f*, These *f (esp Philos)*; *(= claim)* These *f*

e *(= statement of proof)* Beweis *m*; **the two main types of ~** die beiden wichtigsten Beweisarten; **Professor Ayer's ~ is that ...** Professor Ayers These lautet, dass ...; **the Ontological/Teleological Argument** der ontologische/teleologische Gottesbeweis; **all the various ~s for the existence of a god** all die verschiedenen Gottesbeweise; **I don't think that's a valid ~** ich glaube, das ist kein gültiger Beweis; **an interesting ~** eine interessante These

f *(Math)* Argument *nt*

argumentation [ˌɑːgjʊmənˈteɪʃən] N Argumentation *f*, Beweisführung *f*; *(= discussion)* Diskussion *f*; **an ingenious piece of ~** eine geniale Beweisführung

argumentative [ˌɑːgjʊˈmentətɪv] ADJ *person* streitsüchtig

argy-bargy [ˈɑːdʒɪˈbɑːdʒɪ] *(Brit inf)* N Hin und Her *nt (inf)*, Hickhack *m or nt (inf)* VI hin und her reden, endlos debattieren

aria [ˈɑːrɪə] N Arie *f*

Arian[1] [ˈɛərɪən] N ADJ = **Aryan**

Arian[2] *(Astrol)* N Widder *m*; **to be an ~** Widder sein

ARIBA [əˈriːbə] *abbr of* **Associate of the Royal British Institute of Architects** *Mitglied des britischen Architektenverbandes*

arid [ˈærɪd] ADJ *(lit) countryside, soil* dürr; *climate* trocken, arid *(spec)*; *(fig) subject* trocken, nüchtern; *existence* freudlos, öd

aridity [əˈrɪdɪtɪ] N *(of countryside, soil)* Dürre *f*; *(of climate)* Trockenheit *f*, Aridität *f (spec)*; *(fig: of subject)* Trockenheit *f*, Nüchternheit *f*; *(of existence)* Freudlosigkeit *f*, Öde *f*

Aries [ˈɛəriːz] N *(Astrol)* Widder *m*; **she is (an) ~** sie ist Widder

aright [əˈraɪt] ADV recht, wohl *(old)*; **if I understand it ~** wenn ich das recht verstehe

arise [əˈraɪz] *pret* **arose** [əˈrəʊz] *ptp* **arisen** [əˈrɪzn] VI a *(= occur)* sich ergeben, entstehen; *(misunderstanding, argument)* aufkommen, entstehen; *(problem)* aufkommen, sich ergeben; *(clouds of dust)* entstehen, sich bilden; *(protest, cry)* sich erheben; *(question)* sich stellen, aufkommen, sich erheben *(geh)*; *(wind)* aufkommen, sich erheben *(geh)*; **should the need ~** falls sich die Notwendigkeit ergibt b *(= result)* **to ~ out of** *or* **from sth** sich aus etw ergeben c *(old, liter. = get up)* sich erheben *(liter)*; **~ Sir Humphrey** erhebt Euch, Sir Humphrey!

aristocracy [ˌærɪsˈtɒkrəsɪ] N *(system, state)* Aristokratie *f*; *(= class also)* Adel *m*; **~ of wealth** Geldadel *m*, Geldaristokratie *f*

aristocrat [ˈærɪstəkræt] N Aristokrat(in) *m(f)*, Adlige(r) *mf*; **he is too much of an ~ to ...** *(fig)* er ist sich *(dat)* zu fein, um ... zu ...; **the ~ of the dog/cat family** der edelste Vertreter der Hunde-/Katzenfamilie

aristocratic [ˌærɪstəˈkrætɪk] ADJ *(lit)* aristokratisch, adlig; *(fig also)* vornehm

Aristotelian [ˌærɪstəˈtiːlɪən] ADJ aristotelisch N Aristoteliker *m*

Aristotle [ˈærɪstɒtl] N Aristoteles *m*

arithmetic [əˈrɪθmətɪk] N Rechnen *nt*; *(= calculation)* Rechnung *f*; **could you check my ~?** kannst du mal gucken, ob ich richtig gerechnet habe?; **your ~ is wrong** du hast dich verrechnet; **~ book** Rechenfibel *f or* -buch *nt*; *(= exercise book)* Rechenheft *nt*

arithmetical [ˌærɪθˈmetɪkəl] ADJ rechnerisch; **~ genius** Rechenkünstler(in) *m(f)*; **the basic ~ skills** Grundwissen *nt* im Rechnen; **~ progression** arithmetische Reihe

arithmetician [əˌrɪθməˈtɪʃən] N Rechner(in) *m(f)*

arithmetic mean N arithmetisches Mittel

ark [ɑːk] N **a** Arche *f*; **it looks as though it's come out of the ~** *(inf)* das sieht aus wie von anno Tobak *(inf)* **b Ark of the Covenant** Bundeslade *f*

arm¹ [ɑːm] N **a** *(Anat)* Arm *m*; **in one's ~s** im Arm; **under one's ~** unter dem *or* unterm Arm; **he had a bandage on his ~** er hatte einen Verband am Arm *or* um den Arm; **to give sb one's ~** *(Brit)* jdm den Arm geben *or* reichen *(geh)*; **with his ~s full of books** den Arm *or* die Arme voller Bücher; **to have sb/sth on one's ~** *(Brit)* jdn/etw am Arm haben; **to take sb in one's ~s** jdn in die Arme nehmen *or* schließen *(geh)*; **to hold sb in one's ~s** jdn umarmen, jdn in den *or* seinen Armen halten *(geh)*; **to put** *or* **throw one's ~s around sb** jdn umarmen, die Arme um jdn schlingen *(geh)*; **to put an ~ around sb's shoulders** jdm den Arm um die Schulter legen; **~ in ~** Arm in Arm; *(= arms linked)* eingehakt, untergehakt; **at ~'s length** auf Armeslänge; **to keep sb at ~'s length** *(fig)* jdn auf Distanz halten; **to receive** *or* **welcome sb with open ~s** jdn mit offenen Armen empfangen; **to receive** *or* **welcome sth with open ~s** etw mit Kusshand nehmen *(inf)*; **within ~'s reach** in Reichweite; **the long ~ of the law** der lange Arm des Gesetzes; **a list as long as your ~** eine ellenlange Liste; **a criminal with a record as long as your ~** ein Verbrecher mit einer langen Latte von Vorstrafen *(inf)*; **it cost him an ~ and a leg** *(inf)* es kostete ihn ein Vermögen; **to put the ~ on sb** *(dated US inf)* jdn unter Druck setzen

b *(= sleeve)* Ärmel *m*, Arm *m*

c *(of river)* (Fluss)arm *m*; *(of sea)* Meeresarm *m*; *(of armchair)* (Arm)lehne *f*; *(of record player)* Tonarm *m*

d *(= branch)* Zweig *m*; *(Mil)* Truppengattung *f*

arm² VT *person, nation, ship etc* bewaffnen; **to ~ sth with sth** etw mit etw ausrüsten; **to ~ oneself with sth** *(lit, fig)* sich mit etw bewaffnen; *(fig: non-aggressively)* sich mit etw wappnen; **he came ~ed with an excuse** er hatte eine Ausrede parat; **~ed only with her beauty, she …** ihre Schönheit war die einzige Waffe, mit der sie … VI aufrüsten; **to ~ for war** zum Krieg rüsten N *(Mil, Her)* = **arms**

armada [ɑːˈmɑːdə] N Armada *f*; **the Armada** die Armada; *(= battle)* die Armadaschlacht

armadillo [ˌɑːməˈdɪləʊ] N Gürteltier *nt*

Armageddon [ˌɑːməˈgedn] N *(Bibl)* Armageddon *nt*; *(fig also)* weltweite *or* globale Katastrophe

Armalite® [ˈɑːməlaɪt] N *automatisches, sehr leichtes Schnellfeuergewehr*

armament [ˈɑːməmənt] N **a armaments** PL *(= weapons)* Ausrüstung *f* **b** *(= preparation)* Aufrüstung *f no pl*; **much of the national budget is devoted to ~** ein großer Teil des Staatshaushalts geht in die Rüstung

armature [ˈɑːmətjʊəʳ] N *(Elec)* Anker *m*

armband [ˈɑːmbænd] N Armbinde *f*

armchair [ˈɑːmtʃɛəʳ] N Sessel *m*, Lehnstuhl *m* ADJ **~ philosopher** Stubengelehrte(r) *mf*; **~ politician** Stammtischpolitiker(in) *m(f)*; **~ strategist** Stammtisch- *or* Salonstratege *m*/-strategin *f*; **he is an ~ traveller** *(Brit) or* **traveler** *(US)* er reist nur mit dem Finger auf der Landkarte *(inf)*

armed [ɑːmd] ADJ bewaffnet

-armed [-ɑːmd] ADJ *suf* -armig; **one-armed** einarmig

armed: **armed forces, armed services** PL Streitkräfte *pl*; **armed robbery** N bewaffneter Raubüberfall

Armenia [ɑːˈmiːnɪə] N Armenien *nt*

Armenian [ɑːˈmiːnɪən] ADJ armenisch N **a** *(= person)* Armenier(in) *m(f)* **b** *(= language)* Armenisch *nt*

arm: **armful** N Arm *m* voll *no pl*, Ladung *f* *(inf)*; **armhole** N Armloch *nt*

armistice [ˈɑːmɪstɪs] N Waffenstillstand *m*

Armistice Day N 11.11., *Tag des Waffenstillstands (1918)*

arm: **armlet** N **a** = **armband b** *(liter, of sea)* kleiner Meeresarm; **arm-lock** N Armschlüssel *m*; *(by police etc)* Polizeigriff *m*

armor *etc (US)* = **armour** *etc*

armorial [ɑːˈmɔːrɪəl] ADJ Wappen-; **~ plate** Wappenteller *m* N Wappenbuch *nt*

armour, *(US)* **armor** [ˈɑːməʳ] N **a** Rüstung *f*; *(of animal)* Panzer *m*; **suit of ~** Rüstung *f*; *(fig)* Panzer *m*, Rüstung *f*; **to wear ~** eine Rüstung tragen **b** *(no pl: = steel plates)* Panzerplatte(n) *f(pl)* **c** *(= vehicles)* Panzerfahrzeuge *pl*; *(= forces)* Panzertruppen *pl* VT panzern; *(fig)* wappnen

armour-clad, *(US)* **armor-clad** [ˈɑːməˈklæd] ADJ *(Mil, Naut)* gepanzert

armoured, *(US)* **armored** [ˈɑːməd] ADJ Panzer-; *vehicle* gepanzert; **~ car** Panzerwagen *m*; **~ personnel carrier** Schützenpanzer(wagen) *m*

armourer, *(US)* **armorer** [ˈɑːmərəʳ] N *(= maker)* Waffenschmied(in) *m(f)*; *(= keeper)* Waffenmeister(in) *m(f)*

armour, *(US)* **armor**: **armour-piercing** ADJ panzerbrechend; **armour-plated** ADJ gepanzert; **armour plating** N Panzerung *f*

armoury, *(US)* **armory** [ˈɑːmərɪ] N **a** Arsenal *nt*, Waffenlager *nt* **b** *(US: = factory)* Munitionsfabrik *f*

arm: **armpit** N Achselhöhle *f*; *(of garments)* Achsel *f*; **armrest** N Armlehne *f*

arms [ɑːmz] PL **a** *(= weapons)* Waffen *pl*; **to ~!** zu den Waffen!; **to carry ~** Waffen tragen; **to be under ~** unter Waffen stehen; **to take up ~ (against sb/sth)** (gegen jdn/etw) zu den Waffen greifen; *(fig)* (gegen jdn/etw) zum Angriff übergehen; **to be up in ~ (about sth)** *(fig inf)* (über etw *acc*) empört sein; **~ limitation talks** Rüstungsbegrenzungsverhandlungen *pl* **b** *(Her)* Wappen *nt*

arms: **arms control** N Rüstungskontrolle *f*; **arms dealer** N Waffenhändler(in) *m(f)*; **arms race** N Wettrüsten *nt*, Rüstungswettlauf *m*

arm-twist [ˈɑːmtwɪst] VT *(inf)* jdm Daumenschrauben anlegen *(fig)*; **to ~ sb into doing sth** jdn so lange unter Druck setzen, bis er/sie etw tut

arm-twisting [ˈɑːmtwɪstɪŋ] N *(inf)* Überredungskunst *f*; **with a bit of ~ …** wenn man etwas nachhilft …; **it took a lot of/didn't take much ~ to get him to agree** er ließ sich nicht schnell/schnell breitschlagen *(inf)*

arm wrestling N Armdrücken *nt*

army [ˈɑːmɪ] N **a** Armee *f*, Heer *nt*; **~ of occupation** Besatzungsarmee *f*; **to be in the ~** beim Militär sein; *(Ger also)* bei der Bundeswehr sein; *(Aus also)* beim Bundesheer sein; **to join the ~** zum Militär gehen **b** *(fig)* Heer *nt* **c** *(= division)* Armee(korps *nt*) *f attr* Militär-; *discipline* militärisch; **~ doctor** Militär- *or* Stabsarzt *m*/-ärztin *f*; **~ life** Soldatenleben *nt*; **~ officer** Offizier(in) *m(f)* in der Armee; **an ~ type** *(inf)* einer vom Barras *(inf) or* Bund *(Ger inf)*

army: **army ant** N Wanderameise *f*, Treiberameise *f*; **army-issue** ADJ Armee-; **~ rifle** Armeegewehr *nt*; **Army List** N *(Brit)* Rangliste *f*; **army-surplus** ADJ Armee-, Army-; **~ store** Armee- *or* Armyladen *m*

arnica [ˈɑːnɪkə] N *(Bot)* Arnika *f*

A-road [ˈeɪrəʊd] N *(Brit)* ≈ Bundesstraße *f*

aroma [əˈrəʊmə] N Duft *m*, Aroma *nt*

aromatherapist [əˈrəʊməˈθerəpɪst] N Aromatherapeut(in) *m(f)*

aromatherapy [əˌrəʊməˈθerəpɪ] N Aromatherapie *f*

aromatic [ˌærəʊˈmætɪk] ADJ aromatisch, wohlriechend

aromatize [əˈrəʊmətaɪz] VT aromatisieren

arose [əˈrəʊz] *pret of* **arise**

around [əˈraʊnd] ADV herum, rum *(inf)*; **a house with gardens all ~** ein von Gärten umgebenes Haus, ein Haus mit Gärten ringsherum; **I looked all ~** ich sah mich nach allen Seiten um; **books lying all ~** überall herumliegende Bücher; **they came from all ~** sie kamen aus allen Richtungen *or* von überall her; **slowly, he turned ~** er drehte sich langsam um; **for miles ~** meilenweit im Umkreis; **to stroll/travel ~** herumschlendern/-reisen; **is he ~?** ist er da?; **if you want me I'll be ~** ich bin da, falls du mich brauchst; **he must be ~ somewhere** er muss hier irgendwo sein *or* stecken *(inf)*; **I didn't know you were ~** ich wusste nicht, dass du hier bist; **he's been ~!** der kennt sich aus!; **it's been ~ for ages** das ist schon uralt; **he's been ~ for ages** *(inf)* der ist schon ewig hier *(inf)*; **see you ~!** *(inf)* also, bis demnächst!, bis bald!; **where have you been? – (just) ~** wo warst du? – weg!

PREP **a** *(= right round) (movement, position)* um; *(in a circle)* um … herum

b *(= in, through)* **to wander ~ the city** durch die Stadt spazieren; **to travel ~ Scotland** durch Schottland reisen; **to talk ~ a subject** um ein Thema herumreden; **to be** *or* **stay ~ the house** zu Hause bleiben; **I left it ~ your office somewhere** ich habe es irgendwo in deinem Büro gelassen; **the paper must be ~ here somewhere** die Zeitung muss hier irgendwo (he)rumliegen; **the church must be ~ here somewhere** die Kirche muss hier irgendwo sein

c *(= approximately) (with date)* um; *(with time of day)* gegen; *(with weight, price)* etwa, um die *(inf)* → *also* **round**

around the clock ADJ *pred*, **around-the--clock** ADJ *attr* rund um die Uhr *pred*

arousal [əˈraʊsəl] N *(sexual)* Erregung *f*

arouse [əˈraʊz] VT **a** *(lit liter)* aufwecken, erwecken *(liter)* **b** *(fig: = excite)* erregen; *interest, suspicion etc* erregen, erwecken; **to ~ sb from his slumbers** *(fig)* jdn aus dem Schlaf wachrütteln

arpeggio [ɑːˈpedʒɪəʊ] N Arpeggio *nt*

arr *abbr of* **arrival, arrives** Ank.

arrack [ˈærək] N Arrak *m*

arraign [əˈreɪn] VT *(Jur) person* Anklage erheben gegen; *(liter: = denounce)* rügen; **to be ~ed on a charge** angeklagt werden

arraignment [əˈreɪnmənt] N *(Jur)* Anklageerhebung *f*

arrange [əˈreɪndʒ] VT **a** *(= order)* ordnen; *furniture, objects* aufstellen, hinstellen; *items in a collection, books in library etc* anordnen; *flowers* arrangieren; *room* einrichten; *(fig) thoughts* ordnen; **I don't want you arranging my life for me** ich will nicht, dass du mein Leben planst

b *(= fix, see to)* vereinbaren, ausmachen; *details* regeln; *party* arrangieren; **to ~ a mortgage for sb** jdm eine Hypothek beschaffen; **I'll ~ for you to meet him** ich arrangiere für Sie ein Treffen mit ihm; **I have ~d for a car to pick you up** ich habe Ihnen einen Wagen besorgt, der Sie mitnimmt; **can you ~ an interview with the President for me?** können Sie mir ein Interview mit dem Präsidenten besorgen?; **we need some more glasses – I'll ~ that** es sind nicht genug Gläser da – das mache *or* reg(e)le *(inf)* ich; **his manager wants to ~ another fight next month** sein Manager will nächsten Monat noch einen Kampf ansetzen; **to ~ a sale/marriage** einen Verkauf/die Ehe vereinbaren; **an ~d marriage** eine arrangierte Ehe; **I'll ~ the drinks, you get the food** ich besorge die Getränke, und du kümmerst dich um das Essen; **if you could ~ to be ill that morning/there at**

five wenn du es so einrichten kannst, dass du an dem Morgen krank/um fünf Uhr da bist; **I think I could ~ that** ich glaube, das lässt sich machen *or* einrichten; **that's easily ~d** das lässt sich leicht einrichten *or* arrangieren *(inf)*; **how can we ~ it so it looks like an accident?** wie können wir es machen *or* drehen *(inf)*, dass es wie ein Unfall aussieht?; **they'd obviously ~d things between themselves before the meeting started** sie hatten die Dinge offenbar vor Beginn des Treffens untereinander abgesprochen
c *(= settle, decide on)* vereinbaren, abmachen; **nothing definite has been ~d yet** es ist noch nichts Verbindliches vereinbart worden; **a meeting has been ~d for next month** nächsten Monat ist ein Treffen angesetzt!; **good, that's ~d then** gut, das ist abgemacht!; **I don't like having things ~d for me** ich habe es nicht gern, wenn man Dinge für mich entscheidet; **but you ~d to meet me!** aber du wolltest dich doch mit mir treffen!
d *(Mus)* bearbeiten, arrangieren

arrangement [əˈreɪndʒmənt] N **a** Anordnung *f*; *(of room)* Einrichtung *f*; *(inf: = contrivance)* Gerät *nt (inf)*; **a floral** *or* **flower ~** ein Blumenarrangement *nt*; **the very unusual ~ of her hair** ihre sehr ungewöhnliche Haartracht
b *(= agreement)* Vereinbarung *f*; *(to meet)* Verabredung *f*; *(esp shifty)* Arrangement *nt*; **by ~** laut *or* nach Vereinbarung *or* Absprache; **by ~ with** mit freundlicher Genehmigung *(+gen)*; **salary by ~** Gehalt nach Vereinbarung; **a special ~** eine Sonderregelung; **to have an ~ with sb** eine Regelung mit jdm getroffen haben; **he has an ~ with his wife ...** er hat mit seiner Frau ein Arrangement ...; **I've got a nice little ~ going** ich habe da so eine Abmachung *or* Absprache getroffen; **to make an ~ with sb** eine Vereinbarung *or* Absprache mit jdm treffen; **to come to an ~** eine Regelung finden; **to come to an ~ with sb** eine Regelung mit jdm treffen
c *(usu pl) (= plans)* Pläne *pl*; *(= preparations)* Vorbereitungen *pl*; **to make ~s for sb/sth** für jdn/etw Vorbereitungen treffen; **to make ~s for sth to be done** veranlassen, dass etw getan wird; **to make one's own ~s** selber zusehen(, wie ...), es selber arrangieren(, dass ...); **who's in charge of the transport ~s?** wer regelt die Transportfrage?; **seating ~s** Sitzordnung *f*; **"funeral ~s"** „Ausführung von Bestattungen"; **who will look after the funeral ~s?** wer kümmert sich um die Beerdigung?
d *(Mus)* Bearbeitung *f*; *(light music)* Arrangement *nt*

arranger [əˈreɪndʒəʳ] N **a** *(Mus)* Arrangeur(in) *m(f)* **b** *(= organizer)* Organisator(in) *m(f)*

arrant [ˈærənt] ADJ Erz-; **~ coward** Erzfeigling *m*; **~ nonsense** barer Unsinn

arras [ˈærəs] N *(old)* (Arazzo)wandteppich *m*

array [əˈreɪ] VT **a** *(= line up)* aufstellen; *(Mil)* in Aufstellung bringen **b** *(= dress)* schmücken *(geh)*, herausputzen *(hum)* N **a** *(Mil: = arrangement)* Aufstellung *f*; **in battle ~** in Kampfaufstellung, in Schlachtordnung **b** *(= collection)* Ansammlung *f*, Aufgebot *nt (hum)*; *(of objects)* stattliche *or* ansehnliche Reihe **c** *(Comput)* Datenfeld *nt*, Array *nt* **d** *(liter)* Schmuck *m (geh)*; *(= dress)* Staat *m*; **the trees in all their spring ~** die Bäume im Frühlingskleid *(poet)*

arrears [əˈrɪəz] PL Rückstände *pl*; **to be in ~ with sth** im Rückstand mit etw sein; **to get** *or* **fall into ~** in Rückstand kommen; **to have ~ of £5000** mit £ 5000 im Rückstand sein; **to be paid in ~** rückwirkend bezahlt werden

arrest [əˈrest] VT **a** *(= apprehend)* festnehmen; *(with warrant)* verhaften; *(fig) attention* erregen, erheischen *(liter)*; **I am ~ing you** ich muss Sie festnehmen/verhaften
b *(= check)* hemmen; *sth unwanted* (Ein)halt gebieten *(+dat) (geh)*; **~ed development** Entwicklungshemmung *f*
N *(of suspect)* Festnahme *f*; *(with warrant)* Verhaftung *f*; *(of ship)* Aufbringen *nt*; **to be under ~** festgenommen/verhaftet sein; **you are under ~** Sie sind festgenommen/verhaftet; **to put** *or* **place sb under ~** jdn festnehmen/verhaften; **to make an ~** eine Person festnehmen/verhaften; **they hope to make an ~ soon** man hofft, dass es bald zu einer Festnahme/Verhaftung kommt

arrestable [əˈrestəbl] ADJ **to be an ~ offence** *(Brit) or* **offense** *(US)* ein Grund zur Festnahme sein

arresting [əˈrestɪŋ] ADJ **a** *(= striking)* atemberaubend; *features* markant **b the ~ officer** der festnehmende Beamte

arrest warrant N Haftbefehl *m*

arrhythmia [əˈrɪðmɪə] N *(Med)* Arrhythmie *f*

arrival [əˈraɪvəl] N **a** Ankunft *f no pl*; *(of person)* Ankunft *f*, Eintreffen *nt no pl*; *(of goods, news)* Eintreffen *nt no pl*; **our eventual ~ at a decision ...** dass wir endlich zu einer Entscheidung kamen ...; **on ~** bei Ankunft; **he was dead on ~** bei seiner Einlieferung ins Krankenhaus wurde der Tod festgestellt; **~ time, time of ~** Ankunftszeit *f*; **~s and departures** *(Rail)* Ankunft/Abfahrt *f*; *(Aviat)* Ankunft *f*/Abflug *m*
b *(= person)* Ankömmling *m*; **new ~** Neuankömmling *m*; *(at school also)* Neue(r) *mf*; *(in hotel, boarding house)* neu angekommener Gast; *(in firm, office)* neuer Mitarbeiter, neue Mitarbeiterin; **a new ~ on the pop scene** ein neues Gesicht auf der Popszene; **when our firm was still a new ~ in the publishing world** als unsere Firma noch ein Neuling im Verlagswesen war; **the new ~ is a little girl** der neue Erdenbürger ist ein kleines Mädchen; **he was the latest ~** er kam als Letzter

arrivals board [əˈraɪvəlzbɔːd] N *(Rail)* Ankunftstafel *f*; *(Aviat)* Ankunftsanzeige *f*

arrivals lounge [əˈraɪvəlz,laʊndʒ] N Ankunftshalle *f*

arrive [əˈraɪv] ✪ 21.4, 25.2 VI **a** *(= come)* ankommen, eintreffen *(geh)*; *(= be born)* ankommen; **to ~ home** nach Hause kommen; *(esp after journey etc)* zu Hause ankommen; **to ~ at a town/the airport** in einer Stadt/am Flughafen ankommen *or* eintreffen *(geh)*; **the train will ~ at platform 10** der Zug läuft auf Gleis 10 ein; **the great day ~d** der große Tag kam; **a new era has ~d!** ein neues Zeitalter ist angebrochen!; **the time has ~d for sth/to do sth** die Zeit für etw ist gekommen, die Zeit ist reif für etw/etw zu tun; **television has not ~d here yet** das Fernsehen ist noch nicht bis hier durchgedrungen; **to ~ at a decision** zu einer Entscheidung kommen *or* gelangen; **to ~ at the age of ...** das Alter von ... Jahren erreichen; **to ~ at an answer/a conclusion/result** zu einer Antwort/einem Schluss/Ergebnis kommen; **to ~ at a price** auf einen Preis kommen; *(= agree on)* sich auf einen Preis einigen
b *(inf: = succeed)* **then you know you've really ~d** dann weiß man, dass man es geschafft hat

arriviste [,æriːˈviːst] N Emporkömmling *m*, Parvenü *m (geh)*

arrogance [ˈærəgəns] N Arroganz *f*, Überheblichkeit *f*

arrogant [ˈærəgənt] ADJ arrogant, überheblich

arrogantly [ˈærəgəntlɪ] ADV arrogant; **the group had rather ~ assumed themselves to be in command** die Gruppe hatte arroganterweise *or* anmaßenderweise angenommen, dass sie das Kommando hätte

arrogate [ˈærəʊgeɪt] VT **to ~ sth to oneself** etw für sich in Anspruch nehmen; *title* sich *(dat)* etw anmaßen

arrow [ˈærəʊ] N *(= weapon, sign)* Pfeil *m* VT *way, direction* durch Pfeile/einen Pfeil markieren

▶ **arrow in** VT *sep (in text)* durch Pfeil einzeichnen

arrow: **arrow bracket** N spitze Klammer; **arrowhead** N Pfeilspitze *f*; **arrow key** N *(Comput)* Pfeiltaste *f*; **arrowroot** N *(= plant)* Pfeilwurz *f*; *(= flour)* Arrowroot *nt*

arse [ɑːs] *(Brit sl)* N **a** Arsch *m (sl)*; **shift your ~!** *(= move over)* rutsch mal ein Stück *(inf)*; *(= hurry up)* setz mal deinen Arsch in Bewegung! *(sl)*; **get your ~ in gear!** setz mal deinen Arsch in Bewegung! *(sl)*; **tell him to get his ~ into my office** sag ihm, er soll mal in meinem Büro antanzen *(inf)*; **get your ~ out of here!** verpiss dich hier! *(sl)*; **contribution? my ~!** Beitrag? das soll wohl ein Witz sein! *(inf)* **b** *(= fool: also* **silly arse***)* Armleuchter *m (inf)* VT **I can't be ~d** ich hab keinen Bock *(sl)*

▶ **arse about** *or* **around** VI *(Brit inf)* rumblödeln *(inf)*

arse: **arsehole** [ˈɑːshəʊl] N *(Brit sl)* Arschloch *nt (vulg)*; **arse licker** N *(Brit sl)* Arschkriecher(in) *m(f) (inf)*

arsenal [ˈɑːsɪnl] N *(Mil) (= store)* Arsenal *nt*, Zeughaus *nt (old)*; *(= factory)* Waffen-/Munitionsfabrik *f*; *(fig)* Waffenlager *nt*

arsenic [ˈɑːsnɪk] N Arsen *nt*, Arsenik *nt*; **~ poisoning** Arsenvergiftung *f*

arson [ˈɑːsn] N Brandstiftung *f*

arsonist [ˈɑːsənɪst] N Brandstifter(in) *m(f)*

art[1] [ɑːt] N **a** *(= painting etc)* Kunst *f*; **the ~s** die schönen Künste; **~ for ~'s sake** Kunst um der Kunst willen, Kunst als Selbstzweck; *(slogan)* L'art pour l'art → **work N c**
b *(= skill)* Kunst *f*; *(= physical technique)* Geschick *nt*, Kunst *f*; **there's an ~ to driving this car** es gehört ein gewisses Geschick dazu, mit diesem Auto zu fahren; **there's an ~ to it** das ist eine Kunst; **the ~ of war/government** die Kriegs-/Staatskunst; **the ~ of conversation/translation** die Kunst der Unterhaltung/Übersetzung; **~s and crafts** Kunsthandwerk *nt*, Kunstgewerbe *nt*
c *(= human endeavour)* Künstlichkeit *f*; **unspoiled by ~** unverbildet; **are they the products of ~ or nature?** sind sie natürlich oder von Menschenhand geschaffen?; **her beauty owes more to ~ than nature** sie verdankt ihre Schönheit mehr der Kunst als der Natur
d ~s *(Univ)* Geisteswissenschaften *pl*; **~s minister** Kulturminister(in) *m(f)*; **~s subject** geisteswissenschaftliches Fach → **bachelor, liberal arts**
e *(usu pl: = trick)* List *f*, Kunstgriff *m*
ADJ *attr* Kunst-; **~ critic** Kunstkritiker(in) *m(f)*

art[2] *(old) 2nd pers sing present of* **be**

art college N = **art school**

Art Deco [ɑːtˈdekəʊ] N Art déco *f*

Art-Deco [ɑːtˈdekəʊ] ADJ *attr* Art-déco-; **~ design** Art-déco-Design *nt*

artefact *(Brit)*, **artifact** [ˈɑːtɪfækt] N Artefakt *nt*; **are these human ~s?** sind das Schöpfungen von Menschenhand?

arterial [ɑːˈtɪərɪəl] ADJ **a** *(Anat)* arteriell **b ~ road** *(Aut)* Fernverkehrsstraße *f*; **~ line** *(Rail)* Hauptstrecke *f*

arteriosclerosis [ɑːˈtɪərɪəʊsklɪˈrəʊsɪs] N *(Med)* Arteriosklerose *f*, Arterienverkalkung *f*

artery [ˈɑːtərɪ] N **a** *(Anat)* Arterie *f*, Schlag- *or* Pulsader *f* **b** *(also* **traffic artery***)* Verkehrsader *f*

artesian well [ɑːˈtiːzɪənˈwel] N artesischer Brunnen

art form N (Kunst)gattung *or* -form *f*

artful [ˈɑːtfʊl] ADJ *person, trick* raffiniert, schlau; **~ dodger** Schlawiner *m (inf)*

artfully [ˈɑːtfəlɪ] ADV raffiniert

artfulness [ˈɑːtfʊlnɪs] N Raffinesse *f*

art: **art gallery** N Kunstgalerie *f*; **art-house** ADJ *attr* **~ film** Experimentalfilm *m*; **~ cinema** ≈ Programmkino *nt*

arthritic [ɑːˈθrɪtɪk] ADJ arthritisch; **she is ~** sie hat Arthritis

arthritis [ɑːˈθraɪtɪs] N Arthritis *f*, Gelenkentzündung *f*

arthropod [ˈɑːθrəpɒd] N Gliederfüßer *m*; **the ~s** die Arthropoden *pl*

arthrosis [ɑːˈθrəʊsɪs] N Arthrose *f*

Arthur [ˈɑːθəʳ] N Art(h)ur *m*; **King ~** König Artus

Arthurian [ɑːˈθjʊərɪən] ADJ Artus-; **~ knight** Artusritter *m*

artic [ɑːˈtɪk] N (*Brit inf*) (Sattel)schlepper *m*

artichoke [ˈɑːtɪtʃəʊk] N Artischocke *f* → **Jerusalem artichoke**

article [ˈɑːtɪkl] **N** **a** (*= item*) Gegenstand *m*; (*in list*) Posten *m*; (*Comm*) Ware *f*, Artikel *m*; **~ of value** Wertgegenstand *m*; **~ of furniture** Möbelstück *nt*; **~s of clothing** Kleidungsstücke *pl*; **toilet ~s** Toilettenartikel *pl* → **genuine**
b (*in newspaper etc*) Artikel *m*; (*= encyclopedia entry*) Eintrag *m*
c (*of constitution*) Artikel *m*; (*of treaty, contract*) Paragraf *m*; **~s of association** Gesellschaftsvertrag *m*; **~ of faith** Glaubensartikel *m*; (*fig*) Kredo *nt*; **~s of war** (*Hist*) Kriegsartikel *pl*
d (*Gram*) Artikel *m*, Geschlechtswort *nt*
e (*of articled clerk*) **to be under ~s** (Rechts)referendar sein; **to take one's ~s** seine Referendarprüfung machen
VT *apprentice* in die Lehre geben (*to* bei); **to be ~d to sb** bei jdm eine Lehre machen, bei jdm in die Lehre gehen; **to be ~d to sb/sth** an jdn/etw vertraglich gebunden sein; **~d clerk** (*Brit Jur*) ≈ Rechtsreferendar(in) *m(f)*

articulate [ɑːˈtɪkjʊlɪt] **ADJ** **a** *sentence, book* klar; **to be ~** sich gut *or* klar ausdrücken können; **clear and ~** klar und deutlich; **that is amazingly ~ for a five-year-old** das ist erstaunlich gut ausgedrückt für einen Fünfjährigen **b** (*Anat*) gegliedert **VT** [ɑːˈtɪkjʊleɪt] **a** (*= pronounce*) artikulieren **b** (*= state*) *reasons, views etc* darlegen **c** (*Anat*) **to be ~d** zusammenhängen (*to, with* mit) **VI** [ɑːˈtɪkjʊleɪt] artikulieren

articulated bus [ɑːˈtɪkjʊleɪtɪdˈbʌs] N Gelenkbus *m*

articulated lorry (*Brit*), **articulated truck** [ɑːˈtɪkjʊleɪtɪd-] N Sattelschlepper *m*

articulately [ɑːˈtɪkjʊlɪtlɪ] ADV *pronounce* artikuliert; *write, express oneself* klar, flüssig; **an ~ presented argument** eine klar verständlich vorgetragene These

articulateness [ɑːˈtɪkjʊlɪtnɪs] N Fähigkeit *f*, sich gut auszudrücken

articulation [ɑːˌtɪkjʊˈleɪʃən] N **a** Artikulation *f* **b** (*Anat*) Gelenkverbindung *f*

artifact N = **artefact**

artifice [ˈɑːtɪfɪs] N **a** (*= guile*) List *f no pl* **b** (*= stratagem*) (Kriegs)list *f*

artificial [ˌɑːtɪˈfɪʃəl] ADJ **a** (*= synthetic*) künstlich; **~ light** künstliches Licht; **~ manure** Kunstdünger *m*; **~ hair/silk** Kunsthaar *nt*/-seide *f*; **~ heart** Kunstherz *nt*; **~ leather** Kunstleder *nt*; **~ limb** Prothese *f*, Kunstglied *nt* **b** (*fig*: *= not genuine*) künstlich; (*pej*: *= not sincere*) *smile, manner* gekünstelt, unecht; **you're so ~** du bist nicht echt; **if you say it that way it sounds ~** wenn du es so sagst, klingt das unecht

artificial: **artificial horizon** N künstlicher Horizont; **artificial insemination** N künstliche Befruchtung; **artificial intelligence** N künstliche Intelligenz

artificiality [ˌɑːtɪfɪʃɪˈælɪtɪ] N **a** Künstlichkeit *f* **b** (*= insincerity, unnaturalness*) Gekünsteltheit *f*

artificially [ˌɑːtɪˈfɪʃəlɪ] ADV künstlich; (*= insincerely*) gekünstelt

artificial respiration N künstliche Beatmung *f*

artillery [ɑːˈtɪlərɪ] N (*= weapons, troops*) Artillerie *f*

artilleryman [ɑːˈtɪlərɪmən] N *pl* **-men** [-mən] Artillerist *m*

artisan [ˈɑːtɪzæn] N Handwerker(in) *m(f)*

artisanal [ɑːˈtɪzənəl] ADJ kunsthandwerklich

artist [ˈɑːtɪst] N Künstler(in) *m(f)*; (*fig also*) Könner(in) *m(f)*; **~'s impression** Zeichnung *f*; (*of sth planned also*) Entwurf *m*

artiste [ɑːˈtiːst] N Künstler(in) *m(f)*; (*= circus artiste*) Artist(in) *m(f)*; **~s' entrance** Bühneneingang *m*

artistic [ɑːˈtɪstɪk] ADJ künstlerisch; (*= tasteful*) *arrangements* kunstvoll; (*= appreciative of art*) *person* kunstverständig *or* -sinnig (*geh*); **the café has an ~ clientele** in dem Café verkehren Künstler; **~ temperament** Künstlertemperament *nt*; **an ~ life** ein Künstlerleben *nt*; **to look ~** wie ein Künstler aussehen; **she's very ~** sie ist künstlerisch veranlagt *or* begabt/sehr kunstverständig

artistically [ɑːˈtɪstɪkəlɪ] ADV künstlerisch; (*= tastefully*) kunstvoll

artistic director N künstlerischer Direktor, künstlerische Direktorin

artistry [ˈɑːtɪstrɪ] N (*lit, fig*) Kunst *f*

artless ADJ, **artlessly** ADV [ˈɑːtlɪs, -lɪ] unschuldig

artlessness [ˈɑːtlɪsnɪs] N Unschuld *f*

art lover N Kunstliebhaber(in) *m(f) or* freund(in) *m(f)*

Art Nouveau [ˈɑːnuːˈvəʊ] N Jugendstil *m*; **~ movement** Jugendstilbewegung *f*

Art-Nouveau [ˈɑːnuːˈvəʊ] ADJ *attr* Jugendstil-; **~ building** Jugendstilbau *m*

art: **art paper** N Kunstdruckpapier *nt*; **art school** N Kunstakademie *or* -hochschule *f*

Arts [ɑːts]: **Arts Council** N Kulturausschuss *m* (*der britischen Regierung*); **arts degree** N Abschlussexamen *nt* der philosophischen Fakultät; **Arts Faculty**, **Faculty of Arts** N philosophische Fakultät

art student N Kunststudent(in) *m(f)*

artsy [ˈɑːtsɪ] ADJ (*US hum inf*) = **arty**

artwork [ˈɑːtwɜːk] N **a** (*in book*) Bildmaterial *nt*; **this will have to be done as ~** das muss grafisch gestaltet werden **b** (*for advert etc*: *= material ready for printing*) Druckvorlage *f* **c** (*= painting, sculpture*) Kunstwerk *nt*

arty [ˈɑːtɪ] ADJ (+*er*) (*inf*) Künstler-; *type also, tie, clothes* verrückt (*inf*); *person* auf Künstler machend (*pej*); *decoration, style* auf Kunst gemacht (*inf*); *film, novel* geschmäcklerisch; **he was more of an ~ type than his brother** er war mehr ein Künstlertyp als sein Bruder; **she's in publishing/the theatre – oh yes, I knew it was something ~** sie arbeitet im Verlag/Theater – ach ja, ich wusste doch, dass es etwas Künstlerisches war

arty-crafty [ˈɑːtɪˈkrɑːftɪ], (*US*) **artsy-craftsy** [ˈɑːtsɪˈkrɑːftsɪ] ADJ (*inf*) **a** = **arty** **b** *object* kunstgewerblerisch

arty-farty [ˈɑːtɪˈfɑːtɪ] ADJ (*hum inf*) = **arty**

Aryan [ˈɛərɪən] **N** Arier(in) *m(f)* **ADJ** arisch

as [æz, əz] ✪ 5.1, 5.4, 17.1, 26.2, 26.3 **CONJ** **a** (*= when, while*) als; (*two parallel actions*) während, als, indem (*geh*); **he got deafer as he got older** mit zunehmendem Alter nahm seine Schwerhörigkeit zu; **as a child he would …** als Kind hat er immer …
b (*= since*) da
c (*= although*) **rich as he is I won't marry him** obwohl er reich ist, werde ich ihn nicht heiraten; **stupid as he is, he …** so dumm er auch sein mag, … er; **big as he is I'll …** so groß, wie er ist, ich …; **much as I admire her, …** sosehr ich sie auch bewundere, …; **be that as it may** wie dem auch sei *or* sein mag; **try as he might** sosehr er sich auch bemüht/bemühte
d (*manner*) wie; **do as you like** machen Sie, was Sie wollen; **leave it as it is** lass das so; **I did it as he did** ich habe es wie er gemacht; **the first door as you go upstairs/as you go in** die erste Tür oben/, wenn Sie hereinkommen; **knowing him as I do** so wie ich ihn kenne; **as you yourself said …** wie Sie selbst gesagt haben …; **he drinks enough as it is** er trinkt sowieso schon genug; **it is bad enough as it is** es ist schon schlimm genug; **as it is, I'm heavily in debt** ich bin schon tief verschuldet; **as it were** sozusagen, gleichsam; **as you were!** (*Mil*) weitermachen!; (*fig*) lassen Sie sich nicht stören; (*in dictation, speaking*) streichen Sie das; **my husband as was** (*inf*) mein verflossener *or* (*late*) verstorbener Mann
e (*phrases*) **as if** *or* **though** als ob, wie wenn; **he rose as if to go** er erhob sich, als wollte er gehen; **it isn't as if he didn't see me** schließlich hat er mich ja gesehen; **as for him/you** (und) was ihn/dich anbetrifft *or* angeht; **as from** *or* **of the 5th** vom Fünften an, ab dem Fünften; **as from now** von jetzt an, ab jetzt; **so as to** (*= in order to*) um zu +*infin*; (*= in such a way*) so, dass; **be so good as to …** (*form*) hätten Sie die Freundlichkeit *or* Güte, … zu … (*form*); **he's not so silly as to do that** er ist nicht so dumm, das zu tun, so dumm ist er nicht
ADV **as … as** so … wie; **not as … as** nicht so … wie; **twice as old** doppelt so alt; **just as nice** genauso nett; **late as usual!** wie immer zu spät!; **is it as difficult as that?** ist das denn so schwierig?; **if he eats as quickly as that** wenn er so schnell isst; **it is not as good as all that** so gut ist es auch wieder nicht; **you hate it as much as I do** du magst das doch genauso wenig wie ich; **as recently as yesterday** erst gestern; **she is very clever, as is her brother** sie ist sehr intelligent, genau(so) wie ihr Bruder; **she was as nice as could be** (*inf*) sie war so freundlich wie nur was (*inf*); **as many/much as I could** so viele/so viel ich (nur) konnte; **there were as many as 100 people there** es waren bestimmt 100 Leute da; **this one is just as good** diese(r, s) ist genauso gut; **as often happens, he was …** wie so oft, war er …
REL PRON **a** (*with same, such*) der/die/das; (*pl*) die; **the same man as was here yesterday** derselbe Mann, der gestern hier war → **such**
b (*dial*) der/die/das; (*pl*) die; **those as knew him** die ihn kannten
PREP **a** (*= in the capacity of*) als; **to treat sb as a child** jdn als Kind *or* wie ein Kind behandeln; **he appeared as three different characters** er trat in drei verschiedenen Rollen auf
b (*esp*: *= such as*) wie (zum Beispiel); **animals such as cats and dogs** Tiere wie (zum Beispiel) Katzen und Hunde

asap [ˈeɪsæp] *abbr of* **as soon as possible** baldmöglichst, baldmögl.

asbestos [æzˈbestəs] N Asbest *m*

asbestosis [ˌæzbesˈtəʊsɪs] N (*Med*) Asbestose *f*, Asbeststaublunge *f*

ascend [əˈsend] **VI** (*= rise*) aufsteigen; (*Christ*) auffahren; (*= slope upwards*) ansteigen (*to* auf +*acc*); **in ~ing order** in aufsteigender Reihenfolge **VT** *stairs* hinaufsteigen; *mountain, heights of knowledge* erklimmen (*geh*); *throne* besteigen; **to ~ the scale** (*Mus*) die Tonleiter aufwärts singen

ascendancy, **ascendency** [əˈsendənsɪ] N Vormachtstellung *f*; **to gain/have (the) ~ over sb** die Vorherrschaft über jdn gewinnen/haben; **to gain (the) ~ over one's fears** seine Ängste besiegen

ascendant, **ascendent** [əˈsendənt] N **to be in the ~** (*Astrol*) im Aszendenten stehen, aszendieren (*spec*); (*fig*) im Aufstieg begriffen sein; **his star is in the ~** (*fig*) sein Stern ist im Aufgehen

ascender [əˈsendəʳ] N (*Typ*) Oberlänge *f*

Ascension [əˈsenʃən] N **the ~** (Christi) Himmelfahrt *f*

Ascension Day N Himmelfahrt(stag *m*) *nt*

ascent [əˈsent] N Aufstieg *m*; **the ~ of Ben Nevis** der Aufstieg auf den Ben Nevis; **it was his first ~ in an aeroplane** er ist das erste Mal in einem Flugzeug geflogen

ascertain [ˌæsəˈteɪn] VT ermitteln, feststellen

ascertainable [ˌæsəˈteɪnəbl] ADJ feststellbar

ascetic [əˈsetɪk] **ADJ** asketisch **N** Asket *m*; **she's something of an ~** sie lebt ziemlich asketisch

asceticism [əˈsetɪsɪzəm] N Askese *f*; **a life of ~** ein Leben in Askese

ASCII [ˈæskɪ] *abbr of* **American Standard Code for Information Interchange** ASCII *nt*; **~ file** ASCII-Datei *f*

ASCII code N (*Comput*) ASCII-Code *m*

ASCII file N ASCII-Datei *f*

ascorbic acid [əˈskɔːbɪkˈæsɪd] N Askorbinsäure *f*

ascribable [əˈskraɪbəbl] ADJ **to be ~ to sth** einer Sache (*dat*) zuzuschreiben sein

ascribe [əˈskraɪb] VT zuschreiben (*sth to sb* jdm etw); *importance, weight* beimessen (*to sth* einer Sache *dat*)

ascription [əˈskrɪpʃən] N Zuschreibung *f*; **difficulties arising from the ~ of emotions to animals** Schwierigkeiten, die sich ergeben, wenn man Tieren Gefühle zuschreibt

asdic [ˈæzdɪk] N Echo(tiefen)lot *nt*

ASEAN [ˈæzɪən] *abbr of* **Association of South-East Asian Nations**

aseptic [eɪˈseptɪk] ADJ aseptisch, keimfrei; *(fig) atmosphere* steril, klinisch

asexual [eɪˈseksjʊəl] ADJ ungeschlechtlich, geschlechtslos; *person* asexuell; *reproduction* ungeschlechtlich

asexually [eɪˈseksjʊəlɪ] ADV *reproduce* asexuell, ungeschlechtlich

ash[1] [æʃ] N (*also* **ash tree**) Esche *f*

ash[2] N **a** Asche *f*; **~es** Asche *f*; **to reduce sth to ~es** etw total *or* völlig niederbrennen; *(in war etc)* etw in Schutt und Asche legen; **to rise from the ~es** *(fig)* aus den Trümmern wiederauferstehen; **~es to ~es** Erde zu Erde → **sackcloth b ashes** PL *(of the dead)* Asche *f* **c** *(Cricket)* **the Ashes** *Testmatch zwischen Australien und England*

ashamed [əˈʃeɪmd] ADJ beschämt; **to be** *or* **feel ~ (of sb/sth)** sich schämen (für jdn/etw, jds/einer Sache *(geh)*); **it's nothing to be ~ of** deswegen braucht man sich nicht zu genieren *or* schämen; **to be ~ that ...** sich schämen, dass ...; **I felt ~ for him** ich habe mich für ihn geschämt; **he is ~ to do it** es ist ihm peinlich, das zu tun, er schämt sich, das zu tun; **... I'm ~ to say** ..., muss ich leider zugeben; **to be ~ of oneself (for doing sth)** sich schämen(, etw getan zu haben); **you ought to be ~ (of yourself)** du solltest dich (was) schämen!, schäm dich!; **you may well look ~** schäm dich ruhig!

A shares [ˈeɪʃɛəz] PL stimmrechtslose Aktien *pl*

ash: **ash bin** N Asch(en)eimer *m*, Aschentonne *f*; **ash blond** N Aschblonde(r) *m*; **ash blonde** N Aschblonde *f*; **ash-blond(e)** ADJ aschblond; **ashcan** N *(US)* = **ash bin**

ashen [ˈæʃn] ADJ *colour* aschgrau, aschfarben; *face* aschfahl *(geh)*, kreidebleich

ashen-faced [ˌæʃnˈfeɪst] ADJ kreidebleich

ash-grey, *(US)* **ash-gray** ADJ *colour* aschgrau, aschfarben

ashlar [ˈæʃləʳ] N Quaderstein *m*

ashore [əˈʃɔːʳ] ADV an Land; **to run ~** stranden, auf den Strand auflaufen; **to put ~** an Land gehen

ash: **ashpan** N Aschenkasten *m*; **ashtray** N Aschenbecher *m*; **Ash Wednesday** N Aschermittwoch *m*

ashy [ˈæʃɪ] ADJ **a** = **ashen b** *(= covered with ashes)* mit Asche bedeckt

Asia [ˈeɪʃə] N Asien *nt*

Asia Minor N Kleinasien *nt*

Asian [ˈeɪʃn], **Asiatic** [ˌeɪʃɪˈætɪk] ADJ **a** asiatisch; *(= from the Indian subcontinent)* indisch-pakistanisch **b** *(Brit: = from Indian subcontinent)* indopakistanisch N **a** Asiat(in) *m(f)* **b** *(Brit: = person from the Indian subcontinent)* Indopakistaner(in) *m(f)*

Asian-American [ˌeɪʃnəˈmerɪkən] ADJ asiatisch-amerikanisch N Amerikaner(in) *m(f)* asiatischer Herkunft

Asian flu N asiatische Grippe

aside [əˈsaɪd] ADV **a** *(with verbal element)* zur Seite, beiseite; **to set sth ~ for sb** für jdn etw beiseitelegen; **to turn ~** sich zur Seite drehen, sich abwenden *(esp fig)*
b *(Theat etc)* beiseite
c *(esp US)* **~ from** außer; **~ from demanding an extra 10% ...** außer einer Zusatzforderung von 10% ...; **~ from being chairman of this committee he is ...** außer Vorsitzender dieses Ausschusses ist er auch ...; **this criticism, ~ from being wrong, is ...** diese Kritik ist nicht nur falsch, sondern ...
N *(Theat)* Aparte *nt (rare)*; **to say sth in an ~** etw beiseitesprechen; **there are too many ~s to the audience** es wird zu viel zum Publikum gesprochen

A-side [ˈeisaɪd] N *(of record)* A-Seite *f*

asinine [ˈæsɪnaɪn] ADJ idiotisch; **what an ~ thing to do!** wie kann man bloß so ein Esel sein!

ask [ɑːsk] ✪ 4, 6.2, 21.1, 21.4, 26.1 VT **a** *(= inquire)* fragen; *question* stellen; **to ~ sb the way/the time/his opinion** jdn nach dem Weg/der Uhrzeit/seiner Meinung fragen; **to ~ if ...** (nach)fragen, ob ...; **he ~ed me where I'd been** er fragte mich, wo ich gewesen sei *or* wäre *(inf) or* bin *(inf)*; **if you ~ me** wenn du mich fragst; **don't ~ me!** *(inf)* frag mich nicht, was weiß ich! *(inf)*; **I ~ you!** *(inf)* ich muss schon sagen!
b *(= invite)* einladen; *(in dancing)* auffordern; **to ~ sb for** *or* **to lunch** jdn zum (Mittag)essen einladen
c *(= request)* bitten (*sb for sth* jdn um etw); *(= require, demand)* verlangen (*sth of sb* etw von jdm); **to ~ sb to do sth** jdn darum bitten, etw zu tun; **are you ~ing me to believe that?** und das soll ich glauben?; **all I ~ is ...** ich will ja nur ...; **you don't ~ for much, do you?** *(iro)* sonst noch was? *(iro)*, sonst *or* weiter nichts? *(iro)*; **could I ~ your advice?** darf ich Sie um Rat bitten?; **he ~ed to be excused** er bat, ihn zu entschuldigen, er entschuldigte sich; **that's ~ing the impossible** das ist ein Ding der Unmöglichkeit; **he ~s too much of me** er verlangt zu viel von mir; **that's ~ing too much** das ist zu viel verlangt
d *(Comm) price* verlangen, fordern
VI **a** *(= inquire)* fragen; **to ~ about sb/sth** sich nach jdm/etw erkundigen; **~ away!** frag nur!; **I only ~ed** ich habe doch nur gefragt; **and what does that mean, may I ~?** und was soll das bedeuten, wenn ich mal fragen darf?; **well may you ~** das fragt man sich mit Recht
b *(= request)* bitten (*for sth* um etw); **you just have to ~** du musst nur was sagen *(inf)*, du brauchst nur zu fragen; **I'm not ~ing for sympathy** ich will kein Mitleid; **there's no harm in ~ing** Fragen kostet nichts!; **it's yours for the ~ing** du kannst es haben; **you are ~ing for trouble** du willst wohl Ärger haben; **if you do that you're ~ing for trouble** wenn du das tust, dann kriegst du Ärger; **that's ~ing for trouble** das kann ja nicht gut gehen; **you ~ed for it** *(inf)* du hast es ja so gewollt; **he's ~ing for it** *(inf)* er will es ja so, er will es ja nicht anders; **to ~ for Mr X** Herrn X verlangen; **she was ~ing for you** *(Scot)* sie hat sich nach dir erkundigt; **to ~ for sth back** etw wiederhaben wollen

▶ **ask after** VI *+prep obj* sich erkundigen nach; **tell her I was asking after her** grüß sie schön von mir

▶ **ask around** VI herumfragen

▶ **ask back** VT *sep* **a** *(= invite)* zu sich einladen; **he asked us back for a drink** er lud uns zu sich auf einen Drink ein **b they never asked me back again** sie haben mich nie wieder eingeladen **c let me ask you something back** lassen Sie mich eine Gegenfrage stellen

▶ **ask in** VT *sep (to house)* hereinbitten; **she asked her boyfriend in** sie hat ihren Freund mit reingenommen

▶ **ask out** VT *sep* einladen

▶ **ask over** VT SEP zu sich *(dat)* einladen

▶ **ask round** VT SEP *(esp Brit)* = **ask over**

▶ **ask up** VT *sep* heraufbitten; *boyfriend* mit raufnehmen

askance [əˈskɑːns] ADV **to look ~ at sb** jdn entsetzt ansehen; **to look ~ at a suggestion/sb's methods** *etc* über einen Vorschlag/jds Methoden *etc* die Nase rümpfen

askew [əˈskjuː] ADJ ADV schief

asking [ˈɑːskɪŋ] N *no pl* **to be had for the ~** umsonst *or* leicht *or* mühelos zu haben sein; **he could have had it for the ~** er hätte es leicht bekommen können; **she thought the world was hers for the ~** sie dachte, die Welt stehe ihr offen

asking price [ˈɑːskɪŋˌpraɪs] N Verkaufspreis *m*; *(for car, house etc also)* Verhandlungsbasis *f*; **what's your ~?** was verlangen Sie (dafür)?

a/s/l *(Internet etc) abbr of* **age/sex/location** Alter/Geschlecht/Wohnort

aslant [əˈslɑːnt] *(liter)* ADV quer, schräg PREP quer *or* schräg über

asleep [əˈsliːp] ADJ *pred* **a** *(= sleeping)* schlafend; **to be (fast** *or* **sound) ~** (fest) schlafen; **he was sitting there, ~** er saß da und schlief; **to fall ~** einschlafen *(also euph)*; **to lie ~** schlafen; **he is not dead, only ~** er ist nicht tot, er schläft nur *or* liegt nur im Schlaf *(geh)* → **half ADV a b** *(inf: = numb)* eingeschlafen

ASLEF [ˈæzlef] *(Brit) abbr of* **Associated Society of Locomotive Engineers and Firemen** *Eisenbahnergewerkschaft*

ASM *(Theat) abbr of* **assistant stage manager** Assistent(in) *m(f)* des Inspizienten

asocial [eɪˈsəʊʃəl] ADJ ungesellig

asp [æsp] N *(Zool)* Natter *f*

asparagus [əsˈpærəgəs] N *no pl* Spargel *m*

asparagus fern N Spargelkraut *nt*, Asparagus *m*

asparagus tips PL Spargelspitzen *pl*

aspect [ˈæspekt] N **a** *(liter: = appearance)* Anblick *m*, Erscheinung *f*; *(of thing)* Aussehen *nt* **b** *(of question, subject etc)* Aspekt *m*, Seite *f*; **the political ~ of his novel** der politische Aspekt seines Romans; **from the ~ of town planning** aus stadtplanerischer Sicht; **what about the security ~?** was ist mit der Sicherheit? **c** *(of building)* **to have a southerly ~** Südlage haben **d** *(Gram)* Aspekt *m*

aspectual [æˈspektjʊəl] ADJ *(Gram)* im Aspekt

aspen [ˈæspən] N *(Bot)* Espe *f*, Zitterpappel *f*; **to tremble like an ~** *(liter)* zittern wie Espenlaub

aspergillum [ˌæspəˈdʒɪləm] N Weih(wasser) wedel *m*

asperity [æsˈperɪtɪ] N Schroffheit *f no pl*, Schärfe *f no pl*; **the asperities of the winter** *(liter)* der raue Winter *(geh)*

aspersion [əsˈpɜːʃən] N **to cast ~s on sb/sth** abfällige Bemerkungen über jdn/etw machen; **without wishing to cast any ~s** ohne mich abfällig äußern zu wollen

asphalt [ˈæsfælt] N Asphalt *m* VT asphaltieren ADJ *attr* Asphalt-, asphaltiert; **~ jungle** Asphaltdschungel *m*

asphodel [ˈæsfədel] N Asphodelus *m*, Affodill *m*

asphyxia [æsˈfɪksɪə] N Erstickung *f*, Asphyxie *f (spec)*

asphyxiate [æsˈfɪksɪeɪt] VT ersticken; **to be ~d** ersticken VI ersticken

asphyxiation [æsˌfɪksɪˈeɪʃən] N Erstickung *f*

aspic [ˈæspɪk] N *(Cook)* Aspik *m or nt*, Gelee *nt*

aspidistra [ˌæspɪˈdɪstrə] N Aspidistra *f*

aspirant [ˈæspɪrənt] N Anwärter(in) *m(f)* (*to, for* auf *+acc*); *(for job)* Kandidat(in) *m(f)* (*for* für), Aspirant(in) *m(f) (hum)*; *(for sb's hand in marriage)* Bewerber *m* (*for* um)

aspirate [ˈæspəreɪt] N Aspirata *f (spec)*, Hauchlaut *m* VT aspirieren, behauchen

aspiration [ˌæspəˈreɪʃən] N **a** (hohes) Ziel, Aspiration *f (geh)*; **his ~ towards** *(Brit) or* **toward** *(US)* **Lady Sarah's hand** *(liter)* seine Hoffnung auf Lady Sarahs Hand **b** *(Phon)* Aspiration *f*, Behauchung *f*

aspirational [ˌæspəˈreɪʃənl] ADJ *person* auf sozialen Aufstieg bedacht; *product* den sozialen Aufstieg verkörpernd

aspire [əˈspaɪəʳ] VI **to ~ to sth** nach etw streben, etw erstreben; **to ~ to do sth** danach streben, etw zu tun

aspirin [ˈæsprɪn] N Kopfschmerztablette *f*, Aspirin® *nt*

aspiring [əˈspaɪərɪŋ] ADJ aufstrebend

ass[1] [æs] N *(lit, fig inf)* Esel *m*; **silly ~!** blöder Esel!; **don't be an ~!** sei kein Esel!, sei nicht blöd!; **to make an ~ of oneself** sich lächerlich machen, sich blamieren

ass[2] N *(US sl)* Arsch *m (vulg)*; **a nice piece of ~** eine geile Braut *(sl)*; **he was looking for a piece of ~** er wollte eine Frau aufreißen *(inf)*; **this place is just full of ~** hier laufen unwahrscheinlich viele Bräute rum *(sl)*; **to kick ~** *(= get tough)* mit der Faust auf den Tisch hauen *(inf)*; **to work one's ~ off** sich zu Tode schuften *(inf)*; **to kiss ~** *(esp US sl)* ein Arschkriecher sein *(inf)*; **to kiss sb's ~** *(esp US sl)* jdm in den Arsch kriechen *(inf)*; **kiss my ~!** *(esp US sl)* du kannst mich mal am Arsch lecken! *(vulg)* → *also* **arse**

assagai N = **assegai**

assail [ə'seɪl] VT *(lit, fig)* angreifen; *(fig: with questions etc)* überschütten, bombardieren; **a harsh sound ~ed my ears** ein scharfes Geräusch drang an mein Ohr; **to be ~ed by doubts** von Zweifeln befallen sein *or* geplagt werden

assailable [ə'seɪləbl] ADJ *(lit, fig)* angreifbar

assailant [ə'seɪlənt] N Angreifer(in) *m(f)*

assassin [ə'sæsɪn] N Attentäter(in) *m(f)*, Mörder(in) *m(f)*

assassinate [ə'sæsɪneɪt] VT ein Attentat *or* einen Mordanschlag verüben auf *(+acc)*; **JFK was ~d in Dallas** JFK fiel in Dallas einem Attentat *or* Mordanschlag zum Opfer, JFK wurde in Dallas ermordet; **they ~d him** sie haben ihn ermordet

assassination [əˌsæsɪ'neɪʃən] N (geglücktes) Attentat, (geglückter) Mordanschlag (*of* auf *+acc*); **~ attempt** Attentat *nt*; **to plan an ~** ein Attentat planen; **before/after the ~** vor dem Attentat/nach dem (geglückten) Attentat

assault [ə'sɔːlt] **N** **a** *(Mil)* Sturm(angriff) *m* (*on* auf *+acc*); *(fig)* Angriff *m* (*on* gegen); **to make an ~ on sth** einen (Sturm)angriff gegen etw führen **b** *(Jur)* Körperverletzung *f*; **~ and battery** Körperverletzung *f*; **sexual ~** Notzucht *f* → *also* **indecent assault** **VT** **a** *(Jur: = attack)* tätlich werden gegen; *(sexually)* herfallen über *(+acc)*; *(= rape)* sich vergehen an *(+dat)*; **to ~ sb with a stick** jdn mit einem Stock angreifen **b** *(Mil)* angreifen

assault: **assault course** N Übungsgelände *nt*; **getting to the bathroom is like an ~** der Weg zum Badezimmer ist ein wahres Hindernisrennen; **assault craft** N Sturmlandefahrzeug *nt*; **assault rifle** N Maschinengewehr *nt*; **assault troops** PL Sturmtruppen *pl*

assay [ə'seɪ] **N** Prüfung *f* **VT** **a** *mineral, ore, value, sb's worth* prüfen **b** *(liter) (= try)* sich versuchen an *(+dat)*; *(= put to the test) troops* prüfen

ass-backwards [ˌæs'bækwədz] *(US sl)* **ADJ** *(= reversed)* umgekehrt; *(= confused)* verdreht **ADV** *(= in reverse)* rückwärts; *(= in confused manner)* verdreht, verkehrt

assegai ['æsəgaɪ] N Assagai *m*

assemblage [ə'semblɪdʒ] N **a** *(= assembling)* Zusammensetzen *nt*, Zusammenbau *m*; *(esp of car, machine)* Montage *f* **b** *(= collection) (of things)* Sammlung *f*; *(of facts)* Anhäufung *f*; *(of people)* Versammlung *f*

assemble [ə'sembl] **VT** zusammensetzen, zusammenbauen; *car, machine etc also* montieren; *facts* zusammentragen; *Parliament* einberufen, versammeln; *people* zusammenrufen; *team* zusammenstellen **VI** sich versammeln; **we are ~d here today to …** wir haben uns *or* sind heute versammelt, um …

assembler [ə'semblə'] N *(Comput)* Assembler *m*

assembly [ə'semblɪ] N **a** *(= gathering of people, Parl)* Versammlung *f* **b** *(Sch)* Morgenandacht *f*, *tägliche Versammlung* **c** *(= putting together)* Zusammensetzen *nt*, Zusammenbau *m*; *(esp of machine, cars)* Montage *f*; *(of facts)* Zusammentragen *nt* **d** *(= thing assembled)* Konstruktion *f*

assembly: **assembly hall** N *(Sch)* Aula *f*; **assembly language** N *(Comput)* Assemblersprache *f*; **assembly line** N Montageband *nt*; **assemblyman** [ə'semblɪmən] N *(US)* Abgeordnete(r) *m*; **Assembly Member** N Mitglied *nt* des walisischen Parlaments; **assembly plant** N Montagewerk *nt*; **assembly point** N Sammelplatz *m*; **assembly shop** N Montagehalle *f*; **assemblywoman** [ə'semblɪwʊmən] N *(US)* Abgeordnete *f*; **assembly worker** N Montagearbeiter(in) *m(f)*

assent [ə'sent] **N** Zustimmung *f*; **to give one's ~ to sth** seine Zustimmung zu etw geben; **by common ~** mit allgemeiner Zustimmung; **royal ~** königliche Genehmigung **VI** zustimmen; **to ~ to sth** einer Sache *(dat)* zustimmen

assert [ə'sɜːt] VT **a** *(= declare)* behaupten; *one's innocence* beteuern **b** *(= insist on)* **to ~ one's authority** seine Autorität geltend machen; **to ~ one's rights** sein Recht behaupten; **to ~ one's independence** seine Unabhängigkeit demonstrieren; **to ~ oneself** sich behaupten *or* durchsetzen (*over* gegenüber); **if you ~ yourself too much you will lose their support** wenn Sie zu bestimmt auftreten, verlieren Sie ihre Unterstützung

assertion [ə'sɜːʃən] ✪ 26.1 N **a** *(= statement)* Behauptung *f*; *(of innocence)* Beteuerung *f*; **to make ~s/an ~** Behauptungen/eine Behauptung aufstellen **b** *no pl (= insistence)* Behauptung *f*

assertive ADJ, **assertively** ADV [ə'sɜːtɪv, -lɪ] bestimmt

assertiveness [ə'sɜːtɪvnɪs] N Bestimmtheit *f*; **~ training course** Persönlichkeitstrainingskurs *m*

assess [ə'ses] VT **a** *person, chances, abilities, needs* einschätzen; *problem, situation, prospects* beurteilen, einschätzen; *proposal* abwägen; *damage* abschätzen **b** *property* schätzen, taxieren; *person (for tax purposes)* veranlagen (*at* mit); **to ~ sth at its true worth** einer Sache *(dat)* den richtigen Wert beimessen **c** *fine, tax* festsetzen, bemessen (*at* auf *+acc*); *damages* schätzen (*at* auf *+acc*)

assessable [ə'sesəbl] ADJ *(Fin, Tax)* steuer- *or* abgabenpflichtig; **~ income** steuerpflichtiges Einkommen

assessment [ə'sesmənt] N **a** *(= evaluation) (of person, chances, abilities, needs)* Einschätzung *f*; *(of problem, situation, prospects also)* Beurteilung *f*; *(of proposal, advantages also)* Abwägen *nt*; *(of damage)* Schätzung *f*; **in my ~** meines Erachtens; **what's your ~ of the situation?** wie sehen *or* beurteilen Sie die Lage? **b** *(Fin, of property)* Schätzung *f*, Taxierung *f*; *(of person: for tax purposes)* Veranlagung *f* **c** *(Jur) (of fine, tax)* Festsetzung, Bemessung *f*; *(of damages)* Schätzung *f* **d** *(Sch, Univ: of student)* Einstufung *f*; *(Med: of patient)* Beurteilung *f*

assessor [ə'sesə'] N Schätzer(in) *m(f)*, Taxator *m (form)*; *(Insur)* (Schadens)gutachter(in) *m(f)*; *(Univ)* Prüfer(in) *m(f)*

asset ['æset] N **a** *(usu pl)* Vermögenswert *m*; *(on balance sheet)* Aktivposten *m*; **~s** Vermögen *nt*; *(on balance sheet)* Aktiva *pl*; **personal ~s** persönlicher Besitz **b** *(fig)* **it would be an ~ …** es wäre von Vorteil …; **he is one of our great ~s** er ist einer unserer besten Leute; **this player, the club's newest ~** dieser Spieler, die neueste Errungenschaft des Klubs; **he's hardly an ~ to the company** er ist nicht gerade ein Gewinn für die Firma; **good health is a real ~** Gesundheit ist ein großes Kapital; **his appearance is not his best ~** aus seinem Aussehen kann er kein Kapital schlagen

asset-stripping ['æsetstrɪpɪŋ] N Asset-Stripping *nt*, *Aufkauf von finanziell gefährdeten Firmen und anschließender Verkauf ihrer Vermögenswerte*

asseverate [ə'sevəreɪt] VT *(form)* beteuern

asseveration [əˌsevə'reɪʃən] N *(form)* Beteuerung *f*

asshole ['æshəʊl] N *(US sl)* Arschloch *nt (vulg)*

assiduity [ˌæsɪ'djuːɪtɪ] N gewissenhafter Eifer

assiduous ADJ, **assiduously** ADV [ə'sɪdjʊəs, -lɪ] gewissenhaft

assiduousness [ə'sɪdjʊəsnɪs] N Gewissenhaftigkeit *f*

assign [ə'saɪn] **VT** **a** *(= allot)* zuweisen, zuteilen (*to sb* jdm); *(to a purpose) room* bestimmen (*to* für); *(to a word) meaning* zuordnen (*to +dat*); *(= fix) date, time* bestimmen, festsetzen; *(= attribute) cause, novel, play, music* zuschreiben (*to +dat*); **at the time ~ed** zur festgesetzten Zeit; **which class have you been ~ed?** welche Klasse wurde Ihnen zugewiesen?
b *(= appoint)* berufen; *(to a mission, case, task etc)* betrauen (*to* mit), beauftragen (*to* mit); **she was ~ed to this school** sie wurde an diese Schule berufen; **he was ~ed to the post of ambassador** er wurde zum Botschafter berufen; **I was ~ed to speak to the boss** ich wurde damit beauftragt *or* betraut, mit dem Chef zu sprechen
c *(Jur)* übertragen, übereignen (*to sb* jdm)
N *(Jur: also* **assignee***)* Abtretungsempfänger(in) *m(f)*

assignable [ə'saɪnəbl] ADJ **a** *(= ascribable)* bestimmbar **b** *cause* anführbar **c** *(Jur)* übertragbar

assignation [ˌæsɪg'neɪʃən] N **a** Stelldichein *nt*, Rendezvous *nt* **b** = **assignment b-d**

assignment [ə'saɪnmənt] N **a** *(= task)* Aufgabe *f*; *(= mission)* Auftrag *m*, Mission *f*; **to be on (an) ~** einen Auftrag haben **b** *(= appointment)* Berufung *f*; *(to case, task etc)* Betrauung *f* (*to* mit), Beauftragung *f* (*to* mit); **his ~ to the post of ambassador/to this school** seine Berufung zum Botschafter/an diese Schule **c** *(= allocation)* Zuweisung *f*, Zuteilung *f*; *(of room)* Bestimmung *f* (*to* für); *(of meaning)* Zuordnung *f* (*to* zu) **d** *(Jur)* Übertragung *f*, Übereignung *f*

assignor [ˌæsaɪ'nɔː, ˌæsɪ'nɔː] N *(Jur)* Abtretende(r) *mf*, Zedent(in) *m(f) (spec)*

assimilable [ə'sɪmɪləbl] ADJ **a** *(Biol, Ling)* assimilierbar **b** *(= integrable)* angleichbar

assimilate [ə'sɪmɪleɪt] VT *food, information* aufnehmen; *(fig: into society etc also)* integrieren; **newcomers are easily ~d** Neuankömmlinge können leicht integriert werden

assimilation [əˌsɪmɪ'leɪʃən] N *(of food, knowledge)* Aufnahme *f*; *(fig: into society etc also)* Integration *f*; **his powers of ~** seine geistige Aufnahmefähigkeit

assist [ə'sɪst] **VT** helfen *(+dat)*; *(= act as an assistant to)* assistieren *(+dat)*; *growth, progress, development* fördern, begünstigen; **to ~ sb with sth** jdm bei etw helfen *or* behilflich sein; **to ~ sb in doing** *or* **to do sth** jdm helfen, etw zu tun; **… who was ~ing the surgeon** …, der dem Chirurgen assistierte; **in a wind ~ed time of 10.01 seconds** mit Rückenwind in einer Zeit von 10,01 Sekunden; **a man is ~ing the police (with their inquiries)** *(euph)* ein Mann wird von der Polizei vernommen
VI **a** *(= help)* helfen; **to ~ with sth** bei etw helfen; **to ~ in doing sth** helfen, etw zu tun
b *(= be present) (doctor)* assistieren (*at* bei); *(in church)* ministrieren
N *(Sport)* Vorlage *f*

assistance [ə'sɪstəns] N Hilfe *f*; **to give ~ to sb** *(= come to aid of)* jdm Hilfe leisten; **my secretary will give you every ~** meine Sekretärin wird Ihnen in jeder Hinsicht behilflich sein; **to come to sb's ~** jdm zu Hilfe kommen; **to be of ~ to sb** jdm helfen *or* behilflich sein; **can I be of any ~?** kann ich irgendwie helfen *or* behilflich sein?

assistant [ə'sɪstənt] **N** Assistent(in) *m(f)*; *(= shop assistant)* Verkäufer(in) *m(f)*; **are you in charge here? – no, I am just an ~** sind Sie hier der Chef? – nein, ich bin bloß Mitarbeiter **ADJ** *attr manager etc* stellvertretend

assistant: **assistant master/mistress** N Lehrer(in) *m(f) (ohne besondere zusätzliche Verantwortung)*; **assistant priest** N Hilfspriester *m*; **assistant professor** N *(US)* Assistenz-Professor(in) *m(f)*; **assistant referee** N *(Ftbl)* Schiedsrichterassistent(in) *m(f)*

assistantship [əˈsɪstəntʃɪp] N (*Brit*: *at school*) Stelle *f* als Fremdsprachenassistent(in); (*US*: *at college*) Assistentenstelle *f*

assisted [əˌsɪstɪd]: **assisted living** N (*US*) betreutes Wohnen; **assisted place** N (*Brit Sch*) *staatlich finanzierter Platz in einer Privatschule, der für einen Schüler aus bescheidenen Verhältnissen reserviert ist*; **assisted suicide** N aktive Sterbehilfe

assizes [əˈsaɪzɪz] PL (*Brit, dated*) Gerichtstage *pl*, Assisen *pl* (*old*); **at the county ~** während der Bezirksgerichtstage

assn *abbr of* **association**

associate [əˈsəʊʃɪɪt] **N** **a** (= *colleague*) Kollege *m*, Kollegin *f*; (*Comm*: = *partner*) Partner *m*, Kompagnon *m*, Teilhaber(in) *m(f)*; (= *accomplice*) Komplize *m*, Komplizin *f*
b (*of a society*) außerordentliches *or* assoziiertes Mitglied [əˈsəʊʃɪeɪt]
VT in Verbindung bringen, assoziieren (*also Psych*); **to ~ oneself with sb/sth** sich jdm/einer Sache anschließen, sich mit jdm/einer Sache assoziieren; **to be ~d with sb/sth** mit jdm/einer Sache in Verbindung gebracht *or* assoziiert werden; **it is ~d in their minds with …** sie denken dabei gleich an (*+acc*) …; **I don't ~ him with sport** ich assoziiere ihn nicht mit Sport, ich denke bei ihm nicht an Sport; **the Associated Union of …** der Gewerkschaftsverband der …; **~(d) company** Partnerfirma *f* [əˈsəʊʃɪeɪt]
VI **to ~ with** verkehren mit

associate: **associate director** N *Direktor einer Firma, der jedoch nicht offiziell als solcher ernannt wurde*; **associate editor** N Mitherausgeber(in) *m(f)*; **associate member** N außerordentliches *or* assoziiertes Mitglied; **associate partner** N (Geschäfts)partner(in) *m(f)*; **associate professor** N (*US*) außerordentlicher Professor, außerordentliche Professorin

association [əˌsəʊsɪˈeɪʃən] N **a** *no pl* (= *associating*: *with people*) Verkehr *m*, Umgang *m*; (= *cooperation*) Zusammenarbeit *f*; **he has benefited from his ~ with us** er hat von seiner Beziehung zu uns profitiert; **he has had a long ~ with the party** er hat seit langem Verbindung mit der Partei
b (= *organization*) Verband *m*
c (= *connection in the mind*) Assoziation *f* (*with* an *+acc*) (*also Psych*); **~ of ideas** Gedankenassoziation *f*; **to have unpleasant ~s for sb** unangenehme Assoziationen bei jdm hervorrufen; **to be found in ~ with sth** zusammen mit etw vorkommen; **published in ~ with …** in Zusammenarbeit mit … veröffentlicht; **to be guilty/tainted by ~** indirekt schuldig/betroffen sein; **free ~** (*Psych*) freie Assoziation

association football N (*Brit*) Fußball *m*, Soccer *nt*

associative [əˈsəʊʃɪətɪv] ADJ assoziativ

assonance [ˈæsənəns] N Assonanz *f*

assort [əˈsɔːt] VI (*form*) **a** (= *agree, match*) passen (*with* zu) **b** (= *consort*) Umgang pflegen (*with* mit)

assorted [əˈsɔːtɪd] ADJ **a** (= *mixed*) gemischt **b** (= *matched*) zusammengestellt → **ill-assorted**

assortment [əˈsɔːtmənt] N Mischung *f*; (*of goods*) Auswahl *f* (*of* an *+dat*), Sortiment *nt* (*of* von); (*of ideas*) Sammlung *f*; **a whole ~ of boyfriends** ein ganzes Sortiment von Freunden

asst *abbr of* **assistant**

assuage [əˈsweɪdʒ] VT *hunger, thirst, desire* stillen, befriedigen; *anger, fears etc* beschwichtigen; *pain, grief* lindern; *guilt* vermindern; *conscience* erleichtern

assume [əˈsjuːm] ✪ 20.3, 26.1 VT **a** (= *take for granted, suppose*) annehmen; (= *presuppose*) voraussetzen; **let us ~ that you are right** nehmen wir an *or* gehen wir davon aus, Sie hätten recht; **assuming (that) …** angenommen(, dass) …; **assuming (that) this is true …** angenommen *or* vorausgesetzt, (dass) das stimmt …; **Professor X ~s as his basic premise that …** Professor X geht von der Grundvoraussetzung aus, dass …
b *power, control* übernehmen; (*forcefully*) ergreifen
c (= *take on*) *name, title* annehmen, sich (*dat*) zulegen; *guise, shape, attitude* annehmen; **to ~ office** sein Amt antreten; **to ~ a look of innocence/surprise** eine unschuldige/überraschte Miene aufsetzen; **the problem has ~d a new importance** das Problem hat neue Bedeutung gewonnen; **the sky ~d a reddish glow** (*liter*) der Himmel nahm rötliche Glut an (*poet*)

assumed [əˈsjuːmd] ADJ **a** **~ name** angenommener Name; (*for secrecy etc also*) Deckname *m*
b (= *pretended*) *surprise, humility* gespielt, vorgetäuscht; **in the ~ guise of a beggar** als Bettler verkleidet

assuming [əˈsjuːmɪŋ] ADJ anmaßend, überheblich

assumption [əˈsʌmpʃən] N **a** Annahme *f*; (= *presupposition*) Voraussetzung *f*; **to go on the ~ that …** von der Voraussetzung ausgehen, dass …; **the basic ~s of this theory are …** diese Theorie geht grundsätzlich davon aus, dass …
b (*of power, role, office etc*) Übernahme *f*; (*forcefully*) Ergreifen *nt* **c** (*of guise, false name etc*) Annahme *f*; (*insincere*: *of look of innocence etc*) Vortäuschung *f*, Aufsetzen *nt* **d** (*Eccl*) **the Assumption** Mariä Himmelfahrt *f*

assurance [əˈʃʊərəns] N **a** Versicherung *f*; (= *promise*) Zusicherung *f*; **he gave me his ~ that it would be done** er versicherte mir, dass es getan (werden) würde; **do I have your ~ that …?** garantieren Sie mir, dass …?; **you have my ~ that …** Sie können versichert sein, dass … **b** (= *self-confidence*) Sicherheit *f* **c** (= *confidence*) Zuversicht *f* (*in* in *+acc*), Vertrauen *nt* (*in* in *+acc*); **in the ~ that …** (*liter*) im Vertrauen darauf, dass …, in der Zuversicht, dass … **d** (*Brit*: = *life assurance*) Versicherung *f*

assure [əˈʃʊəʳ] ✪ 15.1 VT **a** (= *say with confidence*) versichern (*+dat*); (= *promise*) zusichern (*+dat*); **to ~ sb of sth** (*of love, willingness etc*) jdn einer Sache (*gen*) versichern; (*of service, support, help*) jdm etw zusichern; **to ~ sb that …** jdm versichern/zusichern, dass …; **… I ~ you …** versichere ich Ihnen **b** (= *make certain of*) *success, happiness, future* sichern; **he is ~d of a warm welcome wherever he goes** er kann sich überall eines herzlichen Empfanges sicher sein **c** (*Brit*: = *insure*) *life* versichern; **she ~d her life for £100,000** sie schloss eine Lebensversicherung über £ 100.000 ab

assured [əˈʃʊəd] **N** (*Brit*) Versicherte(r) *mf* **ADJ** sicher; *income, future also* gesichert; (= *self-confident*) sicher; **to rest ~ that …** sicher sein, dass …; **to rest ~ of sth** einer Sache (*gen*) sicher sein

assuredly [əˈʃʊərɪdlɪ] ADV mit Sicherheit; **yes, most ~** ganz sicher

Assyria [əˈsɪrɪə] N Assyrien *nt*

Assyrian [əˈsɪrɪən] **ADJ** assyrisch **N** **a** Assyrer(in) *m(f)* **b** (= *language*) Assyrisch *nt*

aster [ˈæstəʳ] N Aster *f*

asterisk [ˈæstərɪsk] **N** Sternchen *nt* **VT** mit Sternchen versehen

astern [əˈstɜːn] (*Naut*) **ADV** achtern; (= *towards the stern*) nach achtern; (= *backwards*) achteraus **PREP** **~ (of) the ship** achteraus

asteroid [ˈæstərɔɪd] N Asteroid *m*

asthma [ˈæsmə] N Asthma *nt*; **~ attack** Asthmaanfall *m*

asthmatic [æsˈmætɪk] **N** Asthmatiker(in) *m(f)* **ADJ** asthmatisch

asthmatically [æsˈmætɪkəlɪ] ADV asthmatisch

astigmatic [ˌæstɪgˈmætɪk] ADJ astigmatisch

astigmatism [æsˈtɪgmətɪzəm] N Astigmatismus *m*

astir [əˈstɜːʳ] ADJ *pred* **a** (= *in motion, excited*) voller *or* in Aufregung **b** (*old, liter*: = *up and about*) auf den Beinen, auf

ASTM (*US*) *abbr of* **American Society for Testing Materials** amerikanischer Normenausschuss, ≈ DNA *m*

ASTMS [ˈæztəmz] *abbr of* **Association of Scientific, Technical and Managerial Staffs** *Gewerkschaft der Wissenschaftler, Techniker und leitenden Angestellten*

astonish [əˈstɒnɪʃ] VT erstaunen, überraschen; **you ~ me!** (*iro*) das wundert mich aber! (*iro*), was du nicht sagst! (*iro*); **to be ~ed** erstaunt *or* überrascht sein; **I am ~ed** *or* **it ~es me that …** ich bin erstaunt *or* es wundert mich, dass …; **I am ~ed to learn that …** ich höre mit Erstaunen *or* Befremden (*geh*), dass …

astonishing [əˈstɒnɪʃɪŋ] ADJ erstaunlich

astonishingly [əˈstɒnɪʃɪŋlɪ] ADV erstaunlich; **~ (enough)** erstaunlicherweise

astonishment [əˈstɒnɪʃmənt] N Erstaunen *nt*, Überraschung *f* (*at* über *+acc*); **look of ~** erstaunter *or* überraschter Blick; **she looked at me in (complete) ~** sie sah mich (ganz) erstaunt *or* überrascht an; **to my ~** zu meinem Erstaunen

astound [əˈstaʊnd] VT sehr erstaunen, in Erstaunen (ver)setzen; **to be ~ed (at** *or* **by)** höchst erstaunt sein (über *+acc*)

astounding [əˈstaʊndɪŋ] ADJ erstaunlich

astoundingly [əˈstaʊndɪŋlɪ] ADV erstaunlich; **~, an American had won the Tour de France** erstaunlicherweise hatte ein Amerikaner die Tour de France gewonnen

astrakhan [ˌæstrəˈkæn] N Astrachan *m* *attr* Astrachan-; **~ coat** Astrachanmantel *m*

astral [ˈæstrəl] ADJ Stern-; (*in theosophy*) Astral-; **~ matter** Sternmaterie *f*; **~ projection** Astralreise *f*

astray [əˈstreɪ] ADJ verloren; **to go ~** (*person*) (*lit*) vom Weg abkommen; (*fig*: *morally*) vom rechten Weg abkommen, auf Abwege geraten; (*letter, object*) verloren gehen; (= *go wrong*: *in argument etc*) irregehen; **to lead sb ~** (*fig*) jdn vom rechten Weg abbringen; (= *mislead*) jdn irreführen

astride [əˈstraɪd] **PREP** rittlings auf (*+dat*) **ADV** rittlings; *ride* im Herrensitz

astringency [əsˈtrɪndʒənsɪ] N (*fig*) Ätzende(s) *nt*

astringent [əsˈtrɪndʒənt] **ADJ** adstringierend; (*fig*) *remark, humour* ätzend, beißend **N** Adstringens *nt*

astro- [ˈæstrəʊ-] PREF Astro-

astrolabe [ˈæstrəleɪb] N Astrolab(ium) *nt*

astrologer [əsˈtrɒlədʒəʳ] N Astrologe *m*, Astrologin *f*

astrological [ˌæstrəˈlɒdʒɪkəl] ADJ astrologisch; **~ sign** Tierkreiszeichen *nt*

astrologically [ˌæstrəˈlɒdʒɪkəlɪ] ADV astrologisch

astrology [əsˈtrɒlədʒɪ] N Astrologie *f*

astronaut [ˈæstrənɔːt] N Astronaut(in) *m(f)*

astronautics [ˌæstrəʊˈnɔːtɪks] N *sing* Raumfahrt *f*, Astronautik *f*

astronomer [əsˈtrɒnəməʳ] N Astronom(in) *m(f)*

astronomical [ˌæstrəˈnɒmɪkəl] ADJ (*lit, fig*: *also* **astronomic**) astronomisch

astronomical clock N astronomische Uhr

astronomically [ˌæstrəˈnɒmɪkəlɪ] ADV (*lit, fig*) astronomisch

astronomical year N Sternjahr *nt*

astronomy [əsˈtrɒnəmɪ] N Astronomie *f*

astrophysics [ˌæstrəʊˈfɪzɪks] N *sing* Astrophysik *f*

astute [əˈstjuːt] ADJ schlau; *remark also* scharfsinnig; *businessman also* clever (*inf*); *child* aufgeweckt; *mind* scharf; **he's very ~ for one so old** er ist für sein Alter geistig sehr rege

astutely [əˈstjuːtlɪ] ADV *remark, observe* scharfsinnig

astuteness [əsˈtjuːtnɪs] N Schlauheit *f*; (*of remark also*) Scharfsinnigkeit *f*; (*of businessman also*) Cleverness *f* (*inf*); (*of child*) Aufgewecktheit *f*; (*of mind*) Schärfe *f*

asunder [ə'sʌndəʳ] ADV *(liter)* *(= apart)* auseinander; *(= in pieces)* entzwei, in Stücke; **to split ~** spalten; **her heart was rent ~** ihr brach das Herz; **... let no man put ~** ..., soll der Mensch nicht trennen *or* scheiden

asylum [ə'saɪləm] N **a** Asyl *nt*; **to ask for (political) ~** um (politisches) Asyl bitten **b** *(= lunatic asylum)* (Irren)anstalt *f*

asylum-seeker N [ə'saɪləm,siːkəʳ] Asylbewerber(in) *m(f)*

asymmetric(al) [,eɪsɪ'metrɪk(əl)] ADJ asymmetrisch

asymmetric(al) bars PL Stufenbarren *m*

asymmetry [æ'sɪmɪtrɪ] N Asymmetrie *f*

asynchronous [æ'sɪŋkrənəs] ADJ *(also Comput)* asynchron

at [æt] PREP **a** *(position)* an *(+dat)*, bei *(+dat)*; *(with place)* in *(+dat)*; **at a table** an einem Tisch; **at the window** am *or* beim Fenster; **at the corner** an der Ecke; **at the top** an der Spitze; **at home** zu Hause; **at the university** *(US)*, **at university** an *or* auf der Universität; **at school** in der Schule; **at the hotel** im Hotel; **at the zoo** im Zoo; **at my brother's** bei meinem Bruder; **at a party** auf *or* bei einer Party; **to arrive at the station** am Bahnhof ankommen; **he came in at the window** er ist durch das Fenster hereingekommen; **the rain came in at the window** es hat durchs Fenster hineingeregnet; **where are you at with your work?** *(inf)* wie weit sind Sie mit Ihrer Arbeit?; **this is where it's at** *(esp US inf)* da gehts ab *(sl)*, da geht die Post ab *(inf)*; **he doesn't know where he's at** *(inf)* der weiß ja nicht, was er tut *(inf)*

b *(direction)* **to aim/shoot/point** *etc* **at sb/sth** auf jdn/etw zielen/schießen/zeigen *etc*; **to look/growl/swear** *etc* **at sb/sth** jdn/etw ansehen/anknurren/beschimpfen *etc*; **at him!** auf ihn!

c *(time, frequency, order)* **at ten o'clock** um zehn Uhr; **at night/dawn** bei Nacht/beim *or* im Morgengrauen; **at Christmas/Easter** *etc* zu Weihnachten/Ostern *etc*; **at your age/16 (years of age)** in deinem Alter/mit 16 (Jahren); **three at a time** drei auf einmal; **at the start/end of sth** am Anfang/am Ende einer Sache *(gen)*

d *(activity)* **at play** beim Spiel; **at work** bei der Arbeit; **good/bad/an expert at sth** gut/schlecht/ein Experte in etw *(dat)*; **his employees/creditors are at him** seine Angestellten/Gläubiger setzen ihm zu; **while we are at it** *(inf)* wenn wir schon mal dabei sind; **the couple in the next room were at it all night** *(inf)* die beiden im Zimmer nebenan haben es die ganze Nacht getrieben *(inf)*; **the brakes are at it again** *(inf)* die Bremsen mucken schon wieder *(inf)*

e *(state, condition)* **to be at an advantage** im Vorteil sein; **at a loss/profit** mit Verlust/Gewinn; **I'd leave it at that** ich würde es dabei belassen → **best, worst, that**[1]

f *(= as a result of, upon)* auf *(+acc)* ... (hin); **at his request** auf seine Bitte (hin); **at her death** bei ihrem Tod; **at that/this he left the room** daraufhin verließ er das Zimmer

g *(cause: = with)* *angry, annoyed, delighted etc* über *(+acc)*

h *(rate, value, degree)* **at full speed/50 km/h** mit voller Geschwindigkeit/50 km/h; **at 50p a pound** für *or* zu 50 Pence pro *or* das Pfund; **at 5% interest** zu 5% Zinsen; **at a high/low price** zu einem hohen/niedrigen Preis; **when the temperature is at 90** wenn die Temperatur bei *or* auf 90 ist; **with inflation at this level** bei so einer Inflationsrate → **all, cost, rate**[1]

atavism ['ætəvɪzəm] N Atavismus *m*

atavistic [,ætə'vɪstɪk] ADJ atavistisch

ataxia [ə'tæksɪə] N Ataxie *f*

ataxic [ə'tæksɪk] ADJ ataktisch

ATB *abbr of* **all-terrain bike**

ate [eɪt, et] *pret of* **eat**

atheism ['eɪθɪɪzəm] N Atheismus *m*

atheist ['eɪθɪɪst] **N** Atheist(in) *m(f)* **ADJ** *attr* atheistisch

atheistic [,eɪθɪ'ɪstɪk] ADJ atheistisch

Athenian [ə'θiːnɪən] **N** Athener(in) *m(f)* **ADJ** athenisch; *(esp modern)* Athener

Athens ['æθɪnz] N Athen *nt*

athirst [ə'θɜːst] ADJ *(fig liter)* **to be ~ for sth** nach etw *(dat)* dürsten *(liter)*

athlete ['æθliːt] N Athlet(in) *m(f)*; *(= specialist in track and field events)* Leichtathlet(in) *m(f)*; **he is a natural ~** er ist der geborene Sportler

athlete's foot [,æθliːts'fʊt] N Fußpilz *m*

athlete's heart [,æθliːts'hɑːt] N Sportlerherz *nt*

athletic [æθ'letɪk] ADJ sportlich; *(referring to athletics) build* athletisch

athletically [æθ'letɪkəlɪ] ADV sportlich; *built* athletisch

athleticism [æθ'letɪsɪzəm] N Athletentum *nt*

athletics [æθ'letɪks] N *sing or pl* Leichtathletik *f*; **~ meeting** Leichtathletikwettkampf *m*; **~ coach** Leichtathletiktrainer(in) *m(f)*; **sexual ~** Sexualakrobatik *f*

at-home ['æt'həʊm] N Empfang *m* bei sich *(dat)* zu Hause

athwart [ə'θwɔːt] **ADV** quer; *(Naut)* dwars **PREP** quer über; *(Naut)* dwars, quer

Atlantic [ət'læntɪk] **N** *(also* **Atlantic Ocean***)* Atlantik *m*, Atlantischer Ozean **ADJ** *attr* atlantisch; **~ crossing** Atlantiküberquerung *f*; **~ liner** Ozeandampfer *m*

Atlantic Charter N Atlantik-Charta *f*

Atlantic wall N Atlantikwall *m*

atlas ['ætləs] N Atlas *m*

Atlas Mountains PL Atlas(gebirge *nt*) *m*

ATM *abbr of* **automated telling** *or* **teller machine**

atmosphere ['ætməsfɪəʳ] N *(lit, fig)* Atmosphäre *f*; *(fig: of novel also)* Stimmung *f*

atmospheric [,ætməs'ferɪk] ADJ atmosphärisch; *(= full of atmosphere) description* stimmungsvoll

atmospheric pressure N Luftdruck *m*

atmospherics [,ætməs'ferɪks] PL *(Rad)* atmosphärische Störungen *pl*

atoll ['ætɒl] N Atoll *nt*

atom ['ætəm] N **a** Atom *nt* **b** *(fig)* **to powder sth into ~s** etw völlig zertrümmern; **not an ~ of truth** kein Körnchen Wahrheit

atom bomb N Atombombe *f*

atomic [ə'tɒmɪk] ADJ atomar

atomic *in cpds* Atom-; **atomic age** N Atomzeitalter *nt*; **atomic bomb** N Atombombe *f*; **atomic clock** N Atomuhr *f*; **atomic energy** N Atom- *or* Kernenergie *f*; **Atomic Energy Authority** *(Brit)*, **Atomic Energy Commission** *(US)* N Atomkommission *f*; **atomic mass** N Atommasse *f*; **atomic number** N Ordnungszahl *f*; **atomic power** N Atomkraft *f*; *(= propulsion)* Atomantrieb *m*; **atomic-powered** ADJ atomgetrieben; **atomic reactor** N Atomreaktor *m*; **atomic structure** N Atombau *m*; **atomic warfare** N atomare Kriegsführung; **atomic waste** N Atommüll *m*; **atomic weapon** N Atomwaffe *f*; **atomic weight** N Atomgewicht *nt*

atomism ['ætəmɪzəm] N *(Philos)* Atomismus *m*

atomistic [,ætə'mɪstɪk] ADJ *(Philos)* atomistisch

atomize ['ætəmaɪz] VT *liquid* zerstäuben

atomizer ['ætəmaɪzəʳ] N Zerstäuber *m*

atom smasher N Teilchenbeschleuniger *m*

atonal [æ'təʊnl] ADJ atonal

atone [ə'təʊn] VI **to ~ for sth** (für) etw sühnen *or* büßen

atonement [ə'təʊnmənt] N Sühne *f*, Buße *f*; **to make ~ for sth** für etw Sühne *or* Buße tun; **in ~ for sth** als Sühne *or* Buße für etw; **the Atonement** *(Eccl)* das Sühneopfer (Christi)

atop [ə'tɒp] PREP *(liter)* (oben) auf *(+dat)*

A to Z® N Stadtplan *m (mit Straßenverzeichnis, meist in Buchform)*

at-risk ['æt,rɪsk] ADJ Risiko-; **~ group** Risikogruppe *f*; **~ register** *(Social Work)* Register *nt* gefährdeter Kinder

atrium ['eɪtrɪəm] N *(Archit)* Vorhof *m*, Atrium *nt* *(spec)*; *(Roman)* Atrium *nt*

atrocious ADJ, **atrociously** ADV [ə'trəʊʃəs, -lɪ] grauenhaft

atrocity [ə'trɒsɪtɪ] N Grausamkeit *f*; *(act also)* Gräueltat *f*

atrophy ['ætrəfɪ] **N** Atrophie *f (geh)*, Schwund *m* **VT** schwinden lassen **VI** verkümmern, schwinden

at-seat ['æt,siːt] ADJ **~ TV** *(Aviat etc) in die Rückenlehne integrierter kleiner Monitor*

at sign N *(Comput)* at-Zeichen *nt*

att *abbr of* **attorney**

attaboy ['ætəbɔɪ] INTERJ *(esp US inf)* gut gemacht!

attach [ə'tætʃ] **VT** **a** *(= join)* festmachen, befestigen *(to* an *+dat)*; *document to a letter etc* an- *or* beiheften; **please find ~ed ...** beigeheftet ...; **to ~ oneself to sb/a group** sich jdm/einer Gruppe anschließen; **is he/she ~ed?** ist er/sie schon vergeben?; **to ~ conditions to sth** Bedingungen mit etw verknüpfen *or* an etw *(acc)* knüpfen

b **to be ~ed to sb/sth** *(= be fond of)* an jdm/etw hängen

c *(= attribute) importance* beimessen, zuschreiben *(to +dat)*

d *(Mil etc) personnel* angliedern, zuteilen *(to +dat)*

VI **no blame ~es to him** ihm haftet keine Schuld an, ihn trifft keine Schuld; **responsibility ~ing** *or* **~ed to this post** *(esp Brit)* *or* **position** Verantwortung, die dieser Posten mit sich bringt; **great importance ~es to this** dem haftet größte Bedeutung an

attachable [ə'tætʃəbl] ADJ **to be ~** sich befestigen lassen

attaché [ə'tæʃeɪ] N Attaché *m*

attaché case N Aktenkoffer *m*

attachment [ə'tætʃmənt] N **a** *(= act of attaching)* Festmachen *nt*, Befestigen *nt*; *(of document (to a letter etc))* An- *or* Beiheften *nt* **b** *(= accessory: for tool etc)* Zusatzteil, Zubehörteil *nt* **c** *(fig: = affection)* Zuneigung *f (to* zu*)* **d** *(Mil etc: = temporary transfer)* Zuordnung *f*, Angliederung *f*; **to be on ~** angegliedert *or* zugeteilt sein *(to +dat)* **e** *(Comput)* Anlage *f*, Anhang *m*, Attachment *nt*

attack [ə'tæk] **N** **a** *(Mil, Sport, fig)* Angriff *m* *(on* auf *+acc)*; **there have been two ~s on his life** es wurden bereits zwei Anschläge auf sein Leben gemacht *or* verübt; **to be under ~** angegriffen werden; *(fig also)* unter Beschuss stehen; **to go on to the ~** zum Angriff übergehen; **to return to the ~** wieder zum Angriff übergehen; **to launch an ~** einen Angriff vortragen *or* machen *(on* auf *+acc)*; *(on sb's character)* angreifen *(on +acc)*; **~ is the best form of defence** *(Brit)* *or* **defense** *(US)* Angriff ist die beste Verteidigung; **to leave oneself open to ~** Angriffsflächen bieten

b *(Med etc)* Anfall *m*; **an ~ of fever** ein Fieberanfall *m*; **to have an ~ of nerves** plötzlich Nerven bekommen

VT **a** *(Mil, Sport, fig)* angreifen; *(from ambush, in robbery etc)* überfallen

b *(= tackle) task, problem, sonata* in Angriff nehmen

c *(Med, illness)* befallen

VI angreifen; **an ~ing side** eine angriffsfreudige *or* offensive Mannschaft; **ready to ~** zum Angriff bereit

attack dog N Kampfhund *m*

attacker [ə'tækəʳ] N Angreifer(in) *m(f)*

attagirl ['ætəgɜːl] INTERJ *(esp US inf)* gut gemacht!

attain [ə'teɪn] **VT** *aim, rank, age, perfection* erreichen; *knowledge, independence* erlangen; *happiness, prosperity, power* gelangen zu; **he has ~ed his ambitions** er hat sein Ziel erreicht **VI** **to ~ to sth** *(to perfection)* etw erreichen; *to prosperity, power* zu etw gelangen; **to ~ to man's estate** *(form)* das Mannesalter erreichen *(form)*

attainable [ə'teɪnəbl] ADJ erreichbar, zu erreichen; *knowledge, happiness, power* zu erlangen

attainder [əˈteɪndəʳ] N → bill³ h

attainment [əˈteɪnmənt] N **a** *(= act of attaining)* Erreichung *f*, Erreichen *nt*; *(of knowledge, happiness, prosperity, power)* Erlangen *nt*; **difficult/easy** *etc* **of ~** *(form)* schwierig/leicht zu erreichen *or* erlangen **b** *(usu pl: = accomplishment)* Fertigkeit *f*; **a low/high standard of ~** ein niedriger/hoher Leistungsstandard

attempt [əˈtempt] VT versuchen; *smile, conversation* den Versuch machen *or* unternehmen zu; *task, job* sich versuchen an *(+dat)*; **~ed murder** Mordversuch *m*; **~ed suicide** Selbstmordversuch *m*
N Versuch *m*; *(on sb's life)* (Mord)anschlag *m* *(on* auf *+acc)*; **an ~ on Mount Everest/the record** ein Versuch, Mount Everest zu bezwingen/den Rekord zu brechen; **an ~ at a joke/at doing sth** ein Versuch, einen Witz zu machen/etw zu tun; **to make an ~ on sb's life** einen Anschlag auf jdn *or* jds Leben verüben; **to make an ~ at doing sth** *or* **to do sth** versuchen, etw zu tun; **he made no ~ to help us** er unternahm keinen Versuch, uns zu helfen; **at the first ~** auf Anhieb, beim ersten Versuch; **in the ~** dabei

attend [əˈtend] ✪ 19.3, 19.5, 25.1 VT **a** *classes, church, meeting, school etc* besuchen; *wedding, funeral* anwesend *or* zugegen sein bei, beiwohnen *(+dat)* *(geh)*; **the wedding was well ~ed** die Hochzeit war gut besucht
b *(= accompany)* begleiten; *(= wait on) queen etc* bedienen, aufwarten *(+dat)*; **which doctor is ~ing you?** von welchem Arzt werden Sie behandelt?, wer ist Ihr behandelnder Arzt?
VI **a** *(= be present)* anwesend sein; **are you going to ~?** gehen Sie hin?; **to ~ at a birth** bei einer Geburt helfen *or* assistieren; **to ~ (up)on sb** *(old)* jdm aufwarten *(old)*
b *(= pay attention)* aufpassen

▶ **attend to** ✪ 20.7 VI *+prep obj (= see to)* sich kümmern um; *(= pay attention to) work etc* Aufmerksamkeit schenken *or* widmen *(+dat)*; *(= listen to) teacher, sb's remark* zuhören *(+dat)*; *(= heed) advice, warning* hören auf *(+acc)*, Beachtung schenken *(+dat)*; *(= serve) customers etc* bedienen; **are you being attended to?** werden Sie schon bedient?; **that's being attended to** das wird (bereits) erledigt

attendance [əˈtendəns] N **a to be in ~ at sth** bei etw anwesend sein; **to be in ~ on sb** jdm aufwarten, jdn bedienen; **she entered with her maids in ~** sie kam von ihren Hofdamen begleitet herein; **the police are in ~** *(form)* die Polizei ist vor Ort *(form)* **b** *(= being present)* Anwesenheit *f* *(at* bei); **regular ~ at school** regelmäßiger Schulbesuch **c** *(= number of people present)* Teilnehmerzahl *f*; **record ~** eine Rekordteilnehmerzahl, Rekordteilnehmerzahlen *pl*

attendance: **attendance allowance** N *(Brit)* Pflegegeld *nt*; **attendance centre** N *(Brit)* Heim *nt* für jugendliche Straftäter; **attendance officer** N *(Brit) Beamter, der sich um Fälle häufigen unentschuldigten Fehlens in der Schule kümmert*; **attendance record** N *(= school register etc)* Anwesenheitsliste *f*; **he doesn't have a very good ~** er fehlt oft

attendant [əˈtendənt] N *(in retinue)* Begleiter(in) *m(f)*; *(in public toilets)* Toilettenwart *m*, Toilettenfrau *f*; *(in swimming baths)* Bademeister(in) *m(f)*; *(in art galleries, museums)* Aufseher(in) *m(f)*, Wärter(in) *m(f)*; *(= medical attendant)* Krankenpfleger(in) *m(f)*; *(of royalty)* Kammerherr *m*/-frau *f*; **her ~s** ihr Gefolge *nt*
ADJ **a** *problems etc* (da)zugehörig, damit verbunden; **~ circumstances** Begleitumstände *pl*; **old age and its ~ ills** Alter und die damit verbundenen Beschwerden; **to be ~ (up)on sth** mit etw zusammenhängen, etw begleiten
b *(form: = serving)* **to be ~ on sb** *(lady-in-waiting etc)* jdm aufwarten; **there were two ~ nurses** es waren zwei Krankenschwestern anwesend

attendee [əˌtenˈdiː] N *(esp US)* Teilnehmer(in) *m(f)*

attention [əˈtenʃən] ✪ 13, 20.6, 26 N **a** *no pl* *(= consideration, observation, notice)* Aufmerksamkeit *f*; **to call ~ to sth** auf etw *(acc)* aufmerksam machen; **to call** *or* **draw sb's ~ to sth, to call** *or* **draw sth to sb's ~** jds Aufmerksamkeit auf etw *(acc)* lenken, jdn auf etw *(acc)* aufmerksam machen; **to attract sb's ~** jds Aufmerksamkeit erregen, jdn auf sich *(acc)* aufmerksam machen; **to turn one's ~ to sb/sth** jdm/einer Sache seine Aufmerksamkeit zuwenden, seine Aufmerksamkeit auf jdn/etw richten; **to pay ~/no ~ to sb/sth** jdn/etw beachten/nicht beachten; **to pay ~ to the teacher** dem Lehrer zuhören; **to hold sb's ~** jdn fesseln; **can I have your ~ for a moment?** dürfte ich Sie einen Augenblick um (Ihre) Aufmerksamkeit bitten?; **~!** Achtung!; **your ~, please** ich bitte um Aufmerksamkeit; *(official announcement)* Achtung, Achtung!; **it has come to my ~ that …** ich bin darauf aufmerksam geworden, dass …; **it has been brought to my ~ that …** es ist mir zu Ohren gekommen, dass …
b *(Comm)* **~ Miss Smith, for the ~ of Miss Smith** zu Händen von Frau Smith; **your letter will receive our earliest ~** Ihr Brief wird baldmöglichst *or* umgehend bearbeitet; **for your ~** zur gefälligen Beachtung
c *(Mil)* **to stand to** *or* **at ~, to come to ~** stillstehen; **~!** stillgestanden!
d attentions
PL *(= kindnesses)* Aufmerksamkeiten *pl*; **to pay one's ~s to sb** *(dated: = court)* jdm den Hof machen

Attention Deficit Disorder N *(Med)* Aufmerksamkeitsdefizit-Störung *f*

attention-seeking [əˈtenʃənsiːkɪŋ] N Beachtungsbedürfnis *nt* ADJ **to show ~ behaviour** *(Brit) or* **behavior** *(US)* beachtet werden wollen

attention span N Konzentrationsvermögen *nt*; **to have a very short ~** sich nur sehr kurz konzentrieren können

attentive [əˈtentɪv] ADJ aufmerksam; **to be ~ to sb** sich jdm gegenüber aufmerksam verhalten; **to be ~ to sth** einer Sache *(dat)* Beachtung schenken; **to be ~ to sb's needs** sich um jds Bedürfnisse kümmern

attentively [əˈtentɪvlɪ] ADV aufmerksam

attentiveness [əˈtentɪvnɪs] N Aufmerksamkeit *f*

attenuate [əˈtenjʊeɪt] VT *(= weaken)* abschwächen; *statement also* abmildern; *gas* verdünnen; *(= make thinner)* dünn machen; **attenuating circumstances** mildernde Umstände VI *(= get weaker)* schwächer *or* abgeschwächt werden; *(gas)* sich verdünnen; *(= get thinner)* dünner werden ADJ *(Bot)* **~ leaf** lanzettförmiges Blatt

attenuation [əˌtenjʊˈeɪʃən] N *(= weakening)* Abschwächen *nt*, Abschwächung *f*; *(of statement also)* Abmildern *nt*, Abmilderung *f*; *(= making thinner)* Verdünnung *f*

attest [əˈtest] VT **a** *(= certify, testify to) sb's innocence, authenticity* bestätigen, bescheinigen; *signature* beglaubigen; *(on oath)* beschwören; **~ed herd** *(Brit)* tuberkulosefreier Bestand **b** *(= be proof of)* beweisen, bezeugen

▶ **attest to** VI *+prep obj* bezeugen

attestation [ˌætesˈteɪʃən] N **a** *(= certifying)* Bestätigung *f*; *(of signature)* Beglaubigung *f*; *(= document)* Bescheinigung *f* **b** *(= proof: of ability etc)* Beweis *m*

attestor [əˈtestəʳ] N Beglaubiger *m*

Attic [ˈætɪk] ADJ attisch

attic [ˈætɪk] N Dachboden *m*, Speicher *m*; *(lived-in)* Mansarde *f*; **~ room** Dachkammer *f*, Mansarden- *or* Dachzimmer *nt*; **in the ~** auf dem (Dach)boden *or* Speicher

Attica [ˈætɪkə] N Attika *nt*

Attila [ˈætɪlə] N Attila *m*; **~ the Hun** Attila, der Hunnenkönig

attire [əˈtaɪəʳ] VT kleiden *(in* in *+acc)* N *no pl* Kleidung *f*; **ceremonial ~** Festtracht *f*, volles Ornat

attitude [ˈætɪtjuːd] ✪ 6.1 N **a** *(= way of thinking)* Einstellung *f* *(to, towards* zu); *(= way of acting, manner)* Haltung *f* *(to, towards* gegenüber); **~ of mind** Geisteshaltung *f*; **I don't like your ~** ich bin mit dieser Einstellung überhaupt nicht einverstanden; *(= manner)* ich bin mit Ihrem Benehmen überhaupt nicht einverstanden; **well, if that's your ~ …** ja, wenn du SO denkst …; **women with ~** kämpferische Frauen **b** *(= way of standing)* Haltung *f*; **to strike a defensive ~** in Verteidigungsstellung gehen **c** *(in ballet)* Attitüde *f* **d** *(Aviat, Space)* Lage *f*

attitudinal [ˌætɪˈtjuːdɪnəl] ADJ *(form)* die Einstellung betreffend *attr*; **~ change/difference** veränderte/unterschiedliche Einstellung; **social and ~ changes** Veränderungen in Gesellschaft und Einstellung

attitudinize [ˌætɪˈtjuːdɪnaɪz] VI so tun, als ob, posieren *(geh)*

attn *abbr of* **attention** z. Hd(n) von

attorney [əˈtɜːnɪ] N **a** *(Comm, Jur: = representative)* Bevollmächtigte(r) *mf*, Stellvertreter(in) *m(f)*; **letter of ~** (schriftliche) Vollmacht → **power b** *(US: = lawyer)* (Rechts)anwalt *m*/-anwältin *f*

Attorney General N *pl* **Attorneys General** *or* **Attorney Generals** *(US: = public prosecutor) (of state government)* ≈ Generalstaatsanwalt *m*/-anwältin *f*; *(of federal government)* ≈ Generalbundesanwalt *m*/-anwältin *f*; *(Brit)* ≈ Justizminister(in) *m(f)*

attract [əˈtrækt] VT **a** *(Phys, magnet etc)* anziehen **b** *(fig: = appeal to) (person)* anziehen; *(idea, music, place etc)* ansprechen; **she feels ~ed to him** sie fühlt sich von ihm angezogen *or* zu ihm hingezogen; **she feels ~ed to the idea** die Idee reizt sie; **I am not ~ed to her/by it** sie/es reizt mich nicht **c** *(fig: = win, gain) interest, attention etc* auf sich *(acc)* ziehen *or* lenken; *new members, investors etc* anziehen, anlocken; **to ~ publicity/notoriety** (öffentliches) Aufsehen erregen

attraction [əˈtrækʃən] N **a** *(Phys, fig)* Anziehungskraft *f*; *(esp of big city etc)* Reiz *m*; **to lose one's/its ~** seinen Reiz verlieren; **I still feel a certain ~ toward(s) him** ich fühle mich noch immer von ihm angezogen; **to have an ~ for sb** Anziehungskraft *or* einen Reiz auf jdn ausüben; **what are the ~s of this subject?** was ist an diesem Fach reizvoll? **b** *(= attractive thing)* Attraktion *f*

attractive [əˈtræktɪv] ADJ **a** attraktiv; *personality, smile* anziehend; *house, view, furnishings, picture, dress, location* reizvoll; *story, music* nett, ansprechend; *price, idea, offer* reizvoll, verlockend **b** *(Phys)* Anziehungs-; **~ force** Anziehungskraft *f*

attractively [əˈtræktɪvlɪ] ADV attraktiv; *smile* anziehend; *dress, furnish, paint* reizvoll; **~ priced** zum attraktiven *or* verlockenden Preis *(at* von)

attractiveness [əˈtræktɪvnɪs] N Attraktivität *f*; *(of house, furnishing, view etc)* Reiz *m*; **the ~ of her appearance** ihr reizvolles *or* ansprechendes *or* anziehendes Äußeres; **the ~ of the melody** die ansprechende Melodie

attributable [əˈtrɪbjʊtəbl] ADJ **to be ~ to sb/sth** jdm/einer Sache zuzuschreiben sein

attribute [əˈtrɪbjuːt] ✪ 17.2 VT **to ~ sth to sb** *(play, remark etc)* jdm etw zuschreiben; *(= credit sb with sth) intelligence, feelings etc also* jdm etw beimessen; **to ~ sth to sth** *(success, accident, problem, deaths etc)* etw auf etw *(acc)* zurückführen; *(= attach) importance etc* einer Sache *(dat)* etw beimessen [ˈætrɪbjuːt] N Attribut *nt*; *(= quality also)* Merkmal *nt*

attribution [ˌætrɪˈbjuːʃən] N **a** *no pl* **the ~ of this play to Shakespeare** (die Tatsache,) dass man Shakespeare dieses Schauspiel zuschreibt; **the ~ of the accident to mechanical failure** (die Tatsache,) dass man den Unfall auf mechanisches Versagen zurückführt **b** *(= attribute)* Attribut *nt*, Eigenschaft *f*

attributive [əˈtrɪbjʊtɪv] *(Gram)* ADJ attributiv N Attributiv *nt*

attributively [əˈtrɪbjʊtɪvlɪ] ADV attributiv

attrition [əˈtrɪʃən] N *(lit, form)* Abrieb *m*, Zerreibung *f*; *(fig)* Zermürbung *f*; *(Rel)* unvollkommene Reue, Attrition *f (spec)*; **war of ~** *(Mil)* Zermürbungskrieg *m*

attune [əˈtjuːn] VT *(fig)* abstimmen *(to* auf *+acc)*; **to ~ oneself to sth** sich auf etw *(acc)* einstellen; **to become ~d to sth** sich an etw *(acc)* gewöhnen; **the two of them are well ~d to each other** die beiden sind gut aufeinander eingespielt

atwitter [əˈtwɪtəʳ] ADJ *pred (fig)* in heller Aufregung

atypical [ˌeɪˈtɪpɪkəl] ADJ atypisch

atypically [ˌeɪˈtɪpɪkəlɪ] ADV ungewöhnlich; **~, she is very young for this** atypischerweise *or* ungewöhnlicherweise ist sie sehr jung dafür

aubergine [ˈəʊbəʒiːn] N Aubergine *f*; *(= colour)* Aubergine *nt* ADJ aubergine(farben)

auburn [ˈɔːbən] ADJ *hair* rotbraun, rostrot

auction [ˈɔːkʃən] N Auktion *f*, Versteigerung *f*; **to sell sth by ~** etw versteigern; **to put sth up for ~** etw zum Versteigern *or* zur Versteigerung anbieten VT *(also* **auction off***)* versteigern

auction bridge N *(Cards)* Auktionsbridge *nt*

auctioneer [ˌɔːkʃəˈnɪəʳ] N Auktionator(in) *m(f)*

auction: **auction house** N Auktionshaus *nt*; **auction room** N Auktionshalle *f*, Auktionssaal *m*; **auction rooms** PL Auktionshalle *f*; **auction sale** N Auktion *f*, Versteigerung *f*

audacious ADJ, **audaciously** ADV [ɔːˈdeɪʃəs, -lɪ] **a** *(= impudent)* dreist, unverfroren **b** *(= bold)* kühn, wagemutig, verwegen

audacity [ɔːˈdæsɪtɪ], **audaciousness** [ɔːˈdeɪʃəsnɪs] N **a** *(= impudence)* Dreistigkeit *f*, Unverfrorenheit *f*; **to have the ~ to do sth** die Dreistigkeit *or* Unverfrorenheit besitzen, etw zu tun **b** *(= boldness)* Kühnheit, Verwegenheit *f*

audibility [ˌɔːdɪˈbɪlɪtɪ] N Hörbarkeit *f*, Vernehmbarkeit *f*

audible [ˈɔːdɪbl] ADJ hörbar, (deutlich) vernehmbar; **she was hardly ~** man konnte sie kaum hören

audibly [ˈɔːdɪblɪ] ADV hörbar, vernehmlich

audience [ˈɔːdɪəns] N **a** Publikum *nt no pl*; *(Theat, TV)* Zuschauer *pl*, Publikum *nt no pl*; *(of speaker)* Zuhörer *pl*, Publikum *nt no pl*; *(of writer, book)* Leserkreis *m*, Leserschaft *f*; *(Rad)* Zuhörerschaft *f*; **to have a large ~** ein großes Publikum haben *or* ansprechen *(also Rad, TV etc)*; **to have ~ appeal** publikumswirksam sein; **I prefer London ~s** ich ziehe das Publikum in London vor **b** *(= formal interview)* Audienz *f (with* bei)

audio [ˈɔːdɪəʊ] *in cpds* Audio-; **audio book** N Hörbuch *nt*; **audio card** N *(Comput)* Soundkarte *f*; **audio cassette** N Kassette *f*, Audiokassette *f*; **audio equipment** N *(in recording studio)* Tonaufzeichnungsgeräte *pl*, Audiogeräte *pl*; *(= hi-fi)* Stereoanlage *f*; **audio frequency** N Hörfrequenz *f*; **audioguide** N Audioguide *m*, *tragbares Gerät mit Kopfhörer zum Abhören von Infos über Exponate in Museen etc*

audiometer [ˌɔːdɪˈɒmɪtəʳ] N Audiometer *nt*, Gehörmesser *m*

audio: **audio pollution** N Lärmbelästigung *f*; **audio response** N *(Comput)* Sprachausgabe *f*; **audio typist** N Phonotypistin *f*; **audiovisual** ADJ audiovisuell

audit [ˈɔːdɪt] N Bücherrevision *f*, Buchprüfung *f* VT **a** *accounts, company* prüfen **b** *(US Univ)* belegen, ohne einen Schein zu machen, Gasthörer sein bei

audition [ɔːˈdɪʃən] N *(Theat)* Vorsprechprobe *f*; *(of musician)* Probespiel *nt*; *(of singer)* Vorsingen *nt*; **she was asked for ~** sie wurde zum Vorsprechen/Probespiel/Vorsingen eingeladen VT vorsprechen/vorspielen/vorsingen lassen VI vorsprechen/vorspielen/vorsingen

auditor [ˈɔːdɪtəʳ] N **a** *(Comm)* Rechnungsprüfer(in) *m(f)*, Buchprüfer(in) *m(f)* **b** *(US Univ)* Gasthörer(in) *m(f)* **c** *(= listener)* Zuhörer(in) *m(f)*

auditorium [ˌɔːdɪˈtɔːrɪəm] N Auditorium *nt*; *(in theatre, cinema also)* Zuschauerraum *m*; *(in concert hall also)* Zuhörersaal *m*

auditory [ˈɔːdɪtərɪ] ADJ Hör-; **~ ability** Hörfähigkeit *f*; **~ nerve** Gehörnerv *m*

au fait [ˌəʊˈfeɪ] ADJ vertraut; **to be ~ with sth** mit etw vertraut sein

Aug *abbr of* **August** Aug

Augean stables [ɔːˈdʒiːənˈsteɪblz] PL Augiasstall *m*; **to clean out the ~** *(Myth, fig)* den Augiasstall ausmisten

auger [ˈɔːgəʳ] N Stangenbohrer *m*; *(Agr)* Schnecke *f*

aught [ɔːt] N *(old, liter)* irgendetwas; **he might have moved for ~ I know** was weiß ich, vielleicht ist er umgezogen

augment [ɔːgˈment] VT vermehren; *income also* vergrößern VI zunehmen; *(income etc also)* sich vergrößern

augmentation [ˌɔːgmənˈteɪʃən] N Vermehrung *f*; *(of income also)* Vergrößerung *f*; *(in numbers)* Zunahme *f*; *(Mus)* Augmentation *f*; **breast ~** Brustvergrößerung *f*

augmented [ɔːgˈmentɪd] ADJ *(Mus) fourth, fifth* übermäßig

au gratin [ˌəʊˈgrætæŋ] ADV überbacken, au gratin; **cauliflower ~** überbackener Blumenkohl, Blumenkohl *m* au gratin

augur [ˈɔːgəʳ] VI **to ~ well/ill** etwas Gutes/nichts Gutes verheißen VT verheißen N *(= person)* Augur *m*

augury [ˈɔːgjʊrɪ] N *(= sign)* Anzeichen *nt*, Omen *nt*

August [ˈɔːgəst] N August *m* → *also* **September**

august [ɔːˈgʌst] ADJ illuster; *occasion, spectacle* erhaben

Augustan [ɔːˈgʌstən] ADJ augusteisch; **~ age** *(Hist, Art)* augusteisches Zeitalter; *(fig)* Blütezeit *f (einer nationalen Literatur)*

Augustine [ɔːˈgʌstɪn] N Augustinus *m*

Augustinian [ˌɔːgəsˈtɪnɪən] ADJ Augustiner-; **~ monk** Augustinermönch *m* N Augustiner *m*

auk [ɔːk] N *(Zool)* Alk *m*

auld [ɔːld] ADJ *(+er) (Scot)* alt; **Auld Lang Syne** *(song)* Nehmt Abschied, Brüder; **for ~ lang syne** um der alten Zeiten willen

aunt [ɑːnt] N Tante *f*

auntie, **aunty** [ˈɑːntɪ] N *(esp Brit inf)* Tante *f*; **~!** Tantchen!; **Auntie** *(Brit hum)* die BBC *(britische Rundfunk- und Fernsehanstalt)*

Aunt Sally [ˌɑːntˈsælɪ] N *(Brit, lit)* Schießbudenfigur *f*; *(= stall)* Schieß- *or* Wurfbude *f*; *(fig)* Zielscheibe *f*

au pair [ˌəʊˈpɛə] N *pl* **- -s** *(also* **au pair girl***)* Au-pair(mädchen) *nt nt* ADV au pair

aura [ˈɔːrə] N Aura *f (geh)*, Fluidum *nt (geh)*; **he has an ~ of saintliness about him** ihn umgibt eine Aura der Heiligkeit *(geh)*, er steht im Nimbus der Heiligkeit; **she has an ~ of mystery about her** eine geheimnisvolle Aura *(geh) or* ein geheimnisvoller Nimbus umgibt sie; **an ~ of sophistication** ein Flair *nt* von Kultiviertheit; **he has an ~ of calm** er strömt *or* strahlt Ruhe aus; **it gives the hotel an ~ of respectability** es verleiht dem Hotel einen Anstrich von Seriosität

aural [ˈɔːrəl] ADJ Gehör-, aural *(spec)*; **~ sense** Gehörsinn *m*; **~ examination** Hörtest *m*

aureole [ˈɔːrɪəʊl] N *(Astron)* Korona *f*; *(because of haze)* Hof *m*, Aureole *f*; *(Art)* Aureole *f*

auricle [ˈɔːrɪkl] N *(Anat)* Ohrmuschel *f*, Auricula *f (spec)*; *(of heart)* Vorhof *m*, Atrium *nt (spec)*

auricular [ɔːˈrɪkjʊləʳ] ADJ *(Anat)* **a** *(of ear)* aurikular *(spec)*, Ohren-, Hör-; **~ nerve** Hörnerv *m*; **~ confession** Ohrenbeichte *f*, geheime Beichte **b** *(of heart)* aurikular *(spec)*, Aurikular- *(spec)*; **~ flutter** (Herz)vorhofflattern *nt*

aurochs [ˈɔːrɒks] N Auerochse *m*, Ur *m*

aurora australis [ɔːˌrɔːrəɒsˈtreɪlɪs] N *(Astron)* südliches Polarlicht, Südlicht *nt*

aurora borealis [ɔːˌrɔːrəbɔːrɪˈeɪlɪs] N *(Astron)* nördliches Polarlicht, Nordlicht *nt*

auscultate [ˈɔːskəlteɪt] VT abhören, auskultieren *(spec)*

auscultation [ˌɔːskəlˈteɪʃən] N Abhören *nt*

auspices [ˈɔːspɪsɪz] PL **a** *(= sponsorship)* Schirmherrschaft *f*; **under the ~ of** unter der Schirmherrschaft *(+gen)*, unter den Auspizien *(+gen) (geh)* **b** *(= auguries)* Vorzeichen *pl*, Auspizien *pl (geh)*; **under favourable** *(Brit) or* **favorable** *(US)* **~** unter günstigen Vorzeichen *or* Auspizien *(geh)*

auspicious [ɔːsˈpɪʃəs] ADJ günstig; *start* vielverheißend, vielversprechend; **an ~ occasion** ein feierlicher Anlass

auspiciously [ɔːsˈpɪʃəslɪ] ADV verheißungsvoll, vielversprechend

Aussie [ˈɒzɪ] *(inf)* N **a** *(= person)* Australier(in) *m(f)* **b** *(Austral: = country)* Australien *nt*; *(= dialect)* australisches Englisch ADJ australisch

austere [ɒsˈtɪəʳ] ADJ streng; *way of life also* asketisch, entsagend; *style also* schmucklos; *room* schmucklos, karg

austerely [ɒsˈtɪəlɪ] ADV streng; *furnish* karg, schmucklos; *live* asketisch, entsagend

austerity [ɒsˈterɪtɪ] N **a** *(= severity)* Strenge *f*; *(= simplicity)* strenge Einfachheit, Schmucklosigkeit *f*; *(of landscape)* Härte *f* **b** *(= hardship, shortage)* Entbehrung *f*; **after the ~ of the war years** nach den Entbehrungen der Kriegsjahre; **a life of ~** ein Leben der Entsagung; **~ budget** Sparhaushalt *m*; **~ measures** Sparmaßnahmen *pl*

Australasia [ˌɔːstrəˈleɪsjə] N Australien und Ozeanien *nt*

Australasian [ˌɔːstrəˈleɪsjən] N Ozeanier(in) *m(f)* ADJ ozeanisch, südwestpazifisch

Australia [ɒsˈtreɪlɪə] N Australien *nt*

Australian [ɒsˈtreɪlɪən] N Australier(in) *m(f)*; *(= accent)* australisches Englisch ADJ australisch

Austria [ˈɒstrɪə] N Österreich *nt*

Austria-Hungary [ˈɒstrɪəˈhʌŋgərɪ] N Österreich-Ungarn *nt*

Austrian [ˈɒstrɪən] N Österreicher(in) *m(f)*; *(= dialect)* Österreichisch *nt* ADJ österreichisch

Austro- [ˈɒstrəʊ-] PREF österreichisch-; **~Hungarian** österreichisch-ungarisch

aut *abbr of* **automatic**

autarchy [ˈɔːtɑːkɪ] N **a** Selbstregierung *f* **b** = **autarky**

autarky [ˈɔːtɑːkɪ] N Autarkie *f*

authentic [ɔːˈθentɪk] ADJ *signature, manuscript* authentisch; *accent, antique, tears* echt; *claim to title etc* berechtigt

authentically [ɔːˈθentɪkəlɪ] ADV echt; *restored* authentisch

authenticate [ɔːˈθentɪkeɪt] VT bestätigen, authentifizieren *(geh)*; *signature, document* beglaubigen; *manuscript, work of art* für echt befinden *or* erklären; *claim* bestätigen; **it was ~d as being …** es wurde bestätigt, dass es … war

authentication [ɔːˌθentɪˈkeɪʃən] N Bestätigung *f*, Authentifizierung *f (geh)*; *(of signature, document)* Beglaubigung *f*; *(of manuscript, work of art)* Echtheitserklärung *f*

authenticity [ˌɔːθenˈtɪsɪtɪ] N Echtheit *f*, Authentizität *f (geh)*; *(of claim to title etc)* Berechtigung *f*

author [ˈɔːθəʳ] N *(profession)* Autor(in) *m(f)*, Schriftsteller(in) *m(f)*; *(of report, pamphlet)* Verfasser(in) *m(f)*; *(fig)* Urheber(in) *m(f)*; *(of plan)* Initiator(in) *m(f)*; **the ~ of the book** der Autor/die Autorin des Buches; **~'s copy** Autorenexemplar *nt*

authoress [ˈɔːθərɪs] N Schriftstellerin *f*

authorial [ɔːˈθɔːrɪəl] ADJ *(liter)* eines/des Autors

authoritarian [ˌɔːθɒrɪˈtɛərɪən] ADJ autoritär N autoritärer Mensch/Vater/Politiker *etc*; **to be an ~** autoritär sein

authoritarianism [ˌɔːθɒrɪˈteərɪənɪzəm] N Autoritarismus *m*

authoritative [ɔːˈθɒrɪtətɪv] ADJ **a** *(= commanding)* bestimmt, entschieden; *manner* Respekt einflößend; **to sound ~** Respekt einflößen, bestimmt auftreten **b** *(= reliable)* verlässlich, zuverlässig; *(= definitive)* maßgeblich, maßgebend; **I won't accept his opinion as ~** seine Meinung ist für mich nicht maßgeblich *or* maßgebend

authoritatively [ɔːˈθɒrɪtətɪvlɪ] ADV *(= with authority)* bestimmt, mit Autorität; *(= definitively)* maßgeblich *or* maßgebend; *(= reliably)* zuverlässig

authority [ɔːˈθɒrɪtɪ] N **a** *(= power)* Autorität *f*; *(= right, entitlement)* Befugnis *f*; *(= specifically delegated power)* Vollmacht *f*; *(Mil)* Befehlsgewalt *f*; **people who are in ~** Menschen, die Autorität haben; **the person in ~** der Zuständige *or* Verantwortliche; **who's in ~ here?** wer ist hier der Verantwortliche?; **I'm in ~ here!** hier bestimme ich!; **parental ~** Autorität der Eltern; *(Jur)* elterliche Gewalt; **to be in** *or* **have ~ over sb** Weisungsbefugnis gegenüber jdm haben *(form)*; *(describing hierarchy)* jdm übergeordnet sein; **to put sb in ~ over sb** jdm die Verantwortung für jdn übertragen; **those who are put in ~ over us** diejenigen, deren Aufsicht wir unterstehen; **the Queen and those in ~ under her** die Königin und die ihr untergebenen Verantwortlichen; **to be under the ~ of sb** unter jds Aufsicht *(dat)* stehen; *(in hierarchy)* jdm unterstehen; *(Mil)* jds Befehlsgewalt *(dat)* unterstehen; **on one's own ~** auf eigene Verantwortung; **you'll have to ask a teacher for the ~ to take the key** du brauchst die Erlaubnis *or* Genehmigung des Lehrers, wenn du den Schlüssel haben willst; **under** *or* **by what ~ do you claim the right to ...?** mit welcher Berechtigung verlangen Sie, dass ...?; **to have the ~ to do sth** berechtigt *or* befugt sein, etw zu tun; **to have no ~ to do sth** nicht befugt *or* berechtigt sein, etw zu tun; **he was exceeding his area of ~** er hat seinen Kompetenzbereich *or* seine Befugnisse überschritten; **to give sb the ~ to do sth** jdn ermächtigen *(form) or* jdm die Vollmacht erteilen, etw zu tun; **he had my ~ to do it** ich habe es ihm gestattet *or* erlaubt; **to have full ~ to act** volle Handlungsvollmacht haben; **to do sth on sb's ~** etw in jds Auftrag *(dat)* tun; **who gave you the ~ to do that?** wer hat Sie dazu berechtigt?; **who gave you the ~ to treat people like that?** mit welchem Recht glaubst du, Leute so behandeln zu können?

b *(also pl: = ruling body)* Behörde *f*, Amt *nt*; *(= body of people)* Verwaltung *f*; *(= power of ruler)* (Staats)gewalt *f*, Obrigkeit *f*; **the university authorities** die Universitätsverwaltung; **the water ~** die Wasserbehörde; **the local ~** *or* **authorities** die Gemeindeverwaltung; **the Prussian respect for ~** das preußische Obrigkeitsdenken; **the concept of ~ in a state** der Autoritätsgedanke im Staat; **they appealed to the supreme ~ of the House of Lords** sie wandten sich an die höchste Autorität *or* Instanz, das Oberhaus; **this will have to be decided by a higher ~** das muss an höherer Stelle entschieden werden; **to represent ~** die Staatsgewalt verkörpern; **the father represents ~** der Vater verkörpert die Autorität; **you must have respect for ~** du musst Achtung gegenüber Respektspersonen haben

c *(= weight, influence)* Autorität *f*; **to have** *or* **carry (great) ~** viel gelten *(with* bei*)*; *(person also)* (große *or* viel) Autorität haben *(with* bei*)*; **to speak/write with ~** mit Sachkunde *or* mit der Autorität des Sachkundigen sprechen/schreiben; **I/he can speak with ~ on this matter** darüber kann ich mich/kann er sich kompetent äußern; **to give an order with ~** einen Befehl mit der nötigen Autorität geben; **to appeal to the ~ of precedent** auf einen Präzedenzfall zurückgreifen

d *(= expert)* Autorität *f*, Fachmann *m*/-frau *f*; **I'm no ~ but ...** ich bin kein Fachmann/keine Fachfrau, aber ...; **he is an ~ on art** er ist eine Autorität *or* ein Fachmann auf dem Gebiet der Kunst

e *(= definitive book etc)* (anerkannte) Autorität *f*; *(= source)* Quelle *f*; **to have sth on good ~** etw aus zuverlässiger Quelle wissen; **on the best ~** aus bester Quelle; **on whose ~ do you have that?** aus welcher Quelle haben Sie das?

authorization [ˌɔːθəraɪˈzeɪʃən] ✪ 9.3 N Genehmigung *f*; *(= delegation of authority)* Bevollmächtigung *f*, Autorisation *f (geh)*; *(= right)* Recht *nt*

authorize [ˈɔːθəraɪz] ✪ 9.4, 9.5 VT **a** *(= empower)* berechtigen, ermächtigen, autorisieren *(geh)*; *(= delegate authority)* bevollmächtigen; **to be ~d to do sth** *(= have right)* berechtigt sein *or* das Recht haben, etw zu tun; **he was fully ~d to do it** er war voll und ganz befugt, das zu tun; **this licence** *(Brit) or* **license** *(US)* **~s you to drive ...** dieser Führerschein berechtigt Sie zum Fahren von ... **b** *(= permit)* genehmigen; *money, claim etc* genehmigen, bewilligen; *translation, biography etc* autorisieren

authorized [ˈɔːθəraɪzd] ADJ *overdraft* bewilligt; *person, representative, bank* autorisiert, bevollmächtigt; *biography* autorisiert; **"authorized personnel only"** „Zutritt nur für Befugte"; **duly ~** *(Jur, Fin)* ordnungsgemäß bevollmächtigt; **~ dealer** Vertragshändler(in) *m(f)*; **~ signatory** Zeichnungsberechtigte(r) *mf*; **~ signature** Unterschrift *f* eines bevollmächtigten Vertreters

authorized capital N autorisiertes Kapital

Authorized Version N *die englische Bibelfassung von 1611*

authorship [ˈɔːθəʃɪp] N **a** Autorschaft *f*, Verfasserschaft *f*; **of unknown ~** eines unbekannten Autors *or* Verfassers; **he claimed/denied ~ of the article** er bekannte/bestritt, den Artikel verfasst *or* geschrieben zu haben; **there are disagreements as to the ~ of the play** der Autor des Stückes ist umstritten **b** *(= occupation)* Schriftstellerberuf *m*

autism [ˈɔːtɪzəm] N Autismus *m*

autist [ˈɔːtɪst] N Autist(in) *m(f)*

autistic [ɔːˈtɪstɪk] ADJ autistisch

auto [ˈɔːtəʊ] N *(US)* Auto *nt*, PKW *m*, Pkw *m*

auto- [ˈɔːtəʊ-] PREF auto-, Auto-

autobank [ˈɔːtəʊbæŋk] N Geldautomat *m*

autobiographer [ˌɔːtəʊbaɪˈɒgrəfəˈ] N Autobiograf(in) *m(f)*

autobiographical [ˈɔːtəʊˌbaɪəʊˈgræfɪkəl] ADJ autobiografisch

autobiography [ˌɔːtəʊbaɪˈɒgrəfɪ] N Autobiografie *f*

autocade [ˈɔːtəʊkeɪd] N *(US)* Wagenkolonne *f or* -konvoi *m*

autochanger [ˈɔːtəʊˌtʃeɪndʒəˈ] N (automatischer) Plattenwechsler

autocracy [ɔːˈtɒkrəsɪ] N Autokratie *f*

autocrat [ˈɔːtəʊkræt] N Autokrat(in) *m(f)*

autocratic [ˌɔːtəʊˈkrætɪk] ADJ autokratisch

autocross [ˈɔːtəʊkrɒs] N Autocross *nt*

Autocue® [ˈɔːtəʊkjuː] N *(Brit TV)* ≈ Teleprompter® *m*

auto-da-fé [ˈɔːtəʊdɑːˈfeɪ] N *pl* **autos-da-fé** Autodafé *nt*

autodidact [ˈɔːtəʊˌdaɪdækt] N *(form)* Autodidakt(in) *m(f)*

autoerotic [ˌɔːtəʊɪˈrɒtɪk] ADJ autoerotisch

autoeroticism [ˌɔːtəʊɪˈrɒtɪˌsɪzəm] N Autoerotik *f*

autofocus [ˈɔːtəʊfəʊkəs] N *(Phot)* Autofokus *m*

autofunction [ˈɔːtəʊˌfʌŋkʃən] N *(= Comput etc)* automatische Funktion

autograph [ˈɔːtəgrɑːf] **N** *(= signature)* Autogramm *nt*; *(= manuscript)* Originalmanuskript *nt* **VT** signieren; **he ~ed my album** er hat mir ein Autogramm fürs Album gegeben

autograph: **autograph album** N Autogrammalbum *nt*; **autograph book** N Autogrammbuch *nt*; **autograph copy** N handgeschriebenes Manuskript

autohyphenation [ˈɔːtəʊˌhaɪfəˈneɪʃən] N *(Comput)* automatische Silbentrennung

autoimmune [ˌɔːtəʊɪˈmjuːn] ADJ autoimmun; **~ disease** Autoimmunkrankheit *f*

autoinfection [ˌɔːtəʊɪnˈfekʃən] N *(Med)* Autoinfektion *f*

automat [ˈɔːtəmæt] N *(US)* Automatenrestaurant *nt*

automata [ɔːˈtɒmətə] *pl of* **automaton**

automate [ˈɔːtəmeɪt] VT automatisieren; **~d telling** *or* **teller machine** Geldautomat *m*

automatic [ˌɔːtəˈmætɪk] **ADJ** *(lit, fig)* automatisch; **the refund is not ~** Rückerstattung erfolgt nicht automatisch; **he has the ~ right ...** er hat automatisch das Recht ...; **the film star's ~ smile** das Routinelächeln des Filmstars; **you shouldn't need telling, it should be ~** das sollte man dir nicht erst sagen müssen, das solltest du automatisch tun; **~ camera** Automatikkamera *f*; **~ choke** Startautomatik *f*; **~ data processing** automatische Datenverarbeitung; **~ defroster** Abtauautomatik *f*; **~ exposure** *(Phot)* Belichtungsautomatik *f*; **~ gearbox** *or* **transmission** *(Aut)* Automatikgetriebe *nt*; **the ~ model** das Modell mit Automatik; **~ rifle** Schnellfeuergewehr *nt*; **~ weapon** automatische Waffe, Schnellfeuerwaffe *f*

N *(= car)* Automatikwagen *m*; *(= gun)* automatische Waffe, Maschinenwaffe *f*; *(= washing machine)* Waschautomat *m*

automatically [ˌɔːtəˈmætɪkəlɪ] ADV automatisch

automatic writing N automatisches Schreiben

automation [ˌɔːtəˈmeɪʃən] N Automatisierung *f*

automaton [ɔːˈtɒmətən] N *pl* **-s** *or* **automata** [-ətə] *(= robot)* Roboter *m*; *(fig also)* Automat *m*

automobile [ˈɔːtəməbiːl] N Auto(mobil) *nt*, Kraftwagen *m (form)*

automotive [ˌɔːtəˈməʊtɪv] ADJ *vehicle* selbstfahrend, mit Selbstantrieb

automotive engineering N Kfz-Technik *f*

autonomous ADJ, **autonomously** ADV [ɔːˈtɒnəməs, -lɪ] autonom

autonomy [ɔːˈtɒnəmɪ] N Autonomie *f*

autopilot [ˌɔːtəʊˈpaɪlət] N Autopilot *m*; **on ~** *(lit)* mit Autopilot; **to switch onto ~** *(lit, fig inf)* auf Automatik umschalten; **he was on ~** *(fig)* er funktionierte wie automatisch *or* ferngesteuert; **I'm so shattered, I just do everything on ~** ich bin so geschafft, dass ich alles nur noch ganz automatisch mache

autopsy [ˈɔːtɒpsɪ] N Autopsie *f*, Leichenöffnung *f*

autoreverse [ˌɔːtəʊrɪˈvɜːs] N Autoreversefunktion *f*

autoscroll [ˈɔːtəʊˌskrəʊl] N *(Comput)* automatischer Bildlauf

autosuggestion [ˌɔːtəʊsəˈdʒestʃən] N Autosuggestion *f*

autosuggestive [ˌɔːtəʊsəˈdʒestɪv] ADJ autosuggestiv

autotimer [ˈɔːtəʊˌtaɪməˈ] N *(on cooker etc)* Ein-/ /Abschaltautomatik *f*

autotrain [ˈɔːtəʊˌtreɪn] N *(US)* Autoreisezug *m*

autotransfusion [ˌɔːtəʊtrænsˈfjuːʒən] N *(Med)* Eigenbluttransfusion *f*

autumn [ˈɔːtəm] *(esp Brit)* **N** *(lit, fig)* Herbst *m*; **in (the) ~** im Herbst; **two ~s ago** im Herbst vor zwei Jahren **ADJ** *attr* Herbst-, herbstlich; **~ leaves** bunte (Herbst)blätter *pl*

autumnal [ɔːˈtʌmnəl] ADJ herbstlich, Herbst-; **~ weather** Herbstwetter *nt*

auxiliary [ɔːgˈzɪlɪərɪ] **ADJ** Hilfs- *(also Comput)*; *(= additional) engine, generator etc* zusätzlich; **~ note** *(Mus)* Nebennote *f*; **~ nurse** Schwesternhelferin *f*; **~ program** *(Comput)* Hilfsprogramm *nt*; **~ verb** Hilfsverb *nt* **N a** *(Mil, esp pl)* Soldat(in) *m(f)* der Hilfstruppe; **auxiliaries** *pl* Hilfstruppe(n) *f(pl)* **b** *(general: = assistant)* Hilfskraft *f*, Helfer(in) *m(f)*; **teaching ~** (Aus)-hilfslehrer(in) *m(f)*; **nursing ~** Schwesternhelferin *f* **c** *(= auxiliary verb)* Hilfsverb *or* -zeitwort *nt*

AV *abbr of* **Authorized Version**

Av *abbr of* **avenue**

av *abbr of* **average** Durchschn.

avail[1] *abbr of* **available**

avail[2] [ə'veɪl] VR **to ~ oneself of sth** von etw Gebrauch machen; **to ~ oneself of the opportunity of doing sth** die Gelegenheit wahrnehmen *or* nutzen, etw zu tun

VI *(form)* helfen; **nothing could ~ against their superior strength** gegen ihre Überlegenheit war nichts auszurichten

N **of no ~** erfolglos, ohne Erfolg, vergeblich; **of little ~** wenig erfolgreich, mit wenig *or* geringem Erfolg; **his advice was/his pleas were of no/little ~** seine Ratschläge/Bitten haben nicht(s)/wenig gefruchtet; **to no ~** vergebens, vergeblich; **to little ~** ohne großen Erfolg; **of what ~ is it to ...?** *(liter)* was nützt es, zu ...?; **and to what ~?** *(liter)* und zu welchem Behuf? *(old form)*

availability [əˌveɪlə'bɪlɪtɪ] N *(of object)* Erhältlichkeit *f*; *(Comm) (from supplier also)* Lieferbarkeit *f*; *(of stock)* Vorrätigkeit *f*; *(of worker, means, resources)* Verfügbarkeit *f*; **the market price is determined by ~** der Marktpreis richtet sich nach dem vorhandenen Angebot; **because of the greater ~ of their product ...** weil ihr Produkt leichter erhältlich/lieferbar ist ...; **we'd like to sell you one, but it's a question of ~** wir würden Ihnen gern eines verkaufen, das hängt aber davon ab, ob es erhältlich/lieferbar ist; **offer subject to ~ while stocks last** (das Angebot gilt) nur solange der Vorrat reicht; **greater ~ of jobs** größeres Stellenangebot; **because of the limited ~ of seats** weil nur eine begrenzte Anzahl an Plätzen zur Verfügung steht; **to increase the ~ of culture to the masses** breiteren Bevölkerungsschichten den Zugang zu Kultur erleichtern; **his ~ for discussion is, I'm afraid, determined by ...** ob er Zeit für eine Besprechung hat, hängt leider von ... ab

available [ə'veɪləbl] ✪ 19.3 ADJ a *object* erhältlich; *(Comm) (from supplier)* lieferbar, erhältlich; *(= in stock)* vorrätig; *(= free) time, post* frei; *theatre seats etc* frei, zu haben *pred*; *(= at one's disposal) worker, means, resources etc* verfügbar, zur Verfügung stehend; **to be ~** vorhanden sein; *(= at one's disposal)* zur Verfügung stehen; *(person) (= not otherwise occupied)* frei *or* abkömmlich *(form)* sein; *(= can be reached)* erreichbar sein; *(for discussion)* zu sprechen sein; **to make sth ~ to sb** jdm etw zur Verfügung stellen; *(= accessible) culture, knowledge, information* jdm etw zugänglich machen; **to make oneself ~ to sb** sich jdm zur Verfügung stellen; **could you make yourself ~ for discussion between 2 and 3?** könnten Sie sich zwischen 2 und 3 für eine Besprechung freihalten *or* zur Verfügung halten?; **the best dictionary ~, the best ~ dictionary** das beste Wörterbuch, das es gibt; **he caught the next ~ flight home** er nahm den nächsten *or* nächstmöglichen Flug nach Hause; **to try every ~ means (to achieve sth)** nichts unversucht lassen(, um etw zu erreichen); **reference books/consultants are ~** Nachschlagewerke/Berater stehen einem/Ihnen *etc* zur Verfügung; **all ~ staff were asked to help out** das abkömmliche *or* verfügbare *or* zur Verfügung stehende Personal wurde gebeten auszuhelfen; **are you ~ for tennis/a discussion tonight?** können Sie heute Abend Tennis spielen/an einer Diskussion teilnehmen?; **when will you be ~ to start in the new job?** wann können Sie die Stelle antreten?; **I'm not ~ until October** ich bin vor Oktober nicht frei; **a professor should always be ~ to his students** ein Professor sollte stets für seine Studenten da sein *or* seinen Studenten stets zur Verfügung stehen; **he's ~ for consultation on Mondays** er hat montags Sprechzeit; **you shouldn't make yourself so ~ to him** du solltest es ihm nicht so leicht machen; **she's what is known as "available"** es ist bekannt, dass sie „leicht zu haben" ist

b *(form) ticket* gültig

avalanche ['ævəlɑːnʃ] N *(lit, fig)* Lawine *f*

avant-garde ['ævɒŋ'gɑːd] N Avantgarde *f* ADJ avantgardistisch

avarice ['ævərɪs] N Habgier *f*, Habsucht *f*

avaricious [ˌævə'rɪʃəs] ADJ habgierig, habsüchtig

avariciously [ˌævə'rɪʃəslɪ] ADV (hab)gierig

avatar ['ævətɑː'] N *(Rel, fig)* Inkarnation *f*

avdp *abbr of* **avoirdupois**

Ave *abbr of* **avenue**

Ave (Maria) ['ɑːveɪ(mə'rɪə)] N Ave(-Maria) *nt*

avenge [ə'vendʒ] VT rächen; **to ~ oneself on sb (for sth)** sich an jdm (für etw) rächen; **an avenging angel** ein Racheengel *m*

avenger [ə'vendʒə'] N Rächer(in) *m(f)*

avenue ['ævənjuː] N a *(tree-lined)* Allee *f*; *(= broad street)* Boulevard *m* b *(fig: = method)* Weg *m*; **~s of approach** Verfahrensweisen; **an ~ of approach to the problem** ein Weg, das Problem anzugehen; **~ of escape** Ausweg *m*; **to explore every ~** alle sich bietenden Wege prüfen

aver [ə'vɜː'] VT *(form)* mit Nachdruck betonen; *love, innocence* beteuern

average ['ævərɪdʒ] N (Durch)schnitt *m*; *(Math also)* Mittelwert *m*; **to do an ~ of 50 miles a day/3% a week** durchschnittlich *or* im (Durch)schnitt 50 Meilen pro Tag fahren/3% pro Woche erledigen; **what's your ~ over the last six months?** was haben Sie im letzten halben Jahr durchschnittlich geleistet/verdient *etc*?; **on ~** durchschnittlich, im (Durch)schnitt; *(= normally)* normalerweise; **if you take the ~** *(Math)* wenn Sie den (Durch)schnitt *or* Mittelwert nehmen; *(general)* wenn Sie den durchschnittlichen Fall nehmen; **above ~** überdurchschnittlich, über dem Durchschnitt; **below ~** unterdurchschnittlich, unter dem Durchschnitt; **the law of ~s** das Gesetz der Serie; **by the law of ~s** aller Wahrscheinlichkeit nach

ADJ durchschnittlich; *(= ordinary)* Durchschnitts-; *(= not good or bad)* mittelmäßig; **above/below ~** über-/unterdurchschnittlich; **the ~ man, Mr Average** der Durchschnittsbürger; **the ~ Scot** der Durchschnittsschotte; **he's a man of ~ height** er ist von mittlerer Größe

VT a *(= find the average of)* den Durchschnitt ermitteln von

b *(= do etc on average)* auf einen Schnitt von ... kommen; **we ~d 80 km/h** wir kamen auf einen Schnitt von 80 km/h, wir sind durchschnittlich 80 km/h gefahren; **the factory ~s 500 cars a week** die Fabrik produziert durchschnittlich *or* im (Durch)schnitt 500 Autos pro Woche

c *(= average out at)* **sales are averaging 10,000 copies per day** der Absatz beläuft sich auf *or* beträgt durchschnittlich *or* im (Durch)schnitt 10.000 Exemplare pro Tag

▸ **average out** VT *sep* **if you average it out** im Durchschnitt; **it'll average itself out** es wird sich ausgleichen VI durchschnittlich ausmachen *(at, to +acc)*; *(= balance out)* sich ausgleichen; **how does it average out on a weekly basis?** wie viel ist das durchschnittlich *or* im Schnitt pro Woche?

averagely ['ævərɪdʒlɪ] ADV durchschnittlich

averment [ə'vɜːmənt] N Beteuerung *f*

averse [ə'vɜːs] ADJ *pred* abgeneigt; **I am not ~ to a glass of wine** einem Glas Wein bin ich nicht abgeneigt; **I am rather ~ to doing that** es widerstrebt mir, das zu tun

aversion [ə'vɜːʃən] N a *(= strong dislike)* Abneigung *f*, Aversion *f (geh, Psych)* (to gegen); **he has an ~ to getting wet** er hat eine Abscheu davor, nass zu werden b *(= object of aversion)* Gräuel *m*; **smoking is his pet ~** Rauchen ist ihm ein besonderer Gräuel

aversion therapy N *(Psych)* Aversionstherapie *f*

avert [ə'vɜːt] VT a *(= turn away) eyes, gaze* abwenden, abkehren *(geh)* b *(= prevent)* verhindern, abwenden; *suspicion* ablenken; *blow etc* abwehren; *accident* verhindern, verhüten

avgas ['ævgæs] N *(inf: Aviat)* Flugbenzin *nt*

AVI *abbr of* **automatic vehicle identification** automatische Fahrzeugidentifizierung

avian flu [ˌeɪvɪən'fluː], **avian influenza** ['eɪvɪənˌɪnflʊ'enzə] N Vogelgrippe *f*, Geflügel- *or* Hühnerpest *f*

aviary ['eɪvɪərɪ] N Vogelhaus *nt*, Voliere *f*

aviation [ˌeɪvɪ'eɪʃən] N die Luftfahrt; **the art of ~** die Kunst des Fliegens

aviator ['eɪvɪeɪtə'] N Flieger(in) *m(f)*

aviculture ['eɪvɪˌkʌltʃə'] N *(form)* Vogelzucht *f*

avid ['ævɪd] ADJ a *(= desirous)* gierig *(for* nach); *(esp for fame, praise)* süchtig *(for* nach); **~ for fame** ruhmsüchtig b *(= keen)* begeistert, passioniert; *interest* lebhaft, stark; **he is an ~ follower of this series** er verfolgt diese Serie mit lebhaftem Interesse; **as an ~ reader of your column** als eifriger Leser Ihrer Spalte; **I am an ~ reader** ich lese leidenschaftlich gern

avidity [ə'vɪdɪtɪ] N *no pl (liter)* a *(= desire, eagerness)* Begierde *f* (for nach); *(pej)* Gier *f* (for nach); **with ~** begierig, gierig b *(= keenness)* Begeisterung *f*; *(of supporter)* Eifer *m*

avidly ['ævɪdlɪ] ADV a *(= eagerly)* begierig; *(pej)* gierig b *(= keenly)* eifrig; *read* leidenschaftlich gern

avionics [ˌeɪvɪ'ɒnɪks] N *sing* Avionik *f*

avocado [ˌævə'kɑːdəʊ] N *pl* **-s** *(also* **avocado pear**) Avocado(birne) *f*; *(= tree)* Avocadobaum *m*

avocation [ˌævəʊ'keɪʃən] N *(form: = calling)* Berufung *f*

avoid [ə'vɔɪd] ✪ 10.1 VT vermeiden; *damage, accident also* verhüten; *person* meiden, aus dem Weg gehen *(+dat)*; *obstacle* ausweichen *(+dat)*; *difficulty, duty, truth* umgehen; **to ~ danger** *(in general)* die Gefahr meiden; *(on a specific occasion)* der Gefahr *(dat)* entgehen; **in order to ~ being seen** um nicht gesehen zu werden; **he'd do anything to ~ washing the dishes** er würde alles tun, um nur nicht abwaschen zu müssen; **I'm not going if I can possibly ~ it** wenn es sich irgendwie vermeiden lässt, gehe ich nicht; **... you can hardly ~ visiting them** ... dann kommst du wohl kaum darum herum *or* kannst du es wohl schlecht vermeiden, sie zu besuchen; **to ~ sb's eye** jds Blick *(dat)* ausweichen, es vermeiden, jdn anzusehen; **to ~ being noticed** möglichst unbemerkt bleiben

avoidable [ə'vɔɪdəbl] ADJ vermeidbar; **if it's (at all) ~** wenn es sich (irgend) vermeiden lässt

avoidance [ə'vɔɪdəns] N Vermeidung *f*; **the ~ of inheritance tax** die Umgehung der Erbschaftssteuer; **his careful ~ of the truth** sein ständiges Umgehen der Wahrheit; **thanks only to her steady ~ of bad company** nur weil sie konsequent schlechte Gesellschaft mied

avoirdupois [ˌævwɑːdjuː'pwɑː] N Avoirdupois *nt*; *(hum: = excess weight)* Fülligkeit *f*, Üppigkeit *f*; **there's been an increase in her ~** *(hum)* sie ist ziemlich in die Breite gegangen

avow [ə'vaʊ] VT *(liter)* erklären; *belief, faith* bekennen; **to ~ one's love (to sb)** (jdm) seine Liebe erklären *or* gestehen, sich (jdm) erklären; **he ~ed himself to be a royalist** er bekannte (offen), Royalist zu sein

avowal [ə'vaʊəl] N Erklärung *f*; *(of faith)* Bekenntnis *nt*; *(of love)* Geständnis *nt*, Erklärung *f*; *(of belief, interest)* Bekundung *f*

avowed [ə'vaʊd] ADJ erklärt

avowedly [ə'vaʊɪdlɪ] ADV erklärtermaßen

avuncular [ə'vʌŋkjʊlə'] ADJ onkelhaft

aw *abbr of* **atomic weight**

AWACS, Awacs ['eɪwæks] *abbr of* **airborne warning and control system** AWACS-Flugzeug *nt*, Awacs-Flugzeug *nt*, *mit Frühwarnsystem ausgestattetes Aufklärungsflugzeug der US-Luftwaffe*

await [ə'weɪt] ✪ 20.5 VT a *(= wait for)* erwarten; *future events, decision etc* entgegensehen *(+dat)*; **the long ~ed day** der lang ersehnte Tag; **parcels ~ing despatch** zum Versand bestimmte Pakete; **we ~ your reply with interest**

wir sehen Ihrer Antwort mit Interesse entgegen; **to be ~ing trial** *(case)* zur Verhandlung anstehen; **he is ~ing trial** sein Fall steht noch zur Verhandlung an **b** *(= be in store for)* erwarten

awake [ə'weɪk] *pret* **awoke**, *ptp* **awoken** *or* **awaked** [ə'weɪkt] VI *(lit, fig)* erwachen; **to ~ from sleep/a dream** aus dem Schlaf/einem Traum erwachen; **to ~ to sth** *(fig: = realize)* sich *(dat)* einer Sache *(gen)* bewusst werden; *(= become interested)* beginnen, sich für etw zu interessieren; **to ~ to the joys of sth** (plötzlich) Vergnügen an etw *(dat)* finden; **his interest is only beginning to ~** sein Interesse ist erst neu erwacht
VT wecken; *(fig) suspicion, interest etc also* erwecken; **to ~ sb to sth** *(= make realize)* jdm etw bewusst machen; *(= make interested)* jds Interesse für etw wecken
ADJ *pred (lit, fig)* wach; *(= alert also)* aufmerksam; **to be/lie/stay ~** wach sein/liegen/bleiben; **to keep sb ~** jdn wach halten; **wide ~** *(lit, fig)* hellwach; **to be ~ to sth** *(fig)* sich *(dat)* einer Sache *(gen)* bewusst sein **ADV a**

awaken [ə'weɪkən] VTI = **awake**

awakening [ə'weɪknɪŋ] N *(lit, fig)* Erwachen *nt*; **a rude ~** *(lit, fig)* ein böses Erwachen ADJ *(fig)* erwachend

award [ə'wɔːd] VT *prize, penalty, free kick etc* zusprechen *(to sb* jdm), zuerkennen *(to sb* jdm); *(= present) prize, degree, medal etc* verleihen *(to sb* jdm); **to be ~ed damages** Schadenersatz zugesprochen bekommen; **to ~ sb first prize** jdm den ersten Preis zuerkennen N **a** *(= prize)* Preis *m*; *(for bravery etc)* Auszeichnung *f*; *(Jur)* Zuerkennung *f*; **to make an ~ (to sb)** einen Preis (an jdn) vergeben **b** *(Univ)* Stipendium *nt*

award: **award(s) ceremony** N *(Film, Theat, TV)* Preisverleihung *f*; **award-winning** ADJ preisgekrönt

aware [ə'wɛə'] ADJ *esp pred* bewusst; **to be/become ~ of sb/sth** sich *(dat)* jds/einer Sache bewusst sein/werden; *(= notice also)* jdn bemerken/etw merken; **I was not ~ (of the fact) that ...** es war mir nicht klar *or* bewusst, dass ...; **you will be ~ of the importance of this** es muss Ihnen bewusst sein, wie wichtig das ist; **are you ~ that ...?** ist dir eigentlich klar, dass ...?; **not that I am ~ (of)** nicht dass ich wüsste; **as far as I am ~** so viel ich weiß; **we try to remain ~ of what is going on in other companies/the world** wir versuchen, uns auf dem Laufenden darüber zu halten, was in anderen Firmen/auf der Welt vor sich geht; **to make sb ~ of sth** jdm etw bewusst machen *or* zum Bewusstsein bringen; **to make sb more ~** jds Bewusstsein wecken; **for a three-year-old he's very ~** für einen Dreijährigen ist er sehr aufgeweckt; **she's very ~ of language** sie ist sehr sprachbewusst

awareness [ə'wɛənɪs] N Bewusstsein *nt*; **he showed no ~ of the urgency of the problem** er schien sich der Dringlichkeit des Problems nicht bewusst zu sein; **her tremendous ~ of the shades of meaning in the language/of other people's feelings** ihr außerordentlich waches Gespür für die Bedeutungsnuancen der Sprache/für die Empfindungen anderer; **to increase one's ~ of the outer world** seine Umwelt bewusster wahrnehmen

awash [ə'wɒʃ] ADJ *pred decks, rocks etc* überspült; *cellar* unter Wasser; **to be ~ with blood/money** im Blut/Geld schwimmen; **to be ~ with water** unter Wasser stehen; **Rome was ~ with rumours** *(Brit) or* **rumors** *(US)* in Rom kursierten Tausende *or* tausende von Gerüchten

away [ə'weɪ] ADV **a** *(= to or at a distance)* weg; **three miles ~ (from here)** drei Meilen (entfernt) von hier; **lunch seemed a long time ~** es schien noch lange bis zum Mittagessen zu sein; **~ back in the distance/past** weit in der Ferne/vor sehr langer Zeit; **they're ~ behind/out in front/off course** sie sind weit zurück/voraus/ab vom Kurs
b *(motion)* **~!** *(old, liter)* fort!, hinweg! *(old, liter)*; **~ with the old philosophy, in with the new!** fort mit der alten Philosophie, her mit der neuen!; **come, let us ~!** *(liter)* kommt, lasst uns fort von hier *(old)*; **~ with him!** fort mit ihm!; **but he was ~ before I could say a word** aber er war fort *or* weg, bevor ich den Mund auftun konnte; **to look ~** wegsehen; **~ we go!** los (gehts)!; **they're ~!** *(horses, runners etc)* sie sind gestartet; **they're ~ first time** gleich der erste Start hat geklappt
c *(= absent)* fort, weg; **he's ~ from work (with a cold)** er fehlt (wegen einer Erkältung); **he's ~ in London** er ist in London; **when I have to be ~** wenn ich nicht da sein kann
d *(Sport)* **to play ~** auswärts spielen; **they're ~ to Arsenal** sie haben ein Auswärtsspiel bei Arsenal
e *(= out of existence, possession etc)* **to put/give ~** weglegen/weggeben; **to boil/gamble/die ~** verkochen/verspielen/verhallen; **we talked the evening ~** wir haben den Abend verplaudert
f *(= continuously)* unablässig; **to work/knit** *etc* **~** vor sich *(acc)* hin arbeiten/stricken *etc*
g *(= forthwith)* **ask ~!** frag nur!, schieß los *(inf)*; **pull/heave ~!** und los(, zieht/hebt an)!; **right** *or* **straight ~** sofort
h *(inf)* **he's ~ again** *(talking, giggling, drunk etc)* es geht wieder los; **he's ~ with the idea that ...** er hat den Fimmel, dass ... *(inf)*; **~ with you!** ach wo!
ADJ *attr (Sport)* Auswärts-; **~ match** Auswärtsspiel *nt*; **~ win** Auswärtssieg *m*; **~ team** Gastmannschaft *f*
N *(in football pools: = away win)* Auswärtssieg *m*

awe [ɔː] N Ehrfurcht *f*, ehrfürchtige Scheu; **to be** *or* **stand in ~ of sb** Ehrfurcht vor jdm haben; *(= feel fear)* große Furcht vor jdm haben; **to hold sb in ~** Ehrfurcht *or* großen Respekt vor jdm haben; **to strike sb with ~** jdm Ehrfurcht einflößen; *(= make fearful)* jdm Furcht einflößen; **the sight filled me with (a sense of) ~** der Anblick erfüllte mich mit ehrfurchtsvoller Scheu VT Ehrfurcht *or* ehrfürchtige Scheu einflößen *(+dat)*; **~d by the beauty/silence** von der Schönheit/der Stille ergriffen; **in an ~d voice** mit ehrfürchtiger Stimme

awe-inspiring ['ɔːɪn,spaɪərɪŋ] ADJ Ehrfurcht gebietend

awesome ['ɔːsəm] ADJ **a** *(= frightening)* beängstigend; *(= impressive)* beeindruckend **b** *(esp US inf: = excellent)* irre *(inf)*; **she's really ~** sie ist echt cool drauf *(inf)*

awesomely ['ɔːsəmlɪ] ADV *(= frighteningly)* beängstigend; *(= impressively)* unwahrscheinlich, beeindruckend

awe-stricken ['ɔː,strɪkən], **awe-struck** ['ɔː,strʌk] ADJ von Ehrfurcht ergriffen; *voice, expression also* ehrfurchtsvoll; *(= frightened)* von Schrecken ergriffen; **I was quite ~ by its beauty** ich war von seiner Schönheit ergriffen

awful ['ɔːfəl] ADJ **a** *(inf)* schrecklich, furchtbar; **how ~!** das ist wirklich schlimm!; **you are ~!** du bist wirklich schrecklich!; **the film was just too ~ for words** der Film war unbeschreiblich schlecht; **an ~ lot of time/money** furchtbar viel Zeit/Geld; **it's not an ~ lot better** das ist nicht arg viel besser **b** *(old: = awe-inspiring)* Ehrfurcht gebietend ADV *(strictly incorrect)* = **awfully he was crying something ~** er weinte ganz schrecklich *or* furchtbar

awfully ['ɔːflɪ] ADV *(inf)* furchtbar *(inf)*, schrecklich *(inf)*; **it's not ~ important** es ist nicht so schrecklich *or* furchtbar wichtig *(inf)*; **she is rather ~ ~** *(Brit hum)* sie ist furchtbar vornehm *(inf)*; **thanks ~** *(Brit)* vielen, vielen Dank!; **would you mind ~ (waiting for me)?** *(Brit)* würde es Ihnen furchtbar viel ausmachen(, auf mich zu warten)? *(inf)*

awfulness ['ɔːfʊlnɪs] N *(of situation)* Schrecklichkeit *f*, Furchtbarkeit *f*; *(of person)* abscheuliche Art, Abscheulichkeit *f*; **we were shocked by the ~ of it all** wir waren von der Schrecklichkeit *or* Furchtbarkeit des Ganzen überwältigt

awhile [ə'waɪl] ADV *(liter)* eine Weile; **not yet ~!** noch eine ganze Weile nicht!

awkward ['ɔːkwəd] ADJ **a** *(= difficult)* schwierig; *time, moment, angle, shape* ungünstig; **4 o'clock is a bit ~ (for me)** 4 Uhr ist ein bisschen ungünstig *or* schlecht *(inf)* (für mich); **to make things ~ for sb** jdm Schwierigkeiten machen; **~ customer** übler Bursche *(inf)*
b *(= embarrassing)* peinlich
c *(= embarrassed)* verlegen; *(= shamefaced)* betreten; *silence* betreten; **I was at an ~ age** ich war in einem schwierigen Alter; **I feel ~ about that** das ist mir unangenehm; **I feel ~ about doing that** es ist mir unangenehm, das zu tun; **to feel ~ in sb's company** sich in jds Gesellschaft *(dat)* nicht wohlfühlen; **I felt ~ when I had to ...** es war mir unangenehm *or* peinlich, als ich ... musste
d *(= clumsy) person, movement, style* unbeholfen

awkwardly ['ɔːkwədlɪ] ADV **a** *(= clumsily) fall, move, express oneself, translate* ungeschickt; *lie* unbequem; *hang* merkwürdig; **~ placed** an einem ungünstigen Ort; **~ timed** zu einer ungünstigen Zeit **b** *(= embarrassingly)* peinlich **c** *(= embarrassedly)* verlegen; *(= shamefacedly)* betreten **d** *(= clumsily)* unbeholfen

awkwardness ['ɔːkwədnɪs] N **a** *(= difficulty)* Schwierigkeit *f*; *(of time, angle, shape)* Ungünstigkeit *f* **b** *(= discomfort)* Peinlichkeit *f* **c** *(= embarrassment)* Verlegenheit *f*; *(= shamefacedness)* Betretenheit *f* **d** *(= clumsiness)* Unbeholfenheit *f*

awl [ɔːl] N Ahle *f*, Pfriem *m*

awning ['ɔːnɪŋ] N *(on window, of shop)* Markise *f*; *(on boat)* Sonnensegel *nt*; *(of wagon)* Plane *f*; *(= caravan awning)* Vordach *nt*

awoke [ə'wəʊk] *pret of* **awake**

awoken [ə'wəʊkən] *ptp of* **awake**

AWOL ['eɪwɒl] *(Mil) abbr of* **absent without leave**

awry [ə'raɪ] ADJ *pred (= askew)* schief ADV **the picture/hat is ~** das Bild hängt/der Hut sitzt schief; **to go ~** *(plans etc)* schiefgehen

axe, *(US)* **ax** [æks] N Axt *f*, Beil *nt*; *(fig)* (radikale) Kürzung; **to wield the ~ on sth** *(fig)* etw radikal kürzen; **to get** *or* **be given the ~** *(employee)* abgesägt werden; *(project)* eingestellt werden; **the ~ has fallen on the project** das Projekt ist dem Rotstift zum Opfer gefallen; **to have an/no ~ to grind** *(fig)* ein/kein persönliches Interesse haben; **~ murderer** Axtmörder(in) *m(f)* VT *plans, projects, jobs* streichen; *person* entlassen

axiom ['æksɪəm] N Axiom *nt*

axiomatic [,æksɪəʊ'mætɪk] ADJ axiomatisch; **we can take it as ~ that ...** wir können von dem Grundsatz ausgehen, dass ...

axis ['æksɪs] N *pl* **axes** ['æksiːz] Achse *f*; **the Axis (powers)** *(Hist)* die Achse, die Achsenmächte *pl*

axle ['æksl] N Achse *f*

axle: **axle bearing** N Achslager *nt*; **axle box** N Achsgehäuse *nt*; **axle grease** N Achs(en)fett *nt*; **axle housing** N Achsgehäuse *nt*; **axle load** N Achslast *f*; **axle pin** N Achs(en)nagel *m*; **axletree** N Achswelle *f*

ayatollah [,aɪə'tɒlə] N Ayatollah *m*

ay(e) [aɪ] INTERJ *(esp Scot dial)* ja; **aye, aye, Sir** *(Naut)* jawohl, Herr Kapitänleutnant/Admiral *etc* N *(esp Parl)* Jastimme *f*, Ja *nt*; **the ayes** diejenigen, die dafür sind, die dafür; **the ayes have it** die Mehrheit ist dafür

aye [eɪ] ADV *(old, Scot)* immer

azalea [ə'zeɪlɪə] N Azalee *f*

Azerbaijani [,æzəbaɪ'dʒɑːnɪ] ADJ aserbaidschanisch N Aserbaidschaner(in) *m(f)*

Azeri [ə'zɛərɪ] ADJ, N = **Azerbaijani**

azimuth ['æzɪməθ] N *(Astron)* Azimut *nt or m*

Azores [ə'zɔːz] PL Azoren *pl*

AZT *abbr of* **azidothymidine** AZT *nt*

Aztec ['æztek] N Azteke *m*, Aztekin *f* ADJ aztekisch

azure ['æʒə'] N Azur(blau *nt*) *m* ADJ *sky* azurblau; *eyes also* tiefblau; **~ blue** azurblau

B

B, b [biː] N B *nt*, b *nt*; (*Sch: as a mark*) zwei, gut; (*Mus*) H *nt*, h *nt*; **B flat** B *nt*, b *nt*; **B sharp** His *nt*, his *nt* → **natural**

b *abbr of* **born** geb.

BA *abbr of* **Bachelor of Arts**

baa [bɑː] **N** Mähen *nt no pl*; **~!** mäh!; **~-lamb** (*baby-talk*) Bählamm *nt (baby-talk)*, Mähschäfchen *nt (baby-talk)* **VI** mähen, mäh machen (*baby-talk*)

babble [ˈbæbl] **N** **a** Gemurmel *nt*; (*of baby, excited person etc*) Geplapper *nt*; **~ (of voices)** Stimmengewirr *nt* **b** (*of stream*) Murmeln *nt no pl (liter)*, Plätschern *nt no pl* **VI** **a** (*person*) plappern, quasseln (*inf*); (*baby*) plappern, lallen; **don't ~, speak slowly** nicht so schnell, rede langsam; **the other actress tended to ~** die andere Schauspielerin neigte dazu, ihren Text herunterzurasseln **b** (*stream*) murmeln (*liter*), plätschern

▶ **babble away** *or* **on** VI quatschen (*inf*) (*about* über *+acc*), quasseln (*inf*) (*about* von); **she babbled away** *or* **on excitedly** sie quasselte *or* plapperte aufgeregt drauflos (*inf*)

▶ **babble out** VT *sep* brabbeln; *secret* ausplaudern

babbler [ˈbæbləʳ] N Plaudertasche *f (inf)*

babbling [ˈbæblɪŋ] ADJ *brook* murmelnd (*liter*), plätschernd

babe [beɪb] N **a** (*liter*) Kindlein *nt (liter)*; **~ in arms** (*esp Brit*) Säugling *m* **b** (*esp US inf*) Baby *nt (inf)*, Puppe *f (inf)*; **hey Susie/Mike ~!** he du, Susie!/Mike! **c** (*inf: = girl*) Schnalle *f (sl)*, Tussi *f (sl)*, Braut *f (sl)* → *also* **baby e**

Babel [ˈbeɪbəl] N **a** **the Tower of ~** (*story*) der Turmbau zu Babel *or* Babylon; (*edifice*) der Babylonische Turm **b** (*also* **babel**) (*= confusion*) Durcheinander *nt*; (*= several languages*) babylonisches Sprachengewirr

baboon [bəˈbuːn] N Pavian *m*

babuschka [bəˈbuːʃkə] N Kopftuch *nt*

baby [ˈbeɪbɪ] **N** **a** Kind *nt*, Baby *nt*; (*esp in weeks after birth*) Säugling *m*; (*of animal*) Junge(s) *nt*; **to have a ~** ein Kind *or* Baby bekommen; **she's going to have a ~** sie bekommt ein Kind *or* Baby; **I've known him since he was a ~** ich kenne ihn von klein auf *or* von Kindesbeinen an; **the ~ of the family** der/die Kleinste *or* Jüngste, das Nesthäkchen; (*boy also*) der Benjamin; **~ elephant** Elefantenjunge(s) *nt or* -baby *nt*; **he's a big ~** er ist ein großes Kind; **don't be such a ~!** sei nicht so ein Baby! (*inf*), stell dich nicht so an! (*inf*); **to be left holding the ~** (*Brit inf*) der Dumme sein (*inf*), die Suppe ausbaden müssen (*inf*); **the bank cancelled the loan and I was left holding a very expensive ~** (*Brit inf*) als die Bank das Darlehen rückgängig machte, hatte ich eine teure Suppe auszulöffeln; **to throw out the ~ with the bathwater** das Kind mit dem Bade ausschütten; **that encyclopedia is his first ~** (*inf*) das Lexikon ist sein Erstling (*hum*) *or* erstes Kind; **this little ~ cost me a fortune** (*inf*) das (Ding) hat mich ein Vermögen gekostet

b (*= small object of its type*) Pikkolo *m (hum)*

c (*inf: = thing for which one is responsible*) **that's a costing problem, that's Harrison's ~** das ist eine Kostenfrage, das ist Harrisons Problem; **I think this problem's your ~** das ist wohl dein Bier (*inf*)

d (*inf: = girlfriend, boyfriend*) Schatz *m*, Schätzchen *nt*

e (*esp US inf, as address*) Schätzchen *nt (inf)*; (*man to man*) mein Freund, mein Junge; **that's my ~** jawohl, so ists prima (*inf*); **that's great, ~** Mensch, das ist klasse (*inf*); **Mike/Susie ~, listen** du, Mike/Susie, hör mal her!

VT (*inf*) wie einen Säugling behandeln

baby: **baby barrier** N Sicherheitstür *f*, Sicherheitsgitter *nt*; **baby-batterer** N *jd, der Kleinkinder misshandelt*; **baby-battering** N Kindesmisshandlung *f*; **baby blue** N Himmelblau *nt*; **baby-blue** ADJ (*inf*) *eyes, ribbon, car* himmelblau; **baby blues** PL (*inf*) Depressionen *pl* nach der Geburt; **baby bond** N (*US Fin*) Baby Bond *m*; **baby boom** N Babyboom *m*; **baby boomer** N *Person, die während des Babybooms geboren wurde*; **baby bottle** N Saugflasche *f*; **Baby-bouncer®** N Babywippe *f*; **baby boy** N kleiner Junge; (*= son*) Sohn *m*; **baby break** N Babypause *f*; **baby brother** N kleiner Bruder; **baby buggy®** N (*Brit*) Sportwagen *m*; **baby bust** N drastischer Rückgang in der Geburtenziffer; **baby car** N Kleinwagen *m*, Autochen *nt (hum)*; **baby carriage** N (*US*) Kinderwagen *m*; **baby clothes** PL Kindersachen *pl*, Babywäsche *f*; **baby-doll face** N Puppengesicht *nt*; **baby-doll pyjamas**, (*US*) **baby-doll pajamas** PL Babydoll *nt*; **baby-face** N Kindergesicht *nt*; (*of adult male*) Milchgesicht *nt*; **baby-faced** ADJ *person* milchgesichtig; **baby fat** N (*US*) Babyspeck *m (inf)*; **baby food** N Babynahrung *f*; **baby girl** N kleines Mädchen; (*= daughter*) Tochter *f*, Töchterchen *nt*; **baby grand (piano)** N Stutzflügel *m*

babyhood [ˈbeɪbɪhʊd] N frühe Kindheit, Säuglingsalter *nt*

babyish [ˈbeɪbɪɪʃ] ADJ kindisch

baby jogger N (*= pram*) Babyjogger *m*

baby linen N Babywäsche *f no pl*

Babylon [ˈbæbɪlən] N Babylon *nt*

Babylonian [ˌbæbɪˈləʊnɪən] **ADJ** babylonisch **N** Babylonier(in) *m(f)*

baby: **baby-minder** N Tagesmutter *f*, Kinderpfleger(in) *m(f)*; **baby new potatoes** PL neue Kartöffelchen; **baby pool** N (*US*) Planschbecken *nt*; **baby-proof** **ADJ** kindersicher **VT** kindersicher machen

baby's breath N (*Bot*) Schleierkraut *nt*

baby: **baby scales** PL Baby- *or* Säuglingswaage *f*; **baby seat** N (*in car*) Baby(sicherheits)sitz *m*; **baby sister** N kleine Schwester; **baby-sit** *pret, ptp* **baby-sat** VI babysitten; **she ~s for them** sie geht bei ihnen babysitten; **baby-sitter** N Babysitter(in) *m(f)*; **baby-sitting** N Babysitten *nt*, Babysitting *nt*; **baby snatcher** N Kindesentführer(in) *m(f)*; **baby-snatching** N Kindesentführung *f*; **baby stroller** N (*US*) Babyjogger *m*; **baby-talk** N Kindersprache *f*; **baby tooth** N Milchzahn *m*; **baby-walker** N Laufstuhl *m*

baccara(t) [ˈbækərɑː] N Bakkarat *nt*

bacchanalia [ˌbækəˈneɪlɪə] N (*Hist, fig*) Bacchanal *nt (geh)*

bacchanalian [ˌbækəˈneɪlɪən] ADJ bacchantisch (*geh*)

Bacchus [ˈbækəs] N Bacchus *m*

baccy [ˈbækɪ] N (*inf*) Tabak *m*, Knaster *m (inf)*

bachelor [ˈbætʃələʳ] N **a** Junggeselle *m*; **still a ~** immer noch Junggeselle **b** (*Univ*) **Bachelor of Arts/Science** ≈ Magister *m* (der philosophischen/naturwissenschaftlichen Fakultät)

bachelordom [ˈbætʃələdəm] N = **bachelorhood**

bachelor: **bachelor flat** N Junggesellenwohnung *f*; **bachelor girl** N Junggesellin *f*

bachelorhood [ˈbætʃələhʊd] N Junggesellentum *nt*

bacillary [bəˈsɪlərɪ] ADJ (*Med*) bazillär (*spec*); *infection also* durch Bazillen; *form* stäbchenförmig

bacillus [bəˈsɪləs] N *pl* **bacilli** [bəˈsɪlaɪ] Bazillus *m*

back [bæk] **N** **a** (*of person, animal, book*) Rücken *m*; (*of chair*) (Rücken)lehne *f*; **with one's ~ to the engine** (*Brit*) mit dem Rücken zur Fahrtrichtung, rückwärts; **to be on one's ~** (*= be ill*) auf der Nase liegen (*inf*), krank sein; **to wear one's hair down one's ~** überschulterlange Haare haben; **to break one's ~** (*lit*) sich (*dat*) das Rückgrat brechen; (*fig*) sich abrackern, sich abmühen; **we've broken the ~ of the job** (*Brit*) wir sind mit der Arbeit über den Berg (*inf*); **behind sb's ~** (*fig*) hinter jds Rücken (*dat*); **to put one's ~ into sth** (*fig*) sich bei etw anstrengen, bei etw Einsatz zeigen; **to put** *or* **get sb's ~ up** jdn gegen sich aufbringen; **to turn one's ~ on sb** (*lit*) jdm den Rücken zuwenden; (*fig*) sich von jdm abwenden; **when I needed him he turned his ~ on me** als ich ihn brauchte, ließ er mich im Stich; **get these people off my ~** (*inf*) schaff mir diese Leute vom Hals! (*inf*); **get off my ~!** (*inf*) lass mich endlich in Ruhe!; **he's got the boss on his ~ all the time** er hat dauernd seinen Chef auf dem Hals; **the rich have always lived off the ~s of the poor** die Reichen haben immer auf Kosten der Armen gelebt; **to have one's ~ to the wall** (*fig*) in die Enge getrieben sein/werden; **I was pleased to see the ~ of them** (*inf*) ich war froh, sie endlich los zu sein (*inf*)

b (*as opposed to front*) Rück- *or* Hinterseite *f*; (*of hand, dress*) Rücken *m*; (*of house, page, coin, cheque*) Rückseite *f*; (*of material*) linke Seite; **I know London like the ~ of my hand** ich kenne London wie meine Westentasche; **the index is at the ~ of the book** das Verzeichnis ist hinten im Buch; **he drove into the ~ of me** er ist mir hinten reingefahren (*inf*); **on the ~ of his hand** auf dem Handrücken; **the ~ of one's head** der Hinterkopf; **at/on the ~ of the bus** hinten im/am Bus; **in the ~ (of a car)** hinten (im Auto); **one thing was at the ~ of my mind** ich hatte dabei eine Überlegung im Hinterkopf; **there's one other worry at the ~ of my mind** da ist noch etwas, das mich beschäftigt; **right at the ~ of the cupboard** ganz hinten im Schrank; **at the ~ of the stage** im Hintergrund der Bühne; **at the ~ of the garage** (*inside*) hinten in der Garage; (*outside*) hinter der Garage; **at the ~ of beyond** am Ende der Welt, jwd (*hum*); **in ~** (*US*) hinten

c (*Ftbl*) Verteidiger(in) *m(f)*; (*Rugby*) Hinterspieler(in) *m(f)*

ADJ Hinter-; *rent* ausstehend, rückständig; ~

wheel Hinterrad *nt*

ADV **a** *(= to the rear)* **(stand) ~!** zurück(treten)!, (treten Sie) zurück!; **~ and forth** hin und her

b *(= in return)* zurück; **to pay sth ~** etw zurückzahlen

c *(= returning)* zurück; **to come/go ~** zurückkommen/-gehen; **to fly to London and ~** nach London und zurück fliegen; **there and ~** hin und zurück

d *(= again)* wieder; **he went ~ several times** er fuhr noch öfters wieder hin; **I'll never go ~** da gehe ich nie wieder hin; **she is ~ at work** sie arbeitet wieder; **~ in London** zurück in London

e *(= ago: in time phrases)* **a week ~** vor einer Woche; **as far ~ as the 18th century** *(= dating back)* bis ins 18. Jahrhundert zurück; *(point in time)* schon im 18. Jahrhundert; **~ in March, 1987** im März 1987; **far ~ in the past** vor langer, langer Zeit, vor Urzeiten

PREP *(US)* **~ of** hinter

VT **a** *(= support)* unterstützen; **I will ~ you whatever you do** egal was du tust, ich stehe hinter dir; **if the bank won't ~ us** wenn die Bank nicht mitmacht; **to ~ a bill** *(Fin)* einen Wechsel indossieren

b *(Betting)* setzen *or* wetten auf *(+acc)*; **the horse was heavily ~ed** auf das Pferd wurden viele Wetten abgeschlossen

c *(= cause to move) car* zurückfahren *or* -setzen; *cart* zurückfahren; *horse* rückwärts gehen lassen; **he ~ed his car into the tree/garage** er fuhr rückwärts gegen den Baum/in die Garage; **to ~ water** *(Naut)* rückwärts rudern

d *(Mus) singer* begleiten

e *(= put sth behind) picture* mit einem Rücken versehen, unterlegen; *(= stick on)* aufziehen

VI **a** *(= move backwards: car, train)* zurücksetzen *or* -fahren; **the car ~ed into the garage** das Auto fuhr rückwärts in die Garage; **she ~ed into me** sie fuhr rückwärts in mein Auto

b *(Naut, wind)* drehen

▶ **back away** VI zurückweichen *(from* vor *+dat)*

▶ **back down** VI *(fig)* nachgeben, klein beigeben

▶ **back off** VI **a** *(vehicle)* zurücksetzen **b** *(= step back)* zurückweichen; *(crowd)* zurücktreten; *(= withdraw from deal etc)* aussteigen *(inf)*; *(= stop harassing)* sich zurückhalten; **back off!** *(= stop interfering)* verschwinde!

▶ **back on to** VI *+prep obj* hinten angrenzen an *(+acc)*

▶ **back out** VI **a** *(car etc)* rückwärts herausfahren *or* -setzen **b** *(fig: of contract, deal etc)* aussteigen *(of, from* aus) *(inf)* VT *sep vehicle* rückwärts herausfahren *or* -setzen

▶ **back up** VI **a** *(car etc)* zurücksetzen; **to back up to sth** rückwärts an etw *(acc)* heranfahren **b** *(traffic)* sich stauen; *(US: drain)* verstopfen **c** *(Comput)* sichern VT *sep* **a** *(= support)* unterstützen; *(= confirm) story* bestätigen; *knowledge* fundieren; *claim, theory* untermauern; **he backed up the boy's story that ...** er bestätigte den Bericht des Jungen, wonach ...; **he can back me up in this** er kann das bestätigen **b** *car etc* zurückfahren **c** *(Comput)* sichern, sicherstellen

back: **backache** N Rückenschmerzen *pl*; **back alley** N Gasse *f*; **back bench** N *(esp Brit)* Abgeordnetensitz *m*; **the ~es** das Plenum; **backbencher** N *(esp Brit)* Abgeordnete(r) *mf (auf den hinteren Reihen im britischen Parlament)*

> **BACKBENCHER**
>
> Alle britischen Unterhausabgeordneten, die weder in der Regierung noch im Schattenkabinett der Opposition sind, werden als **backbenchers** bezeichnet, da sie nicht in den vorderen Rängen, den **front benches**, des Unterhauses neben dem Premierminister bzw. dem Oppositionsführer sitzen. Da sie kein offizielles Amt innehaben, ist es für die **backbenchers** oft einfacher, sich entgegen der offiziellen Parteilinie zu äußern oder gegen sie zu stimmen. Mit **the back benches** werden generell alle Abgeordneten beider Seiten im Unterhaus bezeichnet, die keine wichtige Stellung innehaben.

back: **back bend** N *(Sport)* Brücke *f*; **backbiting** N Lästern *nt*; **backboard** N *(Basketball)* Korbbrett *nt*; **back boiler** N Warmwasserboiler *m (hinter der Heizung angebracht)*; **backbone** N *(lit, fig)* Rückgrat *nt*; **backbreaking** [ˈbækbreɪkɪŋ] ADJ erschöpfend, ermüdend; **back burner** N *(lit)* hintere Kochplatte; **to put sth on the ~** *(fig inf)* etw zurückstellen; **this project's been on the ~ for years** an diesem Projekt wird seit Jahren nur so nebenbei gearbeitet; **back catalogue** N *(Mus)* ältere Aufnahmen *pl*, Back-Katalog *m*; **backchat** N *no pl (inf)* Widerrede *f*; **none of your ~!** keine Widerrede!; **backcloth** [ˈbækklɒθ] N Prospekt *m*, Hintergrund *m*; **backcomb** VT *hair* toupieren; **back copy** N alte Ausgabe *or* Nummer; **back country, backcountry** *(US)* N **the ~** das Hinterland, die tiefste Provinz ADJ *road* Land-; **~ expedition** Expedition *f* ins Hinterland; **back cover** N *(of book, magazine)* Rückseite *f*; **backdate** VT (zu)rückdatieren; **salary increase ~d to May** Gehaltserhöhung rückwirkend ab Mai; **back door** N *(lit)* Hintertür *f*; *(fig)* Hintertürchen *nt*; **by the ~** *(fig)* durch die Hintertür; **if you use the back-door means of doing it** wenn Sie das durchs Hintertürchen machen; **backdrop** N Prospekt *m*, Hintergrund *m (also fig)*

-backed [-bækt] ADJ *suf* **low/high-backed** mit niedriger/hoher Rückenlehne; **a low-backed dress** ein Kleid mit tiefem Rückenausschnitt; **straight-backed** *(chair)* mit gerader Rückenlehne; *person* mit geradem Rücken

back end N *(= rear)* hinteres Ende; **at the ~ of the year** gegen Ende des Jahres, in den letzten Monaten des Jahres; **she looks like the ~ of a bus** *(inf)* sie ist potthässlich *(inf)*

backer [ˈbækəʳ] N **a** *(= supporter)* **his ~s** (diejenigen,) die ihn unterstützen **b** *(Betting)* Wettende(r) *mf* **c** *(Comm)* Geldgeber(in) *m(f)*

back: **backfile** N alte Akte; **backfire** N **a** *(Aut)* Fehlzündung *f* **b** *(US)* Gegenfeuer *nt* VI **a** *(Aut)* Fehlzündungen haben **b** *(inf, plan etc)* ins Auge gehen *(inf)*; **it ~d on us** der Schuss ging nach hinten los *(inf)*; **back-flip** N Flickflack *m*; **back formation** N *(Ling)* Rückbildung *f*; **back four** N *(+pl vb) (Ftbl)* Viererkette *f*; **backgammon** N Backgammon *nt*; **back garden** N Garten *m* (hinterm Haus)

background [ˈbækgraʊnd] N **a** *(of painting etc, fig)* Hintergrund *m*; **to stay in the ~** im Hintergrund bleiben, sich im Hintergrund halten; **to keep sb in the ~** jdn nicht in den Vordergrund treten lassen; **against a ~ of poverty and disease** vor dem Hintergrund von Armut und Krankheit

b *(of person) (educational etc)* Werdegang *m*; *(social)* Verhältnisse *pl*; *(= family background)* Herkunft *f no pl*; *(Sociol)* Background *m*; **he comes from a ~ of poverty** er kommt aus ärmlichen Verhältnissen; **comprehensive schools take children from all ~s** Gesamtschulen nehmen Kinder aus allen Schichten auf; **what do we know about the main character's ~?** was wissen wir über das Vorleben der Hauptperson?; **what's your educational ~?** was für eine Ausbildung haben Sie?

c *(of case, problem etc)* Zusammenhänge *pl*, Hintergründe *pl*, Hintergrund *m*; **he explained the ~ to the crisis** er erläuterte die Zusammenhänge *or* Hintergründe der Krise

ADJ *reading* vertiefend; **~ music** Hintergrundmusik *f*, Musikuntermalung *f*; **~ noises** *pl* Geräuschkulisse *f*, Geräusche *pl* im Hintergrund; **~ information** Hintergrundinformationen *pl*; **what's the ~ information on this?** welche Hintergründe *or* Zusammenhänge bestehen hierfür?

background program N *(Comput)* Hintergrundprogramm *nt*

background radiation N *(Phys)* natürliche Strahlung *f*

back: **backhand** N *(Sport)* Rückhand *f no pl*, Backhand *f no pl*; *(one stroke)* Rückhandschlag *m* ADJ Rückhand-; **~ stroke** Rückhandschlag *m* ADV mit der Rückhand; **backhanded** ADJ *compliment* zweifelhaft; *writing* nach links geneigt; **~ shot** Rückhandschuss *m*; **backhander** N **a** *(Sport)* Rückhandschlag *m* **b** *(inf: = bribe)* Schmiergeld *nt*; **to give sb a ~** jdn schmieren *(inf)*; **back-heel** N Hackentrick *m*, Absatztrick *m* VT *ball* mit der Hacke *or* dem Absatz spielen

backing [ˈbækɪŋ] N **a** *(= support)* Unterstützung *f*; **~ store** *(Comput)* Ergänzungsspeicher *m* **b** *(Mus)* Begleitung *f*; **~ group** Begleitband *f*; **~ singer** Begleitsänger(in) *m(f)*; **~ vocals** Begleitung *f* **c** *(for picture frame, for strengthening)* Rücken(verstärkung *f*) *m*; *(for carpet, wallpaper etc)* Rücken(beschichtung *f*) *m*

back: **backlash** N **a** *(Tech) (= jarring reaction)* Gegenschlag *m*; *(play)* zu viel Spiel **b** *(fig)* Gegenreaktion *f*; **backless** ADJ *dress* rückenfrei; **backlist** N *(in publishing)* Backlist *f*; **back-lit** ADJ *screen, photograph* hintergrundbeleuchtet; **backlog** N Rückstände *pl*; **I have a ~ of work** ich bin mit der Arbeit im Rückstand; **look at this ~ of typing** sehen Sie sich diesen Berg unerledigter Schreibarbeiten an; **backlot** N *(Film) Hintergelände eines Filmstudios*; **back marker** N *(Sport)* Nachzügler(in) *m(f)*, Schlusslicht *nt*; **the ~s** die Nachhut; **backmost** ADJ hinterste(r, s); **back number** N *(of paper)* alte Ausgabe *or* Nummer; *(fig inf) (= person)* altmodischer Mensch; *(= thing)* veraltetes Ding; **he is a ~** *(inf)* er ist altmodisch; **backpack** N Rucksack *m*; **backpacker** N Wanderer *m*, Wanderin *f*; *(= hitch-hiker)* Rucksacktourist(in) *m(f)*; **backpacking** N Wandern *nt*; *(= hitch-hiking)* Trampen *nt*; **to go ~** auf (Berg)tour gehen; trampen; **back passage** N *(euph Anat)* Mastdarm *m*; **back pay** N Nachzahlung *f*; **back-pedal** VI *(lit)* rückwärts treten; *(fig inf)* einen Rückzieher machen *(inf)* *(on* bei); **back-pedal brake** N Rücktrittbremse *f*; **back pocket** N Gesäßtasche *f*; **back projection** N *(Film)* Rückprojektion *f*; **back rest** N Rückenstütze *f*; **back road** N kleine Landstraße; **back room** N Hinterzimmer *nt*; **back-room boy** N *(inf)* Experte *m* im Hintergrund; **backscratching** N *no pl* gegenseitige Begünstigung, Vetternwirtschaft *f (pej)*; **back seat** N Rücksitz *m*; **to take a ~** *(fig)* sich zurückhalten *or* raushalten *(inf)*; **back-seat driver** N Beifahrer, der dem Fahrer dazwischenredet; **she is a terrible ~** sie redet beim Fahren immer rein; **back shift** N Spätschicht *f*; **backside** N *(Brit inf)* Hintern *m (inf)*, Hinterteil *nt (inf)*; **backsight** N *(on rifle)* Visier *nt*, Kimme *f*; **back-slapping** N *(inf)* Schulterklopfen *nt*; **backslash** N *(Typ, Comput)* Backslash *m*; **backslide** VI *(fig)* rückfällig werden; *(Eccl)* abtrünnig werden; **backslider** N Rückfällige(r) *mf*, Abtrünnige(r) *mf*; **backspace** VTI *(Typing)* zurücksetzen; **backspace key** N Rücktaste *f*; **backspacer** N *(Typing)* Rücktaste *f*; **backstage** ADV ADJ hinter den Kulissen; *(in dressing room area)* in die/der Garderobe; **~ crew** Leute *pl* hinter den Kulissen; *(at pop concert etc)* Backstagetruppe *f*; **backstairs** N *sing* Hintertreppe *f* ADJ **~ deal** Hintertreppendeal *m*; **backstitch** N Steppstich *m*; **backstop** N *(Tennis)* Bande *f*; **back straight** N *(Sport)* Gegengerade *f*; **backstreet** N Seitensträßchen *nt*; **he comes from the ~s of Liverpool** er kommt aus dem ärmeren Teil von Liverpool; **backstreet abortion** N illegale Abtreibung; **~s** Engelmacherei *f (inf)*; **she had a ~** sie war bei einem Engelmacher *(inf)*; **backstreet abortionist** N Engelmacher(in) *m(f) (inf)*; **backstretch** N *(Sport)* Gegengerade *f*; **backstroke** N *(Swimming)* Rückenschwimmen *nt*; **can you do the ~?** können Sie rückenschwimmen?; **backswing** N *(Sport)* Durchschwung *m*; **backtalk** N Widerrede *f*; **back to back** ADV Rücken an Rücken; *(things)* mit den Rückseiten aneinander; **back-to-back** ADJ direkt aufeinanderfolgend *attr*; **back to front** ADV verkehrt herum; *read* von hinten nach vorne; **back tooth** N Backenzahn *m*; **backtrack** VI *(over ground)* denselben Weg zurückgehen *or* zurückverfolgen; *(on policy etc)* einen Rückzieher machen *(on* sth bei etw*)*; **backup** N a Unterstützung *f* b *(Comput)* Sicherungskopie *f*, Backup *nt*, Back-up *nt* ADJ a *services* zur Unterstützung; ~ **troops** Unterstützungstruppen *pl*; ~ **train/plane** Entlastungszug *m*/-flugzeug *nt*; ~ **plan** Ausweichplan *m*; ~ **staff** Reservekräfte *pl*; ~ **service** *(for customer)* Kundendienst *m* b *(Comput)* Sicherungs-, Backup-; ~ **copy** Sicherungs- *or* Backupkopie *f*; **back-up light** [ˈbækʌp,laɪt] N *(US Aut)* Rückfahrscheinwerfer *m*; **back vowel** N *(Phon)* hinterer Vokal, Rachenvokal *m*

backward [ˈbækwəd] ADJ a ~ **and forward movement** Vor-und Zurückbewegung *f*; ~ **flow of information** Rückfluss *m* von Daten; **a ~ glance** ein Blick zurück; **a ~ step** *(fig)* ein Schritt *m* zurück b *(fig) economy, region* rückständig; *(pej: = retarded) child* zurückgeblieben; **to be socially/economically ~** gesellschaftlich/wirtschaftlich rückständig sein ADV = **backwards**

backward-compatible [,bækwədkəmˈpætɪbl] ADJ = **backwards-compatible**

backwardness [ˈbækwədnɪs] N *(mental)* Zurückgebliebenheit *f*; *(of region)* Rückständigkeit *f*

backwards [ˈbækwədz] ADV a rückwärts; **to fall ~** nach hinten fallen; **to walk ~ and forwards** hin und her gehen; **to stroke a cat ~** eine Katze gegen den Strich streicheln; **to lean** *or* **bend over ~ to do sth** *(inf)* sich fast umbringen *or* sich *(dat)* ein Bein ausreißen, um etw zu tun *(inf)*; **I know it ~** *(Brit) or* **~ and forwards** *(US)* das kenne ich in- und auswendig b *(= towards the past)* zurück; **to look ~** zurückblicken

backwards-compatible [,bækwədzkəmˈpætɪbl] ADJ *(Comput, Hi-Fi etc)* abwärtskompatibel *(with* mit*)*

back: **backwash** N *(Naut)* Rückströmung *f*; *(fig)* Nachwirkung *f usu pl*; **those caught up in the ~ of the scandal** diejenigen, die in den Skandal mit hineingezogen wurden; **backwater** N *(lit)* Stauwasser *nt*, totes Wasser; *(fig)* rückständiges Nest; **this town is a cultural ~** kulturell (gesehen) ist diese Stadt tiefste Provinz; **backwoods** PL unterschlossene (Wald)gebiete *pl*; **backwoodsman** N Waldsiedler *m*; *(fig inf)* Hinterwäldler *m*; **back yard** N Hinterhof *m*; **in one's own ~** *(fig)* vor der eigenen Haustür

bacon [ˈbeɪkən] N durchwachsener Speck; **~ and eggs** Eier mit Speck; **to save sb's ~** *(inf)* jds Rettung sein; **to bring home the ~** *(inf: = earn a living)* die Brötchen verdienen *(inf)*

bacteria [bækˈtɪərɪə] *pl of* **bacterium**

bacterial [bækˈtɪərɪəl] ADJ bakteriell

bacteriological [bæk,tɪərɪəˈlɒdʒɪkəl] ADJ bakteriologisch

bacteriologist [bæk,tɪərɪˈɒlədʒɪst] N Bakteriologe *m*, Bakteriologin *f*

bacteriology [bæk,tɪərɪˈɒlədʒɪ] N Bakteriologie *f*

bacterium [bækˈtɪərɪəm] N *pl* **bacteria** [bækˈtɪərɪə] Bakterie *f*, Bakterium *nt (old)*

bad[1] [bæd] ADJ *comp* **worse**, *superl* **worst** a schlecht; *smell* übel; *habit* schlecht, übel; *insurance risk* hoch; *word* unanständig, schlimm; *(= immoral, wicked)* böse; *(= naughty, misbehaved)* unartig, ungezogen; *dog* böse; **it was a ~ thing to do** das hättest du nicht tun sollen; **it was ~ of you to treat her like that** das war gemein von dir, sie so zu behandeln; **he went through a ~ time** er hat eine schlimme Zeit durchgemacht; **I've had a really ~ day** ich hatte einen furchtbaren Tag; **you ~ boy!** du ungezogener Junge!, du Lümmel! *(also iro)*; **he's been a ~ boy** er war unartig *or* böse; **I didn't mean that word in a ~ sense** ich habe mir bei dem Wort nichts Böses gedacht; **it's a ~ business** das ist eine üble Sache; **it's not so ~/not ~ at all** es ist nicht/gar nicht so schlecht; **things are going from ~ to worse** es wird immer schlimmer; **to go ~** schlecht werden, verderben; **he's gone ~** *(US)* er ist auf die schiefe Bahn geraten; **to be ~ for sb/sth** schlecht *or* nicht gut für jdn/etw sein; **he's ~ at French** er ist schlecht in Französisch; **he's ~ at sports** im Sport ist er schlecht *or* nicht gut, er ist unsportlich; **I'm very ~ at telling lies** ich kann schlecht *or* nicht gut lügen; **he speaks very ~ English, his English is very ~** er spricht sehr schlecht(es) Englisch; **to be ~ to sb** jdn schlecht behandeln; **there's nothing ~ about living together** es ist doch nichts dabei, wenn man zusammenlebt; **this is a ~ town for violence** in dieser Stadt ist es wirklich schlimm mit der Gewalttätigkeit; **~ light stopped play** das Spiel wurde aufgrund des schlechten Lichts abgebrochen; **it would not be a ~ thing** das wäre nicht schlecht *or* keine schlechte Idee; **that's not a ~ idea!** das ist keine schlechte Idee!; **(that's) too ~!** *(indignant)* so was!; *(= bad luck!)* Pech!; **it's too ~ of you** das ist wirklich nicht nett von dir; **too ~ you couldn't make it** (es ist) wirklich schade, dass Sie nicht kommen konnten; **to have a ~ hair day** *(inf)* Probleme mit der Frisur haben; *(fig)* total durch den Wind sein *(inf)*; **to be in ~ with sb** *(US)* bei jdm schlecht angeschrieben sein

b *(= serious) wound, sprain* schlimm; *accident, mistake, cold* schlimm, schwer; *headache* stark; **he's got it ~** *(inf)* ihn hats schwer erwischt *(inf)*; **to have it ~ for sb** *(inf)* in jdn schwer *or* unheimlich verknallt sein *(inf)*

c *(= unfavourable) time, day* ungünstig, schlecht; **Thursday's ~, can you make it Friday?** Donnerstag ist ungünstig *or* schlecht, gehts nicht Freitag?

d *(= in poor health, sick) stomach* krank; *leg, knee, hand* schlimm; *tooth (generally)* schlecht; *(now)* schlimm; **he/the economy is in a ~ way** *(Brit)* es geht ihm schlecht/es steht schlecht um die *or* mit der Wirtschaft; **I've got a ~ head** *(Brit)* ich habe einen dicken Kopf *(inf)*; **to feel ~** sich nicht wohlfühlen; **I feel ~** mir geht es nicht gut, mir ist nicht gut; **to be taken ~** *(Brit)* **to take a ~ turn** *(inf)* plötzlich krank werden; **how is he? – he's not so ~** wie geht es ihm? – nicht schlecht; **I didn't know she was so ~** ich wusste nicht, dass es ihr so schlecht geht *or* dass sie so schlimm dran ist *(inf)*

e *(= regretful)* **I feel really ~ about not having told him** es tut mir wirklich leid *or* ich habe ein schlechtes Gewissen, dass ich ihm das nicht gesagt habe; **don't feel ~ about it** machen Sie sich *(dat)* keine Gedanken *or* Sorgen (darüber)

f *debt* uneinbringlich; *voting slip, coin* ungültig; *(= damaged) copies etc* beschädigt

g *(Comput) data format* ungültig; *(= corrupted)* fehlerhaft

N *no pl* a **to take the good with the ~** (auch) die schlechten Seiten in Kauf nehmen; **there is good and ~ in everything/everybody** alles/jeder hat seine guten und schlechten Seiten

b **he's gone to the ~** *(Brit)* er ist auf die schiefe Bahn geraten

bad[2] *pret of* **bid**

bad: **bad-ass** [ˈbædæs] *(US sl)* N knallharter Typ *(inf)* ADJ *attitude* knallhart *(inf)*; **a ~ kid** ein knallharter Bursche *(inf)*; **bad blood** N böses Blut; **there is ~ between them** sie haben ein gestörtes Verhältnis; **bad cheque**, *(US)* **bad check** N *(containing a mistake)* ungültiger Scheck; *(not covered by funds)* ungedeckter Scheck

baddie [ˈbædɪ] N *(inf)* Schurke *m*, Bösewicht *m*

baddish [ˈbædɪʃ] ADJ *(inf)* ziemlich schlecht

bade [beɪd] *pret of* **bid**

badge [bædʒ] N a Abzeichen *nt*; *(made of metal)* Button *m*; *(on car etc)* Plakette *f*; *(= sticker)* Aufkleber *m*; **~ of office** Dienstmarke *f* b *(fig: = symbol)* Merkmal *nt*

badger [ˈbædʒəʳ] N Dachs *m*; **~-baiting** Dachshetzjagd *f* VT zusetzen *(+dat)*, bearbeiten *(inf)*, keine Ruhe lassen *(+dat)*; **don't ~ me** lass mich in Ruhe *or* Frieden; **to ~ sb for sth** jdm mit etw in den Ohren liegen

bad hair day N *(inf)* Scheißtag *m (inf)*, Tag *m*, an dem alles schiefgeht

badlands [ˈbædləndz] PL Ödland *nt*

badly [ˈbædlɪ] ADV a schlecht; **to do ~** *(in election, exam etc)* schlecht abschneiden; *(Fin)* schlecht stehen; *(Comm)* schlecht gehen; **to go ~** schlecht laufen; **to be ~ off** schlecht dran sein

b *wounded, mistaken* schwer; **~ beaten** *(Sport)* vernichtend geschlagen; *person* schwer *or* schlimm verprügelt; **the ~ disabled** die Schwerstbeschädigten

c *(= very much)* sehr; *in debt, overdrawn* hoch; **to want sth ~** etw unbedingt wollen; **I need it ~** ich brauche es dringend; **he ~ needs** *or* **wants a haircut** er muss dringend zum Friseur

d *(= unfavourably)* **to reflect ~ on sb** ein schlechtes Licht auf jdn werfen; **to think ~ of sb** schlecht von jdm denken

bad-mannered [,bædˈmænəd] ADJ ungezogen, unhöflich

badminton [ˈbædmɪntən] N Federball *nt*; *(on court)* Badminton *nt*

bad-mouth [ˈbædmaʊθ] VT *(inf)* herziehen über *(+acc) (inf)*

badness [ˈbædnɪs] N *no pl* a Schlechtheit *f*; *(moral)* Schlechtigkeit *f*; *(= naughtiness)* Unartigkeit *f*, Ungezogenheit *f* b *(= seriousness)* Schwere *f*; *(of headache)* Stärke *f*

bad-tempered [,bædˈtempəd] ADJ schlecht gelaunt *attr*, übellaunig; **to be ~** schlechte Laune haben; *(as characteristic)* ein übellauniger Mensch sein

baffle [ˈbæfl] VT a *(= confound, amaze)* verblüffen; *(= cause incomprehension)* vor ein Rätsel stellen; **a ~d look** ein verdutzter Blick; **the police are ~d** die Polizei steht vor einem Rätsel; **it really ~s me how ...** es ist mir wirklich ein Rätsel, wie ...; **a case that ~d all the experts** ein Fall, der den Experten Rätsel aufgab; **this one's got me ~d** ich stehe vor einem Rätsel b *(Tech) sound* dämpfen N *(also* **baffle plate**: *Aut)* Umlenkblech *nt*

bafflement [ˈbæflmənt] N *(= bewilderment)* Verblüffung *f*, Verwirrung *f*

baffling [ˈbæflɪŋ] ADJ *case* rätselhaft; *complexity* verwirrend; *mystery* unergründlich; *question* verblüffend; **I find it ~** es ist mir ein Rätsel

BAFTA [ˈbæftə] N *(Brit) abbr of* **British Academy of Film and Television Arts** *britische Film- und Fernsehakademie*

bag [bæg] N a Tasche *f*; *(with drawstrings, pouch)* Beutel *m*; *(for school)* Schultasche *f*; *(made of paper, plastic)* Tüte *f*; *(= sack)* Sack *m*; *(= suitcase)* Reisetasche *f*; **~s** (Reise)gepäck *nt*; **to pack one's ~s** seine Sachen packen; **with ~ and ~gage** mit Sack und Pack; **to be a ~ of bones** *(fig inf)* nur Haut und Knochen sein *(inf)*; **the whole ~ of tricks** *(inf)* die ganze Trickkiste *(inf)*; **to be left holding the ~** *(US inf)* der Dumme sein *(inf)*, die Sache ausbaden müssen *(inf)*

b *(Hunt)* **the ~** die (Jagd)beute; **to get a good ~** (eine) fette Beute machen *or* heimbringen; **it's in the ~** *(fig inf)* das habe ich *etc* schon in der Tasche *(inf)*, das ist gelaufen *(inf)*; *(Sport)* wir haben den Sieg in der Tasche *(inf)*

c **~s under the eyes** *(black)* Ringe *pl* unter den Augen; *(of skin)* (hervortretende) Tränensäcke *pl*

d *(inf: = a lot)* **~s of** jede Menge *(inf)*

e *(pej inf: = woman)* **(old) ~** Schachtel *f (pej inf)*; **ugly old ~** Schreckschraube *f (inf)*

f **bags**

PL *(Brit) (= Oxford bags)* weite Hose; *(dated inf: = trousers)* Buxe *f (dated inf)*

VT a in Tüten/Säcke verpacken

b *(Hunt)* erlegen, erbeuten

c *(Brit, sl: = get)* (sich *dat*) schnappen *(inf)*;

~s I have first go! will anfangen!; **I ~s that ice cream!** will das Eis!
VI *(garment)* sich (aus)beulen

bagatelle [ˌbægəˈtel] **N** **a** *(liter: = trifle)* Bagatelle *f* **b** *(= game)* Tivoli *nt*

bagel [ˈbeɪgəl] **N** *kleines, rundes Brötchen*

bagful [ˈbægfʊl] **N a ~ of groceries** eine Tasche voll Lebensmittel

baggage [ˈbægɪdʒ] **N** **a** *(= luggage)* (Reise)gepäck *nt* **b** *(Mil)* Gepäck *nt* **c** *(pej inf: = woman)* Stück *nt (inf)* → **emotional a**

baggage *(esp US)*: **baggage allowance N** Freigepäck *nt*; **baggage car N** Gepäckwagen *m*; **baggage check N** Gepäckkontrolle *f*; **baggage checkroom N** Gepäckaufbewahrung *f*; **baggage claim N** Gepäckausgabe *f*; **baggage handler N** Gepäckmann *m*; **baggage locker N** Gepäckschließfach *nt*; **baggage master N** Beamte(r) *m* am Gepäckschalter; **baggage rack N** *(Rail)* Gepäcknetz *nt*; **baggage reclaim N** Gepäckausgabe *f*; **baggage room N** Gepäckaufbewahrung *f*; **baggage wagon N** Gepäckwagen *m*

bagging [ˈbægɪŋ] **N** *(material)* Sack- *or* Packleinen *nt*

baggy [ˈbægɪ] **ADJ** *(+er)* *(= ill-fitting)* zu weit; *dress* sackartig; *skin* schlaff (hängend); *(= out of shape) trousers, suit* ausgebeult; *jumper* ausgeleiert; **~ trousers are fashionable again** weite (Flatter)hosen sind wieder modern

Baghdad [ˌbægˈdæd] **N** Bagdad *nt*

bag lady N Stadtstreicherin *f (die ihre gesamte Habe in Einkaufstaschen mit sich führt)*

bagpiper [ˈbægpaɪpəʳ] **N** Dudelsackpfeifer(in) *or* -bläser(in) *m(f)*

bagpipe(s) [ˈbægpaɪp(s)] **N(PL)** Dudelsack *m*

bags [bægz] **PL** → **bag N d**

bag-snatcher [ˈbægˌsnætʃəʳ] **N** Handtaschendieb(in) *m(f)*

baguette [bæˈget] **N** Baguette *f or nt*, Stangenbrot *nt*

Bahamas [bəˈhɑːməz] **PL the ~** die Bahamas *pl*

Bahrain, Bahrein [bɑːˈreɪn] **N** Bahrain *nt*

bail¹ [beɪl] **N** *(Jur)* Kaution *f*, Sicherheitsleistung *f (form)*; **to go** *or* **stand** *or* **put up ~ for sb** für jdn (die) Kaution stellen *or* leisten; **to grant/refuse ~** die Freilassung gegen Kaution bewilligen/verweigern; **he was refused ~** sein Antrag auf Freilassung gegen Kaution wurde abgelehnt; **to be (out) on ~** gegen Kaution freigelassen sein; **to let sb out on ~** jdn gegen Kaution freilassen

▶ **bail out VT** *sep* **a** *(Jur)* gegen Kaution *or* Sicherheitsleistung freibekommen, die Kaution stellen für **b** *(fig)* aus der Patsche helfen *(+dat) (inf)* **c** *boat* = **bale out**

bail² VI = **bale²**

bail³ N **a** *(Cricket)* Querholz *nt* **b** *(in stable)* Trennstange *f*

bailable [ˈbeɪləbl] **ADJ** *(Jur)* kautionsfähig

bail: **bail bandit N** *(Brit inf) jd, der eine Straftat begeht, während er gegen Kaution freigelassen ist*; **bail bond N** *(US Jur) (= document)* Verpflichtungserklärung *f*; *(= money)* Kaution *f*; **bail bondsman N** *(US Jur)* Kautionsbürge *m*

bailee [beɪˈliː] **N** *(Jur)* Depositar(in) *m(f) (einer beweglichen Sache), (treuhänderische(r))* Verwahrer(in) *m(f)*

Bailey bridge [ˈbeɪlɪˈbrɪdʒ] **N** Behelfsbrücke *f*

bailiff [ˈbeɪlɪf] **N** **a** *(Jur)* *(Brit: also* **sheriff's bailiff***)* Amtsdiener(in) *m(f)*; *(Brit: for property)* Gerichtsvollzieher(in) *m(f)*; *(US: in court)* Gerichtsdiener(in) *m(f)* **b** *(Brit: on estate)* (Guts)verwalter(in) *m(f)*, Landvogt(in) *m(f) (obs)*

bailor [beɪˈlɔː, ˈbeɪləʳ] **N** *(Jur)* Hinterleger(in) *m(f) (einer beweglichen Sache)*, Deponent(in) *m(f)*

bailout [ˈbeɪlaʊt] **N** *(Econ)* Sanierung *f*; **~ plan** Sanierungsplan *m*

bairn [beən] **N** *(Scot)* Kind *nt*

bait [beɪt] **N** *(lit, fig)* Köder *m*; **to take** *or* **swallow the ~, to rise to the ~** *(lit, fig)* anbeißen; *(fig: = be trapped)* sich ködern lassen **VT** **a** *hook, trap* mit einem Köder versehen, beködern **b** *(= torment) animal* (mit Hunden) hetzen; *person* quälen

baize [beɪz] **N** Fries *m*, Flaus *m*; **green ~** Billardtuch *nt*

bake [beɪk] **VT** **a** *(Cook)* backen; **~d apples** *pl* Bratäpfel *pl*; **~d potatoes** *pl* in der Schale gebackene Kartoffeln *pl* **b** *pottery, bricks* brennen; *(sun) earth* ausdörren **VI** **a** *(Cook)* backen; *(cake)* im (Back)ofen sein **b** *(pottery etc)* gebrannt werden, im (Brenn)ofen sein **c** *(inf)* **I just want to lie in the sun and ~** ich möchte mich in der Sonne braten lassen

bakehouse [ˈbeɪkhaʊs] **N** Backhaus *nt*

Bakelite® [ˈbeɪkəlaɪt] **N** Bakelite® *nt*, Bakelit® *nt*

bake-off [ˈbeɪkɒf] **N** *(US Cook)* Backwettbewerb *m*

baker [ˈbeɪkəʳ] **N** Bäcker(in) *m(f)*; **~'s boy** Bäckerjunge *m*; **~'s (shop)** Bäckerei *f*, Bäckerladen *m*

baker's dozen [ˈbeɪkəzˈdʌzn] **N** 13 (Stück)

bakery [ˈbeɪkərɪ] **N** Bäckerei *f*

bakeware [ˈbeɪkweəʳ] **N** Backformen und -bleche *pl*

Bakewell tart [ˈbeɪkwelˈtɑːt] **N** *(Brit) Törtchen mit Mandel- und Marmeladenfüllung*

baking [ˈbeɪkɪŋ] **N** **a** *(act) (Cook)* Backen *nt*; *(of earthenware)* Brennen *nt*; **it's our own ~** das ist selbst gebacken **b** *(batch: of bread, of bricks etc)* Ofenladung *f*, Schub *m* **ADJ** *(inf: = stifling, roasting)* **I'm ~** ich komme um vor Hitze; **it's ~ (hot) today** es ist eine Affenhitze heute *(inf)*

baking: **baking day N** Backtag *m*; **baking dish N** Backform *f*; **baking mitt N** *(US)* Topfhandschuh *m*; **baking pan N** *(US)* Backblech *nt*; **baking powder N** Backpulver *nt*; **baking sheet N** Back- *or* Plätzchenblech *nt*; **baking soda N** ≈ Backpulver *nt*; **baking tin N** *(Brit)* Backform *f*; **baking tray N** *(Brit)* Kuchenblech *nt*

baksheesh [ˈbækʃiːʃ] **N** Bakschisch *nt*

Balaclava [ˌbæləˈklɑːvə] **N** *(also* **Balaclava helmet***)* Kapuzenmütze *f*

balalaika [ˌbæləˈlaɪkə] **N** Balalaika *f*

balance [ˈbæləns] **N** **a** *(= apparatus)* Waage *f*; **to be** *or* **hang in the ~** *(fig)* in der Schwebe sein; **his life hung in the ~** sein Leben hing an einem dünnen *or* seidenen Faden; **to put sth in the ~** *(= risk)* etw in die Waagschale werfen
b *(= counterpoise)* Gegengewicht *nt (to* zu); *(fig)* Ausgleich *m (to* für)
c *(lit, fig: = equilibrium)* Gleichgewicht *nt*; **sense of ~** Gleichgewichtssinn *m*; **to keep one's ~** das Gleichgewicht (be)halten; **to lose one's ~** aus dem Gleichgewicht kommen, das Gleichgewicht verlieren; **to recover one's ~** wieder ins Gleichgewicht kommen, das Gleichgewicht wiedererlangen; **off ~** aus dem Gleichgewicht; **to throw sb off (his) ~** jdn aus dem Gleichgewicht bringen; **the right ~ of personalities in the team** eine ausgewogene Mischung verschiedener Charaktere in der Mannschaft; **on the ~ of probabilities ...** wenn man die Möglichkeiten gegeneinander abwägt, ...; **the ~ of power** das Gleichgewicht der Kräfte; **~ of terror** Gleichgewicht *nt* des Schreckens; **to strike the right ~ between old and new/import and export** den goldenen Mittelweg zwischen Alt und Neu finden/das richtige Verhältnis von Import zu Export finden; **on ~** *(fig)* alles in allem
d *(= preponderant weight)* Hauptgewicht *nt*; **the ~ of advantage lies with you** der Hauptvorteil ist auf Ihrer Seite
e *(Comm, Fin: = state of account)* Saldo *m*; *(with bank)* Kontostand *m*, Saldo *m*; *(of company)* Bilanz *f*; **~ of trade** Handelsbilanz *f*; **~ in hand** *(Comm)* Kassen(be)stand *m*; **~ carried forward** Saldovortrag *or* -übertrag *m*; **~ due** *(Banking)* Debetsaldo *m*, Soll *nt*; *(Comm)* Rechnungsbetrag *m*; **~ in your favour** *(Brit) or* **favor** *(US)* Salдoguthaben *nt*; **~ of payments/trade** Zahlungs-/Handelsbilanz *f*
f *(= remainder)* Rest *m*; **to pay off the ~** den Rest bezahlen; *(Banking)* den Saldo begleichen; **my father has promised to make up the ~** mein Vater hat versprochen, die Differenz zu (be)zahlen
g *(Art)* Ausgewogenheit *f*
VT **a** *(= keep level, in equilibrium)* im Gleichgewicht halten; *(= bring into equilibrium)* ins Gleichgewicht bringen, ausbalancieren; **to ~ oneself on one foot** auf einem Bein balancieren; **the seal ~s a ball on its nose** der Seehund balanciert einen Ball auf der Nase
b *(in the mind) two arguments* (gegeneinander) abwägen; *interests, needs, demands* abwägen *(against* gegen); **to ~ sth against sth** etw einer Sache *(dat)* gegenüberstellen
c *(= equal, make up for)* ausgleichen
d *(Comm, Fin) account (= add up)* saldieren, abschließen; *(= make equal)* ausgleichen; *(= pay off)* begleichen; *budget* ausgleichen; **to ~ the books** die Bilanz ziehen *or* machen
e *(Aut) wheel* auswuchten
VI **a** *(= be in equilibrium)* Gleichgewicht halten; *(scales)* sich ausbalancieren; *(painting)* ausgewogen sein; **he ~d on one foot** er balancierte auf einem Bein; **with a ball balancing on its nose** mit einem Ball, den er auf der Nase balancierte
b *(Comm, Fin, accounts)* ausgeglichen sein; **the books don't ~** die Abrechnung stimmt nicht; **to make the books ~** die Abrechnung ausgleichen

▶ **balance out VT** *sep* aufwiegen, ausgleichen; **they balance each other out** sie wiegen sich auf, sie halten sich die Waage; *(personalities)* sie gleichen sich aus **VI** sich ausgleichen

balance account N *(Fin)* Ausgleichskonto *nt*

balanced [ˈbælənst] **ADJ** **a** *(= objective) report, account, assessment, picture* ausgewogen **b** *(= well-proportioned) diet, painting, photography, mixture* ausgewogen; **nutritionally ~** vom Nährwert her ausgewogen; **~ budget** ausgeglichener Haushalt **c** *(Psych) person, personality, life* ausgeglichen; *view* vernünftig

balance: **balance sheet N** *(Fin)* Bilanz *f*; *(= document)* Bilanzaufstellung *f*; **balance wheel N** *(in watch)* Unruh *f*

balancing [ˈbælənsɪŋ]: **balancing act** [ˈbælənsɪŋækt] **N** *(lit, fig)* Balanceakt *m*; **balancing trick N** Balancekunststück *nt*

balcony [ˈbælkənɪ] **N** **a** Balkon *m* **b** *(Theat)* oberster Rang

bald [bɔːld] **ADJ** *(+er)* **a** *person* kahl, glatzköpfig; *head, tree* kahl; *bird* federlos; **he is ~** er hat eine Glatze; **to go ~** eine Glatze bekommen, kahl werden; **he is going ~ at the temples** er hat Geheimratsecken; **~ patch** kahle Stelle **b** *(Aut: = worn)* **~ tyre** *(Brit) or* **tire** *(US)* abgefahrener Reifen **c** *style, statement* knapp **d** *(liter: = bare, denuded)* kahl

bald eagle N weißköpfiger Seeadler

balderdash [ˈbɔːldədæʃ] **N** *(dated Brit inf)* Kokolores *m (dated inf)*

bald: **bald-faced ADJ** *(US) lie* unverfroren, unverschämt, schamlos; **baldheaded ADJ** kahl- *or* glatzköpfig

balding [ˈbɔːldɪŋ] **ADJ** **his ~ head** sein schütter werdendes Haar; **a ~ gentleman** ein Herr mit schütterem Haar; **he is ~** er bekommt langsam eine Glatze **N** Haarausfall *m*

baldly [ˈbɔːldlɪ] **ADV** *(fig) (= bluntly)* unverblümt, unumwunden; *(= roughly)* grob, knapp

baldness [ˈbɔːldnɪs] **N** **a** Kahlheit *f* **b** *(of style, statement)* Knappheit *f*

baldy [ˈbɔːldɪ] **N** *(inf)* Glatzkopf *m*

bale¹ [beɪl] **N** *(of hay etc)* Bündel *nt*; *(out of combine harvester, of cotton)* Ballen *m*; *(of paper etc)* Pack *m* **VT** bündeln; zu Ballen verarbeiten

bale² VI *(Naut)* schöpfen

▶ **bale out VI** **a** *(Aviat)* abspringen, aussteigen *(inf)* *(of* aus) **b** *(Naut)* schöpfen **VT** *sep*

(Naut) water schöpfen; *ship* ausschöpfen, leer schöpfen

Balearic [ˌbælɪˈærɪk] ADJ **the ~ Islands** die Balearen *pl*

baleful [ˈbeɪlfʊl] ADJ **a** *(= evil)* böse; *look (of bull etc)* stier **b** *(= sad)* traurig

balefully [ˈbeɪlfəlɪ] ADV *(= vindictively) watch* mit scheelem Blick; *scowl* böse; *(= sadly)* traurig

balk, baulk [bɔːk] **N a** *(= beam)* Balken *m* **b** *(= obstacle)* Hindernis *nt*, Hemmschuh *m* (*to* für) **VT** *person* hemmen; *plan* vereiteln **VI** *(person)* zurückschrecken (*at* vor *+dat*); *(horse)* scheuen, bocken (*at* bei)

Balkan [ˈbɔːlkən] **ADJ** Balkan-; **the ~ Mountains** der Balkan; **the ~ States** die Balkanländer *pl*; **~ syndrome** Balkansyndrom *nt*, *Verseuchung von Soldaten durch Rückstände radioaktiver Munition* **N the ~s** der Balkan, die Balkanländer *pl*

ball[1] [bɔːl] **N a** Ball *m*; *(= sphere)* Kugel *f*; *(of wool, string)* Knäuel *m*; **the cat lay curled up in a ~** die Katze hatte sich zusammengerollt; **~ and chain** Fußfessel *f* (mit Gewicht)
b *(Sport)* Ball *m*; *(Billiards, Croquet)* Kugel *f*
c *(= delivery of a ball)* Ball *m*; *(Tennis, Golf)* Schlag *m*; *(Ftbl, Hockey)* Schuss *m*; *(Cricket)* Wurf *m*; **the backs were giving their strikers a lot of good ~(s)** die Verteidiger spielten den Stürmern gute Bälle zu; **no ~** *(Cricket)* falsch ausgeführter Wurf
d *(= game)* Ball *m*; *(US: = baseball)* Baseball *nt*; **to play ~** Ball/Baseball spielen
e *(fig phrases)* **to keep the ~ rolling** das Gespräch in Gang halten; **to start** *or* **set** *or* **get the ~ rolling** den Stein ins Rollen bringen; **to have the ~ at one's feet** seine große Chance haben; **the ~ is in your court** Sie sind am Ball *(inf)*; **that puts the ~ back in his court** damit ist er wieder am Ball; **to be on the ~** *(inf)* am Ball sein *(inf)*, auf Zack *or* Draht sein *(inf)*; **to keep several ~s in the air** mehrere Eisen im Feuer haben; **to run with the ~** *(US inf)* die Sache mit Volldampf vorantreiben *(inf)* → **play N b VT a**
f *(Anat)* **~ of the foot/thumb** Fuß-/Handballen *m*
g *(sl) (= testicle)* Ei *nt usu pl (sl)*; *(pl)* Eier *pl (sl)*, Sack *m (vulg)*; **~s!** *(= nonsense)* red keinen Scheiß *(inf)*; **~s to him** der kann mich am Arsch lecken *(vulg)*; **~s to the regulations** ich scheiß doch auf die Bestimmungen *(sl)*; **~s** *(inf: = courage)* Schneid *m (inf)*, Mumm *m (inf)*; **he's got us by the ~s** *(sl)* er hat uns in der Zange *(inf)*
h *(old, for gun)* Kugel *f* → **cannonball**
i *(Cook, of meat, fish)* Klößchen *nt*, Klops *m*
VTI *(dated US vulg)* ficken *(vulg)*

ball[2] **N a** *(= dance)* Ball *m* **b** *(inf: = good time)* Spaß *m*; **to have a ~** sich prima amüsieren *(inf)*

ballad [ˈbæləd] N *(Mus, Liter)* Ballade *f*

ball-and-socket joint [ˌbɔːlənˈsɒkɪtdʒɔɪnt] N Kugelgelenk *nt*

ballast [ˈbæləst] **N a** *(Naut, Aviat, fig)* Ballast *m*; **to take in/discharge ~** Ballast aufnehmen/abwerfen **b** *(= stone, clinker)* Schotter *m*; *(Rail)* Bettung(sschotter *m*) *f* **VT** *(Naut, Aviat)* mit Ballast beladen

ball: **ball bearing** N Kugellager *nt*; *(= ball)* Kugellagerkugel *f*; **ball boy** N *(Tennis)* Balljunge *m*; **ball cock** N Schwimmerhahn *m*; **ball control** N Ballführung *f*

ballerina [ˌbæləˈriːnə] N Ballerina *f*; *(principal)* Primaballerina *f*

ballerina shoes PL *(Fashion)* Ballerinaschuhe *pl*, Ballerinas *pl*

ballet [ˈbæleɪ] N Ballett *nt*

ballet dancer N Balletttänzer(in) *m(f)*, Ballettteuse *f*

balletic [bæˈletɪk] ADJ ballettartig

ballet: **ballet master** N Ballettmeister(in) *m(f)*; **ballet pump, ballet shoe** N Ballettschuh *m*; **ballet skirt** N Balletttröckchen *nt*

ball: **ball game** N Ballspiel *nt*; **it's a whole new/different ~** *(fig inf)* das ist eine ganz andere Chose *(inf)*; **ball girl** N *(Tennis)* Ballmädchen *nt*

ballistic [bəˈlɪstɪk] ADJ ballistisch; **to go ~** *(inf)* ausrasten *(inf)*, an die Decke gehen *(inf)*

ballistic missile N Raketengeschoss *nt*

ballistics [bəˈlɪstɪks] N *sing* Ballistik *f*; **~ expert** Schusswaffenfachmann *m*

ball: **ball joint** N *(Tech)* Kugelgelenk *nt*; **ball loss** N *(Sport)* Ballverlust *m*

balloon [bəˈluːn] **N a** *(Aviat)* (Frei)ballon *m*; *(toy)* (Luft)ballon *m*; *(Met)* (Wetter)ballon *m*; **the ~ went up** *(fig inf)* da ist die Bombe geplatzt *(inf)*; **that went down like a lead ~** *(inf)* das kam überhaupt nicht an **b** *(in cartoons)* Sprechblase *f* **c** *(Chem: also* **balloon flask***)* (Rund)kolben *m* **VI a to go ~ing** auf Ballonfahrt gehen **b** *(= swell out)* sich blähen

balloon glass N Kognakglas *nt or* -schwenker *m*

balloonist [bəˈluːnɪst] N Ballonfahrer(in) *m(f)*

balloon tyre, *(US)* **balloon tire** [bəˈluːnˌtaɪəʳ] N Ballonreifen *m*

ballot [ˈbælət] **N a** *(= method of voting)* (geheime) Abstimmung; *(= election)* Geheimwahl *f*; **voting is by ~** die Wahl/Abstimmung ist geheim; **to decide sth by ~** über etw *(acc)* (geheim) abstimmen **b** *(= vote)* Abstimmung *f*; *(= election)* Wahl *f*; **first/second ~** erster/zweiter Wahlgang; **to take** *or* **hold a ~** abstimmen, eine Wahl abhalten, wählen; **they demanded a ~** sie verlangten eine (geheime) Wahl **c** *(numbers)* abgegebene Stimmen; **a large ~** eine hohe Wahlbeteiligung **VI** abstimmen; *(= elect)* eine (geheime) Wahl abhalten **VT** *members* abstimmen lassen

ballot: **ballot box** N Wahlurne *f*; **ballot paper** N Stimm- *or* Wahlzettel *m*; **ballot rigging** N Wahlbetrug *m*, Wahlfälschung *f*

ball: **ballpark** N **a** *(US)* Baseballstadion *nt* **b ~ figure** Richtzahl *f*; **in the ~** in dieser Größenordnung; **am I in the right ~?** bewege ich mich in der richtigen Größenordnung?; **ballplayer** N *(US)* Baseballspieler(in) *m(f)*; **ballpoint (pen)** N Kugelschreiber *m*; **ballroom** N Ball- *or* Tanzsaal *m*; **ballroom dancing** N klassische Tänze *pl*, Gesellschaftstänze *pl*

balls-up [ˈbɔːlzʌp], *(esp US)* **ball up** N *(inf)* Durcheinander *nt*; **he made a complete ~ of the job** er hat bei der Arbeit totale Scheiße gebaut *(sl)*; **the repair was a ~!** das war vielleicht eine Scheißreparatur! *(inf)*

▶ **balls up**, *(esp US)* **ball up** VT *sep (inf)* verhunzen *(inf)*

ballsy [ˈbɔːlzɪ] ADJ *(inf)* mutig, beherzt, unerschrocken; **you're a ~ little runt** du hast zumindest Eier *(sl)*

ball winner N *(esp Ftbl)* zweikampfstarke(r) Spieler(in)

bally [ˈbælɪ] ADJ *(dated Brit inf)* verflixt *(inf)*

ballyhoo [ˌbælɪˈhuː] *(inf)* **N** Trara *(inf)*, Tamtam *(inf) nt*; **to make a lot of ~ about sth** ein großes Trara *or* Tamtam um etw machen *(inf)* **VT** *(US)* marktschreierisch anpreisen

balm [bɑːm] **N a** *(lit, fig)* Balsam *m* **b** *(Bot)* Melisse *f*

balmy [ˈbɑːmɪ] ADJ *(+er)* *(= fragrant)* wohlriechend; *(= mild)* sanft, lind *(geh)*; **~ breezes** sanfte Brisen, linde Lüfte *(geh)*

balneotherapy [ˌbælnɪəˈθerəpɪ] N Balneotherapie *f*, *Behandlung mit Heilbädern und Badekuren*

baloney [bəˈləʊnɪ] **N a** *(inf)* Stuss *m (inf)*, Quatsch *m (inf)*; **she gave me some ~ about having had a difficult childhood** sie faselte was von einer schwierigen Kindheit *(inf)* **b** *(US: = sausage)* Mortadella *f*

balsa [ˈbɔːlsə] N *(also* **balsa wood***)* Balsa(holz) *nt*

balsam [ˈbɔːlsəm] **N a** Balsam *m* **b** *(Bot)* Springkraut *nt*

balsam fir N Balsamtanne *f*

Baltic [ˈbɔːltɪk] **ADJ** Ostsee-; *language (= of Baltic States)* baltisch; **~ port** Ostseehafen *m*; **the ~ States** die baltischen Staaten, das Baltikum **N a the ~** die Ostsee **the ~s PL** das Baltikum, die baltischen Staaten

Baltic Sea N Ostsee *f*

baluster [ˈbæləstəʳ] N Baluster *m*, Balustersäule *f*

balustrade [ˌbæləˈstreɪd] N Balustrade *f*

bamboo [bæmˈbuː] N Bambus *m attr* Bambus-; **~ shoots** *pl* Bambussprossen *pl*; **the Bamboo Curtain** *(Pol)* der Bambusvorhang

bamboozle [bæmˈbuːzl] VT *(inf) (= baffle)* verblüffen, baff machen *(inf)*; *(= trick)* hereinlegen *(inf)*; **he was ~d into signing the contract** sie haben es so getrickst *or* sie haben ihn mit Tricks dazu gebracht, dass er den Vertrag unterschrieben hat *(inf)*

ban [bæn] **N** Verbot *nt*; *(Eccl)* (Kirchen)bann *m*; *(Comm)* Embargo *nt*; **to put a ~ on sth** etw verbieten, etw mit einem Verbot/Embargo belegen *(form)*; **to lift a ~ on sth** das Verbot einer Sache *(gen)*/das Embargo für etw aufheben; **a ~ on smoking** Rauchverbot *nt*; **a ~ on keeping poultry outdoors** Stallpflicht *f* für Geflügel **VT** *(= prohibit)* verbieten; *(Eccl)* auf den Index setzen; *footballer etc* sperren; **to ~ sb from doing sth** jdm verbieten, etw zu tun; **he is ~ned from this bar** er hat hier Lokalverbot; **she was ~ned from driving** ihr wurde Fahrverbot erteilt; **~ned substances** verbotene Substanzen

banal [bəˈnɑːl] ADJ banal

banality [bəˈnælɪtɪ] N Banalität *f*

banana [bəˈnɑːnə] N Banane *f*

banana *in cpds* Bananen-; **banana plantation** N Bananenplantage *f*; **banana republic** N Bananenrepublik *f*

bananas [bəˈnɑːnəz] ADJ *pred (inf: = crazy)* bekloppt *(inf)*, bescheuert *(inf)*, beknackt *(sl)*; **this is driving me ~** das macht mich verrückt *or* ganz krank *(inf)*; **he's ~ about her** er steht voll auf sie *(sl)*; **the whole place went ~** der ganze Saal drehte durch *(inf)*

banana: **banana skin** N Bananenschale *f*; **to slip on a ~** *(fig)* über eine Kleinigkeit stolpern; **banana split** N *(Cook)* Bananensplit *nt*; **banana tree** N Bananenstaude *f*

band[1] [bænd] **N a** *(of cloth, iron)* Band *nt*; *(on barrel)* Fassband *nt*, Reifen *m*; *(over book jacket)* (Einband)streifen *m*; *(of leather)* Band *nt*, Riemen *m*; *(= waistband)* Bund *m*; *(on cigar)* Banderole *f*, Bauchbinde *f*; *(= ring: on bird; US: = wedding band)* Ring *m*; *(on machine)* Riemen *m* **b** *(= stripe)* Streifen *m* **c bands PL** *(Eccl, Univ: = collar)* Beffchen *pl* **d** *(Rad)* Band *nt* → **frequency band, waveband VT** *bird* beringen

band[2] **N a** Schar *f*; *(of robbers etc)* Bande *f*; *(of workers)* Trupp *m*, Kolonne *f* **b** *(Mus)* Band *f*; *(= dance band)* Tanzkapelle *f*; *(in circus, brass band, Mil etc)* (Musik)kapelle *f*

▶ **band together** VI sich zusammenschließen

bandage [ˈbændɪdʒ] **N** Verband *m*; *(= strip of cloth)* Binde *f* **VT** *(also* **bandage up***) cut* verbinden; *broken limb* bandagieren; **with his heavily ~d wrist** mit einem dick verbundenen Handgelenk

Band-Aid® [ˈbændeɪd] *(US)* **N** Heftpflaster *nt* **ADJ** *(also* **band-aid***)* *(inf: = makeshift) solution etc* behelfsmäßig

bandan(n)a [bænˈdænə] N großes Schnupftuch; *(round neck)* Halstuch *nt*

B & B [ˌbiːənˈbiː] N *abbr of* **bed and breakfast**

bandbox [ˈbændbɒks] N Hutschachtel *f*

bandeau top [bænˈdəʊˌtɒp] N *(Fashion)* Bandeautop *nt*, *eng anliegendes Oberteil*

banderol(e) [ˈbændərəʊl] N *(Naut)* Wimpel *m*, Fähnlein *nt*; *(Her)* Fähnchen *nt*; *(Archit)* Inschriftenband *nt*

bandit [ˈbændɪt] N Bandit(in) *m(f)*, Räuber(in) *m(f)*

banditry [ˈbændɪtrɪ] N Banditentum *or* -unwesen *nt*

band: **band leader** N Bandleader(in) *m(f)*; **bandmaster** N Kapellmeister *m*

bandolier [ˌbændəˈlɪəʳ] N Schulterpatronengurt *m*

band saw N Bandsäge *f*

bandsman [ˈbændzmən] N *pl* **-men** [-mən] Musiker *m*, Musikant *m (old)*; **military ~** Mitglied *nt* eines Musikkorps

band: **bandstand** N Musikpavillon *m or* -podium *nt*; **bandwagon** N *(US)* Musikwagen *m*, (Fest)wagen der Musikkapelle; **to jump** *or* **climb on the ~** *(also Brit: fig inf)* sich dranhängen, auf den fahrenden Zug aufspringen; **bandwidth** N *(Rad, Comput)* Bandbreite *f*

bandy[1] [ˈbændɪ] ADJ krumm; **~ legs** *(of people)* O-Beine

bandy[2] VT *jokes* sich *(dat)* erzählen; **to ~ words (with sb)** sich (mit jdm) herumstreiten

▸ **bandy about** *(Brit) or* **around** VT *sep sb's name* immer wieder nennen; *story, secret* herumerzählen, herumtragen; *ideas* verbreiten; *figures, sum, words, technical expressions* um sich werfen mit; **the press have been bandying his name/these words around a lot** die Presse hat seinen Namen/diese Wörter stark strapaziert; **I'd rather you didn't bandy my nickname around the office** es wäre mir lieber, wenn Sie meinen Spitznamen nicht im Büro herumposaunen würden *(inf)*

bandy-legged [ˌbændɪˈlegd] ADJ *(Brit)* mit krummen Beinen; *person* krummbeinig, o-beinig, O-beinig

bane [beɪn] N a *(= cause of distress)* Fluch *m*; **he's/it's the ~ of my life** er/das ist noch mal mein Ende *(inf)* b *(old: = poison)* Gift *nt*

baneful [ˈbeɪnfʊl] ADJ verhängnisvoll

bang[1] [bæŋ] N a *(= noise)* Knall *m*; *(of sth falling)* Plumps *m*; **there was a ~ outside** draußen hat es geknallt; **to go off with a ~** mit lautem Knall losgehen; *(inf: = be a success)* ein Bombenerfolg sein *(inf)*; **to get more ~ for the buck** *or* **more ~s for your bucks** *(esp US)* etwas für sein Geld geboten kriegen *(inf)*

b *(= violent blow)* Schlag *m*; **he gave himself a ~ on the shins** er hat sich *(dat)* die Schienbeine angeschlagen

c *(Brit sl: = sex)* Nummer *f (inf)*; **to have a ~ with sb** mit jdm bumsen *(inf)*

ADV a **to go ~** knallen; *(gun also)* peng machen *(inf)*; *(balloon)* zerplatzen, peng machen *(inf)*

b *(inf: = exactly, directly etc)* voll *(inf)*, genau; **his answer was ~ on** seine Antwort war genau richtig; **is that right? – ~ on** stimmt das? – haargenau; **she came ~ on time** sie war auf die Sekunde pünktlich; **~ up to date** auf dem neuesten Stand; **they came ~ up against fierce opposition** sie stießen auf heftige Gegenwehr; **the whole ~ shoot** *(Brit)* das ganze Zeug *(inf)*; *(people)* die ganze Bande *(inf)*

INTERJ peng; *(of hammer)* klopf; **~ goes my chance of promotion** *(inf)* und tschüs mit der Beförderung *(inf)*, und das wars dann mit der Beförderung *(inf)*; **~ go my dreams of fame and fortune** *(inf)* und das wars dann mit meinen Träumen von Ruhm und Reichtum *(inf)*

VT a *(= thump)* schlagen, knallen *(inf)*; **he ~ed his fist on the table** er schlug *or* haute mit der Faust auf den Tisch; **I'll ~ your heads together if you don't shut up!** *(inf)* wenn ihr nicht ruhig seid, knallts *(inf)*; **I felt like ~ing their heads together** *(inf)* ich hätte ihnen am liebsten ein paar links und rechts geknallt *(inf)*

b *(= shut noisily) door* zuschlagen, zuknallen *(inf)*; **you have to ~ the door to close it** Sie müssen die Tür richtig zuschlagen

c *(= hit, knock) head, shin* sich *(dat)* anschlagen (*on* an *+dat*); **to ~ one's head** *etc* **on sth** sich *(dat)* den Kopf *etc* an etw *(dat)* anschlagen, mit dem Kopf *etc* gegen etw knallen *(inf)*

VI a *(door: = shut)* zuschlagen, zuknallen *(inf)*; *(fireworks, gun)* knallen; **the door was ~ing in the wind** die Tür schlug im Wind

b **to ~ on** *or* **at sth** gegen *or* an etw *(acc)* schlagen

▸ **bang about** *(Brit) or* **around** VI Krach machen; *(heavy noise)* herumpoltern VT *sep* Krach machen mit; *chairs also* herumstoßen

▸ **bang away** VI a *(guns)* knallen; *(persons: = keep firing)* wild (drauflos)feuern *(at* auf *+acc)*, wild (drauflos)ballern *(inf) (at* auf *+acc)*; *(workman etc)* herumklopfen *or* -hämmern *(at* an *+dat)*; **to bang away at the typewriter** auf der Schreibmaschine herumhauen *or* -hämmern *(inf)* b *(inf: = work industriously)* **to bang away (at sth)** sich hinter etw *(acc)* klemmen *(inf)* c *(sl: = have sexual intercourse)* vögeln *(inf)*

▸ **bang down** VT *sep* (hin)knallen *(inf)*; *nail* einschlagen; *(= flatten)* flach schlagen; *lid* zuschlagen, zuknallen *(inf)*; **to bang down the receiver** den Hörer aufknallen *(inf)*

▸ **bang in** VT *sep nail* einschlagen

▸ **bang into** VI *+prep obj* a *(= collide with)* knallen *(inf) or* prallen auf *(+acc)* b *(inf: = meet)* zufällig treffen

▸ **bang on about** VI *+prep obj (Brit inf)* schwafeln von *(inf)*

▸ **bang out** VT *sep* a *nail* herausschlagen, heraushauen *(inf)* b **to bang out a tune on the piano** eine Melodie auf dem Klavier hämmern *(inf)*; **to bang out a letter on the typewriter** einen Brief auf der Schreibmaschine herunterhauen *(inf)*

▸ **bang up** VT SEP *(sl) prisoner* einbuchten *(inf)*

bang[2] N *(US: = fringe)* Pony *m*, Ponyfransen *pl*; **~s** Ponyfrisur *f*

banger [ˈbæŋəʳ] N a *(Brit inf: = sausage)* Wurst *f* b *(inf: = old car)* Klapperkiste *f (inf)* c *(Brit: = firework)* Knallkörper *m*

banging [ˈbæŋɪŋ] ADJ *(US sl)* **that girl is ~** das ist ne scharfe Frau *(inf)*, die ist vielleicht scharf *(inf)*

Bangladesh [ˈbæŋgləˈdeʃ] N Bangladesh *nt*

Bangladeshi [ˌbæŋgləˈdeʃɪ] N Einwohner(in) *m(f)* von Bangladesh, Bangladeshi *mf* ADJ aus Bangladesh

bangle [ˈbæŋgl] N Armreif(en) *m*; *(for ankle)* Fußreif *or* -ring *m*

bang-on [ˌbæŋˈɒn] ADJ *(inf)* **to be ~** haargenau stimmen

bang-up [ˈbæŋʌp] ADJ *(US sl)* klasse *(inf)*, prima *(inf)*

banish [ˈbænɪʃ] VT *person* verbannen; *cares, fear* vertreiben

banishment [ˈbænɪʃmənt] N Verbannung *f*

banister, bannister [ˈbænɪstəʳ] N (*also* **banisters**) Geländer *nt*

banjaxed [ˈbændʒækst] ADJ *(inf) machine* kaputt *(inf)*

banjo [ˈbændʒəʊ] N *pl* **-es** *or (US)* **-s** Banjo *nt*

bank[1] [bæŋk] N a *(of earth, sand)* Wall *m*, Damm *m*; *(Rail)* (Bahn)damm *m*; *(= slope)* Böschung *f*, Abhang *m*; *(on racetrack)* Kurvenüberhöhung *f*; **~ of snow** Schneeverwehung *f* b *(of river, lake)* Ufer *nt*; **we sat on the ~s of a river/lake** wir saßen an einem Fluss/See *or* Fluss-/Seeufer c *(in sea, river)* (Sand)bank *f* d *(of clouds)* Wand *f*, Bank *f* e *(Aviat)* Querlage *f*; **to go into a ~** in den Kurvenflug gehen

VT a *road* überhöhen b *river* mit einer Böschung versehen, einfassen c *plane* in die Querlage bringen VI *(Aviat)* den Kurvenflug einleiten, in die Querlage gehen

▸ **bank up** VT *sep earth etc* aufhäufen, aufschütten; *(= support)* mit einer Böschung stützen; *fire* mit Kohlestaub ab- *or* bedecken *(damit es langsam brennt)* VI *(snow etc)* sich anhäufen; *(clouds also)* sich zusammenballen

bank[2] N a Bank *f* b *(Gambling)* Bank *f*; **to keep** *or* **be the ~** die Bank halten *or* haben c *(Med)* Bank *f* d *(fig)* Vorrat *m (of* an *+dat)* VT *money* zur Bank bringen, einzahlen VI **where do you ~?** bei welcher Bank haben Sie Ihr Konto?; **I ~ with Lloyds** ich habe ein Konto *or* ich bin bei Lloyds

▸ **bank on** VI *+prep obj* sich verlassen auf *(+acc)*, rechnen mit; *sb, sb's help also* zählen *or* bauen auf *(+acc)*; **you mustn't bank on it** darauf würde ich mich nicht verlassen; **I was banking on your coming** ich hatte fest damit gerechnet, dass du kommst

bank[3] N a *(Naut: = rower's bench)* Ruderbank *f* b *(= row of objects, oars)* Reihe *f*; *(on organ, typewriter)* (Tasten)reihe *f*

bankable [ˈbæŋkəbl] ADJ *cheque etc* einzahlbar; **a very ~ film star** *(fig inf)* ein Filmstar, der viel Geld einbringt

bank: **bank acceptance** N Bankakzept *nt*; **bank account** N Bankkonto *nt*; **bank balance** N Kontostand *m*; **bank bill** N a *(Brit: Fin)* Bankwechsel *m*, Banktratte *f* b *(US: = banknote)* Banknote *f*, Geldschein *m*; **bankbook** N Sparbuch *nt*; **bank card** N Scheckkarte *f*; **bank charge** N Kontoführungsgebühr *f*; **bank cheque, bank check** *(US)* N Bankscheck *m*; **bank clerk** N Bankangestellte(r) *mf*; **bank code number** N Bankleitzahl *f*; **bank deposit** N Bankeinlage *f*; **bank draft** N Bankwechsel *m*, Banktratte *f*

banker [ˈbæŋkəʳ] N *(Fin)* Bankier *m*, Bankfachmann *m*/-fachfrau *f*, Banker(in) *m(f) (inf)*; *(gambling)* Bankhalter(in) *m(f)*

banker's: **banker's card** N Scheckkarte *f*; **banker's order** N *(= standing order)* Dauerauftrag *m*; **by ~** durch Dauerauftrag

bank: **bank giro** N Banküberweisung *f*; **bank holiday** N *(Brit)* öffentlicher Feiertag; *(US)* Bankfeiertag *m*

banking[1] [ˈbæŋkɪŋ] N a *(on road, racetrack)* Überhöhung *f* b *(Aviat)* Kurvenflug *m*

banking[2] N Bankwesen *nt*; **the world of ~** die Bankwelt; **he wants to go into ~** er will ins Bankfach *or* Bankgewerbe gehen *attr* Bank-; **the ~ business** das Bankgeschäft; **the ~ side of the business** die Bankangelegenheiten der Firma

banking: **banking hours** PL Schalterstunden *pl*; **banking house** N Bankhaus *nt*; **banking operation, banking transaction** N Bankgeschäft *nt*

bank: **bank loan** N Bankkredit *m*; **to take out a ~** einen Kredit bei der Bank aufnehmen; **bank manager** N Filialleiter(in) *m(f) (einer Bank)*; **my ~** der Filialleiter/die Filialleiterin meiner Bank; **banknote** N Banknote *f*, Geldschein *m*; **bank rate** N *(Brit)* Diskontsatz *m*; **bank reference** N *(for new customer etc)* Bankauskunft *f*; **bank robber** N Bankräuber(in) *m(f)*; **bank robbery** N Bankraub *m*; **bankroll** *(esp US)* N Bündel *nt* Geldscheine; *(fig)* Geld *nt*, Geldmittel *pl* VT *(inf)* **to ~ sb** jdn finanziell unterstützen; **to ~ sth** etw finanzieren

bankrupt [ˈbæŋkrʌpt] N a Gemein- *or* Konkursschuldner(in) *m(f) (Jur)*, Bankrotteur(in) *m(f)* b *(fig)* **to be a moral ~** moralisch bankrott sein ADJ a *(Jur)* bankrott; **to go ~** Bankrott machen, in Konkurs gehen; **to be ~** bankrott *or* pleite *(inf)* sein b *(fig)* bankrott; **they are totally ~ of ideas** sie haben keinerlei Ideen VT *person, country* zugrunde *or* zu Grunde richten, ruinieren; *firm also* in den Konkurs treiben

bankruptcy [ˈbæŋkrəptsɪ] N a *(Jur)* Bankrott *m*, Konkurs *m*; *(instance)* Konkurs *m*; **the possibility of ~** die Möglichkeit eines *or* des Bankrotts *or* Konkurses b *(fig)* Bankrott *m*

bankruptcy: **Bankruptcy Court** N Konkursgericht *nt*; **bankruptcy proceedings** PL Konkursverfahren *nt*

bankrupt's certificate [ˈbæŋkrʌpts-] N Eröffnungsbeschluss *m*

bankrupt's estate N Konkursmasse *f*

bank: **bank sort code** N Bankleitzahl *f*; **bank statement** N Kontoauszug *m*; **bank transfer** N Banküberweisung *f*

banner [ˈbænəʳ] N Banner *nt (also fig)*; *(in processions)* Transparent *nt*, Spruchband *nt*

banner ad N *(Internet)* Bannerwerbung *f*, Banner *nt*

banner headlines ['bænə'hedlaɪnz] N Schlagzeilen *pl*

banning ['bænɪŋ] N Verbot *nt*; **the ~ of cars from city centres** *(Brit)* or **centers** *(US)* das Fahrverbot in den Innenstädten; **the ~ of three athletes from the Olympic Games** der Ausschluss dreier Teilnehmer von den Olympischen Spielen

bannister ['bænɪstəʳ] N = **banister**

banns [bænz] PL *(Eccl)* Aufgebot *nt*; **to read the ~** das Aufgebot verlesen; **where are you having your ~ called?** wo haben Sie das Aufgebot bestellt?

banquet ['bæŋkwɪt] **N** *(= lavish feast)* Festessen *nt*; *(= ceremonial dinner also)* Bankett *nt* **VT** üppig or festlich bewirten *(on* mit); *(ceremoniously)* ein Bankett abhalten für **VI** speisen, tafeln *(geh)*; **to ~ on sth** etw speisen

banquet(ing)-hall ['bæŋkwɪt(ɪŋ)'hɔːl] N Festsaal *m*, Bankettsaal *m*

banquette [,bæŋ'ket] N gepolsterte Bank

banshee [bæn'ʃiː] N *(Ir Myth)* Banshee *f*, Todesfee *f*; **to scream like a ~** gespenstisch heulen

bantam ['bæntəm] N Bantamhuhn *nt*

bantamweight ['bæntəmweɪt] N Bantamgewicht *nt*

banter ['bæntəʳ] **N** Geplänkel *nt*; **enough of this foolish ~** lassen wir das alberne Gerede! **VT** *(old)* verulken, necken

bantering ['bæntərɪŋ] ADJ *(= joking)* scherzhaft; *(= teasing)* neckend, flachsig *(dial)*

Bantu [,bæn'tuː] **N** *(= language)* Bantu *nt*; *(pl: = tribes)* Bantu *pl*; *(= person)* Bantu *mf*, Bantuneger(in) *m(f)* *(neg!)* **ADJ** Bantu-; **~ tribe** Bantustamm *m*

banyan (tree) ['bænɪən(,triː)] N Bengalische Feige, Banyan *m*

BAOR *abbr of* **British Army of the Rhine**

bap (bun) ['bæp(bʌn)] N *(Brit)* weiches Brötchen

baptism ['bæptɪzəm] N Taufe *f*; **~ of fire** *(fig)* Feuertaufe *f*

baptismal [bæp'tɪzməl] ADJ Tauf-; **~ name** Taufname *m*

Baptist ['bæptɪst] N Baptist(in) *m(f)*; **the ~ Church** *(= people)* die Baptistengemeinde; *(= teaching)* der Baptismus

baptize [bæp'taɪz] VT taufen

bar¹ [bɑːʳ] **N** **a** *(of metal, wood)* Stange *f*; *(of toffee etc)* Riegel *m*; *(of electric fire)* Element *nt*; **~ of gold** Goldbarren *m*; **a ~ of chocolate, a chocolate ~** *(= slab)* eine Tafel Schokolade; *(Mars® bar etc)* ein Schokoladenriegel *m*; **a ~ of soap** ein Stück *nt* Seife; **a two-~ electric fire** ein Heizgerät *nt* mit zwei Heizstäben

b *(of window, grate, cage)* (Gitter)stab *m*; *(of door)* Stange *f*; **the window has ~s** das Fenster ist vergittert; **behind ~s** hinter Gittern; **to put sb behind ~s** jdn hinter Gitter or hinter Schloss und Riegel bringen

c *(Sport) (horizontal)* Reck *nt*; *(for high jump etc)* Latte *f*; *(= one of parallel bars)* Holm *m*; **~s** *pl (parallel)* Barren *m*; **(wall) ~s** Sprossenwand *f*; **to exercise on the ~s** am Barren turnen

d *(Ballet)* Stange *f*; **at the ~** an der Stange

e *(Comput)* Leiste *f*

f *(fig: = obstacle)* Hindernis *nt* *(to* für), Hemmnis *nt* *(to* für); **to be a ~ to sth** einer Sache *(dat)* im Wege stehen

g *(of colour)* Streifen *m*; *(of light)* Strahl *m*, Streifen *m*

h *(Jur)* **the Bar** die Anwaltschaft; **to be a member of the Bar** Anwalt vor Gericht sein; **to be called** or *(US)* **admitted to the Bar** als Anwalt (vor Gericht) or Verteidiger zugelassen werden; **to read for the Bar** Jura studieren; **at the ~ of public opinion** *(fig)* vor dem Forum der Öffentlichkeit

i *(for prisoners)* Anklagebank *f*; **to stand at the ~** auf der Anklagebank sitzen; **prisoner at the ~** „Angeklagter!"

j *(for drinks)* Lokal *nt*; *(esp expensive)* Bar *f*; *(part of pub)* Gaststube *f*; *(= counter)* Theke *f*, Tresen *m*; *(at railway station)* Ausschank *m*; **we're going to hit the ~s** *(Brit inf)* **we're going to the ~s** *(US inf)* wir machen eine Kneipentour, wir machen die Kneipen unsicher *(inf)*

k *(Mus)* Takt *m*; *(= bar line)* Taktstrich *m*

l *(Brit: on medal)* **DSO and ~** *zweimal verliehener DSO*

m *(Her)* Balken *m*

n *(Met)* Bar *nt*

o *(in river, harbour)* Barre *f*

VT **a** *(= obstruct) road* blockieren, versperren; **to ~ sb's way** jdm den Weg versperren or verstellen; **to ~ the way to progress** dem Fortschritt im Wege stehen

b *(= fasten) window, door* versperren; **to ~ the door against sb** jdm die Tür versperren

c *(= exclude, prohibit) person, possibility* ausschließen; *action, thing* untersagen, verbieten; **to ~ sb from a competition** jdn von (der Teilnahme an) einem Wettbewerb ausschließen; **to ~ sb from a career** jdm eine Karriere unmöglich machen; **they've been ~red (from the club)** sie haben Klubverbot; **minors are ~red from this club** Minderjährige haben keinen Zutritt zu diesem Klub

bar² PREP **~ none** ohne Ausnahme, ausnahmslos; **~ one** außer einem

barb [bɑːb] **N** **a** *(of hook, arrow)* Widerhaken *m*; *(of barbed wire)* Stachel *m*, Spitze *f*; *(of feather)* Fahne *f*; *(Bot, Zool)* Bart *m* **b** *(fig: of wit etc)* Spitze *f*; *(liter, of remorse)* Stachel *m* **VT** *(lit)* mit Widerhaken versehen

Barbados [bɑː'beɪdɒs] N Barbados *nt*

barbarian [bɑː'beərɪən] **N** *(Hist, fig)* Barbar(in) *m(f)* **ADJ** *(Hist, fig)* barbarisch

barbaric [bɑː'bærɪk] ADJ barbarisch; *guard etc* grausam, roh; *(fig inf) conditions* grauenhaft

barbarically [bɑː'bærɪkəlɪ] ADV barbarisch

barbarism ['bɑːbərɪzəm] N **a** *(Hist, fig)* Barbarei *f* **b** *(Ling)* Barbarismus *m*

barbarity [bɑː'bærɪtɪ] N Barbarei *f*; *(fig)* Primitivität *f*; *(= cruelty: of guard etc)* Grausamkeit *f*, Rohheit *f*; **the barbarities of modern warfare** die Barbarei or die Gräuel *pl* des modernen Krieges

barbarous ['bɑːbərəs] ADJ *(Hist, fig)* barbarisch; *(= cruel)* grausam; *guard etc* roh; *accent* grauenhaft

barbarously ['bɑːbərəslɪ] ADV *(= cruelly)* grausam; *speak also* grauenhaft *(inf)*

Barbary ['bɑːbərɪ] N Berberei *f*

Barbary *in cpds* Berber-; **Barbary ape** N Berberaffe *m*; **Barbary Coast** N Barbareskenküste *f*; **Barbary States** PL Barbareskenstaaten *pl*

barbecue ['bɑːbɪkjuː] **N** **a** *(Cook: = grid)* Grill *m* **b** *(= occasion)* Grillparty *f*, Barbecue *nt* **c** *(= meat)* Grillfleisch *nt*/-wurst *f etc* **VT** *steak etc* grillen, auf dem Rost braten; *animal* am Spieß braten

barbed [bɑːbd] ADJ **a** *arrow* mit Widerhaken **b** *(fig) wit* beißend; *remark* spitz, bissig

barbed: **barbed wire** N Stacheldraht *m*; **barbed-wire fence** N Stacheldrahtzaun *m*

barbel ['bɑːbəl] N *(fish)* Barbe *f*; *(= filament on fish)* Bartel *f*, Bartfaden *m*

barbell [bɑː'bel] N Hantel *f*

barber ['bɑːbəʳ] N (Herren)friseur *m*, Barbier *m* *(old)*; **the ~'s** der Friseur(laden), das (Herren)friseurgeschäft; **at/to the ~'s** beim/zum Friseur

barbershop ['bɑːbəʃɒp] **N** *(US)* (Herren)friseurgeschäft *nt* or -laden *m* **ADJ** **~ quartet** Barbershop-Quartett *nt*

barber's pole [,bɑːbəz'pəʊl] N *Ladenzeichen der Friseure: Stange mit rot-weißer Spirale*

barbican ['bɑːbɪkən] N Außen- or Vorwerk *nt*; *(= tower)* Wachtturm *m*

barbie ['bɑːbɪ] N *(esp Austral inf)* → **barbecue N b**

Barbie (doll)® ['bɑːbɪ(,dɒl)] N Barbie-Puppe® *f*

bar billiards N *(esp Brit) eine Art Billard, das in Pubs gespielt wird*

barbitone ['bɑːbɪtəʊn] N *(Med)* barbiturathaltiges Mittel

barbiturate [bɑː'bɪtjʊrɪt] N Schlafmittel *nt*, Barbiturat *nt*; **a ~ overdose** eine Überdosis an Schlafmitteln

barbs [bɑːbz] PL *(inf) abbr of* **barbiturates**

bar: **bar chart** N Balkendiagramm *nt*, Säulendiagramm *nt*; **bar code** N Strichkode *m*, Bar-Code *m*; **bar-coded** ADJ mit Strichkodierung; **bar code reader** N Strichkodeleser *m*

bard [bɑːd] N **a** *(= minstrel) (esp Celtic)* Barde *m*; *(in Ancient Greece)* (Helden)sänger *m* **b** *(old Liter, hum: = poet)* Barde *m*, Bardin *f*; **the Bard of Avon** Shakespeare

bardic ['bɑːdɪk] ADJ *poetry etc* bardisch

bare [beəʳ] **ADJ** (+er) **a** *(= naked, uncovered) skin, boards, floor* nackt, bloß; *summit, tree, countryside* kahl, nackt; *earth, rock* nackt; *room, garden* leer; *sword* blank; *wire* blank; *style* nüchtern; **he stood there ~ to the waist** er stand mit nacktem Oberkörper da; **~ patch** kahle Stelle; **to sleep on ~ boards** auf blanken Brettern schlafen; **to lay ~ one's heart** sein Innerstes bloßlegen; **the ~ facts** die nackten Tatsachen; **the ~ fact that he ...** allein die Tatsache, dass er ...; **with his ~ hands** mit bloßen Händen; **she told him the ~ bones of the story** sie erzählte ihm die Geschichte in groben Zügen

b *(= scanty, mere)* knapp; **a ~ majority** eine knappe Mehrheit; **a ~ subsistence wage** gerade das Existenzminimum; **a ~ ten centimetres** *(Brit)* or **centimeters** *(US)* knappe or kaum zehn Zentimeter; **with just the ~st hint of garlic** nur mit einer winzigen Spur Knoblauch; **the ~ minimum** das absolute Minimum

VT *breast, leg* entblößen; *(at doctor's)* frei machen; *teeth (in anger)* fletschen; *end of a wire* freilegen; **she ~d her teeth in a forced smile** sie grinste gezwungen; **to ~ one's head** den Hut *etc* ziehen, das Haupt entblößen *(liter)*; **to ~ one's soul** seine Seele entblößen; **to ~ one's heart to sb** jdm sein Herz ausschütten

bare: **bareback** ADV, ADJ ohne Sattel; **a ~ rider** ein Reiter, der/eine Reiterin, die ohne Sattel reitet; **barefaced** ADJ *(fig: = shameless) liar* unverfroren, unverschämt, schamlos; *cheek* unverschämt; **it is ~ robbery** das ist der reine Wucher *(inf)*; **barefoot** **ADV** barfuß **ADJ** barfüßig, barfuß *pred*; **barefooted** **ADJ** barfüßig, barfuß *pred* **ADV** barfuß; **bareheaded** **ADJ** barhäuptig *(geh)*, ohne Kopfbedeckung **ADV** ohne Kopfbedeckung, barhaupt *(geh)*; **barelegged** ADJ mit bloßen Beinen

barely ['beəlɪ] ADV **a** *(= scarcely)* kaum; *(with figures)* knapp, kaum; **we ~ know him** wir kennen ihn kaum; **~ had he started when ...** kaum hatte er angefangen, als ...; **~ concealed horror** kaum verhohlenes Entsetzen; **she was ~ ten years old** sie war kaum or knapp zehn Jahre alt **b** *furnished* dürftig, spärlich

bareness ['beənɪs] N Nacktheit *f*; *(of person also)* Blöße *f*; *(of trees, countryside)* Kahlheit *f*; *(of room, garden)* Leere *f*; *(of style)* Nüchternheit *f*

Barents Sea ['bærənts'siː] N Barentssee *f*

barf [bɑːf] *(esp US inf)* **VI** kotzen *(inf)* **N** Kotze *f* *(inf)*

barf bag N *(esp US inf: Aviat)* Kotztüte *f (inf)*, Spucktüte *f*

barfly ['bɑːflaɪ] N *(inf)* Kneipenhocker(in) *m(f)* *(inf)*

bargain ['bɑːgɪn] **N** **a** *(= transaction)* Handel *m*, Geschäft *nt*; **to make** or **strike a ~** sich einigen; **they are not prepared to make a ~** sie wollen nicht mit sich handeln lassen; **I'll make a ~ with you, if you ...** ich mache Ihnen ein Angebot, wenn Sie ...; **to keep one's side of the ~** sich an die Abmachung halten; **it's a ~!** abgemacht!, einverstanden!; **you drive a hard ~** Sie stellen ja harte Forderungen!; **to offer sb a good ~** jdm ein gutes Angebot machen; **then it started raining into the ~** *(Brit)* or **in the ~** *(US)* dann hat es (obendrein) auch noch angefan-

gen zu regnen; **and she was rich into the ~** *(Brit)* or **in the ~** *(US)* und außerdem war sie reich; **to get the worst/best of the ~** den schlechteren/besseren Teil erwischen
b *(= cheap offer)* günstiges Angebot, Sonderangebot *nt*; *(= thing bought)* Gelegenheitskauf *m*; **this jacket is a good ~** diese Jacke ist wirklich günstig; **a great ~** ein echtes Schnäppchen *(inf)*; **what a ~!** das ist aber günstig!
VI handeln *(for* um); *(in negotiations)* verhandeln; **the traders are not prepared to ~** die Ladenbesitzer lassen nicht mit sich handeln

▶ **bargain away** VT *sep rights, advantage etc* sich *(dat)* abhandeln lassen; *freedom, independence also* veräußern

▶ **bargain for** VI *+prep obj (inf: = expect)* rechnen mit, erwarten; **I hadn't bargained for that** damit hatte ich nicht gerechnet; **I got more than I bargained for** ich habe vielleicht mein blaues Wunder erlebt! *(inf)*; *(in argument also)* ich habe vielleicht eins draufbekommen! *(inf)*

▶ **bargain on** VI *+prep obj* zählen auf *(+acc)*, sich verlassen auf *(+acc)*

bargain: **bargain basement** N *Untergeschoss eines Kaufhauses mit Sonderangeboten*; **bargain buy** N Preisschlager *m (inf)*; **that's a real ~** das ist wirklich günstig; **bargain counter** N Sonder(angebots)tisch *m*

bargainer [ˈbɑːgɪnəʳ] N **to be a good/bad ~** handeln/nicht handeln können; *(in negotiations)* gut/nicht gut verhandeln können; **to be a hard ~** hart handeln or *(in negotiations)* verhandeln

bargain: **bargain hunter** N Schnäppchenjäger(in) *pl (inf)*; **the ~s** Leute *pl* auf der Jagd nach Sonderangeboten; **bargain-hunting** N Jagd *f* nach Sonderangeboten; **to go ~** auf Schnäppchenjagd gehen *(inf)*

bargaining [ˈbɑːgɪnɪŋ] N Handeln *nt*; *(= negotiating)* Verhandeln *nt*; **~ position** Verhandlungsposition *f*; **~ table** Verhandlungstisch *m*

bargain: **bargain offer** N Sonderangebot *nt*, günstiges Angebot; **bargain price** N Sonderpreis *m*; **at a ~** zum Sonderpreis; **bargain rates** PL Sonderpreise *pl*; **bargain sale** N Ausverkauf *m*

barge [bɑːdʒ] **N** **a** *(for freight)* Last- or Frachtkahn *m*; *(unpowered)* Schleppkahn *m*; *(= lighter)* Leichter *m*; *(= ship's boat)* Barkasse *f*; *(= houseboat)* Hausboot *nt*; **the Royal/state ~** die königliche Barkasse/die Staatsbarkasse; *(unpowered)* das königliche Boot/das Staatsboot
b *(= shove)* Stoß *m*, Rempler *m (inf)*
VT **a** **he ~d me out of the way** er hat mich weggestoßen; **he ~d his way into the room** er ist (ins Zimmer) hereingeplatzt *(inf)*; **he ~d his way through the crowd** er hat sich durch die Menge geboxt *(inf)*
b *(Sport)* rempeln; **he ~d him off the ball** er hat ihn vom Ball weggestoßen
VI **a** **to ~ into a room** (in ein Zimmer) herein-/hineinplatzen *(inf)*; **to ~ out of a room** aus einem Zimmer heraus-/hinausstürmen; **he ~d through the crowd** er drängte or boxte *(inf)* sich durch die Menge
b *(Sport)* rempeln

▶ **barge about** *(Brit)* or **around** VI *(inf)* herumpoltern *(inf)*

▶ **barge in** VI *(inf)* **a** *(= enter suddenly)* hinein-/hereinplatzen *(inf)* or -stürzen **b** *(= interrupt)* dazwischenplatzen *(inf)* (on bei); *(= interfere also)* sich einmischen (on in *+acc)*

▶ **barge into** VI *+prep obj* **a** *(= knock against) person* (hinein)rennen in *(+acc) (inf)*; *(= shove)* (an)rempeln; *thing* rennen gegen *(inf)* **b** *(inf) room, party, conversation* (hinein-/herein)platzen in *(+acc) (inf)*

bargee [bɑːˈdʒiː] N Lastschiffer *m*; *(= master)* Kahnführer *m*

bargepole [ˈbɑːdʒpəʊl] N Bootsstange *f*; **I wouldn't touch it/him with a ~** *(Brit inf)* von so etwas/so jemandem lasse ich die Finger *(inf)*; *(out of disgust, distaste)* das/den würde ich noch nicht mal mit der Kneifzange anfassen *(inf)*

bar graph N Balkendiagramm *nt*

bar hopping N *(esp US inf)* Kneipentouren *pl (inf)*; **we're going ~** wir machen eine Kneipentour *(inf)*, wir machen die Kneipen unsicher *(inf)*

baritone [ˈbærɪtəʊn] **N** Bariton *m* **ADJ** Bariton-

barium [ˈbɛərɪəm] N Barium *nt*

barium meal N Bariumbrei *m*

bark[1] [bɑːk] **N** *(of tree)* Rinde *f*, Borke *f*; **to strip the ~ from** or **off a tree** einen Baumstamm schälen **VT** *(= rub off) skin* aufschürfen; *(= knock against)* anstoßen, anschlagen; **to ~ one's shin against the table** sich *(dat)* das Schienbein am Tisch anschlagen

bark[2] **N** *(of dog, seal, gun, cough)* Bellen *nt*; **his ~ is worse than his bite** *(Prov)* Hunde, die bellen, beißen nicht *(Prov)* **VI** bellen; **to ~ at sb** jdn anbellen; *(person also)* jdn anfahren; **to be ~ing up the wrong tree** *(fig inf)* auf dem Holzweg sein *(inf)*

▶ **bark out** VT *sep orders* bellen

bark[3], **barque** N **a** *(poet)* Barke *f (liter)* **b** *(Naut)* Bark *f*

barkeep(er) [ˈbɑːkiːp(əʳ)] N *(US)* Barbesitzer(in) *m(f)*, Gastwirt *m*; *(= bartender)* Barkeeper *m*, Barmann *m*

barker [ˈbɑːkəʳ] N *(outside shop, club)* Anreißer *m (inf)*; *(at fair)* Marktschreier *m (inf)*

barking (mad) [ˈbɑːkɪŋ(ˈmæd)] ADJ *(inf)* total verrückt or übergeschnappt *(inf)*, völlig durchgeknallt *(sl)*

barley [ˈbɑːlɪ] N Gerste *f*

barley: **barleycorn** N Gerstenkorn *nt* → **John**; **barley sugar** N Gersten- or Malzzucker *m*; *(sweet) hartes Zuckerbonbon*; **barley water** N *Art Gerstenextrakt*; **lemon/orange ~** konzentriertes Zitronen-/Orangegetränk; **barley wine** N *(Brit) Art Starkbier*

bar line N *(Mus)* Taktstrich *m*

barm [bɑːm] N (Bier)hefe *f*, Bärme *f*

bar: **barmaid** N Bardame *f*; **barman** N Barkeeper *m*, Barmann *m*

Bar Mitzvah [bɑːˈmɪtsvə] N *(= ceremony)* Bar Mizwa *nt*; *(= boy) Junge, der Bar Mizwa feiert*

barmy [ˈbɑːmɪ] ADJ *(+er) (Brit inf)* bekloppt *(inf)*; *idea etc* blödsinnig *(inf)*

barn [bɑːn] N **a** Scheune *f*, Scheuer *f*; *(in field)* Schober *m (S Ger, Aus)*; **a great ~ of a house** eine große Scheune *(inf)* **b** *(US, for streetcars, trucks)* Depot *nt*, Hof *m*

barnacle [ˈbɑːnəkl] N **a** *(= shellfish)* (Rankenfuß)krebs *m*, Rankenfüßer *m* **b** *(fig, = person)* Klette *f (inf)*

barnacle goose N Nonnengans *f*

barn dance N Bauerntanz *m*

barn door N Scheunentor *nt*; **(as) big as a ~** *(inf)* nicht zu verfehlen

barney [ˈbɑːnɪ] N *(esp Brit inf: = noisy quarrel)* Krach *m (inf)*; *(= punch-up)* Schlägerei *f*, Keilerei *f (inf)*

barn: **barn owl** N Schleiereule *f*; **barnstorm** VI *(esp US Theat)* in der Provinz spielen; *(Pol)* in der Provinz Wahlreden halten; **barnstormer** N *(US Pol)* Wahlredner(in) *m(f)* in der Provinz; *(Theat)* Wanderschauspieler(in) *m(f)*; **barnstorming** ADJ *(Brit) performance* hinreißend; **barnyard** N (Bauern)hof *m*; **~ fowl(s)** *pl* (Haus)geflügel *nt*

barometer [bəˈrɒmɪtəʳ] N *(lit, fig)* Barometer *nt*

barometric [ˌbærəʊˈmetrɪk] ADJ barometrisch, Barometer-

barometric pressure N Atmosphären- or Luftdruck *m*

baron [ˈbærən] N **a** Baron *m* **b** *(fig)* Baron *m*, Magnat *m*; **industrial ~** Industriebaron *m*; **oil ~** Ölmagnat *m*; **press ~** Pressezar *m* **c** *(of beef)* doppeltes Lendenstück

baroness [ˈbærənɪs] N Baronin *f*; *(unmarried)* Baronesse *f*

baronet [ˈbærənɪt] N Baronet *m*

baronetcy [ˈbærənɪtsɪ] N *(= rank)* Baronetstand *m*; *(= title)* Baronetswürde *f*

baronial [bəˈrəʊnɪəl] ADJ *(lit)* Barons-; *(fig)* fürstlich, feudal

barony [ˈbærənɪ] N Baronie *f*

baroque [bəˈrɒk] **ADJ** barock, Barock- **N** *(= style)* Barock *m or nt*; **the ~ period** das or der Barock, die Barockzeit

barouche [bəˈruːʃ] N Landauer *m*

barque [bɑːk] N = **bark[3]**

barrack[1] [ˈbærək] VT *soldiers* kasernieren

barrack[2] **VT** *actor etc* auspfeifen, auszischen **VI** pfeifen, zischen

barracking[1] [ˈbærəkɪŋ] N *(Mil)* Kasernierung *f*

barracking[2] N Pfeifen *nt*, Zischen *nt*, Buhrufe *pl*; **to get a ~** ausgepfiffen werden

barrack-room [ˈbærəkˌruːm] ADJ *attr* rau, roh; **~ language** Landsersprache *f*

barrack-room lawyer N *(pej)* Paragrafenreiter *m (inf)*

barracks [ˈbærəks] **PL** *(often with sing vb, Mil)* Kaserne *f*; *(fig pej also)* Mietskaserne *f*; **to live in ~** in der Kaserne wohnen **ATTR** **~ life** Kasernenleben *nt*; **barrack(s) square** Kasernenhof *m*

barracuda [ˌbærəˈkjuːdə] N Barrakuda *m*, Pfeilhecht *m*

barrage [ˈbærɑːʒ] N **a** *(across river)* Wehr *nt*; *(larger)* Staustufe *f* **b** *(Mil)* Sperrfeuer *nt*; **under this ~ of stones ...** unter diesem Steinhagel ...; **they kept up a ~ of stones** sie bedeckten die Polizei/uns *etc* mit einem Steinhagel **c** *(fig, of words, questions etc)* Hagel *m*; **he faced a ~ of questions** er wurde mit Fragen beschossen

barrage balloon N Sperrballon *m*

barre [bɑːʳ] N *(Ballet)* Stange *f*; **at the ~** an der Stange

barred [bɑːd] ADJ **a** *suf* **five-~ gate** Weidengatter *nt* (mit fünf Querbalken) **b** **~ window** Gitterfenster *nt*

barrel [ˈbærəl] **N** **a** Fass *nt*; *(for oil, tar, rainwater etc)* Tonne *f*; *(= measure: of oil)* Barrel *nt*; **they've got us over a ~** *(inf)* sie haben uns in der Zange *(inf)*; **it wasn't exactly a ~ of laughs** *(inf)* es war nicht gerade komisch; **she wasn't exactly a ~ of laughs** *(inf)* sie war nicht gerade in bester Stimmung; **to pay cash on the ~** *(US)* bar auf den Tisch or die Kralle *(inf)* zahlen → **biscuit, scrape**
b *(of handgun)* Lauf *m*; *(of cannon etc)* Rohr *nt*; **to give sb both ~s** auf jdn aus beiden Läufen feuern; **I found myself looking down the ~ of a gun** ich hatte plötzlich eine Kanone vor der Nase *(sl)* → **lock[2]**
c *(of fountain pen)* Tank *m*
VT *wine etc* (in Fässer) (ab)füllen; *herring* (in Fässer) einlegen; **~led beer** Fassbier *nt*

▶ **barrel along** VI *(inf)* entlangbrausen *(inf)*

barrel: **barrel-chested** ADJ breitbrüstig, mit gewölbter Brust; **to be ~** einen gewölbten Brustkasten haben; **barrelful** N Fass *nt*; *(of oil)* Barrel *nt*; **barrelhead** N **to pay cash on the ~** *(US)* bar auf den Tisch or die Kralle *(inf)* zahlen; **barrelhouse** *(US)* **N** Kneipe *f*; *(= jazz)* Kneipenjazz *m* **ADJ** **~ blues** *alte, in Kneipen gespielte Form des Blues*; **barrel organ** N Drehorgel *f*, Leierkasten *m*; **barrel roll** N *(Aviat)* Rolle *f (im Kunstflug)*; **barrel-shaped** ADJ fass- or tonnenförmig; **~ man/woman** Fass *nt (inf)*/Tonne *f (inf)*; **barrel vault** N Tonnengewölbe *nt*

barren [ˈbærən] **ADJ** **a** unfruchtbar; *land also* karg **b** *(fig) years* unfruchtbar, unproduktiv; *discussion also* fruchtlos; *atmosphere also* steril; *style, subject* trocken; *topic* unergiebig; **the house looks ~ without any furniture** das Haus wirkt ohne Möbel leer; **a government ~ of new ideas** eine Regierung, der neue Ideen fehlen or die keinerlei neue Ideen hat **N** **barrens** **PL** *(esp US)* Ödland *nt*

barrenness [ˈbærənnɪs] N **a** Unfruchtbarkeit *f*; *(of land also)* Kargheit *f* **b** *(fig)* Unfruchtbarkeit *f*, Unproduktivität *f*; *(of discussion also)*

Fruchtlosigkeit *f*; *(of atmosphere also)* Sterilität *f*; *(of style, subject, study)* Trockenheit *f*; *(of topic)* Unergiebigkeit *f*

barrette [bəˈret] N *(US)* (Haar)spange *f*

barricade [ˌbærɪˈkeɪd] N Barrikade *f* VT verbarrikadieren

▸ **barricade in** VT *sep* verbarrikadieren

▸ **barricade off** VT *sep* (mit Barrikaden) absperren

barrier [ˈbærɪəʳ] N **a** *(natural)* Barriere *f*; *(man-made, erected also)* Sperre *f*; *(= railing etc)* Schranke *f*; *(= crash barrier)* (Leit)planke *f* **b** *(fig: = obstacle)* Hindernis *nt*, Barriere *f* *(to* für); *(of class, background, education, between people)* Schranke *f*, Barriere *f*; **trade ~s** Handelsschranken *pl*; **~ of language, language ~** Sprachbarriere *f*; **a ~ to success/progress** *etc* ein Hindernis für den Erfolg/Fortschritt *etc*; **because of the ~ of her shyness** aufgrund *or* auf Grund ihrer Schüchternheit, die ein Hemmnis ist/war *etc*; **to put up/break down ~s** Zäune errichten/niederreißen

barrier: **barrier contraceptive** N mechanisches Verhütungsmittel; **barrier-free** ADJ barrierefrei, ohne Hindernisse; **barrier cream** N Haut(schutz)creme *f*; **barrier reef** N Barriere-, Wallriff *nt*; **the Great Barrier Reef** das Große Barriereriff

barring [ˈbɑːrɪŋ] PREP **~ accidents** falls nichts passiert; **~ one** außer einem

barrister [ˈbærɪstəʳ] N *(Brit)* Rechtsanwalt *m*/-anwältin *f* (bei Gericht), Barrister *m*

barrow[1] [ˈbærəʊ] N Karre(n *m*) *f*; *(= wheel barrow)* Schubkarre(n *m*) *f*; *(Rail: = luggage barrow)* Gepäckkarre(n *m*) *f*; *(esp Brit: costermonger's)* (handgezogener) Obst-/Gemüse-/Fischkarren *etc m*

barrow[2] N *(Archeol)* Hügelgrab *nt*

barrow boy N Straßenhändler *m (mit Karren)*

bar sinister N *(Her)* Bastardfaden *m*

bar stool N Barhocker *m*

Bart. *abbr of* **baronet**

bartender [ˈbɑːtendəʳ] N *(US)* Barkeeper *m*; **~!** hallo!

barter [ˈbɑːtəʳ] VT tauschen *(for* gegen) VI tauschen; *(as general practice also)* Tauschhandel treiben; **to ~ for sth** um etw handeln; **to ~ for peace** über einen Frieden verhandeln N (Tausch)handel *m*

▸ **barter away** VT *sep one's rights* verspielen; **to barter sth away for sth** etw für etw verschachern

barter: **barter economy** N Tauschwirtschaft *f*; **barter exchange** N Tauschbörse *f*; **barter society** N Tauschgesellschaft *f*

basal [ˈbeɪsl] ADJ **a** *(lit, fig)* Grund-, fundamental **b** *(Med)*

basal metabolism N Grundumsatz *m*

basalt [ˈbæsɔːlt] N Basalt *m*

bascule [ˈbæskjuːl] N Brückenklappe *f*; **~ bridge** Klappbrücke *f*

base[1] [beɪs] N **a** *(= lowest part)* Basis *f*; *(= that on which sth stands also)* Unterlage *f*; *(Archit, of column also)* Fuß *m*; *(= support for statue etc)* Sockel *m*; *(of lamp, tree, mountain)* Fuß *m*; *(= undercoat also)* Grundierung *f*; **at the ~ (of)** unten (an *+dat*)

b *(= main ingredient)* Basis *f*, Haupt- *or* Grundbestandteil *m*

c *(of theory)* Basis *f*; *(= starting point also)* Ausgangspunkt *m*; *(= foundation also)* Grundlage *f*

d *(Mil etc, fig, for holidays, climbing etc)* Standort *m*, Stützpunkt *m*; **to return to ~** zur Basis *or* zum Stützpunkt zurückkehren; **~ of operations** Operationsbasis *f*

e *(Baseball)* Mal *nt*, Base *nt*; **at** *or* **on second ~** auf Mal *or* Base 2, auf dem zweiten Mal *or* Base; **to get to first ~** *(fig)* die ersten Erfolge erzielen; **to touch ~** *(US inf)* sich melden *(with* bei); **to touch** *or* **cover all the ~s** *(US fig)* an alles denken

f *(Gram)* Wortstamm *m*, Wortwurzel *f*

g *(Math)* Basis *f*, Grundzahl *f*

h *(Chem)* Lauge *f*, Base *f*

i *(Geometry)* Basis *f*; *(of plane figure also)* Grundlinie *f*; *(of solid also)* Grundfläche *f*

VT **a** *(lit)* stellen; **to be ~d on** ruhen auf *(+dat)*; *(statue)* stehen auf *(+dat)*; **the supports are firmly ~d in concrete** die Stützen sind fest in Beton eingelassen; **you need something to ~ it on** Sie brauchen dafür eine feste *or* stabile Unterlage

b *(fig) opinion, theory* gründen, basieren *(on* auf *+acc)*; *hopes, theory also* setzen *(on* auf *+acc)*; *relationship also* bauen *(on* auf *+acc)*; **to be ~d on sb/sth** auf jdm/etw basieren; *(hopes, theory also)* sich auf jdn/etw stützen; **to ~ one's technique on sb/sth** in seiner Technik von jdm/etw ausgehen; **he tried to ~ his life on this theory** er versuchte, nach dieser Theorie zu leben

c *(Mil)* stationieren; **the company is ~d in London** die Firma hat ihren Sitz in London; **my job is ~d in Glasgow** ich arbeite in Glasgow; **I am ~d in Glasgow but cover all of Scotland** mein Büro ist in Glasgow, aber ich bereise ganz Schottland; **basing country** *(Mil)* Stationierungsland *nt*

base[2] ADJ *(+er)* **a** *motive, character* niedrig; *person, thoughts, action, lie, slander* gemein, niederträchtig **b** *(= inferior) task, level* niedrig; *coin* falsch, unecht; *metal* unedel **c** *(obs) birth (= low)* niedrig *(old)*; *(= illegitimate)* unehelich

baseball [ˈbeɪsbɔːl] N Baseball *m or nt*

> **BASEBALL**
>
> **Baseball** ist ein amerikanischer Nationalsport. Zwei Teams mit neun Spielern spielen auf einem Spielfeld mit vier Markierungen, die als Male **(bases)** bezeichnet werden und in Form einer Raute angeordnet sind. Ein Mitglied des schlagenden Teams **(batter)** versucht, den Ball, der vom Werfer **(pitcher)** geworfen wurde, außerhalb der Reichweite der Fänger **(fielders)** zu schlagen, damit er von Mal zu Mal laufend wieder zu dem Punkt zurückkehren kann, von dem aus er geschlagen hat.
>
> Es gibt zwei wichtige Baseball-Ligen in den USA: die National League und die American League. Die jeweiligen Gewinner beider Ligen spielen dann in mehreren Begegnungen gegeneinander, die als **World Series** bekannt sind.
>
> Einige Aspekte des Spiels, wie z. B. Kameradschaft und Wettbewerb, werden in Filmen häufig als Metaphern für den American Way of Life benutzt. **Baseball** hat nicht nur die beliebte Baseballmütze in den Alltag eingebracht, sondern hat auch die englische Sprache um eine Reihe von Redewendungen bereichert, wie „a ballpark figure" (eine Richtzahl), „a whole new ballgame" (eine ganz andere Chose) und „to get to first base" (die ersten Erfolge erzielen)

baseball cap N Baseballmütze *f*

baseboard [ˈbeɪsbɔːd] N *(US)* Fußleiste *f*, Lambrie *f (S Ger)*

base camp N Basislager *nt*, Versorgungslager *nt*

-based [-beɪst] ADJ *suf* **London-based** mit Sitz in London; **to be computer-based** auf Computerbasis arbeiten

base: **base form** N *(Ling)* Stammform *f*; **base hit** N *(Baseball) Treffer, durch den der Schlagmann sicher das Mal erreichen kann*; **base jumping** N Basejumping *nt*

baseless [ˈbeɪslɪs] ADJ *accusations etc* ohne Grundlage, aus der Luft gegriffen; *fears, suspicion also* unbegründet, grundlos

baseline [ˈbeɪslaɪn] N *(Baseball) Verbindungslinie zwischen zwei Malen (Surv)* Basis *f*, Grundlinie *f*; *(of a diagram, Tennis)* Grundlinie *f*; *(Art)* Schnittlinie *f* von Grundebene und Bildebene

base load N *(Elec)* Grundlast *f*, Grundbelastung *f*

basely [ˈbeɪslɪ] ADV gemein, niederträchtig; *act also* niedrig

baseman [ˈbeɪsmən] N *pl* **-men** [-mən] *(Baseball)* Spieler *m* an einem Mal

basement [ˈbeɪsmənt] N **a** *(in building)* Untergeschoss *nt*, Untergeschoß *nt (Aus)*, Souterrain *nt*; *(in house also)* Keller *m*, Kellergeschoss *nt*, Kellergeschoß *nt (Aus)*; **~ flat** *(Brit) or* **apartment** Souterrainwohnung *f* **b** *(Archit, = foundations)* Fundament *nt*

base metal N unedles Metall

baseness [ˈbeɪsnɪs] N **a** *(of motive, character)* Niedrigkeit *f*; *(of person, thoughts, action, lie, slander)* Gemeinheit *f*, Niederträchtigkeit *f* **b** *(of task)* Niedrigkeit *f*; *(of coin)* Falschheit *f* **c** *(obs: of birth) (= humbleness)* Niedrigkeit *f (old)*; *(= illegitimacy)* Unehelichkeit *f*

base: **base price** N Grundpreis *m*; **base rate** N Leitzins *m*; **base unit** N *(Phys)* Grundeinheit *f*; **base wallah** N *(Mil sl)* Etappenhengst *m (Mil sl)*

bash [bæʃ] *(inf)* N **a** Schlag *m*; **to give sb a ~ on the nose** jdm (eine) auf die Nase hauen *(inf)*; **he gave himself a ~ on the shin** er hat sich *(dat)* das Schienbein angeschlagen; **the door has had a ~** die Tür hat eine Delle abgekriegt *(inf)*

b I'll have a ~ (at it) ich probiers mal *(inf)*; **have a ~** probier mal! *(inf)*

c *(dated inf, = party)* Party *f*

VT *person* (ver)hauen *(inf)*, verprügeln; *ball* knallen *(inf)*, dreschen *(inf)*; *car, wing* eindellen *(inf)*; **to ~ one's head/shin (against** *or* **on sth)** sich *(dat)* den Kopf/das Schienbein (an etw *(dat)*) anschlagen; **I ~ed my shin against the table** ich bin mit dem Schienbein gegen den Tisch geknallt *(inf)*; **to ~ sb on** *or* **over the head with sth** jdm mit etw auf den Kopf hauen

▸ **bash about** VT *sep (esp Brit inf) person* durchprügeln *(inf)*, verdreschen *(inf)*; *objects* demolieren *(inf)*; **he/his luggage got rather bashed about in the accident** er/sein Gepäck ist bei dem Unfall ziemlich lädiert worden *(inf)*

▸ **bash down** VT *sep (inf) door* einschlagen

▸ **bash in** VT *sep (inf) door* einschlagen; *hat, car* eindellen *(inf)*; **to bash sb's head in** jdm den Schädel einschlagen *(inf)*

▸ **bash up** VT *sep (esp Brit inf) person* vermöbeln *(inf)*, verkloppen *(inf)*; *car* demolieren *(inf)*, kaputt fahren *(inf)*

-basher [-bæʃəʳ] *suf (inf)* **Paki-/queer-basher** Pakistaner-/Schwulenklatscher(in) *m(f) (inf)*

bashful [ˈbæʃfʊl] ADJ, **bashfully** [ˈbæʃfəlɪ] ADV schüchtern; *(on particular occasion)* verlegen; **give us a song! ah, he's ~** sing was! ach, er geniert sich!

bashfulness [ˈbæʃfʊlnɪs] N Schüchternheit *f*; *(on particular occasion)* Verlegenheit *f*

bashing [ˈbæʃɪŋ] N *(inf)* Prügel *pl*; **he got a nasty ~** er hat ganz schön was abgekriegt *(inf)*

-bashing *suf (inf)* **Paki-/queer-bashing** *(physical)* Überfälle *pl* auf Pakistaner/Schwule, Pakistaner-/Schwulenklatschen *nt (inf)*; **Tory-bashing** *(verbal)* das Schlechtmachen *or* Heruntermachen *(inf)* der Konservativen → **Bible-bashing**

Basic [ˈbeɪsɪk] *(Comput) abbr of* **beginner's all-purpose symbolic instruction code** BASIC *nt*

basic [ˈbeɪsɪk] ADJ **a** *(= fundamental)* Grund-; *problem also, reason, issue* Haupt-; *points, issues* wesentlich; *(= rudimentary) knowledge, necessities, equipment also* elementar; *character, intention, purpose also* eigentlich; *incompatibility, misconception, indifference, problem* grundsätzlich; **to be ~ to sth** Voraussetzung sein für etw; **there's no ~ difference** es besteht kein grundlegender Unterschied; **he has a ~ mistrust of women** er misstraut Frauen grundsätzlich; **a certain ~ innocence** eine gewisse elementare Unschuld; **he is, in a very ~ sense, …** er ist, im wahrsten Sinne des Wortes, …; **the ~ thing to remember is …** woran man vor allem denken muss, ist …;

must you be so ~! müssen Sie sich denn so direkt ausdrücken?; **his knowledge is rather ~** er hat nur ziemlich elementare Kenntnisse; **the furniture is rather ~** die Möbel sind ziemlich primitiv; **the room is rather ~** es ist ein recht einfaches Zimmer; **you should know that, that's ~** das müssten Sie aber wissen, das ist doch elementar; **this is ~ to the whole subject** das liegt dem Fach zugrunde *or* zu Grunde; **~ salary/working hours** Grundgehalt *nt*/-arbeitszeit *f*; **the four ~ operations** *(Math)* die vier Grundrechenarten; **~ vocabulary** Grundwortschatz *m*
b *(= original)* zugrunde *or* zu Grunde liegend; *theory also, assumption* ursprünglich
c *(= essential)* notwendig; **knowledge of French is/good boots are absolutely ~** Französischkenntnisse/gute Stiefel sind unbedingt nötig *or* sind eine Voraussetzung
d *(Chem)* basisch
PL **the ~s** das Wesentliche; **to get down to (the) ~s** zum Kern der Sache *or* zum Wesentlichen kommen; **to get back to ~s** sich auf das Wesentliche besinnen

basically ['beɪsɪkəlɪ] ✪ 26.3 ADV im Grunde; *(= mainly)* im wesentlichen, hauptsächlich; **is that correct? – ~ yes** stimmt das? – im Prinzip, ja *or* im Grunde schon; **it's ~ finished** es ist praktisch *or* im Grunde fertig; **that's ~ it** das wärs im Wesentlichen

basic: **basic English** N englischer Grundwortschatz, Basic English *nt*; **basic food** N, **basic foodstuffs** PL Grundnahrungsmittel *pl*; **basic industry** N Schlüsselindustrie *f*; **basic rate** N *(of wage)* Grundgehalt *nt*; *(of tax)* Eingangssteuersatz *m*; **the ~ of income tax** der Eingangssteuersatz bei Lohn- und Einkommensteuer; **basic salary** N Grundgehalt *nt*, Fixum *nt*; **basic slag** *(Chem)* N Thomasschlacke *f*; **basic wage** N *usu pl* Grundlohn *m*

basil ['bæzl] N *(Bot)* Basilikum *nt*, Basilienkraut *nt*

basilica [bə'zɪlɪkə] N Basilika *f*

basilisk ['bæzɪlɪsk] N *(Myth, Zool)* Basilisk *m*

basin ['beɪsn] N **a** *(= vessel)* Schüssel *f*; *(= wash basin)* (Wasch)becken *nt*; *(of fountain)* Becken *nt* **b** *(Geog)* Becken *nt*; *(= harbour basin)* Hafenbecken *nt*; *(= yacht basin)* Jachthafen *m*; *(= hollow between mountains also)* Kessel *m*

basinful ['beɪsnfʊl] N Schüssel *f* (voll)

basis ['beɪsɪs] N *pl* **bases** **a** *(of food, mixture etc)* Basis *f*, Grundlage *f* **b** *(fig: = foundation)* Basis *f*; *(for assumption)* Grund *m*; **we're working on the ~ that ...** wir gehen von der Annahme aus, dass ...; **to be on a sound ~** *(business)* auf festen Füßen stehen; *(theory)* auf einer soliden Basis ruhen; **to put sth on a sounder ~** einer Sache *(dat)* eine solidere Basis geben, etw auf eine solidere Basis stellen; **on the ~ of this evidence** aufgrund dieses Beweismaterials; **to approach a problem on a scientific ~** an ein Problem wissenschaftlich herangehen

basis point N *(Fin)* Basispunkt *m*

bask [bɑːsk] VI *(in sun)* sich aalen *(in* in *+dat)*; *(in sb's favour etc)* sich sonnen *(in* in *+dat)*

basket ['bɑːskɪt] N **a** Korb *m*; *(for rolls, fruit etc)* Körbchen *nt*; **a ~ of eggs** ein Korb/Körbchen (voll) Eier; **a ~ of currencies** ein Währungskorb *m* **b** *(Basketball)* Korb *m* **c** *(euph sl, = bastard)* Idiot *m*, Blödmann *m (inf)*

basket: **basketball** N Basketball *m*; **basket case** N *(sl)* hoffnungsloser Fall; **basket chair** N Korbsessel *m*; **basket clause** N *(Jur)* Generalklausel *f*; **basketful** ['bɑːskɪtfʊl] ADJ **a ~ of food** ein Korb voll(er) Essen; **basket-maker** N Korbmacher(in) *m(f)*, Korbflechter(in) *m(f)*

basketry ['bɑːskɪtrɪ] N Korbflechterei *f*

basket: **basket weave** N Leinenbindung *f*; **basketwork** N Korbflechterei *f*; *(= articles)* Korbarbeiten *pl*; **a ~ chair** ein Korbstuhl *m*

basking shark ['bɑːskɪŋʃɑːk] N Riesenhai *m*

Basle [bɑːl] N Basel *nt*

Basque [bæsk] **N** **a** *(= person)* Baske *m*, Baskin *f* **b** *(= language)* Baskisch *nt* **ADJ** baskisch

basque [bæsk] N Bustier *nt*

bas-relief ['bæsrɪ,liːf] N Basrelief *nt*

bass[1] [beɪs] *(Mus)* **N** Bass *m* **ADJ** Bass-

bass[2] [bæs] N *pl* **-(es)** *(= fish)* (Wolfs)barsch *m*

bass [beɪs]: **bass clef** N Bassschlüssel *m*; **bass drum** N große Trommel

basset hound ['bæsɪthaʊnd] N Basset *m*

bassinet [,bæsɪ'net] N Babykorb *m*; *(old: = pram)* Kinderwagen *m*

bassoon [bə'suːn] N Fagott *nt*

bassoonist [bə'suːnɪst] N Fagottbläser(in) *m(f)*, Fagottist(in) *m(f)*

basso profundo [,bæsəʊprə'fʊndəʊ] N tiefer Bass

bass viol [beɪs-] N Gambe *f*

bastard ['bɑːstəd] **N** **a** *(lit)* uneheliches Kind, Bastard *m (old)*; *(fig: = hybrid)* Bastard *m*, Kreuzung *f* **b** *(sl: = person)* Scheißkerl *m (inf)*; **stupid ~** Arschloch *nt (vulg)*; **poor ~** armes Schwein *(inf)*, armer Hund *(inf)* **c** *(sl: = difficult job etc)* **this question is a real ~** diese Frage ist wirklich hundsgemein *(inf)*; **a ~ of a job** *etc* eine Scheißarbeit *etc (inf)* **ADJ** **a** *(lit) child* unehelich **b** *(fig: = hybrid) dog, plant* Bastard-; *language* Misch-

bastard file N *(Tech)* Bastardfeile *f*

bastardize ['bɑːstədaɪz] VT *(fig)* verfälschen

bastard title N *(Typ)* Schmutztitel *m*

bastardy ['bɑːstədɪ] N *(form)* Unehelichkeit *f*; **~ proceedings** *pl (US Jur)* Vaterschaftsprozess *m*

baste[1] [beɪst] VT *(Sew)* heften

baste[2] VT *(Cook)* (mit Fett) beträufeln *or* begießen

basting[1] ['beɪstɪŋ] N *(Sew: = act)* Heften *nt*; *(= stitches)* Heftnaht *f*; **to take out the ~** die Heftfäden herausziehen

basting[2] N *(inf: = beating)* Prügel *pl*; **to give sb a ~** *(team, critics)* jdn fertigmachen *(inf)*

bastion ['bæstɪən] N *(lit, fig)* Bastion *f*; *(= person)* Stütze *f*, Säule *f*

bat[1] [bæt] N *(Zool)* Fledermaus *f*; **to have ~s in the belfry** *(inf)* eine Meise *or* einen Sparren haben *(inf)*; **he ran/drove like a ~ out of hell** er lief/fuhr, wie wenn der Teufel hinter ihm her wäre; **(as) blind as a ~** stockblind *(inf)*; **silly old ~** *(pej inf)* alte Schrulle *(pej inf)*

bat[2] *(Sport)* **N** **a** *(Baseball, Cricket)* Schlagholz *nt*, Keule *f*; *(Table-tennis)* Schläger *m*; **off one's own ~** *(Brit inf)* auf eigene Faust *(inf)*; **right off the ~** *(US)* prompt **b** *(= batsman)* **he is a good ~** er schlägt gut **c** *(inf, = blow)* Schlag *m* **VT** *(Baseball, Cricket)* schlagen; **to ~ sth around** *(US inf: = discuss)* etw bekakeln *(inf)* **VI** *(Baseball, Cricket)* schlagen; **to go (in) to ~ for sb** *(fig)* sich für jdn einsetzen

bat[3] VT **not to ~ an eyelid** *(Brit) or* **eye** *(US)* nicht mal mit der Wimper zucken

bat[4] N **a** *(dated Brit, inf, = speed)* **at a fair old ~** mit 'nem ganz schönen Zahn drauf *(inf)* **b** *(US sl: = binge)* Sauftour *f (inf)*; **to go on a ~** auf Sauftour gehen *(inf)*

batch [bætʃ] N *(of people)* Schwung *m (inf)*; *(of loaves)* Schub *m*; *(of prisoners, recruits also)* Trupp *m*; *(of things dispatched also)* Sendung *f*, Ladung *f*; *(of letters, books, work also)* Stoß *m*, Stapel *m*; *(of dough, concrete etc)* Ladung *f*

batch *(Comput)*: **batch command** N Batchbefehl *m*; **batch file** N Stapeldatei *f*, Batchdatei *f*; **batch job** N Stapelverarbeitung *f*; **batch processing** N Stapelverarbeitung *f*, Batchbetrieb *m*

bated ['beɪtɪd] ADJ **with ~ breath** mit angehaltenem Atem

bath [bɑːθ] **N** **a** Bad *nt*; **to have** *or* **take a ~** baden, ein Bad nehmen *(geh)*; **to give sb a ~** jdn baden → **blood bath, Turkish** *etc*
b *(= bathtub)* (Bade)wanne *f*; **to empty the ~** das Badewasser ablassen; **I was just in my** *or* **the ~** ich war *or* saß gerade im Bad *or* in der Wanne *(inf)*; **a room with ~** ein Zimmer mit Bad → **eyebath, foot bath** *etc*
c **~s** *pl (Hist)* Bäder *pl*, Badeanlagen *pl*; **(swimming) ~s** *pl* (Schwimm)bad *nt*; **(public) ~s** *pl* Badeanstalt *f*, öffentliches Bad
d *(Tech, Chem, Phot)* Bad *nt*; *(= container)* Behälter *m*
e *(Brit)* **the Order of the Bath** der Orden vom Bade
VT *(Brit)* baden
VI *(Brit)* (sich) baden

bath bun N *Hefebrötchen mit Zitronat und Orangeat*

Bath chair N Kranken- *or* Rollstuhl *m*

bath cube N Würfel *m* Badesalz

bathe [beɪð] **VT** **a** *person, feet, eyes, wound etc* baden; *(with cotton wool etc)* waschen; **to ~ one's eyes** ein Augenbad machen; **~d in tears** tränenüberströmt; **to be ~d in light** in Licht gebadet sein; **to be ~d in sweat** in Schweiß gebadet sein, schweißgebadet sein **b** *(US)* = **bath VT** **VI** baden **N** Bad *nt*; **to have** *or* **take a ~** baden

bather ['beɪðə'] N Badende(r) *mf*

bathhouse ['bɑːθhaʊs] N *(old)* Bad(e)haus *nt (old)*

bathing ['beɪðɪŋ] N Baden *nt*

bathing: **bathing beach** N Badestrand *m*; **bathing beauty** N Badeschönheit *f*; **bathing belle** N Badeschönheit *f*; **bathing cap** N Bademütze *f*, Badekappe *f*; **bathing costume** N Badeanzug *m*; **bathing hut** N Badehäuschen *nt*; **bathing machine** N transportable Umkleidekabine; **bathing suit** N *(dated esp US)* = **bathing costume**; **bathing trunks** PL Badehose *f*; **bathing waters** PL Badegewässer *pl*

bathmat ['bɑːθmæt] N Badematte *f or* -vorleger *m*

bathos ['beɪθɒs] N *(= anticlimax)* Abfall *or* Umschlag *m* ins Lächerliche; *(= sentimentality)* falsches Pathos

bathrobe ['bɑːθrəʊb] N Bademantel *m*

bathroom ['bɑːθruːm] N Bad(ezimmer) *nt*; *(euph: = lavatory)* Toilette *f*

bathroom: **bathroom cabinet** N Toilettenschrank *m*; **bathroom fittings** PL Badezimmerausstattung *f*; **bathroom scales** PL Personenwaage *f*

bath: **bath salts** PL Badesalz *nt*; **bath sheet** N großes Badetuch; **bathtowel** N Badetuch *nt*; **bathtub** N Badewanne *f*

bathysphere ['bæθɪsfɪə'] N Tauchkugel *f*, Bathysphäre *f*

batik ['bætɪk] N Batik *m*; *(= cloth)* Batikdruck *m*

batiste [bæ'tiːst] N Batist *m*

batman ['bætmən] N *pl* **-men** [-mən] *(Mil)* (Offiziers)bursche *m*

baton ['bætən, *(US)* bæ'tɒn] N **a** *(Mus)* Taktstock *m*, Stab *m*; *(Mil)* (Kommando)stab *m*; **under the ~ of** *(Mus)* unter der Stabführung von **b** *(of policeman)* Schlagstock *m*; *(for directing traffic)* Stab *m* **c** *(in relay race)* Staffelholz *nt*, Stab *m*; **to hand on** *or* **pass the ~ to sb** *(fig)* die Verantwortung an jdn abgeben

baton: **baton charge** N Schlagstockeinsatz *m*; **to make a ~** Schlagstöcke einsetzen; **baton round** N *(Mil)* Plastikgeschosse *pl*; **baton twirler** N Tambourmajor(in) *m(f)*

bats [bæts] ADJ *pred (inf)* bekloppt *(inf)*; **you must be ~** du spinnst wohl! *(inf)*

batsman ['bætsmən] N *pl* **-men** [-mən] *(Sport)* Schlagmann *m*

battalion [bə'tælɪən] N *(Mil, fig)* Bataillon *nt*

batten ['bætn] **N** **a** Leiste *f*, Latte *f*; *(for roofing)* Dachlatte *f*; *(for flooring)* (Trag)latte *f* **b** *(Naut, for sail)* Segellatte *f*; *(for hatch)* Schalklatte *f* **VT** **a** *roof, floor* mit Latten versehen **b** *(Naut) sail* mit Latten verstärken; *hatch* (ver-)schalken

▶ **batten down** VT *sep* **to batten down the hatches** die Luken schalken *(spec) or* dicht machen; (*fig*: = *close doors, windows*) alles dicht machen; (= *prepare oneself*) sich auf etwas gefasst machen

▶ **batten on** VI +*prep obj* schmarotzen bei

▶ **batten onto** VI +*prep obj idea* sich (*dat*) aneignen

batter[1] [ˈbætəˈ] N (*Cook, for frying*) (Ausback)teig *m*; (*for pancakes, waffles etc*) Teig *m*

batter[2] N (*Sport*) Schlagmann *m*

batter[3] VT **a** (= *hit*) einschlagen auf (+*acc*); (= *strike repeatedly*) *wife, baby* schlagen, (ver)prügeln; (*with battering ram*) berennen; **he ~ed him about the head with an iron bar** er schlug mit einer Eisenstange auf seinen Kopf ein; **the ship was ~ed by the waves** die Wellen krachten unentwegt gegen das Schiff; **the house was ~ed by the wind** der Wind rüttelte unentwegt am Haus
b (= *damage*) böse *or* übel zurichten; *car also, metal* zer- *or* verbeulen; **the town was badly ~ed during the war** die Stadt wurde während des Krieges schwer zerbombt
c (*inf*) *opponent* eins *or* eine draufgeben (+*dat*) (*inf*); **to get ~ed** eins *or* eine draufbekommen (*inf*)
VI schlagen, trommeln (*inf*); **to ~ at the door** an die Tür hämmern *or* trommeln (*inf*)

▶ **batter about** VT *sep* (*esp Brit*) *sb* schlagen, verprügeln; *sth* grob umgehen mit, ramponieren (*inf*)

▶ **batter down** VT *sep wall* zertrümmern; *door also* einschlagen; *resistance* zerschlagen

▶ **batter in** VT *sep door* einschlagen; (*with ram*) einrennen

battered [ˈbætəd] ADJ böse *or* übel zugerichtet, lädiert (*inf*); *wife, baby* misshandelt; *hat, car, teapot also* verbeult; *city* zerbombt; *house, furniture* mitgenommen, ramponiert (*inf*); *nerves* zerrüttet; *image, reputation* ramponiert (*inf*); **~ baby syndrome** Phänomen *nt* der Kindesmisshandlung

batterer [ˈbætərəˈ] N **wife-~** prügelnder Ehemann; **child-~** prügelnder Vater, prügelnde Mutter; **treatment programmes for ~s** Behandlungsprogramme für prügelnde Ehepartner und Eltern

battering [ˈbætərɪŋ] N (*lit*) Schläge *pl*, Prügel *pl*; (*of baby, wife*) Misshandlung *f*; **he/it got** *or* **took a real ~** er/es hat ganz schön was abgekriegt (*inf*), es hat schwer gelitten; **to give sb a ~** jdn verprügeln; **to give sth a ~** etw ramponieren (*inf*) *or* demolieren (*inf*); **he'll give his opponent a ~** er wird es seinem Gegner geben (*inf*)

battering ram N Rammbock *m*, Sturmbock *m*

battery [ˈbætərɪ] N (*all senses*) Batterie *f*; (*fig, of arguments etc*) Reihe *f* → **assault**

battery: **battery acid** N Batteriesäure *f*; **battery charger** N Ladegerät *nt*; **battery compartment** N Batteriefach *nt*; **battery farm** N Legebatterie *f*; **battery farming** N Massentierhaltung; (*of chickens*) Legebatterien *pl*; **battery fire** N (*Mil*) Geschützfeuer *nt*; **battery hen** N (*Agr*) Batteriehuhn *nt*; **battery meter** N (*Comput etc*) Energieanzeige *f*; **battery-powered** ADJ batteriebetrieben; **battery set** N (= *radio*) Batteriegerät *nt*

battle [ˈbætl] N (*lit*) Schlacht *f*; (*fig*) Kampf *m*; **to give/offer/refuse ~** sich zum Kampf *or* zur Schlacht stellen/bereit erklären/den Kampf *or* die Schlacht verweigern; **to fight a ~** eine Schlacht schlagen (*also fig*), einen Kampf führen; **I don't need you to fight my ~s for me** ich kann mich schon alleine durchsetzen; **to do ~ for sb/sth** sich für jdn/etw schlagen, sich für jdn/etw einsetzen; **to win the ~ but lose the war** (*fig*) die Schlacht gewinnen, aber den Krieg verlieren; **killed in ~** (im Kampf) gefallen; **~ of wits** Machtkampf *m*; **~ of words** Wortgefecht *nt*; **~ of wills** geistiger Wettstreit; **to have a ~ of wits** sich geistig messen; **we are fighting the same ~** wir ziehen am selben Strang; **that's half the ~** damit ist schon viel gewonnen; **getting an interview is only half the ~** damit, dass man ein Interview bekommt, ist es noch nicht getan; **~ of the giants** Kampf *m* der Giganten; **~ of the sexes** Geschlechterkampf *m*
VI sich schlagen; (*fig also*) kämpfen, streiten; **to ~ for breath** um Atem ringen; **to ~ through a book** *etc* sich durch ein Buch *etc* (durch)kämpfen
VT (*fig*) **to ~ one's way through difficulties/four qualifying matches** sich (durch Schwierigkeiten)/durch vier Qualifikationsspiele durchschlagen

▶ **battle on** VI (*fig*) weiterkämpfen

▶ **battle out** VT *sep* **to battle it out** sich einen harten Kampf liefern

battle: **battle-axe**, (*US*) **battle-ax** N (= *weapon*) Streitaxt *f*; (*inf*: = *woman*) Drachen *m* (*inf*); **battle cruiser** N Schlachtkreuzer *m*; **battle cry** N Schlachtruf *m*

battledore [ˈbætldɔːˈ] N (Federball)schläger *m*; **~ and shuttlecock** Federball *m*

battle: **battledress** N Kampfanzug *m*; **battle fatigue** N Kriegsmüdigkeit *f*; **battlefield** N Schlachtfeld *nt*; **battle fleet** N Schlachtflotte *f*; **battleground** N Schlachtfeld *nt*; **battle lines** PL Kampflinien *pl*; **the ~ are drawn** (*fig*) die Fronten sind abgesteckt

battlements [ˈbætlmənts] PL Zinnen *pl*

battle: **battle order** N Schlachtordnung *f*; **battle plan** N (*lit, fig*) Schlachtplan *m*; **battle royal** N (*fig*: = *quarrel*) heftige Auseinandersetzung; **battle-scarred** ADJ (*lit*) *person, country* vom Krieg gezeichnet; (*fig*) *furniture* schwer mitgenommen, ramponiert (*inf*); (*inf*) *person* schwer mitgenommen, angeschlagen; **battleship** N Kriegs- *or* Schlachtschiff *nt*; **~s** (= *game*) Schiffeversenken *nt*; **battle song** N Kampf- *or* Kriegslied *nt*; **battle zone** N Kriegs- *or* Kampfgebiet *nt*

batty [ˈbætɪ] ADJ (+*er*) (*Brit inf*) verrückt; *person also* plemplem *pred* (*inf*); **to go ~** überschnappen (*inf*)

bauble [ˈbɔːbl] N Flitter *m no pl*; **~s** Flitterzeug *nt*

baud [bɔːd] N (*Comput*) Baud *nt*; **at 1200 ~** bei 1200 Baud; **~ rate** Baudrate *f*

baulk [bɔːk] N = **balk**

bauxite [ˈbɔːksaɪt] N Bauxit *m*

Bavaria [bəˈvɛərɪə] N Bayern *nt*

Bavarian [bəˈvɛərɪən] N **a** (= *person*) Bayer(in) *m(f)* **b** (= *dialect*) Bayrisch *nt* ADJ bay(e)risch

bawd [bɔːd] N (= *brothel keeper*) Bordellwirtin *f*, Puffmutter *f* (*inf*)

bawdiness [ˈbɔːdɪnɪs] N Derbheit *f*

bawdy [ˈbɔːdɪ] ADJ (+*er*) derb; **~ talk** derbes Gerede

bawl [bɔːl] VI **a** (= *shout*) brüllen, schreien; (= *sing*) grölen (*inf*); **to ~ for help** um Hilfe schreien **b** (*inf*: = *weep*) plärren (*inf*), heulen (*inf*)
VT *order* brüllen, schreien; *song* grölen (*pej inf*)

▶ **bawl out** VT *sep* **a** *order* brüllen; *song* schmettern, grölen (*pej inf*) **b** (*inf*: = *scold*) ausschimpfen

bawling-out [ˈbɔːlɪŋˈaʊt] N (*inf*) Schimpfkanonade *f* (*inf*); **to give sb a ~** jdn zur Schnecke machen (*inf*)

bay[1] [beɪ] N Bucht *f*; (*of sea also*) Bai *f*; **Hudson Bay** die Hudsonbai

bay[2] N (*Bot*) Lorbeer(baum) *m*

bay[3] N **a** (*Archit*) Erker *m* **b** (= *loading bay*) Ladeplatz *m*; (= *parking bay*) Parkbucht *f*; (*Rail*) Abstellgleis *nt* **c** (*Aviat*: = *bomb bay*) Bombenschacht *m* **d** (= *sick bay*) (Kranken)revier *nt*

bay[4] N (*of dogs*) Bellen *nt no pl*; (*Hunt*) Melden *nt no pl*; **to bring to/be at ~** (*fig*) in die Enge treiben/getrieben sein; **to have sb at ~** (*fig*) jdn in der Zange haben (*inf*); **to keep** *or* **hold sb/sth at ~** jdn/etw in Schach halten VI bellen; (*Hunt also*) melden; **to ~ at the moon** den Mond anbellen *or* anheulen; **to ~ for blood** Vergeltung fordern; **to ~ for sb's blood** jds Kopf fordern

bay[5] ADJ *horse* (kastanien)braun N (= *horse*) Braune(r) *m*; **red ~** rötlicher Brauner

bay leaf N Lorbeerblatt *nt*

bayonet [ˈbeɪənɪt] N Bajonett *nt*, Seitengewehr *nt*; **with ~s fixed/at the ready** mit aufgepflanzten/gefällten Bajonetten VT mit dem Bajonett *or* Seitengewehr aufspießen

bayonet fitting N (*Elec*) Bajonettfassung *f*

bayou [ˈbaɪuː] N (*US, of river*) sumpfiger Flussarm; (*of lake*) sumpfiger Ausfluss (*aus einem See*)

bay: **bay rum** N Pimentöl *nt*; **bay tree** N Lorbeerbaum *m*; **bay window** N Erkerfenster *nt*

bazaar [bəˈzɑːˈ] N Basar *m*

bazooka [bəˈzuːkə] N Bazooka *f*, Panzerfaust *f*, Panzerschreck *m*

BB N (*Brit*) *abbr of* **Boys' Brigade** ADJ (*on pencil*) 2B

BBC *abbr of* **British Broadcasting Corporation** BBC *f*

BBFC *abbr of* **British Board of Film Classification**

BBQ *abbr of* **barbecue**

BBS (*Comput*) *abbr of* **bulletin board system** BBS *nt*

BC[1] *abbr of* **before Christ** v. Chr

BC[2] *abbr of* **British Columbia**

BCG *abbr of* **Bacille Calmette Guérin** BCG

BD *abbr of* **Bachelor of Divinity**

be [biː]
pres **am, is, are**, *pret* **was, were**, *ptp* **been**

1 COPULATIVE VERB	3 INTRANSITIVE VERB
2 AUXILIARY VERB	4 IMPERSONAL VERB

1 – COPULATIVE VERB

a [with adjective, noun, pronoun] sein; **to be critical of** kritisch sein *or* sich kritisch äußern über (+*acc*); **be sensible!** sei vernünftig; **who's that? – it's me/that's Mary** wer ist das? – ich bins/das ist Mary; **if I were you** wenn ich Sie *or* an Ihrer Stelle wäre; **he is a soldier/a German** er ist Soldat/Deutscher; **he wants to be a doctor** er möchte Arzt werden

Note that the article is used in German only when the noun is qualified by an adjective.

he's a good student/a true Englishman er ist ein guter Student/ein echter Engländer

b [referring to physical, mental state] **how are you?** wie gehts?; **I'm better now** es geht mir jetzt besser; **she's not at all well** es geht ihr gar nicht gut; **to be hungry/thirsty** Hunger/Durst haben, hungrig/durstig sein; **I am hot/cold/frozen** mir ist heiß/kalt/eiskalt; **they were horrified** sie waren entsetzt

c [age] sein; **he's five** er ist fünf; **how old is she?** wie alt ist sie?; **he'll be three next month** er wird nächsten Monat drei (Jahre alt)

d [= cost] kosten; **how much is that?** wie viel *or* was kostet das?

e [Math] sein; **two times two is** *or* **are four** zwei mal zwei ist *or* sind *or* gibt vier

f [with possessive] gehören (+*dat*); **that book is your brother's/his** das Buch gehört Ihrem Bruder/ihm, das ist das Buch Ihres Bruders/das ist sein Buch

g [in exclamations] **was he pleased to hear it!** er war vielleicht froh, das zu hören!; **but wasn't she glad when ...** hat sie sich vielleicht gefreut, als ...

h [Brit] *inf* **how are you for a beer?** hast du Lust auf ein Bier?

2 – AUXILIARY VERB

a [in continuous tenses]

Note how German uses the simple tense:

what are you doing? was machst du da?; **she's always complaining** sie beklagt sich dauernd; **they're coming tomorrow** sie kommen morgen

Note how German uses the present tense:

I have been waiting for you for half an hour ich warte schon seit einer halben Stunde auf Sie; **will you be seeing her tomorrow?** sehen *or* treffen Sie sie morgen?; **you will be hearing from us** Sie hören von uns, Sie werden von uns hören

Note the use of bei + infinitive:

we're just drinking coffee wir sind (gerade) beim Kaffeetrinken; **I've just been packing my case** ich war gerade beim Kofferpacken; **I was packing my case when …** ich war gerade beim Kofferpacken, als …

b in passive constructions werden; **he was run over** er ist überfahren worden, er wurde überfahren; **the box had been opened** die Schachtel war geöffnet worden; **it is/was being repaired** es wird/wurde gerade repariert; **I will not be intimidated** ich lasse mich nicht einschüchtern

♦ **to be/not to be …**

intention **they are shortly to be married** sie werden bald heiraten; **they were to have been married last week** sie hätten letzte Woche heiraten sollen; **the car is to be sold** das Auto soll verkauft werden; **she was to be/was to have been dismissed but …** sie sollte entlassen werden, aber …/sie hätte entlassen werden sollen, aber …

= ought to be **he is to be pitied/not to be envied** er ist zu bedauern/nicht zu beneiden; **not to be confused with** nicht zu verwechseln mit; **what is to be done?** was ist zu tun?, was soll geschehen?

obligation, command **I am to look after her** ich soll mich um sie kümmern; **I am not to be disturbed** ich möchte nicht gestört werden; **he is not to open it** er soll es nicht öffnen; **I wasn't to tell you his name** ich sollte dir nicht sagen, wie er heißt; *(but I did)* ich hätte Ihnen eigentlich nicht sagen sollen *or* dürfen, wie er heißt

= be destined **she was never to return** sie sollte nie zurückkehren

possibility **he was not to be persuaded** er war nicht zu überreden, er ließ sich nicht überreden; **if it were** *or* **was to snow** falls *or* wenn es schneien sollte; **and were I** *or* **if I were to tell him?** und wenn ich es ihm sagen würde?

c in tag questions/short answers **he's always late, isn't he? – yes he is** er kommt doch immer zu spät, nicht? – ja, das stimmt; **he's never late, is he? – yes he is** er kommt nie zu spät, oder? – oh, doch; **you're not ill, are you? – yes I am/no I'm not** Sie sind doch nicht (etwa) krank? – doch!/nein; **it's all done, is it? – yes it is/no it isn't** es ist also alles erledigt? – ja/nein

3 – INTRANSITIVE VERB

a sein; *(= remain)* bleiben; **I'm going to Berlin – how long will you be there?** ich gehe nach Berlin – wie lange wirst du dort bleiben?; **he is there at the moment but he won't be much longer** im Augenblick ist er dort, aber nicht mehr lange; **we've been here a long time** wir sind schon lange hier; **the powers that be** die zuständigen Stellen; **let me/him be** lass mich/ihn (in Ruhe); **be that as it may** wie dem auch sei; **to be or not to be** Sein oder Nichtsein

b = be situated sein; *(town, forest, papers)* liegen, sein; *(car, tower, chair)* stehen, sein

c = visit, call **I've been to Paris** ich war schon (ein)mal in Paris; **the milkman has already been** der Milchmann war schon da; **he has been and gone** er war da und ist wieder gegangen; **now you've been and done it** *(inf)* jetzt hast du aber was angerichtet! *(inf)*; **I've just been and (gone and) broken it!** jetzt hab ichs tatsächlich kaputt gemacht *(inf)*

d = like to have **who's for coffee/tee/biscuits?** wer möchte (gerne)Kaffee/Tee/Kekse?

♦ **here/there is… here is a book/are two books** hier ist ein Buch/sind zwei Bücher; **here/there you are** *(= you've arrived)* da sind Sie ja; *(= take this)* hier/da, bitte; *(= here/there it is)* hier/da ist es/sind sie doch; **there he was sitting at the table** da saß er nun am Tisch; **nearby there are two churches** in der Nähe sind *or* stehen zwei Kirchen

4 – IMPERSONAL VERB

sein; **it is dark/morning** es ist dunkel/Morgen; **tomorrow is Friday/the 14th of June** morgen ist Freitag/der 14. Juni, morgen haben wir Freitag/den 14. Juni; **it is 5 km to the nearest town** es sind 5 km bis zur nächsten Stadt

♦ **it was us/you** *etc* **who… it was us** *or* **we** *(form)* **who found it** WIR haben das gefunden, wir waren diejenigen, die das gefunden haben; **it was me** *or* **I** *(form)* **who said it first** ICH habe es zuerst gesagt, ich war derjenige, der es zuerst gesagt hat

♦ **were it not … were it not for the fact that I am a teacher, I would …** wenn ich kein Lehrer wäre, dann würde ich …; **were it not for my friendship with him** wenn ich nicht mit ihm befreundet wäre; **were it not for him, if it weren't** *or* **wasn't for him** wenn er nicht wäre; **and even if it were not so** und selbst wenn das *or* dem nicht so wäre

♦ **had it not been for… had it not been** *or* **if it hadn't been for him** wenn er nicht gewesen wäre

B/E *abbr of* **bill of exchange**

beach [biːtʃ] **N** Strand *m*; **on the ~** am Strand **VT** *boat* auf Strand setzen

beach: **beach ball N** Wasserball *m*; **beach buggy N** Strandbuggy *m*; **beach chair N** Liegestuhl *m*; **beachcomber N** Strandgutsammler *m*; *(living rough)* am Strand lebender Einsiedler; **beachhead N** *(Mil)* Landkopf *m*; **beach hut N** Strandhäuschen *nt*; **beach towel N** Strandlaken *or* -tuch*nt*; **beach umbrella N** Sonnenschirm *m*; **beach volleyball N** Beachvolleyball *m*; **beachwear N** Badesachen *pl*, Badezeug *nt (inf)*; *(Fashion)* Strandmode *f*

beacon [ˈbiːkən] **N** *(= fire, light)* Leuchtfeuer *nt*; *(= radio beacon)* Funkfeuer *nt*; *(= one of a series of lights, radio beacons)* Bake *f*

bead [biːd] **N a** Perle *f*; **(string of) ~s** Perlenschnur *f*; *(= necklace)* Perlenkette *f*; **to tell one's ~s** den Rosenkranz beten **b** *(= drop: of dew, sweat)* Perle *f*, Tropfen *m* **c** *(of gun)* Korn *nt*; **to draw a ~ on sb** auf jdn zielen

beaded [ˈbiːdɪd] **ADJ** *(= decorated with pearls)* perlenverziert; **to be ~ with sweat** *(face, forehead)* schweißüberströmt sein

beading [ˈbiːdɪŋ] **N** Perlstab *m*, Perlschnur *f*

beadle [ˈbiːdl] **N** *(old Eccl)* Kirchendiener *m*; *(Univ) Angestellter, der bei Prozessionen den Amtsstab trägt*

beady [ˈbiːdɪ] **ADJ ~ eye** waches Auge; **I've got my ~ eye on you** *(inf)* ich beobachte Sie genau!

beagle [ˈbiːgl] **N** Beagle *m (englischer Spürhund)*

beak [biːk] **N a** *(of bird, turtle)* Schnabel *m* **b** *(inf, of person)* Zinken *m*, Rüssel *m (inf)* **c** *(Brit inf: = judge etc)* Kadi *m (inf)*; *(Brit, Sch sl)* (Di)rex *m (sl)*

beaker [ˈbiːkəʳ] **N** Becher *m*; *(Chem etc)* Becherglas *nt*

be-all and end-all [ˈbiːɔːləndˈendɔːl] **N the ~** das A und O; **it's not the ~** das ist auch nicht alles

beam [biːm] **N a** *(Build, of scales)* Balken *m* **b** *(of light etc)* Strahl *m*; **to drive on full** *or* **high ~** mit Fernlicht fahren; **to be on full** *or* **high ~** das Fernlicht eingeschaltet haben **c** *(= radio beam)* Leitstrahl *m*; **to be on/off ~** auf Kurs sein/vom Kurs abgekommen sein; *(fig inf) (person)* richtigliegen *(inf)*/danebenliegen *(inf)*; *(figures)* stimmen/nicht stimmen; **you're/your guess is way off ~** *(fig inf)* Sie haben total danebengehauen *(inf)*/danebengeraten **d** *(= smile)* Strahlen *nt*; **a ~ of delight** ein freudiges Strahlen **e** *(Naut, = side)* Seite *f*; *(= width)* Breite *f*; **on the ~** querschiffs; **on the port ~** backbords; **the ~ of a ship** die Schiffsbreite; **to be broad in the ~** *(ship)* sehr breit sein; *(person)* breit gebaut sein

VI a *(light)* strahlen; **to ~ down** *(sun)* niederstrahlen **b** *(fig, person, face)* strahlen; **she was ~ing with joy** sie strahlte übers ganze Gesicht

VT *(Rad, TV)* ausstrahlen, senden (*to* in, an +*acc*)

beam-ends [ˈbiːmˈendz] **PL to be on one's ~** *(Naut)* starke Schlagseite haben; *(Brit fig)* auf dem letzten Loch pfeifen *(inf)*

beamer [ˈbiːməʳ] **N** = **beemer**

beaming [ˈbiːmɪŋ] **ADJ** *sun* strahlend; *smile, face* (freude)strahlend

bean [biːn] **N a** Bohne *f*; **the proposals don't amount to a hill** *or* **row of ~s** *(inf)* die Vorschläge sind nicht überwältigend *(inf)*; **he hasn't (got) a ~** *(Brit inf)* er hat keinen roten *or* lumpigen Heller *(inf)*; **calm the ~s!** *(Brit inf: = calm down)* bleib locker! *(inf)*, komm runter! *(inf)* **b** *(fig)* **to be full of ~s** *(inf)* putzmunter sein *(inf)*

bean: **beanbag N a** *(= seat)* Sitzsack *m* **b** *(= toy) mit Bohnen gefülltes Säckchen, das zum Spielen verwendet wird*; **beanburger N** vegetarischer Hamburger *(mit Bohnen)*; **bean-counter N** *(pej inf)* Erbsenzähler(in) *m(f) (inf)*; **bean curd N** Tofu *nt*

beaner [ˈbiːnəʳ] **N** *(pej sl) Latino aus Kalifornien*

beanery [ˈbiːnərɪ] **N** *(US inf)* billiges Speiselokal

beanfeast [ˈbiːnfiːst] **N** *(inf)* Schmaus *m (inf)*

beano [ˈbiːnəʊ] **N** *(dated inf)* Schmaus *m (inf)*

bean: **beanpole N** *(lit, fig)* Bohnenstange *f*; **bean sprout N** Sojabohnensprosse *f*; **beanstalk N** Bohnenstängel *m*

bear[1] [bɛəʳ] ✪ 5.3 *pret* **bore**, *ptp* **borne VT a** *(= carry) burden, arms* tragen; *gift, message* bei sich tragen, mit sich führen; **to ~ away/back** mitnehmen/mit (sich) zurücknehmen; *(through the air)* fort- *or* wegtragen/zurücktragen; **the music was borne/borne away on the wind** *(liter)* die Musik wurde vom Wind weiter-/weggetragen; **he was borne along by the crowd** die Menge trug ihn mit (sich)

b *(= show) inscription, signature* tragen; *mark, traces also, likeness, relation* aufweisen, zeigen → **witness**

c *(= be known by) name, title* tragen, führen

d *(= have in heart or mind) love* empfinden, in sich *(dat)* tragen; *hatred, grudge also* hegen *(geh)*; **the love/hatred he bore her** die Liebe, die er für sie empfand/der Hass, den er gegen sie hegte *(geh) or* empfand → **mind**

e *(lit, fig: = support, sustain) weight, expense, responsibility* tragen; **to ~ examination/comparison** einer Prüfung/einem Vergleich standhalten; **it doesn't ~ thinking about** man darf gar nicht daran denken; **his language doesn't ~ repeating** seine Ausdrucksweise lässt sich nicht wiederholen

f *(= endure, tolerate)* ertragen; *(with neg also)* ausstehen, leiden; *pain* aushalten; *criticism, joking* vertragen; *smell, noise etc* aushalten, vertragen; **she can't ~ flying** sie kann einfach nicht fliegen; **she can't ~ doing nothing** sie kann einfach nicht untätig sein; **she can't ~ being laughed at** sie kann es nicht vertragen, wenn man über sie lacht; **could you ~ to stay a little longer?** können Sie es noch ein bisschen länger hier aushalten?

g *(= produce, yield fruit etc)* tragen → **interest**

h *(= give birth to)* gebären → **born**

VI a *(= move)* **to ~ right/left/north** sich rechts/links/nach Norden halten; **to ~ away** *or* **off** *(Naut)* abdrehen

b *(fruit tree etc)* tragen

c to bring one's energies/powers of persuasion to ~ seine Energie/Überzeugungskraft aufwenden (*on* für); **to bring one's mind to ~ on sth** seinen Verstand *or* Geist für etw anstrengen; **to bring pressure to ~ on sb/sth** Druck auf jdn/etw ausüben

VR sich halten; **he bore himself with dignity** er hat Würde gezeigt

▶ **bear down** VI **a** *(= approach quickly)* sich nahen *(geh)*; *(hawk etc)* herabstoßen; **to bear down on sb/sth** *(driver etc)* auf jdn/etw zuhalten **b** *(woman in labour)* drücken VT *sep* niederdrücken; **he was borne down by poverty** seine Armut lastete schwer auf ihm; **to be borne down by the weight of …** von der Last … *(gen)* gebeugt sein

▶ **bear in (up)on** VT *+prep obj* **to be borne in (up)on sb** jdm zu(m) Bewusstsein kommen

▶ **bear on** VI *+prep obj* = **bear (up)on**

▶ **bear out** VT *sep* bestätigen; **to bear sb out in sth** jdn in etw bestätigen; **you will bear me out that …** Sie werden bestätigen, dass …

▶ **bear up** VI sich halten; **he bore up well under the death of his father** er trug den Tod seines Vaters mit Fassung; **bear up!** Kopf hoch!; **how are you? – bearing up!** wie gehts? – man lebt!

▶ **bear (up)on** VI *+prep obj* **a** *(= relate to)* betreffen; **does this bear (up)on what you were saying?** hat das einen Bezug zu dem, was Sie sagten? **b** **to bear hard (up)on sb** sich hart auf jdn auswirken

▶ **bear with** VI *+prep obj* tolerieren; **if you would just bear with me for a couple of minutes** wenn Sie sich vielleicht zwei Minuten gedulden wollen

bear² N **a** Bär *m*; *(fig: = person)* Brummbär *m (inf)*; **he is like a ~ with a sore head** er ist ein richtiger Brummbär *(inf)* **b** *(Astron)* **the Great/Little Bear** der Große/Kleine Bär *or* Wagen **c** *(St Ex)* Baissespekulant *m*, Baissier *m* VI *(St Ex)* auf Baisse spekulieren

bearable [ˈbɛərəbl] ADJ erträglich, zum Aushalten

bear: **bear-baiting** N Bärenhatz *f*; **bear cub** N Bärenjunge(s) *nt*

beard [bɪəd] N **a** Bart *m*; *(full-face)* Vollbart *m*; **a man with a ~** ein Mann mit Bart; **a two-day** *or* **three-day ~** *(hum)* ein Dreitagebart *m (inf)*; **a week's (growth of) ~** ein eine Woche alter Bart; **small pointed ~** Spitzbart *m* **b** *(of goat, bird)* Bart *m*; *(of fish also)* Barthaare *pl*; *(of grain)* Grannen *pl* VT *(= confront)* ansprechen; **to ~ sb about sth** jdn auf etw *(acc)* hin ansprechen; **to ~ the lion in his den** *(Brit fig)* sich in die Höhle des Löwen wagen

bearded [ˈbɪədɪd] ADJ *man, animal, face* bärtig; **the ~ lady** die Dame mit dem Bart

beardless [ˈbɪədlɪs] ADJ bartlos; **~ youth** Milchbart *m (pej inf)*, Milchgesicht *nt (pej inf)*

bearer [ˈbɛərəʳ] N **a** *(= carrier)* Träger(in) *m(f)*; *(of news, letter, cheque, banknote)* Überbringer *m*; *(of name, title)* Träger(in) *m(f)*, Inhaber(in) *m(f)*; *(of passport)* Inhaber(in) *m(f)*; **~ bond** Inhaberschuldverschreibung *f*; **~ cheque, ~ check** *(US)* Inhaberscheck *m*; **~ securities** *pl* Inhaberpapiere *pl*; **~ share, ~ stock** *(US)* Inhaberaktie *f* **b** *(= tree etc)* **a good ~** ein Baum/Busch *etc*, der gut trägt

bear: **bear garden** N *(Brit)* Tollhaus *nt*; **bear hug** N ungestüme Umarmung; *(Wrestling)* Klammer *f*, Umklammerung *f*

bearing [ˈbɛərɪŋ] N **a** *(= posture)* Haltung *f*; *(= behaviour)* Verhalten *nt*, Auftreten *nt*, Gebaren *nt*
b *(= relevance, influence)* Auswirkung *f* (*on* auf *+acc*); *(= connection)* Bezug *m* (*on* zu); **to have some/no ~ on sth** von Belang/belanglos für etw sein; *(= be/not be connected with)* einen gewissen/keinen Bezug zu etw haben
c *(= endurance)* **to be beyond (all) ~** unerträglich *or* nicht zum Aushalten sein
d *(= direction)* **to take a ~** sich orientieren; **to get a ~ on sth** sich an etw *(dat)* orientieren; **to take a compass ~** den Kompasskurs feststellen; **to get** *or* **find one's ~s** sich zurechtfinden, sich orientieren; **to lose one's ~s** die Orientierung verlieren
e *(Tech)* Lager *nt*

bearish [ˈbɛərɪʃ] ADJ *(St Ex)* zur Baisse neigend *attr*; **to be ~ on sth** bei etw auf Baisse spekulieren

bear: **bear market** N *(St Ex)* Baisse *f*; **bear paw** N *(US inf: Mot)* Park-, Radkralle *f*; **bear-pit** N Bärengehege *nt*

bear's garlic [ˌbɛəzˈgɑːlɪk] N *(Bot)* Bärlauch *m*

bearskin [ˈbɛəskɪn] N *(Mil)* Bärenfellmütze *f*

beast [biːst] N **a** Tier *nt* **b** *(inf: = person)* Biest *nt*, Ekel *nt*; **don't be a ~!** sei nicht so eklig! *(inf)*; **that ~ of a brother-in-law** dieser fiese Schwager *(inf)*; **this (problem) is a ~, it's a ~ (of a problem)** das (Problem) hats in sich *(inf)*; **a good thriller is a rare ~ indeed** ein guter Krimi ist wirklich eine Seltenheit; **TV films are a different ~ (from movies)** Fernsehfilme sind etwas ganz anderes (als Kinofilme)

beastliness [ˈbiːstlɪnɪs] N *(inf)* Scheußlichkeit *f*, Garstigkeit *f*; *(of person, conduct also)* Gemeinheit *f*, Ekligkeit *f (inf)*

beastly [ˈbiːstlɪ] *(inf)* ADJ scheußlich, garstig *(inf)*; *person, conduct also* gemein, eklig *(inf)*; **what ~ weather** so ein Hundewetter; **it's a ~ business** das ist eine üble Angelegenheit; **what a ~ shame!** *(dated)* so ein Jammer! ADV *(dated)* scheußlich; **it's ~ difficult** es ist verteufelt schwierig *(inf)*

beat [biːt] VB *pret* **beat**, *ptp* **beaten**
N **a** *(of heart, pulse, drum, = single beat)* Schlag *m*; *(= repeated beating)* Schlagen *nt*; **the ~ of her heart grew weaker** ihr Herzschlag wurde schwächer; **to the ~ of the drum** zum Schlag der Trommeln; **he answered without missing a ~** er antwortete ohne sich aus der Ruhe *or* Fassung bringen zu lassen
b *(of policeman, sentry)* Runde *f*, Rundgang *m*; *(= district)* Revier *nt*; **to be on** *or* **to patrol the ~** seine Runde machen
c *(Mus, Poet)* Takt *m*; *(of metronome, baton)* Taktschlag *m*; **to have a heavy ~** einen ausgeprägten Rhythmus haben; **on/off the ~** auf dem betonten/unbetonten Taktteil
d *(= beat music)* Beat(musik *f*) *m*
e *(Hunt)* Treibjagd *f*
VT **a** *(= hit)* schlagen; *person, animal also* (ver)prügeln, hauen *(inf)*; *carpet* klopfen; *(= search) countryside, woods* absuchen, abkämmen; **the crocodile ~ the ground with its tail** das Krokodil schlug mit dem Schwanz auf den Boden; **to ~ a/one's way through sth** einen/sich *(dat)* einen Weg durch etw bahnen; **to ~ a path to sb's door** *(fig)* jdm die Bude einrennen *(inf)*; **to ~ a/the drum** trommeln, die Trommel schlagen; **to ~ the air** um sich schlagen, herumfuchteln; **to ~ one's breast** *(lit, fig)* sich *(dat)* an die Brust schlagen; *(ape)* sich *(dat)* gegen die Brust trommeln; **~ it!** *(fig inf)* hau ab! *(inf)*, verschwinde!
b *(= hammer) metal* hämmern; *(= shape also)* treiben; **to ~ sth flat** etw flach *or* platt hämmern
c *(= defeat)* schlagen; *record* brechen; *inflation* in den Griff bekommen; *disease* erfolgreich bekämpfen; **to ~ sb at chess/tennis** jdn im Schach/Tennis schlagen; **his shot/forehand ~ me** ich war dem Schuss/Vorhandschlag nicht gewachsen; **to ~ sb into second place** jdn auf den zweiten Platz verweisen; **you can't ~ these prices** diese Preise sind nicht zu unterbieten; **you can't ~ central heating/real wool** es geht doch nichts über Zentralheizung/reine Wolle; **he ~s the rest of them any day** er steckt sie alle (jederzeit) in die Tasche *(inf)*; **if you can't ~ them, join them** *(inf)* wenn dus nicht besser machen kannst, dann mach es genauso; **coffee ~s tea any day** Kaffee ist allemal besser als Tee; **that ~s everything** das ist doch wirklich der Gipfel *or* die Höhe *(inf)*, das schlägt dem Fass den Boden aus *(inf)*; *(= is very good)* darüber geht nichts; **it ~s me (how/why …)** *(inf)* es ist mir ein Rätsel(, wie/warum …) *(inf)*; **well, can you ~ it!** *(inf)* ist das denn zu fassen? *(inf)*; **he managed to ~ the charge** *(inf)* er wurde (von der Anklage) freigesprochen
d *(= be before) budget, crowds* zuvorkommen *(+dat)*; **to ~ sb to the top of a hill** vor jdm oben auf dem Berg sein *or* ankommen; **I'll ~ you down to the beach** ich bin vor dir am Strand; **to ~ sb home** vor jdm zu Hause sein; **to ~ the deadline** vor Ablauf der Frist fertig sein; **to ~ sb to the draw** schneller ziehen als jd; **to ~ sb to it** jdm zuvorkommen
e *(= move up and down regularly)* schlagen; **the bird ~s its wings** der Vogel schlägt mit den Flügeln
f *(Mus)* **to ~ time (to the music)** den Takt schlagen
g *(Cook) cream, eggs* schlagen
VI **a** *(heart, pulse, drum)* schlagen; **to ~ on the door (with one's fists)** (mit den Fäusten) gegen die Tür hämmern *or* schlagen; **with ~ing heart** mit pochendem *or* klopfendem Herzen; **her heart was ~ing with excitement** ihr Herz schlug vor Aufregung schneller → **bush¹**
b *(wind, waves)* schlagen; *(rain also)* trommeln; *(sun)* brennen
c *(cream)* sich schlagen lassen
ADJ **a** *(inf: = exhausted)* **to be (dead) ~** total kaputt *or* geschafft *or* erledigt sein *(inf)*
b *(inf: = defeated)* **to be ~(en)** aufgeben müssen *(inf)*, sich geschlagen geben müssen; **I'm ~** ich gebe mich geschlagen; **he doesn't know when he's ~(en)** er gibt nicht auf *(inf)*; **we've got him ~** wir haben ihn schachmatt gesetzt; **this problem's got me ~** mit dem Problem komme ich nicht klar *(inf)*

▶ **beat back** VT *sep flames, enemy* zurückschlagen

▶ **beat down** VI *(rain)* herunterprasseln; *(sun)* herunterbrennen VT *sep* **a** *(= reduce) prices* herunterhandeln; *opposition* kleinkriegen *(inf)*; **I managed to beat him down (on the price)** ich konnte den Preis herunterhandeln; **I beat him down to £20 for the chair** ich habe den Stuhl auf £ 20 heruntergehandelt **b** *(= flatten) door* einrennen; *wheat, crop* niederwerfen

▶ **beat in** VT *sep* **a** *door* einschlagen; **to beat sb's brains in** *(inf)* jdm den Schädel einschlagen *(inf)* **b** *(Cook) eggs etc* unterrühren

▶ **beat off** VT *sep* abwehren

▶ **beat out** VT *sep fire* ausschlagen; *metal, dent, wing* aushämmern; *tune, rhythm* schlagen; *(on drum)* trommeln; *plan* ausarbeiten, ausklamüsern *(inf)*, austüfteln *(inf)*; **to beat sb's brains out** *(inf: = kill)* jdm den Schädel einschlagen *(inf)*

▶ **beat up** VT *sep* **a** *person* zusammenschlagen **b** *(Cook) eggs, cream* schlagen

▶ **beat up on** VI *+prep obj (US inf) (= hit)* verhauen *(inf)*, schlagen; *(= bully)* einschüchtern; *(= criticize)* auseinandernehmen *(inf)*

beat bobby N *(Brit inf)* Streifenpolizist(in) *m(f)*

beaten [ˈbiːtn] *ptp of* **beat** ADJ **a** *metal* gehämmert; *egg* geschlagen **b** *earth* festgetreten; *path* ausgetreten; **a well-~ path** ein Trampelpfad *m*; **to be off the ~ track** *(fig)* abgelegen sein **c** *(= defeated)* **a ~ man** ein geschlagener Mann

beater [ˈbiːtəʳ] N **a** *(= carpet beater)* Klopfer *m*; *(= egg beater)* Schneebesen *m* **b** *(Hunt)* Treiber(in) *m(f)*

beat *in cpds* Beat-; **Beat Generation** N Beatgeneration *f*; **beat group** N Beatgruppe *or* -band *f*

beatific [ˌbiːəˈtɪfɪk] ADJ glückselig; *vision* himmlisch

beatification [biːˌætɪfɪˈkeɪʃən] N Seligsprechung *f*

beatify [biːˈætɪfaɪ] VT seligsprechen, beatifizieren *(spec)*

beating [ˈbiːtɪŋ] N **a** *(= series of blows)* Schläge *pl*, Prügel *pl*; **to give sb a ~** jdn verprügeln; *(as punishment also)* jdm eine Tracht Prügel verabreichen *(inf)*; **to get a ~** verprügelt werden; *(as punishment also)* Schläge *or* Prügel bekommen **b** *(of drums, heart, wings)* Schlagen *nt* **c** *(= defeat)* Niederlage *f*; **to take a ~** eine Schlappe einstecken *(inf)*; **to take a ~ (at the hands of sb)** (von jdm) nach allen Regeln der Kunst geschlagen werden **d** **to take some ~** nicht leicht zu übertreffen sein; *(idea, insolence etc)* seines-/ihresgleichen suchen **e** *(Hunt)* Treiben *nt*

beating-up [,bi:tɪŋ'ʌp] N Abreibung *f (inf)*; **to give sb a ~** jdn zusammenschlagen; **to get a ~** zusammengeschlagen werden

beatitude [bi:'ætɪtju:d] N Glückseligkeit *f*; **the Beatitudes** *(Bibl)* die Seligpreisungen *pl*

beatnik ['bi:tnɪk] N Beatnik *m*

beat poetry N Beatlyrik *f*

beats [bi:ts] PL *(Mus)* Techno *m*

beat-up ['bi:t'ʌp] ADJ *(inf)* zerbeult, ramponiert *(inf)*

beau [bəʊ] N *(old)* **a** *(= dandy)* Beau *m (dated)* **b** *(= suitor)* Galan *m (dated)*, Kavalier *m*

Beaufort scale ['bəʊfət,skeɪl] N Beaufortskala *f*

beaut [bju:t] N *(esp Austral inf: = thing)* Prachtexemplar *nt*; **to be a (real) ~** einsame Klasse sein *(inf)*

beauteous ['bju:tɪəs] ADJ *(poet)* wunderschön, prachtvoll

beautician [bju:'tɪʃən] N Kosmetiker(in) *m(f)*

beautiful ['bju:tɪfʊl] ADJ schön; *weather, morning also, idea, meal* herrlich, wunderbar; *(= good) swimmer, swimming, organization, piece of work* hervorragend, wunderbar; **that's a ~ specimen** das ist ein Prachtexemplar; **the ~ people** die Schickeria; **~!** prima! *(inf)*, toll! *(inf)* N **a** **the ~** das Schöne **b** *(inf)* **hello, ~** hallo, schönes Kind

beautifully ['bju:tɪfəlɪ] ADV schön; *warm, prepared, shine, simple* herrlich, wunderbar; *(= well) sew, cook, sing, swim* hervorragend, sehr gut, prima *(inf)*; **that will do ~** das ist ganz ausgezeichnet

beautify ['bju:tɪfaɪ] VT verschönern; **to ~ oneself** *(hum)* sich schönmachen *(hum)*

beauty ['bju:tɪ] N **a** Schönheit *f*; **~ is only skin-deep** *(prov)* der äußere Schein kann trügen; **~ is in the eye of the beholder** *(Prov)* schön ist, was (einem) gefällt **b** *(= beautiful person)* Schönheit *f*; **Beauty and the Beast** die Schöne und das Tier **c** *(= good example)* Prachtexemplar *nt*; **isn't it a ~!** ist das nicht ein Prachtstück *or* Prachtexemplar? **d** *(= pleasing feature)* **the ~ of it is that ...** das Schöne *or* Schönste daran ist, dass ...; **that's the ~ of it** das ist das Schöne daran; **one of the beauties of this job is ...** eine der schönen Seiten dieser Arbeit ist ...

beauty *in cpds* Schönheits-; **beauty care** N Kosmetik *f no pl*, Schönheitspflege *f*; **beauty competition, beauty contest** N Schönheitswettbewerb *m*; **beauty mark** N → **beauty spot**; **beauty parlour**, *(US)* **beauty parlor** N Schönheits- *or* Kosmetiksalon *m*; **beauty queen** N Schönheitskönigin *f*; **beauty salon, beauty shop** N Schönheits- *or* Kosmetiksalon *m*; **beauty sleep** N *(hum)* Schlaf *m*; **beauty specialist** N Kosmetiker(in) *m(f)*; **beauty spot** N **a** Schönheitsfleck *m*; *(= patch also)* Schönheitspflästerchen *nt* **b** *(= place)* schönes *or* hübsches Fleckchen (Erde), schöner *or* hübscher Fleck; **beauty treatment** N kosmetische Behandlung

beaver[1] ['bi:və'] N **a** Biber *m*; **to work like a ~** wie ein Wilder/eine Wilde arbeiten → **eager beaver** **b** *(= fur)* Biber(pelz) *m* **c** *(= hat)* Biber- *or* Kastorhut *m*

▶ **beaver away** VI *(inf)* schuften *(inf) (at* an *+dat)*

beaver[2] N *(of helmet)* Kinnreff *nt*

beaverboard N Hartfaserplatte *f*

becalm [bɪ'kɑ:m] VT **to be ~ed** *(Naut)* in eine Flaute geraten; *(fig)* eine Flaute haben; **the ship lay** *or* **was ~ed for three weeks** das Schiff war *or* befand sich drei Wochen lang in einer Flaute

became [bɪ'keɪm] *pret of* **become**

because [bɪ'kɒz] ✪ 17.1, 20.4, 26.3 CONJ weil; *(= since also)* da; **it was the more surprising ~ we were not expecting it** es war umso überraschender, als wir es nicht erwartet hatten; **if I did it, it was ~ it had to be done** ich habe es nur getan, weil es getan werden musste; **why did you do it? – just ~** *(inf)* warum *or* weshalb hast du das getan? – darum *or* deshalb PREP **~ of** wegen *(+gen or (inf) +dat)*; **I only did it ~ of you** ich habe es nur deinetwegen/Ihretwegen getan

beck [bek] N **to be (completely) at sb's ~ and call** jdm voll und ganz zur Verfügung stehen; **I'm not at your ~ and call** du kannst doch nicht so einfach über mich verfügen; **his wife is completely at his ~ and call** seine Frau muss nach seiner Pfeife tanzen; **to have sb at one's ~ and call** jdn zur ständigen Verfügung haben, ganz über jdn verfügen können

beckon ['bekən] VI winken; **he ~ed to her to follow (him)** er gab ihr ein Zeichen *or* winkte ihr, ihm zu folgen; **opportunities ~ for talented young players** jungen begabten Spielern stehen viele Möglichkeiten offen; **fame/Hollywood ~ed** der Ruhm/Hollywood lockte VT winken; *(fig: fame)* locken; **he ~ed her to follow (him)** er gab ihr ein Zeichen *or* winkte ihr, ihm zu folgen; **he ~ed me in/back/over** er winkte mich herein/zurück/herüber

become [bɪ'kʌm] *pret* **became**, *ptp* **become** VI **a** *(= grow to be)* werden; **it has ~ a rule** es ist jetzt Vorschrift; **it has ~ a habit** es ist zur Gewohnheit geworden; **it has ~ a custom/nuisance** es ist üblich/lästig geworden; **he's becoming a problem** er wird zum Problem; **to ~ interested in sb/sth** anfangen, sich für jdn/etw zu interessieren

b *(= acquire position of)* werden; **to ~ king/a doctor** König/Arzt werden

c **what has ~ of him?** was ist aus ihm geworden?; **what's to ~ of him?** was soll aus ihm werden?; **I don't know what will ~ of him** ich weiß nicht, was aus ihm noch werden soll

VT **a** *(= suit)* stehen *(+dat)*

b *(= befit)* sich schicken für, sich ziemen für *(geh)*

becoming [bɪ'kʌmɪŋ] ADJ **a** *(= suitable, fitting)* schicklich; **it's not ~ (for a lady) to sit like that** es schickt sich (für eine Dame) nicht, so zu sitzen **b** *(= flattering)* vorteilhaft, kleidsam; **that dress is very ~** das Kleid steht ihr/dir *etc* sehr gut

becomingly [bɪ'kʌmɪŋlɪ] ADV **a** *(= suitably)* passend **b** *(= fetchingly)* entzückend

becquerel [,bekə'rel] N Becquerel *nt*

B Ed *abbr of* **Bachelor of Education**

bed [bed] N **a** Bett *nt*; **to go to ~** zu *or* ins Bett gehen; **to put** *or* **get sb to ~** jdn ins *or* zu Bett bringen; **to get into ~** sich ins Bett legen; **to get into ~ with sb** *(lit, fig)* mit jdm ins Bett gehen *or* steigen *(inf)*; **he couldn't get her into ~ with him** er hat sie nicht ins Bett gekriegt *(inf)*; **to go to** *or* **jump into ~ with sb** *(inf)* mit jdm ins Bett gehen *or* steigen *(inf)*; **to be good in ~** gut im Bett sein; **he must have got out of ~ on the wrong side** *(inf)* er ist wohl mit dem linken Fuß zuerst aufgestanden; **to be in ~** im Bett sein; *(through illness also)* das Bett hüten müssen; **a ~ of rice** *(Cook)* ein Reisbett *nt*; **a ~ of nails** ein Nagelbrett *nt*; **life isn't always a ~ of roses** *(prov)* man ist im Leben nicht immer auf Rosen gebettet; **his life is not exactly a ~ of roses** er ist nicht gerade auf Rosen gebettet; **to make the ~** das Bett machen; **as you make your ~ so you must lie on it** *(Brit Prov)* **you make the ~ you lie in** *(US Prov)* wie man sich bettet, so liegt man *(Prov)*; **a ~ for the night** eine Übernachtungsmöglichkeit; **can I have a ~ for the night?** kann ich hier/bei euch *etc* übernachten?; **to put a newspaper to ~** *(Press)* eine Zeitung in Druck geben; **the paper has gone to ~** *(Press)* die Zeitung ist im Druck; **to put sth to ~** *(fig)* bei etw zu einem Abschluss kommen

b *(of ore)* Lager *nt*; *(of coal also)* Flöz *nt*; *(of building, road etc)* Unterbau *m*; **a ~ of clay** Lehmboden *m*

c *(= bottom) (= sea bed)* Grund *m*, Boden *m*; *(= river bed)* Bett *nt*

d *(= oyster bed, coral bed)* Bank *f*

e *(= flower bed, vegetable bed)* Beet *nt*

f *(= base: of engine, lathe, machine)* Bett *nt*

VT **a** *plant* setzen, pflanzen

b *(old, hum, = have sex with)* beschlafen *(old, hum)*

▶ **bed down** VI sein Lager aufschlagen; **to bed down for the night** sein Nachtlager aufschlagen VT *sep* **a** *person* das Bett machen *(+dat)*; *child* schlafen legen; **the soldiers were bedded down in the shed** die Soldaten hatten ihr (Nacht)quartier im Schuppen **b** *animals* einstreuen *(+dat)*

▶ **bed in** VT *sep foundations* einlassen; *machine* betten; *brakes* einfahren VI *(brakes)* eingefahren werden

bed and breakfast N Übernachtung *f* mit Frühstück; *(also* **bed and breakfast place***)* Frühstückspension *f*; **"bed and breakfast"** „Fremdenzimmer"

bedaub [bɪ'dɔ:b] VT beschmieren; *face* anmalen, anschmieren

bedazzle [bɪ'dæzl] VT blenden

bed *in cpds* Bett-; **bed bath** N (Kranken)wäsche *f* im Bett; **to give sb a ~** jdn im Bett waschen; **bedbug** N Wanze *f*; **bedchamber** N *(old)* Schlafgemach *nt (old)*; **bedclothes** PL *(Brit)* Bettzeug *nt*; **bedcover** N *(= bedspread)* Tagesdecke *f*; **~s** *pl (= bedclothes)* Bettzeug *nt*

bedding ['bedɪŋ] N **a** Bettzeug *nt* **b** *(for horses)* Streu *f*

bedding plant N Setzling *m*

beddy-byes ['bedɪbaɪz] PL *(US baby-talk)* **to go ~** Heia machen *(baby-talk)*, in die Heia gehen *(baby-talk)*

bedeck [bɪ'dek] VT schmücken

bedevil [bɪ'devl] VT komplizieren, erschweren; **~led** *(Brit) or* **~ed** *(US)* **by misfortune** vom Schicksal verfolgt; **~led** *(Brit) or* **~ed** *(US)* **by injuries** von Verletzungen heimgesucht

bed: **bedfellow** N **to be** *or* **make strange ~s** *(fig)* eine eigenartige Kombination *or* ein merkwürdiges Gespann sein; **bedframe** N Bettgestell *nt*; **bedhead** N Kopfteil *m* des Bettes; **bed jacket** N Bettjäckchen *nt*

bedlam ['bedləm] N *(fig: = uproar)* Chaos *nt*; **in the classroom it was absolute ~** in der Klasse ging es zu wie im Irrenhaus

bed linen N Bettwäsche *f*

Bedouin ['bedʊɪn] N Beduine *m*, Beduinin *f* ADJ beduinisch

bed: **bedpan** N Bettpfanne *or* -schüssel *f*; **bedplate** N *(Mech)* Grund- *or* Fundamentplatte *f*; **bedpost** N Bettpfosten *m*

bedraggled [bɪ'drægld] ADJ *(= wet)* trief- *or* tropfnass; *(= dirty)* verdreckt; *(= untidy) person, appearance* ungepflegt, schlampig

bedridden ['bedrɪdn] ADJ bettlägerig

bedrock ['bedrɒk] N **a** *(Geol)* Grundgebirge *or* -gestein *nt* **b** *(fig)* **to get down to** *or* **to reach ~** zum Kern der Sache kommen

bedroom ['bedru:m] N Schlafzimmer *nt*

bedroom *in cpds* Schlafzimmer-; **bedroom slipper** N Hausschuh *m*

Beds *abbr of* **Bedfordshire**

beds *abbr of* **bedrooms** Zi.

bed: **bed-settee** ['bedse'ti:] N *(Brit)* Sofabett *nt*; **bed sheet** N Bettlaken *nt*

bedside ['bedsaɪd] N **to be/sit at sb's ~** an jds Bett *(dat)* sein/sitzen

bedside: **bedside lamp** N Nachttischlampe *f*; **bedside manner** N Art *f* mit Kranken umzugehen; **he has a good/bad ~** er kann gut/nicht gut mit den Kranken umgehen; **bedside rug** N Bettvorleger *m*; **bedside table** N Nachttisch *m*

bedsit(ter) ['bedsɪt(ə')] *(inf)*, **bedsitting room** [,bed'sɪtɪŋrʊm] *(geh)* N *(Brit)* **a** *(one-room flat)* Einzimmerappartement *nt* **b** *(rented room)* möbliertes Zimmer **c** Wohnschlafzimmer *nt*; *(for teenager etc)* Jugendzimmer *nt*

bed: **bedsock** N Bettschuh *m*; **bedsore** N aufgelegene *or* wund gelegene Stelle; **to get ~s** sich wund liegen *or* aufliegen; **bed space** N *(in hospital, hotel etc)* Bettenzahl *f*, Bettenkapazität *f*; **bedspread** N Tagesdecke *f*; **bedstead** N Bettgestell *nt*; **bedstraw** N *(Bot)* Labkraut *nt*; **bedtime** N Schlafenszeit *f*; **it's ~** es ist Schlafenszeit; **his ~ is 10 o'clock** er geht um 10 Uhr schlafen; **it's past your ~** du müsstest schon lange im Bett sein; **bedtime story** N Gutenachtgeschichte *f*; **bed-wetter** N Bettnässer(in) *m(f)*; **bed-wetting** N Bettnässen *nt*

bee [bi:] N **a** Biene *f*; **like ~s round a honeypot** wie die Motten ums Licht; **to have a ~ in one's bonnet** *(inf)* einen Fimmel *or* Tick haben *(inf)*; **he's got a ~ in his bonnet about cleanliness** *(inf)* er hat einen Sauberkeitsfimmel *or* -tick *(inf)* **b** *(= sewing bee)* Kränzchen *nt*; *(= competition)* Wettbewerb *m*

Beeb [bi:b] N **the ~** *(Brit inf)* die BBC

beech [bi:tʃ] N **a** *(= tree)* Buche *f* **b** *(= wood)* Buche(nholz *nt*) *f*

beech: **beech mast** N Bucheckern *pl*; **beechnut** N Buchecker *f*; **beech tree** N Buche *f*; **beechwood** N **a** *(= material)* Buchenholz *nt* **b** *(= trees)* Buchenwald *m*

bee-eater ['bi:,i:tə'] N *(Orn)* Bienenfresser *m*

beef [bi:f] **N a** *(= meat)* Rindfleisch *nt* **b** *(inf: = flesh)* Speck *m (pej)*; *(= muscles)* Muskeln *pl*; **to have plenty of ~** jede Menge Bizeps haben *(inf)*; **you'd better get rid of some of this ~** du musst ein bisschen abspecken *(inf)* **c what's his ~?** *(inf)* was hat er zu meckern? *(inf)* **VI** *(inf: = complain)* meckern *(inf)* *(about* über *+acc)*; **what are you ~ing about?** was hast du zu meckern? *(inf)*

▶ **beef up** VT *sep (= make more powerful etc)* aufmotzen *(inf)*

beef: **beefburger** N Hamburger *m*; **beefcake** N *no pl (inf: = male photos)* Männerfleisch *nt (hum)*, Muskelprotze *pl*; **beef cattle** PL Schlachtrinder *pl*; **beefeater** N **a** Beefeater *m* **b** *(US inf)* Engländer(in) *m(f)*; **beef extract** N Fleischextrakt *m*; **beef olive** N Rinderroulade *f*; **beef sausage** N Rindswürstchen *nt*; **beefsteak** N Beefsteak *nt*; **beef tea** N Kraft- *or* Fleischbrühe *f*

beefy ['bi:fɪ] ADJ *(+er)* fleischig

bee: **beehive** **N a** Bienenstock *m*; *(dome-shaped)* Bienenkorb *m* **b** *(= hairstyle)* toupierte Hochfrisur **ADJ ~ hairdo** toupierte Hochfrisur; **beekeeper** N Bienenzüchter(in) *m(f)*, Imker(in) *m(f)*; **beeline** N **to make a ~ for sb/sth** schnurstracks auf jdn/etw zugehen

beemer ['bi:mə'], **beamer** ['bi:mə'] N *(Aut inf)* BMW® *m*

been [bi:n] *ptp of* **be**

beep [bi:p] *(inf)* **N** Tut(tut) *nt (inf)*; **leave your name and number after the ~** hinterlassen Sie Ihren Namen und Ihre Nummer nach dem Signalton *or* Pfeifton **VT to ~ one's horn** hupen **VI** tuten *(inf)*; **~ ~!** tut, tut *(inf)*

beeper ['bi:pə'] N *(= gadget)* Piepser *m (inf)*

beer [bɪə'] N Bier *nt*; **two ~s, please** zwei Bier, bitte; **life is not all ~ and skittles** das Leben ist nicht nur eitel Sonnenschein

> **BEER**
>
> In England und Wales ist das am weitesten verbreitete Fassbier **(draught beer)** ein **bitter**, das so heißt wegen seines vollen, leicht bitteren Geschmacks. Das schottische **heavy** ähnelt dem englischen **bitter**. Außerdem werden in Großbritannien noch andere Biersorten gerne getrunken, so z. B. das **stout**, das stark und sehr dunkel ist, das **mild**, das ähnlich wie ein **bitter** schmeckt, aber mit weniger Hopfen gebraut wird, und das **lager**, ein leichtes Bier, das am ehesten einem deutschen Export entspricht.
>
> Der Begriff **ale** bezeichnete ursprünglich ein Bier, das ohne Hopfen gebraut wurde, wird aber heutzutage auch für **beer** im Allgemeinen benutzt. Beliebte Sorten sind hierbei **light ale** oder auch **pale ale** und **brown ale**, das dunkler, stärker und kräftiger im Geschmack ist.

beer *in cpds* Bier-; **beer belly** N *(inf)* Bierbauch *m (inf)*; **beer bottle** N Bierflasche *f*; **beer bust** N *(US Univ sl: = party)* Bierfete *f (inf)*, Biersause *f (sl)*; *(= drinking spree)* Saufgelage *nt (pej inf)*; **beer can** N Bierdose *f*; **beer cellar** N Bierkeller *m*; **beer garden** N *(Brit)* Biergarten *m*; **beer glass** N Bierglas *nt*; **beer gut** N *(inf)* Bierbauch *m (inf)*; **beer mat** N *(Brit)* Bierdeckel *m*; **beer money** N *(inf)* Geld *nt* für Getränke; **to keep sb in ~** ein nettes Taschengeld für jdn sein; *(extra income)* ein nettes Zubrot für jdn sein; **beer-pull** N Bierpumpengriff *m*; **beer-swilling** ADJ *(pej inf)* Bier saufend *(inf)*

beery ['bɪərɪ] ADJ Bier-; *person* mit einer Bierfahne *(inf)*; *(= tipsy)* bierselig; *face* biergerötet; **to have ~ breath, to smell ~** eine Bierfahne haben *(inf)*, nach Bier riechen

bee sting N Bienenstich *m*

beeswax ['bi:zwæks] N Bienenwachs *nt*

beet [bi:t] N Rübe *f*, Bete *f (form)*

beetle[1] ['bi:tl] N Käfer *m*

▶ **beetle along** VI *(inf)* entlangpesen *(inf)*; *(on foot also)* entlanghasten *(inf)*

▶ **beetle off** VI *(inf)* abschwirren *(inf)*

beetle[2] N *(= tool)* Stampfer *m*; *(for paving, pile-driving also)* Ramme *f*

beetle: **beetle-browed** ['bi:tl'braʊd] ADJ mit buschigen, zusammengewachsenen Augenbrauen; **beetle brows** PL buschige, zusammengewachsene Augenbrauen *pl*; **beetle-crushers** PL *(inf)* Elbkähne *pl (inf)*, Kindersärge *pl (inf)*

beetling ['bi:tlɪŋ] ADJ *cliffs* überhängend; *brow* vorspringend

beet: **beetroot** [bi:tru:t] N Rote Bete *or* Rübe; **beet sugar** N Rübenzucker *m*

befall [bɪ'fɔ:l] *pret* **befell** [bɪ'fel] *ptp* **befallen** [bɪ'fɔ:lən] *(old, liter)* **VI** sich zutragen **VT** widerfahren *(+dat) (geh)*

befit [bɪ'fɪt] VT *(form) sb* anstehen *(+dat) (geh)*, sich ziemen für *(geh)*; *occasion* angemessen sein *(+dat)*, entsprechen *(+dat)*; **it ill ~s him to speak thus** es steht ihm schlecht an *or* ziemt sich nicht für ihn, so zu reden *(geh)*

befitting [bɪ'fɪtɪŋ] ADJ gebührend, geziemend *(dated)*

befog [bɪ'fɒg] VT *(fig) issue* vernebeln; *person, mind* verwirren; *(alcohol, blow)* benebeln; **to be ~ged** *(person)* benebelt sein; *(issue)* verwirrt sein

before [bɪ'fɔ:'] **PREP a** *(= earlier than)* vor *(+dat)*; **the year ~ last/this** vorletztes/letztes Jahr, das vorletzte/letzte Jahr; **the day ~ yesterday** vorgestern; **the day/time ~ that** der Tag/die Zeit davor; **~ Christ** *(abbr* **BC***)* vor Christi Geburt *(abbr v. Chr.)*; **I got/was here ~ you** ich war vor dir da; **that was ~ my time** das war vor meiner Zeit; **he died ~ his time** er ist früh gestorben; **to be ~ sb/sth** vor jdm/etw liegen; **~ then** vorher; **~ now** früher, eher, vorher; **you should have done it ~ now** das hättest du schon (eher) gemacht haben sollen; **~ long** bald; **~ everything else** zuallererst

b *(in order, rank)* vor *(+dat)*; **to come ~ sb/sth** vor jdm/etw kommen; **I believe in honour** *(Brit)* *or* **honor** *(US)* **~ everything** die Ehre geht mir über alles, für mich ist die Ehre das Wichtigste; **ladies ~ gentlemen** Damen haben den Vortritt

c *(in position)* vor *(+dat)*; *(with movement)* vor *(+acc)*; **~ my (very) eyes** vor meinen Augen; **the task ~ us** *(= with which we are dealing)* die uns vorliegende Aufgabe; *(= with which we are confronted)* die Aufgabe, vor der wir stehen; *(= which lies ahead of us)* die uns bevorstehende Aufgabe; **to sail ~ the wind** *(Naut)* vor dem Wind segeln

d *(= in the presence of)* vor *(+dat)*; **he said it ~ us all** er sagte das vor uns allen; **~ God/a lawyer** vor Gott/einem Anwalt; **to appear ~ a court/judge** vor Gericht/einem Richter erscheinen

e *(= rather than)* **death ~ surrender** eher *or* lieber tot als sich ergeben; **he would die ~ betraying his country** er würde eher sterben als sein Land verraten

ADV a *(in time, = before that)* davor; *(= at an earlier time, before now)* vorher; **have you been to Scotland ~?** waren Sie schon einmal in Schottland?; **I have seen/read** *etc* **this ~** ich habe das schon einmal gesehen/gelesen *etc*; **never ~** noch nie; **(on) the evening/day ~** am Abend/Tag davor *or* zuvor *or* vorher; **(in) the month/year ~** im Monat/Jahr davor; **two hours ~** zwei Stunden vorher; **two days ~** zwei Tage davor *or* zuvor; **to continue as ~** *(person)* (so) wie vorher weitermachen; **things continued as ~** alles war wie gehabt; **life went on as ~** das Leben ging seinen gewohnten Gang

b *(= ahead)* **to march on ~** vorausmarschieren

c *(indicating order)* davor; **that chapter and the one ~** dieses Kapitel und das davor

CONJ a *(in time)* bevor; **~ doing sth** bevor man etw tut; **you can't go ~ this is done** du kannst erst gehen, wenn das gemacht ist; **it will be six weeks ~ the boat comes again** das Boot wird erst in sechs Wochen wiederkommen; **it will be a long time ~ he comes back** es wird lange dauern, bis er zurückkommt

b *(= rather than)* **he will die ~ he surrenders** eher will er sterben als sich geschlagen geben

beforehand [bɪ'fɔ:hænd] ADV im Voraus; **you must tell me ~** Sie müssen mir vorher Bescheid sagen

before-tax [bɪ'fɔ:tæks] ADJ *income, profits* vor Steuern

befoul [bɪ'faʊl] VT *(liter: lit, fig)* besudeln; *atmosphere* verpesten

befriend [bɪ'frend] VT *(= help)* sich annehmen *(+gen)*; *(= be friend to)* Umgang pflegen mit; **she seems to have ~ed them** sie scheint sich mit ihnen angefreundet zu haben

befuddle [bɪ'fʌdl] VT **a** *(= make tipsy)* benebeln **b** *(= confuse)* durcheinanderbringen; **he is rather ~d** er ist ziemlich durcheinander *(inf)* *or* verwirrt

beg [beg] **VT a** *money, alms* betteln um

b *(= crave, ask for) forgiveness, mercy, a favour* bitten um; **to ~ sth of sb** jdn um etw bitten; **he ~ged to be allowed to ...** er bat darum, ... zu dürfen; **the children ~ged me to let them go to the circus** die Kinder bettelten, ich solle sie in den Zirkus gehen lassen; **to ~ leave to do sth** um Erlaubnis bitten, etw tun zu dürfen; **I ~ leave to be dismissed** *(form)* gestatten Sie, dass ich mich entferne? *(form)*; **I ~ to inform you ...** *(form)* ich erlaube mir, Sie davon in Kenntnis zu setzen ...; **I ~ to differ** ich erlaube mir, anderer Meinung zu sein → **pardon**

c *(= entreat) sb* anflehen, inständig bitten; **I ~ you!** ich flehe dich an!

d to ~ the question die Frage offenlassen; **sth ~s the question whether ...** etw wirft die Frage auf, ob ...

VI a *(beggar)* betteln; *(dog)* Männchen machen

b *(for help, time etc)* bitten *(for* um)

c *(= entreat)* **to ~ of sb to do sth** jdn anflehen *or* inständig bitten, etw zu tun; **I ~ of you** ich bitte Sie

d to go ~ging *(inf)* noch zu haben sein; *(= be unwanted)* keine Abnehmer finden

began [bɪ'gæn] *pret of* **begin**

beget [bɪ'get] *pret* **begot** *or (obs)* **begat** [bɪ'gæt] *ptp* **begotten** *or* **begot** VT **a** *(obs, Bibl)* zeugen → **begotten b** *(fig) difficulties etc* zeugen *(geh)*; **violence ~s violence** Gewalt erzeugt Gewalt

begetter [bɪ'getə'] N *(form)* Begründer(in) *m(f)*

beggar ['begə'] **N a** Bettler(in) *m(f)*; **~s can't be choosers** *(prov)* in der Not frisst der Teufel Fliegen *(prov)*, wer arm dran ist, kann nicht wählerisch sein **b** *(Brit inf)* Kerl *m (inf)*; **poor ~!** armer Kerl! *(inf)*, armes Schwein! *(inf)*; **a lucky ~** ein Glückspilz *m*; **a funny little ~** ein drolliges Kerlchen; *(= girl)* ein drolliger Fratz **VT** **a** *(= make poor)* an den Bettelstab bringen **b** *(fig)* **to ~ description** jeder Beschreibung *(gen)* spotten; **to ~ belief** nicht zu fassen sein

beggarly [ˈbegəlɪ] ADJ kümmerlich

beggar: beggarman N *(old)* Bettler *m*, Bettelmann *m (old)*; **beggar-my-neighbour, beggar-your-neighbour** N *(Cards) Kartenspiel, bei dem der gewinnt, der zum Schluss alle Karten hat*; **beggarwoman** N *(old)* Bettlerin *f*, Bettelfrau *f (old)*

beggary [ˈbegərɪ] N Bettelarmut *f*; *(= beggars)* Bettler *pl*, Bettelvolk *nt*; **to have been reduced to ~** bettelarm sein

begging [ˈbegɪŋ]: **begging bowl** N Bettlerschale *f*; **to hold out a ~ (to sb)** *(fig)* (bei jdm) betteln gehen; **begging letter** N Bittbrief *m*

begin [bɪˈgɪn] ✪ 26.1 *pret* **began**, *ptp* **begun** **VT** **a** *(= start)* beginnen, anfangen; *conversation also* anknüpfen; *song also* anstimmen; *bottle* anbrechen, anfangen; *book, letter, new cheque book, new page* anfangen; *rehearsals, work* anfangen mit; *task* in Angriff nehmen, sich machen an *(+acc)*; **to ~ to do sth** *or* **doing sth** anfangen *or* beginnen, etw zu tun; **to ~ working** *or* **to work on sth** mit der Arbeit an etw *(dat)* anfangen *or* beginnen; **to ~ an attack** zum Angriff schreiten; **when did you ~ (learning** *or* **to learn) English?** wann haben Sie angefangen, Englisch zu lernen?; **she ~s the job next week** sie fängt nächste Woche (bei der Stelle) an; **he began his speech by saying that ...** er leitete seine Rede damit *or* mit den Worten ein, dass ...; **to ~ school** eingeschult werden, in die Schule kommen; **to ~ life as a ...** als ... anfangen *or* beginnen; **she began to feel tired** sie wurde allmählich *or* langsam müde; **she's ~ning to understand** sie fängt langsam an zu verstehen, sie versteht so langsam; **his mother began to fear the worst** seine Mutter befürchtete schon das Schlimmste; **I'd begun to think you weren't coming** ich habe schon gedacht, du kommst nicht mehr; **that doesn't even ~ to compare with ...** das lässt sich nicht mal annähernd mit ... vergleichen; **they didn't even ~ to solve the problem** sie haben das Problem nicht mal annähernd gelöst; **I couldn't even ~ to count the mistakes** ich konnte die Fehler überhaupt nicht zählen; **I can't ~ to thank you for what you've done** ich kann Ihnen gar nicht genug dafür danken, was Sie getan haben
b *(= initiate, originate)* anfangen; *fashion, custom, policy* einführen; *society, firm, movement* gründen; *(= cause) war* auslösen; **he began the rumour** *(Brit) or* **rumor** *(US)* er hat das Gerücht in die Welt gesetzt
c *(= start to speak)* beginnen, anfangen; **it's late, he began** es ist spät, begann er *or* fing *or* hub *(old)* er an
VI **a** *(= start)* anfangen, beginnen; *(new play etc)* anlaufen; **to ~ by doing sth** etw zuerst (einmal) tun; **he began by saying that ...** er sagte eingangs *or* einleitend, dass ...; **where the hair ~s** am Haaransatz; **before school ~s** vor Schulanfang; **to ~ in business** ins Geschäftsleben eintreten; *(as self-employed)* ein Geschäft aufmachen; **~ning from Monday** ab Montag, von Montag an; **~ning from page 10** von Seite 10 an; **say your names ~ning from the back** nennen Sie Ihre Namen von hinten nach vorn; **it all/the trouble began when ...** es fing alles/der Ärger fing damit an, dass ...; **to ~ with sb/sth** mit jdm/etw anfangen; **~ with me** fangen Sie bei *or* mit mir an; **he began with the intention of writing a thesis** anfänglich wollte er eine Doktorarbeit schreiben; **to ~ with there were only three** anfänglich waren es nur drei; **this is wrong to ~ with** das ist schon einmal falsch; **to ~ with, this is wrong, and ...** erstens einmal ist das falsch, dann ...; **to ~ on sth** mit etw anfangen *or* beginnen; **to ~ on a new venture/project** ein neues Unternehmen/Projekt in Angriff nehmen
b *(= come into being)* beginnen, anfangen; *(custom)* entstehen; *(river)* entspringen; **since the world began** seit (An)beginn *or* Anfang der Welt; **when did this movement ~?** seit wann gibt es diese Bewegung?

beginner [bɪˈgɪnəˈ] N Anfänger(in) *m(f)*; **~'s luck** Anfängerglück *nt*

beginning [bɪˈgɪnɪŋ] N **a** *(= act of starting)* Anfang *m*; **to make a ~** einen Anfang machen
b *(= place, of book etc)* Anfang *m*; *(temporal also)* Beginn *m*; *(of river)* Ursprung *m*; **at the ~** anfänglich, zuerst; **at the ~ of sth** am Anfang *or (temporal also)* zu Beginn einer Sache *(gen)*; **the wedding will be at the ~ of July** die Hochzeit findet Anfang Juli statt; **the ~ of time/the world** der Anbeginn *or* Anfang der Welt; **in the ~** *(Bibl)* am Anfang; **from the ~** von Anfang an; **from the ~ of the week/poem** seit Anfang *or* Beginn der Woche/vom Anfang des Gedichtes an; **read the paragraph from the ~** lesen Sie den Paragrafen von (ganz) vorne; **from ~ to end** von vorn bis hinten; *(temporal)* von Anfang bis Ende; **to start again at** *or* **from the ~** noch einmal von vorn anfangen; **to begin at the ~** ganz vorn anfangen; **the ~ of negotiations** der Beginn der Verhandlungen, der Verhandlungsbeginn
c *(= origin)* Anfang *m*; *(of custom, movement)* Entstehen *nt no pl*; **the shooting was the ~ of the rebellion** die Schießerei bedeutete den Beginn *or* Anfang der Rebellion; **it was the ~ of the end for him** das war der Anfang vom Ende für ihn; **his humble ~s** seine einfachen Anfänge; **from humble ~s** aus einfachen Verhältnissen; **Nazism had its ~s in Germany** der Nazismus hatte seine Anfänge *or* seinen Ursprung in Deutschland; **the ~s of science** die Anfangsgründe der Naturwissenschaft

begone [bɪˈgɒn] VI *imper and infin only (old)* **~!** fort (mit dir/Ihnen); *(esp Rel)* weiche; **they bade him ~** sie befahlen ihm, sich fortzuscheren

begonia [bɪˈgəʊnɪə] N Begonie *f*

begot [bɪˈgɒt] *pret, ptp of* **beget**

begotten [bɪˈgɒtn] *ptp of* **beget**; **the only ~ son** der eingeborene Sohn

begrime [bɪˈgraɪm] VT beschmutzen

begrudge [bɪˈgrʌdʒ] VT **a** *(= be reluctant)* **to ~ doing sth** etw widerwillig tun **b** *(= envy)* missgönnen *(sb sth* jdm etw); **no one ~s you your good fortune** wir gönnen dir ja dein Glück; **he ~s him the air he breathes** er gönnt ihm das Salz in der Suppe nicht **c** *(= give unwillingly)* nicht gönnen *(sb sth* jdm etw); **I wouldn't ~ you the money** ich würde dir das Geld ja gönnen; **I won't ~ you £5** du sollst die £ 5 haben

begrudging [bɪˈgrʌdʒɪŋ] ADJ widerwillig

begrudgingly [bɪˈgrʌdʒɪŋlɪ] ADV widerwillig

beguile [bɪˈgaɪl] VT **a** *(= deceive)* betören *(geh)*; **to ~ sb into doing sth** jdn dazu verführen, etw zu tun **b** *(= charm) person* betören; *(liter) time* sich *(dat)* angenehm vertreiben

beguiling [bɪˈgaɪlɪŋ] ADJ betörend, verführerisch

begun [bɪˈgʌn] *ptp of* **begin**

behalf [bɪˈhɑːf] ✪ 22 N **on** *or* **in** *(US)* **~ of** für, im Interesse von; *(as spokesman)* im Namen von; *(as authorized representative)* im Auftrag von; **I'm not asking on my own ~** ich bitte nicht für mich selbst *or* in meinem eigenen Interesse darum

behave [bɪˈheɪv] **VI** sich verhalten; *(people also)* sich benehmen; *(children also)* sich betragen, sich benehmen; *(= be good)* sich benehmen; **to ~ well/badly** sich gut/schlecht benehmen; **what a way to ~!** was für ein Benehmen!; **to ~ badly/well toward(s) sb** jdn schlecht/gut behandeln; **to ~ irresponsibly toward(s) sb** sich jdm gegenüber verantwortungslos verhalten; **to ~ like an honest man** wie ein ehrlicher Mensch handeln; **to ~ very wisely** sich sehr klug verhalten; **~!** benimm dich!; **can't you make your son/dog ~?** kannst du deinem Sohn/Hund keine Manieren beibringen?; **he knows how to ~ at a cocktail party** er weiß sich bei Cocktailpartys zu benehmen; **how is your car behaving these days?** wie fährt dein Auto zurzeit?
VR **to ~ oneself** sich benehmen; **~ yourself!** benimm dich!; **can't you make your son/dog ~ himself/itself?** kannst du deinem Sohn/Hund keine Manieren beibringen?

behaviour, *(US)* **behavior** [bɪˈheɪvjəˈ] N **a** *(= manner, bearing)* Benehmen *nt*; *(esp of children also)* Betragen *nt*; **to be on one's best ~** sich von seiner besten Seite zeigen, sein bestes Benehmen an den Tag legen **b** *(towards others)* Verhalten *nt* *(to(wards)* gegenüber) **c** *(of car, machine)* Verhalten *nt*

behavioural, *(US)* **behavioral** [bɪˈheɪvjərəl] ADJ *in cpds* Verhaltens-; **behavioural science** N Verhaltensforschung *f*; **behavioural scientist** N Verhaltensforscher(in) *m(f)*

behaviourism, *(US)* **behaviorism** [bɪˈheɪvjərɪzəm] N Behaviorismus *m*

behaviourist, *(US)* **behaviorist** [bɪˈheɪvjərɪst] **N** Behaviorist *m* **ADJ** behavioristisch

behaviour pattern, *(US)* **behavior pattern** N Verhaltensmuster *nt*

behead [bɪˈhed] VT enthaupten, köpfen

beheld [bɪˈheld] *pret, ptp of* **behold**

behemoth [bɪˈhiːmɒθ] N *(liter. = monster)* Moloch *m (geh)*

behest [bɪˈhest] N *(liter)* Geheiß *nt (liter)*; **at his ~/the ~ of his uncle** auf sein Geheiß *(liter)*/auf Geheiß seines Onkels *(liter)*

behind [bɪˈhaɪnd] **PREP** **a** *(= in or at the rear of, stationary)* hinter *(+dat)*; *(with motion)* hinter *(+acc)*; **come out from ~ the door** komm hinter der Tür (her)vor; **he came up ~ me** er trat von hinten an mich heran; **walk close ~ me** gehen Sie dicht hinter mir; **close the door ~ you** mach die Tür hinter dir zu; **put it ~ the books** stellen Sie es hinter die Bücher; **he has the Communists ~ him** er hat die Kommunisten hinter sich *(dat)*; **to be ~ an idea** eine Idee unterstützen; **what is ~ this/this incident?** was steckt dahinter/steckt hinter diesem Vorfall?; **she has years of experience ~ her** sie hat viele Jahre der Erfahrung hinter sich *(dat)*
b *(= more backward than)* **to be ~ sb** hinter jdm zurück sein
c *(in time)* **to be ~ time** *(train etc)* Verspätung haben; *(with work etc)* im Rückstand sein; **to be ~ schedule** im Verzug sein; **to be three hours ~ time** drei Stunden Verspätung haben; **to be ~ the times** *(fig)* hinter seiner Zeit zurück(geblieben) sein; **you must put the past ~ you** Sie müssen Vergangenes vergangen sein lassen, Sie müssen die Vergangenheit begraben; **their youth is far ~ them** ihre Jugend liegt weit zurück
ADV **a** *(= in or at rear)* hinten; *(= behind this, sb etc)* dahinter; **the runner was (lying) a long way ~** der Läufer lag weit hinten *or* zurück; **from ~** von hinten; **to look ~** zurückblicken; **to stand ~** *(= be standing)* dahinterstehen; *(= position oneself)* sich dahinterstellen
b *(= late)* **to be ~ with one's studies/payments** mit seinen Studien/Zahlungen im Rückstand sein; **we are three days ~ with the schedule** wir sind drei Tage im Rückstand *or* Verzug
N *(inf)* Hinterteil *nt (inf)*, Hintern *m (inf)*

behindhand [bɪˈhaɪndhænd] ADV ADJ **a** *(= late)* **to be ~** Verspätung haben **b** *(= in arrears)* **to be ~ with sth** mit etw im Rückstand *or* Verzug sein

behold [bɪˈhəʊld] *pret, ptp* **beheld** VT *(liter)* sehen, erblicken *(liter)*; **~!** und siehe (da); *(Rel)* siehe; **~ thy servant** siehe deinen Diener

beholden [bɪˈhəʊldən] ADJ *(liter)* **to be ~ to sb for sth** jdm für etw verpflichtet sein *(geh)*

behove [bɪˈhəʊv], *(US)* **behoove** [bɪˈhuːv] VT IMPERS *(form)* sich geziemen *(geh)* *(sb to do sth* für jdn, etw zu tun)

beige [beɪʒ] **ADJ** beige **N** Beige *nt*

being [ˈbiːɪŋ] N **a** *(= existence)* Dasein *nt*, Leben *nt*; **to come into ~** entstehen; *(club etc also)* ins Leben gerufen werden; **to bring into ~** ins Leben rufen, (er)schaffen; **then in ~** damals bestehend **b** *(= that which exists)* (Lebe)wesen *nt*, Geschöpf *nt*; **~s from outer space** Wesen *pl* aus dem All **c** *(= essence)* Wesen *nt*; **with all** *or* **every fibre** *(Brit) or* **fiber** *(US)* **of my ~** mit jeder Faser meines Herzens

Beirut [beɪ'ru:t] N Beirut *nt*

bejewelled, *(US)* **bejeweled** [bɪ'dʒu:əld] ADJ mit Edelsteinen geschmückt; **~ with sequins** mit Pailletten besetzt; **~ with dew/stars** *(poet)* mit glitzernden Tautropfen besät/sternenbesät *(poet)*

belabour, *(US)* **belabor** [bɪ'leɪbə'] VT **a** *(= hit)* einschlagen auf *(+acc)* **b** *(fig, with insults etc)* überhäufen; *(with questions)* beschießen, bearbeiten

Belarus ['belərʌs, 'belərʊs,] N *(Geog)* Weißrussland *nt*

belated ADJ, **belatedly** ADV [bɪ'leɪtɪd, -lɪ] verspätet

belay [bɪ'leɪ] VT *(Naut)* belegen, festmachen; *(Mountaineering)* sichern INTERJ *(Naut)* **~ there** aufhören

belaying pin [bɪ'leɪɪŋ,pɪn] N *(Naut)* Belegklampe *f*; *(Mountaineering)* (Kletter)haken *m*

belch [beltʃ] VI *(person)* rülpsen, aufstoßen; *(volcano)* Lava speien *or* ausstoßen; *(smoke, fire)* herausquellen VT *(also* **belch forth** *or* **out***)* *smoke, flames* (aus)speien, ausstoßen N **a** *(= burp)* Rülpser *m (inf)* **b** *(of smoke etc)* Stoß *m*

beleaguer [bɪ'li:gə'] VT belagern; *(fig)* umgeben

belfry ['belfrɪ] N Glockenstube *f* → **bat**[1]

Belgian ['beldʒən] N Belgier(in) *m(f)* ADJ belgisch

Belgium ['beldʒəm] N Belgien *nt*

Belgrade [bel'greɪd] N Belgrad *nt*

belie [bɪ'laɪ] VT **a** *(= prove false) words, proverb* Lügen strafen, widerlegen **b** *(= give false impression of)* hinwegtäuschen über *(+acc)* **c** *(= fail to justify) hopes* enttäuschen

belief [bɪ'li:f] N **a** Glaube *m (in* an *+acc)*; **it is beyond ~** es ist unglaublich *or* nicht zu glauben; **a statement unworthy of your ~** *(form)* eine Aussage, der Sie keinen Glauben schenken sollten
b *(Rel: = faith)* Glaube *m*; *(= doctrine)* (Glaubens)lehre *f*
c *(= convinced opinion)* Überzeugung *f*, Glaube *m no pl*; **what are the ~s of the average citizen today?** woran glaubt der heutige Durchschnittsbürger?; **in the ~ that …** im Glauben, dass …; **acting in this ~** in gutem Glauben, im guten Glauben; **it is my ~ that …** ich bin der Überzeugung, dass …; **it is one of my ~s that …** es ist meine Überzeugung, dass …; **yes, that is my ~** ich glaube schon; **to the best of my ~** meines Wissens
d *no pl (= trust)* Glaube *m (in* an *+acc)*; **to have ~ in** glauben an *(+acc)*

believability [bɪ,li:və'bɪlɪtɪ] N Glaubhaftigkeit *f*, Glaubwürdigkeit *f*

believable [bɪ'li:vəbl] ADJ glaubhaft, glaubwürdig; **hardly ~** wenig glaubhaft

believe [bɪ'li:v] ✪ 26.2 VT **a** *sth* glauben; *sb* glauben *(+dat)*; **I don't ~ you** das glaube ich (Ihnen) nicht; **don't you ~ it** wers glaubt, wird selig *(inf)*; **it's true, please ~ me** es stimmt, bitte glauben Sie mir das; **~ me, I mean it** glauben Sie mir, es ist mir ernst *or* Ernst; **~ you me!** *(inf)* das können Sie mir glauben!; **~ it or not** ob Sies glauben oder nicht; **would you ~ it!** *(inf)* ist das (denn) die Möglichkeit *(inf)*; **I would never have ~d it of him** das hätte ich nie von ihm geglaubt; **he could hardly ~ his eyes/ears** er traute seinen Augen/Ohren nicht; **if he is to be ~d** wenn man ihm glauben darf *or* Glauben schenken kann
b *(= think)* glauben; **he is ~d to be ill** es heißt, dass er krank ist; **I ~ so/not** ich glaube schon/nicht → **make-believe**
VI *(= have a religious faith)* an Gott glauben; **you must ~!** Sie müssen glauben!

▶ **believe in** VI *+prep obj* **a** *God, ghosts* glauben an *(+acc)*
b *(= have trust in) promises* glauben an *(+acc)*; *method also* Vertrauen haben zu; **to believe in oneself** an sich selbst glauben; **the boss/his mother still believes in him** der Chef/seine Mutter glaubt immer noch an ihn; **please believe in me** bitte haben Sie Vertrauen zu mir; **he doesn't believe in medicine/doctors** er hält nicht viel von Medikamenten/Ärzten
c *(= support idea of)* **to believe in sth** (prinzipiell) für etw sein; **he believes in getting up early** er ist überzeugter Frühaufsteher; **he believes in giving people a second chance** er gibt prinzipiell jedem noch einmal eine Chance; **I don't believe in compromises** ich halte nichts von Kompromissen, ich bin gegen Kompromisse

believer [bɪ'li:və'] N **a** *(Rel)* Gläubige(r) *mf*
b **to be a (firm) ~ in sth** (grundsätzlich) für etw sein; **I'm a ~ in doing things properly** ich bin grundsätzlich der Meinung, dass man, was man macht, richtig machen sollte; **he's a (firm) ~ in getting up early** er ist überzeugter Frühaufsteher; **he's not much of a ~ in getting up early** er hält nicht viel vom Frühaufstehen

Belisha beacon [bɪ,li:ʃə'bi:kən] N *(Brit) gelbes Blinklicht an Zebrastreifen*

belittle [bɪ'lɪtl] ✪ 26.3 VT herabsetzen, heruntermachen *(inf)*; *achievement also* schmälern; **to ~ oneself** sich schlechter machen, als man ist

belittlement [bɪ'lɪtlmənt] N Herabsetzung *f*; *(of achievement also)* Schmälerung *f*

Belize [be'li:z] N Belize *nt*

bell[1] [bel] N **a** Glocke *f*; *(small: on toys, pet's collar etc)* Glöckchen *nt*, Schelle *f*; *(= school bell, doorbell, of bicycle)* Klingel *f*, Glocke *f (dated)*; *(= handbell also)* Schelle *f*; *(of typewriter, Telec)* Klingel *f*; **as clear as a ~** *(voice)* glasklar; *picture* gestochen scharf; *hear, sound* laut und deutlich; **as sound as a ~** kerngesund
b *(= sound of bell)* Läuten *nt*; *(of doorbell, school bell, telephone etc)* Klingeln *nt*; *(in athletics)* Glocke *f* zur letzten Runde; **there's the ~** es klingelt *or* läutet; **was that the ~?** hat es gerade geklingelt *or* geläutet?; **the teacher came in on the ~** der Lehrer kam mit dem Klingeln *or* Läuten herein; **he's coming up to the ~** er geht nun in die letzte Runde; **it was 3.02 at the ~** zu Beginn der letzten Runde hatte er eine Zeit von 3.02; **to give sb a ~** *(Brit inf)* jdn anrufen
c *(Naut)* Schiffsglocke *f*; *(= ringing)* Läuten *nt* (der Schiffsglocke); *(for time also)* Glasen *nt (spec)*; **it is eight ~s** es ist acht Glas *(spec)*; **to ring one ~** einmal glasen *(spec)*
d *(of flower)* Glocke *f*, Kelch *m*; *(of trumpet)* Stürze *f*; *(of loudspeaker)* (Schall)trichter *m*
VT eine Glocke/ein Glöckchen umhängen *(+dat)*; **to ~ the cat** *(fig)* der Katze die Schelle umhängen

bell[2] N *(of stag)* Röhren *nt* VI röhren

belladonna [,belə'dɒnə] N *(Bot)* Tollkirsche *f*, Belladonna *f*; *(Med)* Belladonin *nt*

bell: **bell-bottomed trousers** *(esp Brit)*, **bell-bottoms** PL ausgestellte Hosen; **bellboy** N *(esp US)* Page *m*, Hoteljunge *m*; **bell captain** N *(US)* Chef(in) *m(f)* der Hotelpagen

belle [bel] N Schöne *f*, Schönheit *f*; **the ~ of the ball** die Ballkönigin

bell: **bellflower** N *(Bot)* Glockenblume *f*; **bell heather** N Glockenheide *f*; **bellhop** N *(US)* = **bellboy**

bellicose ['belɪkəʊs] ADJ *nation, mood* kriegerisch, kriegslustig; *(= pugnacious)* kampflustig, streitsüchtig

bellicosity [,belɪ'kɒsɪtɪ] N *(of nation, mood)* Kriegslust *f*; *(= pugnacity)* Kampf(es)lust *f*, Streitsüchtigkeit *f*

belligerence, **belligerency** [bɪ'lɪdʒərəns, -sɪ] N *(of nation)* Kriegslust *f*, Kampf(es)lust *f*; *(of person, attitude)* Streitlust *f*; *(of speech)* Aggressivität *f*

belligerent [bɪ'lɪdʒərənt] ADJ **a** *nation* kriegslustig, kampflustig, kriegerisch; *person, attitude* streitlustig, kampflustig; *mood* streitlustig, kämpferisch; *speech* aggressiv **b** *(= waging war)* Krieg führend, streitend; **~ power** Streitmacht *f* N *(= nation)* Krieg führendes Land; *(= person)* Streitende(r) *mf*

belligerently [bɪ'lɪdʒərəntlɪ] ADV *say, act, behave* streitlustig

bell jar N (Glas)glocke *f*

bellow ['beləʊ] VI *(animal, person)* brüllen; *(singing also)* grölen *(inf)*; **to ~ at sb** jdn anbrüllen VT *(also* **bellow out***)* brüllen; *song also* grölen *(inf)* N Brüllen *nt*

bellows ['beləʊz] PL Blasebalg *m*; **a pair of ~** ein Blasebalg

bell: **bell pull** N Klingelzug *m*; **bell push** N Klingel *f*; **bell-ringer** N Glöckner *m*; **bell-ringing** N Glockenläuten *nt*; **bell rope** N *(in church)* Glockenstrang *m*; *(in house)* Klingelzug *m*; **bells and whistles** [,belzənd'wɪslz] PL *(esp Comput inf: = additional features)* Extras *pl*; **bell-shaped** ADJ glockenförmig, kelchförmig

Bell's palsy [,belz'pɔ:lzɪ] N *(Med)* bellsche Lähmung

bell: **bell tent** N Rundzelt *nt*; **bell tower** N Glockenturm *m*; **bellwether** ['bel,weðə'] N Leithammel *m*

belly ['belɪ] N *(general)* Bauch *m*; *(of violin etc)* Decke *f*

▶ **belly out** VT *sep sails* blähen, schwellen lassen VI *(sails)* sich blähen, schwellen

belly: **bellyache** *(inf)* N Bauchweh *nt (inf)*, Bauchschmerzen *pl* VI *(= complain)* murren *(about* über *+acc)*; **bellyaching** N *(inf)* Murren *nt*, Gemurre *nt*; **bellybutton** N *(inf)* Bauchnabel *m*; **belly dance** N Bauchtanz *m*; **belly-dance** VI bauchtanzen; **belly dancer** N Bauchtänzerin *f*; **bellyflop** N Bauchklatscher *m (inf)*; **to do a ~** einen Bauchklatscher machen *(inf)*

bellyful ['belɪfʊl] N **a** *(inf: = more than enough)* **I've had a ~ of him/writing these letters** ich habe die Nase voll von ihm/davon, immer diese Briefe zu schreiben *(inf)* **b** *(inf, of food)* **after a good ~ of beans** nachdem ich mir/er sich *etc* den Bauch mit Bohnen vollgeschlagen hatte *(inf)*

belly: **belly-land** VI bauchlanden; **belly landing** N Bauchlandung *f*; **belly laugh** N dröhnendes Lachen; **he gave a great ~** er lachte lauthals los; **belly up** ADV **to go ~** *(inf, company)* pleitegehen *(inf)*; **his plans went ~** er ging mit seinen Plänen baden *(inf)*

belong [bɪ'lɒŋ] VI **a** *(= be the property of)* gehören *(to sb* jdm*)*; **who does it ~ to?** wem gehört es?; **the parks ~ to everybody** die Parkanlagen sind für alle da
b *(= be part of)* gehören *(to* zu*)*; *(to town: person)* gehören *(to* nach*)*, sich zu Hause fühlen *(to* in *+dat)*; **to ~ together** zusammengehören; **the lid ~s to this box** der Deckel gehört zu dieser Schachtel; **to ~ to a club** einem Klub angehören; **why don't you ~?** warum sind Sie nicht Mitglied?; **concepts that ~ to physics** Begriffe, die in die Physik gehören
c *(= be in right place)* gehören; **I don't ~ here** ich gehöre nicht hierher, ich bin hier fehl am Platze; **to feel that one doesn't ~** das Gefühl haben, dass man fehl am Platze ist *or* dass man nicht dazugehört; **you don't ~ here, so scram** Sie haben hier nichts zu suchen, also verschwinden Sie; **the vase ~s on the mantelpiece** die Vase gehört auf den Sims; **where does this one ~?** wo gehört das hin?; **that doesn't ~ to my area of responsibility** das gehört nicht in meinen Verantwortungsbereich; **this case ~s in the Appeal Court** dieser Fall gehört vor das Berufungsgericht; **that doesn't ~ to this department** das gehört nicht in diese Abteilung; **it ~s under the heading of …** das gehört *or* fällt in die Rubrik der …

belongings [bɪ'lɒŋɪŋz] PL Sachen *pl*, Besitz *m*, Habe *f (geh)*; **personal ~** persönliches Eigentum, persönlicher Besitz; **all his ~** sein ganzes Hab und Gut

beloved [bɪ'lʌvɪd] ADJ geliebt; *memory* lieb, teuer N Geliebte(r) *mf*; **dearly ~** *(Rel)* liebe Brüder und Schwestern im Herrn

below [bɪˈləʊ] PREP **a** *(= under)* unterhalb *(+gen)*; *(with line, level etc also)* unter *(+dat or with motion +acc)*; **on it and ~ it** darauf und darunter; **her skirt comes well ~ her knees** *or* **the knee** ihr Rock geht bis weit unters Knie; **Naples is ~ Rome** *(on the map)* Neapel liegt unterhalb Roms; **the sun disappeared ~ the horizon** die Sonne verschwand hinter dem Horizont; **to be ~ sb** *(in rank)* (rangmäßig) unter jdm stehen
b *(= downstream from)* unterhalb *(+gen)*, nach
c *(= unworthy of)* **or is that ~ you?** oder ist das unter Ihrer Würde?
ADV **a** *(= lower down)* unten; **the cows in the valley ~** die Kühe drunten im Tal; **they live one floor ~** sie wohnen ein Stockwerk tiefer; **the tenants/apartment ~** die Mieter/die Wohnung darunter; *(below us)* die Mieter/Wohnung unter uns; **write the name here with the address ~** schreiben Sie den Namen hierher und die Adresse darunter; **in the class ~** in der Klasse darunter; *(below me)* in der Klasse unter mir; **what's the next rank ~?** was ist der nächstniedere Rang?; **down ~** unten
b *(Naut)* unter Deck; **to go ~** unter Deck gehen
c *(in documents)* (weiter) unten; **see ~** siehe unten
d 15 degrees ~ 15 Grad unter null, 15 Grad minus
e here ~ *(= on earth)* hier unten; **and on earth ~** *(Bibl)* und unten auf der Erde; **down ~** *(= in hell)* dort drunten

below strength ADJ *pred*, **below-strength** ADJ *attr (Sport)* ersatzgeschwächt

Belshazzar [belˈʃæzəʳ] N **~'s Feast** Belsazars Gastmahl *nt*

belt [belt] N **a** *(on clothes)* Gürtel *m*; *(for holding, carrying etc, seat belt)* Gurt *m*; *(Mil etc, on uniform)* Koppel *nt*; *(for cartridges)* Patronengurt *m*; *(= rifle sling)* (Gewehr)riemen *m*; **a blow below the ~** *(lit, fig)* ein Schlag *m* unterhalb der Gürtellinie, ein Tiefschlag; **to hit sb below the ~** *(lit, fig)* jdm einen Schlag unter die Gürtellinie versetzen; **that was below the ~** das war ein Schlag unter die Gürtellinie; **to be a black ~** den schwarzen Gürtel haben; **to get the ~** (mit dem Lederriemen) eine auf die Finger bekommen; **to tighten one's ~** *(fig)* den Gürtel *or* Riemen enger schnallen; **under one's ~** *(fig inf)* auf dem Rücken *(inf)*
b *(Tech)* (Treib)riemen *m*; *(= conveyor belt)* Band *nt*
c *(= tract of land)* Gürtel *m*; **~ of trees** Waldstreifen *m*; *(around house etc)* Baumgürtel *m*; **industrial ~** Industriegürtel *m* → **commuter**
d *(inf: = hit)* Schlag *m*; **to give sb/the ball a ~** jdm eine knallen *(inf)*/den Ball knallen *(inf)*
e *(US: = ring road)* Umgehungsstraße *f*
f *(US inf: = drink)* Schluck *m* aus der Pulle *(inf)*
VT **a** *(= fasten)* den Gürtel zumachen *(sth +gen)*
b *(Sch etc: = thrash)* (mit dem Lederriemen) schlagen
c *(inf: = hit)* knallen *(inf)*; **she ~ed him one in the eye** sie verpasste *or* haute *or* knallte ihm eins aufs Auge *(inf)*
VI *(inf: = rush)* rasen *(inf)*; **to ~ out** hinaus-/herausrasen *(inf)*; **to ~ across** hinüber-/herüberrasen *(inf)*; **we were really ~ing along** wir sind wirklich gerast *(inf)*; **he ~ed off down the street** er raste davon die Straße hinunter *(inf)*; **this novel really ~s along** dieser Roman ist wirklich tempogeladen *(inf)*

▶ **belt down** VT *sep (inf: = drink quickly)* hinunterschütten, hinunterkippen *(inf)*

▶ **belt on** VT *sep sword* umschnallen, sich umgürten mit *(geh)*; *raincoat* anziehen

▶ **belt out** VT *sep (inf) tune* schmettern *(inf)*; *rhythm* voll herausbringen *(inf)*; *(on piano)* hämmern *(inf)*

▶ **belt up** VT *sep jacket* den Gürtel *(+gen)* zumachen VI **a** *(inf)* die Klappe *or* Schnauze halten *(inf)*; *(= stop making noise)* mit dem Krach aufhören *(inf)* **b** *(esp hum: = put seat belt on)* sich anschnallen

belt bag N Gürteltasche *f*

belt buckle N Gürtelschnalle *f*

belt drive N Riemenantrieb *m*

belter [ˈbeltəʳ] N *(inf: = singer)* toller Sänger *(inf)*, tolle Sängerin *(inf)*; *(= song)* Hit *m*; *(= party)* tolle Fete

belting [ˈbeltɪŋ] N *(inf)* Dresche *f (inf)*; **to give sb a good ~** jdn ganz schön verdreschen *(inf)*

belt loop N Gürtelschlaufe *f*

beltway [ˈbeltweɪ] N *(US)* Umgehungsstraße *f*

bemoan [bɪˈməʊn] VT beklagen

bemused [bɪˈmjuːzd] ADJ ratlos; **to be ~ by sth** einer Sache *(dat)* ratlos gegenüberstehen

bemusedly [bɪˈmjuːzɪdlɪ] ADV ratlos

bench [bentʃ] N **a** *(= seat)* Bank *f*; **laughter from the government ~es** *(Brit)* Gelächter von der Regierungsbank
b *(Jur: = office of a judge)* Richteramt *nt*; *(= judges generally)* Richter *pl*; *(= court)* Gericht *nt*; **member of the ~** Richter *m*; **to be raised to the ~** zum Richter bestellt werden; **to be on the ~** *(permanent office)* Richter sein; *(when in court)* der Richter sein, auf dem Richterstuhl sitzen *(geh)*
c *(= workbench)* Werkbank *f*; *(in lab)* Experimentiertisch *m*
d *(Sport: = selected as substitute)* **on the ~** auf der Reservebank
VT *(US Sport)* auf die Strafbank schicken; *(= keep as substitute)* auf die Reservebank setzen

bencher [ˈbentʃəʳ] N *(Brit Jur)* *Vorstandsmitglied eines der Inns of Court*

benchmark [ˈbentʃmɑːk] N *(Surv)* Höhenfestpunkt *m*; *(fig)* Maßstab *m* ADJ *attr* **~ price** Richtpreis *m*; **~ rate** Benchmark *f*; **the ~ machine** die Maschine, die Maßstäbe setzt

benchmarking [ˈbentʃmɑːkɪŋ] N *(Econ)* Benchmarking *nt*

bench: **bench penalty** N *(Ice hockey)* Bankstrafe *f*; **bench press** N *(Sport)* Bankdrücken *nt*; **bench seat** N *(in the car)* Sitzbank *f*; **bench test** N *(Tech)* Test *m* auf dem Prüfstand, Prüfstandtest *m*; **bench warmer** N *(Sport inf)* Ersatzspieler(in) *m(f) (der/die nur selten zum Einsatz kommt)*

bend [bend] VB *pret, ptp* **bent**
N **a** *(in river, tube, etc)* Krümmung *f*, Biegung *f*; *(90°)* Knie *nt*; *(in road also)* Kurve *f*; **there is a ~ in the road** die Straße macht (da) eine Kurve; **~s for 3 miles** 3 Meilen kurvenreiche Strecke; **don't park on the ~** parken Sie nicht in der Kurve; **to go/be round the ~** *(Brit inf)* durchdrehen *(inf)*, verrückt werden/sein *(inf)*; **to drive sb round the ~** *(Brit inf)* jdn verrückt *or* wahnsinnig machen *(inf)*
b *(= knot)* Stek *m*
VT **a** *(= curve, make angular)* biegen; *rod, rail, pipe also* krümmen; *bow* spannen; *arm, knee also* beugen; *leg, arm also* anwinkeln; *(forwards) back also* beugen, krümmen; *head* beugen, neigen; **he can ~ an iron bar with his teeth** er kann mit den Zähnen eine Eisenstange verbiegen; **to ~ sth at right angles** etw rechtwinklig abbiegen *or* abknicken; **to ~ sth out of shape** etw verbiegen; **the bumper got bent in the crash** die Stoßstange hat sich bei dem Zusammenstoß verbogen; **on ~ed knees** auf Knien; *(fig also)* kniefällig; **to go down on ~ed knees** auf die Knie fallen; *(fig also)* einen Kniefall machen
b *(fig) rules, truth* es nicht so genau nehmen mit; **to ~ the law** das Gesetz beugen; **to ~ sb to one's will** sich *(dat)* jdn gefügig machen
c *(= direct) one's steps, efforts* lenken, richten
d *(Naut) sail* befestigen
VI **a** sich biegen; *(pipe, rail also)* sich krümmen; *(forwards also, tree, corn etc)* sich neigen; *(person)* sich beugen; **this metal ~s easily** *(a bad thing)* dieses Metall verbiegt sich leicht; *(a good thing)* dieses Metall lässt sich leicht biegen; **my arm won't ~** ich kann den Arm nicht biegen; **~ing strain** Biegespannung *f*
b *(river)* eine Biegung machen; *(at right angles)* ein Knie machen; *(road also)* eine Kurve machen; **the road/river ~s to the left** die Straße/der Fluss macht eine Linkskurve/-biegung
c *(fig: = submit)* sich beugen, sich fügen *(to +dat)*

▶ **bend back** VI sich zurückbiegen; *(over backwards)* sich nach hinten biegen; *(road, river)* in einer Schleife zurückkommen VT *sep* zurückbiegen

▶ **bend down** VI *(person)* sich bücken; *(branch, tree)* sich neigen, sich nach unten biegen; **she bent down to look at the baby** sie beugte sich hinunter, um das Baby anzusehen VT *sep edges* nach unten biegen

▶ **bend over** VI *(person)* sich bücken; **to bend over to look at sth** sich nach vorn beugen, um etw anzusehen → **backwards** VT *sep* umbiegen

bender [ˈbendəʳ] N *(Brit inf)* Kneipkur *f (hum inf)*; **to go on a ~** *(Brit inf)* sich besaufen *(inf)*; *(= go on pub-crawl)* auf eine Sauftour gehen *(inf)*

bends [bendz] N **the ~** die Taucherkrankheit

bend sinister N *(Her)* Schräglinksbalken *m*

bendy [ˈbendɪ] ADJ *(inf)* **a** *(= flexible)* biegsam **b** *road* kurvenreich, kurvig

bendy bus N *(Mot)* Gelenkbus *m*

beneath [bɪˈniːθ] PREP **a** unter *(+dat or with motion +acc)*; *(with line, level etc also)* unterhalb *(+gen)*; **to marry ~ one** unter seinem Stand heiraten → *also* **below PREP a b** *(= unworthy of)* **it is ~ him** das ist unter seiner Würde; **he regarded the critics as ~ his notice** er fand es unter seiner Würde, von den Kritikern überhaupt Notiz zu nehmen ADV unten → *also* **below ADV a**

Benedictine [ˌbenɪˈdɪktɪn] N **a** *(Eccl)* Benediktiner(in) *m(f)* **b** *(= liqueur)* Benediktiner *m* ADJ Benediktiner-

benediction [ˌbenɪˈdɪkʃən] N **a** *(= blessing)* Segen *m*; *(= act of blessing)* Segnung *f* **b** *(= consecration)* Einsegnung *f*

benefaction [ˌbenɪˈfækʃən] N **a** *(= good deed)* Wohltat *f*, gute Tat **b** *(= gift)* Spende *f*

benefactor [ˈbenɪfæktəʳ] N Wohltäter *m*; *(= giver of money also)* Gönner *m*

benefactress [ˈbenɪfæktrɪs] N Wohltäterin *f*; *(= giver of money also)* Gönnerin *f*

benefice [ˈbenɪfɪs] N Pfründe *f*, kirchliches Benefizium *(spec)*

beneficence [bɪˈnefɪsəns] N *(liter)* Wohltätigkeit *f*

beneficent [bɪˈnefɪsənt] ADJ *(liter)* wohltätig

beneficial [ˌbenɪˈfɪʃəl] ADJ **a** gut *(to* für); *climate also* zuträglich *(geh) (to +dat)*; *influence also* vorteilhaft; *advice, lesson* nützlich *(to* für); *(= advantageous)* günstig, von Vorteil; **the change will be ~ to you** die Veränderung wird Ihnen guttun **b** *(Jur)* **~ owner** Nutznießer(in) *m(f)*

beneficiary [ˌbenɪˈfɪʃərɪ] N **a** Nutznießer(in) *m(f)*; *(of will, insurance etc)* Begünstigte(r) *mf* **b** *(Eccl)* Pfründner *m*

benefit [ˈbenɪfɪt] N **a** *(= advantage)* Vorteil *m*; *(= profit)* Nutzen *m*, Gewinn *m*; **to derive** *or* **get ~ from sth** aus etw Nutzen ziehen; **for the ~ of his family/the poor** zum Wohl *or* für das Wohl seiner Familie/der Armen; **for the ~ of your health** Ihrer Gesundheit zuliebe, um Ihrer Gesundheit willen; **for your ~** Ihretwegen, um Ihretwillen *(geh)*; **this money is for the ~ of the blind** dieses Geld kommt den Blinden zugute; **it is for his ~ that this was done** das ist seinetwegen geschehen; **to give sb the ~ of the doubt** im Zweifelsfall zu jds Gunsten entscheiden; **we should give him the ~ of the doubt** wir sollten das zu seinen Gunsten auslegen
b *(= allowance)* Unterstützung *f*; *(= sickness benefit)* Krankengeld *nt*; *(Brit: = child benefit)* Kindergeld *nt*; *(= social security benefit)* Sozialhilfe *f*; *(Brit: = maternity benefit)* Wochengeld *nt*; *(= insurance benefit)* Versicherungsleistung *f*; **old age ~** Altersrente *f* → **fringe benefits**
c *(= special performance)* Benefizveranstaltung *f*; *(Theat also)* Benefiz(vorstellung *f*) *nt*; *(Sport al-*

so) Benefizspiel *nt*; **it's his ~** es ist eine Benefizvorstellung für ihn
d **without ~ of clergy** ohne kirchlichen Segen
VT guttun *(+dat)*, nützen *(+dat)*, zugutekommen *(+dat)*; *(healthwise)* guttun *(+dat)*
VI profitieren *(from, by* von); *(from experience also)* Nutzen ziehen *(from* aus); **who will ~ from that?** wem wird das nützen?; **but how do we ~?** aber was nützt das uns?; **he would ~ from a week off** eine Woche Urlaub würde ihm guttun; **I think you'll ~ from the experience** ich glaube, diese Erfahrung wird Ihnen nützlich sein *or* von Nutzen sein; **a cure from which many have ~ed** eine Behandlung, die schon manchem geholfen hat

benefit: **benefit concert** N Benefizkonzert *nt*; **benefit match** N Benefizspiel *nt*; **benefit performance** N Benefizveranstaltung *f*

Benelux ['benılʌks] N Benelux-Wirtschaftsunion *f*; **~ countries** Beneluxstaaten *or* -länder *pl*

benevolence [bı'nevələns] N Wohlwollen *nt*; *(of smile, gesture)* Gutmütigkeit *f*; *(as character trait)* Güte *f*; *(of emperor, judge)* Milde *f*

benevolent [bı'nevələnt] ADJ a wohlwollend; *pat, smile, twinkle* gutmütig; *(as character trait)* gütig; *emperor, judge* mild; **Benevolent Despotism** der aufgeklärte Absolutismus b *(= charitable)* **~ fund** Unterstützungsfonds *m*, Unterstützungskasse *f*; **~ institution** Wohltätigkeitseinrichtung *f*; **~ society** Wohltätigkeitsverein *m*

benevolently [bı'nevələntlı] ADV *look, say* wohlwollend; *smile* gutmütig; *(= leniently)* milde

Bengal [beŋ'gɔːl] N Bengalen *nt*

Bengalese [ˌbeŋgə'liːz] N Bengale *m*, Bengalin *f* ADJ bengalisch

Bengali [beŋ'gɔːlı] N *(= language)* Bengali *nt*; *(= person)* Bengale *m*, Bengalin *f* ADJ bengalisch

Bengal light, Bengal match N bengalisches Feuer *or* Hölzchen

Bengal tiger N Bengalischer Tiger, Königstiger *m*

benighted [bı'naıtıd] ADJ a *(fig) person* unbedarft; *country* gottverlassen; *policy etc* hirnrissig b *(lit)* von der Dunkelheit *or* Nacht überfallen *or* überrascht

benign [bı'naın] ADJ a gütig; *planet, influence* günstig; *climate* mild; *(= harmless) substance, process, research* harmlos b *(Med) tumour* gutartig

benny ['benı] N *(sl) dim of* **Benzedrine**

bent [bent] *pret, ptp of* **bend** ADJ a *metal etc* gebogen; *(= out of shape)* verbogen
b *(Brit inf: = dishonest) person* korrupt; *affair* unsauber *(inf)*; **he's ~** er ist ein krummer Hund *(inf)*
c *(Brit pej inf: = homosexual)* andersrum *pred (inf)*
d **to be ~ on sth/doing sth** etw unbedingt *or* partout wollen/tun wollen; **he seemed ~ on self-destruction** er schien von einem Selbstzerstörungstrieb besessen zu sein
N *(= aptitude)* Neigung *f (for* zu); *(= type of mind, character)* Schlag *m*; **to follow one's ~** seiner Neigung folgen; **people with** *or* **of a musical ~** Menschen mit einer musikalischen Veranlagung; **people of his ~** Leute seines Schlags

benumb [bı'nʌm] VT a *limb* gefühllos machen; *person* betäuben; *(with cold also)* erstarren lassen; **he was/his fingers were ~ed with cold** er war/seine Finger waren starr vor Kälte b *(fig) mind* betäuben; *(panic, experience etc)* lähmen; **~ed by alcohol** vom Alkohol benommen

Benzedrine® ['benzıdriːn] N Benzedrin *nt*

benzene ['benziːn] N Benzol *nt*

benzine ['benziːn] N Leichtbenzin *nt*

bequeath [bı'kwiːð] VT a *(in will)* vermachen, hinterlassen *(to sb* jdm) b *(fig) tradition* hinterlassen, vererben *(to sb* jdm)

bequest [bı'kwest] N *(= act of bequeathing)* Vermachen *nt (to* an *+acc)*; *(= legacy)* Nachlass *m*

berate [bı'reıt] VT *(liter)* schelten, auszanken

Berber ['bɜːbə'] N a Berber *m*, Berberfrau *f* b *(= language)* die Berbersprache ADJ berberisch

bereave [bı'riːv] VT a *pret, ptp* **bereft** *(liter, = deprive)* berauben *(geh) (of +gen)* b *pret, ptp* **bereaved** *(= cause loss by death: illness) (sb of sb* jdm jdn) rauben *(geh)*, nehmen; **he was ~d of his son** sein Sohn ist ihm genommen worden *(geh)*

bereaved [bı'riːvd] ADJ leidtragend; **the ~** die Hinterbliebenen *pl*

bereavement [bı'riːvmənt] N a *(= death in family)* Trauerfall *m*; **owing to a/his recent ~** wegen *or* aufgrund eines Trauerfalls/dieses für ihn so schmerzlichen Verlusts; **to sympathize with sb in his ~** jds Leid teilen b *(= feeling of loss)* schmerzlicher Verlust; **to feel a sense of ~ at sth** etw als schmerzlichen Verlust empfinden

bereft [bı'reft] ADJ **to be ~ of sth** einer Sache *(gen)* bar sein *(geh)*; **his life was ~ of happiness** seinem Leben fehlte jegliches Glück

beret ['bereı] N Baskenmütze *f*

berg [bɜːg] N = **iceberg**

beribboned [bı'rıbənd] ADJ mit Bändern geschmückt, bebändert; *general* mit Ordensbändern geschmückt

beriberi ['berı'berı] N Beriberi *f*

Bering ['berıŋ]: **Bering Sea** N Beringmeer *nt*; **Bering Strait** N Beringstraße *f*

berk [bɜːk] N *(Brit inf)* Dussel *m (inf)*

Berks [bɑːks] *abbr of* **Berkshire**

Berlin [bɜː'lın] N Berlin *nt*; **the ~ Wall** die Mauer

Bermuda [bɜː'mjuːdə] N Bermuda *nt (form rare)*; **the ~s** die Bermudas *pl*, die Bermudainseln *pl*; **to go to ~** auf die Bermudas fahren

Bermudas [bɜː'mjuːdəz] PL, **Bermuda shorts** PL Bermudashorts *pl*

Bermuda Triangle N Bermudadreieck *nt*

Bernard ['bɜːnəd] N Bernhard *m*

Berne [bɜːn] N Bern *nt*

Bernese [bɜː'niːz] ADJ Berner; *village* im Berner Oberland

berry ['berı] N a *(= fruit)* Beere *f*; **as brown as a ~** *(Brit)* ganz braun gebrannt b *(Bot)* Beerenfrucht *f*

berrying ['berııŋ] N Beerensammeln *nt*; **to go ~** Beeren sammeln gehen

berserk [bə'sɜːk] ADJ wild; **to go ~** wild werden; *(audience)* aus dem Häuschen geraten *(inf)*, zu toben anfangen; *(= go mad)* überschnappen *(inf)*, verrückt werden

berth [bɜːθ] N a *(on ship)* Koje *f*; *(on train)* Schlafwagenplatz *m* b *(Naut, for ship)* Liegeplatz *m* c *(Naut, = sea-room)* Raum *m*; **to give a wide ~ to a ship** Abstand zu einem Schiff halten; **to give sb/sth a wide ~** *(fig)* einen (weiten) Bogen um jdn/etw machen VI anlegen VT **to ~ a ship** mit einem Schiff (am Kai) anlegen; *(= assign berth to)* einem Schiff einen Liegeplatz zuweisen; **where is she ~ed?** wo liegt es?, wo hat es angelegt?

beryl ['berıl] N Beryll *m*

beseech [bı'siːtʃ] *pret, ptp* **beseeched** *or (liter)* **besought** *(liter)* VT *person* anflehen, beschwören; *forgiveness* flehen um, erflehen *(geh)*

beseeching ADJ, **beseechingly** ADV [bı'siːtʃıŋ, -lı] flehentlich *(geh)*, flehend

beset [bı'set] *pret, ptp* **beset** VT *(difficulties, dangers)* (von allen Seiten) bedrängen; *(doubts)* befallen; *(temptations, trials)* heimsuchen; **to be ~ with difficulties/danger** *(problem, journey etc)* reich an *or* voller Schwierigkeiten/Gefahren sein; **he was ~ with difficulties** er wurde von Schwierigkeiten heimgesucht; **~ by doubts** von Zweifeln befallen

besetting [bı'setıŋ] ADJ **his ~ sin** eine ständige Untugend von ihm; **his one ~ worry** die Sorge, die ihn nicht loslässt

beside [bı'saıd] PREP a *(= at the side of)* neben *(+dat or with motion +acc)*; *(= at the edge of) road, river* an *(+dat or with motion +acc)*; **~ the road** am Straßenrand b *(= compared with)* neben *(+dat)*; **if you put it ~ the original** wenn man es neben dem Original sieht c *(= irrelevant to)* **to be ~ the point** damit nichts zu tun haben d **to be ~ oneself** *(with anger)* außer sich sein *(with* vor); *(with joy also)* sich nicht mehr zu lassen wissen *(with* vor)

besides [bı'saıdz] ADV a *(= in addition)* außerdem, obendrein; **he wrote a novel and several short stories ~** er hat einen Roman und außerdem noch mehrere Kurzgeschichten geschrieben; **many more ~** noch viele mehr; **have you got any others ~?** haben Sie noch andere *or* noch welche? b *(= anyway, moreover)* außerdem PREP a *(= in addition to)* außer; **others ~ ourselves** außer uns noch andere; **there were three of us ~ Mary** Mary nicht mitgerechnet, waren wir zu dritt; **~ which he was unwell** überdies *or* außerdem fühlte er sich nicht wohl b *(= except)* außer, abgesehen von

besiege [bı'siːdʒ] VT a *(Mil) town* belagern b *(fig)* belagern; *(with information, offers)* überschütten, überhäufen; *(= pester: with letters, questions)* bestürmen, bedrängen

besieger [bı'siːdʒə'] N *(Mil)* Belagerer *m*

besmirch [bı'smɜːtʃ] VT *(lit, fig)* beschmutzen, besudeln

besom ['biːzəm] N a (Reisig)besen *m* b *(pej inf: = woman)* Besen *m (pej inf)*

besotted [bı'sɒtıd] ADJ a *(= drunk)* berauscht *(with* von) b *(= infatuated)* völlig vernarrt *(with* in *+acc)*; *(with idea)* berauscht *(with* von)

besought [bı'sɔːt] *(liter) pret, ptp of* **beseech**

bespake [bı'speık] *(old) pret of* **bespeak**

bespangle [bı'spæŋgl] VT besetzen; **~d costume** mit Pailletten besetztes Kostüm; **the sky ~d with …** *(liter)* der mit … übersäte Himmel

bespatter [bı'spætə'] VT bespritzen

bespeak [bı'spiːk] *pret* **bespoke** *or (old)* **bespake**, *ptp* **bespoken** *or* **bespoke** VT a *(= indicate)* verraten, erkennen lassen b *(old, = reserve)* reservieren lassen, bestellen

bespectacled [bı'spektıkld] ADJ bebrillt

bespoke [bı'spəʊk] ADJ *goods* nach Maß; *garment also* Maß-; *service, software* maßgeschneidert, den Kundenbedürfnissen angepasst; **a ~ tailor** ein Maßschneider *m*

bespoken [bı'spəʊkən] *ptp of* **bespeak**

besprinkle [bı'sprıŋkl] VT *(with liquid)* besprengen, bespritzen; *(with powder)* bestäuben

Bess [bes] N *dim of* **Elizabeth**; **good Queen ~** Elisabeth I

Bessemer ['besımə'] *in cpds* Bessemer-; **~ converter** Bessemerbirne *f*

best [best] ✪ 1.1, 2.2, 7.1, 21.3, 23.1, 23.3, 23.5, 24.2, 24.3 ADJ *superl of* **good** beste(r, s) *attr*; *(= most favourable) route, price also* günstigste(r, s) *attr*; **to be ~** am besten/günstigsten sein; **to be ~ of all** am allerbesten/allergünstigsten sein; **that was the ~ thing about her/that could happen** das war das Beste an ihr/, was geschehen konnte; **that would be ~** *or* **the ~ thing for everybody** das wäre für alle das Beste; **the ~ thing to do is to wait, it's ~ to wait** das Beste ist zu warten; **may the ~ man win!** dem Besten der Sieg!; **to put one's ~ foot forward** *(= hurry)* seinen schnellsten Gang anschlagen; *(fig)* sein Bestes geben *or* tun; **the ~ part of the year/my money** fast das ganze Jahr/all mein Geld
ADV *superl of* **well** a am besten; *like* am liebsten *or* meisten; *enjoy* am meisten; **the ~ fitting dress** das am besten passende Kleid; **her ~ known novel** ihr bekanntester Roman; **he was ~ known for …** er war vor allem bekannt für …; **~ of all** am allerbesten/-liebsten/-meisten; **I helped him as ~ I could** ich half ihm, so gut ich konnte; **I thought it ~ to go** ich hielt es für das Beste zu gehen; **do as you think ~** tun Sie, was Sie für richtig halten; **you know ~** Sie müssen es (am besten) wissen
b *(= better)* **you had ~ go now** am besten gehen Sie jetzt

N a *(= person, thing)* **the ~** der/die/das Beste; **the ~ of the bunch** *(inf)* (noch) der/die/das Beste; **his last book was his ~** sein letztes Buch war sein bestes; **with the ~ of intentions** mit den besten Absichten; **they are the ~ of friends** sie sind enge Freunde; **he can sing with the ~ of them** er kann sich im Singen mit den Besten messen
b *(= clothes)* beste Sachen *pl*, Sonntagskleider *pl (inf)*; **to be in one's (Sunday) ~** in Schale sein *(inf)*, im Sonntagsstaat sein
c **to do one's (level) ~** sein Bestes *or* Möglichstes tun; **that's the ~ you can expect** Sie können nichts Besseres erwarten; **do the ~ you can!** machen Sie es so gut Sie können!; **it's not perfect but it's the ~ I can do** es ist nicht perfekt, aber mehr kann ich nicht tun; **what a lame excuse, is that the ~ you can do?** so eine lahme Ausrede, fällt Ihnen nichts Besseres ein?; **to get** *or* **have the ~ of sb** jdn unterkriegen; **to get the ~ out of sb/sth** das Beste aus jdm/etw herausholen; **to get the ~ of the bargain** *or* **of it** am besten dabei wegkommen; **to play the ~ of three/five** nur so lange spielen, bis eine Partei zweimal/dreimal gewonnen hat; **to make the ~ of it/a bad job** das Beste daraus machen; **to make the ~ of one's opportunities** seine Chancen voll nützen; **the ~ of it is that ...** das Beste daran ist, dass ...; **we've had the ~ of the day** der Tag ist so gut wie vorbei; *(= the weather's getting worse)* das schöne Wetter wäre für heute vorbei; **it's all for the ~** es ist nur zum Guten; **I meant it for the ~** ich habe es doch nur gut gemeint; **to do sth for the ~** etw in bester Absicht tun; **to the ~ of my ability** so gut ich kann/konnte; **to the ~ of my knowledge** meines Wissens; **to the ~ of my recollection** *or* **memory** soviel ich mich erinnern kann; **to look one's ~** besonders gut aussehen; **to be at one's ~** *(= on form)* in Hochform sein; **he is at his ~ at about 8 in the evening** so gegen 8 abends ist seine beste Zeit; **roses are at their ~ just now** jetzt ist die beste Zeit für Rosen; **that is Goethe at his ~** das ist Goethe, wie er besser nicht sein könnte; **it's not enough (even) at the ~ of times** das ist schon normalerweise nicht genug; **at ~** bestenfalls; **to wish sb all the ~** jdm alles Gute wünschen; **all the ~ (to you)** alles Gute!
VT schlagen

best: **best-before date** N Haltbarkeitsdatum *nt*; **best boy** N *(Film)* Assistent *m* des Elektromeisters; **best-dressed** ADJ bestgekleidet *attr*

bestial [ˈbestɪəl] ADJ *acts, cruelty* bestialisch, tierisch; *person, look, appearance (= cruel)* brutal; *(= carnal)* tierisch

bestiality [ˌbestɪˈælɪtɪ] N a *(of behaviour)* Bestialität *f*; *(of person)* Brutalität *f* b *(= act)* Gräueltat *f* c *(= sex with animals)* Sodomie *f*

bestiary [ˈbestɪərɪ] N Bestiaire *nt*, Bestiarium *nt*

bestir [bɪˈstɜːˈ] VR *(hum, liter)* sich regen, sich rühren; **to ~ oneself to do sth** sich dazu aufraffen, etw zu tun

best: **best-laid** ADJ **the ~ plans (of mice and men)** noch so wohlbedachte Pläne; **best man** N Trauzeuge *m (des Bräutigams)*

> **BEST MAN**
>
> Bei einer traditionellen Hochzeit ist der **best man** der Trauzeuge des Bräutigams, normalerweise ein enger Freund oder Verwandter, zum Beispiel ein Bruder oder ein Cousin. Der **best man** ist dafür verantwortlich, dass am Hochzeitstag alles glattläuft. Seine Pflichten umfassen so wichtige Aufgaben wie den Bräutigam pünktlich zur Kirche zu bringen, Hochzeitsgäste zu empfangen und sich um die Trauringe zu kümmern. Auf dem Hochzeitsempfang übermittelt er normalerweise die Glückwünsche all derer, die nicht kommen konnten, sagt die Redner an, hält selbst eine humorvolle Rede und bringt einen Toast auf das Brautpaar aus.

bestow [bɪˈstəʊ] VT a *((up)on sb* jdm) *(= grant, give) gift, attention* schenken; *favour, friendship, kiss also* gewähren *(geh)*; *honour* erweisen, zuteilwerden lassen *(geh)*; *title, medal* verleihen b *(old, = place)* verstauen, unterbringen

bestowal [bɪˈstəʊəl] N *((up)on* an *+acc)* *(of gift)* Schenken *nt*; *(of favour, friendship, kiss)* Gewähren *nt*; *(of honour)* Erweisen *f*; *(of title, medal)* Verleihung *f*

bestraddle [bɪˈstrædl] VT = **bestride**

bestride [bɪˈstraɪd] *pret* **bestrode** *or* **bestrid** [bɪˈstrəʊd, bɪˈstrɪd] *ptp* **bestridden** [bɪˈstrɪdn] VT *(= sit astride)* rittlings sitzen auf *(+dat)*; *(= stand astride)* (mit gespreizten Beinen) stehen über *(+dat)*; *(= mount)* sich schwingen auf *(+acc)*; *(fig: = dominate)* beherrschen; **to ~ the world like a Colossus** die Welt beherrschen

best: **bestseller** N Verkaufs- *or* Kassenschlager *m*; *(= book)* Bestseller *m*; *(= author)* Erfolgsautor(in) *m(f)*; **bestselling** ADJ *article* absatzstark, der/die/das am besten geht; *author* Erfolgs-; **a ~ novel** ein Bestseller *m*; **this month's ~ books** die Bestsellerliste dieses Monats

bet [bet] *vb: pret, ptp* **bet** N Wette *f (on* auf *+acc)*; *(= money etc staked)* Wetteinsatz *m*; **to make** *or* **have a ~ with sb** mit jdm wetten, mit jdm eine Wette eingehen; **I have a ~ (on) with him that ...** ich habe mit ihm gewettet, dass ...; **it's a good** *or* **safe/bad ~** das ist ein sicherer/schlechter Tip; **it's a good** *or* **safe ~ he'll be in the bar** er ist bestimmt *or* garantiert in der Kneipe; **Liverpool look a good** *or* **safe ~ for the championship** Liverpool hat gute Aussichten auf den Meistertitel; **he's a bad ~ for the job** er ist nichts für diese Arbeit *(inf)*; **all ~s are off** *(fig)* es ist unmöglich vorauszusagen, was passieren wird
VT a *(Gambling)* wetten, setzen *(against* gegen/*on* auf *+acc)*; **I ~ him £5** ich habe mit ihm (um) £ 5 gewettet; **to ~ ten to one** zehn gegen eins wetten
b *(inf: = wager)* wetten; **I ~ he'll come!** wetten, dass er kommt! *(inf)*; **I'll ~ you anything (you like)** ich gehe mit dir jede Wette (darauf) ein; **~ you!** wetten! *(inf)*; **you can ~ your boots** *or* **your bottom dollar that ...** Sie können Gift darauf nehmen, dass ... *(inf)*; **~ you I can!** *(inf)* wetten, dass ich das kann! *(inf)*
VI wetten; **to ~ on a horse/horses** auf ein Pferd/Pferde setzen *or* wetten, Pferdewetten abschließen; **don't ~ on it** darauf würde ich nicht wetten; **you ~!** *(inf)* und ob! *(inf)*; **(do you) want to ~?** (wollen wir) wetten?

beta [ˈbiːtə] N Beta *nt*; *(Brit Sch)* gut

beta-blocker [ˈbiːtəˌblɒkəˈ] N Betablocker *m*

betake [bɪˈteɪk] *pret* **betook**, *ptp* **betaken** [bɪˈteɪkn] VR *(old, hum)* sich begeben

beta ray N Betastrahl *m*

beta release, **beta version** N *(Comput)* Betaversion *f*

betcha [ˈbetʃə] INTERJ *(inf)* wetten(, dass) *(inf)*

betel [ˈbiːtəl] N Betel *m*

betel nut N Betelnuss *f*

bête noire [betˈnwɑːˈ] N **to be sb's ~** jdm ein Gräuel sein

bethink [bɪˈθɪŋk] *pret, ptp* **bethought** VR *(liter, obs)* **to ~ oneself of sth/that ...** etw bedenken/bedenken, dass ...

Bethlehem [ˈbeθlɪhem] N Bethlehem *nt*

bethought [bɪˈθɔːt] *pret, ptp of* **bethink**

betide [bɪˈtaɪd] VI geschehen; **whatever (may) ~** was immer auch geschehen mag *(geh)* VT geschehen *(+dat)* → **woe**

betimes [bɪˈtaɪmz] ADV *(old, liter)* beizeiten *(geh)*

betoken [bɪˈtəʊkən] VT *(old)* bedeuten, hindeuten auf *(+acc)*

betook [bɪˈtʊk] *pret of* **betake**

betray [bɪˈtreɪ] VT verraten *(to +dat)*; *trust* enttäuschen, brechen; *(= be disloyal to also)* im Stich lassen; *(= be unfaithful to)* untreu werden *(+dat)*; *ideals, principles* untreu werden *(+dat)*, verraten; *(Pol)* verraten *(to* an *+acc)*; **to ~ oneself** sich verraten; **his accent ~ed him as a foreigner** sein Akzent verriet, dass er Ausländer war

betrayal [bɪˈtreɪəl] N *(= act)* Verrat *m (of +gen)*; *(= instance)* Verrat *m (of* an *+dat)*; *(of trust)* Enttäuschung *f*; *(of friends)* Verrat *m (of* an *+dat)*, Untreue *f (of* gegenüber); *(of ideals, principles)* Verrat *m (of +gen)*; **the ~ of Christ** der Verrat an Christus; **a ~ of trust** ein Vertrauensbruch *m*

betrayer [bɪˈtreɪəˈ] N Verräter(in) *m(f) (of* an *+dat)*; *(Pol)* Verräter(in) *m(f)* (an *+dat*)

betroth [bɪˈtrəʊð] VT *(obs, liter)* angeloben *(obs, liter)* *(to sb* jdm), versprechen *(liter)* *(to sb* jdm), verloben *(to sb* mit jdm)

betrothal [bɪˈtrəʊðəl] N *(obs, liter, hum)* Verlobung *f*

betrothed [bɪˈtrəʊðd] N *(obs, liter, hum)* Anverlobte(r) *mf (obs)*

better[1] [ˈbetəˈ] N Wetter(in) *m(f)*

better[2] ✪ 1.1, 2.3, 5.2, 7.2, 7.4, 13, 26.3 ADJ *comp of* **good** besser; *route, way also* günstiger; **he's ~** *(= recovered)* es geht ihm wieder besser; **he's much ~** es geht ihm viel besser; **the patient/his foot is getting ~** dem Patienten/seinem Fuß geht es schon viel besser; **I hope you get ~ soon** hoffentlich sind Sie bald wieder gesund; **~ and ~** immer besser; **that's ~!** *(approval)* so ist es besser!; *(relief etc)* so!; **to be ~ than one's word** mehr tun, als man versprochen hat; **it couldn't be ~** es könnte gar nicht besser sein; **I couldn't be ~** es könnte mir gar nicht besser gehen; **I am none the ~ for it** das hilft mir auch nicht; **she is no ~ than she ought to be** sie ist auch keine Heilige; **the ~ part of an hour/my money/our trip** fast eine Stunde/fast mein ganzes Geld/fast die ganze Reise; **it would be ~ to go early** es wäre besser, früh zu gehen; **you would be ~ to go early** Sie gehen besser früh; **to go one ~** einen Schritt weiter gehen; *(in offer)* höher gehen; **this hat has seen ~ days** dieser Hut hat auch schon bessere Tage gesehen *(inf)*
ADV *comp of* **well** a besser; *like* lieber, mehr; *enjoy* mehr; **they are ~ off than we are** sie sind besser dran als wir; **he is ~ off where he is** für ihn ist es besser, da zu sein, wo er ist, er ist besser dran, wo er ist *(inf)*; **you would do ~** *or* **be ~ advised to go early** Sie sollten lieber früh gehen; **to think ~ of it** es sich *(dat)* noch einmal überlegen; **I didn't think any ~ of him for that** deswegen hielt ich auch nicht mehr von ihm → **know, late**
b **I had ~ go** ich gehe jetzt wohl besser; **you'd ~ do what he says** tun Sie lieber, was er sagt; **I'd ~ answer that letter soon** ich beantworte den Brief lieber *or* besser bald; **I won't touch it – you'd ~ not!** ich fasse es nicht an – das will ich dir auch geraten haben
N a **one's ~s** Leute, die über einem stehen; *(socially also)* Höhergestellte *pl*, höher Gestellte *pl*; **that's no way to talk to your ~s** man muss immer wissen, wen man vor sich *(dat)* hat; **respect for one's ~s** Achtung *f* Respektspersonen gegenüber
b *(= person, object)* **the ~** der/die/das Bessere
c **it's a change for the ~** es ist eine Wendung zum Guten; **to think (all) the ~ of sb** (um so) mehr von jdm halten; **all the ~, so much the ~** umso besser; **it would be all the ~ for a drop of paint** ein bisschen Farbe würde Wunder wirken; **the bigger/sooner the ~** je größer/eher, desto besser; **it's done now, for ~ or worse** so oder so, es ist geschehen; **for ~, for worse** *(in marriage ceremony)* in Freud und Leid; **to get the ~ of sb** *(person)* jdn unterkriegen *(inf)*; *(illness)* jdn erwischen *(inf)*; *(problem etc)* jdm schwer zu schaffen machen
VT *(= improve on)* verbessern; *(= surpass)* übertreffen
VR *(= increase one's knowledge)* sich weiterbilden; *(in social scale)* sich verbessern

better half N *(inf)* bessere Hälfte *(inf)*

betterment [ˈbetəmənt] N **a** Verbesserung *f*; *(educational)* Weiterbildung *f* **b** *(Jur)* Wertsteigerung *f*; *(of land)* Melioration *f*

betting [ˈbetɪŋ] N Wetten *nt*; **the ~ was brisk** das Wettgeschäft war rege; **what is the ~ on his horse?** wie stehen die Wetten auf sein Pferd?

betting: **betting man** N (regelmäßiger) Wetter; **I'm not a ~** ich wette eigentlich nicht; **if I were a ~ I'd say …** wenn ich ja wetten würde, würde ich sagen …; **betting news** N Wettnachrichten *pl*; **betting shop** N Wettannahme *f*; **betting slip** N Wettschein *m*; **betting tax** N Wettsteuer *f*

Betty [ˈbetɪ] N *dim of* **Elizabeth**

between [bɪˈtwiːn] PREP **a** zwischen *(+dat)*; *(with movement)* zwischen *(+acc)*; **I was sitting ~ them** ich saß zwischen ihnen; **sit down ~ those two boys** setzen Sie sich zwischen diese beiden Jungen; **in ~** zwischen *(+dat/acc)*; **~ now and next week we must …** bis nächste Woche müssen wir …; **there's nothing ~ them** *(= they're equal)* sie sind gleich gut; *(no feelings, relationship)* zwischen ihnen ist nichts
b *(= amongst)* unter *(+dat/acc)*; **share the sweets ~ the two children** teilen Sie die Süßigkeiten zwischen den beiden Kindern auf; **divide the sweets ~ the children** verteilen Sie die Süßigkeiten unter die Kinder; **we shared an apple ~ us** wir teilten uns *(dat)* einen Apfel; **~ ourselves** *or* **~ you and me he is not very clever** unter uns *(dat)* gesagt, er ist nicht besonders gescheit; **that's just ~ ourselves** das bleibt aber unter uns
c *(= jointly, showing combined effort)* **~ us/them** zusammen; **we have a car ~ the two/three of us** wir haben zu zweit/dritt ein Auto, wir zwei/drei haben zusammen ein Auto; **~ the two/three of us we have enough** zusammen haben wir (zwei/drei) genug; **we got the letter written ~ us** wir haben den Brief zusammen *or* gemeinsam *or* mit vereinten Kräften geschrieben
d *(= what with, showing combined effect)* neben *(+dat)*; **~ housework and study I have no time for that** neben *or* zwischen Haushalt und Studium bleibt mir keine Zeit dazu
ADV *(place)* dazwischen; *(time also)* zwischendurch; **in ~** dazwischen; **the space/time ~** der Zwischenraum/die Zwischenzeit, der Raum/die Zeit dazwischen

betweentimes [bɪˈtwiːntaɪmz], **betweenwhiles** [bɪˈtwiːnwaɪlz] ADV in der Zwischenzeit

betwixt [bɪˈtwɪkst] PREP *(obs, liter, dial)* = **between** ADV **~ and between** dazwischen

bevel [ˈbevəl] N Schräge *f*, Schrägfläche *f*, Abschrägung *f*; *(also* **bevel edge***)* abgeschrägte Kante, Schrägkante *f*; *(= tool: also* **bevel square***)* Schrägmaß *nt*, Stellwinkel *m* VT abschrägen, schräg abflachen; **~led** *(Brit) or* **~ed** *(US)* **edge** Schrägkante *f*, abgeschrägte Kante; **~led** *(Brit) or* **~ed** *(US)* **mirror** Spiegel *m* mit schräg geschliffenen Kanten

bevel gear N Kegelradgetriebe *nt*

beverage [ˈbevərɪdʒ] N Getränk *nt*

bevvy [ˈbevɪ] N *(Brit inf)* **a** *(= drink)* alkoholisches Getränk; **he fancied a few bevvies** er hatte Lust, einen trinken zu gehen; **to go for a ~** einen trinken gehen **b** *(= drinking session)* **we had a major ~ after the match** nach dem Spiel haben wir ordentlich einen draufgemacht *(inf)* **c to go out on the ~** auf Sauftour gehen *(inf)* VI **to get bevvied** sich vollaufen lassen *(inf)*

bevy [ˈbevɪ] N *(of birds)* Schwarm *m*; *(of girls also)* Schar *f*

bewail [bɪˈweɪl] VT *(= deplore)* beklagen; *(= lament also)* bejammern; *sb's death also* betrauern

beware [bɪˈweəʳ] ✪ 2.3 VI *imper and infin only* **to ~ of sb/sth** sich vor jdm/etw hüten, sich vor jdm/etw in Acht nehmen; **to ~ of doing sth** sich davor hüten, etw zu tun; **~ of falling** passen Sie auf *or* sehen Sie sich vor, dass Sie nicht fallen; **~ of being deceived, ~ lest you are deceived** *(old)* geben Sie acht *or* sehen Sie sich vor, dass Sie nicht betrogen werden; **~ of how you speak** geben Sie acht *or* sehen Sie sich vor, was Sie sagen; **~!** *(old, liter)* gib acht!; **"beware of the dog"** „Vorsicht, bissiger Hund"; **"beware of pickpockets"** „vor Taschendieben wird gewarnt"
VT *imper and infin only* **to ~ sb/sth** sich vor jdm/etw hüten, sich vor jdm/etw in Acht nehmen; **to ~ doing sth** sich davor hüten, etw zu tun

bewigged [bɪˈwɪgd] ADJ mit Perücke, Perücke tragend *attr*

bewilder [bɪˈwɪldəʳ] VT *(= confuse)* verwirren, irremachen; *(= baffle)* verblüffen, verwundern

bewildered [bɪˈwɪldəd] ADJ *(= confused)* verwirrt, durcheinander *pred (inf)*; *(= baffled)* verblüfft, perplex *(inf)*, verwundert

bewildering [bɪˈwɪldərɪŋ] ADJ *(= confusing)* verwirrend; *(= baffling)* verblüffend

bewilderingly [bɪˈwɪldərɪŋlɪ] ADV *(= confusingly)* verwirrend; *(= bafflingly)* verblüffend

bewilderment [bɪˈwɪldəmənt] N *(= confusion)* Verwirrung *f*; *(= bafflement)* Verblüffung *f*, Erstaunen *nt*; **in ~** verwundert; **his ~ was obvious** er war offensichtlich verwirrt/verblüfft

bewitch [bɪˈwɪtʃ] VT verhexen, verzaubern; *(fig)* bezaubern

bewitching ADJ, **bewitchingly** ADV [bɪˈwɪtʃɪŋ, -lɪ] bezaubernd, hinreißend

beyond [bɪˈjɒnd] PREP **a** *(in space, = on the other side of)* über *(+dat)*, jenseits *(+gen) (geh)*; *(= further than)* über *(+acc)* … hinaus, weiter als; **~ the Alps** jenseits der Alpen; **I saw peak ~ snow-capped peak** ich sah schneebedeckte Gipfel bis weit in die Ferne; **~ the convent walls** außerhalb der Klostermauern
b *(in time)* **~ 6 o'clock/next week/the 17th century** nach 6 Uhr/nächster Woche/dem 17. Jahrhundert; **until ~ 6 o'clock** bis nach 6 Uhr; **until ~ next week/the 17th century** bis über nächste Woche/das 17. Jahrhundert hinaus; **~ the middle of June/the week** über Mitte Juni/der Woche hinaus
c *(= surpassing, exceeding)* **a task ~ her abilities** eine Aufgabe, die über ihre Fähigkeiten geht; **it's ~ your authority** das liegt außerhalb Ihrer Befugnis; **that is ~ human understanding** das übersteigt menschliches Verständnis; **~ repair** nicht mehr zu reparieren; **it was ~ her to pass the exam** sie schaffte es nicht, das Examen zu bestehen; **that's ~ me** *(= I don't understand)* das geht über meinen Verstand, das kapiere ich nicht *(inf)* → **compare, grave¹, help** *etc*
d *(with neg, interrog)* außer; **have you any money ~ what you have in the bank?** haben Sie außer dem, was Sie auf der Bank haben, noch Geld?; **~ this/that** sonst; **I've got nothing to suggest ~ this** sonst habe ich keine Vorschläge
ADV *(= on the other side of)* jenseits davon *(geh)*; *(= after that)* danach; *(= further than that)* darüber hinaus, weiter; **India and the lands ~** Indien und die Gegenden jenseits davon; **… a river, and ~ is a small field** … ein Fluss, und danach kommt ein kleines Feld; **the world ~** das Jenseits
N **the great Beyond** das Jenseits; *(= space)* der weite Raum

BF *(euph) abbr of* **bloody fool**

B/F, b/f *abbr of* **brought forward** Übertrag

BFPO *abbr of* **British Forces Post Office**

bhangra [ˈbæŋgrə] N Bhangra *m*

bhp *abbr of* **brake horsepower**

bi [baɪ] *(inf: = bisexual)* ADJ bi *(inf)* N Bisexuelle(r) *m(f)*

bi- [baɪ] PREF bi, Bi-

Biafra [bɪˈæfrə] N *(Hist)* Biafra *nt*

Biafran [bɪˈæfrən] *(Hist)* N Biafraner(in) *m(f)* ADJ Biafra-; **~ war** Biafrakrieg *m*

biannual ADJ, **biannually** ADV [baɪˈænjʊəl, -ɪ] zweimal jährlich; *(= half-yearly)* halbjährlich

bias [ˈbaɪəs] *vb: pret, ptp* **biased** *or (US)* **biassed**
N **a** *(= inclination, of course, newspaper etc)* (einseitige) Ausrichtung *f (towards* auf *+acc)*; *(of person)* Vorliebe *f (towards* für); **to have a ~ against sth** *(course, newspaper etc)* gegen etw eingestellt sein; *(person)* eine Abneigung gegen etw haben; **to have a left-/right-wing ~** *or* **a ~ to the left/right** nach links/rechts ausgerichtet sein, einen Links-/Rechtsdrall haben *(inf)*; **to be without ~** unvoreingenommen sein, ohne Vorurteile sein
b *(Sew)* **on the ~** schräg zum Fadenlauf
c *(Sport, = shape of bowl)* Überhang *m*
VT *report, article etc* (einseitig) färben; *(towards sth)* ausrichten *(towards* auf *+acc)*; *person* beeinflussen; **he ~ed** *(Brit) or* **~sed** *(US)* **his article in favour of a historical approach to the problem** in seinem Artikel ging er das Problem eher aus historischer Sicht an; **to ~ sb toward(s)/against sth** jdn für/gegen etw einnehmen

bias: **bias attack** N *(US)* = **bias incident**; **bias binding** N Schrägband *nt or* -streifen *m*

biased, *(US)* **biassed** [ˈbaɪəst] ADJ voreingenommen, befangen; **… but then I'm ~** … aber ich bin natürlich voreingenommen *or* befangen; **~ toward(s) sb/sth** gegenüber jdm/einer Sache voreingenommen; **~ in favour** *(Brit) or* **favor** *(US)* **of/against** voreingenommen für/gegen

bias incident N *(US)* rassistisch motivierter Vor- *or* Zwischenfall

biathlon [baɪˈæθlən] N Biathlon *nt*

bib [bɪb] N **a** *(for baby)* Latz *m*, Lätzchen *nt* **b** *(on garment)* Latz *m* **c** *(Brit inf)* **in one's best ~ and tucker** in Schale *(inf)*; **she put on her best ~ and tucker** sie warf sich in Schale *(inf)*

Bible [ˈbaɪbl] N Bibel *f*; *(fig also)* Evangelium *nt*

Bible: **Bible-basher** N *(inf)* aufdringlicher Bibelfritze *(sl)*; **Bible-bashing** ADJ *(inf)* **her ~ father** ihr Vater, der fanatisch auf die Bibel schwört/schwörte; **Bible class** N Bibelstunde *f*; **Bible school** N *(US)* Bibelschule *f*; **Bible story** N biblische Geschichte; **Bible-thumper** N *(inf)* aufdringlicher Bibelfritze *(sl)*

biblical [ˈbɪblɪkəl] ADJ biblisch, Bibel-

bibliographer [ˌbɪblɪˈɒgrəfəʳ] N Bibliograf *m*

bibliographic(al) [ˌbɪblɪəʊˈgræfɪk(əl)] ADJ bibliografisch

bibliography [ˌbɪblɪˈɒgrəfɪ] N Bibliografie *f*

bibliomania [ˌbɪblɪəʊˈmeɪnɪə] N Bibliomanie *f*

bibliophile [ˈbɪblɪəʊfaɪl] N Bibliophile(r) *mf*, Büchernarr *m*

bibulous [ˈbɪbjʊləs] ADJ *(form) person* trunksüchtig

bicameral [baɪˈkæmərəl] ADJ *(Pol)* Zweikammer-

bicarb [ˈbaɪkɑːb] N *(inf)* Natron *nt*

bicarbonate of soda [baɪˌkɑːbənɪtəvˈsəʊdə] N *(Cook)* ≈ Backpulver *nt*; *(Chem)* doppeltkohlensaures Natron

bicentenary [ˌbaɪsenˈtiːnərɪ], *(US)* **bicentennial** [ˌbaɪsenˈtenɪəl] N zweihundertjähriges Jubiläum, Zweihundertjahrfeier *f (of +gen)*; **the ~ of Beethoven's birth/death** Beethovens zweihundertster Geburts-/Todestag ADJ Zweihundertjahr-, zweihundertjährig; *celebrations* Zweihundertjahr-

bicephalous [baɪˈsefələs] ADJ *(spec)* dizephal *(spec)*, bikephalisch *(spec)*

biceps [ˈbaɪseps] PL Bizeps *m*

bichromate [baɪˈkrəʊmɪt] N Bichromat *nt*

bicker [ˈbɪkəʳ] VI *(= quarrel)* sich zanken, aneinandergeraten; **they are always ~ing** sie liegen sich dauernd in den Haaren

bickering [ˈbɪkərɪŋ] N Gezänk *nt*

bickie [ˈbɪkɪ] N *(Brit inf)* Keks *m*

bicuspid [baɪˈkʌspɪd] ADJ mit zwei Spitzen, zweihöckrig, bikuspidal *(spec)* N *(Anat)* vorderer Backenzahn

bicycle [ˈbaɪsɪkl] N Fahrrad *nt*; **to ride a ~** Fahrrad fahren, Rad fahren VI mit dem (Fahr)rad fahren

bicycle *in cpds* → **cycle**

bicycle kick N *(Ftbl)* Fallrückzieher *m*

bicyclist [ˈbaɪsɪklɪst] N *(dated)* Radfahrer(in) *m(f)*

bid [bɪd] VT a *pret, ptp* **bid** *(at auction)* bieten *(for* auf *+acc)*
b *pret, ptp* **bid** *(Cards)* reizen, bieten
c *pret* **bade** *or* **bad**, *ptp* **bidden** *(= say)* **to ~ sb good morning** jdm einen guten Morgen wünschen; **to ~ farewell to sb, to ~ sb farewell** von jdm Abschied nehmen, jdm Lebewohl sagen *(geh)*; **to ~ sb welcome** jdn willkommen heißen
d *pret* **bade** *or* **bad**, *ptp* **bidden to ~ sb (to) do sth** *(old, liter)* jdn etw tun heißen *(old)*
VI a *pret, ptp* **bid** *(at auction)* bieten
b *pret, ptp* **bid** *(Cards)* bieten, reizen
c *pret* **bad**, *ptp* **bidden to ~ fair to ...** versprechen zu ...; **everything ~s fair to be successful** es sieht alles recht erfolgversprechend aus
N a *(at auction)* Gebot *nt (for* auf *+acc)*; *(Comm)* Angebot *nt (for* für*)*; **any more ~s?** *(at auction)* wer bietet mehr?
b *(Cards)* Ansage *f*, Gebot *nt*; **to raise the ~** höher bieten *or* reizen, überrufen; **to make no ~** passen; **no ~!** passe!
c *(= attempt)* Versuch *m*; **to make a ~ for power** nach der Macht greifen; **to make a ~ for fame/freedom** versuchen, Ruhm/die Freiheit zu erlangen; **his ~ for fame/freedom failed** sein Versuch, Ruhm/die Freiheit zu erlangen, scheiterte; **rescue ~ fails** Rettungsversuch erfolglos; **the ~ for the summit** der Griff nach dem Gipfel; **she tried acupuncture in a ~ to stop smoking** sie versuchte es mit Akupunktur, um das Rauchen aufzugeben

biddable [ˈbɪdəbl] ADJ *(liter)* fügsam, willfährig *(geh)*

bidden [ˈbɪdn] *ptp of* **bid**

bidder [ˈbɪdəʳ] N Bietende(r) *mf*, Steigerer *m*; **to sell to the highest ~** an den Höchst- *or* Meistbietenden verkaufen; **there were no ~s** niemand hat geboten *or* ein Gebot gemacht

bidding [ˈbɪdɪŋ] N a *(at auction)* Steigern *nt*, Bieten *nt*; **how high did the ~ go?** wie hoch wurde gesteigert?; **to raise the ~** den Preis in die Höhe treiben; **the ~ is closed** es werden keine Gebote mehr angenommen, keine Gebote mehr b *(Cards)* Bieten *nt*, Reizen *nt* c *(= order)* Geheiß *nt (old)*, Gebot *nt*; **at whose ~?** auf wessen Geheiß? *(old)*; **the slave does his master's ~** der Sklave tut, was sein Herr ihn heißt *(old) or* ihm befiehlt; **he needed no second ~** man musste es ihm nicht zweimal sagen

bidding war N *(Fin)* Übernahmeschlacht *f*

biddy [ˈbɪdɪ] N *(inf, = hen)* Huhn *nt*, Henne *f*; *(inf: = old lady)* Muttchen *nt (inf)*, Tantchen *nt (inf)*

bide [baɪd] VT **to ~ one's time** den rechten Augenblick abwarten *or* abpassen; **to ~ awhile** *(old)* verweilen *(geh)*

bidet [ˈbiːdeɪ] N Bidet *nt*

bidirectional [ˌbaɪdɪˈrekʃənəl] ADJ *(Comput) printing* bidirektional

bid price N *(St Ex)* Geldkurs *m*

biennial [baɪˈenɪəl] ADJ *(= every two years)* zweijährlich; *(rare, = lasting two years)* zweijährig N *(Bot)* zweijährige Pflanze

biennially [baɪˈenɪəlɪ] ADV zweijährlich, alle zwei Jahre; *(Bot)* bienn

bier [bɪəʳ] N Bahre *f*

biff [bɪf] N *(inf)* Stoß *m*, Puff *m (inf)*; **a ~ on the nose** eins auf die Nase *(inf)* INTERJ bums VT *(esp Brit inf) person* boxen; *car* eine Beule fahren in *(+acc)*; *door* anschlagen; *lamppost* bumsen an *(+acc) or* gegen *(inf)*; **to ~ sb on the nose** jdm eins auf die Nase geben *(inf)*

bifocal [baɪˈfəʊkəl] ADJ Bifokal- N **bifocals** PL Bifokalbrille *f*

bifurcate [ˈbaɪfɜːkeɪt] VI *(form)* sich gabeln ADJ gegabelt

bifurcation [ˌbaɪfɜːˈkeɪʃən] N Gabelung *f*

big [bɪg] ADJ *(+er)* a *(in size, amount)* groß; *lie also* faustdick *(inf)*; **a ~ man** ein großer, schwerer Mann; **she's a ~ girl** *(inf)* sie hat einen ganz schönen Vorbau *(inf)*; **you ~ girl's blouse!** *(Brit inf)* du Angsthase! *(inf)*; **5 ~ ones** *(inf)* 5 Riesen *(sl)*; **~ with child/young** hochschwanger/trächtig
b *(of age)* groß; **my ~ brother** mein großer Bruder; **you're ~ enough to know better** du bist groß *or* alt genug und solltest es besser wissen
c *(= important)* groß, wichtig; **the Big Four/Five** die Großen Vier/Fünf; **Mr Big** *(inf)* der große Boss; **to look ~** *(inf)* ein bedeutendes Gesicht machen; **to be ~ in publishing/plastics** *(inf)* eine Größe im Verlagswesen/der Plastikproduktion sein; **to be onto something ~** *(inf)* einer großen Sache auf der Spur sein
d *(= great) cheat, bully, liar* groß
e *(= conceited)* **~ talk** Angeberei *f (inf)*, Großspurigkeit *f*; **~ talker** Angeber *m (inf)*, Maulheld *m (inf)*, eingebildeter Schwätzer; **he's getting too ~ for his boots** *(inf, child)* er wird ein bisschen zu aufmüpfig *(inf)*; *(employee)* er wird langsam größenwahnsinnig; **to have a ~ head** *(inf)* eingebildet sein
f *(= generous, iro)* großzügig, nobel *(inf)*; *(= forgiving)* großmütig, nobel *(inf)*; *heart* groß; **few people have a heart as ~ as his** es sind nur wenige so großzügig/großmütig wie er; **he was ~ enough to admit he was wrong** er hatte die Größe zuzugeben, dass er unrecht hatte; **that's really ~ of you** *(iro)* wirklich nobel von dir *(iro)*
g *(inf: = fashionable)* in *(inf)*
h *(fig phrases)* **to earn ~ money** das große Geld verdienen *(inf)*; **to have ~ ideas** große Pläne haben, Rosinen im Kopf haben *(pej inf)*; **to have a ~ mouth** *(inf)* eine große Klappe haben *(inf)*; **to do things in a ~ way** alles im großen (Stil) tun *or* betreiben; **to live in a ~ way** auf großem Fuß *or* in großem Stil leben; **it's no ~ deal** *(inf: = nothing special)* das ist nichts Besonderes; *(= quite all right)* (das ist) schon in Ordnung; **~ deal!** *(iro inf)* na und? *(inf)*; *(= that's not much etc)* das ist ja ergreifend! *(iro)*; **what's the ~ idea?** *(inf)* was soll denn das? *(inf)*; **what's the ~ hurry?** warum denn so eilig?; **our company is ~ on service** *(inf)* unsere Firma ist ganz groß in puncto Kundendienst
ADV **to talk ~** groß daherreden *(inf)*, große Töne spucken *(inf)*; **to act ~** sich aufspielen, großtun; **to think ~** im großen (Maßstab) planen; **to go over** *or* **down ~** *(inf)* ganz groß ankommen *(inf)*, großen Anklang finden *(with* bei*)*; **to make it ~ (as a singer/actor)** (als Sänger(in)/Schauspieler(in)) ganz groß rauskommen *(inf)*

bigamist [ˈbɪgəmɪst] N Bigamist *m*

bigamous [ˈbɪgəməs] ADJ bigamistisch

bigamy [ˈbɪgəmɪ] N Bigamie *f*

big: **Big Apple** N **the ~** *(inf)* New York *nt*; **big band** N Big Band *f* ADJ *attr* Bigband-; **Big Bang** N *(Brit St Ex)* Big Bang *m (Tag der Umstellung der Londoner Börse auf Computerbetrieb)*; **big bang** N *(Astron)* Urknall *m*; **big bang theory** N *(Astron)* Urknalltheorie *f*; **Big Ben** N Big Ben *m*; **Big Bertha** N die Dicke Berta; **big-boned** ADJ breit- *or* grobknochig; **Big Brother** N der große Bruder; **big bug** N *(inf)* hohes Tier *(inf)*; **big business** N a *(= high finance)* Großkapital *nt*, Hochfinanz *f*; **to be ~** das große Geschäft sein b *(baby-talk)* großes Geschäft *(baby-talk)*; **big cat** N Großkatze *f*; **big cheese** N *(inf)* hohes Tier *(inf)*; **big dipper** N a *(Brit, at fair)* Achterbahn *f*, Berg-und-Talbahn *f* b *(US Astron)* **Big Dipper** Großer Bär *or* Wagen; **big end** N *(Tech)* Pleuelfuß *m*, Schubstangenkopf *m*; **big-eyed** ADJ *(pej)* gefräßig, unersättlich; **big game** N *(Hunt)* Großwild *nt*; **big game hunter** N Großwildjäger *m*

biggie [ˈbɪgɪ] N *(inf)* Hit *m (inf)*, Knüller *m (inf)*; *(= important thing)* große Sache *(inf)*; **it's no ~** nicht so schlimm! *(inf)*

biggish [ˈbɪgɪʃ] ADJ ziemlich groß

big: **bighead** N *(inf: = person)* Angeber(in) *m(f) (inf)*, eingebildeter Fatzke *(sl)*; **bigheaded** ADJ *(inf)* eingebildet, angeberisch *(inf)*; **big-hearted** ADJ großherzig, großmütig; *(= forgiving)* weitherzig

bight [baɪt] N *(Geog)* Bucht *f*

big: **Big Issue** N *Obdachlosenzeitschrift in Großbritannien mit Ablegern in den USA, Südafrika, Namibia und Australien*; **bigmouth** N *(inf)* Großmaul *nt (inf)*, Angeber(in) *m(f) (inf)*; *(= blabbermouth)* Schwätzer(in) *m(f) (pej)*; **big name** N *(inf: = person)* Größe *f (in +gen)*; **all the ~s were there** alles, was Rang und Namen hat, war da; **big noise** N *(inf)* hohes Tier *(inf)*

bigot [ˈbɪgət] N Eiferer *m*; *(Rel also)* bigotter Mensch

bigoted ADJ, **bigotedly** ADV [ˈbɪgətɪd, -lɪ] eifernd; *(Rel)* bigott

bigotry [ˈbɪgətrɪ] N eifernde Borniertheit; *(Rel)* Bigotterie *f*

big: **big point** N *(Tennis)* wichtiger *or* entscheidender Punkt; **big shot** N hohes Tier *(inf)*; **he thinks he is a ~ in his new Jag** *(inf)* er hält sich mit seinem neuen Jaguar für den Größten *(inf)*; **big-ticket** ADJ *(US)* **~ item** teure Anschaffung; **big time** N *(inf)* **to make** *or* **hit the ~** groß einsteigen *(inf)*; **once he'd had a taste of the ~** nachdem er einmal ganz oben *or* groß gewesen war; **big-time** *(inf)* ADJ **one of the ~ boys** eine ganz große Nummer *(inf)*; **a ~ politician** eine große Nummer *(inf)* in der Politik ADV **they lost ~** sie haben gewaltig verloren; **to sell ~** *(esp US)* große Mengen verkaufen; **big toe** N große Zehe; **big top** N *(= circus)* Zirkus *m*; *(= main tent)* Hauptzelt *nt*; **big wheel** N a *(US inf)* = **big shot** b *(Brit, at fair)* Riesenrad *nt*; **bigwig** N *(inf)* hohes Tier *(inf)*; **the local ~s** die Honoratioren des Ortes

bijou [ˈbiːʒuː] ADJ *(esp in advertising)* **~ residence** nettes kleines Haus/nette kleine Wohnung

bike [baɪk] *(inf)* N (Fahr)rad *nt*; *(= motorbike)* Motorrad *nt*, Maschine *f (inf)*; **on your ~!** *(Brit inf: = clear off)* verschwinde! *(inf)*, zieh Leine! *(inf)* VI radeln *(inf)*

bike *in cpds* → **cycle**; **bike lane** N Fahrradspur *f*

biker [ˈbaɪkəʳ] N *(inf)* Motorradfahrer *m*; *(= gang member)* Rocker *m*

bike shorts PL *(US)* Radlerhose *f*

bikeway [ˈbaɪkweɪ] N *(esp US)* Radweg *m*

bikini [bɪˈkiːnɪ] N Bikini *m*; **~ line** Bikinilinie *f*; **~ wax** *kosmetische Wachsbehandlung der Bikinizone am Unterleib zur Entfernung von überstehenden Schamhaaren*

bi: **bilabial** N Bilabial *m* ADJ bilabial; **bilateral** ADJ, **bilaterally** [baɪˈlætərəl, -ɪ] ADV bilateral

bilberry [ˈbɪlbərɪ] N Heidelbeere *f*, Blaubeere *f*

bile [baɪl] N a *(Med)* Galle *f* b *(fig: = anger)* Übellaunigkeit *f*; **a man full of ~** ein Griesgram *m*

bilestone [ˈbaɪlstəʊn] N Gallenstein *m*

bilge [bɪldʒ] N a *(Naut)* Bilge *f* b *(also* **bilge water***)* Leckwasser *nt* c *(of cask)* (Fass)bauch *m* d *(Brit inf: = nonsense)* Quatsch *m (inf)*, Mumpitz *m (dated inf)*; **to talk ~** Unsinn verzapfen *(inf)* e *(Sch sl, = biology)* Bio *no art (Sch inf)*

bilharzia [bɪlˈhɑːzɪə] N Bilharziose *f*

bi: **bilinear** ADJ bilinear; **bilingual** ADJ, **bilingually** ADV zweisprachig; **~ secretary** Fremdsprachensekretärin *f*; **bilingualism** N Zweisprachigkeit *f*

bilious [ˈbɪlɪəs] ADJ a *(Med)* Gallen-; **~ attack** Gallenkolik *f* b *(= irritable)* reizbar; **he is very ~** ihm läuft immer gleich die Galle über *(inf)* c *(= sickly) colour* widerlich; **you're looking a bit ~** Sie sind ein bisschen grün um die Nase *(inf)*

biliousness [ˈbɪlɪəsnɪs] N *(Med)* Gallenkrankheit *f*, Gallenleiden *nt*; *(= irritability)* Reizbarkeit *f*; *(= sickliness: of colour)* Widerlichkeit *f*

bilk [bɪlk] VT *(esp US) creditor* prellen *(of* um*)*; *debt* nicht bezahlen

Bill [bɪl] N *dim of* **William**

bill¹ [bɪl] **N** **a** *(of bird, turtle)* Schnabel *m* **b** *(Geog)* Landzunge *f* **VI** *(bird)* schnäbeln; **to ~ and coo** *(birds)* schnäbeln und gurren; *(fig, people)* (miteinander) turteln

bill² **N** **a** *(= statement of charges)* Rechnung *f*; **could we have the ~ please?** *(esp Brit)* zahlen bitte!, wir möchten bitte zahlen
b *(US: = banknote)* Banknote *f*, Schein *m*; **five-dollar ~** Fünfdollarschein *m or* -note *f*
c *(= poster)* Plakat *nt*; *(on notice board)* Anschlag *m*; *(= public announcement)* Aushang *m*; **"post no ~s"** *(Brit)* „Plakate ankleben verboten"
d *(Theat: = programme)* Programm *nt*; **to head** *or* **top the ~, to be top of the ~** Star *m* des Abends/der Saison sein; *(act)* die Hauptattraktion sein
e **~ of fare** Speisekarte *f*
f *(Parl)* (Gesetz)entwurf *m*, (Gesetzes)vorlage *f*; **the ~ was passed** das Gesetz wurde verabschiedet
g *(esp Comm, Fin: = certificate, statement)* **~ of lading** *(Naut)* Seefrachtbrief *m*, Konnossement *nt*; **~ of exchange** Wechsel *m*, Tratte *f*; **~ of sale** Verkaufsurkunde *f*; **~ of health** *(Naut)* Gesundheitsattest *nt*; **to give sb a clean ~ of health** *(lit, fig)* jdm (gute) Gesundheit bescheinigen; **to fit** *or* **fill the ~** *(fig)* der/die/das Richtige sein, passen
h *(Jur)* **~ of attainder** *(Brit Hist) Anklage und Urteil gegen politische Persönlichkeiten in Form eines Gesetzes (US) unmittelbare Bestrafung einer Person durch den Gesetzgeber* **~ of indictment** Anklageschrift *f*
VT **a** *customers* eine Rechnung ausstellen *(+dat)*; **we won't ~ you for that, sir** *(= not charge)* wir werden Ihnen das nicht berechnen *or* in Rechnung stellen *(form)*
b *play, actor* ankündigen; *(fig: = advertise)* anpreisen; **he's ~ed at the King's Theatre** er soll im King's Theatre auftreten; **to ~ oneself as ...** sich anpreisen als ...

bill³ N *(= tool)* = **billhook**

billabong [ˈbɪləbɒŋ] N *(Austral) (of river)* Seitenarm *m* eines Flusses; *(= pool)* stehendes Wasser

billboard [ˈbɪlbɔːd] N Reklametafel *f*

bill broker N *(Fin)* Wechselmakler(in) *m(f)*

billet [ˈbɪlɪt] **N** **a** *(Mil: = document)* Quartierschein *m*; *(= accommodation)* Quartier *nt*, Unterkunft *f* **b** *(fig inf)* **to have a cushy ~** einen schlauen Posten haben **VT** *(Mil) soldier* einquartieren *(on sb* bei jdm); **troops were ~ed on** *or* **in our town** in unserer Stadt wurden/waren Truppen einquartiert

billet-doux [ˌbɪleɪˈduː] N Liebesbrief *m*, Billetdoux *nt (old)*

billeting [ˈbɪlɪtɪŋ] N *(Mil)* Einquartierung *f*; **~ officer** Quartiermeister *m*

bill: **billfold** N *(US)* Brieftasche *f*; **billhead** N *(= heading)* Rechnungskopf *m*; *(= sheet)* Rechnungsformular *nt*; **billhook** N Hippe *f*

billiard [ˈbɪljəd] ADJ *attr* Billard-

billiard [ˈbɪljəd]: **billiard ball** N Billardkugel *f*; **billiard cue** N Queue *nt*, Billardstock *m*

billiards [ˈbɪljədz] N Billard *nt*; **to have a game of ~** Billard spielen

billiard table N Billardtisch *m*

billing [ˈbɪlɪŋ] N **a** *(Theat)* **to get top/second ~** an erster/zweiter Stelle auf dem Programm stehen **b** *(Telec etc)* Abrechnung *f*; **~ unit** Abrechnungstakt *m*

billion [ˈbɪljən] N Milliarde *f*; *(dated Brit)* Billion *f*; **~s of ...** *(inf)* tausende *or* Tausende von ...

billionaire [bɪljəˈnɛəʳ] N *(esp US)* Milliardär(in) *m(f)*

billionth [ˈbɪljənθ] **ADJ** milliardste(r, s); *(dated Brit)* billionste(r, s) **N** Milliardstel *nt*; *(dated Brit)* Billionstel *nt*

Bill of Rights N ≈ Grundgesetz *nt*

BILL OF RIGHTS

Die **Bill of Rights** besteht aus den zehn ursprünglichen **Amendments** (Änderungen oder Zusätzen) zur Verfassung der Vereinigten Staaten von Amerika, die 1791 in Kraft traten. In einer Reihe von durchnummerierten Artikeln listet die **Bill of Rights** die Rechte auf, die jedem amerikanischen Bürger garantiert werden und definiert die verschiedenen Zuständigkeitsbereiche von Staat und Bundesregierung. In der **Bill of Rights** sind Religions-, Versammlungs- und Pressefreiheit **(First Amendment)**, das Recht, eine Waffe zu tragen **(Second Amendment)**, und das Recht auf eine faire Gerichtsverhandlung **(Sixth Amendment)** festgelegt. Zusatzartikel nach 1791 betreffen das Recht auf gleichen Schutz durch das Gesetz für alle Staatsbürger **(Fourteenth Amendment)** und das allgemeine Wahlrecht **(Fifteenth Amendment)** → FIFTH AMENDMENT

billow [ˈbɪləʊ] **N** **a** *(liter, of sea)* Woge *f (geh)* **b** *(fig, of dress etc)* Bauschen *nt no pl*; *(of sail)* Blähen *nt no pl*; *(of smoke)* Schwaden *m* **VI** **a** *(liter, sea)* wogen *(geh)* **b** *(fig, sail)* sich blähen; *(dress etc)* sich bauschen; *(smoke)* in Schwaden vorüberziehen

▶ **billow out** VI *(sail etc)* sich blähen; *(dress etc)* sich bauschen; *(smoke)* sich zu Schwaden formieren

billowy [ˈbɪləʊɪ] ADJ **a** *(liter) sea* wogend *(geh)* **b** *sails, curtains etc* gebläht; *smoke* in Schwaden ziehend

billposter [ˈbɪlpəʊstəʳ], **billsticker** [ˈbɪlstɪkəʳ] N Plakat(an)kleber *m*

Billy [ˈbɪlɪ] N *dim of* **William**

billy [ˈbɪlɪ] N *(also* **billycan**) Kochgeschirr *nt*

billy goat N Ziegenbock *m*

billyo(h) [ˈbɪlɪəʊ] N *(esp Brit inf)* **like ~** wie verrückt *(inf)*

bimbo [ˈbɪmbəʊ] N *(pej inf)* Puppe *f (inf)*, Häschen *nt (inf)*

bi: **bimetallic** ADJ **a** *rod, bar* Bimetall- **b** *(Fin)* **~ currency** Doppelwährung *f*; **bimetallism** N *(Fin)* Doppelwährung *f*; **bimonthly** **ADJ** **a** *(= twice a month)* vierzehntäglich **b** *(= every two months)* zweimonatlich **ADV** **a** *(= twice a month)* zweimal monatlich *or* im Monat **b** *(= every two months)* alle zwei Monate, jeden zweiten Monat

bin [bɪn] N **a** *(esp Brit, for bread)* Brotkasten *m*; *(for coal)* (Kohlen)kasten *m*; *(= rubbish bin)* Mülleimer *m*; *(= dustbin)* Mülltonne *f*; *(= litter bin)* Abfallbehälter *m* **b** *(for grain)* Tonne *f*

binary [ˈbaɪnərɪ] ADJ binär; *(Mus) form* zweiteilig

binary: **binary code** N *(Comput)* Binärkode *m*; **binary fission** N Zellteilung *f*; **binary notation** N *(Comput)* Binärdarstellung *f*, binäre Schreibweise; **binary number** N *(Math)* Dualzahl *f*, binäre Zahl; **binary star** N *(Astron)* Doppelstern *m*; **binary star system** N *(Astron)* Doppelsternsystem *nt*; **binary system** N *(Math)* Dualsystem *nt*, binäres System

bind [baɪnd] *pret, ptp* **bound** **VT** **a** *(= make fast, tie together)* binden *(to* an *+acc)*; *person* fesseln; *(fig)* verbinden *(to* mit); **bound hand and foot** an Händen und Füßen gefesselt *or* gebunden; **the emotions which ~ her to him** ihre emotionale Bindung an ihn
b *(= tie round) wound, arm etc* verbinden; *bandage* wickeln, binden; *artery* abbinden; *(for beauty) waist* einschnüren; *feet* einbinden *or* -schnüren; *hair* binden
c *(= secure edge of) material, hem* einfassen
d *book* binden
e *(= oblige: by contract, promise)* **to ~ sb to sth** jdn an etw *(acc)* binden, jdn zu etw verpflichten; **to ~ sb to do sth** jdn verpflichten, etw zu tun; **to ~ sb as an apprentice** jdn in die Lehre geben *(to* zu) → **bound³**
f *(Med) bowels* verstopfen
g *(= make cohere, Cook)* binden
VI **a** *(= cohere: cement etc)* binden; **stop the soil ~ing by adding some compost** lockern Sie den Boden mit Kompost; **the clay soil tended to ~** der Lehmboden war ziemlich schwer *or* klebte ziemlich; **the grass should help the soil ~** das Gras sollte den Boden festigen
b *(Med, food)* stopfen
c *(= stick: brake, sliding part etc)* blockieren
N *(inf)* **a** **in a ~** in der Klemme *(inf)*
b **to be (a bit of) a ~** *(Brit)* recht lästig sein

▶ **bind on** VT *sep* anbinden *(+prep obj, -to* an *+acc)*; **to bind sth on(to) sth** *(= on top of)* etw auf etw *(acc)* binden

▶ **bind over** VT *sep (Jur)* **to bind sb over (to keep the peace)** jdn verwarnen; **he was bound over for six months** er bekam eine sechsmonatige Bewährungsfrist

▶ **bind together** VT *sep (lit)* zusammenbinden; *(fig)* verbinden

▶ **bind up** VT *sep* **a** *wound* verbinden; *hair* hochbinden **b** *prisoner* fesseln **c** *(fig)* verknüpfen, verbinden; **to be bound up** *(with one another)* verbunden *or* verknüpft sein; **to be bound up with** *or* **in sth** eng mit etw verknüpft sein

binder [ˈbaɪndəʳ] N **a** *(Agr: = machine)* (Mäh)binder *m*, Bindemäher *m*; *(= person)* (Garben)binder(in) *m(f)* **b** *(Typ: = person)* Buchbinder(in) *m(f)*; *(= machine)* Bindemaschine *f* **c** *(for papers)* Hefter *m*; *(for magazines also)* Mappe *f*

bindery [ˈbaɪndərɪ] N Buchbinderei *f*

binding [ˈbaɪndɪŋ] **N** **a** *(of book)* Einband *m*; *(= act)* Binden *nt* **b** *(Sew)* Band *nt* **c** *(on skis)* Bindung *f* **ADJ** **a** *agreement, promise* bindend, verbindlich *(on* für) **b** *(Tech)* bindend, Binde- **c** *(Med) food etc* stopfend

bindweed [ˈbaɪndwiːd] N Winde *f*

binge [bɪndʒ] *(inf)* **N** *(drinking)* (Sauf)gelage *nt (inf)*; *(eating)* (Fress)gelage *nt (inf)*; *(= spending spree)* Großeinkauf *m*; **to go on a ~** auf eine Sauftour gehen *(inf)*; eine Fresstour machen *(inf)*; groß einkaufen gehen **VI** auf eine Sauf-/ /Fresstour gehen *(inf)*; **you'll have to stop ~ing** du musst mit diesen Sauf-/Fressgelagen aufhören *(inf)*

bingo [ˈbɪŋgəʊ] N Bingo *nt*

bin liner N *(Brit)* Mülltüte *f*

binman N *pl* **-men** *(Brit)* Müllmann *m*

binnacle [ˈbɪnəkl] N Kompasshaus *nt*

binoculars [bɪˈnɒkjʊləz] PL Fernglas *nt*; **a pair of ~** ein Fernglas *nt*

bi: **binomial** **ADJ** *(Math)* binomisch **N** Binom *nt*; **binuclear** [baɪˈnjuːklɪəʳ] ADJ binuklear, zweikernig

bio [baɪəʊ]: **biochemical** ADJ biochemisch; **biochemist** N Biochemiker(in) *m(f)*; **biochemistry** N Biochemie *f*; **biodegradable** ADJ biologisch abbaubar; **biodiesel** N Biodiesel *m*; **biodiversity** N Artenvielfalt *f*; **biodynamic** ADJ biodynamisch; **bioengineering** N Biotechnik *f*; **bioethics** N *sing* Bioethik *f*; **biofeedback** N Biofeedback *nt*; **biogenesis** N Biogenese *f*

biographer [baɪˈɒgrəfəʳ] N Biograf(in) *m(f)*

biographic(al) [ˌbaɪəʊˈgræfɪk(əl)] ADJ biografisch

biography [baɪˈɒgrəfɪ] N Biografie *f*, Lebensbeschreibung *f*

biological [ˌbaɪəˈlɒdʒɪkəl] ADJ biologisch; **~ detergent** Biowaschmittel *nt*; **~ diversity** Artenvielfalt *f*; **~ waste** Bioabfall *m*; **~ weapons** biologische Waffen *pl*

biological clock N biologische Uhr

biologically [ˌbaɪəʊˈlɒdʒɪkəlɪ] ADV biologisch

biologist [baɪˈɒlədʒɪst] N Biologe *m*, Biologin *f*

biology [baɪˈɒlədʒɪ] N Biologie *f*

bio: **biomass** N Biomasse *f*; **biomechanics** N *sing* Biomechanik *f*; **biomedical** ADJ biomedizinisch

biometric [baɪəˈmetrɪk] ADJ biometrisch

biometrics [baɪəˈmetrɪks], **biometry** [baɪˈɒmətrɪ] N Biometrie *f*

bionic [baɪˈɒnɪk] ADJ bionisch

bio: **biophysical** ADJ biophysikalisch; **biophysics** [ˌbaɪəʊˈfɪzɪks] N *sing* Biophysik *f*

biopic [ˈbaɪəʊpɪk] N *(inf)* Filmbiografie *f*

biopsy [ˈbaɪɒpsɪ] N Biopsie *f*

bio: **bioresonance, bio-resonance** N Bioresonanz *f*; **biorhythm** N *usu pl* Biorhythmus *m usu sing*; **biosphere** N Biosphäre *f*; **biosynthesis** N Biosynthese *f*; **biotechnology** N Biotechnik *f*; **bioterrorism** N Bioterrorismus *m*

biotope [ˈbaɪətəʊp] N Biotop *nt*

bioweapon [ˈbaɪəʊˌwepən] N Biowaffe *f*

bi: **bipartisan** ADJ Zweiparteien-; **bipartite** ADJ zweiteilig; *(= affecting two parties)* zweiseitig; **biped** N Zweifüßer *m*; *(hum: = human)* Zweibeiner *m* ADJ zweifüßig; **biplane** N Doppeldecker *m*; **bipolar** ADJ zwei- *or* doppelpolig

birch [bɜːtʃ] N **a** Birke *f* **b** *(for whipping)* Rute *f* ATTR Birken- VT (mit Ruten) schlagen

birching [ˈbɜːtʃɪŋ] N *(= act)* Prügeln *nt*; *(Jur)* Prügelstrafe *f*; **to get a ~** mit der Rute geschlagen werden

bird [bɜːd] N **a** Vogel *m*; **~ of paradise/passage** *(lit, fig)* Paradies-/Zugvogel *m*; **to eat like a ~** *(fig inf)* essen wie ein Spatz *(inf)*; **the ~ has flown** *(fig)* der Vogel ist ausgeflogen; **a little ~ told me** *(inf)* das sagt mir mein kleiner Finger; **that's strictly for the ~s** *(inf)* das ist geschenkt *(inf)*; **a ~ in the hand is worth two in the bush** *(Prov)* der Spatz in der Hand ist besser als die Taube auf dem Dach *(Prov)*; **to tell sb about the ~s and the bees** jdm erzählen, wo die kleinen Kinder herkommen → **feather, kill**
b *(Cook)* Vogel *m (hum inf)*
c *(Brit inf: = girl)* Tussi *f (sl)*
d *(inf: = person)* Vogel *m (inf)*; **he's a cunning old ~** er ist ein alter Fuchs
e **to give sb the ~** *(esp Brit inf: = boo)* jdn auspfeifen; *(US sl: = show the finger)* jdm den Stinkefinger zeigen; **to get the ~** *(esp Brit inf)* ausgepfiffen werden; *(US sl)* den Stinkefinger gezeigt bekommen
f *(Brit, inf, = prison term)* Knast *m (inf)*; **to do ~** sitzen *(inf)*

bird: **birdbath** N Vogelbad *nt*; **bird box** N Vogelhäuschen *nt*; **bird brain** N *(inf)* **to be a ~** ein Spatzenhirn haben *(inf)*; **birdcage** N Vogelbauer *nt or* -käfig *m*; **bird call** N Vogelruf *m*; **bird dog** *(US)* N *(lit, fig)* Spürhund *m* VT *(inf)* beschatten *(inf)*

birder [ˈbɜːdəʳ] N Vogelbeobachter(in) *m(f)*

bird: **bird fancier** N Vogelzüchter *m*; **bird flu** N Vogelgrippe *f*, Geflügel- *or* Hühnerpest *f*; **birdhouse** N Vogelhäuschen *nt*

birdie [ˈbɜːdɪ] N **a** *(inf)* Vögelchen *nt*; **watch the ~** gleich kommts Vögelchen raus! **b** *(Golf)* Birdie *nt* VT *(Golf)* **to ~ a hole** ein Birdie spielen

bird: **bird-like** ADJ vogelartig; **birdlime** N Vogelleim *m*; **bird of passage** N *(lit, fig)* Zugvogel *m*; **bird of prey** N Raubvogel *m*; **bird plague** N Geflügel- *or* Hühnerpest *f*; **bird sanctuary** N Vogelschutzgebiet *nt*; **birdseed** N Vogelfutter *nt*

bird's: **bird's-eye view** N Vogelperspektive *f*; **to get a ~ of the town** die Stadt aus der Vogelperspektive sehen; **bird's-foot** N Vogelfuß *m*

birdshot [ˈbɜːdʃɒt] N feiner Schrot

bird's: **bird's nest** N Vogelnest *nt*; **bird's-nest** VI **to go ~ing** Vogelnester ausnehmen; **bird's-nest soup** N Schwalben- *or* Vogelnestersuppe *f*

bird: **birdsong** N Vogelgesang *m*; **bird table** N Futterplatz *m (für Vögel)*; **bird-watcher** N Vogelbeobachter(in) *m(f)*

biretta [bɪˈretə] N Birett *nt*

Biro® [ˈbaɪərəʊ] N *(Brit)* Kugelschreiber *m*, Kuli *m (inf)*

birth [bɜːθ] ✪ 24.1 N **a** Geburt *f*; **the town/country of his ~** seine Geburtsstadt/sein Geburtsland *nt*; **blind/deaf from** *or* **since ~** von Geburt an blind/taub; **within a few minutes of ~** einige Minuten nach der Geburt; **the rights which are ours by ~** unsere angeborenen Rechte; **to give ~ to** gebären; *(woman also)* entbunden werden von; **to give ~** entbinden; *(animal)* jungen; **she's going to give ~!** sie bekommt ihr Kind!
b *(= parentage)* Abstammung *f*, Herkunft *f*; **Scottish by ~** Schotte von Geburt, gebürtiger Schotte; **of good ~** aus gutem Hause *or* guter Familie; **of low** *or* **humble ~** von niedriger Geburt
c *(fig)* Geburt *f*; *(of movement, fashion etc)* Aufkommen *nt*; *(of nation, party, company also)* Gründung *f*, Entstehen *nt*; *(of new era)* Anbruch *m*, Geburt *f (geh)*; *(of star)* Entstehung *f*; **to give ~ to sth** etw schaffen/aufkommen lassen/gründen/anbrechen lassen

birth: **birth canal** N *(Med)* Geburtskanal *m*; **birth certificate** N Geburtsurkunde *f*; **birth control** N Geburtenkontrolle *or* -regelung *f*; **birth-control clinic** N Familienberatungsstelle *f*; **birthdate** N Geburtsdatum *nt*

birthday [ˈbɜːθdeɪ] ✪ 23.3 N Geburtstag *m*; **what did you get for your ~?** was hast du zum Geburtstag bekommen?; **~ celebrations** Geburtstagsfeierlichkeiten *pl*; **on my ~** an meinem Geburtstag → **happy**

birthday: **birthday cake** N Geburtstagskuchen *m or* -torte *f*; **birthday card** N Geburtstagskarte *f*; **Birthday honours** PL *(Brit)* Titel- und Ordensverleihungen *pl (am offiziellen Geburtstag des britischen Monarchen)*; **birthday party** N Geburtstagsfeier *f*; *(with dancing etc)* Geburtstagsparty *f*; *(for child)* Kindergeburtstag *m*; **birthday present** N Geburtstagsgeschenk *nt*; **birthday suit** N *(inf)* Adams-/Evaskostüm *nt (inf)*; **in one's ~** im Adams-/Evaskostüm *(inf)*

birth father N *(= biological father)* leiblicher Vater

birthing [ˈbɜːθɪŋ] *in cpds* Geburts-; **birthing centre,** *(US)* **birthing center** N Geburtshaus *nt*; **birthing pool** N Entbindungsbadewanne *f*; **birthing room** N Entbindungsraum *m*, Kreißsaal *m*; **birthing stool** N Gebärstuhl *m*

birth: **birthmark** N Muttermal *nt*; **birth mother** N *(= biological mother)* biologische Mutter; *(= surrogate mother)* Leihmutter *f*; **birth name** N Geburtsname *m*; **birthplace** N Geburtsort *m*; **birth plan** N Geburtsplan *m*; **birthrate** N Geburtenrate *or* -ziffer *f*; **birthright** N **a** Geburtsrecht *nt* **b** *(= right of first-born)* Erstgeburtsrecht *nt*; **birthstone** N Monatsstein *m*; **birth trauma** N Geburtstrauma *nt*

biryani [bɪrɪˈɑːnɪ] N *indisches Reisgericht*

Biscay [ˈbɪskeɪ] N **the Bay of ~** der Golf von Biskaya *or* Biscaya

biscuit [ˈbɪskɪt] N **a** *(Brit)* Keks *m*; *(= dog biscuit)* Hundekuchen *m*; **that takes/you take the ~!** *(Brit inf)* das übertrifft alles *or (negatively)* schlägt dem Fass den Boden aus **b** *(US)* Brötchen *nt* **c** *(= porcelain: also* **biscuit-ware***)* Biskuitporzellan *nt* **d** *(= colour)* Beige *nt* ADJ *(colour)* beige

biscuit barrel N Keksdose *f*

biscuity [ˈbɪskətɪ] ADJ *texture* keksartig; *colour* beige

bisect [baɪˈsekt] VT in zwei Teile *or (equal parts)* Hälften teilen; *(Math)* halbieren VI sich teilen

bisection [baɪˈsekʃən] N *(Math)* Halbierung *f*

bisector [baɪˈsektəʳ] N *(Math)* Halbierende *f*

bisexual [ˌbaɪˈseksjʊəl] ADJ bisexuell; *(Biol)* zwittrig, doppelgeschlechtig N *(= person)* Bisexuelle(r) *mf*

bisexuality [ˌbaɪˌseksjʊˈælɪtɪ] N Bisexualität *f*; *(Biol)* Zwittrigkeit *f*, Doppelgeschlechtigkeit *f*

bishop [ˈbɪʃəp] N **a** *(Eccl)* Bischof *m*; **thank you, ~** vielen Dank, Herr Bischof **b** *(Chess)* Läufer *m*

bishopric [ˈbɪʃəprɪk] N *(= diocese)* Bistum *nt*; *(= function)* Bischofsamt *nt*

bismuth [ˈbɪzməθ] N Wismut *nt*

bison [ˈbaɪsn] N *(American)* Bison *m*; *(European)* Wisent *m*

bisque [bɪsk] N **a** *(= pottery)* Biskuitporzellan *nt* **b** *(= soup)* Fischcremesuppe *f*

bissextile [bɪˈsekstaɪl] *(form)* N Schaltjahr *nt* ADJ Schalt-

bistable [baɪˈsteɪbl] ADJ *(Tech)* bistabil

bistro [ˈbiːstrəʊ] N Bistro *nt*

bit[1] [bɪt] N **a** *(for horse)* Gebiss(stange *f*) *nt*; **to take the ~ between one's teeth** *(fig)* sich ins Zeug legen → **champ**[1] **b** *(of drill)* (Bohr)einsatz *m*, Bohrer *m*; *(of plane)* (Hobel)messer *nt* **c** *(of key)* (Schlüssel)bart *m*

bit[2] N **a** *(= piece)* Stück *nt*; *(smaller)* Stückchen *nt*; *(of glass also)* Scherbe *f*; *(= section: of book, film, symphony)* Teil *m*; *(part or place in book, drama, text, symphony etc)* Stelle *f*; **a few ~s of furniture** ein paar Möbelstücke; **a ~ of bread** ein Stück Brot; **I gave my ~ to my sister** ich habe meiner Schwester meinen Teil gegeben; **this is the ~ I hate, he said, taking out his wallet** das tue ich gar nicht gern, sagte er und zückte seine Brieftasche; **a ~** *(= not much, small amount)* ein bisschen, etwas; **would you like a ~ of ice cream?** möchten Sie etwas *or* ein bisschen Eis?; **there's a ~ of truth in what he says** daran ist schon etwas Wahres; **a ~ of advice/luck/news** ein Rat *m*/ein Glück *nt*/eine Neuigkeit; **we had a ~ of trouble/excitement** wir hatten ein wenig Ärger/Aufregung; **I only read a ~ of the novel** ich habe nur ein bisschen *or* Stückchen von dem Roman gelesen; **don't you feel the slightest ~ of remorse?** hast du denn nicht die geringsten Gewissensbisse?; **it did me a ~ of good** das hat mir geholfen; **it might be a ~ of help** das könnte eine kleine Hilfe sein; **it wasn't a ~ of help** das war überhaupt keine Hilfe; **I've experienced quite a ~ in my life** ich habe in meinem Leben schon (so) einiges erlebt; **there's quite a ~ of work left to do/bread left** es ist noch eine ganze Menge Arbeit zu erledigen/Brot da; **in ~s and pieces** *(= broken)* in tausend Stücken; *(lit, fig: = come apart)* in die Brüche gegangen; **to do the work in ~s and pieces** die Arbeit stückchenweise machen; **the ~s and pieces** die einzelnen Teile; *(= broken bits)* die Scherben *pl*; **bring all your ~s and pieces** bring deine Siebensachen; **to pick up the ~s and pieces** *(fig)* retten, was zu retten ist; **to come** *or* **fall to ~s** kaputtgehen, aus dem Leim gehen; **to pull** *or* **tear sth to ~s** *(lit)* etw in (tausend) Stücke reißen; *(fig)* keinen guten Faden an etw *(dat)* lassen; **to go to ~s** *(fig inf)* durchdrehen *(inf)* → **bob**[3] **N e**
b *(with time)* **a ~** ein Weilchen *nt*; **he's gone out for a ~** er ist ein Weilchen *or* mal kurz weggegangen
c *(with cost)* **a ~** eine ganze Menge; **it cost quite a ~** das hat ganz schön (viel) gekostet *(inf)*
d **to do one's ~** sein(en) Teil tun; *(= fair share also)* das seine *or* Seine tun; **look, you're not doing your ~** hör mal zu, du setzt dich nicht genügend ein
e **a ~ of a crack/bruise** *etc* ein kleiner Riss/Fleck *etc*; **he's a ~ of a rogue/an expert** er ist ein ziemlicher Schlingel/ein Fachmann; **he's a ~ of a musician** er ist gar kein schlechter Musiker; **she's a ~ of a connoisseur** sie versteht einiges davon; **you're a ~ of an idiot, aren't you?** du bist ganz schön dumm; **he's got a ~ of a nerve!** der hat vielleicht Nerven!; **it's a ~ of a nuisance** das ist schon etwas ärgerlich; **now that's a ~ of an improvement** das ist schon besser
f **~ by ~** Stück für Stück; *(= gradually)* nach und nach; **he's every ~ a soldier/Frenchman** er ist durch und durch Soldat/Franzose; **it/he is every ~ as good as …** es/er ist genauso gut, wie …; **not a ~ of it** keineswegs, keine Spur *(inf)*
g **when it comes to the ~** wenn es drauf ankommt
h *(= coin)* *(Brit)* Münze *f*; **2/4/6 ~s** *(US)* 25/50/

75 Cent(s)
i *(Brit, inf)* Tussi *f (sl)*
ADV **a** ~ ein bisschen, etwas; **were you angry? – a ~** haben Sie sich geärgert? – ja, schon etwas *or* ein bisschen; **wasn't she a little ~ surprised?** war sie nicht etwas erstaunt?; **I'm not a (little) ~ surprised** das wundert mich überhaupt nicht *or* kein bisschen *(inf) or* keineswegs; **he wasn't a ~ the wiser for it** danach war er auch nicht viel klüger *or* schlauer; **quite a ~** ziemlich viel; **that's quite a ~ better** das ist schon besser; **he's improved quite a ~** er hat sich ziemlich gebessert

bit[3] **N** *(Comput)* Bit *nt*

bit[4] *pret of* **bite**

bitch [bɪtʃ] **N** **a** *(of dog)* Hündin *f*; *(of canines generally)* Weibchen *nt*; *(of fox)* Füchsin *f*; *(of wolf)* Wölfin *f*; **terrier ~** weiblicher Terrier
b *(sl: = woman)* Miststück *nt (inf)*, gemeine Zicke *(inf)*; *(spiteful)* Hexe *f*; **silly ~** doofe Ziege *(inf)*; **don't be a ~** sei nicht so gemein *or* gehässig; **she's a mean ~** sie ist ein gemeines Stück *(inf)*; **life's a ~** das Leben kann ganz schön beschissen sein *(inf)*
c *(inf: = complaint)* **to have a ~ (about sb/sth)** (über jdn/etw) meckern *(inf)*; **what's your ~ this time?** was hast du diesmal zu meckern? *(inf)*
VI *(inf: = complain)* meckern *(inf) (about* über *+acc)*

▶ **bitch up** **VT** *sep (sl)* versauen *(inf)*

bitchiness [ˈbɪtʃɪnɪs] **N** Gehässigkeit *f*, Gemeinheit *f*; *(of remark also)* Bissigkeit *f*

bitchy [ˈbɪtʃɪ] **ADJ** *(+er) (inf) woman* gehässig, gemein; *remark also* bissig; **that was a ~ thing to do/say** das war gehässig *or* gemein; **he started getting ~ (about her)** er fing an, bissige *or* gehässige Bemerkungen (über sie) zu machen

bite [baɪt] *vb: pret* **bit**, *ptp* **bitten** **N** **a** Biss *m*; **in two ~s** mit zwei Bissen; **he took a ~ (out) of the apple** er biss in den Apfel; **to get a second** *or* **another ~ at the cherry** *(fig)* eine zweite Chance bekommen
b *(= wound etc) (= dog, snake, flea bite etc)* Biss *m*; *(= insect bite)* Stich *m*; *(= love bite)* (Knutsch)fleck *m (inf)*
c *(Fishing)* **I think I've got a ~** ich glaube, es hat einer angebissen
d *(of food)* Happen *m*; **there's not a ~ to eat** es ist überhaupt nichts zu essen da; **come and have a ~** komm und iss 'ne Kleinigkeit; **do you fancy a ~ (to eat)?** möchten Sie etwas essen?
e **there's a ~ in the air** es ist beißend kalt; **the ~ of the wind** der beißend kalte Wind
f *(of file, saw)* **the file has lost its ~** die Feile ist stumpf geworden; **these screws don't have enough ~** diese Schrauben greifen *or* fassen nicht richtig
g *(of sauce etc)* Schärfe *f*
VT **a** *(person, dog)* beißen; *(insect)* stechen; **to ~ one's nails** an seinen Nägeln kauen; **to ~ one's tongue/lip** *(lit, fig)* sich *(dat)* auf die Zunge/Lippen beißen; **the trapeze artist ~s the rope between her teeth** die Trapezkünstlerin hält das Seil mit den Zähnen fest; **don't worry, he won't ~ you** *(fig inf)* keine Angst, er wird dich schon nicht beißen *(inf)*; **to ~ the dust** *(inf)* dran glauben müssen *(inf)*; **he had been bitten by the travel/music bug** ihn hatte das Reisefieber/das Musikfieber erwischt *(inf)*; **once bitten twice shy** *(Prov)* (ein) gebranntes Kind scheut das Feuer *(Prov)*; **to ~ the hand that feeds you** *(prov)* sich *(dat)* ins eigene Fleisch schneiden; **what's biting you?** *(fig inf)* was ist mit dir los? *(inf)*, was hast du denn?
b *(cold, frost, wind)* schneiden in *(+dat)*
c *(file, saw)* schneiden in *(+acc)*; *(acid)* ätzen
d *(inf: = swindle)* **I've been bitten** ich bin reingelegt worden *(inf)*
VI **a** *(dog etc)* beißen; *(insects)* stechen
b *(fish, fig inf)* anbeißen
c *(cold, frost, wind)* beißen, schneiden
d *(wheels)* fassen, greifen; *(saw, anchor)* fassen; *(screw)* greifen

▶ **bite into** **VI** *+prep obj (person)* (hinein)beißen in *(+acc)*; *(teeth)* (tief) eindringen in *(+acc)*; *(acid, saw)* sich hineinfressen in *(+acc)*; *(screw, drill)* sich hineinbohren in *(+acc)*

▶ **bite off** **VT** *sep* abbeißen; **he won't bite your head off** *(inf)* er wird dir schon nicht den Kopf abreißen; **to bite off more than one can chew** *(prov)* sich *(dat)* zu viel zumuten

▶ **bite on** **VI** *+prep obj* beißen auf *(+acc)*; **give the baby something to bite on** gib dem Kind etwas zum Beißen

▶ **bite through** **VT** *insep* durchbeißen

biter [ˈbaɪtəʳ] **N** **the ~ bitten!** mit den eigenen Waffen geschlagen!; *(in deception also)* der betrogene Betrüger!

bite-size(d) [ˈbaɪtsaɪz(d)] **ADJ** **a** *food, piece* mundgerecht **b** *(fig) information etc* leicht verdaulich

biting [ˈbaɪtɪŋ] **ADJ** beißend; *cold, wind also* schneidend

bit: **bitmap** **N** *(Comput)* **a** *no pl (= mode)* Bitmap *nt* **b** *(also* **bitmapped image**) Bitmap-Abbildung *f*; **bitmapped** **ADJ** *(Comput)* Bitmap-, bit-mapped *pred*; **~ graphics** Bitmapgrafik *f*; **bit part** **N** kleine Nebenrolle; **bit(-part) player** **N** Schauspieler(in) *m(f)* in kleinen Nebenrollen

bitten [ˈbɪtn] *ptp of* **bite**

bitter [ˈbɪtəʳ] **ADJ** *(+er)* **a** *taste* bitter; **it was a ~ pill to swallow** *(fig)* es war eine bittere Pille **b** *cold, winter* bitter; *weather, wind* bitterkalt, eisig; **it's ~ today** es ist heute bitterkalt **c** *enemy, struggle, opposition* erbittert **d** *disappointment, hatred, reproach, remorse, tears* bitter; *criticism* scharf, heftig; **to the ~ end** bis zum bitteren Ende **e** *(= embittered)* bitter; *person also* verbittert; **to be** *or* **feel ~ at sth** über etw *(acc)* bitter *or* verbittert sein **ADV** **~ cold** bitterkalt **N** **a** *(Brit: = beer) halbdunkles obergäriges Bier* **b** **bitters** **PL** Magenbitter *m*; **gin and ~s** Gin *m* mit Bitterlikör

bitter lemon **N** Bitter Lemon *nt*

bitterly [ˈbɪtəlɪ] **ADV** **a** *reproach, disappointed* bitter; *complain also, weep* bitterlich; *oppose* erbittert; *criticize* scharf; *jealous* sehr **b** *cold* bitter **c** *(= showing embitteredness)* verbittert; *criticize* erbittert

bittern [ˈbɪtɜːn] **N** Rohrdommel *f*

bitterness [ˈbɪtənɪs] **N** **a** *(of taste)* Bitterkeit *f* **b** *(of cold, winter)* Bitterkeit *f*; *(of weather, wind)* bittere Kälte **c** *(of struggle, opposition)* Erbittertheit *f* **d** *(of disappointment, hatred, reproach, remorse)* Bitterkeit *f*; *(of criticism)* Schärfe *f*, Heftigkeit *f*; **such was the ~ of his disappointment/jealousy** er war so bitter enttäuscht/derart eifersüchtig **e** *(= anger)* Bitterkeit *f*; *(of person also)* Verbitterung *f*

bittersweet [ˈbɪtəˌswiːt] **ADJ** *(lit, fig)* bittersüß **N** *(Bot)* Kletternder Baumwürger; *(= nightshade)* Bittersüßer Nachtschatten

bitty [ˈbɪtɪ] **ADJ** *(+er) (Brit inf: = scrappy)* zusammengestoppelt *(pej inf) or* -gestückelt *(inf)*

bitumen [ˈbɪtjʊmɪn] **N** Bitumen *nt*

bituminous [bɪˈtjuːmɪnəs] **ADJ** **~ coal** Stein- *or* Fettkohle *f*

bivalent [ˈbaɪˈveɪlənt] **ADJ** bivalent, zweiwertig

bivalve [ˈbaɪvælv] *(Zool)* **N** zweischalige Muschel **ADJ** zweischalig

bivouac [ˈbɪvʊæk] *vb: pret, ptp* **bivouacked** **N** Biwak *nt* **VI** biwakieren

bivvy [ˈbɪvɪ] **N** *(inf)* Biwakzelt *nt* **VI** **to ~ up** biwakieren

biweekly [ˈbaɪˈwiːklɪ] **ADJ** **a** *(= twice a week)* **~ meetings/editions** Konferenzen/Ausgaben, die zweimal wöchentlich *or* in der Woche stattfinden/erscheinen **b** *(= fortnightly)* zweiwöchentlich, vierzehntäglich **ADV** **a** *(= twice a week)* zweimal wöchentlich, zweimal in der Woche **b** *(= fortnightly)* alle vierzehn Tage, vierzehntäglich

biz [bɪz] *(inf) abbr of* **business**

bizarre [bɪˈzɑːʳ] **ADJ** bizarr

BL *abbr of* **Bachelor of Law**

blab [blæb] **VI** quatschen *(inf)*; *(= talk fast, tell secret)* plappern; *(criminal)* singen *(sl)* **VT** *(also* **blab out**) *secret* ausplaudern

blabbermouth [ˈblæbəˌmaʊθ] **N** *(inf)* Klatschmaul *nt (inf)*

black [blæk] **ADJ** *(+er)* **a** *(colour)* schwarz; **~ man/woman** Schwarze(r) *mf*; **~ and blue** grün und blau; **~ and white photography/film** Schwarzweißfotografie *f*/-film *m*; **the situation isn't so ~ and white as that** die Situation ist nicht so eindeutig schwarz-weiß *or* schwarzweiß
b *(= dirty)* schwarz
c *(= wicked) thought, plan, deed* schwarz; **he's not so ~ as he's painted** *(prov)* er ist nicht so schlecht wie sein Ruf
d *future, prospects, mood* düster, finster; **he painted the future in the ~est colours** er malte die Zukunft in den schwärzesten Farben; **things are looking ~ for our project** es sieht für unser Vorhaben ziemlich schwarz *or* düster aus; **maybe things aren't as ~ as they seem** vielleicht ist alles gar nicht so schlimm, wie es aussieht; **in ~ despair** in tiefster Verzweiflung; **this was a ~ day for ...** das war ein schwarzer Tag für ...
e *(fig: = angry) looks* böse; **he looked as ~ as thunder** er machte ein bitterböses Gesicht; **his face went ~** er wurde rot vor Zorn; **to be in a ~ mood** schlechte Laune haben
f *(Brit: during strike)* **to declare a cargo** *etc* **~** eine Ladung *etc* für bestreikt erklären; **~ goods** bestreikte Waren
N **a** *(= colour)* Schwarz *nt*; **he's dressed in ~** er trägt Schwarz; **to wear ~** *(in mourning)* Trauer *or* Schwarz tragen; **it's written down in ~ and white** es steht schwarz auf weiß geschrieben; **a ~ and white** *(Art)* eine Schwarzweißzeichnung; *(= film)* ein Schwarzweißfilm *m*; **a film which oversimplifies and presents everything in ~ and white** ein Film, der durch seine Schwarzweißmalerei alles vereinfacht darstellt; **to swear that ~ is white** schwören, dass zwei mal zwei fünf ist
b *(= black person)* Schwarze(r) *mf*
c **in the ~** *(Fin)* in den schwarzen Zahlen
d *(Chess etc)* Schwarz *nt*; *(Billiards)* schwarzer Ball; *(Roulette)* Schwarz *nt*, Noir *nt*
e *(of night)* Schwärze *f*
VT **a** *(= blacken)* schwärzen; **to ~ one's face** sich *(dat)* das Gesicht schwarz machen; **to ~ sb's eye** jdm ein blaues Auge schlagen *or* verpassen *(inf)*
b *shoes* wichsen
c *(Brit: trade union)* bestreiken; *goods* boykottieren

▶ **black out** **VI** das Bewusstsein verlieren, ohnmächtig werden **VT** *sep* **a** *building, stage, window* verdunkeln **b** *(= not broadcast)* **the technicians have blacked out tonight's programmes** *(Brit) or* **programs** *(US)* durch einen Streik des technischen Personals kann das heutige Abendprogramm nicht ausgestrahlt werden **c** *(with ink, paint)* schwärzen

▶ **black up** **VI** *(Theat inf)* sich schwarz anmalen

Black Africa **N** Schwarzafrika *nt*

blackamoor [ˈblækəmʊəʳ] **N** *(obs)* Mohr *m (obs)*

black: **blackball** **VT** *(= vote against)* stimmen gegen; *(inf: = exclude)* ausschließen; **black beetle** **N** Küchenschabe *f*; **blackberry** **N** Brombeere *f*; **to go ~ing** *(Brit)* Brombeeren pflücken gehen, in die Brombeeren gehen *(inf)*; **blackbird** **N** Amsel *f*; **blackboard** **N** Tafel *f*; **to write sth on the ~** etw an die Tafel schreiben; **black book** **N** **to be in sb's ~s** bei jdm schlecht angeschrieben sein *(inf)*; **little ~** Notizbuch *nt (mit Adressen der Mädchenbekanntschaften)*; **black box** **N** *(Aviat)* Flugschreiber *m*; *(= mysterious device)* Blackbox *f*; **black bread** **N** Schwarzbrot *nt*; **black cab** **N** *(Brit) britisches Taxi*; **blackcap** **N** **a** *(= bird)* Mönchsgrasmücke *f* **b** *(US: = berry)* Barett *nt* **c** *(Jur)* schwarze Kappe *(des Richters* *bei Todesurteilen)*; **black comedy** N schwarze Komödie; **Black Country** N *Industriegebiet in den englischen Midlands*; **blackcurrant** N Schwarze Johannisbeere; **Black Death** N *(Hist)* Schwarzer Tod; **black economy** N Schattenwirtschaft *f*

blacken ['blækən] VT a *(= make black)* schwarz machen; *one's face* schwarz anmalen; **the walls were ~ed by the fire** die Wände waren vom Feuer schwarz b *(fig) character* verunglimpfen; **to ~ sb's name** *or* **reputation** jdn schlechtmachen VI schwarz werden

black: **Black English** N Englisch *nt* der Schwarzen; **black eye** N blaues Auge; **to give sb a ~** jdm ein blaues Auge schlagen *or* verpassen *(inf)*; **black-eyed** ADJ schwarzäugig; **blackfly** N Schwarze Blattlaus; **Black Forest** N Schwarzwald *m*; **Black Forest gateau** N *(esp Brit)* Schwarzwälder Kirschtorte *f*; **black frost** N *strenge, aber trockene Kälte*; **black grouse** N Birkhuhn *nt*

blackguard ['blægɑːd] N *(old)* Bösewicht *m*, (Spitz)bube *m (old)*

blackguardly ['blægɑːdlɪ] ADJ *deed, person* niederträchtig

black: **blackhead** N Mitesser *m*; **black-headed gull** N Schwarzkopfmöwe *f*; **black-hearted** ADJ böse; **black hole** N *(Astron, fig)* schwarzes Loch; **Black Hole of Calcutta** N *(cramped)* Affenstall *m*; *(dirty, dark)* scheußliches Verlies; **black humour**, *(US)* **black humor** N schwarzer Humor; **black ice** N Glatteis *nt*

blacking ['blækɪŋ] N a *(for shoes)* schwarze (Schuh)wichse; *(for stoves)* Ofenschwärze *f* b *(Brit) (by trade union)* Bestreikung *f*; *(of goods)* Boykottierung *f*

blackish ['blækɪʃ] ADJ schwärzlich

black: **blackjack** N a *(= flag)* schwarze (Piraten)flagge b *(Cards: = pontoon)* Siebzehnundvier *nt* c *(US: = weapon)* Totschläger *m* d *(Hist, = drinking vessel)* (lederner) Becher VT *(US: = hit)* prügeln; **black lead** N Grafit *m*, Graphit *m*; *(for stoves)* Schwärze *f*; **black-lead** VT *stove* schwärzen; **blackleg** *(Brit Ind)* N Streikbrecher(in) *m(f)* VI Streikbrecher(in) sein, sich als Streikbrecher(in) betätigen VT *one's fellow workers* sich unsolidarisch verhalten gegen; **blacklist** N schwarze Liste, Negativliste *f* VT auf die schwarze Liste setzen; **black lung** N Staublunge *f*

blackly ['blæklɪ] ADV *(= gloomily)* düster, finster

black: **black magic** N Schwarze Kunst *or* schwarze Magie *f*; **blackmail** N Erpressung *f*; **to use emotional ~ on sb** jds Gefühle brutal ausnutzen; **that's emotional ~!** das ist die reinste Erpressung! VT erpressen; **to ~ sb into doing sth** jdn durch Erpressung dazu zwingen, etw zu tun; **he had ~ed £500 out of her** er hatte £ 500 von ihr erpresst; **blackmailer** N Erpresser(in) *m(f)*; **Black Maria** [ˌblækmə'raɪə] N grüne Minna *(inf)*; **black mark** N Tadel *m*; *(in school register also)* Eintrag *m*; **that's a ~ for** *or* **against him** das ist ein Minuspunkt für ihn; **black market** N Schwarzmarkt *m* ADJ *attr* Schwarzmarkt-; **black marketeer** N Schwarzhändler(in) *m(f)*; **black mass** N schwarze Messe; **Black Muslim** N Black Moslem *m*; **Black Nationalism** N *(US)* schwarzer Nationalismus

blackness ['blæknɪs] N Schwärze *f*; **the ~ of his mood** seine düstere Laune

black: **blackout** N a *(Med)* Ohnmacht(sanfall *m*) *f no pl*; **I must have had a ~** ich muss wohl in Ohnmacht gefallen sein; **he had a ~** ihm wurde schwarz vor Augen b *(= light failure)* Stromausfall *m*; *(Theat)* Blackout *nt*; *(during war)* Verdunkelung *f*; *(TV)* Ausfall *m* c *(= news blackout)* (Nachrichten)sperre *f*; **Black Panther** N Black Panther *m*; **black pepper** N schwarzer Pfeffer; **Black Power** N Black Power *f*; **black pudding** N ≈ Blutwurst *f*; **Black Rod** N *Zeremonienmeister des britischen Oberhauses*; **Black Sea** N Schwarzes Meer; **black sheep** N *(fig)* schwarzes Schaf; **Blackshirt** N Schwarzhemd *nt*; **blacksmith** N (Grob- *or* Huf)schmied *m*; **at/to the ~'s (shop)** beim/zum Schmied; **black spot** N *(also* **accident black spot***)* Gefahrenstelle *f*; **blackthorn** N *(Bot)* Schwarzdorn *m*; **black tie** N *(on invitation)* Abendanzug *m* ADJ *dinner, function* mit Smokingzwang; **is it ~?** ist da Smokingzwang?; **blacktop** N *(US: = substance)* schwarzer Straßenbelag; *(= road)* geteerte Straße; *(paved with asphalt)* Asphaltstraße *f*; **black velvet** N *Sekt mit Starkbier*; **black-water rafting** N Höhlenrafting *nt*; **black widow** N Schwarze Witwe *f*

bladder ['blædəʳ] N a *(Anat, Bot)* Blase *f*; **with all that beer in your ~** mit dem vielen Bier im Bauch b *(Ftbl)* Blase *f*

bladdered ['blædəd] ADJ *(inf: = drunk)* voll *(inf)*, blau *(inf)*; **to get ~** sich volllaufen lassen

bladderwrack ['blædəræk] N Blasentang *m*

blade [bleɪd] N a *(of knife, tool, weapon, razor)* Klinge *f*; *(of pencil sharpener)* Messerchen *nt*; *(of guillotine)* Beil *nt* b *(of tongue)* vorderer Zungenrücken; *(of oar, spade, saw, windscreen wiper)* Blatt *nt*; *(of plough)* Schar *f*; *(of turbine, paddle wheel)* Schaufel *f*; *(of propeller)* Blatt *nt*, Flügel *m* c *(of leaf)* Blatt *nt*, Spreite *f (spec)*; *(of grass, corn)* Halm *m*, Spreite *f (spec)* d *(liter, = sword)* Klinge *f (liter)* e *(old, = dashing fellow)* schmucker Bursch *(old)* f *(Anat)* = **shoulder blade**

-bladed [-bleɪdɪd] ADJ *suf* **a twin-bladed propeller** ein Zweiblattpropeller *m*; **a two-bladed knife** ein Messer *nt* mit zwei Klingen

blaeberry ['bleɪbərɪ] N *(Scot, N Engl)* = **bilberry**

blag [blæg] *(Brit inf)* VT a *(= cadge)* schnorren *(inf)*, abstauben *(inf)*; *(= bluff)* bluffen; **to ~ one's way into a club** sich in einen Klub hineinmogeln *(inf)*; **to ~ one's way out of sth** sich aus etw herausreden; **to ~ (on) about sth** etw total falsch darstellen b *(= steal)* rauben; *bank* ausrauben N a *(= cheating)* Schummelei *f (inf)*; *(= bluff)* Bluff *m* b *(= robbery)* Raubüberfall *m*

blagger ['blægəʳ] N *(Brit inf)* a *(= cadger)* Schnorrer(in) *m(f) (inf)*; *(= cheater)* Schummler(in) *m(f) (inf)* b *(= robber) jd, der Raubüberfälle macht*

blah [blɑː] *(inf)* N *(dated, = nonsense)* Blabla *(inf)*, Geschwafel *(inf) nt* INTERJ **~, ~, ~** blabla *(inf)*

blame [bleɪm] VT a *(= hold responsible)* die Schuld geben *(+dat)*, beschuldigen; **to ~ sb for sth/sth on sb** jdm die Schuld an etw *(dat)* geben, die Schuld an etw *(dat)* auf jdn schieben; **to ~ sth on sth** die Schuld an etw *(dat)* auf etw *(acc)* schieben, einer Sache *(dat)* die Schuld an etw *(dat)* geben; **you only have yourself** *or* **you have no-one but yourself to ~** das hast du dir selbst zuzuschreiben; **I'm to ~ for this** daran bin ich schuld; **who/what is to ~ for this accident?** wer/was ist schuld an diesem Unfall?; **I ~ him for leaving the door open** er ist schuld, dass die Tür aufblieb; **to ~ oneself for sth** sich *(dat)* etw selbst zuzuschreiben haben, selbst an etw *(dat)* schuld sein; *(= feel responsible)* sich für etw verantwortlich fühlen, sich selbst bezichtigen; **he ~s himself for starting the fire** er gibt sich selbst die Schuld daran, dass das Feuer ausgebrochen ist

b *(= reproach)* Vorwürfe machen *(sb for* jdm für *or* wegen); **nobody is blaming you** es macht Ihnen ja niemand einen Vorwurf

c **he decided to turn down the offer – well, I can't say I ~ him** er entschloss sich, das Angebot abzulehnen – das kann man ihm wahrhaftig nicht verdenken; **so I told her to get lost – (I) don't ~ you** da habe ich ihr gesagt, sie soll zum Teufel gehen – da hattest du ganz recht; **so I told him what I really thought, do you ~ me?** da habe ich ihm gründlich meine Meinung gesagt, und doch wohl nicht zu Unrecht, oder?

N a *(= responsibility)* Schuld *f*; **to put the ~ for sth on sb** jdm die Schuld an etw *(dat)* geben; **to take the ~** die Schuld auf sich *(acc)* nehmen; *(for sb's mistakes also)* den Kopf hinhalten; **why do I always have to take the ~?** warum muss denn immer ich an allem schuld sein?; **parents must take the ~ for their children's failings** Eltern haben die Verantwortung für die Fehler ihrer Kinder zu tragen; **we share the ~** wir haben beide/alle Schuld; **the ~ lies with him** er hat Schuld *or* ist schuld (daran)

b *(= censure)* Tadel *m*; **without ~** ohne Schuld; *(= irreproachable) life etc* untadelig

blameable, blamable *(US)* ['bleɪməbl] ADJ tadelnswert, tadelnswürdig

blameless ['bleɪmlɪs] ADJ schuldlos; *life* untadelig

blamelessly ['bleɪmlɪslɪ] ADV unschuldig

blameworthy ['bleɪmwɜːðɪ] ADJ *person* schuldig; *behaviour, action* tadelnswert

blanch [blɑːntʃ] VT *(Hort)* bleichen; *(illness) face* bleich machen; *(fear)* erbleichen lassen; *(Cook) vegetables* blanchieren; *almonds* brühen VI *(with* vor *+dat) (person)* blass werden; *(with fear also)* bleich werden, erbleichen *(geh)*

blancmange [blə'mɒnʒ] N Pudding *m*

bland [blænd] ADJ *(+er) taste, food, diet* fad; *book, film, statement* nichtssagend; *person, character* langweilig, farblos; *expression, look, smile* leer

blandish ['blændɪʃ] VT schönreden *(+dat)*

blandishment ['blændɪʃmənt] N Schmeichelei *f*

blandly ['blændlɪ] ADV *say, reply* regungslos; *smile* vage

blandness ['blændnɪs] N *(of taste, food, diet)* Fadheit *f*; *(of book, film, statement)* Inhaltslosigkeit *f*; *(of person, character)* Farblosigkeit *f*; *(of expression, look, smile)* Leere *f*

blank [blæŋk] ADJ *(+er)* a *piece of paper, page, wall* leer; *silence, darkness* tief; *coin* ungeprägt; **~ space** Lücke *f*; *(on form)* freies Feld; *(Typ)* Zwischenraum *m*, Leerraum *m*; **~ form** Formular (-blatt) *nt*, Vordruck *m*; **please leave ~** *(on form)* bitte frei lassen *or* nicht ausfüllen

b *(= expressionless) face, look* ausdruckslos; *(= stupid)* verständnislos; *(= puzzled)* verdutzt, verblüfft; **he looked at me with ~ incomprehension** er sah mich völlig verständnislos an; **to look ~** *(= expressionless)* eine ausdruckslose Miene aufsetzen; *(= stupid)* verständnislos dreinschauen; *(= puzzled)* ein verdutztes Gesicht machen; **he just looked ~** *or* **gave me a ~ look** er guckte mich nur groß an *(inf)*; **my mind** *or* **I went ~** ich hatte Mattscheibe *(inf)*, ich hatte ein Brett vor dem Kopf *(inf)*; **sorry, I've gone ~** *(inf)* tut mir leid, aber ich habe totale Mattscheibe *(inf)*

c *(= empty) life etc* unausgefüllt, leer; **these ~ and characterless house fronts** diese nackten, charakterlosen Fassaden

N a *(in document)* freier Raum, leere Stelle; *(= blank document)* Vordruck *m*, Formular *nt*; *(= gap)* Lücke *f*

b *(= void)* Leere *f*; **I** *or* **my mind was/went a complete ~** ich hatte totale Mattscheibe *(inf)*

c *(in lottery)* Niete *f*; **to draw a ~** *(fig)* kein Glück haben

d *(in a target)* Scheibenmittelpunkt *m*

e *(= cartridge)* Platzpatrone *f* → *also* **blank cartridge**

f *(= domino)* Blank *nt*

g *(= coin)* Schrötling *m (spec)*; *(= key)* Rohling *m*

VT *(= ignore) person* ignorieren

▶ **blank out** VT *sep feeling, thought etc* ausschalten

blank: **blank book** N Notizbuch *nt*; **blank cartridge** N Platzpatrone *f*; **blank CD** N *(Comput)* Rohling *m*; **blank cheque**, *(US)* **blank check** N Blankoscheck *m*; *(fig)* Freibrief *m*; **to give sb a ~** *(fig)* jdm Carte blanche geben *(geh)*, jdm freie Hand geben

blanket ['blæŋkɪt] N *(lit, fig)* Decke *f*; **a ~ of snow/fog** eine Schnee-/Nebeldecke; **born on the wrong side of the ~** *(hum inf)* unehelich (geboren) ADJ *attr statement* pauschal; *insurance, coverage* umfassend; *ban* generell; *bombing* flächendeckend VT **a** *(snow, smoke)* zudecken; **fog ~ed the town** Nebel hüllte die Stadt ein **b** *(Naut) ship* den Wind abhalten von

blanket: **blanket bath** N Waschen *nt* im Bett; **to give sb a ~** jdn im Bett waschen; **blanket insurance** N Kollektivversicherung *f*; **blanket mortgage** N Gesamthypothek *f*; **blanket stitch** N Langettenstich *m*

blank line N *(Typ)* Leerzeile *f*

blankly ['blæŋklı] ADV *(= expressionlessly)* ausdruckslos; *(= uncomprehendingly)* verständnislos; **she just looked at me ~** sie sah mich nur groß an *(inf)*

blankness ['blænknıs] N *(= emptiness)* Leere *f*; *(of expression)* Ausdruckslosigkeit *f*; *(= not understanding)* Verständnislosigkeit *f*; *(= puzzlement)* Verdutztheit *f*, Verblüffung *f*

blank verse N Blankvers *m*

blare [blεə'] N Plärren *nt*, Geplärr *nt*; *(of car horn)* lautes Hupen; *(of trumpets)* Schmettern *nt* VI plärren; *(car horn)* laut hupen; *(trumpets)* schmettern; **the music/his voice ~d through the hall** die Musik/seine Stimme schallte durch den Saal; **he likes to drive with the music blaring** er dreht die Musik im Auto gern voll auf *(inf)* VT **be quiet!, he ~d** Ruhe!, brüllte er

▶ **blare out** VI *(loud voice, music)* schallen; *(trumpets)* schmettern; *(radio, music also)* plärren; *(car horn)* laut hupen; *(person)* brüllen VT *sep (trumpets) tune* schmettern; *(radio) music* plärren; *(person) order, warning etc* brüllen

blarney ['blɑ:nı] N Schmeichelei *f*, Schmus *m* *(inf)*; **he has kissed the Blarney Stone** *(fig)* der kann einen beschwatzen *(inf)* VT *sb* schmeicheln *(+dat)*; **he could ~ his way out of trouble** er könnte sich aus allem herausreden VI schmeicheln

blaspheme [blæs'fi:m] VT lästern, schmähen *(geh)* VI Gott lästern; **to ~ against sb/sth** *(lit, fig)* jdn/etw schmähen *(geh)*

blasphemer [blæs'fi:mə'] N Gotteslästerer *m*

blasphemous ['blæsfıməs] ADJ *(lit, fig)* blasphemisch; *words also* lästerlich, frevelhaft

blasphemously ['blæsfıməslı] ADV blasphemisch; *speak also* lästerlich, frevlerisch

blasphemy ['blæsfımı] N Blasphemie *f*; *(Rel also)* (Gottes)lästerung *f*; *(= words also)* Schmähung *f (geh)*

blast [blɑ:st] N **a** Windstoß *m*; *(of hot air)* Schwall *m*; **a ~ of wind** ein Windstoß; **an icy ~** ein eisiger Wind; **a ~ from the past** *(inf)* eine Erinnerung an vergangene Zeiten
b *(= sound, of trumpets)* Geschmetter *nt*, Schmettern *nt*; *(of foghorn)* Tuten *nt*; **the ship gave a long ~ on its foghorn** das Schiff ließ sein Nebelhorn ertönen; **to blow a ~ on the bugle** auf dem Horn blasen
c *(= noise, explosion)* Explosion *f*; *(= shock wave)* Druckwelle *f*; **to get the full ~ of sb's anger** jds Wut in voller Wucht abkriegen
d *(in quarrying etc)* Sprengladung *f*
e *(of furnace)* (Blas)wind *m*; **with the radio/heating on (at) full ~** mit dem Radio/der Heizung voll aufgedreht
f *(inf: = enjoyable experience)* **it was a ~** das war echt spitze *(inf)*; **to have a ~** sich blendend amüsieren
VT **a** *(lightning)* schlagen in *(+acc)*; *(with powder)* sprengen
b *(= send) rocket* schießen; *ball* mit Wucht schießen; *air* blasen
c *(= shoot with gun)* schießen auf *(+acc)*; *(= shoot dead)* erschießen; **the police ~ed their way in** die Polizei hat sich den Weg ins Haus frei geschossen *or (with explosives)* frei gebombt
d *(inf: = criticize)* verreißen; *person* heruntерputzen *(inf)*
e *(= blight) plant* vernichten, zerstören; *reputation also, future* ruinieren
VI *(in quarry)* sprengen
INTERJ *(inf)* **~ (it)!** verdammt! *(inf)*, so ein Mist! *(inf)*; **~ what he wants!** das ist doch wurscht, was der will! *(inf)*; **~ him for coming so late** Herrgott, dass er aber auch so spät kommen muss! *(inf)*; **~ this car!** dieses verdammte Auto! *(inf)*

▶ **blast away** VI *(with gun)* drauflosschießen *or* -ballern *(inf)*; *(radio, rock band etc)* dröhnen

▶ **blast off** VI *(rocket, astronaut)* abheben, starten

▶ **blast out** VI *(music)* dröhnen

blasted ['blɑ:stıd] ADJ **a** öde **b** *(inf)* verdammt *(inf)*, Mist- *(inf)*; **he was talking all the ~ time** verdammt, er hat die ganze Zeit geredet *(inf)* ADV *(inf)* verdammt *(inf)*

blast furnace N Hochofen *m*

blasting ['blɑ:stıŋ] N *(Tech)* Sprengen *nt*; **"danger ~ in progress"** „Achtung! Sprengarbeiten!" → **sandblasting**

blastoff ['blɑ:stɒf] N Abschuss *m*

blat [blæt] *(inf esp US)* VI *(sheep)* blöcken VT *(= give away)* ausposaunen *(pej)*

blatancy ['bleıtənsı] N *(= obviousness)* Offensichtlichkeit *f*; *(of injustice, lie also)* Eklatanz *f*; *(of error)* Krassheit *f*, Eklatanz *f*; **the ~ of their disregard for …** ihre unverhohlene *or* offene Missachtung der …

blatant ['bleıtənt] ADJ *(= very obvious)* offensichtlich; *injustice, lie, lack also* eklatant; *error* krass, eklatant; *liar, social climber* unverfroren; *colour* schreiend; *disregard* offen, unverhohlen; **there's no need (for you) to be quite so ~ about it** *(in talking)* Sie brauchen das nicht so herumzuposaunen *(inf)*; *(in doing sth)* Sie brauchen das nicht so deutlich zu tun

blatantly ['bleıtəntlı] ADV offensichtlich; *(= openly)* offen; *(= without respect)* unverfroren; **you don't have to make it quite so ~ obvious** Sie brauchen es nicht so überdeutlich zu zeigen; **she ~ ignored it** sie hat das schlicht und einfach ignoriert

blather ['blæðə'] N VI *(inf)* = **blether**

blaze¹ [bleız] N **a** *(= fire)* Feuer *nt*; *(of building etc also)* Brand *m*; **"blaze at factory"** „Brand in Fabrik"; **six people died in the ~** sechs Menschen kamen in den Flammen um
b *(of guns etc)* Feuer *nt*, Funkeln *nt*; **a ~ of lights** ein Lichtermeer *nt*; **a ~ of colour** *(Brit) or* **color** *(US)* ein Meer *nt* von Farben; **a sudden ~ of light from the watchtower** ein plötzlicher Lichtstrahl vom Wachturm; **he went out in a ~ of glory** er trat mit Glanz und Gloria ab
c *(of fire, sun)* Glut *f*; *(fig, of rage)* Anfall *m*
d *(inf)* **go to ~s** scher dich zum Teufel! *(inf)*; **it can go to ~s** das kann mir gestohlen bleiben *(inf)*; **what/how the ~s …?** was/wie zum Teufel …? *(inf)*; **like ~s** wie verrückt *(inf)*
VI **a** *(sun)* brennen; *(fire also)* lodern; **to ~ with anger** vor Zorn glühen
b *(guns)* feuern; **with all guns blazing** aus allen Rohren feuernd

▶ **blaze abroad** VT *sep (liter)* verbreiten *(throughout* in *+dat)*

▶ **blaze away** VI **a** *(soldiers, guns)* drauflosfeuern *(at* auf *+acc)* **b** *(fire etc)* lodern

▶ **blaze down** VI *(sun)* niederbrennen *(on* auf *+acc)*

▶ **blaze up** VI aufflammen, auflodern

blaze² N *(of horse etc)* Blesse *f*; *(on tree)* Anreißung *f* VT **to ~ a trail** *(lit)* einen Weg markieren; *(fig)* den Weg bahnen

blazer ['bleızə'] N Blazer *m (also Sch)*, Klubjacke *f*

blazing ['bleızıŋ] ADJ **a** *building etc* brennend; *fire, torch* lodernd; *sun, light* grell; *sun (= hot)* brennend **b** *(fig) eyes* funkelnd *(with* vor *+dat)*; *row* furchtbar; **he is ~** *(inf)* er kocht vor Wut *(inf)*, er ist fuchsteufelswild *(inf)*

blazon ['bleızn] N *(Her)* Wappen *nt* VT *(liter: also* **blazon abroad**) *news* verbreiten *(throughout* in *+dat)*

bldg *abbr of* **building**

bleach [bli:tʃ] N **a** Bleichmittel *nt*; *(= household bleach)* Reinigungsmittel *nt* **b** *(act)* Bleichen *nt*; **to give sth a ~** etw bleichen VT *linen, bones, hair, skin* bleichen; *(sun) colour, fabric* verbleichen lassen, ausbleichen VI *(bones)* (ver)bleichen; *(Phot: image)* verblassen

▶ **bleach out** VT *sep* ausbleichen

bleachers ['bli:tʃəz] PL *(US)* unüberdachte Zuschauertribüne

bleaching ['bli:tʃıŋ] N Bleichen *nt*; **they need a good ~** sie müssten richtig gebleicht werden

bleaching agent N Bleichmittel *nt*

bleaching powder N Bleichkalk *m*

bleak [bli:k] ADJ *(+er)* **a** *landscape, place* öde, trostlos **b** *weather, wind* rau, kalt **c** *(fig)* trostlos; *prospects also* trüb; *smile, look, tone of voice* niedergeschlagen; **his face was ~** er sah niedergeschlagen aus; **things look rather ~ for him** es sieht ziemlich trostlos für ihn aus

bleakly ['bli:klı] ADV *look, say, smile* niedergeschlagen

bleakness ['bli:knıs] N **a** *(of landscape)* Öde *f*, Trostlosigkeit *f* **b** *(of weather)* Rauheit *f*, Kälte *f* **c** *(fig)* Trostlosigkeit *f*; *(of prospects also)* Trübheit *f*

blearily ['blıərılı] ADV *look* mit trüben Augen

bleary ['blıərı] ADJ *(+er)* **a** *eyes* trübe; *(after sleep)* verschlafen **b** *(= blurred)* verschwommen

bleary-eyed ['blıərı,aıd] ADJ *(after sleep)* verschlafen; **~ after proofreading** mit ganz trüben Augen nach dem Korrekturlesen

bleat [bli:t] VI **a** *(sheep, calf)* blöken; *(goat)* meckern **b** *(fig inf: = complain, moan)* meckern *(inf)* N **a** *(of sheep, calf)* Blöken *nt*, Geblök *nt*; *(of goat)* Meckern *nt* **b** *(inf, = moan)* Meckern *nt (inf)*, Gemecker *nt (inf)*

bleed [bli:d] *pret, ptp* **bled** [bled] VI **a** *(= lose blood)* bluten; **to ~ to death** verbluten; **my heart ~s for you** *(iro)* ich fang gleich an zu weinen; **our hearts ~ for the oppressed** *(liter)* wir leiden mit den Unterdrückten *(geh)* **b** *(plant)* bluten, schwitzen; *(wall)* schwitzen VT **a** *person* zur Ader lassen **b** *(fig inf)* schröpfen *(inf)* *(for* um), bluten lassen *(inf)*; **to ~ sb dry** *or* **white** jdn total ausnehmen *(inf)* **c** *radiator* (ent)lüften; *(Aut) brakes* lüften

▶ **bleed away** VI *(lit, fig)* ausströmen, verströmen *(geh)*

bleeder ['bli:də'] N **a** *(Med inf)* Bluter *m* **b** *(Brit inf: = person)* Arschloch *nt (vulg)*; *(= thing)* Scheißding *nt (inf)*; **you're a cheeky little ~** du bist ein frecher Hund *(inf)*

bleeding ['bli:dıŋ] N **a** *(= loss of blood)* Blutung *f*; **internal ~** innere Blutungen *pl*
b *(= taking blood)* Aderlass *m*
c *(of plant)* Blutung *f*, Schwitzen *nt*
d *(of brakes)* Lüftung *f*
ADJ **a** *wound, nose, gums* blutend; *(fig) heart* gebrochen
b *(Brit inf)* verdammt *(inf)*, Scheiß- *(inf)*; *(in positive sense) miracle etc* verdammt *(inf)*; **get your ~ hands off** nimm deine Dreckpfoten weg *(inf)*
ADV *(Brit inf)* verdammt *(inf)*; **that's ~ marvellous** das ist ja wieder toll! *(inf)*, na klasse! *(inf)*; **who does he/she think he/she ~ well is?** für was hält sich der Kerl/die Kuh eigentlich? *(inf)*; **not ~ likely** wohl kaum *(inf)*

bleeding heart N *(pej: = person)* Sensibelchen *nt (inf)*

bleeding-heart ['bli:dıŋ'hɑ:t] ADJ sentimental; **~ Liberal** sentimentaler Liberaler, sentimentale Liberale

bleep [bli:p] N *(Rad, TV)* Piepton *m* VI *(transmitter)* piepen VT *(in hospital) doctor* rufen

bleeper ['bli:pə'] N Funkrufempfänger *m*, Piepser *m (inf)*

bleezing ['bli:zıŋ] ADJ *(Brit sl)* total besoffen *(inf)*; **to be totally ~** total strack *or* hacke sein *(sl)*

blemish ['blemıʃ] N *(lit, fig)* Makel *m*; **without (a) ~** makellos, ohne Makel VT *object* beschädigen; *work, beauty* beeinträchtigen; *reputation, honour* beflecken; **~ed skin** unreine Haut; **~ed complexion** unreiner Teint

blench [blentʃ] VI bleich werden, erbleichen *(geh)*

blend [blend] **N** Mischung *f*; *(of whiskies also)* Blend *m*; **a ~ of tea** eine Teemischung
VT **a** *teas, colours etc* (ver)mischen; *cultures* vermischen, miteinander verbinden; **to ~ a building (in) with its surroundings** ein Gebäude seiner Umgebung anpassen
b *(Cook: = stir)* einrühren; *(in blender) liquids* mixen; *semisolids* pürieren
VI **a** *(= mix together, teas, whiskies)* sich vermischen, sich mischen lassen; *(voices, colours)* verschmelzen; **sea and sky seemed to ~ into one another** Meer und Himmel schienen ineinander überzugehen *or* miteinander zu verschmelzen
b *(also* **blend in**: *= go together, harmonize)* harmonieren *(with* mit), passen *(with* zu)

▶ **blend in** **VT** *sep flavouring* einrühren; *colour, tea* daruntermischen; *building* anpassen *(with +dat)* **VI** = **blend VI b**

blended [ˈblendɪd] ADJ **~ whisky** Blended *m*

blender [ˈblendəˈ] N Mixer *m*, Mixgerät *nt*

bless [bles] VT **a** *(God, priest)* segnen; **God ~ (you)** behüt dich/euch Gott; **God ~ America** Gott schütze Amerika; **~ you, my son** Gott segne dich, mein Sohn; **did you buy that for me, ~ you?** *(inf)* hast du das für mich gekauft? das ist aber lieb von dir! *(inf)*; **~ you, darling, you're an angel** *(inf)* du bist wirklich lieb, du bist ein Engel *(inf)*; **~ your little cotton socks** *(inf)* du bist ja ein Schatz *(inf)*; **~ you!** *(to sneezer)* Gesundheit!; **~ me!** *(inf)* **~ my soul!** *(inf)* du meine Güte! *(inf)*; **he's lost it again, ~ him** *(iro)* prima, er hat es wieder mal verloren! *(iro)*; **I'll be ~ed** *or* **blest if I'm going to do that!** *(inf)* das fällt mir ja nicht im Traum ein! *(inf)*; **well, I'll be ~ed!** *(inf)* so was!
b **to ~ sb with sth** jdn mit etw segnen; **to be ~ed with** gesegnet sein mit
c *(Eccl, = adore)* preisen

blessed [ˈblesɪd] **ADJ** **a** *(Rel)* heilig; **the Blessed X** der selige X; **~ be God!** gepriesen sei Gott!; **of ~ memory** seligen Angedenkens
b *(= fortunate)* selig; **~ are the pure in heart** *(Bibl)* selig sind, die reinen Herzens sind
c *(liter, = giving joy)* willkommen
d *(euph inf: = cursed)* verflixt *(inf)*; **I couldn't remember a ~ thing** ich konnte mich an rein gar nichts mehr erinnern *(inf)*; **the whole ~ day** den lieben langen Tag *(inf)*; **every ~ evening** aber auch JEDEN Abend
ADV verflixt *(inf)*; **he's too ~ lazy** er ist einfach zu faul
N **the Blessed, the Blest** die Seligen *pl*

blessedly [ˈblesɪdlɪ] ADV zum Glück

Blessed Virgin N Heilige Jungfrau (Maria)

blessing [ˈblesɪŋ] N *(Rel, fig)* Segen *m*; **he can count his ~s** da kann er von Glück sagen; **you can count your ~s you didn't get caught** du kannst von Glück sagen, dass du nicht geschnappt worden bist; **the ~s of civilization** die Segnungen der Zivilisation; **it was a ~ in disguise** es war schließlich doch ein Segen

blest [blest] **ADJ** *(liter)* = **blessed ADJ b, c** **N** = **blessed**

blether [ˈbleðəˈ] *(Scot inf)* **VI** quatschen *(inf)*, schwätzen *(S Ger inf)* **N** **a** **to have a good ~** einen ordentlichen Schwatz halten *(inf)* **b** *(= person)* Quasselstrippe *f (inf)*

blethering [ˈbleðərɪŋ] N *(inf)* Gequatsche *nt (inf)*

blew [bluː] *pret of* **blow²**

blight [blaɪt] **N** **a** *(on plants)* Braunfäule *f* **b** *(fig)* **to be a ~ on** *or* **upon sb's life/happiness** jdm das Leben/jds Glück vergällen; **these slums are a ~ upon the city** diese Slums sind ein Schandfleck für die Stadt; **scenes of urban ~** verfallene Stadtteile; **this poverty which is a ~ upon our nation** die Armut, mit der unser Volk geschlagen ist **VT** **a** *plants* zerstören **b** *(fig) hopes* vereiteln; *sb's career, future also* verderben; **to ~ sb's life** jdm das Leben verderben

blighter [ˈblaɪtəˈ] N *(Brit inf)* Kerl *m (inf)*; *(= boy)* ungezogener Bengel; *(= girl)* Luder *nt (inf)*; **a poor ~** ein armer Hund *(inf)*; **you ~** du Idiot! *(inf)*; **what a lucky ~!** so ein Glückspilz!

Blighty [ˈblaɪtɪ] N *(Brit Mil sl)* *(= leave)* Heimaturlaub *m*; *(= England)* die Heimat; **he's going back to ~** er geht nach Hause; **a blighty one** *(= wound)* ein Heimatschuss *m*

blimey [ˈblaɪmɪ] INTERJ *(Brit inf)* verflucht *(inf)*, Mensch *(inf)*

blimp [blɪmp] N **a** *(Brit inf)* **(Colonel) Blimp** Stockkonservative(r) *m*, alter Oberst *(inf)* **b** *(Aviat)* Kleinluftschiff *nt* **c** *(Film)* Blimp *m*, Schallschutzgehäuse *nt*

blind [blaɪnd] **ADJ** *(+er)* **a** *(= sightless)* blind; **to go ~** erblinden, blind werden; **a ~ man/woman** ein Blinder/eine Blinde; **~ in one eye** auf einem Auge blind
b *(fig, to beauty, charm etc)* blind *(to* für, gegen); **love is ~** Liebe macht blind; **to be ~ to sb's faults** jds Fehler nicht sehen; **to be ~ to the possibilities** die Möglichkeiten nicht sehen; **to turn a ~ eye to sth** bei etw ein Auge zudrücken; **she remained ~ to the fact that ...** sie sah einfach nicht, dass ...
c *(fig: = lacking judgement) obedience, passion* blind; *fury, panic also* hell; **in a ~ fury** in heller Wut; **~ with passion/rage** blind vor Leidenschaft/Wut; **he came home in a ~ stupor** er kam sinnlos betrunken nach Hause; **~ faith (in sth)** blindes Vertrauen (in etw *acc*); **~ forces** blinde Kräfte
d *(= vision obscured) corner* unübersichtlich → **blind spot**
e *(Brit inf)* **it's not a ~ bit of use trying to persuade him** es hat überhaupt keinen Zweck, ihn überreden zu wollen; **he hasn't done a ~ bit of work** er hat keinen Strich *or* Schlag getan *(inf)*; **but he didn't take a ~ bit of notice** aber er hat sich nicht die Spur darum gekümmert *(inf)*
f *(= false) door, window* blind
g *(= without exit) passage* ohne Ausgang, blind endend *attr*; *(= without windows and doors) wall* ohne Fenster und Türen
VT **a** *(= make blind: light, sun)* blenden; **the explosion ~ed him** er ist durch die Explosion blind geworden; **he was ~ed in the war** er ist kriegsblind; **the war--ed** die Kriegsblinden *pl*
b *(sun, light)* blenden
c *(fig, love, hate etc)* blind machen *(to* für, gegen); *(wealth, beauty)* blenden; **to ~ sb with science** jdn mit Fachjargon beeindrucken (wollen)
N **a** **the ~** die Blinden *pl*; **it's the ~ leading the ~** *(fig)* das hieße, einen Lahmen einen Blinden führen lassen
b *(= window shade, cloth)* Rollo *nt*, Rouleau *nt*; *(slats)* Jalousie *f*; *(outside)* Rollladen *m*
c *(= cover)* Tarnung *f*; **to be a ~** zur Tarnung dienen
d *(fig sl, = booze-up)* Sauferei *f (inf)*
e *(US: = hide)* Versteck *nt*
ADV **a** *(Aviat) fly* blind
b *(Cook)* **to bake sth ~** etw vorbacken
c **~ drunk** *(inf)* sinnlos betrunken

blind: **blind alley** N *(lit, fig)* Sackgasse *f*; **to be up a ~** *(fig)* in einer Sackgasse stecken; **blind date** N Rendezvous *nt* mit einem/einer Unbekannten; *(= person)* unbekannter (Rendezvous)partner, unbekannte (Rendezvous)partnerin

blinder [ˈblaɪndəˈ] N **a** *(US: = blinker)* Scheuklappe *f* **b** *(Brit inf, = drinking spree)* Kneipkur *f (inf)* **c** *(Brit inf)* **to play a ~** *(Sport)* spitzenmäßig spielen *(inf)*

blind flying N *(Aviat)* Blindflug *m*

blindfold [ˈblaɪndfəʊld] **VT** die Augen verbinden *(+dat)* **N** Augenbinde *f* **ADJ** mit verbundenen Augen; **I could do it ~** *(inf)* das mach ich mit links *(inf)*

blinding [ˈblaɪndɪŋ] ADJ *light* blendend; *truth* ins Auge stechend; *headache, pain* furchtbar; **as ~ tears filled her eyes** von Tränen geblendet

blindingly [ˈblaɪndɪŋlɪ] ADV *bright* blendend; **it is ~ obvious** das sieht doch ein Blinder *(inf)*

blind landing N *(Aviat)* Blindlandung *f*

blindly [ˈblaɪndlɪ] ADV *(lit, fig)* blind(lings)

blind man's buff N Blindekuh *no art*, Blindekuhspiel *nt*

blindness [ˈblaɪndnɪs] N *(lit, fig)* Blindheit *f (to* gegenüber)

blind: **blind side** N *(Sport)* ungedeckte Seite; **blind spot** N *(Med)* blinder Fleck; *(Aut, Aviat)* toter Winkel; *(Rad)* tote Zone; **to have a ~ about sth** einen blinden Fleck in Bezug auf etw *(acc)* haben; **he has a ~ where she's concerned** er ist ihr gegenüber absolut blind; **trigonometry was his ~** Trigonometrie war sein schwacher Punkt; **blind staggers** N *sing* Taumelsucht *f*; **blind test** N Blindversuch *m*; **blind trust** N *(Fin)* Blind Trust *m*; **blindworm** N Blindschleiche *f*

bling bling [ˈblɪŋˈblɪŋ] N *(inf: = jewellery)* Schmuck *m*, Brillies *pl (inf)*

blink [blɪŋk] **N** Blinzeln *nt*; **in the ~ of an eye** im Nu; **to be on the ~** *(inf)* kaputt sein *(inf)* **VI** **a** *(person)* blinzeln, zwinkern **b** *(light)* blinken **VT** **to ~ one's eyes** mit den Augen zwinkern

▶ **blink at** VI *+prep obj (= ignore)* hinwegsehen über *(+acc)*

▶ **blink away** VT *sep tears* wegblinzeln *(inf)*

blinker [ˈblɪŋkəˈ] N **a** *(US inf: = light)* Blinker *m* **b** **blinkers** PL Scheuklappen *pl*

blinkered [ˈblɪŋkəd] ADJ **a** *(fig)* engstirnig; **they are all so ~** sie laufen alle mit Scheuklappen herum **b** *horse* mit Scheuklappen

blinking [ˈblɪŋkɪŋ] **ADJ** *(Brit inf)* verflixt *(inf)*, blöd *(inf)*; **what a ~ cheek!** so eine bodenlose Frechheit! *(inf)*; **it's about ~ time too!** das wird aber auch Zeit! *(inf)* **ADV** verflixt *(inf)* **N** **a** *(of eyes)* Blinzeln *nt*, Zwinkern *nt* **b** *(of light)* Blinken *nt*

blintz(e) [blɪnts] N *(US Cook)* dünner Pfannkuchen, Crêpe *f*

blip [blɪp] N leuchtender Punkt (auf dem Radarschirm); *(fig)* kurzzeitiger Tiefpunkt

bliss [blɪs] N Glück *nt*; *(Rel)* (Glück)seligkeit *f*; **a feeling of ~** ein Gefühl *nt* der Wonne; **this is ~!** das ist herrlich *or* eine Wohltat!; **sun, sea, sand, ah sheer ~** Sonne, Meer und Strand, einfach paradiesisch; **ah ~, she sighed** herrlich, seufzte sie; **ignorance is ~** *(prov)* Unwissenheit ist ein Geschenk des Himmels → **domestic ADJ a**

blissful [ˈblɪsfʊl] ADJ *time* herrlich, paradiesisch; *respite also* wohltuend; *feeling also* wonnig; *happiness* höchste(s); *state, look, smile* (glück)selig; *moments* selig; **in ~ ignorance of the facts** *(iro)* in herrlicher Ahnungslosigkeit; **in ~ ignorance of the fact that ...** *(iro)* in keinster Weise ahnend, dass ...

blissfully [ˈblɪsfəlɪ] ADV *stretch* wohlig; *peaceful* paradiesisch, herrlich; *smile* selig; **~ happy** überglücklich; **to be ~ ignorant/unaware** so herrlich ahnungslos/arglos sein; **he remained ~ ignorant of what was going on** er ahnte in keinster Weise, was eigentlich vor sich ging

B list *(inf)* **N** weniger wichtige Personen *pl or* Leute *pl (inf)* **ADJ** **B-list people** B-Promis *pl (inf)*; **B-list star** Star *m* aus der zweiten Reihe *(inf)*, zweitklassiger Star

blister [ˈblɪstəˈ] **N** *(on skin, paint)* Blase *f*; *(Aviat, for gun)* Bordwaffenstand *m* **VI** *(skin)* Blasen bekommen; *(paintwork, metal)* Blasen werfen **VT** *skin, paint* Blasen hervorrufen auf *(+dat)*

blistered [ˈblɪstəd] ADJ **to have ~ skin/feet/hands** Blasen auf der Haut/an den Füßen/an den Händen haben; **to be ~** Blasen haben; **~ paint** Blasen werfende Farbe

blistering [ˈblɪstərɪŋ] ADJ **a** *heat, sun* glühend; *pace* mörderisch **b** *(= scathing) attack, criticism* vernichtend, ätzend

blister pack N (Klar)sichtpackung *f*

blister-packed [ˈblɪstəˌpækt] ADJ klarsichtverpackt

blithe [blaɪð] ADJ *(+er)* *(pej: = casual)* unbekümmert, ungeniert; *(liter: = cheerful)* fröhlich, munter

blithely [ˈblaɪðlɪ] ADV *carry on* munter; *say, announce* unbekümmert; *unaware* erstaunlich; **he ~ ignored the problem** er setzte sich ungeniert *or* unbekümmert über das Problem hinweg

blithering [ˈblɪðərɪŋ] ADJ *(inf)* **a ~ idiot** ein Trottel *m (inf)*; **don't be such a ~ idiot** du bist ja total bescheuert *(inf)*

B Litt *abbr of* **Bachelor of Letters**

blitz [blɪts] **N** **a** Blitzkrieg *m*; *(aerial)* Luftangriff *m*; **the Blitz** *deutscher Luftangriff auf britische Städte 1940-41* **b** *(fig inf)* Blitzaktion *f*; **he had a ~ on his room** er machte gründlich in seinem Zimmer sauber **VT** heftig bombardieren

blitzed [blɪtst] ADJ **a** *area* zerbombt **b** *(inf: = drunk)* voll *(inf)*, zu *(inf)*

blizzard [ˈblɪzəd] N Schneesturm *m*, Blizzard *m*; *(fig: of products, letters, lawsuits)* Flut *f* (*of* von)

bloated [ˈbləʊtɪd] ADJ **a** aufgedunsen; **I feel absolutely ~** *(inf)* ich bin zum Platzen voll *(inf)* **b** *(fig, with pride, self-importance)* aufgeblasen (*with* vor *+dat*)

bloater [ˈbləʊtəˈ] N Räucherhering *m*

blob [blɒb] N *(of water, honey, wax)* Tropfen *m*; *(of ink)* Klecks *m*; *(of paint)* Tupfer *m*; *(of ice cream, mashed potato)* Klacks *m*

bloc [blɒk] N *(Pol)* Block *m*

block [blɒk] **N** **a** Block *m*, Klotz *m*; *(= executioner's block)* Richtblock *m*; *(= engine block)* Motorblock *m*; **~s** *(= toys)* (Bau)klötze *pl*; **huge ugly ~s of concrete** riesige, hässliche Betonklötze; **to be sent to/to go to the ~** dem Henker überantwortet werden/vor den Henker treten; **to put** *or* **lay one's head on the ~** *(fig)* Kopf und Kragen riskieren

b *(= building)* Block *m*; **~ of flats** *(Brit)* Wohnblock *m*; **to take a stroll round the ~** einen Spaziergang um den Block machen; **she lived in the next ~/three ~s from us** *(esp US)* sie wohnte im nächsten Block/drei Blocks *or* Straßen weiter

c *(= division of seats)* Block *m*

d *(= obstruction, in pipe, Med)* Verstopfung *f*; *(mental)* geistige Sperre (*about* in Bezug auf *+acc*), Mattscheibe *f (inf)*; **I've a mental ~ about it** da habe ich totale Mattscheibe *(inf)*

e *(Comput)* Block *m*

f *(of tickets, shares)* Block *m*

g *(inf: = head)* **to knock sb's ~ off** jdm eins überziehen *(inf)*

h *(usu pl: also* **starting block***)* Startblock *m*; **to be first off the (starting) ~s** *(fig)* als Erster aus den Startlöchern kommen; **new kid on the ~** *(inf)* Neuling *m*, Newcomer *m (inf)*

i *(in ballet shoe)* Spitzenverstärkung *f*; *(= ballet shoe)* spitzenverstärkter Ballettschuh

j *(Typ)* Druckstock *m*

VT **a** *road, harbour, wheel, deal, move, sale* blockieren; *plans also* im Wege stehen *(+dat)*; *traffic also, progress* aufhalten; *pipe* verstopfen; *(Ftbl) one's opponent* blocken; *ball* stoppen; **to ~ sb's way/view** jdm den Weg/die Sicht versperren

b *credit* sperren

c *(Comput)* blocken

VI *(Sport)* blocken

▶ **block in** VT *sep* **a** *(Art)* andeuten **b** *(= hem in)* einkeilen

▶ **block off** VT *sep street* absperren; *fireplace* abdecken

▶ **block out** VT *sep* **a** *(= obscure) light* nicht durchlassen; *sun also* verdecken; **the trees are blocking out all the light** die Bäume nehmen das ganze Licht weg **b** *(= obliterate) part of picture, photograph* wegretuschieren **c** *(= ignore) pain, fact, past* verdrängen; *noise (double glazing etc)* unterdrücken; *(person)* ausblenden **d** *(= sketch roughly)* andeuten

▶ **block up** VT *sep* **a** *(= obstruct) gangway* blockieren, versperren; *pipe* verstopfen; **my nose is** *or* **I'm all blocked up** meine Nase ist völlig verstopft **b** *(= close, fill in) window, entrance* zumauern; *hole* zustopfen

blockade [blɒˈkeɪd] **N** **a** *(Mil)* Blockade *f*; **under ~** im Blockadezustand; **to break** *or* **run the ~** die Blockade brechen **b** *(= barrier, obstruction)* Sperre *f*, Barrikade *f* **VT** blockieren, sperren

blockade runner N Blockadebrecher *m*

blockage [ˈblɒkɪdʒ] N Verstopfung *f*; *(in windpipe etc)* Blockade *f*; *(= act)* Blockierung *f*

block: **block and tackle** N Flaschenzug *m*; **block booking** N *(= travel booking)* Gruppenbuchung *f*; *(Theat)* Gruppenbestellung *f*; **block brake** N *(Tech)* Backenbremse *f*; **blockbuster** N **a** *(inf)* Knüller *m (inf)*; *(= film also)* Kinohit *m (inf)* **b** *(Mil)* große Bombe; **block grant** N Pauschalsubvention *f*; **blockhead** N *(inf)* Dummkopf *m*; **blockhouse** N Blockhaus *nt*

blockish [ˈblɒkɪʃ] ADJ *(inf)* dumm, doof *(inf)*

block: **block letters** PL Blockschrift *f*; **block vote** N Stimmenblock *m*

blog [blɒg] **N** *(Internet)* Blog *nt or m*, Weblog *nt or m*, *persönlicher Artikel oder Diskussionsbeitrag im Internet* **VTI** bloggen, *(einen Artikel oder Diskussionsbeitrag) ins Internet stellen*

blogger [ˈblɒgəˈ] N Blogger(in) *m(f)*, *jd, der persönliche Artikel oder Diskussionsbeiträge ins Internet stellt*

bloke [bləʊk] N *(Brit inf)* Kerl *m (inf)*, Typ *m (inf)*

blokey [ˈbləʊkɪ], **blok(e)ish** [ˈbləʊkɪʃ] ADJ *(Brit inf)* kumpelhaft

blond [blɒnd] ADJ *man, hair, beard* blond

blonde [blɒnd] **ADJ** blond; **I want to go ~** ich möchte meine Haare blondieren (lassen) **N** **a** *(= woman)* Blondine *f* **b** *(Brit pej inf)* **you're such a ~!** du bist ein echter Obertrottel!, du bist echt blond! *(inf)*

blonde bombshell N *(inf)* Superblondine *f (inf)*

blood [blʌd] **N** **a** Blut *nt*; **to give ~** Blut spenden; **to spill** *or* **shed ~** *(in conflict, war)* Blut vergießen; **it makes my ~ boil** das macht mich rasend; **his ~ is up** er ist wütend; **she's out for** *or* **after his ~** sie will ihm an den Kragen *(inf)*; **his ~ ran cold** es lief ihm eiskalt über den Rücken; **this firm needs new ~** diese Firma braucht frisches Blut; **it is like trying to get ~ from a stone** *(prov)* das ist verlorene Liebesmüh; **~, sweat and tears** Blut, Schweiß und Tränen; **he has (their) ~ on his hands** an seinen Händen klebt (ihr) Blut → **bad blood**

b *(fig: = lineage)* Blut *nt*, Geblüt *nt (geh)*, Abstammung *f*; **a prince of the ~** ein Prinz von edlem Geblüt *(geh)*; **it's in his ~** das liegt ihm im Blut; **~ is thicker than water** *(prov)* Blut ist dicker als Wasser *(prov)*

c *(old, = dandy)* Geck *m (old)*, Stutzer *m (dated)*

ATTR *(= purebred)* reinrassig

VT *hounds* an Blut gewöhnen

blood *in cpds* Blut-; **blood alcohol** N Blutalkohol *m*; **blood and thunder** N Mord und Totschlag *m*; **blood-and-thunder** ADJ **~ novel** Reißer *m*; **~ speech** melodramatische *or* donnernde Rede; **blood bank** N Blutbank *f*; **blood bath** N Blutbad *nt*; **blood blister** N Blutblase *f*; **blood brother** N Blutsbruder *m*; **blood cell** N Blutkörperchen *nt*; **blood clot** N Blutgerinnsel *nt*; **blood count** N *(Med)* Blutbild *nt*; **bloodcurdling** ADJ grauenerregend; **they heard a ~ cry** sie hörten einen Schrei, der ihnen das Blut in den Adern erstarren ließ *(geh)*; **blood donor** N Blutspender(in) *m(f)*; **blood feud** N Blutfehde *f*; **blood group** N Blutgruppe *f*; **blood guilt**, **blood guiltiness** N Blutschuld *f*; **blood heat** N Körpertemperatur *f*; **bloodhound** N **a** *(Zool)* Bluthund *m* **b** *(fig: = detective)* Schnüffler *m (inf)*, Detektiv *m*

bloodily [ˈblʌdɪlɪ] ADV *defeat, repress, kill* blutig

bloodiness [ˈblʌdɪnɪs] N **a** *(of sight, war etc)* Blutigkeit *f* **b** *(inf, = horribleness)* Grässlichkeit *f*, Abscheulichkeit *f*

bloodless [ˈblʌdlɪs] ADJ *(rare, = without blood)* blutlos; *(= without bloodshed) victory, coup* unblutig; *(= pallid)* blutleer, bleich

bloodlessly [ˈblʌdlɪslɪ] ADV unblutig

bloodlessness [ˈblʌdlɪsnɪs] N *(of victory, coup)* Unblutigkeit *f*; *(= pallidness)* Blutleere *f*, Bleichheit *f*

blood: **blood-letting** N Aderlass *m*; **blood lust** N Blutrünstigkeit *f*; **bloodmobile** N *(US)* Blutspendewagen *m*; **blood money** N Mordgeld *nt*; **blood orange** N Blutorange *f*; **blood plasma** N Blutplasma *nt*; **blood poisoning** N Blutvergiftung *f*; **blood pressure** N Blutdruck *m*; **to have high ~** hohen Blutdruck haben; **blood pudding** N ≈ Blutwurst *f*; **blood-red** ADJ blutrot; **blood relation** N Blutsverwandte(r) *mf*; **blood sample** N *(Med)* Blutprobe *f*; **bloodshed** N Blutvergießen *nt*; **bloodshot** ADJ blutunterlaufen; **blood sports** PL *Jagdsport, Hahnenkampf etc*; **bloodstain** N Blutfleck *m*; **bloodstained** ADJ blutig, blutbefleckt; **bloodstock** N reinrassige Zucht; **bloodstone** N Blutjaspis *m*, Heliotrop *m*; **bloodstream** N Blut *nt*, Blutkreislauf *m*; **bloodsucker** N *(Zool, fig)* Blutsauger *m*; **blood sugar** N Blutzucker *m*; **~ level** Blutzuckerspiegel *m*; **blood test** N Blutprobe *f*; **bloodthirstiness** N *(of tale, regime)* Blutrünstigkeit *f*; *(of person, animal, disposition also)* Blutgier *f*; **bloodthirsty** ADJ *tale, regime* blutrünstig; *person, animal, disposition also* blutgierig; **blood ties** PL Blutsbande *pl (geh)*; **blood transfusion** N Blutübertragung *f*, (Blut)transfusion *f*; **blood type** N Blutgruppe *f*; **blood vessel** N Blutgefäß *nt*; **he almost burst a ~** *(lit)* ihm wäre beinahe eine Ader geplatzt; *(fig inf)* ihn traf fast der Schlag

bloody [ˈblʌdɪ] **ADJ** *(+er)* **a** *(lit) nose, bandage, battle* blutig; **to give sb a ~ nose** *(fig) (in contest)* jdm einen Denkzettel verpassen; *(in war)* jdm eine Niederlage beibringen

b *(Brit inf: = damned)* verdammt *(inf)*, Scheiß- *(inf)*; *(in positive sense) genius, wonder* echt *(inf)*, verdammt *(inf)*; **it was a ~ nuisance/waste of time** Mann *or* Mensch, das war vielleicht ein Quatsch *(inf) or* Scheiß *(inf)*/das war reine Zeitverschwendung; **it was there all the ~ time** Mann *(inf) or* Mensch *(inf) or* Scheiße *(inf)*, das war schon die ganze Zeit da; **I haven't got any ~ time** verdammt noch mal, ich hab keine Zeit *(inf)*; **he hasn't got a ~ hope** Mensch *or* Mann, der hat doch überhaupt keine Chance *(inf)*; **~ hell!** verdammt! *(inf)*, Scheiße! *(inf)*; *(in indignation)* verdammt noch mal! *(inf)*; *(in amazement)* Menschenskind! *(inf)*, meine Fresse! *(sl)*; **he is a ~ marvel** er ist echt *or* verdammt gut *(inf)*

c *(inf, = awful)* gräulich *(inf)*; *person, behaviour* abscheulich

ADV *(Brit inf)* verdammt *(inf)*, saumäßig *(inf)*; *hot, cold, stupid* sau- *(inf)*; *(in positive sense) good, brilliant* echt *(inf)*, verdammt *(inf)*; **that's ~ useless, that's no ~ good** das ist doch Scheiße *(inf)*; **not ~ likely** da ist überhaupt nichts drin *(inf)*; **he can ~ well do it himself** das soll er schön alleine machen, verdammt noch mal! *(inf)*

VT blutig machen

Bloody Mary N *Cocktail aus Tomatensaft und Wodka*

bloody-minded [ˈblʌdɪˈmaɪndɪd] ADJ *(Brit inf)* stur *(inf)*

blooey [ˈbluːɪ] ADJ, ADV *(US inf)* kaputt; **to go ~** *(thing)* kaputtgehen; *(= come apart)* zusammenbrechen; *(plan, = not succeed)* danebengehen *(inf)*

bloom [bluːm] **N** **a** Blüte *f*; **to be in (full) ~** in (voller) Blüte stehen; **to come/burst into ~** aufblühen/plötzlich erblühen **b** *(fig)* **her skin has lost its ~** ihre Haut ist welk geworden; **in the ~ of youth** in der Blüte der Jugend; **in the**

first ~ of love in der ersten Begeisterung ihrer Liebe c *(on fruit)* satter Schimmer; *(on peaches)* Flaum *m* VI *(lit, fig)* blühen

bloomer ['blu:mə'] N *(Brit inf)* grober Fehler; **to make a ~** einen Bock schießen *(inf)*

bloomers ['blu:məz] PL Pumphose *f*

blooming ['blu:mɪŋ] *prp of* **bloom** ADJ *(inf)* verflixt *(inf)*; **it was there all the ~ time** verflixt, das war schon die ganze Zeit da! *(inf)* ADV verflixt *(inf)*

blooper ['blu:pə'] N *(US inf)* Schnitzer *m (inf)*

blossom ['blɒsəm] N Blüte *f*; **in ~** in Blüte VI a *(tree, plant)* blühen b *(fig, relationship)* blühen; *(person, trade etc also)* aufblühen; **to ~ into sth** zu etw aufblühen; *(person also)* zu etw erblühen *(geh)*; *(relationship)* zu etw wachsen

▶ **blossom out** VI *(fig)* aufblühen *(into* zu)

blot [blɒt] N a *(of ink)* (Tinten)klecks *m* b *(fig, on honour, reputation)* Fleck *m (on* auf *+dat)*; **a ~ on his career** ein schwarzer Fleck in seiner Karriere; **a ~ on the landscape** ein Schandfleck *m* in der Landschaft VT a *(= make ink spots on)* beklecksen; **to ~ one's copybook** *(fig)* sich unmöglich machen; *(with sb)* es sich *(dat)* verderben b *(= dry) ink, page* ablöschen; *skin, face etc* abtupfen

▶ **blot out** VT *sep* a *(lit) words* unleserlich machen, verschmieren b *(fig: = hide from view) landscape, sun* verdecken; *(= obliterate) memories* auslöschen; *pain* betäuben

blotch [blɒtʃ] N *(on skin)* Fleck *m*; *(of ink, colour also)* Klecks *m* VT *paper, written work* beklecksen, Flecken machen auf *(+acc)*; *skin* fleckig werden lassen

blotchy ['blɒtʃɪ] ADJ *(+er) skin* fleckig; *drawing, paint* klecksig; **a rather ~ drawing** ein richtiges Klecksbild

blotter ['blɒtə'] N a (Tinten)löscher *m* b *(US: = record book)* Kladde *f*; *(= police blotter)* Polizeiregister *nt*

blotting ['blɒtɪŋ]: **blotting pad** N Schreibunterlage *f*; **blotting paper** N Löschpapier *nt*

blotto ['blɒtəʊ] ADJ *pred (Brit inf: = drunk)* stockbesoffen *(inf)*

blouse [blaʊz] N a Bluse *f* b *(US Mil)* (Feld)-bluse *f* c *(esp US inf)* **he's a big girl's ~** *or* **a bit of a ~ when it comes to pain** bei Schmerzen ist er ein ziemlicher Jammerlappen *(inf)*; **you girl's ~!** du Weichei! *(inf)*

bloused [blaʊzd] ADJ blusig, wie eine Bluse

blouson ['blu:zɒn] N *(Brit)* Blouson *m or nt*

blow[1] [bləʊ] N *(lit, fig)* Schlag *m*; *(fig: = sudden misfortune also)* Schicksalsschlag *m (for, to* für); **to come to ~s** handgreiflich werden; **it came to ~s** es gab Handgreiflichkeiten; **at a (single)** *or* **one ~** *(fig)* mit einem Schlag *(inf)*; **to give sb/sth a ~** jdn/etw schlagen; **to deal sb/sth a ~** *(fig)* jdm/einer Sache einen Schlag versetzen; **to strike a ~ for sth** *(fig)* einer Sache *(dat)* einen großen Dienst erweisen; **without striking a ~** ohne jede Gewalt; **to match sth ~ for ~** etw Schlag auf Schlag kontern; **they matched us ~ for ~** sie haben Schlag auf Schlag gekontert

blow[2] *vb: pret* **blew**, *ptp* **blown** VI a *(wind)* wehen, blasen; **there was a draught** *(Brit) or* **draft** *(US)* **~ing in from the window** es zog vom Fenster her; **the wind was ~ing hard** es wehte ein starker Wind

b *(person)* blasen, pusten *(on* auf *+acc)*; **to ~ on one's soup** auf die Suppe pusten

c *(= move with the wind)* fliegen; *(leaves, hat, papers also)* geweht werden; **the door blew open/shut** die Tür flog auf/zu

d *(= make sound, bugle, horn)* blasen; *(whistle)* pfeifen; **then the whistle blew** *(Sport)* da kam der Pfiff

e *(fuse, light bulb)* durchbrennen; *(gasket)* platzen

f *(whale)* spritzen; **there she ~s!** Wal in Sicht!

g *(= pant)* pusten *(inf)*, schnaufen *(inf)*; *(animal)* schnaufen

h *(inf, = leave)* abhauen *(inf)*

VT a *(= move by blowing, breeze)* wehen; *(strong wind, draught)* blasen; *(gale etc)* treiben; *(person)* blasen, pusten *(inf)*; **the wind blew the ship off course** der Wind trieb das Schiff vom Kurs ab; **to ~ sb a kiss** jdm eine Kusshand zuwerfen

b *(= drive air into) fire* anblasen; *eggs* ausblasen; **to ~ one's nose** sich *(dat)* die Nase putzen

c *(= make by blowing) glass, smoke rings* blasen; *bubbles* machen

d *trumpet* blasen; *(Hunt, Mil) horn* blasen in *(+acc)*; **the referee blew his whistle** der Schiedsrichter pfiff; **to ~ one's own trumpet** *(Brit) or* **horn** *(US) (fig)* sein eigenes Lob singen

e *(= burn out, blow up) safe, bridge etc* sprengen; *valve, gasket* platzen lassen; *transistor* zerstören; **I've ~n a fuse/light bulb** mir ist eine Sicherung/Birne durchgebrannt; **the car blew a tyre** *(Brit) or* **tire** *(US)* an dem Auto ist ein Reifen geplatzt; **to be ~n to pieces** *(bridge, car)* in die Luft gesprengt werden; *(person)* zerfetzt werden

f *(inf: = spend extravagantly) money* verpulvern *(inf)*

g *(inf: = reveal) secret* verraten → **gaff**[2]

h *(Brit inf: = damn)* **~!** Mist! *(inf)*; **~ this rain!** dieser mistige Regen! *(inf)*; **~ the expense/what he likes!** das ist doch wurscht, was es kostet/was er will *(inf)*; **well, I'll be ~ed** Mensch(enskind)! *(inf)*; **I'll be ~ed if I'll do it** ich denke nicht im Traum dran(, das zu tun) *(inf)*; **… and ~ me if he still didn't forget** … und er hat es trotzdem glatt vergessen *(inf)*

i *(inf)* **to ~ one's chances of doing sth** es sich *(dat)* verscherzen, etw zu tun; **I think I've ~n it** ich glaube, ich habs versaut *(inf)*

j *(inf)* → **mind 1**

k *(esp US sl: = fellate)* **to ~ sb** jdm einen blasen *(sl)*

N a *(= expulsion of breath)* Blasen *nt*, Pusten *nt (inf)*; **to give a ~** blasen, pusten *(inf)*; *(when blowing nose)* sich schnäuzen

b *(Brit: = breath of air)* **to go for a ~** sich durchlüften lassen

▶ **blow away** VI *(hat, paper etc)* wegfliegen VT *sep* a wegblasen; *(breeze also)* wegwehen b *(inf: = kill)* abknallen *(inf)* c *(inf: = defeat)* fertigmachen *(inf)*, in die Pfanne hauen *(inf)*

▶ **blow down** VI *(tree etc)* umfallen, umgeweht werden VT *sep (lit)* umwehen; **blow me down!** *(inf)* Mensch(enskind)! *(inf)*

▶ **blow in** VI a *(lit: = be blown down, window etc)* eingedrückt werden; *(= be blown inside, dust etc)* hinein-/hereinfliegen, hinein-/hereingeweht *or* -geblasen werden; *(wind)* hereinwehen, hereinblasen; **there was a draught blowing in** es zog herein b *(inf: = arrive unexpectedly)* hereinschneien *(inf)* (+prep obj, -to in +acc) VT *sep window, door etc* eindrücken; *dust etc* hinein-/hereinblasen *or* -wehen (+prep obj, -to in +acc)

▶ **blow off** VI wegfliegen VT *sep* wegblasen; (+prep obj) blasen von; *(breeze also)* wegwehen; (+prep obj) wehen von; **to blow one's/sb's head off** *(= kill)* sich/jdm eine Kugel durch den Kopf jagen *(inf)* VT *insep (fig) steam* ablassen *(inf)*

▶ **blow out** VI a *(candle etc)* ausgehen b *(Aut: tyre)* platzen; *(Elec, fuse)* durchbrennen c *(gas, oil)* ausbrechen; *(oil well)* einen Ausbruch haben VT *sep* a *candle* ausblasen, löschen b *(= fill with air) one's cheeks* aufblasen c **to blow one's/sb's brains out** sich/jdm eine Kugel durch den Kopf jagen *(inf)* VR *(wind, storm)* sich legen; *(fig, passion)* verpuffen *(inf)*

▶ **blow over** VI a *(tree etc)* umfallen b *(lit, fig, storm, dispute)* sich legen VT *sep tree etc* umstürzen

▶ **blow up** VI a *(= be exploded)* in die Luft fliegen; *(bomb)* explodieren b *(lit, fig, gale, crisis, row)* ausbrechen; **his allegations could blow up in his face** seine Behauptungen könnten nach hinten losgehen c *(fig inf, person)* explodieren *(inf)* VT *sep* a *mine, bridge, person* in die Luft jagen, hochjagen b *tyre, balloon* aufblasen c *photo* vergrößern d *(fig: = magnify, exaggerate) event* aufbauschen *(into* zu)

blow: **blowback** N *(Tech, Mil)* Rückstoß *m*; **blow-by-blow** ADJ *account* detailliert; **blow-dry** N **to have a cut and ~** sich *(dat)* die Haare schneiden und föhnen lassen VT föhnen

blower ['bləʊə'] N a *(= device)* Gebläse *nt* b *(= glass blower)* Glasbläser *m* c *(Brit inf: = telephone)* Telefon *nt*; **to be on the ~** an der Strippe hängen *(inf)*; **to get on the ~ to sb** jdn anrufen

blow: **blowfly** N Schmeißfliege *f*; **blowgun** N *(= weapon)* Blasrohr *nt*; **blowhole** N a *(of whale)* Atemloch *nt* b *(Min)* Abzugsloch *nt*; **blow job** N *(sl)* **to give sb a ~** jdm einen blasen *(sl)*; **blowlamp** N Lötlampe *f*

blown [bləʊn] *ptp of* **blow**[2] ADJ *flower* voll aufgeblüht; *glass* mundgeblasen

blow: **blowout** N a *(inf: = meal)* Schlemmerei *f*; **to have a ~** schlemmen *(inf)* b *(= burst tyre)* **he had a ~** ihm ist ein Reifen geplatzt; **in the case of a ~** wenn ein Reifen platzt c *(Elec)* **there's been a ~** die Sicherung ist durchgebrannt d *(Min)* Ausbruch *m*; *(on oil rig)* Ölausbruch *m* e *(US inf: = clearance sale)* Ausverkauf *m*; **blowpipe** N a *(= weapon)* Blasrohr *nt* b *(Tech)* Gebläsebrenner *m*, Lötrohr *nt* c *(for glassmaking)* Glasbläserpfeife *f*

blowsy ['blaʊzɪ] ADJ = **blowzy**

blow: **blowtorch** N Lötlampe *f*; **blow-up** N a *(inf, = outburst of temper)* Wutausbruch *m* b *(inf, = row)* Krach *m*; **they've had a ~** sie hatten Krach c *(Phot)* Vergrößerung *f*

blowy ['bləʊɪ] ADJ *(+er)* windig

blowzy ['blaʊzɪ] ADJ *(+er) woman* schlampig

BLT [ˌbi:el'ti:] *(US inf) abbr of* **bacon, lettuce, and tomato sandwich**

blub [blʌb] VI *(inf)* heulen *(inf)*, flennen *(inf, pej)*

blubber ['blʌbə'] N a Walfischspeck *m*; *(inf, on person)* Wabbelspeck *m (inf)* b *(inf: = weep)* **to have a ~** flennen *(inf)*, heulen *(inf)* VTI *(inf)* flennen *(inf)*, heulen *(inf)*

▶ **blubber out** VT *sep (inf)* flennen *(inf)*, heulen *(inf)*

blubberer ['blʌbərə'] N *(inf)* Heulsuse *f (inf)*

blubbery ['blʌbərɪ] ADJ a wabb(e)lig *(inf)* b *(inf, = weepy)* verheult *(inf)*

bludgeon ['blʌdʒən] N Knüppel *m*, Keule *f* VT a *(= hit)* verprügeln; **to ~ sb to death** jdn zu Tode prügeln b *(fig)* bearbeiten *(inf)*; **he ~ed me into doing it** er hat mich so lange bearbeitet, bis ich es getan habe *(inf)*; **I don't want to ~ you into it** ich möchte dich nicht dazu zwingen

blue [blu:] ADJ *(+er)* a blau; **~ with cold** blau vor Kälte; **until you're ~ in the face** *(inf)* bis zum Gehtnichtmehr *(inf)*, bis zum Erbrechen *(inf)*; **once in a ~ moon** alle Jubeljahre (einmal); **like a ~ streak** *(inf)* wie ein geölter Blitz *(inf)*; **into the wide** *or* **wild ~ yonder** weit weit weg

b *(inf: = miserable)* melancholisch, trübsinnig; **to feel ~** den Moralischen haben *(inf)*; **to look ~** traurig aussehen

c *(inf: = obscene) language* derb, nicht salonfähig; *joke* schlüpfrig; *film* Porno-, Sex-; **the air was ~ (with oaths)** da habe ich/hat er *etc* vielleicht geflucht *(inf)*

d *(Pol)* konservativ

N a Blau *nt*; **the boys in ~** *(inf: = police)* die Polizei *pl*, die Grünen *pl (dated inf)*

b *(liter, = sky)* Himmel *m*; **out of the ~** *(fig inf)* aus heiterem Himmel *(inf)*

c *(Pol)* Konservative(r) *mf*

d *(inf)* **the blues** PL *(= depression)* der Moralische *(inf)*; **to have the ~s** den Moralischen haben *(inf)*

e *(Mus)* **the blues** PL der Blues; **a ~s** *sing* ein Blues

f *(Univ Sport) Student von Oxford oder Cambridge, der bei Wettkämpfen seine Universität vertritt (oder vertreten hat)*; *(= colours) blaue Mütze, Symbol dafür, dass man seine Universität in Wettkämpfen vertreten hat*

VT *(inf, = spend)* auf den Kopf hauen *(inf)* *(on* für)

blue: **blue baby** N Baby *nt* mit angeborenem Herzfehler; **Bluebeard** N Ritter Blaubart *m*; **bluebell** N Sternhyazinthe *f*; *(Scot: = harebell)* Glockenblume *f*; **blue beret** N Blauhelm *m*; **blueberry** N Blau- *or* Heidelbeere *f*; **bluebird** N Rotkehlhüttensänger *m*; **blue blood** N blaues Blut; **blue-blooded** ADJ blaublütig; **bluebook** N a *(Brit Parl)* Blaubuch *nt* b *(US: = list of prominent people)* ≈ Who's Who *nt* c *(US: = used-car price list)* Gebrauchtwagenpreisliste *f*, ≈ Schwacke-Liste *f*; **bluebottle** N Schmeißfliege *f*; **blue cheese** N Blauschimmelkäse *m*; **blue-chip** ADJ erstklassig; *shares also* Blue-Chip-; *investment* sicher; **~ company** Blue-Chip-Firma *f*, *seriöses Unternehmen mit guter Finanzlage*; **blue-collar** ADJ **~ worker/union/jobs** Arbeiter *m*/Arbeitergewerkschaft *f*/Stellen *pl* für Arbeiter; **blue-eyed** ADJ blauäugig; **sb's ~ boy** *(fig)* jds Liebling(sjunge) *m*; **blue helmet** N Blauhelm *m*; **bluejacket** N *(dated inf)* Matrose *m*; **to join the ~s** zu den blauen Jungs gehen *(dated inf)*; **blue jeans** PL Bluejeans *pl*; **blue line** N *(US: Typ)* Blaupause *f*

blueness ['blu:nɪs] N a *(lit)* Bläue *f* b *(inf: = obscenity, of language)* Derbheit *f*; *(of joke)* Schlüpfrigkeit *f*; *(of film)* Sexgeladenheit *f (inf)*

blue: **Blue Nile** N Blauer Nil; **blue-pencil** VT *(= edit, revise)* korrigieren; *(= delete)* ausstreichen; **blue peter** N *(Naut)* Blauer Peter; **blueprint** N Blaupause *f*; *(fig)* Plan *m*, Entwurf *m*; **do I have to draw you a ~?** *(inf)* muss ich dir erst 'ne Zeichnung machen? *(inf)*; **blue rib(b)and** N Blaues Band; **blue rinse** N **with her ~** mit ihrem silberblau getönten Haar; **bluestocking** N *(fig)* Blaustrumpf *m*

bluesy ['blu:zɪ] ADJ *(Mus)* bluesartig

blue: **bluetit** N Blaumeise *f*; **blue-water** ADJ *(Navy)* **~ fleet/ship** Hochseeflotte *f*/-schiff *nt*; **blue whale** N Blauwal *m*

bluff[1] [blʌf] N *(= headland)* Kliff *nt*; *(inland)* Felsvorsprung *m* ADJ rau aber herzlich *(inf)*; *honesty, answer* aufrichtig

bluff[2] VT bluffen; **he ~ed his way through it** er hat sich durchgeschummelt *(inf)* VI bluffen N Bluff *m*; **to call sb's ~** es darauf ankommen lassen; *(= make prove)* jdn auf die Probe stellen

▶ **bluff out** VT *sep* **to bluff it out** sich rausreden *(inf)*; **to bluff one's way out of sth** sich aus etw rausreden *(inf)*

bluffer ['blʌfəʳ] N Bluffer *m*

bluish ['blu:ɪʃ] ADJ bläulich

blunder ['blʌndəʳ] N (dummer) Fehler, Schnitzer *m (inf)*; *(socially also)* Fauxpas *m*; **to make a ~** einen Bock schießen *(inf)*; *(socially)* einen Fauxpas begehen VI a *(= make a blunder)* einen Bock schießen *(inf)*, Mist bauen *(inf)*; *(socially)* sich blamieren b *(= move clumsily)* tappen *(into* gegen); **to ~ in/out** hinein-/herein-/ /hinaus-/heraustappen; **to ~ into a trap** *(lit, fig)* in eine Falle tappen; **to ~ into war/a life of crime** in einen Krieg/ein kriminelles Leben hineinschlittern; **he ~ed through the poem** er kämpfte sich mühsam durch das Gedicht

blunderbuss ['blʌndəbʌs] N Donnerbüchse *f*

blunderer ['blʌndərəʳ] N Schussel *m (inf)*; *(socially)* Elefant *m (inf)*

blundering ['blʌndərɪŋ] ADJ a *person (= making mistakes)* schusselig *(inf)*; *(socially)* ohne jedes Feingefühl; **~ idiot** Erztrottel *m (inf)* b *(= clumsy)* tollpatschig; *reading* holp(e)rig N Schussligkeit *f (inf)*; *(socially)* gesellschaftliche Schnitzer *pl*

blunt [blʌnt] ADJ *(+er)* a stumpf; **with a ~ instrument** mit einem stumpfen Gegenstand b *(= outspoken) person* geradeheraus *pred*; *speech, warning, message, language* unverblümt; *fact* nackt, unbeschönigt; **he's rather a ~ person** er drückt sich ziemlich unverblümt *or* deutlich aus; **to be ~ about sth** sich unverblümt zu etw äußern; **he was very ~ about it** er hat sich sehr deutlich ausgedrückt; **let me be ~ about this** lassen Sie mich das ganz ohne Umschweife sagen VT *knife etc* stumpf machen; *(fig) palate, senses* abstumpfen; **his wits had been ~ed** er war geistig abgestumpft

bluntly ['blʌntlɪ] ADV *speak* freiheraus, geradeheraus; **he told us quite ~ what he thought** er sagte uns ganz unverblümt seine Meinung

bluntness ['blʌntnɪs] N a *(of blade, needle)* Stumpfheit *f* b *(= outspokenness)* Unverblümtheit *f*

blur [blɜːʳ] N verschwommener Fleck; **the ~ of their faces** ihre verschwommenen Gesichter; **the trees became a ~** man konnte die Bäume nur noch verschwommen erkennen; **a ~ of colours** *(Brit) or* **colors** *(US)* ein buntes Durcheinander von Farben VT a *inscription* verwischen; *writing also* verschmieren; *view* verschleiern; *outline, photograph* unscharf *or* verschwommen machen; *sound* verzerren; **to have ~red vision** nur noch verschwommen sehen; **to be/become ~red** undeutlich sein/werden; *(image etc also)* verschwommen sein/verschwimmen; **her eyes were ~red with tears** ihre Augen schwammen in Tränen; **the tape is ~red here** an dieser Stelle ist die Aufnahme verzerrt b *(fig) senses, mind, judgement* trüben; *memory also, meaning* verwischen; *intention* in den Hintergrund drängen VI *(vision, image)* verschwommen werden, verschwimmen

blurb [blɜːb] N Material *nt*, Informationen *pl*; *(on book cover)* Klappentext *m*, Waschzettel *m*

blurry ['blɜːrɪ] ADJ *(+er) outline, photograph* verschwommen, unscharf; *vision* verschwommen; *view* verschleiert

blurt (out) [blɜːt('aʊt)] VT *sep* herausplatzen mit *(inf)*

blush [blʌʃ] VI a *(= go red)* rot werden, erröten *(with* vor *+dat)* b *(fig: = be ashamed)* sich schämen *(for* für); **I ~ to say so** es ist mir peinlich, das zu sagen N Erröten *nt no pl*; **with a ~** errötend; **without a ~** ohne rot zu werden; **to spare** *or* **save sb's ~es** jdn nicht in Verlegenheit bringen; **to put sb to the ~** *(dated)* jdn in Verlegenheit bringen; **the first ~ of dawn** *(fig)* der zarte Schimmer der Morgenröte; **at first ~** auf den ersten Blick

blusher ['blʌʃəʳ] N Rouge *nt*

blushing ['blʌʃɪŋ] ADJ errötend; **the ~ bride** die sittsame Braut

bluster ['blʌstəʳ] VI a *(wind)* tosen, toben b *(fig: person)* ein großes Geschrei machen; *(angrily also)* toben VT **to ~ one's way out of it/sth** es/etw lautstark abstreiten N *(of person)* großes Geschrei; *(angry also)* Toben *nt*

blustering ['blʌstərɪŋ] ADJ *person* polternd; *manner* stürmisch

blustery ['blʌstərɪ] ADJ *wind, day* stürmisch

Blu-Tack® ['blu:tæk] N Klebmasse *f*

Blvd. *abbr of* **boulevard**

BM a *abbr of* **British Museum** b *abbr of* **Bachelor of Medicine**

BMA *abbr of* **British Medical Association** *britischer Ärzteverband*

B-movie ['bi:ˌmu:vɪ] N *als Beiprogramm gezeigter Kinofilm*, B-Movie *nt (spec)*

B Mus *abbr of* **Bachelor of Music**

BMX *abbr of* **bicycle motocross** *(= sport)* BMX-Radsport *m*, BMX-biking *nt*; *(= bicycle)* BMX-Rad *nt*

BO *(inf) abbr of* **body odour** Körpergeruch *m*

boa ['bəʊə] N Boa *f*; **~ constrictor** Boa constrictor *f*

boar [bɔːʳ] N *(= male pig)* Eber *m*; *(wild)* Keiler *m*; **~'s head** Schweinskopf *m*

board [bɔːd] N a Brett *nt*; *(= blackboard)* Tafel *f*; *(= notice board)* Schwarzes Brett; *(= signboard)* Schild *nt*; *(= floorboard)* Diele(nbrett *nt*) *f*; **the ~s** *(Theat)* die Bretter b *(= provision of meals)* Kost *f*, Verpflegung *f*; **~ and lodging** Kost und Logis; **full/half ~** Voll-/ /Halbpension *f* c *(= group of officials)* Ausschuss *m*; *(= board of inquiry, examiners also)* Kommission *f*; *(with advisory function, = board of trustees)* Beirat *m*; *(= permanent official institution: = gas board, harbour board etc)* Behörde *f*; *(of company: also* **board of directors***)* Vorstand *m*; *(of British/American company)* Verwaltungsrat *m*; *(including shareholders, advisers)* Aufsichtsrat *m*; **to be on the ~, to have a seat on the ~** im Vorstand/Aufsichtsrat sein *or* sitzen; **~ of governors** *(Brit Sch)* Verwaltungsrat *m*; **Board of Trade** *(Brit)* Handelsministerium *nt*; *(US)* Handelskammer *f* d *(Naut, Aviat)* **on ~** an Bord; **to go on ~** an Bord gehen; **on ~ the ship/plane** an Bord des Schiffes/Flugzeugs; **on ~ the bus** im Bus; **he held a party on ~ his yacht** er veranstaltete eine Party auf seiner Jacht e *(= cardboard)* Pappe *f*; *(Typ)* Deckel *m* f *(= board of interviewers)* Gremium *nt* (zur Auswahl von Bewerbern); *(= interview)* Vorstellungsgespräch *nt* (vor einem Gremium); **to be on a ~** einem Gremium zur Auswahl von Bewerbern angehören g *(US St Ex)* Notierung *f*; *(inf: = stock exchange)* Börse *f* h *(fig phrases)* **across the ~** allgemein, generell; *criticize, agree, reject* pauschal; **a wage increase of £10 per week across the ~** eine allgemeine *or* generelle Lohnerhöhung von £ 10 pro Woche; **to go by the ~** *(work, plans, ideas)* unter den Tisch fallen; *(dreams, hopes)* zunichtewerden; *(principles)* über Bord geworfen werden; *(business)* zugrunde *or* zu Grunde gehen; **that's all gone by the ~** daraus ist nichts geworden; **to take sth on ~** *(= understand)* etw begreifen; *(= deal with)* sich einer Sache *(gen)* annehmen VT a *(= cover with boards)* mit Brettern verkleiden b *ship, plane* besteigen, an Bord *(+gen)* gehen/kommen; *train, bus* einsteigen in *(+acc)*; *(Naut, in attack)* entern VI a in Pension sein *(with* bei) b *(Sch)* Internatsschüler(in) *m(f)* sein c *(Aviat)* die Maschine besteigen; **flight ZA173 now ~ing at gate 13** Passagiere des Fluges ZA173, bitte zum Flugsteig 13

▶ **board out** VT *sep person* in Pension schicken *(with* bei) VI in Pension wohnen *(with* bei)

▶ **board up** VT *sep door, window* mit Brettern vernageln

boarder ['bɔːdəʳ] N a Pensionsgast *m*; **to take in ~s** Leute in Pension nehmen b *(Sch)* Internatsschüler(in) *m(f)*; *(= weekly boarder) während der Woche im Internat wohnender Schüler (dated, = day boarder) Tagesschüler, der in der Schule zu Mittag isst* c *(Naut)* Mitglied *nt* eines Enterkommandos

board game N Brettspiel *nt*

boarding ['bɔːdɪŋ]: **boarding card** N Bordkarte *f*; **boarding house** N a Pension *f* b *(Sch)* Wohngebäude *nt* eines Internats; **boarding kennel** N Hundepension *f*, Tierpension *f* für Hunde; **boarding party** N *(Naut)* Enterkommando *nt*; **boarding pass** N Bordkarte *f*; **boarding school** N Internat *nt*

board: **board meeting** N Vorstandssitzung *f*; **boardroom** N Sitzungssaal *m (des Vorstands)*; **he's ~ material** er hat Führungspotenzial *or*-potential; **boardroom floor** N Vorstandsetage *f*; **boardroom politics** PL Firmenklüngel *m (inf)*; **board school** N *(Brit Hist)* staatliche Schule; **boardwalk** N *(US)* Holzsteg *m*; *(on beach)* hölzerne Uferpromenade

boast [bəʊst] N a Prahlerei *f* b *(= source of pride)* Stolz *m*; **it is their ~ that ...** sie rühmen sich, dass ... VI prahlen *(about, of* mit *to sb* jdm gegenüber); **without ~ing, without wishing to ~** ohne zu prahlen VT a *(= possess)* sich rühmen *(+gen) (geh)* b *(= say boastfully)* prahlen

boaster ['bəʊstə'] N Aufschneider(in) *m(f)*, Prahlhans *m (inf)*

boastful ['bəʊstfʊl] ADJ, **boastfully** ['bəʊstfəlɪ] ADV prahlerisch

boastfulness ['bəʊstfʊlnɪs] N Prahlerei *f*

boasting ['bəʊstɪŋ] N Prahlerei *f (about, of* mit)

boat [bəʊt] N **a** *(= small vessel)* Boot *nt*; *(wooden: on lake, river etc also)* Kahn *m*; *(seagoing: = passenger boat)* Schiff *nt*; *(= pleasure steamer etc)* Dampfer *m*; **by ~** mit dem Schiff; **to miss the ~** *(fig inf)* den Anschluss verpassen; **to push the ~ out** *(fig inf: = celebrate)* auf den Putz hauen *(inf)*; **we're all in the same ~** *(fig inf)* wir sitzen alle in einem *or* im gleichen Boot **b** *(= gravy boat)* Sauciere *f*

boat: **boatbuilder** N Bootsbauer *m*; **boatbuilding** N Bootsbau *m*; **boat deck** N Bootsdeck *nt*

boater ['bəʊtə'] N **a** *(= hat)* steifer Strohhut, Kreissäge *f (inf)* **b** *(= person)* Bootsfahrer(in) *m(f)*, Kahnfahrer(in) *m(f)*

boat: **boatful** N Schiffs-/Bootsladung *f*; **boat hire** N Bootsverleih *m*; *(= company)* Bootsverleiher *m*; **boathook** N Bootshaken *m*; **boathouse** N Bootshaus *nt or* -schuppen *m*

boating ['bəʊtɪŋ] N Bootfahren *nt*; **to go ~** Bootsfahrten/eine Bootsfahrt machen; **~ holiday/trip** Bootsferien *pl*/-fahrt *f*

boat: **boatload** N Bootsladung *f*; **boatman** N *(handling boat)* Segler *m*; Ruderer *m*; Paddler *m*; *(working with boats)* Bootsbauer *m*; *(= hirer)* Bootsverleiher *m*; **boat people** PL Bootsflüchtlinge *pl*; **boat race** N Regatta *f*; **boat-shaped** ADJ kahnförmig

boatswain, **bosun**, **bo's'n** ['bəʊsn] N Bootsmann *m*; **~'s mate** Bootsmanngehilfe *m*

boat: **boat train** N Zug *m* mit Fährenanschluss; **boatyard** N Bootshandlung *f*; *(as dry dock)* Liegeplatz *m*

Bob [bɒb] N *dim of* **Robert**; **... and ~'s your uncle!** *(inf)* ... und fertig ist der Lack! *(inf)*

bob[1] [bɒb] VI **a** *(= move up and down)* sich auf und ab bewegen; *(rabbit)* hoppeln; *(bird's tail)* wippen; *(boxer)* tänzeln; **to ~ (up and down) in** *or* **on the water** auf dem Wasser schaukeln; *(cork, piece of wood etc)* sich im Wasser auf und ab bewegen; **he ~bed out of sight** er duckte sich **b** *(= curtsey)* knicksen *(to sb* vor jdm) VT **a** *(= move jerkily) head* nicken mit; *(bird) tail* wippen mit **b** *curtsey* machen; **to ~ a greeting** zum Gruß kurz nicken N **a** *(= curtsey)* Knicks(chen *nt*) *m* **b** *(of head)* Nicken *nt no pl*; *(of bird's tail)* Wippen *nt no pl*

▶ **bob down** VI sich ducken VT *sep one's head* ducken

▶ **bob up** VI *(lit, fig)* auftauchen VT *sep* **he bobbed his head up** sein Kopf schnellte hoch

bob[2] N *pl* **bob** *(dated Brit inf)* Shilling *m*; **that must have cost a ~ or two** das muss schon ein paar Euro gekostet haben *(inf)*; **that must be worth a few ~** das muss eine Stange Geld wert sein *(inf)*; **he must be worth a few ~** er muss eine Stange Geld haben *(inf)*

bob[3] N **a** *(= haircut)* Bubikopf *m* **b** *(= horse's tail)* gestutzter Schwanz **c** *(= weight: on pendulum, plumb line)* Gewicht *nt* **d** *(Fishing, = float)* Schwimmer *m* **e** **a few/various bits and ~s** so ein paar/verschiedene Dinge; **my personal bits and ~s** meine Siebensachen; **the usual plastic bits and ~s** die sonst üblichen Plastikdinger *(inf)*; **to sell bits and ~s** Trödel verkaufen VT **to have one's hair ~bed** sich *(dat)* einen Bubikopf schneiden lassen; **~bed** kurz geschnitten, gestutzt

bob[4] N *(= sleigh)* Bob *m*; *(= runner)* Kufe *f*; **two-/four-man ~** Zweier-/Viererbob *m*

bob-a-job [ˌbɒbə'dʒɒb] N *(Brit) leichte, von Pfadfindern verrichtete Haus- und Gartenarbeit für ein geringes Entgelt*; **~ week** *Woche, in der Pfadfinder leichte Haus- und Gartenarbeiten für ein geringes Entgelt verrichten*

bobbin ['bɒbɪn] N Spule *f*; *(= cotton reel)* Rolle *f*

bobble ['bɒbl] N **a** Bommel *f*, Pompon *m* **b** *(US inf: = mistake)* Schnitzer *m (inf)*

bobble hat N *(Brit)* Pudelmütze *f*

Bobby ['bɒbɪ] N *dim of* **Robert**

bobby ['bɒbɪ] N *(dated Brit inf)* Bobby *m*, Schupo *m (dated)*

bobby: **bobby-dazzler** N *(dated Brit inf) (= object)* Knüller *m (inf)*, Sensation *f*; *(= girl)* Augenweide *f*; **bobby pin** N *(US)* Haarklemme *f*; **bobby sox** PL *(dated US)* kurze Söckchen *pl*; **bobbysoxer** N *(dated US inf)* Teenager *m*, junges Mädchen

bob: **bob cap** N Pudelmütze *f*; **bobcat** N *(US)* Luchs *m*; **bobsleigh**, *(US)* **bobsled** N Bob *m* VI Bob fahren; **bobtail** N gestutzter Schwanz; **bobtail cap**, **bobtail hat** N Bommelmütze *f*; **bobtailed** ADJ *horse, dog* mit gestutztem Schwanz

Boche [bɒʃ] N *(pej inf)* Boche *m*

bod [bɒd] N **a** *(Brit inf: = person)* Mensch *m*; **odd ~** komischer Kerl **b** *(sl: = body)* Body *m (sl)*

bodacious [bəʊ'deɪʃəs] ADJ *(US inf)* toll

bode [bəʊd] VI **to ~ well/ill** ein gutes/schlechtes Zeichen sein VT bedeuten, ahnen lassen; **that ~s no good** das bedeutet nichts Gutes, das lässt Böses ahnen

bodega [bəʊ'di:gə] N *(US)* Bodega *f*

bodge [bɒdʒ] N VT = **botch**

bodice ['bɒdɪs] N **a** Mieder *nt*; *(of dress also)* Oberteil *nt* **b** *(= vest)* Leibchen *nt*

bodice: **bodice ripper** N *(inf)* schwülstiger historischer Film/Roman; **bodice-ripping** ['bɒdɪsrɪpɪŋ] ADJ *attr (inf)* **~ film/novel** schwülstiger historischer Film/Roman

-bodied [-'bɒdɪd] ADJ *suf* -gebaut, von ... Körperbau

bodiless ['bɒdɪlɪs] ADJ körperlos

bodily ['bɒdɪlɪ] ADJ *(= physical)* körperlich; **~ illness** Krankheit *f* des Körpers; **~ needs/wants** leibliche Bedürfnisse *pl*; **~ harm** Körperverletzung *f*; **~ functions/fluids** Körperfunktionen/-flüssigkeiten *pl*; **~ injury** Körperverletzungen *pl* ADV **a** *(= forcibly)* gewaltsam **b** *(= in person)* leibhaftig **c** *(= all together)* geschlossen; *(= in one piece)* ganz

bodkin ['bɒdkɪn] N **a** *(Sew)* Durchziehnadel *f* **b** *(Hist: = hairpin)* lange Haarnadel; *(obs, = dagger)* Dolch *m*

body ['bɒdɪ] N **a** *(of man, animal)* Körper *m*; *(of human also)* Leib *m (geh)*; **the ~ of Christ** der Leib des Herrn; **just enough to keep ~ and soul together** gerade genug, um Leib und Seele zusammenzuhalten; **she was committed, ~ and soul** sie war mit Leib und Seele bei der Sache
b *(= corpse)* Leiche *f*, Leichnam *m (geh)* → **dead**
c *(= main part of structure, of plane, ship)* Rumpf *m*, Körper *m*; *(of string instrument)* Korpus *m*, Schallkörper *m*; *(of church, speech, army: also* **main body**) Hauptteil *m*; **the main ~ of his readers/the students** das Gros seiner Leser/der Studenten; **in the ~ of the House** *(Brit Parl)* im Plenum
d *(= coachwork: of car)* Karosserie *f*
e *(= group of people)* Gruppe *f*; **the student ~** die Studentenschaft; **a ~ of troops** ein Truppenverband *m*; **a great ~ of followers/readers** eine große Anhängerschaft/Leserschaft; **a large ~ of people** eine große Menschenmenge; **in a ~** geschlossen
f *(= organization)* Organ *nt*; *(= committee)* Gremium *nt*; *(= corporation)* Körperschaft *f* → **corporate, politic**
g *(= quantity)* **a ~ of facts/evidence/data** Tatsachen-/Beweis-/Datenmaterial *nt*; **a ~ of laws/legislation** ein Gesetzeskomplex *m*; **a large ~ of water** eine große Wassermasse
h *(inf: = person)* Mensch *m*
i *(Math, Phys, Chem)* Körper *m*
j *(= substance, thickness, of wine)* Körper *m*; *(of soup)* Substanz *f*; *(of paper, cloth)* Festigkeit *f*, Stärke *f*; **this conditioner will add ~ to your hair** diese Pflegespülung gibt Ihrem Haar mehr Volumen
k *(also* **body stocking**) Body *m*

body: **body armour**, *(US)* **body armor** N Schutzkleidung *f*; **body bag** N Leichensack *m*; **body blow** N Körperschlag *m*; *(fig)* Schlag *m* ins Kontor *(to, for* für); **body builder** N **a** *(= food)* Kraftnahrung *f* **b** *(= apparatus)* Heimtrainer *m* **c** *(= person)* Bodybuilder(in) *m(f)*; **body building** N Bodybuilding *nt* ADJ *exercise* muskelkräftigend; *food* stärkend, kräftigend; **bodycheck** N Bodycheck *m*; **body clock** N innere Uhr; **body control** N Körperbeherrschung *f*; **body count** N *(Mil)* Zählung *f* der Toten; **body double** N *(Film, TV)* Körperdouble *nt*; **body drop** N *(Judo)* Körperwurf *m*; **body fascism** N *Diskriminierung aufgrund körperlicher Merkmale*; **body fluids** PL *(Physiol)* Körpersäfte *pl*; **body glitter** N *(Fashion = gel)* Glitzergel *nt*; *(= powder)* Glitterpuder *m or* -pulver *nt*; **body growth** N körperliches Wachstum; **bodyguard** N *(= one person)* Leibwächter *m*; *(= group)* Leibwache *f*; **body heat** N Körperwärme *f*; **body language** N Körpersprache *f*; **body lotion** N Körperlotion *f*; **body mike** N Umhängemikrofon *nt*; **body odour**, **body odor** *(US)* N Körpergeruch *m*; **body piercing** N Piercing *nt*; **body popping** N Breakdance *m*; **body (repair) shop** N Karosseriewerkstatt *f*; **body scanner** N Scanner *m*; **body scissors** N *sing (Wrestling)* über den Körper angelegte Schere; **body search** N Leibesvisitation *f*; **bodyshell** N *(Aut)* Karosserie *f*; **body shop** N **a** = **body (repair) shop** **b** *(in factory)* Karosseriewerk *nt*; **body slam** N *(Wrestling)* Wurf *m*; **body snatcher** N Leichenräuber(in) *m(f)*; **body stocking** N Body(stocking) *m*; **body-surf** VI bodysurfen; **body-surfing** N *no pl* Bodysurfing *nt*; **body swerve** N **to give sb/sth a ~** *(fig inf)* einen weiten Bogen um jdn/etw machen; **body temperature** N Körpertemperatur *f*; **body warmer** N Thermoweste *f*; **body wash** N Duschgel *nt*; **bodywork** N *(Aut)* Karosserie *f*

Boer ['bəʊə'] N Bure *m*, Burin *f* ADJ burisch; **the ~ War** der Burenkrieg

B of E *abbr of* **Bank of England**

boffin ['bɒfɪn] N *(Brit inf)* Eierkopf *m (inf)*, Egghead *m (inf)*

boffo ['bɒfəʊ] ADJ *(US inf)* klasse *(inf)*, super *(inf)*

bog [bɒg] N **a** Sumpf *m*; *(= peat bog)* (Torf)moor *nt* **b** *(Brit inf: = toilet)* Lokus *m (inf)*, Klo *nt (inf)*

▶ **bog down** VT *sep* **to be bogged down** *(lit)* stecken bleiben; *(fig)* stecken geblieben sein, sich festgefahren haben; *(in details)* sich verzettelt haben; **to get bogged down** *(lit)* stecken bleiben; *(fig also)* sich festfahren; *(in details)* sich verzetteln

bogey[1], **bogy** ['bəʊgɪ] N *pl* **bogeys, bogies** **a** *(= spectre, goblin)* Kobold *m*, Butzemann *m* **b** *(fig, = bugbear)* Popanz *m*, Schreckgespenst *nt* **c** *(Brit inf)* (Nasen)popel *m (inf)*

bogey[2] *(Golf)* N Bogey *nt* VT **to ~ a hole** ein Bogey spielen *or* machen

bogeyman ['bəʊgɪmæn] *pl* **bogeymen** [-men] Butzemann *m*, schwarzer Mann

boggle ['bɒgl] VI *(inf)* glotzen *(inf)*, völlig sprachlos sein; **the mind ~s** das ist nicht *or* kaum auszumalen *(inf)*; **stories that make the mind ~** unglaubliche Geschichten

boggy ['bɒgɪ] ADJ *(+er) ground* sumpfig, morastig

bogie ['bəʊgɪ] N **a** *(Rail)* Drehgestell *nt*; *(= trolley)* Draisine *f*, Dräsine *f* **b** *(Brit inf)* (Nasen)popel *m (inf)*

bog paper, **bog roll** N *(Brit inf)* Klopapier *nt (inf)*

bog-standard [ˌbɒg'stændəd] ADJ *(Brit inf)* stinknormal *(inf)*

bogus ['bəʊgəs] ADJ *doctor, lawyer, name* falsch; *pearls also, document* gefälscht; *company, transac-*

tion Schwindel-; *claim* erfunden; **~ asylum seekers** Scheinasylanten *pl (pej)*

bogy [ˈbəʊgɪ] N = **bogey**[1]

Bohemia [bəʊˈhiːmɪə] N *(Geog)* Böhmen *nt; (fig)* Boheme *f*

Bohemian [bəʊˈhiːmɪən] **N** **a** Böhme *m,* Böhmin *f* **b** *(fig)* **bohemian** Bohemien *m* **ADJ** **a** böhmisch **b** *(fig)* **bohemian** *(lifestyle)* unkonventionell, unbürgerlich; *circles, quarter* Künstler-

bohemianism [bəʊˈhiːmɪənɪzəm] N unkonventionelle *or* unbürgerliche Lebensweise

boho [ˈbəʊhəʊ] *(inf)* **N** unkonventioneller Künstler, unkonventionelle Künstlerin **ADJ** unkonventionell

boil[1] [bɔɪl] N *(Med)* Furunkel *m*

boil[2] **VI** **a** *(lit)* kochen; *(water also, Phys)* sieden; **the kettle was ~ing** das Wasser im Kessel kochte; **~ing oil** siedendes Öl; **allow to ~ gently** *(Cook)* langsam kochen; **to let the kettle ~ dry** das Wasser im Kessel verkochen lassen
b *(fig inf: = be hot)* **~ing hot water** kochend heißes Wasser; **it was ~ing (hot) in the office** es war eine Affenhitze im Büro *(inf)*; **I was ~ing (hot)** mir war fürchterlich heiß; **you'll ~ in that sweater** in dem Pullover schwitzt du dich ja tot *(inf)*
c *(fig inf: = be angry)* kochen, schäumen *(with* vor *+dat)*
d *(fig, sea, river)* brodeln, tosen
VT kochen; **~ed/hard ~ed egg** weich/hart gekochtes Ei; **~ed potatoes** Salzkartoffeln *pl*
N **to bring sth to the** *(Brit) or* **a** *(US)* **~** etw aufkochen lassen; **to keep sth on the ~** etw kochen *or* sieden lassen; **to be on/come to/go off the ~** kochen/zu kochen anfangen/aufhören

▶ **boil away** VI **a** *(= go on boiling)* weiterkochen **b** *(= evaporate completely)* verdampfen

▶ **boil down** **VT** *sep* einkochen **VI** **a** *(jam etc)* dickflüssig werden **b** *(fig)* **to boil down to sth** auf etw *(acc)* hinauslaufen; **what it boils down to is that ...** das läuft darauf hinaus, dass ...

▶ **boil over** VI **a** *(lit)* überkochen **b** *(fig, situation, quarrel)* den Siedepunkt erreichen; **he just boiled over** ihm platzte der Kragen *(inf)*

▶ **boil up** VI **a** *(lit)* aufkochen **b** *(fig)* **he could feel the anger boiling up in him** er fühlte, wie die Wut in ihm aufstieg

boiled shirt N *(inf)* weißes Hemd

boiled sweet N Bonbon *nt*

boiler [ˈbɔɪləˈ] N **a** *(domestic)* Boiler *m,* Warmwasserbereiter *m; (in ship, engine)* (Dampf)kessel *m; (old, for washing)* Waschkessel *m* **b** *(= chicken)* Suppenhuhn *nt*

boiler: **boiler house** N Kesselhaus *nt*; **boilermaker** N Kesselschmied *m*; **boilermaking** N Kesselbau *m*; **boilerman** N Heizer *m*; **boilerplate letter** N *(US)* (Brief)rumpf *m*; **boiler room** N Kesselraum *m*; **boiler suit** N *(Brit)* Overall *m,* blauer Anton *(inf),* Blaumann *m (inf)*

boiling [ˈbɔɪlɪŋ]: **boiling fowl** N Suppenhuhn *nt*; **boiling point** N *(lit, fig)* Siedepunkt *m*; **at ~** *(lit, fig)* auf dem Siedepunkt; **to reach ~** *(lit, fig)* den Siedepunkt erreichen; *(feelings also, person)* auf dem Siedepunkt anlangen; **boiling pot** N *(fig: = tumultuous situation)* Tohuwabohu *nt*

boisterous [ˈbɔɪstərəs] ADJ **a** *(= exuberant, noisy) person* ausgelassen; *game, party, dance also* wild **b** *(= rough) wind* tosend; *sea also* aufgewühlt

boisterously [ˈbɔɪstərəslɪ] ADV *shout, sing, laugh* ausgelassen; *play* wild, übermütig

bold [bəʊld] ADJ *(+er)* **a** *(= brave)* kühn *(geh),* mutig; *deed, plan also* verwegen
b *(= impudent, forward)* unverfroren, dreist; **to be** *or* **make so ~ as to ...** sich *(dat)* erlauben, zu ..., sich erkühnen, zu ... *(geh)*; **might I be so ~ as to ...?** wenn ich es mir erlauben darf, zu ...?; **might I make so ~ as to help myself?** darf ich so frei sein und mich bedienen?; **to make ~ with sth** sich *(dat)* die Freiheit herausnehmen, sich bei etw einfach zu bedienen; **as ~ as brass** *(inf)* rotzfrech *(inf)*
c *(= striking) colours, pattern, stripes* kräftig; *checks also* grob; *strokes also* kühn *(geh)*; *handwriting* kraftvoll, kühn *(geh)*; *style* kraftvoll, ausdrucksvoll; **to bring out in ~ relief** stark hervortreten lassen
d *(Typ)* fett; *(= secondary bold)* halbfett; **~ type** Fettdruck *m*; **to set sth in ~ (type)** etw fett/halbfett drucken

boldface [ˈbəʊldfeɪs] *(Typ)* **N** (halb)fette Schrift **ADJ** (halb)fett; **in ~ type** (halb)fett, in (halb)fetter Schrift

boldly [ˈbəʊldlɪ] ADV **a** *(= bravely)* mutig, kühn *(geh)* **b** *(= forthrightly)* unverfroren, dreist **c** *(= strikingly)* auffallend

boldness [ˈbəʊldnɪs] N **a** *(= bravery)* Kühnheit *f (geh),* Mut *m*; *(of deed, plan also)* Verwegenheit *f* **b** *(= impudence, forwardness)* Unverfrorenheit *f,* Dreistigkeit *f* **c** *(of colours, pattern, stripes)* Kräftigkeit *f*; *(of checks also)* Grobheit *f*; *(of strokes also)* Kühnheit *f (geh)*; *(of style)* Ausdruckskraft *f*

bole [bəʊl] N Baumstamm *m*

bolero [bəˈlɛərəʊ] N *(all senses)* Bolero *m*

Bolivia [bəˈlɪvɪə] N Bolivien *nt*

Bolivian [bəˈlɪvɪən] **N** Bolivianer(in) *m(f),* Bolivier(in) *m(f)* **ADJ** bolivianisch, bolivisch

boll [bəʊl] N Samenkapsel *f*

bollard [ˈbɒləd] N *(on quay, road)* Poller *m*

▶ **bollix up** [ˈbɒlɪksˈʌp] VT *(sl)* **to bollix sth up** etw verpfuschen *or* versauen *(inf)*

bollocking [ˈbɒləkɪŋ] N *(Brit sl)* Schimpfkanonade *f (inf)*; **to give sb a ~** jdn zur Sau machen *(inf)*

bollocks [ˈbɒləks] PL *(sl)* **a** Eier *pl (sl)* **b** *(= nonsense)* **(that's) ~!** Quatsch mit Soße! *(inf)*; **he was talking ~** der hat einen Scheiß geredet *(inf)*

boll weevil N Baumwollkapselkäfer *m*

Bollywood [ˈbɒlɪwʊd] N *(inf)* Bollywood *nt (inf, die indische Filmindustrie)*

bologna [bəˈləʊnɪ], **bologna sausage** [bəˌləʊnɪˈsɒsɪdʒ] N *(Cook)* Mortadella *f*

boloney [bəˈləʊnɪ] N = **baloney**

Bolshevik [ˈbɒlʃəvɪk] **N** Bolschewik *m* **ADJ** bolschewistisch

Bolshevism [ˈbɒlʃəvɪzəm] N Bolschewismus *m*

Bolshevist [ˈbɒlʃəvɪst] N ADJ = **Bolshevik**

bolshie, bolshy [ˈbɒlʃɪ] *(inf)* **N** Bolschewik *m* **ADJ** *(+er)* **a** *(Brit fig: = uncooperative)* stur; *(= aggressive)* pampig *(inf),* rotzig *(inf)* **b** *(pej)* bolschewistisch

bolster [ˈbəʊlstəˈ] **N** *(on bed)* Nackenrolle *f* **VT** *(also* **bolster up***: fig) person* Mut machen *(+dat)*; *status* aufbessern; *currency* stützen; *economy, confidence* Auftrieb geben *(+dat)*; *profits, power* erhöhen; *case* untermauern; *support* verstärken; **it ~s my ego** das gibt mir Auftrieb, das baut mich auf; **to ~ (up) sb's morale** jdm Mut machen

bolt [bəʊlt] **N** **a** *(on door etc)* Riegel *m*
b *(Tech)* Schraube *f* (ohne Spitze), Bolzen *m*
c *(of lightning)* Blitzstrahl *m*; **it came/was like a ~ from the blue** *(fig)* das schlug ein/war wie ein Blitz aus heiterem Himmel
d *(of cloth)* Ballen *m*
e *(of crossbow)* Bolzen *m* → **shoot**
f *(of rifle)* Kammer *f*
g *(= sudden dash)* Satz *m (inf)*; **his ~ for freedom** sein Fluchtversuch *m*; **he made a ~ for the door** er machte einen Satz zur Tür; **to make a ~ for it** losrennen
ADV **~ upright** kerzengerade
VI **a** *(horse)* durchgehen; *(person)* Reißaus nehmen *(inf)*; **too late now, the horse has ~ed** *(fig)* zu spät, der Zug ist schon abgefahren
b *(= move quickly)* sausen, rasen, pesen *(inf)*
VT **a** *door, window* zu- *or* verriegeln
b *(Tech) parts* verschrauben *(to* mit), mit Schraubenbolzen befestigen *(to* an *+dat)*; **to ~ together** verschrauben
c *(also* **bolt down***) one's food* hinunterschlingen

▶ **bolt in** **VI** *(= rush in)* herein-/hineinplatzen *or* -stürzen **VT** *sep (= lock in)* einsperren

▶ **bolt on** VT *sep (Tech)* festschrauben *(prep obj,* *-to* an *+dat)*

▶ **bolt out** **VI** *(= rush out)* hinaus-/herausstürzen **VT** *sep (= lock out)* aussperren

bolt hole N Schlupfloch *nt*

bolus [ˈbəʊləs] N *pl* **-es** *(Med)* große Pille

bomb [bɒm] **N** **a** *(= device)* Bombe *f*; **to put a ~ under sb/sth** *(Brit fig inf)* jdn/etw radikal verändern
b *(Brit inf)* **his party went like a ~** seine Party war ein Bombenerfolg *(inf)*; **the car goes like a ~** das ist die reinste Rakete von Wagen *(inf)*; **the car cost a ~** das Auto hat ein Bombengeld gekostet *(inf)*; **to make a ~** eine Stange Geld verdienen *(inf)*; **to go down a ~** Riesenanklang finden *(with* bei) *(inf)*
c *(US inf)* **the play was a real ~** das Stück war ein totaler Reinfall
VT **a** *(lit)* bombardieren; *(not from the air)* ein Bombenattentat verüben auf *(+acc)*
b *(US inf: = fail)* durchfallen bei
VI **a** *(inf: = go fast)* fegen *(inf),* zischen *(inf)*
b *(US inf: = fail)* durchfallen *(inf)*

▶ **bomb along** VI *(inf: = drive fast)* dahinrasen *(inf)*

▶ **bomb out** VT *sep* ausbomben

bomb alert N Bombenwarnung *f*

bombard [bɒmˈbɑːd] VT *(Mil, fig)* bombardieren *(with* mit); *(Phys)* beschießen

bombardier [ˌbɒmbəˈdɪəˈ] N *(Mil)* Artillerieunteroffizier *m*; *(Aviat)* Bombenschütze *m*

bombardment [bɒmˈbɑːdmənt] N *(Mil)* Bombardierung *f (also fig),* Bombardement *nt*; *(Phys)* Beschießen *nt*

bombast [ˈbɒmbæst] N Schwulst *m,* Bombast *m*

bombastic ADJ, **bombastically** ADV [bɒmˈbæstɪk, -əlɪ] schwülstig, bombastisch

bomb attack N Bombenangriff *m*

Bombay [bɒmˈbeɪ] N *(Hist)* Bombay *nt (Hist)* → **Mumbai**

Bombay duck N *kleiner getrockneter Fisch als Beigabe zur indischen Reistafel*

bomb: **bomb bay** N Bombenschacht *m*; **bomb carpet** N Bombenteppich *m*; **bomb crater** N Bombentrichter *m*; **bomb disposal** N Bombenräumung *f*; **bomb disposal expert** N Bombenräumexperte *m*; **bomb disposal squad, bomb disposal unit** N Bombenräumtrupp *m or* -kommando *nt*

bombed [bɒmd] ADJ *(inf)* total zu *(inf)*

bombed out [ˌbɒmˈdaʊt] ADJ *(inf)* **a** *(= exhausted)* völlig fertig *(inf),* fix und foxi *(sl)* **b** *(= drunk, on drugs)* zu *(inf)* **c** **our team's ~** *(= has no chance)* unsere Mannschaft hat keine Chance **d** *(= very busy) pub etc* gerammelt voll *(inf)*

bomber [ˈbɒməˈ] N **a** *(= aircraft)* Bomber *m,* Bombenflugzeug *nt* **b** *(= person, Aviat)* Bombenschütze *m*; *(= terrorist)* Bombenattentäter(in) *m(f)*

bomber: **bomber command** N Bombenverband *m or* -geschwader *nt*; **bomber jacket** N Fliegerjacke *f*; **bomber pilot** N Bomberpilot *m*

bomb factory N Bombenfabrik *f*

bombing [ˈbɒmɪŋ] **N** Bombenangriff *m (of* auf *+acc)*; *(of target also)* Bombardierung *f* **ADJ** *raid, mission* Bomben-

bomb: **bombproof** ADJ bombensicher; **bomb scare** N Bombenalarm *m*; **bombshell** N **a** *(Mil)* Bombe *f* **b** *(fig)* Bombe *f,* plötzliche Überraschung; **this news was a ~** die Nachricht schlug wie eine Bombe ein; **to drop a** *or* **the** *or* **one's ~** die Bombe platzen lassen; **bomb shelter** N Luftschutzkeller *m*; *(specially built)* (Luftschutz)bunker *m*; **bombsight** N Fliegerbombenzielgerät *nt*; **bomb site** N Trümmergrundstück *nt*

bona fide ['bəʊnə'faɪdɪ] ADJ bona fide; *traveller, word, antique* echt; **it's a ~ offer** es ist ein Angebot auf Treu und Glauben

bona fides ['bəʊnə'faɪdi:z] N *sing (form: = trustworthiness)* Vertrauenswürdigkeit *f*

bonanza [bə'nænzə] N **a** *(US, Min)* reiche Erzader **b** *(fig)* Goldgrube *f*; **the oil ~** der Ölboom ADJ *attr year* Boom-

bonbon ['bɒnbɒn] N Bonbon *m or nt*

bonce [bɒns] N *(Brit inf: = head)* Birne *f (inf)*; **curly ~** Krauskopf *m (inf)*

bond [bɒnd] N **a** *(= agreement)* Übereinkommen *nt*
b *(fig: = link)* Band *nt (geh)*, Bindung *f*
c bonds PL *(lit: = chains)* Fesseln *pl*, Bande *pl (liter)*; *(fig: = ties)* Bande *pl (geh)*; *(burdensome)* Fesseln *pl*; **marriage ~s** das Band/die Fesseln der Ehe
d *(Comm, Fin)* Obligation *f*, Pfandbrief *m*, festverzinsliches Wertpapier, Bond *m*; **government ~** Staatsanleihe *f or* -papiere *pl*
e *(Comm: = custody of goods)* Zollverschluss *m*; **to put sth into ~** etw unter Zollverschluss geben; **goods in ~** Zollgut *nt*
f *(= adhesion between surfaces)* Haftfestigkeit *f*, Haftwirkung *f*; **nothing can break the ~ between the two surfaces** die beiden Flächen haften *or* kleben fest und unlösbar aneinander
g *(Build)* Verband *m*
h *(Chem)* Bindung *f*
VT **a** *(Comm) goods* unter Zollverschluss legen *or* nehmen
b *(Build) bricks* im Verband verlegen
VI **a** *(glue)* binden; *(bricks)* einen Verband bilden
b to ~ with one's baby Liebe zu seinem Kind entwickeln; **we ~ed immediately** wir haben uns auf Anhieb gut verstanden, wir waren uns auf Anhieb sympathisch

bondage ['bɒndɪdʒ] N **a** *(lit)* Sklaverei *f*; *(in Middle Ages)* Leibeigenschaft *f*; **in ~ to sb** in Sklaverei/Leibeigenschaft bei jdm, jdm hörig **b** *(fig liter)* vollständige Unterjochung; **in ~ to sth** einer Sache *(dat)* unterworfen; **her stronger will kept him in ~** ihr stärkerer Wille hielt ihn vollständig unterdrückt **c** *(sexual)* Fesseln *nt*; **~ gear/magazine** Sadomasoausrüstung *f*/-heft *nt*

bonded ['bɒndɪd] ADJ *goods* unter Zollverschluss

bonded labour, *(US)* **bonded labor** N Leibeigenschaft *f*

bonded warehouse N Zolllager *nt*, Zolldepot *nt*

bond: bondholder N Pfandbrief- *or* Obligationsinhaber(in) *m(f)*; **bondman, bondsman** N Sklave *m*; *(medieval)* Leibeigene(r) *mf*

bone [bəʊn] N **a** Knochen *m*; *(of fish)* Gräte *f*; **~s** *pl (of the dead)* Gebeine *pl*; **ham off the ~** Schinken *m* vom Knochen; **meat on the ~** Fleisch *nt* am Knochen; **chilled to the ~** völlig durchgefroren; **that was a bit close** *or* **near to the ~** *(fig)* das war hart an der Schmerzgrenze; **to work one's fingers to the ~** sich *(dat)* die Finger abarbeiten; **to cut costs to the ~** Kosten drastisch reduzieren; **~ of contention** Zankapfel *m*; **to have a ~ to pick with sb** *(inf)* mit jdm ein Hühnchen zu rupfen haben *(inf)*; **I'll make no ~s about it, you're/this is ...** *(inf)* du bist/das ist, offen gestanden *or* ehrlich gesagt, ...; **he made no ~s about saying what he thought** *(inf)* er hat mit seiner Meinung nicht hinterm Berg gehalten; **I can feel it in my ~s** das spüre ich in den Knochen; **my old ~s** *(inf)* meine alten Knochen *(inf)*
b *(= substance)* Knochen *m*
c *(of corset)* Stange *f*; *(smaller)* Stäbchen *nt*
d *(Mus)* **bones** PL Klangstäbe *pl*
e *(= dice)* **bones** PL *(inf)* Würfel *pl*, Knöchel *pl (old)*
ADJ *attr (= made of bone)* Bein-, beinern
VT die Knochen lösen aus, ausbeinen *(dial)*; *fish* entgräten

▶ **bone up on** VI +*prep obj (inf) subject* pauken *(inf)*

bone china N feines Porzellan

boned [bəʊnd] ADJ **a** *meat* ohne Knochen; *fish* entgrätet **b** *bodice etc* mit Fischbeinstäbchen

-boned ADJ *suf* -knochig; **to be big-boned** starke Knochen haben

bone: bone dry ADJ *pred*, **bone-dry** ADJ *attr (inf)* knochentrocken; **bonehead** N *(inf)* Dummkopf *m*, Armleuchter *m (inf)*; **boneheaded** ADJ *(inf)* blöd(e) *(inf)*, doof *(inf)*; **bone idle** ADJ *(Brit inf)* stinkfaul *(inf)*; **boneless** ADJ *meat* ohne Knochen; *fish* ohne Gräten; **bone marrow** N Knochenmark *nt*; **~ donor** Knochenmarkspender(in) *m(f)*; **bone meal** N Knochenmehl *nt*

boner ['bəʊnəʳ] N *(US sl)* Schnitzer *m (inf)*, Hammer *m (inf)*

bone: boneshaker N **a** *(inf)* Klapperkiste *f (inf)*, Mühle *f (inf)* **b** *(old: = cycle)* Fahrrad *nt* ohne Gummireifen; **bone structure** N *(of face)* Gesichtszüge *pl*; **boneyard** N *(inf)* Friedhof *m*

bonfire ['bɒnfaɪəʳ] N *(for burning rubbish)* Feuer *nt*; *(as beacon)* Leucht- *or* Signalfeuer *nt*; *(Guy Fawkes)* Guy-Fawkes-Feuer *nt*; *(for celebration)* Freudenfeuer *nt*

bonfire night N 5. November *(Jahrestag der Pulververschwörung)*

bongo ['bɒŋgəʊ] N Bongo *nt or f*

bonhomie ['bɒnɒmi:] N Bonhomie *f (geh)*, Jovialität *f*

bonhomous ADJ, **bonhomously** ADV ['bɒnəməs, -lɪ] jovial

boniness ['bəʊnɪnɪs] N Knochigkeit *f*

bonk [bɒŋk] *(inf)* VT **a** *(= have sex with)* bumsen *(inf)* **b** *(= knock)* **he ~ed his head against the doorframe** er knallte mit dem Kopf gegen den Türrahmen *(inf)* VI bumsen *(inf)* N *(= sex)* **to have a ~** bumsen *(inf)*

bonkers ['bɒŋkəz] ADJ *(esp Brit inf)* meschugge *(inf)*; **to be ~** spinnen *(inf)*; **to go ~** überschnappen *(inf)*; **he's ~ about her** er ist völlig verrückt nach ihr *(inf)*

bonking ['bɒŋkɪŋ] N *(inf)* Bumsen *nt (inf)*

bon mot ['bɒn'məʊ] N Bonmot *nt (geh)*

Bonn [bɒn] N Bonn *nt* ADJ Bonner

bonnet ['bɒnɪt] N **a** *(woman's)* Haube *f*; *(baby's)* Häubchen *nt*; *(esp Scot, man's)* Mütze *f* **b** *(Brit Aut)* Motor- *or* Kühlerhaube *f* **c** *(of chimney)* Schornsteinkappe *f*

bonnie, bonny ['bɒnɪ] ADJ *(esp Scot)* schön; *lassie also* hübsch; *baby* prächtig

bonsai ['bɒnsaɪ] N *pl* - Bonsai *nt*

bonus ['bəʊnəs] N **a** Prämie *f*; *(for output, production also)* Zulage *f*; *(= cost-of-living bonus)* Zuschlag *m*; *(= Christmas bonus)* Gratifikation *f*; **~ scheme** Prämiensystem *nt*; **~ point** *(in game, quiz etc)* Bonuspunkt *m* **b** *(Fin, on shares)* Extradividende *f*, Sonderausschüttung *f* **c** *(inf: = sth extra)* Zugabe *f*

bonus ball N *(Brit, in National Lottery)* Zusatzzahl *f*

bony ['bəʊnɪ] ADJ (+*er*) *(= of bone)* knöchern; *(= like bone)* knochenartig; *person, knee, hips* knochig; *fish* grätig, mit viel Gräten; *meat* mit viel Knochen

bonze [bɒnz] N Bonze *m*

bonzer ['bɒnzəʳ] ADJ *(Austral inf)* klasse *(inf)*

boo[1] [bu:] INTERJ buh; **he wouldn't say ~ to a goose** *(inf)* er ist ein schüchternes Pflänzchen VT *actor, play, speaker, referee* auspfeifen, ausbuhen; **to be ~ed off the stage** ausgepfiffen *or* ausgebuht werden VI buhen N Buhruf *m*

boo[2] [bu:] N *(US inf: = partner, lover)* Schatz *m (inf)*

boob [bu:b] N **a** *(Brit inf: = mistake)* Schnitzer *m (inf)*; **a common ~** ein häufig gemachter Fehler **b** *(inf: = woman's breast)* Brust *f*; **big ~s** große Titten *pl or* Möpse *pl (sl)* VI *(Brit inf)* einen Schnitzer machen *(inf)*; *(= fail)* Mist bauen *(inf)*; **somebody ~ed, I didn't get the letter** da hat jemand was verbockt *(inf)*, ich habe den Brief überhaupt nicht gekriegt

boob job N *(inf)* Busenvergrößerung *or* -verkleinerung *f*

boo-boo ['bu:bu:] N *(inf)* Schnitzer *m (inf)*

boob tube N **a** *(Brit Tex)* Bustier *nt*, Bandeau-Top *nt* **b** *(esp US inf: = television)* Röhre *f (inf)*, Glotze *f (inf)*

booby ['bu:bɪ] N *(inf)* **a** *(= fool)* Trottel *m* **b** = **boob N b**

booby: booby hatch N *(dated US sl)* Klapsmühle *f (inf)*; **booby prize** N *Scherzpreis für den schlechtesten Teilnehmer*; **booby trap** N **a** Falle *f (als Schabernack versteckt angebracht)* **b** *(Mil etc)* versteckte Bombe; **don't open that box, it's a ~** machen Sie die Schachtel nicht auf, da ist eine Bombe drin VT **the suitcase was booby-trapped** in dem Koffer war eine Bombe versteckt

booger ['bu:gəʳ] N *(US inf)* (Nasen)popel *m (inf)*

boogie-woogie ['bu:gɪˌwu:gɪ] N Boogie-Woogie *m*

boohoo [bu:'hu:] INTERJ *(to indicate crying)* huh-huh; *(to mock crying)* schluchz-schluchz

booing ['bu:ɪŋ] N Buhrufen *nt*

book [bʊk] ✪ 21.3 N **a** Buch *nt*; *(= exercise book)* Heft *nt*; *(= division: in Bible, poem etc)* Buch *nt*; **the (good) Book** das Buch der Bücher; **the Book of Genesis** die Genesis, das 1. Buch Mose; **to bring sb to ~** jdn zur Rechenschaft ziehen; **to throw the ~ at sb** *(inf)* jdn nach allen Regeln der Kunst fertigmachen *(inf)*; **by** *or* **according to the ~** nach dem Buchstaben; **he does everything by** *or* **according to the ~** er hält sich bei allem strikt an die Vorschriften; **to go by the ~** sich an die Vorschriften halten; **to be in sb's good/bad ~s** bei jdm gut/schlecht angeschrieben sein *(inf)*; **I can read him like a ~** ich kann in ihm lesen wie in einem Buch; **to close the ~ on sth** das Kapitel einer Sache *(gen)* abschließen; **it's a closed ~ to me** das ist ein Buch mit sieben Siegeln für mich; **he/my life is an open ~** er/mein Leben ist ein offenes Buch; **he knows/used every trick in the ~** *(inf)* er ist/war mit allen Wassern gewaschen *(inf)*; **he'll use every trick in the ~ to get what he wants** *(inf)* er wird alles und jedes versuchen, um zu erreichen, was er will; **that counts as cheating in my ~** *(inf)* für mich ist das Betrug; **I'm in the ~** *(Telec)* ich stehe im Telefonbuch
b *(of tickets)* Heft *nt*; *(thicker)* Block *m*; **~ of stamps/matches** Briefmarken-/Streichholzheftchen *nt*
c books PL *(Comm, Fin)* Bücher *pl*; **to keep the ~s of a firm** die Bücher einer Firma führen; **to do the ~s for sb** jdm die Bücher führen; **I've been doing the ~s** ich habe die Abrechnung gemacht
d *(of club, society)* (Mitglieder)verzeichnis *nt*, Mitgliedsliste *f*; **to be on the ~s of an organization** im Mitgliederverzeichnis *or* auf der Mitgliedsliste einer Organisation stehen
e *(Gambling)* Wettbuch *nt*; **to make** *or* **keep a ~** *(Horseracing)* Buch machen; *(generally)* Wetten abschließen
f *(= libretto: of opera etc)* Textbuch *nt*
g *(Comm)* **~ of samples, sample ~** Musterbuch *nt*
VT **a** *(= reserve)* bestellen; *seat, room also* buchen, reservieren lassen; *artiste* engagieren, verpflichten; *cabaret act* nehmen; *(privately)* sorgen für; **this performance/flight/hotel is fully ~ed** diese Vorstellung ist ausverkauft/dieser Flug ist ausgebucht/das Hotel ist voll belegt; **can I ~ a time to see him?** kann ich einen Termin bei ihm bekommen?; **to ~ sb through to Hull** *(Rail)* jdn bis Hull durchbuchen
b *(Fin, Comm) order* aufnehmen; **to ~ goods to sb's account** jdm Waren in Rechnung stellen
c *(inf) driver etc* aufschreiben *(inf)*, einen

Strafzettel verpassen *(+dat) (inf)*; *footballer* verwarnen; **to be ~ed for speeding** wegen zu schnellen Fahrens aufgeschrieben werden; **let's ~ him** *(said by policeman etc)* den schnappen wir uns *(inf)*

VI bestellen; *(= reserve seat, room also)* buchen; **to ~ through to Hull** bis Hull durchlösen

▶ **book in** VI *(in hotel etc)* sich eintragen; **we booked in at** *or* **into the Hilton** wir sind im Hilton abgestiegen VT *sep* **a** *(= register)* eintragen **b** *(= make reservation for)* **to book sb into a hotel** jdm ein Hotelzimmer reservieren lassen; **we're booked in at** *or* **into the Hilton** unsere Zimmer sind im Hilton bestellt *or* reserviert

▶ **book up** VI buchen VT *sep (usu pass)* reservieren lassen; **to be (fully) booked up** (ganz) ausgebucht sein; *(evening performance, theatre)* (bis auf den letzten Platz) ausverkauft sein

bookable [ˈbʊkəbl] ADJ **a** im Vorverkauf erhältlich **b** *(Sport)* **a ~ offence** *(Brit) or* **offense** *(US)* ein Verstoß *m*, für den es eine Verwarnung gibt

book: **bookbinder** N Buchbinder *m*; **bookbinding** N Buchbinderei *f*; **bookcase** N Bücherregal *nt*; *(with doors)* Bücherschrank *m*; **book claim** N *(Fin)* Buchforderung *f*, buchmäßige Forderung; **book club** N Buchgemeinschaft *f*; **book debt** N *(Fin)* Buchschuld *f*, buchmäßige Schuld; **book end** N Bücherstütze *f*

> **BOOKER PRIZE**
>
> Der **Booker Prize** ist ein Preis, der seit 1969 jährlich für ein Werk der Belletristik aus Großbritannien, Irland oder dem Commonwealth vergeben wird. Es handelt sich dabei um eine hohe Geldprämie, die von der Booker McConnell Maschinenbaugesellschaft ausgesetzt wird. Die Preisverleihung wird in den Medien mit großem Interesse verfolgt und sogar live im Fernsehen übertragen. Die Jury setzt sich normalerweise aus Schriftstellern, Universitätsdozenten und Kritikern zusammen, und ihr Urteil ist manchmal heftig umstritten.

book fair N Buchmesse *f*

bookie [ˈbʊkɪ] N *(inf)* Buchmacher(in) *m(f)*

booking [ˈbʊkɪŋ] ✪ 21.4 N Buchung *f*, Bestellung *f*, Reservierung *f*; *(of artiste, performer)* Engagement *nt*, Verpflichtung *f*; **to make a ~** buchen; **to cancel a ~** den Tisch/die Karte *etc* abbestellen, die Reise/den Flug *etc* stornieren; **to change one's ~** umbuchen; **have you got a ~ for** *or* **in the name of Higgins?** ist bei Ihnen etwas auf den Namen Higgins gebucht?

booking: **booking clerk** N Fahrkartenverkäufer(in) *m(f)*; *(in ticket booth also)* Schalterbeamte(r) *m*, Schalterbeamtin *f*; **booking fee** N Buchungsgebühr *f*, Reservierungsgebühr *f*; **booking office** N *(Rail)* Fahrkartenschalter *m*; *(Theat)* Vorverkaufsstelle *or* -kasse *f*

bookish [ˈbʊkɪʃ] ADJ gelehrt *(pej, hum)*; *(= given to reading)* lesewütig; *(= not worldly)* lebensfremd; *language, expression* buchsprachlich; *(pej)* trocken, papieren; **a ~ word** ein Wort *nt* der Schriftsprache; **he is a very ~ person** er hat die Nase dauernd in einem Buch; *(= not worldly)* er ist ein richtiger Stubengelehrter *(pej)*; **~ style** Buchstil *m*; *(pej)* papierener Stil

book: **book jacket** N Schutzumschlag *m*, Buchhülle *f*; **book-keeper** N Buchhalter(in) *m(f)*; **book-keeping** N Buchhaltung *f*, Buchführung *f*; **book knowledge**, **book-learning** N Bücherweisheit *f*

booklet [ˈbʊklɪt] N Broschüre *f*

book: **book lover** N Bücherfreund *m*; **bookmaker** N Buchmacher(in) *m(f)*; **bookmaking** N Buchmacherei *f*; **~ firm** Buchmacherfirma *f*; **bookmark** N Lesezeichen *nt*; *(Comput)* Lesezeichen *nt*, Bookmark *nt*; **bookmobile** N *(US)* Fahrbücherei *f*; **bookplate** N Exlibris *nt*; **book post** N Büchersendung *f*; **to send sth by ~** etw als Büchersendung schicken; **~ is ...** Büchersendungen sind ...; **bookrest** N Lesepult *nt*; **book review** N Buchbesprechung *f*, Rezension *f*; **bookseller** N Buchhändler *m*; **bookselling** N der Buchhandel; **bookshelf** N Bücherbord *or* -brett *nt*; **bookshelves** PL *(= bookcase)* Bücherregal *nt*; **bookshop** *(esp Brit)*, **bookstore** *(US)* N Buchhandlung *f or* -laden *m*; **bookstall** N Bücherstand *m*; **bookstand** N *(US)* **a** *(= bookrest)* Lesepult *nt* **b** *(= bookcase)* Bücherregal *nt* **c** *(= bookstall: in station, airport)* Bücherstand *m*; **to hit the ~s** in die Buchläden kommen

booksy [ˈbʊksɪ] ADJ *(inf, pej)* hochgestochen *(pej)*, intellektuell

book: **book token** N Buchgutschein *m*; **book trade** N Buchhandel *m*; **book value** N *(Fin)* Buchwert *m*, Bilanzwert *m*; **bookworm** N *(fig)* Bücherwurm *m*

Boolean [ˈbuːlɪən] ADJ *algebra, logic* boolesch *attr*

boom¹ [buːm] N **a** *(= barrier, across river etc)* Sperre *f*; *(at factory gate etc)* Schranke *f* **b** *(Naut)* Baum *m* **c** *(Tech, also* **derrick boom***)* Ladebaum *m*; *(= jib of crane)* Ausleger *m* **d** *(for microphone)* Galgen *m*

boom² N *(of sea, waves, wind)* Brausen *nt*; *(of thunder)* Hallen *nt*; *(of guns)* Donnern *nt*; *(of organ, voice)* Dröhnen *nt* VI **a** *(sea, wind)* brausen; *(thunder)* hallen **b** *(organ, person, voice: also* **boom out***)* dröhnen; *(guns)* donnern INTERJ bum

▶ **boom out** VI = **boom² VI b** VT *sep (person) order* brüllen; **to boom out a command to sb** jdm mit Donnerstimme einen Befehl zubrüllen; **the bass booms out the chorus** der Bass singt den Refrain mit dröhnender Stimme

boom³ VI *(trade, sales)* einen Aufschwung nehmen, boomen *(inf)*; *(prices)* anziehen, in die Höhe schnellen; **business is ~ing** das Geschäft blüht *or* floriert N *(of business, fig)* Boom *m*, Aufschwung *m*; *(= period of economic growth)* Hochkonjunktur *f*; *(of prices)* Preissteigerung *f*; **to undergo a sudden ~** einen plötzlichen Aufschwung nehmen *or* erfahren

boom: **boom box** N *(US inf)* Gettoblaster *m (inf)*; **boom-bust** ADJ *(Econ)* Konjunktur-; **the ~ pattern of the economy in recent years** der Konjunkturzyklus der Wirtschaft in den letzten Jahren; **property is a ~ business** Immobilien sind ein Konjunkturgeschäft; **~ cycle** Kreislauf *m* von Hochkonjunktur und Rezession, Konjunkturzyklus *m*

boomerang [ˈbuːməræŋ] N *(lit, fig)* Bumerang *m*; **to have a ~ effect** einen Bumerangeffekt haben VI *(fig inf, words, actions)* wie ein Bumerang zurückkommen *(on* zu*)*

booming [ˈbuːmɪŋ] ADJ *sound* dröhnend; *surf* brausend

boom: **boom microphone** N Mikrofon *nt or* Mikrophon *nt* am Galgen; **boom-slump** ADJ **~ cycle** Konjunktur-Zyklus *m*; **boom town** N Goldgräberstadt *f*

boon¹ [buːn] N **a** *(= blessing, advantage)* Segen *m*; **it's such a ~** es ist ein wahrer Segen **b** *(obs, = favour, wish)* Gunst *f*, Gnade *f*

boon² ADJ **~ companion** *(old, liter)* lustiger Gesell *(old)*

boondockers [ˈbuːndɒkəz] PL *(US inf: = heavy boots)* (schwere) Stiefel *pl*

boondocks [ˈbuːndɒks] PL *(US inf: = backwoods)* Wildnis *f*; **in the ~** irgendwo, jwd *(inf)*

boondoggle [ˈbuːndɒgl] *(US inf)* VI auf Staatskosten Zeit und Geld verplempern *(inf)* N Zeitverschwendung *f or* Kleinkrämerei *f* auf Staatskosten

boondoggler [ˈbuːndɒgləʳ] N *(US inf)* staatlich angestellte Niete, kleinkarierte Beamtenseele, beamteter Kleinkrämer

boor [bʊəʳ] N Rüpel *m*, Flegel *m*

boorish ADJ, **boorishly** ADV [ˈbʊərɪʃ, -lɪ] rüpelhaft, flegelhaft

boorishness [ˈbʊərɪʃnɪs] N Rüpelhaftigkeit *f*, Flegelhaftigkeit *f*

boost [buːst] N Auftrieb *m no pl*; *(Elec, Aut)* Verstärkung *f*; *(= booster rocket)* Zusatzantrieb *m*; **to give sb/sth a ~** jdm/einer Sache Auftrieb geben, jdn aufmöbeln *(inf)*/etw ankurbeln *or* in Schwung bringen; *(by advertising)* für jdn/etw die Werbetrommel rühren; **to give my bank account a ~** um meinem Bankkonto eine Finanzspritze zu verabreichen; **this device gives the heart a ~** dieser Apparat verstärkt den Herzschlag; **to give a ~ to sb's morale** jdm Auftrieb geben *or* Mut machen; **to give a ~ to sb's confidence** jds Selbstvertrauen stärken

VT *production, output, sales, economy* ankurbeln; *profits, prices, income, chances* erhöhen; *electric charge, engine, heart beat etc* verstärken; *immune system, confidence, sb's ego* stärken; *morale* heben; **that's ~ed my ego** das hat mich aufgebaut, das hat mir Auftrieb gegeben

booster [ˈbuːstəʳ] N **a** *(Elec)* Puffersatz *m*; *(Rad)* Zusatzverstärker *m*; *(TV)* Zusatzgleichrichter *m*; *(Comput: on cable)* Zwischengenerator *m*; *(Aut, = supercharger)* Kompressor *m*; *(for heating)* Gebläse *nt*; *(= booster rocket)* Booster *m*; *(for launching)* Booster *m*, Startrakete *f*; *(Aviat)* Hilfstriebwerk *nt*; *(Space)* Booster *m*, Zusatztriebwerk *nt*; **to act as a ~** zur Verstärkung dienen **b** *(Med: also* **booster shot***)* Wiederholungsimpfung *f*; **~ dose** zusätzliche Dosis

booster: **booster cables** PL *(US Aut)* Starthilfekabel *pl*; **booster cushion** N, **booster seat** N *(Aut)* Kindersitz *m*; **booster shot** N *(Med)* Auffrischungsimpfung *f*

boot¹ [buːt] N **a** Stiefel *m*; **the ~ is on the other foot** *(fig)* es ist genau umgekehrt; **to give sb the (order of the** *(hum)***) ~** *(inf)* jdn rausschmeißen *(inf)*, jdn an die Luft setzen *(inf)*; **to get the ~** *(inf)* rausgeschmissen werden *(inf)*; **it's the ~ for him** *(inf)* der fliegt *(inf)*; **to die with one's ~s on** *(inf)* über der Arbeit *or* in den Sielen sterben; **to quake** *or* **shake** *or* **tremble in one's ~s** vor Angst fast umkommen; **to put the ~ in** *(Brit inf)* kräftig zutreten; *(fig)* zuschlagen; **to put the ~ into sb/sth** *(Brit fig inf)* jdn/etw niedermachen

b *(Brit, of car etc)* Kofferraum *m*

c *(inf: = kick)* **to give sb/sth a ~** jdm/einer Sache einen Tritt geben *or* versetzen; **he gave her the ~** *(fig)* er hat mit ihr Schluss gemacht *(inf)*

d *(Brit, pej inf, = woman)* Schreckschraube *f (inf)*

VT **a** *(inf: = kick)* einen (Fuß)tritt geben *(+dat)*; *ball* kicken

b *(Comput)* starten, booten, hochfahren

VI *(Comput)* starten, booten

▶ **boot out** VT *sep (inf: lit, fig)* rausschmeißen *(inf)*

▶ **boot up** *(Comput)* VT *sep* booten VI booten

boot² ADV *(hum, form)* **to ~** obendrein, noch dazu

boot: **bootblack** N Schuhputzer *m*; **boot boy** N *(Brit inf)* Skinhead *m*; **boot camp** N *(US Mil inf)* Armee-Ausbildungslager *nt*; **boot-cut jeans** PL Boot-cut-Jeans *pl*

bootee [buːˈtiː] N *(baby's)* gestrickter Babyschuh

booth [buːð] N **a** *(at fair)* (Markt)bude *f or* -stand *m*; *(at show)* (Messe)stand *m* **b** *(= telephone booth)* (offene) Zelle *f*; *(= polling booth, in cinema, language laboratory)* Kabine *f*; *(in restaurant)* Nische *f*, Séparée *nt (geh)*, Separee *nt (geh)*

boot: **bootjack** N Stiefelknecht *m*; **bootlace** N Schnürsenkel *m*; **to pull oneself up by one's (own) ~s** *(inf)* sich aus eigener Kraft hocharbeiten; **bootleg** VT **a** *(= make) liquor* schwarzbrennen *(inf)*; *(= sell)* schwarz verkaufen; *(= transport)* schmuggeln **b** *(inf: = produce illegally)* schwarz herstellen; *cassettes etc* schwarz mitschneiden ADJ *whisky etc* schwarzgebrannt; *goods* schwarz hergestellt; *cassettes etc* schwarz mitgeschnitten N *(= product, cassette etc)* Raubkopie *f*; **bootlegger** N Bootlegger *m*; *(= seller also)* Schwarzhändler *m*

bootless [ˈbuːtlɪs] ADJ *(liter)* nutzlos, eitel *(liter)*

boot: **bootlicker** N *(pej inf)* Speichellecker *m (pej inf)*; **bootmaker** N Schuhmacher *m*; **boot polish** N Schuhcreme *f*

boots [buːts] N *sing (Brit)* Hausbursche *or* -diener *m*

bootstrap [ˈbuːtstræp] N a Stiefelschlaufe *f*; **to pull oneself up by one's (own) ~s** sich aus eigener Kraft hocharbeiten; **he's British/a Tory to his ~s** *(inf)* er ist durch und durch ein Brite/Tory b *(Comput)* Bootstrap *m*, Bootstrapping *nt* VT *(Comput) computer, program* booten

booty [ˈbuːtɪ] N *(lit, fig)* Beute *f*

booty art N Beutekunst *f*

booze [buːz] *(inf)* N (= *alcoholic drink*) Alkohol *m*; (= *spirits also*) Schnaps *m*; (= *drinking bout*) Sauftour *f (inf)*; **keep off the ~** lass das Saufen sein *(inf)*; **bring some ~** bring was zu schlucken mit *(inf)*; **he's gone back on the ~ again** er säuft wieder *(inf)* VI saufen *(inf)*; **all this boozing** diese Sauferei *(inf)*; **boozing party** Besäufnis *nt (inf)*; **to go out boozing** saufen gehen *(inf)*

boozed(-up) [ˈbuːzd(ʌp)] ADJ *(inf)* blau *(inf)*, alkoholisiert *(inf)*

boozer [ˈbuːzəˈ] N a *(pej inf: = drinker)* Säufer(in) *m(f) (pej inf)*, Schluckspecht *m (inf)* b *(Brit inf: = pub)* Kneipe *f (inf)*

booze-up [ˈbuːzʌp] N *(inf)* Besäufnis *nt (inf)*

boozy [ˈbuːzɪ] ADJ *(+er) (inf) look, face* versoffen *(inf)*; **a ~ person** ein Schluckspecht *m (inf)*; *(stronger)* ein versoffenes Loch *(sl)*; **to have ~ breath** eine Fahne haben *(inf)*; **~ party** Sauferei *f (inf)*; **~ lunch** Essen *nt* mit reichlich zu trinken

bop [bɒp] N a *(Mus)* Bebop *m* b *(inf: = dance)* Schwof *m (inf)* c *(inf: = blow)* Knuff *(inf)*, Puff *(inf) m*; **to give sb a ~ on the nose** jdm eins auf die Nase geben VI *(inf: = dance)* schwofen *(inf)* VT *(inf)* **to ~ sb on the head** jdm eins auf den Kopf geben

boracic [bəˈræsɪk] ADJ *(Chem)* Bor-, borhaltig

borage [ˈbɒrɪdʒ] N Borretsch *m*

borax [ˈbɔːræks] N Borax *m*

border [ˈbɔːdəˈ] N a (= *edge, side: of woods, field, page*) Rand *m*
b (= *boundary, frontier*) Grenze *f*; **on the French ~** an der französischen Grenze; **on the ~s of France** an der französischen Grenze; **on the ~s of France and Switzerland** an der Grenze zwischen Frankreich und der Schweiz, an der französisch-schweizerischen Grenze; **the Borders** *(Brit Geog) das Grenzgebiet zwischen England und Schottland*; **north/south of the ~** *(Brit)* in/nach Schottland/England
c *(in garden)* Rabatte *f* → **herbaceous border**
d (= *edging, on dress*) Bordüre *f*; *(of carpet)* Einfassung *f*; *(of picture, text)* Umrahmung *f*, Rahmen *m*; **black ~** *(on notepaper)* schwarzer Rand, Trauerrand *m*
VT a (= *line edges of) road, path* säumen; *garden, estate etc* begrenzen; *(on all sides)* umschließen
b *(land etc: = lie on edge of)* grenzen an *(+acc)*

▶ **border on** *or* **upon** VI *+prep obj (lit, fig)* grenzen an *(+acc)*; **it was bordering on being rude** das grenzte an Unhöflichkeit

border dispute N Grenzstreitigkeit *f*; (= *fighting*) Grenzzwischenfall *m*

borderer [ˈbɔːdərəˈ] N Grenzbewohner(in) *m(f)*; *(Brit) Bewohner des Grenzgebiets zwischen England und Schottland*

border: **border guard** N Grenzsoldat *m*; **border incident** N Grenzzwischenfall *m*

bordering [ˈbɔːdərɪŋ] ADJ *country* angrenzend

border: **borderland** N *(lit)* Grenzgebiet *nt*; *(fig)* Grenzbereich *m*; **borderline** N a *(between states, districts)* Grenzlinie *f*, Grenze *f* b *(fig, between categories, classes etc)* Grenze *f*; **to be on the ~** an der Grenze liegen, ein Grenzfall sein; **his marks were on the ~ between a pass and a fail** er stand mit seinen Noten auf der Kippe ADJ *(fig)* **a ~ case** ein Grenzfall *m*; **it was a ~ pass/fail** er *etc* ist ganz knapp durchgekommen/durchgefallen; **he/it is ~** er/es ist ein Grenzfall; **it's too ~** das liegt zu sehr an der Grenze; **border raid** N Grenzüberfall *m*; **border state** N Grenzstaat *m*; **border town** N Grenzstadt *f*

bore¹ [bɔːˈ] VT *hole, well, tunnel* bohren; *rock* durchbohren VI bohren *(for* nach) N *(of shotgun, cannon)* Kaliber *nt*; **a 12 ~ shotgun** eine Flinte vom Kaliber 12

bore² N a (= *person*) Langweiler *m*; **what a ~ he is!** das ist ein Langweiler!, der kann einen langweilen *or* anöden *(inf)*; **the club/office ~** der Langweiler vom Dienst
b (= *thing, profession, situation etc*) **to be a ~** langweilig sein
c (= *nuisance*) **don't be a ~** nun sei doch nicht so (schwierig)!; **he's a ~, he never wants ...** er ist eine Plage, er will nie ...; **it's such a ~ having to go** es ist wirklich zu dumm *or* lästig, dass ich *etc* gehen muss; **oh what a ~!** das ist aber auch zu dumm *or* lästig!
VT langweilen; **to ~ sb stiff** *or* **to death** *or* **to tears, to ~ the pants off sb** *(inf)* jdn zu Tode langweilen; **to be/get ~d** sich langweilen; **I'm ~d** mir ist es langweilig, ich langweile mich; **he is ~d with his job/her** seine Arbeit/sie langweilt ihn; **he was ~d with reading/life** er war des Lesens/Lebens überdrüssig *(geh)*, er hatte das Lesen/Leben über

bore³ *pret of* **bear¹**

bore⁴ N (= *tidal wave*) Flutwelle *f*

boredom [ˈbɔːdəm] N Lang(e)weile *f*; (= *boringness*) Stumpfsinn *m*, Langweiligkeit *f*; **with a look of utter ~ on his face** mit einem völlig gelangweilten Gesichtsausdruck

borehole [ˈbɔːhəʊl] N Bohrloch *nt*

borer [ˈbɔːrəˈ] N *(Tech)* Bohrer *m*; (= *insect*) Bohrkäfer *m*

boric acid [ˈbɔːrɪkˈæsɪd] N *(Chem)* Borsäure *f*

boring¹ [ˈbɔːrɪŋ] N *(Tech, = act)* Bohren *nt*; (= *hole*) Bohrloch *nt* ADJ **~ machine** Bohrmaschine *f*

boring² ADJ langweilig

boringly [ˈbɔːrɪŋlɪ] ADV langweilig

born [bɔːn] *ptp of* **bear¹** VT h; **to be ~** *(person, fig: idea)* geboren werden; *(fig: organization)* entstehen; **I was ~ in 1948** ich bin *or* wurde 1948 geboren; **when were you ~?** wann sind Sie geboren?; **he was ~ Harry Webb** er wurde als Harry Webb geboren; **to be ~ again** wiedergeboren werden; **every baby ~ into the world** jedes Kind, das auf die Welt kommt; **he was ~ to a life of hardship/into a rich family** er wurde in ein schweres Leben/eine reiche Familie hineingeboren; **to be ~ deaf** von Geburt an taub sein; **the baby was ~ dead** das Baby wurde tot geboren *or* war eine Totgeburt; **he was just ~ to be Prime Minister** er war zum Premierminister geboren; **I wasn't ~ yesterday** *(inf)* ich bin nicht von gestern *(inf)*; **there's one ~ every minute!** *(fig inf)* die Dummen werden nicht alle!; **the characteristics which are ~ in us** die uns angeborenen Eigenschaften; **he was ~ of poor parents** er war das Kind armer Eltern; **with that confidence ~ of experience** mit dem aus Erfahrung hervorgegangenen Selbstvertrauen ADJ *suf (= native of)* **he is Chicago-~** er ist ein gebürtiger *or* geborener Chicagoer; **his foreign-/French-~ wife** seine Frau, die Ausländerin/gebürtige Französin ist
ADJ geboren; **he is a ~ poet/teacher** er ist der geborene Dichter/Lehrer; **an Englishman ~ and bred** ein echter *or* waschechter *(inf)* Engländer; **in all my ~ days** *(inf)* mein Lebtag *(dated)*, in meinem ganzen Leben

born-again [ˈbɔːnəˌgen] ADJ *Christian etc* wiedergeboren

borne [bɔːn] *ptp of* **bear¹**

Borneo [ˈbɔːnɪəʊ] N Borneo *nt*

borough [ˈbʌrə] N a *(also* **municipal borough**) Bezirk *m*, Stadtgemeinde *f* b *(Parl)* städtischer Wahlbezirk

borrow [ˈbɒrəʊ] VT a (sich *dat*) borgen, sich *(dat)* leihen *(from* von); *£5000 (from bank), car* sich *(dat)* leihen; *library book* ausleihen; *word* entlehnen; *(fig) idea, methodology* borgen *(inf)*, übernehmen *(from* von); **to ~ money from the bank/another country** Kredit bei der Bank/eine Anleihe bei einem anderen Land aufnehmen; **~ed word** Lehnwort *nt*; **he is living on ~ed time** seine Uhr ist abgelaufen b *(Math, in subtraction)* borgen *(inf)* VI borgen; *(from bank)* Kredit *m* aufnehmen; **~ing country** kreditnehmendes Land

borrower [ˈbɒrəʊəˈ] N Entleiher(in) *m(f)*; *(of capital, loan etc)* Kreditnehmer(in) *m(f)*

borrowing [ˈbɒrəʊɪŋ] N Borgen *nt*, Leihen *nt*; *(of library book)* Ausleihen *nt*; *(of word)* Entlehnung *f*; *(fig, of idea, methodology)* Übernahme *f*; **~ of money from the bank** Kreditaufnahme *f or (short-term)* Geldaufnahme *f* bei der Bank; **government ~** staatliche Kreditaufnahme; **consumer ~** Verbraucherkredit *m*; **~s** *(Fin)* aufgenommene Schulden *pl*; *(of country also)* Anleihen *pl*; **~ requirements** Kreditbedarf *m*

borsch(t) [bɔːʃ(t)] N Borschtsch *m*

borstal [ˈbɔːstl] N *(Brit old)* Jugendheim *nt*, Besserungsanstalt *f*

borzoi [ˈbɔːzɔɪ] N Barsoi *m*

bosh [bɒʃ] N *(dated inf)* Quatsch *m (inf)*, Quark *m (dated inf)*

bo's'n [ˈbəʊsn] N = **boatswain**

Bosnia [ˈbɒznɪə] N Bosnien *nt*

Bosnia and Herzegovina [ˈbɒznɪəændˌhɜːtsəgəʊˈviːnə] N Bosnien und Herzegowina *nt*

Bosnian [ˈbɒznɪən] ADJ bosnisch N Bosnier(in) *m(f)*

bosom [ˈbʊzəm] N a *(lit, fig, of person)* Busen *m*; **to lay bare one's ~ to sb** *(fig liter)* jdm sein Herz erschließen *(liter)*, jdm sein Innerstes offenbaren *(liter)* b *(of dress)* Brustteil *m* c *(fig)* **in the ~ of his family** im Schoß der Familie ADJ *attr friend etc* Busen-

bosomy [ˈbʊzəmɪ] ADJ *(inf)* vollbusig

Bosp(h)orus [ˈbɒsfərəs, ˈbɒspərəs] N **the ~** der Bosporus

boss¹ [bɒs] N Chef *m*, Boss *m (inf)*; **industrial/union ~es** Industrie-/Gewerkschaftsbosse *pl (inf)*; **his wife is the ~** seine Frau hat das Sagen, bei ihm zu Hause bestimmt die Frau; **OK, you're the ~** in Ordnung, du hast zu bestimmen

▶ **boss about** *(Brit) or* **around** VT *sep (inf)* rumkommandieren *(inf)*

boss² N (= *knob on shield*) Buckel *m*; *(Archit)* Schlussstein *m*

bossa nova [ˌbɒsəˈnəʊvə] N Bossa Nova *m*

boss-eyed [bɒsˈaɪd] ADJ *(Brit inf)* schielend *attr*; **to be ~** schielen, einen Knick in der Optik haben *(inf)*

bossiness [ˈbɒsɪnɪs] N Herrschsucht *f*, herrische Art

boss man N *(inf)* Boss *m (inf)*

bossy [ˈbɒsɪ] ADJ *(+er)* herrisch; **don't be ~ with me!** kommandier mich nicht so rum *(inf)*; **he tends to be rather ~** er kommandiert einen gern rum *(inf)*

Boston [ˈbɒstən]: **Boston baked beans** [ˌbɒstənbeɪktˈbiːnz] PL *(US) weiße Bohnen mit gepökeltem Schweinefleisch und Melasse oder braunem Zucker*; **Boston crab** N *(Wrestling)* Beinschraube *f*

bosun [ˈbəʊsn] N = **boatswain**

BOT *(Brit) abbr of* **Board of Trade**

botanic(al) [bəˈtænɪk(əl)] ADJ botanisch, Pflanzen-

botanic(al) gardens [bəˌtænɪk(əl)ˈgɑːdnz] PL botanischer Garten

botanist [ˈbɒtənɪst] N Botaniker(in) *m(f)*

botany [ˈbɒtənɪ] N Botanik *f*, Pflanzenkunde *f*

botch [bɒtʃ] *(inf)* VT *(also* **botch up**) verpfuschen, vermurksen *(inf)*; *plans etc* vermasseln *(inf)*; **a ~ed job** ein Pfusch *m (inf)* N Murks *m (inf)*, Pfusch *m (inf)*; **to make a ~ of sth** etw verpfuschen/vermasseln *(inf)*

botcher ['bɒtʃəʳ] N *(inf)* Murkser *m (inf)*, Pfuscher *m (inf)*

botch-up ['bɒtʃʌp] *(inf)* N Murks *m (inf)*, Pfusch *m (inf)*

botchy ['bɒtʃɪ] ADJ *(inf)* verpfuscht, vermurkst *(inf)*

botel [bəʊ'tel] N Botel *nt (als Hotel ausgebautes Schiff)*

botfly ['bɒtflaɪ] N *(Zool)* Pferdebremse *f*

both [bəʊθ] ✪ 26.2 ADJ beide; **~ (the) boys** beide Jungen
PRON beide; *(two different things)* beides; **~ of them were there, they were ~ there** sie waren (alle) beide da; **two pencils/a pencil and a picture - he took ~** zwei Bleistifte/ein Bleistift und ein Bild - er hat beide/beides genommen; **~ of these answers are wrong** beide Antworten sind falsch; **~ of you are wrong** ihr habt (alle) beide unrecht; **come in ~ of you** kommt beide herein; **I meant ~ of you** ich habe euch beide gemeint
ADV **~ ... and ...** sowohl ..., als auch ...; **~ you and I** wir beide; **John and I ~ came** John und ich sind beide gekommen; **she was ~ laughing and crying** sie lachte und weinte zugleich *or* gleichzeitig; **I'm ~ pleased and not pleased** ich freue mich und auch wieder nicht; **is it black or white? – ~** ist es schwarz oder weiß? – beides; **you and me ~** *(inf)* wir zwei beide *(inf)*

bother ['bɒðəʳ] ✪ 7.5 VT **a** *(= annoy, trouble, person, noise)* belästigen; *(sb's behaviour, tight garment, hat, long hair)* ärgern, stören; *(= cause disturbance to, light, noise, sb's presence, mistakes etc)* stören; *(= give trouble, back, teeth etc)* zu schaffen machen *(+dat)*; *(= worry)* Sorgen machen *(+dat)*; *(matter, problem, question)* beschäftigen, keine Ruhe lassen *(+dat)*; **I'm sorry to ~ you but ...** es tut mir leid, dass ich Sie damit belästigen muss, aber ...; **well I'm sorry I ~ed you** entschuldigen Sie, dass ich (überhaupt) gefragt habe; **don't ~ your head about that** zerbrechen Sie sich *(dat)* darüber nicht den Kopf; **don't ~ yourself about that** machen Sie sich *(dat)* darüber mal keine Gedanken *or* Sorgen; **I wouldn't let it ~ me** darüber würde ich mir keine Sorgen *or* Gedanken machen; **I shouldn't let it ~ you** machen Sie sich mal keine Sorgen; **don't ~ me!** lass mich in Frieden!; **he was always ~ing me to lend him money** er hat mich dauernd um Geld angegangen; **could I ~ you for a light?** dürfte ich Sie vielleicht um Feuer bitten?; **one thing is still ~ing him** eins stört ihn noch; **what's ~ing you?** was haben Sie denn?; **is something ~ing you?** haben Sie etwas? → **hot**
b **I/he can't be ~ed** ich habe/er hat keine Lust; **I can't be ~ed with people like him/with opera** für solche Leute/für Opern habe ich nichts übrig; **I can't be ~ed to do** *or* **with doing that** ich habe einfach keine Lust, das zu machen; **he can't be ~ed about** *or* **with small matters like that** mit solchen Kleinigkeiten gibt er sich nicht ab; **do you want to stay or go? – I'm not ~ed** willst du bleiben oder gehen? – das ist mir egal; **I'm not ~ed about him/the money** seinetwegen/wegen des Geldes mache ich mir keine Gedanken
c *(= take trouble to do)* **don't ~ to do it again** das brauchen Sie nicht nochmals zu tun; **don't ~ to ask** Sie brauchen nicht (zu) fragen; **I won't ~ asking YOU again!** DICH werde ich bestimmt nicht mehr fragen!; **she didn't even ~ to ask/check first** sie hat gar nicht erst gefragt/nachgesehen; **please don't ~ getting up** *or* **to get up** bitte, bleiben Sie doch sitzen; **you needn't ~ to come** Sie brauchen wirklich nicht (zu) kommen
VI sich kümmern *(about* um); *(= get worried)* sich *(dat)* Sorgen machen *(about* um); **don't ~ about me!** machen Sie sich meinetwegen keine Sorgen; *(sarcastic)* ist ja egal, was ich will; **to ~ with sb** sich mit jdm abgeben; **he/it is not worth ~ing about** über ihn/darüber brauchen wir gar nicht zu reden, er/das ist nicht der Mühe wert; **I'm not going to ~ with that** das lasse ich; **I didn't ~ about lunch** ich habe das Mittagessen ausgelassen; **don't ~!** nicht nötig!; **really you needn't have ~ed!** das wäre aber wirklich nicht nötig gewesen!; **don't ~!** nicht nötig!; **really you needn't have ~ed!** das wäre aber wirklich nicht nötig gewesen!
N **a** *(= nuisance)* Plage *f*; **it's such a ~** das ist wirklich lästig *or* eine Plage; **I've forgotten it, what a ~** ich habe es vergessen, wie ärgerlich *or* so was Ärgerliches; **he/the car can be a bit of a ~** er/das Auto kann einem wirklich Schwierigkeiten machen; **I know it's an awful ~ for you but ...** ich weiß, dass Ihnen das fürchterliche Umstände macht, aber ...
b *(= trouble, contretemps etc)* Ärger *m*; *(= difficulties)* Schwierigkeiten *pl*; **she's in a spot of ~** sie hat Schwierigkeiten; **we had a spot** *or* **bit of ~ with the car** wir hatten Ärger mit dem Auto; **I didn't have any ~ getting the visa** es war kein Problem, das Visum zu bekommen; **I'll do it tonight, no ~** *(inf)* kein Problem, das mache ich heute Abend; **that's all right, it's no ~** bitte schön, das tue ich doch gern; **it wasn't any ~** *(= don't mention it)* das ist gern geschehen; *(= not difficult)* das war ganz einfach; **the children were no ~ at all** wir hatten mit den Kindern überhaupt keine Probleme; **to go to a lot of ~ to do sth** sich *(dat)* mit etw viel Mühe geben; **please don't put yourself to any ~ on my account** machen Sie meinetwegen keine Umstände
INTERJ Mist *(inf)*; **~ that man!** zum Kuckuck mit ihm! *(inf)*; **oh ~ this lock!** das ist ein doofes Schloss! *(inf)*

botheration [,bɒðə'reɪʃən] INTERJ verflixt und zugenäht *(inf)*

bothersome ['bɒðəsəm] ADJ lästig; *child* unleidlich; **the cooker has been rather ~ lately** mit dem Herd hatte ich *etc* in letzter Zeit viel Ärger

bothie ['bɒθɪ] N = **bothy**

Bothnia ['bɒθnɪə] N **Gulf of ~** Bottnischer Meerbusen

bothy ['bɒθɪ] N *(Scot)* Schutzhütte *f*

Botox® ['bəʊtɒks] N Botox® *nt*; **she uses ~** sie lässt sich Botox spritzen

Botswana [,bɒt'swɑːnə] N Botswana *nt*

bottle ['bɒtl] N **a** Flasche *f*; **a ~ of wine** eine Flasche Wein **b** *(Brit inf)* Mumm *m* (in den Knochen) *(inf)* **c** *(fig inf: = drink)* Flasche *f (inf)*; **to be off the ~** nicht mehr trinken; **to take to the ~** zur Flasche greifen; **he's too fond of the ~** er trinkt zu gern → **hit** VT **a** in Flaschen abfüllen; **~d in ...** abgefüllt in ... **b** *(Brit inf)* **to ~ it** die Nerven verlieren

▶ **bottle out** VI *(Brit inf: = lose nerve)* die Nerven verlieren

▶ **bottle up** VT *sep emotion* in sich *(dat)* aufstauen, in sich *(acc)* hineinfressen *(inf)*; **there's a lot of hate bottled up inside her** es ist viel aufgestauter Hass in ihr

bottle: **bottle bank** N Altglascontainer *m*; **bottle blonde** N *(inf)* Wasserstoffblondine *f (inf)*

bottled ['bɒtld] ADJ *wine* in Flaschen (abgefüllt); *gas* in Flaschen; *beer* Flaschen-; *fruit* eingemacht

bottle: **bottle-fed** ADJ **he is ~** er wird aus der Flasche ernährt; **a ~ baby** ein Flaschenkind *nt*; **bottle-feed** VT aus der Flasche ernähren; **bottle-green** ADJ flaschengrün; **bottleneck** N *(lit, fig)* Engpass *m*; **bottle-opener** N Flaschenöffner *m*; **bottle party** N Bottleparty *f*

bottler ['bɒtləʳ] N *(= company)* Abfüllbetrieb *m*; *(= person)* Abfüller(in) *m(f)*; *(= machine)* Abfüllmaschine *f*

bottle: **bottle rack** N Flaschengestell *nt*; **bottle top** N Flaschenverschluss *m*; **bottle-washer** N Flaschenreiniger *m*

bottling ['bɒtlɪŋ] N Abfüllen *nt*; *(of fruit)* Einmachen *nt*; **~ plant** Abfüllanlage *f*

bottom ['bɒtəm] N **a** *(= lowest part, of receptacle, box, glass)* Boden *m*; *(of mountain, pillar, spire, printed character)* Fuß *m*; *(of well, canyon)* Grund *m*; *(of page, screen, wall)* unteres Ende; *(of list, road)* Ende *nt*; *(of trousers)* unteres Beinteil; *(of dress)* Saum *m*; **the ~ of the league** das Tabellenende, der Tabellenschluss; **which end is the ~?** wo ist unten?; **the ~ of the tree/wall** *etc* **is ...** der Baum/Wand *etc* ist unten ...; **at the ~ of the page/list/league/hill/wall/tree** *etc* unten auf der Seite/Liste/in der Tabelle/am Berg/an der Wand/am Baum *etc*; **at the ~ of the canyon** unten in der Schlucht; **at the ~ of the mountain/cliff** am Fuß des Berges/Felsens; **to be (at the) ~ of the class** der/die Letzte in der Klasse sein; **he's near the ~ in English** in Englisch gehört er zu den Schlechtesten; **at the ~ of the garden** hinten im Garten; **at the ~ of the table/road** am unteren Ende des Tisches/am Ende der Straße; **~s up!** hoch die Tassen *(inf)*; **from the ~ of my heart** aus tiefstem Herzen; **he took a card from the ~ of the pack** er nahm eine Karte unten aus dem Stapel; **at ~** *(fig)* im Grunde; **the ~ fell out of his world** *(inf)* für ihn brach alles zusammen; **the ~ dropped** *or* **fell out of the market** die Marktlage hat einen Tiefstand erreicht
b *(= underneath, underside)* Unterseite *f*, untere Seite; **on the ~ of the tin/ashtray** unten an der Dose/am Aschenbecher
c *(of sea, lake, river)* Grund *m*, Boden *m*; **at the ~ of the sea** auf dem Meeresboden *or* -grund *(geh)*; **to send a ship to the ~** ein Schiff versenken; **the ship went to the ~** das Schiff sank auf den Grund
d *(of chair)* Sitz *m*, Sitzfläche *f*
e *(of person)* Hintern *m (inf)*, Po *m (inf)*; *(of trousers etc)* Hosenboden *m*
f *(fig, causally)* **to be at the ~ of sth** *(person)* hinter etw *(dat)* stecken; *(thing)* einer Sache *(dat)* zugrunde *or* zu Grunde liegen; **to get to the ~ of sth** einer Sache *(dat)* auf den Grund kommen, hinter etw *(acc)* kommen; **let's get to the ~ of the matter** wir wollen der Sache auf den Grund gehen
g *(Naut, of ship)* Boden *m*; **the ship floated ~ up** das Schiff trieb kieloben
h *(Brit Aut)* **~ (gear)** erster Gang; **in ~ (gear)** im ersten Gang; **we're still in ~ gear** *(inf)* wir sind immer noch nicht richtig auf Touren gekommen *(inf)*
i **bottoms** PL *(US: = low land)* Ebene *f*
j **tracksuit/pyjama** *(Brit) or* **pajama** *(US)* **~s** Trainings-/Schlafanzughose *f*; **bikini ~(s)** Bikiniunterteil *nt*
ADJ *attr (= lower)* untere(r, s); *(= lowest)* unterste(r, s); *price* niedrigste(r, s); *(Fin)* Tiefst-; *pupil* schlechteste(r, s); **~ half** *(of box)* untere Hälfte; *(of list, class)* zweite Hälfte

▶ **bottom out** VI *(= reach lowest point)* die Talsohle erreichen *(at* bei); *(= pass lowest point)* die Talsohle verlassen *or* überwinden

bottom: **bottom drawer** N *(Brit)* **to put sth away in one's ~** etw für die Aussteuer beiseitelegen; **bottom-fermented** ['bɒtəmfə'mentɪd] ADJ *beer* untergärig; **bottomless** ADJ *(lit)* bodenlos; *(fig) funds* unerschöpflich; *despair* tiefste(r, s); **a ~ pit** *(fig)* ein Fass ohne Boden; **she is a ~ pit** sie frisst wie ein Scheunendrescher *(inf)*; **bottom line** N **a** *(of accounts etc)* Saldo *m*; **if the balance sheet shows a healthy ~** wenn die Bilanz einen gesunden Saldo aufweist; **to keep an eye on the ~** auf die Profitabilität achten **b** *(fig)* **that's the ~ (of it)** *(= decisive factor)* das ist das Entscheidende (dabei); *(= what it amounts to)* darauf läuft es im Endeffekt hinaus; **bottom-line** ADJ *attr management, publishing* gewinnorientiert; **bottommost** ADJ allerunterste(r, s); **bottom-up** ADJ *approach, view, analysis* von unten nach oben

botulism ['bɒtjʊlɪzəm] N Nahrungsmittelvergiftung *f*, Botulismus *m*

bouclé [buː'kleɪ] N Bouclé *nt*

boudoir ['buːdwɑːʳ] N Boudoir *nt (old)*

bouffant ['buːfɒŋ] ADJ *hairstyle* aufgebauscht

bougainvillea [ˌbuːgən'vɪlɪə] N Bougainvillea *f*
bough [baʊ] N Ast *m*
bought [bɔːt] *pret, ptp of* **buy**
bouillon ['buːjɒŋ] N Bouillon *f*, klare Fleischbrühe
bouillon cube N *(US)* Brühwürfel *m*
boulder ['bəʊldəʳ] N Felsblock *m*, Felsbrocken *m*
boulder clay N *(Geol)* Geschiebelehm *m*
boulevard ['buːləvɑːʳ] N Boulevard *m*
bounce [baʊns] VI a *(ball etc)* springen; *(Sport: ball)* aufspringen; *(chins, breasts etc)* wackeln; **rubber ~s** Gummi federt; **the child ~d up and down on the bed** das Kind hüpfte auf dem Bett herum; **the car ~d along the bumpy road** das Auto holperte die schlechte Straße entlang; **he came bouncing into the room** er kam munter ins Zimmer; **I gotta ~** *(US sl)* ich mach nen Abgang *(inf)*
b *(inf, cheque)* platzen *(inf)*
VT a *ball* aufprallen lassen, prellen *(Sport)*; *laser beams, light, radio waves* reflektieren; **he ~d the ball against the wall** er warf den Ball gegen die Wand; **he ~d the baby on his knee** er ließ das Kind auf den Knien reiten
b *(inf) cheque* platzen lassen
c *(inf, = throw out)* rausschmeißen *(inf)*
d *(= coerce)* **to ~ sb into doing sth** jdn dazu bringen, etw zu tun
N a *(of ball: = rebound)* Aufprall *m*; **to hit a ball on the ~** den Ball beim Aufprall nehmen; **count the number of ~s** zählen Sie, wie oft der Ball *etc* aufspringt
b *no pl (of ball)* Sprungkraft *f*; *(of hair also, rubber)* Elastizität *f*; *(inf, of person)* Schwung *m* *(inf)*
▶ **bounce back** VT *sep ball* zurückprallen lassen VI abprallen, zurückprallen; *(fig inf: person)* sich nicht unterkriegen lassen *(inf)*; *(to boyfriend)* zurückkommen
▶ **bounce off** VT *always separate* **to bounce sth off sth** etw von etw abprallen lassen; *radio waves etc* etw an etw *(dat)* reflektieren; **to bounce an idea off sb** *(fig inf)* eine Idee an jdm testen *(inf)* VI abprallen; *(radio waves)* reflektieren
bounce pass N *(Basketball)* Bodenpass *m*
bouncer ['baʊnsəʳ] N *(inf)* Rausschmeißer(in) *m(f) (inf)*
bouncing ['baʊnsɪŋ] ADJ **~ baby** strammer Säugling
bouncy ['baʊnsɪ] ADJ (+er) a *ball* gut springend; *mattress, step* federnd; *springs, hair* elastisch; *ride* holpernd b *(fig inf: = exuberant)* vergnügt und munter, quietschvergnügt *(inf)*
bouncy castle® N Hüpfburg *f*
bound¹ [baʊnd] N *usu pl (lit, fig)* Grenze *f*; **to keep within ~s** innerhalb der Grenzen bleiben; **to keep within the ~s of propriety** den Anstand wahren, im Rahmen bleiben; **within the ~s of probability** im Bereich des Wahrscheinlichen; **his ambition knows no ~s** sein Ehrgeiz kennt keine Grenzen; **the bar is out of ~s** das Betreten des Lokals ist verboten; **this part of town is out of ~s** dieser Stadtteil ist Sperrzone VT *usu pass country* begrenzen; *area also* abgrenzen
bound² N Sprung *m*, Satz *m* → **leap** VI springen; *(rabbit)* hoppeln; **to ~ in/away/back** herein-/weg-/zurückspringen; **the dog came ~ing up** der Hund kam angesprungen
bound³ *pret, ptp of* **bind** ADJ a gebunden; **~ hand and foot** an Händen und Füßen gebunden
b *book* gebunden; **~ in board** kartoniert
c *(= sure)* **to be ~ to do sth** etw bestimmt tun; **but then of course he's ~ to say that** das muss er ja sagen; **it's ~ to happen** das muss so kommen
d *(= obliged) person* verpflichtet; *(by contract, word, promise)* gebunden; **but I'm ~ to say ...** *(inf)* aber ich muss schon sagen ...; **if you say X then you're ~ to say that ...** wenn Sie X behaupten, müssen Sie zwangsläufig sagen, dass ...; **I'm not ~ to agree** ich muss nicht zwangsläufig zustimmen → **honour**
e **~ variable** *(Math)* abhängige Variable; **~ form** *(Chem)* gebundene Form
bound⁴ ADJ *pred* **to be ~ for London** *(= heading for)* auf dem Weg nach London sein, nach London unterwegs sein; *(= about to start, ship, plane, lorry etc)* nach London gehen; *(person)* nach London reisen wollen; **the plane/all passengers ~ for London will ...** das Flugzeug/alle Passagiere nach London wird/werden ...; **where are you ~ for?** wohin geht die Reise?, wohin wollen Sie?; **we were northward-/California-~** wir waren nach Norden/Kalifornien unterwegs → **homeward**
boundary ['baʊndərɪ] N Grenze *f*; *(Cricket)* Spielfeldgrenze *f*; **to hit/score a ~** den Ball über die Spielfeldgrenze schlagen/4 oder 6 Punkte für einen Schlag über die Spielfeldgrenze erzielen
boundary: **Boundary Commission** N *(Brit Pol)* Kommission *f* zur Festlegung der Wahlbezirke; **boundary line** N Grenzlinie *f*; *(Sport)* Spielfeldgrenze *f*; **boundary mark** N Grenzmal *nt*; **boundary rider** N *(Austral) Arbeiter, der die Grenzen des Weidelandes abreitet*; **boundary stone** N Grenzstein *m*; **boundary value** N *(Math)* Randwert *m*
bounden ['baʊndən] ADJ **~ duty** *(old, liter)* Pflicht und Schuldigkeit *f (geh)*
bounder ['baʊndəʳ] N *(dated Brit, inf)* Lump *m* *(dated inf)*
boundless ['baʊndlɪs] ADJ *(lit, fig)* grenzenlos
bounteous ['baʊntɪəs], **bountiful** ['baʊntɪfʊl] ADJ großzügig; *sovereign, god* gütig; *harvest, gifts* (über)reich
bounteousness ['baʊntɪəsnɪs], **bountifulness** ['baʊntɪfʊlnɪs] N Großzügigkeit *f*; *(of sovereign, god)* Güte *f*; *(of harvest, gifts)* reiche Fülle *(geh)*
bounty ['baʊntɪ] N a *(= generosity)* Freigebigkeit *f*; *(of nature)* reiche Fülle *(geh)* b *(= gift)* großzügige *or* reiche Gabe *(geh)* c *(= reward money)* Kopfgeld *nt*
bounty: **bounty-fed** ['baʊntɪfed] ADJ *(Econ)* subventioniert; **bounty hunter** N Kopfgeldjäger(in) *m(f)*
bouquet ['bʊkeɪ] N a Strauß *m*, Bukett *nt* *(geh)* b *(of wine)* Bukett *nt*, Blume *f*
bouquet garni ['bʊkeɪgɑː'niː] N *(Cook)* Kräutermischung *f*
Bourbon ['bʊəbən] N *(Hist)* Bourbone *m*, Bourbonin *f*
bourbon ['bɜːbən] N (*also* **bourbon whiskey**) Bourbon *m*
bourgeois ['bʊəʒwɑː] N Bürger(in) *m(f)*, Bourgeois *m (esp Sociol)*; *(pej)* Spießbürger(in) *m(f)*, Spießer *m* ADJ bürgerlich; *(pej)* spießbürgerlich, spießig
bourgeoisie [ˌbʊəʒwɑː'ziː] N Bürgertum *nt*, Bourgeoisie *f*
bout [baʊt] N a *(of flu etc)* Anfall *m*; *(of negotiations)* Runde *f*; **a ~ of fever/rheumatism** ein Fieber-/Rheumaanfall *m*; **a drinking ~** eine Zecherei; **I did another final ~ of revision before the exam** ich habe vor dem Examen noch einmal alles wiederholt b *(Boxing, Wrestling, Fencing)* Kampf *m*; **to have a ~ with sb** einen Kampf mit jdm austragen
boutique [buː'tiːk] N Boutique *f*
bovine ['bəʊvaɪn] ADJ *(lit)* Rinder-; *appearance* rinderartig; *(fig)* stupide, einfältig N Rind *nt*
bovver boots ['bɒvə'buːts] PL *(dated Brit sl)* Rockerstiefel *pl*
bow¹ [bəʊ] N a *(for shooting arrows)* Bogen *m*; **a ~ and arrow** Pfeil und Bogen *pl* b *(Mus)* Bogen *m*; **up/down ~ stroke** Auf-/Abstrich *m*
c *(= knot: of ribbon etc)* Schleife *f* VI *(Mus)* den Bogen führen VT *(Mus)* streichen
bow² [baʊ] N *(with head, body)* Verbeugung *f*; *(by young boy)* Diener *m*; **to make one's ~ to sb** sich vor jdm verbeugen *or* verneigen *(geh)*, jdm seine Reverenz erweisen *(form)*; **to take a ~** sich verbeugen *or* verneigen; **take a ~** *(fig: = take the credit)* das haben wir Ihnen zu verdanken
VI a *(person: with body)* sich verbeugen, sich verneigen *(geh)* *(to sb* vor jdm); *(young boy)* einen Diener machen; **to ~ and scrape** katzbuckeln *(pej)*, liebedienern *(pej)*
b *(= bend: branches etc)* sich biegen *or* beugen
c *(fig: = defer, submit)* sich beugen *(before* vor *+dat, under* unter *+dat, to +dat)*; **to ~ to the majority** sich der Mehrheit beugen; **to ~ to the inevitable** sich in das Unvermeidliche fügen
VT a **to ~ one's head** den Kopf senken; *(in prayer)* sich verneigen
b *(= bend) branches* beugen; **old age had not ~ed him** er war vom Alter ungebeugt *(geh)*
c *(= defeat)* **to be ~ed by sth** von etw schwer getroffen sein
▶ **bow down** VI *(lit)* sich beugen *or* neigen; **to bow down to** *or* **before sb** *(fig)* sich jdm beugen VT *sep* **bowed down with snow/cares** schneebeladen/mit Sorgen beladen
▶ **bow out** VI *(fig)* sich verabschieden; **to bow out of sth** sich aus etw zurückziehen
bow³ [baʊ] N *often pl* Bug *m*; **in the ~s** im Bug; **on the port/starboard ~** backbord(s)/steuerbord(s) voraus; **~ doors** Bugtor *nt*
Bow Bells [ˌbəʊ'belz] PL **he was born within the sound of ~** er ist ein waschechter Cockney *(Londoner)*
bowdlerize ['baʊdləraɪz] VT *book* von anstößigen Stellen säubern, reinigen; **a ~d version** eine zensierte Ausgabe
bowed¹ [bəʊd] ADJ *legs* krumm
bowed² [baʊd] ADJ *person* gebeugt; *shoulders* hängend
bowel ['baʊəl] N *usu pl* a *(Anat, of person)* Eingeweide *nt usu pl*, Gedärm *nt usu pl*; *(of animal also)* Innereien *pl*; **a ~ movement** Stuhl (-gang) *m*; **to move one's ~s** Stuhl(gang) haben; **to control one's ~s** seine Darmentleerung kontrollieren; **he had something wrong with his ~s** mit seiner Verdauung stimmte etwas nicht
b *(fig)* **the ~s of the earth/ship** *etc* das Erdinnere/Schiffsinnere *etc*, das Innere der Erde/der Schiffsbauch *etc*
bower ['baʊəʳ] N Laube *f*
bowing ['bəʊɪŋ] N *(Mus)* Bogenführung *f*
bowl¹ [bəʊl] N a Schüssel *f*; *(smaller, shallow also, fingerbowl)* Schale *f*; *(for sugar etc)* Schälchen *nt*; *(for animals, prisoners also)* Napf *m*; *(= punch bowl)* Bowle *f*; *(= washbowl also)* Becken *nt*; **a ~ of milk** eine Schale/ein Napf Milch b *(of pipe)* Kopf *m*; *(of spoon)* Schöpfteil *m*; *(of lavatory)* Becken *nt*; *(of lamp)* Schale *f*; *(of wineglass)* Kelch *m* c *(Geog)* Becken *nt* d *(US: = stadium)* Stadion *nt*
bowl² N *(Sport: = ball)* Kugel *f* → *also* **bowls** VI a *(Bowls)* Bowling/Boccia/Boule spielen; *(tenpin)* bowlen, Bowling spielen; *(skittles)* kegeln b *(Cricket)* werfen c *(= travel: car, cycle etc)* brausen *(inf)*; **he came ~ing down the street** er kam auf der Straße angerauscht *(inf)* VT a *(= roll) ball* rollen; *hoop also* treiben b *(Cricket) ball* werfen; *batsman* ausschlagen
▶ **bowl along** VI dahergerauscht kommen/dahinrauschen *(prep obj* auf *+dat) (inf)*
▶ **bowl out** VT *sep (Cricket)* ausschlagen
▶ **bowl over** VT *sep* a *(lit, with ball etc)* umwerfen; *(in car etc)* umfahren, über den Haufen fahren *(inf)* b *(fig)* umwerfen, umhauen *(inf)*; **to be bowled over** sprachlos *or* platt *(inf)* sein; **he was bowled over by the news/her/the idea** die Nachricht/sie/die Idee hat ihn (einfach) überwältigt *or* umgehauen *(inf)*
bow [bəʊ]: **bow-legged** [ˌbəʊ'legɪd] ADJ o-beinig, O-beinig; **bowlegs** PL O-Beine *pl*
bowler¹ ['bəʊləʳ] N *(Sport)* a Bowlingspieler(in) *m(f)*; *(of bowls also)* Boccia-/Boulespieler(in) *m(f)* b *(Cricket)* Werfer *m*
bowler² N (*Brit: also* **bowler hat**) Melone *f*; **~ hat brigade** *(hum)* Bürohengste *pl (inf)*

bowline [ˈbəʊlɪn] N Palstek *m*; *(= rope)* Bulin(e) *f*

bowling [ˈbəʊlɪŋ] N **a** *(Cricket)* Werfen *nt*; **renowned for his fast ~** für seine schnellen Bälle berühmt **b** *(= tenpin bowling)* Bowling *nt*; *(= skittles)* Kegeln *nt*; **to go ~** bowlen/kegeln gehen

bowling: **bowling alley** N Bowlingbahn *f*; **bowling green** N Spiel- *or* Rasenfläche *f* für Bowling/Boccia/Boule

bowls [bəʊlz] N Bowling *nt*; *(Italian, German)* Boccia *nt*; *(French)* Boule *nt*

bowman [ˈbəʊmən] N *pl* **-men** [-mən] Bogenschütze *m*

bows [baʊz] PL → **bow[3]**

bowsprit [ˈbəʊsprɪt] N Bugspriet *nt or m*

Bow Street runner [bəʊ-] N *(Brit, Hist)* Büttel *m (der offiziellen Detektei in der Londoner Bow Street)*

bow [bəʊ]: **bowstring** N *(Mus)* (Bogen)bezug *m*; *(in archery)* (Bogen)sehne *f*; **bow tie** N Fliege *f*

bow wave [baʊ-] N Bugwelle *f*

bow window [bəʊ-] N Erkerfenster *nt*

bow-wow [ˈbaʊˈwaʊ] *(baby-talk)* INTERJ wauwau *(baby-talk)* [ˈbaʊwaʊ] N *(= dog)* Wauwau *m (baby-talk)*

box[1] [bɒks] VI *(Sport)* boxen VT *(Sport)* boxen; **to ~ sb's ears** *or* **sb on the ears** jdn ohrfeigen, jdm eine Ohrfeige geben N **a ~ on the ear** *or* **round the ears** eine Ohrfeige, eine Backpfeife *(inf)*

box[2] N *(Bot)* Buchsbaum *m*

box[3] N **a** *(made of wood or strong cardboard)* Kiste *f*; *(= cardboard box)* Karton *m*; *(made of light cardboard, = matchbox)* Schachtel *f*; *(= snuffbox, cigarette box etc, biscuit tin)* Dose *f*; *(of crackers, chocolates etc)* Packung *f*, Schachtel *f*; *(= jewellery box)* Schatulle *f*, Kasten *m*; *(= tool box)* (Werkzeug)kasten *m*; *(= ballot box)* Urne *f*; *(= money box, with lid and lock)* Kassette *f*; *(for saving)* Sparbüchse *or* -dose *f*; *(= collection box)* (Sammel)büchse *f*; *(in church)* Opferbüchse *f*; *(fixed to wall etc)* Opferstock *m*; *(Brit, old, = trunk)* (Schrank)koffer *m*; **to be out of one's ~** *(Brit inf: = drunk, drugged)* total zu sein *(inf)*

b *(on form)* Kästchen *nt*; *(on newspaper page)* Kasten *m*; *(Baseball)* Box *f*; *(Football)* Strafraum *m*; *(in road junction)* *gelb schraffierter Kreuzungsbereich*; **draw a ~ (a)round it** umranden Sie es; **tick the appropriate ~** das entsprechende Kästchen ankreuzen

c *(Theat)* Loge *f*; *(= jury box)* Geschworenenbank *f*; *(= witness box)* Zeugenstand *m*; *(= press box)* Pressekabine *f*; *(outside)* Pressetribüne *f*; *(in court)* Pressebank *f*

d *(Tech: = housing)* Gehäuse *nt*

e *(building, = sentry box)* Schilderhaus *nt*; *(= signal box)* Häuschen *nt*; *(= hunting box)* (Jagd)hütte *f*

f *(= horse box)* Box *f*

g *(Brit: = pillar box)* (Brief)kasten *m*

h *(Brit: = phone box)* Zelle *f*

i *(esp Brit inf: = TV)* Glotze *f (inf)*, Glotzkasten *m (inf)*; **what's on the ~?** was gibts im Fernsehen?; **I was watching the ~** ich habe geglotzt *(inf)*

j *(Brit, = gift of money)* Geldgeschenk *nt*

k *(on stagecoach)* (Kutsch)bock *m*

VT **a** *goods etc* (in eine(r) Schachtel *etc*) verpacken

b to ~ the compass *(Naut)* alle Kompasspunkte der Reihe nach aufzählen

▶ **box in** VT *sep* **a** *player* in die Zange nehmen; *parked car* einklemmen; *(fig)* einengen, keinen *or* zu wenig Spielraum lassen *(+dat)* **b** *bath etc* verkleiden; *(with wood also)* verschalen

▶ **box off** VT *sep* abteilen, abtrennen

▶ **box up** VT *sep* **a** *(= confine)* einsperren **b** *(= put in boxes)* (in Kartons) einpacken

box: **box bed** N Klappbett *nt*; **box calf** N Boxkalf *nt*; **box camera** N Box *f*; **boxcar** N *(US Rail)* (geschlossener) Güterwagen

boxer [ˈbɒksəʳ] N **a** *(Sport)* Boxer *m* **b** *(= dog)* Boxer *m*

boxer shorts PL Boxershorts *pl*

box: **box file** N Flachordner *m*; **box girder** N Kastenträger *m*; **box hedge** N streng geschnittene Hecke

boxing [ˈbɒksɪŋ] N Boxen *nt*

boxing *in cpds* Box-; **Boxing Day** N *(Brit)* zweiter Weihnachts(feier)tag; **boxing match** N Boxkampf *m*; **boxing ring** N Boxring *m*

> **BOXING DAY**
>
> Der **Boxing Day** ist in Großbritannien der zweite Weihnachtsfeiertag. Traditionellerweise finden an diesem Tag auch eine ganze Reihe sportlicher Veranstaltungen statt. Der Name geht auf einen Brauch aus dem 19. Jahrhundert zurück, als Händler und Lieferanten an diesem Tag ein Trinkgeld oder ein Weihnachtsgeschenk, die sogenannte **Christmas box**, erhielten.

box: **box junction** N *(Mot)* gelb schraffierte Kreuzung *(in die bei Stau nicht eingefahren werden darf)*; **box kite** N Kastendrachen *m*; **box lunch** N *(US)* Lunchpaket *nt*; **box number** N Chiffre *f*; *(at post office)* Postfach *nt*; **box office** N Kasse *f*, Theater-/Kinokasse *f*; **to be good ~** ein Kassenschlager sein ATTR **~ success/hit/attraction** Kassenschlager *m*; **box pleat** N Kellerfalte *f*; **boxroom** N *(Brit)* Abstellraum *m*; **box seat** N *(Theat)* Logenplatz *m*; **to be in the ~** *(Austral)* in der besten Position sein; **box spanner** N Steckschlüssel *m*; **box tree** N Buchsbaum *m*; **boxwood** N Buchsbaum(holz *nt*) *m*

boxy [ˈbɒksɪ] ADJ *(usu pej) building, car* kastenförmig

boy [bɔɪ] N **a** *(= male child)* Junge *m*, Bub *m (dial)*; **bad** *or* **naughty ~!** du frecher Bengel; *(to animal)* böser Hund! *etc*; **sit, ~!** *(to dog)* sitz!; **the Jones ~** der Junge von Jones; **~s will be ~s** Jungen sind nun mal so; **a school for ~s** eine Jungenschule; **good morning, ~s** guten Morgen(, Jungs)! → **old boy**

b *(inf: = fellow)* Knabe *m (inf)*; **the old ~** *(= boss)* der Alte *(inf)*; *(= father)* mein *etc* alter Herr

c *(= friend)* **the ~s** meine/seine Kumpels; **our ~s** *(= team)* unsere Jungs; **jobs for the ~s** Vetternwirtschaft *f*

d *(= native servant, liftboy)* Boy *m*; *(= messenger boy, ship's boy)* Junge *m*; *(= butcher's etc boy)* (Lauf)junge *m*; *(= pageboy)* (Hotel)boy *m*; *(= stable boy)* Stalljunge *or (older)* -bursche *m*

e oh ~! *(inf)* Junge, Junge! *(inf)*

boy band N *(Mus)* Boygroup *f*

boycott [ˈbɔɪkɒt] N Boykott *m*; **to impose a ~ on sth** einen Boykott über etw *(acc)* verhängen VT boykottieren

boy: **boyfriend** N Freund *m*; **boyhood** N Kindheit *f*; *(as teenager)* Jugend(zeit) *f*

boyish [ˈbɔɪɪʃ] ADJ jungenhaft; *woman* knabenhaft

boyishly [ˈbɔɪɪʃlɪ] ADV jungenhaft

boyo [ˈbɔɪəʊ] INTERJ *(Welsh)* Junge *m*

Boys' Brigade N *Jugendorganisation*, ≈ Junge Pioniere *pl (Hist DDR)*

boy: **boy scout** N Pfadfinder *m*; **Boy Scouts** N *sing* Pfadfinder *pl*; **boy toy** N *(inf, pej)* **a** *(= woman)* *junge, sexuell anziehende Frau* **b** *(= man)* *junger, besonders für ältere Frauen attraktiver Mann*; **boy wonder** N *(inf)* Wunderkind *nt*, Wunderknabe *m*

bozo [ˈbəʊzəʊ] N *(US)* (primitiver) Kerl *(inf)*

bpi *(Comput) abbr of* **bits per inch** Bits pro Zoll

B-picture N → **B-movie**

bps *(Comput) abbr of* **bits per second** Bits pro Sekunde

BR *abbr of* **British Rail** *die britischen Eisenbahnen*

bra [brɑː] N *abbr of* **brassière** BH *m*

brace[1] [breɪs] N *pl* - *(= pair: of pheasants etc)* Paar *nt*

brace[2] N **a** *(Build)* Strebe *f* **b** *(= tool) (= wheel brace)* Radschlüssel *m*; *(to hold bit)* Bohrwinde *f*; **~ and bit** Bohrer *m* (mit Einsatz) **c** *(on teeth)* Klammer *f*, Spange *f*; *(Med)* Stützapparat *m* **d** *(Typ)* geschweifte Klammer, Akkolade *f* VT **a** *(= support)* (ab)stützen; *(horizontally)* verstreben; *(in vice etc)* verklammern **b** *(climate etc: = invigorate)* stärken, kräftigen VR sich bereithalten; *(fig)* sich wappnen *(geh)*, sich bereit machen; **to ~ oneself for sth** sich auf etw *(acc)* gefasst machen; **~ yourself, I've got bad news for you** mach dich auf eine schlechte Nachricht gefasst

bracelet [ˈbreɪslɪt] N Armband *nt*; *(= bangle)* Armreif(en) *m*; *(= ankle bracelet)* Fußreif(en) *m*; **~s** *(inf: = handcuffs)* Handschellen *pl*

bracer [ˈbreɪsəʳ] N **a** *(inf: = drink)* kleine Stärkung, Schnäpschen *nt* **b** *(Sport)* Armschutz *m*

braces[1] [ˈbreɪsɪz] PL *(Brit)* Hosenträger *pl*; **a pair of ~** (ein Paar) Hosenträger

braces[2] [ˈbreɪsɪz] PL *(Typ)* geschweifte Klammern *pl*

bracing [ˈbreɪsɪŋ] ADJ belebend, anregend; *climate* Reiz-

bracken [ˈbrækən] N Adlerfarn *m*

bracket [ˈbrækɪt] N **a** *(= angle bracket)* Winkelträger *m*; *(for shelf)* (Regal)träger *m*; *(Archit)* Konsole *f*; *(of stone)* Kragstein *m*

b *(Typ, Mus)* Klammer *f*; **round/square/angle** *or* **pointed** *or* **broken ~s** runde/eckige/spitze Klammern *pl*; **open/close ~s** Klammer auf/zu; **in ~s** in Klammern

c *(= gas bracket)* Anschluss *m*; *(for electric light)* (Wand)arm *m*

d *(= group)* Gruppe *f*, Klasse *f*; **the lower income ~** die untere Einkommensgruppe

VT **a** *(= put in brackets)* einklammern

b *(also* **bracket together**, *= join by brackets)* mit einer Klammer verbinden; *(Mus also)* mit einer Akkolade verbinden; *(fig: = group together)* zusammenfassen

brackish [ˈbrækɪʃ] ADJ *water* brackig

bract [brækt] N Tragblatt *nt*

brad [bræd] N Stift *m*

bradawl [ˈbrædɔːl] N Ahle *f*, Pfriem *m*

brae [breɪ] N *(Scot)* Berg *m*

brag [bræg] VI prahlen, angeben (*about, of* mit) VT prahlen; **to ~ that** prahlen, dass, damit angeben, dass N **a** *(= boast)* Prahlerei *f*, Angeberei *f* **b** *(inf)* = **braggart**

braggart [ˈbrægət] N Prahler *m*, Angeber *m*

bragging [ˈbrægɪŋ] N Prahlerei *f*, Angeberei *f*

braid [breɪd] N **a** *(of hair)* Flechte *f (geh)*, Zopf *m* **b** *(= trimming)* Borte *f*; *(self-coloured)* Litze *f* **c** *(Mil)* Tressen *pl*; **gold ~** Goldtressen *pl* **d** *(to tie hair)* (Haar)band *nt* VT **a** *(= plait) hair, straw etc* flechten **b** *(= trim)* mit einer Borte besetzen **c** *(= tie up with braid) hair* binden

Braille [breɪl] N Blinden- *or* Brailleschrift *f* ADJ Blindenschrift-; **~ library** Blindenbücherei *f*; **~ books** Bücher *pl* in Blindenschrift

brain [breɪn] N **a** *(Anat, of machine)* Gehirn *nt*; **he's got sex/cars on the ~** *(inf)* er hat nur Sex/Autos im Kopf; **I've got that tune on the ~** *(inf)* das Lied geht *or* will mir nicht aus dem Kopf

b brains PL *(Anat)* Gehirn *nt*; *(Cook)* Hirn *nt*

c *(= mind)* Verstand *m*; **~s** *pl (= intelligence)* Intelligenz *f*, Grips *m (inf)*, Köpfchen *nt (inf)*; **to have a good ~** einen klaren *or* guten Verstand haben; **he has ~s** er ist intelligent, er hat Grips *(inf) or* Köpfchen *(inf)*; **she's the ~s of the family** sie ist das Familiengenie *(hum)*, sie ist die Schlauste in der Familie; **you're the one with the ~s** du bist doch der Schlaue *or* Intelligente hier; **use your ~s** streng mal deinen Kopf *or* Grips *(inf)* an; **he didn't have the ~s to …** er ist nicht einmal daraufgekommen, zu … VT den Schädel einschlagen (*sb* jdm)

brain: **brain activity** N (Ge)hirntätigkeit *f*; **brainbox** N *(hum inf)* Schlauberger *m (inf)*; **brainchild** N Erfindung *f*; *(= idea)* Geistesprodukt *nt*; **brain damage** N (Ge)hirnschaden *m*; **brain-damaged** ADJ *(lit)* hirngeschädigt; *(fig inf)* (ge)hirnamputiert *(hum inf)*; **brain-dead** ADJ *(lit)* (ge)hirntot; *(fig inf)* gehirnamputiert; *(inf)*; **brain death** N (Ge)hirntod *m*; **brain drain** N Abwanderung *f* von Wissenschaftlern, Braindrain *m*; **brainfag** N geistige Erschöpfung; **brain failure** N *(inf)* Aussetzer *m (inf)*; **brain fart** N *(inf)* Gedankenfurz *m*; **brain fever** N Hirnhautentzündung *f*; **brain fog** N *(inf)* Gehirnnebel *m (inf)*, *eingeschränkte geistige Leistungsfähigkeit*; **brain gain** N Brain Gain *m or nt*, *Gewinn ausländischer Spitzenforscher und -manager*; **brain haemorrhage**, **brain hemorrhage** *(US)* N (Ge)hirnblutung *f*; **brainless** ADJ *plan, idea* hirnlos, dumm; *person also* unbedarft; **brainpower** N Intelligenz *f*; **brain scan** N Computertomografie *f* des Schädels; **brain scanner** N Computertomograf *m (zur Untersuchung des Gehirns)*; **brainstorm** N a *(Brit)* **to have a ~** geistig weggetreten sein *(inf)* b *(US: = brainwave)* Geistesblitz *m* VI ein Brainstorming machen VT gemeinsam erarbeiten; **brainstorming** N gemeinsame Problembewältigung, Brainstorming *nt*; **to have a ~ session** ein Brainstorming veranstalten *or* abhalten

brains trust N *(= discussion)* Podiumsdiskussion *f*; *(= panel)* Gruppe *f* von Sachverständigen *or* Experten

brain: **brain surgeon** N Neurochirurg(in) *m(f)*, Hirnchirurg(in) *m(f)*; **brain-teaser** N Denksportaufgabe *f*; **brain trust** N *(US)* Braintrust *m*, Expertenausschuss *m*; **brain tumour**, *(US)* **brain tumor** N Gehirntumor *m*; **brainwash** VT einer Gehirnwäsche *(dat)* unterziehen; **to ~ sb into believing/accepting** *etc* **that …** jdm (ständig) einreden, dass …; **brainwashing** N Gehirnwäsche *f*; **brainwave** N a *(Brit)* Geistesblitz *m* b **brainwaves** PL *(Physiol)* Gehirnströme *pl*; **brainwork** N Kopfarbeit *f*

brainy [ˈbreɪnɪ] ADJ *(+er) (inf)* gescheit, helle *(inf)*

braise [breɪz] VT *(Cook)* schmoren

brake[1] [breɪk] N *(Tech)* Bremse *f*; **to put the ~s on** *(lit, fig)* bremsen; **to put the ~s on sth** *(fig)* etw bremsen; **to act as a ~** *(lit)* als Bremse wirken *(on* auf *+acc)*; *(fig)* dämpfend wirken *(on* auf *+acc)*, bremsen *(on +acc)* VI bremsen

brake[2] N *(Bot)* (Adler)farn *m*

brake[3] N *(= thicket)* Unterholz *nt*

brake[4] N *(= shooting brake)* Kombi(wagen) *m*

brake *in cpds* Brems-; **brake block** N Bremsbacke *f*; **brake disc** N Bremsscheibe *f*; **brake drum** N Bremstrommel *f*; **brake fluid** N Bremsflüssigkeit *f*; **brake horsepower** N Bremsleistung *f*; **brake light** N Bremslicht *nt*; **brake lining** N Bremsbelag *m*; **brakeman** N *(US Rail)* Bremser *m*; **brake pad** N Bremsklotz *m*; **brake shoe** N Bremsbacke *f*; **brake van** N Bremswagen *m*

braking [ˈbreɪkɪŋ] N Bremsen *nt*

braking: **braking distance** N Bremsweg *m*; **braking power** N Bremskraft *f*

bramble [ˈbræmbl] N a *(= thorny shoot)* dorniger Zweig, Dornenzweig *m* b *(= blackberry)* Brombeere *f*; *(= bush also)* Brombeerstrauch *m*; **~ jam** Brombeermarmelade *f*

bran [bræn] N Kleie *f*

branch [brɑːntʃ] N a *(Bot)* Zweig *m*; *(growing straight from trunk)* Ast *m* b *(of river, pipe, duct)* Arm *m*; *(of road)* Abzweigung *f*; *(of family, race, language)* Zweig *m*; *(of railway)* Abzweig *m*; *(of antler)* Sprosse *f*, Ende *nt* c *(in river, road, railway, pipe, duct)* Gabelung *f* d *(Comm)* Filiale *f*, Zweigstelle *f*; *(of company, bank also)* Geschäftsstelle *f*; **main ~** Haupt(geschäfts)stelle *f*; *(of store)* Hauptgeschäft *nt*; *(of bank)* Hauptgeschäftsstelle *f*, Zentrale *f* e *(= field: of subject etc)* Zweig *m* VI *(= divide, river, road etc)* sich gabeln; *(in more than two)* sich verzweigen

▶ **branch off** VI *(road)* abzweigen; *(driver)* abbiegen

▶ **branch out** VI *(fig, person, company)* sein Geschäft erweitern *or* ausdehnen *(into* auf *+acc)*; **the firm is branching out into cosmetics** die Firma erweitert ihren (Geschäfts)bereich jetzt auf Kosmetika; **to branch out on one's own** sich selbstständig machen

branch: **branch line** N *(Rail)* Zweiglinie *f*, Nebenlinie *f*; **branch manager** N Filialleiter *m*; **branch office** N Filiale *f*, Zweigstelle *f*; **branch road** N *(US)* Nebenstraße *f*

brand [brænd] N a *(= make)* Marke *f* b *(= mark, on cattle)* Brandzeichen *nt*; *(on criminal, prisoner, fig)* Brandmal *nt* c → **branding iron** d *(obs, poet, = sword)* Klinge *f (liter)* VT a *goods* mit seinem Warenzeichen versehen; **~ed goods** Markenartikel *pl*; **~ed company** Markenartikler *m* b *cattle, property* mit einem Brandzeichen kennzeichnen c *(= stigmatize) person* brandmarken

brand: **brand awareness** N Markenbewusstsein *nt*; **brand image** N Markenimage *nt*

branding iron [ˈbrændɪŋˌaɪən] N Brandeisen *nt*

brandish [ˈbrændɪʃ] VT schwingen, fuchteln mit *(inf)*

brand: **brand leader** N führende Marke; **brand loyalty** N Markentreue *f*; **brand manager** N Brandmanager(in) *m(f)*, Markenbetreuer(in) *m(f)*; **brand name** N Markenname *m*; **brand-new** ADJ nagelneu, brandneu *(inf)*

brandy [ˈbrændɪ] N Weinbrand *m*, Brandy *m*

brandy: **brandy butter** N Weinbrandbutter *f*; **brandysnap** N *Gebäckröllchen aus dünnem, mit Ingwer gewürztem Teig*

brash [bræʃ] ADJ *(+er)* nassforsch, dreist; *(= tasteless) colour etc* laut, aufdringlich

brashly [ˈbræʃlɪ] ADV dreist

brashness [ˈbræʃnɪs] N nassforsche Art, Dreistigkeit *f*; *(of colour etc)* Aufdringlichkeit *f*

brasier N = **brazier**

brass [brɑːs] N a Messing *nt* b **the ~** *(Mus)* die Blechbläser *pl*, das Blech *(inf)* c *(= thing made of brass) (= plaque)* Messingtafel *f or* -schild *nt*; *(in church: on tomb)* Grabplatte *f* aus Messing; *(no pl: = brass articles)* Messing *nt*; **to do** *or* **clean the ~(es)** das Messing putzen d *(inf)* **the top ~** die hohen Tiere *(inf)* e *(inf, = impudence)* Frechheit *f* f *(inf: = money)* Kohle *f (inf)* ADJ *(= made of brass)* Messing-, messingen *(rare)*; *(Mus)* Blech-; **~ instrument** Blechblasinstrument *nt*; **~ player** Blechbläser *m*; **~ section** Blech(bläser *pl*) *nt*

brass band N Blaskapelle *f*

brassed off [ˌbrɑːstˈɒf] ADJ **to be ~** *(Brit sl)* die Schnauze voll haben *(inf) (with* von)

brass: **brass farthing** N **he hasn't got a ~** *(Brit inf)* er besitzt keinen Cent; **not to get a ~** *(Brit inf)* keinen Cent bekommen; **it doesn't matter a ~** *(Brit inf)* es ist völlig egal; **brass foundry** N Messinggießerei *f*; **brass hat** N *(Brit Mil sl)* hohes Tier *(inf)*

brassière [ˈbræsɪəˈ] N *(dated, form)* Büstenhalter *m*

brass: **brass knuckles** PL *(inf)* Schlagring *m*; **brass monkey** N **it's cold enough to freeze the balls off a ~** *(Brit hum sl)* es ist arschkalt *(sl)*; **real ~ weather, eh?** *(Brit hum inf)* arschkalt, was? *(sl)*; **brass neck** N **to have a ~** Nerven haben *(inf)*; **brass plaque**, **brass plate** N Messingschild *nt*; *(in church)* Messinggedenktafel *f*; **brass rubbing** N *(= activity)* Durchpausen *or* -zeichnen *nt (des Bildes auf einer Messinggrabtafel)*; *(= result)* Pauszeichnung *f (des Bildes auf einer Messinggrabtafel)*; **brass tacks** PL **to get down to ~** *(inf)* zur Sache kommen

brassy [ˈbrɑːsɪ] ADJ *(+er)* a *metal* messingartig; *hair, blonde* messingfarben; *sound* blechern b *(inf, = impudent)* frech, dreist c *(pej: = flashy) woman* aufgedonnert *(pej inf)*

brat [bræt] N *(pej inf)* Balg *m or nt (inf)*, Gör *nt (inf)*; *(esp girl)* Göre *f (inf)*; **a spoiled ~** eine verzogene Göre *(inf)*

bravado [brəˈvɑːdəʊ] N *(= showy bravery)* Draufgängertum *nt*, Wagemut *m*; *(hiding fear)* gespielte Tapferkeit; **this is just military ~** da lässt das Militär die Muskeln spielen

brave [breɪv] ADJ a *(+er) person, act* mutig, unerschrocken *(geh)*; *(= showing courage, suffering pain)* tapfer; *attack* mutig; *smile* tapfer; **be ~!** nur Mut!; *(more seriously)* sei tapfer! b *(obs, liter, = fine)* schmuck *(dated)*, ansehnlich; **~ new world** schöne neue Welt N *(= American Indian warrior)* Krieger *m* VT die Stirn bieten *(+dat)*; *weather, elements* trotzen *(+dat)*; *death* tapfer ins Auge sehen *(+dat)*

▶ **brave out** VT *sep* **to brave it out** es *or* das durchstehen

bravely [ˈbreɪvlɪ] ADV tapfer

braveness [ˈbreɪvnɪs], **bravery** [ˈbreɪvərɪ] N *(of person, act)* Mut *m*; *(of attempt, smile)* Tapferkeit *f*

bravo [brɑːˈvəʊ] INTERJ bravo! N *pl* **-es** Bravoruf *m*

bravura [brəˈvʊərə] N Bravour *f*; *(Mus)* Bravourstück *nt*

brawl [brɔːl] VI sich schlagen N Schlägerei *f*

brawling [ˈbrɔːlɪŋ] N Schlägereien *pl*

brawn [brɔːn] N a *(Cook)* Presskopf *m*, Sülze *f* b Muskeln *pl*, Muskelkraft *f*; **to have plenty of ~** starke Muskeln haben, ein Muskelpaket *or* Muskelprotz sein *(inf)*; **he's all ~ and no brains** (er hat) Muskeln, aber kein Gehirn

brawny [ˈbrɔːnɪ] ADJ *(+er)* muskulös, kräftig

bray [breɪ] N *(of ass)* (Esels)schrei *m*; *(inf, = laugh)* Wiehern *nt*, Gewieher *nt* VI *(ass)* schreien; *(inf, person)* wiehern

brazen [ˈbreɪzn] ADJ a *(= impudent)* unverschämt, dreist; *lie* schamlos; **to be ~ about sth** klar zu etw stehen; **to be ~ about doing sth** etw ganz dreist tun b *(obs, = of brass)* messingen *(rare)*

▶ **brazen out** VT *sep* **to brazen it out** durchhalten; *(by lying)* sich durchmogeln *(inf)*

brazen-faced [ˈbreɪznˌfeɪst] ADJ schamlos, unverschämt

brazenly [ˈbreɪznlɪ] ADV unverschämt, dreist; *lie* schamlos

brazenness [ˈbreɪznnɪs] N Unverschämtheit *f*, Dreistigkeit *f*; *(of lie)* Schamlosigkeit *f*

brazier [ˈbreɪzɪəˈ] N (Kohlen)feuer *nt* (im Freien); *(= container)* Kohlenbecken *nt*

Brazil [brəˈzɪl] N Brasilien *nt*

brazil [brəˈzɪl] N *(also* **brazil nut**) Paranuss *f*

Brazilian [brəˈzɪlɪən] N Brasilianer(in) *m(f)* ADJ brasilianisch

breach [briːtʃ] N a Verletzung *f (of +gen)*, Verstoß *m* (of gegen); *(of law)* Übertretung *f (of +gen)*, Verstoß *m*; **a ~ of confidence/contract/faith** ein Vertrauens-/Vertrags-/Vertrauensbruch *m*; **a ~ of law** ein Rechtsbruch *m*; **a ~ of rule** eine Regelwidrigkeit *f*; *(Sport)* eine Regelverletzung *f*; **a ~ of security** ein Verstoß *m* gegen die Sicherheitsbestimmungen; **~ of the peace** *(Jur)* öffentliche Ruhestörung; **~ of privilege** Privilegienmissbrauch *m*; **~ of promise** *(Jur)* Bruch *m* des Eheversprechens b *(= estrangement: in friendship etc)* Bruch *m* c *(= gap, in wall etc)* Bresche *f*, Lücke *f*; *(in security)* Lücke *f*; **to make a ~ in the enemy's lines** *(Mil)* eine Bresche in die feindlichen Linien schlagen; **to step into the ~** *(fig)* in die Bresche springen VT a *wall* eine Bresche schlagen in *(+acc)*; *defences, security* durchbrechen b *contract, treaty* verletzen

bread [bred] N a Brot *nt*; **a piece of ~ and butter** ein Butterbrot *nt*; **we just had ~ and butter** wir aßen nur Brot mit Butter; **he was put on (dry) ~ and water** er saß bei Wasser und

(trocken) Brot; **he knows which side his ~ is buttered (on)** er weiß, wo was zu holen ist; **~ and circuses** Brot und Spiele *pl*
b *(= food, livelihood)* **writing is his ~ and butter** er verdient sich seinen Lebensunterhalt mit Schreiben; **to take the ~ out of sb's mouth** *(fig)* jdn seiner Existenzgrundlage *(gen)* berauben; **to break ~ with sb** *(old)* sein Brot mit jdm teilen, das Brot mit jdm brechen *(old)*
c *(inf: = money)* Kohle *f (inf)*
VT panieren

bread: **bread-and-butter letter**, **bread-and-butter note** N Bedankemichbrief *m*; **bread-and-butter pudding** N Brotauflauf *m*; **breadbasket** N **a** Brotkorb *m* **b** *(inf)* Wampe *f (inf)*; **breadbin** N *(Brit)* Brotkasten *m*; **breadboard** N Brot(schneide)brett *nt*; **breadbox** N *(US)* = **breadbin**; **breadcrumb** N Brotkrume *f or* -krümel *m*; **breadcrumbs** PL *(Cook)* Paniermehl *nt*; **in ~** paniert; **breadfruit** N Brotfrucht *f*; **breadknife** N Brotmesser *nt*; **breadline** N *Schlange vor einer Nahrungsmittelausgabestelle* **to be on the ~** *(fig)* nur das Allernotwendigste zum Leben haben; **bread roll** N Brötchen *nt*; **bread sauce** N Brottunke *f*; **breadstick** N Knabberstange *f*

breadth [bretθ] N Breite *f*; *(of ideas, theory)* (Band)breite *f*; **a hundred metres** *(Brit) or* **meters** *(US)* **in ~** hundert Meter breit; **his ~ of outlook** *(= open-mindedness)* seine große Aufgeschlossenheit; *(= variety of interests)* seine große Vielseitigkeit; **the ~ of his comprehension** sein umfassendes Verständnis

breadthways [ˈbretθweɪz], **breadthwise** [ˈbretθwaɪz] ADV in der Breite, der Breite nach

breadwinner [ˈbredwɪnəʳ] N Ernährer(in) *m(f)*, Brotverdiener(in) *m(f)*

break [breɪk]
vb: pret **broke**, *ptp* **broken**

1 NOUN	3 INTRANSITIVE VERB
2 TRANSITIVE VERB	4 PHRASAL VERBS

1 – NOUN

a = fracture *in bone, pipe* Bruch *m*; *(Gram, Typ: = word break)* (Silben)trennung *f*; **... he said with a break in his voice** ... sagte er mit stockender Stimme; **break in the circuit** *(Elec)* Stromkreisunterbrechung *f*
b = gap Lücke *f*; *(in rock)* Spalte *f*, Riss *m*; *(in drawn line)* Unterbrechung *f*; **row upon row of houses without a break** Häuserzeile auf Häuserzeile, ohne Lücke *or* lückenlos
c = pause *also Brit Sch* Pause *f*; *(in journey)* Pause *f*, Unterbrechung *f*; **without a break** ohne Unterbrechung *or* Pause, ununterbrochen; **to take** *or* **have a break** (eine) Pause machen; **at break** *(Sch)* in der Pause; **after the break** *(Rad, TV)* nach der Pause; **give me a break!** *(inf, expressing annoyance)* nun mach mal halblang! *(inf)*
d = end of relations Bruch *m*
e = change Abwechslung *f*; **break in the weather** Wetterumschwung *m*
f = respite Erholung *f*; **the playgroup gives parents a break** die Spielgruppe verschafft den Eltern etwas Erholung
g = holiday Urlaub *m*; **I'm looking forward to a good break** ich freue mich auf einen schönen Urlaub
h **at break of day** bei Tagesanbruch
i = escape *inf* Ausbruch *m*; **they made a break for it** sie versuchten zu entkommen
j = opportunity *inf* **to have a good/bad break** Glück *or* Schwein *(inf) nt*/Pech *nt* haben; **we had a few lucky breaks** wir haben ein paar Mal Glück *or* Schwein *(inf)* gehabt; **she had her first big break in a Broadway play** sie bekam ihre erste große Chance in einem Broadwaystück
k Billiards Break *nt or m*, Serie *f*

2 – TRANSITIVE VERB

a in pieces = *fracture bone* sich *(dat)* brechen; *stick* zerbrechen; *(= smash)* kaputt schlagen, kaputt machen; *glass, cup* zerbrechen; *window* einschlagen; *egg* aufbrechen; **to break sth from sth** etw von etw abbrechen; **to break one's leg** sich *(dat)* das Bein brechen; **break a leg!** *(US: inf)* Hals- und Beinbruch! → **heart**
b = make unusable *toy, chair* kaputt machen
c = violate *promise, treaty, vow* brechen; *law, rule, commandment* verletzen; *appointment* nicht einhalten; **to break bail** die Haftverschonung brechen
d = interrupt *journey, silence, fast* unterbrechen; *spell* brechen; *monotony, routine* unterbrechen, auflockern; **to break a holiday short** *(Brit)* einen Urlaub abbrechen
♦ **to break + habit to break a habit** mit einer Gewohnheit brechen, sich *(dat)* etw abgewöhnen; **he couldn't break the habit of smoking** er konnte sich das Rauchen nicht abgewöhnen; **to break sb of a habit** jdm etw abgewöhnen
e = penetrate *skin* ritzen; *surface, shell* durchbrechen; **his skin is bruised but not broken** seine Haut ist zwar abgeschürft, aber nicht aufgeplatzt; **to break surface** *(submarine, fig)* auftauchen
f = surpass *record* brechen; *sound barrier* durchbrechen
g = open up → **ground**
h = tame *horse* zureiten; *person* brechen
i = destroy *person* kleinkriegen *(inf)*, mürbemachen; *resistance, strike* brechen; *code* entziffern; *(Tennis) serve* durchbrechen; **his spirit was broken by the spell in solitary confinement** die Zeit in Einzelhaft hatte ihn seelisch gebrochen; **this betrayal nearly broke him** dieser Verrat hätte ihn fast zum Wahnsinn getrieben; **to break sb (financially)** jdn ruinieren, jdn bankrott machen; **to break the bank** *(Gambling)* die Bank sprengen; **37p, well that won't exactly break the bank** 37 Pence, na, davon gehe ich/gehen wir noch nicht bankrott; **his service was broken** *(Tennis)* er hat das Aufschlagspiel abgegeben
j = soften *fall* dämpfen, abfangen; **the wall breaks the force of the wind** der Wind bricht sich an der Mauer
k = get out of *jail, one's bonds* ausbrechen aus; **to break step** *(Mil)* aus dem Schritt fallen → **camp, cover, rank**
l = disclose *news* mitteilen; **how can I break it to her?** wie soll ich es ihr sagen?

3 – INTRANSITIVE VERB

a in pieces = *snap, twig, bone* brechen; *(rope)* zerreißen; (= *smash, window)* kaputtgehen; *(cup, glass)* zerbrechen; **breaking strain** Belastbarkeit *f*
b = become useless *watch, toy, chair* kaputtgehen
c = become detached **to break from sth** von etw abbrechen
d = pause (eine) Pause machen, unterbrechen; **to break for lunch** Mittagspause machen
e = change *weather, luck* umschlagen
f = disperse *clouds* aufreißen; *(crowd)* sich teilen
g = give way, *health* leiden, Schaden nehmen; *(stamina)* gebrochen werden; *under interrogation etc* zusammenbrechen; **his spirit broke** sein Mut verließ ihn
h wave sich brechen
i day, dawn anbrechen; *(suddenly: storm)* losbrechen
j voice *with emotion* brechen; **his voice is beginning to break** *(boy)* er kommt in den Stimmbruch
k = become known *story, news, scandal* bekannt werden, an den Tag *or* ans Licht kommen; **the news broke on Wall Street yesterday** gestern platzte diese Nachricht in der Wall Street
l = escape *from jail* ausbrechen *(from* aus) → **loose**
m company **to break even** seine (Un)kosten decken
n Billiards anstoßen
o ball **to break to the right/left** nach rechts/links wegspringen
p = let go *(Boxing etc)* sich trennen; **break!** break!
q = end relations brechen

4 – PHRASAL VERBS

▸ **break away** VI **a** *(chair leg, handle etc)* abbrechen *(from* von); *(railway coaches, boats)* sich losreißen *(from* von) **b** *(= dash away)* weglaufen *(from* von); *(prisoner)* sich losreißen *(from* von); *(Ftbl)* sich absetzen; **he broke away from the rest of the field** er hängte das ganze Feld ab **c** *(= cut ties)* sich trennen *or* lossagen *(from* von); *(US Sport: = start too soon)* fehlstarten, zu früh starten; **to break away from a group** sich von einer Gruppe trennen; **to break away from the everyday routine** aus der täglichen Routine ausbrechen VT *sep* abbrechen *(from* von)

▸ **break down** VI **a** *(vehicle)* eine Panne haben; *(machine)* versagen
b *(= fail, negotiations, plan, marriage)* scheitern; *(communications, law and order, theory)* zusammenbrechen
c *(= give way: resistance)* zusammenbrechen
d *(= start crying, have a breakdown)* zusammenbrechen
e *(= be analysed, expenditure)* sich aufschlüsseln *or* -gliedern; *(theory)* sich unter- *or* aufgliedern (lassen); *(Chem: substance)* sich zerlegen (lassen); *(= change its composition: substance)* sich aufspalten *(into* in +*acc)*
VT *sep* **a** *(= smash down) door* einrennen; *wall* niederreißen
b *(= overcome) opposition* brechen; *hostility, reserve, shyness, suspicion* überwinden
c *(to constituent parts) expenditure* aufschlüsseln, aufgliedern; *argument* auf- *or* untergliedern, aufspalten; *(= change composition of)* umsetzen

▸ **break forth** VI *(liter, light, water)* hervorbrechen; *(storm)* losbrechen

▸ **break in** VI **a** *(= interrupt)* unterbrechen *(on sb/sth* jdn/etw) **b** *(= enter illegally)* einbrechen
VT *sep* **a** *door* aufbrechen **b** *shoes* einlaufen

▸ **break into** VI +*prep obj* **a** *house* einbrechen in (+*acc)*; *safe, car* aufbrechen; **his house has been broken into** bei ihm ist eingebrochen worden; **his car has been broken into** sein Auto ist aufgebrochen worden **b** *(= use part of) savings, £20 note, rations* anbrechen **c** *(= begin suddenly)* **to break into song/a run/a trot** zu singen/laufen/traben anfangen, in Laufschritt/Trab (ver)fallen; **to break into a smile** zu lächeln beginnen **d** *(professionally)* **she finally broke into films** schließlich machte sie sich einen Namen beim Film

▸ **break off** VI **a** *(branch, piece)* abbrechen *(from* von) **b** *(= stop)* abbrechen, aufhören; *(= stop speaking)* abbrechen; *(temporarily)* unterbrechen; **to break off from work** die Arbeit abbrechen VT *sep* **a** *twig, piece of chocolate etc* abbrechen **b** *negotiations, relations* abbrechen; *engagement* lösen; **she's broken it off** sie hat die Verlobung gelöst

▸ **break open** VI aufspringen VT *sep* aufbrechen

▸ **break out** VI **a** *(epidemic, fire, war)* ausbrechen **b** **to break out in a rash/in spots** einen Ausschlag/Pickel bekommen; **he broke out in a sweat** er kam ins Schwitzen, ihm brach der Schweiß aus; **he broke out in a cold sweat** ihm brach der Angstschweiß aus **c** *(= escape)* ausbrechen *(from, of* aus) **d** *(= speak suddenly)* herausplatzen, losplatzen

▸ **break through** VI *(Mil, sun)* durchbrechen
VI +*prep obj defences, barrier, crowd* durchbrechen; **to break through sb's reserve** jdn aus der Reserve locken

▸ **break up** VI **a** *(road, ice)* aufbrechen; *(ship)* *(in storm)* zerbersten; *(on rocks)* zerschellen
b *(clouds)* sich lichten; *(crowd, group)* auseinanderlaufen; *(meeting, partnership)* sich auflösen; *(marriage, relationship)* in die Brüche gehen; *(party)* zum Ende kommen; *(political party)* sich auflösen, auseinandergehen; *(friends, partners)* sich trennen; *(empire)* auseinanderfallen; *(inf, with laughter)* sich totlachen *(inf)*; **to break**

up with sb sich von jdm trennen; **when did the party break up last night?** wie lange ging die Party gestern Abend?
c *(Brit Sch, school, pupils)* aufhören; **when do you break up?** wann hört bei euch die Schule auf?, wann habt ihr Ferien?
d *(on mobile phone)* **you're breaking up** ich kann Sie nicht verstehen
VT *sep* **a** *ground, road* aufbrechen; *oil slick* auflösen; *ship* auseinanderbrechen lassen; *(in breaker's yard)* abwracken
b *estate, country, room* aufteilen; *paragraph, sentence* unterteilen; *empire* auflösen; *lines, expanse of colour* unterbrechen; *(= make more interesting)* auflockern
c *(= bring to an end, disperse) marriage, home* zerstören; *meeting (police etc)* auflösen; *(troublemakers)* sprengen; *crowd (police)* zerstreuen, auseinandertreiben; **he broke up the fight** er trennte die Kämpfer; **break it up!** auseinander!

breakable [ˈbreɪkəbl] **ADJ** zerbrechlich **N** **breakables** **PL** zerbrechliche Ware

breakage [ˈbreɪkɪdʒ] **N** **a** *(in chain, link)* Bruch *m* **b** *(of glass, china)* Bruch *m*; **to pay for ~s** für zerbrochene Ware *or* Bruch bezahlen; **were there any ~s?** hat es Bruch gegeben?, ist irgendetwas kaputtgegangen *or* zu Bruch gegangen?

breakaway [ˈbreɪkəˌweɪ] **N** **a** *(Pol)* Abfall *m*; *(of state also)* Loslösung *f* **b** *(Sport)* Aus- *or* Durchbruch *m* **c** *(US Sport: = false start)* Fehlstart *m* **ADJ** *group* Splitter-

break: **breakbeat** **N** *(Mus)* Breakbeat *m*; **break command** **N** *(Comput)* Unterbrechungsbefehl *m*; **break dance** **VI** Breakdance tanzen; **break dancer** **N** Breakdancetänzer(in) *m(f)*; **break dancing** **N** Breakdance *m*

breakdown [ˈbreɪkdaʊn] **N** **a** *(of machine)* Betriebsschaden *m*; *(of vehicle)* Panne *f*, Motorschaden *m* **b** *(of communications, system)* Zusammenbruch *m* **c** *(Med, physical, mental)* Zusammenbruch *m* **d** *(of figures, expenditure etc)* Aufschlüsselung *f*; *(of thesis, theory etc)* Auf- *or* Untergliederung *f* **e** *(Chem)* Aufspaltung *f*; *(= change in composition)* Umsetzung *f*

breakdown: **breakdown service** **N** Pannendienst *m*; **breakdown truck**, **breakdown van** **N** Abschleppwagen *m*

breaker [ˈbreɪkəʳ] **N** **a** *(= wave)* Brecher *m* **b** *(also* **breaker's (yard)***)* **to send a ship/vehicle to the ~'s (yard)** ein Schiff/Fahrzeug abwracken

breaker box **N** *(US)* Sicherungskasten *m*

breakeven point [breɪkˈiːvənˌpɔɪnt] **N** Gewinnschwelle *f*, Break-even-Punkt *m (spec)*

breakfast [ˈbrekfəst] **N** Frühstück *nt*; **to have ~** frühstücken, Frühstück essen; **for ~** zum Frühstück **VI** frühstücken; **he ~ed on bacon and eggs** er frühstückte Eier mit Speck

breakfast *in cpds* Frühstücks-; **breakfast bar** **N** Frühstücksbar *f*; **breakfast cereal** **N** Cornflakes *pl*, Getreideflocken *pl*; **breakfast meeting** **N** Arbeitsfrühstück *nt*; **breakfast set** **N** Frühstücksservice *nt*; **breakfast television** **N** Frühstücksfernsehen *nt*; **breakfast time** **N** Frühstückszeit *f*

break-in [ˈbreɪkɪn] **N** Einbruch *m*; **we've had a ~** bei uns ist eingebrochen worden

breaking [ˈbreɪkɪŋ] **N** **~ and entering** *(Jur)* Einbruch *m*

breaking point **N** **a** *(Tech)* Festigkeitsgrenze *f* **b** *(fig)* **she is at** *or* **has reached ~** sie ist nervlich völlig am Ende (ihrer Kräfte)

break: **breakneck** **ADJ** **at ~ speed** *(Brit)* mit halsbrecherischer Geschwindigkeit; **break-out** **N** Ausbruch *m*; **break point** **N** *(Tennis)* Breakpunkt *m*; **breakthrough** **N** *(Mil, fig)* Durchbruch *m*; **break-up** **N** **a** *(lit, of ship)* Zerbersten *nt*; *(on rocks)* Zerschellen *nt*; *(of ice)* Bersten *nt* **b** *(fig, of friendship)* Bruch *m*; *(of marriage)* Zerrüttung *f*; *(of empire)* Zerfall *m*; *(of political party)* Zersplitterung *f*; *(of partnership, meeting)* Auflösung *f*; *(by trouble-makers)* Sprengung *f*; **break-up value** **N** *(Fin)* Liquidationswert *m*; **breakwater** **N** Wellenbrecher *m*

bream [briːm] **N** Brasse *f*, Brachsen *m*

breast [brest] **N** **a** *(= chest)* Brust *f*; *(Cook, of chicken, lamb)* Brust(stück *nt*) *f* **b** *(of woman)* Brust *f*; **a child/baby at the ~** ein Kind/Säugling an der Brust **c** *(fig liter)* Brust *f*, Busen *m (liter)* **VT** **a** **to ~ the waves/the storm** gegen die Wellen/den Sturm ankämpfen **b** **to ~ the tape** *(Sport)* durchs Ziel gehen

breast: **breast augmentation** **N** Brustvergrößerung *f*; **breastbone** [ˈbrestbəʊn] **N** Brustbein *nt*; *(of bird)* Brustknochen *m*; **breast cancer** **N** Brustkrebs *m*

-breasted [-ˈbrestɪd] **ADJ** *suf woman* -brüstig; **a double-/single-breasted jacket** ein Einreiher *m*/Zweireiher *m*

breast: **breast enlargement** **N** Brustvergrößerung *f*; **breast-fed** **ADJ** **to be ~** gestillt werden; **~ child** Brustkind *nt*; **breast-feed** **VTI** stillen; **breast-feeding** **N** Stillen *nt*; **breast milk** **N** Muttermilch *f*; **breastplate** **N** *(on armour)* Brustharnisch *m*; *(of high priest)* Brustplatte *f or* -gehänge *nt*; **breast pocket** **N** Brusttasche *f*; **breast reduction** **N** Brustverkleinerung *f*; **breaststroke** **N** Brustschwimmen *nt*; **to swim** *or* **do the ~** brustschwimmen; **breastwork** **N** *(Mil)* Brustwehr *f*

breath [breθ] **N** **a** Atem *m*; **to take a deep ~** einmal tief Luft holen; *(before diving, singing etc)* einmal tief einatmen; **bad** *or* **stinky** *(inf)* **~** Mundgeruch *m*; **to have bad ~** aus dem Mund riechen, Mundgeruch haben; **with one's dying ~** mit dem letzten Atemzug; **to draw one's last ~** *(liter)* seinen letzten Atemzug tun; **out of ~** außer Atem, atemlos; **short of ~** kurzatmig; **to stop for ~** sich verschnaufen, eine Pause zum Luftholen machen; **to get one's ~ back** wieder zu Atem kommen; **in the same ~** im selben Atemzug; **to say sth all in one ~** etw in einem Atemzug sagen; **to take sb's ~ away** jdm den Atem verschlagen; **to say sth under one's ~** etw vor sich *(acc)* hin murmeln; **save your ~** spar dir die Spucke *(inf)*; **you're wasting your ~** du redest umsonst → **fresh air**
b *(= slight stirring)* **~ of wind** Lüftchen *nt*; **there wasn't a ~ of air** es regte sich *or* wehte kein Lüftchen
c *(fig, = whisper)* Hauch *m*, Sterbenswörtchen *nt*

breathable [ˈbriːðəbl] **ADJ** *fabric, garment* atmungsaktiv

breathalyze [ˈbreθəlaɪz] **VT** blasen lassen; **he refused to be ~d** er weigerte sich, (ins Röhrchen) zu blasen

Breathalyzer® [ˈbreθəlaɪzəʳ] **N** Atem(luft)messgerät *nt*, Promillemesser *m (inf)*; **to blow into the ~** ins Röhrchen blasen

breathe [briːð] **VI** *(person, fabric, garment)* atmen; *(inf: = rest)* verschnaufen, Luft holen *or* schöpfen; *(liter, = live)* leben; **now we can ~ again** jetzt können wir wieder frei atmen; *(= have more space)* jetzt haben wir wieder Luft; **to ~ down sb's neck** jdm die Hölle heißmachen *(inf)*; **I don't want him breathing down my neck** ich will nicht, dass er mir die Hölle heißmacht *(inf)*; **red wine should be allowed to ~ before drinking** Rotwein muss atmen, bevor man ihn trinkt
VT **a** *air* einatmen; **to ~ one's last** seinen letzten Atemzug tun; **to ~ the air of one's own country again** wieder auf heimatlichem Boden sein *or* stehen
b *(= exhale)* atmen *(into* in *+acc)*; **he ~d alcohol all over me** er hatte eine solche Fahne; **he ~d garlic all over me** er verströmte einen solchen Knoblauchgeruch; **to ~ fire** Feuer spucken; **he ~d new life into the firm** er brachte neues Leben in die Firma
c *(= utter) prayer* flüstern, hauchen; **to ~ a sigh of relief** erleichtert aufatmen; **don't ~ a word of it!** sag kein Sterbenswörtchen darüber!

▶ **breathe in** **VI VT** *sep* einatmen

▶ **breathe out** **VI VT** *sep* ausatmen

breather [ˈbriːðəʳ] **N** *(= short rest)* Atempause *f*, Verschnaufpause *f*; **to give sb a ~** jdn verschnaufen lassen; **to take** *or* **have a ~** sich verschnaufen

breathing [ˈbriːðɪŋ] **N** *(= respiration)* Atmung *f*; **the child's peaceful ~** die ruhigen Atemzüge des Kindes

breathing: **breathing apparatus** **N** Sauerstoffgerät *nt*; **breathing mask** **N** Atemmaske *f*; **breathing space** **N** *(fig)* Atempause *f*, Ruhepause *f*

breathless [ˈbreθlɪs] **ADJ** atemlos; *(with exertion also)* außer Atem; **he said in a ~ voice** sagte er, nach Luft ringend; **he is rather ~** *(through illness)* er leidet an Atemnot; **~ with excitement/anticipation** ganz atemlos vor Aufregung/Spannung; **it left me ~** *(lit, fig)* es verschlug mir den Atem; **at a ~ pace** atemberaubend schnell

breathlessly [ˈbreθlɪslɪ] **ADV** atemlos; *(from exertion also)* außer Atem

breathlessness [ˈbreθlɪsnɪs] **N** *(due to exertion)* Atemlosigkeit *f*; *(due to illness)* Kurzatmigkeit *f*

breathtaking **ADJ**, **breathtakingly** **ADV** [ˈbreθteɪkɪŋ, -lɪ] atemberaubend

breath test **N** Atemalkoholtest *m*

breath testing **N** Atemalkoholkontrolle *f*

breathy [ˈbreθɪ] **ADJ** *(+er)* rauchig; *(through shyness)* hauchig

bred [bred] *pret, ptp of* **breed**

-bred **ADJ** *suf* -erzogen

breech[1] [briːtʃ] **N** *(of gun)* Verschluss *m*

breech[2] **ADJ** *attr (Med) birth, delivery* Steiß-; **~ presentation** Steißlage *f*; **to be a ~ baby** eine Steißlage sein

breeches [ˈbrɪtʃɪz] **PL** Kniehose *f*; *(= riding breeches)* Reithose *f*; *(for hiking)* (Knie)bundhose *f*

breeches buoy [ˈbriːtʃɪzbɔɪ] **N** Hosenboje *f*

breech-loader [ˈbriːtʃˌləʊdəʳ] **N** *(Mil)* Hinterlader *m*

breed [briːd] *vb: pret, ptp* **bred** **N** *(lit, fig: = species)* Art *f*, Sorte *f*; **they produced a new ~** sie haben eine neue Züchtung hervorgebracht; **a ~ apart** *(fig)* eine besondere *or* spezielle Sorte *or* Gattung **VT** **a** *(= raise, rear) animals, flowers* züchten → **born** **b** *(fig: = give rise to)* erzeugen; **dirt ~s disease** Schmutz verursacht Krankheit, Schmutz zieht Krankheit nach sich **VI** *(animals)* Junge haben; *(birds)* brüten; *(pej, hum, people)* sich vermehren

breeder [ˈbriːdəʳ] **N** **a** *(= person)* Züchter(in) *m(f)* **b** *(Phys: also* **breeder reactor***)* Brutreaktor *m*, Brüter *m*

breeding [ˈbriːdɪŋ] **N** **a** *(= reproduction)* Fortpflanzung *und* Aufzucht *f* der Jungen **b** *(= rearing)* Zucht *f* **c** *(= upbringing, good manners: also* **good breeding***)* gute Erziehung, Kinderstube *f*

breeding: **breeding ground**, **breeding place** **N** *(lit, fig)* Brutstätte *f*; **breeding season** **N** *(of birds)* Brutzeit *f*; *(of animal)* Zeit *f* der Fortpflanzung und Aufzucht der Jungen

breeze [briːz] **N** Brise *f*; **it's a ~** *(esp US inf)* das ist kinderleicht

▶ **breeze in** **VI** fröhlich angetrabt kommen *or* hereinschneien; **he breezed into the room** er kam fröhlich ins Zimmer geschneit

▶ **breeze out** **VI** vergnügt abziehen *(of* aus*)*

▶ **breeze through** **VI** *+prep obj (inf: = do easily)* spielend *or* mit Leichtigkeit schaffen

breeze: **breeze block** **N** *(Brit Build)* Ytong® *m*; **breezeway** **N** *(US)* überdachter Durchgang

breezily [ˈbriːzɪlɪ] **ADV** *(fig)* frisch-fröhlich

breeziness [ˈbriːzɪnɪs] **N** *(fig)* frisch-fröhliche Art

breezy [ˈbriːzɪ] **ADJ** *(+er)* **a** *weather, day* windig; *corner, spot also* luftig **b** *manner, person* frisch-fröhlich; *melody* locker-leicht

brekkie, **brekky** [ˈbrekɪ] **N** *(Austral inf)* Frühstück *nt*

Bren gun ['brengʌn] N *(Mil)* leichtes Maschinengewehr; ~ **carrier, Bren carrier** kleines leichtes Panzerfahrzeug

brer, br'er [brɛə'] N *(old)* Gevatter *m (old)*

brethren ['breðrɪn] PL *(obs, Eccl)* Brüder *pl*

Breton ['bretən] ADJ bretonisch N a Bretone *m*, Bretonin *f* b *(Ling)* Bretonisch *nt*

breve [bri:v] N *(Brit Mus)* Brevis *f*

breviary ['bri:vɪərɪ] N Brevier *nt*

brevity ['brevɪtɪ] N a *(= shortness)* Kürze *f* b *(= conciseness)* Kürze *f*, Bündigkeit *f*, Knappheit *f*; ~ **is the soul of wit** *(Prov)* in der Kürze liegt die Würze *(Prov)*

brew [bru:] N a *(= beer)* Bräu *nt*, Bier *nt* b *(of tea)* Tee *m*, Gebräu *nt (iro)*; *(of herbs)* Kräutermischung *f* → **witches' brew** VT a *beer, ale* brauen; *tea* aufbrühen, aufgießen, kochen b *(fig) scheme, mischief, plot* ausbrüten, aushecken; **to ~ a plot** ein Komplott schmieden VI a *(beer)* gären; *(tea)* ziehen b *(= make beer)* brauen c *(fig)* **there's trouble/a storm ~ing (up)** da braut sich ein Konflikt/ein Sturm zusammen; **there's something ~ing** da braut sich etwas zusammen

▶ **brew up** VI a *(inf: = make tea)* sich *(dat)* einen Tee machen b *(fig)* = **brew VI c**

brewer ['bru:ə'] N Brauer *m*

brewer's droop N *(Brit hum inf)* alkoholbedingte vorübergehende Impotenz; **to get ~** *(Brit hum inf)* alkoholbedingt keinen hochkriegen *(inf)*

brewer's yeast N Bierhefe *f*

brewery ['bru:ərɪ] N Brauerei *f*

brew-up ['bru:ʌp] N *(inf)* **to have a ~** Tee kochen

briar ['braɪə'] N a *(also* **briarwood**) Bruyère(-holz) *nt*; *(also* **briar pipe**) Bruyère(pfeife) *f* b = **brier a**

bribable ['braɪbəbl] ADJ bestechlich

bribe [braɪb] N Bestechung *f*; *(= money also)* Bestechungsgeld *nt*; **as a ~** als Bestechung; **to take a ~** sich bestechen lassen, Bestechungsgeld nehmen; **to offer sb a ~** jdn bestechen wollen, jdm Bestechungsgeld anbieten VT bestechen; **to ~ sb to do sth** jdn bestechen, damit er etw tut

bribery ['braɪbərɪ] N Bestechung *f*; **open to ~** bestechlich

bric-a-brac ['brɪkəbræk] N Nippes *m*, Nippsachen *pl*

brick [brɪk] N a *(Build)* Ziegel- *or* Backstein *m*; **~s and mortar** *(= property)* Immobilien *pl*; **you can't make ~s without straw** *(Prov)* wo nichts ist, kann auch nichts werden; **he came** *or* **was down on me like a ton of ~s** *(inf)* er hat mich unheimlich fertiggemacht *(inf)*; **to drop a ~** *(Brit fig inf)* ins Fettnäpfchen treten; **to drop sb/sth like a hot ~** *(inf)* jdn/etw wie eine heiße Kartoffel fallen lassen b *(= toy)* (Bau)klotz *m*; **box of (building) ~s** Baukasten *m* c *(of ice cream)* Block *m* d *(dated inf)* feiner Kerl *(inf)*; **be a ~!** sei ein Kumpel! e **~s** *(Brit sl: = money)* Kohle *f (inf)*

▶ **brick in** *or* **up** VT *sep door, window* zumauern

brick *in cpds* Backstein-; **brickbat** ['brɪkbæt] N *(= missile)* Backsteinbrocken *m*; *(fig)* Beschimpfung *f*; **brick building** N Backsteinbau *m*

brickie ['brɪkɪ] N *(Brit inf)* Maurer *m*

brick: **brick kiln** N Ziegelofen *m*; **bricklayer** N Maurer *m*; **bricklaying** N Maurerarbeit *f*; *(= trade)* Maurerhandwerk *nt*; **brick-red** ADJ ziegelrot; **brick wall** N *(fig inf)* **I might as well be talking to a ~** ich könnte genauso gut gegen eine Wand reden; **it's like beating** *or* **banging one's head against a ~** es ist, wie wenn man mit dem Kopf gegen die Wand rennt; **to come up against** *or* **hit a ~** plötzlich vor einer Mauer stehen; **brickwork** N Backsteinmauerwerk *nt*; **brickworks** PL, **brickyard** N Ziegelei *f*

bridal ['braɪdl] ADJ Braut-; *procession also, feast* Hochzeits-; ~ **gown/wear** Hochzeitskleid *nt*/-bekleidung *f*; ~ **vow** Eheversprechen *nt* der Braut

bridal party N Angehörige *pl* und Freunde *pl* der Braut

bridal suite N Hochzeitssuite *f*

bride [braɪd] N Braut *f*; **the ~ and (~)groom** Braut und Bräutigam, das Hochzeitspaar; ~ **of Christ** Braut Christi

bridegroom ['braɪdgru:m] N Bräutigam *m*

bridesmaid ['braɪdzmeɪd] N Brautjungfer *f*

bridezilla [braɪd'zɪlə] N *(inf) Braut, die während der Hochzeitsvorbereitung zickig wird,* Brautzilla *f (inf)*

bridge[1] [brɪdʒ] N a *(lit, fig)* Brücke *f*; **to build ~s** *(fig)* Brücken schlagen; **that's all water under the ~** *(fig)* das ist alles Schnee von gestern; **don't cross your ~s before you come to them** *(fig)* lass die Dinge einfach auf dich zukommen b *(Naut)* (Kommando)brücke *f* c *(of nose)* Sattel *m*; *(of spectacles, violin)* Steg *m* d *(Dentistry)* Brücke *f* e *(Billiards)* Steg *m* VT *river, railway* eine Brücke schlagen *or* bauen über *(+acc)*; *(fig)* überbrücken; **to ~ the gap** *(fig)* die Zeit überbrücken; *(between people)* die Kluft überbrücken

bridge[2] N *(Cards)* Bridge *nt*

bridge: **bridge bond** N *(Chem)* Brückenbindung *f*; **bridge-building** N Brückenbau *m*; **bridgehead** N Brückenkopf *m*; **to establish a ~** einen Brückenkopf errichten; **bridgehouse** N Brückenhaus *nt*; **bridge roll** N längliches Brötchen; **bridgework** N *(Dentistry)* Zahnbrücken *pl*; *(of individual)* Zahnbrücke *f*

bridging finance ['brɪdʒɪŋ'faɪnæns] N Zwischenfinanzierung *f*

bridging loan ['brɪdʒɪŋləʊn] N Überbrückungskredit *m*

bridle ['braɪdl] N *(of horse)* Zaum *m* VT a *horse* aufzäumen b *(fig) one's tongue, emotions* im Zaume halten VI sich entrüstet wehren *(at* gegen)

bridle path N Reitweg *m*

brief [bri:f] ADJ (+er) kurz; *(= curt also) manner* kurz angebunden; **in ~** kurz; **the news in ~** Kurznachrichten *pl*; **to be ~** um es kurz zu machen; **could you give me a ~ idea ...** könnten Sie mir kurz erzählen ...
N a *(Jur)* Auftrag *m (an einen Anwalt)*; *(= document)* Unterlagen *pl* zu dem/einem Fall; *(= instructions)* Instruktionen *pl*; **to take a ~** *(Jur)* einen Fall annehmen; **to hold a ~ for sb** *(Jur)* jds Sache vor Gericht vertreten; **I hold no ~ for him** *(fig)* ich will nicht für ihn plädieren
b *(= instructions)* Auftrag *m*
c *(Brit sl: = lawyer)* Rechtsverdreher *m*
VT a *(Jur) lawyer* instruieren; *(= employ)* beauftragen
b *(= give instructions, information to)* instruieren *(on* über *+acc)*; **the pilots were ~ed on what they had to do** die Piloten wurden instruiert, was sie tun sollten

briefcase ['bri:fkeɪs] N (Akten)tasche *f*, (Akten)mappe *f*

briefing ['bri:fɪŋ] N *(= instructions)* Instruktionen *pl*, Anweisungen *pl*; *(also* **briefing session**) Einsatzbesprechung *f*

briefly ['bri:flɪ] ADV kurz

briefness ['bri:fnɪs] N Kürze *f*

briefs [bri:fs] PL Slip *m*; **a pair of ~** ein Slip

brier ['braɪə'] N a *(= wild rose)* wilde Rose; *(= bramble runner)* Ranke *f*; *(= thorny bush)* Dornbusch *m* b = **briar a**

Brig. *abbr of* **brigadier**

brig [brɪg] N a *(= ship)* Brigg *f* b *(US: = cell on ship)* Arrestzelle *f (auf einem Schiff)*; *(Mil sl)* Bunker *m (sl)*

brigade [brɪ'geɪd] N *(Mil)* Brigade *f*

brigadier [ˌbrɪgə'dɪə'] N *(Brit)* Brigadegeneral *m*

brigadier (general) N *(Brit Hist, US)* Brigadegeneral *m*

brigand ['brɪgənd] N *(old)* Räuber *m*, Bandit *m*

bright [braɪt] ADJ (+er) a *light, fire* hell; *colour* leuchtend; *sunshine, star also, eyes, gem* strahlend; *day, weather* heiter; *reflection* stark; *metal* glänzend; ~ **red** knallrot; **it was really ~ outside** es war wirklich sehr hell draußen; ~ **with lights** hell erleuchtet; ~ **intervals** *or* **periods** *(Met)* Aufheiterungen *pl*; **the outlook is ~er** *(Met)* die Aussichten sind etwas freundlicher; *(fig)* es sieht etwas besser aus; **the ~ lights** *(inf)* der Glanz der Großstadt
b *(= cheerful) person, smile* fröhlich, heiter; **I wasn't feeling too ~** es ging mir nicht besonders gut; **~ and early** in aller Frühe → **side**
c *(= intelligent) person* intelligent, schlau; *child* aufgeweckt; *idea* glänzend; *(iro)* intelligent; **I'm not very ~ this morning** ich habe heute Morgen Mattscheibe *(inf)*; **I forgot to tell him – that's ~** *(inf)* ich habe vergessen, ihm das zu sagen – toll! *(inf)*
d *(= favourable) future* glänzend; *prospects also* freundlich; **things aren't looking too ~** es sieht nicht gerade rosig aus

brighten (up) ['braɪtn(ʌp)] VT *sep* a *(= make cheerful) spirits, person* aufmuntern, aufheitern; *room, atmosphere* aufhellen, aufheitern; *conversation* beleben; *prospects, situation* verbessern b *(= make bright) colour, hair* aufhellen; *metal* aufpolieren VI a *(weather, sky)* sich aufklären *or* aufheitern b *(person)* fröhlicher werden; *(face)* sich aufhellen *or* aufheitern; *(eyes)* aufleuchten; *(prospects)* sich verbessern, freundlicher werden; *(future)* freundlicher aussehen

bright-eyed ['braɪtaɪd] ADJ mit strahlenden Augen; **~ and bushy-tailed** *(hum inf)* putzmunter *(inf)*

brightly ['braɪtlɪ] ADV a *shine, burn* hell; *reflected* stark; **~ lit** hell erleuchtet b *(= cheerfully) say, smile* fröhlich, heiter

brightness ['braɪtnɪs] N a *(of light, fire)* Helligkeit *f*; *(of colour)* Leuchten *nt*; *(of sunshine, star also, eyes, gem)* Strahlen *nt*; *(of day, weather)* Heiterkeit *f*; *(of reflection)* Stärke *f*; *(of metal)* Glanz *m*; **~ control** Helligkeitsregler *m* b *(= cheerfulness: of person, smile)* Fröhlichkeit *f*, Heiterkeit *f* c *(= intelligence, of person)* Intelligenz *f*; *(of child)* Aufgewecktheit *f* d *(of prospects)* Freundlichkeit *f*; **the ~ of the future** die glänzende Zukunft

Bright's disease ['braɪtsdɪˌzi:z] N brightsche Krankheit

bright young thing N *(fashionable)* junger Schicki *(inf)*, junge Schicki *(inf)*; *(male also)* Sonnyboy *m*; *(talented)* hoffnungsvolles Talent; **~s** *(recalling the 1920s)* die Jeunesse dorée

brill[1] [brɪl] N Glattbutt *m*

brill[2] ADJ *(Brit inf)* toll *(inf)*

brilliance ['brɪljəns] N a *(= brightness)* heller Glanz, Strahlen *nt*; *(of colour)* Strahlen *nt* b *(fig: = intelligence)* Großartigkeit *f*; *(of scientist, artist, wit, achievement also)* Brillanz *f*; **a man of such ~** ein Mann von so hervorragender Intelligenz

brilliant ['brɪljənt] ADJ a *(fig)* großartig *(also iro)*; *scientist, artist, wit, achievement also* glänzend, brillant; *student* hervorragend; **she is a ~ woman** sie ist eine sehr intelligente Frau; **he is ~ with my children** er versteht sich großartig mit meinen Kindern; **to be ~ at sth/doing sth** etw hervorragend können/tun können b *sunshine, light, eyes, colour* strahlend EXCL *(inf: = great)* super *(inf)*

brilliantine ['brɪljənˌti:n] N Brillantine *f*, Haarpomade *f*

brilliantly ['brɪljəntlɪ] ADV a *shine, lit, illuminated* hell; *sunny* strahlend; **~ coloured** *(Brit) or* **colored** *(US)* in kräftigen Farben b *(= very well, superbly)* großartig; *talented* glänzend; *play, perform* brillant; *funny, witty, simple* herrlich; **a ~ original idea** eine Idee von glänzender Originalität

Brillo pad® ['brɪləʊˌpæd] N Scheuertuch *nt (aus Stahlwolle)*

brim [brɪm] N *(of cup)* Rand *m*; *(of hat also)* Krempe *f*; **full to the ~ (with sth)** *(lit)* randvoll (mit etw); **she is full to the ~ with joy** sie strömt über vor Freude **VI** strotzen *(with* von *or* vor *+dat)*; **her eyes were ~ming with tears** ihre Augen schwammen in Tränen

▶ **brim over** VI *(lit, fig)* überfließen *(with* vor *+dat)*

brimful [ˈbrɪmˈfʊl] ADJ *(lit)* randvoll; *(fig)* voll *(of, with* von); **he is ~ of energy** er sprüht vor Energie; **she is ~ of health** sie strotzt vor Gesundheit

-brimmed [-brɪmd] ADJ *suf hat* -krempig

brimstone [ˈbrɪmstəʊn] N *(= sulphur)* Schwefel *m*

brindled [ˈbrɪndld] ADJ gestreift

brine [braɪn] N **a** *(= salt water)* Sole *f*; *(for pickling)* Lake *f* **b** *(= sea water)* Salzwasser *nt*; *(liter. = sea)* See *f*

bring [brɪŋ] *pret, ptp* **brought** VT **a** bringen; *(also* **bring with one***)* mitbringen; **did you ~ the car/your guitar** *etc*? haben Sie den Wagen/die Gitarre *etc* mitgebracht?; **to ~ sb across/inside** *etc* jdn herüber-/hereinbringen *etc*
b *(= result in, be accompanied by) snow, rain, luck* bringen; **to ~ a blush/tears to sb's cheeks/eyes** jdm die Röte ins Gesicht/die Tränen in die Augen treiben
c *(+infin: = persuade)* **I cannot ~ myself to speak to him** ich kann es nicht über mich bringen, mit ihm zu sprechen
d *(esp Jur: = present for trial, discussion) case, matter* bringen *(before* vor *+acc)*; **the trial will be brought next week** der Prozess findet nächste Woche statt → **action, charge**
e *(= sell for, earn) price, income* (ein)bringen
f *(in phrases, see also relevant nouns)* **to ~ sth to a close** *or* **an end** etw zu Ende bringen; **to ~ sb low** jdn auf null bringen *(inf)*; **to ~ sth to sb's knowledge** jdm etw zur Kenntnis bringen; **to ~ sth to sb's attention** jdn auf etw *(acc)* aufmerksam machen; **to ~ to perfection** perfektionieren, vervollkommnen

▶ **bring about** VT *sep* **a** *(= cause)* herbeiführen, verursachen **b** *(Naut)* wenden; **he brought us about** er wendete

▶ **bring along** VT *sep* **a** *(= bring with one)* mitbringen **b** = **bring on b**

▶ **bring around** VT *sep* = **bring round a, d**

▶ **bring away** VT *sep person* wegbringen; *memories, impression* mitnehmen

▶ **bring back** VT *sep* **a** *(lit) person, object* zurückbringen **b** *(= restore) custom, hanging* wieder einführen; *government* wieder wählen; **a rest will bring him back to normal** ein wenig Ruhe wird ihn wiederherstellen; **to bring sb back to life/health** jdn wieder lebendig/gesund machen; **to bring a government back to power** eine Regierung wieder an die Macht bringen **c** *(= recall) memories* zurückbringen, wecken; *events* erinnern an *(+acc)*

▶ **bring down** VT *sep* **a** *(out of air) (= shoot down) bird, plane* herunterholen; *(= land) plane, kite* herunterbringen; **to bring sb's wrath down (up)on one** sich *(dat)* jds Zorn zuziehen; **you'll bring the boss down on us** da werden wir es mit dem Chef zu tun bekommen **b** *opponent, footballer* zu Fall bringen; *(by shooting) animal* zur Strecke bringen; *person* niederschießen → **house c** *government etc* zu Fall bringen **d** *(= reduce) temperature, prices, cost of living* senken; *swelling* reduzieren, zurückgehen lassen

▶ **bring forth** VT *sep (old, liter)* **a** *fruit* hervorbringen *(geh)*; *child, young* zur Welt bringen *(geh)* **b** *ideas* hervorbringen; *suggestions* vorbringen; *protests* auslösen

▶ **bring forward** VT *sep* **a** *(lit) person, chair* nach vorne bringen **b** *(fig: = present) witness* vorführen; *evidence, argument, proposal* vorbringen, unterbreiten **c** *(= advance time of) meeting* vorverlegen; *clock* vorstellen **d** *(Comm) figure, amount* übertragen; **amount brought forward** Übertrag *m*

▶ **bring in** VT *sep* **a** *(lit) person, object* hereinbringen *(prep obj, -to* in *+acc)*; *harvest* einbringen, bergen *(esp DDR)*; *sails* einziehen; **to bring in the New Year** das neue Jahr begrüßen **b** *(fig: = introduce) fashion, custom* einführen; *(Parl) bill* einbringen; **to bring sth into fashion** etw in Mode bringen **c** *(= involve, call in) police, consultant etc* einschalten *(on* bei); **don't bring him into it** lass ihn aus der Sache raus; **she's bound to bring Freud in** sie wird bestimmt Freud mit hereinbringen; **why bring Freud/that in?** was hat Freud/das damit zu tun? **d** *(Fin) income, money, interest* (ein)bringen *(-to sb* jdm); *(Comm) business* bringen **e** *(Jur, jury) verdict* fällen

▶ **bring into** VT *always separate* **to bring sth into action/blossom/view** etw zum Einsatz bringen/blühen lassen/sichtbar werden lassen

▶ **bring off** VT *sep* **a** *people from wreck* retten, wegbringen *(prep obj* von) **b** *(= succeed with) plan* zustande *or* zu Stande bringen, zuwege *or* zu Wege bringen; **to bring off a coup** ein Ding drehen *(inf)*; **he brought it off!** er hat es geschafft! *(inf)* **c** *(sl, = bring to orgasm)* **to bring sb off** es jdm besorgen *(sl)*

▶ **bring on** VT *sep* **a** *(= cause) illness, quarrel* herbeiführen, verursachen; *attack also* auslösen **b** *(= help develop) pupil, young athlete* weiterbringen; *crops, flowers* herausbringen **c** *(Theat) person* auftreten lassen; *thing* auf die Bühne bringen; *(Sport) player* einsetzen; **to bring sb on the scene** *(fig)* jdn auf die Szene rufen **d to bring sth (up)on oneself** sich *(dat)* etw selbst aufladen; **you brought it (up)on yourself** das hast du dir selbst zuzuschreiben

▶ **bring out** VT *sep* **a** *(lit)* (heraus)bringen *(of* aus); *(of pocket)* herausholen *(of* aus) **b** *(= draw out) person* die Hemmungen nehmen *(+dat)*; **can't you bring him out (of his shell) a bit?** können Sie nichts tun, damit er ein bisschen aus sich herausgeht? **c** *(= elicit) greed, bravery* zum Vorschein bringen; *best qualities also* herausbringen; **to bring out the best/worst in sb** das Beste/Schlimmste in jdm zum Vorschein bringen **d** *(also* **bring out on strike***) workers* auf die Straße schicken **e** *(= make blossom) flowers* herausbringen **f** *(to society) debutante* in die Gesellschaft einführen **g** *(= bring on the market) new product, book* herausbringen **h** *(= emphasize, show up)* herausbringen, hervorheben **i** *(= utter) few words* herausbringen; *cry* ausstoßen **j to bring sb out in spots/a rash** bei jdm Pickel/einen Ausschlag verursachen

▶ **bring over** VT *sep* **a** *(lit)* herüberbringen **b** *(fig, to ideas)* überzeugen *(to* von); *(to other side)* bringen *(to* auf *+acc)*

▶ **bring round** *(esp Brit)* VT *sep* **a** *(to one's house etc)* vorbeibringen **b** *(= steer) discussion, conversation* bringen *(to* auf *+acc)* **c** *unconscious person* wieder zu Bewusstsein bringen **d** *(= convert)* herumkriegen *(inf)*

▶ **bring through** VT *always separate patient, business* durchbringen; **to bring sb through a crisis** jdn durch eine Krise bringen; **to bring sb through an illness** jdm helfen, eine Krankheit zu überstehen

▶ **bring to** VT *always separate* **a** *(Naut)* stoppen **b** *unconscious person* wieder zu Bewusstsein bringen **c to bring sb to himself/herself** jdn wieder zu sich bringen

▶ **bring together** VT *sep* zusammenbringen

▶ **bring under** **VT** *always separate (= subdue)* unterwerfen **VT** *+prep obj (= categorize)* bringen unter *(+dat)*; **this can be brought under four main headings** dies lässt sich in vier Kategorien gliedern → **control**

▶ **bring up** VT *sep* **a** *(to a higher place)* heraufbringen; *(to the front)* her-/hinbringen → **rear b** *(= raise, increase) amount, reserves* erhöhen *(to* auf *+acc)*; *level, standards* anheben; **to bring sb up to a certain standard** jdn auf ein gewisses Niveau bringen **c** *(= rear) child, animal* groß- *or* aufziehen; *(= educate)* erziehen; **a well/badly brought-up child** ein gut/schlecht erzogenes Kind; **to bring sb up to do sth** jdn dazu erziehen, etw zu tun; **he was brought up to believe that ...** man hatte ihm beigebracht, dass ... **d** *(= vomit up)* brechen; *(esp baby, patient)* spucken *(inf)* **e** *(= mention) fact, problem* zur Sprache bringen, erwähnen; **do you have to bring that up?** müssen Sie davon anfangen? **f** *(Jur)* **to bring sb up (before a judge)** jdn (einem Richter) vorführen **g** *(Mil) battalion* heranbringen → **rear h to bring sb up short** jdn innehalten lassen **i to bring sb up against sth** jdn mit etw konfrontieren

▶ **bring upon** VT *sep +prep obj* = **bring on d**

bring-and-buy (sale) [ˈbrɪŋənˈbaɪ(ˌseɪl)] N *(Brit)* Basar *m (wo mitgebrachte Sachen angeboten und verkauft werden)*

brink [brɪŋk] N *(lit, fig)* Rand *m*; **on the ~ of sth** *(lit, fig)* am Rande von etw; **on the ~ of doing sth** *(lit, fig)* nahe daran, etw zu tun

brinkmanship [ˈbrɪŋkmənʃɪp] N *(inf)* Spiel *nt* mit dem Feuer

briny [ˈbraɪnɪ] **ADJ** salzhaltig, salzig **N** *(inf)* See *f*

Bri-nylon® [ˌbraɪˈnaɪlən] N *(Brit) britische Kunstfaser*

brio [ˈbriːəʊ] N *(= vigour)* Feuer *nt*, Schwung *m*

briquet(te) [brɪˈket] N Brikett *nt*

brisk [brɪsk] ADJ *(+er)* **a** *person, way of speaking* forsch; *sales assistant, service* flott, flink; *walk, pace* flott; **to go for a ~ walk** einen ordentlichen Spaziergang machen **b** *(fig) trade, betting, bidding* lebhaft, rege; **business** *etc* **was ~** das Geschäft *etc* ging lebhaft *or* war rege; **voting got off to a ~ start** die Wahl begann mit einer lebhaften Beteiligung **c** *wind, weather* frisch

brisket [ˈbrɪskɪt] N *(Cook)* Bruststück *nt*

briskly [ˈbrɪsklɪ] ADV **a** *speak, act* forsch; *walk* flott **b** *(Comm etc) trade, sell, bid* lebhaft, rege

briskness [ˈbrɪsknɪs] N **a** *(of person, way of speaking)* Forschheit *f*; *(of sales assistant, service)* Flottheit *f*, Flinkheit *f*; *(of walk, pace)* flottes Tempo; **feeling warmed by the ~ of their walk, they ...** durch den flotten Spaziergang aufgewärmt, ... sie ... **b** *(Comm etc, of trade, sales, bidding)* Lebhaftigkeit *f* **c** *(of wind, weather)* Frische *f*

brisling [ˈbrɪzlɪŋ] N Brisling *m*, Sprotte *f*

bristle [ˈbrɪsl] **N** *(of brush, boar etc)* Borste *f*; *(of beard)* Stoppel *f* **VI** **a** *(animal's hair)* sich sträuben; **the dog ~d** dem Hund sträubte sich das Fell **b** *(fig, person)* zornig werden; **to ~ with anger** vor Wut schnauben **c** *(fig)* **to be bristling with people** von *or* vor Leuten wimmeln; **bristling with difficulties** mit Schwierigkeiten gespickt; **the dress was bristling with pins** das Kleid steckte voller Nadeln; **the soldiers ~d with weapons** die Soldaten waren bis an die Zähne bewaffnet

bristly [ˈbrɪslɪ] ADJ *(+er) animal* borstig; *chin* Stoppel-, stoppelig; *hair, beard* borstig

Bristol fashion [ˈbrɪstəlˌfæʃn] ADJ → **shipshape**

bristols [ˈbrɪstəlz] PL *(Brit inf)* Titten *pl (sl)*

Brit [brɪt] N *(inf)* Engländer *m*, Tommy *m (inf)*

Britain [ˈbrɪtən] N Großbritannien *nt*; *(in ancient history)* Britannien *nt*

BRITAIN, GREAT BRITAIN, UNITED KINGDOM

Auch wenn man es häufig hören kann, dass fälschlicherweise von England gesprochen wird, wenn eigentlich ganz Großbritannien gemeint ist, sollte man diesen Fehler nicht nachmachen, da man dadurch Schotten, Waliser und einen Teil der Iren kränkt. **Britain, Great Britain, the United Kingdom** und **the British Isles** sind Bezeichnungen, die man leicht verwechseln kann, und sogar englische Muttersprachler verwenden sie oft nach Gutdünken.

Great Britain, Großbritannien, ist der Name der britischen Hauptinsel mit England, Schottland und Wales. In der Amtssprache sind dabei auch alle Inseln vor der Küste mit eingeschlossen, mit Ausnahme der Isle of Man und der Kanalinseln.
The British Isles, die Britischen Inseln, ist die geografische Bezeichnung für Großbritannien, die Isle of Man, und die Insel Irland. Politisch gesehen umfassen sie zwei souveräne Staaten, nämlich **the United Kingdom of Great Britain and Northern Ireland** und die Republik Irland.
The United Kingdom of Great Britain and Northern Ireland oder auch **UK**, das Vereinigte Königreich, ist eine politische Einheit, die aus Großbritannien und Nordirland besteht. Es ist eine parlamentarische Demokratie mit einer konstitutionellen Monarchie und Mitglied der Europäischen Union.
Um die Verwirrung komplett zu machen, wird **Britain** sowohl als Synonym für **United Kingdom** als auch für **Great Britain** verwendet. Alle Angehörigen des Vereinigten Königreichs haben die britische Staatsbürgerschaft.

Britannia [brɪˈtænɪə] N *(poet: = country)* Britannien *nt*; *(= personification)* Britannia *f*

Britannic [brɪˈtænɪk] ADJ **Her/His ~ Majesty** Ihre/Seine Britannische Majestät

britches [ˈbrɪtʃəz] PL *(US)* = **breeches**

briticism [ˈbrɪtɪsɪzəm] N Britizismus *m*

briticize [ˈbrɪtɪsaɪz] VT anglisieren, britifizieren

British [ˈbrɪtɪʃ] ADJ britisch; **I'm ~** ich bin Brite/Britin; **~ English** britisches Englisch; **and the best of ~ (luck)!** *(inf)* na, dann mal viel Glück! → **luck** N **the ~** *pl* die Briten *pl*

British Council N British Council *m*, *Organisation zu Förderung britischer Kultur im Ausland*

British Empire N **the ~** das Britische Weltreich

Britisher [ˈbrɪtɪʃəʳ] N *(dated US)* Brite *m*, Britin *f*

British: **British Honduras** N Britisch-Honduras *nt*; **British Isles** PL **the ~** die Britischen Inseln; **British Telecom** N British Telecom *f*

Briton [ˈbrɪtən] N Brite *m*, Britin *f*

Britpop [ˈbrɪtpɒp] N *(Brit Mus)* Britpop *m*

Brittany [ˈbrɪtənɪ] N die Bretagne

brittle [ˈbrɪtl] ADJ **a** spröde, zerbrechlich; *old paper* bröcklig; *biscuit* mürbe; **~ bones** schwache Knochen **b** *(fig) nerves* schwach; *person* empfindlich; *voice, laugh* schrill; **to have a ~ temper** aufbrausend sein

brittle bone disease N *(= osteoporosis)* Osteoporose *f*; *(= osteogenesis)* abnorme Knochenbrüchigkeit, mangelhafte Knochenbildung

brittleness [ˈbrɪtlnɪs] N **a** Sprödigkeit *f*, Zerbrechlichkeit *f*; *(of old paper)* Bröckligkeit *f*; *(of biscuit)* Mürbheit *f*; *(of bones)* Schwäche *f* **b** *(fig, of nerves)* Schwäche *f*; *(of person)* Empfindlichkeit *f*; *(of voice, laugh)* Schrillheit *f*

bro [brəʊ] N *(US inf)* **a** *(= friend)* Kumpel *m*; **hi, ~!** hallo, Kumpel! **b** *(= brother)* Bruder *m*

broach [brəʊtʃ] VT **a** *barrel* anstechen, anzapfen **b** *subject, topic* anschneiden

B-road [ˈbiːrəʊd] N *(Brit)* ≈ Landstraße *f*

broad [brɔːd] ADJ *(+er)* **a** *(= wide)* breit; **to grow ~er** breiter werden; *(road, river also)* sich verbreitern; **to make ~er** verbreitern; **it's as ~ as it is long** *(fig)* es ist Jacke wie Hose *(inf)*
b *(= widely applicable) theory* umfassend; *(= general)* allgemein
c *(= not detailed) distinction, idea, outline* grob; *instructions* vage; *sense* weit; **as a very ~ rule** als Faustregel; **to draw** *or* **paint sth in ~ strokes** *(fig)* etw in groben Zügen umreißen
d *(= liberal) mind, attitude, ideas* großzügig, tolerant; **a man of ~ sympathies** ein aufgeschlossener Geist; **a ~ church** ein Sammelbecken *nt* verschiedenster Strömungen *or* Richtungen
e *wink, hint* deutlich; *(= indelicate) humour* derb
f *(= strongly marked) accent* stark; *(= with long vowel sounds also)* breit; **he speaks ~ Scots** er spricht breit(est)es Schottisch *or* starken schottischen Dialekt
N **a** *(= widest part)* **the ~ of the back** die Schultergegend
b **the (Norfolk) Broads** *pl* die Norfolk Broads
c *(sl: = woman)* Tussi *f (sl)*

broad: **broadband** *(Telec)* N Breitband *nt* ADJ Breitband-; **broad-based** ADJ *support* breit; *government* auf breiter Basis; **broad bean** N dicke Bohne, Saubohne *f*; **broad-brush** ADJ *(= general)* grob, allgemein

broadcast [ˈbrɔːdkɑːst] *vb: pret, ptp* **broadcast** N *(Rad, TV)* Sendung *f*; *(of match etc)* Übertragung *f*; **~s** *pl* Programm *nt*, Sendungen *pl* VT **a** *(Rad, TV)* senden, ausstrahlen; *football match, event* übertragen **b** *(fig) news, rumour etc* verbreiten **c** *(Agr) seed* aussäen VI *(Rad, TV, station)* senden; *(person)* im Rundfunk/Fernsehen sprechen; **we're not ~ing tonight** heute Abend strahlen wir kein Programm aus

broadcaster [ˈbrɔːdkɑːstəʳ] N *(Rad, TV: = announcer)* Rundfunk-/Fernsehsprecher(in) *m(f)*; *(= personality)* Rundfunk-/Fernsehpersönlichkeit *f*; **he's not a very good ~** er ist nicht besonders gut im Fernsehen/Rundfunk; **a famous ~** eine vom Rundfunk/Fernsehen bekannte Persönlichkeit

broadcasting [ˈbrɔːdkɑːstɪŋ] N *(Rad, TV)* Sendung *f*; *(of event)* Übertragung *f*; **end of ~** Ende des Programms; **to work in ~** beim Rundfunk/Fernsehen arbeiten; **the early days of ~** die Anfänge des Rundfunks/Fernsehens ATTR *(Rad)* Rundfunk-; *(TV)* Fernseh-

Broadcasting Standards Council N *(Brit)* *Rundfunk- und Fernsehkontrollorgan*

broadcasting station N *(Rad)* Rundfunkstation *f*; *(TV)* Fernsehstation *f*

broadcloth [ˈbrɔːdklɒθ] N merzerisierter Baumwollstoff

broaden (out) [ˈbrɔːdn(aʊt)] VT *sep road etc* verbreitern; *(fig) person, attitudes* aufgeschlossener machen; **to broaden one's mind/one's horizons** *(fig)* seinen Horizont erweitern VI breiter werden, sich verbreitern; *(fig, person, attitudes)* aufgeschlossener werden; *(fig, horizon)* sich erweitern

broad: **broad gauge** N Breitspur *f*; **broad jump** N *(US Sport)* Weitsprung *m*; **broadloom** ADJ *carpet* überbreit

broadly [ˈbrɔːdlɪ] ADV **a** *(= in general terms)* allgemein, in großen Zügen; *outline, describe* grob; *agree, accept* weitgehend; *welcome, support, applicable* allgemein; *differ* beträchtlich; **~ speaking** ganz allgemein gesprochen; **~-based** breit gefächert **b** *grin, smile, laugh* breit; *hint, wink* deutlich

broad: **broad-minded** ADJ großzügig, tolerant; **broad-mindedness** N Großzügigkeit *f*, Toleranz *f*; **broadness** N = **breadth**; **broadsheet** N *(Press) großformatige Zeitung* → *also* **tabloid**; **broad-shouldered** ADJ breitschult(e)rig; **broadside** *(Naut)* N Breitseite *f*; *(fig also)* Attacke *f*; **to fire a ~** eine Breitseite abgeben *or* abfeuern; **he fired a ~ at the manager** *(fig)* er attackierte den Manager scharf ADV **~ on** mit der Breitseite *(to* nach); **broadsword** N breites Schwert

brocade [brəʊˈkeɪd] N Brokat *m* ATTR Brokat-, brokaten

brocaded [brəʊˈkeɪdɪd] ADJ (wie Brokat) verziert *or* bestickt

broccoli [ˈbrɒkəlɪ] N Brokkoli *pl*, Spargelkohl *m*

brochure [ˈbrəʊʃjʊəʳ] N Broschüre *f*, Prospekt *m*

brodie [ˈbrəʊdɪ] N *(US sl)* **a** *(= jump)* Todessprung *m*; **to do a ~** sich in die Tiefe stürzen *(in selbstmörderischer Absicht)*; **to do a ~ from a bridge** sich von einer Brücke stürzen **b** *(= failure)* Pleite *f (inf)*, Reinfall *m (inf)*

brogue¹ [brəʊg] N *(= shoe)* ≈ Haferlschuh *m (Aus)*, Budapester *m*

brogue² N *(= Irish accent)* irischer Akzent

broil [brɔɪl] VTI *(Cook)* grillen

broiler [ˈbrɔɪləʳ] N **a** *(= chicken)* Brathähnchen *nt*, (Gold)broiler *m (dial)* **b** *(= grill)* Grill *m*

broiling [ˈbrɔɪlɪŋ] ADJ *(esp US) sun, summer* brütend heiß

broke [brəʊk] *pret of* **break** ADJ *pred* **a** *(inf)* abgebrannt *(inf)*, pleite *(inf)*; **to go ~** Pleite machen *(inf)*; **to go for ~** alles riskieren **b** **if it ain't ~, don't fix it** *(fig inf)* man sollte ohne Not nichts ändern

broken [ˈbrəʊkən] *ptp of* **break** ADJ **a** kaputt *(inf)*; *twig* geknickt; *bone* gebrochen; *rope also* gerissen; *(= smashed) cup, glass etc* zerbrochen, kaputt
b *(fig) voice* brüchig; *chord* gebrochen; *heart, spirit, man* gebrochen; *health, marriage* zerrüttet; **surely his voice has ~ by now** er muss den Stimmbruch schon hinter sich *(dat)* haben; **from a ~ home** aus zerrütteten Familienverhältnissen
c *promise* gebrochen; *appointment* nicht (ein)gehalten
d *road, surface, ground* uneben; *coastline* zerklüftet; *water, sea* aufgewühlt, bewegt; *set* unvollständig
e *(= interrupted) journey* unterbrochen; *line also* gestrichelt; *sleep also* gestört
f *English, German etc* gebrochen

broken: **broken-down** [ˈbrəʊkənˈdaʊn] ADJ *machine, car, furniture* kaputt *(inf)*; *building* heruntergekommen; **brokenhearted** [ˈbrəʊkənˈhɑːtɪd] ADJ untröstlich; **broken white** N gebrochenes Weiß; **broken-winded** ADJ kurzatmig, dämpfig *(spec)*

broker [ˈbrəʊkəʳ] N *(St Ex, Fin, real estate)* Makler *m*; **yachting ~** Bootshändler *m* VT *deal, agreement* aushandeln

brokerage [ˈbrəʊkərɪdʒ] N **a** *(= commission)* Maklergebühr *f*; *(of insurance broker also)* Maklerlohn *m* **b** *(= trade)* Maklergeschäft *nt*

broking [ˈbrəʊkɪŋ] N Geschäft *nt* eines Maklers

brolly [ˈbrɒlɪ] N *(Brit inf)* (Regen)schirm *m*

bromide [ˈbrəʊmaɪd] N **a** *(Chem)* Bromid *nt*; *(Typ)* Bromsilberdruck *m*; *(Med inf)* Beruhigungsmittel *nt* **b** *(fig, = platitude)* Plattitüde *f*, Allgemeinplatz *m*

bromide paper N *(Phot)* Bromsilberpapier *nt*

bronchia [ˈbrɒŋkɪə] PL Bronchien *pl*

bronchial [ˈbrɒŋkɪəl] ADJ bronchial

bronchial tubes PL Bronchien *pl*

bronchitis [brɒŋˈkaɪtɪs] N Bronchitis *f*

bronchus [ˈbrɒŋkəs] N *pl* **bronchi** [ˈbrɒŋkiː] Bronchus *m*

bronco [ˈbrɒŋkəʊ] N *wildes oder halbwildes Pferd in den USA*

broncobuster [ˈbrɒŋkəʊˌbʌstəʳ] N *(inf) Zureiter wilder oder halbwilder Pferde*

brontosaurus [ˌbrɒntəˈsɔːrəs] N Brontosaurus *m*

Bronx cheer [brɒŋksˈtʃɪəʳ] N *(US inf)* **to get a ~** ausgelacht werden; **to give sb a ~** jdn auslachen

bronze [brɒnz] N *(all senses)* Bronze *f* VI *(person)* braun werden, bräunen VT **a** *metal* bronzieren **b** *face, skin* bräunen ADJ Bronze-

Bronze: **Bronze Age** N Bronzezeit *f*; **Bronze Age man** N der Mensch der Bronzezeit

bronzed [brɒnzd] ADJ *face, person* braun, (sonnen)gebräunt

bronze medallist, *(US)* **bronze medalist** N *(Sport)* Bronzemedaillengewinner(in) *m(f)*

bronzer [ˈbrɒnzəʳ] N Bräunungsmittel *nt*

bronzing [ˈbrɒnzɪŋ] ADJ Bräunungs-; **~ powder** Bräunungspuder *m*; **~ gel** Bräunungsgel *nt*

brooch [brəʊtʃ] N Brosche *f*

brood [bruːd] N *(lit, fig)* Brut *f* VI **a** *(bird)* brüten **b** *(fig, person)* grübeln; *(despondently also)* brüten

▸**brood over** or **(up)on** VI +prep obj nachgrübeln über (+acc); (despondently also) brüten über (+dat)

brooder ['bru:də'] N a (for breeding) Brutapparat m, Brutkasten m b (fig: = thinker) Grübler(in) m(f)

brood mare N Zuchtstute f

broody ['bru:dɪ] ADJ a hen brütig; **the hen is ~** die Henne gluckt; **to be feeling ~** (hum inf) den Wunsch nach einem Kind haben b person grüblerisch; (= sad, moody) schwerblütig

brook¹ [brʊk] N Bach m

brook² VT (liter: = tolerate) dulden; **to ~ no delay** keinen Aufschub dulden

brooklet ['brʊklɪt] N Bächlein nt

broom [bru:m] N a Besen m; **a new ~ sweeps clean** (Prov) neue Besen kehren gut (Prov) b (Bot) Ginster m

broom: **broom cupboard** N Besenschrank m; **broomstick** N Besenstiel m; **a witch on her ~** eine Hexe auf ihrem Besen

Bros PL (Comm) abbr of **Brothers** Gebr.

broth [brɒθ] N Fleischbrühe f; (= thickened soup) Suppe f

brothel ['brɒθl] N Bordell nt, Puff m (inf)

brothel: **brothel creepers** PL (hum) Leisetreter pl (hum); **brothel-keeper** N Bordellwirt(in) m(f)

brother ['brʌðə'] N pl -s or (obs, Eccl) **brethren** a (also Eccl) Bruder m; **they are ~ and sister** sie sind Geschwister, sie sind Bruder und Schwester; **my/his ~s and sisters** meine/seine Geschwister; **the Clarke ~s** die Brüder Clarke; (Comm) die Gebrüder Clarke; **oh ~!** (esp US inf) Junge, Junge! (inf) b (in trade unions) Kollege m c (= fellow man, DDR Pol) Bruder m; **his ~ officers** seine Offizierskameraden; **our ~s** unsere Mitmenschen or Brüder (geh, Eccl)

brother: **brotherhood** N a brüderliches Einvernehmen, Brüderlichkeit f; **sense of ~** (lit) Brudersinn m; (fig) Gefühl nt der Brüderlichkeit b (= organization) Bruderschaft f; **~ of man** Gemeinschaft f der Menschen; **brother-in-arms** N Waffenbruder m; **brother-in-law** N pl **brothers-in-law** Schwager m

brotherliness ['brʌðəlɪnɪs] N Brüderlichkeit f

brotherly ['brʌðəlɪ] ADJ brüderlich

brougham ['bru:əm] N Brougham m

brought [brɔ:t] pret, ptp of **bring**

brouhaha ['bru:hɑ:hɑ:] N usu sing Wirbel m, Tumult m

brow [braʊ] N a (= eyebrow) Braue f b (= forehead) Stirn f c (of hill) (Berg)kuppe f

browbeat ['braʊbi:t] pret **browbeat**, ptp **browbeaten** VT unter (moralischen) Druck setzen; **to ~ sb into doing sth** jdn so unter Druck setzen, dass er etw tut; **I can't ~ you into accepting it** ich kann euch natürlich nicht (dazu) zwingen, es anzunehmen; **I won't be ~en** ich lasse mich nicht tyrannisieren or unter Druck setzen

brown [braʊn] ADJ (+er) braun; (Cook) roast etc also braun gebraten N Braun nt VT (sun) skin, person bräunen; (Cook) (an)bräunen; meat also anbraten VI braun werden

▸**brown off** VT **to be browned off with sb/sth** (esp Brit inf) jdn/etw satthaben (inf); **I was pretty browned off at the time** ich hatte es damals ziemlich satt; **you're looking a bit browned off** du siehst so aus, als hättest du alles ziemlich satt

brown: **brown ale** N Malzbier nt; **brown-bag** VI (US) **to ~ lunch** sein Mittagessen mit zur Arbeit bringen; **brown bear** N Braunbär m; **brown bread** N Grau- or Mischbrot nt; (from wholemeal) Vollkornbrot nt; (darker) Schwarzbrot nt; **brown coal** N Braunkohle f; **brown-eyed** ADJ braunäugig; **brown goods** PL hochwertige Konsumgüter pl (Fernsehgerät, Videorekorder etc); **brown-haired** ADJ braunhaarig

brownie ['braʊnɪ] N a (= chocolate cake) kleiner Schokoladenkuchen b (= fairy) Heinzelmännchen nt c **Brownie** (in Guide Movement) Wichtel m

Brownie points PL Pluspunkte pl; **let's give him ~ for trying** dass er es versucht hat, können wir ihm ja anrechnen; **to score ~ with sb** sich bei jdm beliebt machen

browning ['braʊnɪŋ] N (Cook: = act) Anbraten nt; (= substance) Bratensoße f, Bratenpulver nt

brownish ['braʊnɪʃ] ADJ bräunlich

brown: **brown-nose** (US inf) VI arschkriechen (inf, pej) N Arschkriecher(in) m(f) (inf, pej); **brownout** N (esp US: = blackout) teilweiser Stromausfall; (during war) teilweise Verdunkelung; **brown owl** N a (Orn) Waldkauz m b **Brown Owl** (in Brownies) die weise Eule; **brown paper** N Packpapier nt; **brown rat** N Hausratte f; **brown rice** N geschälter Reis; **brown sauce** N (Brit Cook) braune Soße; **Brown Shirt** N Braunhemd nt (Hist); **brownstone** N (US: = material) rötlich brauner Sandstein; (= house) (rotes) Sandsteinhaus nt; **brown study** N **to be in a ~** (liter) geistesabwesend sein, in Gedanken verloren sein; **brown sugar** N brauner Zucker

browse [braʊz] VI a **to ~ among the books** in den Büchern schmökern; **to ~ through a book** in einem Buch schmökern; **to ~ (around)** sich umsehen b (Comput) browsen, surfen c (cattle) weiden; (deer) äsen VT **to ~ sth** etw durchsehen or -suchen; **to ~ the Internet** im Internet surfen N **to have a ~ (around)** sich umsehen; **to have a ~ through the books** in den Büchern schmökern; **to have a ~ around the bookshops** sich in den Buchläden umsehen

browser ['braʊzə'] N a (Comput) Browser m b (= reader) jd, der in Büchern etc herumblättert c (= customer) jd, der sich in einem Geschäft unverbindlich umsieht

Bruges [bru:ʒ] N Brügge nt

bruin ['bru:ɪn] N (Meister) Petz m

bruise [bru:z] N (on person) blauer Fleck; (more serious) Prellung f, Bluterguss m (esp Med); (on fruit) Druckstelle f

VT person einen blauen Fleck/blaue Flecke(n) schlagen (+dat) or beibringen (+dat); (more seriously) eine Prellung/Prellungen beibringen (+dat); fruit beschädigen; (fig) person, spirit, feelings verletzen; **to ~ oneself** sich stoßen, sich (dat) einen blauen Fleck holen; **to ~ one's elbow** sich (dat) einen blauen Fleck am Ellbogen holen

VI (person, part of body) einen blauen Fleck/blaue Flecke(n) bekommen; (fruit) eine Druckstelle/Druckstellen bekommen; (fig, person, feelings) verletzt werden; **he ~s easily** er bekommt leicht blaue Flecken; (fig) er ist sehr empfindlich

bruised [bru:zd] ADJ a **to be ~** (person) einen blauen Fleck/blaue Flecke haben; (= have severe bruising) Prellungen haben; (fruit, vegetable) eine Druckstelle/Druckstellen haben; **she has a ~ shoulder, her shoulder is ~** sie hat einen blauen Fleck/blaue Flecke auf der Schulter; **I feel ~ all over** mir tuts am ganzen Körper weh b (fig) ego, feelings, pride verletzt; **to feel ~** sich verletzt fühlen

bruiser ['bru:zə'] N (inf) Rabauke m, Räuber m (hum)

bruising ['bru:zɪŋ] N Prellungen pl

brumal ['bru:məl] ADJ winterlich, Winter-

brunch [brʌntʃ] N Brunch m, Frühstück und Mittagessen in einem

Brunei ['bru:naɪ] N Brunei nt

brunette [bru:'net] N Brünette f ADJ brünett

brunt [brʌnt] N **to bear the (main) ~ of the attack** die volle Wucht des Angriffs tragen; **to bear the (main) ~ of the work/costs** die Hauptlast der Arbeit/Kosten tragen; **to bear the ~** das meiste abkriegen

brush [brʌʃ] N a (= object) Bürste f; (= artist's brush, paintbrush, shaving brush, pastry brush) Pinsel m; (= hearth brush) Besen m; (with dustpan) Handbesen or -feger m; (= flue brush) Stoßbesen m; (= flue brush with weight) Sonne f; **to be as daft as a ~** (inf) total meschugge sein (inf)

b (= action) **to give sth a ~** etw bürsten; jacket, shoes etw abbürsten; **to give one's hair a ~** sich die Haare bürsten; **your jacket/hair/teeth could do with a ~** du solltest deine Jacke/dein Haar/deine Zähne mal wieder bürsten

c (= light touch) leichte, flüchtige Berührung, Streifen nt; **I felt the ~ of his lips against my neck** ich fühlte, wie seine Lippen meinen Nacken leicht berührten

d (of fox) Lunte f

e (= undergrowth) Unterholz nt

f (Mil: = skirmish) Zusammenstoß m, Scharmützel nt; (= quarrel, incident) Zusammenstoß m; **to have a ~ with sb** mit jdm aneinandergeraten

g (Elec, of commutator) Bürste f

VT a (= clean, tidy) bürsten; (with hand) wischen; **to ~ one's teeth** sich (dat) die Zähne putzen; **to ~ one's hair** sich (dat) das Haar bürsten

b (= sweep) dirt fegen, kehren; (with hand, cloth) wischen; **to ~ sth into a pile** etw zu einem Haufen zusammenfegen

c (= touch lightly) streifen

d fabric bürsten, aufrauen

▸**brush against** VI +prep obj streifen

▸**brush aside** VT sep obstacle, person (einfach) zur Seite schieben; objections (einfach) abtun; ideas verwerfen

▸**brush away** VT sep (with brush) abbürsten; (with hand, cloth) ab- or wegwischen; insects verscheuchen

▸**brush down** VT sep abbürsten; horse striegeln

▸**brush off** VT sep a mud, snow abbürsten; insect verscheuchen b (inf: = reject) person abblitzen lassen (inf); suggestion, criticism zurückweisen VI (mud etc) sich abbürsten or (with hand, cloth) abwischen lassen

▸**brush past** VI streifen (prep obj +acc); **as he brushed past** als er mich/ihn etc streifte

▸**brush up** VT sep a crumbs, dirt auffegen, aufkehren b wool, nap aufrauen, rauen (form) c (fig: also **brush up on**) subject, one's German auffrischen

brushed nylon [ˌbrʌʃt'naɪlən] N Nylon-Velours m

brush fire N a (= fire) Buschfeuer nt b (= crisis) begrenzter or lokaler Konflikt

brushings ['brʌʃɪŋz] PL Kehricht m no pl

brush: **brushoff** N (inf) Abfuhr f; **to give sb the ~** jdn abblitzen lassen (inf), jdm einen Korb geben (inf); **to get the ~** abblitzen (inf), einen Korb kriegen (inf); **brushstroke** N Pinselstrich m; (= way of painting) Pinselführung f; **brush-up** N (inf) **I must give my Italian a ~** ich muss meine Italienischkenntnisse auffrischen; **brushwood** N a (= undergrowth) Unterholz nt b (= cut twigs) Reisig nt; **brushwork** N (Art) Pinselführung f

brusque [bru:sk] ADJ (+er) person, tone, manner brüsk, schroff; reply schroff

brusquely ['bru:sklɪ] ADV behave brüsk, schroff; speak brüsk, in schroffem Ton; reply schroff

brusqueness ['bru:sknɪs] N Schroffheit f

Brussels ['brʌslz] N Brüssel nt

Brussels: **Brussels lace** N Brüsseler Spitze(n) f(pl); **Brussels sprouts** PL Rosenkohl m

brutal ['bru:tl] ADJ brutal

brutalism ['bru:təlɪzəm] N (Archit) Brutalismus m

brutality [bru:'tælɪtɪ] N Brutalität f

brutalize ['bru:təlaɪz] VT brutalisieren, verrohen lassen

brutally ['bru:təlɪ] ADV brutal; **I'll be ~ frank** ich werde schonungslos offen sein

brute [bru:t] N a Tier nt, Vieh nt (pej) b (= person) brutaler Kerl; (= savage) Bestie f; **drink**

brings out the ~ in him Alkohol bringt das Tier in ihm zum Vorschein **c** (*inf, = thing*) **it's a ~ of a problem** es ist ein höllisches Problem (*inf*); **this nail's a real ~ (to get out)** dieser Nagel geht höllisch schwer raus (*inf*) **ADJ** *attr strength* roh; *passion* tierisch, viehisch (*pej*); **by ~ force** mit roher Gewalt

brutish ['bru:tɪʃ] **ADJ** *person, behaviour* viehisch, brutal

BS (*US inf*) *abbr of* **bullshit**

BSc *abbr of* **Bachelor of Science**

BSc Econ *abbr of* **Bachelor of Economic Science**

BSE *abbr of* **bovine spongiform encephalopathy** BSE *f*, Rinderwahn *m*

BSI *abbr of* **British Standards Institution** *britischer Normenausschuss*

B-side ['bi:saɪd] **N** (*of record*) B-Seite *f*

BST *abbr of* **British Summer Time, British Standard Time**

BT *abbr of* **British Telecom** *britisches Telekommunikationsunternehmen*

Bt. *abbr of* **baronet**

BTA *abbr of* **British Tourist Authority**

BTEC ['bi:tek] (*Brit*) *abbr of* **Business and Technology Education Council** **a** (*= organization*) *Fachschule für Betriebswirtschaft, Naturwissenschaften und Technologie* **b** (*= diploma*) *Diplom in Betriebswirtschaft, Naturwissenschaften und Technologie*

BTW (*inf*) *abbr of* **by the way**

bub [bʌb] **N** (*US inf*) Alte(r) *m* (*inf*), Mann *m* (*inf*)

bubble ['bʌbl] **N** Blase *f*; (*on plane etc*) (Glas)kuppel *f*; **to blow ~s** Blasen machen; **to burst sb's ~** (*fig*) jdn auf den Boden der Tatsachen zurückbringen; **the ~ has burst** (*fig*) alles ist wie eine Seifenblase zerplatzt **VI** **a** (*liquid*) sprudeln; (*heated also*) strudeln; (*wine*) perlen; (*gas*) Blasen/Bläschen machen *or* bilden **b** (*= make bubbling noise*) blubbern (*inf*); (*cooking liquid, geyser etc*) brodeln; (*stream*) plätschern **c** (*fig*) **to ~ with excitement/enthusiasm/confidence** fast platzen vor Aufregung/Begeisterung/Selbstvertrauen

▶ **bubble out** **VI** (*liquid*) heraussprudeln

▶ **bubble over** **VI** (*lit*) überschäumen; (*fig*) übersprudeln (*with* vor *+dat*)

▶ **bubble up** **VI** (*liquid*) aufsprudeln; (*gas*) in Blasen/Bläschen hochsteigen; (*excitement, emotions*) aufsteigen, hochkommen

bubble: **bubble and squeak** **N** (*Brit*) *zusammen gebratene Fleischreste und Gemüse*; **bubble bath** **N** Schaumbad *nt*; **bubble car** **N** (*Brit, opening at the top*) Kabinenroller *m*; (*opening at the front*) Isetta® *f*; **bubble chamber** **N** Blasenkammer *f*; **bubble gum** **N** Bubblegum *m*; **bubblehead** **N** (*esp US pej inf*) Schwachkopf *m* (*inf*); **bubble-jet printer** **N** (*Comput*) Bubblejet-Drucker *m*; **bubble memory** **N** (*Comput*) Blasenspeicher *m*; **bubble pack** **N** (Klar)sichtpackung *f*

bubbler ['bʌblə'] **N** (*US, Austral*) Trinkbrunnen *m*

bubbly ['bʌblɪ] **ADJ** (+*er*) **a** (*lit*) sprudelnd **b** (*fig inf*) *person, personality* temperamentvoll, lebendig; *mood* übersprudelnd **N** (*inf*) Schampus *m* (*inf*)

bubonic plague [bju:'bɒnɪk'pleɪg] **N** Beulenpest *f*

buccaneer [,bʌkə'nɪə'] **N** Seeräuber *m*; (*= ship*) Piratenschiff *nt*

Bucharest [,bju:kə'rest] **N** Bukarest *nt*

buck [bʌk] **N** **a** (*= male deer*) Bock *m*; (*= male rabbit, hare*) Rammler *m*
b (*US inf: = dollar*) Dollar *m*; **20 ~s** 20 Dollar; **to make a ~** Geld verdienen; **to make a fast** *or* **quick ~** (*also Brit*) schnell Kohle machen (*inf*); **to get more bang for the ~** mehr für sein Geld kriegen
c **to pass the ~** (*difficulty, unpleasant task*) den Schwarzen Peter weitergeben; (*responsibility also*) die Verantwortung abschieben; **to pass the ~ to sb** jdm den Schwarzen Peter zuschieben/die Verantwortung aufhalsen; **the ~ stops here** der Schwarze Peter landet bei mir/uns; **the ~ stops with her** der Schwarze Peter landet bei ihr
d (*old, hum, = dandy*) Stutzer *m*, Geck *m* (*old*)
e (*leap by horse*) Bocken *nt*
f (*in gymnastics*) Bock *m*
VI **a** (*horse*) bocken
b (*= resist, object*) sich sträuben (*at* gegen)
VT **a** **you can't ~ the market** gegen den Markt kommt man nicht an; **to ~ the trend** sich dem Trend widersetzen → **system**
b (*horse*) *rider* abwerfen

▶ **buck for** **VI** +*prep obj* (*US inf*) **to buck for promotion** mit aller Gewalt *or* auf Teufel komm raus (*inf*) befördert werden wollen

▶ **buck off** **VT** *sep rider* abwerfen

▶ **buck up** (*inf*) **VI** **a** (*= hurry up*) sich ranhalten (*inf*), rasch *or* fix machen (*inf*); **buck up!** halt dich ran! (*inf*) **b** (*= cheer up*) aufleben; **buck up!** Kopf hoch! **VT** *sep* **a** (*= make hurry*) Dampf machen (*+dat*) (*inf*) **b** (*= make cheerful*) aufmuntern **c** **to buck one's ideas up** sich zusammenreißen (*inf*)

buckaroo [,bʌkə'ru:] **N** (*US inf hum*) Cowboy *m*

buckboard ['bʌkbɔ:d] **N** (*US*) (einfache, offene) Kutsche

bucket ['bʌkɪt] **N** (*also of dredger, grain elevator*) Eimer *m*; (*of excavator, water wheel*) Schaufel *f*; **a ~ of water** ein Eimer *m* Wasser; **to weep** *or* **cry ~s** (*inf*) wie ein Schlosshund heulen (*inf*); **it's coming down in ~s** (*US inf*) es gießt *or* schüttet wie aus *or* mit Kübeln (*inf*) → **kick, drop** **VI** (*Brit inf*) **it's ~ing!, the rain is ~ing (down)!** es gießt *or* schüttet wie aus *or* mit Kübeln (*inf*)

▶ **bucket about** **VT** *sep usu pass* (*Brit inf*) durchrütteln

▶ **bucket along** **VI** (*dated inf*) mit einem Affenzahn dahin-/entlangkutschen (*inf*) *or* -karriolen (*inf*)

▶ **bucket down** **VI** (*Brit inf*) = **bucket VI**

bucket brigade **N** Eimerkette *f*

bucketful ['bʌkɪtfʊl] **N** Eimer *m*; **by the ~** (*fig inf*) tonnenweise (*inf*)

bucket: **bucket seat** **N** Schalensitz *m*; **bucket shop** **N** (*Fin*) unreelle Maklerfirma, Schwindelmakler *m*; (*= travel agency*) Agentur *f* für Billigreisen; **bucketwheel** **N** (*Tech*) Schöpfrad *nt*

buckeye ['bʌkaɪ] **N** (*US*) Rosskastanie *f*; (*= seed*) Kastanie *f*

Buck House ['bʌk,haʊs] **N** (*Brit inf*) = **Buckingham Palace**

Buckingham Palace ['bʌkɪŋəm'pælɪs] **N** Buckingham Palace *m*, der Buckingham-Palast

buckle ['bʌkl] **N** **a** (*on belt, shoe*) Schnalle *f*, Spange *f* **b** (*in metal etc*) Beule *f*; (*concave also*) Delle *f*; **there's a nasty ~ in this girder** dieser Träger ist übel eingebeult *or* (*twisted*) verbogen; **there's a nasty ~ in this wheel** dieses Rad ist übel verbogen **VT** **a** *belt, shoes* zuschnallen **b** *wheel, girder etc* verbiegen; (*= dent*) verbeulen **VI** **a** (*belt, shoe*) mit einer Schnalle *or* Spange geschlossen werden **b** (*wheel, metal*) sich verbiegen

▶ **buckle down** **VI** (*inf*) sich dahinterklemmen (*inf*), sich dranmachen (*inf*); **to buckle down to a task** sich hinter eine Aufgabe klemmen (*inf*), sich an eine Aufgabe machen

▶ **buckle on** **VT** *sep armour* anlegen; *sword, belt* umschnallen

▶ **buckle to** **VI** sich am Riemen reißen (*inf*)

buck-passing ['bʌk,pɑ:sɪŋ] **N** *no pl* (*inf*) *Abwälzen der Verantwortung auf eine andere Person*

buckram ['bʌkrəm] **N** Buckram *m* **ADJ** *attr* Buckram-

Bucks [bʌks] *abbr of* **Buckinghamshire**

bucksaw ['bʌksɔ:] **N** Handsäge *f*

buck's fizz [bʌks'fɪz] **N** Sekt *m* mit Orangensaft

buckshee [bʌk'ʃi:] **ADJ** (*Brit inf*) gratis, umsonst

buck: **buckshot** **N** grober Schrot, Rehposten *m* (*spec*); **buckskin** **N** **a** Wildleder *nt*, Buckskin *m* **b** **buckskins** **PL** Lederhose(n) *f(pl)*; **bucktooth** **N** vorstehender Zahn; **buck-toothed** **ADJ** mit vorstehenden Zähnen; **buckwheat** **N** Buchweizen *m*

bucolic [bju:'kɒlɪk] **ADJ** (*liter*) bukolisch (*liter*)

bud[1] [bʌd] **N** **a** Knospe *f*; **to be in ~** knospen, Knospen treiben **b** (*Anat*) → **taste bud** **VI** (*plant, flower*) knospen, Knospen treiben; (*tree also*) ausschlagen; (*horns*) wachsen

bud[2] **INTERJ** (*US inf*) = **buddy**

Budapest [,bju:də'pest] **N** Budapest *nt*

Buddha ['bʊdə] **N** Buddha *m*

Buddhism ['bʊdɪzəm] **N** Buddhismus *m*

Buddhist ['bʊdɪst] **N** Buddhist(in) *m(f)* **ADJ** buddhistisch

budding ['bʌdɪŋ] **ADJ** knospend; (*fig*) *poet etc* angehend

buddy ['bʌdɪ] **N** (*US inf*) Kumpel *m*; **hey, ~!** he, Kumpel, hör mal!; (*threatening*) hör mal zu, Kumpel *or* Freundchen (*inf*)

buddy-buddy ['bʌdɪbʌdɪ] **ADJ** (*US inf*) **to be ~ with sb** mit jdm dick befreundet sein (*inf*); **to try to get ~ with sb** sich bei jdm anbiedern

buddy system **N** (*US inf*) **to employ** *or* **use the ~** aus Sicherheitsgründen Zweiergruppen bilden (*um sich ggf. gegenseitig zu helfen*)

budge [bʌdʒ] **VI** **a** (*= move*) sich rühren, sich bewegen; **~ up** *or* **over!** mach Platz!, rück mal ein Stückchen! **b** (*fig: = give way*) nachgeben, weichen; **I will not ~ an inch** ich werde keinen Fingerbreit nachgeben *or* weichen; **he is not going to ~** er gibt nicht nach, der bleibt stur (*inf*) **VT** **a** (*= move*) (von der Stelle) bewegen **b** (*= force to give way*) zum Nachgeben bewegen; **we can't ~ him** er lässt sich durch nichts erweichen

budgerigar ['bʌdʒərɪgɑ:'] **N** Wellensittich *m*

budget ['bʌdʒɪt] **N** Etat *m*, Budget *nt*; (*Parl also*) Haushalt(splan) *m* **VI** haushalten, Haus halten, wirtschaften; **responsible for ~ing** für das Budget *or* den Etat *or* (*Parl also*) den Haushalt verantwortlich **VT** **a** *money, time* verplanen **b** (*also* **budget for**) *item* kostenmäßig einplanen; *costs* einplanen; **~ed costs** Vorgabekosten *pl*, vorgesehene Kosten *pl*; **~ed revenue** Sollertrag *m*

▶ **budget for** **VI** +*prep obj* (im Etat) einplanen

> **BUDGET**
>
> Das **Budget** ist die jährliche Verlautbarung der geschätzten Einnahmen und Ausgaben der Regierung, die der britische Finanzminister normalerweise im März im Parlament in Form einer Rede abgibt. Das **Budget** beinhaltet auch Änderungen in der Besteuerung und den Sozialausgaben. Daher wird die Rede in ihrer gesamten Länge im Fernsehen übertragen, damit die Bürgerinnen und Bürger aus erster Hand erfahren, welche Auswirkungen das **Budget** für sie persönlich bei den Steuern für beispielsweise Benzin, Alkohol und Zigaretten haben wird → TREASURY

-budget *suf* **low-budget** mit bescheidenen Mitteln finanziert; **big-budget** aufwendig (finanziert), groß angelegt; **a low-/big-budget film** ein mit bescheidenen Mitteln/aufwendig finanzierter Film, ein Low-Budget-/Big-Budget-Film *m*

budget account **N** Kundenkonto *nt*

budgetary ['bʌdʒɪtrɪ] **ADJ** Etat-, Budget-, Haushalts-; **~ problems** Etat- *or* Budget- *or* Haushaltsprobleme *pl*; **~ constraints** finanzielle Zwänge; **~ policy** Haushaltspolitik *f*

budget: **budget day** **N** (*Parl*) ≈ Haushaltsdebatte *f*; **budget deficit** **N** Haushaltsdefizit *nt*

budgeting ['bʌdʒɪtɪŋ] **N** Kalkulation *f*, Budgetierung *f*

budget speech **N** (*Parl*) Etatrede *f*

budgie ['bʌdʒɪ] N *(inf) abbr of* **budgerigar** Wellensittich *m*

Buenos Aires [,bweɪnɒs'aɪrɪz] N Buenos Aires *nt*

buff¹ [bʌf] N a (= *leather*) (kräftiges, weiches) Leder b **in the ~** nackt, im Adams-/Evaskostüm *(hum)* c (= *polishing disc*) Schwabbelscheibe *f (spec)*, Polierscheibe *f*; (= *cylinder*) Schwabbelwalze *f (spec)* d (= *colour*) Gelbbraun *nt* ADJ a ledern, Leder- b *(colour)* gelbbraun VT *metal* polieren

buff² N *(inf: = movie/theatre etc buff)* Fan *m (inf)*

buffalo ['bʌfələʊ] N *pl* **-es**, *collective pl* **-** Büffel *m*

buffalo grass N *(US)* Büffelgras *nt*

buffer¹ ['bʌfə'] N *(lit, fig, Comput)* Puffer *m*; *(Rail, at terminus)* Prellbock *m*; **to hit the ~s** *(Brit: plan, project)* am Ende sein

buffer² N *(Brit inf)* Heini *m (inf)*

buffering ['bʌfərɪŋ] N *(Comput)* Pufferung *f*

buffer: **buffer solution** N *(Chem)* Puffer *m*, Pufferlösung *f*; **buffer state** N *(Pol)* Pufferstaat *m*; **buffer zone** N Pufferzone *f*

buffet¹ ['bʌfɪt] N (= *blow*) Schlag *m* VT hin und her werfen; **~ed by the wind** vom Wind gerüttelt; **~ing wind** böiger Wind

buffet² ['bʊfeɪ] N Büffet *nt*; *(Brit Rail)* Speisewagen *m*; (= *meal*) Stehimbiss *m*; (= *cold buffet*) kaltes Büffet; **~ lunch/meal/supper** Stehimbiss *m*

buffet car ['bʊfeɪ-] N *(Brit Rail)* Speisewagen *m*

buffeting ['bʌfɪtɪŋ] N heftiges Schaukeln; *(Aviat)* Rütteln *nt*; **to get** *or* **take a ~** hin und her geworfen *or (Aviat)* gerüttelt werden

buffoon [bə'fuːn] N Clown *m*; *(stupid)* Blödmann *m (pej inf)*; **to act** *or* **play the ~** den Clown *or* Hanswurst spielen

buffoonery [bə'fuːnərɪ] N Clownerie *f*

bug [bʌg] N a Wanze *f*; *(inf: = any insect)* Käfer *m*; **~s** *pl* Ungeziefer *nt*
b (= *bugging device*) Wanze *f*
c *(inf: = germ, virus)* Bazillus *f*; **I might get your ~** du könntest mich anstecken; **he picked up a ~ while on holiday** *(esp Brit) or* **vacation** *(US)* er hat sich *(dat)* im Urlaub eine Krankheit geholt; **there must be a ~ going about** das geht zur Zeit um
d *(inf: = obsession)* **now he's got the ~** jetzt hats ihn gepackt *(inf)*; **she's got the travel ~** die Reiselust hat sie gepackt
e *(inf, = snag, defect)* Fehler *m*; **~s** *pl* Mucken *pl (inf)*
f *(Comput)* Programmfehler *m*, Bug *m (inf)*
VT a *room, building* verwanzen *(inf)*, Wanzen *pl* installieren in *(+dat) or* einbauen in *(+acc) (inf)*; *conversation, telephone lines* abhören; **this room is ~ged** hier sind Wanzen *(inf)*, das Zimmer ist verwanzt *(inf)*
b *(inf: = worry)* stören; (= *annoy*) nerven *(inf)*, den Nerv töten *(+dat) (inf)*; **he ~s me** er nervt nich an *inf*; **don't let it ~ you** mach dir nichts draus *(inf)*

bugaboo ['bʌgəbuː] N Schreckgespenst *nt*

bug: **bugbear** ['bʌgbɛə'] N Schreckgespenst *nt*; **bugbite** N Wanzenstich *m*; *(of other insect)* Insektenstich *m*; **bug-eyed** ADJ mit vorstehenden *or* vorquellenden Augen; **bug-free** [bʌg'friː] ADJ *(Comput)* fehlerfrei

bugger ['bʌgə'] N *(inf)* Scheißkerl *m (inf)*, Arschloch *nt (vulg)*; *(when not contemptible)* Kerl *m (inf)*; (= *thing*) Scheißding *nt (inf)*; **this nail's a ~, it won't come out** dieser Scheißnagel geht einfach nicht raus *(inf)*; **you lucky ~!** du hast vielleicht ein Schwein! *(inf)*; **to play silly ~s** *(Brit inf)* Scheiß machen *(sl)*
INTERJ *(Brit inf)* Scheiße *(inf)*; **~ (it)!** Scheiße! *(inf)*; **~ this car!** dieses Scheißauto *(inf)*; **~ the cost!** ich scheiß auf die Kosten! *(sl)*; **~ him** dieser Scheißkerl *(inf)*; (= *he can get lost*) der kann mich mal *(inf)*; **~ me!** *(surprise)* (du) meine Fresse! *(sl)*; *(annoyance)* so'n Scheiß! *(inf)*
VT a *(lit)* anal verkehren mit
b *(Brit, sl)* versauen *(sl)*

▶ **bugger about** *or* **around** *(Brit inf)* VI (= *laze about etc*) rumgammeln *(inf)*; (= *be ineffective*) blöd rummachen *(inf)*; **stop buggering about** *or* **around and get on with it** nun mach mal Nägel mit Köpfen *(inf)*; **to bugger about** *or* **around with sth** an etw *(dat)* rumpfuschen *(inf)* VT *sep* verarschen *(inf)*

▶ **bugger off** VI *(Brit inf)* abhauen *(inf)*, Leine ziehen *(inf)*

▶ **bugger up** VT *sep (Brit inf)* versauen *(inf)*; **I'm sorry if I've buggered you up** tut mir leid, dass ich dich in eine solche Scheißlage gebracht habe *(inf)*

bugger all [,bʌgər'ɔːl] N *(Brit inf: = nothing)* rein gar nichts

buggered ['bʌgəd] ADJ *(Brit inf)* (= *broken, ruined*) *machine, car, pen etc* im Arsch *(sl)*; (= *exhausted*) *person* fix und fertig *(inf)*; **I couldn't be ~** (= *bothered*) es war mir scheißegal *(inf)*; **I'm ~ if I'll do it** ich denke nicht im Traum daran, es zu tun; **well, I'll be ~!** ich glaub, ich krieg mich nicht mehr! *(sl)*

buggery ['bʌgərɪ] N Analverkehr *m*; *(with animals)* Sodomie *f*

bugging ['bʌgɪŋ] N Abhören *nt*; **the use of ~** der Gebrauch von Abhörgeräten; **elaborate ~** raffiniertes Abhörsystem

bugging device N Abhörgerät *nt*, Wanze *f (inf)*

buggy ['bʌgɪ] N *(with horse)* Buggy *m*, leichter Einspänner; **(baby) ~** *(Brit)* Sportwagen *m*; *(US)* Kinderwagen *m*

bugle ['bjuːgl] N Bügelhorn *nt*; **~ call** Hornsignal *nt*

bugler ['bjuːglə'] N Hornist *m*

bug: **bug-proof** ADJ *room, telephone* abhörsicher; **bug report** N *(Comput)* Fehlerbericht *m*; **bug-ridden** ['bʌg,rɪdn] ADJ a *hotel, mattress* von Wanzen befallen, verwanzt *(inf)* b *(Comput) software etc* voller Fehler

build [bɪld] *vb: pret, ptp* **built** N Körperbau *m*
VT a *(generally)* bauen; **the house is being built** das Haus ist im Bau *or* befindet sich im Bau b *(fig) new nation, relationship, career, system etc* aufbauen; *a better future* schaffen VI bauen; **to ~ on a piece of land** auf einem Grundstück bauen; (= *cover with houses etc*) ein Grundstück bebauen

▶ **build in** VT *sep (lit, fig) wardrobe, proviso etc* einbauen; *(fig) extra time* einplanen → **built-in**

▶ **build on** VT *sep* anbauen; **to build sth onto sth** etw an etw *(acc)* anbauen VI *+prep obj* bauen auf *(+acc)*

▶ **build up** VI a *(business)* wachsen; *(anticyclone, atmosphere)* entstehen, sich aufbauen; *(residue)* sich ablagern; (= *increase*) zunehmen; *(Tech, pressure)* sich erhöhen; **the music builds up to a huge crescendo** die Musik steigert sich zu einem gewaltigen Crescendo
b *(traffic)* sich verdichten; *(queue, line of cars)* sich bilden
c **the parts build up into a complete ...** die Teile bilden zusammen ein vollständiges ...
VT *sep* a *business* aufbauen *(into* zu); *finances* aufbessern; **to build up a reputation** sich *(dat)* einen Namen machen
b (= *increase*) *ego, muscles, forces* aufbauen; *production, pressure* steigern, erhöhen; *forces* (= *mass*) zusammenziehen; *health* kräftigen; *sb's confidence* stärken; **porridge builds you up** von Porridge wirst du groß und stark; **growing children need lots of vitamins to build them up** Kinder im Wachstumsalter brauchen viele Vitamine als Aufbaustoffe; **to build up sb's hopes** jdm Hoffnung(en) machen
c (= *cover with houses*) *area, land* (ganz) bebauen
d (= *publicize*) *person* aufbauen; **he wasn't as good as he had been built up to be** er war nicht so gut, wie die Werbung erwarten ließ

builder ['bɪldə'] N (= *worker*) Bauarbeiter(in) *m(f)*; *(of ships)* Schiffsbauer *m*; (= *contractor*) Bauunternehmer *m*; (= *future owner*) Bauherr *m*; *(fig, of state)* Baumeister *m (geh)*, Erbauer *m*; **John Higgins, Builders** Bauunternehmen John Higgins; **~'s labourer** *(Brit) or* **laborer** *(US)* Bauarbeiter *m*; **~'s merchant** Baustoffhändler *m*

building ['bɪldɪŋ] N a Gebäude *nt*; *(usually big or in some way special also)* Bau *m*; **it's the next ~ but one** das ist zwei Häuser weiter; **the ~s in the old town** die Häuser *or* Gebäude in der Altstadt b (= *act of constructing*) Bau *m*, Bauen *nt*; *(of new nation etc)* Aufbau *m*

building: **building block** N *(in toy set)* Bauklotz *m*; *(fig)* Baustein *m*; **building contractor** N Bauunternehmer *m*; **~s** Bauunternehmen *nt*; **building costs** PL Baukosten *pl*; **building estimate** N Baukosten(vor)anschlag *m*; **building firm** N Baufirma *f*; **building freeze** N Baustopp *m*; **building industry** N Bauindustrie *f*; **building land** N Bauland *nt*; **building materials** PL Baumaterial *nt*, Baustoffe *pl*; **building site** N Baustelle *f*; **building society** N *(Brit)* Bausparkasse *f*; **building trade** N Baugewerbe *nt*; **building worker** N Bauarbeiter *m*

build-up ['bɪldʌp] N a *(inf)* Werbung *f*; **publicity ~** Werbekampagne *f*; **they gave the play a good ~** sie haben das Stück ganz groß herausgebracht *(inf)*; **the chairman gave the speaker a tremendous ~** der Vorsitzende hat den Redner ganz groß angekündigt b *(of pressure)* Steigerung *f*; *(Tech also)* Verdichtung *f*; **~ of troops** Truppenmassierungen *pl*; **a traffic ~, a ~ of traffic** eine Verkehrsverdichtung

built [bɪlt] PRET, PTP *of* **build** ADJ **heavily/slightly ~** *(person)* kräftig/zierlich gebaut; **to be ~ like a tank** *(inf: person)* wie ein Schrank gebaut sein; *(object)* grundsolide gebaut sein

built: **built-in** ADJ *cupboard etc* eingebaut, Einbau-; *(fig: = instinctive)* instinktmäßig; **a camera with ~ flash** eine Kamera mit eingebautem Blitzlicht; **built-in obsolescence** N geplanter Verschleiß; **built-up** ADJ a **~ area** (= *urbanized*) bebautes Gebiet; *(Mot)* geschlossene Ortschaft b *shoulders* gepolstert; **~ shoes** Schuhe *pl* mit überhoher Sohle; *(Med)* orthopädische Schuhe *pl*

bulb [bʌlb] N a Zwiebel *f*; *(of garlic)* Knolle *f* b *(Elec)* (Glüh)birne *f* c *(of thermometer etc)* Kolben *m*

bulbous ['bʌlbəs] ADJ *plant* knollig, Knollen-; (= *bulb-shaped*) *growth etc* knotig, Knoten-; **~ nose** Knollennase *f*

Bulgaria [bʌl'gɛərɪə] N Bulgarien *nt*

Bulgarian [bʌl'gɛərɪən] ADJ bulgarisch N a Bulgare *m*, Bulgarin *f* b *(Ling)* Bulgarisch *nt*

bulge [bʌldʒ] N a *(in surface)* Wölbung *f*; *(irregular)* Unebenheit *f*; *(in jug, glass etc also)* Bauch *m*; *(in plaster, metal: accidental)* Beule *f*; *(in line)* Bogen *m*; *(in tyre)* Wulst *m*; **the Battle of the Bulge** die Ardennenoffensive; **what's that ~ in your pocket?** was steht denn in deiner Tasche so vor?
b *(in birth rate etc)* Zunahme *f*, Anschwellen *nt (in +gen)*; **the post-war ~** der Babyboom der Nachkriegsjahre
VI a *(also* **bulge out**, = *swell)* (an)schwellen; *(metal, sides of box)* sich wölben; *(plaster)* uneben sein; (= *stick out*) vorstehen; **his eyes were bulging out of his head** *(lit)* die Augen traten ihm aus dem Kopf; *(fig)* er bekam Stielaugen *(inf)*
b *(pocket, sack)* prall gefüllt sein, gestopft voll sein *(inf) (with* mit); *(cheek)* voll sein *(with* mit); **his notebooks were absolutely bulging with ideas** seine Notizbücher waren berstend *or* zum Bersten voll mit Ideen

bulging ['bʌldʒɪŋ] ADJ *stomach* prall, vorstehend; *pockets, suitcase* prall gefüllt, gestopft voll *(inf)*; **~ muscles** Muskelpakete *pl*; **~ eyes** Glotzaugen *pl*

bulimia [bə'lɪmɪə] N Bulimie *f*

bulimic [bə'lɪmɪk] ADJ bulimisch N Bulimiker(in) *m(f)*

bulk [bʌlk] N a (= *size*) Größe *f*; *(of task)* Ausmaß *nt*; (= *large shape, of thing*) massige Form;

(of person, animal) massige Gestalt; **of great ~** massig b *(also* **great bulk***)* größter Teil; *(of debt, loan also)* Hauptteil *m*; *(of work, mineral deposits also)* Großteil *m*; *(of people, votes also)* Gros *nt*; *(of property, legacy etc also)* Masse *f* c *(Comm)* **in ~** im Großen, en gros VI **to ~ large** eine wichtige Rolle spielen

bulk: **bulk buyer** N Großabnehmer(in) *m(f)*; **bulk buying** [ˌbʌlk'baɪɪŋ] N Mengen- *or* Großeinkauf *m*; **bulk carrier** N *(Naut)* Bulkcarrier *m*, Massengutfrachter *m*; **bulk consumer** N Großverbraucher(in) *m(f)*; **bulk discount** N Mengenrabatt *m*

bulkhead ['bʌlkhed] N Schott *nt*; *(in tunnel)* Spundwand *f*

bulkiness ['bʌlkɪnɪs] N a *(of object)* Sperrigkeit *f*; *(of book)* Dicke *f*; *(of sweater, spacesuit)* Unförmigkeit *f* b *(of person)* Massigkeit *f*, Wuchtigkeit *f*

bulk: **bulk purchase** N Mengen- *or* Großeinkauf *m*; **bulk sale** N Massenverkauf *m*

bulky ['bʌlkɪ] ADJ *(+er)* a *object* sperrig; *book* dick; *sweater, spacesuit* unförmig; **~ goods** Sperrgut *nt* b *person* massig, wuchtig

bull[1] [bʊl] N a Stier *m*; *(for breeding)* Bulle *m*; **to take** *or* **seize the ~ by the horns** *(fig)* den Stier bei den Hörnern packen; **like a ~ in a china shop** *(inf)* wie ein Elefant im Porzellanladen *(inf)*; **with a neck like a ~** stiernackig b *(= male of elephant, whale etc)* Bulle *m*; **a ~ elephant** ein Elefantenbulle *m*; **~ calf** Bullenkalb *nt* c *(St Ex)* Haussier *m*, Haussespekulant(in) *m(f)* d *(Brit Mil sl)* Drill *m* und Routine *f* e *(inf: = nonsense)* Unsinn *m*, Quatsch *m* *(inf)* VI *(St Ex)* auf Hausse spekulieren VT *(St Ex) stocks, shares* hochtreiben; **to ~ the market** die Kurse hochtreiben

bull[2] N *(Eccl)* Bulle *f*

bull bars PL *(Aut)* Kuhfänger *m*

bulldog ['bʊldɒg] N a Bulldogge *f*; **he has the tenacity of a ~** er hat eine zähe Ausdauer b *(Brit, Univ)* Helfer *m* des Proctors

bulldog: **bulldog breed** N **he is one of the ~** er ist ein zäher Mensch; **bulldog clip** N *(Brit)* Papierklammer *f*; **bulldog edition** N Frühausgabe *f (einer Zeitung)*

bulldoze ['bʊldəʊz] VT a *(fig: = force)* **to ~ sb into doing sth** jdn zwingen, etw zu tun, jdn so unter Druck setzen, dass er *etc* etw tut; **to ~ a bill through parliament** eine Maßnahme im Parlament durchpeitschen; **she ~d her way through the crowd** sie boxte sich durch die Menge b **they ~d the rubble out of the way** sie räumten den Schutt mit Bulldozern weg

bulldozer ['bʊldəʊzəʳ] N Planierraupe *f*, Bulldozer *m* ADJ *attr (fig) tactics etc* Holzhammer- *(inf)*

bull dyke N *(pej sl)* kesser Vater *(sl)*

bullet ['bʊlɪt] N a Kugel *f*; **to bite the ~** in den sauren Apfel beißen *(inf)*; **to get** *or* **be given the ~** *(inf)* gefeuert werden *(inf)* b *(Typ, in list)* Aufzählungszeichen *nt*, *(Comput also)* Gliederungspunkt *m*

bullet: **bullet head** N *(pej)* Dickkopf *m*; **bullet-headed** ADJ rundköpfig; **bullet hole** N Einschuss(loch *nt*) *m*

bulletin ['bʊlɪtɪn] N a Bulletin *nt*, amtliche Bekanntmachung; **health ~** Krankenbericht *m*, Bulletin *nt*; **a ~ to the media** ein Pressekommuniqué *nt*, ein Pressekommunikee *nt* b *(of club, society)* Bulletin *nt*

bulletin board N *(US: = notice board, Comput)* Schwarzes Brett

bullet: **bulletproof** ADJ kugelsicher VT kugelsicher machen; **bullet train** N *(japanischer)* Superexpress; **bullet wound** N Schusswunde *or* -verletzung *f*

bull: **bullfight** N Stierkampf *m*; **bullfighter** N Stierkämpfer *m*; **bullfighting** N Stierkampf *m*; **~ is …** der Stierkampf ist …; **bullfinch** N Dompfaff *m*, Gimpel *m*; **bullfrog** N Ochsenfrosch *m*; **bullheaded** ['bʊl'hedɪd] ADJ *person* dickköpfig; **bullhorn** N *(US)* Megafon *nt*, Megaphon *nt*

bullion ['bʊljən] N *no pl* Gold-/Silberbarren *pl*

bullish ['bʊlɪʃ] ADJ a *personality* selbstsicher; **to be ~ about sth** in Bezug auf etw *(acc)* zuversichtlich sein b *(St Ex)* **the market was ~** der Markt war in Haussestimmung

bull market N *(St Ex)* Hausse *f*

bull-necked ['bʊlnekt] ADJ stiernackig

bullock ['bʊlək] N Ochse *m*

bull: **bullpen** N *(US inf)* a *(Baseball) (= area)* Bereich *in dem sich Einwechsel-Werfer aufwärmen (= players)* Einwechsel-Werfer *pl*, Einwechsel-Pitcher *pl* b *(= office)* Großraumbüro *nt* c *(= cell)* Sammelzelle *f*; **bullring** N Stierkampfarena *f*; **bull's-eye** N a *(of target)* Scheibenmittelpunkt *m or* -zentrum *nt*; *(= hit)* Schuss *m* ins Schwarze *or* Zentrum; *(in darts)* Bull's eye *nt*; *(in archery)* Mouche *f*; **to get a** *or* **hit the ~** *(lit, fig)* ins Schwarze treffen; **~!** *(lit, fig)* genau getroffen!, ein Schuss ins Schwarze! b *(= sweet)* hartes Pfefferminzbonbon; **bullshit** *(sl)* N *(lit)* Kuhscheiße *f (vulg)*; *(fig)* Scheiß *m (inf)* INTERJ ach Quatsch *(inf)*; **~, of course you can** red keinen Scheiß, klar kannst du das *(inf)* VI Scheiß erzählen *(inf)* VT **to ~ sb** jdm Scheiß erzählen *(inf)*; **he ~ted his way out of trouble** er hat sich ganz großkotzig aus der Affäre gezogen *(inf)*; **bullshitter** N *(sl)* Dummschwätzer(in) *m(f) (inf)*; **bull terrier** N Bullterrier *m*; **bullwhip** N Lederpeitsche *f* VT auspeitschen

bully[1] ['bʊlɪ] N a Tyrann *m*; *(esp Sch)* Rabauke *m*; **you great big ~** du Rüpel; **to be a bit of a ~** den starken Mann markieren *(inf)*; **don't be a ~ with your little sister** schikaniere *or* tyrannisiere deine kleine Schwester nicht b *(Hockey)* Bully *nt* VT tyrannisieren, schikanieren; *(using violence)* drangsalieren; *(into doing sth)* unter Druck setzen; **to ~ sb into doing sth** jdn so unter Druck setzen, dass er *etc* etw tut

▶ **bully about** VT *sep (Brit)* = **bully around**

▶ **bully around** VT *sep* herumkommandieren, tyrannisieren

▶ **bully off** VI *(Hockey)* das Bully machen

bully[2] INTERJ *(dated)* prima *(inf)*, hervorragend; **~ for you!** *(dated, iro)* gratuliere!

bully: **bully beef** N *(Mil inf)* Cornedbeef *nt*, Corned Beef *nt*; **bullyboy** ['bʊlɪbɔɪ] *(inf)* N Schlägertyp *m (inf)*; **bully-boy** ['bʊlɪbɔɪ] ADJ *attr* Einschüchterungs-; **~ tactics** Einschüchterungstaktik *f*

bullying ['bʊlɪɪŋ] ADJ *person, manner* tyrannisch; *boss, wife also* herrisch N Tyrannisieren *nt*, Schikanieren *nt*; *(with violence)* Drangsalieren *nt*; *(= coercion)* Anwendung *f* von Druck (of auf *+acc*)

bully-off [bʊlɪ'ɒf] N *(Hockey)* Bully *nt*

bulrush ['bʊlrʌʃ] N Rohrkolben *m*; **in the ~es** im Schilfrohr

bulwark ['bʊlwək] N a *(lit, fig)* Bollwerk *nt* b *(Naut)* Schanzkleid *nt*

bum[1] [bʌm] N *(esp Brit inf)* Hintern *m (inf)*, Popo *m (inf)*; **to put ~s on seats** *(pop star etc)* ein Publikumsmagnet *m* sein

bum[2] *(inf)* N *(esp US)* a *(= good-for-nothing)* Rumtreiber *m (inf)*; *(young)* Gammler *m*; *(= down-and-out)* Penner *m (inf)*, Pennbruder *m (inf)*

b *(= despicable person)* Saukerl *m (inf)*

c **to be on the ~** schnorren *(inf)*; **he's always on the ~ for cigarettes** er schnorrt immer Zigaretten *(inf)*

ADJ *(= bad)* beschissen *(inf)*; *trick* hundsgemein *(inf)*; **~ rap** *(US inf)* Gemeinheit *f*, unfaire Kritik; *(= false charge)* falsche Anschuldigung; **to get a ~ rap** unfair behandelt werden; zu Unrecht beschuldigt werden; **to give sb a ~ steer** *(US inf)* jdn auf die falsche Fährte locken

VT a *money, food* schnorren *(inf)* (off sb bei jdm); **could I ~ a lift into town?** kannst du mich in die Stadt mitnehmen?; **could I ~ a smoke?** kann ich 'ne Kippe abstauben *(inf) or* schnorren *(inf)*?

b **he ~med (his way) around Europe** er ist durch Europa gezogen *(inf)*

VI *(= scrounge)* schnorren *(inf)* (off sb bei jdm)

▶ **bum about** *(Brit) or* **around** *(inf)* VI rumgammeln *(inf)* VI *+prep obj* ziehen durch *(inf)*

bum bag N *(Ski)* Gürteltasche *f*

bumbershoot ['bʌmbəʃuːt] N *(US inf)* Musspritze *f (hum inf)*

bumblebee ['bʌmblbiː] N Hummel *f*

bumbledom ['bʌmbldəm] N *(inf)* kleinlicher Bürokratismus

bumbler ['bʌmbləʳ] N Stümper(in) *m(f) (pej)*, Pfuscher(in) *m(f) (pej)*

▶ **bumble through** ['bʌmbl'θruː] VI sich durchwursteln *(inf) or* -mogeln *(inf) (+prep obj* durch)

bumbling ['bʌmblɪŋ] ADJ *(= clumsy)* schusselig *(inf)*; **some ~ idiot** irgend so ein Vollidiot *(inf)*

bumboat ['bʌmbəʊt] N Proviantboot *nt*

bum boy N *(Brit pej sl)* Sexgespiele *m*

bumf [bʌmf] N = **bumph**

bum-fluff ['bʌmflʌf] N *(inf)* Flaumbart *m*

bummer ['bʌməʳ] N *(inf: = person)* Niete *f*; **what a ~** *(= nuisance etc)* so 'ne Scheiße *(inf)*; **this one's a real ~** das kannst du vergessen; **I had a ~ of a day** ich habe einen total beschissenen Tag gehabt *(inf)*

bump [bʌmp] N a *(= blow, noise, jolt)* Bums *m (inf)*; *(of sth falling also)* Plumps *m (inf)*; **to get a ~ on the head** sich *(dat)* den Kopf anschlagen; **I accidentally gave her a ~ on the chin** ich habe sie aus Versehen ans Kinn geboxt *or* gestoßen; **he sat down with a ~** er ließ sich plumpsen *(inf)*; **the car has had a few ~s** mit dem Auto hat es ein paar Mal gebumst *(inf)*; **each ~ was agony as the ambulance …** jede Erschütterung war eine Qual, als der Krankenwagen …; **~ and grind** *(inf)* erotische Zuckungen *pl*; *(= sex)* Bumserei *f (inf)*

b *(on any surface)* Unebenheit *f*, Hubbel *m (inf)*; *(on head, knee etc)* Beule *f*; *(on car)* Delle *f*

c *(Aviat, = rising air current)* Bö *f*

VT a stoßen *(obj* gegen*)*; *car wing etc, one's own car* eine Delle fahren in *(+acc)*; *another car* auffahren auf *(+acc)*; **to ~ one's head/knee** sich *(dat)* den Kopf/das Knie anstoßen *or* anschlagen *(on, against* an *+dat)*; **her father ~ed her up and down on his knee** ihr Vater ließ sie auf den Knien reiten

b *(Sch inf)* hochwerfen

VI *(= move joltingly)* holpern; **he fell and went ~ing down the stairs** er stürzte und fiel polternd die Treppe hinunter; **the economy is continuing to ~ along the bottom** *(Brit)* die Wirtschaft befindet sich noch immer auf der Talsohle

ADV **to go ~** bumsen *(inf)*; **things that go ~ in the night** Geräusche *pl* im Dunkeln *or* in der Nacht

▶ **bump about** *(Brit) or* **around** VI herumpoltern

▶ **bump into** VI *+prep obj* a *(= knock into)* stoßen *or* bumsen *(inf)* gegen; *(driver, car)* fahren gegen; *another car* fahren auf *(+acc)* b *(inf: = meet)* begegnen *(+dat)*, treffen

▶ **bump off** VT *sep (inf)* abmurksen *(inf)*, kaltmachen *(inf)*

▶ **bump up** VT *sep (inf) (to* auf *+acc) prices, total* erhöhen; *salary* aufbessern

▶ **bump up against** VI *+prep obj* treffen

bumper ['bʌmpəʳ] N *(of car)* Stoßstange *f* ADJ **~ crop** Rekordernte *f*; **a special ~ edition** eine Riesensonderausgabe; **~ offer** großes Sonderangebot

bumper: **bumper car** N Boxauto *nt (dial)*, Autoskooter *m*; **bumper sticker** N *(Aut)* Aufkleber *m*; **bumper-to-bumper** ADJ **~ traffic** Stop-and-go-Verkehr *m*

bumph [bʌmf] N *(Brit inf)* a *(= forms)* Papierkram *m (inf)* b *(= toilet paper)* Klopapier *nt (inf)*

bumpiness [ˈbʌmpɪnɪs] N *(of surface)* Unebenheit *f*, Hubbeligkeit *f (inf)*; *(of road, drive)* Holp(e)rigkeit *f*; *(of flight)* Böigkeit *f*

bumpkin [ˈbʌmpkɪn] N *(also* **country bumpkin**, *= man)* (Bauern)tölpel *m*; *(= woman)* Trampel *f* vom Land

bump-start VT *car* anschieben N **to give a car a ~** ein Auto anschieben

bumptious [ˈbʌmpʃəs] ADJ aufgeblasen, wichtigtuerisch

bumptiousness [ˈbʌmpʃəsnɪs] N Aufgeblasenheit *f*, Wichtigtuerei *f*

bumpy [ˈbʌmpɪ] ADJ *(+er) surface* uneben, hubbelig *(inf)*; *road, drive* holp(e)rig; *flight* böig, unruhig; **we had a very ~ drive** auf der Fahrt wurden wir tüchtig durchgerüttelt

bum's rush N *(inf)* **to give sb the ~** jdn abblitzen lassen *(inf)*; **to get** *or* **be given the ~** abblitzen *(inf)*

bun [bʌn] N **a** *(= bread)* Brötchen *nt*; *(= iced bun etc)* süßes Stückchen *or* Teilchen; *(N Engl: = small cake)* Biskuittörtchen *nt*; **to have a ~ in the oven** *(sl)* einen Braten in der Röhre haben *(sl)* **b** *(= hairstyle)* Knoten *m*; **she wears her hair in a ~** sie trägt einen Knoten

bunch [bʌntʃ] N **a** *(of flowers)* Strauß *m*; *(of bananas)* Büschel *nt*; *(of radishes, asparagus)* Bund *nt*; *(of hair)* (Ratten)schwanz *m*, Zöpfchen *nt*; **a ~ of roses** ein Strauß *m* Rosen; **a ~ of flowers** ein Blumenstrauß *m*; **~ of grapes** Weintraube *f*; **~ of keys** Schlüsselbund *m*; **to wear one's hair in ~es** (Ratten)schwänze *pl or* Zöpfchen *pl* haben; **the pick** *or* **best of the ~** die Allerbesten; *(things)* das Beste vom Besten; **to pick the best of the ~** sich *(dat)* die Allerbesten/das Beste aussuchen; **a ~ of fives** *(inf: = fist)* 'ne Faust ins Gesicht *(inf)*
b *(inf, of people)* Haufen *m (inf)*; **a small ~ of tourists** ein Häufchen *nt or* eine kleine Gruppe Touristen
c *(inf: = a lot)* **thanks a ~** *(esp iro)* schönen Dank; **there's still a whole ~ of things to do** es sind noch jede Menge Sachen zu erledigen *(inf)*
VI *(dress)* sich bauschen → **bunch together VI ~ up VI**

▶ **bunch together** VT *sep* zusammenfassen; *(at random)* zusammenwürfeln; **the girls/prisoners were sitting all bunched together** die Mädchen/Gefangenen saßen alle auf einem Haufen VI *(people)* Grüppchen *or* einen Haufen bilden; *(atoms)* Cluster bilden; **they bunched together for warmth** sie kauerten sich aneinander, um sich zu wärmen; **don't bunch together, spread out!** bleibt nicht alle auf einem Haufen, verteilt euch!

▶ **bunch up** VT *sep* **a** *dress, skirt* bauschen **b** *(= put together) objects* auf einen Haufen legen VI **a** *(= bunch together)* Grüppchen *or* Haufen bilden; **don't bunch up so much, spread out!** bleibt nicht alle auf einem Haufen, verteilt euch! **b** *(material)* sich bauschen

bunco [ˈbʌŋkəʊ] N *pl* **buncos** *(US inf) (= trick)* Bauernfängerei *f*; *(= swindle)* Betrug *m*, Schwindel *m*

bundle [ˈbʌndl] N **a** *(= pile)* Bündel *nt*; **to tie sth in a ~** etw bündeln
b *(fig)* **a ~ of** *(= large number of)* eine ganze Menge; **he is a ~ of nerves** er ist ein Nervenbündel; **that child is a ~ of mischief** das Kind hat nichts als Unfug im Kopf; **her little ~ of joy** *(inf)* ihr kleiner Wonneproppen *(inf)*; **a ~ of fun** *(inf)* das reinste Vergnügen; **it cost a ~** *(inf)* das hat eine Stange Geld gekostet *(inf)*; **he didn't go a ~ on clubbing** *(inf)* er stand nicht so auf Nachtklubs *(inf)*
VT **a** *(= tie in a bundle)* bündeln; **~d software** *(Comput)* Softwarepaket *nt*; **it comes ~d with ...** *(Comput)* ... ist im Softwarepaket enthalten → **bundle up**
b *(= put, send hastily) things* stopfen; *people* verfrachten, schaffen; *(into vehicle)* packen *(inf)*, schaffen

▶ **bundle off** VT *sep person* schaffen; **he was bundled off to Australia** er wurde nach Australien verfrachtet

▶ **bundle up** VT *sep (= tie into bundles)* bündeln; *(= collect hastily)* zusammenraffen; **bundled up in his overcoat** in seinen Mantel eingehüllt *or* gemummelt *(inf)*

bun fight N *(dated inf)* Festivitäten *pl (dated)*

bung [bʌŋ] *(Brit)* N **a** *(of cask)* Spund(zapfen) *m* **b** *(inf: = bribe)* Schmiergeld *nt (inf)* VT **a** *cask* spunden, verstopfen **b** *(Brit inf: = throw)* schmeißen *(inf)* **c** *(inf: = bribe)* schmieren *(inf)*

▶ **bung in** VT *sep (Brit inf: = include)* dazutun

▶ **bung out** VT *sep (Brit inf)* rauswerfen *(inf)*

▶ **bung up** VT *sep (inf) pipe* verstopfen; **I'm all bunged up** meine Nase ist verstopft

bungalow [ˈbʌŋgələʊ] N Bungalow *m*

bungee [ˈbʌndʒiː]: **bungee cord** N *(for jumping)* Bungee-Seil *nt*; *(for fastening)* (dehnbarer) Gurt; **bungee jumping** N Bungeespringen *nt*, Bungeejumping *nt*; **bungee rope** N = **bungee cord**

bung-ho [bʌŋˈhəʊ] INTERJ *(dated inf)* famos *(dated inf)*

bunghole [ˈbʌŋhəʊl] N *(Brit)* Spundloch *nt*

bungle [ˈbʌŋgl] VT verpfuschen, vermasseln *(inf)*; **it was a ~d job** die Sache war vermasselt *(inf) or* verpfuscht VI **I see you've ~d again, Higgins** wie ich sehe, haben Sie wieder einmal alles verpfuscht *or* vermasselt *(inf)*, Higgins N verpfuschte Sache, Stümperei *f*

bungler [ˈbʌŋgləʳ] N Nichtskönner *m*, Stümper *m*

bungling [ˈbʌŋglɪŋ] ADJ *person* unfähig, trottelhaft, dusselig *(inf)*; *attempt* stümperhaft; **some ~ idiot has ...** irgendein Trottel hat ... *(inf)* N Stümperei *f*, Dusseligkeit *f (inf)*

bungy jumping [ˈbʌndʒiːˈdʒʌmpɪŋ] N = **bungee jumping**

bunion [ˈbʌnjən] N Ballen *m*

bunk[1] [bʌŋk] N **to do a ~** *(Brit inf)* türmen *(inf)*

▶ **bunk off** VI *(Brit Sch inf)* schwänzen

bunk[2] N *(inf)* Quatsch *m (inf)*

bunk[3] N *(in ship)* Koje *f*; *(in train, dormitory)* Bett *nt*

▶ **bunk down** VI *(inf)* kampieren *(inf)*

bunk beds PL Etagenbett *nt*

bunker [ˈbʌŋkəʳ] N *(Naut, Golf, Mil)* Bunker *m* VT *(Golf) shot* in den Bunker schlagen; **he was ~ed** er hatte den Ball in den Bunker geschlagen

bunk: **bunkhouse** [ˈbʌŋkhaʊs] N Schlafbaracke *f*; **bunkmate** N *(inf)* Bettnachbar(in) *m(f) (im Etagenbett)*

bunkum [ˈbʌŋkəm] N *(inf)* Blödsinn *m*, Quatsch *m (inf)*

bunny [ˈbʌnɪ] N *(also* **bunny rabbit***)* Hase *m*, Häschen *nt*

bunny girl N Häschen *nt*

Bunsen (burner) [ˈbʌnsn(ˈbɜːnəʳ)] N Bunsenbrenner *m*

bunting[1] [ˈbʌntɪŋ] N *(Orn)* Ammer *f* → **corn bunting, reed bunting**

bunting[2] N *(= material)* Fahnentuch *nt*; *(= flags)* bunte Fähnchen *pl*, Wimpel *pl*

buoy [bɔɪ] N Boje *f*; **to put down a ~** eine Boje verankern

▶ **buoy up** VT *sep* **a** *(lit)* über Wasser halten **b** *(fig) person* Auftrieb geben *(+dat)*; *sb's hopes* beleben; **buoyed up by new hope** von neuer Hoffnung beseelt **c** *(Fin) market, prices* Auftrieb geben *(+dat)*

buoyancy [ˈbɔɪənsɪ] N **a** *(of ship, object)* Schwimmfähigkeit *f*; *(of liquid)* Auftrieb *m*; **~ aid** Schwimmhilfe *f*; *(for canoeing)* Kajakweste *f* **b** *(fig: = cheerfulness)* Schwung *m*, Elan *m* **c** *(Fin: of market, prices)* Festigkeit *f*; *(= resilience)* Erholungsfähigkeit *f*

buoyancy chamber N *(Naut)* Trimmtank *m*

buoyancy tank N Luftkammer *f*

buoyant [ˈbɔɪənt] ADJ **a** *ship, object* schwimmend; *liquid* tragend; **fresh water is not so ~ as salt water** Süßwasser trägt nicht so gut wie Salzwasser **b** *(fig) person, mood* heiter; *(= energetic) step* federnd, elastisch **c** *(Fin) market, prices* fest; *(= resilient)* erholungsfähig; *trading* rege

buoyantly [ˈbɔɪəntlɪ] ADV *(fig: = optimistically)* guten Mutes

BUPA [ˈbuːpə] *abbr of* **British United Provident Association** *private Krankenversicherung*

> **BUPA**
>
> Die **BUPA (British United Provident Association)** ist der größte Anbieter privater Gesundheitsfürsorge in Großbritannien und dabei der einzige mit eigenen Krankenhäusern und Kliniken. Obschon alle britischen Staatsbürger ein Anrecht auf kostenlose Gesundheitsfürsorge durch den National Health Service **(NHS)** haben, lässt sich ein zunehmender Trend zur Privatvorsorge feststellen → NHS

buppie, buppy [ˈbʌpɪ] N *(inf) abbr of* **black upwardly mobile professional** schwarzer Yuppie, schwarze Yuppie

bur, burr [bɜːʳ] N *(Bot, fig inf)* Klette *f*; **chestnut ~** Kastanienschale *f*

Burberry® [ˈbɜːbərɪ] N Burberry® *m*, *Regenmantel aus hochwertigem Gabardine*

burble [ˈbɜːbl] VI **a** *(stream)* plätschern, gurgeln **b** *(fig, person)* plappern; *(baby)* gurgeln; **what's he burbling (on) about?** *(inf)* worüber quasselt er eigentlich? *(inf)* N *(of stream)* Plätschern *nt*, Gurgeln *nt*; *(on tape etc)* Gemurmel *nt*

burbot [ˈbɜːbət] N Quappe *f*

burbs, 'burbs [bɜːbz] PL *(US inf)* = **suburbs**

burden[1] [ˈbɜːdn] N **a** *(lit)* Last *f*; **it puts too much of a ~ on him/the engine** das überlastet ihn/den Motor; **beast of ~** Lasttier *nt*
b *(fig)* Belastung *f (on, to* für*)*; **he has such a ~ of responsibility** er hat eine schwere Last an Verantwortung zu tragen; **~ of taxation** steuerliche Belastung, Steuerlast *f*; **I don't want to be a ~ to you** ich möchte Ihnen nicht zur Last fallen; **the ~ of proof is on him** er muss den Beweis dafür erbringen *or* liefern; *(Jur)* er trägt die Beweislast
c *(Naut)* Tragfähigkeit *f*, Tragkraft *f*
VT belasten; **to be ~ed by guilt/regret** von Schuldgefühlen/Bedauern geplagt sein

burden[2] N **a** *(of song)* Refrain *m*, Kehrreim *m* **b** *(of speech, essay etc)* Grundgedanke *m*

burdensome [ˈbɜːdnsəm] ADJ *load* schwer; *condition* lästig; *task* mühsam; **to be ~** eine Belastung darstellen

burdock [ˈbɜːdɒk] N Klette *f*

bureau [bjʊəˈrəʊ] N **a** *(Brit: = desk)* Sekretär *m* **b** *(US: = chest of drawers)* Kommode *f* **c** *(= office)* Büro *nt* **d** *(= government department)* Amt *nt*, Behörde *f*

> **BUREAU OF INDIAN AFFAIRS**
>
> Das **Bureau of Indian Affairs** ist eine Regierungsbehörde der USA, die sich um alle Belange der Nachkommen der amerikanischen Urbevölkerung kümmert. 1824 wurde sie als Teil des Kriegsministeriums eingerichtet und war ursprünglich für die Verwaltung der Indianerreservate verantwortlich. Heute ist sie dem Innenministerium unterstellt, sieht ihre Hauptaufgabe im Schutz des indianischen Landes und seiner Ressourcen und arbeitet mit der Urbevölkerung zusammen, um deren Lebensbedingungen zu verbessern. Dabei werden zum Beispiel Gesundheits- und Sozialpläne erstellt sowie Ausbildungs- und Arbeitsplätze geschaffen. Seit 1960 stellt das Büro für indianische Angelegenheiten auch technische Hilfsmittel und Schulungsmöglichkeiten auf dem Gebiet der Landwirtschaft und der Ressourcengewinnung → NATIVE AMERICAN

bureaucracy [bjʊəˈrɒkrəsɪ] N Bürokratie *f*

bureaucrat [ˈbjʊərəʊkræt] N Bürokrat *m*

bureaucratic ADJ, **bureaucratically** ADV [ˌbjʊərəʊˈkrætɪk, -əlɪ] bürokratisch

bureau de change [ˌbjʊərəʊdɪˈʃɒndʒ] N *pl* **bureaux de change** Wechselstube *f*

burgeon [ˈbɜːdʒən] VI (*liter: also* **burgeon forth**, *flower*) knospen (*liter*); (*plant*) sprießen (*liter*); (*fig*) hervorsprießen (*geh*); **when young love first ~s** wenn die junge Liebe erblüht (*liter*)

burgeoning [ˈbɜːdʒənɪŋ] ADJ *industry, market* boomend; *movement* expandierend; *career* Erfolg versprechend, hoffnungsvoll; *demand* wachsend; *population* ständig wachsend

burger [ˈbɜːgəʳ] N (*inf*) Hamburger *m*

burger bar N Imbissstube *f*, Schnellimbiss *m*

burgess [ˈbɜːdʒɪs] N **a** (freier) Bürger, (freie) Bürgerin **b** (*Hist*) Abgeordnete(r) *mf* **c** (*US*) *Abgeordneter der Volksvertretung der Kolonien Maryland oder Virginia*

burgh [ˈbʌrə] N (*Scot*) freie Stadt

burgher [ˈbɜːgəʳ] N (*old*) Bürger(in) *m(f)*

burglar [ˈbɜːgləʳ] N Einbrecher(in) *m(f)*

burglar alarm N Alarmanlage *f*

burglarize [ˈbɜːgləraɪz] VT (*US*) einbrechen in (+*acc*); **the place/he was ~d** in dem Gebäude/bei ihm wurde eingebrochen

burglarproof [ˈbɜːgləpruːf] ADJ einbruchsicher

burglary [ˈbɜːglərɪ] N Einbruch *m*; (= *offence*) (Einbruchs)diebstahl *m*

burgle [ˈbɜːgl] VT (*Brit*) einbrechen in (+*acc*); **the place/he was ~d** in dem Gebäude/bei ihm wurde eingebrochen

Burgundy [ˈbɜːgəndɪ] N Burgund *nt*; (= *wine*) Burgunder *m*

burial [ˈberɪəl] N Beerdigung *f*, Bestattung *f*; (= *burial ceremony also*) Begräbnis *nt*; (*in cemetery also*) Beisetzung *f* (*form*); **Christian ~** christliches Begräbnis; **~ at sea** Seebestattung *f*

burial: **burial chamber** N Grabkammer *f*; **burial ground** N Begräbnisstätte *f*; **burial mound** N Grabhügel *m*; **burial object** N (*Archeol*) Grabbeigabe *f*; **burial place** N Grabstätte *f*; **burial service** N Trauerfeier *f*

burin [ˈbjʊərɪn] N (*Art*) Stichel *m*

burk [bɜːk] N (*Brit inf*) = **berk**

Burkina Faso [bɜːˌkiːnəˈfæsəʊ] N Burkina Faso *nt*

burlap [ˈbɜːlæp] N Sackleinen *nt*

burlesque [bɜːˈlesk] **N** **a** (= *parody*) Parodie *f*; (*Theat*) Burleske *f*; (*Liter*) Persiflage *f* **b** (*US Theat*) Varieté *nt*, Varietee *nt*; (= *show*) Varietévorstellung *f* **ADJ** **a** (= *parodic*) parodistisch; (*Theat*) burlesk; (*Liter*) persiflierend **b** (*US Theat*) Varieté-; **~ show** Varietévorstellung *f* **VT** parodieren; *book, author, style* persiflieren

burly [ˈbɜːlɪ] ADJ (+*er*) kräftig, stramm

Burma [ˈbɜːmə] N Birma *nt*, Burma *nt*

Burmese [bɜːˈmiːz] **ADJ** birmanisch, burmesisch **N** **a** Birmane *m*, Burmese *m*, Birmanin *f*, Burmesin *f* **b** (*Ling*) Birmanisch *nt*, Burmesisch *nt*

burn¹ [bɜːn] N (*Scot*) Bach *m*

burn² *vb: pret, ptp* **burnt** (*Brit*) *or* **burned** **N** **a** (*on skin*) Brandwunde *f*; (*on material*) verbrannte Stelle, Brandfleck *m*; **severe ~s** schwere Verbrennungen *pl*; **second degree ~s** Verbrennungen zweiten Grades; **cigarette ~** Brandfleck *m* *or* (*hole*) Brandloch *nt or* (*on skin*) Brandwunde *f* von einer Zigarette

b (*Space, of rocket*) Zündung *f*

c (*Sport inf*) **to go for the ~** sich total verausgaben (*inf*)

VT **a** verbrennen; *incense* abbrennen; *village, building* niederbrennen; **he ~ed me with his cigarette** er hat mich mit der Zigarette gebrannt; **to ~ oneself** sich verbrennen; **to be ~ed to death** verbrannt werden; (*in accident*) verbrennen; **to be ~ed alive** bei lebendigem Leibe verbrannt werden *or* (*in accident*) verbrennen; **to ~ a hole in sth** ein Loch in etw (*acc*) brennen; **to ~ one's fingers** (*lit, fig*) sich (*dat*) die Finger verbrennen; **he's got money to ~** (*fig*) er hat Geld wie Heu; **to ~ one's boats** *or* **bridges** (*Brit fig*) alle Brücken hinter sich (*dat*) abbrechen; **to ~ the midnight oil** (*fig*) bis tief in die Nacht arbeiten

b *meat, sauce, toast, cakes* verbrennen lassen; (*slightly*) anbrennen lassen; (*sun*) *person, skin* verbrennen

c (*acid*) ätzen; **the curry ~ed his throat** das Currygericht brannte ihm im Hals

d (= *use as fuel, ship etc*) befeuert werden mit; (= *use up*) *petrol, electricity* verbrauchen

VI **a** (*wood, fire etc*) brennen; **you will ~ in hell** du wirst in der Hölle schmoren; **to ~ to death** verbrennen → **ear¹**

b (*meat, pastry etc*) verbrennen; (*slightly*) anbrennen; **she/her skin ~s easily** sie bekommt leicht einen Sonnenbrand

c (*ointment, curry, sun*) brennen; (*acid*) ätzen; **the acid ~ed into the metal** die Säure fraß sich ins Metall

d (= *feel hot*: *wound, eyes, skin*) brennen; **his face was ~ing (with heat/shame)** sein Gesicht glühte *or* war rot (vor Hitze/Scham); **it's so hot, I'm ~ing** es ist so heiß, ich komm bald um vor Hitze

e **to be ~ing to do sth** darauf brennen, etw zu tun; **he was ~ing to get his revenge** er brannte auf Rache; **he was ~ing with anger** er war wutentbrannt; **he was ~ing with ambition** er war glühend ehrgeizig; **to ~ (with love/desire) for sb** (*liter*) von glühender Liebe/glühendem Verlangen nach jdm verzehrt werden (*liter*)

f (*Space, rockets*) zünden

▶ **burn away** **VI** **a** (= *go on burning*) vor sich hin brennen **b** (*wick, candle, oil*) herunterbrennen; (*part of roof etc*) abbrennen **VT** *sep* abbrennen; (*Med*) wegbrennen

▶ **burn down** **VI** **a** (*house etc*) abbrennen **b** (*fire, candle, wick*) herunterbrennen **VT** *sep* abbrennen

▶ **burn off** VT *sep paint etc* abbrennen

▶ **burn out** **VI** (*fire, candle*) ausbrennen, ausgehen; (*fuse, dynamo etc*) durchbrennen; (*rocket*) den Treibstoff verbraucht haben

VR **a** (*candle, lamp*) herunterbrennen; (*fire*) ab- *or* ausbrennen

b (*fig inf*) **to burn oneself out** sich kaputtmachen (*inf*), sich völlig verausgaben

VT *sep* **a** *enemy troops etc* ausräuchern; **they were burned out of house and home** ihr Haus und Hof war abgebrannt

b *usu pass* **burned out cars/houses** ausgebrannte Autos/Häuser; **he/his talent is burned out** (*inf*) mit ihm/seinem Talent ists vorbei (*inf*), er hat sich völlig verausgabt; **he looked completely burned out** (*inf*) er sah völlig kaputt (*inf*) *or* verbraucht aus

▶ **burn up** **VI** **a** (*fire etc*) auflodern **b** (*rocket etc in atmosphere*) verglühen **VI** +*prep obj* **to burn up the road** die Straße entlangbrettern (*inf*) **VT** *sep* **a** *rubbish* verbrennen; *fuel, energy* verbrauchen; *excess fat also* abbauen **b** **he was burned up with envy** er verzehrte sich vor Neid (*geh*) **c** (*US inf*: = *make angry*) zur Weißglut bringen (*inf*)

burner [ˈbɜːnəʳ] N (*of gas cooker, lamp*) Brenner *m*

burning [ˈbɜːnɪŋ] **ADJ** **a** *candle, town* brennend; *coals also, face* glühend; **I still have this ~ sensation in my mouth/on my skin** mein Mund/meine Haut brennt immer noch; **the ~ bush** (*Bibl*) der brennende Dornbusch **b** (*fig*) *thirst, question, topic* brennend; *desire also, fever, hate, passion, ambition* glühend; **~ issue** brandaktuelles Problem **N** **there is a smell of ~, I can smell ~** es riecht verbrannt *or* (*Cook also*) angebrannt

burning: **burning glass** N Brennglas *nt*; **burning life** N Brenndauer *f*

burnish [ˈbɜːnɪʃ] VT *metal* polieren; (*fig*) *image* aufpolieren

BURNS' NIGHT

Mit der **Burns' Night** wird am 25. Januar der Geburtstag des schottischen Nationaldichters Robert Burns begangen. Auf der ganzen Welt treffen sich Schotten bei einem festlichen Abendessen, dem **Burns' Supper**, um das Leben und Werk Robert Burns' zu feiern. Der Hauptgang, der traditionellerweise feierlich unter Dudelsackbegleitung aufgetragen wird, besteht aus **haggis** (gefülltem Schafsmagen) mit „neeps" und „tatties" (Steckrüben- und Kartoffelpüree). Trinksprüche werden ausgebracht, und nach dem Essen werden Gedichte von Burns aufgesagt und seine Lieder gesungen.

burns unit [ˈbɜːnzjuːnɪt] N (*Med*) Verbrennungsintensivstation *f*

burnt [bɜːnt] ADJ (*Brit*) verbrannt; **there's a ~ smell** es riecht verbrannt *or* brenzlig *or* (*Cook also*) angebrannt; **the coffee has a slightly ~ taste** der Kaffee schmeckt wie frisch geröstet

burnt offering N (*Rel*) Brandopfer *nt*; (*hum*: = *food*) angebranntes Essen

burn-up [ˈbɜːnʌp] N (*Brit inf*) Rennfahrt *f*; **to go for a ~** eine Rennfahrt machen

burp [bɜːp] (*inf*) **VI** rülpsen (*inf*); (*baby*) aufstoßen **VT** *baby* aufstoßen lassen **N** Rülpser *m* (*inf*)

burp gun N (*inf*) MG *nt* (*inf*)

burr¹ [bɜːʳ] N = **bur**

burr² N (*Ling*) *breiige Aussprache (von R)*; **to speak with a ~** breiig sprechen

burrow [ˈbʌrəʊ] **N** (*of rabbit etc*) Bau *m* **VI** (*rabbits, dogs etc*) graben, buddeln (*inf*); (= *make a burrow*) einen Bau graben; **they had ~ed under the fence** sie hatten sich (*dat*) ein Loch *or* (*below ground*) einen Gang unterm Zaun gegraben *or* gebuddelt (*inf*) **VT** *hole* graben, buddeln (*inf*); **to ~ one's way into sth** (*fig*) sich in etw (*acc*) einschleichen

bursar [ˈbɜːsəʳ] N Schatzmeister(in) *m(f)*, Finanzverwalter(in) *m(f)*

bursary [ˈbɜːsərɪ] N **a** (*Brit*: = *grant*) Stipendium *nt* **b** (= *office*) Schatzamt *nt*; (*Univ*) Quästur *f*

burst [bɜːst] *vb: pret, ptp* **burst** **N** **a** (*of shell etc*) Explosion *f*

b (*in pipe etc*) Bruch *m*

c (*of anger, enthusiasm, activity etc*) Ausbruch *m*; (*of flames*) (plötzliches) Auflodern; **~ of laughter** Lachsalve *f*; **~ of applause** Beifallssturm *m*; **~ of speed** Spurt *m*; (*of cars etc*) Riesenbeschleunigung *f* (*inf*); **a ~ of automatic gunfire** eine Maschinengewehrsalve; **give them another ~** verpass ihnen noch eine Salve

VI **a** (*balloon, bubble, tyre*) platzen; **to ~ open** (*box, door etc*) aufspringen; (*buds*) aufbrechen; (*abscess*) aufplatzen; (*wound*) aufbrechen, aufplatzen

b (= *be full to overflowing*: *sack etc*) platzen, bersten; **to fill sth to ~ing point** etw bis zum Platzen *or* Bersten füllen; **to be full to ~ing** zum Platzen *or* Bersten voll sein; **to be ~ing with health** vor Gesundheit strotzen; **to be ~ing with a desire to do sth** vor Begierde brennen, etw zu tun; **to be ~ing with pride** vor Stolz platzen; **if I eat any more, I'll ~** (*inf*) wenn ich noch mehr esse, platze ich (*inf*); **I'm ~ing** (*inf*: = *need the toilet*) ich muss ganz dringend (*inf*); **he was ~ing to tell us** (*inf*) er brannte darauf, uns das zu sagen → **seam**

c (= *start, go suddenly*) **to ~ into tears** in Tränen ausbrechen; **to ~ into flames** in Flammen aufgehen; **he ~ past me** er schoss an mir vorbei; **he ~ into the room** er platzte ins Zimmer; **we ~ through the enemy lines** wir durchbrachen die feindlichen Linien; **the sun ~ through the clouds** die Sonne brach durch die Wolken; **sunlight ~ into the room** Sonnenlicht fiel plötzlich ins Zimmer; **the oil ~ from the well** das Öl brach aus der Quelle; **to ~ into view** plötzlich in Sicht kommen; **to ~ into song** lossingen; **to ~ into bloom** plötzlich aufblühen

VT *balloon, bubble, tyre* zum Platzen bringen,

platzen lassen; *(person)* kaputtmachen *(inf)*; *boiler, pipe, dyke* sprengen; **the river has ~ its banks** der Fluss ist über die Ufer getreten → **blood vessel**

▶ **burst forth** VI *(liter, blood, sun)* hervorbrechen; *(blossoms)* ausbrechen

▶ **burst in** VI hinein-/hereinstürzen; *(on conversation)* dazwischenplatzen (*on* bei); **he burst in on us** er platzte bei uns herein

▶ **burst out** VI **a** *(emotions)* hervorbrechen, herausbrechen; *(lava)* ausbrechen; **she's bursting out of that dress** sie sprengt das Kleid fast **b** **to burst out of a room** aus einem Zimmer stürzen *or* stürmen **c** *(in speech)* losplatzen; **he burst out in fury** er zog plötzlich vom Leder **d** **to burst out laughing/crying** in Gelächter/Tränen ausbrechen, loslachen/losheulen

burthen [ˈbɜːðən] N, VT *(old, liter)* = **burden**[1]

burton [ˈbɜːtn] N *(dated Brit, sl)* **to have gone for a ~** im Eimer sein *(inf)*

bury [ˈberɪ] VT **a** *person, animal, possessions, differences* begraben; *(with ceremony also)* beerdigen, bestatten *(geh)*; *(= hide in earth) treasure, bones* vergraben; *(= put in earth) end of post, roots* eingraben; **where is he buried?** wo liegt *or* ist er begraben?; *(in cemetery also)* wo liegt er?; **to ~ sb at sea** jdn auf See bestatten *(geh)*, jdm ein Seemannsgrab geben; **he is dead and buried** er ist schon lange tot; **that's all dead and buried** *(fig)* das ist schon lange passé *(inf)*; **she has buried three husbands** *(fig)* sie hat schon drei Männer begraben *(inf)*; **buried by an avalanche** von einer Lawine verschüttet *or* begraben; **to be buried in work** *(fig)* bis zum Hals in Arbeit stecken; **to ~ one's head in the sand** *(fig)* den Kopf in den Sand stecken
b *(= conceal) one's face* verbergen; **to ~ one's face in one's hands** das Gesicht in den Händen vergraben; **to ~ oneself under the blankets/(away) in the country** sich unter den Decken/auf dem Land vergraben; **a village buried in the heart of the country** ein im Landesinnern versteckt gelegenes Dorf
c *(= put, plunge) hands, fingers* vergraben (*in* in *+dat*); *claws, teeth* schlagen (*in* in *+acc*); *dagger* stoßen (*in* in *+acc*)
d *(= engross)* **to ~ oneself in one's books** sich in seinen Büchern vergraben

burying ground N Begräbnisstätte *f*

bus[1] [bʌs] **N** *pl* **-es** *or (US)* **-ses** **a** Bus *m*; **by ~** mit dem Bus → **miss**[1] **b** *(inf: = car, plane)* Kiste *f (inf)* **VI** *(inf)* mit dem Bus fahren **VT** *(esp US)* mit dem Bus befördern *or* fahren

bus[2] N *(Comput)* (Daten)bus *m*

bus boy N *(US)* Bedienungshilfe *f*

busby [ˈbʌzbɪ] N hohe Pelzmütze

bus: **bus conductor** N (Omni)busschaffner *m*; **bus conductress** N (Omni)busschaffnerin *f*; **bus depot** N (Omni)busdepot *nt*; **bus driver** N (Omni)busfahrer(in) *m(f)*; **bus garage** N (Omni)bushalle *f*

bush[1] [bʊʃ] N **a** *(= shrub)* Busch *m*, Strauch *m*; *(= thicket: also* **bushes***)* Gebüsch *nt*; **to beat about** *(Brit) or* **around the ~** *(fig)* um den heißen Brei herumreden; *(= not act, take decision etc)* wie die Katze um den heißen Brei herumschleichen **b** *(in Africa, Australia)* Busch *m*; *(Austral: = the country)* freies *or* offenes Land **c** *(fig)* **~ of hair** Haarschopf *m*

▶ **bush out** VI *(hair, tail)* buschig sein

bush[2] N *(Tech)* Buchse *f*

bushbaby [ˈbʊʃˌbeɪbɪ] N Buschbaby *nt*

bushed [bʊʃt] ADJ *(inf: = exhausted)* groggy *(inf)*

bushel [ˈbʊʃl] N Scheffel *m*; **to hide one's light under a ~** *(prov)* sein Licht unter den Scheffel stellen *(prov)*

bushfire [ˈbʊʃfaɪəʳ] N Buschfeuer *nt*

bushiness [ˈbʊʃɪnɪs] N Buschigkeit *f*

bushing [ˈbʊʃɪŋ] N *(US)* = **bush**[2]

bush: **bush league** N *(US)* Provinzliga *f*; **bush leaguer** N *(US)* Provinzspieler *m*; *(fig)* Dilettant *m*; **bushman** N *(Austral) jd, der im Busch lebt und arbeitet*; **Bushman** N *(in S Africa)* Buschmann *m*; **bushranger** N **a** *(Austral)* Bandit *m*, Strauchdieb *m (dated)* **b** *(US, Canada) jd, der in der Wildnis lebt*; **bush telegraph** N *(lit)* Urwaldtelefon *nt*; **I heard it on the ~** *(fig inf)* ich habe da so was läuten gehört *(inf)*, das ist mir zu Ohren gekommen; **bushwhack** **VI** in den Wäldern hausen **VT** *(= ambush)* (aus dem Hinterhalt) überfallen; **bushwhacker** N *(= frontiersman) jd, der in den Wäldern haust (= bandit)* Bandit *m*; *(= guerilla)* Guerilla(kämpfer) *m*

bushy [ˈbʊʃɪ] ADJ *(+er)* buschig

busily [ˈbɪzɪlɪ] ADV *(= actively, eagerly)* eifrig

business [ˈbɪznɪs] N **a** *no pl (= commerce)* Geschäft *nt*; *(= line of business)* Branche *f*; **to be in ~** Geschäftsmann sein; **I am in ~ with him** ich habe geschäftlich mit ihm zu tun; **to go into ~** Geschäftsmann werden; **to go into ~ with sb** mit jdm ein Geschäft gründen; **what line of ~ is she in?** was macht sie beruflich?; **to be in the publishing/insurance ~** im Verlagswesen/der Versicherungsbranche tätig sein; **to set up in ~** ein Geschäft gründen; **to set up in ~ as a butcher/lawyer** *etc* sich als Fleischer/Rechtsanwalt *etc* niederlassen; **to go out of ~** zumachen; **to do ~ with sb** Geschäfte *pl* mit jdm machen; **~ is ~** Geschäft ist Geschäft; **"business as usual"** *(during renovation etc)* das Geschäft bleibt geöffnet; **it's ~ as usual** alles geht wie gewohnt weiter; **how's ~?** wie gehen die Geschäfte?; **~ is good** die Geschäfte gehen gut; **to look for ~** sich nach Aufträgen umsehen; **to go to Paris on ~** geschäftlich nach Paris fahren; **he is here/away on ~** er ist geschäftlich hier/unterwegs; **to know one's ~** seine Sache verstehen; **to get down to ~** zur Sache kommen; **to combine** *or* **mix ~ with pleasure** das Angenehme mit dem Nützlichen verbinden; **you shouldn't mix ~ with pleasure** man sollte Geschäftliches und Vergnügen trennen; **looking for ~?** *(asked by prostitute)* na, Süßer, wie wärs?
b *(fig inf)* **now we're in ~** jetzt kanns losgehen *(inf)*; **to mean ~** es ernst meinen; **it's/she's the ~** das/sie ist spitze *(inf)*
c *(= commercial enterprise)* Geschäft *nt*, Betrieb *m*; **a small ~** ein kleines Unternehmen; **a family ~** ein Familienunternehmen *nt*
d *(= concern)* Sache *f*, Angelegenheit *f*; *(= task, duty also)* Aufgabe *f*; **that's my ~** das ist meine Sache *or* Angelegenheit; **that's no ~ of mine/yours, that's none of my/your ~** das geht mich/dich nichts an; **to make it one's ~ to do sth** es sich *(dat)* zur Aufgabe machen, etw zu tun; **you should make it your ~ to see that all the products ...** Sie sollten sich darum kümmern, dass alle Produkte ...; **you've no ~ doing that** du hast kein Recht, das zu tun; **we are not in the ~ of doing that** es ist nicht unsere Aufgabe, das zu tun; **to send sb about his ~** jdn in seine Schranken weisen; **I must be about my ~** *(form)* ich muss (jetzt) meinen Geschäften nachgehen → **mind**
e *(= difficult job)* Problem *nt*
f *(inf: = affair)* Sache *f*; **I am tired of this protest ~** ich hab genug von dieser Protestiererei *(inf)*; **moving house can be a costly/stressful ~** ein Umzug kann ganz schön teuer/stressig sein → **funny**
g *(Theat)* dargestellte Handlung
h *(inf, = defecation: of dog, child)* Geschäft *nt (inf)*; **to do one's ~** sein Geschäft machen *or* verrichten *(inf)*

business: **business acumen** N Geschäftstüchtigkeit *f*, Geschäftssinn *m*; **business address** N Geschäftsadresse *f*; **business associate** N Geschäftsfreund(in) *m(f)*; *(= business partner)* Geschäftspartner(in) *m(f)*; **business card** N (Visiten)karte *f*; **business centre**, *(US)* **business center** N Geschäftszentrum *nt*; **business class** N Businessclass *f*, Businessklasse *f*; **business college** N Wirtschaftshochschule *f*; **business consultant** N Betriebsberater(in) *m(f)*; **business culture** N Geschäftskultur *f*; **business development loan** N Investitionskredit *m*; **business end** N *(inf, of knife, chisel etc)* scharfes Ende; *(of rifle etc)* Lauf *m*; **business expenses** PL Spesen *pl*; **business hours** PL Geschäftsstunden *pl*, Geschäftszeit *f*; **business letter** N Geschäftsbrief *m*

businesslike [ˈbɪznɪslaɪk] ADJ *person, firm (= good at doing business)* geschäftstüchtig; *person, manner* geschäftsmäßig; *transaction* geschäftlich; *(= efficient) person, prose* kühl und sachlich, nüchtern; **I want something ~** *(when buying clothes)* ich möchte etwas Schickes für die Arbeit

business: **business lunch** N Geschäftsessen *nt*; **businessman** N Geschäftsmann *m*; **business management** N Betriebswirtschaft(slehre) *f*; **business manager** N *(for theatre)* Verwaltungsdirektor(in) *m(f)*; *(of pop star etc)* Manager(in) *m(f)*; **business model** N Geschäftsmodell *nt*; **business park** N Industriegelände *nt*; **business people** PL Geschäftsleute *pl*; **business plan** N Geschäftsplan *m*; **business practices** PL Geschäftsgebaren *nt no pl*; **business proposition** N *(= proposal)* Geschäftsangebot *nt*; *(= idea)* Geschäftsvorhaben *nt*; **business school** N Wirtschaftsschule *f*; **business sense** N Geschäftssinn *m*; **business studies** PL Wirtschaftslehre *f*; **business suit** N Straßenanzug *m*; **business trip** N Geschäftsreise *f*; **businesswoman** N Geschäftsfrau *f*; **business year** N Geschäftsjahr *nt*

busing [ˈbʌsɪŋ] N = **bussing**

busk [bʌsk] VI *als Straßenmusikant vor Kinos, Theatern etc spielen*

busker [ˈbʌskəʳ] N Straßenmusikant *m*

bus: **bus lane** N Busspur *f*; **busload** N **a ~ of children** eine Busladung Kinder; **by the ~** *(inf)* **in ~s** *(inf)* busweise *(inf)*; **busman** N **a ~'s holiday** *(fig)* praktisch eine Fortsetzung der Arbeit im Urlaub; **bus pass** N Seniorenkarte *f* für Busse; *(for the disabled)* Behindertenkarte *f* für Busse; **bus route** N Buslinie *f*; **we're not on a ~** wir haben keine Busverbindungen; **bus service** N Busverbindung *f*; *(= network)* Busverbindungen *pl*; **bus shelter** N Wartehäuschen *nt*

bussing [ˈbʌsɪŋ] N *(esp US) Busbeförderung von Schulkindern in andere Bezirke, um Rassentrennung zu verhindern*

bus: **bus station** N Busbahnhof *m*; **bus stop** N Bushaltestelle *f*

bust[1] [bʌst] N Büste *f*; *(Anat also)* Busen *m*; **~ measurement** Brustumfang *m*, Oberweite *f*

bust[2] *vb: pret, ptp* **bust** *(inf)* **ADJ** **a** *(= broken)* kaputt *(inf)*
b *(= bankrupt)* pleite *(inf)*
ADV *(= bankrupt)* **to go ~** pleitegehen *or* Pleite machen *(inf)*
N *(US: = failure)* Pleite *f (inf)*
VT **a** *(= break)* kaputt machen *(inf)*; **to ~ sth open** etw aufbrechen; **to ~ a gut** sich *(dat)* den Arsch aufreißen *(sl)*; **he just about ~ a gut doing it** er hat sich *(dat)* dabei fast einen abgebrochen *(inf)*; **don't ~ my chops!** *(US: expressing annoyance and disbelief)* na, na, na! *(inf)*, jetzt hör aber auf! *(inf)*
b *(= catch, convict)* hinter Schloss und Riegel bringen; *drugs ring, syndicate* auffliegen lassen *(inf)*; **he got ~ed for driving without a license** *(US)* er ist ohne Führerschein erwischt worden
c *(US Mil: = demote)* degradieren (*to* zu)
VI *(= break)* kaputtgehen *(inf)*

▶ **bust out** *(inf)* **VI** ausbrechen **VT** *sep* herausholen *(inf)*

▶ **bust up** VT *sep (inf) box* kaputt machen *(inf)*; *marriage* kaputtmachen *(inf)*; *meeting* auffliegen lassen *(inf)*; *(by starting fights)* stören; **I hate to bust up the party** tut mir leid, dass ich die traute Runde stören muss

bustard [ˈbʌstəd] N Trappe *f*

buster [ˈbʌstəʳ] N *(esp US inf, as address)* Meister *m (inf)*; *(threatening)* Freundchen *nt (inf)*

-buster *suf (inf)* -brecher; **sanctions-buster** Sanktionsbrecher(in) *m(f)*; **crime-buster** Verbrechensbekämpfer(in) *m(f)*

bus ticket N Busfahrschein *m*

bustier ['bu:stɪeɪ, 'bʌstɪeɪ] N *(Fashion)* Bustier *nt*

bustle[1] ['bʌsl] N Betrieb *m* (*of* in *+dat*); *(of fair, streets also)* geschäftiges *or* reges Treiben (*of* auf *or* in *+dat*) VI **to ~ about** geschäftig hin und her eilen *or* sausen *(inf)*; **to ~ in** geschäftig hinein-/hereineilen *or* -sausen *(inf)*; **to ~ out** geschäftig hinaus-/herauseilen *or* -sausen *(inf)*; **the marketplace was bustling with activity** auf dem Markt herrschte großer Betrieb *or* ein reges Treiben

bustle[2] N *(Fashion)* Turnüre *f*

bustling ['bʌslɪŋ] ADJ *person* geschäftig; *place, scene* belebt, voller Leben

bust-up ['bʌstʌp] N *(inf)* Krach *m (inf)*; **they had a ~** sie haben Krach gehabt *(inf)*; *(= split up)* sie haben sich verkracht *(inf)*

busty ['bʌstɪ] ADJ *(+er) (inf) woman* vollbusig

busway ['bʌsweɪ] N *(US)* Busspur *f*

busy ['bɪzɪ] ✪ 27.3 ADJ *(+er)* **a** *(= occupied) person* beschäftigt; **a very ~ man** ein viel beschäftigter Mann; **are you ~?** haben Sie gerade Zeit?; *(in business)* haben Sie viel zu tun?; **not now, I'm ~** jetzt nicht, ich bin gerade beschäftigt; **the boss is always ~** der Chef hat immer viel zu tun; *(= never available)* der Chef hat nie Zeit; **I'll come back when you're less ~** ich komme wieder, wenn Sie mehr Zeit haben; **to keep sb/oneself ~** jdn/sich selbst beschäftigen; **I was ~ studying when you called** ich war gerade beim Lernen, als Sie kamen; **I was ~ studying all evening** ich war den ganzen Abend mit Lernen beschäftigt; **she's always too ~ thinking about herself** sie ist immer zu sehr mit sich selbst beschäftigt; **they were ~ plotting against him** sie haben eifrig Pläne gegen ihn geschmiedet; **let's get ~** an die Arbeit!
b *(= active) life, time* bewegt; *place, street, town* belebt; *(with traffic)* verkehrsreich; *street* stark befahren; **it's been a ~ day/week** heute/diese Woche war viel los; **have you had a ~ day?** hast du heute viel zu tun gehabt?; **he leads a very ~ life** bei ihm ist immer etwas los; **the shop was ~ all day** im Geschäft war den ganzen Tag viel los
c *(esp US) telephone line* besetzt
d *(= officious) person, manner* (über)eifrig
e *pattern, design, print* unruhig
VR **to ~ oneself doing sth** sich damit beschäftigen, etw zu tun; **to ~ oneself with sth** sich mit etw beschäftigen

busybody ['bɪzɪ'bɒdɪ] N Wichtigtuer *m*, Gschaftlhuber *m (S Ger)*; **don't be such a ~** misch dich nicht überall ein

busy signal, busy tone N *(esp US Telec)* Besetztzeichen *nt*

but [bʌt] CONJ **a** aber; **~ you must know that ...** Sie müssen aber wissen, dass ..., aber Sie müssen wissen, dass ...; **~ HE didn't know that** aber er hat das nicht gewusst, er hat das aber nicht gewusst; **~ he didn't know that** er aber hat das nicht gewusst; **they all went ~ I didn't** sie sind alle gegangen, nur ich nicht
b not X ~ Y nicht X sondern Y
c *(subordinating)* ohne dass; **never a week passes ~ she is ill** keine Woche vergeht, ohne dass sie krank ist; **I would have helped ~ that I was ill** *(old, liter)* ich hätte geholfen, wäre ich nicht krank gewesen *(old)*
d ~ then he couldn't have known that aber er hat das ja gar nicht wissen können; **~ then you must be my brother!** dann müssen Sie ja mein Bruder sein!; **~ then do you mean to say ...** wollen Sie dann etwa sagen ...; **~ then it is well paid** aber dafür wird es gut bezahlt
ADV **she's ~ a child** sie ist doch noch ein Kind; **I cannot (help) ~ think that ...** ich kann nicht umhin zu denken, dass ...; **one cannot ~ admire him/suspect that ...** man kann ihn nur bewundern/nur annehmen, dass ...; **you can ~ try** du kannst es immerhin versuchen; **I had no alternative ~ to leave** mir blieb keine andere Wahl als zu gehen; **she left ~ a few minutes ago** sie ist erst vor ein paar Minuten gegangen; **Napoleon, to name ~ one, lived here** Napoleon, um nur einen zu nennen, hat hier gelebt
PREP **no one ~ me could do it** niemand außer mir *or* nur ich konnte es tun; **who ~ Fred would ...?** wer außer Fred würde ...?; **anything ~ that!** (alles,) nur das nicht!; **it was anything ~ simple** das war alles andere als einfach; **he/it was nothing ~ trouble** er/das hat nichts als *or* nur Schwierigkeiten gemacht; **the last house ~ one/two/three** das vorletzte/vorvorletzte/drittletzte Haus; **the first ~ one** der/die/das Zweite; **the next street ~ one/two/three** die übernächste/überübernächste Straße/vier Straßen weiter; **~ for you I would be dead** ohne Sie wäre ich tot, wenn Sie nicht gewesen wären, wäre ich tot; **I could definitely live in Scotland, ~ for the weather** ich könnte ganz bestimmt in Schottland leben, wenn das Wetter nicht wäre
N **no ~s about it** kein Aber *nt*

but and ben N *(Scot) Hütte bestehend aus Küche und kleiner Schlafkammer*

butane ['bju:teɪn] N Butan *nt*

butch [bʊtʃ] ADJ *(inf) clothes, hairstyle, manner* maskulin

butcher ['bʊtʃəʳ] N **a** Fleischer *m*, Metzger *m (dial)*, Schlachter *m (N Ger)*; **~'s (shop)** Fleischerei *f*, Metzgerei *f (dial)*, Schlachterei *f (N Ger)*; **at the ~'s** beim Fleischer *etc*; **~'s boy** Fleischerjunge *etc m*; **~'s wife** Fleischersfrau *etc f*
b *(fig: = murderer)* Schlächter *m*
c butchers PL *(Brit inf: = look)* **give us a ~s** lass mal gucken *(inf)*; **take** *or* **have a ~s (at that)** guck mal (das an) *(inf)*; **do you want a ~s?** willste mal gucken? *(inf)*
VT *animals* schlachten; *people* abschlachten, niedermetzeln; *(fig) play, piece of music, language* vergewaltigen; **his ~ed body** seine schrecklich zugerichtete Leiche

butchery ['bʊtʃərɪ] N *(= slaughter)* Gemetzel *nt*, Metzelei *f*; **the ~ of millions** das Abschlachten *or* Niedermetzeln von Millionen; **stop the fight, this is ~!** brechen Sie den Kampf ab, das ist ja das reinste Gemetzel!

butler ['bʌtləʳ] N Butler *m*

> **BUTLINS**
>
> **Butlins** ist eine britische Ferienklubkette, die Rundum-Urlaub für die ganze Familie anbietet, wobei Wert auf ein gutes Preis-Leistungs-Verhältnis gelegt wird. Auf einem einzigen Gelände findet man Unterkünfte, Restaurants, Bars und ein breites Freizeitangebot. Für jedes Alter wird etwas geboten, zum Beispiel Sportwettkämpfe, Rummelplätze und Musikkonzerte für die Kinder und Jugendlichen oder Bingo und Tanzveranstaltungen für die älteren Semester. Die Animateure von Butlins werden **redcoats** (Rotröcke) genannt, weil rote Jacken das dominierende Element ihres Outfits sind.

butt[1] [bʌt] N *(for wine)* großes Fass; *(for rainwater)* Tonne *f*

butt[2] N (*also* **butt end**) dickes Ende; *(of rifle)* (Gewehr)kolben *m*; *(of cigar, cigarette)* Stummel *m*

butt[3] N *(US inf: = cigarette)* Kippe *f (inf)*

butt[4] N **a** *(= target)* Schießscheibe *f* **b** *usu pl (on shooting range, behind targets)* Kugelfang *m*; *(in front of targets)* Schutzwall *m*; *(= range itself)* Schießstand *m* **c** *(fig: = person)* Zielscheibe *f*; **she's always the ~ of his jokes** sie ist immer (die) Zielscheibe seines Spottes

butt[5] N (Kopf)stoß *m*; **to give sb a ~** jdn mit dem Kopf stoßen; *(goat also)* jdn mit den Hörnern stoßen VT mit dem Kopf stoßen; *(goat also)* mit den Hörnern stoßen

▶ **butt at** VI *+prep obj (goat)* stoßen gegen

▶ **butt in** VI sich einmischen (*on* in *+acc*), dazwischenfunken *or* -platzen *(inf)* (*on* bei)

▶ **butt into** VI *+prep obj* sich einmischen in *(+acc)*, dazwischenfunken *or* dazwischenplatzen bei *(inf)*

butt[6] N *(US inf: = backside)* Arsch *m (vulg)*; **get up off your ~** setz mal deinen Arsch in Bewegung *(sl)*

butt call N *(US inf) unbeabsichtigter Anruf durch Sitzen auf dem Handy*

butter ['bʌtəʳ] N Butter *f*; **she looks as if ~ wouldn't melt in her mouth** sie sieht aus, als ob sie kein Wässerchen trüben könnte VT *bread etc* mit Butter bestreichen, buttern

▶ **butter up** VT *sep (inf)* schöntun *(+dat)*, um den Bart gehen *(+dat) (inf)*

butter: **butterball** N *(US inf: = fat person)* Fettkloß *m (inf)*; **butter bean** N Mondbohne *f*; **buttercup** N Butterblume *f*, Hahnenfuß *m*; **butter dish** N Butterdose *f*; **butterfingers** N *sing (inf)* Schussel *m (inf)*; **~!** du Schussel! *(inf)*

butterfly ['bʌtəflaɪ] N **a** Schmetterling *m*; **I've got/I get butterflies (in my stomach)** mir ist/wird ganz flau im Magen *(inf)*, mir ist/wird ganz mulmig zumute *or* zu Mute *(inf)* **b** *(Swimming)* Schmetterlingsstil *m*, Butterfly *m*; **can you do the ~?** können Sie Butterfly *or* den Schmetterlingsstil?

butterfly: **butterfly bandage** N Pflasterzugverband *m*; **butterfly kiss** N Schmetterlingskuss *m*; **butterfly net** N Schmetterlingsnetz *nt*; **butterfly nut** N Flügelmutter *f*; **butterfly stroke** N Schmetterlingsstil *m*, Butterfly *m*

butter: **butter icing** N ≈ Buttercreme *f*; **butter knife** N Buttermesser *nt*; **butter mountain** N Butterberg *m*; **buttermilk** N Buttermilch *f*; **butterscotch** N ≈ Karamellbonbon *m* ADJ Karamell-; **butterwort** N *(Bot)* Fettkraut *nt*

buttery ['bʌtərɪ] N Vorratskammer *f*; *(Univ)* Cafeteria *f*

buttock ['bʌtək] N (Hinter)backe *f*, Gesäßhälfte *f (form)*; **~s** *pl* Gesäß *nt*, Hintern *m (inf)*

button ['bʌtn] N **a** Knopf *m*; **not worth a ~** *(inf)* keinen Pfifferling wert *(inf)*; **his answer was right on the ~** *(inf)* seine Antwort hat voll ins Schwarze getroffen *(inf)*; **he arrived right on the ~** *(inf)* er kam auf den Glockenschlag *(inf)*; **to push** *or* **press the right ~s** *(fig inf)* es richtig anstellen *(inf)*; **she knew which ~s to press to get what she wanted** *(fig inf)* sie wusste, wie sie es anstellen musste, um zu bekommen, was sie wollte *(inf)*
b *(= mushroom)* junger Champignon
c ~s *sing (inf, = pageboy)* (Hotel)page *m*
d *(Comput)* Schaltfläche *f*, Button *m*
e *(esp US: = badge)* Sticker *m*, Button *m*
VT *garment* zuknöpfen; **~ your lip** *(inf)* halt den Mund *(inf)*
VI *(garment)* geknöpft werden

▶ **button up** VT *sep* zuknöpfen; **to have a deal all buttoned up** ein Geschäft unter Dach und Fach haben

button cell (battery) N Knopfzelle *f*

button-down ['bʌtndaʊn] ADJ **~ collar** Button-down-Kragen *m*

buttoned-up ['bʌtnd,ʌp] ADJ *(inf: = reserved)* zugeknöpft *(inf)*

button: **buttonhole** N **a** *(in garment)* Knopfloch *nt* **b** *(= flower)* Blume *f* im Knopfloch; **to sell ~s** Blumen fürs Knopfloch verkaufen VT *(fig)* zu fassen bekommen, sich *(dat)* schnappen *(inf)*; **buttonhole stitch** N Knopflochstich *m*; **buttonhook** N *(for boots)* Stiefelknöpfer *m*; **button mushroom** N junger Champignon

buttress ['bʌtrɪs] N *(Archit)* Strebepfeiler *m*; *(fig)* Pfeiler *m* VT *(Archit) wall* (durch Strebepfeiler) stützen; *(fig)* stützen

butty ['bʊtɪ] N *(esp N Engl inf)* Stulle *f (dial)*

buxom ['bʌksəm] ADJ drall

buy [baɪ] *vb: pret, ptp* **bought** VT **a** *(= purchase)* kaufen; *(Rail) ticket also* lösen; **there are some things that money can't ~** es gibt Dinge, die man nicht kaufen kann; **all that money can ~** alles, was man mit Geld kaufen kann; **to ~ and sell goods** Waren an- und verkaufen

b *(fig) victory, fame* sich *(dat)* erkaufen; *time* gewinnen; *(= bribe)* bestechen, kaufen; **the victory was dearly bought** der Sieg war teuer erkauft
c to ~ sth *(inf: = accept)* etw akzeptieren; **I'll ~ that** das ist o.k. *(inf)*; *(= believe)* ja, das glaube ich
d *(inf, = be killed)* **he bought it** den hats erwischt *(inf)*
VI kaufen
N *(inf)* Kauf *m*; **to be a good ~** ein guter Kauf sein; *(clothes also, food)* preiswert sein

▶ **buy back** VT *sep* zurückkaufen

▶ **buy forward** VT *(Fin)* auf Termin kaufen

▶ **buy in** VT *sep (= acquire supply of) goods* einkaufen

▶ **buy into** VI +*prep obj* **a** *(Comm) business, organization, industry* sich einkaufen in *(+acc)* **b** *(fig)* schlucken *(inf)*, akzeptieren

▶ **buy off** VT *sep (inf: = bribe)* kaufen *(inf)*

▶ **buy out** VT *sep* **a** *shareholders etc* auszahlen; *firm* aufkaufen **b** *(from army)* los- *or* freikaufen (*of* von)

▶ **buy over** VT *sep* kaufen; *(= get on one's side)* für sich gewinnen

▶ **buy up** VT *sep* aufkaufen

buy-back [ˈbaɪˌbæk] ADJ **~ option** Rückkaufoption *f*; **~ price** Rückkaufpreis *m*

buyer [ˈbaɪəʳ] N Käufer *m*; *(= agent)* Einkäufer *m*; **~'s market** Käufermarkt *m*

buyout [ˈbaɪaʊt] N Aufkauf *m*

buzz [bʌz] VI **a** *(insect)* summen, brummen; *(smaller or agitated insects)* schwirren; *(device)* summen; **did you ~, sir?** haben Sie nach mir verlangt?; **Miss Jones, I've been ~ing for 10 minutes** Fräulein Jones, ich versuche schon seit 10 Minuten, Sie zu erreichen
b my ears are ~ing mir dröhnen die Ohren; **my head is ~ing** *(with ideas etc)* mir schwirrt der Kopf; *(from noise)* mir dröhnt der Kopf
c the town is ~ing in der Stadt ist was los *(inf) or* herrscht reges Leben; **the city was ~ing with excitement** die Stadt war in heller Aufregung; **the news set the town ~ing** die Nachricht versetzte die Stadt in helle Aufregung
VT **a** *(= call) secretary* (mit dem Summer) rufen
b *(US inf: = telephone)* anrufen
c *(plane) plane, building* dicht vorbeifliegen an *(+dat)*; **we were ~ed** Flugzeuge flogen dicht an uns heran
N **a** *(of insect)* Summen *nt*, Brummen *nt*; *(of smaller or agitated insects)* Schwirren *nt*; *(of device)* Summen *nt*
b *(of conversation)* Stimmengewirr *nt*, Gemurmel *nt*; **~ of excitement/anticipation** aufgeregtes/erwartungsvolles Gemurmel
c *(inf: = telephone call)* Anruf *m*; **to give sb a ~** jdn anrufen; *(= signal) secretary etc* jdn (mit dem Summer) rufen
d *(inf: = thrill)* Kitzel *m*; **driving fast gives me a ~, I get a ~ from driving fast** ich verspüre einen Kitzel, wenn ich schnell fahre

▶ **buzz about** *(Brit) or* **around** VI *(inf)* herumschwirren

▶ **buzz in** VT *(esp US: inf)* **to buzz sb in** jdn per Türöffner hereinlassen *or* ins Haus lassen

▶ **buzz off** VI *(Brit inf)* abzischen *(inf)*

buzzard [ˈbʌzəd] N Bussard *m*

buzz bomb N Fernrakete *f*

buzzed ADJ *(US inf: = drunk)* besoffen *(inf)*, hackedicht *(inf)*

buzzer [ˈbʌzəʳ] N Summer *m*

buzz: buzz phrase N Modeausdruck *m*; **buzz topic** N Modethema *nt*; **buzz word** N Modewort *nt*

b/w *abbr of* **black and white** S/W

by [baɪ] PREP **a** *(= close to)* bei, an *(+dat)*; *(with movement)* an *(+acc)*; *(= next to)* neben *(+dat)*; *(with movement)* neben *(+acc)*; **by the window/fire/river** am *or* beim Fenster/Feuer/Fluss; **by the church** an *or* bei der Kirche; **a holiday** *(esp Brit) or* **vacation** *(US)* **by the sea** Ferien *pl* an der See; **come and sit by me** komm, setz dich neben mich; **she sat by me** sie saß neben mir; **to keep sth by one** etw bei sich haben
b *(= via)* über *(+acc)*
c *(= past)* **to go/rush** *etc* **by sb/sth** an jdm/etw vorbeigehen/-eilen *etc*
d *(time: = during)* **by day/night** bei Tag/Nacht
e *(time: = not later than)* bis; **can you do it by tomorrow?** kannst du es bis morgen machen?; **by tomorrow I'll be in France** morgen werde ich in Frankreich sein; **by the time I got there, he had gone** bis ich dorthin kam, war er gegangen; **but by that time** *or* **by then I had realized that ...** aber bis dahin war mir klar geworden, dass ...; **but by that time** *or* **by then it will be too late** aber dann ist es schon zu spät; **but by that time** *or* **by then he will have forgotten** aber bis dann *or* dahin hat er es schon vergessen; **by now** inzwischen
f *(indicating amount)* **by the inch/kilo/hour/month** zoll-/kilo-/stunden-/monatsweise; **one by one** einer nach dem anderen; **they came in two by two** sie kamen paarweise herein; **letters came in by the hundred** hunderte *or* Hunderte von Briefen kamen
g *(indicating agent, cause)* von; **killed by a bullet** durch eine *or* von einer Kugel getötet; **indicated by an asterisk** durch Sternchen gekennzeichnet; **a painting by Picasso** ein Bild von Picasso; **surrounded by** umgeben von
h *(indicating method, means, manner: see also nouns)* **by bus/car/bicycle** mit dem *or* per Bus/Auto/Fahrrad; **by land and (by) sea** zu Land und zu Wasser; **to pay by cheque** *(Brit) or* **check** *(US)* mit Scheck bezahlen; **made by hand** handgearbeitet; **made by machine** maschinell hergestellt; **by daylight/moonlight** bei Tag(eslicht)/im Mondschein; **to know sb by name/sight** jdn dem Namen nach/vom Sehen her kennen; **to be known by the name of ...** unter dem Namen ... bekannt sein; **to lead sb by the hand** jdn an der Hand führen; **to grab sb by the collar** jdn am Kragen packen; **he had a daughter by his first wife** von seiner ersten Frau hatte er eine Tochter; **by myself/himself** *etc* allein
i by saving hard he managed to ... durch eisernes Sparen *or* dadurch, dass er eisern sparte, gelang es ihm ...; **by turning this knob** durch Drehen dieses Knopfes, wenn Sie an diesem Knopf drehen; **by saying that I didn't mean ...** ich habe damit nicht gemeint ...; **animals which move by wriggling** Tiere, die sich schlängelnd fortbewegen; **he could walk by supporting himself on ...** gestützt auf ... könnte er gehen
j *(according to: see also nouns)* nach; **to judge by appearances** nach dem Äußern urteilen; **by my watch it is nine o'clock** nach meiner Uhr ist es neun; **if you play by the rules** *(fig)* wenn du dich an die Regel hältst; **by the terms of Article I** gemäß *or* nach (den Bestimmungen von) Artikel I; **to call sb/sth by his/its proper name** jdn/etw beim richtigen Namen nennen; **if it's OK by you/him** *etc* wenn es Ihnen/ihm *etc* recht ist; **it's all right by me** von mir aus gern *or* schon
k *(measuring difference)* um; **broader by a foot** um einen Fuß breiter; **it missed me by inches** es verfehlte mich um Zentimeter
l *(Math, Measure)* **to divide/multiply by** dividieren durch/multiplizieren mit; **a room 20 feet by 30** ein Zimmer 20 auf *or* mal 30 Fuß
m *(points of compass)* **South by South West** Südsüdwest
n *(in oaths)* bei; **I swear by Almighty God** ich schwöre beim allmächtigen Gott; **by heaven, I'll get you for this** das sollst *or* wirst du mir, bei Gott, büßen!
o by the right! *(Mil)* rechts, links ...!
p by the way *or* **by(e)** übrigens; **all this is by the way** *or* **by(e)** *(= irrelevant)* das ist alles Nebensache *or* zweitrangig
ADV **a** *(= past)* **to pass/wander/rush** *etc* **by** vorbei- *or* vorüberkommen/-wandern/-eilen *etc*
b *(= in reserve)* **to put** *or* **lay by** beiseitelegen
c *(phrases)* **by and by** irgendwann; *(with past tense)* nach einiger Zeit; **by and large** im Großen und Ganzen

by(e) [baɪ] N **a** *(Cricket) Lauf bei Bällen, die nicht vom Schlagmann geschlagen worden sind* **b bye** *(Sport)* **to get a bye into the second round** spielfrei in die zweite Runde kommen

bye [baɪ] INTERJ *(inf)* tschüs(s); **~ for now!** bis bald!

bye-bye [ˈbaɪˈbaɪ] INTERJ *(inf)* Wiedersehen *(inf)*; **that's ~ £200** (da sind) £ 200 futsch! *(inf)* N **to go (to) ~s** *(Brit baby-talk) or* **~** *(US baby-talk)* in die Heia gehen *(baby-talk)*

by(e): **by(e)-election** [baɪˈlekʃən] N Nachwahl *f*; **by(e)-law** [ˈbaɪlɔː] N **a** *(Brit: of community)* Gemeindeverordnung *f*; *(of town)* städtische Verordnung **b** *(of company, society etc)* Satzung *f*

Byelorussia [ˌbjeləʊˈrʌʃə] N Weißrussland *nt*

Byelorussian [ˌbjeləʊˈrʌʃən] ADJ weißrussisch N **a** Weißrusse *m*, Weißrussin *f* **b** *(Ling)* Weißrussisch *nt*

bygone [ˈbaɪgɒn] ADJ längst vergangen; **in ~ days** in früheren Zeiten N **to let ~s be ~s** die Vergangenheit ruhen lassen

by: bylaw, bye-law N Verordnung *f*; **by-line** N **a** *(Press) Zeile mit dem Namen des Autors* **b** *(Ftbl)* Seitenlinie *f*; *(at goal)* Tor(aus)linie *f*; **byname** N Inbegriff *m* (*for* von); **X is a ~ for tractors** X ist der Name für Traktoren

BYO *abbr of* **bring your own** *Restaurant ohne Schankerlaubnis, in dem mitgebrachte alkoholische Getränke verzehrt werden dürfen*

BYOB *abbr of* **bring your own bottle** *or* **beer** *or (inf)* **booze** alkoholische Getränke sind mitzubringen

bypass [ˈbaɪpɑːs] N *(= road)* Umgehungsstraße *f*; *(Med, Tech: = pipe etc)* Bypass *m*; **he's had a charisma/humour** *(Brit) or* **humor** *(US)* **~** *(inf)* als Charisma/Humor verteilt wurde, haben sie ihn vergessen VT *town, village* umgehen; *(Med)* umgehen; *(Tech) fluid, gas* umleiten; *(fig) person* übergehen; *intermediate stage also* überspringen; *difficulties* umgehen

bypass: bypass operation N Bypassoperation *f*; **bypass surgery** N Bypasschirurgie *f*; **to have ~** sich einer Bypassoperation unterziehen

by: by-play N *(Theat)* Nebenhandlung *f*; **by-product** [ˈbaɪprɒdʌkt] N *(lit, fig)* Nebenprodukt *nt*

byre [ˈbaɪəʳ] N (Kuh)stall *m*

by: byroad N Neben- *or* Seitenstraße *f*; **bystander** N Umstehende(r) *mf*, Zuschauer *m*; **innocent ~** unbeteiligter Zuschauer

byte [baɪt] N *(Comput)* Byte *nt*

by: byway N Seitenweg *m* → **highway**; **byword** N **to become a ~ for sth** gleichbedeutend mit etw werden

Byzantine [baɪˈzæntaɪn] ADJ byzantinisch N Byzantiner(in) *m(f)*

Byzantium [baɪˈzæntɪəm] N Byzanz *nt*

C

C, c [siː] C, c *nt*; **C sharp** Cis *nt*, cis *nt*; **C flat** Ces *nt*, ces *nt* → *also* **major, minor, natural**

C *abbr of* **centigrade** C

c **a** *abbr of* **cent** c, ct **b** *abbr of* **circa** ca

C4 *(Brit TV) abbr of* **Channel Four**

CA **a** *abbr of* **chartered accountant** **b** *abbr of* **Central America**

c/a *abbr of* **current account**

cab [kæb] N **a** *(= taxi)* Taxi *nt*, Taxe *f (inf)*, Droschke *f (form)* **b** *(of railway engine, lorry, crane)* Führerhaus *nt*

cabal [kəˈbæl] N **a** *(= intrigue)* Intrige *f*, Komplott *nt*, Kabale *f (old liter)* **b** *(= group)* Clique *f*, Kamarilla *f (geh)*

cabaret [ˈkæbəreɪ] N Varieté *nt*, Varietee *nt*; *(satirical)* Kabarett *nt*

cabbage [ˈkæbɪdʒ] N **a** Kohl *m*, Kraut *nt (esp S Ger)*; **a head of ~** ein Kohlkopf *m* **b** *(inf: = person)* geistiger Krüppel *(inf)*; **to become a ~** verblöden *(inf)*; *(sick person)* dahinvegetieren

cabbage: **cabbage lettuce** N Kopfsalat *m*; **cabbage rose** N Zentifolie *f*; **cabbage white (butterfly)** N Kohlweißling *m*

cab(b)alistic [ˌkæbəˈlɪstɪk] ADJ kabbalistisch

cabby [ˈkæbɪ] N *(inf, of taxi)* Taxifahrer(in) *m(f)*; *(of horsedrawn vehicle)* Kutscher(in) *m(f)*

cab driver N Taxifahrer(in) *m(f)*

caber [ˈkeɪbəˡ] N *(Scot)* Pfahl *m*, Stamm *m* → **toss**

cabin [ˈkæbɪn] N **a** *(= hut)* Hütte *f* **b** *(Naut)* Kabine *f*, Kajüte *f*; *(= stateroom)* Kabine *f* **c** *(of lorries, buses etc)* Führerhaus *nt* **d** *(Aviat, for passengers)* Passagierraum *m*; *(for pilot)* Cockpit *nt*, (Flug)kanzel *f*

cabin: **cabin attendant** N *(Aviat)* Flugbegleiter(in) *m(f)*; **cabin boy** N Schiffsjunge *m*; *(= steward)* Kabinensteward *m*; **cabin class** N zweite Klasse; **cabin crew** N *(Aviat)* Flugbegleitpersonal *nt*; **cabin cruiser** N Kajütboot *nt*

cabinet [ˈkæbɪnɪt] N **a** Schränkchen *nt*; *(for display)* Vitrine *f*; *(for TV etc)* Schrank *m*, Truhe *f*; *(= loudspeaker cabinet)* Box *f* **b** *(Parl)* Kabinett *nt*, Regierungsmannschaft *f (inf)*

> **CABINET**
>
> In Großbritannien besteht das **Cabinet** aus ungefähr zwanzig Ministern, die vom Premierminister berufen werden. Das Kabinett plant die wichtigsten Gesetze und legt sie dem Parlament vor. In den Debatten verteidigt es die Regierungspolitik.
> Das US-**Cabinet** ist ein Organ, dessen einzige Aufgabe die Beratung des Präsidenten ist. Daher kann es keine politischen Richtlinien festlegen oder Gesetze einbringen. Die Mitglieder des Kabinetts sind entweder Leiter der Ministerien oder andere Regierungsbeamte, müssen aber nicht zwangsläufig Politiker sein. Sie werden vom Präsidenten ausgewählt und mit der Zustimmung des Senats ernannt. Weitere, allerdings inoffizielle Berater des Präsidenten gelten als „kitchen cabinet", als Küchenkabinett.

cabinet: **cabinet edition** N *(= book)* bibliophile Ausgabe; **cabinet-maker** N (Möbel)tischler(in) *m(f)*, (Möbel)schreiner(in) *m(f)*; **cabinet-making** N Tischlern *nt*, Tischlerei *f*; **cabinet meeting** N Kabinettssitzung *f*; **cabinet minister** N ≈ Mitglied *nt* des Kabinetts, Minister(in) *m(f)*; **cabinet reshuffle** N *(Brit Pol)* Kabinettsumbildung *f*; **cabinet-size** ADJ *(Phot)* im Kabinettformat

cabin: **cabin luggage** N Kabinengepäck *nt*; **cabin staff** N Kabinenpersonal *nt*; **cabin trunk** N Schrank- *or* Überseekoffer *m*

cable [ˈkeɪbl] **N** **a** Tau *nt*; *(of wire)* Kabel *nt*, Trosse *f (Naut)* **b** *(Elec)* Kabel *nt*, Leitung *f* **c** *(= cablegram)* Telegramm *nt*; *(from abroad)* (Übersee)telegramm *nt*, Kabel *nt*; **by ~** per Telegramm/Kabel **d** *(= cable television)* Kabelfernsehen *nt* **VT** *information* telegrafisch durchgeben; *(overseas)* kabeln; **to ~ sb** jdm telegrafieren/kabeln **VI** telegrafieren, ein Telegramm/Kabel schicken

cable: **cable car** N *(hanging)* Drahtseilbahn *f*; *(= streetcar)* (gezogene) Straßenbahn; *(= funicular)* Standseilbahn *f*; **cable channel** N *(TV)* Kabelkanal *m*; **cablegram** N = **cable N c**; **cable-knit** ADJ Zopfmuster-; **~ sweater** Zopfmusterpullover *m*; **cable-laying** N Kabelverlegung *f*, Kabellegen *nt*; **cable length** N *(Naut)* Kabellänge *f*; **cable railway** N Bergbahn *f*; **cable stitch** N *(Knitting)* Zopfmuster *nt*; **cable television** N Kabelfernsehen *nt*

cabling [ˈkeɪblɪŋ] N *(= cables)* Kabel *pl*; *(= process)* Verkabelung *f*

caboodle [kəˈbuːdl] N *(inf)* **the whole (kit and) ~** das ganze Zeug(s) *(inf)*, der ganze Kram *(inf)*

caboose [kəˈbuːs] N **a** *(Naut)* Kombüse *f* **b** *(US Rail)* Dienstwagen *m*

cab rank N *(Brit)* Taxistand *m*, Droschkenplatz *m (form)*

cabrio [ˈkæbrɪəʊ] N *(inf)* Cabrio *nt*, Kabrio *nt*

cabriole [ˈkæbrɪəʊl] N *(of table etc)* geschwungenes *or* geschweiftes Bein

cabriolet [ˌkæbrɪəʊˈleɪ] N Cabriolet *nt*

cab stand N *(esp US)* = **cab rank**

cacao [kəˈkɑːəʊ] N *(= tree, bean)* Kakao *m*

cache [kæʃ] **N** **a** Versteck *nt*, geheimes (Waffen-/Proviant)lager **b** *(Comput: also* **cache memory***)* Zwischenspeicher *m*, Cachespeicher *m* **VT** verstecken

cachepot [ˈkæʃpəʊ, -pɒt] N Übertopf *m*

cachet [ˈkæʃeɪ] N Gütesiegel *nt*, Gütezeichen *nt*; **the name has a certain ~ on the French market** der Name gilt auf dem französischen Markt als Gütezeichen; **it had given me a certain ~ in her parents' eyes** dadurch hatte ich bei ihren Eltern ein gewisses Ansehen

cachou [ˈkæʃuː] N Cachou(bonbon) *m or nt*

cack [kæk] N *(Brit sl: lit, fig)* Kacke *f (vulg)*

cack-handed [ˈkækˈhændəd] ADJ *(Brit inf)* tollpatschig *(inf)*

cackle [ˈkækl] **N** *(of hens)* Gackern *nt*; *(= laughter)* (meckerndes) Lachen; *(inf, = chatter)* Geblödel *nt (inf)* **VI** *(hens)* gackern; *(= laugh)* meckernd lachen; *(inf: = talk)* schwatzen

cacophonous [kæˈkɒfənəs] ADJ misstönend, kakophon *(geh)*

cacophony [kæˈkɒfənɪ] N Kakophonie *f (geh)*, Missklang *m*

cactus [ˈkæktəs] N Kaktus *m*

CAD [kæd] *abbr of* **computer-aided design** CAD

cad [kæd] N *(dated)* Schurke *m (old)*, Schuft *m*

cadaver [kəˈdævəˡ] N Kadaver *m*; *(of humans)* Leiche *f*

cadaverous [kəˈdævərəs] ADJ *(= corpse-like)* Kadaver-, Leichen-; *(= gaunt)* ausgezehrt, ausgemergelt; *(= pale)* leichenblass

CAD/CAM [ˈkædˈkæm] *abbr of* **computer-aided design/computer-aided manufacture** CAD/CAM

caddie [ˈkædɪ] *(Golf)* **N** Caddie *m* **VI** Caddie sein *or* spielen *(inf)*

caddie car, caddie cart N *(Golf)* Caddywagen *m*

caddis fly [ˈkædɪsˈflaɪ] N Köcherfliege *f*, Frühlingsfliege *f*

caddish [ˈkædɪʃ] ADJ *(dated)* schurkisch *(old)*, niederträchtig

caddy [ˈkædɪ] N **a** *(= tea caddy)* Behälter *m*, Büchse *f* **b** *(US: = shopping trolley)* Einkaufswagen *m* **c** = **caddie N**

cadence [ˈkeɪdəns] N *(Mus)* Kadenz *f*; *(of voice)* Tonfall *m*, Melodie *f*; *(= rhythm)* Rhythmus *m*, Melodie *f*; **the ~s of his prose** der Duktus seiner Prosa

cadenza [kəˈdenzə] N *(Mus)* Kadenz *f*

cadet [kəˈdet] N **a** *(Mil etc)* Kadett *m*; **~ school** Kadettenanstalt *f* **b** *(old)* jüngerer Sohn/Bruder

cadet corps M *(Mil etc)* Kadettenkorps *nt*

cadge [kædʒ] *(Brit inf)* **VT** (er)betteln, abstauben *(inf)*, schnorren *(inf)* *(from sb* bei *or* von jdm); **could I ~ a lift with you?** könnten Sie mich vielleicht (ein Stück) mitnehmen? **VI** schnorren *(inf)*

cadger [ˈkædʒəˡ] N *(inf)* Schnorrer(in) *m(f) (inf)*, Abstauber(in) *m(f) (inf)*

cadmium [ˈkædmɪəm] N Kadmium *nt*, Cadmium *nt*

cadre [ˈkædrɪ] N *(Mil, fig)* Kader *m*

caecum, *(US)* **cecum** [ˈsiːkəm] N *(Anat)* Blinddarm *m*

Caesar [ˈsiːzəˡ] N Cäsar *m*, Caesar *m*

Caesarean, *(US)* **Cesarean** [siːˈzeərɪən] **ADJ** cäsarisch, Cäsaren-; *(= of Caesar)* cäsarisch **N** *(Med: also* **Caesarean section***)* Kaiserschnitt *m*; **he was a ~** er wurde mit Kaiserschnitt entbunden; **she had a (baby by) ~** sie hatte einen Kaiserschnitt

Caesarian, *(US)* **Cesarian** [siːˈzeərɪən] N = **Caesarean**

caesium, *(US)* **cesium** [ˈsiːzɪəm] N Cäsium *nt*, Zäsium *nt*

caesura, *(US)* **cesura** [sɪˈzjʊərə] N Zäsur *f*

café [ˈkæfeɪ] N Café *nt*

café car N *(US Rail)* Zug-Cafeteria *f*

café society N *no pl* Schickeria *f*

cafeteria [ˌkæfɪˈtɪərɪə] N Cafeteria *f*

cafetière [ˌkæfəˈtjɛəˡ] N Kaffeebereiter *m*

caff [kæf] N *(Brit inf)* Café *nt*

caffein(e) ['kæfi:n] N Koffein *nt*

caftan ['kæftæn] N Kaftan *m*

cag [kæg] N *(Brit inf)* → **cagoule**

cage [keɪdʒ] N **a** Käfig *m*; *(= small birdcage)* Bauer *nt or m*; **~ bird** Käfigvogel *m* **b** *(of lift)* Aufzug *m*; *(Min)* Förderkorb *m* VT *(also* **cage up**) in einen Käfig sperren, einsperren

cagey ['keɪdʒɪ] ADJ *(inf)* vorsichtig; *behaviour, answer also* zugeknöpft *(inf)*; *(= evasive)* ausweichend; **what are you being so ~ about?** warum tust du so geheimnisvoll?; **she was very ~ about her age** sie hat aus ihrem Alter ein großes Geheimnis gemacht; **he was very ~ about his plans** er hat mit seinen Absichten hinterm Berg gehalten

cagily ['keɪdʒɪlɪ] ADV *(inf)* vorsichtig; *(= evasively)* ausweichend

caginess ['keɪdʒɪnɪs] N *(inf)* Vorsicht *f*, Zugeknöpftheit *f (inf)*; *(= evasiveness)* ausweichende Art

cagoule [kə'gu:l] N Windhemd *nt*

cahoots [kə'hu:ts] N *(inf)* **to be in ~ with sb** mit jdm unter einer Decke stecken

CAI *abbr of* = **computer-assisted** *or* **-aided instruction** computergestütztes Lernen

caiman ['keɪmən] N Kaiman *m*

Cain [keɪn] N Kain *m*; **to raise ~** *(inf: = be noisy)* Radau machen *(inf)*, lärmen; *(= protest)* Krach schlagen *(inf)*

cairn [kɛən] N **a** Steinpyramide *f*, Steinhügel *m* **b** *(also* **cairn terrier**) Cairnterrier *m*

Cairo ['kaɪərəʊ] N Kairo *nt*

caisson ['keɪsən] N **a** *(Mil)* Munitionskiste *f*; *(= wagon)* Munitionswagen *m* **b** *(Tech: = underwater caisson)* Senkkasten *m*, Caisson *m*

cajole [kə'dʒəʊl] VT gut zureden *(+dat)*, beschwatzen *(inf)*; **to ~ sb into doing sth** jdn dazu bringen *or* jdn beschwatzen *(inf)*, etw zu tun; **to ~ sb out of doing sth** jdm etw ausreden; **he would not be ~d** er ließ sich nicht beschwatzen *(inf)*

cajolery [kə'dʒəʊlərɪ] N Überredung *f*, Beschwatzen *nt (inf)*

cake [keɪk] N **a** Kuchen *m*; *(= gateau)* Torte *f*; *(= bun, individual cake)* Gebäckstück *nt*, Teilchen *nt (dial)*; **~s and pastries** Gebäck *nt*; **a piece of ~** *(fig inf)* ein Kinderspiel *nt*, ein Klacks *m (inf)*; **he/that takes the ~** *(inf)* das ist das Schärfste *(inf)*; *(negatively also)* das schlägt dem Fass den Boden aus; **to sell like hot ~s** weggehen wie warme Semmeln *(inf)*; **you can't have your ~ and eat it** *(prov)* beides auf einmal geht nicht; **he wants to have his ~ and eat it** *(prov)* er will das eine, ohne das andere zu lassen

b *(of soap)* Stück *nt*, Riegel *m*; *(of chocolate)* Tafel *f*

VT dick einschmieren; **my shoes are ~d with** *or* **in mud** meine Schuhe sind völlig verdreckt *or* dreckverkrustet

VI festtrocknen, eine Kruste bilden

cake: **cake mix** N Backmischung *f*; **cake mixture** N Kuchenteig *m*; **cake pan** N *(US)* Kuchenform *f*; **cake shop** N Konditorei *f*; **cake tin** N *(Brit, for baking)* Kuchenform *f*; *(for storage)* Kuchenbüchse *f*

cakey, caky ['keɪkɪ] ADJ klumpend; *(= lumpy)* klumpig

calabash ['kæləbæʃ] N Kalebasse *f*; **~ tree** Kalebassenbaum *m*

calaboose ['kæləbu:s] N *(US inf)* Kittchen *nt (inf)*

calamine ['kæləmaɪn] N Galmei *m*

calamine lotion N Galmeilotion *f*

calamitous [kə'læmɪtəs] ADJ katastrophal

calamity [kə'læmɪtɪ] N Katastrophe *f*

Calamity Jane N [kə'læmɪtɪ'dʒeɪn] Pechmarie *f*

calcification [,kælsɪfɪ'keɪʃən] N Kalkablagerung *f*; *(Med)* Verkalkung *f*

calcify ['kælsɪfaɪ] VT Kalk *m* ablagern auf/in *(+dat)*, verkalken lassen VI verkalken

calcium ['kælsɪəm] N Kalzium *nt*, Calcium *nt*

calcium carbonate N Kalziumkarbonat *nt*, kohlensaurer Kalk

calculable ['kælkjʊləbl] ADJ berechenbar, kalkulierbar

calculate ['kælkjʊleɪt] VT **a** *(mathematically, scientifically)* berechnen; *costs also* ermitteln **b** *(fig: = estimate critically)* kalkulieren, schätzen **c** **to be ~d to do sth** *(= be intended)* auf etw *(acc)* abzielen; *(= have the effect)* zu etw angetan sein **d** *(US inf: = suppose)* schätzen, annehmen, meinen VI *(Math)* rechnen

▶ **calculate on** VI *+prep obj* rechnen mit; **I had calculated on finishing by this week** ich hatte damit gerechnet, diese Woche fertig zu werden

calculated ['kælkjʊleɪtɪd] ADJ *(= deliberate)* berechnet; **a ~ insult** ein bewusster Affront; **a ~ risk** ein kalkuliertes Risiko

calculating ['kælkjʊleɪtɪŋ] ADJ, **calculatingly** ADV ['kælkjʊleɪtɪŋ, -lɪ] berechnend

calculating machine N Rechenmaschine *f*

calculation [,kælkjʊ'leɪʃən] N Berechnung *f*, Kalkulation *f*; *(= critical estimation)* Schätzung *f*; **to do a quick ~** die Sache schnell überschlagen; **with cold ~** eiskalt berechnend; **you're out in your ~s** du hast dich verrechnet; **by my ~s he will arrive on Sunday** nach meiner Schätzung müsste er Sonntag ankommen

calculator ['kælkjʊleɪtə'] N **a** *(= machine)* Rechner *m* **b** *(= person)* Kalkulator(in) *m(f)*, Rechnungsbeamte(r) *m*/-beamtin *f* **c** *(= table of figures)* Rechentabelle *f*

calculus ['kælkjʊləs] N **a** *(Math)* Infinitesimalrechnung *f*, Differenzialrechnung *f*, Differentialrechnung *f*, Integralrechnung *f* **b** *(Med)* Stein *m*

Calcutta [kæl'kʌtə] N *(Hist)* Kalkutta *nt (Hist)* → **Kolkata**

Caledonia [,kælə'dəʊnɪə] N Kaledonien *nt*

Caledonian [,kælə'dəʊnɪən] ADJ kaledonisch

calefactory [kælə'fæktərɪ] ADJ *(form)* Wärme-

calendar ['kæləndə'] N **a** Kalender *m* **b** *(= schedule)* Terminkalender *m*; *(Jur)* Prozessregister *nt*; **~ of events** Veranstaltungskalender *m*

calendar month N Kalendermonat *m*

calender ['kæləndə'] N Kalander *m* VT kalandern

calf[1] [kɑ:f] N *pl* **calves** **a** Kalb *nt*; **a cow in** *or* **with ~** eine trächtige Kuh **b** *(= young elephant, seal etc)* Junge(s) *nt*, -junge(s) *nt* **c** *(= leather)* Kalb(s)leder *nt*

calf[2] N *pl* **calves** *(Anat)* Wade *f*

calf: **calf love** N (jugendliche) Schwärmerei; **calfskin** ['kɑ:fskɪn] N Kalb(s)leder *nt*

caliber N *(US)* = **calibre**

calibrate ['kælɪbreɪt] VT *gun* kalibrieren; *meter, instrument also* eichen

calibration [,kælɪ'breɪʃən] N **a** *(of gun)* Kalibrieren *nt*; *(of meter, instrument also)* Eichen *nt* **b** *(= mark, on gun)* Kalibrierung *f*; *(on meter, instrument also)* Eichung *f*

calibre, *(US)* **caliber** ['kælɪbə'] N *(lit)* Kaliber *nt*; *(fig also)* Format *nt*; **a man of his ~** ein Mann seines Kalibers, ein Mann von seinem Format

calico ['kælɪkəʊ] N Kattun *m*

California [kælɪ'fɔ:nɪə] N *(abbr* **Cal(if)**) Kalifornien *nt*

Californian [kælɪ'fɔ:nɪən] ADJ kalifornisch N Kalifornier(in) *m(f)*

calipers ['kælɪpəz] PL *(US)* = **callipers**

caliph ['keɪlɪf] N Kalif *m*

calisthenics [,kælɪs'θenɪks] N *(US)* = **callisthenics**

calk[1] [kɔ:k] VT mit Stollen versehen; *shoe also* mit Nägeln beschlagen N Stollen *m*; *(on shoe also)* Nagel *m*

calk[2] VT *drawing, design* durchpausen

calk[3] VT = **caulk**

CALL *abbr of* = **computer-assisted language learning** computergestütztes Sprachlernen

call [kɔ:l] ✪ 27 N **a** *(= shout, cry, of person, bird etc)* Ruf *m*; *(of bugle)* Signal *nt*; **to give sb a ~** jdn (herbei)rufen; *(= inform sb)* jdm Bescheid sagen; *(= wake sb)* jdn wecken; **they came at my ~** sie kamen auf meinen Ruf hin, als ich rief, kamen sie; **within ~** in Rufweite *f*; **a ~ for help** *(lit, fig)* ein Hilferuf *m*

b *(= telephone call)* Gespräch *nt*, Anruf *m*; **to be on ~** telefonisch erreichbar sein; **to give sb a ~** jdn anrufen; **I'll give you a ~** ich rufe Sie an; **to take a ~** ein Gespräch entgegennehmen; **will you take the ~?** nehmen Sie das Gespräch an?

c *(= summons) (for flight, meal)* Aufruf *m*; *(of religion)* Berufung *f*; *(Theat: to actors)* Aufruf *m*; *(fig: = lure)* Ruf *m*, Verlockung *f*; **to be on ~** Bereitschaftsdienst haben; **the doctor had a ~ at midnight** der Arzt wurde um Mitternacht zu einem Patienten gerufen; **that's your ~!** *(Theat)* Ihr Auftritt!; **the ~ of nature** die Stimme der Natur; **to answer a ~ of nature** *(euph)* mal kurz verschwinden gehen *(inf)*; **the Call** *or* **~ came when he was 17** mit 17 Jahren spürte er die Berufung; **the ~ of duty** der Ruf der Pflicht; **he acted above and beyond the ~ of duty** er handelte über die bloße Pflichterfüllung hinaus; **to issue a ~ for unity** zur Einigkeit aufrufen

d *(= visit)* Besuch *m*; **to pay a ~ on sb** jdn besuchen, jdm einen Besuch abstatten *(form)*; **I have several ~s to make** ich muss noch einige Besuche machen; **port of ~** Anlaufhafen *m*; *(fig)* Station *f*; **to pay a ~** *(euph)* mal verschwinden *(inf)*

e *(= demand, claim)* Inanspruchnahme *f*, Beanspruchung *f*; *(Comm)* Nachfrage *f* (*for* nach); **to have many ~s on one's purse/time** finanziell/zeitlich sehr in Anspruch genommen sein; **the sudden rain made for heavy ~s on the emergency services** die plötzlichen Regenfälle bedeuteten eine starke Belastung der Notdienste; **to have first ~ on sth** ein Vorrecht *nt* auf etw *(acc)* haben

f **at** *or* **on ~** *(Fin)* auf Abruf

g *(= need, occasion)* Anlass *m*, Grund *m*, Veranlassung *f*; **there is no ~ for you to worry** es besteht kein Grund zur Sorge, Sie brauchen sich *(dat)* keine Sorgen zu machen

h *(Cards)* Ansage *f*; **to make a ~ of three diamonds** drei Karo ansagen; **whose ~ is it?** wer sagt an?

i *(Tennis)* Entscheidung *f*

VT **a** *(= shout out)* rufen; **the landlord ~ed time** der Wirt rief „Feierabend"; **to ~ spades** *(Cards)* Pik reizen; **the ball was ~ed out** der Ball wurde für „aus" erklärt → **halt**

b *(= name, consider)* nennen; **to be ~ed** heißen; **what's he ~ed?** wie heißt er?; **what do you ~ your cat?** wie nennst du deine Katze?, wie heißt deine Katze?; **she ~s me lazy and selfish** sie nennt mich faul und selbstsüchtig; **to ~ sth by its proper name** etw richtig bezeichnen; **what's this ~ed in German?** wie heißt das auf Deutsch?; **let's ~ it a day** machen wir Schluss *or* Feierabend für heute; **~ it £5** sagen wir £ 5

c *(= summon) person, doctor* rufen; *meeting* einberufen; *elections* ausschreiben; *strike* ausrufen; *(Jur) witness* aufrufen; *(= subpoena)* vorladen; *(= waken)* wecken; **he was ~ed home** *(US) or* **to his maker** *(liter)* er ist in die Ewigkeit abberufen worden → **mind, question, bluff**[2]

d *(= telephone)* anrufen; *(= contact by radio)* rufen

e *(Fin) bond* aufrufen; *loan* abrufen

f *(US Sport: = call off)* abbrechen

VI **a** *(= shout: person, animal)* rufen; **to ~ for help** um Hilfe rufen; **to ~ to sb** jdm zurufen

b *(= visit)* vorbeigehen/-kommen; **she ~ed to see her mother** sie machte einen Besuch bei ihrer Mutter; **the gasman ~ed to read the meter** der Gasmann kam, um die Gasuhr abzulesen

c *(Telec)* anrufen; *(by radio)* rufen; **who's ~ing, please?** wer spricht da bitte?; **London ~ing!**

(Rad) hier ist London; **thanks for ~ing** vielen Dank für den Anruf

▶ **call (a)round** VI *(inf)* vorbeikommen

▶ **call aside** VT *sep person* beiseiterufen

▶ **call at** VI *+prep obj (person)* vorbeigehen bei; *(Rail)* halten in *(+dat)*; *(Naut)* anlaufen; **a train for Lisbon calling at ...** ein Zug nach Lissabon über ...

▶ **call away** VT *sep* weg- *or* abrufen; **I was called away on business** ich wurde geschäftlich abgerufen; **he was called away from the meeting** er wurde aus der Sitzung gerufen

▶ **call back** ✪ 27.4, 27.6 VT *sep* zurückrufen VI zurückrufen

▶ **call down** VT *sep* **a** *(= invoke)* **to call down blessings on sb's head** jdn segnen **b** **to call sb down** *(lit)* jdn herunterrufen; *(US: = reprimand)* jdn ausschimpfen, jdn herunterputzen *(inf)*

▶ **call for** VI *+prep obj* **a** *(= send for) person* rufen; *food, drink* kommen lassen; *(= ask for)* verlangen (nach), fordern; **to call for sb's resignation** jds Rücktritt fordern *or* verlangen **b** *(= need) courage, endurance* verlangen, erfordern; **that calls for a drink!** darauf muss ich/müssen wir einen trinken!, das muss begossen werden!; **that calls for a celebration!** das muss gefeiert werden! **c** *(= collect) person, goods* abholen; *(= come to see)* fragen nach; **"to be called for"** *(goods) (sent by rail)* „bahnlagernd"; *(sent by post)* „postlagernd"; *(in shop)* „wird abgeholt"

▶ **call forth** VI *+prep obj protests* hervorrufen; *abilities etc* wachrufen, wecken

▶ **call in** VT *sep* **a** *doctor* zurate *or* zu Rate ziehen **b** *(= withdraw) faulty goods etc* aus dem Verkehr ziehen; *currency also* aufrufen *(form)*; *hire boats* zurück- *or* aufrufen; *books* an- *or* zurückfordern; **to call in a loan** einen Kredit einfordern *or* kündigen VI *(= visit)* vorbeigehen *or* -schauen *(at, on* bei)

▶ **call off** VT *sep* **a** *(= cancel) appointment, holiday* absagen; *deal* rückgängig machen; *strike* absagen, abblasen *(inf)*; *(= end)* abbrechen; *engagement* lösen; **let's call the whole thing off** blasen wir die ganze Sache ab *(inf)* **b** *dog* zurückrufen; **to call off the dogs** *(fig)* die Angriffe einstellen, die Hetzhunde zurückpfeifen *(inf)* VI absagen

▶ **call on** VI *+prep obj* **a** *(= visit)* besuchen **b** = **call upon**

▶ **call out** VI rufen, schreien VT *sep* **a** *names* aufrufen; *(= announce)* ansagen **b** *doctor* rufen; *troops, fire brigade* alarmieren **c** *(= order to strike)* zum Streik aufrufen

▶ **call out for** VI *+prep obj food* verlangen; *help* rufen um

▶ **call up** VT *sep* **a** *(Brit Mil) reservist* einberufen; *reinforcements* mobilisieren; **called up to go to Vietnam** nach Vietnam einberufen **b** *(Sport)* berufen *(to* in *+acc)* **c** *(Telec)* anrufen **d** *(fig)* (herauf)beschwören; *images, thoughts also* erwecken; *memories also* wachrufen; **to call up the Devil** den Teufel beschwören VI *(Telec)* anrufen

▶ **call upon** VI *+prep obj* **a** *(= ask)* **to call upon sb to do sth** jdn bitten *or* auffordern, etw zu tun; **I now call upon the vicar to say a few words** ich möchte nun den Herrn Pfarrer um ein paar Worte bitten **b** *(= invoke)* **to call upon sb's generosity** an jds Großzügigkeit *(acc)* appellieren; **to call upon God** Gott anrufen

callable [ˈkɔːləbl] ADJ *(Fin) money* abrufbar; *security* kündbar

call: **call alarm** N Notrufgerät *nt (eines Kranken)*; **callback** N *(Comm: = action)* Rückrufaktion *f*; **there were 1,000 ~s** 1.000 wurden zurückbeordert; **call box** N *(Brit)* Telefonzelle *f*, öffentlicher Fernsprecher; **callboy** N *(Theat)* Inspizientengehilfe *m (der die Schauspieler zu ihrem Auftritt ruft)*; **callcard** N *(esp Ir)* Telefonkarte *f*; **call centre** N *(Brit)* Telefoncenter *nt*, Callcenter *nt*

caller [ˈkɔːləʳ] ✪ 27.3 N **a** *(= visitor)* Besuch *m*, Besucher(in) *m(f)* **b** *(Telec)* Anrufer(in) *m(f)*; **hold the line please ~!** bitte bleiben Sie am Apparat!

caller: **caller display** *(Telec)* Rufnummernanzeige *f*; Anruferkennung *f*; **caller ID** N *(Telec)* Anruferkennung *f*; *(of e-mails, text messages etc)* Absenderkennung *f*

call forwarding N *(Telec)* Anrufweiterschaltung *f*

callgirl [ˈkɔːlgɜːl] N Callgirl *nt*

calligraphic [ˌkælɪˈgræfɪk] ADJ kalligrafisch, Schönschreib-

calligraphy [kəˈlɪgrəfɪ] N Kalligrafie *f*

calling [ˈkɔːlɪŋ] N Berufung *f*

calling card N Visitenkarte *f*; **to leave one's ~** *(euph, cats or dogs)* seine Visitenkarte hinterlassen *(hum)*

calliper brake, *(US)* **caliper brake** [ˈkælɪpəˌbreɪk] N Felgenbremse *f*

callipers, *(US)* **calipers** [ˈkælɪpəz] PL Tastzirkel *m*

callisthenics, *(US)* **calisthenics** [ˌkælɪsˈθenɪks] N *sing or pl* Gymnastik *f*, Fitnessübungen *pl*, Kallisthenie *f (dated)*

call: **call loan** N *(Fin)* täglich kündbares Darlehen; **call money** N *(Fin)* Tagesgeld *nt*, tägliches Geld

callous [ˈkæləs] ADJ **a** *(= cruel)* gefühllos, herzlos **b** *(Med)* schwielig, kallös

calloused [ˈkæləst] ADJ schwielig, kallös

callously [ˈkæləslɪ] ADV herzlos

callousness [ˈkæləsnɪs] N Gefühllosigkeit *f*, Herzlosigkeit *f*

call-out charge, **call-out fee** [ˈkɔːlaʊt-] N Anfahrtkosten *pl*

callow [ˈkæləʊ] ADJ unreif; *ideas etc* unausgegoren; **a ~ youth** ein grüner Junge *(inf)*

call: **call sign** N *(Rad)* Sendezeichen *nt*; **call-up** N *(Brit) (Mil)* Einberufung *f*; *(Sport)* Berufung *f (to* in *+acc)*; **call-up papers** PL *(Brit Mil)* Einberufungsbescheid *m*

callus [ˈkæləs] N *(Med)* Schwiele *f*; *(of bone)* Kallus *m*, Knochenschwiele *f*; *(Bot)* Wundholz *nt*, Kallus *m*

callused [ˈkæləst] ADJ = **calloused**

calm [kɑːm] ADJ *(+er)* ruhig; *weather also* windstill; **keep ~!** bleib ruhig!; **the weather grew ~ again after the storm** nach dem Sturm beruhigte sich das Wetter wieder; **(cool,) ~ and collected** ruhig und gelassen; **~er waters** *(lit, fig)* ruhigere Gewässer *pl* N **a** Ruhe *f*, Stille *f*; *(at sea)* Flaute *f*; *(of wind)* Windstille *f*; **a dead ~** absolute Stille, Totenstille *f*; **the ~ before the storm** *(lit, fig)* die Ruhe vor dem Sturm **b** *(= composure)* Ruhe, Gelassenheit *f* VT beruhigen; *pain, itch* lindern; *protests* mildern; **to ~ sb's fears** jds Ängste abbauen, jdn beruhigen VI *(sea)* sich beruhigen; *(wind)* sich legen

▶ **calm down** VT *sep* beruhigen, beschwichtigen VI sich beruhigen; *(wind)* abflauen; **calm down!** beruhigen Sie sich!

calming [ˈkɑːmɪŋ] ADJ beruhigend

calmly [ˈkɑːmlɪ] ADV *speak, act* ruhig, gelassen; **he spoke ~** er redete mit ruhiger Stimme; **she ~ told me that she'd crashed the car** sie erzählte mir seelenruhig, dass sie das Auto kaputt gefahren hatte

calmness [ˈkɑːmnɪs] N *(of person)* Ruhe *f*, Gelassenheit *f*; *(of wind, sea)* Stille *f*

Calor Gas® [ˈkæləgæs] N Butangas *nt*

caloric [ˈkælərɪk] ADJ kalorisch, Wärme-

calorie [ˈkælərɪ] N Kalorie *f*; **low on ~s** kalorienarm

calorie *in cpds* Kalorien-, kalorien-; **calorie-conscious** ADJ kalorienbewusst

calorific [ˌkæləˈrɪfɪk] ADJ wärmeerzeugend

calorific value N Heizwert *m*

calumniate [kəˈlʌmnɪeɪt] VT *(liter)* schmähen *(geh)*, verunglimpfen

calumny [ˈkæləmnɪ] N *(liter)* Schmähung *f (geh)*, Verunglimpfung *f*

Calvary [ˈkælvərɪ] N **a** Golgatha *nt*, Kalvarienberg *m* **b** **calvary** Bildstock *m*, Marterl *nt (S Ger, Aus)*

calve [kɑːv] VI kalben

calves [kɑːvz] *pl of* **calf¹**, *of* **calf²**

Calvin [ˈkælvɪn] N Calvin *m*

Calvinism [ˈkælvɪnɪzəm] N Calvinismus *m*

Calvinist [ˈkælvɪnɪst] N Calvinist(in) *m(f)* ADJ calvinistisch

Calvinistic [ˌkælvɪˈnɪstɪk] ADJ calvinistisch

calypso [kəˈlɪpsəʊ] N Calypso *m*

calyx [ˈkeɪlɪks] N *pl* **calyces** *or* **-es** [ˈkeɪlɪsiːz, ˈkeɪlɪksəz] Blütenkelch *m*

CAM [kæm] *abbr of* **computer-aided manufacture** CAM

cam¹ [kæm] N Nocken *m*

cam² *(inf) abbr of* **camera¹**

camaraderie [ˌkæməˈrɑːdərɪ] N Kameradschaft *f*

camber [ˈkæmbəʳ] N *(of ship, aircraft wing)* Wölbung *f*; *(of road also)* Überhöhung *f*; *(of wheels)* Radsturz *m* VT *road, deck* wölben; **a ~ed wheel** ein Rad *nt* mit Sturz

Cambodia [kæmˈbəʊdɪə] N Kambodscha *nt*

Cambodian [kæmˈbəʊdɪən] ADJ kambodschanisch N **a** Kambodschaner(in) *m(f)* **b** *(Ling)* Kambodschanisch *nt*

cambric [ˈkeɪmbrɪk] N *(Tex)* Kambrik *m*, Cambrai *m*, Kammertuch *nt*

Cambridge [ˈkeɪmbrɪdʒ] N Cambridge *nt*

Cambs [kæmz] *abbr of* **Cambridgeshire**

camcorder [ˈkæmkɔːdəʳ] N Camcorder *m*, Kamerarekorder *m*

came [keɪm] *pret of* **come**

camel [ˈkæməl] N Kamel *nt* ATTR *(= colour) coat* kamelhaarfarben

camel driver N Kameltreiber *m*

camel hair, *(US)* **camel's hair** N Kamelhaar *nt*

camelhair [kæməlhɛəʳ] ADJ *attr* Kamelhaar-; **~ coat** Kamelhaarmantel *m*

camellia [kəˈmiːlɪə] N Kamelie *f*

cameo [ˈkæmɪəʊ] N **a** *(= jewellery)* Kamee *f* **b** *(Liter)* Miniatur *f* **c** *(also* **cameo part**) Miniaturrolle *f*

camera¹ [ˈkæmərə] N Kamera *f*; *(for stills also)* Fotoapparat *m*

camera² N *(Jur)* **in ~** unter Ausschluss der Öffentlichkeit; *(fig)* hinter verschlossenen Türen, in geschlossener Gesellschaft

camera: **camera crane** N Kamerakran *m*; **camera crew** N Kamerateam *nt*; **cameraman** N Kameramann *m*; **camera obscura** [ˈkæmərəəbˈskjʊərə] N *(Opt)* Camera obscura *f*, Lochkamera *f*; **camera operator** N Kameramann *m*/-frau *f*; **camera-ready copy** N Druckvorlage *f*; **camera-shy** ADJ kamerascheu; **camerawoman** N Kamerafrau *f*; **camerawork** N Kameraführung *f*

Cameroons [ˌkæməˈruːnz] PL **the ~** Kamerun *nt*

camiknickers [ˈkæmɪˌnɪkəz] PL Spitzenhemdhöschen *nt*

camisole [ˈkæmɪsəʊl] N Mieder *nt*, Leibchen *nt*

camomile [ˈkæməʊmaɪl] N Kamille *f*; **~ tea** Kamillentee *m*

camouflage [ˈkæməflɑːʒ] N *(Mil)* Tarnung *f*; *(fig)* Tarnung *f*, Camouflage *f (geh)*; **for ~** zur Tarnung; **~ nets** Tarnnetze *pl* VT *(Mil, fig)* tarnen; **she smiled but it didn't ~ her despair** ihr Lächeln konnte nicht über ihre Verzweiflung hinwegtäuschen

camouflage *in cpds* Tarn-

camp¹ [kæmp] N **a** Lager *nt*; *(Mil)* (Feld)lager *nt*; **to be in ~** im Lager leben *or* sein; *(Mil)* im Felde leben; **to pitch ~** Zelte *or* ein Lager aufschlagen; **to strike** *or* **break ~** die Zelte abbauen, das Lager *or* die Zelte abbrechen **b** *(fig)* Lager *nt*; **to have a foot in both ~s** mit beiden Seiten zu tun haben; **the socialist ~** das sozialistische Lager VI zelten, kampieren; *(Mil)* lagern; **to go ~ing** zelten (gehen)

▶ **camp out** VI zelten

camp² ADJ *(= theatrical, stagey)* übertrieben, extrem *(inf)*; *performance* manieriert, geschmäcklerisch; *person's appearance* aufgedonnert, aufgemotzt *(inf)*; *(= effeminate)* tuntenhaft *(inf)*; *(= homosexual)* schwul *(inf)*; **to be as ~ as a row of tents** *(hum)* mächtig schwul sein *(inf)*

▶ **camp up** VT *sep* **to camp sth up** *(= vamp up)* etw aufmöbeln *(inf)*, etw aufmotzen *(inf)*; *(= overact)* etw überziehen, in *or* bei etw zu dick auftragen; **to camp it up** *(= overact, exaggerate)* es zu weit treiben; *(Theat)* es überziehen, zu dick auftragen; *(= act homosexually)* sich tuntenhaft *(inf) or* wie eine Schwuchtel *(inf)* benehmen

campaign [kæmˈpeɪn] N a *(Mil)* Feldzug *m*, Kampagne *f (old)*; **Hitler's Russian ~** Hitlers Russlandfeldzug *m* b *(fig)* Kampagne *f*, Aktion *f*; *(= election campaign)* Feldzug *m*, Kampagne *f*; **~ headquarters** *(Pol)* Wahlkampfzentrale *f* VI a *(Mil)* kämpfen, Krieg führen; **~ing in Ruritania** im Einsatz in Ruritanien b *(fig) (for* für) *(against* gegen) sich einsetzen, sich starkmachen *(inf)*, agitieren; *(outdoors also)* auf die Straße gehen; *(politician, candidate)* im Wahlkampf stehen, den Wahlkampf führen; *(supporters)* Wahlwerbung treiben; **we were out on the streets ~ing** wir waren auf der Straße im Einsatz

campaigner [kæmˈpeɪnəʳ] N a *(Mil)* Krieger *m*; **old ~** alter Kämpe b *(fig, for sth)* Befürworter(in) *m(f) (for +gen)*; *(against sth)* Gegner(in) *m(f) (against +gen)*; *(for politician)* Wahlwerber(in) *m(f)*

campanology [ˌkæmpəˈnɒlədʒɪ] N Kunst *f* des Glockenspiels

camp: **camp bed** N *(Brit)* Campingliege *f*; **camp chair** N Campingstuhl *m*

camper [ˈkæmpəʳ] N a Camper(in) *m(f)* b *(= vehicle: also* **camper van**) Wohnmobil *nt*

camp: **campfire** N Lagerfeuer *nt*; **camp follower** N a Marketender(in) *m(f)* b *(fig)* Anhänger(in) *m(f)*, Mitläufer(in) *m(f) (pej)*; **campground** N *(US)* Campingplatz *m*, Zeltplatz *m*

camphor [ˈkæmfəʳ] N Kampfer *m*

camphorated [ˈkæmfəreɪtɪd] ADJ mit Kampfer präpariert

camphorated oil N Kampferöl *nt*

camping [ˈkæmpɪŋ] N Zelten *nt*, Camping *nt*; **no ~** Zelten verboten!

camping *in cpds* Camping-; **camping gas** N *(US)* Campinggas *nt*; **camping ground** N Zeltplatz *m*; **camping site** N Campingplatz *m*, Zeltplatz *m*; **camping van** N Wohnmobil *nt*

camp: **camp meeting** N *(US Rel)* Campmeeting *nt*; **camp site** N = **camping site**; **camp stool** N Campinghocker *m*

campus [ˈkæmpəs] N Campus *m*, Universitätsgelände *nt*; **to live on ~** auf dem Campus wohnen

campy [ˈkæmpɪ] ADJ *(inf)* = **camp²**

camshaft [ˈkæmʃɑːft] N Nockenwelle *f*

can¹ [kæn] ✪ 3.3, 6.2, 9.2, 9.3, 9.4, 10.4, 12.1, 12.3, 15.4, 16.3, 16.4 *pret* **could** MODAL AUX VB *(defective parts supplied by to be able to)* a *(= be able to)* können; **~ you come tomorrow?** kannst du morgen kommen?; **I ~'t** *or* **~not go to the theatre tomorrow** ich kann morgen nicht ins Theater (gehen); **I'll do it if I ~** wenn ich kann(, tue ich es); **he'll help you all he ~** er wird sein Möglichstes tun, er wird tun, was in seinen Kräften steht; **as soon as it ~ be arranged** sobald es sich machen lässt; **could you tell me ...** können *or* könnten Sie mir sagen, ...; **~ you speak German?** können *or* sprechen Sie Deutsch?; **we ~ but hope that..., we ~ only hope that ...** wir können nur hoffen, dass ...; **they could not (help) but condemn it** sie konnten nicht anders, als das zu verurteilen

b *(= may)* dürfen, können; **~ I come too?** kann ich mitkommen?; **~** *or* **could I take some more?** darf ich mir noch etwas *or* noch einmal nehmen?; **you ~ go now** Sie können jetzt gehen; **~ I help?** darf *or* kann ich Ihnen helfen?; **could I possibly go with you?** könnte *or* dürfte ich vielleicht mitkommen?; **I'd like to go, ~ I? – no, you ~'t** ich würde gerne gehen, darf ich? – nein, du darfst nicht; **~ I use your car? – no, you ~'t** kann *or* darf ich dein Auto nehmen? – nein

c *(expressing surprise etc)* können; **how ~/could you say such a thing!** wie können/konnten Sie nur *or* bloß so etwas sagen!; **where ~ it be?** wo kann das bloß sein?; **where ~ they have gone?** wo können sie denn nur hingegangen sein?; **you ~'t be serious** das kann doch wohl nicht dein Ernst sein

d *(expressing possibility)* können; **it could be that he's got lost** vielleicht hat er sich verlaufen, (es ist) möglich, dass er sich verlaufen hat; **could he have got lost?** ob er sich wohl *or* vielleicht verlaufen hat?; **he could be on the next train** er könnte im nächsten Zug sein; **and it could have been such a good party!** und es hätte so eine gute Party sein können!; **to think he could have become a doctor** wenn man bedenkt, dass er hätte Arzt werden können

e *(with verbs of perception)* können; **~ you hear me?** hören Sie mich?, können Sie mich hören?

f *(= be capable of occasionally)* können; **she ~ be very nice when she wants to** wenn sie will, kann sie sehr nett sein

g *(indicating suggestion)* können; **you could try telephoning him** Sie könnten ihn ja mal anrufen; **you could have been a little more polite** Sie hätten etwas höflicher sein können; **you could have told me** das hätten Sie mir auch sagen können

h *(= feel inclined to)* können; **I could have murdered her** ich hätte sie umbringen können

i **we could do with some new furniture** wir könnten neue Möbel gebrauchen; **I could do with a drink now** ich könnte jetzt etwas zu trinken vertragen; **this room could do with a coat of paint** das Zimmer könnte mal wieder gestrichen werden; **he looks as though he could do with a wash/haircut** ich glaube, er müsste sich mal waschen/er müsste sich *(dat)* mal wieder die Haare schneiden lassen

can² N a *(= container)* Kanister *m*; *(= milk can)* Kanne *f*; *(esp US: = garbage can)* (Müll)eimer *m*; **in the ~** *(Film)* im Kasten; **the contract's in the ~** *(inf)* wir haben den Vertrag in der Tasche *(inf)*; **to carry the ~** *(Brit fig inf)* die Sache ausbaden *(inf)* b *(= tin)* Dose *f*; *(of food also)* Büchse *f*; **a ~ of beer** eine Dose Bier; **a beer ~** eine Bierdose; **a ~ of paint** eine Dose Farbe; *(with handle)* ein Eimer *m* Farbe → **worm N a** c *(US inf: = prison)* Knast *m (inf)* d *(US inf: = lavatory)* Klo *nt (inf)*, Scheißhaus *nt (sl)* VT a *foodstuffs* einmachen, eindosen → **canned** b *(inf)* **~ it!** Klappe! *(inf)*

can *in cpds* Büchsen-, Dosen-

Canaan [ˈkeɪnən] N Kanaan *nt*

Canaanite [ˈkeɪnənaɪt] N Kanaaniter(in) *m(f)*

Canada [ˈkænədə] N Kanada *nt*

Canadian [kəˈneɪdɪən] ADJ kanadisch N Kanadier(in) *m(f)*

Canadian elk N Wapiti(hirsch) *m*

canal [kəˈnæl] N a Kanal *m*; **~ barge** Schleppkahn *m* b *(Anat)* Gang *m*, Kanal *m*

canalization [ˌkænəlaɪˈzeɪʃən] N *(lit)* Kanalisation *f*; *(fig)* Kanalisierung *f*

canalize [ˈkænəlaɪz] VT *(lit, fig)* kanalisieren

canapé [ˈkænəpeɪ] N Cocktail- *or* Appetithappen *m*

canard [kæˈnɑːd] N (Zeitungs)ente *f*

Canaries [kəˈneərɪz] PL = **Canary Isles**

canary [kəˈneərɪ] N a Kanarienvogel *m* b *(old, = wine)* Kanarienwein *m (old)* c *(dated US, sl, = female singer)* Sängerin *f* ATTR *(colour: also* **canary yellow**) kanariengelb

Canary Isles [kəˈneərɪˈaɪlz] PL Kanarische Inseln *pl*

canasta [kəˈnæstə] N Canasta *nt*

can bank N Altblech- *or* Dosencontainer *m*

cancan [ˈkænkæn] N Cancan *m*

cancel [ˈkænsəl] ✪ 20.5, 21.4 VT a *(= call off)* absagen; *(officially)* stornieren; *plans* aufgeben, fallen lassen; *train, bus* streichen; **the last train has been ~led** *(Brit) or* **~ed** *(US)* der letzte Zug fällt aus

b *(= revoke, annul)* rückgängig machen; *command, invitation also* zurücknehmen; *contract also* (auf)lösen; *debt* streichen; *order for goods* stornieren; *magazine subscription* kündigen; *decree* aufheben; *(Comput) program* abbrechen; **no, ~ that** *(in dictation etc)* nein, streichen Sie das

c *(= frank) stamp, ticket, cheque* entwerten, ungültig machen

d *(Math)* kürzen; **this X ~s that one** dieses X hebt das X auf

VI *(= revoke commercial order, contract)* stornieren; *(= call off appointment, holiday)* absagen

▶ **cancel out** VT *sep (Math)* aufheben; *(fig)* zunichtemachen; **to cancel each other out** *(Math)* sich aufheben, sich kürzen lassen; *(fig)* einander aufheben, sich gegenseitig aufheben VI *(Math)* sich aufheben, sich wegkürzen lassen *(inf)*

cancellation [ˌkænsəˈleɪʃən] N a *(= calling off)* Absage *f*; *(official)* Stornierung *f*; *(of plans)* Aufgabe *f*; *(of train, bus)* Streichung *f*, Ausfall *m*; **your appointment may be brought forward in the event of a ~** wir werden möglicherweise im Falle einer Absage auf Sie zurückkommen b *(= annulment)* Rückgängigmachung *f*; *(of command, invitation also)* Zurücknahme *f*; *(of contract also)* Auflösung *f*; *(of debt)* Streichung *f*; *(of order for goods)* Stornierung *f*; *(of magazine subscription)* Kündigung *f*; *(of decree)* Aufhebung *f* c *(= franking: of stamp, ticket, cheque)* Entwertung *f* d *(Math)* Kürzung *f*

cancellation clause N Rücktrittsklausel *f*

cancer [ˈkænsəʳ] N *(Med)* Krebs *m*; *(fig)* Krebsgeschwür *nt*; **~ of the throat** Kehlkopfkrebs *m*; **Cancer** *(Astrol)* Krebs *m*; **he's (a) Cancer** er ist Krebs

cancerous [ˈkænsərəs] ADJ krebsartig; **~ growth** *(lit, fig)* krebsartige Wucherung

cancer: **cancer relief** N Krebshilfe *f*; **cancer research** N Krebsforschung *f*; **cancer screening** N Krebsvorsorgeuntersuchung *f*; **cancer stick** N *(inf: = cigarette)* Sargnagel *m (inf)*

candelabra [ˌkændɪˈlɑːbrə] N Kandelaber *m*, Leuchter *m*

candid [ˈkændɪd] ADJ offen, ehrlich; **he was quite ~ about it** er war ganz offen, er sprach ganz offen darüber; **my ~ opinion is that he ...** ich bin offen gesagt der Meinung, dass er ...

candida [ˈkændɪdə] N *(Med)* Candidose *f*

candidacy [ˈkændɪdəsɪ] N Kandidatur *f*

candidate [ˈkændɪdeɪt] N *(Pol)* Kandidat(in) *m(f)*; *(= exam candidate also)* Prüfling *m*; **to stand as (a) ~** kandidieren; **they are ~s for relegation** *(Sport)* sie sind Abstiegskandidaten; **the obese are prime ~s for heart disease** Fettleibige stehen auf der Liste der Herzinfarktkandidaten ganz oben ADJ *attr* **~ country** *(for EU membership etc)* Beitrittskandidat *f*

candidature [ˈkændɪdətʃəʳ] N *(Brit)* = **candidacy**

candidly [ˈkændɪdlɪ] ADV offen, ehrlich; **quite ~, ...** offen gestanden, ...; **to speak ~** offen *or* ehrlich sein

candidness [ˈkændɪdnɪs] N Offenheit *f*, Ehrlichkeit *f*

candied [ˈkændɪd] ADJ *(Cook)* kandiert, gezuckert; **~ peel** *(of lemon)* Zitronat *nt*; *(of orange)* Orangeat *nt*

candle [ˈkændl] N Kerze *f*; **to burn the ~ at both ends** mit seinen Kräften Raubbau treiben; **he can't hold a ~ to his brother** er kann seinem Bruder nicht das Wasser reichen; **the game is not worth the ~** das ist nicht der Mühe wert

candle *in cpds* Kerzen-; **candle end** N Kerzenstummel *m*; **candle grease** N Kerzenwachs *nt*; **candlelight** N Kerzenlicht *nt*, Kerzenschein *m*; **by ~** im Kerzenschein, bei Kerzenlicht; **a ~ dinner** ein Candlelight-Dinner *nt*, ein Essen *nt* bei Kerzenlicht

Candlemas ['kændlməs] N Mariä Lichtmess *nt*

candle: **candlepower** N (*old Elec*) Lichtstärke *f*; **candlestick** ['kændlstɪk] N Kerzenhalter *m*; **candlewick** N a Kerzendocht *m* b (*Tex*) Frottierplüschmuster *nt* ATTR *bedspread* im Frottierplüschmuster

candour, (*US*) **candor** ['kændəʳ] N Offenheit *f*, Ehrlichkeit *f*

candy ['kændɪ] N (*US*: = *sweet*) Bonbon *m or nt*; (= *sweets*) Süßigkeiten *pl*, Bonbons *pl*; (= *bar of chocolate*) (Tafel *f*) Schokolade *f*; (= *individual chocolate*) Praline *f*; **it's like taking ~ from a baby** das ist kinderleicht VT *sugar* kristallisieren lassen; *fruit etc* kandieren

candy: **candy apple** N (*US*) kandierter Apfel; **candy-ass** N (*US sl*) Weichei *nt* (*pej inf*), Memme *f* (*pej*), Waschlappen *m* (*pej inf*); **candy bar** N (*US*) Schokoladenriegel *m*, Schokoriegel *m*; **candyfloss** N (*Brit*) Zuckerwatte *f*; **candy store** N (*US*) Süßwarenhandlung *f*, Bonbonladen *m* (*inf*); **candy-striped** ADJ bunt gestreift (*auf weißem Hintergrund*)

cane [keɪn] N a (= *stem of bamboo, sugar etc*) Rohr *nt*; (*of raspberry*) Zweig *m*; (*for supporting plants*) Stock *m*; **~ chair** Rohrstuhl *m* b (= *walking stick*) (Spazier)stock *m*; (= *instrument of punishment*) (Rohr)stock *m*; **to use the ~** den Rohrstock benutzen; **to get the ~** Prügel bekommen; (*on hand*) eine auf die Finger bekommen, eine Tatze bekommen (*S Ger*) VT *schoolboy* mit dem Stock schlagen

cane *in cpds* Rohr-; **canebrake** N (*US*) Röhricht *nt*, Rohrdickicht *nt*; **cane sugar** N Rohrzucker *m*

canicular: **canicular days** [kə'nɪkjʊləˌdeɪz] PL Hundstage *pl*; **canicular heat** [kəˌnɪkjʊlə'hi:t] N Hundstagshitze *f*

canine ['keɪnaɪn] N a (= *animal*) Hund *m* b (*also* **canine tooth**) Eckzahn *m* ADJ Hunde-

caning ['keɪnɪŋ] N (= *beating with cane*) Schläge *pl* mit dem Stock, Prügeln *nt* (*inf*); **to give sb a ~** jdm eine Tracht Prügel verabreichen; **to get a ~** (*Sport*) haushoch geschlagen werden; (*new play etc*) verrissen werden

canister ['kænɪstəʳ] N Behälter *m*; (*for tea, coffee etc also*) Dose *f*; **~ shot** (*Mil*) Kartätsche *f*

canker ['kæŋkəʳ] N (*Med*) Mund- *or* Lippengeschwür *nt*; (*Vet*) Hufkrebs *m*, Strahlfäule *f*; (*Bot*) Brand *m*; (*fig*) (Krebs)geschwür *nt*

cankerous ['kæŋkərəs] ADJ (*Med*) entzündet; (*Vet, Bot*) brandig; (*fig*) krebsartig

cannabis ['kænəbɪs] N Cannabis *m*

cannabis resin N Cannabisharz *nt*

canned [kænd] ADJ a (*US*) Dosen-, in Dosen; **~ beer** Dosenbier *nt*; **~ goods** Konserven *pl* b (*inf*) **~ music** Musikberieselung *f* (*inf*); **~ laughter/applause** Gelächter *nt*/Applaus *m* vom Band; **~ heat** Brennspiritus *m* c (*inf*: = *drunk*) blau (*inf*), voll (*sl*)

cannery ['kænərɪ] N (*US*) Konservenfabrik *f*

cannibal ['kænɪbəl] N (= *person*) Kannibale *m*, Kannibalin *f*, Menschenfresser(in) *m(f)*; **these insects are ~s** diese Insekten fressen sich gegenseitig ADJ kannibalisch; *animals* sich gegenseitig auffressend

cannibalism ['kænɪbəlɪzəm] N (*of people*) Kannibalismus *m*, Menschenfresserei *f*

cannibalistic [ˌkænɪbə'lɪstɪk] ADJ kannibalisch; *people also* Menschen fressend

cannibalization [ˌkænɪbəlaɪ'zeɪʃən] N (*Econ*) Kannibalisierung *f*

cannibalize ['kænɪbəlaɪz] VT *old car etc* ausschlachten

cannily ['kænɪlɪ] ADV clever, raffiniert; (*involving money also*) geschäftstüchtig; (*with plans also*) gewieft

canning ['kænɪŋ] N Konservenabfüllung *f*; (= *preserving*) Konservierung *f*; **the ~ of meat** die Herstellung von Fleischkonserven

cannon ['kænən] N a (*Mil*) Kanone *f* b (*Brit, Billiards*) Karambolage *f* VI (*Brit, Billiards*) karambolieren

▶ **cannon into** VI +*prep obj* zusammenprallen mit

cannonade [ˌkænə'neɪd] N Kanonade *f*

cannon: **cannonball** N Kanonenkugel *f*; **cannon fodder** N Kanonenfutter *nt*

cannot ['kænɒt] ✪ 5.3, 10.4, 12.3, 16.3 NEG *of* **can**[1]

cannula ['kænjʊlə] N *pl* **cannulae, cannuli** Kanüle *f*

canny ['kænɪ] ADJ (+*er*) (= *cautious*) vorsichtig; (= *shrewd also*) schlau, clever; (= *careful with money also*) sparsam

canoe [kə'nu:] N Kanu *nt*; **to paddle one's own ~** (*fig*) auf eigenen Füßen *or* Beinen stehen VI Kanu fahren, paddeln

canoeing [kə'nu:ɪŋ] N Kanusport *m*, Kanufahren *nt*

canoeist [kə'nu:ɪst] N Kanufahrer(in) *m(f)*, Kanute *m*, Kanutin *f*

canon[1] ['kænən] N (*all senses*) Kanon *m*

canon[2] N (= *priest*) Kanoniker *m*, Kanonikus *m*

cañon N (*US*) = **canyon**

canonical [kə'nɒnɪkəl] ADJ a (*Eccl*) kanonisch; **~ dress** Priestergewand *nt* b (*fig*, = *accepted*) anerkannt, rechtmäßig

canonization [ˌkænənaɪ'zeɪʃən] N (*Eccl*) Heiligsprechung *f*, Kanonisation *f*, Kanonisierung *f*

canonize ['kænənaɪz] VT (*Eccl*) heiligsprechen, kanonisieren

canon law N (*Eccl*) Kanon *m*, kanonisches Recht

canoodle [kə'nu:dl] VI (*Brit inf*) rumschmusen (*inf*)

can-opener N Dosen- *or* Büchsenöffner *m*

canopy ['kænəpɪ] N a (= *awning*) Markise *f*, Überdachung *f*; (*over entrance*) Vordach *nt*, Pergola *f*; (*of bed, throne*) Baldachin *m*; (*of aircraft*) Kanzeldach *nt*; (*of parachute*) Fallschirmkappe *f* b (*fig liter, of sky, foliage*) Baldachin *m* (*liter*); **the ~ of the heavens** das Himmelszelt (*liter*)

canst [kænst] (*obs*) *2nd pers sing of* **can**[1]

cant[1] [kænt] N a (= *hypocrisy*) Heuchelei *f*, scheinheiliges *or* leeres Gerede b (= *jargon*) Jargon *m*, Kauderwelsch *nt*

cant[2] N (= *tilt*) Schräge *f* VT schräg stellen, kanten; **the wind ~ed the boat** der Wind brachte das Boot zum Kippen VI schräg *or* schief sein, sich neigen; (*boat*) kippen

can't [kɑ:nt] *contr of* **can not**

Cantab ['kæntæb] *abbr of* **Cantabrigiensis** von der Universität Cambridge

cantaloup(e) ['kæntəlu:p] N Honigmelone *f*, Buttermelone *f*

cantankerous [kæn'tæŋkərəs] ADJ mürrisch, knurrig

cantata [kæn'tɑ:tə] N Kantate *f*

canteen [kæn'ti:n] N a (= *restaurant*) Kantine *f*; (*in university*) Mensa *f* b (*Mil*: = *flask*) Feldflasche *f*; (= *mess tin*) Kochgeschirr *nt* c (*Brit*: *of cutlery*) Besteckkasten *m*

canter ['kæntəʳ] N Handgalopp *m*, Kanter *m*; **to go for a ~** einen Ausritt machen VI langsam galoppieren

canticle ['kæntɪkl] N (*Eccl*) Lobgesang *m*; (= *song*) Volksweise *f*; **Canticles** Hohelied *nt*, Hohes Lied

cantilever ['kæntɪli:vəʳ] N Ausleger *m*

cantilever *in cpds* Ausleger-; **cantilever bridge** ['kæntɪli:və'brɪdʒ] N Auslegerbrücke *f*; **cantilever roof** ['kæntɪli:və'ru:f] N (*Archit*) Krag- *or* Auslegerdach *nt*

canto ['kæntəʊ] N (*Liter*) Canto *m*, Gesang *m*

canton ['kæntɒn] N Kanton *m*

Cantonese [ˌkæntə'ni:z] ADJ kantonesisch N a Kantonese *m*, Kantonesin *f* b (*Ling*) Kantonesisch *nt*

cantonment [kən'tu:nmənt] N Truppenunterkunft *f*, Kantonnement *nt* (*old*)

cantor ['kæntɔ:ʳ] N Kantor *m*

Canuck [kə'nʌk] N (*US pej inf*) (Franko)kanadier(in) *m(f)*

Canute [kə'nju:t] N Knut *m*

canvas ['kænvəs] N Leinwand *f*; (*for sails*) Segeltuch *nt*; (= *set of sails*) Segel *pl*; (*for tent*) Zeltbahn *f*; (*Art*: = *material*) Leinwand *f*; (= *painting*) Gemälde *nt*; **under ~** (= *in a tent*) im Zelt; (*Naut*) mit gehisstem Segel; **~ chair** Liegestuhl *m*, Klappstuhl *m*; **~ shoes** Segeltuchschuhe *pl*

canvass ['kænvəs] VT a (*Pol*) *district* Wahlwerbung machen in (+*dat*); *person* für seine Partei zu gewinnen suchen; **to ~ the local electorate** in seinem Wahlkreis Stimmen werben *or* auf Stimmenfang gehen (*inf*) b *customers, citizens etc* ansprechen, werben; *issue* unter die Leute bringen; *district* bereisen; (= *sound out*) *opinions* erforschen VI a (*Pol*) um Stimmen werben (*for sb* für jdn) b (*Comm*) werben, eine Werbekampagne durchführen, Klinken putzen (*inf*) N (*Pol, Comm*) Aktion *f*, Kampagne *f*

canvasser ['kænvəsəʳ] N a (*Pol*) Wahlhelfer(in) *m(f)* b (*Comm*) Vertreter(in) *m(f)*, Klinkenputzer(in) *m(f)* (*inf*)

canvassing ['kænvəsɪŋ] N a (*Pol*) Durchführung *f* des Wahlkampfs, Wahlwerbung *f* b (*Comm*) Von-Haus-zu-Haus-Gehen *nt*, Klinkenputzen *nt* (*inf*); (= *sounding-out*: *of opinions*) Meinungsforschung *f*; **~ by applicants is not allowed** es ist den Bewerbern nicht gestattet, mit Firmenangehörigen Kontakt aufzunehmen, um den Bewerbungsvorgang zu beeinflussen

canyon, (*US*) **cañon** ['kænjən] N Cañon *m*

canyoning ['kænjənɪŋ] N (*Sport*) Canyoning *nt*

cap[1] [kæp] N a (= *hat*) Mütze *f*; (= *soldier's cap also*) Käppi *nt*; (= *nurse's cap*) Haube *f*; (*Jur, Univ*) Barett *nt*; (*for swimming*) Bademütze *or* -kappe *f*; (*of jester*) Kappe *f*; (*of cardinal*) Hut *m*; (= *skullcap*) Käppchen *nt*; **~ in hand** kleinlaut; **if the ~ fits(, wear it)** (*Brit prov*) wem die Jacke passt(, der soll sie sich (*dat*) anziehen); **~ and bells** Schellenkappe *f*; **in ~ and gown** mit Doktorhut und Talar

b (*Brit Sport*) **he has won 50 ~s for Scotland** er ist 50 Mal mit der schottischen Mannschaft angetreten; **Owen is the team's only new ~** Owen ist der einzige Neuzugang in der Mannschaft

c (= *lid, cover, of bottle*) Verschluss *m*, Deckel *m*; (*of fountain pen*) (Verschluss)kappe *f*; (*of valve*) Kappe *f*; (*Mil*: *of shell, fuse*) Kapsel *f*; (*Aut*: = *petrol cap, radiator cap*) Verschluss *m*

d (= *contraceptive*) Pessar *nt*

e (= *explosive*) Platzpatrone *f*; (*for toy gun*) Zündplättchen *nt*

f (*of mushroom*) Hut *m*

g (*Pol*) Kappungsgrenze *f*

VT a (= *put cap on*) *bottle etc* verschließen, zumachen; (*fig*: = *cover top of*) *peaks* bedecken; **to have one's teeth ~ped** sich (*dat*) die Zähne überkronen lassen

b (*Sport*) **he was ~ped four times for England** er wurde viermal für die englische Nationalmannschaft aufgestellt

c (= *do or say better*) überbieten; **and then to ~ it all ...** und, um dem Ganzen die Krone aufzusetzen ...

d (*Scot Univ*) einen akademischen Grad verleihen (+*dat*)

e (*in spending etc*) **they ~ped spending at £50,000** die Ausgaben wurden bei £ 50.000 gedeckelt; **the council was ~ped** (*Brit*) dem Stadtrat wurde von der Regierung ein Höchstsatz für die Kommunalsteuer *etc* auferlegt; **~ped rate mortgage** (*Brit*) Hypothek *f* mit Zinsobergrenze

cap[2] N (*Typ inf*) großer Buchstabe; **in ~s** in Großbuchstaben → *also* **capital N b**

CAP *abbr of* **Common Agricultural Policy** *gemeinsame Agrarpolitik der EG*, GAP *f*

capability [ˌkeɪpəˈbɪlɪtɪ] N **a** *(= potential ability)* Fähigkeit *f*; *(no pl: = capableness also)* Kompetenz *f*; **sth is within sb's capabilities** jd ist zu etw fähig; **sth is beyond sb's capabilities** etw übersteigt jds Fähigkeiten **b** *(Mil)* Potenzial *nt*, Potential *nt*

capable [ˈkeɪpəbl] ADJ **a** *(= skilful, competent)* fähig, kompetent; *mother* gut
b **to be ~ of doing sth** etw tun können; *(person: = have physical, mental ability also)* fähig sein, etw zu tun; **to be ~ of sth** etw können, zu etw fähig sein; **it's ~ of exploding any minute** es kann jede Minute explodieren; **it's ~ of speeds of up to ...** es erreicht Geschwindigkeiten bis zu ...; **he's ~ of better** er ist zu Besserem fähig; **the poem is ~ of several interpretations** das Gedicht lässt mehrere Interpretationsmöglichkeiten zu; **~ of improvement** verbesserungsfähig; **he's quite ~ of changing his mind at the last minute** er bringt es fertig und ändert seine Meinung in der letzten Minute; **thank you but I'm quite ~ of doing that myself** danke, ich kann das durchaus allein

capably [ˈkeɪpəblɪ] ADV kompetent, geschickt

capacious [kəˈpeɪʃəs] ADJ geräumig; *dress* weit

capacitance [kəˈpæsɪtəns] N *(Elec)* Speicherkapazität *f*

capacitor [kəˈpæsɪtəˈ] N Kondensator *m*

capacity [kəˈpæsɪtɪ] ✪ 19.1 N **a** *(= cubic content etc)* Fassungsvermögen *nt*, (Raum)inhalt *m*; *(= maximum output)* Kapazität *f*; *(= maximum weight)* Höchstlast *f*; *(Aut, = engine capacity)* Hubraum *m*; **filled to ~** randvoll; *(hall)* bis auf den letzten Platz besetzt; **seating ~ of 400** 400 Sitzplätze; **to work to ~** voll ausgelastet sein; **working at full ~** voll ausgelastet; **the Stones played to ~ audiences** die Stones spielten vor ausverkauften Sälen
b *(= ability)* Fähigkeit *f*; **his ~ for learning** seine Lern- *or* Aufnahmefähigkeit; **he has a great ~ for work** er kann sehr gut arbeiten; **this work is within/beyond his ~** er ist zu dieser Arbeit fähig/nicht fähig
c *(= role, position)* Eigenschaft *f*, Funktion *f*; **in my ~ as a doctor** (in meiner Eigenschaft) als Arzt; **speaking in his official ~ as mayor, he said ...** er sagte in seiner Eigenschaft als Bürgermeister ...; **in a personal ~** als Privatperson; **they refused to employ him in any ~ whatsoever** sie lehnten es ab, ihn in irgendeiner Form zu beschäftigen
d *(= legal power)* Befugnis *f*

caparison [kəˈpærɪsn] *(liter)* **N** Schabracke *f* *(old)* **VT** mit einer Schabracke bedecken *(old)*

cape¹ [keɪp] N Cape *nt*, Umhang *m*, Pelerine *f* *(old)*

cape² N *(Geog)* Kap *nt*

Cape: **Cape Canaveral** N Kap Canaveral *nt*; **Cape Cod** N Cape Cod *nt*; **Cape Coloured** N Farbige(r) *mf*, Gemischtrassige(r) *mf*; **cape gooseberry** N Kapstachelbeere *f*, Physalis *f*; **Cape Horn** N Kap *nt* Hoorn; **Cape of Good Hope** N Kap *nt* der guten Hoffnung

caper¹ [ˈkeɪpəˈ] **VI** herumtollen **N** **a** *(= skip)* Luft- *or* Freudensprung *m* **b** *(= prank)* Eskapade *f*, Kapriole *f* **c** *(inf: = crime)* Ding *nt* *(sl)*

caper² N *(Bot, Cook)* Kaper *f*; *(= shrub)* Kapernstrauch *m*

capercaillie, capercailzie [ˌkæpəˈkeɪlɪ] N Auerhahn *m*

Cape: **Cape Town** N Kapstadt *nt*; **Cape Verde Islands** PL Kapverdische Inseln *pl*, Kapverden *pl*

capful [ˈkæpfʊl] N **one ~ to one litre of water** eine Verschlusskappe auf einen Liter Wasser

capillary [kəˈpɪlərɪ] **ADJ** kapillar, Kapillar-; **~ attraction** *or* **action** Kapillarwirkung *f* **N** Kapillare *f*, Kapillargefäß *nt*

capital [ˈkæpɪtl] **N** **a** *(also* **capital city***)* Hauptstadt *f*; *(fig: = centre)* Zentrum *nt*
b *(also* **capital letter***)* Großbuchstabe *m*; **large ~s** Großbuchstaben *pl*, Versalien *pl* *(spec)*; **small ~s** Kapitälchen *pl* *(spec)*; **please write in ~s** bitte in Blockschrift schreiben!
c *no pl (Fin, fig: = knowledge, skill)* Kapital *nt*; **to make ~ out of sth** *(fig)* aus etw Kapital schlagen; **~ and labour** Kapital und Arbeit
d *(Archit)* Kapitell *nt*
ADJ **a** *letter* Groß-; **love with a ~ L** die große Liebe; **a car with a ~ C** ein richtiges Auto; **unity with a ~ U** hundertprozentige Einheit
b *(= major)* **of ~ importance** von größter Bedeutung
c *(Jur)* Kapital-; **~ crime** Kapitalverbrechen *nt*; **they will be tried on a ~ charge of instigating the riots** sie werden des Kapitalverbrechens der Anstiftung zum Aufruhr angeklagt werden
d *(dated inf: = excellent)* prächtig *(dated)*, famos *(dated)*

capital *in cpds* Kapital-; **capital account** N Kapitalbilanz *f*; **capital allowance** N Abschreibung *f*; **capital assets** PL Kapitalvermögen *nt*; **capital base** N Kapitalbasis *f*; **capital costs** PL Kapitalkosten *pl*; **capital employed** N Betriebskapital *nt*; **capital equipment** N (Betriebs)anlagen *pl*; **capital expenditure** N Kapitalaufwendungen *pl*; **capital gain** N, **capital gains** PL Kapitalgewinn *m*, Wertzuwachs *m*; **capital gains tax** N Kapitalertragssteuer *f*; **capital goods** PL Investitionsgüter *pl*; **capital growth** N Kapitalzuwachs *m*; **capital-intensive** ADJ kapitalintensiv; **capital investment** N Kapitalanlage *f*

capitalism [ˈkæpɪtəlɪzəm] N Kapitalismus *m*

capitalist [ˈkæpɪtəlɪst] **N** Kapitalist(in) *m(f)* **ADJ** kapitalistisch

capitalistic [ˌkæpɪtəˈlɪstɪk] ADJ kapitalistisch

capitalization [ˌkæpɪtəlaɪˈzeɪʃən] N **a** *(Fin)* Kapitalisierung *f*, Kapitalisation *f* **b** *(Typ)* Großschreibung *f*

capitalize [ˈkæpɪtəˌlaɪz] VT **a** *(Fin)* kapitalisieren **b** *(Typ) word* großschreiben

▶ **capitalize on** VI *+prep (fig)* Kapital schlagen aus

capital: **capital levy** N Vermögens- *or* Kapitalsteuer *f*; **capital loss** N (Kapital)veräußerungsverlust *m*; **capital market** N Kapitalmarkt *m*; **capital offence** N Kapitalverbrechen *nt*; **capital punishment** N die Todesstrafe; **capital reserves** PL Kapitalreserven *pl*; **capital returns tax** N Kapitalertrag(s)steuer *f*; **capital spending** N = **capital expenditure**; **capital stock** N Gesellschaftskapital *nt*; **capital sum** N Kapitalbetrag *m*, Kapital *nt*; **capital transfer tax** N Kapitalverkehrssteuer *f*; *(for inheritance)* Erbschaftssteuer *f*

capitation [ˌkæpɪˈteɪʃən] N Kopfsteuer *f*

Capitol [ˈkæpɪtl] N Kapitol *nt*

capitulate [kəˈpɪtjʊleɪt] VI kapitulieren *(also Mil)* (*to* vor *+dat*), aufgeben (*to* gegenüber)

capitulation [kəˌpɪtjʊˈleɪʃən] N Kapitulation *f*

caplet, Caplet® [ˈkæplɪt] N *(= coated tablet)* Kapsel *f*

capo [ˈkæpəʊ] N Kapodaster *m*

capon [ˈkeɪpən] N Kapaun *m*

cappuccino [ˌkæpʊˈtʃiːnəʊ] N Cappuccino *m*

Capri [kəˈpriː] N Capri *nt*

caprice [kəˈpriːs] N **a** Laune(nhaftigkeit) *f*, Kaprice *f (geh)* **b** *(Mus)* Capriccio *nt*

capricious [kəˈprɪʃəs] ADJ launisch, kapriziös *(geh)*

capriciously [kəˈprɪʃəslɪ] ADV *act, behave* launenhaft; *decide, do sth* einer Laune gehorchend *(geh)*

capriciousness [kəˈprɪʃəsnɪs] N Launenhaftigkeit *f*

Capricorn [ˈkæprɪkɔːn] N Steinbock *m*; **I'm (a) ~** ich bin Steinbock

capries [kəˈpriːz] PL *(US)* Caprihose *f*

capsicum [ˈkæpsɪkəm] N Pfefferschote *f*, Peperoni *pl*

capsize [kæpˈsaɪz] **VI** kentern **VT** zum Kentern bringen

caps lock [ˈkæpslɒk] N *(Comput)* Feststelltaste *f*

capstan [ˈkæpstən] N Poller *m*

capstone [ˈkæpstəʊn] N *(Archit) (lit, fig)* Schlussstein *m*; *(of wall)* Mauerkappe *f*

capsular [ˈkæpsjʊləˈ] ADJ Kapsel-

capsule [ˈkæpsjuːl] N Kapsel *f*

captain [ˈkæptɪn] *(abbr* **Capt***)* **N** *(Mil)* Hauptmann *m*; *(Naut, Aviat, Sport)* Kapitän *m*; *(US, in restaurant)* Oberkellner *m*; **yes, ~!** jawohl, Herr Hauptmann/Kapitän!; **~ of industry** Industriekapitän *m* **VT** *(Sport) team* anführen; *(Naut) ship* befehligen; **he ~ed the team for years** er war jahrelang Kapitän der Mannschaft

captaincy [ˈkæptənsɪ] N Befehligung *f*, Befehl *m*; *(Sport)* Führung *f*; **to get the ~** *(Sport)* zum Mannschaftskapitän ernannt werden; **under his ~** mit ihm als Kapitän

caption [ˈkæpʃən] **N** Überschrift *f*, Titel *m*; *(under cartoon)* Bildunterschrift *f*; *(Film: = subtitle)* Untertitel *m* **VT** betiteln, mit einer Überschrift *or* einem Titel *etc* versehen

captious [ˈkæpʃəs] ADJ *person* überkritisch, pedantisch; *remark* spitzfindig

captivate [ˈkæptɪveɪt] VT faszinieren, entzücken

captivating [ˈkæptɪveɪtɪŋ] ADJ bezaubernd; *personality* einnehmend

captive [ˈkæptɪv] **N** Gefangene(r) *mf*; **to take sb ~** jdn gefangen nehmen; **to hold sb ~** jdn gefangen halten; *(fig)* jdn fesseln, jdn gefangen nehmen **ADJ** *person* gefangen; *animal, bird* in Gefangenschaft; **in a ~ state** in Gefangenschaft *f*; **a ~ audience** ein unfreiwilliges Publikum; **~ breeding** Zucht *f* (von artbedrohten Tieren) in Gefangenschaft

captive balloon N Fesselballon *m*

captive market N Monopol-Absatzmarkt *m*

captivity [kæpˈtɪvɪtɪ] N Gefangenschaft *f*

captor [ˈkæptəˈ] N derjenige, der jdn gefangen nimmt; **his ~s treated him kindly** er wurde nach seiner Gefangennahme gut behandelt; **his ~s were Ruritanian** er wurde von Ruritaniern gefangen genommen; **his ~s later freed him** man ließ ihn später wieder frei

capture [ˈkæptʃəˈ] **VT** **a** *town* einnehmen, erobern; *treasure* erobern; *person* gefangen nehmen; *animal* (ein)fangen; *ship* kapern, aufbringen *(spec)*; **they ~d the town from the enemy** sie eroberten die vom Feind beherrschte Stadt **b** *(fig) votes* erringen, auf sich *(acc)* vereinigen; *prizes* erringen; *(painter etc) atmosphere* einfangen; *attention, sb's interest* erregen **c** *(Comput) data* erfassen **N** Eroberung *f*; *(= thing captured also)* Fang *m*; *(of escapee)* Gefangennahme *f*; *(of animal)* Einfangen *nt*; *(Comput, of data)* Erfassung *f*

capuchin [ˈkæpjʊtʃɪn] N **a** *(= hooded cloak)* Kapuzencape *nt* **b** *(Zool)* Kapuziner(affe) *m* **c** *(Eccl)* **Capuchin** Kapuziner(mönch) *m*

car [kɑːˈ] N **a** Auto *nt*, Wagen *m*; **by ~** mit dem Auto *or* Wagen; **~ ride** Autofahrt *f*, Fahrt *f* mit dem Auto **b** *(esp US Rail: = tram car)* Wagen *m* **c** *(of airship, balloon, cable car)* Gondel *f*; *(US, of elevator)* Fahrkorb *m*

carafe [kəˈræf] N Karaffe *f*

car accident N Autounfall *m*

car alarm N Auto-Alarmanlage *f*

caramel [ˈkærəməl] N *(= substance)* Karamell *m*; *(= sweet)* Karamelle *f*

caramel *in cpds* Karamell-; **caramel-coloured** ADJ hellbraun; **caramel-flavoured** ADJ mit Karamellgeschmack

carapace [ˈkærəpeɪs] N Schale *f*; *(of tortoise etc)* (Rücken)panzer *m*

carat [ˈkærət] N Karat *nt*; **nine ~ gold** neunkarätiges Gold

caravan [ˈkærəvæn] N **a** *(Brit Aut)* Wohnwagen *m*, Caravan *m*; **~ holiday** Ferien *pl* im Wohnwagen **b** *(= gipsy caravan)* Zigeunerwagen *m* **c** *(= desert caravan)* Karawane *f*

caravanning ['kærəvænɪŋ] N Caravaning *nt*, Urlaub *m* im Wohnwagen; **to go ~** Urlaub im Wohnwagen machen

caravanserai [,kærə'vænsə,raɪ] N Karawanserei *f*

caravan site N Campingplatz *m* für Wohnwagen

caravel [kærə'vel] N Karavelle *f*

caraway ['kærəweɪ] N Kümmel *m*

caraway seeds PL Kümmel(körner *pl*) *m*

carb [kɑ:b] N *(inf)* Kohle(n)hydrat *nt*

carbide ['kɑ:baɪd] N Karbid *nt*

carbine ['kɑ:baɪn] N Karabiner *m*

car body N (Auto)karosserie *f*

carbohydrate ['kɑ:bəʊ'haɪdreɪt] N Kohle(n)hydrat *nt*

carbolic [kɑ:'bɒlɪk] ADJ Karbol- N *(also* **carbolic soap**) Karbolseife *f*

carbolic acid N Karbolsäure *f*

car bomb N Autobombe *f*

carbon ['kɑ:bən] N *(Chem)* Kohlenstoff *m*; *(Elec)* Kohle *f*

carbonaceous [,kɑ:bə'neɪʃəs] ADJ Kohlenstoff-, kohlenstoffhaltig

carbonate ['kɑ:bənɪt] N Karbonat *nt*

carbonated ['kɑ:bə,neɪtəd] ADJ mit Kohlensäure (versetzt)

carbon: **carbon copy** N Durchschlag *m*; **to be a ~ of sth** das genaue Ebenbild einer Sache *(gen)* sein; **she's a ~ of her sister** sie sieht ihrer Schwester zum Verwechseln ähnlich; **carbon dating** N Radiokarbonmethode *f*, Kohlenstoffdatierung *f*; **carbon dioxide** N Kohlendioxid *nt*; **carbon fibre** N Kohlenstoffaser *f*; **carbon footprint** N CO^2-Fußabdruck *m*

carbonic [kɑ:'bɒnɪk] ADJ Kohlen-

carbonic: **carbonic acid** N Kohlensäure *f*; **carbonic oxide** N Kohlenmonoxid *nt*

carboniferous [,kɑ:bə'nɪfərəs] ADJ *(Geol)* kohlehaltig

carbonization [,kɑ:bənaɪ'zeɪʃən] N Karbonisation *f*, Verkohlung *f*

carbonize ['kɑ:bənaɪz] VT karbonisieren, verkohlen (lassen)

carbon: **carbonless paper** N selbstdurchschreibendes Papier; **carbon monoxide** N Kohlenmonoxid *nt*; **carbon-neutral** ADJ CO^2-neutral; **carbon paper** N Kohlepapier *nt*

> **CAR-BOOT SALE, GARAGE SALE**
>
> **Car-boot sales** sind in Großbritannien recht beliebte Flohmärkte, bei denen die Leute Dinge, die sie nicht mehr länger benötigen, wie Kleider, Möbel und andere Haushaltsgegenstände, aus den Kofferräumen ihrer Autos heraus verkaufen. Normalerweise werden solche Märkte auf Parkplätzen oder anderen Plätzen im Freien abgehalten, wobei die Autobesitzer eine kleine Gebühr für den Standplatz entrichten müssen.
> In den USA verkaufen Hausbesitzer überflüssigen Hausrat und Kleider, indem sie einen **garage sale** oder auch **yard sale** abhalten und alles, von dem sie sich trennen wollen, im Garten oder in der Garage zum Verkauf anbieten. Manchmal schließen sich auch mehrere Nachbarn zusammen und veranstalten einen gemeinsamen **garage sale**.

carboy ['kɑ:bɔɪ] N Korbflasche *f*

carbuncle ['kɑ:bʌŋkl] N **a** *(Med)* Karbunkel *m* **b** *(= jewel)* Karfunkel(stein) *m*

carburettor, *(US)* **carburetor** [,kɑ:bə'retə'] N Vergaser *m*

carcass ['kɑ:kəs] N **a** *(= corpse)* Leiche *f*; *(of animal)* Kadaver *m*, (Tier)leiche *f*; *(at butcher's)* Rumpf *m*; **move your fat ~!** *(inf)* schwing deinen Arsch weg! *(sl)* **b** *(of ship, house)* Skelett *nt*; *(= remains)* Überbleibsel *pl*, Trümmer *pl*

car chase N Verfolgungsjagd *f (mit dem Auto)*

carcinogen [kɑ:'sɪnədʒen] N Krebserreger *m*, Karzinogen *nt*

carcinogenic [,kɑ:sɪnə'dʒenɪk] ADJ karzinogen, krebserregend, Krebs erregend

carcinoma [,kɑ:sɪ'nəʊmə] N Karzinom *nt*

car: **car coat** N Dreivierteljacke *f*; **car crash** N (Auto)unfall *m*

card[1] [kɑ:d] N **a** *no pl (= cardboard)* Pappe *f* **b** *(= greetings, business card etc)* Karte *f (also Comput)*; *(= cheque/credit card)* (Scheck-/Kredit)karte *f* **c** **cards** PL *(= employment cards)* Papiere *pl*; **he asked for his ~s** *(inf)* er wollte sich *(dat)* seine Papiere geben lassen *(inf)* **d** *(= playing card)* (Spiel)karte *f*; **to play ~s** Karten spielen; **to lose money at ~s** Geld beim Kartenspiel verlieren; **pack of ~s** Karten *pl*, Kartenspiel *nt*; **game of ~s** Kartenspiel *nt*; **house of ~s** *(lit, fig)* Kartenhaus *nt* **e** *(Sport, = programme)* Programm *nt* **f** *(fig)* **to put** *or* **lay one's ~s on the table** seine Karten aufdecken *or* (offen) auf den Tisch legen; **to play one's ~s right/badly** geschickt/ungeschickt taktieren, taktisch geschickt/unklug vorgehen; **to hold all the ~s** alle Trümpfe in der Hand haben; **to play one's last/trump ~** seinen letzten/höchsten Trumpf ausspielen; **to play** *or* **keep one's ~s close to one's chest** *or (US)* **close to the vest** sich *(dat)* nicht in die Karten sehen lassen; **it's on the ~s** das ist zu erwarten **g** *(dated inf, = person)* ulkiger Vogel *(inf)* VT *(US inf)* **to ~ sb** jds Identität kontrollieren; **Jack got ~ed** sie haben Jacks Ausweis kontrolliert

card[2] *(Tex)* N Wollkamm *m*, Krempel *f*, Karde *f* VT *wool, cotton* kämmen, krempeln, karden

cardamom ['kɑ:dəməm] N Kardamom *m or nt*

card: **cardboard** N Karton *m*, Pappe *f* ATTR Papp-; *(fig) character* stereotyp, klischeehaft, schablonenhaft; **cardboard box** N (Papp)karton *m*, Pappschachtel *f*; **card-carrying** ADJ **a ~ member** ein eingetragenes Mitglied; **~ communist** Mitglied *nt* der Kommunistischen Partei; **card catalogue**, **card file** N Zettelkatalog *m*; *(in library)* Katalog(karten *pl*) *m*; **card game** N Kartenspiel *nt*; **card holder** N *(of credit card)* Karteninhaber(in) *m(f)*

cardiac ['kɑ:dɪæk] ADJ Herz-

cardiac arrest N Herzstillstand *m*

cardigan ['kɑ:dɪgən] N Strickjacke *f*

cardinal ['kɑ:dɪnl] N **a** *(Eccl)* Kardinal *m* **b** → **cardinal number** ADJ *(= chief)* Haupt-; *(= utmost)* äußerste(r, s) *attr*

cardinal: **cardinal number** N Kardinalzahl *f*; **cardinal points** PL Himmelsrichtungen *pl*; **cardinal red** N Purpurrot *nt*; **cardinal sin** N Todsünde *f*; **cardinal virtue** N Kardinaltugend *f*

card index N Kartei *f*; *(in library)* Katalog *m*

cardio- ['kɑ:dɪəʊ-] PREF Kardio-; **cardiogram** Kardiogramm *nt*

cardiologist [,kɑ:dɪ'ɒlɪdʒɪst] N Kardiologe *m*, Kardiologin *f*

cardiology [,kɑ:dɪ'ɒlədʒɪ] N Kardiologie *f*

cardiopulmonary [,kɑ:dɪəʊ'pʌlmənərɪ] ADJ Herz-Lungen-; **~ resuscitation** Herz-Lungen--Wiederbelebung *f*

cardiovascular [,kɑ:dɪəʊ'væskjʊlə'] ADJ kardiovaskulär

card: **cardphone** N Kartentelefon *nt*; **card player** N Kartenspieler(in) *m(f)*; **card punch** N Lochkartenmaschine *f*; **card reader** N Lesemaschine *f*; **cardsharp(er)** N Falschspieler(in) *m(f)*, Zinker(in) *m(f) (inf)*; **card table** N Spieltisch *m*; **card trick** N Kartenkunststück *nt*; **card vote** N *(Brit)* ≈ Abstimmung *f* durch Wahlmänner

CARE [kεə'] *abbr of* **Cooperative for American Relief Everywhere**; **~ packet** Carepaket *nt*

care [kεə']

⊙ 7.5

1 NOUN	3 TRANSITIVE VERB
2 INTRANSITIVE VERB	4 PHRASAL VERB

1 – NOUN

a [= worry] Sorge *f* (*of* um); **free of care(s)** ohne Sorgen, frei von Sorge; **he hasn't a care in the world** er hat keinerlei Sorgen; **the cares of the world** die Sorgen des Alltags; **the cares of state** die Staatsgeschäfte *pl*

b [= carefulness] Sorgfalt *f*; **this word should be used with care** dieses Wort sollte sorgfältig *or* mit Sorgfalt gebraucht werden; **paint strippers need to be used with care** Abbeizmittel müssen vorsichtig *or* mit Vorsicht angewandt werden; **driving without due care and attention** fahrlässiges Verhalten im Straßenverkehr; **to drive with due care and attention** sich umsichtig im Straßenverkehr verhalten; **"fragile, with care", "handle with care"** „Vorsicht, zerbrechlich"; **it got broken despite all the care we took** es ist trotz aller Vorsicht kaputtgegangen; **have a care** *(old: = be careful)* gib acht *or* Obacht! *(old)*; *(inf: = be considerate)* nun mach mal einen Punkt! *(inf)*

♦ **to take care** *(= be careful)* aufpassen, vorsichtig sein; **take care when using weedkillers** beim Gebrauch von Unkrautbekämpfungsmitteln sollte man aufpassen *or* vorsichtig sein; **take care he doesn't cheat you** sehen Sie sich vor *or* nehmen Sie sich in Acht, dass er Sie nicht betrügt; **bye-bye, take care** tschüs(s), machs gut

♦ **to take care to do sth/not to do sth** sich bemühen *or* sich *(dat)* Mühe geben, etw zu tun/etw nicht zu tun; **I'll take care not to upset him** ich werde mich bemühen *or* ich werde mir Mühe geben, ihn nicht zu verärgern

♦ **to take care over** *or* **with sth/in doing sth** etw sorgfältig tun; **you should take more care with** *or* **over the details** Sie sollten sich sorgfältiger mit den Einzelheiten befassen

c [= maintenance] *of teeth, skin, car, furniture etc* Pflege *f*; **to take care of sth** *(= maintain)* auf etw *(acc)* aufpassen; *one's appearance, hair, car, furniture* etw pflegen; *(= not treat roughly) car, furniture, health* etw schonen; **to take care of oneself** sich um sich selbst kümmern; *(as regards health)* sich schonen, auf sich *(acc)* aufpassen; *(as regards appearance)* etwas für sich tun, sich pflegen

d [of old people, children] Versorgung *f*, Fürsorge *f*; **medical care** ärztliche Versorgung; **he needs medical care** er muss ärztlich behandelt werden; **he is in the care of Dr Smith** er ist bei Dr. Smith in Behandlung; **to take care of sb** sich um jdn kümmern; *patients* jdn versorgen; *one's family* für jdn sorgen; **they took good care of her in hospital** sie wurde im Krankenhaus gut versorgt

e [= protection] Obhut *f*; **care of** *(abbr* **c/o**) bei; **in** *or* **under sb's care** in jds *(dat)* Obhut; **to take a child into care** ein Kind in Pflege nehmen; **to be taken into care** in Pflege gegeben werden; **children placed in the care of the council** Kinder *pl* in der Obhut des Sozialamtes; **the children/valuables in my care** die mir anvertrauten Kinder/Wertsachen; **to take care of sth** *(valuables etc)* auf etw *(acc)* aufpassen; *plants, animals etc* sich um etw kümmern; *(over longer period)* etw versorgen

♦ **to take care of sb/sth** *(= see to)* sich um jdn/etw kümmern; *of arrangements, affairs etc also* etw erledigen; **that takes care of him/it** er/das wäre abgehakt *(inf)*, das wäre erledigt; **let me take care of that** lassen Sie mich das mal machen, überlassen Sie das mir; **that can take care of itself** das wird sich schon irgendwie geben; **let the housework take care of itself for a while** nun lass doch mal eine Zeit lang die Hausarbeit (sein)

f [= concern] *of person* Anteilnahme *f*, Fürsorglichkeit *f*; *(of state, council)* Interesse *nt* am Mitmenschen; **if the town planners showed more care** wenn die Städteplaner etwas mehr Menschenfreundlichkeit zeigen würden; **if only she showed a little care** wenn sie nur nicht so gleichgültig wäre; **the party has a genuine care for senior citizens** der Partei liegt das Wohl der älteren Mitbürger am Herzen

2 – INTRANSITIVE VERB

(= feel concern) **I don't care** das ist mir egal *or* gleichgültig; **as if I cared** als ob mir das etwas ausmachen würde; **for all I care** meinetwegen, von mir aus; **who cares?** na und?, und wennschon?; **he just doesn't care** das ist ihm so egal; **I didn't know you cared** *(hum)* ich wusste gar nicht, dass ich dir was bedeute; **the company that cares** die Firma mit Herz; **I wish you'd care a bit more** ich wünschte, das wäre dir nicht alles egal *or* gleichgültig

♦ **to care about sth** Wert auf etw *(acc)* legen; **we care about our image** wir legen Wert auf unser Image; **a company that cares about its staff** eine Firma, die sich um ihr Personal kümmert *or* für ihr Personal sorgt; **money is all he cares about** er interessiert sich nur fürs Geld, ihm liegt nur etwas am Geld; **that's all he cares about** alles andere ist ihm egal; **he cares deeply about her/this** sie/das liegt ihm sehr am Herzen; **he doesn't care about her** sie ist ihm gleichgültig; **I know you don't care about me/such things** ich weiß, dass ich dir gleichgültig bin/dass dir so etwas gleichgültig *or* egal ist

3 – TRANSITIVE VERB

a [= mind] **I don't care what people say** es ist mir egal *or* es kümmert mich nicht, was die Leute sagen; **don't you care that half the world is starving?** berührt es Sie überhaupt nicht, dass die halbe Welt hungert?; **what do I care?** was geht mich das an?; **I couldn't care less what people say, I could care less** *(US)* es ist mir doch völlig egal *or* gleich(gültig), was die Leute sagen; **you don't care what happens to me – but I do care** dir ist es ja egal, was mir passiert – nein, das ist mir überhaupt nicht egal; **I didn't think you cared what I do** ich habe gedacht, das ist dir egal, was ich mache

b [= like] **to care to do sth** etw gerne tun mögen *or* wollen; **would you care to take off your coat?** würden Sie gerne Ihren Mantel ablegen?, wollen *or* möchten Sie nicht (Ihren Mantel) ablegen?; **I wouldn't care to meet him/try** ich würde keinen gesteigerten Wert darauf legen, ihn kennenzulernen/das zu probieren; **but I don't care to** ich will aber nicht

4 – PHRASAL VERB

▶ **care for** VI *+prep obj* **a** *(= look after)* sich kümmern um; *hands, furniture etc* pflegen; **well cared-for** *(person)* gut versorgt; *hands, garden, hair, house* gepflegt; **the children are being cared for by their grandmother** die Großmutter kümmert sich um die Kinder

b *(= like)* **I don't care for that suggestion/picture/him** dieser Vorschlag/das Bild/er sagt mir nicht zu; **I don't care for your tone of voice** wie reden Sie denn mit mir?; **would you care for a cup of tea?** hätten Sie gerne eine Tasse Tee?; **care for a drink?** wie wärs mit einem Drink?, etwas zu trinken?; **care for another?** noch einen?; **I've never much cared for his films** ich habe mir noch nie viel aus seinen Filmen gemacht; **I didn't care for the hotel we stayed in** ich fand das Hotel, in dem wir waren, nicht nach meinem Geschmack; **but you know I do care for you** aber du weißt doch, dass du mir viel bedeutest *or* dass du mir nicht egal *or* gleichgültig bist

---

career [kəˈrɪə] N Karriere *f*; *(= profession, job)* Beruf *m*; *(= working life)* Laufbahn *f*; **journalism is his new ~** er hat jetzt die Laufbahn des Journalisten eingeschlagen; **to make a ~ for oneself** Karriere machen ATTR Karriere-; *soldier, diplomat* Berufs-; **a good/bad ~ move** ein karriereförderner/karriereschädlicher Schritt VI rasen; **to ~ along** rasen; **the car ~ed out of control** das Auto geriet außer Kontrolle

career break N Unterbrechung *f* der Berufstätigkeit

career girl, career woman N Karrierefrau *f*

careerist [kəˈrɪərɪst] N Karrierist(in) *m(f)*, Karrieremacher(in) *m(f)*

career-minded ADJ karrierebewusst

careers guidance N Berufsberatung *f*

Careers Officer, Careers Adviser N Berufsberater(in) *m(f)*

carefree [ˈkɛəfriː] ADJ sorglos, unbekümmert; *song* heiter

careful [ˈkɛəfʊl] ✪ 2.3 ADJ sorgfältig; *(= cautious, circumspect)* sorgsam, vorsichtig; *(with money etc)* sparsam; **I gave the matter some ~ thought** ich habe die Sache gründlich überlegt; **~!** Vorsicht!, passen Sie auf!; **to be ~** aufpassen *(of* auf *+acc)*; **be ~ with the glasses** sei mit den Gläsern vorsichtig; **be ~ what you do** sieh dich vor, nimm dich in Acht; **she's very ~ about what she eats** sie achtet genau darauf, was sie isst; **to be ~ about doing sth** es sich gut überlegen, ob man etw tun soll; **be ~ (that) they don't hear you** gib acht *or* sei vorsichtig, damit *or* dass sie dich nicht hören; **be ~ not to drop it** pass auf, dass du das nicht fallen lässt; **he is very ~ with his money** er hält sein Geld gut zusammen; **you can't be too ~ these days** man kann heutzutage nicht zu vorsichtig sein

carefully [ˈkɛəfəlɪ] ADV sorgfältig; *(= cautiously)* sorgsam, vorsichtig; *consider* gründlich; *listen* gut; *read* sorgfältig, gründlich; *drive* vorsichtig; *explain* genau

carefulness [ˈkɛəfʊlnɪs] N Sorgfalt *f*; *(= caution)* Sorgsamkeit *f*, Vorsicht *f*; *(with money etc)* Sparsamkeit *f*

caregiver [ˈkɛəˌɡɪvəʳ] N *(esp US)* → **carer**

care label N Pflegeetikett *nt*

careless [ˈkɛəlɪs] ADJ **a** *(= negligent, heedless) person, worker, work* nachlässig; *driver* unvorsichtig; *driving* leichtsinnig; *remark* gedankenlos; **~ mistake** Flüchtigkeitsfehler *m*; **how ~ of me!** wie dumm von mir; *(= clumsy)* wie ungeschickt von mir; **to be ~ of one's health** nicht auf seine Gesundheit achten; **to be ~ of sb's feelings** nicht an jds Gefühle *(acc)* denken; **to be ~ in one's remarks** gedankenlos daherreden; **to be ~ in one's behaviour** leichtsinnig handeln **b** *(= carefree)* sorglos, unbekümmert **c** *dress, elegance* lässig

carelessly [ˈkɛəlɪslɪ] ADV **a** *(= negligently, heedlessly) leave, discard, place, handle, allow* leichtsinnigerweise, unvorsichtigerweise **b** *(= casually) say* gedankenlos; *throw, toss* achtlos

carelessness [ˈkɛəlɪsnɪs] N **a** *(= negligence, heedlessness, of person, worker, work)* Nachlässigkeit *f*; *(of driver)* Unvorsicht(igkeit) *f*; *(of driving)* Leichtsinn *m*; *(of remark)* Gedankenlosigkeit *f* **b** *(= carefreeness)* Sorglosigkeit *f*, Unbekümmertheit *f*

care order N *(Brit: Jur, Sociol)* Fürsorgeanordnung *f*

carer [ˈkɛərəʳ] N im Sozialbereich Tätige(r) *mf*; **the elderly and their ~s** Senioren und ihre Fürsorgenden

caress [kəˈres] N Liebkosung *f*, Zärtlichkeit *f usu pl*, Streicheln *nt no pl* VT streicheln, liebkosen

caressing [kəˈresɪŋ] ADJ zärtlich, sanft, streichelnd

caret [ˈkærət] N *(Typ)* Einschaltungszeichen *nt*; *(on ruler)* Caret-Zeichen *nt*

care: **caretaker** N Hausmeister(in) *m(f)*; **caretaker government** N geschäftsführende Regierung; **careware** N *(Comput)* Careware *f*, *Software, für deren Nutzung eine Spende etc gefordert wird*; **care worker** N *Heimbetreuer(in) für Kinder, Geisteskranke oder alte Menschen*; **health ~** im Gesundheitswesen Tätige(r) *mf*; **child ~** in der Jugendhilfe Tätige(r) *mf*; **careworn** ADJ von Sorgen gezeichnet

car: **car exhaust fumes** PL Autoabgase *pl*; **carfare** N *(US)* Fahrpreis *m*; **car ferry** N Autofähre *f*

cargo [ˈkɑːɡəʊ] N (Schiffs)fracht *or* -ladung *f*, Kargo *m (spec)*; **~ boat** Frachter *m*, Frachtdampfer *m*, Frachtschiff *nt*

car hire N Autovermietung *f*; **~ booking** Mietwagenbuchung *f*; **~ company** *or* **firm** Mietwagenfirma *f*, Autoverleih *m*

carhop [ˈkɑːhɒp] N *(dated US)* Bedienung *f* in einem Drive-in-Restaurant

Caribbean [ˌkærɪˈbiːən, *(US)* kæˈrɪbiːən] ADJ karibisch; **~ Sea** Karibisches Meer; **a ~ island** eine Insel in der Karibik N Karibik *f*

caribou [ˈkærɪbuː] N Karibu *m*

caricature [ˈkærɪkətjʊəʳ] N Karikatur *f* VT karikieren

caricaturist [ˌkærɪkəˈtjʊərɪst] N Karikaturist(in) *m(f)*

caries [ˈkɛərɪiːz] N Karies *f*

carillon [kəˈrɪljən] N Glockenspiel *nt*

caring [ˈkɛərɪŋ] ADJ *person, attitude* warmherzig, mitfühlend, einfühlsam; *parent, husband* liebevoll; *teacher* engagiert; *government, society* sozial, mitmenschlich; **a child needs a ~ environment** ein Kind braucht Zuwendung *or* braucht eine Umgebung, die sich um es kümmert; **~ profession** Sozialberuf *m*

car insurance N Kfz-Versicherung *f*, Kraftfahrzeugversicherung *f*

carious [ˈkɛərɪəs] ADJ *(Med) teeth* kariös, von Karies befallen *pred*

car: **carjacker** [ˈkɑːˌdʒækəʳ] N Autoräuber(in) *m(f)*, Carjacker(in) *m(f)*; **carjacking** [ˈkɑːˌdʒækɪŋ] N Autoraub *m*, Carjacking *nt*; **car keys** PL Autoschlüssel *pl*; **carload** N **a** *(Aut)* Wagenladung *f* **b** *(US Rail)* Waggonladung *f*

Carmelite [ˈkɑːməlaɪt] N Karmelit(in) *m(f)*, Karmeliter(in) *m(f)*

carmine [ˈkɑːmaɪn] ADJ karm(es)inrot N Karmesin *nt*, Karmin *nt*

carnage [ˈkɑːnɪdʒ] N Blutbad *nt*, Gemetzel *nt*; **a scene of ~** ein blutiges Schauspiel; **fields covered with the ~ of war** mit Toten *or* Leichen übersäte Schlachtfelder *pl*

carnal [ˈkɑːnl] ADJ fleischlich, körperlich; **~ desires** sinnliche Begierden *pl*; **~ lusts** Fleischeslust *f (liter)*; **to have ~ knowledge of sb** mit jdm (Geschlechts)verkehr haben

carnation [kɑːˈneɪʃən] N Nelke *f*

carnival [ˈkɑːnɪvəl] N Volksfest *nt*; *(= village carnival etc)* Schützenfest *nt*; *(based on religion)* Karneval *m* ATTR Fest-, Karnevals-; **~ procession** Fest-/Karnevalszug *m*

carnivore [ˈkɑːnɪvɔːʳ] N *pl* **carnivora** [kɑːˈnɪvərə] *(= animal)* Fleischfresser *m*; *(= plant)* fleischfressende Pflanze

carnivorous [kɑːˈnɪvərəs] ADJ fleischfressend, karnivor

carob [ˈkærəb] N Johannisbrotbaum *m*; *(= fruit)* Johannisbrot *nt*

carol [ˈkærəl] N Lied *nt* VI *(old, liter)* (fröhlich) singen, jubilieren *(old, liter)*; *(bird)* tirilieren *(old, liter)*

carol: **carol singers** PL ≈ Sternsinger *pl*; **carol singing** N Weihnachtssingen *nt*

carom [ˈkærəm] *(US)* N Karambolage *f* VI *(Billiards)* karambolieren; *(= rebound)* abprallen

carotene [ˈkærətiːn] N Karotin *nt*

carotid (artery) [kəˈrɒtɪd(ˈɑːtərɪ)] N Halsschlagader *f*, Karotide *f (spec)*

carousal [kəˈraʊzəl] N *(old)* (Zech)gelage *nt*, Schmaus *m*

carouse [kəˈraʊz] VI *(old)* zechen, Gelage feiern

carousel [ˌkæruːˈsel] N **a** Karussell *nt* **b** *(for slides)* Rundmagazin *nt*

car owner N Autohalter(in) *m(f)*

carp[1] [kɑːp] N *(= fish)* Karpfen *m*

carp[2] VI etwas auszusetzen haben, nörgeln; **to ~ at sb** an jdm etwas auszusetzen haben, an jdm herummeckern *(inf)*; **to ~ at sth** an etw etwas auszusetzen haben, über etw *(acc)* meckern *(inf)*

carpal bone ['kɑːpl'bəʊn] N Handwurzelknochen *m*

carpal tunnel syndrome [ˌkɑːpl-'tʌnlsɪndrəʊm] N *(Med)* Karpaltunnelsyndrom *nt*

car: car park N *(Brit, open-air)* Parkplatz *m*; *(covered)* Parkhaus *nt*; **car parking** N **~ facilities are available** Parkplatz *or* Parkmöglichkeit(en) vorhanden; **car park ticket** N Parkschein *m*

Carpathians [kɑː'peɪθɪənz] PL *(Geog)* Karpaten *pl*

carpel ['kɑːpl] N Fruchtblatt *nt*

carpenter ['kɑːpɪntəʳ] N Zimmermann *m*, Zimmerfrau *f*; *(for furniture)* Tischler(in) *m(f)*

carpentry ['kɑːpɪntrɪ] N Zimmerhandwerk *nt*, (Bau)tischlerei *f*; *(as hobby)* Tischlern *nt*

carpet ['kɑːpɪt] **N** *(lit, fig)* Teppich *m*; *(fitted)* Teppichboden *m*; **the subject on the ~** das Thema, das zurzeit diskutiert wird; **to be on the ~** *(inf)* zur Schnecke *or* Minna gemacht werden *(inf)* **VT** **a** *floor* (mit Teppichen/Teppichboden) auslegen; **the wood ~ed with flowers** der blumenbedeckte Waldboden **b** *(Brit inf: = reprimand)* zur Minna machen *(inf)*

carpet: carpetbag N Reisetasche *f*; **carpetbagger** N **a** *(US Pol inf)* politischer Abenteurer, politische Abenteuerin; *(Hist) politischer Ämterjäger, der mit nichts als einer Reisetasche nach dem Sezessionskrieg in die besetzten Südstaaten kam* **b** *(Fin)* Spekulant(in) *m(f) (der/die Geld bei vielen verschiedenen Hypothekenbanken investiert in der Hoffnung, bei Änderung der Statuten einen Gewinn zu machen)*; **carpet-beater** N Teppich- *or* Ausklopfer *m*; **carpet bombing** N *(Mil)* Flächenbombardierung *f*

carpeting ['kɑːpɪtɪŋ] N Teppiche *pl*

carpet: carpet slippers PL Pantoffeln *pl*, Hausschuhe *pl*; **carpet-sweeper** N Teppichkehrer *m*, Teppichkehrmaschine *f*; **carpet tile** N Teppichfliese *f*

car phone N Autotelefon *nt*

carping ['kɑːpɪŋ] **ADJ** **a ~ old woman** eine alte Meckerziege *(inf)*; **she grew weary of his ~ criticism** sie wurde sein ständiges Nörgeln leid **N** Nörgelei(en) *f(pl)*, Gemecker *nt (inf)*

carpool ['kɑːpuːl] **N** **a** *(= people)* Fahrgemeinschaft *f* **b** *(= vehicles)* Fuhrpark *m* **VI** eine Fahrgemeinschaft bilden *(with* mit)

carport ['kɑːpɔːt] N Einstellplatz *m*

car radio N Autoradio *nt*

carrel ['kærəl] N *(in library etc)* Arbeitsnische *f*, Arbeitsplatz *m*

car rental N *(US)* Autovermietung *f*; **~ company** *or* **firm** Mietwagenfirma *f*, Autoverleih *m*

carriage ['kærɪdʒ] N **a** *(= horse-drawn vehicle)* Kutsche *f*; *(US: = baby carriage)* Kinderwagen *m*; **~ and pair** Zweispänner *m* **b** *(Brit Rail)* Wagen *m* **c** *(Comm: = conveyance)* Beförderung *f*; *(= cost of carriage also)* Beförderungskosten *pl*; **~ forward** Fracht zahlt Empfänger; **~ free** frachtfrei; **~ paid** frei Haus **d** *(Typ)* Wagen *m*; *(Comput)* Return *nt* **e** *(Mil, = gun-carriage)* Lafette *f* **f** *(of person: = bearing)* Haltung *f*

carriage: carriage clock N ≈ Stiluhr *f*; **carriage return** N Wagenrücklauf *m*; **carriageway** N *(Brit)* Fahrbahn *f*

carrier ['kærɪəʳ] N **a** *(= goods haulier)* Spediteur *m*, Transportunternehmer *m*; *(= passenger airline)* Fluggesellschaft *f* **b** *(of disease)* Überträger *m* **c** *(= aircraft carrier)* Flugzeugträger *m*; *(= troop carrier)* Transportflugzeug *nt*/-schiff *nt* **d** *(= luggage rack)* Gepäckträger *m* **e** *(Brit: also* **carrier bag**) Tragetasche *f*, Tragetüte *f* **f** *(also* **carrier pigeon**) Brieftaube *f*; **by ~ (pigeon)** mit der Taubenpost **g** *(Chem)* Träger (-substanz *f*) *m*; *(= catalyst)* Katalysator *m*

carrion ['kærɪən] N Aas *nt*

carrion crow N Rabenkrähe *f*

carrot ['kærət] N Mohrrübe *f*, Karotte *f*, Möhre *f*; *(fig)* Köder *m*; **to dangle a ~ before sb** *or* **in front of sb** jdm einen Köder unter die Nase halten; **the stick and the ~** Zuckerbrot und Peitsche

carrot: carrot-and-stick ADJ **~ policy** Politik *f* von Zuckerbrot und Peitsche; **carrot cake** N Karottenkuchen *m*; **carrot top** N *(hum inf)* Rotkopf *m*, Kupferdach *nt (hum inf)*

carroty ['kærətɪ] ADJ *hair* kupferrot

carrousel [ˌkæruː'sel] N = **carousel**

carry ['kærɪ] **VT** **a** *load, person, object* tragen; *message* (über)bringen

b *(vehicle: = convey)* befördern; *goods also* transportieren; **this coach carries 30 people** dieser Bus kann 30 Personen befördern; **a boat ~ing missiles to Cuba** ein Schiff mit Raketen für Kuba; **the boat was carried along by the wind** der Wind trieb das Boot dahin; **the current carried them along** die Strömung trieb sie mit sich; **the wind carried the sound to him** der Wind trug die Laute zu ihm hin *or* an sein Ohr

c *(= have on person) documents, money* bei sich haben *or* führen *(form)*; *gun, sword* tragen; **to ~ sth about** *or* **around with one** etw mit sich herumtragen; **to ~ money on one** Geld bei sich haben; **to ~ the facts in one's head** die Fakten im Kopf haben; *(= remember)* die Fakten (im Kopf) behalten; **the ship was ~ing too much sail** das Schiff hatte zu viele Segel gesetzt

d *(fig)* **his denial did not ~ conviction** sein Leugnen klang nicht überzeugend; **he carried his audience (along) with him** er riss das Publikum mit, er begeisterte das Publikum; **to ~ interest** *(Fin)* Zinsen tragen *or* abwerfen; **the loan carries 5% interest** das Darlehen wird mit 5% verzinst; **this job carries extra pay/a lot of responsibility** dieser Posten bringt eine höhere Bezahlung/viel Verantwortung mit sich; **the offence carries a penalty of £50** auf dies Vergehen *or* darauf steht eine Geldstrafe von £ 50

e *(bridge etc: = support)* tragen, stützen

f *(Comm) goods, stock* führen, (auf Lager) haben

g *(Tech, pipe) water, oil, electricity* führen; *(wire) sound* (weiter)leiten, übertragen

h *(= extend)* führen, (ver)legen; **they carried the pipes under the street** sie verlegten die Rohre unter der Straße; **to ~ sth too far** *(fig)* etw zu weit treiben; **they carried the war into the enemy's territory** sie trugen den Krieg in feindliches Gebiet; **this theme is carried through the whole book** dies Thema zieht sich durch das ganze Buch

i *(= win)* einnehmen, erobern; **to ~ the day** siegreich sein, den Sieg davontragen; **to ~ all before one** freie Bahn haben; *(hum, woman)* viel Holz vor der Tür haben *(inf)*; **the motion was carried unanimously** der Antrag wurde einstimmig angenommen; **he carried his point** er ist mit diesem Punkt durchgekommen; **he carried all seven states** er hat die Wahl in allen sieben Staaten gewonnen

j **he carries himself well/like a soldier** er hat eine gute/soldatische Haltung; **he carries himself with dignity** er tritt würdig auf; **she carries her head very erect** sie trägt den Kopf sehr aufrecht

k *(Press) story, photo* bringen

l *(Med)* **people ~ing the AIDS virus** Menschen, die das Aidsvirus in sich *(dat)* tragen

m *(= be pregnant with)* erwarten, schwanger gehen mit *(geh)*; **to be ~ing a child** schwanger sein, ein Kind erwarten

n *(Math)* **... and ~ 2** ... übertrage *or* behalte 2, ... und 2 im Sinn *(inf)*

VI **a** *(voice, sound)* tragen; **the sound of the alphorn carried for miles** der Klang des Alphorns war meilenweit zu hören

b *(ball, arrow)* fliegen

▶ **carry away** VT *sep* **a** *(lit)* (hin)wegtragen; *(torrent, flood)* (hin)wegspülen; *(whirlwind, tornado)* hinwegfegen

b *(fig)* **to get carried away** sich nicht mehr bremsen können *(inf)*; **don't get carried away!** übertreibs nicht!, brems dich *(inf)*; **to get carried away by sth** bei etw in Fahrt kommen; **to be carried away by one's feelings** sich (in seine Gefühle) hineinsteigern; **don't get carried away by your success** dass dir dein Erfolg nicht in den Kopf steigt!; **she got carried away by all the excitement** sie wurde von all der Aufregung mitgerissen; **she got carried away with excitement** sie war vor Aufregung ganz aus dem Häuschen *(inf)*

▶ **carry back** VT *sep (fig) person* zurückversetzen (to in +*acc*)

▶ **carry forward** VT *sep (Fin)* vortragen

▶ **carry off** VT *sep* **a** *(= seize, carry away)* wegtragen **b** *(= win) prizes, medals* gewinnen, mit nach Hause nehmen *(inf)* **c** **to carry it off** es hinkriegen *(inf)* **d** *(= kill)* (hin)wegraffen *(geh)*

▶ **carry on** **VI** **a** *(= continue)* weitermachen; *(life)* weitergehen **b** *(inf: = talk)* reden und reden; *(= make a scene)* ein Theater machen *(inf)*; **to carry on about sth** sich über etw *(acc)* auslassen; **they just kept carrying on about it until somebody did something** sie haben so lange weitergebohrt, bis jemand etwas gemacht hat **c** *(= have an affair)* etwas haben *(inf)* *(with sb* mit jdm) **VT** *sep* **a** *(= continue) tradition, family business* fortführen **b** *(= conduct) conversation, correspondence, business* führen; *profession, trade* ausüben

▶ **carry out** VT *sep* **a** *(lit)* heraustragen **b** *(fig) order, rules, job* ausführen; *promises, obligations* erfüllen; *plan, reform, search, experiment* durchführen; *threats* wahr machen

▶ **carry over** VT *sep* **a** *(Fin)* vortragen **b** *(to next meeting etc)* vertagen

▶ **carry through** VT *sep* **a** *(= carry out)* zu Ende führen **b** *(= sustain)* überstehen lassen

▶ **carry up** VT *sep* hinauftragen, hochtragen

carry: carryall N *(US)* (Einkaufs-/Reise)tasche *f*; **carrycot** N *(Brit)* Babytragetasche *f*

carrying: carrying agent ['kærɪɪŋˌeɪdʒənt] N Spediteur(in) *m(f)*; **carrying capacity** ['kærɪɪŋkəˌpæsɪtɪ] N **a** *(of load)* Tragfähigkeit *f*; *(of vehicle)* Ladefähigkeit *f* **b** *(Elec)* Belastbarkeit *f*; **carrying charge** N *(US) (Fin)* Nebenkosten *pl*; *(Mot)* Speditionskosten *pl*, Transportkosten *pl*; **carryings-on** ['kærɪɪŋz'ɒn] PL *(inf)* übles Treiben *(inf)*; **all these ~ next door** was die da nebenan alles so treiben *(inf)*, was sich da nebenan alles so abspielt

carry: carry-on N *(inf)* Theater *nt (inf)*; **carry-out** *(US, Scot)* **N** **a** *(= restaurant)* Imbissstube *f*/Restaurant *nt* für Außer-Haus-Verkauf; *(= bar)* Schalter *m* für Außer-Haus-Verkauf, Gassenschenke *f (S Ger)* **b** *(= meal, drink)* Speisen *pl*/Getränke *pl* zum Mitnehmen; **let's get a ~** kaufen wir uns etwas zum Mitnehmen; **~s aren't allowed in the grounds** auf das Gelände dürfen keine Getränke mitgebracht werden **ADJ** *attr* Außer-Haus-; **the ~ menu is quite different** für Gerichte zum Mitnehmen gibt es eine ganz andere Speisekarte; **carry-over** N Überbleibsel *nt*; *(Fin)* Saldovortrag *m*, Übertrag *m*; *(Math)* Rest *m*

car: carsick ['kɑːsɪk] ADJ **I used to get ~** früher wurde mir beim Autofahren immer übel *or* schlecht; **carsickness** N Übelkeit *f* beim Autofahren

cart [kɑːt] **N** **a** Wagen *m*, Karren *m*; **to put the ~ before the horse** *(prov)* das Pferd beim Schwanz aufzäumen *(prov)* **b** *(= shopping cart US, shopping trolley Brit)* Einkaufswagen *m* **VT** *(fig inf)* mit sich schleppen

▶ **cart away** *or* **off** VT *sep* abtransportieren, wegbringen

cartage ['kɑːtɪdʒ] N *(= act, cost)* Transport *m*

carte blanche ['kɑːt'blɑːnʃ] N *no pl* Blankovollmacht *f*; **to give sb ~** jdm Carte blanche *f (geh) or* eine Blankovollmacht geben

cartel [kɑː'tel] N Kartell *nt*

carter [ˈkɑːtəʳ] N Fuhrmann *m*

Cartesian [kɑːˈtiːzɪən] ADJ kartesianisch, kartesisch N Kartesianer(in) *m(f)*

Carthage [ˈkɑːθɪdʒ] N Karthago *nt*

Carthaginian [ˌkɑːθəˈdʒɪnɪən] ADJ karthagisch N Karthager(in) *m(f)*

carthorse [ˈkɑːthɔːs] N Zugpferd *nt*

cartilage [ˈkɑːtɪlɪdʒ] N Knorpel *m*

cartload [ˈkɑːtləʊd] N Wagenladung *f*

cartographer [kɑːˈtɒgrəfəʳ] N Kartograf(in) *m(f)*

cartographic(al) [ˌkɑːtəʊˈgræfɪk(əl)] ADJ kartografisch

cartography [kɑːˈtɒgrəfɪ] N Kartografie *f*

cartomancy [ˈkɑːtəˌmænsɪ] N Kartenlegen *nt*, Kartomantie *f (spec)*

carton [ˈkɑːtən] N (Papp)karton *m*; *(of cigarettes)* Stange *f*; *(of milk)* Tüte *f*

cartoon [kɑːˈtuːn] N **a** Cartoon *m or nt*; *(= single picture)* Karikatur *f* **b** *(Film, TV)* (Zeichen)trickfilm *m*; **Mickey Mouse ~** Mickymausfilm *m* **c** *(Art: = sketch)* Karton *m*

cartoon character N Comicfigur *f*

cartoonist [ˌkɑːˈtuːnɪst] N **a** Karikaturist(in) *m(f)* **b** *(Film, TV)* Trickzeichner(in) *m(f)*

cartoon strip N Cartoon *m or nt*, Comic *m*, Zeichengeschichte *f*

cartouche [kɑːˈtuːʃ] N Kartusche *f*

cartridge [ˈkɑːtrɪdʒ] N *(for rifle, pen)* Patrone *f*; *(Phot, for tape recorder)* Kassette *f*; *(for record player)* Tonabnehmer *m*

cartridge *in cpds* Patronen-; **cartridge belt** N Patronengurt *or* -gürtel *m*; **cartridge case** N Patronenhülse *f*; **cartridge clip** N Magazin *nt*; **cartridge paper** N Zeichenpapier *nt*

cart: **carttrack** N Feldweg *m*; **cartwheel** N *(lit)* Wagenrad *nt*; *(Sport)* Rad *nt*; **to turn** *or* **do ~s** Rad schlagen

carve [kɑːv] VT **a** *(Art: = cut)* *wood* schnitzen; *stone etc* (be)hauen; **~d out of** *or* **in wood** aus Holz geschnitzt; **~d out of** *or* **in marble** aus Marmor gehauen; **~d in(to) the wood** in das Holz geschnitzt; **~d in(to) the stone** in den Stein gehauen *or* gemeißelt; **to ~ sth on a stone** etw in einen Stein einmeißeln; **to ~ one's initials on a tree** seine Initialen in einen Baum einritzen *or* schnitzen; **a frieze ~d with flowers** ein geschnitzter *or (in stone)* gemeißelter Blumenfries; **the sculptor was still carving the face** der Bildhauer schnitzte *or (in stone)* meißelte noch das Gesicht
b *(Cook)* aufschneiden, zerteilen, tranchieren
c *(fig)* **to ~ a road through the jungle** eine Straße durch den Dschungel schlagen; **to ~ one's way through the crowd** sich *(dat)* seinen Weg durch die Menge bahnen; **to ~ a niche for oneself (as), to ~ oneself a niche (as)** sich *(dat)* seine Sporen verdienen (als)
VI *(Cook)* tranchieren

▶ **carve out** VT *sep* **a** *(in wood)* schnitzen; *(in stone)* meißeln **b** *(fig) piece of land* abtrennen, loslösen **c** **to carve out a career for oneself** sich *(dat)* eine Karriere aufbauen

▶ **carve up** VT *sep* **a** *meat* aufschneiden; *(surgeon)* aufschneiden; *body* zerstückeln **b** *(fig) inheritance* verteilen; *country* aufteilen, zerstückeln; *area of town etc* zerreißen, auseinanderreißen **c** *(inf, with knife) person* (mit dem Messer) böse zurichten *(inf)*; **to carve up sb's face** jdm das Gesicht zerfetzen **d** *(inf, driver)* schneiden

carver [ˈkɑːvəʳ] N *(= knife)* Tranchiermesser *nt*; **a set of ~s** ein Tranchierbesteck *nt*

carvery [ˈkɑːvərɪ] N Buffet *nt*

carve-up [ˈkɑːvʌp] N *(inf, of inheritance)* Verteilung *f*; *(of estate, country)* Zerstückelung *f*

carving [ˈkɑːvɪŋ] N *(Art: = thing carved)* Skulptur *f*; *(in wood also)* (Holz)schnitzerei *f*; *(= relief)* Relief *nt*; *(in wood)* Holzschnitt *m*

carving knife N Tranchiermesser *nt*

carwash [ˈkɑːwɒʃ] N *(= place)* Autowaschanlage *f*, Waschstraße *f*; *(= wash)* Autowäsche *f*

caryatid [ˌkærɪˈætɪd] N Karyatide *f*

cas [kæʒ] ADJ *(US inf: of clothes)* leger, lässig; **I think I'm just gonna go ~** ich glaub, ich zieh einfach was Normales or Lässiges an

casanova [ˌkæsəˈnəʊvə] N *(hum)* Casanova *m (inf)*

cascade [kæˈskeɪd] N Kaskade *f*; *(fig, of lace etc)* (Spitzen)besatz *m*; *(of sparks)* Regen *m*; **a ~ of green sparks** ein grüner Funkenregen VI *(also* **cascade down***)* *(onto* auf *+acc)* (in Kaskaden) herabfallen; *(sparks)* herabsprühen, herabregnen; *(hair)* wallend herabfallen VT *(Comput) windows* überlappend anordnen

cascading menu [kæˈskeɪdɪŋˌmenjuː] N *(Comput)* Untermenü *nt*

case[1] [keɪs] 26.1 N **a** *(= situation)* Fall *m*; **if that's the ~** wenn das der Fall ist, wenn das zutrifft *or* stimmt; **is that the ~ with you?** ist das bei Ihnen der Fall?, trifft das auf Sie zu?; **if it is the ~ that you're right …** sollten Sie wirklich *or* tatsächlich recht haben …, im Fall(e), dass Sie tatsächlich recht haben …; **if it is a ~ of his not having been informed** wenn er nicht benachrichtigt worden ist; **such being the ~** da das der Fall ist, da dem so ist *(geh)*; **as the ~ may be** je nachdem
b *(= instance, police case, Med etc)* Fall *m*; **in most ~s** meist(ens), in den meisten Fällen; **a typical ~ (of)** ein typischer Fall (von); **it's a clear ~ of double standards** das ist ein klarer Fall von Doppelmoral; **in ~** falls; **(just) in ~** für alle Fälle; **in ~ of emergency** im Notfall *m*, bei Gefahr *f*; **in any ~** sowieso; **in this/that ~** in dem Fall; **in no ~** unter keinen Umständen, auf keinen Fall; **in such a ~** in einem solchen Fall; **five ~s of smallpox/pneumonia** fünf Pockenfälle/Fälle von Lungenentzündung *f*
c *(Jur)* Fall *m*; **to win one's ~** seinen Prozess gewinnen; **the ~ for the defence/prosecution** die Verteidigung/Anklage; **what's the ~ for the prosecution?** worauf stützt sich die Anklage?; **could we hear the ~ for the defence?** das Wort hat die Verteidigung; **the Keeler ~** der Fall Keeler; **in the ~ Higgins v Schwarz** in der Sache Higgins gegen Schwarz; **to take a ~ to the High Court** einen Fall vors oberste Gericht bringen; **to make out a good ~ for sth** überzeugende Argumente für etw liefern; **the ~ for/against the abolition of capital punishment** die Argumente für/gegen die Abschaffung der Todesstrafe; **you haven't got a ~** das Belastungsmaterial reicht nicht für ein Verfahren; *(fig)* Sie haben keine Handhabe; **to have a good ~** *(Jur)* gute Chancen haben durchzukommen; **you/they have a good ~** es ist durchaus gerechtfertigt, was Sie/sie sagen; **there's a very good ~ for adopting this method** es spricht sehr viel dafür, diese Methode zu übernehmen; **they do not have a very good ~** sie haben nicht viel Chancen, damit durchzukommen; **to put one's ~** seinen Fall darlegen; **to put the ~ for sth** etw vertreten; **there's a strong ~ for legalizing pot** es spricht viel für die Legalisierung von Hasch; **there's a good ~ for voting Labour** es gibt viele Gründe, Labour zu wählen; **the court decided that there was no ~ against him** das Gericht entschied, dass nichts gegen ihn vorlag; **a ~ of conscience** eine Gewissensfrage *or* -entscheidung
d *(Gram)* Fall *m*, Kasus *m*; **in the genitive ~** im Genitiv
e *(inf: = person)* Witzbold *m*, Type *f (inf)*; **a hopeless/sad ~** ein hoffnungsloser/trauriger Fall; **a hard ~** ein schwieriger Fall
f *(inf)* **to be on sb's ~ (about sth)** jdn (wegen etw) nerven *(inf)*; **to get on sb's ~ (about sth)** an jdm (wegen etw) herummeckern *(inf)*; **get off my ~!** lass mich in Ruhe! *(inf)*

case[2] N **a** *(= suitcase)* Koffer *m*; *(= crate, packing case)* Kiste *f*; *(= display case)* Vitrine *f*, Schau- *or* Glaskasten *m*; **a ~ of champagne** eine Kiste Champagner **b** *(= box)* Schachtel *f*; *(for jewels)* Schatulle *f*, Kästchen *nt*; *(for spectacles)* Etui *nt*, Futteral *nt*; *(= seed case)* Hülse *f*, Hülle *f*; *(for CD, umbrella)* Hülle *f*; *(= pillowcase)* Bezug *m*; *(for musical instrument)* Kasten *m*; *(of watch)* Gehäuse *nt* **c** *(Typ)* **upper/lower ~** groß-/kleingeschrieben VT *(inf)* **to ~ the joint** sich *(dat)* den Laden ansehen *(inf)*

case: **casebook** N *(Med)* (Kranken)fälle *pl*; *(in social work, Jur)* Fallsammlung *f*; **casebound** ADJ *(Typ)* mit Pappeinband; **case conference** N *(Med)* Fallbesprechung *f*; **case ending** N *(Gram)* Endung *f*; **case file** N **~ on X** Akte *f* zum Fall X; **case-harden** VT *metal* verstählen, vereisenen; **case-hardened** ADJ *(fig)* abgebrüht *(inf)*; **case history** N *(Med)* Krankengeschichte *f*; *(Sociol, Psych)* Vorgeschichte *f*; **case law** N *(Jur)* Fallrecht *nt*; **caseload** N **to have a heavy/light ~** viele/wenig Fälle haben

casement [ˈkeɪsmənt] N *(= window)* Flügelfenster *nt*; *(= frame)* Fensterflügel *m*

case: **case-sensitive** ADJ case-sensitive, die Groß-/Kleinschreibung beachtend; **case squad** N Sonderkommission *f*; **case study** N Fallstudie *f*; **casework** N *(Sociol)* ≈ Sozialarbeit *f*; **caseworker** N *(Sociol)* ≈ Sozialarbeiter(in) *m(f)*

cash [kæʃ] N **a** Bargeld *nt*; *(= change also)* Kleingeld *nt*; **~ in hand** Barbestand *m*, Kassenbestand *m*; **to pay (in) ~** bar bezahlen; **ready ~** verfügbares Geld; **how much do you have in ready ~?** wie viel Geld haben Sie verfügbar?
b *(= immediate payment)* Barzahlung *f*; *(= not credit)* Sofortzahlung *f*; **~ down** Barzahlung *f*, Sofortzahlung *f*; **£250 ~ down and the rest over …** £ 250 sofort (zu bezahlen), und der Rest über …; **to pay ~** (in) bar/sofort bezahlen; **~ or charge?** zahlen Sie bar oder mit Karte?; **~ with order** zahlbar bei Bestellung; **~ on delivery** per Nachnahme
c *(= money)* Geld *nt*; **to be short of ~** knapp bei Kasse sein *(inf)*; **I'm out of ~** ich bin blank *(inf)*, ich habe kein Geld
VT *cheque* einlösen

▶ **cash in** VT *sep* einlösen VI **to cash in on sth** aus etw Kapital schlagen, sich *(dat)* etw zunutze *or* zu Nutze machen; **we want to stop others cashing in (on the act)** *(inf)* wir wollen verhindern, dass andere aus der Sache Kapital schlagen

▶ **cash up** VI *(Brit)* Kasse machen

cash: **cash advance** N Vorschuss *m*; **cash-and-carry** ADJ Cash-and-carry-; **~ price** Mitnahmepreis *m* N *(for retailers)* Cash and Carry *m*, Abholmarkt *m*; *(for public)* Verbrauchermarkt *m*; **cashback** N **a** *(with purchases)* Rückerstattung *f*; *(with mortgage)* Barerstattung *f (bei Abschluss bestimmter Hypotheken)*; **"get £5 ~!"** „Sie bekommen £ 5 zurück!" **b** *(at supermarket)* Barauszahlung *f (zusätzlich zu dem Preis der gekauften Ware, wenn man mit Kundenkarte bezahlt)*; **I'd like £10 ~, please** und ich hätte gern zusätzlich £ 10 in bar; **cash balance** N Kassenbestand *m*, Kassensaldo *nt*, Barguthaben *nt*; **cash-book** N Kassenbuch *nt*; **cash box** N (Geld)kassette *f*; **cash business** N Bar(zahlungs)geschäft *nt*, Kassageschäft *nt*; **cash card** N (Geld)automatenkarte *f*; **cash cow** N *(fig inf)* Milchkuh *f (fig)*, Cashcow *f*; **cash crop** N zum Verkauf bestimmte Ernte; **cash desk** N *(Brit)* Kasse *f*; **cash discount** N Skonto *m or nt*, Rabatt *m* bei Barzahlung; **cash dispenser** N *(Brit)* Geldautomat *m*

cashew [kæˈʃuː] N *(= tree)* Nierenbaum *m*; *(= nut)* Cashewnuss *f*

cash: **cash expenditure** N Barausgaben *pl*, Barauslagen *pl*; **cash flow** [ˈkæʃfləʊ] N Cashflow *m* ATTR **cash-flow analysis** Cashflowanalyse *f*; **cash-flow forecast** Cashflowprognose *f*; **cash-flow position** Bruttoertragslage *f*; **cash-flow problems** Liquiditätsprobleme *pl*; **I've got cash-flow problems** *(personal)* ich bin in Geldschwierigkeiten

cashier[1] [kæˈʃɪəʳ] N Kassierer(in) *m(f)*

cashier[2] VT *(Mil)* (unehrenhaft) entlassen, kassieren *(old)*

cashier's check [kæʃɪəz'tʃek] N *(US)* Bankscheck *m*, Banktratte *f*

cashless ['kæʃləs] ADJ bargeldlos

cash machine N *(esp US)* Geldautomat *m*

cashmere ['kæʃmɪəʳ] N Kaschmir *m*; **~ (wool)** Kaschmirwolle *f*

cash: **cash offer** N Bar(zahlungs)angebot *nt*; **cash office** N Kasse *f*, Kassenbüro *nt*; **cash payment** N Barzahlung *f*; **cash point** N *(Brit: = ATM)* Geldautomat *m*; **cash price** N Bar(-zahlungs)preis *m*; **cash purchase** N Barkauf *m*; **cash receipts** PL *(in shop)* Bareinnahmen *pl*; **cash reduction** N = **cash discount**; **cash register** N Registrierkasse *f*; **cash reserves** PL Bargeldreserven *pl*; **cash sale** N Barverkauf *m*; **cash settlement** N Barausgleich *f*, Barabgeltung *f*; **cash transaction** N Bargeldtransfer *m*

casing ['keɪsɪŋ] N *(Tech)* Gehäuse *nt*; *(of cylinder, tyre)* Mantel *m*; *(of sausage)* Haut *f*, Darm *m*

casino [kə'siːnəʊ] N (Spiel)kasino *nt*, Spielbank *f*

cask [kɑːsk] N Fass *nt*

casket ['kɑːskɪt] N Schatulle *f*; *(for cremated ashes)* Urne *f*; *(US: = coffin)* Sarg *m*, Totenschrein *m (geh)*

Caspian Sea ['kæspɪən'siː] N Kaspisches Meer

Cassandra [kə'sændrə] N *(Myth)* Kassandra *f*; **despite all the ~s** *(fig)* allen Kassandrarufen *or* Unkenrufen zum Trotz

cassava [kə'sɑːvə] N Maniok *m*

casserole ['kæsərəʊl] **N** *(Cook)* Schmortopf *m*, Kasserolle *f*; **a lamb ~**, **a ~ of lamb** eine Lammkasserolle **VT** schmoren

cassette [kæ'set] N Kassette *f*

cassette: **cassette deck** N Kassettendeck *nt*; **cassette player**, **cassette recorder** N Kassettenrekorder *m*; **cassette tape** N Kassette *f*

cassock ['kæsək] N Talar *m*, Soutane *f*

cast [kɑːst] *vb: pret, ptp* **cast** **N** **a** *(of dice, net, line)* Wurf *m*
b *(= mould)* (Guss)form *f*; *(= object moulded)* Abdruck *m*; *(in metal)* (Ab)guss *m*
c *(= plaster cast)* Gipsverband *m*
d *(Theat)* Besetzung *f*; **~ (in order of appearance)** Darsteller *pl* (in der Reihenfolge ihres Auftritts *or* Auftretens); **the ~ includes several famous actors** das Stück ist mit mehreren berühmten Schauspielern besetzt; **who's in the ~?** wer spielt mit?
e **the ~ of sb's features** jds Gesichtsschnitt *m*; **~ of mind** *or* **thought** Gesinnung *f*
f *(Med: = squint)* schielender Blick; **to have a ~ in one eye** auf einem Auge schielen
g *(of worm)* aufgeworfene Erde; *(of bird)* Gewölle *nt*
h *(= tinge)* Schimmer *m*
VT **a** *(lit liter, fig: = throw)* werfen; *anchor, net, fishing lines* auswerfen; *horoscope* erstellen; **to ~ one's vote** seine Stimme abgeben; **a picture of the bishop ~ing his vote** ein Bild des Bischofs bei der Stimmabgabe; **to ~ lots** (aus)losen; **to ~ in one's lot with sb** sich auf jds *(acc)* Seite stellen; **to ~ one's eyes over sth** einen Blick auf etw *(acc)* werfen; **to ~ a critical/sceptical eye on sth** etw kritisch/skeptisch begutachten; **to ~ a greedy eye** *or* **greedy eyes on sth** gierige Blicke auf etw *(acc)* werfen; **to ~ the blame on sb** jdm die Schuld geben, die Schuld auf jdn abwälzen; **to ~ a shadow** *(lit, fig)* einen Schatten werfen (*on* auf *+acc*)
b *(= shed)* **to ~ its skin** sich häuten; **to ~ a shoe** ein Hufeisen *nt* verlieren; **to ~ its feathers** *(form)* sich mausern; **to ~ its leaves** *(form)* die Blätter abwerfen; **to ~ its young** *(form)* (Junge) werfen
c *(Tech, Art)* gießen → **mould**[1]
d *(Theat) play* besetzen; *parts also* verteilen; **he was well/badly ~** die Rolle passte gut/schlecht zu ihm; **he was ~ for the part of Hamlet** er sollte den Hamlet spielen; **I don't know why they ~ him as the villain** ich weiß nicht, warum sie ihm die Rolle des Schurken gegeben *or* zugeteilt haben; **to ~ oneself as** sich darstellen als
VI **a** *(Fishing)* die Angel auswerfen
b *(Theat)* die Rollen verteilen, die Besetzung vornehmen

▶ **cast about** *(Brit) or* **around for** VI *+prep obj* zu finden versuchen; *for new job etc also* sich umsehen nach; **he was casting about** *or* **around (in his mind) for something to say/for an excuse** er suchte nach Worten/nach einer Ausrede

▶ **cast aside** VT *sep cares, prejudices, inhibitions, habits* ablegen; *old clothes etc* ausrangieren; *person* fallen lassen

▶ **cast away** VT *sep* wegwerfen; **to be cast away** *(Naut)* gestrandet sein; **he was cast away on a desert island** er wurde auf eine einsame Insel verschlagen

▶ **cast back** **VI** *(fig)* **to cast back (in one's mind)** im Geiste zurückdenken (*to* an *+acc*) **VT** *sep* **to cast one's thoughts** *or* **mind back** seine Gedanken zurückschweifen lassen (*to* in *+acc*)

▶ **cast down** VT *sep eyes* niederschlagen; *(liter, = throw down) weapons* hinwerfen; **to be cast down** *(fig)* niedergeschlagen sein

▶ **cast off** **VT** *sep* **a** *(= get rid of)* abwerfen; *friends* fallen lassen **b** *stitches* abketten **c** *(Naut)* losmachen **VI** **a** *(Naut)* losmachen **b** *(Knitting)* abketten

▶ **cast on** *(Knitting)* **VT** *sep* anschlagen **VI** anschlagen

▶ **cast out** VT *sep (liter)* vertreiben; *demons* austreiben

▶ **cast up** VT *sep* **a** **to cast one's eyes up (to the heavens)** seine Augen (zum Himmel) emporrichten **b** *(= wash up) flotsam, sailors* anspülen; **they were cast up on a desert island** sie wurden auf einer einsamen Insel an Land gespült **c** *(= refer to) sb's misdemeanours etc* aufbringen; **to cast sth up at sb** jdm etw vorhalten

castanets [ˌkæstə'nets] PL Kastagnetten *pl*

castaway ['kɑːstəweɪ] N *(lit, fig)* Schiffbrüchige(r) *mf*

caste [kɑːst] **N** Kaste *f*; **to lose ~** an Rang verlieren, absteigen; **he lost ~ with his friends** er verlor in den Augen seiner Freunde *or* bei seinen Freunden an Ansehen **ADJ** *attr mark, system* Kasten-; **a high/low ~ family** eine Familie, die einer hohen/niedrigen Kaste angehört

castellan ['kæstələn] N Schlossvogt *m*, Kastellan *m*

castellated ['kæstəleɪtɪd] ADJ mit (Türmen und) Zinnen

caster ['kɑːstəʳ] N = **castor**

caster sugar N *(Brit)* Sandzucker *m*

castigate ['kæstɪgeɪt] VT *person (verbally)* geißeln; *(old: physically)* züchtigen

castigation [ˌkæstɪ'geɪʃən] N *(verbal)* Geißelung *f*; *(old: physical)* Züchtigung *f*

Castile [kæ'stiːl] N Kastilien *nt*

Castilian [kæ'stɪljən] **ADJ** kastilisch **N** **a** *(Ling)* Kastilisch *nt* **b** *(= person)* Kastilier(in) *m(f)*

casting ['kɑːstɪŋ] N **a** *(Fishing)* Auswerfen *nt*; *(Tech, Art: = act, object)* (Ab)guss *m*; *(in plaster)* Abdruck *m*, Abguss *m* **b** *(Theat)* Rollenverteilung *f*, Besetzung *f*

casting: **casting couch** N *(hum)* Besetzungscouch *f (hum inf)*; **she got the part through the ~** sie bekam die Rolle, weil sie mit dem Regisseur geschlafen hat; **casting director** N Besetzungsleiter(in) *m(f)*; **casting vote** N ausschlaggebende Stimme; **he used his ~** seine Stimme gab den Ausschlag

cast iron N Gusseisen *nt*

cast-iron [ˌkɑːst'aɪən] ADJ **a** *(lit)* gusseisern **b** *(fig) will, constitution* eisern; *case, alibi* hieb- und stichfest

castle ['kɑːsl] **N** **a** Schloss *nt*; *(= medieval fortress)* Burg *f*; **to build ~s in the air** Luftschlösser bauen **b** *(Chess)* Turm *m* **VI** *(Chess)* rochieren

castling ['kɑːslɪŋ] N *(Chess)* Rochade *f*

cast: **cast-off** ADJ *clothes* abgelegt *attr*; **cast-offs** PL *(Brit inf)* abgelegte Kleider *pl*; **she's one of his ~** *(fig inf)* sie ist eine seiner ausrangierten Freundinnen *(inf)*

castor ['kɑːstəʳ] N **a** *(Brit, for sugar, salt etc)* Streuer *m* **b** *(= wheel)* Rolle *f*, Rad *nt*

castor oil N Rizinus(öl) *nt*

castrate [kæs'treɪt] VT kastrieren; *(fig) text* verstümmeln

castrati [kæs'trɑːtiː] *pl of* **castrato**

castration [kæs'treɪʃən] N Kastration *f*

castrato [kæs'trɑːtəʊ] N *pl* **castrati** Kastrat *m*

casual ['kæʒjʊl] **ADJ** **a** *(= not planned)* zufällig; *acquaintance, glance* flüchtig; **we were in the area, so we paid them a ~ visit** wir waren gerade in der Gegend und haben sie bei der Gelegenheit besucht
b *(= offhand, careless)* lässig; *attitude* gleichgültig; *remark* beiläufig; *(= lacking emotion)* gleichgültig; **it was just a ~ remark** das war nicht so ernst gemeint, das habe ich/hat er *etc* nur so gesagt; **he was very ~ about it** es war ihm offensichtlich gleichgültig; *(in reaction)* das hat ihn kaltgelassen *or* nicht tangiert *(inf)*; **you shouldn't be so ~ about it** du solltest das nicht so leichtnehmen *or* auf die leichte Schulter nehmen; **he tried to sound ~** er tat so, als ob ihm das nichts ausmachen würde; **he had a rather ~ manner for a policeman** für einen Polizisten war er ziemlich salopp *or* lässig; **the ~ observer** der oberflächliche Betrachter
c *(= informal)* zwanglos; *discussion, chat also* ungezwungen; *clothes* leger; **a ~ shirt** ein Freizeithemd *nt*; **~ wear** Freizeitkleidung *f*; **he was wearing ~ clothes** er war leger gekleidet; **I want something ~** *(when buying clothes)* ich möchte etwas Sportliches *or* Lässiges
d *(= irregular) work, worker, labourer* Gelegenheits-; *(= occasional) drug user, sexual partner* gelegentlich; *affair, relationship* locker; **~ drinker** Gelegenheitstrinker(in) *m(f)*; **~ friendship** oberflächliche Freundschaft; **~ sex** Gelegenheitssex *m*, freie Liebe
N **a** **casuals** **PL** *(= shoes)* Slipper *pl*
b *(= casual worker)* Gelegenheitsarbeiter(in) *m(f)*; **~s** Aushilfen *pl*
c *(also* **football casual***)* Fußballrowdy *m*

casually ['kæʒjʊlɪ] ADV *(= without planning)* zufällig; *(= without emotion)* ungerührt; *(= incidentally, in an offhand manner)* beiläufig; *(= without seriousness)* lässig; *(= informally)* zwanglos; *dressed* leger

casualness ['kæʒjʊlnɪs] N *(= informality)* Zwanglosigkeit *f*; *(= carelessness)* Lässigkeit *f*; *(= lack of emotion)* Ungerührtheit *f*, Schnodderigkeit *f (inf)*; *(= offhand nature: of remark)* Beiläufigkeit *f*; **the ~ of his dress** seine legere Kleidung

casualty ['kæʒjʊltɪ] N **a** *(lit, fig)* Opfer *nt*; *(injured also)* Verletzte(r) *mf*; *(killed also)* Tote(r) *mf*; **were there many casualties?** gab es viele Opfer?; *(Mil)* gab es hohe Verluste? **b** *(also* **casualty unit***)* Notaufnahme *f*; **to go to ~** in die Notaufnahme gehen; **to be in ~** in der Notaufnahme sein

casualty: **casualty department** N *(in hospital)* Notaufnahme *f*, Unfallstation *f*; **casualty list** N Verlustliste *f*; **casualty ward** N Unfallstation *f*

casuist ['kæzjʊɪst] N Kasuist *m*

casuistry ['kæzjʊɪstrɪ] N Kasuistik *f*

CAT **a** *(Aviat) abbr of* **clear air turbulence** Turbulenzen *pl* bei klarer Sicht **b** *(Sch) abbr of* **computer-assisted** *or* **-aided testing** computergestützte Tests *pl*

cat[1] [kæt] N **a** Katze *f*; *(= tiger etc)* (Raub)katze *f*; **the (big) ~s** die großen Katzen; **to let the ~ out of the bag** die Katze aus dem Sack lassen; **they fight like ~ and dog** die sind *or* die vertragen sich wie Hund und Katze; **to play a ~-and--mouse game with sb** mit jdm Katz und Maus spielen; **there isn't room to swing a ~** *(inf)* man kann sich nicht rühren(, so eng ist es); **a ~ may look at a king** *(prov)* es wird doch noch erlaubt sein zu gucken!; **to be like a ~ on hot bricks,**

to be like a ~ on a hot tin roof wie auf glühenden Kohlen sitzen; **to look like the ~ that got the cream** sich freuen wie ein Schneekönig *(inf)*; **that's put the ~ among the pigeons!** da hast du *etc* aber was (Schönes) angerichtet!; **he thinks he's the ~'s whiskers** *(Brit inf)* or **the ~'s meow** *(US inf)* er hält sich für wer weiß was; **he doesn't have a ~ in hell's chance of winning** er hat nicht die geringste Chance zu gewinnen; **when** *or* **while the ~'s away the mice will play** *(Prov)* wenn die Katze aus dem Haus ist, tanzen die Mäuse *(Prov)*; **has the ~ got your tongue?** *(inf)* du hast wohl die Sprache verloren?
b *(inf, = woman)* Katze *f*
c *(= whip)* (neunschwänzige) Katze
d *(dated US sl)* Typ *m (inf)*
e *(inf: = caterpillar tractor)* Raupe *f*

cat² [kæt] N *(Aut inf) abbr of* **catalytic converter** Kat *m*

catabolism [kəˈtæbəlɪzm] N Abbaustoffwechsel *m*, Katabolismus *m (spec)*

cataclysm [ˈkætəklɪzəm] N Verheerung *f*; *(fig)* Umwälzung *f*

cataclysmic [ˌkætəˈklɪzmɪk] ADJ verheerend; *(fig)* umwälzend

catacombs [ˈkætəku:mz] PL Katakomben *pl*

catafalque [ˈkætəfælk] N Katafalk *m*

catalepsy [ˈkætəlepsɪ] N Katalepsie *f*, Starrsucht *f*

cataleptic [ˌkætəˈleptɪk] ADJ kataleptisch

catalogue, *(US)* **catalog** [ˈkætəlɒg] **N** Katalog *m* **VT** katalogisieren

catalysis [kəˈtæləsɪs] N Katalyse *f*

catalyst [ˈkætəlɪst] N *(lit, fig)* Katalysator *m*

catalytic [ˌkætəˈlɪtɪk] ADJ *(lit, fig)* katalytisch

catalytic converter N *(Aut)* Katalysator *m*

catamaran [ˌkætəməˈræn] N Katamaran *m*

cat-and-dog ADJ **to lead a ~ life** wie Hund und Katze leben

cat-and-mouse ADJ **to play ~** *or* **a ~ game with sb** mit jdm Katz und Maus spielen

catapult [ˈkætəpʌlt] **N** *(Brit: = slingshot)* Schleuder *f*; *(Mil, Aviat)* Katapult *nt or m*; **~ launching** *(Aviat)* Katapultstart *m* **VT** schleudern, katapultieren; *(Aviat)* katapultieren **VI** geschleudert *or* katapultiert werden

cataract [ˈkætərækt] N **a** *(= rapids)* Katarakt *m* **b** *(Med)* grauer Star

catarrh [kəˈtɑ:ˈ] N Katarr(h) *m*

catarrhal [kəˈtɑ:rəl] ADJ katarr(h)alisch

catastrophe [kəˈtæstrəfɪ] N Katastrophe *f*; **to end in ~** verhängnisvoll *or* in einer Katastrophe enden; **to be heading for ~** auf eine Katastrophe zusteuern; **to be the final ~ for sb** jdm schließlich zum Verhängnis werden

catastrophic [ˌkætəˈstrɒfɪk] ADJ katastrophal; *event, decision, course also* verhängnisvoll

catastrophically [ˌkætəˈstrɒfɪkəlɪ] ADV *fail* katastrophal; **to go ~ wrong** katastrophal schiefgehen

catatonia [ˌkætəˈtəʊnɪə] N Katatonie *f*

catatonic [ˌkætəˈtɒnɪk] *(Med)* **ADJ** katatonisch **N** Katatoniker(in) *m(f)*

cat: **catbird** N *(US)* amerikanische Spottdrossel; **cat burglar** N Fassadenkletterer *m*; **catcall** *(Theat)* **N** **~s** *pl* Pfiffe und Buhrufe *pl* **VI** pfeifen

cat car N Katalysatorauto *nt*

catch [kætʃ] *vb: pret, ptp* **caught** **N** **a** *(of ball etc)* **to make a (good) ~** (gut) fangen; **good ~!** gut gefangen!; **it was a difficult ~** das war schwer zu fangen; **he missed an easy ~** er hat einen leichten Ball nicht gefangen
b *(Fishing, Hunt)* Fang *m*; *(of trawler etc also)* Fischzug *m*; **he didn't get a ~** er hat nichts gefangen; **he's a good ~** *(fig inf)* er ist ein guter Fang; *(for marriage also)* er ist eine gute Partie
c *(= children's game)* Fangen *nt*
d *(= trick, snag)* Haken *m*; **where's the ~?** wo liegt *or* ist (da) der Haken?; **there's a ~ in it somewhere!** die Sache hat irgendwo einen Haken, da ist irgendwo ein Haken dabei; **~ question** Fangfrage *f*
e *(= device for fastening)* Verschluss(vorrichtung *f*) *m*; *(= hook)* Haken *m*; *(= latch)* Riegel *m*
f *(= break in voice)* Stocken *nt*; **with a ~ in one's voice** mit stockender Stimme
g *(Mus) Kanon für Singstimmen mit heiter-komischem Text*
h *(= fragment)* Bruchstück *nt*
VT **a** *object* fangen; *batsman* durch Abfangen des Balls ausscheiden lassen
b *fish, mice* fangen; *thief, offender* fassen, schnappen *(inf)*, erwischen *(inf)*; *escaped animal* (ein)fangen; *(inf: = manage to see)* erwischen *(inf)*; **to ~ sb's arm, to ~ sb by the arm** jdn am Arm fassen; **she held it up to ~ the light** sie hielt es gegen das Licht; **glass which ~es the light** Glas, in dem sich das Licht spiegelt; **to ~ sight/a glimpse of sb/sth** jdn/etw erblicken *or* zu sehen kriegen *(inf)*; **to ~ sb's attention/eye** jdn auf sich *(acc)* aufmerksam machen; **to be caught between two people/alternatives** zwischen zwei Menschen/Möglichkeiten hin und her gerissen sein; **he was caught between envy and admiration** er war zwischen Neid und Bewunderung hin und her gerissen
c *(= take by surprise)* erwischen, ertappen; **to ~ sb at sth** jdn bei etw erwischen; **to ~ sb by surprise** jdn überraschen; **to be caught unprepared** nicht darauf vorbereitet sein; **to ~ sb at a bad time** jdm ungelegen kommen; **I caught him flirting with my wife** ich habe ihn (dabei) erwischt, wie er mit meiner Frau flirtete; **I caught myself feeling sorry for him** ich habe mich dabei ertappt, dass er mir leidtat; **you won't ~ me signing any contract** *(inf)* ich unterschreibe doch keinen Vertrag; **you won't ~ me in that restaurant** *(inf)* in das Restaurant gehe ich garantiert *or* bestimmt nicht; **(you won't) ~ me doing that again!** *(inf)* das mache ich bestimmt nicht wieder!; **you won't ~ me falling for that trick again** *(inf)* auf den Trick falle ich nicht noch einmal herein; **aha, caught you** hab ich dich doch erwischt *(inf)*; *(with question)* ha ha, reingefallen *(inf)*; **caught in the act** auf frischer Tat ertappt; *(sexually)* in flagranti erwischt; **we were caught in a storm** wir wurden von einem Unwetter überrascht; **to ~ sb on the wrong foot** *or* **off balance** *(fig)* jdn überrumpeln
d *(= take) bus, train etc* nehmen
e *(= be in time for) train, bus* erreichen, kriegen *(inf)*; **can I still ~ the post?** kommt der Brief noch mit?; **if you want to ~ the 4 o'clock post ...** wenn das mit der Vieruhrleerung mitsoll ...; **if I hurry I'll ~ the end of the film** wenn ich mich beeile kriege ich das Ende des Films noch mit *(inf)*
f *(= become entangled)* hängen bleiben mit; **a nail caught her dress** ihr Kleid blieb an einem Nagel hängen; **I caught my finger in the car door** ich habe mir den Finger in der Wagentür eingeklemmt; **he caught his foot in the grating** er ist mit dem Fuß im Gitter hängen geblieben
g *(with stitches)* mit ein paar Stichen befestigen; **to ~ a dress (in) at the waist** ein Kleid an der Taille fassen
h *(= understand, hear)* mitkriegen *(inf)*
i **to ~ an illness** sich *(dat)* eine Krankheit zuziehen *or* holen *(inf)*; **he's always ~ing cold(s)** er erkältet sich leicht; **you'll ~ your death (of cold)!** du holst dir den Tod! *(inf)*
j *(= portray) mood, atmosphere etc* einfangen
k **to ~ one's breath** *(after exercise etc)* Luft holen, verschnaufen; **to ~ sb a glancing blow** jdn seitlich erwischen; **the blow/ball caught him on the arm** der Schlag/Ball traf ihn am Arm; **she caught him one on the nose** *(inf)* sie haute ihm auf die Nase; **you'll ~ it!** *(Brit inf)* es setzt was! *(inf)*, du kannst (aber) was erleben! *(inf)*; **he caught it all right!** *(Brit inf) (physically)* der hat vielleicht eine Abreibung bekommen! *(inf)*; *(verbally)* der hat aber was zu hören bekommen! *(inf)*
VI **a** *(with ball)* fangen
b *(fire)* in Gang kommen, brennen; *(wood etc)* Feuer fangen, brennen; *(Cook)* anbrennen
c *(= get stuck)* klemmen, sich verklemmen; *(= get entangled)* hängen bleiben, sich verfangen; **her dress caught in the door** sie blieb mit ihrem Kleid in der Tür hängen

► **catch at** VI +*prep obj (= grab for)* greifen nach; *opportunity* ergreifen

► **catch on** VI *(inf)* **a** *(= become popular)* ankommen; *(fashion also)* sich durchsetzen; *(book etc also)* einschlagen **b** *(= understand)* kapieren *(inf)*

► **catch out** VT *sep (fig)* überführen; *(with trick question etc)* hereinlegen *(inf)*; *(Sport)* abfangen; **I caught you out there!** du bist durchschaut; *(with trick question)* jetzt bist du aber reingefallen *(inf)*; **to catch sb out in a lie** jdn beim Lügen ertappen

► **catch up** **VI** aufholen; **to catch up on one's sleep** Schlaf nachholen; **to catch up on** *or* **with one's work** Arbeit nachholen; **to catch up with sb** *(running, in work etc)* jdn einholen; **hurry, they're catching up!** beeil dich, sie holen auf!; **you've got a lot of catching up to do** du musst noch eine Menge nachholen
VT *sep* **a** **to catch sb up** *(walking, working etc)* jdn einholen
b *(= snatch up)* (vom Boden) hochheben; *hair* hochstecken; **she caught up her skirts** sie raffte *or* schürzte ihre Röcke
c **to get caught up in sth** *(= entangled)* sich in etw *(dat)* verheddern *or* verfangen; *in traffic* in etw *(acc)* kommen; *in discussion* in etw *(acc)* verwickelt werden

catch: **catch-22** N ausweglose Falle, Sackgasse *f*; **a ~ situation** *(inf)* eine Zwickmühle; **catch-all** N **a** *(US: = drawer etc)* Schublade *f* für Krimskrams *(inf)* **b** *(= phrase, clause etc)* allgemeine Bezeichnung/Klausel/allgemeiner Rahmen *etc*; **catch-as-catch-can** N *(Sport)* Catch-as-catch-can *nt*; **catch crop** N Zwischenfrucht *f*

catcher [ˈkætʃəˈ] N Fänger *m*; **he's a good ~** er ist gut im Fangen, er fängt gut

catching [ˈkætʃɪŋ] ADJ *(Med, fig)* ansteckend

catchment area [ˈkætʃməntˈeərɪə] N Einzugsgebiet *nt*, Einzugsbereich *m*

catchment basin [ˈkætʃməntˈbeɪsn] N Einzugsgebiet *nt*

catch: **catchpenny** ADJ *(dated)* publikumswirksam, zugkräftig; **catch phrase** N Schlagwort *nt*, Slogan *m*; **catch question** N *(inf)* Fangfrage *f*; **catch quota** N Fangquote *f*

catchup [ˈkætʃəp] N *(US)* = **ketchup**

catch: **catchweight** ADJ *(Sport)* ohne Gewichtsklasse; **catchword** N Schlagwort *nt*

catchy [ˈkætʃɪ] ADJ (+er) *tune, slogan* eingängig; *title* einprägsam

catechism [ˈkætɪkɪzəm] N *(= instruction)* Katechese *f*; *(fig)* Verhör *nt*; *(= book)* Katechismus *m*

catechize [ˈkætɪkaɪz] VT katechisieren

categorical [ˌkætɪˈgɒrɪkəl] ADJ *statement, denial* kategorisch; **he was quite ~ about it** er hat das mit Bestimmtheit gesagt; **~ imperative** kategorischer Imperativ

categorically [ˌkætɪˈgɒrɪkəlɪ] ADV *state, deny* kategorisch; *say* mit Bestimmtheit

categorization [ˌkætɪgəraɪˈzeɪʃən] N Kategorisierung *f*

categorize [ˈkætɪgəraɪz] VT kategorisieren

category [ˈkætɪgərɪ] N Kategorie *f*, Klasse *f*; **Category A prisoner** *(Brit)* ≈ Schwerverbrecher(in) *m(f)*

cater [ˈkeɪtəˈ] VI *(= provide food)* die Speisen und Getränke liefern

► **cater for** VI +*prep obj* **a** *(= serve with food)* mit Speisen und Getränken versorgen; *coach party etc* (mit Speisen und Getränken) bedienen; **weddings and functions catered for** wir richten Hochzeiten und andere Veranstaltungen aus; **that café caters mainly for students** das Café ist hauptsächlich auf Studenten eingestellt

b *(= provide for)* ausgerichtet *or* eingestellt sein auf *(+acc)*; *(also* **cater to***) needs, tastes* gerecht werden *(+dat)*, etwas zu bieten haben *(+dat)*; **to cater for all tastes** jedem Geschmack gerecht werden, für jeden (Geschmack) etwas zu bieten haben; **a region which caters more for old people** eine Gegend, die mehr für alte Menschen tut *or* die alten Menschen mehr zu bieten hat; **a resort which caters for children** ein kinderfreundlicher Urlaubsort
c *(= expect, be prepared for)* **I hadn't catered for that** darauf bin/war ich nicht eingestellt

cater-corner(ed) [ˌkeɪtəˈkɔːnəʳ(-əd)] ADJ, ADV *(US)* diagonal

caterer [ˈkeɪtərəʳ] N *(= company)* Lieferfirma *f* für Speisen und Getränke; *(for parties etc)* Partyservice *m*; *(= owner, manager)* Gastronom(in) *m(f)*

catering [ˈkeɪtərɪŋ] N Versorgung *f* mit Speisen und Getränken *(for +gen)*; *(= trade)* Gastronomie *f*; **who's doing the ~?** wer liefert das Essen und die Getränke?; **~ service** Partyservice *m*; **~ trade** (Hotel- und) Gaststättengewerbe *nt*

caterpillar [ˈkætəpɪləʳ] N **a** *(Zool)* Raupe *f* **b** ~® *(Tech)* Raupe(nkette) *f*, Gleiskette *f*; *(= vehicle)* Raupenfahrzeug *nt*

caterpillar track® N Raupenkette *f*, Gleiskette *f*

caterpillar tractor® N Raupenfahrzeug *nt*, Gleiskettenfahrzeug *nt*

caterwaul [ˈkætəwɔːl] VI jaulen

caterwauling [ˈkætəwɔːlɪŋ] N Gejaule *nt*

cat: **cat fight** N *(esp US inf, between women)* Gezänk *nt*, Gezerfe *nt*; **catfish** N Wels *m*, Katzenfisch *m*; **cat flap** N Katzenklappe *f*; **catgut** [ˈkætgʌt] N Katgut *nt*

catharsis [kəˈθɑːsɪs] N **a** *(Med)* Darmreinigung *f*, Darmentleerung *f* **b** *(Liter, Philos)* Katharsis *f*, Läuterung *f*

cathartic [kəˈθɑːtɪk] **ADJ** **a** *(Med)* abführend **b** *(Liter, Philos)* kathartisch **N** *(Med)* Abführmittel *nt*

cathedral [kəˈθiːdrəl] N Dom *m*; *(esp in England, France, Spain)* Kathedrale *f*; **~ town/city** Domstadt *f*

Catherine [ˈkæθərɪn] N Katharina *f*

Catherine wheel N Feuerrad *nt*

catheter [ˈkæθɪtəʳ] N Katheter *m*

catheterize [ˈkæθɪtəraɪz] VT katheterisieren

cathode [ˈkæθəʊd] N Kat(h)ode *f*

cathode: **cathode ray** N Kat(h)odenstrahl *m*; **cathode-ray tube** N Kat(h)odenstrahlröhre *f*

Catholic [ˈkæθəlɪk] **ADJ** *(Eccl)* katholisch; **the ~ Church** die katholische Kirche **N** Katholik(in) *m(f)*

catholic [ˈkæθəlɪk] ADJ *(= varied)* vielseitig; **he's a man of very ~ tastes** er ist (ein) sehr vielseitig interessiert(er Mensch)

Catholicism [kəˈθɒlɪsɪzəm] N Katholizismus *m*

cat: **catkin** N *(Bot)* Kätzchen *nt*; **catlick** N *(inf)* Katzenwäsche *f*; **catlike** ADJ katzenhaft, katzengleich; **cat litter** N Katzenstreu *f*; **catmint** N Katzenminze *f*; **catnap** **N** **to have a ~** ein Nickerchen *nt* machen *(inf)* **VI** dösen; **catnip** N Katzenminze *f*; **cat-o'-nine-tails** N neunschwänzige Katze

CAT scan [ˈkætˌskæn] N Computertomografie *f*

cat's cradle N Abnehmespiel *nt*, Fadenspiel *nt*

cat's-eye [ˈkætsˌaɪ] N *(Miner)* Katzenauge *nt*

Catseye® [ˈkætsˌaɪ] N *(Brit Aut)* Katzenauge *nt*, Rückstrahler *m*

cat's-paw [ˈkætspɔː] N Handlanger *m*

cat's pyjamas PL *(US)* → **cat's whiskers**

catsuit [ˈkætsuːt] N einteiliger Hosenanzug

catsup [ˈkætsəp] N *(US)* = **ketchup**

cat's whiskers PL *(inf)* **to be the ~** spitze sein *(inf)*; **he thinks he's the ~** er hält sich für etwas Besonderes

cattail [ˈkætˌteɪl] N *(US)* Rohrkolben *m*, Kanonenputzer *m (inf)*

cattery [ˈkætərɪ] N *(for boarding)* Katzenpension *f*; *(for breeding)* Katzenzucht *f*

cattiness [ˈkætɪnɪs] N *(fig)* Gehässigkeit *f*, Boshaftigkeit *f*

cattle [ˈkætl] PL Rind(vieh) *nt*; **500 head of ~** 500 Rinder, 500 Stück Vieh; **"cattle crossing"** „Vorsicht Viehtrieb!"; **they were treated like ~** sie wurden wie Vieh behandelt

cattle: **cattle breeding** N Rinderzucht *f*; **cattle car** N *(US Rail)* Viehwaggon *m*; **cattle-grid** N Weidenrost *m*, Viehtor *nt*; **cattleman** N Rinderzüchter *m*; **cattle market** N *(lit)* Viehmarkt *m*; *(fig inf) (= beauty contest etc)* Fleischbeschau *f (inf)*; *(for pick-ups)* Abschleppladen *m (inf)*; **cattle prod** N Knüppel *m* zum Viehtreiben; **cattle range** N Weideland *nt*, Viehtrift *f*; **cattle rustler** N Viehdieb *m*; **cattle shed** N Viehstall *m*; **cattle show** N Rinder(zucht)schau *f*; **cattle truck** N *(Aut)* Viehanhänger *m*; *(Rail)* Viehwagen *m*

catty [ˈkætɪ] ADJ *(+er)* gehässig, boshaft

catty-corner(ed) [ˌkætɪˈkɔːnəʳ(-əd)] ADJ, ADV *(US)* = **cater-corner(ed)**

catwalk [ˈkætwɔːk] N Steg *m*, Brücke *f*; *(for models)* Laufsteg *m*

Caucasian [kɔːˈkeɪzɪən] **ADJ** kaukasisch **N** Kaukasier(in) *m(f)*

Caucasus [ˈkɔːkəsəs] N Kaukasus *m*

caucus [ˈkɔːkəs] N *(= committee)* Gremium *nt*, Ausschuss *m*; *(US: = meeting)* Sitzung *f*

caudal [ˈkɔːdl] ADJ Schwanz-, kaudal *(spec)*; **the ~ vertebrae** die Schwanzwirbel *pl*; **the ~ fin** die Schwanzflosse

caught [kɔːt] *pret, ptp of* **catch**

caul [kɔːl] N Glückshaube *f*

cauldron [ˈkɔːldrən] N großer Kessel; *(= witch's cauldron)* (Hexen)kessel *m*

cauliflower [ˈkɒlɪflaʊəʳ] N Blumenkohl *m*

cauliflower cheese N Blumenkohl *m* mit Käsesoße

cauliflower ear N Boxerohr *nt*

caulk [kɔːk] VT *seams, joints* abdichten; *(on ship)* kalfatern

caulking [ˈkɔːkɪŋ] N Material *nt* zum Abdichten; *(Naut)* Teer *m*

causal [ˈkɔːzəl] ADJ kausal, ursächlich; **~ relationship** Kausalzusammenhang *m*

causality [kɔːˈzælɪtɪ] N Kausalität *f*

causally [ˈkɔːzəlɪ] ADV kausal, ursächlich; **they are ~ connected** dazwischen besteht ein Kausalzusammenhang

causation [kɔːˈzeɪʃən] N Kausalität *f*; *(of particular event)* Ursache *f*; **the law of ~** das Kausalgesetz *or* -prinzip

causative [ˈkɔːzətɪv] **ADJ** *factor* verursachend; *(Gram)* kausativ **N** *(Gram)* Kausativ *nt*

cause [kɔːz] ✪ 17.2, 26.3 **N** **a** Ursache *f* (of für); **~ and effect** Ursache und Wirkung; **what was the ~ of the fire?** wodurch ist das Feuer entstanden?
b *(= reason)* Grund *m*, Anlass *m*; **she has no ~ to be angry** sie hat keinen Grund, sich zu ärgern; **the ~ of his failure** der Grund für sein Versagen; **with/without (good) ~** mit (triftigem)/ohne (triftigen) Grund; **not without ~** nicht ohne Grund; **there's no ~ for alarm** es besteht kein Grund *or* Anlass zur Aufregung; **you have every ~ to be worried** du hast allen Anlass zur Sorge; **you have good ~ for complaint** Sie haben allen Grund zur Klage, Sie beklagen sich zu Recht
c *(= purpose, ideal)* Sache *f*; **to make common ~ with sb** mit jdm gemeinsame Sache machen; **to work for** *or* **in a good ~** sich für eine gute Sache einsetzen; **he died for the ~ of peace** er starb für den Frieden *or* für die Sache des Friedens; **in the ~ of justice** für die (Sache der) Gerechtigkeit, im Namen der Gerechtigkeit; **it's all in a good ~** es ist für eine gute Sache
d *(Jur: = action)* Fall *m*, Sache *f*
VT verursachen; **to ~ sb grief** jdm Kummer machen; **to ~ sb to do sth** *(form)* jdn veranlassen, etw zu tun *(form)*

cause célèbre N Cause célèbre *f*

causeway [ˈkɔːzweɪ] N Damm *m*

caustic [ˈkɔːstɪk] ADJ *(Chem)* ätzend, kaustisch; *(fig)* ätzend; *remark* bissig; **he was very ~ about the project** er äußerte sich sehr bissig über das Projekt

caustically [ˈkɔːstɪklɪ] ADV *say, remark* bissig; **his new book is ~ funny** sein neues Buch ist auf bissige Art lustig

caustic soda N Ätznatron *nt*

cauterization [ˌkɔːtəraɪˈzeɪʃən] N *(Med)* Kaustik *f*, Kauterisation *f*

cauterize [ˈkɔːtəraɪz] VT *(Med)* kauterisieren

caution [ˈkɔːʃən] **N** **a** *(= circumspection)* Vorsicht *f*, Umsicht *f*, Bedacht *m*; **"caution!"** „Vorsicht!"; **to act with ~** umsichtig *or* mit Bedacht vorgehen, Vorsicht walten lassen **b** *(= warning)* Warnung *f*; *(official)* Verwarnung *f* **c** *(inf)* **to be a real ~** zum Piepen sein *(inf)* **VT** **to ~ sb** jdn warnen *(against* vor *+dat)*; *(officially)* jdn verwarnen; **to ~ sb against doing sth** jdn davor warnen, etw zu tun

cautionary [ˈkɔːʃənərɪ] ADJ belehrend; *sign* Warn-; **a ~ tale** eine Geschichte mit Moral

caution money N *(Brit)* Kaution *f*

cautious [ˈkɔːʃəs] ADJ vorsichtig; **to play a ~ game** Vorsicht walten lassen; **to give sth a ~ welcome** etw mit Zurückhaltung *or* verhaltener Zustimmung aufnehmen; **~ optimism** vorsichtiger *or* verhaltener Optimismus

cautiously [ˈkɔːʃəslɪ] ADV *move, say, react* vorsichtig; *welcome* verhalten; *accept* mit Vorbehalten; **~ optimistic** verhalten optimistisch

cautiousness [ˈkɔːʃəsnɪs] N Vorsicht *f*

cavalcade [ˌkævəlˈkeɪd] N Kavalkade *f*

cavalier [ˌkævəˈlɪəʳ] **N** *(= horseman, knight)* Kavalier *m*; **Cavalier** *(Hist)* Kavalier *m* **ADJ** **a** **the Cavalier resistance** *(Hist)* der Widerstand der Kavaliere **b** *(= offhand) person, nature, attitude, approach* unbekümmert; *disregard, overruling also* ungeniert, kalt lächelnd; **... he said in his ~ fashion** ... sagte er leichthin; **treat it seriously, don't be so ~** nehmen Sie das ernst, und gehen Sie nicht so leichthin darüber hinweg

cavalierly [ˌkævəˈlɪəlɪ] ADV unbekümmert, kalt lächelnd; *say* leichthin

cavalry [ˈkævəlrɪ] N Kavallerie *f*, Reiterei *f*

cavalry: **cavalryman** N Kavallerist *m*; **cavalry officer** N Kavallerieoffizier *m*; **cavalry twill** N Reitertrikot *m*, *strapazierfähiger Hosenstoff*

cave¹ [ˈkeɪvɪ] N **to keep ~** *(dated Brit Sch sl)* Schmiere stehen *(inf)*

cave² [keɪv] **N** Höhle *f* **VI** **to go caving** auf Höhlenexpedition(en) gehen; **he did a lot of caving in his youth** in seiner Jugend hat er viel Höhlenforschung betrieben

▶ **cave in** VI **a** *(= collapse) (roof, wall)* einstürzen; *(fig: scheme etc)* zusammenbrechen **b** *(inf: = surrender, yield)* nachgeben, kapitulieren

caveat [ˈkævɪæt] N Vorbehalt *m*; **to enter a ~** *(Jur)* Einspruch einlegen

caveat emptor [ˌkævɪætˈemptɔːʳ] N *(Jur)* Ausschluss *m* der Gewährleistung

cave: **cave dweller** N Höhlenbewohner *m*; **cave-in** N Einsturz *m*; *(= place)* Einsturzstelle *f*; **caveman** N Höhlenmensch *m*; *(fig)* Tier *nt (inf)*, Urmensch *m*; **~ instincts** Urinstinkte *pl*; **cave painting** N Höhlenmalerei *f*

caver [ˈkeɪvəʳ] N Höhlenforscher(in) *m(f)*

cavern [ˈkævən] N Höhle *f*

cavernous [ˈkævənəs] ADJ **a** *cellar, pit, darkness* tief; *hole* gähnend; *mouth* riesig; *eyes* tief liegend; *cheeks* eingefallen, hohl; *voice* hohl (tönend); *yawn* herzhaft, breit **b** *mountain etc* höhlenreich, voller Höhlen

CAVES [keɪvz] *abbr of* **Citizens Against Virtually Everything** *Bürger, die gegen jedes Bebauungsprojekt oder jede soziale Veränderung in ihrer Umgebung sind*

caviar(e) ['kævɪɑːˈ] N Kaviar *m*
cavil ['kævɪl] VI kritteln; **to ~ at sth** an etw *(dat)* herumkritteln
cavity ['kævɪtɪ] N Hohlraum *m*, Höhlung *f*; *(in tooth)* Loch *nt*; **nasal/chest ~** *(Anat)* Nasen-/Brusthöhle *f*
cavity block N Hohlraumziegel *m*
cavity wall N Hohlwand *f*; **~ insulation** Schaumisolierung *f*
cavort [kəˈvɔːt] VI tollen, toben; **to ~ about** herumtollen *or* -toben
cavy ['keɪvɪ] N Meerschweinchen *nt*
caw [kɔː] **VI** krächzen **N** (heiserer) Schrei
cawing ['kɔːɪŋ] N Krächzen *nt*, Gekrächz(e) *nt*
cay [keɪ] N (kleine) Insel, Koralleninsel *f*
cayenne pepper ['keɪen'pepəˈ] N Cayennepfeffer *m*
CB *abbr of* **Citizens' Band** CB; **CB radio** CB-Funk *m*
CBA *abbr of* **cost-benefit analysis**
CBC *abbr of* **Canadian Broadcasting Corporation**
CBE *(Brit) abbr of* **Commander of the Order of the British Empire**
CBI *(Brit) abbr of* **Confederation of British Industry** ≈ BDI
CBS *abbr of* **Columbia Broadcasting System** CBS
CC *(Brit)* **a** *abbr of* **County Council** **b** *abbr of* **Cricket Club**
cc[1] *abbr of* **cubic centimetre** cc, cm^3
cc[2] *abbr of* **carbon copy** **N** Kopie *f* **VT** eine Kopie senden an *(+acc)*; **cc: ...** Kopie (an): ...
CCTV N ABBR *of* **closed-circuit television**
CCTV camera N *(TV)* Videoüberwachungskamera *f*
CD **a** *abbr of* **compact disc** CD *f*; **CD burner** CD-Brenner *m*; **CD player** CD-Spieler *m*, CD-Player *m*; **CD case** CD-Hülle *f*; **CD Walkman®** CD-Walkman *(R)*, tragbarer CD-Player; **CD writer** CD-Brenner *m* **b** *abbr of* **corps diplomatique** **c** *abbr of* **civil defence** **d** *(US) abbr of* **Congressional District**
CDC *(US) abbr of* **Centers for Disease Control and Prevention**

> **CDC**
> Die **Centers for Disease Control and Prevention**, kurz **CDC**, bilden eine US-Bundesbehörde, die für viele Aspekte der öffentlichen Gesundheit zuständig ist. Zu ihren Aufgaben gehört das Festlegen und Verschärfen von Schadstoffgrenzwerten und Sicherheitsstandards für Umwelt oder Arbeitsplätze, das Sammeln und Analysieren von Daten, die für das Gesundheitswesen relevant sind, sowie die Vorsorge gegen übertragbare Krankheiten und deren Kontrolle. Der Hauptsitz der **CDC** ist in Atlanta, Georgia. Im Ausland wurde die US-Seuchenkontrollbehörde vor allem durch ihre Vorreiterrolle bei der Beobachtung der Ausbreitung des HIV-Virus und der Identifizierung von dessen Übertragungswegen bekannt.

Cdr *abbr of* **Commander**
CD-ROM [siːdiːˈrɒm] *abbr of* **compact disk - read only memory** CD-ROM *f*; **~ drive** CD-ROM-Laufwerk *nt*
CDT **a** *(US) abbr of* **Central Daylight Time** **b** *(Brit Sch) abbr of* **Craft, Design and Technology** ≈ Arbeitslehre *f*
CDTV *abbr of* **compact disc television** CDTV *nt*
cease [siːs] **VI** enden, aufhören; *(noise, shouting etc)* verstummen; **we shall not ~ from our endeavours** *(liter)* wir werden in unserem Streben nicht nachlassen *(geh)*; **without ceasing** ohne Pause, unaufhörlich; **to ~ from doing sth** *(form)* von etw ablassen *(geh)* **VT** beenden; *fire, payments, production* einstellen; **to ~ doing sth** aufhören, etw zu tun; **to ~ to exist** aufhören zu bestehen; **~ fire!** Feuer halt! **N** **without ~** *(liter)* unaufhörlich, ohne Unterlass *(liter)*
cease-fire [siːsˈfaɪəˈ] N Feuerpause *or* -einstellung *f*; *(longer)* Waffenruhe *f*, Einstellung *f* der Kampfhandlungen; **to give the ~** den Befehl zur Feuereinstellung geben
ceaseless ['siːslɪs] ADJ *(= endless)* endlos, unaufhörlich; *(= relentless) vigilance* unablässig
ceaselessly ['siːslɪslɪ] ADV *(= endlessly)* unaufhörlich; *(= relentlessly)* unablässig
cecum ['siːkəm] N = **caecum**
cedar ['siːdəˈ] N **a** *(= tree)* Zeder *f*; **~ of Lebanon** Libanonzeder *f* **b** *(also* **cedarwood**) Zedernholz *nt*
cede [siːd] VT *territory* abtreten *(to* an *+acc)*; **to ~ a point in an argument** in einem Punkt *or* in einer Sache nachgeben
cedilla [sɪˈdɪlə] N Cedille *f*
Ceefax® ['siːfæks] N *Videotext der BBC*
ceiling ['siːlɪŋ] N **a** (Zimmer)decke *f* **b** *(Aviat: = cloud ceiling)* Wolkenhöhe *f*; *(= aircraft's ceiling)* Gipfelhöhe *f* **c** *(fig: = upper limit)* obere(r, s) Grenze, Höchstgrenze *f*; **price ~** oberste Preisgrenze; **to put a ~ on sth** etw nach oben begrenzen
celadon ['selədɒn] **N** Seladon *nt* **ADJ** seladongrün
celandine ['seləndaɪn] N **a** *(= greater celandine)* Schöllkraut *nt* **b** *(= lesser celandine)* Scharbockskraut *nt*
celeb [sɪˈleb] N *(inf)* Promi *m (inf)*
celebrant ['selɪbrənt] N *(Eccl)* Zelebrant *m*
celebrate ['selɪbreɪt] ✪ 25.1, 25.2 **VT** **a** feiern; *event, birthday also* begehen **b** *(= extol) sb's name, deeds* feiern, preisen *(geh)* **c** *mass, ritual* zelebrieren; *communion* feiern **VI** feiern
celebrated ['selɪbreɪtɪd] ADJ gefeiert *(for* wegen), berühmt *(for* für)
celebration [ˌselɪˈbreɪʃən] N **a** *(= party, festival)* Feier *f*; *(= commemoration, jubilee also)* Gedenkfeier *f*; *(= act of celebrating)* Feiern *nt*; **during the centenary ~s** während der Hundertjahrfeier(n); **in ~ of** zur Feier *(+gen)* **b** *(= praise)* Verherrlichung *f* **c** *(of mass, ritual)* Zelebration *f*; *(of communion)* Feier *f*
celebratory [ˌselɪˈbreɪtəri] ADJ *meal, drink* zur Feier des Tages
celebrity [sɪˈlebrɪtɪ] N Berühmtheit *f*; *(= person also)* berühmte Persönlichkeit
celebutante [sɪˈlebjʊtɑːnt] N *meist aus der höheren Gesellschaftsschicht stammende, meist reiche Person, deren Debüt offentlich war und die intensiv am gesellschaftlichen Leben teilnimmt*
celeriac [səˈlerɪæk] N (Knollen)sellerie *f*
celerity [sɪˈlerɪtɪ] N *(form)* Geschwindigkeit *f*
celery ['selərɪ] N Stangensellerie *m or f*; **three stalks of ~** drei Stangen Sellerie; **~ hearts** Sellerieherzen *pl*
celesta [sɪˈlestə], **celeste** [sɪˈlest] N *(Mus)* Celesta *f*
celestial [sɪˈlestɪəl] ADJ himmlisch; *(Astron)* Himmels-
celibacy ['selɪbəsɪ] N Zölibat *nt or m*; *(fig)* Enthaltsamkeit *f*
celibate ['selɪbɪt] **ADJ** *(Rel)* keusch, zölibatär *(spec)*; *(fig)* enthaltsam **N** **to be a ~** im Zölibat leben
cell [sel] N **a** Zelle *f*; **~ wall** Zellwand *f* **b** *(US inf: = cellphone)* Handy *nt*
cellar ['seləˈ] N Keller *m*; **he keeps an excellent ~** er hat einen ausgezeichneten Weinkeller
cellarage ['selərɪdʒ] N *(= cellar space)* Kellerfläche *f*; *(= storage cost)* Lagerkosten *pl*
cell culture N *(Biol)* Zellkultur *f*
cellist ['tʃelɪst] N Cellist(in) *m(f)*
cello, 'cello ['tʃeləʊ] N Cello *nt*
Cellophane® ['seləfeɪn] N Cellophan® *nt*
cellphone ['selfəʊn] N *(esp US)* Handy *nt*, Mobiltelefon *nt*
cell salts PL *(Med)* Schüßlersalze *pl*, *lebenswichtige Mineralsalze*
cellular ['seljʊləˈ] ADJ **a** zellenförmig, zellular, Zell- **b** *(Tex)* aus porösem Material
cellular phone N Funktelefon *nt*; *(= mobile phone)* Handy *nt*, Mobiltelefon *nt*
cellulite ['seljʊˌlaɪt] N Cellulitis *f*
celluloid ['seljʊlɔɪd] N Zelluloid *nt*; **~ heroes** Zelluloidhelden *pl*; **on ~** auf der Leinwand
cellulose ['seljʊləʊs] **N** Zellulose *f*, Zellstoff *m* **ADJ** Zellulose-
Celsius ['selsɪəs] ADJ Celsius-; **30 degrees ~** 30 Grad Celsius
Celt [kelt, selt] N Kelte *m*, Keltin *f*
Celtic ['keltɪk, 'seltɪk] **ADJ** keltisch **N** *(Ling)* Keltisch *nt*
cembalo ['tʃembələʊ] N *(Mus)* Cembalo *nt*
cement [səˈment] **N** **a** *(Build)* Zement *m*; *(inf: = concrete)* Beton *m* **b** *(= glue)* Leim *m*, Klebstoff *m*; *(for holes etc, fig)* Kitt *m* **c** *(of tooth)* (Zahn-)zement *m* **VT** *(Build)* zementieren; *(= glue)* leimen, kitten; *(fig)* festigen, zementieren
cement mixer N Betonmischmaschine *f*
cemetery ['semɪtrɪ] N Friedhof *m*
cenotaph ['senətɑːf] N Mahnmal *nt*, Ehrenmal *nt*, Kenotaph *m*
censer ['sensəˈ] N *(Eccl)* Rauchfass *nt*
censor ['sensəˈ] **N** Zensor *m* **VT** zensieren; *(= remove) chapter* herausnehmen
censorious [senˈsɔːrɪəs] ADJ *remark, glance* strafend; **he was very ~ of the new policy** er kritisierte die neue Politik scharf
censorship ['sensəʃɪp] N Zensur *f*; **press ~, ~ of the press** Pressezensur *f*
censure ['senʃəˈ] **VT** tadeln **N** Tadel *m*; **vote of ~** Tadelsantrag *m*
census ['sensəs] N Zensus *m*, Volkszählung *f*; *(Bibl)* Schätzung *f*; *(= traffic census)* Verkehrszählung *f*; **to take a ~ (of the population)** eine Volkszählung durchführen
cent [sent] N Cent *m*; **I haven't a ~** *(US)* ich habe keinen Cent; **to put in one's two ~s' worth** *(esp US)* seinen Senf dazugeben *(inf)*
centaur ['sentɔːˈ] N Zentaur *m*
centenarian [ˌsentɪˈnɛərɪən] **ADJ** hundertjährig **N** Hundertjährige(r) *mf*, Zentenar *m (geh)*
centenary [senˈtiːnərɪ] N *(= anniversary)* hundertster Jahrestag; *(= birthday)* hundertster Geburtstag; *(= 100 years)* Jahrhundert *nt*; **she has just celebrated her ~** sie ist gerade hundert Jahre alt geworden; **~ celebrations** Hundertjahrfeier *f*
centennial [senˈtenɪəl] **ADJ** hundertjährig, hundertjährlich **N** *(esp US)* Hundertjahrfeier *f*, Zentenarfeier *f (geh)*
center N *(US)* = **centre**
centesimal [senˈtesɪməl] ADJ zentesimal, hundertteilig
centigrade ['sentɪgreɪd] ADJ Celsius-; **one degree ~** ein Grad Celsius
centigramme, *(US)* **centigram** ['sentɪgræm] N Zentigramm *nt*
centilitre, *(US)* **centiliter** ['sentɪˌliːtəˈ] N Zentiliter *m or nt*
centimetre, *(US)* **centimeter** ['sentɪˌmiːtəˈ] N Zentimeter *m or nt*
centipede ['sentɪpiːd] N Tausendfüßler *m*
central ['sentrəl] **ADJ** **a** zentral, Zentral-; *(= main, chief)* Haupt-; **the ~ area of the city** das Innenstadtgebiet; **~ London** das Zentrum von London; **our house is very ~** unser Haus liegt sehr zentral **b** *(fig)* wesentlich; *importance, figure, issue* zentral; *role* wesentlich, zentral; **to be ~ to sth** das Wesentliche an etw *(dat)* sein; **he plays a ~ role** *or* **part in ...** er spielt eine zentrale *or* wesentliche Rolle bei ... **N** *(US: = exchange, operator)* (Telefon)zentrale *f*, Fernamt *nt*
central: **Central African Republic** N Zentralafrikanische Republik; **Central America** N Mittelamerika *nt*; **Central American** **ADJ** mittelamerikanisch **N** Mittelamerikaner(in) *m(f)*;; **Central Asian** ADJ zentralasiatisch; **central casting** N *(esp US Film)* Castingagentur *f*;

straight out of ~ *(fig)* wie eine klassische Figur aus dem Film; **Central Committee** N *(Pol)* Zentralkomitee *nt*; **Central Europe** N Mitteleuropa *nt*; **Central European** ADJ mitteleuropäisch N Mitteleuropäer(in) *m(f)*; **Central European Time** N mitteleuropäische Zeit; **central government** N Zentralregierung *f*; **central heating** N Zentralheizung *f*

centralism ['sentrəlɪzəm] N *(esp Pol)* Zentralismus *m*

centralist ['sentrəlɪst] ADJ *(esp Pol)* zentralistisch

centrality [sen'trælətɪ] N *(= central location)* zentrale Lage; *(fig: = importance)* zentrale Bedeutung

centralization [,sentrəlaɪ'zeɪʃən] N Zentralisierung *f*

centralize ['sentrəlaɪz] VT zentralisieren

central locking [,sentrəl'lɒkɪŋ] N Zentralverriegelung *f*

centrally ['sentrəlɪ] ADV zentral; **~ heated** zentralbeheizt; **~ planned economy** zentral gesteuerte *or* geplante Wirtschaft

central: **central nervous system** N Zentralnervensystem *nt*; **central processing unit** N *(Comput)* Zentraleinheit *f*; **central reservation** N Mittelstreifen *m*, Grünstreifen *m*; **Central Standard Time** N Central Standard Time *f*; **central station** N Hauptbahnhof *m*; **central unit** N *(Comput)* Zentraleinheit *f*

centre, *(US)* **center** ['sentə'] N **a** *(= chief place)* Zentrum *nt*
b *(= middle, Pol)* Mitte *f*; *(of circle)* Mittelpunkt *m*; *(= town centre)* Stadtmitte *f*; *(= city centre)* Zentrum *nt*, City *f*; **~ of gravity** Schwerpunkt *m*; **~ of attention** *or* **attraction** Hauptanziehungspunkt *m*, Hauptattraktion *f*; *(= person)* Mittelpunkt *m* der Aufmerksamkeit; **she always wants to be the ~ of attraction** sie will immer im Mittelpunkt stehen; **the man at the ~ of the controversy** der Mann im Mittelpunkt der Kontroverse; **left of ~** *(Pol)* links der Mitte; **politician/party of the ~** Politiker(in) *m(f)*/Partei *f* der Mitte; **the ~ of the field** *(Sport)* das Mittelfeld; **let's go into the ~** komm, wir gehen in die Stadt!
c *(= community centre, sports centre, shopping centre)* Zentrum *nt*, Center *nt*
d *(Rugby)* mittlerer Dreiviertelspieler; *(Basketball, Netball)* Center *m*
VT **a** *(also Comput)* zentrieren; **to feel ~d** *(person)* ausgeglichen sein
b *(= concentrate)* konzentrieren; **to be ~d on sth** sich auf etw *(acc)* konzentrieren
c *(Sport) ball* zur Mitte (ab)spielen

▶ **centre up** VT *sep* zentrieren

▶ **centre (up)on** VI *+prep obj (thoughts, problem, talk etc)* kreisen um, sich drehen um

centre, *(US)* **center**: **centre bit** N *(Tech)* Zentrumbohrer *m*; **centreboard**, *(US)* **centerboard** N *(Naut)* (Kiel)schwert *nt*; **centre court**, **center court** *(US)* N *(Tennis)* Centre- *or* Center-Court *m*; **centrefold**, *(US)* **centerfold** N *doppelseitiges Bild in der Mitte einer Zeitschrift (= girl) weibliches Aktmodell, dessen Foto auf den Mittelseiten einer Zeitschrift abgedruckt ist*; **centrefold girl**, *(US)* **centerfold girl** N *weibliches Aktmodell, dessen Foto auf den Mittelseiten einer Zeitschrift abgedruckt ist*; **centre forward** N *(Sport)* Mittelstürmer(in) *m(f)*; **centre half** N *(Sport)* Stopper(in) *m(f)*; **centre line** N Mittellinie *f*, Mitte *f*; **centre party** N Partei *f* der Mitte; **centrepiece**, *(US)* **centerpiece** N *(on table)* Tafelaufsatz *m*; *(fig) (of meeting, talks, treaty, statement)* Kernstück *nt*; *(of novel, work)* Herzstück *nt*; *(of show)* Hauptattraktion *f*; **the ~ of this week's events was ...** im Mittelpunkt des Geschehens dieser Woche stand ...; **centre three-quarter** N *(Rugby)* mittlerer Dreiviertelspieler, mittlere Dreivertelspielerin

centrifugal [,sentrɪ'fjʊgəl] ADJ zentrifugal; **~ force** Zentrifugal- *or* Fliehkraft *f*

centrifuge ['sentrɪfju:ʒ] N *(Tech)* Zentrifuge *f*, Schleuder *f*

centripetal [,sentrɪ'pɪtl] ADJ zentripetal; **~ force** Zentripetalkraft *f*

centrist ['sentrɪst] N Anhänger(in) *m(f)* der politischen Mitte; *(= politician)* Politiker(in) *m(f)* der Mitte

centuries-old ['sentjʊrɪz'əʊld] ADJ jahrhundertealt

centurion [sen'tjʊərɪən] N Zenturio *m*

century ['sentjʊrɪ] N **a** Jahrhundert *nt*; **in the twentieth ~** im zwanzigsten Jahrhundert; *(written)* im 20. Jahrhundert **b** *(Cricket)* Hundert *f*

CEO *(US) abbr of* **chief executive officer**

cep [sep] N *(Bot)* Steinpilz *m*

cephalic [sɪ'fælɪk] ADJ *(form)* Kopf-, Schädel-

ceramic [sɪ'ræmɪk] ADJ keramisch; **~ hob** Glaskeramikkochfeld *nt* N Keramik *f*

ceramics [sɪ'ræmɪks] N **a** *sing (= art)* Keramik *f* **b** *pl (= articles)* Keramik(en *pl*) *f*, Keramikwaren *pl*

cereal ['sɪərɪəl] N **a** *(= crop)* Getreide *nt*; **~ crop** Getreideernte *f*; **the growing of ~s** der Getreideanbau; **maize, rye and other ~s** Mais, Roggen und andere Getreidearten **b** *(= food)* Cornflakes *pl*/Müsli *nt*/Müesli *nt (Sw) etc*

cerebellum [,serɪ'beləm] N Kleinhirn *nt*, Zerebellum *nt (spec)*

cerebral ['serɪbrəl] ADJ *(Physiol)* zerebral; *(= intellectual)* geistig; *person* durchgeistigt, vergeistigt; **~ palsy** zerebrale Lähmung

cerebration [,serɪ'breɪʃən] N *(usu hum)* Reflexion *f*

cerebrum ['serəbrəm] N Großhirn *nt*, Zerebrum *nt (spec)*

ceremonial [,serɪ'məʊnɪəl] ADJ zeremoniell N Zeremoniell *nt*

ceremonially [,serɪ'məʊnɪəlɪ] ADV feierlich, zeremoniell

ceremonious [,serɪ'məʊnɪəs] ADJ förmlich, zeremoniös *(geh)*

ceremoniously [,serɪ'məʊnɪəslɪ] ADV mit großem Zeremoniell

ceremony ['serɪmənɪ] ✪ 24.3 N **a** *(= event etc)* Zeremonie *f*, Feier(lichkeiten *pl*) *f* **b** *(= formality)* Förmlichkeit(en *pl*) *f*; **to stand on ~** förmlich sein

cerise [sə'ri:z] ADJ kirschrot, cerise *pred* N Kirschrot *nt*

cert[1] [sɜ:t] *abbr of* **certificate**

cert[2] [sɜ:t] N *(Brit inf)* **a (dead) ~** eine todsichere Sache *(inf)*; **it's a dead ~ he'll be coming** er kommt todsicher *(inf)*

certain ['sɜ:tən] ✪ 15.1, 16.1, 26.3 ADJ **a** *(= positive, convinced)* sicher; *(= inevitable, guaranteed)* bestimmt, gewiss; **are you ~ of** *or* **about that?** Sind Sie sich *(dat)* dessen sicher?; **is he ~?** weiß er das genau?; **there's no ~ cure for this disease/for inflation** für *or* gegen diese Krankheit/gegen die Inflation gibt es kein sicheres Mittel; **for ~** ganz sicher, ganz genau; **I don't know for ~, but I think ...** ich bin mir nicht ganz sicher, aber ich glaube ...; **I can't say for ~** ich kann das nicht genau *or* mit Sicherheit sagen; **he is ~ to come** er wird ganz bestimmt *or* gewiss kommen; **we are ~ to succeed** wir werden ganz bestimmt Erfolg haben; **to make ~ of sth** *(= check)* sich einer Sache *(gen)* vergewissern, etw nachprüfen; *(= ensure)* für etw sorgen; **to make ~ of a seat** sich *(dat)* einen Platz sichern; **will you please make ~?** vergewissern Sie sich bitte noch einmal; **be ~ to tell him** vergessen Sie bitte nicht, ihm das zu sagen; **there is ~ to be strong opposition to the proposal** es wird sicher starken Widerstand gegen den Vorschlag geben; **that was ~ to happen** das musste ja so kommen; **to my ~ knowledge** ich bin mir ganz sicher
b *attr (= not named or specified)* gewiss; *reason, conditions* bestimmt; **a ~ gentleman** ein gewisser Herr; **to a ~ extent** *or* **degree** in gewisser Hinsicht, zu einem bestimmten Grade; **of a ~ age** in einem gewissen Alter
PRON einige; **~ of you/them** einige von euch/ihnen

certainly ['sɜ:tənlɪ] ✪ 26.1, 26.3 ADV *(= admittedly)* sicher(lich); *(= positively, without doubt)* bestimmt, gewiss *(geh)*; **it is ~ true that ...** es ist sicherlich richtig, dass ...; **~ not!** ganz bestimmt nicht, auf keinen Fall!; **I ~ will not!** ich denke nicht daran!; **~!** sicher!, gewiss! *(geh)*

certainty ['sɜ:təntɪ] N **a** *(= sure fact)* Gewissheit *f*; **to know for a ~ that ...** mit Sicherheit wissen, dass ...; **he was faced with the ~ of defeat** er sah seiner sicheren Niederlage entgegen; **his success is a ~** er wird mit Sicherheit Erfolg haben, sein Erfolg ist gewiss; **the ultimate ~ of death** die letztliche Gewissheit des Todes; **there are no certainties in modern Europe** in einem modernen Europa ist nichts gewiss; **will it happen? – yes, it's a ~** wird das passieren? – ja, mit Sicherheit; **it's a ~ that ...** es ist absolut sicher, dass ... **b** *no pl (= conviction)* Gewissheit *f*, Sicherheit *f*

CertEd *(Brit) abbr of* **Certificate in Education**

certifiable [,sɜ:tɪ'faɪəbl] ADJ **a** *fact, claim* nachweisbar **b** *(Psych)* unzurechnungsfähig; *(inf: = mad)* nicht zurechnungsfähig

certificate [sə'tɪfɪkɪt] N Bescheinigung *f*, Nachweis *m*; *(of qualifications)* Zeugnis *nt*, Urkunde *f*; *(of health)* Zeugnis *nt*; *(= marriage certificate)* Trauschein *m*; *(of baptism)* Taufschein *m*; *(= share certificate)* Zertifikat *nt*; *(Film)* Freigabe *f*

certification [,sɜ:tɪfɪ'keɪʃən] N **a** *(of film)* Klassifizierung *f* **b** *(Jur, = document)* Beglaubigung *f*

certified ['sɜ:tɪfaɪd]: **certified accountant** N *(Brit)* konzessionierte(r) Buchprüfer(in) *m(f)*, konzessionierte(r) Steuerberater(in) *m(f)*; **certified mail** N *(US)* Einschreiben *nt*; **certified milk** N *(US)* Vorzugsmilch *f*; **certified public accountant** N *(US)* geprüfter Buchhalter, geprüfte Buchhalterin

certify ['sɜ:tɪfaɪ] VT **a** *(= confirm)* bescheinigen, bestätigen; *(Jur)* beglaubigen; **this is to ~ that ...** hiermit wird bescheinigt *or* bestätigt, dass ...; **she was certified dead** sie wurde für tot erklärt; **certified as a true copy** beglaubigte Abschrift; **the painting has been certified (as) genuine** das Gemälde wurde als echt erklärt; **certified cheque** *or* *(US)* **check** gedeckter Scheck **b** *(Psych)* für unzurechnungsfähig erklären; *(= put in asylum)* in eine Anstalt einweisen; **he should be certified** *(inf)* der ist doch nicht ganz zurechnungsfähig *(inf)* VI **to ~ to sb/sth** sich für jdn/etw verbürgen

certitude ['sɜ:tɪtju:d] N Gewissheit *f*, Sicherheit *f*

cervical ['sɜ:vɪkəl, sə'vaɪkəl] ADJ zervikal *(spec)*

cervical cancer N Gebärmutterhalskrebs *m*

cervical smear N Abstrich *m*

cervix ['sɜ:vɪks] N *(of uterus)* Gebärmutterhals *m*

Cesarean, Cesarian [si:'zeərɪən] N *(US)* = **Caesarean**

cesium N *(US)* = **caesium**

cessation [se'seɪʃən] N Ende *nt*; *(of hostilities)* Einstellung *f*; **~ of the heartbeat** Herzstillstand *m*

cession ['seʃən] N Abtretung *f*; **~ of land/territory** Gebietsabtretung(en *pl*) *f*

cesspit ['sespɪt] N = **cesspool a**

cesspool ['sespu:l] N **a** Senk- *or* Jauchegrube *f*, Latrine *f* **b** *(fig)* Sumpf *m*; **a ~ of vice** ein Sündenpfuhl *m*

cestode ['sestəʊd], **cestoid** ['sestɔɪd] N *(Zool)* Bandwurm *m*

CET *abbr of* **Central European Time** MEZ

cetacean [sɪ'teɪʃɪən] N Wal *m*, Zetazee *f (spec)* ADJ Wal(fisch)-, Zetazeen- *(spec)*

Ceylon [sɪ'lɒn] N Ceylon *nt*

Ceylonese [sɪlɒ'ni:z] ADJ ceylonesisch N Ceylonese *m*, Ceylonesin *f*

CF *(US) abbr of* **cost and freight** cf

cf *abbr of* **confer** vgl

c/f *abbr of* **carry forward**

CFC *abbr of* **chlorofluorocarbon** FCKW *m*

CFE a *(Brit) abbr of* **college of further education** Weiterbildungseinrichtung *f* b *abbr of* **Conventional Forces in Europe** Konventionelle Streitkräfte *pl* in Europa, CFE

CFI *(US) abbr of* **cost, freight and insurance** cif

CFO *abbr of* **chief financial officer** Finanzdirektor(in) *m(f)*

CFS *(Med) abbr of* **chronic fatigue syndrome** CFS

CG *(US) abbr of* **coastguard**

cg *abbr of* **centigram(s), centigramme(s)** cg

CGA *(Comput) abbr of* **colour graphics adaptor** CGA *m*

ch a *abbr of* **chapter** Kap b *abbr of* **central heating** ZH

cha-cha [ˈtʃɑːtʃɑː] N Cha-Cha-Cha *m* VI Cha-Cha-Cha tanzen

Chad [tʃæd] N der Tschad

chador [ˈtʃɑːdɔːˈ] N Tschador *m*

chafe [tʃeɪf] VT a *(= rub, abrade)* (auf)scheuern, wund scheuern; **his shirt ~d his neck** sein (Hemd)kragen scheuerte (ihn) b *(fig)* aufregen, nervös machen VI a *(= rub)* sich aufscheuern *or* wund scheuern; *(= cause soreness)* scheuern; **her skin ~s easily** ihre Haut wird leicht wund; **the rope was chafing against the railings** das Seil scheuerte an der Reling b *(fig)* sich ärgern *(at, against* über *+acc)*; **he ~d at having to take orders from her** es ging ihm gegen den Strich, dass er von ihr Befehle entgegennehmen musste N wund gescheuerte Stelle

chafer [ˈtʃeɪfəˈ] N Käfer *m*

chaff[1] [tʃɑːf] N a *(= husks of grain)* Spreu *f* → **wheat** b *(= straw)* Häcksel *m or nt*

chaff[2] N *(= banter: also* **chaffing)** Scherze *pl*, Flachserei *f (inf)* VT aufziehen *(about* mit)

chaffinch [ˈtʃæfɪntʃ] N Buchfink *m*

chagrin [ˈʃægrɪn] N Ärger *m*, Verdruss *m (geh)* VT ärgern, verdrießen *(geh)*; **he was much ~ed by the news** die Nachricht bekümmerte *or* verdross *(geh)* ihn sehr

chain [tʃeɪn] N a Kette *f*; **~s** *(lit, fig: = fetters)* Ketten *pl*, Fesseln *pl*; *(Aut)* (Schnee)ketten *pl*; **~ of office** Amtskette *f*; **to keep a dog on a ~** einen Hund an der Kette halten; **to pull** *or* **yank sb's ~** *(esp US fig)* jdn necken; **in ~s** in Ketten
b *(of mountains)* (Berg)kette *f*, (Gebirgs)kette *f*; *(of atoms etc)* Kette *f*; **~ of shops** Ladenkette *f*; **to make a ~** eine Kette bilden; **~ of events** Kette von Ereignissen; **~ of evidence** Beweiskette *f*; **~ of command** *(Mil)* Befehlskette *f*
c *(= measure of length)* Messkette *f*
VT *(lit, fig)* anketten, festketten; *dog* an die Kette legen, anketten; **to ~ sb/sth to sth** jdn/etw an etw *(acc)* ketten

▶ **chain up** VT *sep prisoner* in Ketten legen; *dog* an die Kette legen, anketten

chain *in cpds* Ketten-; **chain bridge** N Ketten- *or* Hängebrücke *f*; **chain drive** N Kettenantrieb *m*, Kettengetriebe *f*; **chain gang** N Trupp*e f* aneinandergeketteter Sträflinge, Sträflingskolonne *f*; **chain letter** N Kettenbrief *m*; **chain lightning** N Linienblitz *m*; **chain-link fence** N Maschendrahtzaun *m*; **chain mail** N Kettenhemd *nt*; **chain reaction** N Kettenreaktion *f*; **chain saw** N Kettensäge *f*; **chain-smoke** VI eine (Zigarette) nach der anderen rauchen, kettenrauchen *infin only*; **chain smoker** N Kettenraucher(in) *m(f)*; **chain stitch** N *(Sew)* Kettenstich *m*; **chain store** N Kettenladen *m*

chair [tʃɛəˈ] N a *(= seat)* Stuhl *m*; *(= armchair)* Sessel *m*; *(= sedan chair)* Sänfte *f*; **please take a ~** bitte nehmen Sie Platz! b *(in committees etc)* Vorsitz *m*; **to be in/take the ~** den Vorsitz führen; **to address the ~** sich an den Vorsitzenden/die Vorsitzende wenden; **all questions through the ~, please** bitte alle Fragen (direkt) an den Vorsitzenden richten! c *(= professorship)* Lehrstuhl *m* (of für) d *(= electric chair)* (elektrischer) Stuhl VT a *meeting* den Vorsitz führen bei b *(Brit, = carry in triumph)* auf den Schultern (davon)tragen

chair: **chairborne** [ˈtʃɛəbɔːn] ADJ **to be ~** *(inf)* einen Schreibtischjob haben; **chairbound** [ˈtʃɛəbaʊnd] ADJ an den Rollstuhl gefesselt; **chairlift** N Sessellift *m*; **chairman** N Vorsitzende(r) *mf*; **Mr/Madam Chairman** Herr Vorsitzender/Frau Vorsitzende; **chairmanship** N Vorsitz *m*; **under the ~ of** unter (dem) Vorsitz von; **chairperson** N Vorsitzende(r) *mf*; **chair umpire** N *(Tennis)* Stuhlschiedsrichter(in) *m(f)*; **chairwoman** N Vorsitzende *f*

chaise [ʃeɪz] N *(Hist)* Einspänner *m*

chaise longue [ʃeɪzˈlɒŋ] N Chaiselongue *f*

chakra [ˈtʃækrə, ˈtʃʌkrə] N Chakra *nt*

chalet [ˈʃæleɪ] N Chalet *nt*; *(in motel etc)* Apartment *nt*

chalice [ˈtʃælɪs] N *(poet, Eccl)* Kelch *m*

chalk [tʃɔːk] N Kreide *f*; *(= limestone also)* Kalkstein *m*; **white as ~** kreidebleich; **not by a long ~** *(Brit inf)* bei Weitem nicht, noch nicht einmal annähernd; **the biggest by a long ~** *(Brit inf)* bei Weitem der Größte; **they're as different as ~ and cheese** *(Brit)* sie sind (so verschieden) wie Tag und Nacht VT *message etc* mit Kreide schreiben; *luggage etc* mit Kreide kennzeichnen; *billiard cue* mit Kreide einreiben

▶ **chalk up** VT *sep* a *(lit)* (mit Kreide) aufschreiben, notieren b *(fig: = gain, win) success, victory* verbuchen; *medal* einheimsen c *(fig: = mark up as credit)* anschreiben *(inf)*

chalk: **chalk dust** N Kreidestaub *m*; **chalkface** N *(Brit Sch hum)* **at the ~** im Klassenzimmer

chalkiness [ˈtʃɔːkɪnɪs] N Kalkigkeit *f*; *(= chalky content)* Kalkhaltigkeit *f*

chalk pit N Kalk(stein)bruch *m*

chalky [ˈtʃɔːkɪ] ADJ *(+er) (= containing chalk)* kalkhaltig, kalkig; *(= like chalk)* kalkartig; *(= covered with chalk)* voller Kalk

challenge [ˈtʃælɪndʒ] N a *(to duel, match etc)* Herausforderung *f (to* an *+acc)*; *(fig: = demands)* Anforderung(en *pl*) *f*; **to issue a ~ to sb** jdn herausfordern; **this job is a ~** bei dieser Arbeit ist man gefordert; **I see this task as a ~** ich sehe diese Aufgabe als Herausforderung; **the ~ of modern life** die Anforderungen des heutigen Lebens; **those who rose to the ~** diejenigen, die sich der Herausforderung stellten; **the office job presented no ~ for him** die Bürotätigkeit stellte keine Ansprüche an ihn *or* forderte ihn nicht; **the ~ of the unknown** der Reiz des Unbekannten
b *(= bid: for leadership etc)* Griff *m (for* nach); **a direct ~ to his authority** eine direkte Infragestellung seiner Autorität
c *(Mil, of sentry)* Anruf *m*, Werdaruf *m*
d *(Jur, of witness)* Ablehnung *f*
VT a *person, champion (to duel, race etc)* herausfordern; *world record etc* überbieten wollen; **to ~ sb to do sth** wetten, dass jd etw nicht (tun) kann; **he ~d her to run a marathon** er wettete, dass sie keinen Marathonlauf machen würde; **to ~ sb to a duel** jdn zum Duell fordern; **to ~ sb to a game** jdn zu einer Partie herausfordern
b *(fig: = make demands on)* fordern
c *(fig) remarks, sb's authority* infrage *or* in Frage stellen, anfechten
d *(sentry)* anrufen
e *(Jur) witnesses* ablehnen; *evidence, verdict* anfechten

challengeable [ˈtʃælɪndʒəbl] ADJ anfechtbar

-challenged [-ˈtʃælɪndʒd] ADJ *suf (usu hum)* **vertically-challenged** zu kurz geraten *(hum)*; **intellectually-challenged** beschränkt, geistig minderbemittelt *(inf)*; **follically-challenged** mit spärlichem Haarwuchs, oben ohne *(hum inf)*

challenger [ˈtʃælɪndʒəˈ] N *(to duel, match etc)* Herausforderer *m*, Herausforderin *f*; **a ~ of traditional beliefs** einer, der überkommene Glaubenssätze infrage *or* in Frage stellt

challenging [ˈtʃælɪndʒɪŋ] ADJ *(= provocative)* herausfordernd; *(= thought-provoking)* reizvoll; *(= demanding)* anspruchsvoll, fordernd; **a ~ idea** eine reizvolle Vorstellung; **I don't find this work very ~** diese Arbeit fordert mich nicht

challengingly [ˈtʃælɪndʒɪŋlɪ] ADV a *(= defiantly)* herausfordernd; **he looked ~ at the doctor** er sah den Arzt herausfordernd an b *(= demandingly)* extrem; **a ~ difficult game** ein schwieriges Spiel, das eine echte Herausforderung darstellt

chamber [ˈtʃeɪmbəˈ] N a *(old: = room)* Gemach *nt (old)*, Raum *m*; *(= bedroom)* Schlafgemach *nt (old)*; **~ of horrors** Horrorkabinett *nt* b *(Brit)* **~s** *pl (of solicitor)* Kanzlei *f*; *(of judge)* Dienst- *or* Amtszimmer *nt* c **Chamber of Commerce** Handelskammer *f*; **the Upper/Lower Chamber** *(Parl)* die Erste/Zweite Kammer d *(Anat)* (Herz)kammer *f* e *(of revolver)* Kammer *f*

chamberlain [ˈtʃeɪmbəlɪn] N Kammerherr *m*

chamber: **chambermaid** N Zimmermädchen *nt*, Kammerzofe *f (old)*; **chamber music** N Kammermusik *f*; **chamber orchestra** N Kammerorchester *nt*; **chamber pot** N Nachttopf *m*

chambray [ˈtʃæmbreɪ] N *(US)* = **cambric**

chameleon [kəˈmiːlɪən] N *(Zool, fig)* Chamäleon *nt*

chamfer [ˈtʃæmfəˈ] N Fase *f*, Schrägkante *f* VT abfasen, abschrägen

chamois [ˈʃæmwɑː] N a *(= leather)* Gamsleder *nt*; **a ~ (leather)** ein Ledertuch *nt*, ein Fensterleder *nt* b *(Zool)* Gämse *f*

champ[1] [tʃæmp] VT **to ~ at the bit** *(lit)* an der Gebissstange kauen; *(fig)* vor Ungeduld fiebern

champ[2] N *(inf)* Meister(in) *m(f)*, Champion *m*; **listen, ~** hör zu, Meister

champagne [ʃæmˈpeɪn] N Sekt *m*, Schaumwein *m*; *(= French champagne)* Champagner® *m*; **~ bucket** Sektkübel *m*, Sektkühler *m*; **~ glass** Sekt-/Champagnerglas *nt*; **~ lifestyle** Luxusleben *nt* ADJ *(also* **champagne-coloured,** *(US)* **champagne-colored)** champagner(farben)

champers [ˈʃæmpəz] N *(dated Brit inf)* Schampus *m (inf)*

champion [ˈtʃæmpjən] N a *(Sport)* Meister(in) *m(f)*, Champion *m*; **~s** *(= team)* Meister *m*; **world ~** Weltmeister(in) *m(f)*; **boxing ~** Boxchampion *m*; **heavyweight ~ of the world** Weltmeister *m* im Schwergewicht b *(of a cause)* Verfechter *m* ADJ a *(= prizewinning)* siegreich; *dog, bull, show animal* preisgekrönt; **~ boxer** erfolgreicher Boxer; **~ horse** *(Racing)* Turfsieger *m*; *(Show-jumping)* siegreiches Turnierpferd b *(N Engl, inf)* klasse *inv (inf)*, prima *inv (inf)* VT *person, action, cause* eintreten für, sich engagieren für

championship [ˈtʃæmpjənʃɪp] N a *(Sport)* Meisterschaft *f* b **championships** PL *(= event)* Meisterschaftskämpfe *pl* c *(= support)* Eintreten *nt*, Engagement *nt (of* für)

chance [tʃɑːns] ✪ 16.2, 16.3 N a *(= coincidence)* Zufall *m*; *(= luck, fortune)* Glück *nt*; **by ~** durch Zufall, zufällig; **a game of ~** ein Glücksspiel *nt*; **would you by any ~ be able to help?** könnten Sie mir wohl *or* vielleicht behilflich sein?; **to leave things to ~** die Dinge dem Zufall überlassen; **to trust to ~** auf sein Glück vertrauen
b *(= possibility)* Aussicht(en *pl*) *f*, Chance(n *pl*) *f*; *(= probability, likelihood)* Möglichkeit *f*; **(the) ~s are that ...** aller Wahrscheinlichkeit nach ..., wahrscheinlich ...; **the ~s are against that happening** vieles spricht dagegen *or* die Wahrscheinlichkeit ist gering, dass das eintritt; **what are the ~s of him agreeing?** wie sind die Aussichten *or* wie stehen die Chancen, dass er zustimmt?; **what are the ~s of his coming?** wie groß ist die Wahrscheinlichkeit, dass er kommt?; **is there any ~ of us meeting again?** könnten wir uns vielleicht wiedersehen?; **is there any ~ he might be lost?** besteht die Mög-

lichkeit, dass er sich verirrt hat?; **on the ~ of finding her at home** in der Hoffnung, sie zu Hause anzutreffen; **he doesn't stand** *or* **hasn't got a ~** er hat keine(rlei) Chance(n); **he doesn't stand a ~ of winning** er hat keine Chance zu gewinnen; **he has a good ~ of winning** er hat gute Aussicht zu gewinnen, er hat gute Siegeschancen; **there will be a ~ of rain on Thursday** am Donnerstag könnte es vereinzelt regnen; **to be in with a ~** eine Chance haben; **no ~!** *(inf)* nee! *(inf)*, ist nicht drin *(inf)*; **will you lend me £50? – sorry, no ~** *(inf)* leihst du mir £ 50? – bedaure, nichts zu machen *or* ist nicht drin *(inf)*
c *(= opportunity)* Chance *f*; **the ~ of a lifetime** eine einmalige Chance; **you won't get another ~ of going there** *or* **to go there** die Gelegenheit, dahin zu fahren, bietet sich (dir) nicht noch einmal; **you won't get another ~** das ist eine einmalige Gelegenheit; **I had the ~ to go** *or* **of going** ich hatte (die) Gelegenheit, dahin zu gehen; **now's your ~!** das ist deine Chance!; **this is my big ~** das ist DIE Chance für mich; **to take one's ~** die Gelegenheit nutzen; **to have an eye to the main ~** *(pej)* nur auf seinen Vorteil bedacht sein; **he never had a ~ in life** er hat im Leben nie eine Chance gehabt; **give me a ~!** nun mach aber mal langsam *(inf)*; **to give sb a ~** jdm eine Chance geben; **you never gave me a ~ to explain** du hast mir ja nie die Chance gegeben, das zu erklären; **~ would be a fine thing!** *(inf)* schön wärs!
d *(= risk)* Risiko *nt*; **to take a ~** es darauf ankommen lassen; **aren't you taking a bit of a ~?** ist das nicht ein bisschen riskant?; **he's not taking any ~s** er geht kein Risiko ein
ATTR zufällig; **~ meeting** zufällige Begegnung
VI it ~d that ... es traf *or* fügte *(geh)* sich, dass ...
VT a to ~ to do sth zufällig etw tun
b I'll ~ it! *(inf)* ich versuchs mal *(inf)*; **to ~ one's arm** *(inf)* (et)was riskieren; **to ~ one's luck** *(= have a try)* sein Glück versuchen; *(= risk)* das Glück herausfordern; **I'll just have to ~ that happening** das muss ich eben riskieren

► **chance (up)on** VI *+prep obj person* zufällig begegnen *(+dat)*, zufällig treffen; *thing* zufällig stoßen auf *(+acc)*

chancel [ˈtʃɑːnsəl] N Chor *m*, Altarraum *m*

chancellery [ˈtʃɑːnsələrɪ] N *(= offices)* Kanzleramt *nt*; *(= position)* Kanzlerschaft *f*

chancellor [ˈtʃɑːnsələʳ] N *(Jur, Pol, Univ)* Kanzler *m*; **Chancellor (of the Exchequer)** *(Brit)* Schatzkanzler(in) *m(f)*, Finanzminister(in) *m(f)*

chancellorship [ˈtʃɑːnsələʃɪp] N Kanzlerschaft *f*

chancer [ˈtʃɑːnsəʳ] N *(inf)* Windhund *m (inf)*

chancery [ˈtʃɑːnsərɪ] N **ward in ~** Mündel *nt* in Amtsvormundschaft

Chancery Division [ˈtʃɑːnsərɪdɪˌvɪʒən] N *(Brit Jur) für Grundstücks-, Erbschaftssachen etc zuständige Abteilung des High Court of Justice*

chancre [ˈʃæŋkəʳ] N Schanker *m*

chancy [ˈtʃɑːnsɪ] ADJ *(+er)* *(inf: = risky)* riskant

chandelier [ˌʃændəˈlɪəʳ] N Kronleuchter *m*

chandler [ˈtʃɑːndləʳ] N *(for candles)* Kerzenmacher *m*; *(= shop)* Kerzenladen *m*; **ship's ~** Schiffsausrüster *m*

change [tʃeɪndʒ] ✪ 19.3 **N a** *(= alteration)* Veränderung *f*; *(= modification also)* Änderung *f* *(to +gen)*; **a ~ for the better** ein Fortschritt *m*, eine Verbesserung; **a ~ for the worse** ein Rückschritt *m*, eine Verschlechterung; **~ of address** Adressen- *or* Anschriftenänderung *f*; **a ~ in the weather** eine Wetterveränderung; **a ~ of air** eine Luftveränderung; **a ~ is as good as a rest** *(prov)* Abwechslung wirkt *or* tut Wunder; **no ~** unverändert; **I need a ~ of scene** ich brauche Tapetenwechsel; **to make ~s (to sth)** (an etw *dat*) (Ver)änderungen *pl* vornehmen; **to make a ~/a major ~ in sth** etw ändern/bedeutend verändern; **save changes** *(Comput)* Änderungen speichern; **the ~ of life** die Wechseljahre; **he needs a ~ of clothes** er müsste sich mal wieder umziehen; **I didn't have a ~ of clothes with me** ich hatte nichts zum Wechseln mit; **a ~ of job** ein Stellenwechsel *m*
b *(= variety)* Abwechslung *f*; **(just) for a ~** zur Abwechslung (mal); **that makes a ~** das ist mal was anderes; *(iro)* das ist ja was ganz Neues!; **it'll make a nice ~** das wäre eine nette Abwechslung → **ring**
c *no pl (= changing)* Veränderung *f*; **those who are against ~** diejenigen, die gegen jegliche Veränderung sind; **the constant ~ will only confuse people** der ständige Wechsel verwirrt die Leute nur
d *(of one thing for another)* Wechsel *m*; **~ of career** Berufswechsel *m*; **a ~ of government** ein Regierungswechsel *m*, ein Wechsel *m* in der Regierung; **a wheel ~** ein Radwechsel *m*
e *no pl (= money)* Wechselgeld *nt*; *(= small change)* Kleingeld *nt*; **can you give me ~ for a pound?** können Sie mir ein Pfund wechseln?; **I haven't got any ~** ich habe kein Kleingeld; **I haven't got ~ for £5** ich kann auf £ 5 nicht rausgeben *or* £ 5 nicht wechseln; **you won't get much ~ out of £5** von £ 5 wird wohl nicht viel übrig bleiben; **keep the ~** der Rest ist für Sie; **you won't get much ~ out of him** *(fig)* aus ihm wirst du nicht viel rauskriegen
f *(St Ex)* **Change** Börse *f*
VT a *(by substitution)* wechseln; *address, name* ändern; **to ~ trains/buses** *etc* umsteigen; **to ~ one's clothes** sich umziehen; **to ~ a wheel/the oil** einen Rad-/Ölwechsel vornehmen, ein Rad/das Öl wechseln; **to ~ a baby's nappy** *(Brit) or* **diaper** *(US)*, **to ~ a baby** (bei einem Baby) die Windeln wechseln, ein Baby wickeln; **to ~ the sheets** *or* **the bed** die Bettwäsche wechseln, das Bett neu beziehen; **to ~ one's seat** den Platz wechseln, sich woanders hinsetzen; **to ~ hands** den Besitzer wechseln; **would you ~ the record?** *(lit, fig)* kannst du (mal) eine andere Platte auflegen?; **to ~ places with sb** mit jdm den Platz tauschen; **she ~d places with him/Mrs Brown** er/Frau Brown und sie tauschten die Plätze; **I wouldn't ~ places with him for the world** ich möchte *or* würde um nichts in der Welt mit ihm tauschen
b *(= alter)* (ver)ändern; *person, ideas* ändern; *(= transform)* verwandeln; **to ~ sb/sth into sth** jdn/etw in etw *(acc)* verwandeln; **you won't be able to ~ her** du kannst sie nicht ändern; **a chameleon can ~ its colour** das Chamäleon kann seine Farbe wechseln
c *(= exchange: in shop etc)* umtauschen; **she ~d the dress for one of a different colour** sie tauschte das Kleid gegen ein andersfarbiges um; **he ~d his Rolls Royce for a Jaguar** er vertauschte seinen Rolls Royce mit einem Mini → **guard**
d *money (into smaller money)* wechseln; *(into other currency)* (ein)wechseln, (um)tauschen
e *(Brit Aut)* **to ~ gear** schalten
VI a *(= alter)* sich ändern; *(town, person also)* sich verändern; **you've ~d!** du hast dich aber verändert!; **he will never ~** er wird sich nie ändern, der ändert sich nie!; **to ~ from sth into ...** sich aus etw in ... *(acc)* verwandeln
b *(= change clothes)* sich umziehen; **she ~d into an old skirt** sie zog sich einen alten Rock an; **I'll just ~ out of these old clothes** ich muss mir noch die alten Sachen ausziehen
c *(= change trains etc)* umsteigen; **you ~ at York** in York müssen Sie umsteigen; **all ~!** Endstation!, alle aussteigen!
d *(Brit Aut: = change gear)* schalten; *(traffic lights)* umspringen *(to* auf *+acc)*
e *(from one thing to another) (seasons)* wechseln; **to ~ to a different system** auf ein anderes System umstellen, zu einem anderen System übergehen; **I ~d to philosophy from chemistry** ich habe von Chemie zu Philosophie gewechselt; **do you want to ~ with me?** *(places)* möchten Sie mit mir tauschen?

► **change around** VT SEP = **change round VT**

► **change down** VI *(Brit Aut)* einen niedrigeren Gang einlegen, in einen niedrigeren Gang schalten, (he)runterschalten

► **change over VI a** *(= change to sth different)* sich umstellen *(to* auf *+acc)*; **we have just changed over from gas to electricity** hier *or* bei uns ist gerade von Gas auf Strom umgestellt worden **b** *(= exchange places, activities etc)* wechseln; *(Sport also)* die Seiten wechseln; **do you mind if I change over?** *(TV)* hast du was dagegen, wenn ich umschalte? **VT** *sep* austauschen

► **change round** *(esp Brit)* **VI** = **change over VI b VT** *sep room* umräumen; *furniture* umstellen; *tyres* austauschen, auswechseln

► **change up** VI *(Brit Aut)* einen höheren Gang einlegen, in einen höheren Gang schalten, höherschalten *(inf)*; **to change up into top** in den höchsten Gang schalten

changeability [ˌtʃeɪndʒəˈbɪlɪtɪ] N Unbeständigkeit *f*, Veränderlichkeit *f*

changeable [ˈtʃeɪndʒəbl] ADJ *person, character* unbeständig; *weather* veränderlich, wechselhaft; *mood, winds* wechselnd

changeless [ˈtʃeɪndʒlɪs] ADJ unveränderlich

changeling [ˈtʃeɪndʒlɪŋ] N *(= child)* Wechselbalg *m*

change machine N Geldwechsler *m*

changeover [ˈtʃeɪndʒəʊvəʳ] N Umstellung *f* *(to* auf *+acc)*; *(of governments)* Regierungswechsel *m*; *(in relay race)* (Stab)wechsel *m*; *(of teams changing ends)* Seitenwechsel *m*

changing [ˈtʃeɪndʒɪŋ] **ADJ** sich verändernd, wechselnd; **the fast-~ market** der sich schnell ändernde Markt **N the ~ of the Guard** die Wachablösung

changing room N *(in store)* Ankleideraum *m*, Kabine *f*; *(Sport)* Umkleideraum *m*, Umkleidekabine *f*

channel [ˈtʃænl] **N a** *(= watercourse)* (Fluss)bett *nt*; *(= strait)* Kanal *m*; *(= deepest part of river etc)* Fahrrinne *f*; **the (English) Channel** der Ärmelkanal
b *(fig, usu pl) (of bureaucracy etc)* Dienstweg *m*; *(of information etc)* Kanal *m*; *(of thought, interest etc)* Bahn *f*; **if you go through the right ~s** wenn Sie sich an die richtigen Stellen wenden; **to go through the official ~s** den Dienstweg gehen; **you'll have to go through ~s** *(US)* Sie werden den Dienstweg einhalten müssen; **through the usual ~s** auf dem üblichen Wege
c *(= groove)* Furche *f*, Rinne *f*
d *(TV, Rad)* Kanal *m*, Programm *nt*
VT a *(= dig out, furrow) way, course* sich *(dat)* bahnen
b *(= direct) water, river* (hindurch)leiten *(through* durch)
c *(fig) efforts, interest* lenken *(into* auf *+acc)*; *energy also* kanalisieren; *crowd also* dirigieren

► **channel off** VT *sep (lit)* ableiten; *(fig)* abzweigen

channel: **channel changer** N *(Brit TV)* Fernbedienung *f*; **Channel ferry** N *(Brit)* Kanalfähre *f*; **channel-hop** VI *(Brit TV inf)* ständig umschalten *or* den Kanal wechseln, zappen *(inf)*; **channel-hopping** N *(Brit TV inf)* ständiges Umschalten, Zappen *nt (inf)*

channelling, *(US)* **channeling** [ˈtʃænəlɪŋ] N Channeling *nt*

channel: **Channel Islander** N Bewohner(in) *m(f)* der Kanalinseln; **Channel Islands** PL Kanalinseln *pl*; **channel-surf** VI *(esp US TV inf)* = **channel-hop**; **channel-surfing** N *(esp US TV inf)* = **channel-hopping**; **Channel Tunnel** N Kanaltunnel *m*

chant [tʃɑːnt] **N** *(Eccl, Mus)* Gesang *m*, Cantus *m*; *(= monotonous song)* Sprechgesang *m*, Singsang *m*; *(of football fans etc)* Sprechchor *m*; **tribal ~s** Stammesgesänge *pl* **VT** im (Sprech)chor rufen; *(Eccl)* singen **VI** Sprechchöre anstimmen; *(Eccl)* singen

chanterelle [ˈtʃæntərel] N Pfifferling *m*

chanticleer [ˈtʃæntɪkliːəʳ] N *(old)* Hahn *m*

chaos ['keɪɒs] N Chaos *nt*, Durcheinander *nt*; **complete ~** ein totales Durcheinander

chaotic [keɪ'ɒtɪk] ADJ chaotisch

chaotically [keɪ'ɒtɪklɪ] ADV chaotisch; **the papers had been scattered ~ about the room** die Papiere lagen kreuz und quer im ganzen Raum verteilt; **such people can be ~ untidy** bei solchen Leuten kann das reinste Chaos herrschen

chap[1] [tʃæp] **N** *(Med, of skin)* **he's got ~s on his hands** seine Hände sind aufgesprungen *or* rau **VI** *(skin)* aufspringen **VT** spröde machen; **~ped lips** aufgesprungene *or* raue Lippen *pl*

chap[2] N *(Brit inf: = man)* Kerl *m (inf)*, Typ *m (inf)*; **old ~** alter Junge *(inf) or* Knabe *(inf)*; **poor little ~** armer Kleiner!, armes Kerlchen!; **now look here (you) ~s** hört mal zu, Jungs *(inf)*

chap[3] *abbr of* **chapter** Kap.

chapel ['tʃæpəl] N **a** Kapelle *f*; *(Sch, Univ: = service)* Andacht *f*; **~ of rest** *Kapelle in einem Bestattungsunternehmen, wo Tote aufgebahrt werden* **b** *(= nonconformist church)* Sektenkirche *f* **c** *(Press, of union) Betriebsgruppe innerhalb der Gewerkschaft der Drucker und Journalisten*

chaperon(e) ['ʃæpərəʊn] **N** **a** *(for propriety)* Anstandsdame *f*, Anstandswauwau *m (hum inf)* **b** *(= escort)* Begleiter(in) *m(f)* **c** *(esp US: = supervisor)* Aufsichts- *or* Begleitperson *f* **VT** **a** *(for propriety)* begleiten, Anstandsdame spielen bei **b** *(= escort)* begleiten **c** *(esp US: = supervise)* beaufsichtigen

chaplain ['tʃæplɪn] N Kaplan *m*

chaplaincy ['tʃæplənsɪ] N Amt *nt or* Stelle *f* eines Kaplans; *(= building)* Diensträume *pl* eines Kaplans

chaplet ['tʃæplɪt] N *(of flowers etc)* Kranz *m*

chappy ['tʃæpɪ] N *(inf)* Kerlchen *nt (inf)*

chaps [tʃæps] PL lederne Reithosen *pl*, Cowboyhosen *pl*

chapstick® ['tʃæpstɪk] N Lippenbalsam *m*, ≈ Labello® *m*

chapter ['tʃæptə'] N **a** *(of book)* Kapitel *nt*; **to give ~ and verse (for sth)** *(fig)* etw genau belegen **b** *(fig)* Kapitel *nt*; **a ~ of accidents** eine Serie von Unfällen **c** *(Eccl)* Kapitel *nt* **d** *(esp US: = branch)* Ortsgruppe *f*

chapterhouse N *(Eccl)* Kapitel(saal *m*) *nt*

char[1] [tʃɑː'] VT *(= burn black)* verkohlen

char[2] *(Brit inf)* **N** *(also* **charwoman, charlady***)* Putzfrau *f* **VI** putzen; **to ~ for sb** bei jdm putzen

char[3] N *(= fish)* Saibling *m*

char[4] N *(Brit inf: = tea)* Tee *m*

charabanc, char-à-banc ['ʃærəbæŋ] N *(old) offener Omnibus für Ausflugsfahrten*

character ['kærɪktə'] N **a** *(= nature)* Charakter *m*; *(of people)* Wesen *nt no pl*, Wesensart *f*; **there's quite a difference in ~ between them** sie sind wesensmäßig sehr verschieden; **to be in ~ for sb** typisch für jdn sein; **it is out of ~ for him to behave like that** solches Benehmen ist untypisch für ihn; **it's out of ~ for him to do that** es ist eigentlich nicht seine Art, so etwas zu tun; **to be of good/bad ~** ein guter/schlechter Mensch sein

b *no pl (= strength of character)* Charakter *m*; **a man of ~** ein Mann von Charakter

c *no pl (= individuality, of towns etc)* Charakter *m*; *(of person)* Persönlichkeit *f*; **she/it has no ~** sie/es hat keine eigene Note; **her face is full of ~** sie hat ein Charaktergesicht

d *(in novel)* (Roman)figur *f*, (Roman)gestalt *f*; *(Theat)* Gestalt *f*

e *(= person in public life)* Persönlichkeit *f*, Gestalt *f*; *(= original person)* Original *nt*; *(inf: = person)* Typ *m (inf)*, Type *f (inf)*

f *(= reference)* Zeugnis *nt*

g *(Typ, Comput)* Zeichen *nt*; *(Chinese etc also)* Schriftzeichen *nt*; **to type 100 ~s per minute** 100 Anschläge pro Minute machen; **Gothic ~s** gotische Schrift

character *in cpds (Theat)* Charakter-; **character actor** N Charakterdarsteller *m*; **character assassination** N Rufmord *m*

characteristic [ˌkærɪktə'rɪstɪk] **ADJ** charakteristisch, typisch (*of* für) **N** (typisches) Merkmal, Charakteristikum *nt*; *(Math)* Charakteristik *f*, Kennziffer *f*; **one of the main ~s of his style is ...** besonders charakteristisch für seinen Stil ist ..., eines der Hauptmerkmale seines Stils ist ...; **he has all the ~s of the true aristocrat** er hat alle Züge des echten Aristokraten

characteristically [ˌkærɪktə'rɪstɪkəlɪ] ADV typisch

characterization [ˌkærɪktəraɪ'zeɪʃən] N *(in a novel etc)* Personenbeschreibung *f*; *(of one character)* Charakterisierung *f*

characterize ['kærɪktəraɪz] VT **a** *(= be characteristic of)* kennzeichnen, charakterisieren **b** *(= describe)* beschreiben

characterless ['kærɪktəlɪs] ADJ *person* nichtssagend, farblos; *room* nichtssagend, nichts Besonderes *pred*; *wine* fade

character: **character map** N *(Comput)* Zeichentabelle *f*; **character mapping** N *(Comput)* Zeichenbelegung *f*; **character part** N Charakterrolle *f*; **character reference** N Referenz *f*; **character set** N *(Comput)* Zeichensatz *m*; **character sketch** N Charakterstudie *f*; **character space** N *(Comput)* Zeichenplatz *m*; **character string** N *(Comput)* Zeichenkette *f*; **character witness** N *(Jur)* Leumundszeuge *m*, Leumundszeugin *f*

charade [ʃə'rɑːd] N Scharade *f*; *(fig)* Farce *f*, Affentheater *nt (inf)*

char-broiled ['tʃɑːˌbrɔɪld] ADJ *(US)* = **char-grilled**

charcoal ['tʃɑːkəʊl] N Holzkohle *f*; *(= drawing)* Kohlezeichnung *f*; *(= pencil)* Kohle(stift *m*) *f*

charcoal: **charcoal-burner** N *(= person)* Köhler *m*, Kohlenbrenner *m (rare)*; *(= stove)* Holzkohlenofen *m*; **charcoal drawing** N Kohlezeichnung *f*; **charcoal grey**, *(US)* **charcoal gray** N Schwarzgrau *nt*; **charcoal-grey**, *(US)* **charcoal-gray** ADJ schwarzgrau

charge [tʃɑːdʒ] **N** **a** *(Jur: = accusation)* Anklage *f* (*of* wegen); **convicted on all three ~s** in allen drei Anklagepunkten für schuldig befunden; **to bring a ~ against sb** gegen jdn Anklage erheben, jdn unter Anklage stellen; **to press ~s (against sb)** (gegen jdn) Anzeige erstatten; **what is the ~?** wessen werde ich/wird er *etc* beschuldigt?; **to be on a murder ~** unter Mordanklage stehen; **he was arrested on a ~ of murder** er wurde wegen *or* unter Mordverdacht festgenommen; **to give sb in ~** *(form)* jdn in polizeilichen Gewahrsam bringen *(form)*; **it was laid to his ~** *(form)* es wurde ihm angelastet *or* zur Last gelegt; **to be on a ~** *(soldier)* eine Disziplinarstrafe verbüßen; **to put a soldier on a ~** über einen Soldaten eine Disziplinarstrafe verhängen, einen Soldaten verknacken *(inf)*; **you're on a ~, Smith!** das gibt eine Disziplinarstrafe, Smith!

b *(= attack: of soldiers, bull etc)* Angriff *m*; *(= trumpet call)* Signal *nt*; **to sound the ~** zum Angriff blasen

c *(= fee)* Gebühr *f*; **what's the ~?** was kostet das?; **what's your ~?** was verlangen Sie?; **to make a ~ (of £5) for sth** (£ 5 für) etw berechnen *or* in Rechnung stellen; **he made no ~ for mending my watch** er hat mir für die Reparatur der Uhr nichts berechnet; **there's an extra ~ for delivery** die Lieferung wird zusätzlich berechnet; **his ~s are quite reasonable** seine Preise sind ganz vernünftig; **free of ~** kostenlos, gratis; **delivered free of ~** Lieferung frei Haus

d *(= explosive charge)* (Spreng)ladung *f*; *(in firearm, Elec, Phys)* Ladung *f*; **to put a battery on ~** eine Batterie aufladen; **to be on ~** aufgeladen werden; **it still gives me a ~** *(fig inf)* das macht mir noch immer Spaß

e *(= position of responsibility)* Verantwortung *f* (*of* für); **to be in ~** verantwortlich sein, die Verantwortung haben; **who is in ~ here?** wer ist hier der Verantwortliche?; **look, I'm in ~ here** hören Sie mal zu, hier bestimme ich!; **to be in ~ of sth** für etw die Verantwortung haben; *of department* jdm etw leiten; **to put sb in ~ of sth** jdm die Verantwortung für etw übertragen; *of department* jdm die Leitung von etw übertragen; **while in ~ of a motor vehicle** *(form)* am Steuer eines Kraftfahrzeuges; **the man in ~** der Verantwortliche, die verantwortliche Person; **the children were placed in their aunt's ~** die Kinder wurden der Obhut der Tante anvertraut; **the children in** *or* **under her ~** die ihr anvertrauten Kinder; **to take ~ of sth** etw übernehmen; **to take ~** das Kommando übernehmen; **he took ~ of the situation** er nahm die Sache in die Hand; **I've been given ~ of this class** diese Klasse wurde mir anvertraut

f *(= ward) (= child)* Schützling *m*; *(of authorities)* Mündel *nt*; *(= patient)* Patient(in) *m(f)*

g *(= financial burden)* **to be a ~ on sb** jdm zur Last fallen

VT **a** *(with +gen) (Jur)* anklagen; *(fig)* beschuldigen; **to ~ sb with doing sth** jdm vorwerfen, etw getan zu haben; **to find sb guilty/not guilty as ~d** jdn im Sinne der Anklage für schuldig/nicht schuldig befinden

b *(= attack)* stürmen; *troops* angreifen; *(bull etc)* losgehen auf *(+acc)*; *(Sport) goalkeeper, player* angehen; **the forwards ~d the defence** die Stürmer griffen die Deckung an

c *(= ask in payment)* berechnen; **I won't ~ you for that** das kostet Sie nichts, ich berechne Ihnen nichts dafür

d *(= record as debt)* in Rechnung stellen; **~ it to the company** stellen Sie das der Firma in Rechnung, das geht auf die Firma *(inf)*; **please ~ all these purchases to my account** bitte setzen Sie diese Einkäufe auf meine Rechnung

e *firearm* laden; *(Phys, Elec) battery* (auf)laden

f *(form: = command)* **to ~ sb to do sth** jdn beauftragen *or* anweisen *(form)*, etw zu tun

g *(form: = give as responsibility)* **to ~ sb with sth** jdn mit etw beauftragen

VI **a** *(= attack)* stürmen; *(at people)* angreifen *(at sb* jdn); *(bull)* losgehen *(at sb* auf jdn); **~!** vorwärts!

b *(inf: = rush)* rennen; **he ~d into a brick wall** er rannte gegen eine Mauer; **he ~d into the room/upstairs** er stürmte ins Zimmer/die Treppe hoch

▸ **charge up** VT *sep* **a** *(= record as debt)* in Rechnung stellen *(to sb* jdm); **I'll charge the expenses up** das geht auf Geschäftskosten **b** *(Elec)* aufladen

chargeable ['tʃɑːdʒəbl] ADJ **a** *(Jur) crime, offence* strafbar; **to be ~ with sth** für etw angeklagt werden können **b** **to be ~ to sb** auf jds Kosten *(acc)* gehen; **are these expenses ~?** geht das auf Geschäftskosten?

charge: **charge account** N Kunden(kredit)konto *nt*; **charge-cap** VT *(Brit)* **the council was ~ped** dem Stadtrat wurde ein Höchstsatz für die Kommunalsteuer auferlegt; **charge-capping** N *(Brit) Festlegung eines Kommunalsteuer-Höchstsatzes durch die Zentralregierung*; **charge card** N Kundenkreditkarte *f*

charged [tʃɑːdʒd] ADJ *(lit, fig)* geladen; *(Elec also)* aufgeladen; **~ with emotion** emotionsgeladen

chargé d'affaires ['ʃɑːʒeɪdæ'fɛə'] N Chargé d'affaires *m*

charge: **charge hand** N Vorarbeiter(in) *m(f)*; **charge nurse** N *(Brit)* Stationsleiter(in) *m(f) (im Pflegedienst)*

charger ['tʃɑːdʒə'] N **a** *(= battery charger)* Ladegerät *nt* **b** *(= horse)* Ross *nt* **c** *(old, = dish)* Platte *f*

charge sheet N Anklageprotokoll *nt*

char-grilled ['tʃɑːˌgrɪld] ADJ *(Brit)* vom Holzkohlengrill

charily ['tʃɛərɪlɪ] ADV vorsichtig

chariness ['tʃɛərɪnɪs] N Vorsicht *f*

chariot ['tʃærɪət] N Wagen *m*, Streitwagen *m (liter)*

charioteer [ˌtʃærɪə'tɪə'] N Wagenlenker *m*

charisma [kæ'rɪzmə] N Charisma *nt*

charismatic [ˌkærɪz'mætɪk] ADJ charismatisch

charitable ['tʃærɪtəbl] ADJ menschenfreundlich, gütig; *(= dispensing charity) trust, organization* Wohltätigkeits-, karitativ; *(= financially generous, tolerant)* großzügig; *thought, remark etc* freundlich; **to have ~ status** als gemeinnützig anerkannt sein; **a ~ deed** eine gute Tat; **he wasn't very ~ about his boss** er äußerte sich nicht gerade schmeichelhaft über seinen Chef; **I'm feeling ~ today, here's £5** ich habe heute meinen sozialen Tag, hier hast du £ 5; **to take a ~ view of sth** etw milde betrachten

charitably ['tʃærɪtəblɪ] ADV großzügig; *say etc* freundlich

charity ['tʃærɪtɪ] N **a** *(= Christian virtue)* tätige Nächstenliebe, Barmherzigkeit *f* **b** *(= tolerance, kindness)* Menschenfreundlichkeit *f*; **for ~'s sake, out of ~** aus reiner Menschenfreundlichkeit; **~ begins at home** *(Prov)* man muss zuerst an seine eigene Familie/sein eigenes Land *etc* denken **c** *(= alms)* **to live on ~** von Almosen leben **d** *(= charitable society)* Wohltätigkeitsverein *m*, karitative Organisation; *(= charitable purposes)* Wohlfahrt *f*; **to work for ~** für die Wohlfahrt arbeiten; **a collection for ~** eine Sammlung für wohltätige *or* karitative Zwecke

charity *in cpds* Wohltätigkeits-

charity shop N *(Brit)* Secondhandladen *m (dessen Ertrag für wohltätige Zwecke verwendet wird)*

charlady ['tʃɑː,leɪdɪ] N *(Brit)* Putz- *or* Reinemachefrau *f*

charlatan ['ʃɑːlətən] N Scharlatan *m*

Charlemagne ['ʃɑːləmeɪn] N Karl der Große

Charles [tʃɑːlz] N Karl *m*

charleston ['tʃɑːlstən] N Charleston *m*

charley horse ['tʃɑːlɪhɔːs] N *(US inf)* steifes Bein

Charlie ['tʃɑːlɪ] N *dim of* **Charles**

charlie ['tʃɑːlɪ] *(Brit)* N **a** *(inf: = fool)* Heini *m (inf)*, Blödmann *m (inf)*; **I felt a real ~** ich kam mir richtig blöd vor *(inf)*; **I must have looked a proper ~** ich muss ziemlich dumm aus der Wäsche geguckt haben *(inf)* **b** *(sl: = cocaine)* Koks *m (inf)*, Candy *m (sl)*

Charlotte ['ʃɑːlət] N **a** Charlotte *f* **b** *(Cook)* **charlotte** Charlotte *f*; **charlotte russe** Charlotte Malakoff

charm [tʃɑːm] **N a** *(= attractiveness)* Charme *m no pl*; *(of person also)* Anziehungskraft *f*; *(of cottage, village, countryside)* Reiz *m*; **feminine ~s** (weibliche) Reize *pl*; **he succumbed to her ~s** er erlag ihrem Charme; **to turn on the ~** seinen (ganzen) Charme spielen lassen
b *(= spell)* Bann *m*; **it worked like a ~** das hat hervorragend geklappt
c *(= amulet)* Talisman *m*; *(= trinket)* Anhänger *m*
VT a *(= attract, please)* bezaubern; **to ~ one's way into sth** sich in etw *(acc)* einschmeicheln; **to ~ one's way out of sth** sich mit Charme vor etw *(dat)* drücken; **to ~ sth out of sb** jdm etw abschmeicheln; **he could ~ the birds out of** *or* **from the trees** *(prov)* er könnte mit seinem Charme alles erreichen
b *(= cast spell on)* bannen; *snakes* beschwören; **to lead a ~ed life** einen Schutzengel haben

▶ **charm away** VT *sep fears, worries etc* zerstreuen

charm bracelet N Armband *nt* mit Anhängern

charmed circle [tʃɑːmd'sɜːkl] N *(liter)* illustrer Kreis

charmer ['tʃɑːmə'] N **to be a real ~** wirklich charmant sein

charming ['tʃɑːmɪŋ] ADJ reizend, charmant; **~!** *(iro)* wie reizend! *(iro)*, na, das ist ja reizend! *(iro)*

charmingly ['tʃɑːmɪŋlɪ] ADV reizend; **she behaved/welcomed us quite ~** sie war/begrüßte uns äußerst charmant

charmless ['tʃɑːmlɪs] ADJ *place* wenig reizvoll; *person* unsympathisch

charm offensive N Charmeoffensive *f*

charnel house ['tʃɑːnlhaʊs] N *(old)* Leichenhalle *f*; *(for bones)* Beinhaus *nt*

chart [tʃɑːt] **N a** Tabelle *f*; *(= graph, diagram)* Schaubild *nt*, Diagramm *nt*; *(= map, weather chart)* Karte *f*; **on a ~** in einer Tabelle/einem Diagramm; **to keep a ~ of sth** etw in eine Tabelle eintragen/in einem Diagramm festhalten **b charts PL** *(= top twenty)* Hitliste *f*, Charts *pl* **VT** *(= make a map of)* kartografisch erfassen; *(= record progress of)* auswerten; *(= keep a chart of)* aufzeichnen, erfassen; *(= plan)* festlegen; **to ~ the progress of a team** den Erfolg eines Teams aufzeichnen **VI** *(= reach pop charts: singer, song)* in die Charts *pl or* die Hitliste kommen

charter ['tʃɑːtə'] **N a** Charta *f*; *(= town charter, Univ also)* Gründungsurkunde *f*; *(of a society)* Satzung *f*; *(= permission to become established)* Charter *f or m*, Freibrief *m* **b** *(Naut, Aviat etc: = hire)* **on ~** gechartert; **the plane is available for ~** das Flugzeug kann gechartert werden **VT** *plane, bus etc* chartern

charter *in cpds* Charter-

chartered accountant [,tʃɑːtədə'kaʊntənt] N *(Brit)* staatlich geprüfter Bilanzbuchhalter, staatlich geprüfte Bilanzbuchhalterin

charter: **charter flight** N Charterflug *m*; **charter party** N Chartergesellschaft *f*; **charter plane** N Charterflugzeug *nt*

chart topper N *(= hit record)* Spitzenreiter *m*

charwoman ['tʃɑː,wʊmən] N *(Brit)* = **charlady**

chary ['tʃɛərɪ] ADJ *(+er)* *(= cautious)* vorsichtig; *(= sparing)* zurückhaltend (of mit); **I'd be ~ of taking lifts from strangers if I were you** an deiner Stelle würde ich nicht so ohne Weiteres mit Fremden mitfahren; **he is ~ of giving praise** er ist mit Lob zurückhaltend

Charybdis [kə'rɪbdɪs] N Charybdis *f*

Chas *abbr of* **Charles**

chase[1] [tʃeɪs] **N** Verfolgungsjagd *f*; *(Hunt)* Jagd *f*; *(Horse Racing: = steeplechase)* Hindernisrennen *nt*; **a (high-speed) car ~** eine Verfolgungsjagd im Auto; **to give ~** die Verfolgung aufnehmen; **to give ~ to sb** jds Verfolgung aufnehmen; **the thrill of the ~** die Jagdlust; **the ~ for the championship** der Kampf um die Meisterschaft; **to cut to the ~** *(esp US inf)* zum Kern der Sache kommen
VT jagen; *(= follow)* verfolgen; *member of opposite sex* hinterherlaufen *(+dat)*, nachlaufen *(+dat)*; **he's been chasing that girl for months** er ist schon seit Monaten hinter der Frau her; **to ~ one's own tail** *(fig)* seine Zeit und Energie verschwenden
VI to ~ after sb hinter jdm herrennen *(inf)*; *(in vehicle)* hinter jdm herrasen *(inf)*; **to ~ around** herumrasen *(inf)*

▶ **chase away** *or* **off VI** losrasen *(inf)*; *(on foot also)* losrennen **VT** *sep* wegjagen; *(fig) sorrow etc* vertreiben

▶ **chase down** VT SEP **a** *(= track down)* aufspüren; *thing* auftreiben **b** *(US: = catch)* aufspüren, erwischen

▶ **chase up** VT *sep person* rankriegen *(inf)*; *information etc* ranschaffen *(inf)*; **we'll have to chase them up a bit (about ...)** wir werden ihnen ein bisschen Dampf machen müssen (wegen ...)

chase[2] VT *(Tech) silver, metal* ziselieren

chaser ['tʃeɪsə'] N **a** *(= pursuer)* Verfolger *m* **b** *(= drink)* **have a whisky ~** trinken Sie einen Whisky dazu

chasm ['kæzəm] N *(Geol)* Spalte *f*, Kluft *f (also fig)*; **a yawning ~** ein gähnender Abgrund; **the future lay before him, a great black ~** die Zukunft tat sich wie ein riesiger dunkler Abgrund vor ihm auf

chassis ['ʃæsɪ] N Chassis *nt*; *(Aut also)* Fahrgestell *nt*

chaste [tʃeɪst] ADJ *(+er)* *(= pure, virtuous)* keusch; *(= simple, unadvanced) style, elegance* schlicht

chastely ['tʃeɪstlɪ] ADV *kiss* keusch, unschuldig; *dress* schlicht

chasten ['tʃeɪsn] VT nachdenklich stimmen, zur Einsicht bringen; *pride, stubborn nature* zügeln; **~ed by ...** durch ... zur Einsicht gelangt

chasteness ['tʃeɪstnɪs] N *(of person, relationship)* Keuschheit *f*; *(= simplicity: of style)* Schlichtheit *f*

chastening ['tʃeɪsnɪŋ] ADJ *thought, experience* ernüchternd

chastise [tʃæs'taɪz] VT *(physically)* züchtigen *(geh)*; *(verbally)* schelten

chastisement ['tʃæstɪzmənt] N *(physical)* Züchtigung *f (geh)*; *(verbal)* Schelte *f*

chastity ['tʃæstɪtɪ] N *(= sexual purity)* Keuschheit *f*; *(= virginity also)* Unberührtheit *f*, Reinheit *f*

chastity belt N Keuschheitsgürtel *m*

chasuble ['tʃæzjʊbl] N Messgewand *nt*, Kasel *f*

chat [tʃæt] **N** Unterhaltung *f*; *(about unimportant things also)* Plauderei *f*, Schwatz *m (inf)*; *(Internet)* Chat *m (inf)*; **could we have a ~ about it?** können wir uns mal darüber unterhalten?; **she dropped in for a ~** sie kam zu einem Schwätzchen rein *(inf)* **VI** plaudern; *(two people also)* sich unterhalten; *(Internet)* chatten *(inf)*

▶ **chat up** VT *sep (Brit inf) person* einreden auf *(+acc)*; *prospective girl-/boyfriend* sich heranmachen an *(+acc)*, anquatschen *(inf)*

chatelaine ['ʃætəleɪn] N **a** *(of castle, = housekeeper)* Schlossverwalterin *f*; *(= owner)* Schlossherrin *f* **b** *(old) Gürtel, an dem ein Schlüsselbund getragen wird*

chat: **chatline** N *(Telec, Internet)* Chatline *f*; **chat room** N *(Comput)* Chatroom *m*; **chat show** N *(Brit)* Talkshow *f*

chattels ['tʃætlz] PL *(Jur)* bewegliches Vermögen, bewegliche Habe; **all his (goods and) ~** seine gesamte Habe

chatter ['tʃætə'] **N** *(of person)* Geschwätz *nt*, Geplapper *nt*; *(of birds, monkeys)* Geschnatter *nt* **VI** *(person)* schwatzen, schwätzen *(esp S Ger)*, plappern; *(birds, monkeys)* schnattern; *(teeth)* klappern

chatterbox ['tʃætəbɒks] N Quasselstrippe *f (inf)*

chattering ['tʃætərɪŋ] **N** Geschwätz *nt* **ADJ the ~ classes** *(Brit pej inf)* das Bildungsbürgertum

chatty ['tʃætɪ] ADJ *(+er) person* geschwätzig, schwatzhaft; **written in a ~ style** im Plauderton geschrieben

chat-up line ['tʃætʌplaɪn] N Anmacherspruch *m*, Aufreiße *f (inf)*

chauffeur ['ʃəʊfə'] N Chauffeur *m*, Fahrer *m*; **~-driven** mit Fahrer *or* Chauffeur; **to be ~-driven** einen Fahrer haben

chauffeuse [ʃəʊ'fɜːz] N Chauffeuse *f*, Fahrerin *f*

chauvinism ['ʃəʊvɪnɪzəm] N Chauvinismus *m*

chauvinist ['ʃəʊvɪnɪst] **N** *(= jingoist)* Chauvinist(in) *m(f)*; *(= male chauvinist)* männlicher Chauvinist **ADJ** chauvinistisch; **(male) ~ pig** Chauvinistenschwein *nt (inf)*

chauvinistic [,ʃəʊvɪ'nɪstɪk] ADJ chauvinistisch

cheap [tʃiːp] **ADJ** *(+er)* **a** **ALSO ADV** *(= inexpensive)* billig; **I got it ~** ich habe es billig gekriegt; **it's going ~** es ist billig zu haben; **it doesn't come ~** es ist nicht billig; **~ and cheerful** preiswert; **it's ~ at the price** es ist spottbillig; **to hold sth ~** etw gering achten; **human life is ~** ein Menschenleben ist nicht viel wert **b** *(= poor quality)* billig, minderwertig; **everything they sell is ~ and nasty** sie verkaufen nur Ramsch
c *(fig: = mean, shallow, sexually cheap) joke, flattery, thrill, girl* billig; *person, behaviour, appearance* ordinär; **to feel ~** sich *(dat)* schäbig vorkommen; **how can you be so ~!** wie kannst du nur so gemein sein!; **to make oneself ~** sich entwürdigen; *(by loose living)* sich wegwerfen
N on the ~ auf die billige Tour *(inf)*; **to buy sth on the ~** *(inf)* etw für einen Pappenstiel *(inf) or* einen Apfel und ein Ei *(inf)* kaufen; **to make sth on the ~** *(inf)* etw ganz billig produzieren

cheapen ['tʃiːpən] **VT** *(lit)* verbilligen, herabsetzen; *(fig)* herabsetzen, schlechtmachen; **to ~**

oneself sich entwürdigen **VI** billiger werden, sich verbilligen

cheapie ['tʃi:pɪ] ADJ *(inf)* = **cheapo**

cheap-jack ['tʃi:pdʒæk] ADJ Ramsch- *(pej)*

cheaply ['tʃi:plɪ] ADV *buy, sell, furnish, decorate* billig; *make, produce, eat, live* günstig

cheapness ['tʃi:pnɪs] N **a** *(= inexpensiveness)* billiger Preis **b** *(= poor quality)* Billigkeit *f*, Minderwertigkeit *f* **c** *(fig, of joke)* Billigkeit *f*; *(of person, behaviour)* ordinäre Art

cheapo ['tʃi:pəʊ] **N** Billigartikel *m*, billiges Ding *(inf)* **ADJ** *(inf)* Billig-; **~ video** Billigvideo *nt*

cheap shot N unfaire Bemerkung; **that was a ~** das war unfair, das ging unter die Gürtellinie *(inf)*

cheapskate ['tʃi:pskeɪt] N *(inf)* Knicker *m*, Knauser *m (inf)*

cheat [tʃi:t] **VT** betrügen; *authorities also* täuschen; **to ~ death** dem Tod von der Schippe springen; **to ~ sb out of sth** jdn um etw betrügen; **to feel ~ed** sich betrogen fühlen **VI** betrügen; *(in exam, game etc)* mogeln *(inf)*, schummeln *(Sch inf)*; *(in card games also)* falschspielen, mogeln *(inf)* **N** **a** *(= person)* Betrüger(in) *m(f)*; *(in exam, game etc)* Mogler(in) *m(f) (inf)*, Schummler(in) *m(f) (Sch inf)*; *(in card games also)* Falschspieler(in) *m(f)*, Mogler(in) *m(f) (inf)*
b *(= dishonest trick)* Betrug *m*, Täuschung *f*
c *(Comput, also* **cheat code***)* Cheat *m*

► **cheat on** VI *+prep obj* betrügen

cheater ['tʃi:tə'] N *(US: = person)* = **cheat N a**

cheating ['tʃi:tɪŋ] **N** Betrügen *nt*, Betrug *m*; *(in exam, game etc)* Mogeln *m (inf)*, Schummeln *nt (Sch inf)*; *(in card games also)* Falschspielen *nt*, Mogeln *nt (inf)* **ADJ** betrügerisch

Chechen ['tʃetʃən] **N** *pl* **Chechens** *or* **Chechen** Tschetschene *m*, Tschetschenin *f* **ADJ** tschetschenisch; **the ~ Republic** die Tschetschenische Republik

Chechenia [tʃe'tʃɛnɪə], **Chechnya** ['tʃetʃnɪə] N Tschetschenien *nt*

check [tʃek] **N** **a** *(= examination)* Überprüfung *f*, Kontrolle *f*; **to give sth a ~** etw überprüfen *or* nachsehen; **to make a ~ on sb/sth** jdn/etw überprüfen, bei jdm/etw eine Kontrolle durchführen; **a random ~** eine Stichprobe; **to keep a ~ on sb/sth** jdn/etw überwachen *or* kontrollieren
b *(= restraint)* Hemmnis *nt*, Erschwernis *f*; *(Mil, to army)* Hindernis *nt*, Sperre *f*; **an efficient ~ on population growth** ein wirksames Mittel zur Eindämmung des Bevölkerungswachstums; **to hold** *or* **keep sb in ~** jdn in Schach halten; **to keep one's temper in ~** sich beherrschen; **(a system of) ~s and balances** ein Sicherungssystem *nt*; **to act as a ~ on sth** etw unter Kontrolle *(dat)* halten
c *(= pattern)* Karo(muster) *nt*; *(= square)* Karo *nt*
d *(Chess)* Schach *nt*; **to be in ~** im Schach stehen
e *(US: = cheque)* Scheck *m*; *(= bill)* Rechnung *f*; **~ please** bitte (be)zahlen
f *(US: = room) (Rail)* Gepäckaufbewahrung *f*; *(Theat)* Garderobe *f*; (= *ticket, Rail*) (Gepäck)schein *m*; *(Theat)* (Garderoben)marke *f*
g *(US: = tick)* Haken *m*
VT **a** *(= examine)* überprüfen, checken *(inf)*; *(in book also)* nachschlagen; *tickets also* kontrollieren; **to ~ whether** *or* **if ...** nachprüfen, ob ...
b *(= act as control on)* kontrollieren; *(= stop) enemy, advance* aufhalten; *anger* unterdrücken, beherrschen; **I was going to say it, but I just managed to ~ myself in time** ich wollte es sagen, aber ich konnte mich gerade noch beherrschen
c *(Chess)* Schach bieten *(+dat)*
d *(Aviat) luggage* einchecken, abfertigen lassen; *(US) coat etc* abgeben; *(US Rail) luggage (= register)* aufgeben; *(= deposit)* abgeben, zur Aufbewahrung geben
e *(US: = tick)* abhaken
f *(Comput) control box* aktivieren
VI **a** *(= make sure)* nachfragen *(with* bei); *(= have a look)* nachsehen, nachgucken; **I was just ~ing** ich wollte nur nachprüfen
b *(= stop, pause)* stocken; *(horse)* scheuen

► **check back** VI *(= look back in records)* zurückgehen *(in* zu), nachsehen *(in* in *+dat)*; *(= re-contact)* rückfragen *(with* bei)

► **check in** **VI** *(at airport)* sich bei der Abfertigung melden, einchecken; *(at hotel)* sich anmelden; **what time do you have to check in?** wann musst du am Flughafen sein? **VT** *sep (at airport) luggage* abfertigen lassen, einchecken; *(at hotel) person* anmelden; **he isn't checked in at this hotel** er wohnt nicht in diesem Hotel; **they checked me in at a first-class hotel** ich wurde in einem erstklassigen Hotel untergebracht

► **check off** VT *sep (esp US)* abhaken

► **check on** VI *+prep obj* = **check up on**

► **check out** **VI** sich abmelden; *(= leave hotel)* abreisen; *(= sign out)* sich austragen; *(= clock out)* stempeln, stechen **VT** *sep* **a** *figures, facts, persons* überprüfen; **check it out with the boss** klären Sie das mit dem Chef ab; **check out our new range** *(inf)* sehen Sie sich *(dat)* unser neues Sortiment an **b** *(hotel) guest* abfertigen

► **check over** VT *sep* überprüfen

► **check through** VT *sep* **a** *account, proofs* durchsehen, durchgehen **b** **they checked my bags through to Berlin** mein Gepäck wurde nach Berlin durchgecheckt

► **check up** VI überprüfen

► **check up on** VI *+prep obj* überprüfen; *person also* Nachforschungen anstellen über *(+acc)*; *(= keep a check on) sb* kontrollieren

checkable ['tʃekəbl] ADJ kontrollierbar, nachprüfbar

checkback ['tʃekbæk] N Rückfrage *f*

checkbook ['tʃekbʊk] N *(US)* Scheckbuch *nt*

check box N *(Comput)* Kontrollkästchen *nt*

checked [tʃekt] ADJ **a** *(in pattern)* kariert; **~ pattern** Karomuster *nt* **b** *(Phon) syllable* geschlossen; *vowel* in geschlossener Silbe (stehend)

checker ['tʃekə'] N **a** *(of documents etc)* Prüfer(in) *m(f)* **b** *(US, in supermarket)* Kassierer(in) *m(f)* **c** *(US, for coats etc)* Garderobenfrau *f*/-mann *m*

checkerboard ['tʃekəbɔ:d] N *(US)* Damebrett *nt*; *(= chessboard)* Schachbrett *nt*

Checker cab® ['tʃekə,kæb] N *(US Aut)* *US-Taxi mit Schachbrettmusterstreifen an den Seiten*

checkered ADJ *(US)* = **chequered**

checkers ['tʃekəz] N *(US)* Damespiel *nt*; **to play ~** Dame spielen

check-in (desk) ['tʃekɪn(,desk)] N Abfertigung *f*, Abfertigungsschalter *m*; *(Aviat)* Abflugschalter *m*; *(US, in hotel)* Rezeption *f*, Anmeldung *f*

checking ['tʃekɪŋ] N Überprüfung *f*, Kontrolle *f*; **it needs more ~** es muss gründlicher überprüft werden; **~ account** *(US)* Girokonto *nt*; **~ slip** Kontrollabschnitt *m*

check: **check list** N Prüf- *or* Checkliste *f*; **checkmate** **N** Schachmatt *nt*; **~!** *(Chess)* matt!; *(fig)* aus!; **he found himself in ~** *(lit, fig)* er war mattgesetzt **VT** matt setzen; **checkout** N **a** *(in supermarket)* Kasse *f* **b** *(= leaving of hotel)* Auschecken *nt no pl*; **checkpoint** N Kontrollpunkt *m*; **Checkpoint Charlie** Checkpoint Charlie *m*, Ausländerübergang *m* Friedrichstraße; **checkroom** N *(US Theat)* Garderobe *f*; *(Rail)* Gepäckaufbewahrung *f*; **checkup** N *(Med)* Untersuchung *f*, Check-up *m*; **to have a ~/go for a ~** einen Check-up machen lassen

> **CHECKS AND BALANCES**
>
> Der Begriff **checks and balances** bezeichnet das der Verfassung der Vereinigten Staaten zugrunde liegende Prinzip der gegenseitigen Kontrolle **(checks)** und des Machtgleichgewichts **(balances)** der Regierungsgewalten, das dem Machtmissbrauch vorbeugen soll: Die Exekutive, die Legislative und die Judikative werden getrennt und sollen sich durch gegenseitige Kontrolle im Gleichgewicht halten. Die Gestalter der US-Verfassung sahen in **checks and balances** die Garantie für Freiheit im Rahmen der Verfassung und entwarfen ein System, in dem die Gewalt des Präsidenten, des Kongresses, der Gerichte und der Regierungen der einzelnen Staaten immer wieder infrage gestellt diskutiert und, wenn nötig, auch aufgehoben werden kann.

cheddar ['tʃedə'] N Cheddar(käse) *m*

> **CHEDDAR**
>
> **Cheddar** ist ein orangegelber Hartkäse aus Kuhmilch, der nach der Gegend im Südwesten Englands benannt wurde, in der er ursprünglich hergestellt wurde. Er wird wegen seines Geschmacks und seiner Konsistenz gern zum Kochen verwendet und ist die bei Weitem beliebteste Käsesorte in Großbritannien. Auch wenn es noch ein paar kleine Käsereien gibt, die Cheddar herstellen, wird überwiegend industriell gefertigte Massenware verkauft, die in Großmolkereien auf den Britischen Inseln, in den USA, Kanada und Australien produziert wird.

cheek [tʃi:k] **N** **a** Backe *f*, Wange *f (liter)*; **to be ~ by jowl (with sb)** Tuchfühlung mit jdm haben, auf Tuchfühlung (mit jdm) sein; **to dance ~ to ~** Wange an Wange tanzen; **~ pouch** Futtertasche *f*; **to turn the other ~** die andere Wange hinhalten
b *(= buttock)* Backe *f*
c *(Brit: = impudence)* Frechheit *f*, Unverschämtheit *f*, Dreistigkeit *f*; **to have the ~ to do sth** die Frechheit *or* Stirn haben, etw zu tun, sich erfrechen, etw zu tun; **they gave him a lot of ~** sie waren sehr frech zu ihm; **enough of your ~!** jetzt reichts aber!; **of all the ~!, the ~ of it!** so eine Frechheit *or* Unverschämtheit!
VT *(Brit)* **to ~ sb** frech sein zu jdm *or* gegen jdn

cheekbone ['tʃi:kbəʊn] N Wangenknochen *m*, Jochbein *nt (spec)*

-cheeked [-'tʃi:kd] ADJ *suf* -backig; **rosy-cheeked** rotbackig

cheekily ['tʃi:kɪlɪ] ADV frech, vorwitzig, dreist

cheekiness ['tʃi:kɪnɪs] N Frechheit *f*, Dreistigkeit *f*, Vorwitz *m (geh)*; *(of person also)* freche Art

cheeky ['tʃi:kɪ] ADJ *(+er) (Brit)* frech, vorwitzig, dreist; *remark, person, smile also* schnippisch; *hat, dress* kess, flott; *driving* schneidig, schnittig, frech; **it's a bit ~ asking for another pay rise so soon** es ist etwas unverschämt, schon wieder eine Gehaltserhöhung zu verlangen; **~ girl** freche Göre

cheep [tʃi:p] **N** Piep *m*, Piepser *m* **VI** piepsen

cheer [tʃɪə'] **N** **a** Hurra- *or* Beifallsruf *m*; *(= cheering)* Hurrageschrei *nt*, Jubel *m*; **to give three ~s for sb** jdn dreimal hochleben lassen, ein dreifaches Hoch auf jdn ausbringen; **three ~s for Mike!** ein dreifaches Hurra für Mike!; **~s!** *(inf: = your health)* prost!; *(Brit inf: = goodbye)* tschüs(s)! *(inf)*; *(Brit inf: = thank you)* danke schön!
b *(= comfort)* Aufmunterung *f*, Ermutigung *f*; **the news gave us some ~** die Nachricht munterte uns auf; **words of ~** aufmunternde Worte, Zuspruch *m*
c *(old)* **be of good ~** seid guten Mutes *or* wohlgemut *(old)*
d *(old, = food etc)* **good ~** Tafelfreude(n *pl*) *f (old)*
VT **a** *person* zujubeln *(+dat)*; *thing, event* bejubeln
b *(= gladden)* aufmuntern, aufheitern, froh machen
VI jubeln, hurra *or* Hurra rufen

► **cheer on** VT *sep* anspornen, anfeuern

► **cheer up** **VT** *sep* aufmuntern, aufheitern; *room, place* aufheitern; **he needed a bit of**

cheering up er brauchte etwas Aufmunterung *or* Aufheiterung; **tell him that, that'll cheer him up** sag ihm das, dann freut er sich **VI** *(person)* vergnügter *or* fröhlicher werden, bessere Laune bekommen; *(things)* besser werden; **cheer up!** lass den Kopf nicht hängen!, nun lach doch mal!; **cheer up, it's not that bad** Kopf hoch *or* nur Mut, so schlimm ist es auch wieder nicht

cheerful ['tʃɪəfʊl] ADJ fröhlich, vergnügt; *person also* gut gelaunt, heiter *(geh)*; *place, colour etc* heiter; *prospect, news* erfreulich; *tune* fröhlich; **to be ~ about sth** in Bezug auf etw optimistisch sein; **you're a ~ one, aren't you?** *(iro)* du bist (mir) vielleicht ein schöner Miesmacher *(inf)*; **that's ~!** *(iro)* das ist ja heiter!

cheerfully ['tʃɪəfəlɪ] ADV fröhlich, vergnügt; **I could ~ strangle him!** den könnte ich glatt umbringen

cheerfulness ['tʃɪəfʊlnɪs] N Fröhlichkeit *f*; *(of person also)* gute Laune, Vergnügtheit *f*, Frohsinn *m (geh)*; *(of place, colour etc)* Heiterkeit *f*; *(of prospect, news)* Erfreulichkeit *f*; *(of tune)* fröhlicher Charakter

cheerily ['tʃɪərɪlɪ] ADV fröhlich, vergnügt; **~ coloured** lustig angemalt

cheering ['tʃɪərɪŋ] **N** Jubel *m*, Jubeln *nt*, Hurrageschrei *nt*; *(= cheering on)* anfeuernde Zurufe *pl* **ADJ** **a** *news, prospect* beglückend **b** *crowds* jubelnd

cheerio ['tʃɪərɪ'əʊ] INTERJ *(esp Brit inf)* **a** *(= goodbye)* Wiedersehen *(inf)*, Servus *(S Ger, Aus)*; *(to friends)* tschüs(s) *(inf)* **b** *(= your health)* prost

cheerleader ['tʃɪəliːdə'] N *(Sport)* Cheerleader *m*

cheerless ['tʃɪəlɪs] ADJ freudlos, trüb; *person* trübselig, trübsinnig; *prospect* trübe, düster, traurig; *scenery* grau

cheers [tʃɪərz] INTERJ → **cheer N a**

cheery ['tʃɪərɪ] ADJ *(+er)* fröhlich, vergnügt; *tune, colour also* lustig

cheese [tʃiːz] N Käse *m*; **a big ~** *(inf)* ein hohes Tier *(inf)*; **hard ~!** *(dated inf)* Künstlerpech! *(inf)*; **say ~!** *(Phot)* bitte recht freundlich, sag „cheese"

cheese *in cpds* Käse-; **cheeseboard** N Käsebrett *nt*; *(= course)* Käseplatte *f*; **cheeseburger** N Cheeseburger *m*; **cheesecake** N *(Cook)* Käsekuchen *m*; *(sl: = female photos)* (nacktes) Fleisch *(inf)*; **cheesecloth** N Käseleinen *nt*, indische Baumwolle *f*

cheesed off [tʃiːzd'ɒf] ADJ *(Brit inf)* angeödet *(inf)*; **I'm ~ with this job/her** diese Arbeit/sie ödet mich an *(inf)* *or* stinkt mir *(inf)*

cheese: cheeseparing **N** Pfennigfuchserei *f* *(inf)*, Knauserei *f* **ADJ** knauserig, knickerig *(inf)*; **cheese straw** N *(Brit)* kleine Käsestange

cheesy ['tʃiːzɪ] ADJ *(+er)* **a** käsig; **to taste ~** nach Käse schmecken; **a ~ taste** ein Käsegeschmack; **a ~ smile** ein Lächeln *nt* wie aus der Zahnpastawerbung *(inf)* **b** *(inf) clothes (= tasteless)* geschmacklos; *(= old-fashioned)* altmodisch, out *(inf)*; **her outfit is totally ~** ihre Klamotten sind total aus der Mode *(inf)* **c** *(inf: = shoddy)* mies *(inf)*

cheetah ['tʃiːtə] N Gepard *m*

chef [ʃef] N Küchenchef *m*; *(as profession)* Koch *m*; *(= head chef)* Chefkoch *m*

Chelsea bun [ˌtʃelsɪ'bʌn] N *(Brit) Hefeteigbrötchen mit Rosinen*

Chelsea Pensioner [ˌtʃelsɪ'penʃənə'] N *(Brit) Armeeangehöriger im Ruhestand, der im „Chelsea Royal Hospital" wohnt*

chemical ['kemɪkəl] **ADJ** chemisch; **~ accident** Chemieunfall *m*; **~ castration** chemische Kastration **N** Chemikalie *f*

chemical: chemical engineer N Chemieingenieur(in) *m(f)*; **chemical engineering** N Chemotechnik *f*; **chemically** ['kemɪkəlɪ] ADV chemisch; **chemical toilet** N Chemietoilette *f*; **chemical warfare** N chemische Krieg(s)führung

chemise [ʃə'miːz] N Unterkleid *nt*

chemist ['kemɪst] N **a** *(= expert in chemistry)* Chemiker(in) *m(f)* **b** *(Brit: in shop)* Drogist(in) *m(f)*; *(dispensing)* Apotheker(in) *m(f)*; **~'s shop** Drogerie *f*; *(dispensing)* Apotheke *f*

chemistry ['kemɪstrɪ] N **a** Chemie *f*; *(= chemical make-up)* chemische Zusammensetzung; **~ set** Chemiebaukasten *m* **b** *(fig)* Verträglichkeit *f*; **the good ~ between them** ihre gute Verträglichkeit; **the ~ between us was perfect** wir haben uns sofort vertragen, es hat sofort zwischen uns gefunkt *(inf)*; **the ~'s all wrong (between us)** wir sind einfach zu verschieden; **the ~ of physical attraction/of love** das Kräftespiel der körperlichen Anziehung/in der Liebe

chemo ['kiːməʊ] *(inf) abbr of* **chemotherapy** Chemo *f (inf)*; **to have/need/undergo ~** (eine) Chemotherapie bekommen/brauchen/machen

chemotherapy [ˌkiːməʊ'θerəpɪ] N Chemotherapie *f*

chenille [ʃə'niːl] N Chenille *f*

cheque, *(US)* **check** [tʃek] ✪ 20.7 N Scheck *m*; **a ~ for £100** ein Scheck über £ 100; **to write out/to cash a ~** einen Scheck ausstellen/einlösen; **to pay by ~** mit (einem) Scheck bezahlen

cheque account N Girokonto *nt*

chequebook, *(US)* **checkbook** ['tʃekbʊk] N Scheckheft *nt*, Scheckbuch *nt*; **~ journalism** Scheckbuchjournalismus *m*

cheque card N Scheckkarte *f*

chequered, *(US)* **checkered** ['tʃekəd] ADJ *(lit)* kariert; *(= dappled)* gefleckt, gesprenkelt; *(fig) career, history, past* bewegt

chequered flag, *(US)* **checkered flag** N *(Motor Racing)* Zielflagge *f*

cherish ['tʃerɪʃ] VT **a** *person* liebevoll sorgen für; **to love and to ~** zu lieben und zu ehren **b** *feelings, hope* hegen; *idea, illusion* sich hingeben *(+dat)*; **I shall always ~ that memory/present** die Erinnerung (daran)/das Geschenk wird mir immer lieb und teuer sein; **to ~ sb's memory** jds Andenken in Ehren halten

cherished ['tʃerɪʃt] ADJ *dream, belief, ambition* lang gehegt, größte(r, s); **this is one of my ~ memories** daran erinnere ich mich gern zurück; **her most ~ possessions** die Dinge, an denen sie am meisten hängt

Cherokee (Indian) ['tʃerəʊkiː(ˈɪndɪən)] N Tscherokese *m*, Tscherokesin *f*

cheroot [ʃə'ruːt] N Stumpen *m*

cherry ['tʃerɪ] **N** Kirsche *f*; *(= colour)* Kirschrot *nt*; **wild ~** Vogelkirsche *f*; **life isn't exactly a bowl of cherries for her right now** das Leben ist für sie im Moment kein Zuckerlecken **ADJ** *(colour)* kirschrot; *(Cook)* Kirsch-

cherry *in cpds* Kirsch-; **cherry blossom** N Kirschblüte *f*; **cherry bomb** N *(US)* Knallerbse *f*; **cherry brandy** N Cherry Brandy *m*; **cherry orchard** N Kirschgarten *m*; **cherry-pick** *(fig inf)* **VT** die Rosinen herauspicken aus *(inf)* **VI** sich *(dat)* die Rosinen herauspicken; **cherry picker** N *(= vehicle)* Bockkran *m*; **cherry-red** ADJ kirschrot; **cherry tomato** N Kirschtomate *f*, Cherrytomate *f*

chert [tʃɜːt] N *(Min)* Kieselschiefer *m*, Feuerstein *m*, Hornstein *m*; *(Build)* Gneiszuschlag(stoff) &, Feingranitzuschlag *m (für Sichtbeton)*

cherub ['tʃerəb] N **a** *pl* **-im** ['tʃerəbɪm] *(Eccl)* Cherub *m* **b** *pl* **-s** *(Art)* Putte *f*, Putto *m (form)*; *(= baby)* Engelchen *nt*

chervil ['tʃɜːvɪl] N Kerbel *m*

Cheshire cat [ˌtʃeʃə'kæt] N **to grin like a ~** breit grinsen

chess [tʃes] N Schach(spiel) *nt*

chess: chessboard N Schachbrett *nt*; **chessman**, **chesspiece** N Schachfigur *f*; **chess piece** N Schachfigur *f*; **chess set** N Schachspiel *nt*

chest¹ [tʃest] N *(for tea, tools etc)* Kiste *f*; *(= piece of furniture, for clothes, money etc)* Truhe *f*; **~ of drawers** Kommode *f*

chest² N *(Anat)* Brust *f*, Brustkorb *m (esp Med)*; **the boxer's broad ~** der breite Brustkasten des Boxers; **to measure sb's ~** jds Brustweite *or* Brustumfang messen; **to get sth off one's ~** *(fig inf)* sich *(dat)* etw von der Seele reden, etw loswerden; **to have a weak ~** schwach auf der Brust sein *(inf)*; **a cold on the ~** *(Brit)* **a ~ cold** Bronchialkatarr(h) *m*; **~ pains** Schmerzen *pl* in der Brust

-chested [-'tʃestɪd] ADJ *suf* -brüstig; **flat-chested** flachbrüstig

chesterfield ['tʃestəfiːld] N Chesterfieldsofa *nt*

chest infection N Lungeninfekt *m*

chestnut ['tʃesnʌt] **N** **a** *(= nut, tree)* Kastanie *f* **b** *(= colour)* Kastanienbraun *nt* **c** *(= horse)* Fuchs *m* **d** *(inf, = old joke)* alte *or* olle Kamelle *(inf)* **ADJ** *(colour) hair* kastanienbraun, rötlich braun; **a ~ horse** ein Fuchs *m*

chest pain N Brustschmerz *m*

chest specialist N Facharzt *m*/-ärztin *f* für Lungenkrankheiten, Lungenfacharzt *m*/-ärztin *f*

chesty ['tʃestɪ] ADJ *(+er)* *(Brit inf) person* erkältet, grippig *(inf)*; *cough* rau, schnarrend; **I'm a bit ~ this morning** ich habs heute etwas auf der Brust *(inf)*

cheval glass [ʃə'vælglɑːs] N Standspiegel *m* (zum Kippen)

chevron ['ʃevrən] N Winkel *m*

chew [tʃuː] **N** Kauen *nt*; **to have a good ~ on sth** auf *or* an etw *(dat)* gründlich herumkauen **VT** kauen; **this meat requires a lot of ~ing** an *or* bei diesem Fleisch muss man viel (herum)kauen; **that dog's been ~ing the carpet again** der Hund hat schon wieder am Teppich genagt; **don't ~ your fingernails** kaue nicht an deinen Nägeln; **she always ~s her nails when she's nervous** immer, wenn sie nervös ist, kaut sie an den Nägeln; **to ~ the fat** *(inf)* tratschen *(inf)* → **cud**

▶ **chew away** **VI** lange herumkauen *(at* an *or* auf *+dat)*; **the rats have been chewing away at the woodwork** die Ratten haben am Holz herumgenagt **VT** *sep* wegfressen

▶ **chew off** *or* **out** VT *sep (US inf)* zur Schnecke machen *(inf)*

▶ **chew on** VI *+prep obj* **a** *(lit)* (herum)kauen auf *(+dat)* **b** *(also* **chew over***: inf) facts, problem* sich *(dat)* durch den Kopf gehen lassen

▶ **chew up** VT *sep* **a** *(lit)* aufessen, fertig essen; *(animal)* auffressen; *pencil etc* zerkauen; *ground, road surface* zerstören; *paper* zerfressen, zermalmen **b** *(inf, = tell off)* fertigmachen *(inf)*, runterputzen *(inf)*

chewing gum ['tʃuːɪŋgʌm] N Kaugummi *m or nt*

chewy ['tʃuːɪ] ADJ *meat* zäh; *pasta* kernig; *sweets* weich

chiaroscuro [kɪˌɑːrəs'kʊərəʊ] N Chiaroscuro *nt*, Helldunkel *nt*

chic [ʃiːk] **ADJ** *(+er)* chic, schick, elegant **N** Schick *m*, Chic *m*

chicane [ʃɪ'keɪn] N *(Sport)* Schikane *f*

chicanery [ʃɪ'keɪnərɪ] N *(= trickery)* Machenschaften *pl*; *(legal)* Winkelzüge *pl*

Chicano [tʃɪ'kɑːnəʊ] N *(= Mexican American) pl* **Chicanos** Chicano *m*

chichi ['tʃiːtʃiː] ADJ *(inf)* todschick *(inf)*, auf schön gemacht *(inf)*; *dress etc* verspielt, niedlich

chick [tʃɪk] N **a** *(of chicken)* Küken *nt*; *(= young bird)* Junge(s) *nt* **b** *(inf: = child)* Kleine(s) *nt* **c** *(inf: = girl)* Mieze *f (inf)*; **she's some ~** sie ist nicht ohne *(inf)*

chicken ['tʃɪkɪn] **N** **a** Huhn *nt*; *(for roasting, frying)* Hähnchen *nt*; **she's no ~** *(inf)* sie ist nicht mehr die Jüngste; **~ liver** Hühner- *or* Geflügelleber *f*; **to run around like a headless ~** wie ein kopfloses Huhn herumlaufen; **don't count your ~s (before they're hatched)** *(Prov)* man soll den Tag nicht vor dem Abend loben *(Prov)*; **it's a ~ and egg situation** *(inf)* das ist eine Zwickmühle **b** *(inf, = coward)* feiges Huhn *(inf)*, Feigling *m* **ADJ** *(inf)* feig; **he's ~** er ist ein Feigling *or* ein feiges Huhn *(inf)*; **he's too ~ to do it** er ist zu feig(e)

▶ **chicken out** VI *(inf)* kneifen *(inf)*

chicken *in cpds* Hühner-; **chicken farmer** N Hühnerzüchter *m*; **chicken feed** N **a** *(lit)* Hühnerfutter *nt* **b** *(inf: = insignificant sum)* ein paar Cent; **they expect us to work for ~** sie erwarten, dass wir für 'n Appel und 'n Ei arbeiten *(inf)*; **chicken flu** N Hühnergrippe *f*; **chicken-hearted, chicken-livered** ADJ feige, hasenherzig *(old, liter)*; **chickenpox** N Windpocken *pl*; **chicken run** N Hühnerhof *m*, Auslauf *m*; **chickenshit** *(US sl)* **N** **a** *(= coward)* Angsthase *m (inf)*, Memme *f (pej inf)* **b** *no pl* **to be ~** *(= be worthless)* Scheiße sein *(sl)*, einen Dreck wert sein *(inf)* **ADJ** **a** *(= cowardly)* feige **b** *(= worthless)* beschissen *(inf)*; **chicken wire** N Hühnerdraht *m*

chick: **chick flick** N *(inf)* Frauenfilm *m*, Schnulze *f (inf pej)*; **chick lit** N *(inf)* Frauenroman *m*, Frauenbuch *nt*; **chickpea** ['tʃɪkpi:] N Kichererbse *f*; **chickweed** N Sternmiere *f*

chicle ['tʃɪkl] N Chiclegummi *m*

chicory ['tʃɪkərɪ] N Chicorée *f or m*, Schikoree *f or m*; *(in coffee)* Zichorie *f*

chide [tʃaɪd] *pret* **chid** *(old) or* **chided** [tʃɪd, 'tʃaɪdɪd] *ptp* **chided** *or* **chidden** *(old)* ['tʃɪdn] VT schelten, rügen

chief [tʃi:f] **N** *pl* **-s** **a** *(of organization)* Leiter(in) *m(f)*, Chef(in) *m(f) (inf)*; *(of clan)* Oberhaupt *nt*; *(of tribe)* Häuptling *m*; *(of gang)* Anführer(in) *m(f)*; *(inf: = boss)* Boss *m (inf)*, Chef *m*; **~ of police** Polizeipräsident(in) *or* -chef(in) *m(f)*; **~ of staff** *(Mil)* Stabschef(in) *m(f)*; **~ of state** Staatschef(in) *m(f)*
b *(Her)* Schildhaupt *nt*
c **in ~** hauptsächlich
ADJ **a** *(= most important)* Haupt-, wichtigste(r, s), bedeutendste(r, s); **the ~ thing** das Wichtigste, die Hauptsache; **~ reason** Hauptgrund *m*
b *(= most senior)* Haupt-, Ober-, erste(r); **~ clerk** Bürochef *m*; **~ executive officer** Hauptgeschäftsführer(in) *m(f)*, Generaldirektor(in) *m(f)*, Vorstandsvorsitzende(r) *m(f)*; **Chief Secretary (to the Treasury)** *(Brit Pol)* stellvertretender Finanzminister, stellvertretende Finanzministerin; **~ of staff** (General)stabschef(in) *m(f)*

chief constable N *(Brit)* Polizeipräsident(in) *m(f) or* -chef(in) *m(f)*

chief justice N *(Brit)* ≈ Oberrichter(in) *m(f)*; *(US)* Oberster Bundesrichter, Oberste Bundesrichterin

chiefly ['tʃi:flɪ] ADV hauptsächlich, in erster Linie, vor allem

chieftain ['tʃi:ftən] N *(of tribe)* Häuptling *m*; *(of clan)* Oberhaupt *nt*, Älteste(r) *m*; *(of robber band)* Hauptmann *m*; **the village ~** der Dorfälteste

> **CHIEF WHIP**
>
> Im britischen Parlamentssystem sind die **Chief Whips** (Fraktionsführer) die Abgeordneten, die für die Einhaltung der Parteidisziplin im Unterhaus sorgen. Sowohl die Regierungspartei wie auch die Opposition haben einen **Chief Whip**, der die Abgeordneten seiner Partei über die Parlamentsgeschäfte auf dem Laufenden hält, der den Parteichef über die Ansichten der Hinterbänkler informiert und der vor allem darauf achtet, dass alle Abgeordneten bei wichtigen Abstimmungen auch anwesend sind und ihre Stimme abgeben. Diese letzte Aufgabe ist gerade dann besonders wichtig, wenn die Regierung nur über eine knappe Mehrheit im Unterhaus verfügt.

chiffon ['ʃɪfɒn] **N** Chiffon *m* **ADJ** Chiffon-

chignon ['ʃi:njɒŋ] N Nackenknoten *m*, Chignon *m*

chihuahua [tʃɪ'waʊwɑ:] N Chihuahua *m*

chilblain ['tʃɪlbleɪn] N Frostbeule *f*

child [tʃaɪld] N *pl* **children** *(lit, fig)* Kind *nt*; **when I was a ~** in *or* zu meiner Kindheit; **she was with ~** *(old, liter)* sie trug ein Kind unter ihrem Herzen *(old, liter)*; **the ~ of ignorance** das Produkt der Unwissenheit

child *in cpds* Kinder-; **child abuse** N Kindesmisshandlung *f*; *(sexually)* Kindesmissbrauch *m*, Notzucht *f* mit Kindern; **child abuser** N *jd, der Kinder misshandelt (sexually)* Kinderschänder(in) *m(f)*; **child allowance** N *(Brit inf)* Kindergeld *nt*; **child-bearing** **N** Mutterschaft *f*, Kinderkriegen *nt (inf)*; **ten years of ~ exhausted her** zehn Jahre mit kleinen Kindern erschöpften sie **ADJ** **of ~ age** im gebärfähigen Alter; **good ~ hips** gebärfreudiges Becken; **child bed** N *(old)* Kind- *or* Wochenbett *nt*; **to be in ~** im Wochenbett liegen; **child benefit** N *(Brit)* Kindergeld *nt*; **childbirth** N Geburt *f*, Gebären *nt*; **to die in ~** bei der Geburt sterben; **child bride** N kindliche *or* sehr junge Braut; **childcare** N Kinderbetreuung *f*; *(= social work department)* Jugendfürsorge *f*, Jugendhilfe *f*; **child-friendly** ADJ kinderfreundlich; **child guidance** N Erziehungsberatung *f*; *(= social work agency)* Erziehungsberatungsstelle *f*; **childhood** N Kindheit *f*; **to be in one's second ~** seine zweite Kindheit erleben

childish ['tʃaɪldɪʃ] ADJ *(pej)* kindisch

childishly ['tʃaɪldɪʃlɪ] ADV *(pej)* kindisch; **~ simple** kinderleicht

childishness ['tʃaɪldɪʃnɪs] N *(pej)* kindisches Gehabe

child: **child labour**, *(US)* **child labor** N Kinderarbeit *f*; **childless** ADJ kinderlos; **childlike** ADJ kindlich; **child lock** N Kindersicherung *f*; **childminder** N *(Brit)* Tagesmutter *f*; **childminding** N *(Brit)* Beaufsichtigung *f* von Kindern; **child molester** N *Person, die Kinder (sexuell) belästigt*; **child prodigy** N Wunderkind *nt*; **childproof** ADJ kindersicher; **Child Protection Register** N *(Brit) von örtlichen Sozialbehörden geführte Liste von Kindern, die dem Kinderschutzprogramm unterstellt sind*; **child reduction** N Kinderermäßigung *f*

children ['tʃɪldrən] *pl of* **child**

children's channel N *(TV)* Kinderkanal *m*

children's department N *(in department store)* Kinderabteilung *f*

child: **child-resistant** ADJ bruchsicher; **child seat** N Kindersitz *m*; **child sex** **N** Kindersex *m* **ADJ** *attr* Kindersex-; **~ tourism** Kindersextourismus *m*; **~ abuser** Kinderschänder(in) *m(f)*; **child's play** N ein Kinderspiel *nt*; **child's seat** N = **child seat**; **Child Support Agency** N *(Brit) staatliche Organisation, die sich um Unterhaltszahlungen für Kinder kümmert*; **child welfare** N Jugendfürsorge *f*; **Child Welfare Centre** Kinderabteilung *f* im Gesundheitsamt

Chile ['tʃɪlɪ] N Chile *nt*

Chilean ['tʃɪlɪən] **ADJ** chilenisch **N** Chilene *m*, Chilenin *f*

chill [tʃɪl] **N** **a** Frische *f*; **there's quite a ~ in the air** es ist ziemlich frisch; **the sun took the ~ off the water** die Sonne hat das Wasser ein bisschen erwärmt; **you should take the ~ off the wine** Sie sollten den Wein nicht so eiskalt servieren
b *(Med)* fieberhafte Erkältung; *(= shiver)* Schauder *m*, Frösteln *nt*; **to catch a ~** sich verkühlen
c *(fig)* **a distinct ~ in East/West relations** eine deutliche Abkühlung der Ost-West-Beziehungen; **his presence cast a ~ over the meeting** durch seine Anwesenheit wurde das Treffen sehr kühl *or* frostig
ADJ *(lit)* kühl, frisch; *(fig liter) reception* kühl, frostig
VT **a** *(lit) wine, meat* kühlen; **I was ~ed to the bone** *or* **marrow** die Kälte ging mir bis auf die Knochen
b *(fig) blood* gefrieren lassen
VI *(inf)* chillen *(sl)*, relaxen *(sl)*

▶ **chill out** VI *(inf)* relaxen *(sl)*

chill cabinet N *(Brit)* Kühlvitrine *f*

chiller ['tʃɪlə'] N *(inf)* Gruselgeschichte *f*; *(= film)* Gruselfilm *m*

chilli, *(US)* **chili** ['tʃɪlɪ] N Peperoni *pl*; *(= spice, meal)* Chili *m*

chill(i)ness ['tʃɪl(ɪ)nɪs] N *(lit)* Kühle *f*, Frische *f*; *(fig)* Kühle *f*, Frostigkeit *f*

chilling ['tʃɪlɪŋ] ADJ *look* frostig, eisig; *prospect, thought* äußerst unerquicklich, beunruhigend; *reminder, message, warning, words* schrecklich, schreckenerregend; *sight, story, account* grauenhaft, schaudererregend

chillingly ['tʃɪlɪŋlɪ] ADV *(+adj)* beunruhigend, beängstigend; *reminiscent, similar* schrecklich; *(+vb)*schaudererregend; **the voice was ~ familiar** die Stimme klang auf beunruhigende Art vertraut; **they have ~ demonstrated how ...** sie haben auf erschreckende Weise gezeigt, wie ...

chill-out ['tʃɪlaʊt] ADJ *(inf) music* zum Relaxen *(inf)*; **~ room** Ruheraum *m (in dem sich die Besucher eines Rave Clubs erholen können)*, Chill-out *m (sl)*

chill pill N *(esp US sl)* Beruhigungsmittel *nt*; **take a ~** reg dich ab *(inf)*, bleib mal locker *(inf)*

chilly ['tʃɪlɪ] ADJ *(+er) weather* kühl, frisch; *manner, look, smile etc* kühl, frostig; **to feel ~** frösteln, frieren; **I feel ~** mich fröstelts, mir ist kühl

chime [tʃaɪm] **N** Glockenspiel *nt*, Geläut *nt*; *(of doorbell)* Läuten *nt no pl* **VT** schlagen **VI** läuten

▶ **chime in** VI *(inf)* sich einschalten

▶ **chime in with** VI *+prep obj (plans)* in Einklang stehen mit

chimera [kaɪ'mɪərə] N Chimäre *f*; *(fig)* Schimäre *f*

chimerical [kaɪ'merɪkəl] ADJ schimärisch

chimney ['tʃɪmnɪ] N Schornstein *m*; *(on factory also)* Schlot *m*; *(= open fireplace)* Kamin *m*; *(of lamp)* Zylinder *m*; *(of stove)* Rauchfang *m*; *(Mountaineering)* Kamin *m*; **to smoke like a ~** *(inf)* wie ein Schlot rauchen *(inf)*

chimney: **chimney breast** N Kaminvorsprung *m*; **chimneypiece** N Kaminsims *m*; **chimneypot** N Schornsteinkopf *m*; **chimney stack** N Schornstein *m*; **chimney sweep** N Schornsteinfeger *m*

chimp [tʃɪmp] *(inf)*, **chimpanzee** [ˌtʃɪmpæn'zi:] N Schimpanse *m*

chin [tʃɪn] **N** Kinn *nt*; **to have a weak/strong ~** wenig Kinn/ein ausgeprägtes Kinn haben; **to keep one's ~ up** die Ohren steifhalten *(inf)*; **keep your ~ up!** Kopf hoch!, nur Mut!; **he took it on the ~** *(fig inf)* er hats mit Fassung getragen **VT** *(Sport)* **to ~ the bar** einen Klimmzug machen

China ['tʃaɪnə] N China *nt*

china ['tʃaɪnə] **N** Porzellan *nt* **ADJ** Porzellan-; **~ cabinet** Porzellanvitrine *f*

china: **china blue** N Kobaltblau *nt*; **china clay** N Kaolin *m*; **Chinaman** N Chinese *m*; *(US pej)* Schlitzauge *nt*; **China Sea** N **East/South ~** Ost-/Südchinesisches Meer; **Chinatown** N Chinesenviertel *nt*; **chinaware** N Porzellanware(n *pl*) *f*

chinchilla [tʃɪn'tʃɪlə] N Chinchilla *f*; *(= fur)* Chinchilla(pelz) *m*

Chinese [tʃaɪ'ni:z] **N** **a** *(= person)* Chinese *m*, Chinesin *f* **b** *(= language, fig: = gibberish)* Chinesisch *nt* **c** *(inf: = restaurant)* Chinarestaurant *nt*; *(= meal)* chinesisches Essen **ADJ** chinesisch; **~ restaurant** Chinarestaurant *nt*

Chinese: **Chinese cabbage** N Chinakohl *m*; **Chinese lantern** N Lampion *m*; **Chinese leaves** N Chinakohl *m*; **Chinese puzzle** N *ein Gegenstand zum Zusammensetzen als Geduldsspiel*; **Chinese red** N Zinnoberrot *nt*; **Chinese studies** PL Sinologie *f*; **Chinese wall** N *(fig)* unüberwindliches Hindernis; **Chi-**

nese whispers N stille Post; **to have a game of ~** stille Post spielen; **Chinese white** N Chinesischweiß *nt*

chink[1] [tʃɪŋk] **N** Riss *m*, Ritze *f*; *(in door)* Spalt *m*; **a ~ of light** ein dünner Lichtstreifen *or* -strahl; **the ~ in sb's armour** *(fig)* jds schwacher Punkt **VT** *(US)* stopfen

chink[2] **N** *(= sound)* Klirren *nt*; *(of coins)* Klimpern *nt* **VT** klirren mit; *coins* klimpern mit **VI** klirren; *(coins)* klimpern

Chink [tʃɪŋk] N *(pej)* Schlitzauge *nt*, Chinese *m*, Chinesin *f*

chinkie ['tʃɪŋkɪ] *(inf)* **N** *(= restaurant)* Chinarestaurant *nt*; *(= meal)* chinesisches Essen **ADJ** *(esp pej) restaurant, meal* chinesisch

chin: **chinless** ADJ **to be ~** *(lit)* ein fliehendes Kinn haben; *(fig)* willensschwach sein; **~ wonder** *(hum)* leicht vertrottelter Vertreter der Oberschicht; **chin rest** N Kinnstütze *f*; **chin strap** N Kinnriemen *m*

chintz [tʃɪnts] **N** Chintz *m* **ATTR** *curtains* Chintz-

chintzy ['tʃɪntsɪ] ADJ *(+er)* schmuck; *(pej)* kitschig

chin-up ['tʃɪnʌp] N Klimmzug *m*

chinwag ['tʃɪnwæg] N *(Brit inf)* Schwatz *m (inf)*

chip [tʃɪp] **N** **a** Splitter *m*; *(of glass also)* Scherbe *f*; *(of wood)* Span *m*; **chocolate ~s** ≈ Schokoladenstreusel *pl*; **he's a ~ off the old block** er ist ganz der Vater; **to have a ~ on one's shoulder** einen Komplex haben (*about* wegen); **sb with a ~ on his shoulder** jd, der sich ständig angegriffen fühlt
b *(Brit: = potato stick)* Pomme frite *m or nt usu pl*; *(US: = potato slice)* Chip *m usu pl*
c *(in crockery, furniture etc)* abgeschlagene *or* abgestoßene Ecke *or* Stelle; **this cup has a ~** diese Tasse ist angeschlagen
d *(in poker etc)* Chip *m*, Spielmarke *f*; **to cash in one's ~s** *(euph)* den Löffel abgeben *(euph inf)*; **he's had his ~s** *(inf)* (d)er hat ausgespielt *(inf)*; **to be in the ~s** *(US inf)* Kleingeld haben *(inf)*, flüssig sein *(inf)*; **when the ~s are down** wenn es drauf ankommt
e **to give the ball a ~** *(Golf, Tennis)* den Ball chippen
f *(Comput: = microchip)* Chip *nt*
VT **a** *cup, stone* anschlagen; *varnish, paint* abstoßen; *wood* beschädigen; *(= chip off)* wegschlagen, abstoßen
b *(Sport) ball* chippen
VI *(cup etc)* angeschlagen werden, Macken/eine Macke bekommen *(inf)*; *(paint)* abspringen; *(stone)* splittern; **this pottery ~s easily** diese Keramik ist schnell angeschlagen

▶ **chip away** **VT** *sep* weghauen; **the woodpecker chipped away the bark** der Specht hackte die Rinde ab **VI** **the sculptor chipped away until ...** der Bildhauer meißelte am Stein herum, bis ...

▶ **chip away at** VI +PREP OBJ *authority, system* unterminieren; *debts* reduzieren, verringern; **to chip away at sb's image** jds Image ankratzen, jdn demontieren

▶ **chip in** VI *(inf)* **a** *(= interrupt)* sich einschalten **b** *(= contribute)* **he chipped in with £3** er steuerte £ 3 bei; **would you like to chip in?** würdest du gerne etwas beisteuern?

▶ **chip off** **VT** *sep paint etc* wegschlagen; *piece of china* abstoßen, abschlagen **VI** *(paint etc)* absplittern

chip basket N Frittiersieb *nt*

chipboard ['tʃɪpbɔːd] N Spanholz *nt*; **piece of ~** Spanplatte *f*

chipmunk ['tʃɪpmʌŋk] N Backenhörnchen *nt*

chipolata [tʃɪpə'lɑːtə] N *(Brit)* Cocktailwürstchen *nt*

chip pan N Fritteuse *f*

chipped [tʃɪpt] ADJ **a** *cup, bone, tooth, enamel, step* angeschlagen, abgestoßen, beschädigt; *paint, nail varnish* abgesplittert; **to be badly ~** stark angeschlagen sein **b** *(Brit Cook)* **~ potatoes** Pommes frites *pl*

Chippendale ['tʃɪpəndeɪl] ADJ Chippendale-; **~ chair** Chippendalestuhl *m*

chipper[1] ['tʃɪpə'] ADJ *(inf)* lebhaft, munter

chipper[2] ['tʃɪpə'] N *(inf: = fish and chip shop)* Fish-and-chips-Imbiss *m*

chippie ['tʃɪpɪ] N = **chippy b**

chippings ['tʃɪpɪŋz] PL Splitter *pl*; *(of wood)* Späne *pl*; *(= road chippings)* Schotter *m*

chippy ['tʃɪpɪ] N *(inf)* **a** *(= joiner)* Schreiner *m* **b** *(= chip shop)* Imbiss- *or* Frittenbude *f (inf)*

chip shop N *(Brit)* Imbiss- *or* Frittenbude *f (inf)*

chip shot N *(Golf)* Chip(shot) *m*; *(Tennis)* Chip *m*

chiromancer ['kaɪərəmænsə'] N Chiromant(in) *m(f)*

chiromancy ['kaɪərəmænsɪ] N Chiromantie *f*

chiropodist [kɪ'rɒpədɪst] N Fußpfleger(in) *m(f)*

chiropody [kɪ'rɒpədɪ] N Fußpflege *f*

chiropractic [,kaɪərə'præktɪk] N Chiropraktik *f*

chiropractor ['kaɪərəʊ,præktə'] N Chiropraktiker(in) *m(f)*

chirp [tʃɜːp] **VI** *(birds)* zwitschern; *(crickets)* zirpen **N** *(of birds)* Piepser *m*; *(= chirping)* Piepsen *nt no pl*, Zwitschern *nt no pl*; *(of crickets)* Zirpen *nt no pl*; **I don't want to hear another ~ out of you** ich möchte keinen Muckser mehr von dir hören *(inf)*

chirpy ['tʃɜːpɪ] ADJ *(+er) (inf)* munter

chirrup ['tʃɪrəp] = **chirp**

chisel ['tʃɪzl] **N** Meißel *m*; *(for wood)* Beitel *m* **VT** meißeln; *(in wood)* stemmen; **her finely ~led features** ihr fein geschnittenes Gesicht

chit[1] [tʃɪt] N junges Ding; **she's a mere ~ of a girl** sie ist ja noch ein halbes Kind

chit[2] N (*also* **chit of paper**) Zettel *m*

chitchat ['tʃɪttʃæt] N *(inf)* Geschwätz *nt*, Gerede *nt*

chivalric ['ʃɪvəlrɪk] ADJ ritterlich

chivalrous ADJ, **chivalrously** ADV ['ʃɪvəlrəs, -lɪ] ritterlich

chivalry ['ʃɪvəlrɪ] N Ritterlichkeit *f*; *(medieval concept)* Rittertum *nt*; **~ is not dead** es gibt noch Kavaliere

chives [tʃaɪvz] N Schnittlauch *m*

chivvy ['tʃɪvɪ] VT *(Brit inf: also* **chivvy along** *or* **up**) antreiben; **to ~ sb into doing sth** jdn dazu antreiben, etw zu tun

chlorate ['klɔːreɪt] N Chlorat *nt*

chloric ['klɔːrɪk] ADJ chlorig, chlorhaltig

chloric acid N Chlorsäure *f*

chloride ['klɔːraɪd] N Chlorid *nt*; **~ of lime** Chlorkalk *m*

chlorinate ['klɒrɪneɪt] VT *water* chloren

chlorination [klɒrɪ'neɪʃən] N *(of water)* Chloren *nt*

chlorine ['klɔːriːn] N Chlor *nt*

chlorofluorocarbon [,klɒrəʊfluərə'kɑːbən] N Chlorfluorkohlenwasserstoff *m*

chloroform ['klɒrəfɔːm] **N** Chloroform *nt* **VT** mit Chloroform betäuben, eine Chloroformnarkose geben *(+dat)*

chlorophyll ['klɒrəfɪl] N Chlorophyll *nt*

choc [tʃɒk] N *(Brit inf)* Praline *f*; **box of ~s** Schachtel *f* Pralinen

choc-ice ['tʃɒkaɪs] N Eismohrle *nt (Eiscreme mit Schokoladenüberzug)*

chock [tʃɒk] **N** Bremskeil *m*, Bremsklotz *m*; *(Naut) (under boat)* Bock *m*; *(for cables)* Lippe *f*, Lippklampe *f*; **~s away** Bremsklötze weg **VT** *wheel* blockieren; *boat* aufbocken

chock-a-block ['tʃɒkəblɒk] ADJ *(esp Brit inf)*, **chock-full** ['tʃɒkfʊl] ADJ *(inf)* knüppelvoll *(inf)*, gerammelt voll *(inf)*

chocoholic [,tʃɒkə'hɒlɪk] N *(inf)* Schokoladensüchtige(r) *mf*; **to be a ~** nach Schokolade süchtig sein

chocolate ['tʃɒklɪt] **N** **a** Schokolade *f*; **(hot *or* drinking) ~** Schokolade *f*, Kakao *m*; **a ~** eine Praline **b** *(= colour)* Schokoladenbraun *nt* **ADJ** Schokoladen-; *(= chocolate-coloured)* schokoladenbraun; **~ pudding** Schokoladenkuchen *m*; *(= whip)* Schokoladenpudding *m*; **~ sauce** Schokoladensoße *f*

chocolate: **chocolate bar** N *(= slab)* Tafel *f* Schokolade; *(= Mars® bar etc)* Schokoladenriegel *m*; **chocolate biscuit** N Schokoladenkeks *m*; **chocolate box** N Pralinenschachtel *f*; **chocolate-box** ADJ *look, picture* Postkarten-; **chocolate cake** N Schokoladenkuchen *m*; **chocolate-coloured** ADJ schokoladenbraun; **chocolate-flavoured** ADJ mit Schokoladengeschmack; **chocolate fudge cake** N Schokoladencremetorte *f*; **chocolate sauce** N Schokoladensoße *f*

choice [tʃɔɪs] ✪ 1.1, 10.1, 18.3 **N** **a** *(= act of, possibility of choosing)* Wahl *f*; **it's your ~** du hast die Wahl; **to make a ~** eine Wahl treffen; **to take one's ~** sich *(dat)* etwas aussuchen; **I didn't do it from ~** ich habe es mir nicht ausgesucht; **he had no *or* little ~ but to obey** er hatte keine (andere) Wahl *or* es blieb ihm nichts anderes übrig, als zu gehorchen; **if I had the ~ I would ...** wenn ich die Wahl hätte, würde ich ...; **the prize is a holiday of your (own) ~** zu gewinnen ist eine Urlaubsreise an einen Ort Ihrer Wahl
b *(= person, thing chosen)* Wahl *f*; **it was your ~** du wolltest es ja so
c *(= variety to choose from)* Auswahl *f* (*of* an *+dat*, von)
ADJ **a** *(Comm) goods, fruit, wine* Qualitäts-, erstklassig
b *language (= elegant)* gewählt; *(euph: = vulgar)* der/die/das sich gewaschen hat *(inf)*

choicest [tʃɔɪsəst] ADJ allerfeinste(r, s), auserlesen

choir ['kwaɪə'] N **a** Chor *m*; **you are singing to the ~** *(US: inf)* du rennst offene Türen ein **b** *(Archit)* Chor(raum) *m*

choir *in cpds* Chor-; **choirboy** N Chor- *or* Sängerknabe *m*; **choir loft** N Chorempore *f*; **choir master** N Chorleiter *m*; **choir practice** N Chorprobe *f*; **choir school** N Konvikt *nt* für Sängerknaben; **choir stall** N Chorstuhl *m*; **choir stalls** PL Chorgestühl *nt*

choke [tʃəʊk] **VT** **a** *person* ersticken; *(= throttle)* (er)würgen, erdrosseln; **don't eat so fast, you'll ~ yourself** iss nicht so schnell, sonst erstickst du daran; **to ~ the life out of sb/sth** *(lit, fig)* jdm/einer Sache den Garaus machen; **in a voice ~d with tears/emotion** mit tränenerstickter/tief bewegter Stimme **b** *(fig) pipe, tube, street* verstopfen; *fire, plants* ersticken **VI** ersticken (*on* an *+dat*); **he was choking with laughter/anger** er erstickte fast *or* halb vor Lachen/Wut **N** *(Aut)* Choke *m*, Starterzug *m*; **give it a bit of ~** zieh den Choke etwas heraus

▶ **choke back** VT *sep feelings, tears, reply* unterdrücken

▶ **choke down** VT *sep* hinunterschlucken

▶ **choke off** VT *sep* **a** *supplies* drosseln; **raising taxes could choke off the recovery** eine Steuererhöhung könnte den Erholungsprozess beeinträchtigen **b** *(inf) person (= interrupt)* das Wort abschneiden *+dat*; *(= put off)* abwimmeln *(inf)* **c** *(inf, = make fed up)* **I'm choked off** mir stinkts! *(inf)*

▶ **choke up** VT *sep* **a** *(= block) pipe, drain etc* verstopfen **b** *(usu pass) voice* ersticken; **you sound a bit choked up** du klingst etwas verschnupft **c** **to get/be choked up** *(inf)* ganz fuchsig *(inf)* werden/sein (*about* wegen)

choke chain N Stachelhalsband *nt*

choked [tʃəʊkt] ADJ *(inf)* pikiert

chokedamp ['tʃəʊkdæmp] N *(Brit)* Ferch *m*, böse *or* giftige Wetter *pl*

choker ['tʃəʊkə'] N *(= collar)* Vatermörder *m*; *(= necklace)* enger Halsreif; *(of velvet etc)* Kropfband *nt*

choking ['tʃəʊkɪŋ] ADJ **a** *smoke, fumes* beißend; **~ dust** Staub *m*, der einem die Luft zum Atmen nimmt **b** *sob, moan, gasp* erstickt

choler ['kɒlə'] N *(old, = bile)* (gelbe) Galle; *(= bad temper)* Zorn *m*

cholera ['kɒlərə] N Cholera *f*

choleric ['kɒlərɪk] ADJ cholerisch, leicht aufbrausend

cholesterol [kɒ'lestərəl] N Cholesterin *nt*

cholesterol inhibitor [kɒ,lestərəlɪn'hɪbɪtə'] N *(Med)* Cholesterinhemmer *m*

chomp [tʃɒmp] VT laut mahlen; *(person)* mampfen *(inf)*

choo-choo ['tʃu:tʃu:] N *(baby-talk: = train)* Puffpuff *f (baby-talk)*

choose [tʃu:z] *pret* **chose**, *ptp* **chosen** VT **a** *(= select)* (aus)wählen, sich *(dat)* aussuchen; **to ~ a team** eine Mannschaft auswählen *or* zusammenstellen; **they chose him as their leader** *or* **to be their leader** sie wählten ihn zu ihrem Anführer; **in a few well-chosen words** in wenigen wohlgesetzten Worten
b *(= decide, elect)* **to ~ to do sth** es vorziehen, etw zu tun; **may I come earlier? – if you ~ to** darf ich früher kommen? – wenn Sie wollen
VI **a** **to ~ (between** *or* **among/from)** wählen *or* eine Wahl treffen (zwischen *+dat*/aus *or* unter *+dat*); **there is nothing** *or* **little to ~ between them** sie sind gleich gut; **there aren't many to ~ from** die Auswahl ist nicht sehr groß
b *(= decide, elect)* **as/if you ~** wie/wenn Sie wollen

choos(e)y ['tʃu:zɪ] ADJ *(+er)* wählerisch

chop[1] [tʃɒp] N **a** *(= blow)* Schlag *m*
b *(Cook)* Kotelett *nt*
c *(Sport)* harter (Kurz)schlag; *(Karate)* Karateschlag *m*
d *(of waves)* Klatschen *nt*, Schlagen *nt*
e *(inf)* **to get the ~** *(= be axed)* dem Rotstift zum Opfer fallen; *(= be fired)* rausgeschmissen werden *(inf)*; **to give sb the ~** jdn rausschmeißen *(inf)*; **to be for the ~** *(= going to be axed)* gestrichen werden; *(= going to be fired)* auf der Abschussliste stehen *(inf)*
VT **a** *(= cut)* hacken; *meat, vegetables etc* klein schneiden; **to ~ one's way through the undergrowth** sich *(dat)* einen Weg durchs Dickicht schlagen
b *(Sport) ball* (ab)stoppen; *(Wrestling etc) opponent* einen Schlag versetzen *(+dat)*

▶ **chop at** VI *+prep obj* hacken *or* schlagen nach; *(with axe)* einhacken auf *(+acc)*

▶ **chop back** VT *sep* zurück- *or* wegschneiden

▶ **chop down** VT *sep tree* fällen

▶ **chop off** VT *sep* abhacken, abschlagen, abhauen

▶ **chop up** VT *sep* zerhacken, zerkleinern; *(fig) country* aufteilen; *company* aufspalten

chop[2] VI **a** *(Naut, wind)* drehen, umspringen
b *(fig)* **to ~ and change (one's mind)** ständig seine Meinung ändern; **if they keep ~ping and changing the team ...** wenn sie ständig die Spieler wechseln ...

chop chop ADV INTERJ *(inf)* hopp, hopp *(inf)*

chophouse ['tʃɒphaʊs] N Steakhaus *nt*

chopper ['tʃɒpə'] N **a** *(= axe)* Hackbeil *nt* **b** *(inf: = helicopter)* Hubschrauber *m* **c** *(= bicycle)* BMX-Rad *nt*; *(inf: = motorcycle)* Maschine *f (inf)*

choppers ['tʃɒpəz] PL *(inf: = teeth)* Beißerchen *pl (inf)*

chopping ['tʃɒpɪŋ]: **chopping block** N Hackklotz *m*; *(for wood, executions etc)* Block *m*; **chopping board** N *(Brit)* Hackbrett *nt*; **chopping knife** N *(Brit)* Hackmesser *nt*; *(with rounded blade)* Wiegemesser *nt*

choppy ['tʃɒpɪ] ADJ *(+er) sea* kabbelig; *wind* böig, wechselhaft

chops [tʃɒps] PL *(of dog)* Lefzen *pl*; *(inf, of person)* Visage *f (inf)*

chop: **chopstick** N Stäbchen *nt*; **chop suey** [tʃɒp'su:ɪ] N Chopsuey *nt*

choral ['kɔ:rəl] ADJ Chor-; **~ society** Gesangverein *m*, Chor *m*

chorale [kɒ'rɑ:l] N Choral *m*

chord [kɔ:d] N **a** *(Mus)* Akkord *m*; **to strike the right ~** *(fig)* den richtigen Ton treffen; **to strike a sympathetic ~** *(fig)* auf Verständnis stoßen **b** *(Geometry)* Sehne *f* **c** *(Anat)* Band *nt*

chordal ['kɔ:dl] ADJ *(Mus)* Akkord-

chore [tʃɔ:'] N lästige Pflicht; **~s** *pl* Hausarbeit *f*; **to do the ~s** den Haushalt machen, die Hausarbeit erledigen

choreograph ['kɒrɪəʊgrɑ:f] VT choreografieren

choreographer [,kɒrɪ'ɒgrəfə'] N Choreograf(in) *m(f)*

choreographic [,kɒrɪəʊ'græfɪk] ADJ choreografisch

choreography [,kɒrɪ'ɒgrəfɪ] N Choreografie *f*

chorister ['kɒrɪstə'] N (Kirchen)chormitglied *nt*; *(= boy)* Chorknabe *m*

chortle ['tʃɔ:tl] VI gluckern, glucksen; **he was chortling over the article** er lachte in sich hinein *or* vor sich hin, als er den Artikel las N Gluckser *m*

chorus ['kɔ:rəs] N **a** *(= refrain)* Refrain *m* **b** Chor *m*; *(of opera)* Opernchor *m*; *(= dancers)* Tanzgruppe *f*; **she's in the ~** sie singt im Chor/sie ist bei der Tanzgruppe; **in ~** im Chor; **he was greeted with a ~ of good morning, sir** als er hereinkam, riefen alle im Chor: Guten Morgen! VI im Chor singen/sprechen/rufen

chorus: **chorus girl** N Revuetänzerin *f or* -girl *nt*; **chorus line** N Revue *f*

chose [tʃəʊz] *pret of* **choose**

chosen ['tʃəʊzn] *ptp of* **choose** ADJ **the ~ people** das auserwählte Volk; **the ~ few** die wenigen Auserwählten

choux pastry ['ʃu:'peɪstrɪ] N Brandteig *m*

chow [tʃaʊ] N *(inf: = food)* was zu mampfen *(inf)*

chow(chow) ['tʃaʊ(tʃaʊ)] N *(= dog)* Chow-Chow *m*

chowder ['tʃaʊdə'] N sämige Fischsuppe

chow mein [tʃaʊ'meɪn] N *gebratene Nudeln mit Pilzen, Fleisch, Shrimps etc*

Christ [kraɪst] N Christus *m* INTERJ *(sl)* Herrgott *(inf)*

christen ['krɪsn] VT **a** *(= baptize)* taufen; **to ~ sb after sb** jdn nach jdm (be)nennen **b** *(inf: = use for first time)* einweihen

Christendom ['krɪsndəm] N *(old)* die Christenheit

christening ['krɪsnɪŋ] N Taufe *f*; **~ robe** Taufkleid *nt*

Christian ['krɪstɪən] N Christ *m* ADJ *(lit, fig)* christlich

Christianity [,krɪstɪ'ænɪtɪ] N **a** *(= faith, religion)* Christentum *nt*, christlicher Glaube; *(= body of Christians)* Christenheit *f* **b** *(= being a Christian)* Christlichkeit *f*, Frömmigkeit *f*; **his ~ did not prevent him from doing it** sein christlicher Glaube hinderte ihn nicht daran(, das zu tun) **c** *(= Christian character)* christliche Haltung *or* Gesinnung

Christianize ['krɪstɪənaɪz] VT christianisieren

Christian: **Christian name** N Vor- *or* Rufname *m*; **to be on ~ terms** sich mit Vornamen anreden; **Christian Science** N Christian Science *f*; **Christian Scientist** N Anhänger(in) *m(f)* der Christian Science

Christlike ['kraɪstlaɪk] ADJ christusgleich

Christmas ['krɪsməs] ✪ 23.2 N Weihnachten *nt*; **are you going home for ~?** fährst du (über) Weihnachten nach Hause?; **what did you get for ~?** was hast du zu Weihnachten bekommen?; **merry** *or* **happy ~!** frohe *or* fröhliche Weihnachten!; **it's as if ~ had come early!** das ist wie Ostern und Weihnachten zusammen

Christmas: **Christmas biscuit**, **Christmas cookie** *(US)* N Weihnachtsplätzchen *nt*; **Christmas bonus** N Weihnachtsgratifikation *f (geh)*, Weihnachtsgeld *nt*; **Christmas box** N *(Brit)* Trinkgeld *nt* zu Weihnachten, ≈ Neujahrsgeld *nt*; **Christmas cake** N *Früchtekuchen mit Zuckerguss zu Weihnachten*; **Christmas card** N Weihnachtskarte *f*; **Christmas carol** N Weihnachtslied *nt*; **Christmas Day** N der erste Weihnachtstag; **on ~** an Weihnachten, am ersten (Weihnachts)feiertag; **Christmas Eve** N Heiligabend *m*; **on ~** Heiligabend; **Christmas Island** N Weihnachtsinsel *f*; **Christmas present** N Weihnachtsgeschenk *nt*; **Christmas pudding** N Plumpudding *m*; **Christmas rose** N Christrose *f*; **Christmas stocking** N *Strumpf, in den Weihnachtsgeschenke gelegt werden*

Christmassy ['krɪsməsɪ] ADJ *(inf)* weihnachtlich

Christmas: **Christmas time** N Weihnachtszeit *f*; **at ~** zur *or* in der Weihnachtszeit; **Christmas tree** N Weihnachtsbaum *m*, Christbaum *m (esp S Ger)*

chromatic [krə'mætɪk] ADJ *(Art, Mus)* chromatisch

chrome [krəʊm] N Chrom *nt*

chrome steel N Chromstahl *m*

chromium ['krəʊmɪəm] N Chrom *nt*

chromium: **chromium plate** N Chromschicht *f*; **chromium-plated** ['krəʊmɪəm,pleɪtɪd] ADJ verchromt; **chromium plating** N Verchromung *f*

chromosome ['krəʊməsəʊm] N Chromosom *nt*

chronic ['krɒnɪk] ADJ **a** *disease, invalid, liar, underfunding, overcrowding etc* chronisch; **Chronic Fatigue Syndrome** chronisches Erschöpfungssyndrom **b** *(inf: = terrible)* schlecht, miserabel *(inf)*

chronically ['krɒnɪklɪ] ADV *ill, depressed, underfunded, overcrowded* chronisch

chronicle ['krɒnɪkl] N Chronik *f*; **Chronicles** *pl (Bibl)* Bücher *pl* der Chronik VT aufzeichnen; *historic events also* eine Chronik *(+gen)* verfassen

chronicler ['krɒnɪklə'] N Chronist *m*

chronograph ['krɒnəgrɑ:f] N Chronograf *m*; *(= stopwatch)* Zeitmesser *m*

chronological [,krɒnə'lɒdʒɪkəl] ADJ chronologisch; **in ~ order** in chronologischer Reihenfolge

chronologically [,krɒnə'lɒdʒɪkəlɪ] ADV chronologisch; **~ arranged** in chronologischer Reihenfolge

chronology [krə'nɒlədʒɪ] N zeitliche Abfolge, Chronologie *f (form)*; *(= list of dates)* Zeittafel *f*

chronometer [krə'nɒmɪtə'] N Chronometer *m*

chrysalis ['krɪsəlɪs] N *pl* **-es** *(Biol)* Puppe *f*; *(= covering)* Kokon *m*

chrysanthemum [krɪ'sænθəməm], **chrysanth** [krɪ'sænθ] *(inf)* N Chrysantheme *f*

chub [tʃʌb] N *pl* - Döbel *m*, Aitel *m*

Chubb lock® ['tʃʌblɒk] N *(Brit)* Sicherheitsschloss *nt*

chubby ['tʃʌbɪ] ADJ *(+er)* pummelig, rundlich; **~ cheeks** Pausbacken *pl*

chubby-cheeked ['tʃʌbɪ'tʃi:kd] ADJ pausbäckig

chuck[1] [tʃʌk] VT *(inf)* **a** *(= throw)* schmeißen *(inf)* **b** *(inf) girlfriend etc* Schluss machen mit; *job* hinschmeißen *(inf)*; **~ it!** *(= stop it)* Schluss jetzt! **c** **to ~ sb under the chin** jdm einen Kinnstüber versetzen N *(inf, = dismissal)* Rausschmiss *m (inf)*; **to give sb the ~** jdn rausschmeißen *(inf)*, jdn an die Luft setzen *(inf)*; **he got the ~** er ist rausgeflogen *(inf)*, den haben sie an die Luft gesetzt *(inf)*

▶ **chuck about** *(Brit) or* **around** VT *sep (inf)* rumschmeißen (mit) *(inf)*

▶ **chuck away** VT *sep (inf: = throw out)* wegschmeißen *(inf)*; *(= waste) money* aus dem Fenster schmeißen *(inf)*

▶ **chuck in** VT *sep (Brit inf) job* hinschmeißen *(inf)*, an den Nagel hängen *(inf)*; **to chuck it (all) in** den Laden hinschmeißen *(inf)*

▶ **chuck out** VT *sep (inf)* rausschmeißen *(inf)*; *useless articles also* wegschmeißen *(inf)*; **to be chucked out** rausfliegen *(of* aus) *(inf)*

▶ **chuck up** VT *sep (Brit inf) job* hinschmeißen *(inf)*

chuck[2] N *(Tech)* Spannfutter *nt*

chuck[3] N *(dated US inf: = food)* Essen *nt*

chucker-out ['tʃʌkər'aʊt] N *(inf)* Rausschmeißer *m (inf)*

chuckle ['tʃʌkl] **N** leises Lachen, Kichern *nt no pl*; **to have a good ~ about sth** sich *(dat)* eins lachen über etw *(acc)* *(inf)* **VI** leise in sich *(acc)* hineinlachen, sich *(dat)* eins lachen *(inf)*; **to ~ away** vor sich hin lachen *or* kichern

chuck wagon N*(dated US inf)* Proviantwagen *m* mit fahrbarer Küche

chuffed [tʃʌft] ADJ *(Brit inf)* vergnügt und zufrieden; *(= flattered)* gebauchpinselt *(inf)* *(about* wegen); **I was dead ~ about it** ich freute mich darüber wie ein Schneekönig *(inf)*; **to be ~ with oneself** auf sich *(acc)* selbst stolz sein; **to look ~ with oneself** sehr zufrieden aussehen

chug [tʃʌg] **N** Tuckern *nt* **VI** tuckern

▶ **chug along** VI entlangtuckern; *(fig inf)* gut vorankommen

chukka, chukker ['tʃʌkəʳ] N *(Polo)* Chukka *nt*, Chukker *nt*

chum [tʃʌm] N *(inf)* Kamerad *m*, Kumpel *m (inf)*, Spezi *m (S Ger)*

▶ **chum up** VI sich anfreunden

chummy ['tʃʌmɪ] ADJ *(+er)* *(inf)* kameradschaftlich; **to be ~ with sb** mit jdm sehr dicke sein *(inf)*; **to get ~ with sb** sich mit jdm anfreunden

chump [tʃʌmp] N **a** *(inf)* Trottel *m*, dummes Stück, Hornochse *m (inf)* **b he's off his ~** *(Brit inf)* der hat 'ne Meise *(inf)*

chump chop N Kotelett *nt*

chunder ['tʃʌndəʳ] VI *(inf)* kotzen *(sl)*

chunk [tʃʌŋk] N großes Stück; *(of meat)* Batzen *m*; *(of stone)* Brocken *m*

chunky ['tʃʌŋkɪ] ADJ *(+er)* *(inf) legs, arms* stämmig; *person also* untersetzt, gedrungen; *knitwear* dick, klobig; *book* kompakt; *glass* massiv; *jewellery* klotzig

Chunnel ['tʃʌnəl] N *(inf)* Kanaltunnel *m*

church [tʃɜːtʃ] N Kirche *f*; *(= service)* die Kirche; **to go to ~** in die Kirche gehen; **the Church Fathers** die Kirchenväter; **the Church of England** die anglikanische Kirche; **he has gone into** *or* **entered the Church** er ist Geistlicher geworden; **Church calendar** Kirchenkalender *m*, Kalendarium *nt*

church *in cpds* Kirchen-; **churchgoer** ['tʃɜːtʃgəʊəʳ] N Kirchgänger(in) *m(f)*; **churchgoing** ['tʃɜːtʃgəʊɪŋ] ADJ **a ~ family** eine Familie, die regelmäßig in die Kirche geht; **church hall** N Gemeindehalle *f*; **churchman** N *(= clergyman)* Geistliche(r), Seelsorger *m*; *(= churchgoer)* Kirchgänger *m*; **church mode** N *(Mus)* Kirchentonart *f*; **church mouse** N **as poor as a ~** arm wie eine Kirchenmaus; **church school** N Konfessionsschule *f*; **church service** N Gottesdienst *m*; **churchwarden** N Gemeindevorsteher *m*

churchy ['tʃɜːtʃɪ] ADJ *(+er)* *(inf) person* kirchlich

churchyard N Friedhof *m*, Kirchhof *m (old, dial)*

churl ['tʃɜːl] N ungehobelter Kerl, Rüpel *m*

churlish ADJ, **churlishly** ADV ['tʃɜːlɪʃ, -lɪ] ungehobelt

churlishness ['tʃɜːlɪʃnɪs] N ungehobeltes Benehmen

churn [tʃɜːn] **N** *(for butter)* Butterfass *nt*; *(Brit: = milk churn)* Milchkanne *f* **VT a to ~ butter** buttern, Sahne buttern **b** *(= agitate) sea, mud etc* aufwühlen **VI** *(water, mud)* wirbeln, strudeln; *(wheels, rage etc)* wühlen; *(propeller)* wirbeln, sich wild drehen; **his stomach was ~ing** sein Magen revoltierte; **the ~ing sea** die stampfende See

▶ **churn away** VI sich wild drehen; *(engine)* stampfen

▶ **churn out** VT *sep* am laufenden Band produzieren

▶ **churn up** VT *sep* aufwühlen

chute [ʃuːt] N **a** Rutsche *f*; *(= garbage chute)* Müllschlucker *m* **b** *(= rapid in river)* Stromschnelle *f* **c** *(inf: = parachute)* Fallschirm *m* **d** *(in playground)* Rutschbahn *f*, Rutsche *f*

chutney ['tʃʌtnɪ] N Chutney *m*

chutzpah ['hʊtspə] N Chuzpe *f*

CI *abbr of* **Channel Islands**

CIA *abbr of* **Central Intelligence Agency** CIA *m*

ciabatta [tʃə'bætə] N Ciabatta *nt*

ciborium [sɪ'bɔːrɪəm] N Ziborium *nt*

cicada [sɪ'kɑːdə] N Zikade *f*

cicatrix ['sɪkətrɪks] N *pl* **cicatrices** [sɪkə'traɪsiːz] wildes Fleisch, Granulationsgewebe *nt (spec)*; *(= scar)* Narbe *f*

cicerone [ˌtʃɪtʃə'rəʊnɪ] N Cicerone *m*

CID *(Brit) abbr of* **Criminal Investigation Department** ≈ Kripo *f*

cider ['saɪdəʳ] N Apfelwein *m*, Cidre *m*; **hard ~** *(US)* Apfelwein *m (voll vergoren)*; **sweet ~** süßer Apfelwein *(teilweise vergoren)*, Rauscher *m (dial)*; **rough ~** Apfelwein *m (mit größerem Alkoholgehalt)*

cider: **cider apple** N Mostapfel *m*; **cider press** N Apfelpresse *f*

cif *abbr of* **cost, insurance and freight** cif

cig [sɪg] N *(inf)* *(= cigarette)* Zigarette *f*; *(= cigar)* Zigarre *f*

cigar [sɪ'gɑːʳ] N Zigarre *f*

cigar: **cigar box** N Zigarrenkiste *f*; **cigar cutter** N Zigarrenabschneider *m*

cigarette [ˌsɪgə'ret] N Zigarette *f*

cigarette: **cigarette box** N Zigarettenschachtel *f*; **cigarette case** N Zigarettenetui *nt*; **cigarette end** N Zigarettenstummel *m*; **cigarette holder** N Zigarettenspitze *f*; **cigarette lighter** N Feuerzeug *nt*; **cigarette machine** N Zigarettenautomat *m*; **cigarette paper** N Zigarettenpapier *nt*

cigarillo [sɪgə'rɪləʊ] N Zigarillo *m or nt*

cigar: **cigar lighter** N *(in car)* Zigarettenanzünder *m*; **cigar-shaped** ADJ zigarrenförmig

ciggie, ciggy ['sɪgɪ] N *(inf)* Glimmstängel *m (inf)*, Kippe *f (inf)*

C-in-C *abbr of* **Commander in Chief**

cinch [sɪntʃ] **N a** *(US: = saddle girth)* Sattelgurt *m* **b** *(inf)* **it's a ~** *(= easy)* das ist ein Kinderspiel *or* ein Klacks *(inf)*; *(esp US: = certain)* es ist todsicher *(inf)* **VT** *(US)* **a to ~ a horse** den Sattelgurt anziehen **b** *(inf) deal* regeln *(sl)*

cinch connector, cinch plug N *(Tech)* Cinch-Stecker *m*

cinder ['sɪndəʳ] N **~s** *pl* Asche *f*; *(lumpy)* Schlacke *f*; *(still burning)* glühendes Kohlestück; **burnt to a ~** *(Brit fig)* verkohlt

Cinderella [ˌsɪndə'relə] N *(lit, fig)* Aschenputtel *nt*

cinder track N Aschenbahn *f*

cineaste ['sɪnɪæst] N Cineast(in) *m(f)*, Kinoliebhaber(in) *m(f)*

cine ['sɪnɪ]: **cine camera** N *(Brit)* (Schmal)filmkamera *f*; **cine film** N *(Brit)* Schmalfilm *m*

cinema ['sɪnəmə] N *(esp Brit)* Kino *nt*; *(= films collectively also)* Film *m*; **at/to the ~** im/ins Kino

cinema *(esp Brit)*: **cinema complex** N Kinocenter *nt*; **cinemagoer** N Kinogänger(in) *m(f)*; **cinema-going** **N the popularity of ~** die Beliebtheit des Kinos **ADJ the ~ public** das Kinopublikum, die Kinogänger *pl*; **cinema-loving** ADJ kinofreudig

Cinemascope® ['sɪnəməskəʊp] N Cinemascope® *nt*

cinematic [sɪnə'mætɪk] ADJ filmisch; **~ art** Filmkunst *f*

cinematograph [ˌsɪnə'mætəgrɑːf] N *(dated)* Kinematograf *m (dated)*

cinephile ['sɪnɪfaɪl] N Kinoliebhaber(in) *m(f)*

Cineplex® ['sɪnɪpleks] N ≈ Mulitplex-Kino *nt*

cine projector N *(Brit)* Filmprojektor *m*

Cinerama® [ˌsɪnə'rɑːmə] N Cinerama® *nt*

cinerary ['sɪnərərɪ] ADJ Aschen-

cinerary urn ['sɪnərərɪ-] N Urne *f*

cinnabar ['sɪnəbɑːʳ] N Zinnober *m*

cinnamon ['sɪnəmən] **N** Zimt *m* **ADJ** *attr* **a** *cake, biscuit* Zimt- **b** *(colour)* zimtfarben

CIO *(US) abbr of* **Congress of Industrial Organizations** *amerikanischer Gewerkschaftsdachverband*

cipher ['saɪfəʳ] **N a** *(= Arabic numeral)* Ziffer *f*, Zahl *f* **b** *(= zero)* Null *f* **c** *(= nonentity)* Niemand *m no pl* **d** *(= code)* Chiffre *f*, Code *m*, Kode *m*; **in ~** chiffriert **e** *(= monogram)* Monogramm *nt*, Namenszeichen *nt* **VT** *(= encode)* verschlüsseln, chiffrieren

cipher clerk N (De)chiffreur(in) *m(f)*

cipher officer N *(army)* Fernmeldeoffizier(in) *m(f)*; *(secret service etc)* (De)chiffreur(in) *m(f)*

circ *abbr of* **circa** ca.

circa ['sɜːkə] PREP circa, zirka

circle ['sɜːkl] **N a** Kreis *m*; **to stand in a ~** im Kreis stehen; **to go round in ever decreasing ~s** *(lit)* Spiralen drehen; *(fig)* sich unablässig im Kreis drehen; **to have come** *or* **turned full ~** *(lit)* sich ganz herumgedreht haben, eine Volldrehung gemacht haben; *(fig)* wieder da sein, wo man angefangen hat; **we're just going round in ~s** *(fig)* wir bewegen uns nur im Kreise; **to come full ~** *(fig)* zum Ausgangspunkt zurückkehren; **things have come full ~** der Kreis hat sich geschlossen; **when the seasons have come full ~** wenn sich der Kreis der Jahreszeiten schließt

b *(of hills etc)* Ring *m*, Kette *f*; *(round the eyes)* Ring *m (round* unter *+dat)*; *(in gymnastics)* Welle *f*; **a Celtic stone ~** ein keltischer Steinkreis

c *(Brit Theat)* Rang *m* → **dress circle, upper circle**

d *(= group of persons)* Kreis *m*, Zirkel *m (geh)*; **a close ~ of friends** ein enger Freundeskreis; **in political ~s** in politischen Kreisen; **the family ~** der engste Familienkreis; **the whole family ~** die ganze Familie; **he's moving in different ~s now** er verkehrt jetzt in anderen Kreisen

VT a *(= surround)* umgeben

b *(= move around)* kreisen um; **the enemy ~d the town** der Feind kreiste die Stadt ein

c *(= draw a circle round)* einen Kreis *or* Kringel machen um; **he ~d several of the addresses** er machte einen Kreis um mehrere der Anschriften; **~d in red** rot umkringelt

VI *(= fly in a circle)* kreisen

▶ **circle around** VI *(people)* umhergehen *or* -wandern; *(birds)* Kreise ziehen; *(vehicle)* kreisen, Runden drehen; *(ship, plane)* kreisen; **the wolves circled around, waiting** die Wölfe kreisten lauernd um uns/sie/das Lager *etc*

circlet ['sɜːklɪt] N Reif *m*

circlip ['sɜːklɪp] N Sicherungsring *m*

circuit ['sɜːkɪt] **N a** *(= journey around etc)* Rundgang *m*/-fahrt *f*/-reise *f (of* um); **to make a ~ of sth** um etw herumgehen/-fahren, einen Rundgang/eine Rundfahrt um etw machen; **three ~s of the racetrack** drei Runden auf der Rennbahn; **they made a wide ~ to avoid the enemy** sie machten einen großen Bogen um den Feind

b *(of judges etc)* Gerichtsbezirk *m*; **to go on ~** den (Gerichts)bezirk bereisen; **he is on the eastern ~** er bereist *or* hat den östlichen (Gerichts)bezirk

c *(Theat)* Theaterring *m or* -kette *f*; **to travel the ~** die Theater (der Reihe nach) bereisen

d *(Elec)* Stromkreis *m*; *(= apparatus)* Schaltung *f*

e *(Sport: = track)* Rennbahn *f*

f the professional golf/tennis ~ die Golf-/ /Tennisturnierrunde (der Berufsspieler)

VT *track, course* eine Runde drehen um

circuit: **circuit board** N *(Tech)* Platine *f*, Leiterplatte *f*; **circuit breaker** N Stromkreisunterbrecher *m*; **circuit court** N *Bezirksgericht, das an verschiedenen Orten eines Gerichtsbezirks Sitzungen abhält*; **circuit diagram** N

Schaltplan *m*; **circuit judge** N Richter *m* an einem Bezirksgericht

circuitous [sɜː'kjʊɪtəs] ADJ umständlich; ~ **path** Schlängelpfad *m*

circuitously [sɜː'kjʊɪtəslɪ] ADV umständlich; **the road winds** ~ die Straße schlängelt sich

circuitousness [sɜː'kjʊɪtəsnɪs] N Umständlichkeit *f*; *(of route)* Gewundenheit *f*

circuitry ['sɜːkətrɪ] N Schaltkreise *pl*

circuit training N Circuittraining *nt*, Zirkeltraining *nt*

circuity [sɜː'kjʊətɪ] N = **circuitousness**

circular ['sɜːkjʊlə'] ADJ *object* kreisförmig, rund; ~ **motion** Kreisbewegung *f*; ~ **tour** Rundfahrt *f*/-reise *f*; **a ~ tour of the island** eine Inselrundfahrt; ~ **argument** Zirkelschluss *m* N *(in firm)* Rundschreiben *nt*, Rundbrief *m*; *(single copy)* Umlauf *m*; *(= printed advertisement)* Wurfsendung *f* → *also* **circular letter**

circularize ['sɜːkjʊləraɪz] VT *person* durch Rundschreiben informieren; *letter, memo* zirkulieren lassen

circular: **circular letter** N Rundschreiben *nt*, Rundbrief *m*; **circular saw** N Kreissäge *f*; **circular stair**, **circular staircase** N Wendeltreppe *f*

circulate ['sɜːkjʊleɪt] VI **a** *(water, blood, money)* fließen, zirkulieren; *(traffic)* fließen; *(news, rumour)* kursieren, in Umlauf sein **b** *(person: at party)* die Runde machen VT *news, rumour* verbreiten, in Umlauf bringen; *memo etc* zirkulieren lassen; *water* pumpen

circulating ['sɜːkjʊleɪtɪŋ]: **circulating capital** N flüssiges Kapital, Umlaufkapital *nt*; **circulating library** N Fahrbücherei *f*; **circulating medium** N *(Fin)* Zahlungs- *or* Umlaufsmittel *nt*

circulation [ˌsɜːkjʊ'leɪʃən] N **a** *(= act of circulating) (Med)* Kreislauf *m*, Zirkulation *f*; *(of traffic)* Ablauf *m*, Fluss *m*; *(of money also)* Umlauf *m*; *(of news, rumour)* Kursieren *nt*; **to have poor** ~ Kreislaufstörungen haben; **to put notes into** ~ Banknoten in Umlauf bringen; **this coin was withdrawn from** *or* **taken out of** ~ diese Münze wurde aus dem Verkehr gezogen; **new words which come into** ~ Wörter, die neu in Umlauf kommen; **he's back in** ~ **now** *(inf)* er mischt wieder mit *(inf)*; **to be out of** ~ *(inf) (person)* von der Bildfläche *or* in der Versenkung verschwunden sein; *(criminal, politician)* aus dem Verkehr gezogen worden sein; **the ideas then in** ~ die Ideen, die damals im Schwang(e) waren

b *(of newspaper etc)* Auflage(nziffer) *f*; **for private** ~ zum privaten Gebrauch

circulatory [ˌsɜːkjʊ'leɪtərɪ] ADJ Kreislauf-; ~ **system** Blutkreislauf *m*

circum- ['sɜːkəm-] PREF um-, um ... herum

circumcise ['sɜːkəmsaɪz] VT beschneiden

circumcision [ˌsɜːkəm'sɪʒən] N Beschneidung *f*; **the Circumcision** *(Eccl)* der Tag der Beschneidung des Herrn

circumference [sə'kʌmfərəns] N Umfang *m*; **the tree is 10 ft in** ~ der Baum hat einen Umfang von 10 Fuß

circumflex ['sɜːkəmfleks] N Zirkumflex *m*

circumlocution [ˌsɜːkəmlə'kjuːʃən] N Weitschweifigkeit *f*; *(= evasiveness)* Umschreibung *f*, Drumherumreden *nt (inf)*

circumlocutory [ˌsɜːkəmlə'kjuːtərɪ] ADJ weitschweifig; *expression* umschreibend

circumnavigate [ˌsɜːkəm'nævɪgeɪt] VT *the globe* umfahren; *(in yacht also)* umsegeln; *cape, island also* umschiffen

circumnavigation ['sɜːkəmˌnævɪ'geɪʃən] N Fahrt *f* (of um); *(in yacht also)* Umseglung *f*; ~ **of the globe** Fahrt *f* um die Welt; Weltumseglung *f*

circumnavigator [ˌsɜːkəm'nævɪgeɪtə'] N ~ **of the globe** Weltumsegler(in) *m(f)*

circumscribe ['sɜːkəmskraɪb] VT **a** *(Math)* einen Kreis umbeschreiben *(+dat)* **b** *(= restrict)* eingrenzen

circumscription [ˌsɜːkəm'skrɪpʃən] N **a** *(= restriction)* Eingrenzung *f* **b** *(on coin)* Umschrift *f*

circumspect ['sɜːkəmspekt] ADJ umsichtig

circumspection [ˌsɜːkəm'spekʃən] N Umsicht *f*

circumspectly ['sɜːkəmspektlɪ] ADV umsichtig

circumstance ['sɜːkəmstəns] N **a** Umstand *m*; **in** *or* **under the ~s** unter diesen Umständen; **in** *or* **under no ~s** unter gar keinen Umständen, auf keinen Fall; **in certain ~s** unter Umständen, eventuell; **what were the ~s surrounding the case?** wie waren die näheren Umstände des Falls?; **a victim of** ~ ein Opfer *nt* der Umstände; **he was forced by** ~ **to do it** die Umstände zwangen ihn, es zu tun **b** **circumstances** PL *(= financial condition)* finanzielle Verhältnisse *pl*, Umstände *pl (form)*; **in poor ~s** in ärmlichen Verhältnissen **c** → **pomp**

circumstantial [ˌsɜːkəm'stænʃəl] ADJ **a** *(= detailed) report, statement* ausführlich, detailliert **b** *(Jur) case* auf Indizienbeweisen beruhend; ~ **evidence** Indizienbeweis *m*; **the case against him is purely** ~ sein Fall beruht allein auf Indizienbeweisen **c** *(= secondary)* nebensächlich

circumstantiate [ˌsɜːkəm'stænʃɪeɪt] VT *(form)* belegen

circumvent [ˌsɜːkəm'vent] VT umgehen

circumvention [ˌsɜːkəm'venʃən] N Umgehung *f*

circus ['sɜːkəs] N Zirkus *m*; *(in place names)* Platz *m*

cirrhosis [sɪ'rəʊsɪs] N Zirrhose *f*

cirrus ['sɪrəs] N *pl* **cirri** ['sɪraɪ] Zirruswolke *f*

CIS *abbr of* **Commonwealth of Independent States** GUS *f*

cisalpine ['siːzælpaɪn] ADJ zisalpin

cissy ['sɪsɪ] N = **sissy**

Cistercian [sɪs'tɜːʃən] N Zisterzienser *m* ADJ Zisterzienser-

cistern ['sɪstən] N Zisterne *f*; *(of WC)* Spülkasten *m*

citable ['saɪtəbl] ADJ anführbar, zitierbar

citadel ['sɪtədl] N Zitadelle *f*

citation [saɪ'teɪʃən] N **a** *(= quote)* Zitat *nt*; *(= act of quoting)* Zitieren *nt* **b** *(Mil)* Belobigung *f*, lobende Erwähnung **c** *(Jur)* Vorladung *f* (vor Gericht)

cite [saɪt] VT **a** *(= quote)* anführen, zitieren **b** *(Mil)* belobigen, lobend erwähnen (*for* wegen) **c** *(Jur)* vorladen; **he was ~d to appear** er wurde vorgeladen, er erhielt eine Vorladung; **he was ~d as the co-respondent** *(= mentioned)* er wurde als der Dritte in der Scheidungssache genannt

citify ['sɪtɪfaɪ] VT verstädtern

citizen ['sɪtɪzn] N **a** Bürger(in) *m(f)* **b** *(of a state)* (Staats)bürger(in) *m(f)*; **French** ~ französischer Staatsbürger, französische Staatsbürgerin, Franzose *m*, Französin *f*; ~ **of the world** Weltbürger(in) *m(f)*

citizenry ['sɪtɪznrɪ] N *(liter)* Bürgerschaft *f*

Citizens' Advice Bureau N *(Brit)* ≈ Bürgerberatungsstelle *f*

> **CITIZENS' ADVICE BUREAU**
>
> 1939 wurden in Großbritannien **Citizens' Advice Bureaux** eingerichtet, die die Bürger über die Kriegssonderregelungen informieren sollten. Nach dem Krieg wurde daraus ein allgemeiner kostenloser Beratungsdienst, der der Öffentlichkeit bei einer ganzen Palette von Problemen mit Rat und Tat zur Seite steht. Heutzutage beschäftigen sich diese Bürgerberatungsstellen überwiegend mit Schuldenproblemen, Wohnungssuche, Sozialhilfe, Sozialdiensten und Verbraucherschutz. Der öffentlich finanzierte Service verfügt über Hunderte von örtlichen Beratungsstellen, die von jeweils einem voll bezahlten leitenden Mitarbeiter sowie speziell geschulten ehrenamtlichen Kräften betrieben werden.

citizen: **citizen's arrest** N *Festnahme durch eine Zivilperson*; **Citizens' Band** N CB-Funk *m*; **Citizen's Charter** N *(Brit) 1991 von der britischen Regierung zur Verbesserung öffentlicher Dienstleistungen eingesetzte Charta*

citizenship ['sɪtɪznʃɪp] N Staatsbürgerschaft *f*

citrate ['sɪtreɪt] N Zitrat *nt*

citric acid ['sɪtrɪk'æsɪd] N Zitronensäure *f*

citron ['sɪtrən] N *(= fruit)* Zitrone *f*; *(= tree)* Zitronenbaum *m*

citrus ['sɪtrəs] N Zitrusgewächs *nt*; ~ **fruits** Zitrusfrüchte *pl*

city ['sɪtɪ] N **a** Stadt *f*, Großstadt *f*; **towns and cities** Städte und Großstädte; **the ~ of Glasgow** die Stadt Glasgow **b** *(in London)* **the City** die City, das Banken- und Börsenviertel

> **CITY NICKNAMES**
>
> Amerikanische Städte haben oft Spitznamen, die auch häufig verwendet werden. New York ist allgemein unter „The Big Apple" bekannt (**apple** ist ein Slangausdruck für eine Großstadt), Chicago ist „The Windy City" (weil hier heftige Winde vom Michigansee her wehen), New Orleans „The Big Easy" (wegen des dortigen Lebensrhythmus), und Detroit ist „Motown" (da es für seine Motorenindustrie bekannt ist).
>
> Einige Städte werden auf ihre Initialen reduziert, wie „LA" für Los Angeles und „Big D" für Dallas. Bei anderen Städten werden Namensteile weggelassen, so bei „Vegas" für Las Vegas, oder zu Kurzversionen zusammengezogen, wie bei „Frisco" statt San Francisco und „Philly" statt Philadelphia.

city: **city boy** N Großstadtkind *nt*, Großstadtjunge *m*; **city-bred** ADJ in der (Groß)stadt aufgewachsen; **city centre**, *(US)* **city center** N Stadtmitte *f*, Stadtzentrum *nt*, Innenstadt *f*, City *f*; **city council** N Stadtrat *m*; **city councillor**, *(US)* **city councilor** [n] Stadtrat *m*/-rätin *f*, Stadtratsmitglied *nt*; **city desk** N *(Brit)* Finanz- und Wirtschaftsabteilung *f (einer Redaktion)*; *(US)* Abteilung *f* für Lokalnachrichten; **city dweller** N Stadtbewohner(in) *m(f)*; **city editor** N *(Brit)* Wirtschaftsredakteur(in) *m(f)*; *(US)* Lokalredakteur(in) *m(f)*; **city father** N Stadtverordnete(r) *m*; **the ~s** die Stadtväter *pl*; **city hall** N Rathaus *nt*; *(US: = municipal government)* Stadtverwaltung *f*; **city life** N (Groß)stadtleben *nt*; **city manager** N *(US)* Oberstadtdirektor(in) *m(f)*; **city page** N *(Brit)* Wirtschaftsseite *f*; **city person** N (Groß)stadtmensch *m*; **cityscape** N (Groß)stadtlandschaft *f*; **city slicker** N *(pej inf)* feiner Pinkel aus der (Groß)stadt *(pej inf)*; *(dishonest)* schlitzohriger Großstädter *(pej inf)*; **city state** N Stadtstaat *m*; **City Technology College** N *(Brit)* ≈ technische Fachschule; **city treasurer** N Stadtkämmerer *m*/-kämmerin *f*; **city type** N (Groß)stadtmensch *m*

civet ['sɪvɪt] N *(= substance)* Zibet *m*; *(= cat)* Zibetkatze *f*

civic ['sɪvɪk] ADJ *rights, virtues* bürgerlich, Bürger-; *duties, responsibilities* als Bürger; *guard, authorities* Stadt-, städtisch; *event, reception* der Stadt

civic centre N *(Brit)* Verwaltungszentrum *nt* einer Stadt

civics ['sɪvɪks] N *sing* Staatsbürgerkunde *f*

civies ['sɪvɪz] PL *(inf)* = **civvies**

civil ['sɪvl] ADJ **a** *(= of society)* bürgerlich; *duties* staatsbürgerlich, Bürger-; *unrest, conflict* in der Bevölkerung **b** *(= polite)* höflich; *(in behaviour also)* aufmerksam, zuvorkommend; **to be ~ to sb** höflich zu jdm sein; **cigar? – very ~ of you** Zigarre? – sehr zuvorkommend (von Ihnen) **c** *(Jur)* zivilrechtlich **d** *(= civilian) aircraft, aviation* zivil

civil: **Civil Aviation Authority** N Behörde *f* für Zivilluftfahrt; **civil ceremony** N standesamtliche Hochzeit; **to get married in a ~** standesamtlich heiraten; **civil defence**, *(US)* **civil defense** N Zivilschutz *m*; ~ **worker** Beauftragte(r) *mf* des Zivilschutzes; **civil disobedience** N ziviler Ungehorsam; ~ **campaign** Kampagne *f* für zivilen Ungehorsam; **civil engineer** N Bauingenieur(in) *m(f)*; **civil engineering** N Hoch- und Tiefbau *m*

civilian [sɪˈvɪlɪən] N Zivilist(in) *m(f)* ADJ zivil, Zivil-; **in ~ clothes** in Zivil; **~ casualties** Verluste *pl* unter der Zivilbevölkerung

civility [sɪˈvɪlɪtɪ] N Höflichkeit *f*

civilization [ˌsɪvɪlaɪˈzeɪʃən] N a (= *civilized world*) Zivilisation *f*; **all ~** die ganze zivilisierte Welt; **~!, the explorer exclaimed** Menschen!, rief der Forscher aus b (= *state: of Greeks etc*) Kultur *f* c (= *act*) Zivilisierung *f*

civilize [ˈsɪvɪlaɪz] VT zivilisieren; *person also* Kultur beibringen (+*dat*)

civilized [ˈsɪvɪlaɪzd] ADJ a zivilisiert; **all ~ nations** alle Kulturnationen b *working hours, conditions, hour* zivil; (= *cultured*) *lifestyle, age etc* kultiviert; **a more ~ place to live in** ein etwas zivilerer Ort zum Leben; **brandy after dinner, very ~** Weinbrand nach dem Essen, sehr gepflegt

civil: **civil law** N Zivilrecht *nt*, bürgerliches Recht; **civil liberty** N Bürgerrecht *nt*; **civil liberties group** Bürgerrechtsgruppe *f*; **civil list** N Zivilliste *f*

civilly [ˈsɪvɪlɪ] ADV (= *politely*) höflich, zuvorkommend

civil: **civil marriage** N standesamtliche Trauung, Ziviltrauung *f*; **civil rights** PL (staats)bürgerliche Rechte *pl* ATTR *march, campaign, demonstration* Bürgerrechts-; **civil servant** N ≈ Staatsbeamte(r) *m*, Staatsbeamtin *f*; **civil service** N ≈ Staatsdienst *m (ohne Richter und Lehrer)*; (= *civil servants collectively*) Beamtenschaft *f*; **civil union** N gleichgeschlechtliche Ehe; **civil war** N Bürgerkrieg *m*

civvies [ˈsɪvɪz] PL (*inf*) Zivil *nt*; **he put his ~ on** er schmiss sich in Zivil (*inf*)

civvy street [ˈsɪvɪˈstriːt] N (*Brit inf*) Zivilleben *nt*; **on ~** im Zivilleben

CJ *abbr of* **chief justice**

CJD *abbr of* **Creutzfeldt-Jakob disease** CJK *f*

cl *abbr of* **centilitre(s)** cl

clack [klæk] N Klappern *nt*, Geklapper *nt* VI klappern

clad [klæd] (*old*) *pret, ptp of* **clothe** ADJ (*liter*) gekleidet; **~ with tiles** mit Ziegeln gedeckt ADJ *suf* **fur-/silk-~** in Pelze/Seide gekleidet; **iron-/steel-~** mit Eisen/Stahl verkleidet; **ivy-~** efeubewachsen; **snow-~** schneebedeckt

claim [kleɪm] ✪ 17.1 VT a (= *demand as one's own or due*) Anspruch *m* erheben auf (+*acc*); *social security, benefits, sum of money* (= *apply for*) beantragen; (= *draw*) beanspruchen; *lost property* abholen; **he ~ed diplomatic immunity** er berief sich auf seine diplomatische Immunität; **to ~ sth as one's own** etw für sich beanspruchen, Anspruch auf etw (*acc*) erheben; **both armies ~ed the victory** beide Armeen nahmen den Sieg für sich in Anspruch; **territories ~ed by the Arabs** von den Arabern beanspruchte Gebiete; **the fighting ~ed many lives** die Kämpfe forderten viele Menschenleben; **does anyone ~ this wallet?** gehört diese Brieftasche jemandem?
b (= *profess, assert*) behaupten; **he ~s to have seen you** er behauptet, Sie gesehen zu haben, er will Sie gesehen haben; **the club can ~ a membership of ...** der Verein kann ... Mitglieder vorweisen; **the advantages ~ed for this technique** die Vorzüge, die man dieser Methode zuschreibt
c *one's attention, interest* in Anspruch nehmen
VI a (*Insur*) Ansprüche geltend machen; (*for damage done by people*) Schadenersatz *m* verlangen
b (*for expenses etc*) **to ~ for sth** sich (*dat*) etw zurückgeben *or* -zahlen lassen; **you can ~ for your travelling expenses** Sie können sich (*dat*) Ihre Reisekosten zurückerstatten lassen
N a (= *demand*) Anspruch *m*; (= *pay claim, Ind*) Forderung *f*; **his ~ to the throne/title/property** *etc* sein Anspruch auf den Thron/Titel/das Grundstück *etc*; **my ~ to fame is that ...** mein Anspruch auf Ruhm begründet sich darauf, dass ...; **I have many ~s on my time** meine Zeit ist *or* ich bin sehr in Anspruch genommen; **you have no ~ on me** du hast keine Ansprüche an mich (zu stellen); **children have first ~ on their parents** die Kinder müssen an erster Stelle stehen, die Kinder müssen vorgehen; **to lay ~ to sth** Anspruch auf etw (*acc*) erheben; **to put in a ~ (for sth)** etw beantragen; (*Insur*) Ansprüche geltend machen; **they put in a ~ for extra pay** sie forderten einen Zuschlag; **we want the ~ back-dated** wir wollen das Geld rückwirkend; **he put in an expenses ~ for £100** er reichte Spesen in Höhe von £ 100 ein; **the ~s were all paid** (*Insur*) der Schaden wurde voll ersetzt
b (= *assertion*) Behauptung *f*; **to make a ~** eine Behauptung aufstellen; **have you heard his ~?** haben Sie gehört, was er behauptet?; **the exaggerated ~s made for the new washing powder** die übertriebenen Eigenschaften, die man diesem neuen Waschpulver zuschreibt; **the book makes no ~ to be original** das Buch erhebt keinen Anspruch auf Originalität; **I make no ~ to be a genius** ich erhebe nicht den Anspruch, ein Genie zu sein
c (*Min*) Claim *m (Anteil an einem Goldfeld etc)* → **stake**

▸**claim back** VT *sep* zurückfordern; **to claim sth back (as expenses)** sich (*dat*) etw zurückzahlen *or* -geben *or* -erstatten lassen

claimant [ˈkleɪmənt] N (*for social security etc*) Antragsteller(in) *m(f)*; (*for inheritance etc*) Anspruchsteller(in) *m(f)* (*to* auf +*acc*); (*Jur*) Kläger(in) *m(f)*; **a ~ to a title/throne** ein Titel-/ /Thronanwärter *m*, eine Titel-/Thronanwärterin

claim form N Antragsformular *nt*

clairvoyance [klɛəˈvɔɪəns] N Hellsehen *nt*, Hellseherei *f*

clairvoyant [klɛəˈvɔɪənt] N Hellseher(in) *m(f)* ADJ hellseherisch; **I'm not ~** ich bin (doch) kein Hellseher!

clam [klæm] N Venusmuschel *f*; **he shut up like a ~** aus ihm war kein Wort mehr herauszubekommen

▸**clam up** VI (*inf*) keinen Piep (mehr) sagen (*inf*); **he clammed up on me** ich habe kein Wort mehr aus ihm herausgekriegt (*inf*)

clambake [ˈklæmbeɪk] N (*US*) Muschelessen *nt* am Strand; (*inf: = party*) Fete *f* (*inf*)

clamber [ˈklæmbəʳ] VI klettern, kraxeln (*esp S Ger*); **to ~ up a hill** auf einen Berg klettern, einen Berg hinaufklettern; **the baby ~ed all over the sofa** das Baby krabbelte auf dem Sofa herum N Kletterei *f*, Kraxelei *f* (*esp S Ger*)

clamminess [ˈklæmɪnɪs] N Feuchtigkeit *f*, Klammheit *f*

clammy [ˈklæmɪ] ADJ (+*er*) feucht, klamm; **a ~ handshake** ein feuchter Händedruck

clamor N (*US*) = **clamour**

clamorous [ˈklæmərəs] ADJ (*liter*) a *mob* lärmend b *demands* lautstark; *applause* tosend

clamour, (*US*) **clamor** [ˈklæməʳ] N a (= *noise*) Lärm *m*, Lärmen *nt*; **the ~ of the battlefield** der Kampf- *or* Schlachtenlärm b (= *demand*) lautstark erhobene Forderung (*for* nach); **a ~ against sth** ein Aufschrei *m* gegen etw; **constant ~ against the EC** ständiges Geschrei gegen die EG VI **to ~ for sth** nach etw schreien; **to ~ against sth** sich gegen etw empören; **the paper ~ed against the government** die Zeitung wetterte gegen die Regierung; **the men were ~ing to go home** die Männer forderten lautstark die Heimkehr

clamp[1] [klæmp] N Schraubzwinge *f*; (*Med, Elec*) Klemme *f*; (*for illegally parked car*) Parkkralle *f* VT (ein)spannen; *illegally parked car* eine Parkkralle befestigen an (+*dat*)

▸**clamp down** VT *sep* (*lit*) festmachen VI (*fig, on expenses etc*) gewaltig bremsen (*inf*); (*police, government*) rigoros durchgreifen

▸**clamp down on** VI +*prep obj person* an die Kandare nehmen; *expenditure, activities* einen Riegel vorschieben (+*dat*); *news broadcasts* unterdrücken; **the government clamped down on private radio stations** die Regierung holte zum Schlag gegen private Rundfunksender aus

clamp[2] N (*Brit, of potatoes*) Miete *f*

clampdown [ˈklæmpdaʊn] N Schlag *m* (*on* gegen); **he ordered a ~ on the porn merchants** er hat dafür gesorgt, dass es den Pornohändlern an den Kragen ging (*inf*); **the ~ has made tax evasion almost impossible** das harte Durchgreifen hat Steuerhinterziehung fast unmöglich gemacht

clan [klæn] N (*lit, fig*) Clan *m*

clandestine [klænˈdestɪn] ADJ geheim; *meeting, society* Geheim-; *rendezvous* heimlich

clandestinely [klænˈdestɪnlɪ] ADV im Geheimen

clang [klæŋ] N Klappern *nt*; (*of hammer*) Hallen *nt*, Dröhnen *nt*; (*of swords*) Klirren *nt* VI klappern; (*hammer*) hallen, dröhnen; (*swords*) klirren VT klappern mit; *cymbal* schlagen; *bell* läuten

clanger [ˈklæŋəʳ] N (*Brit inf*) Fauxpas *m*, Schnitzer *m* (*inf*); **to drop a ~** ins Fettnäpfchen treten (*inf*)

clangor [ˈklæŋgəʳ] N (*US*) = **clangour**

clangorous [ˈklæŋgərəs] ADJ (*liter*) hallend

clangour [ˈklæŋgəʳ] N Hallen *nt*; (*irritating*) Getöse *nt*

clank [klæŋk] N Klirren *nt* VT klirren mit VI klirren

clannish [ˈklænɪʃ] ADJ *group* klüngelhaft, verfilzt (*inf*); *person* cliquenbewusst; **the office staff became unbearably ~** im Büro entwickelte sich eine unerträgliche Cliquenwirtschaft

clansman [ˈklænzmən] N *pl* **-men** [-mən] Clanmitglied *nt*; **all the McTaggart clansmen** alle Mitglieder des Clans McTaggart

clap[1] [klæp] N (*inf*) Tripper *m*; **to catch a dose of the ~** sich (*dat*) was *or* den Tripper (weg)holen (*inf*)

clap[2] N Klatschen *nt no pl*; (*no pl: = applause*) (Beifall)klatschen *nt*; **a ~ of thunder** ein Donnerschlag *m*; **give him a ~!** klatscht ihm Beifall!, alle(s) klatschen!; **the audience gave him a big ~** das Publikum klatschte (ihm) begeistert Beifall; **a ~ on the back** ein Schlag *m* auf die Schulter
VT a (= *applaud*) Beifall klatschen (+*dat*)
b **to ~ one's hands** in die Hände klatschen; **to ~ sb on the back** jdm auf die Schulter klopfen
c (= *put quickly*) **he ~ped his hand over my mouth** er hielt mir den Mund zu; **to ~ sb into prison** jdn ins Gefängnis stecken; **to ~ eyes on sb/sth** (*inf*) jdn/etw zu sehen kriegen (*inf*)
VI (Beifall) klatschen

▸**clap on** VT *sep handcuffs* anlegen (*prep obj* +*dat*); **to clap on one's hat** sich (*dat*) den Hut aufstülpen; **to clap on sail** (*Naut*) Beisegel setzen; **to clap on the brakes** (*Aut*) auf die Bremse latschen (*inf*)

▸**clap to** VT *always separate door* zuklappen VI (*door*) zuklappen

clapboard [ˈklæpbɔːd] N Schindel *f*; **a white ~ structure** ein weißes, mit Schindeln verkleidetes Gebäude

clapped-out [ˈklæptaʊt] ADJ *attr*, **clapped out** [ˈklæptˈaʊt] ADJ *pred* (*inf*) klapprig; **a ~ old car** ein klappriges Auto, eine alte Klapperkiste (*inf*); **I feel really clapped out** (*Brit inf*) ich bin total geschafft (*inf*)

clapper [ˈklæpəʳ] N (*of bell*) (Glocken)klöppel *m*; **to go/drive/work like the ~s** (*Brit inf*) ein Mordstempo draufhaben (*inf*)

clapperboard [ˈklæpəbɔːd] N (*Film*) (Synchron)klappe *f*

clapping [ˈklæpɪŋ] N (Beifall)klatschen *nt*, Beifall *m*

claptrap [ˈklæptræp] N (*inf*) Geschwafel *nt* (*inf*)

claque [klæk] N *(Theat)* Claque *f*, Claqueure *pl*

claret ['klærət] N a (= wine) roter Bordeauxwein b (= colour) Weinrot *nt* ADJ weinrot

clarification [ˌklærɪfɪ'keɪʃən] N a (= explanation) Klarstellung *f*; **the whole issue needs a lot more ~** die Sache bedarf noch der Klärung; **I'd like a little ~ on this point** ich hätte diesen Punkt gerne näher erläutert; **in** *or* **as ~** zur Klarstellung b (of wine) Klärungsprozess *m*

clarificatory [klærɪfɪ'keɪtərɪ] ADJ erklärend

clarified ['klærɪfaɪd] ADJ *butter, sugar* raffiniert; *stock, wine* geklärt

clarify ['klærɪfaɪ] VT a (= explain) klären, klarstellen; *text* erklären; *statement* näher erläutern; **the matter has now clarified itself** die Sache hat sich jetzt geklärt b *butter, sugar* raffinieren; *stock, wine* klären VI (wine) sich klären

clarinet [ˌklærɪ'net] N Klarinette *f*

clarinettist [ˌklærɪ'netɪst] N Klarinettist(in) *m(f)*

clarion ['klærɪən] N *(liter)* Fanfare *f*; **a ~ call for reform** ein Ruf *m* nach Reformen; **a ~ call to action** ein Aufruf *m* zum Handeln

clarity ['klærɪtɪ] N Klarheit *f*

clash [klæʃ] VI a (armies, demonstrators) zusammenstoßen; **the chairman ~ed with the committee at the last meeting** der Vorsitzende hatte auf der letzten Sitzung eine Auseinandersetzung mit dem Komitee; **unions ~ with government over pay** in der Tariffrage gibt es einen Konflikt zwischen Gewerkschaften und Regierung
b (colours) nicht harmonieren, sich beißen; (interests) kollidieren, aufeinanderprallen; (programmes, films) sich überschneiden; **our personalities** *or* **we ~ too much** wir passen einfach nicht zusammen
c (cymbals etc: also **clash together**) aneinanderschlagen; (swords) klirrend aneinanderschlagen
VT *cymbals, swords* schlagen
N a (of armies, demonstrators etc) Zusammenstoß *m*; (between people, parties) Konflikt *m*; **there's bound to be a ~ between the chairman and the vice-chairman** zwischen dem Vorsitzenden und seinem Stellvertreter muss es ja zu einem Zusammenstoß kommen
b (of personalities) grundsätzliche Verschiedenheit, Unvereinbarkeit *f*; **we want to avoid a ~ of personalities in the office** wir wollen keine Leute im Büro, die absolut nicht miteinander harmonieren; **it's such a ~ of personalities** sie sind charakterlich grundverschieden; **I don't like that ~ of red and turquoise** mir gefällt diese Zusammenstellung von Rot und Türkis nicht; **a ~ of interests** eine Interessenkollision
c (of swords) Aufeinanderprallen *nt*

clasp [klɑːsp] N a (on brooch etc) (Schnapp)verschluss *m*
b (with one's arms) Umklammerung *f*; (with hand) Griff *m*
c (Mil, of medals) Ansteckabzeichen *nt*, Metallspange *f* auf dem Ordensband
VT a (= hold) (er)greifen; **to ~ sb's hand** jds Hand ergreifen; **to ~ one's hands (together)** die Hände falten; **with his hands ~ed in prayer** mit zum Gebet gefalteten Händen; **with his hands ~ed behind his back** mit auf dem Rücken verschränkten Händen; **to ~ sb in one's arms** jdn in die Arme nehmen *or* schließen; **they lay ~ed in each other's arms** sie lagen sich in den Armen; **to ~ sb to one's chest** jdn ans Herz drücken
b (= fasten with a clasp) befestigen, zuschnappen lassen; **she ~ed the bracelet round her wrist** sie legte ihr Armband an

clasp knife N Taschenmesser *nt*

class [klɑːs] ✪ 5.2 N a (= group, division) Klasse *f*; **what ~ are you travelling?** in welcher Klasse reisen Sie?; **he's not in the same ~ as his brother** sein Bruder ist eine Klasse besser; **they're just not in the same ~** man kann sie einfach nicht vergleichen; **in a ~ by himself/itself** *or* **of his/its own** weitaus der/das Beste
b (= social rank) gesellschaftliche Stellung, Stand *m (dated)*, Klasse *f (Sociol)*; **the ruling ~** die herrschende Klasse, die Herrschenden *pl*; **considerations of ~** Standeserwägungen *pl (dated)*, Klassengesichtspunkte *pl*; **it was ~ not ability that determined who ...** (die gesellschaftliche) Herkunft und nicht die Fähigkeiten bestimmten wer ...; **what ~ is he from?** aus welcher Schicht *or* Klasse kommt er?; **are you ashamed of your ~?** schämst du dich deines Standes *(dated) or* deiner Herkunft?; **~ and educational background** Klassenzugehörigkeit und Erziehung; **we were talking about ~** wir sprachen über die gesellschaftlichen Klassen
c (Sch, Univ) Klasse *f*; **I don't like her ~es** ihr Unterricht gefällt mir nicht; **you should prepare each ~ in advance** du solltest dich auf jede (Unterrichts)stunde vorbereiten; **to take a Latin ~** Latein unterrichten *or* geben; *(Univ)* ein Lateinseminar *etc* abhalten; **the French ~** (= lesson) die Französischstunde; (= people) die Französischklasse; **an evening ~** ein Abendkurs *m*; **eating in ~** Essen *nt* während des Unterrichts; **the ~ of 1980** der Jahrgang 1980, *die Schul-/ /Universitätsabgänger etc des Jahres 1980*
d (Bot, Zool) Klasse *f*
e (Brit Univ, of degree) Prädikat *nt*; **a first-~ degree** ein Prädikatsexamen *nt*; **second-/third-~ degree** ≈ Prädikat Gut/Befriedigend
f (inf: = quality, tone) Stil *m*; **to have ~** Stil haben, etwas hermachen *(inf)*; (person) Format haben; **that gives the place a bit of ~** das macht (doch) (et)was her *(inf)*; **I see we've got a bit of ~ in tonight, two guys in dinner jackets** heute Abend haben wir ja vornehme *or* exklusive Gäste, zwei Typen im Smoking
ADJ (inf: = excellent) erstklassig, exklusiv; **to be a ~ act** große Klasse sein *(inf)*
VT einordnen, klassifizieren; **he was ~ed with the servants** er wurde genauso eingestuft wie die Diener
VI eingestuft werden, sich einordnen lassen

class: class action N (US Jur) *Klage im Interesse einer Gruppe von Beteiligten*, Gruppenklage *f*; **class-conscious** ADJ standesbewusst, klassenbewusst; **class-consciousness** N Standesbewusstsein *nt*, Klassenbewusstsein *nt*; **class distinction** N gesellschaftlicher Unterschied, Klassenunterschied *m*; **there is too much ~** die gesellschaftlichen Unterschiede/ Klassenunterschiede sind zu groß; **class feeling** N (= antagonism) Klassenantagonismus *m*; (= solidarity) Solidarität *f*, Klassenbewusstsein *nt*

classic ['klæsɪk] ADJ (lit, fig) klassisch; **it was ~!** *(inf)* das war geradezu klassisch!; **a ~ example of sth** ein klassisches Beispiel für etw; **~ car** klassischer Wagen N Klassiker *m*

classical ['klæsɪkəl] ADJ klassisch; (= in the style of classical architecture) klassizistisch; *education* humanistisch; *method, solution also* altbewährt; **~ music** klassische Musik; **the ~ world** die antike Welt; **a ~ scholar** ein Altphilologe *m*

classically ['klæsɪkəlɪ] ADV klassisch

classicism ['klæsɪsɪzəm] N Klassik *f*; (= style of classic architecture) Klassizismus *m*

classicist ['klæsɪsɪst] N Altphilologe *m*/-philologin *f*

classics ['klæsɪks] N *sing (Univ)* Altphilologie *f*

classifiable ['klæsɪfaɪəbl] ADJ klassifizierbar

classification [ˌklæsɪfɪ'keɪʃən] N Klassifizierung *f*, Einteilung *f*

classified ['klæsɪfaɪd] ADJ in Klassen *or* Gruppen eingeteilt; **~ ad(vertisement)** Kleinanzeige *f*; **~ information** (Mil) Verschlusssache *f*; (Pol) Geheimsache *f*; **~ results** (Brit Sport) (Spiel)ergebnisse *pl*; **~ section** (Press) Kleinanzeigenteil *m* N **the ~s** die Kleinanzeigen *pl*

classify ['klæsɪfaɪ] VT a (= categorize) klassifizieren, (nach Klassen *or* Gruppen) ordnen b *information* für geheim erklären

classiness ['klɑːsɪnɪs] N *(inf)* Exklusivität *f*

classism ['klɑːsɪzəm] N Klassendiskriminierung *f*

class: classless ADJ *society* klassenlos; **class list** N (Brit Univ) Benotungsliste *f*; **classmate** N Klassenkamerad(in) *m(f)*, Mitschüler(in) *m(f)*; **class reunion** N Klassentreffen *nt*; **classridden** ADJ *society* von Klassengegensätzen beherrscht; **classroom** N Klassenzimmer *nt*; **classroom assistant** N Assistenzlehrkraft *f*; **class size** N (Sch) Klassenstärke *f*; **class society** N Klassengesellschaft *f*; **class struggle** N Klassenkampf *m*; **class system** N Klassensystem *nt*; **class thinking** N Klassendenken *nt*; **class war(fare)** N Klassenkrieg *m*

> **CLASS SYSTEM**
>
> Auch wenn sich das strenge Klassensystem des Viktorianischen Zeitalters im 20. Jahrhundert etwas gelockert hat, ist die britische Gesellschaft doch noch immer stark von einer Trennung der sozialen Klassen gekennzeichnet. In Großbritannien wird die Zugehörigkeit zu einer Klasse durch Geburt, Ausbildung, Beruf und Vermögen bestimmt, wobei auch Lebensstil und Akzent eine Rolle spielen. Auch wenn die Schaffung einer „klassenlosen Gesellschaft" das erklärte Ziel vieler Politiker ist, findet in der Öffentlichkeit relativ wenig Diskussion über das Klassensystem oder über Strategien zur Überwindung der Klassenschranken statt.

classy ['klɑːsɪ] ADJ (+er) *(inf)* nobel *(inf)*, exklusiv; **~ hotel** eine Nobelherberge *(inf)*; **a ~ woman** eine Klassefrau *(inf)*

clatter ['klætəʳ] N Klappern *nt*, Geklapper *nt*; (of hooves also) Trappeln *nt*, Getrappel *nt*; **her workbox fell with a ~ to the ground** mit lautem Klappern fiel der Nähkasten zu Boden VI klappern; (hooves also) trappeln; **the box of tools went ~ing down the stairs** der Werkzeugkasten polterte die Treppe hinunter; **the cart ~ed over the cobbles** der Wagen polterte *or* rumpelte über das Pflaster VT klappern mit

clause [klɔːz] N a (Gram) Satz *m* b (Jur etc) Klausel *f*

claustrophobia [ˌklɔːstrə'fəʊbɪə] N Klaustrophobie *f*, Platzangst *f (inf)*

claustrophobic [ˌklɔːstrə'fəʊbɪk] ADJ klaustrophob(isch) *(Psych)*; **it's so ~ in here** hier kriegt man Platzangst *(inf)*; **I get this ~ feeling** ich kriege Platzangst *(inf)*; **a room of ~ proportions** ein Zimmer, in dem man Platzangst kriegt *(inf)*

clave [kleɪv] *ptp of* **cleave**[2]

clavichord ['klævɪkɔːd] N Klavichord *nt*

clavicle ['klævɪkl] N Schlüsselbein *nt*

claw [klɔː] N Kralle *f*; (of lions, birds of prey also, of excavator) Klaue *f*; (of lobster etc) Schere *f*, Zange *f*; (of hammer) Nagelklaue *f*; **to show one's ~s** *(fig)* die Krallen zeigen; **to get one's ~s into sb** *(inf)* (dauernd) auf jdm herumhacken; **once a woman like that has got her ~s into a man ...** wenn eine Frau wie die erst einmal einen Mann in den Klauen hat ...
VT kratzen; **badly ~ed** schlimm zerkratzt; **the mole ~s its way through the soil** der Maulwurf wühlt sich durch das Erdreich; **they ~ed their way out from under the rubble** sie wühlten sich aus dem Schutt hervor; **he ~ed his way to the top** *(fig)* er hat sich an die Spitze durchgeboxt; **two women, like cats, ~ing each other** zwei Frauen, die wie Hyänen aufeinander losgingen
VI **to ~ at sth** sich an etw *(acc)* krallen; **he ~ed desperately for the handle** er krallte verzweifelt nach der Klinke

► **claw back** VT *sep* (taxman etc) sich *(dat)* zurückholen

► **claw out** VT *sep* auskratzen

claw: clawback N (for individual) Rückerstattung *f*; **from this sale the government got a £3m ~** aus diesem Verkauf flossen 3 Millionen Pfund in die Staatskasse zurück; **claw hammer** N Tischlerhammer *m*; **claw mark** N Kratzer *m*

clay [kleɪ] N Lehm *m*; **to have feet of ~** *or (US)* **~ feet** einen Makel auf seiner weißen Weste haben → *also* **potter**[1]

clay court N *(Tennis)* Sandplatz *m*

clayey ['kleɪɪ] ADJ lehmig; *soil also* Lehm-

claymore ['kleɪmɔː'] N zweischneidiges Langschwert

clay: **clay pigeon** N Tontaube *f*; **clay pigeon shooting** N Tontaubenschießen *nt*; **clay pipe** N Tonpfeife *f*

clean [kliːn] ADJ *(+er)* **a** *(= not dirty, also bomb)* sauber; **to wash/wipe/brush sth ~** etw abwaschen/-reiben/-bürsten; **to wipe a disk ~** *(Comput)* alle Daten von einer Diskette löschen; **she has very ~ habits, she's a very ~ person** sie ist sehr sauber

b *(= new, not used) sheets, paper* sauber, neu; *(Typ) proof* sauber; **I want to see a nice ~ plate** ich will einen schön leer gegessenen Teller sehen; **the vultures picked the carcass/bone ~** die Geier nagten den Kadaver bis aufs Skelett ab/nagten den Knochen ganz ab; **to make a ~ start** ganz von vorne anfangen; *(in life)* ein neues Leben anfangen; **to have a ~ record** *(with police)* nicht vorbestraft sein, eine weiße Weste haben *(inf)*; **he has a ~ record** gegen ihn liegt nichts vor; **to start again with a ~ sheet** einen neuen Anfang machen, ein neues Kapitel aufschlagen; **a ~ driving licence** ein Führerschein *m* ohne Strafpunkte; **he's been ~ for six months** *(criminal)* er ist seit sechs Monaten sauber; *(from drink)* er ist seit sechs Monaten trocken; *(from drugs)* er ist seit sechs Monaten clean; **he's ~, no guns** *(inf)* alles in Ordnung, nicht bewaffnet

c *(= not obscene) joke* stubenrein; *film* anständig; **keep television ~** das Fernsehen muss sauber *or* anständig bleiben; **good ~ fun** ein harmloser, netter Spaß

d *(= well-shaped) lines* klar

e *(= regular, even) cut* sauber, glatt; **a ~ break** *(also Med)* ein glatter Bruch; *(fig)* ein klares Ende; **a ~ break with the past** ein klarer Bruch mit der Vergangenheit

f *(Sport) fight, match* sauber, fair; *boxer* fair

g *(= acceptable to religion)* rein

h **to make a ~ breast of sth** etw gestehen, sich *(dat)* etw von der Seele reden; **to have ~ hands** *(fig)* eine reine Weste haben → **sweep**

ADV glatt; **I ~ forgot** das habe ich glatt(weg) vergessen *(inf)*; **he got ~ away** er verschwand spurlos; **he got ~ away from the rest of the field** er ließ das übrige Feld weit hinter sich; **the ball/he went ~ through the window** der Ball flog glatt/er flog achtkantig durch das Fenster; **to cut ~ through sth** etw ganz durchschneiden/durchschlagen *etc*; **to come ~** *(inf)* auspacken *(inf)*; **to come ~ about sth** etw gestehen; **we're ~ out (of matches)** es sind keine (Streichhölzer) mehr da

VT sauber machen; *(with cloth also)* abwischen; *carpets also* reinigen; *(= remove stains etc)* säubern; *clothes also* säubern *(form)*; *(= dry-clean)* reinigen; *nails, paintbrush, furniture also, dentures, old buildings* reinigen; *window, shoes* putzen, reinigen *(form)*; *fish, wound* säubern; *chicken* ausnehmen; *vegetables* putzen; *apple, grapes etc* säubern *(form)*; *(= wash)* (ab)waschen; *(= wipe)* abwischen; *cup, plate etc* säubern *(form)*; *car* waschen, putzen; **the cat is ~ing itself** die Katze putzt sich; **to ~ one's hands** *(= wash)* sich *(dat)* die Hände waschen *or (wipe)* abwischen *or (scrape, with grease remover)* säubern; **to ~ one's teeth** sich *(dat)* die Zähne putzen *or (with toothpick)* säubern; **to ~ one's face** *(= wash)* sich *(dat)* das Gesicht waschen *or (wipe)* abwischen; **~ the dirt off your face** wisch dir den Schmutz vom Gesicht!; **~ your shoes before you come inside** putz dir die Schuhe ab, bevor du reinkommst!; **to ~ a room** ein Zimmer sauber machen, in einem Zimmer putzen; **clothes which are easy to ~** pflegeleichte Kleider *pl*

VI reinigen; **this paint ~s easily** diese Farbe lässt sich leicht reinigen; **brand X ~s better** die Marke X reinigt gründlicher

N **to give sth a ~** etw sauber machen, reinigen

▶ **clean down** VT *sep car, lorry* waschen; *walls* abwaschen

▶ **clean off** VT *sep (= wash)* abwaschen; *(= rinse)* abspülen; *(= wipe)* abwischen; *(= scrape, rub)* abreiben; *dirt, barnacles, rust* entfernen, abmachen *(inf)* VI sich abwaschen *etc* lassen

▶ **clean out** VT *sep* **a** *(lit)* gründlich sauber machen; *(with water also)* ausspülen; *stables also* ausmisten; *carburettor* reinigen; *stomach* auspumpen *or* -räumen **b** *(inf) (= to leave penniless) person* ausnehmen (wie eine Weihnachtsgans) *(inf)*; *(= to rob, burgle) bank, house, flat* ausräumen *(inf)*; **to clean out the bank** *(when gambling)* die Bank sprengen; **to be cleaned out** abgebrannt sein *(inf)* **c** *(inf: = buy all stock)* **to clean sb out** jdm alles wegkaufen

▶ **clean up** VT *sep* **a** *(lit)* sauber machen; *old building, old painting* reinigen; *mess* aufräumen; **to clean oneself up** sich sauber machen **b** *(fig)* **the new mayor cleaned up the city** der neue Bürgermeister hat für Sauberkeit in der Stadt gesorgt; **to clean up television** den Bildschirm (von Gewalt, Sex *etc*) säubern → **act N d** VI **a** *(lit)* aufräumen **b** *(inf)* abkassieren *(inf)*, absahnen *(inf)*; **to clean up at the record stores/box office** *(CD/movie)* voll abräumen *(inf)*

clean: **clean-break divorce** N *Scheidung, bei der die Frau auf Unterhaltszahlungen verzichtet und dafür Vermögenswerte wie z.B. das Haus überschrieben bekommt*; **clean-cut** ['kliːn'kʌt] ADJ klar, klar umrissen; *sort of person* gepflegt; **the ~ lines of his new suit** der klare *or* einfache Schnitt seines neuen Anzuges; **~ features** klare Gesichtszüge *pl*

cleaner ['kliːnə'] N **a** *(= person)* Reinemachefrau *f*, Gebäudereiniger *m (form)*; **a firm of office ~s** eine Büroreinigungsfirma; **the ~s come once a week** das Reinigungspersonal kommt einmal pro Woche **b** *(= shop)* **~'s** Reinigung *f*; **to take sb to the ~'s** *(inf: = con, trick)* jdn übers Ohr hauen *(inf)*, jdn reinlegen *(inf)*; *(= defeat easily)* jdn in die Pfanne hauen *(inf)* **c** *(= thing)* Reiniger *m* → **vacuum cleaner** **d** *(= substance)* Reiniger *m*, Reinigungsmittel *nt*

cleaning ['kliːnɪŋ] N **the ladies who do the ~** die Frauen, die (hier) sauber machen; **~ fluid** Reinigungsflüssigkeit *f*

cleaning lady N Reinemachefrau *f*

clean-limbed ['kliːn'lɪmd] ADJ gut gebaut

cleanliness ['klenlɪnɪs] N Reinlichkeit *f*; **~ is next to godliness** *(Prov)* Sauberkeit ist alles!

clean-living ['kliːn'lɪvɪŋ] ADJ anständig, sauber

cleanly[1] ['kliːnlɪ] ADV sauber; **the bone broke ~** es war ein glatter Knochenbruch

cleanly[2] ['klenlɪ] ADJ *(+er)* sauber; *person* reinlich

cleanness ['kliːnnɪs] N **a** Sauberkeit *f* **b** *(of joke)* Anständigkeit *f*, Stubenreinheit *f*; *(of film)* Anständigkeit *f*; *(Typ, of proof)* Sauberkeit *f* **c** *(of outline)* Klarheit *f* **d** *(of break etc)* Sauberkeit *f*, Glätte *f*; **because of the ~ of the break** weil es ein glatter Bruch war

clean-out ['kliːnaʊt] N **to give sth a ~** etw sauber machen

clean room N *(Ind)* Reinraum *m*

cleanse [klenz] VT reinigen; *(spiritually)* läutern (of von)

cleanser ['klenzə'] N *(= detergent)* Reiniger *m*, Reinigungsmittel *nt*; *(for skin)* Reinigungscreme *f*, Reinigungsmilch *f*

clean-shaven ['kliːn'ʃeɪvn] ADJ glatt rasiert

cleansing ['klenzɪŋ] ADJ *agent* Reinigungs-; **~ cream/milk** Reinigungscreme *f*/-milch *f*; **~ lotion** Reinigungslotion *f*

cleansing department N Stadtreinigung *f*

cleanskin ['kliːnskɪn] N *(Brit, Austral inf) Person ohne beweisbaren kriminellen oder terroristischen Hintergrund*

cleanup ['kliːnʌp] N **a** **give yourself a good ~ before you come down to dinner** wasch dich erst einmal, bevor du zum Essen kommst; **to give sth a ~** etw sauber machen; **~ operation/costs** Säuberungsaktion *f*/-kosten *pl* **b** *(by police)* Säuberung *f* **c** *(sl: = profit)* Schnitt *m (inf)*

clear [klɪə']
✪ 26.1, 26.3

1 ADJECTIVE	4 TRANSITIVE VERB
2 NOUN	5 INTRANSITIVE VERB
3 ADVERB	6 PHRASAL VERBS

1 – ADJECTIVE *(+er)*

a [generally] klar; *complexion* rein; *conscience* rein, gut *attr*; *photograph* scharf; **on a clear day** bei klarem Wetter

b [= obvious] klar; **to be clear to sb** jdm klar sein; **it's still not clear to me why** es ist mir immer noch nicht klar, warum, ich bin immer noch im Unklaren (darüber), warum; **a clear case of murder** ein klarer *or* eindeutiger Fall von Mord; **to have a clear advantage** eindeutig *or* klar im Vorteil sein; **you weren't very clear** du hast dich nicht sehr klar ausgedrückt; **is that clear?** alles klar?; **let's get this clear, I'm the boss** eins wollen wir mal klarstellen, ich bin hier der Chef; **as clear as day** sonnenklar; **as clear as mud** *(inf)* klar wie Kloßbrühe *(inf)*

♦ **to make + clear** **to make oneself** *or* **one's meaning clear** sich klar ausdrücken; **do I make myself clear?** habe ich mich klar (genug) ausgedrückt?; **to make it clear to sb that …** es jdm (unmissverständlich) klarmachen, dass …; **to make sth clear to sb** *(= explain)* jdm etw klarmachen; **I wish to make it clear that …** *(= state unequivocally)* ich möchte einmal ganz klar sagen, dass …

c [= sure] **to be clear on** *or* **about sth** (sich *dat*) über etw *(acc)* im Klaren sein; **if you're not clear about something, ask me** falls Ihnen etwas unklar ist *or* falls Sie sich über etwas nicht im Klaren sind, fragen Sie bitte mich

d [= free] **to be clear of sth** frei von etw sein; **I want to keep the weekend clear** ich möchte mir das Wochenende freihalten; **we're now clear of debts** jetzt sind wir schuldenfrei *or* frei von Schulden, jetzt haben wir keine Schulden mehr; **he's clear of all suspicion** er ist frei von jedem Verdacht; **she is clear of cancer** sie hat keinen Krebs mehr

e [= unobstructed] *road, way* frei; **is it clear now?** *(of road)* ist jetzt frei?; **there's not an inch of clear space on his desk** auf seinem Schreibtisch ist überhaupt kein Platz

f [= not touching] **jack the car up until the wheel is clear** heb den Wagen an, bis das Rad nicht mehr den Boden berührt

♦ **clear of**

[= away from] **the bottom of the door should be about 3 mm clear of the floor** zwischen Tür und Fußboden müssen etwa 3 mm Luft sein; **park at least 20 cm clear of the pavement** parken Sie wenigstens 20 cm vom Bürgersteig entfernt; **OK, keep going, you're clear of the wall** in Ordnung, fahr, bis zur Mauer ist noch ein ganzes Stück Platz; **hold his head well clear of the water** den Kopf gut über Wasser halten; **the mortars landed well clear of us** die Mörser schlugen ein ganzes Stück neben uns ein

[= beyond] **the plane climbed until it was clear of the clouds** das Flugzeug stieg auf, bis es aus den Wolken heraus war; **the car was clear of the town** das Auto hatte die Stadt hinter sich gelassen; **at last we were/got clear of the prison walls** endlich hatten wir die Gefängnismauern hinter uns

g [= ahead] *Brit* **Rangers are now three points clear** Rangers liegen jetzt mit drei Punkten Vorsprung an der Spitze; **Rangers are now three points clear of Celtic** Rangers liegt jetzt drei Punkte vor Celtic

h [= complete] voll, vollständig; **three clear days** drei volle Tage

i [= net] klar; **a clear profit** ein Reingewinn *m*; **a clear majority** eine klare Mehrheit; **to have a clear lead** klar führen

2 – NOUN

♦ **in clear** in Klartext

♦ **in the clear** **to be in the clear** *(= free from suspicion)* frei von jedem Verdacht sein; **we're not in the clear yet** *(= not out of debt, difficulties)* wir sind noch nicht aus allem heraus; **this puts Harry in the clear** damit ist Harry entlastet

3 – ADVERB

a [= distinctly] **loud and clear** laut und deutlich

b [= completely] **he got clear away** er verschwand spurlos; **he kicked the ball clear across the field** er schoss den Ball quer über das Spielfeld

c [= away] **he kicked the ball clear** er klärte; **the helicopter lifted him clear** der Hubschrauber brachte ihn außer Gefahr; **he leapt clear of the burning car** er rettete sich durch einen Sprung aus dem brennenden Auto; **I'll come when I get clear of all this work** ich komme, wenn ich diese ganze Arbeit erledigt *or* hinter mir habe

♦ **to steer/keep clear** **to steer** *or* **keep clear of sb** jdm aus dem Wege gehen; **to steer** *or* **keep clear of sth** etw meiden; **to steer** *or* **keep clear of a place** um einen Ort einen großen Bogen machen; **you'd better steer** *or* **keep clear of that pub** um die Kneipe würde ich lieber einen großen Bogen machen; **I prefer to keep clear of town during the rush hour** während der Hauptverkehrszeit meide ich die Stadt nach Möglichkeit; **exit, keep clear** Ausfahrt frei halten!; **dangerous chemicals, keep clear** Vorsicht, giftige Chemikalien!; **keep clear of the testing area** Versuchsgebiet nicht betreten!

♦ **to stand clear** zurücktreten, zurückbleiben; **stand clear of the doors!** bitte von den Türen zurücktreten!

4 – TRANSITIVE VERB

a [= remove obstacles from] *pipe* reinigen; *blockage* beseitigen; *land, road, railway line* räumen; *(Comput) screen* löschen; *one's conscience* erleichtern; **to clear the table** den Tisch abräumen; **to clear the decks (for action)** *(fig)* alles startklar machen; **to clear a space for sth** für etw Platz schaffen; **to clear the way for sb/sth** den Weg für jdn/etw frei machen; **to clear the streets of beggars** die Bettler von den Straßen vertreiben; **to clear a way through the crowd** sich *(dat)* einen Weg durch die Menge bahnen; **to clear a room** *(of people)* ein Zimmer räumen; *(of things)* ein Zimmer ausräumen; **her singing cleared the room in no time** ihr Gesang ließ die Leute fluchtartig den Raum verlassen; **to clear the court** den Gerichtssaal räumen lassen; **to clear the ground for further talks** den Boden für weitere Gespräche bereiten

b [= clear away] *snow, rubbish* räumen; **he cleared all the rubbish off his desk, he cleared his desk of all the rubbish** er räumte den ganzen Kram von seinem Schreibtisch

c [letterbox] leeren

d [= free from guilt] *Jur: = find innocent person* freisprechen; *one's/sb's name* reinwaschen; **that clears him** das beweist seine Unschuld; **he will easily clear himself** er wird seine Unschuld leicht beweisen können

e [= get past or over] **he cleared the bar easily** er übersprang die Latte mit Leichtigkeit; **the horse cleared the gate easily** das Pferd nahm das Gatter mit Leichtigkeit; **the door should clear the floor by 3 mm** zwischen Tür und Fußboden müssen 3 mm Luft sein; **raise the car till the wheel clears the ground** das Auto anheben, bis das Rad den Boden nicht mehr berührt; **the ship's keel only just cleared the reef** der Kiel des Schiffes kam an dem Riff nur um Haaresbreite vorbei

f [= purify] *blood* reinigen; **to clear one's head** [(wieder)] einen klaren Kopf bekommen

g [Ftbl etc] *Brit* **to clear the ball** klären

h [= make profit of] machen, rausholen *(inf)*; **I didn't even clear my expenses** ich habe nicht einmal meine Ausgaben wieder hereinbekommen

i [debt] begleichen, zurückzahlen

j [stock] räumen; **"half price, to clear"** „Restposten zum halben Preis"

k [= approve] abfertigen; *ship* klarieren; *expenses, appointment* bestätigen; *goods* zollamtlich abfertigen; **to clear a cheque** *or (US)* **check** bestätigen, dass ein Scheck gedeckt ist; **you'll have to clear that with management** Sie müssen das mit der Firmenleitung regeln *or* abklären; **cleared by security** von den Sicherheitsbehörden für unbedenklich erklärt; **to clear a plane for take-off** einem Flugzeug die Starterlaubnis erteilen, ein Flugzeug zum Start freigeben

5 – INTRANSITIVE VERB

(weather) aufklaren, schön werden; *(mist, smoke)* sich auflösen

6 – PHRASAL VERBS

► **clear away** VT *sep* wegräumen VI **a** *(mist etc)* sich auflösen, sich legen **b** *(= clear away the dishes)* den Tisch abräumen

► **clear off** VT *sep debts* begleichen, zurückzahlen; *mortgage* abzahlen, abtragen; *arrears of work* aufarbeiten VI *(Brit inf)* abhauen *(inf)*, verschwinden *(inf)*

► **clear out** VT *sep cupboard, room, unwanted objects* ausräumen; **he cleared everyone out of the room** er schickte alle aus dem Zimmer VI *(inf)* **a** *(= leave)* verschwinden *(inf)* **b** *(= leave home etc)* ausziehen, sich absetzen *(inf)*

► **clear up** VT *sep* **a** *point, matter* klären; *mystery, crime* aufklären, aufdecken; *doubts* beseitigen **b** *(= tidy)* aufräumen; *litter* wegräumen VI **a** *(weather)* (sich) aufklären; *(rain)* aufhören **b** *(= tidy up)* aufräumen

---

clearance [ˈklɪərəns] N **a** *(= act of clearing)* Entfernen *nt*, Beseitigung *f* → *also* **slum clearance** **b** *(= free space)* Spielraum *m*; *(= headroom)* lichte Höhe **c** *(Ftbl etc)* **it was a good ~ by the defender** der Verteidiger hat gut geklärt **d** *(of cheque)* Bestätigung *f* der Deckung **e** *(by customs)* Abfertigung *f*; *(by security)* Unbedenklichkeitserklärung *f*; *(= document)* Unbedenklichkeitsbescheinigung *f*; **get your security ~ first** Sie müssen erst noch von den Sicherheitsorganen für unbedenklich erklärt werden; **the despatch was sent to the Foreign Office for ~** der Bericht wurde zur Überprüfung ans Außenministerium geschickt; **~ to land** Landeerlaubnis *f*; **~ for takeoff** Startfreigabe *f* **f** *(Naut)* Klarierung *f*; **~ outwards** Ausklarierung *f*; **~ inwards** Einklarierung *f*

clearance: **clearance certificate** N *(Naut)* Verzollungspapiere *pl*; **clearance sale** N *(Comm)* Räumungsverkauf *m*

clear-cut [ˈklɪəˈkʌt] ADJ **a** *decision, distinction, answer, policy, victory* klar; *issue, problem* klar umrissen **b** *features* scharf

clear-headed [ˈklɪəˈhedɪd] ADJ *person, decision* besonnen

clearing [ˈklɪərɪŋ] N *(in forest)* Lichtung *f*

clearing: **clearing bank** N *(Brit)* Clearingbank *f*; **clearing house** N Clearingstelle *f*

clearly [ˈklɪəlɪ] ✪ 15.1 ADV **a** *(= distinctly)* klar; **~ visible** klar *or* gut zu sehen; **to stand out ~ from the rest** sich deutlich vom Übrigen hervorheben *or* abheben **b** *(= obviously)* eindeutig; **is that so? – ~** ist das der Fall? – natürlich *or* selbstverständlich; **~ we cannot allow …** wir können keinesfalls zulassen …; **this ~ can't be true** das muss eindeutig falsch sein, das kann auf keinen Fall stimmen

clearness [ˈklɪənɪs] N **a** *(of water, soup, sky, head, eyes, weather etc)* Klarheit *f*; *(of complexion, conscience)* Reinheit *f*; *(of colour)* Kräftigkeit *f*; *(of photograph)* Schärfe *f* **b** *(of sound)* Klarheit *f* **c** *(to one's understanding: = distinctness, obviousness)* Klarheit *f*

clear: **clear round** N *(Showjumping)* Null-Fehler-Ritt *m*; **to do a ~** den Parcours fehlerfrei durchreiten; **clear-sighted** ADJ *(fig)* klar- *or* scharfsichtig; **clear-sightedness** N *(fig)* Klar- *or* Scharfsicht *f*; **clear-up rate** N *(Police)* Aufklärungsrate *f*; **clearway** N *(Brit)* Straße *f* mit Halteverbot, Schnellstraße *f*

cleat [kliːt] N *(on shoes)* Stoßplatte *f*; *(made of metal)* Absatzeisen *nt*; *(on gangplank etc)* Querleiste *f*; *(for rope)* Klampe *f*

cleavage [ˈkliːvɪdʒ] N **a** *(= split)* Spalte *f*, Kluft *f (geh)*; *(fig)* Spaltung *f*, Kluft *f* **b** *(of woman's breasts)* Dekolletee *nt*, Dekolleté *nt*

cleave[1] [kliːv] *pret* **clove** *or* **cleft** *or* **cleaved**, *ptp* **cleft** *or* **cloven** VT spalten; **to ~ in two** in zwei Teile spalten; **to ~ a way through sth** sich *(dat)* einen Weg durch etw bahnen VI **a** **to ~ through the waves** die Wellen durchschneiden **b** *(Biol)* sich spalten

cleave[2] VI *pret* **cleaved** *or* **clave**, *ptp* **cleaved** *(= adhere)* festhalten *(to* an *+dat)*, beharren *(to* auf *+dat)*; **through all the difficulties they ~d fast to each other** *(liter)* durch alle Schwierigkeiten hindurch hielten sie fest zusammen

cleaver [ˈkliːvəˈ] N Hackbeil *nt*

clef [klef] N (Noten)schlüssel *m*

cleft [kleft] *pret, ptp of* **cleave**[1] ADJ gespalten; **a ~ chin** ein Kinn *nt* mit Grübchen; **to be in a ~ stick** in der Klemme sitzen *(inf)* N Spalte *f*, Kluft *f (geh)*; *(in chin)* Grübchen *nt*; *(in forehead)* Senkrecht- *or* Skeptikerfalte *f*; *(fig)* Spaltung *f*, Kluft *f*

cleft: **cleft lip** N Hasenscharte *f*; **cleft palate** N Gaumenspalte *f*, Wolfsrachen *m*

clematis [ˈklemətɪs] N Waldrebe *f*, Klematis *f*

clemency [ˈklemənsɪ] N Milde *f (towards sb* jdm gegenüber); **the prisoner was shown ~** dem Gefangenen wurde eine milde Behandlung zuteil

clement [ˈklemənt] ADJ mild *(towards sb* jdm gegenüber)

clementine [ˈkleməntaɪn] N *(= fruit)* Klementine *f*

clench [klentʃ] VT **a** *fist* ballen; *teeth* zusammenbeißen; *(= grasp firmly)* packen; **to ~ sth between one's teeth** etw zwischen die Zähne klemmen; **to ~ sth in one's hands** etw mit den Händen umklammern; **~ed-fist salute** Arbeiterkampfgruß *m* **b** → **clinch VT a**

Cleopatra [ˌkliːəˈpætrə] N Kleopatra *f*

clerestory [ˈklɪəstɔːrɪ] N *(Archit)* Lichtgaden *m*

clergy [ˈklɜːdʒɪ] PL Klerus *m*, Geistlichkeit *f*, die Geistlichen *pl*; **to join the ~** Geistlicher werden

clergyman [ˈklɜːdʒɪmən] N *pl* **-men** [-mən] Geistliche(r) *m*, Pastor *m*, Pfarrer *m*

clergywoman [ˈklɜːdʒɪˌwʊmən] *pl* **-women** [-wɪmɪn] N Geistliche *f*, Pastorin *f*, Pfarrerin *f*

cleric [ˈklerɪk] N Geistliche(r) *m*

clerical [ˈklerɪkəl] ADJ **a** **~ work/job** Schreib- *or* Büroarbeit *f*; **~ worker** Schreib- *or* Bürokraft *f*; **~ staff** Schreibkräfte *pl*, Büropersonal *nt*; **~ error** Versehen *nt*; *(in figures, wording etc)* Schreibfehler *m*; **~ duties** Büroarbeiten *pl*; **~ inaccuracies** Versehen *nt*, Nachlässigkeit *f*; **the ~ branch of the civil service** ≈ die mittlere Beamtenlaufbahn **b** *(Eccl)* geistlich

clerical collar N Stehkragen *m (des Geistlichen)*, Priesterkragen *m*

clericalism [ˈklerɪkəlɪzəm] N Klerikalismus *m*

clerihew [ˈklerɪhjuː] N Clerihew *nt*, witziger Vierzeiler

clerk [klɑːk, *(US)* klɜːrk] N **a** (Büro)angestellte(r) *mf* **b** *(= secretary)* Schriftführer(in) *m(f)*; **Clerk of the Court** *(Brit Jur)* Protokollführer(in) *m(f)*; **~ of works** *(Brit)* Bauleiter(in) *m(f)* **c** *(US: = shop assistant)* Verkäufer(in) *m(f)* **d** *(US, in hotel)* Hotelsekretär(in) *m(f)*

clever ['klevəʳ] ADJ a (= *mentally bright*) schlau; *animal also* klug; **to be ~ at French** gut in Französisch sein; **how ~ of you to remember my birthday!** wie aufmerksam von dir, dass du an meinen Geburtstag gedacht hast! b (= *ingenious, skilful, witty*) klug; *person, move in chess also* geschickt; *idea also* schlau; *device, machine* raffiniert, geschickt; **to be ~ at sth** in etw *(dat)* geschickt sein; **he is ~ at raising money** er ist geschickt, wenn es darum geht, Geld aufzubringen; **to be ~ with one's hands** geschickte Hände haben c (= *cunning, smart*) schlau, clever *(inf)*

clever-clever ['klevəʳ'klevəʳ] ADJ *(inf)* ausgeklügelt; *person* oberschlau *(inf)*

clever clogs ['klevəʳ'klɒgz] N *(inf)* Schlauberger *m (inf)*

clever Dick N *(Brit inf)* Schlaumeier *m (inf)*, Schlaukopf *m (inf)*

cleverly ['klevəlɪ] ADV geschickt; (= *wittily*) schlau, klug; **he very ~ remembered it** schlau wie er war, hat er es nicht vergessen

cleverness ['klevənɪs] N a (= *intelligence*) Schlauheit *f*; *(of animal also)* Klugheit *f* b (= *skill, ingenuity*) Klugheit *f*; *(of person, move in chess also)* Geschicktheit *f*; *(of idea)* Schlauheit *f*; *(of device, machine)* Raffiniertheit *f* c (= *cunning*) Schläue *pl*, Cleverness *f*

clew [kluː] N a *(of thread)* Knäuel *nt* b *(Naut, of sail)* Schothorn *nt*; *(of hammock)* Schlaufe *f* c = **clue** VT a *thread* aufwickeln b *(Naut)* **to ~ (up)** aufgeien

cliché ['kliːʃeɪ] N Klischee *nt*; **~-ridden** voller Klischees

clichéd ['kliːʃeɪd] ADJ klischeehaft

click[1] [klɪk] N Klicken *nt*; *(of joints)* Knacken *nt*; *(of light switch)* Knipsen *nt*; *(of fingers)* Knipsen *nt*, Schnipsen *nt*; *(Comput)* (Maus)klick *m*; *(of latch, key in lock)* Schnappen *nt*; *(tongue, Phon)* Schnalzen *nt*; **he turned with a sharp ~ of his heels** er drehte sich um und klappte zackig die Hacken zusammen

VI a (= *make clicking noise*) klicken; *(joints)* knacken; *(light switch)* knipsen; *(fingers)* knipsen, schnipsen; *(Comput)* klicken; *(latch, key in lock)* schnappen; *(tongue, Phon)* schnalzen; *(high heels)* klappern

b *(inf: = be understood)* funken *(inf)*; **suddenly it all ~ed (into place)** plötzlich hatte es gefunkt *(inf)*

c *(inf: = get on well)* funken *(inf)*; **they ~ed right from the moment they first met** zwischen ihnen hatte es vom ersten Augenblick an gefunkt *(inf)*; **some people you ~ with straight away** mit manchen Leuten versteht man sich auf Anhieb

d *(inf: = catch on)* ankommen *(inf)* *(with* bei*)*

VT *heels* zusammenklappen; *fingers* schnippen mit; *(Comput)* klicken auf *+acc*; *tongue* schnalzen mit; **to ~ a door shut** eine Tür zuklinken; **to ~ sth into place** etw einschnappen lassen

▶ **click on** VI a *(inf, = understand)* es schnallen *(inf)*; **he just didn't click on** er hat es einfach nicht geschnallt *(inf)* b *(Comput)* **to click on the mouse** mit der Maus klicken; **to click on an icon** ein Icon anklicken

click[2] N *usu pl (US inf)* Kilometer *m*

clickable ['klɪkəbl] ADJ *(Comput) icon, image* anklickbar

clicker ['klɪkəʳ] N *(US inf: = remote control)* Fernbedienung *f*

clickstream ['klɪkstriːm] N *(Internet)* Clickstream *m*, *zurückgelegter Weg auf einer Website*

client ['klaɪənt] N a Kunde *m*, Kundin *f*; *(of solicitor)* Klient(in) *m(f)*; *(of barrister)* Mandant(in) *m(f)* b *(US, receiving welfare)* Bezieher(in) *m(f)*

clientele [ˌkliːɒn'tel] N Kundschaft *f*, Klientel *f*; **the regular ~** die Stammkundschaft

client state N *(Pol)* Satellitenstaat *m*

cliff [klɪf] N Klippe *f*; *(along coast also)* Kliff *nt*; *(inland also)* Felsen *m*; **the ~s of Cornwall** die Kliffküste Cornwalls; **the ~s of Dover** die Felsen von Dover

cliff: **cliff dweller** N *vorgeschichtlicher Höhlenbewohner im Colorado-Cañon*; **cliffhanger** N Superthriller *m (inf)*; **cliffhanging** ADJ *conclusion* spannungsgeladen; **clifftop** N Felskuppe *f*; **a house on a ~** ein Haus oben auf einem Felsen ADJ **~ walk** Spaziergang *m* auf der Felskuppe; **~ scenery** Felsenlandschaft *f*

climacteric [klaɪ'mæktərɪk] N *(Med)* Klimakterium *nt*; *(fig)* (Lebens)wende *f*, Wendepunkt *m* (im Leben)

climactic [klaɪ'mæktɪk] ADJ **the conclusion was ~ in the extreme** der Schluss war ein absoluter Höhepunkt; **a ~ scene** ein Höhepunkt

climate ['klaɪmɪt] N *(lit, fig)* Klima *nt*; **the two countries have very different ~s** die beiden Länder haben (ein) sehr unterschiedliches Klima; **America has many different ~s** Amerika hat viele verschiedene Klimazonen; **to move to a warmer ~** in eine wärmere Gegend *or* in eine Gegend mit wärmerem Klima ziehen; **the ~ of public opinion** die Stimmung in der Öffentlichkeit, das öffentliche Klima; **~ conference** *(Pol)* Klimakonferenz *f or* -gipfel *m*

climatic [klaɪ'mætɪk] ADJ klimatisch, Klima-

climatologist [ˌklaɪmə'tɒlədʒɪst] N Klimaforscher(in) *m(f)*

climatology [ˌklaɪmə'tɒlədʒɪ] N Klimatologie *f*, Klimakunde *f*

climax ['klaɪmæks] N *(all senses)* Höhepunkt *m*; *(sexual also)* Orgasmus *m*; **this brought matters to a ~** damit erreichte die Angelegenheit ihren Höhepunkt

climb [klaɪm] VT a *(also* **climb up***)* klettern auf *(+acc)*; *wall also, hill* steigen auf *(+acc)*; *mountains also* besteigen; *ladder, steps* hoch- *or* hinaufsteigen; *pole, cliffs* hochklettern; **my car can't ~ that hill** mein Auto schafft den Berg nicht *or* kommt den Berg nicht hoch; **to ~ a rope** an einem Seil hochklettern

b *(also* **climb over***)* *wall etc* steigen *or* klettern über *(+acc)*

VI klettern; *(as mountaineer)* bergsteigen; *(into train, car etc)* steigen; *(road)* ansteigen; *(aircraft)* (auf)steigen; *(sun)* steigen; *(prices)* steigen, klettern *(inf)*; **when the sun had ~ed to its highest point** als die Sonne am höchsten stand; **he ~ed to the top of his profession** er hat den Gipfel seiner beruflichen Laufbahn erklommen

N a (= *climbing*) **we're going out for a ~** wir machen eine Kletter- *or* Bergtour; *(as mountaineers)* wir gehen bergsteigen; **that was some ~!** das war eine Kletterei!; **Ben Lomond is an easy ~** Ben Lomond ist leicht zu besteigen; **I've never done that ~** den habe ich noch nicht bestiegen

b *(of aircraft)* Steigflug *m*; **the plane went into a steep ~** das Flugzeug zog steil nach oben

▶ **climb down** VI a *(person, from tree, wall)* herunterklettern; *(from horse, mountain)* absteigen; *(from ladder)* heruntersteigen; *(road)* abfallen b (= *admit error*) nachgeben; **it'll be a pleasure to make him climb down** es wird ein Vergnügen sein, ihn von seinem hohen Ross herunterzuholen VT *+prep obj tree, wall* herunterklettern von; *ladder* heruntersteigen; *mountain etc* absteigen

▶ **climb in** VI einsteigen; *(with difficulty also)* hineinklettern

▶ **climb up** VI = **climb** VI VI *+prep obj ladder etc* hinaufsteigen; *tree, wall* hochklettern

climbable ['klaɪməbl] ADJ besteigbar

climb-down ['klaɪmdaʊn] N *(fig)* Abstieg *m*; **it was quite a ~ for the boss to have to admit that he was wrong** der Chef musste ziemlich zurückstecken und zugeben, dass er unrecht hatte

climber ['klaɪməʳ] N a (= *mountaineer*) Bergsteiger(in) *m(f)*; (= *rock climber*) Kletterer(in) *m(f)* b (= *social climber*) sozialer Aufsteiger, soziale Aufsteigerin c (= *plant*) Kletterpflanze *f*

climbing ['klaɪmɪŋ] ADJ a Berg(steiger)-; (= *rock climbing*) Kletter-; *accident, partner* beim Bergsteigen; **we are going on a ~ holiday** wir gehen im Urlaub zum Bergsteigen/Klettern; **~ club** Bergsteiger-/Kletterklub *m*; **~ speed** *(Aviat)* Steiggeschwindigkeit *f* b *plant* Kletter- N a Bergsteigen *nt*; (= *rock climbing*) Klettern *nt*; **to go ~** bergsteigen/klettern gehen, zum Bergsteigen/Klettern gehen; **we did a lot of ~** wir sind viel geklettert b *(pej: also* **social climbing***)* sozialer Aufstieg

climbing: **climbing frame** N Klettergerüst *nt*; **climbing irons** ['klaɪmɪŋ'aɪənz] PL Steigeisen *pl*; **climbing plant** N Kletter- *or* Schlingpflanze *f*; **climbing wall** N Kletterwand *f*

clime [klaɪm] N *(old, liter)* Himmelsstrich *(old, liter)*, Landstrich *(geh) m*; **in these ~s** in diesen Breiten; **he moved to warmer ~s** er zog in wärmere Breiten

clinch [klɪntʃ] VT a *(Tech: also* **clench***)* *nail* krumm schlagen b *argument* zum Abschluss bringen; **to ~ the deal** den Handel perfekt machen, den Handel besiegeln; **that ~es it** damit ist der Fall erledigt VI *(Boxing)* in den Clinch gehen, clinchen N *(Boxing, fig)* Clinch *m*; **in a ~** im Clinch *(inf)*

clincher ['klɪntʃəʳ] N *(inf)* ausschlaggebendes Argument; **that was the ~** das gab den Ausschlag

cling[1] [klɪŋ] *pret, ptp* **clung** VI (= *hold on tightly*) sich festklammern *(to* an *+dat)*, sich klammern *(to* an *+acc)*; *(to opinion also)* festhalten *(to* an *+dat)*; (= *remain close*) sich halten *(to* an *+acc)*; *(clothes, fabric)* sich anschmiegen *(to +dat)*; *(smell)* haften *(to* an *+dat)*, sich setzen *(to* in *+acc)*; **~ on tight!** halt dich gut fest!; **to ~ together** sich aneinanderklammern; *(lovers)* sich umschlingen, sich umschlungen halten; **in spite of all the difficulties they've clung together** trotz aller Schwierigkeiten haben sie zusammengehalten; **she clung around her father's neck** sie hing ihrem Vater am Hals; **the boat clung to the shoreline** das Schiff hielt sich dicht an die Küste; **women who ~** Frauen, die sich an einen klammern

cling[2] N Klingen *nt*; *(of cash register)* Klingeln *nt* VI klingen; *(cash register)* klingeln

clingfilm ['klɪŋfɪlm] N Frischhaltefolie *f*

clinging ['klɪŋɪŋ] ADJ *garment* sich anschmiegend; *smell* lange haftend, hartnäckig; **she's the ~ sort** sie ist wie eine Klette *(inf)*

clinging vine N *(inf)* Klette *f (inf)*

cling(stone) peach ['klɪŋ(stəʊn)'piːtʃ] N Klingstone *m (nicht steinlösende Pfirsichsorte)*

clingwrap ['klɪŋræp] N *(US)* Frischhaltefolie *f*

clingy ['klɪŋɪ] ADJ *(+er) person* anhänglich; *thing* haftend

clinic ['klɪnɪk] N a Klinik *f* b (= *medical course*) klinischer Unterricht, Klinik *f*

clinical ['klɪnɪkəl] ADJ a *(Med)* klinisch; **~ tests** *or* **trials** klinische Tests *pl* b *(fig)* (= *sterile*) *room, atmosphere* steril, kalt; (= *detached, dispassionate*) klinisch, nüchtern; *sb's appearance* streng

clinical depression N klinische Depression

clinically ['klɪnɪkəlɪ] ADV *dead, test, prove, observe* klinisch; *insane, obese* krankhaft; **~ depressed** klinisch depressiv

clinical thermometer N Fieberthermometer *nt*

clink[1] [klɪŋk] VT klirren lassen; (= *jingle*) klimpern mit; **she ~ed a coin against the window** sie schlug mit einer Münze gegen die Scheibe, dass es klirrte; **to ~ glasses with sb** mit jdm anstoßen VI klirren; (= *jingle*) klimpern; **the spoon ~ed against the glass** der Löffel stieß klirrend an das Glas N *no pl* Klirren *nt*, Klimpern *nt*; **the ~ of glasses as they drank to his health** das Klingen der Gläser, als auf sein Wohl getrunken wurde

clink[2] N *(inf: = prison)* Knast *m (inf)*; **in ~** im Knast

clinker ['klɪŋkəʳ] N **a** *(from fire)* Schlacke *f*; **a ~** ein Stück Schlacke **b** *(= brick)* Klinker *m*

clinker-built ['klɪŋkəbɪlt] ADJ *(Naut)* klinkergebaut

clip[1] [klɪp] **N** **a** *(for holding things)* Klammer *f* **b** *(= jewel)* Klips *m* **c** *(of gun)* Ladestreifen *m* **VT** **to ~ on** anklemmen; *papers also* anheften; **to ~ sth onto sth** etw an etw *(acc)* anklemmen/-heften; **to ~ two things together** zwei Dinge zusammenklemmen/-heften **VI** **to ~ on (to sth)** (an etw *acc*) angeklemmt werden; **to ~ together** zusammengeklemmt werden

clip[2] **VT** **a** *(= trim)* scheren; *dog also* trimmen; *hedge also, fingernails* schneiden; *wings* stutzen; **to ~ sb's wings** *(fig)* jdm einen Dämpfer aufsetzen; **they'll find that a young baby will ~ their wings a bit** sie werden merken, dass das Kleinkind sie recht unbeweglich macht
b *(also* **clip out***) article from paper* ausschneiden; *(also* **clip off***) hair* abschneiden; **he ~ped a few seconds off the lap record** er hat den Rundenrekord um ein paar Sekunden unterboten
c *(Brit) ticket* lochen, knipsen, entwerten
d **to ~ (the ends of) one's words** abgehackt sprechen
e *(= hit)* treffen; *(= graze: car, bullet)* streifen; **he ~ped him round the ear** er gab ihm eine Ohrfeige; **the left jab just ~ped his chin** die linke Gerade streifte sein Kinn
N **a** *(= trim)* **to give the sheep a ~** die Schafe scheren; **to give the hedge a ~** die Hecke scheren *or* (be)schneiden; **to give one's fingernails a ~** sich *(dat)* die Fingernägel schneiden
b *(= sound)* Klappern *nt*
c *(= hit)* Schlag *m*; **he gave him a ~ round the ear** er gab ihm eins hinter die Ohren *(inf)*
d *(inf: = high speed)* **at a fair ~** mit einem Mordszahn *(inf)*; **he made off at a fair ~** er legte ganz schön los *(inf)*
e *(from film)* Ausschnitt *m*, Clip *m*

clip: **clip art** N *(Comput)* Clip-Art *f*; **clipboard** N **a** *(= board)* Klemmbrett *nt*, Manuskripthalter *m* **b** *(Comput)* Zwischenablage *f*; **clip-clop** N **the ~ of hooves** das Getrappel der Hufe; **clip frame** N Wechselrahmen *m*; **clip joint** N *(sl)* Nepplokal *nt (inf)*; **clip-on** ADJ *brooch* mit Klips; *tie* zum Anstecken; **~ earrings** Klips *pl*; **~ sunglasses** Sonnenklip *m*, Sonnenvorstecker *m*

clipped [klɪpt] ADJ *accent* abgehackt; **~ form** Kurzform *f*

clipper ['klɪpəʳ] N *(Naut)* Klipper *m*; *(Aviat)* Clipper *m*

clippers ['klɪpəz] PL *(also* **pair of clippers***)* Schere *f*; *(for hedge also)* Heckenschere *f*; *(for hair)* Haarschneidemaschine *f*; *(for fingernails)* Zwicker *m*, Nagelzange *f*

clippie ['klɪpɪ] N *(Brit inf)* Schaffnerin *f*

clipping ['klɪpɪŋ] N *(= newspaper clipping)* Ausschnitt *m*; **nail ~s** abgeschnittene Nägel *pl*

clique [kli:k] N Clique *f*, Klüngel *m (inf)*

cliquish ['kli:kɪʃ] ADJ cliquenhaft, klüngelhaft *(inf)*

cliquishness ['kli:kɪʃnɪs] N Cliquenwirtschaft *f*, Klüngel *m (inf)*

clitoris ['klɪtərɪs] N Klitoris *f*, Kitzler *m*

Cllr *(Brit) abbr of* **Councillor**

cloak [kləʊk] **N** *(lit)* Umhang *m*; *(fig: = disguise)* Deckmantel *m*; *(= veil: of secrecy etc)* Schleier *m*; **under the ~ of darkness** im Schutz der Dunkelheit **VT** *(fig)* verhüllen; **fog ~ed the town** die Stadt war in Nebel gehüllt

cloak: **cloak-and-dagger** ADJ mysteriös, geheimnisumwittert; **~ play** Kriminalstück *nt*; **a ~ operation** eine Nacht-und-Nebel-Aktion; **cloakroom** N **a** *(Brit: for coats)* Garderobe *f* **b** *(Brit euph)* Waschraum *m (euph)*

clobber ['klɒbəʳ] *(inf)* **N** *(Brit: = belongings)* Zeug *nt (inf)*; *(= clothes)* Klamotten *pl (inf)* **VT** **a** *(= hit, defeat)* **to get ~ed** eins übergebraten kriegen *(inf)*; **to ~ sb one** jdm ein paar vor den Latz knallen *(inf)* **b** *(= charge a lot)* schröpfen; **the taxman really ~ed me** das Finanzamt hat mir ganz schön was abgeknöpft *(inf)*

clobbering ['klɒbərɪŋ] N *(inf: = beating, defeat)* Tracht *f* Prügel *(inf)*, Dresche *f (inf)*; **to get a ~** Dresche *(inf) or* eine Tracht Prügel *(inf)* beziehen; *(fig: from the taxman)* ganz schön geschröpft werden *or* was abgeknöpft kriegen *(inf)*

cloche [klɒʃ] N **a** *(= hat)* Topfhut *m* **b** *(for plants)* Folien-/Glasschutz *m*

cloche tunnel N Folientunnel *m*

clock [klɒk] **N** **a** Uhr *f*; **round the ~** rund um die Uhr; **against the ~** *(Sport)* nach *or* auf Zeit; **to work against the ~** gegen die Uhr arbeiten; **to beat the ~** schneller als vorgesehen fertig sein; **to put the ~ back/forward** *or* **on** *(lit)* die Uhr zurückstellen/vorstellen; **to put** *or* **turn the ~ back** *(fig)* die Zeit zurückdrehen; **to watch the ~** *(inf)* dauernd auf die Uhr sehen
b *(inf: = speedometer, milometer)* Tacho *m (inf)*; *(of taxi)* Uhr *f*; **it's got 100,000 miles on the ~** es hat einen Tachostand von 100.000 Meilen
VT **a** *(Sport)* **he ~ed four minutes for the mile** er lief die Meile in vier Minuten; **he's ~ed the fastest time this year** er ist die schnellste Zeit dieses Jahres gelaufen/gefahren
b *(inf: = hit)* **he ~ed him one** er hat ihm eine runtergehauen *(inf)*
c *(Brit inf: = see)* sehen
d *(Brit inf) mileage* **to ~ back** *(in betrügerischer Absicht)* den Meilenzähler zurückdrehen

▶ **clock in** VI *(Sport)* **he clocked in at 3 minutes 56 seconds** seine Zeit war 3 Minuten 56 Sekunden

▶ **clock in** *or* **on** **VI** (den Arbeitsbeginn) stempeln *or* stechen **VT** *sep* **to clock sb on** für jdn stempeln *or* stechen

▶ **clock off** *or* **out** **VI** (das Arbeitsende) stempeln *or* stechen **VT** *sep* **to clock sb out** für jdn stempeln *or* stechen

▶ **clock up** VT *sep* **a** *(athlete, competitor) time* laufen/fahren/schwimmen *etc* **b** *speed, distance* fahren **c** *(inf) success* verbuchen; **that's another successful deal to clock up to Jim** noch ein erfolgreiches Geschäft, das Jim für sich verbuchen kann; **to clock up overtime** Überstunden machen

clock *in cpds* Uhr(en)-; **clock card** N Stechkarte *f*; **clock face** N Zifferblatt *nt*; **clock golf** N Uhrengolf *nt*; **clock hour** N volle Stunde; **clockmaker** N Uhrmacher(in) *m(f)*; **clock radio** N Radiouhr *f*; **clock rate** N *(Comput) (of CPU)* Taktfrequenz *f*; **clock speed** N *(Comput)* = **clock rate**; **clock tower** N Uhrenturm *m*; **clock-watcher** N **she's a terrible ~** sie sieht *or* guckt dauernd auf die Uhr; **clock-watching** N Auf-die-Uhr-Schauen *nt*; **clockwise** ADJ ADV im Uhrzeigersinn; **in a ~ direction** im Uhrzeigersinn; **clockwork** **N** *(of clock)* Uhrwerk *nt*; *(of toy)* Aufziehmechanismus *m*; **driven by ~** zum Aufziehen; **like ~** wie am Schnürchen **ATTR** **a** *train, car* aufziehbar, zum Aufziehen **b** **~ precision** äußerste Genauigkeit; **with ~ regularity** mit der Regelmäßigkeit eines Uhrwerks; **he arrives every day at 9.30 with ~ regularity** er kommt jeden Tag pünktlich auf die Minute um 9.30 Uhr

clod [klɒd] N **a** *(of earth)* Klumpen *m* **b** *(fig: = person, also* **clodpole***)* Trottel *m*; **this silly great ~** dieser Obertrottel *(inf)*

clodhopper ['klɒd,hɒpəʳ] N *(inf)* **a** *(= person)* Trampel *nt (inf)*, Tollpatsch *m* **b** *(= shoe)* Quadratlatschen *m (inf)*

clodhopping ['klɒd,hɒpɪŋ] ADJ *(inf) person* trampelig *(inf)*, tölpelhaft, schwerfällig; **~ shoes/boots** klobige Schuhe *pl*/Stiefel *pl*

clog [klɒg] **N** *(= shoe)* Holzschuh *m*; **~s** *pl (modern)* Clogs *pl*; **~ dance** Holzschuhtanz *m*; **to pop one's ~s** *(Brit inf)* den Löffel abgeben *(inf)* **VT** *(also* **clog up***) pipe, drain etc* verstopfen; *mechanism, wheels* blockieren; **~ged with traffic** verstopft **VI** *(also* **clog up***, pipe etc)* verstopfen; *(mechanism etc)* blockiert werden

cloggy ['klɒgɪ] ADJ *(inf)* klumpig

cloister ['klɔɪstəʳ] **N** **a** *(= covered walk)* Kreuzgang *m* **b** *(= monastery)* Kloster *nt* **VR** **to ~ oneself (away)** sich von der Welt abkapseln

cloistered ['klɔɪstəd] ADJ **a** *(fig)* weltabgeschieden; *way of thinking* weltfremd *or* -fern *(liter)*; **to lead a ~ life** *(= isolated)* in klösterlicher Abgeschiedenheit leben; *(= sheltered)* ein streng *or* klösterlich behütetes Leben führen **b** *(Archit)* **a ~ courtyard** ein Klosterhof *m* mit Kreuzgang

clone [kləʊn] **N** *(also Comput, fig: = person)* Klon *m* **VT** klonen

cloning ['kləʊnɪŋ] N Klonen *nt*; **human ~** Klonen *nt* von Menschen; **therapeutic ~** therapeutisches Klonen

clonk [klɒŋk] *(inf)* **VT** hauen **N** *(= blow)* Schlag *m*; *(= sound)* Plumps *m*

close[1] [kləʊs] **ADJ** *(+er)* **a** *(= near)* nahe *(to +gen)*, in der Nähe *(to +gen*, von); **is Glasgow ~ to Edinburgh?** liegt Glasgow in der Nähe von Edinburgh?; **the buildings which are ~ to the station** die Gebäude in der Nähe des Bahnhofs *or* in Bahnhofsnähe; **in ~ proximity** in unmittelbarer Nähe *(to +gen)*; **in such ~ proximity (to one another)** so dicht zusammen; **you're very ~** *(in guessing etc)* du bist dicht dran; **~ combat** Nahkampf *m*; **at ~ quarters** aus unmittelbarer Nähe; **he chose the ~st cake** er nahm den Kuchen, der am nächsten lag; **we use this pub because it's ~/the ~st** wir gehen in dieses Lokal, weil es in der Nähe/am nächsten ist
b *(in time)* nahe (bevorstehend); **nobody realized how ~ a nuclear war was** es war niemandem klar, wie nahe ein Atomkrieg bevorstand
c *(fig) friend, co-operation, connection etc* eng; *relative* nahe; *resemblance* groß, stark; **they were very ~ (to each other)** sie waren *or* standen sich *or* einander *(geh)* sehr nahe
d *(= not spread out) handwriting, print* eng; *ranks* dicht, geschlossen; *(fig) argument* lückenlos, stichhaltig; *reasoning, game* geschlossen
e *(= exact, painstaking) examination, study* eingehend, genau; *translation* originalgetreu; *watch* streng, scharf; **now pay ~ attention to me** jetzt hör mir gut zu; **you have to pay very ~ attention to the traffic signs** du musst genau auf die Verkehrszeichen achten; **to keep a ~ lookout for sb/sth** scharf nach jdm/etw Ausschau halten
f *(= stuffy)* schwül; *(indoors)* stickig
g *(= almost equal) fight, result* knapp; **a ~ (-fought) match** ein (ganz) knappes Spiel; **a ~ finish** ein Kopf-an-Kopf-Rennen *nt*; **a ~ election** ein Kopf-an-Kopf-Rennen *nt*, eine Wahl mit knappem Ausgang; **it was a ~ thing** *or* **call** das war knapp!; **the vote/election was too ~ to call** der Ausgang der Abstimmung/Wahl war völlig offen
h **~ on** nahezu; **~ on sixty/midnight** an die sechzig/kurz vor Mitternacht
ADV *(+er)* nahe; *(spatially also)* dicht; **~ by** in der Nähe; **~ by us** in unserer Nähe; **stay ~ to me** bleib dicht bei mir; **~ to the water/ground** nahe *or* dicht am Wasser/Boden; **~ to** *or* **by the bridge** nahe (bei) der Brücke; **he followed ~ behind me** er ging dicht hinter mir; **don't stand too ~ to the fire** stell dich nicht zu nahe *or* dicht ans Feuer; **to be ~ to tears** den Tränen nahe sein; **~ together** dicht *or* nahe zusammen; **my exams were so ~ together** meine Prüfungen lagen so kurz hintereinander; **the ~r the exams came the more nervous he got** je näher die Prüfung rückte, desto nervöser wurde er; **that brought the two brothers ~r together** das brachte die beiden Brüder einander näher; **please stand ~r together** bitte rücken Sie näher *or* dichter zusammen; **this pattern comes ~/~st to the sort of thing we wanted** dieses Muster kommt dem, was wir uns vorgestellt haben, nahe/am nächsten; **what does it look like (from) ~ up?** wie sieht es von Nahem

aus?; **if you get too ~ up ...** wenn du zu nahe herangehst ...
N *(in street names)* Hof *m*; *(of cathedral etc)* Domhof *m*; *(Scot: = outside passage)* offener Hausflur

close² [kləʊz] VT a *(= shut)* schließen; *eyes, door, shop, window, curtains also* zumachen; *(permanently) business, shop etc* schließen; *factory* stilllegen; *(= block) opening etc* verschließen; *road* sperren; **"closed"** „geschlossen"; **sorry, we're ~d** tut uns leid, wir haben geschlossen *or* zu; **don't ~ your mind to new ideas** du solltest dich neuen Ideen nicht verschließen; **to ~ one's eyes/ears to sth** sich einer Sache gegenüber blind/taub stellen; **to ~ ranks** *(Mil, fig)* die Reihen schließen; **to ~ the gap between ...** die Diskrepanz zwischen ... beseitigen; **to ~ an application** *(Comput)* eine Anwendung beenden
b *(= bring to an end) church service, meeting* schließen, beenden; *affair, discussion also* abschließen; *bank account etc* auflösen; *sale* abschließen; **the matter is ~d** der Fall ist abgeschlossen
c *(Elec) circuit* schließen
VI a *(= shut, come together)* sich schließen; *(door, window, box, lid, eyes, wound also)* zugehen; *(= can be shut)* schließen, zugehen; *(shop, factory)* schließen, zumachen; *(factory: permanently)* stillgelegt werden; **his eyes ~d** die Augen fielen ihm zu; *(in death)* seine Augen schlossen sich
b *(= come to an end)* schließen; *(tourist season)* aufhören, enden, zu Ende gehen; *(Theat, play)* auslaufen
c *(= approach)* sich nähern, näher kommen; *(boxers etc)* aufeinander losgehen; **the battleship ~d to within 100 metres** das Kriegsschiff kam bis auf 100 Meter heran
d *(Comm: = accept offer)* abschließen, zu einem Abschluss kommen
e *(St Ex)* schließen; **the shares ~d at £5** die Aktien erreichten eine Schlussnotierung von £ 5
N Ende *nt*, Schluss *m*; **to come to a ~** enden, aufhören, zu Ende gehen; **to draw to a ~** sich dem Ende nähern, dem Ende zugehen; **to draw** *or* **bring sth to a ~** etw beenden; **at/towards** *(Brit) or* **toward** *(US)* **the ~ of (the) day** am/gegen Ende des Tages; **at the ~ (of business)** bei Geschäfts- *or (St Ex)* Börsenschluss

▶ **close around** VI *+prep obj* umschließen, sich schließen um; **the waters closed around the drowning man** die Wellen schlugen über dem Ertrinkenden zusammen

▶ **close down** VI a *(business, shop etc)* schließen, zumachen *(inf)*; *(factory: permanently)* stillgelegt werden b *(Rad, TV)* das Programm beenden; **programmes close down at about 12** Sendeschluss (ist) gegen 24 Uhr; **we're now closing down for the night** (und) damit ist unser heutiges Programm beendet VT *sep shop etc* schließen; *factory (permanently)* stilllegen

▶ **close in** VI *(evening, winter)* anbrechen; *(night, darkness)* hereinbrechen; *(days)* kürzer werden; *(enemy etc)* bedrohlich nahe kommen; **the troops closed in around the enemy** die Truppen zogen sich um den Feind zusammen; **to close in on sb** *(gang, individual etc)* jdm auf den Leib rücken; **the walls were slowly closing in on him** die Wände kamen langsam auf ihn zu; **the police are closing in on him** die Polizei zieht das Netz um ihn zu; *(physically)* die Polizisten umzingeln ihn VT *sep* umgeben, umfrieden *(geh)*

▶ **close off** VT *sep* abriegeln, (ab)sperren; *(= separate off) area of office etc* abteilen, abtrennen

▶ **close on** VI *+prep obj* einholen

▶ **close round** VI *+prep obj (esp Brit)* = **close around**

▶ **close up** VI a *(line of people)* aufschließen, zusammenrücken; *(Mil)* aufschließen; *(wound)* (sich) schließen b *(= lock up)* ab- *or* zuschließen, ab- *or* zusperren VT *sep* a *house, shop* zumachen; *house also* verschließen; *shop also* ab- *or* zuschließen, ab- *or* zusperren b *(= block up)* zumachen

▶ **close with** VI *+prep obj* a *enemy* zum Nahkampf übergehen mit; *boxer etc* ringen *or* kämpfen mit b *(= strike bargain with)* handelseinig sein *or* werden mit; *(= accept) offer* eingehen auf

close-cropped [ˌkləʊsˈkrɒpt] ADJ *hair* kurz geschnitten

closed [kləʊzd]: **closed circuit** N geschlossener Stromkreis; **closed-circuit television** N interne Fernsehanlage; *(for supervision)* Fernsehüberwachungsanlage *f*; **closed-door** ADJ *meeting, session* hinter verschlossenen Türen

close-down [ˈkləʊzdaʊn] N a *(of shop, business etc)* (Geschäfts)schließung *f*; *(of factory)* Stilllegung *f* b *(Rad, TV)* Sendeschluss *m*

closed [kləʊzd]: **closed primary** N *(US Pol) Vorwahl mit Fraktionszwang, bei der nur Mitglieder der eigenen Partei gewählt werden können*; **closed scholarship** N an eine bestimmte Schule gebundenes Stipendium; **closed season** N Schonzeit *f*; **closed session** N *(Jur)* Sitzung *f* unter Ausschluss der Öffentlichkeit; **closed set** N *(Math)* abgeschlossene Menge; **closed shop** N Closedshop *m*; **we have a ~** wir haben Gewerkschaftszwang

close [kləʊs]: **close-fisted** ADJ geizig, knauserig *(inf)*; **close-fitting** ADJ eng anliegend, eng sitzend; **close-grained** ADJ fein gemasert; **close-harmony singers** PL Vokalgruppe *f (die im Barbershop-Stil singt)*; **close-harmony singing** N Gesang *m* in geschlossener Harmonie; **close-knit** ADJ *comp* **closer-knit** *community* eng *or* fest zusammengewachsen

closely [ˈkləʊslɪ] ADV a eng, dicht; *work, connect* eng; *woven* fest; *related* nah(e), eng; *follow (in time)* dicht; **he was ~ followed by a policeman** ein Polizist ging dicht hinter ihm; **she held the baby ~** sie drückte das Baby (fest) an sich; **~ reasoned** schlüssig dargestellt *or* -gelegt; **the match was ~ contested** der Spielausgang war hart umkämpft b *(= attentively) watch, listen etc* genau; *study also* eingehend; *guard* scharf, streng; **a ~-guarded secret** ein streng gehütetes Geheimnis

close-mouthed [ˌkləʊsˈmaʊðd] ADJ verschwiegen

closeness [ˈkləʊsnɪs] N a *(= nearness, in time)* Nähe *f*; **she could feel his ~ to her** sie konnte seine Nähe fühlen
b *(fig, of friendship)* Innigkeit *f*; **thanks to the ~ of their co-operation ...** dank ihrer engen Zusammenarbeit ...; **the ~ of their relationship/resemblance caused problems** ihre so enge Beziehung/ihre große Ähnlichkeit verursachte Probleme
c *(fig: of reasoning)* Schlüssigkeit *f*; *(Sport, of game)* Geschlossenheit *f*; **the ~ of the print/weave** die große Druck-/(Ge)webedichte
d *(of examination, interrogation)* Genauigkeit *f*; *(of watch)* Strenge *f*; *(of translation)* Textnähe *f or* -treue *f*
e **the ~ (of the air)** die Schwüle; *(indoors)* die stickige Luft
f *(of race etc)* knapper Ausgang; **the ~ of the finish** der knappe Ausgang des Rennens

close [kləʊs]: **close-run** ADJ *comp* **closer-run** *race* mit knappem Ausgang; **it was a ~ thing** es war eine knappe Sache; **close season** N a *(Ftbl)* Saisonpause *f* b *(Hunt, Fishing)* Schonzeit *f*; **close-set** ADJ *comp* **closer-set** *eyes* eng zusammenstehend; *print* eng; **close-shaven** ADJ glatt rasiert

closet [ˈklɒzɪt] *vb: pret, ptp* **closeted** [ˈklɒzɪtɪd] N a *(US)* Wandschrank *m*; **to come out of the ~** *(fig) (man)* sich als Homosexueller outen; *(woman)* sich als Lesbe outen b *(dated: = water closet)* Klosett *nt* c *(old: = small room)* Kabinett *nt*, Nebenzimmer *nt* VT **to be ~ed** hinter verschlossenen Türen sitzen *(with sb* mit jdm); **I ~ed myself in my study** ich habe mich in meinem Arbeitszimmer vergraben ADJ *attr (= secret)* heimlich

close-up [ˈkləʊsʌp] N Nahaufnahme *f*; **in ~** in Nahaufnahme; *(of face)* in Großaufnahme ATTR *shot, view* Nah-; *lens* für Nahaufnahmen

closing [ˈkləʊzɪŋ] N a *(= shutting)* Schließung *f*; *(of factory: permanently)* Stilllegung *f* b *(St Ex)* Börsenschluss *m* ADJ a *remarks, words etc* abschließend, Schluss-; **~ arguments** *(Jur)* Schlussplädoyers *pl* b *(St Ex)* **~ prices** Schlusskurse *pl*, Schlussnotierungen *pl*

closing: **closing balance sheet** N *(Fin)* Schlussbilanz *f*; **closing date** N *(for competition etc)* Einsendeschluss *m*; **closing-down sale** [ˌkləʊzɪŋˈdaʊnseɪl] N *(Comm)* Räumungsverkauf *m*; **closing scene** N *(Theat, TV)* Schlussszene *f*; **closing time** N Geschäfts- *or* Ladenschluss *m*; *(Brit, in pub)* Polizei- *or* Sperrstunde *f*; **when is ~?** wann schließt die Bank/das Geschäft/der Laden/das Lokal *etc*?

closure [ˈkləʊʒəˈ] N a *(= act of closing)* Schließung *f*; *(of road)* Sperrung *f*; *(of wound, incision)* Schließen *nt*; *(of factory, mine etc also)* Stilllegung *f* b *(Parl)* Schluss *m* der Debatte; **to move the ~** den Schluss der Debatte beantragen; **to apply the ~ to a debate** das Ende einer Debatte erklären

clot [klɒt] N a *(of blood)* (Blut)gerinnsel *nt*; *(of milk)* (Sahne)klumpen *m* b *(Brit inf: = person)* Trottel *m* VT *blood* zum Gerinnen bringen VI *(blood)* gerinnen; *(milk)* dick werden

cloth [klɒθ] N a Tuch *nt*, Stoff *m*; *(as book cover)* Leinen *nt*; **a nice piece of ~** ein schöner Stoff, ein gutes Tuch; **~ of gold** goldenes Tuch b *(= dishcloth, tea cloth etc)* Tuch *nt*; *(for cleaning also)* Lappen *m*; *(= tablecloth)* Tischdecke *f*, Tischtuch *nt* c *no pl (Eccl)* **a man of the ~** ein geistlicher Herr; **the ~** der geistliche Stand, die Geistlichkeit

cloth: **clothbound** ADJ *book* in Leinen (gebunden); **cloth cap** N Schlägermütze *f*

clothe [kləʊð] *pret, ptp* **clad** *(old) or* **clothed** VT a *(usu pass: = dress)* anziehen, kleiden; **she appeared ~d in white** *(liter)* sie erschien (ganz) in Weiß b *(= provide clothes for)* anziehen c *(fig liter)* kleiden *(liter)*; **~d in glory** mit Ruhm bedeckt; **the hills ~d in mist** die nebelverhangenen Hügel

cloth: **cloth-eared** ADJ *(inf)* doof *(inf)*; **cloth-ears** N *sing (inf)* Doofmann *m (inf)*

clothes [kləʊðz] PL a *(= garments)* Kleider *pl*; *(= clothing, outfit also)* Kleidung *f no pl*; **his mother still washes his ~** seine Mutter macht ihm immer noch die Wäsche; **with one's ~ on** angezogen, (voll) bekleidet; **with one's ~ off** ausgezogen; **you can't swim properly with your ~ on** mit *or* in Kleidern kann man nicht richtig schwimmen; **to put on/take off one's ~** sich an-/ausziehen b *(= bedclothes)* Bettzeug *nt*

clothes: **clothes basket** N Wäschekorb *m*; **clothes brush** N Kleiderbürste *f*; **clothes drier, clothes dryer** N Wäschetrockner *m*; **clothes hanger** N Kleiderbügel *m*; **clothes horse** N Wäscheständer *m*; **she's a real ~** *(inf)* sie hat einen Kleiderfimmel *(inf)*; **clothes line** N Wäscheleine *f*; **clothes moth** N Kleidermotte *f*; **clothes peg**, *(US)* **clothes pin** N Wäscheklammer *f*; **clothes pole, clothes prop** N Wäschestütze *f*; **clothes shop** N Bekleidungsgeschäft *nt*

clothier [ˈkləʊðɪəˈ] N *(= seller of clothes, for men)* Herrenausstatter *m*; *(for women)* Modegeschäft *nt or* -salon *m*

clothing [ˈkləʊðɪŋ] N Kleidung *f*

clotted [ˈklɒtɪd] ADJ **hair ~ with mud** mit Schlamm verklebtes Haar

clotted cream [ˈklɒtɪdˈkriːm] N Sahne *f (aus erhitzter Milch)*

clottish [ˈklɒtɪʃ] ADJ *(inf)* trottelig; **a ~ thing to do** eine Eselei

cloud [klaʊd] N a Wolke *f*; **low ~(s) delayed takeoff** tief hängende Wolken verzögerten den Start; **to have one's head in the ~s** in höheren Regionen schweben; *(momentarily)* geistesabwesend sein; **to be up in the ~s** *(inf)* überglücklich sein; **to be on ~ nine** *(inf)* im siebten Himmel sein *or* schweben *(inf)*; **every ~ has a silver lining** *(Prov)* kein Unglück ist so groß, es hat sein Glück im Schoß *(Prov)*

b *(of smoke, dust etc)* Wolke *f*; *(of insects)* Schwarm *m*, Haufen *m*; *(of gas, smoke from fire)* Schwaden *m*; ~ **of dust/smoke** Staub-/Rauchwolke *f*; **a ~ of controversy/confusion surrounded the whole matter** die ganze Angelegenheit wurde von Kontroversen überschattet/nebulöses Durcheinander herrschte in der ganzen Angelegenheit; **the ~ of suspicion hanging over him suddenly dispersed** der Verdacht, der über ihm schwebte, verflog plötzlich; **he's been under a ~ for weeks** *(= under suspicion)* seit Wochen haftet ein Verdacht an ihm; *(= in disgrace)* die Geschichte hängt ihm schon wochenlang nach; **the ~s are gathering** *(lit, fig)* es braut sich etwas zusammen
c *(in liquid, marble)* Wolke *f*
VT a *(lit) sky, view* verhängen *(geh)*; *mirror* trüben; **a ~ed sky** ein bewölkter Himmel
b *(fig: = cast gloom on) prospect, sb's enjoyment* trüben; *face, expression* umwölken *(geh)*; *(= mar, spoil) friendship, sb's future* überschatten; *(= make less clear) mind, judgement, awareness* trüben; *nature of problem* verschleiern; **to ~ the issue** *(= complicate)* es unnötig kompliziert machen; *(= hide deliberately)* die Angelegenheit verschleiern
VI = **cloud over**

▶**cloud over** VI *(sky)* sich bewölken, sich bedecken; *(mirror etc)* (sich) beschlagen, anlaufen; **his face clouded over** seine Stirn umwölkte sich *(geh)*

▶**cloud up** **VI** *(mirror etc)* beschlagen; **it's clouding up** *(weather)* es bezieht sich **VT** *sep* **the steam clouded up the windows** die Fenster beschlugen (vom Dampf)

cloud: **cloud bank** N Wolkenwand *f*; **cloudburst** N Wolkenbruch *m*; **cloud-capped** ADJ *(liter)* **the ~ peaks** die wolkenverhangenen Gipfel; **cloud chamber** N Nebelkammer *f*; **cloud computing** N *(Comput)* Cloud Computing *nt*; **cloud-cuckoo-land** N Wolkenkuckucksheim *nt*; **you're living in ~ if you think ...** du lebst auf dem Mond, wenn du glaubst ... *(inf)*

cloudiness [ˈklaʊdɪnɪs] N **a** *(of sky)* Bewölkung *f* **b** *(of liquid, diamond, glass, plastic etc)* Trübung *f*; *(of eyes)* Trübheit *f* **c** *(of argument, position, point of view)* Unklarheit *f*

cloudless [ˈklaʊdlɪs] ADJ *sky* wolkenlos

cloudy [ˈklaʊdɪ] ADJ *(+er)* **a** *sky* wolkig, bewölkt, bedeckt; *weather* grau; **we had only three ~ days** wir hatten nur drei Tage, an denen es bewölkt war; **it's getting ~** es bewölkt sich; **the weather will be ~** es ist mit Bewölkung zu rechnen **b** *liquid, diamond, glass, eyes etc* trüb **c** *(= unclear) argument, position, point of view* diffus, unklar

clout [klaʊt] **N a** *(inf: = blow)* Schlag *m*; **to give sb a ~** jdm eine runterhauen *(inf)*; **to give sth a ~** auf etw *(acc)* schlagen *or* hauen *(inf)*; **to give sb a ~ round the ears** jdm eine Ohrfeige geben *(inf)*; **to give oneself a ~ on the knee, to give one's knee a ~** sich *(dat)* aufs Knie hauen *(inf)*; *(against door etc)* sich *(dat)* das Knie (an)stoßen *or* anschlagen **b** *(political, industrial)* Schlagkraft *f* **VT** *(inf)* schlagen, hauen *(inf)*; **to ~ sb one** jdm eine runterhauen *(inf)* *or* eins verpassen *(inf)*

clove¹ [kləʊv] N **a** Gewürznelke *f*; **oil of ~s** Nelkenöl *nt* **b ~ of garlic** Knoblauchzehe *f*

clove² *pret of* **cleave¹**

clove hitch N Webeleinstek *m*

cloven [ˈkləʊvn] PTP *of* **cleave¹**

cloven hoof N Huf *m* der Paarhufer *or* -zeher; *(of devil)* Pferdefuß *m*; **pigs have cloven hooves** Schweine sind Paarzeher

clover [ˈkləʊvəˈ] N Klee *m*; **to be/live in ~** wie Gott in Frankreich leben

cloverleaf [ˈkləʊvəliːf] N *(Bot, Mot)* Kleeblatt *nt*

clown [klaʊn] **N** *(in circus etc)* Clown *m*; *(inf) (= foolish person also)* Kasper *m*, Hanswurst *m*; *(pej)* Idiot *m*, Trottel *m*; **to act the ~** den Clown *or* Hanswurst spielen, herumkaspern *(inf)* **VI** *(also* **clown about** *or* **around**) herumblödeln *(inf) or* -kaspern *(inf)*

clownish [ˈklaʊnɪʃ] ADJ albern, clownesk *(geh)*

cloy [klɔɪ] VI *(lit, fig)* zu süßlich sein/werden; *(pleasures)* an Reiz verlieren

cloying [ˈklɔɪɪŋ] ADJ *(lit)* übermäßig süß; **~ sentimentality** gefühlsduselige Sentimentalität

cloyingly [ˈklɔɪɪŋlɪ] ADV süßlich; **~ sentimental** gefühlsduselig sentimental

cloze test [ˈkləʊz,test] N Wortergänzungstest *m*, Lückentest *m*

club [klʌb] **N a** *(= weapon)* Knüppel *m*, Prügel *m*, Keule *f*; *(= golf club)* Golfschläger *m*; *(= Indian club)* Keule *f*
b clubs PL *(Cards)* Kreuz *nt*; **the ace/nine of ~s** (das) Kreuzass/(die) Kreuzneun
c *(= society)* Klub *m*, Verein *m*; *(= tennis club, golf club, gentleman's club, night club)* Klub *m*, Club *m*; *(Ftbl)* Verein *m*; **to be in the ~** *(inf)* in anderen Umständen sein *(inf)*, ein Kind kriegen *(inf)*; **to get sb in the ~** *(inf)* jdm ein Kind machen *(inf)*; **join the ~!** *(inf)* gratuliere! du auch!; **the London ~ scene** das Nachtleben von London
VT einknüppeln auf *(+acc)*, knüppeln
VI to go ~bing Nachtklubs besuchen, tanzen gehen

▶**club together** VI *(Brit)* zusammenlegen

clubbable [ˈklʌbəbl] ADJ geeignet, in einen Klub aufgenommen zu werden; *(= sociable)* gesellschaftsfähig

clubby [ˈklʌbɪ] ADJ *(inf)* gesellig

club: **club class** N *(Aviat)* Klubklasse *f*, Businessklasse *f*; **club foot** N Klumpfuß *m*; **club-footed** ADJ klumpfüßig; **clubhouse** N Klubhaus *nt*; **clubland** N *(of gentlemen's clubs)* Klubviertel *m (vornehmer Stadtteil, in dem sich besonders viele Klubs befinden)*; *(esp Brit: of nightclubs)* Vergnügungsviertel *nt*; **clubman** N **he isn't much of a ~** er interessiert sich nicht besonders für Klubs; **club member** N Vereins- *or* Klubmitglied *nt*; **club room** N Klubraum *nt*; **club sandwich** N Klubsandwich *nt*

cluck [klʌk] **VI** gackern; *(hen: to chicks)* glucken **N** Gackern *nt*; *(of hen to chicks)* Glucken *nt*

clue [kluː] N Anhaltspunkt *m*, Hinweis *m*; *(in police search also: = object)* Spur *f*; *(in crosswords)* Frage *f*; **to find a/the ~ to sth** den Schlüssel zu etw finden; **I'll give you a ~** ich gebe dir einen Tipp; **I haven't a ~!** (ich hab) keine Ahnung!

▶**clue up** VT *sep (inf) person* informieren; **to get clued up on** *or* **about sth** sich mit etw vertraut machen; **to be clued up on** *or* **about sth** über etw *(acc)* im Bilde sein; *(about subject)* mit etw vertraut sein

clueless [ˈkluːlɪs] ADJ *(inf)* ahnungslos, unbedarft *(inf)*; *expression, look* ratlos

cluelessly [ˈkluːlɪslɪ] ADV *(inf)* ratlos

clump [klʌmp] **N a** *(of trees, flowers etc)* Gruppe *f*; *(of earth)* Klumpen *m*; **a ~ of shrubs** ein Gebüsch *nt* **b** *(inf: = blow)* Schlag *m*, Hieb *m* **VT** *(inf: = hit)* schlagen, hauen *(inf)* **VI** trampeln; *(with adv of place)* stapfen; **to ~ about** herumtrampeln; *(in snow, mud etc)* herumstapfen

clumpy [ˈklʌmpɪ] ADJ *shoes* klobig

clumsily [ˈklʌmzɪlɪ] ADV **a** ungeschickt; *(= in an ungainly way)* schwerfällig; *act* ungeschickt **b** *(= inelegantly) written, translated etc* schwerfällig, unbeholfen **c** *(= awkwardly, tactlessly)* ungeschickt, unbeholfen; *compliment also* plump

clumsiness [ˈklʌmzɪnɪs] N **a** Ungeschicklichkeit *f*; *(= ungainliness)* Schwerfälligkeit *f* **b** *(of tool, shape)* Unförmigkeit *f*; *(of prose, translation etc)* Schwerfälligkeit *f*, Unbeholfenheit *f* **c** *(= awkwardness: of apology, excuse etc)* Plumpheit *f*

clumsy [ˈklʌmzɪ] ADJ *(+er)* **a** ungeschickt; *(= all thumbs also)* tollpatschig; *(= ungainly)* schwerfällig **b** *(= unwieldy)* plump; *tool also* wuchtig, klobig; *shape also* unförmig, klobig; *(= inelegant) prose, translation etc* schwerfällig, unbeholfen; *(= careless) mistake* dumm **c** *(= awkward, tactless)* plump, ungeschickt

clung [klʌŋ] *pret, ptp of* **cling¹**

clunk [klʌŋk] **N** dumpfes Geräusch **VI the door ~ed shut** die Tür schloss sich mit einem dumpfen Geräusch

clunker [ˈklʌŋkəˈ] N *(US pej inf: = car)* Kiste *f (pej inf)*, Mühle *f (pej inf)*

clunky [ˈklʌŋkɪ] ADJ klobig

cluster [ˈklʌstəˈ] **N** *(of trees, flowers, houses)* Gruppe *f*, Haufen *m*; *(of islands)* Gruppe *f*; *(of diamonds)* Büschel *nt*; *(of bees, people, grapes)* Traube *f*; *(of diamonds)* Büschel *nt*; *(Phon)* Häufung *f*; *(Comput)* Zuordnungseinheit *f*; **the flowers grow in a ~ at the top of the stem** die Blumen sitzen *or* wachsen doldenförmig am Stängel; *(of roses etc)* mehrere Blüten wachsen am gleichen Stiel **VI** *(people)* sich drängen *or* scharen; **they all ~ed round to see what he was doing** alle drängten *or* scharten sich um ihn, um zu sehen, was er tat

cluster bomb N Splitterbombe *f*

clutch¹ [klʌtʃ] **N a** *(= grip)* Griff *m* **b** *(Aut)* Kupplung *f*; **to let in/out the ~** ein-/auskuppeln; **~ pedal** Kupplungspedal *nt* **c** *(fig)* **to fall into sb's ~es** jdm in die Hände fallen, jdm ins Netz gehen; **to be in sb's ~es** in jds Gewalt *(dat)* sein; **to have sb in one's ~es** jdn im Netz *or* in den Klauen haben; **he escaped her ~es** er entkam ihren Klauen **VT** *(= grab)* umklammern, packen; *(= hold tightly)* umklammert halten; **to ~ sth in one's hand** etw umklammern

▶**clutch at** VI *+prep obj (lit)* schnappen nach *(+dat)*, greifen; *(= hold tightly)* umklammert halten; *(fig)* sich klammern an *(+acc)* → **straw**

clutch² N *(of chickens)* Brut *f*; *(of eggs)* Gelege *nt*

clutch bag, **clutch purse** *(US)* N Unterarmtasche *f*, Tasche *f* ohne Trageriemen

clutter [ˈklʌtəˈ] **N** *(= confusion)* Durcheinander *nt*; *(= disorderly articles)* Kram *m (inf)*; **the ~ of bottles and crockery in the kitchen** das Durcheinander von Flaschen und Geschirr in der Küche; **his desk was in a ~** auf seinem Schreibtisch war ein fürchterliches Durcheinander; **his essay was a ~ of unrelated details** sein Aufsatz war ein Sammelsurium *or* Wirrwarr von zusammenhangslosen Einzelheiten
VT *(also* **clutter up**) zu voll machen *(inf)*/stellen; *painting, photograph* überladen; *mind* vollstopfen; **to be ~ed with sth** *(mind, room, drawer etc)* mit etw vollgestopft sein; *(floor, desk etc)* mit etw übersät sein; *(painting etc)* mit etw überladen sein; **the floor was terribly ~ed** auf dem Fußboden lag alles verstreut; **his desk was dreadfully ~ed** sein Schreibtisch war ganz voll

cm *abbr of* **centimetre** cm

Cmdr *abbr of* **Commander**

CNAA *abbr of* **Council for National Academic Awards**

CND *abbr of* **Campaign for Nuclear Disarmament**

CNN *abbr of* **Cable News Network** CNN *no art*

CO *abbr of* **Commanding Officer**

Co a *abbr of* **company** KG *f* **b** *abbr of* **county**

co- [kəʊ-] PREF Mit-, mit-

c/o a *abbr of* **care of** bei, c/o **b** *abbr of* **carried over** Übertr.

coach [kəʊtʃ] **N a** *(horsedrawn)* Kutsche *f* **b** *(Rail)* (Eisenbahn)wagen *m*, Waggon *m* **c** *(Brit: = motor coach)* (Reise)bus *m*; **by ~** mit dem Bus; **~ travel/journeys** Busreisen *pl*; **~ driver** Busfahrer *m* **d** *(= tutor)* Nachhilfelehrer(in) *m(f)*; *(Sport)* Trainer *m* **e** *(esp US: Aviat)* Economy(klasse) *f*; **to fly ~** (in der) Economyklasse fliegen **VT a** *(Sport)* trainieren **b to ~ sb for an exam** jdn aufs Examen vorbereiten; **he had been ~ed in what to say** man hatte mit ihm eingeübt, was er sagen sollte

coach: **coach box** N (Kutsch)bock *m*; **coach-builder** N *(Brit)* Karosseriebauer *m*; **coach-building** N *(Brit)* Karosseriebau *m*; **coach class** N *(esp US: Aviat)* → **coach N e**; **coach house** N *(old)* Remise *f*

coaching [ˈkəʊtʃɪŋ] N *(Sport)* Trainerstunden *pl*; *(Tennis)* Training *nt*; *(= tutoring)* Nachhilfe *f*

coach: **coachload** N *(Brit)* = **busload**; **coachman** N Kutscher *m*; **coach party** N *(Brit)* Busreisegruppe *f*; **coach station** N *(Brit)* Busbahnhof *m*; **coach trip** N *(Brit)* Busfahrt *f*; **coachwork** N *(Brit)* Karosserie *f*

coagulate [kəʊˈægjʊleɪt] VI *(blood)* gerinnen, koagulieren *(spec)*; *(milk)* dick werden; *(jelly)* fest werden; *(paint)* zähflüssig werden, eindicken VT *blood* gerinnen lassen; *milk* dick werden lassen; *jelly* fest werden lassen

coagulation [kəʊˌægjʊˈleɪʃən] N *(of blood)* Gerinnen *nt*, Gerinnung *f*, Koagulation *f (spec)*; *(of milk)* Dickwerden *nt*; *(of jelly)* Festwerden *nt*; *(of paint)* Eindicken *nt*

coal [kəʊl] N Kohle *f*; **we still burn ~** wir heizen noch mit Kohle; **as black as ~** kohlrabenschwarz; **to carry** *or* **take ~s to Newcastle** *(Brit Prov)* Eulen nach Athen tragen *(Prov)*; **to haul** *(Brit) or* **drag sb over the ~s** jdm eine Standpauke halten, jdm die Leviten lesen; **to heap ~s of fire on sb's head** feurige Kohlen auf jds Haupt *(dat)* sammeln

coal *in cpds* Kohlen-; **coal bed** N Kohlenflöz *m*; **coal bin, coal bunker** N Kohlenkasten *m*; **coal-black** ADJ kohlrabenschwarz; **coal cellar** N Kohlenkeller *m*; **coal dust** N Kohlenstaub *m*, (Kohlen)grus *m*

coalesce [ˌkəʊəˈles] VI *(Phys, Chem)* sich verbinden, eine Verbindung eingehen; *(fig)* sich vereinigen, zusammengehen; *(views, opinions etc)* sich verquicken *(geh)*

coalescence [ˌkəʊəˈlesəns] N *(Phys, Chem)* Verbindung *f*; *(fig)* Vereinigung *f*; *(of views, opinions etc)* Verquickung *f (geh)*

coal: **coalface** N *(Brit)* Streb *m*; **men who work at the ~** Männer, die im Streb *or* vor Ort arbeiten; **workers at the ~** *(fig)* diejenigen, die die Arbeit machen; **coalfield** N Kohlenrevier *nt*; **coal fire** N Kamin *m*; **a ~ heats better** ein Kohlenfeuer wärmt besser; **coal-fired** ADJ Kohle(n)-; **~ power station** Kohlekraftwerk *nt*; **coal hod** N Kohleneimer *m*; **coal hole** N Kohlenbunker *m*

coalition [ˌkəʊəˈlɪʃən] N Koalition *f*; **~ agreement** Koalitionsvereinbarung *f or* -absprache *f*; *(esp written)* Koalitionsvertrag *m*; **~ government** Koalitionsregierung *f*

coal: **coal man** N Kohlenmann *m*; **coal merchant** N Kohlenhändler *m*; **coal mine** N Grube *f*, Zeche *f*, Kohlenbergwerk *nt*; **coal miner** N Bergmann *m*, Kumpel *m (inf)*; **coal-mining** N Kohle(n)bergbau *m*; **the ~ industry** der Kohle(n)bergbau; **~ area** Kohlenrevier *nt*; **coal pit** N = **coal mine**; **coal scuttle** N Kohleneimer *m*, Kohlenkasten *m*; **coal seam** N Kohlenflöz *m*; **coal shed** N Kohlenschuppen *m*; **coal strike** N Bergarbeiterstreik *m*; **coal tar** N Kohlenteer *m*; **coal tar soap** N Teerseife *f*; **coal tip** N *(Brit)* Kohlenhalde *f*; **coal tit** N *(Orn)* Tannenmeise *f*; **coal yard** N Kohlenhof *m*

coarse [kɔːs] ADJ *(+er)* **a** *(= not delicate, in texture)* grob; *sand, sugar also* grobkörnig; *features also* derb; **~ sandpaper** grobes Schmirgelpapier **b** *(= uncouth)* gewöhnlich; *person, manners also* grob, ungehobelt, ungeschliffen; *laugh* derb; *joke* derb, unanständig **c** *(= common) food* derb, einfach; **~ red wine** einfacher (Land)rotwein

coarse: **coarse fish** N Süßwasserfisch *m (mit Ausnahme aller Lachs- und Forellenarten)*; **coarse fishing** N Angeln *nt* von Süßwasserfischen; **coarse-grained** [ˈkɔːsˈgreɪnd] ADJ grobfaserig; **~ fibre** grobe Faser; **~ paper** ungeleimtes Papier, Zeitungspapier *nt*

coarsely [ˈkɔːslɪ] ADV **a** *(= in large pieces) chop, grate, grind* grob; **~ woven cloth** grob gewobener Stoff **b** *(= uncouthly) laugh, joke, speak* derb; *behave* ungehobelt

coarsen [ˈkɔːsn] VT *person* derber machen; *skin* gerben VI *(person)* derber werden; *(skin)* gröber werden

coarseness [ˈkɔːsnɪs] N **a** *(of texture)* Grobheit *f* **b** *(fig: = vulgarity)* Gewöhnlichkeit *f*; *(of person, manners also)* Grobheit *f*, Ungeschliffenheit *f*; *(of joke also)* Unanständigkeit *f*; *(of sb's language)* Derbheit *f*; **the ~ of his laugh** sein derbes Lachen

coast [kəʊst] N Küste *f*, Gestade *nt (poet)*; **at the ~** an der Küste; **on the ~** am Meer; **we're going to the ~** wir fahren an die Küste *or* ans Meer; **the ~ is clear** *(fig)* die Luft ist rein VI **a** *(car, cyclist, in neutral)* (im Leerlauf) fahren; *(= cruise effortlessly)* dahinrollen; *(athlete)* locker laufen; *(US, on sled)* hinunterrodeln **b** *(fig)* **to be ~ing along** mühelos *or* spielend vorankommen; **he was just ~ing up to the exam** er steuerte ohne große Mühe aufs Examen zu

coastal [ˈkəʊstəl] ADJ Küsten-; **~ traffic** Küstenschifffahrt *f*

coaster [ˈkəʊstəʳ] N **a** *(Naut)* Küstenmotorschiff *nt* **b** *(= drip mat)* Untersetzer *m* **c** *(US: = sled)* (Rodel)schlitten *m*; *(= roller-coaster)* Achterbahn *f*, Berg- und Talbahn *f*

coaster brake N *(US)* Rücktrittbremse *f*

coast: **coastguard** N Küstenwache *f*; **the ~s** die Küstenwacht; **~ boat/station** Küstenwachtboot *nt*/-posten *m*; **coastline** N Küste *f*

coat [kəʊt] N **a** *(= outdoor garment)* Mantel *m*; *(= doctor's coat etc also)* (Arzt)kittel *m*; *(= jacket of suit etc)* Jacke *f*; *(for men also)* Jackett *nt*; **~ and skirt** Kostüm *nt*
b *(Her)* **~ of arms** Wappen *nt*
c **~ of mail** Panzerhemd *nt*; *(of chain mail)* Kettenhemd *nt*
d *(of animal)* Fell *nt*; **winter ~** Winterfell *nt*
e *(of paint, tar etc, = application)* Anstrich *m*; *(= actual layer)* Schicht *f*; **give it a second ~** *(of paint)* streich es noch einmal
VT *(with paint etc)* streichen; *(with chocolate, icing etc)* überziehen; **to be ~ed with dust/mud** mit einer Staub-/Schmutzschicht überzogen sein, eine Staub-/Schmutzschicht haben; **my hands were ~ed with grease/flour** meine Hände waren voller Schmiere/Mehl; **his tongue was ~ed** seine Zunge war belegt; **~ed paper** gestrichenes Papier; **the chassis was ~ed with an anti-rust preparation** das Chassis war mit einem Rostschutzmittel beschichtet *or (sprayed)* gespritzt

coat hanger N Kleiderbügel *m*

coating [ˈkəʊtɪŋ] N Überzug *m*, Schicht *f*; *(of paint)* Anstrich *m*

coat: **coatless** ADJ ohne Mantel; **coat stand** N Garderobenständer *m*; **coat-tails** PL Rockschöße *pl*

co-author [ˈkəʊˌɔːθəʳ] N Mitautor(in) *m(f)*, Mitverfasser(in) *m(f)*; **they were ~s of the book** sie haben das Buch gemeinsam geschrieben

coax [kəʊks] VT überreden; **to ~ sb into doing sth** jdn beschwatzen *(inf) or* dazu bringen, etw zu tun; **he ~ed the engine into life** er brachte den Motor mit List und Tücke in Gang; **you have to ~ the fire** du musst dem Feuer ein bisschen nachhelfen; **to ~ sth out of sb** jdm etw entlocken

coaxing [ˈkəʊksɪŋ] N gutes Zureden, Zuspruch *m*; **with a little ~ the engine/fire started** mit etwas List und Tücke kam der Motor/das Feuer in Gang ADJ einschmeichelnd

coaxingly [ˈkəʊksɪŋlɪ] ADV **to ask ~** mit einschmeichelnder Stimme fragen; **however ~ she spoke to him ...** sosehr sie auch versuchte, ihn zu überreden ...

cob [kɒb] N **a** *(= horse) kleines, gedrungenes Pferd* **b** *(= swan)* (männlicher) Schwan **c** *(= corn)* (Mais)kolben *m*; *(= bread)* rundes Brot; **corn on the ~** Maiskolben *m*; **a ~ of coal** ein Stück Eier- *or* Nusskohle **d** *(also* **cobnut***)* (große) Haselnuss

cobalt [ˈkəʊbɒlt] N Kobalt *nt*

cobalt-blue [ˈkəʊbɒltbluː] ADJ kobaltblau

cobber [ˈkɒbəʳ] N *(Austral inf)* Kumpel *m (inf)*

cobble [ˈkɒbl] N *(also* **cobblestone***)* Kopfstein *m* VT **a** *shoe* flicken **b** **a ~d street** eine Straße mit Kopfsteinpflaster

▶ **cobble together** VT *sep (inf) essay etc* zusammenschustern

cobbler [ˈkɒbləʳ] N **a** Schuster *m*, Flickschuster *m* **b** *(= drink)* Cobbler *m*; *(esp US: = fruit pie) Obst mit Teig überbacken*

cobblers [ˈkɒbləz] PL *(Brit inf: = rubbish)* Scheiße *f (inf)*, Mist *m (inf)*; **(what a load of old) ~!** was fürn Haufen Mist! *(inf)*

cobblestone [ˈkɒblstəʊn] N Kopfstein *m*; **~ pavement** Kopfsteinpflaster *nt*

COBOL [ˈkəʊbɒl] *abbr of* **common business oriented language** COBOL

cobra [ˈkəʊbrə] N Kobra *f*

cobweb [ˈkɒbweb] N *(= single thread, threads)* Spinn(en)webe *f*; *(= full cobweb)* Spinnennetz *nt*; **a brisk walk will blow away the ~s** *(fig)* ein ordentlicher Spaziergang und man hat wieder einen klaren Kopf

cobwebbed [ˈkɒbwebd] ADJ voller Spinnweben

coca [ˈkəʊkə] N **a** *(= shrub)* Koka *f* **b** *no pl (= dried leaves)* Kokablätter *pl*, Koka *f*

cocaine [kəˈkeɪn] N Kokain *nt*

coccyx [ˈkɒksɪks] N Steißbein *nt*

cochineal [ˈkɒtʃɪniːl] N *(= insect, colouring)* Koschenille *f*

cochlear [ˈkɒklɪəʳ] ADJ kochlear

cock [kɒk] N **a** *(= rooster)* Hahn *m*; *(= weathercock)* Wetterhahn *m*; **(the) ~ of the walk** *or* **roost** der Größte *(inf)* **b** *(= male bird)* Männchen *nt* **c** *(= tap)* (Wasser)hahn *m* **d** *(of rifle)* Hahn *m* **e** *(of hat)* schiefer Sitz **f** *(Brit, inf: = mate)* Kumpel *m (inf)* **g** *(sl: = penis)* Schwanz *m (sl)* VT **a** **to ~ the gun** den Hahn spannen **b** *ears* spitzen; **the parrot ~ed its head to one side** der Papagei legte seinen Kopf schief *or* auf die Seite; **to ~ a snook at sb** *(Brit) (lit)* jdm eine lange Nase machen; *(fig)* zeigen, dass man auf jdn pfeift

▶ **cock up** VT *sep (Brit inf: = mess up)* versauen *(inf)*

cockade [kɒˈkeɪd] N Kokarde *f*

cock: **cock-a-doodle-doo** N Kikeriki *nt*; **cock-a-hoop** ADJ ganz aus dem Häuschen, außer sich vor Freude; **cock-a-leekie (soup)** N Lauchsuppe *f* mit Huhn

cockamamie [ˌkɒkəˈmeɪmɪ] ADJ *(US inf: = poor quality)* mies *(inf)*

cock-and-bull story [ˌkɒkənˈbʊlˌstɔːrɪ] N Lügengeschichte *f*; **to give sb a ~** jdm eine Lügengeschichte erzählen

cockatoo [ˌkɒkəˈtuː] N Kakadu *m*

cockatrice [ˈkɒkətrɪs] N Basilisk *m*

cockchafer [ˈkɒkˌtʃeɪfəʳ] N Maikäfer *m*

cockcrow [ˈkɒkkrəʊ] N *(old: = dawn)* Hahnenschrei *m*; **at ~** beim ersten Hahnenschrei

cocked [kɒkt] ADJ **~ hat** *(with two points)* Zweispitz *m*; *(with three points)* Dreispitz *m*; **to knock sb into a ~ hat** *(inf) (= beat up)* aus jdm Kleinholz machen; *(= outdo)* jdn total an die Wand spielen; **this painting knocks all the others into a ~ hat** *(inf)* dieses Gemälde stellt alle anderen in den Schatten

cocker [ˈkɒkəʳ] N *(also* **cocker spaniel***)* Cocker(spaniel) *m*

cockerel [ˈkɒkərəl] N junger Hahn

cock: **cockeyed** [ˈkɒkaɪd] ADJ *(inf)* **a** *(= crooked)* schief **b** *(= absurd) idea* verrückt, widersinnig; **cockfight** N Hahnenkampf *m*; **cockhorse** N *(old)* Steckenpferd *nt*

cockily [ˈkɒkɪlɪ] ADV *(inf)* großspurig

cockiness [ˈkɒkɪnɪs] N *(inf)* Großspurigkeit *f*

cockle [ˈkɒkl] N **a** *(= shellfish: also* **cockleshell***)* Herzmuschel *f* **b** *(= boat)* kleines Boot, Nussschale *f* **c** **it warmed the ~s of my heart** es wurde mir warm ums Herz

cockney [ˈkɒknɪ] N **a** *(= dialect)* Cockney *nt* **b** *(= person)* Cockney *m* ADJ Cockney-

COCKNEY

Ein **Cockney** ist jemand, der in Londons East End geboren ist. Traditionellerweise ist er nur dann ein waschechter **Cockney**, wenn seine

Geburt innerhalb der Hörweite der **Bow Bells**, der Kirchenglocken von St Mary-le-Bow in Cheapside im Osten Londons, stattfand. Mit **Cockney** wird auch der Dialekt bezeichnet, der in diesem Teil Londons gesprochen wird; fälschlicherweise wird der Ausdruck oft für jeden Akzent der Londoner Arbeiterklasse verwendet. Ein weltbekanntes Exemplar eines echten **Cockneys** ist der Schauspieler Michael Caine.

cockpit [ˈkɒkpɪt] N **a** *(Aviat, of racing car)* Cockpit *nt*; *(Naut: on yacht)* Plicht *f*, Cockpit *nt* **b** *(for cockfighting)* Hahnenkampfplatz *m*

cockroach [ˈkɒkrəʊtʃ] N Küchenschabe *f*, Kakerlak *m*

cockscomb [ˈkɒkskəʊm] N **a** *(Orn, Bot)* Hahnenkamm *m* **b** = **coxcomb**

cock: **cock sparrow** N (männlicher) Spatz; **cocksucker** [ˈkɒkˌsʌkəˈ] N *(pej, vulgar)* Schwanzlutscher(in) *m(f) (pej)*; **cocksure** ADJ (ganz) sicher, fest überzeugt; **don't you be so ~** sei dir deiner Sache *(gen)* nicht zu sicher; **to be ~ of oneself** von sich *(dat)* selber *or* selbst sehr überzeugt sein

cocktail [ˈkɒkteɪl] N Cocktail *m*; **we're invited for ~s** wir sind zum Cocktail eingeladen

cocktail *in cpds* Cocktail-; **cocktail bar** N Cocktailbar *f*; **cocktail cabinet** N Hausbar *f*; **cocktail lounge** N Cocktailbar *f*; **cocktail stick** N Cocktailspieß *m*; **cocktail tomato** N Cocktailtomate *f*; **cocktail waiter** N *(esp US)* Getränkekellner *m*; **cocktail waitress** N *(esp US)* Getränkekellnerin *f*

cockup [ˈkɒkʌp] N *(Brit inf)* **to be a ~** in die Hose gehen *(inf)*; **to make a ~ of sth** bei *or* mit etw Scheiße bauen *(inf)*

cocky [ˈkɒkɪ] ADJ *(+er) (inf)* anmaßend, großspurig; **he was so ~ before the exams** er tat so großspurig vorm Examen

cocoa [ˈkəʊkəʊ] N Kakao *m*

cocoa bean N Kakaobohne *f*

cocomat [ˈkəʊkəmæt] N Kokosmatte *f*

coconut [ˈkəʊkənʌt] **N** Kokosnuss *f* **ATTR** Kokos-

coconut: **coconut matting** N Kokosläufer *m*; **coconut oil** N Kokosöl *nt*; **coconut palm** N Kokospalme *f*; **coconut shy** N Wurfbude *f*; **coconut tree** N Kokospalme *f*

cocoon [kəˈkuːn] **N** Kokon *m*; *(fig, of scarves, blankets etc)* Hülle *f*; **the old warships were put in ~s** die alten Kriegsschiffe wurden mit Planen abgedeckt **VT** einhüllen; *ship etc* abdecken; **she looks well ~ed against the wind** sie ist gut gegen den Wind eingemummt

cocooning [kəˈkuːnɪŋ] N *(Sociol)* Cocooning *nt*

COD *abbr of* **cash** *(Brit) or* **collect** *(US)* **on delivery**

cod[1] [kɒd] N Kabeljau *m*; *(in Baltic)* Dorsch *m*

cod[2] ADJ *(Brit: = not genuine)* vorgetäuscht

coda [ˈkəʊdə] N Koda *f*

coddle [ˈkɒdl] VT **a** *child, invalid* umhegen, verhätscheln **b** *(Cook) eggs* im Backofen pochieren

code [kəʊd] **N a** *(= cipher)* Code *m*, Kode *m*, Chiffre *f*; **in ~** verschlüsselt, chiffriert; **to put into ~** verschlüsseln, chiffrieren; **to break a secret ~** einen Geheimkode knacken **b** *(Jur)* Gesetzbuch *nt*, Kodex *m* **c** *(= rules, principles)* Kodex *m*; **~ of honour/behaviour** Ehren-/Sittenkodex *m*; **~ of conduct** Verhaltenskodex *m*; **~ of practice** Verfahrensregeln *pl* **d post** *or* **zip** *(US)* **~** Postleitzahl *f* **e** *(Comput)* Code *m*, Kode *m* **f** *(Ling, Sociol)* Code *m*, Kode *m* **VT** verschlüsseln, chiffrieren; *(Comput)* codieren, kodieren

code breaker N Codeknacker *m*

coded [ˈkəʊdɪd] ADJ **a** *(= in code) message, warning, instructions* codiert, verschlüsselt; **in ~ form** in codierter *or* verschlüsselter Form **b** *(= indirect) criticism, attack, reference* versteckt; **in ~ language** in verschlüsselter *or* codierter Sprache **c** *(Telec) signal* codiert

codeine [ˈkəʊdiːn] N Codein *nt*

code: **code letter** N Codebuchstabe *m*; **code name** N Deckname *m*; **code number** N Kennziffer *f*

co-dependent [ˌkəʊdɪˈpendənt] *(esp US Psych)* **N** Koabhängige(r) *mf* **ADJ** koabhängig

code word N Codewort *nt*; *(Comput also)* Passwort *nt*, Kennwort *nt*

codex [ˈkəʊdeks] N *pl* **codices** Kodex *m*

codfish [ˈkɒdfɪʃ] N = **cod**[1]

codger [ˈkɒdʒəˈ] N *(inf)* komischer (alter) Kauz

codices [ˈkɒdɪsiːz] *pl of* **codex**

codicil [ˈkɒdɪsɪl] N Kodizill *nt*

codify [ˈkəʊdɪfaɪ] VT *laws* kodifizieren

coding [ˈkəʊdɪŋ] N **a** Chiffrieren *nt*; **a new ~ system** ein neues Chiffriersystem; **I don't understand the ~** ich verstehe den Code nicht **b** *(Comput: = codes)* Codierung(en *pl*) *f*

cod: **cod-liver oil** [ˈkɒdlɪvərˌɔɪl] N Lebertran *m*; **codpiece** N Hosenbeutel *m*

co-driver [ˈkəʊdraɪvəˈ] N Beifahre(in) *m(f)*

codswallop [ˈkɒdzwɒləp] N *(Brit inf)* Stuss *m (dated inf)*

co-ed, coed [ˈkəʊˈed] **N** *(inf, Brit: = school)* gemischte Schule, Koedukationsschule *f*; *(dated US: = girl student)* Schülerin *f or* Studentin *f* einer gemischten Schule **ADJ** *school* gemischt, Koedukations- **ADV** **to go ~** Koedukation einführen

coedit [ˌkəʊˈedɪt] VT *book* mit herausgeben

coedition [ˌkəʊɪˈdɪʃən] N gemeinsame Ausgabe

coeditor [ˈkəʊˈedɪtəˈ] N Mitherausgeber(in) *m(f)*

coeducation [ˈkəʊˌedjʊˈkeɪʃən] N Koedukation *f*

coeducational [ˈkəʊˌedjʊˈkeɪʃənl] ADJ *teaching* koedukativ; *school* Koedukations-

coefficient [ˌkəʊɪˈfɪʃənt] N *(Math, Phys)* Koeffizient *m*

coerce [kəʊˈɜːs] VT zwingen; **to ~ sb into doing sth** jdn dazu zwingen *or* nötigen *(geh)*, etw zu tun

coercion [kəʊˈɜːʃən] N Zwang *m*; *(Jur)* Nötigung *f*

coercive [kəʊˈɜːsɪv] ADJ Zwangs-

coeval [kəʊˈiːvəl] *(form)* **ADJ** der gleichen Periode *or* Zeit *(with* wie); *manuscripts, authors etc also* zeitgenössisch *attr* **N** Zeitgenosse *m*

coexist [ˌkəʊɪgˈzɪst] VI koexistieren *(Pol, Sociol, geh)*, nebeneinander bestehen; **to ~ with** *or* **alongside sb/sth** neben *or* mit jdm/etw bestehen *or* existieren

coexistence [ˌkəʊɪgˈzɪstəns] N Koexistenz *f*

coexistent [ˌkəʊɪgˈzɪstənt] ADJ koexistent *(geh)*, nebeneinander bestehend; **the two states are now peacefully ~** die beiden Staaten leben jetzt friedlich nebeneinander *or* in friedlicher Koexistenz

coextensive [ˌkəʊɪkˈstensɪv] ADJ *(in time)* zur gleichen Zeit; *(in area)* flächengleich; *(in length)* längengleich; *(fig) concepts* bedeutungs- *or* inhaltsgleich; **to be ~ with sth** mit etw zusammenfallen; *(spatially)* sich mit etw decken

C of E *abbr of* **Church of England**

coffee [ˈkɒfɪ] N Kaffee *m*; **two ~s, please** zwei Kaffee, bitte

coffee *in cpds* Kaffee-; **coffee bar** N Café *nt*; **coffee bean** N Kaffeebohne *f*; **coffee break** N Kaffeepause *f*; **coffee cake** N Mokkakuchen *m*; **coffee cup** N Kaffeetasse *f*; **coffee filter** N Kaffeefilter *m*; **coffee grinder** N Kaffeemühle *f*; **coffee grounds** PL Kaffeesatz *m*; **coffee house** N *(also Hist)* Kaffeehaus *nt*; **coffee machine** N *(= coffee maker)* Kaffeemaschine *f*; *(= vending machine)* Kaffee-Verkaufsautomat *m*; **coffee maker** N Kaffeemaschine *f*; **coffee percolator** N Kaffeemaschine *f*; **coffeepot** N Kaffeekanne *f*; **coffee shop** N Café *nt*, Imbissstube *f*; **coffee table** N Couchtisch *m*; **coffee-table** ADJ **~ book** Bildband *m*; **coffee whitener** N Kaffeeweißer *m*

coffer [ˈkɒfəˈ] N **a** Truhe *f* **b** *(fig)* **the ~s** die Schatulle, das Geldsäckel; *(of state)* das Staatssäckel **c** *(Archit)* Kassette *f*

cofferdam [ˈkɒfədæm] N Caisson *m*

coffin [ˈkɒfɪn] N Sarg *m*

coffin dodger N *(hum inf)* Scheintote(r) *mf (sl)*

cog [kɒg] N *(Tech)* Zahn *m*; *(= cogwheel)* Zahnrad *nt*; **he's only a ~ in the machine** *(fig)* er ist nur ein Rädchen im Getriebe; **each employee is a vital ~ in the company** jeder einzelne Angestellte ist ein wichtiger Teil in der Firma

cogency [ˈkəʊdʒənsɪ] N Stichhaltigkeit *f*

cogent [ˈkəʊdʒənt] ADJ stichhaltig; *argument, reason also* zwingend; *reasoning also* überzeugend

cogently [ˈkəʊdʒəntlɪ] ADV stichhaltig

cogitate [ˈkɒdʒɪteɪt] **VI** *(about, (up)on* über *+acc)* nachdenken, grübeln **VT** nachdenken über *+acc*; *(= devise)* ersinnen

cogitation [ˌkɒdʒɪˈteɪʃən] N Nachdenken *nt*

cognac [ˈkɒnjæk] N Kognak *m*; *(French)* Cognac® *m*

cognate [ˈkɒgneɪt] **ADJ** verwandt; *(Ling)* urverwandt **N** *(Ling)* urverwandtes Wort, urverwandte Sprache; **"night" is a ~ of "Nacht"** „night" ist mit „Nacht" verwandt

cognition [kɒgˈnɪʃən] N Erkenntnis *f*; *(visual)* Wahrnehmung *f*

cognitive [ˈkɒgnɪtɪv] ADJ *powers, faculties* kognitiv

cognizance [ˈkɒgnɪzəns] N *(form)* **a** *(= conscious knowledge, awareness)* Kenntnis *f*; *(= range of perception)* Erkenntnisbereich *m*; **to take ~ of sth** etw zur Kenntnis nehmen **b** *(= jurisdiction)* Zuständigkeit *f*, Befugnis *f*; *(Jur)* Gerichtsbarkeit *f*

cognizant [ˈkɒgnɪzənt] ADJ *(form)* **a** *(= aware, conscious)* **to be ~ of sth** sich *(dat)* einer Sache *(gen)* bewusst sein **b** *(= having jurisdiction)* zuständig

cognoscente [ˌkɒgnəʊˈʃentɪ] N *pl* **cognoscenti** [ˌkɒgnəʊˈʃentiː] Kenner *m*

cog: **cog railway** N *(US)* Zahnradbahn *f*; **cogwheel** N Zahnrad *nt*

cohabit [kəʊˈhæbɪt] VI *(esp Jur)* in nichtehelicher *or* nicht ehelicher Lebensgemeinschaft leben, zusammenleben

cohabitant [kəʊˈhæbɪtənt] N Lebensgefährte *m*/-gefährtin *f*

cohabitation [ˌkəʊhæbɪˈteɪʃən] N eheähnliche Gemeinschaft

cohabitee [ˌkəʊhæbɪˈtiː] N *Partner(in) in einer nichtehelichen Lebensgemeinschaft*

coheir [ˈkəʊˈɛəˈ] N Miterbe *m (to +gen)*; **they were ~s to the fortune** sie waren gemeinsame Erben des Vermögens

coheiress [ˈkəʊˈɛərɪs] N Miterbin *f (to +gen)*

cohere [kəʊˈhɪəˈ] VI **a** *(lit)* zusammenhängen **b** *(fig, community)* ein Ganzes *or* eine Einheit bilden; *(essay, symphony etc)* in sich geschlossen sein; *(argument, reasoning, style)* kohärent *or* zusammenhängend sein

coherence [kəʊˈhɪərəns] N **a** *(lit)* Kohärenz *f* **b** *(of community)* Zusammenhalt *m*; *(of essay, symphony etc)* Geschlossenheit *f*; *(of argument, reasoning, style)* Kohärenz *f*; **his speech lacked ~** seiner Rede *(dat)* fehlte der Zusammenhang **c** *(fig: = comprehensibility)* **after five whiskies he lacked ~** nach fünf Whiskys gab er nur noch unzusammenhängendes Zeug von sich

coherent [kəʊˈhɪərənt] ADJ **a** *(= comprehensible)* zusammenhängend; **incapable of ~ speech** unfähig, zusammenhängend zu sprechen **b** *(= cohesive) logic, reasoning etc* kohärent, schlüssig; *case* schlüssig

coherently [kəʊˈhɪərəntlɪ] ADV **a** *(= comprehensibly)* zusammenhängend **b** *(= cohesively)* kohärent, schlüssig

cohesion [kəʊˈhiːʒən] N *(Sci)* Kohäsion *f*; *(fig also)* Zusammenhang *m*; *(of group)* Zusammenhalt *m*, Geschlossenheit *f*

cohesive [kəʊˈhiːsɪv] ADJ *(Sci)* Binde-, Kohäsiv-; *(fig)* geschlossen

cohesively [kəʊˈhiːsɪvlɪ] ADV *(Sci)* kohäsiv; *(fig) write, argue* im Zusammenhang

cohort [ˈkəʊhɔːt] N Kohorte *f*, Trupp *m*

COHSE [ˈkəʊzɪ] *(Brit dated) abbr of* **Confederation of Health Service Employees** *Gewerkschaft der Angestellten des Gesundheitsdienstes*

coif [kɔɪf] N *(Hist, Eccl)* Haube *f*; *(= skullcap)* Kappe *f*

coiffed [kɔɪft] ADJ frisiert

coiffure [kwɒˈfjʊəʳ] N Haartracht *f*, Coiffure *f (geh)*

coiffured [kwɒˈfjʊəd] ADJ = **coiffed**

coil [kɔɪl] N **a** *(of rope, wire etc)* Rolle *f*; *(in light bulb)* Glühdraht *m*; *(on loop)* Windung *f*; *(of smoke)* Kringel *m*; *(of hair)* Kranz *m*; **she wore her hair in ~s** *(round head)* sie hatte eine Gretchenfrisur; *(round ears)* sie trug ihr Haar in Schnecken; **the sinewy ~s of the snake** die kraftvoll gespannte Spirale des Schlangenkörpers
b *(Elec)* Spule *f*
c *(= contraceptive)* Spirale *f*
VT aufwickeln, aufrollen; *wire* aufspulen, aufwickeln; **to ~ sth round sth** etw um etw wickeln; **the python ~ed itself around the rabbit/(up) in the basket** die Pythonschlange umschlang das Kaninchen/rollte sich im Korb zusammen
VI sich ringeln; *(smoke also)* sich kringeln; *(river)* sich schlängeln *or* winden

coil spring N Sprungfeder *f*

coin [kɔɪn] N **a** Münze *f* **b** *no pl* Münzen *pl*; **in the ~ of the realm** in der Landeswährung; **I'll pay you back in the same ~** *(Brit fig)* das werde ich dir in gleicher Münze heimzahlen; **the other side of the ~** *(fig)* die Kehrseite der Medaille; **they are two sides of the same ~** das sind zwei Seiten derselben Sache VT *(lit, fig) money, phrase* prägen; **he's ~ing money** *or* **it (in)** *(fig inf)* er scheffelt Geld *(inf)*; **..., to ~ a phrase** ..., um mich mal so auszudrücken

coinage [ˈkɔɪnɪdʒ] N **a** *(= act)* Prägen *nt*, Prägung *f*; *(= coins)* Münzen *pl*, Hartgeld *nt no pl*; *(= system)* Währung *f* **b** *(fig)* Prägung *f*, Neuschöpfung *f*

coin box N *(= telephone)* Münzfernsprecher *m*; *(= box)* Geldkasten *m*; *(on telephone, meter)* Münzzähler *m*

coincide [ˌkəʊɪnˈsaɪd] VI *(in time, place)* zusammenfallen; *(in area)* sich decken; *(= agree)* übereinstimmen; **the two concerts ~** die beiden Konzerte finden zur gleichen Zeit statt

coincidence [kəʊˈɪnsɪdəns] N **a** Zufall *m*, Fügung *f (geh)*; **what a ~!** welch ein Zufall!; **it is no ~ that ...** es ist kein Zufall, dass ..., es ist nicht von ungefähr, dass ... **b** *(= occurring or coming together, in time)* Zusammentreffen *nt*; *(in place)* Zusammenfall *m*; *(= agreement)* Übereinstimmung *f*

coincident [kəʊˈɪnsɪdənt] ADJ *(in time)* zusammentreffend; *(in place)* zusammenfallend; *(= agreeing)* übereinstimmend

coincidental ADJ, **coincidentally** ADV [kəʊˌɪnsɪˈdentl, -təlɪ] zufällig

coin-operated [ˈkɔɪnˈɒpəreɪtɪd] ADJ Münz-; **~ machine** Münzautomat *m*

coin slot N Münzeinwurf *m*

coir [kɔɪəʳ] N Kokosfaser *f*, Coir *nt or f*

coital [ˈkɔɪtəl] ADJ *(form)* Koitus-

coition [kəʊˈɪʃən], **coitus** [ˈkɔɪtəs] N *(form)* Koitus *m*, Akt *m*

coitus interruptus [ˈkɔɪtəsˌɪntəˈrʌptəs] N Coitus interruptus *m*

coke[1] [kəʊk] N Koks *m*

coke[2] N *(inf: = cocaine)* Koks *m (inf)*

Coke® [kəʊk] N *(inf)* (Coca-)Cola® *f*, Coke® *nt*

col[1] [kɒl] N Sattel *m*, Pass *m*

col[2] *abbr of* **column** Sp.

Col *abbr of* **Colonel**

COLA [ˈkəʊlə] *(US Fin) abbr of* **cost-of-living adjustment** Dynamisierung *f* auf der Basis veränderter Lebenshaltungskosten

colander [ˈkʌləndəʳ] N Seiher *m*, Sieb *nt*

cold [kəʊld] ✪ 7.5 ADJ *(+er)* **a** kalt; **~ meats** Aufschnitt *m*; **I am ~** mir ist kalt, ich friere; **my hands are ~/are getting ~** ich habe/kriege kalte Hände; **the room is/the nights are getting ~** das Zimmer wird/die Nächte werden kalt; **don't get ~** pass auf, dass du nicht frierst!; **if you get ~** wenn es dir zu kalt wird, wenn du frierst; **your coffee is getting ~** dein Kaffee wird kalt
b *(fig)* kalt; *answer, reception* betont kühl; *colour* kalt; *personality* kühl; *(= dispassionate, not sensual)* kühl; **to be ~ to sb** jdn kühl behandeln; **that leaves me ~** das lässt mich kalt
c *(inf: = unconscious)* bewusstlos; *(= knocked out)* k. o.; **to be out ~** bewusstlos/k. o. sein; **to knock sb out ~** jdn k. o. schlagen
d *(inf, in guessing)* kalt; **you're still ~** immer noch kalt
e *(Hunt) scent* kalt
f *(phrases)* **in ~ blood** kaltblütig; **~ comfort** ein schwacher Trost; **to get/have ~ feet** *(fig inf)* kalte Füße kriegen/haben *(inf)*; **to get/have ~ feet about doing sth** Muffe kriegen/haben, etw zu tun *(inf)*; **he's a ~ fish** er ist ein kalter Fisch *(inf)*; **to give sb the ~ shoulder** *(inf)* jdm die kalte Schulter zeigen; **to be in a ~ sweat** vor Angst schwitzen; **that brought him out in a ~ sweat** dabei brach ihm der kalte Schweiß *or* der Angstschweiß aus; **to throw ~ water on sb's plans** *(inf)* jdm eine kalte Dusche geben; **to throw ~ water on sb's hopes** *(inf)* jds Hoffnungen *(dat)* einen Dämpfer aufsetzen
ADV **to come to sth ~** unvorbereitet an eine Sache herangehen; **to learn/know sth ~** *(US)* etw gut lernen/können; **he stopped ~ when ...** *(US)* er hielt unvermittelt an, als ...; **she quit her job ~** sie hat glatt *or* eiskalt gekündigt *(inf)*; **he was turned down ~** er wurde glatt abgelehnt
N **a** Kälte *f*; **to feel the ~** kälteempfindlich sein; **don't go out in this ~!** geh nicht raus bei dieser Kälte!; **to be left out in the ~** *(fig)* ausgeschlossen werden, links liegen gelassen werden; **to feel left out in the ~** sich ausgeschlossen fühlen
b *(Med)* Erkältung *f*; *(= runny nose)* Schnupfen *m*; **a heavy** *or* **bad ~** eine schwere Erkältung; **to have a ~** erkältet sein; *(= runny nose)* einen Schnupfen haben; **to get** *or* **catch a ~** sich erkälten, sich *(dat)* eine Erkältung holen; **to catch ~** sich erkälten; **~ in the head** *(Brit)*, **head ~** Kopfgrippe *f*; **~ on the chest** *(Brit)* **chest ~** Bronchialkatarr(h) *m*

cold: **cold-blooded** ADJ *(Zool, fig)* kaltblütig; **~ animal** Kaltblüter *m*; **to be ~ about sth** etw kaltblütig tun; **cold-bloodedly** [ˈkəʊldˈblʌdɪdlɪ] ADV kaltblütig; **cold boot** N *(Comput)* Kaltstart *m*; **cold box** N *(Brit)* Kühlbox *f*; **cold call** N *(Comm) (on phone)* Vertreteranruf *m*; *(= visit)* Vertreterbesuch *m*; **cold calling** N *(Comm) (on phone)* Kundenwerbung *f* per Telefon; *(= visiting)* Vertreterbesuche *pl*; **cold case** N ungelöster Kriminalfall; **cold chisel** N Kaltmeißel *m*; **cold cream** N Coldcream *f or nt*, halbfette Feuchtigkeitscreme; **cold cuts** PL *(US)* Aufschnitt *m*; **cold frame** N *(Hort)* Frühbeet *nt*; **cold fusion** N *(Phys)* kalte Fusion; **cold-hearted** ADJ kaltherzig

coldly [ˈkəʊldlɪ] ADV *(lit, fig)* kalt; *answer, receive* betont kühl; **they ~ planned the murder** der Mord wurde von ihnen kaltblütig geplant

coldness [ˈkəʊldnɪs] N *(lit, fig)* Kälte *f*; *(of answer, reception, welcome)* betonte Kühle; **the unexpected ~ of the weather** die unerwartete Kälte; **the ~ with which they planned the murder** die Kaltblütigkeit, mit der sie den Mord planten

cold: **cold room** N Kühlraum *m*; **cold selling** N Cold Selling *nt*; **cold shoulder** N *(inf)* **to give sb the ~** jdm die kalte Schulter zeigen; **cold-shoulder** VT *(inf)* die kalte Schulter zeigen *(+dat)*; **cold snap** N *(Met)* Kälteeinbruch *m*; **cold sore** N *(Med)* Bläschenausschlag *m*; **cold start** N *(Aut, Comput)* Kaltstart *m*; **cold storage** N Kühllagerung *f*; **to put sth into ~** *(lit, food)* etw kühl lagern; *(fig) idea, plan* etw auf Eis legen; **cold store** N Kühlhaus *nt*; **cold turkey** *(inf)* ADJ **a ~ cure** ein kalter Entzug *(sl)* ADV **to come off drugs ~** einen kalten Entzug machen *(sl)*; **cold war** N kalter Krieg; **cold warrior** N kalter Krieger; **cold-weather payment** N *(Brit)* Brennstoffbeihilfe *f*

coleslaw [ˈkəʊlslɔː] N Krautsalat *m*

colic [ˈkɒlɪk] N Kolik *f*

coliseum [ˌkɒlɪˈsiːəm] N Kolosseum *nt*

collaborate [kəˈlæbəreɪt] VI **a** *(= work together)* zusammenarbeiten; **they asked him to ~** sie baten ihn mitzuarbeiten, sie baten um seine Mitarbeit; **to ~ with sb on** *or* **in sth** mit jdm bei etw zusammenarbeiten **b** *(with enemy)* kollaborieren; **he was suspected of collaborating** er wurde der Kollaboration verdächtigt

collaboration [kəˌlæbəˈreɪʃən] N **a** *(= working together)* Zusammenarbeit *f*; *(of one party)* Mitarbeit *f*; **helpful ~** Mithilfe *f* **b** *(with enemy)* Kollaboration *f* **c** *(= piece of work)* Gemeinschaftsproduktion *f*

collaborative [kəˈlæbərətɪv] ADJ gemeinschaftlich

collaboratively [kəˈlæbərətɪvlɪ] ADV gemeinschaftlich; **to work ~** zusammenarbeiten

collaborator [kəˈlæbəreɪtəʳ] N **a** Mitarbeiter(in) *m(f)* **b** *(with enemy)* Kollaborateur(in) *m(f)*

collage [kɒˈlɑːʒ] N Collage *f*

collapse [kəˈlæps] VI **a** *(person)* zusammenbrechen; *(mentally, = have heart attack also)* einen Kollaps erleiden *or* haben; **his health ~d** er hatte einen Kollaps; **they all ~d with laughter** sie konnten sich alle vor Lachen nicht mehr halten; **she ~d onto her bed, exhausted** sie plumpste erschöpft aufs Bett
b *(= fall down, cave in)* zusammenbrechen; *(building, wall, roof also)* einstürzen; *(lungs)* zusammenfallen, kollabieren
c *(fig: = fail)* zusammenbrechen; *(negotiations)* scheitern; *(civilization)* untergehen; *(prices)* stürzen, purzeln *(inf)*; *(government)* zu Fall kommen, stürzen; *(plans)* scheitern, zu Fall kommen; *(hopes)* sich zerschlagen; **his whole world ~d about him** eine ganze Welt stürzte über ihm zusammen; **their whole society ~d** ihre ganze Gesellschaftsordnung brach zusammen
d *(= fold, table, umbrella, bicycle etc)* sich zusammenklappen lassen; *(telescope, walking stick)* sich zusammenschieben lassen; *(life raft)* sich zusammenlegen *or* -falten lassen
VT *table, umbrella, bicycle etc* zusammenklappen; *telescope, walking stick* zusammenschieben; *life raft* zusammenlegen *or* -falten
N **a** *(of person)* Zusammenbruch *m*; *(= nervous breakdown also, heart attack)* Kollaps *m*
b *(of object)* Zusammenbruch *m*; *(of building, wall, roof also)* Einsturz *m*; *(of lungs)* Kollaps *m*
c *(fig: = failure)* Zusammenbruch *m*; *(of negotiations also)* Scheitern *nt*; *(of civilization)* Untergang *m*; *(of government)* Sturz *m*; *(of hopes)* Zerschlagung *f*

collapsible [kəˈlæpsəbl] ADJ *table, bicycle etc* zusammenklappbar, Klapp-; *telescope, walking stick* zusammenschiebbar; *life raft* zusammenlegbar, zusammenfaltbar, Falt-; **~ umbrella** zusammenschiebbarer Schirm, Taschenschirm *m*

collar [ˈkɒləʳ] N **a** Kragen *m*; **he got hold of him by the ~** er packte ihn am Kragen; **~ stud** Kragenknopf *m* **b** *(for dogs)* Halsband *nt*; *(for horses)* Kum(me)t *nt* **c** *(= chain and insignia)* Hals- *or* Ordenskette *f* **d** *(Mech, on pipe etc)* Bund *m* VT *(= capture)* fassen; *(= latch onto)* abfangen, schnappen *(inf)*

collarbone [ˈkɒləˈbəʊn] N Schlüsselbein *nt*

collate [kɒˈleɪt] VT a *data, information* zusammentragen b *(Typ)* kollationieren, zusammentragen c *(printer) copies* sortieren

collateral [kɒˈlætərəl] ADJ a *(= connected but secondary) evidence, questions etc* zusätzlich, Zusatz-; *events* Begleit- b *(= parallel, side by side) states etc* nebeneinanderliegend; *(fig) aims etc* Hand in Hand gehend c *descent, branch of family* seitlich, kollateral *(spec)* d *(Fin) security* zusätzlich N *(Fin)* (zusätzliche) Sicherheit

collateral: **collateral damage** N *(Mil, Pol)* Kollateralschaden *m*; **collateral loan** N *(Fin)* Lombardkredit *m*, Lombarddarlehen *nt*; **collateral security** N *(Fin)* Nebensicherheit *f*, Nebenbürgschaft *f*

collation [kɒˈleɪʃən] N a *(= collating)* Vergleich *m*, Kollationieren *nt*; *(Typ)* Kollationieren *nt*, Zusammentragen *nt* b *(form: = meal)* Imbiss *m*

colleague [ˈkɒliːg] N Kollege *m*, Kollegin *f*; **my ~s at work** meine Arbeitskollegen

collect¹ [ˈkɒlekt] N *(Eccl)* Kirchen- *or* Tagesgebet *nt*

collect² [kəˈlekt] ✪ 27.2 VT a *(= accumulate)* ansammeln; *(furniture) dust* anziehen; *empty glasses, exam papers, tickets etc* einsammeln; *litter* aufsammeln; *prize* bekommen; *belongings* zusammenpacken *or* -sammeln; *(= assemble)* sammeln; *one's thoughts* sammeln, ordnen; *information* sammeln, zusammentragen; **she ~ed a lot of praise/five points for that** das hat ihr viel Lob/fünf Punkte eingebracht *or* eingetragen; **to ~ interest** Zinsen bringen
b *(= pick up, fetch) things, persons* abholen (*from* bei)
c *stamps, coins* sammeln
d *taxes* einziehen; *money, jumble for charity* sammeln; *rent, fares* kassieren; *debts* eintreiben
VI a *(= gather)* sich ansammeln; *(dust)* sich absetzen
b *(= collect money)* kassieren; *(for charity)* sammeln
c *(Comm: = call for goods)* abholen
ADJ *(US)* → **collect cable, collect call**
ADV *(US)* **to pay ~** bei Empfang bezahlen; **to call ~** ein R-Gespräch führen; **to pay ~ on delivery** bei Lieferung bezahlen; *(through post)* per Nachnahme bezahlen

► **collect together** VT *sep* zusammensammeln; *information* zusammentragen; *team of people* auf- *or* zusammenstellen; **the officer collected his men together** der Offizier rief seine Leute zusammen

► **collect up** VT *sep* einsammeln; *litter* aufsammeln; *belongings* zusammenpacken *or* -sammeln

collect cable N *(US)* vom Empfänger bezahltes Telegramm

collect call N *(US)* R-Gespräch *nt*

collected [kəˈlektɪd] ADJ a **the ~ works of Oscar Wilde** Oscar Wildes gesammelte Werke b *(= calm)* ruhig, gelassen

collectedly [kəˈlektɪdlɪ] ADV ruhig, gelassen

collection [kəˈlekʃən] N a *(= group of people, objects)* Ansammlung *f*; *(of stamps, coins etc)* Sammlung *f*; **they're an odd ~ of people** das ist ein seltsamer Verein *(inf)*
b *(= collecting, of facts, information)* Zusammentragen *nt*; *(of goods, person)* Abholung *f*; *(of mail)* Abholung *f*; *(from letter box)* Leerung *f*; *(of stamps, coins)* Sammeln *nt*; *(of money, jumble for charity)* Sammlung *f*; *(in church)* Kollekte *f*; *(of rent, fares)* Kassieren *nt*; *(of taxes)* Einziehen *nt*; *(of debts)* Eintreiben *nt*; **the police organized the ~ of all firearms** die Polizei ließ alle Schusswaffen einsammeln; **to hold a ~ for sb/sth** für jdn/etw eine Sammlung durchführen; **bill for ~** Inkassowechsel *m*
c *(Fashion)* Kollektion *f*

collective [kəˈlektɪv] ADJ a kollektiv, Kollektiv-; *responsibility, agreement, action also* gemeinsam; **~ ticket** Sammelfahrschein *m* b *(= accumulated) wisdom, discoveries, experience* gesamt *attr*; **the ~ unconscious** das kollektive Unbewusste N Kollektiv *nt*; *(= farm also)* Produktionsgenossenschaft *f*

collective bargaining N Tarifverhandlungen *pl*

collective farm N landwirtschaftliche Produktionsgenossenschaft

collectively [kəˈlektɪvlɪ] ADV gemeinsam, zusammen; *(in socialist context also)* kollektiv

collective noun N *(Gram)* Kollektivum *nt*, Sammelbegriff *m*

collective security N *(Pol)* kollektive Sicherheit

collectivism [kəˈlektɪvɪzəm] N Kollektivismus *m*

collectivist [kəˈlektɪvɪst] N Kollektivist(in) *m(f)* ADJ kollektivistisch

collectivize [kəˈlektɪvaɪz] VT kollektivieren

collector [kəˈlektəʳ] N a *(of taxes)* Einnehmer(in) *m(f)*; *(of rent, cash)* Kassierer(in) *m(f)*; *(= ticket collector) Bahnbediensteter, der die abgefahrenen Fahrkarten einsammelt* b *(of stamps, coins etc)* Sammler(in) *m(f)*; **~'s** *(item, piece, price)* Sammler-, Liebhaber-; **~'s car** Liebhaberauto *nt*

colleen [ˈkɒliːn] N *(Ir)* junges Mädchen, Mädel *nt*

college [ˈkɒlɪdʒ] N a *(= part of university)* College *nt*, Institut *nt*; **to go to ~** *(= university)* studieren; **to start ~** sein Studium beginnen; **we met at ~** wir haben uns im Studium kennengelernt b *(of music, agriculture, technology etc)* Fachhochschule *f*; **College of Art** Kunstakademie *f* c *(= body)* **College of Cardinals** Kardinalskollegium *nt*; **College of Physicians/Surgeons** Ärztebund *m*, Ärztekammer *f*

> **COLLEGE**
>
> **College** ist ein allgemeiner Oberbegriff für höhere Bildungsinstitute. In Großbritannien kann er sich auf Einrichtungen beziehen, in denen man in einzelnen Fachbereichen, wie Kunst oder Musik, einen Hochschulabschluss erwerben kann, aber ebenso auf Schulen ohne weiteren Abschluss, z. B. für Sekretärinnen oder Friseure. Einige britische Universitäten, darunter Oxford und Cambridge, setzen sich aus **Colleges** zusammen. In diesen **collegiate universities** sorgen die **Colleges** für die Unterbringung und Ausbildung der Studenten, auch wenn die Universität dann die Abschlüsse verleiht. Zu den bekanntesten **Colleges** zählen wohl das King's College in Cambridge und das Magdalen College in Oxford.
> In den USA werden die Universitäten in Verwaltungseinheiten unterteilt, die als **Colleges** bezeichnet werden: zum Beispiel das „College of Arts and Sciences" oder das „College of Medicine". **Graduate schools**, die normalerweise Teil einer Universität sind, bieten auf dem **bachelor** aufbauende Studiengänge zur weiteren Spezialisierung an. **Junior** oder **community colleges** sind Institute, an denen man nach zweijähriger Studienzeit einen berufsbezogenen Abschluss machen kann; sie bieten auch Weiterbildungen für Berufstätige an → DEGREE, OXBRIDGE

college bar N *(esp US)* College-Bar *f*, Uni-Kneipe *f*

collegiate [kəˈliːdʒɪɪt] ADJ College-; **~ life** das Collegeleben, das Leben auf dem College; **Oxford is a ~ university** Oxford ist eine auf dem College-System aufgebaute Universität

collide [kəˈlaɪd] VI a *(lit)* zusammenstoßen *or* -prallen; *(Naut)* kollidieren; **they ~d head-on** sie stießen frontal zusammen; **to ~ with sb** mit jdm zusammenstoßen; **to ~ with sth** gegen etw prallen b *(fig, person)* eine heftige Auseinandersetzung haben (*with* mit); *(interest, demands)* kollidieren

collie [ˈkɒlɪ] N Collie *m*

collier [ˈkɒlɪəʳ] N a Bergmann *m*, Kumpel *m* *(inf)* b *(= coal ship)* Kohlenschiff *nt*

colliery [ˈkɒlɪərɪ] N Grube *f*, Zeche *f*

collimate [ˈkɒlɪmeɪt] VT kollimieren

collision [kəˈlɪʒən] N *(lit)* Zusammenstoß *m*, Zusammenprall *m*; *(fig)* Zusammenstoß *m*, Konflikt *m*, Kollision *f*; *(Naut)* Kollision *f*; **on a ~ course** *(lit, fig)* auf Kollisionskurs; **to be in ~ with sth** mit etw zusammenstoßen; **to come into ~ with sth** *(lit, fig)* mit etw zusammenstoßen; *(Naut)* mit etw kollidieren

collision damage waiver N *(Insur)* Schadenersatzverzichtklausel *f* bei Kollisionen

collocate [ˈkɒləkeɪt] VT *(Gram)* nebeneinanderstellen; **to be ~d** nebeneinanderstehen

collocation [kɒləˈkeɪʃən] N *(Gram)* Kollokation *f*

colloquial [kəˈləʊkwɪəl] ADJ umgangssprachlich

colloquialism [kəˈləʊkwɪəlɪzəm] N umgangssprachlicher Ausdruck

colloquially [kəˈləʊkwɪəlɪ] ADV umgangssprachlich

colloquium [kəˈləʊkwɪəm] N Kolloquium *nt*

colloquy [ˈkɒləkwɪ] N *(form)* Gespräch *nt*; *(Liter)* Dialog *m*; **in ~** im Gespräch

collude [kəˈluːd] VI gemeinsame Sache machen (*with* mit)

collusion [kəˈluːʒən] N (geheime) Absprache; **they're acting in ~** sie haben sich abgesprochen; **there's been some ~ between those two pupils** diese beiden Schüler haben zusammengearbeitet

collusive [kəˈluːsɪv] ADJ **~ behaviour** geheime Absprachen *pl*; **~ business practices** geheime Geschäftsabsprachen *pl*

collywobbles [ˈkɒlɪˌwɒblz] PL *(inf)* **the ~** *(= upset stomach)* Bauchgrimmen *nt (inf)*; *(= nerves)* ein flaues Gefühl im Magen

Cologne [kəˈləʊn] N Köln *nt* ADJ Kölner, kölnisch

cologne [kəˈləʊn] N Kölnischwasser *nt*, Eau de Cologne *nt*

colon¹ [ˈkəʊlən] N *(Anat)* Dickdarm *m*

colon² N *(Gram)* Doppelpunkt *m*; *(old, Typ)* Kolon *nt*

colonel [ˈkɜːnl] N Oberst *m*; *(as address)* Herr Oberst

colonial [kəˈləʊnɪəl] ADJ Kolonial-, kolonial; **~ architecture** Kolonialstil *m*; **~ type** Typ *m* des Herrenmenschen *(iro)* N Bewohner(in) *m(f)* einer Kolonie/der Kolonien

colonialism [kəˈləʊnɪəlɪzəm] N Kolonialismus *m*

colonialist [kəˈləʊnɪəlɪst] ADJ kolonialistisch N Kolonialist(in) *m(f)*

colonist [ˈkɒlənɪst] N Kolonist(in) *m(f)*, Siedler(in) *m(f)*

colonization [ˌkɒlənaɪˈzeɪʃən] N Kolonisation *f*

colonize [ˈkɒlənaɪz] VT kolonisieren

colonized [ˈkɒlənaɪzd] ADJ kolonisiert

colonnade [ˌkɒləˈneɪd] N Kolonnade *f*, Säulengang *m*

colony [ˈkɒlənɪ] N Kolonie *f*

colophon [ˈkɒləfən] N Kolophon *m*, Signet *nt*

color *etc (US)* = **colour** *etc*

Colorado beetle [ˌkɒləˈrɑːdəʊˈbiːtl] N Kartoffelkäfer *m*

colorant [ˈkʌlərənt] N *(US)* = **colourant**

coloration [ˌkʌləˈreɪʃən] N Färbung *f*

coloratura [kɒlərəˈtʊərə] N Koloratur *f*

color guard N *(US)* = **colour party**

coloscopy [kəˈlɒskəpɪ] N *(Med)* Koloskopie *f*

colossal [kəˈlɒsl] ADJ riesig, ungeheuer, gewaltig; *fool, cheek, mistake* ungeheuer; *car, man, park, lake, city* riesig; *prices, damage, building also* kolossal

colossally [kəˈlɒsəlɪ] ADV *(= immensely) (+adj)* wahnsinnig, unheimlich; *(+vb)* enorm, extrem; **~ expensive** wahnsinnig teuer

colosseum [kɒlɪ'si:əm] N Kolosseum *nt*

colossi [kə'lɒsaɪ] *pl of* **colossus**

Colossians [kə'lɒʃəns] N **(Epistle to the) ~** Kolosserbrief *m*

colossus [kə'lɒsəs] N *pl* **colossi** *or* **-es** *(= statue)* Koloss *m*; *(= person also)* Riese *m*; **this ~ of the world of music** dieser Gigant *or* Titan der Musik

colostomy [kə'lɒstəmɪ] N *(Med)* Kolostomie *f*; **~ bag** Kolostomiebeutel *m*

colour, *(US)* **color** ['kʌlə'] **N** **a** *(lit, fig)* Farbe *f*; **what ~ is it?** welche Farbe hat es?; **red/yellow in ~** rot/gelb; **the film was in ~** der Film war in Farbe; **~ illustration** farbige Illustration; **a good sense of ~** ein guter Farbensinn; **let's see the ~ of your money first** *(inf)* zeig erst mal dein Geld her *(inf)*; **the ~ of a note** *(Mus)* die Klangfarbe eines Tons → **glowing**
b *(= complexion)* (Gesichts)farbe *f*; **to change ~** die Farbe wechseln; **to get one's ~ back** wieder Farbe bekommen; **to bring the ~ back to sb's cheeks** jdm wieder Farbe geben; **to have a high ~** *(Brit)* eine gesunde Gesichtsfarbe haben; *(= look feverish)* rot im Gesicht sein; **he had gone a funny ~** er nahm eine komische Farbe an
c *(racial)* Hautfarbe *f*; **I don't care what ~ he is** seine Hautfarbe interessiert mich nicht; **people of ~** *(dated)* Farbige *pl*
d **colours** **PL** *(= paints)* Farben *pl*; **a box of ~s** ein Mal- *or* Tuschkasten *m*
e *(fig: = bias: of newspaper, report)* Färbung *f*
f *(of place, period etc)* Atmosphäre *f*; **to add ~ to a story** einer Geschichte *(dat)* Farbe geben; **the pageantry and ~ of Elizabethan England** der Prunk und die Farbenpracht des Elisabethanischen England
g *(= appearance of truth)* **to lend ~ to a tale** eine Geschichte ausschmücken
h **colours** **PL** *(= symbols of membership)* Farben *pl*; *(Sport)* (Sport)abzeichen *nt*; *(= flag)* Fahne *f*; **the regimental ~s** die Regimentsfahne; **to serve with/join the ~s** *(old)* der Fahne dienen *(dated)*/den bunten Rock anziehen *(old)*; **to nail one's ~s to the mast** *(fig)* Farbe bekennen; **to nail one's ~s to sb's mast** *(fig)* sich zu jdm bekennen; **to sail under false ~s** *(fig)* unter falscher Flagge segeln; **to show one's true ~s** *(fig)* sein wahres Gesicht zeigen
VT **a** *(lit)* anmalen; *(Art)* kolorieren; *(= dye)* färben
b *(fig)* beeinflussen; *(= bias deliberately)* färben
VI **a** *(leaves)* sich (ver)färben
b *(person: also* **colour up***)* rot werden, erröten

▶ **colour in** VT *sep* anmalen; *(Art)* kolorieren

colourant, *(US)* **colorant** ['kʌlərənt] N Farbstoff *m*

colour, *(US)* **color** *in cpds* Farb-; *(racial)* Rassen-; *(Mil)* Fahnen-; **colour bar** N Rassenschranke *f*; *(in country also)* Rassenschranken *pl*; **to operate a ~** Rassentrennung praktizieren; **colour-blind** ADJ farbenblind; **colour blindness** N Farbenblindheit *f*; **colour-code** VT farbig kennzeichnen *or* kodieren; **colour coordination** N farbliche Abstimmung; **colour copy** N Farbkopie *f*

coloured, *(US)* **colored** ['kʌləd] **ADJ** **a** bunt; *fabric, walls also* farbig **b** *(fig: = biased)* gefärbt; *(= exaggerated)* ausgeschmückt; **a highly ~ account** ein reichlich ausgeschmückter Bericht **c** *person, race* farbig; *(= of mixed blood)* gemischtrassig **N** Farbige(r) *mf*; *(of mixed blood)* Mischling *m*

-coloured, *(US)* **-colored** ADJ *suf* **yellow-/red-coloured** gelb/rot; **straw-/dark-coloured** strohfarben/dunkel

colourfast, *(US)* **colorfast** ['kʌləfɑ:st] ADJ farbecht

colourful, *(US)* **colorful** ['kʌləfʊl] ADJ **a** *(lit)* bunt; *spectacle* farbenfroh *or* -prächtig **b** *(fig) style of writing, account etc* farbig, anschaulich; *life, historical period* (bunt) bewegt; *personality* (bunt) schillernd; **his ~ past** seine bunte *or* bewegte Vergangenheit **c** *(euph: = vulgar) language* derb

colourfully, *(US)* **colorfully** ['kʌləfəlɪ] ADV **a** *(= brightly) dressed, painted, decorated* bunt **b** *(= excitingly) describe, write* anschaulich **c** *(euph: = vulgarly) swear* heftig

colourfulness, *(US)* **colorfulness** ['kʌləfʊlnɪs] N **a** *(lit)* Buntheit *f*; *(of spectacle)* Farbenpracht *f* **b** *(fig, of style of writing, account)* Farbigkeit *f*, Anschaulichkeit *f*; *(of sb's life, historical period)* Bewegtheit *f*; **the ~ of his character** sein schillernder Charakter

colouring, *(US)* **coloring** ['kʌlərɪŋ] N **a** *(= complexion)* Gesichtsfarbe *f*, Teint *m* **b** *(= substance)* Farbstoff *m* **c** *(= painting)* Malen *nt* **d** *(= coloration)* Farben *pl* **e** *(fig, of news, facts etc)* Färbung *f*

colouring book, *(US)* **coloring book** N Malbuch *nt*

colouring set, *(US)* **coloring set** N Mal- *or* Tuschkasten *m*; *(= box of crayons)* Schachtel *f* Buntstifte

colourist, *(US)* **colorist** ['kʌlərɪst] N Farbkünstler(in) *m(f)*

colourless, *(US)* **colorless** ['kʌləlɪs] ADJ *(lit, fig)* farblos; *existence also* grau

colourlessly, *(US)* **colorlessly** ['kʌləlɪslɪ] ADV *(lit)* farblos; *(fig)* neutral

colourlessness, *(US)* **colorlessness** ['kʌləlɪsnɪs] N Farblosigkeit *f*

colour, *(US)* **color**: **colour party** N Fahnenträgerkommando *nt*; **colour photograph** N Farbfoto *nt*; **colour postcard** N bunte Ansichtskarte; **colour retention** N *(of clothes, paint)* Farbechtheit *f*; **colour scheme** N Farbzusammenstellung *f*; **colour sergeant** N *(Mil)* Fahnenträger *m*; **colour supplement** N Farbbeilage *f*, Magazin *nt*; **colour television** N Farbfernsehen *nt*; *(= set)* Farbfernseher *m*; **colour transparency** N Farbdia *nt*; **colourwash**, *(US)* **colorwash** N Farbtünche *f*

colt [kəʊlt] N Hengstfohlen *nt*; *(dated fig: = youth)* junger Dachs *(inf)*

Co Ltd *abbr of* **company limited** GmbH *f*

coltsfoot ['kəʊltsfʊt] N *pl* **-s** *(Bot)* Huflattich *m*

columbine ['kɒləmbaɪn] N *(Bot)* Akelei *f*

Columbus [kə'lʌmbəs] N Kolumbus *m*

Columbus Day N *(US) amerikanischer Feiertag am zweiten Montag im Oktober, an dem die Entdeckung Amerikas durch Kolumbus gefeiert wird*

column ['kɒləm] N **a** *(Archit, of smoke, water etc)* Säule *f*; **~ of mercury** Quecksilbersäule *f* **b** *(of figures, names)* Kolonne *f*; *(= division of page)* Spalte *f*, Kolumne *f (spec)*; *(= article in newspaper)* Kolumne *f* **c** *(of vehicles, soldiers etc)* Kolonne *f* **d** *(Typ)* Spalte *f*

columnist ['kɒləmnɪst] N Kolumnist(in) *m(f)*

coma ['kəʊmə] N Koma *nt*; **to be in a ~** im Koma liegen; **to go** *or* **fall into a ~** ins Koma fallen

comatose ['kəʊmətəʊs] ADJ komatös

comb [kəʊm] **N** **a** *(also Tech, of fowl)* Kamm *m* **b** *(= act)* **to give one's hair a ~** sich kämmen; **your hair could do with a ~** du könntest dich (auch) mal wieder kämmen **c** *(= honeycomb)* Wabe *f* **VT** **a** *hair, wool* kämmen; *horse* striegeln; **to ~ one's hair** sich *(dat)* die Haare kämmen, sich kämmen **b** *(= search)* durchkämmen; *newspapers* durchforsten

▶ **comb out** VT *sep* **a** *hair* auskämmen **b** *mistakes* ausmerzen; *useless stuff* aussortieren

▶ **comb through** VI *+prep obj hair* kämmen; *files, book etc* durchgehen; *shops* durchstöbern

combat ['kɒmbæt] **N** Kampf *m*; **ready for ~** kampfbereit, einsatzbereit **VT** *(lit, fig)* bekämpfen **VI** kämpfen

combatant ['kɒmbətənt] N *(lit, fig)* Kombattant *m*

combat: **combat dress** N Kampfanzug *m*; **combat fatigue** N Kriegsmüdigkeit *f*

combative ['kɒmbətɪv] ADJ *(= pugnacious)* kämpferisch; *(= competitive)* aggressiv

combat: **combat jacket** N Feldjacke *f*, Kampfjacke *f*; **combat knife** N Kampfmesser *nt*; **combat mission** N Kampfeinsatz *m*; **combat plane** N Kampfflugzeug *nt*; **combats** ['kɒmbæts] PL *(inf)* Tarnhose *f*, Kampfhose *f*; **combat troops** PL Kampftruppen *pl*; **combat trousers** PL *(Brit)* Tarnhose *f*, Kampfhose *f*; **combat unit** N *(esp US)* Kampfverband *m*, Kampfeinheit *f*; **combat zone** N Kampfgebiet *nt or* -zone *f*

combination [ˌkɒmbɪ'neɪʃən] N **a** Kombination *f*; *(= combining, of organizations, people etc)* Vereinigung *f*, Zusammenschluss *m*; *(of events)* Verkettung *f*; **in ~** zusammen, gemeinsam; **an unusual colour ~** eine ungewöhnliche Farbzusammenstellung; **pink is a ~ of red and white** Rosa ist eine Mischung aus Rot und Weiß; **those two boys together are a nasty ~** diese beiden Jungen zusammen sind ein übles Duo **b** **combinations** PL *(= undergarment)* Kombination *f*, Hemdhose *f* **c** *(= motorcycle combination)* Motorrad *nt* mit Beiwagen **d** *(for lock)* Kombination *f*

combination: **combination lock** N Kombinationsschloss *nt*; **combination sandwich** N *(US)* gemischt belegtes Sandwich

combine [kəm'baɪn] **VT** kombinieren, verbinden; **couldn't we ~ the two suggestions?** lassen sich die beiden Vorschläge nicht kombinieren *or* miteinander verbinden?; **your plan ~s the merits of the other two** Ihr Plan vereinigt die Vorzüge der beiden anderen **VI** sich zusammenschließen; *(Chem)* sich verbinden; **to ~ against sb** sich gegen jdn verschwören ['kɒmbaɪn] **N** **a** *(Econ)* Firmengruppe *f*, Konzern *m*; *(in socialist countries)* Kombinat *nt* **b** *(Agr: also* **combine harvester***)* Mähdrescher *m*

combined [kəm'baɪnd] ADJ gemeinsam; *talents, efforts* vereint; *forces* vereinigt; **~ with** in Kombination mit; *(esp clothes, furniture)* kombiniert mit; **a ~ clock and wireless** eine Radiouhr; **a ~ radio and tape recorder** Radio *nt* und Tonband *nt* in einem; **~ downhill** *(Ski)* Kombinationsabfahrt *f*; **~ event** *(Sport)* Mehrkampf *m*; *(Ski)* Kombination *f*; **~ honours** *(Brit Univ)* Doppelstudium *nt*; **~ operations** *(Mil)* gemeinsame Operation; **~ time** *(Sport)* Gesamtzeit *f*

combining form [kəm'baɪnɪŋfɔ:m] N Affix *nt*, Wortbildungselement *nt*

combo ['kɒmbəʊ] N **a** *(Mus)* Combo *f* **b** *(US inf: = fast-food meal with drink)* (Spar)menü *nt*

combustibility [kəmˌbʌstɪ'bɪlɪtɪ] N Brennbarkeit *f*

combustible [kəm'bʌstɪbl] **ADJ** brennbar **N** brennbarer Stoff

combustion [kəm'bʌstʃən] N Verbrennung *f*

combustion chamber N Brennkammer *f*

come [kʌm] *pret* **came**, *ptp* **come** **VI** **a** *(= approach)* kommen; **~!** *(form: = come in)* herein!; **~ and get it!** (das) Essen ist fertig!, Essen fassen! *(esp Mil)*; **to ~ and go** kommen und gehen; *(vehicle)* hin- und herfahren; **the picture/sound ~s and goes** das Bild/der Ton geht immerzu weg; **I don't know whether I'm coming or going** ich weiß nicht (mehr), wo mir der Kopf steht *(inf)*; **~ and see me soon** besuchen Sie mich bald einmal; **he has ~ a long way** er hat einen weiten Weg hinter sich; *(fig)* er ist weit gekommen; **the project has ~ a long way** das Projekt ist schon ziemlich weit; **he came running into the room** er kam ins Zimmer gerannt; **he came hurrying into the room** er eilte ins Zimmer; **he came laughing into the room** er kam lachend ins Zimmer; **coming!** ich komme (gleich)!, ich komm ja schon!; **~ ~!, ~ now!** *(fig)* komm(, komm)!, na, na!; **Christmas is coming** bald ist Weihnachten
b *(= arrive)* kommen; *(= reach, extend)* reichen *(to* an/in/bis *etc +acc)*; **they came to a town/castle** sie kamen in eine Stadt/zu einem Schloss; **it came to me that ...** mir fiel ein, dass ...

c *(= have its place)* kommen; **May ~s before June** Mai kommt vor Juni; **the adjective must ~ before the noun** das Adjektiv muss vor dem Substantiv stehen; **where does your name ~ in the list?** an welcher Stelle auf der Liste steht Ihr Name?; **that must ~ first** das muss an erster Stelle kommen; **all the other candidates came far behind** die anderen Bewerber waren weit abgeschlagen
d *(= happen)* geschehen; **~ what may** ganz gleich, was geschieht, komme, was (da) mag *(geh)*; **you could see it coming** das konnte man ja kommen sehen, das war ja zu erwarten; **she had it coming to her** *(inf)* das musste ja so kommen; **you've got it coming to you** *(inf)* mach dich auf was gefasst!; **recovery came slowly** nur allmählich trat eine Besserung ein
e how ~? *(inf)* wieso?, weshalb?; **how ~ you're so late?, how do you ~ to be so late?** wieso *etc* kommst du so spät?
f *(= be, become)* werden; **his dreams came true** seine Träume wurden wahr; **the handle has ~ loose** der Griff hat sich gelockert; **it ~s less expensive to shop in town** es ist *or* kommt billiger, wenn man in der Stadt einkauft; **everything came all right in the end** zuletzt *or* am Ende wurde doch noch alles gut
g *(Comm: = be available)* erhältlich sein; **milk now ~s in plastic bottles** es gibt jetzt Milch in Plastikflaschen
h *(+infin: = be finally in a position to)* **I have ~ to believe him** inzwischen *or* mittlerweile glaube ich ihm; **I'm sure you will ~ to agree with me** ich bin sicher, dass du mir schließlich zustimmst; **(now I) ~ to think of it** wenn ich es mir recht überlege
i the years/weeks to ~ die kommenden *or* nächsten Jahre/Wochen; **in days to ~** in Zukunft; **in time to ~** in künftigen Zeiten; **the life (of the world) to ~** das ewige Leben
j *(inf uses)* **... ~ next week** nächste Woche ...; **I've known him for three years ~ January** im Januar kenne ich ihn drei Jahre; **how long have you been away? – a week ~ Monday** wie lange bist du schon weg? – (am) Montag acht Tage *(inf) or* eine Woche; **a week ~ Monday I'll be ...** Montag in acht Tagen *(inf) or* in einer Woche bin ich ...; **~ again?** wie bitte?; **she is as vain as they ~** sie ist so eingebildet wie nur was *(inf)*
k *(inf: = have orgasm)* kommen *(inf)*
VT *(Brit inf: = act as if one were)* spielen; **don't ~ the innocent with me** spielen Sie hier bloß nicht den Unschuldigen!, kommen Sie mir bloß nicht auf die unschuldige Tour *(inf)*!; **he tried to ~ the innocent with me** er hat versucht, den Unschuldigen zu markieren *(inf)*, er hat es auf die unschuldige Tour versucht *(inf)*; **don't ~ that game** *or* **that (with me)!** kommen Sie mir bloß nicht mit DER Tour! *(inf)*, DIE Masche zieht bei mir nicht! *(inf)*; **that's coming it a bit strong!** das ist reichlich übertrieben
N *(sl: = semen)* Saft *m (sl)*

▸**come about** VI **a** *impers (= happen)* passieren; **how does it come about that you are here?** wie kommt es, dass du hier bist?; **this is why it came about** das ist so gekommen; **this is how it came about ...** das kam so ... **b** *(Naut, wind)* drehen; *(ship)* beidrehen

▸**come across** VI **a** *(= cross)* herüberkommen **b** *(= be understood)* verstanden werden; *(message, speech)* ankommen **c** *(= make an impression)* wirken; **he wants to come across as a tough guy** er mimt gerne den starken Mann *(inf)* **d** *(inf: = do what is wanted)* mitmachen *(inf)* VI *+prep obj (= find or meet by chance)* treffen auf *(+acc)*; **if you come across my watch ...** wenn du zufällig meine Uhr siehst

▸**come across with** VI *+prep obj (inf) information* rausrücken mit *(inf)*; *money* rausrücken *(inf)*

▸**come after** VI *+prep obj* **a** *(= follow in sequence, be of less importance than)* kommen nach; **the noun comes after the verb** das Substantiv steht nach *or* hinter dem Verb **b** *(= pursue)* herkommen hinter *(+dat)* **c** *(= follow later)* nachkommen VI *(= follow later)* nachkommen

▸**come along** VI **a** *(= hurry up, make an effort etc: also* **come on***)* kommen
b *(= attend, accompany)* mitkommen; **come along with me** kommen Sie mal (bitte) mit
c *(= develop: also* **come on***)* **to be coming along** sich machen, vorangehen; *(person)* sich machen; **how is your broken arm? – it's coming along nicely** was macht dein gebrochener Arm? – dem gehts ganz gut *or* prima; **the bulbs are coming along nicely** die Blumenzwiebeln wachsen gut; **the new apprentice is coming along nicely** der neue Lehrling macht sich gut; **my play isn't coming along at all well** mein Stück macht überhaupt keine Fortschritte
d *(= arrive, turn up)* kommen, auftauchen; *(chance etc)* sich ergeben

▸**come apart** VI *(= fall to pieces)* kaputtgehen, auseinanderfallen; *(= be able to be taken apart)* zerlegbar sein; **it just came apart in my hands** es ist in meinen Händen in Stücke gegangen

▸**come (a)round** VI **a the road was blocked and we had to come round by the farm** die Straße war blockiert, so dass *or* sodass wir einen Umweg über den Bauernhof machen mussten
b *(= call round)* vorbeikommen *or* -schauen
c *(= recur)* **your birthday will soon come round again** du hast ja bald wieder Geburtstag; **Christmas has come round again** nun ist wieder Weihnachten
d *(= change one's opinions)* es sich *(dat)* anders überlegen; **eventually he came round to our way of thinking** schließlich machte er sich *(dat)* unsere Denkungsart zu Eigen
e *(= regain consciousness)* wieder zu sich *(dat)* kommen
f to come round to doing sth *(= get round)* dazu kommen, etw zu tun
g *(= throw off bad mood)* wieder vernünftig werden *(inf)*
h *(Naut, boat)* wenden

▸**come at** VI *+prep obj (= attack) sb* losgehen auf *(+acc)*; *(= approach) runway* anfliegen; *problem* angehen

▸**come away** VI **a** *(= leave)* (weg)gehen; **come away with me for a few days** fahr doch ein paar Tage mit mir weg!; **come away from there!** komm da weg!; **come away in!** *(Scot)* kommen Sie doch rein! **b** *(= become detached)* abgehen

▸**come back** VI **a** *(= return)* zurückkommen; *(= drive back)* zurückfahren; **to come back to what I was saying** um noch einmal auf das zurückzukommen, was ich vorhin gesagt habe; **we always come back to the same difficulty** wir stoßen immer wieder auf dieselbe Schwierigkeit; **can I come back to you on that one?** kann ich später darauf zurückkommen?; **the colour is coming back to her cheeks** langsam bekommt sie wieder Farbe; **will his memory ever come back?** wird er je das Gedächtnis wiedererlangen?
b *(= return to one's memory)* **his name is coming back to me** langsam erinnere ich mich wieder an seinen Namen; **ah yes, it's all coming back** ach ja, jetzt fällt mir alles wieder ein; **your German will very quickly come back** du wirst ganz schnell wieder ins Deutsche reinkommen *(inf)*
c *(= become popular again)* wieder in Mode kommen
d *(= make a comeback)* **they thought Sinatra would never come back** man glaubte, Sinatra würde niemals ein Comeback machen; **they came back into the game with a superb goal** sie fanden mit einem wunderbaren Tor ins Spielgeschehen zurück
e *(= reply)* reagieren; **she came back at him with a fierce accusation** sie entgegnete ihm mit einer heftigen Anschuldigung

▸**come before** VT *(Jur, person)* gebracht werden vor *(+acc)*; **his case came before the court** sein Fall wurde vor Gericht gebracht

▸**come between** VI *+prep obj people, lovers* treten zwischen *(+acc)*; **I never let anything come between me and my evening pint** ich lasse mich durch nichts von meinem abendlichen Bier(chen) abhalten; **he tried to come between the two fighting men** er versuchte, die beiden Kampfhähne zu trennen

▸**come by** VI *+prep obj (= obtain)* kriegen; *illness, bruise* sich *(dat)* holen; *idea* kommen auf *(+acc)* VI *(= visit)* vorbeikommen

▸**come close to** VI *+prep obj* = **come near to**

▸**come down** VI **a** *(from ladder, stairs)* herunterkommen; *(aircraft also)* landen; *(from mountain also)* absteigen; *(snow, rain)* fallen; **come down from there at once!** komm da sofort runter!; **we came down to 6,000 metres** wir gingen auf 6.000 m runter
b *(= be demolished: building etc)* abgerissen werden; *(= fall down)* (he)runterfallen
c *(= drop, prices)* sinken, runtergehen *(inf)*; *(seller)* runtergehen *(to* auf *+acc)*
d *(= be a question of)* ankommen *(to* auf *+acc)*; **it all comes down to something very simple** das ist letzten Endes ganz einfach; **when you come** *or* **it comes down to it** letzten Endes
e *(= lose social rank)* sinken, absteigen; **you've come down in the world a bit** du bist aber ganz schön tief gesunken
f *(= reach)* reichen *(to* bis auf *+acc,* zu*)*; **her hair comes down to her shoulders** die Haare gehen *or* fallen ihr bis auf die Schultern; **the dress comes down to her ankles** das Kleid geht ihr bis zu den Knöcheln
g *(= be transmitted: tradition, story etc)* überliefert werden
h *(from university)* **when did you come down?** wann bist du von der Uni runter? *(inf)*, wann haben Sie die Universität verlassen?; *(for vacation)* seit wann habt ihr Semesterferien?
i *(dated US inf: = be about to happen)* **there's a bank robbery coming down next week** für nächste Woche ist ein Banküberfall geplant

▸**come down on** VI *+prep obj* **a** *(= punish, rebuke)* rannehmen *(inf)*, zusammenstauchen *(inf)* → **brick b** *(= decide in favour of)* setzen auf *(+acc)*; **he came down on the side of expansion** er setzte auf Expansion; **you've got to come down on one side or the other** du musst dich so oder so entscheiden

▸**come down with** VI *+prep obj illness* kriegen

▸**come for** VI *+prep obj* kommen wegen

▸**come forward** VI **a** *(= make oneself known)* sich melden **b to come forward with help/money** Hilfe/Geld anbieten; **to come forward with a good suggestion** mit einem guten Vorschlag kommen

▸**come from** VI *+prep obj* kommen aus; *(suggestion)* kommen *or* stammen von; **where does he/it come from?** wo kommt er/das her?

▸**come in** VI **a** *(= enter)* (he)reinkommen; *(person also)* eintreten; **come in!** herein!; **to come in out of the cold** aus der Kälte kommen
b *(= arrive)* ankommen, eintreffen; *(train also)* einfahren; *(ship also)* einlaufen
c *(tide)* kommen
d *(report, information etc)* hereinkommen; **a report has just come in of ...** uns ist gerade eine Meldung über ... zugegangen
e *(= become seasonable)* **when do strawberries come in?** wann ist die Zeit für Erdbeeren?, wann gibt es (frische) Erdbeeren?
f *(fashions, vogue)* aufkommen, in Mode kommen
g *(in a race)* **he came in fourth** er wurde Vierter, er belegte den vierten Platz; **where did he come in?** der Wievielte ist er denn geworden?, welchen Platz hat er belegt?
h *(Pol: = be elected to power)* **when the socialists came in** als die Sozialisten ans Ruder *or* an die Regierung kamen
i *(= be received as income)* **he has £15,000 coming in every year** er kriegt *(inf) or* hat £ 15.000 im Jahr; **we have no money coming in at the moment** im Moment kommt kein Geld herein

j *(= have a part to play)* **where do I come in?** welche Rolle spiele ich dabei?; **... but where does your brother come in?** ... aber was hat dein Bruder mit der ganzen Sache zu tun?; **that will come in handy** *(inf)* *or* **useful** das kann ich/man noch gut gebrauchen
k *(Telec)* **come in, Panda 5** Panda 5, melden!

▶ **come in for** VI *+prep obj attention, admiration* erregen; *criticism etc also* hinnehmen *or* einstecken müssen

▶ **come in on** VI *+prep obj venture, scheme etc* mitmachen bei, sich beteiligen an *(+dat)*

▶ **come into** VI *+prep obj* a *(= inherit) legacy etc* erben b *(= be involved)* **I don't see where I come into all this** ich verstehe nicht, was ich mit der ganzen Sache zu tun habe; **this is a donation, publicity doesn't come into it** es handelt sich hier um eine Spende, Publicity ist dabei nicht im Spiel c *(in fixed collocations)* **to come into one's own** zeigen, was in einem steckt; **to come into being** *or* **existence** entstehen; **to come into bud** zu knospen beginnen; **to come into sb's possession** in jds Besitz *(acc)* gelangen

▶ **come near to** VI *+prep obj* **to come near to doing sth** nahe daran *or* drauf und dran sein, etw zu tun; **he came near to (committing) suicide** er war *or* stand kurz vor dem Selbstmord

▶ **come of** VI *+prep obj* a *(= result from)* **nothing came of it** es ist nichts daraus geworden, es führte zu nichts; **that's what comes of disobeying!** das kommt davon, wenn man nicht hören will! b *(= be descended from)* kommen *or* stammen aus

▶ **come off** VI a *(person: off bicycle etc)* runterfallen
b *(button, handle, paint etc)* abgehen; *(= be removable also)* sich abnehmen lassen
c *(stains, marks)* weg- *or* rausgehen
d *(= take place)* stattfinden; **her wedding didn't come off after all** aus ihrer Hochzeit ist nun doch nichts geworden
e *(plans etc)* klappen *(inf)*; *(attempts, experiments etc also)* glücken, gelingen
f *(= acquit oneself)* abschneiden; **he came off well in comparison to his brother** im Vergleich zu seinem Bruder ist er gut weggekommen; **he always came off badly in fights** bei Schlägereien zog er immer den Kürzeren; **several companies are likely to come off badly with the new tax laws** mehrere Firmen kommen in der neuen Steuergesetzgebung schlecht weg
g *(sl: = have orgasm)* kommen *(inf)*; **eventually he came off** endlich kam es ihm *(sl)*
VI *+prep obj* a *bicycle, horse etc* fallen von
b *(button, paint, stain)* abgehen von
c *case, assignment etc* abgeben; **to come off the gold standard** *(Fin)* vom Goldstandard abgehen
d **to come off sth** *(drugs, medication)* aufhören mit etw
e *(= be removed from price of)* runtergehen von *(inf)*
f *(inf)* **come off it!** nun mach mal halblang! *(inf)*

▶ **come on** VI a *(= follow)* nachkommen
b = **come along a**; **come on!** komm!; **come ON!** komm schon!
c *(= continue to advance)* zukommen *(towards* auf *+acc)*
d *(Brit: = progress, develop)* = **come along c**
e *(= start, night)* hereinbrechen; *(storm)* ausbrechen, einsetzen; **it came on to rain, the rain came on** es begann zu regnen, es fing an zu regnen; **I've a cold coming on** ich kriege eine Erkältung; **winter** *etc* **is coming on** es wird Winter *etc*
f *(Jur, case)* verhandelt werden
g *(Sport: player)* ins Spiel kommen; *(Theat, actor)* auftreten, auf die Bühne kommen; *(play)* gegeben werden
h *(inf)* **she's coming on seventeen** sie wird siebzehn
i *(inf: = make impression, behave)* **he tries to come on like a tough guy** er versucht, den starken Mann zu mimen *(inf)*; **he came on with this bit about knowing the director** er gab damit an, den Direktor zu kennen; **to come on strong** groß auftreten *(inf)*
VI *+prep obj* = **come (up)on**

▶ **come on to** VI *+prep obj (esp US inf: = make advances to)* anmachen *(inf)*

▶ **come out** VI a *(= leave)* (he)rauskommen; **to come out of a room/meeting** *etc* aus einem Zimmer/einer Versammlung *etc* kommen; **can you come out tonight?** kannst du heute Abend weg?; **do you want to come out with me?** gehst du mit mir weg?; **he asked her to come out for a meal/drive** er lud sie zum Essen/einer Spazierfahrt ein; **to come out fighting** *(fig)* sich kämpferisch geben
b *(= be published, marketed, book, magazine)* erscheinen, herauskommen; *(new product)* auf den Markt kommen; *(film)* (in den Kinos) anlaufen; *(= become known, exam results)* herauskommen, bekannt werden; *(news)* bekannt werden
c *(Ind)* **to come out (on strike)** in den Streik treten, streiken
d *(Phot, film, photograph)* **the photo of the hills hasn't come out very well** das Foto von den Bergen ist nicht sehr gut geworden; **let's hope the photos come out** hoffentlich sind die Bilder was geworden *(inf)* *or* gut geworden; **you always come out well in photos** du bist sehr fotogen; **all the details have come out clearly** alle Einzelheiten kommen klar (he)raus
e *(= show itself)* sich zeigen; **his arrogance comes out in everything he says** bei allem, was er sagt, kommt seine Arroganz durch
f *(splinter, stains, dye etc)* (he)rausgehen
g *(Math: problems, divisions etc)* aufgehen
h *(= total, average)* betragen; **the total comes out at £500** das Ganze beläuft sich auf *(+acc)* *or* macht *(inf)* £ 500
i *(in exams etc)* **he came out third in French** er wurde Drittbester in Französisch
j *(stars, sun, flowers)* (he)rauskommen
k *(truth, meaning etc)* (he)rauskommen; **no sooner had the words come out than ...** kaum waren die Worte heraus, als ...
l *(= go into society: girl)* debütieren
m *(= be released: prisoner)* (he)rauskommen
n *(homosexual)* sich outen; *(man also)* sich als Homosexueller bekennen; *(woman also)* sich als Lesbe bekennen
o **his face came out in spots** er bekam lauter Pickel im Gesicht; **he came out in a rash** er bekam einen Ausschlag; **he came out in a sweat** ihm brach der Schweiß aus
p **to come out against/in favour of** *or* **for sth** sich gegen/für etw aussprechen, etw ablehnen/befürworten
q **to come out of sth badly/well** bei etw schlecht/nicht schlecht wegkommen; **she came out of the interview well** sie hat bei dem Vorstellungsgespräch einen guten Eindruck gemacht; **to come out on top** sich durchsetzen, Sieger bleiben

▶ **come out with** VI *+prep obj truth, facts* rausrücken mit *(inf)*; *remarks, nonsense* loslassen *(inf)*

▶ **come over** VI a *(lit)* herüberkommen; **he came over to England** er kam nach England
b *(= change one's opinions, allegiance)* **he came over to our side** er trat auf unsere Seite über; **he came over to our way of thinking** er machte sich unsere Denkungsart zu Eigen
c *(inf: = become suddenly)* werden; **I came over (all) queer** *or* **funny** mir wurde ganz komisch *(inf)* *or* ganz merkwürdig
d *(= be understood)* = **come across VI b**
e *(= make an impression)* = **come across VI c**
VI *+prep obj (feelings)* überkommen; **I don't know what came over her to speak like that!** ich weiß nicht, was über sie gekommen ist, so zu reden!; **what's come over you?** was ist denn (auf einmal) mit dir los?, was ist in dich gefahren?

▶ **come through** VI a *(phone call, order)* durchkommen; **your expenses haven't come through yet** *(= been cleared)* wir haben Ihre Ausgaben noch nicht durchgekriegt; **your papers haven't come through yet** Ihre Papiere sind noch nicht fertig; **his divorce has come through** seine Scheidung ist durch *(inf)* b *(= survive)* durchkommen c *(= be successful)* **to come through for sb** für jdn da sein; **they came through on their promises** sie haben ihre Versprechen gehalten VI *+prep obj (= survive) illness, danger* überstehen

▶ **come to** VI a *(= regain consciousness: also* **come to oneself)** wieder zu sich kommen
b *(Naut)* beidrehen
VI *+prep obj* a **that will never come to much** daraus wird nie etwas werden; **that won't come to much** daraus wird nicht viel werden; **that didn't come to anything** daraus ist nichts geworden
b *impers* **when it comes to mathematics ...** wenn es um Mathematik geht, ...; **when it comes to choosing, he ...** wenn er die Wahl hat *or* vor die Wahl gestellt wird, ...; **if it comes to that we're sunk** wenn es dazu kommt, sind wir verloren; **come to that** *or* **if it comes to that, he's just as good** was das betrifft *or* an(be)langt, ist er genauso gut; **let's hope it never comes to a court case** *or* **to court** wollen wir hoffen, dass es nie zum Prozess kommt; **it comes to the same thing** das kommt *or* läuft auf dasselbe hinaus
c *(price, bill)* **how much does it come to?** wie viel macht das?; **it comes to £20** es kommt auf *or* beläuft sich auf £ 20; **it comes to 50 dollars even** *(US)* *or* **to exactly 50 dollars** es kostet genau 50 Dollar; **it comes to much less/more than I thought** es kommt viel billiger/teurer, als ich dachte
d *(= touch on) point, subject etc* kommen auf *(+acc)*; *(= tackle) problem, job etc* herangehen an *(+acc)*
e *(in certain collocations)* **to come to a decision** zu einer Entscheidung kommen; **it's coming to something when ...** es will schon etwas heißen, wenn ...; **what are things** *or* **what is the world coming to!** wohin soll das noch führen! → **blow**[1], **light** *etc*

▶ **come together** VI zusammenkommen, sich treffen; **he and his wife have come together again** er ist wieder mit seiner Frau zusammen; **it's all coming together for him** *(inf)* es regelt sich jetzt alles für ihn *(inf)*

▶ **come under** VI *+prep obj* a *(= be subject to)* **to come under sb's influence/domination** unter jds Einfluss/Herrschaft geraten; **this shop has come under new management** dieser Laden hat einen neuen Besitzer/Pächter; **this comes under another department** das ist Sache einer anderen Abteilung b *category, heading* kommen unter *(+acc)*

▶ **come up** VI a *(lit)* hochkommen; *(upstairs)* hoch- *or* raufkommen; *(diver, submarine)* nach oben kommen; *(sun, moon)* aufgehen; **do you come up to town often?** kommen Sie oft in die Stadt?; **he came up (to Oxford) last year** *(Univ)* er studiert seit letztem Jahr (in Oxford); **you've come up in the world** du bist ja richtig vornehm geworden!; **he came up to me with a smile** er kam lächelnd auf mich zu
b *(supplies, troops etc)* herangeschafft werden
c *(Jur, case)* verhandelt werden, drankommen *(inf)*; *(accused)* vor Gericht kommen
d *(plants)* herauskommen
e *(matter for discussion)* aufkommen, angeschnitten werden; *(name)* erwähnt werden; **I can't do it as I'm afraid something has come up** ich bin leider verhindert, ich kann leider nicht
f *(number in lottery etc)* gewinnen; **to come up for sale/auction** *etc* zum Verkauf/zur Auktion *etc* kommen; **my contract will soon come up for renewal** mein Vertrag muss bald verlängert werden
g *(post, job)* frei werden
h *(exams, election)* bevorstehen
i *(= be vomited)* wieder hochkommen
j *(= shine, show colour)* herauskommen

▶**come up against** VI *+prep obj* stoßen auf *(+acc)*; *opposing team* treffen auf *(+acc)*; **his plan was doing well until he came up against the directors** sein Vorhaben machte gute Fortschritte, bis er an die Geschäftsleitung geriet; **the new teacher keeps coming up against the headmaster** der neue Lehrer gerät ständig mit dem Direktor aneinander

▶**come (up)on** VI *+prep obj* **a** *(lit: = attack by surprise)* überfallen; *(fig, disaster)* hereinbrechen über *(+acc)* **b** *(= find)* stoßen auf *(+acc)*

▶**come up to** VI *+prep obj* **a** *(= reach up to)* gehen *or* reichen bis zu *or* an *(+acc)*; **the water came up to his knees** das Wasser ging *or* reichte ihm bis an die Knie *or* bis zu den Knien **b** *(= equal) hopes* erfüllen; *expectations* entsprechen *(+dat)* **c** *(inf: = approach)* **she's coming up to twenty** sie wird bald zwanzig; **we're coming up to 150 km/h** wir haben gleich 150 km/h drauf *(inf)*; **it's just coming up to 10 o'clock** es ist gleich 10 Uhr

▶**come up with** VI *+prep obj answer* haben; *idea, solution also* kommen auf *(+acc)*; *plan* sich *(dat)* ausdenken, entwickeln; *suggestion* machen, bringen; **I can't come up with any answers either** ich habe auch keine Antwort; **let me know if you come up with anything** sagen Sie mir Bescheid, falls Ihnen etwas einfällt

come-at-able [kʌm'ætəbl] ADJ *(inf)* leicht erreichbar

comeback ['kʌmbæk] N **a** *(Theat etc, fig)* Comeback *nt*, Come-back *nt*; **to make** *or* **stage a ~** ein Comeback versuchen/machen **b** *(inf: = redress)* Anspruch *m* auf Schadenersatz; *(= reaction)* Reaktion *f*; **we've got no ~ in this situation** wir können da nichts machen

Comecon ['kɒmɪkɒn] *abbr of* **Council for Mutual Economic Aid** Comecon *m or nt*

comedian [kə'miːdɪən] N Komiker(in) *m(f)*; *(fig also)* Witzbold *m*

comedic [kə'miːdɪk] ADJ komisch

comedienne [kəˌmiːdɪ'en] N Komikerin *f*; *(= actress)* Komödiendarstellerin *f*

comedown ['kʌmdaʊn] N *(inf)* Abstieg *m*

comedy ['kɒmɪdɪ] N **a** *(Theat)* Komödie *f*, Lustspiel *nt*; **~ programme** Unterhaltungsprogramm *nt*; **~ writer** Lustspielautor(in) *m(f)* *or (classical)* -dichter(in) *m(f)*; **"Comedy of Errors"** „Komödie der Irrungen"; **the entire deal was just a ~ of errors** *(fig)* bei dem Geschäft ging aber auch alles daneben; **low ~** Klamauk *m*; **high ~** echte *or* gekonnte Komödie; **to act in ~** Komödiendarsteller(in) *m(f)* sein **b** *(fig)* Komödie *f*, Theater *nt (inf)*

come-hither [kʌm'hɪðə'] ADJ *(inf)* **she gave him a ~ look** sie warf ihm einladende *or* aufmunternde Blicke zu

comeliness ['kʌmlɪnɪs] N *(liter)* Wohlgestalt *f (liter)*

comely ['kʌmlɪ] ADJ *(+er)* *(liter)* wohlgestaltet *(geh)*

come-on ['kʌmɒn] N *(inf: = lure, enticement)* Köder *m (fig)*; **to give sb the ~** *(woman)* jdn anmachen *(inf)*

comer ['kʌmə'] N **this competition is open to all ~s** an diesem Wettbewerb kann sich jeder beteiligen; **"open to all ~s"** „Teilnahme für jedermann"

comestible [kə'mestɪbl] N *usu pl* Nahrungsmittel *pl* ADJ essbar; **~ goods** Nahrungsmittel *pl*

comet ['kɒmɪt] N Komet *m*

come-to-bed ['kʌmtəbed] ADJ **she/he has ~ eyes** *(inf)* sie/er hat Schlafzimmeraugen *(inf)*

comeuppance [ˌkʌm'ʌpəns] N *(inf)* **to get one's ~** die Quittung kriegen *(inf)*

comfit ['kɒmfɪt] N *(old)* Konfekt *nt*, Zuckerwerk *(old) nt*

comfort ['kʌmfət] N **a** Komfort *m*, Bequemlichkeit *f*; **relax in the ~ of a leather armchair** entspannen Sie sich in unseren behaglichen Ledersesseln; **he likes his ~s** er liebt seinen Komfort *or* seine Bequemlichkeit; **to live in ~** komfortabel leben; **an apartment with all modern ~s** eine Wohnung mit allem Komfort **b** *(= consolation)* Beruhigung *f*, Trost *m*; **to take ~ from the fact that …** sich mit dem Gedanken *or* sich damit trösten, dass …; **your presence is/you are a great ~ to me** es beruhigt mich sehr, dass Sie da sind; **it is a ~ to know that …** es ist tröstlich *or* beruhigend zu wissen, dass …; **it is no ~** *or* **of little ~ to know that …** es ist nicht sehr tröstlich zu wissen, dass …; **some ~ you are!** *(iro)* das ist ja ein schöner Trost! *(iro)*, du bist gut! *(iro)*; **small ~** schwacher Trost; **a pipe is a great ~** Pfeiferauchen hat etwas sehr Beruhigendes; **your poems brought a little ~ to my life** Ihre Gedichte haben ein wenig Trost in mein Leben gebracht; **too close for ~** bedrohlich nahe

VT *(= console)* trösten; **the child needed a lot of ~ing** es dauerte eine ganze Weile, bis das Kind sich trösten ließ; **he stayed with the injured man to ~ him** er blieb bei dem Verletzten, um ihm Beistand zu leisten; **the hot soup ~ed him a little** nach der heißen Suppe fühlte er sich etwas wohler

comfortable ['kʌmfətəbl] ADJ **a** *armchair, bed, shoes, life, position* bequem; *room, hotel etc* komfortabel; *temperature* angenehm; **to make sb/oneself ~** es jdm/sich bequem machen; *(= make at home)* es jdm/sich gemütlich machen; **the sick man had a ~ night** der Kranke hatte *or* verbrachte eine ruhige Nacht; **the patient/his condition is ~** der Patient/er ist wohlauf; **are you ~?, asked the nurse** liegen/sitzen *etc* Sie bequem?, fragte die Schwester; **are you too hot? – no, I'm just ~** ist es Ihnen zu heiß? – nein, es ist angenehm so

b *(fig) income, pension* ausreichend; *life* geruhsam, angenehm; *majority, lead* sicher; *winner* überlegen; *figure* mollig; **he's very ~ to be with** bei ihm fühlt man sich sehr wohl; **she had quite a ~ feeling about it** sie hatte ein gutes Gefühl dabei; **to feel ~ with sb/sth** sich bei jdm/etw wohlfühlen; **I'm not very ~ about it** mir ist nicht ganz wohl bei der Sache; **I'm not too ~ about giving her the job** mir ist nicht ganz wohl bei dem Gedanken, ihr die Stelle zu geben; **in ~ circumstances** *(= well-off)* gut situiert

comfortably ['kʌmfətəblɪ] ADV **a** *lie, sit, dress, fit etc* bequem; *furnished, upholstered* komfortabel **b** *(fig) win, lead* sicher; *live* geruhsam, angenehm; *afford* gut und gern; *claim, say* ruhig; **they are ~ off** es geht ihnen gut

comfort eating N Frustessen *nt (inf)*

comforter ['kʌmfətə'] N **a** *(= person)* Tröster(in) *m(f)*; **my wife was my ~ in times of stress** in schweren Zeiten war meine Frau mein Beistand **b** *(dated: = scarf)* Wollschal *m* **c** *(= dummy, teat)* Schnuller *m* **d** *(US: = quilt)* Deckbett *nt*

comfort food N Essen *nt*, das als Trost dient

comforting ['kʌmfətɪŋ] ADJ tröstlich, beruhigend; **a ~ cup of tea** eine Tasse Tee zur Beruhigung

comfortless ['kʌmfətlɪs] ADJ **a** *chair etc* unbequem; *room, hotel* ohne Komfort **b** *(fig) person* ungemütlich; *life* unbequem; *thought, prospect* unerfreulich, unangenehm

comfort: **comfort shopping** N Frustkauf *m (inf)*, Frustkäufe *pl (inf)*; **comfort station** N *(US)* Bedürfnisanstalt *f*, öffentliche Toilette; **comfort zone** N *Bereich, in dem man sich sicher fühlt*; **two goals in two minutes put Rangers in the ~** nach zwei Toren in zwei Minuten fühlten Rangers sich sicher; **comfy** ['kʌmfɪ] ADJ *(+er)* *(inf) chair* bequem; *hotel, flat, room* gemütlich; **are you ~?** sitzt/liegst du bequem?; **make yourself ~** machen Sie es sich *(dat)* bequem *or* gemütlich *(inf)*; **comic** ['kɒmɪk] ADJ komisch; **~ actor** Komödiendarsteller(in) *m(f)*, Komöde *m (geh)*; **~ verse** humoristische Gedichte *pl* N **a** *(= person)* Komiker(in) *m(f)* **b** *(= magazine)* Comicheft(chen) *nt* **c** *(US)* **~s** Comics *pl*; **comical** ADJ, **comically** ADV ['kɒmɪkəl, -ɪ] komisch, ulkig

comic: **comic book** N Comicbuch *nt*; **comic opera** N komische Oper; **comic relief** N befreiende Komik; **comic strip** N Comicstrip *m*

coming ['kʌmɪŋ] N Kommen *nt*; **you can sense the ~ of spring** man fühlt *or* spürt das Herannahen des Frühlings; **the first/second ~ (of the Lord)** die Ankunft/Wiederkunft des Herrn; **the ~ of a new manager** die Ankunft eines neuen Geschäftsführers; **~ and going/~s and goings** Kommen und Gehen *nt*; **~ of age** Erreichung *f* der Volljährigkeit ADJ *(lit, fig)* kommend; *year, week also* nächst; **a ~ politician** einer der kommenden Männer in der Politik; **the ~ election** die bevorstehende Wahl; **it's the ~ thing** *(inf)* das ist zurzeit groß im Kommen *(inf)*

coming-out [kʌmɪŋ'aʊt] N gesellschaftliches Debüt, (offizielle) Einführung in die Gesellschaft; *(of homosexual, lesbian)* Coming-out *nt*; **~ party** Debütantinnenparty *f*

comma ['kɒmə] N Komma *nt*

command [kə'mɑːnd] VT **a** *(= order)* befehlen, den Befehl geben *(sb* jdm); **he ~ed that the prisoners be released** er befahl, die Gefangenen freizulassen

b *(= be in control of) army, ship* befehligen, kommandieren

c *(= be in a position to use) money, resources, vocabulary* verfügen über *(+acc)*, gebieten über *(+acc) (geh)*; **to ~ sb's services** jds Dienste *or* Hilfe in Anspruch nehmen

d to ~ sb's admiration/respect jdm Bewunderung/Respekt abnötigen, jds Bewunderung/Respekt erheischen *(geh)*; **antiques ~ a high price** Antiquitäten stehen hoch im Preis

e *(= overlook) valley* überragen; *view* bieten *(of* über *+acc)*

VI **a** *(= order)* befehlen

b *(Mil, Naut: = to be in command)* das Kommando führen

N **a** *(= order)* Befehl *m*; **at/by the ~ of** auf Befehl *+gen*; **at the word of ~** auf Kommando; **on ~** auf Befehl *or* Kommando

b *(Mil: = power, authority)* Kommando *nt*, Befehlsgewalt *f*; **to be in ~** das Kommando *or* den (Ober)befehl haben *(of* über *+acc)*; **to take ~** das Kommando übernehmen *(of +gen)*; **the new colonel arrived to take ~ of his regiment** der neue Oberst kam, um sein Regiment zu übernehmen; **during/under his ~** unter seinem Kommando; **the battalion is under the ~ of …** das Bataillon steht unter dem Kommando von … *or* wird befehligt von …; **to be second in ~** zweiter Befehlshaber sein

c *(Mil) (= troops)* Kommando *nt*; *(= district)* Befehlsbereich *m*; *(= command post)* Posten *m*

d *(Comput)* Befehl *m*

e *(fig: = possession, mastery)* Beherrschung *f*; **~ of the seas** Seeherrschaft *f*; **the gymnast's remarkable ~ over his body** die bemerkenswerte Körperbeherrschung des Turners; **his ~ of English is excellent** er beherrscht das Englische ausgezeichnet; **to have sb/sth at one's ~** über jdn/etw verfügen *or* gebieten *(geh)*; **I am at your ~** ich stehe zu Ihrer Verfügung; **to be in ~ (of oneself)** sich unter Kontrolle haben

commandant [ˌkɒmən'dænt] N *(Mil)* Kommandant(in) *m(f)*

command economy N Kommandowirtschaft *f*

commandeer [ˌkɒmən'dɪə'] VT *(Mil) men* einziehen; *(from another battalion, fig)* abbeordern, abkommandieren; *stores, ship, car etc (lit, fig)* beschlagnahmen, requirieren

commander [kə'mɑːndə'] N **a** Führer(in) *m(f)*; *(Mil, Aviat)* Befehlshaber(in) *m(f)*, Kommandant(in) *m(f)*; *(Naut)* Fregattenkapitän(in) *m(f)*; *(Brit, Police) Distriktleiter der Londoner Polizei* **b** *(of order of chivalry)* Komtur *m*

commander in chief N *pl* **commanders in chief** Oberbefehlshaber(in) *m(f)*

commanding [kə'mɑːndɪŋ] ADJ **a** *(= in charge) position* Befehls- **b** *(= dominant, powerful) position* führend; *personality* gebieterisch; *voice, tone* Kommando- *(pej)*; **to be in a ~ position** eine führende Stellung haben; **to have a ~**

lead überlegen führen **c** *(of place)* beherrschend; **~ heights** Kommandohöhen *pl*

commandingly [kəˈmɑːndɪŋlɪ] ADV *speak* gebieterisch

commanding officer N *(Mil)* befehlshabender Offizier

command language N *(Comput)* Befehlssprache *f*

command line N *(Comput)* Befehlszeile *f*

commandment [kəˈmɑːndmənt] N *(esp Bibl)* Gebot *nt*; **to break a ~** gegen ein Gebot verstoßen

command module N *(Space)* Kommandokapsel *f*

commando [kəˈmɑːndəʊ] N *pl* **-s** *(Mil) (= soldier)* Angehörige(r) *m* eines Kommando(trupp)s; *(= unit)* Kommando(trupp *m*) *nt*

command: **command paper** N *(Brit: Parl) (dem Parlament vorgelegter)* Kabinettsbeschluss *m*; **command performance** N *(Theat)* königliche Galavorstellung; **command post** N *(Mil)* Kommandoposten *m*; **command prompt** N *(Comput)* Eingabeaufforderung *f*

commemorate [kəˈmeməreɪt] VT gedenken *(+gen)*; **a festival to ~ the event** eine Feier zum Gedenken an das Ereignis

commemoration [kəˌmeməˈreɪʃən] N Gedenken *nt*; **in ~ of** zum Gedenken an *(+acc)*

commemorative [kəˈmemərətɪv] ADJ Gedenk-; **~ plaque** Gedenktafel *f*

commence [kəˈmens] *(form)* VI beginnen VT beginnen *(obj* mit *+dat)*; *legal proceedings* eröffnen; **to ~ doing** *or* **to do sth** mit etw anfangen

commencement [kəˈmensmənt] N **a** *(form)* Beginn *m* **b** *(Univ, Cambridge, Dublin, US)* Abschlussfeier *f (zur Verleihung der Diplome etc)*

commend [kəˈmend] VT **a** *(= praise)* loben; *(= recommend)* empfehlen; **it has much/little to ~ it** es ist sehr/nicht sehr empfehlenswert **b** *(= entrust, Bibl) spirit, soul* befehlen *(to +dat)*; **~ me to Mr Smith** *(form)* empfehlen Sie mich Herrn Smith *(form)* VR sich empfehlen *(to +dat)*

commendable [kəˈmendəbl] ADJ lobenswert, löblich

commendably [kəˈmendəblɪ] ADV lobenswerterweise

commendation [ˌkɒmenˈdeɪʃən] N *(no pl: = praise)* Lob *nt*; *(= award)* Auszeichnung *f*; *(= official recognition)* Belobigung *f*

commendatory [kəˈmendətrɪ] ADJ anerkennend

commensurate [kəˈmenʃərɪt] ADJ entsprechend *(with +dat)*; **to be ~ with sth** einer Sache *(dat)* entsprechen; **they made salaries ~ with those in comparable professions** die Gehälter wurden denen in vergleichbaren Berufen angeglichen

commensurately [kəˈmenʃərətlɪ] ADV entsprechend, angemessen

comment [ˈkɒment] ✪ 6.3 N *(= remark)* Bemerkung *f (on,about* über *+acc,* zu); *(official)* Kommentar *m (on* zu); *(no pl: = talk, gossip)* Gerede *nt*; *(= textual or margin note etc)* Anmerkung *f*; **no ~** kein Kommentar!; **to make a ~** eine Bemerkung machen, einen Kommentar abgeben VI sich äußern *(on* über *+acc,* zu), einen Kommentar abgeben *(on* zu); **need I ~?** Kommentar überflüssig! VT bemerken, äußern

commentary [ˈkɒməntərɪ] N Kommentar *m (on* zu); **he used to do commentaries on football matches** früher war er Reporter bei Fußballspielen; **I don't need a running ~ from you** ich brauche deine ständigen Kommentare nicht

commentary box N *(Sport)* Kommentatorenbox *f*

commentate [ˈkɒmenteɪt] VI *(Rad, TV)* Reporter(in) *m(f)* sein *(on* bei)

commentator [ˈkɒmenteɪtəʳ] N **a** *(Rad, TV)* Reporter(in) *m(f)* **b** *(on texts etc)* Interpret(in) *m(f)*; *(of Bible)* Exeget(in) *m(f)*

commerce [ˈkɒmɜːs] N **a** Handel *m*; *(between countries also)* Handelsverkehr *m*; **in the world of ~** im Geschäftsleben; **he is in ~** er ist Geschäftsmann **b** *(form: = dealings)* Verkehr *m*

commercial [kəˈmɜːʃəl] ADJ Handels-; *custom also, ethics, training* kaufmännisch; *language, premises, vehicle* Geschäfts-; *production, radio, project, success, attitude, farming, whaling, fishing* kommerziell; *(pej) film, music etc* kommerziell; **the ~ world** die Geschäftswelt; **of no ~ value** ohne Verkaufswert; **to think in ~ terms** kaufmännisch denken; **it makes good ~ sense** das lässt sich kaufmännisch durchaus vertreten; **has Christmas become too ~?** ist Weihnachten zu kommerziell geworden? N *(Rad, TV)* Werbespot *m*; **during the ~s** während der (Fernseh)-werbung

commercial: **commercial art** N Werbegrafik *f*; **commercial artist** N Werbegrafiker(in) *m(f)*; **commercial bank** N Handelsbank *f*; **commercial break** N Werbepause *f*; **commercial centre**, *(US)* **commercial center** N Handelszentrum *nt*; **commercial college** N Fachschule *f* für kaufmännische Berufe; **commercial court** N Handelsgericht *nt*

commercialese [kəmɜːʃəˈliːz] N Wirtschaftssprache *f*

commercialism [kəˈmɜːʃəlɪzəm] N Kommerzialisierung *f*; *(connected with art, literature also)* Kommerz *m*

commercialization [kəˌmɜːʃəlaɪˈzeɪʃən] N Kommerzialisierung *f*

commercialize [kəˈmɜːʃəlaɪz] VT kommerzialisieren

commercially [kəˈmɜːʃəlɪ] ADV geschäftlich; *manufacture, succeed* kommerziell; **to be ~ minded** kaufmännisch veranlagt *or* kommerziell eingestellt *(usu pej)* sein

commercial: **commercial manager** N kaufmännischer Leiter, kaufmännische Leiterin, Geschäftsführer(in) *m(f)*; **commercial paper** N *(Fin)* kurzfristiges Handelspapier; **commercial television** N kommerzielles Fernsehen; **commercial traveller**, *(US)* **commmercial traveler** N Handelsvertreter(in) *m(f)*; **commercial usage** N Usance *f*, Handelsbrauch *m*; **commercial vehicle** N Nutzfahrzeug *nt*

commie [ˈkɒmɪ] *(pej inf)* N Rote(r) *mf (pej inf)* ADJ rot *(pej inf)*

commingle [kɒˈmɪŋgl] VI *(liter)* sich vermischen; *(colours)* ineinander verschwimmen

commis chef [ˈkɒmɪʃef] N Küchengehilfe *m*, Küchengehilfin *f*

commiserate [kəˈmɪzəreɪt] VI mitfühlen *(with* mit); **we ~ with you on the loss of your husband** wir nehmen Anteil am Tode Ihres Gatten

commiseration [kəˌmɪzəˈreɪʃən] N Mitgefühl *nt no pl*, (An)teilnahme *f no pl*; **my ~s** herzliches Beileid *(on* zu)

commissar [ˈkɒmɪsɑːʳ] N Kommissar *m*

commissariat [ˌkɒmɪˈsɛərɪət] N **a** *(Mil)* Intendantur *f* **b** *(in former USSR etc)* Kommissariat *nt*

commissary [ˈkɒmɪsərɪ] N **a** *(Mil)* Intendant *m* **b** *(= delegate)* Beauftragte(r) *mf* **c** *(US, Comm)* Laden *m* in Lagern/auf Baustellen *etc*

commission [kəˈmɪʃən] N **a** *(= committing)* Begehen *nt (form)*
b *(for building, painting etc)* Auftrag *m*
c *(Comm)* Provision *f*; **on ~, on a ~ basis** auf Provision(sbasis); **to work on ~** auf Provisionsbasis arbeiten; **to charge ~** *(bank etc)* eine Kommission berechnen
d *(Mil)* Patent *nt*
e *(= special committee)* Kommission *f*, Ausschuss *m*; **~ of inquiry** Untersuchungskommission *f or* -ausschuss *m*
f *(Naut, fig: = use)* **to put into ~** in Dienst stellen; **to take out of ~** aus dem Verkehr ziehen; **in/out of ~** in/außer Betrieb
g *(form: = task, errand)* Erledigung *f*; **I was given a ~ to recruit new members** ich wurde (damit) beauftragt, neue Mitglieder zu werben
h **the (EC) Commission** die EG-Kommission
VT **a** *person* beauftragen; *book, painting* in Auftrag geben; **to ~ sb to do sth** jdn damit beauftragen, etw zu tun
b *(Mil) sb* zum Offizier ernennen; *officer* ernennen
c *ship* in Dienst stellen; *power station etc* in Betrieb nehmen; **~ing ceremony** Eröffnungszeremonie *f*

commission agent N Komissionär(in) *m(f)*

commissionaire [kəˌmɪʃəˈnɛəʳ] N Portier *m*

commissioned officer N Offizier *m*

commissioner [kəˈmɪʃənəʳ] N **a** *(= member of commission)* Ausschussmitglied *nt* **b** *(of police)* Polizeipräsident(in) *m(f)* **c** *(Jur)* **~ for oaths** Notar(in) *m(f)*

commissioning editor [kəˈmɪʃənɪŋˈedɪtəʳ] N Redakteur(in) *m(f)*

commit [kəˈmɪt] VT **a** *(= perpetrate)* begehen; **the crimes they ~ted against humanity** ihre Verbrechen gegen die Menschlichkeit
b **to ~ sb (to prison/to a home)** jdn ins Gefängnis/in ein Heim einweisen; **to have sb ~ted (to an asylum)** jdn in eine Anstalt einweisen lassen; **to ~ sb for trial** jdn einem Gericht überstellen; **to ~ sb/sth to sb's care** jdn/etw jds Obhut *(dat)* anvertrauen; **to ~ sth to writing** *or* **to paper** etw zu Papier bringen
c *(= involve, obligate)* festlegen *(to* auf *+acc)*; **to ~ troops to a battle** Truppen in ein Gefecht schicken; **to ~ resources/manpower to a project** Mittel/Arbeitskräfte für ein Projekt einsetzen; **that doesn't ~ you to buying the book** das verpflichtet Sie nicht zum Kauf des Buches
d *(Parl) bill* an den (zuständigen) Ausschuss überweisen
VI **to ~ to sb/sth** sich jdm gegenüber/zu etw verpflichten
VR sich festlegen *(to* auf *+acc)*; **to ~ oneself on an issue** sich in einer Frage festlegen; **you have to ~ yourself totally to the cause** man muss sich voll und ganz für die Sache einsetzen *or* engagieren; **I don't want to ~ myself** ich möchte mich nicht festlegen; **the government has ~ted itself to (undertake) far-reaching reforms** die Regierung hat sich zu weitreichenden *or* weit reichenden Reformen bekannt *or* verpflichtet; **... without ~ting myself to the whole contract** ... ohne damit an den ganzen Vertrag gebunden zu sein

commitment [kəˈmɪtmənt] N **a** *(= obligation)* Verpflichtung *f*; *(= dedication)* Engagement *nt*; **his family ~s** seine familiären Verpflichtungen *pl*; **his teaching ~s** seine Lehrverpflichtungen *pl*; **there's no ~ (to buy)** es besteht kein(erlei) Kaufzwang; **to make a ~ to do sth** *(form)* sich verpflichten, etw zu tun; **the trainer demands one hundred per cent ~ from his team** der Trainer verlangt von seiner Mannschaft hundertprozentigen Einsatz; **his ~ to his job is total** er geht völlig in seiner Arbeit auf; **political/military ~** politisches/militärisches Engagement; **he is frightened of ~** *(in relationship)* er hat Angst davor, sich festzulegen
b *(Parl, of bill)* Überweisung *f* an den (zuständigen) Ausschuss

committal [kəˈmɪtl] N **a** *(to prison, asylum etc)* Einweisung *f*; **his ~ for trial** seine Überstellung ans Gericht; **~ proceedings** gerichtliche Voruntersuchung **b** *(of crime etc)* Begehen *nt (form)* **c** **~ to memory** Auswendiglernen *nt*; *(of single fact)* Sicheinprägen *nt* **d** *(Parl)* = **commitment b**

committed [kəˈmɪtɪd] ADJ *(= dedicated)* engagiert; **he is so ~ to his work that ...** er geht so in seiner Arbeit auf, dass ...; **all his life he has been ~ to this cause** er hat sich sein Leben lang für diese Sache eingesetzt

committee [kəˈmɪtɪ] N Ausschuss *m (also Parl)*, Komitee *nt*; **to be** *or* **sit on a ~** in einem Ausschuss *or* Komitee sein *or* sitzen; **Committee of 100** *(Brit)* Komitee der Hundert; **~ meeting** Ausschusssitzung *f*; **~ member** Ausschussmitglied *nt*

committeeman [kəˈmɪtɪmæn] N *pl* **-men** [-men] *(esp US)* **a** *(= member of committee)* Komiteemitglied *nt* **b** *(Pol)* lokaler Parteiführer

committee stage N *(Brit Parl)* **the bill didn't reach the ~** der Gesetzentwurf ist gar nicht erst an den (zuständigen) Ausschuss gelangt; **the ~ lasted weeks** der Gesetzentwurf wurde mehrere Wochen im Ausschuss verhandelt

committeewoman [kəˈmɪtɪwʊmən] N *pl* **-women** [-wɪmɪn] *(esp US)* **a** *(= member of committee)* Komiteemitglied *nt* **b** *(Pol)* lokale Parteiführerin

commode [kəˈməʊd] N **a** *(= chest of drawers)* Kommode *f* **b** *(= night-commode)* (Nacht)-stuhl *m*

commodious [kəˈməʊdɪəs] ADJ geräumig

commodity [kəˈmɒdɪtɪ] N Ware *f*; *(agricultural)* Erzeugnis *nt*; **basic** *or* **staple commodities** *(natural)* Grundstoffe *pl*; *(St Ex)* Rohstoffe *pl*; *(manufactured)* Bedarfsgüter *pl*; *(= foodstuffs)* Grundnahrungsmittel *pl*; **electricity is a ~ which every country needs** Strom ist ein (Versorgungs)gut, das jedes Land braucht

commodity exchange N *(St Ex)* Warenbörse *f*

commodity futures PL *(St Ex)* Warentermingeschäft *nt*

commodity market N Rohstoffmarkt *m*

commodore [ˈkɒmədɔːʳ] N *(Naut)* Flottillenadmiral *m* *(= senior captain)* Kommodore *m*; *(of yacht club)* Präsident *m*

common [ˈkɒmən] ✪ 5.5 ADJ *(+er)* **a** *(= shared by many)* gemeinsam; *property also* Gemein-, gemeinschaftlich; **~ land** Allmende *f*; **~ prostitute** Straßendirne *f*; **it is ~ knowledge that ...** es ist allgemein bekannt, dass ...; **it is to the ~ advantage that ...** es ist von allgemeinem Nutzen, dass ...; **very little/no ~ ground** kaum eine/keine gemeinsame Basis; **to find ~ ground (with sb)** eine gemeinsame Basis finden (mit jdm); **sth is ~ to everyone/sth** alle haben/etw hat etw gemein
b *(= frequently seen or heard etc)* häufig; *word also* weitverbreitet, weit verbreitet, geläufig; *experience also* allgemein; *animal, bird* häufig *pred*, häufig anzutreffend *attr*; *belief, custom, animal, bird* (weit)verbreitet, weit verbreitet; *(= customary, usual)* normal; **it's quite a ~ sight** das sieht man ziemlich häufig; **it's ~ for visitors to feel ill here** Besucher fühlen sich hier häufig krank; **nowadays it's quite ~ for the man to do the housework** es ist heutzutage ganz normal, dass der Mann die Hausarbeit macht
c *(= ordinary)* gewöhnlich; **the ~ man** der Normalbürger; **the ~ people** die einfachen Leute; **a ~ soldier** ein einfacher *or* gemeiner *(dated)* Soldat; **the ~ run of mankind** die (breite) Masse; **the ~ touch** das Volkstümliche; **he has the ~ touch** er kann gut mit Menschen umgehen; **the Book of Common Prayer** *(Eccl)* die Agende; **it's only ~ decency to apologize** es ist nur recht und billig, dass man sich entschuldigt
d *(= vulgar, low-class)* gewöhnlich; **to be as ~ as muck** *(Brit inf)* schrecklich gewöhnlich *or* ordinär sein
N **a** *(= land)* Anger *m*, Gemeindewiese *f*
b nothing out of the ~ nichts Besonderes
c to have sth in ~ (with sb/sth) etw (mit jdm/etw) gemein haben; **to have a lot/nothing in ~** viel/nichts miteinander gemein haben, viele/keine Gemeinsamkeiten haben; **we do at least have that in ~** wenigstens das haben wir gemein; **in ~ with many other people/towns/countries** (ebenso *or* genauso) wie viele andere (Leute)/Städte/Länder ...; **I, in ~ with ...** ich, ebenso wie ...

Common Agricultural Policy N gemeinsame Agrarpolitik

commonalty [ˈkɒmənəltɪ] N *(form)* **the ~** die Bürgerlichen *pl*

common: **common carrier** N *(Comm: = transport company)* öffentliches Transportunternehmen; *(Telec)* Telefongesellschaft *f*; **common cold** N Schnupfen *m*; **common core** N *(Sch)* Pflichtfächer *pl*; **common currency** N **to be ~** allgemein bekannt sein; *(rumour)* überall umgehen; **to become ~** allgemein bekannt werden; **common denominator** N *(Math, fig)* gemeinsamer Nenner; **lowest ~** *(Math, fig)* kleinster gemeinsamer Nenner; **common divisor** N gemeinsamer Teiler; **Common Entrance (Examination)** N Aufnahmeprüfung *f (für eine britische Public School)*

commoner [ˈkɒmənəʳ] N **a** Bürgerliche(r) *mf* **b** *(Brit, Univ) Student, der kein Universitätsstipendium erhält*

common: **common factor** N gemeinsamer Teiler; **common fraction** N gemeiner Bruch; **common gender** N *(Gram)* doppeltes Geschlecht; **common law** N Gewohnheitsrecht *nt*; **common-law** ADJ **she is his ~ wife** sie lebt mit ihm in eheähnlicher Gemeinschaft; **the law regarded her as his ~ wife** vor dem Gesetz galt ihre Verbindung als eheähnliche Gemeinschaft

commonly [ˈkɒmənlɪ] ADV **a** *(= often)* häufig; *(= widely)* gemeinhin, weithin; **a ~ held belief** eine weitverbreitete *or* weit verbreitete Ansicht; **it is ~ believed that ...** es wird allgemein angenommen, dass ...; **(more) ~ known as ...** besser bekannt als ... **b** *(= vulgarly)* gewöhnlich, ordinär

common: **Common Market** N Gemeinsamer Markt; **Common Marketeer** N Befürworter(in) *m(f)* des Gemeinsamen Marktes; **common multiple** N gemeinsame(s) Vielfache(s); **the lowest** *or* **least ~** das kleinste gemeinsame Vielfache

commonness [ˈkɒmənnɪs] N **a** *(= frequency)* Häufigkeit *f*; *(of word also)* weite Verbreitung, Geläufigkeit *f*; *(of experience also)* Allgemeinheit *f* **b** *(= vulgarity)* Gewöhnlichkeit *f*; *(of person also)* ordinäre Art

common: **common noun** N Gattungsbegriff *m*; **common-or-garden** ADJ *(Brit)* Feld-, Wald- und Wiesen- *(inf)*; *topic, novel etc* ganz gewöhnlich; **commonplace** ADJ alltäglich; *(= banal) remark* banal N Gemeinplatz *m*; **a ~** *(= frequent sight or event)* etwas Alltägliches; **common room** N Aufenthalts- *or* Tagesraum *m*; *(for teachers)* Lehrerzimmer *nt*; *(Univ)* Dozentenzimmer *nt*

Commons [ˈkɒmənz] PL **the ~** *(Parl)* das Unterhaus → **house**

commons [ˈkɒmənz] PL **on short ~** auf Kurzration gesetzt

common: **common sense** N gesunder Menschenverstand; **common-sense** ADJ vernünftig; *attitude also* gesund; **it's the ~ thing to do** das ist das Vernünftigste; **common stock** N *(US St Ex)* Stammaktien *pl*; **common time** N Viervierteltakt *m*; **commonweal** N *(form)* Gemeinwohl *nt*

commonwealth [ˈkɒmənwelθ] N **a** Staat *m*, Gemeinwesen *nt*; *(US) Bezeichnung für die US-Bundesstaaten Kentucky, Massachusetts, Pennsylvania und Virginia*; **the Commonwealth of Australia** der Australische Bund; **the (British) Commonwealth, the Commonwealth of Nations** das Commonwealth; **Commonwealth of Independent States** Gemeinschaft *f* Unabhängiger Staaten **b** *(Hist)* **the Commonwealth** *die englische Republik unter Cromwell*

> **COMMONWEALTH**
>
> Das **Commonwealth**, offiziell **Commonwealth of Nations**, ist ein freiwilliger Zusammenschluss souveräner Staaten, die vormals fast alle britische Kolonien waren. Im Moment gibt es 51 Mitglieder, darunter Großbritannien, Australien, Kanada, Indien, Jamaika, Neuseeland, Pakistan und Südafrika, die zusammen ein Viertel der Weltbevölkerung stellen. Alle Mitgliedsstaaten erkennen den britischen Monarchen als Oberhaupt des Commonwealth an. Bei der jährlichen **Commonwealth Conference** werden verschiedene politische und wirtschaftliche Fragen beraten. Die Mitgliedsstaaten werden in einem anderen Commonwealth-Staat nicht durch eine Botschaft, sondern durch ein Hochkommissariat, genannt **High Commission**, vertreten.

Commonwealth Games PL Commonwealth-Spiele *pl*

commotion [kəˈməʊʃən] N Aufregung *f usu no indef art*; *(= noise)* Lärm *m*, Spektakel *m*; **to cause a ~** Aufsehen erregen; **to make a ~** Theater machen *(inf)*; *(= noise)* Krach machen

comms [kɒmz] N = **communication d**

communal [ˈkɒmjuːnl] ADJ **a** *(= of a community)* Gemeinde-; **~ life** Gemeinschaftsleben *nt* **b** *(= owned, used in common)* gemeinsam; *bathroom, kitchen also* Gemeinschafts-

communally [ˈkɒmjuːnəlɪ] ADV gemeinsam; **to be ~ owned** Gemein- *or* Gemeinschaftseigentum sein

communard [ˈkɒmjʊˌnɑːd] N Kommunarde *m*, Kommunardin *f*

commune[1] [kəˈmjuːn] VI **a** *(= communicate)* Zwiesprache halten; **to ~ with the spirits** mit den Geistern verkehren **b** *(esp US Eccl, Catholic)* kommunizieren, die Kommunion empfangen; *(Protestant)* das Abendmahl empfangen

commune[2] [ˈkɒmjuːn] N Kommune *f*; *(= administrative division also)* Gemeinde *f*

communicable [kəˈmjuːnɪkəbl] ADJ **a** *disease* übertragbar **b** *ideas, knowledge* kommunizierbar, vermittelbar

communicant [kəˈmjuːnɪkənt] N *(Eccl)* Kommunikant(in) *m(f)*

communicate [kəˈmjuːnɪkeɪt] VT *news etc* übermitteln; *ideas, feelings* vermitteln; *illness* übertragen (*to* auf *+acc*) VI **a** *(= be in communication)* in Verbindung *or* Kontakt stehen; **the ship was unable to ~ with the shore** das Schiff konnte keine Verbindung zum Festland herstellen **b** *(= convey or exchange thoughts)* sich verständigen, kommunizieren; **the inability of modern man to ~** die Unfähigkeit des heutigen Menschen zur Kommunikation **c** *(rooms)* verbunden sein; **communicating door** Verbindungstür *f* **d** *(Eccl, Catholic)* kommunizieren; *(Protestant)* das Abendmahl empfangen

communication [kəˌmjuːnɪˈkeɪʃən] N **a** *(= communicating)* Verständigung *f*, Kommunikation *f*; *(of ideas, information)* Vermittlung *f*; *(of disease)* Übertragung *f*; *(= contact)* Verbindung *f*; **system/means of ~** Kommunikationssystem *nt*/-mittel *nt*; **to be in ~ with sb** mit jdm in Verbindung stehen (*about* wegen)
b *(= exchanging of ideas)* Verständigung *f*, Kommunikation *f*; **~ breakdown** Zusammenbruch *m* der Kommunikation
c *(= letter, message)* Mitteilung *f*
d ~s *(= roads, railways, telegraph lines etc)* Kommunikationswege *pl*, Kommunikationsnetz *nt*; **all ~s with the mainland have been cut off** sämtliche Verbindungen zum Festland sind unterbrochen; **they're trying to restore ~s** man versucht, die Verbindung wiederherzustellen
e ~s *(Telec)* Telekommunikation *f*
f *(between rooms etc)* Verbindung *f*

communication: **communication cord** N *(Brit Rail)* ≈ Notbremse *f*; **communication gap** N Kommunikationslücke *f*; **communication problem** N Kommunikationsproblem *nt*; **communication skills** PL Kommunikationsfähigkeit *f*

communications [kəˌmjuːnɪˈkeɪʃənz]: **communications package** N Kommunikationssoftware *f*; **communications satellite** N Kommunikations- *or* Nachrichtensatellit *m*; **communications software** N Kommunikationssoftware *f*; **communications system** N Kommunikationssystem *nt*; **communications technology** N Nachrichtentechnik *f*

communication trench N Verbindungsgraben *m*

communicative [kəˈmjuːnɪkətɪv] ADJ mitteilsam, gesprächig

communicator [kəˈmjuːnɪkeɪtəʳ] N Kommunikator(in) *m(f)*

communion [kəˈmjuːnɪən] N **a** *(= intercourse, exchange of feelings etc)* Zwiesprache *f*; *(with spirits)* Verkehr *m*; **a sense of ~ with nature** ein Gefühl *nt* der Verbundenheit mit der Natur **b** *(= religious group)* Gemeinde *f*; *(= denomination)* Religionsgemeinschaft *f*; **the ~ of saints/the faithful** die Gemeinschaft der Heiligen/Gläubigen **c** *(Eccl: also* **Communion**, *Protestant)* Abendmahl *nt*; *(Catholic)* Kommunion *f*; **to receive** *or* **take ~** die Kommunion/das Abendmahl empfangen

communion: **communion rail** N Kommunionsbank *f*; **communion service** N Abendmahlsgottesdienst *m*; **communion table** N Abendmahlstisch *m*

communiqué [kəˈmjuːnɪkeɪ] N Kommuniqué *nt*, Kommunikee *nt*, (amtliche) Verlautbarung

communism [ˈkɒmjʊnɪzəm] N Kommunismus *m*

communist [ˈkɒmjʊnɪst] **N** Kommunist(in) *m(f)* **ADJ** kommunistisch

Communist China N das Kommunistische China, Rotchina *nt*

communistic [ˌkɒmjʊˈnɪstɪk] ADJ prokommunistisch; *(esp US: = communist)* kommunistisch

Communist Manifesto N Kommunistisches Manifest

Communist Party N kommunistische Partei

community [kəˈmjuːnɪtɪ] N **a** *(= social, cultural etc group)* Gemeinschaft *f*; *(ethnic also)* Bevölkerungsgruppe *f*; **the ~ at large** das ganze Volk; **the great ~ of nations** die große Völkergemeinschaft; **a sense of ~** (ein) Gemeinschaftsgefühl *nt*; **to work in the ~** im Sozialbereich tätig sein **b** *(= the public)* Allgemeinheit *f* **c** *(Eccl, of monks, nuns)* (Ordens)gemeinschaft *f* **d** *(= holding in common)* **the ~ of love** die Liebesgemeinschaft; **they have no ~ of interests** sie haben keine gemeinsamen Interessen

community: **community association** N *(Brit)* Bürgerverein *m*; **community care** N *(Brit Sociol)* **a** *(= home care)* häusliche Pflege **b** *(also* **community care programme**) kommunales Fürsorgeprogramm; **community centre**, *(US)* **community center** N Gemeindezentrum *nt*; **community charge** N *(Brit dated) Kopfsteuer zur Finanzierung der Stadt- und Gemeindeverwaltungen*; **community chest** N *(US)* Wohltätigkeits- *or* Hilfsfonds *m*; **community college** N *(US) College zur Berufsausbildung und Vorbereitung auf ein Hochschulstudium*; **community home** N Fürsorgeanstalt *f*; **community relations** PL das Verhältnis zwischen den Bevölkerungsgruppen; **community service** N *(Jur)* Sozialdienst *m*; **community singing** N gemeinsames Singen; **community spirit** N Gemeinschaftssinn *m*; **community worker** N Sozialberufler(in) *m(f)*

communize [ˈkɒmjʊnaɪz] VT kommunistisch machen

commutable [kəˈmjuːtəbl] ADJ *(Jur)* umwandelbar

commutation [ˌkɒmjʊˈteɪʃən] N **a** *(Jur)* Umwandlung *f* **b** **~ ticket** *(US)* Zeitnetzkarte *f*

commutator [ˈkɒmjʊteɪtəʳ] N *(Elec)* Kommutator *m*

commute [kəˈmjuːt] **VT** *(all senses)* umwandeln **VI** *(= travel as commuter)* pendeln

commuter [kəˈmjuːtəʳ] N Pendler(in) *m(f)*; **the ~ belt** das Einzugsgebiet, der Einzugsbereich; **a ~ belt** ein städtischer Einzugsbereich; **~ traffic** Pendlerverkehr *m*; **~ train** Pendlerzug *m*

commuting [kəˈmjuːtɪŋ] N Pendeln *nt*; *(= commuter traffic)* Pendelverkehr *m*; **I hate ~** ich hasse es zu pendeln; **within ~ distance** nahe genug, um zu pendeln

comp [kɒmp] N *(Typ inf)* Setzer(in) *m(f)*

compact¹ [kəmˈpækt] **ADJ** *(+er)* kompakt; *style of writing, prose also* gedrängt; *soil, snow* fest; **the print is too ~** der Druck ist zu eng, es ist zu eng bedruckt **VT** **a** *snow, soil* festtreten/-walzen/-fahren *etc* **b** *(fig liter)* **to be ~ed of ...** sich aus ... zusammensetzen

compact² [ˈkɒmpækt] N **a** *(= powder compact)* Puderdose *f* **b** *(US: = car)* Kompaktauto *nt or* -wagen *m* **c** *(= camera)* Kompaktkamera *f*

compact³ [ˈkɒmpækt] N *(form: = agreement)* Vereinbarung *f*, Übereinkunft *f*

compact camera N Kompaktkamera *f*

compact disc N Compact Disc *f*, Compact Disk *f*; **~ player** CD-Spieler *m*

compactly [kəmˈpæktlɪ] ADV kompakt; *expressed* gedrängt; *printed* eng

compactness [kəmˈpæktnɪs] N Kompaktheit *f*; *(of style also)* Gedrängtheit *f*; *(of print)* Dichte *f*, Enge *f*

companion [kəmˈpænjən] **N** **a** *(= person with one)* Begleiter(in) *m(f)*; **~s in arms** Kampfgefährten *pl*, Waffenbrüder *pl (geh)*; **my ~s on the journey** meine Reisegefährten *pl*; **travelling/holiday/drinking ~** Reisebegleiter(in) *m(f)*/Urlaubsgefährte *m*, -gefährtin *f*/Zechgenosse *m*, -genossin *f*
b *(= friend)* Freund(in) *m(f)*, Kamerad(in) *m(f)*; **his elder brother is not much of a ~ for him** sein älterer Bruder ist ihm kein richtiger Freund; **a faithful ~ for fifty years** ein treuer Gefährte über fünfzig Jahre
c *(= one of pair of objects)* Pendant *nt*
d *(= lady companion)* Betreuerin *f*
e *(= handbook)* **"the Gardener's Companion"** „der Ratgeber für den Gartenfreund"
f *(of order of knighthood)* Ritter *m*
ATTR passend; *volume* Begleit-; **they have just brought out a ~ set of Dickens** in derselben Reihe ist jetzt eine Dickens-Ausgabe erschienen

companionable [kəmˈpænjənəbl] ADJ freundlich

companionably [kəmˈpænjənəblɪ] ADV vertraut; *smile also* freundlich

companion: **companion piece** N Pendant *nt* *(to* zu); **companion set** N *(= fire irons)* Kaminbesteck *nt*; **companionship** N Gesellschaft *f*; **companionway** N *(Naut)* Niedergang *m*

company [ˈkʌmpənɪ] ✪ 25.1 **N** **a** Gesellschaft *f*; **to keep sb ~** jdm Gesellschaft leisten; **to keep ~ with sb** mit jdm verkehren; **I enjoy ~** ich bin gern in Gesellschaft, ich habe gern Gesellschaft; **I enjoy his ~** ich bin gern mit ihm zusammen; **female ~** Damengesellschaft *f*; **he arrived with female ~** er kam in Damenbegleitung; **he's good ~** seine Gesellschaft ist angenehm; **he came along just for (the) ~** er kam bloß mit, um Gesellschaft zu haben; **he doesn't know how to behave in ~** er weiß nicht, wie man sich in Gesellschaft benimmt; **I/he in ~ with ...** ich/er, genauso wie ...; **she is not fit ~ for your sister** sie ist nicht der richtige Umgang für deine Schwester; **a man is known by the ~ he keeps** *(prov)* sage mir, mit wem du umgehst, so sage ich dir, wer du bist *(prov)*; **she has a cat, it's ~ for her** sie hält sich eine Katze, da hat sie (wenigstens) Gesellschaft; **you'll be in good ~ if ...** wenn du ..., bist du in guter Gesellschaft
b *(= guests)* Besuch *m*
c *(Comm)* Firma *f*, Gesellschaft *f*; **Smith & Company, Smith & Co.** Smith & Co.; **shipping ~** Schifffahrtsgesellschaft *f*, Reederei *f*; **publishing ~** Verlagshaus *nt*, Verlag *m*; **a printing/clothes ~** ein Druckerei-/Textilbetrieb *m*; **that's paid for by the ~** das bezahlt die Firma
d *(Theat)* (Schauspiel)truppe *f*
e *(Naut)* **ship's ~** Besatzung *f*
f *(Mil)* Kompanie *f*
ATTR Firmen-; **he has a ~ BMW** er hat einen BMW als Firmenwagen

company: **company car** N Firmenwagen *m*; **company commander** N *(Mil)* Kompaniechef *m*; **company director** N Direktor(in) *m(f)*, Firmenchef(in) *m(f)*; **company law** N Gesellschaftsrecht *nt*; **company lawyer** N *(for company law)* Gesellschaftsrechtler(in) *m(f)*; *(within company)* Hausjurist(in) *m(f)*; **company loyalty** N Firmentreue *f*; **company man** N treues *or* loyales Firmenmitglied; **company policy** N Geschäftspolitik *f*; **company secretary** N *(Brit Comm)* ≈ Prokurist(in) *m(f)*; **company sergeant major** N *(Mil)* Kompaniefeldwebel *m*; **company time** N Arbeitszeit *f*

comparable [ˈkɒmpərəbl] ADJ vergleichbar *(with, to* mit)

comparably [ˈkɒmpərəblɪ] ADV ähnlich

comparative [kəmˈpærətɪv] **ADJ** **a** *religion, philology etc* vergleichend; **~ literature** vergleichende Literaturwissenschaft, Komparatistik *f* **b** **the ~ form** *(Gram)* der Komparativ, die erste Steigerungsstufe **c** *(= relative)* relativ; **to live in ~ luxury** relativ luxuriös leben **N** *(Gram)* Komparativ *m*

comparatively [kəmˈpærətɪvlɪ] ✪ 5.1 ADV **a** vergleichend **b** *(= relatively)* verhältnismäßig, relativ

compare [kəmˈpeəʳ] ✪ 5.1, 5.3, 26.3 **VT** vergleichen *(with, to* mit); **~d with** *or* **to** im Vergleich zu, verglichen mit; **they cannot be ~d** man kann sie nicht vergleichen, sie lassen sich nicht vergleichen; **his car is not to be** *or* **can't be ~d with my new one** sein Wagen ist überhaupt kein Vergleich zu meinem neuen Auto; **to ~ notes** Eindrücke/Erfahrungen austauschen
VI sich vergleichen lassen *(with* mit); **it ~s badly/well** es schneidet vergleichsweise schlecht/gut ab; **it doesn't ~ very well at all** es schneidet im Vergleich überhaupt nicht gut ab; **how do the two cars ~ in terms of speed?** wie sieht ein Geschwindigkeitsvergleich der beiden Wagen aus?; **the old car can't ~ in terms of speed with the new one** in puncto Geschwindigkeit lässt sich der alte Wagen nicht mit dem neuen vergleichen
N **beyond** *or* **without ~** unvergleichlich; **beautiful beyond ~** unvergleichlich schön

comparison [kəmˈpærɪsn] ✪ 5.2, 5.5, 26.3 N **a** Vergleich *m* *(to* mit); **in** *or* **by ~** vergleichsweise; **in** *or* **by ~ with** im Vergleich zu; **to make** *or* **draw a ~** einen Vergleich anstellen; **to bear** *or* **stand ~** einem Vergleich standhalten, einen Vergleich aushalten; **there's no ~** das ist gar kein Vergleich **b** *(Gram)* Steigerung *f*; **degree of ~** Steigerungsstufe *f*

comparison shopping N *(Comm)* preisbewusstes Einkaufen

compartment [kəmˈpɑːtmənt] N *(in fridge, desk etc)* Fach *nt*; *(Rail)* Abteil *nt*; *(Naut)* Schott *nt*, Schotte *f*; *(fig)* (Schub)fach *nt*

compartmentalize [ˌkɒmpɑːtˈmentəlaɪz] VT aufsplittern

compartmentalized [ˌkɒmpɑːtˈmentəlaɪzd] ADJ *subject* gegliedert; **their excessively ~ view of life** ihre übertrieben genau gegliederte Lebensanschauung

compass [ˈkʌmpəs] **N** **a** Kompass *m*; **by the ~** nach dem Kompass **b** **compasses** **PL** *(also* **pair of compasses**) Zirkel *m* **c** *(fig: = extent)* Rahmen *m*; *(of human mind, experience)* Bereich *m*; *(Mus, of voice)* Umfang *m* **VT** = **encompass** **~ed about with enemies** *(form)* von Feinden umzingelt

compass: **compass bearing** N Kompasspeilung *f*; **compass card** N Kompassscheibe *f*, Windrose *f*; **compass course** N Navigationskurs *m*

compassion [kəmˈpæʃən] N Mitgefühl *nt*, Mitleid *nt* *(for* mit); *(esp Bibl)* Erbarmen *nt* *(on, for* mit)

compassionate [kəmˈpæʃənɪt] ADJ mitfühlend, voller Mitgefühl *or* Mitleid; **on ~ grounds** aus familiären Gründen

compassionate leave N Beurlaubung *f* wegen einer dringenden Familienangelegenheit

compassionately [kəmˈpæʃənɪtlɪ] ADV voll Mitgefühl

compass rose N Windrose *f*

compatibility [kəmˌpætəˈbɪlɪtɪ] N Vereinbarkeit *f*, Kompatibilität *f (geh)*; *(Med)* Verträglichkeit *f*, Kompatibilität *f (spec)*; *(Comput)* Kompatibilität *f*; **their ~/lack of ~ was obvious** es war offensichtlich, dass die beiden gut/schlecht zueinanderpassten

compatible [kəmˈpætɪbl] ADJ vereinbar, kompatibel *(geh)*; *(Med)* verträglich, kompatibel *(spec)*; *people* zueinanderpassend; *colours, furniture* passend; *(Comput)* kompatibel; **to be ~** *(people)* zueinanderpassen; *(colours, furniture)* zusammenpassen; *(plan)* vereinbar sein; **a salary ~ with the dangers of the job** ein Gehalt, das den Gefahren des Berufs entspricht; **such action would not be ~ with democracy** ein solches Vorgehen ist nicht mit dem Demokratieverständnis zu vereinen; **an IBM-~ computer** ein IBM-kompatibler Computer

compatibly [kəmˈpætɪblɪ] ADV **to be ~ matched** gut zueinanderpassen

compatriot [kəmˈpætrɪət] N Landsmann *m*, Landsmännin *f*

compel [kəmˈpel] VT **a** *(= force)* zwingen; **I feel ~led to tell you ...** ich sehe mich (dazu) gezwungen *or* veranlasst, Ihnen mitzuteilen, ... **b** *admiration, respect* abnötigen *(from sb* jdm); *obedience* erzwingen *(from sb* von jdm)

compellable [kəmˈpeləbl] ADJ *(Jur) witness* aussagepflichtig

compelling [kəmˈpelɪŋ] ADJ zwingend; *performance, personality, eyes* bezwingend; **to make a ~ case for sth** schlagende Beweise für etw liefern; **the novel makes ~ reading** der Roman ist äußerst spannend zu lesen

compellingly [kəmˈpelɪŋlɪ] ADV *write, tell* spannend; *persuasive* umwerfend; **~ attractive** unwiderstehlich; **he presented his case ~** er legte seinen Fall mit zwingender Logik dar

compendious [kəmˈpendɪəs] ADJ *notes etc* umfangreich

compendium [kəmˈpendɪəm] N Handbuch *nt*, Kompendium *nt*; **~ of games** Spielemagazin *nt*

compensate [ˈkɒmpənseɪt] VT *(= recompense)* entschädigen; *(Mech)* ausgleichen VI *(Psych)* kompensieren

▶ **compensate for** VI +*prep obj (in money, material goods etc)* ersetzen; *(= make up for, offset)* wieder wettmachen *or* ausgleichen; *(Psych)* kompensieren; **he was awarded £900 to compensate for the damage** er erhielt £ 900 Schadenersatz *or* -ausgleich

compensating [ˈkɒmpənseɪtɪŋ] ADJ ausgleichend, Ausgleichs-; **~ errors** *pl* sich gegenseitig aufhebende Fehler

compensation [ˌkɒmpənˈseɪʃən] N *(= damages)* Entschädigung *f*; *(fig)* Ausgleich *m*; *(Psych)* Kompensation *f*; **he had the ~ of knowing that ...** er hatte die Genugtuung zu wissen, dass ...; **in ~** als Entschädigung/Ausgleich/Kompensation

compensatory [kəmˈpensətərɪ] ADJ kompensierend, ausgleichend; *education* kompensatorisch; *(Psych)* kompensatorisch

comper [ˈkɒmpəʳ] N *(inf) jd, der regelmäßig an Preisausschreiben teilnimmt*

compère [ˈkɒmpɛəʳ] *(Brit)* N Conférencier *m* VT **to ~ a show** bei einer Show der Conférencier sein

compete [kəmˈpiːt] VI **a** *(firm, country)* konkurrieren; **to ~ with each other** sich (gegenseitig) Konkurrenz machen; **to ~ for sth** um etw kämpfen *or (esp Comm)* konkurrieren; **able to ~ industrially** industriell konkurrenzfähig; **his poetry can't ~ with Eliot's** seine Gedichte können sich nicht mit denen Eliots messen; **he can't ~ (any more)** er kann nicht mehr mithalten **b** *(Sport)* teilnehmen; **to ~ for the championship** um die Meisterschaft kämpfen; **to ~ with/against sb** gegen jdn kämpfen *or* antreten

competence [ˈkɒmpɪtəns], **competency** [ˈkɒmpɪtənsɪ] N **a** Fähigkeit *f*; *(of lawyer, scientist etc also, Ling)* Kompetenz *f*; **to do sth with surprising ~** etw mit erstaunlichem Geschick tun; **his ~ in handling money/dealing with awkward clients** sein Geschick im Umgang mit Geld/schwierigen Kunden; **what level of ~ has the class reached in Spanish?** auf welchem Stand ist die Klasse in Spanisch? **b** *(form: = income)* Einkommen *nt* **c** *(Jur)* Zuständigkeit *f*

competent [ˈkɒmpɪtənt] ADJ **a** fähig, befähigt (in zu); *(in a particular field)* kompetent; *(= adequate) knowledge, understanding* angemessen, adäquat; **his English is quite ~** sein Englisch ist recht gut; **to be/feel ~ to do sth** kompetent *or* fähig sein/sich kompetent *or* fähig fühlen, etw zu tun; **to do a ~ job** gute Arbeit leisten **b** *(Jur)* zuständig; *evidence, witness* zulässig **c** *(form: = relevant)* **to be ~/not ~** *(business, question)* von/ohne *or* nicht von Belang sein

competently [ˈkɒmpɪtəntlɪ] ADV geschickt, kompetent

competition [ˌkɒmpɪˈtɪʃən] N **a** *no pl* Konkurrenz *f (for* um); **to keep an eye on the ~** die Konkurrenz beobachten; **unfair ~** unlauterer Wettbewerb; **a spirit of ~** Wettbewerbs- *or* Konkurrenzdenken *nt*; **to be in ~ with sb** mit jdm wetteifern *or (esp Comm)* konkurrieren; **to be driven by ~** unter Konkurrenzdruck stehen **b** *(= contest)* Wettbewerb *m*; *(in newspapers etc)* Preisausschreiben *nt*; **beauty/swimming ~** Schönheitskonkurrenz *f or* -wettbewerb *m*/ Schwimmwettbewerb *m*

competitive [kəmˈpetɪtɪv] ADJ **a** *person, attitude* vom Konkurrenzdenken geprägt; *sport* (Wett)kampf-; **~ advantage/disadvantage** Wettbewerbsvorteil *m*/-nachteil *m*; **~ spirit** Wettbewerbs- *or* Konkurrenzgeist *m*; *(of team)* Kampfgeist *m*; **he's a very ~ sort of person** er genießt Wettbewerbssituationen; *(in job etc)* er ist ein sehr ehrgeiziger Mensch; **the exam system encourages children to be too ~** das Prüfungssystem regt die Kinder zu sehr zum Konkurrenzdenken an; **the recruitment procedure is not ~** die Stellenvergabe erfolgt nicht aufgrund eines Auswahlverfahrens; **to gain a ~ advantage** *or* **edge over sb** jdm gegenüber einen Wettbewerbsvorteil erzielen; **a ~ examination** eine Auswahlprüfung **b** *(Comm) business, prices, salaries* wettbewerbs- *or* konkurrenzfähig; **a highly ~ market** ein Markt mit starker Konkurrenz; **retailing is highly ~** der Einzelhandel ist stark wettbewerbsbetont *or* -orientiert; **~ bidding** Ausschreibungswettbewerb *m*; **~ tendering** freie Ausschreibung

competitively [kəmˈpetɪtɪvlɪ] ADV **a to be ~ priced** im Preis konkurrenzfähig sein **b** *swim, ski, play etc* in Wettkämpfen

competitiveness [kəmˈpetɪtɪvnɪs] N *(= competitive spirit)* Wettbewerbs- *or* Konkurrenzgeist *m*; *(of product, company, prices)* Wettbewerbsfähigkeit *f*

competitor [kəmˈpetɪtəʳ] N **a** *(Sport, in contest)* Teilnehmer(in) *m(f)*; *(for job)* Mitbewerber(in) *m(f)*; **to be a ~** teilnehmen **b** *(Comm)* Konkurrent(in) *m(f)*; **our ~s** unsere Konkurrenz *or* Konkurrenten

compilation [ˌkɒmpɪˈleɪʃən] N Zusammenstellung *f*; *(of material)* Sammlung *f*; *(of dictionary)* Abfassung *f*

compile [kəmˈpaɪl] VT zusammenstellen, erstellen *(form)*; *material* sammeln, zusammentragen; *dictionary* verfassen; *(Comput)* kompilieren

compiler [kəmˈpaɪləʳ] N *(of dictionary)* Verfasser(in) *m(f)*; *(Comput)* Compiler *m*; **who's the ~ of this list?** wer hat diese Liste zusammengestellt?

comping [ˈkɒmpɪŋ] N *(inf)* regelmäßige Teilnahme an Preisausschreiben

complacence [kəmˈpleɪsəns], **complacency** [kəmˈpleɪsnsɪ] N Selbstzufriedenheit *f*, Selbstgefälligkeit *f*

complacent [kəmˈpleɪsənt] ADJ selbstzufrieden *or* -gefällig; **don't get ~ just because ...** jetzt werde bloß nicht selbstgefällig *or* überheblich, nur weil ...

complacently [kəmˈpleɪsəntlɪ] ADV selbstzufrieden *or* -gefällig; **those who ~ accept their parents' beliefs** diejenigen, die die Ansichten ihrer Eltern unreflektiert übernehmen

complain [kəmˈpleɪn] VI sich beklagen, klagen *(about* über *+acc)*; *(= to make a formal complaint)* sich beschweren, Beschwerde einlegen *(form)* *(about* über *+acc, to* bei); **to ~ that ...** sich darüber beklagen/beschweren, dass ...; **(I) can't ~** *(inf)* ich kann nicht klagen *(inf)*; **stop ~ing!** beklag dich nicht dauernd!; **to ~ of sth** über etw *(acc)* klagen; **to ~ of not having enough time** über Zeitmangel klagen; **she's always ~ing** sie muss sich immer beklagen, sie hat immer etwas zu klagen

complainant [kəmˈpleɪnənt] N Beschwerdeführer(in) *m(f)*; *(in court)* Kläger(in) *m(f)*

complaint [kəmˈpleɪnt] N **a** Klage *f*; *(= formal complaint)* Beschwerde *f (to* bei); **I have no cause for ~** ich kann mich nicht beklagen; **I wouldn't have any ~(s) if ...** ich würde mich nicht beklagen, wenn ...; **to lodge a ~ against sb with the police** jdn bei der Polizei anzeigen, gegen jdn Anzeige erstatten **b** *(= illness)* Beschwerden *pl*; **a very rare ~** eine sehr seltene Krankheit, ein sehr seltenes Leiden

complaisance [kəmˈpleɪzəns] N *(liter)* Gefälligkeit *f*

complaisant ADJ, **complaisantly** ADV [kəmˈpleɪzənt, -lɪ] gefällig, entgegenkommend; *smile* wohlwollend

complement [ˈkɒmplɪmənt] N **a** *(= addition)* Ergänzung *f (to +gen)*; *(to perfect sth)* Vervollkommnung *f (to +gen)*; *(= colour)* Komplementärfarbe *f (to* zu)

b *(= full number)* volle Stärke; *(= crew of ship)* Besatzung *f*; **the battalion didn't have its full ~ of soldiers** das Bataillon hatte seine Sollstärke nicht; **we've got our full ~ in the office now** unser Büro ist jetzt komplett *or* voll besetzt

c *(Gram)* Ergänzung *f*

d *(Math: = angle)* Ergänzungswinkel *m*

VT [ˈkɒmplɪment] **a** *(= add to)* ergänzen; *(= make perfect)* vervollkommnen, abrunden; *(colour)* herausbringen; **to ~ each other** sich ergänzen; *(colours)* aufeinander abgestimmt sein

b *(Gram)* die Ergänzung bilden zu

c *(Math)* zu 90° ergänzen

complementary [ˌkɒmplɪˈmentərɪ] ADJ *colour* Komplementär-; *angle* Ergänzungs-; **a ~ pair** ein zusammengehöriges Paar; **two ~ characters** zwei einander ergänzende Charaktere; **they are ~ to each other** sie ergänzen sich *or* einander; **they have ~ interests** ihre Interessen ergänzen sich

complementary: **complementary colour**, *(US)* **complementary color** N Komplementärfarbe *f*; **complementary medicine** N Komplementärmedizin *f*

complete [kəmˈpliːt] ADJ **a** *(= entire, whole)* ganz *attr*; *set also, wardrobe, deck of cards* vollständig, komplett; *(= having the required numbers)* vollzählig; *edition* Gesamt-; **my happiness/disappointment was ~** mein Glück/meine Enttäuschung war perfekt *or* vollkommen; **my life is now ~** mein Leben ist erfüllt; **our victory was ~** unser Sieg war vollkommen; **the ~ works of Shakespeare** die gesammelten Werke Shakespeares; **no classical collection is ~ without Beethoven's ninth symphony** eine Sammlung klassischer Musik wäre ohne Beethovens neunte Sinfonie nicht zu denken; **a very ~ account** ein sehr umfassender *or* detaillierter Bericht; **are we ~?** sind wir vollzählig?

b *attr (= total, absolute)* völlig; *failure, beginner, disaster, flop also, victory* total; *surprise, shambles also* komplett; *satisfaction also, approval* voll; **we were ~ strangers** wir waren uns *or* einander völlig fremd; **we were in ~ agreement** wir stimmten völlig überein

c *(= finished)* fertig; **his novel is not yet ~** sein Roman ist noch nicht abgeschlossen; **my life's work is now ~** mein Lebenswerk ist nun vollbracht

d ~ with komplett mit; **he came ~ with rucksack and boots** er erschien komplett ausgerüstet mit Rucksack und Stiefeln

e *sportsman, gardener etc* perfekt

VT **a** *(= make whole) collection, set* vervollständigen, komplettieren; *team* vollzählig machen; *education, meal* abrunden; **to ~ our numbers** damit wir vollzählig sind; **that ~s my collection** damit ist meine Sammlung vollständig

b *(fig) happiness* vollkommen machen; **and to ~ their misery ...** und zu allem Unglück ...

c *(= finish)* beenden, abschließen, zum Abschluss *or* zu Ende bringen; *building, work* fertigstellen; *prison sentence* verbüßen; **~ this phrase** ergänzen Sie diesen Ausspruch; **it's not ~d yet** es ist noch nicht fertig

d *form, questionnaire* ausfüllen

completely [kəmˈpliːtlɪ] **ADV** völlig, vollkommen; **he's ~ wrong** er irrt sich gewaltig, er hat völlig unrecht; **he's not ~ normal** er ist nicht ganz normal

completeness [kəmˈpliːtnɪs] **N** Vollständigkeit *f*; **the design has a sense of ~ about it** das Design erscheint vollendet *or* vollkommen; **a work which demonstrates the ~ of his talent** ein Werk, das sein vollendetes Talent beweist

completion [kəmˈpliːʃən] **N** **a** *(= finishing)* Fertigstellung *f*; *(of work also)* Beendigung *f*; *(of project, course, education)* Abschluss *m*; *(of prison sentence)* Verbüßung *f*; **to be near ~** kurz vor dem Abschluss stehen; **to bring sth to ~** etw zum Abschluss bringen; **we need more people for the ~ of the work** wir brauchen noch mehr Leute, um die Arbeit zum Abschluss zu bringen; **on ~ of the course** am Ende *or* nach Abschluss des Kurses; **on ~ of the contract/sale** bei Vertrags-/Kaufabschluss; **~ date** Fertigstellungstermin *m*

b *(= making whole)* Vervollständigung *f*; *(of education, meal)* Abrundung *f*; *(of happiness etc)* Vervollkommnung *f*

c *(= filling in: of form etc)* Ausfüllen *nt*

complex [ˈkɒmpleks] **ADJ** **a** komplex; *person, mind, issue, question, problem, poem also* vielschichtig; *theory, task, system also, machine, pattern* differenziert, kompliziert; *situation also, paragraph* verwickelt, kompliziert **b** *(Gram)* **a ~ sentence** ein Satzgefüge *nt* **N** **a** Komplex *m*; **industrial ~** Industriekomplex *m* **b** *(Psych)* Komplex *m*; **he has a ~ about his ears** er hat Komplexe *or* einen Komplex wegen seiner Ohren; **don't get a ~ about it** deswegen brauchst du keine Komplexe zu bekommen

complexion [kəmˈplekʃən] **N** **a** Teint *m*; *(= skin colour)* Gesichtsfarbe *f* **b** *(fig: = aspect)* Anstrich *m*, Aspekt *m*; **to put a new/different** *etc* **~ on sth** etw in einem neuen/anderen *etc* Licht erscheinen lassen; **of a different political/religious ~** mit anderen politischen/religiösen Anschauungen

complexity [kəmˈpleksɪtɪ] **N** Komplexität *f*; *(of person, mind, issue, question, problem, poem also)* Vielschichtigkeit *f*; *(of theory, task, system also, machine, pattern)* Differenziertheit *f*, Kompliziertheit *f*

compliance [kəmˈplaɪəns] **N** Einverständnis *nt*; *(with rules etc)* Einhalten *nt (with +gen)*; *(= submissiveness)* Willfährigkeit *f (geh)*, Fügsamkeit *f*; **in ~ with the law/our wishes** *etc* dem Gesetz/unseren Wünschen *etc* gemäß

compliant [kəmˈplaɪənt] **ADJ** entgegenkommend, gefällig; *(= submissive)* nachgiebig, willfährig *(geh)*

complicate [ˈkɒmplɪkeɪt] **VT** komplizieren

complicated [ˈkɒmplɪkeɪtɪd] **ADJ** kompliziert

complication [ˌkɒmplɪˈkeɪʃən] **N** Komplikation *f*; *(= complicated nature)* Kompliziertheit *f*

complicit [kəmˈplɪsɪt] **ADJ** **a** *(= knowing) look, wink, silence* wissend **b** *(= involved)* **to be ~ in sth** an etw *(dat)* beteiligt *or* in etw *(acc)* verwickelt sein; **he was ~ in allowing it to happen** er war mitverantwortlich dafür, dass es passieren konnte

complicity [kəmˈplɪsɪtɪ] **N** Mittäterschaft *f (in* bei)

compliment [ˈkɒmplɪmənt] **N** **a** Kompliment *nt (on* zu, wegen); **to pay sb a ~** jdm ein Kompliment machen; **that's quite a ~, coming from you** wenn Sie das sagen, heißt das schon etwas *or* ist das wahrhaftig ein Kompliment; **(give) my ~s to the chef** mein Lob *or* Kompliment dem Koch/der Köchin

b compliments **PL** *(form)* Grüße *pl*; **give him my ~s** empfehlen Sie mich ihm *(dated form)*; **to pay one's ~s to sb** *(on arrival)* jdn begrüßen; *(on departure)* sich jdm empfehlen *(dated form)*; *(= visit)* jdm einen Höflichkeitsbesuch abstatten *(form)*; **the ~s of the season** frohes Fest; **"with the ~s of Mr X/the management"** „mit den besten Empfehlungen von Herrn X/der Geschäftsleitung"; **"with the ~s of the publishers"** „zur gefälligen Kenntnisnahme, der Verlag"

VT [ˈkɒmplɪment] ein Kompliment/Komplimente machen *(+dat)* *(on* wegen, zu)

complimentary [ˌkɒmplɪˈmentərɪ] **ADJ** **a** *(= praising)* schmeichelhaft; **~ close** Schlussformel *f*; **to be ~ about sb/sth** sich schmeichelhaft über jdn/etw äußern, jdn/etw loben **b** *(= free) seat, ticket* Frei-; **~ copy** Freiexemplar *nt*; *(of magazine)* Werbenummer *f*

compliments slip [ˈkɒmplɪmənts,slɪp] **N** *(Comm)* Empfehlungszettel *m*

compline [ˈkɒmplɪn] **N** *(Eccl)* Komplet *f*

comply [kəmˈplaɪ] ✪ 11.3 **VI** *(person)* einwilligen; *(object, system etc)* die Bedingungen erfüllen, den Bedingungen entsprechen; **to ~ with sth** einer Sache *(dat)* entsprechen; *(system)* in Einklang mit etw stehen; **to ~ with the terms of a treaty** die Vertragsbedingungen erfüllen; **to ~ with a request/a wish/instructions** einer Bitte/einem Wunsch/den Anordnungen nachkommen *(form)* or entsprechen *(form)*; **to ~ with sb's wishes** sich jds Wünschen *(dat)* fügen; **to ~ with a time limit** eine Frist einhalten; **to ~ with the rules** sich an die Regeln halten

component [kəmˈpəʊnənt] **N** Teil *nt*, Bestandteil *m*; *(Chem, Phys)* Komponente *f* **ADJ** **a ~ part** ein (Bestand)teil *m*; **the ~ parts** die Bestand- *or* Einzelteile *pl*; **the ~ parts of a machine/sentence** die einzelnen Maschinen-/Satzteile *pl*

comport [kəmˈpɔːt] *(form)* **VR** sich verhalten **VI** **to ~ with** sich vereinbaren lassen mit

comportment [kəmˈpɔːtmənt] **N** Verhalten *nt*; **to study ~** Anstandsunterricht nehmen

compose [kəmˈpəʊz] **VT** **a** *music* komponieren; *letter* abfassen, aufsetzen; *poem, e-mail* verfassen; **"compose"** *(e-mail)* „neue Nachricht" **b** *(= constitute, make up)* bilden; **to be ~d of** sich zusammensetzen aus; **water is ~d of ...** Wasser besteht aus ... **c** **to ~ oneself** sich sammeln; **to ~ one's features** sich wieder in die Gewalt bekommen; **to ~ one's thoughts** Ordnung in seine Gedanken bringen **d** *(Typ)* setzen

composed [kəmˈpəʊzd] **ADJ** *(= calm)* beherrscht, gelassen

composedly [kəmˈpəʊzədlɪ] **ADV** beherrscht, gelassen

composer [kəmˈpəʊzəʳ] **N** **a** *(Mus)* Komponist(in) *m(f)* **b** *(of letter, poem etc)* Verfasser(in) *m(f)*

composite [ˈkɒmpəzɪt] **ADJ** **a** zusammengesetzt; **~ motion** Sammelantrag *m*; **~ material** Verbund(werk)stoff *m*; **~ structure** gegliederter Aufbau **b** *(Bot)* Korbblütler-; *flower* zur Familie der Korbblütler gehörig **c** *(Math) number* teilbar **N** **a** *(Bot)* Korbblütler *m* **b** *(= photograph)* Fotomontage *f*

composite photograph **N** Fotomontage *f*

composition [ˌkɒmpəˈzɪʃən] **N** **a** *(= act of composing, of music)* Komponieren *nt*; *(of letter)* Abfassen *nt*, Aufsetzen *nt*; *(of poem)* Verfassen *nt*; **music of his own ~** selbst komponierte Musik; **verse of her own ~** selbst verfasste Verse *pl*

b *(= arrangement, Mus, Art)* Komposition *f*; *(Mus: = theory of composition also)* Kompositionslehre *f*

c *(Sch: = essay)* Aufsatz *m*

d *(= constitution, make-up)* Zusammensetzung *f*; *(of sentence)* Aufbau *m*, Konstruktion *f*; **to change the ~ of sth** die Zusammenstellung einer Sache *(gen)* ändern; **to decide on the ~ of sth** etw zusammenstellen; **this medicine is a ~ of ...** dieses Medikament setzt sich aus ... zusammen; **there is a touch of madness in his ~** *(old, liter)* in ihm findet sich die Anlage zum Wahnsinn

e *(= artificial substance)* Kunststoff *m*

f *(Typ)* Setzen *nt*; **~ by hand** Handsatz *m*, manueller Satz

g *(Jur)* Vergleich *m*

compositional [ˌkɒmpəˈzɪʃənl] **ADJ** Kompositions-; **~ style** Kompositionsstil *m*

composition *in cpds* Kunst-; **composition rubber** **N** synthetischer Kautschuk; **composition sole** **N** Kunststoffsohle *f*

compositor [kəmˈpɒzɪtəʳ] **N** *(Typ)* (Schrift)setzer(in) *m(f)*

compos mentis [ˈkɒmpəsˈmentɪs] **ADJ** **I'm never really ~ first thing in the morning** frühmorgens ist mein Verstand noch nicht so klar *or* bin ich noch nicht voll da *(inf)*; **he's quite ~** er ist voll zurechnungsfähig; **he's not quite ~** er ist nicht voll zurechnungsfähig, er ist nicht ganz bei Trost *(inf)*

compost [ˈkɒmpɒst] **N** Kompost *m*; **~ heap** Komposthaufen *m*

composure [kəmˈpəʊʒəʳ] **N** Beherrschung *f*, Fassung *f*; **to lose one's ~** die Beherrschung verlieren; **to regain one's ~** seine Selbstbeherrschung wiederfinden

compote [ˈkɒmpəʊt] **N** Kompott *nt*

compound[1] [ˈkɒmpaʊnd] **N** *(Chem)* Verbindung *f*; *(Gram)* Kompositum *nt*, zusammengesetztes Wort

ADJ **a** *(Chem)* **~ substance** Verbindung *f*

b *(Gram) tense, word* zusammengesetzt

VT [kəmˈpaʊnd] **a** *(rare, = combine)* verbinden; *(Chem)* mischen; **to be ~ed of ...** *(liter)* sich zusammensetzen aus ...

b *(Jur) debt* begleichen, tilgen; *quarrel* beilegen; **to ~ a crime** ein Verbrechen wegen erhaltener Entschädigung nicht verfolgen

c *(= make worse)* verschlimmern; *problem* verstärken, vergrößern; **this only ~s our difficulties** das erschwert unsere Lage *or* Situation noch zusätzlich

VI [kəmˈpaʊnd] einen Vergleich schließen; *(with creditors)* sich vergleichen; **to ~ with sb for sth** sich mit jdm auf etw *(acc)* einigen

compound[2] [ˈkɒmpaʊnd] **N** *(= enclosed area)* Lager *nt*; *(in prison)* Gefängnishof *m*; *(= living quarters)* Siedlung *f*; *(in zoo)* Gehege *nt*

compound: **compound eye** **N** *(Zool)* Facetten- *or* Netzauge *nt*; **compound fraction** **N** *(Math)* Doppelbruch *m*; **compound fracture** **N** *(Med)* offener *or* komplizierter Bruch

compounding [ˈkɒmpaʊndɪŋ] **N** *(Ling)* Zusammensetzungen *pl*

compound: **compound interest** **N** *(Fin)* Zinseszins *m*; **compound number** **N** *(Math)* zusammengesetzte Zahl; **compound sentence** **N** *(Gram)* Satzgefüge *nt*; *(of two or more main clauses)* Satzreihe *f*, Parataxe *f*

comprehend [ˌkɒmprɪˈhend] **VT** **a** *(= understand)* begreifen, verstehen **b** *(= include)* enthalten, umfassen, einschließen

comprehensibility [ˌkɒmprɪˌhensɪˈbɪlɪtɪ] **N** Verständlichkeit *f*

comprehensible [ˌkɒmprɪˈhensəbl] **ADJ** verständlich; **the graffiti is not ~** das Graffito ist nicht verständlich *or* zu verstehen

comprehension [ˌkɒmprɪˈhenʃən] **N** **a** *(= understanding)* Verständnis *nt*; *(= ability to understand)* Begriffsvermögen *nt*; **that is beyond my ~** das übersteigt mein Begriffsvermögen; *(behaviour)* das ist mir unbegreiflich **b** *(= inclusion)* Aufnahme *f* **c** *(= school exercise)* Fragen *pl* zum Textverständnis

comprehensive [ˌkɒmprɪˈhensɪv] **ADJ** umfassend; **to go ~** *(Brit Sch)* (eine) Gesamtschule werden; **(fully) ~ insurance** Vollkasko(versicherung *f*) *nt*; **are you ~?** *(Insur)* sind Sie vollkaskoversichert?, haben Sie Vollkasko? *(inf)* **N** *(Brit)* Gesamtschule *f*

comprehensively [ˌkɒmprɪˈhensɪvlɪ] ADV umfassend

comprehensiveness [ˌkɒmprɪˈhensɪvnɪs] N Ausführlichkeit *f*; **the ~ of his report** sein umfassender Bericht

comprehensive school N *(Brit)* Gesamtschule *f*

> **COMPREHENSIVE SCHOOL**
> **Comprehensive schools** sind in Großbritannien weiterführende Schulen, an denen alle Kinder aus einem Einzugsgebiet unterrichtet werden und alle Schulabschlüsse gemacht werden können. Diese Gesamtschulen wurden in den Sechzigerjahren von der Labour-Regierung eingeführt, um das vorherige selektive System von **grammar schools** und **secondary modern schools** abzulösen und allen Kindern die gleichen Möglichkeiten zu gewährleisten. Auch wenn es immer noch einige **grammar schools** gibt, sind die meisten staatlichen Schulen in Großbritannien heutzutage **comprehensive schools**.

compress[1] [kəmˈpres] VT *also data* komprimieren (*into* auf *+acc*); *air etc also, data* verdichten; *materials* zusammenpressen (*into* zu) **VI** sich verdichten, sich komprimieren lassen

compress[2] [ˈkɒmpres] N Kompresse *f*, feuchter Umschlag

compressed air [kəmˈprestˈɛəˈ] N Druck- *or* Pressluft *f*

compression [kəmˈpreʃən] N Verdichtung *f*, Kompression *f*; *(of information etc)* Komprimieren *nt*; **the gas is in a state of very high ~** das Gas ist stark verdichtet *or* komprimiert

compression: compression bandage N Druck- *or* Kompressionsverband *m*; **compression ratio** N Verdichtungs- *or* Kompressionsverhältnis *nt*

compressor [kəmˈpresəˈ] N Kompressor *m*, Verdichter *m*; **~ program** *(Comput)* Verdichtungsprogramm *nt*

comprise [kəmˈpraɪz] VT bestehen aus, umfassen

compromise [ˈkɒmprəmaɪz] **N** Kompromiss *m*; **to come to** *or* **reach** *or* **make a ~** zu einem Kompromiss kommen *or* gelangen, einen Kompromiss schließen; **one has to make ~s** man muss auch mal Kompromisse schließen **ADJ** *attr* Kompromiss-; **~ decision** Kompromiss(lösung *f*) *m*; **~ solution** Kompromisslösung *f* **VI** Kompromisse schließen (*about* in *+dat*); **we agreed to ~** wir einigten uns auf einen Kompromiss **VT** **a** *sb* kompromittieren; **to ~ oneself** sich kompromittieren; **to ~ one's reputation** seinem guten Ruf schaden; **to ~ one's principles** seinen Prinzipien untreu werden **b** (= *imperil*) gefährden

compromising [ˈkɒmprəmaɪzɪŋ] ADJ kompromittierend

comptroller [kənˈtrəʊləˈ] N *(form)* Rechnungsprüfer *m*, Bücherrevisor *m*; **Comptroller of the Queen's Household** *Beamter des Rechnungshofes, der die königlichen Finanzen überprüft*

compulsion [kəmˈpʌlʃən] N Zwang *m*, Druck *m*; *(Psych)* innerer Zwang; **under ~** unter Druck *or* Zwang; **you are under no ~** Sie sind nicht gezwungen, niemand zwingt Sie

compulsive [kəmˈpʌlsɪv] ADJ zwanghaft, Zwangs-; *neurosis* Zwangs-; *behaviour* zwanghaft; **the ~ buying of ...** der krankhafte Zwang, ... zu kaufen; **~ buying as a form of disease** Kaufzwang, eine Art Krankheit; **he has a ~ desire to ...** er steht unter dem Zwang, zu ...; **he is a ~ eater/shopper** er hat die Esssucht/Kaufsucht, er leidet an einem Esszwang/Kaufzwang; **he is a ~ liar** er hat einen krankhaften Trieb zu lügen; **she's a ~ talker** sie muss unbedingt reden; **it makes ~ reading/viewing** das muss man einfach lesen/sehen; **this ~ TV-watching ruins every conversation** diese ständige Fernseherei zerstört jede Unterhaltung!

compulsively [kəmˈpʌlsɪvlɪ] ADV **a** *lie, gamble, eat, talk* zwanghaft; **to act ~** unter einem (inneren) Zwang handeln **b** (= *irresistibly*) **~ readable/watchable** faszinierend zu lesen/anzusehen

compulsorily [kəmˈpʌlsərɪlɪ] ADV zwangsweise

compulsory [kəmˈpʌlsərɪ] ✪ 10.3 **ADJ** obligatorisch; *liquidation, measures* Zwangs-; *subject, member* Pflicht-; **that is ~** das ist Pflicht *or* obligatorisch; **education is ~** es besteht (allgemeine) Schulpflicht; **~ registration** Meldepflicht *f*; **~ retirement** Zwangspensionierung *f* **PL the compulsories** *(Ice-Skating etc)* die Pflicht

compulsory: compulsory purchase N Enteignung *f*; **compulsory purchase order** N Enteignungsbeschluss *m*; **to put a ~ on a place** die Enteignung eines Grundstückes verfügen; **compulsory service** N *(US)* Wehrpflicht *f*

compunction [kəmˈpʌŋkʃən] N *(liter)* Schuldgefühle *pl*, Gewissensbisse *pl*; **without the slightest ~** ohne sich im Geringsten schuldig zu fühlen

computation [ˌkɒmpjʊˈteɪʃən] N Berechnung *f*, Kalkulation *f*

computational [ˌkɒmpjʊˈteɪʃənəl] ADJ Computer-

computational linguistics N *sing* Computerlinguistik *f*

compute [kəmˈpjuːt] VT berechnen (*at* auf *+acc*), errechnen

computer [kəmˈpjuːtəˈ] N Computer *m*, Rechner *m*; *(for data processing also)* Datenverarbeitungsanlage *f*; **to put/have sth on ~** etw im Computer speichern/(gespeichert) haben; **it's all done by ~** das geht alles per Computer; **~ skills** Computerkenntnisse *pl*

computer *in cpds* Computer-; **computer age** N Computerzeitalter *nt*; **computer-aided** ADJ computer- *or* rechnergestützt; **computer-aided design** N CAD *nt*, computergestütztes Design; **computer animation** N Computeranimation *f*; **computer-assisted** N computergestützt

computerate [kəmˈpjuːtərɪt] ADJ **to be ~** sich mit Computern auskennen

computer: computer-based ADJcomputergestützt; **computer code** N Maschinenkode *m*; **computer-controlled** ADJ computergestützt, rechnergesteuert; **computer crash** N Computerabsturz *m*; **computer crime** N Computerkriminalität *f*; **computer dating** N Partnervermittlung *f* per Computer; **~ agency** *or* **bureau** Partnervermittlungsbüro *nt* auf Computerbasis; **computer-designed** ADJ am Computer *or* mit Computerunterstützung entworfen; **computer error** N Computerfehler *m*

computerese [kəmˌpjuːtəˈriːz] N *(inf: = jargon)* Computerjargon *m*

computer: computer expert N Computerexperte *m*/-expertin *f*; **computer freak** N *(inf)* Computerfreak *m (inf)*; **computer game** N Computerspiel *nt*; **computer games software** N Software *f* für Computerspiele; **computer-generated** ADJ *image, graphics* computergeneriert; **computer graphics** N *sing* Computergrafik *f*, grafische Datenverarbeitung

computerization [kəmˈpjuːtəraɪˈzeɪʃən] N *(of information etc)* Computerisierung *f*; **the ~ of the factory** die Umstellung der Fabrik auf Computer

computerize [kəmˈpjuːtəraɪz] VT *information* computerisieren; *company, accounting methods* auf Computer *or* EDV umstellen

computerized axial tomography [kəmˈpjuːtəraɪzd ˈæksɪəl təˈmɒgrəfɪ] N Computertomografie *f*

computer: computer language N Computersprache *f*; **computer literacy** N Computerkenntnisse *pl*; **computer literate** ADJ **to be ~** sich mit Computern auskennen; **computer model** N Computermodell *nt*; **computer nerd** N *(pej inf)* Computerfreak *m (sl)*; **computer network** N Computernetzwerk *nt*; *(larger also)* Rechnerverbund *m*; **computer-operated** ADJ computergesteuert; **computer operator** N Operator(in) *m(f)*; **computer peripheral** N Peripheriegerät *nt*; **computer printout** N (Computer)ausdruck *m*; **computer program** N (Computer)programm *nt*; **computer programmer** N Programmierer(in) *m(f)*; **computer projection** N Hochrechnung *f*; **computer science** N Informatik *f*; **computer scientist** N Informatiker(in) *m(f)*; **computer search** N Suche *f* per Computer; *(in criminal contexts)* Rasterfahndung *f*; **computer sex** N Computersex *m*; **computer skills** PL PC-Kenntnisse *pl*; **computer studies** PL Computerwissenschaft *f*; **computer tomography** N *(Med)* Computertomografie *f*; **computer-typeset** VT in Computersatz herstellen; **computer typesetting** N Computersatz *m*; **computer virus** N Computervirus *m*

computing [kəmˈpjuːtɪŋ] **N** **a** (= *subject*) Computerwissenschaft *f*; **her husband's in ~** ihr Mann ist in der Computerbranche **b** (= *act*) Berechnung *f* **ATTR** *problem, task* rechnerisch; **~ speed** Rechen- *or* Operationsgeschwindigkeit *f*

comrade [ˈkɒmrɪd] N Kamerad *m*; *(Pol)* Genosse *m*, Genossin *f*

comrade-in-arms [ˈkɒmrɪdɪnˈɑːmz] N Waffenbruder *m (old)*, Kriegskamerad *m*

comradely [ˈkɒmrɪdlɪ] ADJ kameradschaftlich

comradeship [ˈkɒmrɪdʃɪp] N Kameradschaft(-lichkeit) *f*; **the spirit of ~** der Kameradschaftsgeist

comsat [ˈkɒmsæt] *abbr of* **communications satellite**

Con *(Pol) abbr of* **Conservative**

con[1] [kɒn] VT *(rare: = learn)* sich *(dat)* einprägen

con[2] ADV N → **pro[3]**

con[3] VT *(Naut)* steuern, lenken

con[4] *(inf)* **N** Schwindel *m*, Beschiss *m (inf)*; **it's a ~!** das ist alles Schwindel *or* Beschiss *(inf)* **VT** hereinlegen *(inf)*, bescheißen *(inf)*; **he ~ned her out of all her money** er hat sie um ihr ganzes Geld gebracht; **to ~ sb into doing sth** jdn durch einen faulen Trick dazu bringen, dass er etw tut *(inf)*; **don't let him ~ you into believing it** lass dir das bloß nicht von ihm aufbinden *(inf)* *or* einreden; **he ~ned his way through the security check** er hat sich durch die Sicherheitskontrolle gemogelt *(inf)*

con[5] *(inf) abbr of* **convict** Knastbruder *m (inf)*

con artist N *(inf)* Schwindler(in) *m(f)*

conc *abbr of* **concessions** Erm.

concatenation [kɒnˌkætɪˈneɪʃən] N Verkettung *f*

concave [ˈkɒnkeɪv] ADJ konkav; *mirror* Konkav-, Hohl-

concavity [kɒnˈkævɪtɪ] N Konkavität *f*

concavo-convex [kɒnˌkeɪvəʊkɒnˈveks] ADJ konkav-konvex

conceal [kənˈsiːl] VT (= *hide*) *object, emotions, thoughts* verbergen; (= *keep secret*) verheimlichen (*sth from sb* jdm etw); **why did they ~ this information from us?** warum hat man uns diese Informationen vorenthalten?; **to ~ the fact that ...** (die Tatsache) verheimlichen, dass ...; **the chameleon was completely ~ed against its background** das Chamäleon war nicht mehr von seiner Umgebung zu unterscheiden

concealed [kənˈsiːld] ADJ verborgen; *lighting, wiring, turning, entrance* verdeckt; *camera* versteckt, Geheim-

concealment [kənˈsiːlmənt] N *(of facts)* Verheimlichung *f*; *(of evidence)* Unterschlagung *f*; *(of criminal)* Gewährung *f* von Unterschlupf (*of an +acc*); **to come out of ~** aus dem Versteck auftauchen; **to stay in ~** sich versteckt halten

concede [kənˈsiːd] **VT** **a** (= *yield, give up*) *privilege* aufgeben; *lands* abtreten (*to* an *+acc*); **to ~ a right to sb** jdm ein Recht überlassen; **to ~ victory to sb** vor jdm kapitulieren; **to ~ a**

match *(= give up)* aufgeben, sich geschlagen geben; *(= lose)* ein Match abgeben; **to ~ a penalty** einen Elfmeter verursachen; **to ~ a point to sb** jdm in einem Punkt recht geben; *(Sport)* einen Punkt an jdn abgeben
b *(= admit, grant)* zugeben, einräumen *(form)*; *privilege* einräumen *(to sb* jdm); *right* zubilligen, zugestehen *(to sb* jdm); **it's generally ~d that ...** es ist allgemein anerkannt, dass ...; **to ~ defeat** sich geschlagen geben
VI nachgeben, kapitulieren

conceit [kən'siːt] **N** **a** *(= pride)* Einbildung *f*; **he's full of ~** er ist schrecklich eingebildet **b** **he is wise in his own ~** *(liter)* er dünkt sich weise *(liter)* **c** *(Liter)* Konzetto *nt*

conceited [kən'siːtɪd] **ADJ** eingebildet

conceitedly [kən'siːtɪdlɪ] **ADV** *say* eingebildet; **he ~ claimed ...** eingebildet wie er ist, hat er behauptet ...

conceitedness [kən'siːtɪdnɪs] **N** Eingebildetheit *f*, Einbildung *f*

conceivable [kən'siːvəbl] **ADJ** denkbar, vorstellbar; **it is hardly ~ that ...** es ist kaum denkbar, dass ..., man kann sich *(dat)* kaum vorstellen, dass ...; **it's not ~ that she would have gone without us** ich kann mir nicht vorstellen, dass sie ohne uns gegangen ist

conceivably [kən'siːvəblɪ] **ADV** **she may ~ be right** es ist durchaus denkbar, dass sie recht hat; **will it happen? – ~** wird das geschehen? – das ist durchaus denkbar

conceive [kən'siːv] **VT** **a** *child* empfangen
b *(= imagine)* sich *(dat)* denken *or* vorstellen; *idea, plan* haben; *novel* die Idee haben zu; **it was originally ~d as quite a different sort of book** ursprünglich war das Buch ganz anders geplant *or* konzipiert *(geh)*; **the idea was ~d in a Paris café** die Idee (dazu) wurde in einem Pariser Café geboren; **the way he ~s his role** seine Vorstellung *or* Auffassung von seiner Rolle; **she ~s it to be her duty** sie erachtet *(geh) or* betrachtet es als ihre Pflicht; **I can't ~ why** ich verstehe *or* begreife nicht, warum
c **to ~ a dislike for sb/sth** eine Abneigung gegen jdn/etw entwickeln; **to ~ a passion for sb/sth** seine Leidenschaft für jdn/etw entdecken
VI *(woman)* empfangen

► **conceive of** **VI** *+prep obj* sich *(dat)* vorstellen; **who first conceived of the idea?** wer hatte die Idee zuerst?, wem kam die Idee zuerst?; **he absolutely refuses to conceive of cheating** Betrug käme ihm überhaupt nicht in den Sinn

concentrate ['kɒnsəntreɪt] **VT** **a** konzentrieren *(on* auf *+acc)*; **to ~ all one's energies on sth** sich (voll und) ganz auf etw *(acc)* konzentrieren; **to ~ one's mind on sth** seine Gedanken *or* sich auf etw *(acc)* konzentrieren; **a spell in prison will certainly ~ his mind** eine Gefängnisstrafe wird ihm sicher zu denken geben; **it's amazing how he's ~d so much material into one novel** es ist erstaunlich, wie viel Material er in einem Roman zusammengedrängt hat
b *(Mil) troops* konzentrieren
c *(Chem)* konzentrieren
VI **a** *(= give one's attention)* sich konzentrieren; **to ~ on doing sth** sich darauf konzentrieren, etw zu tun
b *(people)* sich sammeln; *(troops also)* sich konzentrieren
ADJ *(Chem)* konzentriert
N *(Chem)* Konzentrat *nt*

concentrated ['kɒnsəntreɪtɪd] **ADJ** **a** *liquid, substance* konzentriert; **in a ~ form** in konzentrierter Form; **~ orange juice** Orangensaftkonzentrat *nt* **b** *(= concerted) effort, attack* konzentriert

concentration [ˌkɒnsən'treɪʃən] **N** **a** Konzentration *f*; **powers of ~** Konzentrationsfähigkeit *f* **b** *(= gathering)* Ansammlung *f* **c** *(Chem)* Konzentration *f*

concentration camp **N** Konzentrationslager *nt*, KZ *nt*

concentric [kən'sentrɪk] **ADJ** *circles* konzentrisch

concept ['kɒnsept] **N** Begriff *m*; *(= conception)* Vorstellung *f*; **the ~ of evil** der Begriff des Bösen; **our ~ of the world** unser Weltbild *nt*; **his ~ of marriage** seine Vorstellungen von der Ehe; **the ~ behind the play was good** das Stück war gut konzipiert *(geh)*, das Stück war in der Anlage *or* vom Konzept her gut

concept album **N** *(Mus)* Konzeptalbum *nt*

conception [kən'sepʃən] **N** **a** *(= forming ideas)* Vorstellung *f*
b *(= idea)* Vorstellung *f*; *(= way sth is conceived)* Konzeption *f*; **what's your ~ of the ideal life?** was ist Ihrer Vorstellung nach ein ideales Leben?; **the Buddhist ~ of life/nature/morality** die buddhistische Auffassung vom Leben/Vorstellung von der Natur/Moralvorstellung; **the classical ~ of beauty** das klassische Schönheitsideal; **they have a totally different ~ of justice** sie haben eine völlig unterschiedliche Auffassung *or* Vorstellung von Gerechtigkeit; **in their ~ they are ...** sie sind von der Konzeption her ...; **he has no ~ of how difficult it is** er macht sich *(dat)* keinen Begriff davon *or* er hat keine Vorstellung, wie schwer das ist
c *(of child)* die Empfängnis, die Konzeption *(form)*

conceptual [kən'septjʊəl] **ADJ** *thinking* begrifflich; **is this a ~ possibility?** ist ein solcher Begriff überhaupt denkbar?

conceptual art **N** Conceptart *f*, Konzeptkunst *f*

conceptualism [kən'septjʊəlɪzəm] **N** Konzeptualismus *m*

conceptualization [kənˌseptjʊəlaɪ'zeɪʃən] **N** Begriffsbildung *f*; **the ~ of experience** die begriffliche Erfassung der Erfahrung

conceptualize [kən'septjʊəlaɪz] **VT** in Begriffe fassen **VI** begrifflich denken

conceptually [kən'septjʊəlɪ] **ADV** begrifflich; **X is ~ impossible** X ist begrifflich undenkbar; **it only exists ~** das existiert nur in der Vorstellung

concern [kən'sɜːn] ✪ 26.2 **N** **a** *(= relation, connection)* **do you have any ~ with banking?** haben Sie etwas mit dem Bankwesen zu tun?; **to have no ~ with sth** mit etw nichts zu tun haben
b *(= business, affair)* Angelegenheit(en *pl*) *f*; *(= matter of interest and importance to sb)* Anliegen *nt*; **the day-to-day ~s of government** die täglichen Regierungsgeschäfte; **it's no ~ of his** das geht ihn nichts an; **what ~ is it of yours?** was geht Sie das an?
c *(Comm)* Konzern *m* → **going ADJ c**
d *(= share)* Beteiligung *f*
e *(= anxiety)* Sorge *f*, Besorgnis *f*; **a look of ~** ein besorgter *or* sorgenvoller Blick; **the situation in the Middle East is causing ~** die Lage im Nahen Osten ist besorgniserregend; **there's some/no cause for ~** es besteht Grund/kein Grund zur Sorge; **to do sth out of ~ for sb** etw aus Sorge um jdn tun; **he showed great ~ for your safety** er war *or* zeigte sich *(geh)* sehr um Ihre Sicherheit besorgt; **don't you feel any ~ for the starving millions?** berührt Sie die Tatsache, dass Millionen am Verhungern sind, überhaupt nicht?
f *(= importance)* Bedeutung *f*; **a matter of great ~** eine Angelegenheit von immenser Bedeutung; **issues of national ~** Fragen *pl* von nationalem Interesse; **to be of little/great ~ to sb** jdm nicht/sehr wichtig sein
VT **a** *(= be about)* handeln von; **it ~s the following issue** es geht um die folgende Frage; **the last chapter is ~ed with ...** das letzte Kapitel behandelt ...
b *(= be the business of, involve)* angehen, betreffen; *(= affect)* betreffen; **that doesn't ~ you** das betrifft Sie nicht; *(as snub)* das geht Sie nichts an; **to whom it may ~** *(on certificate)* Bestätigung *f*; *(on reference)* Zeugnis *nt*; **the countries ~ed with oil production** die Länder, die mit der Ölproduktion zu tun haben; **where money/honour is ~ed** wenn es um Geld/die Ehre geht; **as far as the money is ~ed** was das Geld betrifft *or* angeht; **is it important? – not as far as I'm ~ed** ist es denn wichtig? – was mich betrifft nicht; **as far as he is ~ed it's just another job, but ...** für ihn ist es nur ein anderer Job, aber ...; **as far as I'm ~ed you can do what you like** von mir aus kannst du tun und lassen, was du willst; **where we are ~ed** wo es um uns geht; *(= in so far as we are affected)* wo wir betroffen sind; **the department ~ed** *(= relevant)* die zuständige Abteilung; *(= involved)* die betreffende Abteilung; **who are the people ~ed in this report?** wer sind die Leute, um die es in diesem Bericht geht?; **the persons ~ed** die Betroffenen, die betroffenen Personen; **my brother is the most closely ~ed** mein Bruder ist am meisten davon betroffen; **the men ~ed in the robbery** die in den Überfall verwickelten Männer
c *(= interest)* **he is only ~ed with facts** ihn interessieren nur die Fakten; *(= is only dealing with)* ihm geht es nur um die Fakten; **to ~ oneself with** *or* **about sth** sich für etw interessieren; **I'm not ~ed now** *or* **I don't want to ~ myself now with the economic aspect of the problem** mir geht es jetzt nicht um den ökonomischen Aspekt des Problems
d *(= have at heart)* **we should be ~ed more with** *or* **about quality** Qualität sollte uns ein größeres Anliegen sein; **a mother is naturally ~ed about the wellbeing of her children** das Wohl ihrer Kinder ist einer Mutter natürlich ein Anliegen; **he's not at all ~ed with** *or* **about her well-being** ihr Wohl kümmert ihn überhaupt nicht; **he's not at all ~ed with** *or* **about her wellbeing** ihr Wohl kümmert ihn überhaupt nicht; **there's no need for you to ~ yourself about that** darum brauchen Sie sich nicht zu kümmern
e *(= worry: usu pass)* **to be ~ed about sth** sich *(dat)* um etw Sorgen machen, um etw besorgt sein; **I was very ~ed to hear about your illness** ich habe mir Sorgen gemacht, als ich von Ihrer Krankheit hörte; **he was ~ed by the news** die Nachricht beunruhigte ihn; **don't ~ yourself** machen Sie sich keine Sorgen; **I was very ~ed about** *or* **for your safety** ich war sehr um Ihre Sicherheit besorgt; **I am ~ed to hear that ...** es beunruhigt mich, dass ...; **~ed parents** besorgte Eltern; **a ~ed look** ein besorgter Blick

concerning [kən'sɜːnɪŋ] **PREP** bezüglich, hinsichtlich, betreffs *(form)* *(all +gen)*; **~ your request ...** apropos Ihrer Anfrage ..., was Ihre Anfrage betrifft ...; **~ what?** worüber?

concert[1] ['kɒnsət] **N** **a** *(Mus)* Konzert *nt*; **were you at the ~?** waren Sie in dem Konzert?; **Madonna in ~** Madonna live **b** *(of voices etc)* **in ~** im Chor, gemeinsam **c** *(fig)* **in ~** gemeinsam; **to work in ~ with sb** mit jdm zusammenarbeiten

concert[2] [kən'sɜːt] **VT** *efforts* vereinen

concerted [kən'sɜːtɪd] **ADJ** *efforts, action, attack* gemeinsam, konzertiert *(esp Pol)*; **with their ~ efforts ...** mit vereinten Kräften ...; **to take ~ action** gemeinsam vorgehen; **to make a ~ attack** gemeinsam *or* geballt angreifen

concert: **concertgoer** **N** Konzertbesucher(in) *m(f) or* -gänger(in) *m(f)*; **concert grand** **N** Konzertflügel *m*; **concert hall** **N** Konzerthalle *f or* -saal *m*

concertina [ˌkɒnsə'tiːnə] **N** Konzertina *f* **VI** sich wie eine Ziehharmonika zusammenschieben

concertmaster ['kɒnsətmæstə'] **N** *(US)* Konzertmeister *m*

concerto [kən'tʃɜːtəʊ] **N** Konzert *nt*, Concerto *nt*

concert: **concert performer** **N** Konzertkünstler(in) *m(f)*; **concert pianist** **N** Pianist(in) *m(f)*; **concert pitch** **N** Kammerton *m*; **concert tour** **N** Konzerttournee *f*

concession [kən'seʃən] **N** Zugeständnis *nt*, Konzession *f* *(to* an *+acc)*; *(Comm)* Konzession *f*; **to make ~s to sb** jdm Konzessionen *or* Zugeständnisse machen

concessionaire [kənˌseʃə'nɛə'] **N** *(Comm)* Konzessionär *m*

concessionary [kən'seʃənərɪ] ADJ *(Comm)* Konzessions-; *(= reduced) rates, fares* verbilligt

concessive [kən'sesɪv] ADJ *(Gram)* konzessiv, Konzessiv-

conch [kɒntʃ] N *große, spiralige Meeresschnecke (used as trumpet)* Trompetenschnecke *f*, Tritonshorn *nt (also Myth)*

conchy ['kɒntʃɪ] N *(pej sl)* Kriegsdienstverweigerer *m*, Drückeberger *m (pej inf)*

concierge ['kɒnsɪɜ:ʒ] N Portier *m*, Portiersfrau *f*

conciliate [kən'sɪlɪeɪt] VT **a** *(= placate)* besänftigen; *(= win the goodwill of) person* versöhnlich stimmen **b** *(= reconcile) opposing views* auf einen Nenner bringen, in Einklang bringen

conciliation [kən,sɪlɪ'eɪʃən] N **a** *(= resolution: of dispute, differences, Pol, Ind)* Schlichtung *f*; **~ board** Schlichtungskommission *f*; **~ procedure** *(Jur)* Güteverfahren *nt*; **~ proceedings** *(Jur: = hearing)* Gütetermin *m* **b** *(= appeasement: of person)* Besänftigung *f*

conciliator [kən'sɪlɪeɪtə'] N Vermittler(in) *m(f)*

conciliatory [kən'sɪlɪətərɪ] ADJ *(= intended to reconcile)* versöhnlich; *(= placatory)* beschwichtigend, besänftigend

concise [kən'saɪs] ADJ präzis(e), exakt; **~ dictionary** Handwörterbuch *nt*

concisely [kən'saɪslɪ] ADV präzis(e), exakt

conciseness [kən'saɪsnɪs], **concision** [kən'sɪʒən] N Präzision *f*, Exaktheit *f*

conclave ['kɒnkleɪv] N **a** Klausur *f*; **in ~** in Klausur; **to meet in ~** eine Klausurtagung abhalten **b** *(Eccl)* Konklave *nt*

conclude [kən'klu:d] ✪ 26.1 VT **a** *(= end) meeting, letter, speech* beenden, schließen; *meal* abschließen, beenden; **this, gentlemen, ~s our business** damit, meine Herren, sind wir mit unserer Besprechung am Ende; **and now, to ~ tonight's programmes** zum Abschluss unseres heutigen Abendprogramms
b *(= arrange) treaty, transaction, deal* abschließen
c *(= infer)* schließen, folgern *(from* aus); **what did you ~?** was haben Sie daraus geschlossen *or* gefolgert?
d *(= decide, come to conclusion)* zu dem Schluss kommen; **what have you ~d about his suggestion?** zu welchem Schluss sind Sie in Bezug auf seinen Vorschlag gekommen?
VI *(meetings, events)* enden; *(letter, speech etc also)* schließen; **to ~ I would like to say …, I would like to ~ by saying …** abschließend möchte ich sagen …

concluding [kən'klu:dɪŋ] ADJ *remarks, words* abschließend, Schluss-; **~ bars/lines** Schlusstakte/-zeilen *pl*; **the ~ stages of the tournament** die letzten Durchgänge des Turniers

conclusion [kən'klu:ʒən] ✪ 26.1, 26.3 N **a** *(= end)* Abschluss *m*; *(of essay, novel etc)* Schluss *m*; **in ~** zum (Ab)schluss, abschließend **b** *(= settling: of treaty etc)* Abschluss *m*, Zustandekommen *nt* **c** Schluss(folgerung *f*) *m*; **what ~ do you draw** *or* **reach from all this?** welchen Schluss *or* welche Schlussfolgerung ziehen Sie daraus *or* aus alldem?; **let me know your ~s** lassen Sie mich wissen, zu welchem Schluss Sie gekommen sind; **a hasty ~** ein voreiliger Schluss; **one is forced to the ~ that …** man kommt unweigerlich zu dem Schluss, dass …
d *(Logic)* Folgerung *f*

conclusive [kən'klu:sɪv] ADJ *(= convincing)* schlüssig, überzeugend; *(= decisive, final)* endgültig; *(Jur) evidence* einschlägig; *proof* schlüssig, eindeutig

conclusively [kən'klu:sɪvlɪ] ADV *(= convincingly)* schlüssig, überzeugend; *(= decisively)* endgültig; *prove* eindeutig, unwiderleglich; **this settles this issue ~** damit ist die Sache endgültig beigelegt

concoct [kən'kɒkt] VT **a** *(Cook etc)* zusammenstellen, (zu)bereiten; *(hum)* kreieren, zurechtzaubern **b** *(fig)* sich *(dat)* zurechtlegen; *scheme, plan also* ausbrüten *or* -hecken; *excuse also* sich *(dat)* ausdenken; *new dress, hat* zaubern

concoction [kən'kɒkʃən] N **a** *(= food)* Kreation *f*, Zusammenstellung *f*; *(= drink)* Gebräu *nt*; **one of her little ~s** eines ihrer Spezialrezepte **b** *(= story etc)* Erdichtung *f*; *(Fashion)* Zauberei *f*, Spielerei *f*; **the plot is an amazing ~ of bizarre events** der Plot ist eine erstaunliche Verkettung der merkwürdigsten Ereignisse

concomitant [kən'kɒmɪtənt] ADJ **to be ~ with sth** von etw begleitet werden N Begleiterscheinung *f*

concord ['kɒŋkɔ:d] N *(= harmony)* Eintracht *f*; *(about decision etc)* Einvernehmen *nt*, Übereinstimmung *f*

concordance [kən'kɔ:dəns] N **a** *(= agreement)* Übereinstimmung *f*; **in ~ with your specifications** *(form)* Ihren Angaben *or* Anweisungen gemäß **b** *(Bibl, Liter)* Konkordanz *f*

concordant [kən'kɔ:dənt] ADJ *(form)* übereinstimmend; **to be ~ with** entsprechen *(+dat)*

concordat [kɒn'kɔ:dæt] N Konkordat *nt*

concourse ['kɒŋkɔ:s] N **a** *(liter, of people)* Menschenmenge *f*, Menschenauflauf *m*; *(of two rivers)* Zusammenfluss *m* **b** *(= place)* Eingangshalle *f*; *(US, in park)* freier Platz; **station ~** Bahnhofshalle *f*

concrete[1] ['kɒŋkri:t] ADJ *object, evidence, example, proposals, measures* konkret; **a chair is a ~ object** ein Stuhl ist gegenständlich *or* etwas Gegenständliches; **could you put your argument in a more ~ form?** könnten Sie etwas konkreter werden?

concrete[2] N *(Build)* Beton *m*; **nothing is set** *or* **embedded in ~ yet** *(fig)* es ist noch nichts definitiv festgelegt ADJ Beton- VT *wall, floor* betonieren

concretely [kən'kri:tlɪ] ADV konkret; **to express sth ~/more ~** etw konkretisieren/konkreter ausdrücken

concrete: **concrete mixer** N Betonmischmaschine *f*; **concrete music** N konkrete Musik; **concrete noun** N Konkretum *nt*; **concrete poetry** N Bilderlyrik *f*

concretion [kən'kri:ʃən] N *(= coalescence)* Verschmelzung *f*; *(Geol also)* Konkretion *f*; *(Med)* Konkrement *nt*

concubine ['kɒŋkjʊbaɪn] N **a** *(old)* Konkubine *f*, Mätresse *f* **b** *(in polygamy)* Konkubine *f*, Nebenfrau *f*

concupiscence [kən'kju:pɪsəns] N Lüsternheit *f*

concupiscent [kən'kju:pɪsənt] ADJ lüstern

concur [kən'kɜ:'] VI **a** *(= agree)* übereinstimmen; *(with a suggestion etc)* beipflichten *(with +dat)*; *(Math)* zusammenlaufen; **John and I ~red** John und ich waren einer Meinung; **I ~ with that** ich pflichte dem bei **b** *(= happen together)* zusammentreffen, auf einmal eintreten

concurrence [kən'kʌrəns] N **a** *(= accordance)* Übereinstimmung *f*; *(= agreement, permission)* Einverständnis *nt*, Zustimmung *f* **b** *(of events)* Zusammentreffen *nt* **c** *(Math)* Schnittpunkt *m*; **at the ~ of the two lines** im Schnittpunkt der beiden Geraden

concurrent [kən'kʌrənt] ADJ **a** *(= occurring at the same time)* gleichzeitig; **to be ~ with sth** mit etw zusammentreffen, zur gleichen Zeit wie etw stattfinden **b** *(= acting together)* vereint, gemeinsam **c** *(= in agreement)* übereinstimmend; *interpretation, statement also* gleichlautend; **to be ~ with sth** mit etw übereinstimmen **d** *(Math)* zusammenlaufend; *(= intersecting)* sich schneidend

concurrently [kən'kʌrəntlɪ] ADV gleichzeitig; **the two sentences to run ~** *(Jur)* unter gleichzeitigem Vollzug beider Freiheitsstrafen

concuss [kən'kʌs] VT *(usu pass)* **to be ~ed** eine Gehirnerschütterung haben

concussion [kən'kʌʃən] N Gehirnerschütterung *f*

condemn [kən'dem] ✪ 26.3 VT **a** *(= censure)* verurteilen
b *(Jur: = sentence)* verurteilen; **to ~ sb to death/10 years' imprisonment** jdn zum Tode/zu 10 Jahren Gefängnis verurteilen; **the ~ed man** der zum Tode Verurteilte; **the ~ed cell** die Todeszelle
c *(fig)* verdammen, verurteilen *(to* zu)
d *(= declare unfit) building, slums* für abbruchreif erklären; *ship* für nicht mehr seetüchtig erklären; **these houses are/should be ~ed** diese Häuser stehen auf der Abrissliste/sollten abgerissen werden; **the fruit was ~ed as unfit for consumption** das Obst wurde für den Verzehr ungeeignet erklärt
e *(US Jur)* beschlagnahmen; *land* enteignen

condemnation [,kɒndem'neɪʃən] ✪ 14 N **a** Verurteilung *f*; *(fig also)* Verdammung *f*; **what a ~** was für ein Armutszeugnis **b** *(of slums, ship)* Kondemnation *f (spec)*; **the new council was responsible for the immediate ~ of some of the old city slums** die neue Stadtverwaltung war dafür verantwortlich, dass einige der alten Slums sofort auf die Abrissliste kamen **c** *(US Jur)* Beschlagnahme *f*; *(of land)* Enteignung *f*

condemnatory [kɒndem'neɪtərɪ] ADJ aburteilend; *frown* missbilligend; *criticism* verdammend; *conclusion* vernichtend

condensation [,kɒnden'seɪʃən] N **a** *(of vapour)* Kondensation *f*; *(= liquid formed)* Kondensat *nt*; *(on window panes etc)* Kondenswasser *nt*; **the windows/walls are covered with ~** die Fenster/Wände sind beschlagen **b** *(= short form)* Kurzfassung *f*; *(= act)* Kondensierung *f*, Zusammenfassung *f*

condense [kən'dens] VT **a** *(= reduce)* kondensieren **b** *(Phys) gas* kondensieren; *(= compress)* verdichten; *rays* bündeln **c** *(= shorten)* zusammenfassen; **in a very ~d form** in sehr gedrängter Form VI *(gas)* kondensieren, sich niederschlagen

condensed milk [kən'denst'mɪlk] N Kondensmilch *f*, Büchsen- *or* Dosenmilch *f*

condenser [kən'densə'] N *(Elec, Phys)* Kondensator *m*; *(Opt)* Kondensor *m*, Sammellinse *f*

condescend [,kɒndɪ'send] VI **a** *(= stoop)* sich herab- *or* herbeilassen; **to ~ to do sth** sich herab- *or* herbeilassen, etw zu tun, geruhen *(geh, iro) or* so gnädig sein, etw zu tun **b to ~ to sb** jdn herablassend behandeln; **he doesn't like being ~ed to** er lässt sich nicht gerne von oben herab behandeln

condescending [,kɒndɪ'sendɪŋ] ADJ *(pej)* herablassend, von oben herab *pred*; **to be ~ to** *or* **toward(s) sb** jdn von oben herab *or* herablassend behandeln

condescendingly [,kɒndɪ'sendɪŋlɪ] ADV *(pej)* herablassend, von oben herab

condescension [,kɒndɪ'senʃən] N *(pej)* Herablassung *f*; *(= attitude also)* herablassende Haltung

condiment ['kɒndɪmənt] N Würze *f*

condition [kən'dɪʃən] N **a** *(= determining factor)* Bedingung *f (also Jur, Comm)*; *(= prerequisite)* Voraussetzung *f*; **~s of sale** Verkaufsbedingungen *pl*; **on ~ that …** unter der Bedingung *or* Voraussetzung, dass …; **on one/this ~** unter einer/der Bedingung *or* Voraussetzung; **on what ~?** zu welchen Bedingungen?, unter welchen Voraussetzungen?; **on no ~** auf keinen Fall; **to make ~s** Bedingungen stellen; **he made it a ~ that …** er machte es zur Bedingung, dass …
b conditions PL *(= circumstances)* Verhältnisse *pl*, Zustände *pl (pej)*; **working ~s** Arbeitsbedingungen *pl*; **living ~s** Wohnverhältnisse *pl*; **weather ~s** die Wetterlage; **in** *or* **under (the) present ~s** bei den derzeitigen Verhältnissen
c *no pl (= state)* Zustand *m*; **he is in good/bad ~** er ist in guter/schlechter Verfassung; **it is in good/bad ~** es ist in gutem/schlechtem Zustand; **not in your ~!** nicht in deinem Zustand!; **he is in a critical ~** sein Zustand ist kritisch; **he is in no ~ to make the journey** er ist nicht reisefähig; **the car is in no ~ to make such a long journey** so wie das Auto ist, kann man damit keine Reise machen; **you're in no ~ to drive** du

bist nicht mehr fahrtüchtig; **to be in/out of ~** eine gute/keine Kondition haben; **to keep in/get into ~** in Form bleiben/kommen; *(Sport also)* seine Kondition beibehalten/sich *(dat)* eine gute Kondition antrainieren; **in an interesting ~** *(dated hum inf)* in anderen Umständen; **to change one's ~** *(old)* sich verehelichen *(dated)*; **the human ~** die Situation des Menschen *or* der Menschen

d *(Med)* Beschwerden *pl*; **heart/thyroid ~** Herz-/Schilddrüsenleiden *nt*; **he has a heart ~** er ist herzkrank

e *(old: = rank)* Stand *m*, Schicht *f*; **in every ~ of life** aus allen Ständen

VT **a** *(esp pass: = determine)* bedingen, bestimmen; **to be ~ed by** bedingt sein durch, abhängen von

b *(= bring into good condition) hair, athlete, animal* in Form bringen; **~ing powder** Aufbaumittel *nt*

c *(Psych etc: = train)* konditionieren; *(= accustom)* gewöhnen; **they have become ~ed to believe it** sie sind so konditioniert, dass sie es glauben; **~ed reflex** *or* **response** bedingter Reflex

conditional [kən'dɪʃənl] **ADJ** **a** mit Vorbehalt, bedingt, vorbehaltlich; *(Comm, Jur) sale* mit Auflagen; **a ~ yes** ein Ja mit Vorbehalt; **to be ~ (up)on sth** von etw abhängen **b** *(Gram)* konditional, Konditional-, Bedingungs-; **the ~ mood/tense** der Konditional **N** *(Gram)* Konditional *m*

conditional access **N** *(TV)* Empfang *m* nur für Abonnenten

conditional discharge **N** *(Jur)* Entlassung *f* auf Bewährung

conditionally [kən'dɪʃnəlɪ] **ADV** unter *or* mit Vorbehalt

conditioner [kən'dɪʃənəʳ] **N** *(for hair)* Pflegespülung *f*; *(for washing)* Weichspüler *m*

conditioning shampoo [kən'dɪʃənɪŋʃæm'puː] **N** Pflegeshampoo *nt*

condo ['kɒndəʊ] **N** *(US inf)* = **condominium**

condole [kən'dəʊl] **VI** **to ~ with sb (on** *or* **upon sth)** jdm (zu etw) sein Mitgefühl aussprechen; *(on death also)* jdm (zu etw) kondolieren

condolence [kən'dəʊləns] **N** Beileid *nt no pl*, Anteilnahme *f*, Kondolenz *f no pl (pej)*; **message/letter of ~** Kondolenzbotschaft *f*/-brief *m*; **book of ~(s)** Kondolenzbuch *nt*; **please accept my ~s on the death of your mother** (meine) aufrichtige Anteilnahme zum Tode Ihrer Mutter

condom ['kɒndɒm] **N** Kondom *nt or m*, Präservativ *nt*

condominium ['kɒndə'mɪnɪəm] **N** **a** *(Pol)* Kondominium *nt*; *(= rule also)* Kondominat *nt* **b** *(US: = apartment house)* ≈ Haus *nt* mit Eigentumswohnungen, Eigentumsblock *m*; *(= single apartment)* ≈ Eigentumswohnung *f*

condone [kən'dəʊn] **VT** *(= overlook)* (stillschweigend) hinwegsehen über *(+acc)*; *(= approve)* (stillschweigend) dulden

condor ['kɒndɔːʳ] **N** Kondor *m*

conduce [kən'djuːs] **VI** **to ~ to** *(form)* förderlich sein *(+dat)*

conducive [kən'djuːsɪv] **ADJ** förderlich, dienlich *(to +dat)*

conduct ['kɒndʌkt] **N** **a** *(= behaviour)* Verhalten *nt*, Benehmen *nt (towards* gegenüber); *(of children also)* Betragen *nt*; *(of prisoner)* Führung *f*; **the rules of ~** die Verhaltensregeln

b *(= management)* Führung *f*; *(of conference, commission of inquiry)* Leitung *f*; *(of investigation)* Durchführung *f*; **his ~ of the war** seine Kriegsführung; **their ~ of the campaign** die Art, wie sie die Kampagne durchführen/durchgeführt haben

VT [kən'dʌkt] **a** *(= guide)* führen; *(ceremoniously)* geleiten *(geh)*; **~ed tour (of)** *(of country)* Gesellschaftsreise *f* (durch); *(of building)* Führung *f* (durch)

b *(= direct, manage) war, campaign, correspondence, conversation* führen; *meeting, business also* leiten; *investigation* durchführen; *private affairs* handhaben; **he ~ed his own defence** er übernahm seine eigene Verteidigung

c *(Mus)* dirigieren

d *(Phys, Physiol)* leiten; *lightning* ableiten, erden

VI [kən'dʌkt] **a** *(Mus)* dirigieren

b *(Phys)* leiten

VR [kən'dʌkt] sich verhalten, sich benehmen; *(prisoner)* sich führen; **her husband ~ed himself abominably** ihr Mann führte sich unmöglich auf

conductible [kən'dʌktɪbl] **ADJ** *(Phys)* leitfähig

conduction [kən'dʌkʃən] **N** *(Phys, Physiol)* Leitung *f (along* durch *or (Physiol)* entlang)

conductive [ˌkɒn'dʌktɪv] **ADJ** leitfähig, leitend

conductivity [ˌkɒndʌk'tɪvɪtɪ] **N** *(Phys, Physiol)* Leitfähigkeit *f*

conductor [kən'dʌktəʳ] **N** **a** *(Mus)* Dirigent(in) *m(f)*; *(of choir also)* Leiter(in) *m(f)* **b** *(= bus, tram conductor)* Schaffner *m*; *(US Rail: = guard)* Zugführer *m* **c** *(Phys)* Leiter *m*; *(= lightning conductor)* Blitzableiter *m*

conductor rail **N** (Fahr)leitung(sschiene) *f*

conductress [kən'dʌktrɪs] **N** *(on bus etc)* Schaffnerin *f*

conduct sheet ['kɒndʌkt-] **N** *(Mil)* militärische Beurteilung

conduit ['kɒndɪt] **N** Leitungsrohr *nt*; *(Elec)* Rohrkabel *nt*

cone [kəʊn] **N** **a** Kegel *m*; *(Geol: of volcano)* (Berg)kegel *m*; *(= storm cone)* Windsack *m*; *(= traffic cone)* Pylon *m (form)*, Leitkegel *m*; *(Space: = nose cone)* Nase *f*; **a ~ of light** ein Lichtkegel *m* **b** *(Bot)* Zapfen *m* **c** *(= ice-cream cone)* (Eis)tüte *f*

▶ **cone off** **VT** *sep* mit Pylonen absperren

cone-shaped ['kəʊn'ʃeɪpt] **ADJ** kegelförmig

cone sugar **N** Hutzucker *m*

coney **N** = **cony**

confab ['kɒnfæb] **N** *(inf)* kleine Besprechung; **we'd better have a quick ~** wir bekakeln das am besten mal schnell *(inf)*

confection [kən'fekʃən] **N** **a** *(= sweets)* Konfekt *nt*, Zucker- *or* Naschwerk *nt (old)* **b** *(Comm: = item of ladies' clothing)* modischer Artikel; **a charming little ~ from Dior** eine bezaubernde kleine Kreation von Dior

confectioner [kən'fekʃənəʳ] **N** *(= maker)* Konditor *m*, Zuckerbäcker *m (old)*; *(= seller also)* Süßwarenverkäufer(in) *m(f)*; **~'s (shop)** Süßwarenladen *m*

confectioner's custard [kən'fekʃənəz-] **N** Puddingmasse *f*

confectioner's sugar **N** *(US)* Puderzucker *m*

confectionery [kən'fekʃənərɪ] **N** Konditorwaren *pl*, Süßwaren *pl*; *(= chocolates)* Konfekt *nt*

confederacy [kən'fedərəsɪ] **N** *(Pol: = confederation)* Bündnis *nt*; *(of nations)* Staatenbund *m*, Konföderation *f*; **the Confederacy** *(US Hist)* die Konföderierten Staaten von Amerika

confederate [kən'fedərɪt] **ADJ** *system* konföderiert; *nations also* verbündet; **the Confederate States** *(US Hist)* die Konföderierten Staaten von Amerika **N** *(Pol: = ally)* Verbündete(r) *m*, Bündnispartner *m*, Bundesgenosse *m*; *(pej: = accomplice)* Komplize *m (pej)*; **the Confederates** *(US Hist)* die Konföderierten *pl*

confederation [kənˌfedə'reɪʃən] **N** **a** *(Pol) (= alliance)* Bündnis *nt*, Bund *m*; *(= system of government)* Staatenbund *m*, Konföderation *f*; **the Swiss Confederation** die Schweizerische Eidgenossenschaft **b** *(= association)* Bund *m*; **Confederation of British Industry** Verband *m* der britischen Industrie

confer [kən'fɜːʳ] **VT** *(on, upon sb* jdm) *title, degree* verleihen; *power also* übertragen **VI** sich beraten, konferieren *(geh)*

conference ['kɒnfərəns] **N** **a** Konferenz *f*; *(more informal)* Besprechung *f*; **to be in a ~ (with)** eine Besprechung *or* Unterredung haben (mit); **to get round the ~ table** sich an den Konferenztisch setzen; **to get sb to the ~ table** jdn an den Konferenztisch bringen; **I'm sorry, he's in ~** tut mir leid, er ist in *or* bei einer Konferenz/Besprechung **b** *(= convention)* Konferenz *f*, Tagung *f*

conference call **N** *(Telec)* Konferenzschaltung *f*

conference room **N** Konferenzzimmer *nt*

conferencing ['kɒnfərənsɪŋ] **N** *(Telec)* Konferenzschaltungen *pl*

conferment [kən'fɜːmənt], **conferral** [kən'fɜːrəl] **N** *(of title, degree)* Verleihung *f*

conferrable [kən'fɜːrəbl] **ADJ** übertragbar

confess [kən'fes] **VT** **a** *(= acknowledge)* gestehen, zugeben; *ignorance, mistake also* bekennen, beichten *(hum inf)* **b** *(Eccl) sins* bekennen; *(to priest)* beichten; *(priest) penitent* die Beichte abnehmen *(+dat)* **VI** **a** *(= admit)* gestehen *(to +acc)*; **to ~ to sth** etw gestehen, sich zu etw bekennen; **if you did it, you might as well ~** wenn du es warst, warum gestehst du es (dann) nicht? **b** *(Eccl)* beichten; **to ~ to sb/to sth** jdm/etw *(acc)* beichten

confessed [kən'fest] **ADJ** *(= admitted) plan* zugegeben, erklärt, eingestanden; *(= having confessed) criminal* geständig; *(= self-confessed) revolutionary* erklärt; *alcoholic, criminal* eigenen Eingeständnisses, nach eigenen Angaben

confessedly [kən'fesɪdlɪ] **ADV** zugegebenermaßen

confession [kən'feʃən] **N** **a** *(= admission)* Eingeständnis *nt*; *(of guilt, crime etc)* Geständnis *nt*; **on his own ~** laut eigener Aussage; **to make a full ~ of sth to sb** *(Jur also)* jdm ein volles Geständnis einer Sache *(gen)* ablegen; **I have a ~ to make** ich muss dir etwas beichten *(inf) or* gestehen; *(Jur)* ich möchte ein Geständnis ablegen; **"confessions of a ... "** „Bekenntnisse eines/einer ...“; **~ magazine** Zeitschrift *f* mit Geschichten, die das Leben schrieb

b *(Eccl: of sins)* Beichte *f*, (Schuld- *or* Sünden)bekenntnis *nt*; **general ~** allgemeines Sündenbekenntnis; **~ of faith** Glaubensbekenntnis *nt*; **to make one's ~** seine Sünden bekennen; **to hear ~** (die) Beichte hören

c *(= faith)* (Glaubens)bekenntnis *nt*, Konfession *f*; **what ~ are you?** welche Konfession *or* Glaubenszugehörigkeit haben Sie?

confessional [kən'feʃənl] **N** Beichtstuhl *m*; **the secrecy of the ~** das Beichtgeheimnis

confessor [kən'fesəʳ] **N** **a** *(Eccl)* Beichtvater *m* **b** **Edward the Confessor** Edward der Bekenner

confetti [kən'fetiː] **N** *no pl* Konfetti *nt*

confidant [ˌkɒnfɪ'dænt] **N** Vertraute(r) *m*

confidante [ˌkɒnfɪ'dænt] **N** Vertraute *f*

confide [kən'faɪd] **VT** anvertrauen *(to sb* jdm)

▶ **confide in** **VI** *+prep obj* **a** *(= tell secrets to)* sich anvertrauen *(+dat)*; **to confide in sb about sth** jdm etw anvertrauen **b** *(old: = trust)* sein Vertrauen setzen in *(+acc)*, bauen auf *(+acc)*

confidence ['kɒnfɪdəns] ✪ 19.4 **N** **a** *(= trust)* Vertrauen *nt*; *(in sb's abilities also)* Zutrauen *nt (in* zu); *(= confident expectation)* Zuversicht *f*; **to have (every/no) ~ in sb/sth** (volles/kein) Vertrauen zu jdm/etw haben *or* in jdn/etw setzen; **they have no ~ in his ability/the future** sie haben kein Vertrauen *or* Zutrauen zu seinen Fähigkeiten/kein Vertrauen in die Zukunft; **I have every ~ that ...** ich bin ganz zuversichtlich, dass ...; **to put one's ~ in sb/sth** auf jdn/etw bauen, sich auf jdn/etw verlassen; **I wish I had your ~** ich wünschte, ich hätte deine Zuversicht(lichkeit); **we look with ~ ...** wir schauen zuversichtlich ...; **can you leave your car here with ~?** kann man hier sein Auto beruhigt abstellen?; **he talked with ~ on the subject** er äußerte sich sehr kompetent zu dem Thema; **I can't talk with any ~ about ...** ich kann nichts Bestimmtes über *(+acc)* ... sagen; **in the full ~ that ...** im festen Vertrauen darauf, dass ...; **issue of ~** *(Parl)* Vertrauensfrage *f*; **to give a vote**

of ~ *(Parl)* das Vertrauen aussprechen; **to ask for a vote of ~** *(Parl)* die Vertrauensfrage stellen; **motion/vote of no ~** Misstrauensantrag *m*/-votum *nt*
b *(= self-confidence)* (Selbst)vertrauen *nt*, Selbstsicherheit *f*
c *(= confidential relationship)* Vertrauen *nt*; **in (strict) ~** (streng) vertraulich; **to take sb into one's ~** jdn ins Vertrauen ziehen; **to be in** *or* **enjoy sb's ~** jds Vertrauen besitzen *or* genießen
d *(= information confided)* vertrauliche Mitteilung

confidence: **confidence building** N Vertrauensbildung *f*; **confidence-building** ADJ vertrauensbildend; **confidence trick** N = **con trick**; **confidence trickster** N = **con man**

confident ['kɒnfɪdənt] ADJ **a** *(= sure)* überzeugt, zuversichtlich *(of +gen)*; *look etc* zuversichtlich; **to be ~ of success** *or* **succeeding** vom Erfolg überzeugt sein, zuversichtlich *or* überzeugt sein, dass man gewinnt; **to be/feel ~ about sth** in Bezug auf etw zuversichtlich sein; **it will happen – are you ~?** es wird geschehen – sind Sie davon überzeugt *or* dessen sicher?; **to be ~ in sb/sth** Vertrauen zu jdm/etw haben, jdm/einer Sache vertrauen; **~ in her love** ihrer Liebe gewiss *(geh)* **b** *(= self-assured)* (selbst)sicher; **to be in a ~ mood** sich seiner sicher fühlen

confidential [ˌkɒnfɪ'denʃəl] ADJ **a** *information, whisper* vertraulich; **to treat sth as ~** etw vertraulich behandeln; **to keep sth ~** etw für sich behalten **b** *(= enjoying sb's confidence)* **~ secretary** Privatsekretär(in) *m(f)*; **~ agent** Sonderbeauftragte(r) *mf* mit geheimer Mission **c** *(= inclined to confide)* vertrauensselig

confidentiality [ˌkɒnfɪˌdenʃɪ'ælɪtɪ] N Vertraulichkeit *f*

confidentially [ˌkɒnfɪ'denʃəlɪ] ADV vertraulich, im Vertrauen

confidently ['kɒnfɪdəntlɪ] ADV **a** zuversichtlich; *look forward also* vertrauensvoll **b** *(= self-confidently)* selbstsicher; *(= with conviction)* mit Überzeugung

confiding [kən'faɪdɪŋ] ADJ vertraulich; **he's not a ~ sort of person** er vertraut sich keinem an

confidingly [kən'faɪdɪŋlɪ] ADV vertraulich

configuration [kənˌfɪgjʊ'reɪʃən] N Konfiguration *f (form)*; *(Geog)* Form *f*, Gestalt *f*; *(Sci)* Struktur *f*, Aufbau *m*; *(Astron)* Anordnung *f*, Aspekt *m (spec)*; *(Comput)* Konfiguration *f*

configure [kən'fɪgəʳ] VT *(Comput)* konfigurieren

confine [kən'faɪn] VT **a** *(= keep in) person, animal* (ein)sperren; *flood* eindämmen; **to be ~d to the house** nicht aus dem Haus können; **to be ~d to barracks/one's room** Kasernen-/Stubenarrest *m* haben
b *(= limit) remarks* beschränken *(to* auf *+acc)*; **to ~ oneself to doing sth** sich darauf beschränken, etw zu tun; **the damage was ~d to …** der Schaden beschränkte *or* erstreckte sich nur auf *(+acc)*…; **he finds the job too confining** er fühlt sich in dem Job beschränkt *or* eingeengt; **lions are ~d to Africa** Löwen gibt es nur in Afrika
c *(dated pass: in childbirth)* **to be ~d** niederkommen *(old)*
PL **confines** ['kɒnfaɪnz] *(of space, thing etc)* Grenzen *pl*; *(of marriage)* Fesseln *pl*; *(of system)* enge Grenzen *pl*

confined [kən'faɪnd] ADJ *space* beschränkt, begrenzt; *atmosphere* beengend

confinement [kən'faɪnmənt] N **a** *(= imprisonment) (= act)* Einsperren *nt*; *(in hospital)* Einweisung *f*; *(of animals)* Gefangenhalten *nt*; *(= state)* Eingesperrtsein *nt*; *(in jail)* Haft *f*; *(of animals)* Gefangenschaft *f*; *(Mil)* Arrest *m (also hum)*; **~ to barracks/one's room** Kasernen-/Stubenarrest *m*; **to put sb in ~** jdn einsperren; **to keep sb in close ~** jdn in strengem Gewahrsam halten **b** *(= restriction)* Beschränkung *f (to* auf *+acc)* **c** *(dated: = childbirth)* Entbindung *f*, Niederkunft *f (old)*

confirm [kən'fɜːm] VT **a** *(= verify)* bestätigen; **this has ~ed me in my decision** das hat meinen Entschluss bekräftigt; **his new play ~s him as our leading playwright** sein neues Stück stellt wieder unter Beweis, dass er unser führender Schauspieldichter ist **b** *(= strengthen)* bestärken; *one's resolve also* bekräftigen **c** *(Eccl)* konfirmieren; *Roman Catholic* firmen

confirmation [ˌkɒnfə'meɪʃən] N **a** Bestätigung *f*; **a letter in ~ (of)** ein Brief *m* zur *or* als Bestätigung *(+gen)* **b** *(Eccl)* Konfirmation *f*; *(of Roman Catholics)* Firmung *f*; **~ classes** Konfirmanden-/Firmunterricht *m*

confirmatory [ˌkɒnfɜː'meɪtərɪ] ADJ bestätigend

confirmed [kən'fɜːmd] ADJ **a** erklärt; *non-smoker, meat-eater, atheist* überzeugt; *bachelor* eingefleischt **b** *booking* bestätigt

confirming bank [kən'fɜːmɪŋˌbæŋk] N bestätigende Bank

confiscate ['kɒnfɪskeɪt] VT beschlagnahmen, konfiszieren; **to ~ sth from sb** jdm etw abnehmen

confiscation [ˌkɒnfɪs'keɪʃən] N Beschlagnahme *f*, Konfiszierung *f*

confiscatory [ˌkɒnfɪs'keɪtərɪ] ADJ **they have ~ powers** sie sind zur Beschlagnahme befugt

conflagration [ˌkɒnflə'greɪʃən] N *(of forest, towns)* Feuersbrunst *f (geh)*; *(of building)* Großbrand *m*

conflate [kən'fleɪt] VT zusammenfassen

conflation [kən'fleɪʃən] N Zusammenfassung *f*

conflict ['kɒnflɪkt] N Konflikt *m*; *(of moral issues, ideas also)* Widerstreit *m*, Zwiespalt *m*; *(between two accounts etc)* Widerspruch *m*; *(= fighting)* Zusammenstoß *m*; **to be in ~ with sb/sth** mit jdm/etw im Konflikt liegen, im Widerspruch zu jdm/etw stehen; **the ego is always in ~ with the id** das Ich ist immer im Widerstreit mit dem Es; **to come into ~ with sb/sth** mit jdm/etw in Konflikt geraten; **open/armed ~** offener Konflikt/bewaffneter Zusammenstoß; **border ~** Grenzkonflikt *m*; **~ of interests/opinions** Interessen-/Meinungskonflikt *m*
VI [kən'flɪkt] im Widerspruch stehen *(with* zu*)*, widersprechen *(with +dat)*; **their opinions on the subject ~** in diesem Punkt stehen ihre Ansichten im Widerspruch zueinander

conflicting [kən'flɪktɪŋ] ADJ widersprüchlich

confluence ['kɒnfluəns] N *(of rivers)* Zusammenfluss *m*

conform [kən'fɔːm] VI **a** *(things: = comply with)* entsprechen *(to +dat)*; *(people: socially)* sich anpassen *(to* an *+acc)*; *(things, people: to rules etc)* sich richten *(to* nach*)*; *(= agree)* übereinstimmen, konform gehen *(with* mit*)* **b** *(Brit, Eccl)* sich (der englischen Staatskirche *dat*) unterwerfen

conformance [kən'fɔːməns] N = **conformity**

conformism [kən'fɔːmɪzəm] N Konformismus *m*

conformist [kən'fɔːmɪst] ADJ konformistisch N Konformist *m (also Brit Eccl)*

conformity [kən'fɔːmɪtɪ] N **a** *(= uniformity)* Konformismus *m* **b** *(= compliance)* Übereinstimmung *f*; *(of manners)* Konformismus *m*; *(socially)* Anpassung *f (with* an *+acc)*; **in ~ with sth** einer Sache *(dat)* entsprechend *or* gemäß; **to be in ~ with sth** einer Sache *(dat)* entsprechen; **to bring sth into ~ with sth** etw mit etw in Einklang *or* Übereinstimmung bringen

confound [kən'faʊnd] VT **a** *(= amaze)* verblüffen **b** *(= throw into confusion)* verwirren, durcheinanderbringen **c** *(liter: = mistake for sth else)* verwechseln **d** *(inf)* **~ it!** vermaledeit *(dated)* *or* verflixt *(inf)* noch mal!; **~ him!** der vermaledeite *(dated)* *or* verflixte *(inf)* Kerl!

confounded [kən'faʊndɪd] ADJ *(inf)* vermaledeit *(dated inf)*, verflixt *(inf)*; *cheek also* verflucht *(inf)*; *noise also* Heiden- *(inf)*; *nuisance* elend *(inf)*

confoundedly [kən'faʊndɪdlɪ] ADV *(dated inf)* verflucht *(inf)*

confront [kən'frʌnt] VT **a** *(= face) danger, enemy, the boss* gegenübertreten *(+dat)*; *(fig) problems, issue also* begegnen *(+dat)*; *(= stand or be confronting) wall of ice etc* gegenüberstehen *(+dat)*; *(problems, decisions)* sich stellen *(+dat)* **b** *(= bring face to face with)* konfrontieren; **to ~ sb with sb/sth** jdn jdm gegenüberstellen, jdn mit jdm/etw konfrontieren; **to be ~ed with sth** mit etw konfrontiert sein, vor etw *(dat)* stehen; **(when) ~ed with** angesichts *(+gen)*

confrontation [ˌkɒnfrən'teɪʃən] N Konfrontation *f (also Pol)*; *(defiant also)* Auseinandersetzung *f*; *(with witnesses, evidence etc)* Gegenüberstellung *f*

Confucian [kən'fjuːʃən] ADJ konfuzianisch N Konfuzianer(in) *m(f)*

Confucianism [kən'fjuːʃənɪzm] N Konfuzianismus *m*

Confucius [kən'fjuːʃəs] N Konfuzius *m*, Konfutse *m*

confuse [kən'fjuːz] VT **a** *(= bewilder, muddle) people* konfus machen, verwirren, durcheinanderbringen; *(= make unclear) situation* verworren machen; **am I confusing you?** bringe ich Sie durcheinander?, verwirrt Sie das?; **don't ~ the issue!** bring (jetzt) nicht alles durcheinander! **b** *(= mix up) people* verwechseln; *matters, issues also* durcheinanderbringen; **to ~ two problems** zwei Probleme durcheinanderbringen *or* miteinander verwechseln

confused [kən'fjuːzd] ADJ **a** *(= muddled)* wirr, konfus; *person also* verwirrt; *(through old age, after anaesthetic etc)* wirr im Kopf; *idea, report, situation also* verworren; *sound, jumble* wirr **b** *(= embarrassed)* verwirrt, verlegen, betreten

confusedly [kən'fjuːzɪdlɪ] ADV verwirrt; *(= in disorder also)* wirr; *(= embarrassedly also)* verlegen, betreten

confusing [kən'fjuːzɪŋ] ADJ verwirrend

confusingly [kən'fjuːzɪŋlɪ] ADV verwirrend; **~, he then contradicted himself** verwirrenderweise widersprach er sich dann

confusion [kən'fjuːʒən] N **a** *(= disorder)* Durcheinander *nt*, Wirrwarr *m*, Unordnung *f*; *(= jumble)* Wirrwarr *m*; **to be in ~** in Unordnung sein, durcheinander sein; **scenes of ~** allgemeines *or* wildes Durcheinander; **to retreat in ~** *(Mil)* einen ungeordneten Rückzug antreten; **to throw everything into ~** alles durcheinanderbringen; **in the ~ of the battle** im Durcheinander der Schlacht; **to run about in ~** wild durcheinanderlaufen
b *(= perplexity)* Verwirrung *f*, Unklarheit *f*; *(= mental confusion, after drugs, blow on head etc)* Verwirrtheit *f*; *(through old age etc)* Wirrheit *f*; **in the ~ of the moment** im Eifer des Gefechts
c *(= embarrassment)* Verlegenheit *f*; *(at being found out)* Betroffenheit *f*; **to be covered in ~** vor Verlegenheit erröten
d *(= mixing up)* Verwechslung *f*

confutation [kɒnfjuː'teɪʃən] N Widerlegung *f*

confute [kən'fjuːt] VT widerlegen

conga ['kɒŋgə] N Conga *f*

congeal [kən'dʒiːl] VI erstarren, starr werden; *(glue, mud)* hart *or* fest werden; *(blood)* gerinnen; *(fig: = with fear)* erstarren VT erstarren lassen *(also fig)*; *glue, mud* hart werden lassen; *blood* gerinnen lassen

congenial [kən'dʒiːnɪəl] ADJ **a** *(= pleasant)* ansprechend; *person also* sympathisch; *place, job also, atmosphere* angenehm; **to be ~ to sb** *(place, atmosphere, environment, work)* jdm zusagen **b** *(liter: = of like nature)* kongenial *(liter)*, geistesverwandt

congenital [kən'dʒenɪtl] ADJ angeboren, kongenital *(spec)*; **~ defect** Geburtsfehler *m*; **~ liar** *(inf)* Erzlügner(in) *m(f) (inf)*

congenitally [kən'dʒenɪtəlɪ] ADV *(Med) deaf, blind, disabled* von Geburt an; *obese* anlagebedingt; *(fig) lazy, incapable, stupid, optimistic, dishonest* von Natur aus

conger ['kɒŋgəʳ] N *(also* **conger eel***)* Seeaal *m*

congeries [kən'dʒiːriːz] N *sing (liter)* Konglomerat *nt*, Ansammlung *f*, Anhäufung *f*

congested [kən'dʒestɪd] ADJ überfüllt; *(with traffic)* verstopft; *(with people also)* voll; *pavement* übervoll; *(= highly populated)* über(be)völkert; **his lungs are ~** in seiner Lunge hat sich Blut angestaut *or* ist es zu einem Blutstau gekommen

congestion [kən'dʒestʃən] N *(= traffic, pedestrians)* Stau *m*, Stockung *f*; *(in corridors etc)* Gedränge *nt*; *(= overpopulation)* Übervölkerung *f*; *(Med)* Blutstau *m*, Blutandrang *m*; **the ~ in the city centre is getting so bad ...** die Verstopfung in der Innenstadt nimmt derartige Ausmaße an ...

congestion charge N Stauabgabe *f or* -gebühr *f*, City-Maut *f*

congestive [kən'dʒestɪv] ADJ *(Med)* Stauungs-; **~ heart failure** Stauungsinsuffizienz *f*

conglomerate [kən'glɒmərɪt] N *(also Geol, Comm)* Konglomerat *nt* ADJ *nation* zusammengewürfelt; *language* Misch-; **~ rock** *(Geol)* Konglomeratgestein *nt* VI [kən'glɒməreɪt] sich zusammenballen, sich vereinigen, verschmelzen

conglomeration [kən,glɒmə'reɪʃən] N Ansammlung *f*, Haufen *m*; *(of ideas)* Gemisch *nt*

Congo ['kɒŋgəʊ] N Kongo *m*; **the Democratic Republic of the ~** die Demokratische Republik Kongo; **the Republic of the ~** die Republik Kongo

Congolese [,kɒŋgəʊ'liːz] ADJ kongolesisch N Kongolese *m*, Kongolesin *f*

congrats [kən'græts] INTERJ *(dated inf)* gratuliere!

congratulate [kən'grætjʊleɪt] VT gratulieren *(+dat) (also on birthday, engagement etc)*, beglückwünschen *(on* zu); **you are to be ~d on not having given up** man kann Ihnen nur gratulieren, dass Sie nicht nachgegeben haben

congratulation [kən,grætjʊ'leɪʃən] ✪ 23.6, 24.1, 24.2, 24.3 N Gratulation *f*, Gratulieren *nt*; **letter/message of ~** Glückwunschbrief *m*/-botschaft *f*, Gratulationsbrief *m*/-botschaft *f*

congratulations [kən,grætjʊ'leɪʃənz] PL Glückwunsch *m*, Glückwünsche *pl*; **to offer/send one's ~** gratulieren, jdn beglückwünschen/jdm gratulieren, jdm seine Glückwünsche senden INTERJ (ich) gratuliere!, herzlichen Glückwunsch!; *(iro)* gratuliere!; **~ on ...!** herzlichen Glückwunsch *or* herzliche Glückwünsche zu ...!

congratulatory [kən'grætjʊlətərɪ] ADJ *card, telegram* Glückwunsch-; *look, tone* anerkennend; **I wrote him a ~ letter on ...** ich gratulierte ihm brieflich zu ...; **she bought me a ~ drink** sie lud mich ein, um mit mir darauf zu trinken *or* anzustoßen

congregate ['kɒŋgrɪgeɪt] VI sich sammeln; *(on a particular occasion)* sich versammeln; **to be ~d in ...** sich sammeln/versammeln in *(+dat)* ...

congregation [,kɒŋgrɪ'geɪʃən] N **a** Versammlung *f*; *(not planned)* Ansammlung *f*; *(= people in cities etc)* Zusammenballung *f* **b** *(Eccl)* Gemeinde *f*; *(of cardinals)* Kongregation *f*

congregational [,kɒŋgrɪ'geɪʃənl] ADJ **a** **Congregational** kongregationalistisch **b** *(of a congregation)* Gemeinde-

Congregationalism [,kɒŋgrɪ'geɪʃənəlɪzəm] N Kongregationalismus *m*

Congregationalist [,kɒŋgrɪ'geɪʃənəlɪst] N Kongregationalist(in) *m(f)*

congress ['kɒŋgres] N **a** *(= meeting)* Kongress *m*, Tagung *f*; *(of political party)* Parteitag *m* **b** **Congress** *(US etc Pol)* der Kongress

congressional [kɒŋ'greʃənl] ADJ *delegate, meeting* Kongress-

Congressional district N *(US Pol)* Kongresswahlbezirk *m*

Congressional Record N *(US Pol)* Veröffentlichung *f* der Kongressdebatten

Congressman ['kɒŋgresmən] N *pl* **-men** [-mən] Kongressabgeordnete(r) *m*

Congresswoman ['kɒŋgres,wʊmən] N *pl* **-women** [-wɪmɪn] Kongressabgeordnete *f*

congruence ['kɒŋgrʊəns] N Kongruenz *f*, Übereinstimmung *f*; *(Geometry)* Deckungsgleichheit *f*, Kongruenz *f*

congruent ['kɒŋgrʊənt] ADJ **a** = **congruous** **b** *(Math) number* kongruent; *(Geometry also)* deckungsgleich

congruity [kəŋ'gruːɪtɪ] N Übereinstimmung *f*, Kongruenz *f (geh)*

congruous ['kɒŋgrʊəs] ADJ **a** *(= corresponding)* sich deckend, übereinstimmend; **to be ~ with sth** sich mit etw decken **b** *(= appropriate, proper)* vereinbar

conic ['kɒnɪk] ADJ **a** *(Math)* Kegel-, konisch **b** *(also* **conical**) kegelförmig, Kegel-, konisch

conic projection N *(Geog)* Kegelprojektion *or* -abbildung *f*

conic section N *(Math)* Kegelschnitt *m*

conifer ['kɒnɪfə'] N Nadelbaum *m*, Konifere *f (spec)*; **~s** Nadelhölzer *pl*

coniferous [kə'nɪfərəs] ADJ *tree, forest* Nadel-

conjectural [kən'dʒektʃərəl] ADJ auf Vermutungen *or* Mutmaßungen beruhend; **a conclusion which must remain ~** ein Schluss, der Vermutung *or* Mutmaßung bleiben muss; **it is entirely ~** es ist reine Vermutung

conjecture [kən'dʒektʃə'] VT vermuten, mutmaßen *(geh)* VI Vermutungen *or* Mutmaßungen anstellen, mutmaßen *(geh)*; **it was just as scientists had ~d** es verhielt sich geradeso, wie es die Wissenschaftler gemutmaßt *or* vermutet hatten N Vermutung *f*, Mutmaßung *f (geh)*; **what will come next is a matter of** *or* **for ~** was folgt, das kann man nur vermuten *or* das bleibt unserer Vermutung überlassen

conjoin [kən'dʒɔɪn] VT *(form)* verbinden

conjoined [kən'dʒɔɪnd] ADJ *(form)* verbunden, verknüpft; *(= at the same time) events* zusammentreffend

conjoint ADJ, **conjointly** ADV [kən'dʒɔɪnt, -lɪ] gemeinsam

conjugal ['kɒndʒʊgəl] ADJ *rights, bliss, duties* ehelich; *state* Ehe-; **~ affection** Gattenliebe *f*

conjugate ['kɒndʒʊgeɪt] VT *(Gram)* konjugieren, beugen VI *(Gram)* sich konjugieren lassen; *(Biol)* konjugieren

conjugation [,kɒndʒʊ'geɪʃən] N *(Gram, Biol)* Konjugation *f*

conjunct [kən'dʒʌŋkt] ADJ *(= joined)* verbunden; *(= combined)* vereint, gemeinsam; *(Jur)* befangen

conjunction [kən'dʒʌŋkʃən] N **a** *(Gram)* Konjunktion *f*, Bindewort *nt* **b** *(= association)* Verbindung *f*; *(= co-occurrence: of events)* Zusammentreffen *nt*; **in ~** zusammen; **in ~ with the new evidence** in Verbindung mit dem neuen Beweismaterial; **the programme was broadcast in ~ with the NBC** die Sendung wurde von NBC übernommen; **the programme was produced in ~ with the NBC** das Programm wurde in Zusammenarbeit mit NBC aufgezeichnet **c** *(Astron)* Konjunktion *f*

conjunctive [kən'dʒʌŋktɪv] ADJ *(Gram, Anat)* Binde-

conjunctivitis [kən,dʒʌŋktɪ'vaɪtɪs] N *(Med)* Bindehautentzündung *f*, Konjunktivitis *f (spec)*

conjuncture [kən'dʒʌŋktʃə'] N Zusammentreffen *nt*

conjure[1] [kən'dʒʊə'] VT *(liter: = appeal to)* beschwören

conjure[2] ['kʌndʒə'] VI zaubern; **a name to ~ with** ein Name, der Wunder wirkt *or* der eine Ausstrahlung hat VT zaubern; *image, memory* heraufbeschwören; **to ~ something out of nothing** etwas aus dem Nichts herbeizaubern

► **conjure away** VT *sep (lit, fig)* wegzaubern

► **conjure up** VT *sep ghosts, spirits* beschwören; *(fig) memories etc* heraufbeschwören; *(= provide, produce)* hervorzaubern; *meal* zusammenzaubern

conjurer ['kʌndʒərə'] N Zauberer, Zauberkünstler(in) *m(f)*

conjuring ['kʌndʒərɪŋ] N Zaubern *nt*; *(= performance)* Zauberei *f*; **~ trick** Zaubertrick *m*, (Zauber)kunststück *nt*

conjuror ['kʌndʒərə'] N = **conjurer**

conk [kɒŋk] *(inf)* N *(esp Brit: = nose)* Zinken *m (inf)* VT *(= hit)* hauen *(inf)*

► **conk out** VI *(inf)* es aufstecken *(inf)*, den Geist aufgeben; *(person, = faint)* umkippen *(inf)*; *(= die)* ins Gras beißen *(inf)*

conker ['kɒŋkə'] N *(Brit inf)* (Ross)kastanie *f*; **~s** *(= game) Spiel, bei dem zwei Spieler mit an Fäden befestigten Kastanien wechselseitig versuchen, die Kastanie des Gegenspielers zu treffen und zu zerstören*

con man N *pl* **con men** *(inf)* Schwindler *m*, Bauernfänger *m (inf)*; *(pretending to have social status)* Hochstapler *m*; *(promising marriage)* Heiratsschwindler *m*

connect [kə'nekt] ✪ 17.2, 27.5 VT **a** *(= join)* verbinden *(to, with* mit); *(Elec etc: also* **connect up**) *appliances, subscribers* anschließen *(to* an *+acc)*; **I'll ~ you** *(Telec)* ich verbinde (Sie); **to be ~ed** *(two things)* miteinander verbunden sein; *(several things)* untereinander verbunden sein; **to ~ to earth** erden; **~ed by telephone** telefonisch verbunden → **parallel**
b *(fig: = associate)* in Verbindung *or* Zusammenhang bringen; **I always ~ Paris with springtime** ich verbinde Paris immer mit Frühling; **these things are ~ed in my mind** diese Dinge gehören für mich zusammen; **I'd never ~ed them** ich hatte sie nie zueinander in Beziehung gesetzt
c *(esp pass: = link) ideas, theories etc* verbinden; **to be ~ed with** eine Beziehung haben zu, in einer Beziehung *or* in Verbindung stehen zu; *(= be related to)* verwandt sein mit; **he's ~ed with the BBC/university** er hat mit der BBC/der Universität zu tun; **to be ~ed by marriage** verschwägert sein; **to be ~ed** *(ideas etc)* in Beziehung zueinander stehen; *(firms)* geschäftlich miteinander verbunden sein; **loosely ~ed facts** lose verknüpfte Fakten
VI **a** *(= join, two rooms)* eine Verbindung haben *(to, with* zu); *(two parts, wires etc)* Kontakt haben; **to ~ with sb/sb's ideas** jdn/jds Gedanken verstehen; **~ing rooms** angrenzende Zimmer *pl (mit Verbindungstür)*
b *(Rail, Aviat etc)* Anschluss haben *(with* an *+acc)*; **~ing flight** Anschlussflug *m*
c *(inf: = hit) (fist etc)* landen *(inf) (with* auf *+dat)*; *(golf club etc)* treffen *(with +acc)*; **he really ~ed** er hat voll getroffen

► **connect up** VT *sep (Elec etc)* anschließen *(to, with* an *+acc)*

connecting [kə'nektɪŋ]: **connecting cord** N *(Elec)* Verbindungsschnur *f*; **connecting flight** N Anschlussflug *m*; **connecting rod** N Pleuel- *or* Kurbelstange *f*

connection [kə'nekʃən] N **a** Verbindung *f (to, with* zu, mit); *(= telephone line also, wire)* Leitung *f*; *(to mains)* Anschluss *m (to* an *+acc)*; *(= connecting part)* Verbindung(sstück *nt*) *f*; **parallel/series ~** Parallel-/Reihenschaltung *f*; **~ charge** *(Telec)* Anschlussgebühr *f*
b *(fig: = link)* Zusammenhang *m*, Beziehung *f (with* zu); **in this ~** in diesem Zusammenhang; **in ~ with** in Zusammenhang mit
c *(= relationship, business connection)* Beziehung *f*, Verbindung *f (with* zu); *(= family connection)* familiäre Beziehung; *(old, form: = relative)* (entfernter) Verwandter, (entfernte) Verwandte; **to have ~s** Beziehungen haben; **there is some family ~** sie/wir *etc* sind weitläufig miteinander verwandt
d *(Rail etc)* Anschluss *m*

connective [kə'nektɪv] N *(Gram)* Bindewort *nt* ADJ verbindend

connective tissue N Bindegewebe *nt*

connector [kə'nektə'] N *(= device)* Verbindungsstück *nt*, Anschluss *m*; *(Elec)* Lüsterklemme *f*

connexion [kə'nekʃən] N = **connection**

conning tower ['kɒnɪŋtaʊə'] N Kommandoturm *m*

connivance [kə'naɪvəns] N *(= tacit consent)* stillschweigendes Einverständnis; *(= dishonest dealing)* Schiebung *f*; **his ~ at the wrongdoing** seine Mitwisserschaft bei dem Vergehen; **to do sth in ~ with sb** etw mit jds Wissen tun; **to be in ~ with sb** mit jdm gemeinsame Sache machen

connive [kə'naɪv] VI **a** *(= conspire)* sich verschwören, gemeinsame Sache machen; **he's a conniving little wretch** *(inf)* er ist ein hinterhältiger Tropf *(inf)* **b** *(= deliberately overlook)* **to ~ at sth** etw stillschweigend dulden; **to ~ at a crime** einem Verbrechen Vorschub leisten

connoisseur [ˌkɒnə'sɜː'] N Kenner *m*, Connaisseur *m (geh)*; **~ of wines/women** Wein-/Frauenkenner *m*

connotation [ˌkɒnəʊ'teɪʃən] N Assoziation *f*, Konnotation *f (spec)*; **the ~s of this word** die mit diesem Wort verbundenen Assoziationen, die Konnotationen dieses Wortes *(spec)*

connotative ['kɒnəteɪtɪv] ADJ *meaning* Neben-, assoziativ, konnotativ *(spec)*

connote [kɒ'nəʊt] VT suggerieren

connubial [kə'njuːbɪəl] ADJ ehelich, Ehe-

conquer ['kɒŋkə'] VT **a** *(lit) country* erobern; *enemy, nation* besiegen **b** *(fig) difficulties, feelings, disease* bezwingen, besiegen; *sb's heart* erobern; *mountain* bezwingen

conquering ['kɒŋkərɪŋ] ADJ *hero* siegreich

conqueror ['kɒŋkərə'] N *(of country, heart)* Eroberer *m*, Eroberin *f*; *(of enemy, difficulties, feelings, disease)* Sieger(in) *m(f)* (of über *+acc*), Besieger(in) *m(f)*; *(of difficulties, feelings, mountains)* Bezwinger(in) *m(f)*; **William the Conqueror** Wilhelm der Eroberer

conquest ['kɒŋkwest] N Eroberung *f*; *(of enemy etc, disease)* Sieg *m* (of über *+acc*), Bezwingung *f*; *(inf: = person)* Eroberung *f*

Cons *abbr of* **Conservative**

consanguinity [ˌkɒnsæŋ'gwɪnɪtɪ] N Blutsverwandtschaft *f*

conscience ['kɒnʃəns] N Gewissen *nt*; **to have a clear/easy/bad/guilty ~** ein reines/gutes/schlechtes/böses Gewissen haben (*about* wegen); **doesn't telling lies give you a guilty ~?** haben Sie keine Gewissensbisse *or* kein schlechtes Gewissen, wenn Sie lügen?; **with an easy ~** mit ruhigem Gewissen, ruhigen Gewissens *(geh)*; **he has no ~ about lying** er macht sich *(dat)* kein Gewissen daraus, zu lügen; **it/he will be on your ~ all your life** Sie werden das/ihn Ihr Leben lang auf dem Gewissen haben; **she/it is on my ~** ich habe ihretwegen/deswegen Gewissensbisse; **it's still on my ~** *(= I still haven't done it)* es steht mir noch bevor; **my ~ won't let me do it** das kann ich mit meinem Gewissen nicht vereinbaren; **in (all) ~** allen Ernstes; **I can't in all ~ ...** ich kann unmöglich ...; **let your ~ be your guide!** hör auf dein Gewissen; **it's between you and your ~** das musst du mit dir selbst *or* mit deinem Gewissen abmachen

conscience: **conscience clause** N *(Jur)* ≈ Gewissensklausel *f*; **conscience money** N **his donation looks like ~** mit der Spende will er wohl sein Gewissen beruhigen; **conscience-stricken** ADJ schuldbewusst

conscientious [ˌkɒnʃɪ'enʃəs] ADJ **a** *(= diligent)* gewissenhaft; *(= conscious of one's duty)* pflichtbewusst **b** *(Mil)* **he refused to go as a ~ objection** er weigerte sich aus Gewissensgründen hinzugehen → **conscientious objector**

conscientiously [ˌkɒnʃɪ'enʃəslɪ] ADV *practise, exercise* gewissenhaft; *obey* pflichtschuldigst

conscientiousness [ˌkɒnʃɪ'enʃəsnɪs] N Gewissenhaftigkeit *f*; *(= sense of duty)* Pflichtbewusstsein *nt*, Pflichtgefühl *nt*

conscientious objector N *(Mil)* Wehrdienst- *or* Kriegsdienstverweigerer *m (aus Gewissensgründen)*

conscious ['kɒnʃəs] ADJ **a** *(Med)* bei Bewusstsein **b** *(= aware)* bewusst *(also Psych)*; **the ~ mind** das Bewusstsein; **to be/become ~ of sth** sich *(dat)* einer Sache *(gen)* bewusst sein/werden; **I was/became ~ that** es war/wurde mir bewusst, dass; **politically ~** politisch bewusst; **environmentally ~** umweltbewusst **c** *(= deliberate) effort etc* bewusst; *humour also* absichtlich

-conscious ADJ *suf* -bewusst; **weight-conscious** gewichtsbewusst

consciously ['kɒnʃəslɪ] ADV bewusst; *(= deliberately also)* absichtlich

consciousness ['kɒnʃəsnɪs] N **a** *(Med)* Bewusstsein *nt*; **to lose ~** das Bewusstsein verlieren, bewusstlos werden; **to regain ~** das Bewusstsein wiedererlangen, wieder zu sich kommen **b** *(= awareness)* Bewusstsein *nt*, Wissen *nt*; **her ~ of her abilities** das Wissen um ihre Fähigkeiten **c** *(= conscious mind)* Bewusstsein *nt*; **to be ~-raising** den Bewusstseinsgrad erhöhen, bewusstseinserweiternd sein

-consciousness N *suf* -bewusstheit *f*

conscript [kən'skrɪpt] VT einziehen, einberufen; *army* ausheben N ['kɒnskrɪpt] *(Brit)* Wehrpflichtige(r) *m*

conscripted [kən'skrɪptɪd] ADJ *soldier* eingezogen, einberufen; *troops* aus Wehrpflichtigen bestehend; *workers, labourers* zwangsverpflichtet

conscription [kən'skrɪpʃən] N Wehrpflicht *f*; *(= act of conscripting)* Einberufung *f*; *(of army)* Aushebung *f*

consecrate ['kɒnsɪkreɪt] VT *(lit, fig)* weihen

consecration [ˌkɒnsɪ'kreɪʃən] N Weihe *f*; *(in Mass)* Wandlung *f*

consecutive [kən'sekjʊtɪv] ADJ **a** aufeinanderfolgend; *numbers* fortlaufend; **on four ~ days** vier Tage hintereinander; **this is the third ~ morning he's been late** er ist jetzt dreimal hintereinander morgens zu spät gekommen **b** *(Gram) clause* Konsekutiv-, Folge-

consecutively [kən'sekjʊtɪvlɪ] ADV nacheinander, hintereinander; *numbered* fortlaufend

consensual [kən'sensjʊəl] ADJ **a** *(Jur)* **to be ~** auf (bloßer) mündlicher Übereinkunft beruhen; **~ contract** obligatorischer Vertrag **b** *(Physiol)* Reflex-, unwillkürlich

consensus [kən'sensəs] N Übereinstimmung *f*; *(= accord also)* Einigkeit *f*; **what's the ~?** was ist die allgemeine Meinung?; **the ~ is that ...** man ist allgemein der Meinung, dass ...; **there's a ~ (of opinion) in favour of ...** die allgemeine Mehrheit ist für ...; **cabinet decisions are based on ~** Entscheidungen des Kabinetts beruhen auf einem Mehrheitsbeschluss; **there was no ~ (among them)** sie waren sich nicht einig, es gab keinen Konsens unter ihnen *(form)*; **~ politics** Politik *f* des Konsensus *or* Miteinander

consent [kən'sent] ✪ 9.3, 11.2 VI zustimmen (*to +dat*), einwilligen (*to* in *+acc*); **to ~ to do sth** sich bereit erklären, etw zu tun; **to ~ to sb doing sth** einwilligen *or* damit einverstanden sein, dass jd etw tut; **homosexuality between ~ing adults** homosexuelle Beziehungen zwischen erwachsenen Männern N Zustimmung *f* (*to* zu), Einwilligung *f* (*to* in *+acc*); **it/he is by common** *or* **general ~ ...** man hält es/ihn allgemein für ...; **to be chosen by general ~** einstimmig gewählt werden; **by mutual** *or* **common ~** in gegenseitigem Einverständnis → **age N c**

consent form N *(Med)* Einverständniserklärung *f*

consequence ['kɒnsɪkwəns] ✪ 26.3 N **a** *(= result, effect)* Folge *f*; *(of actions also)* Konsequenz *f*; **in ~** folglich; **in ~ of** infolge *(+gen)*; **in ~ of which** infolgedessen; **and the ~ is that we have ...** und folglich haben wir ...; **as a ~ of ...** als Folge *(+gen)*; **with the ~ that he ...** was zur Folge hatte *or* mit dem Erfolg, dass er ...; **to face** *or* **take the ~s** die Folgen *or* Konsequenzen tragen
b *(= importance)* Wichtigkeit *f*, Bedeutung *f*; **a person of ~** eine bedeutende *or* wichtige Persönlichkeit; **did he have anything of ~ to say?** hatte er irgend etwas Wichtiges zu sagen?; **he's (a man) of no ~** er hat nichts zu sagen; **it's of no ~** das spielt keine Rolle; **that's of no ~ to me** das ist mir einerlei; **of what ~ is that to you?** was tangiert Sie das? *(inf)*
c consequences SING *(= game) Schreibspiel, bei dem auf gefaltetem Papier ein nicht bekannter Vorsatz ergänzt wird*

consequent ['kɒnsɪkwənt] ADJ *attr* daraus folgend, sich daraus ergebend; *(temporal)* darauf folgend; **to be ~ upon sth** *(form, liter)* sich aus etw ergeben

consequential [ˌkɒnsɪ'kwenʃəl] ADJ **a** = **consequent b** *(= self-important)* wichtigtuerisch; *smile, tone also* überheblich **c** *(= logically consistent)* folgerichtig

consequentially [ˌkɒnsɪ'kwenʃəlɪ] ADV *(= as a result)* daraufhin

consequently ['kɒnsɪkwəntlɪ] ✪ 26.3 ADV folglich

conservancy [kən'sɜːvənsɪ] N **a** *(Brit: = board)* Schutzbehörde *f*; *(for ports, rivers etc)* Wasserschutzamt *nt*; *(for forests)* Forstamt *nt* **b** *(= official conservation)* Erhaltung *f*, Schutz *m*

conservation [ˌkɒnsə'veɪʃən] N **a** *(= preservation)* Erhaltung *f*, Schutz *m*; **~ technology** Umweltschutztechnik *f* **b** *(Phys)* Erhaltung *f*

conservation area N Naturschutzgebiet *nt*; *(in town)* unter Denkmalschutz stehendes Gebiet

conservationist [ˌkɒnsə'veɪʃənɪst] N Umweltschützer(in) *m(f)*; *(as regards old buildings etc)* Denkmalpfleger(in) *m(f)*

conservatism [kən'sɜːvətɪzəm] N Konservatismus *m*

conservative [kən'sɜːvətɪv] ADJ **a** *person, style* konservativ; *(= cautious, moderate)* vorsichtig; **at a ~ estimate** bei vorsichtiger Schätzung; **I want something ~** *(when buying clothes)* ich möchte etwas Gediegenes *or* Unauffälliges **b** *(Pol)* konservativ; **the Conservative Party** *(Brit)* die Konservative Partei N *(Pol: also* **Conservative**) Konservative(r) *mf*; **I'm a ~ in such matters** in solchen Dingen bin ich konservativ

conservatively [kən'sɜːvətɪvlɪ] ADV konservativ; *estimate, invest* vorsichtig

conservatoire [kən'sɜːvətwɑː'] N Konservatorium *nt*

conservatory [kən'sɜːvətrɪ] N **a** Wintergarten *m* **b** *(esp US, Mus etc)* Konservatorium *nt*

conserve [kən'sɜːv] VT erhalten, bewahren, konservieren; *building* erhalten; *one's strength* schonen; *strength, energy* (auf)sparen

conserves [kən'sɜːvz] PL Eingemachte(s) *nt*

consider [kən'sɪdə'] ✪ 21.4, 26.1, 26.3 VT **a** *(= reflect upon) plan, idea, offer* sich *(dat)* überlegen, nachdenken über *(+acc)*; *possibilities* sich *(dat)* überlegen; **I'll ~ the matter** ich werde mir die Sache überlegen *or* durch den Kopf gehen lassen
b *(= have in mind)* in Erwägung ziehen; **we're ~ing a few changes** wir ziehen ein paar Änderungen in Erwägung; **I'm ~ing going abroad** ich spiele mit dem Gedanken, ins Ausland zu gehen, ich erwäge einen Auslandsaufenthalt *(geh)*; **he is being ~ed for the job** er wird für die Stelle in Erwägung *or* Betracht gezogen
c *(= entertain)* in Betracht ziehen; **he refused even to ~ the possibility** er verwarf die Möglichkeit sofort, er weigerte sich, die Möglichkeit überhaupt in Betracht zu ziehen; **I won't even ~ the idea of ...** der Gedanke, zu ..., kommt für mich überhaupt nicht in Betracht; **I won't even ~ it!** ich denke nicht daran!; **would you ~ £500?** hielten Sie £ 500 für angemessen?; **I'm sure he would never ~ doing anything criminal** ich bin überzeugt, es käme ihm nie in den Sinn, etwas Kriminelles zu tun
d *(= think of)* denken an *(+acc)*; **~ George** denken Sie an George; **~ my position** überlegen Sie sich meine Lage; **~ this case, for example** nehmen Sie zum Beispiel diesen Fall; **~ how he must have felt** überlegen Sie sich, wie ihm zumute *or* zu Mute gewesen sein muss; **~ how much you owe him** denken Sie daran *or* bedenken Sie, wie viel Sie ihm schulden; **have**

you ~ed going by train? haben Sie daran gedacht, mit dem Zug zu fahren?
e *(= take into account)* denken an *(+acc)*; *cost, difficulties, dangers also, facts* bedenken, berücksichtigen; *person, feelings also* Rücksicht nehmen auf *(+acc)*; **when one ~s that …** wenn man bedenkt, dass …; **all things ~ed** alles in allem
f *(= regard as, deem)* betrachten als; *person* halten für; **to ~ sb to be** *or* **as …** jdn als … betrachten, jdn für … halten; **to ~ oneself lucky/honoured** sich glücklich schätzen/geehrt fühlen; **~ it (as) done!** schon so gut wie geschehen!; **(you can) ~ yourself sacked** betrachten Sie sich als entlassen; **I ~ it an honour** ich betrachte es als besondere Ehre
g *(= look at)* (eingehend) betrachten

considerable [kən'sɪdərəbl] ADJ beträchtlich, erheblich; *sum of money, achievement also* ansehnlich; *loss also, interest, income* groß; *(used admiringly) number, size, achievement, effort etc* beachtlich; **to a ~ extent** *or* **degree** weitgehend; **to face ~ difficulties** mit beträchtlichen *or* erheblichen *or* gewaltigen Schwierigkeiten konfrontiert sein; **for a** *or* **some ~ time** für eine ganze Zeit

considerably [kən'sɪdərəblɪ] ADV *(in comparisons) changed, older, better, grown* beträchtlich, um einiges; *(= very) upset, impressed* höchst

considerate [kən'sɪdərɪt] ADJ rücksichtsvoll *(to(wards))* gegenüber); *(= kind)* aufmerksam

considerately [kən'sɪdərɪtlɪ] ADV *behave, say* rücksichtsvoll

consideration [kən,sɪdə'reɪʃən] ✪ 26.1 N **a** *no pl (= careful thought)* Überlegung *f*; **I'll give it my ~** ich werde es mir überlegen
b *no pl (= regard, account)* **to take sth into ~** etw bedenken, etw berücksichtigen; *factors also* etw in Erwägung ziehen; **taking everything into ~** alles in allem; **to leave sth out of ~** etw außer Acht lassen; **your request/the matter is under ~** Ihr Gesuch/die Sache wird zurzeit geprüft *(form)*, wir gehen der Sache zurzeit nach; **in ~ of** *(= in view of)* mit Rücksicht auf *(+acc)*, in Anbetracht *(+gen)*; *(= in return for)* als Dank für
c *no pl (= thoughtfulness)* Rücksicht *f* *(for* auf *+acc)*; **to show** *or* **have ~ for sb/sb's feelings** Rücksicht auf jdn/jds Gefühle nehmen; **his lack of ~ (for others)** seine Rücksichtslosigkeit (anderen gegenüber)
d *(= sth taken into account)* Erwägung *f*, Gesichtspunkt *m*, Faktor *m*; **money is a minor ~/not a ~/his first ~** Geld spielt eine unbedeutendere Rolle/keine Rolle/bei ihm die größte Rolle; **it's a ~** das wäre zu überlegen
e *(= reward, payment)* Entgelt *nt*, Gegenleistung *f*, kleine Anerkennung *(hum)*; **for a ~** gegen Entgelt, für eine Gegenleistung *or* kleine Anerkennung *(hum)*

considered [kən'sɪdɪd] ADJ *opinion* ernsthaft

considering [kən'sɪdərɪŋ] PREP für *(+acc)*, wenn man … *(acc)* bedenkt CONJ wenn man bedenkt; **~ (that) he's been ill …** wenn man bedenkt, dass er krank war …, dafür, dass er krank war … ADV eigentlich; **it's not too bad ~** es ist eigentlich gar nicht so schlecht; **yes it is, ~** ach ja, eigentlich schon

consign [kən'saɪn] VT **a** *(Comm: = send)* versenden, verschicken; *(= address)* adressieren *(to* an *+acc)*; **the goods are ~ed to …** die Waren sind für … bestimmt **b** *(= commit)* übergeben *(to +dat)*; *(= entrust also)* anvertrauen; **it was ~ed to the rubbish heap** es landete auf dem Abfallhaufen; **to ~ a child to sb's care** ein Kind in jds Obhut *(acc)* geben

consignee [,kɒnsaɪ'niː] N *(Comm)* Empfänger *m*

consigner [kən'saɪnə'] N = **consignor**

consignment [kən'saɪnmənt] N *(Comm)* **a** *(of goods)* Versendung *f*, Verschickung *f*; **goods for ~ abroad** ins Ausland gehende Ware; **on ~** in Kommission; *(overseas)* in Konsignation **b** *(= goods)* Sendung *f*; *(bigger)* Ladung *f*

consignment note N *(Comm)* Frachtbrief *m*

consignor [kən'saɪnə'] N *(Comm)* Versender *m*

consist [kən'sɪst] VI **a** *(= be composed)* **to ~ of** bestehen aus **b** *(= have as its essence)* **to ~ in sth** in etw *(dat)* bestehen; **his happiness ~s in helping others** sein Glück besteht darin, anderen zu helfen

consistency [kən'sɪstənsɪ] N **a** *no pl* Konsequenz *f*; *(of statements)* Übereinstimmung *f*, Vereinbarkeit *f*; *(of argument)* Logik *f*, Folgerichtigkeit *f*; **his statements lack ~** seine Aussagen widersprechen sich *or* sind nicht miteinander vereinbar **b** *no pl (= uniformity, of quality)* Beständigkeit *f*; *(of performance, results)* Stetigkeit *f*; *(of method, style)* Einheitlichkeit *f* **c** *(of substance)* Konsistenz *f*; *(of liquids also)* Dicke *f*; *(of glue, dough, rubber etc also)* Festigkeit(sgrad *m*) *f*; **beat it to a thick ~** zu einer festen Masse schlagen

consistent [kən'sɪstənt] ADJ **a** konsequent; *statements* übereinstimmend, miteinander vereinbar; *(= logical) argument* logisch, folgerichtig; *(= constant) failure* ständig, stetig **b** *(= uniform) quality* beständig; *performance, results* gleichbleibend, stetig; *method, style* einheitlich **c** *(= in agreement)* **to be ~ with sth** einer Sache *(dat)* entsprechen; **what you're saying now is not ~ with what you said before** was Sie jetzt sagen, widerspricht dem *or* lässt sich mit dem nicht vereinbaren, was Sie davor gesagt haben

consistently [kən'sɪstəntlɪ] ADV **a** *argue, behave* konsequent; *(= constantly) fail* ständig; *refuse, deny, oppose, reject* hartnäckig **b** *(= uniformly)* einheitlich, durchweg **c** *(= in agreement)* entsprechend *(with +dat)*

consolation [,kɒnsə'leɪʃən] N Trost *m no pl*; *(= act)* Tröstung *f*; **it is some ~ to know that …** es ist tröstlich *or* ein Trost zu wissen, dass …; **that's a big ~!** *(iro)* das ist ein schwacher Trost!; **old age has its ~s** das Alter hat auch seine guten Seiten; **a few words of ~** ein paar tröstende Worte

consolation prize N Trostpreis *m*

consolatory [kən'sɒlətərɪ] ADJ tröstlich, tröstend

console[1] [kən'səʊl] VT trösten; **to ~ sb for sth** jdn über etw *(acc)* hinwegtrösten

console[2] ['kɒnsəʊl] N **a** *(= control panel)* (Kontroll)pult *nt*; *(of organ)* Spieltisch *m* **b** *(= cabinet)* Schrank *m*, Truhe *f*; **our TV is a ~ (model)** wir haben eine Fernsehtruhe **c** *(= ornamental bracket)* Konsole *f*

console table N Konsoltischchen *nt*

consolidate [kən'sɒlɪdeɪt] VT **a** *(= confirm)* festigen **b** *(= combine)* zusammenlegen, vereinigen; *companies* zusammenschließen; *funds, debts* konsolidieren; **~d balance sheet** konsolidierte Bilanz

consolidated fund N *(Brit Fin)* konsolidierter Staatsfonds, unablösbare Anleihe

consolidation [kən,sɒlɪ'deɪʃən] N **a** *(= strengthening)* Festigung *f* **b** *(= amalgamation)* Zusammenlegung *f*, Vereinigung *f*; *(of companies)* Zusammenschluss *m*; *(of funds, debts)* Konsolidierung *f*

consoling [kən'səʊlɪŋ] ADJ tröstlich, tröstend

consols ['kɒnsɒlz] PL *(Brit Fin)* Konsols *pl*, konsolidierte Staatsanleihen *pl*

consommé [kɒn'sɒmeɪ] N Kraftbrühe *f*, Konsommee *f (old)*

consonance ['kɒnsənəns] N *(Mus)* Konsonanz *f*; *(Poet)* Konsonantengleichklang *m*; *(fig, of agreement, ideas)* Einklang *m*, Harmonie *f*; *(= consistency)* Übereinstimmung *f*

consonant ['kɒnsənənt] N *(Phon)* Konsonant *m*, Mitlaut *m*; **~ shift** Lautverschiebung *f* ADJ *(Mus)* konsonant *(with* zu); **to be ~ with sth** *(fig)* mit etw in Einklang zu bringen sein

consonantal [,kɒnsə'næntl] ADJ konsonantisch

consort ['kɒnsɔːt] N *(form: = spouse)* Gemahl(in) *m(f)* *(form)*, Gatte *m* *(form)*, Gattin *f* *(form)* → **prince consort** VI [kən'sɔːt] **a** *(form: = associate)* verkehren *(with* mit) **b** *(= be consistent)* passen *(with* zu), sich vereinbaren lassen *(with* mit)

consortium [kən'sɔːtɪəm] N Konsortium *nt*

conspicuous [kən'spɪkjʊəs] ADJ *person, clothes, behaviour* auffällig, auffallend; *(= easily visible) road signs* deutlich sichtbar, auffällig; *(= obvious) lack of sympathy etc* deutlich, offensichtlich, auffallend; *(= outstanding) bravery* bemerkenswert, hervorragend; **to be/make oneself ~** auffallen; **to feel ~** den Eindruck haben aufzufallen; **why don't you put it in a more ~ position?** warum stellen Sie es nicht irgendwohin, wo es eher auffällt?; **to be/not to be ~ for sth** sich/sich nicht gerade durch etw auszeichnen; **he was ~ by his absence** er glänzte durch Abwesenheit; **he showed a ~ lack of tact** er fiel durch sein mangelndes Taktgefühl (unangenehm) auf

conspicuous consumption N Prestigekäufe *pl*

conspicuously [kən'spɪkjʊəslɪ] ADV **a** *(= prominently)* gut sichtbar **b** *(= noticeably) silent, uneasy* auffällig, auffallend; *successful* bemerkenswert; **to be ~ lacking in sth** etw offenkundig nicht haben; **to be ~ absent** *(person)* durch Abwesenheit glänzen; **the government has ~ failed to intervene** es wurde übel vermerkt, dass die Regierung nicht eingegriffen hat

conspicuousness [kən'spɪkjʊəsnɪs] N *(of person, clothes, behaviour)* Auffälligkeit *f*; *(= visibility: of road signs etc)* deutliche Sichtbarkeit, Auffälligkeit *f*; *(= obviousness: of lack of sympathy etc)* Deutlichkeit *f*

conspiracy [kən'spɪrəsɪ] N Verschwörung *f*, Komplott *nt*, Konspiration *f (form)*; *(Jur)* (strafbare) Verabredung; **~ to defraud** Verabredung *f* zum Betrug; **~ to murder** Mordkomplott *nt*; **a ~ of silence** ein verabredetes Schweigen; **he thinks it's all a ~ against him** er meint, man hätte sich gegen ihn verschworen

conspiracy theory N Verschwörungstheorie *f*

conspirator [kən'spɪrətə'] N Verschwörer(in) *m(f)*

conspiratorial ADJ, **conspiratorially** ADV [kən,spɪrə'tɔːrɪəl, -lɪ] ADJ verschwörerisch

conspire [kən'spaɪə'] VI **a** *(people)* sich verschwören, sich zusammentun, konspirieren *(form)* *(against* gegen); **to ~ (together) to do sth** sich verabreden *or* heimlich planen, etw zu tun **b** *(events)* zusammenkommen, sich verschwören *(geh)*; *(fate etc)* sich verschwören *(against* gegen)

constable ['kʌnstəbl] N *(Brit: = police constable)* Polizist(in) *m(f)*; *(in address)* Herr Wachtmeister, Frau Wachtmeisterin

constabulary [kən'stæbjʊlərɪ] N *(Brit)* Polizei *f no pl*

constancy ['kɒnstənsɪ] N **a** *(of support, supporter)* Beständigkeit *f*, Konstanz *f (liter)*; *(of feelings)* Unveränderlichkeit *f*, Unwandelbarkeit *f*;; *(of friend, lover)* Treue *f*; *(also* **constancy of purpose**) Ausdauer *f* **b** *(of temperature etc)* Beständigkeit *f*

constant ['kɒnstənt] ADJ **a** *(= continuous) quarrels, interruptions, noise* dauernd, ständig, konstant *(geh)*; **we have ~ hot water** wir haben ständig heißes Wasser **b** *(= unchanging) temperature* gleichmäßig, gleichbleibend, konstant; **x remains ~ while y …** x bleibt konstant, während y …; **the price is not ~** der Preis bleibt nicht gleich *or* konstant **c** *(= steadfast) affection, devotion* unwandelbar, beständig; *friend, supporter, lover* treu N *(Math, Phys, fig)* Konstante *f*, konstante Größe

constant load N *(Tech)* Grundlast *f*

constantly ['kɒnstəntlɪ] ADV (an)dauernd, ständig

constellation [,kɒnstə'leɪʃən] N Sternbild *nt*, Konstellation *f (also fig)*

consternation [,kɒnstə'neɪʃən] N *(= dismay)* Bestürzung *f*; *(= concern, worry)* Sorge *f*; *(= fear and confusion)* Aufruhr *m*; **to my great ~** zu meiner großen Bestürzung; **in ~** bestürzt; **to cause ~** *(state of £, sb's behaviour)* Grund zur Sorge geben; *(news)* Bestürzung auslösen; **with a look**

of ~ on his face mit bestürzter Miene; **the news filled me with ~** ich war bestürzt, als ich das hörte

constipate ['kɒnstɪpeɪt] VT Verstopfung *f* hervorrufen bei, verstopfen

constipated ['kɒnstɪpeɪtɪd] ADJ *bowels* verstopft; **he is ~** er hat Verstopfung, er ist verstopft *(inf)*; **it'll make you ~** davon bekommst du Verstopfung, das stopft

constipation [ˌkɒnstɪ'peɪʃən] N *no pl* Verstopfung *f*

constituency [kən'stɪtjʊənsɪ] N *(Pol)* Wahlkreis *m*

constituent [kən'stɪtjʊənt] ADJ **a** *(Pol) assembly* konstituierend **b** *attr part, element* einzeln; **~ part** *or* **element** *(of machine, matter)* Bestandteil *m* N **a** *(Pol)* Wähler(in) *m(f)* **b** *(= part, element)* Bestandteil *m* **c** *(Ling)* Satzteil *m*

constitute ['kɒnstɪtju:t] VT **a** *(= make up)* bilden, ausmachen; **society is so ~d that …** die Gesellschaft ist so aufgebaut, dass … **b** *(= amount to)* darstellen; **that ~s a lie** das ist eine glatte Lüge **c** *(= set up, give legal authority to) committee, court* einrichten, konstituieren *(form)* **d** *(form: = appoint)* ernennen *or* bestimmen zu; **he ~d himself my bodyguard** er spielte meinen Leibwächter

constitution [ˌkɒnstɪ'tju:ʃən] N **a** *(Pol)* Verfassung *f*; *(of club etc)* Satzung *f* **b** *(of person)* Konstitution *f*, Gesundheit *f*; **to have a strong/weak ~** eine starke/schwache Konstitution haben **c** *(= way sth is made)* Aufbau *m*; *(= what sth is made of)* Zusammensetzung *f* **d** *(= setting up: of committee etc)* Einrichtung *f*

> **CONSTITUTION**
>
> Großbritannien hat anders als die Bundesrepubik Deutschland oder die Vereinigten Staaten keine niedergeschriebene Verfassung. Stattdessen setzt sich die britische **constitution** aus Gesetzen zusammen, die entweder verabschiedet **(statute law)** oder durch Gerichtsbeschluss entschieden worden sind **(common law)**; außerdem umfasst sie eine Vielzahl von Regeln und Bräuchen, die die Basis für die Regierungsarbeit bilden. Die Gesetze der Verfassung können, wie jedes andere Gesetz, durch Parlamentsbeschlüsse modifiziert oder abgeschafft werden.

constitutional [ˌkɒnstɪ'tju:ʃənl] ADJ **a** *(Pol) reform, crisis, theory* Verfassungs-; *monarchy, monarch* konstitutionell; *government, action* verfassungsmäßig; **~ law** Verfassungsrecht *nt*; **~ change** Verfassungsänderung *f*; **it's not ~** das ist verfassungswidrig **b** *(Med)* konstitutionell *(spec)*, körperlich bedingt; *(fig) dislike etc* naturgegeben *or* -bedingt N *(hum inf)* Spaziergang *m*; **to go for a/one's ~** einen/seinen Spaziergang machen

constitutionally [ˌkɒnstɪ'tju:ʃənəlɪ] ADV *(Pol)* verfassungsmäßig; *(= as the constitution says also)* nach der Verfassung; *(= in accordance with the constitution)* verfassungsgemäß; *(Med)* körperlich; *(fig)* von Natur aus

constrain [kən'streɪn] VT zwingen; *one's temper* zügeln

constrained [kən'streɪnd] ADJ *(= forced)* gezwungen; **to feel ~ by sth** sich durch etw eingeengt sehen; **to be/feel ~ to do sth** gezwungen sein/sich gezwungen sehen, etw zu tun

constraint [kən'streɪnt] N **a** *(= compulsion)* Zwang *m* **b** *(= restriction)* Beschränkung *f*, Einschränkung *f*; **to place ~s on sth** einer Sache *(dat)* Zwänge auferlegen **c** *(in manner etc)* Gezwungenheit *f*; *(= embarrassment)* Befangenheit *f*

constrict [kən'strɪkt] VT **a** *(= compress)* einzwängen, einengen; *muscle* zusammenziehen; *vein* verengen **b** *(= hamper, limit) movements* behindern, einschränken *(also fig)*; *breathing* behindern; *(rules, traditions etc)* einengen; *outlook, view etc* beschränken

constriction [kən'strɪkʃən] N **a** *(of muscles)* Zusammenziehen *nt*; **he had a feeling of ~ in his chest** er hatte ein Gefühl der Enge in der Brust **b** *(= limiting, of movements)* Behinderung *f*; *(caused by rules, traditions etc)* Einengung *f*; *(of outlook, view etc)* Beschränkung *f*

constrictive [kən'strɪktɪv] ADJ *garment* beengend; *environment* einengend; *ideology* eng; *amendments* einschränkend

constrictor [kən'strɪktə'] N **a** *(= muscle)* Schließmuskel *m*, Konstriktor *m (spec)* **b** *(= snake)* Boa (constrictor) *f*

construct [kən'strʌkt] VT bauen; *bridge, machine also* konstruieren; *(Geometry)* konstruieren; *sentence* bilden, konstruieren; *novel, play etc* aufbauen; *theory* entwickeln, konstruieren ['kɒnstrʌkt] N Gedankengebäude *nt*

construction [kən'strʌkʃən] N **a** *(of building, road)* Bau *m*; *(of bridge, machine also, of geometrical figures)* Konstruktion *f*; *(of novel, play etc)* Aufbau *m*; *(of theory)* Entwicklung *f*, Konstruktion *f*; **in course of** *or* **under ~** in *or* im Bau **b** *(= way sth is constructed)* Struktur *f*; *(of building)* Bauweise *f*; *(of machine, bridge)* Konstruktion *f*
c *(= sth constructed)* Bau *m*, Bauwerk *nt*; *(= bridge, machine)* Konstruktion *f*; **primitive ~s** primitive Bauten
d *(= interpretation)* Deutung *f*; **to put a wrong ~ on sth** etw falsch auffassen *or* auslegen; **I don't know what ~ to put on it** ich weiß nicht, wie ich das auffassen soll
e *(Gram)* Konstruktion *f*; **sentence ~** Satzbau *m*

constructional [kən'strʌkʃənl] ADJ baulich; *technique, tool* Bau-; *fault, toy* Konstruktions-

construction: **construction industry** N Bauindustrie *f*; **construction pit** N Baugrube *f*; **construction site** N Baustelle *f*, Baugelände *nt*; **construction vehicle** N Baufahrzeug *nt*; **construction worker** N Bauarbeiter(in) *m(f)*

constructive [kən'strʌktɪv] ADJ konstruktiv; **~ stress** Eustress *m*

constructively [kən'strʌktɪvlɪ] ADV konstruktiv; *critical* auf konstruktive Art; **he suggested, not very ~, that …** er machte den nicht gerade konstruktiven Vorschlag, zu …

construe [kən'stru:] VT **a** *(Gram) words* analysieren; *sentence also* zerlegen; **in English it is ~d as an adjective** im Englischen wird das als Adjektiv betrachtet **b** *(= interpret)* auslegen, auffassen VI *(Gram, sentence)* sich zerlegen *or* aufgliedern *or* analysieren lassen

consubstantiation [ˌkɒnsəbˌstænʃɪ'eɪʃən] N *(Eccl)* Konsubstantiation *f*

consuetude [ˌkɒnswɪ'tju:d] N *(form)* normative Kraft des Faktischen *(form)*

consul ['kɒnsəl] N Konsul *m*

consular ['kɒnsjʊlə'] ADJ konsularisch

consulate ['kɒnsjʊlɪt] N Konsulat *nt*

consul general N *pl* **-s -** Generalkonsul *m*

consulship ['kɒnsəlʃɪp] N Konsulat *nt*

consult [kən'sʌlt] VT **a** *(= ask)* sich besprechen mit, konsultieren; *lawyer, doctor etc* konsultieren, zurate *or* zu Rate ziehen; *dictionary* nachschlagen in *(+dat)*, konsultieren *(geh)*; *map* nachsehen auf *(+dat)*; *oracle* befragen; *horoscope* nachlesen; *clock* sehen auf *(+acc)*; **he might have ~ed me** das hätte er auch mit mir besprechen können, er hätte mich auch konsultieren können; **you don't have to ~ me about every little detail** Sie brauchen mich nicht wegen jeder Kleinigkeit zu fragen; **he did it without ~ing anyone** er hat das getan, ohne jemanden zu fragen
b *(form: = consider)* bedenken
VI *(= confer)* sich beraten, beratschlagen; **to ~ together (over sth)** (etw) gemeinsam beraten; **to ~ with sb** sich mit jdm beraten

consultancy [kən'sʌltənsɪ] N *(= act)* Beratung *f*;*(= business)* Beratungsbüro *nt*

consultant [kən'sʌltənt] N **a** *(Brit Med)* Facharzt *m*/-ärztin *f (am Krankenhaus)*; *(other professions)* Berater(in) *m(f)* **b consultants** PL *(Econ)* Beratungs- *or* Beraterfirma *f*, Unternehmensberatung *f* ADJ *attr* beratend

consultation [ˌkɒnsəl'teɪʃən] N *(= meeting)* Beratung *f*, Besprechung *f*, Konsultation *f (form)*; *(of doctor, lawyer)* Konsultation *f* (of +*gen*), Beratung *f* (of mit); **in ~ with** in gemeinsamer Beratung mit; **to have a ~ with one's doctor/lawyer** seinen Arzt/Rechtsanwalt konsultieren; **to hold a ~ (with sb)** sich (mit jdm) beraten, eine Besprechung (mit jdm) abhalten

consultative [kən'sʌltətɪv] ADJ *document* beratend, konsultativ *(form)*; **in a ~ capacity** in beratender Funktion

consulting [kən'sʌltɪŋ] ADJ *engineer, architect, psychiatrist* beratend

consulting: **consulting firm** N *(Econ)* Beratungs- *or* Beraterfirma *f*, Unternehmensberatung *f*; **consulting hours** PL *(Med)* Sprechstunde *f*; **consulting room** N *(Med)* Sprechzimmer *nt*

consumable [kən'sju:məbl] N Konsumgut *nt*, Verbrauchsgut *nt*; **~s** *(Comput)* Verbrauchsmaterial *nt*

consume [kən'sju:m] VT **a** *food, drink* zu sich nehmen, konsumieren *(form)*; *food also* verzehren *(geh)*, aufessen, vertilgen *(hum inf)*; *(Econ)* konsumieren **b** *(= destroy, fire)* vernichten; *(= use up) fuel, money* verbrauchen; *energy* aufbrauchen, verzehren *(geh)*; *time* in Anspruch nehmen; **he was ~d with desire/jealousy** er wurde von Begierde/Eifersucht verzehrt *(geh)*; **he was ~d with rage** die Wut fraß ihn nahezu auf

consumer [kən'sju:mə'] N Verbraucher(in) *m(f)*, Konsument(in) *m(f) (form)*

consumer *in cpds* Verbraucher-; **consumer advice centre** N Verbraucherzentrale *f*; **consumer credit** N Verbraucherkredit *m*; **consumer demand** N (konsumptive *(spec)*) Nachfrage; **consumer durables** PL (langlebige) Gebrauchsgüter *pl*; **consumer goods** PL Konsumgüter *pl*; **consumer group** N Verbrauchergruppe *f*

consumerism [kən'sju:mərɪzəm] N Konsumismus *m*, Konsumdenken *nt*; **the age of ~** das Konsumzeitalter

consumer: **consumer prices** PL Verbraucherpreise *f*; **consumer protection** N Verbraucherschutz *m*; **consumer research** N Verbraucherbefragung *f*; **consumer resistance** N Kaufunlust *f*; **Consumers' Association** N *(Brit) britischer Verbraucherverband*; **consumer society** N Konsumgesellschaft *f*

consuming [kən'sju:mɪŋ] ADJ *ambition, interest* glühend, brennend; *desire, passion also* verzehrend *(geh)*

consummate [kən'sʌmɪt] ADJ *skill, folly* vollendet, vollkommen; *politician* unübertrefflich; **with ~ ease** mit spielender Leichtigkeit ['kɒnsəmeɪt] VT *marriage* vollziehen

consummately [kən'sʌmɪtlɪ] ADV **a** *(form: = skilfully)* vollendet; **the film is a ~ acted piece** der Film ist schauspielerisch hervorragend umgesetzt **b** *(= supremely)* unübertrefflich; **he's ~ manipulative** er ist ein Meister der Manipulation

consummation [ˌkɒnsə'meɪʃən] N **a** *(of marriage)* Vollzug *m* **b** *(fig, = peak)* Höhepunkt *m*; *(= fulfilment)* Erfüllung *f*

consumption [kən'sʌmpʃən] N **a** *(of fuel etc)* Konsum *m*; *(of food also)* Verzehr *m (geh)*; *(of non-edible products)* Verbrauch *m*; **this letter is for private ~ only** *(inf)* der Brief ist nur für den privaten Gebrauch; **not fit for human ~** zum Verzehr ungeeignet; **world ~ of oil** Weltölverbrauch *m*; **his daily ~ of two bottles of wine** sein täglicher Konsum von zwei Flaschen Wein **b** *(Med old)* Auszehrung *f (old)*, Schwindsucht *f*

consumptive [kən'sʌmptɪv] *(old)* N Schwindsüchtige(r) *mf* ADJ schwindsüchtig

contact [ˈkɒntækt] ✪ 21.1 **N** **a** Kontakt *m*; *(= touching also)* Berührung *f*; *(= communication also)* Verbindung *f*; **to be in ~ with sb/sth** *(= be touching)* jdn/etw berühren; *(= in communication)* mit jdm/etw in Verbindung *or* Kontakt stehen; **to keep in ~ with sb** mit jdm in Kontakt bleiben; **to come into ~ with sb/sth** *(lit, fig)* mit jdm/etw in Berührung kommen; *with disease carrier also* mit jdm in Kontakt kommen; **he has no ~ with his family** er hat keinen Kontakt zu seiner Familie; **frequent ~ with death** häufige Berührung mit dem Tod; **on ~ with air/water** wenn es mit Luft/Wasser in Berührung kommt; **I'll get in ~** ich werde mich melden *(inf)*, ich werde von mir hören lassen; **I'll get in(to) ~ with you** ich werde mich mit Ihnen in Verbindung setzen; **how can we get in(to) ~ with him?** wie können wir ihn erreichen?; **to make ~** *(two things)* sich berühren; *(wires, wheels etc)* in Berührung *or* Kontakt (miteinander) kommen; *(two people, = get in touch)* sich miteinander in Verbindung setzen; *(by radio etc)* eine Verbindung herstellen; *(psychologically)* Kontakt bekommen; **he could make ~ by radio** er konnte sich durch Funk in Verbindung setzen; **as soon as the glue makes ~ (with the surface)** sobald der Klebstoff mit der Fläche in Berührung *or* Kontakt kommt; **to make ~ with sb/sth** *(= touch)* jdn/etw berühren, mit jdm/etw in Berührung kommen; *(wire, wheels etc also)* mit jdm/etw in Kontakt kommen; *(= get in touch with)* sich mit jdm/etw in Verbindung setzen; *(psychologically)* Kontakt zu jdm/etw bekommen; **I finally made ~ with him at his office** ich habe ihn schließlich im Büro erreicht; **to lose ~ (with sb/sth)** den Kontakt *or* die Verbindung (zu jdm/etw) verlieren; **point of ~** *(Math, fig)* Berührungspunkt *m*
b *(Elec) (= act)* Kontakt *m*; *(= equipment)* Kontakt- *or* Schaltstück *nt*; **to make/break ~** den Kontakt herstellen/unterbrechen
c *(= person)* Kontaktperson *f (also Med)*; *(in espionage)* Verbindungsmann *m*, V-Mann *m*; **~s** *pl* Kontakte *pl*, Verbindungen *pl*; **to make ~s** Kontakte herstellen; **he's made a useful ~** er hat einen nützlichen Kontakt hergestellt
VT *person, agent, lawyer* sich in Verbindung setzen mit; *(for help) police* sich wenden an *(+acc)*; **I've been trying to ~ you for hours** ich versuche schon seit Stunden, Sie zu erreichen; **he doesn't want to be ~ed unless it's urgent** er möchte, dass man sich nur in dringenden Fällen mit ihm in Verbindung setzt

contact: **contact allergy** N Kontaktallergie *f*; **contact breaker** N Unterbrecher *m*; **contact flight** N Sichtflug *m*; **contact lens** N Kontaktlinse *f*; **contact man** N Kontakt- *or* Mittelsmann *m*; **contact poison** N Kontakt- *or* Berührungsgift *nt*; **contact print** N *(Phot)* Kontaktabzug *m*; **contact sport** N Kontaktsport *m*

contagion [kənˈteɪdʒən] N *(= contact)* Ansteckung *f*; *(= disease)* Ansteckungskrankheit *f*; *(= epidemic)* Seuche *f (also fig)*; *(fig: = spreading influence)* schädlicher Einfluss

contagious [kənˈteɪdʒəs] ADJ *(Med, fig)* ansteckend; *disease also* direkt übertragbar; **he's not ~** *(Med)* seine Krankheit ist nicht ansteckend; *(hum)* er ist nicht giftig *(inf)*

contain [kənˈteɪn] VT **a** *(= hold within itself)* enthalten; **the envelope ~ed money** im Umschlag befand sich Geld, der Umschlag enthielt Geld **b** *(= have capacity for: box, bottle, room)* fassen **c** *(= control) emotions, oneself* beherrschen; *tears* zurückhalten; *laughter* unterdrücken; *disease, inflation, sb's power* in Grenzen halten; *epidemic, flood* aufhalten, unter Kontrolle bringen; *enemy* in Schach halten; *(Sport)* in Schach halten; *attack* abwehren; **he could hardly ~ himself** er konnte kaum an sich *(acc)* halten **d** *(Math) angle* einschließen

container [kənˈteɪnəʳ] **N** **a** Behälter *m*; *(= bottle, jar etc also)* Gefäß *nt* **b** *(Comm, for transport)* Container *m* **ADJ** *attr* Container-; **by ~ lorry** per Container

containerization [kənˌteɪnəraɪˈzeɪʃən] N *(of goods)* Verpackung *f* in Container; *(of ports)* Umstellung *f* auf Container

containerize [kənˈteɪnəraɪz] VT *freight* in Container verpacken; *port* auf Container umstellen

containment [kənˈteɪnmənt] N *(Mil)* In-Schach-Halten *nt*; *(of attack)* Abwehr *f*; **their efforts at ~ (of the rebels)** ihre Bemühungen, die Rebellen in Schach zu halten

contaminate [kənˈtæmɪneɪt] VT verunreinigen, verschmutzen; *(= poison)* vergiften; *(radioactivity)* verseuchen, kontaminieren *(spec)*; *(fig) mind* verderben; **the oranges were ~d by poison** in den Orangen befanden sich Giftstoffe

contamination [kənˌtæmɪˈneɪʃən] N *no pl* Verunreinigung *f*, Verschmutzung *f*; *(by poison)* Vergiftung *f*; *(by radioactivity)* Verseuchung *f*, Kontaminierung *f (spec)*; *(= substance)* Giftstoffe *pl*; *(fig)* schädlicher Einfluss *(of* auf *+acc)*

contango [kənˈtæŋgəʊ] N *(Fin)* Report *m*

contd *abbr of* **continued** Forts., Fortsetzung *f*

contemplate [ˈkɒntempleɪt] VT **a** *(= look at)* betrachten **b** *(= think about, reflect upon)* nachdenken über *(+acc)*; *(= consider) changes, a purchase, action, accepting an offer* in Erwägung ziehen, erwägen *(geh)*; *a holiday* denken an *(+acc)*; **he ~d the future with some misgivings** er sah der Zukunft mit einem unguten Gefühl entgegen; **he would never ~ violence** der Gedanke an Gewalttätigkeit würde ihm nie kommen; **it's too awful to ~** schon der Gedanke (daran) ist zu entsetzlich **c** *(= expect)* voraussehen **d** *(= intend)* **to ~ doing sth** daran denken, etw zu tun

contemplation [ˌkɒntemˈpleɪʃən] N *no pl* **a** *(= act of looking)* Betrachtung *f* **b** *(= act of thinking)* Nachdenken *nt* (*of* über *+acc*); *(= deep thought)* Besinnung *f*, Betrachtung *f*, Kontemplation *f (esp Rel)*; **a life of ~** ein beschauliches *or* kontemplatives *(esp Rel)* Leben; **deep in ~** in Gedanken versunken **c** *(= expectation)* Erwartung *f*

contemplative [kənˈtemplətɪv] ADJ **a** *(= thoughtful) look, person* nachdenklich; *mood also* besinnlich **b** *life, religious order* beschaulich, kontemplativ

contemplatively [kənˈtemplətɪvlɪ] ADV nachdenklich; *sit also* in Gedanken

contemporaneous [kənˌtempəˈreɪnɪəs] ADJ gleichzeitig stattfindend *attr*; **a manuscript ~ with ...** ein Manuskript aus derselben Zeit *or* Epoche wie ...; **events ~ with the rebellion** Ereignisse zur Zeit des Aufstandes

contemporary [kənˈtempərərɪ] **ADJ** **a** *(= of the same time) events* gleichzeitig; *records, literature, writer* zeitgenössisch; *(= of the same age) manuscript* gleich alt; **records ~ with the invasion** Aufzeichnungen aus der Zeit der Invasion **b** *(= of the present time) life* heutig; *art, design* zeitgenössisch, modern **N** Altersgenosse *m*/-genossin *f*; *(in history)* Zeitgenosse *m*/-genossin *f*; *(at university)* Kommilitone *m*, Kommilitonin *f*

contempt [kənˈtempt] N **a** Verachtung *f*; *(= disregard also)* Geringachtung *f*, Geringschätzung *f* (*for* von); **to hold in ~** verachten; **to bring into ~** in Verruf bringen; **in ~ of public opinion** die öffentliche Meinung außer Acht lassend, ohne Ansehen der öffentlichen Meinung; **beneath ~** unter aller Kritik **b** *(Jur, also* **contempt of court**) Missachtung *f* (der Würde) des Gerichts, Ungebühr *f* vor Gericht; *(through non-appearance)* Ungebühr *f* durch vorsätzliches Ausbleiben; *(by press)* Beeinflussung *f* der Rechtspflege; **to be in ~ (of court)** das Gericht *or* die Würde des Gerichts missachten

contemptible [kənˈtemptəbl] ADJ verachtenswert, verächtlich

contemptuous [kənˈtemptjʊəs] ADJ *manner, gesture, look* geringschätzig, verächtlich; *person* herablassend; *laugh, sneer, remark, reference* verächtlich; **to be ~ of sb/sth** jdn/etw verachten; **she was quite ~ of my offer** sie reagierte ziemlich verächtlich auf mein Angebot

contemptuously [kənˈtemptjʊəslɪ] ADV *say, look, laugh, spit* verächtlich

contend [kənˈtend] **VI** **a** *(= compete)* kämpfen; **to ~ (with sb) for sth** (mit jdm) um etw kämpfen; **then you'll have me to ~ with** dann bekommst du es mit mir zu tun; **but I've got two directors to ~ with** aber ich habe es mit zwei Direktoren zu tun **b** *(= cope)* **to ~ with sb/sth** mit jdm/etw fertig werden **VT** behaupten

contender [kənˈtendəʳ] N Kandidat(in) *m(f)*, Anwärter(in) *m(f)* *(for* auf *+acc)*; *(for job also)* Bewerber(in) *m(f)* *(for* um); *(Sport)* Wettkämpfer(in) *m(f)* *(for* um)

contending [kənˈtendɪŋ] ADJ *emotions* widerstreitend; **the ~ parties** *(in dispute, lawsuit)* die streitenden Parteien *pl*

content[1] [kənˈtent] **ADJ** *pred* zufrieden *(with* mit); **to be/feel ~** zufrieden sein; **she's quite ~ to stay at home** sie bleibt ganz gern zu Hause **N** Zufriedenheit *f* **VT** *person* zufriedenstellen; **to ~ oneself with** sich zufriedengeben *or* begnügen *or* abfinden mit; **to ~ oneself with doing sth** sich damit zufriedengeben *or* begnügen *or* abfinden, etw zu tun

content[2] [ˈkɒntent] N **a** **contents** PL *(of room, one's pocket, book etc)* Inhalt *m*; **(table of) ~s** Inhaltsverzeichnis *nt* **b** *no pl (= substance, component)* Gehalt *m*; *(of speech, book etc also)* Inhalt *m*; **gold/vitamin ~** Gold-/Vitamingehalt *m*

contented, **contentedly** [kənˈtentɪd, -lɪ] ADJ, ADV zufrieden

contentedness [kənˈtentɪdnɪs] N = **contentment**

contention [kənˈtenʃən] N **a** *(= dispute)* Streit *m*; **~s** Streitigkeiten *pl*; **the matter in ~** die strittige Angelegenheit; **that is no longer in ~** das steht nicht mehr zur Debatte **b** *(= argument)* Behauptung *f*; **it is my ~ that ...** ich behaupte, dass ... **c** *(in contest)* **to be in ~ (for sth)** Chancen (auf etw *(acc)*) haben

contentious [kənˈtenʃəs] ADJ *subject, issue* strittig, umstritten; *view* umstritten, kontrovers; *decision, proposal, legislation* umstritten; *person* streitlustig, streitsüchtig

contentiously [kənˈtenʃəslɪ] ADV kontrovers

contentment [kənˈtentmənt] N Zufriedenheit *f*

content provider N *(Comput)* Content Provider *m*

contest [ˈkɒntest] **N** *(for* um) Kampf *m*; *(= competition also)* Wettkampf *m*, Wettstreit *m (geh)*; *(= beauty contest etc)* Wettbewerb *m*; **boxing ~** Boxkampf *m*; **election ~** Wahlkampf *m*; **it's no ~** das ist ein ungleicher Kampf; **it was a real ~ of skill** es kam dabei wirklich aufs Können an
VT [kənˈtest] **a** *(= fight over)* kämpfen um; *(= fight against, oppose)* kämpfen gegen; *(Parl) election* teilnehmen an *(+dat)*; **to ~ a seat** *(Parl)* um einen Wahlkreis kämpfen; **the seat was not ~ed** es gab keinen Kampf um den Wahlkreis
b *(= dispute) statement* bestreiten, angreifen; *measure* angreifen; *(Jur) will, right, legal action* anfechten; **a ~ed measure** eine umstrittene Maßnahme; **to ~ sb's right to do sth** jdm das Recht streitig machen *or* jds Recht anfechten, etw zu tun
VI [kənˈtest] kämpfen *(for* um)

contestant [kənˈtestənt] N (Wettbewerbs)teilnehmer(in) *m(f)*; *(Parl, in quiz)* Kandidat(in) *m(f)*; *(Sport)* (Wettkampf)teilnehmer(in) *m(f)*; *(Mil)* Kämpfende(r) *m*; **the ~s in the election** die Wahlkandidaten

context [ˈkɒntekst] ✪ 26.2 N Zusammenhang *m*, Kontext *m (geh)*; **(taken) out of ~** aus dem Zusammenhang *or* Kontext *(geh)* gerissen; **in the broader European ~** im weiteren europäischen Zusammenhang *or* Kontext *(geh) or* Rahmen; **in this ~** in diesem Zusammenhang; **in an office ~** im Rahmen eines Büros

context menu N *(Comput)* Kontextmenü *nt*

context-sensitive [ˌkɒntekstˈsensɪtɪv] ADJ *(Comput)* kontextsensitiv; **~ menu** Kontextmenü *nt*

contextual [kənˈtekstjʊəl] ADJ kontextuell *(form)*; *meaning* aus dem Zusammenhang *or* Kontext *(geh)* ersichtlich

contextualize [kənˈtekstjʊəlaɪz] VT in einen Zusammenhang *or* Kontext *(geh)* setzen

contiguity [ˌkɒntɪˈgjʊɪtɪ] N (unmittelbare) Nachbarschaft

contiguous [kənˈtɪgjʊəs] ADJ *(form)* aneinandergrenzend, sich berührend; *(in time)* (unmittelbar) aufeinanderfolgend; **the estates are ~** die Grundstücke grenzen aneinander; **~ cull** *(of cattle)* Keulung *f*

continence [ˈkɒntɪnəns] N **a** *(Med)* Kontinenz *f (spec)*, Fähigkeit *f* Stuhl und/oder Urin zurückzuhalten **b** *(= abstinence)* Enthaltsamkeit *f*

continent[1] [ˈkɒntɪnənt] ADJ **the old lady was not ~** *(Med)* die alte Dame konnte ihre Darmtätigkeit/Blasentätigkeit nicht mehr kontrollieren

continent[2] N *(Geog)* Kontinent *m*, Erdteil *m*; *(= mainland)* Festland *nt*; **the Continent (of Europe)** *(Brit)* Kontinentaleuropa *nt*; **on the Continent** in Europa, auf dem Kontinent

continental [ˌkɒntɪˈnentl] ADJ **a** *(Geog)* kontinental **b** *(Brit: = European)* europäisch; *holidays* in Europa N (Festlands)europäer(in) *m(f)*

continental: **continental breakfast** N kleines Frühstück; **continental drift** N *(Geog)* Kontinentaldrift *f*; **continental quilt** N Steppdecke *f*; **continental shelf** N *(Geog)* Kontinentalschelf *m*, Kontinentalsockel *m*

contingency [kənˈtɪndʒənsɪ] N **a** möglicher Fall, Eventualität *f*; **in this ~, should this ~ arise** in diesem Fall, für diesen Fall, sollte dieser Fall eintreten; **to provide for all contingencies** alle Möglichkeiten einplanen, alle Eventualitäten berücksichtigen; **a ~ plan** ein Ausweichplan *m*; **~ planning** Planung *f* für Eventualfälle **b** *(Philos)* Kontingenz *f*

contingency fee N *(US Jur)* Erfolgshonorar *nt*

contingency fund N Eventualfonds *m*

contingent [kənˈtɪndʒənt] ADJ **a ~ upon** *(form)* abhängig von; **to be ~ upon** abhängen von **b** *(Philos)* kontingent N Kontingent *nt*; *(= section)* Gruppe *f*; *(Mil)* Trupp *m*

continual [kənˈtɪnjʊəl] ADJ *(= frequent)* dauernd, ständig; *(= unceasing)* ununterbrochen, pausenlos

continually [kənˈtɪnjʊəlɪ] ADV *(= repeatedly)* (an)dauernd, ständig; *(= ceaselessly)* ununterbrochen, pausenlos

continuance [kənˈtɪnjʊəns] N **a** *(= duration)* Dauer *f* **b** = **continuation a**

continuation [kənˌtɪnjʊˈeɪʃən] N **a** Fortsetzung *f*, Fortführung *f*; **the ~ of the human race** der Weiterbestand *or* Fortbestand der menschlichen Rasse; **the Government's ~ in office** das Verbleiben der Regierung im Amt **b** *(= retention: of arrangement etc)* Beibehaltung *f* **c** *(= resumption)* Fortsetzung *f*, Wiederaufnahme *f* **d** *(= sth continued)* Fortsetzung *f*, Weiterführung *f*

continue [kənˈtɪnju:] VT **a** *(= carry on)* fortfahren mit; *policy, tradition, struggle* fortsetzen, fortführen, weiterführen; *activity, piece of work, meal* fortsetzen, weitermachen mit; **to ~ doing** *or* **to do sth** etw weiter tun, fortfahren, etw zu tun; **to ~ to fight/sing/read/eat, to ~ fighting/singing/reading/eating** weiterkämpfen/-singen/-lesen/-essen; **her condition ~s to improve** ihr Befinden bessert sich ständig
b *(= resume)* fortsetzen; *conversation, work, journey also* wieder aufnehmen; **to be ~d** Fortsetzung folgt; **~d on p 10** weiter *or* Fortsetzung auf Seite 10; **~ (command)** *(Comput)* weiter
c *(= prolong) line* verlängern, weiterführen
VI *(= go on, person)* weitermachen; *(crisis, speech)* fortdauern, (an)dauern; *(influence)* fortdauern, andauern; *(weather)* anhalten; *(road, forest etc)* weitergehen, sich fortsetzen; *(concert etc)* weitergehen; **to ~ on one's way** weiterfahren; *(on foot)* weitergehen; **he ~d after a short pause** er redete/schrieb/las *etc* nach einer kurzen Pause weiter; **to ~ with one's work** seine Arbeit fortsetzen, mit seiner Arbeit weitermachen; **please ~** bitte machen Sie weiter; *(in talking)* fahren Sie fort; **to ~ to be obstinate/cheerful** weiterhin starrköpfig/fröhlich bleiben; **he ~s to be optimistic** er ist nach wie vor optimistisch; **to ~ at university/with a company/as sb's secretary** auf der Universität/bei einer Firma/jds Sekretärin bleiben; **to ~ in office** im Amt verbleiben; **his influence ~d after his death** sein Einfluss überdauerte seinen Tod

continuing [kənˈtɪnju:ɪŋ] ADJ ständig, fortgesetzt; *process* stetig, kontinuierlich *(geh)*

continuity [ˌkɒntɪˈnju:ɪtɪ] N **a** Kontinuität *f*; **the story lacks ~** der Geschichte fehlt der rote Faden **b** *(Film)* Anschluss *m*; *(Rad)* (verbindende) Ansagen *pl*

continuity announcer N *(TV, Rad)* Ansager(in) *m(f)*

continuity girl N Scriptgirl *nt*

continuo [kənˈtɪnjʊəʊ] N Continuo *nt*; **to play the ~** Continuo spielen

continuous [kənˈtɪnjʊəs] ADJ dauernd, ständig, kontinuierlich *(geh)*; *line* durchgezogen, ununterbrochen; *rise, movement etc* stetig, stet *attr (geh)*, gleichmäßig; *(Math) function* stetig; **to be in ~ use** ständig in Benutzung sein; **a ~ stream of people** ein ununterbrochener Andrang von Menschen; **a ~ stream of phone calls** eine ununterbrochene Flut von Anrufen; **~ assessment** Beurteilung *f* der Leistungen während des ganzen Jahres; **~ paper** *(Comput)* Endlospapier *nt*; *(pre-printed)* Endlosformular *nt*; **~ performance** *(Film)* durchgehende Vorstellung; **~ tense** *(Gram)* Verlaufsform *f*; **present/past ~** *(Gram)* erweitertes Präsens/Präteritum; **~ text** Fließtext *m*

continuously [kənˈtɪnjʊəslɪ] ADV *(= repeatedly)* dauernd, ständig, kontinuierlich *(geh)*; *(= ceaselessly)* ununterbrochen; *rise, move* stetig, gleichmäßig

continuum [kənˈtɪnjʊəm] N Kontinuum *nt*

contort [kənˈtɔ:t] VT **a** *one's features, metal* verziehen *(into* zu); *limbs* verrenken, verdrehen; **a face ~ed with pain** ein schmerzverzerrtes Gesicht; **a ~ed smile** ein verkrampftes Lächeln **b** *(fig) words* verdrehen; *report also* verzerren

contortion [kənˈtɔ:ʃən] N *(esp of acrobat)* Verrenkung *f*; *(of features)* Verzerrung *f*; **mental ~s** geistige Verrenkungen *pl or* Klimmzüge *pl*; **he resorted to elaborate verbal ~s to avoid telling the truth** er hat sich gedreht und gewendet, um nicht die Wahrheit sagen zu müssen

contortionist [kənˈtɔ:ʃənɪst] N Schlangenmensch *m*

contour [ˈkɒntʊəˈ] N **a** *(= outline)* Kontur *f*, Umriss *m* **b** **contours** PL *(= shape)* Konturen *pl*; **the ~s of her body** ihre Konturen **c** *(Geog)* Höhenlinie *f* VT *road* der Gegend anpassen; *land* hügelig anlegen; *map* mit Höhenlinien versehen

contoured [ˈkɒntʊəd] ADJ konturenreich, geschwungen; **~ seat** den Körperformen angepasster Sitz

contour *(Geog)*: **contour line** N Höhenlinie *f*; **contour map** N Höhenlinienkarte *f*; **contour sheet** N *(US)* Spannbettlaken *nt*, Spannbetttuch *nt*

contra- [ˈkɒntrə-] PREF Gegen-, Kontra-; *(Mus, = pitched lower)* Kontra-

contraband [ˈkɒntrəbænd] N *no pl (= goods)* Konterbande *f*, Schmuggelware *f*; *(form: = smuggling)* Schleichhandel *m*, Schmuggeln *nt*; **~ of war** Kriegskonterbande *f* ADJ Schmuggel-; **~ goods** Konterbande *f*, Schmuggelware *f*

contraception [ˌkɒntrəˈsepʃən] N Empfängnisverhütung *f*

contraceptive [ˌkɒntrəˈseptɪv] N empfängnisverhütendes Mittel; *(= sheath)* Verhütungsmittel *nt*, Präventivmittel *nt (form)* ADJ empfängnisverhütend; *pill* Antibaby-; *advice* über Empfängnisverhütung

contract[1] [ˈkɒntrækt] N **a** *(= agreement)* Vertrag *m*, Kontrakt *m (old)*; *(= document also)* Vertragsdokument *nt*; *(Comm: = order)* Auftrag *m*; *(= delivery contract)* Liefervertrag *m*; **to enter into** *or* **make a ~ (with sb)** (mit jdm) einen Vertrag eingehen *or* (ab)schließen; **to be under ~** unter Vertrag stehen *(to* bei, mit); **to be bound by ~** vertraglich gebunden sein *(to* an *+acc)*; **to put work out to ~** Arbeiten außer Haus machen lassen; **to take out a ~ on sb** *(to kill)* einen Killer auf jdn ansetzen; **terms of ~** Vertragsbedingungen *or* -bestimmungen *pl*
b *(Bridge)* Kontrakt *m* → **contract bridge**
ADJ *price, date* vertraglich festgelegt *or* vereinbart; **~ work** Auftragsarbeit *f*
VT [kənˈtrækt] **a** *(= acquire) debts* machen, ansammeln; *illness* erkranken an *(+dat)*; *vices, habit* sich *(dat)* zulegen, entwickeln, annehmen; *passion* entwickeln
b *(= enter into) marriage, alliance* schließen, eingehen
VI [kənˈtrækt] **a** *(Comm)* **to ~ to do sth** sich vertraglich verpflichten, etw zu tun
b *(form, = make an arrangement)* sich verbünden

► **contract in** VI sich anschließen *(-to +dat)*; *(into insurance scheme)* beitreten *(-to +dat)*

► **contract out** VI *(= withdraw)* austreten, aussteigen *(inf)* *(of* aus); *(= not join)* sich nicht anschließen *(of +dat)*; *(out of insurance scheme)* nicht beitreten *(of +dat)* VT *sep (Comm) work* außer Haus machen lassen *(to* von), vergeben *(to* an *+acc)*

contract[2] [kənˈtrækt] VT **a** *muscle, metal etc* zusammenziehen **b** *(Ling)* zusammenziehen, kontrahieren *(spec) (into* zu) VI *(muscle, metal etc)* sich zusammenziehen; *(pupil also)* sich verengen; *(fig, influence, business)* (zusammen)schrumpfen

contract bridge N Kontrakt-Bridge *nt*

contracted [kənˈtræktɪd] ADJ zusammengezogen; *(Ling also)* verkürzt; *brow* gerunzelt; *(fig)* engstirnig

contraction [kənˈtrækʃən] N **a** *(of metal, muscles)* Zusammenziehen *nt*, Zusammenziehung *f*; *(fig)* Schrumpfung *f* **b** *(Ling)* Kontraktion *f* **c** *(in childbirth)* **(labour) ~s** (Geburts)wehen *pl*; **the ~s are coming strong** die Wehen sind stark **d** *(form: = acquisition, of debts)* Ansammlung *f*; *(of habit)* Entwicklung *f*, Annahme *f*; **his ~ of polio** seine Erkrankung an Kinderlähmung

contract: **contract killing** N Auftragsmord *m*; **contract law** N *no pl* Vertragsrecht *nt*; **contract note** N *(St Ex)* Schlussschein *m*

contractor [kənˈtræktəˈ] N *(= individual)* Auftragnehmer *m*, beauftragter Elektriker/Monteur *etc*; *(= company also)* beauftragte Firma; *(= building contractor)* Bauunternehmer *m*; *(= company)* Bauunternehmen *nt*, Bauunternehmer *m*; **that is done by outside ~s** damit ist eine andere Firma beauftragt

contractual [kənˈtræktʃʊəl] ADJ vertraglich

contractually [kənˈtræktʃʊəlɪ] ADV vertraglich; **~ binding** vertraglich bindend

contradict [ˌkɒntrəˈdɪkt] ✪ 26.3 VT *(person)* widersprechen *(+dat)*; *(event, action, statement also)* im Widerspruch stehen zu; **to ~ oneself** sich *(dat)* widersprechen; **he ~ed every word I said** er widersprach mir bei jedem Wort; **he can't stand being ~ed** er duldet keinen Widerspruch

contradiction [ˌkɒntrəˈdɪkʃən] N Widerspruch *m (of* zu); *(= act of) contradicting)* Widersprechen *nt*; **full of ~s** voller Widersprüchlichkeiten; **to give a flat ~** einfach *or* rundheraus widersprechen *(+dat)*

contradictory [ˌkɒntrəˈdɪktərɪ] ADJ *person* widersprüchlich; *statements also* (sich) widersprechend; **to be ~ to sth** einer Sache *(dat)* widersprechen, zu etw im Widerspruch stehen; **it is ~ to claim that …** es ist ein Widerspruch, zu behaupten ...; **he was in a ~ mood** er war voller Widerspruchsgeist

contradistinction [ˌkɒntrədɪsˈtɪŋkʃən] N *(form)* **in ~ to** im Gegensatz *or* Unterschied zu

contraflow [ˈkɒntrəfləʊ] *(Mot)* N Gegenverkehr *m* ADJ Gegenverkehrs-

contrail [ˈkɒntreɪl] N *(Aviat)* Kondensstreifen *m*

contraindication [ˌkɒntrəˌɪndɪˈkeɪʃən] N *(Med)* Kontraindikation *f*, Gegenanzeige *f*

contralto [kənˈtræltəʊ] N *(= voice)* Alt *m*; *(= singer also)* Altist(in) *m(f)* ADJ *voice* Alt-; **the ~ part** die Altstimme, der Alt

contraption [kənˈtræpʃən] N *(inf)* Apparat *m (inf)*; *(= vehicle also)* Vehikel *nt (inf)*, Kiste *f (inf)*

contrapuntal [ˌkɒntrəˈpʌntl] ADJ kontrapunktisch

contrarian [kənˈtreərɪən] *(form)* N Querdenker(in) *m(f)*, Nonkonformist(in) *m(f)* ADJ nonkonformistisch

contrarily [kənˈtreərɪlɪ] ADV *(= perversely)* widerborstig; *(of horse etc)* widerspenstig

contrariness [kənˈtreərɪnɪs] N Widerborstigkeit *f*; *(of person also)* Widerspruchsgeist *m*; *(of horse)* Widerspenstigkeit *f*

contrary[1] [ˈkɒntrərɪ] ✪ 22, 26.2, 26.3 ADJ *(= opposite)* entgegengesetzt; *effect, answer also* gegenteilig; *(= conflicting) views, statements also* gegensätzlich; *(= adverse) winds, tides* widrig; **in a ~ direction** in entgegengesetzter Richtung; **sth is ~ to sth** etw steht im Gegensatz zu etw; **it is ~ to our agreement** es entspricht nicht unseren Abmachungen; **to run ~ to sth** einer Sache *(dat)* zuwiderlaufen; **~ to nature** wider die Natur; **~ to our hopes/intentions** wider all unsere Hoffnungen/Absichten, entgegen unseren Hoffnungen/Absichten; **~ to what I expected** entgegen meinen Erwartungen
N Gegenteil *nt*; **on the ~** im Gegenteil; **the ~ of what I expected** das Gegenteil von dem, was ich erwartet hatte; **unless you hear to the ~** sofern Sie nichts Gegenteiliges hören; **statement/evidence to the ~** gegenteilige Aussage/gegenteiliger Beweis; **quite the ~** ganz im Gegenteil

contrary[2] [kənˈtreərɪ] ADJ widerborstig, widerspenstig; *person also* voll Widerspruchsgeist; *horse* widerspenstig

contrast [ˈkɒntrɑːst] ✪ 5.1 N **a** *(= contrasting)* Gegenüberstellung *f*
b Gegensatz *m* (*with, to* zu); *(visual, = striking difference of opposites)* Kontrast *m* (*with, to* zu); **by** *or* **in ~** im Gegensatz dazu; **to be in ~ with** *or* **to sth** im Gegensatz/in Kontrast zu etw stehen; **the red is a good ~** das Rot stellt einen guten Kontrast dar; **she's quite a ~ to her sister** es besteht ein ziemlicher Gegensatz *or* Unterschied zwischen ihr und ihrer Schwester; **the ~ between the state of the £ now and last year** der Unterschied zwischen dem jetzigen Stand des Pfundes und seinem Wert im letzten Jahr; **and now, by way of ~** und nun etwas ganz anderes; **what a ~!** welch ein Gegensatz!
c *(Art, Phot, TV)* Kontrast *m*
VT [kənˈtrɑːst] einen Vergleich anstellen (*with* zwischen *+dat*), gegenüberstellen (*with +dat*)
VI [kənˈtrɑːst] im Gegensatz *or* in Kontrast stehen (*with* zu), kontrastieren (*with* mit); *(colours also)* sich abheben (*with* von), abstechen (*with* von); **to ~ unfavourably with sth** bei einem Vergleich mit *or* im Vergleich zu etw schlecht abschneiden; **his promises and his actions ~ sharply** seine Versprechungen und seine Handlungsweise stehen in scharfem Kontrast *or* Gegensatz zueinander; **blue and yellow ~ nicely** Blau und Gelb ergeben einen hübschen Kontrast

contrasting [kənˈtrɑːstɪŋ] ADJ *opinions, lifestyle etc* gegensätzlich, kontrastierend *(form)*; *colours* kontrastierend, Kontrast-

contrastive [kənˈtrɑːstɪv] ADJ gegenüberstellend; *(Ling)* kontrastiv

contravene [ˌkɒntrəˈviːn] VT *law, custom etc (action, behaviour)* verstoßen gegen, verletzen; *(person also)* zuwiderhandeln *(+dat)*

contravention [ˌkɒntrəˈvenʃən] N Verstoß *m* (*of* gegen), Verletzung *f* (*of +gen*); *(of law also)* Übertretung *f* (*of +gen*); **to be in ~ of ...** gegen ... verstoßen; **to act in ~ of sth** einer Sache *(dat)* zuwiderhandeln

contre-jour [ˈkɒntrəʒʊəˈ] ADJ *(Phot)* Gegenlicht-; **~ shot** Gegenlichtaufnahme *f*

contretemps [ˈkɒntrəˌtɒŋ] N *no pl* Zwischenfall *m*; *(= unexpected hitch also)* kleines Missgeschick

contribute [kənˈtrɪbjuːt] VT beitragen (*to* zu); *food, money, supplies* beisteuern (*to* zu); *(to charity)* spenden (*to* für); *time, talent* zur Verfügung stellen (*to +dat*); *press article also, information* liefern (*to* für), beisteuern (*to +dat*); **to ~ one's share** sein(en) Teil dazu beitragen
VI beitragen (*to* zu); *(to pension fund etc)* einen Beitrag leisten (*to* zu); *(to present)* beisteuern (*to* zu); *(to charity)* spenden (*to* für); *(to newspaper, conference, society etc)* einen Beitrag leisten (*to* zu); *(regularly: to a magazine etc)* mitwirken (*to* an *+dat*); **do you want me to ~?** möchten Sie, dass ich etwas dazu beisteuere *or (to charity)* etwas spende?

contribution [ˌkɒntrɪˈbjuːʃən] N Beitrag *m* (*to* zu); *(= donation also)* Spende *f* (*to* für); **to make a ~ to sth** einen Beitrag zu etw leisten; **the beer is my ~** das Bier stelle ich; **I appreciate the ~ of so much of your time/effort** ich weiß es zu schätzen, dass Sie Ihre Zeit so großzügig zur Verfügung gestellt/solche Anstrengungen unternommen haben

contributor [kənˈtrɪbjʊtəˈ] N *(to magazine etc)* Mitarbeiter(in) *m(f)* (*to* an *+dat*); *(of goods, money)* Spender(in) *m(f)*; **to be a ~ to a newspaper** für eine Zeitung schreiben; **to be a ~ to an appeal** auf einen Appell hin etwas spenden

contributory [kənˈtrɪbjʊtərɪ] ADJ **a** **it's certainly a ~ factor/cause** es ist sicherlich ein Faktor, der dazu beiträgt *or* der mit eine Rolle spielt; **to be a ~ cause of a disease** ein Faktor sein, der zu einer Krankheit beiträgt; **to be ~ to sth** zu etw beitragen **b** *pension scheme* beitragspflichtig

contributory negligence N *(Jur)* Mitverschulden *nt*

con trick N *(inf)* Schwindel *m*

contrite ADJ, **contritely** ADV [kənˈtraɪt, -lɪ] reuig, zerknirscht

contrition [kənˈtrɪʃən] N Reue *f*; **act of ~** *(Eccl)* Buße *f*

contrivance [kənˈtraɪvəns] N **a** *(= device)* Vorrichtung *f*; *(mechanical)* Gerät *nt*, Apparat *m* **b** *(= devising, scheming)* Planung *f*; *(= invention)* Erfindung *f*; *(= inventiveness)* Findigkeit *f*, Erfindungsgabe *f*; **a plan of his ~** ein seinem Kopf entstammender Plan; **a device of his ~** ein von ihm erfundenes Gerät **c** *(= plan, scheme)* List *f*

contrive [kənˈtraɪv] VT **a** *(= devise) plan, scheme* entwickeln, entwerfen, ersinnen; *(= make)* fabrizieren; **to ~ a means of doing sth** einen Weg finden, etw zu tun **b** *(= manage, arrange)* bewerkstelligen, zuwege *or* zu Wege bringen; *meeting also* arrangieren; **to ~ to do sth** es fertigbringen *(also iro) or* zuwege *or* zu Wege bringen, etw zu tun; **can you ~ to be here at three o'clock?** können Sie es so einrichten, dass Sie um drei Uhr hier sind?; **he always ~s to get his own way** er versteht (es) immer, seinen Kopf durchzusetzen

contrived [kənˈtraɪvd] ADJ gestellt; *style also* gekünstelt

control [kənˈtrəʊl] N **a** *no pl (= management, supervision)* Aufsicht *f* (*of* über *+acc*); *(of money, fortune)* Verwaltung *f* (*of +gen*); *(of situation, emotion, language)* Beherrschung *f* (*of +gen*); *(= self-control)* (Selbst)beherrschung *f*; *(= physical control)* (Körper)beherrschung *f* (*of +gen*); *(= authority, power)* Gewalt *f*, Macht *f* (*over* über *+acc*); *(over territory)* Gewalt *f* (*over* über *+acc*); *(= regulation, of prices, disease, inflation)* Kontrolle *f* (*of +gen*); *(of traffic)* Regelung *f* (*of +gen*); *(of pollution)* Einschränkung *f* (*of +gen*); **his ~ of the ball** seine Ballführung; **to be in ~ of sth, to have ~ of sth** *(= be in charge of, business, office)* etw leiten, etw unter sich *(dat)* haben; *money* etw verwalten; **to have ~ of sb** jdn unter Kontrolle haben; *children* jdn beaufsichtigen; **I'm in ~ here** ich habe hier die Leitung; **to be in ~ of sth, to have sth under ~** *(= deal successfully with)* etw in der Hand haben; *class also* etw unter Kontrolle haben; *situation also* Herr einer Sache *(gen)* sein, etw beherrschen; *car, inflation, disease, pollution* etw unter Kontrolle haben; **to be in ~ of oneself** sich in der Hand *or* in der Gewalt haben; **to be in ~ of one's emotions** Herr über seine Gefühle sein, Herr seiner Gefühle sein; **to have some/no ~ over sb/sth** *(= have influence over)* Einfluss/keinen Einfluss auf jdn/etw haben; *over money* Kontrolle/keine Kontrolle über etw *(acc)* haben; **she has no ~ over how the money is spent/what her children do** sie hat keinen Einfluss darauf, wie das Geld ausgegeben wird/was ihre Kinder machen; **to lose ~ (of sth)** etw nicht mehr in der Hand haben, (über etw *acc*) die Gewalt *or* Herrschaft verlieren; *of business* die Kontrolle (über etw *acc*) verlieren; *of car* die Kontrolle *or* Herrschaft (über etw *acc*) verlieren; **to lose ~ of oneself** die Beherrschung verlieren; **to lose ~ of the situation** nicht mehr Herr der Lage sein; **to keep ~ (of oneself)** sich unter Kontrolle halten; **to be/get out of ~** *(child, class)* außer Rand und Band sein/geraten; *(situation)* außer Kontrolle sein/geraten; *(car)* nicht mehr zu halten sein; *(inflation, prices, disease, pollution)* sich jeglicher Kontrolle *(dat)* entziehen/nicht mehr zu halten *or* zu bremsen *(inf)* sein; *(fire)* nicht unter Kontrolle sein/außer Kontrolle geraten; **the car spun out of ~** der Wagen begann sich ganz unkontrollierbar zu drehen; **under state ~** unter staatlicher Kontrolle *or* Aufsicht; **to bring** *or* **get sth under ~** etw unter Kontrolle bringen; *situation* Herr einer Sache *(gen)* werden; *car* etw in seine Gewalt bringen; **to be under ~** unter Kontrolle sein; *(children, class)* sich benehmen; *(car)* (wieder) lenkbar sein; **everything** *or* **the situation is under ~** wir/sie *etc* haben die Sache im Griff *(inf)*; **the situation was beyond their ~** die Sache war ihnen völlig aus der Hand geglitten, sie hatten die Sache nicht mehr in der Hand; **he was beyond his parents' ~** er war seinen Eltern über den Kopf gewachsen; **circumstances beyond our ~** nicht in unserer Hand liegende Umstände
b *(= check)* Kontrolle *f* (*on +gen*, über *+acc*); **wage/price ~s** Lohn-/Preiskontrolle *f*
c *(= control room)* die Zentrale; *(Aviat)* der Kontrollturm
d *(= knob, switch)* Regler *m*; *(of vehicle, machine)* Schalter *m*; **to be at the ~s** *(of spaceship, airliner)* am Kontrollpult sitzen; *(of small plane, car)* die Steuerung haben; **to take over the ~s** die Steuerung übernehmen
e *(Sci: = person)* Kontrollperson *f*; *(= animal)* Kontrolltier *nt*; *(= group)* Kontrollgruppe *f*
f *(Spiritualism)* *Geist einer Persönlichkeit, dessen Äußerungen das Medium wiedergibt*
g *(Comput)* Steuerung *f*; **~-F1** Control-F1
VT **a** *(= direct, manage)* kontrollieren; *business* führen, leiten, unter sich *(dat)* haben; *sea* beherrschen; *organization* in der Hand haben; *animal, child, class* fertig werden mit; *car* steuern, lenken; *traffic* regeln; *emotions, movements* beherrschen, unter Kontrolle halten; *hair* bändigen; **to ~ oneself/one's temper** sich beherrschen; **~ yourself!** nimm dich zusammen!; **please try to ~ your children/dog** bitte sehen Sie zu, dass sich Ihre Kinder benehmen/sich Ihr Hund benimmt
b *(= regulate, check) prices, rents, growth etc* kontrollieren; *temperature, speed* regulieren; *disease* unter Kontrolle bringen; *population* eindämmen, im Rahmen halten

control: **control centre**, *(US)* **control center** N Kontrollzentrum *nt*; **control character**

N *(Comput)* Steuerzeichen *nt*; **control column** N Steuersäule *f (form)*, Steuerknüppel *m*; **control desk** N Steuer- *or* Schaltpult *nt; (TV, Rad)* Regiepult *nt*; **control experiment** N Kontrollversuch *m*; **control freak** N *(inf)* **most men are total ~s** die meisten Männer müssen immer alles unter Kontrolle haben; **control group** N *(Med, Psych)* Kontrollgruppe *f*; **control key** N *(Comput)* Steuerungstaste *f*; **control knob** N *(on TV etc)* Kontrollknopf *m*

controllable [kən'trəʊləbl] ADJ kontrollierbar, zu kontrollieren *pred; child, animal* lenkbar

controlled [kən'trəʊld] ADJ *emotion, movement, voice* beherrscht; *passion* gezügelt; *conditions, rent* kontrolliert; *prices* gebunden; *temperature* geregelt; **~ drugs** *or* **substances** verschreibungspflichtige Medikamente *pl*

controller [kən'trəʊlə'] N **a** *(= director, Rad)* Intendant(in) *m(f)*; *(Aviat)* (Flug)lotse *m*, (Flug)lotsin *f* **b** *(= financial head)* Leiter *m* des Finanzwesens **c** *(for video games etc)* Joypad *nt* **d** *(Comput)* Controller *m*

control: **control lever** N *(Mot, Tech)* Schalthebel *m*; *(Aviat)* Steuerknüppel *m*; **control light** N Kontrolllampe *f*

controlling [kən'trəʊlɪŋ] ADJ *attr factor* beherrschend; *body* Aufsichts-; **~ company** Muttergesellschaft *f*; **~ interest** Mehrheitsanteil *m*

control: **control measures** PL Überwachungsmaßnahmen *pl*; **control menu** N *(Comput)* Systemmenü *nt*; **control panel** N Schalttafel *f*, Schaltblende *f*; *(on aircraft, TV)* Bedienungsfeld *nt*; *(on machine)* Steuer- *or* Bedienungs- *or* Betriebspult *nt*; *(on car)* Armaturenbrett *nt*; *(Comput)* Systemsteuerung *f*; **control point** N Kontrollpunkt *m*, Kontrollstelle *f*; **control rod** N Regelstab *m*; **control room** N Kontrollraum *m*; *(Naut also)* Kommandoraum *m*; *(Mil)* (Operations)zentrale *f*; *(of police)* Zentrale *f*; **control stick** N = **control column**; **control tower** N *(Aviat)* Kontrollturm *m*; **control unit** N *(Comput)* Steuereinheit *f*, Steuerwerk *nt*

controversial [,kɒntrə'vɜːʃəl] ADJ *speech, person, figure etc* kontrovers; *(= debatable) matter, decision also* umstritten, strittig; **it is still ~ whether ...** es ist immer noch umstritten, ob ...; **he is deliberately ~** er gibt sich bewusst kontrovers

controversially [,kɒntrə'vɜːʃəlɪ] ADV kontroverserweise; **more ~, he claims that ...** er behauptet, was noch umstritten ist, dass ...

controversy ['kɒntrəvɜːsɪ, kən'trɒvəsɪ] N Kontroversen *pl*, Streit *m*; **there was a lot of ~ about it** es gab deswegen große Kontroversen *or* Differenzen; **to lead to ~** Anlass zu Kontroversen geben; **statements/facts that are beyond ~** völlig unumstrittene Behauptungen/Tatsachen

controvert ['kɒntrəvɜːt] VT *(form)* anfechten, bestreiten

contumacious [,kɒntjʊ'meɪʃəs] ADJ *(form)* verstockt; *(= insubordinate)* rebellisch

contumaciously [,kɒntjʊ'meɪʃəslɪ] ADV *(form)* verstockt; *(= insubordinately)* rebellisch

contumacy ['kɒntjʊməsɪ] N *(form)* Verstocktheit *f*; *(= insubordination)* Gehorsamsverweigerung *f*

contumely ['kɒntjʊmɪlɪ] N *no pl (form: = abuse)* Schmähen *nt (geh)*; *(= insult)* Schmähung *f (geh)*

contuse [kən'tjuːz] VT *(form)* quetschen, prellen

contusion [kən'tjuːʒən] N Quetschung *f*, Kontusion *f (spec)*

conundrum [kə'nʌndrəm] N *(lit, fig)* Rätsel *nt*

conurbation [,kɒnɜː'beɪʃən] N Ballungsgebiet *nt or* -raum *m or* -zentrum *nt*, Conurbation *f (spec)*

convalesce [,kɒnvə'les] VI genesen *(from, after* von); **while convalescing** während der Genesung(szeit)

convalescence [,kɒnvə'lesəns] N Genesung *f*; *(= period)* Genesungszeit *f*

convalescent [,kɒnvə'lesənt] **N** Rekonvaleszent(in) *m(f) (form)*, Genesende(r) *mf* **ADJ** genesend; **to be ~** auf dem Wege der Besserung sein

convalescent home N Genesungsheim *nt*

convection [kən'vekʃən] N Konvektion *f*

convection oven N *(US)* Umluftherd *m*

convector [kən'vektə'] N *(also* **convector heater***)* Heizlüfter *m*

convene [kən'viːn] **VT** *meeting* einberufen; *group of people* zusammenrufen, versammeln **VI** zusammenkommen, sich versammeln; *(parliament, court)* zusammentreten

convener [kən'viːnə'] N *Person, die Versammlungen einberuft (Brit Ind)* Gewerkschaftsvertreter(in) *m(f) (der für die Vetrauensleute in einem Betrieb zuständig ist)*

convenience [kən'viːnɪəns] N **a** *no pl (= usefulness, advantageousness)* Annehmlichkeit *f*; *(= functionalness)* Zweckmäßigkeit *f*; **for the sake of ~** aus praktischen Gründen; **marriage of ~** Vernunftehe *f*
b *no pl* **for your ~** zum gefälligen Gebrauch; **these chairs are for the ~ of customers** diese Stühle sind für unsere Kunden gedacht; **he did not find that date to his ~** der Termin passte ihm nicht *or* kam ihm nicht gelegen; **at your own ~** zu einem Ihnen angenehmen Zeitpunkt, wann es Ihnen passt *(inf)*; **at your earliest ~** *(Comm)* möglichst bald, baldmöglichst *(form)*
c *(= convenient thing, amenity)* Annehmlichkeit *f*; **a house with all modern ~s** ein Haus mit allem modernen Komfort
d *(Brit form: = public convenience)* (öffentliche) Toilette, Bedürfnisanstalt *f (dated form)*

convenience foods PL Fertiggerichte *pl*

convenient [kən'viːnɪənt] ADJ *(= useful, functional)* zweckmäßig, praktisch; *area, house (for shops etc)* günstig gelegen; *time* günstig, passend; **at a more ~ time** zu einem passenderen *or* günstigeren Zeitpunkt; **if it is ~** wenn es Ihnen (so) passt; **if it is ~ to** *or* **for you** wenn es Ihnen (so) passt, wenn es Ihnen keine Umstände macht; **a place/time ~ for all of us** ein Ort, der/eine Zeit, die uns allen passt *or* für uns alle günstig ist; **is tomorrow ~ (to** *or* **for you)?** passt (es) Ihnen morgen?, geht es morgen?; **he sat down on a ~ chair** er setzte sich auf einen Stuhl, der gerade da stand; **the trams are very ~** *(= nearby)* die Straßenbahnhaltestellen liegen sehr günstig; *(= useful)* die Straßenbahn ist sehr praktisch; **a ~ place to stop** eine geeignete *or* günstige Stelle zum Anhalten; **is there a ~ train?** gibt es einen geeigneten *or* passenden Zug?; **her resignation was most ~ (for him)** ihr Rücktritt kam (ihm) äußerst gelegen; **how ~!** sehr günstig!

conveniently [kən'viːnɪəntlɪ] ADV günstigerweise; *situated* günstig, vorteilhaft; *(= usefully) designed* praktisch, zweckmäßig; **he very ~ arrived home early** er kam früh nach Hause, was äußerst günstig war; **it ~ started to rain** wie bestellt, fing es an zu regnen; **the house is ~ close to the shops** das Haus liegt in praktischer Nähe der Läden; **he ~ forgot to post the letter** *(iro)* er hat praktischerweise vergessen, den Brief aufzugeben

convent ['kɒnvənt] N (Frauen)kloster *nt*; **to enter a ~** ins Kloster gehen

convention [kən'venʃən] N **a** Brauch *m*, Sitte *f*; *(= social rule)* Konvention *f*; **~ requires** *or* **demands that ...** die Sitte *or* der Brauch will es so, dass ...; **it's a ~ that ...** es ist so üblich *or* Sitte *or* Brauch, dass ...; **it's a social ~** es ist gesellschaftlich der Brauch; *(= point of etiquette)* es ist eine gesellschaftliche Konvention; **a disregard for ~** eine Missachtung der Konventionen **b** *(= agreement)* Abkommen *nt* **c** *(= conference)* Tagung *f*, Konferenz *f*; *(Pol)* Versammlung *f*

conventional [kən'venʃənl] ADJ *dress, attitudes, warfare, weapons* konventionell; *person, behaviour also* konventionsgebunden; *philosophy, beliefs, theory, manner, technique* herkömmlich; *theatre, music, style* traditionell; *symbol, mealtimes* normalerweise üblich; **it is ~ to do sth** es ist normalerweise üblich, etw zu tun; **~ medicine** konventionelle Medizin; **in the ~ sense** im herkömmlichen Sinn

Conventional Forces in Europe PL konventionelle Streitkräfte *pl* in Europa

conventionality [kən,venʃə'nælɪtɪ] N *(of dress, attitudes)* Konventionalität *f*; *(of person, behaviour also)* Konventionsgebundenheit *f*; *(of philosophy, beliefs, theory, manner, technique)* Herkömmlichkeit *f*; *(of theatre, music, style)* traditionelle Art

conventionally [kən'venʃnəlɪ] ADV *dress, behave, live* konventionell; *written, built, designed* traditionell; **~ one would be expected to ...** herkömmlicherweise würde erwartet, dass man ...

convention centre, *(US)* **convention center** N Tagungszentrum *nt*, Kongresszentrum *nt*

conventioneer [,kɒnvenʃə'nɪə'] N *(esp US)* Konferenzteilnehmer(in) *m(f)*

convent school N Klosterschule *f*

converge [kən'vɜːdʒ] VI *(roads, lines)* zusammenlaufen *(at* in *or* an *+dat)*; *(rivers also)* zusammenströmen *(at* in *or* an *+dat)*; *(Math, Phys)* konvergieren *(at* in *+dat)*; *(fig, views etc)* sich aneinander annähern, konvergieren *(geh)*; **to ~ on sb/sth/New York** von überallher zu jdm/etw/nach New York strömen

convergence [kən'vɜːdʒəns] N *(of roads, lines)* Zusammenlaufen *nt*; *(of rivers also)* Zusammenströmen *nt*; *(Math, Phys)* Konvergenz *f*; *(fig, of views etc)* Annäherung *f*; **~ criteria** *(in EU)* Konvergenzkriterien *pl*; **point of ~** Schnittpunkt *m*; *(of rays)* Brennpunkt *m*; *(of rivers)* Zusammenfluss *m*

convergent [kən'vɜːdʒənt], **converging** [kən'vɜːdʒɪŋ] ADJ *roads, lines* zusammenlaufend; *rivers also* zusammenströmend; *(Math, Phys)* konvergent *(form)*, konvergierend; *(fig) views etc* sich (aneinander) annähernd

conversant [kən'vɜːsənt] ADJ *pred* **~ with sth** mit etw vertraut

conversation [,kɒnvə'seɪʃən] N Gespräch *nt*, Unterhaltung *f*; *(Sch)* Konversation *f*; **to make ~** sich unterhalten; *(= small talk)* Konversation machen; **to get into/be in ~ with sb** mit jdm ins Gespräch kommen/im Gespräch sein; **deep in ~** ins Gespräch vertieft; **to have a ~/several ~s with sb (about sth)** sich mit jdm/mehrmals mit jdm (über etw *acc*) unterhalten; **he has no ~** mit ihm kann man sich nicht unterhalten; **his ~ is so amusing** er ist ein unterhaltsamer Gesprächspartner; **a subject of ~** ein Gesprächsthema *nt*; **words used only in ~** Wörter, die nur in der gesprochenen Sprache gebraucht werden; **we only mentioned it in ~** wir haben das nur gesprächsweise erwähnt; **the art of ~** die Kunst der gepflegten Konversation *or* Unterhaltung

conversational [,kɒnvə'seɪʃənl] ADJ *tone, style* Unterhaltungs-, Plauder-, leger; **~ German** gesprochenes Deutsch; **his tone was quiet and ~** er sagte es in ruhigem Gesprächston; **that gave him a ~ opening** das ermöglichte es ihm, sich in die Unterhaltung einzuschalten *or (to get talking)* eine Unterhaltung anzufangen

conversationalist [,kɒnvə'seɪʃnəlɪst] N guter Unterhalter *or* Gesprächspartner, gute Unterhalterin *or* Gesprächspartnerin; **not much of a ~** nicht gerade ein Konversationsgenie

conversationally [,kɒnvə'seɪʃnəlɪ] ADV *write* im Plauderton

conversation: **conversation mode** N *(Comput)* Dialogbetrieb *m*; **conversation piece** N Gesprächsgegenstand *m*; **conversation stopper** N **that was a real ~** das brachte die Unterhaltung zum Erliegen

converse[1] [kən'vɜːs] VI *(form)* sich unterhalten, konversieren *(old)*

converse[2] ['kɒnvɜːs] **ADJ** umgekehrt; *(Logic also)* konvers *(spec)*; *opinions etc* gegenteilig **N** *(= opposite)* Gegenteil *nt*; *(Logic: = proposition)* Umkehrung *f*, Konverse *f (spec)*; **the ~ is true** das

Gegenteil trifft zu; **quite the ~** ganz im Gegenteil

conversely [kɒnˈvɜːslɪ] ADV umgekehrt

conversion [kənˈvɜːʃən] N **a** *(= transformation)* Konversion *f (into* in *+acc); (Fin, Sci also)* Umwandlung *f (into* in *+acc); (Rugby)* Verwandlung *f; (of measures)* Umrechnung *f (into* in *+acc); (of van, caravan etc)* Umrüstung *f,* Umbau *m; (= model)* Spezialausführung *f; (of building)* Umbau *m (into* zu*); (of appliances)* Umstellung *f (to* auf *+acc); (Comput: of data)* Konvertierung *f;* **the attic flat is a ~** die Wohnung ist ein ausgebauter Dachstock; **~ rate/table** Umrechnungskurs *f*/-tabelle *f* **b** *(Rel, fig)* Bekehrung *f,* Konversion *f (to* zu*)*

convert [ˈkɒnvɜːt] **N** *(lit, fig)* Bekehrte(r) *mf; (to another denomination)* Konvertit *m;* **to become a ~ to sth** *(lit, fig)* sich zu etw bekehren
VT [kənˈvɜːt] **a** *(= transform)* konvertieren *(into* in *+acc); (Fin, Sci also)* umwandeln *(into* in *+acc); (Rugby)* verwandeln; *measures* umrechnen *(into* in *+acc); van, caravan etc* umrüsten, umbauen *(into* zu*); attic* ausbauen *(into* zu*); building* umbauen *(into* zu*); appliance* umstellen *(to* auf *+acc);* **a sofa that can be ~ed into a bed** ein Sofa, das sich in ein Bett verwandeln lässt; **most of the town has now been ~ed to natural gas** der größte Teil der Stadt ist jetzt auf Erdgas umgestellt
b *(Rel, fig)* bekehren *(to* zu*); (to another denomination)* konvertieren
VI [kənˈvɜːt] sich verwandeln lassen *(into* in *+acc)*

converted [kənˈvɜːtɪd] ADJ *barn, chapel* umgebaut; *loft* ausgebaut → **preach**

converter [kənˈvɜːtəˈ] N *(Elec)* Konverter *m; (for AC/DC)* Stromgleichrichter *m*

convertibility [kənˌvɜːtəˈbɪlɪtɪ] N *(of currency)* Konvertierbarkeit *f,* Konvertibilität *f; (of appliances)* Umstellbarkeit *f*

convertible [kənˈvɜːtəbl] **ADJ** verwandelbar; *currency* konvertibel, konvertierbar; *car* mit aufklappbarem Verdeck; *appliances* umstellbar; **a ~ sofa** ein Sofa, das sich in ein Bett verwandeln lässt **N** *(= car)* Cabrio *nt;* **the ~ season** *(inf)* die Cabriosaison

convex [kɒnˈveks] ADJ *lens, mirror* konvex, Konvex-

convexity [kɒnˈveksɪtɪ] N Konvexität *f*

convey [kənˈveɪ] VT **a** *(= transport)* befördern; *goods* spedieren; *water* leiten **b** *(= make known or felt) opinion, idea* vermitteln; *(= make understood) meaning* klarmachen; *(= transmit) message, order, best wishes* übermitteln, überbringen; **what does this poem/music ~ to you?** was sagt Ihnen dieses Gedicht/diese Musik?; **words cannot ~ what I feel** was ich empfinde, lässt sich nicht mit Worten ausdrücken; **try to ~ to him that he should ...** versuchen Sie doch, ihm klarzumachen, dass er ... sollte **c** *(Jur) property* übertragen *(to* auf *+acc)*

conveyance [kənˈveɪəns] N **a** *(= transport)* Beförderung *f; (of goods also)* Spedition *f;* **~ of goods** Güterverkehr *m;* **mode of ~** Beförderungsmittel *nt* **b** *(old, form, = vehicle)* Gefährt *nt* **c** *(Jur)* (Eigentums)übertragung *f (to* auf *+acc); (= document)* Übertragungsurkunde *f*

conveyancing [kənˈveɪənsɪŋ] N *(Jur)* (Eigentums)übertragung *f*

conveyor [kənˈveɪəˈ] N *(of message etc)* Überbringer(in) *m(f); (Tech)* Förderer *m*

conveyor belt N Fließband *nt; (for transport, supply)* Förderband *nt*

conveyor-belt [kənˈveɪəˈbelt] ADJ *(fig)* Fließband-; **a ~ hospital** ein Krankenhaus, in dem die Patienten wie am Fließband abgefertigt werden

convict [ˈkɒnvɪkt] **N** Sträfling *m,* Zuchthäusler(in) *m(f)* **VT** [kənˈvɪkt] **a** *(Jur) person* verurteilen *(of* wegen*),* für schuldig erklären *(of +gen);* **a ~ed criminal** ein verurteilter Verbrecher, eine verurteilte Verbrecherin; **to get sb ~ed** jds Verurteilung *(acc)* bewirken **b** *(actions etc: = betray)* überführen; **to stand ~ed by one's own actions** durch sein Handeln überführt werden **VI** [kənˈvɪkt] jdn verurteilen; **the jury refused to ~** die Geschworenen lehnten es ab, einen Schuldspruch zu fällen

conviction [kənˈvɪkʃən] N **a** *(Jur)* Verurteilung *f;* **five previous ~s** fünf Vorstrafen; **to get a ~** *(police, prosecution)* einen Schuldspruch erreichen
b *(= belief, act of convincing)* Überzeugung *f;* **to be open to ~** sich gern eines Besseren belehren lassen; **to carry ~** überzeugend klingen; **his speech lacked ~** seine Rede klang wenig überzeugend; **he's a socialist by ~** er ist ein überzeugter Sozialist; **he did it in the ~ that ...** er tat es in der Überzeugung, dass ...; **a man of strong ~s** ein Mann, der feste Anschauungen vertritt; **his fundamental political/moral ~s** seine politische/moralische Gesinnung → **courage**

convince [kənˈvɪns] ✪ 6.2, 15.1, 26.2 VT überzeugen; **I'm trying to ~ him that ...** ich versuche, ihn davon zu überzeugen, dass ...

convinced [kənˈvɪnst] ADJ überzeugt

convincing ADJ, **convincingly** ADV [kənˈvɪnsɪŋ, -lɪ] ✪ 26.1, 26.3 überzeugend

convivial [kənˈvɪvɪəl] ADJ heiter und unbeschwert; *person also* fröhlich; *(= sociable)* gesellig

conviviality [kənˌvɪvɪˈælɪtɪ] N unbeschwerte Heiterkeit; *(of person also)* Fröhlichkeit *f; (= sociability)* Geselligkeit *f*

convocation [ˌkɒnvəˈkeɪʃən] N *(form: = calling together)* Einberufung *f; (= meeting, Eccl)* Versammlung *f*

convoke [kənˈvəʊk] VT *meeting* einberufen; *(Parl also)* zusammentreten lassen

convolute [ˈkɒnvəluːt] ADJ *shell* spiralig aufgewunden; *petal, leaf* eingerollt

convoluted [ˌkɒnvəˈluːtɪd] ADJ **a** *(= involved)* verwickelt; *plot also* verschlungen; *theory also* kompliziert; *style* gewunden **b** *(= coiled)* gewunden; *shell* spiralig aufgewunden

convolution [ˌkɒnvəˈluːʃən] N *usu pl (= coil)* Windung *f; (of plot)* Verschlungenheit *f no pl; (of style)* Gewundenheit *f no pl; (of theory)* Kompliziertheit *f*

convolvulus [kənˈvɒlvjʊləs] N Winde *f*

convoy [ˈkɒnvɔɪ] **N** **a** *(= escort)* Konvoi *m,* Geleit *nt;* **under ~** mit Geleitschutz, unter Konvoi; **one of our ~ was torpedoed** eines unserer Geleitboote *or* Begleitboote wurde torpediert; **to be on ~ duty** als Geleitschutz abgeordnet sein **b** *(= vehicles under escort, fig)* Konvoi *m; (= ships also)* Verband *m;* **in ~** im Konvoi/Verband **VT** Geleitschutz geben *(+dat),* begleiten; **the ships were ~ed across** die Schiffe wurden unter Konvoi hinübergebracht

convulse [kənˈvʌls] VT *(earthquake, war etc) land* erschüttern; *(fig also)* schütteln; *sb's body, muscles* krampfhaft zusammenziehen; **to be ~d with laughter/in pain** sich vor Lachen schütteln/Schmerzen krümmen; **a face ~d with rage** ein vor Wut verzerrtes Gesicht; **a joke which ~d the audience** ein Witz, bei dem sich das Publikum vor Lachen bog

convulsion [kənˈvʌlʃən] N **a** *(Med)* Schüttelkrampf *m no pl,* Konvulsion *f (spec); (of crying)* Weinkrampf *m no pl* **b** *(caused by social upheaval etc)* Erschütterung *f* **c** *(inf, of laughter)* **to go into/be in ~s** sich biegen *or* schütteln vor Lachen; **he had the audience in ~s** er rief beim Publikum wahre Lachstürme hervor

convulsive [kənˈvʌlsɪv] ADJ konvulsiv(isch) *(spec),* Krampf-; *movement also* krampfhaft; **~ laughter** Lachkrämpfe *pl*

convulsively [kənˈvʌlsɪvlɪ] ADV krampfartig; **she sobbed ~** sie wurde von Schluchzern geschüttelt

cony, coney [ˈkəʊnɪ] N **a** *(US)* Kaninchen *nt* **b** *(also* **cony skin***)* Kaninchenfell *nt*

COO *abbr of* **chief operating officer** höchster diensthabender Offizier

coo [kuː] **VI** *(pigeon, fig)* gurren **VT** gurren, girren **N** Gurren *nt,* Girren *nt* **INTERJ** *(Brit, inf)* ui

cooee [ˈkuːiː] **INTERJ** huhu **VI** huhu rufen

cook [kʊk] **N** Koch *m,* Köchin *f;* **she is a good ~/very plain ~** sie kocht gut/einfache Kost; **too many ~s (spoil the broth)** *(Prov)* viele Köche verderben den Brei *(Prov);* **to be chief ~ and bottle-washer** *(inf: = dogsbody)* (das) Mädchen für alles sein *(inf)*
VT **a** *food, meal* machen, zubereiten; *(in water, milk etc)* kochen; *(= fry, roast)* braten; *pie, pancake also* backen; **how are you going to ~ the duck?** wie willst du die Ente zubereiten?; **a ~ed meal/supper** eine warme Mahlzeit/ein warmes Abendessen; **a ~ed breakfast** ein Frühstück *nt* mit warmen Gerichten; **to ~ sb's/one's goose** *(fig inf)* jdm/sich die Tour vermasseln *(inf);* **our goose is ~ed** *(fig inf)* wir sitzen in der Tinte *(inf)*
b *(inf: = falsify) accounts* frisieren *(inf);* **to ~ the books** die Bilanz(en) frisieren *(inf)*
VI *(person, food)* kochen; *(= fry, roast)* braten; *(pie)* backen; **it will ~ quickly** das ist schnell gekocht; **the pie takes half an hour to ~** die Pastete ist in einer halben Stunde fertig; **what's ~ing?** *(fig inf)* was ist los?

▶ **cook up** VT *sep (fig inf) story, excuse* sich *(dat)* einfallen lassen, zurechtbasteln *(inf);* **cooked-up story** Lügenmärchen *nt*

cookbook [ˈkʊkbʊk] N Kochbuch *nt*

cooker [ˈkʊkəˈ] N **a** *(esp Brit: = stove)* Herd *m* **b** *(= apple)* Kochapfel *m*

cooker hood N *(Brit)* Abzugshaube *f*

cookery [ˈkʊkərɪ] N Kochen *nt (also Sch),* Kochkunst *f;* **French ~** französische Küche; **~ classes** Kochkurs *m,* Kochkurse *pl*

cookery book N Kochbuch *nt*

cookhouse [ˈkʊkhaʊs] N *(Naut)* Kombüse *f; (Mil)* Feldküche *f*

cookie, cooky [ˈkʊkɪ] N **a** *(US: = biscuit)* Keks *m,* Plätzchen *nt;* **that's the way the ~ crumbles** *(inf: also Brit)* so ist das nun mal (im Leben), das ist der Lauf der Welt *or* der Dinge; **to get caught with one's hands in the ~ jar** *(fig inf)* ertappt werden *(inf)* **b** *(inf: = smart person)* Typ *m;* **he's a pretty tough ~** er ist ein ziemlich zäher Typ; **smart ~** cleveres Köpfchen **c** *(Comput)* Cookie *nt*

cookie cutter *(US)* **N** *(Cook)* Ausstechform *f* **ADJ** *(fig inf)* einfallslos

cooking [ˈkʊkɪŋ] N Kochen *nt; (= food)* Essen *nt;* **plain ~** einfaches Essen, Hausmannskost *f;* **French ~** die französische Küche, französisches Essen; **his ~ is atrocious** er kocht miserabel

cooking *in cpds* Koch-; **cooking apple** N Kochapfel *m;* **cooking chocolate** N Blockschokolade *f;* **cooking facilities** PL Kochgelegenheit *f;* **cooking foil** N Backfolie *f;* **cooking salt** N Kochsalz *nt*

cook: **cook-off** N *(US)* Kochwettbewerb *m;* **cookout** N *(US)* Kochen *nt* am Lagerfeuer; *(on barbeque)* Grillparty *f;* **cookware** N Kochgeschirr *nt,* Töpfe und Pfannen *pl*

cooky N = **cookie**

cool [kuːl] **ADJ** (+er) **a** *water, weather, drink* kühl; *clothes* luftig, leicht; **serve ~** kalt *or* (gut) gekühlt servieren; **it's nice to slip into something ~** es ist angenehm, in etwas Luftiges *or* Leichtes schlüpfen zu können; **"keep in a ~ place"** „kühl aufbewahren“
b *(= calm, unperturbed) person, manner* besonnen; *voice* kühl; **to keep ~, to keep a ~ head** einen kühlen Kopf behalten; **keep ~!** reg dich nicht auf!, (nur) ruhig Blut!; **as ~ as you please** mit kühler Gelassenheit, in aller Seelenruhe
c *(= audacious)* kaltblütig, unverfroren *(pej),* kaltschnäuzig *(inf);* **as ~ as you please** mit größter Unverfrorenheit *(pej),* seelenruhig; **that was very ~ of him** da hat er sich ein starkes Stück geleistet; **a ~ customer** *(inf)* ein cooler Typ *(inf)*
d *(= unenthusiastic, unfriendly) greeting, reception, look* kühl; **to be ~ to(wards) sb** sich jdm gegenüber kühl verhalten; **play it ~!** immer mit der Ruhe!; **she decided to play it ~** sie entschied sich, ganz auf kühl zu machen

e *colour* kalt; ~ **green** kaltes Grün
f *(inf, with numbers etc)* glatt *(inf)*; **he earns a ~ thirty thousand a year** er verdient glatte dreißigtausend im Jahr *(inf)*
g *(inf: = great, smart) idea, disco, pub, dress etc* stark *(inf)*, cool *(sl)*; *dress* stylish *(inf)*; **to act ~** sich cool geben *(sl)*; **to look ~** cool aussehen *(sl)*
N **a** *(lit, fig)* Kühle *f*; **in the ~ of the evening** in der Abendkühle; **to keep sth in the ~** etw kühl aufbewahren
b *(inf)* **keep your ~!** reg dich nicht auf!, immer mit der Ruhe!; **to lose one's ~** durchdrehen *(inf)*; **he doesn't have the ~ to be a TV announcer** er hat nicht die Nerven für einen Fernsehansager
VT **a** kühlen; *(= cool down)* abkühlen; *wine* kühlen, kalt stellen
b *(inf)* **~ it!** *(= don't get excited)* reg dich ab! *(inf)*, mach mal langsam *(inf)*; *(= don't cause trouble)* mach keinen Ärger! *(inf)*; **tell those guys to ~ it** sag den Typen, sie sollen keinen Ärger machen *(inf)*; **I think we should ~ it** ich glaube wir sollten etwas langsamer treten *(inf)*
VI *(lit, fig)* abkühlen; *(anger)* verrauchen, sich legen; *(enthusiasm, interest)* nachlassen; **he has ~ed toward(s) her** er ist ihr gegenüber kühler geworden

► **cool down** **VI** **a** *(lit)* abkühlen; *(weather also, person)* sich abkühlen **b** *(feelings etc)* sich abkühlen; *(anger also)* verrauchen; *(critical situation, person: = calm down)* sich beruhigen; **look, just cool down will you!** komm, reg dich (bloß wieder) ab! *(inf)*; **to let things cool down** die Sache etwas ruhen lassen **VT** *sep* **a** *food, drink* abkühlen; *(= let cool down)* abkühlen lassen; **to cool oneself down** sich abkühlen **b** *situation* beruhigen; **put him in a cell, that'll cool him down** steck ihn in eine Zelle, dann wird er sich schon wieder beruhigen

► **cool off** **VI** **a** *(liquid, food)* abkühlen; *(person)* sich abkühlen **b** *(fig)* (sich) abkühlen; *(enthusiasm, interest)* nachlassen; *(= become less angry)* sich beruhigen; *(= become less friendly)* kühler werden *(about or towards sb* jdm gegenüber)

coolant ['ku:lənt] **N** Kühlmittel *nt*

cool: **cool bag** **N** Kühltasche *f*; **cool box** **N** Kühlbox *f*

cooler ['ku:ləʳ] **N** **a** *(for milk etc)* Kühlapparat *m*; *(for wine)* Kühler *m* **b** *(inf: = prison)* Bau *m* *(inf)*

cool-headed [ku:l'hedɪd] **ADJ** kühl (und besonnen)

coolie ['ku:lɪ] **N** *(pej)* Kuli *m*

cooling ['ku:lɪŋ] **ADJ** *drink, shower* kühlend; *effect* (ab)kühlend; *affection* abnehmend; *enthusiasm, interest* nachlassend; **~ fan** Lüfter *m*

cooling-off ['ku:lɪŋ'ɒf] **N** *(in relationship etc)* Abkühlung *f*; **there's been a distinct ~ (of interest) about this project** das Interesse an diesem Projekt hat merklich nachgelassen

cooling-off period **N** **a** *(gesetzlich festgelegter) Zeitraum für Schlichtungsverhandlungen (bei Arbeitskämpfen)* **b** *(in relationship etc)* Zeit *f* zur Abkühlung

cooling tower **N** Kühlturm *m*

cool jazz **N** Cooljazz *m*, Cool Jazz *m*

coolly ['ku:lɪ] **ADV** **a** *(= calmly)* ruhig, gefasst, besonnen **b** *(= unenthusiastically, in an unfriendly way)* kühl **c** *(= audaciously)* kaltblütig, unverfroren *(pej)*, kaltschnäuzig *(inf)*

coolness ['ku:lnɪs] **N** **a** *(of water, weather, drink)* Kühle *f*; *(of clothes)* Luftigkeit *f*, Leichtigkeit *f* **b** *(= calmness, of person, manner)* Besonnenheit *f*; *(of voice)* Kühle *f* **c** *(= audacity, impudence)* Kaltblütigkeit *f*, Unverfrorenheit *f* *(pej)*, Kaltschnäuzigkeit *f (inf)* **d** *(= unfriendliness: of greeting, reception, look)* Kühle *f*

coomb [ku:m] **N** Tal(mulde *f*) *nt*

coon [ku:n] **N** **a** *(Zool)* Waschbär *m* **b** *(very offensive sl)* Nigger *m (very offensive)*

coop [ku:p] **N** *(also* **hen coop**) Hühnerstall *m*; **to fly the ~** *(fig inf)* sich aus dem Staub machen *(inf)*

► **coop up** **VT** *sep person* einsperren; *several people* zusammenpferchen *(inf)*

co-op ['kəʊ'ɒp] **N** Genossenschaft *f*; *(= shop)* Coop *m*, Konsum *m*

cooper ['ku:pəʳ] **N** Böttcher *m*, Küfer *m (dial)*

cooperate [kəʊ'ɒpəreɪt] **VI** kooperieren, zusammenarbeiten; *(= go along with, not be awkward)* mitmachen; **to ~ toward(s) a common end** auf ein gemeinsames Ziel hinarbeiten; **even the weather ~d in making it a day to remember** auch das Wetter trug dazu bei, es zu einem denkwürdigen Tag zu machen; **if the weather ~s** wenn das Wetter mitmacht

cooperation [kəʊ,ɒpə'reɪʃən] **N** Kooperation *f*, Zusammenarbeit *f*; *(= help)* Mitarbeit *f*, Kooperation *f*; **we produced this model in ~ with …** wir haben dieses Modell in Gemeinschaftsarbeit *or* Kooperation *or* gemeinsam mit … produziert; **to increase ~ between EC countries** um die Kooperation *or* Zusammenarbeit zwischen EG-Ländern zu fördern; **with the ~ of all members then …** wenn alle Mitglieder mitmachen, dann …

cooperative [kəʊ'ɒpərətɪv] **ADJ** **a** *(= prepared to comply)* kooperativ; *(= prepared to help)* hilfsbereit; **if any member does not have a ~ attitude** wenn ein Mitglied nicht bereit ist mitzumachen **b** *firm* auf Genossenschaftsbasis; **~ farm** Bauernhof *m* auf Genossenschaftsbasis **N** Genossenschaft *f*, Kooperative *f*; *(also* **cooperative farm**) Bauernhof *m* auf Genossenschaftsbasis

cooperative bank **N** *(US)* Genossenschaftsbank *f*

cooperatively [kəʊ'ɒpərətɪvlɪ] **ADV** *(= jointly)* gemeinsam; *(= obligingly)* hilfsbereit; **to work ~ with sb** mit jdm zusammenarbeiten

cooperative society **N** Genossenschaft *f*, Kooperative *f*

coopt [kəʊ'ɒpt] **VT** selbst (hinzu)wählen, kooptieren *(spec)*; **he was ~ed onto the committee** er wurde vom Komitee selbst dazugewählt

coordinate [kəʊ'ɔ:dnɪt] **ADJ** gleichwertig; *(in rank)* gleichrangig; *(Gram)* nebengeordnet *(with* zu) **N** *(Math etc)* Koordinate *f*; *(= equal)* etwas Gleichwertiges; **~s** *(= clothes)* Kleidung *f* zum Kombinieren [kəʊ'ɔ:dɪneɪt] **VT** **a** *movements, muscles, pieces of work* koordinieren; *(two people, firms) operations etc also* aufeinander abstimmen; *thoughts also* ordnen; **to ~ one thing with another** eine Sache auf eine andere abstimmen **b** *(Gram)* nebenordnen, koordinieren; **coordinating conjunction** nebenordnende *or* koordinierende Konjunktion

coordinated [kəʊ'ɔ:dɪneɪtɪd] **ADJ** **a** *person, action, effort, approach, operation* koordiniert; **to be badly ~** *(person)* eine Koordinationsstörung haben **b** *(= matching) clothes, designs* aufeinander abgestimmt; **colour-~** *(clothes)* farblich aufeinander abgestimmt

coordinate geometry [kəʊ'ɔ:dnɪt-] **N** *(Math)* analytische Geometrie

coordination [kəʊ,ɔ:dɪ'neɪʃən] **N** Koordination *f*, Koordinierung *f*; **in ~ with** in Abstimmung mit; **to have little** *or* **no ~** eine Koordinationsstörung haben

coordinator [kəʊ'ɔ:dɪneɪtəʳ] **N** Koordinator(in) *m(f)*; *(Gram)* koordinierende *or* nebenordnende Konjunktion

coot [ku:t] **N** Wasserhuhn *nt*; **bald as a ~** völlig kahl; **to be as bald as a ~** eine Platte haben *(inf)*

cootie ['ku:tɪ] **N** *(US inf)* Laus *f*

co-owner ['kəʊ'əʊnəʳ] **N** Mitbesitzer(in) *m(f)*, Miteigentümer(in) *m(f)*

co-ownership ['kəʊ'əʊnəʃɪp] **N** Mitbesitz *m*

cop [kɒp] **N** **a** *(inf: = policeman)* Polizist(in) *m(f)*, Bulle *m (pej inf)*; **to play ~s and robbers** Räuber und Gendarm spielen **b** *(Brit inf: = arrest)* **it's a fair ~** jetzt hats mich erwischt *(inf)*
c *(Brit inf)* **it's not much ~** das ist nichts Besonderes **VT** *(inf: = catch) sb* schnappen *(inf)*, erwischen *(inf)*; *clout, thump* fangen *(inf)*; **he ~ped one right on the nose** er fing eine genau auf der Nase *(inf)*; **when they found out he didn't have a licence he really ~ped it** *(Brit)* als sie herausfanden, dass er keinen Führerschein hatte, war er dran *(inf)*; **hey, ~ a load of this!** he, hör dir das mal an! *(inf)*

► **cop out** **VI** *(inf)* aussteigen *(inf) (of* aus)

copartner ['kəʊ'pɑ:tnəʳ] **N** Teilhaber(in) *m(f)*, Partner *m*

copartnership ['kəʊ'pɑ:tnəʃɪp] **N** Teilhaberschaft *f*, Partnerschaft *f*

copayment [kəʊ'peɪmənt] **N** *(US)* Zuzahlung *f* *(zu Medikamenten etc)*

cope[1] [kəʊp] **N** **a** *(Eccl)* Pluviale *nt* **b** *(Archit)* = **coping**

cope[2] [kəʊp] **VI** zurechtkommen; *(with work)* es schaffen; **to ~ with** *(problems, children, difficult person)* fertig werden mit, zurechtkommen mit; **how do you ~ all by yourself?** wie werden Sie so allein fertig?, wie kommen Sie so allein zurecht?; **I can't ~ with all this work** ich bin mit all der Arbeit überfordert; **she can't ~ with the stairs any more** sie schafft die Treppe nicht mehr

Copenhagen [,kəʊpn'heɪgən] **N** Kopenhagen *nt*

Copernican [kə'pɜ:nɪkən] **ADJ** kopernikanisch

Copernicus [kə'pɜ:nɪkəs] **N** Kopernikus *m*

copestone ['kəʊpstəʊn] **N** **a** *(Archit)* Abdeckplatte *f* **b** *(fig, of career etc)* Krönung *f*; *(of theory)* Schlussstein *m*

copier ['kɒpɪəʳ] **N** *(= copyist)* Kopist(in) *m(f)*; *(= imitator also)* Nachmacher(in) *m(f)*; *(of writer, painter etc)* Imitator(in) *m(f)*; *(= machine)* Kopiergerät *nt*, Kopierer *m (inf)*

co-pilot ['kəʊpaɪlət] **N** Kopilot(in) *m(f)*

coping ['kəʊpɪŋ] **N** *(Archit)* Mauerkrone *f*

coping: **coping saw** **N** Laubsäge *f*; **coping stone** **N** = **copestone**

copious ['kəʊpɪəs] **ADJ** *supply* groß, reichlich; *information, details, illustrations* zahlreich; *writer* fruchtbar; **~ amounts of sth** reichliche Mengen von etw *or* an etw *(dat)*; **to weep ~ tears** Ströme *or* eine Flut von Tränen vergießen

copiously ['kəʊpɪəslɪ] **ADV** reichlich; **she wept ~** sie vergoss Ströme von Tränen

copiousness ['kəʊpɪəsnɪs] **N** *(of supply)* Größe *f*, Reichlichkeit *f*; *(of information, details)* Fülle *f*, Reichtum *m*; *(of writer)* Fruchtbarkeit *f*

cop-out ['kɒpaʊt] **N** *(inf: = going back on sth)* Rückzieher *m (inf)*; *(= deliberate evasion)* Ausweichmanöver *nt*; **this solution/translation is just a ~** diese Lösung/Übersetzung weicht dem Problem nur aus

copper ['kɒpəʳ] **N** **a** *(= metal)* Kupfer *nt*; **~ ore** Eisenerz *nt*; **~ sulphate** Kupfersulfat *nt*, Kupfervitriol *nt* **b** *(= colour)* Kupferrot *nt* **c** *(esp Brit inf: = coin)* Cent *m*; **~s** Kleingeld *nt* **d** *(inf: = policeman)* Polizist(in) *m(f)*, Bulle *m (pej inf)* **e** *(for boiling clothes etc)* Kupferkessel *f*, Waschkessel *m*

copper: **copper beech** **N** Rotbuche *f*; **copper-bottomed** **ADJ** mit Kupferboden; *(Fin, fig)* gesund; **copper-coloured** **ADJ** kupferfarben; **copper mine** **N** Kupfermine *f*; **coppernob** **N** *(inf)* Rotkopf *m (inf)*; **copperplate** **VT** verkupfern **N** **a** *(= plate for engraving)* Kupferplatte *f*; *(= engraving)* Kupferstich *m* **b** *(= handwriting)* lateinische (Ausgangs)schrift **ADJ** **~ engraving** Kupferstich *m*; *(= process also)* Kupferstechen *nt*; **~ (hand)writing** lateinische (Ausgangs)schrift; **in your best ~ writing** in deiner besten Sonntagsschrift; **copper-plating** **N** Verkupferung *f*; **coppersmith** **N** Kupferschmied *m*

coppery ['kɒpərɪ] **ADJ** kupfern, kupferrot

coppice ['kɒpɪs] **N** = **copse**

copra ['kɒprə] **N** Kopra *f*

coprocessor ['kəʊ'prəʊsesə'] N *(Comput)* Koprozessor *m*; **maths ~** Arithmetikprozessor *m*

co-produce [ˌkəʊprə'dju:s] VT *film, album* koproduzieren

co-production [ˌkəʊprə'dʌkʃən] N Koproduktion *f*

coprophilia ['kɒprəfɪlɪə] N Koprophilie *f*

copse [kɒps] N Wäldchen *nt*

cop shop N *(Brit inf)* Bullerei *f (sl)*, Wache *f*

copter ['kɒptə'] N *(inf)* Hubschrauber *m*

Coptic ['kɒptɪk] ADJ koptisch

copula ['kɒpjʊlə] N Kopula *f*, Satzband *nt*

copulate ['kɒpjʊleɪt] VI kopulieren

copulation [ˌkɒpjʊ'leɪʃən] N Kopulation *f*

copulative ['kɒpjʊlətɪv] *(Gram)* N Kopula *f* ADJ kopulativ

copy ['kɒpɪ] N **a** Kopie *f (also Comput)*; *(of document, separately written or typed also)* Abschrift *f*; *(typed carbon also)* Durchschlag *m*; *(handwritten carbon also)* Durchschrift *f*; *(Phot)* Abzug *m*; **to take** *or* **make a ~ of sth** eine Kopie/Zweitschrift *etc* von etw machen; **to write out a fair ~** etw ins Reine schreiben, eine Reinschrift herstellen
b *(of book etc)* Exemplar *nt*; **have you got a ~ of today's "Times"?** hast du die „Times" von heute?
c *(Press etc: = subject matter)* Stoff *m*; *(= material to be printed)* Artikel *m*; *(Typ)* (Manu)skript *nt*; **that's always good ~** das zieht immer; **this murder story will make good ~** aus diesem Mord kann man etwas machen
d *(in advertising)* Werbetext *m*; **who did the ~ for this campaign?** wer hat den Text/die Texte für diese Werbekampagne gemacht?; **he writes good ~** er schreibt gute Werbetexte
VI *(= imitate)* nachahmen; *(Sch etc)* abschreiben
VT **a** *(= make a copy of)* kopieren *(also Comput)*; *document (separately written/typed)* eine Abschrift anfertigen von; *(typed/handwritten carbon)* einen Durchschlag/eine Durchschrift machen von; *(Phot)* abziehen; *(= write out again)* abschreiben; **to ~ sth to a disk** etw auf eine Diskette kopieren
b *(= imitate)* nachmachen; *gestures, person also* nachahmen; **they always ~ Ford** sie machen Ford immer alles nach
c *(Sch etc) sb else's work* abschreiben; *(by painting)* abmalen; **to ~ Brecht** (von) Brecht abschreiben
d *(= send a copy to)* einen Durchschlag/eine Durchschrift senden an *(+acc)*

copy: **copybook** N Schönschreibheft *nt* → **blot** ADJ *attr* mustergültig, wie es/er/sie im Lehrbuch steht; **a ~ landing** eine Bilderbuchlandung; **copy boy** N *(Press)* Laufjunge *m*; **copycat** N *(inf)* Nachahmer(in) *m(f)*; *(with written work)* Abschreiber(in) *m(f)*; **she's a terrible ~** sie macht immer alles nach; sie schreibt immer ab; **~!** Nachmachen gilt nicht! *(inf)* ADJ *attr* **his was a ~ crime** er war ein Nachahmungstäter; **copy desk** N *(Press)* Redaktionstisch *m*; **copy-edit** VT *(Press)* redigieren; *(in publishing also)* lektorieren, bearbeiten; **copy editor** N *(Press)* Redakteur(in) *m(f)*; *(publishing also)* Lektor(in) *m(f)*, Manuskriptbearbeiter(in) *m(f)*

copyist ['kɒpɪɪst] N Kopist(in) *m(f)*

copy *(Comput)*: **copy-protected** ADJ *disk* kopiergeschützt; **copy protection** N Kopierschutz *m*

copyreader ['kɒpɪri:də'] N = **copy editor**

copyright ['kɒpɪraɪt] N Copyright *nt*, Urheberrecht *nt*; **out of ~** urheberrechtlich nicht mehr geschützt ADJ urheberrechtlich geschützt VT *book* urheberrechtlich schützen; *(author)* urheberrechtlich schützen lassen

copy: **copy typist** N Schreibkraft *f*; **copywriter** ['kɒpɪraɪtə'] N Werbetexter(in) *m(f)*

coquetry ['kɒkɪtrɪ] N Koketterie *f*

coquette [kə'ket] N kokettes Mädchen, kokette Frau

coquettish [kə'ketɪʃ] ADJ kokett, kess

coquettishly [kə'ketɪʃlɪ] ADV kokett

cor [kɔ:'] INTERJ *(Brit inf)* Mensch *(inf)*, Mann *(sl)*

coracle ['kɒrəkl] N *kleines ovales Ruderboot aus mit Leder bezogenem Flechtwerk*

coral ['kɒrəl] N **a** Koralle *f*; **~ necklace** Korallenkette *f* **b** *(= colour)* Korallenrot *nt*

coral *in cpds* Korallen-; **coral-coloured** ADJ korallenfarbig; **coral island** N Koralleninsel *f*; **coral reef** N Korallenriff *nt*; **Coral Sea** N Korallenmeer *nt*; **coral snake** N Korallennatter *f*

cor anglais ['kɔ:r'ɒŋgleɪ] N *(esp Brit)* Englischhorn *nt*

corbel ['kɔ:bəl] N Kragstein *m*, Konsole *f*

cord [kɔ:d] N **a** Schnur *f*; *(for clothes)* Kordel *f*; *(Elec)* Schnur *f* **b cords** PL *(also* **a pair of cords**) Cordhosen *pl* **c** *(Tex)* = **corduroy d** *(Anat)* → **spinal, umbilical, vocal** ATTR *(Brit)* Cord-; **~ jacket** Cordjacke *f*; **~ trousers** Cordhosen *pl*

cordage ['kɔ:dɪdʒ] N *no pl* Tauwerk *nt*

corded ['kɔ:dɪd] ADJ *(= ribbed)* gerippt

cordial ['kɔ:dɪəl] ADJ freundlich, höflich; *dislike* heftig N *(= drink)* Fruchtsaftkonzentrat *nt*; *(alcoholic)* Fruchtlikör *m*

cordiality [ˌkɔ:dɪ'ælɪtɪ] N Freundlichkeit *f*, Höflichkeit *f*

cordially ['kɔ:dɪəlɪ] ADV freundlich, höflich; **~ yours** mit freundlichen Grüßen; **they ~ dislike him** er ist ihnen zutiefst unsympathisch

cordite ['kɔ:daɪt] N Cordit *nt*

cordless ['kɔ:dlɪs] ADJ *telephone* schnurlos

cordon ['kɔ:dn] N **a** Kordon *m*, Postenkette *f*; **to put a ~ round sth** einen Kordon um etw ziehen, etw (hermetisch) abriegeln **b** *(= ribbon of an Order)* Kordon *m*, (Ordens)band *nt* **c** *(Hort)* Kordon *m*, Schnurbaum *m* VT = **cordon off**

▸ **cordon off** VT *sep area, building* absperren, abriegeln

cordon bleu [ˌkɔ:dɒn'blɜ:] N *(Cook, = award)* Meisterkochdiplom *nt*; *(= chef, cook)* Meisterkoch *m*, Meisterköchin *f* ADJ *cook* vorzüglich; *recipe, dish, meal* delikat, exquisit; **she's taking a ~ cookery course** sie macht einen Kochkurs für die feine Küche (mit)

cordon sanitaire [ˌkɔ:dnsanɪ'tɛə'] N *(Med, Pol)* Cordon sanitaire *m*

corduroy ['kɔ:dərɔɪ] N Cordsamt *m*; **~s** Cord(samt)hosen *pl*

corduroy *in cpds* Cord(samt)-; **corduroy road** N Knüppeldamm *m*

CORE [kɔ:'] *(US) abbr of* **Congress of Racial Equality** *Verband zur Bekämpfung von Rassendiskriminierung*

core [kɔ:'] N *(lit, fig)* Kern *m*; *(of apple, pear)* Kernhaus *nt*, Butzen *m (dial)*; *(of rock)* Innere(s) *nt*; *(of nuclear reactor)* Kern *m*; **rotten/English to the ~** *(fig)* durch und durch schlecht/englisch; **shaken/shocked to the ~** zutiefst erschüttert/schockiert; **to get to the ~ of the matter** *(fig)* zum Kern der Sache kommen ADJ *attr issue* Kern-; *(Sch) subject* Haupt-, Pflicht-; *curriculum* Haupt-; **~ (business) activity** *(Comm)* Kerngeschäft *nt* VT *fruit* entkernen; *apple, pear* das Kernhaus *(+gen)* entfernen *or* ausschneiden

corelate VTI = **correlate**

coreligionist ['kəʊrɪ'lɪdʒənɪst] N Glaubensgenosse *m*/-genossin *f*

corer ['kɔ:rə'] N *(Cook)* Apfelstecher *m*

co-respondent ['kəʊrɪs'pɒndənt] N *(Jur)* Mitbeklagte(r) *or* Dritte(r) *mf (im Scheidungsprozess)*, Scheidungsgrund *m (hum)*

core: **core time** N Kernzeit *f*; **core vocabulary** N Grundwortschatz *m*

Corfu [kɔ:'fu:] N Korfu *nt*

corgi ['kɔ:gɪ] N Corgi *m*

coriander [ˌkɒrɪ'ændə'] N Koriander *m*

Corinth ['kɒrɪnθ] N Korinth *nt*

Corinthian [kə'rɪnθɪən] ADJ korinthisch N **a** Korinther(in) *m(f)* **b** *(Eccl)* **~s** *+sing vb* Korinther *pl*

Coriolanus ['kɒrɪə'leɪnəs] N Coriolan *m*

cork [kɔ:k] N **a** *no pl (= substance)* Kork *m* **b** *(= stopper)* Korken *m*; **put a ~ in it!** *(inf)* halt die Klappe! *(inf)* **c** *(Fishing: also* **cork float**) Schwimmer *m* VT *(also* **cork up**) *bottle, wine* zu- *or* verkorken ADJ Kork-, korken *(rare)*; **~ flooring** Kork(fuß)boden *m*

corkage ['kɔ:kɪdʒ] N Korkengeld *nt*

corked [kɔ:kt] ADJ **the wine is ~** der Wein schmeckt nach Kork

corker ['kɔ:kə'] N *(dated inf)* **a ~** einsame Klasse *(inf)*

corking ['kɔ:kɪŋ] ADJ *(dated Brit, inf)* Klasse- *(inf)*; **a ~ game** ein Klassespiel *nt (inf)*

cork: **cork oak** N Korkeiche *f*; **corkscrew** N Korkenzieher *m*; **corkscrew curls** PL Korkenzieherlocken *pl*; **cork shoes** PL Schuhe *pl* mit Korksohlen; **cork tile** N Korkfliese *f*; **cork-tipped** ADJ *cigarette* mit Korkfilter; **cork tree** N Korkbaum *m*

corky ['kɔ:kɪ] ADJ Kork-, korkartig; *taste* Kork-, korkig

corm [kɔ:m] N Knolle *f*

cormorant ['kɔ:mərənt] N Kormoran *m*

Corn *(Brit) abbr of* **Cornwall**

corn[1] [kɔ:n] N **a** *no pl (Brit: = cereal)* Getreide *nt*, Korn *nt* **b** *(= seed of corn)* Korn *nt* **c** *no pl (esp US: = maize)* Mais *m* → **cob**

corn[2] N *(on foot)* Hühnerauge *nt*; **~ plaster** Hühneraugenpflaster *nt*; **to tread on sb's ~s** *(fig)* jdm auf die Hühneraugen treten

corn[3] N *(inf: = sentiment etc)* Kitsch *m*, sentimentales Zeug

corn: **cornball** N *(US inf)* N Gefühlsdusel *m (inf)* ADJ gefühlsduselig *(inf)*, kitschig, schmalzig; **Corn Belt** N *(Geog)* Getreidegürtel *m*; **corn bread** N *(US)* Maisbrot *nt*; **corn bunting** N *(Orn)* Grauammer *f*; **corn chandler** N Kornhändler *m*; **corncob** N Maiskolben *m*; **corn-coloured** ADJ strohfarben, strohgelb; **corncrake** N *(Orn)* Wachtelkönig *m*; **corncrib** N *(US)* Maisspeicher *m*; **corn dodger** N *(US)* Maisfladen *m*; **corn dog** N *(US Cook) mit Maismehl paniertes Bratwürstchen*

cornea ['kɔ:nɪə] N Hornhaut *f*, Cornea *f (spec)*

corneal ['kɔ:nɪəl] ADJ Hornhaut-; **~ lenses** Linsen *pl*

corned beef ['kɔ:nd'bi:f] N Corned Beef *nt*, Cornedbeef *nt*

corner ['kɔ:nə'] N **a** *(generally, Boxing)* Ecke *f*; *(of sheet also)* Zipfel *m*; *(of mouth, eye)* Winkel *m*; *(= sharp bend in road)* Kurve *f*; *(fig: = awkward situation)* Klemme *f (inf)*; **at** *or* **on the ~** an der Ecke; **the teacher made him stand in the ~** der Lehrer stellte ihn in die Ecke; **it's just round the ~** *(= near)* es ist gleich um die Ecke; *(inf: = about to happen)* das steht kurz bevor; *(fig, recovery etc)* das wird bald eintreten; **to turn the ~** *(lit)* um die Ecke biegen; **we've turned the ~ now** *(fig)* wir sind jetzt über den Berg; **the pages are curling up at the ~s** die Seiten haben Eselsohren; **out of the ~ of one's eye** aus dem Augenwinkel (heraus); **he always has a cigarette hanging out of the ~ of his mouth** er hat immer eine Zigarette im Mundwinkel (hängen); **to cut ~s** *(lit)* Kurven schneiden; *(fig)* das Verfahren abkürzen; **to drive** *or* **force sb into a ~** *(fig)* jdn in die Enge treiben; **to fight one's ~** *(esp Brit fig)* für seine Sache kämpfen; **to have sb in one's ~** *(fig)* jdn auf seiner Seite haben; **all four ~s of the world** alle vier Winde; **he has travelled to all four ~s of the world** er hat die ganze Welt bereist; **in every ~ of Europe/the globe/the house** in allen (Ecken und) Winkeln Europas/der Erde/des Hauses; **an attractive ~ of Britain** eine reizvolle Gegend Großbritanniens
b *(= out-of-the-way place)* Winkel *m*; **have you got an odd ~ somewhere where I could store my books?** hast du irgendwo ein Eckchen *or*

Plätzchen, wo ich meine Bücher lagern könnte?
c *(Comm: = monopoly)* Monopol *nt*; **to make/have a ~ in sth** das Monopol für *or* auf etw *(acc)* erwerben/haben
d *(Ftbl)* Ecke *f*, Eckball *m*, Corner *m (Aus)*; **to take a ~** eine Ecke ausführen
VT a *(lit, fig: = trap)* in die Enge treiben
b *(Comm) the market* monopolisieren
VI *(= take a corner: person)* Kurven/die Kurve nehmen; **this car ~s well** dieses Auto hat eine gute Kurvenlage

corner *in cpds* Eck-; **corner cabinet** N Eckschrank *m*; **corner chair** N Eckstuhl *m*

cornered [ˈkɔːnəd] ADJ eckig; *(fig)* in die Ecke getrieben

-cornered [-ˈkɔːnəd] ADJ *suf* -eckig; **three-cornered** dreieckig

corner: **corner flag** N *(Sport)* Eckfahne *f*; **corner hit** N *(Hockey)* Eckschlag *m*

cornering [ˈkɔːnərɪŋ] N *(of car)* Kurvenlage *f*; *(of driver)* Kurventechnik *f*

corner: **corner kick** N *(Ftbl)* Eckstoß *m*; **corner post** N *(Ftbl)* Eckfahne *f*; **corner seat** N *(Rail)* Eckplatz *m*; **corner shop** N Laden *m* an der Ecke; **cornerstone** N *(lit, fig)* Grundstein *m*, Eckstein *m*; **corner store** N *(US)* = **corner shop**; **corner table** N Tisch *m* in der Ecke, Ecktisch *m*; **cornerways, cornerwise** ADV über Eck, diagonal

cornet [ˈkɔːnɪt] N **a** *(Mus)* Kornett *nt* **b** *(= ice-cream cornet)* (Eis)tüte *f*

corn: **corn exchange** N Getreidebörse *f*; **corn-fed** ADJ mit Getreide gefüttert; **cornfield** N *(Brit)* Korn- *or* Weizenfeld *nt*; *(US)* Maisfeld *nt*; **cornflakes** PL Cornflakes *pl*; **cornflour** N *(Brit)* Stärkemehl *nt*; **cornflower** N **a** Kornblume *f* **b** *(= colour)* Kornblumenblau *nt* ADJ *(also* **cornflower blue**) kornblumenblau

cornice [ˈkɔːnɪs] N *(Archit: of wall, column)* (Ge)sims *nt*; *(fig, of snow)* Wechte *f*

corniche [ˈkɔːnɪʃ, kɔːˈniːʃ] N Küstenstraße *f*

Cornish [ˈkɔːnɪʃ] ADJ kornisch, aus Cornwall N *(Ling)* Kornisch *nt*

Cornishman [ˈkɔːnɪʃmən] N *pl* **-men** [-mən] Bewohner *m* Cornwalls

Cornish pasty n *(Brit) Gebäckstück aus Blätterteig mit Fleischfüllung*

Cornishwoman [ˈkɔːnɪʃwʊmən] N *pl* **-women** [-wɪmɪn] Bewohnerin *f* Cornwalls

corn: **cornmeal** N *(US)* Maismehl *nt*; **corn oil** N (Mais)keimöl *nt*; **corn plaster** N Hühneraugenpflaster *nt*; **corn pone** N *(US)* = **corn bread**; **corn poppy** N Klatschmohn *m*, Mohnblume *f*; **corn shock** N (Getreide)garbe *f*; **cornstarch** N *(US)* Stärkemehl *nt*; **corn syrup** N *(US)* (Mais)sirup *m*

cornucopia [kɔːnjʊˈkəʊpɪə] N *(Myth, = horn-shaped container)* Füllhorn *nt*; *(fig: = abundance)* Fülle *f*

Cornwall [ˈkɔːnwəl] N Cornwall *nt*

corn whisky N *(US)* Maiswhisky *m*

corny [ˈkɔːnɪ] ADJ *(+er) (inf) joke* blöd *(inf)*; *(= sentimental)* kitschig; **what a ~ old joke!** der Witz hat (so) einen Bart *(inf)*

corolla [kəˈrɒlə] N *(Bot)* Blumenkrone *f*, Korolla *f (spec)*

corollary [kəˈrɒlərɪ] N (logische) Folge, Korollar *nt (also Math)*; **this would prove, as a ~, that ...** damit würde dann gleichzeitig auch bewiesen, dass ... ADJ Begleit-

corona [kəˈrəʊnə] N *(Astron, of sun, moon etc)* Hof *m*; *(= part of sun's atmosphere)* Korona *f*; *(of tooth)* Krone *f*; *(Bot)* Nebenkrone *f*; *(= cigar)* Corona *f*

coronary [ˈkɒrənərɪ] ADJ *(Med)* Koronar- *(spec)*; **~ failure** Herzversagen *nt (inf)*, Koronarinsuffizienz *f* N Herzinfarkt *m*

coronary: **coronary artery** N *(Med)* Kranzarterie *f*; **coronary thrombosis** N *(Med)* Herzinfarkt *m*; **coronary vessel** N *(Med)* (Herz)kranzgefäß *nt*, Koronargefäß *nt (spec)*

coronation [ˌkɒrəˈneɪʃən] N **a** Krönung *f* **b** *in cpds* Krönungs-; **~ robes** Krönungsgewänder *pl*

coroner [ˈkɒrənəʳ] N *Beamter, der Todesfälle untersucht, die nicht eindeutig eine natürliche Ursache haben*; **~'s inquest** *Untersuchung nicht eindeutig natürlicher Todesfälle*; **~'s jury** *Untersuchungskommission bei nicht eindeutig natürlichen Todesfällen*

coronet [ˈkɒrənɪt] N Krone *f*; *(= jewellery)* Krönchen *nt*

corp. *abbr of* **corporation**

corporal[1] [ˈkɔːpərəl] N *(Mil)* Stabsunteroffizier *m*

corporal[2] ADJ körperlich; *pleasures, needs* leiblich

corporal punishment N Prügel- *or* Körperstrafe *f*

corporate [ˈkɔːpərɪt] ADJ **a** *(= of a group)* gemeinsam, korporativ; **~ action/decision** geschlossenes *or* gemeinsames Vorgehen/gemeinsame Entscheidung; **to work for the ~ good** für das Gemeinwohl arbeiten; **to take out ~ membership of another society** als geschlossene Gruppe Mitglied eines anderen Vereins werden
b *(of a corporation)* korporativ; *(of a company)* Firmen-; *(Jur)* Korporations-; **I'm not a ~ man** ich bin ein Mensch, der sich in großen Firmen nicht wohlfühlt; **the ~ life of an organization** das Leben in einer großen Vereinigung; **I was meaning "we" in the ~ sense** ich meinte „wir" als Firma; **our ~ liabilities** unsere Verbindlichkeiten als Firma; **to move up the ~ ladder** in der Firma aufsteigen; **~ body** Körperschaft *f*; **~ finance** Unternehmensfinanzen *pl*; **~ financing** Unternehmensfinanzierung *f*; **~ planning** Unternehmensplanung *f*

corporate: **corporate hospitality** N *Unterhaltung und Bewirtung von Firmenkunden*; **corporate identity** N Firmenimage *nt*; **corporate law** N Gesellschaftsrecht *nt*; **corporate lawyer** N *(working for corporation)* Firmenanwalt *m*/-anwältin *f*; *(= specialist in corporate law)* Anwalt *m*/Anwältin *f* für Gesellschaftsrecht

corporately [ˈkɔːpərɪtlɪ] ADV **a** *(= collectively)* gemeinsam **b** *(Comm)* körperschaftlich; **to be ~ owned** einer Firma *(dat)* gehören; **he has plenty of capital, both ~ and privately** er hat jede Menge Kapital, sowohl geschäftlich als auch privat

corporate raider N Firmenaufkäufer(in) *m(f)*

corporate tax N Körperschaftsteuer *f*

corporation [ˌkɔːpəˈreɪʃən] N **a** *(= municipal corporation)* Gemeinde *f*, Stadt *f*; **the Mayor and Corporation** der Bürgermeister und die Stadt **b** *(Brit Comm: = incorporated company)* Handelsgesellschaft *f*; *(US Comm: = limited liability company)* Gesellschaft *f* mit beschränkter Haftung; **private ~** *(Comm)* Privatunternehmen *nt*; **public ~** *(Comm)* staatliches Unternehmen **c** *(Brit, hum, = large belly)* Schmerbauch *m*

corporation: **corporation bus** N Stadtbus *m*, städtischer Omnibus; **corporation property** N gemeindeeigener Besitz; **corporation tax** N Körperschaftssteuer *f*; **corporation tram** N städtische Straßenbahn; **corporation transport** N städtisches Verkehrsmittel

corporatism [ˈkɔːpərɪtɪzəm] N **the growth of ~** die steigende Zahl der Großunternehmen; **a sense of ~** ein Zusammengehörigkeitsgefühl *nt* innerhalb des/eines Unternehmens

corporeal [kɔːˈpɔːrɪəl] ADJ körperlich

corps [kɔːʳ] N *pl* - *(Mil)* Korps *nt*

corps de ballet N Corps de Ballet *nt*

corps diplomatique [ˈkɔːˌdɪpləʊmæˈtiːk] N diplomatisches Korps → **diplomatic corps**

corpse [kɔːps] N Leiche *f*, Leichnam *m (geh)* VI *(Theat sl)* einen Lachanfall bekommen

corpulence [ˈkɔːpjʊləns] N Korpulenz *f*

corpulent [ˈkɔːpjʊlənt] ADJ korpulent

corpus [ˈkɔːpəs] N **a** *(= collection)* Korpus *m*; *(of opinions)* Paket *nt* **b** *(= main body)* Großteil *m*; **the main ~ of his work** der Hauptteil seiner Arbeit **c** *(Fin)* Stammkapital *nt*

Corpus Christi [ˈkɔːpəsˈkrɪstɪ] N *(Eccl)* Fronleichnam *m*

corpuscle [ˈkɔːpʌsl] N Korpuskel *nt (spec)*; **blood ~** Blutkörperchen *nt*

corpuscular [kɔːˈpʌskjuːləʳ] ADJ Korpuskular- *(spec)*

corpus delicti [ˈkɔːpəsdəˈlɪktaɪ] N *(Jur)* Corpus Delicti *nt*; *(= corpse)* Leiche *f*

corral [kəˈrɑːl] N Korral *m* VT *cattle* in den Korral treiben

correct [kəˈrekt] ADJ **a** *(= right)* richtig; *answer, pronunciation also* korrekt; *time also* genau; **to be ~** *(person)* recht haben; **to be ~ in one's estimates/assessment** richtig schätzen/einschätzen; **am I ~ in thinking that ...?** gehe ich recht in der Annahme, dass ...?; **~ money** *or* **change only** nur abgezähltes Geld, nur passenden Betrag
b *(= proper, suitable, perfectly mannered)* korrekt; **it's the ~ thing to do** das gehört sich so; **she was ~ to reject the offer** es war richtig, dass sie das Angebot abgelehnt hat
VT a korrigieren; *person, pronunciation, error etc also* berichtigen, verbessern; *bad habit* sich/jdm abgewöhnen; **to ~ proofs** Korrektur lesen; **~ me if I'm wrong** Sie können mich gern berichtigen; **I stand ~ed** ich nehme alles zurück
b *(old, by punishment, scolding)* maßregeln; *(by corporal punishment)* züchtigen

correcting fluid [kəˈrektɪŋˌfluːɪd] N Korrekturflüssigkeit *f*

correction [kəˈrekʃən] N **a** Korrektion *f*, Korrektur *f*; *(of person, pronunciation, error etc also)* Berichtigung *f*, Verbesserung *f*; *(of bad habit)* Abgewöhnung *f*; **~ of proofs** Korrekturlesen *nt*; **I am open to ~** ich lasse mich gerne berichtigen; **to do one's ~s** *(Sch)* die Verbesserung machen; **~ key** Korrekturtaste *f*; **~ tape** *(on typewriter)* Korrekturband *nt* **b** *(old, by punishment, scolding)* Maßregelung *f*; *(by corporal punishment)* Züchtigung *f*; **house of ~** Besserungsanstalt *f*

correctional [kəˈrekʃənəl] ADJ *(US)* **~ officer** Justizvollzugsbeamte(r) *m*/-beamtin *f*; **the ~ system** das Justizvollzugssystem; **~ facility** Justizvollzugsanstalt *f*, Strafanstalt *f*

correction fluid N Korrekturflüssigkeit *f*

correctitude [kəˈrektɪtjuːd] N = **correctness b**

corrective [kəˈrektɪv] ADJ korrigierend; **to take ~ action** korrigierend eingreifen; **to have ~ surgery** sich einem korrigierenden Eingriff unterziehen N *(Pharm, fig)* Korrektiv *nt*

correctly [kəˈrektlɪ] ADV **a** *(= accurately)* richtig; *answer, pronounce also* korrekt; **he had ~ assumed that ...** er hatte richtigerweise angenommen, dass ...; **if I remember ~** wenn ich mich recht entsinne **b** *(= in proper way) behave, speak, dress* korrekt

correctness [kəˈrektnɪs] N **a** *(= accuracy)* Richtigkeit *f* **b** *(of behaviour etc)* Korrektheit *f*

correlate [ˈkɒrɪleɪt] VT *two things* zueinander in Beziehung setzen, korrelieren *(geh)*; **to ~ sth with sth** etw mit etw in Beziehung setzen, etw mit etw korrelieren *(geh)* VI *(two things)* sich entsprechen; **to ~ with sth** mit etw in Beziehung stehen

correlation [ˌkɒrɪˈleɪʃən] N *(= correspondence)* Beziehung *f*; *(= close relationship)* enger *or* direkter Zusammenhang; *(Math, Statistics)* Korrelation *f*

correlative [kɒˈrelətɪv] N Korrelat *nt* ADJ *(= directly related)* entsprechend; *(Gram)* korrelativ

correspond [ˌkɒrɪsˈpɒnd] ✪ 5.4 VI **a** *(= be equivalent)* entsprechen *(to, with +dat)*; *(two or more: to one another)* sich entsprechen; *(= be in accordance also)* sich decken *(with* mit); **your version doesn't ~** Ihre Version deckt sich nicht damit **b** *(= exchange letters)* korrespondieren *(with* mit)

correspondence [ˌkɒrɪsˈpɒndəns] N **a** *(= agreement, equivalence)* Übereinstimmung *f (between* zwischen, *with* mit) **b** *(= letter-writing)* Korrespondenz *f; (= letters also)* Briefe *pl; (in newspaper)* Leserzuschriften *or* -briefe *pl;* **to be in ~ with sb** mit jdm in Korrespondenz stehen *(form)*, mit jdm korrespondieren; *(private)* mit jdm in Briefwechsel stehen, mit jdm korrespondieren *(geh)*

correspondence: **correspondence card** N Briefkarte *f;* **correspondence chess** N Fernschach *nt;* **correspondence column** N *(Press)* Leserbriefspalte *f;* **correspondence course** N Fernkurs *m;* **correspondence school** N Fernlehrinstitut *nt*

correspondent [ˌkɒrɪsˈpɒndənt] **N** **a** *(= letter-writer)* Briefschreiber(in) *m(f);* **to be a good/bad ~** ein eifriger Briefschreiber sein/schreibfaul sein; **according to my ~** wie man mir geschrieben hat **b** *(Press)* Korrespondent(in) *m(f)* **c** *(Comm)* Entsprechung *f*, Gegenstück *nt* **ADJ** entsprechend

corresponding [ˌkɒrɪsˈpɒndɪŋ] ADJ entsprechend

correspondingly [ˌkɒrɪsˈpɒndɪŋlɪ] ADV (dem-)entsprechend

corridor [ˈkɒrɪdɔːˈ] N Korridor *m; (in building also, in train, bus)* Gang *m;* **in the ~s of power** an den Schalthebeln der Macht

corridor train N D-Zug *m*

corrie [ˈkɒrɪ] N *(Geol)* Kar *m*

corrigendum [kɒrɪˈdʒendəm] N *pl* **corrigenda** [kɒrɪˈdʒendə] Corrigendum *nt (geh)*

corroborate [kəˈrɒbəreɪt] VT bestätigen; *theory also* bekräftigen, erhärten, untermauern

corroboration [kəˌrɒbəˈreɪʃən] N Bestätigung *f; (of theory also)* Bekräftigung *f*, Erhärtung *f*, Untermauerung *f;* **in ~ of** zur Untermauerung *or* Unterstützung *(+gen);* **through lack of ~** *(Jur)* mangels unterstützenden Beweismaterials; *(from witnesses)* mangels bestätigender Zeugenaussagen

corroborative [kəˈrɒbərətɪv] ADJ bestätigend; *evidence* erhärtend, untermauernd *all attr;* **to be ~ of sth** etw bestätigen/untermauern

corroboree [kəˈrɒbərɪ] N *(Austral) Tanzritual der Aborigines (fig)* rauschendes Fest

corrode [kəˈrəʊd] **VT** *metal* zerfressen; *(fig)* zerstören **VI** *(metal)* korrodieren

corroded [kəˈrəʊdɪd] ADJ korrodiert

corrosion [kəˈrəʊʒən] N Korrosion *f; (fig)* Zerstörung *f*

corrosive [kəˈrəʊzɪv] **ADJ** korrosiv; *(fig)* zerstörend **N** Korrosion verursachendes Mittel

corrugated [ˈkɒrəgeɪtɪd] ADJ gewellt; **~ cardboard** dicke Wellpappe

corrugated iron N Wellblech *nt*

corrugated paper N Wellpappe *f*

corrugation [ˌkɒrəˈgeɪʃən] N Welle *f*

corrupt [kəˈrʌpt] **ADJ** verdorben, verworfen, schlecht; *(= open to bribery)* korrupt, bestechlich; *text, language* verderbt, korrumpiert; *(Comput) disk* nicht lesbar, kaputt; **morally ~** moralisch verdorben *or* schlecht **VT** *(morally)* verderben; *(ethically)* korrumpieren; *(form: = bribe)* bestechen, korrumpieren; *(Comput) data* kaputt *or* unlesbar machen, zerstören; **to become ~ed** *(text, language)* korrumpiert werden; **to ~ sb's morals** jdn moralisch verderben

corrupted [kəˈrʌptɪd] ADJ *(Comput) file* fehlerhaft, beschädigt

corruptible [kəˈrʌptəbl] ADJ korrumpierbar; *(= bribable also)* bestechlich

corruption [kəˈrʌpʃən] N **a** *(= act, of person)* Korruption *f; (by bribery also)* Bestechung *f; (Comput, of data)* Zerstörung *f* **b** *(= corrupt nature)* Verdorbenheit *f*, Verderbtheit *f; (by bribery)* Bestechlichkeit *f; (of morals)* Verfall *m; (of language, text)* Korrumpierung *f* **c** *(form, = decay of bodies etc)* Zersetzung *f*, Fäulnis *f*

corruptly [kəˈrʌptlɪ] ADV korrupt

corsage [kɔːˈsɑːʒ] N **a** *(= bodice)* Mieder *nt* **b** *(= flowers)* Ansteckblume *f*

corsair [ˈkɔːsɛəˈ] N *(= ship)* Piratenschiff *nt*, Korsar *m; (= pirate)* Pirat *m*, Korsar *m*

corselet [kɔːsəˈlet] N **a** *(= corset)* Korselett *nt* **b** → **corslet**

corset [ˈkɔːsɪt] N, **corsets** *pl* Korsett *nt; (to give wasp waist)* Schnürmieder *nt*

corseted [ˈkɔːsɪtɪd] ADJ geschnürt

corsetry [ˈkɔːsɪtrɪ] N Miederwarenherstellung *f; (= corsets)* Miederwaren *pl*

Corsica [ˈkɔːsɪkə] N Korsika *nt*

Corsican [ˈkɔːsɪkən] **ADJ** korsisch; **~ holiday** Urlaub *m* auf Korsika; **she is ~** sie ist Korsin **N** **a** Korse *m*, Korsin *f* **b** *(Ling)* Korsisch *nt*

corslet, **corselet** [ˈkɔːslɪt] N Brust- (und Rücken)panzer *m*

cortège [kɔːˈteɪʒ] N *(= retinue)* Gefolge *nt; (= procession)* Prozession *f; (= funeral cortège)* Leichenzug *m*

cortex [ˈkɔːteks] N *pl* **cortices** *(Anat, of brain)* Hirnrinde *f; (of kidney)* Nierenrinde *f; (Bot)* Kortex *m*

cortical [ˈkɔːtɪkl] ADJ *(Anat, Bot)* kortikal

cortices [ˈkɔːtɪsiːz] *pl of* **cortex**

cortisone [ˈkɔːtɪzəʊn] N Kortison *nt*, Cortison *nt*

corundum [kəˈrʌndəm] N *(Geol)* Korund *m*

coruscate [ˈkɒrəskeɪt] VI funkeln

coruscating [ˈkɒrəskeɪtɪŋ] ADJ brilliant, geistsprühend

corvette [kɔːˈvet] N *(Naut)* Korvette *f*

cos[1] [kɒz] *abbr of* **cosine** cos

cos[2] [kɒs] N *(also* **cos lettuce**) Romagnasalat *m*, römischer Salat *m*

cos[3] [kəz] CONJ *(inf)* = **because**

cosec [ˈkəʊsek] *abbr of* **cosecant** cosec

cosecant [ˈkəʊsekænt] N Kosekans *m*

cosh [kɒʃ] **VT** auf den Schädel schlagen, eins über den Schädel ziehen *(+dat) (inf)* **N** *(= instrument)* Totschläger *m; (= blow)* Schlag *m* (auf den Kopf)

cosignatory [ˈkəʊˈsɪgnətərɪ] N Mitunterzeichner(in) *m(f)*

cosily, *(US)* **cozily** [ˈkəʊzɪlɪ] ADV **a** *(= snugly) furnished, decorated* behaglich **b** *(= comfortably) sit, settle* behaglich **c** *(= intimately) chat, gossip* gemütlich

cosine [ˈkəʊsaɪn] N Kosinus *m*

cosiness, *(US)* **coziness** [ˈkəʊzɪnɪs] N Gemütlichkeit *f*, Behaglichkeit *f; (= warmth)* mollige Wärme; *(of chat)* Freundschaftlichkeit *f*, Traulichkeit *f (dated)*

COSLA [ˈkɒzlə] *(Scot) abbr of* **Convention of Scottish Local Authorities**

cosmaceuticals, **cosmeceuticals** [kɒzməˈsjuːtɪkəlz] PL Kosmezeutika *pl*, *Produkte, die sowohl pharmazeutische als auch kosmetische Effekte erzielen*

cosmetic [kɒzˈmetɪk] **ADJ** *(lit, fig)* kosmetisch **N** Kosmetikum *nt*, Schönheitspflegemittel *nt*

cosmetician [kɒzməˈtɪʃən] N Kosmetiker(in) *m(f)*

cosmetic surgery N kosmetische Chirurgie; **she's had ~** sie hat eine Schönheitsoperation gehabt

cosmetologist [kɒzməˈtɒlədʒɪst] N Kosmetologe *m*, Kosmetologin *f*

cosmetology [kɒzməˈtɒlədʒɪ] N Kosmetologie *f*

cosmic [ˈkɒzmɪk] ADJ kosmisch; **~ dust** Weltraumnebel *m*

cosmo N *(inf: = drink)* Cosmopolitan *m*

cosmogony [kɒzˈmɒgənɪ] N Kosmogonie *f*

cosmography [kɒzˈmɒgrəfɪ] N Kosmografie *f*

cosmologist [kɒzˈmɒlədʒɪst] N Kosmologe *m*, Kosmologin *f*

cosmology [kɒzˈmɒlədʒɪ] N Kosmologie *f*

cosmonaut [ˈkɒzmənɔːt] N Kosmonaut(in) *m(f)*

cosmopolitan [ˌkɒzməˈpɒlɪtən] **ADJ** kosmopolitisch, international **N** **a** Kosmopolit *m*, Weltbürger *m* **b** *(= drink)* Cosmopolitan *m*

cosmos [ˈkɒzmɒs] N **a** Kosmos *m* **b** *(Bot)* Kosmee *f*

cossack [ˈkɒsæk] **N** Kosak(in) *m(f)* **ADJ** Kosaken-

cossack hat N Kosakenmütze *f*

cosset [ˈkɒsɪt] VT verwöhnen

cossie, **cozzie** [ˈkɒzɪ] N *(Brit inf)* Badeanzug *m*

cost [kɒst] *vb: pret, ptp* **cost** **VT** **a** *(lit, fig)* kosten; **how much does it ~?** wie viel kostet es?; **how much will it ~ to have it repaired?** wie viel kostet die Reparatur?; **it ~ (him) a lot of money** das hat (ihn) viel Geld gekostet; **designer clothes ~ money** Designerkleidung kostet Geld; **driving without a seat belt ~ him dear** Fahren ohne Sicherheitsgurt kam ihn teuer zu stehen; **it ~ him a great effort/a lot of time** es kostete ihn viel Mühe/viel Zeit; **that mistake could ~ you your life** der Fehler könnte dich das Leben kosten; **~ what it may** koste es, was es wolle; **politeness doesn't ~ (you) anything** es kostet (dich) nichts, höflich zu sein; **it'll ~ you** *(inf)* das kostet dich was *(inf)*

b *pret, ptp* **costed** *(= work out cost of) project etc* veranschlagen

c *pret, ptp* **costed** *(Comm: = put a price on) articles for sale* auspreisen *(at* zu)

N **a** *(lit)* Kosten *pl (of* für); **to bear the ~ of sth** die Kosten für etw tragen, für die Kosten von etw aufkommen; **the ~ of electricity/petrol these days** die Strom-/Benzinpreise heutzutage; **to buy sth at great ~** etw zu einem hohen Preis kaufen; **at little ~ to oneself** ohne große eigene Kosten; **to buy sth at ~** etw zum Selbstkostenpreis kaufen; **~ containment** Kostendämpfung *f;* **~ of manufacture** Produktions- *or* Herstellungskosten *pl;* **~ of sales** Verkaufskosten *pl*

b *(fig)* Preis *m;* **at all ~s, at any ~** um jeden Preis; **whatever the ~** kostet es, was es wolle; **at the ~ of one's health/job/marriage** *etc* auf Kosten seiner Gesundheit/Stelle/Ehe *etc;* **at great/little personal ~** unter großen/geringen eigenen Kosten; **he found out to his ~ that …** er machte die bittere Erfahrung, dass …

c **costs** **PL** *(Jur)* Kosten *pl;* **to be ordered to pay ~s** zur Übernahme der Kosten verurteilt werden

▶ **cost out** VT *sep* (kostenmäßig) kalkulieren

Costa Brava [ˈkɒstəˈbrɑːvə] N Costa Brava *f*

cost: **cost accountant** N Kostenbuchhalter(in) *m(f);* **cost accounting** N Kalkulation *f*

Costa del Sol [ˈkɒstədelˈsɒl] N Costa del Sol *f*

co-star [ˈkəʊstɑːˈ] **N** *(Film, Theat)* einer der Hauptdarsteller; **Burton and Taylor were ~s** Burton und Taylor spielten die Hauptrollen **VT** **the film ~s R. Burton** der Film zeigt R. Burton in einer der Hauptrollen **VI** als Hauptdarsteller auftreten

Costa Rica [ˈkɒstəˈriːkə] N Costa Rica *nt*

Costa Rican [ˈkɒstəˈriːkən] **ADJ** costa-ricanisch **N** Costa Ricaner(in) *m(f)*

cost: **cost-benefit analysis** N Kosten-Nutzen-Analyse *f;* **cost centre** N Kostenstelle *f;* **cost clerk** N Angestellte(r) *mf* in der Kostenbuchhaltung; **cost-conscious** ADJ kostenbewusst; **cost-covering** ADJ *(Fin)* kostendeckend; **cost-cutting** **N** Kostenverringerung *f* **ADJ** *attr* **~ exercise** kostendämpfende Maßnahmen *pl;* **cost-effective** ADJ rentabel, kosteneffizient *(spec);* **cost-effectively** ADV rentabel; **cost-effectiveness** N Rentabilität *f*, Kosteneffizienz *f (spec)*

coster(monger) [ˈkɒstə(ˌmʌŋgəˈ)] N *(Brit)* Straßenhändler *m*

costing [ˈkɒstɪŋ] N Kalkulation *f;* **~ department** Kostenbuchhaltung *f*, betriebliches Rechnungswesen

costive ['kɒstɪv] ADJ *(form: = constipated)* verstopft; *(= constipating)* stopfend

costliness ['kɒstlɪnɪs] N Kostspieligkeit *f*; *(in business, industry)* hoher Kostenaufwand; **the ~ of buying a new car** die mit dem Kauf eines neuen Wagens verbundenen hohen Kosten

costly ['kɒstlɪ] ADJ teuer, kostspielig; *tastes, habits* teuer; **~ in terms of time/labour** zeitaufwendig *or* -aufwändig/arbeitsintensiv; **running a car is a ~ business** ein Auto zu unterhalten ist eine teure Angelegenheit

cost: **cost of living** N Lebenshaltungskosten *pl*; **cost-of-living adjustment** N *(US Fin)* Dynamisierung *f* auf der Basis veränderter Lebenshaltungskosten; **cost-of-living bonus** N Lebenshaltungskostenzuschlag *m*; **cost-of--living index** N Lebenshaltungsindex *m*; **cost-plus** ADJ **calculated on a ~ basis** unter Einbeziehung einer Gewinnspanne berechnet; **cost price** N Selbstkostenpreis *m*; **cost-saving** ADJ kostensparend

costume ['kɒstjuːm] N Kostüm *nt*; *(= bathing costume)* Badeanzug *m*

costume: **costume ball** N Kostümfest *nt*; **costume drama** N **a** *(= play)* Schauspiel *nt* in historischen Kostümen; *(= film)* Kostümfilm *m*, Historienfilm *m*; *(= series)* Serie *f* in historischen Kostümen **b** *(= genre, Theat)* Schauspiele *pl* in historischen Kostümen; *(Film)* Kostümfilme *pl*; *(TV)* Serien *pl* in historischen Kostümen; **costume jewellery** N Modeschmuck *m*; **costume piece**, **costume play** N Schauspiel *nt* in historischen Kostümen; **costume ring** N Modeschmuckring *m*

costumier [kɒs'tjuːmɪə'], *(US)* **costumer** [kɒs'tjuːmə'] N **a** *(= theatrical costumier)* Kostümverleih *m* **b** *(form, = dressmaker)* Schneider(in) *m(f)*

cosy, *(US)* **cozy** ['kəʊzɪ] ADJ *(+er) room, atmosphere, restaurant* gemütlich, behaglich; *(= warm)* mollig warm; *(fig) chat* gemütlich, traulich *(dated)*; *relationship* traut; **to feel ~** *(person)* sich wohl- und behaglich fühlen; *(room etc)* einen behaglichen *or* gemütlichen Eindruck machen; **I'm very ~ here** ich fühle mich hier sehr wohl, ich finde es hier sehr gemütlich; **a ~ little tête--à-tête** *(fig)* ein trautes Tete-a-tete *or* Tête-à-tête; **warm and ~** mollig warm N *(= tea cosy, egg cosy)* Wärmer *m* VI **to ~ up to sb** *(inf)* mit jdm auf Schmusekurs gehen *(inf)*

cot [kɒt] N *(esp Brit: = child's bed)* Kinderbett *nt*; *(US: = camp bed)* Feldbett *nt*

cot death N *(Brit)* Krippentod *m*, plötzlicher Kindstod

cote [kəʊt] N *(= dovecote)* Taubenschlag *m*; *(= sheepcote)* Schafstall *m*

coterie ['kəʊtərɪ] N Clique *f*; *(= literary coterie)* Zirkel *m*

cotill(i)on [kə'tɪljən] N Kotillon *m*

cotta ['kɒtə] N *(Eccl)* Chorhemd *nt*

cottage ['kɒtɪdʒ] N **a** Cottage *nt*, Häuschen *nt*; *(US, in institution)* Wohneinheit *f* **b** *(sl: for gays)* Klappe *f (sl)*

cottage: **cottage cheese** N Hüttenkäse *m*; **cottage hospital** N *(Brit) kleines Krankenhaus für leichtere Fälle*; **cottage industry** N Manufaktur *f*, Heimindustrie *f*; **cottage loaf** N *(Brit) eine Art rundes, hohes Weißbrot*; **cottage pie** N *Hackfleisch mit Kartoffelbrei überbacken*

cottager ['kɒtɪdʒə'] N *(Brit)* Cottagebewohner(in) *m(f)*

cotter (pin) ['kɒtə(,pɪn)] N Splint *m*

cotton ['kɒtn] N Baumwolle *f*; *(= plant)* Baumwollstrauch *m*; *(= fibre)* Baumwollfaser *f*; *(= fabric)* Baumwollstoff *m*; *(= sewing thread)* (Baumwoll)garn *nt* ADJ Baumwoll-, baumwollen; *clothes, fabric also* aus Baumwolle

▶ **cotton on** VI *(Brit inf)* es kapieren *(inf)*, es schnallen *(inf)*; **to cotton on to sth** etw checken *(inf)*; **has he cottoned on yet?** hat er es endlich kapiert *(inf) or* geschnallt? *(inf)*

▶ **cotton to** VI *+prep obj (US inf) plan, suggestion* gut finden

cotton *in cpds* Baumwoll-; **cotton batting** N *(US)* Gaze *f*; **Cotton Belt** N *(Geog)* Baumwollzone *f*; **cotton bud** N *(Brit)* Wattestäbchen *nt*; **cotton cake** N Futtermittel *nt*; **cotton candy** N *(US)* Zuckerwatte *f*; **cotton gin** N Entkörnungsmaschine *f* (für Baumwolle); **cotton grass** N Wollgras *nt*; **cotton mill** N Baumwollspinnerei *f*; **cotton pad** N Wattepad *nt*; **cotton picker** N Baumwollpflücker(in) *m(f)*; *(= machine)* Baumwollpflückmaschine *f*; **cotton-picking** ADJ *(US inf)* verflucht *(inf)*; **cotton plant** N Baumwollstaude *f or* -strauch *m*; **cotton print** N *(= fabric)* bedruckter Baumwollstoff; **cottonseed** N Baumwollsamen *m*; **cottonseed cake** N = **cotton cake**; **cottonseed oil** N Baumwollsamenöl *nt*; **cottontail** N *(US)* Kaninchen *nt*, Karnickel *nt*; **cottonwood** N Pyramidenpappel *f*; **cotton wool** N *(Brit)* Watte *f*; **to wrap sb (up) in ~** *(fig)* jdn in Watte packen; **my brain feels like ~** ich kann überhaupt nicht klar denken; **cotton-wool ball** N Wattebausch *m*

cotyledon [,kɒtɪ'liːdən] N Keimblatt *nt*

couch [kaʊtʃ] N Sofa *nt*; *(= studio couch)* Schlafcouch *f*; *(= doctor's couch)* Liege *f*; *(= psychiatrist's couch)* Couch *f*; *(poet, = bed)* Lager *nt* VT **a** *(= put in words) request* formulieren, abfassen **b** *(= lower) spear, lance* anlegen VI *(liter, lion, cat etc)* lauern, auf der Lauer liegen

couchant ['kuːʃənt] ADJ *(Her)* liegend

couchette [kuː'ʃet] N *(Rail)* Liegewagen(platz) *m*

couch grass N Quecke *f*

couch potato N *(inf)* Dauerglotzer(in) *m(f) (inf)*, Couch-Potato *f*

cougar ['kuːgə'] N Puma *m*, Kuguar *m*

cough [kɒf] N Husten *m*; **he has a bit of a ~** er hat etwas Husten; **to give a warning ~** sich warnend räuspern; **a smoker's ~** Raucherhusten *m* VI husten VT *blood* husten

▶ **cough out** VT *sep* aushusten, ausspucken

▶ **cough up** VT *sep (lit)* aushusten VT *insep (fig inf) money* rausrücken *(inf)*, ausspucken *(inf)*, rüberkommen mit *(sl)* VI *(fig inf)* blechen *(inf)*, ausspucken *(inf)*

cough: **cough drop** N Hustenpastille *f*; **cough mixture** N Hustensaft *m or* -mittel *nt*; **cough sweet** N *(Brit)* Hustenbonbon *nt*; **cough syrup** N Hustensaft *m*

could [kʊd] ✪ 1.1, 1.2, 2.2, 4, 9.1, 15.3, 26.3 *pret of* **can**[1]

couldn't ['kʊdnt] *contr of* **could not**

coulomb ['kuːlɒm] N Coulomb *nt*

council ['kaʊnsl] N *(= body of representatives)* Rat *m*; *(= meeting)* Sitzung *f*, Beratung *f*; **city/town ~** Stadtrat *m*; **to be on the ~** im Rat sitzen, Ratsmitglied sein; **to hold ~** Beratungen abhalten, Rat halten *(old)*; **~ of war** Kriegsrat *m*; **Council of Europe** Europarat *m*; **Council of Ministers** *(Pol)* Ministerrat *m* ADJ *attr* **~ meeting** Ratssitzung *f*

council *(Brit)*: **council chamber** N Sitzungssaal *m* des Rats; **council estate** N Sozialwohnungssiedlung *f*; **council flat** N Sozialwohnung *f*; **council house** N Sozialwohnung *f*; **council housing** N sozialer Wohnungsbau

councillor, *(US)* **councilor** ['kaʊnsələ'] N Ratsmitglied *nt*; *(= town councillor)* Stadtrat *m*/-rätin *f*; **~ Smith** Herr Stadtrat/Frau Stadträtin Smith

council tax N *(Brit)* Kommunalsteuer *f*

council tenant N *(Brit)* Bewohner(in) *m(f)* einer Sozialwohnung

counsel ['kaʊnsəl] N **a** *(form: = advice)* Rat (-schlag) *m*; **to hold ~ with sb over** *or* **about sth** mit jdm etw beraten *or* beratschlagen; **to keep one's own ~** seine Meinung für sich behalten, mit seiner Meinung zurückhalten; **~s of perfection** schlaue Ratschläge **b** *pl - (Jur)* Rechtsanwalt *m*; **~ for the defence/prosecution** Verteidiger(in) *m(f)*/Vertreter(in) *m(f)* der Anklage, ≈ Staatsanwalt *m*/-anwältin *f*; **~ on both sides** Verteidigung und Anklage VT **a** *(form) person* beraten; *course of action* empfehlen, raten zu; **to ~ sb to do sth** jdm raten *or* empfehlen, etw zu tun **b** *(in social work etc)* beraten

counselling, *(US)* **counseling** ['kaʊnsəlɪŋ] N Beratung *f*; *(Sociol)* soziale Beratung; *(by therapist)* Therapie *f*; **to need ~** professionelle Hilfe brauchen; **to go for** *or* **have ~** zur Beratung/Therapie gehen; **to give sb ~** jdm professionelle Hilfe zukommen lassen, jdn beraten/therapieren

counsellor, *(US)* **counselor** ['kaʊnsələ'] N **a** *(= adviser)* Berater(in) *m(f)* **b** *(US, Ir: = lawyer)* Rechtsanwalt *m*/-anwältin *f*

count[1] [kaʊnt] N **a** *(with numbers)* Zählung *f*; *(Sport)* Auszählen *nt*; *(of votes)* (Stimmen)zählung *f*, (Stimmen)auszählung *f*; **I'll have a ~** ich zähle es mal (ab); **she lost ~ when she was interrupted** sie kam mit dem Zählen durcheinander, als sie unterbrochen wurde; **I've lost all ~ of her boyfriends** ich habe die Übersicht über ihre Freunde vollkommen verloren; **to keep ~ (of sth)** (etw) mitzählen; *(= keep track)* die Übersicht (über etw *(acc)*) behalten; **she couldn't keep ~ of them** sie verlor die Übersicht; **at the last ~ there were twenty members** bei der letzten Zählung waren es zwanzig Mitglieder; **all together now, on the ~ of three** und jetzt alle zusammen, bei drei gehts los; **I'll come and look for you after a ~ of ten** ich zähle bis zehn und dann komme und suche ich dich; **he was out for the ~, he took the ~** *(fig)* er war k. o.; **he took a ~ of eight** *(Sport)* er ging bis acht zu Boden

b *(Jur: = charge)* Anklagepunkt *m*; **on that ~** *(fig)* in dem Punkt; **you're wrong on both ~s** Sie haben in beiden Punkten unrecht; **on all ~s** in jeder Hinsicht

c *no pl (= notice)* **don't take any ~ of what he says** hören Sie nicht auf das, was er sagt; **she never takes much/any ~ of him** sie nimmt wenig/keine Notiz von ihm

VT **a** *(with numbers)* (ab)zählen; *(= count again)* nachzählen; *votes* (aus)zählen; **to ~ ten** bis zehn zählen; **I only ~ed ten people** ich habe nur zehn Leute gezählt; **to ~ the cost** *(lit)* auf die Kosten achten, jeden Pfennig umdrehen; **she'll help anyone without ~ing the cost to herself** sie hilft jedem, ohne an sich selbst zu denken

b *(= consider)* ansehen, betrachten; *(= include)* mitrechnen, mitzählen; **to ~ sb (as) a friend/among one's friends** jdn als Freund ansehen/zu seinen Freunden zählen; **you should ~ yourself lucky to be alive** Sie sollten froh und glücklich sein *or* Sie können noch von Glück sagen, dass Sie noch leben; **ten people (not) ~ing the children** zehn Leute, die Kinder (nicht) mitgerechnet *or* eingerechnet; **to ~ sth against sb** etw gegen jdn anrechnen

VI **a** *(with numbers)* zählen; **to ~ to ten** bis zehn zählen; **~ing from today** von heute an (gerechnet)

b *(= be considered)* betrachtet *or* angesehen werden; *(= be included)* mitgerechnet *or* mitgezählt werden; *(= be important)* wichtig sein; **the children don't ~** die Kinder zählen nicht; **he doesn't ~ amongst her friends** er zählt nicht zu ihren Freunden; **that doesn't ~** das zählt nicht; **every minute/it all ~s** jede Minute ist/das ist alles wichtig; **appearance ~s a lot** es kommt sehr auf die äußere Erscheinung an; **to ~ against sb** gegen jdn sprechen

▶ **count down** VI den Countdown durchführen; **they started counting down last night** sie haben gestern abend mit dem Countdown angefangen; **to count down to blast-off** bis zum Abschuss (der Rakete) rückwärtszählen VT *sep* **to count a rocket down** den Countdown (für eine Rakete) durchführen

▶ **count for** VI *+prep obj* **to count for a lot** sehr viel bedeuten; **to count for nothing** nichts gelten

▶ **count in** VT *sep* mitzählen; *person also* mitrechnen, berücksichtigen, einplanen; **to count**

sb in on sth davon ausgehen *or* damit rechnen, dass jd bei etw mitmacht; **you can count me in!** Sie können mit mir rechnen, da mache ich mit

▶ **count off** VT *sep* VI abzählen

▶ **count on** VI *+prep obj (= depend on)* rechnen mit, sich verlassen auf *(+acc)*; **to count on doing sth** die Absicht haben, etw zu tun; **to count on being able to do sth** damit rechnen, etw tun zu können; **you can count on him to help you** du kannst auf seine Hilfe zählen

▶ **count out** VT *sep* **a** *(Sport)* auszählen **b** *money, books etc* abzählen **c** *(Brit, Parl)* **to count the House out** *eine Sitzung des Unterhauses wegen zu geringer Abgeordnetenzahl vertagen* **d** *(inf: = exclude)* **(you can) count me out (of that)!** ohne mich!, da mache ich nicht mit!; **count him out of it** plane ihn besser nicht ein

▶ **count up** VT *sep* zusammenzählen *or* -rechnen

▶ **count upon** VI *+prep obj* = **count on**

count² N Graf *m*

countable [ˈkaʊntəbl] ADJ zählbar *(also Gram)*

countdown [ˈkaʊntdaʊn] N Countdown *m*, Count-down *m*; **to start the ~** mit dem Countdown beginnen

countenance [ˈkaʊntɪnəns] N **a** *(old, form: = face)* Angesicht *nt (old, Eccl)*, Antlitz *nt (old)*; *(= expression)* Gesichtsausdruck *m*; **to keep one's ~** *(fig)* die Fassung *or* Haltung bewahren; **to lose ~** *(fig)* das Gesicht verlieren; **to put sb out of ~** jdn aus der Fassung bringen **b** *(= support)* **to give/lend ~ to sth** etw ermutigen/unterstützen VT *behaviour* gutheißen; *plan, suggestion also, person* unterstützen

counter [ˈkaʊntəʳ] N **a** *(in shop)* Ladentisch *m*, Tresen *m (N Ger)*; *(in café)* Theke *f*; *(in bank, post office)* Schalter *m*; **to sell/buy sth under/over the ~** etw unter dem/über den Ladentisch verkaufen/bekommen; **medicines which can be bought over the ~** Medikamente, die man rezeptfrei bekommt; **under-the-~ deals** *(fig)* dunkle Geschäfte *pl*, Schiebereien *pl*
b *(= small disc for games)* Spielmarke *f*
c *(Tech)* Zähler *m*
d *(Sport, Fencing)* Parade *f*; *(Boxing also)* Konter *m*
e *(= reply)* Entgegnung *f*, Erwiderung *f*, Replik *f (geh)*
f *(= opposing force)* Gegengewicht *nt (to* zu)
VT *(= retaliate against)* antworten auf *(+acc)*, kontern *(also Sport)*; **how dare you ~ my orders!** *(= countermand)* wie können Sie es wagen, meine Anweisungen *or (Mil)* Befehle aufzuheben; **to ~ the loss** den Verlust wettmachen *or* ausgleichen
VI kontern *(also Sport)*
ADV **~ to** gegen *(+acc)*; **to go** *or* **run ~ to sb's wishes** jds Wünschen *(dat)* zuwiderlaufen; **the results are ~ to expectations** die Ergebnisse widersprechen den Erwartungen

counter-: **counteract** VT *(= make ineffective)* neutralisieren; *(= act in opposition to)* entgegenwirken *(+dat)*; *disease* bekämpfen; **counteraction** N *(= making ineffective)* Neutralisierung *f*; *(= offsetting)* Gegenwirkung *f*; *(against disease)* Bekämpfung *f*; **counteractive** ADJ entgegenwirkend, Gegen-; **~ measures** Gegenmaßnahmen *pl*; **counterargument** N Gegenargument *nt*; **counterattack** N Gegenangriff *m*; *(esp Sport)* Konter *m* VT einen Gegenangriff starten gegen; *(= argue against)* kontern, beantworten VI einen Gegenangriff starten, zurückschlagen; **counterattraction** N Gegenattraktion *f (to* zu); *(on TV etc)* Konkurrenzprogramm *nt*; **counterbalance** N Gegengewicht *nt* VT ausgleichen; **counterblast** N *(fig: = reaction)* heftige Gegenreaktion *(to* auf *+acc)*; **countercharge** N **a** *(Jur)* Gegenklage *f* **b** *(Mil)* Gegenattacke *f*; **countercheck** N Gegenkontrolle *f*; **counterclaim** N *(Jur)* Gegenanspruch *m*; **counter clerk** N *(in bank, booking office etc)* Angestellte(r) *mf* im Schalterdienst; *(in post office etc)* Schalterbeamte(r) *m*/-beamtin *f*; **counterclockwise** ADJ ADV *(US)* = **anticlockwise**; **counterculture** N Gegenkultur *f*; **counterespionage** N Gegenspionage *f*, Spionageabwehr *f*; **counterexample** N Gegenbeispiel *nt*

counterfeit [ˈkaʊntəfiːt] ADJ gefälscht; *(fig)* falsch; **~ money/coins** Falschgeld *nt* N Fälschung *f* VT fälschen; *(fig)* vortäuschen

counterfoil [ˈkaʊntəfɔɪl] N Kontrollabschnitt *m*

counter-: **counterinflationary** ADJ *(Econ)* antiinflationär; **counterinsurgency** N Kampf *m* gegen Aufständische; **~ measures** Maßnahmen *pl* gegen Aufständische; **counterinsurgent** N Antiguerillakämpfer(in) *m(f)*; **counterintelligence** N = **counterespionage**; **counterirritant** N *(Med)* Gegenreizmittel *nt*; **counterman** N *(US, in restaurant)* Mann *m* an der Theke

countermand [ˌkaʊntəˈmɑːnd] VT *order* aufheben, widerrufen; *attack, plan* rückgängig machen; **unless ~ed** bis auf gegenteilige Anweisung *or (Mil)* Order

counter-: **countermarch** *(Mil)* N Rückmarsch *m* VI zurückmarschieren; **countermeasure** N Gegenmaßnahme *f*; **counteroffensive** N *(Mil)* Gegenoffensive *f*; **counteroffer** N Gegenangebot *nt*; **counterpane** N Tagesdecke *f*; **counterpart** N *(= equivalent)* Gegenüber *nt*; *(= complement)* Gegenstück *nt*, Pendant *nt*; **counterplot** N Gegenanschlag *m* VI einen Gegenanschlag planen; **counterpoint** N *(Mus, fig)* Kontrapunkt *m* VT *(fig)* einen Kontrapunkt bilden zu; **counterpoise** N **a** *(= weight)* Gegengewicht *nt*; *(= force, fig)* Gegenkraft *f* **b** *no pl (= equilibrium, fig)* Gleichgewicht *nt*; **to be in ~** im Gleichgewicht sein VT *(lit, fig)* ausgleichen; **counterproductive** ADJ unsinnig, widersinnig; *criticism, measures, policies* destruktiv, kontraproduktiv; **that wouldn't help us at all, in fact it would be ~** das würde uns nicht weiterbringen, sondern sogar das Gegenteil bewirken *or* es wäre sogar kontraproduktiv; **Counter-Reformation** N *(Hist)* Gegenreformation *f*; **counter-revolution** N Gegen- *or* Konterrevolution *f*; **counter-revolutionary** ADJ konterrevolutionär; **countershaft** N *(Tech)* Vorgelegewelle *f*; **countersign** N *(Mil)* Parole *f*, Kennwort *nt* VT *cheque etc* gegenzeichnen; **countersignature** N Gegenunterschrift *f*; **countersink** N *(= tool)* Versenker *m*, Spitzsenker *m* VT *hole* senken; *screw* versenken; **counter staff** PL *(in shop)* Verkäufer *pl*; **counterstroke** N Gegenschlag *m*; **countersunk** ADJ *screw* Senk-; **countertenor** N *(Mus)* Kontratenor *m*; **counterterrorism** N Terrorismusbekämpfung *f*; **counterweight** N Gegengewicht *nt*; **counterwoman** N *(US, in restaurant)* Frau *f* an der Theke

countess [ˈkaʊntɪs] N Gräfin *f*

counting house [ˈkaʊntɪŋhaʊs] N *(old)* Kontor *nt*

countless [ˈkaʊntlɪs] ADJ unzählig *attr*, zahllos *attr*; **~ millions of ...** unzählige *or* zahllose Millionen von ...

count palatine N *pl* **-s -** Pfalzgraf *m*

countrified [ˈkʌntrɪfaɪd] ADJ ländlich, bäuerlich

country [ˈkʌntrɪ] N **a** *(= state)* Land *nt*; *(= people also)* Volk *nt*; **his own ~** seine Heimat; **to die for one's ~** für sein Land sterben; **to go to the ~** Neuwahlen ausschreiben **b** *no pl (as opposed to town)* Land *nt*; *(= scenery, countryside also)* Landschaft *f*; **in/to the ~** auf dem/aufs Land; **the surrounding ~** das umliegende Land, die Umgebung; **this is good hunting/fishing ~** das ist eine gute Jagd-/Fischgegend; **this is mining ~** dies ist ein Bergbaugebiet; **we're back in familiar ~ again** *(fig)* wir befinden uns wieder auf vertrautem Boden

country *in cpds* Land-; **country and western** N Country-und-Western-Musik *f*; **country-and-western** ADJ Country- und Western-; **country-born** ADJ auf dem Land geboren; **country-bred** ADJ auf dem Land aufgewachsen; *animals* auf dem Land gezogen; **country bumpkin** N *(pej)* Bauerntölpel *(inf)*, Bauer *(pej inf) m*; *(= girl)* Bauerntrampel *nt (inf)*; **country club** N *Klub auf dem Lande*; **country code** N **a** *(= telephone prefix)* Landeskennzahl *f*, internationale Vorwahl **b** *(Brit: = set of rules)* Verhaltenskodex *m* für Besucher auf dem Lande; **country cousin** N Vetter *m*/Base *f* vom Lande; **country dance** N Volkstanz *m*; **country dancing** N Volkstanz *m*; **to go ~** zum Volkstanz gehen; **country dweller** N Landbewohner(in) *m(f)*; **country folk** PL Leute *pl* vom Lande; **country gentleman** N Landbesitzer *m*; **country gentry** PL Landadel *m*; **country house** N Landhaus *nt*; **country life** N das Landleben, das Leben auf dem Lande; **countryman** N **a** *(= compatriot)* Landsmann *m*; **his fellow countrymen** seine Landsleute **b** *(= country dweller)* Landmann *m*; **country mile** N *(US inf)* **to miss sth by a ~** etw um Längen verpassen; **country music** N Countrymusik *f*; **country people** PL Leute *pl* vom Land(e); **country road** N Landstraße *f*; **country seat** N Landsitz *m*; **countryside** N *(= scenery)* Landschaft *f*, Gegend *f*; *(= rural area)* Land *nt*; **it's beautiful ~** das ist eine herrliche Landschaft *or* Gegend; **to live in the middle of the ~** mitten auf dem Land leben; **Countryside Commission** N *(Brit)* Kommission *f* zum Schutz ländlicher Gebiete; **country town** N Kleinstadt *f*; **country-wide** ADJ landesweit, im ganzen Land; **countrywoman** N **a** *(= compatriot)* Landsmännin *f* **b** *(= country dweller)* Landfrau *f*

county [ˈkaʊntɪ] N *(Brit)* Grafschaft *f*; *(US)* (Verwaltungs)bezirk *m* ADJ *(Brit) family* zum Landadel gehörend; *accent, behaviour* vornehm; *occasion* für den Landadel; **the ~ set** die feinen Pinkel *(inf)*

county: **county borough** N *(Brit) Stadt mit grafschaftlichen Rechten*; **county council** N *(Brit)* Grafschaftsrat *m*; **county court** N *(Brit)* Grafschaftsgericht *nt*; **county seat** N *(US) Hauptstadt eines Verwaltungsbezirkes*; **county town** N *(Brit) Hauptstadt einer Grafschaft*

coup [kuː] N **a** *(= successful action)* Coup *m* **b** *(= coup d'état)* Staatsstreich *m*, Coup d'Etat *m*

coup: **coup de grâce** [ˌkuːdəˈgrɑːs] N *(lit, fig)* Gnadenstoß *m*; *(with gun)* Gnadenschuss *m*; **coup d'état** [ˈkuːdeɪˈtɑː] N = **coup b**

coupé [ˈkuːpeɪ] N *(= car)* Coupé *nt*, Kupee *nt*

couple [ˈkʌpl] N **a** *(= pair)* Paar *nt*; *(= married couple)* Ehepaar *nt*; **courting ~s** Liebespaare *pl*; **in ~s** paarweise → **happy a**
b *(inf)* **a ~** *(= two)* zwei; *(= several)* ein paar, einige; **a ~ of letters/friends** *etc*, **a ~ letters/friends** *etc (US)* ein paar *or* einige Briefe/Freunde *etc*; **we had a ~ in the pub** wir haben in der Kneipe ein paar getrunken; **a ~ of times** ein paar Mal; **it took a ~ of minutes/hours** es hat einige *or* ein paar Minuten/ungefähr zwei Stunden gedauert
VT **a** *(= link) names, circuit* verbinden; *carriages etc* koppeln; **smoking ~d with poor diet ...** Rauchen in Verbindung mit schlechter Ernährung ...
b *(= mate) animals* paaren
VI *(= mate)* sich paaren

▶ **couple on** VT *sep* anhängen

▶ **couple up** VT *sep* ankoppeln

coupler [ˈkʌpləʳ] N *(Comput)* Koppler *m*

couples therapy N *(US)* Eheberatung *f*

couplet [ˈkʌplɪt] N Verspaar *nt*

coupling [ˈkʌplɪŋ] N **a** *(= linking)* Verbindung *f*; *(of carriages etc)* Kopplung *f*; **the continual ~ of his name with ...** dass sein Name ständig mit ... in Verbindung gebracht wird/wurde **b** *(= mating)* Paarung *f* **c** *(= linking device)* Kupplung *f*

coupon [ˈkuːpɒn] N **a** *(= voucher)* Gutschein *m*; *(= ration coupon)* (Zuteilungs)schein *m* **b** *(Ftbl)* Totoschein *m*, Wettschein *m* **c** *(Fin)* Kupon *m*

courage [ˈkʌrɪdʒ] N Mut *m*, Courage *f (inf)*; **I haven't the ~ to refuse** ich habe einfach nicht den Mut, nein *or* Nein zu sagen; **take ~!** *(liter)* nur Mut!; **to take ~ from sth** sich durch etw ermutigt fühlen; **to lose one's ~** den Mut verlieren; **to have/lack the ~ of one's convictions** Zivilcourage/keine Zivilcourage haben; **to take one's ~ in both hands** sein Herz in beide Hände nehmen

courageous [kəˈreɪdʒəs] ADJ mutig; *(= with courage of convictions)* couragiert

courageously [kəˈreɪdʒəslɪ] ADV *fight, resist* mutig; *criticize, denounce* couragiert

courgette [kʊəˈʒet] N *(Brit)* Zucchini *f*

courier [ˈkʊrɪəˈ] N **a** *(= messenger)* Kurier *m*; **by ~** per Kurier **b** *(= tourist guide)* Reiseleiter(in) *m(f)*

course[1] [kɔːs] ✪ 9.2, 11.3 N **a** *(= direction, path, of plane, ship)* Kurs *m*; *(of river)* Lauf *m*; *(fig, of illness, relationship)* Verlauf *m*; *(of history)* Lauf *m*; *(of action etc, = way of proceeding)* Vorgehensweise *f*; **to set (one's) ~ for a place** Kurs auf einen Ort nehmen; **to change** *or* **alter ~** den Kurs wechseln *or* ändern; **to be on/off ~** auf Kurs sein/vom Kurs abgekommen sein; **to be on ~ for sth** *(fig)* gute Aussichten auf etw *(acc)* haben; **to let sth take** *or* **run its ~** einer Sache *(dat)* ihren Lauf lassen, etw *(acc)* seinen Lauf nehmen lassen; **the affair has run its ~** die Angelegenheit ist zu einem Ende gekommen; **the ~ of true love ne'er did run smooth** *(prov)* Liebe geht oft seltsame Wege *(prov)*; **which ~ of action did you take?** wie sind Sie vorgegangen?; **that was an unwise ~ of action** es war unklug, so vorzugehen; **the best ~ (of action) would be …** das Beste wäre …; **we have no other ~ (of action) but to …** es bleibt uns nicht anderes übrig als zu …; **to take a middle ~** einen gemäßigten Kurs einschlagen
b in the ~ of his life/the next few weeks/the meeting *etc* während seines Lebens/der nächsten paar Wochen/der Versammlung *etc*; **in the ~ of time/the conversation** im Laufe der Zeit/Unterhaltung; **it's in the ~ of being done** es wird gerade gemacht; **in the ~ of shaving** beim Rasieren; **in the ordinary ~ of things, you could expect …** unter normalen Umständen könnte man erwarten …; **to be in the ~ of nature** in der Natur der Sache liegen → **due**
c of ~ *(= admittedly)* natürlich; *(= naturally, obviously also)* selbstverständlich; **of ~!** natürlich!, selbstverständlich!, klar! *(inf)*; **of ~ I will!** aber natürlich *or* selbstverständlich!; **of ~ I'm coming** natürlich *or* selbstverständlich komme ich, klar, ich komme; **don't you like me? – of ~ I do** magst du mich nicht? – doch, natürlich; **he's rather young, of ~, but …** er ist natürlich ziemlich jung, aber …
d *(Sch, Univ)* Studium *nt*; *(= summer course etc)* Kurs(us) *m*; *(at work)* Lehrgang *m*; *(Med, of treatment)* Kur *f*; **to go on a French ~** einen Französischkurs(us) besuchen; **a ~ in first aid** ein Kurs über Erste Hilfe, ein Erste-Hilfe-Kurs; **a ~ of lectures, a lecture ~** eine Vorlesungsreihe; **a ~ of pills/treatment** eine Pillenkur/eine Behandlung
e *(Sport: = race course)* Kurs *m*; *(= golf course)* Platz *m*; **to stay** *or* **last the ~** *(fig)* bis zum Ende durchhalten
f *(Cook)* Gang *m*; **first ~** erster Gang; **a three-~ meal** ein Essen *nt* mit drei Gängen
g *(Build)* Schicht *f*
h *(Naut, = sail)* Untersegel *nt*

course[2] VT *(Hunt) hare, stag* hetzen, jagen VI **a** *(blood, tears)* strömen **b** *(Hunt, fig)* hetzen, jagen; **to go coursing** auf Hetzjagd gehen

courser [ˈkɔːsəˈ] N **a** *(= dog)* Hatz- *or* Hetzhund *m* **b** *(poet: = horse)* (schnelles) Ross *(liter)*

coursing [ˈkɔːsɪŋ] N *(Sport)* Hetzjagd *f*, Hatz *f*, Hetze *f*

court [kɔːt] N **a** *(Jur, also* **court of justice** *or* **law***)* Gericht *nt*; *(= body of judges also)* Gerichtshof *m*; *(= room)* Gerichtssaal *m*; **Court of Session** *(Scot) höchstes schottisches Zivilgericht*; **Court of Auditors** *(in EU)* Rechnungshof *m*; **to appear in ~** vor Gericht erscheinen; **the evidence was ruled out of ~** das Beweismaterial wurde nicht zugelassen; **his suggestion was ruled out of ~** *(fig)* sein Vorschlag wurde verworfen; **to take sb to ~** jdn verklagen *or* vor Gericht bringen; **to go to ~ over a matter** eine Sache vor Gericht bringen, mit einer Sache vor Gericht gehen; **the case comes up in ~ next week** der Fall wird nächste Woche verhandelt; **Sir James is still in ~** Sir James ist noch beim Gericht; **to give sb his/her day in ~** *(inf)* jdm die Möglichkeit geben, sich zur Sache zu äußern; **to be laughed out of ~** *(inf)* verlacht werden → **settle**
b *(royal)* Hof *m*; **to be presented at ~** bei Hofe vorgestellt werden; **the Court of St James** der englische Königshof; **to hold ~ in …** *(film star etc)* Hof halten in …
c *(Sport)* Platz *m*; *(for squash)* Halle *f*; *(= marked-off area)* Spielfeld *nt*; *(= service court etc)* Feld *nt*; **grass/hard ~** Rasen-/Hartplatz *m*; **on ~** auf dem Platz/in der Halle; **out of the ~** außerhalb des Spielfeldes
d *(= courtyard, Univ: = quadrangle)* Hof *m*; **inner ~** Innenhof *m*
e *(old form, = courtship)* Hof *m*; **to pay ~ to a woman** einer Frau *(dat)* den Hof machen
VT **a** *(dated) woman* umwerben, werben um, den Hof machen *(+dat)*
b *(fig) person's favour* werben um, buhlen um *(pej)*; *danger, defeat* herausfordern
VI *(dated)* **they were ~ing at the time** zu der Zeit gingen sie zusammen; **she's ~ing** sie hat einen Freund; **are you ~ing?** hast du jemanden?

> **COURT**
>
> In England, Wales und Nordirland werden Schwerverbrechen und Verfahren, bei denen der Angeklagte auf „nicht schuldig" plädiert, im **Crown Court** vor einem Richter und zwölf Geschworenen verhandelt. Weniger schwere Straftaten werden in einem **magistrates' court** vor einem **magistrate** ohne Geschworene verhandelt. Die meisten Zivilfälle werden vor lokalen Gerichten behandelt, wobei sich der **High Court** mit den schwerwiegenderen oder komplexeren Zivilrechtsangelegenheiten befasst. Berufungen können sowohl in Straf- wie in Zivilfällen beim **Court of Appeal** eingelegt werden, und kommen in letzter Instanz vor das Oberhaus.
>
> Die schottische Rechtsprechung ist anders angelegt. Hier befasst sich der **High Court of Justiciary** mit den Schwerverbrechen und **sheriff courts** mit den weniger schweren Straftaten. Der oberste Gerichtshof für Zivilrecht ist der **Court of Session**.
>
> In den USA kümmern sich Bundesgerichte um Straftaten gegen das Bundesrecht; hier werden Fälle aus verschiedenen Staaten behandelt. Straftaten gegen die Gesetze eines Bundesstaates werden dagegen vor Gerichten im jeweiligen Staat verhandelt. Jeder Staat hat sein eigenes Rechtssystem und kann eigene Gesetze erlassen, mit der Einschränkung, dass diese nicht gegen die Verfassung der USA oder Bundesgesetze verstoßen dürfen. Es gibt keine unterschiedlichen Gerichte für Straf- und Zivilangelegenheiten. Die meisten Bundesstraffälle werden in **district courts** verhandelt, zwölf **Courts of Appeal** sind zuständig für die Berufungsfälle der untergeordneten Bundesgerichte. Oberste Gerichtshöfe für sowohl Bundes- wie Staatsrecht sind die **Supreme Courts**, einer in jedem Staat und einer für den Bund. Im Bundesstaatsrecht sind diesen **Appelate Courts** (Berufungsgerichte) untergeordnet, darunter **county** oder **city courts**, die sich mit Fällen der allgemeinen Rechtsprechung befassen.

court: **court battle** N *(Jur)* Rechtsstreit *m*, gerichtliche Auseinandersetzung; **court card** N *(Brit)* Bildkarte *f*; **court case** N *(Jur)* Gerichtsverfahren *nt*, Prozess *m*; **court circular** N Hofnachrichten *pl*; **court correspondent** N *(Brit Press)* Hofberichterstatter(in) *m(f)*; **court dress** N Hoftracht *f*

courteous ADJ, **courteously** ADV [ˈkɜːtɪəs, -lɪ] höflich

courtesan [ˌkɔːtɪˈzæn] N Kurtisane *f*

courtesy [ˈkɜːtɪsɪ] N Höflichkeit *f*; **(by) ~ of** freundlicherweise zur Verfügung gestellt von; **the air was fresh (by) ~ of a large hole in the roof** die Luft war ziemlich frisch, was einem großen Loch im Dach zu verdanken war; **would you do me the ~ of shutting up!** würden Sie mir den Gefallen tun und den Mund halten!

courtesy: **courtesy bus** N gebührenfreier Bus, Hotelbus *m*; **courtesy light** N *(Aut)* Innenleuchte *f*; **courtesy title** N Höflichkeitstitel *m*; **courtesy visit** N Höflichkeitsbesuch *m*

court: **court fees** PL Gerichtskosten *pl*; **court fine** N Ordnungsgeld *nt*; **to issue/face a ~** ein Ordnungsgeld verhängen/zu zahlen haben; **court guide** N Hofkalender *m*; **court hearing** N *(Jur)* Gerichtsverhandlung *f*; **courthouse** [ˈkɔːthaʊs] N *(Jur)* Gerichtsgebäude *nt*

courtier [ˈkɔːtɪəˈ] N Höfling *m*

courtliness [ˈkɔːtlɪnɪs] N *(= politeness)* Höflichkeit *f*; *(= refinement)* Vornehmheit *f*

courtly [ˈkɔːtlɪ] ADJ *manners* höflich; *grace, elegance* vornehm; **~ love** Minne *f*

court: **court martial** N *pl* **court martials** *or* **courts martial** *(Mil)* Militärgericht *nt*; *(in wartime also)* Kriegsgericht *nt*; **to be tried by ~** vor das/ein Militär-/Kriegsgericht gestellt werden *or* kommen; **court-martial** VT vor das/ein Militär-/Kriegsgericht stellen *(for* wegen*)*; **court order** N *(Jur)* gerichtliche Verfügung; **I'll get a ~** ich werde eine gerichtliche Verfügung beantragen; **court reporter** N **a** *(Jur: = stenographer)* Gerichtsschreiber(in) *m(f)* **b** *(Brit Press)* = **court correspondent**; **courtroom** N *(Jur)* Gerichtssaal *m*

courtship [ˈkɔːtʃɪp] N *(dated)* (Braut)werbung *f* *(dated)* (of um); **during their ~** während er um sie warb *or* freite *(dated)*

court: **court shoe** N Pumps *m*; **court tennis** N *(US)* Tennis *nt*; **courtyard** N Hof *m*

couscous [ˈkuːskuːs] N Couscous *m*

cousin [ˈkʌzn] N *(male)* Cousin *m*, Vetter *m (dated)*; *(female)* Cousine *f*, Kusine *f*, Base *f (old)*; **Kevin and Susan are ~s** Kevin und Susan sind Cousin und Cousine

cousinly [ˈkʌznlɪ] ADJ verwandtschaftlich

couture [kuːˈtjʊəˈ] N Couture *f*

couturier [kuːˈtjʊərɪəˈ] N Couturier *m*

cove[1] [kəʊv] N *(Geog)* (kleine) Bucht

cove[2] N *(dated Brit inf, = fellow)* Kerl *m (inf)*; **odd ~** komischer Kauz

coven [ˈkʌvn] N Hexenzirkel *m*; *(= meeting)* Hexensabbat *m*

covenant [ˈkʌvɪnənt] N Schwur *m*; *(Bibl)* Bund *m*; *(Jur)* Verpflichtung *f* zu regelmäßigen Spenden; **to swear a solemn ~ that …** feierlich schwören, dass … VT **to ~ to do sth** durch ein Abkommen versprechen, etw zu tun; *(Jur)* sich vertraglich verpflichten, etw zu tun VI ein Abkommen/einen Bund schließen

Coventry [ˈkɒvəntrɪ] N **to send sb to ~** *(Brit inf)* jdn schneiden *(inf)*

cover [ˈkʌvəˈ] N **a** *(= lid)* Deckel *m*; *(of lens)* (Schutz)kappe *f*; *(= loose cover: on chair)* Bezug *m*; *(= cloth: for typewriter, umbrella etc)* Hülle *f*; *(on lorries, tennis court)* Plane *f*; *(= sheet: over merchandise, shop counter)* Decke *f*, Tuch *nt*; *(= blanket, quilt)* (Bett)decke *f*; **he put a ~ over her/it** er deckte sie/es zu; **she pulled the ~s up to her chin** sie zog die Decke bis ans Kinn (hoch)
b *(of book)* Einband *m*; *(of magazine)* Umschlag *m*; *(= dust cover)* (Schutz)umschlag *m*; **to read a book from ~ to ~** ein Buch von Anfang bis Ende *or* von der ersten bis zur letzten Seite lesen; **on the ~** auf dem Einband/Umschlag; *(of magazine)* auf der Titelseite, auf dem

Titel(blatt)
c (*Comm*: = *envelope*) Umschlag *m*; **under separate ~** getrennt; **under plain ~** in neutralem Umschlag
d *no pl* (= *shelter, protection*) Schutz *m* (*from* vor *+dat*, gegen); (*Mil*) Deckung *f* (*from* vor *+dat*, gegen); **to take ~** (*from rain*) sich unterstellen, Schutz suchen (*from* vor *+dat*); (*Mil*) in Deckung gehen (*from* vor *+dat*); **under the ~ of the trees** im Schutz der Bäume; **these plants/the car should be kept under ~** diese Pflanzen sollten/das Auto sollte abgedeckt sein *or* (*under roof*) durch ein Dach geschützt sein; **to get oneself under ~** sich unterstellen; (*for longer period*) Unterschlupf finden; **under ~ of darkness** im Schutz(e) der Dunkelheit; **to give sb ~** (*Mil*) jdm Deckung geben
e (*Hunt*) Deckung *f*; **to break ~** aus der Deckung hervorbrechen
f (*Brit*: = *place at meal*) Gedeck *nt*; **she laid ~s for six** sie deckte für sechs Personen, sie legte sechs Gedecke auf
g (*Brit*) (*Comm, Fin*) Deckung *f*; (= *insurance cover*) Versicherung *f*; **to operate without ~** ohne Deckung arbeiten; **to take out ~ for a car** ein Auto versichern; **to take out ~ against fire** eine Feuerversicherung abschließen; **to get ~ for sth** etw versichern (lassen); **do you have adequate ~?** sind Sie ausreichend versichert?
h (= *assumed identity*) Tarnung *f*; (= *front organization also*) Deckung *f*; **under ~ as** getarnt als; **to operate under ~** als Agent tätig sein; **to blow sb's ~** jdn enttarnen
i (*Mus*: *also* **cover version**) Coverversion *f*
VT a (= *put cover on*) bedecken; (= *cover over*) zudecken; (*with loose cover*) *chair etc* beziehen; **a ~ed wagon/way** ein Planwagen *m*/überdachter Weg; **to ~ one's head** den Kopf bedecken; **the car ~ed us in mud** das Auto bespritzte uns von oben bis unten mit Schlamm; **the mountain was ~ed with** *or* **in snow** der Berg war schneebedeckt *or* mit Schnee bedeckt; **you're all ~ed with dog hairs** du bist voller Hundehaare; **to ~ oneself in** *or* **with glory** Ruhm ernten; **to ~ oneself with ridicule** sich lächerlich machen; **~ed in** *or* **with shame** zutiefst beschämt
b (= *hide*) *surprise* verbergen; *mistake, tracks also* verdecken; **to ~ one's face in** *or* **with one's hands** sein Gesicht in den Händen verstecken *or* verbergen
c (= *protect*) decken; **to ~ one's back** *or* **rear** *or* (*US inf*) **ass** (*fig*) sich absichern; **he only said that to ~ himself** er hat das nur gesagt, um sich abzudecken *or* zu decken
d (= *point a gun at etc*) *door etc* sichern; *sb* decken; (= *be on guard near*) sichern; **to keep sb ~ed** jdn in Schach halten; **I've got you ~ed!** (*with gun etc*) ich hab auf dich angelegt; (*fig, Chess etc*) ich hab dich
e (*Fin*) *loan* decken; *expenses, costs also* abdecken; (*Insur*) versichern; **will £30 ~ the drinks?** reichen £ 30 für die Getränke?; **he gave me £30 to ~ the drinks** er gab mir £ 30 für Getränke
f (= *take in, include*) behandeln; (*law also*) erfassen; (= *allow for, anticipate*) *possibilities, eventualities* vorsehen; **what does your travel insurance ~ you for?** was deckt deine Reiseversicherung ab?; **to ~ the waterfront** (*esp US*) einen weiten Bereich abdecken
g (*Press*: = *report on*) berichten über (*+acc*)
h (= *travel*) *miles, distance* zurücklegen
i (*salesman etc*) *territory* zuständig sein für
j (*Mus*) *song* neu interpretieren
k (*animals*: = *copulate with*) decken
l (= *play a higher card than*) überbieten
▶ **cover for** VI *+prep obj* **a** *absent person* vertreten, einspringen für **b** (= *protect*) decken
▶ **cover in** VT *sep* **a** (= *fill in*) *grave etc* auffüllen, zuschütten **b** (= *roof in*) überdachen
▶ **cover over** VT *sep* (= *put a cover over*) zudecken; (*for protection*) *tennis court* abdecken; (= *roof over*) überdachen
▶ **cover up** **VI a** (= *wrap up*) sich einmummen **b** (= *conceal a fact*) alles vertuschen *or* verheimlichen; **don't try to cover up** versuchen Sie nicht, Ihren Fehler zu vertuschen; **to cover up for sb** jdn decken **VT** *sep* **a** *child* zudecken; *object also, tennis court* abdecken **b** (= *hide*) *truth, facts* vertuschen, verheimlichen

coverage [ˈkʌvərɪdʒ] N *no pl* **a** (*in media*) Berichterstattung *f* (*of* über *+acc*); **to give full ~ to an event** ausführlich über ein Ereignis berichten; **the games got excellent TV ~** die Spiele wurden ausführlich im Fernsehen gebracht **b** (*Insur*) Versicherung *f*; **this policy gives you full ~ for …** diese Versicherung bietet Ihnen volle Deckung bei …

cover: **cover address** N Deckadresse *f*; **coverall** N *usu pl* (*US*) Overall *m*; **cover charge** N Kosten *pl* für ein Gedeck

covered market [ˌkʌvəd ˈmɑːkɪt] N überdachter Markt

cover girl N Titel(bild)mädchen *nt*, Covergirl *nt*

covering [ˈkʌvərɪŋ] N Decke *f*; (= *floor covering*) Belag *m*; **a ~ of dust/snow** eine Staub-/Schneedecke; **what kind of ~ did you put over the hole?** womit haben Sie das Loch ab- *or* zugedeckt?

covering: **covering agreement** N Mantelvertrag *m*; **covering letter** N (*Brit*) Begleitbrief *m*

coverlet [ˈkʌvəlɪt] N Tagesdecke *f*

cover letter N (*US*) = **covering letter**

cover: **cover note** N Deckungszusage *f*, vorläufiger Versicherungsschein; **cover organization** N Deckorganisation *f*; **cover page** N Titelseite *f*; *of fax etc* Deckblatt *nt*; **cover price** N Einzel(exemplar)preis *m*; **cover shot** N (*Phot*) Totale *f*; (*for magazine*) Titelfoto *nt*; **cover story** N (*of paper*) Titelgeschichte *f*; (*of spy*) Geschichte *f*

covert [ˈkʌvət] **ADJ** *threat, attack* versteckt; *glance also* verstohlen; *surveillance* heimlich **N** Versteck *nt* → **draw²**

covertly [ˈkʌvətlɪ] ADV *threaten, attack* versteckt; *glance also* verstohlen; *film, watch* heimlich

cover-up [ˈkʌvərʌp] N Vertuschung *f*, Verschleierung *f*; **the Watergate ~** die Vertuschung von Watergate

cover version N (*Mus*) Coverversion *f*

covet [ˈkʌvɪt] **VT** begehren **VI** begehrlich *or* begierig sein

covetable [ˈkʌvɪtəbl] ADJ begehrenswert

covetous [ˈkʌvɪtəs] ADJ begehrlich; **to be ~ of sth** (*liter*) etw begehren

covetously [ˈkʌvɪtəslɪ] ADV begehrlich

covetousness [ˈkʌvɪtəsnɪs] N Begierde *f* (*of* auf *+acc*), Begehren *nt* (*of* nach)

covey [ˈkʌvɪ] N (*of partridges*) Kette *f*

coving [ˈkəʊvɪŋ] N Wölbung *f*

cow¹ [kaʊ] N **a** Kuh *f*; **a ~ elephant** eine Elefantenkuh; **till the ~s come home** (*fig inf*) bis in alle Ewigkeit (*inf*); **you'll be waiting till the ~s come home** (*fig inf*) da kannst du warten, bis du schwarz wirst (*inf*); **to have a ~** (*US inf*) die Fassung verlieren, sich aufregen **b** (*pej inf*: = *woman, stupid*) Kuh *f* (*inf*); (*nasty*) gemeine Ziege (*inf*); **cheeky/lazy/nosey ~!** freches/faules/neugieriges Stück! (*inf*)

cow² VT *person, animal* einschüchtern, verschüchtern; **she had a ~ed look about her** sie machte einen eingeschüchterten *or* verschüchterten Eindruck; **to ~ sb into submission** jdn (durch Einschüchterung) gefügig machen

coward [ˈkaʊəd] N Feigling *m*

cowardice [ˈkaʊədɪs], **cowardliness** [ˈkaʊədlɪnɪs] N Feigheit *f*

cowardly [ˈkaʊədlɪ] ADJ feig(e)

cow: **cowbell** N Kuhglocke *f*; **cowboy** N **a** Cowboy *m*; **to play ~s and Indians** Indianer spielen; **the little boy was wearing a ~ outfit** der kleine Junge war als Cowboy verkleidet **b** (*fig inf, incompetent*) Pfuscher *m*; (*dishonest*) Gauner *m* (*inf*); **a ~ outfit** ein windiges Unternehmen (*inf*); **cowboy hat** N Cowboyhut *m*; **cowcatcher** N (*Rail*) Schienenräumer *m*; **cow dung** N Kuhmist *m*

cower [ˈkaʊəʳ] VI sich ducken; (*squatting*) kauern; **to ~ before sb** vor jdm ducken; **he stood ~ing in a corner** er stand geduckt in einer Ecke; **the ~ing peasants** die geduckten Bauern
▶ **cower away** VI (furchtsam) ausweichen (*from* +*dat*)
▶ **cower down** VI sich niederkauern

cow: **cowgirl** N Cowgirl *nt*; **cowhand** N Hilfscowboy *m*; (*on farm*) Stallknecht *m*; **cowherd** N Kuhhirte *m*; **cowhide** N **a** (*untanned*) Kuhhaut *f*; (*no pl*: = *leather*) Rindsleder *nt* **b** (*US*: = *whip*) Lederpeitsche *f*

cowl [kaʊl] N **a** (= *monk's hood*) Kapuze *f* **b** (= *chimney cowl*) (Schornstein)kappe *f*

cowlick [ˈkaʊlɪk] N Tolle *f*

cowling [ˈkaʊlɪŋ] N (*Aviat*) Motorhaube *f*

cowl neck N Schalrollkragen *m*

cowman [ˈkaʊmən] N *pl* **-men** [-mən] (= *farm labourer*) Stallbursche *m*; (*US*: = *cattle rancher*) Viehzüchter *m*

co-worker [ˈkəʊˈwɜːkəʳ] N Kollege *m*, Kollegin *f*

cow: **cow parsley** N Wiesenkerbel *m*; **cowpat** N Kuhfladen *m*; **cowpoke** N (*US inf*) Kuhheini *m* (*pej inf*), Cowboy *m*; **cowpox** N Kuhpocken *pl*; **cowpuncher** N (*US inf*) Cowboy *m*

cowrie, cowry [ˈkaʊrɪ] N Kaurischnecke *f*

cow: **cowshed** N Kuhstall *m*; **cowslip** N (*Brit*: = *primrose*) Schlüsselblume *f*; (*US*: = *kingcup*) Sumpfdotterblume *f*

cox [kɒks] **N** Steuermann *m* **VT** *crew* Steuermann sein für **VI** steuern

coxcomb [ˈkɒkskəʊm] N (*old*) Stutzer *m* (*old*)

coxless [ˈkɒkslɪs] ADJ ohne Steuermann

coxswain [ˈkɒksn] N **a** (*in rowing*) = **cox N** **b** (*Naut*: *of lifeboat etc*) Boot(s)führer *m*

coy [kɔɪ] ADJ (+*er*) (= *affectedly shy*) verschämt; (= *coquettish*) neckisch, kokett; (= *evasive*) zurückhaltend; **to be ~ about sth** (= *shy*) in Bezug auf etw (*acc*) verschämt tun; (= *evasive*) sich ausweichend zu etw äußern

coyly [ˈkɔɪlɪ] ADV (= *shyly*) *smile, look* schüchtern, verschämt; (= *evasively*) *say, answer, refuse* ausweichend

coyness [ˈkɔɪnɪs] N (= *shyness*) Verschämtheit *f*; (= *coquettishness*) neckisches *or* kokettes Benehmen; (= *evasiveness*) ausweichende Haltung

coyote [kɔɪˈəʊtɪ] N Kojote *m*

coypu [ˈkɔɪpuː] N Sumpfbiber *m*

cozy ADJ (*US*) = **cosy**

cozzie [ˈkɒzɪ] N (*Brit inf*) = **cossie**

CP *abbr of* **Communist Party** KP *f*

cp *abbr of* **compare** vgl.

CPA (*US*) *abbr of* **certified public accountant**

CPI (*US*) *abbr of* **Consumer Price Index**

cpi *abbr of* **characters per inch** cpi

Cpl *abbr of* **Corporal**

CP/M *abbr of* **control program/monitor** CP/M

CPO *abbr* **a** (*Naut*) *of* **chief petty officer** Oberfähnrich *m* zur See **b** (*Police*) *of* **crime prevention officer**

CPR *abbr of* **cardiopulmonary resuscitation** HLW *f*

cps *abbr of* **characters per second** cps, Zeichen *pl* pro Sekunde

CPU *abbr of* **central processing unit** CPU *f*, Zentraleinheit *f*

crab¹ [kræb] N **a** Krabbe *f*; (*small also*) Krebs *m*; (*as food*) Krabbe *f*; **to catch a ~** (*Rowing*) einen Krebs fangen **b** (= *crab louse*) Filzlaus *f* **c** (*Gymnastics*) Brücke *f*

crab² VI nörgeln

crab apple N (= *fruit*) Holzapfel *m*; (= *tree*) Holzapfelbaum *m*

crabbed [ˈkræbd] ADJ **a** = **crabby** **b** *handwriting* kritzelig, unleserlich

crabby [ˈkræbɪ] ADJ (+*er*) *person* griesgrämig, mürrisch

crab: **crab grass** N Fingerhirse *f*; **crab louse** N Filzlaus *f*; **crabmeat** ['kræbmiːt] N Krabbenfleisch *nt*; **crabwise** ADV seitwärts

crack [kræk] **N** **a** Riss *m*; *(between floorboards etc)* Ritze *f*; *(= wider hole etc)* Spalte *f*; *(= fine line: in pottery, glass etc)* Sprung *m*; **leave the window open a ~** lass das Fenster einen Spalt offen; **at the ~ of dawn** in aller Frühe; **to fall** *or* **slip through the ~s** *(US fig)* durch die Maschen schlüpfen
b *(= sharp noise, of wood etc breaking)* Knacks *m*; *(of gun, whip)* Knall(en *nt no pl*) *m*; *(of thunder)* Schlag *m*; **at the ~ of doom** beim Jüngsten Gericht
c *(= sharp blow)* Schlag *m*; **to give sb a ~ on the head** jdm eins auf den Kopf geben; **to give oneself a ~ on the head** sich *(dat)* den Kopf anschlagen
d *(inf: = gibe)* Stichelei *f*; *(= joke)* Witz *m*; **to make a ~ about sb/sth** einen Witz über jdn/etw reißen
e *(inf: = attempt)* **to have a ~ at sth** etw mal probieren *(inf)*
f *(Drugs)* Crack *nt*
g *(Ir, Brit inf)* tolle Zeit; **tourists come to Ireland for the ~** die Touristen kommen wegen der tollen Atmosphäre nach Irland
h *(Brit vulg: = vagina)* Fotze *f (vulg)*
ADJ *attr* erstklassig; *(Mil)* Elite-; **~ shot** Meisterschütze *m*, Meisterschützin *f*
VT **a** *(= make a crack in) glass, china, pottery* einen Sprung machen in *(+acc)*; *bone* anbrechen, anknacksen *(inf)*; *skin, ground* rissig machen; *ground, ice* einen Riss/Risse machen in *(+acc)*; **to ~ a rib** sich *(dat)* eine Rippe anbrechen
b *(= break) nuts, safe* knacken; *(fig inf) code* knacken; *case, problem* lösen; **to ~ (open) a bottle** einer Flasche *(dat)* den Hals brechen; **I've ~ed it** *(= solved it)* ich habs!
c *joke* reißen
d *whip* knallen mit; *finger, joint* knacken mit; **to ~ the whip** *(fig)* die Peitsche schwingen, ein strenges Regiment führen
e *(= hit sharply)* schlagen; **he ~ed his head against the pavement** er krachte mit dem Kopf aufs Pflaster
f *(= distil) petroleum* kracken; **~ing plant** Krackanlage *f*
VI **a** *(= get a crack, pottery, glass)* einen Sprung/Sprünge bekommen, springen; *(ice, road)* einen Riss/Risse bekommen; *(lips, skin)* spröde *or* rissig werden; *(bones)* einen Knacks bekommen *(inf)*; *(= break)* brechen; **at last his stern face ~ed and he laughed** schließlich verzog sich seine ernste Miene zu einem Lachen
b *(= make a cracking sound, twigs, joints)* knacken, krachen; *(whip, gun)* knallen
c *(= hit sharply)* schlagen, krachen
d *(= break: voice) (with emotion)* versagen; **his voice is ~ing/beginning to ~** *(boy)* er ist im/kommt in den Stimmbruch
e *(inf)* **to get ~ing** loslegen *(inf)*, sich daranmachen; **to get ~ing with** *or* **on sth** mit etw loslegen *(inf)*, sich an etw *(acc)* machen; **get ~ing!** los jetzt!; *(= speed up)* mach(t) mal ein bisschen Dampf! *(inf)*
f = **crack up VI**; **he ~ed under the strain** er ist unter der Belastung zusammengebrochen

▶ **crack down** VI **a** *(whip)* niederknallen, niederkrachen **b** *(= clamp down)* hart durchgreifen *(on* bei)

▶ **crack open** VT *sep* aufbrechen; **to crack open the champagne** die Sektkorken knallen lassen

▶ **crack up** **VI** **a** *(= break into pieces)* zerbrechen; *(road surface, lips)* aufspringen, rissig werden; *(ice)* brechen; *(machine, plane)* auseinanderbrechen, auseinanderfallen; *(make-up)* rissig werden
b *(fig inf, person)* durchdrehen *(inf)*; *(under strain)* zusammenbrechen; *(= have a mental breakdown)* einen Nervenzusammenbruch haben; *(organization)* auseinanderfallen, zusammenbrechen; *(= lose ability, strength: athlete etc)* abbauen; **I/he must be cracking up** *(hum)* so fängts an *(inf)*; **she cracked up in the witness box** sie brach auf der Zeugenbank zusammen
VT *sep (inf)* **he's/it's not all he's/it's cracked up to be** so toll ist er/es dann auch wieder nicht; **he's cracked up to be some sort of genius** er wird als eine Art Genie gepriesen

crackajack N ADJ *(US)* = **crackerjack**

crackbrained ['krækbreɪnd] ADJ *(inf)* verrückt, irre

crackdown N *(inf)* scharfes Durchgreifen; **to order a ~ on sth** anordnen, bei etw scharf durchzugreifen

cracked [krækt] ADJ **a** *glass, plate, ice* gesprungen; *rib, bone* angebrochen, angeknackst *(inf)*; *(= broken)* gebrochen; *surface, walls, make-up* rissig; *lips, skin* aufgesprungen **b** *(Brit inf: = mad)* übergeschnappt *(inf)*

cracked wheat N Weizenschrot *m or nt*

cracker ['krækəʳ] N **a** *(= biscuit)* Kräcker *m* **b** *(= firecracker)* Knallkörper *m*; *(= Christmas cracker)* Knallbonbon *nt* **c** **crackers** PL *(= nut crackers)* Nussknacker *m* **d** *(Brit inf) (= woman)* tolle Frau *(inf)*; *(= man)* toller Mann *(inf)*; *(= thing)* tolles Ding *(inf)*

crackerjack, *(US)* **crackajack** ['krækədʒæk] **N** *(= person)* Kanone *f (inf)*; *(= thing)* Knüller *m (inf)* **ADJ** bombig *(inf)*

crackers ['krækəz] ADJ *pred (Brit inf)* übergeschnappt *(inf)*; **to go ~** überschnappen *(inf)*

crack house N Bezugsstelle *f* für Crack, Crackhaus *nt*

cracking ['krækɪŋ] ADJ *(inf) pace* scharf; *(dated: = good) novel* klasse *inv (inf)*, fantastisch, phantastisch

crackjaw ['krækdʒɔː] *(inf)* **ADJ** *attr word, name* zungenbrecherisch **N** Zungenbrecher *m*

crackle ['krækl] **VI** *(dry leaves)* rascheln; *(paper also)* knistern; *(fire)* knistern, prasseln; *(twigs, telephone line)* knacken; *(machine gun)* knattern; *(bacon)* brutzeln; **the line was crackling so much** es knackte so stark in der Leitung **VT** *paper* rascheln *or* knistern mit **N** **a** *(= crackling noise, of dry leaves)* Rascheln *nt*; *(of paper also)* Knistern *nt*; *(of fire also)* Knistern *nt*, Prasseln *nt*; *(of twigs, telephone line)* Knacken *nt*; *(of machine gun)* Knattern *nt*; *(of bacon)* Brutzeln *nt* **b** *(on china, porcelain)* Craquelé *m or nt*, Krakelee *m or nt*

crackleware ['kræklwɛəʳ] N Krakeleeporzellan *nt*, Craqueléporzellan *nt*

crackling ['kræklɪŋ] N *no pl* **a** = **crackle N** **b** *(Cook)* Kruste *f (des Schweinebratens)*

cracknel ['kræknl] N (harter) Keks

crackpot ['krækpɒt] *(inf)* **N** Spinner(in) *m(f) (inf)*, Irre(r) *mf* **ADJ** verrückt, irre

cracksman ['kræksmən] N *pl* **-men** [-mən] *(sl)* Safeknacker *m (inf)*

crackup ['krækʌp] N *(inf)* Zusammenbruch *m*

cradle ['kreɪdl] **N** *(= cot, fig: = birthplace)* Wiege *f*; *(= support, of phone)* Gabel *f*; *(for invalids)* Schutzgestell *nt (zum Abhalten des Bettzeugs von Verletzungen)*; *(for ship)* (Ablauf)schlitten *m*; *(Build, for window-cleaners)* Hängegerüst *nt*; *(in sea rescues)* Hosenboje *f*; *(for mechanic under car)* Schlitten *m*; **from the ~ to the grave** von der Wiege bis zur Bahre; **right from the ~** von klein auf, von Kindesbeinen an
VT **a** *(= hold closely)* an sich *(acc)* drücken; **he was cradling his injured arm** er hielt sich *(dat)* seinen verletzten Arm; **to ~ sb/sth in one's arms/lap** jdn/etw fest in den Armen/auf dem Schoß halten; **the baby lay ~d in her lap** das Baby lag (geborgen) in ihrem Schoß; **he ~d the telephone under his chin** er klemmte sich *(dat)* den Hörer unters Kinn; **the way he ~s the guitar** wie er die Gitarre zärtlich hält
b *receiver* auflegen

cradle: **cradle cap** N Milchschorf *m*; **cradle snatcher** N *(inf)* **what a ~ he/she is!** *(fig)* der könnte ja ihr Vater/sie könnte ja seine Mutter sein!; **cradle-snatching** N *(inf)* **she is known for ~** sie angelt sich dauernd viel jüngere Männer *(inf)*; **cradlesong** N Wiegenlied *nt*

craft [krɑːft] N **a** *(= handicraft)* Kunsthandwerk *nt*; *(as trade)* Kunstgewerbe *nt*; *(= trade)* Handwerk *nt*, Gewerbe *nt*; **it's a real ~** das ist eine echte Kunst → **art¹** **b** *(= guild)* (Handwerker)-innung *f*, (Handwerks)zunft *f (Hist)* **c** *no pl (= skill)* Kunst *f* **d** *no pl (= cunning)* List *f*; **to obtain sth by ~** sich *(dat)* etw erlisten, etw durch List bekommen **e** *pl* **craft** *(= boat)* Boot *nt*

craft fair N Kunstgewerbemarkt *m*

craftily ['krɑːftɪlɪ] ADV schlau, clever

craftiness ['krɑːftɪnɪs] N Schlauheit *f*, Cleverness *f*

craftsman ['krɑːftsmən] N *pl* **-men** [-mən] Kunsthandwerker *m*; **he's a real ~** er ist ein echter Künstler

craftsmanship ['krɑːftsmənʃɪp] N Handwerkskunst *f*; *(of person also)* handwerkliches Können, Kunstfertigkeit *f*; **there's no ~ left these days** heutzutage gibt es einfach keine Handwerkskunst mehr

craftsperson ['krɑːftspɜːsən] N *pl* **-people** [-piːpl] Kunstgewerbler(in) *m(f)*, Kunsthandwerker(in) *m(f)*

craftswoman ['krɑːftswʊmən] N *pl* **-women** [-wɪmɪn] Kunsthandwerkerin *f*

craft union N Handwerkergewerkschaft *f*

crafty ['krɑːftɪ] ADJ *(+er)* schlau, clever; **he's a ~ one** *(inf)* er ist ein ganz Schlauer *(inf)*; **he's as ~ as a fox** er ist ein schlauer Fuchs; **he took a ~ glance at ...** er riskierte einen verstohlenen Blick auf *(+acc)* ...

crag [kræg] N Fels *m*

craggy ['krægɪ] ADJ *(+er) (= rocky)* felsig; *(= jagged)* zerklüftet; *face* kantig; **he was good-looking in a ~ sort of way** er sah auf eine herbe, kantige Art gut aus

cragsman ['krægzmən] N *pl* **-men** [-mən] Kletterer *m*, geübter Bergsteiger

crake [kreɪk] N Ralle *f*

cram [kræm] **VT** **a** *(= fill)* vollstopfen, vollpacken; *(= stuff in)* hineinstopfen *(in(to)* in *+acc)*; *people* hineinzwängen *(in(to)* in *+acc)*; **the room was ~med (with furniture)** der Raum war (mit Möbeln) vollgestopft; **we were all ~med into one room** wir waren alle in einem Zimmer zusammengepfercht; **he ~med his hat (down) over his eyes** er zog sich *(dat)* den Hut tief ins Gesicht **b** *(for exam) Latin verbs etc* pauken *(inf)*, büffeln *(inf)*; *(= teach for exam) pupil* pauken mit *(inf)* **VI** *(= swot)* pauken *(inf)*, büffeln *(inf)*

▶ **cram in** VI *(people)* sich hinein-/hereindrängen *or* -quetschen *or* -zwängen (-to in *+acc*)

cram-full ['kræmfʊl] ADJ *(inf)* vollgestopft *(of* mit), gestopft voll *(inf)*

crammer ['kræməʳ] N *(= tutor)* Einpauker *m*; *(= student)* Büffler(in) *m(f) (inf)*; *(= book)* Paukbuch *nt*; *(= school)* Paukschule *f*

cramp¹ [kræmp] **N** *(Med)* Krampf *m*; **to have ~ in one's leg** einen Krampf im Bein haben; **to have the ~s** *(US)* Krämpfe haben **VT** **a** *(also* **cramp up***) persons* zusammenpferchen, einpferchen; *writing* eng zusammenkritzeln **b** *(fig: = hinder)* behindern; **to ~ sb's style** jdm im Weg sein **c** *(= give cramp to)* Krämpfe *pl* verursachen in *(+dat)*

cramp² **N** *(also* **cramp iron***)* Bauklammer *f* **VT** klammern

cramped [kræmpt] ADJ **a** *space* eng, beschränkt; *flat, accommodation, room* beengt; *coach, train, plane* überfüllt; **we are very ~ (for space)** wir sind räumlich sehr beschränkt **b** *position, person, muscle, limb* verkrampft **c** *handwriting* eng zusammengekritzelt

crampon ['kræmpən] N Steigeisen *nt*

cranberry ['krænbərɪ] N Preiselbeere *f*, Kronsbeere *f*; **~ sauce** Preiselbeersoße *f*

crane [kreɪn] **N** **a** Kran *m*; **~ driver** Kranführer(in) *m(f)* **b** *(Orn)* Kranich *m* **VT** **to ~ one's neck** den Hals recken, sich *(dat)* fast den Hals verrenken *(inf)* **VI** *(also* **crane forward***)* den Hals *or* den Kopf recken

cranefly ['kreɪnflaɪ] N Schnake *f*

cranesbill ['kreɪnzbɪl] N *(Bot)* Storchschnabel *m*

crania ['kreɪnɪə] *pl of* **cranium**

cranial ['kreɪnɪəl] ADJ *(Anat)* Schädel-, kranial *(spec)*

cranium ['kreɪnɪəm] N *pl* **crania** ['kreɪnɪə] *(Anat)* Schädel *m*, Cranium *nt (spec)*

crank¹ [kræŋk] N *(= eccentric person)* Spinner(in) *m(f) (inf)*; *(US: = cross person)* Griesgram *m*

crank² N *(Mech)* Kurbel *f* VT *(also* **crank up***)* ankurbeln

crankcase ['kræŋkkeɪs] N *(Aut)* Kurbelgehäuse *nt*

crankiness ['kræŋkɪnɪs] N **a** *(= eccentricity)* Verrücktheit *f* **b** *(esp US: = bad temper)* Griesgrämigkeit *f*

crankshaft ['kræŋkʃɑːft] N *(Aut)* Kurbelwelle *f*

cranky ['kræŋkɪ] ADJ *(+er)* **a** *(= eccentric)* verrückt **b** *(esp US: = bad-tempered)* griesgrämig

cranny ['krænɪ] N Ritze *f*, Spalte *f* → **nook**

crap [kræp] N **a** *(sl)* Scheiße *f (vulg)*; **to go for a ~** scheißen gehen *(vulg)*; **to have** *or* **take a ~** scheißen *(vulg)* **b** *(inf: = rubbish)* Scheiße *f (inf)*; **a load of ~** große Scheiße *(inf)* VI *(sl)* scheißen *(vulg)* ADJ *attr (inf) joke, job etc* Scheiß- *(inf)*

▶ **crap out** VI *(inf)* kneifen *(of* vor *+dat)*

crap game N *(US)* Würfelspiel *nt (mit zwei Würfeln)*

crappy ['kræpɪ] ADJ *(+er) (inf)* beschissen *(inf)*, Scheiß- *(inf)*

craps [kræps] N *(US)* Würfelspiel *nt*; **to shoot ~** Würfel spielen

crapshooter ['kræpʃuːtəʳ] N Würfelspieler(in) *m(f)*

crash [kræʃ] N **a** *(= noise)* Krach(en *nt no pl*) *m no pl*; *(of thunder, cymbals also, of drums)* Schlag *m*; **there was a ~ upstairs** es hat oben gekracht; **the vase fell to the ground with a ~** die Vase fiel krachend zu Boden; **a ~ of thunder** ein Donnerschlag *m*; **the ~ of the waves against …** das Krachen der Wellen gegen …
b *(= accident)* Unfall *m*, Unglück *nt*; *(= collision also)* Zusammenstoß *m*; *(with several cars)* Karambolage *f*; *(= plane crash)* (Flugzeug)unglück *nt*; **to be in a (car) ~** in einen (Auto)unfall verwickelt sein; **to have a ~** (mit dem Auto) verunglücken, einen (Auto)unfall haben; *(= cause it)* einen Unfall verursachen *or* bauen *(inf)*; **the impact of the ~** die Wucht des Aufpralls; *(into another car)* die Wucht des Zusammenstoßes
c *(Fin)* Zusammenbruch *m*; *(St Ex)* Börsenkrach *m*
d *(Comput)* Crash *m (inf)*, Absturz *m*
ADV krach; **he went ~ into a tree** er krachte gegen einen Baum; **~, bang, wallop!** *(inf)* bums! *(inf)*, krach! *(inf)*
VT **a** *car, bicycle* einen Unfall haben mit; *plane* abstürzen mit; **if you let him use your car he's bound to ~ it** wenn du ihm dein Auto gibst, fährt er es dir bestimmt kaputt *(inf)*; **to ~ one's car into sth** mit dem Auto gegen etw krachen *or* knallen *(inf)*; **the car was found ~ed** das Auto wurde demoliert aufgefunden
b *(with particle: = bang)* **stop ~ing the plates around** hör auf, mit den Tellern zu scheppern *(inf)*; **he ~ed the cymbals together** er schlug scheppernd die Becken zusammen; **he ~ed his head against the windscreen** er krachte mit dem Kopf gegen die Windschutzscheibe; **he ~ed the car through the barrier** er fuhr mit dem Auto voll durch die Absperrung *(inf)*
c *(inf: = gatecrash)* **to ~ a party** uneingeladen zu einer Party gehen, in eine Party hineinplatzen
VI **a** *(= have an accident)* verunglücken, einen Unfall haben; *(plane, computer)* abstürzen; **to ~ into sth** gegen etw *(acc)* krachen *or* knallen *(inf)*
b *(with particle: = move with a crash)* krachen; **to ~ to the ground/through sth** zu Boden/durch etw krachen; **they went ~ing through the undergrowth** sie brachen krachend durchs Unterholz; **his fist ~ed into Tom's face** seine Faust landete krachend in Toms Gesicht; **the whole roof came ~ing down (on him)** das ganze Dach krachte auf ihn herunter; **his whole world ~ed about him** *or* **his ears** seine ganze Welt brach zusammen
c *(Fin)* Pleite machen *(inf)*; *(Comput)* abstürzen; **when Wall Street ~ed** als Wall Street zusammenbrach, beim Börsenkrach der Wall Street
d *(inf: also* **crash out***)* *(= sleep)* knacken *(sl)*; *(= fall asleep)* einknacken *(sl)*; *(= become unconscious)* zusammenklappen *(inf)*

crash: **crash barrier** N Leitplanke *f*; **crash course** N Schnell- *or* Intensivkurs *m*; **crash diet** N Radikalkur *f*; **crash dive** N Schnelltauchmanöver *nt*; **crash-dive** VI schnelltauchen; **crash helmet** N Sturzhelm *m*

crashing ['kræʃɪŋ] ADJ *(dated inf)* **he's/it's a ~ bore** er/es ist fürchterlich *or* zum Einschlafen langweilig *(inf)*

crashingly ['kræʃɪŋlɪ] ADV *(dated inf)* schrecklich

crash: **crash-land** VI eine Bruchlandung machen, bruchlanden VT eine Bruchlandung machen mit, bruchlanden mit; **crash-landing** N Bruchlandung *f*; **crash programme** N Intensivprogramm *nt*

crass [krɑːs] ADJ *(+er)* *(= stupid, unsubtle)* krass; *ignorance also* haarsträubend; *(= coarse) behaviour* unfein, derb; **must you be so ~ about it?** müssen Sie sich so krass ausdrücken?

crassly ['krɑːslɪ] ADV krass; *behave* unfein

crassness ['krɑːsnɪs] N *(= insensitivity)* Krassheit *f*; *(= coarseness)* Derbheit *f*

crate [kreɪt] N *(also inf: = car, plane)* Kiste *f*; *(= beer crate, milk crate)* Kasten *m* VT *goods* (in Kisten/eine Kiste) (ver)packen

crater ['kreɪtəʳ] N Krater *m*

cravat(te) [krə'væt] N Halstuch *nt*

crave [kreɪv] VT *(liter: = beg)* erbitten; *mercy also* erflehen; *(= desire) attention, drink etc* sich sehnen nach; **to ~ sb's pardon** *(form)* jdn um Verzeihung anflehen; **ladies and gentlemen, may I ~ your indulgence?** *(form)* meine Damen und Herren, darf ich um Ihre werte Aufmerksamkeit bitten?; **may I ~ your indulgence a moment longer?** *(form)* darf ich Ihre Geduld noch etwas länger in Anspruch nehmen?

▶ **crave for** VI *+prep obj* sich sehnen nach

craven ['kreɪvən] *(liter)* ADJ feig(e); **a ~ coward** ein elender Feigling, eine feige Memme *(geh)* N Memme *f (geh)*

cravenly ['kreɪvənlɪ] ADV *(liter)* feige, feigherzig *(old)*

craving ['kreɪvɪŋ] N Verlangen *nt*; **to have a ~ for sth** Verlangen nach etw haben; **I have a ~ for ice cream** ich hab total Lust auf ein Eis *(inf)*; **pregnant women have strange ~s** schwangere Frauen haben eigenartige Gelüste

crawfish ['krɔːfɪʃ] N = **crayfish b**

crawl [krɔːl] N **a** *(on hands and knees)* Kriechen *nt*; *(= slow speed)* Schnecken- *or* Kriechtempo *nt*; *(Brit inf: = pub-crawl)* Kneipenbummel *m*; **it was a long ~** wir mussten lange kriechen; *(in car)* wir sind lange nur im Kriechtempo vorangekommen; **we could only go at a ~** wir kamen nur im Schnecken- *or* Kriechtempo voran; **to join the ~ to the coast** sich der (Auto)schlange zur Küste anschließen
b *(= swimming stroke)* Kraul(stil) *m*, Kraulen *nt*; **to do the ~** kraulen; **she's very fast at the ~** sie ist sehr schnell im Kraulen
VI **a** *(person, traffic)* kriechen; *(baby, insects also)* krabbeln; *(time also)* schleichen; **he tried to ~ away** er versuchte wegzukriechen
b *(= be infested)* wimmeln *(with* von*)*; **the meat was ~ing with flies** das Fleisch wimmelte nur so von Fliegen; **the street was ~ing with police** auf der Straße wimmelte es von Polizisten
c spiders make/he makes my flesh *or* **skin ~** wenn ich Spinnen/ihn sehe, kriege ich eine Gänsehaut
d *(inf: = suck up)* kriechen *(to* vor *+dat)*; **he went ~ing to teacher** er ist gleich zum Lehrer gerannt

crawler ['krɔːləʳ] N **a** *(Brit inf: = sycophant)* Kriecher(in) *m(f)* **b crawlers** PL *(= rompers)* Spielanzug *m*

crawler lane N *(Brit Aut)* Kriechspur *f*

crawling ['krɔːlɪŋ] ADJ *insect, movement* kriechend, krabbelnd; **a baby at the ~ stage** ein Baby im Krabbelalter → *also* **crawl**

crawl space N *(US)* niedriger Keller; *(under roof)* Zwischendecke *f*

crayfish ['kreɪfɪʃ] N **a** *(freshwater)* Flusskrebs *m* **b** *(saltwater: also* **crawfish***)* Languste *f*

crayon ['kreɪən] N **a** *(= pencil)* Buntstift *m*; *(= wax crayon)* Wachs(mal)stift *m*; *(= chalk crayon)* Pastellstift *m*, Malkreide *f* **b** *(= picture)* Pastell *nt*, Kreide- *or* Pastellzeichnung *f* VTI (mit Bunt-/Wachsmal-/Pastellstiften) zeichnen *or* malen

▶ **crayon in** VT *sep drawing* ausmalen

craze [kreɪz] N Fimmel *m (inf)*; **it's all the ~** *(inf)* das ist große Mode; **there's a ~ for collecting old things just now** es ist zurzeit große Mode, alte Sachen zu sammeln VT **a** *(= make insane)* **a ~d gunman** ein Amokschütze *m*; **to be half ~d with grief** vor Schmerz halb wahnsinnig sein; **he had a ~d look on his face** er hatte den Gesichtsausdruck eines Wahnsinnigen **b** *pottery, glazing* rissig machen VI *(pottery)* rissig werden

crazily ['kreɪzɪlɪ] ADV **a** *skid, bounce, whirl* wie verrückt; *lean, tilt* unwahrscheinlich **b** *(= madly)* verrückt

craziness ['kreɪzɪnɪs] N Verrücktheit *f*

crazy ['kreɪzɪ] ADJ *(+er)* **a** verrückt *(with* vor *+dat)*; **to send** *or* **drive sb ~** jdn verrückt *or* wahnsinnig machen; **to go ~** verrückt *or* wahnsinnig werden; **to act ~** sich wie verrückt *or* wahnsinnig aufführen; **that's ~** das ist doch verrückt!; **like ~** *(inf)* wie verrückt *(inf)*; **it/you would be ~ to do that** es wäre/du wärst verrückt, das zu tun **b** *(inf: = enthusiastic)* verrückt *(inf)*; **to be ~ about sb/sth** ganz verrückt *or* wild auf jdn/etw sein *(inf)*; **football-~** fußballverrückt *(inf)*; **to be ~ for sb** verrückt nach jdm sein *(inf)* **c** *angle, tilt* unwahrscheinlich

crazy: **crazy bone** N *(US)* Musikantenknochen *m*; **crazy golf** N *(Brit)* Minigolf *nt*; **crazy house** N *(US inf)* Irrenhaus *nt*; **crazy paving** N Mosaikpflaster *nt*; **crazy quilt** N *(US)* Flickendecke *f*

CRC *abbr of* **camera-ready copy**

CRE N *(Brit) abbr of* **Commission for Racial Equality** Kommission *f* für Rassengleichheit

creak [kriːk] N Knarren *nt no pl*; *(of hinges, bed springs)* Quietschen *nt no pl*; *(of knees etc)* Knacken *nt no pl*; **to give a loud ~** laut knarren/quietschen/knacken; **a series of ~s** knarrende/quietschende/knackende Geräusche VI knarren; *(hinges, bed springs)* quietschen; *(knees etc)* knacken

creaky ['kriːkɪ] ADJ *(+er)* **a** *(lit)* knarrend; *hinges, bed springs* quietschend; *knees etc* knackend **b** *(fig) plot, thriller etc* verstaubt

cream [kriːm] N **a** Sahne *f*, Rahm *m (S Ger)*; *(= cream pudding, artificial cream)* Creme *f*, Krem *f*; **~ of asparagus/tomato/chicken soup** Spargel-/Tomaten-/Hühnercremesuppe *f*; **~ of tartar** Weinstein *m*
b *(= lotion)* Creme *f*
c *(= colour)* Creme(farbe *f*) *nt*; **a skirt in a pale shade of ~** ein blass-cremefarbener Rock
d *(fig: = best)* die Besten; *(of society also)* Creme *f*, Elite *f*; **our rivals take the ~ of the applicants** unsere Konkurrenz sahnt die besten Bewerber ab; **the ~ of the crop** *(= people)* die Elite; *(= things)* das Nonplusultra; **the ~ of society** die Creme der Gesellschaft; **to take the ~** den Rahm abschöpfen
ADJ **a** *(colour)* creme *inv*, cremefarben *or* -farbig

b *(= made with cream)* Sahne-, Creme-; **~ soups** Cremesuppen *pl*
VT **a** *(= put cream on) face etc* eincremen
b *butter, eggs etc* cremig rühren; *potatoes* pürieren; **~ed potatoes** Kartoffelpüree *nt*
c *(= skim) milk* entrahmen
d *(= allow to form a cream) milk* aufrahmen lassen
e *(US inf: = defeat easily)* in die Pfanne hauen *(inf)*
VI *(milk)* aufrahmen

▶ **cream off** VT *sep (lit)* abschöpfen; *(fig) profits also, the best* absahnen

cream: **cream bun** N Eclair *nt*; **cream cake** N Sahnetorte *f*, Cremetorte *f*; *(small)* Sahnetörtchen *nt*, Cremetörtchen *nt*; **cream cheese** N (Doppelrahm)frischkäse *m*

creamer ['kri:mə'] N **a** *(US: = jug)* Sahnekännchen *nt* **b** *(= skimming machine)* Milchzentrifuge *or* -schleuder *f* **c** *(= dried milk)* Milchpulver *nt*

creamery ['kri:mərı] N Molkerei *f*; *(= shop)* Milchgeschäft *nt*

cream: **cream puff** N Windbeutel *m*; **cream soda** N Sodawasser *nt* mit Vanillegeschmack; **cream tea** N Nachmittagstee *m*

creamy ['kri:mı] ADJ *(+er)* **a** *(= tasting of cream)* sahnig; *(= smooth)* cremig; **a ~ complexion** ein zarter Teint **b** *(= cream-coloured)* creme(farben *or* -farbig)

crease [kri:s] **N** **a** Falte *f*; *(= deliberate fold, in material also)* Kniff *m*; *(in paper also)* Falz *m*, Kniff *m*; *(ironed: in trousers etc)* (Bügel)falte *f*; **to be a mass of ~s** völlig zerknittert sein; **to put a ~ in a pair of trousers** eine Falte in eine Hose bügeln **b** *(Sport)* Linie *f* **VT** *(deliberately) clothes* Falten/eine Falte machen in *(+acc)*; *material, paper* Kniffe/einen Kniff machen in *(+acc)*; *paper* falzen; *(unintentionally)* zerknittern; **smartly ~d trousers** Hosen mit sauberen Bügelfalten **VI** knittern; **his face ~d with laughter** er fing an zu lachen

▶ **crease up** VI *(inf, with laughter)* sich kringeln *(inf)*

crease-proof ['kri:spru:f], **crease-resistant** ['kri:srızıstənt] ADJ knitterfrei

create [kri:'eıt] **VT** **a** *(= bring into existence)* schaffen; *new style, fashion also* kreieren; *the world, man* erschaffen; *draught, noise, fuss* verursachen; *difficulties* machen; *problems (person)* schaffen; *(action, event)* verursachen, hervorbringen; *impression* machen; *(Comput) file* anlegen, erstellen; **to ~ a sensation** eine Sensation sein; **to ~ a fuss** Theater machen *(inf)*
b *(= appoint) peer* ernennen; **peers can only be ~d by the reigning monarch** nur der regierende Monarch kann jemanden in den Adelsstand erheben; **to ~ sb baron** jdn zum Baron erheben *or* ernennen
VI *(Brit inf)* Theater machen *(inf)*

creation [kri:'eıʃən] N **a** *no pl (= bringing into existence)* Schaffung *f*; *(of new style, fashion also)* Kreation *f*; *(of the world, man)* Erschaffung *f*; *(of draught, noise, fuss)* Verursachung *f*; *(of problems, by person)* Schaffen *nt*; *(by action, event)* Verursachung *f* **b** *no pl (= appointment: of peer)* Erhebung *f*, Ernennung *f* **c** *no pl* **the Creation** die Schöpfung; **all ~, the whole of ~** die Schöpfung, alle Kreatur *f*, alle Geschöpfe *pl* **d** *(= created object, Art)* Werk *nt*; *(Fashion)* Kreation *f*

creationism [kri:'eıʃənızəm] N Kreationismus *m*

creationist [kri:'eıʃənıst] **N** Kreationist(in) *m(f)* **ADJ** kreationistisch

creative [kri:'eıtıv] ADJ *power, skill etc* schöpferisch; *approach, attitude, person* kreativ; **the ~ use of language** kreativer Sprachgebrauch

creative accounting N kreative Buchführung *f (um einen falschen Eindruck vom erzielten Gewinn zu erwecken)*

creatively [kri:'eıtıvlı] ADV kreativ

creativeness [ˌkri:'eıtıvnıs], **creativity** [ˌkri:eı'tıvıtı] N schöpferische Begabung *or* Kraft; *(of person also, of approach, attitude)* Kreativität *f*

creative thinking N kreatives Denken

creative toys PL Spielzeug *nt* zum Gestalten und Werken

creative writing N dichterisches Schreiben

creativity [ˌkri:eı'tıvıtı] N schöpferische Begabung *or* Kraft; *(of person also, of approach, attitude)* Kreativität *f*

creator [kri:'eıtə'] N Schöpfer(in) *m(f)*

creature ['kri:tʃə'] N **a** Geschöpf *nt*, (Lebe)wesen *nt*, Kreatur *f*; **what a beautiful ~!** welch ein herrliches Geschöpf!; **all dumb ~s** die stumme Kreatur; **she's a funny ~** sie ist ein komisches Geschöpf; **there wasn't a ~ in sight** nirgends regte sich etwas, kein Lebewesen war zu sehen **b** *(= subordinate person)* Geschöpf *nt*

creature comforts PL leibliches Wohl

crèche [kreıʃ] N **a** *(Brit: = day nursery)* (Kinder)krippe *f* *or* -hort *m*; *(esp US: = children's home)* Kinderheim *nt* **b** *(= crib)* Krippe *f*

cred [kred] → **street cred**

credence ['kri:dəns] N **a** *no pl (= belief)* Glaube *m*; **to lend ~ to sth** etw glaubwürdig erscheinen lassen *or* machen; **worthy of ~** glaubwürdig; **to give** *or* **attach ~ to sth** einer Sache *(dat)* Glauben schenken; **letter of ~** Beglaubigungsschreiben *nt* **b** *(Eccl: also* **credence table***)* Kredenz *f*

credentials [krı'denʃəlz] PL *(= references)* Referenzen *pl*, Zeugnisse *pl*; *(= identity papers)* (Ausweis)papiere *pl*; **to present one's ~** seine Papiere vorlegen

credibility [ˌkredə'bılıtı] N Glaubwürdigkeit *f*; **his ~ rating is pretty low** er wird als nicht sehr glaubwürdig eingestuft

credibility gap N Glaubwürdigkeitslücke *f*; **his ~ widened** er verlor immer mehr an Glaubwürdigkeit

credible ['kredıbl] ADJ glaubwürdig

credibly ['kredıblı] ADV glaubhaft

credit ['kredıt] **N** **a** *no pl (Fin)* Kredit *m*; *(in pub, hotel, shop etc)* Stundung *f*; **the bank will let me have £5,000 ~** die Bank räumt mir einen Kredit von £ 5.000 ein; **to buy on ~** auf Kredit kaufen; **to sell on ~** gegen Kredit verkaufen; **his ~ is good** er ist kreditwürdig; *(in small shop)* er ist vertrauenswürdig; **to give sb (unlimited) ~** jdm (unbegrenzt) Kredit geben; **we can't give you ~** *(bank)* wir können Ihnen keinen Kredit geben; *(corner shop etc)* wir können Ihnen nichts stunden; **pubs do not usually give ~** in Lokalen bekommt man normalerweise nichts gestundet; **letter of ~** Kreditbrief *m*, Akkreditiv *nt*
b *(Fin: = money possessed by person, firm)* (Gut)haben *nt*; *(Comm: = sum of money)* Kreditposten *m*; **to be in ~** Geld *nt* auf dem Konto haben; **to keep one's account in ~** sein Konto nicht überziehen; **the ~s and debits** Soll und Haben *nt*; **how much have we got to our ~?** wie viel haben wir auf dem Konto?; **~ arrangements** Kreditvereinbarungen *pl*
c *no pl (= standing)* Ansehen *nt*; **a man of good ~** ein angesehener Mann
d *no pl (= honour)* Ehre *f*; *(= recognition)* Anerkennung *f*; *(Sch, Univ: = distinction)* Auszeichnung *f*; **he's a ~ to his family** er macht seiner Familie Ehre; **that's to his ~** das ehrt ihn; **well, all ~ to you for not succumbing** alle Achtung, dass Sie nicht nachgegeben haben; **at least he has this to his ~** das spricht immerhin für ihn; **her generosity does her ~** ihre Großzügigkeit macht ihr alle Ehre; **to reflect great ~ on sb** jdm große Ehre machen; **to come out of sth with ~** ehrenvoll aus etw hervorgehen; **to get all the ~** die ganze Anerkennung *or* Ehre einstecken; **I do all the work and he gets all the ~** ich mache die Arbeit, und ihm wird es als Verdienst angerechnet; **the ~ for that should go to him** das ist sein Verdienst; **to take the ~ for sth** das Verdienst für etw in Anspruch nehmen; **~ where ~ is due** *(prov)* Ehre, wem Ehre gebührt *(prov)*
e *no pl (= belief)* Glaube *m*; **to give ~ to sth** etw glauben, einer Sache *(dat)* Glauben schenken; **to lend ~ to sth** etw glaubwürdig erscheinen lassen *or* machen; **to gain ~** an Glaubwürdigkeit gewinnen; **I gave you ~ for more sense** ich habe Sie für vernünftiger gehalten; **worthy of ~** glaubwürdig
f *(esp US Univ)* Schein *m*; **to take** *or* **do ~s** Scheine machen
g **credits** **PL** *(Film etc)* Vor-/Nachspann *m*; *(in book)* Herausgeber- und Mitarbeiterverzeichnis *nt*
VT **a** *(= believe)* glauben; **would you ~ it!** ist das denn zu glauben!, ist das denn die Möglichkeit!
b *(= attribute)* zuschreiben *(+dat)*; **I ~ed him with more sense** ich habe ihn für vernünftiger gehalten; **he was ~ed with having invented it** die Erfindung wurde ihm zugeschrieben; **he was ~ed with having found the solution** es wurde als sein Verdienst angerechnet *or* es wurde ihm zugutegehalten, diese Lösung gefunden zu haben; **it's ~ed with (having) magic powers** ihm werden Zauberkräfte zugeschrieben
c *(Fin)* gutschreiben; **to ~ a sum to sb's account** jds Konto *(dat)* einen Betrag gutschreiben (lassen); **he/his account had been ~ed with £100** ihm/seinem Konto waren £ 100 gutgeschrieben worden

creditable ['kredıtəbl] ADJ **a** *(= praiseworthy)* lobenswert, anerkennenswert **b** *(= credible)* glaublich

creditably ['kredıtəblı] ADV löblich

credit: **credit account** N Kreditkonto *nt*; **credit agency** N *(giving credit)* Finanzierungsinstitut *nt*; *(for credit investigation)* Kreditschutzverein *m*; **credit balance** N Kontostand *m*, Saldo *m*; **credit bureau** N *(US)* = **credit agency**; **credit card** N Kreditkarte *f*; **credit check** N Überprüfung *f* der Kreditwürdigkeit; **to run a ~ on sb** jds Kreditwürdigkeit überprüfen; **credit control** N Kreditüberwachung *f*; **credit entry** N Gutschrift *f*; **credit facilities** PL Kreditmöglichkeiten *pl*; **credit hour** N *(US: Univ)* anrechenbare (Vorlesungs)stunde; **credit interest** N Habenzinsen *pl*; **credit limit** N Kreditgrenze *f*; **credit line** N **a** *(Fin)* Kreditrahmen *m* **b** *(= sources)* Herkunfts- *or* Quellenangabe *f*; **credit note** N Gutschrift *f*

creditor ['kredıtə'] N Gläubiger *m*

credit: **credit page** N Herausgeber- und Mitarbeiterverzeichnis *nt*; **credit rating** N Kreditwürdigkeit *f*; **to have a good/bad ~** als kreditwürdig/als nicht kreditwürdig eingestuft werden; **credit-rating agency** N Kreditschutzverein *m*, ≈ Schufa *f*; **credit report** N Kreditauskunft *f*; **credit risk** N Kreditrisiko *nt*, Gegenparteirisiko *nt*; **to be a good/poor ~** ein geringes/großes Kreditrisiko darstellen; **credit sales** PL Kreditkäufe *pl*; **credit side** N *(lit, fig)* Habenseite *f*; **on the ~ he's young** für ihn spricht, dass er jung ist; **credit slip** N Einzahlungsschein *m*; **credit squeeze** N Kreditbeschränkung *or* -knappheit *f*; **credit standing** N Kreditwürdigkeit *f*; **credit terms** PL Kreditbedingungen *pl*; **credit titles** PL *(Film)* = **credit N g**; **credit transfer** N *(Brit)* (Geld)überweisung *f*; **credit union** N Kreditgenossenschaft *f*; **creditworthiness** N Kreditwürdigkeit *f*; **creditworthy** ADJ kreditwürdig

credo ['kreıdəʊ] N *(lit, fig)* Kredo *nt*, Credo *nt*, Glaubensbekenntnis *nt*

credulity [krı'dju:lıtı] N *no pl* Leichtgläubigkeit *f*

credulous, **credulously** ADJ, ADV ['kredjʊləs, -lı] leichtgläubig

creed [kri:d] N *(Eccl: = prayer)* Glaubensbekenntnis *nt*; *(as part of service, fig also)* Kredo *nt*, Credo *nt*

creek [kri:k] N *(esp Brit: = inlet)* (kleine) Bucht; *(US: = brook)* Bach *m*; **to be up the ~ (without a paddle)** *(inf: = be in trouble)* in der Tinte sitzen *(inf)*; *(= be completely wrong)* auf dem falschen Dampfer sein *(inf)*

creel [kri:l] N Korb *m*

creep [kri:p] *vb: pret, ptp* **crept** VI **a** *(= move quietly or slowly)* schleichen; *(with the body close to the ground, insects)* kriechen; *(plants, horizontally)* kriechen; *(vertically)* klettern, sich ranken; **ivy is a ~ing plant** Efeu ist eine Kletterpflanze; **~ing paralysis** schleichende Lähmung; **~ing inflation** schleichende Inflation; **the water level crept higher and higher** der Wasserspiegel kletterte immer höher
b the story made my flesh ~ bei der Geschichte überlief es mich kalt *or* bekam ich eine Gänsehaut
N **a** *(inf: = unpleasant person)* Widerling *m (inf)*, widerlicher *or* fieser Typ *(inf)*; **you little ~!** du fieser Typ *(inf)*
b *(inf)* **he gives me the ~s** er ist mir nicht geheuer; **this old house gives me the ~s** in dem alten Haus ist es mir nicht geheuer

▶ **creep in** VI (sich) hinein-/hereinschleichen (*-to* in *+acc*); *(mistakes, doubts)* sich einschleichen (*-to* in *+acc*)

▶ **creep over** VI *+prep obj (feeling, doubt etc)* beschleichen, überkommen; *(pleasant feeling)* überkommen

▶ **creep up** VI **a** *(person)* sich heranschleichen (*on* an *+acc*); *(prices, inflation)* (in die Höhe) klettern **b to creep up on sb** *(time, exam)* langsam auf jdn zukommen; **old age is creeping up on him** er wird langsam alt

creeper ['kri:pəʳ] N **a** *(= plant, along ground)* Kriechpflanze *f*; *(upwards)* Kletterpflanze *f* **b** *(= bird)* Baumläufer *m* **c creepers** PL *(US)* *Schuhe mit dicken Gummisohlen*, Leisetreter *pl (inf)*

creepy ['kri:pɪ] ADJ *(+er) (= frightening)* unheimlich; *story, place also* gruselig

creepy-crawly ['kri:pɪ'krɔ:lɪ] *(inf)* ADJ *insect* krabbelig *(inf)*, kribbelnd, krabbelnd; *feeling* unheimlich N Krabbeltier *nt*

cremate [krɪ'meɪt] VT einäschern, kremieren *(rare)*

cremation [krɪ'meɪʃən] N Einäscherung *f*, Kremation *f*

crematorium [ˌkremə'tɔ:rɪəm], *(esp US)* **crematory** ['kreməˌtɔ:rɪ] N Krematorium *nt*

crème de la crème ['kremdəlæ'krem] N Crème de la Crème *f*

crème de menthe ['kremdə'mɒnθ] N Pfefferminzlikör *m*

crenellated ['krenɪleɪtɪd] ADJ *battlements* mit Zinnen versehen, kreneliert *(spec)*; *moulding, pattern* zinnenartig

crenellation [ˌkrenɪ'leɪʃən] N *usu pl (on castle)* Zinnen *pl*, Krenelierung *f (spec)*; *(on moulding)* Zinnenmuster *nt*

Creole ['kri:əʊl] N **a** *(Ling)* Kreolisch *nt* **b** *(= person)* Kreole *m*, Kreolin *f* ADJ kreolisch; **he is ~** er ist Kreole

creolized ['kreɪəlaɪzd] ADJ kreolisiert

creosote ['krɪəsəʊt] N Kreosot *nt* VT mit Kreosot streichen

crêpe [kreɪp] N **a** *(Tex)* Krepp *m*, Crêpe *f* **b** *(Cook)* Crêpe *m* **c** = **crêpe rubber d** = **crêpe paper** ADJ *(= made of crêpe)* Krepp-

crêpe: **crêpe bandage** N elastische Binde, elastischer Verband; **crêpe de Chine** [ˌkrepdə'ʃi:n] N Crêpe de Chine *m*, Chinakrepp *m*; **crêpe paper** N Krepppapier *nt*; **crêpe rubber** N Kreppgummi *m* ADJ Kreppgummi-; **crêpe-soled** [kreɪp'səʊld] ADJ mit Kreppsohle(n), Krepp-; **crêpe suzette** [ˌkreɪpsu:'zet] N Crêpe Suzette *f*

crepitate ['krepɪteɪt] VI *(liter)* prasseln

crept [krept] *pret, ptp of* **creep**

crepuscular [krɪ'pʌskjʊləʳ] ADJ *(liter)* dämmerig; **~ animals** *(Zool)* Dämmerungstiere *pl*

crescendo [krɪ'ʃendəʊ] N *(Mus)* Crescendo *nt*; *(fig)* Zunahme *f*; **~ of excitement** Anschwellen *nt* der Aufregung VI *(Mus, fig)* anschwellen

crescent ['kresnt] N Halbmond *m*; *(in street names)* Weg *m (halbmondförmig verlaufende Straße)* ADJ **the ~ moon** die Mondsichel

crescent-shaped ['kresnt'ʃeɪpt] ADJ halbmond- *or* sichelförmig

cress [kres] N (Garten)kresse *f*; *(= watercress)* Brunnenkresse *f*

crest [krest] N **a** *(of bird)* Haube *f*; *(of cock)* Kamm *m*; *(on hat etc)* Federbusch *m*; *(= plume on helmet)* Helmbusch *m* **b** *(Her)* Helmzierde *f*; *(= coat of arms)* Wappen *nt* **c** *(of wave, hill, Anat: of horse etc)* Kamm *m*; *(fig: of excitement, popularity)* Höhepunkt *m*, Gipfel *m*; *(Phys, of oscillation)* Scheitel(punkt) *m*; **he's riding on the ~ of a wave** *(fig)* er schwimmt im Augenblick oben VT *(= reach the crest of)* erklimmen

crested ['krestɪd] ADJ *notepaper, seal* verziert; *(Orn)* Hauben-; **~ coot** Kammblessralle *f*

crested tit N Haubenmeise *f*

crestfallen ['krestˌfɔ:lən] ADJ geknickt, niedergeschlagen

cretaceous [krɪ'teɪʃəs] ADJ Kreide-, kretazeisch *(spec)*; **the ~ age** *(Geol)* die Kreide(zeit)

Cretan ['kri:tən] ADJ kretisch N Kreter(in) *m(f)*

Crete [kri:t] N Kreta *nt*

cretin ['kretɪn] N *(Med)* Kretin *m*; *(inf)* Schwachkopf *m (inf)*

cretinism ['kretɪnɪzəm] N *(Med)* Kretinismus *m*; *(inf)* Schwachsinn *m*, Idiotie *f*

cretinous ['kretɪnəs] ADJ *(Med)* kretinoid; *(inf)* schwachsinnig

cretonne [kre'tɒn] N Cretonne *f or m*

Creutzfeldt-Jakob disease [ˌkrɔɪtsfelt'jækɒbdɪˌzi:z] N *no pl* Creutzfeldt-Jakob-Krankheit *f*

crevasse [krɪ'væs] N (Gletscher)spalte *f*

crevice ['krevɪs] N Spalte *f*

crew¹ [kru:] N **a** Mannschaft *f*; *(also Sport)* Crew *f*; *(including officers: of ship also, of plane, tank)* Besatzung *f*, Crew *f*; **50 passengers and 20 ~** 50 Passagiere und 20 Mann Besatzung; **the ground ~** *(Aviat)* das Bodenpersonal; **is Mary your ~?** macht Mary Vorschotmann? **b** *(Brit inf: = gang)* Bande *f*; **they were a motley ~** sie waren ein bunt zusammengewürfelter Haufen *(inf)* VT **to ~ for sb** bei jdm den Vorschotmann machen VT *yacht* die Mannschaft *or* Crew sein von

crew² *(old) pret of* **crow**

crew: **crew cut** N Bürstenschnitt *m*; **crew member** N Mitglied *nt* der Mannschaft, Besatzungsmitglied *nt*; **crew neck** N runder Halsausschnitt; *(also* **crew-neck pullover** *or* **sweater***)* Pullover *m* mit rundem Halsausschnitt

crib [krɪb] N **a** *(= cradle)* Krippe *f*; *(US: = cot)* Kinderbett *nt* **b** *(= manger)* Krippe *f*, Raufe *f*; *(fig: = nativity scene)* Krippe *f* **c** *(US: = maize bin)* Trockengerüst *nt* für Maiskolben **d** *(esp Brit Sch: = cheating aid)* Spickzettel *m (inf)*; *(inf: = plagiarism)* Anleihe *f (inf)* VI *(esp Brit Sch inf)* abschreiben *(inf)*, spicken *(inf)*; **to ~ from sb** von jdm abschreiben *(inf)* VT *(esp Brit Sch inf)* abschreiben *(inf)*; **to ~ sth from sb** etw von jdm abschreiben *(inf)*

cribbage ['krɪbɪdʒ] N Cribbage *nt*

crib death N *(US)* Krippentod *m*, plötzlicher Kindstod

crick [krɪk] N **a ~ in one's neck/back** ein steifes Genick/ein steifer Rücken VT **to ~ one's neck/back** sich *(dat)* ein steifes Genick/einen steifen Rücken zuziehen

cricket¹ ['krɪkɪt] N *(= insect)* Grille *f*

cricket² N *(Sport)* Kricket *nt*; **that's not ~** *(fig inf)* das ist nicht fair

CRICKET

Cricket wird oft als typisch englisches Spiel angesehen, obwohl es in ganz Großbritannien und dem Commonwealth sehr beliebt ist. Es wird überwiegend im Sommer auf großen Spielfeldern im Freien, den sogenannten **cricket pitches**, gespielt. Dabei treten zwei Teams mit jeweils elf Spielern gegeneinander an. Das Regelwerk ist ziemlich komplex. Jedes Team schlägt abwechselnd den Ball möglichst weit weg und versucht dann, mit **runs** Punkte zu erzielen. Die gegnerische Mannschaft, die **fielders**, versuchen dabei, den Ball zu fangen oder abzustoppen, damit der **batsman**, der Schlagmann, keinen Punkt machen kann. Wenn der Ball das Tor des Schlagmanns berührt oder gefangen wird, ohne nach dem Abschlag den Boden berührt zu haben, ist der Schlagmann draußen und muss ersetzt werden. Sind alle zehn Schlagmänner im Aus, wechseln die Mannschaften die Rollen; jetzt muss das andere Team aufschlagen. Die Mannschaft, die die meisten **runs** punkten konnte, gewinnt. Wie bei Baseball in den USA, wird Kricket oft als Metapher für viele Aspekte des englischen Lebensstils herangezogen. Zahlreiche Ausdrücke haben Eingang in die Alltagssprache gefunden, z. B. „to be on a sticky wicket" (in der Klemme sein) und „to knock someone for six" (jemanden umhauen).

cricket *in cpds* Kricket-; **cricket bat** N (Kricket)schlagholz *nt*

cricketer ['krɪkɪtəʳ] N Kricketspieler(in) *m(f)*

cricketing ['krɪkɪtɪŋ] ADJ Kricket-; **England's ~ heroes** Englands Kricketthelden

cricket: **cricket match** N Kricketspiel *nt*; **cricket pitch** N Kricketfeld *nt*

cri de c"oe)ur ['kri:də'kɜ:ʳ] N verzweifelter Stoßseufzer

crier ['kraɪəʳ] N *(= town crier)* Ausrufer *m*; *(= court crier)* Gerichtsdiener *m*

crikey ['kraɪkɪ] INTERJ *(dated Brit, inf)* Mann *(inf)*

crime [kraɪm] N **a** Straftat *f*; *(= murder, robbery with violence etc also, fig)* Verbrechen *nt*; **it's not a ~!** das ist nicht verboten; **it's a ~ to throw away all that good food** es ist eine Sünde *or* eine Schande, all das gute Essen wegzuwerfen **b** *no pl* Verbrechen *pl*; **~ and punishment** Verbrechen und Verbrechensverfolgung; **to lead a life of ~** kriminell leben; **~ is on the increase** die Zahl der Verbrechen nimmt zu; **~ doesn't pay** Verbrechen lohnen sich nicht

Crimea [kraɪ'mɪə] N *(Geog)* Krim *f*; *(inf: = Crimean War)* der Krimkrieg

Crimean [kraɪ'mɪən] N *(= person)* Krimbewohner(in) *m(f)* ADJ Krim-; **she's ~** sie kommt von der Krim

crime: **crime fighter** N Kriminalitätsbekämpfer(in) *m(f)*; **crime fighting** N Kriminalitätsbekämpfung *f*; **crime-fighting** ADJ Kriminalitätsbekämpfungs-, zur Kriminalitätsbekämpfung; **crime of passion** N Mord *m* aus Eifersucht; **crime prevention** N Verbrechensverhütung *f*, präventive Verbrechensbekämpfung *(form)*, Kriminalitätsprävention *f*; **crime prevention officer** N Beamte(r) *m*/Beamtin *f* für Kriminalitätsprävention *or* Verbrechensverhütung; **crime rate** N Verbrechensrate *f*; **crime spree** N **to go on a ~** auf Verbrechenstour gehen; **crime story** N Kriminalgeschichte *f*, Krimi *m (inf)*; **crime wave** N Verbrechenswelle *f*

criminal ['krɪmɪnl] N Straftäter(in) *m(f) (form)*, Kriminelle(r) *mf*; *(guilty of capital crimes also, fig)* Verbrecher(in) *m(f)* ADJ **a** kriminell, verbrecherisch; *action also* strafbar; **~ law** Strafrecht *nt*; **to take ~ proceedings against sb** strafrechtlich gegen jdn vorgehen; **to have a ~ record** vorbestraft sein **b** *(fig)* kriminell; **it's ~ to stay in in this weather** es ist eine Schande, bei diesem Wetter drinnen zu bleiben

criminal: **criminal assault** N Körperverletzung *f*; **criminal charge** N Anklage *f* wegen eines Verbrechens; **she faces ~s** sie wird eines Verbrechens angeklagt, sie muss sich vor Gericht wegen eines Verbrechens verantworten; **criminal code** N Strafgesetzbuch *nt*; **crimi-**

nal court N Strafkammer *m*, Gericht *nt* für Strafsachen; **criminal damage** N strafbare Sachbeschädigung *f*; **Criminal Investigation Department** N *(Brit)* Kriminalpolizei *f*

criminality [ˌkrɪmɪˈnælɪtɪ] N Kriminalität *f*

criminalization [ˌkrɪmɪnəlaɪˈzeɪʃən] N Kriminalisierung *f*

criminalize [ˈkrɪmɪnəlaɪz] VT kriminalisieren

criminal lawyer N Anwalt *m*/Anwältin *f* für Strafsachen; *(specializing in defence)* Strafverteidiger(in) *m(f)*

criminally [ˈkrɪmɪnəlɪ] ADV kriminell, verbrecherisch; **~ liable** *(Jur)* strafrechtlich verantwortlich, schuldfähig; **he thought she behaved quite ~** *(fig)* seiner Meinung nach hat sie sich kriminell verhalten

criminal: **criminal negligence** N grobe Fahrlässigkeit, Fahrlässigkeitsdelikt *nt*; **criminal offence**, *(US)* **criminal offense** N strafbare Handlung; **criminal profile** N Täterprofil *nt*; **Criminal Records Office** N Kriminaldienststelle *f* zur Führung der Verbrecherkartei; **criminal responsibility** N Strafbarkeit *f*; *(= accountability)* Zurechnungsfähigkeit g; **age of ~** Strafmündigkeit *f*

criminologist [ˌkrɪmɪˈnɒlədʒɪst] N Kriminologe *m*, Kriminologin *f*

criminology [ˌkrɪmɪˈnɒlədʒɪ] N Kriminologie *f*

crimp [krɪmp] VT *hair* (mit der Brennschere) wellen

Crimplene® [ˈkrɪmpliːn] N ≈ knitterfreies Trevira®

crimson [ˈkrɪmzn] ADJ purpurn, purpurrot; *sky* blutrot, purpurrot; *(through blushing)* knallrot *(inf)*, dunkelrot; **to turn** *or* **go ~** *(person, face)* knallrot *(inf)* *or* dunkelrot werden *or* anlaufen; *(sky)* sich blutrot färben N Purpur *nt*, Purpurrot *nt*

cringe [krɪndʒ] VI **a** *(= shrink back)* zurückschrecken *(at* vor *+dat)*; *(fig)* schaudern; **to ~ before sb** vor jdm zurückweichen *or* -schrecken; **he ~d at the thought** er *or* ihn schauderte bei dem Gedanken; **he ~d when she mispronounced his name** er zuckte zusammen, als sie seinen Namen falsch aussprach **b** *(= humble oneself, fawn)* katzbuckeln, kriechen *(to* vor *+dat)*; **to go cringing to sb** zu jdm gekrochen kommen; **a cringing person** ein Kriecher *m*; **cringing behaviour** kriecherisches Benehmen

cringe-making [ˈkrɪndʒˌmeɪkɪŋ] ADJ extrem peinlich

crinkle [ˈkrɪŋkl] N (Knitter)falte *f*; *(in skin)* Fältchen *nt* VT *paper, foil, dress etc* (zer)knittern; *cardboard, plastic etc* knicken; *edge of paper* wellen VI *(= wrinkle, paper, foil, dress etc)* knittern; *(face, skin)* (Lach)fältchen bekommen; *(edges of paper)* sich wellen, wellig werden; *(= curl: hair)* sich krausen; **his eyes ~d when he smiled** er bekam tausend Fältchen um die Augen, wenn er lächelte

crinkled [ˈkrɪŋkld] ADJ *leaf, paper, clothes* zerknittert, zerknautscht; *face* faltig, runzelig; **the paper was all ~** das Papier war ganz zerknittert

crinkly [ˈkrɪŋklɪ] ADJ *(+er)* *(inf: = wrinkled) paper, foil etc* zerknittert; *edges* wellig; *hair* krauselig *(inf)*

crinoline [ˈkrɪnəlɪn] N Krinoline *f*

cripes [kraɪps] INTERJ *(dated Brit, inf)* Mann *(inf)*

cripple [ˈkrɪpl] N Krüppel *m* VT *person* zum Krüppel machen; *arm, legs etc* verkrüppeln; *ship, plane* aktionsunfähig machen; *(fig) industry, exports* lahmlegen, lähmen; *person* lähmen; **the ship was ~d** das Schiff war nicht mehr aktionsfähig; **~d with rheumatism** von Rheuma praktisch gelähmt; **to be ~d for life** lebenslang ein Krüppel sein; **to be emotionally ~d** ein emotionaler Krüppel sein

crippling [ˈkrɪplɪŋ] ADJ *pain* lähmend; *guilt, depression* lähmend; *taxes, repayments* erdrückend; *strikes* alles lähmend *attr*; **a ~ disease** ein Leiden, das einen bewegungsunfähig macht; **a ~ blow** *(lit, fig)* ein schwerer Schlag

cripplingly [ˈkrɪplɪŋlɪ] ADV *expensive* unerschwinglich

crisis [ˈkraɪsɪs] N *pl* **crises** [ˈkraɪsiːz] Krise *f* *(also Med)*; **to reach ~ point** den Höhepunkt erreichen; **that was a ~ in his life** *(= decisive moment)* das war ein entscheidender Punkt in seinem Leben; *(= emotional crisis)* das war eine Krise in seinem Leben; **at this time of ~** in dieser krisenreichen *or* schweren Zeit; **in times of ~** in Krisenzeiten

crisis: **crisis centre** N Einsatzzentrum *nt (für Krisenfälle)*; **rape ~** Beratungsstelle *f (für Frauen, die Opfer einer Vergewaltigung geworden sind)*; **crisis management** N Krisenmanagement *nt*

crisp [krɪsp] ADJ *(+er) apple, lettuce* knackig, fest; *bread, biscuits, bacon* knusprig; *snow* verharscht; *leaves* trocken; *appearance* adrett, frisch; *curls, clothes* steif; *manner, voice, style of writing, remark* knapp; *air, weather, colour* frisch; *sound* klar; *(Sport) shot* sauber; *ten-pound note* brandneu; **a ~ dry white wine** ein leichter, trockener Weißwein; **a ~ spring morning** ein frischer Frühlingsmorgen

N *(Brit: = potato crisp)* Chip *m*; **to burn sth to a ~** etw verbrutzeln lassen; *toast* etw verkohlen lassen; **burned** *or* **blackened to a ~** völlig verbrutzelt; *toast* völlig verkohlt

VT *(also* **crisp up***) bread* aufbacken

crispbread [ˈkrɪspbred] N Knäckebrot *nt*

crispen (up) [ˈkrɪspn(ˈʌp)] VT *sep bread* aufbacken; *blouse etc* auffrischen

crisper [ˈkrɪspəˈ] N *(in fridge)* Gemüsefach *nt*

crisply [ˈkrɪsplɪ] ADV knackig; *baked, fried* knusprig; *starched* steif; *dressed* adrett, frisch; *write, speak* knapp; **the snow crunched ~ under his feet** der Schnee knirschte unter seinen Füßen; **the notes rang out ~** die Töne kamen klar

crispness [ˈkrɪspnɪs] N *(of apple, lettuce)* Knackigkeit *f*, Festheit *f*; *(of bread, biscuits, bacon)* Knusprigkeit *f*; *(of snow)* Verharschtheit *f*; *(of leaves)* Trockenheit *f*; *(of clothes)* Steifheit *f*; *(of manner, voice, style of writing)* Knappheit *f*; *(of air, weather)* Frische *f*; *(of sound)* Klarheit *f*; *(Sport, of shot)* Sauberkeit *f*

crispy [ˈkrɪspɪ] ADJ *(+er) (inf)* knusprig

crisscross [ˈkrɪskrɒs] N Kreuzundquer *nt* ADJ *pattern* Kreuz- ADV kreuz und quer VT mit einem Kreuzmuster versehen

crit [krɪt] N *(inf, of book etc)* Kritik *f*

criterion [kraɪˈtɪərɪən] N *pl* **criteria** [kraɪˈtɪərɪə] Kriterium *nt*; **then, by the same ~, he is guilty too** dann ist er ebenso schuldig

critic [ˈkrɪtɪk] N Kritiker(in) *m(f)*; **literary ~** Literaturkritiker(in) *m(f)*; **he's a terrible ~** *(= very critical)* er ist schrecklich kritisch; **he's his own worst ~** er kritisiert sich selbst am meisten, er ist sein schlimmster Kritiker; **she is a strong/constant ~ of the government** sie kritisiert die Regierung heftig/ständig *or* heftig/ständig an der Regierung

critical [ˈkrɪtɪkəl] ADJ **a** *(= fault-finding, discriminating)* kritisch; **the book was a ~ success** das Buch kam bei den Kritikern an; **the book met with ~ acclaim** das Buch fand Anklang bei den Kritikern *or* wurde in den Kritiken gelobt; **~ reviews** Kritiken *pl*; **~ edition** kritische Ausgabe; **to cast a ~ eye over sth** sich *(dat)* etw kritisch ansehen; **to be ~ of sb/sth** jdn/etw kritisieren **b** *(= dangerous, Sci)* kritisch; *(= crucial also)* entscheidend; *(Med) person* in kritischem Zustand; **it is ~ (for us) to understand what is happening** es ist (für uns) von entscheidender Bedeutung zu wissen, was vorgeht; **of ~ importance** von entscheidender Bedeutung; **to be on the ~ list** *(Med)* in kritischem Zustand sein

critically [ˈkrɪtɪkəlɪ] ADV **a** *(= finding fault)* kritisch **b** *ill* schwer **c** *(= crucially)* **to be ~ important** von entscheidender Bedeutung sein **d** *(Art, Liter etc)* **~ acclaimed** in den Kritiken gelobt

critical mass N *(Phys)* kritische Masse; *(fig)* Mindestanforderung *f*; **to reach ~** *(fig)* einen kritischen Punkt erreichen

critical path N kritischer Pfad; **~ analysis** kritische Pfadanalyse

criticism [ˈkrɪtɪsɪzəm] ✪ 26.3 N Kritik *f*; **literary ~** Literaturkritik *f*; **to come in for a lot of ~** schwer kritisiert werden; **the decision is open to ~** das ist eine sehr anfechtbare Entscheidung

criticize [ˈkrɪtɪsaɪz] ✪ 26.3 VI kritisieren VT kritisieren; **to ~ sb for sth** jdn für etw kritisieren; **I ~d her for always being late** ich kritisierte sie dafür, dass sie immer zu spät kommt

critique [krɪˈtiːk] N Kritik *f*

critter [ˈkrɪtəˈ] N *(US dial)* = **creature**

croak [krəʊk] N *(of frog)* Quaken *nt no pl*; *(of raven, person)* Krächzen *nt no pl* VI *(frog)* quaken; *(raven, person)* krächzen VT **a** *(person)* krächzen **b** *(inf: = die)* **he ~ed it** er ist abgekratzt *(inf)*

croaky [ˈkrəʊkɪ] ADJ *(+er) (inf) voice* krächzend; **you sound a bit ~** du klingst etwas heiser

Croat [ˈkrəʊæt] N *(= person)* Kroate *m*, Kroatin *f*; *(Ling)* Kroatisch *nt*

Croatia [krəʊˈeɪʃɪə] N Kroatien *nt*

Croatian [krəʊˈeɪʃɪən] N = **Croat** ADJ kroatisch; **she is ~** sie ist Kroatin

crochet [ˈkrəʊʃeɪ] N *(also* **crochet work***)* Häkelei *f*; **~ hook** Häkelnadel *f*; **to do a lot of ~** viel häkeln VTI häkeln

crock[1] [krɒk] N *(= jar)* Topf *m*; **what a ~ of shit!** *(US sl)* was für ein Haufen Scheiße *(sl)*

crock[2] N *(inf) (= vehicle)* Kiste *f (inf)*; *(= person)* Wrack *nt (inf)*; *(= horse)* Klepper *m*; **an old ~s race** ein Oldtimerrennen *nt*

crocked [krɒkt] ADJ *(US inf)* breit *(sl)*

crockery [ˈkrɒkərɪ] N *(Brit)* Geschirr *nt*

crocodile [ˈkrɒkədaɪl] N **a** Krokodil *nt* **b** *(Brit Sch)* **to walk in a ~** zwei und zwei hintereinandergehen; **the long ~ of little girls** der lange Zug kleiner Mädchen, die zwei und zwei hintereinandergehen

crocodile: **crocodile clip** N Krokodilklemme *f*; **crocodile tears** PL Krokodilstränen *pl*; **to shed ~** Krokodilstränen vergießen

crocus [ˈkrəʊkəs] N Krokus *m*

Croesus [ˈkriːsəs] N Krösus *m*; **to be as rich as ~** ein (richtiger) Krösus sein

croft [krɒft] N *(esp Scot)* kleines Pachtgrundstück; *(= house)* Kate *f*

crofter [ˈkrɒftəˈ] N *(esp Scot)* Kleinpächter(in) *m(f)*

crofting [ˈkrɒftɪŋ] *(esp Scot)* N *Bewirtschaftung von kleinen Pachtgrundstücken* ADJ *attr community* von Kleinpächtern

Crohn's disease [ˈkrəʊnzdɪˌziːz] N *(Med)* Morbus Crohn *m*

croissant [ˈkrwɑːsɒŋ] N Hörnchen *nt*

crone [krəʊn] N Tante *f (inf)*

crony [ˈkrəʊnɪ] N Freund(in) *m(f)*, Spießgeselle *(hum) m*

cronyism [ˈkrəʊnɪɪzəm] N *no pl (pej)* Vetternwirtschaft *f (pej)*

crook[1] [krʊk] N **a** *(= dishonest person)* Gauner *m (inf)* **b** *(= staff, of shepherd)* Hirtenstab *m*, Krummstab *m*; *(of bishop also)* Bischofsstab *m* → **hook** **c** *(= bend: in arm)* Beuge *f* VT *finger* krümmen; *arm* beugen; **she only has to ~ her (little) finger and he comes running** sie braucht nur mit dem kleinen Finger zu winken und schon kommt er angerannt

crook[2] ADJ *(Austral inf)* **a** *(= sick)* krank; **he's ~ with the flu/a cold** er hat die Grippe/eine Erkältung; **he feels ~** er fühlt sich mies *(inf)* *or* lausig *(inf)*; **he is ~** es geht ihm mies *(inf)* **b** *(= not functioning)* kaputt *(inf)*; *(= not good)* mies *(inf)* **c** *(= angry)* wild *(inf)*; **to go ~ at** *or* **on sb** wegen jdm wild werden

crooked [ˈkrʊkɪd] ADJ *(lit: = bent)* krumm; *(= tilted, sloping also) smile* schief; *(fig inf: = dishonest) method* krumm; *person* unehrlich; **your hat's ~** dein Hut sitzt schief

crookedly ['krʊkɪdlɪ] ADV *hang, smile, grin* schief

croon [kru:n] VT *(= sing softly)* leise *or* sanft singen; *(usu pej, sentimentally)* gefühlvoll *or* schmalzig *(pej inf)* singen VI *(= sing softly)* leise *or* sanft singen; *(usu pej, sentimentally)* Schnulzen *(pej inf) or* sentimentale Lieder singen

crooner ['kru:nəʳ] N Sänger *m* (sentimentaler Lieder), Schnulzensänger *m (pej inf)*

crop [krɒp] N **a** *(= produce)* Ernte *f*; *(= species grown)* (Feld)frucht *f*, Nutzpflanze; *(fig: = large number)* Schwung *m*; **the cereal ~s were destroyed** die Getreideernte wurde zerstört; **the barley ~ is looking good** die Gerste steht gut; **a good ~ of fruit/potatoes** eine gute Obst-/Kartoffelernte; **the beef ~** die Rindfleischproduktion; **to be in** *or* **under/out of ~** bebaut/nicht bebaut sein; **he grows a different ~ every year** er baut jedes Jahr etwas anderes an; **to bring the ~s in** die Ernte einbringen; **a ~ of students/problems** *(inf)* eine Reihe von Studenten/Problemen
b *(of bird)* Kropf *m*
c *(of whip)* Stock *m*; *(= hunting crop)* Reitpeitsche *f*
d *(= hairstyle)* Kurzhaarschnitt *m*; **to give sb a close ~** jdm die Haare gehörig stutzen
VT *hair* stutzen; *horse's or dog's tail also* kupieren; **her husband was ~ped from the photograph** ihr Mann war auf dem Foto weggeschnitten; **it's best to keep the grass ~ped short** man sollte das Gras kurz halten; **the goat ~ped the grass** die Ziege fraß das Gras ab; **~ped hair, hair ~ped short** kurz geschnittenes Haar

▶ **crop out** VI auftauchen; *(minerals)* zutage *or* zu Tage treten

▶ **crop up** VI aufkommen; **something's cropped up** es ist etwas dazwischengekommen; **he was ready for anything that might crop up** er war auf alle Eventualitäten gefasst

crop: **crop circle** N Kornkreis *m*; **crop-dusting** ['krɒpdʌstɪŋ] N Schädlingsbekämpfung *f (aus dem Flugzeug)*; **crop failure** N Missernte *f*

cropped [ˌkrɒpt] ADJ *(Fashion)* **~ top** bauchfreies Shirt; **~ trousers** *(Brit)* Caprihose *f*

cropper ['krɒpəʳ] N **a** *(= person)* Anbauer *m*; **these plants are poor ~s** diese Pflanzen bringen nicht viel Ertrag **b** *(Brit inf)* **to come a ~** *(lit: = fall)* hinfliegen *(inf)*; *(fig: = fail)* auf die Nase fallen

crop: **crop rotation** N Fruchtwechsel *m*; **crop-sprayer** N *(= person)* Schädlingsbekämpfer(in) *m(f)*; *(= plane)* Schädlingsbekämpfungsflugzeug *nt*; *(= tractor)* Schädlingsbekämpfungsfahrzeug *nt*, Besprühungsfahrzeug *nt*; **crop-spraying** N Schädlingsbekämpfung *f (durch Besprühen)*

croquet ['krəʊkeɪ] N Krocket(spiel) *nt*; **~ lawn** Krocketrasen *m*

croquette [krəʊ'ket] N Krokette *f*

crosier, crozier ['krəʊʒɪəʳ] N Bischofsstab *m*, Hirtenstab *m*, Krummstab *m*

cross[1] [krɒs] ✪ 27.7 N **a** Kreuz *nt*; **to make one's ~** sein Kreuz(chen) machen *or* setzen; **to make the sign of the Cross** das Kreuzzeichen machen *or* schlagen; **the Cross and the Crescent** Kreuz und Halbmond; **to bear/take up one's ~** *(fig)* sein Kreuz tragen/auf sich *(acc)* nehmen; **we all have our ~ to bear** wir haben alle unser Kreuz zu tragen
b *(= bias)* **on the ~** schräg; **to be cut on the ~** schräg geschnitten sein
c *(= hybrid)* Kreuzung *f*; *(fig)* Mittelding *nt*; **a ~ between a laugh and a bark** eine Mischung aus Lachen und Bellen
d *(Ftbl)* Flanke *f*; **to hit a ~ to sb** jdm zuflanken
e *(Boxing)* Seitwärtshaken *m*
ATTR *(= transverse) street, line etc* Quer-
VT **a** *(= go across) road, river, mountains* überqueren; *(on foot) picket line etc* überschreiten; *country, desert, room* durchqueren; **to ~ the road** über die Straße gehen, die Straße überqueren; **to ~ sb's path** *(fig)* jdm über den Weg laufen; **it ~ed my mind that ...** es fiel mir ein, dass ..., mir kam der Gedanke, dass ...; **a smile ~ed her lips** ein Lächeln kam über ihre Lippen; **don't ~ your bridges until you come to them** *(prov)* lass die Probleme auf dich zukommen; **we'll ~ that bridge when we come to it** lassen wir das Problem mal auf uns zukommen, das sind ungelegte Eier *(inf)*; **they have clearly ~ed the boundary into terrorism** sie haben eindeutig die Grenze zum Terrorismus überschritten
b *(= put at right-angles, intersect)* kreuzen; **to ~ one's legs** die Beine übereinanderschlagen; **to ~ one's arms** die Arme verschränken; **the lines are ~ed, we have a ~ed line** *(Telec)* die Leitungen überschneiden sich; **line AB ~es line CD at point E** AB schneidet CD in E; **to ~ sb's palm with silver** jdm ein Geldstück in die Hand drücken; **keep your fingers ~ed for me!** *(inf)* drück *or* halt mir die Daumen! *(inf)*; **I'm keeping my fingers ~ed (for you)** *(inf)* ich drücke *or* halte (dir) die Daumen *(inf)*
c *(= put a line across) letter, t* einen Querstrich machen durch; *(Brit) cheque* ≈ zur Verrechnung ausstellen; **a ~ed cheque** ein Verrechnungsscheck *m*; **to ~ sth through** etw durchstreichen → **dot**
d *(= make the sign of the Cross)* **to ~ oneself** sich bekreuzigen; **~ my/your heart** *(inf)* Ehrenwort, Hand aufs Herz
e *(= mark with a cross)* ankreuzen
f *(= go against) plans* durchkreuzen; **to ~ sb** jdn verärgern; **to be ~ed in love** in der Liebe enttäuscht werden
g *animal, fruit* kreuzen
VI **a** *(across road)* hinübergehen, die Straße überqueren; *(across Channel etc)* hinüberfahren; **"cross now"** „gehen"; **to ~ at the green light** bei Grün über die Straße gehen
b *(= intersect)* sich kreuzen; *(lines also)* sich schneiden; **our paths have ~ed several times** *(fig)* unsere Wege haben sich öfters gekreuzt
c *(letters etc)* sich kreuzen

▶ **cross off** VT *sep* streichen *(prep obj* aus, von)

▶ **cross out** VT *sep* ausstreichen

▶ **cross over** VI **a** *(= cross the road)* hinübergehen, die Straße überqueren **b** *(= change sides)* übergehen, überwechseln *(to* zu) VI *+prep obj road, street* überqueren

cross[2] ADJ *(+er)* böse, sauer *(inf)*; **to be ~ with sb** mit jdm *or* auf jdn böse sein

cross: **cross-action** N *(Jur)* Widerklage *f*; **crossbar** N *(of bicycle)* Stange *f*; *(Sport)* Querlatte *f*; **crossbeam** N *(= girder)* Querbalken *m*; *(Sport)* Schwebebalken *m*; **cross-bench** N *usu pl (Parl) Bank, wo die weder zur Regierungs- noch zur Oppositionspartei gehörenden Abgeordneten sitzen*; **cross-bencher** ['krɒsbentʃəʳ] N *(Parl) Abgeordneter, der weder der Regierungs- noch der Oppositionspartei angehört*; **crossbill** N *(Orn)* Kreuzschnabel *m*; **crossbones** PL gekreuzte Knochen *pl (unter einem Totenkopf)* → **skull**; **crossbow** N (Stand)armbrust *f*; **cross brace** N Kreuz- *or* Querverstrebung *f*; **crossbred** ADJ *(Zool, Biol)* gekreuzt; **crossbreed** *(Zool, Biol)* N Kreuzung *f* VT kreuzen; **cross-Channel** ADJ *attr ferries, swimmer* Kanal-; **a ~ swim** ein Durchschwimmen *nt* des Kanals; **crosscheck** N Gegenprobe *f* VT *facts, figures* überprüfen; *equation* die Gegenprobe machen bei; **cross-compiler** N *(Comput)* Crosscompiler *m*; **cross-country** ADJ Querfeldein-; **~ ski** Langlaufski *m*; **~ skier** Langläufer(in) *m(f)*; **~ skiing** Langlauf *m*; **~ ski track** (Langlauf)loipe *f* ADV querfeldein N *(= race)* Querfeldeinrennen *nt*; **cross-court** *(Tennis)* ADV *hit* cross, diagonal über den Platz ADJ **to hit** *or* **play a ~ forehand** die Vorhand cross schlagen; **cross-cultural** ADJ multikulturell; **crosscurrent** N Gegenströmung *f*; **cross-dress** VI sich als Transvestit kleiden; **cross-dresser** N Transvestit *m*; **cross-dressing** N Transvestismus *m*; **cross-examination** N Kreuzverhör *nt* (of über *+acc*); **cross-examine** VT ins Kreuzverhör nehmen; **cross-eyed** ADJ schielend; **to be ~** schielen; **cross-fertilization** N *no pl (Bot)* Kreuzbefruchtung *f*, Fremdbestäubung *f*; *(fig)* gegenseitige Befruchtung; **cross-fertilize** VT *(Bot)* kreuzbefruchten; **crossfield** ADJ **~ pass** *(Ftbl, Hockey)* Querpass *m*; **crossfire** N Kreuzfeuer *nt*; **to be caught in the ~** *(lit, fig)* ins Kreuzfeuer geraten; **cross-gartered** ADJ *(old)* mit kreuzweise geschnürten Waden; **cross-grained** ADJ *wood* quer gefasert; *(= grumpy)* mürrisch; *(= perverse)* querköpfig; **cross hairs** PL Fadenkreuz *nt*; **crosshatch** VT mit Kreuzlagen schattieren; **crosshatching** N Kreuzschattierung *f*

crossing ['krɒsɪŋ] N **a** *(= act)* Überquerung *f*; *(= sea crossing)* Überfahrt *f* **b** *(= crossing place)* Übergang *m*; *(= crossroads)* Kreuzung *f*

crossing point N *(of border)* Grenzübergang *m*

cross: **cross-keys** PL *(Her)* gekreuzte Schlüssel *pl*; **crosskick** N *(Ftbl)* Querpass *m* (nach innen); **cross-legged** [ˌkrɒs'leg(ɪ)d] ADJ ADV mit gekreuzten Beinen; *(on ground)* im Schneidersitz; **cross liability** N *(Jur)* beiderseitige Haftpflicht

crossly ['krɒslɪ] ADV böse, verärgert

cross: **cross-match** VT *(Med)* kreuzen; **cross-matching** N *(Med)* Kreuzprobe *f*; **crossover** N *(Rail)* Gleiskreuzung *f*; *(Mus)* Crossover *m*; **a jazz-rap ~** ein Jazz-Rap-Cross-over *m*; **cross-party** ADJ *(Pol) talks* zwischen den Parteien, parteienübergreifend; *support, committee* überparteilich; **crosspatch** N *(inf)* Brummbär *m (inf)*; **crosspiece** N *(= bar)* Querstange *f*; **cross-ply** ADJ Diagonal- N *(inf)* Diagonalreifen *m*;; **cross-pollinate** VT fremdbestäuben; **cross-pollination** N Fremdbestäubung *f*; **cross-purposes** PL **to be** *or* **talk at ~** aneinander vorbeireden; **he was at ~ with her** sie haben aneinander vorbeigeredet; **cross-question** VT = **cross-examine**; **cross-rate** N *(St Ex)* Kreuznotierung *f*, Kreuzkurs *m*; **cross-refer** VT verweisen *(to* auf *+acc)*; **cross-reference** N (Quer)verweis *m (to* auf *+acc)* VT = **cross-refer**; **crossroads** N *sing or pl (lit)* Kreuzung *f*; *(fig)* Scheideweg *m*; **cross section** N Querschnitt *m*; **to draw sth in ~** etw im Querschnitt zeichnen; **a ~ of the population** ein Querschnitt durch die Bevölkerung; **cross-stitch** N *(Sew)* Kreuzstich *m* VT im Kreuzstich arbeiten; **cross sum** N *(Math)* Quersumme *f*; **crosstalk** N *no pl* **a** *(witty)* Wortgefecht *nt*, Wortgefechte *pl* **b** *(Telec)* Nebensprechen *nt*; **cross-town** ADJ *(US)* quer durch die Stadt; **crosswalk** N *(US)* Fußgängerüberweg *m*; **crossways** ADV = **crosswise**; **crosswind** N Seitenwind *m*; **crosswise** ADV quer; **crossword (puzzle)** N Kreuzworträtsel *nt*; **crosswort** N Kreuzlabkraut *nt*

crotch [krɒtʃ] N **a** *(in tree etc)* Gabelung *f* **b** *(of trousers)* Schritt *m*; *(Anat)* Unterleib *m*; **a kick in the ~** ein Tritt zwischen die Beine; **she wears her skirts about an inch below the ~** ihre Röcke reichen nur ein Paar Zentimeter über den Po *(inf)*

crotchet ['krɒtʃɪt] N **a** *(Brit Mus)* Viertelnote *f*; **~ rest** Viertelpause *f* **b** *(inf: = cross person)* Miesepeter *m (inf)*

crotchety ['krɒtʃɪtɪ] ADJ *(inf: = cross)* schlecht gelaunt, miesepetrig *(inf)*; *child* quengelig *(inf)*

crouch [kraʊtʃ] VI sich zusammenkauern, kauern; **to ~ down** sich niederkauern N Hocke *f*; *(of animal)* Kauerstellung *f*

croup[1] [kru:p] N *no pl (Med)* Krupp *m*, Kehlkopfdiphtherie *f*

croup[2] N *(of horse)* Kruppe *f*

croupier ['kru:pɪeɪ] N Croupier *m*

crouton ['kru:tɒn] N Croûton *m*

crow[1] [krəʊ] N **a** *(Orn)* Krähe *f*; **as the ~ flies** (in der) Luftlinie; **to eat ~** *(US inf)* zu Kreuze kriechen **b** *(inf)* = **crowbar**

crow[2] N *(of cock, baby)* Krähen *nt no pl*; *(of person)* J(a)uchzer *m*; **a ~ of delight** ein Freudenjauchzer *m* VI **a** *pret* **crowed** *or (old)* **crew**, *ptp* **crowed** *(cock)* krähen **b** *pret, ptp* **crowed** *(fig:*

= boast) sich brüsten, angeben *(about* mit); *(= exult)* hämisch frohlocken *(over* über *+acc)*

crow: **crowbar** ['krəʊbɑː'] N Brecheisen *nt*; **crowberry** N Krähenbeere *f*

crowd [kraʊd] **N** **a** Menschenmenge *f*; *(Sport, Theat)* Zuschauermenge *f*; **to be swept along by the ~** von der *or* in der Menge mitgerissen werden; **to get lost in the ~(s)** in der Menge verloren gehen; **~s of people** Menschenmassen *pl*, große Menschenmengen *pl*; **that would pass in a ~** *(fig)* das geht (durch), wenn man nicht zu genau hinsieht; **to get a good ~ at a match** bei einem Spiel eine Menge Zuschauer haben; **there was quite a ~** es waren eine ganze Menge Leute da; **a whole ~ of us** ein ganzer Haufen von uns *(inf)*
b *(= set of people, clique)* Clique *f*, Haufen *m* *(inf)*; **the university ~** der Uni-Haufen *(inf)*, die Uni-Clique; **the usual ~** die üblichen Leute; **I'm not one of that ~** ich gehöre nicht zu diesem Haufen *(inf) or* zu denen; **they're a nice ~** sie sind ein netter Haufen *(inf)*
c *no pl (= the masses)* **the ~** die (breite) Masse; **to go with** *or* **follow the ~** mit der Herde laufen; **she hates to be just one of the ~** sie geht nicht gern in der Masse unter
VI (sich) drängen; **to ~ (a)round** sich herumdrängen; **to ~ together** sich zusammendrängen; **to ~ in** (sich) hereindrängen; **to ~ (a)round sb/sth** (sich) um jdn/etw herumdrängen
VT **a** **to ~ the streets** die Straßen bevölkern; **to ~ a room with furniture** ein Zimmer mit Möbeln vollstopfen; **it will really ~ the office having three new people** mit drei neuen Leuten wird es im Büro sicherlich eng werden; **to ~ things together** Dinge eng zusammendrängen
b *(inf: = harass)* **to ~ sb** jdn drängeln, jdm auf den Füßen stehen *(inf)*; *(creditors)* jdn bedrängen

► **crowd out** VT *sep (= not let in)* wegdrängen; *(= make leave)* herausdrängen; *(Press) article etc* verdrängen; **the pub was crowded out** das Lokal war gerammelt voll *(inf) or* proppenvoll *(inf)*

crowd control N *no pl* **~ was becoming difficult** die Kontrolle der Massen wurde schwierig; **expert in ~** Sicherheitsexperte *m*/-expertin *f*

crowded ['kraʊdɪd] ADJ **a** *(= filled with people) train, shop etc* überfüllt; **the streets/shops/trains are ~** es ist voll auf den Straßen/in den Geschäften/in den Zügen; **~ with people** voller Menschen; **a room ~ with children** ein Zimmer voller Kinder; **to play to a ~ house** *(Theat)* vor vollem Haus spielen; **the holiday was ~ with incidents** die Ferien waren sehr ereignisreich; **a mind ~ with facts** eine Ansammlung von Faktenwissen (im Kopf)
b *(= overpopulated) city, district* überbevölkert; *conditions* beengt; **it's a ~ profession** es ist ein überfüllter Berufszweig

crowd: **crowd pleaser** ['kraʊdpliːzə'] N *(= person)* Publikumsliebling *m*; *(= event etc)* Publikumserfolg *m*; **crowd puller** ['kraʊdpʊlə'] N Kassenmagnet *m*; **crowd scene** N *(Theat)* Massenszene *f*; **crowd trouble** N *no pl* Massenausschreitungen *pl*

crowfoot ['krəʊfʊt] N *(Bot)* Hahnenfuß *m*

crown [kraʊn] **N** **a** *(for royalty)* Krone *f*; **~ of thorns** Dornenkrone *f*; **the Crown** die Krone; **to wear the ~** auf dem Thron sitzen; **to be heir to the ~** Thronfolger(in) *m(f)* sein; **to succeed to the ~** die Thronfolge antreten
b *(= coin)* Krone *f*
c *(= top) (of head)* Wirbel *m*; *(= skull)* Schädel *m*; *(= head measurement)* Kopf(umfang) *m*; *(of hat)* Kopf *m*; *(of road)* Wölbung *f*; *(of arch)* Scheitelpunkt *m*; *(of roof)* First *m*; *(of tooth, tree)* Krone *f*; *(of hill)* Kuppe *f*
d *(= size of paper) englisches Papierformat (ca. 45 × 38 cm²)*
e *(fig: = climax, completion)* Krönung *f*
VT **a** *king, queen* krönen; **he was ~ed king** er ist zum König gekrönt worden
b *(= top)* **the hill is ~ed with trees** die Bergkuppe ist mit Bäumen bewachsen; **the cake was ~ed with marzipan decorations** der Kuchen war zur Krönung des Ganzen (noch) mit Marzipanfiguren geschmückt; **to be ~ed with success** *(fig)* von Erfolg gekrönt sein
c *(fig: = form climax to)* krönen; **to ~ it all it began to snow** *(inf)* zur Krönung des Ganzen begann es zu schneien; **that ~s everything!** *(inf)* das ist doch der Gipfel *or* die Höhe! *(inf)*
d *(in draughts etc)* eine Dame bekommen mit
e *tooth* eine Krone machen für; **the tooth had been ~ed before** der Zahn hatte schon vorher eine Krone gehabt
f *(inf: = hit)* eine runterhauen *(+dat) (inf)*

crown: **Crown Agent** N *(Brit Pol) Mitglied des Entwicklungshilfeausschusses*; **crown cap** N = **crown cork**; **crown colony** N Kronkolonie *f*; **crown cork** N Kron(en)korken *m*; **crown court** N *Bezirksgericht für Strafsachen*

crowned head [ˌkraʊnd'hed] N gekröntes Haupt

crown green bowling N *(Brit)* ≈ Boule *nt*

crowning ['kraʊnɪŋ] **N** Krönung *f* **ADJ** *success, achievement* krönend; **her hair was her ~ glory** ihr Haar war ihre größte Zierde; **that symphony was his ~ glory** diese Sinfonie war die Krönung seines Werkes

crown: **crown jewels** PL Kronjuwelen *pl*; **crown lands** PL königliche Ländereien *pl*, Ländereien *pl* der Krone; **Crown law** N *(Brit: Jur)* Strafrecht *nt*; **crown prince** N Kronprinz *m*; **crown princess** N Kronprinzessin *f*; **crown wheel** N Kronenrad *nt*, Kammrad *nt*; **crown witness** N Zeuge *m*/Zeugin *f* der Anklage

crow's: **crow's feet** PL Krähenfüße *pl*; **crow's nest** N *(Naut)* Mastkorb *m*; *(on foremast)* Krähennest *nt*, Ausguck *m*

crozier N = **crosier**

crucial ['kruːʃəl] ADJ **a** *(= decisive)* entscheidend *(to* für) **b** *(= very important)* äußerst wichtig **c** *(Med) incision etc* kreuzförmig

crucially ['kruːʃəlɪ] ADV ausschlaggebend; *different* bedeutend; **~ important** von entscheidender Bedeutung; **~, he is 10 years older than she is** von entscheidender Bedeutung ist, dass er 10 Jahre älter ist als sie

cruciate ['kruːʃɪeɪt] ADJ kreuzförmig; **~ ligament** Kreuzband *nt*

crucible ['kruːsɪbl] N (Schmelz)tiegel *m*

crucible steel N Tiegelgussstahl *m*

crucifix ['kruːsɪfɪks] N Kruzifix *nt*

crucifixion [ˌkruːsɪ'fɪkʃən] N Kreuzigung *f*

cruciform ['kruːsɪfɔːm] ADJ kreuzförmig

crucify ['kruːsɪfaɪ] VT **a** *(lit)* kreuzigen **b** *(fig inf) play, author* verreißen; *person* in der Luft zerreißen *(inf)* **c** *(= mortify) the flesh* abtöten

crud [krʌd] N *(inf)* **a** *(= dirt)* Dreck *m (lit, fig)* **b** *(pej: = person)* Scheißkerl *m (pej)*

cruddy ['krʌdɪ] ADJ *(+er) (inf)* blöd *(inf)*, bescheuert *(inf)*

crude [kruːd] **ADJ** *(+er)* **a** *(= unprocessed)* Roh-, roh **b** *(= vulgar) expression, story etc* ordinär, derb **c** *(= unsophisticated) method, model, implement* primitiv; *sketch* grob; *manners* ungehobelt, grob; *attempt* unbeholfen **N** Rohöl *nt*

crudely ['kruːdlɪ] ADV **a** *(= vulgarly)* ordinär, derb **b** *(= unsophisticatedly)* primitiv; *behave* ungehobelt; *(= approximately) estimate, draw* grob; **to put it ~** um es ganz grob auszudrücken

crudeness ['kruːdnɪs], **crudity** ['kruːdɪtɪ] N **a** *(= vulgarity)* Derbheit *f* **b** *(= lack of sophistication) (of method, model, implement)* Primitivität *f*; *(of sketch)* Grobheit *f*; *(of manners)* Ungehobelte(s) *nt (of +gen, in +dat)*; *(of attempt)* Unbeholfenheit *f*

crude oil N Rohöl *nt*

crudités ['kruːdɪteɪz] PL *rohes Gemüse, serviert mit Dips*

cruel ['krʊəl] ADJ grausam *(to* zu); *remark, wit, critic, winter also* unbarmherzig; **to be ~ to animals** ein Tierquäler sein; **to be ~ to one's dog** seinen Hund quälen; **that is ~ to animals** das ist Tierquälerei; **don't be ~!** sei nicht so gemein!; **sometimes you have to be ~ to be kind** manchmal ist es letzten Endes besser, wenn man hart ist

cruelly ['krʊəlɪ] ADV *(+vb)* grausam; *(+adj)* auf grausame Art

cruelty ['krʊəltɪ] N Grausamkeit *f (to* gegenüber); *(of remark, critic also)* Unbarmherzigkeit *f*; **~ to children** Kindesmisshandlung *f*; **~ to animals** Tierquälerei *f*; **physical ~** Grausamkeit *f*; **mental ~** seelische Grausamkeit

cruelty-free ADJ *cosmetics* nicht an Tieren getestet

cruet ['kruːɪt] N **a** *(= set)* Gewürzständer *m*, Menage *f*; *(for oil)* Krügchen *nt*; **would you pass the ~?** könnten Sie mir bitte die Gewürze reichen? **b** *(Eccl)* Krügchen *nt*

cruise [kruːz] **VI** **a** *(person)* eine Kreuzfahrt machen; *(ship)* kreuzen, eine Kreuzfahrt machen
b *(= travel at cruising speed) (car)* Dauergeschwindigkeit fahren; *(aircraft)* (mit Reisegeschwindigkeit) fliegen; *(athlete)* locker laufen; *(= drive around)* herumfahren; **the car ~s happily along at 90** 90 ist eine ideale Fahrgeschwindigkeit für das Auto; **we were cruising along the road** wir fuhren (gemächlich) die Straße entlang; **we are now cruising at a height/speed of ...** wir fliegen nun in einer Flughöhe/mit einer Reisegeschwindigkeit von ...; **the cyclist ~d down the hill** der Radfahrer rollte den Berg hinunter
c *(fig)* **to ~ to victory** einen leichten Sieg erringen
VT *(ship)* befahren; *(car) streets* fahren auf *(+dat)*; *area* abfahren
N Kreuzfahrt *f*; **to go on** *or* **for a ~** eine Kreuzfahrt machen

cruise control N *(Aut)* Tempomat *m*, Tempostat *m*

cruise missile N Cruisemissile *nt*, Marschflugkörper *m*

cruiser ['kruːzə'] N *(Naut)* Kreuzer *m*; *(= pleasure cruiser)* Vergnügungsjacht *f*

cruiserweight ['kruːzəweɪt] N *(Boxing)* Halbschwergewicht *nt*

cruising ['kruːzɪŋ] N Kreuzfahrten *pl*; **to go ~** eine Kreuzfahrt/Kreuzfahrten machen

cruising: **cruising altitude** N Reiseflughöhe *f*; **cruising speed** N Reisegeschwindigkeit *f*; **cruising yacht** N Vergnügungsjacht *f*

cruller ['krʌlə'] N *(US Cook) eine Art Berliner*

crumb [krʌm] **N** **a** *(of bread etc)* Krümel *m*, Krume *f*, Brösel *m*; *(inside of loaf)* Krume *f*; **can you spare a ~?** haben Sie eine Scheibe Brot für einen hungrigen Menschen?; **~s from the rich man's/master's table** Brosamen, die von des Reichen/des Herren Tisch fallen; **a few ~s of information** ein paar Informationsbrocken; **that's one ~ of comfort** das ist (wenigstens) ein winziger Trost **b** *(inf) (= fool)* Depp *m (inf)*; *(= brute)* Lump *m (inf)* **INTERJ** **~s!** *(inf)* Mensch! *(inf)*, Mensch Meier! *(inf)* **VT** *(Cook) fish etc* panieren

crumble ['krʌmbl] **VT** zerkrümeln, zerbröckeln; **to ~ sth into/onto sth** etw in/auf etw *(acc)* krümeln *or* bröckeln **VI** *(brick, earth)* bröckeln; *(bread, cake etc)* krümeln; *(also* **crumble away***)* *(earth, building)* zerbröckeln; *(fig) (resistance, opposition)* sich auflösen, schmelzen; *(hopes)* schwinden; *(plans)* ins Wanken geraten **N** *(Brit Cook)* Obst *nt* mit Streusel; *(= topping)* Streusel *pl*; **apple/rhubarb ~** *mit Streuseln bestreutes, überbackenes Apfel-/Rhabarberdessert*

crumbly ['krʌmblɪ] ADJ *(+er) stone, earth* bröckelig; *cake, bread* krümelig, bröselig

crummy ['krʌmɪ] ADJ *(+er) (inf)* mies *(inf)*, Scheiß- *(sl)*

crumpet ['krʌmpɪt] N a *(Cook)* *süßes, pfannkuchenartiges Gebäck* b *(dated esp Brit inf: = women)* Miezen *pl (inf)*; **he fancied a bit of ~** ihm war nach ein bisschen Sex; **she's a nice bit of ~** sie ist sehr sexy

crumple ['krʌmpl] VT *(also* **crumple up***)* *paper, dress, fabric (= crease)* zer- *or* verknittern, zerknautschen; *(= screw up)* zusammenknüllen; *metal* eindrücken; **the force of the impact ~d the bonnet/car** die Wucht des Aufpralls drückte die Kühlerhaube ein/quetschte das Auto zusammen VI *(lit, fig: = collapse)* zusammenbrechen; *(= get creased: paper)* krumpeln, knittern; *(car, metal)* zusammengedrückt werden; **her face ~d** ihr Gesicht verzog sich (zum Weinen)

crumple zone N Knautschzone *f*

crunch [krʌntʃ] VT a *biscuit etc* mampfen *(inf)*
b **he ~ed the beetle/ice/gravel underfoot** der Käfer zerknackte/das Eis zersplitterte/der Kies knirschte unter seinen Füßen; **to ~ the gears** *(Aut)* die Gänge reinwürgen *(inf)*
c *(Comput) numbers* verarbeiten
VI a *(gravel, snow etc)* knirschen; *(gears)* krachen; **he ~ed across the gravel** er ging mit knirschenden Schritten über den Kies
b **he was ~ing on a carrot** er mampfte eine Möhre *(inf)*; **he ~ed into the apple** er biss knackend in den Apfel
N a *(= sound)* Krachen *nt*; *(of footsteps, gravel etc)* Knirschen *nt*; **the two cars collided with a ~** die zwei Autos krachten zusammen *(inf)*; **~!** Krach!
b *(inf: = car crash)* Zusammenstoß *m*
c *(inf: = moment of reckoning)* **the ~** der große Krach; **when it comes to the ~** wenn der entscheidende Moment kommt; **this is the ~** jetzt ist der spannende Moment; **it's/we've come to the ~** jetzt kommt es drauf an, jetzt geht es hart auf hart
d **crunches** PL *(in fitness centre)* Bauchpressen *pl*

▶ **crunch up** VT *sep (= eat) carrot etc* zerbeißen; *(= crush noisily) garbage etc* (krachend) zermahlen

crunch machine N *(in fitnss centre)* Bauchmuskelmaschine *f*

crunchy ['krʌntʃɪ] ADJ *(+er) apple* knackig; *biscuit* knusprig; *snow* verharscht

crupper ['krʌpəʳ] N a *(of harness)* Schweifriemen *m* b *(= hindquarters)* Kruppe *f*

crusade [kruː'seɪd] N *(Hist, fig)* Kreuzzug *m*; *(= evangelical crusade)* Missions- *or* Glaubensfeldzug *m* VI *(Hist, fig)* einen Kreuzzug/Kreuzzüge führen; *(as evangelist)* missionieren

crusader [kruː'seɪdəʳ] N *(Hist)* Kreuzfahrer *m*, Kreuzritter *m*; *(fig)* Apostel *m*; *(= evangelical crusader)* Glaubensjünger(in) *m(f)*

crush [krʌʃ] N a *(= crowd)* Gedrängel *nt*; **it'll be a bit of a ~** es wird ein bisschen eng werden
b *(inf) (= infatuation)* Schwärmerei *f*; *(= object of infatuation)* Schwarm *m*; **to have a ~ on sb** für jdn schwärmen, in jdn verschossen sein *(inf)*; **schoolgirl ~** Schulmädchenschwärmerei *f*
c *(= drink)* Saftgetränk *nt*
VT a *(= squeeze, press tightly)* quetschen; *(= damage) soft fruit etc* zerdrücken, zerquetschen; *finger, toes etc* quetschen; *(rock, car etc) sb* zerquetschen; *(= kill)* zu Tode quetschen; *(= grind, break up) spices, garlic* (zer)stoßen; *ice* stoßen; *ore, stone* zerkleinern, zerstampfen; *scrap metal, garbage* zusammenpressen; *(= crease) clothes, paper* zerknittern, zerdrücken; *(= screw up) paper* zerknüllen; **~ed pineapple** *klein geschnetzelte Ananas*; **I was ~ed between two enormous men in the plane** ich war im Flugzeug zwischen zwei fetten Männern eingequetscht *or* eingeklemmt; **she ~ed the child to her breast** sie drückte das Kind fest an die Brust; **to ~ sb into sth** jdn in etw *(acc)* quetschen; **to ~ sth into sth** etw in etw *(acc)* stopfen
b *(fig) enemy, hopes, self-confidence, sb* vernichten; *revolution, opposition* niederschlagen; *(= oppress) people, peasants* unterdrücken; **she ~ed him with one glance** sie sah ihn vernichtend an, sie warf ihm einen vernichtenden Blick zu; **to ~ sb's spirit** jdn brechen
VI a *(crowd)* (sich) drängen; **they ~ed into the car** sie quetschten *or* drängten sich in das Auto
b *(clothes, fabric)* knittern, knautschen *(inf)*

▶ **crush in** VT *sep* hineinstopfen *(prep obj, -to* in *+acc)* VI (sich) hineindrängen

▶ **crush out** VT *sep juice etc* auspressen, ausquetschen *(inf)*

▶ **crush up** VT *sep* a *(= pulverize)* zerstoßen b *(= pack tightly together)* zusammendrücken *or* -quetschen; **we were (sitting) all crushed up** wir saßen alle zusammengequetscht

crush barrier N Absperrung *f*, Barrikade *f*

crushing ['krʌʃɪŋ] ADJ *defeat* zerschmetternd; *blow, look, reply* vernichtend; *experience* niederschmetternd

crushingly ['krʌʃɪŋlɪ] ADV schrecklich

crush-resistant ['krʌʃrɪzɪstənt] ADJ knitterfrei

crust [krʌst] N *(all senses)* Kruste *f*; **the earth's ~** die Erdkruste; **to earn a ~** *(inf)* seinen Lebensunterhalt verdienen VI verkrusten; **~ed port** Portwein *m* mit Kruste

crustacean [krʌs'teɪʃən] N Schalentier *nt*, Krustazee *f (spec)* ADJ *characteristics, class* der Schalentiere *or* Krustazeen *(spec)*; *appearance* krebsähnlich

crusted ['krʌstɪd] ADJ mit einer Kruste überzogen, krustig; *blood* verkrustet

crustily ['krʌstɪlɪ] ADV *(fig)* barsch

crusty ['krʌstɪ] ADJ *(+er)* knusprig; *(fig: = irritable)* barsch

crutch [krʌtʃ] N a *(for walking)* Krücke *f*; **to use sb/sth as a ~** *(fig)* sich an jdn/etw klammern b *(Naut)* Baumstütze *f*, Baumschere *f* c = **crotch**

crux [krʌks] N *(of matter, problem)* Kern *m*; **this is the ~ (of the matter)** das ist der springende Punkt

cry [kraɪ] N a *(= inarticulate shout)* Schrei *m*; *(= call)* Ruf *m*; **to give** *or* **utter a ~** (auf)schreien, einen Schrei ausstoßen; **a ~ of fear/pain** ein Angst-/Schmerzensschrei *m*; **a ~ for help** ein Hilferuf *m*; **he gave a ~ for help** er rief um Hilfe → **far**
b *(of animal)* Schrei *m*; *(Hunt: of hounds)* Geheul *nt*, Gebell *nt*; **the pack is in full ~** die Meute hetzt laut bellend *or* heulend hinter der Beute her; **to be in full ~** voll in Aktion sein *(inf)*; **to be in full ~ after sb** *(fig)* sich mit großem Geheul auf jdn stürzen
c *(= slogan)* Parole *f*; *(= battle cry)* Schlachtruf *m*
d *(= outcry)* **a ~ for sth** ein Ruf *m* nach etw; **a ~ against sth** ein Protest *m* gegen etw
e *(= weep)* **a ~ will do you good** weine ruhig, das wird dir guttun; **to have a good ~** sich einmal richtig ausweinen *or* ausheulen *(inf)*; **to have a little ~** ein bisschen weinen
VI a *(= weep)* weinen, heulen *(inf)*; *(baby)* schreien; **she was ~ing for her teddy bear** sie weinte nach ihrem Teddy; **... or I'll give you something to ~ about** ... und dann weißt du, warum du heulst *(inf)*
b *(= call)* rufen; *(louder)* schreien; *(Hunt: hounds)* heulen; *(animal, bird)* schreien; **to ~ for help** um Hilfe rufen/schreien; **she cried for a nurse/for somebody to come** sie rief/schrie nach einer Krankenschwester/nach jemandem
VT a *(= shout out)* rufen; *(louder)* schreien; **to ~ mercy** *(old, liter)* um Gnade flehen; **he cried to me to go away** er rief mir zu, dass ich verschwinden sollte → **crying, wolf**
b *(= announce)* ausrufen
c *(= weep) bitter tears etc* weinen; **to ~ one's eyes/heart out** sich *(dat)* die Augen ausweinen/herzzerreißend weinen; **to ~ oneself to sleep** sich in den Schlaf weinen; **to ~ on sb's shoulder** sich an jds Schulter *or* bei jdm ausweinen

▶ **cry down** VT *sep (= decry)* herabsetzen

▶ **cry off** VI *(Brit)* einen Rückzieher machen, aussteigen *(inf)*; **to cry off from sth** aus etw aussteigen *(inf)*, etw (wieder) abblasen *(inf)*

▶ **cry out** VI a *(= call out)* aufschreien; **to cry out to sb** jdm etwas zuschreien; **he cried out to me to fetch help** er schrie mir zu, ich sollte Hilfe holen; **well, for crying out loud!** *(inf)* na, das darf doch wohl nicht wahr sein! *(inf)* b *(fig)* **to be crying out for sth** nach etw schreien; *(= be suitable for also)* sich (geradezu) zu etw anbieten; **that building is just crying out to be turned into a pub** dieses Gebäude schreit (geradezu) danach, dass man es in ein Lokal verwandelt

▶ **cry up** VT *sep* **it's/he's not all it's/he's cried up to be** so großartig ist es/er dann auch wieder nicht

crybaby ['kraɪbeɪbɪ] N *(inf)* Heulsuse *f (inf)*

crying ['kraɪɪŋ] ADJ *(fig: = outrageous) injustice*schreiend; *need* dringend; **it is a ~ shame** es ist jammerschade *or* ein Jammer N *(= weeping)* Weinen *nt*; *(of baby)* Schreien *nt*

cryogen ['kraɪədʒən] N Kühlmittel *nt*

crypt [krɪpt] N Krypta *f*; *(= burial crypt)* Gruft *f*

cryptic ['krɪptɪk] ADJ *remark etc* hintergründig, rätselhaft, schleierhaft; *clue, riddle etc* verschlüsselt; **you're being very ~** du drückst dich sehr rätselhaft *or* schleierhaft aus

cryptically ['krɪptɪkəlɪ] ADV hintergründig, rätselhaft, schleierhaft; **~ worded** *(letter, remark)* hintergründig *etc* formuliert; *clue* verschlüsselt formuliert

crypto- ['krɪptəʊ-] PREF Krypto-, krypto-

cryptogram ['krɪptəʊgræm] N Kryptogramm *nt*

cryptographer [krɪp'tɒgrəfəʳ] N Kryptograf(in) *m(f)*

cryptographic [ˌkrɪptəʊ'græfɪk] ADJ kryptografisch, in Geheimschrift verschlüsselt

cryptography [krɪp'tɒgrəfɪ] N Kryptografie *f*

crystal ['krɪstl] N *(Chem, Rad)* Kristall *m*; *(on watch)* (Uhr)glas *nt*; *(= crystal glass)* Kristall *nt*; *(= quartz)* (Quarz)kristall *m* ADJ a *(= crystalline)* Kristall-, kristallin; *(= like a crystal)* kristallartig; *(= crystal-glass)* Kristall-, kristallen; *(= quartz)* Quarzkristall- b *(fig) waters* kristallklar, glasklar

crystal: **crystal ball** N Glaskugel *f*; **I don't have a ~** *(inf)* ich bin (doch) kein Hellseher; **you didn't see that in your ~, did you?** *(inf)* das hast du wohl nicht vorausgesehen?; **crystal-ball gazer** N Hellseher(in) *m(f)*; **crystal-ball gazing** N Hellseherei *f*; **crystal-clear** ADJ *(lit, fig)* glasklar, völlig klar, vollständig klar; **crystal detector** N *(Rad)* Kristalldetektor *m*; **crystal gazer** N Hellseher(in) *m(f)*; **crystal gazing** N Hellseherei *f* ADJ **all these crystal-gazing so-called experts** alle diese sogenannten Experten, die aus dem Kaffeesatz wahrsagen; **crystal lattice** N Kristallgitter *nt*

crystalline ['krɪstəlaɪn] ADJ kristallin; **~ lens** (Augen)linse *f*

crystallization [ˌkrɪstəlaɪzeɪʃən] N a *(lit)* Kristallisierung *f*; *(out of another substance)* Auskristallisierung *f* b *(fig)* (Heraus)kristallisierung *f*; *(= crystallized form)* kristallisierte Form; **after the ~ of these ideas into a theory** nachdem sich aus diesen Gedanken eine Theorie herauskristallisiert hatte

crystallize ['krɪstəlaɪz] VT *(lit)* zum Kristallisieren bringen; *(= separating out)* auskristallisieren; *fruit* kandieren; *(fig)* (feste) Form geben *(+dat)* VI *(lit)* kristallisieren; *(= separate out)* (sich) auskristallisieren; *(fig)* feste Form annehmen; **this theory ~d out of many years' research** diese Theorie hat sich nach jahrelanger Forschung herauskristallisiert

crystallized ['krɪstəlaɪzd] ADJ kristallisiert; *fruit* kandiert

crystallography [ˌkrɪstə'lɒgrəfɪ] N Kristallografie *f*

crystal: **crystal meth** [ˌkrɪstl'meθ] N *(inf: = drug)* Thai-Pille *f*; **crystal set** N *(Rad)* Detek-

torempfänger *m*; **crystal therapy** N Edelsteintherapie *f*
crystal speed N (*inf*: = *drug*) Thai-Pille *f*
CSA (*Brit*) *abbr of* **Child Support Agency**
CSE (*Brit*) *abbr of* **Certificate of Secondary Education**
C section [ˌsiːˈsekʃən] N (*inf*) Kaiserschnitt *m*
CS gas N ≈ Tränengas *nt*
CSM *abbr of* **context-sensitive menu**
CST *abbr of* **Central Standard Time**
ct **a** *abbr of* **cent** **b** *abbr of* **carat**
cu *abbr of* **see you** (*in text message etc*) bis dann, bis später
cub [kʌb] **N** **a** (*of animal*) Junge(s) *nt* **b** **Cub** (= *Cub Scout*) Wölfling *m* **c** (= *cub reporter*) junger Reporter, junge Reporterin **d** (*inf*, = *boy*) grüner Junge **VI** werfen
Cuba [ˈkjuːbə] N Kuba *nt*
Cuban [ˈkjuːbən] **ADJ** kubanisch **N** Kubaner(in) *m(f)*
Cuban heel N Blockabsatz *m*
cubbyhole [ˈkʌbɪhəʊl] N **a** (= *compartment*) Fach *nt* **b** (= *room*) Kabäuschen *nt*, Kabuff *nt*
cube [kjuːb] **N** **a** (= *shape, object*) Würfel *m* **b** (*Math*: = *power of three*) dritte Potenz; **the ~ of 3 is 27** die dritte Potenz von 3 ist 27, 3 hoch 3 ist 27 **VT** **a** (*Math*) in die dritte Potenz erheben, hoch 3 nehmen; **four ~d** vier hoch drei **b** (*Cook*) würfelig *or* in Würfel schneiden
cube: **cube root** N Kubikwurzel *f*; **cube sugar** N Würfelzucker *m*
cubic [ˈkjuːbɪk] ADJ **a** (*of volume*) Kubik-, Raum-; **~ content** Raum- *or* Kubikinhalt *m*; **~ metre/foot** Kubikmeter *m or nt*/Kubikfuß *m* **b** (*Math*) kubisch; **~ equation** Gleichung *f* dritten Grades
cubic capacity N Fassungsvermögen *nt*; (*of engine*) Hubraum *m*
cubicle [ˈkjuːbɪkəl] N Kabine *f*; (*in dormitory etc also*) Alkoven *m*; (*in toilets*) (Einzel)toilette *f*
cubic measure N Raum- *or* Kubikmaß *nt*
cubiform [ˈkjuːbɪfɔːm] ADJ (*form*) kubisch, würfelförmig
cubism [ˈkjuːbɪzəm] N Kubismus *m*
cubist [ˈkjuːbɪst] **N** Kubist(in) *m(f)* **ADJ** kubistisch
cubit [ˈkjuːbɪt] N Elle *f*
cub: **Cub mistress** N Wölflingsmutter *f*; **cub reporter** N junger Reporter, junge Reporterin; **Cub Scout** N Wölfling *m*
cuckold [ˈkʌkəld] **N** Hahnrei *m* (*old*), betrogener Ehemann **VT** zum Hahnrei machen (*old*), betrügen, Hörner aufsetzen (*+dat*)
cuckoo [ˈkʊkuː] **N** Kuckuck *m*; (= *insect*) Schaumzikade *f* **ADJ** *pred* (*inf*) meschugge (*inf*); **to go ~** überschnappen (*inf*)
cuckoo: **cuckoo clock** N Kuckucksuhr *f*; **cuckoopint** [ˈkʊkuːpaɪnt] N (*Bot*) Gefleckter Aronsstab; **cuckoo spit** N (= *secretion*) Kuckucksspeichel *m*
cucumber [ˈkjuːkʌmbəʳ] N (Salat)gurke *f*; **as cool as a ~** seelenruhig
cud [kʌd] N wiedergekäutes Futter; **to chew the ~** (*lit*) wiederkäuen; (*fig*) vor sich hin grübeln, sinnieren
cuddle [ˈkʌdl] **N** Liebkosung *f*; **to give sb a ~** jdn in den Arm nehmen; **to need a ~** Zärtlichkeit brauchen, geknuddelt (*inf*) *or* liebkost werden wollen; **to have a ~** schmusen **VT** in den Arm nehmen; (*amorously also*) schmusen mit **VI** schmusen
▶ **cuddle down** VI sich kuscheln
▶ **cuddle up** VI sich kuscheln (*to, against* an *+acc*); **to cuddle up beside sb** sich neben jdm zusammenkuscheln; **to cuddle up in bed** sich im Bett zusammenkuscheln, sich ins Bett kuscheln; **I'm cold – well, cuddle up then** mir ist kalt – na, dann kuschel dich ran (*inf*); **we all had to cuddle up in the tent to keep warm** wir mussten uns alle im Zelt aneinanderkuscheln, um es warm zu haben
cuddlesome [ˈkʌdlsəm] ADJ = **cuddly**
cuddly [ˈkʌdlɪ] ADJ (*+er*) (= *wanting a cuddle*) verschmust (*inf*), anschmiegsam; (= *good to cuddle*) *toy, doll* zum Liebhaben, knuddelig (*inf*); *person* knuddelig (*inf*); **to be in a ~ mood** in einer verschmusten Laune *or* in Schmuselaune sein
cuddly toy N Schmusetier *nt* (*inf*)
cudgel [ˈkʌdʒəl] **N** (*Brit*) Knüppel *m*; **to take up the ~s for** *or* **on behalf of sb/sth** (*fig*) für jdn/etw eintreten *or* eine Lanze brechen, für jdn/etw auf die Barrikaden gehen **VT** prügeln; **to ~ one's brains** (*fig*) sich (*dat*) das (Ge)hirn zermartern
cue [kjuː] **N** **a** (*Theat, fig*) Stichwort *nt*; (*action*) (Einsatz)zeichen *nt*; (*Film, TV*) Zeichen *nt* zum Aufnahmebeginn; (*Mus*) Einsatz *m*; (*written*: = *preceding bars*) Hilfsnoten *pl*; **to give sb his ~** (*Theat*) jdm das *or* sein Stichwort geben; (*action*) jdm das (Einsatz)zeichen geben; (*Mus*) jdm den Einsatz geben; **that sounds like a ~ for a song** das hört sich ganz nach einem Lied an; **whenever he hears the word "strike" that's his ~ to launch into an attack on the unions** das Wort „Streik" ist für ihn jedesmal (das) Stichwort für einen Angriff auf die Gewerkschaften; **to take one's ~ from sb** sich nach jdm richten; **right on ~** (*Theat*) genau aufs Stichwort; (*fig*) wie gerufen
b (*Billiards*) Queue *nt*
VT (*Theat*) das Stichwort geben (*+dat*); (*with gesture etc*) das Einsatzzeichen geben (*+dat*); (*Film, TV*) *scene* abfahren lassen; (*Mus*) *player* den Einsatz geben (*+dat*); *trumpet flourish etc* den Einsatz geben für; **~!** (*Film, TV*) ab!
▶ **cue in** VT *sep* den Einsatz geben (*+dat*); (*Film, TV*) *scene* abfahren lassen; *tape etc* (zur rechten Zeit) einspielen
cue: **cue ball** N Spielball *m*; **cue card** N (*TV*) Neger *m* (*spec*); **cue rest** N Stütze *f* für das Queue
cuff¹ [kʌf] N **a** Manschette *f*; **off the ~** aus dem Handgelenk, aus dem Stegreif **b** (*US*: *of trousers*) (Hosen)aufschlag *m* **c** *usu pl* (*inf*: = *handcuff*) Handschelle *f* **d** (*dated US inf*: = *credit*) **on the ~** auf Stottern (*inf*)
cuff² **VT** (= *strike*) einen Klaps geben (*+dat*), eins um die Ohren geben (*+dat*) (*inf*) **N** (= *blow*) Klaps *m*
cuff link N Manschettenknopf *m*
cu.ft. *abbr of* **cubic foot/feet**
cu.in. *abbr of* **cubic inch(es)**
cuirass [kwɪˈræs] N Kürass *m*, Brustharnisch *m*
cuirassier [ˌkwɪrəˈsɪəʳ] N Kürassier *m*
cuisine [kwɪˈziːn] N Küche *f*
cul-de-sac [ˈkʌldəsæk] N Sackgasse *f*
culinary [ˈkʌlɪnərɪ] ADJ kulinarisch; *skill, talents etc* im Kochen
cull [kʌl] **N** **a** (= *selection*) Auswahl *f* **b** (= *killing of surplus*) *Erlegen überschüssiger Tierbestände*, Reduktionsabschuss *m*; **~ of seals** Robbenschlag *m* **c** (= *rejected item*) Ausschuss *m* **VT** **a** (= *collect*) entnehmen (*from +dat*); *legends* (zusammen)sammeln (*from* aus) **b** (= *kill as surplus*) (als überschüssig) erlegen; **to ~ seals** Robbenschlag *m* betreiben **c** (= *pick*) *flowers* pflücken
cullender N = **colander**
cullet [ˈkʌlɪt] N Bruchglas *nt*
culminate [ˈkʌlmɪneɪt] **VI** (*Astron*) kulminieren, den *or* seinen Höchst-/Tiefststand erreichen; (*fig*) (= *reach a climax*: *career, music etc*) gipfeln, kulminieren (*geh*) (*in* in *+dat*); (= *end*) herauslaufen (*in* auf *+acc*), enden (*in* mit) **VT** (*US*) den Höhepunkt *or* Gipfel (*+gen*) darstellen
culmination [ˌkʌlmɪˈneɪʃən] N (*Astron*) Kulminationspunkt *m*, Höchst-/Tiefststand *m*; (*fig*) (= *high point*: *of career etc*) Höhepunkt *m*; (= *end*) Ende *nt*, Ausgang *m*
culottes [kjuːˈlɒts] PL Hosenrock *m*; **a pair of ~** ein Hosenrock
culpability [ˌkʌlpəˈbɪlɪtɪ] N (*form*) Schuld *f*
culpable [ˈkʌlpəbl] ADJ (*form*) schuldig
culpable homicide N (*Jur*) fahrlässige Tötung
culpable negligence N (*Jur*) grobe Fahrlässigkeit
culprit [ˈkʌlprɪt] N Schuldige(r) *mf*; (*Jur*) Täter(in) *m(f)*; (*inf*) (= *person causing trouble*) Übeltäter(in) *m(f)*; (= *thing causing trouble*) Übeltäter *m*
cult [kʌlt] **N** (*Rel, fig*) Kult *m*; **to make a ~ of sth** (einen) Kult mit etw treiben **ATTR** Kult-
cultivable [ˈkʌltɪvəbl] ADJ kultivierbar
cultivate [ˈkʌltɪveɪt] VT **a** (*lit*) kultivieren; *soil* bebauen, kultivieren; *crop, fruit etc* anbauen; *beard* wachsen lassen **b** (*fig*) *friendship, links etc* pflegen, kultivieren; *art, skill, taste* entwickeln; *sb* sich (*dat*) warmhalten (*inf*), die Beziehung zu … pflegen; **a connection like that is definitely worth cultivating** es lohnt sich bestimmt, so eine Verbindung aufrechtzuerhalten; **to ~ one's mind** sich bilden
cultivated [ˈkʌltɪveɪtɪd] ADJ (*Agr, fig*) kultiviert
cultivation [ˌkʌltɪˈveɪʃən] N **a** (*lit*) Kultivieren *nt*, Kultivierung *f*; (*of crop, fruit etc*) Anbau *m*; **to be under ~** bebaut werden **b** (*fig*) (*of friendship, links etc*) Pflege *f* (*of* von); (*of art, skill*) Entwicklung *f*; (*of person*) Bemühung *f* (*of* um); **his constant ~ of influential friendships** seine ständigen Bemühungen um einflussreiche Freunde **c** (= *cultivated state*) Kultiviertheit *f*
cultivator [ˈkʌltɪveɪtəʳ] N **a** (= *machine*) Kultivator *m*, Grubber *m* **b** (= *person*) **a ~ of the soil/of new friendships** jemand, der den Boden bebaut/neue Freundschaften pflegt
cult movie N Kultfilm *m*
cultural [ˈkʌltʃərəl] ADJ Kultur-; *resemblances, events* kulturell; **~ differences** kulturelle Unterschiede *pl*, Kulturunterschiede *pl*; **what sort of ~ activities are there?** was wird kulturell geboten?; **we enjoyed a very ~ evening** wir hatten einen kulturell sehr anspruchsvollen Abend; **could you not do something a little more ~ with your spare time?** könntest du deine Freizeit nicht etwas kultivierter gestalten *or* verbringen?; **culture channel** (*TV, Rad*) Kulturkanal *m*; **(world) ~ heritage** (Welt)kulturerbe *nt*
culturally [ˈkʌltʃərəlɪ] ADV kulturell
culture [ˈkʌltʃəʳ] **N** **a** Kultur *f*; **physical ~** (*dated*) Körperkultur *f* (*dated*); **a man of ~/of no ~** ein kultivierter/unkultivierter Mann, ein Mann mit/ohne Kultur; **to study German ~** die deutsche Kultur studieren; **a ~ of dependency, a dependency ~** eine Kultur der Abhängigkeit; **the company ~** die Unternehmenskultur **b** (*Agr, Biol, Med*) Kultur *f*; (*of animals*) Zucht *f* **VT** (*Biol, Med*) eine Kultur anlegen von
culture area N Kulturraum *m*
cultured [ˈkʌltʃəd] ADJ kultiviert; (*Agr, Biol, Med*) gezüchtet
culture dish N (*Biol, Med*) Kulturschale *f*
cultured pearl N Zuchtperle *f*
culture: **culture fluid** N (*Biol, Med*) Nährlösung *f*; **culture gap** N Kulturlücke *f*; **culture medium** N (*Biol, Med*) Kulturmedium *nt*, (künstlicher) Nährboden; **culture shock** N Kulturschock *m*; **culture vulture** N (*hum*) Kulturfanatiker(in) *m(f)*
culvert [ˈkʌlvət] N unterirdischer Kanal, (Abwasser)kanal *m*; (*for cables*) Kabeltunnel *m*
cum [kʌm] PREP in einem, gleichzeitig; **a sort of sofa-~-bed** eine Art von Sofa und Bett in einem
cumbersome [ˈkʌmbəsəm] ADJ *clothing, coat* (be)hinderlich; *spacesuit, movements, gesture, style, piece of music* schwerfällig; *vehicle* unhandlich (*inf*), schwer zu manövrieren; *suitcases, parcels* sperrig, unhandlich; *procedure, regulations* beschwerlich, mühselig; **it's so ~ having to wear all this heavy clothing** es ist so lästig, dass man alle diese schweren Kleidungsstücke tragen muss

cumbersomely [ˈkʌmbəsəmlɪ] ADV *move, write* schwerfällig; *phrased also* umständlich; *dressed* hinderlich

cumbrous [ˈkʌmbrəs] ADJ = **cumbersome**

cumin [ˈkʌmɪn] N Kreuzkümmel *m*

cummerbund [ˈkʌməbʌnd] N Kummerbund *m*

cumulation [ˌkjuːmjʊˈleɪʃən] N Anhäufung *f*, Häufung *f*

cumulative [ˈkjuːmjʊlətɪv] ADJ gesamt, kumulativ *(geh)*; **the ~ debts of ten years** die Schulden, die sich im Lauf von zehn Jahren angehäuft haben/hatten

cumulative evidence N *(Jur)* Häufung *f* von Beweisen/Zeugenaussagen

cumulative interest N *(Fin)* Zins und Zinseszins

cumulatively [ˈkjuːmjʊlətɪvlɪ] ADV kumulativ

cumulative voting N Wählen *nt* durch Kumulieren *or* Stimmenhäufung *or* nach dem Kumulierungssystem

cumulonimbus [ˈkjuːmjələʊˈnɪmbəs] N Kumulonimbus *m*

cumulus [ˈkjuːmjələs] N Kumulus *m*

cuneiform [ˈkjuːnɪfɔːm] ADJ keilförmig; *characters, inscription* in Keilschrift; **~ writing** Keilschrift *f* N Keilschrift *f*

cunnilingus [ˌkʌnɪˈlɪŋgəs] N Cunnilingus *m*

cunning [ˈkʌnɪŋ] N *(= cleverness)* Schlauheit *f*, Listigkeit *f*, Gerissenheit *f*; *(liter: = skill)* (Kunst)fertigkeit *f*, Geschick *nt* ADJ a *plan* schlau; *person* schlau, gerissen; *smile, expression* verschmitzt, verschlagen *(pej)*; *(= ingenious) gadget* schlau *or* clever *(inf)* ausgedacht b *(US inf)* drollig

cunningly [ˈkʌnɪŋlɪ] ADV schlau; *(with reference to people also)* gerissen; *smile, look* verschmitzt, verschlagen *(pej)*; *(= ingeniously)* geschickt; **a ~ designed little gadget** ein geschickt *or* clever ausgedachtes Ding

cunt [kʌnt] N *(vulg) (= vagina)* Fotze *f (vulg)*, Möse *f (vulg)*; *(= intercourse)* Fick *m (vulg)*; *(term of abuse)* Arsch *m (vulg)*; **she's a nice bit of ~** das ist eine geile Fotze *(vulg)*

cup [kʌp] N a Tasse *f*; *(= goblet)* Pokal *m*, Kelch *m*; *(= mug)* Becher *m*; *(Eccl)* Kelch *m*; **in his ~s** *(dated inf)* angezecht
b *(= cupful)* Tasse *f*; *(Cook, standard measure)* 8 fl oz = 0,22 l; **a ~ of tea/water** eine Tasse Tee/Wasser; **that's just/that's not my ~ of tea** *(fig inf)* das ist genau/ist nicht mein Fall; **she's not everyone's ~ of tea** ihre Art gefällt nicht jedem
c *(= prize, football cup etc)* Pokal *m*; **they're out of the Cup** sie sind aus dem Pokal(wettbewerb) ausgeschieden
d *(= drink)* Mix *m*, Becher *m*
e *(Bot: of flower)* Kelch *m*; *(of bra)* Körbchen *nt*; *(Golf)* Metallbüchse *f (im Loch)*; *(Med: = cupping glass)* Schröpfkopf *m*
f *(fig liter: = portion)* Kelch *m*; **to drain the ~ of sorrow (to the dregs)** den Kelch des Leidens (bis zur Neige) leeren *(liter)*; **my ~ is overflowing** *or (liter)* **runneth over** *(Bibl)* ich bin über alle Maßen glücklich, mein Glück ist vollkommen
VT a *hands* hohl machen; **~ped hand** hohle Hand; **he ~ped his hands and blew into them** er blies sich *(dat)* in die Hände; **to ~ sth in one's hands** etw in der hohlen Hand halten; **he ~ped his chin in his hand** er stützte das Kinn in die Hand; **to ~ one's** *or* **a hand to one's ear** die Hand ans Ohr halten; **to ~ one's hands around sth** etw mit der hohlen Hand umfassen
b *(Med)* schröpfen
c *(Golf)* einlochen mit

cup: cup-and-ball N Fangbecherspiel *nt*; **cupbearer** N Mundschenk *m*

cupboard [ˈkʌbəd] N Schrank *m*

cupboard love N fauler Schmus *(inf)*, Zweckfreundlichkeit *f*

cup: cupcake N *kleiner, runder Kuchen*; **Cup Final** N Pokalendspiel *nt*; *(international also)* Cupfinale *nt*; **Cup Finalist** N Teilnehmer(in) *m(f)* am Pokalendspiel; **cupful** N *pl* **cupsful, cupfuls** Tasse *f* (voll)

cupid [ˈkjuːpɪd] N Amorette *f*; **Cupid** Amor *m*; **Cupid's dart** *(liter)* Amors Pfeil *m (liter)*, Liebespfeil *m*

cupidity [kjuːˈpɪdɪtɪ] N *(liter)* Begierde *f (pej)*, Gier *f (pej)*

Cupid's bow [ˈkjuːpɪdzˈbəʊ] ADJ bogenförmig geschwungen; **~ mouth** Kussmund *m*, Herzmund *m*

cup match N Pokalspiel *nt*

cupola [ˈkjuːpələ] N *(Archit)* Kuppel *f*; *(roof also)* Kuppeldach *nt*; *(= furnace)* Kupolofen *m*

cuppa [ˈkʌpə] N *(Brit inf)* Tasse Tee *f*, Tässchen Tee *nt (inf)*

cupping [ˈkʌpɪŋ] N *(Med)* Schröpfen *nt*

cupping glass N *(Med)* Schröpfkopf *m*

cupreous [ˈkjuːprɪəs] ADJ kupfern

cuprite [ˈkjuːpraɪt] N Kupferoxid *nt*, Rotkupfererz *nt*

cupronickel [ˈkjuːprəʊˈnɪkl] N Kupfernickel *nt*, Kupfer-Nickel-Legierung *f*

cuprous [ˈkjuːprəs] ADJ kupfern

cup: cup size N *(of bra)* Körbchengröße *f*; **cup tie** N Pokalspiel *nt*

cupule [ˈkjuːpjuːl] N *(Bot)* Becher *m*, Cupula *f (spec)*

Cup Winner N Pokalsieger(in) *m(f)*; **~s' Cup** *(Ftbl)* Europapokal *m* der Pokalsieger

cur [kɜːʳ] N *(pej) (= dog)* Köter *m (pej)*; *(old, = man)* Kanaille *f (dated pej)*, Hundsfott *m (dated pej)*

curability [ˌkjʊərəˈbɪlɪtɪ] N Heilbarkeit *f*

curable [ˈkjʊərəbl] ADJ heilbar

Curaçao [ˌkjuːrəˈsəʊ] N Curaçao *m*

curacy [ˈkjʊərəsɪ] N *(Catholic)* Anstellung *f* als Kurat; *(Protestant)* Anstellung *f* als Vikar(in)

curate [ˈkjʊərɪt] N *(Catholic)* Kurat *m*; *(Protestant)* Vikar(in) *m(f)*; **it's like the ~'s egg** es ist streckenweise gar nicht so schlecht

curative [ˈkjʊərətɪv] ADJ Heil-, heilend; **~ powers** Heilkräfte *pl* N Heilmittel *nt*

curator [kjʊəˈreɪtəʳ] N a *(of museum etc)* Kustos *m* b *(Jur: = guardian)* Kurator *m*, Vormund *m*

curatorial [ˌkjʊərəˈtɔːrɪəl] ADJ **the museum's ~ team** die Kustoden *pl* des Museums

curb [kɜːb] N a *(of harness) (= bit)* Kandare *f*; *(= chain)* Kinnkette *f*, Kandarenkette *f* b *(fig)* Behinderung *f*; **to put a ~ on sb** *(esp Brit)* jdn im Zaum *or* in Schranken halten; **to put a ~ on sth** etw einschränken; **this acted as a ~ on his musical development** das (be)hinderte seine musikalische Entwicklung c *(esp US: = curbstone)* = **kerb** VT a *horse* zügeln b *(fig)* zügeln; *immigration, investment etc* in Schranken halten, bremsen *(inf)*

curb: curb bit N Kandare *f*; **curb market** N *(US St Ex)* Freiverkehr *m*; **curb rein** N Kandarenzügel *m*; **curb roof** N *(Archit)* Mansardendach *nt*; **curb service** N *(US)* Bedienung *f* am Fahrzeug; **curbside** N *(US)* Straßenrand *m*; **~ pickup** *(of takeaway food etc)* Einkauf *m* direkt vom Straßenrand aus; **curbstone** N *(esp US)* = **kerbstone**

curcuma [ˈkɜːkjʊmə] N *(Bot)* Kurkuma *f*, Gelbwurz *f*

curd [kɜːd] N *(often pl)* Quark *m* VT gerinnen lassen VI gerinnen

curd cheese N Weißkäse *m*

curdle [ˈkɜːdl] VT *(lit, fig)* gerinnen lassen; **to ~ sb's blood** jdm das Blut in den Adern gerinnen lassen VI gerinnen; **his blood ~d** das Blut gerann ihm in den Adern

curdy [ˈkɜːdɪ] ADJ *(= coagulated)* geronnen, dick; *(= lumpy)* klumpig

cure [kjʊəʳ] VT a *(Med) illness, person* heilen, kurieren *(inf)*; **to be/get ~d (of sth)** (von etw) geheilt *or* kuriert *(inf)* sein/werden; **he used to be an alcoholic but he's been ~d** er war früher Alkoholiker, aber jetzt ist er geheilt *or* kuriert *(inf)*
b *(fig) inflation, ill etc* abhelfen *(+dat)*; **to ~ sb of sth** jdm etw austreiben, jdn von etw kurieren; **I'll ~ him!** dem werde ich das schon austreiben!
c *food* haltbar machen; *(= salt)* pökeln; *(= smoke)* räuchern; *(= dry)* trocknen; *skins, tobacco* trocknen
VI a *(= be healed)* heilen
b *(food, bacon, fish)* **it is left to ~** *(= to salt)* es wird zum Pökeln eingelegt; *(= to smoke)* es wird zum Räuchern aufgehängt; *(= to dry)* es wird zum Trocknen aufgehängt *or* ausgebreitet
N a *(Med) (= remedy)* (Heil)mittel *nt (for* gegen); *(= treatment)* Heilverfahren *nt (for sb* für jdn, *for sth* gegen etw); *(= recovery)* Heilung *f*; *(= health cure)* Kur *f*; *(fig: = remedy)* Mittel *nt (for* gegen); **to take the ~** zur *or* in Kur gehen, eine Kur machen; **beyond ~** *(patient)* unheilbar krank; *illness* unheilbar; *(fig) state of affairs, laziness etc* hoffnungslos; **there's no ~ for that** *(lit)* das ist unheilbar; *(fig)* dagegen kann man nichts machen
b *(Eccl: = spiritual care)* **the ~ of souls** die Seelsorge

cure-all [ˈkjʊərɔːl] N *(lit, fig)* Allheilmittel *nt*

cureless [ˈkjʊəlɪs] ADJ unheilbar

curettage [ˈkjʊərətɪdʒ] N *(Med)* Ausschabung *f*, Kürettage *f*

curet(te) [kjʊəˈret] N *(Med)* Kürette *f*

curfew [ˈkɜːfjuː] N Ausgangssperre *f*, Ausgehverbot *nt*; *(old: = evening bell)* Abendglocke *f*; **to be under ~** unter Ausgangssperre *or* Ausgehverbot stehen; **to impose a ~** eine Ausgangssperre *or* ein Ausgehverbot verhängen; **to lift the ~** die Ausgangssperre *or* das Ausgehverbot aufheben; **is the ~ still on?** ist noch Ausgangssperre?

Curia [ˈkjʊərɪə] N Kurie *f*

curie [ˈkjʊərɪ] N *(Phys)* Curie *nt*

curio [ˈkjʊərɪəʊ] N Kuriosität *f*

curiosity [ˌkjʊərɪˈɒsɪtɪ] N a *no pl (= inquisitiveness)* Neugier *f*; *(for knowledge)* Wissbegier(de) *f*; **out of** *or* **from ~** aus Neugier; **~ killed the cat** *(Prov)* sei nicht so neugierig b *(= object, person)* Kuriosität *f*

curiosity shop N Kuriositätenladen *m*

curious [ˈkjʊərɪəs] ADJ a *(= inquisitive)* neugierig; **I'm ~ to know what he'll do** ich bin mal gespannt, was er macht; **I'm ~ to know how he did it** ich bin neugierig zu erfahren, wie er das gemacht hat; **I'd be ~ to know how you got on** ich wüsste (ganz) gern, wie du zurechtgekommen bist; **the neighbours were ~ to know ...** die Nachbarn wollten (nur) zu gerne wissen ...; **I'm ~ about him** ich möchte gern mehr über ihn erfahren *or* herausfinden; **why do you ask? – I'm just ~** warum fragst du? – nur so
b *(= odd)* sonderbar, seltsam, eigenartig; **how ~!** wie seltsam!; **it's ~ the way he already knew that** sonderbar *etc*, dass er das schon gewusst hat

curiously [ˈkjʊərɪəslɪ] ADV a *(= inquisitively)* neugierig b *(= oddly) behave, speak etc* seltsam, eigenartig, merkwürdig, sonderbar; *disappeared* auf sonderbare *or* seltsame Weise; *unconcerned* seltsam, merkwürdig; **they are ~ similar** sie ähneln sich merkwürdig *or* auf seltsame Weise; **it was ~ quiet** es war merkwürdig ruhig; **any sense of humour is ~ absent** seltsamerweise *or* eigenartigerweise fehlt jeglicher Sinn für Humor; **~ enough** merkwürdigerweise; **~ (enough), he didn't object** merkwürdigerweise hatte er nichts dagegen

curiousness [ˈkjʊərɪəsnɪs] N a = **curiosity a** b *(= oddness)* Merkwürdigkeit *f*, Sonderbarkeit *f*

curl [kɜːl] N *(of hair)* Locke *f*; **in ~s** in Locken, gelockt; *(tight)* gekräuselt, kraus; **a ~ of smoke** ein Rauchkringel *m*; **with a ~ of his lip** mit gekräuselten Lippen; **its tail was just a little ~** es hatte nur ein kleines Kringelschwänzchen
VT *hair* locken; *(with curlers)* in Locken legen; *(in tight curls)* kräuseln; *lip (person)* kräuseln; *(animal)* hochziehen; *edges* umbiegen; **he ~ed the ball into the back of the net** er zirkelte den

Ball mit einem Bogenschuss ins Netz
VI **a** *(hair)* sich locken; *(tightly)* sich kräuseln; *(naturally)* lockig sein; *(paper)* sich wellen; *(wood)* sich verziehen; *(road)* sich schlängeln, sich winden; **his lip ~ed** er kräuselte die Lippen; **it's enough to make your hair ~** *(fig inf)* da stehen einem ja die Haare zu Berge *(inf)*
b *(Sport)* Curling spielen

▶**curl up** **VI** **a** *(animal, person)* sich zusammenrollen *or* -kugeln; *(hedgehog)* sich einigeln; *(paper)* sich wellen; *(metal)* sich rollen; *(leaf)* sich hochbiegen; **his moustache curls up at the ends** sein Schnurrbart ist nach oben gezwirbelt; **to curl up in bed/in an armchair** sich ins Bett/in einen Sessel kuscheln; **to curl up with a good book** es sich *(dat)* mit einem guten Buch gemütlich machen
b **the smoke curled up** der Rauch ringelte sich hoch
c *(inf)* **the way he behaves just makes me want to curl up** es macht mich krank, wie er sich benimmt *(inf)*; **I just wanted to curl up and die** *(out of embarrassment etc)* ich wäre am liebsten im Boden versunken
VT *sep ends of moustache, piece of paper etc* wellen; *metal* rollen; *edges* hochbiegen; **to curl oneself/itself up** sich zusammenkugeln/zusammenringeln

curl cloud N *(Met)* Cirruswolke *f*

curler ['kɜːləˈ] N **a** *(= hair curler)* Lockenwickel *m*, Lockenwickler *m*; **to put one's ~s in** sich *(dat)* die Haare eindrehen *or* auf (Locken)wickler drehen; **have you never seen her in ~s?** hast du sie noch nie mit Lockenwickeln gesehen?; **my hair was in ~s, I had my ~s in** ich hatte Lockenwickel *or* Lockenwickler im Haar
b *(Sport)* Curlingspieler(in) *m(f)*

curlew ['kɜːljuː] N Brachvogel *m*

curlicue ['kɜːlɪkjuː] N Schnörkel *m*

curling ['kɜːlɪŋ] N *(Sport)* Curling *nt*, Eisschießen *nt*; **~ stone** Curlingstein *m*, Eisstock *m*

curling tongs ['kɜːlɪŋ,tɒŋz], *(US)* **curling iron** ['kɜːlɪŋ,aɪən] PL Lockenschere *f*, Brennschere *f*; *(electric)* Lockenstab *m*

curlpaper ['kɜːlpeɪpəˈ] N (Papier)lockenwickel *m*

curly ['kɜːlɪ] **ADJ** *(+er) hair* lockig; *(tighter)* kraus; *tail* geringelt; *lettuce* kraus; *leaf* gewellt; *pattern, writing* verschnörkelt; **she was much curlier** ihr Haar war viel lockiger **N** *(inf, = person)* Krauskopf *m*

curly: **curly bracket** N geschweifte Klammer *f*; **curly-haired** ADJ lockig, lockenköpfig; *(tighter)* krausköpfig; **curly-head** N *(inf)* Lockenkopf *m*; *(tighter)* Krauskopf *m*; **curly-headed** ADJ = **curly-haired**

currant ['kʌrənt] N **a** *(= dried fruit)* Korinthe *f*
b *(Bot)* Johannisbeere *f*; **~ bush** Johannisbeerstrauch *m*

currant bun N Rosinenbrötchen *nt*

currency ['kʌrənsɪ] N **a** *(Fin)* Währung *f*; **foreign ~** Devisen *pl* **b** Verbreitung *f*; *(of word, expression)* Gebräuchlichkeit *f*; **to gain ~** sich verbreiten, um sich greifen; **to give ~ to a rumour/theory** ein Gerücht/eine Theorie verbreiten *or* in Umlauf setzen

currency: **currency appreciation** N Geldaufwertung *f*; **currency depreciation** N Geldabwertung *f*; **currency market** N Devisenmarkt *m*; **currency scam** N *(inf)* Währungsschwindel *m or* -betrug *m*; **currency snake** N Währungsschlange *f*; **currency speculator** N Währungsspekulant(in) *m(f)*; **currency trader** N Devisenhändler(in) *m(f)*; **currency trading** N Devisenhandel *m*

current ['kʌrənt] **ADJ** *(= present)* augenblicklich, gegenwärtig; *policy, price* aktuell; *research, month, week* laufend; *edition* letzte(r, s); *(= prevalent) opinion* verbreitet; *spelling, word* gebräuchlich; **to be no longer ~** nicht mehr aktuell sein; *(coins)* nicht mehr in Umlauf sein; **a ~ rumour** ein Gerücht, das zurzeit in Umlauf ist; **~ affairs** Tagespolitik *f*, aktuelle Fragen *pl*, Aktuelle(s) *nt*; **in ~ use** allgemein gebräuchlich
N **a** *(of water)* Strömung *f*, Strom *m*; *(of air)* Luftströmung *f*, Luftstrom *m*; **with/against the ~** mit dem/gegen den Strom; **air/ocean ~** Luft-/Meeresströmung *f or* -strom *m*
b *(Elec)* Strom *m*
c *(fig: of events, opinions etc)* Tendenz *f*, Trend *m*; **to go against the ~ of popular opinion** gegen den Strom *or* die Strömung der öffentlichen Meinung anschwimmen; **to go with the ~ of popular opinion** mit dem Strom *or* der Strömung der öffentlichen Meinung schwimmen; **if you try to go against the ~ of events** wenn Sie versuchen, gegen den Strom der Ereignisse anzuschwimmen; **the ~ of public feeling is now in favour of/against ...** die öffentliche Meinung tendiert zur Befürwortung/Ablehnung von ...; **a politician who ignores the ~ of popular opinion** ein Politiker, der die Tendenz(en) der öffentlichen Meinung *or* den Trend (in) der öffentlichen Meinung unbeachtet lässt

current: **current account** N Girokonto *nt*; **current assets** PL Umlaufvermögen *nt*; **current-carrying** ['kʌrənt,kærɪɪŋ] ADJ *(Elec)* Strom führend; **current collector** N *(Rail etc)* Stromabnehmer *m*; **current expenses** PL laufende Ausgaben *pl*; **current liabilities** PL kurzfristige Verbindlichkeiten *pl*

currently ['kʌrəntlɪ] ADV momentan, zurzeit, gegenwärtig; **it is ~ thought that ...** die aktuelle Meinung ist, dass ...

current meter N *(Elec)* Stromzähler *m*

current price N *(Fin)* Tages- *or* Marktpreis *m*; *(St Ex)* Tageskurs *m*

curricle ['kʌrɪkl] N offener Zweispänner

curricula [kə'rɪkjʊlə] *pl of* **curriculum**

curricular [kə'rɪkjʊləˈ] ADJ *activities* lehrplanmäßig

curriculum [kə'rɪkjʊləm] N *pl* **curricula** Lehrplan *m*; **to be on the ~** auf dem Lehrplan stehen

curriculum vitae [kə'rɪkjʊləm'viːtaɪ] N *(Brit)* Lebenslauf *m*

currish ['kɜːrɪʃ] ADJ *(dated) behaviour* hundsföttisch *(dated)*

curry[1] ['kʌrɪ] *(Cook)* **N** *(= spice)* Curry *m or nt*; *(= dish)* Curry *nt*; **~ sauce** Currysauce *f* **VT** mit Curry zubereiten

curry[2] VT **to ~ favour (with sb)** sich (bei jdm) einschmeicheln *or* lieb Kind machen

currycomb ['kʌrɪkəʊm] **N** Striegel *m* **VT** striegeln

curry powder N Currypulver *nt*

curse [kɜːs] **N** **a** *(= malediction)* Fluch *m*; **to be under a ~** unter einem Fluch stehen; **to put sb under a ~** jdn mit einem Fluch belegen, einen Fluch über jdn aussprechen; **a ~ *or* a thousand ~s on this pen/him!** *(old, hum)* den Füller/den soll doch der Kuckuck holen! *(inf)*, dieser vermaledeite Füller/Mensch! *(old)*; **~s!** *(inf)* verflucht! *(inf)*
b *(= swearword)* Fluch *m*
c *(fig: = affliction)* Fluch *m*; *(inf: = nuisance)* Plage *f (inf)*; **it's the ~ of my life** das ist der Fluch meines Lebens; **the ~ of drunkenness** der Fluch des Alkohols; **the ~** *(inf: = menstruation)* die Tage *pl (inf)*; **she has the ~** *(inf)* sie hat ihre Tage *(inf)*
VT **a** *(= put a curse on)* verfluchen; **~ you/it!** *(inf)* verflucht! *(inf)*, verdammt! *(inf)*, Mist! *(inf)*; **I could ~ you for forgetting it** ich könnte dich verwünschen, dass du das vergessen hast; **where is he now, ~ the man *or* ~ him!** *(inf)* wo steckt er jetzt, der verfluchte Kerl! *(inf)*; **~ these trains!** *(inf)* diese verfluchten Züge! *(inf)*
b *(= swear at or about)* fluchen über *(+acc)*
c *(fig: = afflict)* **to be ~d with sb/sth** mit jdm/etw geschlagen *or* gestraft sein
VI fluchen; **he started cursing and swearing** er fing an, wüst zu schimpfen und zu fluchen

cursed ['kɜːsɪd] ADJ *(inf)* verflucht *(inf)*

cursive ['kɜːsɪv] **ADJ** kursiv, Kursiv-; **~ writing** Kursivschrift *f* **N** Kursivschrift *f*

cursively ['kɜːsɪvlɪ] ADV kursiv

cursor ['kɜːsəˈ] N *(Comput)* Cursor *m*; **~ control** Cursorsteuerung *f*; **~ movements** Cursorbewegungen *pl*

cursorily ['kɜːsərɪlɪ] ADV *glance* flüchtig; *inspect, investigate also* oberflächlich

cursoriness ['kɜːsərɪnɪs] N *(of glance)* Flüchtigkeit *f*; *(of inspection, investigation also)* Oberflächlichkeit *f*

cursory ['kɜːsərɪ] ADJ *glance* flüchtig; *inspection, investigation also* oberflächlich

curst [kɜːst] ADJ *(inf)* = **cursed**

curt [kɜːt] ADJ *(+er) person* kurz angebunden, barsch; *verbal reply also* knapp; *letter, nod, refusal* kurz, knapp; **to be ~ with sb** zu jdm kurz angebunden sein

curtail [kɜː'teɪl] VT kürzen

curtailment [kɜː'teɪlmənt] N Kürzung *f*

curtain ['kɜːtn] **N** **a** Vorhang *m*; *(= net curtain)* Gardine *f*; **to draw *or* pull the ~s** *(= open)* den Vorhang/die Vorhänge aufziehen; *(= close)* den Vorhang/die Vorhänge zuziehen
b *(Theat)* Vorhang *m*; **to drop the ~** den Vorhang fallen lassen; **the ~ rises/falls *or* drops** der Vorhang hebt sich/fällt; **the ~ rises on a scene of domestic harmony** der Vorhang hebt sich und gibt den Blick auf eine Szene häuslichen Glücks frei; **to take the ~** *(inf)* vor den Vorhang treten; **to bring the ~ down on sth** *(fig)* den Vorhang endgültig über etw *(acc)* fallen lassen
c *(fig: of mystery)* Schleier *m*; **a ~ of smoke/flames/rain** eine Rauch-/Flammen-/Regenwand; **if you get caught it'll be ~s for you** *(inf)* wenn sie dich erwischen, ist für dich der Ofen aus *(inf) or* bist du weg vom Fenster *(inf)*
VT mit Vorhängen/einem Vorhang ausstatten; **a ~ed bed** ein Himmelbett *nt*

▶**curtain off** VT *sep* durch einen Vorhang/Vorhänge abtrennen

curtain: **curtain call** N *(Theat)* Vorhang *m*; **to take a ~** vor den Vorhang treten; **curtain hook** N Gardinengleithaken *m*; **curtain pole** N Vorhangstange *f*; **curtain rail** N Vorhangschiene *f*; **curtain-raiser** N *(Theat)* kurzes Vorspiel; **curtain ring** N Gardinenring *m*; **curtain rod** N Gardinenstange *f*; **curtain runner** N Vorhangschiene *f*; *(for curtain rings)* Gardinenstange *f*

curtly ['kɜːtlɪ] ADV *reply, nod* kurz, knapp; *refuse* kurzerhand

curtness ['kɜːtnɪs] N *(of person)* Barschheit *f*; *(of remark, reply, letter, refusal)* Kürze *f*, Knappheit *f*

curtsey, *(US)* **curtsy** ['kɜːtsɪ] **N** Knicks *m*; *(to royalty)* Hofknicks *m*; **to drop a curts(e)y** einen Knicks/Hofknicks machen **VI** knicksen *(to* vor *+dat)*

curvaceous [kɜː'veɪʃəs] ADJ üppig; *figure also* kurvenreich

curvaceously [kɜː'veɪʃəslɪ] ADV üppig, prall

curvature ['kɜːvətʃəˈ] N Krümmung *f*; *(misshapen)* Verkrümmung *f*; **~ of the spine** *(normal)* Rückgratkrümmung *f*; *(abnormal)* Rückgratverkrümmung *f*; **the ~ of space** die Raumkrümmung

curve [kɜːv] **N** Kurve *f*; *(of body, vase etc)* Rundung *f*, Wölbung *f*; *(of river)* Biegung *f*; *(of archway)* Bogen *m*; **there's a ~ in the road** die Straße macht einen Bogen; **the price ~** die Preiskurve; **her ~s** *(inf)* ihre Kurven *or* Rundungen *pl (inf)*
VT biegen; *(= build with a curve) arch, roof, side of ship* wölben; **gravity ~s the path of light** die Gravitation krümmt den Lichtweg; **he ~d the ball around the wall** er zirkelte den Ball um die Mauer herum
VI **a** *(line, road)* einen Bogen machen; *(river)* eine Biegung machen; **her lips ~d into a smile** ihre Lippen verzogen sich zu einem Lächeln; **the road ~s around the city** die Straße macht einen Bogen um die Stadt; **to make a ball ~ (through the air)** einen Ball anschneiden, einem Ball einen Drall geben
b *(= be curved) (space, horizon)* gekrümmt sein;

(side of ship, surface, arch) sich wölben; *(hips, breasts)* sich runden; *(metal strip etc)* sich biegen

curveball ['kɜːvbɔːl] N *(US Baseball)* *Ball, der bogenförmig vom Werfer zum Schlagmann geworfen wird*

curved [kɜːvd] ADJ *line* gebogen; *table legs etc also* geschwungen; *horizon* gekrümmt; *surface, arch, sides of ship* gewölbt; *hips* rund; **space is ~** der Raum ist gekrümmt

curvet [kɜː'vet] N Kruppade *f* VI eine Kruppade springen

curvilinear ['kɜːvɪ'lɪnɪəʳ] ADJ *(= full of curves) tracery etc* mit vielen Rundungen *or* Kurven; *(= curved) motion, course* gewunden; *(Geometry) figure* krummlinig begrenzt

curvy ['kɜːvɪ] ADJ *(+er)* *(inf) road, figure* kurvenreich

cushion ['kʊʃən] N Kissen *nt*; (= *pad, fig:* = *buffer*) Polster *nt*; *(Billiards)* Bande *f*; **a stroke off the ~** ein Stoß *m* gegen die Bande; **a ~ of air/moss** ein Luftkissen *nt*/Moospolster *nt*; **~ cover** Kissenüberzug *m*, Kissenbezug *m* VT **a** (= *absorb, soften) fall, blow* auffangen, dämpfen; *(fig) disappointment* dämpfen **b** *(fig:* = *protect)* **to ~ sb against sth** jdn gegen etw abschirmen, jdn vor etw *(dat)* behüten; **he ~ed the vase against his chest** er barg die Vase an seiner Brust **c** *(Billiards) ball* gegen die Bande spielen

cushioned ['kʊʃənd] ADJ **a** (= *padded*) Polster-, gepolstert **b** *(fig:* = *comfortable)* bequem

cushioning ['kʊʃənɪŋ] ADJ **to have a ~ effect** (stoß)dämpfend wirken; *(fig)* mildernd wirken

cushy ['kʊʃɪ] ADJ *(+er)* *(inf)* bequem; **to have a ~ time of it, to be onto a ~ number** eine ruhige Kugel schieben *(inf)*; **a ~ job** ein gemütlicher *or* ruhiger Job; **that job is a ~ number** in dem Job reißt man sich *(dat)* kein Bein aus *(inf)*

cusp [kʌsp] N *(of tooth)* Höcker *m*; *(of moon)* Spitze *f* (der Mondsichel); *(Astrol)* Eintritt *m* in ein neues Zeichen; **on the ~ of** *(fig)* an der Schwelle zu

cuspid ['kʌspɪd] N Eckzahn *m*

cuspidor ['kʌspɪdɔːʳ] N *(US)* Spucknapf *m*

cuss [kʌs] *(inf)* N **a** (= *person*) Kauz *m (inf)* **b he's not worth a (tinker's) ~** der ist keinen roten Heller wert *(inf)*; **he doesn't care a (tinker's) ~ (about it)** das ist ihm völlig Wurst *(inf) or* schnuppe *(inf)* **c** (= *oath*) Fluch *m* VI fluchen; **to ~ and swear** schimpfen und fluchen

cussed ['kʌsɪd] ADJ *(inf)* stur

cussedness ['kʌsɪdnɪs] N *(inf)* Sturheit *f*; **out of sheer ~** aus lauter *or* reiner Sturheit

cussword ['kʌswɜːd] N *(US inf)* Kraftausdruck *m*, Schimpfwort *nt*

custard ['kʌstəd] N (= *pouring custard*) ≈ Vanillesoße *f*; (= *set custard*) ≈ Vanillepudding *m*

custard: **custard apple** N *(Bot)* Zimt- *or* Rahmapfel *m*; **custard cream (biscuit)** N Doppelkeks *m* (mit Vanillecremefüllung); **custard pie** N *(in slapstick)* Sahnetorte *f*; **custard powder** N *(for pouring custard)* ≈ Vanillesoßenpulver *nt*; *(for set custard)* ≈ Vanillepuddingpulver *nt*; **custard tart** N ≈ Puddingtörtchen *nt*

custodial [kʌs'təʊdɪəl] ADJ *(form)* **a** *duties etc* als Aufseher **b ~ sentence** Gefängnisstrafe *f*

custodian [kʌs'təʊdɪən] N *(of building, park, museum)* Aufseher(in) *m(f)*, Wächter(in) *m(f)*; *(of treasure, tradition, cultural heritage, world peace etc)* Hüter(in) *m(f)*

custody ['kʌstədɪ] N **a** (= *keeping, guardianship*) Obhut *f*; *(of person)* Obhut *f*, Aufsicht *f* (of über +*acc*); *(of object)* Obhut *f*, Aufbewahrung *f* (of +*gen*, with bei); *(Jur, of children)* Sorgerecht *nt* (of für, über +*acc*); (= *guardianship*) Vormundschaft *f* (of für, über +*acc*); **to put** *or* **place sth in sb's ~** etw jdm zur Aufbewahrung anvertrauen, etw in jds Obhut *(acc) or* Gewahrsam *(acc)* geben; **the mother was awarded ~ of the children after the divorce** der Mutter wurde bei der Scheidung das Sorgerecht für *or* über die Kinder zugesprochen; **he is in the ~ of his aunt** seine Tante hat die Vormundschaft für *or* über ihn; **the country's future is placed in the ~ of its teachers** die Zukunft des Landes liegt in den Händen der Lehrer; **whilst these goods are in the ~ of the police** während sich die Gegenstände in Polizeiaufbewahrung befinden **b** (= *police detention*) (polizeilicher) Gewahrsam, Haft *f*; **to take sb into ~** jdn verhaften; **he will be kept in ~ until ...** er wird inhaftiert bleiben, bis ...

custom ['kʌstəm] N **a** (= *established behaviour, convention*) Sitte *f*, Brauch *m*; **~ demands ...** es ist Sitte *or* Brauch ...; **as ~ has it** wie es Sitte *or* (der) Brauch ist; **our ~s** unsere Bräuche *pl*, unsere Sitten und Gebräuche *pl*

b (= *habit*) (An)gewohnheit *f*; **it was his ~ to rest each afternoon** er pflegte am Nachmittag zu ruhen *(geh)*; **as was his ~** wie er es gewohnt war, wie er es zu tun pflegte *(geh)*

c *no pl* (*Comm:* = *patronage*) Kundschaft *f*; **to get sb's ~** jdn als Kunden gewinnen; **to take one's ~ elsewhere** (als Kunde) anderswo hingehen, woanders Kunde werden; **we get a lot of ~ from tourists** wir haben viele Touristen als Kunden, viele unserer Kunden sind Touristen

d customs PL (= *duty, organization*) Zoll *m*; **(the) Customs** der Zoll; **the Customs and Excise Department** die britische Zollbehörde; **to go through ~s** durch den Zoll gehen; **to get sth through the ~s** etw durch den Zoll bekommen

e *(Jur)* Gewohnheitsrecht *nt*; **that is ~ and practice** das ist allgemein üblich

ADJ **a** *(US) suit, shoes* maßgefertigt; *carpenter* auf Bestellung arbeitend; **~ tailor** Maßschneider(in) *m(f)*

b *(Comput)* benutzerdefiniert

customarily ['kʌstəmərəlɪ] ADV normaler- *or* üblicherweise

customary ['kʌstəmərɪ] ADJ (= *conventional*) üblich; (= *habitual*) gewohnt; **it's ~ to apologize** man entschuldigt sich normalerweise *or* gewöhnlich; **it's ~ to wear a tie** man trägt normalerweise *or* gewöhnlich eine Krawatte; **~ laws** Gewohnheitsrecht *nt*

custom-built ['kʌstəmbɪlt] ADJ speziell angefertigt

custom car N speziell angefertigtes Auto, Spezialauto *nt*

customer ['kʌstəməʳ] N **a** (*Comm:* = *patron*) Kunde *m*, Kundin *f*; **our ~s** unsere Kundschaft; **the ~ is always right** der Kunde ist König **b** (*inf:* = *person*) Kunde *m (inf)*

customer: **customer base** N Kundenstamm *m*; **customer service(s)** N Kundendienst *m*; **~ department** Kundendienstabteilung *f*; **customer support** N Kundenbetreuung *f*, Kundenservice*m*

custom house N *(esp Hist)* Zollamt *nt*

customize ['kʌstəmaɪz] VT *car etc* individuell aufmachen; *(Comput)* anpassen

custom-made ['kʌstəmmeɪd] ADJ *clothes, shoes* maßgefertigt, nach Maß; *furniture, car* speziell angefertigt

customs: **customs clearance** N Zollabfertigung *f*; **to get ~ for sth** etw zollamtlich abfertigen lassen; **customs declaration** N Zollerklärung *f*; **customs duty** N Zoll(abgabe *f*) *m*; **customs house** N Zollamt *nt*; **customs inspection** N Zollkontrolle *f*; **customs officer** N Zollbeamte(r) *m*, Zollbeamtin *f*; **customs union** N Zollunion *f*

cut [kʌt]
vb: pret, ptp **cut**

1 NOUN	4 INTRANSITIVE VERB
2 ADJECTIVE	5 PHRASAL VERBS
3 TRANSITIVE VERB	

1 – NOUN

a [= result of cutting] Schnitt *m*; (= *wound*) Schnittwunde *f*, Schnitt *m*; **he was treated for minor cuts and bruises** er wurde wegen kleinerer Schnittwunden und Prellungen behandelt; **to make a cut in sth** in etw *(acc)* einen Einschnitt machen

b [= act of cutting] Schnitt *m*; *(with sword, whip)* Hieb *m*, Schlag *m*; **I need a cut** ich muss mir die Haare schneiden lassen; **his hair could do with a cut** seine Haare könnten mal wieder geschnitten werden; **a cut from his sword** ein Schlag mit seinem Schwert; **he's/it's a cut above the rest of them** er/es ist den anderen um einiges überlegen; **the cut and thrust of politics/publishing** das Spannungsfeld der Politik/der Trubel des Verlagswesens; **the cut and thrust of the debate** die Hitze der Debatte

c [= reduction] *in prices* Senkung *f*, Herabsetzung *f*; *(in quality)* Verminderung *f*; *(in quantity, length etc)* Verringerung *f*; *(in expenses, salaries, expenditure, budget etc)* Kürzung *f*; *(in working hours, holidays)* (Ver)kürzung *f*; *(in programme, text, film)* Kürzung *f*; *(in production, output)* Einschränkung *f*; **a cut in prices/taxes** eine Senkung der Preise/Steuern *(gen)*, eine Preis-/Steuersenkung; **a 1% cut in interest rates** eine 1%ige Senkung des Zinssatzes; **he had to take a cut in (his) salary** er musste eine Gehaltskürzung hinnehmen; **the censor had made so many cuts** die Zensur hatte so viel gestrichen

d [of clothes, hair] Schnitt *m*; *(of jewel)* Schliff *m*

e [of meat] Stück *nt*

f [= share] *inf* Anteil *m*, Teil *m*; **to get one's cut** seinen Teil *or* Anteil bekommen; **to take one's cut** sich *(dat)* seinen Teil *or* Anteil nehmen; **a cut of the profits/proceeds** ein Teil *m* der Gewinne/Einnahmen

g [= gibe] Spitze *f*, spitze Bemerkung; **that remark was a cut at me** diese Bemerkung war auf mich gemünzt; **the unkindest cut of all** *(prov)* der schlimmste Schlag

h [Mus] Track *m*; **a cut from her forthcoming album** ein Track *m* von ihrem nächsten Album

i [= route, waterway = short route] Abkürzung *f*; (= *connecting alleyway etc*) Verbindungsweg *m*; (= *canal*) Kanal *m*

j [= woodcut] Holzschnitt *m*

k [Elec] Unterbrechung *f* (in +*gen*); *(planned)* Sperre *f*; **power/electricity cut** Stromausfall *m*; *(planned)* Stromsperre *f*

l [Cards] Abheben *nt*; **it's your cut** du hebst ab

m [Sport] **to give a cut to the ball** den Ball anschneiden

2 – ADJECTIVE

geschnitten; *bread* (auf)geschnitten; *grass* gemäht; *prices* ermäßigt, herabgesetzt; **to have a cut finger/hand/lip** eine Schnittwunde am Finger/an der Hand/an der Lippe haben; **finely cut features** fein geschnittene Züge *pl*; **a well-cut dress** ein gut geschnittenes Kleid; **cut flowers** Schnittblumen *pl*; **hand-cut crystal** handgeschliffenes Kristall; **the cut version of a film** die gekürzte *or* (= *censored also*) zensierte Fassung eines Films → **half-cut**

3 – TRANSITIVE VERB

a [= make cut in] *with knife, scissors* schneiden; *fabric* zuschneiden; *cake* anschneiden; *rope* durchschneiden; *(Naut)* kappen; *grass* mähen; **to cut one's finger/lip/leg** sich *(dat)* am Finger/an der Lippe/am Bein schneiden; *(with knife, razor etc also)* sich *(dat)* in den Finger/in die Lippe/ins Bein schneiden; **to cut one's nails** sich *(dat)* die Nägel schneiden; **to cut oneself (shaving)** sich (beim Rasieren) schneiden; **to cut sth in half/three** etw halbieren/dritteln, etw in zwei/drei Teile schneiden; **the road cuts the village in two** die Straße schneidet das Dorf in zwei Teile; **to cut a hole in sth** ein Loch in etw *(acc)* schneiden; **to cut to pieces** zerstückeln; *sb's reputation* zerstören; **to cut open** aufschneiden; **he cut his head open** er hat sich *(dat)* den Kopf aufgeschlagen; **to have** *or* **get one's hair cut** sich *(dat)* die Haare schneiden lassen; **to cut sb free/loose** jdn losschneiden

b [= cut off] abschneiden; *(with sword, axe)* abschlagen, abhacken

c [= make by cutting] *steps* schlagen, hauen; *channel, trench* graben, ausheben; *figure (in wood)* schnitzen *(in* aus); *(in stone)* hauen *(in* aus); *glass, crystal, diamond* schleifen; *suit, dress, skirt* zuschneiden; *key* anfertigen; **to cut one's coat according to one's cloth** *(prov)* sich nach der Decke strecken; **to cut a fine/sorry figure** eine gute/schlechte Figur machen *or* abgeben
d [= break off] *electricity* abstellen; *gas* (ab)sperren, abstellen; *power supply* unterbrechen; *ties, links* abbrechen; **to cut all one's ties** *(fig)* alle Verbindungen abbrechen *(with* zu)
e [= skip] *lecture, class* schwänzen *(inf)*; **to cut school** die Schule schwänzen *(inf)*
f [= intersect] *line* schneiden; *(path, road)* kreuzen
g [= reduce] *prices* senken, herabsetzen; *quality* vermindern; *quantity* reduzieren; *working hours, holidays* (ver)kürzen; *expenses, salary, text, programme, film* kürzen; *production, output* verringern, einschränken
h [= remove] *part of programme, text, film* streichen; **to cut and paste text** *(Comput) text etc* ausschneiden ; **they cut him from the team** sie warfen ihn aus dem Team
i [= censor] *film* Teile streichen aus
j [= cause pain or suffering to] schmerzen; **the wind cut his face** der Wind schnitt ihm ins Gesicht → **quick N a**
k [Cards] **to cut the cards/the pack** abheben
l [Sport] *ball* (an)schneiden
m [= edit] *film* schneiden, cutten
n [Mus] *record* pressen; *(singer)* machen
o [= stop] *engine* abstellen; *(inf) noise* aufhören mit; **cut the crap!** *(sl)* hör mit dem Scheiß auf! *(inf)*
p [= divide] **if we cut the profits three ways** wenn wir den Gewinn dritteln *or* unter drei verteilen *or* aufteilen
q [= manage] *inf* **he can't cut it** er bringts nicht *(inf)*
r [set structures]
♦ **to cut sb/sth short to cut sb short** jdm das Wort abschneiden; **to cut sth short** etw vorzeitig abbrechen; **to cut a long story short** kurz und gut, der langen Rede kurzer Sinn
♦ **to cut sb dead** *(Brit)* jdn wie Luft behandeln
♦ **to cut a deal** *(esp US inf)* ein Geschäft machen
♦ **to cut a tooth** zahnen, einen Zahn bekommen; **to cut one's teeth on sth** *(fig)* sich *(dat)* die (ersten) Sporen mit *or* an etw *(dat)* verdienen
♦ **to cut it fine** *(Brit)* knapp bemessen *or* kalkulieren ; **don't cut it too fine with your essay** lass es mit deinem Aufsatz nicht auf die letzte Minute ankommen; **£10 would be cutting it rather fine** £ 10 wären etwas knapp (bemessen); **2.20 would be cutting it a bit fine** 2.20 Uhr wäre ein bisschen knapp; **aren't you cutting it a bit fine?** ist das nicht ein bisschen knapp?
♦ **to cut one's losses** eine Sache abschließen, ehe der Schaden (noch) größer wird

4 – INTRANSITIVE VERB

a [instrument, knife, scissors] schneiden; *(lawn mower)* mähen, schneiden; **to cut loose** *(Naut)* losmachen; *(fig)* sich losmachen; *(US inf)* loslegen *(inf)*
♦ **to cut both ways** *(fig)* ein zweischneidiges Schwert sein
♦ **to cut and run** abhauen *(inf)*, die Beine in die Hand nehmen *(inf)*
b [material] **paper cuts easily** Papier lässt sich leicht schneiden
c [= intersect] *lines, roads* sich schneiden
d [Film] *= change scenes* überblenden *(to* zu); *(= stop filming)* aufhören, abbrechen; **cut!** Schnitt!, aus! → **chase**
e [Cards] abheben; **to cut for dealer** den Geber auslosen *(durch Ziehen einer Karte)*
f [Sport] den Ball/die Bälle (an)schneiden; **to cut at a ball** einen Ball anschneiden

5 – PHRASAL VERBS

► **cut across** VI *+prep obj* **a** *(lit)* hinübergehen/-fahren *etc (prep obj* über *+acc)*; **you can cut across here** Sie können hier hinüber; **if you cut across the fields** wenn Sie über die Felder gehen; **to cut across country** querfeldein gehen/fahren *etc* **b** *(fig) theory etc* widersprechen *(prep obj +dat)*; **this problem cuts across all ages** dieses Problem betrifft alle Altersgruppen

► **cut away** VT *sep* wegschneiden; **the dress was cut away at the back** das Kleid war hinten *or* im Rücken (tief) ausgeschnitten

► **cut back** VI **a** *(= go back)* zurückgehen; *(in car)* zurückfahren; *(Film)* zurückblenden **b** *(= reduce expenditure etc)* sich einschränken; **to cut back on expenses** *etc* die Ausgaben *etc* einschränken; **to cut back on production** die Produktion zurückschrauben; **to cut back on smoking/sweets** weniger rauchen/Süßigkeiten essen VT *sep* **a** *plants* zurückschneiden **b** *production* zurückschrauben; *outgoings* einschränken; *programme* kürzen

► **cut down** VT *sep* **a** *tree* fällen; *corn* schneiden; *person (with sword)* (mit dem Schwert) niederstrecken
b *(= make smaller) number, expenses* einschränken; *text* zusammenstreichen *(to* auf *+acc)*; **to cut sb down to size** jdn auf seinen Platz verweisen
c *usu pass (= kill)* dahinraffen *(geh)*; **a young man cut down in his prime** ein junger Mann, der im Frühling seiner Jahre dahingerafft wurde *(liter)*
VI *(= reduce intake, expenditure etc)* sich einschränken; **to cut down on sth** etw einschränken; **to cut down on smoking** das Rauchen einschränken; **to cut down on sweets** weniger Süßigkeiten essen

► **cut in** VI **a** *(= interrupt)* sich einschalten *(on* in *+acc)*; **to cut in on sb** jdn unterbrechen; **to cut in on sth** sich in etw *(acc)* einschalten
b *(= cut towards the centre) (blade)* einschneiden; **to cut in on sb's market** sich in jds Revier *(acc)* drängen *(inf)*; **he cut in to the centre of the pitch** er zog ins Mittelfeld herüber
c *(Aut: = swerve in front)* sich direkt vor ein anderes/das andere Auto hineindrängen; **to cut in in front of sb** jdn schneiden; **he cut in so sharply that the car behind had to swerve** er zog so schnell herüber, dass das nachfolgende Auto ausweichen musste
VT *sep* **to cut sb in on sth** jdn an etw *(dat)* beteiligen

► **cut into** VI *+prep obj* **a** *(= make a cut in) cake, meat* anschneiden **b** *(= swerve into) line of traffic* sich drängeln in *(+acc)*; *woods, alleyway* schnell einbiegen in *(+acc)* **c** *(= interrupt) conversation* fallen in *(+acc)* **d** *(fig: = make inroads into) savings* ein Loch reißen in *(+acc)*; *holidays* verkürzen

► **cut off** VT *sep* **a** *(with knife etc)* abschneiden; *(with sword etc)* abschlagen; **to cut off sb's head** jdm den Kopf abschlagen
b *town, supply* abschneiden; *allowance* sperren; **to cut off the enemy's retreat/supplies** dem Feind den Rückzug/die Zufuhr abschneiden; **his deafness cut him off from others** seine Taubheit schnitt ihn von der Umwelt ab; **we're very cut off out here** wir leben hier draußen sehr abgeschieden; **that's it, you're cut off** *(US inf: = no more alcohol)* okay, dir reichts für heute *(inf)*
c *(= disinherit)* enterben; **to cut sb off without a penny** jdn enterben
d *(= disconnect) gas, telephone etc* abstellen; **we've been cut off** *(Telec)* wir sind unterbrochen worden
e *(= break off) discussion, relations* abbrechen; **to cut sb off in the middle of a sentence** jdn mitten im Satz unterbrechen

► **cut out** VI *(engine, radio transmission)* aussetzen
VT *sep* **a** *(= remove by cutting)* ausschneiden; *malignant growth* herausschneiden
b *(= form by cutting) coat, dress* zuschneiden; **they had cut out a path through the jungle** sie hatten (sich *dat*) einen Weg durch den Dschungel geschlagen *or* gebahnt
c *(= delete)* (heraus)streichen; *(= not bother with)* verzichten auf *(+acc)*, sich *(dat)* schenken; *smoking, swearing etc* aufhören mit, sein lassen *(inf)*; **double glazing cuts out the noise** Doppelfenster verhindern, dass der Lärm hereindringt; **cut it out!** *(inf)* hör auf damit!, lass das (sein)! *(inf)*; **cut out the nonsense** lass den Unsinn; **and you can cut out the self-pity for a start!** und mit Selbstmitleid brauchst du gar nicht erst zu kommen *or* anzufangen!
d *(fig)* **to be cut out for sth** zu etw geeignet *or* gemacht sein; **to be cut out to be sth** dazu geeignet sein, etw zu sein *or* zu werden; **he's not cut out to be a doctor** er ist nicht zum Arzt geeignet, er hat nicht das Zeug zum Arzt
e **to have one's work cut out** alle Hände voll zu tun haben

► **cut through** VT *sep* **he couldn't cut his way through** es gelang ihm nicht durchzukommen; **we cut through the housing estate** wir gingen/fuhren durch die Siedlung; **the boat cut through the waves** das Boot bahnte sich seinen Weg durch die Wellen

► **cut up** VI **to cut up rough** *(Brit inf)* Krach schlagen *(inf)* VT *sep* **a** *meat* aufschneiden; *wood* spalten; *(fig) enemy, army* vernichten **b** *(Aut)* **to cut sb up** jdn schneiden

---

cut-and-dried [ˌkʌtənˈdraɪd] ADJ *(fig)* festgelegt; **~ opinions** festgelegte Meinungen *pl*; **as far as he's concerned the whole issue is now ~** für ihn ist die ganze Angelegenheit erledigt; **it's not quite ~** so eindeutig ist das nicht

cut-and-paste [ˌkʌtənˈpeɪst] ADJ *(US)* **a ~ job** eine zusammengestückelte Arbeit *(usu pej)*

cutaneous [kjuːˈteɪnɪəs] ADJ kutan *(spec)*

cutaway [ˈkʌtəweɪ] N Cut(away) *m* ADJ **~ coat** Cut(away) *m*; **~ drawing** Schnittdiagramm *nt*

cutback [ˈkʌtbæk] N **a** Kürzung *f* **b** *(Film)* Rückblende *f*

cute [kjuːt] ADJ *(+er)* **a** *(inf: = sweet)* süß, niedlich **b** *(esp US inf: = clever) idea, gadget* dufte *(inf)*, prima *(inf)*; *(= shrewd) person, move* schlau, gerissen, clever *(inf)*; **that was pretty ~ of him** das hat er ganz schön schlau hingekriegt *(inf)*

cutely [ˈkjuːtlɪ] ADV **a** *(= sweetly)* süß, niedlich **b** *(= cleverly) designed, made* prima *(inf)*, toll *(inf)*; *(= shrewdly)* schlau, gerissen

cutesy [ˈkjuːtsɪ] ADJ *(pej inf) person* zuckersüß; *painting, clothes* kitschig

cutey [ˈkjuːtɪ] N → **cutie**

cut glass N geschliffenes Glas

cut-glass [ˈkʌtglɑːs] ADJ **a** *(lit)* aus geschliffenem Glas **b** *accent* vornehm

cuticle [ˈkjuːtɪkl] N *(of nail)* Nagelhaut *f*; *(Anat)* Epidermis *f*; *(Bot)* Kutikula *f*; **~ remover** Nagelhautentferner *m*

cutie [ˈkjuːtɪ] N *(esp US inf) (= attractive person)* flotter Käfer *(inf)*, dufte Biene *(inf)*; *(= child)* süßer Fratz *(inf)*; *(= shrewd person)* gewitzter Typ, Schlitzohr *m (pej)*

cutie-pie [ˈkjuːtɪpaɪ] N *(esp US inf)* süßer Fratz *(inf)*

cutlass [ˈkʌtləs] N Entermesser *nt*

cutler [ˈkʌtləʳ] N Messerschmied *m*

cutlery [ˈkʌtlərɪ] N *no pl (esp Brit)* Besteck *nt*

cutlet [ˈkʌtlɪt] N *(= boneless chop)* Schnitzel *nt*; *(= fish fillet)* (Fisch)schnitzel *nt*; *(of chopped meat)* (paniertes) Hacksteak

cut: **cut loaf** N aufgeschnittenes Brot; **cutoff** N **a** *(Tech, device)* Ausschaltmechanismus *m* **b** *(also* **cutoff point)** Trennlinie *f*; **cutout** N **a** *(= model)* Ausschneidemodell *nt*; *(= figure, doll)* Ausschneidepuppe *f*; **his characters are just cardboard ~s** seine Figuren sind einfach nur oberflächlich; **~ book** Ausschneidebogen *m* **b** *(of engine)* Aussetzen *nt*; **it has an automatic ~** es setzt automatisch aus **c** *(Elec)* Sperre *f* ADJ **a** *model etc* zum Ausschneiden **b** *(Elec)* Abschalt-; **~ device** Abschaltautomatik *f*; **cut-price** ADJ zu Schleuderpreisen; **~ offer** Billigangebot *nt*; **~ retailer** *(Comm)* Discounter *m*; **cut-rate** ADJ zu verbilligtem Tarif; **cut sheet feed** N *(Comput)* Einzelblatteinzug *m*

cutter ['kʌtəʳ] N **a** *(= tool)* Messer *nt*; **a pair of (wire) ~s** eine Drahtschere; *(Elec)* ein Seitenschneider *m* **b** *(of clothes)* Zuschneider(in) *m(f)*; *(of jewel)* Schleifer(in) *m(f)*; *(of glass)* Glasschneider(in) *m(f)*; *(Film)* Cutter(in) *m(f)* **c** *(= boat)* Kutter *m*; *(US: = coastguard's boat)* Boot *nt* der Küstenwache **d** *(US: = sleigh)* leichter Pferdeschlitten

cut-throat ['kʌtθrəʊt] N *(= murderous type)* Verbrechertyp *m* ADJ **a** *competition, business* unbarmherzig, mörderisch **b** **~ razor** (offenes) Rasiermesser

cutting ['kʌtɪŋ] N **a** Schneiden *nt*; *(of grass)* Mähen *nt*; *(of cake)* Anschneiden *nt*; *(of rope)* Durchschneiden *nt*, Kappen *nt*; *(of garment)* Zuschneiden *nt*, Zuschnitt *m*; *(= cutting off)* Abschneiden *nt*; *(with sword)* Abschlagen *nt*
b *(= shaping) (of steps)* Schlagen *nt*; *(of channel, trench)* Graben *nt*; *(of figure) (in wood)* Schnitzen *nt* *(in* aus); *(in stone)* Hauen *nt* *(in* aus); *(of glass, crystal, jewel)* Schliff *m*; *(of key)* Anfertigung *f*; *(of record)* Pressen *nt*, Herstellung *f*
c *(= snubbing: of person)* Schneiden *nt*; *(of lecture, class)* Schwänzen *nt (inf)*
d *(= reduction, of prices)* Senkung *f*, Herabsetzung *f*; *(of quality)* Verminderung *f*; *(of quantity)* Reduzierung *f*; *(of working hours)* Verkürzung *f*; *(of expenses, salary)* Kürzung *f*
e *(= editing, Film)* Schnitt *m*; *(of production)* Drosselung *f*; *(of part of text)* Streichung *f*
f *(Brit: = road cutting, railway cutting)* Durchstich *m*
g *(Brit: = clipping) (from newspaper)* Ausschnitt *m*; *(of cloth)* Schnipsel *m*, Stückchen (Stoff) *nt*
h *(Hort)* Ableger *m*; **to take a ~** einen Ableger nehmen
ADJ **a** *blade, edge* scharf; **to be at the ~ edge of sth** in etw *(dat)* führend sein
b *(fig) wind, cold* schneidend; *remark, tongue* scharf, spitz; **to be ~ to sb** jdm gegenüber spitze Bemerkungen machen

cutting: **cutting board** N *(US)* = **chopping board**; **cutting edge** N **a** *(= blade)* Schneide *f*, Schnittkante *f* **b** *no pl (= most advanced stage)* letzter Stand *(of gen)*; **cutting room** N *(Film)* Schneideraum *m*; **to end up on the ~ floor** *(fig)* im Papierkorb enden

cuttlebone ['kʌtlbəʊn] N Schulp *m*

cuttlefish ['kʌtlfɪʃ] N Tintenfisch *m*, Sepie *f*, Kuttelfisch *m*

cut up ADJ *(inf: = upset)* **he was very ~ about it** das hat ihn schwer getroffen *or* ziemlich mitgenommen

CV *abbr of* **curriculum vitae**

CWIS *(Comput) abbr of* **campus-wide information system** Campusnetz *nt*

cwm [ku:m] N Kar *nt*

CWO *abbr of* **cash with order**

cwt *abbr of* **hundredweight**

cyanide ['saɪənaɪd] N Zyanid *nt*, Blausäuresalz *nt*; **~ poisoning** Blausäurevergiftung *f*

cyber- ['saɪbə-] *(Comput)*: **cyberattack** N Cyberangriff *m*; **cyberbullying** N Cyber-Bullying *nt*; **cybercafé** N Internetcafé *nt*, Cybercafé *nt*; **cybermall** N Cybermall *f*, virtuelles Einkaufszentrum; **cybernetic** ADJ kybernetisch; **cybernetics** N *sing* Kybernetik *f*; **cyberpet** N Tamagotchi *m*, elektronisches Haustier; **cyberpunk** N *(Liter)* Cyberpunk *m*; **cybersecurity** N Computer- und Netzsicherheit *f*; **cybersex** N Cybersex *m*; **cyberspace** N Cyberspace *m*

cyborg ['saɪbɔ:g] N Cyborg *m*, Robotermensch *m*

cyclamen ['sɪkləmən] N Alpenveilchen *nt*, Zyklamen *nt (spec)*

cycle ['saɪkl] N **a** Zyklus *m*, Kreislauf *m*; *(of events)* Gang *m*; *(of poems, songs)* Zyklus *m*; *(Elec)* Periode *f*; **life ~** Lebenszyklus *or* -kreislauf *m*; **the moon's ~** der Mondwechsel **b** *(= bicycle)* (Fahr)rad *nt*; *(inf: = motorbike)* Maschine *f (sl)* VI mit dem (Fahr)rad fahren

cycle: **cycle cab** N Fahrradtaxi *nt*; **cycle clip** N Fahrradklammer *f*; **cycle lane** N (Fahr)radweg *m*; **cycle path** N (Fahr)radweg *m*

cycler ['saɪkləʳ] N *(US)* = **cyclist**

cycle: **cycle race** N Radrennen *nt*; **cycle rack** N Fahrradständer *m*; **cycle shed** N Fahrradstand *m*; **cycle track** N *(= path)* (Fahr)radweg *m*; *(for racing)* Radrennbahn *f*; **cycleway** N (Fahr)radweg *m*

cyclic(al) ['saɪklɪk(əl)] ADJ zyklisch; *(Elec)* periodisch

cycling ['saɪklɪŋ] N Radfahren *nt*; **I enjoy ~** ich fahre gern Rad

cycling: **cycling cape** N Radmantel *m*, Radcape *nt*; **cycling holiday** N Urlaub *m* mit dem Fahrrad; **cycling shorts** PL Radlerhose *f*; **cycling tour** N Radtour *f*

cyclist ['saɪklɪst] N (Fahr)radfahrer(in) *m(f)*; *(= motor cyclist)* Motorradfahrer(in) *m(f)*

cyclometer [saɪ'klɒmɪtəʳ] N Kilometerzähler *m*

cyclone ['saɪkləʊn] N Zyklon *m*; **~ cellar** *(US) tiefer Keller zum Schutz vor Zyklonen*

cyclonic [saɪ'klɒnɪk] ADJ zyklonartig

cyclopaedia [,saɪkləʊ'pi:dɪə] N Enzyklopädie *f*

Cyclops ['saɪklɒps] N Zyklop *m*

cyclorama [,saɪklə'rɑ:mə] N Rundhorizont *m*

cygnet ['sɪgnɪt] N Schwanjunge(s) *nt*

cylinder ['sɪlɪndəʳ] N *(Math, Aut)* Zylinder *m*; *(of revolver, typewriter)* Walze *f*; **a four-~ car** ein Vierzylinder *m*, ein vierzylindriges Auto; **to be firing on all ~s** *(lit)* auf allen Zylindern laufen; *(fig)* in Fahrt sein; **he's only firing on two ~s** *(fig)* er bringt nicht seine volle Leistung

cylinder: **cylinder block** N *(Aut)* Zylinderblock *m*; **cylinder capacity** N *(Aut)* Hubraum *m*; **cylinder head** N *(Aut)* Zylinderkopf *m*; **cylinder head gasket** N *(Aut)* Zylinderkopfdichtung *f*

cylindrical [sɪ'lɪndrɪkəl] ADJ, **cylindrically** ADV [sɪ'lɪndrɪkəl,ɪ] zylindrisch

cymbal ['sɪmbəl] N Beckenteller *m*; **~s** Becken *nt*; **to play the ~s** das Becken schlagen

cynic ['sɪnɪk] N **a** Zyniker(in) *m(f)*; **don't be such a ~** sei nicht so zynisch **b** **Cynic** *(Philos)* Kyniker *m*, Zyniker *m*

cynical ['sɪnɪkəl] ADJ **a** zynisch; **he was very ~ about it** er äußerte sich sehr zynisch dazu **b** **Cynical** *(Philos)* kynisch, zynisch

cynically ['sɪnɪklɪ] ADV zynisch

cynicism ['sɪnɪsɪzəm] N **a** *no pl* Zynismus *m* **b** *(= cynical remark)* zynische Bemerkung **c** **Cynicism** *(Philos)* Kynismus *m*, Zynismus *m*

cynosure ['saɪnəʃʊəʳ] N **to be the ~ of all eyes** *(liter)* alle Blicke auf sich ziehen *or* vereinigen

cypher N VT = **cipher**

cypress ['saɪprɪs] N Zypresse *f*

Cyprian ['sɪprɪən] N *(old)* = **Cypriot**

Cypriot ['sɪprɪət] ADJ zypriotisch, zyprisch N Zypriot(in) *m(f)*, Zyprer(in) *m(f)*

Cyprus ['saɪprəs] N Zypern *nt*

Cyrillic ['sɪrɪlɪk] ADJ kyrillisch

cyst [sɪst] N Zyste *f*

cystic fibrosis [,sɪstɪkfaɪ'brəʊsɪs] N Mukoviszidose *f*

cystitis [sɪs'taɪtɪs] N Blasenentzündung *f*, Zystitis *f (spec)*

cytology [saɪ'tɒlədʒɪ] N Zytologie *f*, Zellenlehre *f*

cytoplasm ['saɪtəʊplæzm] N Zytoplasma *nt*, Zellplasma *nt*

CZ *(US) abbr of* **Canal Zone** Kanalzone *f*, *Gebiet um den Panamakanal*

czar [zɑ:ʳ] N Zar *m*

czarevitch ['zɑ:rəvɪtʃ] N Zarewitsch *m*

czarina [zɑ:'ri:nə] N Zarin *f*

czarism ['zɑ:rɪzəm] N Zarismus *m*

czarist ['zɑ:rɪst] ADJ zaristisch N Zarist(in) *m(f)*

Czech [tʃek] ADJ tschechisch N **a** Tscheche *m*, Tschechin *f* **b** *(Ling)* Tschechisch *nt*

Czechoslovak [tʃekəʊ'sləʊvæk] *(Hist)* ADJ tschechoslowakisch N Tschechoslowake *m*, Tschechoslowakin *f*

Czechoslovakia [tʃekəʊslə'vækɪə] N *(Hist)* die Tschechoslowakei

Czechoslovakian [tʃekəʊslə'vækɪən] ADJ N *(Hist)* = **Czechoslovak**

Czech Republic N Tschechische Republik, Tschechien *nt*

D

D, d [diː] N D *nt*, d *nt*; (*Sch, as a mark*) ausreichend; **D sharp** Dis *nt*, dis *nt*; **D flat** Des *nt*, des *nt* → *also* **major, minor, natural**

D (*US Pol*) *abbr of* **Democratic** dem.

d a (*Brit old*) *abbr of* **pence** b *abbr of* **died** gest.

'd = **had, would**

DA (*US*) *abbr of* **District Attorney**

D/A *abbr of* **deposit account**

dab[1] [dæb] N a (*= small amount*) Klecks *m*; (*applied with puff, of cream etc*) Tupfer *m*; (*of liquid, perfume, glue etc*) Tropfen *m*; (*of butter*) Klacks *m*; **a ~ of powder/ointment** *etc* etwas *or* ein bisschen Puder/Salbe *etc*; **to give sth a ~ of paint** etw überstreichen b **dabs** PL (*Brit inf: = fingerprints*) Fingerabdrücke *pl* VT (*with powder etc*) betupfen; (*with towel etc*) tupfen; **to ~ one's eyes** sich (*dat*) die Augen tupfen; **she ~bed ointment/powder on her face/the wound** sie betupfte sich (*dat*) das Gesicht/die Wunde mit Salbe/Puder

▶ **dab at** VI +*prep obj* betupfen

▶ **dab off** VT *sep* abtupfen

▶ **dab on** VT *sep* auftragen (*prep obj* auf +*acc*)

dab[2] N (*= fish*) Kliesche *f*, Scharbe *f*

dab[3] ADJ (*inf*) **to be a ~ hand at sth** gut in etw (*dat*) sein; **to be a ~ hand at doing sth** sich darauf verstehen, etw zu tun

dabble ['dæbl] VT **to ~ one's hands/feet in the water** mit den Händen/Füßen im Wasser plan(t)schen VI a (*with hands, feet*) plan(t)schen b (*fig*) **to ~ in/at sth** sich (nebenbei) mit etw beschäftigen; **are you a serious photographer? – no, I only ~ (in it)** beschäftigen Sie sich ernsthaft mit der Fotografie? – nein, nur so nebenbei; **he ~s in stocks and shares/antiques** er versucht sich an der Börse/in Antiquitäten

dabbler ['dæblə'] N Amateur(in) *m(f)*

dabchick ['dæbtʃɪk] N Steißfuß *m*

da capo [dɑː'kɑːpəʊ] ADV (*Mus*) da capo, noch einmal

dace [deɪs] N *pl* - Weißfisch *m*

dacha ['dætʃə] N Datscha *f*, Datsche *f*

dachshund ['dækshʊnd] N Dackel *m*, Dachshund *m* (*rare*)

Dacron® ['dækrɒn] N (*US*) Dacron® *nt*

dactyl ['dæktɪl] N (*Zool*) Zehe *f*, Finger *m*; (*Liter*) Daktylus *m*

dactylic [dæk'tɪlɪk] ADJ daktylisch

dad [dæd] N (*inf*) Vater *m*; (*affectionately also*) Vati *m* (*inf*), Papa *m* (*inf*)

Dada ['dɑːdɑː] N (*Art*) Dada *m*

Dadaism ['dɑːdɑːɪzm] N (*Art*) Dadaismus *m*

daddy ['dædɪ] N (*inf*) Papa *m* (*inf*), Vati *m* (*inf*); **the ~ of them all** (*inf*) der Größte; **~'s boy/girl** (*pej*) Papis Liebling *m* (*inf*)

daddy-longlegs [ˌdædɪ'lɒŋlegz] N *pl* - (*Brit*) Schnake *f*; (*US*) Weberknecht *m*

dado ['deɪdəʊ] N (*of pedestal*) Basis *f*; (*of wall*) Paneel *nt*

daemon ['diːmən] N (*liter*) = **demon**

daff [dæf] N (*Brit inf*) = **daffodil**

daffodil ['dæfədɪl] N Osterglocke *f*, Narzisse *f*

daffy ['dæfɪ] ADJ (+*er*) (*inf*) = **daft**

daft [dɑːft] ADJ (+*er*) doof, blöd, bekloppt (*all inf*); **~ in the head** (*inf*) blöd (*inf*), bekloppt (*inf*); **what a ~ thing to do** so was Doofes *or* Blödes *or* Beklopptes (*all inf*); **he's ~ about her/about football** (*inf*) er ist verrückt nach ihr/nach Fußball (*inf*); **to go ~** verblöden; **he's ~ enough to believe anything** er ist so blöd, er glaubt alles

daftie ['dɑːftɪ] N (*Brit inf*) Dussel *m* (*inf*)

daftness ['dɑːftnɪs] N (*inf*) Blödheit *f*, Doofheit *f* (*both inf*)

dag [dæg] N (*inf: = shred*) Zottel *m*, Zipfel *m*, Fetzen *m* (*all inf, pej*)

dagger ['dægə'] N a Dolch *m*; **to be at ~s drawn with sb** (*fig*) mit jdm auf (dem) Kriegsfuß stehen; **to look ~s at sb** (*Brit*) jdn mit Blicken durchbohren b (*Typ*) Kreuz *nt*

dago ['deɪgəʊ] N (*pej*) Südländer(in) *m(f)*, Kanake *m* (*pej sl*), *verächtliche Bezeichnung für Spanier, Portugiesen oder Südamerikaner*

daguerreotype [də'gerəʊtaɪp] N Daguerreotypie *f* VT nach dem Daguerreotypieverfahren fotografieren

dahlia ['deɪlɪə] N Dahlie *f*

Dáil Éireann [daɪl'ɛərən] N *Unterhaus der Republik Irland*

daily ['deɪlɪ] ADJ täglich; **~ newspaper** Tageszeitung *f*; **~ wage** Tageslohn *m*; **~ grind** täglicher Trott; **~ life** der Alltag; **he is employed on a ~ basis** er ist tageweise angestellt; (*labourer*) er ist als Tagelöhner beschäftigt, er steht im Tagelohn ADV täglich; **three times ~** dreimal täglich N a (*= newspaper*) Tageszeitung *f* b (*also* **daily help, daily woman**) Putzfrau *f*

daily bread N (*fig: = livelihood*) tägliches Brot; **to earn one's ~** sich (*dat*) sein Brot verdienen

daily dozen N (*inf*) Morgengymnastik *f*

daintily ['deɪntɪlɪ] ADV zierlich; *hold, walk, move* anmutig

daintiness ['deɪntɪnɪs] N Zierlichkeit *f*; (*of movement, manners etc*) Anmutigkeit *f*, Geziertheit *f* (*pej*)

dainty ['deɪntɪ] ADJ (+*er*) a zierlich; *lace, handkerchief* fein; *movement, music* anmutig; **she has ~ little ways** bei *or* an ihr ist alles fein und zierlich b *food* appetitlich; **~ morsel** Appetithappen *m* c (*= refined*) geziert, etepetete (*inf*) N Leckerei *f*

daiquiri ['daɪkərɪ] N *Cocktail aus Rum, Limonensaft und Zucker*

dairy ['deərɪ] N Molkerei *f*; (*on farm*) Milchkammer *f*; (*= shop*) Milchgeschäft *nt*

dairy: **dairy butter** N Markenbutter *f*; **dairy cattle** PL Milchvieh *nt*; **dairy cow** N Milchkuh *f*; **dairy farm** N auf Milchviehhaltung spezialisierter Bauernhof; **dairy farming** N Milchviehhaltung *f*; **dairy herd** N Herde *f* Milchkühe; **dairy husbandry** N Milchwirtschaft *f*; **dairy ice cream** N Milchspeiseeis *nt*

dairying ['deərɪɪŋ] N Milchwirtschaft *f*

dairy: **dairymaid** N Melkerin *f*; (*= worker*) Molkereiangestellte *f*; **dairyman** N Melker *m*; (*= worker*) Molkereiangestellte(r) *m*; (*= milkman*) Milchmann *m*; **dairy produce** N, **dairy products** PL Milch- *or* Molkereiprodukte *pl*

dais ['deɪɪs] N Podium *nt*

daisy ['deɪzɪ] N Gänseblümchen *nt*; **to be pushing up the daisies** (*inf*) sich (*dat*) die Radieschen von unten besehen (*hum*)

daisy chain N Kette *f* aus Gänseblümchen

daisywheel ['deɪzɪwiːl] N (*Typ, Comput*) Typenrad *m*; **~ typewriter** Typenradschreibmaschine *f*

daisywheel printer N Typenraddrucker *m*

dale [deɪl] N (*N Engl liter*) Tal *nt*

dalesman ['deɪlzmən] N *pl* **-men** [-mən], **daleswoman** ['deɪlzwʊmən] N *pl* **-women** [-wɪmɪn] *Bewohner(in) des Gebiets der Dales in Yorkshire*

dalliance ['dælɪəns] N (*liter*) Tändelei *f* (*liter*)

dally ['dælɪ] VI a (*= waste time*) (herum)trödeln, bummeln; **without ~ing** ohne zu trödeln *or* bummeln b (*= flirt*) **to ~ with sb** mit jdm schäkern; **to ~ with an idea** mit einem Gedanken liebäugeln

Dalmatia [dæl'meɪʃə] N Dalmatien *nt*

Dalmatian [dæl'meɪʃən] ADJ dalmatinisch, dalmatisch N a (*= person*) Dalmatiner(in) *m(f)* b (*= dog*) Dalmatiner *m*

daltonism ['dɔːltənɪzəm] N Farbenblindheit *f*, Daltonismus *m* (*dated spec*), Rotgrünblindheit *f*

dam[1] [dæm] N (*lit, fig*) Damm *m*; (*= reservoir*) Stausee *m* VT (*also* **dam up**) a *river, lake* (auf)stauen; *valley* eindämmen b (*fig*) *flow of words* eindämmen; *feelings* aufstauen

dam[2] N (*= mother*) Muttertier *nt*

damage ['dæmɪdʒ] N a Schaden *m* (*to* an +*dat*); **to do a lot of ~** großen Schaden anrichten; **to do sb/sth a lot of ~** jdm/einer Sache (*dat*) großen Schaden zufügen; **the ~ to his pride/ego/reputation** die Verletzung seines Stolzes/Erschütterung seines Selbstbewusstseins/Schädigung seines Rufs; **it did no ~ to his reputation** das hat seinem Ruf nicht geschadet; **the ~ is done** (*fig*) es ist passiert b **damages** PL (*Jur*) Schaden(s)ersatz *m* (*inf: = cost*) **what's the ~?** was kostet der Spaß? (*inf*)
VT schaden (+*dat*); *health, reputation, relations also* schädigen; *machine, car, furniture, fruit, tree* beschädigen; **to ~ one's eyesight** sich (*dat*) die Augen verderben; **smoking can ~ your health** Rauchen ist gesundheitsschädlich, Rauchen schadet Ihrer Gesundheit; **to ~ one's chances** sich (*dat*) die Chancen verderben

damaged ['dæmɪdʒd] ADJ beschädigt, schadhaft (*geh*); (*= broken*) defekt

damage control, damage limitation N Schadensbegrenzung *f*

damaging ['dæmɪdʒɪŋ] ADJ schädlich; *remarks* abträglich; **to be ~ to sb/sth** sich auf jdn/etw schädigend *or* schädlich auswirken, schädlich für jdn/etw sein; **that was a ~ blow to his pride** das hat seinem Stolz einen empfindlichen Schlag versetzt

damascene ['dæməsiːn] VT damaszieren; **~d blades** Damaszener Klingen *pl*

Damascus [də'mɑːskəs] N Damaskus *nt*; **~ steel** Damaszener Stahl *m*

damask ['dæməsk] N **a** Damast *m* **b** ~ **(steel)** Damaszener Stahl *m* ADJ **a** Damast-, aus Damast; ~ **tablecloth** Damasttischdecke *f* **b** (*liter: colour*) rosig

damask rose N Damaszenerrose *f*

Dam Buster N *jd, der während des 2. Weltkriegs mit speziell angefertigten Bomben Staudämme zerstörte*

dame [deɪm] N **a** **Dame** (*Brit*) *Titel der weiblichen Träger des „Order of the British Empire"* **b** (*= old lady*) Dame *f*; **Dame Fortune** (*esp Brit*) Frau Fortuna *f* **c** (*Theat, in pantomime*) (komische) Alte **d** (*US inf*) Weib *nt* (*inf*)

damfool ['dæm'fu:l] ADJ *attr* (*inf*) idiotisch (*inf*)

dammit ['dæmɪt] INTERJ (*inf*) verdammt (*inf*), Teufel noch mal (*inf*); **it weighs 2 kilos as near as** ~ es wiegt so gut wie 2 Kilo

damn [dæm] INTERJ (*inf*) verdammt (*inf*)
N (*inf*) **he doesn't care** *or* **give a** ~ er schert sich den Teufel *or* einen Dreck (darum) (*inf*); **I don't give a** ~ das ist mir piepegal (*inf*) *or* scheißegal (*inf*); **it's not worth a** ~ das ist keinen Pfifferling wert
ADJ *attr* (*inf*) verdammt; **it's one** ~ **thing after another** verdammt noch mal, da kommt aber auch eins nach dem andern; **it's a** ~ **nuisance** das ist ein verdammter Mist (*inf*), das ist wirklich zu blöd (*inf*); **a** ~ **sight better/worse** verdammt viel besser/schlechter (*inf*); **I can't see a** ~ **thing** verdammt (noch mal), ich kann überhaupt nichts sehen (*inf*); **I couldn't see a** ~ **thing** das war vielleicht ein Mist, ich konnte überhaupt nichts sehen (*inf*)
ADV (*inf*) verdammt; **I should** ~ **well hope/think so** das will ich aber auch stark hoffen/ich doch stark annehmen; **pretty** ~ **good/quick** verdammt gut/schnell (*inf*); **you're** ~ **right** du hast völlig recht; ~ **all** nicht die Bohne (*inf*); **I've done** ~ **all today** ich hab heute null Komma nichts gemacht (*inf*)
VT **a** (*Rel*) verdammen
b (*= bring condemnation, ruin on*) das Genick brechen (*+dat*); (*evidence*) überführen
c (*= judge and condemn*) verurteilen; *book etc* verreißen; **to** ~ **sb/sth with faint praise** jdn/etw auf eine Weise loben, die ihn/es bloßstellt
d (*inf*) ~ **him/you!** (*annoyed*) verdammt! (*inf*); (*indifferent*) der kann/du kannst mich mal! (*inf*); ~ **him for forgetting** so ein (verdammter) Mist, er hats vergessen (*inf*); ~ **Richard, he's pinched my book** der verdammte Richard hat mein Buch geklaut (*inf*); ~ **it!** verdammt (noch mal)! (*inf*); ~ **it all!** zum Donnerwetter! (*inf*); (*in surprise*) Donnerwetter! (*inf*), Teufel auch! (*inf*); **well, I'll be ~ed!** Donnerwetter! (*inf*); **I'll be ~ed if I'll go there** ich denk nicht (im Schlaf) dran, da hinzugehen (*inf*); **I'll be ~ed if I know** weiß der Teufel (*inf*)

damnable ADJ, **damnably** ADV ['dæmnəbl, -ɪ] grässlich

damnation [dæm'neɪʃən] N (*Eccl*) (*= act*) Verdammung *f*; (*= state of damnation*) Verdammnis *f* INTERJ (*inf*) verdammt (*inf*)

damned [dæmd] ADJ **a** *soul* verdammt **b** (*inf*) = **damn ADJ** ADV = **damn ADV** N (*Eccl, liter*) **the** ~ *pl* die Verdammten *pl*

damnedest ['dæmdɪst] N **to do** *or* **try one's** ~ (*inf*) verdammt noch mal sein Möglichstes tun (*inf*)

damning ['dæmɪŋ] ADJ vernichtend; *evidence* belastend; **he was pretty** ~ **about it** er hat sich ziemlich vernichtend darüber geäußert

Damocles ['dæməkli:z] N **sword of** ~ Damoklesschwert *nt*

damp [dæmp] ADJ (*+er*) feucht; **a** ~ **smell** ein modriger Geruch; **a** ~ **squib** (*fig*) ein Reinfall *m*
N **a** (*= dampness*) Feuchtigkeit *f* **b** (*Min*) (*= chokedamp*) Schlagwetter *nt*; (*= firedamp*) Grubengas *nt* VT **a** befeuchten, anfeuchten **b** (*fig*) *enthusiasm etc* dämpfen **c** *sounds, vibrations* dämpfen; (*also* **damp down**) *fire* ersticken

damp course N Dämmschicht *f*

dampen ['dæmpən] VT = **damp VT a, b**

damper ['dæmpə'] N **a** (*of chimney*) (Luft)klappe *f*; (*of piano*) Dämpfer *m* **b** **to put a** ~ **on sth** einer Sache (*dat*) einen Dämpfer aufsetzen **c** (*Austral: = bread*) Fladenbrot *nt*

dampish ['dæmpɪʃ] ADJ etwas feucht

damply ['dæmplɪ] ADV feucht

dampness ['dæmpnɪs] N Feuchtigkeit *f*

damp-proof ['dæmppru:f] ADJ feuchtigkeitsbeständig; ~ **course** Dämmschicht *f*

damsel ['dæmzəl] N (*obs, liter*) Maid *f* (*obs, liter*)

damselfly ['dæmzəlflaɪ] N Seejungfer *f*, Schlankjungfer *f*

damson ['dæmzən] N (*= fruit*) Damaszenerpflaume *f*; (*= tree*) Damaszenerpflaumenbaum *m*

Dan [dæn] N (*Sport*) Dan *m*

dance [dɑ:ns] N **a** (*= movement*) Tanz *m*; ~ **class** Tanzstunde *f*; **the Dance of Death** der Totentanz; **may I have the next ~?** darf ich um den nächsten Tanz bitten?; **she's led him a merry** ~ sie hat ihn ja ganz schön an der Nase herumgeführt; (*= caused a lot of trouble*) ihretwegen hat er sich (*dat*) die Hacken abgelaufen
b (*= ball*) Tanz *m*, Tanzabend *m*; **public** ~ öffentliche Tanzveranstaltung; **end-of-term** ~ Semesterball *m*; **to give** *or* **hold a** ~ einen Tanz (-abend) veranstalten; (*privately*) eine Tanzparty geben; **to go to a** ~ tanzen gehen, zum Tanzen gehen
VT tanzen; **to** ~ **attendance on sb** jdn von hinten und vorn bedienen (*inf*)
VI **a** (*= perform dance*) tanzen; **would you like to ~?** möchten Sie tanzen?
b (*= move here and there*) **to** ~ **about** (herum)tänzeln; **to** ~ **up and down** auf- und abhüpfen; **to** ~ **for joy** einen Freudentanz aufführen
c (*fig*) tanzen; (*boat on waves*) schaukeln

dance *in cpds* Tanz-; **dance band** N Tanzkapelle *f*; **dance floor** N Tanzboden *m*; (*in restaurant*) Tanzfläche *f*; **dance hall** N Tanzsaal *m*; **dance music** N Tanzmusik *f*

dancer ['dɑ:nsə'] N Tänzer(in) *m(f)*; **you ~!** (*Brit inf: = well done*) super gemacht! (*inf*)

dance theatre, (*US*) **dance theater** N Tanztheater *nt*

dancing ['dɑ:nsɪŋ] N Tanzen *nt* ATTR Tanz-; ~ **dervish** tanzender Derwisch; ~ **shoe** Tanzschuh *m*; **put on your** ~ **shoes!** (*fig*) mach dich hübsch *or* zurecht!

dancing: **dancing girl** N Tänzerin *f*; **dancing master** M Tanzlehrer *m*; **dancing partner** N Tanzpartner(in) *m(f)*; **dancing step** N Tanzschritt *m*

D and C *abbr of* **dilation and curettage** Dilation und Kürettage *f* (*spec*), Ausschabung *f*

dandelion ['dændɪlaɪən] N Löwenzahn *m*

dandelion clock ['dændɪlaɪən,klɒk] N Pusteblume *f*

dander ['dændə'] N (*inf*) **to get sb's** ~ **up** jdn auf die Palme bringen (*inf*); **to get one's** ~ **up** seine *or* die Borsten aufstellen (*inf*)

dandified ['dændɪfaɪd] ADJ stutzerhaft

dandle ['dændl] VT schaukeln (*on* auf *+dat*)

dandruff ['dændrəf] N Schuppen *pl*

dandruffy ['dændrəfɪ] ADJ *hair* schuppig

dandy ['dændɪ] N Dandy *m*, Stutzer *m* (*dated*), Geck *m* (*dated*) ADJ (*dated esp US inf*) prima (*inf*)

Dane [deɪn] N Däne *m*, Dänin *f*

dang [dæŋ] (*dated inf*) ADJ, ADB, VT = **damn ADJ, ADV, VT d**

danger ['deɪndʒə'] N **a** Gefahr *f*; **he loves** ~ er liebt die Gefahr; **the ~s of smoking** die mit dem Rauchen verbundenen Gefahren; **to put sb/sth in** ~ jdn/etw in Gefahr bringen, jdn/etw gefährden; **to run into** ~ in Gefahr geraten; **to be in** ~ **of doing sth** Gefahr laufen, etw zu tun; **the species is in** ~ **of extinction** die Art ist vom Aussterben bedroht; **out of** ~ außer Gefahr; **there is a** ~ **of fire** es besteht Feuergefahr; **there is a** ~ **of his getting lost** es besteht die Gefahr, dass er sich verirrt; **he ran the** ~ **of being recognized** er lief Gefahr, erkannt zu werden; **there is no** ~ **of that** die Gefahr besteht nicht; **to be a** ~ **to sb/sth** für jdn/etw eine Gefahr bedeuten; **he's a** ~ **to himself** er bringt sich selbst in Gefahr
b **"danger"** „Achtung, Lebensgefahr!"; (*Mot*) „Gefahrenstelle"; **"danger, high-tension cables"** „Achtung, Hochspannung!"; **"danger, ice"** „Glatteisgefahr"; **"danger, keep out"** „Zutritt verboten, Lebensgefahr!"; **the signal was at** ~ (*Rail*) das Signal stand auf Rot

danger: **danger area** N Gefahrenzone *f or* -bereich *m*; **danger list** N **on/off the** ~ in/außer Lebensgefahr; **danger money** N Gefahrenzulage *f*; **to get** ~ eine Gefahrenzulage kriegen

dangerous ['deɪndʒrəs] ADJ gefährlich; *driving* rücksichtslos; **these prisoners are not** ~ **to the public** diese Gefangenen stellen keine Gefahr für die Öffentlichkeit dar; **the Bronx can be a** ~ **place** die Bronx kann gefährlich sein; ~ **drugs** gefährliche Medikamente; (*= illegal*) Drogen *pl*; **the lion was injured but still** ~ der Löwe war verletzt, aber er stellte immer noch eine Gefahr dar; **to be** ~ **to health** gesundheitsgefährdend sein; **to be a** ~ **driver** rücksichtslos fahren; **this is a** ~ **game we're playing** wir spielen hier gefährlich; **a little knowledge** *or* **learning is a** ~ **thing** (*prov*) Halbwissen ist gefährlich

dangerously ['deɪndʒrəslɪ] ADV gefährlich; *low, high* bedenklich; *drive* rücksichtslos; **the deadline is getting** ~ **close** der Termin rückt bedenklich nahe; **she was** ~ **ill** sie war todkrank, sie schwebte in Lebensgefahr; **let's live** ~ **for once** lass uns einmal etwas riskieren

danger: **danger point** N Gefahrengrenze *f*; **to reach** ~ die Gefahrengrenze erreichen; **danger signal** N (*lit, fig*) Warnsignal *nt*; (*Rail*) Deckungssignal *nt* vor Gefahr (*spec*); **danger zone** N Gefahrenzone *f*

dangle ['dæŋgl] VT baumeln lassen; **to** ~ **sth in front of** *or* **before sb** (*fig*) jdm etw verlockend in Aussicht stellen VI baumeln

dangling ['dæŋglɪŋ] ADJ baumelnd; ~ **participle** (*Gram*) *Partizip mit falschem Bezug*

Danish ['deɪnɪʃ] ADJ dänisch N (*= language*) Dänisch *nt*; **the** ~ *pl* (*= people*) die Dänen

Danish blue (cheese) N Blauschimmelkäse *m*

Danish pastry N Plundergebäck *nt*

dank [dæŋk] ADJ (unangenehm) feucht

Dante ['dæntɪ] N Dante *m*

Dantean ['dæntɪən] ADJ dantisch

Dantesque [dæn'tesk] ADJ dantesk

Danube ['dænju:b] N Donau *f*

dapper ['dæpə'] ADJ gepflegt, gediegen

dapple ['dæpl] VT sprenkeln

dappled ['dæpld] ADJ **a** (*= patchy*) *light* gefleckt; ~ **with sunlight** mit Sonnenlicht gesprenkelt; ~ **shade** Halbschatten *m* **b** (*= mottled*) *horse* scheckig

dapple grey (horse), (*US*) **dapple gray (horse)** N Apfelschimmel *m*

DAR *abbr of* **Daughters of the American Revolution** Töchter *pl* der amerikanischen Revolution

Darby and Joan ['dɑ:bɪən'dʒəʊn] PL *glückliches, älteres Ehepaar*; ~ **club** Altenklub *m*

Dardanelles [,dɑ:də'nelz] PL Dardanellen *pl*

dare [dɛə'] ✪ 14 VI (*= be bold enough*) es wagen; (*= have the confidence*) sich trauen; **you/he wouldn't ~!** du wirst dich/er wird sich schwer hüten; **you ~!** untersteh dich!; **how ~ you!** was fällt dir ein!
VT **a** **to** ~ **(to) do sth** (es) wagen, etw zu tun, sich trauen, etw zu tun; **I didn't** ~ **(to) go upstairs** ich habe mich nicht getraut, die Treppe hinaufzugehen, ich habe mich nicht die Treppe hinauf getraut; **he wouldn't** ~ **say anything bad about his boss** er wird sich hüten *or* sich unterstehen, etwas Schlechtes über seinen Chef zu sagen; **he** ~ **not** *or* **~n't do it** das wagt er nicht!; **she ~s to dress differently (from the**

others) sie hat den Mut, sich anders (als die anderen) anzuziehen; **how ~ you say such things?** wie kannst du es wagen *or* was unterstehst du dich, so etwas zu sagen?; **don't you ~ say that to me** untersteh dich, das zu mir zu sagen; **~ you do it?** trauen Sie sich?
b **I ~ say it gets quite cold here** ich könnte mir denken, dass es hier ziemlich kalt wird; **I ~ say he'll be there** es kann (gut) sein, dass er dort sein wird; **he's bound to be there – I ~ say** er ist sicher dort – das kann gut sein; **he was very sorry – I ~ say** es tat ihm sehr leid – das glaube ich gerne
c *(= challenge)* **go on, I ~ you!** (trau dich doch, du) Feigling!; **are you daring me?** wetten, dass? *(inf)*; **(I) ~ you to jump off** spring doch, du Feigling!
d *(rare, = face the risk of)* riskieren; *danger* trotzen *(+dat)*
N Mutprobe *f*; **to do sth for a ~** etw als Mutprobe tun

daredevil [ˈdɛəˌdevl] **N** Waghals *m* **ADJ** waghalsig

daresay [ˌdɛəˈseɪ] *(esp Brit)* = **dare say**, → **dare VT b**

daring [ˈdɛərɪŋ] **ADJ** **a** *(= courageous) person, move* mutig, kühn *(geh)*; *attempt* kühn *(geh)*; *escape* waghalsig; **at least she was ~ enough to attempt it** sie hat sich wenigstens getraut, es zu versuchen **b** *(= audacious) person* wagemutig; *writer, clothes, film, book* gewagt; **a ~ low-cut dress** ein Kleid mit gewagtem Ausschnitt **N** Wagemut *m*, Kühnheit *f (geh)*; *(of statement)* Gewagtheit *f*

daringly [ˈdɛərɪŋlɪ] **ADV** mutig, kühn *(geh)*; **a ~ low-cut dress** ein Kleid mit einem gewagten Ausschnitt

dark [dɑːk] ✪ 16.1 **ADJ** *(+er)* **a** *room, house, street, cloud, colour, hair, eyes, skin* dunkel; **it will not be ~ for half an hour yet** es wird erst in einer halben Stunde dunkel; **it's getting ~** es wird dunkel; **~ blue/grey** dunkelblau/-grau; **a ~ blue** ein dunkles Blau
b *(= sad, gloomy) days, period, mood* düster, finster; **to think ~ thoughts** düsteren Gedanken nachhängen
c *(= sinister) corner, secret* dunkel; *forces* dunkel, finster; *look, threat* finster; **from ~est Peru** aus dem finstersten Peru; **the ~ side of sth** die Schattenseite einer Sache *(gen)*; **she flashed a ~ glance at me** sie warf mir einen finsteren Blick zu; **to drop ~ hints** dunkle Andeutungen machen; **~ deed** Übeltat *f*
d *(old, = secret)* geheim; **to keep sth ~** etw geheim halten
e *(Phon)* velar, dunkel
N **a** **the ~** *(= darkness)* die Dunkelheit; **he was sitting in the ~** er saß im Dunkeln; **they aren't afraid of the ~** sie haben keine Angst im Dunkeln *or* vor der Dunkelheit; **after/before ~** nach/vor Einbruch der Dunkelheit; **until ~** bis zum Einbruch der Dunkelheit; **we'll be back after ~** wir kommen wieder, wenn es dunkel ist
b *(fig)* **to be in the ~ (about sth)** keine Ahnung (von etw) haben; **to keep** *or* **leave sb in the ~ (about sth)** jdn (über etw *acc*) im Dunkeln lassen; **we must keep him in the ~** er darf nichts davon wissen; **to work in the ~** im Dunkeln tappen

dark: **dark age** **N** *(= era)* dunkles Zeitalter; **the Dark Ages** das frühe Mittelalter; **to be living in the ~s** *(pej)* im finstersten Mittelalter leben; **dark chocolate** **N** Zartbitterschokolade *f*; **dark-complexioned** [ˌdɑːkkəmˈplekʃənd] **ADJ** mit dunklem Teint; **Dark Continent** **N** **the ~** der Schwarze Erdteil

darken [ˈdɑːkən] **VT** **a** *(lit)* dunkel machen; *sky* verdunkeln; *(before storm)* verfinstern; **to ~ one's hair/eyelashes** sich *(dat)* die Haare/Wimpern dunkel färben; **the sun ~ed her skin** die Sonne hat ihre Haut gebräunt **b** *(fig)* trüben; *future* trüben, verdüstern; **never ~ my door again!** lassen Sie sich hier nicht mehr blicken!
VI **a** *(lit)* dunkel werden; *(sky)* sich verdunkeln; *(before storm)* sich verfinstern **b** *(fig, atmosphere, mood)* sich trüben, sich verdüstern; *(face, eyes)* sich verfinstern

dark: **dark-eyed** **ADJ** dunkeläugig; **dark glasses** **PL** Sonnenbrille *f*; *(of blind person)* dunkle Brille; **dark horse** **N** *(fig)* stilles Wasser; *(= unexpected winner)* unbekannte Größe

darkie, darky [ˈdɑːkɪ] **N** *(pej inf)* Schwarze(r) *mf*

darkish [ˈdɑːkɪʃ] **ADJ** *colour, complexion* ziemlich dunkel; **the car was a ~ colour/~ green** der Wagen hatte eine dunkle/dunkelgrüne Farbe

darkly [ˈdɑːklɪ] **ADV** *(+vb)* düster, finster; *(+adj)* auf finstere Weise; **to mutter/hint ~** dunkle Bemerkungen/Andeutungen machen; **a ~ comic novel** ein finster-komischer Roman

dark matter **N** *(Astron)* dunkle Materie, Dunkelmaterie *f*

darkness [ˈdɑːknɪs] **N** **a** *(lit)* Dunkelheit *f*; *(of night)* Finsternis *f*, Dunkelheit *f*; **in total ~** in totaler *or* völliger Dunkelheit, in tiefem Dunkel *(geh)*; **the house was in ~** das Haus lag im Dunkeln **b** *(fig: = sinisterness)* Finsterkeit *f* **c** *(fig: = gloominess, sadness)* Düsterkeit *f*

dark: **darkroom** **N** *(Phot)* Dunkelkammer *f*; **dark-skinned** **ADJ** dunkelhäutig

darky **N** *(pej inf)* = **darkie**

darling [ˈdɑːlɪŋ] **N** **a** Schatz *m*; *(esp child)* Schätzchen *nt*; **he is mother's ~/the ~ of the crowds** er ist Mamas Liebling/der Publikumsliebling; **she's a little ~** sie ist ein süßer kleiner Schatz; **that cat is a little ~** diese Katze ist ein liebes kleines Tierchen; **be a ~ and …** sei so lieb *or* nett und …, sei ein Schatz und … **b** *(form of address)* Liebling *m*, Schatz *m*, Schätzchen *nt* **ADJ** *cat, dress etc* süß, goldig; *wife etc* lieb; *house* reizend

darn[1] [dɑːn] *(Sew)* **N** gestopfte Stelle **VT** stopfen

darn[2] *(also* **darned***)* *(inf)* **ADJ** *cheek, nerve* verdammt *(inf)*; **a ~ sight better/worse** ein ganzes Ende besser/schlechter *(inf)*
ADV verdammt *(inf)*, verflixt *(inf)*; **he'd better make ~ sure** er sollte verdammt noch mal dafür sorgen *(inf)*; **pretty ~ quick** verdammt schnell *(inf)*; **you're ~ right** du hast völlig recht; **you know ~ed well what I mean** du weißt verdammt genau, was ich meine *(inf)*; **we'll do just as we ~ well please** wir machen genau das, was wir wollen; **~ near impossible** so gut wie unmöglich
VT **~ it!** verflixt noch mal! *(inf)*; **~ him!** zum Kuckuck mit ihm!
N **I don't give a ~** das ist mir völlig schnurz *(inf)*

darned [dɑːnd] **ADJ, ADV** *(inf)* = **darn**[2] **ADJ, ADV**

darner [ˈdɑːnəʳ] **N** **a** *(= needle)* Stopfnadel *f* **b** *(= darning egg)* Stopfei *nt*; *(= darning mushroom)* Stopfpilz *m*

darning [ˈdɑːnɪŋ] **N** Stopfen *nt*; *(= things to be darned)* Flick- *or* Stopfsachen *pl*, Flickarbeit *f*; **I've a lot of ~ to do** ich habe viel zu stopfen

darning mushroom **N** Stopfpilz *m*

darning needle **N** Stopfnadel *f*

dart [dɑːt] **N** **a** *(movement)* Satz *m*; **the fish made a ~ for the shelter of the weeds** der Fisch schnellte ins schützende Seegras; **with a ~ of its tongue the chameleon caught its prey** die Zunge schnellte heraus, und das Chamäleon hatte seine Beute gefangen; **he felt a ~ of pain when he thought of her** ein plötzlicher Schmerz durchzuckte ihn, als er an sie dachte
b *(= weapon)* Pfeil *m*; *(fig: of sarcasm etc)* Spitze *f*; *(Sport)* (Wurf)pfeil *m*
c *(liter, of serpent)* (Gift)zahn *m*; *(of bee)* Stachel *m*
d *(Sew)* Abnäher *m*
VI flitzen; *(fish)* schnellen; **to ~ out** *(person)* hinausflitzen; *(fish, tongue)* herausschnellen; **to ~ in** *(person)* hereinstürzen; *(into water: otter etc)* sich hineinstürzen; **he ~ed behind a bush** er hechtete hinter einen Busch; **he ~ed off** *or* **away** er flitzte davon; **her eyes ~ed round the room** ihre Blicke schossen blitzschnell im Zimmer hin und her; **her thoughts were ~ing about** ihre Gedanken schwirrten umher
VT *look* werfen; **to ~ a glance at sb** jdm einen Blick zuwerfen; **to ~ a glance at sth** einen Blick auf etw *(acc)* werfen; **the snake ~ed its tongue out** die Schlange ließ ihre Zunge hervorschnellen

dart board **N** Dartscheibe *f*

darting [ˈdɑːtɪŋ] **ADJ** blitzschnell

darts [dɑːts] **N** *sing* Darts *nt*, Pfeilwurfspiel *nt*; **a game of ~** ein Dartspiel *nt*

Darwinian [dɑːˈwɪnɪən] **N** Darwinist(in) *m(f)* **ADJ** darwinistisch

Darwinism [ˈdɑːwɪnɪzəm] **N** Darwinismus *m*

dash [dæʃ] **N** **a** *(= sudden rush)* Jagd *f*; **he made a ~ for the door/across the road** er stürzte auf die Tür zu/über die Straße; **she made a ~ for it** sie rannte, so schnell sie konnte; **to make a ~ for freedom** versuchen, in die Freiheit zu entkommen; **his ~ for freedom was unsuccessful** sein Versuch, in die Freiheit zu entkommen, war vergeblich; **it was a mad ~ to the hospital** wir/sie *etc* eilten Hals über Kopf zum Krankenhaus
b *(= hurry)* Hetze *f*
c *(= style, vigour)* Schwung *m*, Elan *m*; **to cut a ~** eine schneidige Figur machen
d *(= small amount)* **a ~ of** etwas, ein bisschen; *(of vinegar, spirits)* etwas, ein Schuss *m*; *(of seasoning etc)* etwas, eine Prise; *(of lemon)* ein Spritzer *m*; **a ~ of colour** *(Brit) or* **color** *(US)* ein Farbtupfer *m*; **a ~ of mystery** etwas Geheimnisvolles
e *(Typ)* Gedankenstrich *m*
f *(in morse)* Strich *m*
g *(Aut)* Armaturenbrett *nt*
VT **a** *(= throw violently)* schleudern; **to ~ sth to pieces** etw in tausend Stücke zerschlagen; **he ~ed his head on the floor when he fell** er schlug beim Hinfallen mit dem Kopf auf dem Boden auf; **the ship was ~ed against the rocks** das Schiff wurde gegen die Klippen geschleudert
b *(= discourage) sb's hopes* zunichtemachen; **that ~ed his spirits** das hat ihn völlig geknickt
c *(inf)* = **darn**[2] **VT**
VI **a** *(= rush)* sausen *(inf)*; **to ~ into/across a room** in ein Zimmer/quer durch ein Zimmer stürzen *or* stürmen; **to ~ away/back/up** fort-/zurück-/hinaufstürzen
b *(= knock, be hurled)* schlagen; *(waves)* peitschen
INTERJ **~ (it)!** *(inf)* verflixt! *(inf)*, (verflixter) Mist! *(inf)*

▶ **dash off** **VI** losstürzen; **sorry to have to dash off like this** es tut mir leid, dass ich so forthetzen muss **VT** *sep letter, essay* hinwerfen; *drawing also* mit ein paar Strichen hinwerfen

dashboard [ˈdæʃbɔːd] **N** Armaturenbrett *nt*

dashed [dæʃt] **ADJ ADV** = **darn**[2] **ADV, VT**

dashing [ˈdæʃɪŋ] *(dated)* **ADJ** **a** *(= showy, stylish) person* schneidig, flott; *moustache, clothes* schneidig; **to cut a ~ figure** flott *or* schneidig aussehen **b** *(= spirited) person* temperamentvoll; *(= dynamic)* dynamisch; *action* unerschrocken; **a ~ young officer** ein zackiger junger Offizier

dashpot [ˈdæʃpɒt] **N** *(Tech)* Pralltopf *m*

dastardly [ˈdæstədlɪ] **ADJ** niederträchtig, gemein

DAT **N** *abbr of* **digital audio tape** DAT *nt*; **~ cassette** DAT-Kassette *f*

data [ˈdeɪtə] *pl of* **datum** *usu with sing vb* Daten *pl*; **the actual ~ is quite surprising** die eigentlichen Daten sind recht erstaunlich; **a piece of ~** eine Angabe; *(Math)* ein (Zahlen)wert *m*; **we have a significant amount of ~ on …** wir haben einen beträchtlichen Datenbestand über … *(+acc)*

data: **data analysis** **N** Datenanalyse *f*; **data bank** **N** Datenbank *f*; **database** **N** Datenbank *f*; **we have a large ~ of …** wir haben große Datenbestände an … *(dat)*; **to set up a ~** eine Datenbank aufbauen; **~ manager** Datenbankmanager(in) *m(f)*; **data bit** **N** Datenbit *nt*; **data block** **N** Datenblock *m*; **data buf-**

fer N Datenpuffer *m*; **data capture** N Datenerfassung *f*; **data carrier** N Datenträger *m*; **data collection** N Datenerfassung *f*; **data communication** N, **data communications** PL *(Comput)* Datenkommunikation *f or* -übermittlung *f*; **data file** N Datei *f*; **data-handling system** N Datenerfassungssystem *nt*; **data input** N Dateneingabe *f*; **data medium** N *(Comput)* Datenträger *m*; **data network** N Datennetz *nt*; **data pen** N *(Comput)* Lichtgriffel *or* -stift *m*; **data processing** N Datenverarbeitung *f*; **data protection** N Datenschutz *m*; **data protection act** N Datenschutzgesetz *m*; **data rate** N Datenrate *f*; **data retrieval** N Datenabruf *m*; **data switch** N Datenschalter *m*; **data switching** N Datenvermittlung *f*; **data transfer** N Datentransfer *m*; **data transmission** N Datenübertragung *f*

dataveillance [ˌdeɪtəˈveɪləns] N Datenüberwachung *f*, Überwachung *f* von Kunden- und Personendaten

date[1] [deɪt] N *(= fruit)* Dattel *f*; *(= tree)* Dattelpalme *f*

date[2] **N** **a** *(= time of event)* Datum *nt*; *(= historical date)* Geschichts- *or* Jahreszahl *f*; *(for appointment)* Termin *m*; **~ of birth** Geburtsdatum *nt*; **what's the ~ today?** der Wievielte ist heute?, welches Datum haben wir heute?; **what ~ is Easter this year?** auf welches Datum fällt Ostern dieses Jahr?; **what is the ~ of that letter?** von wann ist der Brief datiert?; **to fix** *or* **set a ~ (for sth)** einen Termin (für etw) festsetzen; **to ~** bis heute, bis dato *(form, dated)*; **the band's UK tour ~s are: …** die Band tritt an den folgenden Daten in Großbritannien auf: …
b *(on coins, medals etc)* Jahreszahl *f*
c *(= appointment)* Verabredung *f*; *(with girlfriend etc)* Rendezvous *nt*; **who's his ~?** mit wem trifft er sich?; **his ~ didn't show up** diejenige, mit der er ausgehen wollte, hat ihn versetzt *(inf)*; **to make a ~ with sb** sich mit jdm verabreden; **she's out on a ~** sie hat eine Verabredung *or* ein Rendezvous; **I've got a lunch ~ today** *(with friend)* ich habe mich heute zum Mittagessen verabredet; *(on business)* ich muss heute Mittag an einem Arbeitsessen teilnehmen
VT **a** *(= put date on)* mit dem Datum versehen; *letter etc also* datieren; **a letter ~d the seventh of August** ein vom siebten August datierter Brief; **a coin ~d 1390** eine Münze von 1390
b *(= establish age of) work of art etc* datieren; **that hat really ~s you** an dem Hut sieht man, wie alt Sie sind
c *(= take out) girlfriend etc* ausgehen mit; *(regularly)* gehen mit *(inf)*
VI **a** **to ~ back to** zurückdatieren auf *(+acc)*; **to ~ from** zurückgehen auf *(+acc)*; *(antique etc)* stammen aus
b *(= become old-fashioned)* veralten
c *(= have boyfriend etc)* einen Freund/eine Freundin haben; *(couple)* miteinander gehen; **he didn't ~ much when he was at school** in seiner Schulzeit ging er nur selten mit Mädchen aus

date change N Datumswechsel *m*

dated [ˈdeɪtɪd] ADJ altmodisch; *clothes, manners also* überholt

date: **date format** N Datumsformat *nt*; **dateless** ADJ **a** *manuscript* undatiert, ohne Jahreszahl **b** *(= never old-fashioned)* zeitlos; **date line** N *(Geog)* Datumsgrenze *f*; *(Typ)* Datumszeile *f*; **date palm** N Dattelpalme *f*; **date rape** N *Vergewaltigung nach einem Rendezvous*; **date-rape drug** N Date-Rape-Droge *f*, Vergewaltigungsdroge *f*; **date stamp** **N** Datumsstempel *m* **VT** mit Datumsstempel versehen; **date style** N Datumsformat *nt*; **date sugar** N Palmzucker *m*

dating bar N *(US) Lokal, in dem sich Singles treffen*

dative [ˈdeɪtɪv] **N** Dativ *m*; **in the ~** im Dativ **ADJ** Dativ-, dativisch; **~ object** Dativobjekt *nt*; **the ~ case** der Dativ

datum [ˈdeɪtəm] N *pl* **data** *(rare)* Faktum *nt*, Datum *nt*

daub [dɔːb] **VT** *walls, canvas, face* beschmieren; *paint, slogans, make-up* schmieren; *(= coat with grease etc) axle* einschmieren; *(= coat with mud, clay) walls* bewerfen; *(= spread on) grease, mud, clay* streichen **N** **a** *(Build)* Bewurf *m* **b** *(pej, = bad picture)* Kleckserei *f*

dauber [ˈdɔːbəʳ] N *(pej)* Kleckser(in) *m(f)*

daughter [ˈdɔːtəʳ] N *(lit, fig)* Tochter *f*

daughterboard [ˈdɔːtəˌbɔːd] N *(Comput)* Zusatzplatine *f*

daughter-in-law [ˈdɔːtərɪnlɔː] N *pl* **daughters-in-law** Schwiegertochter *f*

daunt [dɔːnt] VT entmutigen; **to be ~ed by sth** sich von etw entmutigen lassen; **nothing ~ed** unverzagt

daunting [ˈdɔːntɪŋ] ADJ entmutigend

dauntless [ˈdɔːntlɪs] ADJ unerschrocken, beherzt; *courage* unbezähmbar

davenport [ˈdævnpɔːt] N **a** *(esp US: = sofa)* Sofa *nt*, Couch *f* **b** *(Brit: = desk)* Sekretär *m*

David [ˈdeɪvɪd] N David *m*

davit [ˈdævɪt] N *(Naut)* Davit *m or nt*

Davy [ˈdeɪvɪ] N *dim of* **David**

Davy Jones' locker [ˈdeɪvɪˈdʒəʊnzɪzˈlɒkəʳ] N der Meeresgrund

Davy lamp N (Gruben)sicherheitslampe *f*

dawdle [ˈdɔːdl] VI *(= be too slow)* trödeln; *(= stroll)* bummeln; **to ~ on the way** unterwegs trödeln; **to ~ over one's work** bei der Arbeit bummeln *or* trödeln

▶ **dawdle along** VI dahinbummeln; *(+prep obj)* entlangbummeln

▶ **dawdle away** VT *sep time* vertrödeln

dawdler [ˈdɔːdləʳ] N Trödler(in) *m(f)*; *(as regards work also)* Bummelant(in) *m(f)* *(inf)*

dawdling [ˈdɔːdlɪŋ] ADJ **we were stuck behind a ~ lorry** wir saßen hinter einem Lastwagen fest, der im Bummeltempo fuhr

dawn [dɔːn] **N** *(lit, fig)* (Morgen)dämmerung *f*, Morgenröte *f* *(liter)*; *(no art: time of day)* Tagesanbruch *m*, Morgengrauen *nt*; **at ~** bei Tagesanbruch, im Morgengrauen; **it's almost ~** es ist fast Morgen, es dämmert schon bald; **from ~ to dusk** von morgens bis abends **VI** **a** **day was already ~ing** es dämmerte schon; **the day ~ed rainy** der Tag fing mit Regen an; **the day will ~ when …** *(fig)* der Tag wird kommen, wo … **b** *(fig, new age etc)* dämmern, anbrechen; *(hope)* erwachen **c** *(inf)* **to ~ (up)on sb** jdm dämmern, jdm zum Bewusstsein kommen; **it ~ed on him that …** es wurde ihm langsam klar, dass …, es dämmerte ihm, dass …

dawn: **dawn chorus** N Morgenkonzert *nt* der Vögel; **dawn patrol** N *(Aviat)* Morgenpatrouille *f*; **dawn raid** N **a** *(by police)* Razzia *f (in den frühen Morgenstunden)*; *(Mil)* Überraschungsangriff *m* **b** *(Fin) plötzlicher Aufkauf von Aktien*

day [deɪ] N **a** Tag *m*; **he's coming in three ~s' time** *or* **in three ~s** er kommt in drei Tagen; **it will arrive any ~ now** es muss jeden Tag kommen; **what ~ is it today?** welcher Tag ist heute?, was haben wir heute?; **what ~ of the month is it?** der Wievielte ist heute?; **twice a ~** zweimal täglich *or* am Tag; **the ~ before yesterday** vorgestern; **the ~ after/before, the following/previous ~** am Tag danach/zuvor, am (darauf)folgenden/vorhergehenden Tag; **the ~ after tomorrow** übermorgen; **this ~ week** *(Brit inf)* heute in acht Tagen *(inf)*; **from that ~ on (-wards)** von dem Tag an; **from this ~ forth** *(old)* von diesem Tage an; **two years ago to the ~** auf den Tag genau vor zwei Jahren; **one ~** eines Tages; **one ~ we went swimming, and the next …** einen Tag gingen wir schwimmen, und den nächsten …; **one of these ~s** irgendwann (einmal), eines Tages; **~ in, ~ out** tagein, tagaus; **they went to London for the ~** sie machten einen Tagesausflug nach London; **for ~s on end** tagelang; **~ after ~** Tag für Tag, tagtäglich; **~ by ~** jeden Tag, täglich; **the other ~** neulich; **at the end of the ~** *(fig)* letzten Endes; **to live from ~ to ~** von einem Tag auf den andern leben; **today of all ~s** ausgerechnet heute; **some ~ soon** demnächst; **I remember it to this ~** daran erinnere ich mich noch heute; **he's fifty if he's a ~** *(esp Brit)* er ist mindestens *or* wenigstens fünfzig; **all ~** den ganzen Tag; **to travel during the ~** *or* **by ~** tagsüber *or* während des Tages reisen; **at that time of ~** zu der Tageszeit; **to work ~ and night** Tag und Nacht arbeiten; **good ~!** guten Tag!; *(= goodbye)* auf Wiedersehen!; **(the) ~ is done** *(liter)* der Tag ist vorüber; **to be paid by the ~** tageweise bezahlt werden; **let's call it a ~** machen wir Schluss; **some time during the ~** irgendwann im Laufe des Tages; **to have a nice ~** einen schönen Tag verbringen; **to have a lazy ~** einen Tag faulenzen; **have a nice ~!** viel Spaß!; *(esp US, said by storekeeper etc)* schönen Tag noch!; **did you have a nice ~?** wars schön?; **did you have a good ~ at the office?** wie wars im Büro?; **to have a good/bad ~** einen guten/schlechten Tag haben; **what a ~!** *(terrible)* so ein fürchterlicher Tag!; *(lovely)* so ein herrlicher Tag!; **on a wet/dry ~** an einem regnerischen/trockenen Tag; **to work an eight-hour ~** einen Achtstundentag haben, acht Stunden am Tag arbeiten; **it's all in the** *or* **a ~'s work!** das ist (doch) selbstverständlich; **that'll be the ~** das möcht ich sehen *or* erleben → **make 1 g**
b *(period of time: often pl)* **these ~s** heute, heutzutage; **what are you doing these ~s?** was machst *or* treibst du denn so?; **in this ~ and age** heutzutage; **the talking point of the ~** das Tagesgespräch; **in ~s to come** künftig, in künftigen Zeiten *or* Tagen *(geh)*; **from his young ~s** von Kindesbeinen *or* frühester Jugend an; **in his younger ~s** als er noch jünger war; **in Queen Victoria's ~, in the ~s of Queen Victoria** zu Königin Viktorias Zeiten; **the happiest ~s of my life** die glücklichste Zeit meines Lebens; **those were the ~s** das waren noch Zeiten; **in the old ~s** früher; **in the good old ~s** in der guten alten Zeit; **it's early ~s yet** es ist noch zu früh; **during the early ~s of the war** in den ersten Kriegstagen; **he/this material has seen better ~s** er/dieser Stoff hat (auch) schon bessere Zeiten *or* Tage gesehen; **to end one's ~s in misery** im Elend sterben
c *(with poss adj: = lifetime, best time)* **famous in her ~** in ihrer Zeit berühmt; **it has had its ~** das hat seine Glanzzeit überschritten; **his ~ will come** sein Tag wird kommen; **everything has its ~** für alles kommt einmal die richtige Zeit
d *no pl (= contest, battle)* **to win** *or* **carry the ~** den Sieg bringen; **to lose/save the ~** den Kampf verlieren/retten

day: **day bed** N Ruhebett *nt*; **day boarder** N *(Brit Sch)* Externe(r) *mf*; **daybook** N *(Comm)* Journal *nt*, Tagebuch *nt*; **day boy** N *(Sch)* Externe(r) *m*; **daybreak** N Tagesanbruch *m*; **at ~** bei Tagesanbruch; **daycare** N **to be in ~** *(child)* in einer Tagesstätte untergebracht sein; *(old person)* in einer Altentagesstätte untergebracht sein; **day(care) centre**, *(US)* **day(care) center** N *(for children)* Tagesstätte *f*; *(for old people)* Altentagesstätte *f*; **day coach** N *(US)* (Eisenbahn)personenwagen *m*; **daydream** **N** Tagtraum *m*, Träumerei *f* **VI** (mit offenen Augen) träumen; **day excursion** N Tagesausflug *m*; **dayfly** N Eintagsfliege *f*; **day girl** N *(Sch)* Externe *f*; **day hospital** N Tagesklinik *f*; **day job** N Hauptberuf *m*; **don't give up the ~** *(hum)* häng deinen Beruf nicht gleich an den Nagel *(inf)*; **day labourer**, *(US)* **day laborer** N Tagelöhner(in) *m(f)*

daylight [ˈdeɪlaɪt] N **a** *(= daybreak)* Tagesanbruch *m* **b** Tageslicht *nt*; **it is still ~** es ist noch hell; **it was broad ~** es war heller *or* helllichter Tag; **in broad ~** am hellen *or* helllichten Tage; **I'd like to get there in ~** ich möchte gern bei Tag ankommen; **to beat the living ~s out of sb** *(inf)* jdn windelweich schlagen *(inf)*; **to scare the living ~s out of sb** *(inf)* jdm einen fürchterlichen Schreck einjagen *(inf)*

daylight: **daylight robbery** N *(Brit inf)* Halsabschneiderei *f (inf)*, Nepp *m (inf)*; **daylight saving time** N *(esp US)* Sommerzeit *f*

day: **daylong** ADJ den ganzen Tag dauernd; **day nurse** N Tagesschwester *f*; **day nursery** N Kindertagesstätte *f*; *(in private house)* Kinderzimmer *nt*; **day-old** ADJ *baby* einen Tag alt; *strike, ceasefire* seit einem Tag andauernd; *food, newspaper* vom Vortag; **day pupil** N *(Sch)* Externe(r) *mf*; **dayrate** N Tagessatz *m*; **day release** N *(Brit) tageweise Freistellung von Angestellten zur Weiterbildung*; **day release course** N *(Brit)* Tageskurs *m* für Berufstätige; **day return (ticket)** N *(Brit Rail)* Tagesrückfahrkarte *f*

days [deɪz] ADV *(esp US)* tagsüber

day: **day school** N Tagesschule *f*; **day shift** N Tagschicht *f*; **to be on** *or* **work ~** Tagschicht arbeiten; **day spa** N Day Spa *nt*, *Hotel etc, das eintägige Wellnessprogramme anbietet*; **day ticket** N *(Brit Rail)* Tagesrückfahrkarte *f*

daytime ['deɪtaɪm] **N** Tag *m*; **in the ~** bei Tage, tagsüber, während des Tages **ATTR** am Tage; *raid* am hellen *or* hellichten Tage; **what's your ~ phone number?** unter welcher Nummer sind Sie tagsüber erreichbar?; **~ course** Tageskurs *m*; **~ job** Tagesjob *m*; **~ television** Fernsehen *nt* während des Tages, Vor- und Nachmittagsprogramm *nt*

daytimes ['deɪtaɪmz] ADV *(US)* am Tag, bei Tag

day: **day-to-day** ADJ täglich; *occurrence* alltäglich; **on a ~ basis** tageweise; **day trader** N *(St Ex)* Tagesspekulant(in) *m(f)*, Daytrader(in) *m(f)*; **day trading** N *(St Ex)* Tagesspekulation *f*, Daytrading *nt*; **day trip** N Tagesausflug *m*; **day-tripper** N Tagesausflügler(in) *m(f)*

daze [deɪz] **N** Benommenheit *f*; **in a ~** ganz benommen **VT** benommen machen

dazed [deɪzd] ADJ benommen

dazzle ['dæzl] VT *(lit, fig)* blenden

dazzler ['dæzləʳ] N *(fig)* Blender(in) *m(f)*, Angeber(in) *m(f)*

dazzling ['dæzlɪŋ] ADJ *(lit)* blendend

dazzlingly ['dæzlɪŋlɪ] ADV *(lit, fig)* blendend; **~ beautiful** strahlend schön

dB *abbr of* **decibel** dB

d. b. a. *(Comm) abbr of* **doing business as** firmierend unter

DC **a** *abbr of* **direct current** **b** *abbr of* **District of Columbia**

DCC® N *abbr of* **digital compact cassette** DCC *f*

DCI N *(Brit Police) abbr of* **Detective Chief Inspector**

DD **a** *abbr of* **Doctor of Divinity** Dr. theol. **b** *abbr of* **designated driver**

D/D *abbr of* **direct debit**

D-day ['di:deɪ] N *(Hist, fig)* der Tag X

DDT® *abbr of* **dichloro-diphenyl-trichloroethane** DDT® *nt*

deacon ['di:kən] N Diakon *m*; *(= elder)* Kirchenälteste(r) *m*

deaconess ['di:kənes] N Diakonin *f*; *(= elder)* Kirchenälteste *f*

deaconry ['di:kənrɪ] N Diakonat *nt*

deactivate [di:'æktɪˌveɪt] VT entschärfen

dead [ded] **ADJ** **a** tot; *plant* abgestorben, tot; **he has been ~ for two years** er ist seit zwei Jahren tot; **to drop (down)** *or* **fall down ~** tot umfallen; **to shoot sb ~** jdn erschießen *or* totschießen *(inf)*; **over my ~ body** *(inf)* nur über meine Leiche *(inf)*; **you're ~ meat (if you come back here)** *(inf)* du bist ein toter Mann(, wenn du noch mal hierhin zurückkommst) *(inf)*

b *(= not sensitive) limbs* abgestorben, taub; **my hand's gone ~** ich habe kein Gefühl in meiner Hand; **to be ~ from the neck up** *(inf)* nur Stroh im Kopf haben *(inf)*; **to be ~ to the world** tief und fest schlafen

c *(= without activity etc) town, season* tot; *business* flau

d *(Elec) cable* stromlos; *(Telec)* tot; **to go ~** ausfallen

e *(= burned out) fire* aus *pred*; *match* abgebrannt

f *(inf: = finished with) (Typ) copy* abgesetzt; **are these glasses/bottles ~?** können diese Gläser/Flaschen weg?

g *(Sport) ball* tot

h *(= obsolete) language etc* tot; *custom* ausgestorben; **to be ~ and buried, to be ~ in the water** tot und begraben sein

i *(= absolute, exact)* total, völlig; **~ silence** Totenstille *f*; **~ calm** *(Naut)* absolute *or* totale Windstille; **the ~ centre** die genaue *or* exakte Mitte; **she was in a ~ faint** sie war völlig bewusstlos; **to come to a ~ stop** völlig zum Stillstand kommen; **he's the ~ spit of his father** *(sl)* er ist seinem Vater wie aus dem Gesicht geschnitten → **cert, set**

j *colour* tot, stumpf, matt; *sound* dumpf

k *(Typ)* **~ key** unbelegte Taste *f*

l *(inf: = exhausted)* tot *(inf)*, völlig kaputt *(inf)*; **she looked half ~** sie sah völlig kaputt *or* fertig aus *(inf)*; **I'm ~ on my feet** ich bin zum Umfallen kaputt *(inf)*

ADV **a** *(= exactly)* genau; **~ straight** schnurgerade; **to be ~ on time** auf die Minute pünktlich kommen; *(clock)* auf die Minute genau gehen; **their arrows were ~ on target** ihre Pfeile trafen genau ins Ziel

b *(Brit inf: = very)* total *(inf)*, völlig; **~ drunk** total betrunken, stockvoll *(inf)*; **~ tired** todmüde; **you're ~ right** Sie haben völlig recht; **he was ~ lucky** er hat Schwein gehabt *(inf)*, er hat irrsinnig Glück gehabt; **~ slow** ganz langsam; **"dead slow"** „Schritt fahren"; **to be ~ certain about sth** *(inf)* bei etw todsicher sein; **he's ~ against it** er ist total dagegen

c **to stop ~** abrupt stehen bleiben *or (talking)* innehalten

N **a** **the ~** *pl* die Toten *pl*

b **in the** *or* **at ~ of night** mitten in der Nacht; **in the ~ of winter** mitten im Winter

dead: **dead account** N *(Fin)* umsatzloses *or* unbewegtes Konto; **dead-and-alive** ADJ *(inf) party, place* tot, langweilig; **dead-ball line** N *(Rugby)* Feldauslinie *f*; **dead beat** ADJ *(Brit inf)* völlig kaputt *(inf)*, total fertig *(inf)*; **deadbeat** **N** *(= down-and-out)* Gammler(in) *m(f)*; *(= failure)* Versager(in) *m(f)* **ADJ** **~ dad** *Vater, der seiner Unterhaltspflicht nicht nachkommt*; **dead centre**, *(US)* **dead center** N genaue Mitte; **to hit sth ~** etw genau in die Mitte treffen; **dead duck** N **to be a ~** passé sein; **politically he's/it's a ~** politisch ist er/es gestorben *(inf)*

deaden ['dedn] VT *shock* auffangen; *pain* mildern; *force, blow* abschwächen; *nerve, passions* abtöten; *sound, noise* dämpfen; *mind, feeling* abstumpfen

dead: **dead end** N Sackgasse *f*; **to come to a ~** *(lit, road)* in einer Sackgasse enden; *(driver)* an eine Sackgasse kommen; *(fig)* in eine Sackgasse geraten; **dead-end** ADJ *attr* **~ street** *(esp US)* Sackgasse *f*; **to be in ~ street** *(fig)* keine Chancen haben; **~ kids** Gassenkinder *pl*; **a ~ job** ein Job *m* ohne Aufstiegsmöglichkeiten; **dead hand** N **the ~ of bureaucracy/the state** die schwere Last der Bürokratie/des Staates; **dead heat** N totes Rennen; **dead leg** N *(inf)* taubes Bein; **dead letter** N *(lit)* unzustellbarer Brief; *(Jur)* toter Buchstabe; **deadline** N (letzter) Termin; **to fix** *or* **set a ~** eine Frist setzen; **to work to a ~** auf einen Termin hinarbeiten; **he was working to a six o'clock ~** um sechs Uhr musste er die Arbeit fertig haben; **can you meet the ~?** können Sie den Termin *or* die Frist einhalten?; **copy ~** *(Press)* Redaktionsschluss *m*

deadliness ['dedlɪnɪs] N *(of poison, weapon)* tödliche Wirkung; *(of wit, sarcasm)* vernichtende Wirkung; *(inf, = boringness)* tödliche Langeweile; *(= awfulness)* Entsetzlichkeit *f*

deadlock ['dedlɒk] N **to reach (a) ~** in eine Sackgasse geraten; **to end in ~** sich festfahren; **to break the ~** aus der Sackgasse herauskommen

deadlocked ['dedlɒkt] ADJ *negotiations, talks* festgefahren

deadly ['dedlɪ] **ADJ** *(+er)* **a** *(= lethal) poison, weapon, disease, attack, force* tödlich; **to be ~ to sb** tödliche Folgen für jdn haben; **a ~ combination of ...** eine tödliche Mischung von ...; **assault with a ~ weapon** *(Jur)* Körperverletzung *f* mit einer gefährlichen Waffe; **to play a ~ game** ein tödliches Spiel spielen

b *(= devastating) logic, look* vernichtend; *(= unerring) accuracy* tödlich; *bowler, striker* treffsicher

c *(inf: = boring)* todlangweilig *(inf)*

d *(= complete) silence, enemies, rivals* tödlich; **to be in ~ earnest** es todernst meinen; **their ~ enemy** ihr Todfeind *m*; **that made the competition even deadlier** dadurch wurde die Konkurrenz noch mörderischer; **the (seven) ~ sins** *(Bibl)* die (sieben) Todsünden *pl*

ADV *(= extremely)* **~ dull** todlangweilig *(inf)*; **he was ~ serious** er meinte es todernst; **~ cold** eisig kalt; **~ pale** totenbleich; **~ poisonous** tödlich

deadly nightshade N Tollkirsche *f*

dead: **dead man's handle** N SIFA-Schalttaste *f*, Totmannkurbel *f*; **dead march** N Totenmarsch *m*; **dead men's shoes** N **to wait for ~** warten, bis eine Stelle frei wird

deadness ['dednɪs] N *(of limbs)* Taubheit *f*; *(of colour)* Langweiligkeit *f*; **nothing compares with the ~ of Blackpool in winter** nichts ist so öde wie Blackpool im Winter

dead: **dead nettle** N *(Bot)* Taubnessel *f*; **deadpan** **ADJ** *face* unbewegt; *style, humour* trocken; **with a ~ expression** mit unbeweglicher Miene **N** *(= face, expression)* unbewegliche Miene; **dead reckoning** N *(Naut)* Koppelung *f*; **Dead Sea** N Totes Meer; **~ scrolls** *pl* Schriftrollen *pl* vom Toten Meer; **dead spot** N *(Telec)* Funkloch *nt*; **dead weight** N *(Tech)* Eigengewicht *nt*, Totgewicht *nt*; **the box/she was a ~** die Kiste/sie war furchtbar schwer; **Dead White (European) Male** N *(esp US) abwertender Ausdruck für (das Kulturleben dominierende) Weiße (europäischer Abstammung)*; **deadwood** N *(lit)* morsches Holz; *(Naut)* Totholz *nt*; *(fig)* Ballast *m*; **to get rid of the ~** *(people)* die Nieten loswerden *(inf)*

deaf [def] **ADJ** *(+er) (lit, fig)* taub; **as ~ as a (door)post** stocktaub; **he was ~ to her pleas** er blieb gegen alle ihre Bitten taub, er verschloss sich ihren Bitten; **to turn a ~ ear to sb/sth** sich jdm/einer Sache *(dat)* gegenüber taub stellen; **our pleas fell on ~ ears** unsere Bitten fanden kein Gehör **N** **the ~** *pl* die Tauben *pl*

deaf: **deaf aid** N Hörgerät *nt*; **deaf-and-dumb** ADJ taubstumm; **~ language** Taubstummensprache *f*

deafen ['defn] VT *(lit)* taub machen; *(fig)* betäuben

deafening ['defnɪŋ] ADJ *noise* ohrenbetäubend; *row* lautstark; **a ~ silence** ein eisiges Schweigen

deaf-mute ['def'mju:t] N Taubstumme(r) *mf*

deafness ['defnɪs] N *(lit, fig)* Taubheit *f (to gegenüber)*

deal[1] [di:l] ✪ 26.1 **N** *(= amount)* Menge *f*; **a good** *or* **great ~ of** eine Menge, (ziemlich) viel; **not a great ~ of** nicht (besonders) viel; **there's still a (good** *or* **great) ~ of work left to do** es ist noch ein schönes Stück *or* eine Menge Arbeit zu tun; **there's a good** *or* **great ~ of truth in what he says** es ist schon ziemlich viel Wahres an dem, was er sagt; **it says a good ~ for him (that ...)** es spricht sehr für ihn(, dass ...); **and that's saying a great ~** und damit ist schon viel gesagt; **to mean a great ~ to sb** jdm viel bedeuten

ADV **a good** *or* **great ~** viel; **not a great ~** nicht viel; **to learn/travel/talk a great ~** viel lernen/reisen/reden; **did you swim much? – not a great ~** seid ihr viel geschwommen? – nicht besonders viel; **a good ~ more important** viel wichtiger

deal[2] *vb: pret, ptp* **dealt** **N** **a** *(also* **business deal)** Geschäft *nt*, Handel *m*; *(= arrangement)*

Handel *m*, Abkommen *nt*, Deal *m (inf)*; **to do** *or* **make a ~ with sb** mit jdm ein Geschäft *or* einen Deal *(inf)* machen, mit jdm ein Geschäft abschließen; **it's a ~** abgemacht!; **it's a done ~** *(US)* es ist beschlossene Sache; **I'll make** *or* **do a ~ with you** ich schlage Ihnen ein Geschäft vor; **I never make ~s** ich lasse mich nie auf Geschäfte ein; **are you forgetting our ~?** hast du unsere Abmachung vergessen? → **big**
b *(inf)* **to give sb a fair ~** jdn anständig behandeln; **the workers have always had a bad ~** die Arbeiter sind immer schlecht behandelt worden; **a better ~ for the lower paid** bessere Bedingungen für die schlechter bezahlten Arbeiter; **the management offered us a new ~** die Firmenleitung hat uns ein neues Angebot gemacht; **it's no big ~** *(= doesn't matter)* ist nicht so schlimm *(inf)*, passt schon *(inf)*
c *(Cards)* **it's your ~** Sie geben
VT a *(also* **deal out***)* *cards* geben, austeilen
b *drugs* dealen *(inf)*
c → **blow**[1]
VI a *(Cards)* geben, austeilen
b *(in drugs)* dealen *(inf)*

▶ **deal in VI** *+prep obj (Comm) goods, stolen property, pornography* handeln mit; **this is an organization dealing in terror** diese Organisation hat sich dem Terror verschrieben; **we deal only in facts** wir beschränken uns auf die Tatsachen
VT *sep (Cards) player* Karten geben *(+dat)*

▶ **deal out VT** *sep* verteilen *(to* an *+acc)*; *cards* (aus)geben *(to +dat)*; **to deal out punishment** Strafen verhängen; **to deal out criticism** Kritik üben

▶ **deal with** ✪ 26.3 **VI** *+prep obj* **a** *(= do business with)* verhandeln mit
b *(= manage, handle)* sich kümmern um; *job* sich befassen mit; *emotions* umgehen mit; *(successfully)* fertig werden mit; *(Comm) orders* erledigen; *(= be responsible for)* zuständig sein für; **let's deal with the adjectives first** behandeln wir zuerst die Adjektive; **to know how to deal with sb** wissen, wie man mit jdm fertig wird *or* mit jdm umgeht; **you bad boy, I'll deal with you later** *(inf)* dich knöpf *or* nehm ich mir später vor, du Lausebengel! *(inf)*; **the problem has been successfully dealt with** man ist gut mit dem Problem fertig geworden; **if we don't deal with the problem soon** wenn wir uns nicht bald mit dem Problem befassen; **to deal with a case** *(judge)* einen Fall verhandeln; *(lawyer)* sich mit einem Fall befassen
c *(= be concerned with, book, film etc)* handeln von; *(author)* sich beschäftigen *or* befassen mit

deal[3] **N** *(= wood)* Kiefern- *or* Tannenholz *nt*
ADJ *attr* aus Kiefern- *or* Tannenholz

dealer [ˈdiːləˈ] **N a** *(Comm)* Händler(in) *m(f)*; *(= wholesaler)* Großhändler(in) *m(f)*; **a ~ in furs** ein Pelzhändler **b** *(in drugs)* Dealer(in) *m(f) (inf)* **c** *(Cards)* Kartengeber *m*

dealing [ˈdiːlɪŋ] **N a** *(= trading)* Handel *m*; *(on stock exchange)* Handel *m*, Transaktionen *pl*; *(in drugs)* Dealen *nt*; **he is involved in drug ~** er ist in den Drogenhandel verwickelt **b** *(of cards)* Geben *nt*, Aus- *or* Verteilen *nt* **c dealings PL** *(Comm)* Geschäfte *pl*; *(generally)* Umgang *m*; **to have ~s with sb** mit jdm zu tun haben; *(Comm also)* Geschäftsbeziehungen zu jdm haben; **he had secret ~s with the Mafia** er stand heimlich mit der Mafia in Verbindung

dealing room N *(Fin)* Geschäftsraum *m* für Devisengeschäfte

dealt [delt] *pret, ptp of* **deal**[2]

dean [diːn] **N** *(Eccl, Univ)* Dekan(in) *m(f)*

deanery [ˈdiːnərɪ] **N a** Dekanat *nt* **b** *(Eccl: = house)* Dekanei *f*

deanship [ˈdiːnʃɪp] **N** *(Eccl, Univ)* Dekanat *nt*

dear [dɪəˈ] **ADJ** *(+er)* **a** *(= loved)* lieb, teuer *(liter)*; **I hold him/it ~** er/es ist mir lieb und teuer; **she is a ~ friend of mine** sie ist eine sehr gute Freundin von mir; **it is ~ to my heart** es liegt mir sehr am Herzen; **that is my ~est wish** das ist mein sehnlichster *or* innigster Wunsch; **my ~ fellow** mein lieber Freund; **you are very ~ to me** du bist mir lieb und teuer; **these memories are very ~ to him** diese Erinnerungen sind ihm teuer
b *(= lovable, sweet) child* lieb, süß, reizend; *thing* süß, entzückend, reizend; **what a ~ little dress/baby/kitten** was für ein süßes *or* entzückendes Kleidchen/Kind/Kätzchen!
c *(in letter-writing etc)* **~ Daddy/John** lieber Vati/John!; **~ Sir** sehr geehrter Herr X!; **~ Madam** sehr geehrte Frau X!; **~ Sir or Madam** sehr geehrte Damen und Herren!; **~ Mr Kemp** sehr geehrter Herr Kemp!; *(less formal)* lieber Herr Kemp!; **Dear John letter** *(esp US inf)* Abschiedsbrief *m*
d *(= expensive) goods, shop* teuer; *prices* hoch; **to get ~er** *(goods)* teuer werden
INTERJ ~ ~!, ~ me! (ach) du liebe Zeit!, (du) meine Güte!; **oh ~!** oje!, ach du meine Güte *or* du liebe Zeit!
N hello/thank you ~ hallo/vielen Dank; **Robert ~** (mein lieber) Robert; **yes, ~** *(husband to wife etc)* ja, Schätzchen *or* Liebling; **Edward, my ~** mein lieber Edward; **my ~est** meine Teuerste *(geh)*, mein Teuerster *(geh)*, (meine) Liebste, (mein) Liebster; **are you being served, ~?** *(inf)* werden Sie schon bedient?; **give it to me, there's a ~** *(Brit inf)* gib es mir, sei (doch) so lieb *or* gut; **be a ~** *(inf)* sei so lieb *or* gut; **poor ~** die Arme, der Arme; **your mother is a ~** *(inf)* deine Mutter ist ein Engel *(inf) or* richtig lieb; **her little boy is such a ~** ihr kleiner Junge ist so ein süßer Knopf *(inf)*; **this old ~ came up to me** *(Brit)* dieses Muttchen kam zu mir her *(inf)*
ADV *(lit, fig) buy, pay, sell* teuer; **this will cost them ~** das wird sie teuer zu stehen kommen

dearie, deary [ˈdɪərɪ] **N** *(inf) usu not translated (woman to child)* Kleine(r, s); **thanks for your help, ~** *(to child)* vielen Dank für deine Hilfe, mein Kind

dearly [ˈdɪəlɪ] **ADV a** *(= greatly) love* von ganzem Herzen; *hope* sehr; **~ beloved** *(form, Eccl)* geliebt; *(addressing congregation)* liebe Gemeinde, liebe Brüder und Schwestern; **I would ~ love to marry** ich würde liebend gern heiraten; **I ~ wish I had more money** ich wünschte, ich hätte mehr Geld; **I should ~ love** *or* **like to live here** ich würde für mein Leben gern hier wohnen **b** *(fig)* **he paid ~ (for it)** er hat es teuer bezahlt; **~ bought** teuer erkauft; **to cost sb ~** jdn teuer zu stehen kommen

dearness [ˈdɪənɪs] **N a** *(= expensiveness)* hoher Preis **b** *(= being loved)* **her ~ to him** dass sie ihm lieb und teuer war

dearth [dɜːθ] **N** Mangel *m (of* an *+dat)*; **~ of ideas** Gedankenarmut *f*; **there is no ~ of young men** an jungen Männern ist *or* herrscht kein Mangel

deary N = **dearie**

death [deθ] ✪ 24.4 **N** Tod *m*; *(of plans, hopes etc)* Ende *nt*; **~ by drowning/hanging** Tod durch Ertrinken/Erhängen; **~ to all traitors!** Tod allen Verrätern!; **in ~ as in life** im Tod wie im Leben; **to be afraid of ~** sich vor dem Tod fürchten; **to be burned to ~** verbrennen; *(at stake)* verbrannt werden; **to starve to ~** verhungern; **to bleed to ~** verbluten; **to freeze to ~** erfrieren; **how many ~s were there?** wie viele Tote *or* Todesfälle gab es?; **to die a hero's ~** den Heldentod sterben; **she died a horrible ~** sie starb einen schrecklichen Tod; **a fight to the ~** ein Kampf auf Leben und Tod; **to put sb to ~** jdn hinrichten; **to do sb to ~** *(old)* jdn umbringen; **this type of novel has been done to ~** diese Art von Roman ist schon zu Tode geritten worden; **to drink oneself to ~** sich zu Tode trinken; **to work oneself to ~** sich totarbeiten; **he works his men to ~** er schindet seine Leute zu Tode; **to be at ~'s door** an der Schwelle des Todes stehen; **it will be the ~ of you** *(inf)* das wird dein Tod sein; **he will be the ~ of me** *(inf: = he's so funny)* ich lach mich noch einmal tot über ihn *(inf)*; *(= he's annoying)* er bringt mich noch ins Grab; **to catch one's ~ (of cold)** *(inf)* sich *(dat)* den Tod holen; **I am sick to ~ of all this** *(inf)* das alles hängt mir gründlich zum Halse raus, ich bin das alles gründlich satt *or* leid; **he looked like ~ warmed up** *(Brit inf) or* **over** *(US inf)* er sah wie der Tod auf Urlaub aus *(inf)*

death: **death agony N** Todeskampf *m*; **deathbed N** Sterbebett *nt*; **to be on one's ~** auf dem Sterbebett liegen; **deathbed scene N** Szene *f* am Sterbebett; **death bell N** Totenglocke *f*; **death benefit N** *(Insur)* Versicherungsprämie *f* im Todesfall; **deathblow N** *(lit, fig)* Todesstoß *m*; **death camp N** Vernichtungslager *nt*; **death cell N** *(Brit)* Todeszelle *f*; **death certificate N** Sterbeurkunde *f*, Totenschein *m*; **death chair N** elektrischer Stuhl; **death cup N** *(Bot)* Grüner Knollenblätterpilz; **death-dealing ADJ** *blow, missile* tödlich; **death-defying ADJ** todesverachtend, todesmutig; **death duties PL** *(Brit)* Erbschaftssteuern *pl*; **death grant N** *(Brit Hist)* Sterbegeld *nt*; **death instinct N** *(Psych)* Todestrieb *m*; **death knell N** *(fig)* Todesstoß *m* → **knell**; **deathless ADJ** unsterblich; **deathlike ADJ** totenähnlich

deathly [ˈdeθlɪ] **ADJ ~ hush** *or* **silence** Totenstille *f*; **~ pallor** Totenblässe *f* **ADV ~ pale** totenblass; **~ cold** eiskalt; **~ quiet** totenstill

death: **death mask N** Totenmaske *f*; **death metal N** *(Mus)* Death Metal *nt*; **death penalty N** Todesstrafe *f*; **death rate N** Sterbeziffer *f*; **death rattle N** Todesröcheln *nt*; **death ray N** Todesstrahl *m*; **death roll N** Verlust- *or* Gefallenenliste *f*; **death row N** Todestrakt *m*; **death sentence N** Todesurteil *nt*; **death's head N** *(on flag etc)* Totenkopf *m*; **death's head moth N** Totenkopf *m*, Totenkopfschwärmer *m*; **death squad N** Todeskommando *nt*; **death taxes PL** *(US)* = **death duties**; **death threat N** Morddrohung *f*; **death throes PL** *(lit, fig)* Todeskampf *m*; **in his ~** im Todeskampf; **death toll N** Zahl *f* der (Todes)opfer *or* Toten; **deathtrap N** Todesfalle *f*; **death warrant N** Hinrichtungsbefehl *m*; *(fig)* Todesurteil *nt*; **to sign one's own ~** *(fig)* sein eigenes Todesurteil unterschreiben *or* unterzeichnen; **deathwatch N** Totenwache *f*; **deathwatch beetle N** Totenuhr *f*, Klopfkäfer *m*; **death wish N** Todestrieb *m*

deb [deb] **N** *(inf)* Debütantin *f*

débâcle [deˈbɑːkl] **N** Debakel *nt (over* bei*)*

debag [ˌdiːˈbæg] **VT** *(Brit inf)* die Hosen runterziehen *(+dat)*

debar [dɪˈbɑːˈ] **VT** *(from club, competition)* ausschließen *(from* von*)*; **to ~ sb from doing sth** jdn davon ausschließen, etw zu tun

debark [dɪˈbɑːk] **VI** sich ausschiffen, an Land gehen **VT** ausschiffen; *troops* landen

debarkation [ˌdiːbɑːˈkeɪʃən] **N** Ausschiffung *f*, Landung *f*; *(of troops)* Landen *nt*

debarment [dɪˈbɑːmənt] **N** Ausschluss *m*; **his ~ from the club** sein Ausschluss aus dem Klub

debase [dɪˈbeɪs] **VT a** *person* erniedrigen, entwürdigen **b** *virtues, qualities* mindern, herabsetzen **c** *metal* verschlechtern; *coinage* den Wert mindern *(+gen)*

debased [dɪˈbeɪst] **ADJ** verderbt; *quality, value* minderwertig; *word, expression* abgegriffen

debasement [dɪˈbeɪsmənt] **N a** *(of person)* Erniedrigung *f*, Entwürdigung *f* **b** *(of virtues, qualities)* Minderung *f*, Herabsetzung *f* **c** *(of metal)* Verschlechterung *f*; *(of coinage)* Wertminderung *f*

debatable [dɪˈbeɪtəbl] **ADJ** fraglich; *frontier* umstritten; **it's a ~ point whether …** es ist fraglich, ob …

debate [dɪˈbeɪt] **VT** *question* debattieren, diskutieren **VI** debattieren, diskutieren *(with* mit, *about* über *acc)*; **he was debating with himself whether or not to go** er überlegte hin und her, ob er gehen sollte **N** Debatte *f*; **after much ~** nach langer Debatte; **the ~ was on** *or* **about …** die Debatte ging über … *(acc)*; **the death penalty was under ~** zur Debatte stand die Todesstrafe; **to be open to ~** zur Debatte stehen

debater [dɪˈbeɪtəˈ] **N** Debattierer(in) *m(f)*

debating [dɪˈbeɪtɪŋ] N Debattieren *nt*, Diskutieren *nt* ADJ *attr* Debattier-; **~ society** Debattierklub *m*

debauch [dɪˈbɔːtʃ] VT verderben N Orgie *f*

debauched [dɪˈbɔːtʃt] ADJ *person, look* verderbt; *life* zügellos, ausschweifend

debauchee [ˌdebɔːˈtʃiː] N Wüstling *m*, Lüstling *m*

debauchery [dɪˈbɔːtʃərɪ] N Ausschweifung *f*, Debauche *f (old)*; **a life of ~** ein zügelloses *or* ausschweifendes Leben

debenture [dɪˈbentʃəʳ] N *(Fin)* Schuldschein *m*; *(Customs)* Rückzollschein *m*

debenture: **debenture bond** N Schuldverschreibung *f*, Obligation *f*; **debenture holder** N Obligationär(in) *m(f)*; **debenture stock** N Schuldverschreibungen *pl*, Obligationen *pl*

debilitate [dɪˈbɪlɪteɪt] VT schwächen

debilitating [dɪˈbɪlɪteɪtɪŋ] ADJ schwächend; *lack of funds, war, depression etc* lähmend; *shyness, self-doubt* hinderlich, hemmend; **to have a ~ effect on sb/sth** jdn/etw schwächen

debility [dɪˈbɪlɪtɪ] N Schwäche *f*

debit [ˈdebɪt] N Schuldposten *m*, Debet *nt*; **~ account** Debetkonto *nt*; **~ balance** Debetsaldo *m*; **~ and credit** Soll *nt* und Haben *nt*; **to enter sth to the ~ side of an account** etw auf der Sollseite verbuchen; **on the ~ side** *(fig)* auf der Minusseite VT **to ~ sb/sb's account (with a sum), to ~ (a sum) to sb/sb's account** jdn/jds Konto (mit einer Summe) belasten *or* debitieren *(form)*

debit: **debit card** N Kundenkarte *f*; **debit entry** N Abbuchung *f*

deboard [dɪˈbɔːd] *(US)* VI *(from train, bus, plane)* aussteigen; *(from boat)* ausschiffen VT *train, bus, plane* aussteigen aus; *boat* ausschiffen aus

debonair [ˌdebəˈneəʳ] ADJ flott

debone [diːˈbəʊn] VT *meat* vom Knochen lösen; *fish* entgräten

debouch [dɪˈbaʊtʃ] VI *(troops)* hervorbrechen, debouchieren *(old)*; *(river)* münden, sich ergießen

Debrett [dəˈbret] N ≈ Gotha *m*

debrief [ˌdiːˈbriːf] VT befragen; **to be ~ed** Bericht erstatten

debriefing [ˌdiːˈbriːfɪŋ] N *(also* **debriefing session***)* Einsatzbesprechung *f* (nach dem Flug *etc*)

debris [ˈdebriː] N Trümmer *pl*, Schutt *m*; *(Geol)* Geröll *nt*

debt [det] N *(= money owed, obligation)* Schuld *f*; **~ of honour** *(Brit) or* **honor** *(US)* Ehrenschuld *f*, Verschuldung *f* der öffentlichen Hand; **to be in ~** verschuldet sein (*to* gegenüber); **to be £5 in ~** £ 5 Schulden haben (*to* bei); **he is in my ~** *(for money)* er hat Schulden bei mir; *(for help etc)* er steht in meiner Schuld; **to run** *or* **get into ~** Schulden machen, sich verschulden; **to get out of ~** aus den Schulden herauskommen; **to be out of ~** schuldenfrei sein; **to repay a ~** *(lit, fig)* eine Schuld begleichen; **I shall always be in your ~** ich werde ewig in Ihrer Schuld stehen
ATTR Schulden-; **~ relief/forgiveness** Schuldenerlass *m*; **~ burden** Schulden *pl*

debt: **debt collection agency** N Inkassobüro *nt*; **debt collector** N Inkassobeauftragte(r) *mf*, Schuldeneintreiber(in) *m(f) (inf)*

debtor [ˈdetəʳ] N Schuldner(in) *m(f)*

debt: **debt relief** N Schuldenerleichterung *m*; **debt rescheduling** [ˈdetrɪˈʃedʒʊəlɪŋ] N Umschuldung *f*

debug [ˌdiːˈbʌg] VT **a** *mattress* entwanzen **b** *(= remove technical faults from)* die Fehler beseitigen bei **c** *(= remove bugging equipment from)* entwanzen **d** *(Comput)* debuggen; **~ging program** Fehlerkorrekturprogramm *nt*, Debugger *m*

debugger [ˌdiːˈbʌgəʳ] N *(Comput)* Debugger *m*

debunk [ˌdiːˈbʌŋk] VT *claim* entlarven; *myth* aufdecken; *politician* vom Sockel stoßen

debus [diːˈbʌs] VTI aus dem/einen Bus aussteigen

début [ˈdeɪbjuː] N *(lit, fig)* Debüt *nt*; **to make one's ~** *(in society)* in die Gesellschaft eingeführt werden; *(Theat)* debütieren, sein Debüt geben; *(fig)* sein Debüt geben; **~ album** Debütalbum *nt* VI *(Theat)* debütieren, sein Debüt geben; *(fig)* sein Debüt geben

débutante [ˈdebjʊtɑːnt] N Debütantin *f*

Dec *abbr of* **December** Dez.

dec *abbr of* **deceased** gest.

decade [ˈdekeɪd] N **a** *(= ten years)* Jahrzehnt *nt*, Dekade *f* **b** *(Eccl, of rosary)* Gesätz *nt*

decadence [ˈdekədəns] N Dekadenz *f*

decadent [ˈdekədənt] ADJ dekadent N *(Liter)* Vertreter(in) *m(f)* der Dekadenz, Décadent *m (geh)*

decaf(f) [ˈdiːkæf] N *abbr of* **decaffeinated** *(inf)* Koffeinfreie(r) *m (inf)*

decaffeinated [ˌdiːˈkæfɪneɪtɪd] ADJ koffeinfrei, entkoffeiniert

decagramme, *(US)* **decagram** [ˈdekəgræm] N Dekagramm *nt*

decal [dɪˈkæl] N *(US)* Abziehbild *nt*; *(process)* Abziehen *nt*

decalcify [ˌdiːˈkælsɪfaɪ] VT entkalken

decalitre, *(US)* **decaliter** [ˈdekəˌliːtəʳ] N Dekaliter *m or nt*

decalogue [ˈdekəlɒg] N Dekalog *m*

decametre, *(US)* **decameter** [ˈdekəˌmiːtəʳ] N Dekameter *nt*

decamp [dɪˈkæmp] VI **a** *(Mil)* das Lager abbrechen **b** *(inf)* verschwinden, sich aus dem Staube machen *(inf)*

decant [dɪˈkænt] VT umfüllen, dekantieren *(form)*

decanter [dɪˈkæntəʳ] N Karaffe *f*

decapitate [dɪˈkæpɪteɪt] VT enthaupten *(geh)*, köpfen, dekapitieren *(form)*; **she was ~d in the accident** bei dem Unfall wurde ihr der Kopf abgetrennt

decapitation [dɪˌkæpɪˈteɪʃən] N Enthauptung *f (geh)*

decarbonization [ˈdiːˌkɑːbənaɪˈzeɪʃən] N *(Aut)* Entkohlung *f*, Dekarbonisierung *f*

decarbonize [ˌdiːˈkɑːbənaɪz] VT *pistons etc* dekarbonisieren, entkohlen

decasyllable [ˈdekəsɪləbl] N Zehnsilber *m*

decathlete [dɪˈkæθliːt] N Zehnkämpfer *m*

decathlon [dɪˈkæθlən] N Zehnkampf *m*

decay [dɪˈkeɪ] VI **a** *(lit)* verfallen; *(Phys)* zerfallen; *(= rot, dead body, flesh, vegetable matter)* verwesen; *(food)* schlecht werden, verderben; *(tooth)* faulen, verfallen; *(bones, wood)* verfallen, morsch werden
b *(fig)* verfallen; *(health also)* sich verschlechtern; *(beauty also)* verblühen, vergehen; *(civilization, race)* untergehen; *(friendship)* auseinandergehen, zerfallen; *(one's faculties)* verkümmern; *(business, family)* herunterkommen
VT *food* schlecht werden lassen, verderben; *tooth* faulen lassen, schlecht werden lassen; *wood* morsch werden lassen
N **a** *(lit: = action)* Verfall *m*; *(Phys)* Zerfall *m*; *(= rotting, of dead body, flesh, vegetable matter)* Verwesung *f*; *(of food)* Schlechtwerden *nt*; *(of bones, wood)* Morschwerden *nt*; **tooth ~** Zahnfäule *f*, Karies *f*; **to fall into ~** in Verfall geraten, verfallen
b *(= decayed part or area)* Fäule *f*, Fäulnis *f*
c *(fig)* Verfall *m*; *(of friendship, civilization)* Zerfall *m*; *(of race, family, business)* Untergang *m*; *(of faculties)* Verkümmern *nt*

decayed [dɪˈkeɪd] ADJ *wood etc* morsch; *tooth* faul; *food* schlecht; *body, vegetable matter* verwest

decd *abbr of* **deceased** gest.

decease [dɪˈsiːs] *(Jur, form)* N Ableben *nt (form)* VI sterben, verscheiden *(geh)*

deceased [dɪˈsiːst] *(Jur, form)* ADJ ge- *or* verstorben; **John Brown, ~** der verstorbene John Brown N **the ~** der/die Tote *or* Verstorbene; *(pl)* die Toten *or* Verstorbenen *pl*

deceit [dɪˈsiːt] N Betrug *m no pl*, Täuschung *f*; **these unending ~s** diese endlosen Täuschungsmanöver; **a character full of ~** ein durch und durch falscher Charakter

deceitful [dɪˈsiːtfʊl] ADJ falsch, betrügerisch

deceitfully [dɪˈsiːtfəlɪ] ADV betrügerischerweise; *behave* betrügerisch; **she had ~ lured him to her house** sie hatte ihn auf hinterlistige Weise in ihr Haus gelockt

deceitfulness [dɪˈsiːtfʊlnɪs] N Falschheit *f*; *(= deceitful acts)* Betrügereien *pl*

deceivable [dɪˈsiːvəbl] ADJ leicht zu täuschen(d)

deceive [dɪˈsiːv] VT täuschen, trügen *(geh)*; *one's wife, husband* betrügen; **to ~ sb into doing sth** jdn durch Täuschung dazu bringen, etw zu tun; **are my eyes deceiving me - is it really you?** täuschen mich meine Augen, oder bist du es wirklich?; **to ~ oneself** sich *(dat)* selbst etwas vormachen VI trügen *(geh)*, täuschen

deceiver [dɪˈsiːvəʳ] N Betrüger(in) *m(f)*

decelerate [diːˈseləreɪt] VI *(car, train)* langsamer werden; *(driver)* die Geschwindigkeit herabsetzen; *(production)* sich verlangsamen VT verlangsamen

deceleration [ˈdiːˌseləˈreɪʃən] N *(of car, train)* Langsamerwerden *nt*; *(by driver)* Herabsetzung *f* der Geschwindigkeit; *(of production)* Verlangsamung *f*

December [dɪˈsembəʳ] N Dezember *m* → *also* **September**

decency [ˈdiːsənsɪ] N *(= good manners etc)* Anstand *m*; *(of dress etc)* Anständigkeit *f*; *(of behaviour)* Schicklichkeit *f*; **~ demands that …** der Anstand fordert, dass …; **it's only common ~ to …** es gehört sich einfach, zu …; **have you no sense of ~?** haben Sie denn kein Anstandsgefühl!; **for ~'s sake** anstandshalber; **he could have had the ~ to tell me** er hätte es mir anständigerweise auch sagen können; **I hope you'll have the ~ to tell me** ich hoffe, du wirst die Anständigkeit besitzen, es mir zu sagen

decent [ˈdiːsənt] ADJ *(all senses)* anständig; **are you ~?** *(inf)* bist du schon salonfähig? *(inf)*; **to do the ~ thing** das einzig Anständige tun; **it was ~ of you to come** es war sehr anständig von Ihnen zu kommen; **to give sb a ~ burial** jdn ordentlich begraben

decently [ˈdiːsəntlɪ] ADV *treat, pay, live* anständig; *dress also* schicklich *(geh)*; *bury* richtig, mit Anstand; **you can't ~ ask him to do it now** Sie können ihn jetzt kaum bitten, es zu tun

decentralization [ˈdiːˌsentrəlaɪˈzeɪʃən] N Dezentralisierung *f*

decentralize [diːˈsentrəlaɪz] VTI dezentralisieren

decentralized [diːˈsentrəlaɪzd] ADJ dezentral

deception [dɪˈsepʃən] N **a** *(= act of deceiving)* Täuschung *f*, Betrug *m no pl* (*of an +dat*); *(of wife etc)* Betrug *m* **b** *(= state of being deceived)* Täuschung *f* **c** *(= that which deceives)* Täuschung *f*

deceptive [dɪˈseptɪv] ADJ irreführend; *similarity* täuschend; *simplicity* trügerisch; **to be ~** täuschen, trügen *(geh)*; **appearances are** *or* **can be ~** der Schein trügt

deceptively [dɪˈseptɪvlɪ] ADV *simple, easy* täuschend; *strong, powerful* überraschend; *gentle, mild* trügerisch, täuschend; **to look ~ like sb/sth** jdm/einer Sache täuschend ähnlich sehen

deceptiveness [dɪˈseptɪvnɪs] N Täuschende(s) *nt*; **the ~ of the effects of perspective** die trügerischen Effekte der Perspektive; **beware of the ~ of statistics** Vorsicht, Statistiken sind irreführend

decibel [ˈdesɪbel] N Dezibel *nt*

decide [dɪˈsaɪd] ✪ 8.2 VT **a** *(= come to a decision)* (sich) entscheiden; *(= take it into one's head)* beschließen, sich entschließen; **what did**

you ~? *(yes or no)* wie habt ihr euch entschieden?; *(what measures)* was habt ihr beschlossen?; **did you ~ anything?** habt ihr irgendwelche Entscheidungen getroffen?; **you must ~ what to do** du musst (dich) entscheiden, was du tun willst; **you can't suddenly ~ you're going to leave home** du kannst nicht plötzlich beschließen, dass du einfach von zu Hause weggehst; **I have ~d we are making a big mistake** ich bin zu der Ansicht gekommen, dass wir einen großen Fehler machen; **I'll ~ what we do!** ich bestimme, was wir tun!; **she always wants to ~ everything** sie will immer alles bestimmen; **the car seems to have ~d it's not going to start** das Auto scheint beschlossen zu haben, nicht anzuspringen; **the weather hasn't ~d what it's going to do yet** das Wetter hat (sich) noch nicht entschlossen, was es will

b *(= settle) question, war etc* entscheiden; **to ~ sb's fate** jds Schicksal bestimmen, (über) jds Schicksal entscheiden

c to ~ sb to do sth jdn veranlassen, etw zu tun; **that eventually ~d me** das hat schließlich für mich den Ausschlag gegeben

VI (sich) entscheiden; **I don't know, YOU ~** ich weiß nicht, entscheiden *or* bestimmen SIE!; **I don't know, I can't ~** ich kann mich nicht entscheiden; **to ~ for/ against sth** (sich) für/gegen etw entscheiden; **to ~ for** *or* **in favour** *(Brit) or* **favor** *(US)* **of/against sb** *(Jur)* zu jds Gunsten/Ungunsten *or* für/gegen jdn entscheiden

▶ **decide on** VI *+prep obj* sich entscheiden für

decided [dɪˈsaɪdɪd] ADJ **a** *(= clear, definite) improvement* entschieden; *difference, advantage* deutlich **b** *(= determined) manner* entschlossen, bestimmt; **he is a man of ~ views** er hat sehr fest gefügte Ansichten

decidedly [dɪˈsaɪdɪdlɪ] ADV entschieden; **she is ~ lazy** sie ist (ganz) entschieden faul; **he's ~ uncomfortable about it** es ist ihm gar nicht wohl dabei; **~ dangerous** ausgesprochen gefährlich; **a ~ different view** eine ganz andere Ansicht; **she was ~ unhappy about it** sie war wirklich nicht glücklich damit

decider [dɪˈsaɪdəʳ] N *(Brit)* **a the ~ was that ...** was den Ausschlag gab, war dass ..., ausschlaggebend war, dass ... **b** *(= game)* Entscheidungsspiel *nt*; *(= goal)* Entscheidungstreffer *m*

deciding [dɪˈsaɪdɪŋ] ADJ entscheidend; *factor also* ausschlaggebend; **the ~ game** das Entscheidungsspiel

deciduous [dɪˈsɪdjʊəs] ADJ *leaves* die jedes Jahr abfallen; *antlers* das abgeworfen wird; **~ tree/forest** Laubbaum *m*/-wald *m*

decimal [ˈdesɪməl] **ADJ** Dezimal-; **to three ~ places** auf drei Dezimalstellen; **to go ~** sich auf das Dezimalsystem umstellen **N** Dezimalzahl *f*; **~s** Dezimalzahlen *pl*

decimal currency N Dezimalwährung *f*

decimalization [ˌdesɪməlaɪˈzeɪʃən] N Umstellung *f* auf das Dezimalsystem, Dezimalisierung *f (form)*

decimalize [ˈdesɪməlaɪz] VT *system, currency* auf das Dezimalsystem umstellen, dezimalisieren *(form)*

decimal: **decimal point** N Komma *nt*; **decimal symbol** N Dezimaltrennzeichen *nt*; **decimal system** N Dezimalsystem *nt*

decimate [ˈdesɪmeɪt] VT dezimieren

decipher [dɪˈsaɪfəʳ] VT *(lit, fig)* entziffern

decipherable [dɪˈsaɪfərəbl] ADJ *(lit, fig)* entzifferbar

decision [dɪˈsɪʒən] N **a** Entscheidung *f* (*on* über *+acc*), Entschluss *m*; *(esp of committee etc)* Beschluss *m*; *(of judge)* Entscheidung *f*; **to make a ~** eine Entscheidung treffen *or* fällen, einen Entschluss/Beschluss fassen; **she always wants to make all the ~s** sie will immer über alles bestimmen; **I can't make your ~s for you** ich kann nicht für dich entscheiden; **it's your ~** das musst du entscheiden; **I can't give you a ~ now** ich kann das jetzt nicht entscheiden; **to come to a ~** zu einer Entscheidung kommen; **I've come to the ~ that it's a waste of time** ich bin zu dem Schluss gekommen, dass es Zeitverschwendung ist; **~s, ~s!** immer diese Entscheidungen!

b *no pl (of character)* Entschlusskraft *f*, Entschlossenheit *f*; **a man of ~** ein Mann von Entschlusskraft; **to act with ~** entschlossen handeln

decision: **decision-maker** N Entscheidungsträger(in) *m(f)*; **decision-making** **N** Entscheidungsfindung *f*; **to show an aptitude for ~** Entschlusskraft zeigen; **he's hopeless at ~** er kann einfach keine Entscheidungen treffen **ADJ** *attr* **~ skills** *or* **abilities** Entschlusskraft *f*; **the ~ process** der Prozess der Entscheidungsfindung

decisive [dɪˈsaɪsɪv] ADJ **a** *(= crucial)* entscheidend; *factor* ausschlaggebend, entscheidend; *rejection* entschieden **b** *(= resolute) manner, answer* bestimmt, entschlossen; *person* entschlussfreudig

decisively [dɪˈsaɪsɪvlɪ] ADV **a** *(= crucially, conclusively) change, influence* entscheidend; *defeat* deutlich; *reject* entschieden **b** *(= resolutely) say* bestimmt, entschlossen; *act* entschlossen

decisiveness [dɪˈsaɪsɪvnɪs] N **a** *(= crucial importance)* entscheidende Bedeutung; **a victory of such ~** ein so entscheidender Sieg **b** *(= resoluteness)* Bestimmtheit *f*, Entschlossenheit *f*

deck [dek] **N a** *(Naut)* Deck *nt*; **on ~** auf Deck; **to go up on ~** an Deck gehen; **to go (down) below ~(s)** unter Deck gehen **b** *(of bus, plane)* Deck *nt*; **top** *or* **upper ~** Oberdeck *nt* **c** *(inf: = floor)* Boden *m* **d** *(Cards)* **a ~ of cards** ein Kartenspiel *nt* **e** *(of record player)* Laufwerk *nt*; *(= part of hi-fi unit)* Plattenspieler *m* **f** *(esp US: = veranda)* Veranda *f* **VT** *(also* **deck out***)* schmücken; **to ~ oneself out in one's Sunday best** sich in seinen Sonntagsstaat werfen *(inf)*, sich herausputzen; **all ~ed out in his Sunday best** ganz fesch in seinem Sonntagsstaat

deck: **deck cabin** N Deckkabine *f*; **deck cargo** N Deckladung *f*; **deck chair** N Liegestuhl *m*

-decker [-ˈdekəʳ] N *suf* -decker *m*; *(Naut)* **a three-decker** ein Dreidecker *m* → **single-decker, double-decker**

deck: **deck hand** N Deckshelfer(in) *m(f)*; **deckhouse** N Deckshaus *nt*

decking [ˈdekɪŋ] N *(esp US: = wooden flooring)* Deck *nt*

deckle edge [ˈdekledʒ] N Büttenrand *m*

deckle-edged [ˈdekledʒd] ADJ mit Büttenrand; *paper* Bütten-

deck tennis N Decktennis *nt*

declaim [dɪˈkleɪm] **VI** deklamieren; **to ~ against sth** gegen etw wettern **VT** deklamieren, vortragen

declamation [ˌdekləˈmeɪʃən] N Deklamation *f*; *(against sth)* Tirade *f*

declamatory [dɪˈklæmətərɪ] ADJ deklamatorisch, pathetisch

declarable [dɪˈkleərəbl] ADJ *goods* verzollbar

declaration [ˌdekləˈreɪʃən] N Erklärung *f*; *(Cards)* Ansage *f*; *(Customs)* Deklaration *f (form)*; **~ of intent** Absichtserklärung *f*; **~ of love** Liebeserklärung *f*; **~ of bankruptcy** Konkursanmeldung *f*; **to make/sign a ~** eine Erklärung abgeben/unterzeichnen; **~ of war** Kriegserklärung *f*; **~ of the results** *(Pol)* Bekanntgabe *f* des Ergebnisses/der Ergebnisse

declare [dɪˈkleəʳ] ✪ 26.2 **VT a** *intentions* erklären, kundtun *(geh)*; *results* bekannt geben, veröffentlichen; *goods* angeben, deklarieren *(form)*; **have you anything to ~?** haben Sie etwas zu verzollen?; **to ~ one's income** sein Einkommen angeben; **to ~ one's love (for sb)** (jdm) eine Liebeserklärung machen; **to ~ one's support (for sb/sth)** seine Unterstützung (für jdn/etw) zum Ausdruck bringen; **to ~ war (on sb)** (jdm) den Krieg erklären; **to ~ a state of emergency** den Notstand erklären *or* ausrufen; **to ~ independence** sich für unabhängig erklären; **to ~ sb bankrupt** jdn für bankrott erklären; **I ~ this motorway officially open** ich erkläre diese Autobahn für offiziell eröffnet; **he ~d the meeting closed** er erklärte die Sitzung für geschlossen; **to ~ sb the winner** jdn zum Sieger erklären; **he ~d himself fit to play** er erklärte sich für spielfähig

b *(= assert)* erklären, beteuern, versichern

VI a to ~ for/against sb/sth sich für/gegen jdn/etw erklären; **well I (do) ~!** *(dated)* ist es denn die Möglichkeit!

b *(Sport)* die Runde für beendet erklären

declared [dɪˈkleəd] ADJ erklärt

declaredly [dɪˈkleərɪdlɪ] ADV erklärtermaßen

déclassé, déclassée [deɪˈklæseɪ] ADJ heruntergekommen; *(in status)* sozial abgesunken

declassification [dɪˌklæsɪfɪˈkeɪʃən] N *(of information)* Freigabe *f*

declassify [diːˈklæsɪfaɪ] VT *information* freigeben

declension [dɪˈklenʃən] N *(Gram)* Deklination *f*

declinable [dɪˈklaɪnəbl] ADJ *(Gram)* deklinierbar

decline [dɪˈklaɪn] ✪ 12.3 **N a** *(in standards, birthrate, business, sales, prices)* Rückgang *m*; *(of empire, a party's supremacy)* Untergang *m*, Niedergang *m*; **~ in performance** *(Sport)* Leistungsabfall *m*; **to be on the** *or* **in ~, to go** *or* **fall into ~** *(business)* zurückgehen; *(empire)* verfallen

b *(Med)* Verfall *m*; **she went into a ~** es ging bergab mit ihr

VT a *invitation, honour* ablehnen; **he ~d to come** er hat es abgelehnt, zu kommen

b *(Gram)* deklinieren

VI a *(empire)* verfallen; *(fame)* verblassen; *(health)* sich verschlechtern; *(prices, business)* zurückgehen; *(importance, significance, value)* geringer werden; *(custom)* aussterben; *(popularity, enthusiasm, interest)* abnehmen; *(population, influence)* abnehmen, zurückgehen; **cases of real poverty are declining** Fälle von echter Armut gibt es immer weniger

b *(= refuse, say no)* ablehnen

c *(= slope: ground)* abfallen

d *(sun)* untergehen; *(liter, life, day)* zur Neige gehen *(liter)*; **in his declining years** gegen Ende seiner Tage *(liter)*

e *(Gram)* dekliniert werden

declivity [dɪˈklɪvɪtɪ] N Abschüssigkeit *f*

declutch [ˌdiːˈklʌtʃ] VI auskuppeln

decoction [dɪˈkɒkʃən] N Abkochung *f*, Absud *m*; *(Pharm)* Dekokt *nt (spec)*

decode [ˌdiːˈkəʊd] VT decodieren, dechiffrieren, entschlüsseln; *(Comput, TV)* dekodieren

decoder [ˌdiːˈkəʊdəʳ] N *(Comput, TV)* Decoder *m*, Dekoder *m*, Decodierer *m*

decoke [diːˈkəʊk] VT entrußen

decollate [ˈdiːkɒleɪt] VT *(Comput)* trennen

decollator [ˈdiːkɒleɪtəʳ] N *(Comput)* Formulartrenner *m*, Trennmaschine *f*

décolletage [deɪˈkɒltɑːʒ], **décolleté**[1] [deɪˈkɒlteɪ] N Dekolleté *nt*, Dekolletee *nt*, (tiefer) Ausschnitt

décolleté[2] ADJ dekolletiert, (tief) ausgeschnitten

decolonize [diːˈkɒlənaɪz] VT entkolonisieren

decommission [ˌdiːkəˈmɪʃən] VT *power plant* stilllegen; *arms* ausmustern; *warship* außer Dienst nehmen

decommissioning [ˌdiːkəˈmɪʃənɪŋ] N *(of arms)* Ausmusterung *f*

decompose [ˌdiːkəmˈpəʊz] **VT** *(Chem, Phys)* zerlegen; *(= rot)* zersetzen **VI** zerlegt werden; *(= rot)* sich zersetzen

decomposed [ˌdiːkəmˈpəʊzd] ADJ *(= rotten)* verfault, faul; *corpse* verwest; *food* verfault

decomposition [ˌdiːkɒmpəˈzɪʃən] N *(Phys: of light)* Zerlegung *f*; *(Chem also)* Abbau *m*; *(= rotting)* Zersetzung *f*, Verfaulen *nt*

decompress [ˌdiːkəmˈpres] **VT a** *diver* einer Dekompression *(dat)* unterziehen **b** *picture,* *signal, data* dekomprimieren VI sich einer Dekompression *(dat)* unterziehen

decompression [ˌdi:kəmˈpreʃən] N Dekompression *f*, Druckverminderung *f*

decompression: decompression chamber N Dekompressionskammer *f*; **decompression sickness** N Dekompressions- *or* Taucherkrankheit *f*

decongestant [ˌdi:kənˈdʒestənt] ADJ abschwellend N abschwellendes Mittel; *(drops etc)* Nasentropfen *pl*/-spray *nt*

deconsecrate [ˌdi:ˈkɒnsɪkreɪt] VT dekonsekrieren

deconstruct [ˌdi:kənˈstrʌkt] VT *(esp Liter)* dekonstruieren

decontaminate [ˌdi:kənˈtæmɪneɪt] VT entgiften, dekontaminieren; *(from radioactivity)* entseuchen

decontamination [ˈdi:kənˌtæmɪˈneɪʃən] N Entgiftung *f*, Dekontamination *f*; *(from radioactivity)* Entseuchung *f*, Dekontamination *f*

decontextualize [ˌdi:kənˈtekstjʊəlaɪz] VT *(form)* aus dem Zusammenhang nehmen

decontrol [ˌdi:kənˈtrəʊl] VT *(Comm) trade, prices* freigeben

décor [ˈdeɪkɔ:ʳ] N *(in room)* Ausstattung *f*; *(Theat)* Dekor *m or nt*; **he did his front room with Victorian ~** er richtete sein vorderes Zimmer im viktorianischen Stil ein

decorate [ˈdekəreɪt] VT **a** *cake, hat* verzieren; *street, building, Christmas tree* schmücken; *room* tapezieren; *(= paint)* (an)streichen; *(for special occasion)* dekorieren **b** *soldier* dekorieren, auszeichnen

decorating [ˈdekəreɪtɪŋ] N Tapezieren *nt*; *(= painting)* Streichen *nt*

decoration [ˌdekəˈreɪʃən] N **a** *(of cake, hat)* Verzierung *f*; *(of street, building, Christmas tree)* Schmücken *nt*; *(of room)* Tapezieren *nt*; *(= painting)* (An)streichen *nt*; *(for special occasion)* Dekoration *f* **b** *(= ornament, on cake, hat etc)* Verzierung *f*; *(on Christmas tree, building, in street)* Schmuck *m no pl*; **Christmas ~s** Weihnachtsdekorationen *pl or* -schmuck *m*; **interior ~** Innenausstattung *f*; **his secretary is just for ~** seine Sekretärin ist nur zur Dekoration da **c** *(Mil)* Dekoration *f*, Auszeichnung *f*

decorative [ˈdekərətɪv] ADJ dekorativ

decorator [ˈdekəreɪtəʳ] N *(Brit)* Maler(in) *m(f)*

decorous [ˈdekərəs] ADJ *action, behaviour* geziemend, schicklich; *dress* schicklich

decorously [ˈdekərəslɪ] ADV *behave* geziemend, schicklich; *dress* schicklich

decorum [dɪˈkɔ:rəm] N Anstand *m*, Dekorum *nt (old, form)*; **to have a sense of ~** Gefühl für Anstand haben; **to behave with ~** sich mit gebührendem Anstand benehmen

decouple [ˌdi:ˈkʌpl] VT entkoppeln

decoy [ˈdi:kɔɪ] N *(lit, fig)* Köder *m*; *(person)* Lockvogel *m*; **to act as a ~** als Köder fungieren, Lockvogel spielen; **police ~** Lockvogel *m* der Polizei; **~ manoeuvre** *(Brit) or* **maneuver** *(US)* Falle *f* VT *person* locken; **to ~ sb into doing sth** jdn durch Lockmittel dazu bringen, etw zu tun

decrease [di:ˈkri:s] VI abnehmen; *(figures, output, life expectancy, birth rate, production)* zurückgehen, abnehmen; *(strength, enthusiasm, intensity)* nachlassen; *(in knitting)* abnehmen; **in decreasing order of importance** in der Reihenfolge ihrer Bedeutung; **it ~s in value** es verliert an Wert VT verringern, reduzieren N [ˈdi:kri:s] Abnahme *f*; *(in figures, output, life expectancy, birth rate, production)* Rückgang *m*; *(in strength, enthusiasm, intensity)* Nachlassen *nt*; **~ in speed** Verminderung *or* Abnahme *f* der Geschwindigkeit; **to be on the ~** abnehmen

decreasingly [di:ˈkri:sɪŋlɪ] ADV immer weniger; **~ popular** immer unbeliebter

decree [dɪˈkri:] N Anordnung *f*, Verordnung *f*, Verfügung *f*; *(Pol: of king etc)* Erlass *m*; *(Eccl)* Dekret *nt*; *(Jur)* Verfügung *f*; *(of tribunal, court)* Entscheid *m*, Urteil *nt*; **by royal ~** auf königlichen Erlass; **by government ~** auf Erlass der Regierung; **to issue a ~** einen Erlass herausgeben VT verordnen, verfügen; **he ~d an annual holiday on 1st April** er erklärte den 1. April zum (ständigen) Feiertag

decree absolute N *(Jur)* endgültiges Scheidungsurteil

decree nisi [dɪˌkri:ˈnaɪsaɪ] N *(Jur)* vorläufiges Scheidungsurteil

decrepit [dɪˈkrepɪt] ADJ *staircase, car etc* altersschwach; *building* baufällig, heruntergekommen; *industry* heruntergekommen; *person* altersschwach, klapprig *(inf)*

decrepitude [dɪˈkrepɪtju:d] N *(of staircase, car etc)* Altersschwäche *f*; *(of building)* Baufälligkeit *f*; *(of person)* Altersschwäche *f*, Klapprigkeit *f (inf)*; *(of industry)* heruntergekommener Zustand

decriminalization [ˌdi:krɪmɪnəlaɪˈzeɪʃən] N Entkriminalisierung *f*

decriminalize [di:ˈkrɪmɪnəlaɪz] VT entkriminalisieren

decry [dɪˈkraɪ] VT schlechtmachen

decrypt [di:ˈkrɪpt] VT *(Comput, Telec)* entschlüsseln

dedicate [ˈdedɪkeɪt] VT **a** *church* weihen **b** *book, music, song* widmen (*to sb* jdm); **to ~ oneself** *or* **one's life to sb/sth** sich *or* sein Leben jdm/einer Sache widmen, sich einer Sache hingeben; **~d to the memory of ...** zum Gedenken an ...

dedicated [ˈdedɪkeɪtɪd] ADJ **a** *attitude* hingebungsvoll; *service, fans* treu; *(in one's work)* engagiert; **a ~ nurse/teacher** *etc* eine Krankenschwester/eine Lehrerin *etc*, die mit Leib und Seele bei der Sache ist; **to become a top-class dancer you have to be really ~** um ein erstklassiger Tänzer zu werden, muss man wirklich mit Leib und Seele dabei sein; **he is completely ~, he thinks of nothing but his work** er hat sich völlig seiner Arbeit verschrieben, er denkt an nichts anderes; **it's very ~ of you to stay on this late, Robinson** das ist sehr aufopfernd von Ihnen, so lange zu bleiben, Robinson; **she's ~ to her students** sie engagiert sich sehr für ihre Studenten; **to be a ~ follower of fashion** immer mit der neuesten Mode gehen; **he is a ~ follower of football** er ist ein ausgesprochener Fußballanhänger
b **~ word processor** dediziertes Textverarbeitungssystem

dedicated line N *(Telec, Comput)* Standleitung *f*

dedicatee [ˌdedɪkəˈti:] N *Person, der etwas gewidmet wird*

dedication [ˌdedɪˈkeɪʃən] N **a** *(= quality)* Hingabe *f* (*to* an +*acc*) **b** *(= act: of church)* Einweihung *f*, Weihe *f*; **they admired his ~ of his life to helping the poor** sie bewunderten, dass er sein Leben in den Dienst der Armen stellte **c** *(in book)* Widmung *f*

dedicator [ˈdedɪkeɪtəʳ] N Widmende(r) *mf*, Zueigner(in) *m(f) (geh)*

deduce [dɪˈdju:s] VT folgern, schließen (*from* aus); *(Logic)* deduzieren (*from* von)

deducible [dɪˈdju:sɪbl] ADJ zu schließen, ableitbar (*from* aus); *(Logic)* deduzierbar (*from* von)

deduct [dɪˈdʌkt] VT abziehen (*from* von); *(from wages also)* einbehalten; **to ~ sth from the price** etw vom Preis ablassen; **to ~ sth for expenses** etw für Spesen zurückbehalten; **to ~ income tax at source** Einkommenssteuer einbehalten; **after ~ing 5%** nach Abzug von 5%

deductible [dɪˈdʌktəbl] ADJ abziehbar; *(= tax deductible)* absetzbar

deduction [dɪˈdʌkʃən] N **a** *(= act of deducting)* Abziehen *nt*, Abzug *m*; *(= sth deducted, from price)* Nachlass *m* (*from* für, auf +*acc*); *(from wage)* Abzug *m* **b** *(= act of deducing)* Folgern *nt*, Folgerung *f*; *(= sth deduced)* (Schluss)folgerung *f*; *(Logic)* Deduktion *f*; **by a process of ~** durch Folgern

deductive [dɪˈdʌktɪv] ADJ deduktiv

deed [di:d] N **a** Tat *f*, Handlung *f*; *(= feat)* Tat *f*, Leistung *f*; **good ~** gute Tat; **evil ~** Übeltat *f*; **in word and ~** in Wort und Tat **b** **in ~** tatsächlich, in der Tat; **he is master in ~ if not in name** er ist der eigentliche *or* tatsächliche Herr, wenn auch nicht offiziell *or* nach außen hin **c** *(Jur)* Übertragungsurkunde *f*; **the ~s of a house** die Übertragungsurkunde eines Hauses; **~ of covenant** Vertragsurkunde *f* VT *(US)* überschreiben (*to* auf +*acc*)

deed poll N (einseitige) Absichtserklärung

deejay [ˈdi:dʒeɪ] N *(inf)* Discjockey *m*

deem [di:m] VT **to ~ sb/sth (to be) sth** jdn/etw für etw erachten *(geh) or* halten; **it was ~ed necessary** es wurde für nötig gehalten, man hielt es für nötig; **he was ~ed worthy of the award** *(geh)* er wurde des Preises für würdig erachtet *(geh) or* gehalten; **he was ~ed too ill to leave hospital** man hielt ihn für zu krank, um das Krankenhaus zu verlassen

deep [di:p] ADJ (+*er*) **a** *water, hole, wound* tief; **the pond/snow was 4 feet ~** der Teich war/der Schnee lag 4 Fuß tief; **a two-foot ~ trench** ein zwei Fuß tiefer Graben; **two feet ~ in snow** mit zwei Fuß Schnee bedeckt; **two feet ~ in water** zwei Fuß tief unter Wasser; **the ~ end** *(of swimming pool)* das Tiefe; **to go off (at) the ~ end** *(fig inf)* auf die Palme gehen *(inf)*; **to go** *or* **jump in at the ~ end** *(fig)* sich kopfüber in die Sache stürzen; **to be thrown in at the ~ end** *(fig)* gleich zu Anfang richtig ranmüssen *(inf)*
b *shelf, cupboard* tief; *(= wide) border, edge* breit; **a plot of ground 15 metres ~** ein 15 Meter tiefes Stück Land; **the spectators stood ten ~** die Zuschauer standen zu zehnt hintereinander
c *voice, sound, note, colour* tief
d *breathing, sigh* tief
e *(fig) mystery, sleep, secret, mourning* tief; *(= profound) thinker, book, remark, writer* tiefsinnig; *(= heartfelt) concern, relief, interest* groß; *sorrow* tief (empfunden); *(= devious) person* verschlagen, hintergründig; *dealings* undurchsichtig; **~est sympathy** aufrichtiges Beileid; **~ down, she knew he was right** im Innersten wusste sie, dass er recht hatte; **~ in conversation** ins Gespräch vertieft; **~ in thought/a book** in Gedanken/in ein Buch vertieft *or* versunken; **~ in debt** hoch verschuldet; **~ in recession** mitten in einer Rezession; **we had a ~ and meaningful relationship** wir hatten eine tiefer gehende und sinnvolle Beziehung; **to be in ~ trouble** in großen Schwierigkeiten sein
ADV (+*er*) tief; **~ into the night** bis tief in die Nacht hinein; **~ in enemy territory** tief auf feindlichem Gebiet; **to breathe ~** tief atmen; **he's in it pretty ~** *(inf)* er steckt *or* hängt ganz schön tief da drin *(inf)*; **passions are running ~** die Gefühle schlagen hohe Wellen
N **a** *(liter)* **the ~** das Meer, die See
b **in the ~ of winter** mitten im tiefsten Winter

deepen [ˈdi:pən] VT *(lit, fig)* vertiefen; *concern, sorrow* vergrößern, vertiefen; *love, friendship* vertiefen, verstärken; *colour* dunkler machen; *mystery* vergrößern; *crisis, recession* verschärfen; *sound* tiefer machen VI *(lit, fig)* sich vergrößern, tiefer werden; *(sorrow, concern, interest)* zunehmen, größer werden; *(colour, sound, voice)* tiefer werden; *(mystery)* größer werden; *(rift, divisions)* sich vertiefen; *(crisis, recession)* sich verschärfen

deepening [ˈdi:pənɪŋ] ADJ *sorrow, concern etc* zunehmend, wachsend; *friendship, love also* sich vertiefend; *crisis, recession* sich verschärfend; *colour, mystery* sich vertiefend, tiefer werdend N *(of hole, mystery)* Vergrößerung *f*; *(of sorrow, interest, concern)* Zunahme *f*; *(of friendship, love)* Vertiefung *f*; *(of crisis, recession)* Verschärfung *f*

deep: deep-dyed [ˈdi:pˈdaɪd] ADJ *(inf)* eingefleischt, unverbesserlich, Erz-; **deep-fat fryer** N Fritteuse *f*; **deep-freeze** VT einfrieren; **deepfreeze** [ˌdi:pˈfri:z] N Tiefkühltruhe *f*; *(upright)* Gefrierschrank *m*; **deep-freezing** N Einfrieren *nt*, Tiefgefrieren *nt*; **deep-frozen** ADJ tiefgefroren; **~ foods** Tiefkühlkost *f*;

deep-fry VT frittieren, im schwimmenden Fett backen; **deep grammar** N Tiefengrammatik *f*; **deep kiss** N Zungenkuss *m*; **deep-laid** ADJ *comp* **deeper-laid** *plot* (sorgfältig) ausgetüftelt *(inf) or* ausgearbeitet

deeply ['di:plɪ] ADV **a** *(lit)* tief; ~ **embedded** *or* **ingrained dirt** tief sitzender Schmutz **b** *(fig)* tief; *concerned, worried* zutiefst, äußerst; *unhappy, suspicious, unpopular* äußerst; *regret, move, shock, involved, grateful* zutiefst; *interested* höchst; *love* sehr, innig; *think* gründlich; ~ **religious** tiefreligiös; ~ **committed** stark engagiert; **they are ~ embarrassed by it** es ist ihnen äußerst peinlich; **to be ~ in love** sehr verliebt sein; **to fall ~ in love** sich sehr verlieben; ~ **in debt** hoch verschuldet; **a ~ ingrained prejudice** ein fest verwurzeltes Vorurteil; **to go ~ into a matter** sich gründlich mit einer Sache befassen

deepness ['di:pnɪs] N *(lit, fig)* Tiefe *f*; *(of border, edge)* Breite *f*; *(= profundity, of thinker, remark etc)* Tiefsinnigkeit *f*; *(of concern, relief, interest)* Größe *f*

deep: **deep-pan pizza** [ˌdi:ppæn'pi:tsə] N Pfannenpizza *f*; **deep-ray therapy** N Tiefenbestrahlung *f*; **deep-rooted** ADJ *comp* **deeper-rooted** *(fig)* tief verwurzelt; **deep-sea** ADJ Tiefsee-; ~ **drilling** Tiefseebohrung *f*; **deep-sea diver** N Tiefseetaucher(in) *m(f)*; **deep-sea fishery, deep-sea fishing** N Hochseefischerei *f*; **deep-seated** ADJ *comp* **deeper-seated** tief sitzend; **deep-set** ADJ *comp* **deeper-set** tief liegend; **Deep South** N Tiefer Süden; **deep space** N der äußere Weltraum; **deep structure** N *(Ling)* Tiefenstruktur *f*; **deep-throated** ['di:pˌθrəʊtɪd] ADJ kehlig

deer [dɪəʳ] N *pl* - *(= roe deer)* Reh *nt*; *(= stag)* Hirsch *m*; *(collectively)* Rotwild *nt*; **there are a lot of ~ in the forest** im Wald gibt es viel Rotwild

deer: **deerhound** N Deerhound *m*; **deer park** N Wildpark *m*; **deerskin** N Hirsch-/Rehleder *nt*; **deerstalker** N **a** *(= person) jd, der auf die Pirsch geht* **b** *(= hat)* ≈ Sherlock-Holmes-Mütze *f*; **deerstalking** N Pirschen *nt*, Pirsch *f*; **to go ~** auf die Pirsch gehen

de-escalate [ˌdi:'eskəleɪt] VT deeskalieren

de-escalation [ˌdi:eskə'leɪʃən] N Deeskalation *f*

deface [dɪ'feɪs] VT verunstalten

de facto [deɪ'fæktəʊ] ADJ ADV de facto

defamation [ˌdefə'meɪʃən] N Diffamierung *f*, Verleumdung *f*; ~ **of character** Rufmord *m*

defamatory [dɪ'fæmətərɪ] ADJ diffamierend, verleumderisch

defame [dɪ'feɪm] VT diffamieren, verleumden

default [dɪ'fɔ:lt] N **a** *(= failure to appear, Jur)* Nichterscheinen *nt* vor Gericht; *(Sport)* Nichtantreten *nt*; *(= failure to perform duty)* Versäumnis *f*; *(= failure to pay)* Nichtzahlung *f*; **judgement by ~** *(Jur)* Versäumnisurteil *nt*; **to win by ~** kampflos gewinnen **b** *(= lack, absence)* Mangel *m*; **in ~ of, due to ~ of** in Ermangelung *+gen* **c** ['di:fɔ:lt] *(Comput)* Default *m*, Standard(-wert) *m*, Voreinstellung *f*
VI *(= not appear, Jur)* nicht erscheinen; *(Sport)* nicht antreten; *(= not perform duty, not pay)* säumig sein; **to ~ in one's payments** seinen Zahlungsverpflichtungen nicht nachkommen; **it always ~s to the C drive** *(Comput)* es wird immer das Laufwerk C angesprochen
ATTR ['di:fɔ:lt] *(Comput) parameter* voreingestellt; ~ **drive** Standardlaufwerk *nt*

defaulter [dɪ'fɔ:ltəʳ] N *(Jur)* nicht erscheinende Partei; *(Sport)* nicht antretender Spieler, nicht antretende Spielerin; *(on payment)* Säumige(r) *mf*, säumiger Zahler; *(Mil, Naut)* Straffällige(r) *mf*

default: **default printer** N Standarddrucker *m*; **default value** N Standardwert *m*

defeat [dɪ'fi:t] N *(= defeating)* Besiegung *f*, Sieg *m* (of über *+acc*); *(of motion, bill)* Ablehnung *f*; *(of hopes, plans)* Vereitelung *f*; *(= being defeated)* Niederlage *f*; **their ~ of the enemy** ihr Sieg über den Feind; **their ~ by the enemy** ihre Besiegung *or* Niederlage durch den Feind; **to admit ~** sich geschlagen geben; **to suffer a ~** eine Niederlage erleiden
VT *army, team* besiegen, schlagen; *government* eine Niederlage beibringen *(+dat)*, besiegen; *motion, bill* ablehnen; *hopes, plans* vereiteln; **to ~ one's own ends** *or* **object** sich *(dat or acc)* ins eigene Fleisch schneiden; **that would be ~ing the purpose of the exercise** dann verliert die Übung ihren Sinn; **it ~s me why …** *(inf)* es will mir einfach nicht in den Kopf, warum … *(inf)*

defeatism [dɪ'fi:tɪzəm] N Defätismus *m*

defeatist [dɪ'fi:tɪst] N Defätist *m* ADJ defätistisch

defecate ['defəkeɪt] VI den Darm entleeren, defäkieren *(form)*

defecation [ˌdefə'keɪʃən] N Entleerung *f* des Darms, Defäkation *f (form)*

defect[1] ['di:fekt] N Fehler *m*, Schaden *m*; *(in mechanism also)* Defekt *m*; **physical ~** körperlicher Schaden *or* Defekt; **hearing ~** Gehörfehler *m*, Gehörschaden *m*; **sight ~** Sehfehler *m*, Sehschwäche *f*; **character ~** Charakterfehler *m*

defect[2] [dɪ'fekt] VI *(Pol)* sich absetzen; *(fig)* abtrünnig werden, abfallen; **to ~ to the enemy** zum Feind überlaufen

defection [dɪ'fekʃən] N *(Pol)* Überlaufen *nt*; *(fig)* Abtrünnigkeit *f*, Abfall *m*

defective [dɪ'fektɪv] ADJ **a** *material, goods etc* fehlerhaft; *machine, gene* defekt; *(fig) reasoning etc* fehlerhaft; *hearing, sight* mangelhaft, gestört; **he has a ~ heart valve** er hat einen Herzklappenfehler **b** *(Gram)* unvollständig, defektiv **c** **(mentally)** ~ geistesgestört N **a** *(Gram)* Defektivum *nt* **b** *(= retarded person)* Geistesgestörte(r) *mf*

defence, *(US)* **defense** [dɪ'fens] N **a** *no pl* Verteidigung *f no pl*; **in his ~** zu seiner Verteidigung; **to come to sb's ~** jdn verteidigen; **to put up** *or* **make a spirited ~ of sb/sth** jdn/etw mutig verteidigen; **his only ~ was …** seine einzige Rechtfertigung war … **b** *(= form of protection)* Abwehr- *or* Schutzmaßnahme *f*; *(Mil: = fortification etc)* Befestigung *f*, Verteidigungsanlage *f*; **as a ~ against** als Schutz gegen; **his ~s were down** er war wehrlos; **she caught me when my ~s were down** sie erwischte mich in einem schwachen Augenblick *(inf)* **c** *(Jur, Sport)* Verteidigung *f*; **to play in ~** in der Verteidigung spielen

defence, *(US)* **defense**: **defence counsel** N Verteidiger(in) *m(f)*; **defence expenditure** N Verteidigungsausgaben *pl*; **defenceless**, *(US)* **defenseless** ADJ schutzlos; **defenceman** [dɪ'fensmən] N *pl* **-men** *(Ice hockey)* Verteidiger *m*; **defence mechanism** N *(Physiol, Psych)* Abwehrmechanismus *m*; **defence minister** N Verteidigungsminister(in) *m(f)*; **defence system** N *(Biol)* Abwehrsystem *nt*; **defence witness** N Zeuge *m*/Zeugin *f* der Verteidigung, Entlastungszeuge(in) *m(f)*

defend [dɪ'fend] VT verteidigen *(also Jur)* *(against* gegen); **to ~ oneself** sich verteidigen

defendant [dɪ'fendənt] N Angeklagte(r) *mf*; *(in civil cases)* Beklagte(r) *mf* ADJ angeklagt, beklagt

defender [dɪ'fendəʳ] N Verteidiger(in) *m(f)*; **Defender of the Faith** Fidei Defensor *m*

defending [dɪ'fendɪŋ] ADJ ~ **counsel** Verteidiger(in) *m(f)*; **the ~ champions** die Titelverteidiger *pl*

defenestration [di:ˌfenɪ'streɪʃən] N *(form, hum)* Fenstersturz *m*; **the Defenestration of Prague** der Prager Fenstersturz

defense *etc (US)* = **defence** *etc*

defensible [dɪ'fensɪbl] ADJ **a** *(lit)* wehrhaft; **because of its position the town wasn't ~** die Stadt war wegen ihrer Lage nicht zu verteidigen **b** *(= justifiable) behaviour, argument* vertretbar, zu verteidigen *pred*

defensive [dɪ'fensɪv] ADJ defensiv *(also fig)*; **a good ~ player** ein guter Verteidiger N *(Mil)* Verteidigungs- *or* Abwehraktion *f*; **to be on the ~** *(Mil, fig)* in der Defensive sein; **to put sb on the ~** *(fig)* jdn in die Defensive drängen; **to go onto the ~** *(fig)* sich in die Defensive begeben

defensively [dɪ'fensɪvlɪ] ADV *(also Sport)* defensiv

defer[1] [dɪ'fɜ:ʳ] VT *(= delay)* verschieben; *event also* verlegen; **to ~ doing sth** es verschieben, etw zu tun

defer[2] VI *(= submit)* **to ~ to sb** sich jdm beugen *or* fügen; **to ~ to sb's wishes** sich jds Wünschen *(dat)* fügen

deference ['defərəns] N Achtung *f*, Respekt *m*; **out of** *or* **in ~ to** aus Achtung *(dat) or* Respekt *(dat)* vor; **with all due ~ to you** bei aller schuldigen Achtung *or* allem schuldigen Respekt Ihnen gegenüber

deferential [ˌdefə'renʃəl] ADJ ehrerbietig, respektvoll; **to be ~ to sb** jdm mit Respekt *or* Achtung begegnen

deferentially [ˌdefə'renʃəlɪ] ADV ehrerbietig, respektvoll

deferment [dɪ'fɜ:mənt] N Verschiebung *f*; *(of event also)* Verlegung *f*

deferred [dɪ'fɜ:d]: **deferred annuity** N nach bestimmter Zeit fällige Rente; **deferred pay** N *(Mil)* einbehaltener Sold; *(Naut)* einbehaltene Heuer; **deferred payment** N Ratenzahlung *f*; **deferred shares** PL Nachzugsaktien *pl*; **deferred taxation** N Steuerrückstellung *f*; **deferred terms** PL *(US)* Abzahlungssystem *nt*; **on ~** auf Abzahlung *or* Raten

defiance [dɪ'faɪəns] N Trotz *m* (of *sb* jdm gegenüber); *(of order, law, death, danger)* Missachtung *f* (of *+gen*); **an act of ~** eine Trotzhandlung; **in ~ of sb/sth** jdm/etw zum Trotz; **his ~ of my orders caused an accident** weil er meine Anordnungen missachtete, gab es einen Unfall; **that is in ~ of gravity/logic** das widerspricht den Gesetzen der Schwerkraft/Logik

defiant [dɪ'faɪənt] ADJ *child, answer* trotzig; *(= rebellious)* aufsässig; *(= challenging) attitude* herausfordernd

defiantly [dɪ'faɪəntlɪ] ADV *declare, announce, stare* trotzig, herausfordernd; *reject* trotzig; *resist* standhaft

defibrillator [di:'fɪbrɪleɪtəʳ] N *(Med)* Defibrillator *m*

deficiency [dɪ'fɪʃənsɪ] N *(= shortage)* Mangel *m*; *(Fin)* Defizit *nt*, Fehlbetrag *m*; *(= defect: in character, system)* Schwäche *f*; **vitamin/iron ~** Vitamin-/Eisenmangel *m*

deficiency: **deficiency disease** N *(Med)* Mangelkrankheit *f*; **deficiency guarantee** N *(Fin)* Ausfallbürgschaft *f*; **deficiency payment** N *(Fin)* Ausgleichszahlung *f*

deficient [dɪ'fɪʃənt] ADJ unzulänglich; **sb/sth is ~ in sth** jdm/einer Sache fehlt es an etw *(dat)*; **a diet ~ in iron** eine Ernährung, die nicht genug Eisen enthält → **mentally**

deficit ['defɪsɪt] N Defizit *nt*

deficit financing N *(Fin)* Defizitfinanzierung *f*, Finanzierung *f* durch Staatsverschuldung

deficit spending N *(Fin)* Deficit-Spending *nt*

defile[1] ['di:faɪl] N Hohlweg *m* VI hintereinandermarschieren

defile[2] [dɪ'faɪl] VT *(= pollute, sully)* verschmutzen, verunreinigen; *(= desecrate)* schänden, entweihen

defilement [dɪ'faɪlmənt] N Verschmutzung *f*, Verunreinigung *f*; *(= desecration)* Schändung *f*, Entweihung *f*

definable [dɪ'faɪnəbl] ADJ definierbar; *conditions, boundaries, duties etc* bestimmbar

define [dɪ'faɪn] VT **a** *(= describe)* definieren; *conditions, boundaries, powers, duties* bestimmen, festlegen; **~ custom colours** *(Comput)* Farbe(n) definieren **b** *(= show in outline)* betonen; **clearly ~d** scharf; **the path is not very well ~d** der Weg ist nicht sehr deutlich; **to be clearly ~d against the sky** sich klar *or* scharf gegen den Himmel abzeichnen

definite [ˈdefɪnɪt] ADJ **a** *(= fixed, concrete, explicit)* definitiv; *answer, decision* klar, eindeutig; *agreement, date, plan, intention, wish* fest, definitiv; *command, request* bestimmt; **is that ~?** ist das sicher?; *(= agreed by contract etc also)* steht das fest?; **there has been an improvement, that's ~** es ist eindeutig eine Verbesserung eingetreten; **for ~** *(say, know)* mit Bestimmtheit **b** *(= distinct, pronounced) mark, stain, lisp* deutlich; *advantage, improvement* klar, eindeutig; *problem, possibility* echt **c** *(= positive, decided) tone, manner* bestimmt; **she was very ~ about it** sie war sich *(dat)* sehr sicher **d** *(Gram)* definitiv

definite article N *(Gram)* bestimmter Artikel

definitely [ˈdefɪnɪtlɪ] ✪ 8.2 ADV **a** *(= finally) decide, say* endgültig; **it's not ~ arranged/agreed yet** es steht noch nicht fest **b** *(= clearly)* eindeutig; *(= certainly)* bestimmt; *(= whatever happens)* auf jeden Fall; **~ not** auf keinen Fall; **she has ~ put on weight** sie hat eindeutig zugenommen; **he ~ wanted to come** er wollte bestimmt kommen; **that is ~ wrong** das ist bestimmt nicht richtig; **that's ~ an improvement/an advantage** das ist ganz sicherlich eine Verbesserung/ein Vorteil **c** *(= emphatically) say* nachdrücklich, bestimmt

definiteness [ˈdefɪnɪtnɪs] N Bestimmtheit *f*; *(of answer, decision)* Klarheit *f*, Eindeutigkeit *f*

definition [ˌdefɪˈnɪʃən] N **a** *(of word, concept)* Definition *f*; **by ~** per definitionem, definitionsgemäß **b** *(of powers, duties, boundaries)* Festlegung *f*, Bestimmung *f* **c** *(Phot, TV)* Bildschärfe *f*; *(Rad)* Tonschärfe *f*; *(Opt, of lens)* Schärfe *f*

definitive [dɪˈfɪnɪtɪv] ADJ *(= decisive) victory, answer* entschieden; *(= authoritative) book* maßgeblich *(on* für); *(= defining) term* beschreibend; **~ laws** Rahmengesetze *pl* N *(= stamp)* Briefmarke *f* einer Dauerserie

definitively [dɪˈfɪnɪtɪvlɪ] ADV definitiv

deflate [ˌdiːˈfleɪt] VT *tyre, balloon* die Luft ablassen aus; **to ~ the currency** *(Fin)* eine Deflation herbeiführen; **to ~ sb's confidence/ego** jds Selbstvertrauen/Ego *(dat)* einen Dämpfer aufsetzen; **he felt a bit ~d when …** es war ein ziemlicher Dämpfer für ihn, dass … VI *(Fin)* eine Deflation herbeiführen

deflation [ˌdiːˈfleɪʃən] N *(of tyre, ball)* Luftablassen *nt* *(of* aus); *(Fin)* Deflation *f*

deflationary [ˌdiːˈfleɪʃənərɪ] ADJ *(Fin)* Deflations-, deflationistisch; **~ policy** Deflationspolitik *f*

deflect [dɪˈflekt] VT ablenken; *ball* ablenken, abfälschen; *steam, air current* ableiten, ablenken; *(Phys) light* beugen VI *(compass needle)* ausschlagen; *(projectile)* abweichen

deflection [dɪˈflekʃən] N Ablenkung *f*; *(of ball)* Ablenkung *f*, Abfälschung *f*; *(of air current)* Ableitung *f*; *(Phys, of light)* Beugung *f*

deflective [dɪˈflektɪv] ADJ ablenkend; *(Phys)* beugend

deflector [dɪˈflektəʳ] N Deflektor *m*, Ablenkvorrichtung *f*

defloration [ˌdiːflɔːˈreɪʃən] N *(liter, of girl)* Entjungferung *f*, Defloration *f*

deflower [ˌdiːˈflaʊəʳ] VT *(liter) girl* entjungfern, deflorieren

defog [ˌdiːˈfɒg] NT *windscreen* frei machen

defogger [ˌdiːˈfɒgəʳ] N *(Aut)* Gebläse *nt*

defoliant [ˌdiːˈfəʊlɪənt] N Entlaubungsmittel *nt*

defoliate [ˌdiːˈfəʊlɪeɪt] VT entlauben, entblättern

defoliation [ˌdiːfəʊlɪˈeɪʃən] N Entlaubung *f*

deforest [ˌdiːˈfɒrɪst] VT entwalden

deforestation [diːˌfɒrɪˈsteɪʃən] N Entwaldung *f*

deform [dɪˈfɔːm] VT deformieren, verunstalten; *(Tech)* verformen; *mind, tastes* verderben

deformation [ˌdiːfɔːˈmeɪʃən] N Deformierung *f*, Deformation *f*, Verunstaltung *f*; *(Tech)* Verformung *f*

deformed [dɪˈfɔːmd] ADJ deformiert, verunstaltet; *(Tech)* verformt; *person* deformiert, missgestaltet; *mind* krankhaft

deformity [dɪˈfɔːmɪtɪ] N Deformität *f*, Verunstaltung *f*; *(of person)* Deformität *f*, Missgestalt *f*; *(of mind)* Krankhaftigkeit *f*

defragment [diːfrægˈment] VT *(Comput) hard disk* defragmentieren

defraud [dɪˈfrɔːd] VT betrügen, hintergehen; **to ~ sb of sth** jdn um etw betrügen *or* bringen

defrauder [dɪˈfrɔːdəʳ] N Betrüger(in) *m(f)*

defray [dɪˈfreɪ] VT tragen, übernehmen

defrayal [dɪˈfreɪəl], **defrayment** [dɪˈfreɪmənt] N Übernahme *f*

defrock [ˌdiːˈfrɒk] VT aus dem Priesteramt verstoßen

defrost [ˌdiːˈfrɒst] VT *fridge* abtauen; *food* auftauen VI *(fridge)* abtauen; *(food)* auftauen

defroster [ˌdiːˈfrɒstəʳ] N Defroster *m*, Entfroster *m*

deft [deft] ADJ *(+er)* flink, geschickt

deftly [ˈdeftlɪ] ADV geschickt

deftness [ˈdeftnɪs] N Flinkheit *f*, Geschicktheit *f*

defunct [dɪˈfʌŋkt] ADJ *person* verstorben; *(fig) institution etc* eingegangen; *idea* untergegangen; *law* außer Kraft

defuse [ˌdiːˈfjuːz] VT *(lit, fig)* entschärfen

defy [dɪˈfaɪ] VT **a** *(= refuse to submit to, disobey) person* sich widersetzen *(+dat)*; *(esp child)* trotzen *(+dat)*; *orders, law, death, danger* verachten, trotzen *(+dat)* **b** *(fig: = make impossible)* widerstehen *(+dat)*; **to ~ definition** nicht definiert werden können; **to ~ description** jeder Beschreibung spotten; **that defies belief!** das ist ja unglaublich!; **to ~ gravity/logic** den Gesetzen der Schwerkraft/Logik widersprechen; **to ~ the odds to do sth** etw entgegen allen Erwartungen tun; **she defies her age** *or* **the years and wears the latest fashions** sie trägt ihrem Alter zum Trotz die neueste Mode **c** *(= challenge)* **I ~ you to do it/to buy one more cheaply** machen Sie es doch/kaufen Sie doch einen Billigeren, wenn Sie können

degeneracy [dɪˈdʒenərəsɪ] N Degeneration *f*

degenerate [dɪˈdʒenərɪt] ADJ degeneriert; *people, morals also* entartet N degenerierter Mensch [dɪˈdʒenəreɪt] VI degenerieren; *(people, morals also)* entarten; **the demonstration ~d into violence** die Demonstration artete in Gewalttätigkeiten aus

degenerateness [dɪˈdʒenərɪtnɪs] N Degeneration *f*

degeneration [dɪˌdʒenəˈreɪʃən] N Degeneration *f*; *(of people, morals also)* Entartung *f*

degenerative [dɪˈdʒenərətɪv] ADJ *(Med)* degenerativ *(spec)*

degradable [dɪˈgreɪdəbl] ADJ *waste* abbaubar

degradation [ˌdegrəˈdeɪʃən] N Erniedrigung *f*; *(Geol)* Erosion *f*; *(Chem)* Abbau *m*; **the appalling ~ of the jails** die schrecklich entwürdigenden Zustände in den Gefängnissen

degrade [dɪˈgreɪd] VT erniedrigen; *(esp Mil: = lower in rank)* degradieren; *(Geol)* erodieren; *(Chem)* abbauen; **to ~ oneself** sich erniedrigen; **I wouldn't ~ myself by doing that** ich würde mich nicht dazu erniedrigen, das zu tun VI *(Chem: = break down)* sich abbauen

degrading [dɪˈgreɪdɪŋ] ADJ erniedrigend

degree [dɪˈgriː] N **a** *(= unit of measurement)* Grad *m no pl*; **an angle of 90 ~s** ein Winkel *m* von 90 Grad; **it was 35 ~s in the shade** es waren 35 Grad im Schatten **b** *(= extent: of risk, uncertainty etc)* Maß *nt*; **some** *or* **a certain ~ of** ein gewisses Maß an *(+dat)*; **to some ~, to a (certain) ~** einigermaßen, zu einem gewissen Grad, in gewissem Maße; **to a high ~** in hohem Maße; **to such a ~ that …** so sehr *or* in solchem Maße, dass …; **to what ~ was he involved?** wie weit *or* in welchem Maße war er verwickelt? **c** *(= step in scale)* Grad *m*; **by ~s** nach und nach; **first ~ murder** *(Jur)* Mord *m*; **second ~ murder** *(Jur)* Totschlag *m* **d** *(Univ)* akademischer Grad; **first ~** erster akademischer Grad; **to get one's ~** seinen akademischen Grad erhalten; **to do a ~** studieren; **when did you do your ~?** wann haben Sie das Examen gemacht?; **I'm taking** *or* **doing a language ~** *or* **a ~ in languages** ich studiere Sprachwissenschaften; **I've got a ~ in Business Studies** ich habe einen Hochschulabschluss in Wirtschaftslehre **e** *(= position in society)* Rang *m*, Stand *m*

> **DEGREE**
>
> Mit **degree** bezeichnet man in den englischsprachigen Ländern den Grad der universitären Ausbildung. Der erste erreichbare Grad ist dabei ein **bachelor degree** nach einem vierjährigen Studium, der mit dem Magisterabschluss in Deutschland vergleichbar ist. Die am häufigsten verliehenen Grade sind der **Bachelor of Arts (BA** oder auch manchmal in den USA **AB)** für Geisteswissenschaften, und **Bachelor of Science (BSc** in Großbritannien, **BS** in den USA) für Naturwissenschaften.
>
> Den meisten Hochschulabsolventen in Großbritannien wird ein **honours degree** verliehen. Wenn man die dafür notwendige Note nicht erreicht hat oder sich für einen verkürzten Studiengang eingeschrieben hat, bekommt man einen **ordinary** oder **pass degree**. Die **honours degrees** werden in den folgenden Abstufungen verliehen: **first class** für die Note 1, **upper second** (2-1), **lower second** (2-2) und **third** für die Note 3. In den USA werden die Hochschulabschlüsse zwar nicht benotet, doch bekommen die besten Studenten Ehrentitel **(cum laude, magna cum laude** oder **summa cum laude)**. Wenn man lieber einen praxisorientierten und berufsspezifischen Studiengang absolvieren möchte, kann man nach einer zweijährigen Ausbildung an einem **junior** oder **community college** einen **associate degree** erwerben.
>
> Nach einem **bachelor degree** kann man in einem stärker wissenschafts- und forschungsorientierten Studiengang einen höheren akademischen Titel erwerben, einen sogenannten **master's degree**. Der höchste Titel, der verliehen werden kann, ist ein **doctorate**. Meist wird er in Geisteswissenschaften erworben, und die Doktoranden dürfen ihren Namen dann mit einem **PhD** oder **DPhil** schmücken.

degree: **degree ceremony** N *(Brit Univ)* Graduierungsfeier *f*; **degree course** N *Universitätskurs, der mit dem ersten akademischen Grad abschließt*; **degree day** N Tag *m* der Gradverleihung

dehumanize [ˌdiːˈhjuːmənaɪz] VT entmenschlichen

dehydrate [ˌdiːhaɪˈdreɪt] VT Wasser entziehen *(+dat)*, dehydrieren *(spec)*

dehydrated [ˌdiːhaɪˈdreɪtɪd] ADJ dehydriert *(spec)*; *foods also* getrocknet; *eggs also* pulverisiert; *person, skin* dehydriert *(spec)*, ausgetrocknet; **~ milk** Trockenmilch *f*; **~ vegetables** Dörrgemüse *nt*

dehydration [ˌdiːhaɪˈdreɪʃən] N Austrocknung *f*, Dehydration *f (spec)*; *(of vegetables, milk etc)* Trocknung *f*, Dehydration *f (spec)*

de-ice [ˌdiːˈaɪs] VT enteisen

de-icer [ˌdiːˈaɪsəʳ] N Enteiser *m*; *(= spray for cars)* Defroster *m*

deictic [ˈdaɪktɪk] ADJ *(Ling)* deiktisch

deification [ˌdiːɪfɪˈkeɪʃən] N Vergötterung *f*

deify [ˈdiːɪfaɪ] VT vergöttern

deign [deɪn] VT **to ~ to do sth** geruhen *or* sich herablassen, etw zu tun; **he didn't ~ to** er ließ sich nicht dazu herab

deinstall [ˌdiːɪnˈstɔːl] VT *software* deinstallieren

deism ['di:ɪzəm] N Deismus *m*

deist ['di:ɪst] N Deist(in) *m(f)*

deity ['di:ɪtɪ] N Gottheit *f*; **the Deity** Gott *m*

deixis ['daɪksɪs] N *(Ling)* Deixis *f*

déjà vu ['deɪʒɑ:'vu:] N Déjà-vu-Erlebnis *nt*; **a feeling** *or* **sense of ~** das Gefühl, das schon einmal gesehen zu haben

deject [dɪ'dʒekt] VT deprimieren

dejected ADJ, **dejectedly** ADV [dɪ'dʒektɪd, -lɪ] niedergeschlagen, deprimiert

dejection [dɪ'dʒekʃən] N Niedergeschlagenheit *f*, Depression *f*

de jure [ˌdi:'dʒʊərɪ] ADJ ADV de jure

dekko ['dekəʊ] N *(Brit inf)* kurzer Blick *(at* auf *+acc)*; **let's have a ~ (at it)** *(= show me)* lass (das) mal sehen; *(= let's go and see it)* gucken wir uns das mal an

delay [dɪ'leɪ] VT a *(= postpone)* verschieben, aufschieben; *orgasm* hinauszögern; **to ~ doing sth** es verschieben *or* aufschieben, etw zu tun; **he ~ed paying until ...** er wartete so lange mit dem Zahlen, bis ...; **he ~ed writing the letter** er schob den Brief auf; **rain ~ed play** der Beginn des Spiels verzögerte sich wegen Regens
b *(= hold up) person, train, traffic* aufhalten
VI *(= wait)* warten; **if you ~ too long in booking** wenn Sie zu lange mit der Buchung warten; **to ~ in doing sth** es verschieben *or* aufschieben, etw zu tun; **he ~ed in paying the bill** er schob die Zahlung der Rechnung hinaus; **don't ~!** verlieren Sie keine Zeit!, tun Sie es unverzüglich!; **don't ~ in sending it in** senden Sie es unverzüglich ein
N *(= hold-up)* Aufenthalt *m*; *(to traffic)* Stockung *f*; *(to train, plane)* Verspätung *f*; *(= time lapse)* Verzögerung *f*; **roadworks are causing ~s of up to 1 hour** Straßenbauarbeiten verursachen Staus bis zu 1 Stunde; **"delays possible (until ...)"** „Staugefahr! (bis ...)"; **there are ~s to all flights** alle Flüge haben Verspätung; **a split second's ~** eine Verzögerung von einem Bruchteil einer Sekunde; **without ~** unverzüglich; **without further ~** ohne weitere Verzögerung

delayed [dɪ'leɪd] ADJ *(= postponed)* verschoben, aufgeschoben, hinausgezögert; *(= late)* verspätet; *(TV, Rad) broadcast* zeitversetzt

delayed-action [dɪ'leɪdˌækʃən] ADJ *attr bomb, mine* mit Zeitzünder; **~ shutter release** *(Phot)* Selbstauslöser *m*

delayer [dɪ'leɪəʳ] N a *(= person) jd, der Zeit zu gewinnen sucht* b *(= reason for delay)* Verzögerungsgrund *m*

delaying [dɪ'leɪɪŋ] ADJ *action* verzögernd, hinhaltend, Verzögerungs-; **~ tactics** Verzögerungs- *or* Hinhaltetaktik *f*

dele ['di:lɪ] VT streichen, tilgen *(geh)* N Deleatur *nt*, Deleaturzeichen *nt*

delectable [dɪ'lektəbl] ADJ köstlich; *(fig)* reizend

delectation [ˌdi:lek'teɪʃən] N **for sb's ~** als besonderen Genuss für jdn

delegate ['delɪgeɪt] VT *person* delegieren; *authority, power* übertragen *(to sb* jdm); *responsibility, job* delegieren *(to sb* an jdn); **to ~ sb to do sth** jdn dazu abordnen *or* damit beauftragen, etw zu tun VI delegieren; **you must ~ more** Sie sollten mehr delegieren ['delɪgət] N Delegierte(r) *mf*

delegation [ˌdelɪ'geɪʃən] N a *(of responsibility etc)* Delegation *f*; **he's no good at ~** er kann einfach nicht delegieren b *(= group of delegates)* Delegation *f*, Abordnung *f*

delete [dɪ'li:t] VT streichen *(from* von); *(Comput) file, data* löschen; **"delete where applicable"** „Nichtzutreffendes *or* nicht Zutreffendes (bitte) streichen"

delete key N *(Comput)* Löschtaste *f*

deleterious [ˌdelɪ'tɪərɪəs] ADJ *(form)* schädlich *(to* für)

deletion [dɪ'li:ʃən] N Streichung *f*; *(Comput)* Löschung *f*; **to make a ~** etwas streichen; **he made several ~s in the text** er strich mehrere Stellen im Text; **who made those ~s?** wer hat das gestrichen?

delft [delft] N Delfter Fayencen *pl*

deli ['delɪ] N *(inf)* = **delicatessen**

deliberate [dɪ'lɪbərɪt] ADJ a *(= intentional)* absichtlich; *action, attempt, insult, lie* bewusst; **spot the ~ mistake** suchen Sie den versteckten Fehler b *(= cautious, thoughtful)* besonnen; *action, decision, judgement* (wohl)überlegt; *(= slow) movement, step, voice* bedächtig [dɪ'lɪbəreɪt] VI *(= ponder)* nachdenken *(on, upon* über *+acc)*; *(= discuss)* sich beraten *(on, upon* über *+acc*, wegen) [dɪ'lɪbəreɪt] VT *(= ponder)* bedenken, überlegen; *(= discuss)* beraten

deliberately [dɪ'lɪbərɪtlɪ] ✪ 18.4 ADV a *(= intentionally)* bewusst, absichtlich; *plan* vorsätzlich; **it looks as if the blaze was started ~** es sieht so aus, als sei der Brand vorsätzlich gelegt worden b *(= cautiously, thoughtfully) act* überlegt; *(= steadily) move* bedächtig

deliberateness [dɪ'lɪbərɪtnɪs] N a *(= intentional nature)* Absichtlichkeit *f* b *(= thoughtfulness, cautiousness)* Besonnenheit *f*; *(of action)* Überlegtheit *f*; *(= slowness)* Bedächtigkeit *f*

deliberation [dɪˌlɪbə'reɪʃən] N a *(= consideration)* Überlegung *f* *(on* zu); **after due/careful ~** nach reiflicher/sorgfältiger Überlegung b **deliberations** PL *(= discussions)* Beratungen *pl* *(of, on* in *+dat*, über *+acc)* c *(= purposefulness, slowness)* Bedächtigkeit *f*

deliberative [dɪ'lɪbərətɪv] ADJ *speech* abwägend; **~ body** Beratungsorgan *nt*; **~ assembly** beratende Versammlung; **~ process** Beratungsprozess *m*

delicacy ['delɪkəsɪ] N a = **delicateness** b *(= food)* Delikatesse *f*, Leckerbissen *m*

delicate ['delɪkɪt] ADJ a *(= fine, dainty)* fein; *colour* zart; *food* delikat; *flavour* fein; *(= fragile) person, bones, china* zerbrechlich; *fabric, flower, stomach* empfindlich; *health, person* zart; **in a ~ condition** *(dated euph)* in anderen Umständen; **she's feeling a bit ~ after the party** nach der Party fühlt sie sich etwas angeschlagen
b *(= sensitive) person* feinfühlig; *manner* feinfühlig, delikat; *instrument* empfindlich; *task* fein; *playing* gefühlvoll; **he has a ~ touch** *(pianist, artist)* er hat sehr viel Gefühl
c *(= requiring skilful handling) operation, subject, situation* heikel, delikat **delicates**
PL *(= fabrics)* Feinwäsche *f*

delicately ['delɪkɪtlɪ] ADV a *(= daintily)* zart; **she took it ~ from him** sie nahm es ihm mit einer grazilen Bewegung ab; **a ~ pretty girl** ein zartes, hübsches Mädchen b *(= subtly) spiced, scented* fein; *coloured* zart; **~ flavoured** *(Brit) or* **flavored** *(US)* mit einem delikaten Geschmack; **a soup ~ flavoured** *(Brit) or* **flavored with nutmeg** *(US)* eine fein mit Muskat gewürzte Suppe c *(= tactfully)* taktvoll d *(= with precision)* fein; **she picked her way ~ over the rocks** vorsichtig suchte sie sich einen Weg über die Felsen

delicateness ['delɪkɪtnɪs] N a *(= daintiness)* Zartheit *f*; *(= fragility)* Zerbrechlichkeit *f*; *(of fabric, flower, liver)* Empfindlichkeit *f*; *(of health, person)* Zartheit *f* b *(= sensitivity, of person)* Feinfühligkeit *f*; *(of instrument)* Empfindlichkeit *f*; *(of task)* Feinheit *f*; **the ~ of his playing** sein gefühlvolles Spiel c *(of operation, subject, situation)* heikle Natur d *(= subtlety: of flavour)* Feinheit *f*

delicatessen [ˌdelɪkə'tesn] N Feinkostgeschäft *nt*

delicious [dɪ'lɪʃəs] ADJ a *food etc* köstlich, lecker *(inf)* b *(= delightful)* herrlich; **in ~ anticipation** voll herrlicher Vorfreude

deliciously [dɪ'lɪʃəslɪ] ADV a *(= tastily) tender, creamy* köstlich b *(= delightfully) warm, fresh, fragrant* herrlich

delight [dɪ'laɪt] N Freude *f*; **to my ~** zu meiner Freude; **he takes great ~ in doing that** es bereitet ihm große Freude, das zu tun; **to give sb great ~** jdn hoch erfreuen; **he's a ~ to watch, it's a ~ to watch him** es ist eine Freude, ihm zuzusehen VT *person, ear, eye etc* erfreuen → **delighted** VI sich erfreuen *(in* an *+dat)*; **she ~s in doing that** es bereitet ihr große Freude, das zu tun

delighted [dɪ'laɪtɪd] ✪ 3.2, 11.3, 13, 19.5, 24.1, 24.3, 25.1 ADJ *(with* über *+acc)* erfreut, entzückt; **to be ~** sich sehr freuen *(at* über *+acc, that* dass); **absolutely ~** hocherfreut, ganz entzückt; **~ to meet you!** sehr angenehm!; **we will be ~ to accept (your invitation)** wir nehmen Ihre Einladung gern an; **I'd be ~ to help you** ich würde Ihnen sehr gern helfen

delightful [dɪ'laɪtfʊl] ADJ reizend; *weather, party, meal* wunderbar

delightfully [dɪ'laɪtfəlɪ] ADV wunderbar

delimit [di:'lɪmɪt] VT abgrenzen

delimitation [ˌdi:lɪmɪ'teɪʃən] N Abgrenzung *f*

delimiter [di:'lɪmɪtəʳ] N *(Comput)* Trennzeichen *nt*, Delimiter *m*

delineate [dɪ'lɪnɪeɪt] VT *(= draw)* skizzieren; *boundary, border* einzeichnen; *(= describe)* beschreiben, darstellen

delineation [dɪˌlɪnɪ'eɪʃən] N Skizzierung *f*; *(of boundary, border)* Einzeichnung *f*; *(= description)* Beschreibung *f*, Darstellung *f*

delinquency [dɪ'lɪŋkwənsɪ] N Kriminalität *f*, Delinquenz *f (spec)* → **juvenile delinquency**

delinquent [dɪ'lɪŋkwənt] ADJ a straffällig b *bill* überfällig; *account* rückständig N Delinquent(in) *m(f)* → **juvenile delinquent**

delirious [dɪ'lɪrɪəs] ADJ *(Med)* im Delirium; *(fig)* im Taumel; **to be ~ with joy** im Freudentaumel sein

deliriously [dɪ'lɪrɪəslɪ] ADV a *(= ecstatically) scream, cheer* ekstatisch; **~ happy** euphorisch; **I fell ~ in love with her** ich verliebte mich unsterblich in sie b *(Med) rave* im Delirium

delirium [dɪ'lɪrɪəm] N *(Med)* Delirium *nt*; *(fig)* Taumel *m*

delirium tremens [dɪ'lɪrɪəm'tremenz] N Delirium tremens *nt*, Säuferwahn(sinn) *m*

delist [ˌdi:'lɪst] VT streichen *(von einer Liste)*; *(St Ex)* aus der Notierung streichen

deliver [dɪ'lɪvəʳ] VT a *goods* liefern; *note, message* zustellen, überbringen; *(on regular basis) papers etc* zustellen; *(on foot)* austragen; *(by car)* ausfahren; **to ~ sth to sb** jdm etw liefern/überbringen/zustellen; **he ~ed the goods to the door** er lieferte die Waren ins Haus; **~ed free of charge** frei Haus (geliefert); **to ~ sb/sth into sb's care** jdn/etw in jds Obhut *(acc)* geben; **to ~ the goods** *(fig inf)* es bringen *(sl)*, es schaffen
b *(liter: = rescue)* befreien; **~ us from evil** *(Bibl)* erlöse uns von dem Übel *or* Bösen
c *(= pronounce) speech, sermon, lecture* halten; *ultimatum* stellen; *verdict* sprechen, verkünden; *warning* aussprechen
d *(Med) baby* zur Welt bringen; *(old) woman* entbinden; **to be ~ed of a son** *(old)* eines Jungen genesen *(old)*
e *(= hand over: also* **deliver up***)* aushändigen, übergeben; **to ~ a town into the hands of the enemy** eine Stadt dem Feind ausliefern → **stand**
f *(= aim, throw) blow* versetzen, landen *(inf)*; *ball* werfen; **Ali ~ed a punch to Bugner's jaw** Ali landete einen Schlag an Bugners Kinn *(inf)*; **to ~ a broadside** eine Breitseite abfeuern
VI a *(lit)* liefern
b *(fig inf: = be good enough)* es bringen *(sl)*; **they didn't ~** sie brachtens nicht *(sl)*

deliverable [dɪ'lɪvərəbl] ADJ *goods* lieferbar

deliverance [dɪ'lɪvərəns] N *(liter)* Befreiung *f* *(from* von), Erlösung *f* *(from* von)

deliverer [dɪ'lɪvərəʳ] N a *(Comm)* Lieferant *m* b *(liter, = rescuer)* Erlöser *m*, Retter *m*

delivery [dɪ'lɪvərɪ] ✪ 20.5 N a *(of goods)* (Aus)lieferung *f*; *(of parcels, letters)* Zustellung *f*; **please allow 28 days for ~** die Lieferzeit kann bis zu 28 Tagen betragen; **to take ~ of a package** ein Paket in Empfang nehmen b *(Med)* Entbindung *f* c *(of speaker)* Vortrag *m*, Vortragsweise *f* **d** *(liter, = rescue)* Rettung *f*, Befreiung *f* **e** *(of punch, blow)* Landung *f (inf)*; *(Cricket)* Wurf *m*

delivery: **delivery boy** N Bote *m*; *(for newspapers)* Träger *m*; **delivery charge** N Lieferkosten *pl*; *(for mail)* Zustellgebühr *f*; **delivery contract** N Liefervertrag *m*; **delivery man** N Lieferant *m*; **delivery note** N Lieferschein *m*; **delivery output** N Förderleistung *f*; **delivery room** N Kreißsaal *m*, Entbindungssaal *m*; **delivery service** N Zustelldienst *m*; **delivery time** N Lieferzeit *f*; **delivery van** N Lieferwagen *m*

dell [del] N kleines bewaldetes Tal

delouse [ˌdiːˈlaʊs] VT entlausen

Delphic [ˈdelfɪk] ADJ *(lit, fig)* delphisch; **the ~ oracle** das Delphische Orakel, das Orakel von Delphi

delphinium [delˈfɪnɪəm] N Rittersporn *m*

delta [ˈdeltə] N Delta *nt*

delta: **delta ray** N *(Phys)* Deltastrahl *m*; **delta rhythm**, **delta wave** N *(Physiol)* Deltawelle *f*; **delta wing** N *(Aviat)* Deltaflügel *m*

delude [dɪˈluːd] VT täuschen, irreführen *(with* mit); **to ~ sb into thinking sth** jdn dazu verleiten, etw zu glauben; **to ~ oneself** sich *(dat)* Illusionen machen, sich *(dat)* etwas vormachen; **stop deluding yourself that …** hör auf, dir vorzumachen, dass …; **don't ~ yourself that …** mach dir doch nicht vor, dass …

deluded [dɪˈluːdɪd] ADJ voller Illusionen; **poor ~ girl** arme Irre

deluge [ˈdeljuːdʒ] **N** *(lit)* Überschwemmung *f*; *(of rain)* Guss *m*; *(fig, of complaints, letters etc)* Flut *f*; **the Deluge** *(Bibl)* die Sintflut **VT** *(lit, fig)* überschwemmen, überfluten

delusion [dɪˈluːʒən] N Illusion *f*, Irrglaube *m no pl*; *(Psych)* Wahnvorstellung *f*; **to be** *or* **labour** *(Brit)* *or* **labor** *(US)* **under a ~** in einem Wahn leben; **to have ~s of grandeur** den Größenwahn haben

delusive [dɪˈluːsɪv], **delusory** [dɪˈluːsərɪ] ADJ irreführend, täuschend, trügerisch

de luxe [dɪˈlʌks] ADJ Luxus-, De-Luxe-; **~ hotel/model** Luxushotel/-modell *nt*; **~ version** De-Luxe-Ausführung *f*

delve [delv] VI *(into subject)* sich eingehend befassen *(into* mit); *(into book)* sich vertiefen *(into* in *+acc*); **to ~ in(to) one's pocket/a drawer** tief in die Tasche/eine Schublade greifen; **to ~ into the past** die Vergangenheit erforschen

Dem *(US Pol)* *abbr of* **Democratic**

demagnetize [ˌdiːˈmægnɪtaɪz] VT entmagnetisieren

demagogic [ˌdeməˈgɒgɪk] ADJ demagogisch

demagogue, *(US)* **demagog** [ˈdeməgɒg] N Demagoge *m*, Demagogin *f*

demagoguery [ˌdeməˈgɒgərɪ], **demagogy** [ˈdeməgɒgɪ] N Demagogie *f*

demand [dɪˈmɑːnd] ✪ 10.1 **VT** verlangen, fordern *(of, from* von); *(situation, task etc)* erfordern, verlangen; *time* beanspruchen; **they ~ed his resignation** sie forderten seinen Rücktritt; **he ~ed money** er wollte Geld haben; **he ~ed to know what had happened** er verlangte zu wissen, was passiert war; **he ~ed to see my passport** er wollte meinen Pass sehen

N **a** *(= firm request)* Forderung *f*, Verlangen *nt (for* nach); *(= claim for better pay, of kidnapper etc)* Forderung *f (for* nach); **by popular ~** auf allgemeinen Wunsch; **to be available on ~** auf Wunsch erhältlich sein; **abortion on ~** Abtreibung *f* auf Wunsch; **to make ~s on sb** Forderungen *or* Ansprüche an jdn stellen; **he makes too many ~s on my time** er nimmt mich zu sehr in Beschlag *(inf)*; **he makes too many ~s on my pocket** er liegt mir zu sehr auf der Tasche *(inf)*

b *no pl (Comm)* Nachfrage *f*; **to create (a) ~ for a product** Nachfrage für ein Produkt schaffen; **there's no ~ for it** es ist nicht gefragt, es besteht keine Nachfrage danach; **to be in (great) ~** *(article, person)* sehr gefragt sein

demand: **demand bill** N *(Fin)* Sichtwechsel *m*; **demand deposit** N *(Fin)* Sichteinlage *f*, kurzfristige Einlage

demander [dɪˈmɑːndəʳ] N **a** *(= requester)* Fordernde(r) *mf* **b** *(= buyer)* Käufer(in) *m(f)*

demanding [dɪˈmɑːndɪŋ] ADJ *child, job* anstrengend; *task also, teacher, boss* anspruchsvoll; **physically/mentally ~** körperlich/geistig anstrengend

demand: **demand management** N Steuerung *f* der Nachfrage; **demand note** N Zahlungsaufforderung *f*

de-manning [ˌdiːˈmænɪŋ] N *(Brit, of industry)* Personal- *or* Stellenabbau *m*

demarcate [ˈdiːmɑːkeɪt] VT abgrenzen, demarkieren

demarcation [ˌdiːmɑːˈkeɪʃən] N Abgrenzung *f*, Demarkation *f*; **~ line** Demarkationslinie *f*; **~ dispute** Streit *m* um den Zuständigkeitsbereich

démarche [ˈdeɪmɑːʃ] N Demarche *f*

dematerialize [ˌdiːməˈtɪərɪəlaɪz] **VT** entmaterialisieren **VI** sich entmaterialisieren

demean [dɪˈmiːn] **VR** **a** *(= lower)* sich erniedrigen; **I will not ~ myself by doing that** ich werde mich nicht dazu hergeben, das zu tun **b** *(= behave)* sich benehmen *or* verhalten **VT** erniedrigen

demeaning [dɪˈmiːnɪŋ] ADJ erniedrigend

demeanour, *(US)* **demeanor** [dɪˈmiːnəʳ] N *(= behaviour)* Benehmen *nt*, Auftreten *nt*; *(= bearing)* Haltung *f*

demented [dɪˈmentɪd] ADJ verrückt, wahnsinnig; **~ with worry** verrückt vor Angst

dementia [dɪˈmenʃɪə] N Schwachsinn *m*, Demenz *f (spec)*; **~ praecox** Jugendirresein *nt*, Dementia praecox *f (spec)*

demerara (sugar) [ˌdeməˈrɛərə(ˈʃʊgəʳ)] N brauner Rohrzucker

demerge [ˌdiːˈmɜːdʒ] VT *company* entflechten

demerger [ˌdiːˈmɜːdʒəʳ] N *(Comm)* Abspaltung *m*, Demerger *m*

demerit [diːˈmerɪt] N Schwäche *f*, Fehler *m*; *(dated US: = black mark)* Minuspunkt *m*

demesne [dɪˈmeɪn] N Grundbesitz *m*; **to hold sth in ~** etw in Besitz haben

demi [ˈdemɪ] PREF Halb-, halb-; **~god** Halbgott *m*, Halbgöttin *f*

demijohn [ˈdemɪdʒɒn] N Demijohn *m*; *(in wickerwork)* bauchige Korbflasche

demimonde [ˌdemɪˈmɒnd] N Halbwelt *f*

demilitarization [ˈdiːˌmɪlɪtəraɪˈzeɪʃən] N Entmilitarisierung *f*

demilitarize [ˌdiːˈmɪlɪtəraɪz] VT entmilitarisieren; **~d zone** entmilitarisierte Zone

demise [dɪˈmaɪz] N *(= death)* Tod *m*; *(of person also)* Ableben *nt (geh)*; *(fig, of institution, newspaper etc)* Ende *nt*

demisemiquaver [ˌdemɪsemɪˈkweɪvəʳ] N Zweiunddreißigstelnote *f*

demission [dɪˈmɪʃən] N *(of office, function)* Niederlegung *f*; *(of minister)* Demission *f (geh)*, Rücktritt *m*

demist [ˌdiːˈmɪst] VT *windscreen* frei machen

demister [ˌdiːˈmɪstəʳ] N Gebläse *nt*

demitasse [ˈdemɪtæs] N *(US: = cup)* Mokkatasse *f*; *(= coffee)* Kaffee *m*

demi-vegetarian [ˌdemɪvedʒɪˈtɛərɪən] N Halbvegetarier(in) *m(f)*

demiworld N Halbwelt *f*

demo [ˈdeməʊ] **N** *abbr of* **demonstration** Demo(nstration) *f* **ADJ** *attr* **~ disk** Demodiskette *f*; **~ tape** Demoband *nt*

demob [ˌdiːˈmɒb] *(Brit)* **N** *abbr of* **demobilization** Entlassung *f* aus dem Kriegsdienst **VT** *abbr of* **demobilize** aus dem Kriegsdienst entlassen, demobilisieren

demobilization [ˈdiːˌməʊbɪlaɪˈzeɪʃən] N *(of army)* Demobilmachung *f*, Demobilisierung *f*; *(of soldier)* Entlassung *f* aus dem Kriegsdienst, Demobilisierung *f*

demobilize [diːˈməʊbɪlaɪz] VT aus dem Kriegsdienst entlassen, demobilisieren

democracy [dɪˈmɒkrəsɪ] N Demokratie *f*

democrat [ˈdeməkræt] N Demokrat(in) *m(f)*

democratic [ˌdeməˈkrætɪk] ADJ **a** demokratisch; **the Social Democratic Party** die Sozialdemokratische Partei; **the Christian Democratic Party** die Christlich-Demokratische Partei **b** **Democratic** *(US Pol, candidate, nomination, convention)* der Demokratischen Partei; **the Democratic Party** die Demokratische Partei

democratically [ˌdeməˈkrætɪkəlɪ] ADV demokratisch; **~ accountable** dem Volk verantwortlich; **Democratically controlled** *(US Pol)* von den Demokraten kontrolliert

democratize [dɪˈmɒkrətaɪz] VT demokratisieren

demographer [dɪˈmɒgrəfəʳ] N Demograf(in) *m(f)*

demographic [ˌdeməˈgræfɪk] ADJ demografisch

demography [dɪˈmɒgrəfɪ] N Demografie *f*

demolish [dɪˈmɒlɪʃ] VT *building* ab- *or* einreißen, abbrechen; *fortifications* niederreißen; *(fig) opponent, theory* zunichtemachen, vernichten; *myth* zerstören; *(hum) cake etc* vertilgen

demolition [ˌdeməˈlɪʃən] N Abbruch *m*

demolition: **demolition area** N = **demolition zone**; **demolition squad** N Abbruchkolonne *f*; **demolition work** N Abbrucharbeiten *pl*; **demolition zone** N Abbruchgebiet *nt*

demon [ˈdiːmən] N *(= evil spirit)* Dämon *m*; *(fig: = person)* Dämon(in) *m(f)*; *(inf: = child)* Teufel *m*; **to work like a ~** wie besessen arbeiten; **he's a ~ player** er ist ein teuflisch guter Spieler *(inf)*; **the Demon Drink** König Alkohol *m*

demoniac [dɪˈməʊnɪæk] **ADJ** dämonisch **N** Besessene(r) *mf*

demoniacal [ˌdiːməʊˈnaɪəkəl] ADJ dämonisch

demonic [dɪˈmɒnɪk] ADJ dämonisch

demonize [ˈdiːmənaɪz] VT dämonisieren

demonstrable [ˈdemənstrəbl] ADJ beweisbar, offensichtlich

demonstrably [ˈdemənstrəblɪ] ADV nachweislich

demonstrate [ˈdemənstreɪt] **VT** **a** *truth, emotions, needs, goodwill, skill, bravery* zeigen, beweisen; *(by experiment, example)* demonstrieren, zeigen **b** *appliance etc* vorführen; *operation* vorführen, demonstrieren **VI** *(Pol etc)* demonstrieren

demonstration [ˌdemənˈstreɪʃən] **N** **a** *(of truth, emotions, needs, goodwill, skill, bravery)* Beweis *m*; *(by experiment, example)* Demonstration *f*; *(of appliance etc)* Vorführung *f*; *(of operation)* Vorführung *f*, Demonstration *f*; **to give a ~ of sth** *(by experiment, example)* etw demonstrieren; *of operation also, of gadget* etw vorführen; **he gave us a ~** er zeigte es uns **b** *(Pol etc)* Demonstration *f*; **to hold/break up a ~** eine Demonstration veranstalten *or* durchführen/auflösen **ATTR** **~ project** Demonstrationsprojekt *nt*

demonstration car N Vorführwagen *m*

demonstration model N Vorführmodell *m*

demonstrative [dɪˈmɒnstrətɪv] ADJ demonstrativ

demonstrator [ˈdemənstreɪtəʳ] N **a** *(Comm)* Vorführer(in) *m(f)* (von technischen Geräten), Propagandist(in) *m(f)*; *(Sch, Univ)* Demonstrator *m* **b** *(Pol)* Demonstrant(in) *m(f)*

demoralization [dɪˌmɒrəlaɪˈzeɪʃən] N Entmutigung *f*; *(of troops etc)* Demoralisierung *f*

demoralize [dɪˈmɒrəlaɪz] VT entmutigen; *troops etc* demoralisieren

demoralizing [dɪˈmɒrəlaɪzɪŋ] ADJ entmutigend; *(for troops etc)* demoralisierend

demote [dɪˈməʊt] VT *(Mil)* degradieren *(to* zu); *(in business etc)* zurückstufen; **to be ~d** *(Sport)* absteigen; **~d to captain** zum Hauptmann degradiert

demotic [dɪˈmɒtɪk] ADJ **a** *Greek* demotisch **b** *(= of the people)* volkstümlich

demotion [dɪˈməʊʃən] N *(Mil)* Degradierung *f*; *(in business etc)* Zurückstufung *f*; *(Sport)* Abstieg *m*

demotivate [ˌdiːˈməʊtɪveɪt] VT demotivieren

demount [ˌdiːˈmaʊnt] VT *(= take to pieces)* auseinandernehmen, zerlegen; *machinery* abmontieren

demur [dɪˈmɜːˈ] **VI** Einwände erheben, Bedenken haben *(to, at* gegen); *(Jur)* Einspruch erheben *or* einlegen **N** *(form)* Einwand *m*, Bedenken *pl*; *(Jur)* Einspruch *m*; **without ~** widerspruchslos

demure [dɪˈmjʊəˈ] ADJ *(+er)* sittsam

demurely [dɪˈmjʊəlɪ] ADV sittsam

demureness [dɪˈmjʊənɪs] N Sittsamkeit *f*

demurrage [dɪˈmʌrɪdʒ] N *(Comm: = charge)* (Über)liegegeld *nt*; *(= time)* Überliegezeit *f*

demutualize [ˌdiːˈmjuːtjʊəlaɪz] VI *(Fin)* sich in eine Kapitalgesellschaft umwandeln

demystification [ˌdiːmɪstɪfɪˈkeɪʃən] N Entmystifizierung *f*

demystify [diːˈmɪstɪfaɪ] VT entmystifizieren

demythologize [ˈdiːmɪˈθɒlədʒaɪz] VT entmythologisieren

den [den] N **a** *(of lion, tiger etc)* Höhle *f*, Versteck *nt*; *(of fox)* Bau *m* **b** **~ of iniquity** *or* **vice** Lasterhöhle *f*; **~ of thieves** Spelunke *f*, Räuberhöhle *f (hum)* → **gambling den, opium den** **c** *(= study)* Arbeitszimmer *nt*; *(= private room)* gemütliches Zimmer, Bude *f (inf)*

denationalization [ˈdiːˌnæʃnəlaɪˈzeɪʃən] N Entstaatlichung *f*

denationalize [ˌdiːˈnæʃnəlaɪz] VT entstaatlichen

denature [ˌdiːˈneɪtʃəˈ] VT denaturieren; *(= make unfit for eating, drinking also)* ungenießbar machen

denazification [ˈdiːˌnætsɪfɪˈkeɪʃən] N Entnazifizierung *f*

denazify [ˌdiːˈnætsɪfaɪ] VT entnazifizieren

dendrite [ˈdendraɪt] N Dendrit *m*

deniability [dɪˌnaɪəˈbɪlɪtɪ] N *(esp US Pol)* Möglichkeit *f* zu leugnen *or* alles abzustreiten; **a way of preserving ~** eine Möglichkeit, ein Hintertürchen offenzulassen

deniable [dɪˈnaɪəbl] ADJ bestreitbar

denial [dɪˈnaɪəl] N **a** *(of accusation, guilt)* Leugnen *nt*; **~ of (the existence of) God** Gottesleugnung *f*; **the government issued an official ~** die Regierung gab ein offizielles Dementi heraus; **to be in ~ about sth** etw abstreiten; **to be in ~** *(Psych)* sich der Realität verschließen **b** *(= refusal, of request etc)* Ablehnung *f*, abschlägige Antwort; *(official)* abschlägiger Bescheid; *(of rights)* Verweigerung *f* **c** *(= disowning)* Verleugnung *f*; **Peter's ~ of Christ** die Verleugnung des Petrus **d** *(= self-denial)* Selbstverleugnung *f*

denier [ˈdenɪəˈ] N *(of stockings)* Denier *nt*

denigrate [ˈdenɪgreɪt] VT verunglimpfen

denigration [ˌdenɪˈgreɪʃən] N Verunglimpfung *f*

denim [ˈdenɪm] **N** **a** Jeansstoff *m*, Köper *m* **b** **denims** **PL** Bluejeans *pl*, Jeans *pl* **ADJ** *attr* Jeans-; **~ jacket** Jeansjacke *f*; **~ suit** Jeansanzug *m*

denitrification [ˌdiːnaɪtrɪfɪˈkeɪʃən] N Entstickung *f*

denizen [ˈdenɪzn] N Bewohner(in) *m(f)*; *(= person)* Einwohner(in) *m(f)*; **~s of the forest** Waldbewohner *pl*; **~s of the deep** Bewohner *pl* der Tiefe

Denmark [ˈdenmɑːk] N Dänemark *nt*

denominate [dɪˈnɒmɪneɪt] VT benennen, bezeichnen

denomination [dɪˌnɒmɪˈneɪʃən] N **a** *(Eccl)* Konfession *f* **b** *(= name, naming)* Benennung *f*, Bezeichnung *f* **c** *(of money)* Nennbetrag *m*; *(of weight, measures)* Einheit *f* **d** *(= class, kind)* Klasse *f*, Gruppe *f*

denominational [dɪˌnɒmɪˈneɪʃənl] ADJ *(Eccl)* konfessionell, Konfessions-; **~ school** Konfessionsschule *f*

denominator [dɪˈnɒmɪneɪtəˈ] N *(Math)* Nenner *m*

denotation [ˌdiːnəʊˈteɪʃən] N **a** *(Philos, of term, concept)* Denotation *f*, Begriffsumfang *m*; *(of word)* Bedeutung *f* **b** *(= name: of object)* Bezeichnung *f*; *(= symbol)* Symbol *nt*

denotative [dɪˈnəʊtətɪv] ADJ *(Ling)* denotativ

denote [dɪˈnəʊt] VT bedeuten; *symbol, word* bezeichnen; *(Philos)* den Begriffsumfang angeben von

dénouement [deɪˈnuːmɒŋ] N *(Theat, Liter)* (Auf)lösung *f*; *(fig)* Ausgang *m*

denounce [dɪˈnaʊns] VT **a** *(= accuse publicly)* anprangern, brandmarken; *(= inform against)* anzeigen, denunzieren *(sb to sb* jdn bei jdm) **b** *(= condemn as evil) alcohol, habit etc* verurteilen, denunzieren *(geh)* **c** *treaty* (auf)kündigen

denouncement [dɪˈnaʊnsmənt] N = **denunciation**

dense [dens] ADJ *(+er)* **a** *(= thick) fog, smoke, forest* dicht *(also Phys)*; *crowd* dicht gedrängt **b** *prose, language, style, book, film (= concentrated)* gedrängt; *(= over-complex)* überladen **c** *(inf) person (= of low intellect)* beschränkt *(inf)*; *(= slow)* begriffsstutzig *(inf)*, schwer von Begriff *(inf)*

densely [ˈdenslɪ] ADV *populated, wooded* dicht; **~ packed** *(crowd)* dicht gedrängt

denseness [ˈdensnɪs] N **a** *(= thickness)* Dichte *f* **b** *(= concentrated nature)* Gedrängtheit *f*; *(= excessive complexity)* Überladenheit *f*

densify [ˈdensɪfaɪ] **VT** verdichten **VI** sich verdichten

density [ˈdensɪtɪ] N Dichte *f*; **population ~** Bevölkerungsdichte *f*

dent [dent] **N** *(in metal)* Beule *f*, Delle *f (inf)*; *(in wood)* Kerbe *f*, Delle *f (inf)*; **that made a ~ in his savings** *(inf)* das hat ein Loch in seine Ersparnisse gerissen; **that made a bit of a ~ in his pride/confidence** *(inf)* das hat seinen Stolz/sein Selbstbewusstsein ganz schön angeknackst *(inf)*

VT *hat, car, wing* einbeulen, verbeulen; *wood, table* eine Delle machen in *(+acc)*; *(inf) pride, confidence* anknacksen *(inf)*; *image, reputation* schaden *(+dat)*; *hopes, profits* dahinschwinden lassen; **~ed cans are usually cheaper** eingebeulte Dosen sind meist billiger

VI *(metal etc)* sich einbeulen; *(wood, table)* eindellen

dental [ˈdentl] **ADJ** **a** Zahn-; *treatment* zahnärztlich; *training* zahnmedizinisch *(form)* **b** *(Ling)* Dental-, dental; **~ sound** Dentallaut *m* **N** *(Ling)* Dental *m*, Zahnlaut *m*

dental: **dental assistant** N Zahnarzthelfer(in) *m(f)*; **dental floss** N Zahnseide *f*; **dental hygiene** N Zahnpflege *f*; **dental hygienist** [ˌdentlhaɪˈdʒiːnɪst] N zahnmedizinischer Fachhelfer, zahnmedizinische Fachhelferin; **dental implant** [ˌdentlˈɪmplɑːnt] N Zahnimplantat *nt*; **dental nurse** N Zahnarzthelfer(in) *m(f)*; **dental surgeon** N Zahnarzt *m*/-ärztin *f*; **dental technician** N Zahntechniker(in) *m(f)*

dentifrice [ˈdentɪfrɪs] N Zahnpasta *f*

dentist [ˈdentɪst] N Zahnarzt *m*, Zahnärztin *f*; **at the ~('s)** beim Zahnarzt

dentistry [ˈdentɪstrɪ] N Zahnmedizin *f*, Zahnheilkunde *f*

dentition [denˈtɪʃən] N *(= process of teething)* Zahnen *nt*, Dentition *f (spec)*; *(= arrangement of teeth)* Gebissform *f*

dentures [ˈdentʃəz] PL Zahnprothese *f*; *(full)* Gebiss *nt*

denude [dɪˈnjuːd] VT *(of trees etc)* entblößen *(of +gen)*; *(fig also)* berauben *(of +gen)*

denunciation [dɪˌnʌnsɪˈeɪʃən] N *(= accusation)* Anprangerung *f*, Brandmarkung *f*; *(= informing)* Denunziation *f*; *(= condemnation)* Verurteilung *f*; *(of treaty)* (Auf)kündigung *f*; **the book is a sustained ~ of ...** das Buch ist eine einzige Anklage gegen ...

Denver boot [ˌdenvəˈbuːt] N *(inf: = car clamp)* Parkkralle *f*

deny [dɪˈnaɪ] ✪ 15.1, 26.3 VT **a** *charge, accusation etc* bestreiten, abstreiten, (ab)leugnen; *existence of God* leugnen; *(officially)* dementieren; **do you ~ having said that?** bestreiten *or* leugnen Sie, das gesagt zu haben?; **there's no ~ing it** das lässt sich nicht bestreiten *or* leugnen; **I ~ that there is a real need for it** ich bestreite, dass ein echtes Bedürfnis danach besteht; **to ~ liability** keine Haftung übernehmen

b *(= refuse)* **to ~ sb's request** jdm seine Bitte abschlagen; **to ~ sb his rights** jdm seine Rechte vorenthalten; **to ~ sb aid/a privilege** jdm Hilfe/ein Privileg versagen; **to ~ sb access (to sth)** jdm den Zugang (zu etw) verwehren; **to ~ sb credit** jdm den Kredit verweigern; **I can't ~ her anything** ich kann ihr nichts abschlagen; **I had to ~ myself the pleasure of seeing him** ich musste mir das Vergnügen, ihn zu sehen, versagen; **why should I ~ myself these little comforts?** warum sollte ich mir das bisschen Komfort nicht gönnen?

c *(= disown) leader, religion, principles* verleugnen

d **to ~ oneself** sich selbst verleugnen

deodorant [diːˈəʊdərənt] **ADJ** desodor(is)ierend **N** Deodorant *nt*; **~ spray** Deospray *nt*

deodorize [diːˈəʊdəraɪz] VT desodor(is)ieren

deontology [ˌdiːɒnˈtɒlədʒɪ] N Pflichtethik *f*, Deontologie *f*

deoxidize [diːˈɒksɪdaɪz] VT desoxidieren

deoxygenate [ˌdiːˈɒksɪdʒəneɪt] VT Sauerstoff entziehen *(+dat)*; **~d blood** sauerstoffarmes Blut

deoxyribonucleic acid [dɪˈɒksɪˌraɪbəʊnjuːˈkleɪɪkˌæsɪd] N Desoxyribonukleinsäure *f*

dep. *abbr of* **departs, departure** *(in timetables etc)* Abf.

depart [dɪˈpɑːt] **VI** **a** *(= go away)* weggehen; *(on journey)* abreisen; *(by bus, car etc)* wegfahren; *(train, bus etc)* abfahren; **he ~s for Rome tomorrow morning** er reist morgen früh nach Rom ab; **the bus ~s from the bus station** der Bus fährt vom *or* am Busbahnhof ab; **the train at platform 6 ~ing for ...** der Zug auf Bahnsteig 6 nach ...; **guests are asked to sign the register before they ~** Gäste werden gebeten, vor der Abreise einen Meldezettel auszufüllen; **to be ready to ~** *(person)* start- *or* abfahrbereit sein; **the visitors were about to ~** die Gäste waren im Begriff aufzubrechen; **to ~ on one's way** *(liter, old)* sich aufmachen, aufbrechen

b *(= deviate: from opinion etc)* abweichen *(from* von)

VT **a** *(train, bus etc)* abfahren aus

b *(liter)* **to ~ this earth** *or* **life** aus dieser Welt *or* diesem Leben scheiden *(liter)*

departed [dɪˈpɑːtɪd] **ADJ** **a** *(liter: = dead)* verstorben, verschieden *(geh)* **b** *(= bygone) friends* verloren **N** **the (dear) ~** der/die (liebe) Verstorbene; *(pl)* die (lieben) Verstorbenen *pl*

department [dɪˈpɑːtmənt] N **a** *(generally)* Abteilung *f*; *(Geog: in France)* Departement *nt*; *(in civil service)* Ressort *nt*; **Department of Employment** *(Brit)* **Department of Labor** *(US)* Arbeitsministerium *nt*; **Department of State** *(US)* Außenministerium *nt*; **that's not my ~** *(fig)* dafür bin ich nicht zuständig **b** *(Sch, Univ)* Fachbereich *m*

departmental [ˌdiːpɑːtˈmentl] ADJ Abteilungs-; *(Sch, Univ)* Fachbereichs-; *(in civil service) committee* des Ressorts; **~ manager** Abteilungsleiter(in) *m(f)*; **~ head** *(Sch, Univ)* Fachbereichsleiter(in) *m(f)*; **the minister's new ~ responsibilities** das neue Ressort des Ministers; **the money for ~ budgets** das Geld für die Haushalte der einzelnen Abteilungen

departmentalism [ˌdiːpɑːtˈmentəlɪzəm] N Gliederung *f* in Abteilungen

departmentalize [ˌdiːpɑːtˈmentəlaɪz] VT in Abteilungen einteilen *or* (auf)gliedern

departmentally [ˌdiːpɑːtˈmentəlɪ] ADV abteilungsweise

department store N Kaufhaus *nt*, Warenhaus *nt*

departure [dɪˈpɑːtʃəʳ] N **a** *(of person)* Weggang *m*; *(on journey)* Abreise *f* *(from* aus); *(of vehicle)* Abfahrt *f*; *(of plane)* Abflug *m*; **to be on the point of ~** im Aufbruch (begriffen) sein; **there are three ~s daily for Stockholm** *(by plane)* es gibt täglich drei Flüge nach Stockholm; **"departures"** „Abfahrt"; *(at airport)* „Abflug"; **at the hour of our ~ from this life** *(liter)* in der Stunde unseres Dahinscheidens *(liter)* **b** *(fig, from custom, principle, truth)* Abweichen *nt* *(from* von), Abgehen *nt* *(from* von) **c** *(fig: = change in policy etc)* neue Richtung *f*; **this marks a significant ~ from his previous way of life** hiermit ändert sich sein bisheriger Lebensstil grundlegend

departure: **departure board** N *(Rail)* Abfahrtstafel *f*; *(Aviat)* Abfluganzeige *f*; **departure gate** N Flugsteig *m*, Ausgang *m*; **departure language** N *(Ling)* Ausgangssprache *f*; **departure lounge** N Abflughalle *f*; *(for single flight)* Warteraum *m*; **departure signal** N Abfahrtssignal *nt*; **departure time** N *(Aviat)* Abflugzeit *f*; *(Rail, bus)* Abfahrtzeit *f*

depend [dɪˈpend] ✪ 6.3 VI **a** *(= be determined by)* abhängen *(on sb/sth* von jdm/etw); **the price ~s on the quantity you buy** der Preis hängt von der Menge ab, die Sie kaufen; **it ~s on what you mean by reasonable** es kommt darauf an, was Sie unter vernünftig verstehen; **how long are you staying? – it ~s** wie lange bleiben Sie? – das kommt darauf an; **it all ~s on …** das kommt ganz auf … an; **~ing on his mood** je nach seiner Laune; **~ing on how late we arrive** je nachdem, wie spät wir ankommen **b** *(= rely)* sich verlassen *(on, upon* auf *+acc)*; **you may ~ (up)on his coming** Sie können sich darauf verlassen, dass er kommt; **you can ~ (up)on it!** darauf können Sie sich verlassen!; **you can ~ (up)on it that he'll forget** du kannst dich darauf verlassen, dass er es vergisst **c** *(person: = be dependent on)* **to ~ on** abhängig sein von, angewiesen sein auf *(+acc)*; **they have to ~ on the grandparents for childcare** sie sind darauf angewiesen, dass die Großeltern sich um die Kinder kümmern

dependability [dɪˌpendəˈbɪlɪtɪ] N Zuverlässigkeit *f*, Verlässlichkeit *f*

dependable [dɪˈpendəbl] ADJ zuverlässig, verlässlich

dependably [dɪˈpendəblɪ] ADV zuverlässig, verlässlich

dependant, dependent [dɪˈpendənt] N Abhängige(r) *mf*; **do you have ~s?** haben Sie (abhängige) Angehörige?

dependence [dɪˈpendəns] N Abhängigkeit *f* *(on, upon* von); **drug/alcohol ~** Drogen-/Alkoholabhängigkeit *f*

dependency [dɪˈpendənsɪ] N **a** *(= country)* Schutzgebiet *nt*, Kolonie *f* **b** = **dependence**

dependent [dɪˈpendənt] ADJ **a** *(= reliant, also Gram, Math)* abhängig; **financially ~** finanziell abhängig; **~ on insulin** insulinabhängig; **to be ~ on** *or* **upon sb/sth** von jdm/etw abhängig sein; **heavily ~ on the tourist trade** stark vom Tourismus abhängig; **to be ~ on charity/sb's goodwill** auf Almosen/jds Wohlwollen angewiesen sein; **to be ~ on** *or* **upon sb/sth for sth** für etw auf jdn/etw angewiesen sein; **to be ~ on** *or* **upon sb/sth to do sth** auf jdn/etw angewiesen sein, um etw zu tun; **to have ~ children** Kinder haben, für deren Unterhalt man aufkommen muss **b** **to be ~ on** *or* **upon sb/sth** *(= determined by)* von jdm/etw abhängen; **your success is ~ (up)on the effort you put in** der Erfolg hängt davon ab, wie viel Mühe du dir gibst **N** = **dependant**

depeople [ˌdiːˈpiːpl] VT entvölkern

depersonalize [diːˈpɜːsənəlaɪz] VT entpersönlichen, depersonalisieren *(Psych)*

depict [dɪˈpɪkt] VT darstellen; *(in words also)* beschreiben

depiction [dɪˈpɪkʃən] N Darstellung *f*; *(in words also)* Beschreibung *f*

depilatory [dɪˈpɪlətərɪ] ADJ enthaarend, Enthaarungs-; **~ cream** Enthaarungscreme *f* N Enthaarungsmittel *nt*

deplane [diːˈpleɪn] VT *(aus dem Flugzeug)* ausladen VI *(aus dem Flugzeug)* aussteigen, von Bord gehen

deplenish [dɪˈplenɪʃ] VT *supplies etc* verringern

deplete [dɪˈpliːt] VT **a** *(= exhaust)* erschöpfen; *(= reduce)* vermindern, verringern; *funds* verringern; **certain substances ~ the ozone layer** bestimmte Stoffe bauen die Ozonschicht ab; **our supplies are somewhat ~d** unsere Vorräte sind ziemlich erschöpft; **the larder is rather ~d** die Speisekammer ist ziemlich leer; **the audience had become somewhat ~d** die Zuschauerreihen hatten sich ziemlich gelichtet **b** *(Med)* **to ~ the body of sth** dem Körper etw entziehen

depletion [dɪˈpliːʃən] N **a** *(= exhausting)* Erschöpfung *f*; *(= reduction)* Verminderung *f*, Verringerung *f*; *(of funds)* Verringerung *f*; *(of stock, membership)* Abnahme *f* **b** *(Med)* Mangel *m* (of an *+acc*)

deplorable [dɪˈplɔːrəbl] ADJ *(= dreadful)* schrecklich; *(= disgraceful)* schändlich; **this joke is in ~ taste** dieser Witz ist schrecklich geschmacklos; **it is ~ that …** es ist eine Schande *or* unerhört, dass …

deplorably [dɪˈplɔːrəblɪ] ADV schrecklich; **the press are acting ~** es ist eine Schande, wie die Presse sich verhält; **it is in ~ bad taste** es zeugt von bedauernswert schlechtem Geschmack

deplore [dɪˈplɔːʳ] VT *(= regret)* bedauern, beklagen; *(= disapprove of)* missbilligen; **his attitude is to be ~d** seine Haltung ist bedauerlich

deploy [dɪˈplɔɪ] VT **a** *(Mil: = use, employ)* einsetzen; *(= position)* aufstellen; **the number of troops/missiles ~ed in Germany** die Zahl der in Deutschland stationierten Streitkräfte/Raketen **b** *(fig) resources, staff, arguments* einsetzen VI *(Mil)* sich aufstellen, aufmarschieren

deployment [dɪˈplɔɪmənt] N **a** *(Mil: = using)* Einsatz *m*; *(= positioning)* Aufstellung *f*, Stationierung *f* **b** *(fig, of resources, staff, arguments)* Einsatz *m*

deplume [ˌdiːˈpluːm] VT *bird* rupfen

depoliticize [ˈdiːpɒˈlɪtɪsaɪz] VT entpolitisieren

deponent [dɪˈpəʊnənt] N *(Ling)* Deponens *nt*; *(Jur)* vereidigter Zeuge ADJ **~ verb** Deponens *nt*

depopulate [ˌdiːˈpɒpjʊleɪt] VT entvölkern

depopulation [ˈdiːˌpɒpjʊˈleɪʃən] N Entvölkerung *f*

deport [dɪˈpɔːt] VT *prisoner* deportieren; *foreign national* abschieben VR *(= behave)* sich benehmen *or* verhalten

deportation [ˌdiːpɔːˈteɪʃən] N *(of prisoner)* Deportation *f*; *(of foreign national)* Abschiebung *f*

deportation order N Abschiebungsanordnung *f*

deportee [dɪpɔːˈtiː] N Deportierte(r) *mf*; *(= alien awaiting deportation)* Abzuschiebende(r) *mf*

deportment [dɪˈpɔːtmənt] N Haltung *f*; *(= behaviour)* Verhalten *nt*, Benehmen *nt*; **lessons in ~** Haltungsschulung *f*, Anstandsunterricht *m*

depose [dɪˈpəʊz] VT absetzen; *sovereign also* entthronen VI *(Jur)* unter Eid aussagen

deposit [dɪˈpɒzɪt] VT **a** *(= put down)* hinlegen; *(upright)* hinstellen; **the turtle ~s her eggs in the sand** die Schildkröte legt ihre Eier im Sand ab **b** *money, valuables* deponieren *(in or with* bei); **I ~ed £500 in my account** ich zahlte £ 500 auf mein Konto ein **c** *(Geol)* ablagern N **a** *(Fin, in bank)* Einlage *f*, Guthaben *nt*; **to have £500 on ~** ein Guthaben *or* eine Einlage von £ 500 haben **b** *(Comm: = part payment)* Anzahlung *f*; *(= returnable security)* Sicherheit *f*, Kaution *f*; *(for bottle)* Pfand *nt*, Depot *nt (Sw)*; **to put down a ~ of £1000 on a car** eine Anzahlung von £ 1000 für ein Auto leisten, £ 1000 für ein Auto anzahlen; **to leave a ~** eine Sicherheit *or* Kaution hinterlegen; **to lose one's ~** *(Pol)* seine Kaution verlieren **c** *(Chem: in wine, Geol)* Ablagerung *f*; *(= accumulation of ore, coal, oil)* (Lager)stätte *f*; **to form a ~** sich ablagern; **calcium ~s** Kalziumvorräte *pl*; **fat ~s** Fettablagerungen *pl*

deposit account N Sparkonto *nt*

depositary [dɪˈpɒzɪtərɪ] N Treuhänder(in) *m(f)*

deposit copy N *(= book)* Belegexemplar *nt* *(für öffentliche Bibliotheken)*

deposition [ˌdiːpəˈzɪʃən] N **a** *(of sovereign)* Entthronung *f*, Absetzung *f*; *(of official)* Absetzung *f* **b** *(Jur)* Aussage *f* unter Eid **c** *(Art, Rel)* **~ from the cross** Kreuzabnahme *f*

depositor [dɪˈpɒzɪtəʳ] N Deponent(in) *m(f)*, Einzahler(in) *m(f)*

depository [dɪˈpɒzɪtərɪ] N Verwahrungsort *m*; *(= warehouse)* Lagerhaus *nt*

deposit slip N Einzahlungsbeleg *m*

depot [ˈdepəʊ] N **a** *(= bus garage etc)* Depot *nt*; *(= store)* Lager(haus) *nt*, Depot *nt* **b** *(US Rail)* Bahnhof *m*

depot ship N Versorgungsschiff *nt*

depravation [ˌdeprəˈveɪʃən] N **a** *(= depraving)* Verderbung *f* **b** *(= depravity)* Verderbtheit *f*, Verworfenheit *f*

deprave [dɪˈpreɪv] VT verderben

depraved [dɪˈpreɪvd] ADJ verderbt, verkommen, verworfen

depravity [dɪˈprævɪtɪ] N Verderbtheit *f*, Verworfenheit *f*

deprecate [ˈdeprɪkeɪt] VT *(form)* missbilligen

deprecating ADJ, **deprecatingly** ADV [ˈdeprɪkeɪtɪŋ, -lɪ] missbilligend

deprecation [deprɪˈkeɪʃən] N *(form)* Missbilligung *f*

deprecatory [ˈdeprɪkətərɪ] N = **deprecating**

depreciable [dɪˈpriːʃɪəbl] ADJ *(Fin)* abschreibbar

depreciate [dɪˈpriːʃɪeɪt] VT **a** *value* mindern; *exchange rate* abwerten; **to ~ a currency** die Kaufkraft einer Währung mindern; **to ~ a property** den Wert einer Immobilie mindern **b** *(= belittle)* herabsetzen, herabwürdigen VI an Wert verlieren; *(currency)* an Kaufkraft verlieren; *(exchange rate)* fallen, sinken; **the pound has ~d by 8%** das Pfund ist um 8% gefallen

depreciation [dɪˌpriːʃɪˈeɪʃən] N **a** *(of property, value)* Wertminderung *f*; *(in accounting)* Abschreibung *f*; *(of currency)* Kaufkraftverlust *m* **b** *(= belittlement)* Herabsetzung *f*, Herabwürdigung *f*

depreciatory [dɪˈpriːʃɪətərɪ] ADJ abschätzig, herabsetzend

depredate [ˈdeprɪdeɪt] VT *(= plunder)* plündern; *(= vandalize)* verwüsten

depredation [ˌdeprɪˈdeɪʃən] N *usu pl* Verwüstung *f*

depress [dɪˈpres] VT **a** *person* deprimieren; *immune system* schwächen; *(= discourage)* entmutigen **b** *(= press down) lever* niederdrücken, herunterdrücken; *push button* drücken, betätigen **c** *(Comm) market* schwächen; *prices* fallen lassen; *sales* zurückgehen lassen

depressant [dɪˈpresnt] N Beruhigungsmittel *nt*, Sedativ(um) *nt (spec)* ADJ beruhigend, dämpfend, sedativ *(spec)*

depressed [dɪˈprest] ADJ **a** *(= despondent)* deprimiert *(about* über *+acc)*; *(Med)* depressiv; **to look ~** niedergeschlagen *or* bedrückt aussehen; **to feel ~** sich deprimiert *or* niedergeschlagen fühlen **b** *(Econ: = run-down) market* flau, schleppend; *economy, industry* geschwächt; *re-*

gion Not leidend; *share prices* fallend; *sales* rückläufig; **~ area** Notstandsgebiet *nt*; **the ~ state of the property market** die schlechte Marktlage bei Immobilien **c** *(form: = sunken)* tief liegend

depressing [dɪˈpresɪŋ] ADJ deprimierend, bedrückend; **these figures make ~ reading** es ist deprimierend, diese Zahlen zu lesen

depressingly [dɪˈpresɪŋlɪ] ADV deprimierend; **it all sounded ~ familiar** es hörte sich alles nur zu vertraut an; **~, the costs are too high** deprimierenderweise sind die Kosten zu hoch

depression [dɪˈpreʃən] N **a** Depression *f*; *(Med)* Depressionen *pl* **b** *(of lever)* Herunter- or Niederdrücken *nt*; *(of key, push button)* Drücken *nt*, Betätigen *nt*, Betätigung *f* **c** *(in ground)* Vertiefung *f*, Senke *f*, Mulde *f* **d** *(Met)* Tief(druckgebiet) *nt*; **a deep ~** ein ausgedehntes Tief(druckgebiet) **e** *(Econ)* Flaute *f*; *(St Ex)* Baisse *f*; **the Depression** die Weltwirtschaftskrise

depressive [dɪˈpresɪv] ADJ depressiv N an Depressionen Leidende(r) *mf*; **to be a ~** depressiv sein

depressurize [diːˈpreʃəraɪz] VT den Druck herabsetzen in *(+dat)*; **should the cabin become ~d …** bei Druckverlust in der Kabine …

deprivation [ˌdeprɪˈveɪʃən] N **a** *(= depriving)* Entzug *m*; *(= loss)* Verlust *m*; *(Psych)* Deprivation *f*; *(of rights)* Beraubung *f* **b** *(= state)* Entbehrung *f*; *(= lack of necessities)* Mangel *m*; **the ~s of the war** die Entbehrungen des Krieges

deprive [dɪˈpraɪv] VT **to ~ sb of sth** *(of sth one has)* jdn einer Sache *(gen)* berauben; *(of sth to which one has a right)* jdm etw vorenthalten; **we were ~d of our rights/freedom** wir wurden unserer Rechte/Freiheit beraubt; **they were ~d of a decent education** ihnen wurde eine anständige Erziehung vorenthalten; **I wouldn't want to ~ you of the pleasure of seeing her** ich möchte dir das Vergnügen, sie zu sehen, nicht vorenthalten; **the team was ~d of the injured Owen** die Mannschaft musste ohne den verletzten Owen auskommen; **she was ~d of sleep/oxygen** sie litt an Schlafmangel/Sauerstoffmangel; **they are ~d of any sense of national identity** ihnen fehlt jedes Gefühl für nationale Identität; **to ~ oneself of sth** sich *(dat)* etw nicht gönnen

deprived [dɪˈpraɪvd] ADJ *person, background* benachteiligt; *childhood* arm; *area* (wirtschaftlich) benachteiligt; **the ~ areas of the city** die Armenviertel der Stadt

deprogramme, *(US)* **deprogram** [diːˈprəʊgræm] VT *cult member* entprogrammieren

dept *abbr of* **department** Abt.

depth [depθ] N **a** Tiefe *f*; **the ~s of the ocean** die Tiefen des Ozeans; **at a ~ of 3 feet** in einer Tiefe von 3 Fuß, in 3 Fuß Tiefe; **don't go out of your ~** geh nicht zu tief rein!; **to be out of one's ~** *(lit)* den Boden unter den Füßen verlieren; *(fig also)* ins Schwimmen geraten
b *(of knowledge, feeling, colour)* Tiefe *f*; **the ~ of his feelings for her** die Tiefe seiner Gefühle für sie; **he had no idea of the ~ of feeling against him** er hatte keine Ahnung, wie abgrundtief die Abneigung gegen ihn war; **they now understood the ~ of feeling on this issue** sie wussten jetzt, wie sehr dieses Thema die Gemüter bewegte; **he has ~ of character** er hat Charakterstärke; **the wine has ~ of character** der Wein hat viel Charakter; **in ~** eingehend, intensiv; *interview* ausführlich → **in-depth**
c *(fig)* **~(s)** Tiefen *pl*; **in the ~s of despair** in tiefster Verzweiflung; **in the ~s of winter/the forest** im tiefsten Winter/Wald; **in the ~s of the countryside** auf dem flachen Land; **in the ~s of recession** mitten in der Rezession; **from the ~s of the earth** aus den Tiefen der Erde *(geh)*; **to sink to new ~s** so tief wie nie zuvor sinken

depth charge N Wasserbombe *f*

depthless [ˈdepθlɪs] ADJ unermesslich tief, unendlich; *(fig)* oberflächlich

depth: **depth of field** N *(Phot)* Tiefenschärfe *f*; **depth psychology** N Tiefenpsychologie *f*

deputation [ˌdepjʊˈteɪʃən] N *(= act)* Abordnung *f*; *(= people also)* Delegation *f*

depute [dɪˈpjuːt] VT *person* abordnen, delegieren; **to be ~d to do sth** dazu abgeordnet *or* delegiert werden, etw zu tun

deputize [ˈdepjʊtaɪz] VI vertreten *(for sb* jdn), als Vertreter(in) fungieren *(for sb* für jdn) VT ernennen, abordnen

deputy [ˈdepjʊtɪ] N **a** Stellvertreter(in) *m(f)* **b** *(in deputation)* Delegierte(r) *mf* **c** *(also* **deputy sheriff**) Hilfssheriff *m* **d** *(in France)* Deputierte(r) *mf*; *(US, in foreign parliaments)* Abgeordnete(r) *mf* ADJ *attr* stellvertretend

derail [dɪˈreɪl] VT zum Entgleisen bringen, entgleisen lassen; *(fig) plan, negotiations* scheitern lassen; **to be ~ed** entgleisen VI entgleisen

derailleur gears [dɪˈreɪljəˈgɪəz], **derailleurs** [dɪˈreɪljəz] *(inf)* PL Kettenschaltung *f*

derailment [dɪˈreɪlmənt] N Entgleisung *f*

derange [dɪˈreɪndʒ] VT **a** *(= make insane)* verrückt *or* wahnsinnig machen; *mind, senses* verwirren **b** *plan* durcheinanderbringen, umwerfen

deranged [dɪˈreɪndʒd] ADJ *mind* gestört, verwirrt, verstört; *person, gunman* geistesgestört

derangement [dɪˈreɪndʒmənt] N **a** Geistesgestörtheit *f* **b** *(of order)* Unordnung *f*, Durcheinander *nt*

Derby [ˈdɑːbɪ, *(US)* ˈdɜːbɪ] N **a** *(US: also* **Derby hat**) Melone *f* **b** *(= local Derby)* (Lokal)derby *nt* **c** *(Racing)* Derby *nt*

deregulate [diːˈregjʊleɪt] VT deregulieren; *buses etc* dem freien Wettbewerb überlassen

deregulation [ˌdiːregjʊˈleɪʃən] N Deregulierung *f*; *(of buses etc)* Wettbewerbsfreiheit *f* (*of* für)

derelict [ˈderɪlɪkt] ADJ *(= abandoned)* verlassen, aufgegeben; *(= ruined)* verfallen, heruntergekommen N **a** *(Naut)* (treibendes) Wrack **b** *(= person)* Obdachlose(r) *mf*

dereliction [ˌderɪˈlɪkʃən] N **a** *(= state: of property)* Verfall *m*, Heruntergekommenheit *f* **b** **~ of duty** Pflichtversäumnis *nt*

derestricted [ˌdiːrɪˈstrɪktɪd] ADJ *road, area* ohne Geschwindigkeitsbegrenzung *or* -beschränkung

deride [dɪˈraɪd] VT sich lustig machen über *(+acc)*, verspotten

derider [dɪˈraɪdəʳ] N Verspotter(in) *m(f)*, Spötter(in) *m(f)*

deriding [dɪˈraɪdɪŋ] ADJ spöttisch, höhnisch

de rigueur [dərɪˈgɜːʳ] ADJ *pred* unerlässlich

derision [dɪˈrɪʒən] N Hohn *m*, Spott *m*; **object of ~** Zielscheibe *f* des Spotts; **to be greeted with ~** spöttisch *or* mit Spott aufgenommen werden

derisive [dɪˈraɪsɪv] ADJ spöttisch, höhnisch; *(= malicious)* hämisch, verächtlich

derisively [dɪˈraɪsɪvlɪ] ADV spöttisch, höhnisch; *(= maliciously)* verächtlich

derisory [dɪˈraɪsərɪ] ADJ **a** *amount, offer* lächerlich **b** = **derisive**

derivable [dɪˈraɪvəbl] ADJ *(Ling, Philos, Chem)* ableitbar

derivation [ˌderɪˈveɪʃən] N Ableitung *f*; *(Chem)* Derivation *f*; **this text has its ~ from Kafka's novels** dieser Text basiert auf Kafkas Romanen; **whatever the true ~ of this story may be** woher diese Geschichte auch immer ursprünglich stammt

derivative [dɪˈrɪvətɪv] ADJ abgeleitet; *(Ling, Chem)* abgeleitet, derivativ; *(fig) style, composition, literary work etc* nachgeahmt, imitiert; **~ markets** *(Fin)* Markt *m* für Derivate; **~ products** *(Fin)* Derivate *pl* N **a** Ableitung *f*; *(Ling also, Chem)* Derivat *nt* **b** *(Fin)* Derivat *nt*

derive [dɪˈraɪv] VT *idea, name, origins* her- *or* ableiten (*from* von); *profit, benefit* ziehen (*from* aus); *satisfaction, comfort, pleasure, energy* gewinnen (*from* aus); *income* beziehen (*from* aus); **this word is ~d from the Greek** dieses Wort stammt aus dem Griechischen VI **to ~ from** sich her- *or* ableiten von; *(power, fortune)* beruhen auf *(+dat)*, herkommen *or* -rühren von; *(ideas)* kommen *or* stammen von; **this ~s from the fact that …** das beruht auf der Tatsache, dass …

dermatitis [ˌdɜːməˈtaɪtɪs] N Hautentzündung *f*, Dermatitis *f*

dermatologist [ˌdɜːməˈtɒlədʒɪst] N Hautarzt *m*, Hautärztin *f*, Dermatologe *m*, Dermatologin *f*

dermatology [ˌdɜːməˈtɒlədʒɪ] N Dermatologie *f*; **~ clinic** Hautklinik *f*

dermatosis [ˌdɜːməˈtəʊsɪs] N Hautkrankheit *f*, Dermatose *f (spec)*

derogate [ˈderəgeɪt] VI **to ~ from sth** *(form)* einer Sache *(dat)* Abbruch tun

derogation [ˌderəˈgeɪʃən] N *(form, of power, dignity etc)* Beeinträchtigung *f*, Schmälerung *f*, Abbruch *m (of, from gen)*

derogatory [dɪˈrɒgətərɪ] ADJ abfällig, abschätzig

derrick [ˈderɪk] N Derrickkran *m*, Montagekran *m*; *(above oil well)* Bohrturm *m*

derring-do [ˈderɪŋˈduː] N *(old)* Verwegenheit *f*, Tollkühnheit *f*; **deeds of ~** verwegene *or* tollkühne Taten

derringer [ˈderɪndʒəʳ] N Derringer *m or f*

derv [dɜːv] N *(Brit)* Diesel(kraftstoff) *m*, Dieselöl *nt*

dervish [ˈdɜːvɪʃ] N Derwisch *m*

DES *abbr of* **Department of Education and Science** Bildungs- und Wissenschaftsministerium *nt*

desalinate [diːˈsælɪneɪt] VT entsalzen

desalination [diːˌsælɪˈneɪʃən], **desalinization** [diːˌsælɪnaɪˈzeɪʃən] N Entsalzung *f*

desalination plant N Meerwasserentsalzungsanlage *f*

desalinize [diːˈsælɪnaɪz] VT entsalzen

desalt [diːˈsɔːlt] VT *(esp US)* entsalzen

desalting plant [diːˈsɔːltɪŋplɑːnt] N *(esp US)* Meerwasserentsalzungsanlage *f*

descale [diːˈskeɪl] VT entkalken

descant [ˈdeskænt] N *(Mus)* Diskant *m*; **~ recorder** Sopranflöte *f* VI [desˈkænt] sich auslassen *or* verbreiten (*upon* über *+acc*), ausgiebig kommentieren

descend [dɪˈsend] VI **a** *(= go down, person)* hinuntergehen, hinabschreiten *(geh)*; *(lift, vehicle)* hinunterfahren; *(road)* hinunterführen, hinuntergehen; *(hill)* abfallen; *(from horse)* absteigen; *(Astron)* untergehen; **in ~ing order of importance** nach Wichtigkeit geordnet
b *(= have as ancestor)* abstammen (*from* von)
c *(= pass by inheritance, property)* übergehen (*from* von, *to* auf *+acc*); *(customs)* überliefert werden (*from* von, *to* auf *+acc*); *(rights)* vererbt werden (*from* von, *to* auf *+acc*)
d *(= attack suddenly)* herfallen (*on, upon* über *+acc*), überfallen (*on, upon sb* jdn); *(disease, illness)* heimsuchen (*on, upon sb* jdn); *(= come over, sadness etc)* befallen (*on, upon sb* jdn); *(silence)* sich senken (*on, upon* über *+acc*)
e *(inf: = visit)* **to ~ (up)on sb** jdn überfallen *(inf)*; **thousands of fans are expected to ~ on the city** man erwartet, dass tausende *or* Tausende von Fans die Stadt überlaufen
f *(= lower oneself)* **to ~ to sth** sich zu etw herablassen; **I'd never ~ to sarcasm** ich würde mich nicht dazu herablassen, sarkastisch zu werden; **he even ~ed to bribery** er scheute selbst vor Bestechung nicht zurück; **to ~ into anarchy/chaos/civil war** in Anarchie/Chaos/einen Bürgerkrieg versinken
VT **a** *stairs* hinuntergehen *or* -steigen, hinabschreiten *(geh)*
b **to be ~ed from** abstammen von

descendant [dɪˈsendənt] N **a** Nachkomme *m* **b** *(Astron, Astrol)* **in the ~** im Deszendenten

descender [dɪˈsendəʳ] N *(Typ)* Unterlänge *f*

descent [dɪˈsent] N **a** *(= going down, of person)* Hinuntergehen *nt*, Absteigen *nt*; *(from moun-*

tain, of plane, into underworld) Abstieg *m*; *(of gymnast)* Abgang *m*; (= *slope: of road)* Abfall *m*; **during the ~ of the mountain** während des Abstiegs vom Berg; **the road made a sharp ~** die Straße fiel steil ab; **~ by parachute** Fallschirmabsprung *m*; **the ~ from the cross** *(Art, Rel)* die Kreuzabnahme
b (= *ancestry)* Abstammung *f*, Herkunft *f*; **of noble ~** von adliger Abstammung *or* Herkunft; **he claims direct ~ from ...** er behauptet, direkt von ... abzustammen
c *(of property)* Vererbung *f*, Übertragung *f* *(to* auf *+acc)*; *(of customs)* Überlieferung *f* *(to* auf *+acc)*
d *(Mil, fig, = attack)* Überfall *m* *(on* auf *+acc)*
e *(inf: = visit)* Überfall *m* *(inf)*
f *(fig, into crime etc)* Absinken *nt* *(into* in *+acc)*; *(into chaos, civil war, madness)* Versinken *nt* *(into* in *+acc)*

descramble [diːˈskræmbl] VT *(Telec)* entschlüsseln

describe [dɪˈskraɪb] VT **a** (= *give description of)* beschreiben, schildern; **~ him for us** beschreiben Sie ihn uns *(dat)*; **which cannot be ~d** was unbeschreiblich ist; **to ~ oneself/sb as ...** sich/jdn als ... bezeichnen; **he ~s himself as an intellectual** er bezeichnet sich als Intellektueller; **the police ~ him as dangerous/a terrorist** die Polizei bezeichnet ihn als gefährlich/(einen) Terroristen; **he is ~d as being tall with short fair hair** er wird als groß mit kurzen blonden Haaren beschrieben **b** *(Math)* beschreiben

description [dɪˈskrɪpʃən] N **a** Beschreibung *f*; *(of event, situation)* Schilderung *f*, Beschreibung *f*; **she gave a detailed ~ of what had happened** sie beschrieb ausführlich, was vorgefallen war; **this is beyond ~** das ist ja unbeschreiblich; **to answer (to)** *or* **fit the ~ of ...** der Beschreibung als ... entsprechen; **they answer** *or* **fit the ~ of the suspects** auf sie trifft die Beschreibung der Verdächtigen zu; **do you know anyone of this ~?** kennen Sie jemanden, der dieser Beschreibung entspricht *or* auf den diese Beschreibung zutrifft?
b (= *sort)* Art *f*; **vehicles of every ~** *or* **of all ~s** Fahrzeuge aller Art
c *(Math)* Beschreibung *f*

descriptive [dɪˈskrɪptɪv] ADJ **a** beschreibend; *account, adjective, passage* anschaulich; **~ writing** Beschreibung *f*; **his ~ powers** sein Talent zur Beschreibung; **to be ~ of sth** etw beschreiben **b** *linguistics, science etc* deskriptiv

descriptively [dɪsˈkrɪptɪvlɪ] ADV anschaulich; *(Sci, Ling)* deskriptiv; **the name is not ~ accurate** der Name ist keine genaue Beschreibung; **it is known, ~, as ...** es ist anschaulicherweise unter dem Namen ... bekannt

descriptivism [dɪˈskrɪptɪvɪzəm] N *(Ling, Philos)* Deskriptivismus *m*

descriptivist [dɪˈskrɪptɪvɪst] *(Ling, Philos)* **N** Deskriptivist(in) *m(f)* **ADJ** deskriptivistisch

descry [dɪˈskraɪ] VT *(form, liter)* gewahren *(geh)*, erblicken

desecrate [ˈdesɪkreɪt] VT entweihen, schänden

desecration [ˌdesɪˈkreɪʃən] N Entweihung *f*, Schändung *f*

desecrator [ˈdesɪkreɪtəʳ] N Schänder(in) *m(f)*; *(of graves)* Grabschänder(in) *m(f)*

desegregate [ˌdiːˈsegrɪgeɪt] VT *schools, sport* desegregieren; **~d schools** gemischtrassige Schulen *pl*

desegregation [ˈdiːˌsegrɪˈgeɪʃən] N Aufhebung *f* der Rassentrennung *(of* in *+dat)*, Desegregation *f*

deselect [ˌdiːsɪˈlekt] **VT** *MP etc* nicht wieder (als Kandidat) aufstellen **VI** *(Comput)* eine Markierung aufheben

desensitize [ˌdiːˈsensɪtaɪz] VT *(Phot)* lichtunempfindlich machen; *(Med)* desensibilisieren; **to become ~d to sth** *(fig)* einer Sache *(dat)* gegenüber abstumpfen

desert¹ [ˈdezət] **N** *(lit, fig)* Wüste *f* **ADJ** *attr* Wüsten-; **~ landscape** Wüstenlandschaft *f*; **~ warfare** Wüstenkrieg *m*

desert² [dɪˈzɜːt] **VT** (= *leave)* verlassen; (= *abandon) person, cause, party* im Stich lassen; **by the time the police arrived the place was ~ed** als die Polizei eintraf, war niemand mehr da; **in winter the place is ~ed** im Winter ist der Ort verlassen; **to ~ the army** von der Armee desertieren **VI** *(Mil, fig)* desertieren, Fahnenflucht begehen; **to ~ from the army** von der Armee desertieren; **to ~ to the rebels** zu den Rebellen überlaufen

desert boots [ˈdezət-] PL Boots *pl*

deserted [dɪˈzɜːtɪd] ADJ (= *abandoned)* verlassen; *place* unbewohnt, (wie) ausgestorben; *street* menschenleer; (= *lonely) person* verlassen, einsam

deserter [dɪˈzɜːtəʳ] N *(Mil, fig)* Deserteur(in) *m(f)*

desertion [dɪˈzɜːʃən] N **a** (= *act)* Verlassen *nt*; *(Jur: of wife, family)* böswilliges Verlassen; *(Mil)* Desertion *f*, Fahnenflucht *f*; *(fig)* Fahnenflucht *f*; **~ to the enemy** Überlaufen *nt* zum Feind **b** (= *state)* Verlassenheit *f*

desert island [ˈdezət-] N einsame *or* verlassene Insel

desert rat [ˈdezət-] N *(Brit fig inf)* Wüstensoldat *m*

deserts [dɪˈzɜːts] PL Verdienste *pl*; (= *reward: also iro)* verdiente Belohnung; (= *punishment)* verdiente Strafe; **according to one's ~** nach seinen Verdiensten; **to get one's just ~** bekommen, was man verdient hat, seine gerechte Belohnung bekommen

deserve [dɪˈzɜːv] **VT** verdienen; **he ~s to win** er verdient den Sieg; **he ~s to be punished** er verdient es, bestraft zu werden; **she ~s better** sie hat etwas Besseres verdient; **to get what one ~s** bekommen, was man verdient hat **VI** **he ~s well of his country** *(form)* sein Land ist ihm zu Dank verpflichtet

deserved [dɪˈzɜːvd] ADJ (wohl)verdient

deservedly [dɪˈzɜːvɪdlɪ] ADV verdientermaßen; **and ~ so** und das zu Recht

deserving [dɪˈzɜːvɪŋ] ADJ *person, action, cause* verdienstvoll; *winner* verdient; **the ~ poor** die Bedürftigen; **to be ~ of sth** etw verdient haben

deshabille [ˌdezəˈbiːl] N = **dishabille**

desiccate [ˈdesɪkeɪt] VT trocknen

desiccated [ˈdesɪkeɪtɪd] ADJ getrocknet; *(fig)* vertrocknet

desiccation [ˌdesɪˈkeɪʃən] N Trocknung *f*, Trocknen *nt*

desideratum [dɪˌzɪdəˈrɑːtəm] N *pl* **desiderata** [dɪˌzɪdəˈrɑːtə] Desiderat(um) *nt* *(liter)*, Erfordernis *nt*

design [dɪˈzaɪn] **N** **a** (= *planning, shaping etc, of building, book, picture etc)* Entwurf *m*; *(of dress)* Design *nt*, Entwurf *m*; *(of car, machine, plane etc)* Konstruktion *f*; **it's still at the ~ stage** es befindet sich noch in der Konstruktion *or* im Konstruktionsstadium; **it was a good/faulty ~** es war gut/schlecht konstruiert; **a new ~** *(Aut)* ein neues Modell
b *no pl (as subject: = art of designing)* Design *nt*
c (= *pattern: on pottery, material)* Muster *nt*
d (= *intention)* Plan *m*, Absicht *f*; **evil ~s** böse Absichten; **by ~ (rather than accident)** absichtlich (und nicht zufällig); **to have ~s on sb/sth** mit jdm/etw etwas im Sinn haben, es auf jdn/etw abgesehen haben; **he has ~s on her** er hat etwas mit ihr vor
VT **a** (= *plan, draw)* entwerfen; *machine* konstruieren; **a well ~ed machine** eine gut durchkonstruierte Maschine; **car seats ~ed for maximum safety** Autositze, die für maximale Sicherheit konstruiert sind
b (= *intend)* **to be ~ed for sb/sth** für jdn/etw bestimmt *or* konzipiert sein; **the dictionary is ~ed for beginners** das Wörterbuch ist für Anfänger bestimmt *or* konzipiert; **a peace plan ~ed to end the civil war** ein Friedensplan, der den Bürgerkrieg beenden soll; **this magazine is ~ed to appeal to young people** diese Zeitschrift soll junge Leute ansprechen; **the legislation is ~ed as a consumer protection measure** die Gesetzgebung soll dem Verbraucherschutz dienen
VI planen, Pläne *or* Entwürfe machen
ADJ *attr* Design-; **~ technology** Designtechnik *f*

designate [ˈdezɪgneɪt] **VT** **a** (= *name)* kennzeichnen, benennen; (= *appoint)* bestimmen, ernennen, designieren *(form)*; **to ~ sb as sth** jdn zu etw ernennen **b** (= *indicate, specify, mark)* festlegen, bestimmen; **to be ~d for sth** für etw bestimmt sein; **smoking is permitted in ~d areas** Rauchen ist in den dafür bestimmten Bereichen erlaubt; **to be the ~d driver** als Fahrer bestimmt sein [ˈdezɪgnɪt] **ADJ** **the Prime Minister ~** der designierte Premierminister

designation [ˌdezɪgˈneɪʃən] N **a** (= *naming)* Kennzeichnung *f*, Benennung *f*; (= *appointment)* Bestimmung *f*, Ernennung *f* **b** (= *indicating)* Bestimmung *f*, Festlegung *f*

designedly [dɪˈzaɪnɪdlɪ] ADV absichtlich, vorsätzlich

design engineer N Designingenieur(in) *m(f)*

designer [dɪˈzaɪnəʳ] **N** Designer(in), Gestalter(in) *m(f)*; (= *fashion designer)* Modeschöpfer(in) *m(f)*; *(of machines etc)* Konstrukteur(in) *m(f)*; *(Theat)* Bühnenbildner(in) *m(f)* **ADJ** *attr* Designer-; **~ clothes** Designerkleider *pl*, Designerklamotten *pl (pej)*

designer: designer baby N Designerbaby *nt*; **designer drug** N Modedroge *f*, Designerdroge *f*; **designer stubble** N *(hum)* Dreitagebart *m (inf)*

design fault N Designfehler *m*

designing [dɪˈzaɪnɪŋ] ADJ intrigant, hinterhältig

desirability [dɪˌzaɪərəˈbɪlɪtɪ] N Wünschbarkeit *f*; **they discussed the ~ of launching the product in July** sie erörterten, ob es wünschenswert sei, das Produkt im Juli auf den Markt zu bringen; **in his eyes this only increased her ~** das machte sie in seinen Augen umso begehrenswerter; **in order to increase the ~ of these houses** um die Attraktivität dieser Häuser zu erhöhen

desirable [dɪˈzaɪərəbl] ADJ **a** wünschenswert; *action, progress* erwünscht; *goal* erstrebenswert **b** *position, offer, house, area* reizvoll, attraktiv **c** *woman* begehrenswert

desirably [dɪˈzaɪərəblɪ] ADV *located* reizvoll; *equipped, furnished* attraktiv; *male, sexy, feminine* begehrenswert

desire [dɪˈzaɪəʳ] ✪ 8.3 **N** Wunsch *m* *(for* nach); (= *longing)* Sehnsucht *f* *(for* nach); *(sexual)* Verlangen *nt* *(for* nach), Begehren *nt* *(for* nach); **her sexual ~s** ihre sexuellen Wünsche; **a ~ for peace/revenge** ein Verlangen *nt* nach Frieden/Rache; **the ~ to please** der Wunsch zu gefallen; **heart's ~** Herzenswunsch *m*; **I have no ~ to see him** ich habe kein Verlangen, ihn zu sehen; **I have no ~ to cause you any trouble** ich möchte Ihnen keine Unannehmlichkeiten bereiten
VT wünschen; *object* sich *(dat)* wünschen; *woman* begehren; *peace* haben wollen, verlangen nach; **if ~d** auf Wunsch; **to have the ~d effect** die gewünschte Wirkung haben; **cut the wood to the ~d length** das Holz auf die gewünschte Länge zuschneiden; **it leaves much** *or* **a lot to be ~d** das lässt viel *or* einiges zu wünschen übrig; **it leaves something to be ~d** es lässt zu wünschen übrig; **to ~ sb to do sth** *(form: = request)* jdn bitten *or* ersuchen, etw zu tun

desirous [dɪˈzaɪərəs] ADJ *(form)* **to be ~ of sth** etw wünschen; **to be ~ of doing sth** den Wunsch haben, etw zu tun

desist [dɪˈzɪst] VI *(form)* Abstand nehmen, absehen *(from doing sth* davon, etw zu tun, *from sth* von etw)

desk [desk] N Schreibtisch *m*; *(for pupils, master)* Pult *nt*; *(in shop, restaurant)* Kasse *f*; *(in hotel)* Empfang *m*; *(Press)* Ressort *nt*

desk: desk-bound ADJ an den Schreibtisch gebunden; **desk clerk** N *(US)* Empfangschef *m*, Empfangsdame *f*; **desk diary** N Tischkalender *m*; **desk editor** N Lektor(in) *m(f)*,

Manuskriptbearbeiter(in) *m(f)*; *(Press)* Ressortchef(in) *m(f)*

deskill [ˌdiːˈskɪl] VT *job* vereinfachen *(sodass die Arbeit keine oder kaum Fachkenntnisse mehr erfordert)*

desk: **desk job** N Bürojob *m*; **desk lamp** N Schreibtischlampe *f*; **desk pad** N Schreibunterlage *f*

desktop [ˈdesktɒp] N **a** Arbeitsfläche *f* **b** *(Comput)* Desktop *m* *(= computer)* = **desktop computer**

desktop: **desktop computer** N Desktop-computer *m*, Desktop-Computer *m*, Tischrechner *m*; **desktop copier** N Tischkopierer *f*; **desktop publishing** N Desktop-Publishing *nt*

desk work N Schreibarbeit *f*

desolate [ˈdesəlɪt] ADJ **a** *place (= bleak)* trostlos; *(= devastated)* verwüstet; *landscape* trostlos, öde; *beauty* einsam **b** *(= lonely, sad) person* trostlos; *feeling, cry* verzweifelt; **she looked ~** sie wirkte trostlos; **he was ~ without her** ohne sie fühlte er sich einsam und verlassen [ˈdesəleɪt] VT *(liter) place* verwüsten

desolately [ˈdesəlɪtlɪ] ADV trostlos

desolation [ˌdesəˈleɪʃən] N **a** *(of country by war)* Verwüstung *f* **b** *(of landscape)* Trostlosigkeit *f* **c** *(= grief)* Trostlosigkeit *f*; *(= friendlessness)* Verlassenheit *f*

despair [dɪˈspɛəˈ] N Verzweiflung *f (about, at* über *+acc)*; **he was filled with ~** Verzweiflung überkam *or* ergriff ihn; **to be in ~** verzweifelt sein; **she looked at him in ~** sie sah ihn verzweifelt *or* voller Verzweiflung an; **in ~, she gave up** in ihrer Verzweiflung gab sie auf; **his ~ of ever being able to return home** seine Verzweiflung darüber, vielleicht nie mehr nach Hause zurückkehren zu können; **to be the ~ of sb** jdn zur Verzweiflung bringen

VI verzweifeln, alle Hoffnung aufgeben; **to ~ of doing sth** alle Hoffnung aufgeben, etw zu tun; **to ~ of sth** alle Hoffnung auf etw *(acc)* aufgeben; **I ~ of you** du bringst *or* treibst mich zur Verzweiflung; **I ~ at their incompetence** mit ihrer Unfähigkeit bringen *or* treiben sie mich (noch) zur Verzweiflung; **to make sb ~** jdn zur Verzweiflung bringen *or* treiben

despairing ADJ, **despairingly** ADV [dɪsˈpɛərɪŋ, -lɪ] verzweifelt

despatch [dɪˈspætʃ] VT N *(esp Brit)* = **dispatch**

desperado [ˌdespəˈrɑːdəʊ] N *pl* **-(e)s** Desperado *m*

desperate [ˈdespərɪt] ADJ **a** verzweifelt; *criminal* zum Äußersten entschlossen; *measure, situation* verzweifelt, extrem; *solution* extrem; **don't do anything ~!** mach keine Dummheiten!; **to get** *or* **grow ~** verzweifeln, in Verzweiflung geraten; **I haven't had a cigarette for hours, I'm getting ~** *(inf)* ich habe schon seit Stunden keine mehr geraucht, jetzt brauche ich aber dringend eine; **things are ~** die Lage ist extrem; **the company's ~ financial position** die extrem gespannte Finanzlage der Firma; **the ~ plight of the refugees** die schreckliche Not der Flüchtlinge; **to be ~ to do sth** etw unbedingt tun wollen; **to be ~ for sb to do sth** unbedingt wollen, dass jd etw tut; **to be ~ for sth** etw unbedingt *or* dringend brauchen

b *(= urgent) need, shortage* dringend; **her ~ need to be liked** ihr verzweifeltes Bedürfnis, gemocht zu werden; **to be in ~ need of sth** etw dringend brauchen; **a building in ~ need of repair** ein Gebäude, das dringend repariert werden muss

c *(inf hum)* **are you going out with Jane? you must be ~!** du gehst mit Jane aus? dir muss es ja wirklich schlecht gehen!; **I'm not that ~!** so schlimm ist es auch wieder nicht!

desperately [ˈdespərɪtlɪ] ADV **a** *(= frantically) fight, look for, hope, try* verzweifelt

b *(= urgently) need* dringend; *want* unbedingt; **to be ~ in need of sb/sth** jdn/etw dringend brauchen; **he ~ wanted to become a film maker** er wollte unbedingt Filmemacher werden

c *(= extremely) difficult* extrem; *important, sad* äußerst; **~ ill** schwer krank; **his son was ~ ill with cancer** sein Sohn war schwer krebskrank; **to be ~ worried (about sth)** sich *(dat)* (über etw *acc*) schreckliche Sorgen machen; **I'm not ~ worried** ich mache mir keine allzu großen Sorgen; **to be ~ keen to do sth** etw unbedingt tun wollen; **I'm not ~ keen on ...** ich bin nicht besonders scharf auf *(acc)* ...; **~ unhappy** todunglücklich; **to try ~ hard to do sth** verzweifelt versuchen, etw zu tun; **to be ~ in love (with sb)** unsterblich (in jdn) verliebt sein

desperation [ˌdespəˈreɪʃən] N Verzweiflung *f*; **an act of ~** eine Verzweiflungstat; **in (sheer) ~** aus (reiner) Verzweiflung; **to drive sb to ~** jdn zur Verzweiflung bringen *or* treiben

despicable [dɪˈspɪkəbl] ADJ verabscheuungswürdig; *person* verachtenswert, widerwärtig, ekelhaft

despicably [dɪˈspɪkəblɪ] ADV *(+vb)* abscheulich; *(+adj)* verachtenswert

despise [dɪˈspaɪz] VT verachten; *food also* verschmähen; **to ~ oneself (for sth)** sich selbst (wegen etw) verachten; **she ~d herself for deceiving him** sie verachtete sich selbst dafür, dass sie ihn betrogen hatte

despising ADJ, **despisingly** ADV [dɪˈspaɪzɪŋ, -lɪ] verächtlich, voller Verachtung, verachtungsvoll

despite [dɪˈspaɪt] PREP trotz *(+gen)*; **in ~ of** *(old, liter)* trotz, ungeachtet *(+gen)*; **~ his warnings** seinen Warnungen zum Trotz; **~ what she says** trotz allem, was sie sagt; **I smiled ~ myself** ich konnte mir ein Lächeln nicht verkneifen

despoil [dɪˈspɔɪl] VT *person* berauben *(of gen)*; *countryside* ausplündern

despondence [dɪˈspɒndəns], **despondency** [dɪˈspɒndənsɪ] N Niedergeschlagenheit *f*, Mutlosigkeit *f*

despondent [dɪˈspɒndənt] ADJ niedergeschlagen, mutlos; **to be** *or* **feel ~ about sth** über etw *(acc)* bedrückt sein; **to grow ~** den Mut verlieren

despondently [dɪˈspɒndəntlɪ] ADV niedergeschlagen, mutlos; *say* bedrückt

despot [ˈdespɒt] N *(lit, fig)* Despot(in) *m(f)*

despotic ADJ, **despotically** ADV [desˈpɒtɪk, -əlɪ] *(lit, fig)* despotisch, herrisch

despotism [ˈdespətɪzəm] N Despotie *f*; *(as ideology)* Despotismus *m*

des res [ˈdezˈrez] N *(hum inf)* attraktiver Wohnsitz

dessert [dɪˈzɜːt] N Nachtisch *m*, Dessert *nt*; **for ~** als *or* zum Nachtisch

dessert: **dessert apple** N Dessertapfel *m*; **dessert plate** N Dessertteller *m*; **dessertspoon** N Dessertlöffel *m*; **dessert wine** N Dessertwein *m*

destabilization [ˌdiːsteɪbɪlaɪˈzeɪʃən] N Destabilisierung *f*

destabilize [diːˈsteɪbɪlaɪz] VT destabilisieren

destination [ˌdestɪˈneɪʃən] N *(of person)* Reiseziel *nt*; *(of goods)* Bestimmungsort *m*; *(fig, of person)* Bestimmung *f*; *(of money)* Zweck *m*; **port of ~** Bestimmungshafen *m*; **to know one's ~ in life** seine Bestimmung kennen

destination: **destination drive** N *(Comput)* Ziellaufwerk *nt*; **destination file** N *(Comput)* Zieldatei *f*

destine [ˈdestɪn] VT **a** *(= set apart, predestine) person* bestimmen, aussehen; *object* bestimmen; **to be ~d to do sth** dazu bestimmt *or* ausersehen sein, etw zu tun; **to be ~d for sth** zu etw bestimmt sein **b** *usu pass (= be fated)* **we were ~d to meet** das Schicksal hat es so gewollt, dass wir uns begegnen; **I was ~d never to see them again** ich sollte sie nie (mehr) wiedersehen

destined [ˈdestɪnd] ADJ **~ for** *(ship, person)* unterwegs nach; *goods* für; **where is the cargo ~ for?** wo geht diese Fracht hin?

destiny [ˈdestɪnɪ] N **a** *no art (= determining power)* Schicksal *nt*, Vorsehung *f*; **Destiny** das Schicksal, die Vorsehung **b** *(= individual fate, fated event)* Schicksal *nt*, Geschick *nt*, Los *nt*; **the destinies of Germany during this period** die Geschicke Deutschlands während dieser Zeit; **to control one's own ~** sein Schicksal selbst in die Hand nehmen; **it was his ~** es war sein Schicksal *or* Los; **will it be our ~ to meet again?** wird uns das Schicksal (je) wieder zusammenführen?

destitute [ˈdestɪtjuːt] ADJ **a** *(= poverty-stricken)* mittellos; **to be utterly ~** bettelarm sein **b** *(= lacking)* bar *(of +gen)* N **the ~** *pl* die Mittellosen, die, die im Elend leben

destitution [ˌdestɪˈtjuːʃən] N (bittere) Not, Elend *nt*; *(esp financial)* Mittellosigkeit *f*

destroy [dɪˈstrɔɪ] VT **a** *(lit: = wreck, ruin)* zerstören; *box, toy, watch etc* kaputt machen; *documents, trace* vernichten; **to ~ oneself** sich zugrunde *or* zu Grunde richten; **to be ~ed by fire** durch Brand vernichtet werden **b** *(= kill)* vernichten; *animal* einschläfern **c** *(fig: = put an end to)* zerstören; *influence, hopes, chances* zunichtemachen, vernichten; *reputation, mood, beauty* ruinieren; *morals* zersetzen; **to ~ sb** jdn zugrunde *or* zu Grunde richten

destroyer [dɪˈstrɔɪəˈ] N *(Naut)* Zerstörer *m*

destruct [dɪˈstrʌkt] VI *(esp Space)* sich selbst zerstören

destruct button N Knopf *m* zur Selbstzerstörung

destructible [dɪˈstrʌktəbl] ADJ vernichtbar

destruction [dɪˈstrʌkʃən] N **a** *(= destroying, of town, building, hope)* Zerstörung *f*; *(of enemy, people, insects, documents)* Vernichtung *f*; *(of reputation)* Ruinierung *f*, Zerstörung *f*; *(of character, soul)* Zerstörung *f*, Zersetzung *f* **b** *(= damage: caused by war, fire)* Verwüstung *f*, Zerstörung *f*

destructive [dɪˈstrʌktɪv] ADJ **a** *(lit) power, nature, war, wind* zerstörerisch; *effect* zerstörend; *person, behaviour, tendencies* destruktiv; **~ weapon** Vernichtungswaffe *f*; **the ~ force** *or* **power of ...** die Zerstörungskraft von ...; **~ urge** *(Psych)* Destruktionstrieb *m*; **to be ~ of** *or* **to sth** *(also fig)* etw zerstören; **these air strikes are highly ~ of human life** diese Luftangriffe fordern viele Menschenleben; **environmentally ~ projects** umweltzerstörende Projekte

b *(fig) power, emotion, influence, behaviour, criticism* destruktiv; **the ~ power of gossip** die Destruktivität von Tratsch; **a mutually ~ relationship** eine Beziehung, in der sich beide gegenseitig zerstören; **the economically ~ effect of inflation** die schädliche Auswirkung der Inflation auf die Wirtschaft

destructively [dɪˈstrʌktɪvlɪ] ADV destruktiv; **to be ~ critical** destruktive Kritik üben

destructiveness [dɪˈstrʌktɪvnɪs] N **a** *(of fire, war)* zerstörende Wirkung; *(of weapon)* Zerstörungskraft *f*; *(of person, child etc)* Destruktivität *f (esp Psych)*, Zerstörungswut *f* **b** *(of criticism)* Destruktivität *f*, zersetzende Wirkung

destructor [dɪˈstrʌktəˈ] N *(Tech: also* **refuse destructor**) Müllverbrennungsanlage *f*

desuetude [dɪˈsjʊɪtjuːd] N *(form)* **to fall into ~** außer Gebrauch kommen

desulphurization, *(US)* **desulfurization** [ˌdiːsʌlfəraɪˈzeɪʃən] N Entschwefelung *f*; **~ plant** Entschwefelungsanlage *f*

desultorily [ˈdesəltərɪlɪ] ADV halbherzig; *chat, talk, dance* zwanglos; *announce, answer, point out* beiläufig; **they walked ~ toward(s) the house** sie schlenderten auf das Haus zu

desultoriness [ˈdesəltərɪnɪs] N *(of manner, approach, attempt)* Halbherzigkeit *f*; *(of conversation)* Zwanglosigkeit *f*; *(of reading)* Flüchtigkeit *f*

desultory [ˈdesəltərɪ] ADJ *reading* flüchtig; *manner, approach, attempt* halbherzig; *firing* vereinzelt, sporadisch; *applause* schwach; **to have a ~ conversation** eine zwanglose Unterhaltung führen; **in (a) ~ fashion** halbherzig

detach [dɪˈtætʃ] VT **a** *(= separate, unfasten) rope, cart* loslösen *(from* von); *section of form, document* abtrennen *(from* von); *part of machine, wooden leg, collar, hood* abnehmen *(from* von); *lining* herausnehmen *(from* aus); *coach from train* abhängen *(from* von); **to ~ oneself from a group** sich von einer Gruppe lösen *or* trennen; **a section became ~ed from ...** ein Teil löste sich von ... **b** *(Mil, Naut)* abkommandieren

detachable [dɪˈtætʃəbl] ADJ *part of machine, collar, legs* abnehmbar; *section of document* abtrennbar *(from* von); *lining* ausknöpfbar; *(with zip)* ausreißbar; ~ **hood** abnehmbare Kapuze

detached [dɪˈtætʃt] ADJ **a** *(= unbiased) opinion* distanziert, unvoreingenommen; *(= unemotional) manner, person, expression* kühl, distanziert **b** *(Brit)* ~ **house** allein stehendes Haus, Einzelhaus *nt*

detachment [dɪˈtætʃmənt] N **a** *(= act of separating, of part of machine)* Abnehmen *nt*; *(of section of form, document)* Abtrennen *nt*; *(of rope, cart)* Loslösen *nt* **b** *(= lack of emotion)* Distanz *f*; *(= objectivity)* Abstand *m* **c** *(Mil)* Sonderkommando *nt*, Abordnung *f*

detail [ˈdiːteɪl] ✪ 19.1, 20.1, 21.3, 26.3 N **a** Detail *nt*; *(particular)* Einzelheit *f*; *(= part of painting, photo etc)* Ausschnitt *m*; *(= insignificant circumstance)* unwichtige Einzelheit; **in ~** im Detail, in Einzelheiten; **in great ~** in allen Einzelheiten, ausführlich; **in every ~** mit *or* in allen Einzelheiten; **every ~ was taken care of** jede Kleinigkeit wurde beachtet; **there's one little ~ you've forgotten** eine Kleinigkeit haben Sie (noch) vergessen; **please send me further ~s** bitte schicken Sie mir nähere *or* weitere Einzelheiten; **I didn't want to hear the ~s** ich wollte die Einzelheiten (gar) nicht hören; **to go into ~s** auf Einzelheiten eingehen, ins Detail gehen; **his attention to ~** seine Aufmerksamkeit für das Detail
b *(Mil)* Sondertrupp *m*
VT **a** *facts, story* ausführlich *or* genau berichten; **the specifications are fully ~ed on page 3** die genaue Ausführung wird auf Seite 3 aufgeführt
b *(Mil) troops* abkommandieren *(for* zu, *to do* um zu tun)

detail drawing N Detailzeichnung *f*

detailed [ˈdiːteɪld] ADJ *information, description, discussion, instructions* ausführlich; *report, account, plan, proposal* ausführlich, detailliert; *analysis, study, examination* eingehend; *investigation* eingehend, gründlich; *knowledge, work, results, map, picture* detailliert; *(= precise)* genau; **~ accounts** *(Fin)* genau geführte Geschäftsbücher; **they gave a more ~ account of what they had seen** sie beschrieben ausführlicher, was sie gesehen hatten; **he demanded ~ accounts of her spending** er verlangte eine genaue Aufstellung ihrer Ausgaben; **to have a ~ look at sth** etw genau untersuchen

detain [dɪˈteɪn] VT *(= keep back)* aufhalten; *(police)* in Haft nehmen; **to be ~ed** *(= be arrested)* verhaftet werden; *(= be in detention)* sich in Haft *or* in polizeilichem Gewahrsam befinden; **to ~ sb for questioning** jdn zur Vernehmung festhalten

detainee [dɪteɪˈniː] N Häftling *m*

detect [dɪˈtekt] VT entdecken, herausfinden; *(= see, make out)* ausfindig machen; *crime* aufdecken; *disease* feststellen; *a tone of sadness, movement, noise* wahrnehmen; *mine, gas* aufspüren; **do I ~ a note of irony?** höre ich da nicht eine gewisse Ironie (heraus)?

detectable [dɪˈtektəbl] ADJ *(= able to be found) trace* feststellbar; *(= discernible)* wahrnehmbar; *effect, sign* erkennbar; **no ~ difference** kein erkennbarer Unterschied

detection [dɪˈtekʃən] N **a** *(of criminal)* Entlarvung *f*; *(of crime)* Entdeckung *f*, Aufdeckung *f*; *(of fault)* Entdeckung *f*, Feststellung *f*; *(of disease)* Feststellung *f*; *(= detective work)* Ermittlungsarbeit *f*; **to avoid** *or* **escape ~** nicht entdeckt werden; *(criminal)* nicht gefasst werden, nicht dingfest gemacht werden; *(mistake)* der Aufmerksamkeit *(dat)* entgehen; **he tried to escape ~ by ...** er versuchte, unentdeckt zu bleiben, indem ...; **a brilliant piece of ~** ein glänzendes Stück Detektivarbeit **b** *(of gases, mines)* Aufspürung *f*

detective [dɪˈtektɪv] N Detektiv(in) *m(f)*; *(= police detective)* Kriminalbeamte(r) *m*/-beamtin *f*

detective: detective agency N Detektivbüro *nt*, Detektei *f*; **detective chief inspector** N *(Brit)* Kriminaloberinspektor(in) *m(f)*; **detective chief superintendent** N *(Brit)* Kriminalhauptkommissar(in) *m(f)*; **detective constable** N *(Brit)* Kriminalbeamte(r) *m*/-beamtin *f*; **detective inspector** N Kriminalinspektor(in) *m(f)*; **detective sergeant** N Kriminalmeister(in) *m(f)*; **detective story** N Kriminalgeschichte *f*, Kriminalroman *m*, Krimi *m (inf)*; **detective superintendent** N *(Brit)* Kriminalkommissar(in) *m(f)*; **detective work** N kriminalistische Arbeit

detector [dɪˈtektəʳ] N *(Rad, Tech)* Detektor *m*

detector van N *(Rad, Tech)* Funkmesswagen *m*

détente [deɪˈtɑːnt] N Entspannung *f*, Détente *f*

detention [dɪˈtenʃən] N **a** *(= captivity)* Haft *f*, Gewahrsam *m*; *(= act)* Festnahme *f*; *(Mil)* Arrest *m*; *(Sch)* Nachsitzen *nt*; **to give a pupil two hours' ~** einen Schüler zwei Stunden nachsitzen lassen; **he's in ~** *(Sch)* er sitzt nach **b** *(= being held up, delayed)* Verzögerung *f*, Aufenthalt *m*

detention centre, *(US)* **detention center** N Jugendstrafanstalt *f*

deter [dɪˈtɜːʳ] VT *(= prevent)* abhalten, hindern; *(= discourage)* abschrecken; **to ~ sb from sth** jdn von etw abhalten *or* an etw *(dat)* hindern; **to ~ sb from doing sth** jdn davon abhalten *or* daran hindern, etw zu tun; **he won't be ~red (by the cost)** er lässt sich (von den Kosten) nicht abschrecken; **don't let him ~ you** lassen Sie sich nicht von ihm abhalten *or* abbringen

detergent [dɪˈtɜːdʒənt] N Reinigungs- *or* Säuberungsmittel *nt*; *(= soap powder etc)* Waschmittel *nt* ADJ reinigend

deteriorate [dɪˈtɪərɪəreɪt] VI sich verschlechtern; *(materials)* verderben; *(species)* entarten; *(morals, brickwork)* verfallen

deterioration [dɪˌtɪərɪəˈreɪʃən] N Verschlechterung *f*; *(of materials)* Verderben *nt*; *(of species)* Entartung *f*; *(of morals, brickwork)* Verfall *m*

determent [dɪˈtɜːmənt] N Abschreckung *f* *(from* von); *(= means)* Abschreckungsmittel *nt*

determinable [dɪˈtɜːmɪnəbl] ADJ **a** *quantity* bestimmbar **b** *(Jur)* befristet

determinant [dɪˈtɜːmɪnənt] ADJ determinierend *attr*, entscheidend N ausschlaggebender Faktor; *(Math, Biol etc)* Determinante *f*

determinate [dɪˈtɜːmɪnɪt] ADJ *number, period etc* bestimmt, begrenzt; *concept* festgelegt; *direction* bestimmt

determination [dɪˌtɜːmɪˈneɪʃən] N **a** *(= firmness of purpose)* Entschlossenheit *f*; **he has great ~** er ist ein Mensch von großer Entschlusskraft; **he showed fierce ~** er zeigte wilde Entschlossenheit; **there is an air of ~ about him** er hat etwas Entschlossenes an sich **b** *(= determining)* Determinierung *f*; *(of character, future)* Bestimmung *f*, Determinierung *f*; *(of cause, nature, position)* Ermittlung *f*, Bestimmung *f*; *(of frontiers)* Festlegung *f*, Festsetzung *f*

determinative [dɪˈtɜːmɪnətɪv] *(Gram)* N Determinativ(um) *nt* ADJ determinativ

determine [dɪˈtɜːmɪn] VT **a** *(= be a decisive factor in) sb's character, future etc* bestimmen, determinieren **b** *(= settle, fix) conditions, price* festlegen, festsetzen **c** *(= ascertain) cause, nature, position* ermitteln, bestimmen **d** *(= resolve)* beschließen **e** *(Jur) contract* beenden

► **determine on** VI +*prep obj course of action, alternative* sich entschließen zu; **to determine on doing sth** beschließen *or* sich entschließen, etw zu tun

determined [dɪˈtɜːmɪnd] ✪ 8.2 ADJ entschlossen; *look* fest entschlossen; **he is a ~ opponent/supporter of capital punishment** er ist ein entschiedener Gegner/Befürworter der Todesstrafe; **to make a ~ effort** *or* **attempt to do sth** sein Möglichstes tun, um etw zu tun; **he is ~ that ...** er hat (fest) beschlossen, dass ...; **to be ~ to do sth** fest entschlossen sein, etw zu tun, etw unbedingt tun wollen; **they are ~ to see that the people responsible are brought to justice** sie wollen unbedingt dafür sorgen, dass die Verantwortlichen vor Gericht gebracht werden; **he's ~ to make me lose my temper** er legt es darauf an, dass ich wütend werde; **you seem ~ to exhaust yourself** du scheinst dich mit aller Gewalt kaputtmachen zu wollen

determinedly [dɪˈtɜːmɪndlɪ] ADV *(+vb)* entschlossen; *say* bestimmt, resolut; *(+adj)* entschieden; *(= stubbornly)* beharrlich; **Brian remained ~ optimistic** Brian ließ sich seinen Optimismus nicht nehmen

determiner [dɪˈtɜːmɪnəʳ] N *(Gram)* Bestimmungswort *nt*

determining [dɪˈtɜːmɪnɪŋ] ADJ entscheidend, bestimmend

determinism [dɪˈtɜːmɪnɪzəm] N Determinismus *m*

determinist [dɪˈtɜːmɪnɪst] ADJ deterministisch N Determinist(in) *m(f)*

deterministic [dɪˌtɜːmɪˈnɪstɪk] ADJ deterministisch

deterrence [dɪˈterəns] N Abschreckung *f*

deterrent [dɪˈterənt] N *(also Mil)* Abschreckungsmittel *nt*; **to act as a ~** als Abschreckung(smittel) dienen *(to* für); **to be a ~** abschrecken ADJ abschreckend, Abschreckungs-; **~ effect** Abschreckungseffekt *m*

detest [dɪˈtest] VT verabscheuen, hassen; **I ~ having to get up early** ich hasse es, früh aufstehen zu müssen

detestable [dɪˈtestəbl] ADJ widerwärtig, abscheulich; *character also* verabscheuungswürdig

detestably [dɪˈtestəblɪ] ADV widerwärtig, abscheulich

detestation [ˌdiːtesˈteɪʃən] N Abscheu *m* *(of* vor +*dat)*

dethrone [diːˈθrəʊn] VT entthronen

dethronement [diːˈθrəʊnmənt] N Entthronung *f*

detonate [ˈdetəneɪt] VI *(fuse)* zünden; *(bomb)* detonieren VT zur Explosion bringen; **detonating device** Detonator *m*

detonation [ˌdetəˈneɪʃən] N Zündung *f*

detonator [ˈdetəneɪtəʳ] N Zünd- *or* Sprengkapsel *f*; *(Rail)* Nebelsignal *nt*

detour [ˈdiːtʊəʳ] N **a** *(in road, also fig)* Umweg *m*; *(in river)* Schleife *f*, Bogen *m*; *(from a subject)* Abschweifung *f*; **to make a ~** einen Umweg machen **b** *(for traffic)* Umleitung *f* VT *traffic* umleiten VI *(= make a detour)* einen Umweg machen

detox [ˈdiːtɒks] *(inf)* N *(= treatment)* Entzug *m (inf)*; **~ centre** *(Brit) or* **center** *(US)* Entzugsklinik *f*; **~ programme** *(Brit) or* **program** *(US)* Entzugsprogramm *nt (inf)* VI Entzug machen *(inf)*

detoxification [ˌdiːtɒksɪfɪˈkeɪʃən] N Entgiftung *f*; *(for drug addict)* Entziehungskur *f*

detoxify [diːˈtɒksɪfaɪ] VT entgiften

detract [dɪˈtrækt] VI **to ~ from sth** etw beeinträchtigen, einer Sache *(dat)* Abbruch tun; *from pleasure, merit also* etw schmälern

detraction [dɪˈtrækʃən] N Beeinträchtigung *f* *(from gen)*, Schmälerung *f (from gen)*

detractor [dɪˈtræktəʳ] N Kritiker(in) *m(f)*

detrain [diːˈtreɪn] VT ausladen VI *(troops)* aussteigen

detribalize [diːˈtraɪbəlaɪz] VT die Stammesstruktur auflösen in (+*dat*); **as Africa becomes increasingly ~d** mit dem zunehmenden Verfall der Stammesstruktur in Afrika

detriment [ˈdetrɪmənt] N Schaden *m*, Nachteil *m*; **to the ~ of sth** zum Schaden einer Sache *(gen)*, zum Schaden von etw; **to sb's ~** zu jds

Nachteil; **I don't know anything to his ~** ich weiß nichts Nachteiliges über ihn; **without ~ to** ohne Schaden für

detrimental [ˌdetrɪˈmentl] ADJ *(to health, reputation)* schädlich *(to dat)*; *effect* nachteilig, schädlich *(to* für*)*; *influence* schädlich; *(to case, cause, one's interest)* abträglich *(to dat)*; **to be ~ to sb/sth** jdm/einer Sache *(dat)* schaden; **this could have a ~ effect** das könnte sich nachteilig auswirken

detritus [dɪˈtraɪtəs] N *(Geol)* Geröll *nt*; *(fig)* Müll *m*

de trop [dəˈtrəʊ] ADJ fehl am Platz, überflüssig

detumescent [ˌdiːtjʊˈmesnt] ADJ *(form)* abschwellend

deuce[1] [djuːs] N **a** *(Cards)* Zwei *f* **b** *(Tennis)* Einstand *m*; **after ten ~s** nachdem es zehnmal Einstand gegeben hatte; **to be at ~** den Einstand erreicht haben

deuce[2] N *(dated inf)* Teufel *m* → **devil N c**

deuced [ˈdjʊsɪd] *(dated inf)* ADJ verteufelt *(dated inf)*, verdammt *(inf)*; **that ~ dog** dieser verdammte Hund *(inf)* ADV **it was ~ difficult** es war verteufelt schwierig *(dated inf)*

deucedly [ˈdjuːsɪdlɪ] ADV *(dated inf)* verteufelt *(dated inf)*

deus ex machina [ˈdeɪəseksˈmækɪnə] N Deus ex Machina *m*

deuterium [djuːˈtɪərɪəm] N Deuterium *nt*

Deuteronomy [ˌdjuːtəˈrɒnəmɪ] N das fünfte Buch Mose(s), Deuteronomium *nt (spec)*

Deutschmark [ˈdɔɪtʃmɑːk], **Deutsche Mark** [ˌdɔɪtʃəˈmɑːk] N *(Hist)* D-Mark *f*, Deutsche Mark *f*

devaluate [diːˈvæljʊeɪt] VT = **devalue**

devaluation [ˌdɪvæljʊˈeɪʃən] N Abwertung *f*

devalue [diːˈvæljuː] VT abwerten

devastate [ˈdevəsteɪt] VT **a** *(lit) town, land* verwüsten; *(fig) opposition* vernichten; *economy* zugrunde *or* zu Grunde richten **b** *(inf: = overwhelm)* umhauen *(inf)*; **I was ~d** das hat mich umgehauen *(inf)*; **they were ~d by the news** die Nachricht hat sie tief erschüttert

devastating [ˈdevəsteɪtɪŋ] ADJ **a** *(= destructive) consequence, war, attack, storm, disease* verheerend; **to be ~ to** *or* **for sth, to have a ~ effect on sth** verheerende Folgen für etw haben **b** *(fig) effect* schrecklich; *news* niederschmetternd; *criticism, report, attack, performance* unschlagbar; *defeat* vernichtend; *woman, wit* umwerfend *(inf)*; **a ~ blow/loss** ein vernichtender Schlag/Verlust; **to be ~ to** *or* **for sb** jdn niederschmettern; **to be in ~ form** in unschlagbarer Form sein

devastatingly [ˈdevəsteɪtɪŋlɪ] ADV *(lit)* vernichtend; *(fig) attractive, effective, witty, funny* umwerfend *(inf)*; *accurate, frank* verheerend; **the author demolished these arguments ~** der Autor machte diese Argumente total zunichte

devastation [ˌdevəˈsteɪʃən] N Verwüstung *f*

develop [dɪˈveləp] VT **a** *mind, body* entwickeln
b *argument, thesis, outlines* (weiter)entwickeln, weiter ausführen; *original idea* (weiter)entwickeln; *plot of novel (= unfold)* entfalten; *(= fill out)* weiterentwickeln, ausbauen; *(Mus) theme* durchführen
c *natural resources, region, ground, new estate* erschließen; *old part of a town* sanieren; *new series, new model* entwickeln; *business (from scratch)* aufziehen; *(= expand)* erweitern, ausbauen; **they plan to ~ this area into a ...** es ist geplant, dieses Gebiet als ... zu erschließen
d *liking, taste, talent* entwickeln; *cold* sich *(dat)* zuziehen
e *(Phot, Math)* entwickeln
VI **a** *(person, region, country)* sich entwickeln; **to ~ into sth** sich zu etw entwickeln, etw werden
b *(illness, tendency, feeling)* sich entwickeln; *(talent, plot etc)* sich entfalten
c *(Phot)* entwickelt werden
d *(event, situation)* sich entwickeln; **it later ~ed that he had never seen her** später stellte sich heraus *or* zeigte es sich, dass er sie nie gesehen hatte

developer [dɪˈveləpəˈ] N **a** = **property developer b** *(Phot)* Entwickler *m* **c late ~** Spätentwickler(in) *m(f)*

developing [dɪˈveləpɪŋ] ADJ *crisis, storm* aufkommend; *industry* neu entstehend; *interest* wachsend; *foetus, embryo* sich entwickelnd; *society, economy* sich entwickelnd; **the ~ world** die Entwicklungsländer *pl* N **a** = **development a, d b** *(Phot)* Entwickeln *nt*

developing: **developing bath** N Entwicklerbad *nt*; **developing country** N Entwicklungsland *nt*; **developing tank** N Entwicklerschale *f*

development [dɪˈveləpmənt] N **a** *(of person, mind, body)* Entwicklung *f*
b *(= way subject, plot etc is developed)* Ausführung *f*; *(of interests)* Entfaltung *f*; *(of argument etc)* (Weiter)entwicklung *f*; *(Mus)* Durchführung *f*
c *(= change in situation)* Entwicklung *f*; **new ~s in ...** neue Entwicklungen in ...; **to await (further) ~s** neue Entwicklungen abwarten
d *(of area, site, new town)* Erschließung *f*; *(of old part of town)* Sanierung *f*; *(of industry, from scratch)* Entwicklung *f*; *(= expansion)* Ausbau *m*; **industrial ~** Gewerbegebiet *nt*; **residential ~** Wohnsiedlung *f*; **office ~** Bürokomplex *m*; **business ~** Geschäftszentrum *nt*; **we live in a new ~** wir leben in einer neuen Siedlung; **unauthorized ~** illegale Baumaßnahmen *pl*
e *(Phot, Math)* Entwicklung *f*

development aid N Aufbauhilfe *f*, Entwicklungshilfe *f*

developmental [dɪveləpˈmentl] ADJ Entwicklungs-; **~ stage** Entwicklungsphase *f*; **~ assistance** Aufbauhilfe *f*, Entwicklungshilfe *f*

development: **development area** N Entwicklungsgebiet *nt*; *(in town)* Erschließungsgebiet *nt*; *(in old town)* Sanierungsgebiet *nt*; **development company** N (Wohnungs)baugesellschaft *f*; **development costs** PL Erschließungskosten *pl*; **development cycle** N *(Comm, Biol)* Entwicklungszyklus *m*; **development grant** N Entwicklungsförderung *f*

deviancy [ˈdiːvɪənsɪ] N abweichendes Verhalten, Devianz *f*

deviant [ˈdiːvɪənt] ADJ *behaviour* abweichend, deviant *(spec)* N *jd, der von der Norm abweicht*, Deviant *m (spec)*

deviate [ˈdiːvɪeɪt] VI **a** *(person: from truth, former statement, routine)* abweichen *(from* von*)*
b *(ship, plane, projectile)* vom Kurs abweichen *or* abkommen; *(deliberately)* vom Kurs abgehen

deviation [ˌdiːvɪˈeɪʃən] N Abweichen *nt*, Abweichung *f*; **~ from the norm** Abweichung *f* von der Norm

deviationism [ˌdiːvɪˈeɪʃənɪzəm] N Abweichlertum *nt*

deviationist [ˌdiːvɪˈeɪʃənɪst] ADJ abweichend N Abweichler(in) *m(f)*

device [dɪˈvaɪs] N **a** *(= gadget etc)* Gerät *nt*; *(= extra fitment)* Vorrichtung *f*; **(explosive) ~** Sprengkörper *m*; **nuclear ~** atomarer Sprengkörper; **a rhetorical ~** ein rhetorischer Kunstgriff **b to leave sb to his own ~s** jdn sich *(dat)* selbst überlassen **c** *(= emblem)* Emblem *nt*; *(= motto)* Motto *nt*, Devise *f*

device driver N *(Comput)* Gerätetreiber *m*

devil [ˈdevl] N **a** *(= evil spirit)* Teufel *m*
b *(inf: = person, child)* Teufel *m (inf)*; *(= object, screw etc)* Plage *f*; *(= daring person)* Teufelskerl *m*; **you poor ~!** (du) armer Teufel!; **you little ~!** du kleiner Satansbraten!; **shall I have another? – go on, be a ~** soll ich noch einen trinken *etc*? – los, nur zu, riskiers! *(inf)*; **be a ~ and say yes** riskier mal was und sag ja *or* Ja
c *(inf, as intensifier)* **I had a ~ of a job getting here** es war verdammt schwierig, hierherzukommen *(inf)*; **he had a ~ of a time selling his car** er hatte schreckliche Schwierigkeiten, sein Auto zu verkaufen; **I live a ~ of a long way away** ich wohne verdammt weit weg; **the ~ of it is ...** das Ärgerliche daran ist ... *(inf)*; **how/what/why/who the ~ ...?** wie/was/warum/wer zum Teufel *or* in drei Teufels Namen ...?; **to work like the ~** wie ein Pferd schuften *(inf)*; **to run/drive like the ~** wie ein geölter Blitz sausen/fahren *(inf)*; **there will be the ~ to pay** das dicke Ende kommt nach
d *(in expressions)* **(to be) between the Devil and the deep blue sea** (sich) in einer Zwickmühle (befinden); **go to the ~!** *(inf)* scher dich zum Teufel! *(inf)*; **the ~ take him/it** *(old inf)* der Teufel soll ihn/es holen *(old inf)*, hols der Teufel *(inf)*; **the ~ finds work for idle hands** *(Prov)* Müßiggang ist aller Laster Anfang *(Prov)*; **he has the ~ in him today** ihn reitet heute der Teufel; **to sell one's soul to the ~** dem Teufel seine Seele verkaufen; **speak** *or* **talk** *(Brit)* **of the ~!** wenn man vom Teufel spricht!; **give the ~ his due** das muss der Neid ihm lassen; **to have the ~'s own luck** *or* **the luck of the ~** *(inf)* ein Schweineglück *(inf) or* unverschämtes Glück haben; **better the ~ you know (than the ~ you don't)** *(prov)* von zwei Übeln wählt man besser das, was man schon kennt; **(the) ~ take the hindmost** den Letzten beißen die Hunde *(Prov)*
VI *(Jur, Typ, Liter etc)* Handlangerdienste tun
VT *(Cook) kidneys* scharf gewürzt grillen

devil fish N *(= ray)* Rochen *m*; *(= octopus)* Tintenfisch *m*

devilish [ˈdevlɪʃ] ADJ teuflisch; *chuckle, grin* schalkhaft, verschmitzt ADV *(dated inf, = extremely)* verteufelt *(dated inf)*; **~ funny** urkomisch

devilishly [ˈdevlɪʃlɪ] ADV **a** = **devilish ADV b** *chuckle, grin* schalkhaft, verschmitzt

devilishness [ˈdevlɪʃnɪs] N Teuflische(s) *nt (of* an *+dat)*; *(of chuckle, grin)* Schalkhaftigkeit *f*, Verschmitztheit *f*

devil-may-care [ˌdevlmeɪˈkeəˈ] ADJ leichtsinnig, vollständig unbekümmert; **he's got a ~ attitude to life** seine Lebenseinstellung ist „Nach mir die Sintflut"

devilment [ˈdevlmənt] N (grober) Unfug; **just for ~** aus lauter Übermut; **her eyes twinkled with ~** ihre Augen blitzten voller Übermut

devilry [ˈdevlrɪ] N **a** *(= mischief)* (grober) Unfug **b** *(= black magic)* Teufelskunst *f* **c** *(= extreme wickedness, cruelty)* Teufelei *f*

devil: **devil's advocate** N des Teufels Advokat *m*, Advocatus Diaboli *m*; **to play ~** den Advocatus Diaboli spielen; **devil's food cake** N *(esp US)* schwere Schokoladentorte; **devils-on-horseback** [ˌdevlzɒnˈhɔːsbæk] PL *(Cook) mit Speckscheiben umwickelte Backpflaumen auf Toast*

devious [ˈdiːvɪəs] ADJ **a** *(= deceitful, sly) person* verschlagen, hinterhältig; *means, method* hinterhältig, krumm *(inf)*; *business, plan, game, attempt* trickreich; **by ~ means** auf die krumme Tour *(inf)*; **to have a ~ mind** *(= be cunning)* ganz schön schlau sein; **his/her ~ mind** seine/ihre verschlungenen Gehirnwindungen **b** *(= tortuous) route, way* gewunden; **by a ~ route** auf einem Umweg

deviously [ˈdiːvɪəslɪ] ADV *(+vb)* mit List und Tücke

deviousness [ˈdiːvɪəsnɪs] N **a** *(= deceitfulness)* Verschlagenheit *f*, Hinterhältigkeit *f*; **the ~ of his mind** seine verschlungenen Gedankengänge *pl* **b** *(= tortuousness)* Gewundenheit *f*

devise [dɪˈvaɪz] VT **a** *scheme, style* sich *(dat)* ausdenken; *way, means* finden; *plan* schmieden; *strategy, policy* ausarbeiten **b** *(Jur)* hinterlassen, vermachen N *(Jur)* Vermächtnis *nt*, Hinterlassenschaft *f*

devitalization [diːˌvaɪtəlaɪˈzeɪʃən] N Schwächung *f*

devitalize [diːˈvaɪtəlaɪz] VT schwächen

devoid [dɪˈvɔɪd] ADJ **~ of** bar *+gen*, ohne

devoir [dəˈvwɑː] N *(form, liter)* **a** *(= duty)* Pflicht *f*; **to do one's ~** seine Pflicht tun **b** *(= respect)* Höflichkeit *f*

devolution [ˌdiːvəˈluːʃən] N **a** *(of power)* Übertragung *f (from … to* von … auf *+acc); (Pol)* Dezentralisierung *f* **b** *(Jur, of property, = active devolving)* Übertragung *f; (= being devolved)* Übergang *m* **c** *(Biol)* Rückentwicklung *f*, Degeneration *f*

> **DEVOLUTION**
>
> Innerhalb des politischen Systems Großbritanniens bezieht sich der Begriff **devolution** auf den Dezentralisierungsprozess, das Delegieren von Machtbefugnissen aus dem traditionellen Regierungssitz in London in die Hauptstädte von Schottland (Edinburgh) und Wales (Cardiff). Allerdings ist heftig umstritten, wie weit dieser Prozess gehen soll. Einige hätten am liebsten eigene gesetzgebende Versammlungen für Schottland und Wales innerhalb des Verbandes von Großbritannien, während die Nationalisten anstelle der **devolution** absolute Unabhängigkeit und Eigenstaatlichkeit fordern.

devolve [dɪˈvɒlv] *(on, upon* auf *+acc)* **VI** *(duty, property etc)* übergehen; **the cost of the operation ~s upon the patient** die Kosten für die Operation muss der Patient tragen; **it ~d on me to take the final decision** die endgültige Entscheidung fiel mir zu; **the union ~d into a looser confederation of states** die Union löste sich in einen lockeren Staatenbund auf **VT** *duty, power etc* übertragen; **a ~d government** eine dezentralisierte Regierung

devote [dɪˈvəʊt] VT *time, life, oneself, book, chapter, attention* widmen *(to dat); thought* verwenden *(to* auf *+acc); one's energies* konzentrieren *(to* auf *+acc); building* verwenden *(to* für*); resources* bestimmen *(to* für*)*

devoted [dɪˈvəʊtɪd] ADJ *wife, husband, mother, father* liebend; *servant, follower, fan* treu; *admirer* eifrig; **~ care** hingebungsvolle Pflege; **30 years of ~ service** dreißig Jahre treuer Dienste *(gen)*; **to be ~ to sb** jdn innig lieben; *(servant, fan)* jdm treu ergeben sein; **they are ~ to one another** sie lieben sich innig; **to be ~ to a cause** sich völlig für eine Sache engagieren; **to be ~ to one's family** in seiner Familie völlig aufgehen

devotedly [dɪˈvəʊtɪdlɪ] ADV hingebungsvoll; *serve, follow* treu; *support* eifrig

devotee [ˌdevəʊˈtiː] N Anhänger(in) *m(f); (of a writer)* Verehrer(in) *m(f); (of music, poetry)* Liebhaber(in) *m(f)*

devotion [dɪˈvəʊʃən] N **a** *(to friend, wife etc)* Ergebenheit *f (to* gegenüber*); (to work)* Hingabe *f (to an +acc)*; **~ to duty** Pflichteifer *m* **b** *(of part of building, time etc) (to* für*)* Verwendung *f; (of resources)* Bestimmung *f* **c devotions** PL *(Rel)* Andacht *f*; **to be at one's ~s** in Andacht versunken sein

devotional [dɪˈvəʊʃənl] ADJ *book, literature* religiös; **~ objects** Devotionalien *pl*

devour [dɪˈvaʊəʳ] VT *(lit, fig)* verschlingen; **I could ~ you** ich habe dich zum Fressen gern, du bist wirklich zum Fressen; **to be ~ed by jealousy/an all-consuming passion** von Eifersucht/einer unersättlichen Leidenschaft verzehrt werden

devouring [dɪˈvaʊərɪŋ] ADJ *hunger, passion* verzehrend

devout [dɪˈvaʊt] **ADJ** *person, Christian, Muslim* fromm; *Christianity, Catholicism, Marxist, environmentalist, follower* überzeugt; *supporter* treu; *opponent* eingeschworen; **it was my father's ~ wish/hope that …** es war der inständige Wunsch/die sehnliche Hoffnung meines Vaters, dass …, mein Vater wünschte sich inständig/hoffte sehnlich, dass … **N the ~** die Frommen

devoutly [dɪˈvaʊtlɪ] ADV **a** *(Rel, +adj)* tief; *(+vb)* fromm; **~ religious** tiefreligiös; **a ~ Christian prince** ein frommer christlicher Prinz; **he ~ followed the Catholic faith** er blieb dem katholischen Glauben treu **b** *(= sincerely) believe* ernsthaft; *wish* sehnlich; *hope* inständig

dew [djuː] N Tau *m*

dewater [ˌdiːˈwɔtəʳ] VT entwässern

dew: **dewberry** [ˈdjuːbərɪ] N Brombeere *f*; **dewclaw** N Afterkralle *f*, Afterklaue *f*; **dewdrop** N Tautropfen *m*; **dewfall** N *(poet, liter)* Taufall *m; (= film of dew)* Tauschleier *m (poet)*; **dewlap** N *(on cow)* Wamme *f*; *(hum, on person)* Doppelkinn *nt*; **dew point** N *(Phys)* Taupunkt *m*; **dew pond** N *flacher Teich, der sich aus Regenwasser bildet*

dewy [ˈdjuːɪ] ADJ *(+er) grass, morning* taufeucht; *skin* taufrisch; **her eyes were ~** ihre Augen hatten einen feuchten Schimmer

dewy-eyed [ˈdjuːɪaɪd] ADJ *(= innocent, naive)* naiv; *(= trusting)* vertrauensselig; **to go** *or* **get all ~** feuchte Augen bekommen

dexterity [deksˈterɪtɪ] N Geschick *nt*

dexterous, **dextrous** [ˈdekstrəs] ADJ geschickt

dexterously [ˈdekstrəslɪ] ADV geschickt

dextrose [ˈdekstrəʊz] N Dextrose *f*, Traubenzucker *m*

DFC *abbr of* **Distinguished Flying Cross** *Militärorden für hervorragende Piloten*

DFE *(Brit) abbr of* **Department for Education** Ministerium *nt* für Bildung und Erziehung

dg *abbr of* **decigram(s), decigramme(s)** dg

dhow [daʊ] N D(h)au *f*

DHSS *(Brit, old) abbr of* **Department of Health and Social Security** Ministerium *nt* für Gesundheit und Soziales

diabesity [ˌdaɪəˈbiːsətɪ] N *(Med)* Diabetes *f* wegen Fettleibigkeit

diabetes [ˌdaɪəˈbiːtiːz] N Zuckerkrankheit *f*, Diabetes *m*, Zucker *no art (inf)*

diabetic [ˌdaɪəˈbetɪk] **ADJ** **a** zuckerkrank, diabetisch *(spec)*; **~ patient** Diabetespatient(in) *m(f)*; **~ coma** Diabetikerkoma *nt* **b** *beer, chocolate, drugs, clinic* für Diabetiker **N** Zuckerkranke(r) *mf*, Diabetiker(in) *m(f)*

diabolic [ˌdaɪəˈbɒlɪk], **diabolical** [ˌdaɪəˈbɒlɪkəl] ADJ **a** *(form: = satanic) forces* diabolisch *(geh)*, teuflisch; **with ~al cunning** mit ungeheurer Gerissenheit; **~ possession** Besessenheit *f* durch den Teufel **b** *(inf: = appalling)* entsetzlich; **~al weather** Sauwetter *nt (inf)*

diabolically [ˌdaɪəˈbɒlɪkəlɪ] ADV **a** *(inf: = incredibly) clever, difficult* teuflisch *(inf)*; *cunning* ungeheuer; **~ bad** entsetzlich (schlecht) **b** *(= wickedly) grin, smile* boshaft

diachronic [ˌdaɪəˈkrɒnɪk] ADJ diachron

diacritic [ˌdaɪəˈkrɪtɪk] **ADJ** diakritisch **N** diakritisches Zeichen

diacritical [ˌdaɪəˈkrɪtɪkəl] ADJ diakritisch

diadem [ˈdaɪədem] N Diadem *nt*

diaeresis, *(US)* **dieresis** [daɪˈerɪsɪs] N Diärese *f*; *(= sign)* Trema *nt*

diagnose [ˈdaɪəgnəʊz] VT *(Med, fig)* diagnostizieren

diagnosis [ˌdaɪəgˈnəʊsɪs] N *pl* **diagnoses** [ˌdaɪəgˈnəʊsiːz] Diagnose *f*; **to make a ~** eine Diagnose stellen

diagnostic [ˌdaɪəgˈnɒstɪk] ADJ diagnostisch; **~ test bay** Diagnosestand *m*

diagnostician [ˌdaɪəgnɒsˈtɪʃən] N Diagnostiker(in) *m(f)*

diagnostics [ˌdaɪəgˈnɒstɪks] N *sing or pl* Diagnose *f*; **~ program** *(Comput)* Diagnoseprogramm *nt*

diagonal [daɪˈægənl] **ADJ** diagonal **N** Diagonale *f*

diagonally [daɪˈægənəlɪ] ADV diagonal; *(loosely: = crossways)* schräg; **he crossed the street ~** er ging schräg über die Straße; **~ across sth** *(walk)* schräg über etw *(acc)*; *be placed* schräg über etw *(dat)*; **~ across from** *or* **opposite sb/sth** jdm/einer Sache *(dat)* schräg gegenüber

diagram [ˈdaɪəgræm] N *(Math)* Diagramm *nt*; *(of machine etc)* Diagramm *nt*, Schaubild *nt*; *(= chart: of figures etc)* grafische Darstellung; **as shown in the ~** wie das Diagramm/die grafische Darstellung zeigt

diagrammatic [ˌdaɪəgrəˈmætɪk] ADJ diagrammatisch; **in ~ form** in einem Schaubild *or* Diagramm dargestellt; *(chart)* grafisch dargestellt

dial [ˈdaɪəl] ✪ 27.1, 27.2, 27.7 **N** **a** *(of clock)* Zifferblatt *nt*; *(of speedometer, pressure gauge)* Skala *f*; *(Telec)* Wähl- *or* Nummernscheibe *f*; *(on radio etc)* (Frequenzbereich-)Einstellskala *f* **b** *(inf, = face)* Visage *f (inf)* **VT** *(Telec)* wählen; **to ~ direct** durchwählen; **you can ~ London direct** man kann nach London durchwählen; **to ~ 999** den Notruf wählen; **to ~ a wrong number** eine falsche Nummer wählen, sich verwählen **VI** *(Telec)* wählen

dialect [ˈdaɪəlekt] **N** Dialekt *m*; *(local, rural also)* Mundart *f*; **the country people spoke in ~** die Landbevölkerung sprach Dialekt; **the play is in ~** das Stück ist in Dialekt *or* Mundart geschrieben **ATTR** Dialekt-; **~ word** Dialektausdruck *m*

dialectal [ˌdaɪəˈlektl] ADJ dialektal; *(local, rural also)* mundartlich

dialectical [ˌdaɪəˈlektɪkəl] ADJ dialektisch; **~ materialism** dialektischer Materialismus

dialectician [ˌdaɪəlekˈtɪʃən] N Dialektiker(in) *m(f)*

dialectic(s) [ˌdaɪəˈlektɪk(s)] N *with sing vb* Dialektik *f*

dialer [ˈdaɪələʳ] N *(Telec, Internet)* Dialer *m*

dialling [ˈdaɪəlɪŋ]: **dialling code** N *(Brit Telec)* Vorwahl(nummer) *f*, Ortsnetzkennzahl *f (form)*; **dialling tone** N *(Brit Telec)* Amts- *or* Freizeichen *nt*

dialogue, *(US)* **dialog** [ˈdaɪəlɒg] N *(all senses)* Dialog *m*; **~ box** *(Comput)* Dialogfeld *nt*; **~ coach** Dialogregisseur(in) *m(f)*

dial tone N *(US Telec)* Amts- *or* Freizeichen *nt*

dial-up [ˈdaɪəlʌp] ADJ *attr (Comput)* Wähl-; **~ link** Wählverbindung *f*; **~ modem** (Wähl)modem *nt*; **~ networking** DFÜ-Netzwerk *nt*

dialysis [daɪˈæləsɪs] N Dialyse *f*

diamanté [ˌdaɪəˈmæntɪ] N Strass *m*; *(rare, = fabric) mit Pailletten besetzter Stoff*

diameter [daɪˈæmɪtəʳ] N Durchmesser *m*; **to be one foot in ~** einen Durchmesser von einem Fuß haben; **what's its ~?** welchen Durchmesser hat es?, wie groß ist es im Durchmesser?

diametrical [ˌdaɪəˈmetrɪkəl] ADJ *(Math, fig)* diametral

diametrically [ˌdaɪəˈmetrɪkəlɪ] ADV **~ opposed (to sth)** (einer Sache *dat*) völlig *or* diametral *(geh)* entgegengesetzt; **their views are ~ opposed** sie haben völlig entgegengesetzte Ansichten

diamond [ˈdaɪəmənd] N **a** Diamant *m* → **rough diamond** **b diamonds** PL *(Cards)* Karo *nt*; **the ace/seven of ~s** das Karoass/die Karosieben **c** *(Baseball)* Innenfeld *nt* **d** *(Math: = rhombus)* Raute *f*

diamond *in cpds* Diamant-; **~ bracelet** Diamantarmband *nt*; **diamond cutter** N Diamantschneider(in) *m(f)*; *(Ind)* Diamantschleifer(in) *m(f)*; **diamond cutting** N Diamantschleifen *nt*; **diamond drill** N Diamantbohrer *m*; **diamond jubilee** N 60-jähriges Jubiläum; **diamond lane** N *(US) mit Raute gekennzeichnete Fahrspur, auf der nur Busse, Taxis und Privatautos mit mehr als einem Insassen fahren dürfen*; **diamond merchant** N Diamantenhändler(in) *m(f)*; **diamond-shaped** ADJ rautenförmig; **diamond wedding** N diamantene Hochzeit

Diana [daɪˈænə] N Diana *f*

dianthus [daɪˈænθəs] N *pl* **dianthuses** *(Bot)* Nelke *f*

diapason [ˌdaɪəˈpeɪzən] N *(also Mus)* Diapason *m or nt*; **open ~** Prinzipal *nt*; **stopped ~** gedacktes Prinzipal

diaper [ˈdaɪəpəʳ] N *(US)* Windel *f*

diaphanous [daɪˈæfənəs] ADJ durchscheinend

diaphragm [ˈdaɪəfræm] N *(Anat, Phys, Chem)* Diaphragma *nt*; *(abdominal)* Zwerchfell *nt*, Diaphragma *nt*; *(Phot)* Blende *f*; *(in telephone)* Membran *f*; *(= contraceptive)* Pessar *nt*

diarist ['daɪərɪst] N *(of personal events)* Tagebuchschreiber(in) *m(f)*; *(of contemporary events)* Chronist(in) *m(f)*

diarrhoea, *(US)* **diarrhea** [ˌdaɪə'riːə] N Durchfall *m*, Diarrhö(e) *f*; **verbal ~** geistiger Dünnschiss *(sl)*; **the speaker had verbal ~** der Redner hatte geistigen Dünnschiss *(sl)*

diary ['daɪərɪ] N *(of personal experience)* Tagebuch *nt*; *(for noting dates)* (Termin)kalender *m*; **to keep a ~** Tagebuch führen; **desk/pocket ~** Schreibtisch-/Taschenkalender *m*; **I've got it in my ~** es steht in meinem (Termin)kalender

diaspora [daɪ'æspərə] N Diaspora *f*

diastole [daɪ'æstəlɪ] N Diastole *f*

diastolic [daɪə'stɒlɪk] ADJ *(Physiol) blood pressure* diastolisch

diatonic [ˌdaɪə'tɒnɪk] ADJ diatonisch

diatribe ['daɪətraɪb] N Schmährede *f*

dibble ['dɪbl] N Pflanzholz *nt*, Setzholz *nt* VT *plant* setzen, pflanzen; *hole* machen, graben

dibs [dɪbz] PL *(sl)* **a** *(= claim)* Recht *nt*, Anspruch *m*; **I have ~ on that piece of cake** das Stück Kuchen steht mir zu **b** *(= money)* Knete *f (inf)*

dice [daɪs] N *pl* - Würfel *m*; **to play ~** Würfel spielen, würfeln; **to roll the ~** würfeln; **~ cup** *or* **box** Würfelbecher *m*; **no ~** *(esp US inf)* (das) ist nicht drin *(inf)* VI würfeln; **to ~ with death/danger** mit dem Tode/der Gefahr spielen VT *(Cook)* würfelig *or* in Würfel schneiden

dicey ['daɪsɪ] ADJ *(inf)* riskant

dichotomy [dɪ'kɒtəmɪ] N Trennung *f*, Dichotomie *f*

dick [dɪk] N **a** *(inf: = detective)* Schnüffler(in) *m(f) (inf)*; **private ~** Privatdetektiv(in) *m(f)* → **clever Dick b** *(sl: = bastard)* Wichser *m (sl)* **c** *(sl: = penis)* Schwanz *m (sl)*

dickens ['dɪkɪnz] N *(euph inf: = devil)* Teufel *m* → **devil N c**

Dickensian [dɪ'kenzɪən] ADJ *character, novel* dickenssch *attr*; *(= old-fashioned) building, style* antiquiert; **it's all very ~** das ist alles wie aus einem Roman von Dickens

dicker ['dɪkə'] VI *(US)* feilschen

dickey, dicky ['dɪkɪ] N **a** *(inf, on shirt)* Hemdbrust *f*; *(= bow tie)* Fliege *f* **b** *(also* **dickey seat***)* Notsitz *m (in einem Zweisitzer)*

dickhead ['dɪkhed] N *(sl pej)* Idiot *m (pej)*

dicky ['dɪkɪ] ADJ *(inf) heart* angeknackst *(inf)*; **I feel a bit ~** *(dated)* ich bin ziemlich ab *(inf) or* erschossen *(inf)* N = **dickey**

dickybird ['dɪkɪbɜːd] N *(Brit, baby-talk)* Piepmatz *m (baby-talk)*; **I haven't heard a ~ from him** *(inf)* ich habe keinen Ton von ihm gehört

dicta ['dɪktə] *pl of* **dictum**

Dictaphone® ['dɪktəfəʊn] N Diktaphon *nt*, Diktafon *nt*

dictate [dɪk'teɪt] VT diktieren; **reason/common sense ~s that …** die Vernunft/der gesunde Menschenverstand sagt uns, dass … VI diktieren ['dɪkteɪt] N *usu pl* Diktat *nt*; *(of reason)* Gebote *pl*

▶ **dictate to** VI *+prep obj person* diktieren *(+dat)*, Vorschriften machen *(+dat)*; **I won't be dictated to** ich lasse mir nicht diktieren, ich lasse mir keine Vorschriften machen

dictation [dɪk'teɪʃən] N *(also Sch)* Diktat *nt*; **to take (down) ~** ein Diktat aufnehmen; **to read at ~ speed** in Diktiertempo lesen

dictator [dɪk'teɪtə'] N **a** *(Pol, fig)* Diktator(in) *m(f)* **b** *(of letter, passage)* Diktierende(r) *mf*

dictatorial ADJ, **dictatorially** ADV [ˌdɪktə'tɔːrɪəl, -ɪ] diktatorisch

dictatorship [dɪk'teɪtəʃɪp] N *(Pol, fig)* Diktatur *f*

diction ['dɪkʃən] N **a** *(Liter)* Diktion *f*; **poetic ~** poetische Sprache **b** *(= way of speaking)* Diktion *f*

dictionary ['dɪkʃənrɪ] N Wörterbuch *nt*

dictum ['dɪktəm] N *pl* **dicta** Diktum *nt*

did [dɪd] PRET *of* **do**[2]

didactic [dɪ'dæktɪk] ADJ didaktisch

didactically [dɪ'dæktɪkəlɪ] ADV didaktisch

diddle ['dɪdl] VT *(Brit inf)* übers Ohr hauen *(inf)*, beschummeln; **you have been ~d** man hat Sie übers Ohr gehauen; **to ~ sb out of sth** jdm etw abgaunern *(inf)*

diddler ['dɪdlə'] N *(inf)* Spitzbube *m*, Gauner *m*

diddly-squat ['dɪdlɪ'skwɒt] N *(US inf)* nix *(inf)*; **he knows diddly squat about cooking** er hat keinen blassen Schimmer vom Kochen *(inf)*; **I don't think any of these films mean ~** ich glaube nicht, dass diese Filme irgendwas bedeuten

diddums ['dɪdəmz] INTERJ *(inf)* du Armer/Arme

didn't ['dɪdənt] = **did not**, → **do**[2]

didst [dɪdst] *(obs)* = **didst thou** → **do**[2]

die[1] [daɪ] VI **a** *(lit)* sterben; *(soldier)* fallen, sterben; *(motor, engine)* absterben; *(planet)* vergehen; **to ~ of** *or* **from hunger/pneumonia/grief** vor Hunger/an Lungenentzündung/vor *or* aus Kummer sterben; **to ~ for one's country** für sein Land sterben; **he ~d from his injuries** er erlag seinen Verletzungen; **to ~ by one's own hand** von eigener Hand sterben, Hand an sich *(acc)* legen; **he ~d of a broken heart** er starb an einem gebrochenen Herzen; **he ~d happy/a hero** er starb glücklich/als Held; **to be dying** im Sterben liegen; **never say ~!** nur nicht aufgeben!; **to ~ laughing** *(inf)* sich totlachen *(inf)*; **I'd rather** *or* **sooner ~!** *(inf)* lieber würde ich sterben!; **a dress to ~ for** *(inf)* ein unwiderstehliches *or* umwerfendes *(inf)* Kleid

b *(fig inf: = long)* **to be dying to do sth** darauf brennen, etw zu tun, brennend gern etw tun wollen; **I'm dying to know what happened** ich bin schrecklich gespannt zu hören, was passiert ist; **he's dying to meet you** er möchte Sie brennend gern kennenlernen; **she's dying to get home** sie brennt darauf, heimzukommen; **I'm dying for a cigarette** ich brauche jetzt unbedingt eine Zigarette; **I'm dying of thirst** ich verdurste fast; **I'm dying for him to visit** ich kann seinen Besuch kaum noch abwarten

c *(fig, love)* vergehen, ersterben *(geh)*, erlöschen *(geh)*; *(memory)* (ver)schwinden; *(custom)* aussterben; *(empire)* untergehen; **the secret ~d with him** er nahm das Geheimnis mit ins Grab; **old habits ~ hard** alte Gewohnheiten legt man nur schwer ab

VT **to ~ a hero's/a violent death** den Heldentod/eines gewaltsamen Todes sterben; **to ~ the death** *(plan etc)* sterben *(inf)*

▶ **die away** VI *(sound, voice)* schwächer *or* leiser werden; *(wind)* nachlassen, sich legen; *(anger)* sich legen, vergehen

▶ **die back** VI absterben

▶ **die down** VI nachlassen; *(fire)* herunterbrennen; *(flames)* kleiner werden; *(storm, wind)* sich legen, nachlassen; *(noise)* leiser werden, schwächer werden; *(emotion also)* sich legen; *(quarrel, protest)* nachlassen, schwächer werden

▶ **die off** VI (hin)wegsterben; *(animals, people also)* (der Reihe nach) sterben

▶ **die out** VI aussterben

die[2] N **a** *pl* **dice** *(form)* Würfel *m*; **the ~ is cast** *(prov)* die Würfel sind gefallen → *also* **dice b** *pl* **-s** *(Tech)* Gesenk *nt*, Gussform *f*; *(in minting)* Prägestempel *m*

die casting N *(= article)* Spritzguss *m*, Spritzgussstück *nt*; *(= process)* Spritzgussverfahren *nt*

die-hard ['daɪhɑːd] N zäher Kämpfer, zähe Kämpferin; *(= resistant to change)* Ewiggestrige(r) *mf* ADJ zäh; *(pej)* reaktionär

dielectric [ˌdaɪɪ'lektrɪk] ADJ dielektrisch

dieresis N *(US)* = **diaeresis**

diesel ['diːzəl] N *(= train)* Dieseltriebwagen *m*; *(= car)* Diesel *m*; *(= fuel)* Dieselöl *nt*, Diesel *no art*

diesel: **diesel-electric** ADJ dieselelektrisch; **diesel engine** N Dieselmotor *m*; **diesel oil** N Dieselöl *nt*; **diesel train** N Dieseltriebwagen *m*

die: **die sinker** N Werkzeugmacher(in) *m(f)*; **die stamp** N Prägestempel *m*

diet[1] ['daɪət] N Nahrung *f*; *(= special diet)* Diät *f*; *(= slimming diet)* Schlankheitskur *f*; **there's nothing wrong with my ~** meine Ernährung ist völlig in Ordnung; **to put sb on a ~/a special ~** jdm eine Schlankheitskur/eine Diät verordnen; **to be/go on a ~** eine Schlankheitskur machen; **high protein ~** proteinreiche Diät; **he lives on a ~ of hamburgers and chips** er ernährt sich von Hamburgern und Pommes frites; **to be fed (on) a ~ of sth** *(fig)* etw dauernd eingetrichtert bekommen; **she lives on a ~ of TV soap operas** sie macht nichts anderes als sich Fernsehserien anzusehen VI eine Schlankheitskur machen

diet[2] N *(= assembly)* Abgeordnetenversammlung *f*; **the German/Japanese ~** der deutsche/japanische Reichstag; **the Diet of Worms** der Reichstag zu Worms

dietary ['daɪətərɪ] ADJ Ernährungs-; **~ habits** Ernährungsgewohnheiten *pl*; **~ deficiency** ernährungsbedingte Mangelerscheinung

dietary fibre, *(US)* **dietary fiber** N Ballaststoff *m*

dietetic [ˌdaɪə'tetɪk] ADJ Diät-, diätetisch; **~ foods** Diätnahrungsmittel *pl*

dietetics [ˌdaɪə'tetɪks] N *sing* Diätlehre *f*, Diätetik *f*

dietician [ˌdaɪə'tɪʃən] N Diätist(in) *m(f)*, Ernährungswissenschaftler(in) *m(f)*

diet sheet N Diät-/Schlankheits(fahr)plan *m*

differ ['dɪfə'] VI **a** *(= be different)* sich unterscheiden *(from* von*)*; **tastes ~** die Geschmäcker sind verschieden; **I ~ from you in that …** ich unterscheide mich von Ihnen darin, dass … **b** *(= disagree)* **to ~ with sb on** *or* **over sth** über etw *(acc)* anderer Meinung sein als jd; **we ~ed sharply over that** darin waren wir völlig verschiedener Meinung → **agree, beg**

difference ['dɪfrəns] ✪ 5.4 N **a** Unterschied *m*; *(in age)* (Alters)unterschied *m (in, between* zwischen *+dat)*; **that makes a big ~ to me** das ist für mich ein großer Unterschied; **to make a ~ to** *or* **in sth** einen Unterschied bei etw machen; **that makes a big** *or* **a lot of ~, that makes all the ~** das ändert die Sache völlig, das gibt der Sache *(dat)* ein ganz anderes Gesicht; **co-operation makes all the ~** Zusammenarbeit macht viel aus; **a bottle of wine would make all the ~** es fehlt nur noch eine Flasche Wein dazu; **it makes all the ~ in the world** da liegt der entscheidende Unterschied; **what ~ does it make if …?** was macht es schon, wenn …?; **what ~ is that to you?** was macht dir das aus?; **it makes no ~, it doesn't make any ~** es ist egal; **it makes no ~ to me** das ist mir egal *or* einerlei; **for all the ~ it makes** obwohl es ja eigentlich egal ist; **I can't tell the ~** ich kann keinen Unterschied erkennen; **a job with a ~** *(inf)* ein Job, der mal was anderes ist

b *(between numbers, amounts)* Differenz *f*; **to pay the ~** die Differenz *or* den Rest(betrag) bezahlen; **to split the ~** sich *(dat)* die Differenz *or* den Rest(betrag) teilen

c *(= quarrel)* Differenz *f*, Auseinandersetzung *f*; **a ~ of opinion** eine Meinungsverschiedenheit; **to settle** *or* **resolve one's ~s** die Differenzen *or* Meinungsverschiedenheiten beilegen

different ['dɪfrənt] ADJ **a** andere(r, s), anders *pred (from, to* als*)*; *two people, things* verschieden, unterschiedlich; **completely ~** völlig verschieden; *(= changed)* völlig verändert; **that's ~!** das ist was anderes!; **in what way are they ~?** wie unterscheiden sie sich?; **to feel (like) a ~ person** ein ganz anderer Mensch sein; **to do something ~** etwas anderes tun; **that's quite a ~ matter** das ist etwas völlig anderes; **she's quite ~ from what you think** sie ist ganz anders, als Sie denken; **he wants to be ~** er will unbedingt anders sein *or* etwas Besonderes sein

b *(= various)* verschieden

ADV *think* anders; **he doesn't know any ~** er kennt es nicht anders; *(with behaviour)* er weiß es nicht besser

differential [ˌdɪfəˈrenʃəl] ADJ *(= different) rates of pay, treatment, diagnosis, effects* unterschiedlich; *(= distinguishing) feature* unterscheidend; ~ **pricing** *(Comm)* Preisdiskriminierung *f* N a *(= difference)* Unterschied *m* *(between* zwischen); *(Math)* Differenzial *nt*, Differential *nt*; **wage/salary** ~ Lohn-/Gehaltsunterschiede *or* -differenzen *pl* b *(Aut)* Differenzial(getriebe) *nt*, Differential(getriebe) *nt*

differential: **differential calculus** N *(Math)* Differenzialrechnung *f*, Differentialrechnung *f*; **differential coefficient** N *(Math)* Ableitung *f*; **differential equations** PL *(Math)* Differenzialgleichungen *pl*, Differentialgleichungen *pl*; **differential gear** N *(Aut)* Differenzial(getriebe) *nt*, Differential(getriebe) *nt*

differentially [ˌdɪfəˈrenʃəlɪ] ADV *(Tech)* differenzial, differential

differentiate [ˌdɪfəˈrenʃɪeɪt] ✪ 5.1 VT unterscheiden; *(Math)* differenzieren; **to ~ x and y/x from y** x und y voneinander/x von y unterscheiden VI unterscheiden, einen Unterschied machen, differenzieren; *(two things: = become different)* sich unterschiedlich *or* anders entwickeln; **to ~ between people** einen Unterschied zwischen Menschen machen

differentiation [ˌdɪfərenʃɪˈeɪʃən] N Unterscheidung *f*, Differenzierung *f*

differently [ˈdɪfrəntlɪ] ADV anders *(from* als); *(from one another)* unterschiedlich; **I was never treated ~ from the men** ich wurde nie anders als die Männer behandelt; **we all react ~ to stress** wir reagieren alle anders *or* unterschiedlich auf Stress; **~ priced seating areas** unterschiedlich teure Sitzbereiche; **~ priced books** Bücher mit unterschiedlichen Preisen

differently-abled [ˌdɪfrəntlɪˈeɪbld] ADJ *(euph)* behindert

difficult [ˈdɪfɪkəlt] ✪ 5.1, 26.3 ADJ a *(= hard) question, task, time* schwer, schwierig; *situation, writer, book* schwierig; **there's nothing ~ about it** das ist doch gar nicht schwer; **the ~ thing is that ...** die Schwierigkeit liegt darin, dass ...; **it was a ~ decision to make** es war eine schwere *or* schwierige Entscheidung; **it is not ~ to imagine** es ist nicht schwer, sich *(dat)* das vorzustellen; **it was ~ for him to leave her** es fiel ihm schwer, sie zu verlassen; **it's ~ for youngsters** *or* **youngsters find it ~ to get a job** junge Leute haben Schwierigkeiten, eine Stelle zu finden; **it's ~ to see what they could have done** es lässt sich schwer vorstellen, was sie hätten tun können; **it's ~ to deny that** es lässt sich kaum leugnen; **he's ~ to get on with** es ist schwer, mit ihm auszukommen; **it's ~ being a man today** es ist schwer, heute ein Mann zu sein; **to make it ~ for sb (to do sth)** es jdm nicht leicht machen(, etw zu tun); **to have a ~ time (doing sth)** Schwierigkeiten haben(, etw zu tun); **she's having a ~ time now she's on her own** jetzt, wo sie allein ist, hat sie es schwer; **to put sb in a ~ position** jdn in eine schwierige Lage bringen b *(= awkward) person, child* schwierig; **to be ~ (about sth)** (wegen etw) Schwierigkeiten machen; **he's just trying to be ~** er will nur Schwierigkeiten machen

difficulty [ˈdɪfɪkəltɪ] N Schwierigkeit *f*; **with/without ~** mit/ohne Schwierigkeiten; **he had ~ (in) setting up in business** es fiel ihm schwer *or* nicht leicht, sich selbstständig zu machen; **she had great ~ (in) breathing** sie konnte kaum atmen; **there was some ~ (in) finding him** es war schwierig *or* nicht leicht, ihn zu finden; **the ~ is (in) choosing** *or* **to choose** die Wahl ist nicht leicht; **they hadn't appreciated the ~ of finding somewhere to live** sie hatten nicht bedacht, wie schwierig es sein würde, eine Wohnung zu finden; **in ~** *or* **difficulties** in Schwierigkeiten; **to get into difficulties** in Schwierigkeiten geraten; **to get out of difficulties** Schwierigkeiten überwinden

diffidence [ˈdɪfɪdəns] N Bescheidenheit *f*, Zurückhaltung *f*; *(of smile)* Zaghaftigkeit *f*

diffident [ˈdɪfɪdənt] ADJ zurückhaltend, bescheiden; *smile* zaghaft; **he was ~ about offering his help** er hat zaghaft seine Hilfe angeboten

diffidently [ˈdɪfɪdəntlɪ] ADV zaghaft

diffract [dɪˈfrækt] VT beugen

diffraction [dɪˈfrækʃən] N Diffraktion *f*, Beugung *f*

diffuse [dɪˈfjuːz] VT *light, heat, gas, rays* ausstrahlen, verbreiten; *fluid* ausgießen, ausschütten; *(Chem)* diffundieren, verwischen; *perfume* verbreiten, verströmen; *(fig) knowledge, custom, news* verbreiten; *tension* verringern, abbauen VI ausstrahlen, sich ver- *or* ausbreiten; *(fluid)* sich ausbreiten; *(Chem)* diffundieren, sich verwischen; *(perfume, odour)* ausströmen; *(fig, custom, news)* sich verbreiten; *(tension)* sich verringern [dɪˈfjuːs] ADJ a *gas, rays, light* diffus; *feeling* undeutlich, vage b *(= verbose) style, writer* langatmig, weitschweifig

diffused [dɪˈfjuːzd] ADJ verbreitet; *lighting* indirekt

diffuseness [dɪˈfjuːsnɪs] N *(of style)* Weitschweifigkeit *f*

diffuser [dɪˈfjuːzəʳ] N *(for light)* (Licht)diffusor *m*

diffusion [dɪˈfjuːʒən] N *(of light, heat, rays, fluid etc)* Ausbreitung *f*; *(Chem)* Diffusion *f*; *(of perfume, odour)* Ausströmung *f*; *(of knowledge, custom, news)* Verbreitung *f*

dig [dɪg] *vb: pret, ptp* **dug** VT a *ground* graben; *garden* umgraben; *grave* ausheben; *trench, hole, tunnel etc* graben, ausheben; **to ~ potatoes** Kartoffeln roden; **they dug their way out of prison** sie gruben sich *(dat)* einen (Flucht)tunnel aus dem Gefängnis
b *(= poke, thrust)* bohren *(sth into sth* etw in etw *acc)*; **to ~ sb in the ribs** jdm *or* jdn in die Rippen stoßen
c *(inf: = enjoy)* stehen auf *(+dat) (inf)*; *(= understand)* kapieren *(inf)*
VI a *(person)* graben; *(dog, pig)* wühlen, graben; *(Tech)* schürfen; *(Archeol)* (aus)graben, Ausgrabungen machen; **to ~ for minerals** Erz schürfen; **to ~ in one's pockets for sth** in seinen Taschen nach etw suchen *or* wühlen; **to ~ deep** *(Sport, fig)* auf seine letzten Reserven zurückgreifen; *(fig, in one's memory)* lange überlegen; *(= investigate)* gründlich nachforschen
b *(inf, = taunt)* **to ~ at sb** jdn anschießen *or* anmotzen *(inf)*
N a *(Brit: with hand, elbow)* Puff *m*, Stoß *m*; **to give sb a ~ in the ribs** jdm einen Rippenstoß geben
b *(Brit: = sarcastic remark)* Seitenhieb *m*, Spitze *f*; **to have a ~ at sb/sth** eine spitze Bemerkung über jdn/etw machen
c *(Archeol)* (Aus)grabung *f*; *(= site)* Ausgrabungsstätte *f*

▶ **dig around** VI *(inf)* herumsuchen

▶ **dig in** VI a *(also* **dig oneself in**: *Mil, fig)* sich eingraben; **the pickets are digging in for a long strike** die Streikposten stellen sich auf einen langen Streik ein b *(inf: = eat)* reinhauen *(inf)* VT *sep* a *compost* unter- *or* eingraben b *(Mil) troops, tanks* eingraben c **to dig one's heels in** *(lit)* die Hacken in den Boden stemmen; *(fig)* sich auf die Hinterbeine stellen *(inf)*

▶ **dig into** VI *+prep obj* a *(inf) cake, pie* herfallen über *(+acc) (inf)* b *sb's past* wühlen in *(+dat)* c **to dig (deep) into one's pockets** *or* **purse** *(fig)* tief in die Tasche greifen

▶ **dig out** VT *sep (lit, fig)* ausgraben (*of* aus)

▶ **dig over** VT *sep soil, garden* umgraben

▶ **dig up** VT *sep* a *earth* aufwühlen; *lawn, garden* umgraben b *plants, treasure, body, idea* ausgraben; *weeds* (aus)jäten; *(fig) fact, information* ausgraben, auftun; *solution* finden; **where did you dig her up?** *(inf)* wo hast du die denn aufgegabelt? *(inf)*

digest [daɪˈdʒest] VT *(lit, fig)* verdauen VI verdauen N [ˈdaɪdʒest] a *(of book, facts)* Digest *m or nt*, Auswahl *f* b *(Jur)* Gesetzessammlung *f*

digestible [dɪˈdʒestɪbl] ADJ verdaulich

digestion [dɪˈdʒestʃən] N Verdauung *f*

digestive [dɪˈdʒestɪv] ADJ Verdauungs- N a *(US: = aperitif)* Aperitif *m* b *(Brit)* = **digestive biscuit**

digestive biscuit N *(Brit) Keks aus Roggenmehl*

digestive system Verdauungsapparat *m or* -system *nt*

digger [ˈdɪgəʳ] N a *(person, = miner)* Bergmann *m*, Goldgräber *m*; *(= navvy)* Straßenarbeiter *m*; *(Tech: = excavator)* Bagger *m* b *(inf)* australischer/neuseeländischer Soldat; *(Austral, inf, = pal)* Kumpel *m*

diggings [ˈdɪgɪŋz] PL a *(Min)* Bergwerk *nt*; *(= minerals)* Funde *pl*; *(Archeol)* Grabungsort *m* b *(dated US)* = **digs**

digicam [ˈdɪdʒɪkæm] N *(Comput)* Digitalkamera *f*, Digicam *f*

digit [ˈdɪdʒɪt] N a *(= finger)* Finger *m*; *(= toe)* Zehe *f* b *(Math)* Ziffer *f*; **a four-~ number** eine vierstellige Zahl

digital [ˈdɪdʒɪtəl] ADJ a *clock, computer* Digital-; **~ display** Digitalanzeige *f*; **~ technology** Digitaltechnik *f* b *(Anat)* Finger- N *(of piano, organ)* Taste *f*

digital: **digital audio tape** N DAT-Band *nt*; **digital cable** N *(TV)* Digitalkabel *nt*; **digital camera** N digitale Kamera, Digitalkamera *f*; **digital compact cassette** N digitale Compactkassette *f*, DCC *f*

digitalin [ˌdɪdʒɪˈteɪlɪn] N Digitalis *nt*

digitalis [ˌdɪdʒɪˈteɪlɪs] N Digitalis *f*

digitalization [ˌdɪdʒɪtəlaɪˈzeɪʃən] N Digitalisierung *f*

digitally [ˈdɪdʒɪtəlɪ] ADV digital; **~ remastered** digital aufbereitet; **~ recorded** im Digitalverfahren aufgenommen

digital: **digital photo** N digitales Foto, Digitalfoto *nt*; **digital projector** N Beamer *m*; **digital radio** N digitales Radio; **digital recording** N Digitalaufnahme *f*; **digital television**, **digital TV** N digitales Fernsehen; **digital video recorder** N digitaler Videorekorder

digitize [ˈdɪdʒɪtaɪz] VT *(Comput)* digitalisieren

digitizer [ˈdɪdʒɪtaɪzəʳ] N *(Comput)* Digitalisierer *m*

dignified [ˈdɪgnɪfaɪd] ADJ *person* (ehr)würdig; *behaviour, manner, face* würdevoll; **he maintained a ~ silence** er schwieg würdevoll; **she made a ~ exit** sie machte einen würdevollen Abgang

dignify [ˈdɪgnɪfaɪ] VT ehren, auszeichnen; **to ~ sb/sth with the name of ...** jdn/etw mit dem anspruchsvollen Namen ... belegen

dignitary [ˈdɪgnɪtərɪ] N Würdenträger(in) *m(f)*; **the local dignitaries** die Honoratioren am Ort

dignity [ˈdɪgnɪtɪ] N a *(of person, occasion, work)* Würde *f*; **to die with ~** in Würde sterben; **to stand on one's ~** förmlich sein; **to lose one's ~** sich blamieren; **that would be beneath my ~** das wäre unter meiner Würde b *(= high rank, post)* Rang *m*, (hohe) Stellung; *(= title)* Würde *f*

digraph [ˈdaɪgræf] N Digraph *m*

digress [daɪˈgres] VI abschweifen

digression [daɪˈgreʃən] N Abschweifung *f*, Exkurs *m*; **this by way of a ~** aber das nur nebenbei

digressive [daɪˈgresɪv] ADJ abschweifend, abweichend

digs [dɪgz] PL *(Brit)* Bude *f (inf)*; **to be** *or* **live in ~** ein möbliertes Zimmer *or* eine Bude *(inf)* haben

dihedral [daɪˈhiːdrəl] ADJ zweiflächig N V-Winkel *m*; *(Aviat)* V-Stellung *f*

dike [daɪk] N VT = **dyke**

dilapidated [dɪˈlæpɪdeɪtɪd] ADJ *building* verfallen, heruntergekommen, baufällig; *book, clothes* schäbig

dilapidation [dɪˌlæpɪˈdeɪʃən] N a *(of building)* Baufälligkeit *f*, Verfall *m*; *(of book, clothes)* Schäbigkeit *f*; **in a state of ~** in schlechtem Zustand b *(Geol)* Verwitterung *f*

dilatation [ˌdaɪləˈteɪʃən], **dilation** [daɪˈleɪʃən] N Ausdehnung *f*, Erweiterung *f*; *(of pupils)* Erweiterung *f*; **~ and curettage** Dilation und Kürettage *f (spec)*, Ausschabung *f*

dilate [daɪˈleɪt] VT weiten, dehnen; **~d pupils** erweiterte Pupillen *pl* VI sich weiten, sich dehnen; *(pupils)* sich erweitern; **to ~ (up)on** *(= talk at length)* sich verbreiten über *(+acc)*

dilation [daɪˈleɪʃən] N Ausdehnung *f*, Erweiterung *f*; *(of pupils)* Erweiterung *f*

dilatoriness [ˈdɪlətərɪnɪs] N Langsamkeit *f*, Zögern *nt (in doing sth* etw zu tun)

dilatory [ˈdɪlətərɪ] ADJ a *person* langsam; *reply* verspätet; **to be ~** sich *(dat)* Zeit lassen; **he was rather ~ in answering** er ließ sich mit der Antwort Zeit b *(= delaying)* **~ policy** Hinhaltepolitik *f*; **~ tactics** Hinhalte- *or* Verzögerungstaktik *f*

dildo [ˈdɪldəʊ] N Godemiché *m*

dilemma [daɪˈlemə] N Dilemma *nt*; **to be in a ~** sich in einem Dilemma befinden, in der Klemme sitzen *(inf)*; **to place sb in a ~** jdn in eine Klemme *(inf) or* ein Dilemma bringen; **he is faced with a serious ~** er steht vor einem ernsten Dilemma

dilettante [ˌdɪlɪˈtæntɪ] N *pl* **dilettanti** [ˌdɪlɪˈtæntɪ] Amateur(in) *m(f)*, Dilettant(in) *m(f)*; *(Art)* Kunstliebhaber(in) *m(f)* ADJ amateurhaft, stümperhaft

dilettantism [ˌdɪlɪˈtæntɪzəm] N Dilettantismus *m*, Kunstliebhaberei *f*

diligence [ˈdɪlɪdʒəns] N *(in work etc)* Fleiß *m*; *(= keenness)* Eifer *m*

diligent [ˈdɪlɪdʒənt] ADJ *person (in work etc)* fleißig; *(= keen)* eifrig; *search, work* sorgfältig, genau; **to be ~ in doing sth** etw eifrig tun

diligently [ˈdɪlɪdʒəntlɪ] ADV fleißig; *(= keenly)* eifrig; *(= carefully)* sorgfältig

dill [dɪl] N Dill *m*

dill pickle N saure Gurke *(mit Dill eingelegt)*

dilly-dally [ˈdɪlɪdælɪ] VI *(over work etc)* trödeln; *(when walking also)* bummeln; **without ~ing** ohne zu trödeln/bummeln; **no ~ing!** ein bisschen dalli!

dilute [daɪˈluːt] VT *orange juice, milk etc* verdünnen; *colour* dämpfen, abschwächen; *(fig)* mildern, (ab)schwächen; *power, influence* schwächen; **~ to taste** nach Geschmack verdünnen ADJ verdünnt

dilution [daɪˈluːʃən] N *(of orange juice, milk etc)* Verdünnung *f*; *(of colour)* Dämpfung *f*, Abschwächung *f*; *(fig)* Milderung *f*; *(of power, influence)* Schwächung *f*

diluvial [daɪˈluːvɪəl], **diluvian** [daɪˈluːvɪən] ADJ (Sint)flut-, sintflutartig

dim [dɪm] ADJ *(+er)* a *(= not bright) light, lamp* schwach, trüb; *metal* matt, glanzlos; *(= badly lit) room* dämmerig, dunkel; **the room grew ~** im Zimmer wurde es dunkel
b *(= vague) figure, shape* undeutlich; *outline* schwach, undeutlich; *memory, recollection* dunkel; **I have a ~ memory** *or* **recollection of it** ich erinnere mich nur (noch) dunkel daran; **to have a ~ awareness of sth** sich *(dat)* einer Sache *(gen)* nur undeutlich bewusst sein
c *(= gloomy) prospects, outlook* schlecht; **it's a ~ lookout for him** es sieht sehr schlecht für ihn aus; **to take a ~ view of sth** mit etw gar nicht einverstanden sein
d *(inf: = stupid)* beschränkt *(inf)*, schwer von Begriff *(inf)*
e *(liter) eyes* trüb *(liter)*
VT a *(= turn down) light* dämpfen; *lamp* verdunkeln; **to ~ the lights** *(Theat)* das Licht langsam ausgehen lassen; **to ~ one's headlights** *(esp US)* abblenden
b *(= make dull) colour* dämpfen, decken; *sound* dämpfen; *metal* mattieren; *sight, mind, senses, memory* trüben; *beauty* verblassen lassen; *glory* beeinträchtigen
VI a *(light)* schwach *or* trübe werden; *(lamp)* verlöschen, dunkler werden
b *(= become dull, colour)* gedämpft *or* matter werden; *(sound)* leiser werden; *(metal)* mattiert werden; *(memory)* nachlassen; *(beauty)* verblassen; *(glory)* verblassen, vergehen; *(sight)* nachlassen, getrübt werden

▶ **dim out** VT *sep (US) city* verdunkeln

dime [daɪm] N *(US)* Zehncentstück *nt*; **it's not worth a ~** *(inf)* das ist keinen (roten) Heller *or* keine fünf Pfennig wert; **they're a ~ a dozen** *(inf)* das ist Dutzendware; **~ novel** Groschen- *or* Schundroman *m*; **to drop a ~ on sb** *(inf)* jdn verraten

dimension [daɪˈmenʃən] N Dimension *f*; *(= measurement)* Abmessung(en *pl*) *f*, Maß *nt*; **a problem of vast ~s** ein Problem größten Ausmaßes; **this adds a new ~ to his work** das gibt seiner Arbeit eine neue Dimension

-dimensional [-daɪˈmenʃənl] ADJ *suf* -dimensional; **one-/two-/three-dimensional** ein-/zwei-/dreidimensional

dime store N *(US)* Billigladen *m*, Billigkaufhaus *nt*

diminish [dɪˈmɪnɪʃ] VT a *(= reduce)* verringern; *price, authority* herabsetzen; *value, strength* (ver)mindern, verringern; *number* verkleinern; *enthusiasm* dämpfen; *reputation* schmälern; *power* einschränken
b *(Mus)* (um einen Halbton) vermindern; **~ed** vermindert
VI *(= be reduced)* sich verringern; *(speed, authority, strength)* abnehmen, sich vermindern; *(price)* fallen, sinken; *(value)* sich vermindern, sich verringern; *(number)* sich verkleinern; *(enthusiasm)* nachlassen; *(reputation)* schlechter werden; **law of ~ing returns** *(Econ)* Gesetz *nt* von der fallenden Profitrate; **to ~ in size** kleiner werden; **to ~ in value** im Wert sinken, an Wert verlieren

diminishable [dɪˈmɪnɪʃəbl] ADJ reduzierbar

diminished responsibility [dɪˌmɪnɪʃtrɪspɒnsəˈbɪlɪtɪ] N *(Jur)* verminderte Zurechnungsfähigkeit

diminuendo [dɪˌmɪnjʊˈendəʊ] ADV diminuendo N Diminuendo *nt*

diminution [ˌdɪmɪˈnjuːʃən] N *(in general)* Verringerung *f*; *(of reputation)* Schmälerung *f*; *(in enthusiasm)* Nachlassen *nt*

diminutive [dɪˈmɪnjʊtɪv] ADJ winzig, klein; *(Gram)* diminutiv N *(Gram)* Verkleinerungsform *f*, Diminutiv(um) *nt*; *(of name)* Kurzform *f*

dimity [ˈdɪmɪtɪ] N Dimitz *m*

dimly [ˈdɪmlɪ] ADV a *shine* schwach; **~ lit** schwach beleuchtet b *(= vaguely)* undeutlich; *see* verschwommen; **the peninsula was ~ visible** man konnte die Halbinsel gerade noch ausmachen; **I was ~ aware that …** es war mir undeutlich bewusst, dass …; **she ~ remembered it** sie erinnerte sich (noch) dunkel daran; **in the ~-remembered past** in dunkler Vorzeit

dimmer [ˈdɪməʳ] N *(Elec)* Dimmer *m*; *(US Aut)* Abblendschalter *or* -hebel *m*; **~s** *pl (US Aut)* Abblendlicht *nt*; *(= sidelights)* Begrenzungsleuchten *pl*

dimmer switch N Dimmer *m*

dimness [ˈdɪmnɪs] N a *(of light)* Schwäche *f*, Trübheit *f*; *(of metal)* Mattheit *f*; **the ~ of the room** das Halbdunkel *or* Dämmerlicht im Zimmer b *(= vagueness, of figure, shape)* Undeutlichkeit *f*; *(of outline, eyesight, memory)* Schwäche *f*; *(of eyes)* Trübheit *f* c **the ~ of his prospects** seine schlechten Aussichten *pl* d *(inf: = stupidity)* Beschränktheit *f (inf)*

dim-out [ˈdɪmaʊt] N *(US)* Verdunkelung *f*

dimple [ˈdɪmpl] N *(on cheek, chin)* Grübchen *nt*; *(= depression)* Delle *f*, Vertiefung *f*; *(on water)* Kräuselung *f* VI *(cheeks)* Grübchen bekommen; *(person)* Grübchen zeigen; *(surface)* sich einbeulen; *(water)* sich kräuseln VT **a smile ~d her cheeks** sie lächelte und zeigte dabei ihre Grübchen

dimpled [ˈdɪmpld] ADJ *cheek, chin* mit Grübchen; **she gave him a ~ smile** als sie ihn anlächelte, sah man ihre Grübchen

dimply [ˈdɪmplɪ] ADJ *face* voll(er) Grübchen

dim: **dimwit** N *(inf)* Schwachkopf *m (inf)*; **dim-witted** ADJ *(inf)* blöd *(inf)*, dämlich *(inf)*, beschränkt *(inf)*

din [dɪn] N Lärm *m*, Getöse *nt*; **an infernal ~** ein Höllenlärm *or* -spektakel *m* VT **to ~ sth into sb** jdm etw einbläuen VI **the noise was still ~ning in his ears** der Lärm dröhnte ihm immer noch in den Ohren

dinar [ˈdiːnɑː] N Dinar *m*

din-dins [ˈdɪndɪnz] N *(baby-talk)* Happi(-Happi) *nt (baby-talk)*; **your ~ is ready** jetzt gibts Happi(-Happi); **what's for ~?** was gibts zu füttern? *(inf)*

dine [daɪn] VI speisen, dinieren *(old, geh) (on* etw); **they ~d on caviare every night** sie aßen jeden Abend Kaviar; **to ~ in** zu Hause essen; **to ~ out** außer Haus *or* auswärts speisen; **he ~d out on that story for months** diese Geschichte hat ihm monatelang Einladungen zum Essen verschafft VT bewirten, beköstigen → *also* **wine VT**

diner [ˈdaɪnəʳ] N a *(= person)* Speisende(r) *mf*; *(in restaurant)* Gast *m* b *(= café etc)* Esslokal *nt* c *(Rail)* Speisewagen *m*

diner-out [ˌdaɪnerˈaʊt] N *pl* **diners-out** *jd, der auswärts isst*

dinette [daɪˈnet] N Essecke *f*

ding-a-ling [ˈdɪŋəˈlɪŋ] N a Klingeling *nt*; *(= fire engine)* Tatütata *nt* b *(US inf: = fool)* Depp *m (inf)*

dingbats [ˈdɪŋbæts] PL *(Austral sl: = delirium tremens)* Säuferwahn *m (hum)*, Wahnvorstellungen *pl*; **to give sb the ~** jdn nervös machen

ding-dong [ˈdɪŋˈdɒŋ] N Bimbam *nt* ADJ *(fig) battle* hin und her wogend

ding(e)y, dinghy [ˈdɪŋgɪ] N Ding(h)i *nt*; *(collapsible)* Schlauchboot *nt*

dinginess [ˈdɪndʒɪnɪs] N Unansehnlichkeit *f*

dingle [ˈdɪŋgl] N baumbestandene Mulde

dingo [ˈdɪŋgəʊ] N Dingo *m*, australischer Wildhund

dingy[1] [ˈdɪndʒɪ] ADJ *(+er) building, room, street, area* düster; *(= dirty)* schmuddelig; *colour* schmutzig; **wallpaper with ~ yellow stripes** Tapeten mit schmutzig gelben Streifen

dingy[2] [ˈdɪŋgɪ] N = **ding(e)y**

dining [ˈdaɪnɪŋ]: **dining car** N Speisewagen *m*; **dining chair** N Esszimmerstuhl *m*; **dining hall** N Speisesaal *m*; **dining room** N Esszimmer *nt*; *(in hotel)* Speiseraum *m*; **dining table** N Esstisch *m*

dink [dɪŋk] N a *(inf) abbr of* **double income, no kids**; **~s** *pl* Doppelverdiener *pl* ohne Kinder b *(dated US pej: = Vietnamese)* Vietnamese *m*, Vietnamesin *f*

dinkum [ˈdɪŋkəm] *(Austral inf)* ADJ echt; **a (fair) ~ Aussie** ein waschechter Australier, eine waschechte Australierin ADV echt

dinky[1] [ˈdɪŋkɪ] ADJ a *(Brit inf: = cute)* schnuckelig *(inf)* b *(US inf: = small)* winzig c *(also* **Dinky**)® Modell-; **~ car** Modellauto *nt*

dinky[2] N *(inf) abbr of* **double income, no kids yet**; **dinkies** *pl* noch kinderlose Doppelverdiener *pl*

dinky-di [ˈdɪŋkɪˈdaɪ] ADJ *(Austral)* typisch, echt

dinner [ˈdɪnəʳ] ✪ 25.1, 25.2 N *(= evening meal)* (Haupt)mahlzeit *f*, Abendessen *nt*; *(formal)* (Abend)essen *nt*; *(= lunch)* Mittagessen *nt*; *(for cat, dog)* Fressen *nt*; **to be at ~** beim Essen sein, (gerade) essen; **to be eating** *or* **having one's ~** zu Abend/Mittag essen; *(dog, cat)* (gerade) fressen; **we're having people to ~** wir haben Gäste zum Essen; **~'s ready** das Essen ist fertig; **to finish one's ~** zu Ende essen; **what time do you finish ~?** wann bist du mit dem Essen fertig?; **to go out to ~** *(in restaurant)* auswärts *or* außer Haus essen (gehen); *(at friends')* zum Essen eingeladen sein; **to give a ~ in sb's honour** ein Essen zu jds Ehren geben; **a formal ~** ein offizielles Essen

dinner: **dinner bell** N (Essens)glocke *f*; **the ~ has gone** es hat (zum Essen) geläutet; **dinner-**

dance N *Abendessen mit Tanz*; **dinner dress** N kleines Abendkleid; **dinner duty** N **to do ~** Tischaufsicht haben; **dinner jacket** N Smokingjacke *f*; **dinner knife** N Tafelmesser *nt*; **dinner money** N (*Brit Sch*) Essensgeld *nt*; **dinner party** N Abendgesellschaft *f* (mit Essen); **to have** *or* **give a small ~** ein kleines Essen geben; **dinner plate** N Tafelteller *m*; **dinner service**, **dinner set** N Tafelservice *nt*; **dinner suit** N Smoking *m*; **dinner table** N Tafel *f*; **we were already sitting at the ~** wir hatten schon zum Essen Platz genommen; **dinner theater** N (*US*) *Restaurant mit Theatervorführung*; **dinnertime** N Essenszeit *f*; **dinner trolley**, **dinner wagon** N Servierwagen *m*

dinosaur ['daɪnəsɔː'] N Dinosaurier *m*

dinosaurian [ˌdaɪnə'sɔːriːən] ADJ Dinosaurier-; **~ fossils** Dinosaurierfossilien *pl*

dint [dɪnt] N **a** **by ~ of** durch, kraft (*+gen*); **we succeeded by ~ of working 24 hours a day** wir schafften es, indem wir 24 Stunden pro Tag arbeiteten **b** = **dent** VT = **dent**

diocesan [daɪ'ɒsɪsən] ADJ Diözesan-; **~ bishop** Diözesanbischof *m*

diocese ['daɪəsɪs] N Diözese *f*, Bistum *nt*

diode ['daɪəʊd] N Diode *f*

Dionysian [ˌdaɪə'nɪzɪən] ADJ dionysisch

Dionysus [ˌdaɪə'naɪsɪs] N Dionysos *m*

dioptre, (*US*) **diopter** [daɪ'ɒptə'] N Dioptrie *f*

diorama [ˌdaɪə'rɑːmə] N Diorama *nt*

dioxide [daɪ'ɒksaɪd] N Dioxid *nt*

dioxin [daɪ'ɒksɪn] N Dioxin *nt*

Dip *abbr of* **diploma**

dip [dɪp] VT **a** (*in(to)* in *+acc*) (*into liquid*) tauchen; *pen, hand, brush* (ein)tauchen; *bread* (ein)tunken, stippen (*inf*); *candles* ziehen; *sheep* in Desinfektionslösung baden, dippen; **to ~ sth in flour/egg** etw in Mehl/Ei wälzen
b (*into bag, basket*) *hand* stecken
c (*Brit Aut*) *headlights* abblenden; **~ped headlights** Abblendlicht *nt*; **her lights are ~ped** sie fährt mit Abblendlicht
d **to ~ one's flag** (*Naut*) die Flagge dippen
VI (*ground*) sich senken; (*temperature, pointer on scale, prices*) fallen, sinken; (*boat*) tauchen; **the sun ~ped behind the mountains** die Sonne verschwand hinter den Bergen
N **a** (*= swim*) **to go for a** *or* **to have a ~** kurz *or* schnell mal schwimmen gehen, kurz reinspringen; **after a** *or* **her ~ she lay and sunbathed** nach einem kurzen Bad sonnte sie sich
b (*= liquid, for cleaning animals*) Desinfektionslösung *f*; (*Tech*) Lösung *f*
c (*in ground, = hollow*) Bodensenke *f*; (*= slope*) Abfall *m*; **the road took a ~** die Straße fiel ab
d (*in prices etc*) Fallen *nt*, Sinken *nt*; **to take a ~** fallen, sinken
e (*Phys: also* **angle of dip**) Inklination *f*, Neigungswinkel *m*
f (*Naut, of flag*) Dippen *nt*
g (*Cook*) Dip *m*; **a garlic ~** ein Knoblauchdip → **lucky dip**
h (*= candle*) gezogene Kerze
i (*Sport*) Beugestütz *m*
j (*inf, = pickpocket*) Taschendieb *m*, Langfinger *m* (*inf*)

▶ **dip into** VI *+prep obj* **a** (*lit*) **she dipped into her bag for her keys** sie griff in ihre Tasche, um ihre Schlüssel zu holen **b** (*fig*) **to dip into one's pocket** tief in die Tasche greifen; **to dip into one's savings** seine Ersparnisse angreifen, an seine Ersparnisse gehen **c** *book* einen kurzen Blick werfen in (*+acc*)

Dip. Ed. ['dɪp'ed] (*Brit Univ*) *abbr of* **Diploma in Education** Diplom *nt* in Pädagogik *or* Erziehungswissenschaften

diphtheria [dɪf'θɪərɪə] N Diphtherie *f*

diphthong ['dɪfθɒŋ] N Diphthong *m*

diphthongize ['dɪfθɒŋaɪz] VTI diphthongieren

diploid ['dɪplɔɪd] ADJ (*Biol*) *cell, nucleus* diploid

diploma [dɪ'pləʊmə] N Diplom *nt*; **teacher's ~** Lehrerdiplom *nt*; **to hold a ~ in** ein Diplom haben in (*+dat*)

diplomacy [dɪ'pləʊməsɪ] N (*Pol, fig*) Diplomatie *f*; **to use ~** diplomatisch vorgehen

diplomat ['dɪpləmæt] N (*Pol, fig*) Diplomat(in) *m(f)*

diplomatic [ˌdɪplə'mætɪk] ADJ (*lit, fig*) diplomatisch

diplomatically [ˌdɪplə'mætɪkəlɪ] ADV (*lit, fig: = tactfully*) diplomatisch; (*= by diplomatic means*) auf diplomatischem Wege; (*= at a diplomatic level*) auf diplomatischer Ebene

diplomatic: **diplomatic bag** N (*Brit*) Diplomatenpost *f*; **diplomatic corps** N diplomatisches Korps; **diplomatic immunity** N Immunität *f*; **diplomatic pouch** N (*US*) = **diplomatic bag**; **diplomatic service** N diplomatischer Dienst

diplomatist [dɪ'pləʊmətɪst] N = **diplomat**

dip needle N Inklinationsnadel *f*

dipolar [daɪ'pəʊlə'] ADJ zweipolig

dipole ['daɪpəʊl] N Dipol *m*

dipper ['dɪpə'] N **a** (*= ladle*) Schöpflöffel *m*, Kelle *f* **b** (*Tech, = person*) Eintaucher(in) *m(f)* **c** (*Orn*) Taucher *m*, Tauchente *f* **d** (*Tech, = bulldozer*) Bagger *m*; (*= scoop*) Schaufel *f* **e** (*at fair: also* **Big Dipper**) Achterbahn *f* **f** (*Brit, Aut, for headlamps*) Abblendschalter *m* **g** (*US Astron*) **the Big** *or* **Great/Little Dipper** der Große/Kleine Wagen *or* Bär

dipping shot N (*Ftbl*) Aufsetzer *m*

dippy ['dɪpɪ] ADJ (*inf*) plemplem (*inf*), meschugge (*inf*)

dip rod N (*US*) = **dipstick**

dipso ['dɪpsəʊ] N *abbr of* **dipsomaniac**

dipsomania [ˌdɪpsəʊ'meɪnɪə] N Trunksucht *f*

dipsomaniac [ˌdɪpsəʊ'meɪnɪæk] N Trunksüchtige(r) *mf*

dipstick ['dɪpstɪk] N Ölmessstab *m*

DIP switch ['dɪpswɪtʃ] N (*Comput*) DIP-Schalter *m*

dip switch N (*Aut*) Abblendschalter *m*

diptera ['dɪptərə] PL Dipteren *pl* (*spec*), Zweiflügler *pl*

dipterous ['dɪptərəs] ADJ zweiflüg(e)lig

diptych ['dɪptɪk] N Diptychon *nt*

dire [daɪə'] ADJ **a** (*= serious*) *consequences* verheerend; *warning, prediction, threat* unheilvoll; *effects* katastrophal; *situation* miserabel; (*= desperate*) verzweifelt; **the ~ state of the property market** die miserable Lage auf dem Immobilienmarkt; **in ~ poverty** in äußerster Armut; **to do sth out of ~ necessity** etw aus dringender Notwendigkeit tun; **to be in ~ need of sth** etw dringend brauchen; **to be in ~ straits** in einer ernsten Notlage sein; **the economy is in ~ straits** die Wirtschaftslage ist katastrophal **b** (*inf: = awful*) mies (*inf*); **the standard is pretty ~** das Niveau ist unter aller Kritik (*inf*)

direct [daɪ'rekt] ✪ 27.1, 27.3 ADJ **a** direkt; *link, result, heir, contact* direkt, unmittelbar; *responsibility, cause, danger* unmittelbar; *train* durchgehend; *opposite* genau; **as a ~ result of** als eine unmittelbare Folge von; **~ line of descent** Abstammung *f* in direkter Linie; **to be a ~ descendant of sb** von jdm in direkter Linie abstammen, ein direkter Nachkomme von jdm sein; **to pay by ~ debit** (*Brit*) *or* **deposit** (*US*) per Einzugsauftrag bezahlen; **to impose ~ rule (on the Irish/from London)** (Irland/von London aus) direkt regieren; **~-grant school** (*Brit*) *Privatschule mit staatlicher Unterstützung*; **avoid ~ sunlight** direkte Sonneneinstrahlung meiden; **to take a ~ hit** einen Volltreffer einstecken; **they are willing to hold ~ talks with the government** sie sind bereit, mit der Regierung direkt zu verhandeln
b (*= blunt*) *person, remark* direkt, offen; *refusal, denial* glatt
c (*Gram*) **~ speech** (*Brit*) *or* **discourse** (*US*) direkte Rede
VT **a** (*= address, aim*) *remark, letter* richten (*to* an *+acc*); *efforts, look* richten (*towards* auf *+acc*); *anger* auslassen (*towards* an *+acc*); *money* zufließen lassen (*to +dat*); **the violence was ~ed against the police** die Gewalttätigkeiten richteten sich gegen die Polizei; **to ~ sb's attention to sb/sth** jds Aufmerksamkeit auf jdn/etw lenken; **can you ~ me to the town hall?** können Sie mir den Weg zum Rathaus sagen?
b (*= supervise, control*) *person's work, business* leiten, lenken; *traffic* regeln
c (*= order*) anweisen (*sb to do sth* jdn, etw zu tun); (*Jur*) *jury* Rechtsbelehrung erteilen (*+dat*); **to ~ that sth (should) be done** anordnen, dass etw getan wird; **the judge ~ed the jury to ...** der Richter belehrte die Schöffen darüber, dass ...; **to be taken as ~ed by your doctor** (*Med*) nach ärztlicher Verordnung einzunehmen
d *film, play* Regie führen bei; *group of actors* dirigieren; *radio/TV programme* leiten
ADV direkt

direct: **direct access** N (*Comput*) Direktzugriff *m*; **direct action** N direkte Aktion; **to take ~** direkt handeln; **direct current** N (*Elec*) Gleichstrom *m*; **direct-debit mandate** N (*Fin*) Abbuchungsauftrag *m*; **direct dialling** N Durchwahl *f*; **direct flight** N Direktflug *m*; **direct hit** N (*Mil, fig*) Volltreffer *m*

direction [dɪ'rekʃən] N **a** (*lit, fig: = way*) Richtung *f*; **in every ~/all ~s** in jede Richtung/alle Richtungen; **in the wrong/right ~** (*lit, fig*) in die falsche/richtige Richtung; **in the ~ of Hamburg/the hotel** in Richtung Hamburg/des Hotels; **what ~ did he go in?** in welche Richtung ist er gegangen/gefahren?; **a sense of ~** (*lit*) Orientierungssinn *m*; (*fig*) ein Ziel *nt* im Leben; **new ~s in modern philosophy** neue Wege in der modernen Philosophie
b (*= management: of company etc*) Leitung *f*, Führung *f*
c (*of film, actors*) Regie *f*; (*of play also*) Spielleitung *f*; (*of radio/TV programme*) Leitung *f*; **under the ~ of** unter der Regie von
d **directions** PL (*= instructions*) Anweisungen *pl*; (*to a place*) Angaben *pl*; (*for use*) (Gebrauchs)anweisung *or* -anleitung *f*; (*in recipe etc*) Hinweise *pl*

directional [dɪ'rekʃənl] ADJ Richtungs-; **~ stability** Richtungsstabilität *f*

directional: **directional antenna** N Richtantenne *f*; **directional microphone** N Richtmikrofon *nt*; **directional radio** N Richtfunk *m*, Peilfunk *m*

direction: **direction finder** N Peilantenne *f*; **direction indicator** N (*Aut*) Winker *m*; (*flashing*) Blinker *m*; **direction key** N (*Comput*) Richtungstaste *f*

directionless [dɪ'rekʃənlɪs] ADJ *activity* ziellos; *person* unschlüssig, unentschlossen

directive [dɪ'rektɪv] N Direktive *f*, Weisung *f*

direct line N (*Telec*) Durchwahl *f*

directly [dɪ'rektlɪ] ADV **a** direkt; *above, below, opposite, related* direkt, unmittelbar; **to be ~ linked** *or* **connected (to sth)** in einem direkten *or* unmittelbaren Zusammenhang (mit etw) stehen; **A is not ~ related to B** zwischen A und B besteht kein direkter Zusammenhang; **he is ~ descended from X** er stammt in direkter Linie von X ab; **~ responsible** unmittelbar verantwortlich **b** (*= bluntly*) *say* direkt, offen; *refuse, deny* glatt **c** (*= at once*) sofort; (*= shortly*) gleich CONJ (*= as soon as*) sobald; **he'll come ~ he's ready** er kommt, sobald er fertig ist

direct-mail advertising [daɪ'rekt'meɪl'ædvətaɪzɪŋ] N Postwurfsendungen *pl*

direct marketing N Direktmarketing *nt*

directness [daɪ'rektnɪs] N Direktheit *f*

direct object N (*Gram*) direktes Objekt, Akkusativobjekt *nt*

director [dɪ'rektə'] N **a** (*of company, institution*) Direktor(in) *m(f)*, Leiter(in) *m(f)*; (*Univ*) Rektor(in) *m(f)*; **~ of studies** Studienberater(in) *m(f)*; **~ of music** Musikdirektor(in) *m(f)*; **~ of Public Prosecutions** Oberstaatsanwalt *m*/-anwältin *f* **b** *(Rad, TV)* Direktor(in) *m(f)*; *(Film, Theat)* Regisseur(in) *m(f)* **c** *(Mil)* Richtgerät *nt*

directorate [daɪˈrektərɪt] N *(= period of office)* Dienstzeit *f* als Direktor; *(= board of directors)* Aufsichtsrat *m*

director general N Generaldirektor(in) *m(f)*

director's chair N *(Film)* Regiestuhl *m*

director's cut N *(Film)* vom Regisseur geschnittene Fassung

directorship [dɪˈrektəʃɪp] N Direktorstelle *f or* -posten *m*; **under his ~** unter seiner Leitung

directory [dɪˈrektərɪ] ✪ 27.1 N **a** Adressbuch *nt*; *(= telephone directory)* Telefonbuch *nt*; *(= trade directory)* Branchenverzeichnis *nt*; **~ inquiries** *(Brit) or* **assistance** *(US)* *(Telec)* (Fernsprech)auskunft *f* **b** *(Comput)* Verzeichnis *nt*, Directory *nt*; **to change directories** das Directory wechseln **c** *(Hist)* **the Directory** das Direktorium

direct: **direct product** N *(Math)* Skalarprodukt *nt*; **direct taxation** N direkte Besteuerung

dirge [dɜːdʒ] N Grab- *or* Trauer- *or* Klagegesang *m*

dirigible [ˈdɪrɪdʒɪbl] N (lenkbares) Luftschiff ADJ lenkbar

dirk [dɜːk] N *(Scot)* Dolch *m*

dirt [dɜːt] N **a** Schmutz *m*; *(= soil)* Erde *f*; *(= excrement)* Dreck *m*; **to be covered in ~** völlig verschmutzt sein; **to eat ~** *(fig)* sich widerspruchslos demütigen *or* beleidigen lassen; **to treat sb like ~** jdn wie (den letzten) Dreck behandeln *(inf)*; **he looked at me as though I was a piece of ~** er sah mich an, als wäre ich ein Stück Dreck *(inf)* **b** *(fig: = obscenity)* Schmutz *m*; **to dig up** *or* **dig (the) ~ on sb** *(inf)* jdn in den Schmutz ziehen; **he wanted to get all the ~ he could on his opponent** er wollte seinen Gegner so schlecht wie möglich machen

dirt: **dirt-cheap** ADJ, ADV *(inf)* spottbillig *(inf)*; **it was going ~** es war spottbillig zu haben; **dirt farmer** N *(US)* Kleinbauer *m*, Kleinbäuerin *f*

dirtily [ˈdɜːtɪlɪ] ADV **a** schmutzig **b** *(fig: = meanly)* gemein, schäbig; *(= obscenely)* schmutzig

dirtiness [ˈdɜːtɪnɪs] N Schmutzigkeit *f*; *(of story also)* Unanständigkeit *f*

dirt: **dirt road** N unbefestigte Straße; **dirt track** N Feldweg *m*; *(Sport)* Aschenbahn *f*; **dirt-track racing** N Aschenbahnrennen *nt*

dirty [ˈdɜːtɪ] ADJ *(+er)* **a** *(lit)* schmutzig; **to get sth ~** etw schmutzig machen; **~ mark** Schmutzfleck *m*

b *(with colours)* schmutzig; **~ grey** schmutzig grau; **~ white** schmutzig weiß; **~ green** olivgrün

c *(pej: = underhand)* *job, business, dealings* schmutzig; *player, competitor* unfair; *(emph inf: = despicable)* gemein; **~ play** Foulspiel *nt*; **to do the ~ deed** *(Brit usu hum)* die Übeltat vollbringen

d *(= obscene, smutty)* *book, film, word* unanständig; *joke* schmutzig; *person* obszön; **a ~ mind** eine schmutzige Fantasie; **~ old man** *(pej, hum)* alter Lustmolch *(inf)*; **people for whom "liberalism" is a ~ word** Leute, für die „Liberalismus" ein Schimpfwort ist

e **to give sb a ~ look** *(inf)* jdm einen bösen *or* giftigen *(inf)* Blick zuwerfen

VT *(= soil)* beschmutzen; *(Brit: = foul up)* *machine parts, spark plugs* verschmutzen

N **to do the ~ on sb** *(Brit inf)* jdn reinlegen *(inf)*

dirty: **dirty trick** N gemeiner Trick; **~s campaign** Diffamierungskampagne *f*; **dirty weekend** N *(hum inf)* Liebeswochenende *nt*; **dirty work** N **to do sb's ~** *(lit)* die Schmutzarbeit für jdn machen; *(fig)* sich *(dat)* für jdn die Finger schmutzig machen

dis, diss [dɪs] VT *(sl)* **to ~ sb** jdn blöd anreden *(inf)*

disability [ˌdɪsəˈbɪlɪtɪ] N **a** *(= handicap, injury etc)* Behinderung *f* **b** *(Jur)* Rechtsunfähigkeit *f*

disability living allowance N *(Brit)* Beihilfe *f* für Erwerbsunfähige

disability pension N Erwerbsunfähigkeitsrente *f*

disable [dɪsˈeɪbl] VT **a** *person* zum/zur Behinderten machen **b** *tank, gun* unbrauchbar machen; *ship* kampfunfähig machen **c** *(Jur: = make incapable)* rechtsunfähig machen **d** *(esp Comput)* ausschalten; *control box* deaktivieren

disabled [dɪsˈeɪbld] ADJ **a** behindert; **severely/partially ~** schwerbehindert/leicht behindert; **physically ~** körperbehindert; **mentally ~** geistig behindert; **~ ex-serviceman** Kriegsversehrte(r) *m*; **~ toilet** Behindertentoilette *f* **b** *tank, gun* unbrauchbar; *ship* nicht seetüchtig **c** *(Jur)* nicht rechtsfähig PL **the ~** die Behinderten *pl*; **the war ~** die Kriegsversehrten *pl*

disablement [dɪsˈeɪblmənt] N **a** Behinderung *f* **b** *(of tank, gun, ship)* Unbrauchbarmachen *nt*

disabuse [ˌdɪsəˈbjuːz] VT **to ~ sb of sth** jdn von etw befreien

disaccord [ˌdɪsəˈkɔːd] N *(= disagreement)* Uneinigkeit *f*; *(= contradiction)* Widerspruch *m* VI *(= disagree)* nicht übereinstimmen

disaccustom [ˌdɪsəˈkʌstəm] VT **to ~ sb to sth** jdm etw abgewöhnen

disadvantage [ˌdɪsədˈvɑːntɪdʒ] N Nachteil *m*; *(= detriment also)* Schaden *m*; **to be at a ~** benachteiligt *or* im Nachteil sein; **he felt at a ~** er fühlte sich benachteiligt; **to put sb at a ~** jdn benachteiligen; **to show oneself at a ~** sich von einer ungünstigen *or* unvorteilhaften Seite zeigen; **it would be to your ~** es wäre zu Ihrem Nachteil

disadvantaged [ˌdɪsədˈvɑːntɪdʒd] ADJ benachteiligt

disadvantageous ADJ, **disadvantageously** ADV [ˌdɪsædvɑːnˈteɪdʒəs, -lɪ] nachteilig

disaffected [ˌdɪsəˈfektɪd] ADJ entfremdet; **to become ~** sich entfremden

disaffection [ˌdɪsəˈfekʃən] N Entfremdung *f* *(with von)*

disagio [dɪsˈædʒɪəʊ] N *(Fin)* Disagio *nt*, Abschlag *m*

disagree [ˌdɪsəˈgriː] ✪ 12.1 VI **a** *(with person, views)* nicht übereinstimmen; *(with plan, suggestion etc)* nicht einverstanden sein; *(two people)* sich *(dat)* nicht einig sein **b** *(= quarrel)* eine Meinungsverschiedenheit haben **c** *(= be different: figures, reports)* nicht übereinstimmen **d** *(climate, food)* **to ~ with sb** jdm nicht bekommen; **garlic ~s with me** ich vertrage keinen Knoblauch, Knoblauch bekommt mir nicht

disagreeable [ˌdɪsəˈgriːəbl] ADJ unangenehm; *person* unsympathisch

disagreeableness [ˌdɪsəˈgriːəblnɪs] N Unangenehme(s) *nt*, unangenehme Art; *(of person)* unsympathische Art

disagreeably [ˌdɪsəˈgriːəblɪ] ADV unangenehm

disagreement [ˌdɪsəˈgriːmənt] N **a** *(with opinion, between opinions)* Uneinigkeit *f*; **to be in ~ with sb** mit jdm nicht einer Meinung sein; **we are in ~** wir sind verschiedener Meinung; **there is still ~** es herrscht noch Uneinigkeit **b** *(= quarrel)* Meinungsverschiedenheit *f* **c** *(between figures, reports)* Diskrepanz *f*

disallow [ˌdɪsəˈlaʊ] VT *evidence, expenses* nicht anerkennen; *claim* zurückweisen, nicht anerkennen; *plan etc* ablehnen; *(Sport)* *goal* nicht anerkennen, nicht geben

disambiguate [ˌdɪsæmˈbɪgjʊeɪt] VT *text etc* eindeutig machen, disambiguieren *(spec)*

disappear [ˌdɪsəˈpɪəʳ] VI verschwinden; *(worries, fears, difficulties)* verschwinden, sich in nichts auflösen; *(memory)* schwinden; *(objections)* sich zerstreuen; **he ~ed from sight** er verschwand; **to make sth ~** etw verschwinden lassen; **to do a ~ing trick** *(inf)* sich verdünnisieren *(inf)*, sich verdrücken *(inf)*; **to ~ into thin air** sich in Luft auflösen VT *(esp Pol inf)* verschwinden lassen PL **the ~ed** die Verschwundenen *pl*

disappearance [ˌdɪsəˈpɪərəns] N Verschwinden *nt*

disappoint [ˌdɪsəˈpɔɪnt] VT enttäuschen

disappointed [ˌdɪsəˈpɔɪntɪd] ✪ 14 ADJ enttäuscht; **she was ~ to find/learn that ...** sie war enttäuscht, als sie feststellte/erfuhr, dass ...; **to be ~ that ...** enttäuscht (darüber) sein, dass ...; **to be ~ in** *or* **with** *or* **by sb/sth** von jdm/etw enttäuscht sein; **he was ~ in love** er erlebte eine Enttäuschung in der Liebe; **he was ~ at having to pull out of the race** er war enttäuscht (darüber), dass er aus dem Rennen ausscheiden musste

disappointing [ˌdɪsəˈpɔɪntɪŋ] ADJ enttäuschend; **how ~!** so eine Enttäuschung!

disappointingly [ˌdɪsəˈpɔɪntɪŋlɪ] ADV enttäuschend; *(introducing sentence)* leider; **she performed ~** sie enttäuschte; **rather ~, he didn't have the opportunity** es war ziemlich enttäuschend, dass er keine Gelegenheit dazu hatte, leider hatte er keine Gelegenheit dazu

disappointment [ˌdɪsəˈpɔɪntmənt] N Enttäuschung *f*; *(of ambition)* Nichterfüllung *f*

disapprobation [ˌdɪsæprəˈbeɪʃən] N Missbilligung *f*

disapproval [ˌdɪsəˈpruːvl] N Missbilligung *f*; **murmur of ~** missbilligendes Gemurmel

disapprove [ˌdɪsəˈpruːv] VT missbilligen VI dagegen sein; **if you don't ~, I'd like to ...** wenn Sie nichts dagegen haben, würde ich gerne ...; **to ~ of sb** jdn ablehnen; **to ~ of sth** etw missbilligen; **he ~s of children smoking** er missbilligt es, wenn Kinder rauchen

disapproving [ˌdɪsəˈpruːvɪŋ] ADJ *look, glance, person* missbilligend; **to make ~ noises** sein Missfallen zum Ausdruck bringen; **to be ~ of sb/sth** jdn/etw missbilligen

disapprovingly [ˌdɪsəˈpruːvɪŋlɪ] ADV missbilligend

disarm [dɪsˈɑːm] VT *(lit, fig)* entwaffnen VI *(Mil)* abrüsten

disarmament [dɪsˈɑːməmənt] N Abrüstung *f*

disarmer [dɪsˈɑːməʳ] N Abrüstungsbefürworter(in) *m(f)*

disarming [dɪsˈɑːmɪŋ] ADJ entwaffnend

disarmingly [dɪsˈɑːmɪŋlɪ] ADV entwaffnend; **~ simple** verblüffend einfach

disarrange [ˈdɪsəˈreɪndʒ] VT durcheinanderbringen

disarranged [ˈdɪsəˈreɪndʒd] ADJ unordentlich

disarrangement [ˌdɪsəˈreɪndʒmənt] N Unordnung *f*

disarray [ˌdɪsəˈreɪ] N Unordnung *f*; **to be in ~** *(troops)* in Auflösung (begriffen) sein; *(thoughts, organization, political party)* durcheinander *or* in Unordnung sein; *(person)* aufgelöst sein; *(clothes)* in unordentlichem Zustand sein VT in Unordnung bringen

disassemble [ˈdɪsəˈsembl] VT auseinandernehmen; *prefabricated building* abbauen

disassociate [ˈdɪsəˈsəʊʃɪeɪt] VT = **dissociate**

disaster [dɪˈzɑːstəʳ] N Katastrophe *f*; *(Aviat, Min, Rail)* Unglück *nt*, Katastrophe *f*; *(= fiasco)* Fiasko *nt*, Desaster *nt*; **doomed to ~** zum Untergang verdammt *or* verurteilt → *also* **recipe**

disaster: **disaster area** N Katastrophengebiet *nt*; *(fig inf: = person)* Katastrophe *f*; **disaster fund** N Katastrophenfonds *m*; **disaster movie** N Katastrophenfilm *m*

disastrous [dɪˈzɑːstrəs] ADJ *earthquake, flood, accident* katastrophal, verheerend; *marriage, day, consequence* katastrophal; **dinner was ~** das Abendessen war eine Katastrophe; **to be ~ for sb/sth** katastrophale Folgen für jdn/etw haben

disastrously [dɪˈzɑːstrəslɪ] ADV katastrophal; **it all went ~ wrong** es was eine Katastrophe; **we performed ~** unsere Leistung war katastrophal (schlecht); **they fared ~ in the elections** sie schnitten bei den Wahlen katastrophal schlecht ab

disavow [ˈdɪsəˈvaʊ] VT verleugnen; *one's words* ableugnen

disavowal [ˌdɪsəˈvaʊəl] N Verleugnung *f*; *(of one's words)* Ableugnung *f*

disband [dɪsˈbænd] VT auflösen VI *(army, club)* sich auflösen; *(soldiers, club members)* auseinandergehen

disbar [dɪsˈbɑːʳ] VT *(Jur)* die Lizenz entziehen *(+dat)*

disbelief [ˈdɪsbəˈliːf] N Ungläubigkeit *f*; *(Rel)* Unglaube *m*; **in ~** ungläubig

disbelieve [ˈdɪsbəˈliːv] VT nicht glauben

disbeliever [ˈdɪsbəˈliːvəʳ] N Ungläubige(r) *mf*

disbelieving ADJ, **disbelievingly** ADV [ˈdɪsbəˈliːvɪŋ, -lɪ] ungläubig

disburden [dɪsˈbɜːdn] VT *(lit, fig)* entlasten

disburse [dɪsˈbɜːs] VT aus(be)zahlen

disbursement [dɪsˈbɜːsmənt] N Auszahlung *f*

disc, *(esp US)* **disk** [dɪsk] N a *(= flat, circular object)* (runde) Scheibe; *(Anat)* Bandscheibe *f*; *(Mil, = identity disc)* (Erkennungs)marke *f* → **slip** b *(= record, Comput)* Platte *f*; *(= CD)* CD *f* → *also* **disk**

discard [dɪˈskɑːd] VT a *unwanted article, person* ausrangieren; *idea, plan* verwerfen; *(Comput) changes in file* verwerfen; *(= take off) coat* ausziehen; *antlers, leaves* abwerfen b *(Cards)* abwerfen VI *(Cards)* abwerfen N a *(Cards)* Abwerfen *nt* b *(Ind, Comm)* Ausschuss *m*, Ausschussware *f*

disc: **disc brake** N Scheibenbremse *f*; **disc camera** N Disc-Kamera *f*

discern [dɪˈsɜːn] VT *(with senses)* wahrnehmen; *(mentally)* erkennen; **he was too young to ~ right from wrong** er war zu jung, um Recht von Unrecht unterscheiden zu können

discernible [dɪˈsɜːnəbl] ADJ *(with senses)* wahrnehmbar; *(mentally)* erkennbar

discernibly [dɪˈsɜːnəblɪ] ADV erkennbar

discerning [dɪˈsɜːnɪŋ] ADJ *clientele, reader* anspruchsvoll, kritisch; *eye, ear* fein

discernment [dɪˈsɜːnmənt] N a *(= ability to discern, observation)* feines Gespür; *(discriminating taste)* kritisches Urteilsvermögen b *(= act of discerning, with senses)* Wahrnehmung *f*; *(mentally)* Erkennen *nt*

discharge [dɪsˈtʃɑːdʒ] VT a *employee, prisoner, patient* entlassen; *accused* freisprechen; **he ~d himself (from hospital)** er hat das Krankenhaus auf eigene Verantwortung verlassen
b *(= emit, Elec)* entladen; *liquid, gas (pipe etc)* ausstoßen; *workers* ausströmen lassen; *(Med)* ausscheiden, absondern; **the factory was discharging toxic gas into the atmosphere** aus der Fabrik strömten giftige Gase in die Atmosphäre; **the tanker was discharging oil into the Channel** das Öl lief aus dem Tanker in den (Ärmel)kanal; **how much oil has been ~d?** wie viel Öl ist ausgelaufen?; *(deliberately)* wie viel Öl hat man abgelassen?
c *(= unload) ship, cargo* löschen; **the bus ~d its passengers** die Passagiere stiegen aus dem Bus aus
d *(gun)* abfeuern
e *debt* begleichen; *duty* nachkommen *(+dat)*; *function, obligations* erfüllen; **~d bankrupt** entlasteter Konkursschuldner
VI *(wound, sore)* eitern
N [ˈdɪstʃɑːdʒ] a *(= dismissal, of employee, prisoner, patient)* Entlassung *f*; *(of accused)* Freispruch *m*; *(of soldier)* Abschied *m*
b *(Elec)* Entladung *f*; *(of gas)* Ausströmen *nt*; *(of liquid: Med) (vaginal)* Ausfluss *m*; *(of pus)* Absonderung *f*
c *(of cargo)* Löschen *nt*
d *(of debt)* Begleichung *f*; *(of duty, function)* Erfüllung *f*; *(of bankrupt)* Entlastung *f*

disc harrow N Scheibenegge *f*

disciple [dɪˈsaɪpl] N *(lit)* Jünger *m*; *(fig)* Schüler(in) *m(f)*, Jünger(in) *m(f) (usu iro)*

disciplinarian [ˌdɪsɪplɪˈneərɪən] N Zuchtmeister(in) *m(f)*; **to be a strict ~** eiserne Disziplin halten

disciplinary [ˌdɪsɪˈplɪnərɪ] ADJ Disziplinar-; *matters* disziplinarisch; **~ proceedings** *or* **procedures** Disziplinarverfahren *nt*; **~ measures/powers** Disziplinarmaßnahmen *pl*/-gewalt *f*; **he has no ~ problems in his class** in seiner Klasse hat er keine Schwierigkeiten mit der Disziplin; **the worst ~ record in the League** das längste Disziplinarstrafregister in der Liga; **a school with a firm ~ code** eine Schule mit einer strengen Disziplin; **to take ~ action** Disziplinarmaßnahmen ergreifen; **they face ~ action/charges** gegen sie werden Disziplinarmaßnahmen ergriffen/wird ein Disziplinarverfahren eröffnet

discipline [ˈdɪsɪplɪn] N *(all senses)* Disziplin *f*; *(= punishment)* disziplinarische Maßnahmen *pl*; **to maintain ~** die Disziplin aufrechterhalten VT a *(= train, make obedient)* disziplinieren; *reactions, emotions* in Zucht *or* unter Kontrolle halten; **to ~ oneself to do sth** sich dazu anhalten *or* zwingen, etw zu tun b *(= punish)* bestrafen; *(physically)* züchtigen

disciplined [ˈdɪsɪplɪnd] ADJ diszipliniert; **we gave a ~ performance** wir spielten diszipliniert

disc jockey N Discjockey *m*

disclaim [dɪsˈkleɪm] VT a *(= deny)* abstreiten, (weit) von sich *(dat)* weisen; **to ~ all** *or* **any responsibility** jede Verantwortung von sich weisen b *(Jur) a right* verzichten auf *(+acc)*

disclaimer [dɪsˈkleɪməʳ] N a Dementi *nt*; **to issue a ~** eine Gegenerklärung abgeben b **to put in a ~ of sth** *(Jur)* eine Verzichterklärung auf etw *(acc)* abgeben

disclose [dɪsˈkləʊz] VT *secret* enthüllen; *intentions, news, details, identity* bekannt geben

disclosure [dɪsˈkləʊʒəʳ] N a *(of secret)* Enthüllung *f*; *(of intentions, news, details, identity)* Bekanntgabe *f* b *(= fact etc revealed)* Mitteilung *f*

Discman® [ˈdɪskmən] N Discman® *m*, tragbarer CD-Player

disco [ˈdɪskəʊ] N Disco *f*, Disko *f*; **~ dancing** Discotanzen *nt*

discography [dɪsˈkɒgrəfɪ] N Diskografie *f*

discolor VTI *(US)* = **discolour**

discoloration [dɪsˌkʌləˈreɪʃən] N Verfärben *nt*; *(= mark)* Verfärbung *f*

discolour, *(US)* **discolor** [dɪsˈkʌləʳ] VT verfärben VI sich verfärben

discoloured, *(US)* **discolored** [dɪsˈkʌləd] ADJ verfärbt; **his left temple was bruised and ~** an seiner linken Schläfe hatte er einen Bluterguss

discombobulate [ˌdɪskəmˈbɒbjʊleɪt] VT *(= esp US hum)* irritieren, verunsichern, aus dem Konzept bringen

discomfit [dɪsˈkʌmfɪt] VT Unbehagen verursachen *(+dat)*

discomfiture [dɪsˈkʌmfɪtʃəʳ] N Unbehagen *nt*

discomfort [dɪsˈkʌmfət] N *(lit)* Beschwerden *pl*; *(fig: = uneasiness, embarrassment)* Unbehagen *nt*; **to feel some ~** sich nicht wohlfühlen; **the injury gives me a little ~ now and again** die Verletzung verursacht mir ab und zu leichte Beschwerden; **much to my ~ he offered to pay** es war mir sehr unangenehm, dass er zahlen wollte; **the ~s of camping** die Unannehmlichkeiten des Zeltens

discompose [ˈdɪskəmˈpəʊz] VT *(form)* a *(= disarrange)* in Unordnung bringen; *(fig) person* durcheinanderbringen b *(= agitate)* (völlig) aus der Fassung bringen, verwirren

disconcert [ˌdɪskənˈsɜːt] VT beunruhigen

disconcerting [ˌdɪskənˈsɜːtɪŋ] ADJ beunruhigend

disconcertingly [ˌdɪskənˈsɜːtɪŋlɪ] ADV beunruhigend; *(introducing sentence)* irritierenderweise

disconnect [ˈdɪskəˈnekt] VT *pipe etc* trennen; *(Comput) modem, network drive etc* Verbindung zum/zur ... trennen; *TV, iron* ausschalten; *(= cut off supply of) gas, electricity* abstellen; **to ~ a call** *(Telec)* ein Gespräch unterbrechen; **I've been ~ed** *(for nonpayment)* man hat mir das Telefon/den Strom/das Gas *etc* abgestellt

disconnected [ˌdɪskəˈnektɪd] ADJ a unzusammenhängend; *phrases, sentences* unzusammenhängend, zusammenhanglos; **~ events** nicht miteinander zusammenhängende Ereignisse b *(Tech, Comput)* getrennt

disconsolate [dɪsˈkɒnsəlɪt] ADJ untröstlich; *(= gloomy)* niedergeschlagen; **to grow ~** verzweifeln, verzagen

disconsolately [dɪsˈkɒnsəlɪtlɪ] ADV untröstlich; *(= gloomily)* niedergeschlagen

discontent [ˈdɪskənˈtent] N Unzufriedenheit *f*

discontented [ˈdɪskənˈtentɪd] ADJ unzufrieden *(with, about* mit)

discontentedly [ˌdɪskənˈtentɪdlɪ] ADV unzufrieden

discontentment [ˈdɪskənˈtentmənt] N Unzufriedenheit *f*

discontinuation [dɪskənˌtɪnjʊˈeɪʃən] N Aufgabe *f*; *(of class, conversation, treatment)* Abbruch *m*; *(Comm, of line)* (Produktions)einstellung *f*; *(of production, Jur, of case, proceedings)* Einstellung *f*

discontinue [ˈdɪskənˈtɪnjuː] VT aufgeben; *class, conversation, treatment* abbrechen; *project* abbrechen, aufgeben; *use* beenden; *(Comm) line* auslaufen lassen, die Produktion einstellen von; *production* einstellen; *(Jur) case, proceedings* einstellen; **a ~d line** *(Comm)* eine ausgelaufene Serie

discontinuity [ˌdɪskɒntɪˈnjuːɪtɪ] N mangelnde Kontinuität, Diskontinuität *f (geh)*; **a certain amount of ~** ein gewisser Mangel an Kontinuität; **to reduce any ~ to a minimum** die Kontinuität möglichst wenig unterbrechen

discontinuous ADJ, **discontinuously** ADV [ˌdɪskənˈtɪnjʊəs, -lɪ] nicht kontinuierlich

discord [ˈdɪskɔːd] N a Uneinigkeit *f* b *(Mus)* Disharmonie *f*

discordance [dɪsˈkɔːdəns] N a Uneinigkeit *f* b *(of colours, sounds, music)* Disharmonie *f*

discordant [dɪsˈkɔːdənt] ADJ *opinions, colours* nicht miteinander harmonierend; *sound* misstönend; *meeting, atmosphere* unharmonisch; *(Mus)* disharmonisch; **to strike a ~ note** *(fig)* einen falschen Ton anschlagen

discotheque [ˈdɪskəʊtek] N Diskothek *f*

discount [ˈdɪskaʊnt] ✪ 20.3 N a *(on article)* Rabatt *m*; *(for cash)* Skonto *nt or m*; **to give a ~ on sth** Rabatt *or* Prozente *(inf)* auf etw *(acc)* geben; **to give sb a 5% ~** jdm 5% Rabatt/Skonto geben; **at a ~** auf Rabatt/Skonto; **~ for cash** Skonto *or* Rabatt bei Barzahlung b **to be at a ~** *(Fin)* unter pari sein; *(fig)* nicht *or* wenig gefragt sein VT a *(Comm) sum of money* nachlassen; *bill, note* diskontieren; **~ed bill** Diskontwechsel *m* b [dɪsˈkaʊnt] *person's opinion* unberücksichtigt lassen; **to ~ sth as an exaggeration/as untrue** etw als Übertreibung/als unwahr abtun

discountable [dɪsˈkaʊntəbl] ADJ *(Fin)* diskontfähig, diskontierbar

discount broker N Wechselmakler(in) *m(f)*

discounter [ˈdɪskaʊntəʳ] N *(= Comm)* Discounter *m*

discount: **discount house** N a *(Fin)* Diskontbank *f* b *(= store)* Discountgeschäft *nt or* -laden *m*; **discount market** N *(Fin)* Diskontmarkt *m*; **discount rate** N *(Fin)* Diskontsatz *m*; **discount retailer** N *(= Comm)* Discounter *m*; **discount store** N Discounter *m*, Discountgeschäft *nt or* -laden *m*

discourage [dɪsˈkʌrɪdʒ] VT a *(= dishearten)* entmutigen; **to become ~d (by)** entmutigt werden (von); *(= generally disheartened)* mutlos werden (durch) b *(= dissuade)* **to ~ sb from doing sth** jdm abraten, etw zu tun; *(successfully)* jdn davon abbringen, etw zu tun c *(= deter, hinder)* abhalten; *friendship, advances, plan, speculation, investment* zu verhindern suchen; *praise, evil* abwehren; *pride* nicht ermutigen; *smoking* unterbinden; **the weather ~d people from going away** das Wetter hielt die Leute davon ab wegzufahren

discouragement [dɪsˈkʌrɪdʒmənt] N a *(= depression)* Mutlosigkeit *f* b *(= dissuasion)* Abraten *nt*; *(with success)* Abbringen *nt* c *(= deter-*

rence, hindrance) Abhaltung *f*; *(of friendship)* Verhinderung *f*; *(of praise)* Abwehr *f* **d** *(= discouraging thing)* **to be a ~** entmutigend sein

discouraging [dɪsˈkʌrɪdʒɪŋ] ADJ entmutigend; **he was rather ~ about her chances** er äußerte sich ziemlich entmutigend über ihre Chancen

discouragingly [dɪsˈkʌrɪdʒɪŋlɪ] ADV entmutigend

discourse [ˈdɪskɔːs] **N** Diskurs *m (geh)* **VI** einen Diskurs geben *(geh)*; *(= converse)* einen Diskurs führen *(geh)*

discourse analysis N *(Ling)* Diskursanalyse *f*

discourteous ADJ, **discourteously** ADV [dɪsˈkɜːtɪəs, -lɪ] unhöflich; **we were ~ ignored** wir wurden unhöflicherweise ignoriert

discourteousness [dɪsˈkɜːtɪəsnɪs], **discourtesy** [dɪsˈkɜːtɪsɪ] N Unhöflichkeit *f*

discover [dɪsˈkʌvəˈ] VT entdecken; *culprit* finden; *secret, truth* herausfinden; *cause* feststellen; *(after search) house, book* ausfindig machen, entdecken; *(= notice) mistake, loss* feststellen, bemerken; **did you ever ~ who ...?** haben Sie jemals herausgefunden, wer ...?

discoverer [dɪsˈkʌvərəˈ] N Entdecker(in) *m(f)*

discovery [dɪsˈkʌvərɪ] N Entdeckung *f*

discredit [dɪsˈkredɪt] **VT** **a** *(= cast slur/doubt on)* diskreditieren **b** *(= disbelieve)* keinen Glauben schenken *(+dat)* **N** **a** *no pl (= dishonour, disbelief)* Misskredit *m*; **to bring ~ (up)on sb/sth** jdn/etw in Misskredit bringen **b** **to be a ~ to sb** eine Schande für jdn sein

discreditable [dɪsˈkredɪtəbl] ADJ diskreditierend; **to be ~ to sb** jdn diskreditieren, jdn in Misskredit bringen

discreditably [dɪsˈkredɪtəblɪ] ADV diskreditierend

discredited [dɪsˈkredɪtɪd] ADJ diskreditiert

discreet [dɪˈskriːt] ADJ diskret; *inquiry* diskret, taktvoll; *account* taktvoll; *elegance* unaufdringlich; *jewellery, tie, dress, decoration* dezent; **at a ~ distance** in einer diskreten Entfernung; **to maintain a ~ presence** eine unauffällige Präsenz aufrechterhalten; **to keep** *or* **maintain a ~ silence** diskret schweigen; **to be ~ about sth** etw diskret behandeln

discreetly [dɪˈskriːtlɪ] ADV diskret; *dressed, decorated* dezent; **~, she said nothing** taktvollerweise sagte sie nichts

discreetness [dɪˈskriːtnɪs] N Diskretheit *f*; *(of account)* taktvolle Art; *(of jewellery, tie, dress, decoration)* dezente Art

discrepancy [dɪˈskrepənsɪ] N Diskrepanz *f (between* zwischen *+dat)*

discrete [dɪˈskriːt] ADJ diskret

discretion [dɪˈskreʃən] N **a** Diskretion *f*; **~ is the better part of valour** *(Brit Prov)* Vorsicht ist die Mutter der Porzellankiste *(inf)* **b** *(= freedom of decision)* Ermessen *nt*; **to leave sth to sb's ~** etw in jds Ermessen *(acc)* stellen; **use your own ~** Sie müssen nach eigenem Ermessen handeln; **to be at sb's ~** in jds Ermessen *(dat)* stehen; **to do sth at one's ~** etw nach eigenem Ermessen tun

discretionary [dɪˈskreʃənərɪ] ADJ Ermessens-; **~ powers** Ermessensspielraum *m*

discriminate [dɪˈskrɪmɪneɪt] **VI** **a** *(= be discriminating)* kritisch sein; *(= distinguish)* unterscheiden *(between* zwischen *+dat)* **b** *(= make unfair distinction)* Unterschiede machen *(between* zwischen *+dat)*; **to ~ in favour** *(Brit) or* **favor** *(US)* **of/against sb** jdn bevorzugen/benachteiligen **VT** unterscheiden, einen Unterschied machen zwischen *(+dat)*; **to ~ good from bad** Gut und Böse unterscheiden können

▶ **discriminate against** VI *+prep obj* diskriminieren; **they were discriminated against** sie wurden diskriminiert

discriminating [dɪˈskrɪmɪneɪtɪŋ] ADJ **a** *(= discerning) person* anspruchsvoll, kritisch; *judgement, eye* kritisch; *palate* fein; **a ~ ear** ein feines Gehör **b** *(Fin) tax, tariff* diskriminierend

discrimination [dɪˌskrɪmɪˈneɪʃən] N **a** *(= differential treatment)* Diskriminierung *f*; **racial ~** Rassendiskriminierung *f*; **sex(ual)/religious ~** Diskriminierung *f* aufgrund des Geschlechts/der Religion **b** *(= differentiation)* Unterscheidung *f (between* zwischen *+dat)* **c** *(= discernment)* kritisches Urteilsvermögen

discriminatory [dɪˈskrɪmɪnətərɪ] ADJ diskriminierend

discursive [dɪˈskɜːsɪv] ADJ **a** *style* weitschweifig **b** *(Philos)* diskursiv

discus [ˈdɪskəs] N Diskus *m*; **in the ~** *(Sport)* im Diskuswerfen; **~ thrower** Diskuswerfer(in) *m(f)*

discuss [dɪˈskʌs] VT besprechen; *politics, theory* diskutieren; *in essay, speech etc* erörtern, diskutieren; **I don't want to ~ it any further** ich möchte darüber nicht weiter reden, ich möchte das nicht weiter diskutieren; **I am not willing to ~ it** ich bin nicht gewillt, darüber zu diskutieren

discussant [dɪˈskʌsənt] N *(US)* Diskussionsteilnehmer(in) *m(f)*

discussion [dɪˈskʌʃən] N Diskussion *f (of, about* über *+acc)*; *(= meeting)* Besprechung *f*; **after much** *or* **a lot of ~** nach langen Diskussionen; **to be under ~** zur Diskussion stehen; **that is still under ~** das ist noch in der Diskussion; **open to ~** zur Diskussion gestellt; **a subject for ~** ein Diskussionsthema *nt*; **to come up for ~** zur Diskussion gestellt werden; **~ document** *or* **paper** Diskussionspapier *nt*; **~ group** Diskussionsgruppe *f*

disdain [dɪsˈdeɪn] **VT** *sb* verachten; *sth also* verschmähen; **he ~ed to notice them** er hielt es für unter seiner Würde, ihnen Beachtung zu schenken **N** Verachtung *f*; **with ~** verächtlich

disdainful [dɪsˈdeɪnfʊl] ADJ, **disdainfully** [dɪsˈdeɪnfəlɪ] ADV herablassend; *look* verächtlich

disease [dɪˈziːz] N *(lit, fig)* Krankheit *f*

diseased [dɪˈziːzd] ADJ *(lit, fig)* krank; *tissue, plant* befallen

disembark [ˌdɪsɪmˈbɑːk] **VT** ausschiffen **VI** von Bord gehen

disembarkation [ˌdɪsembɑːˈkeɪʃən] N Landung *f*

disembodied [ˈdɪsɪmˈbɒdɪd] ADJ körperlos; *voice* geisterhaft; *head, hand* (vom Körper) abgetrennt

disembowel [ˌdɪsɪmˈbaʊəl] VT die Eingeweide herausnehmen *(+dat)*; *(= murder)* den Bauch aufschlitzen *(+dat)*

disempower [ˌdɪsɪmˈpaʊəˈ] VT entkräften

disenchant [ˈdɪsɪnˈtʃɑːnt] VT ernüchtern; **he became ~ed with her/it** sie/es ernüchterte ihn

disenfranchise [ˈdɪsɪnˈfræntʃaɪz] VT **a** *person* die bürgerlichen Ehrenrechte aberkennen *(+dat)*; *town* das Recht nehmen, einen Abgeordneten ins Parlament zu senden *(+dat)* **b** *(Comm)* die Konzession entziehen *(+dat)*

disenfranchisement [ˈdɪsɪnˈfræntʃaɪzmənt] N *(of person)* Aberkennung *f* der bürgerlichen Ehrenrechte; *(of town)* Entzug *m* des Rechts, einen Abgeordneten ins Parlament zu senden

disengage [ˌdɪsɪnˈɡeɪdʒ] **VT** **a** *(= extricate)* losmachen, lösen *(from* aus) **b** *(Tech)* ausrücken *(form)*; **to ~ the clutch** *(Aut)* auskuppeln **c** *(Mil, from country)* abziehen; *(from battle)* abziehen, abrücken lassen **VI** **a** *(Tech)* ausrücken *(form)* **b** *(Mil)* auseinanderrücken; *(opponents)* sich trennen **c** *(Fencing)* sich (aus seiner Bindung) lösen

disengagement [ˌdɪsɪnˈɡeɪdʒmənt] N **a** *(= extrication)* Lösung *f* **b** *(Tech)* Ausrücken *nt (form)*; **~ of the clutch** das Auskuppeln **c** *(Mil)* Abzug *m*

disentail [ˈdɪsɪnˈteɪl] VT *(Jur)* das Fideikommiss *(+gen)*, auflösen

disentangle [ˈdɪsɪnˈtæŋɡl] VT *(lit, fig)* entwirren; *problem, mystery also* enträtseln; **to ~ oneself (from sth)** *(lit)* sich (aus etw) lösen; *(fig)* sich (von etw) lösen

disestablish [ˌdɪsɪsˈtæblɪʃ] VT *the Church* vom Staat trennen

disestablishment [ˌdɪsɪsˈtæblɪʃmənt] N Trennung *f* (vom Staat)

disfavour, *(US)* **disfavor** [dɪsˈfeɪvəˈ] N **a** *(= displeasure)* Ungnade *f*; *(= dislike)* Missfallen *nt*; **to fall into/be in ~ (with)** in Ungnade fallen/sein (bei); **to look with ~ (up)on sb/sth** jdn/etw mit Missfallen betrachten **b** *(= disadvantage)* **in/to his ~** zu seinen Ungunsten

disfigure [dɪsˈfɪɡəˈ] VT verunstalten; *person also* entstellen; *city, landscape* verschandeln

disfigurement [dɪsˈfɪɡəmənt] N Verunstaltung *f*; *(of person also)* Entstellung *f*; *(of city, landscape)* Verschandelung *f*

disfranchise [dɪsˈfræntʃaɪz] VT = **disenfranchise**

disfranchisement [dɪsˈfræntʃaɪzmənt] N = **disenfranchisement**

disgorge [dɪsˈɡɔːdʒ] **VT** *food* ausspucken, ausspeien; *(stomach)* ausstoßen; *(fig: = spew forth)* ausspeien; *(river) waters* ergießen; *(= give up)* her(aus)geben *or* herausrücken; **the train ~d its passengers** die Passagiere strömten aus dem Zug; **the ship is disgorging its cargo of weapons** aus dem Schiff werden Waffen ausgeladen **VI** *(river)* aus einer Schlucht austreten

disgrace [dɪsˈɡreɪs] **N** **a** *no pl (= dishonour, shame)* Schande *f*; **in ~** mit Schimpf und Schande; *(as a punishment)* zur Strafe; **to bring ~ (up)on sb** jdm Schande machen *or* bringen; **to be in/fall into ~** in Ungnade (gefallen) sein/fallen *(with* bei)
b *(= cause of shame, thing)* Schande *f (to* für), Blamage *f (to* für); *(person)* Schandfleck *m (to +gen)*; **you're a complete ~!** mit dir kann man sich wirklich nur blamieren!; **the cost of rented accommodation is a ~** es ist eine Schande, wie teuer Mietwohnungen sind
VT Schande machen *(+dat)*; *country, family* Schande bringen über *(+acc)*; **don't ~ us!** mach uns keine Schande!, blamier uns nicht!; **to ~ oneself** sich blamieren; *(child, dog)* sich schlecht benehmen; **he ~d himself by losing his temper** zu seiner Schande verlor er die Beherrschung; **to be ~d** blamiert sein; *(politician, officer etc)* in Unehre gefallen sein

disgraceful [dɪsˈɡreɪsfʊl] ADJ erbärmlich (schlecht); *behaviour, scenes, negligence* skandalös; **it's quite ~ how/that ...** es ist wirklich eine Schande, wie/dass ...

disgracefully [dɪsˈɡreɪsfəlɪ] ADV schändlich; **~ low wages** erbärmlich niedrige Löhne

disgruntle [dɪsˈɡrʌntl] VT verstimmen

disgruntled [dɪsˈɡrʌntld] ADJ verstimmt

disgruntlement [dɪsˈɡrʌntlmənt] N Verstimmung *f*

disguise [dɪsˈɡaɪz] **VT** unkenntlich machen; *voice* verstellen; *vehicle, aircraft, building* tarnen; *fear, dislike* verbergen; *taste* kaschieren; *facts, mistakes, interest* verschleiern; **to ~ oneself/sb as** sich/jdn verkleiden als; **superstition ~d as faith** Aberglaube, der unter dem Deckmantel des Glaubens daherkommt **N** *(lit)* Verkleidung *f*; *(of vehicle, aircraft, building)* Tarnung *f*; *(fig)* Deckmantel *m*; **in ~** verkleidet, getarnt; **in the ~ of** verkleidet als/getarnt als/unter dem Deckmantel von

disgust [dɪsˈɡʌst] **N** Ekel *m*; *(at sb's behaviour)* Entrüstung *f*, Empörung *f*; **in ~** voller Ekel/Empörung; **much to his ~ they left** sehr zu seiner Empörung gingen sie **VT** *(person, sight)* anekeln, anwidern; *(actions)* empören

disgusted [dɪsˈɡʌstɪd] ADJ angeekelt; *(at sb's behaviour)* empört; **to be ~ with sb** empört über jdn sein; **to be ~ with sth** angewidert von etw sein; **I was ~ with myself** ich war mir selbst zuwider

disgustedly [dɪsˈɡʌstɪdlɪ] ADV angewidert; *(= angrily)* empört

disgusting [dɪsˈɡʌstɪŋ] ADJ **a** *(= revolting) behaviour* widerlich; *(= physically nauseating)* ekelhaft; *taste, smell, person* widerlich, ekelhaft; **it looks ~** es sieht widerlich *or* ekelhaft aus **b**

(= offensive) book, film, photo anstößig, widerlich; *(= obscene)* obszön; **don't be ~** sei nicht so ordinär **c** *(= disgraceful)* unerhört; **it's ~ that…** es ist unerhört *or* eine Schande, dass …

disgustingly [dɪsˈɡʌstɪŋlɪ] ADV widerlich, ekelhaft; **~ rich** stinkreich

dish [dɪʃ] **N a** Schale *f*; *(for serving)* Schüssel *f*, Schale *f* **b dishes** PL *(= crockery)* Geschirr *nt*; **to do the ~es** Geschirr spülen, abwaschen **c** *(= food)* Gericht *nt*; **fish/pasta ~es** Fisch-/ /Nudelgerichte *pl* **d** *(Elec)* Parabolreflektor *m*; *(also* **dish aerial** *(Brit) or* **antenna** *(US))* Parabolantenne *f*, Schüssel *f (inf)* **e** *(US inf: = inside knowledge, secret)* **have you heard the latest ~?** weißt du schon das Neueste? **f** *(inf, girl)* klasse Frau *(inf)*, scharfe Braut *(sl)*; *(man)* toller Typ *(inf)*, scharfer Typ *(sl)* **VT a** *(= serve)* anrichten **b to ~ the dirt on sb** *(inf)* jdn in den Dreck ziehen *(inf)*

▶ **dish out** VT *sep (inf)* austeilen; **he can really dish it out** er kann ganz schön austeilen *(inf)*

▶ **dish up VT** *sep* **a** *(lit)* auf dem Teller anrichten; *(in bowls)* auftragen **b** *(fig inf) story, news* auftischen *(inf)* **VI** anrichten

dishabille [ˌdɪsəˈbiːl] N *(form)* **in various degrees of ~** mehr oder weniger hüllenlos

disharmony [ˈdɪsˈhɑːmənɪ] N *(lit, fig)* Disharmonie *f*

dish: **dishcloth** [ˈdɪʃklɒθ] N *(for drying)* Geschirrtuch *nt*; *(for washing)* Spüllappen *m or* -tuch *nt*; **dish drainer** [ˈdɪʃˌdreɪnəʳ] N Abtropfständer *m*

dishearten [dɪsˈhɑːtn] VT entmutigen; **don't be ~ed!** nun verlieren Sie nicht gleich den Mut!, nur Mut!

disheartening ADJ, **dishearteningly** ADV [dɪsˈhɑːtnɪŋ, -lɪ] entmutigend

dished [dɪʃt] ADJ *(Tech)* konkav (gewölbt); *wheels* gestürzt

dishevelled, *(US)* **disheveled** [dɪˈʃevəld] ADJ unordentlich; *hair* zerzaust; *person, appearance* ungepflegt; **to be in a ~ state** ziemlich mitgenommen aussehen

dish mop N Spülbürste *f*

dishonest [dɪsˈɒnɪst] ADJ unehrlich; *(= cheating) businessman* unredlich, unehrlich; *(= lying)* verlogen; *plan, scheme* unlauter

dishonestly [dɪsˈɒnɪstlɪ] ADV *(= not truthfully)* unehrlich; *pretend, claim* unehrlicherweise; *(= deceitfully)* betrügerisch; *(= with intent to deceive)* in betrügerischer Absicht; **to obtain money ~** sich auf betrügerische Weise Geld verschaffen

dishonesty [dɪsˈɒnɪstɪ] N Unehrlichkeit *f*; *(= cheating: of businessman)* Unredlichkeit *f*, Unehrlichkeit *f*; *(= lying)* Verlogenheit *f*; *(of plan, scheme)* Unlauterkeit *f*

dishonour, *(US)* **dishonor** [dɪsˈɒnəʳ] **N** Schande *f*, Unehre *f*; **to bring ~ (up)on sb** Schande über jdn bringen **VT a** *(= disgrace)* schänden, entehren; *family* Schande machen *(+dat)* **b** *(Comm, Fin) cheque* nicht honorieren; *bill* nicht bezahlen **c** *agreement* nicht einhalten; *promise* nicht einlösen *or* einhalten

dishonourable, *(US)* **dishonorable** [dɪsˈɒnərəbl] ADJ unehrenhaft; **it was ~ of him to do that** es war unehrenhaft, dass er das getan hat

dishonourable discharge, *(US)* **dishonorable discharge** N *(Mil)* unehrenhafte Entlassung; **to be given a ~** *(Mil)* unehrenhaft entlassen werden

dishonourableness, *(US)* **dishonorableness** [dɪsˈɒnərəblnɪs] N Unehrenhaftigkeit *f*

dishonourably, *(US)* **dishonorably** [dɪsˈɒnərəblɪ] ADV unehrenhaft

dish: **dishpan** N *(US)* Abwaschschüssel *f*; **dishpan hands** PL raue und rissige Hände *pl*; **dishrack** N Geschirrständer *m*; *(in dishwasher)* (Einsatz)korb *m*; **dishtowel** N *(US, Scot)* Geschirrtuch *nt*; **dishwasher** N *(= person)* Tellerwäscher(in) *m(f)*, Spüler(in) *m(f)*; *(= machine)* (Geschirr)spülmaschine *f*; **dishwasher-proof** ADJ spülmaschinenfest; **dishwater** N Abwasch- *or* Spülwasser *nt*; **this coffee tastes like ~** der Kaffee schmeckt wie Abwasch- *or* Spülwasser

dishy [ˈdɪʃɪ] ADJ *(+er) (inf) woman, man* scharf *(sl)*, toll *(inf)*

disillusion [ˌdɪsɪˈluːʒən] **VT** desillusionieren; **I hate to ~ you, but …** es tut mir leid, Ihnen Ihre Illusionen rauben *or* Sie desillusionieren zu müssen, aber … **N** Desillusion *f*

disillusionment [ˌdɪsɪˈluːʒənmənt] N Desillusionierung *f*

disincentive [ˌdɪsɪnˈsentɪv] N Entmutigung *f*; **to be a ~ to sth** keinen Anreiz für etw bieten; **to be a ~ to do sth** keinen Anreiz dafür bieten, etw zu tun; **it acts as a ~** es hält die Leute ab

disinclination [ˌdɪsɪnklɪˈneɪʃən] N Abneigung *f*, Unlust *f*

disinclined [ˈdɪsɪnˈklaɪnd] ADJ abgeneigt

disinfect [ˌdɪsɪnˈfekt] VT desinfizieren

disinfectant [ˌdɪsɪnˈfektənt] **N** Desinfektionsmittel *nt* **ADJ** desinfizierend, Desinfektions-

disinfection [ˌdɪsɪnˈfekʃən] N Desinfektion *f*

disinformation [ˌdɪsɪnfɔːˈmeɪʃən] N Desinformation *f*

disingenuous [ˌdɪsɪnˈdʒenjʊəs] ADJ unaufrichtig

disingenuously [ˌdɪsɪnˈdʒenjʊəslɪ] ADV unaufrichtig, unehrlich; *say, remark* unaufrichtigerweise; **the finance ministry claims ~ that it did not know this was going on** das Finanzministerium behauptet wider besseren Wissens, dass es über die Vorgänge nicht informiert gewesen sei

disingenuousness [ˌdɪsɪnˈdʒenjʊəsnɪs] N Unaufrichtigkeit *f*

disinherit [ˈdɪsɪnˈherɪt] VT enterben

disinheritance [ˈdɪsɪnˈherɪtəns] N Enterbung *f*

disintegrate [dɪsˈɪntɪɡreɪt] **VI** zerfallen; *(rock, cement)* auseinanderbröckeln; *(road surface)* rissig werden; *(car)* sich in seine Bestandteile auflösen; *(group, institution)* sich auflösen; *(marriage, society, theory)* zusammenbrechen; *(family)* auseinandergehen; **to ~ into civil war/chaos** in den Bürgerkrieg/ins Chaos versinken **VT** zerfallen lassen; *rock, cement* auseinanderbröckeln lassen; *road surface* brüchig werden lassen; *group, institution* auflösen; *theory* zusammenbrechen lassen

disintegration [dɪsˌɪntɪˈɡreɪʃən] N Zerfall *m*; *(of rock, cement)* Auseinanderbröckeln *nt*; *(of road surface)* Rissigkeit *f*; *(of group, institution, family)* Auflösung *f*; *(of marriage, society, theory)* Zusammenbruch *m*

disinter [ˌdɪsɪnˈtɜːʳ] VT ausgraben

disinterest [dɪsˈɪntrəst] N Desinteresse *nt (in an +dat)*

disinterested [dɪsˈɪntrɪstɪd] ADJ **a** *(= impartial)* unvoreingenommen, unparteiisch **b** *(= uninterested)* desinteressiert

disinterestedly [dɪsˈɪntrɪstɪdlɪ] ADV **a** *(= impartially)* unvoreingenommen, unparteiisch; **we reason ~ from the facts we observe** wir urteilen unvoreingenommen auf Grundlage der von uns beobachteten Fakten **b** *(= uninterestedly)* desinteressiert; *look, say* gelangweilt; **I watched ~ as the train pulled into the station** ich beobachtete gelangweilt, wie der Zug in den Bahnhof einfuhr

disinterestedness [dɪsˈɪntrɪstɪdnɪs] N **a** *(= impartiality)* Unvoreingenommenheit *f* **b** *(= lack of concern)* Desinteresse *nt*

disinterment [ˌdɪsɪnˈtɜːmənt] N Ausgrabung *f*

disjointed [dɪsˈdʒɔɪntɪd] ADJ **a** *(= incoherent) sentences, words, thoughts* unzusammenhängend, zusammenhanglos; *film, programme* unzusammenhängend **b** *(= disunited) society* zerrissen; *team* uneinig; *play* unzusammenhängend

disjointedly [dɪsˈdʒɔɪntɪdlɪ] ADV unzusammenhängend, zusammenhanglos

disjointedness [dɪsˈdʒɔɪntɪdnɪs] N **a** *(= incoherence)* Zusammenhanglosigkeit *f* **b** *(= disunity, of society)* Zerrissenheit *f*; *(of team)* Uneinigkeit *f*

disjunctive [dɪsˈdʒʌŋktɪv] *(Gram)* **ADJ** disjunktiv **N** Disjunktion *f*

disk N *(Comput)* Platte *f*; *(= floppy disk)* Diskette *f*; **on ~** auf Platte/Diskette

disk *(Comput)*: **disk access** N Datenträgerzugriff *m*; **disk cleanup** N Datenträgerbereinigung *f*; **disk controller** N Plattencontroller *m*; **disk drive** N (Festplatten)laufwerk *nt*; *(= floppy disk drive)* Diskettenlaufwerk *nt*

diskette [dɪsˈket] N *(Comput)* Diskette *f*

disk: **diskless** [ˈdɪsklɪs] ADJ *(Comput)* plattenlos; **disk operating system** N *(Comput)* Betriebssystem *nt*; **disk space** N *(Comput)* Speicherkapazität *f*

dislike [dɪsˈlaɪk] **VT** nicht mögen, nicht gernhaben; **to ~ doing sth** etw ungern *or* nicht gern tun; **to ~ sb doing sth** es nicht gernhaben *or* gern sehen, wenn jd etw tut; **I ~ him/it intensely** ich mag ihn/es überhaupt nicht; **I don't ~ it** ich habe nichts dagegen **N** Abneigung *f (of* gegen); **likes and ~s** Vorlieben und Abneigungen; **to take a ~ to sb/sth** eine Abneigung gegen jdn/etw entwickeln; **he had taken an instant ~ to John** er konnte John auf Anhieb nicht leiden

dislocate [ˈdɪsləʊkeɪt] VT *(Med)* verrenken, ausrenken; *(fig) plans* durcheinanderbringen; **to ~ one's shoulder** sich *(dat)* den Arm auskugeln

dislocation [ˌdɪsləʊˈkeɪʃən] N *(Med)* Verrenkung *f*; *(of shoulder)* Auskugeln *nt*; *(fig, of plans)* Durcheinanderbringen *nt*

dislodge [dɪsˈlɒdʒ] VT *obstruction, stone* lösen; *(= prise, poke out)* herausstochern; *(= knock out)* herausschlagen *or* -klopfen; *person* verdrängen; *(Mil) enemy* verdrängen; **a few stones have been ~d** einige Steine haben sich gelöst

disloyal [dɪsˈlɔɪəl] ADJ illoyal; **to be ~ to sb** jdm gegenüber nicht loyal sein

disloyalty [dɪsˈlɔɪəltɪ] N Illoyalität *f (to* gegenüber)

dismal [ˈdɪzməl] ADJ **a** *(= depressing) place, building, day, prospect, weather* trostlos; *thought* trüb; **it makes ~ reading** es ist bedrückend zu lesen; **the ~ science** *(= economics)* politische Ökonomie **b** *(= poor) performance* kläglich, miserabel; *prospects* miserabel; **the ~ state of the economy** die miserable Wirtschaftslage; **to be a ~ failure** kläglich scheitern

dismally [ˈdɪzməlɪ] ADV **a** *(= depressingly) say, think, look* trübselig; *grey, monotonous* trostlos; **morale was ~ low** die Moral war deprimierend schlecht **b** *(= badly) fail* kläglich; **the world champion performed ~** der Weltmeister zeigte eine klägliche Leistung

dismantle [dɪsˈmæntl] VT *(= take to pieces)* auseinandernehmen; *scaffolding* abbauen; *(permanently) ship* abwracken; *arms factory, machinery* demontieren; *(fig) apartheid etc* demontieren

dismast [dɪsˈmɑːst] VT entmasten

dismay [dɪsˈmeɪ] **N** Bestürzung *f*; **in ~** bestürzt; **to my ~ I discovered that …** zu meiner Bestürzung stellte ich fest, dass … **VT** bestürzen

dismember [dɪsˈmembəʳ] VT *(lit) animal, body* zerstückeln; *(Med)* zergliedern; *(fig) empire* zersplittern

dismemberment [dɪsˈmembəmənt] N *(lit)* Zergliederung *f*; *(fig)* Zersplitterung *f*

dismire [dɪsˈmaɪəʳ] VT *(= dislike)* nicht mögen, ablehnen

dismiss [dɪsˈmɪs] VT **a** *(from job)* entlassen **b** *(= allow to go)* entlassen; *assembly* auflösen, aufheben; **~!** wegtreten!; **"class ~ed"** „ihr dürft gehen" **c** *(= brush aside) point, objection, speculation, claims* abtun; **to ~ sth from one's mind** etw verwerfen; **to ~ sb from one's mind** sich *(dat)* jdn aus dem Kopf schlagen; **to ~ sth out of hand** etw pauschal abtun **d** *(Jur) accused* entlassen; *appeal* abweisen; **to ~ a case** die Klage abweisen; **to ~ charges against sb** die Klage gegen jdn abweisen **e** *(Sport) batsman, team* ausschlagen; **he was ~ed for 52 runs** er wurde nach 52 Läufen ausgeschlagen

dismissal [dɪsˈmɪsəl] N **a** (= *firing: from job*) Entlassung *f* **b** (= *permission to leave*) Entlassung *f*; (*of assembly*) Auflösung *f* **c** (= *brushing aside: of point, objection, speculation, claim*) Abtun *nt* **d** (*Jur, of accused*) Entlassung *f*; (*of appeal*) Abweisung *f*, Einstellung *f*; (*of case, charges*) Abweisung *f* **e** (*Sport, of batsman, team*) Ausschlagen *nt*

dismissal pay N Abfindung *f*

dismissive [dɪsˈmɪsɪv] ADJ *remark* wegwerfend; *gesture* abweisend; **to be ~ of sb** jdn heruntermachen; **to be ~ of sth** etw abtun

dismissively [dɪsˈmɪsɪvlɪ] ADV abweisend; *say* abweisend, wegwerfend

dismount [dɪsˈmaʊnt] VI absteigen VT **a** *rider* abwerfen **b** (*Tech*) *machine, gun* abmontieren

disobedience [ˌdɪsəˈbiːdɪəns] N Ungehorsam *m* (to gegenüber)

disobedient [ˌdɪsəˈbiːdɪənt] ADJ ungehorsam

disobey [ˌdɪsəˈbeɪ] VT *parents, teacher* nicht gehorchen (+*dat*); *officer* den Gehorsam verweigern (+*dat*); *rule, law* übertreten

disoblige [ˌdɪsəˈblaɪdʒ] VT keinen Gefallen tun (+*dat*)

disobliging ADJ, **disobligingly** ADV [ˌdɪsəˈblaɪdʒɪŋ, -lɪ] ungefällig

disorder [dɪsˈɔːdəʳ] N **a** Durcheinander *nt*; (*in room etc*) Unordnung *f*, Durcheinander *nt*; **in ~** durcheinander, in Unordnung; **to retreat in ~** (*Mil*) einen ungeordneten Rückzug antreten **b** (*Pol: = rioting*) Unruhen *pl* **c** (*Med*) Funktionsstörung *f*; **eating ~** Störung *f* des Essverhaltens; **kidney ~** Nierenleiden *nt*; **mental ~** Geistesstörung *f*; **sleep ~** Schlafstörung *f*; **stomach ~** Magenbeschwerden *pl* VT **a** (= *mess up*) durcheinanderbringen; *room* in Unordnung bringen **b** (*Med*) angreifen

disordered [dɪsˈɔːdəd] ADJ **a** (= *untidy*) *room* unordentlich; *hair, plans, papers* wirr; (*fig: = disorderly*) *life, world, existence* ungeordnet **b** (= *disturbed*) *mind, behaviour, imagination* gestört; **mentally ~** geistesgestört

disorderliness [dɪsˈɔːdəlɪnɪs] N **a** (= *untidiness, of room, desk*) Unordentlichkeit *f*; (*of queue, process, row*) Ungeordnetheit *f* **b** (= *unruliness, of person*) Wildheit *f*; (*of crowd, event*) Undiszipliniertheit *f*; (*of conduct*) Ungehörigkeit *f*

disorderly [dɪsˈɔːdəlɪ] ADJ **a** (= *untidy*) *room, desk* unordentlich; *queue, row* ungeordnet **b** (= *unruly*) *person* wild; *crowd, event* undiszipliniert; *conduct, behaviour* ungehörig; **~ yobbos** (*inf*) randalierende Halbstarke; **to become ~** (*person, crowd*) außer Rand und Band geraten; **the rally became ~** bei der Kundgebung kam es zu Ausschreitungen → *also* **drunk ADJ a c** (= *badly organized*) *process* ungeordnet

disorderly: **disorderly behaviour**, (*US*) **disorderly behavior** N (*Jur*) ungebührliches *or* ungehöriges Benehmen; **disorderly conduct** N = **disorderly behaviour**; **disorderly house** N (*Jur: = brothel*) öffentliches Haus; (= *gambling den*) Spielhölle *f*; **to keep a ~** ein öffentliches Haus unterhalten

disorganization [dɪsˌɔːɡənaɪˈzeɪʃən] N Desorganisation *f*; (= *state of confusion*) Durcheinander *nt*

disorganize [dɪsˈɔːɡənaɪz] VT durcheinanderbringen

disorganized [dɪsˈɔːɡənaɪzd] ADJ systemlos; *life, person* chaotisch; *filing system etc* durcheinander *pred*, ungeordnet; **he/the office is completely ~** bei ihm/im Büro geht alles drunter und drüber

disorient [dɪsˈɔːrɪent], **disorientate** [dɪsˈɔːrɪənteɪt] VT (*lit, fig*) verwirren, desorientieren

disorientation [dɪsˌɔːrɪənˈteɪʃən] N Verwirrung *f*, Desorientierung *f*

disown [dɪsˈəʊn] VT verleugnen; *signature* nicht (als seine eigene) anerkennen; *suggestion* nicht wahrhaben wollen; **I'll ~ you if you go out in that hat** wenn du mit dem Hut ausgehst, tue ich so, als ob ich nicht zu dir gehöre

disparage [dɪˈspærɪdʒ] VT herabsetzen; *work, achievements also* schmälern

disparagement [dɪˈspærɪdʒmənt] N Herabsetzung *f*; (*of work, achievements also*) Schmälerung *f*

disparaging ADJ, **disparagingly** ADV [dɪˈspærɪdʒɪŋ, -lɪ] abschätzig, geringschätzig

disparate [ˈdɪspərɪt] ADJ ungleich, disparat (*geh*)

disparity [dɪˈspærɪtɪ] N Ungleichheit *f*, Disparität *f* (*geh*)

dispassion [dɪsˈpæʃən] N Objektivität *f*

dispassionate [dɪsˈpæʃənɪt] ADJ (= *impartial*) unvoreingenommen, objektiv; (= *unemotional*) unbewegt, leidenschaftslos

dispassionately [dɪsˈpæʃənɪtlɪ] ADV (= *impartially*) unvoreingenommen, objektiv; (= *unemotionally*) unbewegt, leidenschaftslos

dispatch [dɪˈspætʃ] VT **a** (= *send*) *letter, goods etc* senden, schicken; *person, troops etc* (ent)senden, schicken
b (= *deal with*) *job etc* (prompt) erledigen
c (= *kill*) töten
d (*inf*) *food* fertig werden mit (*inf*)
N [dɪˈspætʃ, ˈdɪspætʃ] **a** (*of letter, goods etc*) Senden *nt*, Schicken *nt*; (*of person, troops etc*) Entsendung *f*; **date of ~** Absendedatum *nt*
b (= *message, report*) Depesche *f*; (*Press*) Bericht *m*; **to be mentioned in ~es** (*Mil*) in den Kriegsberichten erwähnt werden
c (= *dealing with: of job etc*) prompte Erledigung
d (= *promptness*) Promptheit *f*; **with ~** prompt

dispatch: **dispatch box** N (*Brit Parl*) Depeschenkassette *f*; **dispatch documents** PL (*Comm*) Versandpapiere *pl*; **dispatch goods** PL Eilgut *nt*; **dispatch note** N (*in advance*) Versandanzeige *f*; (*with goods*) Begleitschein *m*; **dispatch rider** N (= *motorcyclist*) Melder(in) *m(f)*, Meldefahrer(in) *m(f)*

dispel [dɪˈspel] VT *clouds, fog* auflösen, vertreiben; *doubts, fears, gloom* zerstreuen; *sorrows* vertreiben; *myth* zerstören; *impression, notion* ein Ende machen (+*dat*)

dispensability [dɪˌspensəˈbɪlɪtɪ] N Entbehrlichkeit *f*

dispensable [dɪˈspensəbl] ADJ entbehrlich

dispensary [dɪˈspensərɪ] N (*in hospital*) (Krankenhaus)apotheke *f*; (*in chemist's*) Apothekenabteilung *f*; (= *clinic*) Dispensarium *nt*

dispensation [ˌdɪspenˈseɪʃən] N **a** (= *handing out*) Verteilung *f*; (*of charity*) Austeilung *f*; **~ of justice** Rechtsprechung *f* **b** (= *exemption*) Dispensation *f*; (*Eccl*) Dispens *f*; **special ~** Sonderregelung *f* **c** (= *system, regime*) System *nt*; (*Rel*) Glaubenssystem *nt*; **~ of Providence** Fügung *f* der Vorsehung *or* des Schicksals

dispense [dɪˈspens] VT **a** verteilen, austeilen (to an +*acc*); *advice* erteilen; (*machine*) *product, money* ausgeben; **to ~ justice** Recht sprechen **b** (*Pharm*) *medicine* abgeben; *prescription* zubereiten **c** (*form, = exempt*) dispensieren, befreien; **to ~ sb from doing sth** jdn davon befreien *or* dispensieren, etw zu tun VI (*Pharm*) Medizin abgeben, dispensieren (*form*)

▶ **dispense with** VI +*prep obj* verzichten auf (+*acc*); **I could/couldn't dispense with that** ich könnte darauf gut/nicht verzichten, ich könnte ohne das auskommen/nicht auskommen; **that can be dispensed with** das ist entbehrlich

dispenser [dɪˈspensəʳ] N **a** (*Pharm*) Apotheker(in) *m(f)* **b** (= *container*) Spender *m*; (= *slot machine*) Automat *m*

dispensing chemist's [dɪˌspensɪŋˈkemɪsts] N Apotheke *f*

dispersal [dɪˈspɜːsəl] N (= *scattering*) Verstreuen *nt*; (*Bot: of seed*) Verteilung *f*; (= *dispelling: of crowd, mist*) Zerstreuung *f*, Auflösung *f*; (*of oil slick*) Auflösung *f*; (*Opt: of light*) Streuung *f*; (*Chem: of particles*) Dispersion *f*; (*fig*) (*of knowledge etc*) Verbreitung *f*; (*of efforts*) Verzettelung *f*, Zersplitterung *f*

dispersant [dɪˈspɜːsənt] N Lösungsmittel *nt*

disperse [dɪˈspɜːs] VT (= *scatter widely*) verstreuen; (*Bot*) *seed* verteilen; (= *dispel*) *crowd, mist* zerstreuen, auflösen; *oil slick* auflösen; (*Opt*) *light* streuen; (*Chem*) *particles* dispergieren; (*fig*) *knowledge etc* verbreiten VI sich zerstreuen *or* auflösen; (*oil slick*) sich auflösen

dispersion [dɪˈspɜːʃən] N = **dispersal**

dispirit [dɪˈspɪrɪt] VT entmutigen

dispirited ADJ, **dispiritedly** ADV [dɪˈspɪrɪtɪd, -lɪ] entmutigt

dispiriting ADJ, **dispiritingly** ADV [dɪˈspɪrɪtɪŋ, -lɪ] entmutigend

displace [dɪsˈpleɪs] VT **a** (= *move*) verschieben; *people* vertreiben **b** (= *replace*) ablösen, ersetzen **c** (*Naut, Phys*) *water, air etc* verdrängen **d** (*in office*) verdrängen, ausbooten (*inf*)

displaced: **displaced emotion** N verlagertes Gefühl; **displaced person** [dɪsˌpleɪstˈpɜːsn] N Vertriebene(r) *mf*

displacement [dɪsˈpleɪsmənt] N **a** (= *act of moving*) Verschiebung *f*; (*of people*) Vertreibung *f*; (*Naut, Phys: of air, water*) Verdrängung *f*; (= *volume displaced, Phys*) verdrängte Menge; (*Naut*) Verdrängung *f* **b** (= *replacement*) Ablösung *f*, Ersatz *m* **c** (= *distance sth is moved*) Verschiebung *f*; (*Geol, of rocks*) Dislokation *f*

displacement: **displacement activity** N (*Psych*) Ersatzbefriedigung *f*; **displacement ton** N (*Naut*) Verdrängungstonne *f*

display [dɪˈspleɪ] VT **a** (= *show*) *object* zeigen; (*Comput*) anzeigen; *interest, courage* zeigen, beweisen; *ignorance* an den Tag legen, beweisen; (*ostentatiously*) *new clothes etc* vorführen; *feelings* zur Schau stellen; *power* demonstrieren; *exam results, notice* aushängen
b (*Comm*) *goods* ausstellen
c (*Typ, Press*) hervorheben
VI Imponiergehabe zeigen; (*birds*) balzen
N **a** (*of object*) Zeigen *nt*; (*of interest, courage*) Zeigen *nt*, Beweis *m*; (*of ignorance*) Beweis *m*; (*ostentatious, of new clothes etc*) Vorführung *f*; (*of feelings*) Zurschaustellung *f*; (*of power*) Demonstration *f*; **to make a great ~ of sth** etw groß zur Schau stellen; **to make a great ~ of doing sth** etw betont auffällig tun; **to be/go on ~** ausgestellt sein/werden; **the painting goes on public ~ today** das Gemälde wird heute öffentlich ausgestellt; **these are only for ~** die sind nur zur Ansicht; **I hope we don't have another ~ (of temper) like that** ich hoffe, wir kriegen nicht noch einmal denselben Tanz *or* dieselbe Schau (*inf*); **she was not given to public ~s of emotion** sie zeigte ihre Gefühle nicht gerne in der Öffentlichkeit
b (= *exhibition of paintings etc*) Ausstellung *f*; (= *dancing display etc*) Vorführung *f*; (= *military, air display*) Schau *f*; **firework ~** (öffentliches) Feuerwerk
c (*Comm*) Auslage *f*, Display *nt*
d (*Zool*) Imponiergehabe *nt*; (*of bird*) Balz *f*
e (= *visual display*) Anzeige *f*

display: **display advertisement** N Displayanzeige *f*; **display advertising** N Displaywerbung *f*; **display cabinet** N Schaukasten *m*; **display case** N Vitrine *f*; **display pack** N Displaypackung *f*; **display unit** N (*Comput*) (Daten)sichtgerät *nt*, Bildschirmgerät *nt*; **display window** N Schaufenster *nt*

displease [dɪsˈpliːz] VT missfallen (+*dat*), nicht gefallen (+*dat*); (= *annoy*) verstimmen, verärgern; **to be ~d with sth** verärgert über etw (*acc*) sein; **he was rather ~d to hear that …** er hörte nur sehr ungern, dass …; **I was not ~d with my efforts** ich war mit meinen Bemühungen nicht unzufrieden

displeasing [dɪsˈpliːzɪŋ] ADJ unangenehm; **to be ~ to sb** jdm missfallen *or* nicht gefallen; (= *annoy*) jdn verstimmen *or* verärgern; **the idea was not ~ to her** der Gedanke war ihr gar nicht so unangenehm

displeasure [dɪsˈpleʒəʳ] N Missfallen *nt (at* über *+acc)*

disport [dɪˈspɔːt] VR *(old)* sich ergötzen *(old)*

disposability [dɪˌspəʊzəˈbɪlɪtɪ] N (freie) Verfügbarkeit

disposable [dɪˈspəʊzəbl] ADJ **a** *(= throwaway)* Wegwerf-; **~ razor** Wegwerfrasierer *m*; **~ nappy** *(Brit)* Wegwerfwindel *f*; **~ syringe/needle** Einwegspritze *f*/-nadel *f*; **all acupuncture needles are now ~** alle Akupunkturnadeln werden heute nach Gebrauch weggeworfen; **~ contact lenses** Kontaktlinsen *pl* zum Wegwerfen **b** *(fig, = unimportant) person, music, art* unbedeutend **c** *(= available)* verfügbar N **disposables** PL *(= containers)* Einwegbehälter *pl*; *(= nappies)* Wegwerfwindeln *pl*

disposable assets PL *(Fin)* disponibles *(spec) or* frei verfügbares Vermögen

disposable income N verfügbares Einkommen

disposal [dɪˈspəʊzəl] N **a** Loswerden *nt*; *(by selling also)* Veräußerung *f*; *(of unwanted person or goods, of litter, body)* Beseitigung *f*; *(of question, matter)* Erledigung *f*, Regelung *f*
b *(= control: over resources, funds, personnel)* Verfügungsgewalt *f*; **the means at sb's ~** die jdm zur Verfügung stehenden Mittel; **to put sth at sb's ~** jdm etw zur Verfügung stellen; **to be at sb's ~** jdm zur Verfügung stehen; **we had the entire staff/building at our ~** die ganze Belegschaft/das ganze Gebäude stand uns zur Verfügung
c *(form: = arrangement, of ornaments, furniture)* Anordnung *f*, Arrangement *nt*; *(Mil, of troops)* Aufstellung *f*

dispose [dɪˈspəʊz] VT **a** *(form: = arrange) shrubs, ornaments* anordnen; *people, troops* aufstellen; *papers* ordnen **b** *(= make willing)* **to ~ sb to do sth** jdn geneigt machen, etw zu tun VI → **propose VI b**

▶ **dispose of** VI *+prep obj* **a** *(= get rid of) furniture* loswerden; *(by selling)* veräußern, loswerden; *unwanted person, goods* beseitigen, loswerden; *litter, body* beseitigen; *opponent, difficulties* aus dem Weg schaffen; *question, matter* erledigen, regeln **b** *(= have at disposal) fortune, time* verfügen über *(+acc)* **c** *(= kill)* eliminieren

disposed [dɪˈspəʊzd] ADJ *(form)* **a** **to be ~ to do sth** *(= prepared)* bereit sein, etw zu tun; *(= inclined)* etw tun wollen; **to be well** *or* **favourably** *(Brit) or* **favorably** *(US)* **~ to(wards) sb** jdm wohlgesinnt sein; **to be well** *or* **favourably** *(Brit) or* **favorably** *(US)* **~ to(wards) sth** einer Sache *(dat)* wohlwollend gegenüberstehen → *also* **ill-disposed b** *(form, = arranged)* angeordnet; **the choir was ~ in the most original way** der Chor war sehr originell aufgestellt

disposition [ˌdɪspəˈzɪʃən] N **a** *(form: = arrangement) (of buildings, ornaments)* Anordnung *f*; *(of forces)* Aufstellung *f*; *(Jur: of money, property)* Verfügung *f* **b** *(= temperament)* Veranlagung *f*; **her cheerful/friendly ~** ihre fröhliche/freundliche Art

dispossess [ˌdɪspəˈzes] VT enteignen

dispossession [ˌdɪspəˈzeʃən] N Enteignung *f*

disproportion [ˌdɪsprəˈpɔːʃən] N Missverhältnis *nt*

disproportionate [ˌdɪsprəˈpɔːʃnɪt] ADJ **to be ~ (to sth)** in keinem Verhältnis (zu etw) stehen; **a ~ amount of money** ein unverhältnismäßig hoher Geldbetrag; **a ~ amount of time** eine unverhältnismäßig lange Zeit

disproportionately [ˌdɪsprəˈpɔːʃnɪtlɪ] ADV *(+adj)* unverhältnismäßig; *affect* unverhältnismäßig stark; *suffer* unverhältnismäßig viel; **~ large numbers of ...** unverhältnismäßig viele ...; **immigrants were ~ represented** Einwanderer stellten einen unverhältnismäßig großen Anteil dar; **the new tax will fall ~ on the poor** die neue Steuer wird die Armen unverhältnismäßig stark belasten

disprovable [dɪsˈpruːvəbl] ADJ widerlegbar

disprove [dɪsˈpruːv] ✪ 26.3 VT widerlegen

disputable [dɪˈspjuːtəbl] ADJ sehr zweifelhaft, disputabel

disputant [dɪˈspjuːtənt] N Disputant(in) *m(f)*

disputation [ˌdɪspjuːˈteɪʃən] N Disput *m*, Kontroverse *f*

disputatious [ˌdɪspjuːˈteɪʃəs] ADJ streitbar, streitlustig

dispute [dɪˈspjuːt] VT **a** *(= argue against) statement* bestreiten, anfechten; *claim to sth, will* anfechten; **I would ~ that** das möchte ich bestreiten
b *(= debate) question, subject* sich streiten über *(+acc)*; **the issue was hotly ~d** das Thema wurde hitzig diskutiert
c *(= contest) championship, possession* kämpfen um; *territory* beanspruchen
VI *(= argue)* streiten
N [dɪˈspjuːt, ˈdɪspjuːt] **a** *no pl (= arguing, controversy)* Disput *m*, Kontroverse *f*; **to be beyond ~** außer Frage stehen; **there is some ~ about which horse won** es ist umstritten, welches Pferd gewonnen hat; **the two countries are in ~ over boundaries** zwischen den beiden Ländern gibt es Grenzstreitigkeiten; **a territory in** *or* **under ~** ein umstrittenes Gebiet; **to be open to ~** anfechtbar *or* umstritten sein; **the case is in** *or* **under ~** *(Jur)* der Fall wird verhandelt
b *(= quarrel, argument)* Streit *m*
c *(Ind)* Auseinandersetzung *f*; **the union is in ~ with the management** zwischen Gewerkschaft und Betriebsleitung bestehen Unstimmigkeiten; **wages ~** Tarifauseinandersetzungen *pl*

disqualification [dɪsˌkwɒlɪfɪˈkeɪʃən] N **a** Ausschluss *m*; *(Sport)* Disqualifikation *f*; **~ (from driving)** Führerscheinentzug *m* **b** *(= disqualifying factor)* Grund *m* zur Disqualifikation

disqualify [dɪsˈkwɒlɪfaɪ] VT *(= make ineligible)* untauglich *or* ungeeignet machen *(from* für); *(Sport etc)* disqualifizieren, ausschließen; **to ~ sb from driving** jdm den Führerschein entziehen; **that disqualifies you from criticizing him** das nimmt Ihnen jedes Recht, ihn zu kritisieren

disquiet [dɪsˈkwaɪət] VT beunruhigen N Unruhe *f*

disquisition [ˌdɪskwɪˈzɪʃən] N (lange, ausführliche) Abhandlung *or (speech)* Rede *(on* über *+acc)*

disregard [ˈdɪsrɪˈgɑːd] VT ignorieren; *remark, feelings also* nicht beachten; *danger, advice, authority also* missachten N Nichtbeachtung *f (for gen)*, Missachtung *f (for gen)*; *(for danger)* Missachtung *f*; *(for money)* Geringschätzung *f (for gen)*; **to show complete ~ for sth** etw völlig außer Acht lassen

disrelish [dɪsˈrelɪʃ] *(form)* N Abneigung *f*, Widerwillen *m (for* gegen) VT einen Widerwillen haben gegen

disrepair [ˈdɪsrɪˈpɛəʳ] N Baufälligkeit *f*; **in a state of ~** baufällig; **to fall into ~** verfallen

disreputable [dɪsˈrepjʊtəbl] ADJ *person, hotel, bar* verrufen; *clothes* schäbig; *conduct* unehrenhaft; *area* anrüchig, verrufen; **~ woman** leichtes Mädchen

disreputably [dɪsˈrepjʊtəblɪ] ADV *behave (= dishonourably)* übel, gemein; *(= not respectably)* anstößig

disrepute [ˈdɪsrɪˈpjuːt] N schlechter Ruf; **to bring sth into ~** etw in Verruf bringen; **to fall into ~** in Verruf kommen *or* geraten

disrespect [ˌdɪsrɪsˈpekt] N Respektlosigkeit *f (for* gegenüber); **to show ~ for sth** keinen Respekt vor etw *(dat)* haben; **I don't mean any ~, but ...** ich will nicht respektlos sein, aber ...; **no ~ to ...** bei allem Respekt vor *(+dat)* ...

disrespectful [ˌdɪsrɪsˈpektfʊl] ADJ respektlos *(to* gegenüber)

disrespectfully [ˌdɪsrɪsˈpektfəlɪ] ADV respektlos; **I don't mean that ~** das ist nicht respektlos gemeint

disrobe [dɪsˈrəʊb] VI *(judge)* seine Gewänder ablegen; *(form, hum: = undress)* sich entkleiden, sich entblättern *(hum inf)* VT *(form, hum, = undress)* entkleiden

disrupt [dɪsˈrʌpt] VT stören; *lesson, meeting, conversation, train service also* unterbrechen; **their lives were ~ed (by it)** das brachte ihr Leben durcheinander, das stellte ihr Leben auf den Kopf

disruption [dɪsˈrʌpʃən] N Störung *f*; *(of lesson, meeting, conversation, train service also)* Unterbrechung *f*

disruptive [dɪsˈrʌptɪv] ADJ *behaviour, influence* störend; *effect* zerstörerisch; **~ pupils** Schüler, die den Schulbetrieb stören; **to be a ~ influence** einen störenden Einfluss ausüben; **to be ~ to sb/sth** sich störend auf jdn/etw auswirken; **~ action** *(Ind)* Störaktionen *pl*

diss VT = **dis**

dissatisfaction [ˈdɪsˌsætɪsˈfækʃən] N Unzufriedenheit *f*

dissatisfied [dɪsˈsætɪsfaɪd] ADJ unzufrieden *(with* mit)

dissect [dɪˈsekt] VT *plant* präparieren; *animal* sezieren, präparieren; *(fig) report, theory* sezieren, zergliedern

dissection [dɪˈsekʃən] N **a** *(= act) (of plant)* Präparation *f*; *(of animal)* Sektion *f*; *(fig, of report, theory)* Zergliederung *f* **b** *(= plant or animal dissected)* Präparat *nt*

dissemble [dɪˈsembl] VT *(= cover up)* verbergen; *(= feign)* vortäuschen, heucheln VI *(liter)* sich verstellen; *(= feign illness)* simulieren

dissembler [dɪˈsembləʳ] N Heuchler(in) *m(f)*

disseminate [dɪˈsemɪneɪt] VT verbreiten

dissemination [dɪˌsemɪˈneɪʃən] N Verbreitung *f*

dissension [dɪˈsenʃən] N Meinungsverschiedenheit *f*, Differenz *f*; **to cause ~** zu Meinungsverschiedenheiten *or* Differenzen führen; *(person)* Meinungsverschiedenheiten *or* Differenzen verursachen

dissent [dɪˈsent] VI **a** *(= oppose)* anderer Meinung sein, differieren *(geh)*; **I strongly ~ from what he says** ich muss dem, was er sagt, entschieden widersprechen **b** *(Eccl)* sich weigern, die Staatskirche anzuerkennen N **a** *(= opposition)* Dissens *m (geh)*, Nichtübereinstimmung *f*; **to voice/express one's ~ (with sth)** erklären, dass man (mit etw) nicht übereinstimmt; **there was remarkably little ~** es gab bemerkenswert wenig Widerspruch **b** *(Eccl)* Weigerung *f* die (englische) Staatskirche anzuerkennen

dissenter [dɪˈsentəʳ] N Abweichler(in) *m(f)*; *(Eccl also)* Dissenter *m*

dissentient [dɪˈsenʃɪənt] ADJ *(form)* = **dissenting**

dissenting [dɪˈsentɪŋ] ADJ *attr opinion* abweichend; **there was not a single ~ voice** es wurde keine Gegenstimme laut

dissert [dɪˈsɜːt], **dissertate** [ˈdɪsəteɪt] VI *(form) (in writing)* eine Abhandlung schreiben *(on* über *+acc)*; *(in speech)* einen Vortrag halten *(on* über *+acc)*

dissertation [ˌdɪsəˈteɪʃən] N wissenschaftliche Arbeit; *(for PhD)* Dissertation *f*; *(fig)* Vortrag *m*

disservice [dɪsˈsɜːvɪs] N **to do oneself/sb a ~** sich/jdm einen schlechten Dienst erweisen

dissidence [ˈdɪsɪdəns] N Opposition *f*; *(Pol)* Dissidententum *nt*

dissident [ˈdɪsɪdənt] N Dissident(in) *m(f)*, Regimekritiker(in) *m(f)* ADJ dissident, regimekritisch

dissimilar [dɪˈsɪmɪləʳ] ADJ unterschiedlich, verschieden *(to* von); *two things* verschieden; **not ~ (to sb/sth)** (jdm/einer Sache) nicht ungleich *or (in appearance)* nicht unähnlich

dissimilarity [ˌdɪsɪmɪˈlærɪtɪ] N Unterschiedlichkeit *f*, Verschiedenheit *f*; *(in appearance also)* Unähnlichkeit *f*

dissimulate [dɪˈsɪmjʊleɪt] VT verbergen VI sich verstellen

dissimulation [dɪˌsɪmjʊˈleɪʃən] N Verstellung *f*, Heuchelei *f*

dissipate [ˈdɪsɪpeɪt] VT a *(= dispel) fog* auflösen; *heat* ableiten; *doubts, fears* zerstreuen; *tension* lösen b *energy, efforts* verschwenden, vergeuden; *fortune* verschwenden VI *(clouds, fog)* sich auflösen; *(crowd, doubts, fear also)* sich zerstreuen; *(tension)* sich lösen

dissipated [ˈdɪsɪpeɪtɪd] ADJ *person, behaviour, society* zügellos; *life, activity* ausschweifend; *face* verlebt

dissipation [ˌdɪsɪˈpeɪʃən] N a *(= debauchery)* Ausschweifung *f*; **a life of ~** ein ausschweifendes Leben b *(= dispersal: of doubts, fears)* Zerstreuung *f* c *(= wasting, of energy, efforts)* Verschwendung *f*, Vergeudung *f*; *(of fortune)* Verschwendung *f*

dissociate [dɪˈsəʊʃɪeɪt] ✪ 26.2 VT trennen, dissoziieren *(geh, Chem)* *(from* von); **to ~ oneself from sb/sth** sich von jdm/etw distanzieren; **two aspects which have become largely ~d** zwei Aspekte, die sich weitgehend voneinander gelöst haben

dissociation [dɪˌsəʊsɪˈeɪʃən] N Trennung *f*, Dissoziation *f (geh, Chem, Psych)*

dissoluble [dɪˈsɒljʊbl] ADJ *(Chem)* löslich, dissolubel *(spec)*

dissolute [ˈdɪsəluːt] ADJ *person* zügellos; *way of life* ausschweifend, zügellos; *appearance* verlebt

dissoluteness [ˈdɪsəluːtnɪs] N *(of person, way of life)* Zügellosigkeit *f*; *(of appearance)* Verlebtheit *f*

dissolution [ˌdɪsəˈluːʃən] N a *(Chem, Jur, Pol)* Auflösung *f* b *(of relationship)* Auflösung *f*; *(of faith)* Abbröckeln *nt*

dissolve [dɪˈzɒlv] VT a *(lit, Jur, Pol, fig)* auflösen; *marriage* scheiden, auflösen b *(Film)* überblenden *(into* in *or* auf *+acc)* VI a *(lit, Jur, Pol)* sich (auf)lösen; *(fig)* sich in nichts auflösen; **it ~s in water** es ist wasserlöslich, es löst sich in Wasser; **to ~ into tears** in Tränen zerfließen; **to ~ into laughter** in Lachen ausbrechen b *(Film)* überblenden *(into* in *or* auf *+acc)* N *(Film)* Überblendung *f*

dissolvent [dɪˈzɒlvənt] ADJ lösend N Lösungsmittel *nt*

dissonance [ˈdɪsənəns] N *(Mus, fig)* Dissonanz *f*

dissonant [ˈdɪsənənt] ADJ *(Mus)* dissonant; *(fig) opinions, temperaments* unvereinbar; *colours* disharmonisch

dissuade [dɪˈsweɪd] VT **to ~ sb from sth** jdn von etw abbringen, jdm etw ausreden; **to ~ sb from doing sth** jdn davon abbringen *or* jdm ausreden, etw zu tun; **he wouldn't be ~d** er ließ sich nicht davon abbringen, er ließ sich das nicht ausreden

dissuasion [dɪˈsweɪʒən] N Abraten *nt*

dissuasive [dɪˈsweɪsɪv] ADJ abratend; **he was very ~** er riet sehr davon ab

dissuasiveness [dɪˈsweɪsɪvnɪs] N *(of person)* Abraten *nt*; **the ~ of his tone** sein abratender Ton; **the ~ of his arguments** seine abratenden Argumente

distaff [ˈdɪstɑːf] N a *(in spinning)* Spinnrocken *m*, Kunkel *f* b **on the ~ side** mütterlicherseits

distance [ˈdɪstəns] N a *(in space)* Entfernung *f*; *(= gap, interval)* Abstand *m*, Distanz *f (geh)*; *(= distance covered)* Strecke *f*, Weg *m*; **we now measure ~ in feet** wir geben Entfernungen jetzt in Fuß an; **at a ~ of two feet** in zwei Fuß Entfernung; **stopping ~** Bremsweg *m*; **the ~ between the eyes/railway lines** der Abstand zwischen den Augen/Eisenbahnschienen; **at an equal ~ from the middle** gleich weit von der Mitte entfernt; **the ~ between London and Glasgow is …** die Entfernung zwischen London und Glasgow beträgt …; **what's the ~ between London and Glasgow?** wie weit ist es von London nach Glasgow?; **I don't know the exact ~** ich weiß nicht genau, wie weit es ist; **we covered the ~ between London and Glasgow in five hours** wir haben für die Strecke London-Glasgow fünf Stunden gebraucht; **he went with me (for) part of the ~** er ging einen Teil der Strecke *or* des Weges mit mir; **in the (far) ~** (ganz) in der Ferne, (ganz) weit weg; **to gaze into the ~** in die Ferne starren; **he admired her at** *or* **from a ~** *(fig)* er bewunderte sie aus der Ferne; **it's within walking ~** es ist zu Fuß erreichbar; **it's no ~** es ist überhaupt nicht weit, es ist nur ein Katzensprung *(inf)*; **a short ~ away** ganz in der Nähe; **it's quite a ~ (away)** es ist ziemlich weit (entfernt *or* weg); **we drove 600 miles – that's quite a ~** wir sind 600 Meilen gefahren – das ist eine ganz schöne Strecke; **the race is over a ~ of 3 miles** das Rennen geht über eine Distanz von 3 Meilen; **to go the ~** durchhalten, es durchstehen; **the fight went the ~** der Kampf ging über alle Runden; **to keep one's ~ (from sb/sth)** Abstand (von jdm/etw) halten

b *(in time)* **from** *or* **at a ~ of 400 years** aus einem Abstand von 400 Jahren; **at this ~ in time** nach einem so langen Zeitraum

c *(fig, in social rank)* Unterschied *m*; **to keep sb at a ~** jdn auf Distanz halten; **to keep one's ~ (from sb)** *(= be aloof)* auf Distanz (zu jdm) bleiben, Abstand *or* Distanz (zu jdm) wahren *(geh)*

VT a *(Sport etc)* = **outdistance**

b **to ~ oneself/sb from sb/sth** sich/jdn von jdm/etw distanzieren; **television may ~ the public from reality** das Fernsehen kann die Öffentlichkeit der Wirklichkeit entfremden

distanced [ˈdɪstənst] ADJ *(lit, fig)* distanziert

distance: **distance event** N Langstreckenlauf *m*; **distance learning** N Fernunterricht *f*; **~ course** Fernjurs *m*; **distance runner** N Langstreckenläufer(in) *m(f)*

distant [ˈdɪstənt] ADJ a *(in space) horizon, land, region, mountains* fern; *galaxies* weit entfernt; *sound* entfernt; *relative, resemblance* entfernt; **with views of the ~ mountains** mit Aussicht auf die Berge in der Ferne; **we had a ~ view of the church** wir sahen die Kirche in der Ferne; **he is somewhat ~ from the day-to-day operations** er hat mit dem täglichen Betrieb ziemlich wenig zu tun; **I felt so ~ from her** ich fühlte mich so weit weg von ihr; **to come** *or* **finish a ~ second/third (to sb/sth)** *(in race, competition)* weit abgeschlagen auf dem zweiten/dritten Platz (hinter jdm/etw) landen; **profits came a ~ second to preserving jobs** Gewinne lagen an zweiter Stelle, weit hinter der Arbeitsplatzerhaltung

b *(in time, age) past, future* fern; *memory* entfernt, schwach; *days* weit zurückliegend; **it's a ~ prospect** *(fig)* es liegt noch in weiter Ferne; **in the not too** *or* **very ~ future** in nicht allzu ferner Zukunft

c *(= reserved) person, voice* distanziert; **they are emotionally ~ from their families** sie haben ein emotional distanziertes Verhältnis zu ihren Familien

d *(= distracted) person, look, mind* abwesend; **there was a ~ look in her eyes** sie hatte einen abwesenden Blick

ADV *(in time, space)* entfernt; **a mile ~ from our house** eine Meile von unserem Haus entfernt; **dawn was still an hour ~** es war noch eine Stunde bis zum Morgengrauen

distantly [ˈdɪstəntlɪ] ADV a **~ related (to sb)** entfernt *or* weitläufig (mit jdm) verwandt b *(= far away) hear* entfernt, weit weg; *see* in der Ferne; *(fig) remember* entfernt; **a buzzer sounded ~** weit weg war ein Summer zu hören; **to be ~ aware of sth** sich *(dat)* einer Sache *(gen)* vage bewusst sein c *(= unemotionally)* distanziert d *(= distractedly)* abwesend

distaste [dɪsˈteɪst] N Widerwille *m (for* gegen)

distasteful [dɪsˈteɪstfʊl] ADJ *task* unangenehm; *photo, magazine* geschmacklos; **to be ~ to sb** jdm zuwider *or* unangenehm sein; **he found the idea ~** der Gedanke war ihm zuwider

distastefully [dɪsˈteɪstfəlɪ] ADV angewidert

distemper[1] [dɪsˈtempəʳ] N *(= paint)* Temperafarbe *f* VT mit Temperafarbe streichen

distemper[2] N a *(Vet)* Staupe *f* b *(old, = ill temper)* Verstimmung *f*

distend [dɪˈstend] VT *balloon* (auf)blasen; *sails, stomach* (auf)blähen VI sich blähen

distension [dɪˈstenʃən] N Blähen *nt*; *(of stomach)* (Auf)blähung *f*

distil, *(US)* **distill** [dɪˈstɪl] VT a *(Chem)* destillieren; *whisky etc* brennen, destillieren; *(fig)* herausarbeiten, (heraus)destillieren b *(= drip slowly)* tropfenweise ausscheiden *or* absondern VI a *(Chem)* sich herausdestillieren; *(whisky)* gebrannt werden; *(fig)* sich herauskristallisieren b *(= drip slowly)* langsam heraustropfen, herauströpfeln

distillate [ˈdɪstɪlɪt] N *(Chem, Ind)* Destillat *nt*

distillation [ˌdɪstɪˈleɪʃən] N a *(Chem etc: = act)* Destillation *f*; *(of whisky etc also)* Brennen *nt*; *(= product)* Destillat *nt* b *(fig: = act)* Verarbeitung *f*; *(= product)* Destillat *nt*

distilled [dɪˈstɪld] ADJ destilliert; *spirits also* gebrannt; *essence* (heraus)destilliert; *(fig) wisdom* herausdestilliert

distiller [dɪˈstɪləʳ] N Destillateur *m*, (Branntwein)brenner *m*

distillery [dɪˈstɪlərɪ] N Destillerie *f*, (Branntwein)brennerei *f*

distinct [dɪˈstɪŋkt] ADJ a *(= different) parts, groups, types, areas, phases* verschieden, unterschiedlich; **~ from** anders als; **to be ~ from sth** sich von etw unterscheiden; **disciplines ~ from one another** voneinander getrennte Disziplinen; **to keep A ~ from B** A und B auseinanderhalten *or* voneinander trennen; **as ~ from** im Unterschied zu; **what he thinks, as ~ from what he says** was er denkt, im Unterschied dazu, was er sagt

b *(= definite) sign, change, memory, lack, improvement* deutlich; *flavour* bestimmt; *image, sound* klar, deutlich; **to have ~ memories of sb/sth** sich deutlich an jdn/etw erinnern; **to get the ~ idea** *or* **impression that …** den deutlichen Eindruck bekommen, dass …; **to have the ~ feeling that …** das bestimmte Gefühl haben, dass …; **to have a ~ advantage (over sb)** (jdm gegenüber) klar *or* deutlich im Vorteil sein; **there is a ~ possibility that …** es besteht eindeutig die Möglichkeit, dass …; **a ~ personality** eine ausgeprägte Persönlichkeit

distinction [dɪˈstɪŋkʃən] N a *(= difference)* Unterschied *m*; *(= act of distinguishing)* Unterscheidung *f*; **to make** *or* **draw a ~ (between two things)** (zwischen zwei Dingen) unterscheiden *or* einen Unterschied machen

b *no pl (= preeminence)* (hoher) Rang *m*, Distinktion *f (dated geh)*; *(= refinement)* Vornehmheit *f*; **she has an air of ~ about her** sie hat etwas Vornehmes *or* Distinguiertes *(geh)* (an sich); **a pianist of ~** ein Pianist von Rang; **he has the ~ of being the oldest living person** er zeichnet sich dadurch aus, dass er der älteste Mensch ist

c *(Sch, Univ: = grade)* Auszeichnung *f*; **he got a ~ in French** er hat das Französischexamen mit Auszeichnung bestanden; **he was awarded several academic ~s** ihm sind mehrere akademische Auszeichnungen verliehen worden

distinctive [dɪˈstɪŋktɪv] ADJ *style, flavour, smell, gesture, walk etc* unverwechselbar, unverkennbar; *feature, pattern* unverkennbar; *sound* typisch, unverkennbar; *voice, dress (= characteristic)* charakteristisch; *(= unmistakable)* unverwechselbar; *(= striking) colour, plumage* auffällig; **~ features** *(of person)* besondere Kennzeichen; **she had a very ~ voice** sie hatte eine ganz unverwechselbare *or* besondere Stimme; **with his ~ irony** mit der ihm eigenen *or* für ihn charakteristischen Ironie; **there's something ~ about them** an ihnen ist etwas Besonderes; **~ to sb/sth** charakteristisch für jdn/etw

distinctively [dɪˈstɪŋktɪvlɪ] ADV unverwechselbar; **~ dressed** auffällig gekleidet; **music which is ~ American** Musik mit ausgeprägt amerikanischen Zügen; **there is nothing ~ Christian**

about this philosophy an dieser Philosophie ist nichts ausgesprochen Christliches

distinctiveness [dɪsˈtɪŋktɪvnɪs] N *(= unmistakableness)* Unverwechselbarkeit *f*; *(= characteristic nature)* charakteristische Art; *(= striking nature)* Auffälligkeit *f*

distinctly [dɪˈstɪŋktlɪ] ADV **a** *(= clearly) remember, hear, see, speak* deutlich **b** *(= decidedly) different, better* entschieden, eindeutig; *American, English, modern* ausgeprägt; *odd, uncomfortable, uneasy, nervous* ausgesprochen; *limited, cool, unhappy* eindeutig; *possible* durchaus; **he is ~ lacking in imagination** ihm mangelt es eindeutig an Fantasie

distinctness [dɪˈstɪŋktnɪs] N **a** *(= difference)* Verschiedenheit *f*, Unterschiedlichkeit *f*; *(= separateness)* Getrenntheit *f* **b** *(= clarity)* Deutlichkeit *f*

distinguish [dɪˈstɪŋgwɪʃ] **VT** **a** *(= make different)* unterscheiden; **only the length of their hair ~es the twins** die Zwillinge unterscheiden sich nur durch ihre Haarlänge **b** *(= tell apart)* unterscheiden, auseinanderhalten; **he can't ~ green from** *or* **and red** er kann Rot nicht von Grün unterscheiden, er kann Rot und Grün nicht auseinanderhalten **c** *(= make out) landmark, shape* erkennen, ausmachen; *(amongst others) voice* heraushören **VI** **to ~ between** unterscheiden zwischen *(+dat)*, einen Unterschied machen zwischen *(+dat)* **VR** sich auszeichnen, sich hervortun

distinguishable [dɪˈstɪŋgwɪʃəbl] ADJ **a** *(= easily told apart)* unterscheidbar; **to be (barely) ~ from sth** (kaum) von etw zu unterscheiden sein; **to be ~ by sth** an etw *(dat)* erkennbar sein; **it is easily** *or* **readily ~** es ist leicht zu unterscheiden; *(= recognizable)* es ist leicht *or* gut zu erkennen; **the two types are easily/no longer ~** die beiden Arten sind leicht/nicht mehr auseinanderzuhalten *or* voneinander zu unterscheiden **b** *(= discernible) shape, voice, words, figure* erkennbar, zu erkennen

distinguished [dɪˈstɪŋgwɪʃt] ADJ **a** *(= eminent) guest, professor* angesehen; *scholar, writer* namhaft, angesehen; *career* glänzend; *history* ruhmreich; **~ service** verdienstvolle Laufbahn; *(Mil)* Dienst *m* mit Auszeichnung; **the ~ company of …** die hervorragende Gesellschaft *(+gen)* …; **to be ~ for sth** sich durch etw auszeichnen **b** *(= refined) person, appearance* distinguiert *(geh)*; **to look ~** distinguiert *(geh)* *or* vornehm aussehen

distinguishing [dɪˈstɪŋgwɪʃɪŋ] ADJ kennzeichnend, charakteristisch; **he has no ~ features** er hat keine besonderen Kennzeichen; **the ~ feature of his work is …** was seine Arbeit auszeichnet *or* kennzeichnet, ist …

distort [dɪˈstɔːt] **VT** verzerren *(also Phys)*; *truth, words* verdrehen; *reality, history* verzerrt darstellen; *facts* verzerrt darstellen, verdrehen; *judgement* trüben, beeinträchtigen **VI** verzerrt werden

distorted [dɪsˈtɔːtɪd] ADJ **a** *(= unclear, inaccurate) sound, view, picture, report* verzerrt; **she has an entirely ~ impression of events** sie sieht die Ereignisse völlig verzerrt; **she has a ~ image of what is normal** sie hat ein verzerrtes Bild davon, was normal ist **b** *(= deformed, twisted) joints, bones, plants* verformt; *mouth, face* entstellt

distortion [dɪˈstɔːʃən] N Verzerrung *f* *(also Phys)*; *(of truth, words)* Verdrehung *f*; *(of reality, history)* verzerrte Darstellung; *(of facts)* verzerrte Darstellung, Verdrehung *f*; *(of judgement)* Trübung *f*, Beeinträchtigung *f*

distract [dɪˈstrækt] VT **a** *(= divert attention of)* ablenken; **to ~ sb's attention** jdn ablenken **b** *(old, = amuse)* zerstreuen, die Zeit vertreiben *(+dat)*

distracted [dɪˈstræktɪd] ADJ *(= preoccupied)* abwesend, zerstreut; *(= worried, anxious)* besorgt, beunruhigt; *(= grief-stricken, distraught)* außer sich (*with* vor *+dat*); **she screamed like one ~** sie schrie wie eine Irre

distractedly [dɪˈstræktɪdlɪ] ADV abwesend, zerstreut; *(= in distress)* verzweifelt

distraction [dɪˈstrækʃən] N **a** *no pl (= lack of attention)* Unaufmerksamkeit *f* **b** *(= interruption: from work etc)* Ablenkung *f* **c** *(= entertainment)* Zerstreuung *f* **d** *(= anxiety)* Ruhelosigkeit *f*, Unruhe *f*; *(= distraught state)* Verstörung *f*; **to love sb to ~** jdn wahnsinnig lieben; **to drive sb to ~** jdn zum Wahnsinn *or* zur Verzweiflung treiben

distrain [dɪˈstreɪn] VI *(Jur)* **to ~ upon sb's goods** jds Eigentum beschlagnahmen

distraint [dɪˈstreɪnt] N *(Jur)* Beschlagnahmung *f*, Beschlagnahme *f*; **~ order** Beschlagnahmungsverfügung *f*

distraught [dɪˈstrɔːt] ADJ verzweifelt, außer sich *(dat) pred*; *look, voice* verzweifelt

distress [dɪˈstres] **N** **a** Verzweiflung *f*; *(physical)* Leiden *nt*; *(mental, cause of distress)* Kummer *m*, Sorge *f*; **to be in great ~** sehr leiden; **to cause sb ~** jdm Sorge/starke Schmerzen bereiten **b** *(= great poverty)* Not *f*, Elend *nt* **c** *(= danger)* Not *f*; **to be in ~** *(ship)* in Seenot sein; *(plane)* in Not sein; **~ call** Notsignal *nt* **VT** *(= worry)* Kummer machen *(+dat)*, Sorge bereiten *(+dat)*; **don't ~ yourself** machen Sie sich *(dat)* keine Sorgen!; **the thought ~ed him enormously** der Gedanke bekümmerte ihn sehr

distressed [dɪˈstrest] ADJ **a** *(= upset)* bekümmert; *(= grief-stricken)* erschüttert (*about* von) **b** *(= poverty-stricken)* **~ area** Notstandsgebiet *nt*

distressing [dɪˈstresɪŋ] ADJ *(= upsetting)* besorgniserregend; *(stronger)* erschreckend; *(= regrettable)* betrüblich

distressingly [dɪˈstresɪŋlɪ] ADV *(= unfortunately)* leider, bedauerlicherweise; *common, familiar, high, low* erschreckend; *groan* mitleiderregend; **~, it took him six hours to die** es dauerte sechs quälende Stunden, bis er gestorben war

distress: **distress rocket** N Notrakete *f*; **distress signal** N Notsignal *nt*

distributable [dɪˈstrɪbjuːtəbl] ADJ verteilbar, austeilbar

distributary [dɪˈstrɪbjʊtərɪ] **N** *(Geog)* Nebenarm *m*, Flussarm *m* eines Deltas **ADJ** Verteiler-; **~ network** Verteilernetz *nt*

distribute [dɪˈstrɪbjuːt] VT verteilen (*to* an *+acc*); *information* verbreiten; *(Comm) goods* vertreiben (*to, among* an *+acc*); *drugs* handeln mit (*to* bei); *films* verleihen (*to* an *+acc*); *dividends* ausschütten (*to* an *+acc*); **the cells are widely ~d throughout the body** die Zellen sind im ganzen Körper verbreitet; **your weight should be evenly ~d** Ihr Gewicht sollte gleichmäßig verteilt sein

distributing agent N (Groß)handelsvertreter(in) *m(f)*

distribution [ˌdɪstrɪˈbjuːʃən] N **a** *(= act)* Verteilung *f*; *(of information)* Verbreitung *f*; (*Comm: of goods*) Vertrieb *m*; (*= dealing: of drugs*) Handel *m*; (*of* mit) *(of films)* Verleih *m*; *(of dividends)* Ausschüttung *f*; **~ network** Vertriebsnetz *nt*; **~ rights** Vertriebsrechte *pl* **b** *(= spread)* Verbreitung *f*; **geographical ~** geografische Verteilung

distribution management N *(Comm)* Vertriebscontrolling *nt*

distribution box N *(Elec)* Verteilerkasten *m*, Abzweigdose *f*

distributive [dɪˈstrɪbjʊtɪv] *(Gram)* **ADJ** distributiv **N** Distributivum *nt*

distributor [dɪˈstrɪbjʊtəʳ] N **a** Verteiler(in) *m(f)*; (*Comm: = wholesaler*) Großhändler *m*; *(= retailer)* Händler(in) *m(f)*; *(of films)* Verleih(er) *m*; **~ discount** Händlerrabatt *m* **b** *(Aut)* Verteiler *m*

distributorship [dɪsˈtrɪbjʊtəʃɪp] N (*Comm: = company*) Vertriebsgesellschaft *f*; *(= right to supply)* Vertrieb *m*

district [ˈdɪstrɪkt] N *(of country)* Gebiet *nt*; *(of town)* Stadtteil *m*, Viertel *nt*; *(= geographical area)* Gegend *f*; *(= administrative area)* (Verwaltungs)bezirk *m*; **shopping/business ~** Geschäftsviertel *nt*

> **DISTRICT OF COLUMBIA**
>
> Der **District of Columbia** ist der Sitz der Regierung der Vereinigten Staaten von Amerika. Er gehört zu keinem Staat, sondern ist ein vollständig autonomer Bezirk im Osten des Landes. Er umfasst ungefähr 180 km^2, genau die Fläche, über die sich die Landeshauptstadt Washington erstreckt. Die Abkürzung DC wird daher hinter den Namen der Hauptstadt gestellt: Washington, DC.

district: **district attorney** N *(US)* Bezirksstaatsanwalt *m*/-anwältin *f*; **District Commissioner** N *hoher Regierungsbeamter in einer Kolonie*; **district council** N *(Brit)* Bezirksregierung *f*; **district court** N *(US Jur)* Bezirksgericht *nt*; **district judge** N *(US)* Richter(in) *m(f)* an einem (Bundes)bezirksgericht; **district manager** N *(Comm)* Bezirksdirektor(in) *m(f)*; **district nurse** N *(Brit)* Gemeindeschwester *f*; **district surveyor** N Bauinspektor(in) *m(f)*, Beamte(r) *m*/Beamtin *f* des regionalen Bauaufsichtsamtes

distrust [dɪsˈtrʌst] **VT** misstrauen *(+dat)* **N** Misstrauen *nt* (*of* gegenüber)

distrustful [dɪsˈtrʌstfʊl] ADJ misstrauisch (*of* gegenüber)

disturb [dɪˈstɜːb] **VT** **a** *(= interrupt) person, sleep, silence, balance* stören; **the pain ~ed my sleep** vor Schmerzen habe ich schlecht geschlafen; **sorry to ~ you** entschuldigen Sie bitte die Störung **b** *(= alarm) person* beunruhigen **c** *waters* bewegen; *sediment* aufwirbeln; *papers* durcheinanderbringen; *(fig) peace of mind* stören; **to ~ the peace** die Ruhe stören **VI** stören; **"please do not ~"** „bitte nicht stören“

disturbance [dɪˈstɜːbəns] N **a** *(political, social)* Unruhe *f*; *(in house, street)* (Ruhe)störung *f*; **to cause** *or* **create a ~** Unruhe *or* eine Ruhestörung verursachen; **~ of the peace** Störung *f* des Friedens **b** (*= interruption: in work, routine*) Störung *f* **c** *no pl (= disarranging, of papers)* Durcheinanderbringen *nt*; *(of liquid)* Bewegung *f*; *(fig, of peace of mind)* Störung *f*; **emotional ~** seelische Störung **d** *no pl (= alarm, uneasiness)* Unruhe *f*; **I don't want to cause any ~ but …** ich will Sie ja nicht beunruhigen, aber …

disturbed [dɪˈstɜːbd] ADJ **a** *(= interrupted, turbulent) night, times* unruhig; **pregnant women tend to have more ~ sleep than other people** Schwangere schlafen oft unruhiger als andere Menschen; **separate beds can eliminate ~ sleep** getrennte Betten können Schlafstörungen verhindern **b** (*Psych: = unbalanced, unhappy*) *person, behaviour, childhood, background* gestört; **emotionally/mentally ~** seelisch/geistig gestört **c** *(= worried) person* beunruhigt, besorgt (*about, at, by* über *+acc*); **he was ~ that …** es beunruhigte *or* besorgte ihn, dass …; **I was ~ to hear of his accident** ich war beunruhigt, als ich von seinem Unfall erfuhr

disturber [dɪˈstɜːbəʳ] N Störer(in) *m(f)*, Störenfried *m*; *(= troublemaker)* Unruhestifter(in) *m(f)*

disturbing [dɪˈstɜːbɪŋ] ADJ *(= alarming)* beunruhigend; *(= distracting)* störend; **some viewers may find these scenes ~** einige Zuschauer könnten an diesen Szenen Anstoß nehmen

disturbingly [dɪˈstɜːbɪŋlɪ] ADV beunruhigend; *(introducing sentence)* beunruhigenderweise

disulphide, *(US)* **disulfide** [daɪˈsʌlfaɪd] N Disulfid *nt*

disunite [ˈdɪsjuːˈnaɪt] VT spalten, entzweien

disunity [ˌdɪsˈjuːnɪtɪ] N Uneinigkeit *f*

disuse [ˈdɪsˈjuːs] N **to fall into ~** nicht mehr benutzt werden; *(custom)* außer Gebrauch kommen; **rusty from ~** wegen mangelnder Benutzung verrostet

disused [ˈdɪsˈjuːzd] ADJ *building* leer stehend; *mine, quarry, railway line* stillgelegt; *vehicle, machine* nicht mehr benutzt

disyllabic [ˌdaɪsɪˈlæbɪk] ADJ *word* zweisilbig

ditch [dɪtʃ] **N** **a** Graben *m* **b** *(Aviat inf)* Bach *m (sl)* **VT** *(inf: = get rid of) person* abhängen *(inf)*; *employee, boyfriend* abservieren *(inf)*; *plan, project* baden gehen lassen *(inf)*; *car* stehen lassen; *old manuscript, unwanted object* wegschmeißen *(inf)*; **to ~ a plane** eine Maschine im Bach landen *(sl)* **VI** *(Aviat inf)* in den Bach gehen

ditchwater [ˈdɪtʃˌwɔːtəʳ] N abgestandenes, fauliges Wasser; **(as) dull as ~** *(inf)* stinklangweilig *(inf)*

dither [ˈdɪðəʳ] **N** **to be all of a ~, to be in a ~** ganz aufgeregt *or* am Rotieren *(inf)* sein **VI** zaudern, schwanken; **to ~ over sth** mit etw zaudern; **to ~ over how/whether …** schwanken, wie/ob …; **stop ~ing (about) and get on with it!** jetzt lass doch dieses ewige Hin und Her und fang endlich mal an!

dithering [ˈdɪðərɪŋ] **nj** *(Comput: graphics mode)* Farbmischung *f*

dithery [ˈdɪðərɪ] ADJ *(inf)* unentschlossen

dithyrambs [ˈdɪθɪræmz] PL Dithyramben *pl*

ditsy [ˈdɪtsɪ] ADJ *(esp US inf)* = **ditzy**

ditto [ˈdɪtəʊ] N **I'd like coffee – ~ (for me)** *(inf)* ich möchte Kaffee – dito *or* ich auch; **the restaurants are expensive here, and ~ the cinemas** die Restaurants hier sind teuer und die Kinos auch; **~ mark, ~ sign** *(Typ)* Wiederholungszeichen *nt*

ditty [ˈdɪtɪ] N Liedchen *nt*, Weise *f*

ditzy [ˈdɪtsɪ] ADJ *(esp US inf)* **a** *(= silly)* albern; *blonde* doof *(inf)* **b** *(= scatterbrained)* schusselig *(inf)*

diuretic [ˌdaɪjʊəˈretɪk] **ADJ** harntreibend, diuretisch *(spec)* **N** harntreibendes Mittel, Diuretikum *nt (spec)*

diurnal [daɪˈɜːnl] **ADJ** *(liter: = of the daytime)* Tages-; **the earth's ~ rotation** die tägliche Umdrehung der Erde **N** *(Eccl)* Diurnal(e) *nt*

div *abbr of* **dividend**

diva [ˈdiːvə] N Diva *f*, Primadonna *f*

divan [dɪˈvæn] N Diwan *m*; **~ bed** Liege *f*

dive [daɪv] *vb: pret* **dived** *or (US)* **dove**, *ptp* **dived**
N **a** *(by swimmer)* Sprung *m*; *(by plane)* Sturzflug *m*; *(Ftbl)* Hechtsprung *m*; **~rs are only allowed to make two ~s a day** Taucher dürfen nur zweimal am Tag unter Wasser; **that was the deepest ~ yet** das war die bisher größte Tauchtiefe; **to make a ~ for sth** *(fig inf)* sich auf etw *(acc)* stürzen; **to take a ~** *(inf) (pound, dollar etc)* absacken *(inf)*; *(confidence, hopes)* sich in nichts auflösen; *(Ftbl)* eine Schwalbe machen *(sl)*
b *(pej inf: = club etc)* Spelunke *f (inf)*; **~ bar** *(esp US inf)* Schmuddelkneipe *f*
VI **a** *(person, from diving board)* springen; *(from side of lake, pool etc)* (mit dem Kopf voraus) springen, hechten; *(under water)* tauchen; *(submarine)* untertauchen; *(plane)* einen Sturzflug machen; *(birds, from air)* einen Sturzflug machen; *(in water)* tauchen; *(prices)* stürzen; **to ~ for pearls** nach Perlen tauchen; **the goalkeeper ~d for the ball** der Torwart hechtete nach dem Ball; **~!** *(Naut)* auf Tauchstation!
b *(inf)* **he ~d into the crowd** er tauchte in der Menge unter; **he ~d under the table** er verschwand blitzschnell unter dem Tisch; **to ~ for cover** eilig in Deckung gehen; **he ~d into a taxi** er stürzte (sich) in ein Taxi; **he ~d into his bag** er fischte eilig in seiner Tasche

▶ **dive in** VI **a** *(swimmer)* (mit dem Kopf voraus) hineinspringen **b** *(inf: = start to eat)* **dive in!** hau(t) rein! *(inf)*

dive: **dive-bomb** VT im Sturzflug bombardieren; **dive bomber** N Sturzkampfbomber *m*, Stuka *m*; **dive bombing** N Sturzkampfbombardierung *f*

diver [ˈdaɪvəʳ] N **a** Taucher(in) *m(f)*; *(off high board)* Turmspringer(in) *m(f)*; *(off springboard)* Kunstspringer(in) *m(f)* **b** *(bird)* Taucher *m*

diverge [daɪˈvɜːdʒ] VI abweichen *(from* von), divergieren *(geh, Math)*; *(two things)* voneinander abweichen

divergence [daɪˈvɜːdʒəns] N Divergenz *f (geh, Math)*, Auseinandergehen *nt*; *(from a standard etc)* Abweichung *f*

divergent [daɪˈvɜːdʒənt] ADJ *views* unterschiedlich, auseinandergehend; *interests* unterschiedlich, voneinander abweichend; **to take** *or* **follow ~ paths** unterschiedliche Wege gehen; **to be ~ from sth** von etw abweichen; **~ response** *(Psych)* divergente Reaktion

divergent thinking N *(Psych)* divergentes Denken

divers [ˈdaɪvɜːz] ADJ *attr* mehrere, diverse

diverse [daɪˈvɜːs] ADJ **a** *(with singular noun) group* gemischt, bunt zusammengewürfelt; *society, population* gemischt; *range, selection* breit, vielfältig **b** *(with plural noun) people, areas, elements, backgrounds* verschieden, unterschiedlich; *interests* vielfältig; **celebrities as ~ as …** so verschiedene *or* unterschiedliche Berühmtheiten wie …

diversification [daɪˌvɜːsɪfɪˈkeɪʃən] N *(= change, variety)* Abwechslung *f*; *(of business etc)* Diversifikation *f*

diversified [daɪˈvɜːsɪfaɪd] ADJ *(= varied)* verschieden, verschiedenartig; *risk* verteilt; *company* diversifiziert

diversify [daɪˈvɜːsɪfaɪ] **VT** abwechslungsreich(er) gestalten; *interests* breit(er) fächern; *business etc* diversifizieren **VI** *(Comm)* diversifizieren; **to ~ into new products** sich auf neue Produkte umstellen

diversion [daɪˈvɜːʃən] N **a** *(of traffic, stream)* Umleitung *f* **b** *(= relaxation)* Unterhaltung *f*; **for ~** zur Unterhaltung *or* Zerstreuung; **it's a ~ from work** es ist eine angenehme Abwechslung von der Arbeit **c** *(Mil, fig: = sth that distracts attention)* Ablenkung *f*; **to create a ~** ablenken; **as a ~** um abzulenken

diversionary [daɪˈvɜːʃnərɪ] ADJ Ablenkungs-; **~ attack** *or* **raid** Ablenkungsangriff *m*; **~ manoeuvre** Ablenkungsmanöver *nt*

diversity [daɪˈvɜːsɪtɪ] N Vielfalt *f*; **~ of opinion** Meinungsvielfalt *f*; **the ~ of her interests** die Vielfältigkeit ihrer Interessen

divert [daɪˈvɜːt] VT **a** *traffic, stream* umleiten; *attention* ablenken; *conversation* in eine andere Richtung lenken; *blow* abwenden; *money* abzweigen; *resources, investment* umlenken **b** *(= amuse)* unterhalten

diverting [daɪˈvɜːtɪŋ] ADJ unterhaltsam, kurzweilig

divest [daɪˈvest] VT **a** *(of clothes, leaves)* berauben; **to ~ oneself of sth** sich einer Sache *(gen)* entledigen; **to ~ sb of sth** jdn einer Sache *(gen)* berauben; **to be ~ed of sth** einer Sache *(gen)* entledigt/beraubt werden; **to ~ a site of nuclear material** ein Gelände von Strahlenmaterial befreien; **he ~ed her of her coat** *(hum, form)* er nahm ihr den Mantel ab **b** **to ~ sb of office/(his) rank** jdn des *or* seines Amtes/seiner Würden entkleiden *(geh)*

divestiture [daɪˈvestɪtʃəʳ], **divestment** [daɪˈvestmənt] N *(form)* **a** *(= deprivation) (of clothes)* Entkleidung *f*, Entblößung *f*; *(of rights)* Beraubung *f* **b** *(Fin: of investment)* Veräußerung *f*

dividable [dɪˈvaɪdəbl] ADJ teilbar

divide [dɪˈvaɪd] **VT** **a** *(= separate)* trennen
b *(= split into parts: also* **divide up**, *) money, work, property, kingdom, room* teilen *(into* in *+acc)*; *(in order to distribute)* aufteilen; **the river ~s the city into two** der Fluss teilt die Stadt; **~ the pastry in half** den Teig in zwei Hälften teilen; **she ~d the cake into five pieces** sie teilte den Kuchen in fünf Stücke (auf); **the book can be ~d into three main parts** das Buch kann in drei Hauptteile gegliedert werden
c *(= share out) money, time, food* verteilen; **she ~d the food evenly among the children** sie verteilte das Essen gleichmäßig an die Kinder
d *(Math)* dividieren, teilen; **to ~ 6 into 36, to ~ 36 by 6** 36 durch 6 teilen *or* dividieren; **what is 12 ~d by 3?** was ist 12 (geteilt *or* dividiert) durch 3?
e *(= cause disagreement among) friends* entzweien
f *(Brit, Parl)* **to ~ the House** durch Hammelsprung abstimmen lassen
VI **a** *(river, road, room, cells)* sich teilen; *(book etc)* sich gliedern *(into* in *+acc)*; **to ~ into groups** sich in Gruppen aufteilen; *(= be classified)* sich gliedern lassen; **the policy of ~ and rule/conquer** die Politik des „divide et impera“/Teilen und Besiegens
b *(Math, number)* sich teilen *or* dividieren lassen *(by* durch); **we're learning to ~** wir lernen Teilen *or* Dividieren; **he's no good at dividing** er kann nicht teilen *or* dividieren
c *(Brit, Parl)* **the House ~d** das Parlament stimmte durch Hammelsprung ab; **~, ~!** abstimmen!
N *(Geog)* Wasserscheide *f*; **the Great Divide** *(Geog)* die (nord)amerikanische Wasserscheide; *(fig)* die Kluft; *(= death)* der Tod; **to cross the Great Divide** *(fig)* den Schritt über die Schwelle tun; *(= die)* die Schwelle des Todes überschreiten; **the racial/social/cultural ~** die Kluft zwischen den Rassen/Gesellschaftsschichten/Kulturen

▶ **divide off** **VI** sich (ab)trennen; *(= be separable)* sich (ab)trennen lassen **VT** *sep* (ab)trennen

▶ **divide out** VT *sep* aufteilen *(among* unter *+acc or dat)*

▶ **divide up** **VI** = **divide VI a** **VT** *sep* = **divide VT b, c**

divided [dɪˈvaɪdɪd] ADJ **a** *(= partitioned) city, country* geteilt; **~ skirt** Hosenrock *m* **b** *(= disunited) nation, country, society* geteilt, gespalten; *government, opposition* zerstritten; *opinion* geteilt; **to have ~ loyalties** nicht zu vereinbarende Pflichten haben; **children of divorced parents have ~ loyalties** Scheidungskinder fühlen sich zwischen den Eltern hin- und hergerissen; **my mind is ~** ich kann mich nicht entscheiden; **to be ~ on** *or* **over sth** *(people)* sich in etw *(dat) or* über etw *(acc)* nicht einig sein; **opinion was ~ (on whether …)** die Meinungen waren geteilt (darüber, ob …)

divided highway N *(US)* ≈ Schnellstraße *f*

dividend [ˈdɪvɪdend] N **a** *(Fin)* Dividende *f*; **to pay ~s** *(fig)* sich bezahlt machen **b** *(Math)* Dividend *m*

dividend coupon, dividend warrant N *(Fin)* Dividendenschein *m*, Gewinnanteilschein *m*

dividers [dɪˈvaɪdəz] PL Stechzirkel *m*

dividing [dɪˈvaɪdɪŋ] ADJ (ab)trennend

dividing line N *(lit, fig)* Trenn(ungs)linie *f*

dividing wall N Trennwand *f*

divination [ˌdɪvɪˈneɪʃən] N Prophezeiung *f*, Weissagung *f*

divine [dɪˈvaɪn] **ADJ** *(Rel, fig inf)* göttlich; **~ worship** Anbetung *f* Gottes **N** Theologe *m*; *(= priest)* Geistliche(r) *m* **VT** **a** *(= foretell) the future* weissagen, prophezeien **b** *(liter: = make out) sb's intentions* erahnen, erspüren *(liter)* **c** *(= find) water, metal* aufspüren

divinely [dɪˈvaɪnlɪ] ADV **a** *(Rel, by God) appointed, inspired* von Gott; **~ ordained** von Gott gewollt; **~ noble/wise** göttlich edel/weise **b** *(fig inf) funny, decadent etc* göttlich *(inf)*

diviner [dɪˈvaɪnəʳ] N **a** *(of future)* Wahrsager(in) *m(f)* **b** = **water diviner**

diving [ˈdaɪvɪŋ] N *(under water)* Tauchen *nt*; *(into water)* Springen *nt*; *(Sport)* Wasserspringen *nt*

diving: **diving bell** N Taucherglocke *f*; **diving board** N (Sprung)brett *nt*; **diving header** N *(Ftbl)* Flug- *or* Hechtkopfball *m*; **diving suit** N Taucheranzug *m*

divining rod [dɪˈvaɪnɪŋˈrɒd] N Wünschelrute *f*

divinity [dɪˈvɪnɪtɪ] N **a** *(= divine quality)* Göttlichkeit *f* **b** *(= theology)* Theologie *f*; *(Sch)* Religion *f*; **doctor of ~** *(Brit)* Doktor der Theologie **c** *(= divine being)* göttliches Wesen, Gottheit *f*

divisible [dɪˈvɪzəbl] ADJ teilbar *(by* durch)

division [dɪˈvɪʒən] N **a** *(= act of dividing, state of being divided)* Teilung *f*; *(Math)* Teilen *nt*, Division *f*; **we're learning ~** wir lernen Teilen *or* Dividieren; **he can't do ~** er kann nicht teilen

or dividieren; **the ~ of labour** *(Brit) or* **labor** *(US)* die Arbeitsteilung
b *(Mil)* Division *f*
c *(= result of dividing, in administration)* Abteilung *f*; *(in box, case)* Fach *nt*; *(= part)* Teil *m*; *(= category)* Kategorie *f*; **the bank's European ~** die für Europa zuständige Abteilung der Bank; **the sales ~** die Verkaufsabteilung
d *(= that which divides: in room)* Trennwand *f*; *(fig: between social classes etc)* Schranke *f*; *(= dividing line: lit, fig)* Trennungslinie *f*
e *(fig: = discord)* Uneinigkeit *f*
f *(Brit, Parl)* **to call for a ~** eine Abstimmung durch Hammelsprung verlangen
g *(Sport)* Liga *f*

Divisional Court [dɪˌvɪʒənl'kɔːt] N *(Brit Jur) Berufungsgericht mit zwei oder mehr Richtern*

division bell [dɪ'vɪʒənˌbel] N *(Parl) Klingel, mit der die Abgeordneten zur Abstimmung gerufen werden*

division sign N *(Math)* Teilungszeichen *nt*

divisive [dɪ'vaɪsɪv] ADJ *issue, figure* kontrovers, umstritten; *influence, effect* polarisierend; **to be ~** Uneinigkeit schaffen; **a ~ general election** eine Wahl, die das Land in zwei Lager spaltet

divisor [dɪ'vaɪzə'] N *(Math)* Divisor *m*

divorce [dɪ'vɔːs] **N** *(Jur)* Scheidung *f* *(from* von); *(fig)* Trennung *f*; **he wants a ~** er will sich scheiden lassen; **to get a ~ (from sb)** sich (von jdm) scheiden lassen **VT** **a** *husband, wife* sich scheiden lassen von; **to get ~d** sich scheiden lassen **b** *(fig)* trennen **VI** sich scheiden lassen; **they ~d last year** sie haben sich letztes Jahr scheiden lassen

divorcé [dɪ'vɔːseɪ] N geschiedener Mann, Geschiedene(r) *m*

divorce court N Scheidungsgericht *nt*

divorced [dɪ'vɔːst] ADJ *(Jur)* geschieden *(from* von); **to be ~ from sth** *(fig)* keine(rlei) Beziehung zu etw haben; **she's completely ~ from reality** sie ist völlig wirklichkeitsfremd

divorcee [dɪˌvɔː'siː] N Geschiedene(r) *mf*, geschiedener Mann, geschiedene Frau; **she is a ~** sie ist geschieden

divorce proceedings PL Scheidungsprozess *m*

divorce settlement N *(mutually agreed)* Scheidungsvergleich *m*; *(imposed by court)* Scheidungsurteil *nt*

divot ['dɪvɪt] N *vom Golfschläger etc ausgehacktes Rasenstück*

divulge [daɪ'vʌldʒ] VT preisgeben *(sth to sb* jdm etw)

divvy ['dɪvɪ] *(Brit inf) dim of* **dividend** Dividende *f*

▶ **divvy up** *(inf)* **VT** *sep (= divide up)* aufteilen **VI** aufteilen

Diwali [dɪ'wɑːlɪ] N Diwali *nt*

Dixie ['dɪksɪ] **N** *(also* **Dixieland**) Dixie(land) *m* **ADJ** der Südstaaten

> **DIXIE**
>
> **Dixie** ist der Spitzname für die Südstaaten der USA. Insbesondere wird er für die elf Staaten verwandt, die sich vormals während des amerikanischen Bürgerkrieges zu den Konföderierten Staaten von Amerika zusammengeschlossen hatten: Alabama, Arkansas, Georgia, Florida, Louisiana, Mississippi, North Carolina, South Carolina, Tennessee, Texas und Virginia. **Dixie** wird auch adjektivisch eingesetzt, wenn man Besonderheiten der Südstaaten und ihrer Einwohner beschreiben möchte: „Scarlett O'Hara was the epitome of Dixie femininity" (etwa: „ ... war der Inbegriff einer Südstaatenschönheit").
> Der Name **Dixie** stammt ursprünglich wohl aus Louisiana, weil dort auf der Rückseite der Zehn-Dollar-Noten die Zahl auf französisch mit „dix" angegeben war. Andere Mutmaßungen verweisen auf die imaginäre Mason-Dixon Linie, die einst den Norden vom Süden trennte → MASON-DIXON LINE

dixie ['dɪksɪ] N *(Brit Mil sl)* Gulaschkanone *f* *(inf)*; *(for eating)* Essgeschirr *nt*

Dixie cup® N *(US)* Pappbecher *m*

DIY [diːaɪ'waɪ] *(Brit) abbr of* **do-it-yourself** **N** Do-it-yourself *nt*, Heimwerken *nt*; **she was doing some ~ over the weekend** sie machte am Wochenende einige Heimwerkerarbeiten
ADJ *product* für Heimwerker; **~ chain** Baumarktkette *f*; **~ fan** *or* **enthusiast** Heimwerker(in) *m(f)*, Do-it-yourself-Fan *m*; **~ kit** *(for household jobs)* Heimwerkerausrüstung *f*; *(for businesses etc)* Starterpaket *nt*; *(for car etc)* Bausatz *m*; **~ work** Heimwerkerarbeiten *pl*; **this is an easy ~ job** das kann man leicht selber machen; **you can tell it's a ~ job** man kann sehen, dass hier ein Heimwerker am Werk war; **~ home improvements** eigenhändige Modernisierung; **they opted for a ~ divorce** sie entschieden sich, ihre Scheidung selbst zu vereinbaren; **~ justice** Selbstjustiz *f*

DIY centre, DIY shop, DIY store N Baumarkt *m*, Heimwerkermarkt *m*

dizzily ['dɪzɪlɪ] ADV **a** *(= giddily)* benommen; **my head spun ~** mir war entsetzlich schwindelig; **share prices rose ~** die Aktienkurse stiegen auf schwindelerregende Höhen **b** *(fig inf: = foolishly)* dümmlich

dizziness ['dɪzɪnɪs] N Schwindel *m*; **bout** *or* **fit of ~** Schwindelanfall *m*

dizzy ['dɪzɪ] **ADJ** (+er) **a** *(= giddy)* schwindelig; **I'm (feeling) ~** mir ist schwindelig *(from* von); **she started to feel ~** ihr wurde schwindelig; **~ spell** Schwindelanfall *m*; **it makes me ~ to think of it** mir wird ganz schwindelig bei dem Gedanken; **she was ~ with success** der Erfolg hatte sie benommen gemacht; **when you're ~ with desire** wenn dir vor Begehren ganz schwindelig ist
b *(fig) height, speed* schwindelerregend; **to rise to ~ heights** zu schwindelerregenden Höhen aufsteigen
c *(= foolish) person* hirnlos; *action* verrückt; **delightfully ~** herrlich verrückt; **a ~ blonde** ein dummes Blondchen *(inf)*
VT *person* verwirren

DJ **a** *abbr of* **dinner jacket** **b** *abbr of* **disc jockey**

dl **a** *abbr of* **decilitre(s)** dl **b** *(esp US inf) abbr of* **down-low**; **this is on the dl** das ist supergeheim *(inf)*

D Lit *abbr of* **Doctor of Letters** Dr. phil.

DLP *abbr of* **digital light processing**; **~ projector** Beamer *m*

DM **a** *(Hist) abbr of* **Deutschmark** DM **b** *abbr of* **Doctor of medicine** Dr. med.

dm *abbr of* **decimetre(s)** dm

D-Mark ['diːmɑːk] N *(Hist) abbr of* **Deutschmark** D-Mark *f*

D Mus *abbr of* **Doctor of Music**

DMZ *abbr of* **demilitarized zone** entmilitarisierte Zone

DNA *abbr of* **de(s)oxyribonucleic acid** DNS *f*

DNA: DNA fingerprinting, DNA profiling N = **genetic fingerprinting**; **DNA test** N *(Med)* Gentest *m*; **DNA testing** N DNS-Tests *pl*

DNF *(Athletics) abbr of* **did not finish**

D-notice ['diːnəʊtɪs] N *(Brit Pol) offizielles Verbot an die Presse, bestimmte für die innere Sicherheit wichtige Informationen zu veröffentlichen*

DNS *(Athletics) abbr of* **did not start**

do¹ [dəʊ] N *(Mus)* Do *nt*

do² [duː]

vb: pret **did**, *ptp* **done**

1 AUXILIARY VERB	4 NOUN
2 TRANSITIVE VERB	5 PLURAL NOUN
3 INTRANSITIVE VERB	6 PHRASAL VERBS

1 – AUXILIARY VERB

> There is no equivalent in German to the use of *do* in questions, negative statements and negative commands.

a *interrogative, negative* **do you understand?** verstehen Sie?; **I don't** *or* **do not understand** ich verstehe nicht; **what did he say?** was hat er gesagt?; **didn't you** *or* **did you not know?** haben Sie das nicht gewusst?; **don't be silly!** sei nicht albern!

b *in question tags* oder; **you know him, don't you?** Sie kennen ihn doch?, Sie kennen ihn (doch), oder?; **you don't know him, do you?** Sie kennen ihn also nicht, oder?; **so you know them, do you?** *(in surprise)* Sie kennen sie also wirklich *or* tatsächlich!; **he does understand, doesn't he?** das versteht er doch, oder?; **he didn't go, did he?** er ist (doch) nicht gegangen, oder?

c *substitute for another verb* **you speak better German than I do** Sie sprechen besser Deutsch als ich; **he likes cheese and so do I** er isst gern Käse und ich auch; **he doesn't like cheese and neither do I** er mag keinen Käse und ich auch nicht; **I don't like cheese but he does** ich mag keinen Käse, aber er schon; **they said he would go and he did** sie sagten, er würde gehen und das tat er (dann) auch

d *in tag responses* **do you see them often? – yes, I do/no, I don't** sehen Sie sie oft? – ja/nein; **do you serve food? – yes, we do** gibts bei Ihnen Essen? – ja; **you didn't go, did you? – yes, I did** Sie sind nicht gegangen, oder? – doch; **they speak French – oh, do they?** sie sprechen Französisch – ja?, ach, wirklich *or* tatsächlich?; **they speak German – do they really?** sie sprechen Deutsch – wirklich?; **may I come in? – do!** darf ich hereinkommen? – ja, bitte; **shall I open the window? – no, don't!** soll ich das Fenster öffnen? – nein, bitte nicht!; **who broke the window? – I did** wer hat das Fenster eingeschlagen? – ich

e *for emphasis* **DO come!** *(esp Brit)* kommen Sie doch (bitte)!; **DO shut up!** *(esp Brit)* (nun) sei doch (endlich) ruhig!; **do tell him that ...** *(esp Brit)* sagen Sie ihm doch (bitte), dass ...; **well do I remember him!** und ob ich mich an ihn erinnere!; **it's very expensive, but I DO like it** es ist zwar sehr teuer, aber es gefällt mir nun mal; **so you DO know them!** Sie kennen sie also doch!

2 – TRANSITIVE VERB

a tun, machen; **I've done a stupid thing** ich habe da was Dummes gemacht *or* getan; **to do sth again** etw noch (ein)mal tun *or* machen; **sorry, it's impossible, it can't be done** tut mir leid, (ist) ausgeschlossen, es lässt sich nicht machen; **can you do it by yourself?** schaffst du das allein?, kannst du das allein machen?; **we did the journey in eight hours** wir haben die Fahrt in acht Stunden geschafft

♦ **do** *+noun phrase* **to do the housework/one's homework** die Hausarbeit/seine Hausaufgaben machen; **who did the choreography/the cover design?** wer hat die Choreografie/den Umschlagentwurf gemacht?; **we'll have to get someone to do the roof** wir müssen jemanden bestellen, der das Dach macht *(inf)*

> Note that a more specific verb may be required in German.

could you do this letter please tippen Sie bitte diesen Brief; **you do the painting and I'll do the papering** du streichst an und ich tapeziere; **he does the film crits for the magazine** er schreibt die Filmkritiken für die Zeitschrift; **to do the flowers** die Blumen arrangieren; **to do one's make-up** sich schminken; **to do one's hair** sich frisieren, sich *(dat)* die Haare (zurecht)machen *(inf)*; **to do one's nails** sich *(dat)* die Nägel schneiden *or (varnish)* lackieren; **to do one's teeth** *(Brit)* sich *(dat)* die Zähne putzen; **to do the dishes** spülen, den Abwasch machen; **to do the washing** Wäsche waschen; **to do the ironing** bügeln

♦ **do + anything/something** **he knows it's a mistake but he can't do anything about it** er weiß, dass es ein Fehler ist, aber er kann nichts dagegen machen *or* daran ändern; **are you doing anything this evening?** haben Sie heute Abend schon etwas vor?; **we'll have to do something about this/him** wir müssen da/wir müssen mit ihm etwas tun *or* unternehmen; **do something for me, will you … shut up** tu mir bloß den (einen) Gefallen und halt den Mund; **does that do anything for you?** macht dich das an? *(inf)*; **Brecht doesn't do anything for me** Brecht lässt mich kalt *(inf) or* sagt mir nichts

♦ **do + everything I've done everything I can** ich habe alles getan, was ich kann

♦ **do + nothing I've got nothing to do** ich habe nichts zu tun; **I shall do nothing of the sort** ich werde nichts dergleichen tun; **he does nothing but complain** er nörgelt immer nur, er tut nichts als nörgeln *(inf)*

♦ **do** *with wh- phrase* **what's to be done?** was ist da zu tun?; **but what can you do?** aber was kann man da machen?; **what do you want me to do (about it)?** und was soll ich da tun *or* machen?; **well, do what you can** mach *or* tu (eben), was du kannst; **what have you done to him?** was haben Sie mit ihm gemacht?; **now what have you done!** was hast du jetzt bloß wieder angestellt *or* gemacht?; **what are you doing on Saturday?** was machen *or* tun Sie am Sonnabend?; **what do I have to do to get through to him?** was muss ich tun, um zu ihm durchzukommen?; **what shall we do for money?** wie machen wir es mit Geld?; **how do you do it?** wie macht man das?; *(in amazement)* wie machen Sie das bloß?

♦ **that's done it** *(inf)* so, da haben wirs!, da haben wir die Bescherung! *(inf)*

♦ **that does it!** jetzt reichts mir!

b as job, profession **what does your father do?** was macht Ihr Vater (beruflich)?

c = provide service, product **what can I do for you?** was kann ich für Sie tun?; *(by shop assistant)* was darfs sein?; **sorry, we don't do lunches** wir haben leider keinen Mittagstisch; **we do a wide range of herbal teas** wir führen eine große Auswahl an Kräutertees; **we only do one style of gloves** *(= sell)* wir haben *or* führen nur eine Sorte Handschuhe; *(= produce)* wir stellen nur eine Sorte Handschuhe her; **who did the food for your reception?** wer hat bei Ihrem Empfang für das Essen gesorgt?

d = complete, finish *in pret, ptp only* **the work's done now** die Arbeit ist gemacht *or* getan *or* fertig; **what's done cannot be undone** was geschehen ist, kann man nicht ungeschehen machen; **I haven't done** *(Brit) or* **I'm not done telling you what I think of you** mit dir bin ich noch lange nicht fertig; **done!** *(= agreed)* abgemacht!; **are you done?** *(inf)* bist du endlich *or* schon *(iro)* fertig?

♦ **over and done with it's all over and done with** *(= is finished)* das ist alles erledigt; *(= has happened)* das ist alles vorbei *or* überstanden

e = study, cover durchnehmen, haben; **we've done Milton** wir haben Milton gelesen *or* durchgenommen; **I've never done any German** ich habe nie Deutsch gelernt *or* gehabt

f Cook machen *(inf)*; **to do the cooking** kochen; **how do you like your steak done?** wie möchten Sie Ihr Steak?; **well done** durch(gebraten); **is the meat done?** ist das Fleisch fertig (gebraten) *or* durch?

g = solve lösen; *sum, crossword, puzzle etc* lösen, machen

h = take customer drannehmen; **the barber said he'd do me next** der Friseur sagte, er würde mich als Nächsten drannehmen

i Theat, Film *part* spielen; **to do Hamlet** den Hamlet spielen; **to do a play** *(= put on)* ein Stück aufführen; **to do a film** *(= produce)* einen Film machen *or* drehen

j = take off, mimic nachmachen; **he does a brilliant Charlie Chaplin** er kann Charlie Chaplin hervorragend nachmachen; **she does the worried mother very convincingly** sie spielt die besorgte Mutter sehr überzeugend

k = visit, see sights of *city, country, museum* besuchen, abhaken *(inf)*

l Aut etc fahren, machen *(inf)*; **this car does** *or* **can do** *or* **will do 100** das Auto fährt *or* macht *(inf)* 100

m = treat *(Brit inf)* **they do you very well at that hotel** in dem Hotel ist man gut untergebracht *or* aufgehoben; **they do you very well at that restaurant** in dem Restaurant isst man sehr gut

♦ **to do oneself well** es sich *(dat)* gut gehen lassen

n = be suitable for *inf* passen (*sb* jdm); *(= be sufficient for)* reichen (*sb* jdm); **that will do me nicely** das reicht dicke *(inf) or* allemal

o = cheat *inf* übers Ohr hauen *(inf)*, reinlegen *(inf)*; **you've been done!** du bist reingelegt *or* übers Ohr gehauen worden *(inf)*; **I was done for £80** mit £ 80 hat man mich ganz schön übers Ohr gehauen *(inf)*

p = burgle *inf* einbrechen in *(+acc)*; **the office was done last night** im Büro ist gestern Nacht ein Bruch gemacht worden *(sl)*

q = hurt *Brit inf* **I'll do you!** dir besorg ichs noch! *(inf)*

r = tire out *(inf)* **I'm absolutely done (in)!** ich bin völlig geschafft *or* erledigt *or* fertig *(all inf)*

s = take *inf drugs* nehmen

t in prison *inf 6 years etc* sitzen, abreißen *(inf)*

u = translate *(old, liter)* **done into (the) English by …** ins Englische übertragen von …

3 – INTRANSITIVE VERB

a = act **do as I do** mach es wie ich; **he did well to take advice** er tat gut daran, sich beraten zu lassen; **he did right** er hat richtig gehandelt, es war richtig von ihm; **he did right/well to go** es war richtig/gut, dass er gegangen ist

b = get on, fare **how are you doing?** wie gehts (Ihnen)?; **I'm not doing so badly** es geht mir gar nicht so schlecht; **the patient is doing very well** dem Patienten geht es recht ordentlich; **he's doing well at school** er ist gut in der Schule; **his business is doing well** sein Geschäft geht gut; **the roses are doing well this year** die Rosen stehen dieses Jahr gut; **when my uncle died I did quite well** als mein Onkel starb, bin ich ganz gut dabei weggekommen

♦ **how do you do?** *(on introduction)* guten Tag/Abend!, angenehm! *(form)*

♦ **what's doing?** *(inf)* was ist los?

c = be suitable gehen; **that will never do!** das geht nicht!; **this room will do** das Zimmer geht *(inf) or* ist in Ordnung; **will it do if I come back at 8?** geht es, wenn ich um 8 Uhr zurück bin?; **it doesn't do to keep a lady waiting** es gehört sich nicht *or* es geht nicht, dass man eine Dame warten lässt; **will she/it do?** geht sie/das?

d = be sufficient reichen; **can you lend me some money? – will £10 do?** können Sie mir etwas Geld leihen? – reichen £ 10?; **yes, that'll do** ja, das reicht

♦ **to make do you'll have to make do with £10** £ 10 müssen Ihnen reichen, Sie werden mit £ 10 auskommen müssen

♦ **that'll do!** jetzt reichts aber!

4 – NOUN *(Brit inf)*

a = event Veranstaltung *f*, Sache *f (inf)*; *(= party)* Fete *f (inf)*; **she had a big do for her eighteenth birthday** an ihrem achtzehnten Geburtstag stieg bei ihr eine Riesenfete *(inf)*

b = swindle *(Brit)* Schwindel *m*; **the whole thing was a do from start to finish** die ganze Sache war von vorne bis hinten ein Schwindel

c = hairdo *esp US* Frisur *f*, Schnitt *m*

5 – dos PLURAL NOUN

the dos and don'ts was man tun und nicht tun sollte; **fair dos** *(inf)* gleiches Recht für alle

6 – PHRASAL VERBS

▶ **do away with** VI *+prep obj* **a** *custom, law, nuclear weapons* abschaffen; *document* vernichten; *building* abreißen; **to do away with the need for sth** etw überflüssig *or* unnötig machen; **it does away with the need to wear protective clothing** das macht Schutzkleidung überflüssig *or* unnötig **b** *(inf: = kill)* umbringen

▶ **do by** VI *+prep obj* **to do well/badly by sb** jdn gut/schlecht behandeln; **do as you would be done by** *(Prov)* was du nicht willst, dass man dir tu, das füg auch keinem andern zu *(Prov)* → **hard ADV b**

▶ **do down** VT *sep (Brit)* heruntermachen, schlechtmachen

▶ **do for** VI *+prep obj (inf)* **a** *(= finish off) person* fertigmachen *(inf)*; *project* zunichtemachen; **to be done for** *(person)* erledigt *or* fertig *(inf)* sein; *(project)* gestorben sein *(inf)*; **she got done for driving without a licence** *(Brit inf)* sie ist ohne Führerschein erwischt worden *(inf)* **b** *(charlady)* putzen für *or* bei

▶ **do in** VT *sep (inf)* **a** *(= kill)* um die Ecke bringen *(inf)* **b** *(usu pass: = exhaust)* **to be** *or* **feel done in** fertig *or* geschafft sein *(inf)*

▶ **do out** VT *sep* **a** *room* auskehren *or* -fegen **b to do sb out of a job** jdn um eine Stelle bringen; **to do sb out of £100** jdn um £ 100 bringen *or* erleichtern *(inf)*

▶ **do over** VT *sep* **a** *(= redecorate)* (neu) herrichten **b** *(inf: = beat up)* zusammenschlagen; *(= rob, burgle)* ausrauben **c** *(US: = do again)* noch einmal machen

▶ **do up** VI *(dress etc)* zugemacht werden VT *sep* **a** *(= fasten)* zumachen; *tie* binden **b** *(= parcel together) goods* zusammenpacken; **books done up in brown paper** in Packpapier eingewickelte Bücher **c** *house, room* (neu) herrichten; **her hair was done up in ringlets** ihr Haar war in Ringellocken gelegt

▶ **do with** VI *+prep obj* **a** *(= need)* brauchen; **do you know what I could do with?** weißt du, was ich jetzt brauchen könnte?; **I could do with a cup of tea** ich könnte eine Tasse Tee gebrauchen *or* vertragen *(inf)*; **it could do with a clean** es müsste mal sauber gemacht werden **b** *(inf: = tolerate)* ausstehen, vertragen; **I can't be doing with this noise** ich kann den Lärm nicht vertragen *or* ausstehen

c he has to do with the steel industry er hat mit der Stahlindustrie zu tun; **what has that got to do with it?** was hat das damit zu tun?; **I won't have anything to do with it!** ich möchte nichts damit zu tun haben!; **that has** *or* **is nothing to do with you!** das geht Sie gar nichts an!; **it has something to do with money** es hat etwas mit Geld zu tun; **it has something to do with her being adopted** es hat etwas damit zu tun, dass sie adoptiert wurde; **it/this debate has to do with …** dabei/in dieser Debatte geht es um …; **money has a lot to do with it** Geld spielt eine große Rolle dabei

d what have you done with my gloves/your hair? was hast du mit meinen Handschuhen/deinem Haar gemacht?

e he doesn't know what to do with himself er weiß nicht, was er mit sich anfangen soll; **the children can always find something to do with themselves** die Kinder finden immer etwas, womit sie sich beschäftigen können

f to be done with sb/sth *(= finished)* mit jdm/etw fertig sein

▶ **do without** VI *+prep obj* auskommen ohne; **I can do without your advice** Sie können sich Ihren Rat sparen; **I could have done without that!** das hätte mir (wirklich) erspart bleiben können; **you'll have to do without** Sie müssen ohne auskommen

---

do³ *written abbr of* **ditto**

DOA *abbr of* **dead on arrival**

doable [ˈduːəbl] ADJ *(inf)* machbar

d.o.b. *abbr of* **date of birth**

Doberman (pinscher) [ˈdəʊbəmən(ˈpɪnʃəˈ)] N Dobermann(pinscher) *m*

doc [dɒk] N *(inf) abbr of* **doctor** *(as address)* Herr/Frau Doktor

docile [ˈdəʊsaɪl] ADJ sanftmütig; *animal* fromm; *acceptance* widerstandslos

docilely [ˈdəʊsaɪlɪ] ADV sanftmütig

docility [dəʊˈsɪlɪtɪ] N Sanftmut *f*

dock[1] [dɒk] N Dock *nt*; *(for berthing)* Pier *m*, Kai *m*; **~s** *pl* Hafen *m*; **my car is in ~** *(inf)* mein Wagen ist in der Werkstatt VT docken *(spec)*; *(Space also)* ankoppeln *(with* an *+acc)* VI a *(Naut)* anlegen b *(Space, two spacecraft)* docken *(spec)*, ankoppeln; **the space shuttle ~ed with Russia's space station** die Raumfähre koppelte *or* dockte *(spec)* an die russische Raumstation an

dock[2] N *(Jur)* Anklagebank *f*; **to stand in the ~** auf der Anklagebank sitzen; **"prisoner in the ~"** „Angeklagte(r)"

dock[3] VT a *dog's tail* kupieren; *horse's tail* stutzen b *wages* kürzen; *points* abziehen; **to ~ £50 off sb's wages** jds Lohn um £ 50 kürzen; **he was ~ed 6 points for cheating** ihm wurden 6 Punkte wegen Mogeln abgezogen N kupierter Schwanz; *(of horse)* gestutzter Schweif

dock[4] N *(Bot)* Ampfer *m*

docker [ˈdɒkəʳ] N *(Brit)* Hafenarbeiter *m*, Docker *m*

docket [ˈdɒkɪt] N a *(on document, parcel etc)* Warenbegleitschein *m*, Laufzettel *m* b *(Jur: = judgements register)* Urteilsregister *nt*; *(= list of cases) Liste der Gerichtstermine* c *(= customs certificate)* Zollinhaltserklärung *f* VT a *contents, judgement, information etc* zusammenfassen, eine Kurzfassung geben *or* herstellen von b *contents* angeben; *(= put docket on) crate* mit einem Warenbegleitschein *or* Laufzettel versehen

dock gates PL Hafeneingang *m*; *(in water)* Docktor *nt*

docking [ˈdɒkɪŋ] N *(Space)* Docking *nt (spec)*, Ankoppelung *f*

docking: **docking manoeuvre** N *(Space)* (An)koppelungsmanöver *nt*; **docking station** PL a *(Space)* (Welt)raumstation *f* b *(for digital camera)* Dockingstation *f*; **docking techniques** PL *(Space)* (An)koppelungstechnik *f*; **docking time** N Liegezeit *f*

dock: **dock labourer** N Hafenarbeiter *m*; **dockland** N Hafenviertel *nt*; **dock strike** N Hafenarbeiterstreik *m*; **dock worker** N Hafenarbeiter *m*; **dockyard** N Werft *f*

Doc Martens® [dɒkˈmɑːtənz] PL Springerstiefel *pl*

doctor [ˈdɒktəʳ] N a *(Med)* Arzt *m*, Ärztin *f*, Doktor(in) *m(f) (inf)*; **Doctor Smith** Doktor Smith; **yes, ~** ja, Herr/Frau Doktor; **the ~'s** *(= surgery)* der Arzt; **to go to the ~** zum Arzt gehen; **to send for the ~** den Arzt holen; **he is a ~** er ist Arzt; **a woman ~** eine Ärztin; **he's under a ~ in London** *(inf)* er ist bei einem Arzt in London in Behandlung; **to be under ~'s orders** in ärztlicher Behandlung sein; **it's just what the ~ ordered** *(fig inf)* das ist genau das Richtige
b *(Univ etc)* Doktor *m*; **to get one's ~'s degree** promovieren, seinen Doktor machen; **~ of Law/of Science** *etc* Doktor der Rechte/der Naturwissenschaften *etc*; **Dear Doctor Smith** Sehr geehrter Herr Dr./Sehr geehrte Frau Dr. Smith
VT a *cold* behandeln; **to ~ oneself/sb** an sich *(dat)*/jdm herumdoktern
b *(inf: = castrate)* kastrieren
c *(= tamper with) accounts* frisieren; *text* verfälschen; **the food's/wine's been ~ed** dem Essen/Wein ist etwas beigemischt worden

doctoral thesis [ˈdɒktərəlˈθiːsɪs] N Doktorarbeit *f*

doctorate [ˈdɒktərɪt] N Doktorwürde *f*; **~ in science/philosophy** Doktor(titel) *m* in Naturwissenschaften/Philosophie; **to gain one's ~** die Doktorwürde verliehen bekommen; **to take one's ~** seinen Doktor machen; **he's still doing his ~** er sitzt immer noch an seiner Doktorarbeit

doctor's surgery [ˌdɒktəzˈsɜːdʒərɪ] N Arztpraxis *f*

doctrinaire [ˌdɒktrɪˈneəʳ] ADJ doktrinär

doctrinal [dɒkˈtraɪnl] ADJ doktrinell; **on ~ matters** in Sachen der Doktrin

doctrine [ˈdɒktrɪn] N Doktrin *f*, Lehre *f*

docudrama [ˈdɒkjʊˌdrɑːmə] N Dokumentarspiel *nt*

document [ˈdɒkjʊmənt] N Dokument *nt*, Urkunde *f* VT a *history, fact, life* dokumentieren; *case* beurkunden, (urkundlich) belegen; **the theory is well ~ed** die Theorie ist gut belegt b *ship* mit Papieren versehen

documentary [ˌdɒkjʊˈmentərɪ] ADJ a dokumentarisch, urkundlich b *(Film, TV)* **a ~ film** ein Dokumentarfilm *m*; **in ~ form** in Form einer Dokumentation N *(Film, TV)* Dokumentarfilm *m*

documentary credit N *(Fin)* Dokumentenakkreditiv *nt*

documentary evidence N *(Jur)* urkundliche Beweise *pl*

documentation [ˌdɒkjʊmenˈteɪʃən] N Dokumentation *f*

docu-soap [ˈdɒkjʊsəʊp] N *(TV)* Dokusoap *f*

DOD *(US) abbr of* **Department of Defense** Verteidigungsministerium *nt*

dodder [ˈdɒdəʳ] VI tapern

dodderer [ˈdɒdərəʳ] N *(esp Brit inf)* Tattergreis *m (inf)*

doddering [ˈdɒdərɪŋ], **doddery** [ˈdɒdərɪ] ADJ *(esp Brit) person* taperig

doddle [ˈdɒdl] N *(Brit inf)* **it was a ~** es war ein Kinderspiel

dodge [dɒdʒ] N a *(lit)* Sprung *m* zur Seite, rasches Ausweichen; *(Ftbl, Boxing)* Ausweichen *nt*
b *(= trick)* Trick *m*, Kniff *m*; *(= ingenious plan)* Glanzidee *f (inf)*; **to know all the ~s** mit allen Wassern gewaschen sein
VT *blow, ball, question, difficulty* ausweichen *(+dat)*; *tax* umgehen; *(= shirk) work, military service* sich drücken vor *(+dat)*; **to ~ the issue** der (eigentlichen) Frage ausweichen *or* aus dem Weg gehen
VI ausweichen; **to ~ out of sight** blitzschnell verschwinden, sich blitzschnell verdrücken *(inf)*; **to ~ out of the way** *(of car, blow)* zur Seite springen; **to ~ behind a tree** hinter einen Baum springen; **to ~ through the traffic** sich durch den Verkehr schlängeln

dodgem [ˈdɒdʒəm] N (Auto)skooter *m*; **did you go on the ~s?** bist du (Auto)skooter gefahren?

dodger [ˈdɒdʒəʳ] N a *(= trickster)* Schlawiner *m (inf)* → **artful** b *(Naut)* Wetterschutz *m*

dodgery [ˈdɒdʒərɪ] N *(= trick)* Kniff *m*, Trick *m*; *(= fib)* Schwindel *m*

dodgy [ˈdɒdʒɪ] ADJ *(Brit inf)* a *(= dubious, uncertain) person* zweifelhaft, zwielichtig; *deal, business, practices* zwielichtig; *area, loan* zweifelhaft; *plan* unsicher; *situation* vertrackt *(inf)*, verzwickt *(inf)*; *weather* unbeständig; **there's something ~ about him** er ist nicht ganz koscher *(inf)*; **there's something ~ about this business** die Sache ist nicht ganz astrein *(inf)*; **it's a ~ business** *(= uncertain)* es ist eine unsichere Sache; **he's on ~ ground** er befindet sich auf unsicherem Boden
b *(= weak) back, heart* schwach; *(= damaged) tyre, car/boat etc part* defekt; **he has a ~ stomach from eating oysters** er hat Austern gegessen und sich damit den Magen verdorben
c *(= near-the-knuckle) remark* anstößig

dodo [ˈdəʊdəʊ] N a Dodo *m*, Dronte *f*; **as dead as a ~** mausetot b *(US inf: = silly person)* Trottel *m (inf)*

DOE a *(Brit) abbr of* **Department of the Environment** Umweltministerium *nt* b *(US) abbr of* **Department of Energy** Energieministerium *nt*

doe [dəʊ] N *(roe deer)* Reh *nt*, Ricke *f*; *(red deer)* Hirschkuh *f*; *(rabbit)* (Kaninchen)weibchen *nt*; *(hare)* Häsin *f*

doer [ˈduːəʳ] N a *(= author of deed)* Täter(in) *m(f)*; **he's a great ~ of crosswords** *(inf)* er macht sehr gerne Kreuzworträtsel b *(= active person)* Mann *m*/Frau *f* der Tat, Macher(in) *m(f) (inf)*; **he's more of a ~ than a thinker** er ist eher ein Mann der Tat als der Theorie

does [dʌz] *3rd pers sing of* **do**[2]

doeskin [ˈdəʊskɪn] N Rehfell *nt*; *(treated)* Rehleder *nt*

doesn't [ˈdʌznt] *contr of* **does not**

doff [dɒf] VT *hat* ziehen, lüften; *(old) garment* ablegen

dog [dɒg] N a Hund *m*; **the ~s** *(Brit Sport)* das Hunderennen
b *(fig)* **it's a ~'s life** es ist ein Hundeleben; **to go to the ~s** *(person, business, district, institution)* vor die Hunde gehen *(inf)*; **give a ~ a bad name (and hang him)** wer einmal ins Gerede *or* in Verruf kommt(, dem hängt das sein Leben lang an); **~ in the manger** *(Brit)* Spielverderber(in) *m(f)*; **~-in-the-manger attitude** *(Brit)* missgünstige Einstellung; **every ~ has his day** jeder hat einmal Glück im Leben; **it's (a case of) ~ eat ~** es ist ein Kampf aller gegen alle; **~-eat-~ society** Ellenbogengesellschaft *f*; **you can't teach an old ~ new tricks** der Mensch ist ein Gewohnheitstier; **let sleeping ~s lie** schlafende Hunde soll man nicht wecken; **to put on the ~** *(dated US inf)* auf fein machen *(inf)*; **~'s dinner** *or* **breakfast** *(inf)* Schlamassel *m (inf)*; **he made a complete ~'s breakfast of it** *(inf)* er hat dabei totalen Mist gebaut *(inf)*; **to work like a ~** *(inf)* wie ein Pferd arbeiten *(inf)*
c *(= male fox, wolf)* Rüde *m*
d *(inf: = man)* **lucky ~** Glückspilz *m*; **dirty ~** gemeiner Hund; **sly ~** gerissener Hund *(inf)*; **there's life in the old ~ yet** noch kann man ihn nicht zum alten Eisen werfen; **Tom Jones, you old ~!** Tom Jones, du alter Schwerenöter! → **top dog**
e *(Tech, = clamp)* Klammer *f*
f *(US, inf, = failure)* Pleite *f (inf)*
g *(inf) (= unattractive woman)* Schreckschraube *f (inf)*; *(= tart)* Schlampe *f (inf)*, Flittchen *nt (inf)*; *(= unfaithful man)* Schwein *nt (inf)*
VT a *(= follow closely)* **to ~ sb** *or* **sb's footsteps** jdm hart auf den Fersen sein/bleiben
b *(= harass)* verfolgen; **~ged by controversy/injury** von Kontroversen/Verletzungen verfolgt

dog: **dog basket** N Hundekorb *m*; **dog biscuit** N Hundekuchen *m*; **dog breeder** N Hundezüchter(in) *m(f)*; **dog breeding** N Hundezucht *f*; **dogcart** N Dogcart *m*; **dog-cheap** ADJ, ADV *(inf)* spottbillig *(inf)*; **dog collar** N *(lit)* Hundehalsband *nt*; *(vicar's)* Kollar *nt*; **dog days** PL Hundstage *pl*; **dog-eared** [ˈdɒgɪəd] ADJ mit Eselsohren; **dog-end** N *(inf)* Kippe *f (inf)*; **dog fancier** N Hundefreund(in) *m(f)*; *(= breeder, seller)* Hundezüchter(in) *m(f)*; **dogfight** N *(Aviat)* Luftkampf *m*; **dogfish** N Hundshai *m*; **dog food** N Hundefutter *nt*; **dog fox** N Fuchsrüde *m*

dogged [ˈdɒgɪd] ADJ *person* zäh, beharrlich; *determination, resistance, pursuit, battle, refusal* hartnäckig; *persistence* zäh; **they have been ~ in their search** sie haben beharrlich gesucht

doggedly [ˈdɒgɪdlɪ] ADV beharrlich; *fight also* hartnäckig; **~ determined** hartnäckig

doggedness [ˈdɒgɪdnɪs] N Beharrlichkeit *f*, Zähigkeit *f*; *(of resistance, pursuit, refusal)* Hartnäckigkeit *f*

doggerel [ˈdɒgərəl] N *(also* **doggerel verse***)* Knittelvers *m*

doggie, doggy [ˈdɒgɪ] N *(inf)* kleiner Hund, Hündchen *nt* ADJ Hunde-; *(= dog loving)* hundenärrisch; **I'm not really a ~ person** ich bin kein großer Freund von Hunden; **~ smell** Hundegeruch *m*

doggie bag N *(Beutel für) Essensreste, die nach Hause mitgenommen werden*

doggo [ˈdɒgəʊ] ADV *(inf)* **to lie ~** sich nicht mucksen *(inf)*; *(= go underground)* von der Bildfläche verschwinden *(inf)*

doggone [ˌdɒgˈgɒn] INTERJ *(US inf)* **~ (it)!** verdammt noch mal! *(inf)*

doggoned [ˌdɒgˈgɒn(d)] ADJ *(US inf)* verdammt *(inf)*

doggy N *(inf)* = **doggie**

doggy fashion ADV *(inf) have sex* wie die Hunde

doggy paddle N **to do (the) ~** paddeln, Hundepaddeln machen

dog: **dog handler** N Hundeführer(in) *m(f)*; **doghouse** N Hundehütte *f*; **he's in the ~** *(inf)* er ist in Ungnade; *(with wife)* bei ihm hängt der Haussegen schief; **dog iron** N Kaminbock *m*; **dog Latin** N Küchenlatein *nt*; **doglead** N Hundeleine *f*; **dogleg** N Knick *m*; *(in road also)* scharfe Kurve; *(in pipe also)* starke Krümmung; **dog licence**, *(US)* **dog license** N Hundemarke *f*; **a ~ costs ...** die Hundesteuer beträgt ...; **doglike** ADJ hundeähnlich; **~ devotion** hündische Ergebenheit

dogma ['dɒgmə] N Dogma *nt*

dogmatic [dɒg'mætɪk] ADJ dogmatisch; **~ theology** Dogmatik *f*; **to be very ~ about sth** in etw *(dat)* sehr dogmatisch sein

dogmatically [dɒg'mætɪkəlɪ] ADV dogmatisch

dogmatism ['dɒgmətɪzəm] N Dogmatismus *m*

dogmatize ['dɒgmətaɪz] VTI *(Rel, fig)* dogmatisieren

do-gooder [ˈduːˈgʊdəʳ] N *(pej)* Weltverbesserer *m*, Weltverbesserin *f*

dog: **dog paddle** N = **doggy paddle**; **dog rose** N Hundsrose *f*

dogsbody ['dɒgzbɒdɪ] N *(Brit)* **she's/he's the general ~** sie/er ist (das) Mädchen für alles

dog: **dog show** N Hundeausstellung *f*; **dogsled** N Hundeschlitten *m*; **Dog Star** N Hundsstern *m*, Sirius *m*; **dog's-tooth check** [ˌdɒgztuːθ'tʃek], **dog-tooth check** N Hahnentrittmuster *nt*; **dog tag** N *(US Mil inf)* Erkennungsmarke *f*, Hundemarke *f (inf)*; **dog-tired** ADJ hundemüde; **dogtooth** N *(Archit)* Hundszahn *m*; **dog track** N Hunderennbahn *f*; **dogtrot** N gemächlicher *or* leichter Trott; **dogwatch** N *(Naut)* Hundewache *f*; **dogwood** N Hartriegel *m*, Hornstrauch *m*

doily ['dɔɪlɪ] N (Spitzen- *or* Zier)deckchen *nt*

doing ['duːɪŋ] N **a** Tun *nt*; **this is your ~** das ist dein Werk; **it was none of my ~** ich hatte nichts damit zu tun; **that takes some ~** da gehört (schon) etwas dazu; **there is a difference between ~ and saying** zwischen Taten und Worten besteht ein Unterschied **b** **doings** PL *(inf)* Handlungen *pl*, Taten *pl* **c** **doings** PL *(inf Brit: = thing)* Dingsbums *nt (inf)*

do-it-yourself ['duːɪtjə'self] ADJ N = **DIY**

dol *abbr of* **dollar**

Dolby® ['dɒlbɪ] N Dolby® *nt*

doldrums ['dɒldrəmz] PL **a** *(Geog, area)* Kalmengürtel *m or* -zone *f*; *(weather)* Windstille *f*, Kalme *f* **b** **to be in the ~** *(people)* Trübsal blasen; *(business etc)* in einer Flaute stecken

dole [dəʊl] N *(Brit inf)* Arbeitslosenunterstützung *f*, Alu *f (inf)*, Stütze *f (inf)*; **to go/be on the ~** stempeln (gehen)

▶ **dole out** VT *sep* austeilen, verteilen

doleful ['dəʊlfʊl] ADJ *person, face, look, expression* tieftraurig, trübselig; *eyes, voice, sigh* tieftraurig; *song* klagend

dolefully ['dəʊlfəlɪ] ADV tieftraurig, trübselig

dole money N *(Brit inf)* Arbeitslosenunterstützung *f*, Stütze *f (inf)*

dolichocephalic ['dɒlɪkəʊse'fælɪk] ADJ dolichozephal

doll [dɒl] N **a** Puppe *f*; **~'s pram** *(Brit) or* **baby carriage** *(US)* Puppenwagen *m* **b** *(dated esp US inf: = girl)* Mädchen *nt*; *(= pretty girl)* Puppe *f (inf)*; **thanks Betty, you're a ~** danke Betty, du bist klasse *(inf)*

▶ **doll up** VT *sep (inf)* herausputzen; **to doll oneself up, to get dolled up** sich aufdonnern *(inf)*; **she was dolled up for the party** sie war für die Party aufgedonnert *(inf)*

dollar ['dɒləʳ] N Dollar *m*

dollar: **dollar area** N Dollarraum *m*, Dollarblock *m*; **dollar bill** N Dollarnote *f*; **dollar diplomacy** N Finanzdiplomatie *f*; **dollar gap** N Dollarlücke *f*; **dollar rate** N Dollarkurs *m*; **dollar sign** N Dollarzeichen *nt*

dollish ['dɒlɪʃ] ADJ puppenhaft

dollop ['dɒləp] N *(inf)* Schlag *m (inf)*

doll's house, *(US)* **doll house** N Puppenhaus *nt*

dolly ['dɒlɪ] N **a** *(inf: = doll)* Püppchen *nt* **b** *(= wheeled frame)* (Transport)wagen *m*; *(Film, TV)* Dolly *m*, Kamerawagen *m*; *(Rail)* Schmalspurrangierlokomotive *f* **c** *(for washing clothes)* Wäschestampfer *m* **d** *(Tech, for rivet)* Gegenhalter *m* **e** *(inf: = girl)* Puppe *f* **f** *(Sport inf)* lahmer Ball *(inf)* ADJ *(Sport inf) shot* lahm; *catch* leicht

▶ **dolly in** *(Film, TV)* VT *sep* vorfahren VI vorfahren

▶ **dolly out** *(Film, TV)* VT *sep* zurückfahren VI zurückfahren

dolly bird N *(dated Brit inf)* Puppe *f* ADJ *attr* puppig

dolman ['dɒlmən] N Dolman *m*; **~ sleeve** angeschnittener Ärmel

dolomite ['dɒləmaɪt] N Dolomit *m*; **the Dolomites** die Dolomiten *pl*

dolphin ['dɒlfɪn] N Delfin *m*, Delphin *m*

dolphinarium [ˌdɒlfɪ'nɛərɪəm] N Delfinarium *nt*, Delphinarium *nt*

dolt [dəʊlt] N Tölpel *m*

doltish ['dəʊltɪʃ] ADJ tölpelhaft, dumm

domain [dəʊ'meɪn] N **a** *(lit: = estate)* Gut *nt*; *(belonging to state, Crown)* Domäne *f*; **the Crown ~s** die Ländereien der Krone **b** *(fig)* Domäne *f* → **public c** *(Math)* Funktionsbereich *m* **d** *(Comput)* Domäne *f*, Domain *nt*

domain name N *(Comput)* Domainname *m*

dome [dəʊm] N **a** *(Archit, on building)* Kuppel *f* **b** *(of heaven, skull)* Gewölbe *nt*; *(of hill)* Kuppe *f*; *(of branches)* Kuppel *f* **c** *(lid, cover etc)* Haube *f*

domed [dəʊmd] ADJ *forehead, ceiling* gewölbt; *roof* kuppelförmig; **~ stadium** Stadion *nt* mit Kuppeldach

domestic [də'mestɪk] ADJ **a** *(= household)* häuslich; **the ~ arrangements** die häusliche Situation; **~ chores** *or* **duties** Hausarbeit *f*; **his wife has always taken care of his ~ needs** seine Frau hat zu Hause immer alles für ihn gemacht; **everything of a ~ nature** alles, was den Haushalt angeht; **she was never very ~, she was never a very ~ sort of person** sie war nie ein sehr häuslicher Mensch; **~ activities** *or* **things take up a lot of time** der Haushalt nimmt viel Zeit in Anspruch; **in the interests of ~ harmony** im Interesse des Familienfriedens; **~ bliss** häusliches Glück; **~ quarrel** Ehekrach *m*; **~ appliances** Haushaltsgeräte *pl*; **for ~ use** für den Hausgebrauch; **~ rubbish** *(Brit) or* **garbage** *(US)* Hausmüll *m*

b *(esp Pol, Comm: = within a country) consumption, production, spending, sales, demand etc* inländisch, im Inland; *currency* inländisch; *problems* im Inland; *news* aus dem Inland; *issues, affairs* innenpolitisch; **he was more interested in foreign affairs than in ~ affairs** er interessierte sich mehr für Außenpolitik als für Innenpolitik

N **a** *(= servant)* Hausangestellte(r) *mf*

b *(inf: = quarrel)* Ehekrach *m*

domestically [də'mestɪkəlɪ] ADV **a** *(esp Pol, Comm)* inländisch; *grown, produced* im Inland; **to be ~ owned** inländische/einen inländischen Besitzer haben; **~ and internationally** im In- und Ausland **b** *(= in the home)* im Haushalt; **~ inclined** häuslich veranlagt

domestic animal N Haustier *nt*

domesticate [də'mestɪkeɪt] VT *wild animal* domestizieren; *(hum) person* domestizieren; *(= house-train) dog, cat* stubenrein machen

domesticated [də'mestɪkeɪtɪd] ADJ *animal, species* domestiziert; *person* häuslich

domestication [dəmestɪ'keɪʃən] N *(of wild animal, hum: of person)* Domestikation *f*, Domestizierung *f*; **the ~ of cats doesn't take long** es dauert nicht lange, bis man Katzen stubenrein gemacht hat

domestic: **domestic cat** N Hauskatze *f*; **domestic dog** N Haushund *m*; **domestic economy** N *(Pol)* Binnenwirtschaft *f*; **domestic flight** N Inlandflug *m*; **domestic fuel** N Brennstoff *m* für private Haushalte

domesticity [ˌdəʊmes'tɪsɪtɪ] N häusliches Leben

domestic: **domestic market** N *(Pol, Comm)* Binnenmarkt *m*; **domestic policy, domestic politics** N Innenpolitik *f*; **domestic rates** PL *(Brit Econ, Hist)* Kommunalabgaben *pl*; **domestic science** N *(esp old Brit Sch)* Hauswirtschaftslehre *f*; **~ college/teacher** *(esp old Brit Sch)* Hauswirtschaftsschule *f*/-lehrer(in) *m(f)*; **domestic servant** N Hausangestellte(r) *mf*; **domestic service** N Arbeit *f* als Hausangestellte(r); **to be in ~** als Hausangestellte(r) arbeiten; **domestic staff** N Hauspersonal *nt*; **domestic supply** N Hausanschluss *m*; **they had no ~ of water** sie hatten keinen Wasseranschluss im Haus; **domestic violence** N Gewalt *f* in der Familie; **one in ten women is a victim of ~** eine von zehn Frauen ist Opfer häuslicher Gewalt *or* wird zu Hause misshandelt

domicile ['dɒmɪsaɪl] *(form)* N *(Admin)* Wohnsitz *m*; *(Fin)* Zahlungs- *or* Erfüllungsort *m* VT *(Admin)* unterbringen *(with* bei, in *+dat)*; *(Fin)* domizilieren *(at* bei); **he is currently ~d in Berlin** er ist zurzeit in Berlin wohnhaft *(form)*

domiciliary [ˌdɒmɪ'sɪlɪərɪ] ADJ *care* häuslich, im Haus; **~ visit** *(of doctor)* Hausbesuch *m*; **~ expenses** Haushaltskosten *pl*

dominance ['dɒmɪnəns] N Vorherrschaft *f (over* über *+acc)*, Dominanz *f (over* über *+acc) (also Biol)*

dominant ['dɒmɪnənt] ADJ **a** *person, role, class, feature* dominierend; *partner, figure, position, issue, personality* dominierend, beherrschend; *nation, culture, ideology, species, trend, theme* dominierend, vorherrschend; *gene* dominant; **the ~ factor** der wichtigste *or* dominierende Faktor; **to be ~** *or* **the ~ force in sth** etw dominieren; **they are ~ in the world market** sie beherrschen den Weltmarkt; **~ male** *(animal)* männliches Leittier; *(fig hum, man)* Platzhirsch *m*

b *(Mus)* dominant; **~ seventh** Dominantseptakkord *m*

N **a** *(Biol)* dominantes Gen

b *(Mus)* Dominante *f*

dominate ['dɒmɪneɪt] VI dominieren VT beherrschen; *(colour, feature)* beherrschen, dominieren; *(species, gene)* dominieren

domination [ˌdɒmɪ'neɪʃən] N (Vor)herrschaft *f*; **under the ~ of the Romans** unter römischer Herrschaft; **his ~ of his younger brothers** sein dominierendes Verhalten seinen jüngeren Brüdern gegenüber; **her ~ of the conversation/game** die Tatsache, dass sie die Unterhaltung/das Spiel beherrschte

dominatrix [ˌdɒmɪ'neɪtrɪks] N *pl* **dominatrices** *or* **dominatrixes** Domina *f*

domineer [ˌdɒmɪ'nɪəʳ] VI tyrannisieren *(over sb* jdn)

domineering [ˌdɒmɪ'nɪərɪŋ] ADJ herrisch; *mother-in-law, husband etc also* herrschsüchtig

Dominican[1] [də'mɪnɪkən] *(Geog)* ADJ dominikanisch N Dominikaner(in) *m(f)*

Dominican[2] *(Eccl)* N Dominikaner *m* ADJ Dominikaner-, dominikanisch; **~ monastery** Dominikanerkloster *nt*

Dominican Republic N Dominikanische Republik

dominion [də'mɪnɪən] N **a** *no pl* Herrschaft *f (over* über *+acc)*; **to have ~ over sb** Macht über jdn haben **b** *(= territory)* Herrschaftsgebiet *nt*; **overseas ~s** überseeische Gebiete *pl*; **the Dominion of Canada** das Dominion Kanada

Dominion Day N *gesetzlicher Feiertag in Kanada zur Erinnerung an die Übertragung der vollen politischen Autonomie*

domino ['dɒmɪnəʊ] N *pl* **-es** **a** Domino(stein) *m*; **a game of ~es** ein Dominospiel *nt*; **to play ~es** Domino spielen **b** *(= costume, mask)* Domino *m*

domino effect N Dominowirkung *f or* -effekt *m*

domino theory N Dominoeffekt *m*

don¹ [dɒn] N *(Brit Univ)* *Universitätsdozent(in) besonders in Oxford und Cambridge*

don² VT *garment* anziehen, anlegen *(dated)*; *hat* aufsetzen

donate [dəʊ'neɪt] **VT** *money, blood, kidney* spenden; *gifts to a charity also* stiften; *time* zur Verfügung stellen **VI** spenden; **to ~ to charity** für wohltätige Zwecke spenden

donation [dəʊ'neɪʃən] N *(= act of giving: of money, gifts, blood)* Spenden *nt*; *(= gift)* Spende *f*; **to make a ~ of 50p/£10,000** 50 Pence/£ 10.000 spenden

done [dʌn] *ptp of* **do²** ADJ **a** *(= finished) work* erledigt; *(= cooked) vegetables* gar; *meat* durch; *cake* durchgebacken; **to get sth ~** *(= finished)* etw fertig kriegen; **is it ~ yet?** ist es schon erledigt?; **~!** *(= agreed)* abgemacht!; **a ~ deal** *(US)* eine abgekartete Sache **b** *(Brit inf: = tired out)* **I'm ~ (in)** ich bin geschafft *(inf) or* fertig **c** **it's not the ~ thing, that's not ~** das tut man nicht **d** *(inf: = used up)* **the butter is (all) ~** die Butter ist alle

donee [dəʊ'niː] N *(Jur)* Schenkungsempfänger(in) *m(f)*, Beschenkte(r) *mf*

doner kebab ['dɒnəkə'bæb] N Döner(kebab) *m*

dong [dɒŋ] N **a** *(= sound of bell)* Bimbam *nt* **b** *(= currency)* Dong *m* **c** *(sl: = penis)* Apparat *m (inf)*

dongle ['dɒŋgl] N *(Comput)* Dongle *m*, Kopierschutzstecker *m*

Don Juan [ˌdɒn'dʒuːən] N *(lit, fig)* Don Juan *m*

donkey ['dɒŋkɪ] N Esel *m*

donkey: **donkey derby** N Eselrennen *nt*; **donkey engine** N *(Rail)* (kleines) Hilfsaggregat; **donkey jacket** N *dicke (gefütterte) Jacke*; **donkey ride** N Ritt *m* auf dem/einem Esel, Eselsritt *m*

donkey's years ['dɒŋkɪzˌjɪəz] PL *(inf)* ewig und drei Tage *(inf)*, eine Ewigkeit; **she's been here for ~** *(inf)* sie ist schon ewig und drei Tage *(inf) or* eine Ewigkeit hier

donkey-work ['dɒŋkɪwɜːk] N Routinearbeit *f*, Dreckarbeit *f (inf)*

donnish ['dɒnɪʃ] *(Brit: usu pej)* ADJ professoral; **a ~ type** ein typischer Gelehrter

donor ['dəʊnə'] N *(Med, to charity)* Spender(in) *m(f)*

donor card N Organspenderausweis *m*

donor conference N *(= Pol, Econ)* Geberkonferenz *f*

donor fatigue N Spendenmüdigkeit *f*

donor organ N Spenderorgan *nt*

do-nothing ['duːˌnʌθɪŋ] **N** Faulenzer(in) *m(f)*, Nichtstuer(in) *m(f)* **ADJ** faul

don't [dəʊnt] *contr of* **do not**

don't-know [ˌdəʊnt'nəʊ] N *(in opinion poll)* **30% were ~s** 30% hatten keine Meinung

donut ['dəʊnʌt] N *(esp US)* = **doughnut**

doobee ['duːbiː] N *(sl: = cannabis)* Dope *nt*

doodah ['duːdɑː], *(US)* **doodad** ['duːdæd] N *(inf)* Dingsbums *nt (inf)*, Dingsda *nt (inf)*

doodle ['duːdl] **VI** Männchen malen **VT** kritzeln **N** Gekritzel *nt*

doodlebug ['duːdlbʌg] N **a** *(Brit: = bomb)* V1--Rakete *f* **b** *(US: = larva)* Ameisenlarve *f*

doofer ['duːfə'] N *(Brit inf: = remote control)* Fernbedienung *f*

doofus ['duːfəs] N *(US inf)* doofer Typ, Blödmann *m*

doohickey ['duːhɪkɪ] N *(US inf: = thingummy)* Dings(bums) *nt*

doolally [duː'lælɪ] ADJ *(inf)* plemplem *pred (inf)*

doom [duːm] **N** *(= fate)* Schicksal *nt*; *(= ruin)* Verhängnis *nt*; **to go to one's ~** seinem Verhängnis entgegengehen; **to send sb to his ~** jdn ins Verhängnis stürzen; **he met his ~** das Schicksal ereilte ihn; **~ and gloom** tiefster Pessimismus; **it's all ~ and gloom with him at the moment** er sieht zurzeit alles nur schwarz; **it's not all gloom and ~** so schlimm ist es ja alles gar nicht

VT verurteilen, verdammen; **to be ~ed** verloren sein; **the project was ~ed from the start** das Vorhaben war von Anfang an zum Scheitern verurteilt; **the ~ed ship** das dem Untergang geweihte Schiff; **~ed to die** dem Tode geweiht; **~ed to failure** zum Scheitern verurteilt; **this country was ~ed to become a second-rate nation** dieses Land war dazu verdammt, zur Zweitrangigkeit abzusinken

doomsday ['duːmzdeɪ] N der Jüngste Tag; **... otherwise we'll be here till ~** *(inf)* ... sonst sind wir in zwanzig Jahren noch hier; **~ cult** *or* **group** Weltuntergangssekte *f*

door [dɔː'] N **a** Tür *f*; *(= entrance: to cinema etc)* Eingang *m*; **there's someone at the ~** da ist jemand an der Tür; **was that the ~?** hat es geklingelt/geklopft?; **to answer the ~** die Tür aufmachen; **to see sb to the ~** jdn zur Tür bringen; **to stand in the ~** in der Tür stehen; **to be on the ~** *(bouncer etc)* Türsteher sein; *(collecting ticket money etc)* Türdienst haben; **to pay at the ~** *(Theat etc)* an der (Abend)kasse zahlen; **"doors open 2.20"** „Einlass 14.20 Uhr"; **to go from ~ to ~** *(salesman etc)* von Tür zu Tür gehen, Klinken putzen *(inf)*; **he lives three ~s away** er wohnt drei Häuser weiter; **it takes 7 hours from ~ to ~** man braucht 7 Stunden von Tür zu Tür

b *(phrases)* **by** *or* **through the back ~** durch ein Hintertürchen; **to have a foot** *or* **toe in the ~** mit einem Fuß *or* Bein drin sein; **to lay sth at sb's ~** jdm etw vorwerfen *or* anlasten; **to be at death's ~** an der Schwelle des Todes stehen *(geh)*; **to leave the ~ open to** *or* **for further negotiations** die Tür zu weiteren *or* für weitere Verhandlungen offenlassen; **to open the ~ to sth** einer Sache *(dat)* Tür und Tor öffnen; **to show sb the ~** jdm die Tür weisen; **to shut** *or* **slam the ~ in sb's face** jdm die Tür vor der Nase zumachen; **to shut** *or* **close the ~ on sth** etw ausschließen; **we don't want to shut any ~s** wir möchten uns *(dat)* keine Möglichkeiten verbauen; **when one ~ shuts, another ~ opens** *(prov)* irgendwie geht es immer weiter; **out of ~s** im Freien; **behind closed ~s** hinter verschlossenen Türen

door *in cpds* Tür-; **doorbell** N Türglocke *or* --klingel *f*; **there's the ~** es hat geklingelt; **door chain** N Sicherheitskette *f*

do-or-die ['duːɔː'daɪ] ADJ verbissen

door: **doorframe** N Türrahmen *m*; **doorhandle** N Türklinke *f*; *(= knob)* Türknauf *m*; **doorkeeper** N *(of hotel, block of flats)* Portier *m*; **doorknob** N Türknauf *m*; **doorknocker** N Türklopfer *m*; **doorman** N Portier *m*; **doormat** N Fußmatte *f*, Abtreter *m*; *(fig)* Fußabtreter *m*; **door money** N Eintrittsgeld *nt*; **doornail** N **as dead as a ~** mausetot; **door opener** N Türöffner *m*; **doorplate** N Türschild *nt*; **doorpost** N Türpfosten *m*; **deaf as a ~** stocktaub; **doorscraper** N Kratzeisen *nt*, Fußabstreifer *m (aus Metall)*; **doorstep** **N** Eingangsstufe *f*; *(hum: = hunk of bread)* dicke Scheibe Brot; **the bus stop is just on my ~** *(fig)* die Bushaltestelle ist direkt vor meiner Tür **VT** *(Brit Press)* zu Hause aufsuchen und interviewen; *(Pol)* zu Hause besuchen, um Wahlwerbung zu machen; **doorstepping** ['dɔːstepɪŋ] N *no pl (Brit Press) agressive Interviewtechnik, bei der Journalisten unangemeldet und ungebeten jdn zu Hause aufsuchen*; *(Pol) Methode der Wahlwerbung, bei der Politiker von Haus zu Haus gehen, um die Bewohner für ihre Partei zu gewinnen*; **doorstop(per)** N Türstopper *m*; **door-to-door** ADJ *attr*, **door to door** ADJ *pred* **a** **~ salesman** Vertreter *m* **b** *delivery* von Haus zu Haus; **how's that for ~ service?** na, ist das nicht ein Service?; **police are carrying out ~ inquiries** die Polizei befragt alle Anwohner; **doorway** N *(of room)* Tür *f*; *(of building, shop)* Eingang *m*; *(fig, to success etc)* Weg *m*

dopamine ['dəʊpəmiːn] N *(Chem)* Dopamin *nt*

dope [dəʊp] **N** **a** *no pl (inf: = drugs)* Rauschgift *nt*, Stoff *m (inf)*, Drogen *pl*; *(Sport)* Anregungs- *or* Aufputschmittel *nt*; **to smoke ~** Haschisch rauchen; **he failed a ~ test** er fiel bei der Dopingkontrolle auf **b** *no pl (inf, = information)* Information(en) *f(pl)*; **to have ~ on sb** Informationen über jdn haben **c** *(inf: = stupid person)* Esel *m (inf)*, Trottel *m (inf)* **d** *(= varnish)* Lack *m* **e** *(for explosives)* Benzinzusatz(mittel *nt*) *m* **VT** *horse, person* dopen; *food, drink* präparieren, ein Betäubungsmittel untermischen *(+dat)*

► **dope out** VT *(esp US inf: = find out)* herausfinden

► **dope up** VT **to be doped up on** *or* **with Valium®** *(inf)* mit Valium® vollgestopft sein *(inf)*

dope: **dopehead** N *(inf)* Junkie *m (inf)*; **dope peddler**, **dope pusher** N Drogenhändler(in) *m(f)*, Dealer(in) *m(f) (inf)*

dopester ['dəʊpstə'] N *(esp US inf, also* **inside dopester***)* (bestens informierter) Insider

dope test N *(inf Sport)* Dopingkontrolle *f*

dopey, **dopy** ['dəʊpɪ] ADJ *(+er)* *(inf: = stupid)* bekloppt *(inf)*, blöd *(inf)*; *(= sleepy, half-drugged)* benommen, benebelt *(inf)*

doping ['dəʊpɪŋ] N *(Sport)* Doping *nt*; **~ problem** Dopingproblem *nt*

Doppler effect ['dɒplərɪˌfekt] N Dopplereffekt *m*

Doric ['dɒrɪk] ADJ *(Archit)* dorisch

dork [dɔːk] N *(inf pej)* Idiot *m*, Trottel *m (both inf pej)*

dorm [dɔːm] *(inf) abbr of* **dormitory**

dormancy ['dɔːmənsɪ] N *(form: = inactivity) (of volcano)* Untätigkeit *f*; *(of plant)* Ruhe *f*; *(of virus)* Inaktivität *f*

dormant ['dɔːmənt] ADJ *volcano* untätig; *animal, plant, bud* ruhend; *(Banking) account* ruhend; *energy* verborgen, latent; *passion* schlummernd; **~ state** Ruhezustand *m*; **to remain ~** ruhen; *(disease, virus)* schlummern; **the ~ season** die Ruhezeit; **to lie ~** *(project, idea, work of art)* brachliegen; **to let a matter lie ~** eine Sache ruhen *or* liegen lassen

dormer (window) ['dɔːmə('wɪndəʊ)] N Mansardenfenster *nt*

dormice ['dɔːmaɪs] *pl of* **dormouse**

dormitory ['dɔːmɪtrɪ] N Schlafsaal *m*; *(US: = building)* Wohnheim *nt*; **~ suburb** *or* **town** Schlafstadt *f*

Dormobile® ['dɔːməbiːl] N Wohnmobil *nt*, Campingbus *m*

dormouse ['dɔːmaʊs] N *pl* **dormice** Haselmaus *f*; **edible** *or* **fat dormouse** Siebenschläfer *m*; **common ~** Gemeiner Siebenschläfer

Dors *(Brit) abbr of* **Dorset**

dorsal ['dɔːsl] **ADJ** Rücken-, dorsal *(spec)* **N** *(Phon)* Dorsal(laut) *m*

dorsal fin N Rückenflosse *f*

dory ['dɔːrɪ] N *(US)* *Ruderboot mit spitzem Bug und schmalem Heck*

DOS [dɒs] *(Comput) abbr of* **disk operating system** DOS *nt*

dosage ['dəʊsɪdʒ] N Dosis *f*; *(= giving of medicine)* Dosierung *f*; **~ meter** Dosimeter *nt*

dose [dəʊs] **N** **a** *(Med)* Dosis *f*; *(fig, of punishment etc)* Ration *f*; **give him a ~ of medicine** gib ihm Medizin; **he needs a ~ of his own medicine** *(fig)* man sollte es ihm mit gleicher Münze heimzahlen; **in small/large ~s** *(fig)* in kleinen/großen Mengen; **she's all right in small ~s** sie ist nur (für) kurze Zeit zu ertragen

b *(inf, = venereal disease)* Tripper *m*; **to catch a ~** sich *(dat)* etwas holen *(inf)*, sich *(dat)* den Tripper holen

c *(inf: = bout of illness)* Anfall *m*; **she's just had a ~ of the flu** sie hat gerade Grippe gehabt

VT *person* Arznei geben *(+dat)*; **I've tried dosing myself with cough mixture** ich habe versucht, mich mit Hustensaft zu kurieren

dosh [dɒʃ] N *(inf: = money)* Moos *nt (sl)*, Knete *f (sl)*

doss [dɒs] *(Brit inf)* N Schlafplatz *m*, Bleibe *f (inf)* VI *(also* **doss down***)* pennen *(inf)*, sich hinhauen *(inf)*; **to ~ down for the night** sich für die Nacht einquartieren *(inf)*

dosser ['dɒsəʳ] N *(Brit inf)* Penner(in) *m(f) (inf)*, Stadtstreicher(in) *m(f)*

dosshouse ['dɒshaʊs] N *(Brit inf)* Penne *f (inf)*, Obdachlosenheim *nt*

dossier ['dɒsɪeɪ] N Dossier *m or nt*; **they are keeping a ~ on him** sie haben ein Dossier über ihn angelegt

dost [dʌst] *(obs) 2nd pers sing of* **do²**

DOT *(US) abbr of* **Department of Transportation** Verkehrsministerium *nt*

dot [dɒt] N a Punkt *m*; *(on material)* Tupfen *m*, Punkt *m*; **morse code is made up of ~s and dashes** das Morsealphabet besteht aus kurzen und langen Signalen; **~, dash, ~** *(morse)* kurz, lang, kurz; **~, ~, ~** *(in punctuation)* drei Punkte
b *(phrases)* **to arrive on the ~** auf die Minute pünktlich (an)kommen; **on the ~ of 9pm** um Punkt 21 Uhr; **at 3 o'clock on the ~** haargenau *or* auf die Minute genau um 3 Uhr; **she has lived here since the year ~** *(Brit inf)* sie lebt schon ewig *or* schon seit ewigen Zeiten hier
VT a **to ~ an i** einen i-Punkt setzen; **to ~ one's i's and cross one's t's** *(fig)* peinlich genau *or* penibel sein; **a ~ted bow tie** eine gepunktete Fliege; **~ted line** punktierte Linie; **to tear along the ~ted line** an der *or* entlang der punktierten Linie abtrennen; **to sign on the ~ted line** *(fig)* seine formelle Zustimmung geben, formell zustimmen
b *(= sprinkle)* verstreuen; **a field ~ted with flowers** ein mit Blumen übersätes Feld; **hotels ~ted around the island** über die Insel verstreute Hotels; **pictures ~ted around the room** im Zimmer verteilte Bilder
c **to ~ sb one** *(inf)* jdm eine langen *(inf)*

dotage ['dəʊtɪdʒ] N Senilität *f*, Altersschwäche *f*; **to be in one's ~** in seiner zweiten Kindheit sein, senil sein; **he's spending his ~ in the south of France** er verbringt seinen Lebensabend in Südfrankreich

dotcom, dot.com [dɒt'kɒm] N *(Comput)* Internetfirma *f*

dot command N *(Comput)* Punktbefehl *m*

dote on ['dəʊtɒn] VI *+prep obj* abgöttisch lieben

dotgone, dot.gone ['dɒtgɒn] N *(Comput)* gescheiterte Internetfirma

doth [dʌθ] *(obs) 3rd pers sing of* **do²**

doting ['dəʊtɪŋ] ADJ **her ~ parents** ihre sie abgöttisch liebenden Eltern; **a ~ old fool** ein vernarrter alter Trottel

dot matrix (printer) N Matrixdrucker *m*, Nadeldrucker *m*

dottle ['dɒtl] N Tabakrest *m*

dotty ['dɒtɪ] ADJ *(+er) (Brit inf)* kauzig, schrullig; **to be ~ about sb/sth** *(= like)* nach jdm/etw verrückt sein

double ['dʌbl] ADV a *(= twice as much) charge, cost, pay* doppelt so viel; *count* doppelt; **~ the size (of)** doppelt so groß (wie); **~ the amount** doppelt so viel; **we paid her ~ what she was getting before** wir zahlten ihr das Doppelte von dem, was sie vorher bekam; **they charge ~ what they used to** sie berechnen doppelt so viel wie früher; **he took ~ the time it took me** er brauchte doppelt so lange wie ich; **he's ~ your age** er ist doppelt so alt wie du; **~ six is twelve** zweimal sechs ist zwölf; **to see ~** doppelt sehen
b **to bend ~** sich krümmen; **she was bent ~ with laughter/pain** sie krümmte sich vor Lachen/Schmerzen; **to fold sth ~** etw einmal falten
ADJ a *(= twice as much)* doppelt; **to pay a ~ amount** das Doppelte bezahlen; **a ~ gin/whisky** *etc* ein doppelter Gin/Whisky *etc*
b *(= having two similar parts, in pairs)* Doppel-; **~ bottom** doppelter Boden; **the egg had a ~ yolk** das Ei hatte zwei Dotter; **it is spelled with a ~ 'p'** es wird mit Doppel-p *or* mit zwei p geschrieben; **my phone number is 9, ~ 3, 2, 4** meine Telefonnummer ist neun drei drei zwei vier *or* neun dreiunddreißig vierundzwanzig
c *(Bot) flower* gefüllt
N a *(= twice a quantity, number, size etc)* das Doppelte, das Zweifache; **~ or quits** doppelt oder nichts; **he earns the ~ of what I do** er verdient doppelt so viel wie ich
b *(= person)* Ebenbild *nt*, Doppelgänger(in) *m(f)*; *(Film, Theat: = stand-in)* Double *nt*; *(= actor taking two parts)* Schauspieler, der eine Doppelrolle spielt; **I saw your ~** ich habe einen Doppelgänger/eine Doppelgängerin von dir gesehen; **I've got the ~ of that clock** ich habe genau die gleiche Uhr
c **at the ~** *(also Mil)* im Laufschritt; *(fig)* im Eiltempo; **on the ~** *(fig)* auf der Stelle
d *(Cards, = increase)* Verdoppelung *f*; *(Bridge)* Kontra *nt*; *(= hand) Blatt, das die Verdoppelung/das Kontra rechtfertigt (in racing)* Doppelwette *f*; *(in dice)* Pasch *m*; *(in dominoes)* Doppelstein *m*, Pasch *m*
VT a *(= increase twofold)* verdoppeln
b *(= fold in two) piece of paper* (einmal) falten
c *(Film, Theat)* **he ~s the roles of courtier and hangman** er hat die Doppelrolle des Höflings und Henkers; **the producer decided to ~ the parts of pimp and judge** der Produzent beschloss, die Rollen des Zuhälters und des Richters mit demselben Schauspieler zu besetzen
d *(Naut, = sail round)* umsegeln
e *(Cards)* verdoppeln; *(Bridge)* kontrieren
VI a *(= increase twofold)* sich verdoppeln
b *(Mus)* zwei Instrumente spielen; **he ~s on flute and clarinet** er spielt Flöte und Klarinette
c *(Film, Theat)* **to ~ for sb** jds Double sein, jdn doubeln; **who is doubling for him?** wer doubelt ihn?, wer ist sein Double?; **he ~s as the butler and the duke** er hat die Doppelrolle des Butlers und Herzogs; **this bedroom ~s as a study** dieses Schlafzimmer dient auch als Arbeitszimmer
d *(Cards)* verdoppeln; *(Bridge)* kontrieren

▸**double back** VI *(person)* kehrtmachen, zurückgehen/-fahren; *(animal)* kehrtmachen, zurücklaufen; *(road, river)* sich zurückwinden *or* -schlängeln VT *sep blanket* umschlagen; *page* umknicken

▸**double over** VI = **double up VI a** VT *sep* = **double back VT**

▸**double up** VI a *(= bend over)* sich krümmen; *(with laughter)* sich biegen, sich kringeln *(inf)*; **he doubled up when the bullet hit him** er klappte *(inf) or* brach zusammen, als die Kugel ihn traf
b *(= share room)* das Zimmer/Büro *etc* gemeinsam benutzen; *(= share bed)* in einem Bett schlafen; **you'll have to double up with Mary** du musst dir ein Zimmer mit Mary teilen
c *(esp Brit, Betting) den Einsatz bis zum ersten Gewinn verdoppeln*
d *(= have two roles)* **to double up as ...** auch als ... dienen
VT *sep* a *paper* falten, knicken; *blanket* zusammenlegen
b **the bullet/blow doubled him up** von der Kugel/dem Schlag getroffen, brach er zusammen

double: **double act** N *(esp Theat: = performers)* Zweigespann *nt*; *(= performance)* Zweiershow *f*; **double-acting** ADJ doppelt wirksam; **double agent** N Doppelagent(in) *m(f)*; **double album** N *(Mus)* Doppelalbum *nt*; **double bar** N *(Mus)* Doppelstrich *m*; **double-barrelled**, *(US)* **double-barreled** [ˌdʌbl'bærəld] ADJ Doppel-; **double-barrelled name**, *(US)* **double-barreled name** N Doppelname *m*; **double-barrelled shotgun**, *(US)* **double-barreled shotgun** N doppelläufiges Gewehr, Zwilling *m*; **double bass** N Kontrabass *m*; **double bassoon** N Kontrafagott *nt*; **double bed** N Doppelbett *nt*; **double bend** N S-Kurve *f*; **double bill** N Vorstellung *f* mit zwei Filmen/Stücken; **double bind** N Zwickmühle *f*; **double-blind** ADJ *(Sci)* Doppelblind-; **~ experiment** Doppelblindversuch *m*; **double bluff** N *(= deception)* doppelter Bluff; **double boiler** N *(US)* Turmtopf *m*; **double-book** VT *room, seat* zweimal reservieren; *flight* zweimal buchen; **I'm very sorry, I've ~ed your seat** es tut mir sehr leid, ich habe einen Platz für Sie reserviert, der schon vergeben war; **double-breasted** ADJ zweireihig; **~ jacket/suit** Zweireiher *m*; **double check** N doppelte Überprüfung; **in spite of all his ~s** obwohl er alles doppelt *or* noch einmal überprüft hatte; **double-check** VTI noch einmal (über)prüfen; **double chin** N Doppelkinn *nt*; **double click** N *(Comput)* Doppelklick *m*; **double-click** *(Comput)* VT doppelklicken VI doppelklicken *(on* auf *+acc)*; **double-clutch** VI *(US)* = **double-declutch**; **double consonant** N Doppelkonsonant *m*; **double cream** N Schlagsahne *f*; **double-cross** *(inf)* VT ein Doppelspiel *or* falsches Spiel treiben mit; **the ~ing swines!** diese falschen Hunde! *(inf)* N Doppelspiel *nt*; **double-crosser** N *(inf)* falscher Freund *or* Hund *(inf)*; **double-date** VT **he's double-dating me** er trifft sich außer mit mir noch mit einer anderen; **double-dealer** N Betrüger(in) *m(f)*; **double-dealing** N Betrügerei(en) *f(pl)* ADJ betrügerisch; **double-decker** N *(all senses)* Doppeldecker *m*; **double-declutch** VI *(Aut)* mit Zwischengas schalten; **double density** ADJ *(Comput) disk* mit doppelter Dichte; **double doors** PL Flügeltür *f*; **double Dutch** N *(esp Brit)* Kauderwelsch *nt*; **to talk ~** Unsinn *or* Kauderwelsch reden; **it was ~ to me** das waren für mich böhmische Dörfer; **double eagle** N *(US) alte amerikanische Goldmünze mit einem Wert von 20 Dollar*; **double-edged** ADJ *(lit, fig) remark, compliment* zweischneidig; **tourism is ~** *or* **is a ~ sword** der Tourismus ist ein zweischneidiges Schwert; **double entendre** ['du:blɑ̃:n'tɑ̃:ndr] N *(esp Brit)* Zweideutigkeit *f*; **double-entry bookkeeping** N doppelte Buchführung; **double exposure** N doppelt belichtetes Foto; **double fault** N *(Tennis)* Doppelfehler *m*; **double feature** N Programm *nt* mit zwei Hauptfilmen; **double figures** PL zweistellige Zahlen *pl*; **double first** N *(Brit Univ)* **he got a ~** er bestand beide Fächer mit „sehr gut“; **double flat** N *(Mus)* Doppel-b *nt*; **double glaze** VT mit Doppelverglasung versehen; **double glazing** N Doppelfenster *pl*; **double Gloucester** N *englische Käsesorte*; **double-header** N *(US Sport)* Doppelspieltag *m*; **double helix** N *(Chem)* Doppelhelix *f*; **double honours (course)** N *(Brit Univ)* ≈ Doppelstudium *nt*; **double indemnity** N *(US Insur) Verdoppelung der Lebensversicherungssumme bei Unfalltod*; **double jeopardy** N *(US Jur)* doppelte Strafverfolgung wegen derselben Tat; **double-jointed** ADJ äußerst elastisch, sehr gelenkig; **double knitting (wool)** N Sportwolle *f*; **double knot** N Doppelknoten *m*; **double life** N Doppelleben *nt*; **double lock** N Doppelschloss *nt*; **double-lock** VT zweimal abschließen; **double meaning** N **it has a ~** es ist doppeldeutig; **double negative** N doppelte Verneinung; **double pack** N Doppelpack *m*, Doppelpackung *f*; **double-page spread** N Doppelseite *f*; **double-park** VI in der zweiten Reihe parken; **double parking** N Parken *nt* in der zweiten Reihe; **double pneumonia** N doppelseitige Lungenentzündung; **double-quick** *(inf)* ADV im Nu, in null Komma nichts *(inf)* ADJ **in ~ time** im Nu, in null Komma nichts *(inf)*; **double reed** N *(Mus)* doppeltes Rohrblatt; **double room** N Doppelzimmer *nt*

doubles ['dʌblz] N *sing or pl (Sport)* Doppel *nt*; **to play ~** im Doppel spielen

double: **double saucepan** N Turmtopf *m*; **double sharp** N *(Mus)* Doppelkreuz *nt*; **double-sided** ADJ *(Comput) disk* zweiseitig; *poster* doppelseitig; **~ (adhesive) tape** Doppelklebeband *nt*; **double slash** N *(Typ)* Doppelschrägstrich *m*, doppelter Schrägstrich; **double-space** VT *(Typ)* mit doppeltem Zeilenabstand drucken; **double spacing** N doppelter Zeilenabstand; **doublespeak** N *(pej)* doppelzüngiges Gerede; **double standard** N Doppelmoral *f*; **society applies ~s** die Gesellschaft misst mit zweierlei Maß; **double star** N Doppelstern *m*; **double stop** N *(Mus)* Doppelgriff *m* VI mit Doppelgriff spielen; **double stopping** N *(Mus)* Doppelgriffe *pl*; **double strike** N *(Comput, printing)* Doppeldruck *m*

doublet [ˈdʌblɪt] N **a** Wams *nt* **b** *(Ling)* Dublette *f*

double: **double take** N **he did a ~** er musste zweimal hingucken; **double talk** N *(ambiguous)* zwei- *or* doppeldeutiges Gerede; *(deceitful)* doppelzüngiges Gerede; **double taxation** N Doppelbesteuerung *f*; **doublethink** N widersprüchliches Denken; **double ticket** N Eintrittskarte *f* für zwei Personen; **double time** N *(Mil)* Laufschritt *m*; **double-tongue** VI *(Mus)* mit Doppelzunge blasen; **double-tonguing** N Doppelzunge *f*; **double vision** N *(Med)* Doppeltsehen *nt*; **he suffered from ~** er sah doppelt; **double wedding** N Doppelhochzeit *f*; **double whammy** N Doppelschlag *m*; **double windows** PL Doppelfenster *pl*; **double yellow lines** PL *gelbe Doppellinie am Fahrbahnrand zur Kennzeichnung des absoluten Halteverbots*; **it is illegal in Britain to park on ~** in Großbritannien ist es verboten, auf gelben Doppellinien zu parken

doubloon [dʌˈbluːn] N Dublone *f*

doubly [ˈdʌblɪ] ADV doppelt; **to work ~ hard** doppelt so hart arbeiten; **to make ~ sure (that ...)** ganz sichergehen(, dass ...); **~ so** umso mehr; **this road is dangerous, ~ so when it's icy** diese Straße ist gefährlich, umso mehr bei Glatteis

doubt [daʊt] ✪ 15.1, 16.1, 26.3 N Zweifel *m*; **to have one's ~s as to** *or* **about sth** (so) seine Bedenken hinsichtlich einer Sache *(gen)* haben; **I have my ~s about her** ich habe bei ihr (so) meine Bedenken; **I have no ~s about taking the job** ich habe keine Bedenken, die Stelle anzunehmen; **there's no ~ about it** daran gibt es keinen Zweifel; **I have no ~ about it** ich bezweifle das nicht; **I have ~s whether he will come** ich bezweifle, dass er kommt; **to cast ~ on sth** etw in Zweifel ziehen; **there is room for ~** es ist durchaus nicht sicher; **to be open to ~** fragwürdig sein; **his reputation is in ~** sein Ruf wird infrage *or* in Frage gestellt; **to be in (some) ~ about sth** Zweifel an etw *(dat)* haben; **to be in little ~ as to sth** keine Bedenken hinsichtlich einer Sache *(gen)* haben; **I am in no ~ as to what** *or* **about what he means** ich bin mir völlig im Klaren darüber, was er meint; **the outcome is still in ~** das Ergebnis ist noch ungewiss; **when in ~** im Zweifelsfall; **no ~ he will come tomorrow** höchstwahrscheinlich kommt er morgen; **without (a) ~** ohne Zweifel; **I knew beyond ~ that ...** ich wusste ohne jeden Zweifel, dass ...; **it must be proved beyond reasonable ~** es muss ganz unzweifelhaft bewiesen werden
VT bezweifeln; *sb's honesty, truth of statement* anzweifeln, Zweifel haben an *(+dat)*; **to ~ sb's word** jds Wort anzweifeln; **I'm sorry I ~ed you** *(what you said)* es tut mir leid, dass ich dir nicht geglaubt habe; *(your loyalty etc)* es tut mir leid, dass ich an dir gezweifelt habe; **I ~ it (very much)** das möchte ich (doch stark) bezweifeln, das bezweifle ich (sehr); **I don't ~ it** das bezweifle ich (auch gar) nicht; **I ~ whether he will come** ich bezweifle, dass er kommen wird
VI Zweifel haben *or* hegen

doubter [ˈdaʊtəʳ] N Skeptiker(in) *m(f)*, Zweifler(in) *m(f)*

doubtful [ˈdaʊtfʊl] ✪ 16.1, 16.2 ADJ **a** *(usu pred: = unconvinced) person* unsicher; **I'm still ~** ich habe noch Bedenken; **to be ~ about sth** an etw *(dat)* zweifeln; **to be ~ about doing sth** Bedenken haben, ob man etw tun soll; **I was ~ whether I could ever manage it** ich bezweifelte, ob ich es je schaffen könnte; **to be ~ of sb/sth** jdm/einer Sache *(dat)* nicht trauen
b *(= unlikely) reconciliation, improvement, victory* unwahrscheinlich; **it is ~ that...** es ist unsicher *or* zweifelhaft, ob ...
c *(= questionable, dubious) reputation* zweifelhaft, fragwürdig; *future, outcome* ungewiss; *joke, taste, quality, value* zweifelhaft; **information of ~ reliability/origin** zweifelhafte Informationen; **it is ~ whether this could be managed** es ist fraglich, ob es zu schaffen wäre
d *(Sport: = unlikely to play)* **he is ~ for tonight's match** es ist fraglich, ob er heute Abend spielen kann; **she is a ~ starter for Saturday's race** es ist fraglich, ob sie in dem Rennen am Samstag starten wird

doubtfully [ˈdaʊtfəlɪ] ADV **a** *(= uncertainly)* unsicher **b** *(= questionably, dubiously) attributed* fraglicherweise

doubtfulness [ˈdaʊtfʊlnɪs] N **a** *(= uncertainty, of person)* Unsicherheit *f* **b** *(= unlikeliness, of improvement, victory)* Unwahrscheinlichkeit *f* **c** *(= dubiousness)* Zweifelhaftigkeit *f*, Fragwürdigkeit *f*; *(of future, outcome)* Ungewissheit *f*; *(of joke, taste)* Zweifelhaftigkeit *f*

doubting Thomas [ˌdaʊtɪŋˈtɒməs] N ungläubiger Thomas

doubtless [ˈdaʊtlɪs] ✪ 26.3 ADV sicherlich; **this is ~ true** das stimmt sicherlich

douche [duːʃ] N Spülung *f*, Irrigation *f (spec)*; *(= instrument)* Irrigator *m* VI eine Spülung machen VT spülen

douchebag [ˈduːʃbæg] N *(US pej sl)* Trottel *m (inf)*, Idiot *m (inf)*

dough [dəʊ] N **a** Teig *m* **b** *(inf: = money)* Kohle *f (inf)*

dough: **doughball** N Kloß *m*; **doughboy** N *(dated US Mil sl)* Landser *m (inf)*; **dough hook** N *(Cook)* Knethaken *m*; **doughnut** [ˈdəʊnʌt] N *(Brit)* Berliner (Pfannkuchen) *m*, Krapfen *m (S Ger, Aus)*; **doughnutting** [ˈdəʊnʌtɪŋ] N *(Brit Parl inf) Situation, in der sich wenige anwesende Abgeordnete im Unterhaus um den Redner gruppieren, um im Fernsehen den Eindruck eines vollen Hauses zu vermitteln*

doughty [ˈdaʊtɪ] ADJ *(liter)* kühn, tapfer

doughy [ˈdəʊɪ] ADJ **a** *consistency* zäh, teigig; *(pej) bread* klitschig, nicht durchgebacken **b** *(pej) complexion* käsig

Douglas fir [ˌdʌgləsˈfɜːʳ], **Douglas pine** [-ˈpaɪn] N Douglastanne *f*

dour [ˈdʊəʳ] ADJ *(= silent, unfriendly)* verdrießlich; *struggle* hart, hartnäckig

dourly [dʊəlɪ] ADV verdrießlich; *(= stubbornly)* hartnäckig

douse [daʊs] VT **a** *(= pour water over)* Wasser schütten über *(+acc)*; *(= put into water)* ins Wasser tauchen; *plants* reichlich wässern; **to ~ sb/sth in** *or* **with petrol** jdn/etw mit Benzin übergießen **b** *light* ausmachen, löschen

dove[1] [dʌv] N *(lit, fig)* Taube *f*

dove[2] [dəʊv] *(US) pret of* **dive**

dove [dʌv-]: **dove-coloured**, *(US)* **dove-colored** ADJ taubenblau; **dovecot(e)** N [ˈdʌvkɒt] Taubenschlag *m*; **dove-grey** ADJ taubengrau

Dover sole [ˌdəʊvəˈsəʊl] N Seezunge *f*

dovetail [ˈdʌvteɪl] N Schwalbenschwanz *m*; **~ joint** Schwalbenschwanzverbindung *f* VT (schwalbenschwanzförmig) überblatten; *(fig) plans* koordinieren VI *(plans)* übereinstimmen

dowager [ˈdaʊədʒəʳ] N (adlige) Witwe; **~ duchess** Herzoginwitwe *f*

dowdiness [ˈdaʊdɪnɪs] N absoluter Mangel an Schick

dowdy [ˈdaʊdɪ] ADJ *(+er)* ohne jeden Schick

dowel [ˈdaʊəl] N Dübel *m*

dower house [ˈdaʊəhaʊs] N *Haus für eine Witwe*

Dow-Jones average [ˌdaʊˈdʒəʊnzˈævərɪdʒ] N Dow-Jones-Index *m*

down[1] [daʊn]

1 ADVERB
2 PREPOSITION
3 NOUN
4 ADJECTIVE
5 TRANSITIVE VERB

1 – ADVERB

When *down* is an element in a phrasal verb, eg *get down, sit down, stand down, write down*, look up the verb.

a [indicating movement towards speaker] herunter; *(away from speaker)* hinunter; *(downstairs)* nach unten; **to jump down** herunter-/hinunterspringen; **on his way down from the summit** auf seinem Weg vom Gipfel herab/hinab; **on the way down to London** auf dem Weg nach London runter *(inf)*; **all the way down to the bottom** bis ganz nach unten; **down!** *(to dog)* Platz!

♦ **down with ...!** nieder mit ...!

b [indicating static position] unten; **down there** da unten; **I'll stay down here** ich bleibe hier unten; **down in the valley** unten im Tal; **it needs a bit of paint down at the bottom** es muss unten herum neu gestrichen werden; **don't kick a man when he's down** *(fig)* man soll jemanden nicht fertigmachen, wenn er schon angeschlagen ist *or* wenns ihm dreckig geht *(inf)*; **head down** mit dem Kopf nach unten; **the sun was down** die Sonne war untergegangen; **the blinds were down** die Jalousien waren unten *or* heruntergelassen; **John isn't down yet** *(= still in bed)* John ist noch nicht unten; **I'll be down in a minute** ich komme sofort runter; **to be down for the count** *(Boxing)* ausgezählt werden; **I've been down with flu** ich habe mit Grippe (im Bett) gelegen → **dump N d**

c [= to or in another place] *usu not translated* **he came down from London yesterday** er kam gestern aus London; **he's down in London/at his brother's** er ist in London/bei seinem Bruder; **he lives down South** er wohnt im Süden; **we're going down South** wir fahren in den Süden; **we're going down to the seaside/to Dover** wir fahren an die See/nach Dover

d [= below previous level] **his temperature is down** sein Fieber ist zurückgegangen; **his shoes were worn down** seine Schuhe waren abgetragen; **the price of meat is down on last week** der Fleischpreis ist gegenüber der letzten Woche gefallen; **interest rates are down to/by 3%** der Zinssatz ist auf/um 3% gefallen; **I'm £20 down on what I expected** ich habe £ 20 weniger als ich dachte; **he's down to his last £10** er hat nur noch £ 10; **they're still three goals down** sie liegen immer noch mit drei Toren zurück → **luck**

e [in writing] **I've got it down in my diary** ich habe es in meinem Kalender notiert; **let's get it down on paper** schreiben wir es auf, halten wir es schriftlich fest; **when you see it down on paper** wenn man es schwarz auf weiß sieht; **to be down for the next race** für das nächste Rennen gemeldet sein; **it's down for next month** es steht für nächsten Monat auf dem Programm

f [indicating range or succession usu not translated] **from the biggest down** vom Größten angefangen; **down through the ages** von jeher

♦ **down to** *(= until)* bis zu; **from 1700 down to the present** seit 1700 bis zur Gegenwart; **right down to the present day** bis zum heutigen Tag; **from the chairman (all the way) down to the doorman** vom Vorsitzenden bis (herunter) zum Pförtner

g [indicating responsibility]

♦ **to be down to sb/sth** *(= caused by)* an jdm/etw liegen; **any mistakes are down to us** irgendwelche Fehler liegen an uns; **it's down to**

you to decide *(= your responsibility)* die Entscheidung liegt bei Ihnen

h [as deposit] **to pay £20 down** £ 20 anzahlen; **I've put down a deposit on a new bike** ich habe eine Anzahlung für ein neues Fahrrad gemacht; **how much do they want down?** was verlangen sie als Anzahlung?

2 – PREPOSITION

a [indicating movement downwards] **to go/come down the hill/the stairs** *etc* den Berg/die Treppe *etc* hinuntergehen/herunterkommen; **he ran his finger down the list** er ging (mit dem Finger) die Liste durch; **her hair fell loose down her back** sie trug ihr Haar offen über die Schultern

b [at a lower part of] **he's already halfway down the hill** er ist schon auf halbem Wege nach unten; **the other skiers were further down the slope** die anderen Skifahrer waren weiter unten; **she lives just down the street** sie wohnt ein Stückchen weiter die Straße entlang

c [= along] **he was walking/coming down the street** er ging/kam die Straße entlang; **if you look down this road, you can see ...** wenn Sie diese Straße hinunterblicken, können Sie ... sehen

d [= throughout] **down the centuries** durch die Jahrhunderte (hindurch)

e [= to, in, at] *Brit inf* **he's gone down the pub** er ist in die Kneipe gegangen; **she's down the shops** sie ist einkaufen gegangen; **he works down the garage** er arbeitet in der Autowerkstatt

3 – NOUN *(= dislike)*

♦ **to have a down on sb** *(inf)* jdn auf dem Kieker haben *(inf)* → **up**

4 – ADJECTIVE *(inf)*

a [= depressed] **he was (feeling) a bit down** er fühlte sich ein wenig down *(inf)* or niedergeschlagen

b [= not working] **to be down** außer Betrieb sein; *(Comput)* abgestürzt sein

5 – TRANSITIVE VERB

opponent niederschlagen, zu Fall bringen; *enemy planes* abschießen, (he)runterholen *(inf)*; *(Ftbl etc, inf) player* legen *(inf)*; *beer etc* runterkippen or -schütten *(inf)*; **to down tools** die Arbeit niederlegen

down[2] N *(= feathers)* Daunen *pl*, Flaumfedern *pl*; *(= fine hair)* Flaum *m*

down[3] N *usu pl (Geog)* Hügelland *nt no pl*; **on the ~(s)** im Hügelland

down: **down-and-out** N *(= tramp)* Penner(in) *m(f) (inf)* ADJ heruntergekommen; *appearance also* abgerissen; **down arrow** N *(Comput)* Abwärtspfeil *m*; **downbeat** N *Taktstockführung, die den ersten betonten Taktteil anzeigt*, erster Taktteil ADJ *(fig) ending* undramatisch; *mood* gedrückt; **down-bow** N *(Mus)* Abstrich *m*; **downcast** ADJ **a** *(= depressed) person, expression* niedergedrückt, entmutigt **b** *eyes* niedergeschlagen; *look* gesenkt N *(Min)* Wetterschacht *m*; **downdraught**, *(US)* **downdraft** N *(Met)* Fallwind *m*; *(Tech)* Fallstrom *m*

downer ['daʊnəʳ] N **a** *(Drugs inf)* Downer *m (sl)*, Beruhigungsmittel *nt* **b** *(inf: = depressing experience)* **for divorced people, Christmas can be a ~** für Geschiedene kann Weihnachten einen Tiefpunkt bedeuten; **she's on a real ~ just now** sie ist zurzeit richtig depressiv

down: **downfall** N **a** Sturz *m*, Fall *m*; *(of empire)* Fall *m*, Untergang *m*; *(= cause of ruin: drink etc)* Ruin *m* **b** *(of rain)* heftiger Niederschlag, Platzregen *m*; **downgrade** N *(Rail)* Gefälle *nt*; **to be on the ~** *(fig)* auf dem absteigenden Ast sein; *(health, quality)* sich verschlechtern VT *hotel, job, work* herunterstufen; *person* degradieren; **down-hearted** ADJ niedergeschlagen, entmutigt; **downhill** ADV *(lit, fig)* bergab; **to go ~** *(road)* bergab führen or gehen; *(vehicle)* herunterfahren; *(person on foot)* heruntergehen; **he/his health/the economy is going ~** mit ihm/seiner Gesundheit/der Wirtschaft geht es bergab; **things just went steadily ~** es ging immer mehr bergab ADJ **a** *road, path* bergab führend; **~ slope** Abhang *m*; **the path is ~ for two miles** der Weg führt zwei Meilen bergab; **the ~ path to drug addiction** der abschüssige Weg in die Drogensucht; **they had not noticed her gradual ~ path** sie hatten nicht bemerkt, wie es mit ihr langsam bergab ging; **it's all ~ (after thirty)** *(= gets worse)* es geht (ab dreißig) nur noch bergab; **it was ~ all the way** or **all ~ after that** *(= got easier)* danach wurde alles viel einfacher **b** *(Ski)* **~ competition** or **race** Abfahrtslauf *m*; **~ course** Abfahrtsstrecke *f*; **~ skiing** Abfahrtslauf *m* N *(Ski)* Abfahrtslauf *m*

Downing Street ['daʊnɪŋ,stri:t] N die Downing Street; *(= the government)* die britische Regierung

> **DOWNING STREET**
>
> **Downing Street** ist die Straße in London, in der sich der offizielle Wohnsitz des britischen Premierministers (Nr. 10) und der des Finanzministers (Nr. 11) befinden. **Downing Street**, oder auch **Number Ten** oder **Ten Downing Street** wird in den Medien häufig als Synonym für den Premierminister, die Regierung oder das Kabinett verwendet: „Downing Street has strenuously denied these allegations", „A statement from Number Ten is expected later this afternoon".

down: **downlighter** N Deckenstrahler *m*; **down line** N *(Rail) Eisenbahnlinie von der Stadt aufs Land oder aus der Hauptstadt heraus*; **download** *(Comput)* VT (herunter)laden VI **it won't ~** Runterladen ist nicht möglich N *(= downloading)* Herunterladen *nt*, Download *m (inf)* ATTR *font, character* ladbar; **downloadable** ADJ *(Comput)* ladbar; **down-low** ADJ *(esp US inf)* geheim; **down-market** ADJ *product* für den Massenmarkt; *service* weniger anspruchsvoll; **this restaurant is more ~** dieses Restaurant ist weniger exklusiv ADV **to go ~** sich auf den Massenmarkt ausrichten; **down payment** N *(Fin)* Anzahlung *f*; **downpipe** N Abflussrohr *nt*, Fallrohr *nt*; **downplay** VT herunterspielen *(inf)*, bagatellisieren; **downpour** N Platzregen *m*, Wolkenbruch *m*; **downright** ADV *dangerous, silly, hostile, dull etc* ausgesprochen; *rude, disgusting* geradezu ADJ **a ~ lie** eine glatte Lüge; **his ~ rudeness** seine ausgesprochene Unverschämtheit; **downriver** ADV flussabwärts *(from* von); **~ from Bonn** unterhalb von Bonn; **downscale** *(esp US)* VT *workforce etc* reduzieren, verkleinern ADJ *goods, products* minderwertig, wenig anspruchsvoll; *service* mangelhaft; *restaurant, hotel* der unteren Preisklasse; **downshift** VI *in eine schlechter bezahlte Stelle überwechseln*, runterschalten *(inf)*; **downside** N Kehrseite *f*; **downsize** ['daʊnsaɪz] VT *business, workforce* verkleinern; **~d economy** *durch Rationalisierung und Stellenabbau gekennzeichnete wirtschaftliche Lage* VI *(company)* sich verkleinern; **downsizing** *(Comput)* N Downsizing *nt*; *(Comm also)* Stellenabbau *m*; **downspout** N Abflussrohr *nt*, Fallrohr *nt*

Down's syndrome ['daʊnz'sɪndrəʊm] *(Med)* N Downsyndrom *nt* ATTR **a ~ baby** ein an Downsyndrom leidendes Kind

down: **downstage** ADV *(= towards the front of the stage)* zum vorderen Teil der Bühne; *(= at the front of the stage)* im vorderen Teil der Bühne; **downstairs** ADV *go, come* nach unten, die Treppe hinunter; *fall* die Treppe hinunter; *be, sleep, eat etc* unten ['daʊnsteəz] ADJ **the ~ phone/rooms** das Telefon/die Zimmer unten; **~ flat** *(Brit)* or **apartment** Parterrewohnung *f*; **our ~ neighbours** *(Brit)* or **neighbors** *(US)* die Nachbarn unter uns; **the woman/the people ~** die Frau/die Leute von unten N **the ~** das Erdgeschoss; **downstate** *(US)* ADJ im Süden (des Bundesstaates); **in ~ Illinois** im Süden von Illinois ADV *move, go* in den Süden (des Bundesstaates); *live, be situated* im Süden (des Bundesstaates) N der Süden (des Bundesstaates); **downstream** ADV flussabwärts, stromabwärts *(from* von); **downstroke** N *(in writing)* Abstrich *m*; *(Mech, of piston)* Ansaugtakt *m*; **downswept** ADJ *wings* abwärtsgerichtet; **downswing** N Abwärtsschwingen *nt*; **down-the-line** ADJ *(inf: = uncompromising)* vorbehaltlos; **downtime** N Ausfallzeit *f*; **down-to-earth** ADJ *attitude, approach* nüchtern; **he's very ~** *(= practical)* er steht mit beiden Füßen auf der Erde; **downtown** *(esp US)* ADV *go* in die (Innen)stadt, ins Stadtzentrum; *live, be situated* in der (Innen)stadt, im Stadtzentrum ADJ **~ Chicago** die Innenstadt *or* das Stadtzentrum von Chicago; **the ~ area** das Stadtzentrum; **down train** N *Zug, der von der Stadt aufs Land fährt oder von der Hauptstadt abgeht*; **downtrend** N *(Econ)* Abwärtstrend *m*; **to be in** *or* **on a ~** sich im Abwärtstrend befinden; **downtrodden** ADJ *people* unterdrückt, geknechtet; **downturn** N *(in prices, business)* Rückgang *m*, Abflauen *nt*; **to take a ~** zurückgehen, abflauen; **his fortunes took a ~** sein Glücksstern sank; **down under** *(inf)* N *(= Australia)* Australien *nt*; *(= New Zealand)* Neuseeland *nt* ADV *be, live* in Australien/Neuseeland; *go* nach Australien/Neuseeland

downward ['daʊnwəd] ADV *(also* **downwards)** *look, point, extend, move* nach unten; **to work ~(s)** sich nach unten vorarbeiten; **to slope gently ~(s)** sanft abfallen; **face ~(s)** *(person)* mit dem Gesicht nach unten; *(book)* mit der aufgeschlagenen Seite nach unten; **movement ~(s)** *(in price, value)* Rückgang *m*; **to move ~(s)** *(figure, rate)* sinken, fallen; **everyone from the Queen ~(s)** jeder, bei der Königin angefangen; **our estimates have been revised ~(s)** unsere Kalkulation wurde nach unten korrigiert; **to spiral ~(s)** *(prices)* stürzen; **the economy is spiralling** *(Brit)* or **spiraling** *(US)* **~(s)** mit der Wirtschaft geht es rapide bergab ADJ *stroke* nach unten; **~ compatibility** Abwärtskompatibilität *f*; **~ compatible** abwärtskompatibel; **she made a bold ~ stroke with the paintbrush** sie machte einen kühnen Pinselstrich nach unten; **~ movement** Abwärtsbewegung *f*; **apply foundation in a ~ direction** tragen Sie die Grundierung von oben nach unten auf; **~ slope** Abhang *m*; **~ gradient** *(Brit)* or **grade** *(US)* Gefälle *nt*; **~ trend** Abwärtstrend *m*; **~ spiral** stetiger Rückgang; **he's on the ~ path** *(fig)* mit ihm gehts bergab; **the dollar resumed its ~ path** or **slide against the yen** der Dollar fiel weiter gegen den Yen; **a ~ slide in prices** ein Preisrutsch *m*; **to take a ~ turn** sich zum Schlechteren wenden; **to put ~ pressure on wages/prices** die Löhne/Preise (nach unten) drücken

downwind ['daʊnwɪnd] ADV *move, drift* mit dem Wind; *sail* vor dem Wind; *stand, be* in Windrichtung *(of, from +gen)*

downy ['daʊnɪ] ADJ *(+er)* **a** *(= filled with feathers)* daunengefüllt; *(= covered with feathers)* flaumig **b** *(fig) skin, hair, leaf, peach* flaumig; **fine ~ hair** ein feiner Flaum

dowry ['daʊrɪ] N Mitgift *f*

dowse[1] [daʊs] VT = **douse**

dowse[2] [daʊz] VI *(= divine)* mit einer Wünschelrute suchen

dowser ['daʊzəʳ] N Wünschelrutengänger(in) *m(f)*

dowsing rod ['daʊzɪŋrɒd] N Wünschelrute *f*

doxology [dɒk'sɒlədʒɪ] N Lobpreisung *f*, Verherrlichung *f* Gottes

doyen ['dɔɪən] N Nestor *m*; *(of diplomatic corps)* Doyen *m*

doyenne ['dɔɪen] N Nestorin *f*; *(of diplomatic corps)* Doyenne *f*

doz *abbr of* **dozen**

doze [dəʊz] N Nickerchen *nt*; **to have a ~** dösen, ein Nickerchen machen VI (vor sich hin) dösen

▸ **doze off** VI einschlafen, einnicken

dozen ['dʌzn] N Dutzend *nt*; **80p a ~** 80 Pence das Dutzend; **two ~ eggs** zwei Dutzend Eier; **half a ~** sechs, ein halbes Dutzend; **~s** jede Menge; *(fig inf)* eine ganze Menge; **~s of times** *(inf)* x-mal *(inf)*, tausendmal; **there are ~s like that** *(inf)* das gibts wie Sand am Meer; **there were ~s of incidents like this one** *(inf)* es gab dutzende *or* Dutzende solcher Vorfälle; **~s of people came** *(inf)* dutzende *or* Dutzende von Leuten kamen

dozily ['dəʊzɪlɪ] ADV verschlafen, schläfrig

doziness ['dəʊzɪnɪs] N Verschlafenheit *f*, Schläfrigkeit *f*

dozy ['dəʊzɪ] ADJ *(+er)* **a** *(= sleepy)* schläfrig, verschlafen **b** *(Brit inf: = stupid)* dösig *(inf)*

DP *abbr of* **data processing** DV *f*

D Phil *abbr of* **Doctor of Philosophy** Dr. phil.

dpi *(Comput) abbr of* **dots per inch** dpi

DPP *abbr of* **Director of Public Prosecutions**

DPT [ˌdiːpiːˈtiː] N *(Med)* Dreifachimpfung *f* gegen Diphtherie, Keuchhusten und Wundstarrkrampf

dpt *abbr of* **department** Abt

DQ *(Athletics) abbr of* **Disqualified**

Dr *abbr of* **doctor** Dr.

drab [dræb] ADJ *(+er)* trist; *life, activities* eintönig; **~ brown** graubraun N **a** *no pl (Tex)* grober, graubrauner Wollstoff **b** → **dribs and drabs**

drably ['dræblɪ] ADV *dressed* trist; *painted* in tristen Farben; **~ uniform** deprimierend eintönig

drabness ['dræbnɪs] N Tristheit *f*; *(of life, activities)* Eintönigkeit *f*

drachma ['drækmə, *(pl)* 'drækmiː] N *pl* **-e** *or* **-s** Drachme *f*

draconian [drə'kəʊnɪən] ADJ drakonisch

draft [drɑːft] N **a** *(= rough outline)* Entwurf *m* *(also Comput)*
b *(Fin, Comm)* Wechsel *m*, Tratte *f*
c *(Mil, = group of men)* Sonderkommando *nt*
d *(US Mil: = group of conscripts)* Rekruten *pl*; *(= conscription)* Einberufung (zum Wehrdienst)
e *(US)* = **draught**
f *(Comput)* Entwurf *m*; *(printer command)* Entwurfsqualität *f*, Draft(druck) *m*
VT **a** *letter, speech, bill, contract* entwerfen
b *(US Mil) conscript* einziehen, einberufen *(into* zu); **to ~ sb to do sth** *(Mil)* jdn zu etw abkommandieren, etw zu tun; *(fig)* jdn beauftragen, etw zu tun; **he was ~ed into the England squad** er wurde für die englische Nationalmannschaft aufgestellt
ATTR *(Comput)* Draft-; **~ mode** Draft-Modus *m*, Draftmodus *m*

draft: **draft board** N *(US Mil)* Einberufungsbehörde *f*; *(= panel)* Einberufungsausschuss *m*; **draft call** N *(US Mil)* Einberufungsbescheid *m*; **draft card** N *(US Mil)* Wehrpass *m*; **draft dodger** N *(US Mil)* *Wehrpflichtiger, der sich vor dem Wehrdienst drückt*, Drückeberger *m* *(pej inf)*

draftee [drɑː'fiː] N *(US Mil)* Wehrpflichtige(r) *m(f)*

draftiness *etc (US)* = **draughtiness** *etc*

draft: **draft letter** N Entwurf *m* eines/des Briefes; **draft quality** N *(of printout)* Entwurfsqualität *f*; **draft version** N Entwurf *m*

drag [dræg] N **a** *(= object pulled along, for dredging etc)* Suchanker *m*; *(Naut: = cluster of hooks)* Dregganker *m*, Draggen *m*; *(Naut: = dragnet)* Schleppnetz *nt*; *(= heavy sledge)* Lastschlitten *m*; *(Agr, = harrow)* schwere Egge
b *(= resistance, Aviat)* Luft- *or* Strömungswiderstand *m*; *(Naut)* Wasserwiderstand *m*
c *(brake)* Hemmklotz *m*, Hemmschuh *m*
d *(= slow laborious progress)* **it was a long ~ up to the top of the hill** es war ein langer, mühseliger Aufstieg zum Gipfel, der Aufstieg auf den Gipfel war ein furchtbarer Schlauch *(inf)*
e *(inf, = burden)* **to be a ~ on sth** eine Belastung für etw sein
f *(inf)* **what a ~!** *(boring)* Mann, ist der/die/das langweilig! *(inf)*; *(nuisance)* so'n Mist *(inf)*; **what a ~ having to go back!** so'n Mist, dass wir zurückmüssen *(inf)*; **the film was a real ~** der Film war stinklangweilig *(inf)*; **she thought his girlfriend was a real ~** sie fand, dass seine Freundin echt langweilig war *(inf)*
g *(inf: = pull on cigarette)* Zug *m* *(on, at* an *+dat)*; **give me a ~** lass mich mal ziehen, gib mir mal 'n Zug *(inf)*; **he took a long ~ on his cigarette** er zog lange an seiner Zigarette
h *(inf: = women's clothing worn by men)* (von Männern getragene) Frauenkleidung *f*; **in ~** in Frauenkleidung, im Fummel *(sl)*, als Tunte *(inf)*
i *(dated US inf: = influence)* Einfluss *m*; **to use one's ~** seinen Einfluss ausüben
j *(US inf: = street)* **the main ~** die Hauptstraße
VT **a** *person, object* schleppen, schleifen, ziehen;*(Comput: with mouse button pressed)* ziehen; **he ~ged her out of/into the car** er zerrte sie aus dem/in das Auto; **she ~ged me to the library every Friday** sie schleppte mich jeden Freitag in die Bücherei; **the dog was ~ging its broken leg (behind it)** der Hund schleifte sein gebrochenes Bein hinter sich her; **to ~ one's feet** *or* **heels** *(fig)* die Sache schleifen lassen; **she accused the government of ~ging its feet on reforms** sie beschuldigte die Regierung, die Reformen zu verzögern; **to ~ anchor** *(Naut)* vor Anker treiben
b *river* absuchen
VI **a** *(= trail along)* schleifen; *(feet)* schlurfen; *(Naut, anchor)* treiben
b *(= lag behind: person)* hinterherhinken
c *(fig, time, work)* sich hinziehen; *(play, book)* sich in die Länge ziehen; *(conversation)* sich (mühsam) hinschleppen

▶ **drag along** VT *sep person* mitschleppen; **to drag oneself along** sich mühsam dahinschleppen

▶ **drag apart** VT *sep* auseinanderzerren, trennen

▶ **drag away** VT *sep (lit, fig)* wegschleppen *or* -ziehen; **you'll have to drag him away from the television** den muss man mit Gewalt vom Fernsehen wegziehen; **if you can drag yourself away from the television for a second ...** wenn du dich vielleicht mal für eine Sekunde vom Fernsehen losreißen könntest ...

▶ **drag behind** VT *+prep obj* **to drag sb/sth behind one** jdn/etw hinter sich *(dat)* herschleppen *or* herschleifen VI *(fig)* zurückbleiben, hinterherhinken

▶ **drag down** VT *sep (lit)* herunterziehen; *(fig)* mit sich ziehen; **he is trying to drag me down with him** er versucht, mich mit sich zu ziehen; **to drag sb down to one's own level** *(fig)* jdn auf sein eigenes Niveau herabziehen; **he was dragged down by the scandal** der Skandal führte fast zu seinem Ruin; **his illness is dragging him down** seine Krankheit macht ihn fertig *(inf)*; **you shouldn't let these things drag you down so** du solltest dich dadurch nicht so entmutigen lassen

▶ **drag in** VT *sep* **a** *(lit)* hineinziehen; **look what the cat's dragged in** *(fig inf)* sieh mal, wer da kommt **b** *(fig) subject* aufs Tapet bringen; *remark* anbringen

▶ **drag off** VT *sep (lit)* wegzerren *or* -ziehen; *(fig)* wegschleppen; **to drag sb off to a concert** jdn in ein Konzert schleppen

▶ **drag on** VI sich in die Länge ziehen; *(meeting, lecture also)* sich hinziehen; *(conversation)* sich hinschleppen; **it dragged on for 3 hours** es zog sich über 3 Stunden hin

▶ **drag out** VT *sep* **a** *meeting, discussion etc* in die Länge ziehen **b** *(= extract)* **eventually I had to drag it out of him** schließlich musste ich es ihm aus der Nase ziehen *(inf)*

▶ **drag up** VT *sep* **a** *scandal, story* ausgraben; *person* aufgabeln *(inf)*, auftun *(inf)* **b** *(inf) child* mehr schlecht als recht aufziehen

drag: **drag and drop** N *(Comput)* Drag-and-Drop *nt*, Drag & Drop *nt*; **drag artist** N *(inf)* Travestiekünstler(in) *m(f)*; **drag coefficient** N Luftwiderstandsbeiwert *m*

dragée ['dræʒeɪ] N *(Med: = sweet)* Dragee *nt*

drag factor N Widerstandsbeiwert *m*

draggy ['drægɪ] ADJ *(inf)* anödend *(inf)*

drag: **drag lift** N *(Ski)* Schlepplift *m*; **dragline** N Schleppleine *f*, Schleppseil *nt*

dragnet ['drægnet] N *(for fish)* Schleppnetz *nt*; *(= police hunt)* groß angelegte Polizeiaktion

dragoman ['drægəʊmən] N Dragoman *m*

dragon ['drægən] N *(lit, fig inf)* Drache *m*

dragonfly ['drægənˌflaɪ] N Libelle *f*

dragoon [drə'guːn] N *(Mil)* Dragoner *m* VT **to ~ sb into doing sth** jdn zwingen *or* mit Gewalt dazu bringen, etw zu tun

drag: **drag queen** N *(inf)* Tunte *f* *(inf)*; **drag race** N Beschleunigungsrennen *nt*; **dragrope** N Schlepptau *nt*; **drag show** N Transvestitenshow *f*

dragster ['drægstəʳ] N Dragster *m* *(sl)*

drain [dreɪn] N **a** *(= pipe)* Rohr *nt*; *(under sink etc)* Abfluss(rohr *nt*) *m*; *(under the ground)* Kanalisationsrohr *nt*; *(= drain cover)* Rost *m*; **open ~** (Abfluss)rinne *f*; **to pour money down the ~** *(fig inf)* das Geld zum Fenster hinauswerfen; **this country/company is going down the ~** *(inf)* dieses Land/diese Firma geht vor die Hunde *(inf)*; **I had to watch all our efforts go down the ~** ich musste zusehen, wie alle unsere Bemühungen zunichte(gemacht) wurden; **to laugh like a ~** *(Brit inf)* sich kaputtlachen
b *(on resources, finances etc)* Belastung *f* *(on +gen)*; **looking after her father has been a great ~ on her energy** die Pflege ihres Vaters hat sehr an ihren Kräften gezehrt → **brain drain**
VT **a** *(lit)* drainieren; *land, marshes* entwässern; *vegetables* abgießen; *(= let drain)* abtropfen lassen; *mine* auspumpen; *reservoir* trockenlegen; *boiler, radiator* das Wasser ablassen aus; *engine oil* ablassen
b *(fig)* **such emotions ~ our energy** solche Gefühle zehren an unseren Kräften; **to feel ~ed** sich ausgelaugt fühlen; **to ~ a country of resources** ein Land auslaugen *or* auspowern; **to ~ sb dry** jdn ausnehmen *(inf)*
c *(= empty) glass* austrinken, leeren
VI **a** *(vegetables, dishes)* abtropfen; *(land into river)* entwässert werden
b *(fig)* **the blood/colour** *(Brit)* *or* **color** *(US)* **~ed from his face** das Blut/die Farbe wich aus seinem Gesicht; **his face ~ed of all colour** *(Brit)* *or* **color** *(US)* er wurde wachsbleich

▶ **drain away** VI *(liquid)* ablaufen; *(strength)* dahinschwinden; *(tension)* sich lösen VT *sep liquid* ableiten

▶ **drain off** VT *sep* abgießen; *(= let drain)* abtropfen lassen

drainage ['dreɪnɪdʒ] N **a** *(= draining)* Dränage *f*, Drainage *f*; *(of land)* Entwässerung *f* **b** *(= system)* Entwässerungssystem *nt*; *(in house, town)* Kanalisation *f* **c** *(= sewage)* Abwasser *nt* **d** *(Geol)* Dränierung *f*, Drainierung *f* *(spec)*, Entwässerung *f*

drainage: **drainage area, drainage basin** N *(Geol)* Einzugsgebiet *f*; **drainage channel** N *(Build)* Entwässerungsgraben *m*, Abzugsgraben *m*; **drainage tube** N *(Med)* Drain *m*, Drän *m*

drainer ['dreɪnəʳ] N *(for dishes)* Abtropfständer *m*, Abtropfbrett *nt*

drain: **drain hose** N *(of washing machine)* Abflussschlauch *m*; **draining board**, *(US)* **drain board** N Ablauf *m*; **drainpipe** N Abflussrohr *nt*; **drainpipes, drainpipe trousers** PL Röhrenhosen *pl*

drake [dreɪk] N Erpel *m*, Enterich *m* → **duck**[1]

dram [dræm] N **a** *(= measure, Pharm)* ≈ Drachme *f* *(old)* **b** *(Brit: = small drink)* Schluck *m* (Whisky)

drama ['drɑːmə] N *(= art, play, incident)* Drama *nt*; *(no pl: = quality of being dramatic)* Dramatik *f*; **18th-century German ~** das deutsche Drama des 18. Jahrhunderts; **family ~** *(= TV series)* Familienserie *f*; **to make a ~ out of a crisis** eine Krise dramatisieren

drama: **drama critic** N Theaterkritiker(in) *m(f)*; **drama-doc** N *(TV)* Dokumentarspiel *nt*; **drama festival** N Theaterfestival *nt*; **drama queen** N *(pej inf)* Schauspielerin *f (pej inf)*; **drama school** N Schauspielschule *f*; **drama student** N Schauspielschüler(in) *m(f)*

dramatic [drəˈmætɪk] ADJ **a** dramatisch; *change* einschneidend, dramatisch; **there was a ~ improvement (in it)** es verbesserte sich dramatisch **b** *(Theat)* dramatisch; **~ works** dramatische Werke *pl*, Dramen *pl*; **~ criticism** Theaterkritik *f*; **his ~ ability** seine schauspielerischen Fähigkeiten; **~ art** Theater *nt*; **the ~ arts** das Theater; **~ film** Filmdrama *nt* N **dramatics** PL **a** *(= theatricals)* Theater *nt* **b** *(= histrionics)* **his/her** *etc* **~s** sein/ihr *etc* theatralisches Getue

dramatically [drəˈmætɪkəlɪ] ADV **a** *(= radically) increase, improve, fall, reduce* dramatisch, enorm; *change* dramatisch, einschneidend; *different* radikal; *effective* extrem; *worse, better* dramatisch; **this plan is ~ different from the last one** dieser Plan unterscheidet sich radikal *or* dramatisch vom letzten; **a country of ~ changing landscapes** ein Land, in dem sich die Landschaft immer wieder dramatisch verändert **b** *(= theatrically)* theatralisch; **he paused ~** er machte eine theatralische Pause **c** *(Theat)* dramatisch; **~, it was very effective** dramatisch gesehen war es sehr wirkungsvoll

dramatis personae [ˈdræmətɪspɜːˈsəʊnaɪ] PL Personen *pl* der Handlung, dramatis personae *pl (old)*

dramatist [ˈdræmətɪst] N Dramatiker(in) *m(f)*

dramatization [ˌdræmətaɪˈzeɪʃən] N Bühnen-/ /Fernsehbearbeitung *f*, Dramatisierung *f*

dramatize [ˈdræmətaɪz] VT **a** *novel* für die Bühne/das Fernsehen bearbeiten, dramatisieren **b** *(= make vivid) event* dramatisieren VI **a** *(novel etc)* sich für die Bühne/das Fernsehen bearbeiten lassen **b** *(= exaggerate)* übertreiben

drank [dræŋk] *pret of* **drink**

drape [dreɪp] VT drapieren; *window* mit Vorhängen versehen; *person* hüllen; *altar* drapieren, behängen; **to ~ sth over sth** etw über etw *(acc)* drapieren; **she ~d herself over the sofa** *(inf)* sie drapierte sich malerisch auf das Sofa; **she opened the door ~d only in a towel** sie machte die Tür auf, nur in ein Badetuch gehüllt N **a drapes** PL *(US)* Gardinen *pl* **b** *(= way sth hangs)* Fall *m*

draper [ˈdreɪpəʳ] N *(Brit)* Textilkaufmann *m*/-frau *f*; **~'s (shop)** Textilgeschäft *nt*

drapery [ˈdreɪpərɪ] N **a** *(Brit: = cloth etc)* Stoff *m*; *(= business: also* **drapery shop**) Stoffladen *m* **b** *(= hangings)* Draperie *f (old)*; *(on wall)* Behang *m*; *(around bed etc)* Vorhänge *pl*; *(clothing, fig liter)* Gewand *nt*

drastic [ˈdræstɪk] ADJ drastisch; *solution* radikal, drastisch; *consequences* schwerwiegend, schwer wiegend; *surgery* radikal; *change, reform* einschneidend, radikal; *improvement* einschneidend; **to make ~ changes in sth** etw radikal ändern; **to take ~ action** *or* **measures** drastische Maßnahmen ergreifen

drastically [ˈdræstɪkəlɪ] ADV drastisch; *change, different* radikal; **to go ~ wrong** total schiefgehen; **they're ~ short of supplies** ihre Vorräte sind bedrohlich knapp

drat [dræt] INTERJ *(inf)* **~ (it)!** verflixt! *(inf)*; **~ that child!** dieses verflixte Kind! *(inf)*

dratted [ˈdrætɪd] ADJ *(inf)* verflixt *(inf)*

draught, *(US)* **draft** [drɑːft] N **a** (Luft)zug *m*; *(= through draught)* Durchzug *m*; *(for fire)* Zug *m*; **there's a terrible ~ in here** hier zieht es fürchterlich; **I'm sitting in a ~** ich sitze im Zug; **are you in a ~?** ziehts Ihnen?; **there's a ~ blowing round the back of my neck** mir ziehts im Genick; **open the flues to increase the ~** mach die Klappen auf, damit der Ofen mehr Zug bekommt; **he's beginning to feel the ~** *(fig inf)* ihm wird allmählich das Geld knapp **b** *(= swallow, drink)* Zug *m*; **a ~ of mead** ein Schluck *m* Met **c** *(= draught beer)* Fassbier *nt*; **on ~** vom Fass **d** *(Naut)* Tiefgang *m* **e** *(Med)* **sleeping ~** Schlaftrunk *m* **f** *(of fish)* Fischzug *m* **g draughts** PL *(Brit: = game)* Damespiel *nt*; *(+pl vb: = pieces)* Damesteine *pl* **h** *(= rough sketch)* = **draft N a**

draught, *(US)* **draft**: **draught animal** N Zugtier *nt*; **draught beer** N Fassbier *nt*, Bier *nt* vom Fass

draughtboard N *(Brit)* Damebrett *nt*

draught excluder N *(Brit)* Dichtungsmaterial *nt*

draughtiness, *(US)* **draftiness** [ˈdrɑːftɪnɪs] N Zugigkeit *f*

draught net N *(for fishing)* Zugnetz *nt*

draughtproof, *(US)* **draftproof** [ˈdrɑːftpruːf] ADJ *windows, doors* dicht; *room* gegen Zugluft geschützt

draughtproofing, *(US)* **draftproofing** [ˈdrɑːftˌpruːfɪŋ] N Zugluftisolierung *f*; *(= material)* Isoliermaterial *nt* gegen Zugluft

draughtsman, *(US)* **draftsman** [ˈdrɑːftsmən] N *pl* **-men** [-mən] **a** *(of plans)* Zeichner *m*; *(of documents, treaty etc)* Verfasser *m* **b** *(Brit, in game)* Damestein *m*

draughtsmanship, *(US)* **draftsmanship** [ˈdrɑːftsmənʃɪp] N **his brilliant ~** sein hervorragendes zeichnerisches Können; **the power of his ~ shows that ...** an der Qualität seiner Zeichnung kann man sehen, dass ...

draughtswoman, *(US)* **draftswoman** [ˈdrɑːftswʊmən] N *pl* **-women** [-wɪmɪn] *(of plans)* Zeichnerin *f*; *(of documents, treaty etc)* Verfasserin *f*

draughty, *(US)* **drafty** [ˈdrɑːftɪ] ADJ *(+er)* zugig; **it's ~ in here** hier zieht es

draw[1] [drɔː] *pret* **drew**, *ptp* **drawn** VT *(lit, fig)* zeichnen; *line* ziehen; **we must ~ the line somewhere** *(fig)* irgendwo muss Schluss sein; **I ~ the line at cheating** *(personally)* Mogeln kommt für mich nicht infrage; *(in others)* beim Mogeln hörts bei mir auf; **some people just don't know where to ~ the line** *(fig)* manche Leute wissen einfach nicht, wie weit sie gehen können; **to ~ a line between** *(fig)* einen Unterschied machen zwischen VI zeichnen

draw[2] [drɔː]
vb: pret **drew**, *ptp* **drawn**

1 TRANSITIVE VERB	3 NOUN
2 INTRANSITIVE VERB	4 PHRASAL VERBS

1 – TRANSITIVE VERB

a [= move by pulling] ziehen; *bolt* zurückschieben; *bow* spannen; *curtains (= open)* aufziehen; *(= shut)* zuziehen; **he drew his chair nearer the fire** er rückte seinen Stuhl näher an den Kamin heran; **he drew her close to him** er zog sie an sich; **he drew his finger along the edge of the table** er fuhr mit dem Finger die Tischkante entlang; **he drew the smoke into his lungs** er machte einen (tiefen) Lungenzug

b [= move by pulling behind] *coach, cart* ziehen

c [= bring] bringen; **her shouts drew me to the scene** ihr Rufen brachte mich an den Ort des Geschehens; **to draw sth to a close** etw zu Ende bringen, etw beenden

d [= extract] *teeth, sword, gun* ziehen; *knife* ziehen, zücken; *cork* herausziehen; **with drawn sword** mit gezogenem *or* gezücktem Schwert; **it was like drawing teeth** *(fig)* es war Schwerstarbeit

e [= take] holen; *wine (from barrel)* zapfen; **to draw water from a well** Wasser aus einem Brunnen holen; **to draw a (deep) breath** (tief) Luft holen; **to draw a long breath** einmal tief Luft holen; **to draw inspiration from sb/sth/somewhere** sich von jdm/von etw/von irgendwas inspirieren lassen; **to draw strength from sth** Kraft aus etw schöpfen; **to draw comfort from sth** sich mit etw trösten; **he's bitten her – has he drawn blood?** er hat sie gebissen – blutet sie?

♦ **to draw money/a salary/a pension to draw money from the bank** Geld (vom Konto) abheben; **to draw the dole/a big salary** Arbeitslosenunterstützung/ein großes Gehalt beziehen; **to draw one's pension** seine Rente bekommen

f [= elicit] **her singing drew tears from the audience** ihr Singen rührte die Zuschauer zu Tränen; **her singing drew tremendous applause from the audience** ihr Singen rief brausenden Beifall hervor; **the play has drawn a lot of criticism** das Theaterstück hat viel Kritik auf sich *(acc)* gezogen; **to draw a smile/a laugh from sb** jdm ein Lächeln/ein Lachen entlocken; **my letter drew an angry reply from him** auf meinen Brief reagierte er mit einer ungehaltenen Antwort

♦ **to be drawn** *(person)* **he refuses to be drawn** *(= will not speak)* aus ihm ist nichts herauszubringen; *(= will not be provoked)* er lässt sich auf nichts ein; **I won't be drawn on that issue** zu dem Thema möchte ich mich nicht äußern

g [= attract] *interest* erregen; *customer, crowd* anlocken; **to draw fire** *(lit, fig)* unter Feuer genommen werden; **to feel drawn toward(s) sb** sich zu jdm hingezogen fühlen; **to draw sb into sth** jdn in etw *(acc)* hineinziehen *or* verwickeln; **to draw sb away from sb/sth** jdn von jdm/etw weglocken → **attention a**

h [= formulate] *conclusion, comparison* ziehen; *distinction* treffen; **you can draw whatever conclusion you like** du kannst daraus schließen, was du willst

i [Naut] **the boat draws 4 metres** das Boot hat 4 Meter Tiefgang

j [= tie] *Sport* **to draw a match** sich unentschieden trennen, unentschieden spielen

k [= choose at random] ziehen; **the first correct entry drawn from the hat** die erste richtige Einsendung, die gezogen wird; **we've been drawn (to play) away/at home** wir sind für ein Auswärtsspiel/Heimspiel gezogen worden; **France has been drawn against Scotland** Frankreich ist für ein Spiel gegen Schottland gezogen worden; **to draw a raffle** eine Auslosung vornehmen

l [Cards] **to draw a card from the pack** eine Karte vom Haufen abheben *or* nehmen; **to draw trumps** Trümpfe herauszwingen

m [Cook] *fowl* ausnehmen → **hang VT e**

n [Hunt] *fox* aufstöbern; **to draw a covert** ein Tier aus seinem Versteck aufstöbern *or* aufjagen

2 – INTRANSITIVE VERB

a [= move] *person, time, event* kommen; **he drew to one side** er ging/fuhr zur Seite; **to draw round the table** sich um den Tisch versammeln; **to draw to an end** *or* **to a close** zu Ende gehen; **he drew ahead of the other runners** er zog den anderen Läufern davon; **the two horses drew level** die beiden Pferde zogen gleich

♦ **to draw near** herankommen *(to* an *+acc)*; **he drew nearer** *or* **closer (to it)** er kam (immer) näher (heran); **Christmas is drawing nearer** Weihnachten rückt näher

b [= allow airflow] *chimney, pipe* ziehen

c [= tie] *Sport* unentschieden spielen; **they drew 2-2** sie trennten sich *or* sie spielten 2:2 unentschieden; **the teams drew for second place** im Kampf um den 2. Platz trennten sich die Mannschaften unentschieden; **Scotland drew with Ireland** Schottland und Irland trennten sich *or* spielten unentschieden

d [Cards] **to draw for partners** die Partner durch Kartenziehen bestimmen

e [= infuse] *tea* ziehen

3 – NOUN

a [= random selection = lottery] Ziehung *f*, Ausspielung *f*; *(for sports competitions)* Auslosung *f*, Ziehung *f* → **luck**

b [= tie] *Sport* Unentschieden *nt*; **the match ended in a draw** das Spiel endete unentschieden *or* mit einem Unentschieden; **the team had five**

wins and two draws die Mannschaft hat fünfmal gewonnen und zweimal unentschieden gespielt

c [= attraction] *play, film etc* (Kassen)schlager *m*, Knüller *m (inf)*; *(person)* Attraktion *f*; **the pay was the big draw of the job** die Bezahlung war das Attraktive an der Stelle

d [in shooting]

♦ **the draw to be quick on the draw** *(lit)* schnell mit der Pistole sein, schnell (den Revolver) ziehen; *(fig)* schlagfertig sein; **to beat sb to the draw** schneller sein als jd; *(lit: cowboy etc)* schneller ziehen als jd

4 – PHRASAL VERBS

▶ **draw alongside** VI heranfahren/-kommen (*+prep obj* an *+acc*)

▶ **draw apart** VI *(= move away)* sich lösen; *(couple)* sich auseinanderleben; *(from political party etc)* abrücken

▶ **draw aside** VT *sep person* beiseitenehmen; *curtains* zur Seite ziehen

▶ **draw away** VI **a** *(= move off, car etc)* losfahren; *(procession)* sich entfernen **b** *(= move ahead: runner etc)* davonziehen *(from sb* jdm) **c** *(= move away: person)* sich entfernen; **she drew away from him when he put his arm around her** sie rückte von ihm ab, als er den Arm um sie legte VT *sep person* weglocken; *object* wegnehmen

▶ **draw back** VI zurückweichen VT *sep* zurückziehen; *curtains also* aufziehen

▶ **draw down** VT *sep blinds* herunterlassen; **to draw sth down on oneself** *(fig)* etw auf sich *(acc)* ziehen

▶ **draw in** VI **a** *(train)* einfahren; *(car)* anhalten **b** *(= get shorter: days)* kürzer werden; **the nights are starting to draw in** die Abende werden wieder länger VT *sep* **a** *breath, air* einziehen **b** *(= attract, gain) crowds* anziehen **c to draw in one's claws** *(lit, fig)* die Krallen einziehen → **horn d** *(= pull on) reins* anziehen

▶ **draw into** VT *sep (= involve)* hineinziehen; **I don't want to be drawn into your problems** ich möchte nicht in Ihre Probleme verwickelt *or* hineingezogen werden; **the country is refusing to be drawn into the war** das Land lässt sich nicht in den Krieg hineinziehen; **I tried to draw him into the conversation** ich versuchte, ihn am Gespräch zu beteiligen

▶ **draw off** VI *(car)* losfahren VT *sep* **a** *gloves, garment* ausziehen **b** *excess liquid* abgießen

▶ **draw on** VI **as the night drew on** mit fortschreitender Nacht; **time is drawing on** es wird spät VI *+prep obj (= use as source: also* **draw upon**) sich stützen auf *(+acc)*; **you'll have to draw on your powers of imagination** Sie müssen Ihre Fantasie *or* Phantasie zu Hilfe nehmen; **the author draws on his experiences in the desert** der Autor schöpft aus seinen Erfahrungen in der Wüste VT *sep (= put on) stockings, gloves* anziehen

▶ **draw out** VI **a** *(train)* ausfahren; *(car)* herausfahren *(of* aus) **b** *(= become longer: days)* länger werden VT *sep* **a** *(= take out)* herausziehen; *money* abheben **b** *(= make longer)* ziehen **c** *(= prolong)* in die Länge ziehen, hinausziehen; **a long-drawn-out meeting** eine sehr in die Länge gezogene Besprechung **d** *(= cause to speak)* **to draw sb out of his shell** jdn aus der Reserve locken

▶ **draw over** VI **the policeman told the driver to draw over (to the side of the road)** der Polizist sagte dem Autofahrer, er solle an den Straßenrand fahren

▶ **draw together** VT *sep threads* miteinander verknüpfen; *bits of argument also* in einen Zusammenhang bringen

▶ **draw up** VI *(= stop: car)* (an)halten VT *sep* **a** *(= formulate)* entwerfen; *contract, agreement* entwerfen, aufsetzen; *will* aufsetzen; *list* aufstellen **b** *chair* heranziehen; *boat* aufschleppen *(spec)*, an Land ziehen; **to draw oneself up (to one's full height)** sich (zu seiner vollen Größe) aufrichten **c** *(= set in line) troops* aufstellen **d** *(= make stop)* **this thought drew him up short** dieser Gedanke ließ ihn mit einem Ruck innehalten

▶ **draw upon** VI *+prep obj* = **draw on VI** *+prep obj*

---

drawback [ˈdrɔːbæk] N Nachteil *m*

drawbridge [ˈdrɔːbrɪdʒ] N Zugbrücke *f*

drawee [drɔːˈiː] N *(Fin)* Bezogene(r) *mf*, Trassat *m (spec)*

drawer N **a** [drɔːˈ] *(in desk etc)* Schublade *f* → **chest**[1] **b** [ˈdrɔːəˈ] *(person: of pictures)* Zeichner(in) *m(f)* **c** [ˈdrɔːəˈ] *(of cheque etc)* Aussteller(in) *m(f)*, Trassant *m (spec)* **d drawers** [drɔːz] PL *(dated, hum, for men)* Unterhose(n) *f(pl)*; *(for women also)* Schlüpfer *m*

drawing [ˈdrɔːɪŋ] N Zeichnung *f*; **I'm no good at ~** ich bin nicht gut im Zeichnen, ich kann nicht gut zeichnen

drawing: **drawing board** N Reißbrett *nt*; **the project is still on the ~** *(fig)* das Projekt ist noch in der Planung; **it's back to the ~** *(fig)* das muss noch einmal ganz neu überdacht werden; **drawing paper** N Zeichenpapier *nt*; **drawing pen** N Zeichenfeder *f*; **drawing pin** N *(Brit)* Reißzwecke *f*; **drawing room** N Wohnzimmer *nt*; *(in mansion)* Salon *m*; **drawing table** N Zeichentisch *m*

drawl [drɔːl] VI schleppend sprechen VT schleppend aussprechen N schleppende Sprache; **a Texan ~** schleppendes Texanisch; **a southern ~** ein schleppender südlicher Dialekt

drawn [drɔːn] *ptp of* **draw**[1], *of* **draw**[2] ADJ **a** *curtains* zugezogen; *blinds* heruntergezogen **b** *(= haggard, from tiredness)* abgespannt; *(from worry)* abgehärmt **c** *game, match* unentschieden

drawn butter N *(Cook)* Buttersoße *f*

drawstring [ˈdrɔːstrɪŋ] N Kordel *f* zum Zuziehen

dray [dreɪ] N Rollwagen *f*

dray: **drayhorse** N Zugpferd *nt*; *(in brewery)* Brauereipferd *nt*; **drayman** N Rollkutscher *m*

dread [dred] VT sich fürchten vor *(+dat)*, große Angst haben vor *(+dat)*; **I'm ~ing Christmas this year** dieses Jahr graut es mir schon vor Weihnachten; **a ~ed disease** eine gefürchtete Krankheit; **and now the ~ed moment, here are the exam results** der mit Schrecken erwartete Augenblick ist da, hier sind die Examensergebnisse; **I ~ to think what may happen** ich wage nicht daran zu denken, was passieren könnte; **I ~** *or* **I'm ~ing seeing her again** ich denke mit Schrecken an ein Wiedersehen mit ihr; **he ~s going to the dentist** er hat schreckliche Angst davor, zum Zahnarzt zu gehen
N **a sense of ~** ein Angstgefühl *nt*; **the thought filled me with ~** bei dem Gedanken wurde mir angst und bange; **to live in ~ of the secret police** in ständiger Angst vor der Geheimpolizei leben; **to live in ~ of being found out** in ständiger Angst davor leben, entdeckt zu werden
ADJ *(liter)* gefürchtet

dreadful [ˈdredfʊl] ✪ 7.3 ADJ schrecklich, furchtbar; *person* schrecklich; *weather* scheußlich, furchtbar; **a ~ business** eine schreckliche Angelegenheit; **what a ~ thing to happen** wie entsetzlich *or* furchtbar, dass das passieren musste; **to feel ~** *(= ill)* sich elend fühlen; **I feel ~ (about it)** *(= mortified)* es ist mir schrecklich peinlich; **I feel ~ about letting you down** es ist mir schrecklich unangenehm, Sie im Stich zu lassen

dreadfully [ˈdredfəlɪ] ADV schrecklich; *behave also* furchtbar; **to treat sb ~** jdn scheußlich behandeln; **something was ~ wrong** etwas stimmte ganz und gar nicht

dreadlocks [ˈdredlɒks], **dreads** [dredz] *(inf)* PL Dreadlocks *pl*

dreadnought [ˈdrednɔːt] N *(Naut)* Dreadnought *m*

dream [driːm] ✪ 12.3 *vb: pret, ptp* **dreamt** *(Brit) or* **dreamed** N **a** Traum *m*; **to have a bad ~** schlecht träumen; **the whole business was like a bad ~** die ganze Angelegenheit war wie ein böser Traum; **sweet ~s!** träum was Schönes!, träume süß!; **to have a ~ about sb/sth** von jdm/etw träumen; **to see sb/sth in a ~** jdn/etw im Traum sehen; **life is a ~** das Leben ist nur ein Traum; **it worked like a ~** *(inf)* das ging wie im Traum
b *(when awake)* **lost in ~s** traumverloren; **she goes round in a ~** sie lebt wie im Traum; **to be in a ~** (mit offenen Augen) träumen
c *(= fantasy, vision)* Traum *m*; **the house/woman of his ~s** das Haus/die Frau seiner Träume, sein Traumhaus/seine Traumfrau; **she was happy beyond her wildest ~s** sie war so glücklich, wie sie es in ihren kühnsten Träumen nicht für möglich gehalten hätte; **never in my wildest ~s did I think I'd win** ich hätte in meinen kühnsten Träumen nicht gedacht, dass ich gewinnen würde; **in your ~s!** *(inf)* das hättest du wohl gern!; **to have ~s of becoming rich** davon träumen, reich zu werden; **to make a ~ come true for sb, to make sb's ~ come true** jdm einen Traum erfüllen; **all his ~s came true** all seine Träume gingen in Erfüllung; **it was a ~ come true** es war ein Traum, der wahr geworden war; **I have a ~ of a better world** ich träume von einer besseren Welt; **it's just idle ~s** das sind nichts als Wunschträume
d *(inf)* Schatz *m*; **darling, you're a ~!** Liebling, du bist ein Schatz; **a ~ of a hat** ein traumhaft schöner Hut; **a ~ of a girl** ein Schatz *m* von einem Mädchen; **a ~ of a father** ein toller Vater; **in your ~s!** *(inf)* vegiss es! *(inf)*
VI *(lit, fig)* träumen *(about, of* von); **I'm sorry, I was ~ing** es tut mir leid, ich habe geträumt; **~ on!** *(inf)* träum du nur weiter!
VT *(lit, fig)* träumen; *dream* haben; **he ~s of being free one day** er träumt davon, eines Tages frei zu sein; **I would never have ~ed of doing such a thing** ich hätte nicht im Traum daran gedacht, so etwas zu tun; **I wouldn't ~ of it** das würde mir nicht im Traum einfallen; **I wouldn't ~ of telling her** es fiele mir nicht im Traum ein, es ihr zu erzählen; **who would have ~ed it would be so complicated** wer hätte es sich träumen lassen, dass es so kompliziert sein würde; **I never ~ed (that) he would come** ich hätte mir nie *or* nicht träumen lassen, dass er kommen würde
ADJ *attr* Traum-; **~boat** *(dated sl)* Traummann *m*; **~ job** Traumjob *m*; **~land** Traumland *nt*; **~ world** Traumwelt *f*

▶ **dream away** VT *sep time* verträumen; *one's life* mit Träumen verbringen

▶ **dream up** VT *sep (inf) idea* sich *(dat)* einfallen lassen *or* ausdenken; **where did you dream that up?** wie bist du denn bloß darauf gekommen?

dreamer [ˈdriːməˈ] N Träumer(in) *m(f)*

dreamily [ˈdriːmɪlɪ] ADV verträumt

dreaminess [ˈdriːmɪnɪs] N Verträumtheit *f*

dreamless [ˈdriːmlɪs] ADJ *sleep* traumlos

dreamlike [ˈdriːmlaɪk] ADJ traumähnlich; *music* traumhaft; **~ quality** Verträumtheit *f*

dreamt [dremt] *(Brit) pret, ptp of* **dream**

dream: **dream ticket** N *(inf: Pol etc, individual)* ideale Besetzung; *(pair)* Traumpaar *nt*; *(group)* ideales Team; **dream world** N Traumwelt *f*

dreamy [ˈdriːmɪ] ADJ *(+er)* **a** *smile, look, music, voice, person* verträumt; *idea* versponnen; **a ~ look came into the mother's eyes** der Blick der Mutter wurde verträumt **b** *(inf: = lovely)* traumhaft

drear [drɪəˈ] ADJ *(poet)* = **dreary**

drearily [ˈdrɪərɪlɪ] ADV *(+vb)* eintönig; *say* monoton; *stare* trüb; *(+adj)* trostlos; **it rained ~ all day** es war trostlos, wie es den ganzen Tag regnete; **it was ~ familiar** es war nur allzu vertraut

dreariness [ˈdrɪərɪnɪs] N Trostlosigkeit *f*; *(of job, life)* Eintönigkeit *f*

dreary [ˈdrɪərɪ] ADJ *(+er) place* trostlos; *hour, day, month* trostlos, öde; *job, life* eintönig, monoton; *clothes* langweilig; *play, book* langweilig, öde

dredge[1] [dredʒ] N Bagger *m*; *(net)* Schleppnetz *nt*; *(vessel)* = **dredger**[1] VT *river, canal* ausbaggern, schlämmen

▸ **dredge up** VT *sep (lit)* ausbaggern; *(fig) unpleasant facts, painful memories* ans Licht holen, hervorkramen

dredge² VT *(Cook)* bestäuben, bestreuen

dredger¹ [ˈdredʒəˈ] N *(= ship)* Schwimmbagger *m*; *(= machine)* Bagger *m*

dredger² N *(Cook)* Streuer *m*; *(also* **sugar dredger***)* Zuckerstreuer *m*

dredging¹ [ˈdredʒɪŋ] N Ausbaggern *nt*

dredging² N *(Cook)* Bestreuen *nt*

dregs [dregz] PL **a** (Boden)satz *m*; **to drink the ~ of sth** etw bis auf den letzten Tropfen austrinken **b** *(fig)* Abschaum *m*; **the ~ of society** der Abschaum der Gesellschaft

drench [drentʃ] VT **a** *(= soak)* durchnässen; **I'm absolutely ~ed** ich bin durch und durch nass; **to be ~ed in sweat** schweißgebadet sein; **to be ~ed in blood** vor Blut triefen; **to get ~ed to the skin** bis auf die Haut nass werden **b** *(Vet)* Arznei einflößen *(+dat)*

drenching [ˈdrentʃɪŋ] N **to get a ~** bis auf die Haut nass werden ADJ **he's been working out in the ~ rain all day** er hat den ganzen Tag draußen im strömenden Regen gearbeitet

Dresden [ˈdrezdən] N *(also* **Dresden china***)* ≈ Meißner Porzellan *nt*

dress [dres] N **a** *(for woman)* Kleid *nt*
b *no pl (= clothing)* Kleidung *f*; **articles of ~** Kleidungsstücke *pl*; **to be in eastern ~** orientalisch gekleidet sein
c *no pl (= way of dressing)* Kleidung *f*, Kleider *pl*; **to be outrageous/careless in one's ~** sich ausgefallen/nachlässig kleiden
VT **a** *(= clothe) child* anziehen; *family* kleiden; *recruits etc* einkleiden; **to get ~ed** sich anziehen; **are you ~ed?** bist du schon angezogen?; **he's old enough to ~ himself** er ist alt genug, um sich allein anzuziehen; **to ~ sb in sth** jdm etw anziehen; **she ~es herself with great fastidiousness** sie kleidet sich sehr sorgfältig; **~ed in black** in Schwarz, schwarz gekleidet; **~ed in a sailor's uniform** im Matrosenanzug; **he was ~ed in a suit** er trug einen Anzug; **to be ~ed for the country/for the town/for tennis** fürs Land/für die Stadt/zum Tennisspielen angezogen sein; **~ed to kill** *(inf)* todschick aufgemacht *(inf)*
b *(Theat) play* Kostüme entwerfen für
c *(= arrange, decorate) (Naut) ship* beflaggen; *(Comm) shop window* dekorieren; **to ~ sb's hair** jdm das Haar frisieren
d *(Cook) salad* anmachen; *food for table* anrichten; *chicken* brat- *or* kochfertig machen; **~ed crab** farcierter Krebs
e *skins* gerben; *material* appretieren; *timber* hobeln; *stone* schleifen
f *wound* verbinden
g *troops* ausrichten
h *(Agr) fields* vorbereiten
VI **a** sich anziehen *or* kleiden; **to ~ in black** sich schwarz kleiden; **she ~es very well** sie kleidet sich sehr gut; **to ~ for dinner** sich zum Essen umziehen
b *(soldiers)* sich ausrichten; **right, ~!** rechts, richt't euch!

▸ **dress down** VT *sep* **a** *horse* striegeln **b** **to dress sb down** jdn herunterputzen *(inf)* VI sich betont lässig kleiden

▸ **dress up** VI **a** *(in smart clothes)* sich fein machen, sich schön anziehen **b** *(in fancy dress)* sich verkleiden; **he came dressed up as Santa Claus** er kam als Weihnachtsmann (verkleidet); **to dress up as a pirate** sich als Pirat verkleiden VT *sep* **a** *(= disguise)* verkleiden; **it's just his old plan dressed up in a new way** das ist bloß sein alter Plan in einem neuen Gewand **b** *(= smarten) person* herausputzen; **dress yourself up a bit!** mach dich ein bisschen schön!

dressage [ˈdresɑːʒ] N Dressur *f*

dress: **dress circle** N erster Rang; **dress coat** N Frack *m*; **dress code** N Kleiderordnung *f*; **dress designer** N Modezeichner(in) *m(f)*

dresser¹ [ˈdresəˈ] N **a** *(Theat)* Garderobier *m*, Garderobiere *f* **b** *(Med)* **his ~** sein Assistent bei der Operation **c** *(tool, for wood)* Hobel *m*; *(for stone)* Schleifstein *m* **d** *(Comm: also* **window-dresser***)* Dekorateur(in) *m(f)* **e** **she's a stylish ~** sie kleidet sich stilvoll; **Pat is a great ~** Pat ist immer sehr gut gekleidet

dresser² N **a** Anrichte *f* **b** *(US: = dressing table)* Frisierkommode *f*

dress form N Schneiderpuppe *f*

dressing [ˈdresɪŋ] N **a** *(= act)* Anziehen *nt*, Ankleiden *nt* **b** *(Med: = bandage, ointment)* Verband *m* **c** *(Cook)* Soße *f*, Dressing *nt* **d** *(Agr)* Dünger *m*; **a ~ of phosphate** Phosphatdünger *m* **e** *(of material)* Appretieren *nt*; *(of stone)* Schleifen *nt*; *(of leather)* Gerben *nt*; *(of wood)* Hobeln *nt*; *(for material)* Appreturmittel *nt*; *(for leather)* Gerbmittel *nt*

dressing: **dressing-down** N *(inf)* Standpauke *f (inf)*; **to give sb a ~** jdn herunterputzen *(inf)*, jdm eine Standpauke halten *(inf)*; **to get a ~** eins auf den Deckel *or* das Dach kriegen *(inf)*; **dressing gown** N Morgenrock *m*, Morgenmantel *m*; *(in towelling)* Bademantel *m*; **dressing room** N *(in house)* Ankleidezimmer *nt*; *(Theat)* (Künstler)garderobe *f*; *(Sport)* Umkleidekabine *f*; **dressing station** N Verbandsplatz *m*; **dressing table** N Frisiertoilette *or* -kommode *f*; **dressing-table set** N Toilettengarnitur *f*

dress: **dressmaker** N (Damen)schneider(in) *m(f)*; **dressmaking** N Schneidern *nt*; **dress parade** N *(Mil)* Parade *f* in Galauniform; **dress pattern** N *(Sew)* Schnittmuster *nt*; **dress rehearsal** N *(lit, fig)* Generalprobe *f*; **dress sense** N *(esp Brit)* Modebewusstsein *nt*; **he has no ~ at all** er hat bei Kleidung keinen Geschmack; **her ~ is appalling** sie zieht sich fürchterlich an; **dress shield** N Arm- *or* Schweißblatt *nt*; **dress shirt** N Frackhemd *nt*; **dress suit** N Abendanzug *m*; **dress uniform** N Galauniform *f*; **dress watch** N elegante Uhr

dressy [ˈdresɪ] ADJ *(+er) (inf) clothes* elegant; *person* elegant angezogen; *event* vornehm; **do you think I look/a long skirt would be too ~?** meinst du, dass ich zu fein angezogen bin/ein langer Rock übertrieben wäre?

drew [druː] *pret of* **draw¹**, *of* **draw²**

dribble [ˈdrɪbl] VI **a** *(liquids)* tropfen **b** *(baby, person)* sabbern; *(animal)* geifern **c** *(Sport)* dribbeln **d** *(people)* **to ~ back/in** *etc* kleckerweise zurückkommen/hereinkommen *etc (inf)* VT **a** *(Sport)* **to ~ the ball** mit dem Ball dribbeln **b** *(baby etc)* kleckern; **to ~ saliva** sabbern; **he ~d milk down his chin** er kleckerte sich *(dat)* Milch übers Kinn N **a** *(of water)* ein paar Tropfen; **a slow ~ of water was still coming out of the pipe** es tröpfelte immer noch etwas aus der Leitung **b** *(of saliva)* Tropfen *m* **c** *(Sport)* Dribbling *nt*

dribbler [ˈdrɪbləˈ] N **a** *(Sport)* Dribbelkünstler(in), Dribbler(in) *m(f)* **b** **he's a terrible ~** *(baby)* er kleckert ständig *(inf)*

driblet [ˈdrɪblɪt] N *(= drop)* Tropfen *m*; **in ~s** kleckerweise *(inf)*; **~s of intelligence began to come through** Informationen fingen an durchzusickern

dribs and drabs [ˈdrɪbzənˈdræbz] PL **in ~** kleckerweise *(inf)*

dried [draɪd] *pret, ptp of* **dry** ADJ *vegetables, herbs, apricots etc* getrocknet; *blood* eingetrocknet; **~ yeast** Trockenhefe *f*; **~ egg** Trockenei *nt*, Eipulver *nt*; **~ milk** Trockenmilch *f*, Milchpulver *nt*

dried: **dried flowers** PL Trockenblumen *pl*; **dried fruit** N Dörrobst *nt*, Backobst *nt*

dried-up [draɪdˈʌp] ADJ **a** *(pej inf: = wizened)* verhutzelt; **a ~ old spinster** eine vertrocknete alte Jungfer **b** *(= stale) food* eingetrocknet **c** *river bed, oasis* ausgetrocknet; *well* versiegt → *also* **dry up**

drier N = **dryer**

drift [drɪft] VI **a** *(Naut, Aviat, snow)* treiben; *(sand)* wehen; *(Rad)* verschwimmen; **to ~ off course** abtreiben; **rally drivers have a technique of ~ing round corners** Rallyefahrer haben eine Technik, sich durch Kurven tragen zu lassen
b *(fig, person)* sich treiben lassen; **to let things ~** die Dinge treiben lassen; **he ~ed into marriage/crime** er schlitterte in die Ehe/in eine kriminelle Laufbahn hinein *(inf)*; **he ~ed from job to job** er ließ sich planlos von Job zu Job treiben; **he was ~ing aimlessly along** *(in life etc)* er lebte planlos in den Tag hinein, er ließ sich plan- und ziellos treiben; **the nation was ~ing toward(s) a crisis** das Land trieb auf eine Krise zu; **young people are ~ing away from the villages** junge Leute wandern aus den Dörfern ab; **to ~ apart** *(people)* sich auseinanderleben; **we're ~ing apart** wir leben uns immer mehr auseinander; **the audience started ~ing away** das Publikum begann wegzugehen
VT treiben; *(wind) snow also* vor sich her treiben
N **a** *(of air, water current)* Strömung *f*; **the ~ of the current** *(speed)* die (Stärke der) Strömung; *(direction)* die Strömung(srichtung)
b *(= mass caused by drifting, of sand, fallen snow)* Verwehung *f*; *(of leaves)* Haufen *m*
c *(of ship, aircraft)* (Ab)drift *f*, Abweichung *f*; **to allow for ~** Abdriften *or* Abweichungen (mit) einkalkulieren
d *(Geol: = deposits)* Geschiebe *nt*; **glacial ~** Moräne *f*
e *(= tendency)* **the ~ towards the cities** der Drang in die Städte; **the ~ of policy away from this reform** das grundsätzliche Abrücken von dieser Reform; **the ~ of support away from him** die nachlassende Unterstützung für ihn
f *(= general meaning: of questions)* Richtung *f*, Tendenz *f*; **I caught the ~ of what he said** ich verstand, worauf er hinauswollte; **if you get my ~** wenn Sie mich richtig verstehen
g *(Ling)* Tendenz *f*

▸ **drift off** VI **to drift off (to sleep)** einschlafen; *(= doze)* eindämmern

drift anchor N *(Naut)* Treibanker *m*

drifter [ˈdrɪftəˈ] N **a** *(= person)* Gammler(in) *m(f)*; **he's a bit of a ~** ihn hälts nirgends lange **b** *(boat)* Drifter *m*

drift ice N Treibeis *nt*

drifting [ˈdrɪftɪŋ] N *(= drifting snow)* Schneeverwehungen *pl*

drifting mine N Treibmine *f*

drift: **drift net** N Treibnetz *nt*; **drift sand** N Treibsand *m*; **driftwood** N Treibholz *nt*

drill¹ [drɪl] N *(for metal, wood, oil, dentist's)* Bohrer *m* VT bohren; *teeth* anbohren VI bohren; **to ~ for oil** nach Öl bohren; **have they started ~ing yet?** haben sie schon mit den Bohrungen angefangen?

▸ **drill down** VI (in die Tiefe) bohren; **we kept drilling down until we hit oil** wir bohrten bis wir auf Öl stießen; **we drilled down 500 feet** wir bohrten in eine Tiefe von 500 Fuß

drill² N **a** *no pl (esp Mil, also fig)* Drill *m*; *(= marching etc)* Exerzieren *nt*; **we get ~ every morning** jeden Morgen müssen wir exerzieren
b *(in grammar etc)* Drillübung *f*; **pattern ~** Patterndrill *m*
c *(inf: = procedure)* **they went through the ~** sie übten den Ablauf; **they all knew the ~** sie wussten alle, was sie tun mussten; **he doesn't know the ~** er weiß nicht, wie der Laden läuft *(inf)* or wie die Sache angefasst werden muss
VT **a** *soldiers* drillen; *(in marching etc)* exerzieren
b **to ~ pupils in grammar** mit den Schülern Grammatik pauken
c **manners were ~ed into me as a child** man hat mir als Kind gute Manieren eingedrillt *(inf)*; **I ~ed into him that …** ich habe es ihm eingebläut, dass … *(inf)*
VI *(Mil)* gedrillt werden; *(marching etc)* exerzieren

drill³ *(Agr)* N **a** *(= furrow)* Furche *f* **b** *(= machine)* Drillmaschine *f* VT drillen

drill[4] N *(Tex)* Drillich *m*

drill: **drill bit** N Bit *nt*, Bohrspitze *f*; **drill-driver, drill driver** N Bohrschrauber *m*; **drill ground** N Exerzierplatz *m*

drilling ['drɪlɪŋ] N *(for oil)* Bohrung *f*; *(by dentist)* Bohren *nt*; **when does ~ start?** wann fangen die Bohrungen an?; **~ operations begin next week** die Bohrungen fangen nächste Woche an

drilling: **drilling platform** N Bohrplattform *f*; **drilling rig** N Bohrturm *m*; *(at sea)* Bohrinsel *f*

drill sergeant N Ausbilder *m*

drily ['draɪlɪ] ADV **a** *(= with dry humour) say, laugh* trocken; *(= unemotionally) say* nüchtern; **~ witty** trocken-geistreich; **~ ironic** trocken-ironisch **b** *cough, kiss* trocken

drink [drɪŋk] *vb: pret* **drank**, *ptp* **drunk** **N** **a** *(= liquid to drink)* Getränk *nt*; **food and ~** Essen und Getränke; **may I have a ~?** kann ich etwas zu trinken haben?; **would you like a ~ of water?** möchten Sie etwas Wasser?; **to give sb a ~** jdm etwas zu trinken geben; **~s can** Getränkedose *f*

b *(= glass of alcoholic drink)* Glas *nt*, Drink *m*; **have a ~!** trink doch was *or* einen!; **can I get you a ~?** kann ich Ihnen etwas zu trinken holen?; **let's have a ~** trinken wir was; **I need a ~!** ich brauche was zu trinken!; **he likes a ~** er trinkt gern (einen); **he's had a good ~** *(inf)* er hat ein paar über den Durst getrunken; **the ~s are on me** die Getränke zahle *or* spendiere ich; **the ~s are on the house** die Getränke gehen auf Kosten des Hauses; **to ask friends in for ~s** Freunde auf ein Glas *or* einen Drink einladen

c *no pl (= alcoholic liquor)* Alkohol *m*; **the ~ problem** der Alkoholismus; **he has a ~ problem** er trinkt; **~ caused his downfall** der Alkohol hat ihn ruiniert; **to be the worse for ~** betrunken sein; **to take to ~** zu trinken anfangen; **his worries drove him to ~** vor lauter Sorgen fing er an zu trinken; **she drove him to ~** sie war der Grund, warum er zu trinken anfing; **it's enough to drive you to ~!** da könnte man wirklich zum Trinker werden

d *(esp Naut, Aviat inf, = sea)* Bach *m (sl)*; **three planes went down into the ~** drei Flugzeuge gingen in den Bach *(sl)*

VT trinken; **would you like something to ~?** möchten Sie etwas zu trinken (haben)?; **is the water fit to ~?** ist das Trinkwasser?, kann man das Wasser trinken?; **he ~s all his wages** er vertrinkt seinen ganzen Lohn; **to ~ oneself silly** sich dumm und dämlich trinken *(inf) or* saufen *(inf)*; **to ~ oneself into a stupor** sich sinnlos besaufen *(inf)*; **this car ~s petrol** dieses Auto säuft das Benzin nur so *(inf)*; **they drank the pub dry** *(Brit)* sie tranken die Kneipe leer → **table N a**

VI trinken; **he doesn't ~** er trinkt nicht, er trinkt keinen Alkohol; **his father drank** sein Vater hat getrunken *or* war Trinker; **to go out ~ing** einen trinken gehen; **one shouldn't ~ and drive** nach dem Trinken soll man nicht fahren; **~ing and driving** Alkohol am Steuer; **to ~ to sb** auf jdn trinken; *(to one's neighbour at table etc)* jdm zuprosten *or* zutrinken; **to ~ to sth** auf etw *(acc)* trinken; **I'll ~ to that** darauf trinke ich

▶ **drink away** VT *sep fortune* vertrinken; *sorrows* im Alkohol ersäufen

▶ **drink down** VT *sep* hinuntertrinken, hinunterschlucken

▶ **drink in** VT *sep* **a** *(plants etc) water* aufsaugen; *(person) air* einsaugen, einatmen; *sunshine* in sich *(acc)* aufsaugen **b** *(fig) a sight, his words etc* (begierig) in sich aufnehmen

▶ **drink off** VT *sep* austrinken, leeren; **he drank off the wine in one long gulp** er trank den Wein in einem Zug aus

▶ **drink up** **VI** austrinken; **drink up!** trink aus! **VT** *sep* austrinken

drinkable ['drɪŋkəbl] ADJ **a** *(= not poisonous)* trinkbar; **~ water** Trinkwasser *nt* **b** *(= palatable)* genießbar, trinkbar; **a very ~ little wine** ein sehr süffiges Weinchen

drink: **drink-driver** N *(Brit)* angetrunkener Autofahrer, angetrunkene Autofahrerin; **drink-driving** *(Brit)* **N** Trunkenheit *f* am Steuer **ATTR** *charge, conviction* wegen Trunkenheit am Steuer; *campaign* gegen Trunkenheit am Steuer; **the number of ~ offences** die Zahl der Fälle von Trunkenheit am Steuer

drinker ['drɪŋkəʳ] N Trinker(in) *m(f)*; **he's a heavy ~** er ist ein starker Trinker

drinking ['drɪŋkɪŋ] **N** Trinken *nt*; **there had been some heavy ~ at the party** auf der Party war viel getrunken worden; **his ~ caused his marriage to break up** an seiner Trunksucht ging seine Ehe in die Brüche; **underage ~** der Alkoholkonsum von Minderjährigen

ADJ Trink-, Sauf- *(inf)*; **~ habits** Trinkgewohnheiten *pl*; **~ session** *or* **binge** *(inf)* Trinkgelage *nt*; **~ bout** *or* **spree** Sauftour *f (inf)*; **when his wife died he went on a ~ bout for three months** als seine Frau starb, hat er drei Monate lang nur getrunken; **they are ~ friends** sie gehen oft zusammen einen trinken *(inf)*; **I'm not really a ~ man** ich trinke eigentlich nicht viel Alkohol

drinking: **drinking age** N *Mindestalter für den Alkoholkonsum in der Öffentlichkeit*; **drinking chocolate** N Trinkschokolade *f*; **drinking club** N *Klub, in dem Alkohol ausgeschenkt wird*; **drinking companion** N Zechkumpan(in) *m(f)*; **drinking den** N Kaschemme *f (pej)*; **drinking fountain** N Trinkwasserbrunnen *m*; **drinking glass** N Trinkglas *nt*; **drinking horn** N Trinkhorn *nt*; **drinking laws** PL *Gesetze über den Alkoholkonsum*; **drinking problem** N Alkoholproblem *nt*; **drinking song** N Trinklied *nt*; **drinking station** N *(at marathon)* Verpflegungsstation *f*; **drinking straw** N Trinkhalm *m*, Strohhalm *m*; **drinking trough** N Wassertrog *m*; **drinking-up time** N *(Brit) die letzten zehn Minuten vor der Polizeistunde*; **drinking water** N Trinkwasser *nt*

drinks machine N Getränkeautomat *m*

drink-up time N *(Brit) Zeit, innerhalb derer Gäste ihre Getränke nach Schließung des Lokals austrinken können*

drip [drɪp] **VI** *(water, tap)* tropfen; **to be ~ping with sweat** schweißüberströmt *or* schweißgebadet sein; **to be ~ping with blood** vor Blut triefen; **sweat was ~ping off his forehead** der Schweiß triefte ihm von der Stirn; **the walls were ~ping with water** die Wände waren triefnass; **his voice was ~ping with sarcasm** seine Stimme triefte nur so vor *or* von Sarkasmus; **she was ~ping with jewellery** *(Brit) or* **jewelry** *(US)* sie strotzte nur so von Schmuck

VT *liquid* träufeln, tropfen; **he was ~ping water/blood all over the carpet** Wasser/sein Blut tropfte überall auf den Teppich; **his clothes were ~ping water all over the carpet** von seinen Kleidern tropfte Wasser überall auf den Teppich; **careful, you're ~ping paint on my coat** pass auf, die Farbe tropft mir auf den Mantel!

N **a** *(= sound: of water, rain, tap)* Tropfen *nt*

b *(= drop)* Tropfen *m*

c *(Med)* Infusionsapparat *m*, Tropf *m (inf)*; **to be on a ~** eine Infusion bekommen, am Tropf hängen *(inf)*

d *(inf: person)* Waschlappen *m (inf)*

drip: **drip coffee** N *(US)* Filterkaffee *m*; **drip-dry** **ADJ** *shirt* bügelfrei **VT** tropfnass aufhängen **VI** bügelfrei sein; **"drip-dry"** *(on label)* „bügelfrei"; **let it ~** hängen Sie es tropfnass auf; **drip-feed** *(Med)* **N** künstliche Ernährung **VT** künstlich ernähren

dripping ['drɪpɪŋ] **ADJ** **a** *(= soaking)* **~ (wet)** tropfnass **b** *tap* tropfend; *gutter* undicht **N** **a** *(Brit Cook)* Bratenfett *nt* **b** *(= action of water etc)* Tropfen *nt*

dripping pan N *(Cook)* Fettpfanne *f*

drippy ['drɪpɪ] ADJ *(+er) (inf)* **a** *person* doof *(inf)*; *singer, film, novel* schmalzig **b** *(US: = rainy) day* regnerisch

drivability [ˌdraɪvə'bɪlɪtɪ] N *(Aut: = performance)* Fahreigenschaften *pl*; *(= ease of handling)* Fahrkomfort *m*

drive [draɪv] *vb: pret* **drove**, *ptp* **driven** **N** **a** *(Aut: = journey)* (Auto)fahrt *f*; **to go for a ~** ein bisschen (raus)fahren; **to go for a ~ to the coast** ans Meer fahren; **he took her for a ~ in his new car** er machte mit ihr eine Spazierfahrt in seinem neuen Auto; **it's about one hour's ~ from London** es ist etwa eine Stunde Fahrt von London (entfernt)

b *(into house: also* **driveway***)* Einfahrt *f*; *(longer)* Auffahrt *f*, Zufahrt *f*

c *(Golf, Tennis)* Treibschlag *m*

d *(Psych etc)* Trieb *m*; **sex ~** Geschlechts- *or* Sexualtrieb *m*

e *(= energy)* Schwung *m*, Elan *m*, Tatendrang *m*; **you're losing your ~** Ihr Elan *or* Schwung lässt nach; **he has no ~** er hat keinen Elan *or* Schwung

f *(Comm, Pol etc)* Aktion *f*; **this is part of a ~ to attract new members** das ist Teil einer Mitgliederwerbeaktion; **recruitment ~** Anwerbungskampagne *f*; **fundraising ~** Sammelaktion *f*; **the ~ toward(s) democracy** die starke Entwicklung zur Demokratie hin → **export VI**

g *(Mil: = offensive)* kraftvolle Offensive

h *(Mech: = power transmission)* Antrieb *m*; **front-wheel/rear-wheel ~** Vorderrad-/Hinterradantrieb *m*

i *(Aut)* Steuerung *f*; **left-hand ~** Linkssteuerung *f*

j *(Cards)* → **whist**

k *(Comput)* Laufwerk *nt*

VT **a** *(= cause to move) people, animals, dust, clouds etc* treiben; **to ~ sb out of the country** jdn aus dem Land (ver)treiben; **to ~ a nail/stake into sth** einen Nagel/Pfahl in etw *(acc)* treiben; **the gale drove the ship off course** der Sturm trieb das Schiff vom Kurs ab

b *cart, car, train* fahren; **he ~s a taxi (for a living)** er ist Taxifahrer, er fährt Taxi *(inf)*

c *(= convey in vehicle) person* fahren; **I'll ~ you home** ich fahre Sie nach Hause; **could you ~ us there?** können Sie uns dahin fahren?

d *(= provide power for, operate) motor (belt, shaft)* antreiben; *(electricity, fuel)* betreiben; *(Comput)* steuern; **a car ~n by electricity** ein Auto *nt* mit Elektroantrieb

e *(Tennis, Golf) ball* driven *(spec)*; **to ~ the ball** einen Treibball spielen

f *(= cause to be in a state or to become)* treiben; **to ~ sb round the bend** *(Brit inf) or* **mad** jdn verrückt machen; **to ~ sb to murder** jdn zum Mord treiben; **I was ~n to it** ich wurde dazu getrieben; **who/what drove you to do that?** wer/was trieb *or* brachte Sie dazu(, das zu tun)?

g *(= force to work hard) person* hart herannehmen, schinden *(pej)*; **he ~s himself very hard** er fordert sich selbst sehr stark

h *tunnel* treiben; *well* ausheben; *nail* schlagen

VI **a** *(= travel in vehicle)* fahren; **can you** *or* **do you ~?** fahren Sie Auto?; **he's learning to ~** er lernt Auto fahren; **to ~ at 50 km an hour** mit (einer Geschwindigkeit von) 50 km in der Stunde fahren; **to ~ on the right** rechts fahren; **did you come by train? – no, we drove** sind Sie mit der Bahn gekommen? – nein, wir sind mit dem Auto gefahren; **it's cheaper to ~** mit dem Auto ist es billiger; **driving while intoxicated** *(US)* Fahren *nt* in betrunkenem Zustand, Trunkenheit *f* am Steuer

b *(= move violently)* schlagen, peitschen; **the rain was driving into our faces** der Regen peitschte uns *(dat)* ins Gesicht

▶ **drive along** **VI** *(vehicle, person)* dahinfahren **VT** *sep (wind, current) person, boat* (voran)treiben

▶ **drive at** VI *+prep obj (fig: = intend, mean)* hinauswollen auf *(+acc)*; **what are you driving at?** worauf wollen Sie hinaus?

▶ **drive away** **VI** *(car, person)* wegfahren **VT** *sep (lit, fig) person, cares* vertreiben

▶ **drive back** **VI** *(car, person)* zurückfahren **VT** *sep* **a** *(= cause to retreat) person* zurückdrängen; *enemy* zurücktreiben, zurückdrängen **b** *(= convey back in vehicle) person* zurückfahren

▶ **drive home** VT *sep nail* einschlagen, einhämmern; *argument* einhämmern; **she drove home her point that …** sie legte eindringlich und überzeugend dar, dass …; **how can I drive it home to him that it's urgent?** wie kann ich (es) ihm nur klarmachen, dass es dringend ist?

▶ **drive in** VI *(car, person)* (hinein)fahren; **he drove into the garage** er fuhr in die Garage VT *sep nail* (hin)einschlagen, (hin)einhämmern; *screw* (r)eindrehen

▶ **drive off** VI **a** *(person, car)* weg- *or* abfahren **b** *(Golf)* abschlagen VT *sep* **a** *person, enemy* vertreiben **b** **she was driven off in a big Mercedes** sie fuhr in einem großen Mercedes weg; **he was driven off in an ambulance** er wurde in einem Krankenwagen weggebracht *or* abtransportiert

▶ **drive on** VI *(person, car)* weiterfahren VT *sep (= incite, encourage) person* antreiben; *(to do sth bad)* anstiften

▶ **drive out** VI heraus-/hinausfahren; **he drove out onto the street** er fuhr auf die Straße (hinaus) VT *sep person* hinaustreiben *or* jagen; *evil thoughts* austreiben

▶ **drive over** VI hinüberfahren VT *always separate (in car) person* hinüberfahren; **he drove his family over to see us** er hat seine Familie (mit dem Auto) zu uns gebracht VI *+prep obj dog* überfahren

▶ **drive up** VI *(car, person)* vorfahren; **a car drove up outside the house** ein Auto fuhr vor dem Haus vor

drive: **drive belt** N Treibriemen *m*; **drive-by** ADJ *shooting, crime, murder* aus dem fahrenden Auto heraus (begangen); **drive-in** ADJ **~ cinema** *(esp Brit)* Autokino *nt*; **~ bank** Bank *f* mit Autoschalter; **~ restaurant** Drive-in-Restaurant *nt*; **to watch a ~ movie** sich *(dat)* einen Film im Autokino ansehen N *(= restaurant)* Drive--in-Restaurant *nt*

drivel [ˈdrɪvl] N *(pej)* Blödsinn *m*, Kokolores *m (inf)*; **what a lot of ~!** das ist ja kompletter Blödsinn!; **mindless ~** leeres Gefasel VI *(pej)* Unsinn reden; **what's he ~ling** *(Brit) or* **~ing** *(US)* **(on) about?** was faselt er da?, worüber labert er da? *(inf)*

drive letter N *(Comput)* Laufwerksbuchstabe *m*

driven [ˈdrɪvn] *ptp of* **drive**

-driven [ˈdrɪvn] ADJ *suf* -betrieben; **battery-driven** batteriebetrieben; **computer-driven** computergesteuert; **steam-driven train** Zug *m* mit Dampflokomotive

driver [ˈdraɪvəʳ] N **a** *(of car, taxi, lorry, bus)* Fahrer(in) *m(f)*; *(Brit: of locomotive)* Führer(in) *m(f)*; *(of coach)* Kutscher(in) *m(f)*; **~'s seat** *(lit)* Fahrersitz *m*; **to be in the ~'s seat** *(fig)* das Steuer führen, die Zügel in der Hand haben **b** *(of animals)* Treiber(in) *m(f)* **c** *(= golf club)* Driver *m* **d** *(Comput)* Treiber *m*

driver's license N *(US)* Führerschein *m*

drive: **drive shaft** N Antriebswelle *f*; *(Aut)* Kardanwelle *f*; **drive-through**, *(esp US)* **drive--thru** N Drive-thru *m* ADJ *restaurant* mit Drive--thru; *drugstore* mit Autoschalter; **driveway** N Auffahrt *f*; *(longer)* Zufahrtsstraße *f or* -weg *m*; **drive wheel** N Antriebsrad *nt*, Treibrad *nt*

driving [ˈdraɪvɪŋ] N Fahren *nt*; **his ~ is awful** er fährt schrecklich schlecht; **I do a lot of ~ in my job** in meinem Beruf muss ich sehr viel fahren; **~ is her hobby** Autofahren ist ihr Hobby; **I don't like ~** ich fahre nicht gern (Auto); **~ position** Fahrposition *f* ADJ **a** *(= motivating) ambition* brennend; **to be the ~ force behind sth** die treibende Kraft bei etw sein **b** **~ rain** peitschender Regen; **~ snow** Schneetreiben *nt*

driving: **driving ban** N Führerscheinentzug *m*; **he was given a two-year ~** ihm wurde der Führerschein für zwei Jahre entzogen; **driving conditions** PL Straßenverhältnisse *pl*; **driving distance** N **to be within easy ~** mit dem Auto leicht erreichbar sein; **driving experience** N Fahrpraxis *f*; **driving instructor** N Fahrlehrer(in) *m(f)*; **driving iron** N *(Golf)* Driving-Iron *m*; **driving lesson** N Fahrstunde *f*; **driving licence** N *(Brit)* Führerschein *m*

> **DRIVING LICENCE, DRIVER'S LICENSE**
>
> In Großbritannien erhält ein Führerscheinanwärter erst einmal eine vorübergehende Fahrerlaubnis, die **provisional licence**. Der Besitzer einer **driving licence** ist nicht verpflichtet, das Papier beim Fahren mit sich zu führen, allerdings muss es auf Verlangen innerhalb von sieben Tagen auf der Polizeiwache vorgelegt werden. Eine volle Fahrerlaubnis behält ihre Gültigkeit bis zum siebzigsten Geburtstag des Inhabers und muss danach alle drei Jahre erneuert werden.
>
> In den USA ist es von Staat zu Staat verschieden, ab wann man einen Führerschein, die **driver's license**, erwerben darf - von 15 bis 21 reicht die Spanne. Allerdings können Führerscheinanwärter schon davor **learners' permits** oder **junior licenses** erhalten, mit denen Jugendlichen das Autofahren unter bestimmten Umständen erlaubt ist, zum Beispiel für den Schulweg. Der Führerschein muss immer mitgeführt werden, da er häufig dazu dient, Identität oder Alter des Inhabers auszuweisen. Normalerweise gilt die **driver's license** vier bis sechs Jahre und muss danach erneuert werden.

driving: **driving mirror** N Rückspiegel *m*; **driving offence**, *(US)* **driving offense** N Verkehrsdelikt *nt*; **driving range** N *(Golf)* Drivingrange *nt*; **driving school** N Fahrschule *f*; **driving seat** N Fahrersitz *m*; **to be in the ~** *(fig)* das Steuer führen, die Zügel in der Hand haben; **to put sb in the ~** *(fig)* jdm die Führung übergeben; **we need to put our party back in the ~** wir müssen unsere Partei wieder an die Macht bringen; **driving style** N Fahrweise *f*; **driving test** N Fahrprüfung *f*; **to take/fail/pass one's ~** die Fahrprüfung machen/nicht bestehen/bestehen; **driving wheel** N *(Brit)* Antriebsrad *nt*

drizzle [ˈdrɪzl] N Nieselregen *m*, Sprühregen *m* VI nieseln VT *(pour over)* träufeln; **~ oil over the salad** Öl auf den Salat träufeln

drizzly [ˈdrɪzlɪ] ADJ **~ weather** Nieselwetter *nt*; **it's ~** es nieselt

droll ADJ, **drolly** ADV [drəʊl, -lɪ] komisch, amüsant

dromedary [ˈdrɒmɪdərɪ] N Dromedar *nt*

drone [drəʊn] N **a** *(= bee, fig)* Drohne *f* **b** *(= sound, of bees)* Summen *nt*; *(of engine, aircraft)* Brummen *nt* **c** *(= monotonous way of speaking)* monotone Stimme **d** *(Mus, = bass voice part)* Bass *m*; *(of bagpipes)* Brummer *m*; *(sound)* Bordun(ton) *m* **e** *(Aviat, = robot plane)* ferngesteuertes Flugzeug VI **a** *(bee)* summen; *(engine, aircraft)* brummen **b** *(= speak monotonously: also* **drone away** *or* **on**) eintönig sprechen; *(in reciting)* leiern; **he ~d on and on for hours** er redete stundenlang in seinem monotonen Tonfall; **we had to listen to him droning on about politics** wir mussten seinem monotonen Geschwafel über Politik zuhören *(inf)*

▶ **drone out** VT *sep speech* monoton vortragen; *(reciting)* leiern

drongo [ˈdrɒŋgəʊ] N **a** *(esp Austral pej inf: = person)* Schwachkopf *m (pej inf)* **b** *(= bird)* Drongo *m*

drool [druːl] VI sabbern; *(animal)* geifern

▶ **drool over** VI *+prep obj* richtig verliebt sein in *(+acc)*; **everyone is drooling over the huge reward offered** alle sind scharf auf die hohe Belohnung; **he sat there drooling over a copy of Playboy** er geilte sich an einem Playboyheft auf *(sl)*

droop [druːp] VI **a** *(lit, person)* vornübergebeugt stehen, krumm stehen, sich schlecht halten; *(shoulders)* hängen; *(head)* herunterfallen; *(eyelids)* herunterhängen; *(with sleepiness)* zufallen; *(flowers)* die Köpfe hängen lassen; *(feathers, one's hand, breasts)* schlaff herunterhängen; *(rope, roof etc)* durchhängen **b** *(fig, one's interest, energy)* erlahmen; *(audience etc)* erschlaffen, schlaff werden; **his spirits were beginning to ~** sein Mut begann zu schwinden *or* sinken; **the heat made him ~** die Hitze machte ihn schlaff *or* matt VT *head* hängen lassen N *(lit, of body)* Gebeugtsein *nt*; *(of eyelids)* Schwere *f*; **I recognized her by the familiar ~ of her shoulders** ich habe sie an ihren hängenden Schultern erkannt

drooping [ˈdruːpɪŋ] ADJ **a** *head, shoulders, breasts, feathers, leaves, tail* hängend; *hand, branches* herunterhängend; *moustache* nach unten hängend; *flowers* welk; *eyelids* herunterhängend; *(with sleep)* schwer; *roof* durchhängend **b** **a drink to revive his ~ spirits** ein Schluck, um seine (geschwundenen) Lebensgeister wieder zu wecken

droopy [ˈdruːpɪ] ADJ **a** schlaff; *tail* herabhängend; *moustache* nach unten hängend; *eyelids* herunterhängend; *(with sleep)* schwer **b** *(inf, = tired, weak)* schlaff, schlapp *(inf)*

drop [drɒp]

1 NOUN	3 INTRANSITIVE VERB
2 TRANSITIVE VERB	4 PHRASAL VERBS

1 – NOUN

a [of liquid] Tropfen *m*; **drop by drop** tropfenweise; **a drop of blood** ein Blutstropfen *m*, ein Tropfen *m* Blut; **just a drop for me** für mich nur einen Tropfen; **a drop of wine?** ein Schlückchen *nt* Wein?; **it's a drop in the ocean** *or* **bucket** *(fig)* das ist ein Tropfen auf den heißen Stein; **eye drops** Augentropfen *pl*

b [= fall] *in temperature, prices* Rückgang *m (in gen)*; *(sudden)* Sturz *m (in gen)*; *(in blood pressure)* Absinken *nt (in gen)*; **a drop in prices** ein Preisrückgang *m*/-sturz *m*; **20% is quite a drop** 20%, das ist stark gefallen; **he took a big drop in salary when he changed jobs** als er die Stelle wechselte, nahm er eine beträchtliche Gehaltsverschlechterung in Kauf; **a sudden/noticeable drop in temperature** ein plötzlicher/merklicher Temperaturabfall

c [= vertical distance = difference in level] Höhenunterschied *m*; *(= fall)* Sturz *m*, Fall *m*; **a drop of ten feet** ein Höhenunterschied von zehn Fuß; **there's a drop of ten feet down to the ledge** bis zu dem Felsvorsprung geht es zehn Fuß hinunter; **it's a nasty drop** es geht tief hinunter; **it was a sheer drop from the top of the cliff into the sea** die Klippen fielen schroff zum Meer ab

d [= delivery] *of supplies, arms* Abwurf *m*; *(of drugs etc)* Lieferung *f*; *(= parachute jump)* (Ab)sprung *m*; **the Red Cross made a drop of medical supplies into the flood zone** das Rote Kreuz warf Medikamente über dem Überschwemmungsgebiet ab

e [of gallows] Falltür *f*

f [Theat] *(also* **drop curtain**) Vorhang *m*

g [= hiding place] *for secret mail* toter Briefkasten

h [= advantage] **to have the drop on sb** jdn ausstechen können; **to get the drop on sb** sich *(dat)* einen Vorteil gegenüber jdm verschaffen

i [= sweet] Drops *m*

2 – TRANSITIVE VERB

a [= cause to fall in drops] *liquid* tropfen

b [= allow to fall] fallen lassen; *bomb, supplies, pamphlets, burden* abwerfen; *parachutist* absetzen; *voice* senken; *curtsy* machen; *(Knitting) stitch* fallen lassen; *(= lower) hemline* herunterlassen; *(Theat) curtain* herunterlassen; **I dropped my watch** meine Uhr ist runtergefallen; **don't drop it!** lass es nicht fallen!; **he dropped his heavy**

cases on the floor er setzte *or* stellte seine schweren Koffer auf dem Boden ab; **drop that gun!** lass die Pistole fallen!; **to drop a letter in the postbox** *(Brit) or* **mailbox** *(US)* einen Brief einwerfen *or* in den Briefkasten werfen; **the boys dropped their trousers** *(Brit) or* **pants** die Jungen ließen ihre Hosen herunter

c [= kill] *bird* abschießen; *(sl) person* abknallen *(inf)*

d [= set down] *from car person* absetzen; *thing* abliefern; *(Comput: after dragging with mouse)* ablegen; *(from boat) cargo* löschen

e [= utter casually] *remark, name* fallen lassen; *clue* geben; *hint* machen; **he let drop that he was going to get married** *(by mistake)* es rutschte ihm raus, dass er heiraten wollte *(inf)*; *(deliberately)* er erwähnte so nebenbei, dass er heiraten wollte

f [= send] *postcard, note, line* schreiben; **to drop sb a note** *or* **a line** jdm ein paar Zeilen schreiben

g [= omit] *word, reference* auslassen; *(deliberately)* weglassen *(from* in *+dat)*; *programme* absetzen; **this word drops the "e" in the plural** bei diesem Wort fällt das „e" im Plural weg; **the paper refused to drop the story** die Zeitung weigerte sich, die Geschichte fallen zu lassen; **he drops his aitches** er verschluckt immer das „h"

h [= abandon] *work, habit, lifestyle* aufgeben; *idea, plan* fallen lassen, aufgeben; *discussion, conversation* abbrechen; *candidate, minister, friend* fallen lassen; *girlfriend* Schluss machen mit; *(Jur) case* niederschlagen; **you'll find it hard to drop the habit** es wird Ihnen schwerfallen, sich *(dat)* das abzugewöhnen; **you'd better drop the idea** schlagen Sie sich *(dat)* das aus dem Kopf; **to drop sb from a team** jdn aus einer Mannschaft nehmen; **let's drop the subject** lassen wir das Thema; **let's drop it!** lassen wir das!; **drop it!** *(inf)* hör auf (damit)!; **drop everything (and come here immediately)!** *(inf)* lass alles stehen und liegen (und komm sofort her)!

i [= lose] *money* verlieren, loswerden *(inf)*; **she dropped the first three games** *(Tennis)* sie gab die ersten drei Spiele ab

j [= give birth to] *(animal)* werfen

3 – INTRANSITIVE VERB

a [= drip] *liquid* (herunter)tropfen

b [= fall] *object* (herunter)fallen; *(Theat: curtain)* fallen; *(rate, temperature etc)* sinken; *(wind)* sich legen; *(voice)* sich senken; **don't let it drop** lass es nicht fallen; **to drop astern** *(Naut)* zurückfallen; **Britain has dropped from fifth to tenth in the league** Großbritannien ist vom fünften auf den zehnten Ligaplatz (zurück)gefallen → **penny, pin**

c [to the ground] *person* fallen; *(= collapse)* umfallen, umkippen *(inf)*; **to drop to the ground** sich zu Boden fallen lassen; **to drop to one's knees** auf die Knie fallen *or* sinken; **she dropped into an armchair** sie sank in einen Sessel, sie ließ sich in einen Sessel fallen; **I'm ready to drop** *(inf)* ich bin zum Umfallen müde *(inf)*; **she danced till she dropped** *(inf)* sie tanzte bis zum Umfallen *(inf) or* Gehtnichtmehr *(inf)*; **to drop dead** tot umfallen; **drop dead!** *(inf, expressing contempt)* geh zum Teufel! *(inf)*; **small businesses were dropping like flies in the recession** *(inf)* während der Rezession gingen kleine Geschäfte massenweise ein *(inf)*

d [= end] *conversation etc* aufhören; **to let sth drop** etw auf sich beruhen lassen; **you can't just let the matter drop** Sie können die Sache nicht einfach auf sich beruhen lassen; **shall we let it drop?** sollen wir es darauf beruhen lassen?

4 – PHRASAL VERBS

▶ **drop across** *or* **around** VI *(inf)* vorbeikommen/-gehen; **we dropped around to see him** wir sind bei ihm vorbeigegangen; **drop around and see us some time** kommen Sie doch mal (bei uns) vorbei

▶ **drop away** VI **a** *(= become fewer: numbers)* **people have been dropping away at recent meetings** in letzter Zeit sind immer weniger Leute zu den Versammlungen gekommen **b** *(cliffs)* jäh *or* steil *or* schroff abfallen

▶ **drop back** VI zurückfallen

▶ **drop behind** VI zurückfallen VI *+prep obj* **to drop behind sb** hinter jdn zurückfallen

▶ **drop by** VI *(inf)* vorbeikommen, hereinschauen

▶ **drop down** VI *(= fall)* herunterfallen; **he dropped down behind the hedge** er duckte sich hinter die Hecke; **he dropped down onto his knees** er sank in *or* fiel auf die Knie; **to drop down dead** tot umfallen; **the cliffs drop down to the sea** die Klippen fallen jäh *or* steil zum Meer (hin) ab; **he has dropped down to eighth overall** er ist insgesamt auf den achten Platz zurückgefallen VT *sep* fallen lassen

▶ **drop in** VI *(inf: = visit casually)* vorbeikommen, hereinschauen; **I've just dropped in for a minute** ich wollte nur mal kurz hereinschauen; **drop in on the Smiths** schauen Sie doch mal bei den Smiths herein; **to drop in at the pub** der Kneipe *(dat)* einen Besuch abstatten

▶ **drop off** VI **a** *(= fall down)* abfallen; *(= come off: handle etc)* abgehen **b** *(= fall asleep)* einschlafen; *(for brief while)* einnicken **c** *(sales)* zurückgehen; *(speed, interest, popularity)* nachlassen, zurückgehen VT *sep (= set down from car etc) person* absetzen; *parcel* abliefern

▶ **drop out** VI **a** *(of box etc)* herausfallen *(of* aus) **b** *(from competition etc)* ausscheiden *(of* aus); **to drop out of a race** *(before it)* an einem Rennen nicht teilnehmen; *(during it)* aus dem Rennen ausscheiden; **he dropped out of the philosophy course** er gab den Kurs in Philosophie auf; **to drop out of society** aus der Gesellschaft aussteigen *(inf)*; **to drop out of school** *(Brit)* die Schule vorzeitig verlassen; *(US: out of university)* die Universität vorzeitig verlassen; **he decided to drop out** er beschloss auszusteigen *(inf)* **c** **the "t" drops out** das „t" fällt weg

▶ **drop over** VI *(inf)* = **drop across**

---

drop: **drop ball** N *(Ftbl)* Schiedsrichterball *m*; **drop bottom** N Bodenklappe *f*; **drop ceiling** N Hängedecke *f*; **drop cloth** N *(US: = dust cover)* Staubdecke *f*; **drop curtain** N *(Theat)* (Fall)vorhang *m*; **drop-dead gorgeous** ADJ *(inf)* umwerfend *(inf)*; **drop-down menu** N *(Comput)* Dropdown-Menü *nt*; **drop forge** VT *(Metal)* gesenkschmieden; **drop goal** N *(Rugby)* Tor *nt* durch Dropkick; **drop hammer** N Fallhammer *m*; **drop handlebars** PL Rennlenker *m*; **drop-in centre** N *(Brit)* Tagesstätte *f*; **drop kick** N *(Rugby)* Dropkick *m*; **drop-leaf table** N Tisch *m* mit herunterklappbaren Seitenteilen

droplet [ˈdrɒplɪt] N Tröpfchen *nt*

droplet infection N *(Med)* Tröpfcheninfektion *f*

dropout [ˈdrɒpaʊt] N *(from society)* Aussteiger(in) *m(f) (inf)*; *(pej)* Asoziale(r) *mf*; *(= university dropout)* Studienabbrecher(in) *m(f)*; **the ~ rate at universities** die Zahl der Studienabbrecher

dropper [ˈdrɒpəˈ] N *(Med)* Pipette *f*; *(on bottle)* Tropfer *m*

droppings [ˈdrɒpɪŋz] PL Kot *m*; *(of horse)* Äpfel *pl (inf)*; *(of sheep)* Bohnen *pl*, Köttel *pl (inf)*

drop: **drop scene** N *(Theat)* (Zwischen)vorhang *m*; **drop seat** N Klappsitz *m*; **drop shot** N *(Tennis)* Stoppball *m*

dropsical [ˈdrɒpsɪkəl] ADJ wassersüchtig

dropsy [ˈdrɒpsɪ] N Wassersucht *f*

drop zone N *(for supplies)* Abwurfgebiet *nt*; *(for parachutists)* Absprunggebiet *nt*

drosophila [drəˈsɒfɪlə] N Drosophila *f*, Taufliege *f*

dross [drɒs] N *no pl (Metal)* Schlacke *f*; *(fig)* Schund *m*; **money is but ~** Geld ist eitel und nichtig

drought [draʊt] N Dürre *f*; **three ~s in as many years** drei Dürrekatastrophen in ebenso vielen Jahren

drove[1] [drəʊv] N *(of animals)* Herde *f*; *(of people)* Schar *f*; **they came in ~s** sie kamen in hellen Scharen

drove[2] *pret of* **drive**

drover [ˈdrəʊvəˈ] N Viehtreiber(in) *m(f)*

drown [draʊn] VI ertrinken VT **a** *person, animal* ertränken; **to be ~ed** ertrinken; **he looks like a ~ed rat** *(inf)* er sieht wie eine gebadete Maus aus *(inf)*; **to ~ one's sorrows (in drink)** seine Sorgen (im Alkohol) ertränken; **to ~ one's whisky** seinen Whisky verwässern **b** *(= submerge, flood) land* überschwemmen, überfluten **c** *(= render inaudible: also* **drown out**) *noise, voice* übertönen; *speaker* niederschreien

drowning [ˈdraʊnɪŋ] ADJ *person* ertrinkend; **a ~ man will clutch at a straw** *(Prov)* dem Verzweifelten ist jedes Mittel recht N Ertrinken *nt*; **there were three ~s here last year** im letzten Jahr sind hier drei Leute ertrunken

drowse [draʊz] VI (vor sich *(acc)* hin) dösen *or* dämmern N Halbschlaf *m*, Dämmerschlaf *m*

▶ **drowse off** VI eindämmern, eindösen *(inf)*

drowsily [ˈdraʊzɪlɪ] ADV schläfrig; *(after sleep)* verschlafen

drowsiness [ˈdraʊzɪnɪs] N Schläfrigkeit *f*; *(after sleep)* Verschlafenheit *f*; **to cause ~** schläfrig machen

drowsy [ˈdraʊzɪ] ADJ *(+er)* **a** *(= sleepy) person* schläfrig; *(after sleep)* verschlafen; *voice* verschlafen; **to grow** *or* **become ~** schläfrig werden; **to feel ~** sich schläfrig fühlen; **she was still ~ with sleep** sie war noch verschlafen **b** *(= soporific) afternoon* träge; *countryside* schläfrig; **I spent a ~ evening in front of the telly** ich habe den Abend vor dem Fernseher verdöst

drub [drʌb] VT *(= thrash) person* (ver)prügeln, schlagen; *(= defeat)* schlagen

drubbing [ˈdrʌbɪŋ] N **a** *(= thrashing)* Prügel *pl*; **to give sb a ~** jdm eine Tracht Prügel verpassen **b** *(= defeat)* Niederlage *f*; **to take a good ~** ganz schön Prügel kriegen *(inf)*; **they suffered a 5-0 ~** sie wurden vernichtend mit 5:0 geschlagen

drudge [drʌdʒ] N *(= person)* Arbeitstier *nt (inf)*; *(= job)* stumpfsinnige Plackerei *or* Schufterei *(inf)*; **some see a lexicographer as a harmless ~** manche sehen Lexikografen als Menschen, die nur brav vor sich hin schuften *(inf)* VI sich placken, schuften *(inf)*

drudgery [ˈdrʌdʒərɪ] N stumpfsinnige Plackerei *or* Schufterei *(inf)*; **it's sheer ~** es ist eine einzige Plackerei

drug [drʌg] N **a** *(Med, Pharm)* Medikament *nt*, Arzneimittel *nt*; *(inducing unconsciousness)* Betäubungsmittel *nt*; *(Sport)* Dopingmittel *nt*; **he's on ~s** *(Med)* er muss Medikamente nehmen; **to put sb on ~s** jdm Medikamente verordnen **b** *(= addictive substance)* Droge *f*, Rauschgift *nt*; **to be on ~s** drogen- *or* rauschgiftsüchtig sein; **to take ~s** Drogen *or* Rauschgift nehmen; **to get off the ~** von den Drogen loskommen → **hard drug, soft j** **c** *(Comm, = unsaleable goods)* **a ~ on the market** *(old)* eine unverkäufliche Ware; *(in shop)* ein Ladenhüter *m*

VT **a** *(Med) patient* Medikamente geben *(+dat)*; *(= render unconscious) person, animal* betäuben; **to ~ oneself up to the eyeballs on tranquillizers** *(Brit inf)* sich mit Beruhigungsmitteln vollpumpen *(inf)* **b** **to ~ sth** *(food, drink)* ein Betäubungsmittel in etw *(acc)* mischen

drug: **drug abuse** N Drogenmissbrauch *m*; **~ prevention** Drogenprävention *f*; **drug abuser** N **to be a ~** Drogenmissbrauch *m* betreiben; **drug addict** N Drogen- *or* Rauschgiftsüchtige(r), Drogen- *or* Rauschgiftabhängige(r) *mf*; **drug addiction** N Rauschgiftsucht *f*, Drogenabhängigkeit *or* -sucht *f*; **drug baron** N Drogenbaron *m*; **drug company** N Pharmaunternehmen *nt*; **drug culture** N Drogenkultur *f*;

drug dealer N Drogenhändler(in) *m(f)*, Dealer(in) *m(f) (inf)*; **drug dependency** N Drogenabhängigkeit *f*

drugged [drʌgd] ADJ *food, drink* mit einem Betäubungsmittel versetzt; **to be ~** *(person)* unter Beruhigungsmitteln stehen; **he seemed ~** er schien wie betäubt; **her whisky was ~** in ihrem Whisky waren K.O.-Tropfen; **he awoke from a long ~ sleep** er erwachte aus einer langen, tiefen Betäubung; **~ with sleep** schlaftrunken; **~ with fatigue** vor Müdigkeit ganz benommen

druggie ['drʌgɪ] N *(inf)* Drogenkonsument(in) *m(f)*, Drogi *m (inf)*

druggist ['drʌgɪst] N *(US)* Drogist(in) *m(f)*

drug: **drug industry** N *(Pharm)* Arzneimittelindustrie *f*; **drug pusher** N Dealer(in) *m(f) (inf)*; **drug runner** N Drogenschmuggler(in) *m(f)*; **drug squad** N Rauschgiftdezernat *nt*, Drogenfahndung *f*; **~ officer** Drogenfahnder(in) *m(f)*

drugs: **drugs raid** N Drogenrazzia *f*; **drugs ring** N Drogen(händler)ring *m*; **drugs test** N Dopingtest *m*; **drugs testing** N Dopingkontrolle *f*

drug: **drugstore** N *(US)* Drugstore *m*; **drug taker** N **to be a ~** Drogen *or* Rauschgift nehmen; **drug taking** N Einnehmen *nt* von Drogen *or* Rauschgift; **drug test** N *(Sport)* Dopingkontrolle *f*; **drug traffic**, **drug trafficking** N Drogenhandel *m*; **drug trafficker** N Drogenschieber(in) *m(f)*; **drug treatment** N *(Med)* medikamentöse Behandlung; **drug user** N Drogenbenutzer(in) *m(f)*

druid ['dru:ɪd] N Druide *m*

drum [drʌm] **N** **a** *(Mus)* Trommel *f*; **Joe Jones on ~s** am Schlagzeug: Joe Jones; **the ~s** die Trommeln *pl*; *(pop, jazz)* das Schlagzeug; **to beat** *or* **bang the ~ for sb/sth** *(fig)* die Trommel für jdn/etw rühren **b** *(for oil, petrol)* Tonne *f*; *(cylinder for wire)* Trommel *f*, Rolle *f*; (*Tech*: *= machine part*) Trommel *f*, Walze *f*; *(Phot)* Entwicklertrommel *f*; *(Archit)* *(= wall)* Tambour *m*, Trommel *f*; *(= shaft)* Säulentrommel *f* **c** (*Anat*: *also* **ear drum**) Trommelfell *nt* **VI** *(Mus, fig, rain etc)* trommeln **VT** **to ~ one's fingers on the table** mit den Fingern auf den Tisch trommeln

▸ **drum into** VT *always separate* **to drum sth into sb** jdm etw eintrichtern *(inf) or* einpauken *(inf)*; *tidiness etc* eindrillen *(inf)*

▸ **drum out** VT *sep (out of army, club)* ausstoßen

▸ **drum up** VT *sep enthusiasm, interest* wecken; *support, customers* auftreiben; **to drum up business** Aufträge an Land ziehen *(inf)*

drum: **drumbeat** N Trommelschlag *m*; **drum brake** N Trommelbremse *f*; **drumfire** N *(Mil)* Trommelfeuer *nt*; **drumhead** N Trommelfell *nt*; **drumhead court martial** N Standgericht *nt*; **drum kit** N Schlagzeug *nt*; **drum major** N Tambourmajor *m*; **drum majorette** N *(US)* Tambourmajorin *f*

drummer ['drʌmə'] N **a** *(in orchestra)* Trommelschläger(in) *m(f)*; *(in band, pop group)* Schlagzeuger(in) *m(f)*; *(Mil, in parade etc)* Trommler(in) *m(f)* **b** *(US inf)* Vertreter(in) *m(f)*

drummer boy N Trommler *m*

drumstick ['drʌmstɪk] N **a** *(Mus)* Trommelschlägel *or* -stock *m* **b** *(on chicken etc)* Keule *f*

drunk [drʌŋk] *ptp of* **drink** **ADJ** *(+er)* **a** *(= inebriated)* betrunken; **he was slightly ~** er war leicht betrunken *or* etwas angetrunken; **to get ~** betrunken werden *(on* von); *(on purpose)* sich betrinken *(on* mit); **to be ~ on wine** von Wein betrunken sein; **to be as ~ as a lord** *or* **skunk** *(inf)* blau wie ein Veilchen sein *(inf)*; **to be ~ and disorderly** *(Jur)* durch Trunkenheit öffentliches Ärgernis erregen **b** *(fig)* **to be ~ with** *or* **on success** vom Erfolg berauscht sein; **to be ~ with** *or* **on power/freedom/joy** im Macht-/Freiheits-/Freudenrausch sein **N** Betrunkene(r) *mf*; *(habitual)* Trinker(in) *m(f)*, Säufer(in) *m(f) (inf)*

drunkard ['drʌŋkəd] N Trinker(in) *m(f)*, Säufer(in) *m(f) (inf)*

drunk driver N *(esp US)* angetrunkener Autofahrer, angetrunkene Autofahrerin

drunk driving, **drunken driving** N *(esp US)* Trunkenheit *f* am Steuer

drunken ['drʌŋkən] ADJ *person* betrunken; *(habitually)* versoffen *(inf)*; *state, voice* betrunken; *night, evening, party* feuchtfröhlich; **a ~ man** ein Betrunkener; **~ violence** Gewalttätigkeiten *pl* unter Alkoholeinfluss; **a ~ brawl** eine Schlägerei zwischen Betrunkenen; **a ~ argument** ein Streit *m* im Suff *(inf)*; **in a ~ rage** *or* **fury** in einem Wutanfall im Vollrausch; **in a ~ stupor** im Vollrausch, sinnlos betrunken

drunkenly ['drʌŋkənlɪ] ADV betrunken; *behave* wie ein Betrunkener/eine Betrunkene

drunkenness ['drʌŋkənnɪs] N *(= state)* Betrunkenheit *f*; *(= habit, problem)* Trunksucht *f*

drunkometer [drʌŋ'kɒmɪtə'] N *(US)* = **Breathalyzer®**

dry [draɪ] **VT** *pret, ptp* **dried** trocknen; *fruit also* dörren; *skin* abtrocknen; **to ~ oneself** sich abtrocknen; **he dried his hands/feet** er trocknete sich *(dat)* die Hände/Füße ab, er trocknete seine Hände/Füße ab; **to ~ the dishes** das Geschirr abtrocknen; **to ~ one's eyes** sich *(dat)* die Tränen abwischen

VI **a** *(= become dry)* trocknen; **the washing was hanging up to ~ in the sun** die Wäsche trocknete in der Sonne

b *(= dry dishes)* abtrocknen

ADJ **a** *thing, weather, period, country* trocken; *soil, river, lake* ausgetrocknet; *well* versiegt; **to run ~** *(river)* austrocknen; *(well)* versiegen; **~ period** *or* **spell** Trockenperiode *f*; **the ~ season** die Trockenzeit; **to rub oneself ~** sich abrubbeln; **to rub sth ~** etw abtrocknen *or* trocken reiben; **to wipe sth ~** etw abtrocknen *or* trocken wischen; **as ~ as a bone** knochentrocken; **~ shampoo** Trockenshampoo *nt* → **high ADJ a**

b *mouth, throat, lips, eyes, cough* trocken; **to feel/be ~** (*inf*: *= thirsty*) Durst haben, eine trockene Kehle haben; **there wasn't a ~ eye in the house** es blieb kein Auge trocken

c *(Cook) ingredients* trocken; **~ mustard** Senfpulver *nt*; **~ bread** trocken Brot

d *cow* trockenstehend; **her breasts are ~** sie hat keine Milch

e (*inf*: *= anti-alcohol*) *state, country* alkoholfrei

f *(= ironic, wry) humour, wit* trocken

g *voice* ausdruckslos; *sound* trocken; **her voice was harsh and ~** ihre Stimme klang hart und trocken

h *(= uninspired, dull) book, speech, lecture* trocken; **as ~ as dust** todlangweilig, knochentrocken *(inf)*

i *wine, sherry, cider* trocken

N **in the ~** im Trockenen; **come into the ~** komm ins Trockene; **to give sth a ~** etw trocknen

▸ **dry off** **VI** *(clothes etc)* trocknen, trocken werden **VT** *sep* abtrocknen

▸ **dry out** **VI** **a** *(clothes)* trocknen; *(ground, skin etc)* austrocknen **b** *(inf, alcoholic)* eine Entziehungskur machen **VT** *sep clothes* trocknen; *ground, skin* austrocknen

▸ **dry up** **VI** **a** *(stream, well)* austrocknen, versiegen; *(moisture)* trocknen; *(inspiration, source of income)* versiegen; *(author)* keine Ideen mehr haben; **then business started drying up** dann wurden die Aufträge immer spärlicher **b** *(= dry dishes)* abtrocknen **c** *(actor)* stecken bleiben *(inf)*; *(speaker)* den Faden verlieren **d** (*inf*: *= be quiet*) **dry up!** halt den Mund! *(inf)* **VT** *sep mess* aufwischen; *dishes* abtrocknen; *(sun) well, river bed* austrocknen

dryad ['draɪæd] N Dryade *f*

dry: **dry-as-dust** ADJ fürchterlich trocken, staubtrocken; **dry battery** N *(Elec)* Trockenbatterie *f*; **dry cell** N *(Elec)* Trockenelement *nt*; **dry cell battery** N Trockenbatterie *f*; **dry-clean** **VT** chemisch reinigen; **to have a dress ~ed** ein Kleid chemisch reinigen lassen; **"dry-clean only"** *(on label)* chemisch reinigen! **VI** **will it ~?** lässt es sich chemisch reinigen?; **dry-cleaner's** N chemische Reinigung; **dry-cleaning** N chemische Reinigung; **dry dock** N *(Naut)* Trockendock *nt*

dryer ['draɪə'] N *(for clothes)* Wäschetrockner *m*; *(= spin dryer)* Wäscheschleuder *f*; *(for hands)* Händetrockner *m*; *(for hair)* Föhn *m*, Haartrockner *m*; *(over head)* Trockenhaube *f*; *(in paint)* Trockenstoff *m*

dry: **dry farming** N Trockenfarmsystem *nt*; **dry-fly fishing** N Trockenfliegenfischen *nt*; **dry ginger** N *(mixer)* Ingwerlimonade *f*; **dry goods** PL *(Comm)* Kurzwaren *pl*; **dry ice** N Trockeneis *nt*

drying ['draɪɪŋ]: **drying cupboard** N (Wäsche)trockenschrank *m*; **drying room** N Trockenboden *m*, Trockenkeller *m*; **drying-up** N Abtrocknen *nt*; **to do the ~** abtrocknen

dry land N fester Boden; **I'll be glad to be on ~ again** ich bin froh, wenn ich wieder festen Boden unter den Füßen habe

dryly ['draɪlɪ] ADV = **drily**

dry measure N Trockenmaß *nt*

dryness ['draɪnɪs] N *(all senses)* Trockenheit *f*

dry: **dry nurse** N Säuglingsschwester *f*; **dry-roasted** ADJ *peanuts* trocken geröstet; **dry rot** N (Haus- *or* Holz)schwamm *m*; **dry run** N Probe *f*; *(Mil)* Trockentraining *nt*; **dry-shod** ADJ, ADV mit trockenen Füßen; **to cross sth ~** etw trockenen Fußes überqueren; **dry ski slope** N Trockenskipiste *f*; **dry-stone wall** N Bruchsteinmauer *f*; **dry valley** N Trockental *nt*; **dry weight** N Trockengewicht *nt*

DS *(Brit Police) abbr of* **Detective Sergeant**

DSC *abbr of* **Distinguished Service Cross** *Auszeichnung für besondere Verdienste*

DSc *abbr of* **Doctor of Science** Dr. rer. nat.

DSL *(Comput, Internet) abbr of* **digital subscriber line** DSL *nt*; **~ connection/operator/service** DSL-Anschluss *m*/-Betreiber *m*/-Service *m*

DSM *abbr of* **Distinguished Service Medal** *Auszeichnung für besondere Verdienste*

DSO *(Brit) abbr of* **Distinguished Service Order** *Auszeichnung für besondere Verdienste*

DST *(esp US) abbr of* **daylight saving time**

DTI *(Brit) abbr of* **Department of Trade and Industry** ≈ Wirtschaftsministerium *nt*

DTP *abbr of* **desktop publishing** DTP *nt*

DTs ['di:'ti:z] *abbr of* **delirium tremens**; **to have the ~** vom Saufen den Tatterich haben *(inf)*

dual ['djʊəl] ADJ *(= double)* doppelt, Doppel-; *(= two kinds of)* zweierlei; **in his ~ role as ...** in seiner Doppelrolle als ...; **it has a ~ function** es hat doppelte *or* zweierlei Funktion

dual: **dual carriageway** N *(Brit) Straße mit Mittelstreifen und Fahrbahnen in beiden Richtungen*, ≈ Schnellstraße *f*; **dual citizenship** N doppelte Staatsangehörigkeit; **dual controls** PL *(Aut)* Doppelsteuerung *f*; **dual display** N *(of prices)* doppelte Preisangabe *or* -auszeichnung; **dual economy** N duale Volkswirtschaft

dualism ['djʊəlɪzəm] N Dualismus *m*

dualist ['djʊəlɪst] N Dualist(in) *m(f)*

dualistic [,djʊə'lɪstɪk] ADJ dualistisch

duality [djʊ'ælɪtɪ] N Dualität *f*

dual: **dual nationality** N doppelte Staatsangehörigkeit; **dual personality** N *(Psych)* gespaltene Persönlichkeit; **dual pricing** N deglomerative Preisdifferenzierung; *(for two currencies)* doppelte Preisauszeichnung; **dual-purpose** ADJ zweifach verwendbar

duathlon [djʊ'æθlɒn] N *(Sport)* Duathlon *nt*

dub[1] [dʌb] VT **a** **to ~ sb a knight** jdn zum Ritter schlagen **b** *(= nickname)* taufen **c** *film* synchronisieren; **the film was ~bed into French** der Film war französisch synchronisiert

▸ **dub in** VT *sep (Film) sound* synchron (zum Bild) aufnehmen

dub[2] N *(US inf)* Tollpatsch *m*

dub[3] N *(Mus)* Dub *nt*

Dubai [du:'baɪ] N Dubai *nt*

dubber ['dʌbəʳ] N *(Film)* Synchronsprecher(in) *m(f)*

dubbin ['dʌbɪn] N Lederfett *nt*

dubbing ['dʌbɪŋ] N *(Film)* Synchronisation *f*

dubiety [dju:'baɪətɪ] N *(form)* Zweifel *pl*

dubious ['dju:bɪəs] ADJ **a** *(= questionable) reputation, person* zweifelhaft; *business deal* fragwürdig, zweifelhaft; *idea, claim, statement, basis* fragwürdig; *attribution* fraglich; **it seems ~ that…** es erscheint fragwürdig, dass …; *(= suspicious)* es erscheint verdächtig, dass …; **of ~ origin** zweifelhaften Ursprungs; **of ~ benefit/quality** von zweifelhaftem Nutzen/zweifelhafter Qualität; **it sounds ~ to me** ich habe da meine Zweifel; **to have the ~ honour** *(Brit) or* **honor** *(US) or* **distinction/pleasure of doing sth** *(usu iro)* die zweifelhafte Ehre/das zweifelhafte Vergnügen haben, etw zu tun
b *(= uncertain, unconvinced)* unsicher; **I was ~ at first, but he convinced me** ich hatte zuerst Bedenken, aber er überzeugte mich; **I was ~ that** *or* **whether …** ich bezweifelte, dass …; **he's ~ whether he should come** er weiß nicht *or* ist im Zweifel, ob er kommen soll; **to be ~ about sth** etw anzweifeln; **I'm very ~ about it** ich habe da doch starke Zweifel; **he sounded ~** er klang zweifelnd *or* skeptisch; **she looked ~** sie blickte skeptisch drein; **he gave me a ~ look** er sah mich zweifelnd an

dubiously ['dju:bɪəslɪ] ADV **a** *(= questionably, +vb)* fraglicherweise; *(+adj)* fragwürdig; **costly and ~ effective treatment** teure Behandlungen von zweifelhafter Wirksamkeit **b** *(= uncertainly) look* zweifelnd, skeptisch; *say, suggest* zweifelnd, unsicher

dubiousness ['dju:bɪəsnɪs] N **a** *(= questionable nature, of reputation, origin)* Zweifelhaftigkeit *f*; *(of deal, claim, statement etc)* Fragwürdigkeit *f* **b** *(= uncertainty: of person)* Unsicherheit *f*; **there was a certain ~ in his voice** es lag ein gewisser Zweifel in seiner Stimme

ducal ['dju:kəl] ADJ herzoglich; **~ palace** Herzogspalast *m*

ducat ['dʌkɪt] N *(Hist)* Dukaten *m*

duchess ['dʌtʃɪs] N Herzogin *f*

duchy ['dʌtʃɪ] N Herzogtum *nt*

duck¹ [dʌk] **N a** *(bird)* Ente *f*; **wild ~** Wildente *f*; **roast ~** gebratene Ente, Entenbraten *m*; **to play ~s and drakes** *(Brit)* Steine (über das Wasser) springen lassen; **to play ~s and drakes with sth** *(Brit: = squander)* mit etw furchtbar aasen *(inf)*; **to take to sth like a ~ to water** bei etw gleich in seinem Element sein; **it's (like) water off a ~'s back to him** das prallt alles an ihm ab
b *(Brit, inf)* = **duckie**
c a funny-looking old ~ *(dated esp Brit inf)* eine komische alte Tante *(inf)*
d *(Mil inf)* Amphibienfahrzeug *nt*
e *(Cricket)* **he made** *or* **scored a ~** er hat keinen Punkt gemacht; **to be out for a ~** ohne Punktgewinn aus sein
VI a *(also* **duck down***)* sich ducken; **he ~ed down out of sight** er duckte sich, so dass *or* sodass man ihn nicht mehr sehen konnte; **he ~ed under the water** er tauchte (im Wasser) unter; **they ~ed for cover** sie duckten sich, um in Deckung zu gehen
b he ~ed out of the room er verschwand aus dem Zimmer; **she ~ed out of the rain** sie suchte Schutz vor dem Regen; **to ~ and dive** *or* **weave** *(also fig)* Ausweichmanöver machen
VT a *(= push under water)* untertauchen
b to ~ one's head den Kopf einziehen
c *(= avoid) difficult question, blow, challenge* ausweichen *(+dat)*; *responsibility* sich drücken vor *(+dat) (inf)*

▶ **duck out of** VI *+prep obj (= back out of)* sich drücken vor *(+dat) (inf)*

duck² N **a** *(Tex)* Segeltuch *nt* **b ducks** PL Segeltuchhosen *pl*

duck: duckbill ['dʌkbɪl], **duck-billed platypus** [ˌdʊkbɪld'plætɪpəs] N Schnabeltier *nt*; **duckboard** N Lattenrost *m*; **duck-egg blue** N zartes Blau

duckie ['dʌkɪ] N *(dated Brit inf) often not translated*, Süße(r) *mf*; **are you all right, ~?** na, alles in Ordnung?

ducking ['dʌkɪŋ] N *(in water)* Untertauchen *nt*, Tauchen *nt*; **to give sb a ~** jdn untertauchen *or* tunken

ducking: ducking and diving N *(inf)* Ausweichmanöver *pl*; *(verbal also)* Ausflüchte *pl*; **~ is all part of political life** Ausweichmanöver gehören zur Politik; **ducking stool** N *Sitz auf einem Balken, mit dem Übeltäter zur Strafe ins Wasser getaucht wurden*

duckling ['dʌklɪŋ] N Entenküken, Entlein *nt*; **roast ~** gebratene junge Ente → **ugly duckling**

duck pond N Ententeich *m*

ducks [dʌks] N *(Brit, inf)* = **duckie**

duck: duck shooting N Entenjagd *f*; **duck soup** N *(US inf fig)* Kinderspiel *nt (inf)*; **to be ~** ein Kinderspiel sein *(for* für); **duckweed** N Entenflott *nt*, Entengrütze *f*, Wasserlinse *f*

ducky N *(Brit, inf)* = **duckie**

duct [dʌkt] N **a** *(Anat)* Röhre *f*; **tear ~** Tränenkanal *m* **b** *(for liquid, gas)* (Rohr)leitung *f*, Rohr *nt*; *(Elec)* Rohr *nt*, Röhre *f*

ductile ['dʌktaɪl] ADJ **a** *metal* hämmerbar; *(= stretchable)* dehnbar, streckbar **b** *(fig liter) person* leicht lenkbar

ductless gland ['dʌktlɪs'glænd] N endokrine *or* innersekretorische Drüse

dud [dʌd] *(inf)* **ADJ a** *(= useless)* nutzlos; *(= worthless) person* unfähig; *company* völlig unrentabel; *script* mies *(inf)*; **~ mine/shell/bomb/bullet** Blindgänger *m*; **~ equipment/batteries** Geräte/Batterien, die nichts taugen; **a ~ scheme** ein totaler Reinfall
b *(= counterfeit) note, coin, antique* gefälscht; *cheque, loan* ungedeckt; **a ~ note** *(Brit) or* **bill** *(US)* eine Blüte *(inf)*; **~ £10 notes** *(Brit)* falsche *or* gefälschte 10-Pfund-Scheine
N *(= bomb, shell, grenade)* Blindgänger *m*; *(= coin)* Fälschung *f*; *(= note)* Blüte *f (inf)*; *(= person)* Niete *f (inf)*, Versager(in) *m(f)*; **this watch/battery is a ~** diese Uhr/Batterie taugt nichts

dude [dju:d] N *(US)* **a** *(inf: = man)* Kerl *m (inf)*; **yo ~!** *(sl: = hi)* hi Alter! *(inf)*, hey Dicker! *(inf)* **b** *(dated: = dandy)* Dandy *m* **c** *(dated: = city type)* Städter *m*, feiner Stadtpinkel *(pej inf)*

dude ranch N *(US)* Touristenranch *f*, Ferienranch *f*

> **DUDE RANCH**
>
> Eine **dude ranch** ist eine Ranch im Westen der USA, auf der man als Tourist den Wilden Westen hautnah erleben kann. Die Ranch kann noch wirklich bewirtschaftet werden, es kann sich aber auch um ein reines Freizeitunternehmen handeln. Wer echte Cowboyluft schnuppern möchte, kann zu Pferde durch die Prärie reiten, bei der Rancharbeit helfen und am Lagerfeuer deftige Mahlzeiten einnehmen. **Dude** bezeichnet im amerikanischen Slang einen geschniegelten Städter oder Ostküstenbewohner. In der Filmkomödie „City Slickers" von 1991 mit Billy Crystal geht es genau um solch eine Gruppe Städter von der Ostküste, die auf einer **dude ranch** richtige Abenteuer erleben wollen.

dudgeon ['dʌdʒən] N **in high ~** sehr empört, sehr aufgebracht

duds [dʌdz] PL *(inf: = clothes)* Klamotten *pl (inf)*

due [dju:] ✪ 17.2 **ADJ a** *(= expected, scheduled)* fällig; **to be ~** *(plane, train, bus)* ankommen sollen; *(elections, results)* anstehen; **the train was ~ ten minutes ago/is ~ to arrive at 10.32** der Zug sollte vor 10 Minuten ankommen/soll um 10.32 Uhr ankommen; **when is the baby ~?** wann soll das Baby kommen?; **the results are ~ at the end of the month** die Ergebnisse stehen Ende des Monats an *or* sind Ende des Monats fällig; **he is ~ back in London tomorrow** er soll morgen nach London zurückkommen; **to be ~ in** *(train, bus)* ankommen sollen; *(ferry)* einlaufen sollen; **to be ~ out** *(magazine, CD)* herauskommen sollen; **he is ~ to speak about now** er müsste jetzt gerade seine Rede halten; **the building is ~ to be demolished** das Gebäude soll demnächst abgerissen werden; **he is ~ for a rise** *(Brit) or* **raise** *(US)* ihm steht eine Gehaltserhöhung zu; **she is ~ for promotion** sie ist mit einer Beförderung an der Reihe; **the prisoner is ~ for release** *or* **~ to be released** der Gefangene soll jetzt entlassen werden; **the car is ~ for a service** das Auto muss zur Inspektion; **you look ~ for a haircut** du müsstest mal zum Friseur gehen; **the carpet looks ~ for a clean** der Teppich müsste gereinigt werden; **~ date** *(Fin)* Fälligkeitstermin *m*; *(for baby)* erwarteter Geburtstermin
b *(= proper) attention, consideration* gebührend; *care* nötig; **after ~ consideration** nach reiflicher Überlegung; **to drive with ~ care and attention** mit der gebotenen Vorsicht fahren; **driving without ~ care and attention** *(Jur)* fahrlässiges Verhalten im Straßenverkehr; **in ~ course** *or* **time** *(= eventually)* zu gegebener Zeit; **every home will have a computer in ~ course** auf die Dauer wird jeder Haushalt einen Computer besitzen; **~ credit** die gebührende Anerkennung; **~ credit for his achievements** die Anerkennung, die ihm für seine Leistungen gebührt; **the council, to give them ~ credit, have tried their best to plan ahead** die Stadt, das muss man ihr lassen, hat ihr Bestes getan, um vorauszuplanen; **with (all) ~ respect** bei allem Respekt *(to* für) → **credit N d**
c *(= owed)* **to be ~** *(money)* ausstehen; **to be ~ to sb** *(money, leave, respect)* jdm zustehen; **to fall ~** *(Fin: loan, debt)* fällig werden; **I'm ~ some leave, I've got some leave ~ to me** mir steht etwas Urlaub zu; **the respect ~ to his age** der seinem Alter gebührende Respekt; **the respect ~ from a son to his father** der Respekt, den ein Sohn seinem Vater schuldet; **my thanks are ~ to Mr Dobbs** mein Dank gilt Herrn Dobbs; **to be ~ a couple of days off** ein paar freie Tage verdient haben
d ~ to *(= owing to)* aufgrund *+gen*, auf Grund *+gen*, wegen *+gen*; *(= caused by)* durch; **what's it ~ to?** worauf ist es zurückzuführen?; **closed ~ to repairs** wegen Reparaturarbeiten geschlossen; **his death was ~ to natural causes** er ist eines natürlichen Todes gestorben; **his failure was entirely ~ to himself/his carelessness** an seinem Versagen war nur er selbst/seine Nachlässigkeit schuld
N a dues PL *(= subscription, fees)* (Mitglieds)beitrag *m*; **to pay one's ~s** *(fig)* seinen Verpflichtungen nachkommen
b to give him his ~, he did at least try eins muss man ihm lassen, er hat es wenigstens versucht; **to give him his ~, he had no idea about it** man muss gerechterweise zugeben, dass er davon keine Ahnung hatte → **devil N d**
ADV *(= precisely)* **~ north/south/east/west** direkt nach Norden/Süden/Osten/Westen; **~ east of the village** in Richtung Osten des Dorfes

due diligence N *(Jur, Comm)* **a** Sorgfaltspflicht *f*, gebührende Sorgfalt **b** *(also* **due diligence analysis***)* Due Diligence *f*

duel ['djʊəl] **N** *(lit, fig)* Duell *nt*; **~ of wits** geistiger Wettstreit **VI** sich duellieren; *(German students)* eine Mensur schlagen; **~ling** *(Brit) or* **~ing** *(US)* **pistols** Duellierpistolen *pl*

duellist, *(US)* **duelist** ['djʊəlɪst] N Duellant *m*

due process N *(Jur)* **a ~ (of law)** *(US)* ordentliches Gerichtsverfahren **b ~ of law** ordnungsgemäßes Verfahren

duet [dju:'et] N Duo *nt*; *(for voices)* Duett *nt*; **violin ~** Geigenduo *nt*

duff¹ [dʌf] N *(Cook)* Mehlpudding *m*

duff² **ADJ** *(Brit inf) machine, watch (= useless)* nutzlos; *(= broken)* kaputt *(inf)*; *idea* blöd *(inf)*; *film, book, record, job* mies *(inf)*; *loan* faul *(inf)*; *company* unrentabel; *opponent* unfähig; **I'll bet you**

it's a ~ one ich wette, dass es nichts taugt **N** *(esp US inf: = buttocks)* Hintern *m (inf)*, Arsch *m (vulg)*; **to get off one's ~** seinen Arsch in Bewegung setzen *(sl)*

▶ **duff up** VT *sep (Brit inf)* zusammenschlagen *(inf)*

duffel [ˈdʌfl]: **duffel bag** N Matchbeutel *or* -sack *m*; **duffel coat** N Dufflecoat *m*

duffer [ˈdʌfəʳ] N *(Brit inf)* **a** *(esp Sch)* Blödmann *m (inf)*; **to be a ~ at football/French** eine Niete im Fußball/in Französisch sein *(inf)* **b** *(= silly old man)* (alter) Trottel *(inf)*

dug¹ [dʌg] N *(of animal)* Zitze *f*

dug² *pret, ptp of* **dig**

dugout [ˈdʌgaʊt] N *(Mil)* Schützengraben *m*, Unterstand *m*; *(also* **dugout canoe**) Einbaum *m*

duh [dʌ:, dɜ:] INTERJ *(esp US iro)* na klar, logisch, ach wirklich?

duke [dju:k] N Herzog *m*

dukedom [ˈdju:kdəm] N *(= territory)* Herzogtum *nt*; *(= title)* Herzogswürde *f*

dukes [dju:ks] PL *(dated sl, = fists)* Fäuste *pl*; **put up your ~** zeig mal deine Fäuste *(inf)*

dulcet [ˈdʌlsɪt] ADJ *(liter, hum, iro)* wohlklingend, melodisch; **so nice to hear her/his ~ tones again** *(hum, iro)* wie nett, ihre liebliche/seine sonore Stimme wieder zu hören *(hum, iro)*

dulcimer [ˈdʌlsɪməʳ] N Cymbal *nt*, Hackbrett *nt*

dull [dʌl] ADJ (+er) **a** *(= not bright or shiny) light* trüb; *glow* schwach; *colour* matt, trüb; *eyes* matt, glanzlos; *hair, skin, metal, paintwork* stumpf, matt; *weather, day* trüb, grau; *sky* bedeckt; **the sea was a ~ grey** das Meer war mattgrau; **it will be ~ at first** *(weather forecast)* es wird anfangs bewölkt

b *(= boring)* langweilig; **deadly ~, as ~ as ditchwater** *or* **dishwater** todlangweilig; **there's never a ~ moment** man langweilt sich keinen Augenblick

c *(= vague, muffled) sound, thud, ache, sensation* dumpf; **he fell to the ground with a ~ thud** er schlug dumpf auf den Boden auf

d *(= listless) person, mood* träge; *gaze, expression* lustlos; *(St Ex, Comm) market* flau; *trading* schleppend; **I felt ~ and sleepy** ich fühlte mich träge und müde

e *(= slow-witted)* langsam; **the ~est boy in the class** der schwächste Schüler in der Klasse; **his senses/intellectual powers are growing ~** seine Sinne/geistigen Kräfte lassen langsam nach

f *(form, = blunt) knife, blade* stumpf

VT **a** *(= lessen) pain* betäuben; *grief* lindern; *senses, mind, sensitivity* abstumpfen; *vision, hearing* trüben, schwächen; *impression* schwächen; *pleasure* dämpfen; **emotionally ~ed** (emotional) abgestumpft

b *(= make less bright) light, colour* dämpfen; *metal, paintwork* stumpf werden lassen

c *(= muffle) sound* dämpfen

d *(form, = blunt) knife, blade* stumpf machen

VI *(light)* schwächer werden; *(colour)* verblassen; *(eyes)* sich trüben

dullard [ˈdʌləd] N Dummkopf *m*

dullness [ˈdʌlnɪs] N **a** *(of light)* Trübheit *f*; *(of colours, eyes)* Mattheit *f*; *(of hair, paintwork, metal)* Stumpfheit *f*; *(of weather, day)* Trübheit *f*; *(of sky)* Bedecktheit *f* **b** *(= boring nature)* Langweiligkeit *f* **c** *(of sound, thud)* Dumpfheit *f* **d** *(= listlessness, of person)* Trägheit *f*; *(of expression)* Lustlosigkeit *f*; (*St Ex, Comm, of market)* Flauheit *f* **e** *(= slow-wittedness)* Langsamkeit *f* **f** *(form, = bluntness)* Stumpfheit *f*

dully [ˈdʌllɪ] ADV **a** *(= dimly) gleam, glint* matt, schwach **b** *(= without enthusiasm) say, look* lustlos **c** *(= vaguely) throb, ache, feel* dumpf **d** *(= boringly)* langweilig

duly [ˈdju:lɪ] ADV **a** *(= properly) elect, note, sign* ordnungsgemäß, vorschriftsmäßig; **to be ~ grateful/sympathetic/impressed** gebührend dankbar/mitfühlend/beeindruckt sein; **I was ~ surprised** ich war entsprechend überrascht **b** *(= as expected)* wie erwartet; *(= in due course)* dann auch; **he ~ obliged** wie erwartet tat er es auch, er tat es dann auch; **she ~ went to China in April** wie erwartet fuhr sie im April nach China, so fuhr sie dann im April nach China

dumb [dʌm] ADJ (+er) **a** *(= mute)* stumm; *(= silent, speechless)* sprachlos; *(liter: = silent) rage, recognition* wortlos, stumm; **~ animals** (unsere stummen Freunde,) die Tiere; **she was struck ~** *(fig)* es verschlug ihr die Sprache; **she was struck ~ with fear/shock** die Angst/der Schock verschlug ihr die Sprache; **he was in a ~ rage** er war stumm vor Wut; **don't give me that ~ insolence!** sieh mich nicht so unverschämt an!

b *(esp US inf: = stupid)* dumm, doof *(inf)*; **that was a ~ thing to do/say** wie kann man nur so etwas Dummes machen/sagen!; **he did one ~ thing after another** er machte eine Dummheit nach der anderen; **to act** *or* **play ~** sich dumm stellen

▶ **dumb down** VT *sep* das Niveau *(gen)* herunterfahren; *(= simplify)* vereinfachen VI das Niveau herunterfahren; *(= simplify)* vereinfachen

dumb: **dumbass** [ˈdʌmæs] N *(US sl)* Idiot *m (inf)*, Nullchecker(in) *m(f) (inf)*; **dumbbell** [ˈdʌmbel] N *(Sport)* Hantel *f*; **dumb blonde** N *(pej inf)* dümmliche Blondine *f (pej)*; **dumb cluck** N *(inf: = fool)* Doofi *m (inf)*

dumbfound [dʌmˈfaʊnd] VT verblüffen; **I'm ~ed!** ich bin sprachlos!

dumbing down [ˌdʌmɪŋˈdaʊn] N Niveauverlust *m*; *(= simplification)* Vereinfachung *f*

dumbly [ˈdʌmlɪ] ADV stumm

dumbness [ˈdʌmnɪs] N **a** Stummheit *f* **b** *(esp US inf: = stupidity)* Doofheit *f (inf)*, Dummheit *f*

dumbo [ˈdʌmbəʊ] N *(inf: = stupid person)* Doofkopp *m (inf)*

dumb: **dumb show** N *(Theat) pantomimische Einlage in einem Stück*; **in ~** in Mimik; **dumb terminal** N *(Comput)* Einfachterminal *nt*, unintelligente Datenstation; **dumb waiter** N Speiseaufzug *m*; *(= trolley)* Serviertisch *m*, stummer Diener

dum-dum [ˈdʌmdʌm] N *(inf)* Doofie *m (inf)*

dumdum (bullet) [ˈdʌmdʌm(ˈbʊlɪt)] N Dumdum(geschoss) *nt*

dummy [ˈdʌmɪ] N **a** *(= sham object)* Attrappe *f*; *(Comm)* Schaupackung *f*, Attrappe *f*; *(for clothes)* (Schaufenster- *or* Kleider)puppe *f*; *(of book)* Blindband *m* → **ventriloquist's dummy, tailor's dummy** **b** *(Brit: = baby's teat)* Schnuller *m* **c** *(Cards: = person)* Dummy *m*; *(= cards)* Tisch *m* **d** *(inf: = fool)* Dummkopf *m*, Idiot *m (inf)*, Doofie *m (inf)* **e** *(Ftbl etc)* Finte *f*; **to sell sb a ~** jdn antäuschen ADJ *attr (= not real)* unecht; **it's just a ~ grenade** das ist nur die Attrappe einer Granate; **a ~ company** eine Scheinfirma; **a ~ bomb/weapon** eine Bomben-/ /Waffenattrappe; **~ pills** Placebos *pl*

dummy run N Probe *f*; *(of air attack)* Übung *f*

dump [dʌmp] N **a** *(Brit: = pile of rubbish)* Schutthaufen *m*, Abfallhaufen *m*; *(= place)* Müllplatz *m*, Müllkippe *f*

b *(Mil)* Depot *nt*

c *(pej inf) (= town)* Kaff *nt (inf)*; *(= house, building)* Dreckloch *nt (pej inf)*; *(= school etc)* Sauladen *m (pej inf)*

d *(inf)* **to be (down) in the ~s** deprimiert *or* down *(inf)* sein

e *(Comput)* Dump *m*, Speicherabzug *m*

f *(sl)* **to go for** *(Brit)* *or* **take a ~** auf Scheißhaus gehen *(sl)*

VT **a** *(= get rid of) rubbish* abladen; **they ~ed the waste/bodies overboard** sie warfen den Abfall/die Leichen über Bord

b *(= put down, let fall) load, rubbish* abladen; *bags etc (= drop)* fallen lassen; *(= leave)* lassen; **where can I ~ these books?** wo kann ich diese Bücher lassen?; **to ~ sb/sth on sb** jdn/etw bei jdm abladen

c *(inf: = abandon, get rid of) person, girlfriend* abschieben; *car* abstellen, loswerden; *sth unwanted* abladen; **she ~ed him** sie hat mit ihm Schluss gemacht *(inf)*

d *(Comm) goods* zu Dumpingpreisen verkaufen

e *(Comput)* ausgeben, abziehen, dumpen

▶ **dump down** VT *sep* fallen lassen

▶ **dump off** VT *sep (inf)* **will you dump me off on the way home?** kannst du mich auf der Rückfahrt absetzen?

▶ **dump on** VI *+prep obj (inf)* **to dump on sb** *(= mistreat)* jdn von oben herab behandeln; *(= offload problems)* seine ganzen Probleme bei jdm abladen *(inf)*

dumper [ˈdʌmpəʳ] N *(= dump truck)* Kipper *m*

dumping [ˈdʌmpɪŋ] N **a** *(of load, rubbish)* Abladen *nt*; **"no ~"** *(Brit)* „Schuttabladen verboten!" **b** *(Comm)* Dumping *nt*

dumping: **dumping ground** N Müllkippe *f*, Schuttabladeplatz *m*; *(fig)* Abladeplatz *m*; **dumping price** N *(Comm)* Dumpingpreis *m*

dumpling [ˈdʌmplɪŋ] N **a** *(Cook)* Kloß *m*, Knödel *m* **b** *(inf: = person)* Dickerchen *nt (inf)*

Dumpster® [ˈdʌmpstəʳ] N *(US)* (Müll)container *m*

dump truck N Kipper *m*

dumpy [ˈdʌmpɪ] ADJ pummelig; *glasses* klein und massiv

dun¹ [dʌn] ADJ graubraun N Graubraun *nt*

dun² VT mahnen; **to ~ sb for payment** bei jdm eine Zahlung anmahnen

dunce [dʌns] N *(Sch)* langsamer Lerner *or* Schüler; *(= stupid person)* Dummkopf *m*; **to be a ~ at maths** eine Niete *or* schlecht in Mathe sein *(inf)*; **the ~ of the class** das Schlusslicht der Klasse; **~'s cap** *spitzer Papierhut, der früher zur Strafe dem schlechtesten Schüler aufgesetzt wurde*

dunderhead [ˈdʌndəhed] N Dummkopf *m*, Dummerjan *m (inf)*

dune [dju:n] N Düne *f*

dung [dʌŋ] N Dung *m*; *(of birds)* Dreck *m*; *(Agr: = manure)* Mist *m*, Dünger *m* VT *field* düngen, misten

dungarees [ˌdʌŋgəˈri:z] *(esp Brit)* PL *(workman's, child's)* Latzhose *f*; **a pair of ~** eine Latzhose

dung: **dung beetle** N Mistkäfer *m*; **dung cart** N Mistkarren *m*

dungeon [ˈdʌndʒən] N Verlies *nt*, Kerker *m*

dung: **dung fork** N Mistgabel *f*; **dung heap, dunghill** [ˈdʌŋhɪl] N Mist- *or* Dunghaufen *m*

dunk [dʌŋk] VT (ein)tunken

dunning letter [ˈdʌnɪŋˌletəʳ] N Mahnbrief *m*

dunno [ˈdʌnəʊ] = **(I) don't know**

duo [ˈdju:əʊ] N Duo *nt*

duodenal [ˌdju:əʊˈdi:nl] ADJ **~ ulcer** Zwölffingerdarmgeschwür *nt*

duodenum [ˌdju:əʊˈdi:nəm] N Zwölffingerdarm *m*, Duodenum *nt (spec)*

dupe [dju:p] VT betrügen, überlisten, übertölpeln; **he was ~d into believing it** er fiel darauf rein N Betrogene(r) *mf*

duple [ˈdju:pl] ADJ *(Mus)* **~ time** Zweiertakt *m*

duplex [ˈdju:pleks] ADJ *(Elec, Tech)* doppelt; *(Comput)* Duplex-; **~ operation** Duplexbetrieb *m* N *(esp US)* = **duplex apartment, duplex house**

duplex apartment N *(esp US)* zweistöckige Wohnung

duplex house N *(US)* Zweifamilienhaus *nt*

duplicate [ˈdju:plɪkeɪt] VT **a** *(= make a copy of) document* ein Duplikat *nt or* eine Zweitschrift anfertigen von

b *(= make copies of: on machine)* kopieren, vervielfältigen

c *(= repeat) action etc* wiederholen, noch einmal machen; *(wastefully)* doppelt *or* zweimal machen; *success* wiederholen; **that is merely duplicating work already done** da wird doch nur schon Erledigtes noch einmal gemacht [ˈdju:plɪkɪt]

N *(of document)* Duplikat *nt*, Kopie *f*; *(of work of art)* Kopie *f*; *(of key etc)* Zweitschlüssel *m*; **in**

~ in doppelter Ausfertigung ['dju:plɪkɪt] **ADJ** doppelt, zweifach; **a ~ copy of the text** ein Duplikat *nt or* eine Kopie des Textes; **a ~ receipt** eine Empfangsbescheinigung in doppelter Ausfertigung; **a ~ key** ein Zweitschlüssel *m*

duplicating machine ['dju:plɪkeɪtɪŋməʃi:n] **N** Vervielfältigungsapparat *m*

duplication [,dju:plɪ'keɪʃən] **N** *(of documents, act)* Vervielfältigung *f*; *(= duplicate)* Kopie *f*; *(= double)* Doppel *nt*; *(of efforts, work)* Wiederholung *f*; **save expenses by avoiding ~ of effort** tun Sie nichts zweimal, sparen Sie Kosten

duplicator ['dju:plɪkeɪtəʳ] **N** = **duplicating machine**

duplicitous [dju:'plɪsɪtəs] **ADJ** falsch, betrügerisch

duplicity [dju:'plɪsɪtɪ] **N** Doppelspiel *nt*

durability [,djʊərə'bɪlɪtɪ] **N a** *(of product, material, finish)* Strapazierfähigkeit *f*, Haltbarkeit *f* **b** *(of peace, relationship)* Dauerhaftigkeit *f*

durable ['djʊərəbl] **ADJ a** *(= tough) product, material, finish* strapazierfähig, haltbar; **CDs are more ~ than tapes** CDs halten länger als Kassetten **b** *(= lasting) peace, solution, relationship* dauerhaft

durable goods PL langlebige Güter *pl*

duration [djʊə'reɪʃən] **N** *(of play, war etc)* Länge *f*, Dauer *f*; **for the ~ of** für die Dauer *(+gen)*, während *(+gen)*; **of long/short ~** von langer/kurzer Dauer; **after a struggle of six years' ~** nach sechsjährigem Kampf; **he joined up for the ~** er hat sich bis zum Ende verpflichtet; **it looks as though we are here for the ~** *(inf)* es sieht so aus, als ob wir bis zum Ende hier sind

duress [djʊə'res] **N** Zwang *m*; **he signed the form under ~** er hat die Unterschrift unter Zwang geleistet

Durex® ['djʊəreks] **N** *(= condom)* Gummi *m (inf)*

during ['djʊərɪŋ] **PREP** während *(+gen)*

durst [dɜ:st] *(obs) pret of* **dare**

durum ['djʊərəm] **N**, **durum wheat N** Hartweizen *m*

dusk [dʌsk] **N** *(= twilight)* (Abend)dämmerung *f*; *(= gloom)* Finsternis *f*; **at/shortly after ~** bei/kurz nach Einbruch der Dunkelheit

duskiness ['dʌskɪnɪs] **N** Dunkelheit *f*

dusky ['dʌskɪ] **ADJ** *(+er) (liter) room, evening, skin, colour* dunkel; *person* dunkelhäutig; *light* schwach; **the light in the room was ~** es war dämmerig im Zimmer; **~ pink** altrosa

dust [dʌst] **N** *no pl* **a** Staub *m*; **covered in ~** staubbedeckt; **to make** *or* **raise a lot of ~** *(lit, fig)* eine Menge Staub aufwirbeln; **to gather ~** *(lit, fig)* verstauben; **a speck of ~** ein Körnchen *nt* Staub; **clouds of interstellar ~** staubförmige interstellare Materie; **when the ~ had settled** *(fig)* als sich die Wogen wieder etwas geglättet hatten; **we'll let the ~ settle first** *(fig)* wir warten, bis sich die Wogen geglättet haben → **bite VT a**
b to give sth a ~ etw abstauben
VT a *furniture* abstauben; *room* Staub wischen in *(+dat)*; **it's (all) done and ~ed** *(Brit fig inf)* das ist (alles) unter Dach und Fach
b *(Cook)* bestäuben
c *(Police)* **to ~ sth for prints** etw zur Abnahme von Fingerabdrücken einstauben
VI *(housewife etc)* Staub wischen; **she spent the morning ~ing** sie verbrachte den Morgen mit Staubwischen

▶ **dust down VT** *sep person, sb's clothes (with brush)* abbürsten; *(with hand)* abklopfen; *(fig)* herunterputzen; **to dust oneself down** sich abbürsten, sich *(dat)* den Staub abklopfen; *(fig)* sich reinwaschen

▶ **dust off VT** *sep dirt* abwischen, wegwischen; *table, surface, person* abstauben; **to dust oneself off** sich *(dat)* den Staub abklopfen; *(fig)* sich reinwaschen

▶ **dust out VT** *sep cup* auswischen

dust: **dust bag N** Staubbeutel *m*; **dust-bath N** Staubbad *nt*; **dustbin N** *(Brit)* Mülltonne *f*; **dustbin man N** *(Brit)* = **dustman**; **dust bowl N** Trockengebiet *nt*; **dustcart N** *(Brit)* Müllwagen *m*; **dust cloud N** Staubwolke *f*; **dust-cloth N** Staubtuch *nt*, Staublappen *m*; **dust coat N** Kittel *m*; **dust cover N** *(on book)* (Schutz)umschlag *m*; *(on furniture)* Schonbezug *m*; **dust devil N** kleiner Wirbelsturm

duster ['dʌstəʳ] **N a** Staubtuch *nt*; *(Sch)* (Tafel)schwamm *m* **b** *(Naut)* Schiffsflagge → **red duster c** *(US: also* **duster coat**) Kittel *m*

dust-free ['dʌstfri:] **ADJ** staubfrei

dustiness ['dʌstɪnɪs] **N** Staubigkeit *f*

dusting ['dʌstɪŋ] **N a** Staubwischen *nt*; **to do the ~** Staub wischen; **when I've finished the ~** wenn ich mit Staubwischen fertig bin **b** *(Cook etc: = sprinkling)* (Be)stäuben *nt*; **a ~ of snow** eine dünne Schneedecke

dusting-powder ['dʌstɪŋ,paʊdəʳ] **N** Talkpuder *m*

dust: **dust jacket N** (Schutz)umschlag *m*; **dustman N** *(Brit)* Müllmann *m*; **the dustmen come on Fridays** freitags ist Müllabfuhr; **dustpan N** Kehr- *or* Müllschaufel *f*; **dust-proof ADJ** staubdicht; **dustsheet N** *(Brit)* Tuch *nt (zum Abdecken von Möbeln)*; **dust storm N** Staubsturm *m*; **dust trap N** Staubfänger *m*; **dust-up N** *(dated inf)* Streit *m*, (handgreifliche) Auseinandersetzung

dusty ['dʌstɪ] **ADJ** *(+er)* **a** *(= full of dust, covered in dust)* staubig; *furniture, book, photograph* verstaubt **b** *colour* schmutzig; **~ reds and browns** schmutzige Rot- und Brauntöne; **~ blue** graublau; **~ pink** altrosa **c** *(inf) answer* schroff **d not too** *or* **so ~** *(inf)* gar nicht so übel *(inf)*

Dutch [dʌtʃ] **ADJ** niederländisch *(esp form)*, holländisch; **~ cheese** Holländer Käse; **a ~ man** ein Niederländer *m (esp form)*, ein Holländer *m*; **a ~ woman** eine Niederländerin *(esp form)*, eine Holländerin; **he is ~** er ist Niederländer *(esp form) or* Holländer; **she is ~** sie ist Niederländerin *(esp form) or* Holländerin; **~ master** *(Art)* Meister *m* der Holländischen Schule; **the ~ School** *(Art)* die Holländische Schule
N a *(= people)* **the ~** die Niederländer *(esp form) or* Holländer *pl*
b *(= language)* Niederländisch *nt*, Holländisch *nt*; **to be in ~ (with sb)** *(US inf)* (bei jdm) schlecht angeschrieben sein → *also* **double Dutch, English**
ADV to go ~ (with sb) *(inf: = share the cost)* (mit jdm) getrennte Kasse machen; **she insisted upon going ~** sie bestand darauf, dass wir getrennte Kasse machen *or* dass jeder für sich bezahlt

Dutch: **Dutch auction N** *Versteigerung mit stufenweise erniedrigtem Ausbietungspreis*; **Dutch barn N** *(Brit)* offene Scheune; **Dutch cap N** *(= diaphragm)* Pessar *nt*; **Dutch courage N** *(inf)* **to get** *or* **give oneself ~** sich *(dat)* Mut antrinken *(from* mit); **I can't do it without some ~** ich kann es nicht, ohne mir vorher ein bisschen Mut anzutrinken; **all they need is a bit of ~** sie müssen sich nur ein bisschen Mut antrinken; **Dutch door N** *(US)* quer geteilte Tür; **Dutch East Indies PL** Niederländisch-Ostindien *nt*; **Dutch elm disease N** Ulmensterben *nt*; **Dutchman N** Niederländer *m (esp form)*, Holländer *m*; **if he's a professional footballer, then I'm a ~** *(Brit inf)* wenn er ein Profifußballer ist, dann fresse ich einen Besen *(inf)*; **Dutch metal N** unechtes Blattgold, Rauschgold *nt*; **Dutch oven N** Schmortopf *m*; **Dutch Reformed Church N** Niederländische Reformierte Kirche; **Dutch treat N** *(inf) Kinobesuch/Essen etc mit getrennter Kasse*; **we settled on a ~** wir einigten uns darauf, getrennte Kasse zu machen; **Dutch uncle N to talk to sb like a ~, to be sb's ~** jdm eine Standpauke halten *(inf)*; **Dutchwoman N** Niederländerin *f (esp form)*, Holländerin *f*

dutiable ['dju:tɪəbl] **ADJ** zollpflichtig

dutiful ['dju:tɪfʊl] **ADJ** *child* gehorsam; *husband, employee* pflichtbewusst; **a ~ visit** ein Pflichtbesuch *m*; **your ~ son** *(old, form, in letters)* Dein treuer Sohn *(old, form)*; **with a ~ nod** mit einem gehorsamen Nicken

dutifully ['dju:tɪfəlɪ] **ADV** pflichtbewusst; *(= obediently)* treu und brav; **we all laughed ~** wir alle lachten brav

duty ['dju:tɪ] ✪ 10.1, 19.2, 19.5 **N a** Pflicht *f*; **to do one's ~** seine Pflicht tun; **to do one's ~ by sb** seine Pflicht gegenüber jdm tun *or* erfüllen; **it is my ~ to say** *or* **I am (in) ~ bound to say that ...** es ist meine Pflicht zu sagen, dass ...; **one's ~ to one's parents** seine Pflicht (und Schuldigkeit) seinen Eltern gegenüber; **it is my painful ~ to admit ...** ich habe die schwere *or* traurige Pflicht, Ihnen zu gestehen ...; **you don't know? but it's your ~ to know!** du weißt das nicht? aber es ist deine verdammte Pflicht und Schuldigkeit, es zu wissen!; **to make it one's ~ to do sth** es sich *(dat)* zur Pflicht machen, etw zu tun
b *(= responsibility)* Aufgabe *f*, Pflicht *f*; **to take up one's duties** seine Pflichten aufnehmen; **to report for ~** sich zum Dienst melden; **to be on ~** *(doctor etc)* im Dienst sein; *(Sch etc)* Aufsicht haben; **who's on ~ tomorrow?** wer hat morgen Dienst/Aufsicht?; **he went on ~ at 9** sein Dienst fing um 9 an; **to be off ~** nicht im Dienst sein; **he comes off ~ at 9** sein Dienst endet um 9; **I'm off ~ on Tuesday** Dienstag habe ich dienstfrei; **he was called for overseas ~** er wurde nach Übersee eingezogen; **to return to ~** den Dienst wieder aufnehmen; **night ~** Nachtdienst *m*; **he's been neglecting his duties as a husband** er hat seine ehelichen Pflichten vernachlässigt; **the box does ~ for a table** die Kiste dient als Tisch
c *(Fin: = tax)* Zoll *m*; **to pay ~ on sth** Zoll auf etw *(acc)* zahlen → **estate duty**

duty call N a ~ ein Höflichkeitsbesuch *m*

duty-free [dju:tɪ'fri:] **ADJ** zollfrei **ADV** zollfrei **N ~s** *pl (inf)* zollfreie Waren *pl*

duty-free: **duty-free allowance N** *Warenmenge, die man zollfrei einführen kann*; **duty-free shop N** Duty-free-Shop *m*, Dutyfreeshop *m*; **duty-free shopping N** Einkauf *m* von zollfreien Waren

duty: **duty NCO N** UvD *m*; **duty officer N** Offizier *m* vom Dienst; **duty roster N** Dienstplan *m*

duvet ['dju:veɪ] **N a** *(= quilt)* Steppdecke *f* **b** *(also* **duvet jacket**) Daunenjacke *f*

DV *abbr of* **deo volente** so Gott will

DV cam N *(Comput)* digitale Videokamera, DV-Cam *f*

DVD N ABBR *of* **digital versatile** *or* **video disc** DVD *f*

DVD: **DVD burner N** DVD-Brenner *m*; **DVD player N** DVD-Player *m*; **DVD recorder N** DVD-Rekorder *m*; **DVD-Rom N** DVD-Rom *f*; **DVD writer N** DVD-Brenner *m*

DVLA *(Brit) abbr of* **Driver and Vehicle Licensing Agency** Kfz-Steuer- und Führerscheinbehörde *f*

DVR *abbr of* **digital video recorder**

dwarf [dwɔ:f] **N** *pl* **dwarves** [dwɔ:vz] Zwerg *m*; *(= tree)* Zwergbaum *m*; *(= star)* Zwerg(stern) *m* **ADJ** *person* zwergenhaft; **~ shrubs** Zwergsträucher *pl* **VT a** *(skyscraper, person)* klein erscheinen lassen, überragen; *(through achievements, ability etc)* in den Schatten stellen; **to be ~ed by sb/sth** neben jdm/etw klein erscheinen **b** *(Hort) tree* klein züchten

dwarf galaxy N Zwerggalaxie *f*

dwarf star N Zwerg(stern) *m*

dweeb [dwi:b] **N** *(esp US inf)* trübe Tasse *(inf)*, Blödmann *m (inf)*

dwell [dwel] *pret, ptp* **dwelt VI a** *(liter: = live)* weilen *(geh)*, leben, wohnen **b** *(fig)* **the memory dwelt in his mind** die Erinnerung haftete in seinem Gedächtnis

▶ **dwell (up)on** VI *+prep obj* **a** *(= spend time on)* verweilen bei, sich länger aufhalten bei; *(in thought)* verweilen bei, länger nachdenken über *(+acc)*; **to dwell (up)on the past** sich ständig mit der Vergangenheit befassen; **let's not dwell (up)on it** wir wollen uns nicht (länger) damit aufhalten **b** *(Mus) note* halten

dweller [ˈdwelə'] N Bewohner(in) *m(f)*

dwelling [ˈdwelɪŋ] N *(form: also* **dwelling place***)* Wohnsitz *m (form)*, Wohnung *f*; ~ **house** Wohnhaus *nt*

dwelt [dwelt] *pret, ptp of* **dwell**

DWEM [dwem] N *(esp US) abbr of* **Dead White (European) Male**

DWI *(US Mot inf) abbr of* **driving while intoxicated**; **he got a ~** er ist betrunken am Steuer erwischt worden *(inf)*

dwindle [ˈdwɪndl] VI *(strength, relevance)* schwinden, abnehmen; *(interest)* nachlassen; *(numbers, audiences)* zurückgehen, abnehmen; *(supplies, stocks)* schrumpfen, zur Neige gehen

▶ **dwindle away** VI *(strength, person)* dahinschwinden; *(supplies)* zusammenschrumpfen

dwindling [ˈdwɪndlɪŋ] ADJ schwindend; *interest* nachlassend; *population, numbers, audiences* zurückgehend; *stocks, supplies* schwindend; **the prime minister's ~ popularity** die sinkende Beliebtheit des Premierministers N Schwinden *nt*; *(of stocks, population)* Rückgang *m*; *(of interest)* Nachlassen *nt*

dye [daɪ] N Farbstoff *m*; **hair ~** Haarfärbmittel *nt*; **food ~** Lebensmittelfarbe *f*; **the ~ will come out in the wash** die Farbe geht bei der Wäsche heraus VT färben; **~d blonde hair** blond gefärbtes Haar VI *(cloth etc)* sich färben lassen

dyed-in-the-wool [ˈdaɪdɪnðəˌwʊl] ADJ Erz-, durch und durch *pred*; *attitude* eingefleischt; **he's a ~ conservative/romantic** er ist ein Erzkonservativer/-romantiker, er ist durch und durch konservativ/romantisch

dyer [ˈdaɪə'] N Färber(in) *m(f)*; **~'s and cleaner's** Färberei und Reinigung *f*

dye: **dyestuffs** [ˈdaɪstʌfs] PL Farbstoffe *pl*; **dyeworks** N *sing or pl* Färberei *f*

dying [ˈdaɪɪŋ] *prp of* **die** ADJ **a** *(lit) person* sterbend; *animal* verendend, sterbend; *plant* eingehend; *(= last) breath, wish, words* letzte(r, s); **until** *or* **till** *or* **to one's ~ day** bis an sein Lebensende **b** *(fig: = declining) tradition, industry, art* aussterbend; *(= final) days, minutes* letzte(r, s); *fire, embers* verglühend; **to be a ~ breed** langsam aussterben; **regular customers are a ~ breed** regelmäßige Kunden gibt es fast nicht mehr; **the ~ minutes of the game** die letzten Spielminuten N **the ~** *pl* die Sterbenden

dyke, *(US)* **dike** [daɪk] N **a** *(= channel)* (Entwässerungs)graben *m*, Kanal *m* **b** *(= barrier)* Deich *m*, Damm *m*; *(= causeway)* Fahrdamm *m* **c** *(sl: = lesbian)* Lesbe *f (inf)* VT *land* eindeichen; *river* eindämmen

dykey [ˈdaɪkɪ] ADJ *(inf)* lesbisch

dynamic [daɪˈnæmɪk] ADJ *(also Phys)* dynamisch N Dynamik *f*

dynamically [daɪˈnæmɪkəlɪ] ADV *(also Phys)* dynamisch

dynamics [daɪˈnæmɪks] N *sing or pl* Dynamik *f*

dynamism [ˈdaɪnəmɪzəm] N Dynamismus *m*; *(of person)* Dynamik *f*

dynamite [ˈdaɪnəmaɪt] N *(lit)* Dynamit *nt*; *(fig)* Zünd- *or* Sprengstoff *m*; **she is ~** sie ist eine Wucht *(inf)*; **that story is pure ~** diese Geschichte ist der reinste Zündstoff VT *rocks, bridge* sprengen

dynamo [ˈdaɪnəməʊ] N Dynamo *m*; *(Aut)* Lichtmaschine *f*; **she's a human ~** sie steckt voller Dynamik

dynastic [daɪˈnæstɪk] ADJ dynastisch

dynasty [ˈdɪnəstɪ] N Dynastie *f*

dysentery [ˈdɪsɪntrɪ] N Dysenterie *f*, Ruhr *f*

dysfunction [dɪsˈfʌŋkʃən] N Funktionsstörung *f*, Fehlfunktion *f*; **liver ~** Funktionsstörung *f* der Leber

dysfunctional [dɪsˈfʌŋkʃənəl] ADJ *family, background* dysfunktional; *childhood* zerrüttet

dyslexia [dɪsˈleksɪə] N Legasthenie *f*

dyslexic [dɪsˈleksɪk] ADJ legasthenisch; **she is ~** sie ist Legasthenikerin N Legastheniker(in) *m(f)*

dysmenorrhoea [ˌdɪsmenəˈrɪə] N Dysmenorrhö *f*

dyspepsia [dɪsˈpepsɪə] N Dyspepsie *f*, Verdauungsstörung *f*; **nervous ~** nervöse Magenbeschwerden *pl*

dyspeptic [dɪsˈpeptɪk] ADJ dyspeptisch N jd, der an Dyspepsie leidet

dysphasia [dɪsˈfeɪzɪə] N Dysphasie *f*

dystopia [dɪsˈtəʊpɪə] N Dystopie *f*

dystrophy [ˈdɪstrəfɪ] N Dystrophie *f*, Ernährungsstörung *f*

E

E, e [iː] N E *nt*, e *nt*; *(Mus)* E *nt*, e *nt*; **E flat** Es *nt*, es *nt*; **E sharp** Eis *nt*, eis *nt* → **minor**

E **a** *abbr of* **east** O **b** *abbr of* **ecstasy** Ecstasy *nt*

e- [iː] PREF *(= electronic)* E-, e-

each [iːtʃ] ADJ jede(r, s); **~ one of us** jeder von uns; **~ and every one of us** jeder Einzelne von uns; **~ and every boy** jeder einzelne Junge (ohne Ausnahme)
PRON **a** jede(r, s); **~ of them gave their** *or* **his opinion** sie sagten alle ihre Meinung, jeder (von ihnen) sagte seine Meinung; **a little of ~ please** ein bisschen von jedem, bitte; **we ~ had our own ideas about it** jeder von uns hatte seine eigene Vorstellung davon
b **~ other** sich, einander *(geh)*; **they haven't seen ~ other for a long time** sie haben sich *or* einander lange nicht gesehen; **they wrote (to) ~ other** sie haben sich *(dat) or* einander geschrieben; **we visit ~ other** wir besuchen uns (gegenseitig), wir besuchen einander; **they were sorry for ~ other** sie bedauerten sich gegenseitig, sie bedauerten einander; **the respect they have for ~ other** die Achtung, die sie voreinander haben; **the love they have for ~ other** die Liebe, die sie füreinander empfinden; **you must help ~ other** ihr müsst einander helfen *or* euch gegenseitig helfen; **on top of ~ other** aufeinander; **next to ~ other** nebeneinander; **they went to ~ other's houses** sie besuchten einander zu Hause
ADV je; **we gave them one apple ~** wir haben ihnen je einen Apfel gegeben; **two classes of 20 pupils ~** zwei Klassen mit je 20 Schülern; **the books are £10 ~** die Bücher kosten je £ 10; **carnations at one euro ~** Nelken zu einem Euro das Stück

each way *(Brit Horseracing etc)* ADJ **~ bet** Wetteinsatz *m* auf alle drei Gewinnplätze ADV **to bet on** *or* **back a horse ~** auf alle drei Gewinnplätze setzen; **I had £10 ~ on Black Velvet** ich hatte £ 10 auf Black Velvet auf allen drei Gewinnplätzen gesetzt

eager [ˈiːgəʳ] ADJ *person, discussion, pursuit* eifrig; *face, eyes* erwartungsvoll; *response* begeistert; **the ~ looks on their faces** der erwartungsvolle Ausdruck in ihren Gesichtern; **in ~ anticipation** voll gespannter Erwartung; **to be ~ to do sth** darauf erpicht sein, etw zu tun, etw unbedingt tun wollen; **he was ~ to help** er war äußerst willig zu helfen; **children who are ~ to learn** Kinder, die lerneifrig *or* lernbegierig *or* lernwillig sind; **she is ~ to please** sie ist darum bemüht, alles richtig zu machen; **he was ~ to please her** er war eifrig bedacht, sie zufriedenzustellen; **to be ~ for sth** auf etw *(acc)* erpicht *or* aus sein; **~ for knowledge** wissbegierig; **he was ~ for work** er wollte unbedingt Arbeit haben; **to be ~ for sb to do sth** unbedingt wollen, dass jd etw tut; **to be ~ for sth to happen** es kaum erwarten können, dass etw geschieht

eager beaver N *(inf)* Arbeitstier *nt (inf)*

eagerly [ˈiːgəlɪ] ADV eifrig; *await, anticipate* gespannt; *accept, agree* bereitwillig; **~ awaited** mit Spannung erwartet; **we look forward ~ to the day when ...** wir warten ungeduldig auf den Tag, an dem ...

eagerness [ˈiːgənɪs] N Eifer *m*; **with ~** eifrig; **~ for power/vengeance** Macht-/Rachgier *f*; **~ for combat** Kampflust *f*; **~ for friendship** Suchen *nt* nach Freundschaft; **such was his ~ to please ...** er war so darauf bedacht zu gefallen, ...; **such was his ~ to help ...** seine Bereitwilligkeit zu helfen war so groß, ...

eagle [ˈiːgl] N **a** Adler *m*; **to keep an ~ eye on sb/sth** ein wachsames Auge auf jdn/etw werfen; **under the ~ eye of ...** unter dem wachsamen Blick *(+gen)* ...; **nothing escapes her ~ eye** nichts entgeht ihrem wachsamen Blick **b** *(Golf)* Eagle *nt* VT *(Golf)* **to ~ a hole** ein Eagle *nt* spielen

eagle-eyed [ˈiːglaɪd] ADJ **the ~ detective** der Detektiv mit seinen Adleraugen

Eagle Scout N *(US: = person) ein Pfadfinder des höchsten Ranges in den USA (= rank) höchster Rang für Pfadfinder in den USA*

eaglet [ˈiːglɪt] N Adlerjunge(s) *nt*

E & OE *abbr of* **errors and omissions excepted**

ear[1] [ɪəʳ] N **a** *(Anat, fig)* Ohr *nt*; **to keep one's ~s open** die Ohren offen halten; **to keep an ~ to the ground** die Ohren aufsperren *or* offen halten; **to be all ~s** ganz Ohr sein; **she was listening with only half an ~** sie hörte nur mit halbem Ohr zu; **your ~s must have been burning** Ihnen müssen die Ohren geklungen haben; **to lend an ~** zuhören; **to lend an ~ to sb** jdm sein Ohr leihen; **to find a sympathetic ~** ein offenes Ohr finden; **to lend a sympathetic ~** verständnisvoll zuhören; **if that came to** *or* **reached his ~s** wenn ihm das zu Ohren kommt; **he has the ~ of the prime minister** der Premierminister hört auf ihn; **it goes in one ~ and out the other** das geht zum einen Ohr hinein und zum anderen wieder hinaus; **to be up to one's ~s in debt/work** bis über beide *or* die Ohren in Schulden/Arbeit stecken; **he's got money/houses** *etc* **coming out of his ~s** *(inf)* er hat Geld/Häuser *etc* ohne Ende *(inf)*; **it all came crashing down around his ~s** *(fig)* um ihn herum brach alles zusammen; **he'll be out on his ~** *(inf)* dann fliegt er raus *(inf)*; **to bend sb's ~** *(inf)* jdn vollquatschen *(inf)*, jdn vollsülzen *(sl)*
b *(= sense of hearing)* Gehör *nt*, Ohr *nt*; **to have a good ~ for music** ein feines Gehör für Musik haben; **to play by ~** *(lit)* nach (dem) Gehör spielen; **to play it by ~** *(fig)* improvisieren

ear[2] N *(of grain, plant)* Ähre *f*; *(of maize)* Kolben *m*

ear: **earache** N Ohrenschmerzen *pl*; **eardrops** PL *(Med)* Ohrentropfen *pl*; **eardrum** N Trommelfell *nt*

-eared [-ɪəd] ADJ *suf* **long-/short-eared** lang-/kurzohrig

ear: **earflap** N Ohrenschützer *m*; **earful** N *(inf)* **to get an ~** mit einer Flut von Beschimpfungen überschüttet werden; **to give sb an ~** jdn herunterputzen *(inf)*, jdn zusammenstauchen *(inf)*; **earhole** N *(Brit inf)* Ohr *nt*, Löffel *m (inf)*; **to give sb a clip** *or* **clout round the ~** jdm ein paar *or* eins hinter die Löffel geben *(inf)*

earl [ɜːl] N Graf *m*

earldom [ˈɜːldəm] N *(= land)* Grafschaft *f*; *(= title)* Grafentitel *m*; *(= rank)* Grafenstand *m*

earlier [ˈɜːlɪəʳ] ADJ *comp of* **early** früher; **in ~ times** früher, in vergangenen Zeiten; **at an ~ date** früher, eher; **in his/her ~ years he/she had ...** in jüngeren Jahren hatte er/sie ...; **her ~ dislike gave way to hatred** aus ihrer anfänglichen Abneigung wurde Hass
ADV **~ (on)** früher; *(= just now)* vorhin; **~ (on) in the novel** an einer früheren Stelle in dem Roman; **this is what we talked about ~ (on)** darüber haben wir vorhin schon gesprochen; **her parents had died four years ~** ihre Eltern waren vier Jahre früher *or* vorher *or* zuvor gestorben; **~ (on) today** heute (vor einigen Stunden); **~ (on) this month/year** früher in diesem Monat/in diesem Jahr; **I cannot do it ~ than Thursday** ich kann es nicht vor Donnerstag *or* eher als Donnerstag machen

ear lobe N Ohrläppchen *nt*

early [ˈɜːlɪ] ADV **a** **~ (on)** früh; **~ in 1915/in February** Anfang 1915/Februar; **~ (on) in the year/(the) winter** Anfang des Jahres/des Winters; **~ (on) in the war** in der Anfangsphase des Krieges; **~ (on) in his/her/their** *etc* **life** in jungen Jahren; **~ (on) in the race** zu Anfang des Rennens; **~ (on) in the evening/morning** am frühen Abend/Morgen; **he got up very ~ in the morning** er stand sehr früh (am Morgen) auf; **as ~ as** *(= already)* schon; **she learned to read as ~ as four** sie lernte schon mit vier Jahren lesen; **~ this month/year** Anfang des Monats/Jahres; **~ next month/year** Anfang nächsten Monats/Jahres; **~ today/this morning** heute früh; **the earliest he can come is tomorrow** er kann frühestens morgen kommen
b *(= before the expected time)* früher (als erwartet); *(= before the appointed time)* zu früh; *(= earlier than usual)* früh; **she left ten minutes ~** sie ist zehn Minuten früher gegangen; **to be five minutes/an hour ~** fünf Minuten/eine Stunde zu früh kommen; **he was ~ for the meeting** er kam zu früh zu der Besprechung; **he left school ~** *(went home)* er ging früher von der Schule nach Hause; *(finished education)* er ging vorzeitig von der Schule ab; **to get up/go to bed ~** früh aufstehen/ins Bett gehen; **good morning, you're ~ today** guten Morgen, Sie sind heute ja früh dran; **~ to bed, ~ to rise (makes a man healthy, wealthy and wise)** *(Prov)* früh ins Bett und früh heraus, frommt dem Leib, dem Geist, dem Haus *(Prov)* → **bright b**
ADJ *(+er)* **a** früh; **it was ~ evening when we finished** wir waren am frühen Abend fertig; **we went for an ~ morning drive** *or* **a drive in the ~ morning** wir machten eine Spritztour am frühen Morgen; **we had an ~ lunch** wir aßen früh zu Mittag; **in ~ summer/autumn** zu Sommer-/Herbstanfang, im Frühsommer/Frühherbst; **in ~ spring/winter** zu Frühlings-/Winteranfang; **the ~ years/months/days** die ersten Jahre/Monate/Tage; **~ January/August** *etc* Anfang Januar/August *etc*; **in the ~ 60s/1980s** *etc* Anfang der sechziger/achtziger *etc* Jahre *or* Sechziger-/Achtzigerjahre *etc*; **to have an ~ night** früh ins Bett gehen; **to keep ~ hours** früh ins Bett gehen und früh aufstehen; **the ~ hours** die frühen Morgenstunden; **until** *or* **into the ~ hours** bis in die frühen Morgenstunden; **her ~ life** ihre jungen Jahre; **his ~ work** seine frühen Werke, sein Frühwerk *nt*; **at an ~ age** in jungen Jahren;

from an ~ age von klein auf; **since ~ childhood** seit seiner/ihrer *etc* frühen Kindheit; **in his ~ teens** im frühen Teenageralter; **to be in one's ~ thirties/forties** *etc* Anfang dreißig/vierzig *etc* sein; **it's too ~ to say/to say whether …** es ist noch zu früh, um etwas zu sagen/um zu sagen, ob …; **it is too ~ to know what his motives are** man weiß noch nicht, welche Motive er hat; **it's too ~ for a final decision** es ist zu früh, um eine endgültige Entscheidung zu fällen; **only her voice has changed from those ~ days** nur ihre Stimme ist anders als damals zu Anfang; **it's ~ days (yet)** *(esp Brit)* wir/sie *etc* sind noch im Anfangsstadium; **~ identification** *(Med)* Früherkennung *f*

b *(= before expected time) flowers* früh blühend; *cabbage, peas etc, crop* früh; *death* vorzeitig; *marriage* früh; *menopause* verfrüht; **~ vegetables** Frühgemüse *nt*; **an ~ spring** ein zeitiger Frühling

c *(from historical perspective) settlers, man* frühgeschichtlich; **the ~ church** die Urkirche; **~ Christians** Urchristen *pl*; **an ~ form of hypnotherapy** eine Frühform der Hypnotherapie; **~ baroque** Frühbarock *m*

d *(= soon)* **at an ~ date** bald; **at the earliest possible moment** so bald wie irgend möglich; **to promise ~ delivery** baldige Lieferung versprechen → **convenience b**

early: **early bath** N **to send sb for an ~** *(Brit Ftbl, Rugby)* jdn vom Feld schicken; **to take an ~** *(Brit fig: = withdraw)* sich frühzeitig zurückziehen; **early bird** N *(in morning)* Frühaufsteher(in) *m(f)*; *(arriving etc)* Frühankömmling *m*; **it's the ~ that catches the worm** *(Prov)* Morgenstund hat Gold im Mund *(Prov)*; **early closing** N **it's ~ today** die Geschäfte haben or sind heute nachmittag geschlossen; **early retirement** N vorgezogener *or* vorzeitiger Ruhestand; **to take ~** vorzeitig in den Ruhestand gehen; **to have taken ~** Frührentner(in) *m(f)* sein; **~ benefits** Vorruhestandsleistungen *pl*; **early riser** N Frühaufsteher(in) *m(f)*; **early warning (sign** *or* **signal)** N Vorwarnung *f*; **early warning system** N Frühwarnsystem *nt*

ear: **earmark** N *(on animal)* Ohrmarke *f* VT *(fig)* vorsehen, bestimmen; **ear-minded** [ˈɪəˌmaɪndɪd] ADJ *(Psych)* auditiv, *vorwiegend mit Gehörsinn begabt*; **earmuffs** PL Ohrenschützer *pl*

earn [ɜːn] VT *money, praise, rest* verdienen; *(Fin) interest* bringen; **to ~ one's keep/a living** Kost und Logis/seinen Lebensunterhalt verdienen; **to ~ a** *or* **one's crust** *(Brit)* seine Brötchen verdienen *(inf)*; **this ~ed him a lot of money/respect** das trug ihm viel Geld/große Achtung ein, damit verdiente er sich *(dat)* viel Geld/große Achtung; **he's ~ed it** das hat er sich *(dat)* verdient; **~ing capacity** Verdienstmöglichkeiten *pl*; **~ing value** Ertragswert *m*

earned income [ˈɜːndˈɪnkʌm] N Arbeitseinkommen *nt*

earner [ˈɜːnəʳ] N **a** *(= person)* Verdiener(in) *m(f)*; **big ~s** Großverdiener *pl* **b** *(Brit inf)* Einnahmequelle *f*; **that video shop is a nice little ~** der Videoladen wirft ganz schön was ab *(inf)*

earnest [ˈɜːnɪst] ADJ *person* ernst, ernsthaft; *voice* ernst; *hope, desire* aufrichtig, innig; *conversation, discussion* ernsthaft; **it shall be my ~ prayer that …** ich werde aufrichtig dafür beten, dass …; **they were in ~ conversation** sie unterhielten sich ernsthaft

N **a in ~** *(= for real)* richtig; **then she started crying in ~** dann fing sie erst an richtig zu weinen; **to be in ~ about sth** *(= serious)* etw ernst meinen; **is he in ~ about it?** ist es ihm ernst damit?; **this time I'm in ~** diesmal meine ich es ernst, diesmal ist es mein Ernst

b ~ (money) *(Jur, = deposit)* Handgeld *nt*

c *(= guarantee)* Pfand *nt* (of +*gen*); **an ~ of one's good intentions** ein (Unter)pfand seiner guten Absichten

earnestly [ˈɜːnɪstlɪ] ADV *say, ask* ernst, ernsthaft; *talk, discuss, work, try* ernsthaft; *explain* im Ernst, ernsthaft; *hope* aufrichtig, innig; *look* ernst

earnestness [ˈɜːnɪstnɪs] N Ernsthaftigkeit *f*; *(of voice)* Ernst *m*; *(of desire, prayer)* Innigkeit *f*

earnings [ˈɜːnɪŋz] PL *(of person)* Verdienst *m*; *(of a business)* Ertrag *m*

ear: **ear, nose and throat** ADJ *attr* Hals-Nasen-Ohren-; **~ specialist** Hals-Nasen-Ohren-Facharzt *m*/-ärztin *f*; **earphones** PL Kopfhörer *pl*; **earpiece** N Hörer *m*; **ear piercing** N Durchstechen *nt* der Ohrläppchen; **ear-piercing** ADJ *scream* ohrenbetäubend; **earplug** N Ohrwatte *f*, Ohropax® *nt*; **earring** N Ohrring *m*; **earset** N *(Telec)* Earset *nt*, Ohrhörer *m*; **earshot** N **out of/within ~** außer/in Hörweite; **ear-splitting** ADJ *sound, scream* ohrenbetäubend

earth [ɜːθ] N **a** *(= world)* Erde *f*; **the ~, Earth** die Erde; **on ~** auf der Erde, auf Erden *(liter)*; **to the ends of the ~** bis ans Ende der Welt; **where/who** *etc* **on ~ …?** *(inf)* wo/wer *etc* … bloß?; **what on ~ …?** *(inf)* was in aller Welt …? *(inf)*; **nothing on ~ will stop me now** keine Macht der Welt hält mich jetzt noch auf; **there's no reason on ~ why …** es gibt keinen erdenklichen Grund, warum …; **heaven on ~** der Himmel auf Erden; **did the ~ move for you, darling?** *(hum inf)* war es wahnsinnig schön für dich, Liebling? *(hum inf)*; **it cost the ~** *(Brit inf)* das hat eine schöne Stange Geld gekostet *(inf)*; **it won't cost the ~** *(Brit inf)* es wird schon nicht die Welt kosten *(inf)*; **to pay the ~** *(Brit inf)* ein Vermögen bezahlen

b *(= ground)* Erde *f*; **to fall to ~** zur Erde fallen; **to come back** *or* **down to ~ (again)** *(fig)* wieder auf den Boden der Tatsachen (zurück)kommen; **to bring sb down to ~ (with a bump)** *(fig)* jdn (unsanft) wieder auf den Boden der Tatsachen zurückholen

c *(= soil)* Erde *f*

d *(Brit Elec)* Erde *f*

e *(of fox, badger etc)* Bau *m*; **to go to ~** *(Brit) (fox)* im Bau verschwinden; *(criminal etc)* untertauchen; **to run sb/sth to ~** *(Brit fig)* jdn/etw ausfindig machen *or* aufstöbern

VT *(Brit Elec)* erden

▸ **earth up** VT *sep plant* ausgraben

earth: **earthbound** [ˈɜːθbaʊnd] ADJ erdgebunden; **earth closet** N Trockenabort *m*

earthen [ˈɜːθən] ADJ irden

earthenware [ˈɜːθənwɛəʳ] N *(= material)* Ton *m*; *(= dishes etc)* Tongeschirr *nt* ADJ aus Ton, Ton-; **~ crockery** Tongeschirr *nt*

ear thermometer N *(Med)* Ohrthermometer *nt*

earthiness [ˈɜːθɪnɪs] N Derbheit *f*; *(of person)* Urtümlichkeit *f*

earthling [ˈɜːθlɪŋ] N *(pej)* Erdenwurm *m*

earthly [ˈɜːθlɪ] ADJ **a** *(= of this world)* irdisch **b** *(inf: = possible)* **there is no ~ reason to think …** es besteht nicht der geringste Grund für die Annahme …; **there's no ~ reason why …** es gibt nicht den geringsten Grund, warum …; **this thing is of no ~ use** das Ding hat nicht den geringsten Nutzen N *(inf)* **she doesn't stand an ~** sie hat nicht die geringste Chance

earth: **earthman** N *(Sci-Fi)* Erdenmensch *m*, Terraner(in) *m(f)*; **earth mother** N *(Myth)* Erdmutter *f*; *(fig)* Urmutter *f*; **earth-moving equipment** N Maschinen *pl* für Erdbewegungen; **earthperson** N *(Sci-Fi)* Erdbewohner(in) *m(f)*; **earthquake** N Erdbeben *nt*; **earth sciences** PL Geowissenschaften *pl*; **earth-shattering** ADJ *(fig)* welterschütternd; **earth tremor** N Erdstoß *m*; **earthward** ADJ in Richtung Erde; **in an ~ direction** in Richtung Erde ADV (*also* **earthwards**) in Richtung Erde; **earthwork** N *(Build)* Erdarbeiten *pl*; *(Mil)* Schanzwerk *nt*, Schanze *f*; **earthworm** N Regenwurm *m*

earthy [ˈɜːθɪ] ADJ **a** *colour* erdfarben; *flavour, smell* erdig; **~ browns** erdfarbene Brauntöne *pl*

b *(fig) person* urtümlich; *humour, language, book, play* derb; *approach* robust

ear: **ear trumpet** N Hörrohr *nt*; **earwax** N Ohrenschmalz *nt*; **earwig** N Ohrwurm *m*; **earwitness** N Ohrenzeuge *m*/-zeugin *f* (*to gen*)

ease [iːz] N **a** *(= freedom from discomfort)* Behagen *nt*; **I never feel at ~ in this dress** ich fühle mich in diesem Kleid nie ganz wohl; **I've never felt at ~ with computers** Computer waren mir nie so richtig geheuer; **I am never at ~ in his company** in seiner Gesellschaft fühle ich mich immer befangen *or* fühle ich mich nie frei und ungezwungen; **to be** *or* **feel at ~ with oneself** sich (in seiner Haut) wohlfühlen; **to put** *or* **set sb at (his/her) ~** jdm die Befangenheit nehmen; **to put** *or* **set sb's mind at ~** jdn beruhigen; **my mind is at ~ now** jetzt bin ich beruhigt; **to take one's ~** es sich *(dat)* bequem machen; **(stand) at ~!** *(Mil)* rührt euch! → **ill-at-ease**

b *(= absence of difficulty)* Leichtigkeit *f*; **with (the greatest of) ~** mit (größter) Leichtigkeit; **for ~ of use/access/reference** um die Benutzung/den Zugang/das Nachschlagen zu erleichtern

c *(= absence of work)* Muße *f*; **he lives a life of ~** er führt ein Leben der Muße

VT **a** *(= relieve) pain* lindern; *mind* erleichtern; **to ~ the burden on sb** jdm eine Last abnehmen

b *(= make less, loosen) rope, strap* lockern, nachlassen; *dress etc* weiter machen; *pressure, tension* verringern; *situation* entspannen; *fears* zerstreuen; *problem* abhelfen (+*dat*)

c to ~ a key into a lock einen Schlüssel behutsam in ein Schloss stecken *or* einführen; **to ~ off the clutch** *(Aut)* die Kupplung behutsam kommen lassen; **he ~d the car into gear** er legte behutsam einen Gang ein; **he ~d the lid off** er löste den Deckel behutsam ab; **he ~d his broken leg up onto the stretcher** er hob sein gebrochenes Bein behutsam auf die Trage; **he ~d his way toward(s) the door** *(= slowly)* er bewegte sich langsam zur Tür; *(= unobtrusively)* er bewegte sich unauffällig zur Tür; **he ~d his way through the hole** er schob sich vorsichtig durch das Loch

VI nachlassen; *(situation)* sich entspannen; *(prices)* nachgeben; **he ~d down into second gear** er schaltete behutsam in den zweiten Gang zurück

▸ **ease off** *or* **up** VI **a** *(= slow down, relax)* langsamer werden; *(driver)* verlangsamen; *(situation)* sich entspannen; **ease up a bit!** (etwas) langsamer!, sachte, sachte!; **the doctor told him to ease up a bit at work** der Arzt riet ihm, bei der Arbeit etwas kürzer zu treten; **things usually ease up a little just after Christmas** nach Weihnachten wird es normalerweise etwas ruhiger *or* geruhsamer; **there'll be no easing up until we've finished!** es wird keine Ruhepause geben, bis wir fertig sind **b** *(pain, rain)* nachlassen

easel [ˈiːzl] N Staffelei *f*

easily [ˈiːzɪlɪ] ADV **a** *(= without difficulty)* leicht; **~ accessible** *(place)* leicht zu erreichen; **they now have ~ available travel** sie können jetzt ohne Schwierigkeiten reisen; **he learnt to swim ~** er lernte mühelos schwimmen

b *(= possibly) can, may* leicht; *could, might* gut; **dishwashers can ~ ruin hand-painted china** Spülmaschinen können handbemaltes Porzellan leicht ruinieren; **she might/could ~ decide to cancel** es könnte gut sein, dass sie sich entscheidet abzusagen; **it could just as ~ happen here** es könnte genauso gut hier passieren

c *(= unquestionably, with figures)* gut und gerne; (+ *superl*) eindeutig, mit Abstand; **it's ~ 25 miles** es sind gut und gerne 25 Meilen; **they are ~ the best** sie sind eindeutig *or* mit Abstand die Besten

d *(= in a relaxed manner) talk, breathe* ganz entspannt

easiness [ˈiːzɪnɪs] N Leichtigkeit *f*

east [i:st] **N** **the ~, the East** *(also Pol)* der Osten; **in the ~** im Osten; **to the ~** nach *or* gen *(liter)* Osten; **to the ~ of** östlich von, im Osten von; **the wind is coming from the ~** der Wind kommt von Ost(en) *or* aus (dem) Osten; **the ~ of France** der Osten Frankreichs, das östliche Frankreich; **the south and ~ of the square** die Südseite und die Ostseite des Platzes; **East-West relations** Ost-West-Beziehungen *pl*; **of/between East and West** von/zwischen Osten und Westen → *also* **Far East, Middle East, Near East**
ADV *(= eastward)* nach Osten, ostwärts; **the kitchen faces ~** die Küche liegt nach Osten; **~ of Paris/the river** östlich von Paris/des Flusses
ADJ Ost-; **~ coast** Ostküste *f*; **~ wind** Ostwind *m*; **~ window** Ostfenster *nt*; **Salford East** Salford Ost

east: **East Africa** N Ostafrika *nt*; **East Anglia** N *die englischen Grafschaften Norfolk und Suffolk sowie Teile von Essex und Cambridgeshire*; **East Asia** N Ostasien *nt*; **East Berlin** N Ostberlin *nt*; **East Berliner** N Ostberliner(in) *m(f)*; **eastbound** **ADJ** (in) Richtung Osten; **the ~ carriageway of the M4** *(Brit)* die M4 in Richtung Osten; **to be ~** nach Osten unterwegs sein, ostwärts fahren **ADV** nach Osten, (in) Richtung Osten; **East End** N **the ~** der (Londoner) Osten; **East Ender** N Bewohner(in) *m(f)* des Londoner Ostens

Easter ['i:stəʳ] **N** Ostern *nt*; **at ~** an *or* zu Ostern
ADJ *attr* Oster-

Easter: **Easter bunny** N Osterhase *m*; **Easter Day** N Ostersonntag *m*; **Easter egg** N Osterei *nt*; **Easter Island** N Osterinsel *f*

easterly ['i:stəlɪ] **ADJ** östlich, Ost-; **an ~ wind** ein Ostwind *m*, ein Wind *m* aus östlicher Richtung; **in an ~ direction** in östlicher Richtung **N** *(= wind)* Ostwind *m*, Ost *m (poet)*
ADV nach Osten

Easter Monday N Ostermontag *m*

eastern ['i:stən] ADJ Ost-, östlich; *attitude* orientalisch; **the Eastern bloc** *(Hist)* der Ostblock *(Hist) (neg!)*; **Eastern Europe** Osteuropa *nt*

easterner ['i:stənəʳ] N *(esp US)* Oststaatler(in) *m(f)*; **he's an ~** er kommt aus dem Osten

easternmost ['i:stənməʊst] ADJ östlichste(r, s)

Easter Sunday N Ostersonntag *m*

east: **East Europe** N *(esp US)* Osteuropa *nt*; **East European** **ADJ** osteuropäisch **N** Osteuropäer(in) *m(f)*; **East German** **ADJ** ostdeutsch; **the ~ government** *(Hist)* die Regierung der DDR **N** Ostdeutsche(r) *mf*; **East Germany** N Ostdeutschland *nt*; *(= GDR)* die DDR; **East Indian** ADJ ostindisch; *(= East Caribbean)* ostkaribisch; **East Indies** PL Ostindien *nt (old)*, die Malaiische Archipel; **east-northeast** **N** Ostnordosten *m* **ADV** nach Ostnordosten; **~ of Munich/the lake** ostnordöstlich von München/des Sees; **East Side** N **the (Lower) ~** die East Side *(der Osten von Manhattan)*; **east-southeast** **N** Ostsüdosten *m* **ADV** nach Ostsüdosten; **~ of Munich/the lake** ostsüdöstlich von München/des Sees; **East Timor** N Osttimor *nt*; **eastward** **ADV** *(also* **eastwards***)* ostwärts, nach Osten, (in) Richtung Osten **ADJ** *direction* östlich; *route* nach Osten, (in) Richtung Osten; **eastwardly** ADV ADJ = **eastward**

easy ['i:zɪ] **ADJ** *(+er)* **a** *(= simple)* leicht; *task, job* leicht, einfach; *option, solution, answer* einfach; **finding somewhere to eat is an ~ task** es ist leicht *or* einfach, ein Restaurant zu finden; **it's no ~ task** es ist nicht einfach; **it's ~ to forget that ...** man vergisst leicht, dass ...; **it's ~ for her** sie hat es leicht; **it's ~ for her to do it** sie kann es leicht tun; **that's ~ for you to say** du hast gut reden; **to make ~ reading** leicht zu lesen sein; **he was an ~ winner** er hat mühelos gewonnen; **to be far from ~** *or* **none too ~** alles andere als leicht sein, nicht gerade leicht sein; **that's the ~ part** das ist das Einfache; **it's an ~ (enough) mistake to make** den Fehler kann man leicht machen, das kann einem leicht passieren; **to be within ~ reach of sth** etw leicht erreichen können; **in** *or* **by ~ stages** *(= step by step)* Schritt für Schritt; *(= gradually)* nach und nach; **as ~ as pie** *or* **as ABC** *or* **as falling off a log** kinderleicht; **easier said than done** leichter gesagt als getan; **~ credit** leicht erhältliche Kredite; **on ~ terms** *(Comm)* zu günstigen Bedingungen; **to go for the ~ option, to take the ~ way out** es sich *(dat)* leicht machen; **she is ~ to work with/get on with** mit ihr kann man gut arbeiten/auskommen; **she opted for the ~ life** sie machte sich *(dat)* das Leben leicht; **~ living** ein sorgenfreies Leben; **to have it ~, to have an ~ time (of it)** es leicht haben; **to have an ~ ride** es leicht haben; **he will not be given an ~ ride** man wird es ihm nicht leicht machen; **~ prey** eine leichte Beute; **to be ~ meat** *(inf)* eine leichte Beute sein
b *(= not harsh)* **to be ~ on the eye/ear** angenehm anzusehen/anzuhören sein; **he/she is ~ on the eye** *(inf)* er/sie sieht gut aus; **to be ~ on the stomach** leicht verdaulich sein
c *(= relaxed) temperament, conversation, laugh, smile, voice* ungezwungen; *relationship* unbefangen; *tone* lässig; **at an ~ pace** in gemütlichem Tempo; **he had a quick and ~ laugh** er lachte schnell und ungezwungen; **to be on ~ terms with sb** mit jdm auf vertrautem Fuß stehen; **I'm ~** *(Brit inf)* mir ist alles recht, ist mir egal *(inf)*; **stand ~!** *(Brit Mil)* rührt euch!; **I don't feel ~ about it** *(= uncomfortable)* es ist mir nicht recht, mir ist dabei nicht wohl
d *(pej inf: = promiscuous)* **she's ~** sie ist immer zu haben; **she wasn't like the ~ girls he had known** sie war anders als die leichten Mädchen, die er gekannt hatte; **to be an ~ make** *(US) or* **lay** *(sl)* jeden ranlassen *(inf)*; **woman of ~ virtue** *(dated euph, = prostitute)* Freudenmädchen *nt*
ADV *(inf)* **to go ~ on sb** nicht so streng mit jdm sein; **to go ~ on sth** mit etw sparsam umgehen; **to go ~ on the brakes/one's liver** die Bremsen/seine Leber schonen; **to take it ~, to take things ~** *(= rest)* sich schonen; **take it ~!** *(= calm down)* immer mit der Ruhe!; *(esp US, when saying goodbye)* machs gut!; **~ does it** immer sachte

easy: **easy-care** ADJ pflegeleicht; **easy chair** N Sessel *m*; **easy come, easy go** INTERJ wie gewonnen, so zerronnen *(Prov)*; **easy-come easy-go** ADJ unbekümmert; **easy-going** ADJ *(= not anxious)* gelassen; *(= lax)* lax, lässig; **easy listening** N leichte Musik, Unterhaltungsmusik *f*; **easy-listening** ADJ *album, CD* mit leichter Musik, mit Unterhaltungsmusik; **~ music** leichte Musik, Unterhaltungsmusik *f*; **easy money** N leicht verdientes Geld; **you can make ~** Sie können leicht Geld machen; **easy-on-the-pocket** ADJ erschwinglich; **easy-peasy** [,i:zɪ'pi:zɪ] ADJ *(Brit inf, baby-talk)* kinderleicht; **easy street** N *(inf)* **to be on ~** im Wohlstand leben; **easy touch** N **to be an ~** *(inf)* nicht nein *or* Nein sagen können

eat [i:t] *vb: pret* **ate**, *ptp* **eaten** **VT** *(person)* essen, fressen *(pej inf)*; *(animal)* fressen; **to ~ one's breakfast** frühstücken; **to ~ one's lunch/dinner** zu Mittag/Abend essen; **he ate his way through ...** er aß sich durch ...; **he's ~ing us out of house and home** *(inf)* der isst *or* frisst uns noch arm *or* die Haare vom Kopf *(inf)*; **to ~ one's words** (alles,) was man gesagt hat, zurücknehmen; **he was forced to ~ his words** er musste alles zurücknehmen; **he won't ~ you** *(inf)* er wird dich schon nicht fressen *(inf)*; **what's ~ing you?** *(inf)* was hast du denn? → **alive a**
VI essen, fressen *(pej inf)*; *(animal)* fressen; **I haven't ~en for ages** ich habe schon ewig nichts mehr gegessen
N *(inf)* **eats** **PL** Fressalien *pl (inf)*; **time for ~s!** Fütterung der Raubtiere! *(inf)*

▸ **eat away** VT *sep (sea)* auswaschen; *(acid)* zerfressen

▸ **eat away at** VI *+prep obj* **a** *(waves, sea)* auswaschen; *(acid, rust, pest)* anfressen; *(rot, damp)* angreifen **b** *(fig) revenue* auffressen; *finances* angreifen; *society* zerstören

▸ **eat into** VI *+prep obj metal* anfressen; *capital* angreifen; *market share, profits* verringern; *life, time* verkürzen

▸ **eat out** **VI** zum Essen ausgehen **VT** *sep* **to eat one's heart out** Trübsal blasen, sich vor Gram verzehren *(geh)*; **Michael Parkinson, eat your heart out** Michael Parkinson, da kannst du vor Neid erblassen

▸ **eat out of** VI *+prep obj* **she had them eating out of her hand** *(fig)* sie fraßen ihr aus der Hand

▸ **eat up** **VT** *sep* **a** *(lit)* aufessen; *(animal)* auffressen **b** *(fig: = use up, consume)* verbrauchen, fressen *(inf)*; **this car eats up the miles** der Wagen gibt ganz schön was her *(inf)* **c** **he was eaten up with envy** der Neid nagte *or* zehrte an ihm **VI** aufessen

eatable ['i:təbl] ADJ essbar, genießbar

eat-by date ['i:tbaɪdeɪt] N Haltbarkeitsdatum *nt*

eaten ['i:tn] *ptp of* **eat**

eater ['i:təʳ] N **a** Esser(in) *m(f)* **b** *(= apple)* Essapfel *m*

eatery ['i:tərɪ] N *(hum inf: = restaurant etc)* Esslokal *nt*, Fresslokal *nt (hum inf)*

eating ['i:tɪŋ] N Essen *nt*; **to make good ~** gut zum Essen sein

eating: **eating apple** N Essapfel *m*; **eating disorder** N Essstörung *f*; **eating house** N Gasthaus *nt*; **eating place** N Esslokal *nt*

eau de Cologne ['əʊdəkə'ləʊn] N Kölnischwasser *nt*, Eau de Cologne *nt*

eaves ['i:vz] PL Dachvorsprung *m*

eavesdrop ['i:vzdrɒp] VI (heimlich) lauschen; **to ~ on a conversation** ein Gespräch belauschen

eavesdropper ['i:vzdrɒpəʳ] N Lauscher(in) *m(f)*

eavesdropping ['i:vzdrɒpɪŋ] N heimliches Lauschen *or* Horchen; **electronic ~** *(esp Pol)* Lauschangriff *m* *(on* auf *+acc)*, Lauschoperation *f* *(on* gegen)

ebb [eb] **N** Ebbe *f*; **the tide is on the ~** es ist Ebbe; **~ and flow** Ebbe und Flut *f*; *(fig)* Auf und Ab *nt*; **at a low ~** *(fig)* auf einem Tiefstand; **their popularity is at its lowest ~** ihre Beliebtheit hat einen absoluten Tiefpunkt erreicht **VI** **a** *(tide)* zurückgehen; **to ~ and flow** *(lit, fig)* kommen und gehen **b** *(fig: also* **ebb away***, enthusiasm etc)* abebben, verebben; *(life)* zu Ende gehen

ebb tide N Ebbe *f*

EBIT *(Econ, Comm) abbr of* **earnings before interest and taxes** EBIT, Ebit *nt*, Ergebnis *nt* vor Zinsen und Steuern

EBITDA *(Econ, Comm) abbr of* **earnings before interest, taxes, depreciation and amortization** EBITDA, Ebitda *nt*, Ergebnis *nt* vor Zinsen, Steuern, Abschreibungen auf Sachanlagen und Abschreibungen auf immaterielle Vermögenswerte

Ebola [ɪ'bəʊlə], **Ebola virus** N *(Med)* Ebola-Virus *nt or m*, Eboloavirus *nt or m*

ebonite ['ebənaɪt] N Ebonit *nt*

ebony ['ebənɪ] **N** Ebenholz *nt* **ADJ** *colour* schwarz wie Ebenholz; *material* aus Ebenholz; *hair, face* ebenholzfarben

e-book ['i:bʊk] N Onlinebuch *nt*

EBT *(Econ, Comm) abbr of* **earnings before taxes** EBT *nt*, Ergebnis *nt* vor Steuern

ebullience [ɪ'bʌlɪəns] N Überschwänglichkeit *f*

ebullient [ɪ'bʌlɪənt] ADJ *person* überschwänglich; *spirits, mood* übersprudelnd; *optimism* unbändig

e-business [,i:'bɪznɪs] N **a** *(= company)* Internetfirma *f* **b** *(= commerce)* E-Business *nt*, elektronischer Geschäftsverkehr

EC *abbr of* **European Community** EG *f*

e-card ['i:kɑ:d] N *abbr of* **electronic card** E-Card *f*, elektronische Grußkarte

e-cash [ˈi:kæʃ] N E-Cash *nt*, elektronische Geldüberweisung

ECB *abbr of* **European Central Bank** EZB *f*

eccentric [ɪkˈsentrɪk] **ADJ** *(also Tech)* exzentrisch; *taste* ausgefallen **N** **a** *(= oddball)* Exzentriker(in) *m(f)* **b** *(Tech)* Exzenter *m*

eccentrically [ɪkˈsentrɪkəlɪ] ADV *(also Tech)* exzentrisch; *dress, decorate* ausgefallen; **she ~ rejected it** merkwürdigerweise war sie dagegen

eccentricity [ˌeksənˈtrɪsɪtɪ] N *(all senses)* Exzentrizität *f*

Eccles cake [ˈekəlzˌkeɪk] N *(Brit) mit Dörrobst gefülltes Gebäck*

Ecclesiastes [ɪˌkli:zɪˈæsti:z] N (der Prediger) Salomo *m*

ecclesiastic [ɪˌkli:zɪˈæstɪk] N Kleriker *m*

ecclesiastical [ɪˌkli:zɪˈæstɪkəl] ADJ kirchlich

ECG *abbr of* **electrocardiogram** EKG *nt*

echelon [ˈeʃəlɒn] N *(Mil, = formation)* Staffelung *f*, Echelon *m (old)*; **the higher ~s** die höheren Ränge *pl*

echo [ˈekəʊ] **N** Echo *nt*, Widerhall *m*; *(fig)* Anklang *m (of* an *+acc)*; *(Comput: command)* Echo *nt*; **he was cheered to the ~** er bekam brausenden *or* rauschenden Beifall **VT** *sound* zurückwerfen; *(fig)* wiedergeben **VI** *(sounds)* widerhallen; *(room, footsteps)* hallen; **to ~ with sth** von etw widerhallen; **her words ~ed in his ears** ihre Worte hallten ihm in den Ohren

echo: echo chamber N Hallraum *m*; *(for electric guitar)* Nachhallerzeuger *m*; **echolocation** [ˌekəʊləʊˈkeɪʃən] N Echoortung *f*; **echo sounder** N Echolot *nt*

ECJ N ABBR *of* **European Court of Justice** Europäischer Gerichtshof

éclair [eɪˈklɛəˈ] N Eclair *nt*, Liebesknochen *m*

eclampsia [ɪˈklæmpsɪə] N *(Med)* Eklampsie *f*

eclectic [ɪˈklektɪk] ADJ eklektisch

eclecticism [ɪˈklektɪsɪzəm] N Eklektizismus *m*

eclipse [ɪˈklɪps] **N** *(Astron)* Eklipse *f (spec)*, Finsternis *f*; *(fig) (of fame, theory)* Verblassen *nt*; *(of person)* Niedergang *m*; **~ of the sun/moon** Sonnen-/Mondfinsternis *f*; **to be in ~** *(sun, moon)* verfinstert sein; *(fig)* in der Versenkung verschwunden sein **VT** *(fig)* in den Schatten stellen

eco- [ˈi:kəʊ-] PREF Öko-, öko-

ecocide [ˈi:kəʊsaɪd] N Umweltzerstörung *f*

ecoconscious [ˌi:kəʊˈkɒnʃəs] ADJ ökobewusst, umweltbewusst

ecofriendly [ˌi:kəʊˈfrendlɪ] ADJ *(Brit)* umweltfreundlich

ecohome [ˈi:kəʊhəʊm] N Ökohaus *nt*

eco label N Ökosiegel *nt*

E.coli [i:ˈkəʊlaɪ] N *(Med)* E-coli *f*

ecological [ˌi:kəʊˈlɒdʒɪkəl] ADJ *problem, balance, impact* ökologisch; **~ disaster** Umweltkatastrophe *f*; **~ damage** Umweltschäden *pl*; **~ system** Ökosystem *nt*; **~ group** Umweltorganisation *f*; **~ party** Umweltpartei *f*

ecologically [ˌi:kəʊˈlɒdʒɪkəlɪ] ADV ökologisch; **~ harmful** umweltschädlich; **~ minded/aware** umweltbewusst

ecologist [ɪˈkɒlədʒɪst] N Ökologe *m*, Ökologin *f*

ecology [ɪˈkɒlədʒɪ] N Ökologie *f*

e-commerce [ˈi:ˈkɒmɜ:s] N Onlinehandel *m*, E-Commerce *m*

economic [ˌi:kəˈnɒmɪk] ADJ **a** *(= financial)* Wirtschafts-; **~ crisis** Wirtschaftskrise *f*; **~ growth** Wirtschaftswachstum *nt*; **~ news** Nachrichten *pl* aus der Wirtschaft; **~ policy** Wirtschaftspolitik *f*; **~ recovery** Wirtschaftsaufschwung *m*, wirtschaftlicher Aufschwung; **~ system** Wirtschaftssystem *nt* **b** *(= cost-effective) price, rent* wirtschaftlich; *system* wirtschaftlich, rentabel; **it is not ~ to do this** es ist nicht rentabel, das zu tun; **to be ~ for sb** sich für jdn rentieren

economic aid N Wirtschaftshilfe *f*

economical [ˌi:kəˈnɒmɪkəl] ADJ sparsam, wirtschaftlich; **to be ~ with sth** mit etw haushalten *or* Haus halten, mit etw sparsam umgehen; **they were ~ with the truth** sie haben es mit der Wahrheit nicht so genau genommen; **an ~ style** *(Liter)* ein prägnanter Stil

economically [ˌi:kəˈnɒmɪkəlɪ] ADV **a** *(= financially) depressed, powerful, important* wirtschaftlich; **after the war, the country suffered ~** nach dem Krieg litt die Wirtschaft des Landes; **we can't compete ~** unsere Wirtschaft ist nicht konkurrenzfähig; **~ viable** rentabel; **the most ~ powerful state** die größte Wirtschaftsmacht **b** *(= thriftily)* sparsam; **to use sth ~** mit etw wirtschaftlich *or* sparsam umgehen **c** *(= in few words)* prägnant; **to get the point across ~** das Argument knapp fassen

economic indicator N Wirtschaftsindikator *m*

economic migrant, economic refugee N Wirtschaftsflüchtling *m (neg!)*

economics [ˌi:kəˈnɒmɪks] N **a** *sing or pl* Volkswirtschaft *f*, Wirtschaftswissenschaften *pl*; *(= social economics)* Volkswirtschaft *f*; *(in management studies)* Betriebswirtschaft *f* **b** *pl (= economic aspect)* Wirtschaftlichkeit *f*, Ökonomie *f*; **the ~ of the situation** die wirtschaftliche Seite der Situation

economist [ɪˈkɒnəmɪst] N Wirtschaftswissenschaftler(in) *m(f)*; *(= social economist)* Volkswirt(in) *m(f)*, Volkswirtschaftler(in) *m(f)*; *(in management studies)* Betriebswirt(in) *m(f)*, Betriebswirtschaftler(in) *m(f)*

economize [ɪˈkɒnəmaɪz] VI sparen

▶ **economize on** VI *+prep obj* sparen

economy [ɪˈkɒnəmɪ] N **a** *(system)* Wirtschaft *f no pl*; *(from a monetary aspect)* Konjunktur *f*; **what is the state of the ~?** wie ist die Wirtschaftslage/Konjunktur? **b** *(= saving: in time, money)* Sparmaßnahme *f*, Einsparung *f*; **fuel ~** geringer Kraftstoffverbrauch; **a false ~** falsche Sparsamkeit; **economies of scale** Einsparungen *pl* durch erhöhte Produktion; **to make economies** zu Sparmaßnahmen greifen, Einsparungen machen **c** *(= thrift)* Sparsamkeit *f*; **to practise** *(Brit) or* **practice** *(US)* **~** Sparsamkeit walten lassen; **~ of language/expression** knappe Sprache/Ausdrucksweise; **with ~ of effort** mit sparsamem Kräfteaufwand

economy: economy class N Touristenklasse *f*; **economy drive** N Sparmaßnahmen *pl*; **we'll have to have an ~** wir werden Sparmaßnahmen ergreifen müssen; **economy rate** N Spartarif *m*; **economy size** N Sparpackung *f*

eco: ecosphere N Ökosphäre *f*; **ecosystem** N Ökosystem *nt*; **ecotourism** N Ökotourismus *m*; **eco-warrior** N *(inf)* Ökokämpfer(in) *m(f)*

ecru [eˈkru:] ADJ naturfarben, ekrü

ecstasy [ˈekstəsɪ] N **a** Ekstase *f*, Verzückung *f*; **to be in ~** ekstatisch *or* verzückt sein; **to go into ecstasies over sth** über etw *(acc)* in Ekstase *or* Verzückung geraten; **~! she sighed** welche Wonne! seufzte sie **b** *(= drug)* Ecstasy *nt*

ecstatic ADJ [eksˈtætɪk] ekstatisch, verzückt

ecstatically [eksˈtætɪkəlɪ] ADV ekstatisch; *listen also* verzückt; **~ happy** überglücklich

ECT *abbr of* **electroconvulsive therapy** Elektroschock *m*, Elektrokrampftherapie *f*

ectomorph [ˈektəʊmɔ:f] N ektomorpher Konstitutionstyp

ectopic [ekˈtɒpɪk] ADJ **~ pregnancy** ektopische *or* ektope Schwangerschaft

ectoplasm [ˈektəʊplæzəm] N Ektoplasma *nt*

ECU, ecu [ˈeɪkju:] N *abbr of* **European Currency Unit** ECU *m*, Ecu *m*

Ecuador [ˈekwədɔ:ˈ] N Ecuador *nt*, Ekuador *nt*

Ecuador(i)an [ˌekwəˈdɔ:r(ɪ)ən] **ADJ** ecuadorianisch, ekuadorianisch **N** Ecuadorianer(in) *m(f)*, Ekuadorianer(in) *m(f)*

ecumenical [ˌi:kjʊˈmenɪkəl] ADJ *(form)* ökumenisch; **~ council** Ökumenischer Rat

ecumenically [ˌi:kjʊˈmenɪkəlɪ] ADV *(form)* ökumenisch; *(introducing a sentence)* vom ökumenischen Standpunkt aus

ecumenicism [ˌi:kjʊˈmenɪsɪzm] N *(form)* Ökumenismus *m*

eczema [ˈeksɪmə] N Ekzem *nt*, (Haut)ausschlag *m*

ED [i:ˈdi:] *abbr of* **emergency department**

ed **a** *abbr of* **editor** Hrsg., Herausgeber(in) *m(f)* **b** *abbr of* **edition** Ausg., Ausgabe *f* **c** *abbr of* **edited** hg., herausgegeben

Edam [ˈi:dæm] N Edamer (Käse) *m*

eddy [ˈedɪ] **N** Wirbel *m*; *(of water also)* Strudel *m*; **the wind swept up eddies of dust** der Wind wirbelte Staubwolken auf **VI** wirbeln; *(water also)* strudeln

edelweiss [ˈeɪdlvaɪs] N Edelweiß *nt*

edema [ɪˈdi:mə] N *(esp US)* Ödem *nt*

Eden [ˈi:dn] N *(also fig)* **Garden of ~** Garten *m* Eden

edge [edʒ] **N** **a** *(of knife, razor)* Schneide *f*; **to take the ~ off sth** *(fig, sensation)* etw der Wirkung *(gen)* berauben; *pain* etw lindern; **that took the ~ off my appetite** das nahm mir erst einmal den Hunger; **the noise sets my teeth on ~** das Geräusch geht mir durch und durch; **his arrogance sets my teeth on ~** seine Arroganz bringt mich auf die Palme *(inf)*; **to be on ~** nervös sein; **my nerves are on ~** ich bin schrecklich nervös; **there was an ~ to his voice** seine Stimme klang ärgerlich; **to have the ~ on sb/sth** jdm/etw überlegen sein; **but the professional had the ~** aber der Profi war eben besser; **it gives her/it that extra ~** darin besteht eben der kleine Unterschied; **to lose one's ~** seine Überlegenheit verlieren

b *(= outer limit)* Rand *m*; *(of brick, cube)* Kante *f*; *(of lake, river)* Ufer *nt*, Rand *m*; *(of sea)* Ufer *nt*; *(of estates etc)* Grenze *f*; **a book with gilt ~s** ein Buch mit Goldschnitt; **the trees at the ~ of the road** die Bäume am Straßenrand; **the film had us on the ~ of our seats** der Film war unheimlich spannend; **to be on the ~ of disaster** am Rande des Untergangs stehen; **to live life on the ~** gefährlich leben; **rough ~s** *(fig)* kleine Mängel *pl*

VT **a** *(= put a border on)* besetzen, einfassen; **to ~ a coat with fur** einen Mantel mit Pelz verbrämen; **~d in black** mit einem schwarzen Rand

b *(= sharpen) tool, blade* schärfen, schleifen, scharf machen

c **to ~ one's way toward(s) sth** *(slowly)* sich allmählich auf etw *(acc)* zubewegen; *(carefully)* sich vorsichtig auf etw *(acc)* zubewegen; **she ~d her way through the crowd** sie schlängelte sich durch die Menge; **the prisoner ~d his way along the wall** der Gefangene schob sich langsam an der Wand entlang

VI sich schieben; **to ~ toward(s) the door** sich zur Tür stehlen; **to ~ away** sich davonstehlen; **to ~ away from sb/sth** sich allmählich immer weiter von jdm/etw entfernen; **to ~ up to sb** sich an jdn heranmachen; **he ~d past me** er drückte *or* schob sich an mir vorbei

▶ **edge out** **VT** *sep (of job, position etc)* beiseitedrängen; **Germany edged England out of the final** Deutschland verdrängte England aus dem Endspiel **VI** **she edged out onto the balcony** sie tastete sich auf den Balkon vor; **the driver edged out onto the main road** der Fahrer fuhr vorsichtig auf die Hauptstraße

▶ **edge up** **VT** *sep prices etc* hochdrücken **VI** *(prices etc)* hochgehen

edgeways [ˈedʒweɪz] ADV mit der Schmalseite voran; **I couldn't get a word in ~** ich bin überhaupt nicht zu Wort gekommen

edginess [ˈedʒɪnɪs] N Nervosität *f*

edging [ˈedʒɪŋ] N Borte *f*, Einfassung *f*

edging shears PL Rasenschere *f*

edgy [ˈedʒɪ] ADJ *(+er) person* nervös

edibility [ˌedɪˈbɪlɪtɪ] N Essbarkeit *f*, Genießbarkeit *f*

edible [ˈedɪbl] ADJ essbar, genießbar; **very ~!** durchaus genießbar!

edict [ˈiːdɪkt] N Erlass *m*; *(Hist)* Edikt *nt*

edification [ˌedɪfɪˈkeɪʃən] N Erbauung *f*; **for the ~ of …** zur Erbauung des/der …

edifice [ˈedɪfɪs] N *(lit, fig)* Gebäude *nt*; *(fig also)* Gefüge *nt*

edify [ˈedɪfaɪ] VT erbauen

edifying [ˈedɪfaɪɪŋ] ADJ erbaulich; **this is not a very ~ spectacle** das ist kein besonders erbaulicher Anblick

Edinburgh [ˈedɪnbərə] N Edinburg(h) *nt*

> **EDINBURGH FESTIVAL**
>
> Das **Edinburgh Festival** findet jedes Jahr im August statt. Es dauert drei Wochen und ist mittlerweile eines der größten Kunst- und Theaterfestivals der Welt. Neben dem offiziellen Festivalprogramm, in dem Künstler internationalen Ranges präsentiert werden, gibt es auch noch das Edinburgh Festival **Fringe**, wo man eine riesige Palette der verschiedensten Kunstformen vom Traditionellen über das Abenteuerliche bis hin zum Bizarren erleben kann. Zur selben Zeit wie das Internationale Festival und das **Fringe** findet im Edinburgh Castle der **Military Tattoo**, ein Treffen internationaler Dudelsackgruppen, statt.

edit [ˈedɪt] VT *series, author, newspaper, magazine* herausgeben, edieren; *newspaper story, book, text* redigieren, bearbeiten; *film, tape* schneiden, cutten; *(Comput)* editieren, bearbeiten; **~ed by: …** *(Film)* Schnitt: … VI redigieren, redaktionell arbeiten

► **edit out** VT *sep* herausnehmen; *(from film, tape)* herausschneiden; *character (from story)* herausstreichen

editable [ˈedɪtəbl] ADJ *(Comput) file* editierbar

editing [ˈedɪtɪŋ] N *(of series, author, newspaper, magazine)* Herausgabe *f*, Edieren *nt*; *(of newspaper story, book, text)* Redaktion *f*, Bearbeitung *f*; *(of film, tape)* Schnitt *m*; *(Comput)* Editieren *nt*

edition [ɪˈdɪʃən] N Ausgabe *f*, Edition *f*; *(= impression)* Auflage *f*

editor [ˈedɪtəʳ] N *(of text, newspaper, magazine, series, author)* Herausgeber(in) *m(f)*; *(publisher's)* (Verlags)lektor(in) *m(f)*; *(Film)* Cutter(in) *m(f)*; *(Comput)* Editor *m*; **political ~** politischer Redakteur *m*, politische Redakteurin *f*; **sports ~** Sportredakteur(in) *m(f)*; **~ in chief** Herausgeber(in) *m(f)*; *(of newspaper)* Chefredakteur(in) *m(f)*; **the ~s in our educational department** die Redaktion unserer Schulbuchabteilung; **the ~ of this passage obviously misunderstood** der, der diese Stelle redigierte, hat offensichtlich nicht richtig verstanden

editorial [ˌedɪˈtɔːrɪəl] ADJ **a** *(= editing) work, task, budget, board* redaktionell; **~ department** *or* **office** Redaktion *f*; **~ staff** Redaktionsangestellte *pl*; *(= department)* Redaktion *f*; **~ meeting** Redaktionsbesprechung *f* **b** *(= involving opinions) control, problems, questions* redaktionell; **~ page** Kommentarseite *f*; **the ~ pages** der Kommentarteil; **the paper's ~ policy** die redaktionelle Linie der Zeitung N **a** *(= article)* Leitartikel *m* **b** *(= department)* Redaktion *f*

editorial assistant N Redaktionsassistent(in) *m(f)*

editorial comment N *(Press)* Kommentare *pl* der Redaktion; *(= leaders)* Leitartikel *pl*

editorially [ˌedɪˈtɔːrɪəlɪ] ADV redaktionell; *(= as an editor)* als Redakteur(in); **we are not able to comment ~** wir können keine redaktionellen Kommentare abgeben; **~ the paper will focus on Europe** in ihren Kommentaren wird die Zeitung sich auf Europa konzentrieren

editorship [ˈedɪtəʃɪp] N *(of newspaper, magazine)* Chefredaktion *f*; **under the ~ of …** unter … als Herausgeber(in)

EDP *abbr of* **electronic data processing** EDV *f*

EDT *(US) abbr of* **Eastern Daylight Time** *östliche Sommerzeit in den USA und Kanada*

educable [ˈedjʊkəbl] ADJ erziehbar; *(academically)* ausbildbar

educate [ˈedjʊkeɪt] VT **a** *(Sch, Univ)* erziehen; **the parents' role in educating their children** die Rolle der Eltern bei der Erziehung ihrer Kinder; **he's hardly ~d at all** er ist ziemlich ungebildet; **he was ~d at Eton** er ist in Eton zur Schule gegangen **b** *public* informieren; **we need to ~ our children about drugs** wir müssen dafür sorgen, dass unsere Kinder über Drogen Bescheid wissen **c** *the mind* schulen; *one's tastes* (aus)bilden

educated [ˈedjʊkeɪtɪd] ADJ gebildet; **to make an ~ guess** eine fundierte *or* wohlbegründete Vermutung anstellen; **an ~ mind** ein gebildeter Geist

education [ˌedjʊˈkeɪʃən] N Erziehung *f*; *(= studies, training)* Ausbildung *f*; *(= knowledge, culture)* Bildung *f*; **Ministry of Education** Ministerium *nt* für Erziehung und Unterricht, Kultusministerium *nt*; **lecturer in ~** Dozent(in) *m(f)* für Pädagogik; **College of Education** pädagogische Hochschule; *(for graduates)* Studienseminar *nt*; **(local) ~ authority** Schulbehörde *f*; **to study ~** Pädagogik *or* Erziehungswissenschaften studieren; **if the government neglects ~** wenn die Regierung das Erziehungs- und Ausbildungswesen vernachlässigt; **the ~ budget** der Etat für das Erziehungs- und Ausbildungswesen; **~ is free** die Schulausbildung ist kostenlos; **his ~ was interrupted** seine Ausbildung wurde unterbrochen; **to get an ~** eine Ausbildung bekommen; **the ~ he received at school** seine Schulbildung; **she had a university ~** sie hatte eine Universitätsausbildung; **a literary/scientific ~** eine literarische/naturwissenschaftliche Bildung; **she had little ~** sie war ziemlich ungebildet

educational [ˌedjʊˈkeɪʃənl] ADJ **a** *(= academic) needs* erzieherisch; *(at school level) needs, achievement* schulisch; **~ system** *(= institutions)* Bildungswesen *nt*; *(= structure)* Bildungssystem *nt*; **~ opportunities** Ausbildungschancen *pl*; **~ institution** *or* **establishment** Bildungsanstalt *f*; **~ standards** *(in schools)* Unterrichtsniveau *nt*; *(of country)* Bildungsniveau *nt*; **~ qualification** (Ausbildungs)abschluss *m*
b *(= teaching) issue* pädagogisch; **~ theory** Pädagogik *f*, Unterrichtstheorie *f*; **~ method** *or* **methodology** Erziehungsmethode *f*; **~ supplies** Unterrichtsmaterial *nt*
c *(= educative, instructive) experience, video* lehrreich; *day also* informativ; **~ trip** *(= school trip)* Klassenfahrt *f*; *(for adults)* Bildungsreise *f*; **~ leave** Bildungsurlaub *m*; **~ film** Lehrfilm *m*; **~ book** Lehrbuch *nt*; *(for schools)* Schulbuch *nt*; **~ experience** lehrreiche Erfahrung; **~ toy** pädagogisch wertvolles Spielzeug; **~ game** Lernspiel *nt*; **~ material** Lehrmittel *pl*

educational adviser N *(Brit Sch, Admin)* Unterrichtsberater(in) *m(f)*

educationalist [ˌedjʊˈkeɪʃnəlɪst] N Pädagoge *m*, Pädagogin *f*, Erziehungswissenschaftler(in) *m(f)*

educationally [ˌedjʊˈkeɪʃnəlɪ] ADV pädagogisch; *(= relating to school)* schulisch; **~ subnormal** lernbehindert; **to stimulate the youngsters ~** die Jugendlichen durch Lernen stimulieren

educational: **educational park** N *(US)* Gesamtschulanlage *f*; **educational psychologist** N Schulpsychologe *m*/-psychologin *f*; **educational psychology** N Schulpsychologie *f*; **educational publisher** N Schulbuchverlag *m*; **educational television** N Schulfernsehen *nt*; *(for adults)* Bildungssendungen *pl*

educationist [ˌedjʊˈkeɪʃnɪst] N = **educationalist**

educative [ˈedjʊkətɪv] ADJ erzieherisch

educator [ˈedjʊkeɪtəʳ] N Pädagoge *m*, Pädagogin *f*, Erzieher(in) *m(f)*; **an ~ of the young** ein Erzieher *m*/eine Erzieherin der Jugend

educe [ɪˈdjuːs] VT *(form)* ableiten *(from sth* von etw), entlocken *(from sb* jdm)

edutainment [ˌedjʊˈteɪnmənt] N Edutainment *nt*

Edward [ˈedwəd] N Eduard *m*

Edwardian [edˈwɔːdɪən] ADJ *house, furniture, clothes* Edwardianisch, aus der Zeit Eduards VII.; **the ~ era** die Edwardianische Zeit, die Zeit Eduards VII.; **~ England** England in der Zeit Eduards VII. N *(= person)* Zeitgenosse *m*/Zeitgenossin *f* Eduards VII.

EEC N *(dated) abbr of* **European Economic Community** EG *f*, EWG *f (dated)*

EEG *abbr of* **electroencephalogram** EEG *nt*

eek [iːk] INTERJ i, igitt

eel [iːl] N Aal *m* → **slippery**

e'en [iːn] ADV *(poet) contr of* **even**[1]

EENT *(US Med) abbr of* **eye, ear, nose and throat**; **~ specialist** Augen- und HNO-Arzt *m*/-Ärztin *f*

e'er [ɛəʳ] ADV *(poet) contr of* **ever**

eerie, eery [ˈɪərɪ] ADJ *(+er)* unheimlich

eerily [ˈɪərɪlɪ] ADV *(+vb)* unheimlich; *(+adj)* auf unheimliche Weise; **the whole town was ~ quiet** in der ganzen Stadt herrschte eine unheimliche Stille; **sometimes they were ~ similar** manchmal bestand eine unheimliche Ähnlichkeit zwischen ihnen

EET *abbr of* **Eastern European Time** OEZ *f*

efface [ɪˈfeɪs] VT auslöschen; **to ~ oneself** sich zurückhalten

effect [ɪˈfekt] N **a** *(= result)* Wirkung *f*, Effekt *m*; *(= repercussion)* Auswirkung *f*; **the ~ of an acid on metal** die Wirkung einer Säure auf Metall; **alcohol has the ~ of dulling your senses** Alkohol bewirkt eine Abstumpfung der Sinne; **the ~ of this rule will be to prevent …** diese Regelung wird die Verhinderung von … bewirken *or* zur Folge haben; **the ~ of this is that …** das hat zur Folge, dass …; **the ~s of radioactivity on the human body** die Auswirkungen radioaktiver Strahlen auf den menschlichen Körper; **to feel the ~s of the recession** die Auswirkungen der Rezession spüren; **to feel the ~s of the drugs** die Wirkung der Drogen spüren; **to no ~** erfolglos, ergebnislos; **to such good ~ that …** so wirkungsvoll, dass …; **to have an ~ on sb/sth** eine Wirkung auf jdn/etw haben; **to have a good ~ (on sb/sth)** eine gute Wirkung (auf jdn/etw) haben; **to have no ~** keine Wirkung haben; **to take ~** *(measures)* wirksam werden; **to take ~** *(drug)* wirken; **with immediate ~** mit sofortiger Wirkung; **with ~ from 3 March** mit Wirkung vom 3. März
b *(= impression)* Wirkung *f*, Effekt *m*; **to create an ~** eine Wirkung *or* einen Effekt erzielen; **~s of light** *(Art)* Lichteffekte *pl*; **the sword was only for ~** der Degen war nur zum Effekt da; **he paused for ~** er machte eine effektvolle Pause
c *(= meaning)* **his letter is to the ~ that …** sein Brief hat zum Inhalt, dass …; **we received a letter to the ~ that …** wir erhielten ein Schreiben des Inhalts, dass …; **he used words to that ~** sinngemäß drückte er sich so aus; **… or words to that ~** … oder etwas in diesem Sinne *or* etwas Ähnliches
d **effects** PL *(= property)* Effekten *pl*
e *(= reality)* **in ~** in Wirklichkeit, im Effekt
f *(of laws)* **to be in ~** gültig *or* in Kraft sein; **to come into** *or* **take ~** in Kraft treten; **to put sth into ~** etw in Kraft setzen; **to remain in ~** in Kraft bleiben
VT **a** bewirken, herbeiführen; **to ~ change** Veränderungen herbeiführen; **to ~ an entry** *(form)* sich *(dat)* Zutritt verschaffen; **to ~ an escape** fliehen
b *(form) sale, purchase* tätigen; *payment* leisten; *insurance* abschließen; *settlement* erzielen

effective [ɪˈfektɪv] ADJ **a** *(= successful) way, method, action, measures* effektiv, wirksam; *means, treatment, vaccine, deterrent* wirksam; *strategy, policy, government, politician* effektiv; **to be ~ in pain relief** Schmerzlinderung bewirken; **to be ~ in doing sth** bewirken, dass etw geschieht; **to be ~ against sth** *(drug)* gegen etw wirken
b *(= striking) decoration, pattern, combination*

wirkungsvoll; **to look ~** wirkungsvoll aussehen, gut wirken **c** *(= actual) control, increase* effektiv, tatsächlich; *(Econ, Fin) demand, interest rate* effektiv, tatsächlich; *leader* eigentlich; *income* wirklich, tatsächlich; **they have ~ control of the area** sie haben das Gebiet praktisch unter Kontrolle **d** *(= operative)* wirksam, in Kraft; **a new law, ~ from** *or* **becoming ~ on 1 August** ein neues Gesetz, das am 1. August in Kraft tritt; **~ date** Inkrafttreten *nt* **e** *(Mil) troops* einsatzbereit

effectively [ɪ'fektɪvlɪ] ADV **a** *(= successfully)* wirksam; *function, work, teach* effektiv **b** *(= strikingly)* wirkungsvoll **c** *(= in effect)* effektiv, praktisch

effectiveness [ɪ'fektɪvnɪs] N **a** *(= successfulness)* Wirksamkeit *f*; *(of strategy, government, politician)* Effektivität *f* **b** *(= striking effect)* Wirkung *f*

effectual ADJ, **effectually** ADV [ɪ'fektjʊəl, -ɪ] *(form)* wirksam; **we solved the problem more ~ly** wir haben das Problem besser gelöst

effectuate [ɪ'fektjʊeɪt] VT bewirken

effeminacy [ɪ'femɪnəsɪ] N feminines Wesen, Effemination *f (geh)*

effeminate [ɪ'femɪnɪt] ADJ feminin, effeminiert *(geh)*

effervesce [ˌefə'ves] VI sprudeln; *(fig, person)* überschäumen

effervescence [ˌefə'vesns] N *(lit)* Sprudeln *nt*; *(fig)* Überschäumen *nt*, überschäumendes Temperament

effervescent [ˌefə'vesnt] ADJ sprudelnd; *(fig)* überschäumend

effete [ɪ'fi:t] ADJ schwach; *person* saft- und kraftlos

efficacious [ˌefɪ'keɪʃəs] ADJ *(form)* wirksam; **to be ~ for/against sth** bei etw wirksam sein; **to prove ~ in the treatment of sth** sich in der Behandlung von etw als wirksam erweisen

efficacy ['efɪkəsɪ] N Wirksamkeit *f*

efficiency [ɪ'fɪʃənsɪ] N *(of person)* Fähigkeit *f*, Tüchtigkeit *f*; *(of machine, factory, organization, system)* Leistungsfähigkeit *f*; *(of method)* Wirksamkeit *f*;; *(of engine) (= power)* Leistungsfähigkeit *f*; *(= economy)* Sparsamkeit *f*; *(of service)* Effizienz *f (geh)*; *(of use)* Rationalität *f*; **jobs were lost as part of an ~ drive** Stellen wurden wegrationalisiert; **software that improves the ~ of translators** Software, die die Leistungsfähigkeit von Übersetzern erhöht

efficient [ɪ'fɪʃənt] ADJ *person* fähig, tüchtig; *system, machine, company, organization* leistungsfähig; *car, engine (= powerful)* leistungsfähig; *(= economical)* sparsam, verbrauchsarm; *service* gut, effizient *(geh)*; *method* wirksam; *way, use* rationell; **work is organized in the most logical and ~ way** die Arbeit wird so logisch und rationell wie möglich organisiert; **to be ~ in** *or* **at (doing) sth** etw gut können; **she's ~ at dealing with difficult customers** sie kann gut mit schwierigen Kunden umgehen; **the body is remarkably ~ at dealing with such things** der Körper wird mit diesen Dingen bemerkenswert gut fertig; **they are less ~ at turning sunlight into electricity** bei der Umwandlung von Sonnenlicht in elektrischen Strom sind sie weniger effektiv

efficiently [ɪ'fɪʃəntlɪ] ADV effektiv; **to work more ~** rationeller arbeiten; **quickly and ~** schnell und effizient *(geh)*

effigy ['efɪdʒɪ] N Bildnis *nt*; **to burn sb in ~** jds Puppe verbrennen

effing ['efɪŋ] *(euph sl)* ADJ Scheiß- *(inf)* N **~ and blinding** Fluchen *nt*, Geschimpfe *nt* VI *(only in -ing form)* **he was ~ and blinding** er erging sich in wüsten Schimpfereien

efflorescent [ˌeflɔ:'resnt] ADJ *(Chem)* ausblühend, effloreszierend *(spec)*; *(Bot)* aufblühend

effluence ['efluəns] N Abwasser *nt*

effluent ['efluənt] ADJ ausfließend; *gas* ausströmend N *(from a lake)* Ausfluss *m*; *(= sewage)* Abwasser *nt*

effluvium [e'flu:vɪəm] N Ausdünstung *f*

▶ **eff off** ['efɒf] VI *(euph sl)* sich verpissen *(sl)*

effort ['efət] N **a** *(= attempt)* Versuch *m*; *(= strain, hard work)* Anstrengung *f*, Mühe *f*; *(Mech)* Leistung *f*; **to make an ~ to do sth** den Versuch unternehmen, etw zu tun, sich bemühen, etw zu tun; **to make the ~ to do sth** sich *(dat)* die Mühe machen, etw zu tun; **to make every ~** *or* **a great ~ to do sth** sich sehr bemühen *or* anstrengen, etw zu tun; **to make every possible ~ to do sth** jede nur mögliche Anstrengung *or* große Anstrengungen unternehmen *or* machen, etw zu tun; **to make little ~ to do sth** sich *(dat)* wenig Mühe geben, etw zu tun; **he made no ~ to be polite** er machte sich *(dat)* nicht die Mühe, höflich zu sein; **it's an ~ (to get up in the morning)** es kostet einige Mühe *or* Anstrengung(, morgens aufzustehen); **getting up was an ~** das Aufstehen kostete einige Mühe *or* Anstrengung; **he had to double his ~s** er musste seine Anstrengungen verdoppeln; **if it's not too much of an ~ for you** *(iro)* wenn es dir nicht zu viel Mühe macht; **with an ~** mühsam; **with a great ~ of will** mit einer gewaltigen Willensanstrengung; **come on, make an ~** komm, streng dich an; **it's well worth the ~** die Mühe lohnt sich wirklich **b** *(= campaign)* Aktion *f*; **the famine relief ~** die Hilfsaktion gegen die Hungersnot **c** *(inf)* Unternehmen *nt*; **it was a pretty poor ~** das war eine ziemlich schwache Leistung; **it's not bad for a first ~** das ist nicht schlecht für den Anfang; **what did you think of his latest ~?** was halten Sie von seinem jüngsten Unternehmen?; **his first ~ at making a film** sein erster Versuch, einen Film zu drehen; **best film went to a strange Swedish ~** die Auszeichnung für den besten Film ging an ein merkwürdiges schwedisches Machwerk

effortless ['efətlɪs] ADJ *movement, victory, ease, style* mühelos; *charm, elegance* natürlich, ungezwungen; **~ superiority** natürliche Überlegenheit

effortlessly ['efətlɪslɪ] ADV mühelos; *chat* ungezwungen

effortlessness ['efətlɪsnɪs] N Mühelosigkeit *f*

effrontery [ɪ'frʌntərɪ] N Unverschämtheit *f*; **how can you have the ~ to deny the charge?** dass Sie die Frechheit besitzen, den Vorwurf abzustreiten!

effusion [ɪ'fju:ʒən] N *(lit, fig)* Erguss *m*

effusive [ɪ'fju:sɪv] ADJ überschwänglich; *(= gushing)* exaltiert; **to be ~ in one's praise of** *or* **for sb** jdn überschwänglich loben

effusively [ɪ'fju:sɪvlɪ] ADV überschwänglich

effusiveness [ɪ'fju:sɪvnɪs] N Überschwänglichkeit *f*

E-fit ['i:fɪt] N Computer-Phantombild *nt*

EFL *abbr of* **English as a Foreign Language** Englisch als Fremdsprache; **~ teacher** Lehrer(in) *m(f)* für Englisch als Fremdsprache

EFT *abbr of* **electronic funds transfer** elektronische Geldüberweisung

EFTA ['eftə] *abbr of* **European Free Trade Association** EFTA *f*

EFTPOS ['eftpɒs] *abbr of* **electronic funds transfer at point of sale**

eg *abbr of* **exempli gratia** *(= for example)* z. B.

EGA *(Comput) abbr of* **enhanced graphics adapter** EGA *m*

egad [ɪ'gæd] INTERJ *(old, hum)* fürwahr *(old, hum)*

egalitarian [ɪˌgælɪ'teərɪən] ADJ egalitär; **an ~ relationship between teacher and students** eine gleichberechtigte Beziehung zwischen Lehrer und Schülern N Verfechter(in) *m(f)* des Egalitarismus

egalitarianism [ɪˌgælɪ'teərɪənɪzəm] N Egalitarismus *m*

egg [eg] N Ei *nt*; **to put all one's ~s in one basket** *(prov)* alles auf eine Karte setzen; **as sure as ~s is ~s** *(inf)* so sicher wie das Amen in der Kirche *(inf)*; **to have ~ on** *or* **all over one's face** *(fig inf)* dumm dastehen *(inf)*; **he's a good/bad ~** *(dated inf)* er ist ein famoser Kerl *(dated)*/ein übler Kunde

▶ **egg on** VT *sep* anstacheln; **don't egg him on!** jetzt stachel ihn doch nicht auch noch an!

egg: **egg and dart** N Eierstab *m (spec)*; **egg-and-spoon race** N Eierlauf *m*; **eggbeater** N Schneebesen *m*; **egg cosy**, *(US)* **egg cozy** N Eierwärmer *m*; **egg cup** N **a** Eierbecher *m* **b** *(Brit inf: = small breasts)* zwei Mückenstiche *(inf)*; **egg custard** N Eiercreme *f*; **egg flip** N Ei-Flip *m*; **egghead** N *(pej inf)* Intellektuelle(r) *mf*, Eierkopf *m (inf)*; **eggplant** N *(esp US)* Aubergine *f*; **egg rack** M *(in fridge)* Eierleiste *f*; **egg roll** N Eibrötchen *nt*; **egg sandwich** N Sandwich *nt* mit Ei; **eggs Benedict** N *no pl (Cook) pochierte Eier und Schinken auf Toast mit Sauce hollandaise*; **eggshell** N Eierschale *f*; **he acts as if he's walking on ~s** er führt einen wahren Eiertanz auf ADJ Eierschalen-; **eggshell-blue** ADJ eierschalenblau; **egg slicer** N Eierschneider *m*; **egg spoon** N Eierlöffel *m*; **egg timer** N Eieruhr *f*; **egg tooth** N *(Zool)* Eierzahn *m*; **egg whisk** N Schneebesen *m*; **egg white** N Eiweiß *nt*; **egg yolk** N Eidotter *m*, Eigelb *nt*

egis ['i:dʒɪs] N *(US)* = **aegis**

eglantine ['egləntaɪn] N Weinrose *f*

ego ['i:gəʊ] N *(Psych)* Ego *nt*, Ich *nt*; *(= self-esteem)* Selbstbewusstsein *nt*; *(= conceit)* Einbildung *f*; **this will boost his ~** das wird sein Selbstbewusstsein stärken, das wird ihm Auftrieb geben; **he has a monstrously big ~** er hat ein total übersteigertes Selbstbewusstsein; **his ~ won't allow him to admit he is wrong** sein Stolz lässt ihn nie zugeben, dass er unrecht hat; **to need one's ~ stroked** Streicheleinheiten für sein Ego brauchen *(inf)*

egocentric(al) [ˌegəʊ'sentrɪk(əl)] ADJ egozentrisch, ichbezogen

egoism ['egəʊɪzəm] N Egoismus *m*, Selbstsucht *f*

egoist ['egəʊɪst] N Egoist(in) *m(f)*, selbstsüchtiger Mensch

egoistical [ˌegəʊ'ɪstɪkəl] ADJ egoistisch, selbstsüchtig, eigennützig

egomania [ˌi:gəʊ'meɪnɪə] N Egomanie *f*, übersteigerte Ichbezogenheit

egomaniac [ˌi:gəʊ'meɪnɪæk] N Egomane *m*, Egomanin *f*

egotism ['egəʊtɪzəm] N Ichbezogenheit *f*, Egotismus *m*

egotist ['egəʊtɪst] N Egotist(in) *m(f)*, ichbezogener Mensch

egotistic(al) [ˌegəʊ'tɪstɪk(əl)] ADJ von sich eingenommen, ichbezogen, egotistisch

ego trip N *(inf)* Egotrip *m (inf)*; **to be on an ~** auf einem Egotrip sein

egregious [ɪ'gri:dʒəs] ADJ ausgemacht, ungeheuerlich

egret ['i:grɪt] N *(Orn)* Reiher *m*; *(= ornament)* Reiherfeder *f*

Egypt ['i:dʒɪpt] N Ägypten *nt*

Egyptian [ɪ'dʒɪpʃən] ADJ ägyptisch N **a** Ägypter(in) *m(f)* **b** *(Ling)* Ägyptisch *nt*

Egyptology [ˌi:dʒɪp'tɒlədʒɪ] N Ägyptologie *f*

eh [eɪ] INTERJ **a** *(inviting repetition)* **I've found a gold mine – eh?** ich habe eine Goldmine entdeckt – was? *or* hä? *(inf)* **b** *(inviting agreement)* **it's good, eh?** gut, nicht?

EIB *abbr of* **European Investment Bank**

eider ['aɪdə'] N Eiderente *f*

eiderdown ['aɪdədaʊn] N *(= quilt)* Federbett *nt*, Daunendecke *f*; *(= feathers)* Daunen *pl*, Flaumfedern *pl*

eidetic [aɪ'detɪk] ADJ eidetisch

eight [eɪt] ADJ acht; **to be behind the ~ ball** *(US inf)* in der Patsche sitzen *(inf)* → **six** N **a**

Acht *f* → **six** b *(Rowing)* Achter *m* c **to have had one over the ~** *(inf)* einen über den Durst *or* einen zu viel getrunken haben *(inf)*

eighteen [ˈeɪˈtiːn] ADJ achtzehn N Achtzehn *f*

eighteenth [ˈeɪˈtiːnθ] ADJ achtzehnte(r, s) N *(= fraction)* Achtzehntel *nt; (of series)* Achtzehnte(r, s) → **sixteenth**

eighth [eɪtθ] ADJ achte(r, s) N *(= fraction)* Achtel *nt; (of series)* Achte(r, s) → **sixth**

eighth note N *(US Mus)* Achtelnote *f*, Achtel *nt*

eightieth [ˈeɪtɪəθ] ADJ achtzigste(r, s) N *(= fraction)* Achtzigstel *nt; (of series)* Achtzigste(r, s) → **sixtieth**

eightsome (reel) [ˈeɪtsəm(ˈriːl)] N *schottischer Volkstanz für 8 Tänzer*

eighty [ˈeɪtɪ] ADJ achtzig N Achtzig *f* → **sixty**

Eire [ˈɛərə] N Irland *nt*, Eire *nt*

either [ˈaɪðəʳ, ˈiːðəʳ] ✪ 26.2 ADJ PRON a *(= one or other)* eine(r, s) (von beiden); **there are two boxes on the table, take ~ (of them)** auf dem Tisch liegen zwei Schachteln, nimm eine davon; **if on ~ side of the road there is a line of trees** wenn eine Straßenseite mit Bäumen bestanden ist

b *(= each, both)* jede(r, s), beide *pl*; **~ day would suit me** beide Tage passen mir; **which bus will you take? – ~ (will do)** welchen Bus wollen Sie nehmen? – das ist egal; **she offered me tea and coffee, but I don't drink ~ (of them)** sie bot mir Tee und Kaffee an, aber ich trinke keines von beiden *or* ich trinke beides nicht; **on ~ side of the street** auf beiden Seiten der Straße; **it wasn't in ~ (box)** es war in keiner der beiden (Kisten)

ADV CONJ a *(after neg statement)* auch nicht; **he sings badly and he can't act ~** er ist ein schlechter Sänger, und spielen kann er auch nicht; **I have never heard of him – no, I haven't ~** ich habe noch nie von ihm gehört – ich auch nicht

b **~ … or** entweder … oder; *(after a negative)* weder … noch; **he must be ~ lazy or stupid** er muss entweder faul oder dumm sein; **~ be quiet or go out!** entweder bist du ruhig oder du gehst raus!; **I have never been to ~ Paris or Rome** ich bin weder in Paris noch in Rom gewesen

c *(= moreover)* **she inherited some money and not an insignificant amount ~** sie hat Geld geerbt, und (zwar) gar nicht so wenig

ejaculate [ɪˈdʒækjʊleɪt] VT a *(= utter)* ausstoßen, ausrufen b *(Physiol)* ejakulieren, ausspritzen VI a *(= cry out)* aufschreien b *(Physiol)* ejakulieren N [ɪˈdʒækjʊlɪt] Ejakulat *m*

ejaculation [ɪˌdʒækjʊˈleɪʃən] N a *(= cry)* Ausruf *m* b *(Physiol)* Ejakulation *f*, Samenerguss *m*

ejaculatory [ɪˈdʒækjʊlətərɪ] ADJ *style, language* stoßhaft; *(Physiol)* Ejakulations-; **~ control** Ejakulationskontrolle *f*

eject [ɪˈdʒekt] VT a *(= throw out) heckler, tenant* hinauswerfen b *cartridge* auswerfen; *(Tech)* ausstoßen, auswerfen; *pilot* herausschleudern VI *(pilot)* den Schleudersitz betätigen

ejecta [ɪˈdʒektə] PL *(Geol, Astrol)* Auswurf *m*; *(of vulcano)* ausgeschleuderte Materie

ejection [ɪˈdʒekʃən] N Hinauswurf *m*; *(of cartridge)* Auswerfen *nt*; *(Tech)* Ausstoß *m*; **~ is the pilot's last resort** Betätigung des Schleudersitzes ist die letzte Rettung für den Piloten

ejectment [ɪˈdʒektmənt] N Hinauswurf *m*; *(Jur)* Herausgabeklage *f*

ejector [ɪˈdʒektəʳ] N *(on gun)* Auswerfer *m*, Ejektor *m*

ejector seat [ɪˈdʒektəʳsiːt], *(US)* **ejection seat** N *(Aviat)* Schleudersitz *m*

eke out [ˈiːkaʊt] VT *sep food, supplies* strecken, verlängern; *money, income* aufbessern; **to ~ a living** sich (recht und schlecht) durchschlagen

EKG N *(US)* = **ECG**

el [el] N *(US) abbr of* **elevated railroad** Hochbahn *f*

elaborate [ɪˈlæbərɪt] ADJ a *(= complex, over-complex) machine, equipment, procedure, ritual, system, network* kompliziert; *(= sophisticated)* ausgeklügelt; *scheme* groß angelegt; *precautions, efforts, plans* umfangreich; *(= sophisticated) preparations* ausführlich; *cooking, ceremony, design* aufwendig, aufwändig; **an ~ meal** ein großes Menü; **an ~ hoax/plot** ein ausgeklügelter Schwindel/Plan

b *(= lavish, ornate) costume, design, furniture, style* kunstvoll

VT [ɪˈlæbəreɪt] a *(= expand in words) statement, remark* weiter ausführen; **to ~ sth further** auf etw *acc* näher eingehen

b *(= develop) system, plan, theory* ausarbeiten; *(= refine)* verfeinern, ausfeilen

VI [ɪˈlæbəreɪt] **would you care to** *or* **could you ~ on that?** könnten Sie darauf näher eingehen?; **there's no need to ~** Sie brauchen nichts weiter zu sagen; **it isn't a statement I want to ~ on** zu dieser Feststellung möchte ich mich nicht weiter äußern

elaborately [ɪˈlæbərɪtlɪ] ADV a *(= carefully)* sorgfältig; *(= in detail)* ausführlich; *(= complexly)* kompliziert; **an ~ staged press conference** eine mit großem Aufwand veranstaltete Pressekonferenz; **~ casual** betont lässig b *(= ornately, lavishly)* kunstvoll; **~ costumed** aufwendig *or* aufwändig kostümiert

elaborateness [ɪˈlæbərɪtnɪs] N a *(= comply)* Kompliziertheit *f*; *(of cooking, ceremony, design)* Aufwändigkeit *f*, Aufwendigkeit *f*; *(of scheme)* groß angelegte Art; *(of precautions, plan)* Umfang *m*; *(= sophisticated nature: of plans, preparations)* Ausführlichkeit *f* b *(= ornateness, lavishness)* kunstvolle Art

elaboration [ɪˌlæbəˈreɪʃən] N *(of system, plan, theory, = working out)* Ausarbeitung *f*; *(= refinement)* Verfeinerung *f*, Ausfeilung *f*; *(= description: of details etc)* nähere Ausführung; *(= that which elaborates: details etc)* Ausschmückung *f*; **an author who goes in for a great deal of tedious ~** ein Schriftsteller, der eine Menge langatmiger Beschreibungen bringt

élan [eɪˈlæn] N Elan *m*

elapse [ɪˈlæps] VI vergehen, verstreichen

elastic [ɪˈlæstɪk] ADJ *(lit, fig)* elastisch; **~ waist** Taille *f* mit Gummizug N Gummi(band *nt*) *m*; *(US: = rubber band)* Gummi *m*; **a piece of ~** ein Gummiband *nt*

elasticated [ɪˈlæstɪkeɪtɪd] ADJ elastisch; **~ waist** Gummibund *m*; *(of garment)* Taille *f* mit Gummizug

elastic band N *(esp Brit)* Gummiband *nt*

elasticity [ˌiːlæsˈtɪsɪtɪ] N Elastizität *f*

elastic stockings PL Gummistrümpfe *pl*

Elastoplast® [ɪˈlæstəʊplɑːst] N *(Brit)* ≈ Hansaplast® *nt*

elate [ɪˈleɪt] VT begeistern, in Hochstimmung versetzen

elated [ɪˈleɪtɪd] ADJ begeistert

elation [ɪˈleɪʃən] N Begeisterung *(at* über *+acc)*, Hochstimmung *f*; *(of crowd)* Jubel *m*, Begeisterung *f*; **a mood of such ~** eine solche Hochstimmung

elbow [ˈelbəʊ] N a Ellbogen *m*; **since he's been rubbing ~s with senators** *(esp US)* seit er sich in Senatorenkreisen bewegt b *(of pipe, river, road)* Knie *nt* VT **to ~ one's way forward** sich durchdrängen; **he ~ed his way through the crowd** er boxte sich durch die Menge; **to ~ sb aside** jdn beiseitestoßen; **he ~ed me in the stomach** er stieß mir *or* mich mit dem Ellbogen in den Magen; **to ~ one's way to the top** *(fig)* sich nach oben durchboxen *(inf)*, die Ellbogen gebrauchen, um an die Spitze zu kommen

▶ **elbow out** VT *sep (fig)* hinausdrängeln

elbow grease N *(inf)* Muskelkraft *f*

elbowing [ˈelbəʊɪŋ] N *(Ice hockey)* Ellbogencheck *m*

elbow: elbow rest N Armstütze *f*; **elbowroom** N *(inf: lit, fig)* Ellbogenfreiheit *f (inf)*

elder¹ [ˈeldəʳ] ADJ *attr comp of* **old** a *(= older) brother etc* ältere(r, s) b *(= senior)* **Pliny the ~** Plinius der Ältere, der ältere Plinius N a **respect your ~s and betters** du musst Respekt vor Älteren haben b *(of tribe, Church)* Ältestе(r) *m* c *(Presbyterian)* Gemeindeälteste(r) *mf*, Presbyter(in) *m(f)*

elder² N *(Bot)* Holunder *m*

elderberry [ˈeldəˌberɪ] N Holunderbeere *f*; **~ wine** Holunderwein *m*

elderflower [ˈeldəflaʊəʳ] N Holunder *m*, Holunderblüte *f*

elderly [ˈeldəlɪ] ADJ ältlich, ältere(r, s) *attr*

elder statesman N (alt)erfahrener Staatsmann

eldest [ˈeldɪst] ADJ *attr superl of* **old** älteste(r, s) N **the ~** der/die/das Älteste; *(pl)* die Ältesten *pl*; **the ~ of four children** das älteste von vier Kindern; **my ~** *(inf: = son)* mein Ältester; *(= daughter)* meine Älteste

El Dorado, eldorado [ˌeldəˈrɑːdəʊ] N *pl* **-dos** (El)dorado *nt*, Paradies *nt (fig)*

elec a *abbr of* **electricity** b *abbr of* **electric** elektr.

elect [ɪˈlekt] VT a *(by vote)* wählen; **he was ~ed chairman/MP** er wurde zum Vorsitzenden/Abgeordneten gewählt; **to ~ sb to the Senate** jdn in den Senat wählen b *(= choose)* (er)wählen, sich entscheiden für; **to ~ to do sth** sich dafür entscheiden, etw zu tun; **to ~ French nationality** sich für die französische Staatsangehörigkeit entscheiden ADJ **the president ~** der designierte *or* künftige Präsident PL *(esp Rel)* **the ~** die Auserwählten *pl*

elected [ɪˈlektɪd] ADJ gewählt

election [ɪˈlekʃən] N Wahl *f*; **his ~ to the chairmanship** seine Wahl zum Vorsitzenden; **~ debacle** Wahldebakel *nt*

election *in cpds* Wahl-; **~ victory/defeat** Wahlsieg *m*/-niederlage *f*; **election campaign** N Wahlkampf *m*

electioneer [ɪˌlekʃəˈnɪəʳ] VI als Wahlhelfer arbeiten, Wahlhilfe leisten; **he's just ~ing for X** er macht nur Wahlpropaganda für X

electioneering [ɪˌlekʃəˈnɪərɪŋ] N *(= campaign)* Wahlkampf *m*; *(= propaganda)* Wahlpropaganda *f* ADJ Wahl-; **~ campaign** Wahlkampf *m*; **~ speech** Wahlkampfrede *f*

elective [ɪˈlektɪv] ADJ a *democracy* mit Wahlen; **~ assembly** Wahlversammlung *f*; **~ dictatorship** gewählte Diktatur; **~ office/post** *Amt, das/Posten, der durch Wahl besetzt wird*; **he has never won/held ~ office** er ist noch nie zu einem Amt gewählt worden b *(Med) surgery* nicht unbedingt notwendig; *abortion* nicht medizinisch indiziert c *(US: Sch, Univ: = optional) course* wahlfrei; **~ subject** Wahlfach *nt* N *(US: Sch, Univ)* Wahlfach *nt*

elector [ɪˈlektəʳ] N a Wähler(in) *m(f)* b *(Hist)* **Elector** Kurfürst *m* c *(US)* Wahlmann *m*

electoral [ɪˈlektərəl] ADJ Wahl-; **~ boundaries** Grenzen *pl* der Wahlbezirke; **~ defeat/victory** Wahlniederlage *f*/-sieg *m*; **~ fraud** Wahlbetrug *m*; **~ process** Wahlverfahren *nt*; **~ support** Unterstützung *f* durch die Wähler; **~ system** Wahlsystem *nt*; **the ~ map** *(lit)* die Aufteilung der Wahlbezirke; *(fig)* die Stimmenverteilung in den Wahlbezirken

electoral college N Wahlausschuss *m*; **the ~, the Electoral College** *(US, in presidential election)* das Wahlmännergremium

ELECTORAL COLLEGE

Amerikaner wählen ihren Präsidenten und Vizepräsidenten nicht direkt; stattdessen werden **electors** gewählt, Wahlmänner, die sich verpflichtet haben, für bestimmte Kandidaten zu stimmen. Zusammen bilden die Wahlmänner das von der Verfassung vorgeschriebene **electoral college**. In diesem Gremium hat jeder Staat so viele Stimmen, wie die Gesamtzahl seiner Senatoren und Abgeordneten. Jede Partei wählt eine Gruppe von Wahlmännern, und am Tag der Präsidentschaftswahl stimmt die amerikanische Öffentlichkeit für die Gruppe, die den Kandidaten unterstützt, den sie als Sieger sehen möchte. Da die siegreiche Gruppe dann alle Stimmen eines Staates für den Kandidaten ihrer Partei abgibt, wäre es theoretisch möglich, dass ein Kandidat die Mehrheit der Stimmen aus der Bevölkerung erhält und trotzdem die Präsidentschaftswahl verliert, da zu wenige Wahlmänner für ihn stimmen.

electoral district N Wahlbezirk *m*

electoral law N Wahlrecht *nt*

electorally [ɪ'lektərəlɪ] ADV *(= in the election)* bei der Wahl; *(= with the electorate)* bei den Wählern

electoral register, electoral roll N Wählerverzeichnis *nt*

electoral vote N *(US Pol)* Stimme *f* für die Präsidentschaftswahl

electorate [ɪ'lektərɪt] N Wähler *pl*, Wählerschaft *f*

Electra complex [ɪ'lektrə,kɒmpleks] N *(Psych)* Elektrakomplex *m*

electric [ɪ'lektrɪk] ADJ **a** *(lit: = powered by electricity, generated)* elektrisch; *(= carrying electricity)* Strom-; **~ car/vehicle** Elektroauto *nt*; **~ razor** Elektrorasierer *m*; **~ mixer/kettle** elektrischer Mixer/Wasserkocher **b** *(fig: = exciting) atmosphere, mood* wie elektrisiert; **the effect was ~** das hatte eine tolle Wirkung N **a** *(inf: = electricity)* Elektrizität *f*, Elektrik *f (inf)* **b** **electrics** PL Strom *m*; *(Aut)* Elektrik *f*

electrical [ɪ'lektrɪkəl] ADJ *components, fault, power, failure, activity, signal* elektrisch; **~ equipment/goods** Elektrogeräte *pl*; **~ appliance** Elektrogerät *nt*; **~ system** Elektrik *f*; **~ fittings** Elektroinstallationen *pl*

electrical: **electrical energy** N Elektroenergie *f*, elektrische Energie; **electrical engineer** N Elektrotechniker(in) *m(f)*; *(with degree)* Elektroingenieur(in) *m(f)*; **electrical engineering** N Elektrotechnik *f*; **the ~ industry** die elektrotechnische Industrie; **electrical fitter** N Elektromonteur(in) *m(f)*

electrically [ɪ'lektrɪkəlɪ] ADV elektrisch; **an ~ powered car** ein Wagen *m* mit Elektroantrieb; **~ operated/controlled** elektrisch betätigt/gesteuert

electrical storm N Gewitter *nt*

electric: **electric-arc welding** N Lichtbogenschweißung *f*; **electric bill** N *(inf)* Stromrechnung *f*; **electric blanket** N Heizdecke *f*; **electric blue** N Stahlblau *nt*; **electric-blue** ADJ stahlblau; **electric cable** N Stromkabel *nt*; **electric chair** N elektrischer Stuhl; **electric charge** N elektrische Ladung; **electric circuit** N Stromkreislauf *m*; **electric cooker** N Elektroherd *m*; **electric current** N elektrischer Strom; **electric eel** N Zitteraal *m*; **electric eye** N Fotozelle *f*; **electric fence** N Elektrozaun *m*; **electric field** N elektrisches Feld; **electric fire** N elektrisches Heizgerät; **electric furnace** N *(= blast furnace)* elektrischer Hochofen; *(= kiln)* elektrischer Brennofen; **electric guitar** N elektrische Gitarre, E-Gitarre *f*; **electric heater** N elektrisches Heizgerät

electrician [ɪlek'trɪʃən] N Elektriker(in) *m(f)*

electricity [ɪlek'trɪsɪtɪ] N Elektrizität *f*; *(= electric power for use)* (elektrischer) Strom; **to have ~ connected** Stromanschluss *or* elektrischen Strom bekommen; **to turn on/off the ~** den Strom an-/abschalten

electricity: **electricity (generating) board** *(Brit)* N Elektrizitätswerk *nt*; **electricity meter** N Stromzähler *m*; **electricity price** N Strompreis *m*; **electricity production** N Stromproduktion *f*, Stromerzeugung *f*; **electricity rate** N Stromtarif *m*; **electricity strike** N Streik *m* in den Elektrizitätswerken

electric: **electric light** N elektrisches Licht; **electric lighting** N elektrische Beleuchtung; **electric motor** N Elektromotor *m*; **electric organ** N elektrische Orgel; **electric plug** N (Strom)stecker *m*; **electric ray** N *(Zool)* Zitterrochen *m*; **electric shock** N elektrischer Schlag, Stromschlag *m*; *(Med)* Elektroschock *m* ADJ *attr* **~ treatment** Elektroschocktherapie *f*; **to give sb ~ treatment** jdn mit Elektroschock behandeln; **electric socket** N (Strom)steckdose *f*; **electric storm** N Gewitter *nt*; **electric toothbrush** N elektrische Zahnbürste; **electric train** N Elektrozug *m*; *(= model train set)* elektrische Eisenbahn; **electric window** N *(Aut)* elektrischer Fensterheber; **electric wiring** N Stromleitungen *pl*, elektrische Leitungen *pl*

electrification [ɪ,lektrɪfɪ'keɪʃən] N Elektrifizierung *f*

electrify [ɪ'lektrɪfaɪ] VT **a** *(Rail)* elektrifizieren **b** *(= charge with electricity)* unter Strom setzen **c** *(fig)* elektrisieren

electrifying [ɪ'lektrɪfaɪɪŋ] ADJ *(fig)* elektrisierend

electro- [ɪ'lektrəʊ-] PREF Elektro-

electro: **electrocardiogram** [ɪ,lektrəʊ'kɑːdɪəʊgræm] N Elektrokardiogramm *nt*; **electrocardiograph** [ɪ,lektrəʊ'kɑːdɪəʊgrɑːf] N Elektrokardiograf *m*; **electrochemical** [ɪ,lektrəʊ'kemɪkəl] ADJ elektrochemisch; **electroconvulsive therapy** [ɪ,lektrəʊkən'vʌlsɪv-'θerəpɪ] N Elektroschocktherapie *f*

electrocute [ɪ'lektrəkjuːt] VT durch einen (Strom)schlag töten; *(= execute)* durch den *or* auf dem elektrischen Stuhl hinrichten

electrocution [ɪ,lektrə'kjuːʃən] N Tötung *f* durch Stromschlag; *(= execution)* Hinrichtung *f* durch den elektrischen Stuhl

electrode [ɪ'lektrəʊd] N Elektrode *f*

electro: **electrodynamics** N Elektrodynamik *f*; **electroencephalogram** N Elektroenzephalogramm *nt*; **electroencephalograph** N Elektroenzephalograf *m*

electrolysis [ɪlek'trɒlɪsɪs] N Elektrolyse *f*

electrolyte [ɪ'lektrəʊlaɪt] N Elektrolyt *m*

electro: **electromagnet** N Elektromagnet *m*; **electromagnetic** ADJ elektromagnetisch; **electromagnetism** N Elektromagnetismus *m*

electron [ɪ'lektrɒn] N Elektron *nt*

electron: **electron beam** N Elektronenstrahl *m*; **electron camera** N Elektronenkamera *f*; **electron gun** N Elektronenkanone *f*

electronic [ɪlek'trɒnɪk] ADJ elektronisch; *information* elektronisch gespeichert; **the ~ age** das elektronische Zeitalter

electronically [ɪlek'trɒnɪkəlɪ] ADV elektronisch; **to be available ~** in elektronischer Form vorhanden sein

electronic: **electronic banking** N elektronischer Geldverkehr; **electronic brain** N Elektronen(ge)hirn *nt*; **electronic cash** N E-Cash *nt*, elektronische Geldüberweisung; **electronic commerce** N E-Commerce *m*, elektronischer Handel; **electronic data processing** N *(Comput)* elektronische Datenverarbeitung; **electronic engineering** N Elektronik *f*; **~ company** Elektronikfirma *f*; **electronic flash** N *(Phot)* Elektronenblitz *m*; **electronic funds transfer** N elektronische (Geld)überweisung; **~ system** elektronisches Überweisungssystem; **electronic game** N Elektronikspiel *nt*; **electronic keyboard** N *(Mus)* elektronisches Keyboard; *(on computer)* elektronische Tastatur; **electronic mail** N elektronische Post; **electronic mailbox** N elektronischer Briefkasten; **electronic music** N elektronische Musik; **electronic news gathering** N elektronischer Nachrichtendienst; **electronic point of sale** N elektronisches Kassenterminal; **~ system** System *nt* mit elektronischen Kassenterminals; **electronic publishing** N elektronisches Publizieren

electronics [ɪlek'trɒnɪks] N **a** *sing (subject)* Elektronik *f* **b** *pl (of machine etc)* Elektronik *f*

electronic: **electronic surveillance** N elektronische Überwachung; **electronic tag** N elektronische Marke, elektronisches Kennzeichen; *(for prisoner)* elektronische Fußfessel; **electronic tagging** N elektronische Markierung *or* Kennzeichnung; *(for prisoners)* elektronische Fußfesseln *pl*; **electronic transfer of funds** N elektronische (Geld)überweisung

electron microscope N Elektronenmikroskop *nt*

electroplate [ɪ'lektrəʊpleɪt] VT galvanisieren N *no pl* Galvanisierung *f*; **is it silver? – no, ~** ist das Silber? – nein, nur versilbert

electroplated [ɪ'lektrəʊpleɪtɪd] ADJ (galvanisch) versilbert/verchromt *etc*

electroscope [ɪ'lektrəʊskəʊp] N Elektroskop *nt*

electroshock therapy [ɪ,lektrəʊʃɒk'θerəpɪ] N Elektroschocktherapie *or* -behandlung *f*

electrostatic [ɪ'lektrəʊ'stætɪk] ADJ elektrostatisch

electrotherapy [ɪ,lektrəʊ'θerəpɪ] N *(Med)* Elektrotherapie *f*

elegance ['elɪgəns] N Eleganz *f*

elegant ['elɪgənt] ADJ elegant; *style also* gewandt; *book* elegant geschrieben; **an ~ solution** eine elegante Lösung

elegantly ['elɪgəntlɪ] ADV elegant; *shaped also* harmonisch; *written also* gewandt; **~ simple** bestechend einfach

elegiac [,elɪ'dʒaɪək] ADJ elegisch N *usu pl (Liter)* elegischer Vers, Vers *m* im elegischen Versmaß

elegize ['elɪdʒaɪz] VI (in Elegien) klagen *(upon* über *+acc)*

elegy ['elɪdʒɪ] N Elegie *f*

element ['elɪmənt] N *(all senses)* Element *nt*; **the ~s of mathematics** die Grundbegriffe *pl or* Anfangsgründe *pl (geh)* der Mathematik; **one of the key ~s of the peace plan** einer der grundlegenden Bestandteile des Friedensplans; **an ~ of danger** ein Gefahrenelement *nt*; **the ~ of chance** das Zufallselement; **an ~ of truth** eine Spur *or* ein Element *nt* von Wahrheit; **the personal ~** das persönliche Element; **a hooligan/criminal ~** ein paar Rowdys/Kriminelle; **the (four) ~s** die (vier) Elemente; **to be in one's ~** in seinem Element sein; **to be out of one's ~** *(with group of people)* sich fehl am Platze fühlen; *(with subject)* sich nicht auskennen

elemental [,elɪ'mentl] ADJ **a** *(liter) truth, life, feeling, drive* elementar; *art* urwüchsig; **~ force** Elementargewalt *f*, Naturgewalt *f*; **~ powers** Elementarkräfte *pl*; **the ~ energies** *(of the four elements)* die Energien *pl* der vier Elemente **b** *(Chem)* elementar

elementary [,elɪ'mentərɪ] ADJ **a** *(= simple) rules* einfach, elementar; *(= basic) idea, fact, precautions* grundlegend; **a few ~ rules** einige Grundregeln; **sometimes the cause is quite ~** manchmal ist die Ursache ganz einfach *or* simpel; **~ mistake** Grundfehler *m*, grober Fehler; **~, my dear Watson** elementar, lieber Watson **b** *(pej: = rudimentary)* primitiv; **his acting is about as ~ as you can get** primitiver als er kann man gar nicht spielen **c** *(Sch) level* elementar; **~ skills/knowledge** Grundkenntnisse *pl*; **~ reading and writing** Grundkenntnisse *pl* im Lesen und Schreiben; **~ computer skills** grundlegende Computerkenntnisse *pl*; **~ maths** Elementarmathematik *f*; **a rather ~ knowledge of science** einige Grundkenntnisse in Naturwissenschaften

elementary: **elementary education** N Grundschulbildung *f*; **elementary particle** N *(Phys)* Elementarteilchen *nt*; **elementary particle physics** N *(Phys)* Elementarteilchenphysik *f*; **elementary school** N *(US: = primary school)* Grundschule *f*; **elementary schooling** N *(US)* Grundschulbildung *f*; **elementary student** N *(US)* Grundschüler(in) *m(f)*; **elementary teacher** N *(US)* Grundschullehrer(in) *m(f)*

elephant ['elɪfənt] N Elefant *m* → **pink[1] ADJ a, white elephant**

elephantiasis [,elɪfən'taɪəsɪs] N Elefantiasis *f*, Elephantiasis *f*

elephantine [ˌelɪˈfæntaɪn] ADJ *(= heavy, clumsy)* schwerfällig, wie ein Elefant; *(= large)* riesig, elefantös *(hum)*; **~ memory** Elefantengedächtnis *nt (inf)*

elephant seal N *(Zool)* See-Elefant *m*

elevate [ˈelɪveɪt] VT **a** *(= raise)* heben; *(= increase) blood pressure etc* erhöhen; **by elevating the house a full 3 feet above ...** indem man das Haus ganze 3 Fuß über *(+acc)* ... setzt **b** *(fig) mind* erbauen; *soul* erheben; **elevating reading** erbauliche Lektüre; **an elevating prospect** eine erfreuliche Aussicht; **to ~ the condition of the people** die Lebensbedingungen des Volkes verbessern **c to ~ sb to the peerage** jdn in den Adelsstand erheben; **since he's been ~d to top management** *(hum)* seit er ins Spitzenmanagement berufen worden ist

elevated [ˈelɪveɪtɪd] ADJ **a** *(= raised) situation, platform, level, pressure, rate* erhöht; **~ train, ~ railway** *(Brit) or* **railroad** *(US)* Hochbahn *f*; **an ~ monorail track** eine Einschienenhochbahn; **the ~ section of the M4** die als Hochstraße gebaute Strecke der M4 **b** *(= exalted, lofty) status, tone, style, language* gehoben; *thoughts* erhaben

elevation [ˌelɪˈveɪʃən] N **a** *(lit)* Hebung *f*; *(to higher rank)* Erhebung *f (to* in *+acc)*; *(Eccl)* Elevation *f* **b** *(of thought)* Erhabenheit *f*; *(of position, style)* Gehobenheit *f* **c** *(above sea level)* Höhe *f* über dem Meeresspiegel *or* über N.N.; *(hill etc)* (Boden)erhebung *f*, Anhöhe *f* **d angle of ~** Höhen- *or* Elevationswinkel *m* **e** *(of gun)* Elevation *f*, Erhöhung *f* **f** *(Archit: = drawing)* Aufriss *m*; **front ~** Frontansicht *f*, Fassadenaufriss *m*

elevator [ˈelɪveɪtəʳ] N **a** *(US)* Fahrstuhl *m*, Lift *m*, Aufzug *m* **b** *(= storehouse)* Silo *m* **c** *(Aviat)* Höhenruder *nt* **d** *(with buckets etc)* Aufzug *m*; *(= hoist)* Winde *f*

elevator shoe N Schuh *m* mit Plateausohle

eleven [ɪˈlevn] **N a** *(= number)* Elf *f*; **the ~ plus** *(old Brit, Sch) Aufnahmeprüfung in eine weiterführende Schule* **b** *(Sport)* Elf *f*; **the German ~** die deutsche (National)elf; **the second ~** die zweite Mannschaft **ADJ** elf → *also* **six**

elevenses [ɪˈlevnzɪz] N *sing or pl (Brit)* zweites Frühstück

eleventh [ɪˈlevnθ] **ADJ** elfte(r, s); **at the ~ hour** *(fig)* in letzter Minute, fünf Minuten vor zwölf **N** *(= fraction)* Elftel *nt*, Elfte(r, s); *(of series)* Elfte(r, s) → *also* **sixth**

elf [elf] N *pl* **elves** Elf *m*, Elfe *f*; *(mischievous)* Kobold *m*

elfin [ˈelfɪn] ADJ **a** *(= attractive)* elfenhaft **b** *(Myth)* elfisch

elfish [ˈelfɪʃ] ADJ elfenhaft; *(= mischievous)* koboldhaft

elicit [ɪˈlɪsɪt] VT entlocken *(from sb* jdm*)*; *support* gewinnen *(from sb* jds*)*; **to ~ public sympathy** die Sympathie der Öffentlichkeit gewinnen

elide [ɪˈlaɪd] **VT** elidieren, auslassen **VI** elidiert werden, wegfallen

eligibility [ˌelɪdʒəˈbɪlɪtɪ] N **a** Berechtigung *f*; **because of his undoubted ~ for the post** da er für die Stelle zweifelsohne infrage kommt/kam **b** Wählbarkeit *f*

eligible [ˈelɪdʒəbl] ADJ **a** infrage *or* in Frage kommend; *(for competition etc)* teilnahmeberechtigt; *(for student flights, grants etc)* berechtigt; *(for membership)* aufnahmeberechtigt; **to be ~ for parole** für Bewährung infrage *or* in Frage kommen; **to be ~ for a job/an office** für einen Posten/ein Amt infrage *or* in Frage kommen; **to be ~ for a pension** pensionsberechtigt sein; **an ~ bachelor** ein begehrter Junggeselle **b** *(= able to be elected)* wählbar

eliminate [ɪˈlɪmɪneɪt] VT **a** *(= remove)* ausschließen; *competitor* ausschalten; *inflation, poverty, waste* ein Ende machen *(+dat)*; *danger, problem* beseitigen; *(Physiol)* ausscheiden, eliminieren; *(Math)* eliminieren; **our team/candidate was ~d in the second round** unsere Mannschaft/unser Kandidat schied in der zweiten Runde aus **b** *(= kill) enemy* ausschalten, eliminieren

elimination [ɪˌlɪmɪˈneɪʃən] N **a** *(= removal)* Ausschluss *m*, Ausscheidung *f*; *(of competitor)* Ausschaltung *f*; *(of inflation, poverty, waste)* Beendung *f*; *(of danger, problem)* Beseitigung *f*; *(Physiol)* Ausscheidung *f*, Elimination *f (spec)*; *(Math)* Elimination *f*; **by (a) process of ~** durch negative Auslese; **our ~ by the German team** die Ausschaltung unserer Mannschaft durch die deutsche **b** *(= killing: of enemy)* Ausschaltung *f*, Eliminierung *f*

elision [ɪˈlɪʒən] N Elision *f*

elite [eɪˈliːt] **N** *(often pej)* Elite *f* **ADJ** Elite-; **~ group** Elitegruppe *f*, Elite *f*; **~ unit** Eliteeinheit *f*; **~ force** Elitetruppe *f*; **~ troops** Elitetruppen *pl*; **an ~ group of scholars** eine Elite der Gelehrten

elitism [eɪˈliːtɪzəm] N Elitedenken *nt*

elitist [eɪˈliːtɪst] **ADJ** elitär **N** elitär Denkende(r) *mf*; **he's an ~** er denkt elitär

elixir [ɪˈlɪksəʳ] N Elixier *nt*, Auszug *m*; **~ of life** Lebenselixier *nt*

Elizabeth [ɪˈlɪzəbəθ] N Elisabeth *f*

Elizabethan [ɪˌlɪzəˈbiːθən] **ADJ** elisabethanisch **N** Elisabethaner(in) *m(f)*

elk [elk] N Elch *m*

ellipse [ɪˈlɪps] N Ellipse *f*

ellipsis [ɪˈlɪpsɪs] N *pl* **ellipses** [ɪˈlɪpsiːz] *(Gram)* Ellipse *f*

elliptic(al) [ɪˈlɪptɪk(əl)] ADJ **a** *(Math etc) orbit, path* elliptisch **b** *(fig) account, reference* andeutungsweise; *style* unklar; *essay, book, play* kryptisch *(geh)*; **she gives an elliptical account of the tragedy** sie berichtet nur andeutungsweise von der Tragödie

elliptically [ɪˈlɪptɪkəlɪ] ADV **a** *(Math)* elliptisch; **planets move round ~** die Planeten haben eine elliptische Umlaufbahn **b** *(fig) speak* andeutungsweise; *write* kryptisch *(geh)*

elm [elm] N Ulme *f*

El Niño [elˈniːnjəʊ] N El Niño *m*

elocution [ˌeləˈkjuːʃən] N Sprechtechnik *f*; **teacher of ~** Sprecherzieher(in) *m(f)*; **~ lessons** Sprechunterricht *m*

elocutionist [ˌeləˈkjuːʃənɪst] N Sprecherzieher(in) *m(f)*

elongate [ˈiːlɒŋgeɪt] **VT** verlängern; *(= stretch out)* lang ziehen, strecken **VI** länger werden

elongated [ˈiːlɒŋgeɪtɪd] ADJ *(= extra length added)* verlängert; *(= stretched) neck* ausgestreckt; *shape* länglich; *body* lang gestreckt; *orbit* elliptisch

elongation [ˌiːlɒŋˈgeɪʃən] N Verlängerung *f*; *(= stretching)* Ausstrecken *nt*

elope [ɪˈləʊp] VI durchbrennen *or* ausreißen, um zu heiraten *(inf)*

elopement [ɪˈləʊpmənt] N Durchbrennen *nt (inf) or* Ausreißen *nt (inf)*, um zu heiraten

eloquence [ˈeləkwəns] N *(of person)* Redegewandtheit *f*; *(of speech, words)* Gewandtheit *f*; *(of statement, tribute, plea)* Wortgewandtheit *f*;; *(fig, of testimony, gesture, silence)* Beredtheit *f*; **phrased with such ~** so gewandt ausgedrückt

eloquent [ˈeləkwənt] ADJ **a** *(= persuasive) speech, words* gewandt; *statement, tribute, plea* wortgewandt; *person* redegewandt; **his lawyer made an ~ plea for leniency** sein Anwalt bat mit gewandten Worten um Milde; **to be ~ about** *or* **on sth** mit schönen Worten über etw *(acc)* reden; **to be ~ in describing/recommending sth** etw mit gewandten *or* schönen Worten beschreiben/empfehlen; **to wax ~ (about** *or* **on sth)** (von etw) schwärmen **b** *(fig) hands, voice* ausdrucksvoll; *gesture* beredt; *silence* beredt, vielsagend; **to be** *or* **give ~ testimony to sth** ein beredtes Zeugnis für etw sein, etw beredt bezeugen; **to be ~ proof of sth** ein überzeugender Beweis für etw sein

eloquently [ˈeləkwəntlɪ] ADV **a** *(= persuasively) speak, express, write* mit beredten Worten; *demonstrate* deutlich; **very ~ put** *or* **phrased** sehr gewandt ausgedrückt **b** *(fig) gesture, smile* beredt

else [els] ADV **a** *(after pron)* andere(r, s); **anybody ~ would have done it** jeder andere hätte es gemacht; **is there anybody ~ there?** *(in addition)* ist sonst (noch) jemand da?; **since John doesn't want it, does anybody ~ want it?** da John es nicht will, will jemand anders es haben?; **somebody ~** sonst jemand, jemand anders; **is there somebody ~?, she asked** ist da jemand anders?, fragte sie; **I'd prefer something ~** ich möchte lieber etwas anderes; **I'd prefer anything ~** alles andere wäre mir lieber; **have you anything ~ to say?** haben Sie sonst noch etwas zu sagen?; **do you find this species anywhere ~?** findet man die Gattung sonst wo *or* auch anderswo?; **but they haven't got anywhere ~ to go** aber sie können sonst nirgends anders hingehen; **this is somebody ~'s umbrella** dieser Schirm gehört jemand anders; **something ~** etwas anderes, sonst etwas; **that car is something ~** *(inf)* das Auto ist einfach Spitze *(inf)*; **if all ~ fails** wenn alle Stricke reißen; **above all ~** vor allen Dingen; **will there be anything ~, sir?** *(in shop)* darf es sonst noch etwas sein?; *(butler)* haben Sie sonst noch Wünsche?; **everyone/everything ~** alle anderen/alles andere; **everywhere ~** überall sonst

b somewhere *or* **someplace** *(esp US)* **~** woanders, anderswo; *(with motion)* woandershin, anderswohin; **from somewhere ~** anderswoher, woandersher, von woanders

c *(after pron, neg)* **nobody ~, no one ~** sonst niemand, niemand anders; **nobody ~ understood** sonst hat es niemand verstanden, niemand anders hat es verstanden; **nothing ~** sonst nichts, nichts anderes; **nothing ~ would be good enough** alles andere wäre nicht gut genug; **what do you want? – nothing ~, thank you** was möchten Sie? – danke, nichts weiter; **that this is a result of the cold and nothing ~** dass dies allein auf die Kälte zurückzuführen ist; **if nothing ~, you'll enjoy it** auf jeden Fall wird es dir Spaß machen; **there's nothing ~ for it but to ...** da gibt es keinen anderen Ausweg, als zu ...; **nowhere ~** sonst nirgends *or* nirgendwo, nirgendwo anders; *(with motion)* sonst nirgendwohin, nirgendwo anders hin; **there's not much ~** *or* **there's little ~ we can do** wir können kaum etwas anderes tun; **I can think of little ~** ich kann fast an nichts anderes mehr denken

d *(after interrog)* **where ~?** wo sonst?, wo anders?; **who ~?** wer sonst?; **who ~ but John could have done a thing like that?** wer anders als John hätte so etwas tun können?; **what ~?** was sonst?; **how ~ can I do it?** wie kann ich es denn sonst *or* anders machen?; **what ~ could I have done?** was hätte ich sonst tun können?

e *(adv of quantity)* **they sell books and toys and much ~** *(Brit)* sie führen Bücher, Spielzeug und vieles andere; **there is little ~ to be done** da bleibt nicht viel zu tun übrig

f *(= otherwise, if not)* sonst, andernfalls; **do it now (or) ~ you'll be punished** tu es jetzt, sonst setzt es Strafe *or* oder es setzt Strafe; **do it or ~ ...!** mach das, sonst *or* oder ...!; **he's either a genius or ~ he's completely mad** er ist entweder ein Genie oder aber völlig verrückt

elsewhere [ˌelsˈweəʳ] ADV woanders, anderswo *(inf)*; **to go ~** woandershin gehen; **her thoughts were ~** sie war mit ihren Gedanken woanders

ELT *abbr of* **English Language Teaching**, → *also* **TEFL**

elucidate [ɪˈluːsɪdeɪt] VT *text* erklären; *issue* Licht werfen auf *(+acc)*, erhellen; *situation* erhellen; *point* näher ausführen; *mystery* aufklären, aufhellen

elucidation [ɪˌluːsɪˈdeɪʃən] N *(of text)* Erklärung *f*; *(of issue, situation)* Erhellung *f*; *(of point)* nähere Ausführung; *(of mystery)* Aufklärung *f*, Aufhellung *f*

elucidatory [ɪˈluːsɪdeɪtərɪ] ADJ erklärend

elude [ɪ'lu:d] VT *observation, justice* sich entziehen *(+dat)*; *sb's gaze* ausweichen *(+dat)*; *police, enemy* entkommen *(+dat)*, entwischen *(+dat)*; **to ~ capture** entkommen; **the principle ~d his grasp** er konnte das Prinzip nicht erfassen; **sleep ~d her** sie konnte keinen Schlaf finden; **the name ~s me** der Name ist mir entfallen; **the title still ~s him** der Titel fehlt ihm immer noch

elusive [ɪ'lu:sɪv] ADJ **a** *truth* schwer fassbar; *goal, target, success* schwer erreichbar; *(= unattainable)* unerreichbar; **happiness seems to be an ~ state for some people** Glück scheint für manche Menschen ein unerreichbarer Zustand zu sein; **there was an ~ quality about Robert** Robert hatte etwas schwer Fassbares an sich *(dat)*; **financial success proved ~** der finanzielle Erfolg wollte sich nicht einstellen; **his answer to my question was ~** er antwortete mir ausweichend **b** *person* schwer zu erreichen; *animal* scheu; *prey* schwer zu fangen; **he remained ~** er blieb unauffindbar

elusively [ɪ'lu:sɪvlɪ] ADV *(+adj)* auf undefinierbare Art; *(+vb)* undefinierbar; *answer* ausweichend

elusiveness [ɪ'lu:sɪvnɪs] N *(of thoughts)* Flüchtigkeit *f*; *(of happiness)* Unerreichbarkeit *f*; **the ~ of this concept** die Schwierigkeit, diesen Begriff zu definieren; **the ~ of his answer** seine ausweichende Antwort

elves [elvz] *pl of* **elf**

Elysian [ɪ'lɪzɪən] ADJ **a** *(Myth)* elysisch; **the ~ fields** *pl* Elysium *nt* **b** *(fig)* paradiesisch, himmlisch

'em [əm] PRON *(inf)* = **them**

emaciated [ɪ'meɪsɪeɪtɪd] ADJ abgezehrt, ausgezehrt, stark abgemagert; **to become ~** stark abmagern

emaciation [ɪ,meɪsɪ'eɪʃən] N Auszehrung *f*, starke Abmagerung

e-mail, email ['i:meɪl] **N** E-Mail *f* **VT to ~ sb** jdm eine E-Mail schicken; **to ~ sth** etw per E-Mail schicken, etw mailen *(inf)*

e-mail address N E-Mail-Adresse *f*

emanate ['eməneɪt] VI ausgehen *(from* von); *(odour)* ausströmen, ausgehen *(from* von); *(documents, instructions)* stammen *(from* aus); **according to instructions emanating from regional headquarters** *(form)* nach Anweisungen der Bezirksstelle

emanation [,emə'neɪʃən] N Ausgehen *nt*; *(of odour)* Ausströmen *nt*, Ausgehen *nt*; *(Rel)* Emanation *f*

emancipate [ɪ'mænsɪpeɪt] VT *women* emanzipieren; *slaves* freilassen; *country, people* befreien; *(fig)* emanzipieren, befreien, frei machen; **to ~ oneself** sich emanzipieren

emancipated [ɪ'mænsɪpeɪtɪd] ADJ *woman, outlook* emanzipiert; *slave* freigelassen

emancipation [ɪ,mænsɪ'peɪʃən] N *(lit, fig)* Emanzipation *f*; *(of slave)* Freilassung *f*; *(of country, people)* Befreiung *f*

emasculate [ɪ'mæskjʊleɪt] VT **a** *(= weaken)* entkräften **b** *(lit) man* entmannen

emasculated [ɪ'mæskjʊleɪtɪd] ADJ *style etc* (saftund) kraftlos

emasculation [ɪ,mæskjʊ'leɪʃən] N **a** *(= weakening)* Entkräftung *f*, Schwächung *f* **b** *(lit)* Entmannung *f*, Kastration *f*

embalm [ɪm'bɑ:m] VT *corpse* einbalsamieren

embalming fluid [ɪm'bɑ:mɪŋ,flu:ɪd] N Balsamierflüssigkeit *f*

embank [ɪm'bæŋk] VT *river* eindämmen, eindeichen

embankment [ɪm'bæŋkmənt] N (Ufer)böschung *f*; *(along path, road)* Böschung *f*; *(for railway)* Bahndamm *m*; *(holding back water)* (Ufer)damm *m*, Deich *m*; *(= roadway beside a river)* Ufer(straße *f*) *nt*

embargo [ɪm'bɑ:gəʊ] **N** *pl* **-es a** Embargo *nt* *(against* gegen); **oil/arms/trade ~** Öl-/Waffen-/ /Handelsembargo *nt*; **to impose** *or* **place** *or* **put an ~ on sth** etw mit einem Embargo belegen, ein Embargo über etw *(acc)* verhängen; **to lift an ~ on sth** ein Embargo über etw *(acc)* aufheben; **the country is under an economic ~** über das Land wurde ein Wirtschaftsembargo verhängt **b** *(fig)* Sperre *f*; **to put an ~ on further spending** alle weiteren Ausgaben sperren **VT** *trade, goods* mit einem Embargo belegen

embark [ɪm'bɑ:k] **VT** einschiffen; *goods also* verladen **VI a** *(Naut)* sich einschiffen; *(troops)* eingeschifft werden **b** *(fig)* **to ~ up(on) sth** etw anfangen, etw beginnen

embarkation [,embɑ:'keɪʃən] N **a** Einschiffung *f* **b** *(of cargo)* Verladung *f*, Übernahme *f*

embarkation officer N Verladeoffizier *m*

embarkation papers N Bordpapiere *pl*

embarrass [ɪm'bærəs] VT **a** in Verlegenheit bringen, verlegen machen; *(generosity etc)* beschämen; **she was ~ed by the question** die Frage war ihr peinlich **b** *(obs, = hamper)* **he was ~ed by his cumbersome greatcoat** er wurde durch seinen unförmigen Übermantel behindert

embarrassed [ɪm'bærəst] ADJ verlegen; **he looked a bit ~** er sah etwas verlegen aus; **I am/feel so ~ (about it)** es ist mir so peinlich; **she was ~ to be seen with him** *or* **about being seen with him** es war ihr peinlich, mit ihm gesehen zu werden; **it's nothing to be ~ about, there's no need to feel ~ (about it)** das braucht einem nicht peinlich zu sein; **I was ~ for him** es war mir seinetwegen peinlich; **to be financially ~** in einer finanziellen Verlegenheit sein

embarrassing [ɪm'bærəsɪŋ] ADJ peinlich; *generosity etc* beschämend

embarrassingly [ɪm'bærəsɪŋlɪ] ADV auf peinliche Weise; *(introducing sentence)* peinlicherweise; **the play flopped ~** das Stück war ein peinlicher Reinfall; **it was ~ bad** es war so schlecht, dass es schon peinlich war; **~ candid remarks** Bemerkungen von peinlicher Offenheit; **~ for him, his wife came in at the wrong moment** es war peinlich für ihn, dass seine Frau im falschen Moment hereinkam

embarrassment [ɪm'bærəsmənt] N Verlegenheit *f*; *(through generosity also)* Beschämung *f*; **to cause ~ to sb** jdn in Verlegenheit bringen, jdn verlegen machen; **to be a constant source of ~ to sb** jdn ständig in Verlegenheit bringen; **to my great ~ she ...** sie ..., was mir sehr peinlich war; **she's an ~ to her family** sie blamiert die ganze Familie *(inf)*; **financial ~** finanzielle Verlegenheit; **an ~ of riches** ein verwirrender Reichtum

embassy ['embəsɪ] N Botschaft *f*

embattled [ɪm'bætld] ADJ **a** *(= besieged)* belagert; *(= fought over)* umkämpft; *(= fighting)* kämpfend **b** *(fig) person, government* bedrängt

embed [ɪm'bed] VT **a** einlassen; **the car was firmly ~ded in the mud** das Auto steckte im Schlamm fest; **the bullet ~ded itself in the wall** die Kugel bohrte sich in die Wand; **to be (deeply) ~ded in sth** *(fig)* (tief) in etw *(dat)* verwurzelt sein **b** *(Comput)* **~ded commands** eingebettete Befehle **c** *(Ling)* einschieben; **~ded clauses** eingeschobene Gliedsätze

embellish [ɪm'belɪʃ] VT *(= adorn)* schmücken, verschönern; *(fig) tale, account* ausschmücken; *truth* beschönigen

embellishment [ɪm'belɪʃmənt] N Schmuck *m*; *(= act)* Verschönerung *f*; *(of story)* Ausschmückung *f*; *(of truth)* Beschönigung *f*; *(of handwriting)* Verzierung *f*, Schnörkel *m*; *(Mus)* Verzierung *f*

embers ['embəz] PL Glut *f* → **fan**[1]

embezzle [ɪm'bezl] VT unterschlagen, veruntreuen *(from +dat)*

embezzlement [ɪm'bezlmənt] N Unterschlagung *f*

embezzler [ɪm'bezlə'] N *jd, der Unterschlagungen/eine Unterschlagung begangen hat* **he admitted to being an ~** er gab zu, Geld unterschlagen *or* veruntreut zu haben

embitter [ɪm'bɪtə'] VT *person* verbittern; *relations* trüben, vergiften

emblazon [ɪm'bleɪzən] VT **a** *(Her)* schmücken, (ver)zieren **b** *(= display boldly) name* stolz hervorheben; **the name "Jones" was ~ed on the cover** der Name „Jones" prangte auf dem Umschlag **c** *(= extol)* überschwänglich preisen

emblem ['embləm] N Emblem *nt*; *(of political party, trade also)* Wahrzeichen *nt*

emblematic [,emblə'mætɪk] ADJ emblematisch *(of* für)

embodiment [ɪm'bɒdɪmənt] N **a** Verkörperung *f*; **to be the ~ of evil** das Böse in Person sein **b** *(= inclusion)* Aufnahme *f*, Eingliederung *f*

embody [ɪm'bɒdɪ] VT **a** *(= give form to) one's thoughts* ausdrücken, Ausdruck geben *(+dat)*, in Worte kleiden **b** *spirit, principles, one's ideal* verkörpern **c** *(= include)* enthalten

embolden [ɪm'bəʊldən] VT ermutigen, Mut machen *(+dat)*; **to ~ sb to do sth** jdn dazu ermutigen *or* jdm Mut machen, etw zu tun; **to be ~ed to do sth** dazu ermutigt werden, etw zu tun

embolism ['embəlɪzəm] N *(Med)* Embolie *f*

embonpoint [,ɒmbɒm'pwɑ:ŋ] N *(hum euph)* Embonpoint *m or nt (dated)*, Leibesfülle *f*

emboss [ɪm'bɒs] VT *metal, leather* prägen; *silk, velvet* gaufrieren; **the cover is ~ed with his name** sein Name ist auf den Einband aufgeprägt

embossed [ɪm'bɒst] ADJ *lettering, paper, leather* geprägt; *design* erhaben; **an ~ silver tray** ein Silbertablett *nt* mit Relief; **~ with a design** mit aufgeprägtem Muster; **~ in silver** mit Silberprägung; **~ wallpaper** Prägetapete *f*

embouchure ['ɒmbʊʃʊə'] N *(Mus)* Mundstück *nt*; *(of player)* Mundstellung *f*

embrace [ɪm'breɪs] ✪ 26.3 **VT a** *(= hug)* umarmen, in die Arme schließen; **they ~d each other** sie umarmten sich *or* einander
b *(= seize eagerly) religion* annehmen; *opportunity* wahrnehmen, ergreifen; *cause* sich annehmen *(+gen)*; *offer* annehmen, ergreifen; **he ~d the idea of an integrated Europe** er machte sich *(dat)* den Gedanken eines integrierten Europas zu eigen
c *(= include)* umfassen, erfassen; **an all-embracing role** eine allumfassende Rolle
VI sich umarmen
N *(= hug)* Umarmung *f*; **a couple locked in a tender ~** ein Paar in zärtlicher Umarmung; **he held her in his ~** er hielt sie umschlungen; **his ~ of the Catholic faith** sein Bekenntnis zum katholischen Glauben; **death's ~** *(liter)* die Arme des Todes

embracery [ɪm'breɪsərɪ] N *(Jur)* Bestechungsversuch *m*

embrasure [ɪm'breɪʒə'] N *(in parapet)* Schießscharte *f*; *(of door, window)* Laibung *f*

embrocation [,embrəʊ'keɪʃən] N Einreibemittel *nt*

embroider [ɪm'brɔɪdə'] **VT** *cloth* besticken; *pattern* sticken; *(fig) facts, truth* ausschmücken; **to ~ a design on sth** ein Muster auf etw *(acc)* (auf)sticken **VI** sticken

embroidered [ɪm'brɔɪdəd] ADJ **a** *(lit) material, cushion, tablecloth etc* bestickt *(with* mit); *design* (auf)gestickt *(on* auf *+acc)*; **~ in gold** goldbestickt; **a design ~ in silk and wool** ein mit Wolle und Seide gesticktes Muster **b** *(fig: = embellished) story, version* ausgeschmückt

embroidery [ɪm'brɔɪdərɪ] N **a** Stickerei *f* **b** *(fig)* Ausschmückungen *pl*

embroidery: embroidery frame N Stickrahmen *m*; **embroidery thread** N Stickgarn *nt*

embroil [ɪm'brɔɪl] VT **to ~ sb in sth** jdn in etw *(acc)* hineinziehen; **to become ~ed in a dispute** in einen Streit verwickelt *or* hineingezogen werden

embroilment [ɪm'brɔɪlmənt] N Verwicklung *f* *(in* in *+acc)*

embryo ['embrɪəʊ] N Embryo *m*; *(esp fig)* Keim *m*; **in ~** *(lit, fig)* im Keim; *(animal)* als Embryo

embryologist [ˌembrɪˈɒlədʒɪst] N Embryologe *m*, Embryologin *f*

embryology [ˌembrɪˈɒlədʒɪ] N Embryologie *f*

embryonic [ˌembrɪˈɒnɪk] ADJ embryonisch; *(esp fig)* keimhaft

emcee [ˈemˈsiː] **N** Conférencier *m*; *(on TV also)* Showmaster(in) *m(f)*; *(at private functions)* Zeremonienmeister(in) *m(f)* **VT** *show* als Conférencier *etc* leiten

emend [ɪˈmend] VT *text* verbessern, korrigieren

emendation [ˌiːmenˈdeɪʃən] N Verbesserung *f*, Korrektur *f*

emerald [ˈemərəld] **N** **a** *(= stone)* Smaragd *m* **b** *(= colour)* Smaragdgrün *nt* **ADJ** smaragden, Smaragd-; *(colour also)* smaragdgrün; **~ ring** Smaragdring *m*

Emerald Isle N **the ~** die Grüne Insel

emerge [ɪˈmɜːdʒ] ✪ 17.2 VI **a** *(= come out)* auftauchen; **he ~d from behind the shed** er tauchte hinter dem Schuppen auf; **one arm ~d from beneath the blanket** ein Arm tauchte unter der Decke hervor; **he ~d from the house/a meeting** er kam aus dem Haus/aus einer Besprechung; **we ~d into the bright daylight** wir kamen heraus in das helle Tageslicht; **the country is emerging from civil war** das Land hat den Bürgerkrieg überwunden; **the economy is starting to ~ from the recession** die Wirtschaft beginnt sich von der Rezession zu erholen; **to ~ unscathed** ungeschoren davonkommen; **to ~ victorious** siegreich hervorgehen; **he ~d (as) the winner** er ging als Sieger hervor
b *(= come into being: life, new nation)* entstehen
c *(truth, nature of problem etc)* sich herausstellen, herauskommen *(from* bei); *(facts)* sich herausstellen, an den Tag kommen; **it ~s that ...** es stellt sich heraus, dass ...; **signs are emerging that ...** es gibt Anzeichen dafür, dass ...; **but what will ~ from all this?** aber was wird sich aus all dem ergeben?

emergence [ɪˈmɜːdʒəns] N Auftauchen *nt*; *(of new nation etc)* Entstehung *f*; *(of theory, school of thought)* Aufkommen *nt*

emergency [ɪˈmɜːdʒənsɪ] **N** *(= crisis)* Notfall *m*; *(particular situation)* Notlage *f*; **in an ~, in case of ~** im Notfall; **to be prepared for any ~** für den Notfall vorbereitet sein; **state of ~** Notstand *m*; **to declare a state of ~** den Notstand erklären *or* ausrufen; **to declare a state of ~ in an area** eine Gegend zum Notstandsgebiet erklären; **the doctor's been called out on an ~** der Arzt ist zu einem Notfall gerufen worden
ADJ **a** *(= in/for an emergency)* Not-; *meeting, talks, debate* außerordentlich; *repair* notdürftig; **~ regulations** Notverordnung *f*; **~ appeal** Notaufruf *m*; **~ committee** Notkomitee *nt*; **~ rations** Notverpflegung *f*; **an ~ repair has been done on the car** das Auto ist notdürftig repariert worden; **we had an ~ meeting in the garden** wir hielten schnell eine Lagebesprechung im Garten ab; **to undergo ~ surgery** sich einer Notoperation unterziehen; **to be given ~ treatment** *(in hospital)* auf der Unfallstation behandelt werden; **~ plan/procedure** Plan *m*/Maßnahmen *pl* für den Notfall; **for ~ use only** nur für den Notfall
b *(= for a disaster)* Katastrophen-; **~ aid** *or* **relief** Katastrophenhilfe *f*; **~ fund** Katastrophenfonds *m*; **~ airlift** Luftbrücke *f*
c *(= for state of emergency)* Notstands-; **~ measures** *or* **action** Notstandsmaßnahmen *pl*; **~ powers** Notstandsvollmachten *pl*; **~ law** Notstandsgesetz *nt*

emergency *in cpds* Not-; **emergency brake** N Notbremse *f*; **emergency call** N Notruf *m*; **emergency centre**, *(US)* **emergency center** N Rettungszentrum *nt* des Noteinsatzes; **emergency clause** N Dringlichkeits- *or* Notklausel *f*; **emergency cord** N *(Rail)* Notbremse *f*; **emergency department** N Unfallstation *f*, Unfallambulanz *f*; **emergency doctor** N Notarzt *m*/-ärztin *f*; **emergency exit** N Notausgang *m*; **emergency landing** N Notlandung *f*; **emergency number** N *(Telec)* Notruf *m*; *(after plane crash etc)* Sondertelefon *nt*; *(for technical help)* Hotline *f*; **emergency room** N *(US)* Unfallstation *f*; **emergency service** N Notdienst *m*, Rettungsdienst *m*; **emergency services** PL Notdienst *m*, Notdienste *pl*; **emergency stop** N *(Aut)* Vollbremsung *f*; **emergency telephone** N Notruftelefon *nt*; **emergency telephone number** N *(Telec)* Notrufnummer *f*; *(after plane crash etc)* Nummer *f* des Sondertelefons; *(of individual)* Nummer *f* für dringende Notfälle; *(for technical help)* Hotlinenummer *f*; **emergency ward** N Unfallstation *f*

emergent [ɪˈmɜːdʒənt] ADJ *(form) democracy, nation, country* jung, aufstrebend; *movement, group* aufstrebend; *sexuality, womanhood* erwachend

emeritus [ɪˈmerɪtəs] ADJ emeritiert; **~ professor, professor ~** Professor emeritus *m*

emery [ˈemərɪ] N Schmirgel *m*

emery [ˈemərɪ]: **emery board** N Papiernagelfeile *f*; **emery cloth** N Schmirgelleinwand *f*; **emery paper** N Schmirgelpapier *nt*

emetic [ɪˈmetɪk] **N** Brechmittel *nt*, Emetikum *nt (spec)* **ADJ** Brechreiz erregend, emetisch *(spec)*

emigrant [ˈemɪgrənt] **N** Auswanderer *m*, Auswanderin *f*; *(esp for political reasons)* Emigrant(in) *m(f)* **ADJ** *attr* Auswanderer-, Emigranten-; **~ country** Auswandererland *nt*

emigrate [ˈemɪgreɪt] VI auswandern; *(esp for political reasons)* emigrieren

emigration [ˌemɪˈgreɪʃən] N Auswanderung *f*; *(esp for political reasons)* Emigration *f*

émigré [ˈemɪgreɪ] N Emigrant(in) *m(f)*

eminence [ˈemɪnəns] N **a** *(= distinction)* hohes Ansehen; **doctors of ~** (hoch) angesehene Ärzte *pl*; **to achieve ~** hohes Ansehen erlangen **b** *(of ground)* Erhebung *f*, Anhöhe *f* **c** *(Eccl)* **His/Your Eminence** Seine/Eure Eminenz

éminence grise [ˈemɪnənsˈgriːz] N graue Eminenz

eminent [ˈemɪnənt] ADJ **a** *(= distinguished, prominent) person* angesehen, bedeutend; **to be ~ in a particular field** auf einem bestimmten Gebiet führend sein **b** *(form: = notable)* ausgesprochen; **you showed ~ good sense in coming to us** es war ausgesprochen vernünftig von Ihnen, zu uns zu kommen; **in an ~ degree** in ausgesprochen hohem Maße

eminently [ˈemɪnəntlɪ] ADV *(= extremely) sensible, readable* ausgesprochen; *practical* äußerst; *desirable* überaus; **~ suitable** *or* **suited** vorzüglich geeignet; **~ respectable** hoch angesehen; **an ~ forgettable speech** eine Rede, die man getrost vergessen kann; **it seems to me ~ reasonable** ich finde es durchaus berechtigt; **to be ~ qualified for sth/to do sth** sich vorzüglich für etw eignen/dazu eignen, etw zu tun; **to be ~ capable of sth** eindeutig zu etw fähig sein

emir [eˈmɪəʳ] N Emir m

emirate [ˈemɪrɪt] N Emirat *nt*

emissary [ˈemɪsərɪ] N Emissär *m*, Abgesandte(r) *mf*

emission [ɪˈmɪʃən] N Ausstrahlung *f*, Abstrahlung *f*; *(of fumes, X-rays)* Emission *f (spec)*; *(of gas, smell)* Verströmen *nt*, Ausströmen *nt*; *(of liquid)* Ausströmen *nt*; *(gradual)* Absonderung *f*, Abscheidung *f*; *(of vapour, smoke: continuous)* Abgabe *f*; *(of lava)* Ausstoßen *nt*; *(of sparks)* Versprühen *nt*

emissions trading N *(St Ex)* Emissionshandel *m*

emit [ɪˈmɪt] VT **a** *light* ausstrahlen, abstrahlen; *radiation* aussenden, emittieren *(spec)*; *sound* abgeben; *gas, smell* verströmen, ausströmen; *vapour, smoke (continuously)* abgeben; *lava, cry* ausstoßen; *liquid (gradually)* absondern, abscheiden; *sparks* versprühen **b** *banknotes* ausgeben

Emmy [ˈemɪ] N *(= award)* Emmy *f*

emollient [ɪˈmɒlɪənt] *(Med)* **N** Linderungsmittel *nt* **ADJ** lindernd

emolument [ɪˈmɒljʊmənt] N *usu pl (form)* Vergütung *f*; *(= fee)* Honorar *nt*; *(= salary)* Bezüge *pl*

emote [ɪˈməʊt] VI seine Gefühle ausdrücken; *(actor)* Gefühle mimen

emoticon [ɪˈməʊtɪkən] N *(Comput)* Smiley *nt*, Emoticon *nt*

emotion [ɪˈməʊʃən] N **a** Gefühl *nt*, Emotion *f*, Gefühlsregung *f*; **to dissociate ~ from reason** Verstand und Gefühl trennen **b** *no pl (= state of being moved)* (Gemüts)bewegung *f*, Bewegtheit *f*; **to show no ~** unbewegt bleiben; **in a voice full of ~** mit bewegter Stimme; **there was absolutely no ~ in his voice** seine Stimme war völlig emotionslos

emotional [ɪˈməʊʃənl] ADJ **a** *(= related to emotions, psychological) needs, security, involvement, detachment, reaction, energy* emotional; *problem, stress, trauma, abuse* seelisch; *support, development* psychologisch; **to go through ~ turmoil/an ~ upheaval** einen Aufruhr der Gefühle erleben; **~ state** Gemütszustand *m*; **his ~ wellbeing** sein seelisches Wohl; **~ life** Seelenleben *nt*; **~ intensity** Gefühlsintensität *f*; **on an ~ level** auf emotionaler Ebene; **to be on an ~ high** in Hochstimmung sein; **to be at an ~ low** ein seelisches Tief durchmachen; **~ wreck** seelisches Wrack
b *(= emotive) issue, impact, experience, situation* emotional
c *(= influenced by feelings) person, behaviour (characteristically)* emotional, gefühlsbetont; *(in particular situation)* emotional, gefühlvoll; *decision* gefühlsmäßig; *scene, response, reaction* emotional; *farewell, welcome* gefühlvoll; *appeal, speech* emotional, gefühlsbetont; **he made an ~ appeal to his wife** er appellierte gefühlsbetont an seine Frau; **the ~ appeal of a product** die gefühlsmäßige Anziehungskraft einer Ware; **to be ~ about sth** sich über etw *(acc)* erregen *or* aufregen; **to become** *or* **get ~** sich erregen *or* aufregen; **~ outburst** Gefühlsausbruch *m*

emotional: **emotional baggage** N seelischer Ballast; **emotional blackmail** N psychologische Erpressung; **emotional cripple** N emotionaler Krüppel

emotionalism [ɪˈməʊʃnəlɪzəm] N Gefühlsbetontheit *f*, Rührseligkeit *f*

emotionally [ɪˈməʊʃnəlɪ] ADV **a** *(= psychologically)* seelisch; *(= from an emotional point of view) involved* gefühlsmäßig; **I don't want to get ~ involved (with her)** ich will mich (bei ihr) nicht ernsthaft engagieren; **~ disturbed** seelisch gestört; **an ~ deprived child** ein Kind ohne Nestwärme; **~ I was a wreck** ich war ein seelisches Wrack; **physically and ~** körperlich und seelisch **b** *(= emotively, in an emotional manner)* emotional; **~ charged** *(atmosphere, debate)* spannungsgeladen

emotionless [ɪˈməʊʃənlɪs] ADJ *face, voice etc* ausdruckslos; *person* gefühllos, emotionslos

emotive [ɪˈməʊtɪv] ADJ *issue* emotional; *language, word* emotional gefärbt

empanel VT = **impanel**

empathize [ˈempəθaɪz] VI sich hineinversetzen *or* einfühlen *(with* in *+acc)*

empathy [ˈempəθɪ] N Einfühlungsvermögen *nt*, Empathie *f*

emperor [ˈempərəʳ] N Kaiser *m*; *(in Rome also)* Imperator *m*

emperor penguin N Kaiserpinguin *m*

emphasis [ˈemfəsɪs] N **a** *(= vocal stress)* Betonung *f*; **the ~ is on the first syllable** die Betonung *or* der Ton liegt auf der ersten Silbe; **to lay** *or* **put ~ on a word** ein Wort betonen; **to say sth with ~** etw mit Nachdruck *or* nachdrücklich betonen
b *(= importance)* Betonung *f*, (Schwer)gewicht *nt*; **to lay ~** *or* **place** *or* **put the ~ on sth** etw betonen; **to lay ~** *or* **place** *or* **put the ~ on doing sth** Wert darauf legen, etw zu tun; **this year the ~ is on femininity** dieses Jahr liegt der Akzent *or* die Betonung auf Weiblichkeit; **there is too much ~ on research** die Forschung steht zu sehr im Vordergrund; **a change of ~** eine Akzentverschiebung

emphasize [ˈemfəsaɪz] ✪ 26.3 VT *word, syllable, hips* betonen; *point, importance, difference, need al-*

so hervorheben; **it cannot be too strongly ~d that …** man kann gar nicht genug betonen, dass …

emphatic [ɪmˈfætɪk] ADJ **a** *(= forceful)* entschieden; *response* nachdrücklich, entschieden; *denial* energisch; *tone, stress, gesture* nachdrücklich; **his response was immediate and ~** er antwortete sofort und mit Nachdruck; **the accused responded with an ~ denial** in seiner Antwort leugnete der Angeklagte es energisch *or* entschieden; **the answer is an ~ no** die Antwort lautet ganz entschieden nein; **their answer was an ~ yes** sie bejahten es mit Nachdruck; **to be ~ (that …)** *(person)* darauf bestehen(, dass …); **to be ~ about sth** auf etw *(dat)* bestehen; **he was ~ in his defence of it** er verteidigte es mit Nachdruck; **they were ~ in denying their involvement** sie leugneten entschieden *or* energisch, dass sie daran beteiligt waren
b *(= decisive) victory, win, winner* klar, überzeugend; *defeat* schwer; *result, approval* eindeutig

emphatically [ɪmˈfætɪkəlɪ] ADV **a** *(= forcefully) say* nachdrücklich, mit Nachdruck; *nod* nachdrücklich, entschieden; *reply, reject* entschieden; *deny* energisch, entschieden; **most ~** mit allem Nachdruck **b** *(= definitely)* eindeutig; **most ~** ganz eindeutig; **~ not** auf (gar) keinen Fall

empire [ˈempaɪəʳ] **N** **a** Reich *nt*; *(worldwide)* Weltreich *nt*, Imperium *nt*; **the Holy Roman Empire** das Heilige Römische Reich (deutscher Nation); **the British Empire** das Britische Weltreich, das Empire **b** *(fig, esp Comm)* Imperium *nt*; **his business/publishing ~** sein Geschäfts-/Verlagsimperium *nt* **ADJ** *attr* **Empire** Empire-; **Empire style/furniture** Empirestil *m*/-möbel *pl*

empire: **empire-builder** N *(fig)* jd, der sich ein kleines Imperium aufbaut; **empire-building** N *(fig)* Schaffung *f* eines eigenen kleinen Imperiums

empiric [emˈpɪrɪk] **ADJ** = **empirical** **N** Empiriker(in) *m(f)*

empirical ADJ, **empirically** ADV [emˈpɪrɪkəl, -ɪ] empirisch

empirically [emˈpɪrɪkəlɪ] ADV empirisch; *(introducing sentence)* empirisch gesehen

empiricism [emˈpɪrɪsɪzəm] N Empirismus *m*; *(method)* Empirie *f*

empiricist [emˈpɪrɪsɪst] N Empiriker(in) *m(f)*

emplacement [ɪmˈpleɪsmənt] N *(Mil)* Stellung *f*

employ [ɪmˈplɔɪ] **VT** **a** *person* beschäftigen; *(= take on)* anstellen; *private detective* beauftragen; **he has been ~ed with us for 15 years** er ist schon seit 15 Jahren bei uns
b *(= use) means, method, tactics, skill, force, cunning* anwenden, einsetzen; *word, concept* verwenden; *time* verbringen; **you can surely find a better way of ~ing your time** Sie können doch bestimmt Besseres mit Ihrer Zeit anfangen; **they ~ed the services of a chemist to help them** sie zogen einen Chemiker heran, um ihnen zu helfen
c **to be ~ed in doing sth** damit beschäftigt sein, etw zu tun
N **to be in the ~ of sb** *(form)* bei jdm beschäftigt sein, in jds Diensten stehen *(geh)*

employable [ɪmˈplɔɪəbl] ADJ *person* anstellbar, zu beschäftigen *pred*

employee [ˌɪmplɔɪˈiː] N Angestellte(r) *mf*; **~s and employers** Arbeitnehmer und Arbeitgeber; **the ~s** *(of one firm)* die Belegschaft, die Beschäftigten *pl*; **~ rights** Arbeitnehmerrechte *pl*

employer [ɪmˈplɔɪəʳ] N Arbeitgeber(in) *m(f)*, Brötchengeber *m (hum inf)*; *(Comm, Ind)* Unternehmer(in) *m(f)*, Arbeitgeber(in) *m(f)*; *(of domestics, servants, civil servants)* Dienstherr(in) *m(f)*; **~s' federation** Arbeitgeberverband *m*; **~'s contribution** Arbeitgeberanteil *m*; **~'s liability insurance plan** Arbeitgeberhaftpflichtversicherung *f*

employment [ɪmˈplɔɪmənt] N **a** (An)stellung *f*, Arbeit *f*; **to take up ~ with sb** eine Stelle bei jdm annehmen; **to be without ~** stellungslos *or* ohne Arbeit sein; **to seek ~** Arbeit *or* eine Stelle suchen; **to seek ~ with sb** sich bei jdm bewerben; **to leave one's ~** seine Stelle aufgeben; **out of ~** stellungslos, arbeitslos; **how long is it since you were last in ~?** wann hatten Sie Ihre letzte Stellung?; **conditions/contract/place of ~** Arbeitsbedingungen *pl*/-vertrag *m*/-platz *m*; **~ market** Arbeits- *or* Stellenmarkt *m*; **to find ~ for sb** Arbeit *or* eine Anstellung für jdn finden; **what kind of ~ are you looking for?** welche Art von Tätigkeit suchen Sie?
b *(= act of employing)* Beschäftigung *f*; *(= taking on)* Anstellung *f*, Einstellen *nt*
c *(= use, of means, method, skill, force, cunning)* Anwendung *f*, Einsatz *m*; *(of word, concept)* Verwendung *f*

employment: **employment agency** N Stellenvermittlung *f*; **employment exchange** N *(dated)* = **employment office**; **employment office** N Arbeitsamt *nt*; **employment programme**, *(US)* **employment program** N Beschäftigungsprogramm *nt*

emporium [emˈpɔːrɪəm] N Warenhaus *nt*

empower [ɪmˈpaʊəʳ] VT **a** **to ~ sb to do sth** jdn ermächtigen, etw zu tun; *(Jur)* jdm (die) Vollmacht erteilen, etw zu tun; **to be ~ed to do sth** ermächtigt *or* befugt sein, etw zu tun; *(Jur)* die Vollmacht haben, etw zu tun **b** *(= make powerful) women, minorities etc* stärken

empress [ˈemprɪs] N Kaiserin *f*

emptiness [ˈemptɪnɪs] N Leere *f*, Leerheit *f*; *(of life etc)* Leere *f*

empty [ˈemptɪ] **ADJ** (+er) **a** leer; *(= unoccupied) house* leer stehend *attr*; *seat, chair, space, place* frei; **apart from them the room was ~** außer ihnen war niemand im Zimmer; **there were no ~ seats on the bus** im Bus waren keine Plätze frei; **she was staring into ~ space** sie starrte ins Leere; **the house was just an ~ shell** das Haus bestand nur aus nackten Mauern; **on an ~ stomach** mit leerem Magen; *take drug, drink alcohol* auf leeren Magen; **to be running on ~** *(person, organization etc)* am Ende sein; **my car is running on ~** ich habe kein Benzin mehr; **~ vessels make the most sound** *(Prov)* die am wenigsten zu sagen haben, reden am meisten → *also* **empty-headed, empty-handed**
b *(= devoid)* **the parks are ~ of children** in den Parks sind keine Kinder; **she was left ~ of feeling** sie hatte keine Gefühle mehr; **a sentence ~ of sense** ein sinnloser Satz; **~ of all expression** völlig ausdruckslos
c *(fig: = meaningless, dreary) words, phrase, marriage, gesture, promise, threat, feeling* leer; *dream, hope* verloren; *life, days, weeks* leer, unausgefüllt; *(= expressionless) face, expression, eyes* leer, ausdruckslos; **~ rhetoric** leeres Gerede; **an ~ exercise** eine leere Formalität; **to feel ~** ein leeres Gefühl *or* ein Gefühl *nt* der Leere haben; **that ~ feeling** dieses leere Gefühl, dieses Gefühl der Leere
N *usu pl* **empties** Leergut *nt*
VT **a** leeren; *container* (ent)leeren; *box, room* ausräumen; *house* räumen; *glass, bottle* leeren; *(by drinking)* austrinken; *pond, tank* ablassen, leeren; *lorry* abladen; **her singing emptied the hall in ten minutes flat** mit ihrem Singen schaffte sie es, dass der Saal innerhalb von zehn Minuten leer war; **the burglars emptied the shop** die Einbrecher haben den Laden ausgeräumt
b *(= pour) liquid, contents* ausgießen, leeren; **he emptied it into another container** er goss es in ein anderes Gefäß um
VI *(water)* auslaufen, abfließen; *(rivers)* münden, sich ergießen *(liter)* (into in *+acc*); *(theatre, streets)* sich leeren; **the sink is not ~ing properly** der Ausguss läuft nicht richtig ab

▶ **empty out** VT *sep* ausleeren

empty: **empty-handed** ADJ **to return ~** mit leeren Händen zurückkehren, unverrichteter Dinge zurückkehren; **empty-headed** ADJ strohdumm; **she's an ~ girl** sie hat Stroh im Kopf; **empty nesters** PL *Eltern, deren Kinder erwachsen und aus dem Haus sind*; **empty nest syndrome** N *Syndrom bei Eltern, wenn ihre Kinder (erwachsen und) aus dem Haus sind*

Empyrean [ɛmpɪˈriːən] N **the ~** *(liter)* das Empyreum *nt (liter)*

EMS *abbr of* **European Monetary System** EWS *nt*

EMU *abbr of* **European Monetary Union** EWU *nt*

emu [ˈiːmjuː] N Emu *m*

emulate [ˈemjʊleɪt] VT **a** *(= imitate)* nacheifern *(+dat)*, nachstreben *(+dat)*; **I tried to ~ his success** ich versuchte, es ihm gleichzutun **b** *(Comput)* emulieren

emulation [ˌemjʊˈleɪʃən] N **a** Nacheiferung *f*; **in ~ of sb** in dem Bestreben, es jdm gleichzutun **b** *(Comput)* Emulation *f*

emulsifier [ɪˈmʌlsɪfaɪəʳ] N Emulgator *m*

emulsify [ɪˈmʌlsɪfaɪ] **VT** emulgieren, zu einer Emulsion verbinden **VI** emulgieren

emulsion [ɪˈmʌlʃən] N **a** Emulsion *f* **b** *(also* **emulsion paint**) Emulsionsfarbe *f*

enable [ɪˈneɪbl] VT **a** *(= make able)* **to ~ sb to do sth** es jdm ermöglichen *or* möglich machen, etw zu tun, jdn in den Stand setzen, etw zu tun *(geh)*; **what ~s the seal to stay under water so long?** wodurch ist der Seehund fähig, so lange unter Wasser zu bleiben? **b** *(Jur. = authorize) measures, reforms* anordnen; **to ~ sb to do sth** jdn (dazu) ermächtigen, etw zu tun **c** *(Comput)* aktivieren

enabling [ɪˈneɪblɪŋ] ADJ **a** **~ legislation** Ermächtigungsgesetze *pl*; **~ act/law** Ermächtigungsgesetz *nt* **b** *(= empowering)* **to play an ~ role in sth** etw möglich machen; **~ technology** Hilfstechnologie *f*

enact [ɪˈnækt] VT **a** *(Pol) law* erlassen; **it is hereby ~ed that …** es wird hiermit verfügt, dass … **b** *(= perform) play* aufführen; *role* darstellen, spielen; **the scene which was ~ed yesterday** *(fig)* die Szene, die sich gestern abgespielt hat

enactment [ɪˈnæktmənt] N *(of law)* Erlass *m*; *(of regulation)* Verordnung *f*, Verfügung *f*; *(of play)* Aufführung *f*

enamel [ɪˈnæməl] **N** Email *nt*, Emaille *f (inf)*; *(= paint)* Email(le)lack *m*; *(of tiles etc)* Glasur *f*; *(of teeth)* Zahnschmelz *m*; *(= nail enamel)* Nagellack *m* **VT** emaillieren **ADJ** *pot, pan* Email(le)-; **~ paint** Email(le)lack *m*

enamelled, *(US)* **enameled** [ɪˈnæməld] ADJ emailliert; **~ jewellery** *(Brit)* **enameled jewelry** *(US)* Email(le)schmuck *m*

enamelware [ɪˈnæməlˌwɛəʳ] N Email(le)waren *pl*

enamour, *(US)* **enamor** [ɪˈnæməʳ] VT **to be ~ed of sb** *(= in love with)* in jdn verliebt sein; **to be ~ed of sth** *(= taken by)* von etw angetan *or* entzückt sein; **she was not exactly ~ed of the idea** sie war von der Idee nicht gerade begeistert

en bloc [ˌɑ̃ˈblɒk] ADV en bloc; **to resign ~** geschlossen zurücktreten

enc = **enc(l)**

encamp [ɪnˈkæmp] **VI** das Lager aufschlagen **VT** **where the troops were ~ed** wo die Truppen ihr Lager bezogen hatten

encampment [ɪnˈkæmpmənt] N Lager *nt*

encapsulate [ɪnˈkæpsjʊleɪt] VT *(Pharm)* in Kapseln abfüllen; *(fig: = express in condensed form)* zusammenfassen

encase [ɪnˈkeɪs] VT verkleiden (*in* mit); *wires* umgeben (*in* mit); *(Cook) cake* überziehen (*in* mit); *(in pastry etc)* einhüllen (*in* in *+acc*); **her arms were ~d in plaster** ihre Arme waren eingegipst *or* in einem Gipsverband

encash [ɪnˈkæʃ] VT *cheque etc* einlösen

encashment [ɪnˈkæʃmənt] N *(of cheque etc)* Einlösung *f*

encephalitis [ˌensefəˈlaɪtɪs] N Gehirnentzündung *f*

enchain [ɪnˈtʃeɪn] VT *(lit)* in Ketten legen; **to be ~ed** *(fig)* gefangen sein

enchant [ɪnˈtʃɑːnt] VT **a** *(= delight)* bezaubern, entzücken; **to be ~ed by sth** von etw *or* über etw *(acc)* entzückt sein **b** *(= put under spell)* verzaubern; **the ~ed wood** der Zauberwald

enchanting ADJ, **enchantingly** ADV [ɪnˈtʃɑːntɪŋ, -lɪ] bezaubernd, entzückend

enchantment [ɪnˈtʃɑːntmənt] N **a** *(= delight)* Entzücken *nt* **b** *(= charm)* Zauber *m*

enchantress [ɪnˈtʃɑːntrɪs] N Zauberin *f*; *(= enchanting woman)* bezaubernde Frau

enchilada [entʃɪlɑːdə] N **a** *(= tortilla)* Enchilada *f* **b** *(US) inf* **the whole ~** das ganze Drum und Dran, (das) alles; **the big ~** der große Boss *(inf)*

encipher [ɪnˈsaɪfəʳ] VT chiffrieren

encircle [ɪnˈsɜːkl] VT *(= surround)* umgeben, umfassen; *(belt)* umschließen, umfassen; *(troops)* einkreisen, umfassen; *building* umstellen; **his arm ~d her waist** er hielt ihre Taille umfasst; **the house is ~d by trees** das Haus ist von Bäumen umstanden

encirclement [ɪnˈsɜːklmənt] N *(Mil)* Einkreisung *f*, Umfassung *f*; *(in a valley)* Einkesselung *f*; *(of building)* Umstellung *f*

encircling [ɪnˈsɜːklɪŋ] **N** *(Mil)* Umfassung *f*, Einkreisen *nt*; *(in valley)* Einkesseln *nt*; *(of building)* Umstellung *f* **ADJ** *walls etc* umgebend; *hills, forest* umliegend *(liter)*; *gloom* allumfassend; **~ war** Einkesselungskrieg *m*; **~ movement** *(Mil)* Einkreisungs- *or* Umfassungsmanöver *nt*

enc(l) *abbr of* **enclosure(s)** Anl.

enclave [ˈenkleɪv] N Enklave *f*

enclitic [ɪnˈklɪtɪk] N Enklitikon *nt*

enclose [ɪnˈkləʊz] ✪ 20.2, 20.3, 20.7, 21.1 VT **a** *(= shut in)* einschließen; *(= surround)* umgeben; *(with fence etc) ground* einzäunen, einfrieden *(geh)* **b** *(in a parcel, envelope)* beilegen *(in, with dat)*, beifügen *(in, with dat)*; **to ~ sth in a letter** einem Brief etw beilegen; **I am enclosing the original with the translation** anbei die Übersetzung sowie der Originaltext; **I ~d your letter with mine** ich habe Ihren Brief mit meinem mitgeschickt

enclosed [ɪnˈkləʊzd] ADJ **a** *(= confined) space, area* geschlossen; *garden* abgeschlossen, eingefriedet *(geh)*; *waters* von Land umschlossen **b** *(in letter, parcel) form, cheque, photo, details* beiliegend; **~ with** *or* **in the letter** dem Brief beigelegt; **a phot was ~ in the letter** dem Brief lag ein Foto bei; **please find ~ a cheque for the sum of £25** *(Brit) or* **a check for the sum of 25 dollars** *(US)* in der Anlage *or* beiliegend finden Sie einen Scheck über £ 25/25 dollars **c** *(= separate, sheltered) existence* behütet; *community* geschlossen

enclosed order N *(Rel)* geschlossener Orden

enclosure [ɪnˈkləʊʒəʳ] N **a** *(= ground enclosed)* eingezäuntes Grundstück *or* Feld, Einfriedung *f*; *(for animals)* Gehege *nt*; **the ~** *(on racecourse)* der Zuschauerbereich **b** *(act)* Einzäunung *f*, Einfried(ig)ung *f (geh)* **c** *(= fence etc)* Umzäunung *f*; **~ wall** Umfassungsmauer *f* **d** *(= document etc enclosed)* Anlage *f*

encode [ɪnˈkəʊd] VT *(also Comput)* codieren

encoder [ɪnˈkəʊdəʳ] N *(also Comput)* Codierer *m*, Codiergerät *nt*

encomium [ɪnˈkəʊmɪəm] N *(form)* Lobrede *f*, Laudatio *f (geh)*

encompass [ɪnˈkʌmpəs] VT **a** *(liter. = surround)* umfassen *(by* mit) **b** *(= include)* umfassen **c** *(liter, = bring about) downfall* herbeiführen

encore [ˈɒŋkɔːʳ] **INTERJ** da capo, Zugabe **N** Zugabe *f*, Dakapo *nt*, Dacapo *nt*; **to call for/give an ~** eine Zugabe verlangen/geben **VT** *piece* als Zugabe verlangen; *artiste* um eine Zugabe bitten **VI** eine Zugabe geben

encounter [ɪnˈkaʊntəʳ] **VT** *enemy, opposition* treffen *or* stoßen auf *(+acc)*; *difficulties, resistance* stoßen auf *(+acc)*; *danger* geraten in *(+acc)*; *(liter) person* begegnen *(+dat)*, treffen; **to ~ enemy fire** unter feindlichen Beschuss geraten **N** Begegnung *f*, Treffen *nt*; *(in battle)* Zusammenstoß *m*; **chance ~** zufällige Begegnung; **sexual ~** sexuelle Erfahrung; **close ~** *(Space: = near miss)* Beinahezusammenstoß *m*; *(with aliens)* unheimliche Begegnung

encounter group N *(Psych)* Selbsterfahrungsgruppe *f*

encourage [ɪnˈkʌrɪdʒ] VT *person* ermutigen, ermuntern; *(= motivate)* anregen; *(= give confidence)* Mut machen *(+dat)*, ermutigen; *arts, industry, projects, investments* fördern; *(Sport) team, competitor* anfeuern, anspornen; *bad habits* unterstützen; **to ~ participation** zum Mitmachen anregen; **we don't want to ~ suspicion** wir wollen keinen Verdacht erregen; **to be ~d by sth** durch etw neuen Mut schöpfen; **he's lazy enough as it is, please don't ~ him** er ist schon faul genug, bitte ermuntern *or* unterstützen Sie ihn nicht noch; **that will ~ bad habits** das wird zu schlechten Gewohnheiten führen; **to ~ sb to do sth** jdn ermutigen *or* ermuntern, etw zu tun; **you'll only ~ him to think ...** er wird dann nur noch eher glauben, dass ...; **this ~s me to think that maybe ...** das lässt mich vermuten, dass vielleicht ...

encouragement [ɪnˈkʌrɪdʒmənt] N Ermutigung *f*, Ermunterung *f*; *(= motivation)* Anregung *f*; *(= support)* Unterstützung *f*, Förderung *f*; **to give sb (a lot of) ~** jdn (sehr) ermuntern; **he doesn't need any ~** ihn braucht man nicht zu ermuntern; **an ~ to buy** ein Kaufanreiz *m*

encouraging [ɪnˈkʌrɪdʒɪŋ] ADJ ermutigend; **I found him very ~** er hat mir sehr viel Mut gemacht

encouragingly [ɪnˈkʌrɪdʒɪŋlɪ] ADV *smile, nod, say, speak* ermutigend; *(+adj)* erfreulich; *(introducing sentence)* erfreulicherweise; **more/less ~, they ...** es ist ermutigender/weniger ermutigend, dass sie ...

encroach [ɪnˈkrəʊtʃ] VI **to ~ (up)on** *(land)* vordringen in *(+acc)*; *sphere, rights* eingreifen in *(+acc)*; *privileges* übergreifen auf *(+acc)*; *time* in Anspruch nehmen

encroachment [ɪnˈkrəʊtʃmənt] N *(on land)* Vordringen *nt*; *(on rights)* Eingriff *m*; *(on privileges)* Übergriff *m*; *(on time)* Beanspruchung *f*

encrust [ɪnˈkrʌst] VT *(fig, with pearls)* besetzen; **~ed with earth/cement** erd-/zementverkrustet; **a jewel-~ed brooch** eine juwelenbesetzte Brosche; **~ed with ice** vereist

encrustation [ɪnˌkrʌsˈteɪʃən] N Kruste *f*, Verkrustung *f*; *(fig, with diamonds, pearls, lace)* Besatz *m*; *(with ice etc)* Überzug *m*

encrypt [ɪnˈkrɪpt] VT *(Comput, Telec, TV)* verschlüsseln

encryption [ɪnˈkrɪpʃən] N *(Comput, Telec, TV)* Verschlüsselung *f*; **~ program/system** Verschlüsselungsprogramm *nt*/-system *nt*

encumber [ɪnˈkʌmbəʳ] VT beladen; *(with debts)* belasten; **~ed property** *(Fin)* belasteter Grundbesitz

encumbrance [ɪnˈkʌmbrəns] N *(also Jur)* Belastung *f*; *(person)* Last *f*; **to be an ~ to sb** *(luggage)* jdn behindern; *(person)* eine Last für jdn sein; *(dependent, responsibility)* eine Belastung für jdn sein

encyclical [ɪnˈsɪklɪkəl] N Enzyklika *f*

encyclop(a)edia [ɪnˌsaɪkləʊˈpiːdɪə] N Lexikon *nt*, Enzyklopädie *f*

encyclop(a)edic [ɪnˌsaɪkləʊˈpiːdɪk] ADJ enzyklopädisch

end [end] **N** **a** Ende *nt*; *(of finger)* Spitze *f*; **at the ~ of the procession** am Schluss *or* Ende der Prozession; **our house is the fourth from the ~** unser Haus ist das viertletzte; **to the ~s of the earth** bis ans Ende der Welt; **from ~ to ~** von einem Ende zum anderen; **who'll meet you at the other ~?** wer holt dich ab, wenn du ankommst?; **Lisa's on the other ~ (of the phone)** Lisa ist am Telefon; **to keep one's ~ up** *(inf: = stay cheerful)* sich nicht unterkriegen lassen *(inf)*; *(= do one's share)* das seine *or* Seine tun; **to stand on ~** *(barrel, box etc)* hochkant stehen; *(hair)* zu Berge stehen; **for hours on ~** stundenlang ununterbrochen; **the ships collided ~ on** *(Brit)* die Schiffe fuhren aufeinander auf; **~ to ~** mit den Enden aneinander; **to change ~s** *(Sport)* die Seiten wechseln; **to make (both) ~s meet** *(fig)* zurechtkommen *(inf)*, sich über Wasser halten; **to see no further than the ~ of one's nose** nicht weiter sehen als seine Nase (reicht); **how are things at your ~?** wie sieht es bei Ihnen aus?; **we've got some problems at this ~** wir haben hier *or* bei uns einige Probleme; **to have one's ~ away** *(Brit sl)* kräftig durchziehen *(sl)* → **rope, tether N**

b *(= remnant, of rope)* Ende *nt*, Rest *m*; *(of candle, cigarette)* Stummel *m*; **just a few odd ~s left** nur noch ein paar Reste

c *(= conclusion)* Ende *nt*; **at the ~** schließlich; **the ~ of the month** das Monatsende; **at/toward(s) the ~ of December** Ende/gegen Ende Dezember; **at the ~ of (the) winter/the war** am Ende des Winters/des Krieges; **at the ~ of the opera/the book** am Schluss der Oper/des Buches; **at the ~ of three weeks** nach drei Wochen; **they'll be paid at the ~ of the job** sie werden bezahlt, wenn sie mit der Arbeit fertig sind; **at the ~ of the day** *(fig)* letzten Endes, schließlich und endlich; **until** *or* **to the ~ of time** bis ans Ende aller Tage; **is there no ~ to this?** hört das denn nie auf?; **as far as I'm concerned, that's the ~ of the matter!** für mich ist die Sache erledigt; **we shall never hear the ~ of it** das werden wir noch lange zu hören kriegen; **to be at an ~** zu Ende sein; **to be at the ~ of one's patience/strength** mit seiner Geduld/seinen Kräften am Ende sein; **to watch a film to the ~** einen Film bis zu Ende ansehen; **to read a book to the ~** ein Buch bis zu Ende lesen; **that's the ~ of him** er ist erledigt *or* fertig *(inf)*; **that's the ~ of that** das ist damit erledigt; **to bring to an ~** zu Ende bringen, beenden; *relations* ein Ende setzen *(+dat)*, beenden; **to come to an ~** zu Ende gehen; **to get to the ~ of the road/book** ans Ende der Straße/zum Schluss des Buches kommen; **this is the ~ of the road for the government** das bedeutet das Ende für die Regierung; **at the ~ of the road** *or* **line many businesses will go bankrupt** letzten Endes werden viele Firmen Pleite machen *(inf)*; **in the ~** schließlich, zum Schluss; **to put an ~ to sth** einer Sache *(dat)* ein Ende setzen; **to come to a bad ~** ein böses Ende nehmen; **to meet one's ~** den Tod finden; **he met a violent ~** er starb einen gewaltsamen Tod; **were you with him at the ~?** warst du zum Schluss *or* am Ende bei ihm?

d *(inf phrases)* **we met no ~ of famous people** *(esp Brit)* wir trafen viele berühmte Leute; **to think no ~ of sb** *(esp Brit)* große Stücke auf jdn halten; **it pleased her no ~** *(esp Brit)* das hat ihr maßlos *or* irrsinnig *(inf)* gefallen; **you're the ~** *(Brit) (= annoying)* du bist der letzte Mensch *(inf)*; *(= funny)* du bist zum Schreien *(inf)*

e *(= purpose)* Ziel *nt*, Zweck *m*; **with this ~ in view** mit diesem Ziel vor Augen; **to what ~?** *(form)* zu welchem Zweck?; **an ~ in itself** Selbstzweck *no art*; **the ~ justifies the means** *(prov)* der Zweck heiligt die Mittel *(prov)*

ADJ *attr* letzte(r, s); **the ~ house** das Endhaus, das letzte Haus

VT beenden; *speech, one's days also* beschließen; **the novel to ~ all novels** der größte Roman aller Zeiten; **the deal to ~ all deals** das beste Geschäft aller Zeiten; **to ~ it all** *(= commit suicide)* Schluss machen

VI enden; **we'll have to ~ soon** wir müssen bald Schluss machen; **we ~ed with a song** zum Schluss sangen wir ein Lied; **to be ~ing** zu Ende gehen; **to ~ by doing sth** schließlich etw tun; **where's it all going to ~?** wo soll das nur hinführen?; **to ~ in an "s"** auf „s" enden; **each leg ~s in a claw** jedes Bein läuft in einer Klaue aus; **an argument which ~ed in a fight** ein Streit, der mit einer Schlägerei endete

▸ **end off** VT *sep* abschließen, beschließen

▸ **end up** VI enden, landen *(inf)*; **to end up doing sth** schließlich etw tun; **to end up (as) a lawyer** schließlich Rechtsanwalt werden; **to end up (as) an alcoholic** als Alkoholiker enden; **to end up a criminal** schließlich zum Verbrecher werden; **we ended up at Joe's** wir waren *or* landeten *(inf)* schließlich bei Joe; **you'll end up in trouble** Sie werden noch Ärger bekommen

endanger [ɪnˈdeɪndʒəʳ] VT gefährden

endangered [ɪnˈdeɪndʒəd] ADJ *species, animal, plant* vom Aussterben bedroht

end consumer N End- *or* Letztverbraucher(in) *m(f)*

endear [ɪnˈdɪəʳ] VT beliebt machen (*to* bei); **to ~ oneself to sb** sich bei jdm beliebt machen

endearing [ɪnˈdɪərɪŋ] ADJ *person, quality* liebenswert; *habit, trait, manner* nett, liebenswert; *smile* gewinnend

endearingly [ɪnˈdɪərɪŋlɪ] ADV liebenswert; *smile* gewinnend

endearment [ɪnˈdɪəmənt] N **term of ~** Kosename *m*, Kosewort *nt*; **words of ~** liebe Worte *pl*

endeavour, *(US)* **endeavor** [ɪnˈdevəʳ] N *(= attempt)* Anstrengung *f*, Bemühung *f*; *(liter. = striving)* (Be)streben *nt no pl (geh)*; **all human ~** das gesamte Streben des Menschen; **to make an ~ to do sth** sich nach Kräften bemühen, etw zu tun; **in an ~ to please her** um ihr eine Freude zu machen VI sich anstrengen, sich bemühen, bestrebt sein *(geh)*

endemic [enˈdemɪk] ADJ *(lit, fig)* endemisch; **~ to** endemisch in *(dat)*; **petty embezzling seems to be ~ here** kleine Unterschlagungen scheinen hier eine Krankheit zu sein

endgame [ˈendgeɪm] N Endspiel *nt*

ending [ˈendɪŋ] N *(of story, book, events)* Ausgang *m*; *(of day)* Abschluss *m*; *(= last part)* Ende *nt*, Schluss *m*; *(of word)* Endung *f*; **a story with a happy ~** eine Geschichte mit einem Happy End *or* Happyend; **the dispute had a happy ~** der Streit ging gut aus

endive [ˈendaɪv] N (Winter)endivie *f*, Endiviensalat *m*

endless [ˈendlɪs] ADJ **a** *(= interminable, unlimited) period, stream, series, talk, patience* endlos; *variety* unendlich; *supply* unbegrenzt; **an ~ round of meetings** Besprechungen, die kein Ende nehmen wollen; **the list is ~** die Liste nimmt kein Ende **b** *(= countless) meetings, arguments, questions, problems* unzählig; **the possibilities are ~** es gibt unendlich viele Möglichkeiten **c** *(= continuous) road, stretch* endlos (lang); *queue* endlos lang; *expanse* unendlich; *desert, forest* endlos, unendlich

endlessly [ˈendlɪslɪ] ADV **a** *(= without stopping) talk, discuss, argue* endlos; *listen, play, sit* ewig **b** *(= again and again) repeat, recycle* endlos, immer wieder **c** *(= without limit) stretch* endlos; *fascinating, curious, long* unendlich

endocrine [ˈendəʊkraɪn] ADJ endokrin; **~ gland** endokrine Drüse

endocrinologist [ˌendəʊkraɪˈnɒlədʒɪst] N Endokrinologe *m*, Endokrinologin *f*

endocrinology [ˌendəʊkraɪˈnɒlədʒɪ] N Endokrinologie *f*

endomorph [ˈendəʊmɔːf] N Pykniker(in) *m(f)*

endomorphic [ˈendəʊmɔːfɪk] ADJ pyknisch

endorphin [ˌenˈdɔːfɪn] N Endorphin *nt*

endorse [ɪnˈdɔːs] ✪ 11.1 VT **a** *document, cheque* auf der Rückseite unterzeichnen, indossieren **b** *(Brit Jur) driving licence* eine Strafe vermerken auf *(+dat)*; **I had my licence ~d** ich bekam einen Strafvermerk auf meinem Führerschein **c** *(= approve)* billigen, unterschreiben *(inf)*; *product, company* empfehlen; **I ~ that** dem stimme ich zu, dem pflichte ich bei

endorsee [ɪnˌdɔːˈsiː] N *(Fin)* Indossatar *m*

endorsement [ɪnˈdɔːsmənt] N **a** *(on cheque, bill of exchange)* Indossament *nt*; *(on policy)* Zusatz *m*, Nachtrag *m* **b** *(Brit Jur, on driving licence)* Strafvermerk *m* auf dem Führerschein **c** *(of opinion)* Billigung *f*; *(for product, company)* Empfehlung *f*; **the committee's ~ of the idea** die Billigung der Idee durch das Komitee

endorser [ɪnˈdɔːsəʳ] N *(Fin)* Indossar *m*

endoscope [ˈendəʊˌskəʊp] N Endoskop *nt*

endoscopy [ˌenˈdɒskəpɪ] N Endoskopie *f*

endow [ɪnˈdaʊ] VT **a** *institution, church* eine Stiftung machen an *(+acc)*; *(Univ, Sch) prize, chair* stiften; **an ~ed school** *eine mit Stiftungsgeldern gebaute und finanzierte Schule* **b** *(fig) usu pass* **to ~ sb with sth** jdm etw geben *or* schenken; **to be ~ed with a natural talent for singing** ein sängerisches Naturtalent sein; **the poor lad is not very well ~ed** *(inf: with intelligence)* mit dem armen Bengel ist nicht viel los; **she's well ~ed** *(hum)* sie ist von der Natur reichlich ausgestattet (worden)

endowment [ɪnˈdaʊmənt] N **a** Stiftung *f*; **~s** Stiftungsgelder *pl* **b** *(= natural talent etc)* Begabung *f*; **his/her physical ~s** *(hum)* womit ihn/sie die Natur ausgestattet hat

endowment: **endowment assurance** N Versicherung *f* auf den Erlebensfall, Erlebensversicherung *f*; **endowment mortgage** N Hypothek *f* mit Lebensversicherung; **endowment policy** N Lebensversicherungspolice *f*

end: **endpapers** PL Vorsatzblätter *pl*; **end product** N Endprodukt *nt*; *(fig)* Produkt *nt*; **end result** N Endergebnis *nt*; **end table** N *(for couch)* kleiner Tisch; **end terrace** N *(Brit)* Reiheneckhaus *nt*

endue [ɪnˈdjuː] VT versehen, begaben *(liter)*; **to be ~d with sth** über etw *(acc)* verfügen, mit etw begabt sein

endurable [ɪnˈdjʊərəbl] ADJ erträglich

endurance [ɪnˈdjʊərəns] N Durchhaltevermögen *nt*; **to have great powers of ~** großes Durchhaltevermögen haben; **what a feat of ~** welche Ausdauer!; **he was tried beyond ~** er wurde über die Maßen gereizt; **his suffering was beyond ~** sein Leiden war unerträglich

endurance: **endurance race** N *(Sport) Rennen, bei dem es vor allem auf die Ausdauer ankommt*; **endurance test** N Belastungsprobe *f*; *(fig)* Durchhaltetest *m*

endure [ɪnˈdjʊəʳ] VT **a** *(= undergo) pain, insults, losses, tribulations, hardship* erleiden **b** *(= put up with)* ertragen; *agony* aushalten, ertragen; **it was more than I could ~** ich konnte es nicht mehr ertragen; **she can't ~ being laughed at** sie kann es nicht vertragen *or* haben *(inf)*, wenn man über sie lacht VI bestehen; *(work, memories also)* Bestand haben

enduring [ɪnˈdjʊərɪŋ] ADJ dauerhaft; *love, belief* beständig, dauerhaft; *popularity* bleibend

end user N *(esp Comput)* Endbenutzer *m*, Endverbraucher(in) *m(f)*

endways [ˈendweɪz], **endwise** [ˈendwaɪz] ADV mit dem Ende nach vorne *or* zuerst; *(= end to end)* mit den Enden aneinander; **put it ~ on** legen Sie es mit dem Ende *or* der Spitze an

ENE *abbr of* **east-north-east** ONO

enema [ˈenɪmə] N Klistier *nt*, Einlauf *m*; *(= syringe)* Klistierspritze *f*

enemy [ˈenəmɪ] N *(lit, fig)* Feind(in) *m(f)*; **to make enemies** sich *(dat)* Feinde machen *or* schaffen; **to make an ~ of sb** sich *(dat)* jdn zum Feind(e) machen; **he is his own worst ~** er schadet sich *(dat)* selbst am meisten ADJ *attr* feindlich; *position, advance, morale* des Feindes; **destroyed by ~ action** vom Feind *or* durch Feindeinwirkung *(form)* zerstört

enemy-occupied [ˌenəmɪˈɒkjʊpaɪd] N vom Feind besetzt

energetic [ˌenəˈdʒetɪk] ADJ **a** *person (= enthusiastic, lively)* energiegeladen; *(= active)* aktiv; **to be more/very ~** mehr/viel Energie haben; **if I'm feeling ~** wenn ich die Energie habe **b** *activity (= full of action)* energiegeladen; *(= strenuous)* anstrengend; *performance* schwungvoll; *campaign* aktiv; *action, effort* energisch, entschlossen; **~ sport** Bewegungssport *m*; **do something ~** machen Sie etwas Aktives

energetically [ˌenəˈdʒetɪkəlɪ] ADV **a** *deny, protest, campaign, work* energisch **b** *run, dance, jump* voller Energie; **she nodded her head ~** sie nickte nachdrücklich

energize [ˈenədʒaɪz] VT *rocket motor, particle* Antrieb geben *(+dat)*; *(Elec)* unter Strom setzen; *(fig) person* neue Energie geben *(+dat)*; *economy* ankurbeln; **to be ~d by sth** *(fig)* von etw in Schwung gebracht werden

energy [ˈenədʒɪ] N Energie *f*; **he put his speech over with a lot of ~** er hielt seine Rede mit viel Schwung; **chocolate gives you ~** Schokolade gibt neue Energie; **to concentrate one's energies on doing sth** seine ganze Kraft dafür aufbieten, etw zu tun; **to devote all one's energies to sth** seine ganze Energie *or* Kraft für etw einsetzen; **I haven't the ~** mir fehlt die Energie dazu; **to conserve one's energies** mit seinen Kräften haushalten *or* Haus halten *or* sparsam umgehen; **to save one's ~ for sth** seine Kräfte für etw aufsparen

energy: **energy balance** N *(of body)* Energiehaushalt *m*; **energy conservation** N Energieeinsparung *f*; **energy crisis** N Energiekrise *f*; **energy efficiency** N Energieeffizienz *f*; **energy-efficient** ADJ energieeffizient; **energy-giving** ADJ *food* Energie spendend; **energy-intensive** ADJ energieintensiv; **energy-saving** ADJ Energie sparend; **~ feature** Energiesparfunktion *f*; **~ measures** Energiesparmaßnahmen *pl*; **energy supplies** PL Energievorräte *pl*

enervate [ˈenɜːveɪt] VT *(physically)* entkräften, schwächen; *(mentally)* entnerven, enervieren *(geh)*

enervating [ˈenɜːveɪtɪŋ] ADJ strapazierend

enfant terrible [ˌɒnfɒnteˈriːblə] N *pl* **-s -s** Enfant terrible *nt*

enfeeble [ɪnˈfiːbl] VT schwächen; **~d by** geschwächt durch

enfeeblement [ɪnˈfiːblmənt] N Schwächung *f*

enfold [ɪnˈfəʊld] VT einhüllen (*in* in *+acc*); **to ~ sb in one's arms** jdn in die Arme schließen

enforce [ɪnˈfɔːs] VT **a** durchführen, Geltung verschaffen *(+dat)*; *one's claims, rights* geltend machen; *discipline* sorgen für, schaffen; *decision, policy, ban, ruling* durchsetzen; *measures* durchführen; *sanctions* verhängen; **the police ~ the law** die Polizei sorgt für die Einhaltung der Gesetze; **to ~ silence/obedience** sich *(dat)* Ruhe/Gehorsam verschaffen; **to ~ sth (up)on sb** jdm etw aufzwingen **b** *(rare, = give force to) demand* Nachdruck verschaffen *(+dat)*; *argument* stützen, untermauern

enforceable [ɪnˈfɔːsəbl] ADJ durchsetzbar

enforcement [ɪnˈfɔːsmənt] N *(of law, policy, ruling)* Durchführung *f*; *(of obedience)* Erzwingung *f*

enfranchise [ɪnˈfræntʃaɪz] VT **a** *(= give vote to)* das Wahlrecht geben *or* erteilen *(+dat)*; **to be ~d** wahlberechtigt sein **b** *(= set free) slaves* freilassen

enfranchisement [ɪnˈfræntʃɪzmənt] N **a** *(Pol)* Erteilung *f* des Wahlrechts; **after the ~ of women** nachdem die Frauen das Wahlrecht erhalten hatten **b** *(of slave)* Freilassung *f*

engage [ɪnˈgeɪdʒ] VT **a** *servant, workers* anstellen, einstellen; *singer, performer* engagieren; *lawyer* sich *(dat)* nehmen; **to ~ the services of sb** jdn anstellen/engagieren; *of lawyer* sich *(dat)* jdn nehmen

b *room* mieten, sich *(dat)* nehmen

c *attention, interest* in Anspruch nehmen; **to ~ sb in conversation** jdn in ein Gespräch verwickeln

d **to ~ oneself to do sth** *(form)* sich verpflichten, etw zu tun

e *the enemy* angreifen, den Kampf eröffnen gegen

f *(Tech) gear wheels* ineinandergreifen lassen; **to ~ a gear** *(Aut)* einen Gang einlegen; **to ~ the clutch** (ein)kuppeln; **to ~ four-wheel drive** den Allradantrieb zuschalten

VI **a** *(form, = promise)* sich verpflichten (*to do* zu tun)

b *(gear wheels)* ineinandergreifen; *(clutch)* fassen

c **to ~ in sth** sich an etw *(dat)* beteiligen; **to**

~ in conversation sich unterhalten; **to ~ in politics** sich politisch betätigen; **to ~ with sb/sth** mit jdm/etw in Beziehung treten; **to ~ in competition with sb** in Wettbewerb mit jdm treten **d** *(Mil)* angreifen; **to ~ with the enemy** den Feind angreifen

engaged [ɪnˈgeɪdʒd] ✪ 24.2, 27.3 ADJ **a** *(= betrothed)* **~ (to be married)** verlobt (*to* mit); **the ~ couple** die Verlobten *pl*; **to get** *or* **become ~ (to sb)** sich (mit jdm) verloben
b *toilet, seat, taxi* besetzt; *(Brit Telec) line, number, telephone* besetzt
c *(form: = busy) person* beschäftigt; **to be otherwise ~** *(at future time)* etwas anderes vorhaben; *(at present)* anderweitig beschäftigt sein; **to be ~ in sth** mit etw beschäftigt sein; *in criminal activities* in etw *(acc)* verwickelt sein; **the parties ~ in the dispute** die am Streit beteiligten Parteien; **to be ~ in doing sth** dabei sein, etw zu tun; **we are actively ~ in trying to find a solution** wir bemühen uns aktiv um eine Lösung; **to be ~ on sth** mit etw befasst *or* beschäftigt sein

engaged tone N *(Telec)* Besetztzeichen *nt*

engagement [ɪnˈgeɪdʒmənt] ✪ 24.2, 25.2 N **a** *(= appointment)* Verabredung *f*; *(of actor etc)* Engagement *nt*; **public/social ~s** öffentliche/gesellschaftliche Verpflichtungen *pl*; **a dinner ~** eine Verabredung zum Essen **b** *(= betrothal)* Verlobung *f* **c** *(form, = undertaking)* Verpflichtung *f* **d** *(Mil)* Gefecht *nt*, Kampf *m* **e** *(of parts of machine)* Ineinandergreifen *nt*

engagement: **engagement diary** N Terminkalender *m*; **engagement ring** N Verlobungsring *m*

engaging [ɪnˈgeɪdʒɪŋ] ADJ *person* angenehm; *smile* gewinnend; *character, personality* einnehmend; *manner* einnehmend, angenehm; **he is such an ~ character** er hat so ein einnehmendes Wesen

en garde [ɒŋˈgɑːd] INTERJ en garde

engender [ɪnˈdʒendəʳ] VT *(fig)* erzeugen

engenderment [ɪnˈdʒendəmənt] N Erzeugung *f*

engine [ˈendʒɪn] N **a** Maschine *f*; *(of car, plane etc)* Motor *m*; *(of ship)* Maschine *f* **b** *(Rail)* Lokomotive *f*, Lok *f* **c** *(Comput: = search engine)* Suchmaschine *f*

engine: **engine block** N Motorblock *m*; **engine compartment** N Motorraum *m*

-engined [-ˈendʒɪnd] ADJ *suf* -motorig; **single-/twin-engined** ein-/zweimotorig; **front-/rear-/diesel-engined** mit Front-/Heck-/Dieselmotor

engine driver N *(Brit)* Lok(omotiv)führer(in) *m(f)*

engineer [ˌendʒɪˈnɪəʳ] N **a** *(Tech)* Techniker(in) *m(f)*; *(with university degree etc)* Ingenieur(in) *m(f)*; **the Engineers** *(Mil)* die Pioniere *pl* **b** *(Naut, on merchant ships)* Maschinist(in) *m(f)*; *(in Navy)* (Schiffs)ingenieur(in) *m(f)* **c** *(US Rail)* Lokführer(in) *m(f)* **d** *(fig, of scheme)* Arrangeur(in) *m(f)* VT **a** *(Tech)* konstruieren **b** *(fig) election, campaign, coup* organisieren; *downfall, plot* arrangieren, einfädeln; *success, victory* in die Wege leiten; *(Sport) goal* einfädeln; **to ~ a scheme** einen Plan aushecken

engineering [ˌendʒɪˈnɪərɪŋ] N **a** *(Tech)* Technik *f*; *(= mechanical engineering)* Maschinenbau *m*; *(= engineering profession)* Ingenieurwesen *nt*; **the ~ of the building** die Konstruktion des Gebäudes; **he's in ~** er ist Ingenieur; **a brilliant piece of ~** eine Meisterkonstruktion; **a triumph of ~** ein Triumph *m* der Technik **b** *(fig, of election, campaign, coup)* Organisation *f*; *(of downfall, plot)* Arrangement *nt*; *(= manoeuvring)* Arrangements *pl*

engineering: **engineering department** N technische Abteilung; *(mechanical)* Abteilung *f* für Maschinenbau; **engineering faculty** N *(Univ)* Fakultät *f* für Maschinenbau; **engineering industries** PL Maschinenindustrie *f*; **engineering worker** N Techniker(in) *m(f)*; **engineering works** N *sing or pl* Maschinenfabrik *f*

engineer officer N technischer Offizier, technische Offizierin

engine: **engine mountings** PL Motoraufhängung *f*; **engine oil** N Motoröl *nt*; **engine room** N *(Naut)* Maschinenraum *m*; **engine shed** N*(Brit)* Lokomotivschuppen *m*

England [ˈɪŋglənd] N England *nt* ADJ *attr* **the ~ team** die englische Mannschaft

English [ˈɪŋglɪʃ] ADJ englisch; **he is ~** er ist Engländer; **he's an ~ teacher** *(teaching English)* er ist Englischlehrer; *(English by nationality)* er ist ein englischer Lehrer; **~ translator** englischer Übersetzer, englische Übersetzerin; *(foreign)* Übersetzer(in) *m(f)* für Englisch; **(full) ~ breakfast** englisches Frühstück
N **a** **the ~** *pl* die Engländer *pl*
b *(Ling)* Englisch *nt*; *(= the English language in general, English grammar)* Englisch *nt*, das Englische; *(as university subject)* Anglistik *f*; **can you speak ~?** können Sie Englisch?; **he doesn't speak ~** er spricht kein Englisch; **"English spoken"** „hier wird Englisch gesprochen"; **they were speaking ~** sie unterhielten sich auf Englisch; **he speaks very good ~** er spricht ein sehr gutes Englisch; **in ~** auf *or* in *(inf)* Englisch; **in good/modern-day ~** in gutem/modernem Englisch; **to translate sth into/from ~** etw ins Englische/aus dem Englischen übersetzen; **is that ~?** *(= correct)* ist das richtig?; **that's not ~** das ist verkehrt, das ist falsches Englisch; **~/teaching ~ as a foreign language** *(abbr* **EFL/TEFL**) Englisch als Fremdsprache; **the King's/Queen's ~** die englische Hochsprache → **Old English, plain ADJ b**

> **ENGLISH**
>
> In Großbritannien ist die hochsprachliche Standardaussprache des Englischen unter dem Begriff **Received Pronunciation** (oder auch **RP**) bekannt. Sie entwickelte sich aus dem Akzent des Südostens Englands, ist die vorherrschende Aussprache der Ober- und Mittelschicht und ist in den Medien allgemein verbreitet, auch wenn regionale Dialekte immer höhere Akzeptanz finden. Mit **Standard English** bezeichnet man die aktuelle Form der englischen Sprache, die allgemein in den Schulen unterrichtet wird.
> Amerikanisches Englisch unterscheidet sich von britischem Englisch überwiegend in der Aussprache, auch wenn die Schreibweise manchmal etwas variiert und es für einiges durchaus verschiedene Bezeichnungen gibt. In den Medien ist eine Standardversion des Amerikanischen gebräuchlich, die sich als **Network Standard** eingebürgert hat. In Großbritannien wird der Akzent besonders stark mit der sozialen Schichtzugehörigkeit des Sprechenden verbunden, während in den Vereinigten Staaten kein so enger Bezug zwischen Akzent und Klasse hergestellt wird.

English: **English Channel** N Ärmelkanal *m*; **English flute** N*(Mus)* Blockflöte *f*; **English Heritage** N *(Brit) Organisation für die Pflege von Denkmälern und historischen Bauwerken in England*; **English horn** N *(Mus: = cor anglais)* Englischhorn *nt*; **Englishman** N Engländer *m*; **an ~'s home is his castle** *(Prov)* für den Engländer ist sein Haus seine Burg; **English muffin** N *(US Cook) flaches Milchbrötchen, das meist getoastet gegessen wird*; **English speaker** N Englischsprachige(r) *mf*; **English-speaking** ADJ englischsprachig; **Englishwoman** N Engländerin *f*

Eng Lit [ˈɪŋˈlɪt] *abbr of* **English Literature** engl. Lit.

engorged [ɪnˈgɔːdʒd] ADJ angeschwollen; **sth is ~ with blood** in etw *(dat)* staut sich das Blut; **the blood vessels that allow the penis to become ~** die Blutgefäße, die den Penis anschwellen lassen

engraft [ɪnˈgrɑːft] VT **a** *(Bot)* aufpfropfen (*into, on, upon* auf *+acc*) **b** *(fig geh) principles* verankern (*into* in *+dat*)

engrave [ɪnˈgreɪv] VT *glass, metal, stone, wood* gravieren; *design, letter, names* eingravieren; *(fig)* einprägen

engraved [ɪnˈgreɪvd] ADJ *glass, metal, plaque* graviert; *design, letter, name* eingraviert; **~ plates** *(Typ)* (Kupfer)stiche *pl*; **beautifully ~ with flowers** mit einem hübschen eingravierten Blumenmuster; **her name is ~ on my heart** ich werde ihren Namen immer im Herzen bewahren; **it is ~ on my memory** es hat sich mir unauslöschlich eingeprägt

engraver [ɪnˈgreɪvəʳ] N Graveur(in) *m(f)*; *(on stone)* Steinhauer(in) *m(f)*; *(on wood)* Holzschneider(in) *m(f)*

engraving [ɪnˈgreɪvɪŋ] N **a** *(= process)* Gravieren *nt*; *(on rock, stone)* Einmeißeln *nt*; *(on wood)* Einschnitzen *nt*, Einkerben *nt*; **~ needle** Graviernadel *f* **b** *(= copy)* (Kupfer-/Stahl)stich *m*; *(from wood)* Holzschnitt *m*; *(= design)* Gravierung *f*; *(on wood, stone)* eingemeißelte Verzierung/Schrift *etc*

engross [ɪnˈgrəʊs] VT *person, attention* gefangen nehmen; **to become ~ed in one's book/one's work** sich in sein Buch/seine Arbeit vertiefen; **to be ~ed in one's (own) thoughts/in conversation** in Gedanken/ins Gespräch vertieft sein

engrossing [ɪnˈgrəʊsɪŋ] ADJ fesselnd

engulf [ɪnˈgʌlf] VT verschlingen; *(fig: feeling, pain)* übermannen; **to be ~ed by flames** in Flammen stehen

enhance [ɪnˈhɑːns] VT verbessern; *price, value, attraction, chances* erhöhen

enigma [ɪˈnɪgmə] N Rätsel *nt*

enigmatic [ˌenɪgˈmætɪk] ADJ rätselhaft

enigmatically [ˌenɪgˈmætɪkəlɪ] ADV rätselhaft; **he replied somewhat ~** er gab eine etwas rätselhafte Antwort; **he describes himself, ~, as an old man** er beschreibt sich rätselhafterweise als einen alten Mann

enjambement [ɪnˈdʒæmmənt] N *(Poet)* Enjambement *nt*

enjoin [ɪnˈdʒɔɪn] VT *(form)* **to ~ sb to silence/caution, to ~ silence/caution on sb** jdn eindringlich zur Ruhe/zur Vorsicht mahnen; **to ~ on sb the need for sth** jdm die Notwendigkeit einer Sache eindringlich vor Augen stellen; **to ~ sb to do sth/from doing sth** jdn eindringlich mahnen, etw zu tun/etw nicht zu tun

enjoy [ɪnˈdʒɔɪ] ✪ 7.2 VT **a** *(= take pleasure in)* genießen; **he ~s swimming/reading** er schwimmt/liest gern, Lesen/Schwimmen macht ihm Spaß; **he ~s being rude to people** es macht ihm Spaß *or* ihm macht es Spaß, zu Leuten unhöflich zu sein; **he ~ed writing the book** es hat ihm Freude gemacht, das Buch zu schreiben; **I've ~ed talking to you** es war mir eine Freude, mich mit Ihnen zu unterhalten, es war nett, sich mit Ihnen zu unterhalten; **I ~ed the book/concert** das Buch/Konzert hat mir gefallen; **he ~ed the meal** das Essen hat ihm gut geschmeckt; **I ~ your company/the company of women** ich bin gerne mit Ihnen/mit Frauen zusammen; **I didn't ~ it at all** es hat mir überhaupt keinen Spaß gemacht; **the author didn't mean his book to be ~ed** dem Verfasser ging es nicht darum, dass man an seinem Buch Spaß *or* Vergnügen haben sollte; **to ~ life** das Leben genießen; **I ~ed a very pleasant weekend in the country** ich habe ein sehr angenehmes Wochenende auf dem Land verbracht; **did you ~ your meal?** hat Ihnen das Essen gefallen?; **I really ~ed my meal** ich habe das Essen richtig genossen
b *rights, freedom, advantages, respect, confidence* genießen; *income, success* haben; *good health, reputation, support* sich erfreuen *(+gen) (geh)*
VR **to ~ oneself** sich amüsieren; **~ yourself!** viel Spaß!, amüsieren Sie sich gut!

enjoyable [ɪnˈdʒɔɪəbl] ADJ nett; *film, book* unterhaltsam, nett; *evening, meal* angenehm

enjoyably [ɪnˈdʒɔɪəblɪ] ADV *(= pleasantly)* auf angenehme Art; *(= entertainingly)* unterhaltsam; *(= with enjoyment)* mit Vergnügen

enjoyment [ɪnˈdʒɔɪmənt] N **a** Vergnügen *nt*, Spaß *m* (*of* an *+dat*); **he got a lot of ~ from the book** das Buch machte ihm großen Spaß; **she gets a lot of ~ from reading** Lesen macht ihr großen Spaß *or* bringt ihr viel Freude **b** (*of rights, income, fortune*) Genuss *m*

enlarge [ɪnˈlɑːdʒ] VT vergrößern; *hole, field of knowledge* erweitern; *organ, pore* vergrößern, erweitern; *membership, majority also* erhöhen VI **a** sich vergrößern **b** **to ~ (up)on sth** auf etw (*acc*) näher eingehen

enlarged [ɪnˈlɑːdʒd] ADJ vergrößert; *organ, pore also, community* erweitert; **an ~ force** verstärkte Truppen *pl*; **an ~ print** (*Phot*) eine Vergrößerung; **~ edition** erweiterte Ausgabe

enlargement [ɪnˈlɑːdʒmənt] N **a** (*Phot*) Vergrößerung *f* **b** (*= process*) Vergrößerung *f*; (*of hole, field of knowledge*) Erweiterung *f*; (*Med*: *of organ*) Erweiterung *f*, Vergrößerung *f*; (*of membership, majority*) Erhöhung *f*

enlarger [ɪnˈlɑːdʒəʳ] N (*Phot*) Vergrößerungsapparat *m*

enlighten [ɪnˈlaɪtn] VT aufklären (*on, as to, about* über *+acc*); (*spiritually*) erleuchten; **let me ~ you** darf ich es Ihnen erklären?

enlightened [ɪnˈlaɪtnd] ADJ *person, society* aufgeklärt; (*= progressive*) *person, approach, policy* progressiv, fortschrittlich; **in this ~ age, in these ~ times** (*usu iro*) in diesem aufgeklärten Zeitalter

enlightening [ɪnˈlaɪtnɪŋ] ADJ aufschlussreich

enlightenment [ɪnˈlaɪtnmənt] N Aufklärung *f*; (*spiritual*) Erleuchtung *f*; **the Enlightenment** die Aufklärung; **the age of Enlightenment** das Zeitalter der Aufklärung

enlist [ɪnˈlɪst] VI (*Mil etc*) sich melden (*in* zu) VT *soldiers, recruits* einziehen; *supporters, collaborators* anwerben, gewinnen; *assistance, sympathy, support* gewinnen; **could I ~ your aid?** darf ich Sie um Hilfe bitten?; **I had to ~ his help** ich musste seine Hilfe in Anspruch nehmen

enlisted man [ɪnˈlɪstɪdˈmæn] *pl* **enlisted men** N (*US*) gemeiner Soldat

enlistment [ɪnˈlɪstmənt] N (*of soldiers, recruits, = enlisting*) Meldung *f*; (*= being enlisted*) Einziehung *f*; (*of supporters, collaborators*) Anwerbung *f*, Gewinnung *f*; (*of assistance, support*) Gewinnung *f*

enliven [ɪnˈlaɪvn] VT beleben

en masse [ˌɑ̃ˈmæs] ADV **a** (*= everybody together*) alle zusammen; **to resign ~** geschlossen zurücktreten **b** (*= in large numbers, things*) in großen Mengen; (*people*) in großen Gruppen; **the flowers looked lovely ~** die vielen Blumen sahen schön zusammen aus

enmesh [ɪnˈmeʃ] VT (*lit*) in einem Netz fangen; (*fig*) verstricken; **to get ~ed in sth** in etw (*acc*) verstrickt werden

enmity [ˈenmɪtɪ] N Feindschaft *f*

ennoble [ɪˈnəʊbl] VT (*lit*) adeln, in den Adelsstand erheben; (*fig*) *mind, person* erheben (*geh*)

ennui [ˈɒnwiː] N *no pl* (*liter*) Ennui *m* (*liter*)

enormity [ɪˈnɔːmɪtɪ] N **a** *no pl* (*of action, offence*) ungeheures Ausmaß **b** (*of crime*) Ungeheuerlichkeit *f*

enormous [ɪˈnɔːməs] ADJ *object* enorm, riesig; *animal* riesig; *person* (*= fat*) ungeheuer dick; (*= tall*) riesig groß; *amount, success, profits, losses, range, choice* riesig; *number, quantity, variety, effort, relief* ungeheuer; *difference* riesig, gewaltig; **an ~ great thing** (*inf*) ein Riesending *nt* (*inf*); **she was wearing an ~ great ruby** sie trug einen riesig großen Rubin; **he has ~ talent/an ~ talent for ...** er hat enorm viel Talent/ein enorm großes Talent für ...; **~ amounts** *or* **sums of money** Unsummen *pl*; **an ~ amount of work** eine Unmenge Arbeit; **an ~ amount of pain** ungeheure Schmerzen *pl*; **it means an ~ amount to me** es bedeutet mir ungeheuer viel; **an ~ number of, ~ numbers of** ungeheuer viele; **he was a lovely lad with ~ potential** er war ein netter Junge, aus dem enorm viel hätte werden können

enormously [ɪˈnɔːməslɪ] ADV (*+vb*) enorm; (*+adj*) ungeheuer

enough [ɪˈnʌf] ADJ **a** (*before noun*) (*= sufficient*) genug; **~ sugar/apples** genug *or* genügend Zucker/Äpfel; **~ trouble/problems** (*= more would be unwelcome*) genug Ärger/Probleme **b** (*after noun*: *form*) **proof ~** Beweis genug

PRON genug (*of* von); **I had not seen ~ of his work** ich hatte noch nicht genug von seiner Arbeit gesehen; **I hope it's ~** ich hoffe, es reicht *or* genügt; **two years was ~** zwei Jahre reichten, zwei Jahre waren lange genug; **have you ~ to pay the bill?** haben Sie genug, um die Rechnung zu bezahlen?; **we have ~ to live on** wir haben genug zum Leben, es reicht uns zum Leben; **this noise is ~ to drive me mad** dieser Lärm macht mich noch ganz verrückt; **one song was ~ to show he couldn't sing** ein Lied genügte, um zu zeigen, dass er nicht singen konnte; **it is ~ for us to know that ...** es genügt uns zu wissen, dass ...; **I've got ~ to worry about** ich habe genug Sorgen; **we've made ~ of a mess here** wir haben hier genug angerichtet; **~ is ~** was zu viel ist, ist zu viel; **~ said** mehr braucht man nicht zu sagen; **to have had ~** (*= be fed up*) genug haben (*of* von); **I've had ~** ich habe genug; (*in exasperation*) jetzt reichts mir aber (*inf*); **one can never have ~ of this music** von dieser Musik kann man nie genug kriegen; **that's ~!** jetzt reicht es aber!, jetzt ist es aber genug!

ADV **a** (*= sufficiently*) genug; **to be punished ~** genug bestraft sein; **he is good ~ to win** er ist gut genug, um zu gewinnen; **he knows well ~ what I said** er weiß ganz genau, was ich gesagt habe

b (*= reasonably, fairly*) **it is common ~ for children to overeat** es kommt durchaus häufig vor, dass Kinder zu viel essen; **to be happy ~** einigermaßen zufrieden sein; **to be happy ~ to do sth** etw so weit ganz gern tun; **she sounded sincere ~** sie schien so weit ganz ehrlich; **easy ~** nicht allzu schwer; **it is easy ~ to make them yourself** man kann sie ohne Weiteres selbst machen; **he drove off happily ~** er ist ganz fröhlich weggefahren; **I like it well ~** es gefällt mir so weit ganz gut; **easily ~** ohne größere Schwierigkeiten → *also* **fair**[1] **ADJ a**

c **oddly** *or* **funnily ~** komischerweise; **interestingly ~** interessanterweise → *also* **sure ADV b**

en passant [ˌɑ̃ˈpæsɑ̃] ADV **a** (*liter*) *mention, refer to* beiläufig, nebenbei; **it can be dealt with ~** es kann nebenbei erledigt werden **b** (*introducing remark*) nebenbei bemerkt

enquire *etc* [ɪnˈkwaɪəʳ] = **inquire** *etc*

enquirer [ɪnˈkwaɪərəʳ] N = **inquirer**

enquiring [ɪnˈkwaɪərɪŋ] ADJ = **inquiring**

enquiringly [ɪnˈkwaɪərɪŋlɪ] ADV = **inquiringly**

enquiry [ɪnˈkwaɪərɪ] ✪ 20.2 N = **inquiry**

enrage [ɪnˈreɪdʒ] VT wütend machen; **it ~s me to think that ...** es macht mich wütend, wenn ich daran denke, dass ...

enraged [ɪnˈreɪdʒd] ADJ wütend, aufgebracht (*at, by* über *+acc*); **he was ~ to see that ...** er war wütend, als er sah, dass ...

enrapture [ɪnˈræptʃəʳ] VT entzücken, bezaubern

enraptured [ɪnˈræptʃəd] ADJ hingerissen, entzückt (*at, by* von)

enrich [ɪnˈrɪtʃ] VT bereichern; *soil, food* anreichern; **to ~ oneself** sich bereichern; **to ~ one's life** sein Leben bereichern

enriched [ɪnˈrɪtʃt] ADJ (*also Phys*) angereichert; *person* bereichert; **~ with vitamins** mit Vitaminen angereichert

enrichment [ɪnˈrɪtʃmənt] N Bereicherung *f*; (*of soil*) Anreicherung *f*

enrol, (*US*) **enroll** [ɪnˈrəʊl] VT einschreiben; *members* aufnehmen; *schoolchild* (*school, headmaster*) aufnehmen; (*parents*) anmelden; (*Univ*) immatrikulieren VI sich einschreiben; (*in the army*) sich melden (*in* zu); (*for course, at school*) sich anmelden; (*Univ*) sich immatrikulieren *or* einschreiben

enrolment, (*US*) **enrollment** [ɪnˈrəʊlmənt] N **a** (*= enrolling*) Einschreibung *f*; (*of members*) Aufnahme *f*; (*of schoolchild, by school, headmaster*) Aufnahme *f*; (*by parents*) Anmeldung *f*; (*Univ*) Immatrikulation *f* **b** (*= being enrolled*) Einschreibung *f*; (*in the army*) Meldung *f*; (*for course, at school*) Anmeldung *f*; (*Univ*) Immatrikulation *f*, Einschreibung *f* **c** **to have an ~ of X** (*evening class*) eine (Gesamt)teilnehmerzahl von X haben; (*university*) X immatrikulierte Studenten haben; (*school*) eine (Gesamt)schülerzahl von X haben

en route [ɒŋˈruːt] ADV unterwegs; **~ to/for/from** auf dem Weg zu/nach/von

ensconce [ɪnˈskɒns] VR sich niederlassen, sich häuslich niederlassen (*in* in *+dat*); **he was ~d in the front room** er hatte sich in dem vorderen Zimmer (häuslich) niedergelassen

ensemble [ɑ̃ːnˈsɑ̃ːmbl] N **a** (*Mus, Theat*) Ensemble *nt*; **~ acting** *or* **playing** schauspielerisches Zusammenspiel **b** (*Fashion*) Ensemble *nt* **c** (*= collection*: *of people, things*) Ansammlung *f*

enshrine [ɪnˈʃraɪn] VT (*fig*) bewahren

enshroud [ɪnˈʃraʊd] VT (*liter*: *= shroud*) (*lit*) einhüllen; (*fig*) umgeben; **the case remains ~ed in mystery** der Fall bleibt weiterhin von einem Geheimnis umgeben

ensign [ˈensaɪn] N **a** (*= flag*) Nationalflagge *f* **b** (*Mil Hist*) Fähnrich *m* **c** (*US Naut*) Fähnrich *m* zur See

enslave [ɪnˈsleɪv] VT zum Sklaven machen; **he is ~d by the system** das System hat ihn zum Sklaven gemacht; **she is ~d by her routine** sie ist zur Sklavin ihrer Routine geworden

enslavement [ɪnˈsleɪvmənt] N (*lit*) Versklavung *f*; (*fig*) sklavische Abhängigkeit (*to* von)

ensnare [ɪnˈsnɛəʳ] VT (*lit*) fangen; (*fig, woman*) umgarnen; (*charms*) berücken, bestricken; **his leg became ~d in the ropes** sein Bein verfing sich in den Seilen

ensue [ɪnˈsjuː] VI folgen (*from, on* aus); **it ~s that ...** daraus folgt, dass...; **I don't know what ~d** ich weiß nicht, was daraufhin geschah

ensuing [ɪnˈsjuːɪŋ] ADJ darauf folgend *attr*; *months, weeks also* folgend *attr*

en suite [ˈɒnˈswiːt] ADJ **room with ~ bathroom, ~ room** Zimmer *nt* mit eigenem Bad

ensure [ɪnˈʃʊəʳ] VT sicherstellen; (*= secure*) sichern; **will you ~ that I get a seat?** sorgen Sie dafür, dass ich einen Platz bekomme?

ENT *abbr of* **ear, nose and throat**; **~ department** HNO-Abteilung *f*; **~ specialist** HNO-Arzt *m*/Ärztin *f*

entablature [ɪnˈtæblətʃʊəʳ] N Gebälk *nt*

entail [ɪnˈteɪl] VT **a** *expense, inconvenience, changes* mit sich bringen; *risk, difficulty, loss* verbunden sein mit, mit sich bringen; (*= involve*) *work* erforderlich machen; **what is ~ed in buying a house?** was ist zum Hauskauf alles erforderlich?; **this will ~ (my) buying a new car** das bringt mit sich *or* macht es erforderlich, dass ich mir ein neues Auto kaufen muss

b (*Logic*) **if x = y, not x ~s not y** wenn x = y ist, so folgt daraus, dass nicht x nicht = y ist

c (*Jur*) **to ~ an estate** ein Gut als Fideikommiss vererben; **~ed estate** unveräußerliches Erbgut, Fideikommiss *nt*

entangle [ɪnˈtæŋgl] VT **a** (*= catch up*) verfangen; **to become ~d in sth** sich in etw (*dat*) verfangen; **their feet were ~d in the ropes** sie hatten sich mit den Füßen in den Seilen verfangen **b** (*= get into a tangle*) *hair* verwirren; *wool, thread, ropes* verwickeln, verwirren; **to become ~d** sich verwirren, sich verwickeln *or* verheddern (*inf*) **c** (*fig, in affair etc*) verwickeln, verstricken (*in* in *+acc*); **he became ~d in his own words** er verhaspelte sich (*inf*)

entanglement [ɪnˈtæŋglmənt] N **a** (*lit, no pl*: *= enmeshing*) Verfangen *nt*; (*= tangle, of ropes etc*) Durcheinander *nt*; (*esp Mil, of barbed wire*) Verhau *m* **b** (*fig, in affair etc*) Verwicklung *f*; **legal ~** Rechtskonflikt *m*; **he wanted to avoid**

any ~ with domestic politics er wollte sich aus der Innenpolitik heraushalten; **she didn't want any romantic ~** sie wollte nicht in eine Romanze verwickelt werden

enter ['entə'] VT **a** *(towards speaker)* hereinkommen in *(+acc)*; *(away from speaker)* hineingehen in *(+acc)*; *(= walk into) building etc* betreten, eintreten in *(+acc)*; *(= drive into) car park, motorway* einfahren in *(+acc)*; *(= turn into) road etc* einbiegen in *(+acc)*; *(= flow into: river, sewage etc)* münden in *(+acc)*; *(= penetrate: bullet etc)* eindringen in *(+acc)*; *(= climb into) train* einsteigen in *(+acc)*; *(= cross border of) country* einreisen in *(+acc)*; **to ~ harbour** (in den Hafen) einlaufen; **the dispute is ~ing its fifth year** die Auseinandersetzung zieht sich jetzt schon ins fünfte Jahr hin; **the thought never ~ed my head** *or* **mind** so etwas wäre mir nie eingefallen; **that idea HAD ~ed my mind** *(iro)* auf diesen Gedanken bin ich tatsächlich gekommen
b *(= join, become a member of)* eintreten in *(+acc)*; **to ~ the Army/Navy** zum Heer/zur Marine gehen; **to ~ the Church** Geistlicher werden; **to ~ a school** in eine Schule eintreten; **to ~ university** ein Studium beginnen; **to ~ a profession** einen Beruf ergreifen
c *(= record)* eintragen *(in* in *+acc)*; *(Comput) data* eingeben; **to ~ sb's/one's name** jdn/sich eintragen; **~ these purchases under my name** *(Comm)* tragen Sie diese Käufe auf meinen Namen ein
d *(= enrol, for school, exam etc) pupil* anmelden; *(for race, contest etc) horse* melden; *competitor* anmelden; **I ~ed him in the competition** ich meldete ihn zu dem Wettbewerb an
e *(= go in for) race, contest* sich beteiligen an *(+dat)*; **only amateurs could ~ the race** es konnten nur Amateure an dem Rennen teilnehmen
f *(= submit) appeal, plea* einlegen; **to ~ an action against sb** *(Jur)* gegen jdn einen Prozess anstrengen *or* einleiten
g *(Comput) text etc* eingeben
VI **a** *(towards speaker)* hereinkommen; *(away from speaker)* hineingehen; *(= walk in)* eintreten; *(into bus etc)* einsteigen; *(= drive in)* einfahren; *(= penetrate: bullet etc)* eindringen; *(= into country)* einreisen
b *(Theat)* auftreten
c *(for race, exam etc)* sich melden *(for* zu)
N *(Comput)* **hit ~** Enter drücken

▶ **enter into** VI *+prep obj* **a** *relations, negotiations, discussions* aufnehmen; *contract, alliance* schließen, eingehen; **to enter into conversation with sb** ein Gespräch mit jdm anknüpfen; **to enter into correspondence with sb** mit jdm in Briefwechsel treten → **spirit b** *(= figure in)* eine Rolle spielen bei

▶ **enter up** VT *sep* eintragen

▶ **enter (up)on** VI *+prep obj career, duties* antreten; *new era* eintreten in *(+acc)*; *subject* eingehen auf *(+acc)*; *transaction* abschließen

enteric [en'terɪk] ADJ Darm-; **~ infection** Darmentzündung *f*

enteric fever N (Unterleibs)typhus *m*

enteritis [ˌentə'raɪtɪs] N Dünndarmentzündung *f*

enter key N *(Comput)* Enter-Taste *f*

enterprise ['entəpraɪz] N **a** *no pl (= initiative, ingenuity)* Initiative *f*; *(= adventurousness)* Unternehmungsgeist *m* **b** *(= project, undertaking, Comm: = firm)* Unternehmen *nt*; **free/public/private ~** *(system)* freies/öffentliches/privates Unternehmertum

enterprise zone N wirtschaftliches Fördergebiet

enterprising ['entəpraɪzɪŋ] ADJ *person (= adventurous)* unternehmungslustig; *(= resourceful)* einfallsreich; *company* geschäftstüchtig; *idea, scheme* einfallsreich, originell; **that was ~ of her** da war sie aber unternehmungslustig/einfallsreich

enterprisingly ['entəpraɪzɪŋlɪ] ADV *(= adventurously)* unternehmungslustig; *(= resourcefully)* einfallsreich; **he very ~ started his own business** unternehmungslustig, wie er war, machte er sein eigenes Geschäft auf

entertain [ˌentə'teɪn] VT **a** *(= offer hospitality to)* einladen; *(to meal)* bewirten; **to ~ sb to dinner** jdn zum Essen einladen **b** *(= amuse)* unterhalten; *(humorously, with jokes)* belustigen **c** *thought, intention* sich tragen mit; *suspicion, doubt* hegen; *hope* nähren; *suggestion, proposal, offer, possibility* in Erwägung ziehen VI **a** *(= have visitors)* Gäste haben **b** *(comedian, conjurer etc)* unterhalten

entertainer [ˌentə'teɪnə'] N Unterhalter(in) *m(f)*, Entertainer(in) *m(f)*

entertaining [ˌentə'teɪnɪŋ] ADJ *(= fun)* unterhaltsam; *(= amusing)* amüsant N die Bewirtung von Gästen; **she does a lot of ~** sie hat oft Gäste; **business ~** die Bewirtung von Geschäftspartnern

entertainingly [ˌentə'teɪnɪŋlɪ] ADV *(= in a fun way)* unterhaltsam; *(= amusingly)* amüsant

entertainment [ˌentə'teɪnmənt] N **a** *(= amusement)* Unterhaltung *f*; *(professional)* Entertainment *nt*; **for my own ~** nur so zum Vergnügen, zu meinem Privatvergnügen; **the cinema is a great form of ~** das Kino bietet tolle Unterhaltung; **the film is good ~** der Film ist sehr unterhaltsam; **the world of ~** die Unterhaltungsbranche **b** *(= performance)* Darbietung *f*

entertainment: **entertainment allowance** N ≈ Aufwandspauschale *f*; **entertainment tax** N Vergnügungssteuer *f*; **entertainment value** N **to have good ~** großen Unterhaltungswert haben; *(person)* sehr unterhaltend sein

enthral, **enthrall** *(US)* [ɪn'θrɔːl] VT begeistern, berücken *(geh)*; *(exciting story etc also)* packen, fesseln; **he was (held) ~led by her beauty** er war von ihrer Schönheit gefesselt *or* bezaubert *or* berückt *(geh)*

enthralling [ɪn'θrɔːlɪŋ] ADJ spannend; *story also* packend

enthrone [ɪn'θrəʊn] VT inthronisieren; *bishop* feierlich einsetzen; **to sit ~d** thronen

enthronement [ɪn'θrəʊnmənt] N Inthronisation *f*, Inthronisierung *f*; *(of bishop)* Einsetzung *f*

enthuse [ɪn'θjuːz] VI schwärmen *(over* von)

enthusiasm [ɪn'θjuːzɪæzəm] N **a** Begeisterung *f*, Enthusiasmus *m (for* für); **she showed little ~ for the scheme** sie zeigte sich von dem Plan nicht sehr begeistert; **she has great ~ for life** sie hat sehr viel Lebensfreude; **I can't work up any ~ for going out** ich kann mich gar nicht dafür begeistern, auszugehen; **I can't work up any ~ for the idea** ich kann mich für die Idee nicht begeistern; **the idea filled her with ~** die Idee begeisterte sie
b *(= interest)* Interesse *nt*; *(= passion)* Leidenschaft *f*; **photography is one of her many ~s** Fotografieren ist eines ihrer vielen Interessen/Leidenschaften; **he has many ~s** er kann sich für viele Dinge begeistern

enthusiast [ɪn'θjuːzɪæst] N Enthusiast(in) *m(f)*; **he's a sports/football/rock-and-roll ~** er ist begeisterter Sportler/Fußballfreund *m*/Rock 'n' Roll-Anhänger *m*

enthusiastic [ɪnˌθjuːzɪ'æstɪk] ✪ 7.3, 14 ADJ begeistert, enthusiastisch; **he was very ~ about the plan** er war von dem Plan äußerst begeistert; **to be ~ about doing sth** etw mit Begeisterung tun; *(in future)* sich darauf freuen, etw zu tun; **he was ~ in his praise of it** er lobte es begeistert; **they had been a little too ~ when buying the ingredients** sie waren beim Einkaufen der Zutaten ein bisschen über das Ziel hinausgeschossen; **to be less than ~ (about sth)** nicht gerade (von etw) begeistert sein; **to be less than ~ about doing sth** nicht gerade wild darauf sein, etw zu tun; **to wax ~ (about sth)** (über etw *acc*) in Begeisterung geraten

enthusiastically [ɪnˌθjuːzɪ'æstɪkəlɪ] ADV begeistert, mit Begeisterung

entice [ɪn'taɪs] VT locken; *(= lead astray)* verführen, verleiten; **to ~ sb to do sth** *or* **into doing sth** jdn dazu verführen *or* verleiten, etw zu tun; **to ~ sb away** jdn weglocken

enticement [ɪn'taɪsmənt] N *(= act)* Lockung *f*; *(= leading astray)* Verführung *f*; *(= lure)* Lockmittel *nt*; *(fig)* Verlockung *f*

enticing [ɪn'taɪsɪŋ] ADJ verlockend; *look* verführerisch

enticingly [ɪn'taɪsɪŋlɪ] ADV verlockend, verführerisch; **the wine is ~ aromatic** der Wein hat ein verlockendes Aroma; **they have an ~ simple way of life** sie haben einen beneidenswert einfachen Lebensstil

entire [ɪn'taɪə'] ADJ **a** *(= whole, complete)* ganz; *cost, career* gesamt **b** *(= intact)* vollständig **c** *(= uncastrated)* nicht kastriert

entirely [ɪn'taɪəlɪ] ADV **a** *(= exclusively) depend, devote* ganz, ausschließlich; **the accident was ~ the fault of the other driver** der andere Fahrer hatte die ganze Schuld an dem Unfall; **to be made ~ of ...** ganz *or* ausschließlich aus ... bestehen; **he lived ~ on bread and milk** er lebte ausschließlich *or* nur von Brot und Milch; **that is ~ a matter for the police/the school authorities** dafür ist allein die Polizei/die Schulbehörde zuständig
b *(emph: = totally)* völlig; **I agree ~** ich stimme voll und ganz zu; **I don't agree ~** ich bin nicht ganz der (gleichen) Meinung; **~ free (of charge)** ganz umsonst; **it has been ~ free of serious problems** damit hat es keinerlei ernste Probleme gegeben; **~ possible** durchaus möglich; **to be ~ convinced by sb/sth** von jdm/etw völlig *or* ganz überzeugt sein; **to be another matter ~** *or* **an ~ different matter** etwas ganz *or* völlig anderes sein

entirety [ɪn'taɪərətɪ] N Gesamtheit *f*; **in its ~** in seiner Gesamtheit

entitle [ɪn'taɪtl] VT **a** *book* betiteln; **it is ~d ...** es hat den Titel ... **b** *(= give the right)* **to ~ sb to sth** jdn zu etw berechtigen; *to compensation, legal aid, holiday* jdm den Anspruch auf etw *(acc)* geben; **to ~ sb to do sth** jdn dazu berechtigen, etw zu tun; **to be ~d to sth** das Recht auf etw *(acc)* haben; *to compensation, legal aid, holiday* Anspruch auf etw *(acc)* haben; **to be ~d to do sth** das Recht haben, etw zu tun; **I'm ~d to my own opinion** ich kann mir meine eigene Meinung bilden; **to be ~d to vote** wählen können, das Wahlrecht haben

entitlement [ɪn'taɪtlmənt] N Berechtigung *f (to* zu); *(to compensation, legal aid, holiday etc)* Anspruch *m (to* auf *+acc)*; **what is your holiday ~?** *(Brit)* wie viel Urlaub steht Ihnen zu?

entity ['entɪtɪ] N Wesen *nt* **a legal ~** juristische Person; **living ~** Lebewesen *nt*; **as a separate ~** als ein eigenständiges Gebilde **b** *(Comput)* Entität *f*, Entity *f (inf)*, (separate) Informationseinheit

entomb [ɪn'tuːm] VT beisetzen, bestatten; **the mausoleum which ~s his body** das Mausoleum, in dem er beigesetzt ist

entomologist [ˌentə'mɒlədʒɪst] N Entomologe *m*, Entomologin *f*

entomology [ˌentə'mɒlədʒɪ] N Entomologie *f*, Insektenkunde *f*

entourage [ˌɒntʊ'rɑːʒ] N Gefolge *nt*, Entourage *f (geh)*

entr'acte ['ɒntrækt] N Zwischenspiel *nt*

entrails ['entreɪlz] PL *(lit)* Eingeweide *pl*; *(fig, of watch etc)* Innereien *pl (hum)*

entrain [ɪn'treɪn] VT *troops* (in Eisenbahnwaggons) verladen VI (in den Zug) einsteigen

entrance[1] [ɪn'trɑːns] VT in Entzücken *or* Verzückung versetzen; **to be ~d** verzückt sein; **to be ~d by/with sth** von etw entzückt sein

entrance[2] ['entrəns] N **a** *(= way in)* Eingang *m*; *(for vehicles)* Einfahrt *f*; *(= hall)* Eingangshalle *f*, Entree *nt (geh)*
b *(= entering)* Eintritt *m*; *(Theat)* Auftritt *m*; **on his ~** bei seinem Eintritt/Auftritt; **to make an ~** in Erscheinung treten; **he likes to make an ~** er setzt sich gern in Szene; **to make one's ~** *(Theat)* auftreten; *(fig)* erscheinen; **his ~ into**

equine ['ekwaɪn] ADJ Pferde-; ~ **sports** Pferdesport *m*

equinoctial [ˌiːkwɪ'nɒkʃəl] ADJ *gales, tides* äquinoktial

equinox ['iːkwɪnɒks] N Tagundnachtgleiche *f*, Äquinoktium *nt*; **the spring/autumn ~** die Frühjahrs-/Herbst-Tagundnachtgleiche

equip [ɪ'kwɪp] VT *ship, soldier, astronaut, army, worker* ausrüsten; *household, kitchen* ausstatten; **the building is also ~ped as a sports hall** das Gebäude ist auch als Sporthalle ausgestattet; **to ~ sb for life** *(fig)* jdm das (nötige) Rüstzeug fürs Leben mitgeben; **to ~ oneself with sth** sich mit etw ausrüsten; **to ~ oneself with a good education** sich *(dat)* eine gute Ausbildung verschaffen; **he is well ~ped for the job** *(fig)* er hat die nötigen Kenntnisse *or* das nötige Rüstzeug für die Stelle; **you are better ~ped than I to tackle chemistry translations** du bringst für Chemieübersetzungen das bessere Rüstzeug mit

equipage ['ekwɪpɪdʒ] N Equipage *f*

equipment [ɪ'kwɪpmənt] N *no pl* **a** *(= objects) (of person)* Ausrüstung *f*; **laboratory ~** Laborausstattung *f*; **office ~** Büroeinrichtung *f*; **electrical ~** Elektrogeräte *pl*; **kitchen ~** Küchengeräte *pl* **b** *(= action of equipping: of ship, soldier, astronaut, army, worker)* Ausrüstung *f* **c** *(mental, intellectual)* (geistiges) Rüstzeug

equipoise ['ekwɪpɔɪz] N *(form: = equilibrium)* Gleichgewicht *nt*

equitable ['ekwɪtəbl] ADJ fair, gerecht, recht und billig

equitableness ['ekwɪtəblnɪs] N Fairness *f*, Billigkeit *f*

equitably ['ekwɪtəblɪ] ADV gerecht

equity ['ekwɪtɪ] N **a** Fairness *f*, Billigkeit *f* **b equities** PL *(Fin)* Stammaktien *pl*, Dividendenpapiere *pl*; **equities market** Aktienmarkt *m* **c** *(Jur)* Billigkeitsrecht *nt*, billiges Recht; **~ of redemption** Ablösungsrecht *nt* des Hypothekenschuldners **d** *(Brit, Theat)* **Equity** *britische Schauspielergewerkschaft*

equity: **equity capital** N *(Fin)* Eigenkapital *nt*, Nettoanteil *m*; **Equity card** N *(Brit Theat) Mitgliedskarte der Schauspielergewerkschaft*; **equity stake** N *(Fin)* Kapitalbeteiligung *f*

equivalence [ɪ'kwɪvələns] N Äquivalenz *f*, Entsprechung *f*

equivalent [ɪ'kwɪvələnt] ADJ **a** *(= equal)* gleich, gleichwertig, äquivalent; **that's ~ to saying ...** das ist gleichbedeutend damit, zu sagen ...; **to be ~ in meaning** die gleiche Bedeutung haben

b *(= corresponding)* entsprechend, äquivalent; **the ~ institution in America** die entsprechende Einrichtung in Amerika, das amerikanische Äquivalent dazu; **an ~ salary in 1985 would have been ...** ein entsprechendes Gehalt wäre im Jahre 1985 ... gewesen; **it is ~ to £30** das entspricht £ 30; **... or the ~ value in francs** ... oder der Gegenwert in Francs

c *(Chem)* gleichwertig; *(Geometry)* äquivalent

d that's ~ to lying das ist so viel wie gelogen; **as an au pair she is ~ to nanny and maid** als Aupair ist sie Kindermädchen und Dienstmädchen in einer Person

N Äquivalent *nt*; *(= counterpart)* Gegenstück *nt*, Pendant *nt*; *(= person)* Pendant *nt*; **that is the ~ of ...** das entspricht ... *(dat)*; **what is the ~ in euros?** was ist der Gegenwert in Euro?; **the American ~ of the British public school** das amerikanische Gegenstück *or* Pendant zur britischen Public School; **the German ~ of the English custom** die deutsche Entsprechung zu dem englischen Brauch; **... or the ~ in cash** ...oder der Gegenwert in bar

equivocal [ɪ'kwɪvəkəl] ADJ *(form)* **a** *(= ambiguous, vague) reply, response* zweideutig; *statement, comment* unklar, vage; *position* unklar, unbestimmt; *results, research* unklar; *evidence* nicht schlüssig; **she was ~** sie legte sich nicht fest; **he was more ~** er drückte sich unklarer aus **b** *(= ambivalent) attitude* zwiespältig, ambivalent; *person* ambivalent; *(= undecided)* unentschieden; **to be ~ about sth** keine klare Meinung zu etw haben; **public opinion is ~ about it** die öffentliche Meinung ist darüber geteilt

equivocally [ɪ'kwɪvəkəlɪ] ADV **a** *(= ambiguously)* zweideutig **b** *(= unclearly)* unklar

equivocate [ɪ'kwɪvəkeɪt] VI ausweichen, ausweichend antworten

equivocation [ɪˌkwɪvə'keɪʃən] N Ausflucht *f*, doppelsinnige *or* ausweichende Formulierung; **without ~** ohne Ausflüchte

ER **a** *abbr of* **Elizabeth Regina** **b** *(US) abbr of* **emergency room**

ERA *(US) abbr of* **Equal Rights Amendment** *Verfassungsartikel zur Gleichberechtigung*

era ['ɪərə] N Ära *f*, Epoche *f*; *(Geol)* Erdzeitalter *nt*; **the Christian ~** (die) christliche Zeitrechnung; **the end of an ~** das Ende einer Ära

eradicate [ɪ'rædɪkeɪt] VT ausrotten

eradication [ɪˌrædɪ'keɪʃən] N Ausrottung *f*

erasable [ɪ'reɪzəbl] ADJ löschbar; **~ programmable read only memory** *(Comput)* löschbarer programmierbarer Festwertspeicher

erase [ɪ'reɪz] VT ausradieren; *(from tape, Comput)* löschen; *(from the mind)* streichen *(from* aus); *(sl: = kill)* erledigen *(sl)*

eraser [ɪ'reɪzə'] N Radiergummi *nt or m*

erasure [ɪ'reɪʒə'] N *(= act)* Auslöschen *nt*, Ausradieren *nt*; *(from tape)* Löschen *nt*; *(= sth erased)* ausradierte Stelle, Radierstelle *f*; *(on tape)* gelöschte Stelle

ere [ɛə'] *(old, poet)* PREP ehe, bevor; **~ now** bisher; **~ long** binnen Kurzem CONJ ehe, bevor

e-reader N eReader *m*

erect [ɪ'rekt] VT *wall, building* bauen; *statue, memorial, altar* errichten *(to sb* jdm); *machinery, traffic signs, collapsible furniture* aufstellen; *scaffolding* aufstellen, aufbauen; *tent* aufschlagen; *mast, flagpole* aufrichten; *(fig) barrier* errichten, aufbauen; *system* aufstellen ADJ **a** *(= upright) person, posture, plant* aufrecht; *head* hoch erhoben; *stem* gerade; *tail* erhoben; *ears* aufgestellt; **to stand ~** gerade stehen; **to walk ~** aufrecht gehen **b** *(Physiol) penis* erigiert, steif; *clitoris, nipples* erigiert, aufgerichtet

erectile [ɪ'rektaɪl] ADJ Schwell-, erektil; **~ tissue** Schwellkörper *m*

erection [ɪ'rekʃən] N **a** *(= act of erecting, of wall, building)* (Er)bauen *nt*; *(of statue, memorial, altar)* Errichten *nt*; *(of machinery, traffic signs, collapsible furniture)* Aufstellen *nt*; *(of scaffolding)* Aufstellen *nt*, Aufbauen *nt*; *(of tent)* Aufschlagen *nt*; *(of mast, flagpole)* Aufrichten *nt*; *(fig, of barrier)* Errichten *nt*, Aufbauen *nt*; *(of system)* Aufstellen *nt* **b** *(= building)* Gebäude *nt*, Bau *m* **c** *(Physiol)* Erektion *f*

erectly [ɪ'rektlɪ] ADV aufrecht

e-retailer N E-Retailer *m*, Internet-Einzelhändler *m*

erg [ɜːg] N Erg *nt*

ergo ['ɜːgəʊ] ADV *(form, hum)* ergo, also

ergonomic ADJ, **ergonomically** ADV [ˌɜːgəʊ'nɒmɪk, -əlɪ] ergonomisch

ergonomics [ˌɜːgəʊ'nɒmɪks] N *sing* Ergonomie *f*, Arbeitswissenschaft *f*

ergot ['ɜːgət] N Mutterkorn *nt*, Hungerkorn *nt*

ergotism ['ɜːgətɪzəm] N *(Med)* Mutterkornvergiftung *f*, Ergotismus *m*

erica ['erɪkə] N *(Bot)* Erika *f*, Heidekraut *nt*

Erin ['ɪərɪn] N *(poet)* Irland *nt*

ERM N *abbr of* **exchange rate mechanism**

ermine ['ɜːmɪn] N *(= animal)* Hermelin *nt*; *(= fur)* Hermelin *m*

Ernie ['ɜːnɪ] *abbr of* **Electronic Random Number Indicator Equipment**

erode [ɪ'rəʊd] VT *(glacier, water, sea)* auswaschen, erodieren *(spec)*; *(acid)* ätzen; *(rust)* wegfressen, anfressen; *(fig) confidence, power, values, beliefs* untergraben; *authority* unterminieren; *differentials* aushöhlen; *value* abtragen, untergraben VI *(value)* abgetragen werden

erogenous [ɪ'rɒdʒənəs] ADJ erogen; **~ zones** erogene Zonen *pl*

erosion [ɪ'rəʊʒən] N *(by water, glaciers, rivers)* Erosion *f*, Abtragung *f*; *(by acid)* Ätzung *f*; *(fig, of love etc)* Schwinden *nt*; *(of power, values, beliefs)* Untergrabung *f*; *(of authority)* Unterminierung *f*; *(of differentials)* Aushöhlen *nt*; *(of value)* Abtragung *f*, Untergrabung *f*; **an ~ of confidence in the pound** ein Vertrauensverlust *m or* -schwund *m* des Pfundes

erosive [ɪ'rəʊzɪv] ADJ *effect of sea etc* abtragend; *effect of acid* ätzend

erotic [ɪ'rɒtɪk] ADJ erotisch; *love also* sinnlich; *pose also* aufreizend; **an ~ dancer** ein Erotiktänzer *m*, eine Erotiktänzerin *f*; **he's a very ~ person** er ist sehr erotisch

erotica [ɪ'rɒtɪkə] PL Erotika *pl*

erotically [ɪ'rɒtɪkəlɪ] ADV erotisch; **~ charged** erotisch geladen

eroticism [ɪ'rɒtɪsɪzəm] N Erotik *f*

eroticize [ɪ'rɒtɪsaɪz] VT erotisieren

err [ɜː'] VI **a** *(= be mistaken)* sich irren; **to ~ in one's judgement** in seinem Urteil fehlgehen, sich in seinem Urteil irren; **to ~ is human(, to forgive divine)** *(Prov)* Irren ist menschlich(, Vergeben göttlich) *(Prov)*; **it is better to ~ on the side of caution** man sollte im Zweifelsfall lieber zu vorsichtig sein **b** *(= sin)* sündigen, Verfehlungen begehen **c** *(Rel, = stray)* abgehen, in die Irre gehen

errand ['erənd] N *(= shopping etc)* Besorgung *f*; *(to give a message etc)* Botengang *m*; *(= task)* Auftrag *m*; **to send sb on an ~** jdn auf Besorgungen/einen Botengang schicken; **to go on** *or* **run ~s (for sb)** (für jdn) Besorgungen/Botengänge machen; **to be out on an ~** Besorgungen/einen Botengang machen, etwas erledigen; **~ of mercy** Rettungsaktion *f*

errand boy N Laufbursche *m*, Laufjunge *m*

errant ['erənt] ADJ *(= erring) ways* sündig, verfehlt; *husband etc* untreu; *members* abtrünnig; *(hum) Marxist, Freudian* fehlgeleitet, auf Irrwegen

errata [e'rɑːtə] *pl of* **erratum**

erratic [ɪ'rætɪk] ADJ unberechenbar; *progress, pattern, rhythm, pulse, breathing* ungleichmäßig; *performance* variabel; *movement* unkontrolliert; **to be (very) ~** *(sales, figures)* (stark) schwanken; **~ mood swings** starke Stimmungsschwankungen *pl*; **his ~ driving** sein unberechenbarer Fahrstil; **his work is rather ~** er ist in seiner Arbeit recht wechselhaft; **public transport here is very ~** die öffentlichen Verkehrsmittel verkehren hier nur sehr unregelmäßig; **we work ~ hours** wir haben unregelmäßige Arbeitszeiten

erratically [ɪ'rætɪkəlɪ] ADV *behave, drive* unberechenbar; **to work ~** *(person)* ungleichmäßig arbeiten; *(machine)* unregelmäßig arbeiten; **the ~ brilliant hockey team** die hervorragende, jedoch sehr wechselhaft spielende Hockey-Mannschaft

erratum [e'rɑːtəm] N *pl* **errata** Erratum *nt*

erring ['ɜːrɪŋ] ADJ = **errant**

erroneous [ɪ'rəʊnɪəs] ADJ falsch; *assumption, belief, impression* irrig

erroneously [ɪ'rəʊnɪəslɪ] ADV fälschlicherweise

error ['erə'] ✪ 18.3, 20.6, 20.7 N **a** *(= mistake)* Fehler *m*; **~ in calculation** Rechenfehler *m*; **compass ~** (magnetische) Abweichung; **~s and omissions excepted** *(Comm)* Irrtum vorbehalten; **a pilot ~** ein Fehler *m* des Piloten; **the ~ rate** die Fehlerquote, die Fehlerrate; **~ in fact** *(Jur)* Tatsachenirrtum *m*; **~ in form** *(Jur)* Formfehler *m*; **~ in law** *(Jur)* Rechtsirrtum *m* → **margin** **b** *(= wrongness)* Irrtum *m*; **to be in ~** im Irrtum sein, sich im Irrtum befinden; **in ~** *(= wrongly, accidentally)* irrtümlicherweise; **to see the ~ of one's ways** seine Fehler einsehen

error diffusion N *(Comput: graphics)* Fehlerstreuung *f*

error message N *(Comput)* Fehlermeldung *f*

ersatz ['ɛəzæts] ADJ Ersatz-; **~ religion** Ersatzreligion *f*; **~ coffee** Kaffee-Ersatz *m* N Ersatz *m*

Erse [ɜːs] N *no pl* Gälisch *nt*

erstwhile [ˈɜːstwaɪl] ADJ *(old, liter)* vormalig, einstig, ehemalig ADV *(old, liter)* vormals, ehedem, einst

eructate [ɪˈrʌkteɪt] VI *(hum, form)* aufstoßen

eructation [ˌɪrʌkˈteɪʃən] N *(hum)* Aufstoßen *nt;* **an ~** ein Rülpser *m (inf)*

erudite [ˈerʊdaɪt] ADJ gelehrt; *person also* gebildet, belesen

eruditely [ˈerʊdaɪtlɪ] ADV gelehrt

erudition [ˌerʊˈdɪʃən] N Gelehrsamkeit *f;* **a work of great ~** ein sehr gelehrtes Werk

erupt [ɪˈrʌpt] VI *(volcano, war, quarrel)* ausbrechen; *(spots)* zum Vorschein kommen; *(fig, person)* explodieren; **to ~ in(to) violence** in Gewalttätigkeit ausarten; **the district ~ed in riots** in dem Bezirk brachen Unruhen aus; **the crowd ~ed into applause/laughter** die Menge brach in Applaus/Gelächter aus; **he ~ed in anger** er bekam einen Wutanfall; **her face had ~ed in spots** sie hatte im ganzen Gesicht Pickel bekommen

eruption [ɪˈrʌpʃən] N *(of volcano, anger, war, violence)* Ausbruch *m;* *(Med, of spots, rash)* Eruption *f (spec),* Ausbruch *m,* Auftreten *nt;* *(= rash etc)* Hautausschlag *m,* Eruption *f (spec)*

erysipelas [ˌerɪˈsɪpɪləs] N (Wund)rose *f*

ESA *(Space) abbr of* **European Space Agency**

escalate [ˈeskəleɪt] VT *war* ausweiten, eskalieren; *costs* sprunghaft erhöhen VI sich ausweiten, um sich greifen, eskalieren; *(costs)* eskalieren, in die Höhe schnellen

escalation [ˌeskəˈleɪʃən] N Eskalation *f*

escalator [ˈeskəleɪtəʳ] N Rolltreppe *f*

escalator clause N Gleitklausel *f*

escalope [ɪˈskæləp] N Schnitzel *nt*

escapable [ɪˈskeɪpəbl] ADJ vermeidbar

escapade [ˌeskəˈpeɪd] N Eskapade *f*

escape [ɪˈskeɪp] VI **a** *(= get away)* flüchten, fliehen *(from* aus), entfliehen *(geh) (from +dat)*; *(from pursuers, captivity)* entkommen *(from +dat)*; *(from prison, camp, cage, stall etc)* ausbrechen *(from* aus); *(bird)* entfliegen *(from +dat)*; *(water)* auslaufen *(from* aus); *(gas)* ausströmen *(from* aus); **to stop the prisoners escaping** um Gefängnisausbrüche zu verhindern; **he was shot dead while trying to ~** er wurde bei einem Fluchtversuch erschossen; **an ~d prisoner/tiger** ein entflohener Häftling/entsprungener Tiger; **he ~d from the fire** er ist dem Feuer entkommen; **I've got you now, she said, and I won't let you ~** jetzt habe ich dich, sagte sie, und du entkommst mir so schnell nicht; **I just feel I have to ~ from this place** ich habe einfach das Gefühl, dass ich hier wegmuss; **she has to be able to ~ from her family sometimes** sie muss ab und zu die Möglichkeit haben, ihrer Familie zu entfliehen; **a room which I can ~ to** ein Zimmer, in das ich mich zurückziehen kann; **to ~ from oneself** vor sich *(dat)* selber fliehen; **it's no good trying to ~ from the world** es hat keinen Zweck, vor der Welt fliehen zu wollen; **he's trying to ~ from life on the streets** er versucht, von dem Leben auf der Straße wegzukommen; **to ~ from reality** der Wirklichkeit entfliehen *(geh)*; **to ~ from poverty** der Armut entkommen

b *(= get off, be spared)* davonkommen; **these cuts will affect everyone, nobody will ~** diese Kürzungen betreffen alle, keiner wird ungeschoren davonkommen; **the others were killed, but he ~d** die anderen wurden getötet, aber er kam mit dem Leben davon

VT **a** *pursuers* entkommen *(+dat)*

b *(= avoid) consequences, punishment, disaster, detection* entgehen *(+dat)*; **no department will ~ these cuts** keine Abteilung wird von diesen Kürzungen verschont bleiben; **he narrowly ~d injury** er ist gerade noch unverletzt davongekommen; **he narrowly ~d death** er ist dem Tod mit knapper Not entronnen; **he narrowly ~d being run over** er wäre um ein Haar *or* um Haaresbreite überfahren worden; **to ~ the worst** vom Schlimmsten verschont bleiben; **but you can't ~ the fact that ...** aber du kannst nicht leugnen *or* abstreiten, dass ...

c *(= be unnoticed, forgotten by)* **his name ~s me** sein Name ist mir entfallen; **nothing ~s him** ihm entgeht nichts; **to ~ notice** unbemerkt bleiben; **it had not ~d her (attention)** es war ihr *or* ihrer Aufmerksamkeit nicht entgangen

d the thoughtless words which ~d me die unbedachten Worte, die mir herausgerutscht *or* entfahren sind

N **a** *(from prison etc)* Ausbruch *m,* Flucht *f;* *(= attempted escape)* Ausbruchsversuch *m,* Fluchtversuch *m;* *(from a country)* Flucht *f (from* aus); *(fig, from reality, one's family etc)* Flucht *f (from* vor); **to make one's ~** ausbrechen, entfliehen; **the ~ was successful** der Ausbruchs- *or* Fluchtversuch glückte *or* war erfolgreich; **the increasing number of ~s** die zunehmende Zahl von Ausbruchsfällen; **with this security system ~ is impossible** dieses Sicherheitssystem macht Ausbrechen unmöglich; **what are their chances of ~?** wie sind ihre Fluchtmöglichkeiten?, wie sind ihre Chancen zu entkommen?; **there's been an ~ from London Zoo** aus dem Londoner Zoo ist ein Tier ausgebrochen; **to have a miraculous ~** *(from accident, illness)* auf wunderbare Weise davonkommen; **fishing/music is his ~** Angeln/Musik ist seine Zuflucht; **otherwise I don't get any ~ from the demands of my family** sonst habe ich überhaupt keine Abwechslung von den Ansprüchen meiner Familie; **there's no ~** *(fig)* es gibt keinen Ausweg *or* kein Entrinnen *(geh)* → **lucky**

b *(of water)* Ausfließen *nt;* *(of gas)* Ausströmen *nt;* *(of steam, gas, in a machine)* Entweichen *nt;* **due to an ~ of gas** aufgrund *or* auf Grund ausströmenden Gases

c *(Comput)* **hit ~** Escape drücken

escape: **escape artist** N Entfesselungskünstler(in) *m(f)*; **escape attempt, escape bid** N Fluchtversuch *m;* **escape chute** N *(on plane)* Notrutsche *f;* **escape clause** N *(Jur)* Rücktrittsklausel *f*

escapee [ɪskeɪˈpiː] N entflohener Häftling

escape: **escape hatch** N *(Naut)* Notluke *f;* **escape key** N *(Comput)* Escapetaste *f;* **escape mechanism** N Abwehrmechanismus *m*

escapement [ɪˈskeɪpmənt] N *(of clock)* Hemmung *f*

escape: **escape pipe** N Überlaufrohr *nt;* *(for gas, steam)* Abzugsrohr *nt;* **escape plan** N Fluchtplan *m;* **escape-proof** ADJ ausbruchsicher; **escape road** N Ausweichstraße *f;* **escape route** N Fluchtweg *m;* **escape valve** N Sicherheitsventil *nt;* **escape velocity** N *(Space)* Fluchtgeschwindigkeit *f*

escapism [ɪˈskeɪpɪzəm] N Wirklichkeitsflucht *f,* Eskapismus *m (spec)*

escapist [ɪˈskeɪpɪst] N jd, der vor der Wirklichkeit flieht, Eskapist(in) *m(f)* ADJ eskapistisch; **~ fantasy** unrealistische Fantasien *or* Phantasien *pl*

escapologist [ˌeskəˈpɒlədʒɪst] N Entfesselungskünstler(in) *m(f)*

escarpment [ɪˈskɑːpmənt] N Steilhang *m;* *(Geol)* Schichtstufe *f;* *(as fortification)* Böschung *f*

eschatological [ˌeskətəˈlɒdʒɪkəl] ADJ eschatologisch

eschatology [ˌeskəˈtɒlədʒɪ] N Eschatologie *f*

eschew [ɪsˈtʃuː] VT *(old, liter)* scheuen, (ver)meiden; *wine etc* sich enthalten *(+gen)*; *temptation* aus dem Wege gehen *(+dat)*

escort [ˈeskɔːt] N **a** Geleitschutz *m;* *(escorting vehicles, ships etc)* Eskorte *f,* Geleitschiff *nt/*-schiffe *pl;* *(= police escort)* Begleitmannschaft *f,* Eskorte *f;* *(= guard of honour)* Eskorte *f;* **under ~** unter Bewachung; **motorcycle ~** Motorradeskorte *f* **b** *(= male companion)* Begleiter *m;* *(= hired female)* Hostess *f* VT [ɪˈskɔːt] begleiten; *(Mil, Naut) general* eskortieren, Geleit(schutz) geben *(+dat)*

escort: **escort agency** N Hostessenagentur *f;* **escort duty** N Geleitdienst *m;* **to be on ~** Geleitschutz geben; **escort fighter** N *(Aviat)* Begleitjäger *m;* **escort party** N Eskorte *f;* **escort vessel** N *(Naut)* Geleitschiff *nt*

escrow [ˈeskrəʊ] N **~ account** Anderkonto *nt;* **to put money in ~** Geld auf ein Anderkonto legen

escutcheon [ɪˈskʌtʃən] N Wappen *nt;* **it is a blot on his ~** das ist ein Fleck auf seiner weißen Weste

ESE *abbr of* **east-south-east** OSO

e-shopper N E-Shopper(in) *m(f),* Internetkunde *m*/-kundin *f*

Eskimo [ˈeskɪməʊ] *(pej)* ADJ Eskimo-, eskimoisch N **a** Eskimo *m,* Eskimofrau *f* **b** *(Ling)* Eskimosprache *f*

Eskimo dog N Eskimohund *m*

ESL *abbr of* **English as a Second Language**

ESN *abbr of* **educationally subnormal**

esophagus N *(esp US)* = **oesophagus**

esoteric [ˌesəʊˈterɪk] ADJ esoterisch

ESP *abbr of* **extrasensory perception** ASW *f*

esp. *abbr of* **especially** bes.

espadrille [ˌespəˈdrɪl] N Espadrille *f*

espalier [ɪˈspæljəʳ] N Spalier *nt;* *(= tree)* Spalierbaum *m;* *(method)* Anbau *m* von Spalierobst

espécial [ɪˈspeʃəl] ADJ besondere(r, s)

especially [ɪˈspeʃəlɪ] ✪ 26.3 ADV **a** *(= particularly)* besonders; **I ~ liked the beginning** der Anfang hat mir besonders gut gefallen; **to try ~ hard** sich besonders viel Mühe geben; **not ~** nicht besonders; **(more) ~ as ...** besonders *or* vor allem, weil ...; **~ in summer** vor allem im Sommer; **you ~ ought to know** gerade du solltest das wissen; **why Jim ~?** warum ausgerechnet *or* gerade Jim? **b** *(= specifically)* speziell, eigens; **I came ~ to see you** ich bin eigens gekommen, um dich zu sehen; **to do sth ~ for sb/sth** etw speziell *or* extra für jdn/etw tun

Esperanto [ˌespəˈræntəʊ] N Esperanto *nt*

espionage [ˌespɪəˈnɑːʒ] N Spionage *f*

esplanade [ˌespləˈneɪd] N (Strand)promenade *f*

espousal [ɪˈspaʊzəl] N **a** *(old, = marriage)* Vermählung *f;* *(= betrothal)* Verlobung *f* **b** *(of cause etc)* Parteinahme *f (of* für)

espouse [ɪˈspaʊz] VT **a** *(old, form) woman* sich vermählen mit, zur Frau nehmen; *(= get betrothed to)* sich anverloben *(+dat) (old)*; **to become ~d to sb** jdm angetraut/anverlobt werden **b** *(fig) cause, views* Partei ergreifen für, eintreten für; *violence* befürworten

espresso [eˈspresəʊ] N **~ (coffee)** Espresso *m;* **~ bar** Espresso(bar *f*) *nt*

esprit de corps [eˈspriːdəˈkɔː] N Korpsgeist *m*

espy [ɪˈspaɪ] VT *(old, liter)* erspähen, erblicken

esquire [ɪˈskwaɪəʳ] N *(abbr* **Esq**) *(Brit: on envelope) als Titel nach dem Namen, wenn kein anderer Titel angegeben wird* **James Jones, Esq** Herrn James Jones

essay[1] [eˈseɪ] *(form)* VT *(= try)* (aus)probieren N Versuch *m*

essay[2] [ˈeseɪ] N Essay *m or nt;* *(esp Sch)* Aufsatz *m*

essayist [ˈeseɪɪst] N Essayist(in) *m(f)*

essayistic [ˌeseɪˈɪstɪk] ADJ essayistisch

essence [ˈesəns] N **a** *(Philos)* Wesen *nt,* Essenz *f;* *(= substratum)* Substanz *f*

b *(= most important quality)* Wesen *nt,* Wesentliche(s) *nt,* Kern *m;* **in ~ the theories are very similar** die Theorien sind im Wesentlichen *or* in ihrem Kern *or* essenziell *(geh) or* essentiell *(geh)* sehr ähnlich; **how would you describe the situation, in ~?** wie würden Sie die Situation im Wesentlichen beschreiben?; **speed/time is of the ~** Geschwindigkeit/Zeit ist von entscheidender Bedeutung; **the ~ of his thought** der Kern *or* die Essenz seines Denkens; **the note contained the ~ of what he had said** die Notiz enthielt den Kern dessen, was er gesagt hatte; **he embodies the very ~ of Japanese spirit** er verkörpert den Inbegriff des ja-

panischen Geistes; **the novel captures the ~ of life in the city** der Roman fängt das Leben in der Stadt perfekt ein; **the ~ of Liberalism** die Essenz des Liberalismus
c (= *extract*: *Chem, Cook*) Essenz *f*

essential [ɪ'senʃəl] ✪ 10.1 **ADJ** **a** (= *necessary, vital*) (unbedingt *or* absolut) erforderlich *or* notwendig; *services, supplies* lebenswichtig; **it is ~ to act quickly** schnelles Handeln ist unbedingt *or* absolut erforderlich; **it is ~ that he come(s)** es ist absolut *or* unbedingt erforderlich, dass er kommt, er muss unbedingt kommen; **it is ~ that you understand this** du musst das unbedingt verstehen; **do it now – is it really ~?** mach es jetzt – ist das wirklich unbedingt nötig?; **this is of ~ importance** dies ist von entscheidender Bedeutung; **certain vitamins are ~ for good health** bestimmte Vitamine sind für die Gesundheit unerlässlich; **she's become ~ to me** sie ist mir unentbehrlich geworden; **the ~ thing is to ...** wichtig ist vor allem, zu ...
b (= *of the essence, basic*) wesentlich, essenziell *(geh)*, essentiell *(geh)*; *(Philos)* essenziell, essentiell, wesenhaft; *question, role* entscheidend; **~ features** wesentliche Eigenschaften *pl*; **the ~ feature of his personality** der Grundzug *or* der grundlegende Zug seiner Persönlichkeit; **I don't doubt his ~ goodness** ich zweifle nicht an, dass er im Grunde ein guter Mensch ist; **to establish the ~ nature of the problem** feststellen, worum es im Kern bei diesem Problem eigentlich geht; **to establish the ~ nature of the disease** feststellen, worum es sich bei dieser Krankheit eigentlich handelt
N **a** (= *necessary thing*) **a compass is an ~ for mountain climbing** ein Kompass ist unbedingt notwendig zum Bergsteigen; **the first ~ is to privatize the industry** als Erstes muss die Industrie unbedingt privatisiert werden; **just bring the ~s** bring nur das Allernotwendigste mit; **with only the bare ~s** nur mit dem Allernotwendigsten ausgestattet
b **essentials** **PL** (= *most important points*) wichtige Punkte *pl*, Essentials *pl*; **the ~s of German grammar** die Grundlagen *pl or* die Grundzüge *pl* der deutschen Grammatik

essentially [ɪ'senʃəlɪ] **ADV** (= *fundamentally*) im Wesentlichen; (= *basically, at heart*) im Grunde genommen; **~, they are saying that ...** im Wesentlichen sagen sie, dass ...; **she was an ~ good woman** im Grunde genommen war sie eine gute Frau

essential oils [ɪ'senʃəl'ɔɪlz] **PL** *(Chem)* ätherische Öle *pl*

EST *(US) abbr of* **Eastern Standard Time** Ostküstenzeit *f*

est **a** *abbr of* **established** gegr. **b** *abbr of* **estimated** gesch.

establish [ɪ'stæblɪʃ] ✪ 15.1 **VT** **a** (= *found, set up*) gründen; *government* bilden; *laws* geben, schaffen; *custom, new procedure* einführen; *relations* herstellen, aufnehmen; *links* anknüpfen; *post* einrichten, schaffen; *power, authority* sich *(dat)* verschaffen; *peace* stiften; *order* (wieder) herstellen; *list (in publishing)* aufstellen, zusammenstellen; *reputation* sich *(dat)* verschaffen; *precedent* setzen; *committee* einsetzen; **once he had ~ed his power as Emperor** als er seine Macht als Kaiser begründet hatte; **his father ~ed him in business** sein Vater ermöglichte ihm den Start ins Geschäftsleben; **to ~ one's reputation as a scholar/writer** sich *(dat)* einen Namen als Wissenschaftler(in)/Schriftsteller(in) machen
b (= *prove) fact, innocence* beweisen, nachweisen; *claim* unter Beweis stellen; **we have ~ed that ...** wir haben bewiesen *or* gezeigt, dass ...
c (= *determine) identity, facts* ermitteln, feststellen
d (= *gain acceptance for) product, theory, ideas* Anklang *or* Anerkennung finden für; *one's rights* Anerkennung finden für; **if we can ~ our product on the market** wenn wir unser Produkt auf dem Markt etablieren können
VR *(in business, profession)* sich etablieren, sich niederlassen; **he has now firmly ~ed himself in the company** er ist jetzt in der Firma fest etabliert; **he seems to have ~ed himself as an expert** er scheint sich *(dat)* einen Ruf als Experte verschafft zu haben

established [ɪ'stæblɪʃt] **ADJ** *order, authority, religion* bestehend, etabliert; *rules* bestehend; *business, company* etabliert, eingeführt; *clientele* fest; *reputation* gesichert; *tradition* althergebracht; *name, brand* etabliert; **it's an ~ practice** *or* **custom** es ist allgemein üblich; **this is our ~ procedure** so gehen wir normalerwise vor; **firmly ~** *(reputation, peace)* völlig gesichert; *company, name* fest etabliert; **a well ~ business** ein fest etabliertes *or* gut eingeführtes Geschäft; **well** *or* **firmly ~ as sth** (= *recognized)* allgemein als etw anerkannt; **Indian food is now firmly ~ as a favourite** *(Brit) or* **favorite** *(US)* die indische Küche hat sich einen festen Platz als Lieblingsessen erobert; **it's an ~ fact that ...** es steht fest, dass ...; **this is ~ truth** das ist die unbestrittene Wahrheit; **~ 1850** *(Comm etc)* gegründet 1850

Established Church **N** Staatskirche *f*

establishing shot [ɪ'stæblɪʃɪŋʃɒt] **N** *(Film)* Eröffnungsszene *f*

establishment [ɪ'stæblɪʃmənt] **N** **a** (= *setting up, of relations, links)* Aufnahme *f*, Herstellung *f*; *(of committee)* Bildung *f*, Einsetzung *f*; *(of post)* Schaffung *f*, Einrichtung *f*; *(of peace)* Herstellung *f*; *(of order)* Herstellung *f*, Schaffung *f*; *(of publisher's list)* Bildung *f*; *(of power, authority)* Festigung *f*, (Wieder)herstellung *f*; *(of reputation)* Begründung *f*
b (= *proving)* Beweis *m*; **the lawyer devoted a lot of time to the ~ of a few basic facts** der Rechtsanwalt verwandte viel Zeit darauf, ein paar Tatsachen unter Beweis zu stellen
c (= *determining)* Ermittlung *f*; **~ of the truth** Wahrheitsfindung *f*
d (= *institution etc)* Institution *f*; (= *hospital, school etc)* Anstalt *f*, Institution *f*; **the school is a very modest ~** die Schule ist sehr bescheiden; **commercial ~** kommerzielles Unternehmen
e (= *household)* Haus *nt*, Haushalt *m*; **to keep up a large ~** ein großes Haus führen
f *(Mil, Naut etc: personnel)* Truppenstärke *f*; **war/peace ~** Kriegs-/Friedensstärke *f*
g **the Establishment** das Establishment; **~ person** (Erz)konservative(r) *mf*; **~ figure** Mitglied *nt or* Angehörige(r) *mf* des Establishments

estate [ɪ'steɪt] **N** **a** (= *land)* Gut *nt*; **country ~** Landgut *nt*; **family ~** Familienbesitz *m* **b** *(Jur: = possessions)* Besitz *m*, Besitztümer *pl*, Eigentum *nt*; *(of deceased)* Nachlass *m*, Erbmasse *f*; **to leave one's ~ to sb** jdm seinen ganzen Besitz vermachen *or* hinterlassen; **personal ~** persönliches Eigentum → **real ADJ c** **c** *(esp Brit: = housing estate)* Siedlung *f*; (= *trading estate)* Industriegelände *nt* **d** (= *order, rank)* Stand *m*; **the three ~s** die drei Stände; **person of high ~** *(old)* Standesperson *f (old)*; **the holy ~ of matrimony** *(Brit Rel)* der heilige Stand der Ehe **e** *(Brit)* = **estate car**

estate: **estate agent** **N** *(Brit)* Grundstücks- *or* Immobilienmakler(in) *m(f)*; **estate-bottled** **ADJ** *wine* vom Erzeuger abgefüllt; **"estate bottled"** Erzeugerabfüllung *f*; **estate car** **N** *(Brit)* Kombi(wagen) *m*; **estate duty** **N** Erbschaftssteuer *f*

esteem [ɪ'stiːm] **VT** **a** (= *consider)* ansehen, betrachten **b** (= *think highly of) person* hoch schätzen; *qualities* schätzen; **my ~ed colleague** *(form)* mein verehrter Herr Kollege *(form)*, meine verehrte Frau Kollegin *(form)* **N** Wertschätzung *f*; **to hold sb/sth in (high) ~** jdn/etw (hoch) schätzen, von jdm/etw eine hohe Meinung haben; **to be held in low/great ~** wenig/sehr geschätzt werden; **he went down in my ~** er ist in meiner Achtung gesunken

ester ['estə] **N** *(Chem)* Ester *m*

esthete *etc (esp US)* **N** = **aesthete** *etc*

Est(h)onia [e'stəʊnɪə] **N** Estland *nt*

Est(h)onian [e'stəʊnɪən] **ADJ** estnisch **N** **a** Este *m*, Estin *f* **b** *(Ling)* Estnisch *nt*

estimable ['estɪməbl] **ADJ** **a** (= *deserving respect)* schätzenswert **b** (= *that can be estimated)* (ab)schätzbar

estimate ['estɪmɪt] **N** **a** (= *approximate calculation)* Schätzung *f*; (= *valuation: by antique dealer etc)* Taxierung *f*; **what's your ~ of our chances of success?** wie schätzen Sie unsere Erfolgschancen ein?; **£100/it is just an ~** £ 100/das ist nur geschätzt; **at a rough ~** grob geschätzt, über den Daumen gepeilt *(inf)*; **at a conservative ~** vorsichtig geschätzt; **at the lowest ~** mindestens, wenigstens
b *(Comm, of cost)* (Kosten)voranschlag *m*; **to get an ~** einen (Kosten)voranschlag einholen
c **estimates** **PL** (= *government costs)* Haushalt *m*, Budget *nt* ['estɪmeɪt]
VT *cost, price* (ein)schätzen; *distance, speed* schätzen; **his wealth is ~d at ...** sein Vermögen wird auf ... geschätzt; **I ~ she must be 40** ich schätze sie auf 40, ich schätze, dass sie 40 ist; **~d time of arrival** voraussichtliche Ankunft; **~d time of departure** voraussichtliche Abfahrt; *(Aviat)* voraussichtlicher Abflug ['estɪmeɪt]
VI schätzen; **I'm just estimating** das schätze ich nur

estimation [ˌestɪ'meɪʃən] **N** **a** Einschätzung *f*; **in my ~** meiner Einschätzung nach **b** (= *esteem)* Achtung *f*; **to hold sb in high ~** jdn hoch achten, viel von jdm halten; **he went up/down in my ~** er ist in meiner Achtung gestiegen/gesunken

estimator ['estɪmeɪtə'] **N** *(Insur etc)* Schätzer(in) *m(f)*

estivate *etc (US)* **VB** = **aestivate** *etc*

Estonia *etc* = **Est(h)onia** *etc*

estoppel [ɪ'stɒpl] **N** *(Jur)* rechtshemmender Einwand

estragon ['estrəgɒn] **N** *(Bot)* Estragon *m*

estrange [ɪ'streɪndʒ] **VT** *person* entfremden *(from +dat)*; **to be/become ~d from sb/sth** sich jdm/etw entfremdet haben/entfremden; **they are ~d** *(married couple)* sie haben sich auseinandergelebt; **his ~d wife** seine von ihm getrennt lebende Frau

estrangement [ɪ'streɪndʒmənt] **N** Entfremdung *f (from* von)

estrogen ['iːstrəʊdʒən] **N** *(US)* = **oestrogen**

estuary ['estjʊərɪ] **N** Mündung *f*

estuary English **N** *(Brit) (von Jugendlichen) in Südengland gesprochene Variante des Cockney*

ET *(US) abbr of* **Eastern Time** Ostküstenzeit *f*

ETA *abbr of* **estimated time of arrival** voraussichtliche Ankunft

e-tail ['iːteɪl], **e-tailing** ['iːteɪlɪŋ] **N** E-Tailing *nt*, elektronischer Einzelhandel

et al [et'æl] **ADV** et al

etcetera [ɪt'setərə] **ADV** *(abbr* **etc**) und so weiter, et cetera

etch [etʃ] **VI** ätzen; *(in copper)* in Kupfer stechen; *(in other metals)* radieren **VT** ätzen; *(in copper)* in Kupfer stechen; *(in other metals)* radieren; **the windows were ~ed with the vehicle registration number** das Autokennzeichen war in die Scheiben eingeätzt; **the event was ~ed on her mind** das Ereignis hatte sich ihr ins Gedächtnis eingegraben

etching ['etʃɪŋ] **N** **a** (= *picture)* Ätzung *f*; *(in copper)* Kupferstich *m*; *(in other metals)* Radierung *f*; **come up and see my ~s** *(hum)* wollen Sie noch mit heraufkommen und sich *(dat)* meine Briefmarkensammlung ansehen? *(hum)*
b (= *process)* Ätzen *nt*; *(in copper)* Kupferstechen *nt*; *(in other metals)* Radieren *nt*

ETD *abbr of* **estimated time of departure** voraussichtliche Abfahrt; *(Aviat)* voraussichtlicher Abflug

eternal [ɪ'tɜːnl] **ADJ** **a** (= *everlasting, immutable)* ewig; **the Eternal City** die Ewige Stadt; **the ~ triangle** das Dreiecksverhältnis **b** (= *incessant)* endlos, ewig *(inf)*; **can't you stop this ~ quar-**

relling? könnt ihr nicht mit der ewigen Streiterei aufhören? *(inf)* N **the Eternal** *(Rel)* das Ewige; *(= God)* der Ewige

eternally [ɪˈtɜːnəlɪ] ADV ewig; *optimistic, cheerful* immer; **damned ~** auf ewig verdammt; **to be ~ grateful (to sb/for sth)** (jdm/für etw) ewig dankbar sein

eternity [ɪˈtɜːnɪtɪ] N *(lit, fig: inf)* Ewigkeit *f*; *(Rel: = the future life)* das ewige Leben; **from here to ~** bis in alle Ewigkeit; **for all ~** in alle Ewigkeit; **it seemed an ~** es kam mir wie eine Ewigkeit vor

eternity ring N Memoryring *m*

ethane [ˈiːθeɪn] N Äthan *nt*

ethanol [ˈeθənɒl] N Äthanol *nt*

ether [ˈiːθəˈ] N *(Chem, poet)* Äther *m*

ethereal [ɪˈθɪərɪəl] ADJ **a** *(= light, delicate, spiritual)* ätherisch **b** *(= of the upper air) regions* himmlisch

ethic [ˈeθɪk] N Ethik *f*, Ethos *nt*

ethical [ˈeθɪkəl] ADJ **a** *(= morally right)* ethisch *attr*; *(of ethics)* Moral-; **~ philosophy** Moralphilosophie *f*; **~ values** moralische Werte *pl*; **it is not ~ to ...** es ist unethisch *or* unmoralisch, zu ...; **~ behaviour** *(Brit) or* **behavior** *(US)* ethisch einwandfreies Verhalten **b** *(= available only on prescription) medicine etc* verschreibungspflichtig

ethically [ˈeθɪkəlɪ] ADV ethisch; *(= with correct ethics) act, behave etc* ethisch einwandfrei

ethics [ˈeθɪks] N **a** *sing (= study, system)* Ethik *f* **b** *pl (= morality)* Moral *f*; **the ~ of abortion** die moralischen *or* ethischen Aspekte *pl* der Abtreibung

Ethiopia [ˌiːθɪˈəʊpɪə] N Äthiopien *nt*

Ethiopian [ˌiːθɪˈəʊpɪən] ADJ äthiopisch N Äthiopier(in) *m(f)*

ethnic [ˈeθnɪk] ADJ **a** *(= racial)* ethnisch; **~ clashes** ethnische Konflikte *pl*; **~ violence** Rassenkrawalle *pl*; **~ Germans** Volksdeutsche *pl* **b** *(= traditional) atmosphere* urtümlich; *fabric, clothes* folkloristisch; **~ music** Folklore *f*; **in Zambia she bought several pairs of ~ earrings** in Sambia kaufte sie mehrere Paare der dort typischen Ohrringe; **books on ~ food** Bücher über das Essen in verschiedenen Kulturen N **ethnics** PL Mitglieder *pl* einer ethnischen Gruppe

ethnically [ˈeθnɪklɪ] ADV ethnisch

ethnic cleansing N *(euph)* ethnische Säuberung

ethnographer [eθˈnɒgrəfəˈ] N Völkerkundler(in) *m(f)*

ethnography [eθˈnɒgrəfɪ] N (beschreibende) Völkerkunde, Ethnografie *f*

ethnologist [eθˈnɒlədʒɪst] N Ethnologe *m*, Ethnologin *f*

ethnology [eθˈnɒlədʒɪ] N (vergleichende) Völkerkunde, Ethnologie *f*

ethologist [ɪˈθɒlədʒɪst] N Verhaltensforscher(in) *m(f)*

ethology [ɪˈθɒlədʒɪ] N Verhaltensforschung *f*, Ethologie *f*

ethos [ˈiːθɒs] N Gesinnung *f*, Ethos *nt*

ethyl [ˈiːθaɪl] N Äthyl *nt*

ethylene [ˈeθɪliːn] N Äthylen *nt*

e-ticket N E-Ticket *nt*, elektronische Eintritts-/Fahrkarte *etc*

etiolate [ˈiːtɪəʊleɪt] VT *(Bot)* etiolieren *(spec)*; *(= enfeeble)* auszehren

etiology *etc (esp US)* N = **aetiology** *etc*

etiquette [ˈetɪket] N Etikette *f*; **rules of ~** Verhaltensregeln *pl*; **a breach of ~** ein Verstoß *m* gegen die Etikette; **court ~** Hofetikette *f*; **that's not in accordance with medical ~** das entspricht nicht dem Berufsethos eines Arztes

Eton [ˈiːtən]: **Eton collar** N *breiter, steifer, weißer Umlegekragen*; **Eton crop** N Bubikopf *m*, Herrenschnitt *m*

Etonian [iːˈtəʊnɪən] *(Brit)* N Schüler *m* am Eton College ADJ des Eton College

Etruscan [ɪˈtrʌskən] ADJ etruskisch N **a** Etrusker(in) *m(f)* **b** *(Ling)* Etruskisch *nt*

et seq. *abbr of* **et sequentia** f., und folgende

ETV *(US) abbr of* **Educational Television** ≈ Schulfernsehen *nt*

etymological ADJ, **etymologically** ADV [ˌetɪməˈlɒdʒɪkəl, -ɪ] etymologisch

etymology [ˌetɪˈmɒlədʒɪ] N Etymologie *f*

EU *abbr of* **European Union** EU *f*

eucalyptus [ˌjuːkəˈlɪptəs] N Eukalyptus *m*; **~ (oil)** Eukalyptusöl *nt*

Eucharist [ˈjuːkərɪst] N *(Eccl: = service)* Abendmahlsgottesdienst *m*; **the ~** das (heilige) Abendmahl, die Eucharistie

Eucharistic [ˌjuːkəˈrɪstɪk] ADJ eucharistisch; **the ~ liturgy** die Abendmahlsliturgie; **the ~ sacrament** das Sakrament des heiligen Abendmahls

Euclid [ˈjuːklɪd] N Euklid *m*

Euclidean [juːˈklɪdɪən] ADJ euklidisch

EU country N EU-Land *nt*, EU-Staat *m*

eugenics [juːˈdʒenɪks] N *sing* Eugenik *f*

EU law N EU-Gesetz *nt*; *(= system)* EU-Recht *nt*

eulogistic [ˌjuːləˈdʒɪstɪk] ADJ *(form)* lobrednerisch

eulogize [ˈjuːlədʒaɪz] VT eine Lobesrede halten auf *(+acc)*

eulogy [ˈjuːlədʒɪ] N Lobesrede *f*, Eloge *f (liter)*

eunuch [ˈjuːnək] N Eunuch *m*

euphemism [ˈjuːfəmɪzəm] N Euphemismus *m*, Hüllwort *nt*; **a ~ for sth** ein Euphemismus *m* *or* verhüllender Ausdruck für etw

euphemistic [ˌjuːfəˈmɪstɪk] ADJ euphemistisch, verhüllend

euphemistically [ˌjuːfəˈmɪstɪkəlɪ] ADV euphemistisch, verhüllend; **to be ~ described/known as ...** beschönigend als ... bezeichnet werden/bekannt sein

euphonic [juːˈfɒnɪk], **euphonious** [juːˈfəʊnɪəs] ADJ euphonisch, wohlklingend

euphonium [juːˈfəʊnɪəm] N Euphonium *nt*

euphony [ˈjuːfənɪ] N *(Mus, Ling)* Euphonie *f*, Wohlklang *m*

euphoria [juːˈfɔːrɪə] N Euphorie *f*

euphoric [juːˈfɒrɪk] ADJ euphorisch

Euphrates [juːˈfreɪtiːz] N Euphrat *m*

Eurailpass [ˈjʊəreɪlpɑːs] N *Dauerfahrkarte, die Nicht-Europäer zur Benutzung aller (west)-euopäischen Eisenbahnen berechtigt*

Eurasia [jʊəˈreɪʃə] N Eurasien *nt*

Eurasian [jʊəˈreɪʃn] ADJ eurasisch N Eurasier(in) *m(f)*

Euratom [jʊəˈrætəm] *abbr of* **European Atomic Energy Community** Euratom *f*

EU regulation N EU-Bestimmung *f*

eureka [jʊəˈriːkə] INTERJ heureka

eurhythmics [juːˈrɪðmɪks] N *sing* Eurhythmie *f*

euro [ˈjʊərəʊ] N *(= currency)* Euro *m*

Euro-, **euro-** [ˈjʊərəʊ] PREF Euro-, euro-; **Eurocentric** eurozentrisch

Eurobond [ˈjʊərəʊbɒnd] N Eurobond *m*

eurocent [ˈjʊərəʊsent] N Eurocent *m*

Eurocheque, *(US)* **Eurocheck** [ˈjʊərəʊtʃek] N Euroscheck *m*

Eurocorps [jʊərəʊkɔːˈ] N *(Mil)* Eurokorps *nt*

Eurocrat [ˈjʊərəʊkræt] N Eurokrat(in) *m(f)*

eurocurrency [ˈjʊərəʊˌkʌrənsɪ] N Euro-Währung *f*

Eurodollar [ˈjʊərəʊdɒləˈ] N Eurodollar *m*

Euroland [ˈjʊərəʊlænd] N *(inf)* Eurozone *f*, Euroland *nt (inf)*

Euro MP N *(inf)* Europaabgeordnete(r) *mf*

Europe [ˈjʊərəp] N Europa *nt*

European [ˌjʊərəˈpiːən] ADJ europäisch; **~ standard** *(Ind)* europäische Norm N Europäer(in) *m(f)*

European: **European Central Bank** N Europäische Zentralbank; **European Commission** N Europäische Kommission; **European Community** N Europäische Gemeinschaft; **European Court of Justice** N Europäischer Gerichtshof; **European Cup** N *(Sport)* Europacup *m*; **European Currency Unit** N Europäische Währungseinheit; **European Economic Community** N Europäische Wirtschaftsgemeinschaft; **European elections** PL Europawahlen *pl*; **European Free Trade Area**, **European Free Trade Association** N Europäische Freihandelszone; **European Investment Bank** N Europäische Investitionsbank; **European Monetary Union** N Europäische Währungsunion; **European Parliament** N Europäisches Parlament, Europaparlament *nt*; **European Union** N Europäische Union

Euro-sceptic [ˈjʊərəʊˌskeptɪk] N Euroskeptiker(in) *m(f)*

euro sign, **euro symbol** N Eurozeichen *nt or* -symbol *nt*

Eurotunnel [ˈjʊərəʊˌtʌnl] N Eurotunnel *m*, Kanaltunnel *m*

Eurovision [ˈjʊərəʊvɪʒn] N Eurovision *f*; **~ Song Contest** Eurovisions-Schlagerwettbewerb *m*

Eustachian tube [juːˈsteɪʃənˈtjuːb] N eustachische Röhre

EU standard [ˌiːjuːˈstændəd] N EU-Norm *f*

euthanasia [ˌjuːθəˈneɪzɪə] N Euthanasie *f*

EU-wide ADJ EU-weit

evacuate [ɪˈvækjʊeɪt] VT **a** *(= leave) fort, house* räumen **b** *(= clear) danger area* räumen; *civilians, women, children* evakuieren *(from* aus, *to* nach) **c** *bowels* entleeren VI **all the villagers had to ~** alle Bewohner mussten das Dorf räumen

evacuation [ɪˌvækjʊˈeɪʃən] N *(of fort, house, danger area)* Räumung *f*; *(of civilians, women, children)* Evakuierung *f*

evacuee [ɪˌvækjʊˈiː] N Evakuierte(r) *mf*

evade [ɪˈveɪd] VT **a** *blow* ausweichen *(+dat)*; *pursuit, pursuers* sich entziehen *(+dat)*, entkommen *(+dat)* **b** *obligation, justice, capture* sich entziehen *(+dat)*; *military service* umgehen, sich entziehen *(+dat)*; *question, issue* ausweichen *(+dat)*; *difficulty, person, sb's glance* ausweichen *(+dat)*, (ver)meiden; *sb's vigilance* entgehen *(+dat)*; **to ~ taxes** Steuern hinterziehen; **he successfully ~d the authorities for several years** mehrere Jahre kamen die Behörden ihm nicht auf die Spur; **if you try to ~ paying import duty** wenn Sie versuchen, den Einfuhrzoll zu umgehen; **a concept which somehow ~s precise definition** ein Begriff, der sich einer genauen Definition entzieht

evaluate [ɪˈvæljʊeɪt] VT *house, painting, worth etc* schätzen *(at* auf *+acc)*; *damages* festsetzen *(at* auf *+acc)*; *chances, situation, effectiveness, usefulness* einschätzen, beurteilen; *evidence, results* auswerten; *pros and cons* (gegeneinander) abwägen; *contribution, achievement, work, performance* beurteilen; *(Med) patient* untersuchen (und die Diagnose stellen)

evaluation [ɪˌvæljʊˈeɪʃən] N *(of house, painting, worth etc)* Schätzung *f*; *(of damages)* Festsetzung *f*; *(of situation, chances, effectiveness, usefulness)* Einschätzung *f*, Beurteilung *f*; *(of evidence, results)* Auswertung *f*; *(of pros and cons)* Abwägung *f*; *(of contribution, achievement, work, performance)* Beurteilung *f*; *(Med: of patient)* Untersuchung (und Diagnosestellung) *f*; **in my ~** nach meiner Schätzung; **on ~ of the evidence it became clear that ...** die Auswertung *or* Sichtung des Beweismaterials machte klar, dass ...

evaluative [ɪˌvæljʊətɪv] ADJ *(form)* wertend

evanescence [ˌiːvəˈnesəns] N *(Liter)* Vergänglichkeit *f*

evanescent [ˌiːvəˈnesənt] ADJ *(Liter)* vergänglich

evangelic(al) [ˌiːvænˈdʒelɪk(əl)] ADJ evangelikal

evangelist [ɪˈvændʒəlɪst] N *(Bibl)* Evangelist(in) *m(f)*; *(= preacher)* Prediger(in) *m(f)*; *(= itinerant)* Wanderprediger(in) *m(f)*

evangelize [ɪ'vændʒəlaɪz] VT evangelisieren, bekehren VI das Evangelium predigen

evaporate [ɪ'væpəreɪt] VI a *(liquid)* verdampfen, verdunsten b *(fig: = disappear)* sich in nichts *or* in Luft auflösen; *(hopes)* sich zerschlagen, schwinden VT *liquid* verdampfen *or* verdunsten (lassen); **evaporating dish** Abdampfschale *f*

evaporated milk [ɪ'væpəreɪtɪd'mɪlk] N Kondens- *or* Büchsenmilch *f*

evaporation [ɪˌvæpə'reɪʃən] N Verdampfung *f*, Verdampfen *nt*; *(fig)* Schwinden *nt*

evasion [ɪ'veɪʒən] N a *(of question etc)* Ausweichen *nt* (of vor *+dat*) b *(= evasive answer etc)* Ausflucht *f*

evasive [ɪ'veɪsɪv] ADJ ausweichend; **he was (very) ~** er wich (dauernd) aus; **they were ~ about it** sie redeten drum herum; **she was ~ about her intentions** sie war ausweichend, was ihre Absichten betraf; **to take ~ action** ein Ausweichmanöver machen

evasively [ɪ'veɪsɪvlɪ] ADV ausweichend

evasiveness [ɪ'veɪsɪvnɪs] N ausweichendes Verhalten; *(of answers)* ausweichende Antworten *pl*, Herumgerede *nt (pej)*

Eve [iːv] N Eva *f*

eve[1] [iːv] N Vorabend *m*; **on the ~ of** am Tage vor *(+dat)*, am Vorabend von *or +gen*

eve[2] N *(obs, poet)* Abend *m*

even[1] ['iːvən] ✪ 26.1, 26.3 ADJ a *surface, ground* eben; **to make sth ~** *(ground, earth)* etw ebnen; **the concrete has to be ~ with the ground** der Beton muss eben mit dem Boden abschließen

b *(= regular) layer etc, voice* gleichmäßig; *progress* stetig; *breathing, pulse* regelmäßig, gleichmäßig; *temper* ausgeglichen

c *quantities, distances, values* gleich; **they are an ~ match** sie sind einander ebenbürtig; **I will get ~ with you for that** das werde ich dir heimzahlen; **that makes us ~** *(in game)* damit steht es unentschieden; *(fig)* damit sind wir quitt; **the odds** *or* **chances are about ~** die Chancen stehen etwa fifty-fifty *(inf)*; **he has an ~ chance of winning** seine Gewinnchancen stehen fifty--fifty *(inf)*; **to break ~** die Kosten decken; **to give sb an ~ break** *(esp US)* jdm eine Chance geben; **never give a sucker an ~ break** *(dated US inf)* gib einem Trottel keine Chance *(inf)*

d *number* gerade; **~ money** *Wette, bei der die doppelte Einsatzsumme als Gewinn ausgezahlt wird*; **I'll give you ~ money he's late** *(inf)* ich gehe jede Wette mit dir ein, dass er zu spät kommt

e *(= exact)* genau; **let's make it an ~ hundred** nehmen wir eine runde Zahl und sagen 100

ADV a sogar, selbst; **that's good going, ~ for you** sogar *or* selbst für dich ist das allerhand; **they ~ denied its existence** sie leugneten sogar seine Existenz; **it'll be difficult, impossible ~** das wird schwierig sein, wenn nicht (so)gar unmöglich

b *(with comp adj)* sogar noch; **that's ~ better/more beautiful** das ist sogar (noch) besser/schöner

c *(with neg)* **not ~** nicht einmal; **without ~ a smile** ohne auch nur zu lächeln; **he didn't ~ answer the letter** er hat den Brief (noch) nicht einmal beantwortet

d **~ if** sogar *or* selbst wenn; **~ though** obwohl; **~ if you were a millionaire** sogar *or* selbst wenn du ein Millionär wärst; **~ though I live alone I'm not lonely** obwohl ich allein lebe, bin ich nicht einsam; **but ~ then** aber sogar *or* selbst dann; **~ as I spoke someone knocked at the door** noch während ich redete, klopfte es an der Tür; **~ as ... so** *(old)* genau wie ... so; **~ so** (aber) trotzdem

VT *surface* glatt *or* eben machen, glätten

▶ **even out** VI a *(prices)* sich einpendeln b *(ground)* eben werden, sich ebnen VT *sep* a *prices* ausgleichen b *ground, cement* ebnen, glätten c *tax burden, wealth* gleichmäßig verteilen; **that should even things out a bit** dadurch müsste ein gewisser Ausgleich erzielt werden; **that will even things out between us** damit sind wir wohl wieder quitt

▶ **even up** VT *sep sum* aufrunden *(to* auf *+acc)*; **that will even things up** das wird die Sache etwas ausgleichen VI *(= pay off debt)* Schulden begleichen *(with* bei*)*; **can we even up later?** können wir später abrechnen?

even[2] N *(obs, poet)* Abend *m*

even-handed ADJ, **even-handedly** ADV [ˌiːvn'hændɪd, -lɪ] gerecht, fair

evening ['iːvnɪŋ] N Abend *m*; **in the ~** abends, am Abend; **this/ tomorrow/yesterday ~** heute/morgen/gestern Abend; **that ~** an jenem Abend; **that ~ was ...** jener Abend war ...; **on the ~ of the twenty-ninth** am Abend des 29., am 29. abends; **one ~ as I ...** eines Abends, als ich ...; **every Monday ~** jeden Montagabend; **all ~** den ganzen Abend (lang *or* über); **the ~ of his life** *(liter)* sein Lebensabend

evening: **evening class** N Abendkurs *m*; **to go to** *or* **take ~es** *or* **an ~ in French** einen Abendkurs in Französisch besuchen; **evening dress** N *(men's)* Abendanzug *m*, Gesellschaftsanzug *m*; *(women's)* Abendkleid *nt*; **evening gown** N Abendkleid *nt*; **evening meal** N *(Brit)* Abendessen *nt*; **evening paper** N Abendzeitung *f*; **evening star** N Abendstern *m*

evenly ['iːvənlɪ] ADV a *(= unvaryingly, equally)* gleichmäßig; *divide* in gleiche Teile; **the contestants were ~ matched** die Gegner waren einander ebenbürtig; **your weight should be ~ balanced (between your two feet)** Sie sollten Ihr Gewicht gleichmäßig (auf beide Füße) verteilen; **to be ~ divided between A and B** *(property)* zu gleichen Teilen zwischen A und B aufgeteilt sein; **my time is ~ divided between work and leisure activities** meine Zeit ist zu gleichen Teilen in Arbeit und Freizeit aufgeteilt; **public opinion seems to be ~ divided** die öffentliche Meinung scheint in zwei gleich große Lager gespalten zu sein

b *(= calmly) say, look at* gelassen

evenness ['iːvənnɪs] N a *(of ground)* Ebenheit *f* b *(= regularity)* Gleichmäßigkeit *f*; *(of progress)* Stetigkeit *f*; *(of breathing, pulse)* Regelmäßigkeit *f*, Gleichmäßigkeit *f*; *(of temper)* Ausgeglichenheit *f*

evens ['iːvənz] ADJ **it's ~ that ...** *(inf)* die Chancen stehen fifty-fifty, dass ... *(inf)*

evensong ['iːvənsɒŋ] N Abendgottesdienst *m*

event [ɪ'vent] N a *(= happening)* Ereignis *nt*; **~s are taking place in Belfast which ...** in Belfast geschehen *or* ereignen sich Dinge, die ...; **in the normal course of ~s** normalerweise; **~s have proved us right** die Ereignisse haben uns recht gegeben; **it's quite an ~** das ist wirklich ein Ereignis; **it's easy to be wise after the ~** hinterher ist man immer klüger → **happy event**

b *(= organized function)* Veranstaltung *f*; *(Sport)* Wettkampf *m*; **what is your best ~?** in welcher Disziplin sind Sie am besten?

c *(= case)* Fall *m*; **in the ~ of her death** im Falle ihres Todes; **in the ~ of war/fire** im Falle eines Krieges/Brandes, im Kriegs-/Brandfall; **in the ~ of my not returning, ...** sollte ich nicht wiederkommen, ...; **in the unlikely ~ that ...** falls, was sehr unwahrscheinlich ist, ...; **he said he wouldn't come, but in the ~ he did** er sagte, er würde nicht kommen, aber er kam dann schließlich doch; **but in any ~ I can't give you my permission** aber ich kann dir jedenfalls nicht meine Erlaubnis geben; **but in any ~ you have my permission** aber Sie haben auf alle Fälle meine Erlaubnis; **in either ~** in jedem Fall; **at all ~s** auf jeden Fall

even-tempered ['iːvən'tempəd] ADJ ausgeglichen

eventer [ɪ'ventə'] N *(Sport)* Militaryreiter(in) *m(f)*

eventful [ɪ'ventfʊl] ADJ ereignisreich; *life, period also* bewegt

eventide ['iːvəntaɪd] N *(obs, poet)* Abendzeit *f*

eventide home N Altenheim *nt*

eventing [ɪ'ventɪŋ] N *(Sport)* Military *f*

eventual [ɪ'ventʃʊəl] ADJ **the decline and ~ collapse of the Roman Empire** der Niedergang und schließlich vollkommene Zerfall des Römischen Reiches; **he predicted the ~ fall of the government** er hat vorausgesagt, dass die Regierung am Ende *or* schließlich zu Fall kommen würde; **the ~ success of the project is not in doubt** es besteht kein Zweifel, dass das Vorhaben letzten Endes Erfolg haben wird; **he lost to the ~ winner** er verlor gegen den späteren Gewinner

eventuality [ɪˌventʃʊ'ælɪtɪ] N (möglicher) Fall, Eventualität *f*; **in the ~ of fire** im Brandfall; **be ready for any ~** sei auf alle Eventualitäten gefasst

eventually [ɪ'ventʃʊəlɪ] ADV schließlich; *(= one day)* eines Tages; *(= in the long term)* auf lange Sicht; **they will take decisions on savings and ~ on redundancies** sie werden Entscheidungen über Einsparungen und schließlich auch Entlassungen treffen; **~ your child will leave home** eines Tages wird Ihr Kind von zu Hause weggehen; **this will ~ cause problems** das bringt auf lange Sicht Probleme

ever ['evə'] ADV a je(mals); **not ~** nie; **nothing ~ happens** es passiert nie etwas; **it hardly ~ snows here** hier schneit es kaum (jemals); **if I ~ catch you doing that again** wenn ich dich noch einmal dabei erwische; **if you ~ see her** wenn Sie sie je sehen sollten; **seldom, if ~** selten, wenn überhaupt; **he's a rascal if ~ there was one** er ist ein richtiggehender kleiner Halunke; **as if I ~ would** als ob ich das jemals täte; **don't you ~ say that again!** sag das ja nie mehr!; **neither of us had ~ ridden a horse** keiner von uns war schon jemals geritten; **have you ~ been to Glasgow?** bist du schon einmal in Glasgow gewesen?; **have you ~ known him tell a lie?** haben Sie ihn (schon) jemals lügen hören?; **did you ~ see** *or* **have you ~ seen anything so strange?** hast du schon jemals so etwas Merkwürdiges gesehen?; **more beautiful than ~ (before)** schöner denn je (zuvor); **the best soup I have ~ tasted** die beste Suppe, die ich je(mals) gekostet habe; **the first ... ~** der *etc* allererste ...; **the first man ~ to walk on the moon** der erste Mensch, der je(mals) den Mond betrat; **I'll never, ~ forgive myself** das werde ich mir nie im Leben verzeihen

b *(= at all times)* **~ since I was a boy** seit ich ein Junge war; **~ since I have lived here ...** seitdem ich hier lebe ...; **~ since (then)** seit der Zeit, seitdem; **for ~** für immer, für alle Zeit(en); **it seemed to go on for ~ (and ~)** es schien ewig zu dauern; **for ~ and a day** für alle Zeiten, ewig und drei Tage *(inf)*; **~ increasing power** ständig wachsende Macht; **an ~ present feeling** ein ständiges Gefühl; **he was ~ the troublemaker** er war ein ewiger Unruhestifter; **all she ~ does is complain** sie tut nichts anderes als sich ständig zu beschweren

c *(intensive)* **be he ~ so charming** wenn er auch noch so liebenswürdig ist, sei er auch noch so liebenswürdig; **come as quickly as ~ you can** komm so schnell du nur kannst; **she's the best grandmother ~** sie ist die beste Großmutter, die es gibt; **did you ~!** *(inf)* also so was!

d **what ~ shall we do?** was sollen wir bloß machen?; **when ~ will they come?** wann kommen sie denn bloß *or* endlich?; **why ~ not?** warum denn bloß nicht? → **whatever, wherever** *etc*

e *(inf)* **~ so/such** unheimlich; **~ so slightly drunk** ein ganz klein wenig betrunken; **he's ~ such a nice man** er ist ein ungemein netter Mensch; **I am ~ so sorry** es tut mir schrecklich leid; **thank you ~ so much** ganz herzlichen Dank

f *(old, = always)* allzeit *(old, liter)*

g *(in letters)* **yours ~** *or* **~ yours, Wendy** viele Grüße, Ihre Wendy

Everest ['evərest] N **(Mount) ~** der (Mount) Everest

Everglades ['evəgleɪdz] N **the ~** die Everglades

evergreen ['evəgri:n] ADJ *trees, shrubs, leaves* immergrün; *(fig) topic* immer aktuell N Nadelbaum *m*, immergrüner Busch

evergreen facility N *(Fin)* Revolvingkredit *m*

everlasting [,evə'lɑ:stɪŋ] ADJ a *God, life, torment* ewig; *gratitude* immerwährend; *glory* unvergänglich; **to his ~ shame** zu seiner ewigen Schande b *(inf: = constant)* ewig *(inf)* N **from ~ to ~ thou art God** Du bist Gott von Ewigkeit zu Ewigkeit

everlasting flower N Strohblume *f*, Immortelle *f*

everlastingly [,evə'lɑ:stɪŋlɪ] ADV *(liter)* ewig

evermore [,evə'mɔ:'] ADV a *(liter: = always)* auf immer und ewig; **for ~** in alle Ewigkeit b *(= increasingly)* zunehmend; *rise, fall* immer mehr; **it becomes ~ the responsibility of the individual** dafür wird der Einzelne zunehmend selbst verantwortlich

every ['evrɪ] ADJ a jede(r, s); **you must examine ~ one** Sie müssen jeden (Einzelnen) untersuchen; **~ man for himself** jeder für sich; **in ~ way** *(= in all respects)* in jeder Hinsicht; *(= by every means)* mit allen Mitteln; **he is ~ bit as clever as his brother** er ist ganz genauso schlau wie sein Bruder; **~ bit as much** ganz genauso viel; **~ single time** jedes einzelne Mal; **~ single time I ...** immer wenn ich ...
b *(= all possible)* **I have ~ confidence in him** ich habe unbedingtes *or* uneingeschränktes Vertrauen zu ihm; **I have/there is ~ hope that ...** ich habe allen Grund/es besteht aller Grund zu der Hoffnung, dass ...; **we wish you ~ success/happiness** wir wünschen Ihnen alles (nur erdenklich) Gute/viel Glück und Zufriedenheit; **there was ~ prospect of success** es bestand alle Aussicht auf Erfolg; **to make ~ effort to do sth** sich alle Mühe geben *or* sich sehr bemühen, etw zu tun
c *(indicating recurrence)* **~ fifth day, ~ five days** jeden fünften Tag, alle fünf Tage; **~ other day** jeden zweiten Tag, alle zwei Tage; **write on ~ other line** bitte eine Zeile Zwischenraum lassen; **write on ~ other page** bitte jede zweite Seite beschreiben; **once ~ week** einmal jede *or* pro Woche; **one in ~ twenty people** jeder zwanzigste Mensch; **~ so often, ~ once in a while, ~ now and then** *or* **again** hin und wieder, ab und zu, gelegentlich
d *(after poss adj)* **they catered to his ~ whim** sie erfüllten ihm jeden Wunsch; **his ~ word** jedes seiner Worte, jedes Wort, das er sagte

everybody ['evrɪbɒdɪ] PRON jeder(mann), alle *pl*; **~ has finished** alle sind fertig; **it's not ~ who can afford a video recorder** nicht jeder kann sich *(dat)* einen Videorekorder leisten; **~ knows ~ else here** hier kennt jeder jeden; **~ knows that** das weiß (doch) jeder

everyday ['evrɪdeɪ] ADJ alltäglich; *reality* täglich; **~ clothes** Alltagskleidung *f*; **to be an ~ occurrence** (all)täglich vorkommen; **for ~ use** für den täglichen Gebrauch; **words in ~ use** Wörter *pl* der Alltagssprache; **~ language** Alltagssprache *f*; **~ people** ganz normale Menschen; **~ life** *or* **living** der Alltag; **~ world** Alltagswelt *f*

everyman ['evrɪmæn] N Durchschnittsmensch *m*; **language that ~ and everywoman can understand** eine Sprache, die der Durchschnittsmensch verstehen kann

everyone ['evrɪwʌn] ✪ 26.2 PRON = **everybody**

everything ['evrɪθɪŋ] N alles; **~ possible/old** alles Mögliche/Alte; **~ you have** alles, was du hast; **is ~ all right?** ist alles in Ordnung?; **time is ~** Zeit ist kostbar; **money isn't ~** Geld ist nicht alles; **money is ~ to him** Geld bedeutet ihm alles → **mean**³ **a**

everywhere ['evrɪweə'] ADV überall; *(with direction)* überallhin; **from ~** überallher, von überall; **~ you look there's a mistake** wo man auch hinsieht, findet man Fehler

evict [ɪ'vɪkt] VT *tenants, squatters* zur Räumung zwingen *(from +gen)*; **they were ~ed** sie wurden zum Verlassen ihrer Wohnung gezwungen

eviction [ɪ'vɪkʃən] N Ausweisung *f*

eviction order N Räumungsbefehl *m*

evidence ['evɪdəns] N a Beweis *m*, Beweise *pl*; **show me your ~** welche Beweise haben Sie?; **what ~ is there to support this theory?** welche Anhaltspunkte gibt es, die diese Theorie untermauern?; **according to the ~ of our senses** nach dem, was wir mit unseren Sinnen erkennen können; **there is no ~ of ...** es deutet nichts auf ... hin; **there is no ~ that ...** es deutet nichts darauf hin, dass ...; **these marks are ~ of life on Mars** diese Spuren sind Beweis *or* ein Zeichen *nt* dafür, dass es auf dem Mars Leben gibt; **a scratch was the only ~ of the fight** ein Kratzer war der einzige Beweis für den Kampf; **the car bore ~ of having been in an accident** das Auto trug deutliche Spuren eines Unfalls
b *(Jur)* Beweismaterial *nt*; *(object, dagger etc)* Beweisstück *nt*; *(= testimony)* Aussage *f*; **the lawyers are still collecting ~** die Anwälte holen immer noch Beweise ein; **we haven't got any ~** wir haben keinerlei Beweise; **there wasn't enough ~** die Beweise *or* Indizien reichten nicht aus; **for lack of ~** aus Mangel an Beweisen, mangels Beweisen *(form)*; **on the ~ available ...** aufgrund *or* auf Grund des vorhandenen Beweismaterials ...; **not admissible as ~** als Beweismittel nicht zulässig; **all the ~ was against him** alles sprach *or* die Tatsachen sprachen gegen ihn; **to give ~ (for/against sb)** (für/gegen jdn) aussagen; **to give ~ for the defence** *(Brit) or* **defense** *(US)***/prosecution** für die Verteidigung/die Anklage aussagen; **piece of ~** *(= statement)* Zeugenaussage *f*; *(= object)* Beweisstück *or* -mittel *nt* → **queen's evidence, state's evidence**
c **to be in ~** sichtbar sein; **poverty was still (very) much in ~** es gab immer noch sichtlich viel Armut; **his father was nowhere in ~** sein Vater war nirgends zu sehen; **she likes to be very much in ~** sie hat es gern, gesehen und beachtet zu werden; **a statesman very much in ~ at the moment** ein Staatsmann, der zur Zeit stark beachtet wird
VT zeugen von

evident ADJ, **evidently** ADV ['evɪdənt, -lɪ] offensichtlich

evil ['i:vl] N a Böse(s) *nt*; **good and ~ in Victorian England** das Gute und das Böse im viktorianischen England; **the conflict between good and ~** der Kampf zwischen Gut und Böse; **there was never any trace of ~ in her** an ihr war nie etwas Böses; **the ~ in the universe** das Übel in der Welt; **to wish sb no ~** jdm nichts Böses wünschen; **to speak ~ of sb** schlecht von jdm reden
b *(= bad thing or activity)* Übel *nt*; **a necessary ~** ein notwendiges Übel; **the lesser/greater of two ~s** das kleinere/größere Übel; **social ~s** soziale Missstände *pl*; **a sermon on the ~s of drink** eine Predigt über das Laster des Trinkens
ADJ a *(= bad, wicked) person, tongue* böse; *example, influence, reputation* schlecht; **~ deed** Übeltat *f*; **the country's most ~ terrorists** die schlimmsten Terroristen des Landes; **with ~ intent** mit *or* aus böser Absicht; **the ~ weed** *(hum: = tobacco)* das Kraut *(inf)*; *(= smoking)* das Rauchen; **to put off the ~ day/moment** den schrecklichen Tag/Augenblick hinauszögern
b *(= devilish) spirit, spell, power* böse; *place* verhext
c *(= unpleasant) smell, taste* übel

evil: evildoer N Übeltäter(in) *m(f)*, Bösewicht *m (dated)*; **evil eye** N **the ~** der böse Blick; **to give sb the ~** jdn mit dem bösen Blick ansehen

evilly ['i:vɪlɪ] ADV bösartig; **~ motivated** durch das Böse motiviert

evil: evil-minded [,i:vl'maɪndɪd] ADJ bösartig; **evil-smelling** ADJ übel riechend

evince [ɪ'vɪns] VT an den Tag legen; *surprise, desire also* bekunden

eviscerate [ɪ'vɪsəreɪt] VT ausnehmen; *person* entleiben

evocation [,evə'keɪʃən] N Heraufbeschwören *nt*, Wachrufen *nt*

evocative [ɪ'vɒkətɪv] ADJ atmosphärisch; *name* wohlklingend; **scent can be very ~** ein Duft kann viele Erinnerungen heraufbeschwören; **to be ~ of sth** etw heraufbeschwören

evocatively [ɪ'vɒkətɪvlɪ] ADV atmosphärisch; **the islands ~ known as the South Seas** die Inseln, die unter dem atmosphärischen Namen Südsee bekannt sind

evoke [ɪ'vəʊk] VT heraufbeschwören; *memory also* wachrufen; *admiration, response* hervorrufen

evolution [,i:və'lu:ʃən] N a *(= development, Biol)* Evolution *f*, Entwicklung *f*; **the ~ of events in Vietnam** die Entwicklung in Vietnam; **theory of ~** Evolutionstheorie *f* b *often pl (of troops)* Bewegung *f*; *(of dancers, skaters)* Figur *f*, Bewegung *f*

evolutionary [,i:və'lu:ʃnərɪ] ADJ evolutionär; **~ theory** Evolutionstheorie *f*

evolutionism [,i:və'lu:ʃənɪzəm] N Evolutionismus *m*

evolutionist [,i:və'lu:ʃənɪst] N Evolutionist(in) *m(f)* ADJ evolutionistisch

evolve [ɪ'vɒlv] VT *system, theory, plan* entwickeln VI sich entwickeln, sich herausbilden

ewe [ju:] N Mutterschaf *nt*

ewer ['ju:ə'] N Wasserkrug *m*

ex[1] [eks] N *(inf)* Verflossene(r) *mf (inf)*

ex[2] *abbr of* **example** Bsp., Beispiel *nt*

ex- [eks-] PREF a ehemalig, Ex-; **~president** früherer Präsident, frühere Präsidentin, Expräsident(in) *m(f)*; **~wife** frühere Frau, Exfrau *f*; **~Yugoslavia** das frühere Jugoslawien b **~factory** ab Werk → **ex officio, ex works**

exacerbate [ek'sæsəbeɪt] VT *person* verärgern; *pain, disease, problem* verschlimmern; *hate* vergrößern; *resentment, discontent* vertiefen; *situation, crisis, tensions* verschärfen

exacerbation [ek,sæsə'beɪʃən] N *(of pain, disease, problem)* Verschlimmerung *f*; *(of situation, crisis, tensions)* Verschärfung *f*

exact [ɪg'zækt] ADJ a *(= precise)* genau; *translation* wörtlich; **to be ~ about sth** etw genau darlegen; **do you have the ~ amount?** haben Sie es passend?; **please have the ~ fare ready** bitte Fahrgeld abgezählt bereithalten; **they won't know the ~ nature of the problem until tomorrow** sie werden erst morgen erfahren, worum es sich bei dem Problem genau handelt; **until this ~ moment** bis genau zu diesem Augenblick; **the ~ thing I want** genau das, was ich will; **the ~ same thing** genau das gleiche; **the ~ opposite** das genaue Gegenteil; **he's 47 to be ~** er ist 47, um genau zu sein; **they evolved from reptiles, dinosaurs to be ~** sie stammen von Reptilien ab, genau(er) gesagt, von Dinosauriern; **or to be more ~** oder, genauer gesagt
b *(= meticulous) person* genau, exakt; **to be very ~ in one's work** peinlich genau arbeiten; **~ science** *(lit, fig)* exakte Wissenschaft
VT *(form) money, obedience, revenge* fordern; *payment* eintreiben; *promise* abverlangen *(from sb* jdm); *guarantee, assurance* verlangen *(from* von); **to ~ a high price** *(fig)* einen hohen Preis fordern

exacting [ɪg'zæktɪŋ] ADJ *person, work, task* anspruchsvoll; *standards, demands* hoch; *detail* peinlich genau; **to be very ~** sehr viel verlangen; **he's very ~ about cleanliness** er ist peinlich genau, was Sauberkeit angeht, er nimmt es mit der Sauberkeit sehr genau

exactingness [ɪg'zæktɪŋnɪs] N **because of his ~ as a teacher** da er ein so anspruchsvoller Lehrer ist

exaction [ɪg'zækʃən] N a *(= act, of money)* Eintreiben *nt*; *(of promises)* Abverlangen *nt*; *(of obedience)* Fordern *nt* b *(= money exacted)* Forderung *f*; *(= excessive demand)* überzogene Forderung

exactitude [ɪg'zæktɪtju:d] N Genauigkeit *f*, Exaktheit *f*

exactly [ɪg'zæktlɪ] ✪ 17.2 ADV genau; **I wanted to know ~ where my mother was buried** ich wollte genau wissen, wo meine Mutter begraben war; **that's ~ what I was thinking** genau das habe ich auch gedacht; **at ~ five o'clock** um Punkt fünf Uhr; **at ~ 9.43 a.m./the right time** genau um 9.43 Uhr/zur richtigen Zeit; **I want to get things ~ right** ich will es ganz richtig machen; **who ~ will be in charge?** wer wird eigentlich die Verantwortung haben?; **that's not ~ what I mean** das ist nicht genau das, was ich meine; **~ the same** genau der/die/das Gleiche; **you mean we are stuck? – ~** wir sitzen also fest? – stimmt genau; **is she sick? – not ~** ist sie krank? – eigentlich nicht; **not ~** (*iro: = hardly*) nicht gerade; **his father was not ~ poor/pleased** sein Vater war nicht gerade arm/erfreut; **it's not ~ a comedy** es ist nicht gerade eine Komödie

exactness [ɪg'zæktnɪs] N Genauigkeit *f*

exaggerate [ɪg'zædʒəreɪt] VT **a** (*= overstate*) übertreiben; **he ~d what really happened** er hat das, was wirklich geschehen war, übertrieben dargestellt; **he tends to ~ his own importance** er neigt dazu, sich wichtigzutun **b** (*= intensify*) *effect* verstärken; *similarity* hervorheben VI übertreiben

exaggerated [ɪg'zædʒəreɪtɪd] ADJ übertrieben; **to have an ~ view of sth** etw überschätzen; **to have an ~ sense of one's own importance** eine übertrieben hohe Meinung von sich haben

exaggeratedly [ɪg'zædʒəreɪtɪdlɪ] ADV übertrieben

exaggeration [ɪg,zædʒə'reɪʃən] ✪ 26.1 N Übertreibung *f*; **a bit of an ~** eine leichte Übertreibung, leicht übertrieben

exalt [ɪg'zɔːlt] VT **a** (*in rank or power*) erheben **b** (*= praise*) preisen

exaltation [,egzɔːl'teɪʃən] N (*= feeling*) Begeisterung *f*, Exaltation *f* (*liter*)

exalted [ɪg'zɔːltɪd] ADJ **a** *position, style* hoch; **at** *or* **on a less ~ level** auf nicht ganz so gehobener Ebene; **the ~ ranks of …** die erhabenen Ränge der …; **to be in ~ company** sich in gehobener Gesellschaft befinden; **she moves only in the most ~ circles** sie bewegt sich nur in den besten Kreisen **b** *mood, person* exaltiert, überschwänglich

exam [ɪg'zæm] N Prüfung *f*

examination [ɪg,zæmɪ'neɪʃən] N **a** (*Sch etc*) Prüfung *f*; (*Univ*) Examen *nt*, Prüfung *f*; **geography ~** Geografieprüfung *f*; **~ nerves** *pl* Prüfungsangst *f*
b (*= study, inspection*) Prüfung *f*, Untersuchung *f*; (*of machine, premises, passports*) Kontrolle *f*; (*of question*) Untersuchung *f*; (*of accounts*) Prüfung *f*; **on closer ~** bei genauer(er) Prüfung *or* Untersuchung; **it was found on ~ that …** die Untersuchung ergab, dass …; **the matter is still under ~** die Angelegenheit wird noch geprüft *or* untersucht
c (*Med*) Untersuchung *f*; **she underwent a thorough ~** sie wurde gründlich untersucht
d (*Jur, of suspect, accused, witness*) Verhör *nt*; (*of case, documents*) Untersuchung *f*; **legal ~** Verhör *nt*

examine [ɪg'zæmɪn] ✪ 26.1 VT **a** (*for* auf *+acc*) untersuchen; *documents, accounts* prüfen; *machine, passports, luggage* kontrollieren; **you need (to have) your head ~d** (*inf*) du solltest dich mal auf deinen Geisteszustand untersuchen lassen **b** *pupil, candidate* prüfen (*in* in *+dat*, *on* über *+acc*) **c** (*Med*) untersuchen **d** (*Jur*) *suspect, accused, witness* verhören

examinee [ɪg,zæmɪ'niː] N (*Sch*) Prüfling *m*; (*Univ*) (Examens)kandidat(in) *m(f)*

examiner [ɪg'zæmɪnəʳ] N (*Sch, Univ*) Prüfer(in) *m(f)*; **board of ~s** Prüfungsausschuss *m*

example [ɪg'zɑːmpl] ✪ 26.1, 26.2 N Beispiel *nt*; **for ~** zum Beispiel; **to set a good/bad ~** ein gutes/schlechtes Beispiel geben, mit gutem/schlechtem Beispiel vorangehen; **his conduct should be an ~ to us** sein Verhalten sollte uns ein Beispiel sein; **a leader who is an ~ to his men** ein Führer, der seinen Männern als Beispiel dient *or* mit leuchtendem Beispiel vorangeht; **to follow sb's ~** jds Beispiel folgen; **to take sth as an ~** sich (*dat*) an etw ein Beispiel nehmen; **to make an ~ of sb** an jdm ein Exempel statuieren; **to punish sb as an ~ to others** jdn exemplarisch bestrafen

exasperate [ɪg'zɑːspəreɪt] VT zur Verzweiflung bringen, auf die Palme bringen (*inf*); **to become** *or* **get ~d** verzweifeln (*with* an *+dat*), sich aufregen (*with* über *+acc*); **~d by his lack of attention** verärgert über seine mangelnde Aufmerksamkeit

exasperating [ɪg'zɑːspəreɪtɪŋ] ADJ ärgerlich; *delay, difficulty, job* leidig *attr*; *person* nervig (*inf*); **it's so ~ not to be able to buy a newspaper** es ist wirklich zum Verzweifeln, dass man keine Zeitung bekommen kann; **she can be so ~!** sie kann einen wirklich zur Verzweiflung *or* auf die Palme (*inf*) bringen!

exasperatingly [ɪg'zɑːspəreɪtɪŋlɪ] ADV **this train/student is ~ slow** es ist zum Verzweifeln, wie langsam dieser Zug fährt/dieser Student ist

exasperation [ɪg,zɑːspə'reɪʃən] N Verzweiflung *f* (*with* über *+acc*); **he cried out in ~** er schrie verzweifelt auf

excavate ['ekskəveɪt] VT *ground* ausschachten; (*machine*) ausbaggern; (*Archeol*) *remains* ausgraben; *site* Ausgrabungen machen auf (*+dat*); *trench, graves* ausheben VI (*Archeol*) Ausgrabungen machen

excavation [,ekskə'veɪʃən] N **a** (*Archeol*) (Aus)grabung *f*; **~s** (*= site*) Ausgrabungsstätte *f* **b** (*of tunnel etc*) Graben *nt*

excavator ['ekskəveɪtəʳ] N (*= machine*) Bagger *m*; (*Archeol: = person*) Ausgräber(in) *m(f)*

exceed [ɪk'siːd] VT **a** (*in value, amount, length of time*) übersteigen, überschreiten (*by* um); **the guests ~ed 40 in number** die Zahl der Gäste überstieg 40; **to ~ 5 kilos in weight** das Gewicht von 5 kg übersteigen *or* überschreiten; **a fine not ~ing £500** eine Geldstrafe bis zu £ 500 **b** (*= go beyond*) hinausgehen über (*+acc*); *expectations, desires* übertreffen, übersteigen; *limits, powers, speed limit* überschreiten

exceedingly [ɪk'siːdɪŋlɪ] ADV (*+adj, adv*) äußerst, ausgesprochen; **we had an ~ good lunch** wir aßen ausgesprochen gut zu Mittag; **my aunt felt the cold ~** meine Tante litt außerordentlich unter der Kälte

excel [ɪk'sel] VI sich auszeichnen, sich hervortun VT übertreffen (*in* in *+dat*, an *+dat*); **to ~ oneself** (*often iro*) sich selbst übertreffen

excellence ['eksələns] N **a** (*= high quality*) hervorragende Qualität, Vorzüglichkeit *f*; **artistic/academic ~** höchste künstlerische/wissenschaftliche Qualität; **the ~ of the essay** der ausgezeichnete *or* hervorragende Aufsatz; **we strive for ~** wir streben hervorragende Qualität an **b** (*= excellent feature*) Vorzug *m*, hervorragende Eigenschaft

Excellency ['eksələnsɪ] N Exzellenz *f*; **Your/His ~** Eure/Seine Exzellenz

excellent ✪ 19.2 ADJ ausgezeichnet, hervorragend; **I passed my exams – ~!** ich habe meine Prüfungen bestanden – ausgezeichnet!

excellently ['eksələntlɪ] ADV ausgezeichnet, hervorragend

excelsior [ek'selsɪɔːʳ] N (*US: = shavings*) Holzwolle *f*

except [ɪk'sept] PREP **a** außer (*+dat*); **what can they do ~ wait?** was können sie (anders) tun als warten?; **who could have done it ~ him?** wer hätte es außer ihm denn getan?
b **~ for** abgesehen von, bis auf (*+acc*); **~ that …** außer *or* nur dass …; **~ for the fact that** abgesehen davon, dass …; **~ if** es sei denn(, dass), außer wenn; **~ when** außer wenn
CONJ **a** (*= only*) doch; **I'd refuse ~ I need the money** ich würde ablehnen, doch ich brauche das Geld
b (*old, form, = unless*) es sei denn(, dass); **~ he be a traitor** es sei denn, er wäre ein Verräter
VT ausnehmen; **to ~ sb from sth** jdn bei etw ausnehmen; **none ~ed** ohne Ausnahme

excepting [ɪk'septɪŋ] PREP außer; **not ~ X** ohne X auszunehmen *or* auszuschließen, X nicht ausgenommen; **always ~ …** natürlich mit Ausnahme (*+gen*) …

exception [ɪk'sepʃən] N **a** Ausnahme *f*; **to make an ~** eine Ausnahme machen; **to make an ~ of/for sb** eine Ausnahme bei jdm/für jdn machen; **without ~** ohne Ausnahme; **with the ~ of** mit Ausnahme von; **this case is an ~ to the rule** dieser Fall ist eine Ausnahme, das ist ein Ausnahmefall; **the ~ proves the rule, this is the ~ that proves the rule** (*prov*) Ausnahmen bestätigen die Regel (*prov*); **these strokes of luck are the ~** diese Glückstreffer sind die Ausnahme; **with this ~** mit der einen Ausnahme; **sb/sth is no ~** jd/etw ist *or* bildet keine Ausnahme **b** **to take ~ to sth** Anstoß *m* an etw (*dat*) nehmen

exceptionable [ɪk'sepʃənəbl] ADJ (*form*) **a** (*= arguable*) anfechtbar, bestreitbar **b** (*= objectionable*) anstößig

exceptional [ɪk'sepʃənl] ADJ **a** (*= outstanding*) *person, talent, achievement* außergewöhnlich, außerordentlich; (*= outstandingly good*) *teacher, quality, performance etc* hervorragend; (*= outstandingly high*) *value, amount* außergewöhnlich hoch; **of ~ quality/talent/value/courage** außergewöhnlich gut/talentiert/wertvoll/mutig; **an ~ amount of money** außergewöhnlich viel Geld; **it takes ~ courage** dazu gehört außergewöhnlich viel Mut; **his work is ~ in its poetic quality** seine Werke sind von einer außergewöhnlichen Poesie
b (*= unusual*) *circumstances, situation, powers* außergewöhnlich; *person, weather* ungewöhnlich; **~ case** Ausnahmefall *m*; **in ~ cases, in** *or* **under ~ circumstances** in Ausnahmefällen; **~ child** (*US Sch*) hochbegabtes Kind

exceptionally [ɪk'sepʃənəlɪ] ADV **a** (*= extraordinarily*) außergewöhnlich, außerordentlich **b** (*= unusually, as an exception*) ausnahmsweise

exception error N (*esp Comput*) Ausnahmefehler *m*

excerpt ['eksɜːpt] N Auszug *m*, Exzerpt *nt* VT (*Liter, Mus*) exzerpieren

excess [ɪk'ses] N **a** Übermaß *nt* (*of* an *+dat*); **an ~ of caution** allzu viel Vorsicht; **an ~ of details** allzu viele Einzelheiten; **to eat/drink to ~** übermäßig essen/trinken; **to carry sth to ~** etw übertreiben; **don't do anything to ~** man soll nichts übertreiben; **he does everything to ~** er übertreibt bei allem
b **excesses** PL Exzesse *pl*; (*drinking, sex etc*) Ausschweifungen *pl*; (*brutalities*) Ausschreitungen *pl*
c (*= amount left over*) Überschuss *m*; **~ of demand over supply** Nachfrageüberschuss *m*
d **to be in ~ of** hinausgehen über (*+acc*), überschreiten; **a figure in ~ of …** eine Zahl über (*+dat*) …
e (*esp Brit Insur*) Selbstbeteiligung *f*
ADJ *water, salt, energy* überschüssig; *alcohol* zu viel; **~ fat** Fettpolster *nt*, überschüssiges Fett

excess: **excess baggage** N Übergewicht *nt*; **excess capacity** N Überkapazität *f*; **excess charge** N zusätzliche Gebühr; (*for letter etc*) Nachgebühr *f*; **excess demand** N Nachfrageüberschuss *m*; **excess fare** N Nachlösegebühr *f*; **I had to pay an ~** ich musste nachlösen; **excess freight** N Überfracht *f*

excessive [ɪk'sesɪv] ADJ übermäßig; *price, profits, speed* überhöht; *demands* übertrieben; **an ~ amount of, ~ amounts of** übermäßig viel; **to spend an ~ amount of time on sth** übermäßig viel Zeit auf etw (*acc*) verwenden; **~ levels of lead** ein zu hoher Bleigehalt; **~ drinking** übermäßiger Alkoholgenuss; **~ use of the clutch** zu häufiger Gebrauch der Kupplung; **avoid ~ exposure to the sun** setzen Sie sich nicht zu lange der Sonne aus; **that's (a bit) ~!** das geht (etwas) zu weit!, das ist (etwas) übertrieben!

excessively [ɪk'sesɪvlɪ] ADV (*+vb*) übermäßig; *drink, eat* zu viel; (*+adj*) allzu; *bright, boring, ugly* äußerst, ausgesprochen; **to worry ~** sich übermäßig große Sorgen machen; **~ so** allzu sehr; **he's confident, perhaps ~ so** er ist selbstbewusst, vielleicht sogar zu selbstbewusst

excess: **excess postage** N Nachgebühr *f*, Strafporto *nt (inf)*; **excess production** N Überproduktion *f*; **excess profit** N Übergewinn *m*; **~s tax** *(Econ)* Übergewinnsteuer *f*; **excess supply** N Angebotsüberschuss *m*; **excess weight** N Übergewicht *nt*; **to lose ~** überflüssige Pfunde abnehmen

exchange [ɪks'tʃeɪndʒ] **VT** *books, glances, seats* tauschen; *foreign currency* wechseln, umtauschen (*for* in *+acc*); *information, views, secrets, experiences, hostages, phone numbers* austauschen; **to ~ words** einen Wortwechsel haben; **to ~ letters** einen Briefwechsel führen; **to ~ blows** sich schlagen; **to ~ fire (with)** einen Schusswechsel haben (mit); **to ~ greetings** sich grüßen; **to ~ insults** sich gegenseitig beleidigen; **to ~ gifts** sich (gegenseitig) beschenken; **to ~ one thing for another** eine Sache gegen eine andere austauschen *or (in shop)* umtauschen
N **a** *(of goods, stamps)* Tausch *m*; *(of prisoners, views, secrets, diplomatic notes)* Austausch *m*; *(of one bought item for another)* Umtausch *m*; **an ~ of fire** ein Schusswechsel *m*; **in ~** dafür; **in ~ for money** gegen Geld *or* Bezahlung; **in ~ for a table** für einen Tisch; **in ~ for lending me your car** dafür, dass Sie mir Ihr Auto geliehen haben; **that's not a fair ~ for my bike** das ist kein fairer Tausch für mein Rad; **to lose by the ~** einen schlechten Tausch machen; **fair ~ is no robbery** *(Prov)* Tausch ist kein Raub *(Prov)*
b *(Fin: = act)* Wechseln *nt*; *(= place)* Wechselstube *f*
c *(St Ex)* Börse *f*
d **(telephone) ~** Fernvermittlungsstelle *f (form)*, Fernamt *nt*; *(in office etc)* (Telefon)zentrale *f*
e *(= altercation)* Wortwechsel *m*

exchangeable [ɪks'tʃeɪndʒəbl] **ADJ** austauschbar (*for* gegen); *goods bought* umtauschbar (*for* gegen); **goods bought in the sale are not ~** Ausverkaufsware ist vom Umtausch ausgeschlossen

exchange: **exchange broker** N *(St Ex)* Devisenmakler(in) *m(f)*; **exchange control** N *(Fin)* Devisenkontrolle *f*; **exchange market** N *(Fin)* Devisenmarkt *m*; **exchange rate** N Wechselkurs *m*; **Exchange Rate Mechanism** N *(Fin)* Wechselkursmechanismus *m*; **exchange student** N Austauschstudent(in) *m(f)*; **exchange teacher** N Austauschlehrer(in) *m(f)*; **exchange value** N Tauschwert *m*; **exchange visit** N *(Sch etc)* Austauschbesuch *m*; **to be on an ~** einen Austauschbesuch machen

exchequer [ɪks'tʃekə'] N Finanzministerium *nt*; *(esp in GB)* Schatzamt *nt*; *(inf, personal)* Finanzen *pl (inf)* → **chancellor**

excisable [ek'saɪzəbl] **ADJ** steuerpflichtig

excise[1] ['eksaɪz] N **a** Verbrauchssteuer *f* (*on* auf *+acc*, für); **~ on beer/tobacco** Bier-/Tabaksteuer *f* **b** *(Brit: = department)* *Verwaltungsabteilung für indirekte Steuern*

excise[2] [ek'saɪz] **VT** *(Med)* herausschneiden, entfernen *(also fig)*

excise ['eksaɪz]: **excise duties** PL Verbrauchssteuern *pl*; **excise licence** N *(Brit)* Schankkonzession *f*; **exciseman** N Steuereinnehmer *m*; **excisewoman** N Steuereinnehmerin *f*

excision [ek'sɪʒən] N *(Med, fig)* Entfernung *f*

excitability [ɪk,saɪtə'bɪlɪtɪ] N Erregbarkeit *f*; *(Med)* Reizbarkeit *f*

excitable [ɪk'saɪtəbl] **ADJ** **a** *person, animal* leicht erregbar; **in an ~ state** erregt; **to become** *or* **get ~** erregt werden **b** *(Med)* reizbar

excite [ɪk'saɪt] **VT** **a** *person, animal* aufregen, aufgeregt machen; *(= rouse enthusiasm in)* begeistern; **the news had clearly ~d him** er war wegen der Nachricht sichtlich aufgeregt; **the whole village was ~d by the news** das ganze Dorf war über die Nachricht in Aufregung; **the prospect doesn't exactly ~ me** ich finde die Aussicht nicht gerade begeisternd **b** *(Physiol) nerve* reizen; *(sexually)* erregen **c** *sentiments, passion, admiration* erregen; *interest, curiosity* wecken, erregen; *imagination, appetite* anregen; **the issue has ~d a great deal of fierce debate** das Thema hat viele heiße Debatten ausgelöst

excited [ɪk'saɪtɪd] **ADJ** **a** aufgeregt; *(= agitated)* erregt; *(= enthusiastic)* begeistert; **(sexually) ~** (sexuell) erregt; **he was ~ to hear of this development** er wurde aufgeregt, als er von dieser Entwicklung erfuhr; **to be ~ that...** begeistert darüber sein, dass ...; **to be ~ about sth** von etw begeistert sein; *(= looking forward)* sich auf etw *(acc)* freuen; **to become** *or* **get ~ (about sth)** sich (über etw *acc*) aufregen; *(= enthuse)* sich (über etw *acc*) begeistern; **to get ~** *(sexually)* erregt werden; **aren't you ~ about what's going to happen?** sind Sie nicht gespannt, was passieren wird?; **it was nothing to get ~ about** es war nichts Besonderes; **he is ~ at the prospect of working for himself** er freut sich darauf, selbstständig zu arbeiten
b *(Phys) atom* angeregt

excitedly [ɪk'saɪtɪdlɪ] **ADV** aufgeregt

excitement [ɪk'saɪtmənt] N **a** Aufregung *f*; **there was great ~ when ...** es herrschte große Aufregung, als ...; **a mood of ~** eine Spannung; **a shriek of ~** ein aufgeregter Schrei; **in the ~ of the match** in der Aufregung des Spiels, im Eifer des Gefechts; **she only did it for (a bit of) ~** sie hat es nur getan, um ein bisschen Aufregung zu haben; **what's all the ~ about?** wozu die ganze Aufregung?; **to be in a state of high ~** in heller Aufregung sein; **his novel has caused great ~** sein Roman hat große Begeisterung ausgelöst; **he enjoys paragliding and other such ~s** Paragliding und ähnlich aufregende Dinge machen ihm Spaß
b *(Physiol)* Reizung *f*; *(sexual)* Erregung *f*

exciting [ɪk'saɪtɪŋ] **ADJ** aufregend; *player, artist* sensationell; *prospect* reizvoll; *(= full of suspense)* spannend; *(sexually)* erregend; **it's very ~ to find new talent** es ist sehr aufregend *or* spannend, neue Talente zu entdecken; **there is something ~ about this** das hat etwas Aufregendes an sich; **~ for** *or* **to sb** aufregend für jdn; **visually ~** visuell reizvoll

excitingly [ɪk'saɪtɪŋlɪ] **ADV** *(+adj)* aufregend; *(+vb)* auf aufregende Weise; **the film ~ portrays the last days of the war** der Film ist eine spannende Darstellung der letzten Kriegstage

excl **a** *abbr of* **excluding** **b** *abbr of* **exclusive** exkl.

exclaim [ɪk'skleɪm] **VI** **he ~ed in surprise when he saw it** er schrie überrascht auf, als er es sah; **she ~ed at the sight of such extravagance** beim Anblick solcher Extravaganz entfuhr ihr ein Aufschrei **VT** ausrufen; **at last! she ~ed** endlich! rief sie (aus)

exclamation [,eksklə'meɪʃən] N Ausruf *m (also Gram)*; **an ~ of horror** ein Schreckensschrei *m*

exclamation mark, *(US)* **exclamation point** N Ausrufezeichen *nt*

exclamatory [ɪk'sklæmətərɪ] **ADJ** exklamatorisch; **~ remarks** Ausrufe *pl*

exclude [ɪk'sklu:d] **VT** ausschließen; **to ~ sb from the team/an occupation** jdn aus der Mannschaft/von einer Beschäftigung ausschließen; **to ~ a child from school** ein Kind vom Schulunterricht ausschließen; **to ~ sb from doing sth** jdn davon ausschließen, etw zu tun; **if we don't ~ the possibility that ...** wenn wir die Möglichkeit nicht ausschließen, dass ...; **the price ~s VAT** *(Brit)* der Preis versteht sich ausschließlich Mehrwertsteuer; **£200 excluding VAT** *(Brit)* £ 200 ohne Mehrwertsteuer; **the meal costs £15 excluding wine** das Essen kostet £ 15 ohne Wein; **everything excluding the house** alles außer *or* ausgenommen das Haus

exclusion [ɪk'sklu:ʒən] N Ausschluss *m* (*from* von); *(from school)* Ausschluss *m* von Unterricht; **she thought about her job to the ~ of everything else** sie dachte ausschließlich an ihre Arbeit

exclusionary [ɪks'klu:ʒənərɪ] **ADJ** *(form)* ausschließend

exclusion: **exclusion clause** N *(Insur)* Haftungsausschlussklausel *f*; **exclusion order** N *(Jur, against suspected terrorist, football hooligan)* Einreiseverbot *nt*; *(against spouse)* Hausverbot *nt*

exclusive [ɪk'sklu:sɪv] **ADJ** **a** *(= select)* exklusiv **b** *(= unshared, unique) use, control* alleinig, ausschließlich; *story* exklusiv; **~ interview** Exklusivinterview *nt*; **~ offer** Exklusivangebot *nt*; **an offer ~ to our readers/to Smith's** ein Exklusivangebot für unsere Leser/bei Smith; **~ property** Alleineigentum *nt*; **~ rights to sth** Alleinrechte *pl* an etw *(dat)*; *(Press)* Exklusivrechte *pl* an etw *(dat)*; **~ rights to coverage of the Olympic Games** Exklusivrechte für die Berichterstattung bei den Olympischen Spielen; **to have ~ use of a room** einen Raum für sich allein haben; **this is the ~ preserve of the privileged** das ist die ungeteilte Domäne der Privilegierten
c *(= not inclusive)* exklusive *inv*; **our terms are ~** unsere Bedingungen verstehen sich exklusive; **~ of taxes/postage and packing** *(Comm)* exklusive Steuern/Porto und Verpackung; **mutually ~** einander ausschließend; **they are mutually ~** sie schließen einander aus
N *(Press: = story)* Exklusivbericht *m*; *(= interview)* Exklusivinterview *nt*; **the story was a Times ~** die Geschichte wurde exklusiv von der Times gebracht

exclusively [ɪk'sklu:sɪvlɪ] **ADV** ausschließlich; *(Press)* exklusiv; **details were ~ revealed by Hello** Einzelheiten wurden exklusiv in Hello enthüllt; **an (almost) ~ white population** eine (fast) ausschließlich weiße Bevölkerung; **to be available ~ (from/to)** ausschließlich *or* exklusiv (bei/für) erhältlich sein

exclusiveness [ɪk'sklu:sɪvnɪs] N Exklusivität *f*

exclusivity [,ɪksklu:'sɪvɪtɪ] N Exklusivität *f*

excommunicate [,ekskə'mju:nɪkeɪt] **VT** exkommunizieren

excommunication ['ekskə,mju:nɪ'keɪʃən] N Exkommunikation *f*

ex-convict [,eks'kɒnvɪkt] N ehemaliger Häftling

excoriate [ɪk'skɔ:rɪeɪt] **VT** *(form: = criticize severely) person, organization* attackieren; *idea* verurteilen

excrement ['ekskrɪmənt] N Kot *m*, Exkremente *pl*

excrescence [ɪks'kresns] N Gewächs *nt*, Auswuchs *m (also fig)*

excreta [ɪk'skri:tə] **PL** Exkremente *pl*

excrete [ɪk'skri:t] **VT** ausscheiden, absondern

excretion [ɪk'skri:ʃən] N *(= act)* Ausscheidung *f*, Exkretion *f*; *(= substance)* Exkret *nt*

excruciating [ɪk'skru:ʃɪeɪtɪŋ] **ADJ** **a** *(lit: = unbearable) pain, noise, silence* unerträglich; *cramp, headache also, sight, experience* fürchterlich, entsetzlich; *death* qualvoll; **I was in ~ pain** ich hatte unerträgliche Schmerzen **b** *(fig) experience, boredom* unerträglich; *joke* entsetzlich; *detail* schrecklich; **an ~ pun** ein entsetzlicher Kalauer

excruciatingly [ɪk'skru:ʃɪeɪtɪŋlɪ] **ADV** **a** *(lit: = unbearably) painful* unerträglich; **walking was ~ painful** das Gehen bereitete unerträgliche Schmerzen **b** *(fig: = extremely)* fürchterlich, entsetzlich; **~ funny** urkomisch, zum Schreien *(inf)*

exculpate ['ekskʌlpeɪt] **VT** *(form) person* freisprechen, exkulpieren *(liter)* (*from* von); **to ~ oneself** sich rechtfertigen

excursion [ɪk'skɜ:ʃən] N Ausflug *m*; *(fig, into a subject also)* Exkurs *m*; **to go on an ~** einen Ausflug machen

excursionist [ɪk'skɜ:ʃənɪst] N Ausflügler(in) *m(f)*

excursion: **excursion ticket** N verbilligte Fahrkarte (zu einem Ausflugsort); **excursion train** N Sonderzug *m*

excusable [ɪk'skju:zəbl] ADJ verzeihlich, entschuldbar

excuse [ɪk'skju:z] VT **a** *(= seek to justify) action, person* entschuldigen; **such rudeness cannot be ~d** so eine Unhöflichkeit ist nicht zu entschuldigen; **to ~ oneself** sich entschuldigen *(for sth* für *or* wegen etw); **he ~d himself for being late** er entschuldigte sich, dass er zu spät kam; **he ~d himself by saying that his English wasn't very good** zu seiner Entschuldigung sagte er, er spreche nicht gut Englisch
b *(= pardon)* **to ~ sb** jdm verzeihen; **to ~ sb for having done sth** jdm verzeihen, dass er etw getan hat; **well, I think I can be ~d for believing him** nun, man kann es mir wohl nicht übel nehmen, dass ich ihm geglaubt habe; **~ me for interrupting** entschuldigen *or* verzeihen Sie bitte die Störung; **if you will ~ the expression** wenn Sie mir den Ausdruck gestatten; **~ me!** *(= sorry, to get attention, go past, after sneezing etc)* Entschuldigung!, entschuldigen Sie!; *(indignant)* erlauben Sie mal!; **well, ~ me for asking!** entschuldige, dass ich gefragt habe!
c *(= set free from obligation)* **to ~ sb from (doing) sth** jdn von einer Sache befreien, jdm etw erlassen; **he is ~d attendance** er muss nicht unbedingt anwesend sein; *(pupil)* er ist vom Schulbesuch befreit; **you are ~d** *(to children)* ihr könnt gehen; **can I be ~d?** darf ich mal verschwinden *(inf)*?; **he ~d himself and left the room** er entschuldigte sich und ging aus dem Zimmer; **and now if you will ~ me I have work to do** und nun entschuldigen Sie mich bitte, ich habe zu arbeiten
N [ɪks'kju:s] **a** *(= justification)* Entschuldigung *f*; **there's no ~ for it** dafür gibt es keine Entschuldigung; **they had no ~ for attacking him** sie hatten keinen Grund, ihn anzugreifen; **to give sth as an ~** etw zu seiner Entschuldigung anführen *or* vorbringen; **he gave two reasons as an ~ for his action** er gab zwei Gründe zur Entschuldigung für seine Tat an
b *(= pretext)* Ausrede *f*, Entschuldigung *f*; **to make ~s for sb/sth** jdn/etw entschuldigen; **they made ~s for not having done anything about it** sie brachten Ausreden an, warum sie nichts dagegen unternommen hatten; **I have a good ~ for not going** ich habe eine gute Ausrede *or* Entschuldigung, warum ich nicht hingehen kann; **it was raining – well, that's your ~** es hat geregnet – das ist wohl deine Ausrede *or* Entschuldigung; **~s, ~s!** nichts als Ausreden!; **you're full of ~s** du hast immer eine Ausrede; **he's only making ~s** er sucht nur nach einer Ausrede; **a good ~ for a party** ein guter Grund, eine Party zu feiern
c **excuses** PL *(= apology)* Entschuldigung *f*; **to offer one's ~s** sich entschuldigen
d **an ~ for a steak** ein jämmerliches *or* armseliges Steak

excuse-me [ɪk'skju:zmi:] N *(= dance)* Tanz *m* mit Abklatschen

ex-directory [,eksdaɪ'rektərɪ] ADJ *(Brit)* **to be ~** nicht im Telefonbuch stehen

ex dividend ADV *(St Ex)* ohne Anrecht auf Dividende

ex-dividend [,eks'dɪvɪdend] ADJ *(St Ex)* **~ share** Aktie *f* ohne Anrecht auf Dividende

execrable ADJ, **execrably** ADV ['eksɪkrəbl, -ɪ] scheußlich, abscheulich

execrate ['eksɪkreɪt] VT **a** *(= hate)* verabscheuen **b** *(= curse)* verfluchen, verwünschen

execration [,eksɪ'kreɪʃən] N **a** *(= hatred)* Abscheu *m* **b** *(= curse)* Fluch *m*, Verwünschung *f*

executable ['eksɪkju:təbl] ADJ ausführbar; **~ file** *(Comput)* ausführbare Datei, Programmdatei *f*

executant [ɪg'zekjʊtənt] N Ausführende(r) *mf*

execute ['eksɪkju:t] VT **a** *plan, order, task etc* durchführen, ausführen; *movement, dance* ausführen; *duties* erfüllen, wahrnehmen; *purpose* erfüllen; *(Comput) command* ausführen **b** *(Mus: = perform)* vortragen; *cadenza etc* ausführen; *(Art)* ausführen **c** *criminal* hinrichten **d** *(Jur) will* vollstrecken, ausführen; *contract* ausfertigen; *(= sign) document* unterzeichnen

execution [,eksɪ'kju:ʃən] N **a** *(= carrying out, of plan, order, task etc)* Durchführung *f*, Ausführung *f*; *(of movement, dance)* Ausführung *f*; *(of duties)* Erfüllung *f*, Wahrnehmung *f*; **to put sth into ~** etw ausführen; **in the ~ of his duties** bei der Ausübung seines Amtes **b** *(Mus)* Vortrag *m*; *(= musician's skill)* Ausführung *f*; *(Art)* Ausführung *f* **c** *(as punishment)* Hinrichtung *f*, Exekution *f* **d** *(Jur, of will, judgement)* Vollstreckung *f*; *(of contract)* Ausfertigung *f*; *(= signing)* Unterschreiben *nt*

executioner [,eksɪ'kju:ʃnə'] N Henker *m*, Scharfrichter *m*

executive [ɪg'zekjʊtɪv] N **a** *(Admin, Comm: = person)* leitender Angestellter, leitende Angestellte, Manager(in) *m(f)*; **junior ~** leitender Angestellter, leitende Angestellte; **senior ~** Geschäftsführer(in) *m(f)*; **he's a Shell ~** er ist ein leitender Angestellter bei Shell; **business ~s** leitende Geschäftsleute *pl*
b *(Comm, Pol: = managing group)* Vorstand *m*; **the party's/union's National Executive (Committee)** der Partei-/Gewerkschaftsvorstand; **to be on the ~** Vorstandsmitglied *or* im Vorstand sein
c **the ~** *(Pol, part of government)* die Exekutive
ADJ **a** *(= managerial) position, post* leitend; **~ power** Exekutivgewalt *f*; **the ~ branch (of government)** die Exekutive (der Regierung); **~ decision** Managemententscheidung *f*; **~ function** Führungsfunktion *f*; **~ role** Führungsrolle *f*; **~ ability** Führungsqualität *f*; **he has ~ ability** er hat das Zeug zum Manager; **~ pay** *or* **salaries** Gehälter *pl* der leitenden Angestellten
b *(= luxury, for executives)* für gehobene Ansprüche

executive: **executive assistant** N *(esp US)* Assistent(in) *m(f)* des Geschäftsführers; **executive board** N *(Admin, Comm)* Vorstand *m*; **executive briefcase** N Diplomatenkoffer *m*; **executive burnout** N Managerkrankheit *f*; **executive car** N Wagen *m* der gehobenen Mittelklasse; **executive chair** N Chefsessel *m*; **executive chairman** N Vorstandsvorsitzender *m*; **executive committee** N Vorstand *m*; **executive council** N Vorstand *m*; **the Executive Council** *(Pol)* der Exekutivrat; **executive director** N Vorstandsmitglied *nt*; **executive jet** N Privatjet *m* (für Manager); **executive lounge** N *(at airport)* VIP-Salon *m*; **executive mansion** N **the Executive Mansion** *(US: = White House)* der Amtssitz des Präsidenten; *(= State Governor's house)* der Amtssitz des Gouverneurs; **executive member** N Vorstandsmitglied *nt*; **executive officer** N Erster Offizier; **executive order** N *(US)* Rechtsverordnung *f*; **executive president** N Präsident(in) *m(f)* mit Exekutivgewalt; **executive producer** N *(Film, Theat)* geschäftsführender Produzent, geschäftsführende Produzentin; **executive relief** N *(euph) Sex für leitende Angestellte*; **executive secretary** N Direktionssekretär(in) *m(f)*; **executive session** N *(US Parl)* Senatssitzung *f (unter Ausschluss der Öffentlichkeit)*; **executive suite** N *(in office)* Vorstandsetage *f*; **executive toy** N Managerspielzeug *nt*

EXECUTIVE PRIVILEGE

Das **executive privilege** ist das Recht des US-Präsidenten, bestimmte Informationen über die Aktivitäten seines Büros vor dem Kongress oder der Justiz geheim zu halten. Es wird normalerweise im Interesse der nationalen Sicherheit angewandt oder um private Regierungsgespräche vertraulich zu behandeln. Dieses Privileg kann nicht aus persönlichen Gründen angeführt werden. Einige Präsidenten haben versucht, für ihre Amtszeit das absolute **executive privilege** zu erhalten, was ihnen jedoch von den Gerichten verwehrt wurde. Im Watergate-Skandal berief sich Präsident Nixon auf dieses Privileg, um Bandmitschnitte von Telefongesprächen nicht einem Untersuchungsausschuss des US-Senats übergeben zu müssen, doch der oberste Gerichtshof hob in diesem Fall das Recht auf.

executor [ɪg'zekjʊtə'] N *(of will)* Testamentsvollstrecker *m*

executrix [ɪg'zekjʊtrɪks] N Testamentsvollstreckerin *f*

exegesis [,eksɪ'dʒi:sɪs] N Exegese *f*, Auslegung *f*

exegetical [,eksɪ'dʒetɪkəl] ADJ exegetisch

exemplary [ɪg'zemplərɪ] ADJ **a** *(= excellent)* vorbildlich, beispielhaft *(in sth* in etw *dat)* **b** *(= as a deterrent) punishment, sentence* exemplarisch

exemplary damages PL *(Jur) über den verursachten Schaden hinausgehende Entschädigung*, Bußgeld *nt*

exemplification [ɪg,zemplɪfɪ'keɪʃən] N Erläuterung *f*, Veranschaulichung *f*, Exemplifizierung *f (geh)*

exemplify [ɪg'zemplɪfaɪ] VT erläutern, veranschaulichen

exempt [ɪg'zem*p*t] ADJ befreit *(from* von); **diplomats are ~** Diplomaten sind ausgenommen; **could I be made ~ (from that)?** könnte ich davon befreit werden? VT *person, business* befreien; **to ~ sb from doing sth** jdn davon befreien, etw zu tun; **to ~ sth from a ban** etw von einem Verbot ausnehmen

exemption [ɪg'zem*p*ʃən] N Befreiung *f*; **~ from taxes** Steuerfreiheit *f*

exercise ['eksəsaɪz] N **a** *no pl (of right)* Wahrnehmung *f*; *(of physical, mental power)* Ausübung *f*; *(of patience, mental faculties)* Übung *f*; *(of imagination)* Anwendung *f*; **in the ~ of his duties** bei der Ausübung seiner Pflichten
b *(bodily or mental, drill, Mus etc)* Übung *f*; **stomach ~s** Übungen *pl* für die Bauchmuskeln; **to do one's ~s in the morning** Morgengymnastik machen
c *no pl (physical)* Bewegung *f*; **physical ~** (körperliche) Bewegung; **to do some ~** ein bisschen Sport machen; **a dog needs a lot of ~** ein Hund braucht viel Bewegung; **people who don't take** *or* **get enough ~** Leute, die sich nicht genug bewegen *or* die nicht genug Bewegung bekommen; **I need to get some ~** ich brauche ein wenig Bewegung; **what form of ~ do you do?** wie halten Sie sich fit?
d *(= activity)* **it was a pointless ~** es war völlig sinnlos; **it was a useful ~ in public relations** für die Public Relations war es nützlich; **that's just an ~ in window-dressing** *(fig)* das ist alles nur Schau
e *(Mil) usu pl* Übung *f*; **to go on ~s** eine Übung machen
f **exercises** PL *(US: = ceremonies)* Feierlichkeiten *pl*
VT **a** *body, mind* üben, trainieren; *horse* bewegen; *dog* spazieren führen; **I'm not saying this just to ~ my voice** ich sage das nicht zum Spaß
b *(= use) one's authority, control, power* ausüben; *a right* geltend machen, ausüben; *patience, tact, discretion* üben; *influence* ausüben *(on* auf *+acc)*; *talents* Gebrauch machen von; **to ~ care in doing sth** Vorsicht walten lassen, wenn man etw tut
VI **if you ~ regularly ...** wenn Sie sich viel bewegen ...; **you don't ~ enough** du hast zu wenig Bewegung; **he was exercising on the parallel bars** er turnte (gerade) am Barren

exercise: **exercise bike** N Heimtrainer *m*; **exercise book** N Heft *nt*

exerciser ['eksəsaɪzə'] N *(= machine)* Trainingsgerät *nt*; *(bigger)* Fitness-Center *nt*; *(= person)* Trainer(in) *m(f) (inf)*

exercise yard N Hof *m*

exercycle ['eksəsaɪkl] N Heimtrainer *m*

exert [ɪg'zɜ:t] VT *pressure, influence, power, control* ausüben *(on* auf *+acc)*; *authority* aufbieten, einsetzen *(on* bei); *force* gebrauchen, anwenden;

to ~ a force on sth eine Kraft auf etw *(acc)* ausüben VR sich anstrengen

exertion [ɪɡˈzɜːʃən] N **a** *(= effort)* Anstrengung *f*; **by one's own ~s** durch eigene Anstrengungen **b** *(of force, strength)* Anwendung *f*, Einsatz *m*; *(of authority)* Aufgebot *nt*, Einsatz *m*; *(of influence, power, control)* Ausübung *f*; **the ~ of force/pressure on sth** die Ausübung von Kraft/Druck auf etw *(acc)*; **rugby requires strenuous physical ~** Rugby fordert unermüdlichen körperlichen Einsatz; **after the day's ~s** nach des Tages Mühen

exeunt VI [ˈeksɪʌnt] *(Theat)* ab; **~ Brutus and Cassius** Brutus und Cassius ab

exfoliate [eksˈfəʊlɪeɪt] VT *skin* durch Peeling entfernen, abschleifen VI Peeling *nt* machen

exfoliation [eksˌfəʊlɪˈeɪʃən] N Peeling *nt*

ex gratia [eksˈɡreɪʃə] ADJ *payment* ohne Anerkennung der Rechtspflicht

exhalation [ˌekshəˈleɪʃən] N *(of breath)* Ausatmen *nt*; *(of gas)* Verströmen *nt*

exhale [eksˈheɪl] VT **a** *(= breathe out)* ausatmen **b** *(= give off) smoke* abgeben; *gas, vapour* ablassen, abgeben VI ausatmen

exhaust [ɪɡˈzɔːst] VT **a** *(= use up completely)* erschöpfen; **we have ~ed the subject** wir haben das Thema erschöpfend behandelt **b** *(= tire)* erschöpfen; **the children are/this job is ~ing me** die Kinder sind/diese Arbeit ist eine Strapaze für mich N **a** *(esp Brit Aut etc)* Auspuff *m* **b** *no pl (= gases)* Auspuffgase *pl*

exhausted [ɪɡˈzɔːstɪd] ADJ **a** *(= very tired)* erschöpft *(from* von); **~ from laughing and singing** vom Lachen und Singen erschöpft; **she was ~ from digging the garden** sie war erschöpft, weil sie den Garten umgegraben hatte **b** *(= finished, used up) supplies, resources, funds, oilfield, mine* erschöpft; *ammunition, savings* aufgebraucht; **his patience was ~** er war mit seiner Geduld am Ende

exhaust fumes PL Auspuffgase *pl*, Abgase *pl*

exhausting [ɪɡˈzɔːstɪŋ] ADJ anstrengend; *activity, work, journey also* strapaziös; **grief is ~** Trauern ist erschöpfend

exhaustion [ɪɡˈzɔːstʃən] N Erschöpfung *f*

exhaustive [ɪɡˈzɔːstɪv] ADJ umfassend, erschöpfend; *list* vollständig; *search* gründlich

exhaustively [ɪɡˈzɔːstɪvlɪ] ADV *research, cover, prove, speak, describe* erschöpfend, ausführlich; *complete, thorough* äußerst

exhaust: **exhaust pipe** N *(esp Brit)* Auspuffrohr *nt*; **exhaust system** N *(esp Brit)* Auspuff *m*

exhibit [ɪɡˈzɪbɪt] VT **a** *paintings etc, goods* ausstellen; *membership card* vorzeigen, vorweisen **b** *skill, ingenuity* zeigen, beweisen, an den Tag legen; *reaction* zeigen VI ausstellen N **a** *(in an exhibition)* Ausstellungsstück *nt* **b** *(Jur)* Beweisstück *nt*

exhibition [ˌeksɪˈbɪʃən] N **a** *(of paintings, furniture etc)* Ausstellung *f*; *(of articles for sale)* Auslage *f* **b** *(= act of showing: of a technique, film etc)* Vorführung *f* **c** **what an ~ of bad manners!** was für schlechte Manieren!; **did you see her at the party last night? - what an ~!** hast du sie auf der Party gestern Abend gesehen? - die hat sich vielleicht aufgeführt!; **to make an ~ of oneself** ein Theater machen *(inf)*; **am I making an ~ of myself?** benehm ich mich daneben? **d** *(Brit, Univ, = grant)* Stipendium *nt*

exhibition centre, *(US)* **exhibition center** N Ausstellungszentrum *nt*; *(for trade fair)* Messegelände *nt*

exhibitioner [ˌeksɪˈbɪʃənəʳ] N *(Brit Univ)* Stipendiat(in) *m(f)*

exhibitionism [ˌeksɪˈbɪʃənɪzəm] N Exhibitionismus *m*

exhibitionist [ˌeksɪˈbɪʃənɪst] N Exhibitionist(in) *m(f)* ADJ exhibitionistisch

exhibition match N *(Sport)* Schaukampf *m*

exhibitor [ɪɡˈzɪbɪtəʳ] N Aussteller(in) *m(f)*

exhilarate [ɪɡˈzɪləreɪt] VT in Hochstimmung versetzen; *(news also)* (freudig) erregen; *(sea air etc)* beleben, erfrischen

exhilarated [ɪɡˈzɪləreɪtɪd] ADJ *laugh* erregt, aufgeregt; **to feel ~** in Hochstimmung sein

exhilarating [ɪɡˈzɪləreɪtɪŋ] ADJ *experience* erregend, aufregend; *activity* aufregend; *feeling, sensation* berauschend; *air, breeze* belebend; **it is ~ to run along an empty beach** es ist berauschend, einen leeren Strand entlangzulaufen

exhilaration [ɪɡˌzɪləˈreɪʃən] N Hochgefühl *nt*; **the ~ of flying** das Hochgefühl beim Fliegen

exhort [ɪɡˈzɔːt] VT ermahnen

exhortation [ˌeɡzɔːˈteɪʃən] N Ermahnung *f*

exhumation [ˌeksh*j*uːˈmeɪʃən] N Exhumierung *f*

exhume [eksˈhjuːm] VT exhumieren

exigence [ˈeksɪdʒəns], **exigency** [ɪɡˈzɪdʒənsɪ] N **a** *usu pl (= requirement)* (An)forderung *f*; *(of situation)* Erfordernis *nt* **b** *(= emergency)* Notlage *f* **c** *(= urgency)* Dringlichkeit *f*

exigent [ˈeksɪdʒənt] ADJ *(= urgent)* zwingend, dringend; *(= exacting) master* streng, gestreng *(old)*

exiguity [ˌeɡzɪˈɡjuːɪtɪ] N *(form)* Winzigkeit *f*; *(= meagreness)* Knappheit *f*

exiguous [ɪɡˈzɪɡjʊəs] ADJ *(form) savings, income, revenue* knapp, dürftig

exile [ˈeksaɪl] N **a** *(= person)* Verbannte(r) *mf* **b** *(= banishment)* Exil *nt*, Verbannung *f*; **to go into ~** ins Exil gehen; **in ~** im Exil VT verbannen *(from* aus), ins Exil schicken; **the ~d former president** der im Exil lebende frühere Präsident

exist [ɪɡˈzɪst] VI **a** *(= to be)* existieren, bestehen; **does God ~?** existiert Gott?; **everything that ~s** alles, was ist *or* existiert; **it only ~s in her imagination** das gibt es *or* das existiert nur in ihrer Fantasie; **I want to live, not just ~** ich möchte leben, nicht einfach nur existieren; **it doesn't ~** das gibt es nicht; **to cease to ~** zu bestehen aufhören; **to continue to ~** fortbestehen, weiter bestehen; **doubts still ~** noch bestehen Zweifel; **the understanding which ~s between the two countries** das Einvernehmen zwischen den beiden Ländern; **there ~ many people who ...** es gibt viele Leute, die ...; **there ~s a tradition that ...** es gibt den Brauch, dass ...; **there ~s the possibility** *or* **the possibility ~s that ...** es besteht die Möglichkeit, dass ...
b *(= live)* existieren, leben *(on* von); **we cannot ~ without water** wir können ohne Wasser nicht leben *or* existieren; **can life ~ on Mars?** kann auf dem Mars Leben existieren?; **she ~s on very little** sie kommt mit sehr wenig aus; **is it possible to ~ on such a small salary?** kann man denn von so einem kleinen Gehalt leben?
c *(= be found)* vorkommen; **the natural resources which ~ in the Antarctic** die Bodenschätze, die in der Antarktis vorkommen

existence [ɪɡˈzɪstəns] N **a** Existenz *f*; *(of custom, tradition, institution)* Bestehen *nt*, Existenz *f*; **to be in ~** existieren, bestehen; **to come into ~** entstehen; *(person)* auf die Welt kommen; **to go out of ~** zu bestehen *or* existieren aufhören; **do you believe in the ~ of God?** glauben Sie daran, dass Gott existiert?, glauben Sie an die Existenz Gottes?; **the continued ~ of slavery** das Weiterbestehen *or* der Fortbestand der Sklaverei; **the only one in ~** der Einzige, den es gibt
b *(= life)* Leben *nt*, Dasein *nt*, Existenz *f*; **a miserable ~** ein elendes Leben, ein trostloses Dasein; **means of ~** Lebensunterhalt *m*

existent [ɪɡˈzɪstənt] ADJ existent; *conditions, laws* bestehend; **to be ~** existieren; **dinosaurs are no longer ~** Dinosaurier gibt es nicht mehr

existential [ˌeɡzɪsˈtenʃəl] ADJ existenziell, existentiell

existentialism [ˌeɡzɪsˈtenʃəlɪzəm] N Existenzialismus *m*, Existentialismus *m*

existentialist [ˌeɡzɪsˈtenʃəlɪst] N Existenzialist(in) *m(f)*, Existentialist(in) *m(f)* ADJ existenzialistisch, existentialistisch

existing [ɪɡˈzɪstɪŋ] ADJ bestehend; *circumstances* gegenwärtig; *(esp Comput)* vorhanden

exit [ˈeksɪt] N **a** *(from stage, life)* Abgang *m*; *(from room)* Hinausgehen *nt (from* aus); *(from competition)* Ausscheiden *nt*; *(from sb's life)* Scheiden *nt (geh)*; **to make an/one's ~** *(from stage)* abgehen; *(from room)* hinausgehen; **he made a very dramatic ~** sein Abgang war sehr dramatisch
b *(= way out)* Ausgang *m*; *(for vehicles)* Ausfahrt *f*
VI hinausgehen; *(from stage)* abgehen; *(from competition)* ausscheiden; *(Comput)* das Programm/die Datei *etc* verlassen, aussteigen *(inf)*; **~ the king** *(Theat)* der König (tritt) ab
VT **a** *(US) train* verlassen, aussteigen aus; *place* hinausgehen aus
b *(Comput) program, file* beenden, aussteigen aus *(inf)*

exit: **exit permit** N Ausreisegenehmigung *f*; **exit poll** N *bei Wahlen unmittelbar nach Verlassen der Wahllokale durchgeführte Umfrage*; **exit survey** N *(US)* Meinungsbefragung *f (nach Verlassen einer Institution, eines Geschäfts etc)*

exitus [ˈeksɪtəs] N *(Med)* Exitus *m (spec)*, Tod *m*

exit visa N Ausreisevisum *nt*

exodus [ˈeksədəs] N **a** *(from a country)* Abwanderung *f*; *(Bibl: of Hebrews, also fig)* Exodus *m*; **general ~** allgemeiner Aufbruch **b** **~ of capital** Kapitalabwanderung *f* **c** *(Bibl)* **Exodus** 2. Buch Mosis *or* Mose, Exodus *m*

ex officio [ˌeksəˈfɪʃɪəʊ] *(form)* ADJ **an ~ member** ein Mitglied von Amts wegen ADV von Amts wegen

exonerate [ɪɡˈzɒnəreɪt] VT entlasten *(from* von)

exoneration [ɪɡˌzɒnəˈreɪʃən] N Entlastung *f (from* von)

exorbitance [ɪɡˈzɔːbɪtəns] N *(of price)* Unverschämtheit *f*; *(of demands also)* Maßlosigkeit *f*, Übertriebenheit *f*

exorbitant [ɪɡˈzɔːbɪtənt] ADJ überhöht; *price also* unverschämt; *demand* maßlos, übertrieben; **that's ~!** das ist Wucher!

exorbitantly [ɪɡˈzɔːbɪtəntlɪ] ADV **~ priced** *or* **expensive** maßlos teuer; **they are paid ~** sie werden unverschämt gut bezahlt; **they charge ~** sie verlangen unverschämte Preise

exorcism [ˈeksɔːsɪzəm] N Geisterbeschwörung *f*, Exorzismus *m*, Austreibung *f* böser Geister

exorcist [ˈeksɔːsɪst] N Exorzist(in) *m(f)*

exorcize [ˈeksɔːsaɪz] VT exorzieren; *evil spirit also* austreiben

exoskeleton [ˌeksəʊˈskelɪtən] N Außenskelett *nt*

exoteric [ˌeksəʊˈterɪk] ADJ exoterisch

exotic [ɪɡˈzɒtɪk] ADJ exotisch; **~ dancer** exotischer Tänzer, exotische Tänzerin; **~ holidays** *(esp Brit) or* **vacation** *(US)* Urlaub *m* in exotischen Ländern N *(Bot)* exotische Pflanze, Exot(e) *m*

exotica [ɪɡˈzɒtɪkə] PL Exotika *pl*; **a museum of ~** *(fig)* ein Raritätenkabinett *nt*

exotically [ɪɡˈzɒtɪkəlɪ] ADV exotisch; **~ named** mit exotischem Namen

exoticism [ɪɡˈzɒtɪsɪzəm] N Exotik *f*, Exotische *nt*

expand [ɪkˈspænd] VT *metal, gas, liquid, empire, chest* ausdehnen, expandieren; *business, trade, production* erweitern, expandieren; *knowledge, mind, algebraic formula, membership* erweitern; *influence, experience* vergrößern; *summary, notes* weiter ausführen; *ideas* entwickeln
VI *(solids, gases, liquids, universe)* sich ausdehnen, expandieren; *(business, trade, economy, empire)* expandieren, wachsen; *(volume of trade, exports, production)* zunehmen, expandieren; *(knowledge, experience, influence)* zunehmen, wachsen; *(fields of knowledge, study, mind)* breiter werden; *(horizons)* sich erweitern; **we want to ~** wir wollen expandieren *or* (uns) vergrößern;

the market is ~ing der Markt wächst; **we've ~ed into the European market** wir sind in den europäischen Markt vorgedrungen; **~ing watchstrap** Gliederarmband *nt*

▸ **expand (up)on** VT *subject* weiter ausführen; **could you expand on that?** könnten Sie das weiter ausführen?

expandable [ɪk'spændəbl] ADJ erweiterbar

expanded memory [ɪk'spændɪd-] N *(Comput)* Expansionsspeicher *m*

expanded polystyrene [ɪk'spændɪd-] N Styropor® *nt*

expander [ɪk'spændəʳ] N Expander *m*

expanse [ɪk'spæns] N Fläche *f*; *(of ocean etc)* Weite *f no pl*; **a vast ~ of grass** eine riesige Grasfläche; **an ~ of woodland** ein Waldgebiet *nt*

expansion [ɪk'spænʃən] N *(of liquid, gas, metal, universe, property)* Ausdehnung *f*, Expansion *f*; *(of business, trade, production)* Erweiterung *f*, Expansion *f*; *(territorial, economic, colonial)* Expansion *f*; *(of subject, idea)* Entwicklung *f*; *(Math, of knowledge, membership)* Erweiterung *f*; *(of experience, influence)* Vergrößerung *f*; *(of summary, notes)* Ausweitung *f*

expansion *(Comput)*: **expansion board** N Erweiterungsplatine *f*; **expansion card** N Erweiterungskarte *f*

expansionism [ɪk'spænʃənɪzəm] N Expansionspolitik *f*

expansionist [ɪk'spænʃənɪst] **ADJ** expansionistisch, Expansions-; **~ policy** Expansionspolitik *f* **N** Expansionspolitiker(in) *m(f)*

expansion: **expansion joint** N *(Tech)* Dehn(ungs)fuge *f*; **expansion slot** N *(Comput)* Erweiterungssteckplatz *m*

expansive [ɪk'spænsɪv] ADJ **a** *(= communicative) person, mood* mitteilsam; *welcome* herzlich; **to be in an ~ mood** in gesprächiger Stimmung sein **b** *(form: = broad, extensive) area, lawn* ausgedehnt; *view* weit; *gesture* ausladend; *role* umfassend **c** *(= expanding, growing) economy* expandierend; *business* expansiv; **~ phase** Expansionsphase *f*; **to have ~ ambitions (for sth)** Expansionspläne (für etw) haben **d** *(Phys)* expansiv

expansively [ɪk'spænsɪvlɪ] ADV **a** *(= warmly) say* herzlich; *smile* breit; *(= enthusiastically)* begeistert **b** *(= in detail)* ausführlich

ex parte [,eks'pɑːtɪ] ADJ, ADV *(Jur)* einseitig, (seitens) einer Partei

expat ['eks'pæt] N ADJ = **expatriate N, ADJ**

expatiate [ɪk'speɪʃɪeɪt] VI sich verbreiten *(on* über *+acc)*

expatiation [ɪk,speɪʃɪ'eɪʃən] N weitläufige Erörterung

expatriate [eks'pætrɪət] **N** im Ausland Lebende(r) *mf*; **British ~s** im Ausland lebende Briten; **the ~s in Abu Dhabi** die Ausländer in Abu Dhabi; **I'm an ~ too** ich bin hier auch im Exil *(hum)* **ADJ** *person, family* im Ausland lebend; **~ workers** ausländische Arbeitskräfte; **~ community** Ausländergemeinde *f* **VT** [eks'pætrɪeɪt] *person* ausbürgern, expatriieren *(geh)*

expect [ɪk'spekt] ✪ 6.2, 8.1, 10.2, 16.2, 26.3 **VT** **a** *(= anticipate)* erwarten; *esp sth bad* rechnen mit; **that was to be ~ed** das war zu erwarten, damit war zu rechnen; **I know what to ~** ich weiß, was mich erwartet; **we were ~ing war in 1939** 1939 haben wir mit Krieg gerechnet; **to ~ the worst** mit dem Schlimmsten rechnen; **I ~ed as much** das habe ich erwartet, damit habe ich gerechnet; **he failed as (we had) ~ed** er fiel, wie erwartet, durch; **he got first prize as was to be ~ed** wie erwartet, bekam er den ersten Preis; **to ~ to do sth** erwarten *or* damit rechnen, etw zu tun; **I didn't ~ to gain his sympathy** ich habe kein Mitleid von ihm erwartet; **he ~s to be elected** er rechnet damit, gewählt zu werden; **it is ~ed that ...** es wird erwartet, dass ..., man rechnet damit, dass ...; **it is hardly to be ~ed that ...** es ist kaum zu erwarten *or* damit zu rechnen, dass ...; **the talks are ~ed to last two days** die Gespräche sollen zwei Tage dauern; **she is ~ed to resign tomorrow** es wird erwartet, dass sie morgen zurücktritt; **I was ~ing him to come** ich habe eigentlich erwartet, dass er kommt; **you can't ~ me to agree to that!** Sie erwarten doch wohl nicht, dass ich dem zustimme!; **I'll ~ to see you tomorrow then** dann sehen wir uns also morgen; **at that price, what did you ~?** was hast du denn zu dem *or* für den Preis erwartet?

b *(= suppose)* denken, glauben; **will they be on time? – yes, I ~ so/no, I ~ not** kommen sie pünktlich? – ja, ich glaube schon *or* ich denke doch/nein, ich glaube nicht; **this work is very tiring – yes, I ~ it is** diese Arbeit ist sehr anstrengend – (ja,) das glaube ich; **I ~ it will rain** höchstwahrscheinlich wird es regnen, es wird wohl regnen; **I ~ you'd like a drink** Sie möchten sicher etwas trinken, ich nehme an, Sie möchten etwas trinken; **I ~ you're tired** Sie werden sicher müde sein; **I ~ he turned it down** er hat wohl abgelehnt, ich nehme an, er hat abgelehnt; **well, I ~ he's right** er wird schon recht haben; **well, I ~ it's all for the best** das ist wohl nur gut so; **I ~ it was your father who phoned** ich nehme an, es war dein Vater, der angerufen hat

c *(= demand)* **to ~ sth of** *or* **from sb** etw von jdm erwarten; **to ~ sb to do sth** erwarten, dass jd etw tut; **I ~ you to be obedient** ich erwarte von dir Gehorsam; **what do you ~ me to do about it?** was soll ich da tun?; **don't ~ me to feel sorry** erwarte von mir kein Mitleid; **are we ~ed to tip the waiter?** müssen wir dem Kellner Trinkgeld geben?

d *(= await) person, thing, action, baby* erwarten; **I will be ~ing you tomorrow** ich erwarte dich morgen; **I am ~ing them for supper** ich erwarte sie zum Abendessen; **we'll ~ you when we see you** *(inf)* wenn ihr kommt, dann kommt ihr *(inf)*; **you'll have to ~ me when you see me** *(inf)* wenn ich da bin, bin ich da! *(inf)*

VI **she's ~ing** sie ist in anderen Umständen, sie bekommt *or* erwartet ein Kind

expectancy [ɪk'spektənsɪ] N Erwartung *f*

expectant [ɪk'spektənt] ADJ **a** *(= eagerly waiting)* erwartungsvoll **b** *(= future) mother, father, parents* werdend

expectantly [ɪk'spektəntlɪ] ADV erwartungsvoll; *wait* gespannt

expectation [,ekspek'teɪʃən] N **a** *(= act of expecting)* Erwartung *f*; **in ~ of** in Erwartung *(+gen)*; **in the confident ~ of an easy victory** fest mit einem leichten Sieg rechnend **b** *(= that expected)* Erwartung *f*; **against** *or* **contrary to all ~(s)** wider Erwarten; **to exceed all ~(s)** alle Erwartungen übertreffen; **to come up to sb's ~s** jds Erwartungen *(dat)* entsprechen **c** *(= prospect)* Aussicht *f* **d** **~ of life** Lebenserwartung *f*

expected [ɪk'spektɪd] ADJ erwartet; *relief, profit also* erhofft; **the contract will provide an ~ 900 new jobs** es wird erwartet, dass der Auftrag 900 Arbeitsplätze schaffen wird

expectorant [ɪk'spektərənt] N Expektorans *nt* *(spec)*

expectorate [ɪk'spektəreɪt] VTI *(form)* ausspeien

expedience [ɪk'spiːdɪəns], **expediency** [ɪk'spiːdɪənsɪ] N **a** *(= self-interest)* Zweckdenken *nt*, Berechnung *f* **b** *(of measure etc, = politic nature)* Zweckdienlichkeit *f*; *(= advisability)* Ratsamkeit *f*

expedient [ɪk'spiːdɪənt] **ADJ** *(= politic)* zweckdienlich; *(= advisable)* angebracht, ratsam **N** Notbehelf *m*, Hilfsmittel *nt*

expediently [ɪk'spiːdɪəntlɪ] ADV zweckmäßigerweise

expedite ['ekspɪdaɪt] VT **a** *(= hasten)* beschleunigen, vorantreiben; **see what you can do to ~ matters** sehen Sie zu, ob Sie die Sache beschleunigen können **b** *(rare) letters* expedieren *(spec)*

expedition [,ekspɪ'dɪʃən] N **a** Expedition *f*; *(Mil)* Feldzug *m*; **shopping ~** Einkaufstour *f*; **to go on an ~** auf (eine) Expedition *or* Forschungsreise gehen; **to go on a shopping ~** eine Einkaufstour machen **b** *no pl (old, form, = speed)* Eile *f*; **with ~** eilends *(old, form)*

expeditionary [,ekspɪ'dɪʃənrɪ] ADJ Expeditions-; **~ force** *(Mil)* Expeditionskorps *nt*

expeditious [,ekspɪ'dɪʃəs] ADJ schnell, prompt

expeditiously [,ekspɪ'dɪʃəslɪ] ADV schnell, prompt; **as ~ as possible** so schnell wie möglich, schnellstens

expel [ɪk'spel] VT **a** *person* vertreiben; *(officially, from country)* ausweisen, ausschaffen *(Sw)* *(from* aus); *(from school)* verweisen *(from* von, *+gen)*; *(from society)* ausstoßen, ausschließen; *evil* austreiben **b** *gas, liquid* ausstoßen; **to ~ one's breath** ausatmen

expend [ɪk'spend] VT **a** *(= spend, employ) money* ausgeben, verwenden; *time, energy, care* aufwenden *(on* für, *on doing sth* um etw zu tun), verwenden *(on* auf *+acc*, *on doing sth* darauf, etw zu tun) **b** *(= use up) resources* verbrauchen

expendability [ɪk,spendə'bɪlɪtɪ] N *(form, of device, object)* Entbehrlichkeit *f*; *(of person also)* Überflüssigkeit *f*

expendable [ɪk'spendəbl] *(form)* **ADJ** *device, object* entbehrlich; *person also* überflüssig; **an ~ luxury** ein überflüssiger Luxus **N** *usu pl* **~s** entbehrliche Dinge *pl*

expenditure [ɪk'spendɪtʃəʳ] N **a** *(= money spent)* Ausgaben *pl* **b** *(= spending, of money)* Ausgabe *f*; *(of time, energy)* Aufwand *m* *(on* an *+dat)*; **the ~ of money on ...** Geld auszugeben für ...; **~ of time/energy** Zeit-/Energieaufwand *m*

expense [ɪk'spens] N **a** Kosten *pl*; **at my ~** auf meine Kosten; **at public ~** auf Staatskosten; **at great ~** mit hohen Kosten; **it's a big ~** es ist eine große Ausgabe; **to go to the ~ of buying a car** (viel) Geld für ein Auto anlegen; **they went to the ~ of installing a lift** sie gaben viel Geld dafür aus, einen Lift einzubauen; **to go to great ~ to repair the house** es sich *(dat)* etwas kosten lassen, das Haus instand *or* in Stand zu setzen

b *(Comm, usu pl)* Spesen *pl*; **to incur ~s** Unkosten haben; **your ~s will be covered** Ihre Unkosten werden Ihnen vergütet; **put it on ~s** schreiben Sie es auf die Spesenrechnung; **it's all on ~s** das geht alles auf Spesen

c *(fig)* **at sb's ~, at the ~ of sb** auf jds Kosten *(acc)*; **at the ~ of sth** auf Kosten einer Sache *(gen)*; **to get rich at the ~ of others/the poor** sich auf Kosten anderer/der Armen bereichern; **at the ~ of quality** auf Kosten der Qualität

expense: **expense account** N Spesenkonto *nt*; **this will go on his ~** das geht auf Spesen; **expense-account** ADJ *attr* **~ lunch** Mittagessen *nt* auf Spesen; **~ lifestyle** Leben *nt* auf Spesen; **it's only ~ people who stay in this hotel** *(inf)* in diesem Hotel wohnen nur Spesenreiter *(inf)*; **expenses form** N Formular *nt* zur Spesenabrechnung; **expenses-paid** ADJ auf Geschäftskosten; **an all-~ holiday** ein Gratisurlaub *m*

expensive [ɪk'spensɪv] ADJ teuer; **the least ~ seats** die billigsten Plätze; **they were too ~ for most people to buy** die meisten Leute konnten sie sich nicht leisten; **childcare is an ~ business** Kinderbetreuung ist eine teure *or* kostspielige Angelegenheit; **to have ~ tastes** einen teuren Geschmack haben

expensively [ɪk'spensɪvlɪ] ADV teuer; **both boys had been privately, and ~, educated** beide Jungen hatten teure Privatschulen besucht; **she lived ~ but quietly** sie lebte ein aufwendiges *or* aufwändiges, aber ruhiges Leben; **~ priced** teuer

expensiveness [ɪk'spensɪvnɪs] N *(of goods, travel, services etc)* hoher Preis, Kostspieligkeit *f*; *(of living somewhere)* Kostspieligkeit *f*; **the ~ of her tastes** ihr teurer Geschmack; **the increasing ~**

of basic commodities die ständige Verteuerung von Grundbedarfsmitteln

experience [ɪk'spɪərɪəns] ✪ 19.2 **N** **a** *(= knowledge, wisdom acquired)* Erfahrung *f*; **~ of life** Lebenserfahrung *f*; **~ shows** *or* **proves that …** die Erfahrung lehrt, dass …; **to know sth from ~** etw aus Erfahrung wissen; **to learn/speak from ~** aus eigener Erfahrung lernen/sprechen; **from my own personal ~** aus eigener Erfahrung; **he has no ~ of grief** er hat nie Kummer erfahren *or* erlebt; **he has no ~ of living in the country** er kennt das Landleben nicht; **I gained a lot of useful ~** ich habe viele nützliche Erfahrungen gemacht; **to have an ~** eine Erfahrung machen
b *(= practice, skill)* Erfahrung *f*; **he has had no practical ~** ihm fehlt die Praxis, er hat keine praktischen Kenntnisse *or* keine praktische Erfahrung; **to have ~ of a technique** Erfahrung in einer Methode haben; **have you had any ~ of driving a bus?** haben Sie Erfahrung im Busfahren?; **~ in a job/in business** Berufs-/Geschäftserfahrung *f*; **to have a lot of teaching ~** große Erfahrung als Lehrer(in) haben; **he lacks ~** ihm fehlt die Praxis *or* praktische Erfahrung; **he is working in a factory to gain ~** er arbeitet in einer Fabrik, um praktische Erfahrungen zu sammeln
c *(= event experienced)* Erlebnis *nt*; **I had a nasty ~** mir ist etwas Unangenehmes passiert; **the trial was a very nasty ~** der Prozess war eine sehr unangenehme Sache; **it was a painful ~** es war schmerzlich *(geh)*; **to suffer some terrible ~s** viel durchmachen; **what an ~!** das war vielleicht was!; **it was a new ~ for me** es war völlig neu für mich
VT **a** *(= suffer, undergo) pain, grief, hunger* erfahren, erleben; *difficult times, recession* durchmachen; *problems, symptoms* haben; **to ~ difficulties** auf Schwierigkeiten stoßen, Schwierigkeiten haben
b *(= feel)* fühlen, spüren, empfinden

experienced [ɪk'spɪərɪənst] **ADJ** *person* erfahren; *staff, teacher, driver etc also* mit Erfahrung; **we need someone more ~** wir brauchen jemanden mit mehr Erfahrung *or* jemanden, der mehr Erfahrung hat; **an ~ eye** ein geschulter Blick; **to be ~ in sth** in etw *(dat)* Erfahrung haben *or* erfahren sein; **they are ~ in helping elderly people** sie haben Erfahrung darin, älteren Leuten zu helfen

experiential [ɪkˌspɪərɪ'enʃəl] **ADJ** auf Erfahrung beruhend

experiment [ɪk'sperɪmənt] **N** *(Chem, Phys, fig)* Versuch *m*, Experiment *nt*; **to do an ~** einen Versuch *or* ein Experiment machen; **as an ~** versuchsweise, als Versuch **VI** *(Chem, Phys, fig)* experimentieren *(on, with* mit)

experimental [ɪkˌsperɪ'mentl] **ADJ** *(also Sci, Med, Tech etc)* experimentell; **~ theatre** *(Brit) or* **theater** *(US)***/cinema** Experimentiertheater *nt*/-kino *nt*; **~ physics/psychology** Experimentalphysik *f*/-psychologie *f*; **~ laboratory/period** Versuchslabor *nt*/-zeit *f*; **to be at an** *or* **in the ~ stage** sich im Versuchs- *or* Experimentierstadium befinden; **on an ~ basis** versuchsweise; **he argued for an ~ lifting of the ban** er argumentierte dafür, das Verbot versuchsweise aufzuheben

experimentally [ɪkˌsperɪ'mentəlɪ] **ADV** **a** *(= as an experiment)* versuchsweise **b** *(Chem, Phys etc, = by experiment)* experimentell; *use* in Versuchen

experimentation [ɪkˌsperɪmen'teɪʃən] **N** Experimentieren *nt*

expert ['ekspɜːt] **N** Experte *m*, Expertin *f*; *(= professional)* Fachmann *m*, Fachfrau *f*; *(Jur)* Sachverständige(r) *mf*; **he is an ~ on the subject/at that sort of negotiation** er ist Fachmann *or* Experte auf diesem Gebiet/für solche Verhandlungen; **~ in geology** Fachmann *m*/Fachfrau *f* für Geologie, Geologieexperte *m*/-expertin *f*; **an ~ at chess** ein Schachexperte *m*, eine Schachexpertin; **she is an ~ on wines/oriental philosophy** sie ist eine Weinexpertin/eine Expertin auf dem Gebiet der orientalischen Philosophie; **with the eye of an ~** mit fachmännischem Blick; **to get the advice of ~s** Experten/Sachverständige zurate *or* zu Rate ziehen; **~'s report** Sachverständigenbericht *m*, Gutachten *nt*; **OK, you do it, you're the ~** gut, machen Sies, Sie sind der Fachmann; **he's an ~ at saying the wrong thing** *(iro)* er versteht es meisterhaft, genau das Falsche zu sagen
ADJ **a** *(= skilled) driver, carpenter, accountant etc* meisterhaft; **she's an ~ typist** sie ist perfekt im Maschineschreiben; **he is ~ at** *or* **in skiing** er ist ein perfekter Skifahrer; **he is ~ at forgeries** *or* **an ~ forger** er kann meisterhaft fälschen; **he is ~ at this operation** er führt diese Operation meisterhaft aus; **to be ~ at** *or* **in doing sth** es hervorragend verstehen, etw zu tun; **people sufficiently ~ in interpreting the data** Leute, die sich in der Interpretation der Daten genügend auskennen
b *(= specialist, of an expert) approach, work, job, advice, help, attention, treatment* fachmännisch; *opinion* eines Fachmanns; *(Jur)* eines Sachverständigen; **his ~ hands** seine erfahrenen Hände; **an ~ eye** der Blick des Fachmanns; **to run** *or* **cast an ~ eye over sth** etw fachmännisch begutachten; **we need your ~ touch** wir brauchen Ihr fachmännisches Können; **an ~ opinion** ein Gutachten *nt*; **what's your ~ opinion?** *(also iro)* was meinen Sie als Fachmann *or* Experte dazu?

expertise [ˌekspə'tiːz] **N** Sachverstand *m*, Sachkenntnis *f* *(in* in *+dat*, auf dem Gebiet *+gen)*; *(= manual skills)* Geschick *nt* *(in* bei)

expertly ['ekspɜːtlɪ] **ADV** *(= skilfully)* meisterhaft; *drive, manoeuvre* geschickt, gekonnt; *repair* fachmännisch; *(= using expert knowledge) judge, examine* sachverständig; **the job was ~ done** die Arbeit wurde fachmännisch ausgeführt

expert system **N** *(Comput)* Expertensystem *nt*

expert witness **N** Sachverständige(r) *mf*

expiate ['ekspɪeɪt] **VT** sühnen

expiation [ˌekspɪ'eɪʃən] **N** **in ~ of** als Sühne für

expiatory ['ekspɪətərɪ] **ADJ** Sühne-; **~ offering** Sühneopfer *nt*

expiration [ˌekspaɪə'reɪʃən] **N** **a** = **expiry** **b** *(of breath)* Ausatmen *nt*, Ausatmung *f*

expire [ɪk'spaɪə'] **VI** **a** *(lease, passport)* ablaufen, ungültig werden; *(time limit)* ablaufen, zu Ende gehen **b** *(liter. = die)* seinen Geist aufgeben *(liter)* **c** *(= breathe out)* ausatmen

expiry [ɪk'spaɪərɪ] **N** Ablauf *m*; **on the ~ of** nach Ablauf *(+gen)*; **date of ~**, **~ date** Ablauftermin *m*; *(of voucher, special offer)* Verfallsdatum *nt*

explain [ɪk'spleɪn] ✪ 26.3 **VT** erklären *(to sb* jdm); *motives, situation, thoughts* erläutern, erklären; *mystery* aufklären; **it's all right, I can ~ everything** schon gut, ich kann das alles erklären; **that is easy to ~, that is easily ~ed** das lässt sich leicht erklären; **he wanted to see me but wouldn't ~ why** er wollte mich sehen, sagte aber nicht, warum *or* aus welchem Grunde; **so that ~s why he didn't react** ach, das erklärt, warum er nicht reagiert hat
VR *(= justify)* sich rechtfertigen; **he'd better ~ himself** ich hoffe, er kann das erklären; **I think you'd better start ~ing yourself** was hast du zu deiner Entschuldigung zu sagen?; **~ yourself!** was soll das?, kannst du das erklären?
VI es erklären; **please ~** bitte erklären Sie das; **I think you've got some ~ing to do** ich glaube, Sie müssen da einiges erklären

▸ **explain away** **VT** *sep* eine Erklärung finden für

explainable [ɪk'spleɪnəbl] **ADJ** erklärlich; **this is easily ~** das lässt sich leicht erklären; **that is ~ by …** das lässt sich durch … erklären

explanation [ˌeksplə'neɪʃən] ✪ 26.1 **N** **a** Erklärung *f*; *(of motives, situation, thoughts)* Erläuterung *f*, Erklärung *f*; *(of mystery)* Aufklärung *f*; **it needs some/a little ~** es bedarf einer Erklärung/einer kurzen Erklärung, man muss das etwas/ein wenig erklären; **he gave a long ~ of what he meant** er erklärte lange, was er meinte; **what is the ~ of this?** wie ist das zu erklären?
b *(= justification)* Erklärung *f*, Rechtfertigung *f*; **has he anything to say in ~ of his conduct?** kann er irgendetwas zur Erklärung seines Verhaltens vorbringen?

explanatory [ɪk'splænətərɪ] **ADJ** erklärend; **a few ~ notes** ein paar Anmerkungen zur Erklärung

expletive [ɪk'spliːtɪv] **N** *(= exclamation)* Ausruf *m*; *(= oath)* Kraftausdruck *m*, Fluch *m*; *(Gram: = filler word)* Füllwort *nt* **ADJ** **~ word** *(Gram)* Füllwort *nt*

explicable [ɪk'splɪkəbl] **ADJ** erklärbar

explicate ['eksplɪkeɪt] **VT** *(form)* erläutern, ausführen

explication [ˌeksplɪ'keɪʃən] **N** *(form)* Erläuterung *f*, Ausführung *f*

explicit [ɪk'splɪsɪt] **ADJ** *person, statement, description* (klar und) deutlich; *orders* eindeutig; *instructions, commitment, agreement, support, reference* ausdrücklich; *(esp sexually) details, description, picture, photograph* eindeutig; **sexually ~** sexuell explizit; **in ~ detail** in allen Einzelheiten; **there is no ~ mention of it** es wird nicht ausdrücklich erwähnt; **speaking to MPs, he was more ~** als er zu den Abgeordneten sprach, ging er näher darauf ein; **he was ~ about his intentions** er machte seine Absichten ganz deutlich; **he was very ~ in his explanations** seine Erklärungen waren sehr deutlich; **she was quite ~ in discussing details of the operation** sie diskutierte die Einzelheiten der Operation in aller Deutlichkeit; **in ~ terms** klar und deutlich

explicitly [ɪk'splɪsɪtlɪ] **ADV** **a** *state, say* deutlich, ausdrücklich **b** *forbid, reject, mention, acknowledge* ausdrücklich; *(+adj)* eindeutig; **~ political activities** eindeutig politische Aktivitäten; **~ anti-Semitic** unverhohlen antisemitisch; **~ sexual photographs** sexuell explizite Fotos

explode [ɪk'spləʊd] **VI** **a** *(lit)* explodieren **b** *(fig)* explodieren; **to ~ with anger** vor Wut platzen *(inf)*, in die Luft gehen *(inf)*; **to ~ with laughter** in schallendes Gelächter ausbrechen, losplatzen *(inf)*; **to ~ into life** *(engine, game)* plötzlich in Gang kommen; *(crisis)* plötzlich aufflammen **VT** **a** *bomb, plane* sprengen; *dynamite, gas* zur Explosion bringen **b** *(fig) theory* zu Fall bringen; **to ~ a myth** einen Mythos entlarven

exploded [ɪk'spləʊdɪd] **ADJ** **~ diagram** Explosionszeichnung *f*; **~ view** Einzelteildarstellung *f*, Explosionsdarstellung *f*

exploit ['eksplɔɪt] **N** *(heroic)* Heldentat *f*; **~s** *(= adventures)* Abenteuer *pl* **VT** [ɪk'splɔɪt] **a** *(= use unfairly) workers* ausbeuten; *friend, sb's credulity, good nature, weakness* ausnutzen **b** *(= make use of) talent, the situation, opportunity* ausnutzen, ausnützen *(dial)*; *coal seam* ausbeuten; *land, natural resources, technology* nutzen

exploitation [ˌeksplɔɪ'teɪʃən] **N** **a** *(= unfair treatment, of workers)* Ausbeutung *f*; *(of friend, sb's credulity, good nature, weakness)* Ausnutzung *f* **b** *(= utilization, of land, natural resources, technology)* Nutzung *f*; *(of coal seam)* Ausbeutung *f*; *(of talent, situation, opportunity)* Ausnutzung *f*

exploiter [ɪk'splɔɪtə'] **N** *(lit, fig)* Ausbeuter(in) *m(f)*

exploration [ˌeksplɔː'reɪʃən] **N** *(of country, area)* Erforschung *f*, Exploration *f* *(geh)*; *(of small area, town)* Erkundung *f*; *(of topic, possibilities)* Untersuchung *f*, Sondierung *f*; *(Med)* Untersuchung *f*, Exploration *f*; **a voyage of ~** *(lit, fig)* eine Entdeckungsreise; **on his ~s** auf seinen Erkundungen

exploratory [ɪk'splɒrətərɪ] **ADJ** *approach, stage* exploratorisch; **~ talks** *or* **discussions/meeting** Sondierungsgespräche *pl*/-gespräch *nt*; **he emphasized that the talks were only ~** er betonte, dass es sich nur um Sondierungsgespräche handelte; **~ trip/expedition** Erkundungsfahrt *f*/-expedition *f*; **~ digging/drilling** Probegrabungen *pl*/-bohrungen *pl*; **~ work** Vorarbeiten *pl*; **~ surgery, an ~ operation** *(Med)* eine Explorationsoperation

explore [ɪk'splɔːʳ] **VT** **a** *country, forest, unknown territory* erforschen, erkunden, explorieren *(geh)*; *(Med)* untersuchen **b** *(fig) question, implications, prospects* untersuchen, sondieren; *possibilities, options* prüfen, sondieren; **to ~ common ground** Gemeinsamkeiten herausarbeiten **VI** **to go exploring** auf Entdeckungsreise gehen; **he went off into the village to ~** er ging auf Entdeckungsreise ins Dorf

explorer [ɪk'splɔːrəʳ] **N** Forscher(in) *m(f)*, Forschungsreisende(r) *mf*

explosion [ɪk'spləʊʒən] **N** **a** Explosion *f*; *(= noise)* Knall *m*, Explosion *f* **b** *(fig, of anger)* Wutausbruch *m* **c** *(fig, in prices, figures etc)* Explosion *f*

explosive [ɪk'spləʊzɪv] **N** Sprengstoff *m* **ADJ** **a** *(lit) gas, mixture* explosiv; **~ device** Sprengsatz *m*; **~ charge** Sprengladung *f*; **~ power** *or* **force** Sprengkraft *f* **b** *(fig: = volatile) situation, issue, problem, mixture* explosiv, brisant; *argument, reaction* heftig; *person, temper* aufbrausend **c** *(fig) (= sudden) noise, applause* explosionsartig; *start* explosiv; *(= rapid) growth* explosionsartig **d** *(Phon)* Verschluss-, explosiv

explosively [ɪk'spləʊsɪvlɪ] **ADV** **a** *(lit) react, erupt* explosiv **b** *(fig) grow* explosionsartig; *say, ask* wütend; *laugh* schallend; **his dance is ~ energetic** er tanzt mit einer explosionsartigen Energie

expo ['ekspəʊ] **N** *abbr of* **exposition** Ausstellung *f*

exponent [ɪk'spəʊnənt] **N** **a** *(of theory)* Vertreter(in) *m(f)*, Exponent(in) *m(f)* **b** *(Math)* Exponent *m*, Hochzahl *f*

exponential [ˌekspəʊ'nenʃəl] **ADJ** *growth* exponentiell; *(Math)* Exponential-; **~ function** Exponentialfunktion *f*; **~ series** Exponentialreihe *f*

exponentially [ˌekspəʊ'nenʃəlɪ] **ADV** *grow, increase* exponentiell

export [ɪk'spɔːt] **VT** exportieren *(also Comput)*, ausführen; **countries which ~ oil** Öl exportierende Länder *pl* **VI** exportieren, ausführen; **~ or die** wer nicht exportiert, geht unter **VI** exportieren, ausführen **N** ['ekspɔːt] Export *m*, Ausfuhr *f*; **ban on ~s** Exportverbot *nt*, Ausfuhrverbot *nt* ['ekspɔːt] **ADJ** *attr* Export-, Ausfuhr-; **~ ban** Exportverbot *nt*, Ausfuhrverbot *nt*

exportable [ɪk'spɔːtəbl] **ADJ** exportfähig

exportation [ˌekspɔː'teɪʃən] **N** Export *m*, Ausfuhr *f*

export ['ekspɔːt]: **export director** **N** Exportdirektor(in) *m(f)*; **export drive** **N** Exportkampagne *f*; **export duty** **N** Export- *or* Ausfuhrzoll *m*

exporter [ɪk'spɔːtəʳ] **N** Exporteur *m* (of von); *(= country)* Exportland *nt* (of für)

export ['ekspɔːt]: **export licence**, *(US)* **export license** **N** Ausfuhrgenehmigung *f*, Ausfuhrlizenz *f*, Exportgenehmigung *f*; **export manager** **N** Exportleiter(in) *m(f)*; **export permit** **N** Ausfuhrerlaubnis *f*, Exporterlaubnis *f*; **export regulations** **PL** Ausfuhrbestimmungen *pl*; **export trade** **N** Exporthandel *m*

expose [ɪk'spəʊz] **VT** **a** *(= uncover) rocks, remains* freilegen; *electric wire* freilegen; *(fig) nerve* bloß legen*or* freilegen **b** *(to danger, rain, sunlight, radiation)* aussetzen *(to dat)*; **not to be ~d to heat** vor Hitze (zu) schützen; **to ~ oneself to criticism** sich der Kritik aussetzen **c** *(= display) one's ignorance* offenbaren; *one's wounds* (vor)zeigen; **to ~ oneself** *(indecently)* sich entblößen; **darling, you're exposing yourself** du zeigst etwas (zu) viel, Liebling **d** *(= reveal) abuse, treachery* aufdecken; *scandal, plot* enthüllen, aufdecken; *person, imposter, murderer, thief* entlarven; **to ~ sb/sth to the press** jdn/etw der Presse ausliefern **e** *(Phot)* belichten

exposé [ek'spəʊzeɪ] **N** Exposé *nt*, Exposee *nt*; *(of scandal etc)* Aufdeckung *f*

exposed [ɪk'spəʊzd] **ADJ** **a** *(= unprotected) position, location, hillside, garden* ungeschützt; *(Mil) troops, flank* ungedeckt; *(Mil, fig) position* exponiert; **the house is very ~** *or* **in a very ~ position** das Haus steht sehr frei *or* ungeschützt; **~ to the wind** dem Wind ausgesetzt; **to feel ~** sich verletzlich fühlen; **to be ~ to sth** *(person)* einer Sache *(dat)* ausgesetzt sein; **the troops were ~ to attack** die Truppen waren nicht gegen einen Angriff gedeckt **b** *(= bare) skin, part of body* unbedeckt; *nerve* freigelegt; *wiring, engine parts, brickwork* frei liegend; **to be ~ to view** sichtbar sein; **a dress which leaves the back ~** ein Kleid, bei dem der Rücken frei bleibt; **to feel ~** *(fig: = insecure)* sich allen Blicken ausgesetzt fühlen

exposition [ˌekspə'zɪʃən] **N** **a** *(of facts, theory)* Darlegung *f*, Exposition *f (geh)*; *(explanatory)* Erklärung *f*, Erläuterung *f*; *(of literature, text)* Kommentar *m* (of zu), Erläuterung *f*; *(Mus)* Exposition *f* **b** *(= exhibition)* Ausstellung *f*

expository [ɪk'spɒzɪtərɪ] **ADJ** darlegend

expostulate [ɪk'spɒstjʊleɪt] **VI** protestieren; **to ~ with sb** mit jdm disputieren

expostulation [ɪkˌspɒstjʊ'leɪʃən] **N** Protest *m*

exposure [ɪk'spəʊʒəʳ] **N** **a** *(to sunlight, air, danger)* Aussetzung *f (to +dat)*; **doctors are warning against excessive ~ of the skin to sunlight** die Ärzte warnen davor, die Haut zu sehr dem Sonnenlicht auszusetzen; **to be suffering from ~** *(Med)* an Unterkühlung leiden; **to die of ~** *(Med)* erfrieren **b** *(= displaying)* Entblößung *f* **c** *(= unmasking, of person, thief, murderer)* Entlarvung *f*; *(of abuses, plots, vices, scandals, crime)* Aufdeckung *f*; **to threaten sb with ~** drohen, jdn zu entlarven **d** *(= position of building)* Lage *f*; **southern ~** Südlage *f* **e** *(Phot)* Belichtung(szeit) *f* **f** *(Media)* Publicity *f*; **his new film has been given a lot of ~** sein neuer Film hat viel Publicity bekommen

exposure meter **N** *(Phot)* Belichtungsmesser *m*

expound [ɪk'spaʊnd] **VT** *theory, one's views* darlegen, erläutern

express [ɪk'spres] ✪ 6.3, 24.4, 26.3 **VT** **a** ausdrücken, zum Ausdruck bringen; *(in words) wish, one's sympathy, appreciation also* aussprechen *(to sb* jdm); **to ~ oneself** sich ausdrücken; **this ~es exactly the meaning of the phrase** das gibt genau die Bedeutung dieses Ausdrucks wieder; **I haven't the words to ~ my thoughts** mir fehlen die Worte, um meine Gedanken auszudrücken; **if I may ~ my opinion** wenn ich meine Meinung äußern darf; **the thought/feeling which is ~ed here** der Gedanke, der/das Gefühl, das hier zum Ausdruck kommt; **it is hard to ~ how delighted I am/how much I hate him** es ist schwer, in Worte zu fassen, wie sehr ich mich freue/wie sehr ich ihn hasse **b** *(= be expressive of)* ausdrücken; **a face which ~es candour/pride** ein Gesicht, das Aufrichtigkeit/Stolz ausdrückt **c** *juice, breast milk* auspressen, ausdrücken **d** *letter etc* per Express *or* als Eilsendung schicken **ADJ** **a** *(= explicit) order, instruction, direction, permission* ausdrücklich; *(= specific) purpose, intention* bestimmt; **on ~ orders from the Prime Minister** auf ausdrückliche Anordnung des Premierministers; **with the ~ intention of doing sth** mit der bestimmten Absicht, etw zu tun **b** *(= fast)* **~ letter** Eilbrief *m*; **by ~ mail** per Eilzustellung; **~ service** Express- *or* Schnelldienst *m*; **an ~ laundry service** ein Wäscheschnelldienst *m* **ADV** **to send a letter/package ~** einen Brief/ein Paket als Eilsendung *or* per Express schicken **N** **a** *(= train)* Schnellzug *m*; **the Orient Express** der Orientexpress; **to send goods by ~** Waren als Eilgut schicken **b** *(= bus, coach)* Schnellbus *m*

express: **express company** **N** *(US)* Spedition *f* (für Expressgut); **express delivery** **N** Eilzustellung *f*; **express goods** **PL** Eilfracht *f*, Eilgut *nt*

expression [ɪk'spreʃən] **N** **a** *(= expressing: of opinions, friendship, affection, joy)* Äußerung *f*, Ausdruck *m*; **as an ~ of our gratitude** zum Ausdruck unserer Dankbarkeit; **to give ~ to sth** etw zum Ausdruck bringen; **from Cairo came ~s of regret at the attack** Kairo brachte Bedauern über den Angriff zum Ausdruck; **popular discontent which found ~ in acts of violence** allgemeine Unzufriedenheit, die sich in Gewalttaten äußerte **b** *(= feeling: in music, art etc)* Ausdruck *m*; **you need to put more ~ into it** Sie müssen das ausdrucksvoller spielen; **to play sth with ~** etw ausdrucksvoll spielen **c** *(= phrase etc)* Ausdruck *m* **d** *(of face)* (Gesichts)ausdruck *m*; **you could tell by his ~ that …** man konnte an seinem Gesichtsausdruck erkennen, dass …; **a face devoid of ~** ein ausdrucksloses Gesicht **e** *(Math)* Ausdruck *m*

expressionism [ɪk'spreʃənɪzəm] **N** Expressionismus *m*

expressionist [ɪk'spreʃənɪst] **N** Expressionist(in) *m(f)* **ADJ** expressionistisch

expressionistic [ɪkˌspreʃə'nɪstɪk] **ADJ** expressionistisch

expressionless [ɪk'spreʃənlɪs] **ADJ** *person* unbewegt; *face, eyes, look, voice* ausdruckslos

expressive [ɪk'spresɪv] **ADJ** *eyes, face, voice* ausdrucksvoll; *glance, look* vielsagend; *gestures, painting, music* ausdrucksvoll, expressiv *(geh)*; *language* ausdrucksstark; **~ dance** Ausdruckstanz *m*; **your eyes are your most ~ feature** deine Augen sind das Ausdrucksvollste an dir; **to be ~ of sth** *(form)* etw ausdrücken; **the French term seemed more ~ of what she felt** das französische Wort schien ihre Gefühle besser auszudrücken *or* genauer wiederzugeben; **~ powers/abilities** Ausdrucksfähigkeit *f or* -vermögen *nt*

expressively [ɪk'spresɪvlɪ] **ADV** ausdrucksvoll, expressiv *(geh)*

expressiveness [ɪk'spresɪvnɪs] **N** Ausdruckskraft *f*; *(of face also)* Ausdrucksfähigkeit *f*

expressly [ɪk'spreslɪ] **ADV** **a** *(= explicitly) forbid, state, exclude, allow* ausdrücklich; **not ~ illegal** nicht ausdrücklich verboten **b** *(= specifically) design, write, make* speziell; **he did it ~ to annoy me** *(= intentionally)* er hat es absichtlich *or* bewusst getan, um mich zu ärgern

express: **express train** **N** Schnellzug *m*; **expressway** **N** Schnellstraße *f*

expropriate [eks'prəʊprɪeɪt] **VT** enteignen

expropriation [eksˌprəʊprɪ'eɪʃən] **N** Enteignung *f*, Expropriation *f (dated)*

expulsion [ɪk'spʌlʃən] **N** *(from a country)* Ausweisung *f (from* aus); *(driving out)* Vertreibung *f (from* aus); *(from school)* Verweisung *f* (von der Schule); *(of evil)* Austreibung *f (from* aus)

expulsion order **N** Ausweisungsbefehl *m*

expunge [ɪk'spʌndʒ] **VT** *(form)* ausstreichen *(from* aus); *(from records also)* auslöschen *(from* aus)

expurgate ['ekspɜːgeɪt] **VT** zensieren, die anstößigen Stellen entfernen aus; **~d edition** gereinigte Fassung

exquisite [ɪk'skwɪzɪt] **ADJ** **a** *(= very fine) object, ornament, jewellery, elegance* exquisit, erlesen; *food, wine, humour* exquisit, köstlich; *craftsmanship, painting, sculpture* vorzüglich, erlesen; *face, features, building, town, view* bezaubernd; *manners, taste* ausgesucht, erlesen; *tact, politeness* feinste(r, s); **in ~ detail** im allerfeinsten Detail **b** *(= intense) pleasure, pain, irony* köstlich; *relief* überwältigend; **with ~ care** mit größter Sorgfalt

exquisitely [ɪk'skwɪzɪtlɪ] **ADV** **a** *(= beautifully, delightfully) dress* ausgesucht, erlesen; *carved, crafted, made* aufs kunstvollste *or* Kunstvollste; *decorate* mit erlesenem Geschmack; **~ detailed** aufs feinste *or* Feinste detailliert; **she danced ~** sie tanzte ganz hervorragend; **it was ~ timed**

der Zeitpunkt war hervorragend gewählt; **~ beautiful** bezaubernd schön; **~ elegant** von exquisiter Eleganz **b** *(= intensely, extremely) sensitive, delicate* überaus, außerordentlich; *painful, funny* köstlich; *polite* ausgesucht

ex-serviceman [eks'sɜːvɪsmən] N *pl* **-men** [-mən] Exsoldat *m*, Veteran *m*

ex-servicewoman [eks'sɜːvɪswʊmən] N *pl* **-women** [-wɪmɪn] Exsoldatin *f*, Veteranin *f*

ext *abbr of* **extension** App.

extant [ek'stænt] ADJ (noch) vorhanden *or* existent

extemporaneous [ɪkˌstempə'reɪnɪəs], **extemporary** [ɪk'stempərɪ] ADJ unvorbereitet, aus dem Stegreif

extempore [ɪks'tempərɪ] ADV *speak* aus dem Stegreif, unvorbereitet ADJ *prayer* improvisiert; **to give an ~ speech** eine Rede aus dem Stegreif halten, extemporieren *(geh)*

extemporize [ɪk'stempəraɪz] VTI aus dem Stegreif sprechen, extemporieren *(geh)*; *(Mus)* improvisieren

extend [ɪk'stend] ✪ 22 VT **a** *(= stretch out) arms* ausstrecken; **to ~ one's hand** die Hand ausstrecken; **to ~ one's hand to sb** jdm die Hand reichen; **to ~ a wire between two posts** einen Draht zwischen zwei Pfosten spannen
b *(= prolong) street, line, visit, passport, holidays, deadline, lease* verlängern; **her tender care doubtless ~ed his life** ihre liebevolle Pflege hat sein Leben zweifellos verlängert
c *(= enlarge) research, powers, franchise* ausdehnen, erweitern; *knowledge* erweitern, vergrößern; *influence* ausbauen; *scheme* ausweiten; *house* anbauen an *(+acc)*; *property* vergrößern, erweitern; *limits* erweitern; *frontiers of a country* ausdehnen; **to ~ one's lead** seine Führung ausbauen; **in an ~ed sense of the term** im weiteren Sinne des Wortes
d *(= offer)* (to sb jdm) *help* gewähren; *hospitality, friendship* erweisen; *invitation, thanks, condolences, congratulations* aussprechen; **to ~ a welcome to sb** jdn willkommen heißen
e *(usu pass: = make demands on) person, pupil, athlete* fordern
VI **a** *(wall, estate, garden)* sich erstrecken, sich ausdehnen (*to, as far as* bis); *(ladder, table)* sich ausziehen lassen; *(meetings etc: over period of time)* sich ausdehnen *or* hinziehen; **a career that ~ed from 1974 to 1990** eine Laufbahn, die sich von 1974 bis 1990 erstreckte
b *(= reach to)* **enthusiasm which ~s even to the children** Begeisterung, die sich sogar auf die Kinder überträgt; **does that ~ to (include) me?** betrifft das auch mich?

extendable [ɪk'stendɪbl], **extensible** [ɪk'stensɪbl] ADJ *object* ausziehbar

extended [ɪk'stendɪd]: **extended credit** N *(Fin)* verlängerter Kredit; **extended family** N Großfamilie *f*; **extended memory** N *(Comput)* erweiterter Arbeitsspeicher; **extended-play record** N Schallplatte *f* mit verlängerter Spielzeit

extension [ɪk'stenʃən] ✪ 27.4, 27.5, 27.7 N **a** *(of property)* Vergrößerung *f*; *(of business, knowledge)* Erweiterung *f*, Vergrößerung *f*; *(of powers, franchise, research, frontiers)* Ausdehnung *f*; *(of road, line, period of time)* Verlängerung *f*; *(of house)* Anbau *m*; *(of time limit)* Verlängerung *f*, Aufschub *m* **b** *(= addition to length of sth, of road, line, table, holidays, leave etc)* Verlängerung *f*; *(of house)* Anbau *m* **c** *(Telec)* (Neben)anschluss *m*; **~ 3714** Apparat 3714 **d** *(Logic, of word, concept)* Extension *f* **e** *(Comput)* Erweiterung *f*, Extension *f*; *(of file name)* Dateiendung *or* -erweiterung *f*

extension: **extension cable** N Verlängerungskabel *nt*; **extension course** N *(Univ)* weiterführender Kurs; **extension ladder** N Ausziehleiter *f*; **extension lead** N Verlängerungsschnur *f*

extensive [ɪk'stensɪv] ADJ *area, land, forest, settlement, tour* ausgedehnt; *plans, reforms, influence, powers, rights* weitreichend, weit reichend; *research, range, menu, collection, alterations, repairs, surgery* umfangreich; *burns, rash* großflächig; *damage* beträchtlich; *knowledge* umfassend, umfangreich; *experience* reich, groß; *network* weitverzweigt; *view* weit; **the facilities available are very ~** es steht eine Vielzahl von Einrichtungen zur Verfügung; **the story got** *or* **was given ~ coverage in the papers** über diese Geschichte wurde in der Presse ausführlich berichtet; **we had fairly ~ discussions** wir haben es ziemlich ausführlich diskutiert; **to make ~ use of sth** etw häufig *or* viel benutzen

extensively [ɪk'stensɪvlɪ] ADV *travel, write, work* viel; *use, grow* häufig; *research, report, write, discuss, quote* ausführlich; *modify, alter* beträchtlich; *restore* zum großen Teil; **the clubhouse was ~ damaged** an dem Klubhaus entstand ein größerer *or* beträchtlicher Schaden; **the chassis was ~ modified** am Chassis wurden umfangreiche Änderungen vorgenommen; **this edition has been ~ revised** diese Ausgabe ist grundlegend überarbeitet worden; **I have quoted ~ from the article** ich habe umfangreiche Zitate aus dem Artikel verwendet; **the ~ reported** *or* **covered trial** der Prozess, über den ausführlich berichtet wurde

extensor [ɪk'stensə'] N Streckmuskel *m*

extent [ɪk'stent] N **a** *(= length)* Länge *f*; *(= size)* Ausdehnung *f*
b *(= range, scope, of knowledge, alterations, power, activities, commitments)* Umfang *m*; *(of damage, losses)* Ausmaß *nt*, Umfang *m*; **debts to the ~ of £5,000** Schulden in Höhe von £ 5.000
c *(= degree)* Grad *m*, Maß *nt*; **to some ~** bis zu einem gewissen Grade; **to what ~** inwieweit; **to a certain ~** in gewissem Maße; **to a large/lesser ~** in hohem/geringerem Maße; **she was involved only to the ~ of investing a small amount** ihre Beteiligung beschränkte sich auf die Investition einer kleinen Summe; **to such an ~ that ...** dermaßen *or* derart, dass ...; **he was ruined to the ~ that he had to sell everything** er war dermaßen ruiniert, dass er alles verkaufen musste; **such was the ~ of the damage** so groß war der Schaden

extenuate [ɪk'stenjʊeɪt] VT *guilt* verringern, mindern; *offence, conduct* beschönigen; **extenuating circumstances** mildernde Umstände

extenuation [ɪkˌstenjʊ'eɪʃən] N *(= act)* Verringerung *f*, Minderung *f*, Beschönigung *f*; *(= extenuating factor)* mildernde Umstände *pl*

exterior [ɪk'stɪərɪə'] N **a** *(of house, box etc)* Außenseite *f*, Äußere(s) *nt*; *(of person)* Äußere(s) *nt*; **on the ~** außen **b** *(Film)* Außenaufnahme *f* ADJ Außen-; *surface also* äußere(r, s); **~ wall** Außenwand *f*; **~ lighting** Außenbeleuchtung *f*; **~ shots** Außenaufnahmen *pl*; **~ view** Außenansicht *f*; **~ decoration/paintwork** Außenanstrich *m*; **~ paint** Farbe *f* für Außenanstriche

exterior angle N *(Math)* Außenwinkel *m*

exterminate [ɪk'stɜːmɪneɪt] VT ausrotten, vernichten; *disease, beliefs, ideas* ausrotten

extermination [ɪkˌstɜːmɪ'neɪʃən] N Ausrottung *f*, Vernichtung *f*; *(of disease, beliefs, ideas)* Ausrottung *f*

exterminator [ɪk'stɜːmɪneɪtə'] N *(= person: of rats etc, pests)* Kammerjäger(in) *m(f)*; *(= poison etc)* Vernichtungsmittel *nt*

external [ek'stɜːnl] ADJ **a** *(= outer) layer, covering, similarity etc* äußere(r, s); *dimensions, angle, diameter* Außen-; *injury* äußerlich; *gills* außen liegend; **the ~ walls of the house** die Außenwände des Hauses; **~ appearance** Aussehen *nt*; **~ surface** Außenfläche *f*; **~ skeleton** Außenskelett *nt*; **for ~ use** *(Pharm)* zur äußerlichen Anwendung
b *(fig: = from outside) influence, factor, event, reality* äußere(r, s), extern *(geh)*; **~ pressures** Druck *m* von außen; **~ cause** äußerer Anlass; **the ~ world** die Außenwelt; **to be ~ to sth** außerhalb einer Sache liegen; *(= not part of sth)* nicht zu etw gehören; **reasons both internal and ~ to the company** Ursachen, die sowohl innerhalb als auch außerhalb des Unternehmens zu finden sind
c *(= foreign) affairs, relations, policy* auswärtig; **the European commissioner for ~ affairs** der EG-Kommissar für auswärtige Angelegenheiten; **MI6, the ~ security service** MI6, der militärische Abschirmdienst
d *(= independent) examiner, auditor, assessor, evaluator* extern
N **externals**
PL *(form)* Äußerlichkeiten *pl*

external: **external borders** PL *(of country)* Landesgrenzen *pl*; *(of area)* Außengrenzen *pl*; **external debt** N Auslandsverschuldung *f*; **external degree** N *(Brit Univ)* *Abschluss nach einem Fernstudium*

externalize [ek'stɜːnəlaɪz] VT externalisieren

externally [ek'stɜːnəlɪ] ADV **a** *apply, use* äußerlich; **zinc helps healing both internally and ~** Zink fördert den innerlichen sowie äußerlichen Heilprozess
b *(= on the outside)* außen; *(of person, appearance)* äußerlich; *(= to the outside)* nach außen; *(= from the outside)* von außen; *(Comm: = outside the firm)* außer Haus; **~ mounted cameras** außen angebrachte Kameras; **~ imposed conditions** von außen auferlegte Bedingungen; **the two models are ~ identical** die beiden Modelle sind äußerlich identisch; **he remained ~ calm** er blieb nach außen hin *or* äußerlich ruhig
c *(Pol: = in foreign policy)* außenpolitisch

external trade N Außenhandel *m*

extinct [ɪk'stɪŋkt] ADJ **a** *(= gone forever) animal, species, tribe, custom, art form, type of person etc* ausgestorben; *(fig) way of life, empire* untergegangen; *language* tot; **that fish has been ~ for thousands of years** dieser Fisch ist schon seit tausenden *or* Tausenden von Jahren ausgestorben; **to be made ~** ausgerottet werden; **to become ~** *(also fig)* aussterben; **is the English gentleman ~?** gibt es den englischen Gentleman überhaupt noch? **b** *volcano* erloschen

extinction [ɪk'stɪŋkʃən] N *(of race, family, animal, species, tribe)* Aussterben *nt*; *(= annihilation)* Ausrottung *f*; **threatened with** *or* **faced with** *or* **in danger of ~** vom Aussterben bedroht; **this animal was hunted to ~** diese Tierart wurde durch Jagen ausgerottet

extinguish [ɪk'stɪŋgwɪʃ] VT *fire, candle* (aus)löschen; *cigarette* ausmachen; *light* löschen; *hopes, passion* zerstören; *debt* tilgen

extinguisher [ɪk'stɪŋgwɪʃə'] N Feuerlöscher *m*, Löschgerät *nt*

extirpate ['ekstɜːpeɪt] VT *(lit, fig)* (mit der Wurzel) ausrotten, (gänzlich) beseitigen

extirpation [ˌekstə'peɪʃən] N *(lit, fig)* Ausrottung *f*

extol [ɪk'stəʊl] VT preisen, rühmen

extort [ɪk'stɔːt] VT *money* erpressen (*from* von); *confession* erzwingen (*from* von); *secret* abpressen (*from +dat*)

extortion [ɪk'stɔːʃən] N *(of money)* Erpressung *f*; *(of signature)* Erzwingung *f*; **this is sheer ~!** *(inf)* das ist ja Wucher!

extortionate [ɪk'stɔːʃənɪt] ADJ *charge, rate, sum, amount* horrend; *tax, rent, bill* maßlos hoch; **~ prices** Wucherpreise *pl*, horrende *or* unverschämte *or* astronomische *(inf)* Preise *pl*; **~ rates of interest** Wucherzinsen *pl*; **I was charged an ~ amount for a ticket** ich musste einen Wucherpreis für eine Karte bezahlen

extortioner [ɪk'stɔːʃənə'] N Erpresser(in) *m(f)*; *(charging high prices)* Wucherer(in) *m(f)*

extra ['ekstrə] ADJ *(= additional)* zusätzlich; **take an ~ pair of shoes (just in case)** nimm ein zusätzliches Paar Schuhe (als Reserve) mit; **we need an ~ chair** wir brauchen noch einen Stuhl; **I have set an ~ place at table** ich habe noch ein Gedeck aufgelegt; **if you're cold put an ~ pullover on** wenn du frierst, zieh dir noch einen Pullover an; **to work ~ hours** Überstunden machen; **to make an ~ effort** sich besonders anstrengen; **~ police/troops were called in** es wurde Verstärkung gerufen; **to go to ~ expense** sich zusätzlich in Unkosten stürzen; **take ~ care!** sei besonders vorsichtig!; **for ~**

safety für den speziellen *or* besonderen Schutz; **for ~ whiteness** für ein (noch) strahlenderes Weiß; **an ~ £3 a week** £ 3 mehr pro Woche; **send 75p ~ for postage and packing** schicken Sie zusätzlich 75 Pence für Porto und Verpackung; **we make an ~ charge** wir berechnen einen Zuschlag; **there is an ~ charge/no ~ charge for breakfast** das Frühstück wird zusätzlich/nicht zusätzlich berechnet; **ask if there will be any ~ costs** fragen Sie, ob noch zusätzliche Kosten hinzukommen; **available at ~ cost/at no ~ cost** gegen einen Aufpreis/ohne Aufpreis erhältlich; **~ bus** Sonderbus *m*

ADV **a** *(= more money) pay, cost, charge* mehr; **you have to pay ~ for breakfast, breakfast costs ~** das Frühstück wird zusätzlich berechnet; **post and packing ~** zuzüglich Porto und Verpackung; **to charge ~** einen Zuschlag berechnen

b *(= especially)* besonders; **he wanted to do ~ well in the exam** er wollte bei der Prüfung besonders gut abschneiden

N **a** *(= special request)* Sonderwunsch *m*

b extras PL *(= extra expenses)* zusätzliche Kosten *pl*, Nebenkosten *pl*; *(in restaurant)* zusätzliche Beilagen *pl*; *(for machine)* Zubehör *nt*; *(for car)* Extras *pl* → **optional**

c *(Film, Theat)* Statist(in) *m(f)*, Komparse *m*, Komparsin *f*

d *(= remainder)* **what shall we do with the ~?** was sollen wir mit dem Rest machen?

extra- PREF **a** *(= outside)* außer-; **~parliamentary** außerparlamentarisch **b** *(= especially)* besonders, extra; **~dry** *(wine)* herb; *champagne* extra dry; **~large** *(eggs, tomatoes)* besonders *or* extra groß; *T-shirt, underpants* übergroß; **an ~large size** eine Übergröße; **~smart** besonders schick, todschick *(inf)*

extract [ɪk'strækt] VT **a** *(= take out)* herausnehmen; *cork etc* (heraus)ziehen *(from* aus); *juice, minerals, oil, DNA, energy* gewinnen *(from* aus); *tooth* ziehen, extrahieren *(spec)*; *bullet, foreign body* entfernen; **she ~ed herself from his arms** sie befreite sich aus seinen Armen

b *(fig) information, secrets* entlocken *(from +dat)*; *confession, money* herausholen *(from* aus); *permission, promise, concession* abringen *(from +dat)*, erlangen *(from* von); *the meaning/moral of a book* herausarbeiten *(from* aus); **he is able to ~ himself from difficult situations** er kann sich aus schwierigen Lagen befreien

c *(Math) square root* ziehen

d *quotation, passage* herausziehen, exzerpieren *(geh)*

N ['ekstrækt] **a** *(from book etc)* Auszug *m*, Exzerpt *nt*

b *(Med, Cook)* Extrakt *m*

extraction [ɪk'strækʃən] N **a** *(= process of extracting)* Herausnehmen *nt*; *(of cork etc)* (Heraus)ziehen *nt*; *(of juice, minerals, oil, DNA, energy)* Gewinnung *f*; *(of bullet, foreign body)* Entfernung *f*; *(of information, secrets)* Entlocken *nt*; *(of confession, money)* Herausholen *nt*; *(of permission, promise, concession)* Abringen *nt*, Erlangen *nt*

b *(Dentistry: = act of extracting)* (Zahn)ziehen *nt*, Extraktion *f (spec)*; **he had to have an ~** ihm musste ein Zahn gezogen werden **c** *(= descent)* Herkunft *f*, Abstammung *f*; **of Spanish ~** spanischer Herkunft *or* Abstammung

extractor [ɪk'stræktəʳ] N *(for juice)* Presse *f*, Entsafter *m*; *(in kitchen)* Dunstabzug *m*; *(for dust)* Sauganlage *f*; *(of gun)* Auszieher *m*

extractor fan N Sauglüfter *m*

extractor hood N Dunstabzugshaube *f*

extracurricular ['ekstrəkə'rɪkjʊləʳ] ADJ außerhalb des Stundenplans; **~ activity** *(esp hum: in spare time)* Freizeitaktivität *f (hum)*

extraditable ['ekstrədaɪtəbl] ADJ *offence* auslieferungsfähig; *person* auszuliefern *pred*, auszuliefernd *attr*

extradite ['ekstrədaɪt] VT ausliefern

extradition [ˌekstrə'dɪʃən] N Auslieferung *f*

extradition: **extradition order** N *(= request)* Auslieferungsantrag *m*; **extradition treaty** N Auslieferungsvertrag *m*; **extradition warrant** N Auslieferungsantrag *m*

extramarital ['ekstrə'mærɪtl] ADJ außerehelich

extramural ['ekstrə'mjʊərəl] ADJ *(Brit Univ)* **~ department** *selbstständige Abteilung für Teilzeitkurse, die allen zugänglich sind*; **I took an ~ course at the university** ich besuchte einen Teilzeitkurs an der Universität; **~ studies** *Teilzeitstudium außerhalb des normalen Universitätsprogramms*; **~ activity** Zeitvertreib *m* neben dem Studium; *(esp hum: in spare time)* Freizeitaktivität *f (hum)*

extraneous [ɪk'streɪnɪəs] ADJ *(form)* **a** *(= from outside) noise* von außen; *influence* äußere(r, s), extern *(geh)*; **~ matter** *(Tech, Med)* Fremdstoffe *pl*; *(solid)* Fremdkörper *pl* **b** *(= not relevant) matter, material, issue, detail, thought* irrelevant, unwesentlich; **~ matters/issues** Unwesentliches *nt*; **to avoid all ~ issues** alles vermeiden, was nicht zur Sache gehört; **to feel ~** *(person)* sich *(dat)* überflüssig vorkommen; **~ to sth** für etw irrelevant

extraordinaire [eks,trɔːdɪ'nɛəʳ] ADJ unvergleichlich; **George Kuchar, film maker ~** George Kuchar, der unvergleichliche Filmemacher

extraordinarily [ɪk'strɔːdnrɪlɪ] ADV außerordentlich; *(= unusually) high, low, good, difficult, well* ungemein; *(introducing sentence)* erstaunlicherweise

extraordinary [ɪk'strɔːdnrɪ] ADJ **a** *(= exceptional) person, career, quality* außergewöhnlich; *success, courage, skill* außerordentlich; *(= unusual, strange) behaviour, appearance, dress, action, speech* merkwürdig, eigenartig; *tale, adventure* seltsam; *(= amazing) insults, violence* erstaunlich; **there's nothing ~ about that** daran ist nichts Ungewöhnliches; **it's ~ to think that ...** es ist (schon) eigenartig, wenn man denkt, dass ...; **what an ~ thing to say!** wie kann man nur so etwas sagen!; **it's ~ how much he resembles his brother** es ist erstaunlich, wie sehr er seinem Bruder ähnelt

b *(Brit form: = special) measure, party, congress* außerordentlich; **~ meeting** Sondersitzung *f*

extraordinary general meeting N außerordentliche Hauptversammlung

extrapolate [ek'stræpəleɪt] VTI extrapolieren *(from* aus)

extrapolation [ekˌstræpə'leɪʃən] N Extrapolation *f*

extrasensory ['ekstrə'sensərɪ] ADJ außersinnlich; **~ perception** außersinnliche Wahrnehmung

extra-special ['ekstrə'speʃəl] ADJ ganz besondere(r, s); **to take ~ care over sth** sich *(dat)* besonders viel Mühe mit etw geben; **to make something ~ to eat** etwas ganz Besonderes zu essen machen

extraterrestrial ['ekstrətɪ'restrɪəl] ADJ außerirdisch, extraterrestrisch N außerirdisches Lebewesen

extraterritorial ['ekstrəˌterɪ'tɔːrɪəl] ADJ exterritorial

extra time N *(Sport)* Verlängerung *f*; **we had to play ~** der Schiedsrichter ließ nachspielen

extrauterine pregnancy ['ekstrəˌjuːtəraɪn'pregnənsɪ] N *(Med)* Bauchhöhlenschwangerschaft *f*

extravagance [ɪk'strævəgəns] N **a** Luxus *m no pl*; *(= wastefulness)* Verschwendung *f*; **her ~** ihre Verschwendungssucht; **if you can't forgive her little ~s** wenn Sie es ihr nicht verzeihen können, dass sie sich ab und zu einen kleinen Luxus leistet; **the ~ of her tastes** ihr kostspieliger *or* teurer Geschmack; **the ~ of her daily life** ihr luxuriöses Alltagsleben; **a life of such ~** ein derart luxuriöser Lebensstil; **the ~ of a big wedding** der Aufwand einer großen Hochzeitsfeier

b *(of ideas, theories)* Extravaganz *f*, Ausgefallenheit *f*; *(of claim, demand)* Übertriebenheit *f*

c *(= extravagant action or notion)* Extravaganz *f*

extravagant [ɪk'strævəgənt] ADJ **a** *(= wasteful) person* verschwenderisch; *taste, habit* teuer; **to be ~ with electricity** verschwenderisch mit Strom umgehen, Strom verschwenden; **your ~ spending habits** deine Angewohnheit, das Geld mit vollen Händen auszugeben; **cooking a whole chicken may seem ~** es scheint vielleicht übertrieben, ein ganzes Huhn zu kochen; **it isn't really ~ to rent a car** es ist eigentlich kein Luxus, einen Mietwagen zu nehmen; **she judged it unnecessarily ~** sie hielt es für einen überflüssigen Luxus

b *(= lavish) gift, luxury* teuer, extravagant; *price* überhöht; *lifestyle* aufwendig, aufwändig, luxuriös; *party, entertainment* aufwendig, aufwändig; *designs, style, dress* ausgefallen, extravagant

c *(= flamboyant) person* extravagant; *behaviour, gesture, praise, contempt, claim, promise* übertrieben; *(= absurd) idea, theory* abwegig; **to be ~ in one's praise of sb/sth** jdn/etw übertrieben loben; **an obituary ~ in its praise** ein Nachruf voller übertriebener Bewunderung

extravagantly [ɪk'strævəgəntlɪ] ADV **a** *(= lavishly) entertain* aufwendig, aufwändig; *live* luxuriös; **~ expensive** maßlos teuer **b** *(= extremely)* übertrieben; *gifted* überaus; *praise, thank* überschwänglich; **his ~ eccentric behaviour** sein extravagantes *or* übertriebenes Verhalten **c** *(= flamboyantly) dress, behave* extravagant

extravaganza [ɪkˌstrævə'gænzə] N fantastische Dichtung *or (Mus)* Komposition; *(= show)* Ausstattungsstück *nt*

extravehicular [ˌekstrəviː'hɪkjʊləʳ] ADJ *(Space)* außerhalb des Raumfahrzeugs

extravert ['ekstrəˌvɜːt] N, ADJ = **extrovert**

extreme [ɪk'striːm] ADJ **a** *caution, courage, pleasure, kindness, simplicity* äußerste(r, s); *discomfort, sensitivity, concern, joy, danger* größte(r, s); *example, conditions, behaviour, temperatures* extrem; *(Pol) right, left, views* extrem; *measures, method* drastisch; *difficulty, pressure* ungeheuer; *rudeness* maßlos; *poverty* bitterste(r, s); **to proceed with ~ caution** mit äußerster Vorsicht vorgehen; **to suffer ~ discomfort** größte Beschwerden haben; **in ~ old age** in äußerst hohem Alter; **of ~ importance/urgency** äußerst wichtig/dringend; **~ case** Extremfall *m*; **~ left-wing anarchists** linksextremistische Anarchisten; **fascists of the ~ right** extrem rechts stehende Faschisten; **the weather was pretty ~** es herrschten recht extreme Wetterbedingungen; **the ~ unction** *(Rel)* die Letzte Ölung

b *(= furthest) end, tip, edge, north, south* äußerste(r, s); **the room at the ~ end of the corridor** das Zimmer ganz am Ende des Korridors; **at the ~ left of the picture** ganz links im Bild

N Extrem *nt*; **the ~s of happiness and despair** höchstes Glück und tiefste Verzweiflung; **between these two ~s** zwischen diesen beiden Extremen; **~s of temperature** extreme Temperaturen *pl*; **in the ~** im höchsten Grade; **it is bewildering in the ~** es ist höchst *or* im höchsten Grade verwirrend; **to go from one ~ to the other** von einem Extrem ins andere fallen; **to go to ~s** es übertreiben; **I wouldn't go to that ~** so weit würde ich nicht gehen; **to take** *or* **carry sth to ~s** etw bis zum Extrem treiben; **to drive sb to ~s** jdn zum Äußersten treiben

extremely [ɪk'striːmlɪ] ADV äußerst; *important, high, low* extrem; **was it difficult? – ~!** war es schwierig? – sehr!

extreme sport N Extremsport *m*

extremism [ɪk'striːmɪzəm] N Extremismus *m*

extremist [ɪk'striːmɪst] N Extremist(in) *m(f)* ADJ *organization, element, view* extremistisch; *violence* von Extremisten; **~ leader** Extremistenführer(in) *m(f)*; **~ group** Extremistengruppe *f*; **right-wing ~ organisations** rechtsextremistische Organisationen

extremity [ɪk'stremɪtɪ] N **a** *(= furthest point)* äußerstes Ende; **at the northerly ~ of the continent** am nördlichsten Zipfel des Kontinents **b extremities** PL *(= hands and feet)* Extremitäten *pl* **c** *(= extreme degree)* **in the ~ of his despair** in tiefster *or* äußerster Verzweiflung

d *(= state of need, distress)* Not *f*; **he was reduced to the ~ of having to sell his business** er musste zum äußersten Mittel schreiten und sein Geschäft verkaufen
e *(= extreme actions)* **to resort to extremities** zu äußersten *or* extremen Mitteln greifen; **to drive sb to extremities** jdn zum Äußersten treiben

extricable [ɪk'strɪkəbl] ADJ herausziehbar *(from* aus), zu befreien(d) *(from* aus, von)

extricate ['ekstrɪkeɪt] VT befreien; *(fig)* retten; **to ~ oneself from sth** *(lit, fig)* sich aus etw befreien

extrication [ˌekstrɪ'keɪʃən] N *(lit)* Befreiung *f* *(from* aus); *(fig)* Rettung *f*

extrinsic [ek'strɪnsɪk] ADJ äußerlich; *factor, reason* äußere(r, s); *considerations* nicht hereinspielend

extroversion [ˌekstrəʊ'vɜːʃən] N Extravertiertheit *f*

extrovert ['ekstrəʊvɜːt] ADJ extravertiert N extravertierter Mensch, Extravertierte(r) *mf*

extroverted ['ekstrəʊˌvɜːtɪd] ADJ *(esp US)* extravertiert

extrude [ɪk'struːd] VT *sb, sth* ausstoßen; *metal* herauspressen; *plastic* extrudieren VI herausstehen *(from* aus)

extrusion [ɪk'struːʒən] N *(Tech, of metal)* Fließpressen *nt*; *(of plastic)* Extrudieren *nt*

exuberance [ɪg'zuːbərəns] N **a** *(of person)* Überschwänglichkeit *f*; *(of joy, youth, feelings)* Überschwang *m*; *(= joy)* überschwängliche Freude *(at* über *+acc)*; **in his ~** *(= rejoicing)* in seiner überschwänglichen Freude, im Überschwang der Gefühle; **in their youthful ~** *(= high spirits)* in ihrem jugendlichen Überschwang **b** *(= vitality: of prose, style)* Vitalität *f* **c** *(= abundance)* Fülle *f*, Reichtum *m*

exuberant [ɪg'zuːbərənt] ADJ **a** *(= irrepressible, energetic) person, personality* überschwänglich; *esp child* übermütig; *mood* überschäumend; *voice* jubelnd; *style* übersprudelnd; *painting* lebhaft; *film, music, show* mitreißend; **he was/felt ~ (about his success)** er freute sich unbändig (über seinen Erfolg); **they were ~ after their victory** nach ihrem Sieg waren sie in Jubelstimmung; **rugs in ~ colours** *(Brit) or* **colors** *(US)* farbenfrohe Teppiche **b** *growth, foliage, flowers* üppig

exuberantly [ɪg'zjuːbərəntlɪ] ADV überschwänglich; *(esp of child)* übermütig; *grow, decorate*$eyebath üppig; **~ happy** überglücklich

exude [ɪg'zjuːd] VI *(liquid)* austreten *(from* aus); *(blood, pus etc)* abgesondert werden *(from* von) VT **a** *liquid* ausscheiden; *dampness, sap* ausscheiden, ausschwitzen; *smell* ausströmen **b** *(fig: = radiate) confidence, charisma* ausstrahlen; *optimism* verströmen; *enthusiasm* verbreiten; *(pej) charm* triefen vor

exult [ɪg'zʌlt] VI frohlocken; **~ing in his freedom** seine Freiheit genießend

exultant [ɪg'zʌltənt] ADJ *person, tone* jubelnd; *expression, smile, cry* triumphierend; **he was ~** er jubelte, er war in Jubelstimmung; **~ mood** Jubelstimmung *f*; **the mood was less than ~** es herrschte nicht gerade Jubelstimmung

exultantly [ɪg'zʌltəntlɪ] ADV jubelnd; *laugh* triumphierend

exultation [ˌegzʌl'teɪʃən] N Jubel *m*; **sing in ~** *(Rel)* jauchzet und frohlocket; **their ~ at the prospect** ihr Jubel über die Aussicht

ex works ADV *(Brit)* ab Werk

ex-works [eks'wɜːks] ADJ *(Brit)* **~ prices** Preise *pl* ab Werk

eye [aɪ] N **a** *(of human, animal, electronic)* Auge *nt*; **with tears in her ~s** mit Tränen in den Augen; **a gleam in sb's ~** ein Glitzern in jds Augen *(dat)*; **with one's ~s closed/open** *(lit, fig)* mit geschlossenen/offenen Augen; **an ~ for an ~** Auge um Auge; **~s right!** *(Mil)* (die) Augen rechts!; **~s front!** *(Mil)* Augen geradeaus!; **as far as the ~ can see** so weit das Auge reicht; **to be all ~s** große Augen machen; **that's one in the ~ for him** *(inf)* da hat er eins aufs Dach gekriegt *(inf)*; **to cast** *or* **run one's ~ over sth** etw überfliegen; **to cast one's ~s round a room** seine Blicke durch ein Zimmer wandern *or* schweifen lassen; **his ~ fell on a small door** sein Blick fiel auf eine kleine Tür; **to rest one's ~ on sth** seine Augen *or* den Blick auf etw *(dat)* ruhen lassen; **to look sb (straight) in the ~** jdm in die Augen sehen; **to set** *or* **clap** *(inf)* **~s on sb/sth** jdn/etw zu Gesicht bekommen; **a strange sight met our ~s** ein seltsamer Anblick bot sich uns; **(why don't you) use your ~s!** hast du keine Augen im Kopf?; **with one's own ~s** mit eigenen Augen; **in front of** *or* **before my very ~s** (direkt) vor meinen Augen; **it was there all the time right in front of my ~s** es lag schon die ganze Zeit da, direkt vor meiner Nase; **under the watchful ~ of the guard/their mother** unter der Aufsicht des Wächters/ihrer Mutter; **your ~s are bigger than your stomach** deine Augen sind größer als dein Magen; **you need ~s in the back of your head** da muss man hinten und vorne Augen haben; **I don't have ~s in the back of my head** ich hab doch hinten keine Augen; **to keep an ~ on sb/sth** *(= look after)* auf jdn/etw aufpassen; **the police are keeping an ~ on him** *(= have him under surveillance)* die Polizei beobachtet ihn; **to keep one's ~ on the ball/main objective** sich auf den Ball/die Hauptsache konzentrieren; **to take one's ~s off sb/sth** die Augen *or* den Blick von jdm/etw abwenden; **don't take your ~ off the ball** konzentrier dich auf den Ball; **don't take your ~s off the magician's left hand** lassen Sie die linke Hand des Zauberkünstlers nicht aus den Augen; **to have one's ~s fixed on sth** etw nicht aus den Augen lassen; **to keep one's ~s open** *or* **peeled** *(inf) or* **skinned** *(inf)* die Augen offen halten; **to keep an ~ open** *or* **out for sth** nach etw Ausschau halten; **to keep a watchful ~ on the situation** die Sache im Auge behalten; **to keep an ~ on expenditure** auf die Ausgaben achten *or* aufpassen; **to open sb's ~s to sb/sth** jdm die Augen über jdn/etw öffnen; **to close** *or* **shut one's ~s to sth** die Augen vor etw *(dat)* verschließen; **to see ~ to ~ with sb** mit jdm einer Meinung sein; **to make ~s at sb** jdm schöne Augen machen; **to catch sb's ~** jds Aufmerksamkeit erregen; **the dress caught my ~** das Kleid fiel *or* stach mir ins Auge; **she would buy anything that caught her ~** sie kaufte alles, was ihr ins Auge fiel; **he was a monster in their ~s** in ihren Augen war er ein Scheusal; **in the ~s of the law** in den Augen des Gesetzes; **through sb's ~s** durch *or* mit jds Augen; **to look at a question through the ~s of an economist** eine Frage mit den Augen *or* aus der Sicht eines Volkswirts betrachten; **with a critical/an uneasy ~** mit kritischem/besorgtem Blick; **with an ~ to the future** im Hinblick auf die Zukunft; **with an ~ to buying sth** in der Absicht, etw zu kaufen; **to have an ~ to** *or* **for the main chance** jede Gelegenheit ausnutzen; **I've got my ~ on you** ich beobachte dich genau; **to have one's ~ on sth** *(= want)* auf etw *(acc)* ein Auge geworfen haben; **the ~s of the world** *or* **all ~s are on the police/the conference** die Polizei/die Konferenz steht im Blickpunkt der Öffentlichkeit; **I only have ~s for you** ich habe nur Augen für dich; **to have a keen ~ for sth** ein scharfes Auge für etw haben, einen scharfen Blick für etw haben; **she has an ~ for a bargain** sie hat einen Blick *or* ein Auge für günstige Käufe; **he has no ~ for beauty** ihm fehlt der Blick für Schönheit; **he has a good ~ for form** er hat ein Auge für Form; **you need an ~ for detail** man muss einen Blick fürs Detail haben; **to get one's ~ in** *(shooting)* sich einschießen; *(playing tennis etc)* sich einspielen; **to be up to one's ~s in work** *(Brit inf)* in Arbeit ersticken *(inf)*; **to be up to one's ~s in debt** *(Brit inf)* bis über beide Ohren verschuldet sein *(inf)*; **he's in it up to the ~s** *(inf)* er steckt bis zum Hals drin *(inf)*; **my ~!** *(inf)* Unsinn!; **dry your ~s** *(Brit inf)* hör auf rumzujammern *(inf)*
b *(of needle)* Öhr *nt*; *(of potato, on peacock's tail)* Auge *nt*; *(of hurricane)* Auge *nt*; **in the ~ of the wind** *(Naut)* in *or* gegen den Wind; **the minister in the ~ of the storm** *(fig)* der Minister im Mittelpunkt der Kontroverse → **hook and eye**
VT anstarren; **to ~ sb up and down** jdn von oben bis unten mustern

► **eye up** VT *sep girls, boys* mustern, begutachten

eye: **eye appeal** N attraktive Gestaltung, optische Wirkung; **eyeball** N Augapfel *m*; **to be ~ to ~** sich Auge in Auge gegenüberstehen; **drugged up to the ~s** *(esp Brit inf)* total zugedröhnt *(inf)* VT *(inf)* aggressiv anstarren; **eyebath** N Augenbad *nt*; *(= container)* Augenbadewanne *f*; **eyebrow** N Augenbraue *f*; **to raise one's ~s** die Augenbrauen hochziehen; *(fig)* die Stirn runzeln *(at sth* über etw *acc)*; **he never raised an ~** er hat sich nicht einmal gewundert; **that will raise a few ~s, there will be a few raised ~s (at that)** da werden sich einige wundern; **eyebrow pencil** N Augenbrauenstift *m*; **eye booger** ['aɪbuːgəʳ] N *(US sl)* **you've got some ~s** du hast noch Schlaf in den Augen; **eye candy** N *(inf)* Augenschmaus *m*, was fürs Auge *(inf)*; **that's just ~** *(images, graphics etc)* das hat keinen Tiefgang; **eye-catcher** N *(thing)* Blickfang *m*; **she's quite an ~** sie zieht alle Blicke auf sich; **eye-catching** ADJ auffallend; *publicity, poster* auffällig, ins Auge springend; **that's very ~** das fällt *or* springt wirklich ins Auge; **eye contact** N Blickkontakt *m*; **to make/avoid ~ with sb** Blickkontakt mit jdm aufnehmen/vermeiden; **eyecup** N *(US)* Augenbadewanne *f*

-eyed [-aɪd] ADJ *suf* -äugig; **green-eyed** grünäugig; **sad-eyed** mit traurigen Augen

eyedrops ['aɪdrɒps] PL Augentropfen *pl*

eyeful ['aɪfʊl] N **he got an ~ of soda water** er bekam Selterswasser ins Auge; **she's quite an ~** *(inf)* sie hat allerhand zu bieten *(inf)*; **I opened the bathroom door and got quite an ~** ich öffnete die Badezimmertür und sah allerhand *(inf)*

eye: **eyeglass** N *(old)* Augenglas *nt (old)*; **eyeglasses** PL *(US: = spectacles)* Brille *f*; **eye gook** ['aɪgʊk] N *(US sl)* **you've got some ~** du hast noch Schlaf in den Augen*nt (Tech)* kleine, runde Öffnung; **eyehole** N Guckloch *nt*; *(Tech)* kleine, runde Öffnung; **eyelash** N Augenwimper *f*; **~ curler** Wimpernzange *f*; **eyelet** ['aɪlɪt] N Öse *f*; **eyelevel** ADJ *attr grill* in Augenhöhe; **eyelid** N Augenlid *nt*; **eye lift** N Augenstraffung *f*; **eyeliner** ['aɪlaɪnəʳ] N Eyeliner *m*; **eye-minded** ADJ visuell, *vorwiegend mit Gesichtssinn begabt*; **eye-opener** N **a that was a real ~ to me** das hat mir die Augen geöffnet **b** *(US inf: = drink)* (alkoholischer) Muntermacher; **eye patch** N Augenklappe *f*; **eyepiece** N Okular *nt*; **eyeshade** N Augenblende *f*, Schild *m*; **eye shadow** N Lidschatten *m*; **eyeshot** N Sicht- *or* Sehweite *f*; **within/out of ~** in/außer Sichtweite; **we are out of his ~** er kann uns nicht mehr sehen; **eyesight** N Sehkraft *f*, Sehvermögen *nt*; **to have good/poor ~** gute/schlechte Augen haben; **to lose one's ~** das Augenlicht verlieren *(geh)*, erblinden; **his ~ is failing** seine Augen lassen nach, sein Sehvermögen lässt nach; **eye socket** N *(Anat)* Augenhöhle *f*; **eyesore** N Schandfleck *m*; **this settee is a real ~** dieses Sofa sieht fürchterlich aus; **eyestrain** N Überanstrengung *f or* Ermüdung *f* der Augen; **eye test** N Augentest *m or* -untersuchung *f*

Eyetie ['aɪtaɪ] N *(Brit pej sl)* Spag(h)ettifresser(in) *m(f) (pej inf)*, Itaker *m (pej inf)*

eye: **eyetooth** N Eckzahn *m*, Augenzahn *m*; **I'd give my eyeteeth for that** darum würde ich alles geben; **eyewash** N *(Med)* Augenwasser *or* -bad *nt*; *(fig inf)* Gewäsch *nt (inf)*; *(= deception)* Augenwischerei *f*; **eyewater** N *(Physiol)* Augenflüssigkeit *f*; **eyewitness** N Augenzeuge *m*/-zeugin *f*

eyrie ['ɪərɪ] N Horst *m*

Ezekiel [ɪ'ziːkɪəl] N *(Bibl)* Hesekiel *m*, Ezechiel *m*

e-zine ['iːziːn] N *(Comput)* Onlinemagazin *nt*, Internetmagazin *nt*

F

F, f [ef] N F *nt*, f *nt*; **F sharp** Fis *nt*, fis *nt*; **F flat** Fes *nt*, fes *nt* → **natural**

F *abbr of* **Fahrenheit** F

f **a** *abbr of* **foot, feet** **b** *abbr of* **feminine** f **c** *abbr of* **female** *(in Internet chat etc)* Girl *nt*

FA *abbr of* **Football Association**

fa [fɑː] N *(Mus)* Fa *nt*

fab [fæb] ADJ *(dated inf) abbr of* **fabulous** toll *(inf)*, dufte *(dated inf)*

fable ['feɪbl] N Fabel *f*; *(= legend, body of legend)* Sage *f*; *(fig: = lie)* Märchen *nt*; **is it fact or ~?** ist es wahr oder erfunden?

fabled ['feɪbld] ADJ sagenhaft; **Cleopatra, ~ for her beauty** Kleopatra, berühmt für ihre Schönheit

fabric ['fæbrɪk] N **a** *(Tex)* Stoff *m* **b** *(= basic structure: of building)* Bausubstanz *f* **c** *(fig: of society etc)* Gefüge *nt*, Struktur *f*

fabricate ['fæbrɪkeɪt] VT **a** *(= invent) story* erfinden, ersinnen *(geh)*; *quotation* erfinden; *evidence, confession* fälschen **b** *(= manufacture)* herstellen, fabrizieren

fabrication [ˌfæbrɪ'keɪʃən] N **a** *(= act of inventing)* Erfindung *f*; *(of evidence, confession)* Fälschung *f*; *(= story invented)* Erfindung *f*, Lügenmärchen *nt*; **it's (a) pure ~** das ist ein reines Märchen *or* (eine) reine Erfindung **b** *(= manufacture)* Herstellung *f*, Fabrikation *f*

Fabrikoid® ['fæbrɪkɔɪd] N *(US)* Kunstleder *nt*, Skai® *nt*

fabulist ['fæbjʊlɪst] N *(Liter: = writer of fables)* Fabeldichter(in) *m(f)*; *(= writer of fantastical literature)* Fabulant(in) *m(f)*; *(fig: = liar)* Fabulierer(in) *m(f)*, Fabulant(in) *m(f)*

fabulous ['fæbjʊləs] ADJ sagenhaft *(inf)*; *(inf: = wonderful also)* toll *(inf)*, fabelhaft

fabulously ['fæbjʊləslɪ] ADV *wealthy, expensive* sagenhaft *(inf)*; *(inf: = wonderfully)* fabelhaft, fantastisch *(inf)*; **~ beautiful** hinreißend schön; **you can eat ~ well there** man kann dort fantastisch *(inf) or* fabelhaft essen

façade [fə'sɑːd] N *(lit, fig)* Fassade *f*

face [feɪs] **N** **a** Gesicht *nt*; **to go red in the ~** rot anlaufen; **I don't want to see your ~ here again** ich möchte Sie hier nie wieder sehen; **we were standing ~ to ~** wir standen einander Auge in Auge *or* von Angesicht zu Angesicht *(geh)* gegenüber; **next time I see him ~ to ~** das nächste Mal, wenn ich ihm begegne; **to bring sb ~ to ~ with sb/sth** jdn mit jdm/etw konfrontieren; **to bring two people ~ to ~** zwei Leute einander gegenüberstellen *or* miteinander konfrontieren; **to come ~ to ~ with sb** jdn treffen; **to come ~ to ~ with sth** einer Sache *(dat)* ins Auge sehen; **he told him so to his ~** er sagte ihm das (offen) ins Gesicht; **he shut the door in my ~** er schlug mir die Tür vor der Nase zu; **he laughed in my ~** er lachte mir ins Gesicht; **the plan blew up in his ~** der Plan ging ins Auge; **to look sb in the ~** jdn ansehen; **to be able to look sb in the ~** jdm in die Augen sehen können; **to throw sth back in sb's ~** jdm etw wieder vorhalten; **get outta my ~!** *(US inf)* lass mich in Ruhe!; **in the ~ of great difficulties/much opposition** *etc* angesichts *or (= despite)* trotz größter Schwierigkeiten/starker Opposition *etc*; **courage in the ~ of the enemy** Tapferkeit vor dem Feind; **to be off** *or* **out of one's ~** *(Brit inf: = drunk, on drugs)* total zu sein *(inf)* → **flat**[1]

b *(= expression)* Gesicht(sausdruck *m*) *nt*; **to make** *or* **pull a ~** das Gesicht verziehen; **to make** *or* **pull ~s/a funny ~** Gesichter *or* Grimassen/eine Grimasse machen *or* schneiden *(at sb* jdm); **to put a good ~ on it** gute Miene zum bösen Spiel machen; **to put a brave ~ on it** sich *(dat)* nichts anmerken lassen; *(= do sth one dislikes)* (wohl oder übel) in den sauren Apfel beißen; **he has set his ~ against that** er stemmt sich dagegen

c *(= prestige)* **loss of ~** Gesichtsverlust *m*; **to save (one's) ~** das Gesicht wahren; **to lose ~** das Gesicht verlieren

d *(of clock)* Zifferblatt *nt*; *(= rock face)* (Steil)wand *f*; *(= coalface)* Streb *m*; *(= typeface)* Schriftart *f*; *(of playing card)* Bildseite *f*; *(of coin)* Vorderseite *f*; *(of house)* Fassade *f*; **to put sth ~ up(-wards)/down(wards)** etw mit der Vorderseite nach oben/unten legen; **to be ~ up(wards)/down(wards)** *(person)* mit dem Gesicht nach oben/unten liegen; *(thing)* mit der Vorderseite nach oben/unten liegen; *(book)* mit der aufgeschlagenen Seite nach oben/unten liegen; **to work at the (coal) ~** vor Ort arbeiten; **to change the ~ of the world** die Welt völlig verändern; **the changing ~ of politics** das sich wandelnde Gesicht der Politik; **the unacceptable ~ of capitalism** die unannehmbare Seite des Kapitalismus; **he/it vanished off the ~ of the earth** *(inf)* er/es war wie vom Erdboden verschwunden; **I'm the luckiest person on the ~ of the earth** *(inf)* ich bin der glücklichste Mensch auf der Welt; **on the ~ of it** so, wie es aussieht

e *(inf: = effrontery)* **to have the ~ to do sth** die Stirn haben, etw zu tun

VT **a** *(= be opposite, have one's face towards)* gegenüber sein *(+dat)*, gegenüberstehen/-liegen *etc (+dat)*; *(window, door) north, south* gehen nach; *street, garden etc* liegen zu; *(building, room) north, south* liegen nach; *park, street* liegen zu; **to ~ the wall/light** zur Wand gekehrt/dem Licht zugekehrt sein; *(person)* mit dem Gesicht zur Wand/zum Licht stehen/sitzen *etc*; **sit down and ~ the front!** setz dich und sieh nach vorn!; **~ this way!** bitte sehen Sie hierher!; **he was facing me at dinner** er saß mir beim Essen gegenüber; **the picture/wall facing you** das Bild/die Wand Ihnen gegenüber; **facing one another** einander gegenüber; **to sit facing the front of the bus** in Fahrtrichtung sitzen

b *(fig) possibility, prospect* rechnen müssen mit; **to ~ death** dem Tod ins Auge sehen; **to ~ trial** vor Gericht gestellt werden; **to ~ financial ruin** vor dem finanziellen Ruin stehen; **to be ~d with sth** sich einer Sache *(dat)* gegenübersehen; **the problem facing us** das Problem, dem wir gegenüberstehen *or* mit dem wir konfrontiert sind; **you'll ~ a lot of criticism if you do that** Sie setzen sich großer Kritik aus, wenn Sie das tun; **to be ~d with a bill for £100** eine Rechnung über £ 100 präsentiert bekommen; **he is facing a charge of murder** er steht unter Mordanklage, er ist wegen Mordes angeklagt; **he ~s life in prison if convicted** wenn er für schuldig befunden wird, muss er mit lebenslänglich rechnen

c *(= meet confidently) situation, danger, criticism* sich stellen *(+dat)*; *person, enemy* gegenübertreten *(+dat)*; **he ~d defeat bravely** er hat sich tapfer mit der Niederlage abgefunden; **to ~ (the) facts** den Tatsachen ins Auge blicken *or* sehen; **let's ~ it** machen wir uns doch nichts vor; **you'd better ~ it, you're not going to get the job** du musst dich wohl damit abfinden, dass du die Stelle nicht bekommst

d *(inf: = put up with, bear)* verkraften *(inf)*; *another drink, cake etc* runterkriegen *(inf)*; **I can't ~ another of these arguments** ich halte noch so einen Streit einfach nicht aus; **I can't ~ seeing anyone** ich kann einfach niemanden sehen; **I can't ~ it** *(inf)* ich bringe es einfach nicht über mich

e *building, wall* verblenden, verkleiden; *(Sew) garment* (mit Besatz) verstürzen

f *(Cards)* aufdecken

g *stone* glätten, (plan) schleifen

VI *(house, room)* liegen *(towards park* dem Park zu, *onto road* zur Straße, *away from road* nicht zur Straße); *(window)* gehen *(onto, towards* auf *+acc*, zu, *away from* nicht auf *+acc*); **he was sitting facing away from me** er saß mit dem Rücken zu mir; **they were all facing toward(s) the window** sie saßen alle mit dem Gesicht zum Fenster (hin); **the house ~s south/toward(s) the sea** das Haus liegt nach Süden/zum Meer hin; **in which direction was he facing?** in welche Richtung stand er?; **you've parked facing in the wrong direction** Sie haben in der falschen Richtung geparkt; **the side of the house that ~s onto the road** die der Straße zugekehrte Seite des Hauses; **why was the house built facing away from the park?** warum wurde das Haus nicht mit Blick auf den Park gebaut?; **right ~!** *(Mil)* rechts um!

▶ **face about** VI *(US Mil)* kehrtmachen

▶ **face out** VT *sep* durchstehen

▶ **face up to** VI *+prep obj fact, truth* ins Gesicht sehen *(+dat)*; *danger* ins Auge sehen *or* blicken *(+dat)*; *possibility* sich abfinden mit; *reality, problems* sich auseinandersetzen mit; *responsibility* auf sich *(acc)* nehmen; **he won't face up to the fact that …** er will es nicht wahrhaben, dass …

face: **face card** N Bildkarte *f*; **face cloth** N Waschlappen *m*; **face cream** N Gesichtscreme *f*; **face flannel** N *(Brit)* Waschlappen *m*; **face frame** N *(US inf: = hairstyle) Haarschnitt, der das Gesicht einrahmt*; **face guard** N Schutzmaske *f*; **faceless** ADJ *drawing* gesichtslos; *(fig)* anonym; **face-lift** N *(lit)* Gesichts(haut)straffung *f*, Facelift(ing) *nt*; *(fig, for car, building etc)* Verschönerung *f*; **to have a ~** sich *(dat)* das Gesicht liften *or* straffen lassen; *(fig)* ein neues Aussehen bekommen; **to give the house a ~** das Haus renovieren, das Haus einer Verschönerungsaktion unterziehen; **face mask** N **a** *(of diver etc)* (Gesichts)maske *f* **b** *(Cosmetics)* Gesichtsmaske *f or* -packung *f*; **face-off** N **a** *(= confrontation)* Konfrontation *f* **b** *(Ice hockey)* Bully *nt*; **face pack** N Gesichtspackung *f*; **face paints** PL Gesichtsfarbe *f*; **face powder** N Gesichtspuder *m*

facer ['feɪsəʳ] N *(Brit inf: = difficulty)* harte Nuss *(inf)*

face: **face-saver** N Ausrede *f* um das Gesicht zu wahren; **face-saving** ADJ **a ~ measure/solu-**

tion/tactic eine Maßnahme/Lösung/Taktik, die dazu dient, das Gesicht zu wahren

facet ['fæsɪt] N *(lit)* Facette *f*; *(fig)* Seite *f*, Aspekt *m*

faceted ['fæsɪtɪd] ADJ facettiert, fassettiert

face time N *(US)* Zeit *f* für ein persönliches Gespräch

faceting ['fæsɪtɪŋ] N *(Miner)* Facettenschliff *m*, Fassettenschliff *m*

facetious [fə'siːʃəs] ADJ *remark, speech, tone* witzelnd, spöttisch, mokant; **to be ~ (about sth)** (über etw *(acc)*) Witze machen, sich (über etw *(acc)*) mokieren; **~ humour** Blödeleien *pl*; **if satire is merely ~** wenn Satire zur Blödelei wird; **I was just being ~** das war doch nur ein Witz *or* so eine Blödelei *(inf)*

facetiously [fə'siːʃəslɪ] ADV witzelnd; *(= mockingly)* spöttisch

face: **face tissue** N Kosmetiktuch *nt*; **face-to-face** ADJ persönlich; *confrontation, contact* direkt; **face value** N *(Fin)* Nennwert *m*, Nominalwert *m*; **to take sth at (its) ~** *(fig)* etw für bare Münze nehmen; **to take sb at ~** jdm unbesehen glauben; **face worker** N *(Min)* Hauer *m*

facial ['feɪʃəl] **ADJ** Gesichts-; **~ hair** Gesichtsbehaarung *f*; **~ expression** Gesichtsausdruck *m*; **~ features** Gesichtszüge *pl*; **~ injuries** Gesichtsverletzungen *pl*, Verletzungen *pl* im Gesicht **N** kosmetische Gesichtsbehandlung; **to have a ~** zur Gesichtsbehandlung gehen

facially ['feɪʃəlɪ] ADV *alike* vom Gesicht her; **to be ~ disfigured** entstellte Gesichtszüge haben; **~ disfigured people** Menschen mit entstellten Gesichtszügen; **~, she has changed little** ihr Gesicht hat sich kaum verändert

facile ['fæsaɪl] ADJ *(pej) person, mind, work of art* oberflächlich; *optimism* blind; *task* simpel; *question* vordergründig; *comparison, answer* billig; *solution* billig, simpel; *remark* nichtssagend; *style* flüssig; **it is ~ to suggest that...** es lässt sich natürlich leicht sagen, dass ...

facilitate [fə'sɪlɪteɪt] VT erleichtern; *(= make possible)* ermöglichen; **it would ~ matters** es würde die Sache erleichtern

facilitator [fə'sɪlɪteɪtəʳ] N Vermittler(in) *m(f)*; **the role of teachers as ~s** die Vermittlerrolle von Lehrern

facility [fə'sɪlɪtɪ] N **a** Einrichtung *f*; **to give sb every ~** jdm jede Möglichkeit bieten; **you will have every ~ for study** es wird Ihnen alles zur Verfügung stehen, was Sie zum Studium brauchen; **we have no ~** *or* **facilities for disposing of toxic waste** wir haben keine Möglichkeit zur Beseitigung von Giftmüll; **a computer with the ~ to reproduce text** ein Computer, der Text wiedergeben kann; **a large hotel with all facilities** ein großes Hotel mit allem Komfort; **facilities for the disabled** Einrichtungen *pl* für Behinderte; **cooking facilities** Kochgelegenheit *f*; **toilet facilities** Toiletten *pl* **b** *no pl (= ease)* Leichtigkeit *f*; *(= dexterity)* Gewandtheit *f*; **he has a great ~ for languages/maths** Sprachen fallen/Mathematik fällt ihm sehr leicht

facing ['feɪsɪŋ] **N a** *(on wall)* Verblendung *f*, Verkleidung *f* **b** *(Sew)* Besatz *m* **ADJ on the ~ page** auf der gegenüberliegenden Seite

facsimile [fæk'sɪmɪlɪ] N Faksimile *nt*; *(Telec)* Faksimileübertragung *f*

fact [fækt] ✪ 15.1, 26 N **a** Tatsache *f*, Faktum *nt (geh)*; *(historical, geographical etc)* Faktum *nt*; **hard ~s** nackte Tatsachen *pl*; **the true ~s** der wahre Sachverhalt; **~s and figures** Fakten und Zahlen; **he accepts the ~ that I don't eat meat** er akzeptiert es, dass ich kein Fleisch esse; **in view of the ~ that ...** angesichts der Tatsache, dass ...; **despite the ~ that ...** der Tatsache zum Trotz, dass ...; **to know for a ~ that** (es) ganz genau *or* sicher wissen, dass; **the ~ (of the matter) is that ...** die Sache ist die, dass ...; **the ~ remains that ...** es lässt sich nicht bestreiten, dass ...; **to stick to the ~s** bei den Tatsachen bleiben, sich an die Tatsachen *or* Fakten halten; **to look (the) ~s in the face** der Wirklichkeit *or* den Tatsachen *(dat)* ins Auge sehen; **the ~s of the case** *(Jur)* der Tatbestand, der Sachverhalt; **... and that's a ~** ... darüber besteht kein Zweifel!, ... Tatsache! *(inf)*; **is that a ~?** tatsächlich?, Tatsache? *(inf)* → **face VT c**
b *no pl (= reality)* Wirklichkeit *f*, Realität *f*; **~ and fiction** Dichtung und Wahrheit; **based/founded on ~** auf Tatsachen beruhend
c in (point of) ~, in actual ~ eigentlich; *(= in reality)* tatsächlich, in Wirklichkeit; *(= after all)* (dann) doch; *(to make previous statement more precise)* nämlich; **in ~, as a matter of ~** eigentlich; *(to intensify previous statement)* sogar; **I don't suppose you know him? – in (actual) ~** *or* **as a matter of ~ I do** Sie kennen ihn nicht zufällig? – doch, eigentlich schon; **do you know him? – in (actual) ~** *or* **as a matter of ~ I do** kennen Sie ihn? – jawohl; **it sounds simple, but in (actual) ~** *or* **in point of ~ it's very difficult** es hört sich so einfach an, aber in Wirklichkeit ist es sehr schwer; **I'd meant to do some work but in ~ I was too tired** ich wollte eigentlich etwas arbeiten, war aber dann zu müde; **I thought I could give you a lift, but in (actual) ~ I won't be going** ich dachte, ich könnte dich mitnehmen, aber ich gehe doch nicht; **I'm going soon, in (actual) ~ tomorrow** ich reise bald ab, nämlich morgen; **it won't be easy, in ~** *or* **as a matter of ~ it'll be very difficult** es wird nicht einfach sein, es wird sogar sehr schwierig sein; **does it hurt? – as a matter of ~ it's very painful** tuts weh? – ja, und sogar ganz schön; **I bet you haven't done that! – as a matter of ~ I have!** du hast das bestimmt nicht gemacht! – und ob, aber ja doch!; **as a matter of ~ we were just talking about you** wir haben (nämlich) eben von Ihnen geredet; **do you know Sir Charles? – as a matter of ~ he's my uncle/yes, in ~ he's my uncle** kennen Sie Sir Charles? – ja, und er ist sogar/ja, er ist nämlich mein Onkel
d *(Jur)* **to be an accessory before/after the ~** sich der Beihilfe/Begünstigung schuldig machen

fact-based ['fæktbeɪst] ADJ auf Tatsachen beruhend

fact-finding ['fæktfaɪndɪŋ] ADJ **~ mission** Erkundungsmission *f*; **~ tour** Informations- *or* Erkundungsreise *f*; **~ team** Erkundungsgruppe *f*

faction ['fækʃən] N **a** *(= group)* (Partei)gruppe *f*; *(Pol)* Fraktion *f*; *(= splinter group)* Splittergruppe *f* **b** *no pl (= strife)* interne Unstimmigkeiten *pl*

factionalism ['fækʃənlɪzəm] N interne Streitigkeiten *pl or* Querelen *pl*

factious ['fækʃəs] ADJ *(liter)* streitsüchtig, händelsüchtig; *quarrelling* kleinlich, engherzig

factitious [fæk'tɪʃəs] ADJ künstlich, unecht; *demand for goods* hochgespielt

fact of life N **a** *(= reality)* harte Tatsache; **that's just a ~** so ist es nun mal im Leben **b facts of life** PL *(sexual)* Aufklärung *f*; **to tell** *or* **teach sb the facts of life** jdn aufklären; **to know the facts of life** aufgeklärt sein

factor ['fæktəʳ] ✪ 26.1 **N a** Faktor *m*; **the scandal was a contributing ~ in his defeat** der Skandal trug zu seiner Niederlage bei; **to be a ~ in determining/deciding sth** etw mitbestimmen/mitentscheiden **b** *(of sun cream)* Faktor *m*; **I use ~ 10** ich verwende (Lichtschutz)faktor 10 **c** *(= agent)* Makler(in) *m(f)* **d** *(Comm, for debts)* Kommissionär(in) *m(f)* **e** *(Math)* Faktor *m*; **by a ~ of two/three** *etc* mit einem Faktor von zwei/drei *etc* **f** *(Biol)* Erbfaktor *m* **VI** *(Comm)* Schulden aufkaufen

▶ **factor in** VT SEP *(esp US)* berücksichtigen; **to factor sth into sth** etw in etw *(acc)* mit einbeziehen

factorize ['fæktəraɪz] VT in Faktoren zerlegen, faktorisieren

factory ['fæktərɪ] N Fabrik *f*; *(plant also)* Werk *nt*

factory: **Factory Act** N Arbeitsschutzgesetz *nt*; **factory farm** N industrieller Viehzuchtbetrieb, Großmästerei *f*; **factory farming** N industriell betriebene Viehzucht; **factory hand** N Fabrikarbeiter(in) *m(f)*; **factory inspector** N Gewerbeaufsichtsbeamte(r) *m*, Gewerbeaufsichtsbeamtin *f*; **factory outlet (store)** N *(esp US)* Factoryoutlet-Laden *m*, Fabrikverkauf *m*; **factory price** N Fabrikpreis *m*; **factory ship** N Fabrikschiff *nt*; **factory shop** N *(Brit)* Factoryoutlet-Laden *m*, Fabrikverkauf *m*; **factory worker** N Fabrikarbeiter(in) *m(f)*

factotum [fæk'təʊtəm] N Faktotum *nt*

factsheet ['fæktʃiːt] N Informationsblatt *nt*

factual ['fæktjʊəl] ADJ *evidence* auf Tatsachen beruhend; *account, speech* sachlich; **~ information** Sachinformationen *pl*; *(= facts)* Fakten *pl*; **~ error** Sachfehler *m*; **~ knowledge** Faktenwissen *nt*; **~ report** Tatsachenbericht *m*; **to have a ~ basis** auf Tatsachen beruhen; **the book is largely ~** das Buch beruht zum größten Teil auf Tatsachen

factually ['fæktjʊəlɪ] ADV *write, speak* sachlich; **~ accurate** sachlich richtig

faculty ['fækəltɪ] N **a** *(= power of mind)* Vermögen *nt*, Fähigkeit *f*, Kraft *f*; *(= ability, aptitude)* Begabung *f*, Talent *nt*; **mental faculties** geistige Fähigkeiten *pl*, Geisteskräfte *pl*; **~ of reason** Vernunft *f*; **~ of hearing/sight** Hör-/Sehvermögen *nt*; **to be in (full) possession of (all) one's faculties** im Vollbesitz seiner Kräfte sein; **to have a ~ for doing sth** ein Talent dafür haben, etw zu tun **b** *(Univ)* Fakultät *f*; **the medical ~, the ~ of medicine** die medizinische Fakultät; **the Faculty** *(= staff)* der Lehrkörper **c** *(Eccl)* Vollmacht *f*

fad [fæd] N Fimmel *m*, Tick *m (inf)*; *(= fashion)* Masche *f (inf)*; **it's just a ~** das ist nur ein momentaner Fimmel *(inf) or* Tick *(inf)*; **that's the latest fashion ~** das ist die neuste Modemasche *(inf)*; **her latest food ~** ihr neuester Fimmel in puncto Ernährung *(inf)*; **her ~ for caviar** ihr Kaviarfimmel *(inf)*; **his ~ for wearing an earring** sein Tick *or* Fimmel, einen Ohrring zu tragen *(inf)*

faddish ['fædɪʃ], **faddy** ['fædɪ] *(inf)* ADJ wählerisch

fade [feɪd] **VI a** *(= lose colour)* verblassen; *(material, colour)* verbleichen, verblassen; *(on exposure to light)* verschießen; *(flower)* verblühen; *(= lose shine)* seinen Glanz verlieren; **guaranteed not to ~** garantiert farbecht
b *(fig, memory)* verblassen; *(sight, strength, inspiration, feeling)* nachlassen, schwinden *(geh)*; *(hopes)* zerrinnen; *(smile)* vergehen, verschwinden; *(beauty)* verblühen; *(sound)* verklingen, verhallen; *(radio signal)* schwächer werden; **hopes are fading of finding any more survivors** die Hoffnung, noch weitere Überlebende zu finden, wird immer geringer; **he ~d into obscurity** er geriet langsam in Vergessenheit; **to ~ into the background** *(person)* sich im Hintergrund halten; *(fears)* in den Hintergrund rücken
c *(Rad, TV, Film) scene* ausgeblendet werden; *(cameraman)* ausblenden; **to ~ to another scene** (allmählich) zu einer anderen Szene überblenden
d *(Tech, brakes)* nachlassen
VT a *(= cause to lose colour)* ausbleichen
b *(Rad, TV, Film)* ausblenden; **to ~ one scene (in)to another** von einer Szene (allmählich) in eine andere überblenden
N *(Rad, TV, Film)* Abblende *f*

▶ **fade away** VI *(sight)* schwinden; *(memory)* verblassen, schwinden; *(hopes)* schwinden, zerrinnen; *(interest, strength, inspiration)* nachlassen; *(sound)* verklingen, verhallen; *(person)* immer weniger *or* schwächer werden; *(from memory of the public)* aus dem Gedächtnis schwinden

▶ **fade in** *(Rad, TV, Film)* **VI** allmählich eingeblendet werden **VT** *sep* allmählich einblenden

▶ **fade out VI a** *(Rad, TV, Film)* abblenden **b to fade out of sb's life** aus jds Leben verschwinden **VT** *sep (Rad, TV, Film)* abblenden

▸ **fade up** VT *sep (Rad, TV, Film)* aufblenden; *sound* lauter werden lassen, anschwellen lassen

faded ['feɪdɪd] ADJ *photograph, grandeur* verblasst; *colour, material* verblasst, verblichen; *(after exposure to light)* verschossen; *flowers, beauty* verblüht; **a pair of ~ jeans** verblichene Jeans *pl*

fade: **fade-in** N *(Rad, TV, Film)* Auf- *or* Einblendung *f*; **fadeless** ['feɪdlɪs] ADJ licht- *or* farbecht; *(fig: = eternal)* unvergänglich; **fade-out** N *(Rad, TV, Film)* Abblende *f*

faecal, *(US)* **fecal** ['fiːkəl] ADJ fäkal

faeces, *(US)* **feces** ['fiːsiːz] PL Kot *m*

faerie ['fɛərɪ] *(old)* N Fee *f* ADJ Elfen-; **~ king/queen** Elfenkönig *m*/-königin *f*

Faeroes ['fɛərəʊz] PL = **Faroes**

faery ['fɛərɪ] N, ADJ *(old)* = **faerie**

faff about ['fæfəˌbaʊt], **faff around** ['fæfəˌraʊnd] VI *(Brit inf)* herumbosseln *(inf)*

fag [fæg] *(inf)* N **a** *no pl (Brit = drudgery)* Schinderei *f*, Plackerei *f* **b** *(Brit: = cigarette)* Kippe *f (inf)*, Glimmstängel *m (dated inf)* **c** *(Brit, Sch) junger Internatsschüler, der einem älteren bestimmte Dienste zu leisten hat* **d** *(esp US sl: = homosexual)* Schwule(r) *m (inf)* VT *(Brit inf: also* **fag out***)* erschöpfen, schlauchen *(inf)*; **to be ~ged (out)** kaputt *or* geschafft sein *(inf)* VI *(Brit)* **a** *(also* **fag away***)* sich abrackern *(inf)*, sich abplagen **b** *(Sch) einem älteren Schüler Dienste leisten*

fag end N *(Brit)* **a** *(inf: = cigarette end)* Kippe *f (inf)*, Stummel *m* **b** *(inf: = last part)* letztes Ende; **the ~s of old policies** die kümmerlichen Reste der alten Politik

fag hag N *(US sl)* Schwulenfreundin *f (inf)*

fagot ['fægət] N *(esp US sl: = homosexual)* Schwule(r) *m (inf)*

Fahrenheit ['færənhaɪt] N Fahrenheit *nt*

FAI N ABBR *of* **Football Association of Ireland**

fail [feɪl] VI **a** *(= be unsuccessful)* keinen Erfolg haben; *(in mission, life etc)* versagen, scheitern; *(campaign, efforts, negotiations, plan, experiment, marriage)* fehlschlagen, scheitern; *(undertaking, attempt)* fehlschlagen, misslingen, missglücken; *(applicant, application)* nicht angenommen werden; *(election candidate, Theat: play)* durchfallen; *(business)* eingehen; *(charm, attempts at persuasion etc)* vergeblich *or* umsonst sein; **he ~ed in his attempt to take control of the company** sein Versuch, die Leitung der Firma zu übernehmen, schlug fehl *or* blieb erfolglos *or* missglückte; **he ~ed in his application for the post** seine Bewerbung wurde nicht angenommen; **to ~ in one's duty** seine Pflicht nicht tun; **to ~ by 5 votes** *(motion)* mit 5 Stimmen Mehrheit abgelehnt werden; *(person)* um 5 Stimmen geschlagen werden; **if all else ~s** wenn alle Stricke reißen; **to ~ miserably** *or* **dismally** kläglich scheitern

b *(= not pass exam)* durchfallen; **he ~ed in Latin** er fiel in Latein durch

c *(= fall short)* **where he/the essay ~s is in not being detailed enough** sein Fehler/der Fehler des Aufsatzes ist, dass er nicht ausführlich genug ist; **this report ~s in that it comes up with no clear proposals** dieser Bericht lässt es an klaren Vorschlägen fehlen; **where you ~ is that you lack relevant experience** Ihnen fehlt es an der notwendigen Erfahrung

d *(= grow feeble, health)* sich verschlechtern; *(hearing, eyesight)* nachlassen; *(invalid)* schwächer werden; **he is ~ing fast** sein Zustand verschlechtert sich zusehends

e *(= stop working, be cut off etc, generator, battery, radio, electricity, pump, engine)* ausfallen; *(brakes)* versagen; *(supply, wind)* ausbleiben; *(heart etc)* versagen, aussetzen; **the crops ~ed** es gab ein Missernte; *(completely)* die Ernte fiel aus

VT **a** *candidate* durchfallen lassen; *subject* durchfallen in *(+dat)*; **to ~ an exam** eine Prüfung nicht bestehen, durch eine Prüfung fallen; **to ~ Latin** in Latein durchfallen

b *(= let down, person, memory)* im Stich lassen; *(= not live up to sb's expectations)* enttäuschen; **his heart ~ed him** sein Herz setzte aus; **words ~ me** mir fehlen die Worte

c to ~ to do sth etw nicht tun; *(= neglect)* (es) versäumen, etw zu tun; **she ~ed to lose weight** es gelang ihr nicht abzunehmen; **he ~ed to win support for his proposal** er konnte keine Unterstützung für seinen Vorschlag finden; **she never ~s to amaze me** sie versetzt mich immer wieder in Erstaunen; **I ~ to see why** es ist mir völlig unklar, warum; *(indignantly)* ich sehe gar nicht ein, warum; **I ~ed to understand how/what ...** ich konnte nicht verstehen, wie/was ...

N **a without ~** ganz bestimmt, auf jeden Fall; *(= inevitably)* garantiert, grundsätzlich

b *(= failed candidate, exam)* **there were ten ~s** zehn sind durchgefallen *or* durchgerasselt *(inf)*; **she got a ~ in history** in Geschichte ist sie hängen geblieben *(inf) or* durchgefallen

failed [feɪld] ADJ *attempt, coup, marriage, bid* gescheitert; *bank, company* bankrott; *exam candidate* durchgefallen; *writer, actor* verhindert

failing ['feɪlɪŋ] N Schwäche *f*, Fehler *m* PREP **~ an answer** mangels (einer) Antwort *(geh)*; **ask John if he knows, ~ him try Harry** fragen Sie John (danach), und wenn er es nicht weiß, versuchen Sie es bei Harry; **~ this/that** (oder) sonst, und wenn das nicht möglich ist; **~ which** ansonsten, widrigenfalls *(form)*

fail-safe ['feɪlseɪf] ADJ (ab)gesichert; *method* hundertprozentig sicher; *mechanism, system* störungssicher

failure ['feɪljə'] N **a** *(= lack of success)* Misserfolg *m*; *(of campaign, efforts, negotiations, plan, experiment, marriage)* Fehlschlag *m*, Scheitern *nt*; *(of undertaking, attempt)* Fehlschlag *m*; *(of application)* Ablehnung *f*; *(in exam, Theat: of play)* Misserfolg *m*, Durchfall *m*; *(of business)* Eingehen *nt*; **~ to do sth** vergeblicher Versuch, etw zu tun; **~ rate** *(in exams)* Misserfolgsquote *f*; *(of machine)* Fehlerquote *f*

b *(= unsuccessful person)* Versager(in) *m(f)*, Niete *f (inf)* (at in *+dat*); *(= unsuccessful thing)* Misserfolg *m*, Reinfall *m (inf)*, Pleite *f (inf)*; **I'm a bit of a ~ at making my own clothes** ich bin eine ziemliche Niete, wenn es darum geht, meine eigenen Kleider zu nähen *(inf)*

c *(= omission, neglect)* **because of his ~ to reply/act** weil er nicht geantwortet/gehandelt hat, weil er es versäumt *or* unterlassen hat zu antworten/zu handeln; **his ~ to notice anything** weil er nichts bemerkt hat; **~ to pay will result in prosecution** im Nichteinbringungsfall erfolgt Anzeige *(form)*; **~ to perform one's duty** Nichterfüllung *f* seiner Pflicht; **~ to appear** Nichterscheinen *nt (form)*

d *(of health)* Verschlechterung *f*; *(of hearing, eyesight)* Nachlassen *nt*; *(of invalid)* Nachlassen *nt* der Kräfte

e *(= breakdown, of generator, engine, electricity, pump, engine)* Ausfall *m*; *(of brakes)* Versagen *nt*; *(of supply, wind)* Ausbleiben *nt*; **heart/kidney/liver ~** Herz-/Nieren-/Leberversagen *nt*; **~ of crops** Missernte *f*; *(complete)* Ernteausfall *m*

fain [feɪn] ADV *(obs)* **I would ~ ...** ich möchte ...

faint [feɪnt] ADJ *(+er)* **a** *(= weak, not pronounced)* schwach; *tracks, line, outline* undeutlich; *mark, stain, photocopy* blass; *colour* verblasst; *sound, call, steps, suspicion, hope, smile* leise; *resemblance* entfernt; *chance* gering; **the colours have gone ~** die Farben sind verblichen; **your voice is very ~** *(on telephone)* man hört dich kaum; **I never felt the ~est desire to cry** ich verspürte absolut nicht das Bedürfnis zu weinen; **I have a ~ memory** *or* **recollection of that day** ich kann mich schwach an den Tag erinnern; **she made a ~ attempt at a laugh** sie versuchte zaghaft zu lachen; **I haven't the ~est idea** *(emph)* ich habe nicht die leiseste *or* geringste Ahnung; **the ~ hearts** die Zaghaften *pl*, die Hasenfüße *pl (inf)*; **~ heart never won fair lady** *(Prov)* wer nicht wagt, der nicht gewinnt *(Prov)* → *also* **damn VT c**

b *pred (Med)* **she was** *or* **felt ~** sie war einer Ohnmacht nahe; **he was concerned that I might become ~** er machte sich Sorgen, dass ich ohnmächtig werden könnte; **he began to feel ~** ihm wurde schwach; **she was ~ with hunger** ihr war ganz schwach vor Hunger

VI *(Med: = pass out)* ohnmächtig werden, in Ohnmacht fallen *(with, from* vor *+dat)*; **to ~ at the sight of blood** beim Anblick von Blut ohnmächtig werden

N *(Med)* Ohnmacht *f*; **she fell to the ground in a (dead) ~** sie fiel ohnmächtig zu Boden

faint-hearted [feɪnt'hɑːtɪd] ADJ zaghaft; **it's not for the ~** es ist nichts für ängstliche Gemüter *or* für Angsthasen *(inf)*

faint-heartedness [feɪnt'hɑːtɪdnɪs] N Zaghaftigkeit *f*

fainting fit ['feɪntɪŋfɪt] N Ohnmachtsanfall *m*

faintly ['feɪntlɪ] ADV **a** *(= weakly) glow, shine, burn* schwach; *smell, smile* leicht; *(= quietly) sound, speak, say, sigh* leise; **the words are just ~ visible** die Worte sind gerade noch sichtbar; **I could hear the siren ~** ich konnte die Sirene gerade noch hören **b** *(= slightly) absurd, condescending, disappointed, suspicious* leicht; **she felt ~ ridiculous** sie kam sich etwas lächerlich vor; **~ familiar** entfernt vertraut; **I do remember him ~** ich kann mich schwach an ihn erinnern

faintness ['feɪntnɪs] N **a** Schwäche *f*; *(of tracks, line)* Undeutlichkeit *f*; **such was the ~ of the photocopy that ...** die Fotokopie war so blass, dass ...; **such was the ~ of his voice that ...** seine Stimme war so schwach, dass ...; **due to the ~ of the sound** weil der Ton so leise war; **the ~ of his resemblance to his father** seine entfernte Ähnlichkeit mit seinem Vater; **despite the ~ of her hope** obwohl sie nur eine leise Hoffnung hatte; **~ of heart** *(liter)* Verzagtheit *f* **b** *(= dizziness)* flaues Gefühl, Schwächegefühl *nt*

fair[1] [fɛə'] ADJ *(+er)* **a** *(= just) person, fight, game, player, competition, price* fair (to *or* on sb jdm gegenüber, gegen jdn); *trial, conclusion* gerecht; **he tried to be ~ to everybody** er versuchte, allen gegenüber gerecht zu sein *or (give everybody their due)* allen gerecht zu werden; **that is a (very) ~ point** *or* **comment** das lässt sich (natürlich) nicht abstreiten; **it wouldn't be ~ to disturb the children's education** es wäre unfair, die Ausbildung der Kinder zu unterbrechen; **it is ~ to say that ...** man kann wohl sagen, dass ...; **to be ~, ...** man muss (fairerweise) dazusagen, dass ...; **it's only ~ for her to earn more than us** es ist doch nur gerecht *or* fair, dass sie mehr verdient als wir; **it's only ~ to ask him/to give him a hand** man sollte ihn fairerweise fragen/ihm fairerweise helfen; **it's only ~ to expect ...** man kann doch wohl zu Recht erwarten, ...; **~ enough!** na schön *or* gut, in Ordnung; **that's ~ enough** das ist nur recht und billig; **as is (only) ~** was nur recht und billig ist; **~'s ~** wir wollen doch fair bleiben; **by ~ means or foul** mit allen Mitteln, egal wie *(inf)*

b *(= quite considerable) sum* ziemlich groß; **a ~ amount of money** ziemlich viel Geld; **to have a ~ degree of competence** ziemlich kompetent sein; **to be a ~ size** ziemlich groß sein; **we were doing a ~ speed** wir fuhren ziemlich schnell; **it's a ~ distance** *or* **way** es ist ziemlich weit; **a ~ number of students** ziemlich viele Studenten; **a ~ chance of success** ziemlich gute Erfolgsaussichten

c *(= reasonable, shrewd) guess, assessment, idea* ziemlich gut; **he's a ~ judge of character** er hat eine ziemlich gute Menschenkenntnis; **to have a ~ knowledge of a subject** sich auf einem Gebiet ziemlich gut auskennen; **I had a pretty ~ idea of the answer to the question** ich wusste ziemlich genau, was die Antwort auf diese Frage war; **I've a ~ idea that he's going to resign** ich bin mir ziemlich sicher, dass er zurücktreten wird; **it's a ~ guess that he'll never agree** man kann ziemlich sicher annehmen, dass er nie zustimmen wird; **that's a ~ sample of ...** das ist ziemlich typisch für ...

d *(= average)* mittelmäßig; **how are you? – ~ to middling** *(Brit)* wie gehts dir? – mittelprächtig

tig *(inf) or* so einigermaßen
e *(= fair-haired) person, hair* blond; *(= fair-skinned) person* hellhäutig; *skin* hell
f *(old, poet, = lovely) person* hold *(dated)*; *place* schön; **the ~ sex** *(dated, hum)* das schöne Geschlecht
g *(= fine and dry) weather* heiter, schön; **the weather is set ~** das Wetter bleibt weiterhin schön
ADV a to play ~ fair sein; *(Sport)* fair spielen; **to play ~ with** *or* **by sb** sich jdm gegenüber fair verhalten → *also* **fair play**
b ~ and square *(win, lose)* ganz klar; **they beat us ~ and square** sie haben uns deutlich geschlagen
c *(dial, = pretty well)* ganz schön *(inf)*, vielleicht *(inf)*; **it ~ took my breath away** das hat mir glatt den Atem verschlagen

fair² N (Jahr)markt *m*; *(= funfair)* Volksfest *nt*; *(Comm)* Messe *f*

fair: **fair copy** N Reinschrift *f*; **to write out a ~ of sth** etw ins Reine schreiben; **fair game** N *(lit)* jagdbares Wild; *(fig)* Freiwild *nt*; **the grouse is ~ between the months of …** das Moorhuhn darf in den Monaten … bejagt *(spec) or* gejagt werden; **fairground** N *(for funfair)* Festplatz *m*; **~ showman** Schausteller(in) *m(f)*; **fair-haired** ADJ *comp* **fairer-haired** blond; **fair-haired boy** N *(dated US)* Lieblingskind *nt*, Liebling *m*

fairing [ˈfɛərɪŋ] N *(Aviat, Aut)* Stromlinienverkleidung *f*

fairly [ˈfɛəlɪ] ADV **a** *(= moderately)* ziemlich; **~ recently** erst kürzlich **b** *(= justly) treat* gerecht, fair; *(= justifiably) claim* zu Recht; *describe, blame* gerechterweise; *(= equally) share* gerecht **c** *(= positively, really)* geradezu; **we ~ flew along** wir sausten nur so dahin

fair-minded [ˈfɛəmaɪndɪd] ADJ gerecht

fairness [ˈfɛənɪs] N **a** *(= justice)* Gerechtigkeit *f*, Fairness *f*; **in all ~** gerechterweise, fairerweise; **in (all) ~ to him we should wait** wir sollten so fair sein und noch warten **b** *(= lightness, of hair)* Blondheit *f*; **the ~ of her skin** ihre Hellhäutigkeit

> **FAIRNESS DOCTRINE**
> Die **Fairness Doctrine**, die Ausgewogenheitsdoktrin, ist ein amerikanisches Prinzip, das von der **Federal Communications Commission (FCC)** erstellt wurde. Es besagt, dass Rundfunk- und Fernsehsender immer eine ausgeglichene Darstellung der Standpunkte zu wichtigen lokalen und nationalen Themen liefern müssen. Die Doktrin wurde 1949 von der FCC aufgestellt und vom Kongress bestätigt, auch wenn sie kein Gesetz ist. Darin eingeschlossen ist das Anrecht auf zeitlich gleich lange Berichterstattung über die Hauptkandidaten im Wahlkampf.

fair: **fair play** N *(Sport, fig)* faires Verhalten, Fairplay *nt*, Fair Play *nt*; **that's not ~** *(fig)* das ist nicht fair *or* gerecht; **fair-sized** ADJ recht groß; **fair-spoken** ADJ *(geh)* freundlich, höflich; **fair trade** N fairer Handel *(mit Entwicklungsländern)*; *(US)* Preisbindung *f*; **fairway** N **a** *(Naut)* Fahrwasser *nt or* -rinne *f* **b** *(Golf)* Fairway *nt*; **fair-weather** ADJ **a ~ friend** ein Freund, der nur in guten Zeiten ein Freund ist

fairy [ˈfɛərɪ] N **a** Fee *f*; **good ~** gute Fee; **he's away with the fairies** *(inf)* der hat einen Schaden *(inf)* **b** *(pej inf: = homosexual)* Homo *m (dated inf)*, Schwule(r) *m (inf)*

fairy: **fairy cycle** N Kinderfahrrad *nt*; **fairy footsteps** PL *(iro inf)* Stapfen *nt*; **fairy godmother** N *(lit, fig)* gute Fee; **fairyland** N Märchenland *nt*; **fairy lights** PL bunte Lichter *pl*; **fairy-like** ADJ feenhaft; **fairy queen** N Elfenkönigin *f*; **fairy ring** N Hexentanzplatz *m*; *(of mushrooms)* Hexenring *m*; **fairy story, fairy tale** N *(lit, fig)* Märchen *nt*; **fairy-tale** ADJ *(fig) romance, ending* märchenhaft

fait accompli [ˌfetəˈkɒmpliː] N vollendete Tatsache, Fait accompli *nt (geh)*; **to present sb with a ~** jdn vor vollendete Tatsachen stellen

faith [feɪθ] N **a** *(= trust)* Vertrauen *nt (in* zu); *(in human nature, medicine, science etc, religious faith)* Glaube *m (in* an *+acc)*; **~ in God** Gottvertrauen *nt*; **to have ~ in sb** jdm (ver)trauen; **to have ~ in sth** Vertrauen in etw *(acc)* haben; **act of ~** Vertrauensbeweis *m*; **it was more an act of ~ than a rational decision** das war mehr auf gut Glück gemacht als eine rationale Entscheidung
b *(= religion)* Glaube *m no pl*, Bekenntnis *nt*
c *(= promise)* **to keep/break ~ with sb** jdm treu bleiben/untreu werden, jdm die Treue halten/brechen *(geh)*
d *(= sincerity, loyalty)* Treue *f*; **to act in good/bad ~** in gutem Glauben/böser Absicht handeln

faith cure N Heilung *f* durch Gesundbeten

faithful [ˈfeɪθfʊl] **ADJ a** *(= loyal) person, animal, car, service* treu; **to be/remain ~ to sb/sth** jdm/einer Sache treu sein/bleiben; **to be ~ to one's promise** sein Versprechen treu halten; **to be ~ to sb's wishes** jds Wünsche treu erfüllen; **she is ~ to her own culture and religion** sie bleibt ihrer eigenen Kultur und Religion treu; **they are ~ to each other** sie sind einander treu
b *(= accurate) adaptation, reproduction, copy* originalgetreu; *translation* genau; **the translation is ~ to the original/the spirit of the original** die Übersetzung hält sich genau an das Original/an den Geist des Originals
N a *(= stalwart)* treuer Anhänger, treue Anhängerin; **the party ~(s)** die treuen Anhänger der Partei
b the ~ *pl (Rel)* die Gläubigen *pl*

faithfully [ˈfeɪθfəlɪ] ADV **a** *(= loyally)* treu; *(= conscientiously)* gewissenhaft; *(= steadfastly)* standhaft; **to promise ~** ganz fest versprechen; **Yours ~** *(Brit: on letter)* hochachtungsvoll **b** *(= accurately) restore* originalgetreu; *report, reflect, translate, reproduce* genau

faithfulness [ˈfeɪθfʊlnɪs] N **a** *(= loyalty)* Treue *f (to* zu) **b** *(= accuracy, of translation)* Genauigkeit *f*; *(of reproduction)* Originaltreue *f*

faith: **faith healer** N Gesundbeter(in) *m(f)*; **faith healing** N Gesundbeten *nt*; **faithless** ADJ treulos; **faithlessness** N Treulosigkeit *f*

fake [feɪk] **ADJ** unecht; *certificate, banknote, painting* gefälscht; **~ fur** Pelzimitation *f*; **a ~ suntan** Bräune *f* aus der Flasche **N** *(= object)* Fälschung *f*; *(jewellery)* Imitation *f*; *(= person, trickster)* Schwindler(in) *m(f)*; *(feigning illness)* Simulant(in) *m(f)*; **the passport/painting was a ~** der Pass/das Gemälde war gefälscht **VT** vortäuschen; *picture, document, results, evidence etc* fälschen; *bill, burglary, crash* fingieren; *jewellery* imitieren, nachmachen; *elections* manipulieren; **to ~ an illness** (eine Krankheit) simulieren *or* vortäuschen

► **fake up** VT *sep story* erfinden; *picture, passport* fälschen

fakir [ˈfɑːkɪəʳ] N Fakir *m*

falcon [ˈfɔːlkən] N Falke *m*

falconer [ˈfɔːlkənəʳ] N Falkner(in) *m(f)*

falconry [ˈfɔːlkənrɪ] N Falknerei *f*; *(= sport)* Falkenjagd *or* -beize *f*

Falkland Islands [ˈfɔːklændˌaɪləndz], **Falklands** [ˈfɔːkləndz] PL Falklandinseln *pl*

fall [fɔːl] *vb: pret* **fell**, *ptp* **fallen** **N a** *(lit, fig: = tumble)* Fall *m no pl*, Sturz *m*; *(= decline: of empire etc)* Untergang *m*; **the Fall (of Man)** *(Eccl)* der Sündenfall; **to break sb's ~** jds Fall auffangen; **to have a ~** (hin)fallen, stürzen; **he had several ~s** er ist mehrmals hingefallen *or* gestürzt; **she had a bad ~** sie ist schwer gestürzt; **to head** *or* **ride for a ~** in sein Verderben rennen
b *(= defeat, of town, fortress etc)* Einnahme *f*, Eroberung *f*; *(of Troy)* Fall *m*; *(of country)* Zusammenbruch *m*; *(of government)* Sturz *m*
c ~ of rain/snow Regen-/Schneefall *m*; **~ of rock** Steinschlag *m*; **there was another heavy ~ (of snow) last night** es hat heute Nacht wieder viel geschneit
d *(of night)* Einbruch *m*
e *(= lowering)* Sinken *nt*; *(in temperature)* Abfall *m*, Sinken *nt*; *(sudden)* Sturz *m*; *(of barometer)* Fallen *nt*; *(sudden)* Sturz *m*; *(in wind)* Nachlassen *nt*; *(in revs, population, membership)* Abnahme *f*; *(in graph)* Abfall *m*; *(in morals)* Verfall *m*; *(of prices, currency, gradual)* Sinken *nt*; *(sudden)* Sturz *m*; **~ in demand** *(Comm)* Nachfragerückgang *m*
f *(= slope: of roof, ground)* Gefälle *nt*; *(steeper)* Abfall *m*
g *(= waterfall: also* **falls**) Wasserfall *m*; **the Niagara Falls** der Niagarafall
h *(Wrestling)* Schultersieg *m*
i *(= hang, of curtains etc)* Fall *m*
j *(US: = autumn)* Herbst *m*; **in the ~** im Herbst
VI a *(lit, fig: = tumble)* fallen; *(Sport, from a height, badly)* stürzen; *(object, to the ground)* herunterfallen; **to ~ to one's death** tödlich abstürzen; **to ~ into a trap** in die Falle gehen
b *(= hang down: hair, clothes etc)* fallen; **her hair kept ~ing into her eyes** ihr fielen dauernd die Haare in die Augen
c *(snow, rain)* fallen
d *(= drop, temperature, price)* fallen, sinken; *(population, membership etc)* abnehmen; *(voice)* sich senken; *(wind)* sich legen, nachlassen; *(land)* abfallen; *(graph, curve, rate)* abnehmen; *(steeply)* abfallen; **her eyes fell** sie schlug die Augen nieder *(geh)*; **his face fell** er machte ein langes Gesicht; **to ~ in sb's estimation** *or* **eyes** in jds Achtung *(dat)* sinken
e *(= be defeated, country)* eingenommen werden; *(city, fortress)* fallen, erobert *or* eingenommen werden; *(government, ruler)* gestürzt werden; **to ~ to the enemy** vom Feind eingenommen werden; *(fortress, town also)* vom Feind erobert werden
f *(= be killed)* fallen; **to ~ in battle** fallen
g *(night)* hereinbrechen; *(silence)* eintreten
h *(Bibl)* den Sündenfall tun; *(old, girl)* die Unschuld *or* Ehre verlieren *(dated)*; **when Adam fell** nach Adams Sündenfall
i *(= occur, birthday, Easter etc)* fallen *(on* auf *+acc)*; *(accent)* liegen *(on* auf *+dat)*; *(= be classified)* gehören *(under* in *+acc)*, fallen *(under* unter *+acc)*; **it ~s under another category** das gehört in *or* fällt in eine andere Kategorie; **that ~s within/outside the scope of …** das fällt in/nicht in den Bereich *+gen* …, das liegt innerhalb/außerhalb des Bereichs *+gen* …
j *(= be naturally divisible)* zerfallen, sich gliedern *(into* in *+acc)*; **to ~ into three sections** sich in drei Teile gliedern; **to ~ into categories** sich in Kategorien gliedern lassen
k *(fig)* **her eyes fell on a strange object** ihr Blick fiel auf einen merkwürdigen Gegenstand; **where do you think the responsibility/blame for that will ~?** wem wird Ihrer Meinung nach die Verantwortung dafür/die Schuld daran gegeben?
l *(= become)* werden; **to ~ asleep** einschlafen; **to ~ ill** krank werden, erkranken *(geh)*; **to ~ in love with sb** sich in jdn verlieben; **to ~ out of love with sb** aufhören, jdn zu lieben; **she's forever ~ing in and out of love** sie verliebt sich dauernd neu
m *(= pass into a certain state)* **to ~ into decline** *(building)* verkommen; *(economy)* schlechter werden; **to ~ into ruin** (zur Ruine) verfallen; **to ~ into decay** verfallen; **to ~ into a deep sleep** in tiefen Schlaf fallen *or* sinken; **to ~ into temptation** in Versuchung geraten; **to ~ into conversation (with sb)** (mit jdm) ins Gespräch kommen; **to ~ into a state of unconsciousness** das Bewusstsein verlieren, in Ohnmacht fallen; **to ~ into a coma** in ein Koma fallen; **to ~ into disarray** in Unordnung geraten; **to ~ into bad habits** in schlechte Gewohnheiten verfallen; **to ~ apart** *or* **to pieces** *(chairs, cars, book etc)* aus dem Leim gehen *(inf)*; *(clothes, curtains)* sich in Wohlgefallen auflösen *(inf)*; *(house)* verfallen; *(system, company, sb's life)* aus den Fugen geraten *or* gehen; **I fell apart when he left me** meine Welt brach zusammen, als er mich verließ

n **to ~ to doing sth** *(= start)* anfangen, etw zu tun
o *(in set constructions see also n, adj etc)* **to ~ into the hands of sb** jdm in die Hände fallen; **to ~ among thieves** unter die Räuber fallen *or* geraten

▶ **fall about** *(also* **fall about laughing***)* VI *(Brit inf)* sich kranklachen *(inf)*

▶ **fall away** VI **a** *(ground)* abfallen **b** *(= come away, crumble: plaster, bricks, river bank)* abbröckeln *(from* von*)* **c** = **fall off b** **d** *(anxiety, fears)* weichen *(geh) (from* von*)* **e** *(from party, church)* abfallen

▶ **fall back** VI zurückweichen *(also Mil)*

▶ **fall back (up)on** VI *+prep obj* zurückgreifen auf *(+acc)*

▶ **fall behind** VI **a** *(in race, at school etc)* zurückbleiben *(prep obj* hinter *+dat)*, zurückfallen *(prep obj* hinter *+acc)* **b** *(with rent, work etc)* in Rückstand *or* Verzug geraten

▶ **fall down** VI **a** *(person)* hinfallen; *(statue, vase)* herunterfallen; *(= collapse: house, scaffolding etc)* einstürzen **b** *(down stairs, cliff face)* hinunterfallen *(prep obj +acc)*; **he fell right down to the bottom** er ist bis ganz nach unten gefallen **c** *(fig: = be inadequate: person, theory, plan)* versagen; **where he/the plan falls down is ...** woran es ihm/dem Plan fehlt, ist ..., woran es bei ihm/dem Plan hapert, ist ... *(inf)*; **that was where we fell down** daran sind wir gescheitert

▶ **fall for** VI *+prep obj* **a** **I really fell for him/it** er/es hatte es mir angetan **b** *(= be taken in by) sales talk, propaganda* hereinfallen auf *(+acc)*

▶ **fall in** VI **a** *(into water etc)* hineinfallen **b** *(= collapse)* einstürzen **c** *(Mil, troops)* (in Reih und Glied) antreten; *(one soldier)* ins Glied treten; **fall in!** antreten!; **to fall in beside** *or* **alongside sb** sich jdm anschließen **d** *(= make friends)* **it didn't take long for us to fall in again** es dauerte nicht lange, bis wir uns wieder versöhnten

▶ **fall in with** VI *+prep obj* **a** *(= meet, join up with)* sich anschließen *(+dat)*; *bad company* geraten in *(+acc)* **b** *(= agree to)* mitmachen bei; *request* unterstützen **c** *(= make friends with)* **I didn't fall back in with her for a year** ich habe mich ein Jahr lang nicht mit ihr versöhnt

▶ **fall off** VI **a** *(lit, person, object etc)* herunterfallen *(prep obj* von*)* **b** *(= decrease)* zurückgehen, abnehmen; *(supporters)* abfallen; *(speed)* sich verringern, abnehmen; *(support, enthusiasm)* nachlassen

▶ **fall on** VI *+prep obj* **a** *(= trip on) stone* fallen über *(+acc)* **b** *(= be the responsibility of, be borne by, duty, decision, task)* zufallen *(+dat)*; *(blame)* treffen *(+acc)*; **the responsibility falls on your shoulders** Sie tragen *or* haben die Verantwortung **c** *(= attack)* herfallen über *(+acc)* **d** *(= find)* stoßen auf *(+acc)*

▶ **fall out** VI **a** *(of bed, boat, window)* herausfallen; **to fall out of sth** aus etw fallen **b** *(= quarrel)* sich (zer)streiten; **the two countries fell out over the question of borders** zwischen den beiden Ländern kam es wegen Grenzstreitigkeiten zum Bruch **c** *(Mil)* wegtreten **d** *(= happen)* sich ergeben; **just wait and see how things fall out** wart erst mal ab, wie alles wird

▶ **fall over** **VI** *(person)* hinfallen; *(= collapse)* umfallen; *(statue, vase)* umfallen, umkippen **VI** *+prep obj* **a** *(= trip over) stone, sb's legs* fallen über *(+acc)*; **they were falling over each other to get the book** sie drängelten sich, um das Buch zu bekommen **b** **to fall over oneself to do sth** sich (fast) umbringen *(inf) or* sich *(dat)* die größte Mühe geben, etw zu tun; **to fall over backwards to do sth** sich (förmlich) überschlagen, etw zu tun *(inf)*

▶ **fall through** VI *(plan)* ins Wasser fallen, fehlschlagen

▶ **fall to** VI **a** *(inf: = start eating)* sich dranmachen *(inf)*, reinhauen *(inf)*; *(= start fighting, working)* loslegen *(inf)* **b** *(= be the responsibility of)* zufallen *(+dat)*, obliegen *(+dat) (geh)*

▶ **fall upon** VI *+prep obj* = **fall on b-c**

fallacious [fəˈleɪʃəs] ADJ irrig; *argument* trugschlüssig

fallacy [ˈfæləsɪ] N Irrtum *m*; *(in logic)* Fehlschluss *m*, Trugschluss *m*; **a popular ~** ein weitverbreiteter Irrtum

fall-back position [ˈfɔːlbækpəˌzɪʃən] N Rückfallposition *f*

fallen [ˈfɔːlən] *ptp of* **fall** **ADJ** *women, soldier, angel* gefallen; *leaf* abgefallen; *tree* umgestürzt; **~ idol** gefallener Götze; **~ arches** *pl (Med)* Senkfüße *pl* **PL** **the Fallen** *(Mil)* die Gefallenen *pl*

fall guy N *(esp US inf: = victim)* armes Opfer, Angeschmierte(r) *mf (inf)*; *(= scapegoat)* Sündenbock *m*

fallibility [ˌfælɪˈbɪlɪtɪ] N Fehlbarkeit *f*

fallible [ˈfæləbl] ADJ fehlbar, nicht unfehlbar

falling [ˈfɔːlɪŋ] ADJ *(= dwindling) prices, profits, rate, temperature, standards* sinkend, fallend; *population, membership* abnehmend

falling: **falling-off** N = **fall-off**; **falling-out** N *(= quarrel)* Streit *m*; **falling sickness** N *(old)* Fallsucht *f (old)*; **falling star** N Sternschnuppe *f*

fall: **fall line** N *(Sci)* Fall-Linie *f*; **fall-off** N Rückgang *m*, Abnahme *f*; *(in numbers, attendances)* Abfall *m*; *(in speed)* Verringerung *f*; *(in enthusiasm, support)* Nachlassen *nt*

Fallopian tube [fəˈləʊpɪənˈtjuːb] N Eileiter *m*

fallout [ˈfɔːlaʊt] N radioaktiver Niederschlag, Fallout *m*, Fall-out *m (spec)*; *(fig)* Auswirkungen *pl (from +gen)*; **~ shelter** Atomschutzbunker *m*

fallow[1] [ˈfæləʊ] ADJ **a** *(Agr: = unused)* brachliegend; **most of the fields are (lying) ~** die meisten Felder liegen brach; **to leave land ~, to let land lie ~** Land brachliegen lassen **b** *(fig: = inactive) period* unproduktiv

fallow[2] ADJ falb, gelbbraun

fallow deer N Damwild *nt*

false [fɔːls] **ADJ** *(+er)* **a** *(= wrong)* falsch; **to put a ~ interpretation on sth** etw falsch auslegen *or* deuten; **to prove ~** sich als falsch erweisen; **a ~ sense of security** ein falsches Gefühl der Sicherheit; **~ accounting** *(Jur)* Bücherfälschung *f*; **that's a ~ economy** das ist am falschen Ort gespart; **~ imprisonment/arrest** willkürliche Inhaftierung/Festnahme; **~ judgement** Fehlurteil *nt*; **~ statement** Falschaussage *f*; **under** *or* **by ~ pretences** *(Brit) or* **pretenses** *(US)* unter Vorspiegelung falscher Tatsachen; **~ god/prophet** falscher Gott/Prophet; **to bear ~ witness** *(old)* falsches Zeugnis ablegen *(Bibl, old)*, eine falsche Aussage machen
b *(= artificial, fake) nose, beard* falsch; *blood, eyelashes* künstlich; *papers* gefälscht; **~ bottom** *(of suitcase)* doppelter Boden; **~ ceiling** Zwischendecke *f*
c *(pej: = insincere) laughter, enthusiasm* gekünstelt; **~ modesty** falsche Bescheidenheit; **to ring ~** nicht echt klingen
d *(= disloyal) friend, lover, wife, husband, servant* treulos; **to be ~ to sb** jdm untreu sein; *(= deceive)* jdn hintergehen
ADV **to play sb ~** mit jdm ein falsches Spiel treiben

false: **false alarm** N falscher *or* blinder Alarm; **false beginner** N *Lernende(r) mit Vorkenntnissen, der/die noch einmal von vorne anfängt*; **false ceiling** N *(Archit)* Zwischen- *or* Unterdecke *f*; **false dawn** N **a** *(Astron)* Zodiakal- *or* Tierkreislicht *nt* **b** *(fig)* **the boom was a ~** der Aufschwung erweckte falsche Hoffnungen; **false friend** N *(Ling)* falscher Freund; **false front** N **a** *(Archit, also fig)* falsche Fassade **b** *(fig)* bloße Fassade, Mache *f (inf, pej)*; **false-hearted** ADJ falsch, treulos

falsehood [ˈfɔːlshʊd] N **a** *(= lie)* Unwahrheit *f* **b** *no pl (of statement etc)* Unwahrheit *f*

false key N Dietrich *m*, Nachschlüssel *m*

falsely [ˈfɔːlslɪ] ADV **a** *(= wrongly) interpret, understand* falsch; *accused, convicted, imprisoned* zu Unrecht **b** *(= untruthfully, mistakenly) claim, report, think* fälschlicherweise **c** *(+adj: = artificially)* künstlich

false: **False Memory Syndrome** N *(Psych)* False-Memory-Syndrom *nt*; **false move** N falsche Bewegung; *(fig: = mistake)* Fehler *m*; **one ~ and you're dead** eine falsche Bewegung und du bist tot; **one ~, and ...** *(fig)* ein kleiner Fehler und ...; **false negative** N *(Med)* **~ (result)** falsch negative Diagnose

falseness [ˈfɔːlsnɪs] N **a** *(of statement etc)* Unrichtigkeit *f*, Falschheit *f*; *(of promise)* Unaufrichtigkeit *f*, Falschheit *f* **b** *(= artificiality: of pearls, eyelashes etc)* Unechtheit *f* **c** *(= unfaithfulness: of lover etc)* Untreue *f*, Treulosigkeit *f*

false: **false positive** N *(Med)* **~ (result)** falsch positive Diagnose; **false pregnancy** N *(Med)* Scheinschwangerschaft *f*; **false rib** N falsche Rippe; **false start** N Fehlstart *m*; **false teeth** PL (künstliches) Gebiss, falsche Zähne *pl*

falsetto [fɔːlˈsetəʊ] **N** *(= voice)* Fistelstimme *f*; *(Mus)* Falsett *nt*; *(= person)* Falsettist *m* **ADJ** **~ voice** Fistelstimme *f*; *(Mus)* Falsettstimme *f* **ADV** *sing* im Falsett; *speak* mit einer Fistelstimme

falsies [ˈfɔːlsɪz] PL *(inf)* Gummibusen *m (inf)*

falsifiable [ˈfɔːlsɪfaɪəbl] ADJ *(= disprovable)* widerlegbar, falsifizierbar *(spec)*

falsification [ˌfɔːlsɪfɪˈkeɪʃən] N **a** (Ver)fälschung *f* **b** *(= disproving)* Widerlegung *f*, Falsifikation *f (spec)*

falsify [ˈfɔːlsɪfaɪ] VT **a** *records, evidence, history* fälschen; *report* entstellen; *results, tests* verfälschen **b** *(= disprove)* widerlegen, falsifizieren *(spec)*

falsity [ˈfɔːlsɪtɪ] N *(= incorrectness)* Unrichtigkeit *f*; *(= artificiality: of smile)* Falschheit *f*; *(= unfaithfulness)* Treulosigkeit *f*

falter [ˈfɔːltəʳ] VI *(speaker)* stocken; *(steps, horse)* zögern

faltering [ˈfɔːltərɪŋ] ADJ *voice* stockend, stammelnd; *(= hesitating, wavering)* zögernd; *(= unsteady)* taumelnd; *economy* geschwächt; *campaign* halbherzig; *recovery* zögernd

falteringly [ˈfɔːltərɪŋlɪ] ADV *say* stockend, stammelnd; *(= hesitantly)* zögernd; *(= unsteadily) move, walk* taumelnd

fame [feɪm] N Ruhm *m*; **~ and fortune** Ruhm und Reichtum; **of ill ~** von üblem Ruf, berüchtigt; **to come to ~** Ruhm erlangen, zu Ruhm kommen; **to win ~ for sth** sich *(dat)* durch etw einen Namen machen; **is that the Joseph Heller of "Catch-22" ~?** ist das der berühmte Joseph Heller, der „Catch-22" geschrieben hat?; **Borg of Wimbledon 1979 ~** Borg, der sich 1979 in Wimbledon einen Namen gemacht hat

famed [feɪmd] ADJ berühmt

familial [fəˈmɪlɪəl] ADJ familiär

familiar [fəˈmɪljəʳ] **ADJ** **a** *(= usual, well-known) surroundings, sight, scene* gewohnt, vertraut; *figure, voice* vertraut; *street, person, feeling* bekannt; *phrase, title, song* geläufig, bekannt; *complaint, event, protest* häufig; *(= customary) form, course, pattern* üblich; **his face is ~** das Gesicht ist mir bekannt; **surrounded by ~ faces** von vertrauten Gesichtern umgeben; **the problems are all too ~** die Probleme sind nur allzu vertraut; **to be/seem ~ to sb** jdm bekannt sein/vorkommen; **it looks very ~** es kommt mir sehr bekannt vor; **to sound ~** sich bekannt anhören *(to sb* jdm*)*; **that sounds ~** das habe ich doch schon mal gehört; **to be on ~ ground** Bescheid wissen; **to follow a ~ pattern** *(visit)*$fan outwie gewohnt verlaufen; *(negotiations)* den gewohnten Verlauf nehmen; *(interview)* wie üblich ablaufen
b *(= conversant)* **I am ~ with the word/the town** das Wort/die Stadt ist mir bekannt *or (more closely)* vertraut; **I'm not ~ with computer language** ich bin mit der Computersprache nicht vertraut; **are you ~ with these modern techniques?** wissen Sie über diese modernen Techniken Bescheid?; **is he ~ with our customs?** ist er mit unseren Bräuchen vertraut?; **to make sb ~ with sth** jdn mit etw vertraut machen

c *(= friendly) tone* familiär; *greeting* freundschaftlich; *gesture* familiär, vertraulich; *(= overfriendly)* familiär, plumpvertraulich; **the ~ form of address** die Anrede für Familie und Freunde, die vertraute Anrede; **to be on ~ terms with sb** mit jdm auf vertrautem Fuß stehen; **we're all on pretty ~ terms** wir haben ein ziemlich ungezwungenes Verhältnis zueinander; **~ language** Umgangssprache *f*; **~ expressions** umgangssprachliche Ausdrücke *pl*; **they're not the kind of people one wishes to become too ~ with** mit solchen Leuten möchte man sich nicht unbedingt näher einlassen

N **a** *(liter, = friend)* Vertraute(r) *mf (liter)*

b *(of witch etc)* Hausgeist *m*

familiarity [fəˌmɪlɪˈærɪtɪ] **N** **a** *no pl* Vertrautheit *f* **b** *(between people)* vertrautes Verhältnis; *(between colleagues etc)* ungezwungenes *or* familiäres Verhältnis; *(of tone etc)* Familiarität *f*; *(of greeting)* Freundschaftlichkeit *f*; *(of gesture)* Vertraulichkeit *f*, Familiarität *f*; *(pej: = overfriendliness)* plumpe Vertraulichkeit, Familiarität *f*; **the ~ with which she greeted the head waiter** der vertraute Ton, in dem sie den Oberkellner begrüßte; **~ breeds contempt** *(Prov)* allzu große Vertrautheit erzeugt Verachtung **c** *usu pl (= overfriendly action)* (plumpe) Vertraulichkeit

familiarization [fəˌmɪlɪəraɪˈzeɪʃən] **N** **(process of) ~** Gewöhnungsprozess *m*; **he is responsible for the ~ of all new employees with the procedures** er ist dafür verantwortlich, dass alle neuen Angestellten mit der Verfahrensweise vertraut gemacht werden

familiarize [fəˈmɪlɪəraɪz] **VT to ~ sb/oneself with sth** jdn/sich mit etw vertraut machen; **once you've ~d yourself with the job** wenn Sie sich eingearbeitet haben

familiarly [fəˈmɪljəlɪ] **ADV** **a** *(= informally)* familiär; *(= in a friendly way)* vertraulich; **he slapped me rather too ~ on the back** er klopfte mir plumpvertraulich auf den Rücken; **~ known as** *or* **called X** von Freunden und Verwandten X genannt **b** *(+adj)* gewohnt; **the ~ drab streets** die gewohnt tristen Straßen

family [ˈfæmɪlɪ] **N** **a** Familie *f*; *(including cousins, aunts etc)* Verwandtschaft *f*; *(= lineage)* Familie *f*, Haus *nt*, Geschlecht *nt (geh)*; **to start a ~** eine Familie gründen; **they plan to add to their ~** sie planen Familienzuwachs; **has he any ~?** hat er Familie?; **it runs in the ~** das liegt in der Familie; **of good ~** aus guter Familie, aus gutem Hause; **he's one of the ~** er gehört zur Familie; **with just the immediate ~** im engsten Familienkreis; **a ~ of four** eine vierköpfige Familie

b *(of plants, animals, languages etc)* Familie *f*; **the ~ of man** die Menschheit

ATTR Familien-; **~ business** Familienunternehmen *nt*; **a ~ friend** ein Freund/eine Freundin des Hauses *or* der Familie; **the ~ house** das Haus der Familie; **a ~ house** ein Einfamilienhaus *nt*; **the ~ silver** das Tafelsilber; **she's in the ~ way** *(inf)* sie ist in anderen Umständen; **~ conference** Familienrat *m*; **~ resemblance** Familienähnlichkeit *f*; **~ values** Familienwerte *pl*, familiäre Werte *pl*

family: **family allowance** **N** *(dated)* ≈ Kindergeld *nt*; **family business** **N** Familienbetrieb *m*; **family butcher** **N D. Crosby, Family Butcher** D. Crosby, Fleischermeister; **our/the ~** unsere/die Stammfleischerei; **family circle** **N** **a** *(= family members)* Familienkreis *m* **b** *(US Theat)* zweiter Rang; **family company** **N** Familienunternehmen *nt or* -betrieb *m*; **family credit** **N** *(Brit)* *Sozialleistung für Geringverdiener, um das Familieneinkommen auf einen Mindestbetrag anzuheben*; **Family Division** **N** *(Brit Jur) für Familienrecht zuständige Abteilung des obersten Gerichts*, ≈ Familiengericht *nt*; **family doctor** **N** Hausarzt *m*/-ärztin *f*; **Family Health Services Authority** **N** *(Brit) regionale Gesundheitsbehörde*, ≈ Gesundheitsamt *nt*; **family hotel** **N** Familienpension *f*; **Family Income Supplement** **N** *(dated)* Beihilfe *f* (zum Lebensunterhalt) *(für Familien)*; **family man** **N** *(home-loving)* häuslich veranlagter Mann; *(with a family)* Familienvater *m*; **family name** **N** Familienname *m*, Nachname *m*; **family planning** **N** Familienplanung *f*; **family planning clinic** **N** Familienberatungsstelle *f*; **family reunion** **N** Familientreffen *nt*; **family room** **N** **a** *(esp US: in house)* Wohnzimmer *nt* **b** *(Brit) (in pub) für Kinder zugelassener Raum in einem Lokal (in hotel)* Familienzimmer *nt*; **family-size** **ADJ** in Haushaltsgröße; *car, packet* Familien-; *house* Einfamilien-; **family tree** **N** Stammbaum *m*

famine [ˈfæmɪn] **N** *(lit)* Hungersnot *f*; *(fig)* Knappheit *f*; **to die of ~** verhungern

famine relief **N** Hungerhilfe *f*

famish [ˈfæmɪʃ] **VI** *(inf)* verhungern; **I'm ~ed** ich bin total ausgehungert *(inf)*

famished [ˈfæmɪʃt] **ADJ** *(inf)* verhungert, ausgehungert; **I'm absolutely ~** ich sterbe vor Hunger *(inf)*

famous [ˈfeɪməs] **ADJ** **a** berühmt (*for* durch, für); **so when's this ~ party going to be?** *(iro)* und wann soll diese tolle Party stattfinden? *(inf)*; **~ last words!** *(inf)* man soll es nicht beschreien **b** *(dated: = excellent)* famos *(dated)*

famously [ˈfeɪməslɪ] **ADV** **a** *(= notoriously)* bekanntermaßen; **as X ~ declared** in den berühmten Worten von X; **the man who ~ said "no"** der Mann mit dem berühmten „nein"; **she was married eight times, most ~ to Paul Hassett** sie war achtmal verheiratet, wobei Paul Hassett der bekannteste ihrer Ehemänner war **b** *(dated inf: = excellently)* glänzend; **to get on** *or* **along ~ (with sb)** sich (mit jdm) glänzend verstehen; **they get on ~** sie kommen glänzend miteinander aus; **to do ~** sehr erfolgreich sein; **to go ~** bestens laufen

famulus [ˈfæmjʊləs] **N** Famulus *m*

fan[1] [fæn] **N** **a** *(hand-held)* Fächer *m*; *(mechanical: = extractor fan, Aut: to cool engine)* Ventilator *m*; **then the shit will really hit the ~** *(sl)* dann ist die Kacke echt am Dampfen *(sl)*

b *(of peacock, fig)* Fächer *m*; **to spread sth out in a ~** etw fächerförmig ausbreiten

VT **a** *(wind)* umwehen; *(person)* fächeln *(+dat)*; **to ~ sb/oneself** jdm/sich (Luft) zufächeln; **to ~ the embers** die Glut anfachen; **to ~ the flames** *(lit)* das Feuer anfachen; *(fig)* Öl ins Feuer gießen; **to ~ the flames of resentment/violence** den Groll/die Gewalt schüren

b *cards* fächerförmig ausbreiten; **the peacock ~ned its tail** der Pfau schlug ein Rad

▶ **fan out** **VI** *(searchers etc)* ausschwärmen **VT** *sep feathers* fächerförmig aufstellen; *cards* fächerförmig ausbreiten

fan[2] **N** *(= supporter)* Fan *m*, Anhänger(in) *m(f)*; **I'm quite a ~ of yours** ich bin ein richtiger Verehrer von Ihnen

fan-assisted [ˈfænəˌsɪstɪd] **ADJ** **~ oven** Umluftherd *m*

fanatic [fəˈnætɪk] **N** Fanatiker(in) *m(f)* **ADJ** = **fanatical**

fanatical [fəˈnætɪkəl] **ADJ** fanatisch; **he is ~ about it/them** es geht/sie gehen ihm über alles; **I'm ~ about fitness** ich bin ein Fitnessfanatiker; **there was a ~ gleam in her eye** ihre Augen glänzten fanatisch

fanatically [fəˈnætɪkəlɪ] **ADV** *(+adj) loyal, hostile* auf fanatische Weise; *(+vb) train, cheer* fanatisch; **to be ~ against sth** *or* **opposed to sth** ein fanatischer Gegner von etw sein

fanaticism [fəˈnætɪsɪzəm] **N** Fanatismus *m*

fan base **N** Fangemeinde *f*

fan belt **N** Keilriemen *m*

fanciable [ˈfænsɪəbl] **ADJ** *(Brit: = attractive)* attraktiv, anziehend

fancied [ˈfænsɪd] **ADJ** *(= imaginary)* eingebildet

fancier [ˈfænsɪəˈ] **N** Liebhaber(in) *m(f)*

fanciful [ˈfænsɪfʊl] **ADJ** *story, idea* fantastisch, phantastisch, abstrus; *(= fancy) costume* reich verziert; *pattern, animal etc* fantasievoll, phantasievoll; *(= unrealistic) plan etc* unrealistisch; *visions* überspannt; **I think you're being somewhat ~** ich glaube, das ist etwas weit hergeholt; **and I don't think it's ~ to claim that ...** und ich glaube nicht, dass es verstiegen ist zu behaupten, dass ...

fancifulness [ˈfænsɪfʊlnɪs] **N** *(of story etc)* Seltsamkeit *f*; *(of person)* blühende Fantasie *or* Phantasie; *(of costume)* reiche Verzierung; *(of pattern)* Fantasiereichtum *m*, Phantasiereichtum *m*

fan club **N** Fanklub *m*

fancy [ˈfænsɪ] **VT** **a** *(= like, be attracted by)* **I ~ that car/the idea** *(= like)* das Auto/die Idee gefällt mir *or* hat es mir angetan; **he fancies a house on Crete** *(= would like to have)* er hätte gern ein Haus auf Kreta; **I don't ~ a house in Glasgow** ich möchte kein Haus in Glasgow haben; **I didn't ~ that job/that party** die Stelle/die Party hat mich nicht gereizt; **do you ~ a walk/steak/beer?** hast du Lust zu einem Spaziergang/auf ein Steak/auf ein Bier?; **she fancies (the idea of) doing that** *(= would like to)* sie würde *or* möchte das gern tun; *(= feels like it)* sie hätte Lust, das zu tun; **count me out, I don't ~ the idea** ohne mich, das ist nichts für mich; **I don't ~ the idea, but I'll have to do it** ich habe gar keine Lust dazu, aber ich muss es ja wohl tun; **I don't ~ THAT (idea)!** nur das nicht; **he fancies her as a wife** er hätte sie gern zur Frau; **he really fancies her** *(sexually)* er ist scharf auf sie *(inf)*; **I don't ~ him** *(sexually)* ich finde ihn nicht attraktiv; **he fancies his chances** er meint, er hätte Chancen; **I don't ~ my chances of getting that job** ich rechne mir keine großen Chancen aus, die Stelle zu bekommen; **a bit of what you ~ does you good** man muss sich auch mal was Gutes gönnen

b *(= imagine)* meinen, sich *(dat)* einbilden; *(= think)* glauben; **he fancied he heard footsteps** er meinte, Schritte zu hören; **I rather ~ he has gone out** ich glaube, er ist weggegangen; **how long? – not long, I ~** wie lange? – nicht lange, denke *or* glaube ich

c *(in exclamations)* **~ doing that!** so was(, das) zu tun!; **~ him doing that!** nicht zu fassen, dass er das getan hat *or* tut!; **~ that!** *(inf)* **(just) ~!** *(inf)* (nein) so was!, denk mal an! *(inf)*; **just ~, he ...** *(inf)* stell dir vor, er ...; **~ seeing you here!** so was, Sie hier zu sehen!; **~ him winning!** wer hätte gedacht, dass er gewinnt!

VR von sich eingenommen sein, sich für Wunder was halten *(inf)*; **he fancies himself as an actor/expert** er hält sich für einen (guten) Schauspieler/einen Experten; **do you ~ yourself as a teacher?** kannst du dir dich als Lehrer vorstellen?; **they ~ themselves to be Europeans** sie halten sich für Europäer

N **a** *(= liking)* **to have a ~ for sth** Lust zu etw haben; *(for food or drink)* Lust auf etw *(acc)* haben; **she had a ~ for sports cars** sie hatte eine Vorliebe für Sportwagen; **a passing ~** nur so eine Laune; **he's taken a ~ to her/this car/the idea** sie/das Auto/die Idee hat es ihm angetan; **they took a ~ to each other** sie fanden sich sympathisch; **to take** *or* **catch sb's ~** jdn ansprechen, jdm gefallen; **they took a ~ to go swimming** sie bekamen Lust, schwimmen zu gehen; **to tickle sb's ~** jdn reizen; **just as the ~ takes me/you** *etc* ganz nach Lust und Laune; **he only works when the ~ takes him** er arbeitet nur, wenn ihm gerade danach ist

b *no pl (= imagination)* Fantasie *f*, Phantasie *f*; **to separate fact from ~** die Wirklichkeit von der Fantasie trennen; **that was just his ~** das hat er sich *(dat)* nur eingebildet

c *(= notion, whim)* **I have a ~ that ...** ich habe so ein Gefühl, dass ...; **he had a sudden ~ to go to Spain** ihn überkam eine plötzliche Laune, nach Spanien zu fahren

ADJ *(+er)* **a** *(inf: = elaborate) clothes, shoes* ausgefallen; *pattern, hairdo, manoeuvre* kunstvoll; *food, gadget* raffiniert; *word, language* hochtrabend; **nothing ~** nichts Ausgefallenes; **you won't get anything ~ there** dort be-

kommst du nur etwas ganz Einfaches; **I want something ~** *(when buying clothes)* ich möchte etwas Schickes *or* Ausgefallenes; **he uses such ~ language** er drückt sich so gewählt aus; **how do you like our new computer? – very ~!** wie gefällt dir unser neuer Computer? – sehr beeindruckend!; **~ trick** toller Trick *(inf)*; **~ footwork** *(Ftbl)* geschickte Beinarbeit; *(in dancing)* komplizierte Schritte *pl*; *(fig)* raffinierte Manöver *pl*
b *(often pej inf: = smart) house, car, clothes, shop* schick *(inf)*; *school, restaurant* nobel, schick *(inf)*; **a ~ car** ein toller Schlitten *(inf)*
c *(inf: = high) price* überhöht, gepfeffert *(inf)*

fancy: **fancy dress** N (Masken)kostüm *nt*; **is it ~?** geht man da verkleidet hin?; **they came in ~** sie kamen verkleidet *or* kostümiert; **fancy-dress** ATTR **~ ball** Maskenball *m*; **~ party** Kostümfest *nt*; **fancy-free** ADJ → **footloose**; **fancy goods** PL Geschenkartikel *pl*; **fancy man** N *(= pimp)* Zuhälter *m*; *(= lover)* Liebhaber *m*; **fancy woman** N Freundin *f*, Weibchen *nt* *(inf)*; **fancywork** N feine Handarbeit

fandango [fæn'dæŋgəʊ] N Fandango *m*

fanfare ['fænfɛə'] N Fanfare *f*; **trumpet ~** Trompetenstoß *m*; **with a ~ of publicity** mit einer aufsehenerregenden Werbekampagne

fanfold paper ['fænfəʊld'peɪpə'] N *(Comput)* Endlospapier *nt*

fang [fæŋ] N *(of snake)* Giftzahn *m*; *(of wolf, dog)* Fang *m*; *(of vampire)* Vampirzahn *m*; *(hum, of person)* Hauer *m* *(hum)*

fan: **fan heater** N Heizlüfter *m*; **fanlight** N Oberlicht *nt*; **fan mail** N Verehrerpost *f*

fanny ['fænɪ] N **a** *(esp US inf)* Po *m* *(inf)* **b** *(Brit sl)* Möse *f* *(vulg)*

fanny bag N *(US)* Gürteltasche *f*, Wimmerl *nt* *(dial)*

fan oven N Umluftherd *m*

fan-shaped ['fænʃeɪpt] ADJ fächerförmig

fantabulous [fæn'tæbjʊləs] ADJ *(inf)* super(klasse)toll *(inf)*

fantail N *(= pigeon)* Pfautaube *f*

fantasia [fæn'teɪzɪə] N Fantasie *f*

fantasize ['fæntəsaɪz] VI fantasieren, phantasieren; *(= dream)* Fantasie- *or* Phantasievorstellungen haben *(about* von)

fantastic [fæn'tæstɪk] INTERJ *(inf)* fantastisch!, toll! *(inf)*; **you're pregnant? ~!** du bist schwanger? (das ist ja) toll! *(inf)*
ADJ **a** *(inf: = wonderful)* fantastisch, toll *(inf)*; **it was a ~ success** es war ein Riesenerfolg; **to look ~** fantastisch *or* fabelhaft aussehen; **to sound ~** sich fantastisch anhören
b *(inf: = terrific, huge) range, profit* fantastisch; **a ~ amount of, ~ amounts of** unwahrscheinlich *or* wahnsinnig viel *(inf)*; **at a ~ speed** unwahrscheinlich *or* wahnsinnig schnell *(inf)*
c *(= fantastical, exotic) creature* fantastisch, phantastisch; **~ world** Fabelwelt *f* → **trip VT c**
d *(= unbelievable, improbable) story* unwahrscheinlich; *truth* unglaublich; **~ though that may seem** so unglaublich das auch scheinen mag; **it all seems a bit too ~ to me** es kommt mir alles etwas zu unglaublich vor

fantastical [fæn'tæstɪkl] ADJ *(liter) story, place, world* fantastisch, phantastisch; *account, architecture* seltsam, skurril *(geh)*

fantastically [fæn'tæstɪkəlɪ] ADV **a** *(inf: = extraordinarily) high, large, expensive, well etc* unwahrscheinlich *(inf)*, wahnsinnig *(inf)* **b** *(= strikingly)* auffallend; *(= imaginatively)* fantasievoll, phantasievoll; *(= elaborately)* kunstvoll; **~ coloured** fantastisch *or* phantastisch bunt

fantasy ['fæntəsɪ] N **a** *(= imagination)* Fantasie *f*, Phantasie *f* **b** *(= illusion)* Fantasie *f*, Hirngespinst *nt* *(pej)*; **that's pure ~** *or* **a ~** das ist reine Fantasie *or* bloß ein Hirngespinst **c** *(Mus, Liter)* Fantasie *f*

fan: **fan tracery** N fächerförmiges Maßwerk; **fan vaulting** N Fächergewölbe *nt*

fanzine ['fænziːn] N Fanmagazin *nt*

FAO *abbr of* **for the attention of** z. Hd.

FAQ N *(Comput) abbr of* **frequently asked questions** häufig gestellte Fragen *pl*

far [fɑː'] ✪ 26.2 *comp* **further, farther**, *superl* **furthest, farthest** ADV **a** *(in distance)* weit; **we don't live ~** *or* **we live not ~ from here** wir wohnen nicht weit von hier; **I'll go with you as ~ as the gate** ich begleite dich bis zum Tor; **~ and wide** weit und breit; **from ~ and near** *or* **wide** von nah und fern; **~ above** hoch *or* weit über *(+dat)*; **~ away** weit entfernt *or* weg; **I won't be ~ off** *or* **away** ich bin ganz in der Nähe; **~ away in the distance** weit in der Ferne; **I was** *or* **my thoughts were ~ away** ich war mit meinen Gedanken weit weg; **~ into the jungle** weit in den Dschungel hinein; **~ out** weit draußen; **have you come ~?** kommen Sie von weit her?
b *(in time)* **as ~ back as I can remember** so weit ich (zurück)denken *or* mich erinnern kann; **as ~ back as 1945** schon (im Jahr) 1945; **~ into the night** bis spät in die Nacht; **~ into the future** bis weit in die Zukunft
c *(in degree, extent)* weit; **how ~ have you got with your plans?** wie weit sind Sie mit Ihren Plänen (gekommen)?; **~ longer/better** weit länger/besser; **it's ~ beyond what I can afford** das übersteigt meine Mittel bei Weitem
d *(in set phrases)* **as** *or* **so ~ as I'm concerned** was mich betrifft; **it's all right as ~ as it goes** das ist so weit ganz gut; **in so ~ as** insofern als; **~ and away the best, by ~ the best, the best by ~** bei Weitem *or* mit Abstand der/die/das Beste; **better by ~** weit besser; **~ from satisfactory** alles andere als befriedigend; **~ from liking him I find him quite unpleasant** ich mag ihn nicht, ich finde ihn (im Gegenteil) sogar ausgesprochen unsympathisch; **~ from it!** ganz und gar nicht, (ganz) im Gegenteil; **~ be it from me to …** es sei mir ferne, zu …; **so ~** *(= up to now)* bisher, bis jetzt; *(= up to this point)* so weit; **so ~ this week I've seen him once/three times** diese Woche habe ich ihn erst einmal/schon dreimal gesehen; **so ~ this week I haven't seen him at all** diese Woche habe ich ihn noch nicht gesehen; **so ~ so good** so weit, so gut; **so ~ and no further** bis hierher und nicht weiter; **to go ~** *(money, supplies, measures etc)* weit reichen; *(= last a long time also)* lange reichen; *(person: = succeed)* es weit bringen; **these measures won't go very ~ toward(s) stemming rising costs** diese Maßnahmen werden nicht viel dazu beitragen, die steigenden Kosten einzudämmen; **I would go so ~ as to say …** ich würde so weit gehen zu sagen …; **that's going too ~** das geht zu weit; **to carry a joke too ~** einen Spaß zu weit treiben; **that's carrying a joke too ~** da hört der Spaß auf; **not ~ out** *(in guess)* nicht schlecht; **~ out** *(= avant-garde, art)* hypermodern; *ideas* ausgefallen; *(inf: = fantastic)* echt geil *(sl)*; **not ~ off** *(in space)* nicht weit; *(in guess, aim)* fast (getroffen); *(= almost)* nicht viel weniger; **the weekend isn't ~ off now** es ist nicht mehr lang bis zum Wochenende; **~ gone** *(inf)* schon ziemlich hinüber *(inf)*
ADJ **a** *(= more distant of two)* weiter entfernt, hintere(r, s); **the ~ end of the room** das andere Ende des Zimmers; **the ~ window/door** das Fenster/die Tür am anderen Ende des Zimmers; **the ~ wall** die Wand am anderen Ende; **on the ~ side of** auf der anderen Seite von; **when he reached the ~ bank** als er am anderen Ufer ankam; **which of these cars is yours? – the ~ one** welches ist dein Auto? – das, das weiter weg ist; **which bed will you have? – the ~ one** welches Bett möchtest du? – das da drüben
b *(= far-off) country, land* weit entfernt; **in the ~ distance** in weiter Ferne; **it's a ~ cry from …** *(fig)* das ist etwas ganz anderes als …

Faraday cage ['færədeɪ,keɪdʒ] N *(Phys)* faradayscher Käfig

faraway, far-away ['fɑːrəweɪ] ADJ **a** *(= distant) place* entlegen; *town, region, country* fern; *sound, voice, person* weit entfernt; **a tiny, ~ voice** ein kleines Stimmchen in der Ferne; **a ~ relative** ein in der Ferne lebender Verwandter **b** *(= dreamy) look, voice* verträumt, versonnen

farce [fɑːs] N *(Theat, fig)* Farce *f*; **the election campaign degenerated into ~** der Wahlkampf wurde zur Farce

farcemeat ['fɑːsmiːt] N = **forcemeat**

farcical ['fɑːsɪkl] ADJ *(Theat)* possenhaft; *(fig: = absurd)* absurd, grotesk

fare [fɛə'] N **a** *(= charge)* Fahrpreis *m*; *(on plane)* Flugpreis *m*; *(on boat)* Preis *m* für die Überfahrt; *(= money)* Fahrgeld *nt*; **what is the ~?** was kostet die Fahrt/der Flug/die Überfahrt?; **~s, please!** noch jemand ohne *(inf)*, noch jemand zugestiegen?; **have you got the right ~?** haben Sie das Fahrgeld passend?; **he gave me (the cost of/money for) the ~** er gab mir das Fahrgeld
b *(= passenger)* Fahrgast *m*
c *(old, form: = food)* Kost *f*; **traditional Christmas ~** ein traditionelles Weihnachtsessen; **vegetarian dishes are now standard ~ in most restaurants** vegetarische Gerichte gehören jetzt in den meisten Restaurants zum Angebot
VI **he ~d well** es ging *or* erging *(geh)* ihm gut; **the dollar ~d well on the stock exchange today** der Dollar schnitt heute an der Börse gut ab; **~ thee well** *(old)* leb(e) wohl *(old)*

Far East N **the ~** der Ferne Osten

Far Eastern ADJ fernöstlich; **~ politics** Fernostpolitik *f*; **~ travel** Fernostreisen *pl*

fare: **fare-dodger** N Schwarzfahrer(in) *m(f)*; **fare stage** N Fahrzone *f*, Teilstrecke *f*, Zahlgrenze *f*

farewell [fɛə'wel] N Abschied *m*; **to say** *or* **make one's ~s** sich verabschieden; *(before a longer absence)* Abschied nehmen; **to bid sb ~** jdm Auf Wiedersehen *or* Lebewohl *(old)* sagen; **to say ~ to sth** *(fig)* von etw Abschied nehmen INTERJ *(old)* lebt wohl *(old)*; *(to friend, sweetheart)* leb(e) wohl *(old)*

farewell *in cpds* Abschieds-; **~ speech** Abschiedsrede *f*

fare zone N Tarifzone *f*

far: **far-fetched** ADJ weit hergeholt, an den Haaren herbeigezogen; **far-flung** ADJ **a** *(= distant)* abgelegen **b** *(= widely spread)* weit auseinandergezogen; **far gone** ADJ *night* weit fortgeschritten; *person* erschöpft, schwach; *clothes* abgetragen; *shoes* abgetreten → *also* **far**

farinaceous [,færɪ'neɪʃəs] ADJ mehlhaltig

farm [fɑːm] N Bauernhof *m*; *(bigger)* Gutshof *m*; *(in US, Australia, = health farm)* Farm *f*; *(= fish farm)* Fischzucht *f*, Teichwirtschaft *f* *(form)*; *(= mink farm etc)* (Pelztier)zuchtfarm *f*; **pig/chicken ~** Schweine-/Hühnerfarm *f*; **trout ~** Forellenzucht *f* ATTR landwirtschaftlich; **~ labourer** *(Brit)* *or* **laborer** *(US)* Landarbeiter(in) *m(f)*; **~ animals** Tiere *pl* auf dem Bauernhof VT *land* bebauen; *livestock* halten; *trout, mink etc* züchten VI Landwirtschaft betreiben; **man has been ~ing for thousands of years** der Mensch (be)treibt schon seit Jahrtausenden Ackerbau und Viehzucht

▶ **farm out** VT *sep work* vergeben *(on, to* an *+acc)*; *children* in Pflege geben *(to +dat* bei)

farmer ['fɑːmə'] N Bauer *m*, Bäuerin *f*, Landwirt(in) *m(f)*; *(in US, Australia)* Farmer(in) *m(f)*; *(= mink farmer)* Züchter(in) *m(f)*; *(= fish farmer)* Teichwirt(in) *m(f)* *(form)*; *(= gentleman farmer)* Gutsherr *m*; *(= tenant farmer)* Pächter(in) *m(f)*; **~'s wife** Bäuerin *f*; **~'s co-operative** landwirtschaftliche Genossenschaft

farm: **farmhand** N Landarbeiter(in) *m(f)*; **farmhouse** N Bauernhaus *nt*; **farmhouse loaf** N *(Brit) großes, in einer Kastenform gebackenes Weißbrot*

farming ['fɑːmɪŋ] N Landwirtschaft *f*; *(of crops also)* Ackerbau *m*; *(of animals also)* Viehzucht *f*

farm: **farmland** N Ackerland *nt*; **farm prices** PL Agrarpreise *pl*; **farmstead** N Bauernhof *m*, Gehöft *nt*; **farmyard** N Hof *m*

Far North N **the ~** der hohe Norden

faro ['fɛərəʊ] N Phar(a)o *nt*

Faroe Islands ['fɛərəʊ,aɪləndz], **Faroes** ['fɛərəʊz] PL Färöer *pl*

Faroese [ˌfɛərəʊˈiːz] N a (= person) Färöer(in) *m(f)* b (Ling) Färöisch(e) *nt* ADJ färöisch; **the ~ people** die Färöer *pl*

far-off [ˈfɑːrɒf] ADJ a *days, time (in the past)* lange vergangen, weit zurückliegend; *(in the future)* weit entfernt b *place, country* fern, weit entfernt ADV in der Ferne

farrago [fəˈrɑːgəʊ] N Gemisch *nt*, Allerlei *nt*

far-reaching ADJ weitreichend, weit reichend

farrier [ˈfærɪəˈ] N Hufschmied *m*

farrow [ˈfærəʊ] VT *piglets* werfen VI ferkeln N Wurf *m*

far-seeing ADJ weitblickend, weit blickend

Farsi [ˈfɑːsiː] N Farsi *nt*

far: **far-sighted** ADJ a *(lit)* weitsichtig b *(fig) person, policy* weitblickend, weit blickend; *(= taking precautionary measures)* umsichtig; *measures* auf weite Sicht geplant; **far-sightedness** N a *(lit)* Weitsichtigkeit *f* b *(fig: of person, policy)* Weitblick *m*

fart [fɑːt] *(inf)* N a Furz *m (inf)* b *(= person)* **he's a boring old ~** er ist ein langweiliger alter Knacker *(inf)* VI furzen *(inf)*

▸ **fart about** *(Brit)* or **around** VI a *(= rush around)* hin und her sausen *(inf)* b *(= loaf around)* herumbummeln *(inf)* c *(inf) (= mess around)* herumalbern *(inf)*; **stop farting about** or **around and do some work** jetzt halte dich nicht länger auf und arbeite mal was *(inf)*; **to fart about** or **around with sth** an etw *(dat)* herumfummeln *(inf)*

farther [ˈfɑːðəˈ] *comp of* **far** ADV = **further ADV a** ADJ weiter entfernt, hintere(r, s); **at the ~ end** am anderen Ende

farthermost [ˈfɑːðəməʊst] ADJ = **furthermost**

farthest [ˈfɑːðɪst] ADJ ADV *superl of* **far**; **the ~ point of the island** der am weitesten entfernte Punkt der Insel → **furthest ADV, ADJ**

farthing [ˈfɑːðɪŋ] N Farthing *m (ein Viertelpenny)*

farthingale [ˈfɑːðɪŋgeɪl] N Reifrock *m*, Krinoline *f*

fas *abbr of* **free alongside ship** frei Kai

fascia [ˈfeɪʃə] N *(Brit Aut)* Armaturentafel *f*

fascicle [ˈfæsɪkl], **fascicule** [ˈfæsɪkjuːl] N a *(Bot)* Büschel *nt*; *(Anat)* Bündel *nt* b *(of book)* Lieferung *f*, Faszikel *(old) m*

fascinate [ˈfæsɪneɪt] VT faszinieren; *(= enchant: skill, beauty, singer etc also)* begeistern, bezaubern; *(= hold spellbound: book, film, magician also)* fesseln; **old houses ~/this subject ~s me** ich finde alte Häuser/dieses Gebiet hochinteressant or faszinierend; **the audience watched/listened ~d** das Publikum sah/hörte gebannt zu; **it ~s me how well he does these things** ich finde es erstaunlich, wie gut er das macht

fascinating [ˈfæsɪneɪtɪŋ] ADJ faszinierend, hochinteressant; *beauty* bezaubernd

fascinatingly [ˈfæsɪneɪtɪŋlɪ] ADV faszinierend; *talk, describe* hochinteressant; *beautiful* bezaubernd; *(introducing sentence)* faszinierenderweise; **~ interesting** hochinteressant

fascination [ˌfæsɪˈneɪʃən] N Faszination *f*; *(= fascinating quality also)* Reiz *m*; **to listen/watch in ~** gebannt zuhören/zusehen; **to have** or **hold a ~ for sb** auf jdn einen besonderen Reiz ausüben; **his ~ with the cinema** der Reiz, den das Kino für ihn hat, die Faszination, die das Kino auf ihn ausübt; **I don't understand the ~ of this book** ich verstehe nicht, was an diesem Buch so faszinierend ist; **she developed a ~ for Impressionist painting** impressionistische Malerei begann sie zu faszinieren

fascism [ˈfæʃɪzəm] N Faschismus *m*

fascist [ˈfæʃɪst] N Faschist(in) *m(f)* ADJ faschistisch

fascistic [fəˈʃɪstɪk] ADJ faschistisch

fash [fæʃ] VT *(Scot: = trouble)* ärgern; *(= worry)* aufregen

fashion [ˈfæʃən] N a *no pl (= manner)* Art (und Weise) *f*; **(in the) Indian ~** auf Indianerart, nach Art der Indianer; **in the usual ~** wie üblich; **in a similar ~** auf ähnliche Weise; **to behave in a strange ~** sich merkwürdig verhalten; **did it work/have you translated it? – after a ~** hat es geklappt/hast du es übersetzt? – so einigermaßen; **to do sth after** or **in a ~** etw recht und schlecht machen; **I can cook after a ~** ich kann so einigermaßen kochen; **a novel after** or **in the ~ of D.H. Lawrence** ein Roman im Stil von D. H. Lawrence; **in this ~** auf diese Weise, so

b *(in clothing: = latest style)* Mode *f*; **(back) in ~** (wieder) modern; **it's the/all the ~** es ist Mode/große Mode; **to come into/go out of ~** in Mode/aus der Mode kommen; **a man of ~** ein modischer Herr; **the Paris ~s** die Pariser Mode; **she always wears the latest ~s** sie ist immer nach der neuesten Mode gekleidet; **~s in women's clothes** die Damenmode; **to set a ~** eine Mode aufbringen; **the ~ world** die Welt der Mode

c *(= custom, of society)* Sitte *f*, Brauch *m*; *(of individual)* Gewohnheit *f*; **it was the ~ in those days** das war damals Sitte or Brauch

VT formen, gestalten; **to ~ sth after sth** etw einer Sache *(dat)* nachbilden

fashionable [ˈfæʃnəbl] ADJ *clothes, look, person* modisch; *restaurant, shop, area* schick; *idea, artist* zurzeit beliebt; **~ colour** *(Brit)* or **color** *(US)* Modefarbe *f*; **~ writer** Modeschriftsteller(in) *m(f)*; **to become ~** in Mode kommen, modern werden; **it's ~ to do that** es ist modern or (in) Mode, das zu tun; **Michelle is super ~** *(inf)* Michelle hat supermoderne Klamotten *(inf)*; **the ~ set** or **people** die Schickeria

fashionably [ˈfæʃnəblɪ] ADV modisch

fashion-conscious ADJ modebewusst

fashion designer N Modezeichner(in) *m(f)*

fashionista [ˌfæʃəˈniːstə] N *(= fashion lover)* Modefreak *m*; *(= designer)* Modemacher(in) *m(f)*; *(= journalist)* Modejournalist(in) *m(f)*

fashion: **fashion magazine** N Modeheft *nt* or -zeitschrift *f*; **fashion model** N Mannequin *nt*; *(= man)* Dressman *m*; **fashion parade** N Mode(n)schau *f*; **fashion plate** N Modezeichnung *f*; **she looked like a ~** sie sah aus wie aus der Modezeitung; **fashion sense** N *(esp US)* Modebewusstsein *nt*; **Tom has no ~** Tom hat bei Kleidung keinen Geschmack; **fashion show** N Mode(n)schau *f*; **fashion victim** N *(pej inf)* Modesklave *m*/-sklavin *f (inf)*, Modesfreak *m (inf)*; **fashionwear** [ˈfæʃənwɛəˈ] N Modeartikel *pl*

fast[1] [fɑːst] ADJ *(+er)* a *(= quick)* schnell; **she's a ~ runner/reader** sie kann schnell laufen/lesen; **he's a ~ worker** *(lit)* er arbeitet schnell; *(fig)* er geht mächtig ran *(inf)*; **to pull a ~ one (on sb)** *(inf)* jdn übers Ohr hauen *(inf)*; **the ~ life** das hektische Leben; **~ train** *(Brit)* D-Zug *m*

b **to be ~** *(clock, watch)* vorgehen; **to be five minutes ~** fünf Minuten vorgehen

c *tennis court, squash ball etc* schnell

d *(Phot) film* hochempfindlich; *lens* lichtstark

e *(fig: = immoral) behaviour, person* locker, flott, ausschweifend *(pej)*; **~ woman** leichtlebige Frau

ADV a schnell

b *(fig)* **to live ~** flott or locker leben

c *(old)* **to follow ~ on sth** dicht auf etw *(acc)* folgen

fast[2] ADJ a *(= firm, secure)* fest; **to make a boat ~** ein Boot festmachen b *colour, dye* farbecht c *(= staunch) friend* gut ADV a *(= firmly, securely)* fest; **to stick ~** festsitzen; *(with glue)* festkleben; **to stand ~** standhaft or fest bleiben; **to stand ~ by sb** (treu) zu jdm stehen; **to stand ~ by sth** an etw *(dat)* festhalten; **to hold ~ to sth** an etw *(dat)* festhalten; **to play ~ and loose with sb** mit jdm ein falsches or doppeltes Spiel treiben b *(= soundly)* **to be ~ asleep** tief or fest schlafen

fast[3] VI *(= not eat)* fasten N Fasten *nt*; *(= period of fasting)* Fastenzeit *f*; **~ day** Fasttag *m*; **to break one's ~** das Fasten brechen

fast: **fastback** N (Wagen *m* mit) Fließheck *nt*; **fast-breeder reactor** N Schneller Brüter

fasten [ˈfɑːsn] VT a *(= attach)* festmachen, befestigen *(to, onto* an *+dat)*; *(= do up) parcel etc* zuschnüren; *buttons, buckle, dress etc* zumachen; *(= tighten) screw etc* anziehen; *(= lock) door* (ab)-schließen; **to ~ one's seat belt** sich anschnallen; **to ~ two things together** zwei Dinge zusammenmachen *(inf)* or aneinander befestigen

b *(fig) thoughts, attention* zuwenden *(on sb* jdm); **to ~ the blame on sb** die Schuld auf jdn schieben, jdm die Schuld in die Schuhe schieben *(inf)*; **to ~ one's hopes on sb/sth** seine Hoffnungen auf jdn/etw setzen; **to ~ one's eyes on sb/sth** die Augen or den Blick auf jdn/etw heften

VI sich schließen lassen; **the dress ~s at the back** das Kleid wird hinten zugemacht; **the door won't ~** die Tür lässt sich nicht schließen; **these two pieces ~ together** diese zwei Teile werden miteinander verbunden

▸ **fasten down** VT *sep* festmachen

▸ **fasten in** VT *sep* festschnallen (*+prep obj* in *+dat*)

▸ **fasten on** VT *sep* befestigen, festmachen (*+prep obj, -to* an *+dat*); *flower, badge* anheften (*+prep obj, -to* an *+dat*) VI *+prep obj (= concentrate on) person, subject* herumhacken auf *(+dat) (inf)*; **his eyes fastened on mine** er heftete seine Augen auf meine

▸ **fasten onto** VI *+prep obj (fig)* **to fasten onto sth** sich in etw *(acc)* verbeißen

▸ **fasten up** VT *sep dress etc* zumachen; **could you fasten me up?** *(inf)* kannst du mir zumachen? *(inf)*

fastener [ˈfɑːsnəˈ], **fastening** [ˈfɑːsnɪŋ] N Verschluss *m*

fast food N Fast Food *nt*, Fastfood *nt*; **he lives mainly on ~** er ernährt sich hauptsächlich von Fast Food or von Schnellgerichten

fast-food [ˈfɑːstfuːd]: **fast-food chain** N Fast-Food-Kette *f*, Fastfoodkette *f*, Schnellimbisskette *f*; **fast-food joint** N *(US)* Fast-Food-Restaurant *nt* or -Laden *m (inf)*; **fast-food outlet** N Fast-Food-Lokal *nt*, Schnellimbiss *m*; **fast-food place, fast-food restaurant** N Fast-Food-Restaurant *nt* or -Laden *m (inf)* Schnellimbiss *m*

fast: **fast forward** N *(on tape deck)* Vorspultaste *f*; **fast-forward** [fɑːstˈfɔːwəd] VTI vorspulen

fastidious [fæsˈtɪdɪəs] ADJ genau *(about* in Bezug auf *+acc)*; *(pej)* pingelig *(inf) (about* in Bezug auf *+acc)*

fastidiously [fæsˈtɪdɪəslɪ] ADV a *(= meticulously) check, copy, examine* mit äußerster Sorgfalt; **~ tidy** *(place)* sorgfältigst aufgeräumt; *person* penibel ordentlich; **~ clean** peinlich sauber b *(pej: = fussily)* pingelig *(inf)*; **he wrinkled his nose ~** er rümpfte angewidert die Nase

fastidiousness [fæsˈtɪdɪəsnɪs] N Sorgfalt *f*; *(pej: = fussiness)* Pingeligkeit *f (inf)*

fasting [ˈfɑːstɪŋ] N Fasten *nt*

fast lane N Überholspur *f*; **life in the ~** *(fig)* das hektische Leben; **those in the ~ of life** diese dynamischen Erfolgstypen *(inf)*

fastness [ˈfɑːstnɪs] N a *(= stronghold)* Feste *f*; **mountain ~** Bergfeste *f* b *(of colours)* Farbechtheit *f* c *(= immorality)* Liederlichkeit *f*

fast track N schnellster Weg; **~ carrier** Senkrechtkarriere *f*

fat [fæt] ADJ *(+er)* a *(= overweight) person, animal, stomach, arms, thighs* dick, fett *(pej)*; **to get** or **become ~** dick werden; **to grow ~ (on sth)** *(fig, person, company, town)* (durch etw) reich werden; **it's** or **the show's not over until the ~ lady sings** *(hum inf)* das ist noch nicht das Ende

b *(= thick) book, pile* dick; *(fig inf) profit, fee, salary* üppig, fett *(inf)*; *wallet, cheque(book)* dick; *(= prosperous) year, period* fett

c *(= fatty) meat* fett

d *(inf: = stupid)* **can't you get it into your ~ head (that) …** hast du Idiot es denn noch immer nicht gecheckt, dass … *(inf)*; **they can't get it into their silly ~ heads that …** diesen

Idioten will es nicht in den Kopf, dass … *(inf)* → *also* **fathead**

e *(iro inf)* **that's a ~ lot of good** *or* **use** das bringt doch überhaupt nichts; **a ~ lot of good thieving did you** das Stehlen hat dir überhaupt nichts gebracht *(inf)*; **~ lot of help she was** sie war 'ne schöne Hilfe! *(iro inf)*; **~ chance!** schön wärs!; **~ chance of that!** das kannst du dir abschminken! *(inf)*

N *(Anat, Cook, Chem)* Fett *nt*; **reduce the ~ in your diet** reduzieren Sie den Fettgehalt Ihrer Ernährung; **to put on ~** Speck ansetzen *(inf)*; **to run to ~** in die Breite gehen *(inf)*; **to live off the ~ of the land** *(fig)* wie Gott in Frankreich *or* wie die Made im Speck leben; **the ~'s in the fire** *(fig)* jetzt ist der Teufel los *(inf)*

fatal ['feɪtl] ADJ **a** *(= causing death)* tödlich *(to, for* für); **he had a ~ accident** er ist tödlich verunglückt; **the illness is invariably ~** die Krankheit verläuft immer tödlich; **possibly ~ delays** Verzögerungen *pl*, die möglicherweise tödliche Folgen haben werden; **to prove ~** sich als tödlich erweisen; **~ accident inquiry** *(Scot)* Untersuchung *f* zur Unfallursache *(bei Unfällen mit Todesfolge)*

b *(fig: = disastrous) mistake, weakness, flaw, consequences* fatal, verhängnisvoll; *(Comput) error* schwer; *(= fateful) day, decision* verhängnisvoll; **to be** *or* **prove ~ to** *or* **for sb/sth** das Ende für jdn/etw bedeuten *or* sein; **it proved ~ to their diplomatic relations** es hatte verhängnisvolle Folgen für ihre diplomatischen Beziehungen; **in the end such methods will prove ~** solche Methoden werden sich letztendlich als verhängnisvoll herausstellen; **it's ~ to ask him, he always forgets** frag ihn bloß nicht, er vergisst es immer; **it would be ~ to do that** es wäre verhängnisvoll, das zu tun; **it was a ~ blow to our hopes** es hat unsere Hoffnungen zunichtegemacht; **her ~ attraction for him** die unheilvolle Anziehungskraft, die sie auf ihn ausübte

fatalism ['feɪtəlɪzəm] N Fatalismus *m*

fatalist ['feɪtəlɪst] N Fatalist(in) *m(f)*

fatalistic ADJ, **fatalistically** ADV [ˌfeɪtə'lɪstɪk, -əlɪ] fatalistisch

fatality [fə'tælɪtɪ] N **a** Todesfall *m*; *(in accident, war etc)* (Todes)opfer *nt*; **there were no fatalities** es gab keine Todesopfer **b** *(liter: = inevitability)* Unabwendbarkeit *f*

fatally ['feɪtəlɪ] ADV **a** *(= mortally) wounded, injured* tödlich; **~ ill** todkrank; **they were ~ stabbed** sie wurden erstochen; **she overdosed ~** sie nahm eine tödliche Überdosis **b** *(= irrevocably) undermine, damage, weaken* unwiderruflich; *(= disastrously)* verheerend; **the ~ incriminating tape** das Band mit dem fatalen Belastungsmaterial; **I was ~ attracted to him/it** er/es übte eine unheilvolle Anziehungskraft auf mich aus; **to be ~ flawed** fatale Mängel aufweisen

Fata Morgana ['fɑːtəmɔː'gɑːnə] N Fata Morgana *f*

fat-ass ['fætæs] *(US pej sl)* **N** Fettsack *m (pej inf)*, fettes Schwein *(pej inf)* **ADJ** fett *(pej)*

fat cat N *(fig inf)* überbezahlter Topmanager, überbezahlte Topmanagerin, fette Katze *(inf)*

fate [feɪt] N Schicksal *nt*; **the Fates** *(Myth)* die Parzen *pl*; **the examiners meet to decide our ~ next week** die Prüfer kommen nächste Woche zusammen, um über unser Schicksal zu entscheiden; **to leave sth to ~** etw dem Schicksal überlassen; **to leave sb to his ~** jdn seinem Schicksal überlassen; **to go to meet one's ~** seinem Schicksal entgegentreten; **to meet one's ~** vom Schicksal heimgesucht *or* ereilt *(geh)* werden; **to face a similar ~** einem ähnlichen Schicksal entgegensehen; **to meet with** *or* **suffer the same ~** das gleiche Schicksal haben *or* erleiden; **as sure as ~ it will go wrong** das geht garantiert schief; **as sure as ~ it went wrong** das ist natürlich prompt schiefgegangen

fated ['feɪtɪd] ADJ unglückselig; *project, plan* zum Scheitern verurteilt; **to be ~** unter einem ungünstigen Stern stehen; **to be ~ to fail** *or* **to be unsuccessful** zum Scheitern verurteilt sein; **their plans were ~ to be forgotten** ihre Pläne waren dazu verurteilt, vergessen zu werden; **they were ~ never to meet again** es war ihnen bestimmt, sich nie wiederzusehen

fateful ['feɪtfʊl] ADJ *day, night, moment, meeting, journey* schicksalhaft; *decision, consequence* verhängnisvoll; *words* schicksalsschwer; **to be ~ for sb** jds Schicksal besiegeln

fat-free ['fætˌfriː] ADJ *food* fettfrei

fathead ['fæthed] N *(Brit inf)* Dummkopf *m*, Blödmann *m (inf)*

fatheaded [ˌfæt'hedɪd] ADJ *(Brit inf)* dumm, blöd *(inf)*

father ['fɑːðə'] **N a** *(lit, fig)* Vater *m (to sb* jdm); **from ~ to son** vom Vater auf den Sohn; **like ~ like son** der Apfel fällt nicht weit vom Stamm; **(Old) Father Time** die Zeit *(als Allegorie)*

b ~s *pl (= ancestors)* Väter *pl*

c *(= founder)* Vater *m*; *(= leader)* Führer *m*, Vater *m (liter)*; **the Fathers of the Church** die Kirchenväter *pl*

d *(= God)* **(our) Father** Vater *m* (unser)

e *(= priest)* Pater *m*; **the Holy Father** der Heilige Vater

VT a *child, cub etc* zeugen; *(= admit paternity)* die Vaterschaft anerkennen für; *(fig) idea, plan* Urheber *(+gen)* sein

b *(= saddle with responsibility)* **to ~ sth on sb** jdm die Verantwortung für etw aufhalsen *(inf) or* aufbürden

father: **Father Christmas** N *(Brit)* der Weihnachtsmann; **father confessor** N *(Rel)* Beichtvater *m*; **father figure** N Vaterfigur *f*; **fatherhood** N Vaterschaft *f*; **father-in-law** N *pl* **fathers-in-law** Schwiegervater *m*; **fatherland** N Vaterland *nt*; **fatherless** ADJ vaterlos

fatherly ['fɑːðəlɪ] ADJ väterlich, wie ein Vater

Father's Day N Vatertag *m*

fathom ['fæðəm] **N** Faden *m* **VT a** *(lit)* ausloten **b** *(= understand)* ermessen *(geh)*; *(inf: also* **fathom out***)* verstehen; **I just can't ~ him (out)** er ist mir ein Rätsel; **I couldn't ~ it (out)** ich kam der Sache nicht auf den Grund, ich kam nicht dahinter *(inf)*; **we're trying to ~ (out) what …** wir versuchen zu ergründen, was …

fathomable ['fæðəməbl] ADJ *(fig)* fassbar; **less ~** weniger verständlich

fathomless ['fæðəmlɪs] ADJ *(lit)* abgrundtief; *(fig: = boundless)* unermesslich; *(= incomprehensible)* unergründlich

fatigue [fə'tiːg] **N a** Abspannung *f*, Erschöpfung *f*, Ermüdung *f*; **battle ~** Kampfmüdigkeit *f*; **compassion ~** Verdrossenheit *f* mit immer neuen Spendenaufrufen; **donor ~** Spendenmüdigkeit *f* **b** *(Tech: = metal fatigue)* Ermüdung *f* **c** *(Mil, = fatigue duty)* Arbeitsdienst *m*; **to be on ~** Arbeitsdienst haben **d fatigues** PL *(Mil)* Arbeitsanzug *m*; **in ~s** im Arbeitsanzug **VT a** *(= tire)* ermüden; *(= exhaust)* erschöpfen **b** *(Tech) metal* ermüden **VI** ermüden

fatigue: **fatigue dress** N Arbeitsanzug *m*; **in ~** im Arbeitsanzug; **fatigue duty** N Arbeitseinsatz *m*, Arbeitsdienst *m*; **fatigue party** N Arbeitskommando *nt*

fatiguing [fə'tiːgɪŋ] ADJ *(= tiring)* ermüdend; *(= exhausting)* erschöpfend

fatless ['fætlɪs] ADJ fettfrei, ohne Fett

fatling ['fætlɪŋ] N junges Masttier

fatness ['fætnɪs] N **a** *(= overweight)* Dicke *f*, Fettheit *f (pej)* **b** *(= thickness, of book, pile, wad)* Dicke *f*, Umfang *m*; *(fig inf, of wallet, chequebook)* Dicke *f*; *(of profit, fee, salary)* Üppigkeit *f*, Fettheit *f (inf)* **c** *(fig, of land)* Fruchtbarkeit *f*

fatso ['fætsəʊ] N *(inf)* Dicke(r) *mf (inf)*, Fettsack *m (pej inf)*

fat: **fat-soluble** ADJ *(Chem)* fettlöslich; **fat stock** N Mastvieh *nt*; **fat tax** N Fettsteuer *f*

fatted ['fætɪd] ADJ **to kill the ~ calf** einen Willkommensschmaus veranstalten

fatten ['fætn] **VT** *(also* **fatten up***) animals* mästen; *people* herausfüttern *(inf)*; *(fig) profits* erhöhen; *budget* aufstocken; **are you trying to ~ me up?** *(inf)* du willst mich wohl mästen? *(inf)* **VI** *(also* **fatten up** *or* **out**, *animal)* fett werden; *(person)* dick werden; *(through overeating)* sich mästen *(inf)*

fattener ['fætnə'] N Dickmacher *m*

fattening ['fætnɪŋ] ADJ *food* dick machend; **chocolate is ~** Schokolade macht dick

fatty ['fætɪ] **ADJ** *(+er)* fett; *(= greasy)* fettig; **~ deposits** Fettablagerungen *pl*; **~ tissue** Fettgewebe *nt*; **~ tumour** Fettgeschwulst *f*; **they have a fattier diet than us** sie ernähren sich fettreicher als wir **N** *(inf)* Dickerchen *nt (inf)*

fatty acid N Fettsäure *f*

fatty degeneration N *(Med)* Verfettung *f*

fatuity [fə'tjuːɪtɪ] N Albernheit *f*; *(= remark, action also)* törichte Bemerkung/Tat *(geh)*

fatuous ['fætjʊəs] ADJ töricht *(geh)*, albern

faucet ['fɔːsɪt] N *(US)* Hahn *m*

faugh [fɔː] INTERJ *(old)* pfui

fault [fɔːlt] ✪ 18.3 **N a** *(= mistake, defect)* Fehler *m*; *(Tech)* Defekt *m*; **generous to a ~** übermäßig großzügig; **to find ~ with sb/sth** etwas an jdm/etw auszusetzen haben; **he was at ~** er war im Unrecht; **my memory was at ~** mein Gedächtnis hat mich getrogen; **you were at ~ in not telling me** es war nicht recht von Ihnen, dass Sie mir das nicht gesagt haben

b *no pl* **it won't be my/his ~ if …** es ist nicht meine/seine Schuld, wenn …, ich bin/er ist nicht schuld,wenn …; **whose ~ is it?** wer ist schuld (daran)?; **it's all your own ~** das ist Ihre eigene Schuld, Sie sind selbst schuld; **through no ~ of her own, she …** es war nicht ihre eigene Schuld, dass sie …

c *(Geol)* Verwerfung *f*

d *(Tennis, Horseriding)* Fehler *m*

VT a Fehler finden an *(+dat)*, etwas auszusetzen haben an *(+dat)*; **I can't ~ it/him** ich habe nichts daran/an ihm auszusetzen

b *(Geol)* eine Verwerfung verursachen in *(+dat)*

VI *(Geol)* sich verwerfen

fault: **fault-finder** N Krittler(in) *m(f)*; **fault-finding** ['fɔːltfaɪndɪŋ] **ADJ** krittelig **N** Krittelei *f*

faultily ['fɔːltɪlɪ] ADV falsch

faultless ['fɔːltlɪs] ADJ **a** *(= without mistakes)* fehlerlos; *English* fehlerfrei, fehlerlos **b** *(= immaculate) appearance* tadellos, einwandfrei

faultlessly ['fɔːltlɪslɪ] ADV **a** *(= without mistakes) speak, copy, translate* fehlerfrei, fehlerlos **b** *(= perfectly) dressed, executed* tadellos; *work, run, perform* einwandfrei; *fluent, loyal* vollkommen

fault: **fault line** N *(Geol)* Verwerfungslinie *f*; **fault-tolerant** [fɔːlt'tɒlərənt] ADJ *(Tech, Comput)* fehlertolerant

faulty ['fɔːltɪ] ADJ *(+er) (Tech, Biol)* defekt; *(Comm)* fehlerhaft; *reasoning, logic* falsch, fehlerhaft

faun [fɔːn] N *(Myth)* Faun *m*

fauna ['fɔːnə] N Fauna *f*

faux pas [fəʊ'pɑː] N Fauxpas *m*

fava bean ['fɑːvəbiːn] N *(US)* dicke Bohne, Saubohne *f*

favorite son N *(US Pol)* regionaler Spitzenkandidat

favour, *(US)* **favor** ['feɪvə'] ✪ 11.2 **N a** *no pl (= goodwill)* Gunst *f*, Wohlwollen *nt*; **to win/lose sb's ~** jds Gunst *(acc)* erlangen *(geh)*/verscherzen; **to find ~ with sb** bei jdm Anklang finden; **to look with ~ on sth** einer Sache *(dat)* wohlwollend gegenüberstehen; **to be in ~ with sb** bei jdm gut angeschrieben sein; *(fashion, pop star, writer etc)* bei jdm beliebt sein, bei jdm gut ankommen; **to be/fall out of ~** in Ungnade (gefallen) sein/fallen; *(fashion, pop star, writer etc)* nicht mehr ankommen *or* beliebt sein *(with* bei)

b to be in ~ of sth für etw sein; **to be in ~ of doing sth** dafür sein, etw zu tun; **a point in his**

~ ein Punkt zu seinen Gunsten, ein Punkt, der für ihn spricht; **the judge ruled in his ~** der Richter entschied zu seinen Gunsten; **he's got everything in his ~** es spricht alles für ihn; **circumstances were all working in her ~** die Umstände waren alle günstig für sie; **all those in ~ raise their hands** alle, die dafür sind, Hand hoch; **he rejected socialism in ~ of the market economy** er lehnte den Sozialismus ab und bevorzugte statt dessen die Marktwirtschaft → **balance N f**

c *(= partiality)* Vergünstigung *f*; **to show ~ to sb** jdn bevorzugen

d *(= act of kindness)* Gefallen *m*, Gefälligkeit *f*; **to ask a ~ of sb** jdn um einen Gefallen bitten; **to do sb a ~** jdm einen Gefallen tun; **do me a ~!** *(inf)* sei so gut!; **would you do me the ~ of returning my library books?** wären Sie bitte so freundlich und würden meine Bücher in die Bücherei zurückbringen?; **do me the ~ of shutting up!** *(inf)* tu mir einen Gefallen und halt den Mund!; **as a ~** aus Gefälligkeit; **as a ~ to him** ihm zuliebe; **to sell sexual ~s** *(old, hum)* Liebesgünste verkaufen *(old, hum)*

e *(old, = ribbon etc)* Schleife *f*

f *(on wedding cake)* Verzierung *f*, (Kuchen)dekoration *f*; *(to take home)* *Tüllbeutel mit Zuckermandeln*

VT **a** *idea (= be in favour of)* für gut halten; *(= prefer)* bevorzugen; **I ~ the second proposal** ich bin für den zweiten Vorschlag

b *(= show preference)* bevorzugen; *(king etc)* begünstigen

c *(= oblige, honour)* beehren *(form)*; **to ~ sb with a smile** jdm gütigerweise ein Lächeln gewähren *(geh)*

d *(= be favourable for)* begünstigen

e *(US: = resemble)* ähneln *(+dat)*

favourable, *(US)* **favorable** [ˈfeɪvərəbl] ✪ 13 **ADJ** **a** *(= positive) response, reaction* positiv; *opinion, review, impression* positiv, günstig; **I haven't heard one ~ opinion on it** ich habe noch keine einzige positive Meinung dazu gehört; **her request met with a ~ response** ihre Bitte stieß auf Zustimmung; **most people were ~ to the idea** die meisten Leute standen der Idee positiv gegenüber; **she got a ~ mention in the report** sie wurde in dem Bericht lobend erwähnt

b *(= beneficial) terms, position, deal* günstig, vorteilhaft; *comparison* vorteilhaft; *mood* positiv; *climate, weather, conditions* günstig (*to* für); **to be given ~ treatment** bevorzugt behandelt werden; **to show sth in a ~ light** etw in einem günstigen Licht zeigen; **an atmosphere ~ to expansion** ein günstiges Klima für Expansion; **on ~ terms** zu günstigen Bedingungen; **conditions are ~ for development** für die Entwicklung herrschen günstige Bedingungen

favourableness, *(US)* **favorableness** [ˈfeɪvərəblnɪs] **N** Günstigkeit *f*; **the ~ of his attitude** seine positive Einstellung

favourably, *(US)* **favorably** [ˈfeɪvərəblɪ] **ADV** **a** *(= approvingly) respond* positiv; *receive, regard, think, judge* wohlwollend; **he was ~ impressed by it** er war davon sehr angetan; **her application had impressed him very ~** ihre Bewerbung hatte ihn sehr beeindruckt; **to look ~ (up)on sb/sth** jdn/etw wohlwollend behandeln; **to be ~ disposed** *or* **inclined to(wards) sb/sth** jdm/einer Sache gewogen sein *(geh)* **b** *(= advantageously)* günstig; **to compare ~ (with sth)** im Vergleich (mit etw) gut abschneiden

favoured, *(US)* **favored** [ˈfeɪvəd] **ADJ** **a ~ few** einige (wenige) Auserwählte; **a ~ friend** ein besonderer Freund

favourite, *(US)* **favorite** [ˈfeɪvərɪt] ✪ 7 **N** **a** *(= person)* Liebling *m*; *(Hist, pej)* Günstling *m*; **he is a universal ~** er ist allgemein beliebt; **which of her children is her ~?** welches Kind mag sie am liebsten *or* ist ihr Liebling?

b *(= thing)* **this one is my ~** das habe ich am liebsten; **this book/dress is my ~** das ist mein Lieblingsbuch/-kleid; **we sang all the old ~s** wir haben all die alten Lieder gesungen

c *(Sport)* Favorit(in) *m(f)*; **Chelsea are the ~s** Chelsea ist (der) Favorit

d *(Internet)* Favorit *m*; **to add/organize ~s** Favoriten hinzufügen/verwalten

ADJ *attr* Lieblings-; **my ~ book/dress** mein Lieblingsbuch *nt*/-kleid *nt*

favouritism, *(US)* **favoritism** [ˈfeɪvərɪtɪzəm] **N** Vetternwirtschaft *f (inf)*, Günstlingswirtschaft *f*; *(in school)* Schätzchenwirtschaft *f (inf)*, Lieblingswirtschaft *f*

fawn[1] [fɔːn] **N** **a** Hirschkalb *nt*; *(of roe deer)* Rehkitz *nt* **b** *(= colour)* Beige *nt* **ADJ** *(colour)* beige

fawn[2] **VI** *(fig, person)* katzbuckeln (*on, upon or over* vor *+dat*), herumscharwenzeln (*on, upon or over* um)

fawning [ˈfɔːnɪŋ] **ADJ** *person, manner* kriecherisch, liebedienernd; *dog* schwanzwedelnd

fax [fæks] **N** **a** (*also* **fax machine**) Fax *nt*, Telefax *nt*, Fernkopierer *m*; **to send sth by ~** etw per Fax *or* Telefax senden, etw faxen **b** *(= message, document)* Fax *nt*, Telefax *nt* **VT** faxen; **can you ~ us?** können Sie uns *(dat)* faxen?

▶ **fax back** **VT** *sep document* zurückfaxen; **can you fax me back?** können Sie mir per Fax antworten?

fax: **fax board** **N** Faxkarte *f*; **fax bureau** **N** Faxbüro *nt*; **fax card** **N** = **fax board**; **fax machine** **N** = **fax N a**; **fax message** **N** Fax *nt*, Telefax *nt*; **fax number** **N** (Tele)faxnummer *f*; **faxshot** **N** Direktwerbung *f* per Fax; **to send out a ~** Werbemitteilungen per Fax senden **VT** Werbemitteilungen per Fax senden an *(+acc)*

fay [feɪ] **N** *(liter, = fairy)* Fee *f*

faze [feɪz] **VT** *(inf)* **a** *(= take aback)* verdattern *(inf)*; **the question didn't ~ me at all** die Frage brachte mich keineswegs aus der Fassung **b** *(= daunt)* entmutigen; **do not be ~d by the entrance exam** lass dich von der Aufnahmeprüfung nicht abschrecken

FBI *(US) abbr of* **Federal Bureau of Investigation** FBI *nt*

FC *abbr of* **football club** FC *m*

> **FDA**
>
> Die **Food and Drug Administration,** kurz **FDA**, ist die älteste Verbraucherschutzbehörde in den USA. In ihren Aufgabenbereich fällt die Kontrolle von Nahrungsmitteln, Lebensmittelzusätzen, Medikamenten und Kosmetikartikeln sowie die Entscheidung darüber, ob deren Verzehr bzw. Gebrauch ungefährlich für den Verbraucher ist. Im Ausland ist die FDA besonders für ihre Vorreiterrolle bei der Prüfung von Ungefährlichkeit und Wirksamkeit neuer Arzneimittel bekannt, aber auch für die kontinuierliche Überwachung der Anwendung nach der Markteinführung.

FDD *(Comput) abbr of* **floppy disk drive**

FDR *(Aviat) abbr of* **flight-data recorder** Flug(daten)schreiber *m*

fealty [ˈfiːəltɪ] **N** *(Hist)* Lehnstreue *f*

fear [fɪəʳ] **N** **a** Angst *f*, Furcht *f* (*for* vor *+dat*); **~s for the future** Zukunftsängste *pl*; **~ of death/failure** Todes-/Versagensangst *f*; **~ of flying** Flugangst *f*, Angst *f* vorm Fliegen; **~ of heights** Höhenangst *f*; **he has ~s for his sister's safety** er fürchtet für *or* um die Sicherheit seiner Schwester; **there are ~s that ...** es wird befürchtet, dass ...; **have no ~** *(old, hum)* fürchte dich nicht *(old, hum)*; **with ~ and trembling** mit schlotternden Knien; **to be in ~ of sb/sth** Angst vor jdm/etw haben; **to go** *or* **live in ~ of sb/sth** in (ständiger) Angst vor jdm/etw leben; **he lived in ~ of being discovered** er lebte in ständiger Angst davor, entdeckt zu werden; **to be in ~ of one's life** um sein Leben bangen; **for ~ that ...** aus Angst, dass ...; **she talked quietly for ~ of waking the baby** sie sprach leise, um das Baby nicht aufzuwecken; **without ~ or favour** *(Brit) or* **favor** *(US)* ganz gerecht

b *no pl (= risk, likelihood)* **no ~!** *(inf)* nie im Leben! *(inf)*; **there's no ~ of that happening again** keine Angst, das passiert so leicht nicht wieder; **there's not much ~ of his coming** wir brauchen kaum Angst zu haben, dass er kommt

c *(= awe: of God)* Scheu *f*, Ehrfurcht *f*; **to put the ~ of God into sb** *(inf)* jdm gewaltig Angst einjagen *(inf)*

VT **a** *(= be afraid of)* (be)fürchten; **I ~ the worst** ich befürchte das Schlimmste; **he's a man to be ~ed** er ist ein Mann, den man fürchten muss; **many women ~ to go out at night** viele Frauen haben Angst davor, abends auszugehen

b *(= feel awe for) God* Ehrfurcht haben vor *(+dat)*

VI **to ~ for** fürchten für *or* um; **never ~!** keine Angst!

fearful [ˈfɪəfʊl] **ADJ** **a** *(= apprehensive)* ängstlich, bang; **he was ~ lest he fail/be discovered** *(old)* ihm bangte davor zu versagen/entdeckt zu werden; **to be ~ for one's/sb's life** um sein/jds Leben fürchten; **to be ~ of sb/sth** Angst vor jdm/etw *(dat)* haben; **I was ~ of waking her** ich befürchtete, dass ich sie aufwecken würde **b** *(= frightening)* furchtbar, schrecklich *(inf)* **c** *(dated inf: = terrible)* furchtbar, schrecklich *(inf)*

fearfully [ˈfɪəfəlɪ] **ADV** **a** *(= apprehensively)* ängstlich **b** *(dated inf: = terribly) expensive, hot, loud etc* furchtbar *(inf)*, schrecklich *(inf)*

fearfulness [ˈfɪəfʊlnɪs] **N** *(= apprehension)* Ängstlichkeit *f*

fearless [ˈfɪəlɪs] **ADJ** furchtlos; **~ of sth** ohne Angst *or* Furcht vor etw *(dat)*; **to be ~ of heights/the consequences** keine Höhenangst/keine Angst vor den Folgen haben, Höhen/die Folgen nicht fürchten

fearlessly [ˈfɪəlɪslɪ] **ADV** furchtlos

fearlessness [ˈfɪəlɪsnɪs] **N** Furchtlosigkeit *f*

fearsome [ˈfɪəsəm] **ADJ** furchterregend; **he was in a ~ rage** er hatte einen fürchterlichen Wutanfall

fearsomely [ˈfɪəsəmlɪ] **ADV** *efficient, powerful* erschreckend; **~ equipped with an array of weapons** mit einem Furcht einflößenden Waffenarsenal ausgerüstet

feasibility [ˌfiːzəˈbɪlɪtɪ] **N** **a** *(of plan etc)* Durchführbarkeit *f*, Machbarkeit *f*; **the ~ of doing sth** die Möglichkeit, etw zu tun; **I doubt the ~ of doing that** ich glaube nicht, dass das möglich *or* machbar ist **b** *(= plausibility: of story etc)* Wahrscheinlichkeit *f*

feasibility study **N** Machbarkeitsstudie *f*

feasible [ˈfiːzəbl] **ADJ** **a** *(= practicable)* möglich, machbar; *plan, proposition, alternative* durchführbar; *route* gangbar, möglich; **economically ~** wirtschaftlich machbar **b** *(= plausible) excuse, story, theory* plausibel, wahrscheinlich

feasibly [ˈfiːzəblɪ] **ADV** **a** *(= practicably)* **if it can ~ be done** wenn es machbar ist *or* praktisch möglich ist **b** *(= plausibly)* plausibel; **that could ~ be true** das könnte durchaus stimmen; **he could ~ still be alive** es ist durchaus möglich, dass er noch lebt

feast [fiːst] **N** **a** *(= banquet)* Festmahl *nt*, Festessen *nt*; **a wedding ~** ein Hochzeitsmahl *nt (geh)*; **a ~ for the eyes** eine Augenweide; **a ~ of entertainment** erstklassige Unterhaltung; **it's ~ or famine** *(fig)* alles oder nichts

b *(Eccl, Rel)* Fest *nt*; **~ day** Festtag *m*, Feiertag *m*; **movable/immovable ~** beweglicher/unbeweglicher Feiertag

VI *(lit)* Festgelage *pl*/ein Festgelage halten; **to ~ on sth** sich an etw *(dat)* gütlich tun; *(person also)* in etw *(dat)* schwelgen; *(fig)* sich an etw *(dat)* weiden

VT **a** *guest* festlich bewirten; **to ~ oneself** sich gütlich tun (*on* an *+dat*); *(person also)* schwelgen (*on* in *+dat*)

b **to ~ one's eyes on sb/sth** seine Augen an jdm/etw weiden

feat [fiːt] **N** Leistung *f*; *(heroic, courageous etc)* Heldentat *f*; *(skilful)* Kunststück *nt*, Meisterleistung *f*; **a ~ of courage/daring** eine mutige/wagemutige Tat

feather ['feðəʳ] N Feder *f*; **~s** *(= plumage)* Gefieder *nt*; **~ headdress** Kopfschmuck *m* aus Federn; **as light as a ~** federleicht; **that's a ~ in his cap** das ist ein Ruhmesblatt *nt* für ihn; **you could have knocked me down with a ~** *(inf)* ich war wie vom Donner gerührt; **that'll make the ~s fly** das wird die Gemüter bewegen; **they are birds of a ~** sie sind vom gleichen Schlag; **birds of a ~ stick** *or* **flock together** *(Prov)* Gleich und Gleich gesellt sich gern *(Prov)* → **white feather**
VT a *arrow etc* mit Federn versehen; **to ~ one's nest** *(fig)* sein Schäfchen ins Trockene bringen
b *(Aviat) propeller* auf Segelstellung bringen
c *(Rowing) oar* flach drehen
VI *(Rowing)* das Ruderblatt flach drehen

feather: **feather bed** N mit Federn gefüllte Matratze; **featherbed** VT *(fig) person* verhätscheln; *(Ind, with grants)* verhätscheln; *(by overmanning)* unnötige Arbeitskräfte zugestehen *(+dat)*; **featherbedding** N *(fig)* Hätscheln *nt*; *(with subsidies)* unnötige Subventionierung; **featherbrain** N Spatzenhirn *nt*; **featherbrained** ADJ dümmlich; **feather cut** N *(= hairstyle)* Stufenschnitt *m*; **feather duster** N Staubwedel *m*

feathered ['feðəd] ADJ gefiedert

featherweight ['feðəweɪt] N *(Boxing)* Federgewicht *nt*; *(fig)* Leichtgewicht *nt*; **~ champion** Meister *m* im Federgewicht

feathery ['feðərɪ] ADJ *(+er)* fed(e)rig; *feel, flakes* zart; **~ cloud** Federwolke *f*

feature ['fi:tʃəʳ] N a *(facial)* (Gesichts)zug *m*; **to have strong/delicate ~s** markante/feine Gesichtszüge haben
b *(= characteristic)* Merkmal *nt*, Kennzeichen *nt*, Charakteristikum *nt*; *(of sb's character)* Grundzug *m*; **a ~ of his style is …** sein Stil ist durch … gekennzeichnet; **a ~ of this book is …** das Buch zeichnet sich durch … aus; **special ~** Besonderheit *f*; **new ~** Neuheit *f*; **the main ~ of the recession** das Kennzeichnende an der Rezession
c *(= focal point: of room, building etc)* besonderes *or* herausragendes Merkmal; **~ fireplace** offener Kamin; **to make a ~ of sth** etw besonders betonen, etw zur Geltung bringen; **the main ~ of the new shopping mall** die Hauptattraktion des neuen Einkaufszentrums; **the old volcano, the dominant ~ of the island, …** der die Insel dominierende alte Vulkan …
d *(Press)* (Sonder)beitrag *m*, Feature *nt*; *(Rad, TV)* (Dokumentar)bericht *m*, Feature *nt*
e *(= film)* Spielfilm *m*
VT a *(Press) story, picture* bringen
b **this film ~s an English actress** in diesem Film spielt eine englische Schauspielerin mit; **the album ~s their latest hit single** auf dem Album ist auch ihre neueste Hitsingle; **the room ~s a large fireplace** eine Besonderheit des Zimmers ist der große Kamin
VI a *(= occur)* vorkommen; **the story ~d on all today's front pages** die Geschichte war heute auf allen Titelseiten
b *(Film)* (mit)spielen

feature: **feature article** N Sonderbeitrag *m*, Feature *nt*; **feature film** N Spielfilm *m*; **feature-length** ADJ *film* mit Spielfilmlänge; **featureless** ADJ ohne besondere Merkmale; **feature story** N Sonderbericht *m*, Feature *nt*; **feature writer** N Feuilletonist(in) *m(f)*

Feb *abbr of* **February** Febr.

febrile ['fi:braɪl] ADJ fiebrig, fieberhaft

February ['februərɪ] N Februar *m* → **September**

fecal ['fi:kəl] ADJ *(US)* = **faecal**

feces ['fi:si:z] PL *(US)* = **faeces**

feckless ['feklɪs] ADJ nutzlos

fecund ['fi:kənd] ADJ *(lit, fig)* fruchtbar

fecundate ['fi:kəndeɪt] VT befruchten

fecundity [fɪ'kʌndɪtɪ] N *(lit, fig)* Fruchtbarkeit *f*

fed¹ [fed] *pret, ptp of* **feed**

fed² N *(US inf)* FBI-Agent(in) *m(f)*

Fedayeen [fedɑ:'ji:n] PL Freischärler *pl*

federal ['fedərəl] ADJ Bundes-; *system etc* föderalistisch; *(US Hist)* föderalistisch; **~ state** Bundesstaat *m*; **~ bureau** Bundesamt *nt*; **the Federal Republic of Germany** die Bundesrepublik Deutschland; **Federal Insurance Contributions Act** *(US) Gesetz über die Einbehaltung von Sozialversicherungsbeiträgen* N *(US)* a *(Hist)* Föderalist *m* b *(inf: in FBI)* FBI-Agent(in) *m(f)*

> **FEDERAL**
>
> In den USA besagt der Begriff **federal** vor den Namen von Regierungsbehörden und Verantwortungsbereichen, dass diese Bundesbehörden und -kompetenzen sind und somit der US-Regierung in Washington unterstehen, nicht etwa den Regierungen der einzelnen Staaten. So verfolgt zum Beispiel das **Federal Bureau of Investigation**, besser bekannt als **FBI**, Verstöße gegen Bundesrecht, **federal law**.

federalism ['fedərəlɪzəm] N Föderalismus *m*

federalist ['fedərəlɪst] ADJ föderalistisch N Föderalist *m*

Federal Reserve Board N *(US)* Zentralbankrat *m*

Federal Trade Commission N *(US) Bundesbehörde zur Bekämpfung des unlauteren Wettbewerbs und zur Durchführung der Kartellgesetze*

federate ['fedəreɪt] VT zu einem Bund vereinigen *or* zusammenschließen, föderieren *(rare)*
VI sich zu einem Bund zusammenschließen
ADJ ['fedərɪt] verbündet, föderiert

federated ['fedəreɪtəd] ADJ *state* föderiert

federation [,fedə'reɪʃən] N a *(= act)* Zusammenschluss *m*, Föderation *f (rare)* b *(= league)* Föderation *f*, Bund *m*

fedora [fɪ'dɔ:rə] N Filzhut *m*

fed up ✪ 7.3 ADJ *(inf)* **I'm ~** ich habe die Nase voll *(inf)*; **I'm ~ with him/it** er/es hängt mir zum Hals heraus *(inf)*, ich habe ihn/es satt; **you look pretty ~** du siehst so aus, als hättest du die Nase voll *(inf)*; **I'm ~ waiting for him** ich habe es satt *or* ich bin es leid, auf ihn zu warten

fee [fi:] N a Gebühr *f*; *(of doctor, lawyer, artist, tutor)* Honorar *nt*; *(of stage performer)* Gage *f*; *(of director, administrator etc)* Bezüge *pl*; *(= membership fee)* Beitrag *m*; **(school) ~s** Schulgeld *nt*; **on payment of a small ~** gegen geringe Gebühr
b **land held in ~ simple** *(Jur)* unbeschränkt vererbbares Land

feeble ['fi:bl] ADJ *(+er)* a *(= weak) person* schwach, schwächlich; *light, voice* schwach b *(pej: = pathetic) person, effort, applause, support, smile* schwach; *attempt, performance* kläglich; *explanation, argument, idea* wenig überzeugend; *excuse* faul *(inf)*; *joke* lahm *(inf)*; *response* halbherzig; **don't be so ~!** sei nicht so ein Waschlappen *(inf)*

feeble-minded [,fi:bl'maɪndɪd] ADJ dümmlich

feebleness ['fi:blnɪs] N a *(= weakness, of person)* Schwäche *f*, Schwächlichkeit *f*; *(of light, voice)* Schwäche *f* b *(pej: = pathetic nature)* Kläglichkeit *f*; *(of person, effort, applause, support)* Schwäche *f*; *(of excuse)* Faulheit *f (inf)*; *(of joke)* Lahmheit *f (inf)*; *(of response)* Halbherzigkeit *f*; **the ~ of his argument** sein wenig überzeugendes Argument

feebly ['fi:blɪ] ADV *shine, move, attempt, resist, applaud* schwach; *smile* kläglich; *say, explain* wenig überzeugend; **he performed ~** er zeigte eine klägliche Leistung

feed [fi:d] *vb: pret, ptp* **fed** N a *(= meal, of animals)* Fütterung *f*; *(of baby, inf: of person)* Mahlzeit *f*; *(= food, of animals)* Futter *nt*; *(inf, of person)* Essen *nt*; **when is the baby's next ~?** wann wird das Baby wieder gefüttert?; **to have a good ~** *(inf)* tüchtig futtern *(inf)*; **he's off his ~** *(hum)* er hat keinen Appetit; **~ additives** *(Chem)* Futtermitteladditive *pl*
b *(Theat)* Stichwort *nt*
c *(Tech, to machine)* Versorgung *f (to +gen)*; *(to furnace)* Beschickung *f (to +gen)*; *(to computer)* Eingabe *f (into* in *+acc)*
VT a *(= provide food for) person, army* verpflegen; *family* ernähren; **I have three hungry mouths to ~** ich habe drei hungrige Münder zu stopfen *(inf)*; **to ~ oneself** sich selbst verpflegen; **he ~s himself well** er isst gut
b *(= give food to) baby, invalid, animal* füttern; *plant* düngen; **to (be able to) ~ oneself** *(child)* allein *or* ohne Hilfe essen (können); **to ~ sth to sb/an animal** jdm etw zu essen/einem Tier etw zu fressen geben; **they were fed to the lions** sie wurden den Löwen zum Fraß vorgeworfen
c *(= supply) machine* versorgen; *furnace* beschicken; *computer* füttern; *meter* Geld einwerfen in *(+acc)*, füttern *(hum)*; *fire* unterhalten, etwas legen auf *(+acc)*; *(fig) hope, imagination, rumour* nähren, Nahrung geben *(+dat)*; **two rivers ~ this reservoir** dieses Reservoir wird von zwei Flüssen gespeist; **he steals to ~ his heroin habit** er stiehlt, um sich mit Heroin zu versorgen; **blood vessels that ~ blood to the brain** Blutgefäße, die das Gehirn mit Blut versorgen; **to ~ sth into a machine** etw in eine Maschine geben; **to ~ information (in)to a computer** Informationen in einen Computer eingeben; **to ~ information to sb, to ~ sb (with) information** jdn mit Informationen versorgen; **to ~ sb lies** jdn systematisch belügen
d *(Tech: = insert)* führen; **to ~ sth along/through a tube** etw an einem Röhrchen entlang/durch ein Röhrchen führen
e *(Theat, fig)* **to ~ sb (with) the right lines** jdm die richtigen Stichworte geben
VI *(animal)* fressen; *(baby)* gefüttert werden; *(hum, person)* futtern *(inf)*

▶ **feed back** VT *sep facts, information* zurückleiten *(to* an *+acc)*; *money* zurückfließen lassen; *(Elec)* rückkoppeln; **by the time the information had been fed back to him** als die Informationen schließlich zu ihm zurückkamen; **to feed sth back into the computer** dem Computer etw wieder eingeben

▶ **feed in** VT *sep tape, wire etc* einführen *(prep obj* in *+acc)*; *facts, information* eingeben *(prep obj* in *+acc)*

▶ **feed on** VI *+prep obj* sich (er)nähren von; *(fig)* sich nähren von VT *sep +prep obj* **to feed sb on sth** *(animal, baby)* jdn mit etw füttern; *person* jdn mit etw ernähren

▶ **feed up** VT *sep animal* mästen; **to feed sb up** jdn aufpäppeln → *also* **fed up**

feed: **feedback** N *(Psych, Comput)* Feedback *nt*, Feed-back *nt*, Rückmeldung *f*; *(Elec)* Rückkoppelung *f*; *(fig)* Reaktion *f*, Feedback *nt*, Feed-back *nt*; **~ of information** Rückinformation *f*; **everyone should try to get as much ~ as possible from the others** jeder sollte von den anderen möglichst viel Feedback *or* Feed-back bekommen; **to provide more ~ on sth** ausführlicher über etw *(acc)* berichten; **feedbag** N *(US)* Futtersack *m*; **to put on the ~** *(inf)* eine Mahlzeit einlegen

feeder ['fi:dəʳ] N a *(= bottle)* Flasche *f*; *(for birds)* Futterhalter *m*; *(= net)* Futternetz *nt*; **automatic ~** Futterautomat *m*
b *(= eater)* Esser(in) *m(f)*; **the cow is a good ~** die Kuh frisst gut; **peonies are quite heavy ~s** *(= need water/plant food)* Pfingstrosen brauchen viel Wasser/Dünger
c *(= device supplying machine)* Zubringer *m*
d *(= contributory source) (= river)* Zu(bringer)fluss *m*; *(= road)* Zubringer(straße *f*) *m*; *(= air, bus, rail service)* Zubringerlinie *f*; *(Elec)* Speiseleitung *f*, Feeder *m*
ATTR Zubringer-; **~ road** Zubringerstraße *f*; **~ pipe** Zuleitungsrohr *nt*; **~ line** *(Rail, Aviat)* Zubringerlinie *f*, Zubringerstrecke *f*; **~ service** Zubringerdienst *m*

feeding ['fi:dɪŋ]: **feeding bottle** N Flasche *f*; **feeding cup** N Schnabeltasse *f*; **feeding frenzy** N a *(lit)* Futterstreit *m* b *(fig)* **the**

press was in a ~ die Presse riss sich um die Story; **feeding ground** N Futterplatz *m*; **feeding time** N *(for animal)* Fütterungszeit *f*; *(for baby)* Zeit *f* für die Mahlzeit; **the baby's ~ was still an hour away** die nächste Mahlzeit des Säuglings war erst in einer Stunde fällig

feel [fi:l] ✪ 3.1, 6.2, 7.1, 8.4 *vb: pret, ptp* **felt** VT **a** *(= touch)* fühlen; *(examining)* befühlen; **to ~ one's way** sich vortasten; **I'm still ~ing my way (in my new job)** ich versuche noch, mich (in meiner neuen Stelle) zurechtzufinden; **to ~ one's way into sth** *(fig)* sich in etw *(acc)* einfühlen
b *(= be aware of by touching, feeling) prick, sun etc* fühlen, spüren; **I can't ~ anything in my left leg** ich habe kein Gefühl im linken Bein; **I felt it move** ich spürte, wie es sich bewegte
c *(= be conscious of in oneself) regret, joy, fear etc* fühlen, empfinden; *effects* spüren; **I felt myself blush** ich merkte *or* spürte, dass ich rot wurde; **he felt a sense of regret** er empfand Bedauern; **can't you ~ the sadness in this music?** können Sie nicht empfinden, wie traurig diese Musik ist?; **she felt his eyes on her** sie merkte *or* spürte, wie er sie ansah
d *(= be affected by) heat, cold, insult, loss* leiden unter *(+dat)*; **I don't ~ the cold as much as he does** die Kälte macht mir nicht so viel aus wie ihm; **a right hook which he really felt** ein rechter Haken, der saß; **she's fallen, I bet she felt that!** sie ist hingefallen, das hat bestimmt wehgetan!; **I felt that!** *(pain)* das hat wehgetan!
e *(= think)* glauben; **what do you ~ about him/it?** was halten Sie von ihm/davon?; **it was felt that …** man war der Meinung, dass …; **he felt it necessary** er hielt es für notwendig; **don't ~ you have to …** glauben Sie nicht, Sie müssten …; **I can't help ~ing that …** ich kann mir nicht helfen, ich glaube, dass …
VI **a** *(indicating physical or mental state: person)* sich fühlen; **to ~ well/ill/apprehensive** sich wohlfühlen/elend/unsicher fühlen; **I ~ sick** mir ist schlecht; **how do you ~ today?** wie fühlen Sie sich heute?; **to ~ convinced/certain** überzeugt/sicher sein; **to ~ hungry/thirsty/sleepy** hungrig/durstig/müde sein; **I ~ hot/cold** mir ist heiß/kalt; **I felt very touched by his remarks** ich war sehr gerührt von seinen Bemerkungen; **I ~ much better** ich fühle mich viel besser, es geht mir viel besser; **you'll ~ (all) the better for a bath** ein Bad wird Ihnen guttun; **he doesn't ~ quite himself today** er ist heute nicht ganz auf der Höhe; **I felt sad/strange** mir war traurig/komisch zumute *or* zu Mute; **I felt as though I'd never been away** mir war, als ob ich nie weg gewesen wäre; **I felt as if I was going to be sick** ich dachte, mir würde schlecht werden; **how do you ~ about him?** *(emotionally)* was empfinden Sie für ihn?; **you can imagine what I felt like** *or* **how I felt** Sie können sich *(dat)* vorstellen, wie mir zumute *or* zu Mute war
b *(= feel to the touch: material, ground, bricks etc)* sich anfühlen; **to ~ hard/soft/rough** *etc* sich hart/weich/rau *etc* anfühlen; **the room/air ~s warm** das Zimmer/die Luft kommt einem warm vor; **my skin ~s tight** mir spannt die Haut; **the shirt ~s as though it's made of silk** das Hemd fühlt sich so an, als sei es aus Seide
c *(= think, have opinions)* meinen; **how do you ~ about him/the idea/going for a walk?** was halten Sie von ihm/der Idee/von einem Spaziergang?; **how do you ~ about these developments?** was meinen Sie zu dieser Entwicklung?; **that's just how I ~** das meine ich auch, ich bin genau derselben Meinung
d **to ~ like** *(= have desire for)* Lust haben auf *(+acc)*; *food also* Appetit haben auf *(+acc)*; **I ~ like something to eat** ich möchte jetzt gern etwas essen; **I ~ like going for a walk** ich habe Lust spazieren zu gehen; **I felt like screaming/crying/giving up** ich hätte am liebsten geschrien/geheult/aufgegeben, ich hätte schreien/heulen/aufgeben können; **if you ~ like it** wenn Sie Lust haben, wenn Sie wollen *or* gern möchten
e *impers* **what does it ~ like** *or* **how does it ~ to be all alone?** wie fühlt man sich *or* wie ist das so ganz allein?; **what does it ~ like** *or* **how does it ~ to be the boss?** wie fühlt man sich als Chef?, was ist das für ein Gefühl, Chef zu sein?; **it ~s like flying** es ist wie Fliegen
N *no pl* **a** **let me have a ~ (of it)!** lass (mich) mal fühlen!
b *(= quality when touched)* **it has a velvety/papery ~** es fühlt sich samten/wie Papier an; **he loved the ~ of her skin** er liebte es, wie sich ihre Haut anfühlte; **he recognizes things by their ~** er erkennt Dinge daran, wie sie sich anfühlen; **I don't like the ~ of wool against my skin** ich mag Wolle nicht auf der Haut; **I like the ~ of the sun on my face** ich spüre gerne die Sonne im Gesicht
c *(= quality)* **the room has a cosy ~** das Zimmer hat eine gemütliche Atmosphäre; **there's a nostalgic ~ to his music** seine Musik klingt nostalgisch
d *(fig)* **to get/have a ~ for sth** ein Gefühl *nt* für etw bekommen/haben; **to get the ~ for sth** ein Gefühl *nt* für etw bekommen; **you must get the ~ of the poem** Sie müssen sich in das Gedicht einfühlen

► **feel about** *(Brit) or* **around** VI umhertasten; *(in drawer, bag etc)* herumsuchen, herumtasten

► **feel for** VI *+prep obj* **a** *(= sympathize with)* (mit)fühlen mit, Mitgefühl haben mit; **I feel for you** Sie tun mir leid **b** *(= search or grope for)* tasten nach; *(in pocket, bag etc)* kramen nach

► **feel up** VT *sep (esp US inf: sexually)* befummeln *(inf)*

► **feel up to** VI *+prep obj* sich gewachsen fühlen *(+dat)*

feel-bad ['fi:lbæd] ADJ **~ factor** Frustfaktor *m (inf)*

feeler ['fi:lə'] N **a** *(Zool)* Fühler *m*; *(of sea animal)* Tentakel *m or nt* **b** *(fig)* Fühler *m*; **to put out ~s** seine Fühler ausstrecken **c** **feelers** PL *(also* **feeler gauge***)* Fühl(er)lehre *f*

feel-good ['fi:lgʊd] ADJ *film, song* Feelgood-; **the ~ factor** *(Pol)* der Feelgood-Faktor

feeling ['fi:lɪŋ] N **a** *(= sense of touch)* Gefühl *nt*, Empfindung *f*; **I've lost all ~ in my right arm** ich habe kein Gefühl mehr im rechten Arm
b *(= physical, mental sensation, emotion)* Gefühl *nt*; **a ~ of pain/warmth** ein Gefühl *nt* des Schmerzes/der Wärme; **I had a ~ of isolation** ich kam mir ganz isoliert vor; **he doesn't have much ~ for his sister** er hat nicht viel für seine Schwester übrig; **his voice trembled with ~** seine Stimme bebte vor Gefühl; **I know the ~** ich weiß, wie das ist
c *(= presentiment)* (Vor)gefühl *nt*; **I've a funny ~ she won't come** ich hab so das Gefühl, dass sie nicht kommt
d *(= opinion: also* **feelings***)* Meinung *f*, Ansicht *f (on* zu*)*; **there was a general ~ that …** man war allgemein der Ansicht, dass …; **ill** *or* **bad ~** Verstimmung *f*; **good ~** Wohlwollen *nt*; **there's been a lot of bad ~ about this decision** wegen dieser Entscheidung hat es viel böses Blut gegeben
e *(= talent)* Gefühl *nt*
f **~s** Gefühle *pl*; **to have ~s for sb** Gefühle für jdn haben; **you've hurt his ~s** Sie haben ihn verletzt; **no hard ~s!** ich nehme es dir nicht übel; **no hard ~s?** nimm es mir nicht übel

feet [fi:t] *pl of* **foot**

FEFC *(Brit) abbr of* **Further Education Funding Council** *Organisation, die über die Finanzierung der Erwachsenenbildung entscheidet*

feign [feɪn] VT vortäuschen; *friendship, interest, sympathy, feelings also* heucheln; **to ~ illness/madness** simulieren, sich krank/verrückt stellen; **to ~ sleep/death** sich schlafend/tot stellen

feigned [feɪnd] ADJ vorgeblich *attr*; *illness also* simuliert; *interest, sympathy etc also* vorgetäuscht, geheuchelt

feint [feɪnt] N *(Sport)* Finte *f*; **to make a ~** eine Finte anwenden *(at* gegenüber*)*; **he made a ~ to the left and shot to the right** er hat links angetäuscht und rechts geschossen VI *(Sport)* fintieren, eine Finte anwenden *(also fig)*; **he ~ed with the left and hit with the right** er hat links angetäuscht und rechts zugeschlagen

feint(-ruled) ['feɪnt(ru:ld)] ADJ fein liniert

feisty ['faɪstɪ] ADJ *(+er) (= spirited)* robust; *(inf: = lively)* lebhaft, lebendig

felicitate [fɪ'lɪsɪteɪt] VT *(form)* beglückwünschen *(sb on sth* jdn zu etw*)*, gratulieren *(sb on sth* jdm zu etw*)*

felicitation [fɪˌlɪsɪ'teɪʃən] N *usu pl (form)* Glückwunsch *m*; **my ~s** herzliche Glückwünsche, ich gratuliere

felicitous ADJ, **felicitously** ADV [fɪ'lɪsɪtəs, -lɪ] *(form)* glücklich

felicity [fɪ'lɪsɪtɪ] N *(form)* **a** *(= happiness)* Glück *nt*, Glückseligkeit *f (geh)* **b** *(= aptness)* **he expresses himself with ~** er drückt sich sehr glücklich aus; **the ~ of the expression** die glückliche Wahl des Ausdrucks

feline ['fi:laɪn] ADJ *(lit)* Katzen-; *species* der Katzen; *(fig) grace, suppleness* katzenartig, katzenhaft; **~ eyes** Katzenaugen *pl* N Katze *f*

fell[1] [fel] *pret of* **fall**

fell[2] N *(= skin)* Fell *nt*, Balg *m*

fell[3] ADJ *(liter)* fürchterlich → **swoop**

fell[4] VT *tree* fällen, schlagen; *person* niederstrecken, zu Boden strecken; *animal* zur Strecke bringen

fell[5] N *(N Engl: = mountain)* Berg *m*; *(= moor)* Moorland *nt*

fellah ['felɑ:] N **a** Fellache *m*, Fellachin *f* **b** = **fellow**[1] **a**

fellatio [fɪ'leɪʃɪəʊ] N Fellatio *f*

fellow[1] ['feləʊ] N **a** Mann *m*, Kerl *m (usu pej)*, Typ *m (inf)*; *(inf, = boyfriend)* Freund *m*, Typ *m (inf)*; **a nice/friendly ~** ein netter/freundlicher Kerl; **a clever ~** ein gescheiter Bursche, ein cleverer Typ *(inf)*; **poor ~!** der Arme!; **listen to me, ~** *(US inf)* hör mal her, Mann *(inf)*; **an old ~** ein alter Mann *or* Knabe *(inf)*; **look here, old ~** hör mal her, alter Junge *(inf)*; **young ~** junger Bursche; **this journalist ~** dieser komische Journalist; **my dear ~** mein lieber Freund *or* Mann *(inf)*; **who is this ~?** wer ist denn der Typ *(inf) or* Kerl da?; **this ~ here** dieser Herr, dieser Typ *(inf)*; *(rude)* dieser Kerl hier; **I'm not the sort of ~ who …** ich bin nicht der Typ, der … *(sl)*; **a ~ needs a bit of rest sometimes** *(inf)* man braucht doch auch mal 'ne Pause *(inf)*
b *(= comrade)* Kamerad *m*, Kumpel *m (inf)*; *(= colleague)* Kollege *m*, Kollegin *f*; **~s in distress** Leidensgenossen *pl*; **to get together with one's ~s** mit seinesgleichen zusammenkommen
c *(Univ)* Fellow *m* → **research fellow**
d *(of a society)* Mitglied *nt*
e *(of things: = one of a pair)* Gegenstück *nt*

fellow[2] PREF **our ~ bankers/doctors** unsere Kollegen *pl* (im Bankwesen/in der Ärzteschaft), unsere Berufskollegen *pl*; **our ~ guests** die anderen Gäste; **~ inmates** Mitinsassen *pl*; **~ member** *(in club)* Klubkamerad(in) *m(f)*; *(in party)* Parteigenosse *m*/-genossin *f*; **~ passenger** Mitreisende(r) *mf*; **~ student** Kommilitone *m*, Kommilitonin *f*; **~ sufferer** Leidensgenosse *m*/-genossin *f*; **~ worker** Kollege *m*, Kollegin *f*, Mitarbeiter(in) *m(f)*; **~ writers** Schriftstellerkollegen *pl*; **our ~ communists** unsere kommunistischen Gesinnungsgenossen; **he is a ~ lexicographer** er ist auch Lexikograf; **"fellow Americans…"** „meine lieben amerikanischen Mitbürger…"

fellow: **fellow being** N Mitmensch *m*; **fellow citizen** N Mitbürger(in) *m(f)*; **fellow countryman** N *(= man)* Landsmann *m*; *(= woman)* Landsmännin *f*, Landsfrau *f*; **fellow countrymen** PL Landsleute *pl*; **fellow creature** N Mitmensch *m*; **fellow feeling** N Mitgefühl *nt*; *(= togetherness)* Zusammengehörigkeitsgefühl *nt*; **fellow men** PL Mitmenschen *pl*

fellowship [ˈfeləʊʃɪp] N **a** *no pl* Kameradschaft *f*; *(= company)* Gesellschaft *f*; *(Eccl)* Gemeinschaft *f*; **… who lived without the ~ of other men** …, der keinen Umgang mit anderen Menschen hatte; **there's no sense of ~ here** hier herrscht kein kameradschaftlicher Geist **b** *(Univ: = scholarship)* Forschungsstipendium *nt*; *(= job)* Position eines Fellow

fellow traveller, *(US)* **fellow traveler** N **a** *(lit)* Mitreisende(r) *mf* **b** *(Pol)* Sympathisant(in) *m(f)*

fell runner [ˈfelrʌnəʳ] N Geländeläufer(in) *m(f) (über bergiges Gebiet)*

felon [ˈfelən] N (Schwer)verbrecher(in) *m(f)*

felonious [fɪˈləʊnɪəs] ADJ verbrecherisch

felony [ˈfelənɪ] N (schweres) Verbrechen

felspar [ˈfelspɑːʳ] N Feldspat *m*

felt[1] [felt] *pret, ptp of* **feel**

felt[2] N Filz *m* → **roofing** ADJ *attr* Filz-; **~ hat** Filzhut *m* VI *(wool etc)* (ver)filzen

felt-tip (pen) [ˈfelttɪp(ˈpen)] N Filzstift *m*, Filzschreiber *m*

felucca [feˈlʌkə] N Feluke *f*

female [ˈfiːmeɪl] ADJ **a** weiblich; *labour, rights* Frauen-; **a ~ doctor/student/dog** eine Ärztin/Studentin/Hündin; **~ bear** Bärenweibchen *nt*; **a ~ companion** eine Gesellschafterin; **a ~ football team** eine Damenfußballmannschaft; **a typical ~ attitude** typisch Frau **b** *(Tech) connector, plug* weiblich, Innen-; **~ screw** (Schrauben)mutter *f*, Mutterschraube *f*; **~ thread** Mutter- *or* Innengewinde *nt* N **a** *(= animal)* Weibchen *nt* **b** *(inf: = woman)* Frau *f*; *(pej)* Weib *nt (pej)*, Weibsbild *nt (pej inf)*; **a typical ~** eine typische Frau; **to eye up all the ~s** die Frauen *or* Miezen *(inf)* beäugen

female: **female condom** N Femidom® *nt*, Kondom *nt* für die Frau; **female impersonator** N Damen-Imitator *m*

Femidom® [ˈfemɪdɒm] N Femidom® *nt*, Kondom *nt* für die Frau

feminine [ˈfemɪnɪn] ADJ **a** *person, clothes, look, perfume, voice* feminin; *beauty, role, qualities, nature* weiblich; *(Anat, Biol)* weiblich; **a ~ occupation** ein Frauenberuf *m*; **~ wiles** weibliche Listen *pl*; **his ~ side** seine weibliche *or* feminine Seite **b** *(Gram) noun, pronoun, ending* weiblich, feminin *(spec)* N *(Gram)* Femininum *nt*

feminine hygiene N Monatshygiene *f*; **~ products** Monatshygieneartikel *pl*

femininity [ˌfemɪˈnɪnɪtɪ] N Weiblichkeit *f*

feminism [ˈfemɪnɪzəm] N Feminismus *m*, Frauenrechtlertum *nt*

feminist [ˈfemɪnɪst] N Feminist(in) *m(f)* ADJ feministisch; **I've always been fairly ~** ich war schon immer ziemlich feministisch eingestellt; **the ~ movement** die Frauenbewegung

feminize [ˈfemɪnaɪz] VT weiblich machen, eine weibliche Note verleihen

femme fatale [ˌfæmfəˈtɑːl] N *pl* **femmes fatales** Femme fatale *f*

femur [ˈfiːməʳ] N Oberschenkelknochen *m*

fen [fen] N Moor- *or* Sumpfland *nt*; **the Fens** *die Niederungen in East Anglia*

fence [fens] N **a** Zaun *m*; *(Sport)* Hindernis *nt*; **to sit on the ~** *(fig: = be neutral)* neutral bleiben, nicht Partei ergreifen; *(= be irresolute)* unschlüssig sein, zaudern; **on the wrong/other side of the ~** *(fig)* auf der verkehrten/anderen Seite; **to mend ~s** *(fig)* die Dinge bereinigen

b *(inf: = receiver of stolen goods)* Hehler(in) *m(f)*

c *(Tech)* Anschlag *m*

VT **a** *(also* **fence in***) land* einzäunen, umzäunen

b *(Sport)* fechten gegen

c *(inf)* hehlen; **until we find somebody to ~ stolen cars …** bis wir einen Hehler für gestohlene Autos finden …

VI **a** *(Sport)* fechten

b *(fig)* ausweichen; **to ~ with sb** sich *(dat)* mit jdm ein Wortgefecht liefern; *(evading questions)* jdm ausweichen

c *(inf: = receive stolen goods)* hehlen, mit Diebesgut handeln

▶ **fence in** VT *sep* **a** *(lit)* einzäunen, umzäunen, mit einem Zaun umgeben **b** *(fig)* **to fence sb in** jdn in seiner Freiheit einschränken *or* beschränken, jds Freiheit beschneiden *or* einengen; **don't fence me in** lass mir meine Freiheit; **to feel fenced in by restrictions** sich von Beschränkungen eingeengt fühlen

▶ **fence off** VT *sep piece of land* abzäunen; **to fence oneself off (from sb)** *(fig)* sich (von jdm) absondern

fenced [fenst] ADJ eingezäunt, umzäunt; *(fig)* abgeschottet; **~ community** bewachtes Wohnviertel, bewachte Wohnanlage

fence-mending [ˈfensˌmendɪŋ] N *(esp Pol fig)* Bereinigung *f* der Lage

fencer [ˈfensəʳ] N Fechter(in) *m(f)*

fencing [ˈfensɪŋ] N **a** *(Sport)* Fechten *nt*; **~ instructor** Fechtlehrer(in) *or* -meister(in) *m(f)*; **~ school** Fechtschule *f* **b** *(= fences, material)* Zaun *m*, Einzäunung *f*

fend [fend] VI **to ~ for oneself** *(= provide)* für sich (selbst) sorgen, sich allein durchbringen; *(= defend)* sich (selbst) verteidigen; **could she ~ for herself in the city?** konnte sie sich in der Stadt allein durchschlagen?

▶ **fend off** VT *sep* abwehren; *attacker also* vertreiben; *criticism* zurückweisen; *competition* ausschalten

fender [ˈfendəʳ] N **a** *(in front of fire)* Kamingitter *nt* **b** *(US) (on car)* Kotflügel *m*; *(on bicycle etc)* Schutzblech *nt* **c** *(Naut)* Fender *m* **d** *(US, on train, streetcar)* Puffer *m*

fender-bender [ˈfendəˌbendəʳ] N *(US inf)* kleiner Blechschaden

fenestration [ˌfenɪsˈtreɪʃən] N **a** *(Archit)* Fensteranordnung *f* **b** *(Med)* Fensterungsoperation *f*

fen fire N Irrlicht *nt*

feng shui [ˌfeŋˈʃuːɪ] N Feng Shui *nt*

fennel [ˈfenl] N *(Bot)* Fenchel *m*

feoff [fiːf] N *(old, form, = land)* Lehen *nt*

feral [ˈferəl] ADJ *attr animal, child* verwildert; *(fig) features, quickness* wild; **~ cat** Wildkatze *f*

ferment [ˈfɜːment] N **a** *(= fermentation)* Gärung *f*; *(= substance)* Ferment *nt*, Gärstoff *m* **b** *(fig)* Unruhe *f*, Erregung *f*; **the city was in ~** es brodelte *or* gärte in der Stadt VI [fəˈment] *(lit, fig)* gären; *(plan also)* (aus)reifen VT [fəˈment] *(lit)* fermentieren, zur Gärung bringen; *(fig)* anwachsen lassen

fermentation [ˌfɜːmenˈteɪʃən] N **a** Gärung *f*; *(fig, of plan etc)* Ausreifen *nt* **b** *(fig, = excitement)* Aufregung *f*, Unruhe *f*

fermentation lock N Gärventil *nt*

fern [fɜːn] N Farn(kraut *nt*) *m*

ferocious [fəˈrəʊʃəs] ADJ **a** *(= fierce) animal, person, appearance* wild; *dog* äußerst bissig; *(= trained to attack)* scharf; *look, glare* grimmig; *battle, war* erbittert; *debate, argument* heftig; *attack* brutal; *competition, criticism* scharf, heftig; **a ~ beast** eine reißende Bestie; **to have a ~ temper** zu heftigen Wutanfällen neigen; **he came under ~ attack from the Opposition** er wurde von der Opposition aufs schärfste *or* Schärfste angegriffen

b *(= vicious-looking) knife, dagger, teeth* furchterregend

c *(= extreme) heat* glühend; *storm* heftig; *climate* unerträglich; *thirst* brennend; *energy* grimmig

ferociously [fəˈrəʊʃəslɪ] ADV **a** *(= violently) hit, fight, resist, argue* heftig; *criticize, attack* aufs schärfste *or* Schärfste; *glare* grimmig; *bark, roar* wütend; **~ determined** wild entschlossen; **the market is ~ competitive** auf dem Markt herrscht ein gnadenloser Wettbewerb **b** *(emph, = extremely) tough, difficult* äußerst

ferocity [fəˈrɒsɪtɪ] N *(of animal)* Wildheit *f*; *(of dog)* Bissigkeit *f*; *(of appearance, look, glare)* Grimmigkeit *f*; *(of battle, war, debate, argument, competition, criticism)* Heftigkeit *f*; *(of attack)* Brutalität *f*

ferret [ˈferɪt] N Frettchen *nt* VI **a** *(Sport: also* **go ferreting***)* mit dem Frettchen jagen **b** *(also* **ferret about** *or* **around***)* herumstöbern *or* -schnüffeln *(pej)*; **she was ~ing (about** *or* **around) among my books** sie schnüffelte in meinen Büchern (herum); **he was ~ing (around) for information** er schnüffelte nach Informationen (herum)

▶ **ferret out** VT *sep (Brit inf)* aufstöbern, aufspüren

ferric [ˈferɪk] ADJ Eisen-; **~ oxide** Eisenoxid *nt*

Ferris wheel [ˈferɪsˌwiːl] N Riesenrad *nt*

ferrite [ˈferaɪt] N Ferrit *m*; **~ rod** Ferritstab *m*

ferrite-rod aerial [ˈferaɪtˌrɒdˈeərɪəl] N Ferritantenne *f*

ferroconcrete [ˈferəʊˈkɒŋkriːt] N Eisen- *or* Stahlbeton *m*

ferrous [ˈferəs] ADJ Eisen-; **~ chloride** Eisenchlorid *nt*

ferrule [ˈferuːl] N *(of umbrella, cane)* Zwinge *f*, Ring *m*

ferry [ˈferɪ] N Fähre *f* VT **a** *(also* **ferry across** *or* **over***) (by boat)* übersetzen; *(by plane, car etc)* transportieren, bringen; **to ~ sb across** *or* **over a river** jdn über einen Fluss setzen; **to ~ sb/sth back and forth** jdn/etw hin- und herbringen; **he ferried voters to and from the polls** er fuhr Wähler zum Wahllokal und wieder nach Hause **b** *(= deliver) plane* überführen

ferry: **ferryboat** N Fährboot *nt*; **ferryman** N Fährmann *m*

fertile [ˈfɜːtaɪl] ADJ **a** *(Agr, Biol) land, region, woman, man, animal* fruchtbar; *soil* ergiebig; *egg, ovum* befruchtungsfähig; **the ~ period** *or* **time** die fruchtbaren Tage **b** *(fig: = productive) mind, brain* produktiv; *imagination, period* fruchtbar; **the idea fell on ~ ground** der Gedanke fiel auf fruchtbaren Boden; **this is ~ ground for racists/ethnic hatred** das ist fruchtbarer Boden für Rassisten/Rassenhass

fertility [fəˈtɪlɪtɪ] N *(lit, fig)* Fruchtbarkeit *f*; *(of soil, seed also)* Ergiebigkeit *f*; *(fig, of mind, brain)* Produktivität *f*

fertility: **fertility cult** N Fruchtbarkeitskult *m*; **fertility drug** N Fruchtbarkeitspille *f*; **fertility symbol** N Fruchtbarkeitssymbol *nt*

fertilization [ˌfɜːtɪlaɪˈzeɪʃən] N Befruchtung *f*; *(of soil)* Düngung *f*

fertilize [ˈfɜːtɪlaɪz] VT *animal, egg, flower* befruchten; *land, soil* düngen

fertilizer [ˈfɜːtɪlaɪzəʳ] N Dünger *m*, Düngemittel *nt*; **artificial ~** Kunstdünger *m*

ferule [ˈferuːl] N **a** Stock *m* **b** = **ferrule**

fervency [ˈfɜːvənsɪ] N = **fervour**

fervent [ˈfɜːvənt] ADJ *supporter, belief, advocate, nationalist, socialist* leidenschaftlich; *admirer* glühend; *hope, prayer, wish, desire* inbrünstig *(geh)*; **she is a ~ believer in free trade** sie glaubt leidenschaftlich an den freien Handel

fervently [ˈfɜːvəntlɪ] ADV leidenschaftlich; *hope, wish, pray* inbrünstig *(geh)*; **~ religious** tiefreligiös

fervid [ˈfɜːvɪd] ADJ *(form)* = **fervent**

fervidly [ˈfɜːvɪdlɪ] ADV *(form)* = **fervently**

fervour, *(US)* **fervor** [ˈfɜːvəʳ] N Leidenschaftlichkeit *f*; *(of public speaker)* Leidenschaft *f*; *(of hope, prayer, wish)* Inbrunst *f (geh)*

fest [fest] N *(inf)* Festival *nt*; **film/jazz ~** Film-/Jazzfestival *nt*; **gore ~** *(= film)* blutrünstiger Film

fester [ˈfestəʳ] VI eitern, schwären *(old)*; *(fig, insult, resentment etc)* nagen, fressen; **~ing sore** *(fig)* Eiterbeule *f*

festival [ˈfestɪvəl] N **a** *(Eccl etc)* Fest *nt*; **Church ~s** kirchliche Feste *pl*, kirchliche Feiertage *pl*; **Festival of Lights** Lichterfest *nt* **b** *(cultural)* Festspiele *pl*, Festival *nt*; **the Edinburgh Festival** das Edinburgher Festival; **the Salzburg Festival** die Salzburger Festspiele *pl*

festive ['festɪv] ADJ festlich; the ~ season die Festzeit; he was in (a) ~ mood er war in festlicher Stimmung or in Festtagslaune

festivity [fe'stɪvɪtɪ] N a (= gaiety) Feststimmung f, Feiertagsstimmung f; there was an air of ~ in the office im Büro herrschte Feststimmung f b (= celebration) Feier f; festivities pl (= festive proceedings) Feierlichkeiten pl, Festivitäten pl (hum)

festoon [fe'stu:n] N Girlande f; (in curtain etc, Archit) Feston m VT to ~ sb with sth jdn mit etw behängen; to ~ sth with sth etw mit etw schmücken or verzieren; to be ~ed with sth mit etw behängt sein; lace curtains ~ed the windows Spitzengardinen schmückten die Fenster

feta (cheese) ['fetə('tʃi:z)] N Feta(käse) m

fetal ['fi:tl] ADJ (esp US) = foetal

fetch [fetʃ] VT a (= bring) holen; (= collect) person, thing abholen; would you ~ a handkerchief for me or ~ me a handkerchief? kannst du mir ein Taschentuch holen (gehen)?; I'll ~ her from the station ich hole sie vom Bahnhof ab; she ~ed in the washing sie holte die Wäsche herein; he's upstairs, I'll ~ him down er ist oben, ich hole ihn herunter
b (= bring in) £10 etc (ein)bringen
c (inf) to ~ sb a blow jdm eine langen (inf); (accidentally: with rucksack etc) jdn erwischen (inf)
VI a to ~ and carry for sb bei jdm Mädchen für alles sein
b (Naut) Kurs halten; (= change course) Kurs nehmen

▶ **fetch up** VI (inf) landen (inf) VT sep (Brit, = vomit) wieder von sich geben, erbrechen

fetching ['fetʃɪŋ] ADJ attraktiv, reizend; smile gewinnend, einnehmend

fetchingly ['fetʃɪŋlɪ] ADV attraktiv, reizend; smile gewinnend; pretty bezaubernd

fête [feɪt] N Fest nt; village ~ Dorffest nt VT (= make much of) sb, sb's success feiern; to ~ sb (= entertain) zu jds Ehren ein Fest geben; a much ~d actress eine gefeierte Schauspielerin

fetid ['fetɪd] ADJ übel riechend

fetidness ['fetɪdnɪs] N Gestank m

fetish ['fetɪʃ] N Fetisch m; to have a ~ for leather/cleanliness einen Leder-/Sauberkeitstick haben (inf), ein Leder-/Sauberkeitsfetischist m sein; to make a ~ of sth einen Kult mit etw treiben, etw zum Fetisch machen or erheben

fetishism ['fetɪʃɪzəm] N Fetischismus m

fetishist ['fetɪʃɪst] N Fetischist(in) m(f)

fetishistic [,fetɪ'ʃɪstɪk] ADJ fetischistisch

fetlock ['fetlɒk] N Fessel f; (joint) Fesselgelenk nt

fetter ['fetə'] VT prisoner fesseln; goat anpflocken; (fig) in Fesseln legen N ~s pl (Fuß)fesseln pl; (fig) Fesseln pl; to put a prisoner in ~s einen Gefangenen in Fesseln legen

fettle ['fetl] N to be in fine or good ~ in bester Form sein; (as regards health also) in bester Verfassung or topfit (inf) sein

fettucine [,fetə'tʃi:nɪ] N no pl Fettucine pl

fetus ['fi:təs] N (US) = foetus

feu [fju:] N (Scot) Lehen nt

feud [fju:d] (lit, fig) N Fehde f; to have a ~ with sb mit jdm in Fehde liegen VI sich befehden, in Fehde liegen

feudal ['fju:dl] ADJ Feudal-, feudal; ~ system Feudalsystem nt; ~ landowner Feudal- or Lehnsherr m

feudalism ['fju:dəlɪzəm] N Feudalismus m, Lehnswesen nt

feu duty N (Scot) Lehnsabgabe f

fever ['fi:və'] N a Fieber nt no pl; tropical ~s tropische Fieberkrankheiten pl; to have a ~ eine Fieberkrankheit haben; (= high temperature) Fieber haben b (fig) Aufregung f, Erregung f, Fieber nt; election ~ Wahlfieber nt, Wahlrausch m; in a ~ of excitement in fieberhafter Erregung

feverish ['fi:vərɪʃ] ADJ a (= frenzied, frantic) excitement, activity, haste, pace, effort fieberhaft; speculation wild; atmosphere, expectation fiebrig; to be ~ with excitement vor Aufregung fiebern; to work at a ~ pace in fieberhafter Eile arbeiten b (Med) person fiebrig; condition, illness fieberhaft; to be ~ Fieber haben; ~ dream Fiebertraum m; ~ sweat Fieberschweiß m

feverishly ['fi:vərɪʃlɪ] ADV a (= frantically) work, try fieberhaft; (= agitatedly) await erregt; ~ impatient fiebernd vor Ungeduld; the market is ~ busy auf dem Markt herrscht eine fieberhafte Tätigkeit b sleep, toss fiebrig; talk im Fieber

feverishness ['fi:vərɪʃnɪs] N a (= frantic nature) Fieberhaftigkeit f b (Med) Fiebrigkeit f

fever pitch N at ~ auf dem Siedepunkt; to reach ~ am Siedepunkt angelangt sein, den Siedepunkt erreichen; to be working at ~ auf Hochtouren arbeiten

few [fju:] ADJ (+er) a (= not many) wenige; ~ people come to see him nur wenige Leute besuchen ihn; with ~ exceptions mit wenigen Ausnahmen; we are very ~ wir sind nur sehr wenige or nur ein kleines Häufchen; ~ and far between dünn gesät; as ~ as ten cigarettes a day can be harmful schon or bereits zehn Zigaretten am Tag können schädlich sein; as ~ as six objections bloß sechs Einwände, nicht mehr als sechs Einwände; how ~ they are! wie wenige das sind!; so ~ books so wenige Bücher; too ~ cakes zu wenige Kuchen; there were 3 too ~ es waren 3 zu wenig da; 10 would not be too ~ 10 wären nicht zu wenig; he is one of the ~ people who ... er ist einer der wenigen, die ...; the exceptions are ~ es gibt nur wenige Ausnahmen; such occasions are ~ solche Gelegenheiten sind selten or rar
b a ~ ein paar; a very ~ nur ganz wenige; a ~ more days noch ein paar Tage; a ~ times ein paar Male; there were quite a ~ waiting ziemlich viele warteten; he has quite a ~ girlfriends er hat eine ganze Menge or ziemlich viele Freundinnen; he's had a ~ (too many) er hat einen über den Durst getrunken; quite a ~ books ziemlich viele Bücher, eine ganze Menge Bücher; I saw a good ~ or quite a ~ people ich habe ziemlich viele Leute or eine ganze Menge Leute gesehen; not a ~ people nicht wenige Leute; we'll go in a ~ minutes wir gehen in ein paar Minuten; in the next/past ~ days in den nächsten/letzten paar Tagen; every ~ days alle paar Tage
PRON a (= not many) wenige; ~ of them came wenige von ihnen kamen; some ~ gar nicht so wenige; the Few *Kampfflieger, die an der Luftschlacht um England im zweiten Weltkrieg teilnahmen*; the lucky ~ die wenigen Glücklichen; opera used to be an experience for the ~ Opern waren früher einer privilegierten Minderheit vorbehalten; as ~ as you genauso wenig wie du; how ~ there are! wie wenige das sind!; however ~ there may be wie wenig auch immer da ist; I've got so/too ~ as it is ich habe sowieso schon so/zu wenig(e); so ~ have been sold so wenige sind bis jetzt verkauft worden; there are too ~ of you ihr seid zu wenige
b a ~ ein paar; I'll just take a ~ ich nehme nur ein paar; a ~ more ein paar mehr; quite a ~ eine ganze Menge; quite a ~ did not believe him eine ganze Menge Leute or ziemlich viele Leute glaubten ihm nicht; some ~ einige; there are always the ~ who ... es gibt immer einige wenige Leute or ein paar Leute, die ...; the ~ who knew him die wenigen, die ihn kannten

fewer ['fju:ə'] ADJ PRON comp of few weniger; no ~ than nicht weniger als

fewest ['fju:ɪst] superl of few ADJ die wenigsten PRON die wenigsten, am wenigsten

fey [feɪ] ADJ (Scot) todgeweiht; (= clairvoyant) hellseherisch

fez [fez] N Fes m

ff abbr of following ff

FHSA (Brit) abbr of Family Health Services Authority ≈ Gesundheitsamt nt

fiancé [fɪ'ɑ̃:ŋseɪ] N Verlobte(r) m

fiancée [fɪ'ɑ̃:ŋseɪ] N Verlobte f

fiasco [fɪ'æskəʊ] N pl -s, (US also) -es Fiasko nt

fiat ['faɪæt] N a (= decree) Befehl m, Erlass m, Anordnung f; nothing can be done by ~ nichts geschieht so einfach auf Befehl b (= authorization) Billigung f, Plazet nt

fiat money N Papiergeld nt ohne Deckung

fib [fɪb] (inf) N Flunkerei f (inf), Schwindelei f (inf); that's a ~! das ist geflunkert! (inf); don't tell ~s flunker or schwindel nicht! (inf) VI flunkern (inf), schwindeln (inf)

fibber ['fɪbə'] N (inf) Flunkerer m (inf), Schwindler(in) m(f) (inf)

fibbing ['fɪbɪŋ] N (inf) Flunkerei f (inf)

fibre, (US) **fiber** ['faɪbə'] N a Faser f b (= roughage) Ballaststoffe pl c (fig) moral ~ Charakterstärke f; he has no moral ~ er hat keinen inneren Halt, er hat kein Rückgrat; with every ~ of one's being mit jeder Faser seines Herzens

fibre, (US) **fiber**: **fibreboard**, (US) **fiberboard** N Faserplatte f; **fibreglass**, (US) **fiberglass** N Fiberglas nt, Glasfaser f ADJ aus Fiberglas or Glasfaser; ~-reinforced glasfaserverstärkt; **fibreoptic cable**, (US) **fiberoptic cable** N faseroptisches Kabel; **fibre optics** N sing Faseroptik f; **fibre-tip pen** N (Brit) Faserschreiber m

fibroid ['faɪbrɔɪd] ADJ fibrös N Fibromyom nt

fibrositis [,faɪbrə'saɪtɪs] N Bindegewebsentzündung f

fibrous ['faɪbrəs] ADJ faserig

fibula ['fɪbjʊlə] N Wadenbein nt

FICA (US) abbr of Federal Insurance Contributions Act (Jur) *Gesetz über die Einbehaltung von Sozialversicherungsbeiträgen*; a third of Jack's salary went to ~ ein Drittel von Jacks Gehalt ging an die Sozialversicherung

fickle ['fɪkl] ADJ unbeständig, launenhaft; person also wankelmütig; weather also wechselhaft

fickleness ['fɪklnɪs] N Wechselhaftigkeit f, Unbeständigkeit f; (of person also) Wankelmütigkeit f

fiction ['fɪkʃən] N a no pl (Liter) Erzähl- or Prosaliteratur f; you'll find that under ~ das finden Sie unter Belletristik; work of ~ Erzählung f; (longer) Roman m; light ~ (leichte) Unterhaltungsliteratur; romantic ~ Liebesromane pl b (= invention) (freie) Erfindung, Fiktion f; that's pure ~ das ist frei erfunden; total recycling is a ~ das totale Recycling gibt es nicht

fictional ['fɪkʃənl] ADJ a (= invented) erfunden; (Liter) character, hero, heroine, setting, account erfunden, fiktiv; film, drama fiktional; entirely ~ rein fiktiv, frei erfunden; the party's unity was ~ die Einheit der Partei war eine Fiktion b (= relating to fiction) work erzählerisch; his ~ writing seine erzählenden Schriften; a clever ~ device ein geschickter erzählerischer Trick; a ~ representation of historical events eine dichterische Darstellung historischer Ereignisse

fictitious [fɪk'tɪʃəs] ADJ a (= false, nonexistent) name, address falsch; loan, case fingiert; the job in the advertisement turned out to be ~ es stellte sich heraus, dass es die ausgeschriebene Stelle gar nicht gab b (Liter. = imaginary) character, setting, story, event erfunden; all characters in this film are (entirely) ~ alle Gestalten in diesem Film sind (frei) erfunden

fiddle ['fɪdl] N a (Mus inf) Fiedel f (inf), Geige f; to play second ~ die zweite Geige spielen; to play second ~ to sb (fig) in jds Schatten (dat) stehen; he refuses to play second ~ (fig) er will immer die erste Geige spielen; as fit as a ~ kerngesund
b (Brit inf: = cheat, swindle) Manipulation f, Schiebung f; (with money) faule Geschäfte pl (inf); it's a ~ das ist Schiebung!; there are so many ~s going on es wird so viel getrickst (inf) or manipuliert; the accountants were well aware there had been some sort of ~ die Buchprüfer wussten ganz genau, dass da irgendetwas manipuliert or frisiert (inf) worden war;

tax ~ Steuermanipulation *f*; **to be on the ~** faule Geschäfte *or* krumme Dinger machen *(inf)*
c **it's a bit of a ~** *(Brit: = quite tricky)* es ist eine ziemliche Fummelei *(inf)*
VI **a** *(Mus inf)* fiedeln *(inf)*, geigen
b *(= fidget, play around)* herumspielen; **don't ~ with the engine if you don't know what you're doing** spiel nicht am Motor herum, wenn du dich damit nicht auskennst; **he sat there nervously fiddling with his tie/cigarette lighter** er saß da und spielte nervös an seinem Schlips herum/spielte mit seinem Feuerzeug herum; **put that thing down and stop fiddling!** leg das Ding weg und hör endlich mit der Fummelei auf! *(inf)*
c *(= split hairs, be overprecise etc)* Haare spalten, pingelig sein *(inf)*
VT **a** *(Brit inf) accounts, results* frisieren *(inf)*; *election* manipulieren; **he ~d it so that ...** er hat es so hingebogen *or* getrickst *(inf)*, dass ...
b *tune* fiedeln *(inf)*, geigen
INTERJ ach du liebe Zeit, ach du liebes Lottchen *(hum inf)*

▸ **fiddle about** *(Brit) or* **around** **VI** **to fiddle about** *or* **around with sth** an etw *(dat)* herumspielen *or* herumfummeln *(inf)*; *(= fidget with)* mit etw herumspielen; **he dived under the bonnet and fiddled about** *or* **around for a while** er verschwand unter der Kühlerhaube und fummelte eine Weile herum *(inf)*; **I'm not spending all day just fiddling around with this one little job!** ich werde doch nicht den ganzen Tag damit zubringen, an dieser einen Kleinigkeit rumzufummeln! *(inf)*

fiddle-faddle [ˈfɪdlfædl] **INTERJ** *(dated, = nonsense)* Quatsch *(inf)*

fiddler [ˈfɪdləʳ] **N** **a** *(Mus inf)* Geiger(in) *m(f)* **b** *(inf: = cheat)* Schwindler(in) *m(f)*, Betrüger(in) *m(f)*

fiddler crab **N** Winkerkrabbe *f*

fiddlesticks [ˈfɪdlstɪks] **INTERJ** *(= nonsense)* Unsinn, Quatsch *(inf)*; *(= bother)* du liebe Zeit, du liebes Lottchen *(hum inf)*

fiddliness [ˈfɪdlɪnɪs] **N** *(Brit inf: = intricacy)* Kniffligkeit *f (inf)*; *(= awkwardness in use)* Umständlichkeit *f*

fiddling [ˈfɪdlɪŋ] **ADJ** *(= trivial)* läppisch

fiddly [ˈfɪdlɪ] **ADJ** *(+er) (Brit) (= intricate) job, task* knifflig *(inf)*; *(= awkward to use) object, controls etc* umständlich; **it is ~ to use** es ist (in der Benutzung) zu umständlich; **little ~ bits** umständliche Kleinteile *pl*

fidelity [fɪˈdelɪtɪ] **N** **a** Treue *f (to* zu) **b** *(of translation etc)* Genauigkeit *f*; *(Rad etc)* Klangtreue *f*

fidget [ˈfɪdʒɪt] **VI** *(also* **fidget about** *or* **around**: *= be restless)* zappeln; **to ~ with sth** mit etw herumspielen *or* herumfummeln *(inf)*; **don't ~** zappel nicht so rum; **he sat there ~ing in his chair** er rutschte auf seinem Stuhl hin und her **N** **a** *(= person)* Zappelphilipp *m (inf)* **b** *(inf)* **to get the ~s** zappelig werden; **have you got the ~s?** was bist du für ein Zappelphilipp! *(inf)*

fidgety [ˈfɪdʒɪtɪ] **ADJ** zappelig; *audience etc, legs, feet, hands* unruhig

fiduciary [fɪˈdjuːʃɪərɪ] **ADJ** treuhänderisch; *currency* ungedeckt; **~ company** Treuhandgesellschaft *f* **N** Treuhänder(in) *m(f)*

fie [faɪ] **INTERJ** *(old)* pfui; **~ on you!** pfui!, schämen Sie sich!

fief [fiːf] **N** *(Hist)* Lehen *nt*

field [fiːld] **N** **a** *(Agr)* Feld *nt*, Acker *m*; *(= area of grass)* Weide *f*; *(for cows, horses etc)* Weide *f*; **corn/wheat ~** Getreide-/Weizenfeld *nt*; **potato ~** Kartoffelacker *m*; **we had a picnic in a ~** wir machten auf einer Wiese Picknick; **he's working in the ~s** er arbeitet auf dem Feld *or* Acker; **the farm has 20 ~s** der Hof hat 20 Felder; **beasts of the ~** Feldtiere *pl*; **to cut across the ~s** quer über die Felder gehen
b *(= coalfield, icefield, oilfield etc)* Feld *nt*
c *(for football etc: = ground)* Platz *m*; **sports** *or* **games ~** Sportplatz *m*; **to take the ~** auf den Platz kommen, einlaufen
d *(Mil)* Feld *nt*; **~ of battle** Schlachtfeld *nt*; **noted for his bravery in the ~** für seine Tapferkeit im Feld bekannt; **to take the ~** zur Schlacht antreten
e *(of study, work etc)* Gebiet *nt*, Feld *nt*; **to be first in the ~ with sth** *(Comm)* als Erster etw auf den Markt bringen; **to lead the ~ (in sth)** (in etw *dat*) das Feld anführen; **in all the ~s of human endeavour** *(liter)* im gesamten menschlichen Trachten *(liter)*; **studies in the ~ of medicine** Studien auf dem Gebiet der Medizin; **this is, of course, a very broad ~** das ist natürlich ein weites Feld; **what ~ are you in?** auf welchem Gebiet *or* in welchem Feld arbeiten Sie?; **his ~ is Renaissance painting** sein Spezialgebiet ist die Malerei der Renaissance
f *(= area of practical observation or operation)* Praxis *f*; **when a salesman goes out into the ~** wenn ein Verkäufer in den Außeneinsatz geht; **work in the ~** Feldforschung *f*; *(of sales rep)* Außendienst *m*; **to test sth in the ~** etw in der Praxis *or* vor Ort ausprobieren
g *(Phys, Opt)* Feld *nt*; **~ of vision** Blick- *or* Gesichtsfeld *nt*; **gravitational ~** Gravitationsfeld *nt*, Schwerefeld *nt*; **~ of force** Kraftfeld *nt*; **magnetic ~** Magnetfeld *nt*, magnetisches Feld
h *(Sport: = competitors)* Feld *nt*; *(Cricket, Baseball)* Fängerpartei *f*; **the rest of the ~** *(in race)* der Rest des Feldes, die übrigen Läufer; **there's quite a strong ~ for the race** das Teilnehmerfeld für das Rennen ist ziemlich stark; **to hold off a strong ~** sich gegen ein starkes Feld behaupten
i *(Comput)* Datenfeld *nt*; *(on punch card)* Feld *nt*
j *(on flag, Her)* Feld *nt*, Grund *m*
k **to play the ~** *(inf)* eine Beziehung nach der anderen haben
VT **a** *(Cricket, Baseball etc) ball* auffangen und zurückwerfen; *(fig) question etc* abblocken, abwehren; **he had to ~ calls from irate customers** er musste wütende Kunden am Telefon abwimmeln *(inf)*
b *team, side* aufs Feld *or* auf den Platz schicken
c *(Pol) candidate* aufstellen
VI *(Cricket, Baseball etc)* als Fänger spielen; **when we go out to ~** wenn wir die Fänger(partei) stellen

field: **field ambulance** **N** *(Mil)* Sanka *m*, Sanitätskraftwagen *m*; **field artillery** **N** Feldartillerie *f*; **field day** **N** **a** Manöver *nt* **b** *(US: for school sports)* (Schul)sportfest *nt* **c** *(fig)* **I had a ~** ich hatte meinen großen Tag; **with the score at 6-0 the Scots are having a ~ against the English** beim Stand von 6:0 machen die Schotten jetzt die Engländer nach allen Regeln der Kunst fertig *(inf)*

fielder [ˈfiːldəʳ] **N** *(Cricket, Baseball etc)* Fänger(in) *m(f)*

field: **field event** **N** *(Athletics) Disziplin, die nicht auf der Aschenbahn ausgetragen wird*; **field games** **PL** Feldspiele *pl*; **field glasses** **PL** Feldstecher *m*; **field goal** **N** *(US Basketball)* Korbwurf *m* aus dem Spielgeschehen; *(Ftbl)* Fieldgoal *nt*, Feldtor *nt*; **field gun** **N** *(Mil)* Feldgeschütz *nt*; **field hockey** **N** *(US)* Hockey *nt*; **field hospital** **N** *(Mil)* (Feld)lazarett *nt*; **field kitchen** **N** *(Mil)* Feldküche *f*; **field marshal** **N** *(Mil)* Feldmarschall *m*; **fieldmouse** **N** Feldmaus *f*; **field officer** **N** *(Mil)* Stabsoffizier *m*; **fieldpiece** **N** *(Mil)* Feldgeschütz *nt*; **field service** **N** *(Comm)* Außendienst *m*

fieldsman [ˈfiːldzmən] **N** *pl* **-men** [-mən] *(Cricket)* Fänger *m*

field: **field sports** **PL** **a** Sport *m* im Freien *(Jagen und Fischen)* **b** = **field games**; **field staff** **N** *(Comm)* Außendienstmitarbeiter(in) *m(f)*; **field study** **N** Feldforschung *f*; **a ~** eine Feldstudie; **field test** **N** Feldversuch *m*; **field-test** **VT** in einem Feldversuch/in Feldversuchen testen; **field trip** **N** Exkursion *f*; **field work** **N** **a** *(of geologist, surveyor etc)* Arbeit *f* im Gelände; *(of sociologist etc)* Feldarbeit *f*, Feldforschung *f* **b** *(Mil)* Feldbefestigung *f*, Schanze *f*; **field worker** **N** Praktiker(in) *m(f)*

fiend [fiːnd] **N** **a** *(= evil spirit)* Teufel *m*, Dämon *m*; *(= person)* Teufel *m*; **the Fiend** der böse Feind; **"sex ~ strikes again"** „Sexbestie schlägt wieder zu" **b** *(inf: = addict)* Fanatiker(in) *m(f)*; **tennis ~** Tennisnarr *m*; **she's a fresh-air ~** sie ist Frischluftfanatikerin

fiendish [ˈfiːndɪʃ] **ADJ** **a** *(= cruel) person, act, look* teuflisch; *delight, glee, laughter* hämisch; **he took a ~ delight in doing it** es machte ihm eine höllische Freude, es zu tun **b** *(inf: = cunning) plan, device, gadget* höllisch raffiniert *or* clever *(inf)* **c** *(inf: = very difficult) problem* verzwickt *(inf)*, höllisch schwer *(inf)*

fiendishly [ˈfiːndɪʃlɪ] **ADV** **a** *(inf: = very) difficult, clever, complicated* höllisch *(inf)*, verteufelt *(inf)*; *funny* wahnsinnig *(inf)*; **it's ~ simple** es ist verblüffend einfach **b** *(= evilly) mean, ambitious, laugh, grin* teuflisch

fierce [fɪəs] **ADJ** *(+er) animal* wild, aggressiv; *dog* böse; *person, look, appearance* grimmig; *fighting, battle, opposition, resistance, opponent, critic, rivals* erbittert, heftig; *debate, argument, storm* heftig; *attack, competition, criticism* scharf; *determination* wild; *loyalty* unerschütterlich; *pride, ambition, independence* leidenschaftlich; *heat, sun* glühend; **the troops came under ~ attack** die Truppen wurden scharf angegriffen; **he has a ~ temper** er braust schnell *or* leicht auf

fiercely [ˈfɪəslɪ] **ADV** *contest, oppose, fight, deny* heftig; *criticize* scharf; *defend, argue* leidenschaftlich; *say* böse, grimmig; *independent, competitive, proud, loyal* äußerst; **to be ~ critical of sth** etw scharf kritisieren; **~ determined** wild entschlossen; **to oppose sth ~, to be ~ opposed to sth** einer Sache *(dat)* heftigen Widerstand entgegensetzen, heftigen Widerstand gegen etw leisten; **TV and radio stations compete ~ with one another** Fernseh- und Radiosender stehen in scharfem Wettbewerb miteinander; **the fire was burning ~** es brannte lichterloh

fierceness [ˈfɪəsnɪs] **N** *(of animal)* Wildheit *f*; *(of dog)* Bösartigkeit *f*; *(of person, look, appearance)* Grimmigkeit *f*; *(of temper)* aufbrausende Art; *(of fighting, battle, debate, opposition, rivalry, storm)* Heftigkeit *f*; *(of attack, competition, criticism)* Schärfe *f*; *(of sun)* Gluthitze *f*; **the ~ of the heat** die Gluthitze, die glühende Hitze

fieriness [ˈfaɪərɪnɪs] **N** **a** *(of temperament, character)* Hitzigkeit *f*; *(of person)* Hitzköpfigkeit *f*, Hitzigkeit *f*; *(of speech, performance)* Feurigkeit *f* **b** *(= spiciness: of food)* Feurigkeit *f*

fiery [ˈfaɪərɪ] **ADJ** *(+er)* **a** *(= burning) inferno, furnace, heat* glühend **b** *colour, orange* leuchtend; *sunset* rot glühend; *hair* feuerrot; **~ red** feuerrot **c** *(Cook: = spicy) food, drink* feurig **d** *(= passionate) temperament, character* hitzig; *person* hitzköpfig; *speech, performance* feurig; **a ~ redhead** ein hitziger Rotschopf; **to have a ~ temper** ein Hitzkopf *m* sein

fiesta [fɪˈestə] **N** Fiesta *f*

FIFA [ˈfiːfə] *abbr of* **Federation of International Football Associations** FIFA *f*

fife [faɪf] **N** *(Mus)* Querpfeife *f*

fifteen [ˈfɪfˈtiːn] **ADJ** fünfzehn **N** **a** Fünfzehn *f* **b** **a rugby ~** eine Rugbymannschaft; **the Welsh ~** die Rugbynationalmannschaft von Wales

fifteenth [ˈfɪfˈtiːnθ] **ADJ** fünfzehnte(r, s) **N** Fünfzehnte(r, s); *(= part, fraction)* Fünfzehntel *nt* → *also* **sixteenth**

fifth [fɪfθ] **ADJ** fünfte(r, s); **~ rate** fünftrangig **N** Fünfte(r, s); *(= part, fraction)* Fünftel *nt*; *(Mus)* Quinte *f*; **to take the ~** *(US inf)* die Aussage verweigern → *also* **sixth**

FIFTH AMENDMENT

Im **Fifth Amendment**, dem fünften Zusatz zur Verfassung der USA, wurden verschiedene Grundrechte zum Schutz der Bürger vor Übergriffen des Staates festgeschrieben. Es besagt unter anderem, dass niemand ohne

Gerichtsverhandlung inhaftiert werden darf, dass niemandes Eigentum ohne ordentliches Gerichtsurteil gepfändet werden kann, dass niemand zweimal wegen desselben Verbrechens angeklagt werden darf und dass niemand gegen sich selbst aussagen muss. Wenn jemand die Aussage verweigert, um sich nicht selbst zu belasten, so nennt man das auch „he/she is taking the Fifth". Während der antikommunistischen Untersuchungen unter Leitung von Senator McCarthy in den 50er-Jahren wurden Personen, die sich auf das **Fifth Amendment** beriefen, häufig des unamerikanischen Verhaltens für schuldig befunden → BILL OF RIGHTS

fifth: **fifth column** N fünfte Kolonne; **fifth columnist** N Angehörige(r) *mf* der fünften Kolonne, Kollaborateur(in) *m(f)*

fiftieth ['fɪftɪɪθ] ADJ fünfzigste(r, s) N Fünfzigste(r, s); *(= part, fraction)* Fünfzigstel *nt* → *also* **sixth**

fifty ['fɪftɪ] ADJ fünfzig N Fünfzig *f* → *also* **sixty**

fifty-fifty ['fɪftɪ'fɪftɪ] ADV halbe-halbe *(inf)*, fifty-fifty *(inf)*; **to go ~ (with sb)** (mit jdm) halbe-halbe *or* fifty-fifty machen *(inf)* ADJ **it was a ~ deal** bei dem Handel sollte fifty-fifty geteilt werden *(inf)*; **they had ~ shares in the business** sie waren zu fünfzig Prozent an der Firma beteiligt; **he has a ~ chance of survival/victory** er hat eine fünfzigprozentige Überlebens-/Gewinnchance

fig [fɪg] N Feige *f*; **I don't care** *or* **give a ~** *(Brit inf)* ich kümmere mich einen Dreck darum *(inf)*; **I don't give a ~ what he thinks!** *(Brit inf)* seine Meinung kümmert mich einen (feuchten) Dreck *(inf)*

fig. *abbr of* **figure(s)** Abb.

fight [faɪt] *vb: pret, ptp* **fought** N a *(lit, fig)* Kampf *m*; *(= fist fight, scrap)* Rauferei *f*, Prügelei *f*, Schlägerei *f*; *(Mil)* Gefecht *nt*; *(= argument, row)* Streit *m*; **to have a ~ with sb** sich mit jdm schlagen; *(= argue)* sich mit jdm streiten; **to give sb a ~** *(lit, fig)* jdm einen Kampf liefern; **to put up a ~** *(lit, fig)* sich zur Wehr setzen; **to put up a good ~** *(lit, fig)* sich tapfer zur Wehr setzen, sich tapfer schlagen; **do you want a ~?** willst du was?, du willst dich wohl mit mir anlegen?; **if he wants a ~, then …** *(lit, fig)* wenn er Streit sucht, dann …; **a politician who enjoys a good ~** ein streitlustiger Politiker; **he won't give in without a ~** er ergibt sich nicht kampflos; **in the ~ against disease** im Kampf gegen die Krankheit; **the ~ for survival** der Kampf ums Überleben; **he lost his ~ for life** er verlor den Kampf um sein Leben; **the big ~** *(Boxing)* der große Kampf

b *(= fighting spirit)* Kampfgeist *m*; **there was no ~ left in him** sein Kampfgeist war erloschen; **to show ~** Kampfgeist zeigen

VI kämpfen; *(= have punch-up etc)* raufen, sich prügeln, sich schlagen; *(= argue: with wife etc)* sich streiten *or* zanken; **the dogs were ~ing over a bone** die Hunde rauften um einen Knochen; **to ~ against disease** Krankheiten bekämpfen; **to ~ for sb/sth** um jdn/etw kämpfen; **to ~ for what one believes in** für seine Überzeugungen eintreten *or* streiten; **to ~ for one's life** um sein Leben kämpfen; **to ~ for breath** nach Atem ringen; **to go down ~ing** sich nicht kampflos ergeben; **to ~ shy of sth** einer Sache *(dat)* aus dem Weg gehen; **I've always fought shy of claiming that …** ich habe immer bewusst vermieden, zu behaupten …

VT a *person* kämpfen mit *or* gegen; *(= have punch-up with)* sich schlagen mit, sich prügeln mit; *(in battle)* kämpfen mit, sich *(dat)* ein Gefecht *nt* liefern mit; **I'm prepared to ~ him/the government** *(= argue with, take on)* ich bin bereit, das mit ihm/der Regierung durchzukämpfen; **I'll ~ him on that one** dazu nehme ich es mit ihm auf; **you can't ~ the whole company** du kannst es nicht mit der ganzen Firma aufnehmen

b *fire, disease, cuts, policy, crime, inflation* bekämpfen; *decision* ankämpfen gegen; *corruption* angehen gegen; **there's no point in ~ing it, you can't win** es hat keinen Zweck, dagegen anzukämpfen, es ist aussichtslos; **she fought the urge to giggle** sie versuchte, sich das Kichern zu verkneifen

c **to ~ a duel** ein Duell *nt* austragen, sich duellieren; **to ~ pitched battles** sich *(dat)* offene Gefechte liefern; **to ~ political battles** politische Kämpfe austragen; **to ~ an action** *(Jur)* einen Prozess durchkämpfen *or* durchfechten; **to ~ one's way through the crowd** sich durch die Menge kämpfen → *also* **battle N**

d *(Mil, Naut, = control in battle) army, ships* kommandieren

▶ **fight back** VI *(in fight)* zurückschlagen; *(Mil)* sich verteidigen, Widerstand leisten; *(in argument)* sich wehren, sich zur Wehr setzen; *(after illness)* zu Kräften kommen; *(Sport)* zurückkämpfen VT *sep tears, doubts etc* unterdrücken; **he fought his way back into the match/to the top** er hat sich ins Spiel/wieder an die Spitze zurückgekämpft

▶ **fight down** VT *sep anxiety, anger* unterdrücken

▶ **fight off** VT *sep (Mil, fig) attack, disease, attacker* abwehren; *sleep* ankämpfen gegen; **I'm still trying to fight off this cold** ich kämpfe immer noch mit dieser Erkältung; **she has to keep fighting men off** sie muss dauernd Männer abwimmeln

▶ **fight on** VI weiterkämpfen

▶ **fight out** VT *sep* **to fight it out** es untereinander ausfechten

fightback ['faɪtbæk] N Come-back *nt*, Comeback *nt*

fighter ['faɪtəʳ] N a Kämpfer(in) *m(f)*, Streiter(in) *m(f)*; *(Boxing)* Fighter *m*; **he's a ~** *(fig)* er ist eine Kämpfernatur b *(Aviat: = plane)* Jagdflugzeug *nt*, Jäger *m*

fighter: **fighter-bomber** N Jagdbomber *m*; **fighter interceptor** N Abfangjäger *m*; **fighter pilot** N Jagdflieger *m*

fighting ['faɪtɪŋ] N *(Mil)* Kampf *m*, Gefecht *nt*; *(= punch-ups, scrapping etc)* Prügeleien *pl*, Raufereien *pl*; *(= arguments between husband and wife etc)* Streit *m*, Zank *m*; **~ broke out** Kämpfe brachen aus → **street fighting** ADJ *attr person* kämpferisch, streitlustig; **~ troops, ~ forces** Kampftruppen *pl*; **~ line** Front *f*; **~ man** Krieger *m*, Kämpfer *m*; **~ strength** *(Mil)* Kampf- *or* Einsatzstärke *f*

fighting: **fighting dog** N Kampfhund *m*; **fighting chance** N faire Chancen *pl*; **he's in with** *or* **he has a ~ (of winning)** er hat eine Chance (zu gewinnen), wenn er sich anstrengt; **at least that gives you a ~** damit hast du wenigstens eine Chance; **fighting cock** N *(lit, fig)* Kampfhahn *m*; **fighting fit** ADJ *(Brit inf)* topfit *(inf)*; **fighting spirit** N Kampfgeist *m*; **to have tremendous ~** ungeheuren Kampfgeist haben; **fighting weight** N *(Boxing)* Kampfgewicht *nt*

fig leaf N *(lit, fig)* Feigenblatt *nt*

figment ['fɪgmənt] N **a ~ of the imagination** pure Einbildung, ein Hirngespinst *nt*; **it's all a ~ of his imagination** das ist alles eine Ausgeburt seiner Fantasie *or* Phantasie

fig tree N Feigenbaum *m*

figurative ['fɪgjʊrətɪv] ADJ a *(= metaphorical) language* bildlich; *use, sense* übertragen; **in a ~ sense** im übertragenen Sinn b *(Art) art, painting, sculpture, artist* gegenständlich

figuratively ['fɪgjʊrətɪvlɪ] ADV im übertragenen Sinn; **~ speaking** bildlich gesprochen; **I'm speaking ~ there** das ist natürlich nicht wörtlich gemeint

figure ['fɪgəʳ] N a *(= number)* Zahl; *(= digit)* Ziffer *f*; *(= sum)* Summe *f*; **to put a ~ on sth** etw konkret in Zahlen angeben; **could you put some sort of ~ on the salary?** können Sie mir die ungefähre Höhe des Gehaltes mitteilen?; **he didn't want to put a ~ on it** er wollte keine Zahlen nennen; **name your ~** nennen Sie Ihren Preis; **he's good at ~s** er ist ein guter Rechner; **a mistake in the ~s** eine Unstimmigkeit in den Zahlen; **have you seen last year's ~s?** haben Sie die Zahlen vom Vorjahr gesehen?; **Miss Jones, could you bring in the ~s for the Fotheringham contract?** Fräulein Jones, könnten Sie das Zahlenmaterial zum Fotheringham-Vertrag bringen?; **to reach double ~s** in die zweistelligen Zahlen gehen; **a three-~ sum** eine dreistellige Summe; **to sell for a high ~** für eine hohe Summe verkauft werden; **he earns well into six ~s** er hat gut und gern ein sechsstelliges Einkommen; **government ~s show that …** die Zahlen der Regierung zeigen, dass …; **the ~s work** *(inf)* es rechnet sich *(inf)*

b *(in geometry, dancing, skating)* Figur *f*; **~ (of) eight** Acht *f*

c *(= human form)* Gestalt *f*

d *(= shapeliness)* Figur *f*; **she has a good ~** sie hat eine gute Figur; **I'm dieting to keep my ~** ich lebe Diät, um meine Figur zu behalten; **to lose one's ~** seine Figur verlieren; **to get one's ~ back** seine alte Figur wiederbekommen; **what a ~!** (was für) eine tolle Figur!; **she's a fine ~ of a woman** sie ist eine stattliche Frau; **he's a fine ~ of a man** er ist ein Bild von einem Mann

e *(= personality)* Persönlichkeit *f*; *(= character in novel etc)* Gestalt *f*; **the great ~s of history** die Großen der Geschichte; **a key public ~** eine Schlüsselfigur des öffentlichen Lebens; **~ of fun** Witzfigur *f*, lächerliche Erscheinung

f *(= statuette, model etc)* Figur *f*

g *(Liter)* **~ of speech** Redensart *f*, Redewendung *f*; **it's just a ~ of speech** das ist doch nur eine (leere) Redensart, das sagt man doch nur so

h *(Mus)* Figur *f*, Phrase *f*; *(= notation)* Ziffer *f*

i *(= illustration)* Abbildung *f*

VT a *(= decorate) silk etc* bemalen, mustern; **~d velvet** bedruckter Samt

b *(Mus) bass* beziffern; *melody* verzieren

c *(= imagine)* sich *(dat)* vorstellen, sich *(dat)* denken

d *(esp US inf: = think, reckon)* glauben, schätzen *(inf)*

e *(US inf: = figure out)* schlau werden aus, begreifen

VI a *(= appear)* erscheinen, auftauchen; **where does pity ~ in your scheme of things?** wo rangiert Mitleid in deiner Weltordnung?; **he ~d in a play** er trat in einem Stück auf; **he ~d prominently in my plans** er spielte eine bedeutende Rolle in meinen Plänen

b *(inf: = make sense)* hinkommen *(inf)*, hinhauen *(inf)*; **that ~s** das hätte ich mir denken können; **it doesn't ~** das passt *or* stimmt nicht zusammen

▶ **figure on** VI *+prep obj (esp US)* rechnen mit

▶ **figure out** VT *sep* a *(= understand, make sense of)* begreifen, schlau werden aus; **I can't figure him out at all** ich werde überhaupt nicht schlau aus ihm; **I can't figure it out** ich werde daraus nicht schlau b *(= work out)* ausrechnen; *answer, how to do sth* herausbekommen; *solution* finden; **figure it out for yourself** das kannst du dir (leicht) selbst ausrechnen

figure: **figure-conscious** ADJ figurbewusst; **he's very ~** er achtet sehr auf seine Figur; **figurehead** N *(Naut, fig)* Galionsfigur *f*; **figure-hugging** ADJ figurbetont; **figure-skate** VI Eiskunst laufen; **figure skater** N Eiskunstläufer(in) *m(f)*; **figure skating** N Eiskunstlaufen *nt*

figurine [fɪgə'riːn] N Figurine *f*

Fiji ['fiːdʒiː] N Fidschiinseln *pl*

Fijian [fɪ'dʒiːən] ADJ fidschianisch N a Fidschiinsulaner(in) *m(f)* b *(Ling)* Fidschianisch *nt*

filament ['fɪləmənt] N *(Elec)* (Glüh- *or* Heiz)faden *m*; *(Bot)* Staubfaden *m*

filbert ['fɪlbət] N *(Bot) (= tree)* Haselnussstrauch *m*; *(= nut)* Haselnuss *f*

filch [fɪltʃ] VT *(inf)* filzen, mopsen, mausen *(all inf)*

file[1] [faɪl] N *(= tool)* Feile *f* VT feilen; **to ~ one's (finger)nails** sich *(dat)* die Fingernägel feilen

▶ **file down** VT *sep* abfeilen

file² N a *(= holder)* (Akten)hefter *m*, Aktenordner *m*; *(for card index)* Karteikasten *m*; **would you fetch it from the ~s** könnten Sie es bitte aus der Ablage holen; **it's in the ~s somewhere** das muss irgendwo bei den Akten sein
b *(= documents, information)* Akte *f (on sb* über jdn, *on sth* zu etw); **on ~** aktenkundig, bei den Akten; **have we got that on ~?** haben wir das bei den Akten?; **to open** *or* **start a ~ on sb/sth** eine Akte über jdn/zu etw anlegen; **to have/keep a ~ on sb/sth** eine Akte über jdn/zu etw haben/führen; **to keep sb/sth on ~** jds Unterlagen/die Unterlagen über etw *(acc)* zurückbehalten; **to close the ~ on sb/sth** jds Akte/die Akte zu einer Sache schließen; **the Kowalski ~** die Akte Kowalski
c *(Comput)* Datei *f*, File *nt*; **data on ~** gespeicherte Daten; **to have sth on ~** etw im Computer gespeichert haben; **to activate/insert a ~** eine Datei aufrufen/einfügen; **to attach a ~** eine Datei (als Attachment) anhängen
d *(TV)* Archivbilder *pl*
VT a *(= put in file) letters* ablegen, abheften; *(Comput) text* abspeichern; **it's ~d under "B"** das ist unter „B" abgelegt
b *(Press) report* einsenden
c *(Jur) complaint* einreichen, erheben; *(law)suit* anstrengen; **to ~ a petition with a court** einen Antrag bei Gericht einreichen
VI **to ~ for divorce** die Scheidung einreichen; **to ~ for bankruptcy** Konkurs anmelden; **to ~ for custody (of the children)** das Sorgerecht (für die Kinder) beantragen

▶ **file away** VT *sep papers* zu den Akten legen; **to file sth away in one's memory** etw im Gedächtnis behalten

file³ N *(= row)* Reihe *f*; **in Indian** *or* **single ~** im Gänsemarsch; *(Mil)* in Reihe → **rank¹** VI **to ~ in** hereinmarschieren *or* -kommen; **they ~d out of the classroom** sie gingen hintereinander *or* nacheinander aus dem Klassenzimmer; **the procession ~d under the archway** die Prozession zog unter dem Torbogen hindurch; **they ~d through the turnstile** sie kamen nacheinander durch das Drehkreuz; **the troops ~d past the general** die Truppen marschierten *or* defilierten am General vorbei; **the children ~d past the headmaster** die Kinder gingen in einer Reihe am Direktor vorbei

file: **file attribute** N *(Comput)* Dateiattribut*nt*; **file cabinet** N *(US)* Aktenschrank *m*; **file-card** N Karteikarte *f*; **file clerk** N *(US)* Angestellte(r) *mf* in der Registratur; **file management** N *(Comput)* Dateiverwaltung *f*; **file manager** N *(Comput)* Dateimanager *m*; **file name** N *(Comput)* Dateiname *m*; **file number** N Aktenzeichen *nt*; **file server** N *(Comput)* Fileserver *m*, Dateiserver *m*; **file sharing** N *(Internet)* File-Sharing *nt*; **file size** N *(Comput)* Dateigröße *f or* -umfang *m*

filet [fɪ'leɪ] N *(US)* = **fillet**

file transfer protocol N *(Comput)* Dateitransferprotokoll *nt*

filial ['fɪlɪəl] ADJ *duties* des Kindes, als Kind; *piety, affection* kindlich; **with due ~ respect** mit dem Respekt, den eine Tochter/ein Sohn schuldig ist

filibuster ['fɪlɪbʌstəʳ] *(esp US)* N a *(= speech)* Obstruktion *f*, Dauerrede *f* b *(= person)* = **filibusterer** VI filibustern, Obstruktion betreiben

filibusterer ['fɪlɪbʌstərəʳ] N *(esp US)* Filibuster *m*, Dauerredner(in) *m(f)*, Obstruktionist(in) *m(f)*

filibustering ['fɪlɪbʌstərɪŋ] N *(esp US)* Verschleppungstaktik *f*, Obstruktionismus *m*

filigree ['fɪlɪgriː] N Filigran *nt* ADJ Filigran-; **~ jewellery** Filigranschmuck *m*

filing ['faɪlɪŋ] N a *(of documents)* Ablegen *nt*, Abheften *nt*; **who does your ~?** wer ist bei Ihnen für die Ablage zuständig?; **have you done the ~?** haben Sie die Akten schon abgelegt?
b *(Jur)* Einreichung *f*

filing: **filing cabinet** N Aktenschrank *m or* -regal *nt*; **filing clerk** N *(esp Brit)* Angestellte(r) *mf* in der Registratur

filings ['faɪlɪŋz] PL Späne *pl*

filing tray N Ablagekorb *m*

Filipino [fɪlɪ'piːnəʊ] N Filipino *m*, Filipina *f* ADJ philippinisch

fill [fɪl] VT a *bottle, bucket, hole* füllen; *pipe* stopfen; *teeth* plombieren; *(wind) sails* blähen; *(fig)* (aus)füllen; **I had three teeth ~ed** ich bekam drei Zähne plombiert *or* gefüllt; **I need something to ~ my day** ich brauche etwas, um meinen Tag auszufüllen
b *(= permeate)* erfüllen; **~ed with anger/admiration** voller Zorn/Bewunderung, von Zorn/Bewunderung erfüllt *(geh)*; **~ed with emotion** gefühlsgeladen; **the thought ~ed him with horror/hope** der Gedanke erfüllte ihn mit Entsetzen/Hoffnung
c *post, position (employer)* besetzen; *(employee, = take up)* einnehmen; *(= be in)* innehaben; *need* entsprechen *(+dat)*; *role* übernehmen; **we are looking for a young man to ~ the post of assistant editor** wir suchen einen jungen Mann, der den Posten eines Redaktionsassistenten einnehmen soll; **I think she will ~ the job very nicely** ich denke, sie wird die Stelle sehr gut ausfüllen; **the position is already ~ed** die Stelle ist schon besetzt *or* vergeben
d *theatre, seats* füllen; **the lecture room was ~ed to capacity** der Hörsaal war bis auf den letzten Platz besetzt
VI sich füllen; **his eyes ~ed with tears** Tränen traten ihm in die Augen
N **to drink one's ~** seinen Durst löschen; **to eat one's ~** sich satt essen; **to have had one's ~** gut satt sein; **I've had my ~ of him/it** *(inf)* ich habe von ihm/davon die Nase voll *(inf)*, ich habe ihn/das satt; **she's had her ~ of disappointments** sie hat mehr als genug Enttäuschungen erlebt

▶ **fill in** VI **to fill in for sb** für jdn einspringen VT *sep* a *hole* auffüllen; *door, fireplace* zumauern; **to fill in the gaps in one's knowledge** seine Wissenslücken stopfen; **he's just filling in time until he gets another job** er überbrückt nur die Zeit, bis er eine andere Stelle bekommt b *form* ausfüllen; *name, address, missing word* eintragen; **could you fill in the details for me?** könnten Sie mir die Einzelheiten nennen? c **to fill sb in (on sth)** jdn (über etw *acc*) aufklären *or* ins Bild setzen

▶ **fill out** VI a *(sails etc)* sich blähen b *(= become fatter, person)* fülliger werden; *(cheeks, face)* runder *or* voller werden VT *sep form* ausfüllen; *essay, article etc* strecken

▶ **fill up** VI a *(Aut)* (auf)tanken b *(hall, barrel etc)* sich füllen VT *sep* a *tank, cup* vollfüllen; *(driver)* volltanken; *hole* füllen, stopfen; **to fill sth right up** etw bis zum Rand (an)füllen; **he filled the glass up to the brim** er füllte das Glas randvoll; **fill her up!** *(Aut inf)* volltanken bitte!; **that pie has really filled me up** ich fühle mich wirklich voll nach dieser Pastete; **you need something to fill you up** du brauchst was Sättigendes b *form* ausfüllen

filler ['fɪləʳ] N a *(= funnel)* Trichter *m* b *(Build: = paste for cracks)* Spachtelmasse *f* c *(Press, TV)* Füllsel *nt*, (Lücken)füller *m* d *(Chem, for plastics)* Füllstoff *m* e *(Ling)* **~ (word)** Füllwort *nt*

filler cap N *(Brit)* Tankdeckel *m*

fillet ['fɪlɪt] N a *(Cook, of beef, fish)* Filet *nt*; **~ of beef/lamb** Rinder-/Lammfilet *nt* b *(for the hair)* (Haar)band *nt* VT *(Cook)* filetieren; **~ed sole** Seezungenfilet *nt*

fillet steak N Filetsteak *nt*

filling ['fɪlɪŋ] N a *(in tooth)* Füllung *f*, Plombe *f*; **my ~'s come out** ich hab eine Füllung *or* Plombe verloren; **I had to have three ~s** ich musste mir drei Zähne plombieren *or* füllen lassen b *(Cook, in pie, tart)* Füllung *f* ADJ *food* sättigend

filling station N Tankstelle *f*

fillip ['fɪlɪp] N *(fig)* Ansporn *m*, Aufmunterung *f*; **to give sb a ~** jdn aufmuntern *or* anspornen; **to give sth a ~** einer Sache *(dat)* (neuen) Schwung geben; **this gave a ~ to our business** dadurch hat unser Geschäft einen Aufschwung genommen

fill-up ['fɪlʌp] N *(inf)* **do you want a ~?** soll ich nachschenken?

filly ['fɪlɪ] N Stutfohlen *nt*; *(dated inf)* Mädel *nt (dated)*

film [fɪlm] N a *(= motion picture)* Film *m*; **to make** *or* **shoot a ~** einen Film drehen *or* machen; **to make a ~** *(actor)* einen Film machen; **to go to (see) a ~** ins Kino gehen; **he's in ~s** er ist beim Film; **to go into ~s** zum Film gehen
b *(Phot)* Film *m*; **get your holiday on ~** bannen Sie Ihre Ferien auf Film; **I wish I'd got that on ~** ich wünschte, ich hätte das aufnehmen können; **to take a ~ of sth** einen Film über etw *(acc)* drehen *or* machen
c *(= layer)* Film *m*; *(of dust)* Schicht *f*; *(of ice on water)* Schicht *f*; *(of mist, on the eye)* Schleier *m*; *(= thin membrane)* Häutchen *nt*; *(on teeth)* Belag *m*; *(= fine web)* feines Gewebe
VT *play* verfilmen; *scene* filmen; *people* einen Film machen von; **he didn't know he was being ~ed** er wusste nicht, dass er gefilmt wurde
VI filmen, drehen; **we start ~ing** *or* **~ing starts tomorrow** die Dreharbeiten fangen morgen an

▶ **film over** *or* **up** VI *(mirror, glass)* anlaufen

film: **film archives** PL Filmarchiv(e *pl*) *nt*; **film camera** N Filmkamera *f*; **film clip** N Filmausschnitt *m*; **film fan** N Filmliebhaber(in) *m(f)*, Filmfan *m*; **film festival** N Filmfestival *nt*, Filmfestspiele *pl*; **filmgoer** N Kinogänger(in) *m(f)*, Kinobesucher(in) *m(f)*; **film library** N Cinemathek *f*; **film maker** N Filmemacher(in) *m(f)*; **film rights** PL Filmrechte *pl*; **film script** N Drehbuch *nt*; **film sequence** N Filmsequenz *f*; **film set** N Filmset *nt*, Filmdekoration *f*; **filmset** VT *(Brit Typ)* lichtsetzen, fotosetzen; **filmsetting** N *(Brit Typ)* Lichtsatz *m*, Fotosatz *m*; **film star** N Filmstar *m*; **film strip** N Filmstreifen *m*; **film studio** N Filmstudio *nt*; **film test** N Probeaufnahmen *pl*; **to give sb a ~** Probeaufnahmen von jdm machen; **film version** N Verfilmung *f*

filmy ['fɪlmɪ] ADJ *(+er) clothing, fabric, curtains* hauchdünn

Filofax® ['faɪləʊfæks] N Filofax® *m*, Terminplaner *m*

filo pastry ['fiːləʊ-] N Blätterteiggebäck *nt*

filter ['fɪltəʳ] N a Filter *m*; *(Phot, Rad, Mech)* Filter *nt or m* b *(Brit, for traffic)* grüner Pfeil *(für Abbieger)* VT *liquids, air* filtern; *sunlight* durchschimmern lassen; *information* vorsortieren VI a *(light)* durchscheinen, durchschimmern; *(liquid, sound)* durchsickern b *(Brit Aut)* sich einordnen; **to ~ to the left** sich links einordnen

▶ **filter back** VI *(refugees etc)* allmählich zurückkommen

▶ **filter in** VI *(people)* langsam *or* allmählich eindringen; *(news)* durchsickern

▶ **filter out** VI *(people)* einer nach dem anderen herausgehen; *(news)* durchsickern VT *sep (lit)* herausfiltern; *(fig)* heraussieben

▶ **filter through** VI *(liquid, sound, news)* durchsickern; *(light)* durchschimmern, durchscheinen

filter: **filter bag** N Kaffeefilter *m*; **filter bed** N Klärbecken *nt*; **filter coffee** N Filterkaffee *m*; **filter lane** N *(Brit)* Spur *f* zum Einordnen, Abbiegespur *f*; **filter paper** N Filterpapier *nt*; **filter tip** N Filter *m*; **filter-tipped** ADJ **~ cigarette** Filterzigarette *f*

filth [fɪlθ] N *(lit)* Schmutz *m*, Dreck *m*; *(fig)* Schweinerei *f (inf)*, Sauerei *f (inf)*; *(= people)* Dreckspack *nt (inf)*, (Lumpen)gesindel *nt*; **the ~** *(pej sl: = police)* die Bullen *pl (sl)*; **all the ~ they wrote about him in the papers** all der Unflat, der über ihn in der Zeitung geschrieben wurde; **less of your ~!** nicht so viele Schweinereien, bitte!; **she screamed ~ down the phone** sie rief Schweinereien ins Telefon *(inf)*

filthy ['fɪlθɪ] ADJ *(+er)* **a** *(= dirty)* dreckig, verschmutzt; **the kitchen is ~** die Küche starrt vor Dreck; **the room was ~ dirty** *(inf)* das Zimmer war völlig verdreckt *(inf)*; **you're ~!** du bist ja ganz dreckig!; **to be ~ with mud** *(clothes, person)* mit Schlamm verschmutzt sein; **to live in ~ conditions** im Dreck leben

b *(= disgusting) substance, habit* ekelhaft, widerlich; **whisky is ~ stuff** Whisky ist ein ekelhaftes *or* widerliches Zeug; **you ~ liar!** du gemeiner Lügner!; **you ~ little slut!** *(sl)* du dreckige kleine Schlampe!; **~ rich** *(pej inf)* stinkreich *(inf)* → **lucre**

c *(= obscene) joke* dreckig, schmutzig; *language, expression* zotig; *book, magazine* obszön; **you've got a ~ mind!** du hast eine schmutzige Fantasie *or* Phantasie!

d *(= angry) look* bitterböse; **she gave me a ~ look** sie warf mir einen bitterbösen Blick zu; **he has a ~ temper** er kann sehr unangenehm werden; **to be in a ~ mood** eine miese Laune haben *(inf)*

e *(inf: = bad) night* scheußlich; **~ weather** Sauwetter *nt (inf)*

fin [fɪn] N **a** *(of fish)* Flosse *f* **b** *(Aviat)* Seitenleitwerk *nt*, Seitenflosse *f*; *(of bomb, rocket, ship)* Stabilisierungsfläche *f* **c** *(Aut, of radiator)* Kühlrippe *f* **d** *(for swimming)* Schwimmflosse *f*

finagle [fɪ'neɪgəl] VT *(inf)* deichseln *(inf)*; **to ~ sth out of sb** jdm etw abluchsen; **to ~ one's way out of sth** sich aus einer Sache herausmogeln

final ['faɪnl] **ADJ** **a** *(= last)* letzte(r, s); **~ round/match** letzte Runde/letztes Spiel; *(in a tournament)* Endrunde *f*/-spiel *nt*; **~ bend/stretch** *(in stadium)* Zielkurve *f*/-gerade *f*; **~ stage(s)** Endstadium *nt*; **~ vowel/consonant** Schlussvokal *m*/-konsonant *m*; **~ act/scene/chapter** Schlussakt *m*/-szene *f*/-kapitel *nt*; **~ chord** Schlussakkord *m*; **~ curtain** *(Theat)* Schlussvorhang *m*

b *(= definitive) result, outcome, decision, approval, version* endgültig; **~ verdict** Endurteil *nt*; **~ state** Endzustand *m*; **~ score** Schlussstand *m*, Endergebnis *nt*; **the ~ results of their work** das Endergebnis ihrer Arbeit; **that's my ~ offer** das ist mein letztes Angebot; **the judges' decision is ~** die Preisrichter haben das letzte Wort; **that's not ~ yet** das steht noch nicht endgültig fest; **... and that's ~!** ... und damit basta! *(inf)* → **analysis a**, → *also* **say 2 b**

c *(= ultimate) humiliation* größte(r, s); **this is the ~ insult** das ist der Gipfel; **the ~ irony is that he died two days before the book was completed** die Ironie des Schicksals wollte es schließlich, dass er zwei Tage vor Fertigstellung des Buchs starb; **he paid the ~ penalty for his crime** er bezahlte sein Verbrechen mit dem Leben

N **a** *(esp Sport)* Finale *nt*; *(of quiz, field event)* Endrunde *f*; *(= game)* Endspiel *nt*; *(= race)* Endlauf *m*; **to get to the ~** ins Finale kommen; **World Cup Final** *(Ftbl)* Endspiel *nt* der Fußballweltmeisterschaft; **the Olympic high jump ~** das olympische Finale im Hochsprung; **the ~s** das Finale, die Endrunde

b **finals** **PL** *(Brit Univ: = examinations)* Abschlussprüfung *f*

c *(Press)* **the late (night) ~** die letzte (Nacht)-ausgabe

final: **final clause** N *(Gram)* Finalsatz *m*; **final curtain** N *(Theat)* **ten minutes before the ~** zehn Minuten vor Vorstellungsschluss; **the ~ falls on a horrific scene** bei Vorstellungsschluss bietet sich ein Bild des Schreckens; **final demand** N letzte Mahnung *f*; **final disposal** N *(of radioactive waste)* Endlagerung *f*; **~ site** Endlager *nt*; **final dividend** N *(Fin)* (Jahres)-schlussdividende *f*

finale [fɪ'nɑːlɪ] N *(Mus, in opera)* Finale *nt*; *(Theat)* Schlussszene *f*; *(fig)* Finale *nt (geh)*, (Ab)-schluss *m*

final: **final edition** N *(Press)* letzte Ausgabe; **final examination** N Abschlussprüfung *f*; **Final Four** PL **the ~** *(US Basketball)* die letzten Vier *(in der Basketballmeisterschaft)*; **they have always played in the ~** sie waren immer unter den letzten Vier

finalist ['faɪnəlɪst] N *(Sport)* Endrundenteilnehmer(in) *m(f)*, Finalist(in) *m(f)*; *(Univ)* Examenskandidat(in) *m(f)*

finality [faɪ'nælɪtɪ] N *(of decision etc)* Endgültigkeit *f*; *(of tone of voice)* Entschiedenheit *f*, Bestimmtheit *f*

finalization [ˌfaɪnəlaɪ'zeɪʃən] N Beendigung *f*; *(of plans, arrangements, details)* endgültige Festlegung; *(of deal, negotiations, sale)* endgültiger Abschluss; *(of draft)* endgültige Formgebung

finalize ['faɪnəlaɪz] VT fertig machen, beenden; *(= determine) plans, arrangements, details* endgültig festlegen; *deal, sale, negotiations* zum Abschluss bringen; *draft* die endgültige Form geben *(+dat)*; **to ~ a decision** eine endgültige Entscheidung treffen

finally ['faɪnəlɪ] ✪ 26.1, 26.2 ADV **a** *(= eventually)* schließlich; *(= at last, expressing relief)* endlich **b** *(= lastly)* zum Schluss; *(= in conclusion, introducing a final point)* abschließend, zum Abschluss; **and ~ I must say ...** und abschließend möchte ich sagen ... **c** *(= definitively) decide, settle* endgültig

final: **final score** N *(Sport)* Endstand *m*; **Final Solution** N *(NS)* Endlösung *f*; **final whistle** N *(Ftbl)* Schlusspfiff *m*; **to blow the ~** das Spiel abpfeifen

finance [faɪ'næns] **N** **a** Finanzen *pl*, Finanz- *or* Geldwesen *nt*; **high ~** Hochfinanz *f*; **to study ~** *(academically)* Finanzwissenschaft studieren; *(as training)* eine Finanzfachschule besuchen **b** *(= money)* Geld *nt*, (Geld)mittel *pl*; **it's a question of ~** das ist eine Geldfrage *or* Frage der Finanzen; **~s** Finanzen *pl*, Finanz- *or* Einkommenslage *f*; **his ~s aren't sound** seine Finanzlage ist nicht gesund, seine Finanzen stehen nicht gut **VT** finanzieren

finance: **finance company** N Finanz(ierungs)gesellschaft *f*; **finance director** N Leiter(in) *m(f)* der Finanzabteilung; **finance plan** N Finanzierungsplan *m*

financial [faɪ'nænʃəl] ADJ **a** *problems, difficulties, help, support* finanziell; **it makes good** *or* **sound ~ sense** es ist finanziell sinnvoll; **~ resources** Geldmittel *pl* **b** *(St Ex, Econ)* Finanz-; **~ crisis/policy** Finanzkrise *f*/-politik *f*; **~ investment** Geldanlage *f*; **on the ~ markets** auf den Finanzmärkten; **~ news** Wirtschaftsnachrichten *pl*; **~ sector** Finanzsektor *m*; **~ adjustment** Finanzausgleich *m*; **~ status** Finanz- *or* Vermögenslage *f*

financial: **financial accounting** N *(Comm)* Finanzbuchhaltung *f*; **financial adviser** N Finanzberater(in) *m(f)*; **financial director** N *(Comm)* Leiter(in) *m(f)* der Finanzabteilung; **financial institution** N Geldinstitut *nt*, Finanzinstitut *nt*

financially [faɪ'nænʃəlɪ] ADV finanziell; *(introducing sentence)* finanziell gesehen; **the ~ troubled company** die in finanzielle Schwierigkeiten geratene Firma; **~ sound** finanziell solide; **the company is ~ sound** die Finanzlage der Firma ist gesund; **~ viable** rentabel; **to be ~ embarrassed** in Geldverlegenheit sein; **she's been struggling ~ for years** sie kommt seit Jahren finanziell kaum über die Runden; **~, things are a bit tight for me this month** diesen Monat bin ich etwas knapp bei Kasse *(inf)*

financial: **financial management** N *(Comm)* Finanzmanagement *nt*; **financial services** PL Finanzdienstleistungen *pl*; **financial statement** N *(Comm)* Abschluss *m*; *(annual)* Jahresabschluss *m*; **financial system** N Finanzwesen *nt*; **financial year** N *(Brit)* Geschäftsjahr *nt*, Finanzjahr *nt*

financier [faɪ'nænsɪəʳ] N Finanzier *m*

finch [fɪntʃ] N Fink *m*

find [faɪnd] *vb: pret, ptp* **found** **VT** **a** finden; *(Comput: search command)* suchen; **it's nowhere to be found** es lässt sich nirgendwo finden *or* auftreiben *(inf)*; **to ~ sb out** *or* **away** *(= not at home)* jdn nicht (zu Hause) antreffen; **hoping this letter ~s you in good health** in der Hoffnung, dass Sie gesund sind; **to ~ pleasure in sth** Freude an etw *(dat)* haben; **to ~ comfort in sth** Trost in etw *(dat)* finden; **we left everything as we found it** wir haben alles so gelassen, wie wir es vorgefunden haben; **he was found dead in bed** er wurde tot im Bett aufgefunden; **I can never ~ anything to say to him** ich weiß nie, was ich zu ihm sagen soll; **where am I going to ~ the money/time?** wo nehme ich nur das Geld/die Zeit her?; **you must take us as you ~ us** Sie müssen uns so nehmen, wie wir sind; **if you can ~ it in you to ...** wenn Sie es irgend fertigbringen, zu ...; **~ next** *(Comput: search command)* weitersuchen

b *(= supply)* besorgen *(sb sth* jdm etw); **go and ~ me a needle** hol mir doch mal eine Nadel; **did you ~ him what he wanted?** haben Sie bekommen, was er wollte?; **we'll have to ~ him a desk/secretary** wir müssen einen Schreibtisch/eine Sekretärin für ihn finden

c *(= discover, ascertain)* feststellen; *cause* herausfinden; **we found the car wouldn't start** es stellte sich heraus, dass das Auto nicht ansprang; **I ~ I'm unable to ...** ich stelle fest, dass ich ... nicht kann; **you will ~ that I am right** Sie werden sehen, dass ich recht habe; **it has been found that this is so** es hat sich herausgestellt, dass es so ist

d *(= consider to be)* finden; **I ~ Spain too hot** ich finde Spanien zu heiß; **I don't ~ it easy to tell you this** es fällt mir nicht leicht, Ihnen das zu sagen; **he always found languages easy/hard** ihm fielen Sprachen immer leicht/schwer; **I found all the questions easy** ich fand, dass die Fragen alle leicht waren; **did you ~ her a good worker?** fanden Sie, dass sie gut arbeitet?; **I ~ it impossible to understand him** ich kann ihn einfach nicht verstehen

e **I found myself smiling** ich musste unwillkürlich lächeln; **I found myself wondering** ich machte mir so meine Gedanken; **I found myself thinking that ...** ich ertappte mich bei dem Gedanken, dass ...; **I ~ myself in an impossible situation/in financial difficulties** ich befinde mich in einer unmöglichen Situation/in finanziellen Schwierigkeiten; **one day he suddenly found himself out of a job** eines Tages war er plötzlich arbeitslos; **he awoke to ~ himself in prison/hospital** er erwachte und fand sich im Gefängnis/Krankenhaus wieder; **quite by accident I found myself in the park** ganz zufällig fand ich mich im Park wieder; **I found myself quite able to deal with it** ich stellte fest, dass ich durchaus fähig war, damit zurechtzukommen; **I found myself forced to turn back** ich sah mich gezwungen umzukehren

f **this flower is found all over England** diese Blume findet man in ganz England, diese Blume ist in ganz England vorzufinden; **you don't ~ bears here any more** man findet hier keine Bären mehr, hier gibt es keine Bären mehr; **do you know where there is a florist's to be found?** wissen Sie, wo hier ein Blumenladen ist?

g **£200 per week all found** £ 200 pro Woche, (und freie) Kost und Logis

h *(Jur)* **to ~ sb guilty/not guilty** jdn für schuldig/nicht schuldig befinden, jdn schuldig sprechen/freisprechen; **how do you ~ the accused?** wie lautet Ihr Urteil?; **the court has found that ...** das Gericht hat befunden, dass ...

i *(Comput)* suchen; **~ and replace** suchen und ersetzen

VI *(Jur)* **to ~ for/against the accused** den Angeklagten freisprechen/verurteilen, für/gegen den Angeklagten entscheiden

N Fund *m*

▶ **find out** **VT** *sep* **a** *answer, sb's secret* herausfinden

b *(= discover the misdeeds etc of) person* erwischen; *(= come to know about)* auf die Schliche kommen *(+dat) (inf)*; **his wife has found him out** seine Frau ist dahintergekommen; **don't get found out** lass dich nicht erwischen; **you've been found out** du bist entdeckt *or* ertappt *(inf)*; **your sins will find you out** *(liter)* die Sonne bringt es an den Tag *(prov)*

VI **a** es herausfinden; *(= discover misdeeds, dishonesty etc also)* dahinterkommen; **where is it? – find out for yourself!** wo ist es? – sieh doch selbst nach!

b **to find out about sb/sth** *(= discover existence of)* jdn/etw entdecken; **to help children find out about other countries** Kindern dabei helfen, etwas über andere Länder herauszufinden

finder ['faɪndəʳ] **N** **a** *(of lost object)* Finder(in) *m(f)*; **~s keepers** *(inf)* wers findet, dem gehörts **b** *(of telescope)* Sucher *m*

finding ['faɪndɪŋ] **N** **a** **~s** *pl* Ergebnis(se) *nt(pl)*; *(medical)* Befund *m*; **the ~s of the commission were as follows** die Kommission kam zu folgendem Ergebnis **b** *(Jur, = verdict)* Urteil(sspruch *m*) *nt*

fine[1] [faɪn] **ADV in ~** *(liter)* kurz und gut, kurzum

fine[2] [faɪn] **N** *(Jur)* Geldstrafe *f*; *(for less serious offences)* Geldbuße *or* -strafe *f*; *(driving)* Bußgeld *nt*; *(for minor traffic offences)* (gebührenpflichtige) Verwarnung

VT *(Jur)* zu einer Geldstrafe verurteilen, mit einer Geldstrafe/-buße belegen; *(for driving offences also)* Bußgeld verhängen gegen; *(for minor traffic offences)* eine (gebührenpflichtige) Verwarnung erteilen *(+dat)*; **he was ~d £100** er musste £ 100 Strafe bezahlen; **he was ~d for speeding** er hat einen Strafzettel für zu schnelles Fahren bekommen; **she was ~d for possession (of drugs)** sie wurde wegen Drogenbesitz zu einer Geldstrafe verurteilt

fine[3] **ADJ** *(+er)* **a** *(= excellent) piece of work, example, painting, book, museum* ausgezeichnet; *building, town, view* herrlich; *person* fein, trefflich *(geh)*; *performance, performer, player* großartig, ausgezeichnet; **you're doing a ~ job** Sie machen Ihre Sache ganz ausgezeichnet; **they're in ~ health** sie erfreuen sich bester Gesundheit; **this is even ~r than her previous recording** das ist noch besser als ihre letzte Aufnahme; **she's a ~ woman** sie ist eine bewundernswerte *or (in stature)* stattliche Frau; **he is the ~st actor of our day** er ist der größte Schauspieler unserer Zeit; **the ~st English painting of its time** das beste *or* großartigste englische Gemälde seiner Zeit; **the ~st beaches in Spain** die herrlichsten *or* schönsten Strände Spaniens; **their ~st hour** ihre größte Stunde → **fettle, figure N d, form N i**

b *(= acceptable: of things)* in Ordnung; **my coffee was ~** mein Kaffee war in Ordnung; **any more? – no, that's ~** *or* **it'll be ~** noch etwas? – nein, danke *or* es ist gut so; **everything's (just) ~** alles in (bester) Ordnung; **everything's going to be just ~** es wird schon alles gut gehen; **how was I? – you were ~** wie war ich? – gut; **these apples are ~ for cooking** diese Äpfel eignen sich (gut) zum Kochen; **it's ~ (for you) to interrupt me** Sie dürfen mich gerne unterbrechen; **it's ~ for men to cry** Männer dürfen auch weinen, es ist durchaus in Ordnung, wenn Männer weinen; **the doctor said it was ~ for me to play** der Arzt sagte, ich dürfte ohne Weiteres spielen; **you look/the wallpaper looks ~ (to me)** (ich finde,)du siehst/die Tapete sieht gut aus; **your idea sounds ~** Ihre Idee hört sich gut an; **shall we have another beer? – sounds ~ to me** sollen wir noch ein Bier trinken? – ja, gute Idee; **he/she is ~** *(= managing OK)* er/sie kommt gut zurecht; *(= in good health)* es geht ihm/ihr gut; *(= things are going well)* mit ihm/ihr ist alles in Ordnung; **how are you? – ~, thanks** wie geht es Ihnen? – danke, gut; **a glass of water and I'll be ~** nach einem Glas Wasser wird es mir wieder gut gehen; **he's ~, he's done it before** es schafft es schon, er hat es schon einmal gemacht; **any questions? no? ~** noch Fragen? nein? gut; **that's ~ with** *or* **by me** ich habe nichts dagegen; **it'll take me a couple of days – that's ~ with me** ich werde ein paar Tage dafür brauchen – das ist in Ordnung; **anything she wanted was usually ~ with him** was sie auch immer wollte, er hatte meist nichts dagegen

c *(= high-quality) food* fein; *wine* erlesen, edel; *furniture, jewellery, clothes* ausgesucht; *china, porcelain, fabric* erlesen, ausgesucht; **the ~st ingredients** die erlesensten Zutaten

d *(= refined) lady, gentleman, manners* fein; *(= smart, large) house* vornehm; **she likes to play at being the ~ lady** sie spielt sich gern als feine Dame auf

e *weather, day* schön; **when it is/was ~** bei schönem Wetter; **all areas will be ~ tomorrow** morgen wird es überall schön; **one ~ day** eines schönen Tages

f *(iro) excuse, state, friend etc* schön *(iro)*; **a ~ reward for all my work!** eine schöne Belohnung für meine ganze Mühe!; **a ~ friend you are!** du bist mir ja ein schöner Freund!; **a ~ time to remember that!** ein feiner Augenblick, dich daran zu erinnern!; **that's all very ~, but ...** das ist ja alles schön und gut, aber ...; **that's ~ for you to say** du hast gut reden; **you're a ~ one to talk!** du kannst gerade reden!; **~ words** schöne Worte *pl*

g *(= thin) needle, thread* dünn, fein; *fabric, material* dünn; *hair, grain* fein; *handwriting* fein, zierlich; *sieve, net, mesh, weave* fein(maschig); **a net with a ~ mesh** ein feinmaschiges Netz; **~ nib** spitze Feder; **a paper with very ~ grain** ein sehr feinkörniges Papier

h *(= in small particles) powder, dust, sand, mist* fein; **a ~ rain** Nieselregen *m*; **a ~ dusting of snow/flour** eine dünne Schneedecke/Mehlschicht; **~ dust levels** Feinstaubwerte *pl*

i *(= delicate) china, fabric* fein; *features* fein, zart

j *(= subtle, small) adjustment, detail, distinction, difference* fein; *print* klein; **in ~ print** klein gedruckt; **to read the ~ print** das Kleingedruckte lesen; **the ~r points of English grammar** die Feinheiten der englischen Grammatik; **not to put too ~ a point on it** um ganz offen zu sein; **there's a ~ line between genius and madness** es besteht ein feiner Unterschied zwischen Genie und Wahnsinn

k *gold, silver* fein; **gold 98% ~** Gold mit 98% Feingehalt

ADV **a** *(= well) work* tadellos; **you're doing ~** Sie machen Ihre Sache gut; *(healthwise)* Sie machen gute Fortschritte; **we get on ~** wir kommen ausgezeichnet miteinander aus

b *(= thinly) cut, slice* fein, dünn → **cut 3 q**

► **fine down** **VT** *sep wood etc* glätten; *text, novel etc* straffen *(to* zu); *theory* reduzieren *(to* auf *+acc)*

fine: **fine art** **N** **a** *usu pl* schöne Künste *pl* **b** *(= skill)* Kunststück *nt*, echte Kunst; **he's got it down to a ~** er hat den Bogen heraus *(inf)*; **fine cut** **N** *(= tobacco)* Feinschnitt *m*; **fine-drawn** **ADJ** **a** *thread* fein gesponnen *or (synthetic)* gezogen; *wire* fein gezogen **b** *features* fein (geschnitten); **fine dust** **N** Feinstaub *m*; **fine-food shop** **N** Feinkostgeschäft *nt*; **fine-grain, fine-grained** **ADJ** *wood, rock* fein gemasert; *(Phot) film, paper* feinkörnig

finely ['faɪnlɪ] **ADV** **a** *(= exquisitely) crafted, detailed, carved* fein

b *(= thinly, in small pieces) chop, grate, grind* fein; *slice* dünn; **~ ground coffee** fein gemahlener Kaffee; **~ diced** fein gewürfelt, in feine Würfel geschnitten; **~ sliced** fein geschnitten, in dünne Scheiben geschnitten

c *(= subtly, delicately)* fein; **the case is ~ balanced** der Fall kann sich so oder so entscheiden; **a ~ judged speech** eine wohl ausgewogene Rede; **~ drawn distinctions** feine Unterschiede; **~ tuned** *(engine, machine)* genau eingestellt; *(fig) military/party/administrative machine* gut geölt; *(= ultrasensitive)* hochempfindlich

fine-mesh [faɪn'meʃ] **ADJ** *net* eng- *or* feinmaschig

fineness ['faɪnnɪs] **N** **a** *(= beauty, pleasantness)* Schönheit *f* **b** *(= high quality)* Güte *f*; *(of mind, novel)* Großartigkeit *f*; *(= elegance, delicacy)* Feinheit *f*; *(of material)* Zartheit *f* **c** *(of sieve, net, mesh)* Feinmaschigkeit *f*; *(of dust, sand)* Feinheit *f* **d** *(= thinness)* Feinheit *f*, Dünnheit *f*; *(of nib)* Spitze *f*; **the ~ of the print** die kleine Schrift **e** *(of metal)* Feingehalt *m* **f** *(of adjustment, distinction)* Feinheit *f*

finery ['faɪnərɪ] **N** **a** *(of dress)* Staat *m*; *(liter, of nature etc)* Pracht *f*; **she had never seen so much ~** sie hatte noch nie eine solche Pracht gesehen; **wedding guests in all their ~** Hochzeitsgäste in vollem Staat **b** *(Metal, = furnace)* Frischofen *m*

finesse [fɪ'nes] **N** **a** *(= skill, diplomacy)* Gewandtheit *f*, Geschick *nt* **b** *(= cunning)* Schlauheit *f*, Finesse *f* **c** *(Cards)* Schneiden *nt* **VI** *(Cards)* schneiden **VT** **a** *(= do with finesse) problem* geschickt lösen; *(= avoid)* ausweichen *(+dat)* **b** *(Cards)* schneiden

fine-tooth comb ['faɪntuːθ'kəʊm] **N** **to go over sth with a ~** etw genau unter die Lupe nehmen; *area* etw durchkämmen; *room* etw gründlich durchsuchen

fine: **fine-tune** **VT** *engine* fein abstimmen; *(fig) projection etc* fein abstimmen; **fine-tuning** **N** *(lit)* Feinabstimmung *f*; *(fig also)* Detailarbeit *f*

finger ['fɪŋgəʳ] **N** **a** Finger *m*; **she can twist him round her little ~** sie kann ihn um den (kleinen) Finger wickeln; **to have a ~ in every pie** überall die Finger drin *or* im Spiel haben *(inf)*, überall mitmischen *(inf)*; **I forbid you to lay a ~ on him** ich verbiete Ihnen, ihm auch nur ein Härchen zu krümmen; **I didn't lay a ~ on her** ich habe sie nicht angerührt; **he wouldn't lift a ~ to help me** er würde keinen Finger rühren, um mir zu helfen; **he didn't lift a ~ (around the house)** er hat (im Haus) keinen Finger krumm gemacht *(inf)*; **to point one's ~ at sb** mit dem Finger auf jdn zeigen; **to point the ~** *or* **an accusing ~ at sb** *(fig)* mit Fingern auf jdn zeigen; **to point the ~ of suspicion/blame at sb** jdn verdächtigen/beschuldigen; **I can't put my ~ on it, but ...** ich kann es nicht genau ausmachen, aber ...; **you've put your ~ on it there** da haben Sie den kritischen Punkt berührt; **to put the ~ on sb** *(inf)* jdn verpfeifen *(inf)*; **to get** *or* **pull one's ~ out** *(Brit inf)* Nägel mit Köpfen machen *(inf)*; **pull your ~ out!** *(Brit inf)* es wird Zeit, dass du Nägel mit Köpfen machst! *(inf)*; **to give sb the ~** *(esp US inf)* jdm den Stinkefinger zeigen *(inf)* → **cross**

b *(of whisky etc)* Fingerbreit *m*

VT **a** *(= touch)* anfassen; *(= toy, meddle with)* befingern, herumfingern an *(+dat)*

b *(inf: = inform on)* verpfeifen

c *(Mus, = mark for fingering)* mit einem Fingersatz versehen; **to ~ the keys/strings** in die Tasten/Saiten greifen

finger: **finger alphabet** **N** Fingeralphabet *nt*; **fingerboard** **N** Griffbrett *nt*; **finger bowl** **N** Fingerschale *f*; **finger buffet** **N** Buffet *nt* mit Appetithappen; **finger-dry** **VT** **to ~ one's hair** sich *(dat)* die Haare mit den Fingern trocknen; **finger exercise** **N** Fingerübung *f*; **finger food** **N** Appetithappen *pl*; **finger hole** **N** *(in flute etc)* Griffloch *nt*

fingering ['fɪŋgərɪŋ] **N** **a** *(Mus, in the notation)* Fingersatz *m*; *(of keys, strings)* (Finger)technik *f*; **the ~ is very difficult** die Griffe sind sehr schwierig **b** *(of goods in shop etc)* Anfassen *nt*, Berühren *nt*; *(= toying, meddling)* Befingern *nt (of, with +gen)*, Herumfingern *nt (of, with* an *+dat)* **c** *(Tex)* Strumpfwolle *f*

finger: **fingermark** **N** Fingerabdruck *m*; **fingernail** **N** Fingernagel *m*; **finger paint** **N** Fingerfarbe *f*; **finger-paint** **VT** mit Fingerfarben malen; **fingerprint** **N** Fingerabdruck *m*; **to take sb's ~s** jdm Fingerabdrücke abnehmen **VT** **to ~ sb/sth** jdm/von etw Fingerabdrücke nehmen; **fingerprint expert** **N** Sachverständige(r) *mf* für Fingerabdrücke; **fingerstall** **N** Fingerling *m*; **fingertip** **N** Fingerspitze *f*; **to have sth at one's ~s** *(fig: = know very well)* etw aus dem Effeff kennen *(inf)*; *(= have at one's immediate disposal)* etw im kleinen Finger *(inf) or* parat haben; **everything you need is at your ~s** alles, was Sie brauchen, steht Ihnen zur Verfügung; **to one's ~s** *(fig)* durch und durch; **fingertip control** N *(of steering wheel etc)* mühelose Steuerung; **to have ~** sich mühelos bedienen lassen; **fingertip search** N Durchkämmungsaktion *f*

finickiness [ˈfɪnɪkɪnɪs] N *(of person)* Pingeligkeit *f (inf)*; *(about language also)* Haarspalterei *f*; *(of task)* Kniff(e)ligkeit *f (inf)*; **because of his ~ about what he eats** weil er so wählerisch beim Essen ist

finicky [ˈfɪnɪkɪ] ADJ *person* schwer zufriedenzustellen, pingelig *(inf)*; *(about food, clothes etc)* wählerisch, pingelig *(inf)*; *work, job* kniff(e)lig *(inf)*; *detail* winzig; **he's a ~ eater** er ist beim Essen sehr wählerisch

finish [ˈfɪnɪʃ] N **a** *(= end)* Schluss *m*, Ende *nt*; *(of race)* Finish *nt*; *(= finishing line)* Ziel *nt*; **they never gave up, right to the ~** sie haben bis zum Schluss nicht aufgegeben; **from start to ~** von Anfang bis Ende; **he's got a good ~** *(Sport)* er hat einen starken Endspurt; **to be in at the ~** *(fig)* beim Ende dabei sein; **to fight to the ~** *(fig)* bis zum letzten Augenblick kämpfen
b *(= perfection, of manners)* Schliff *m*; *(of things)* Verarbeitung *f*, Ausfertigung *f*; **they lack the ~ of handmade ones** sie sind nicht so sorgfältig *or* sauber verarbeitet wie handgemachte; **it has a poor ~** die Verarbeitung *or* Ausfertigung ist schlecht
c *(of industrial products)* Finish *nt*; *(= final coat of paint)* Deckanstrich *m*; *(of material)* Appretur *f*; *(of paper)* Oberflächenfinish *nt*; *(of pottery)* Oberfläche *f*; *(= ornamental work)* Verzierung *f*; **paper with a gloss/matt ~** Hochglanz-/Mattglanzpapier *nt*; **paint with a gloss/matt ~** Farbe *f* mit Hochglanzeffekt/mattem Glanz; **highly polished to give it a good ~** auf Hochglanz poliert
VT **a** beenden; *education, course* abschließen; *piece of work, business* erledigen, abschließen; *(Comput: command)* fertigstellen; **he's ~ed the painting/job** er ist mit dem Bild/der Arbeit fertig; **to have ~ed doing sth** damit fertig sein, etw zu tun; **when I ~ eating ...** wenn ich mit dem Essen fertig bin, ...; **I've ~ed ironing** ich bin mit dem Bügeln fertig; **to ~ writing/reading sth** etw zu Ende schreiben/lesen, etw fertig schreiben/lesen; **let me ~ eating** lass mich zu Ende essen, lass mich fertig essen; **to have ~ed sth** etw fertig haben; *task, course* mit etw fertig sein, etw beendet haben; **when do you ~ work?** wann machen Sie Feierabend *or* Schluss?; **I'm in a hurry to get this job ~ed** ich möchte diese Sache so schnell wie möglich zu Ende bringen; **she never lets him ~ (what he's saying)** sie lässt ihn nie ausreden; **Daddy, will you ~ (telling) that story?** Papa, erzählst du die Geschichte zu Ende *or* fertig?; **can I have that book when you've ~ed it?** kann ich das Buch haben, wenn du es ausgelesen hast?; **give me time to ~ my drink** lass mich austrinken; **~ what you're doing and we'll go** mach fertig, was du angefangen hast, und dann gehen wir; **the dollar ~ed the day up against the pound** bei Börsenschluss war der Dollar gegenüber dem Pfund gestiegen
b *(= ruin)* ruinieren; *(= kill, inf: = exhaust)* kaputtmachen *(inf)*, den Rest geben *(+dat) (inf)*; **another strike could ~ the firm** noch ein Streik könnte das Ende für die Firma bedeuten; **that last mile nearly ~ed me** *(inf)* diese letzte Meile hat mir beinahe den Rest gegeben *(inf)*
c *(= put finishing touches to)* den letzten Schliff geben *(+dat)*; *piece of handiwork* verarbeiten; *(= give a surface treatment to) surface, industrial product* fertig bearbeiten, ein Finish geben *(+dat)*; *(= paint)* anstreichen; *car etc* lackieren; **to ~ sth with a coat of varnish** etw zum Schluss (mit Firnis) lackieren; **the paintwork isn't very well ~ed** die Malerarbeiten wurden nicht sehr gut ausgeführt; **the metal is ~ed with a high-speed disc** das Metall wird mit einer schnell rotierenden Scheibe poliert; **the paper is ~ed on the glazing rollers** das Papier wird mit dem Kalander nachbearbeitet
VI **a** zu Ende *or* aus sein; *(person: with task etc)* fertig sein; *(= come to an end, finish work)* aufhören; *(piece of music, story etc)* enden; **when does the film ~?** wann ist der Film aus?; **my course ~es this week** mein Kurs geht diese Woche zu Ende; **we'll ~ by singing a song** wir wollen mit einem Lied schließen, zum Schluss singen wir ein Lied; **I've ~ed** ich bin fertig
b *(Sport)* das Ziel erreichen; **to ~ first/second** als erster/zweiter durchs Ziel gehen

▶ **finish off** VI **a** *(= come to end)* aufhören, Schluss machen
b **to finish off with a glass of brandy** zum (Ab)schluss ein Glas Weinbrand trinken; **we finished off by singing ...** wir schlossen mit dem Lied ..., wir sangen zum (Ab)schluss ...
VT *sep* **a** *piece of work* fertig machen; *job* erledigen; **to finish off a painting** ein Bild zu Ende malen; **to finish off a letter** einen Brief zu Ende schreiben
b *food, meal* aufessen; *drink* austrinken
c *(= kill) wounded animal, person* den Gnadenstoß geben *(+dat)*; *(by shooting)* den Gnadenschuss geben *(+dat)*
d *(= do for) person* den Rest geben *(+dat)*, erledigen *(inf)*; **the last mile just about finished me off** *(inf)* die letzte Meile hat mich ziemlich geschafft *(inf) or* fertiggemacht *(inf)*

▶ **finish up** VI **a** = **finish off VI a, b** **b** *(= end up in a place)* landen *(inf)*; **he finished up a nervous wreck** er war zum Schluss ein Nervenbündel; **he finished up in third place** er landete auf dem dritten Platz *(inf)*; **you'll finish up wishing you'd never started** du wünschst dir bestimmt noch, du hättest gar nicht erst angefangen; **I'll just finish up having to do it all again** zum Schluss muss ich doch alles noch mal machen VT *sep* = **finish off VT b**

▶ **finish with** VI *+prep obj* **a** *(= no longer need)* nicht mehr brauchen; **I've finished with the paper/book** ich bin mit der Zeitung/dem Buch fertig **b** *(= want no more to do with)* **I've finished with him** ich will nichts mehr mit ihm zu tun haben, ich bin fertig mit ihm *(inf)*; *(with boyfriend)* ich habe mit ihm Schluss gemacht **c** **you wait till I've finished with you!** *(inf)* warte nur, dich knöpfe ich mir noch vor *(inf)*

finished [ˈfɪnɪʃt] ADJ **a** *person* fertig; **I'm nearly ~** ich bin fast fertig *or* so weit; **to be ~ doing sth** *(US)* damit fertig sein, etw zu tun; **when I was ~ eating** *(US)* als ich mit dem Essen fertig war; **to be ~ with sb/sth** mit jdm/etw fertig sein; *(= fed up)* von jdm/etw nichts mehr wissen wollen; **I won't be ~ with him/it for some time yet** ich werde noch eine Weile mit ihm/damit zu tun haben; **I'm ~ with politics** mit der Politik ist es für mich vorbei
b *(= used up) things* aufgebraucht, alle *(N Ger inf)*; *(= over) activity, performance, trial* zu Ende; **the wine is ~** es ist kein Wein mehr da; **when work was ~, we often dined out together** nach der Arbeit gingen wir oft zusammen essen; **those days are ~** die Zeiten sind vorbei
c *(inf: = having no future)* **to be ~** *(jobholder, politician, sportsperson etc)* erledigt sein *(inf)* (as als); **we're ~, it's ~ between us** es ist aus zwischen uns; **my career is ~** mit meiner Karriere ist es vorbei, meine Karriere ist am Ende; **the printed word is ~** das gedruckte Wort hat keine Zukunft mehr
d *(= treated) product* fertig bearbeitet; *(with paint)* gestrichen; *(with lacquer, varnish)* lackiert; *(with polish)* poliert; *clothing* verarbeitet; **beautifully ~ wood** wunderschön verarbeitetes Holz; **the room is ~ in red** das Zimmer ist rot gestrichen
e *(= fully made) product, work of art, film, building, dish, size* fertig; **~ goods/products** Fertigprodukte *pl*; **the ~ result** das Endergebnis; **the ~ article** *(= object)* das fertige Produkt; *(= piece of writing, work of art)* die endgültige Version; *(= accomplished performer)* der perfekte Künstler, die perfekte Künstlerin; **they are not yet the ~ article** es fehlt ihnen noch einiges zur Perfektion

finisher [ˈfɪnɪʃəʳ] N **a** *(Ftbl, Rugby, Hockey etc)* **a good ~** ein guter Torschütze **b** *(Athletics, Cycling etc)* **to be a fast/strong ~** einen schnellen/starken Endspurt haben; **he is renowned as a fast ~** er ist für seinen schnellen Endspurt bekannt

finishing [ˈfɪnɪʃɪŋ] N **his ~ is excellent** *(Ftbl, Rugby, Hockey etc)* er ist ein ausgezeichneter Torschütze; *(Cycling, Athletics)* er ist ein ausgezeichneter Sprinter

finishing [ˈfɪnɪʃɪŋ]: **finishing industry** N *(Tech)* verarbeitende Industrie, Veredelungsindustrie *f*; **finishing line** N Ziellinie *f*; **finishing process** N *(Tech)* Veredelungsverfahren *nt*; **finishing school** N (Mädchen)pensionat *nt*

finite [ˈfaɪnaɪt] ADJ **a** *(= limited) set, amount, time, resources* begrenzt; *universe* endlich; **a ~ number** eine begrenzte Zahl; *(Math)* eine endliche Zahl; **coal and oil are ~ resources** Kohle und Öl sind nicht erneuerbare Ressourcen; **there is a ~ limit to the weight a human can lift** ein Mensch kann höchstens ein bestimmtes Gewicht heben **b** *(Rel, Philos) being, world* endlich **c** *(Gram) verb, clause* finit

fink [fɪŋk] *(dated US sl)* N **a** *(= strikebreaker)* Streikbrecher(in) *m(f)* **b** *(= contemptible person)* Saftsack *m (inf)* VI **to ~ on sb** jdn verpfeifen *(inf)*

Finland [ˈfɪnlənd] N Finnland *nt*

Finn [fɪn] N Finne *m*, Finnin *f*

Finnish [ˈfɪnɪʃ] ADJ finnisch; **he is ~** er ist Finne; **she is ~** sie ist Finnin N *(Ling)* Finnisch *nt*

Finno-Ugric [ˈfɪnəʊˈjuːgrɪk], **Finno-Ugrian** [ˈfɪnəʊˈjuːgrɪən] ADJ *(Ling)* finnisch-ugrisch, finnougrisch

fiord [fjɔːd] N Fjord *m*

fir [fɜːʳ] N Tanne *f*; *(= wood)* Tanne(nholz *nt*) *f*

fir cone N Tannenzapfen *m*

fire [faɪəʳ] N **a** Feuer *nt*; **the house was on ~** das Haus brannte; **to set ~ to sth, to set sth on ~** etw anzünden; *(so as to destroy)* etw in Brand stecken; **he'll never set the world** *or* **the Thames** *(Brit) or* **the heather** *(Scot)* **on ~** von ihm sind keine Sensationen zu erwarten; **to catch ~** Feuer fangen *(also fig)*; *(building, forest etc also)* in Brand geraten; **"keep away from ~"** „von Feuer fernhalten"; **when man discovered ~** als der Mensch das Feuer entdeckte; **you're playing with ~** *(fig)* du spielst mit dem Feuer; **to fight ~ with ~** *(fig)* mit den gleichen Waffen kämpfen; **to go through ~ and water** *(fig)* durchs Feuer gehen → **house**
b *(= house fire, forest fire etc)* Brand *m*; **there was a ~ next door** nebenan hat es gebrannt; **~!** Feuer!, feurio *(old)*; **Glasgow has more ~s than any other city** in Glasgow brennt es häufiger als in anderen Städten; **to insure oneself against ~** eine Feuerversicherung abschließen
c *(in grate)* (Kamin)feuer *nt*; *(= electric fire, gas fire)* Ofen *m*; **they have an open ~** sie haben einen offenen Kamin
d *(Mil)* Feuer *nt*; **~!** Feuer!; **to open ~ on sb** das Feuer auf jdn eröffnen; **to be caught between two ~s** *(lit, fig)* zwischen zwei Feuer geraten; **to come under ~** *(lit, fig)* unter Beschuss geraten; **he came under ~ from the critics** er wurde von den Kritikern unter Beschuss genommen; **to draw ~ from sb** *(lit)* von jdm unter Feuer genommen werden; *(fig)* jds Kritik auf sich *(acc)* ziehen; **to be in the line of ~** *(lit, fig)* in der Schusslinie stehen
e *(= passion)* Feuer *nt*; **he spoke with ~** er sprach mit Leidenschaft; **to have ~ in one's belly** von leidenschaftlicher Begeisterung erfüllt sein; **to be on ~** *(fig)* brennen (*with* vor *+dat*)
VT **a** *(= burn to destroy)* in Brand stecken
b *pottery* brennen
c *furnace* befeuern → **oil-fired, gas-fired**
d *(fig) imagination* beflügeln; *passions* entzünden, entfachen *(geh)*; *enthusiasm* befeuern; **to ~ sb with enthusiasm** jdn begeistern, jdn in Begeisterung versetzen
e *gun, arrow* abschießen; *shot* abfeuern, abgeben; *rocket* zünden, abfeuern; **to ~ a gun at sb** auf jdn schießen; **to ~ a salute** Salut schießen;

she ~d an elastic (band) at me sie schoss ein Gummiband auf mich ab; **to ~ questions at sb** Fragen auf jdn abfeuern
f (*inf:* = *dismiss*) feuern (*inf*)
VI **a** (= *shoot*) feuern, schießen (*at* auf +*acc*); **~!** (gebt) Feuer!
b (*engine*) zünden; **the engine is only firing on three cylinders** der Motor läuft nur auf drei Zylindern

▸ **fire away** VI (*inf:* = *begin*) losschießen (*inf*)

▸ **fire off** VT *sep gun, round, shell, questions* abfeuern; *letter* loslassen

▸ **fire up** VT *sep machine, computer* starten; **to be all fired up (about sth)** (*esp US*) (von etw) ganz begeistert sein

fire: **fire alarm** N Feueralarm *m*; (= *apparatus*) Feuermelder *m*; **fire appliance** N Feuerwehrfahrzeug *nt*; **firearm** N Feuer- *or* Schusswaffe *f*; **fireball** N **a** (*of nuclear explosion*) Feuerball *m*; (= *lightning*) Kugelblitz *m* **b** (= *meteor*) Feuerkugel *f* **c** (*fig inf:* = *person*) Energiebündel *nt* (*inf*); **firebomb** N Brandbombe *f*; **firebrand** N **a** Feuerbrand *m* (*old*) **b** (= *mischief-maker*) Unruhestifter(in) *m(f)*, Aufwiegler(in) *m(f)*; **firebreak** N (= *strip of land*) Feuerschneise *f*; (= *wall*) Brandmauer *f*; (= *sandbags etc*) (Schutz)wall *m* (*gegen die Ausbreitung eines Feuers*); **firebrick** N Schamottestein *m*; **fire brigade** N (*Brit*) Feuerwehr *f*; **firebug** N (*inf*) Feuerteufel *m* (*inf*), Brandstifter(in) *m(f)*; **fire chief** N (*esp Brit*) Feuerwehrhauptmann *m*; **fire clay** N Schamotte *f*; **firecracker** N Knallkörper *m*; **firedamp** N (*Min*) Grubengas *nt*, schlagende Wetter *pl*; **fire department** N (*US*) Feuerwehr *f*; **firedog** N Kaminbock *m*; **fire door** N Feuertür *f*; **fire drill** N Probealarm *m*; (*for firemen*) Feuerwehrübung *f*; **fire-eater** N Feuerfresser *or* -schlucker *m*; **fire engine** N Feuerwehrauto *nt*; **fire escape** N (= *staircase*) Feuertreppe *f*; (= *ladder*) Feuerleiter *f*; **fire exit** N Notausgang *m*; (= *external stairs*) Feuertreppe *f*; **fire-extinguisher** N Feuerlöscher *m*; **firefight** N (*Mil*) Schusswechsel *m*; **firefighter** N (= *fireman*) Feuerwehrmann *m*/-frau *f*; (= *voluntary helper*) freiwilliger Helfer/freiwillige Helferin (bei der Feuerbekämpfung); **firefighting** ADJ *attr techniques, team* zur Feuerbekämpfung; **~ equipment** Feuerlöschgeräte *pl*; **~ operation** Feuerlöschaktion *f*; **firefly** N Leuchtkäfer *m*; **fireguard** N (Schutz)gitter *nt* (*vor dem Kamin*); **fire hazard** N **to be a ~** feuergefährlich sein; **these old houses are a ~** bei diesen alten Häusern besteht Brandgefahr; **fire hose** N Feuerwehrschlauch *m*; **firehouse** N (*US*) Feuerwache *f*, Feuerwehrzentrale *f*; **fire hydrant** N Hydrant *m*; **fire insurance** N Feuer- *or* Brandversicherung *f*; **fire irons** PL Kaminbesteck *nt*; **firelight** N Schein *m* des Feuers *or* der Flammen; **firelighter** N Feueranzünder *m*; **fireman** N **a** Feuerwehrmann *m*/-frau *f*; **to give sb a ~'s lift** jdn im Feuerwehrgriff tragen, *jdn hochheben bzw tragen, indem man ihn über die Schulter wirft* **b** (*Rail*) Heizer *m*;; **fire marshal** N (*US*) Feuerwehrhauptmann *m*; **fireplace** N Kamin *m*; **fireplug** N (*dated US*) Hydrant *m*; **firepower** N (*of guns, aircraft, army*) Feuerkraft *f*; **fire prevention** N Brandschutz *m*; **fireproof** ADJ feuerfest VT *materials* feuerfest machen; **fire raiser** N (*esp Brit*) Brandstifter(in) *m(f)*; **fire raising** N (*esp Brit*) Brandstiftung *f*; **fire regulations** PL Brandschutzbestimmungen *pl*; **fire retardant** ADJ feuerhemmend N Feuerhemmer *m*; **fire risk** N Brandrisiko *nt*; **fire sale** N Ausverkauf *m* von Waren mit Brandschäden; **fire screen** N Ofenschirm *m*; **Fire Service** N Feuerwehr *f*; **fireside** N **to sit by the ~** am Kamin sitzen; **~ chair** Lehnsessel *m*; **fire station** N Feuerwache *f*, Feuerwehrzentrale *f*; **firestorm** N Feuersturm *m*; **firetrap** N Feuerfalle *f*; **fire truck** N (*US*) = **fire engine**; **firewall** N **a** (*Comput*) Firewall *f* **b** (= *wall*) Brandmauer *f*; **firewarden** N Feuerwache *f*; **firewater** N (*hum inf*) Feuerwasser *nt* (*inf*); **firewoman** N Feuerwehrfrau *f*; **firewood** N Brennholz *nt*; **fireworks** PL Feuerwerkskörper *pl*; (= *display*) Feuerwerk *nt*; **there's going to be ~ at the meeting** (*fig inf*) bei dem Treffen werden die Funken fliegen

firing ['faɪrɪŋ] N **a** (*of pottery*) Brennen *nt* **b** (*Mil*) Feuer *nt*; (*of gun, shot, rocket*) Abfeuern *nt*; **the ~ of a salute** Salutschüsse *pl* **c** (*inf:* = *dismissal*) Rausschmiss *m* (*inf*) **d** (*Aut, of engine*) Zündung *f*

firing: **firing line** N (*Mil*) Feuer- *or* Schusslinie *f*; (*fig*) Schusslinie *f*; **to be in the ~** (*lit, fig*) in der Schusslinie stehen; **firing pin** N Schlagbolzen *m*; **firing squad** N Exekutionskommando *nt*

firm[1] [fɜːm] N Firma *f*; **~ of lawyers** Rechtsanwaltsbüro *nt*; **the Firm** (*inf*) die Mafia

firm[2] ADJ (+*er*) **a** (= *solid*) *mattress, pillow, fruit, foundation etc* fest; *stomach, thighs* straff; **the cake should be ~ to the touch** der Kuchen sollte sich fest anfühlen; **~ ground** *or* **going** (*Horse Racing*) harter Boden
b (= *strong*) *hold, grip* fest, sicher; *handshake* fest; (= *steady*) *support, chair, ladder* stabil; **to get** *or* **take a ~ hold on sth** etw festhalten; **to keep a ~ grip** *or* **hold on sth/oneself** (*fig*) etw fest/sich gut im Griff haben; **to have ~ control of sth** etw fest unter Kontrolle haben; **Liverpool took ~ control of the game** Liverpool beherrschte das Spiel; **to have a ~ grasp/understanding of sth** etw gut beherrschen/verstehen; **to gain a ~ foothold** (*fig*) festen Fuß fassen; **to have a ~ foothold** (*fig*) eine sichere Ausgangsposition haben; **you need a ~ base** *or* **foundation in any career** für jede Karriere braucht man eine stabile Basis *or* eine feste Grundlage; **they have no ~ foundations on which to build** sie haben keine feste Grundlage, auf der sie bauen können; **to put sth on a ~ footing** *or* **foundation** (*economy, company etc*) etw auf eine sichere Basis stellen
c (= *definite*) *agreement, promise, commitment, belief, support* fest; *decision* endgültig; *evidence, information, conclusion* sicher; *news* bestätigt; *step* entschlossen; **to set a ~ date for sth** einen festen Termin für etw vereinbaren; **it is my ~ belief** *or* **conviction that ...** ich bin der festen Überzeugung, dass ...; **to be a ~ believer in sth/that ...** fest an etw (*acc*) glauben/daran glauben, dass ...; **he's a ~ supporter** *or* **advocate of capital punishment** er ist ein entschiedener Befürworter der Todesstrafe; **~ Conservative supporters** überzeugte Anhänger der konservativen Partei
d (= *strict*) *leader, father* stark; *leadership, policy, voice* fest; *manner, action* entschlossen; *measure* durchgreifend; **this demands ~ leadership** das erfordert eine feste Führung; **to be ~ about sth** auf etw (*dat*) bestehen; **to be ~ with sb** jdm gegenüber bestimmt auftreten; **she's ~ with the children** sie ist streng mit den Kindern; **to take a ~ hand with sb** streng mit jdm umgehen; **children need a ~ hand** Kinder brauchen eine feste Hand; **to take a ~ stand** *or* **line** klar Stellung beziehen; **to take a ~ stand** *or* **line against sth** energisch gegen etw vorgehen
e **~ friends** enge Freunde; **they are ~ friends** sie sind eng befreundet; **to become ~ friends with sb** sich eng mit jdm befreunden; **to be a ~ favourite** (*Brit*) *or* **favorite** (*US*) **(with sb)** (bei jdm) sehr beliebt sein; **this restaurant is one of my ~ favourites** (*Brit*) *or* **favorites** (*US*) dies ist eines meiner Lieblingsrestaurants; **to be the ~ favourite** (*Brit*) *or* **favorite** (*US*) hoher Favorit sein; **the ~ favourite** (*Brit*) *or* **favorite** (*US*) **for a job** der aussichtsreichste Kandidat für einen Posten
f (*Fin*) *price, currency* stabil; **the pound was fairly ~ against the dollar** das Pfund blieb dem Dollar gegenüber relativ stabil
ADV **to hold sth ~** etw festhalten; **to hold ~** (*Fin: prices, shares, currency*) stabil bleiben; **to stand** *or* **hold ~** (= *not give up*) fest *or* standhaft bleiben; **you should stand ~ against such threats** Sie sollten sich durch solche Drohungen nicht beirren lassen
VT *soil* festdrücken

▸ **firm up** VT *sep muscles* kräftigen; *thighs* straffen; *deal etc* unter Dach und Fach bringen

firmament ['fɜːməmənt] N Firmament *nt*

firmly ['fɜːmlɪ] ADV **a** (= *securely*) *place, hold, anchored, shut, established, set, stuck* fest; *fix* sicher; **bake until ~ set** so lange backen, bis es fest (geworden) ist; **she had her sights ~ set on a career in politics** sie hatte sich eine Karriere in der Politik fest vorgenommen; **it was held ~ in place with a pin** es wurde von einer Nadel festgehalten; **these novels were ~ based on reality** diese Romane beruhten vollständig auf tatsächlichen Ereignissen; **~ established/in place** (*fig*) fest etabliert; **to be ~ in control of sth** etw fest in der Hand haben; **she is ~ opposed to the proposal/to doing it** sie ist strikt gegen den Vorschlag/dagegen, es zu tun; **to be ~ committed to sth/to doing sth** sich voll für etw einsetzen/dafür einsetzen, etw zu tun; **~ held opinions** feste Ansichten
b (= *definitely*) *say, tell* bestimmt; *reject* entschieden; *deny* energisch; **I shall tell her quite ~ that ...** ich werde ihr klipp und klar sagen, dass ...

firmness ['fɜːmnɪs] N **a** (= *solidity, of mattress, pillow, fruit, foundation etc*) Festigkeit *f*; (*of stomach, thighs*) Straffheit *f* **b** (= *strength: of hold, grip, handshake*) Festigkeit *f*; (= *steadiness: of support, chair, ladder*) Stabilität *f* **c** (*fig, of agreement, promise, commitment, belief, support*) Festigkeit *f*; (*of person, action, manner*) Entschlossenheit *f*; (= *strictness*) Strenge *f*; **~ of character** Charakterstärke *f*; **it was thanks to his ~ of leadership** es war seiner festen Führung zu verdanken

firmware ['fɜːmwɛəʳ] N (*Comput*) Firmware *f*

first [fɜːst] ✪ 19.2, 26.1, 26.2 ADJ erste(r, s); **his ~ novel** sein Erstlingsroman *m*; **he was ~ in the queue** (*Brit*) *or* **in line** (*US*) er war der Erste in der Schlange; **he was ~ in Latin** er war der Beste in Latein; **who's ~?** wer ist der Erste?; **I'm ~, I've been waiting longer than you** ich bin zuerst an der Reihe, ich warte schon länger als Sie; **the ~ time I saw her ...** als ich sie zum ersten Mal sah, ...; **is it your ~ time?** machst du das zum ersten Mal?; **there always has to be a ~ time** einmal ist immer das erste Mal; **we managed it the very ~ time** wir haben es auf Anhieb geschafft; **in ~ place** (*Sport etc*) an erster Stelle; **to be** *or* **lie in ~ place** an erster Stelle liegen; **in the ~ place** zunächst *or* erstens einmal; **why didn't you say so in the ~ place?** warum hast du denn das nicht gleich gesagt?; **~ time around** beim ersten Mal
ADV **a** zuerst; (= *before all the others*) *arrive, leave* als erste(r, s); **~, take three eggs** zuerst *or* als Erstes nehme man drei Eier; **that's not what you said ~** zuerst hast du etwas anderes gesagt; **~ come ~ served** (*prov*) wer zuerst kommt, mahlt zuerst (*Prov*); **on a ~ come ~ served basis** nach dem Prinzip „wer zuerst kommt, mahlt zuerst"; **women and children ~** Frauen und Kinder zuerst; **ladies ~** Ladies first!, den Damen der Vortritt; **you (go) ~** nach Ihnen; **he says ~ one thing then another** er sagt mal so, mal so; **before he says anything I want to get in ~ with a few comments** bevor er irgendetwas sagt, möchte ich einige Bemerkungen anbringen; **what comes ~ in your order of priorities?** was steht bei Ihnen an erster Stelle?, was ist Ihnen am wichtigsten?; **but, darling, you know you always come ~** aber, mein Schatz, du weißt doch, dass du bei mir immer an erster Stelle stehst; **he always puts his job ~** seine Arbeit kommt bei ihm immer vor allen anderen Dingen
b (= *before all else*) als Erstes, zunächst; (*in listing*) erstens; **~ of all** (= *before all else, mainly*) vor allem; **~ (of all) I'm going for a swim** als Erstes *or* zu(aller)erst gehe ich schwimmen; **why can't I? – well, ~ of all** *or* **~ off** (*inf*), **it's not yours and secondly ...** warum denn nicht? – nun, zunächst *or* erstens einmal gehört es nicht dir und zweitens ...; **~ and foremost** zunächst; **~ and foremost, he is a writer** zuallererst ist er Schriftsteller; **~ and last he is an Englishman** er

ist durch und durch Engländer
c (= *for the first time*) zum ersten Mal, das erste Mal; **when did you ~ meet him?** wann haben Sie ihn das erste Mal *or* zum ersten Mal getroffen?; **when this model was ~ introduced** zu Anfang *or* zuerst, als das Modell herauskam; **when it ~ became known that …** als erstmals bekannt wurde, dass …; **this work was ~ performed/published in 1997** dieses Werk wurde 1997 uraufgeführt/erstveröffentlicht
d (= *before: in time*) (zu)erst; **I must finish this ~** ich muss das erst fertig machen; **think ~ before you sign anything** überlegen Sie es sich, bevor Sie etwas unterschreiben
e (*in preference*) eher, lieber; **I'd die ~!** eher *or* lieber würde ich sterben!
f (*Naut, Rail*) **to travel ~** erster Klasse reisen
N a **the ~** der/die/das Erste; (= *former*) der/die/das Erstere; **he was among the (very) ~ to arrive** er war unter den Ersten *or* Allerersten, die ankamen; **they were the ~ to congratulate me** sie gratulierten mir als Erste; **he was the ~ home/to finish** er war als Erster zu Hause/fertig; (*in race*) er ging als Erster durchs Ziel; **she wore a blouse and a skirt, but the ~ was too tight and the second too baggy** sie trug eine Bluse und einen Rock, aber erstere war zu eng und letzterer zu weit
b **this is the ~ I've heard of it** das ist mir ja ganz neu; **the ~ he knew about it was when he saw it in the paper** er hat erst davon erfahren, als er es in der Zeitung las
c **at ~** zuerst, zunächst; **from the ~** von Anfang an; **from ~ to last** von Anfang bis Ende
d (*Brit Univ*) Eins *f*, Note *f* „Eins"; **he got a ~** er bestand (sein Examen) mit „Eins" *or* „sehr gut"; **he was supposed to get a ~** er war ein Einserkandidat
e **it's a ~** (= *first time ever done*) es ist das allererste Mal(, das so was gemacht wird); **it's a ~ for me/the firm** (= *new experience*) ich habe/die Firma hat noch nie so etwas gemacht; **this is a ~ for the city** das passiert zum ersten Mal in der Stadt
f (*Aut*) **~ (gear)** der erste (Gang); **in ~** im ersten (Gang)
g (*US Baseball*) erstes Base *or* Mal → *also* **sixth**

first: **first aid** N Erste Hilfe; **to give ~** Erste Hilfe leisten; **first-aid box** N (*Brit*) Verband(s)kasten *m*; **first-aid kit** N Verband(s)kasten *m*; **first-aid post, first-aid station** N Sanitätswache *f*; **first-born** ADJ erstgeboren N Erstgeborene(r) *mf*; **first class** N (*Rail, Post etc*) erste Klasse ADJ PRED (= *excellent*) **he's ~ at cooking/tennis** er ist ein erstklassiger Koch/Tennisspieler; **that's absolutely ~!** das ist einfach Spitze! (*inf*); **first-class** ADJ ATTR a (= *excellent*) erstklassig; **he's a ~ cook** er ist ein erstklassiger Koch b (*Rail, Aviat, Tourism*) *flight, train, ticket, cabin* erster Klasse; **a ~ hotel** ein Erste-Klasse-Hotel *nt*, ein Hotel *nt* erster Klasse; **~ travel** Reisen *pl* erster Klasse; **a ~ ticket** eine Fahrkarte erster Klasse; **a ~ compartment** ein Erste-Klasse-Abteil *nt*; **~ passengers** Reisende *pl* in der ersten Klasse c (*Post*) **~ mail** *bevorzugt beförderte Post*; **~ postage/stamp** *Porto/Briefmarke für die bevorzugt beförderte Post*; **~ letter** *bevorzugt beförderter Brief* d (*Brit Univ*) **~ (honours) degree** Examen *nt* mit „Eins" *or* „sehr gut"; **he graduated with ~ honours** er machte sein Examen mit „Eins" *or* „sehr gut" e (*Sport*) *career, innings etc* in der obersten Spielklasse; **~ cricket** *die oberste Kricket-Spielklasse* **to play ~ cricket** *in der obersten Kricket-Spielklasse spielen* ADV a (*Aviat, Naut, Rail*) *travel, fly* erster Klasse b (*Post*) **to send sth ~** etw mit der bevorzugt beförderten Post schicken; **first costs** PL (*Comm*) Selbstkosten *pl*, Gestehungskosten *pl*; **first cousin** N Vetter *m* *or* Cousin *m*/Cousine *f* *or* Kusine *f* ersten Grades; **first-day cover** N Ersttagsbrief *m*; **first-degree burn** N Verbrennung *f* ersten Grades; **first edition** N Erstausgabe *f*; **first-foot** VT (*Scot*) einen Neujahrsbesuch abstatten (*+dat*); **first form** N (*Brit Sch*) erste Klasse; **first-former** N (*Brit Sch*) Erstklässler(in) *m(f)*; **first-generation** ADJ *citizen, computer* der ersten Generation; **first-hand** ADJ *information, experience, knowledge* aus erster Hand; **to have ~ knowledge of sth** etw aus eigener Erfahrung kennen; **they have ~ experience of charitable organizations** sie haben persönlich Erfahrungen mit Wohlfahrtsverbänden gemacht ADV *hear, learn, experience, witness* persönlich, aus erster Hand; *see* mit eigenen Augen; **they experienced police brutality ~** *or* **at first hand** sie haben die Brutalität der Polizei am eigenen Leibe erfahren; **First Lady** N First Lady *f*; **first language** N Muttersprache *f*; **first lieutenant** N Oberleutnant *m*; **first light** N Tagesanbruch *m*, Morgengrauen *nt*; **at ~** bei Tagesanbruch, im Morgengrauen

firstly [ˈfɜːstlɪ] ✪ 26.1, 26.2 ADV (= *in the first place*) zuerst; **they felt that their duty was ~ to the police** sie fühlten sich in erster Linie der Polizei verpflichtet; **why can't I? – well, ~ it's not yours and secondly …** warum denn nicht? – nun, zunächst *or* erstens einmal gehört es nicht dir und zweitens …

first: **first mate** N (*Naut*) Erster Offizier, Erste Offizierin; (*on small boats*) Bestmann *m*; **First Minister** N (*Brit Pol*) Erster Minister, Erste Ministerin; **first name** N Vorname *m*; **they're on ~ terms** sie reden sich mit Vornamen an; **first night** N (*Theat*) Premiere *f*; **~ nerves** Premierenfieber *nt*; **first-nighter** N Premierenbesucher(in) *m(f)*; **first offender** N Ersttäter(in) *m(f)*; **he is a ~** er ist nicht vorbestraft; **first officer** N (*Naut*) Erster Offizier, Erste Offizierin; **first-past-the-post system** N (*Pol*) Mehrheitswahlrecht *nt*; **first performance** N (*Theat*) Uraufführung *f*; (*Mus also*) Erstaufführung *f*; **first person** N erste Person; **the ~ plural** die erste Person Plural; **the story is in the ~** die Geschichte ist in der ersten Person geschrieben *or* wird von einem Icherzähler/einer Icherzählerin erzählt; **first-person** ADJ **~ narrator** Icherzähler(in) *m(f)*; **~ narrative** Icherzählung *f*; **first principles** PL Grundprinzipien *pl*; **to go back** *or* **return to ~** zu den Grundlagen zurückkehren; **first-rate** ADJ erstklassig; **the orchestra was ~** das Orchester hat ausgezeichnet gespielt; **they did a ~ job** sie haben erstklassige *or* ausgezeichnete Arbeit geleistet; **first refusal** N Vorkaufsrecht *nt*; **to give sb (the) ~** jdm das Vorkaufsrecht einräumen; **to have (the) ~ on** das Vorkaufsrecht haben für; **first responder** N *usu pl* Ersthelfer *m*, *Rettungskräfte wie Feuerwehr, Polizei etc, die als erste am Unglücksort eintreffen*; **first school** N (= *Brit*) Grundschule *f*; **first-strike weapon** N Erstschlagwaffe *f*; **first thing** N **she just says the ~ that comes into her head** sie sagt einfach das, was ihr zuerst einfällt; **you don't have to buy the ~ you see** du brauchst nicht das zu kaufen, was du zuerst siehst; **the ~ (to do) is to …** als Erstes muss man …; **the ~ I knew about it was when James told me** ich erfuhr es erst, als James es mir erzählte; **the ~ I knew he'd taken the lot** ehe ich michs versah, hatte er alles genommen; **the ~ to remember is that she hates formality** man muss vor allem daran denken, dass sie Förmlichkeit nicht mag; **~s first** eins nach dem anderen, immer (hübsch) der Reihe nach; (= *most important first*) das Wichtigste zuerst; **you have to put ~s first** du musst wissen, was am wichtigsten ist; **he doesn't know the ~ about it/cars** davon/von Autos hat er nicht die geringste Ahnung ADV gleich; **I'll go ~ in the morning/when I get back** ich gehe gleich morgen früh/gleich, wenn ich wieder da bin; **I'm not at my best ~ (in the morning)** früh am Morgen bin ich nicht gerade in Hochform; **do it ~ before you forget** mach es gleich, ehe du es vergisst; **first-time buyer** N *jd, der zum ersten Mal ein Haus/eine Wohnung kauft*, Erstkäufer(in) *m(f)*; **first-timer** N (*inf*) a (= *novice*) Neuling *m* b (*Comm*) Erstkäufer(in) *m(f)*; **first violin** N erste Geige; **he plays ~** er spielt erste Geige; **First World War** N **the ~** der Erste Weltkrieg

firth [fɜːθ] N (*Scot*) Förde *f*, Meeresarm *m*

fir tree N Tannenbaum *m*

fiscal [ˈfɪskəl] ADJ finanziell; *measures* finanzpolitisch; **~ crisis/policy** Finanzkrise/-politik *f*; **~ reform** Steuerreform *f* N (*Scot Jur*) Staatsanwalt *m*/-anwältin *f*

fiscal year N (*Fin*) Geschäftsjahr *nt*

fish [fɪʃ] N *pl* - *or* (*esp for different types*) **-es** Fisch *m*; **~ and chips** Fisch und Pommes frites; **to drink like a ~** (*inf*) wie ein Loch saufen (*inf*); **to have other ~ to fry** (*fig inf*) Wichtigeres zu tun haben; **like a ~ out of water** wie ein Fisch auf dem Trockenen; **neither ~ nor fowl** (*fig*) weder Fisch noch Fleisch; **he's a queer ~** (*Brit inf*) er ist ein komischer Kauz; **there are plenty more ~ in the sea** (*fig inf*) es gibt noch mehr (davon) auf der Welt; **he's a big ~ in a small** *or* **little pond** er ist ein großes Tier am Ort (*inf*); **a little ~ in a big pond** nur einer von vielen; **The Fishes** (*Astron*) die Fische *pl*
VI fischen; (*with rod also*) angeln; **to go ~ing** fischen/angeln gehen; **to go salmon ~ing** auf Lachsfang gehen
VT fischen; (*with rod also*) angeln; **to ~ a river** in einem Fluss fischen/angeln; **to ~ a river dry** einen Fluss abfischen

▶ **fish for** VI *+prep obj* a (*lit*) fischen; (*with rod also*) angeln b (*fig*) *compliments* fischen nach; **they were fishing for information** sie waren auf Informationen aus

▶ **fish out** VT *sep* herausfischen *or* -angeln (*of or from sth* aus etw); **he fished it out from behind the cupboard** er angelte es hinter dem Schrank hervor

▶ **fish up** VT *sep* auffischen, herausziehen; (*fig, from memory etc*) hervorkramen *or* -holen

fish: **fish-and-chip shop** N (*Brit*) Fish-and-chips-Imbiss *m*; **fishbone** N (Fisch)gräte *f*; **fishbowl** N Fischglas *nt*; **fish cake** N Fischfrikadelle *f*

fisher [ˈfɪʃəʳ] N a (*old*, = *fisherman*) Fischer *m*; **~s of men** (*Bibl*) Menschenfischer *pl* (*Bibl*) b (= *animal*) Fischfänger *m*

fisherman [ˈfɪʃəmən] N *pl* **-men** [-mən] Fischer *m*; (*amateur*) Angler *m*; (= *boat*) Fischereiboot *nt*

fishery [ˈfɪʃərɪ] N (= *area*) Fischereizone *f* *or* -gewässer *nt*; (= *industry*) Fischerei *f*

fish: **fisheye lens** N (*Phot*) Fischauge *nt*; **fish farm** N Fischzucht(anlage) *f*; **fish farmer** N Fischzüchter(in) *m(f)*; **fish farming** N Fischzucht *f*; **fishfinger** N Fischstäbchen *nt*; **fish flour** N Fischmehl *nt*; **fish glue** N Fischleim *m*; **fish-hook** N Angelhaken *m*

fishing [ˈfɪʃɪŋ] N Fischen *nt*; (*with rod*) Angeln *nt*; (*as industry*) Fischerei *f*; **~ (is) prohibited** Angeln verboten!

fishing: **fishing boat** N Fischerboot *nt*; **fishing fleet** N Fischereiflotte *f*; **fishing industry** N Fischindustrie *f*; **fishing line** N Angelschnur *f*; **fishing net** N Fischnetz *nt*; **fishing pole** N (*US*) Angelrute *f*; **fishing port** N Fischereihafen *m*; **fishing rod** N Angelrute *f*; **fishing tackle** N (*for sport*) Angelgeräte *pl*; (*for industry*) Fischereigeräte *pl*; **fishing village** N Fischerdorf *nt*

fish: **fish knife** N Fischmesser *nt*; **fish ladder** N Fischleiter *f*; **fish market** N Fischmarkt *m*; **fishmonger** [ˈfɪʃmʌŋgəʳ] N (*Brit*) Fischhändler(in) *m(f)*; **fishmonger's** N (*Brit*) Fischgeschäft *nt*; **fishnet stockings** PL Netzstrümpfe *pl*; **fish paste** N Fischpaste *f*; **fishplate** N (*Rail*) Lasche *f*; **fish pond** N Fischteich *m*; **fish shop** N (*Brit*) a Fischladen *m* b = **fish-and-chip shop**; **fish slice** N (*for serving*) Fischvorlegemesser *nt*; **fish stick** N (*US*) = **fishfinger**; **fish story** N (*US inf*) Seemannsgarn *nt*; **fish supper** N (*esp Scot, N Engl*) Fisch *m* mit Pommes (*inf*), Fish-and-chips *pl*; **fishtail** (*Mot*) N Schleuderbewegung *f* des Hecks VI (mit dem Heck) seitlich ausbrechen; **fish tank** N (*in house*) Aquarium *nt*; (*on fish farm*) Fischteich *m*; **fishwife** N Fischfrau *f*; (*fig pej*) Marktweib *nt*

fishy [ˈfɪʃɪ] ADJ (*+er*) a **~ smell** Fischgeruch *m*; **it smells rather ~** es riecht ziemlich nach Fisch

b *(inf)* verdächtig; *excuse, story* faul *(inf)*; **there's something ~ about his story** an seiner Geschichte ist was faul *(inf)*; **something ~ is going on** hier ist was faul *(inf)*

fissile ['fɪsaɪl] ADJ spaltbar; **~ material** Spaltmaterial *nt*

fission ['fɪʃən] N *(Phys)* Spaltung *f*; *(Biol)* (Zell)teilung *f*

fissionable ['fɪʃnəbl] ADJ spaltbar

fission bomb N (konventionelle) Atombombe

fissure ['fɪʃəʳ] N Riss *m*; *(deep)* Kluft *f*; *(narrow)* Spalt *m*, Spalte *f*

fissured ['fɪʃəd] ADJ rissig; *(= with deep fissures)* zerklüftet

fist [fɪst] N Faust *f*; **to put one's ~s up** die Fäuste hochnehmen, in (Box)kampfstellung gehen

fistful ['fɪstfʊl] N Handvoll *f*; **a ~ of pound coins** eine Handvoll Pfundmünzen

fisticuffs ['fɪstɪkʌfs] PL *(dated inf: = fighting)* Handgreiflichkeiten *pl*; *(= boxing)* Boxen *nt*; **I'm not much good at ~** ich tauge nicht viel mit den Fäusten; **resorting to ~ is no solution** handgreiflich (zu) werden ist keine Lösung

fit[1] [fɪt] ADJ *(+er)* **a** *(= suitable, suited for sth)* geeignet; *time, occasion* günstig; **~ to eat** essbar; **~ to drink** trinkbar; **is this meat still ~ to eat?** kann man dieses Fleisch noch essen?; **~ for (human) consumption** zum Verzehr (durch Menschen) geeignet; **~ for habitation** *or* **to live in** bewohnbar; **to be ~ to be seen** sich sehen lassen können; **she's not ~ to be a mother** sie ist als Mutter völlig ungeeignet; **this coat is ~ for the dustbin** *(Brit)* *or* **trash can** *(US)* dieser Mantel gehört in den Mülleimer

b *(= deserving)* **a man like that is not ~ to have such a good wife** ein Mann wie er verdient so eine gute Frau nicht *or* ist eine so gute Frau nicht wert; **you're not ~ to be spoken to** du bist es nicht wert *or* verdienst es nicht, dass man sich mit dir unterhält

c *(= right and proper)* richtig, angebracht; **I'll do as I think** *or* **see ~** ich handle, wie ich es für richtig halte; **to see ~ to do sth** es für richtig *or* angebracht halten, etw zu tun; **he did not see ~ to cooperate** er hat es nicht für nötig gehalten zu kooperieren; **as is only ~** wie es sich gebührt; **it is only ~** es ist nur recht und billig

d *(in health)* gesund; *sportsman etc* fit, in Form; **she is not yet ~ to travel** sie ist noch nicht reisefähig; **only the ~test survive** nur die Geeignetsten überleben; *(people)* nur die Gesunden überleben; *(in business etc)* nur die Starken können sich halten

e **to laugh ~ to burst** vor Lachen beinahe platzen; **to be ~ to drop** *(Brit)* zum Umfallen müde sein

f *(Brit sl: = sexy) girl, boy* scharf *(inf)*

N *(of clothes)* Passform *f*; **it is a very good/bad ~** es sitzt *or* passt wie angegossen/nicht gut; **it's a bit of a tight ~** *(clothes)* es ist etwas eng; *(timing, parking)* es geht gerade (noch)

VT **a** *(cover, sheet, nut etc)* passen auf *(+acc)*; *(key etc)* passen in *(+acc)*; *(clothes etc)* passen *(+dat)*; **this coat ~s you better** dieser Mantel passt Ihnen besser *or* sitzt bei Ihnen besser; **"one size ~s all"** „Einheitsgröße"; **that part won't ~ this machine** das Teil passt nicht für diese Maschine; **the washing machine won't ~ this space** die Waschmaschine passt nicht in diese Lücke; **to make a ring ~ sb** jdm einen Ring anpassen

b *(= be suitable for) sb's plans, a theory etc* passen in *(+acc)*; *needs* erfüllen; *mood* passen zu

c **she was ~ted for her wedding dress** ihr Hochzeitskleid wurde ihr angepasst

d *(= put on, attach)* anbringen *(to* an *+dat)*; *tyre, lock* montieren, anbringen; *double glazing* einsetzen, anbringen; *(= put in)* einbauen *(in* in *+acc)*; *(= furnish, provide with)* ausstatten; **to ~ a key in the lock** einen Schlüssel ins Schloss stecken; **to ~ a bulb in its socket** eine Glühbirne in die Fassung drehen *or* schrauben; **to ~ a bolt to a door** eine Tür mit einem Riegel versehen; **to ~ a car with an alarm** eine Alarmanlage in ein Auto einbauen, ein Auto mit einer Alarmanlage ausstatten; **to have a new kitchen ~ted** eine neue Küche einbauen lassen

e *(= match) description, facts, circumstances* entsprechen *(+dat)*; **to make the punishment ~ the crime** eine dem Vergehen angemessene Strafe verhängen

VI **a** *(= be right size, shape: dress etc, key)* passen; **my CV ~s on one page** mein Lebenslauf passt auf eine Seite *or* hat auf einer Seite Platz

b *(= correspond)* zusammenstimmen *or* -passen; **the facts don't ~** die Fakten sind widersprüchlich; **it all ~s** es passt alles zusammen; **there's still one piece of evidence that doesn't ~** da ist immer noch ein Indiz, das nicht dazupasst

▸ **fit in** VT *sep* **a** *(= find space for)* unterbringen; **you can fit five people into this car** in diesem Auto haben fünf Personen Platz

b *(= find time for) person* einen Termin geben *(+dat)*; *meeting* unterbringen; *(= squeeze in)* einschieben; **Sir Charles could fit you in at 3 o'clock** um 3 Uhr hätte Sir Charles Zeit für Sie; **can you fit this meeting in(to) your schedule?** können Sie diese Konferenz noch in Ihrem Terminkalender unterbringen?

c *(= make harmonize)* **to fit sth in with sth** etw mit etw in Einklang bringen

d *(= fit, put in)* einsetzen, einbauen

VI **a** *(= go into place)* hineinpassen; **will we all fit in?** passen wir alle hinein?; **I can't get all the toys to fit in** ich kann die ganzen Spielsachen nicht hineinbekommen; **the clothes won't fit in(to) the case** die Sachen passen nicht in den Koffer

b *(plans, ideas, word)* passen; *(facts etc)* übereinstimmen; *(= match)* dazupassen; **there is one fact that doesn't fit in** da ist ein Punkt, der nicht ins Ganze passt; **how does this fit in?** wie passt das ins Ganze?; **I see, it all fits in now** jetzt passt alles zusammen; **suddenly everything fitted into place** plötzlich wurde alles klar; **to fit in with sth** *(plans, ideas)* in etw *(acc)* passen; *(facts)* mit etw übereinstimmen; *(= match)* zu etw passen; **does that fit in with your plans?** lässt sich das mit Ihren Plänen vereinbaren?; **he wants everybody to fit in with him/his plans** er will, dass sich jedermann nach ihm/seinen Plänen richtet

c *(people: = harmonize)* **he doesn't fit in here/with the others/with such a firm** er passt nicht hierhin/zu den anderen/in eine solche Firma; **she's the sort who fits in easily in any group** sie ist der Typ, der sich in jede Gruppe leicht einfügt; **the new director didn't fit in** der neue Direktor hat nicht in die Firma gepasst *or* nicht reingepasst *(inf)*; **try to fit in (with the others)** versuche dich den anderen anzupassen; **she has problems fitting in** sie kann sich nicht gut anpassen

▸ **fit on** VI **a** *(= be right size, shape)* passen; **will it fit on?** passt es (darauf)? **b** *(= be fixed)* befestigt *or* angebracht sein; **where does this part fit on?** wo gehört dieses Teil drauf?, wo wird dieses Teil befestigt? VT *sep* **a** *dress* anprobieren; *(tailor)* anpassen *(prep obj +dat)* **b** *(= put in place, fix on)* anbringen

▸ **fit out** VT *sep expedition* ausrüsten; *ship* ausstatten; *person (for an expedition)* ausrüsten; *(with clothes etc)* ausstatten; **they've fitted one room out as an office** sie haben eines der Zimmer als Büro eingerichtet

▸ **fit up** VT *sep* **a** *(= fix up)* anbringen; *(= assemble)* zusammensetzen *or* -bauen **b** *(= supply with)* ausstatten; *(with implements, weapons etc)* ausrüsten, ausstatten; **to fit sb/sth up with sth** jdn/etw mit etw versehen *or* ausstatten

fit[2] N *(Med, fig)* Anfall *m*; **~ of coughing/anger** Husten-/Wutanfall *m*; **in a ~ of anger** in einem Anfall von Wut; **~ of remorse** Anwandlung *f or* Anfall *m* von Reue; **in** *or* **by ~s and starts** stoßweise; **he wrote this novel in ~s and starts** er hat diesen Roman in mehreren Anläufen geschrieben; **to be in ~s (of laughter)** sich vor Lachen biegen *or* kugeln *(inf)*; **he'd have a ~** *(fig inf)* er würde (ja) einen Anfall kriegen *(inf)*

f. i. t. *abbr of* **free of income tax** einkommensteuerfrei

fitful ['fɪtfʊl] ADJ unbeständig; *working, progress* stoßweise; *sleep* unruhig; *sun* launenhaft *(geh)*; *enthusiasm* sporadisch

fitfully ['fɪtfəlɪ] ADV *sleep* unruhig; *progress* stoßweise; *work* sporadisch; **the sun shone ~** die Sonne kam vereinzelt durch; **she slept only ~** sie wachte immer wieder auf

fitment ['fɪtmənt] N *(Brit: = furniture)* Einrichtungsgegenstand *m*; *(of machine, car)* Zubehörteil *nt*

fitness ['fɪtnɪs] N **a** *(= health)* Gesundheit *f*; *(= condition)* Fitness *f*, Kondition *f*; **~ instructor** Fitnesstrainer(in) *m(f)*; **~ training** Fitness- *or* Konditionstraining *nt*; **~ fanatic** *or* **freak** *(inf)* Fitnessfanatiker(in) *m(f)*; **~ test** *(Sport)* Fitness- *or* Konditionstest *m* **b** *(= suitability)* Eignung *f*; *(of remark etc)* Angemessenheit *f*; **~ for work** Erwerbsfähigkeit *f*; **~ for service** *(esp Mil)* Dienstfähigkeit *f*/-tauglichkeit *f*

fitted ['fɪtɪd] ADJ **a** **to be ~ with sth** *(room, vehicle)* mit etw ausgestattet sein; **a car ~ with a catalytic converter/an alarm** ein Auto mit (eingebautem) Katalysator/(eingebauter) Alarmanlage; **to be ~ as standard** zur serienmäßigen Ausstattung gehören

b *(= built-in)* Einbau-; *bedroom, bathroom* mit Einbauelementen; **~ wardrobe/cupboard** Einbauschrank *m*; **~ units** Einbauelemente *pl*; **~ kitchen** Einbauküche *f*

c *(= tailored) jacket, shirt* tailliert; **~ carpet** *(Brit)* Teppichboden *m*; **~ sheet** Spannbetttuch *nt*

d *(form: = suited)* **to be ~ to do sth** sich dazu eignen, etw zu tun; **he is well/ill ~ to be king** er eignet sich gut/schlecht zum König; **to be ~ for** *or* **to a task** sich für eine Aufgabe eignen; **these school-leavers are ill ~ for work** diese Schulabgänger sind nicht auf das Arbeitsleben vorbereitet

fitter ['fɪtəʳ] N **a** *(for clothes)* Schneider(in) *m(f)* **b** *(Tech, of engines)* Monteur(in) *m(f)*; *(for machines)* (Maschinen)schlosser(in) *m(f)*; *(not specially qualified)* Montagearbeiter(in) *m(f)*; *(of pipes etc)* Installateur(in) *m(f)*

fitting ['fɪtɪŋ] ADJ *(= suitable)* passend; *punishment, reward* angemessen; *expression also* angebracht; *(= seemly, becoming)* schicklich *(dated)*; **it is not ~ for a young lady ...** es schickt sich nicht *or* ist nicht schicklich *(dated)* für eine junge Dame ... N **a** Anprobe *f*; **to go in for a ~** zur Anprobe gehen **b** *(= part)* Zubehörteil *nt*; **~s** Ausstattung *f*; *(= furniture also)* Einrichtung *f*; *(= pipes)* Installation *f*; **bathroom/office ~s** Badezimmer-/Büroeinrichtung *f*; **electrical ~s** Elektroinstallationen *pl*

fittingly ['fɪtɪŋlɪ] ADV *(+adj)* angemessen; *name, translate* passend; *(introducing sentence)* passenderweise; **a song ~ titled "Goodbye"** ein Lied mit dem passenden Titel „Goodbye"

fitting room N Anproberaum *m*; *(= cubicle)* Anprobekabine *f*

five [faɪv] ADJ fünf N Fünf *f* → *also* **six**

five: **five-and-dime, five-and-ten** N *(US)* billiges Kaufhaus; **five-a-side** ADJ *football* mit fünf Spielern pro Mannschaft; **~ team** Fünfermannschaft *f*, Fünf *f*; **fivefold** ADJ *increase, rise* fünffach ADV *increase, rise* um das Fünffache; **five-o'clock shadow** N *nachmittäglicher Anflug von Bartstoppeln*

fiver ['faɪvəʳ] N *(inf)* Fünfpfund-/Fünfdollarschein *m*

five: **five-spot** N *(US inf)* Fünfdollarschein *m*; **five-star hotel** N Fünf-Sterne-Hotel *nt*; **five-year plan** N Fünfjahresplan *m*

fix [fɪks] VT **a** *(= make firm)* befestigen, festmachen *(sth to sth* etw an/auf etw *dat)*; *(= put on, install) new aerial, new dynamo* anbringen; *(fig) ideas, images* verankern, festsetzen; **to ~ a stake in the ground** einen Pfahl im Boden verankern; **to ~ the blame on sb** die Schuld auf jdn schieben, jdm die Schuld geben; **this image was firmly ~ed in his memory** diese Vorstellung war fest in seinem Gedächtnis verankert; **to ~**

sth in one's mind sich *(dat)* etw fest einprägen; **to ~ bayonets** die Bajonette aufpflanzen
b *eyes, attention* richten *(on, upon* auf *+acc)*; *gun, camera, radar* richten *(on* auf *+acc)*; **all eyes were/everybody's attention was ~ed on her** alle sahen sie wie gebannt an; **to ~ sb with an angry stare** *(liter)* jdn mit wütenden Blicken durchbohren; **to ~ sb with a look of concern** *(liter)* einen besorgten Blick auf jdn richten
c *date, price, limit* festsetzen, festlegen; *(= agree on)* ausmachen, beschließen; **nothing has been ~ed yet** es liegt noch nichts fest, es ist noch nichts fest (ausgemacht *or* beschlossen worden)
d *(= arrange)* arrangieren; *tickets, taxi etc* besorgen, organisieren *(inf)*; **have you got anything ~ed for tonight?** haben Sie (für) heute Abend schon etwas vor?; **I ~ed it so that he could go to the concert** ich habe es arrangiert, dass er zu dem Konzert gehen kann
e *(= straighten out, sort out)* in Ordnung bringen, regeln; **don't worry, I'll ~ things with him** mach dir keine Gedanken, ich regle das mit ihm *or* ich bringe das in Ordnung
f *(inf: = get even with, sort out)* **I'll ~ him** dem werd ichs besorgen *(inf)*; **the Mafia will ~ him** den wird sich *(dat)* die Mafia vornehmen *(inf) or* vorknöpfen *(inf)*
g *(= repair)* in Ordnung bringen, (ganz) machen *(inf)*; *(= put in good order, adjust)* machen *(inf)*
h *drink, meal* machen; **to ~ one's hair/face** sich frisieren/schminken
i *(inf: = arrange dishonestly) race, fight, jury* manipulieren; *prices* absprechen; **the whole thing was ~ed** das war eine abgekartete Sache *(inf)*
j *(Chem, Phot)* fixieren
k *(Naut, Aviat) position* bestimmen; *submarine etc* orten
VI *(US inf: = intend)* vorhaben; **I'm ~ing to get married soon** ich habe vor, bald zu heiraten
N a *(inf: = tricky situation)* Patsche *f (inf)*, Klemme *f (inf)*; **to be in a ~** in der Patsche *or* Klemme sitzen *(inf)*; **to get oneself into a ~** sich *(dat)* eine schöne Suppe einbrocken *(inf)*
b *(Naut)* Position *f*, Standort *m*; **to take a ~ on sth** etw orten; **to get a ~ on sb/sth** *(fig: = get clear about)* sich *(dat)* Klarheit über jdn/etw verschaffen
c *(inf: of drugs)* Druck *m (sl)*; **to give oneself a ~** sich *(dat)* einen Schuss setzen *(inf)*, sich *(dat)* einen Druck verpassen *(sl)*; **I need my daily ~ of chocolate** *(inf)* ich brauche meine tägliche Schokoladenration
d *(inf)* **the fight/competition was a ~** der Kampf/Wettbewerb war eine abgekartete Sache *(inf)*

▶ **fix down** VT *sep* befestigen

▶ **fix on** VT *sep* festmachen *(prep obj* auf *+dat)*; *badge etc also* anheften, anstecken; *(= fit on)* anbringen VI *+prep obj (= decide on)* sich entscheiden für

▶ **fix together** VT *sep* zusammenmachen *(inf)*

▶ **fix up** VT *sep* **a** *shelves* anbringen; *tent* aufstellen **b** *(= arrange)* arrangieren; *holidays etc* festmachen; *(= book) organized tour, hotel etc* buchen; **have you got anything fixed up for this evening?** haben Sie (für) heute Abend schon etwas vor? **c to fix sb up with sth** jdm etw besorgen *or* verschaffen; **we fixed them up for the night** wir haben sie für die Nacht untergebracht; **I stayed with him until I got myself fixed up (with a room)** ich habe bei ihm gewohnt, bis ich ein Zimmer hatte **d** *(= straighten out, sort out)* in Ordnung bringen, regeln **e** *room, house* einrichten

fixated [fɪk'seɪtɪd] ADJ fixiert *(on* auf *+acc)*

fixation [fɪk'seɪʃən] N **a** *(Psych)* Fixierung *f*; **she has a ~ about** *or* **on cleanliness** sie hat einen Sauberkeitsfimmel *(inf)* **b** *(Chem)* Fixierung *f*

fixative ['fɪksətɪv] N Fixativ *nt*

fixative cream N *(for dentures)* Haftcreme *f*

fixed [fɪkst] ADJ **a** *(= invariable) amount, time* fest(gesetzt); *position* unveränderlich; **at ~ intervals** in festen Abständen; **there's no ~ agenda** es gibt keine feste Tagesordnung; **of no ~ abode** *or* **address** *(Jur)* ohne festen Wohnsitz; **~ exchange rate** *(Fin)* fester Wechselkurs; **~ conversion rates** *(Fin)* feste Umrechnungskurse *pl*; **~ menu** Tagesmenü *nt*; **~ point** *(Comput)* Festkomma *nt*;; **~ price** Festpreis *m*
b *idea* fest; *smile, grin* starr; **to have a ~ idea** *or* **belief that …** fest davon überzeugt *or* nicht davon abzubringen sein, dass …; **a ~ stare** ein starrer Blick
c *(= rigged) election, game, match, race* manipuliert; **it's a ~ trial, the trial is ~** der Prozess ist eine abgekartete Sache; **the interview was ~** das Interview war gestellt; **the whole thing was ~** das war eine abgekartete Sache *(inf)*
d *(inf)* **how are we ~ for time?** wie siehts mit der Zeit aus?; **how are you ~ for food/money** *etc***?** wie siehts bei dir mit Essen/Geld *etc* aus?; **how are you ~ for tonight?** was hast du (für) heute Abend vor?

fixed: **fixed assets** PL *(Comm)* feste Anlagen *pl*; **fixed capital** N Anlagevermögen *nt*; **fixed costs** PL *(Comm)* Fixkosten *pl*; **fixed-interest** ADJ Festzins-; *stocks, investments* festverzinslich; **~ loan** Festzinsanleihe *f*

fixedly ['fɪksɪdlɪ] ADV *stare, look* starr, unverwandt

fixed: **fixed-rate** ['fɪkstreɪt] ADJ Festzins-; **~ mortgage** Festzinshypothek *f*; **fixed star** N Fixstern *m*; **fixed-term contract** N Zeitvertrag *m*, befristeter Vertrag; **fixed-wing** ADJ **~ aircraft** Starrflügelflugzeug *nt*

fixer ['fɪksəʳ] N *(Phot)* Fixiermittel *nt*

fixing [fɪksɪŋ] N *(Fin)* Fixing *nt*, Festlegung *f*

fixing bath ['fɪksɪŋ,bɑːθ] N Fixierbad *nt*

fixings ['fɪksɪŋz] PL *(US Cook)* Beilagen *pl*

fixity ['fɪksɪtɪ] N *(liter)* **his ~ of purpose** seine Zielstrebigkeit

fixture ['fɪkstʃəʳ] N **a** *(of a building etc)* **~s** Ausstattung *f*, unbewegliches Inventar *(form)*; **~s and fittings** Anschlüsse und unbewegliches Inventar *(form)*; **lighting ~s** elektrische Anschlüsse; **to be a ~** *(fig hum, person)* zum Inventar gehören **b** *(Brit Sport)* Spiel *nt*

fixture list N *(Brit Sport)* Spielplan *m*

fizz [fɪz] VI *(champagne etc)* perlen, sprudeln, moussieren N **a** *(of champagne etc)* Perlen *nt*, Moussieren *nt* **b** *(= drink)* Sprudel *m*; *(flavoured)* Limonade *f*, Brause *f* **c** *(dated Brit, inf, = champagne)* Schampus *m (dated inf)*

▶ **fizz up** VI (auf)sprudeln

fizzle ['fɪzl] VI zischen, spucken *(inf)*

▶ **fizzle out** VI *(firework, enthusiasm)* verpuffen; *(rocket)* vorzeitig verglühen; *(plan)* im Sande verlaufen

fizzy ['fɪzɪ] ADJ *(+er)* sprudelnd; **to be ~** sprudeln; **it's too ~** da ist zu viel Kohlensäure drin; **the soda water makes it ~** durch das Sodawasser sprudelt es; **a ~ drink** eine Brause

fjord [fjɔːd] N Fjord *m*

flab [flæb] N *(inf)* Speck *m*; **to fight** *or* **beat the ~** *(hum)* etwas für die schlanke Linie tun, Fitnesstraining machen

flabbergast ['flæbəgɑːst] VT *(inf)* verblüffen, umhauen *(inf)*; **I was ~ed to see him/at the price** ich war platt *or* von den Socken, als ich ihn sah/als ich den Preis erfuhr *(inf)*

flabbergasting ['flæbəgɑːstɪŋ] ADJ *pred (inf)* unglaublich

flabbily ['flæbɪlɪ] ADV schlaff; *written* schwammig

flabbiness ['flæbɪnɪs] N *(of thighs, stomach, muscles, skin)* Schlaffheit *f*; *(of person)* Schwabbeligkeit *f (inf)*; *(fig: = ineffectual nature)* Schlaffheit *f*

flabby ['flæbɪ] ADJ *(+er) thighs, stomach, muscles, skin* schlaff; *person also* schwabbelig *(inf)*; *(fig: = ineffectual)* schlaff; **he's getting ~ (round the middle)** er setzt (um die Taille) Speck an

flaccid ['flæksɪd] ADJ *(liter)* schlaff; *prose* saft- und kraftlos

flag[1] [flæg] N **a** Fahne *f*; *(small, on map, chart etc)* Fähnchen *nt*; *(national)* Fahne *f*, Flagge *f*; *(Naut)* Flagge *f*; *(for semaphore)* Signalflagge *or* -fahne *f*; **to fly the ~ (for)** *(fig)* die Fahne hochhalten (für); **to keep the ~ flying** *(lit, fig)* die Stellung halten; **to show the ~** seine Präsenz *or (fig also)* seine Anwesenheit dokumentieren; **~ of convenience** *(Naut)* Billigflagge *f* **b** *(for charity)* Fähnchen *nt* **c** *(of taxi)* **the ~ was down** das Taxi war besetzt; **he put the ~ down** er stellte auf „besetzt" **d** *(= paper marker)* Kennzeichen *nt* VT beflaggen

▶ **flag down** VT *sep taxi etc, person* anhalten

▶ **flag up** VT *sep (inf: = mark, indicate)* markieren

flag[2] VI erlahmen; *(interest, enthusiasm, strength etc also)* nachlassen; **he's ~ging** er lässt nach; *(= he is tiring)* er wird müde; **their spirits ~ged** ihr Mut sank; **the film starts ~ging toward(s) the middle** der Film lässt zur Mitte hin nach

flag[3] N *(Bot)* Schwertlilie *f*; *(= sweet flag)* Kalmus *m*

flag[4] N *(also* **flagstone***)* Steinplatte *f*; *(for floor also)* Fliese *f* VT mit Steinplatten/Fliesen belegen; *floor also* fliesen

flag day N **a** *(Brit) Tag, an dem eine Straßensammlung für einen wohltätigen Zweck durchgeführt wird* **b Flag Day** *(US) 14. Juni, Gedenktag der Einführung der amerikanischen Nationalflagge*

flagellant ['flædʒələnt] N **a** *(Rel)* Flagellant *m* **b** *(form, for sexual gratification)* Flagellant *m*

flagellate ['flædʒəleɪt] VT geißeln

flagellation [,flædʒə'leɪʃən] N Geißelung *f*

flagged [flægd] ADJ **a** *ship* beflaggt **b** *floor* gefliest

flag officer N *(Naut)* Flaggoffizier *m*

flagon ['flægən] N *(= bottle)* Flasche *f*; *(= jug)* Krug *m*

flagpole ['flægpəʊl] N Fahnenstange *f*; **to run an idea/a proposal up the ~** *(inf)* eine Idee/einen Vorschlag testen

flagrance ['fleɪgrəns], **flagrancy** ['fleɪgrənsɪ] N eklatante *or* krasse Offensichtlichkeit; *(of affair, defiance, disregard)* Unverhohlenheit *f*; **such was the ~ of this injustice …** das war eine derart eklatante *or* krasse *or* himmelschreiende Ungerechtigkeit …; **the unabashed ~ of his abuse of privilege** die unverhohlene Art, mit der er seine Privilegien missbraucht

flagrant ['fleɪgrənt] ADJ eklatant, krass; *injustice, crime also* himmelschreiend; *breach, violation* eklatant, flagrant *(geh)*; *disregard, defiance, affair* unverhohlen, offenkundig

flagrantly ['fleɪgrəntlɪ] ADV *violate, abuse, disregard* ganz eindeutig *or* offensichtlich; *flirt* unverhohlen; **he is ~ indiscreet** er begeht offene Indiskretionen; **this is ~ unjust** das ist eine himmelschreiende Ungerechtigkeit

flag: **flagship** N *(lit, fig)* Flaggschiff *nt* ADJ *attr* Vorzeige-; **~ store** Vorzeigeladen *m*; **flagstaff** N Fahnen- *or* Flaggenmast *m*; **flag stop** N *(US)* Bedarfshaltestelle *f*; **flagstone** N (Stein)platte *f*; *(on floor also)* Fliese *f*; **flag-waver** N Hurrapatriot(in) *m(f)*, Chauvinist *m*; **flag-waving** N Hurrapatriotismus *m*, Chauvinismus *m* ADJ *speech* chauvinistisch

flail [fleɪl] N (Dresch)flegel *m* VT dreschen; **he ~ed his arms about** *or* **around wildly** er schlug wild (mit den Armen) um sich VI **to ~ (about)** herumfuchteln; **the dying deer with its legs ~ing in all directions** das verendende Reh, das mit seinen Läufen nach allen Richtungen ausschlug

flail tank N Minenräumpanzer *m*

flair [flɛəʳ] N *(for selecting the best etc)* Gespür *nt*, (feine) Nase *(inf)*, Riecher *m (inf)*; *(= talent)* Talent *nt*; *(= stylishness)* Flair *nt*; **his great ~ for business** sein großes Geschäftstalent

flak [flæk] N **a** Flakfeuer *nt* **b** *(fig)* **he's been getting a lot of ~ (for it)** er ist (dafür) mächtig unter Beschuss geraten *(inf)*; **I'm not taking the ~ for this** ich lass mich deswegen nicht zur Sau machen *(inf)*

flake [fleɪk] N (*of snow, soap*) Flocke *f*; (*of paint, rust*) Splitter *m*; (*of plaster*) abgebröckeltes Stückchen; (*of metal, wood*) Span *m*; (*of skin*) Schuppe *f*; (*of fish*) Stückchen *nt* Fischfleisch; (*of almond*) Blättchen *nt*; (*of chocolate*) Raspel *m*; **~s of paint/plaster were falling off the ceiling** die Farbe blätterte/der Gips bröckelte von der Decke ab VI (*stone, plaster etc*) abbröckeln; (*paint*) abblättern VT (*Cook*) *chocolate, almonds* raspeln; *fish* in Stücke zerteilen

▶ **flake off** VI (*plaster*) abbröckeln; (*paint, rust etc*) abblättern, absplittern; (*skin*) sich schälen, sich abschuppen

▶ **flake out** VI (*inf*: = *become exhausted*) abschlaffen (*inf*); (= *pass out*) umkippen; (= *fall asleep*) einschlafen, einpennen (*inf*)

flak jacket N kugelsichere Weste

flaky [ˈfleɪkɪ] ADJ (+*er*) a *potatoes* flockig; *paint, plaster etc* brüchig; *crust* blättrig; *skin* schuppig b (*esp US*: = *mad, eccentric*) verrückt

flaky pastry N Blätterteig *m*

flamboyance [flæmˈbɔɪəns] N Extravaganz *f*; (*of lifestyle also*) Üppigkeit *f*

flamboyant [flæmˈbɔɪənt] ADJ extravagant; *lifestyle also* üppig, aufwendig, aufwändig; *plumage* farbenprächtig; *colours* prächtig; *gesture* großartig; **~ style** (*Archit*) Flamboyantstil *m*; (*of person*) extravagante Art; **in the ~ court of Louis XIV** am prunkvollen Hof Ludwigs XIV

flamboyantly [flæmˈbɔɪəntlɪ] ADV extravagant

flame [fleɪm] N a Flamme *f*; **the house was in ~s** das Haus stand in Flammen b (*of passion*) Flamme *f* (*geh*), Feuer *nt no pl* c (*inf*: = *sweetheart*) Flamme *f* (*inf*); **she's an old ~ of his** sie ist eine alte *or* ehemalige Flamme von ihm (*inf*) d (*Comput*) Flame *nt*, beleidigende E-Mail VI (*fire*) lodern, flammen (*geh*); (*fig*: *face, cheeks*) glühen VT (*Comput*) **to ~ sb** jdm eine Flame schicken

▶ **flame up** VI a (*fire*) auflodern b (*fig, person*) in Wut *or* Rage geraten; (*anger etc*) aufflammen, auflodern

flame-coloured [ˈfleɪmkʌləd] ADJ feuerfarben

flamenco [fləˈmeŋkəʊ] N Flamenco *m* ADJ Flamenco-; **~ dancer** Flamencotänzer(in) *m(f)*

flame: **flame mail** N (= *Comput*) Flame *nt*, beleidigende E-Mail; **flameproof** [ˈfleɪmpru:f] ADJ feuerfest, feuersicher; *textiles* flammensicher; **flame-red** ADJ feuerrot; **flame retardant** ADJ, N = **fire retardant**; **flame test** N Flammprobe *f*; **flame-thrower** N Flammenwerfer *m*

flaming [ˈfleɪmɪŋ] ADJ a brennend, lodernd; (*fig*) *colour* leuchtend; *rage* hell; *passion* glühend; **he has ~ red hair** er hat feuerrotes Haar; **she was absolutely ~** (*Brit inf*: = *angry*) sie kochte (vor Wut) (*inf*); **to have a ~ row (with sb)** sich (mit jdm) streiten, dass die Fetzen fliegen (*inf*) b (*Brit inf*: = *bloody*) verdammt (*inf*), Scheiß- (*inf*); **it's a ~ nuisance** Mensch, das ist vielleicht ein Mist (*inf*); **it's a ~ waste of time** das ist eine verdammte Zeitverschwendung (*inf*); **it was there all the ~ time** Mensch *or* Scheiße, das war die ganze Zeit da (*inf*); **who does he ~ well think he is?** verdammt noch mal, für wen hält der sich eigentlich? (*inf*)

flamingo [fləˈmɪŋgəʊ] N *pl* **-(e)s** Flamingo *m*

flammable [ˈflæməbl] ADJ leicht entzündbar, feuergefährlich

flan [flæn] N Kuchen *m*; **fruit ~** Obstkuchen *m*

flan case N Tortenboden *m*

Flanders [ˈflɑ:ndəz] N Flandern *nt*

Flanders poppy N (*Bot*) Klatschmohn *m*

flange [flændʒ] N (*on wheel etc*) Spurkranz *m*; (*Tech*: = *ring, collar*) Flansch *m*

flanged [flændʒd] ADJ gebördelt; *tube etc also* geflanscht

flank [flæŋk] N (*of animal, Mil*) Flanke *f*; (*of mountain, building*) Seite *f*, Flanke *f* (*old*) VT a (= *be at side of*) flankieren b (*Mil*) *the enemy* seitlich umgehen; **~ing movement** Flankenbewegung *f*

flannel [ˈflænl] N a Flanell *m* b (*Brit*: = *face flannel*) Waschlappen *m* c (*Brit inf*: = *waffle*) Geschwafel *nt* (*inf*), Gelaber *nt* (*inf*) d **flannels** PL (= *trousers*) Flanellhose *f* ADJ Flanell-; **~ trousers** Flannellhose *f* VI (*Brit inf*: = *waffle*) schwafeln (*inf*), labern (*inf*)

flannelette [ˌflænəˈlet] N (*Brit*) Baumwollflanell *m*; **~ sheet** Biberbetttuch *nt*

flap [flæp] N a (*of pocket*) Klappe *f*; (*of table*) ausziehbarer Teil; (*of tent*) Eingang *m*; (*Aviat*) (Lande)klappe *f*; **a ~ of skin** ein Hautfetzen *m*; (*Med*) ein Hautlappen *m* b (= *sound, of sails, sheeting etc*) Flattern *nt*, Knattern *nt*; (*of wings*) Schlagen *nt* c (= *motion*) **to give sth a ~** leicht auf etw (*acc*) klatschen d (*Brit inf*) helle Aufregung, Panik *f*; **to get in(to) a ~** in helle Aufregung geraten, ins Flattern geraten (*inf*) e (*Phon*) geschlagener Laut VI a (*wings*) schlagen; (*door, shutters*) schlagen, klappern; (*sails, tarpaulin etc*) flattern; **his coat ~ped about his legs** der Mantel schlackerte ihm um die Beine (*inf*); **his ears were ~ping** (*inf*) er spitzte die Ohren b (*Brit inf*) in heller Aufregung sein; **to start to ~** in helle Aufregung geraten; **don't ~** reg dich nicht auf; **there's no need to ~** (das ist) kein Grund zur Aufregung; **she's been ~ping around all morning** sie rennt schon den ganzen Morgen wie ein aufgescheuchtes Huhn durch die Gegend (*inf*) VT **to ~ its wings** mit den Flügeln schlagen; **to ~ one's arms** mit den Armen rudern; **he ~ped the newspaper at the fly** er schlug *or* klatschte mit der Zeitung nach der Fliege

▶ **flap away** VI (*bird*) davonfliegen

flapjack [ˈflæpdʒæk] N (*US*) Pfannkuchen *m*; (*Brit*) Haferkeks *m*

flapper [ˈflæpəʳ] N *modisches Mädchen in den 20er Jahren*

flare [fleəʳ] N a Auflodern *nt*; (*fig, of anger*) Aufbrausen *nt* b (= *signal*) Leuchtsignal *nt*; (*from pistol etc*) Leuchtrakete *f*, Leuchtkugel *f*; (= *fire, landing flare*) Leuchtfeuer *nt* c (*Fashion*) ausgestellter Schnitt; **a skirt with a slight ~** ein leicht ausgestellter Rock; **(a pair of) ~s** (*Brit inf*) eine Hose mit Schlag, eine Schlaghose d (= *solar flare*) Sonneneruption *f*, Fackel *f* e (*Phot*) Reflexlicht *nt* VI a (*match, torch*) aufleuchten; (*sunspot*) aufblitzen b (*trousers, skirts*) ausgestellt sein c (*nostrils*) sich blähen d (*fig, trouble, violence*) ausbrechen, aufflammen; **tempers ~d** die Gemüter erhitzten sich VT *nostrils* aufblähen

▶ **flare up** VI (*lit, fig*: *situation, affair*) aufflackern, auflodern; (*fig, person*) aufbrausen, auffahren; (*injury*) wieder Schwierigkeiten machen; (*fighting, epidemic*) ausbrechen; (*anger*) zum Ausbruch kommen; **his acne flared up** seine Akne trat wieder auf; **she flared up at me** sie fuhr mich an

flared [fleəd] ADJ *trousers, skirt* ausgestellt; **~ nostrils** geblähte Nüstern

flare: **flare path** N (*Aviat*) Leuchtpfad *m*; **flare pistol** N Leuchtpistole *f*; **flare-up** [ˈfleərʌp] N (*of situation*) Aufflackern *nt*, Auflodern *nt*; (*of person*) Aufbrausen *nt*; (*of fighting, epidemic*) Ausbruch *m*; (= *sudden dispute*) (plötzlicher) Krach

flash [flæʃ] N a (*of light*) Aufblinken *nt no pl*; (*very bright*) Aufblitzen *nt no pl*; (*of metal, jewels etc*) Blitzen *nt*, Blinken *nt no pl*; (*Mot*) Lichthupe *f no pl*; **there was a sudden ~ of light** plötzlich blitzte es hell auf; **to give sb a ~** (*Mot*) jdn (mit der Lichthupe) anblinken; **~ of lightning** Blitz *m*; **he gave two quick ~es with his torch** er blinkte zweimal kurz mit der Taschenlampe; **the ~es come at regular intervals** es blinkt in regelmäßigen Abständen; **three short ~es is the Morse sign for S** dreimal kurz blinken ist *or* drei kurze Blinkzeichen sind das Morsezeichen für S b (*fig*) (= *newsflash*) Kurzmeldung *f*; **~ of anger** Wutausbruch *m*; **~ of colour** (*Brit*) *or* **color** (*US*) Farbtupfer *m*; **~ of wit/inspiration** Geistesblitz *m*; **in a ~** blitzartig, wie der Blitz; **as quick as a ~** blitzschnell; **a ~ in the pan** (*inf*) ein Strohfeuer *nt* c (*Mil, on uniform*) Abzeichen *nt* d (*Phot*) Blitz(licht *nt*) *m*; **to use a ~** Blitzlicht benutzen e (*US inf*: = *torch*) Taschenlampe *f* VI a (*light*) aufblinken; (*very brightly*) aufblitzen; (*repeatedly*: *indicators etc*) blinken; (*metal, jewels, teeth*) blitzen; (*Mot*) die Lichthupe benutzen; **to ~ on and off** immer wieder aufblinken; **her eyes ~ed (with anger)** ihre Augen blitzten (wütend); **a message ~ed (up) onto the screen** eine Nachricht blinkte auf dem Bildschirm auf b (= *move quickly*: *vehicle, person*) sausen, schießen, flitzen (*all inf*); **a smile ~ed across his face** ein Lächeln huschte über sein Gesicht; **to ~ past** *or* **by** vorbeisausen *etc*; (*holidays etc*) vorbeifliegen; **the time ~ed past** die Zeit verflog im Nu; **the thought ~ed through my mind that …** mir kam plötzlich der Gedanke, dass …, es schoss mir durch den Kopf, dass … VT a *light* aufblitzen *or* aufleuchten lassen; *SOS, message* blinken; **to ~ a torch on sb** jdn mit der Taschenlampe anleuchten; **to ~ a torch in sb's face** jdm mit der Taschenlampe ins Gesicht leuchten; **to ~ one's headlights** die Lichthupe betätigen; **to ~ one's headlights at sb, to ~ sb** jdn mit der Lichthupe anblinken; **she ~ed him a look of contempt** sie blitzte ihn verächtlich an; **he ~ed his famous smile** er ließ sein berühmtes Lächeln aufblitzen b (*inf*: = *show, wave*: *also* **flash around**) schwenken (*inf*), protzen mit; *diamond ring* blitzen lassen; *identity card* kurz vorzeigen; **don't ~ all that money around** wedel nicht so mit dem vielen Geld herum (*inf*); **those images were ~ed across television screens all around the world** diese Bilder wurden auf Fernsehschirmen in der ganzen Welt gezeigt ADJ (*inf*: = *showy*) protzig (*pej*); (= *smart*) schick

▶ **flash back** VI (*Film*) zurückblenden (*to* auf +*acc*); **his mind flashed back to the events of the last year** er erinnerte sich plötzlich an die Ereignisse des letzten Jahres

flash: **flashback** N (*Film*) Rückblende *f*; **flashbulb** N (*Phot*) Blitzbirne *f*; **flash burn** N Verbrennung *f* (*durch kurzzeitige Strahlungshitze*); **flash card** N (*Sch*) Leselernkarte *f*; **flashcube** N (*Phot*) Blitzwürfel *m*; **flash drive** N (*Comput*) Flashlaufwerk *nt*

flasher [ˈflæʃəʳ] N a (*Mot*) Lichthupe *f* b (*inf*: = *person exposing himself/herself*) Exhibitionist(in) *m(f)*

flash: **flash flood** N flutartige Überschwemmung; **flashforward** N (*Film*) Zeitsprung *m* (nach vorn); **flash gun** N Elektronenblitzgerät *nt*; **flash Harry** N (*Brit inf*) Lackaffe *m* (*pej inf*)

flashily [ˈflæʃɪlɪ] ADV auffallend, auffällig

flashing [ˈflæʃɪŋ] N (*Build*) Verwahrung *f*, Kehlblech *nt*

flash: **flashlight** N a (*Phot*) Blitzlicht *nt* b (*esp US*: = *torch*) Taschenlampe *f* c (= *signal lamp*) Leuchtfeuer *nt*; **flash mob** N Flash Mob *m*, *über das Internet verabredete Menschenansammlung, die eine gemeinsame Aktion durchführt und sich unmittelbar danach wieder auflöst*; **flash photography** N Blitz(licht)fotografie *f*; **flash point** N (*Chem*) Flammpunkt *m*; (*fig*) Siedepunkt *m*

flashy [ˈflæʃɪ] ADJ (+*er*) auffallend, auffällig; **Helen's outfit is totally ~** (*inf*) Helens Klamotten sind total schrill *or* grell *or* flashig (*inf*)

flask [flɑ:sk] N Flakon *m*; (*Chem*) Glaskolben *m*; (*for spirits, carried in pocket*) Flachmann *m* (*inf*), Reiseflasche *f*; (= *vacuum flask*) Thermosflasche *f*

flat[1] [flæt] ADJ (+*er*) a flach; *tyre, nose, feet* platt; *surface* eben; **he stood ~ against the wall** er stand platt gegen die Wand gedrückt; **as ~**

as a pancake *(inf, tyre)* total platt; *(countryside)* total flach; **~ roof** Flachdach *nt*; **to fall ~ on one's face** auf die Nase fallen; **to lie ~** flach *or* platt liegen

b *(fig)* fade; *painting, photo* flach, kontrastarm; *colour* matt, stumpf, glanzlos; *joke, remark* abgedroschen, öde, müde; *trade, market* lau, lahm, lustlos; *battery* leer; *(= stale) beer, wine* schal, abgestanden; **in a ~ voice** mit ausdrucksloser Stimme; **she felt a bit ~** sie fühlte sich ein bisschen daneben *(inf)*, sie hatte zu nichts Lust; **to fall ~** *(joke)* nicht ankommen; *(play etc)* durchfallen

c *refusal, denial* glatt, deutlich; **and that's ~** und damit basta

d *(Mus: = out of tune) instrument* zu tief (gestimmt); *voice* zu tief

e *(Comm)* Pauschal-; **~ rate** Pauschale *f*; *(Internet)* Flatrate *f*; **to charge a ~ rate of interest** einen pauschalen Zinssatz berechnen; **to get a ~ rate of pay** pauschal bezahlt werden; **~ fare** Einheitstarif *m*

ADV a *turn down, refuse* rundweg, kategorisch; **he told me ~ (out) that …** er sagte mir klipp und klar, dass …

b *(Mus)* **to sing/play ~** zu tief singen/spielen

c in ten seconds ~ in sage und schreibe (nur) zehn Sekunden

d ~ broke *(inf)* total pleite *(inf)*

e ~ out *(inf: = exhausted)* total erledigt *(inf)*; *(= asleep, drunk)* hinüber *(inf)*; **to go ~ out** voll aufdrehen *(inf)*; *(in car also)* Spitze fahren *(inf)*; **to work** *or* **go ~ out** auf Hochtouren arbeiten; **to be lying ~ out** platt am Boden liegen

N a *(of hand)* Fläche *f*; *(of blade)* flache Seite

b *(Geog)* Ebene *f*; **on the ~** *(= on the plain)* in der Ebene; *(= on a flat surface)* auf ebener Fläche

c *(Mus)* Erniedrigungszeichen *nt*, b *nt*

d *(Aut)* Platte(r) *m (inf)*, (Reifen)panne *f*

e *(Theat)* Kulisse *f*

f *(Sport)* **the ~** das Flachrennen; *(= season)* die Flachrennsaison

flat² N *(esp Brit)* Wohnung *f*

flat: **flat-bed lorry** N Tieflader *m*; **flat bench** N *(in fitness centre)* Flachbank *f*; **flatboat** N Prahm *m*, Flachboot *nt*; **flat-bottomed** ['flæt,bɒtəmd] ADJ *boat, bowl* flach; **flat-chested** ADJ flachbrüstig; **flat dweller** N *(Brit)* Wohnungsbewohner(in) *m(f)*; **flat feet** PL Plattfüße *pl*; **flatfish** N Plattfisch *m*; **flatfoot** N *(inf: = policeman)* Polyp *m (inf)*; **flat-footed** ADJ plattfüßig; **flat-hunting** N *(Brit)* Wohnungssuche *f*; **to go/be ~** auf Wohnungssuche gehen/sein; **flatiron** N *(old)* Plätteisen *nt*; **flatlet** N *(Brit)* kleine Wohnung

flatly ['flætlɪ] ADV **a** *(= completely) refuse, deny, reject* kategorisch, rundweg; *contradict* aufs Schärfste; **to be ~ against** *or* **opposed to sth** etw rundweg ablehnen; *(in principle)* kategorisch gegen etw sein; **to be ~ opposed to doing sth** kategorisch dagegen sein, etw zu tun **b** *(= unemotionally) say, state* ausdruckslos, nüchtern

flatmate ['flætmeɪt] N *(Brit)* Mitbewohner(in) *m(f)*

flatness ['flætnɪs] N **a** Flachheit *f*; *(of nose)* Plattheit *f*; *(of surface)* Ebenheit *f* **b** *(fig)* Fadheit *f*; *(of painting, photo)* Flachheit *f*, Kontrastarmut *f*; *(of colour)* Stumpfheit *f*; *(of joke, remark)* Abgedroschenheit *f*; *(of trade, market)* Lustlosigkeit *f*; *(of beer, wine)* Schalheit *f* **c** *(of refusal, denial)* Deutlichkeit *f*, Direktheit *f*

flat: **flat pack** N *(Brit: = furniture)* flaches Paket; **it arrives as a ~** es kommt flach verpackt an; **flat-pack** ADJ **~ furniture** Möbel *pl* zur Selbstmontage; **flat paint** N Grundierfarbe *f*; **flat race** N Flachrennen *nt*; **flat racing** N Flachrennen *nt*; **flat-rate** ADJ pauschal; **~ internet access** Flatrate *f*; **flat screen** *(Comput)* N Flachbildschirm *m* ADJ **flat-screen monitor** Flachbildschirm *m*; **flat season** N Flachrennsaison *f*

flatten ['flætn] VT **a** *path, road, field* ebnen, planieren; *metal* flach *or* platt hämmern *or* schlagen; *(storm etc) crops* zu Boden drücken, niederdrücken; *trees* umwerfen; *town* dem Erdboden gleichmachen **b** *(fig: = defeat)* vernichtend schlagen; *(= knock down)* niederschlagen; *(= demoralize, snub)* zu nichts reduzieren; **that'll ~ him** das wird bei ihm die Luft rauslassen *(inf)* VR **to ~ oneself against sth** sich platt gegen *or* an etw drücken

▶ **flatten out** VI *(countryside)* flach(er) *or* eben(er) werden; *(road)* eben(er) werden; *(Aviat)* ausschweben; *(fig, inflation, demand)* abflachen; *(prices)* nicht mehr so stark steigen VT *sep path* ebnen; *metal* glatt hämmern; *map, paper, fabric* glätten

flatter ['flætəʳ] VT schmeicheln *(+dat)*; **it ~s your figure** das ist sehr vorteilhaft; **I was very ~ed by his remark** ich fühlte mich von seiner Bemerkung sehr geschmeichelt; **you can ~ yourself on being …** Sie können sich *(dat)* etwas darauf einbilden, dass Sie …; **he ~s himself he's a good musician** er bildet sich *(dat)* ein, ein guter Musiker zu sein; **don't ~ yourself!** bilde dir ja nichts ein!

flatterer ['flætərəʳ] N Schmeichler(in) *m(f)*

flattering ['flætərɪŋ] ADJ **a** *(= complimentary) remark* schmeichelhaft; *person* schmeichlerisch; **she was very ~ about you** sie hat sich sehr schmeichelhaft über Sie geäußert; **this was hardly ~ to her** das war nicht gerade schmeichelhaft für sie **b** *(= becoming, attractive) clothes, colour* vorteilhaft; *photograph* schmeichelhaft; **lighter hair shades are more ~ to your complexion** hellere Haarfarben sind vorteilhafter für Ihren Teint

flatteringly ['flætərɪŋlɪ] ADV **a** *say, write* schmeichlerisch **b** *(= becomingly, attractively) posed, dressed* vorteilhaft

flattery ['flætərɪ] N *(= compliments)* Schmeicheleien *pl*; **~ will get you nowhere** mit Schmeicheln kommst du nicht weiter

flattop N *(US inf: = aircraft carrier)* Flugzeugträger *m*

flatulence ['flætjʊləns] N Blähung(en) *f(pl)*, Flatulenz *f (spec)*; **to cause ~** Blähungen verursachen, blähen

flatulent ['flætjʊlənt] ADJ aufgebläht; *food* blähend

flat: **flatware** ['flætwɛəʳ] N *(US: = cutlery)* Besteck *nt*; *(= plates etc)* Geschirr *nt*; **flatwork** N *(US)* Mangelwäsche *f*; **flatworm** N Plattwurm *m*

flaunt [flɔːnt] VT *wealth, knowledge* zur Schau stellen, protzen mit; **she ~ed her body in front of him** sie stellte ihren Körper vor ihm zur Schau; **he ~ed his freedom before her** er prahlte vor ihr mit seiner Freiheit; **to ~ oneself** sich groß in Szene setzen

flautist ['flɔːtɪst] N Flötist(in) *m(f)*

flavour, *(US)* **flavor** ['fleɪvəʳ] N *(= taste)* Geschmack *m*; *(= flavouring)* Aroma *nt*; *(fig)* Beigeschmack *m*; **strawberry-~ ice cream** Eis *nt* mit Erdbeergeschmack; **with a lemon ~** mit Zitronengeschmack; **20 different ~s** 20 verschiedene Geschmackssorten; **the film gives the ~ of Paris in the twenties** der Film vermittelt die Atmosphäre des Paris der zwanziger Jahre *or* Zwanzigerjahre; **he/it is ~ of the month** *(inf)* er/es ist diesen Monat in *(inf)* VT Geschmack verleihen *(+dat) or* geben *(+dat)*; **pineapple-~ed** mit Ananasgeschmack

flavouring, *(US)* **flavoring** ['fleɪvərɪŋ] N *(Cook)* Aroma(stoff *m*) *nt*; **vanilla/rum ~** Vanille-/Rumaroma *nt*

flavourless, *(US)* **flavorless** ['fleɪvəlɪs] ADJ fad(e), geschmacklos

flaw [flɔː] N *(lit)* Fehler *m*; *(fig also)* Mangel *m*; *(in sb's character also)* Mangel *m*, Defekt *m*; *(Jur, in contract etc)* (Form)fehler *m* VT **her argument was ~ed by lack of evidence** ihr Argument wurde durch Mangel an Beweisen entkräftet; **her beauty was not ~ed by the slightest imperfection** ihre Schönheit wurde durch keinen Mangel getrübt

flawed [flɔːd] ADJ fehlerhaft; **his logic was ~** seine Logik enthielt Fehler

flawless ['flɔːlɪs] ADJ *performance* fehlerlos; *behaviour* untadelig, tadellos; *complexion* makellos; *diamond* lupenrein; **~ English** fehlerloses *or* einwandfreies *or* tadelloses Englisch; **the weather was ~** das Wetter war ideal

flax [flæks] N *(Bot)* Flachs *m*

flaxen ['flæksən] ADJ *hair* flachsfarben; *(Tex)* flächse(r)n

flaxen-haired ['flæksən'hɛəd] ADJ flachsblond

flay [fleɪ] VT **a** *(= skin) animal* abziehen, häuten; *person* die Haut abziehen *+dat*; *(= beat)* verdreschen; *(= whip)* auspeitschen; **to ~ sb alive** jdn gründlich verdreschen **b** *(fig: = criticize)* kein gutes Haar lassen an *(+dat)*, heruntermachen *(inf)*

flea [fliː] N Floh *m*; **to send sb off with a ~ in his/her ear** *(inf)* jdn wie einen begossenen Pudel abziehen lassen *(inf)*

flea: **fleabag** N **a** *(US inf: = hotel)* Flohbude *f (inf)*, Absteige *f* **b** *(inf, = person)* Schrulle *f (inf)*; **fleabite** N Flohbiss *m*; **it's just a ~** *(fig)* das ist eine Kleinigkeit; **flea-bitten** ADJ voller Flohbisse; *(inf)* vergammelt *(inf)*; **flea circus** N Flohzirkus *m*; **flea collar** N Flohhalsband *nt*; **flea market** N Flohmarkt *m*; **fleapit** N *(Brit inf)* Flohkino *nt (inf)*

fleck [flek] N *(of red etc)* Tupfen *m*; *(of mud, paint) (= blotch)* Fleck(en) *m*; *(= speckle)* Spritzer *m*; *(of fluff, dust)* Teilchen *nt*, Flöckchen *nt* VT sprenkeln; *(with mud etc)* bespritzen; **~ed wool** melierte Wolle; **blue ~ed with white** blau mit weißen Tupfen *or* Punkten, blau und weiß gesprenkelt; **the sky was ~ed with little clouds** der Himmel war mit Schäfchenwolken übersät

flection ['flekʃən] N *(Gram)* Flexion *f*, Beugung *f*

flectional ['flekʃənəl] ADJ **~ ending** Flexionsendung *f*

fled [fled] *pret, ptp of* **flee**

fledged [fledʒd] ADJ *bird* flügge → **fully fledged**

fledgling ['fledʒlɪŋ] N *(Orn: = young bird)* Jungvogel *m* ADJ *democracy, organization, business* jung; *person* frischgebacken *(inf)*; **~ artist** Nachwuchskünstler(in) *m(f)*; **~ teacher/writer** Junglehrer(in) *m(f)*/-autor(in) *m(f)*; **their feminist movement is ~ at best** ihre Feministenbewegung steckt noch in den Kinderschuhen; **they began their ~ career on a shoestring** sie haben ganz klein mit sehr wenig Geld angefangen

flee [fliː] *pret, ptp* **fled** VI fliehen, flüchten *(from* vor *+dat)*; **to ~ from temptation** der Versuchung entfliehen VT *town, country* fliehen *or* flüchten aus; *temptation, danger* entfliehen *(+dat)*

fleece [fliːs] N Vlies *nt*, Schaffell *nt*; *(= fabric, natural)* Schaffell *nt*; *(artificial)* Webpelz *m*, Flausch *m* VT **a** *sheep* scheren **b** *(fig inf)* **to ~ sb (out of his/her money)** jdn schröpfen

fleecy ['fliːsɪ] ADJ **a** *sheep, blanket, lining, garment* flauschig **b** *(fig) snow* flockig; **~ clouds** Schäfchenwolken *pl*

fleet¹ [fliːt] N **a** *(Naut)* Geschwader *nt*; *(= entire naval force)* Flotte *f*; **Fleet Air Arm** Marineluftwaffe *f*; **merchant ~** Handelsflotte *f* **b** *(of cars, coaches, buses etc)* (Fuhr)park *m*; **he owns a ~ of trucks/taxis** er hat einen Lastwagenpark/ein Taxiunternehmen; **~ business** Firmenwagengeschäft *nt*

fleet² ADJ *(+er)* schnell, flink; **~ of foot, ~-footed** schnell- *or* leichtfüßig

fleet admiral N *(US)* Großadmiral *m*

fleetness ['fliːtnɪs] N **a** *(= quickness)* Schnelligkeit *f* **b** *(fig poet: = transience)* Flüchtigkeit *f (geh)*, Vergänglichkeit *f*

fleeting ['fliːtɪŋ] ADJ *moment, thought* flüchtig; **a ~ visit** eine Stippvisite *(inf)*; **to catch** *or* **get a ~ glimpse of sb/sth** einen flüchtigen Blick auf jdn/etw werfen können; **to make a ~ appearance** sich kurz sehen lassen; *(on TV)* kurz auftreten

fleetingly [ˈfliːtɪŋlɪ] ADV *wonder, smile, think, see* flüchtig; *visible* ganz kurz; **they were ~ here** sie waren ganz kurz hier

Fleet Street N *(Brit)* Fleet Street *f*; **he had a job on ~** er hatte einen Job als Journalist

Fleming [ˈflemɪŋ] N Flame *m*, Flämin *f*

Flemish [ˈflemɪʃ] ADJ flämisch N a **the ~** *pl* die Flamen *pl* b *(Ling)* Flämisch *nt*

flesh [fleʃ] N a Fleisch *nt*; *(of fruit)* (Frucht)-fleisch *nt*; *(of vegetable)* Mark *nt*; **to put on ~** *(animals)* zunehmen; *(person also)* Fleisch auf die Rippen bekommen *(inf)*; **all that bare ~ on the beach** diese Fleischbeschau am Strand
b *(fig)* **one's own ~ and blood** sein eigen(es) Fleisch und Blut; **it was more than ~ and blood could bear** das war einfach nicht zu ertragen; **I'm only ~ and blood** ich bin auch nur aus Fleisch und Blut; **in the ~** in Person, in natura; **he's gone the way of all ~** er ist den Weg allen Fleisches gegangen; **to press the ~** *(inf)* Hände drücken; **to put ~ on an idea/a proposal** eine Idee/einen Vorschlag ausgestalten
c *(Rel)* Fleisch *nt*; **sins of the ~** Sünden *pl* des Fleisches

▶ **flesh out** VT *sep idea, proposal, thesis etc* ausgestalten; *details* eingehen auf *(+acc)*

flesh: **flesh colour**, *(US)* **flesh color** N Fleischfarbe *f*; **flesh-coloured**, *(US)* **flesh-colored** [ˈfleʃkʌləd] ADJ fleischfarben; **flesh-eating** ADJ fleischfressend

flesher [ˈfleʃəʳ] N a *(= knife)* Ausfleischmesser *nt* b *(esp Scot: = butcher)* Fleischer(in) *m(f)*, Metzger(in) *m(f)*

fleshings [ˈfleʃɪŋz] PL *(= tights)* Trikotstrumpfhose(n *pl*) *f*

fleshly [ˈfleʃlɪ] ADJ *(+er)* a *(= corporeal)* fleischlich, leiblich b *(fig: = sensual) pleasures, sin* fleischlich *(fig)*, sinnlich c *(= worldly)* irdisch, menschlich

flesh wound N Fleischwunde *f*

fleshy [ˈfleʃɪ] ADJ *(+er)* a *(= fat) face, cheeks, nose* fleischig; *person* füllig b *(= consisting of flesh)* fleischern, aus Fleisch bestehend; *(= similar to flesh)* fleischartig; **~ tones** fleischfarbene Töne *pl*; *(in painting)* Fleischtöne *pl* c *(Bot) fruit, leaves* fleischig

fletch [fletʃ] VT *arrow* befiedern

fletcher [ˈfletʃəʳ] N Pfeilmacher(in) *m(f)*

fleur de lys [ˌflɜːdəˈliː] N *pl* **-s - -** [ˌflɜːdəˈliːz] bourbonische Lilie

flew [fluː] *pret of* **fly**[2]

flex [fleks] N a *(Brit)* Schnur *f*; *(heavy duty)* Kabel *nt* b *(inf, also* **flex tool***)* Flex® *f*, Trennschleifer *m* VT *body, knees, arm etc* beugen; **to ~ one's muscles** *(lit, fig)* seine Muskeln spielen lassen

flexibility [ˌfleksɪˈbɪlɪtɪ] N a *(lit)* Biegsamkeit *f*, Elastizität *f* b *(fig)* Flexibilität *f*; *(of engine)* Elastizität *f*

flexible [ˈfleksəbl] ADJ a *(lit) material, object, limbs, joints, body* biegsam, elastisch; **~ coupling** *(Tech)* elastisches Gelenk b *(fig) person, approach, attitude, timetable, system* flexibel; *engine* elastisch; **~ working hours** gleitende Arbeitszeit, Gleitzeit *f*; **to work ~ hours** gleitende Arbeitszeit haben, Gleitzeit arbeiten; **to be ~ in one's approach** eine flexible Einstellung haben; **to be ~ about sth** in Bezug auf etw *(acc)* flexibel sein

flexibly [ˈfleksəblɪ] ADV a *(lit) connected, mounted* elastisch b *(fig) use, respond, interpret, work* flexibel

flexion [ˈflekʃən] N = **flection**

flexional [ˈflekʃənəl] ADJ = **flectional**

flex(i)time [ˈfleks(ɪ)taɪm] N Gleitzeit *f*

flexor (muscle) [ˈfleksə(mʌsl)] N Beuger *m*

flibbertigibbet [ˌflɪbətɪˈdʒɪbɪt] N (junges) Gänschen

flick [flɪk] N *(with finger)* Schnipsen *nt no pl*; *(of tail)* kurzer Schlag; *(with whip)* Schnalzen *nt no pl*; **with a ~ of his fingers/the whip** mit einem Finger-/Peitschenschnalzen; **a ~ of the wrist** eine schnelle Drehung des Handgelenks
VT *whip* schnalzen *or* knallen mit; *fingers* schnalzen mit; *(with whip) horse etc* leicht schlagen; *(with fingers) switch* anknipsen; *dust, ash* wegschnipsen; *(with cloth)* wegwedeln; **she ~ed her hair out of her eyes** sie strich sich *(dat)* die Haare aus den Augen; **I'll just ~ a duster round the sitting room** *(inf)* ich wedel *or* geh eben mal mit dem Staubtuch durchs Wohnzimmer *(inf)*; **she ~ed the light on** sie knipste das Licht an; **he ~ed the piece of paper onto the floor** er schnipste das Papier auf den Fußboden
VI **the snake's tongue ~ed in and out** die Schlange züngelte

▶ **flick off** VT *sep* wegschnippen; *(with duster)* wegwedeln

▶ **flick through** VI *+prep obj book* (schnell) durchblättern; *pages* (schnell) umblättern; *TV channels* (schnell) wechseln

flicker [ˈflɪkəʳ] VI *(flame, candle, light)* flackern; *(TV)* flimmern; *(needle on dial)* zittern; *(eyelid)* flattern, zucken; **the snake's tongue ~ed in and out** die Schlange züngelte; **a smile ~ed across his face** ein Lächeln huschte über sein Gesicht; **his eyes ~ed toward(s) the door** er blickte kurz zur Tür N *(of flame, candle, light)* Flackern *nt*; *(of TV)* Flimmern *nt*; *(of needle on dial)* Zittern *nt*; *(of eyelid)* Flattern *nt*; **a ~ of hope** ein Hoffnungsschimmer *m*; **without so much as the ~ of a smile** ohne (auch nur) den Anflug eines Lächelns

flicker-free [ˈflɪkəˈfriː] ADJ *screen etc* flimmerfrei

flick knife N *(Brit)* Klappmesser *nt*, Schnappmesser *nt*

flicks [flɪks] PL *(inf)* Kintopp *m (inf)*; **to/at the ~** in den/im Kintopp *(inf)*

flier [ˈflaɪəʳ] N a *(Aviat: = pilot)* Flieger(in) *m(f)*; **to be a good/bad ~** *(person)* das Fliegen gut/nicht vertragen; *(bird)* ein guter/schlechter Flieger sein b *(dated US) (= train)* Schnellzug *m*; *(= fast coach)* Expressbus *m* c **to take a ~** *(Brit, = leap)* einen Riesensprung *or* -satz machen; *(= fall)* der Länge nach hinfallen d *(Brit: = flying start)* fliegender Start; **he got a ~** er hat einen fliegenden Start gemacht e *(= leaflet)* Flugblatt *nt*

flies [flaɪz] PL *(Brit: on trousers)* (Hosen)schlitz *m*

flight[1] [flaɪt] N a Flug *m*; **in ~** *(bird)* im Flug; *(Aviat)* in der Luft; **to take ~** *(bird)* davonfliegen, auffliegen; **the principles of ~** die Prinzipien des Fliegens; **I'm getting the next ~ to Glasgow** ich nehme den nächsten Flug *or* das nächste Flugzeug nach Glasgow
b *(group, of birds)* Schwarm *m*, Schar *f*; *(of aeroplanes)* Geschwader *nt*, Formation *f*; **to be in the top ~** *(fig)* zur Spitze gehören; **the top ~ of world tennis** die weltbesten Tennisspieler
c *(of imagination)* Höhenflug *m*; **~ of fancy** geistiger Höhenflug
d **~ (of stairs)** Treppe *f*; **he lives six ~s up** er wohnt sechs Treppen hoch; **a ~ of hurdles** eine Gruppe von Hürden; **he fell at the second ~** er fiel bei der zweiten Hürde
e *(on dart, arrow)* Steuerfeder *f*

flight[2] N Flucht *f*; **to put the enemy to ~** den Feind in die Flucht schlagen; **to take (to) ~** die Flucht ergreifen; **the ~ of capital abroad** die Kapitalflucht ins Ausland; **to be in full ~** Hals über Kopf auf der Flucht sein; *(fig)* auf Hochtouren sein

flight: **flight attendant** N Flugbegleiter(in) *m(f)*; **flight bag** N Schultertasche *f*; **flight case** N Bordcase *m*; **flight control** N *(Aviat)* Flugsicherung *f*; *(in aircraft)* Flugsteuerung *f*, Steuerfläche *f*; **flight controller** N Fluglotse *m*, Fluglotsin *f*; **flight crew** N Flugbesatzung *f*; **flight deck** N a *(Naut)* Flugdeck *nt* b *(Aviat)* Cockpit *nt*; **flight engineer** N Bordingenieur(in) *m(f)*; **flight feather** N Schwungfeder *f*; **flightless** ADJ nicht flugfähig; **flight lieutenant** N *(Brit Aviat)* Oberleutnant *m* der Luftwaffe; **flight log** N Bordbuch *nt*; **flight mechanic** N Bordmechaniker(in) *m(f)*; **flight number** N Flugnummer *f*; **flight path** N Flugbahn *f*; *(= route)* Flugroute *f*; **flight plan** N Flugablaufplan *m*; **flight recorder** N Flugschreiber *m*; **flight safety** N Flugsicherheit *f*; **flight sergeant** N Haupt- *or* Oberfeldwebel *m* (der Luftwaffe); **flight simulator** N Simulator *m*; **flight test** N Flugtest *m*; **flight-test** VT im Flug testen, flugtesten

flighty [ˈflaɪtɪ] ADJ *(+er) (= fickle)* unbeständig, flatterhaft; *(= empty-headed)* gedankenlos

flimflam [ˈflɪmflæm] N *(inf: = rubbish)* Blödsinn *m*; *(= lies)* Schwindel *m*

flimsily [ˈflɪmzɪlɪ] ADV *built, constructed* leicht, nicht solide; **a ~ bound book** ein schlecht gebundenes Buch

flimsiness [ˈflɪmzɪnɪs] N a *(= weak construction)* leichte *or* wenig solide Bauweise; *(of book)* schlechte *or* billige Aufmachung; **in spite of the ~ of the wings** trotz der leichten Bauweise der Tragflächen b *(= thinness: of material, garment)* Dünne *f* c *(fig, of excuse)* Fadenscheinigkeit *f*; *(of reason)* mangelnde Stichhaltigkeit; *(of evidence)* Dürftigkeit *f*

flimsy [ˈflɪmzɪ] ADJ *(+er)* a *(= fragile) structure* leicht gebaut, wenig solide; *material, cup, paper* dünn; *box* instabil; **of ~ construction** nicht sehr stabil gebaut b *(= thin) material, garment* dünn, leicht; **a ~ dress** ein Fähnchen *nt* c *(fig) evidence* dürftig; *excuse* fadenscheinig; *reason* wenig stichhaltig; **on ~ grounds** ohne stichhaltige Gründe N *(= paper)* Durchschlagpapier *nt*; *(= document)* Durchschlag *m*

flinch [flɪntʃ] VI a *(= wince)* zurückzucken; **without ~ing** ohne mit der Wimper zu zucken b *(fig)* **to ~ from sth** vor etw *(dat)* zurückschrecken; **he ~ed from telling her the truth** er scheute sich, ihr die Wahrheit zu sagen

fling [flɪŋ] *vb: pret, ptp* **flung** N a *(= act of flinging)* Wurf *m*, Schleudern *nt no pl*
b *(fig inf)* Anlauf *m*; **to give sth a ~** sich an etw *(dat)* versuchen, etw (aus)probieren; **youth must have its ~** die Jugend muss sich austoben; **to have a ~** *(= enjoy oneself)* sich austoben; **to have a last** *or* **final ~** sich noch einmal richtig austoben
c *(inf: = relationship)* **to have a ~ (with sb)** eine Affäre (mit jdm) haben, etwas mit jdm haben *(inf)*
d = **Highland fling**
VT *(lit, fig)* schleudern; **to ~ the window open** das Fenster aufstoßen; **the door was flung open** die Tür flog auf; **to ~ one's arms round sb's neck** jdm die Arme um den Hals werfen; **she flung herself into his arms** sie warf sich in seine Arme; **to ~ a coat round one's shoulders** sich *(dat)* einen Mantel über die Schulter(n) werfen; **to ~ oneself into a task** sich in eine Aufgabe stürzen; **to ~ oneself out of the window/off a bridge** sich aus dem Fenster/von einer Brücke stürzen; **to ~ oneself into a chair/to the ground** sich in einen Sessel/auf den Boden werfen; **you shouldn't just ~ yourself at him** *(fig inf)* du solltest dich ihm nicht so an den Hals werfen

▶ **fling away** VT *sep* wegwerfen, wegschmeißen *(inf)*; *(fig) money* vergeuden, verschwenden

▶ **fling back** VT *sep one's head* zurückwerfen; *door* aufwerfen

▶ **fling down** VT *sep (lit)* runterschmeißen *(inf)*; **to fling down the gauntlet** den Fehdehandschuh hinwerfen *or* hinschleudern

▶ **fling off** VT *sep (lit) coat* abwerfen; *opponent* abschütteln; *(fig) remark* hinwerfen; *restraints* von sich werfen

▶ **fling out** VT *sep unwanted object* wegwerfen, wegschmeißen *(inf)*; *person* hinauswerfen, rausschmeißen *(inf)*

▶ **fling up** VT *sep* a *(= throw up)* hochwerfen; **to fling one's arms up in horror** entsetzt die Hände über dem Kopf zusammenschlagen b *(fig inf)* **to fling sth up at sb** jdm etw unter die Nase reiben

flint [flɪnt] N a *(for cigarette lighter)* Feuerstein *m* b *(= stone)* Feuerstein *m*, Flint(stein) *m*

flint: **flint axe** N (Feuer)steinbeil *nt*; **flint glass** N Flintglas *nt*; **flintlock** N Steinschlossgewehr *nt*

flinty [ˈflɪntɪ] ADJ *(+er)* **a** *(= hardhearted) person* hartherzig; *heart* steinern; *eyes, gaze* hart **b** *soil, ground* feuersteinhaltig

flip [flɪp] **N** **a** Schnipser *m*; **by the ~ of a coin** durch Hochwerfen einer Münze **b** *(= somersault)* Salto *m*; **backward ~** Salto rückwärts **c** *(Aviat inf)* Rundflug *m* **d** *(= drink)* Flip *m* **ADJ** *(inf: = flippant)* schnodderig *(inf)* **VT** schnippen, schnipsen; *switch* knipsen; *(inf) record* rumdrehen *(inf)*; **to ~ the pages (of a book)** die Seiten (in einem Buch) umblättern; **to ~ a coin** eine Münze werfen; **to ~ one's lid** *(inf)* durchdrehen *(inf)*, aus dem Häuschen geraten *(inf)* **VI** *(inf)* durchdrehen *(inf)* **INTERJ** *(Brit, inf)* verflixt *(inf)*

▶ **flip off** VT *sep* wegschnipsen; *top, catch* aufklappen

▶ **flip out** VI *(inf)* ausflippen *(inf)*

▶ **flip over** **VT** *sep* umdrehen; *pages of book* wenden **VI** sich (um)drehen; *(plane)* sich in der Luft (um)drehen

▶ **flip through** VI *+prep obj book* durchblättern; *pages* umblättern

flip chart [ˈflɪptʃɑːt] N Flipchart *f*

flip-flop [ˈflɪpflɒp] N **a** *(Sport)* Flickflack *m* **b** *(Elec)* Flipflop *m* **c** *(Brit: = sandal)* Gummilatsche *f (inf)*

flip pack N Klappschachtel *f*

flippancy [ˈflɪpənsɪ] N Leichtfertigkeit *f*; *(= disrespectfulness)* Schnodd(e)rigkeit *f*

flippant [ˈflɪpənt] ADJ *person, tone, attitude* leichtfertig; *remark also* hingeworfen; *(= disrespectful)* schnodd(e)rig *(inf)*; **to sound ~** sich leichtfertig anhören

flippantly [ˈflɪpəntlɪ] ADV *answer, say* leichtfertig; *(= disrespectfully)* schnodd(e)rig *(inf)*

flipper [ˈflɪpəʳ] N Flosse *f*; *(of diver)* (Schwimm)flosse *f*

flipping [ˈflɪpɪŋ] ADJ, ADV *(Brit inf emph)* verdammt *(inf)*

flip: **flip side** N *(of record)* B-Seite *f*; **flip switch** N Kippschalter *m*; **flip top** N Klappdeckel *m*; **flip-top bin** N Abfalleimer *m* mit Klappdeckel

flirt [flɜːt] **VI** flirten; **to ~ with an idea** mit einem Gedanken liebäugeln *or* spielen; **to ~ with danger/disaster** die Gefahr/das Unglück herausfordern **N** **he/she is just a ~** er/sie will nur flirten; **I'm a bit of a ~** ich flirte (für mein Leben) gern

flirtation [flɜːˈteɪʃən] N Flirt *m*; *(= flirting)* Flirten *nt*; **his ~ with death/danger** sein Spiel mit dem Tod/der Gefahr

flirtatious [flɜːˈteɪʃəs] ADJ *woman, behaviour* kokett; **she is very ~** sie flirtet gern

flirty [ˈflɜːtɪ] ADJ **a** *woman, behaviour* kokett **b** *clothes* sexy

flit [flɪt] **VI** **a** *(bats, butterflies etc)* flattern, huschen; *(ghost, person, image)* huschen; **to ~ in and out** *(person)* rein- und rausflitzen; **an idea ~ted through my mind** ein Gedanke schoss mir *or* huschte mir durch den Kopf **b** *(Brit, = move house secretly)* bei Nacht und Nebel ausziehen, sich bei Nacht und Nebel davonmachen **c** *(Scot, N Engl: = move house)* umziehen **N** *(Brit)* **to do a (moonlight) ~** bei Nacht und Nebel umziehen

flitch [flɪtʃ] N Speckseite *f*; *(of halibut)* Heilbuttschnitte *f*

float [fləʊt] **N** **a** *(on fishing line, in cistern, carburettor, on aeroplane)* Schwimmer *m*; *(= anchored raft)* (verankertes) Floß, Schwimmplattform *f*; *(as swimming aid)* Schwimmkork *m*; *(of fish)* Schwimmblase *f*; *(on trawl net)* Korken *m*

b *(= vehicle, in procession)* Festwagen *m*; *(for deliveries)* kleiner Elektrolieferwagen

c *(= ready cash: in till)* Wechselgeld *nt no indef art (zu Geschäftsbeginn)*; *(= loan to start business)* Startkapital *nt*; *(= advance on expenses)* Vorschuss *m*

VI **a** *(on water)* schwimmen; *(= move gently)* treiben; *(in air)* schweben; **the body ~ed (up) to the surface** die Leiche kam an die Wasseroberfläche; **it ~ed downriver** es trieb flussabwärts; **she ~ed down the aisle in a dream** sie schwebte wie im Traum zum Traualtar

b *(Comm, currency)* floaten

VT **a** *boat* zu Wasser bringen; **they ~ed the logs downstream** sie flößten die Baumstämme flussabwärts

b *(Comm, Fin) company* gründen; *loan* lancieren; *shares* auf den Markt bringen; *bond issue* ausgeben; *currency* freigeben, floaten lassen; *(fig) ideas, suggestion* in den Raum stellen, zur Debatte stellen

▶ **float around** VI *(rumour, news)* im Umlauf sein; *(person)* herumschweben *(inf)*; *(things)* herumfliegen *(inf)*

▶ **float away** *or* **off** VI *(on water)* abtreiben, wegtreiben; *(in air)* davonschweben; *(fig, person)* hinwegschweben

▶ **float round** VI = **float around**

floatable [ˈfləʊtəbl] ADJ schwimmfähig; *river* flößbar

floatel [fləʊˈtel] N *(inf)* schwimmendes Hotel

floating [ˈfləʊtɪŋ] **ADJ** **a** *raft, logs* treibend; **~ hotel/restaurant** schwimmendes Hotel/Restaurant **b** *(fig) population* wandernd **c** *(Fin) currency* freigegeben; **~ exchange rate** floatender *or* frei schwankender Wechselkurs **d** *(Math, Comput)* Gleit-; **~ accent** *(Comput)* fliegender Akzent; **~ point** *(Comput)*, Fließ- *or* Gleitkomma *nt* **e** *(Med) kidney* Wander-; *rib* frei **N** *(of currency)* Freigabe *f*, Floating *nt*

floating: **floating bridge** N Schiffsbrücke *f*; **floating capital** N Umlauf- *or* Betriebskapital *nt*; **floating debt** N schwebende Schuld; **floating dock** N Schwimmdock *nt*; **floating ice** N Treibeis *nt*; **floating light** N *(= ship)* Leuchtschiff *nt*; *(= buoy)* Leuchtboje *f*; **floating voter** N *(fig)* Wechselwähler *m*

flock[1] [flɒk] **N** **a** *(of sheep, geese, also Eccl)* Herde *f*; *(of birds)* Schwarm *m*, Schar *f* **b** *(of people)* Schar *f*, Haufen *m (inf)* **VI** in Scharen kommen; **to ~ in** hineinströmen *or* -drängen; **to ~ out** hinausströmen *or* -drängen; **to ~ around sb** sich um jdn scharen *or* drängen

flock[2] N *(Tex)* Flocke *f*

flock wallpaper N Velourstapete *f*

floe [fləʊ] N Treibeis *nt*, Eisscholle *f*

flog [flɒg] VT **a** *(= beat)* prügeln, schlagen; *thief, mutineer* auspeitschen; **you're ~ging a dead horse** *(esp Brit inf)* Sie verschwenden Ihre Zeit **b** *(Brit inf: = sell)* verkloppen, verscherbeln, losschlagen *(all inf)*

▶ **flog off** VT *sep (Brit inf)* verscheuern *(inf)*, verkloppen *(inf)*

flogging [ˈflɒgɪŋ] N Tracht *f* Prügel; *(Jur)* Prügelstrafe *f*; *(of thief, mutineer)* Auspeitschen *nt*; **to bring back ~** die Prügelstrafe wieder einführen; **a public ~** eine öffentliche Auspeitschung

flood [flʌd] **N** **a** *(of water)* Flut *f*; **~s** Überschwemmung *f*, Hochwasser *nt*; *(in several places)* Überschwemmungen *pl*, Hochwasser *nt*; **the Flood** die Sintflut; **the river is in ~** der Fluss führt Hochwasser; **she had a ~ in the kitchen** ihre Küche stand unter Wasser

b *(fig)* Flut *f*, Schwall *m*; **she was in ~s of tears** sie war in Tränen gebadet; **the scene was bathed in a ~ of light** die Szene war lichtüberflutet

c *(also* **flood tide***)* Flut *f*

VT **a** *fields, roads, town* überschwemmen, unter Wasser setzen; **the village/cellar was ~ed** das Dorf/der Keller war überschwemmt *or* stand unter Wasser; **to ~ the engine** den Motor absaufen lassen *(inf)*

b *(storm, rain) river, stream* über die Ufer treten lassen

c *(fig)* überschwemmen, überfluten; **~ed with calls/complaints** mit Anrufen/Beschwerden überhäuft; **~ed with light** lichtdurchflutet, von Licht durchflutet; **she was ~ed with relief** Erleichterung wallte in ihr auf

d *(Comm)* **to ~ the market** den Markt überschwemmen

VI **a** *(river)* über die Ufer treten; *(bath etc)* überfließen, überlaufen; *(cellar)* unter Wasser stehen; *(garden, land)* überschwemmt werden

b *(people)* strömen, sich ergießen *(geh)*; **the crowd ~ed into the streets** die Menge strömte auf die Straßen

▶ **flood back** VI *(memories, feelings)* wieder aufwallen

▶ **flood in** VI *(people, sunshine)* hineinströmen; *(water also)* hineinfließen; **the letters just flooded in** wir/sie *etc* hatten eine Flut von Briefen

▶ **flood out** VT *sep house* überfluten, unter Wasser setzen; **the villagers were flooded out** die Dorfbewohner wurden durch das Hochwasser obdachlos

flood: **flood control** N Hochwasserschutz *m*; **flood disaster** N Flutkatastrophe *f*; **floodgate** N Schleusentor *nt*; **to open the ~s** *(fig)* Tür und Tor öffnen *(to +dat)*

flooding [ˈflʌdɪŋ] N Überschwemmung *f*

flood: **floodlight** *vb: pret, ptp* **floodlit** **VT** *buildings* anstrahlen; *football pitch* mit Flutlicht beleuchten; *(fig, = light brightly)* beleuchten **N** *(= device)* Scheinwerfer *m*; *(= light)* Flutlicht *nt*; **under ~s** unter *or* bei Flutlicht; **floodlighting** N **a** Flutlicht(anlage *f*) *nt* **b** *(of building etc)* Beleuchtung *f*; **floodlit** ADJ **~ football match** Fußballspiel *nt* bei *or* unter Flutlicht; **flood plain** N Schwemmebene *f*; **flood protection** N Hochwasserschutz *m*; **flood tide** N Flut *f*; **flood victim** N *(= person)* Flutopfer *nt*

floor [flɔːʳ] **N** **a** Boden *m*; *(of room)* (Fuß)boden *m*; *(= dance floor)* Tanzboden *m*, Tanzfläche *f*; **ocean ~** Meeresgrund *m*; **valley ~** Talboden *m*; **stone/tiled ~** Stein-/Fliesenboden *m*; **to take to the ~** *(= dance)* aufs Parkett *or* auf den Tanzboden gehen; **to take the ~** *(= speak)* das Wort ergreifen; **to be given the ~** *(= speak)* das Wort erhalten; **to hold** *or* **have the ~** *(speaker)* das Wort haben

b *(= storey: in apartment block etc)* Stock *m*, Stockwerk *nt*; **first ~** *(Brit)* erster Stock; *(US)* Erdgeschoss *nt*, Erdgeschoß *nt (Aus)*; **on the second ~** *(Brit)* im zweiten Stock; *(US)* im ersten Stock

c *(of prices etc)* Minimum *nt*; **property prices have fallen** *or* **dropped through the ~** die Immobilienpreise sind in den Keller gefallen *(inf)*

d *(= main part of chamber)* Plenar- *or* Sitzungssaal *m (also Parl)*; *(of stock exchange)* Parkett *nt*; *(= people present)* Zuhörerschaft *f*; *(Parl)* Abgeordnete *pl*, Haus *nt*; **a question from the ~** eine Frage aus der Zuhörerschaft; *(Brit Parl)* eine Frage aus dem Haus; **~ of the House** *(Brit Parl)* Plenarsaal *m* des Unterhauses; **to cross the ~** *(Brit Parl)* die Partei wechseln

VT **a** *room etc* mit einem (Fuß)boden versehen

b *(= knock down) opponent* zu Boden schlagen

c *(= bewilder)* verblüffen; *(= defeat: question, problem etc)* schaffen *(inf)*; **he looked completely ~ed** er sah völlig perplex aus

floor: **floor area** N Bodenfläche *f*; **floorboard** N Diele *f*, Bohle *f*; **floor cloth** N Scheuer- *or* Putzlappen *m*; **floor covering** N Bodenbelag *m*; **floor debate** N *(Parl)* Plenardebatte *f*; **floor exercise** N Bodenübung *f*

flooring [ˈflɔːrɪŋ] N **a** *(= floor)* (Fuß)boden *m* **b** *(= material)* Fußbodenbelag *m*

floor: **floor lamp** N Stehlampe *f*; **floor leader** N *(US: Parl)* Fraktionsführer(in) *m(f)*; **floor manager** N *(in store)* Abteilungsleiter(in) *m(f) (im Kaufhaus)*; *(TV)* Aufnahmeleiter(in) *m(f)*; **floor model** N (verbilligtes) Ausstellungsstück; **floor plan** N Grundriss *m* (eines Stockwerkes); **floor polish** N Bohnerwachs *nt*; **floor polisher** N *(= tool)* Bohnerbesen *m*; **floor show** N Show *f*, Vorstellung *f (im Nachtklub oder Kabarett)*; **floor space** N Stellraum *m*; **if you've got a sleeping bag we have plenty of ~** wenn du einen Schlafsack hast, wir haben viel Platz auf dem Fußboden; **floor tile** N (Fuß)bodenfliese *f*/-platte *f*;

floor trader N *(St Ex)* Parketthändler(in) *m(f)*; **floor trading** N *(St Ex)* Parketthandel *m*; **floorwalker** N *(US Comm)* Ladenaufsicht *f*; **floor wax** N Bohnerwachs *nt*

floozie, floozy ['flu:zɪ] N *(inf)* Flittchen *nt (inf)*, Schickse *f (inf)*

flop [flɒp] VI **a** *(person: = collapse)* sich fallen lassen; *(heavily)* sich hinplumpsen lassen *(inf)*; **she ~ped into an armchair/onto the bed** sie ließ sich in einen Sessel/aufs Bett plumpsen *(inf)*; **let's ~ now** *(inf)* komm, wir hauen uns in die Falle *(inf)*
b *(thing: = fall)* fallen; *(heavily)* plumpsen
c *(inf: = fail) (scheme, plan)* fehlschlagen, ein Reinfall *nt* sein *(inf)*; *(play, book)* durchfallen; **the show ~ped completely** die Show war ein totaler Reinfall; **he ~ped as Hamlet** als Hamlet war er ein Reinfall
N **a** *(inf: = failure)* Reinfall *m*, Flop *m (inf)*; **a disastrous ~** ein totaler Reinfall
b *(= movement)* Plumps *m* → **bellyflop**

▶ **flop around** VI herumzappeln; *(person: in slippers etc)* herumschlappen

flophouse ['flɒphaʊs] N *(dated US inf)* billige Absteige, Penne *f*

floppy ['flɒpɪ] ADJ *(+er)* schlaff, schlapp; *movement* schlaksig; *clothes* weit; *hair* wallend; *bow* weich; **~ hat** Schlapphut *m*; **~ ears** Schlappohren *pl* N *(= disk)* Floppy Disk *f*, Diskette *f*

floppy disk N *(Comput)* Floppy Disk *f*, Diskette *f*; **~ drive** Diskettenlaufwerk *nt*

flora ['flɔ:rə] N Flora *f*

floral ['flɔ:rəl] ADJ **a** *fabric, print, wallpaper* geblümt; *fragrance, scent* blumig; **~ design** *or* **pattern** Blumenmuster *nt* **b** *(= made of flowers)* Blumen-; **~ arrangement/display** Blumenarrangement *nt*/-gesteck *nt*; **~ tribute** Blumengruß *m*

Florence ['flɒrəns] N Florenz *nt*

Florentine ['flɒrəntaɪn] ADJ florentinisch

florescence [flə'resəns] N Blüte *f*

floret ['flɒrət] N *(of flower)* (Einzel)blütchen *nt*; *(of cauliflower)* Röschen *nt*

florid ['flɒrɪd] ADJ **a** *(usu pej: = ornate) language* blumig, schwülstig *(pej)*; *wallpaper, tie* überladen; *music, architecture* reich verziert **b** *(= ruddy) person* rotgesichtig; *face, complexion* gerötet

florin ['flɒrɪn] N Florin *m*; *(Dutch)* Gulden *m*; *(dated Brit)* Zweishillingstück *nt*

florist ['flɒrɪst] N Blumenhändler(in) *m(f)*, Florist(in) *m(f)*; **~'s (shop)** Blumengeschäft *nt*

floss [flɒs] N Flockseide *f*, Schappe *f*; *(= thread)* Florettgarn *nt*, ungezwirntes Seidengarn; *(= dental floss)* Zahnseide *f* VT *teeth* mit Zahnseide reinigen VI sich *(dat)* die Zähne mit Zahnseide reinigen

floss silk N Schappeseide *f*, Florettseide *f*

flotation [fləʊ'teɪʃən] N *(of ship)* Flottmachen *nt*; *(of log)* Flößen *nt*; *(Comm: of firm)* Gründung *f*; *(Metal)* Flotation *f*, Schwimmaufbereitung *f*

flotation collar N *(Space)* Schwimmkragen *m*

flotilla [fləʊ'tɪlə] N Flotille *f*

flotsam ['flɒtsəm] N Treibgut *nt*; **he was another of the city's ~** er gehörte auch zu den Gestrandeten der Stadt; **~ and jetsam** *(floating)* Treibgut *nt*; *(washed ashore)* Strandgut *nt*; **the ~ and jetsam of our society** die Gestrandeten *pl or* das Strandgut unserer Gesellschaft

flounce¹ [flaʊns] VI stolzieren; **to ~ in/out/around** herein-/heraus-/herumstolzieren N **she turned on her heel with a ~** sie drehte sich pikiert auf dem Absatz um

flounce² N *(= frill)* Volant *m*, Rüsche *f* VT mit einem Volant/Volants *or* Rüschen besetzen

flounced [flaʊnst] ADJ *skirt, dress* mit Volants *or* Rüschen besetzt

flounder¹ ['flaʊndə'] N *(= fish)* Flunder *f*

flounder² VI **a** *(lit)* sich abstrampeln, sich abzappeln; **a stranded whale ~ing on the beach** ein gestrandeter Wal, der sich am Strand abquält; **we ~ed about in the mud** wir quälten uns mühselig im Schlamm **b** *(fig)* sich abzappeln *(inf)*, sich abstrampeln *(inf)*; **the company/economy was ~ing** der Firma/Wirtschaft ging es schlecht; **his career ~ed** mit seiner Karriere ging es abwärts; **to start to ~** ins Schwimmen kommen; **to ~ through sth** sich durch etw wursteln *or* mogeln *(inf)*; **he ~ed on** er wurstelte weiter

flour ['flaʊə'] N Mehl *nt* VT *(Cook) dough, rolling pin, one's hands* mit Mehl bestäuben

flour: **flour bin** N Mehlbüchse *f*; **flour dredger** N Mehlstreuer *m*

flourish ['flʌrɪʃ] VI *(plants etc, person)* (prächtig) gedeihen; *(business)* blühen, florieren; *(type of literature, painting etc)* seine Blütezeit haben; *(writer, artist etc)* großen Erfolg haben, erfolgreich sein; **crime ~ed in poor areas** in den armen Gegenden gedieh das Verbrechen
VT *(= wave about) stick, book etc* herumwedeln *or* -fuchteln mit, schwenken
N **a** *(= curve, decoration etc)* Schnörkel *m*
b *(= movement)* schwungvolle Bewegung, eleganter Schwung; **with a ~ of his stick** seinen Stock schwenkend; **she did/said it with a ~** sie tat es mit einer schwungvollen Bewegung/sagte es mit viel Schwung
c *(Mus: = fanfare)* Fanfare *f*; *(= decorative passage)* Verzierung *f*; **with a ~ of trumpets** mit einem Fanfarenstoß

flourishing ['flʌrɪʃɪŋ] ADJ florierend *attr*; *business also* gut gehend *attr*; *career* erfolgreich; *garden, plant* prächtig gedeihend *attr*; **how are you? – ~** wie gehts? – ausgezeichnet

flour: **flour mill** N (Korn)mühle *f*; **flour shaker** N Mehlstreuer *m*

floury ['flaʊərɪ] ADJ *face, hands, potatoes* mehlig

flout [flaʊt] VT sich hinwegsetzen über *(+acc)*, missachten; *convention, society* pfeifen auf *(+acc)*

flow [fləʊ] VI **a** *(lit, fig)* fließen; *(tears)* strömen, fließen; *(prose)* flüssig sein; **where the river ~s into the sea** wo der Fluss ins Meer mündet; **tears were ~ing down her cheeks** Tränen liefen *or* flossen *or* strömten ihr übers Gesicht; **the wine ~ed freely all evening** der Wein floss den ganzen Abend in Strömen; **to make the conversation ~** ein lebhaftes Gespräch in Gang bringen; **to keep the traffic ~ing** den Verkehr nicht ins Stocken kommen lassen; **his words ~ed readily** er redete sehr flüssig; **to ~ in/out** *(water, people, money etc)* hinein-/herausströmen; **a surge of hatred ~ed through me** Hass wallte in mir auf
b *(dress, hair etc)* fließen, wallen
c *(tide)* steigen, hereinkommen
N **a** Fluss *m*; *(of people)* Strom *m*; **the ~ of blood/traffic/information** der Blut-/Verkehrs-/ /Informationsfluss; **against the ~ of the river** gegen den Strom; **to go with the ~** *(fig)* mit dem Strom schwimmen
b **the tide is on the ~** die Flut kommt
c *(of words etc)* Redefluss *m*; **the powerful ~ of his prose** seine wortgewaltige Prosa; **the ~ of conversation** der Gesprächsfluss; **he was in full ~** er war richtig in Fahrt

flow chart N Flussdiagramm *nt*

flower ['flaʊə'] N **a** Blume *f*; *(= blossom)* Blüte *f*; **"say it with ~s"** „lasst Blumen sprechen"; **no ~s by request** wir bitten von Blumenspenden abzusehen; **to be in ~** blühen, in Blüte stehen; **to come into ~** zu blühen anfangen **b** *no pl (fig)* Blüte *f*; **to be in the (full) ~ of youth** in der Blüte seiner Jugend stehen; **the ~ of British manhood** die Zierde der britischen Männer **c** *(Chem)* **~s of sulphur** Schwefelblume *or* -blüte *f*
VI *(lit, fig)* blühen

flower: **flower arrangement** N Blumengesteck *nt*; **flower arranging** N Blumenstecken *nt*, Fertigen *nt* von Blumenarrangements; **flowerbed** N Blumenbeet *nt*; **flower child** N Blumenkind *nt*

flow[illegible] ['flaʊəd] ADJ *shirt, wallpaper* geblümt

flower: **flower garden** N Blumengarten *m*; **flower girl** N **a** *(= seller)* Blumenmädchen *nt* **b** *(at wedding etc)* Streukind *nt*; **flower head** N Blütenkopf *m*

flowering ['flaʊərɪŋ] ADJ Blüten-; **~ plant** Blütenpflanze *f*; **~ season** Blütezeit *f*; **~ shrub** Zierstrauch *m* N *(fig, of idea etc)* Blüte *f*

flower: **flower people** PL Blumenkinder *pl*; **flowerpot** N Blumentopf *m*; **flower power** N Flowerpower *f*, Flower-Power *f*; **flower-seller** N Blumenverkäufer(in) *m(f)*; **flower shop** N Blumenladen *m*, Blumengeschäft *nt*; **flower show** N Blumenschau *f*; **flower stalk** N Blütenstiel *m*

flowery ['flaʊərɪ] ADJ **a** *fabric, clothes, wallpaper* geblümt; *fragrance, perfume, scent* blumig; **a ~ field/meadow** ein Feld *nt*/eine Wiese voller Blumen **b** *(fig: = elaborate) speech, language* blumig

flowing ['fləʊɪŋ] ADJ **a** *water* fließend **b** *(= long and loose) hair, beard, robe, gown* wallend; *skirt* fließend **c** *(= moving freely) movement, style, football* flüssig; *(= graceful) lines* fließend; **the ~ lines of the car** die schnittigen Linien des Autos

flown [fləʊn] *ptp of* **fly²**

fl. oz. *abbr of* **fluid ounce(s)**

flu, 'flu [flu:] N Grippe *f*; **to get** *or* **catch/have (the) ~** (die *or* eine) Grippe bekommen/haben

flub [flʌb] *(US inf)* VT verpfuschen, verpatzen *(both inf)* VI pfuschen, stümpern *(both inf)* N Schnitzer *m (inf)*, grober Fehler

fluctuate ['flʌktjʊeɪt] VI schwanken; *(in number also)* fluktuieren

fluctuation [,flʌktjʊ'eɪʃən] N Schwankung *f*, Schwanken *nt no pl*; *(in number also)* Fluktuation *f*; *(fig, of opinions)* Schwanken *nt no pl*

flue [flu:] N Rauchfang *m*, Rauchabzug *m*; *(Mus: of organ, = pipe)* Labialpfeife *f*; *(= opening)* Kernspalt *m*; **~ brush** Stoßbesen *m*

fluency ['flu:ənsɪ] N **a** *(in a foreign language)* fließendes Sprechen; **this job requires ~ in German** für diese Stelle ist fließendes Deutsch Voraussetzung; **~ in two foreign languages is a requirement** die Beherrschung von zwei Fremdsprachen ist Voraussetzung; **his ~ in English is inadequate** er spricht Englisch nicht fließend genug **b** *(in one's native language, of speaker, writer)* Gewandtheit *f*; *(of style)* Flüssigkeit *f* **c** *(of movement)* Flüssigkeit *f*

fluent ['flu:ənt] ADJ **a** *(in a foreign language)* **to be ~** die Sprache fließend sprechen; **to be ~ in German** fließend Deutsch sprechen; **she is ~ in six languages** sie beherrscht sechs Sprachen fließend; **his English is not totally ~** er spricht nicht ganz fließend Englisch; **he is a ~ Japanese speaker, he speaks ~ Japanese** er spricht fließend Japanisch
b *(in one's native language) writer, talker, debater* gewandt; *style* flüssig; *reader* fließend; **rage was making him ~** die Wut beflügelte seine Worte; **she speaks in ~ sentences** sie spricht in fließenden *or* flüssigen Sätzen
c *(= moving freely) movement, action* flüssig; **Black Velvet is not the most ~ of jumpers** Black Velvet springt nicht besonders flüssig; **the match contained little ~ football** die Begegnung enthielt nur wenig flüssiges Spiel

fluently ['flu:əntlɪ] ADV **a** *speak, write (in a foreign language)* fließend; *(in one's native language)* flüssig; **to communicate ~ in Hebrew** sich fließend auf Hebräisch verständigen **b** *(= moving freely) jump, play* flüssig

fluey ['flu:ɪ] ADJ *(Brit inf)* **to feel ~** das Gefühl haben, dass man Grippe hat

fluff [flʌf] N *no pl (on birds, young animals)* Flaum *m*; *(from material)* Fusseln *pl*; *(= dust)* Staubflocken *pl*; **a bit of ~** eine Fussel/eine Staubflocke; *(hum inf)* eine Mieze *(inf)* VT **a** *(also* **fluff out**) *feathers* aufplustern; *pillow* aufschütteln **b** *opportunity, lines in play, entrance* vermasseln *(inf)*

▶ **fluff up** VT *sep pillow etc* aufschütteln

fluffy ['flʌfɪ] ADJ *(+er)* **a** *(= soft) wool, slippers, sweater, towel* flauschig; *hair* locker; *kitten, rabbit* flaumweich; **a large ~ dog** ein großer, wolliger Hund; **~ white clouds** weiße Schäfchenwolken; **~ animal** *or* **toy** *(= soft toy)* Kuscheltier *nt* **b** *(= light) omelette, rice, mashed potatoes* locker; *egg, cake mixture* schaumig; **whip the eggs until ~** die Eier schaumig schlagen

fluid ['flu:ɪd] **N** Flüssigkeit *f*; **loss of ~s** Flüssigkeitsverlust *m*; **she can only take ~s** sie kann nur flüssige Nahrung zu sich *(dat)* nehmen **ADJ** **a** *(lit)* flüssig **b** *(fig) movement* flüssig; *shape, painting* fließend **c** *(fig: = variable) situation* ungewiss; **his plans are still ~** seine Pläne stehen noch nicht fest

fluid assets [ˌflu:ɪd'æsets] **PL** *(US Fin)* Umlaufvermögen *nt*

fluidity [flu:'ɪdɪtɪ] **N** **a** *(lit, fig, of movement)* Flüssigkeit *f*; **the ~ of the painting** die fließenden Linien des Gemäldes **b** *(fig: = variability: of situation, plans)* Ungewissheit *f*

fluid ounce **N** *Flüssigkeitsmaß (Brit: =28,4 ml, US: =29,6 ml)*

fluish ['flu:ɪʃ] **ADJ** = **fluey**

fluke[1] [flu:k] **N** *(inf)* Dusel *m (inf)*, Schwein *nt (inf)*; **by a ~** durch Dusel *(inf)*; **it was a (pure) ~** das war (einfach) Dusel *(inf)*

fluke[2] **N** *(Naut)* Flunke *m*; *(of a whale's tail)* Fluke *f*; *(Fishing: = flounder)* Flunder *f*; *(Zool: = flatworm)* Plattwurm *m*

fluky ['flu:kɪ] **ADJ** *(inf) wind* wechselnd; **that was a ~ goal** das war ein Zufallstreffer

flume [flu:m] **N** **a** *(= ravine)* Klamm *f* **b** *(= channel)* Kanal *m* **c** *(in swimming pool)* schlauchförmige Wasserrutsche

flummox ['flʌməks] **VT** *(inf) person* durcheinanderbringen, aus dem Konzept bringen *(inf)*; **to be ~ed** durcheinander sein; **to be ~ed by sth** durch etw verwirrt sein, durch etw aus dem Konzept gebracht werden *(inf)*

flung [flʌŋ] *pret, ptp of* **fling**

flunk [flʌŋk] *(inf)* **VI** durchfallen *(inf)*, durchrasseln *(inf)*, durch die Prüfung fliegen *(inf)* **VT** *test* verhauen *(inf)*; *candidate* durchfallen *or* durchrasseln lassen *(inf)*; **to ~ German/an exam** in Deutsch/bei einer Prüfung durchfallen *(inf)*

flunk(e)y ['flʌŋkɪ] **N** Lakai *m*; *(= flatterer)* Radfahrer(in) *m(f) (inf)*

fluorescence [flʊə'resəns] **N** Fluoreszenz *f*

fluorescent [flʊə'resənt] **ADJ** *(= luminous) colour* leuchtend; *dye, paint, clothes* fluoreszierend; **~ display/screen** Leuchtanzeige *f*/-schirm *m*

fluorescent: **fluorescent bulb** **N** Leuchtstoffbirne *f*; **fluorescent light** **N** Leuchtstofflampe *f*, Neonlampe *f*; **fluorescent lighting** **N** Neonbeleuchtung *f*, Neonröhre *f*; **fluorescent tube** **N** Leuchtstoffröhre *f*

fluoridate ['flʊərɪdeɪt] **VT** mit Fluor versetzen, fluorieren

fluoridation [ˌflʊərɪ'deɪʃən] **N** Fluorzusatz *m (of* zu)

fluoride ['flʊəraɪd] **N** Fluorid *nt*; **~ toothpaste** Fluorzahnpasta *f*

fluorine ['flʊəri:n] **N** Fluor *nt*

fluorocarbon [ˌflʊərəʊ'kɑ:bən] **N** Fluorkohlenwasserstoff *m*

fluorspar ['flʊəspɑ:] **N** → **fluoride**

flurried ['flʌrɪd] **ADJ** **to become ~** sich aufregen, nervös werden

flurry ['flʌrɪ] **N** **a** *(of snow)* Gestöber *nt*; *(of rain)* Guss *m*; *(of wind)* Stoß *m*; **a ~ of blows** ein Hagel *m* von Schlägen **b** *(fig)* Aufregung *f*, Nervosität *f*; **in a ~** ganz aufgescheucht, in großer Aufregung; **a ~ of activity** eine Hektik; **a ~ of excitement** hektische Aufregung **VT** nervös machen, aufregen → **flurried**

flush[1] [flʌʃ] **N** **a** *(= lavatory flush)* (Wasser)spülung *f* **b** *(= blush)* Röte *f*; **the ~ of colour** *(Brit) or* **color** *(US)* **in her cheeks** die Farbe in ihren Wangen **c** *(of beauty, youth)* Blüte *f*; *(of excitement, enthusiasm, panic)* Welle *f*; **in the (first) ~ of victory** im (ersten) Siegestaumel; **in the first ~ of youth** in der ersten Jugendblüte **VI** **a** *(person, face)* rot werden, rot anlaufen *(with* vor *+dat)*; **to ~ crimson** dunkelrot anlaufen *or* werden **b** *(lavatory)* spülen **VT** spülen; *(also* **flush out***) drain* durch- *or* ausspülen; **to ~ the lavatory** *or* **toilet** spülen, die Wasserspülung betätigen; **to ~ sth down the toilet** etw die Toilette hinunterspülen

▸ **flush away** **VT** *sep waste matter etc* wegspülen

▸ **flush out** **VT** *sep* **a** *(with water) sink, bottle* ausspülen, auswaschen; *dirt* wegspülen, wegschwemmen **b** *thieves, spies* aufstöbern, aufspüren; **they flushed them out of their hiding places** sie jagten sie aus ihren Verstecken

flush[2] **ADJ** *pred* **a** bündig; **cupboards ~ with the wall** Schränke, die mit der Wand abschließen; **to be ~ against the wall** direkt an der Wand stehen; **~ left/right** *(text)* links-/rechtsbündig **b** *(inf)* **to be ~** gut bei Kasse sein *(inf)*

flush[3] **VT** *game, birds* aufstöbern, aufscheuchen

flush[4] **N** *(Cards)* Flöte *f*, Sequenz *f*; *(Poker)* Flush *m*

flushed [flʌʃt] **ADJ** *(= red) face, cheeks* rot, gerötet; **to be ~** *(person)* rot im Gesicht sein; **she arrived ~** sie kam mit einem roten Kopf an; **if your child is ~ and feverish** wenn Ihr Kind rot aussieht und Fieber hat; **~ with excitement/embarrassment/anger** rot vor Aufregung/Verlegenheit/Wut; **to be ~ with success/happiness** über seinen Erfolg/vor Glück strahlen; **white flowers ~ with pink** weiße, stellenweise rosa getönte Blüten

flushing ['flʌʃɪŋ] **N** *(for lavatory)* (Wasser)spülung *f*

fluster ['flʌstə'] **VT** nervös machen; *(= confuse)* durcheinanderbringen; **don't ~ me!** machen Sie mich nicht nervös!; **she got ~ed** sie wurde nervös, das brachte sie durcheinander; **to be ~ed** nervös *or* aufgeregt sein, durcheinander sein **N** **in a ~** nervös, aufgeregt; *(= confused)* durcheinander

flute [flu:t] **N** **a** *(Mus)* Querflöte *f*; *(= organ stop)* Flötenregister *nt* **b** **~ (glass)** Flöte *f* **VT** *column, pillar* kannelieren **VI** *(person, voice)* flöten

fluted ['flu:tɪd] **ADJ** *column, pillar* kanneliert; *border, edge* bogenförmig; **~ glass** (Sekt)flöte *f*

fluting ['flu:tɪŋ] **N** *(Archit)* Kannelierung *f*, Kanneluren *pl*; *(of border, edge)* Bogenform *f*

flutist ['flu:tɪst] **N** *(US)* = **flautist**

flutter ['flʌtə'] **VI** **a** *(flag, bird, butterfly)* flattern *(also Med)*; **her heart ~ed as he entered the room** sie bekam Herzklopfen, als er das Zimmer betrat; **to ~ away** *or* **off** davonflattern **b** *(person)* tänzeln; *(nervously)* flatterig sein; **to ~ around** herumtänzeln, nervös herumfuhrwerken *(inf)*; **she ~ed into/out of the room** sie tänzelte ins Zimmer/aus dem Zimmer **VT** *fan, piece of paper* wedeln mit; *(birds) wings* flattern mit; *one's eyelashes* klimpern mit *(hum inf)*; **to ~ one's eyelashes at sb** mit den Wimpern klimpern *(hum)*, jdn mit einem tollen Augenaufschlag bezirzen **N** **a** Flattern *nt (also Med)*; **this caused a ~ among the audience** dies verursachte leichte Unruhe im Publikum **b** *(= nervousness)* **(all) in** *or* **of a ~** in heller Aufregung; **~ of anxiety/excitement** besorgte/aufgeregte Unruhe **c** *(Brit inf)* **to have a ~** *(= gamble)* sein Glück (beim Wetten) versuchen; **he likes his little ~ on a Friday night** er versucht freitagabends gern sein Glück beim Wetten **d** *(Aviat)* Flattern *nt*

flutter kick **N** Wechselschlag *m (beim Kraulen)*

fluty ['flu:tɪ] **ADJ** *(+er) voice* flötend

fluvial ['flu:vɪəl] **ADJ** in Flüssen, fluvial *(spec)*; **~ water** Flusswasser *nt*

flux [flʌks] **N** **a** *(= state of change)* Fluss *m*; **things are in a state of ~** die Dinge sind im Fluss; **to be in constant ~** ständig im Fluss sein **b** *(Med: no pl)* Ausfluss *m*; *(Phys)* Fluss *m* **c** *(Metal)* Flussmittel *nt*

fly[1] [flaɪ] **N** Fliege *f*; **they were dying like flies** sie starben wie die Fliegen; **small retailers are dropping like flies** kleine Einzelhändler gehen massenweise ein *(inf)*; **he wouldn't hurt** *or* **harm a ~** er könnte keiner Fliege etwas zuleide *or* zu Leide tun; **that's the only ~ in the ointment** *(inf)* das ist das einzige Haar in der Suppe; **he's the ~ in the ointment** er ist Sand im Getriebe; **there are no flies on him** *(Brit inf)* ihn legt man nicht so leicht rein *(inf)*; **to be a ~ on the wall** Mäuschen sein *or* spielen

fly[2] *vb: pret* **flew**, *ptp* **flown** **VI** **a** *(person, bird, insect, aircraft etc)* fliegen **b** *(= move quickly, time)* (ver)fliegen; *(people)* sausen *(inf)*, fliegen; *(sparks)* stieben, fliegen; **time flies!** wie die Zeit vergeht!; **the company is ~ing high** die Firma will hoch hinaus; **I'm already late, I must ~** ich bin schon spät dran, ich muss jetzt wirklich sausen *(inf)*; **the door flew open** die Tür flog auf; **to ~ to sb's side** an jds Seite eilen; **to ~ into a rage** einen Wutanfall bekommen; **to ~ at sb** *(inf)* auf jdn losgehen; **to let ~ at sb** auf jdn losgehen; **he really let ~** er legte kräftig los; *(verbally also)* er zog kräftig vom Leder; **to knock** *or* **send sb/sth ~ing** jdn/etw umschmeißen *(inf) or* umwerfen; **he sent the ball ~ing over the wall** er schleuderte *or* schmiss *(inf)* den Ball über die Mauer; **to go ~ing** *(person)* hinfallen; *(object)* runterfallen; **stories are ~ing around the office** im Büro gehen Geschichten um **c** **to ~ in the face of authority/tradition** sich über jede Autorität/alle Traditionen hinwegsetzen; **to ~ in the face of reason** *(person, organization)* sich über jede Vernunft hinwegsetzen; *(idea, theory etc)* jeder Vernunft entbehren **d** *(flag, hair)* wehen **VT** **a** *aircraft* fliegen; *kite* steigen lassen **b** *passengers, route, plane* fliegen; *Atlantic* überfliegen **c** *flag* führen, wehen lassen → **flag**[1] **N** **to go for a ~** fliegen

▸ **fly away** **VI** *(bird)* weg- *or* fortfliegen; *(plane, person also)* abfliegen; *(fig, thoughts)* wandern; *(to* zu)

▸ **fly in** **VI** *(troops, president, rescue plane etc)* einfliegen; **we flew into Heathrow at night** wir sind abends in Heathrow angekommen; **she flew in from New York this morning** sie ist heute Morgen mit dem Flugzeug aus New York angekommen **VT** *sep supplies, troops* einfliegen

▸ **fly off** **VI** **a** *(plane, person)* abfliegen, wegfliegen; *(bird)* wegfliegen, fortfliegen; **to fly off to the south** nach Süden fliegen; **a search plane flew off to look for them** ein Suchflugzeug flog los, um nach ihnen Ausschau zu halten; **as the plane flew off into the sunset** während das Flugzeug der untergehenden Sonne entgegenflog **b** *(= come off, hat, lid etc)* wegfliegen; *(button)* abspringen

▸ **fly out** **VI** *(troops, president, troop plane)* ausfliegen; **as we flew out of Heathrow** als wir von Heathrow abflogen; **I'll fly out and come back by ship** ich werde hin fliegen und mit dem Schiff zurückkommen **VT** *sep troops (to an area)* hinfliegen; *(out of an area)* ausfliegen; **troops were flown out to the area** Truppen wurden in das Gebiet geflogen; **the company will fly you out** *(into area)* die Firma wird Sie hinfliegen; *(out of area)* die Firma wird Sie ausfliegen

▸ **fly past** **VI** **a** *(car, person)* vorbeisausen *or* -flitzen *(inf)* **b** *(ceremonially)* vorbeifliegen **c** *(time)* verfliegen **VI** *+prep obj* **to fly past sth** an etw *(dat)* vorbeifliegen

fly[3] *pret* **flew**, *ptp* **flown** **VI** *(= flee)* fliehen, flüchten; **to ~ for one's life** um sein Leben laufen/fahren *etc* **VT** **to ~ the country** aus dem Land flüchten

fly[4] **N** **a** *(on trousers)* (Hosen)schlitz *m* **b** = **fly sheet** **c** **flies** **PL** *(Theat)* Obermaschinerie *f* **d** = **flywheel**

fly[5] *(Brit inf)* ADJ clever, gerissen N **on the ~** *(= quickly)* schnell, prompt; *(= spontaneously)* spontan; *(= while moving)* in Bewegung, aus der Bewegung heraus

fly: **flyaway** ADJ *hair* fliegend, schwer zu bändigen; **fly-by-night** N a *(= irresponsible man)* Windhund *m (inf)*; *(= woman)* leichtsinniges Ding *(inf)* b *(= decamping debtor)* flüchtiger Schuldner, flüchtige Schuldnerin ADJ a *person* unzuverlässig, unbeständig b *(Fin, Comm) firm, operation* zweifelhaft, windig *(inf)*; **fly-catcher** N a Fliegenschnäpper *m* b *(= trap for flies)* Fliegenfänger *m*; **fly-fishing** N Fliegenfischen *nt*; **fly half** N *(Rugby)* Halbspieler *m*

flying ['flaɪɪŋ] ADJ *animal* fliegend; *glass, debris* herumfliegend N Fliegen *nt*; **he likes ~** er fliegt gerne; **he's afraid of ~** er hat Angst vorm Fliegen *or* Flugangst

flying: **flying ambulance** N *(= helicopter)* Rettungshubschrauber *m*; *(= plane)* Rettungsflugzeug *nt*; **flying boat** N Flugboot *nt*; **flying bomb** N V-Rakete *f*; **flying buttress** N *(Archit)* Strebebogen *m*; **flying colours**, *(US)* **flying colors** PL **to pass with ~** glänzend abschneiden; **flying doctor** N fliegender Arzt *(esp in Australien)*; **Flying Dutchman** N **The ~** der Fliegende Holländer; **flying exhibition** N Wanderausstellung *f*; **flying fish** N Fliegender Fisch; **flying fox** N Flughund *m*; **flying insect** N Fluginsekt *nt*; **flying jacket** N Fliegerjacke *f*; **flying leap** N (großer) Satz; **to take a ~** einen großen Satz machen; **flying machine** N *(old, hum)* Flugmaschine *f*; **flying officer** N *(Brit)* Oberleutnant *m*; **flying picket** N mobiler Streikposten; **flying saucer** N fliegende Untertasse; **flying squad** N Bereitschaftsdienst *m*; **flying start** N *(Sport)* fliegender Start; **to get off to a ~** *(Sport)* hervorragend wegkommen *(inf)*; *(fig)* einen glänzenden Start haben; **flying suit** N Pilotenanzug *m*; **flying time** N Flugzeit *f*; **flying trapeze** N Trapez *nt*, Schwebereck *nt*; **flying visit** N Blitzbesuch *m*, Stippvisite *f*

fly: **flyleaf** N Vorsatzblatt *nt*; **flyover** N Überführung *f*; *(US: = fly-past)* Luftparade *f*; **flypaper** N Fliegenfänger *m*; **fly-past** N *(Brit)* Luftparade *f*; **flyposting** N illegales Plakatekleben; **fly sheet** N *(= entrance)* Überdach *nt*; *(= outer tent)* Überzelt *nt*; **fly spray** N Fliegenspray *m*; **fly swat(ter)** N Fliegenklatsche *f*; **fly-tipping** N illegales Müllabladen; **flytrap** N *(Bot)* Fliegenfalle *f*; **flyway** N *(Orn)* Zuglinie *f*; **flyweight** N *(Boxing)* Fliegengewicht *nt*; **flywheel** N Schwungrad *nt*

FM *abbr* a *of* **frequency modulation** FM b *of* **field marshal** c *of* **foreign minister**

f-number ['ef,nʌmbə'] N *(Phot)* Blende *f*, Blendenzahl *f*

FO *abbr of* **Foreign Office**

foal [fəʊl] N Fohlen *nt*, Füllen *nt*; **in ~** trächtig VI fohlen

foam [fəʊm] N Schaum *m*; *(of sea also)* Gischt *f* VI schäumen; **to ~ at the mouth** *(lit)* Schaum vorm Mund *or (animal)* Maul haben; *(fig, person)* schäumen

▶ **foam up** VI *(liquid in container)* schäumen

foam: **foam machine** N Schaumkanone *f or* -maschine *f*; **foam rubber** N Schaumgummi *m*; **foam sprayer** N Schaumlöscher *m*

foamy ['fəʊmɪ] ADJ a *(+er) (= frothy) waves, beer* schäumend b *(liter, = resembling foam)* schaumig

fob[1] [fɒb] VT *(esp Brit)* **to ~ sb off (with promises)** jdn (mit leeren Versprechungen) abspeisen; **to ~ sth off on sb, to ~ sb off with sth** jdm etw andrehen N *(old: also* **fob pocket***)* Uhrtasche *f*

fob[2] [,efəʊ'bi:] *abbr of* **free on board**

fob watch N Taschenuhr *f*

focal ['fəʊkəl] ADJ *(fig)* im Brennpunkt (stehend), fokal *(geh)*

focal: **focal length** N Brennweite *f*; **focal plane** N Brennebene *f*; **focal point** N *(lit, fig)* Brennpunkt *m*; **his family is the ~ of his life** seine Familie ist der Mittelpunkt seines Lebens, sein ganzes Leben dreht sich um seine Familie

fo'c'sle ['fəʊksl] N = **forecastle**

focus ['fəʊkəs] N *pl* **foci** ['fəʊkɪ] *(Phys, Math, fig)* Brennpunkt *m*; *(of storm)* Zentrum *nt*; *(of earthquake, Med)* Herd *m*; **in ~** *(camera)* (scharf) eingestellt; *photo* scharf; **to bring sth into ~** *(lit)* etw klar *or* scharf einstellen; *(fig) topic* etw in den Brennpunkt rücken; **out of ~** *(lit, camera)* unscharf eingestellt; *photo* unscharf; *(fig) ideas* vage; **to come into ~** ins Blickfeld rücken; **to keep sth in ~** *(lit)* etw scharf eingestellt im Suchfeld behalten; *(fig)* etw im Blickfeld behalten; **he/the new proposal was the ~ of attention** er/der neue Vorschlag stand im Mittelpunkt

VT *instrument* einstellen (*on* auf *+acc*); *light, heat rays* bündeln; *(fig) one's efforts, resources, energy* konzentrieren (*on* auf *+acc*); **to ~ one's eyes on sb/sth** den Blick auf jdn/etw richten; **to ~ one's attention/mind** sich konzentrieren; **I should like to ~ your attention (up)on a new problem** ich möchte Ihre Aufmerksamkeit auf ein neues Problem lenken

VI *(light, heat rays)* sich bündeln; **to ~ on sth** sich auf etw *(acc)* konzentrieren; **his eyes ~ed on the book** sein Blick richtete sich auf das Buch; **I can't ~ properly** ich kann nicht mehr klar sehen

focus group N Fokusgruppe *f*

focus(s)ed ['fəʊkəst] ADJ *(fig)* fokussiert

f. o. d. *(Comm) abbr of* **free of damage** unbeschadigt

fodder ['fɒdə'] N *(lit, fig)* Futter *nt*

foe [fəʊ] N *(liter)* Feind(in) *m(f)*, Widersacher(in) *m(f) (geh)*

FoE *abbr of* **Friends of the Earth**

foetal, *(esp US)* **fetal** ['fi:tl] ADJ fötal

foetid ['fi:tɪd] ADJ = **fetid**

foetus, *(esp US)* **fetus** ['fi:təs] N Fötus *m*, Fetus *m*

fog [fɒg] N a Nebel *m*; **I am still in a ~** *(dated inf)* ich blicke immer noch nicht durch *(inf)* b *(Phot)* (Grau)schleier *m* VT a *(also* **fog up** *or* **over***) mirror, glasses* beschlagen b *(Phot)* verschleiern c *(fig)* **to ~ the issue** die Sache vernebeln VI a *(also* **fog up** *or* **over***: mirror, glasses)* beschlagen b *(Phot, negative)* einen Grauschleier bekommen

fog: **fog bank** N Nebelbank *f*; **fogbound** ADJ *ship, plane* durch Nebel festgehalten; *airport* wegen Nebel(s) geschlossen; **the main road to Edinburgh is ~** auf der Hauptstraße nach Edinburgh herrscht dichter Nebel

fogey ['fəʊgɪ] N *(inf)* **old ~** alter Kauz *(inf)*; *(= woman)* Schrulle *f (inf)*; **young ~** *junger Mensch, der sich bewusst konventionell benimmt und kleidet*, Junggreis *m (inf)*

foggy ['fɒgɪ] ADJ *(+er)* a *(= misty) day, weather, conditions* neb(e)lig b *(fig: = confused) brain* verwirrt; **in my ~ state** in meiner Verwirrung; **I haven't the foggiest (idea)** *(inf)* ich habe keinen blassen Schimmer *(inf)*

Foggy Bottom N *(US hum inf) Scherzname für das amerikanische Außenministerium*

fog: **foghorn** N *(Naut)* Nebelhorn *nt*; **a voice like a ~** *(inf)* eine dröhnende Stimme; **fog lamp**, **fog light** N Nebellampe *f*; *(Aut)* Nebelscheinwerfer *m*; **rear ~** *(Aut)* Nebelschlussleuchte *f*; **fog signal** N *(Naut, Rail)* Nebelsignal *nt*

FOIA *(US) abbr of* **Freedom of Information Act**

foible ['fɔɪbl] N Eigenheit *f*

foil[1] [fɔɪl] N a *(= metal sheet)* Folie *f* → **cooking foil, kitchen foil** b *(fig)* Hintergrund *m*, Folie *f*; **to act as a ~ to sth** einer Sache *(dat)* als Hintergrund *or* Folie dienen

foil[2] N *(Fencing)* Florett *nt*

foil[3] VT *plans* durchkreuzen; *attempts* vereiteln; *person* einen Strich durch die Rechnung machen *(+dat)*; **~ed again!** *(hum)* wieder nichts!; **he was ~ed in his attempts** ihm wurde ein Strich durch die Rechnung gemacht

foist [fɔɪst] VT a **to ~ sth (off) on sb** *(goods)* jdm etw andrehen; *task, responsibility* etw auf jdn abschieben; *opinions* jdm etw aufdrängen b **to ~ oneself on(to) sb** sich jdm aufdrängen

fold[1] [fəʊld] N Falte *f*; *(Geol, of the earth)* (Boden)falte *f*; **~s of skin** Hautfalten *pl*; **~s of fat** Fettwülste *pl*

VT a *(= bend into folds) paper* (zusammen)falten; *blanket* zusammenlegen *or* -falten; **to ~ a newspaper in two/four** eine Zeitung falten/zweimal falten; **to ~ sth flat** etw flach zusammenfalten

b **to ~ one's arms** die Arme verschränken; **she ~ed her hands in her lap** sie faltete die Hände im Schoß zusammen

c *(= wrap up)* einwickeln, einschlagen (*in* in *+acc*); **he ~ed the book in some paper** er schlug das Buch in Papier ein

d **to ~ sb in one's arms** jdn in die Arme schließen

VI a *(chair, table)* sich zusammenklappen lassen; *(accidentally)* zusammenklappen

b *(= close down: business)* eingehen

▶ **fold away** VI *(table, bed)* zusammenklappbar sein, sich zusammenklappen lassen VT *sep table, bed* zusammenklappen; *clothes* zusammenlegen; *newspaper* zusammenfalten

▶ **fold back** VT *sep shutters, door* zurückfalten; *sheet, bedclothes* auf- *or* zurückschlagen VI *(shutters, door)* zurückfalten, sich zurückfalten lassen

▶ **fold down** VT *sep chair* zusammenklappen; *corner* kniffen

▶ **fold in** VT *sep (Cook) flour, sugar* unterziehen, unterheben; **to fold sth into sth** etw unter etw *(acc)* heben *or* ziehen

▶ **fold over** VT *sep paper* umknicken; *blanket* umschlagen

▶ **fold up** VT *sep paper* zusammenfalten; *blanket also* zusammenlegen

fold[2] N *(= pen)* Pferch *m*; **to return to the ~** *(fig)* in den Schoß der Gemeinde zurückkehren

foldaway ['fəʊldəweɪ] ADJ *attr* zusammenklappbar

folded ['fəʊldɪd] ADJ a *paper* (zusammen)gefaltet; *clothes, blanket, towel* (zusammen)gefaltet, zusammengelegt; *petal, leaf* geschlossen; **~ into a rectangle** zu einem Rechteck gefaltet b *(= crossed) hands* gefaltet; *arms* verschränkt; **to stand with one's arms ~** mit verschränkten Armen dastehen

folder ['fəʊldə'] N a *(for papers)* Aktendeckel *m*, Aktenmappe *f* b *(Comput)* Ordner *m* c *(= brochure)* Informationsblatt *nt*

folding ['fəʊldɪŋ] ADJ *attr* Klapp-; **~ bed** Klappbett *nt*; **~ chair** Klappstuhl *m*; *(= grille on lift)* Scherengittertür *f*; **~ table** Klapptisch *m*

folding: **folding doors** PL Falttür *f*; **folding money** N *(inf)* Papiergeld *nt*; **folding screen** N spanische Wand

foldout ['fəʊldaʊt] ADJ *attr section of book etc* ausklappbar

foliage ['fəʊlɪɪdʒ] N Blätter *pl*; *(of tree also)* Laub(werk) *nt*

foliation [,fəʊlɪ'eɪʃən] N a *(Bot)* Blattanordnung *f*; *(= development)* Blattbildung *f* b *(of book)* Foliierung *f*, Blattzählung *f* c *(Geol)* Schichtung *f* d *(Archit)* Laubwerk *nt*

folic acid [,fəʊlɪk'æsɪd] N Folsäure *f*

folio ['fəʊlɪəʊ] N a *(= sheet)* Folio *nt* b *(= volume)* Foliant *m*

folk [fəʊk] PL a *(also* **folks***: inf: = people)* Leute *pl*; *(= people in general)* die Leute, man; **a lot of ~(s) believe ...** viele (Leute) glauben ...; **there were a lot of ~ at the concert** es waren eine Menge Leute bei dem Konzert; **come on, ~s** *(inf)* na los, Leute!; **the young/old ~** die Jungen/Alten; **old ~ can't …** alte Menschen können nicht … **b** *(inf: = relatives: also* **folks)** **my ~s** meine Leute *(inf)*; **the old ~(s) stayed at home** die alten Herrschaften blieben zu Haus

folk: **folk dance** N Volkstanz *m*; **folklore** N Folklore *f*, Volkskunde *f*; **folk medicine** N Volksmedizin *f*; **folk memory** N (im Volk) lebendig gehaltene Überlieferungen *pl*; **folk music** N Volksmusik *f*; **folk singer** N Sänger(in) *m(f)* von Volksliedern; *(modern songs)* Folksänger(in) *m(f)*; **folk song** N Volkslied *nt*; *(modern)* Folksong *m*

folksy ['fəʊksɪ] ADJ **a** *(= rustic) music, culture, charm* volkstümlich; *clothes* bäuerlich; *furniture* rustikal **b** *(pej: = fake rustic)* auf rustikal gemacht *(pej)* **c** *(US: = affable, informal) person, manner* freundlich, herzlich; *speech, comment* volkstümlich

folk tale N Volksmärchen *nt*

follicle ['fɒlɪkl] N Follikel *nt*

follow ['fɒləʊ] ✪ 11.3 VT **a** *person, car, road, sign* folgen *(+dat)*, nachgehen/-fahren *etc (+dat)*; *(= pursue also)* verfolgen; *(= succeed)* folgen *(+dat)*, kommen nach; **he ~ed me about** er folgte mir überallhin; **he ~ed me out** er folgte mir nach draußen; **~ me** folgen Sie mir; *(by car also)* fahren Sie mir nach; **we're being ~ed** wir werden verfolgt; **to have sb ~ed** jdn verfolgen lassen; **his eyes ~ed her, he ~ed her with his eyes** er folgte ihr mit den Augen; **he arrived first, ~ed by the ambassador** er kam als Erster, gefolgt vom Botschafter; **he ~ed his father into the business** er folgte seinem Vater im Geschäft; **the earthquake was ~ed by looting** auf das Erdbeben folgte Plünderung; **the dinner will be ~ed by a concert** im Anschluss an das Essen findet ein Konzert statt; **the toast was ~ed by a vote of thanks** auf den Trinkspruch folgten Worte des Dankes; **to ~ the hounds** (mit den Hunden) auf die Jagd gehen; **~ that (if you can)!** *(said after a good performance etc)* das soll mir/ihm *etc* erst mal einer nachmachen!; **how do you ~ that?** das ist kaum zu überbieten; **I love lasagne ~ed by ice cream** besonders gern mag ich Lasagne und danach Eis; **potatoes are the most popular food, ~ed by white bread** Kartoffeln sind das beliebteste Essen, und an zweiter Stelle steht Weißbrot

b *(= keep to) road, path* folgen *(+dat)*, entlanggehen/-fahren *etc*; **the boat ~ed the coast** das Boot fuhr die Küste entlang; **the road ~s the valley** die Straße folgt dem Tal

c *(= understand)* folgen *(+dat)*; **do you ~ me?** können Sie mir folgen?

d *profession* ausüben, nachgehen *(+dat)*; *course of study, career* verfolgen; **to ~ the sea** *(liter)* zur See fahren

e *(= conform to) fashion* mitmachen; *advice, instructions* befolgen, folgen *(+dat)*; *party line* folgen *(+dat)*; **to ~ (the dictates of) one's heart/conscience** auf die Stimme seines Herzens/Gewissens hören

f *(= read, watch regularly) serial* verfolgen; *strip cartoon* regelmäßig lesen; *(= take an interest in) progress, development, news* verfolgen; *athletics, swimming etc* sich interessieren für; *(= listen to attentively) speech* (genau) verfolgen; **to ~ the horses** sich für Pferderennen interessieren; **which team do you ~?** für welchen Verein sind Sie?; **the film ~s the fortunes of two women** der Film verfolgt das Schicksal zweier Frauen

VI **a** *(= come after)* folgen *(on sth* auf etw *acc)*; **as ~s** wie folgt; **his argument was as ~s** er argumentierte folgendermaßen; **to ~ in sb's footsteps** *(fig)* in jds Fußstapfen *(acc)* treten; **what is there to ~?** *(at meals)* was gibt es noch *or (planning the meal)* hinterher *or* anschließend?; **what ~s** das Folgende

b *(results, deduction)* folgen *(from* aus); **it ~s from this that …** hieraus folgt, dass …; **it doesn't ~ that …** daraus folgt nicht, dass …; **that doesn't ~** nicht unbedingt!

c *(= understand)* folgen; **I don't ~** das verstehe ich nicht, da komme ich nicht mit

▶ **follow on** VI **a** *(= come after)* später folgen *or* kommen; *(person)* nachkommen, später kommen **b** *(results)* folgen, sich ergeben *(from* aus) **c** *(= continue)* **the story follows on from his death** die Geschichte geht nach seinem Tod weiter; **she will follow on from where he left off** sie wird da weitermachen, wo er aufgehört hat **d** *(Cricket)* zwei Innenrunden hintereinander spielen

▶ **follow out** VT *sep idea, plan* zu Ende verfolgen, durchziehen

▶ **follow through** VT *sep argument* durchdenken, (zu Ende) verfolgen; *idea, plan, undertaking* (zu Ende) verfolgen, durchziehen VI **a** *(Sport)* durchschwingen **b** **to follow through with sth** *(with plan)* etw zu Ende verfolgen; *(with threat)* etw wahr machen

▶ **follow up** VT *sep* **a** *(= pursue, take further action on) request* nachgehen *(+dat)*; *offer, suggestion* nachgehen *(+dat)*, aufgreifen

b *(= investigate further)* sich näher beschäftigen *or* befassen mit; *suspect* Erkundigungen einziehen über *(+acc)*; *candidate* in die engere Wahl nehmen; *matter* weiterverfolgen, sich näher befassen mit; *rumour* nachgehen *(+dat)*; *patient* nachuntersuchen; *(= not lose track of) matter* im Auge behalten

c *(= reinforce) success, victory* fortsetzen, ausbauen; **to follow up words with deeds** auf Worte Taten folgen lassen; **he followed up the remark by punching him** er versetzte ihm zur Bekräftigung einen Schlag

d *(= get further benefit from) advantage* ausnutzen

VI **a** **to follow up with sth** etw folgen lassen **b** *(Sport)* nachziehen

follower ['fɒləʊəʳ] N *(= disciple)* Anhänger(in) *m(f)*, Schüler(in) *m(f)*; *(old, = servant)* Gefolgsmann *m*; **to be a ~ of fashion** sehr modebewusst sein; **he's a ~ of Blair** er ist Blair-Anhänger *or* ein Anhänger von Blair

following ['fɒləʊɪŋ] ✪ 20.2, 20.3, 26.2 ADJ **a** folgend; **the ~ day** der nächste *or* (darauf)folgende Tag; **he made the ~ remarks** er bemerkte Folgendes **b** **a ~ wind** Rückenwind *m* N **a** *(= followers)* Anhängerschaft *f*, Gefolgschaft *f* **b** **he said the ~** er sagte Folgendes; **see the ~ for an explanation** *(in documents etc)* Erläuterungen hierzu finden Sie im Folgenden, Erklärungen im Folgenden; **the ~ is of note** Folgendes ist wichtig PREP nach

follow-my-leader ['fɒləʊmaɪ'li:dəʳ], *(US)* **follow-the-leader** ['fɒləʊðə'li:dəʳ] N *Spiel, bei dem alle nachmachen müssen, was einer vormacht*

follow-through [ˌfɒləʊ'θru:] N *(Sport)* Durchziehen *nt*

follow-up ['fɒləʊˌʌp] N **a** Weiterverfolgen *nt*, Weiterführen *nt*; *(= event, programme etc coming after)* Fortsetzung *f (to +gen)* **b** *(= letter)* Nachfassschreiben *nt*; *(Press)* Fortsetzung *f* **c** *(Med)* Nachuntersuchung *f*

follow-up: **follow-up action** N Folgemaßnahmen *pl*; **follow-up advertising** N Nachfasswerbung *f*; **follow-up album** N Nachfolgealbum *nt*; **follow-up care** N *(Med)* Nachbehandlung *f*; **follow-up interview** N zweites Vorstellungsgespräch; **follow-up meeting** N Folgetreffen *nt*; **follow-up operation** N *(Police)* Nachfassoperation *f*; *(Med)* zweite Operation; **follow-up phone call** N Anruf *m* zur Nachfrage *or* um nachzufragen; **follow-up question** N Folgefrage *f*; **follow-up study** N Nachfolgestudie *f*; **follow-up treatment** N *(Med)* Nachbehandlung *f*; **follow-up visit** N *(Med)* Nachuntersuchung *f*

folly ['fɒlɪ] N *(= foolishness, foolish thing)* Torheit *f*, Verrücktheit *f*; *(= building) exzentrischer, meist völlig nutzloser Prachtbau*; **it is sheer ~ (to do that)** es ist der reinste Wahnsinn(, das zu tun)

foment [fəʊ'ment] VT *trouble, discord* schüren; *(Med)* mit feuchten Umschlägen behandeln

fomentation [ˌfəʊmen'teɪʃən] N *(of trouble, discord)* Schüren *nt*; *(Med)* feuchte Umschläge *pl*

fond [fɒnd] ADJ *(+er)* **a** **to be ~ of sb** jdn gernhaben *or* mögen; **to be ~ of sth** etw mögen; **she is very ~ of animals** sie hat Tiere sehr gern, sie ist sehr tierlieb(end); **I'm not enormously ~ of Shaw's plays** ich bin kein großer Freund von Shaws Stücken; **the two were very ~ of each other** die beiden hatten *or* mochten einander sehr gern; **I am ~er of Michael than James, but I am ~est of Adrian** ich habe Michael lieber als James, aber Adrian habe ich am liebsten; **to become** *or* **grow ~ of sb/sth** jdn/etw lieb gewinnen; **he became very ~ of the garden** der Garten ist ihm sehr lieb geworden *or* sehr ans Herz gewachsen; **to be ~ of doing sth** etw gern tun; **she was ~ of shopping** sie ging gern einkaufen; **he is very ~ of telling us about the war** er erzählt uns mit Vorliebe vom Krieg

b *(= loving) husband, parent, relative, look, smile* liebevoll; *friend* lieb; **she gave him a ~ smile** sie lächelte ihn liebevoll an; **to bid sb a ~ farewell** sich liebevoll von jdm verabschieden; **they're saying their ~ farewells** sie nehmen zärtlich voneinander Abschied; **to have ~ memories of sth** schöne Erinnerungen an etw *(acc)* haben, sich gern an etw *(acc)* erinnern; **~est regards** mit lieben Grüßen → **absence a**

c *(= fervent) hope, dream, wish* sehnlich; **his ~est wish** sein sehnlichster Wunsch, sein Herzenswunsch

d *(= foolish, vain) belief* naiv; *hope* töricht *(geh)*; **in the ~ hope/belief that …** in der vergeblichen Hoffnung, dass …; **he has ~ hopes of winning** er bildet sich *(dat)* tatsächlich ein, gewinnen zu können

fondant ['fɒndənt] N Fondant *m*

fondle ['fɒndl] VT (zärtlich) spielen mit; *(= stroke)* streicheln; *person* schmusen mit

fondly ['fɒndlɪ] ADV **a** *(= affectionately)* liebevoll; **to remember sb ~** jdn in bester Erinnerung behalten; **to remember sth ~** sich gern an etw *(acc)* erinnern **b** *(= naively) imagine, believe* naiverweise; *hope* törichterweise *(geh)*

fondness ['fɒndnɪs] N *(for people)* Zuneigung *f*, Liebe *f (for* zu); *(for food, place, writer etc)* Vorliebe *f (for* für); *(for music, art)* Liebe *f (for* zu); **his ~ for** *or* **of swimming** seine Vorliebe fürs Schwimmen; **to remember sth/past times with great ~** sehr gern an etw *(acc)*/an vergangene Zeiten zurückdenken

fondue ['fɒndu:] N Fondue *nt*; **~ set** Fondueset *nt*

font [fɒnt] N **a** *(Eccl)* Taufstein *m* **b** *(Typ)* Schrift *f*

fontanel(le) [ˌfɒntə'nel] N *(Physiol)* Fontanelle *f*

font: **font size** N *(Typ)* Schriftgrad *m*, Schriftgröße *f*; **font style** N *(Typ)* Schriftschnitt *m*; **font type** N *(Typ)* Schriftart *f*

food [fu:d] N **a** Essen *nt*; *(for animals)* Futter *nt*; *(= nourishment)* Nahrung *f*; *(= foodstuff)* Nahrungsmittel *nt*; *(= groceries)* Lebensmittel *pl*; **the ~ is awful here** das Essen hier ist scheußlich; **dog and cat ~** Hunde- und Katzenfutter; **~ and drink** Essen und Trinken; **milk is a ~ rather than a drink** Milch ist eher ein Nahrungsmittel als ein Getränk; **canned ~s** Konserven *pl*; **I haven't any ~ in the house** ich habe nichts zu essen im Haus; **to be off one's ~** keinen Appetit haben; **they also do ~ at the pub** in der Kneipe gibt es auch Essen; **the very thought of ~ made her ill** wenn sie nur ans Essen dachte, wurde ihr schon schlecht **b** *(fig)* Nahrung *f*; **~ for thought** Stoff *m* zum Nachdenken

food: **food additives** PL chemische Zusätze *pl*; **food aid** N Lebensmittelhilfe *f*; **food chain** N Nahrungskette *f*; **to get into the ~** in die Nahrungskette gelangen; **food combining** N Trennkost *f*; **food court** N *(US)* Imbiss-Bereich *m (in einem Einkaufszentrum etc)*

foodie ['fu:dɪ] N *(inf)* **a** *(= gourmet)* Gourmet *m*, Feinschmecker(in) *m(f)* **b** *(= food fanatic)* Kochfreak *m (inf)*

food: **food parcel** N Lebensmittelpaket *nt*; **food poisoning** N Lebensmittelvergiftung *f*; **food processor** N Küchenmaschine *f*; **food rationing** N Lebensmittelrationierung *f*; **food safety** N Lebensmittelsicherheit *f*; **food stamp** N *(US)* Lebensmittelmarke *f*; **foodstuff** N Nahrungsmittel *nt*; **food value** N Nährwert *m*

fool[1] [fu:l] **N** **a** Dummkopf *m*, Narr *m*, Närrin *f*; **don't be a ~!** sei nicht (so) dumm!; **some ~ of a civil servant** irgend so ein blöder *or* doofer Beamter *(inf)*; **I was a ~ not to realize** wie konnte ich nur so dumm sein und das nicht merken; **have I been a ~!** war ich vielleicht dumm *or* blöd!, ich Idiot!; **he was a ~ not to accept** es war dumm von ihm, nicht anzunehmen; **to be ~ enough to ...** so dumm *or* blöd *(inf)* sein, zu ...; **to play** *or* **act the ~** Unsinn machen, herumalbern; **he made himself look a ~ in front of everyone** er machte sich vor allen lächerlich; **to make a ~ of sb** *(with ridicule)* jdn lächerlich machen; *(with a trick)* jdn zum Besten *or* zum Narren haben; **he made a ~ of himself at the party** er hat sich bei der Party blamiert; **to go on a ~'s errand** einen nutzlosen Gang tun; **to live in a ~'s paradise** in einem Traumland leben; **there's no ~ like an old ~** *(Prov)* Alter schützt vor Torheit nicht *(Prov)*; **~s rush in (where angels fear to tread)** *(Prov)* blinder Eifer schadet nur *(Prov)* → **more, nobody**
b *(= jester)* Narr *m*
ADJ *(esp US inf)* doof *(inf)*, schwachsinnig *(inf)*
VI herumalbern, Blödsinn machen; **to ~ with sb/sth** mit jdm/etw spielen; **stop ~ing (around)!** lass den Blödsinn!; **I was only ~ing** das war doch nur Spaß
VT zum Narren haben *or* halten; *(= trick)* hereinlegen *(inf)*; *(disguise, phoney accent etc)* täuschen; **you won't ~ me so easily** so leicht können Sie mich nicht hereinlegen *(inf)*; **I was completely ~ed** ich bin vollkommen darauf hereingefallen; **you had me ~ed** ich habe das tatsächlich geglaubt; **who are you trying to ~?** wem willst du das weismachen?; **they ~ed him into believing that ...** sie haben ihm weisgemacht, dass ...; **they ~ed him into believing it** er hat es ihnen tatsächlich abgenommen

▶ **fool about** *(Brit) or* **fool around** VI **a** *(= waste time)* herumtrödeln; **he spends his time fooling about** *or* **around with his friends** er verschwendet seine ganze Zeit mit seinen Freunden **b** *(= play the fool)* herumalbern **c** **to fool about** *or* **around with sth** mit etw Blödsinn machen **d** *(sexually)* **he's fooling around with my wife** er treibt seine Spielchen mit meiner Frau; **she was fooling around** sie hat sich mit anderen eingelassen

fool[2] N *(Brit Cook)* *Sahnespeise aus Obstpüree*

foolery ['fu:lərɪ] N Albernheit *f*

foolhardiness ['fu:l,hɑ:dɪnɪs] N Tollkühnheit *f*

foolhardy ['fu:l,hɑ:dɪ] ADJ tollkühn

foolish ['fu:lɪʃ] ADJ *person, decision, statement, action, mistake* dumm, töricht *(geh)*; *question* dumm, blöd *(inf)*; **he said his action had been ~** er sagte, dass er sich dumm verhalten *or* eine Dummheit gemacht hatte; **don't do anything ~** mach keinen Unsinn; **she had done something ~** sie hatte eine Dummheit gemacht; **what a ~ thing to do** wie kann man nur so dumm sein *or* so etwas Dummes tun; **to feel ~** sich *(dat)* dumm *or* lächerlich vorkommen; **to look ~** dumm aussehen, sich lächerlich machen; **he's afraid of looking ~** er will sich nicht lächerlich machen *or* sich nicht blamieren; **to make sb look ~** jdn blamieren; **it made him look ~** dadurch hat er sich blamiert

foolishly ['fu:lɪʃlɪ] ADV *(= unwisely) behave, act* unklug, töricht *(geh)*; *grin* dumm; *say* dummerweise; *(introducing sentence)* unklugerweise, törichterweise *(geh)*; **you're being ~ romantic about it** deine romantische Einstellung dazu ist dumm

foolishness ['fu:lɪʃnɪs] N Dummheit *f*; **enough of this ~** lassen wir diese Dummheiten

foolproof ['fu:lpru:f] ADJ *(= infallible) method, system, test* unfehlbar; *(= idiot-proof) camera, recipe* narrensicher, idiotensicher *(inf)*

foolscap ['fu:lskæp] N *(also* **foolscap paper***)* ≈ Kanzleipapier *nt*, *britisches Papierformat (13¼ × 16½ Zoll)*

fool's gold ['fu:lz'gəʊld] N Katzengold *nt*

foosball ['fu:sbɔ:l] N *(esp US)* Tischfußball *m*, Kicker *nt*

foot [fʊt] **N** *pl* **feet** **a** Fuß *m*; **to be on one's feet** *(lit, fig)* auf den Beinen sein; **to help sb back (on)to their feet** jdm wieder auf die Beine helfen; **to get back on one's feet** *(lit, fig)* wieder auf die Beine kommen; **the country is starting to get back on its feet again** das Land kommt langsam wieder auf die Beine; **on ~** zu Fuß; **to set ~ on dry land** den Fuß auf festen Boden setzen, an Land gehen; **I'll never set ~ here again!** hier kriegen mich keine zehn Pferde mehr her! *(inf)*; **the first time he set ~ in the office** als er das erste Mal das Büro betrat; **to get** *or* **rise to one's feet** aufstehen; **to jump to one's feet** aufspringen; **to put one's feet up** *(lit)* die Füße hochlegen; *(fig)* es sich *(dat)* bequem machen; **he never puts a ~ wrong** *(gymnast, dancer)* bei ihm stimmt jeder Schritt; *(fig)* er macht nie einen Fehler; **to catch sb on the wrong ~** *(Sport)* jdn auf dem falschen Fuß erwischen; *(fig)* jdn überrumpeln; **to be dying** *or* **dead on one's feet** *(inf)* todmüde sein
b *(fig uses)* **to put one's ~ down** *(= act with decision or authority)* ein Machtwort sprechen; *(= forbid, refuse)* es strikt verbieten; *(Aut)* Gas geben; **to put one's ~ in it** ins Fettnäpfchen treten; **to put one's best ~ forward** *(= hurry)* die Beine unter den Arm nehmen; *(= do one's best)* sich anstrengen; **to find one's feet** sich eingewöhnen, sich zurechtfinden; **to fall on one's feet** auf die Beine fallen; **to have one's** *or* **both feet (firmly) on the ground** mit beiden Beinen (fest) auf der Erde stehen; **to keep one's feet on the ground** *(fig)* beide Beine auf der Erde halten; **to have one ~ in the grave** mit einem Bein im Grabe stehen; **to get/be under sb's feet** jdm im Wege stehen *or* sein; *(children also)* jdm vor den Füßen herumlaufen; **to get off on the right/wrong ~** einen guten/schlechten Start haben; **to have/get one's** *or* **a ~ in the door** einen Fuß in der Tür haben/in die Tür bekommen; **to get one's feet under the table** *(Brit inf)* sich etablieren; **to stand on one's own two feet** auf eigenen Füßen *or* Beinen stehen; **to sit at sb's feet** *(fig)* jds Jünger sein; **a nice area, my ~!** *(inf)* und das soll eine schöne Gegend sein!
c *(of stocking, list, page, stairs, hill, sewing machine etc)* Fuß *m*; *(of bed)* Fußende *nt*
d *(Measure)* Fuß *m*; **3 ~** *or* **feet wide/long** 3 Fuß breit/lang; **he's 6 ~ 3** ≈ er ist 1,90 m
e *(Poet)* (Vers)fuß *m*
f *no pl (Mil)* Infanterie *f*; **the 15th ~** das 15. Infanterieregiment; **ten thousand ~** *(Brit)* zehntausend Fußsoldaten *pl*
VT **a** **to ~ it** *(inf: = walk)* marschieren *(inf)*
b *bill* bezahlen, begleichen

footage ['fʊtɪdʒ] N **a** *(= length)* Gesamtlänge *f* *(in Fuß)* **b** *(of film)* Filmmeter *pl*

foot-and-mouth (disease) ['fʊtən'maʊθ(dɪ,zi:z)] N *(Brit)* Maul- und Klauenseuche *f*

football ['fʊtbɔ:l] N **a** Fußball *m*; *(= American football)* (American) Football *m* **b** *(= ball)* Fußball *m*, Leder *nt (inf)*

football: **football boot** N Fußballschuh *m*, Fußballstiefel *m*; **football casual** N Fußballprolo *m (inf)*; **football coupon** N *(Brit)* Tippzettel *m*, Totoschein *m*

footballer ['fʊtbɔ:lə^r] N **a** *(Brit)* Fußball(spiel)er(in) *m(f)* **b** *(in American football)* Footballspieler *m*

football: **football fan** N Fußballfan *m*; **football hooligan** N Fußballrowdy *or* -hooligan *m*; **football hooliganism** N Fußballkrawalle *pl*

footballing ['fʊtbɔ:lɪŋ] ADJ Fußball-; **~ career** Fußballkarriere *f*; **~ countries** Fußball spielende Länder *pl*; **his ~ achievements** seine fußballerischen Leistungen

football pools PL Fußballtoto *nt or m* → **pool[2] c**

football shorts PL *(Brit)* Fußballhose *f*

foot: **foot bath** N Fußbad *nt*; **footboard** N *(Rail, on coach)* Trittbrett *nt*; **foot brake** N Fußbremse *f*; **footbridge** N Fußgängerbrücke *f*

-footed [-fʊtɪd] ADJ *suf* -füßig; **four-footed** vierfüßig

footer ['fʊtə^r] N *(Comput)* Fußzeile *f*

foot: **footfall** N Schritt *m*; **foot fault** N *(Tennis)* Fußfehler *m*; **footgear** N Fußbekleidung *f*; **foothills** PL (Gebirgs)ausläufer *pl*; **foothold** N Stand *m*, Halt *m*; *(fig)* sichere (Ausgangs)position; **he got** *or* **gained a ~ on the rock** er fand mit den Füßen Halt am Felsen; **to establish** *or* **gain a ~** *(fig)* Fuß fassen; **to lose one's ~** *(lit, fig)* den Halt verlieren

footie ['fʊtɪ] N *(Brit inf)* Fußball *m*

footing ['fʊtɪŋ] N **a** *(lit)* Stand *m*, Halt *m*; **to lose one's ~** den Halt verlieren; **to miss one's ~** danebentreten
b *(fig) (= foundation, basis)* Basis *f*; *(= relationship)* Beziehung *f*, Verhältnis *nt*; **the business was on a secure ~** das Geschäft stand auf einer sicheren Basis; **we are trying to put training on a more scientific ~** wir versuchen, die Ausbildung wissenschaftlicher zu fundieren; **to be on a friendly ~ with sb** mit jdm auf freundschaftlichem Fuße stehen; **we want to put Britain on the same ~ as the rest of Europe** wir wollen Großbritannien mit dem restlichen Europa gleichstellen; **on an equal ~ (with each other)** auf gleicher Basis; **to be on a war ~** sich im Kriegszustand befinden
c *(Archit)* Sockel *m*

footle ['fu:tl] VI **to ~ about** *(inf)* herumpusseln

footless ['fʊtlɪs] ADJ **a** *(= with no feet)* ohne Füße **b** *(fig: = unsubstantial)* nicht stichhaltig, nicht fundiert **c** *(inf: = inept)* ungeschickt

footlights ['fʊtlaɪts] PL *(Theat)* Rampenlicht *nt*; **the lure of the ~** *(fig)* die Anziehungskraft der Bühne *or* der Bretter

footling ['fu:tlɪŋ] ADJ albern, dumm, läppisch

foot: **footloose** ADJ ungebunden, unbeschwert; **~ and fancy-free** frei und ungebunden; **footman** N Lakai *m*; **footmark** N Fußabdruck *m*; **footnote** N Fußnote *f*; *(fig)* Anmerkung *f*; **footpace** N Schritttempo *nt*; **at a ~** im Schritt; **footpath** N **a** *(= path)* Fußweg *m* **b** *(Brit: = pavement)* Bürgersteig *m*; **footplate** N Führerstand *m*; **footplate men, footplate workers** PL Lokomotivführer *pl*; **foot-pound** N *britische Maßeinheit für Drehmoment und Energie*; **footprint** N Fußabdruck *m*; *(fig, of machine)* Stellfläche *f*, Grundfläche *f*; **footprints** PL Fußspuren *pl*; **foot pump** N Fußpumpe *f*, Blasebalg *m*; **footrest** N Fußstütze *f*; **foot rot** N *(Vet)* Fußfäule *f*; **foot save** N *(Sport)* Fußabwehr *f*

footscraper N Fußabstreifer *m (aus Metall)*

Footsie ['fʊtsɪ] N *(Fin inf)* Footsie(-Index) *m (inf)*, Financial-Times-100-Index *m*

footsie ['fʊtsɪ] N *(inf)* **to play ~ with sb** mit jdm füßeln

foot: **footslog** VI *(inf)* latschen *(inf)*, marschieren; **footslogger** N *(Mil sl)* Fußsoldat *m*, Infanterist *m*; **~s** *(Mil sl)* Fußvolk *nt*; *(inf: = walkers)* Spaziergänger *pl*, Tippler *pl (inf)*; **foot soldier** N Fußsoldat *m*, Infanterist *m*; **footsore** ADJ **to be ~** wunde Füße haben; **footstalk** N *(Bot)* Stängel *m*, Stiel *m*; **footstep** N Schritt *m* → **follow**; **footstool** N Schemel *m*, Fußbank *f*; **footwear** N Schuhe *pl*, Schuhwerk *nt*; **footwork** N *no pl (Sport)* Beinarbeit *f*; *(fig)* Manöver *pl*

footy ['fʊtɪ] N *(Brit inf)* Fußball *m*

foozball ['fu:zbɔ:l] N *(esp US)* Tischfußball *m*, Kicker *nt*

fop [fɒp] N *(dated)* Geck *m*, Stutzer *m (dated)*

foppish [ˈfɒpɪʃ] ADJ *(dated) man* geckenhaft *(pej)*; *clothes* stutzerhaft

for[1] [fɔːˈ] PREP **a** *(intention)* für; *(purpose)* zu, für; *(destination)* nach; **a letter ~ me** ein Brief für mich; **clothes ~ children** Kleidung *f* für Kinder, Kinderkleidung *f*; **destined ~ greatness** zu Höherem bestimmt; **what ~?** wofür?, wozu?; **what is this knife ~?** wozu dient dieses Messer?; **he does it ~ pleasure** er macht es zum *or* aus Vergnügen; **what did you do that ~?** warum *or* wozu haben Sie das getan?; **a room ~ working in/sewing** ein Zimmer zum Arbeiten/Nähen; **a bag ~ carrying books (in)** eine Tasche, um Bücher zu tragen; **fit ~ nothing** zu nichts nutze *or* zu gebrauchen; **to get ready ~ a journey** sich für eine Reise fertig machen; **ready ~ anything** zu allem bereit; **this will do ~ a hammer** das kann man als Hammer nehmen; **to go to Spain ~ one's holidays** nach Spanien in Urlaub fahren; **the train ~ Stuttgart** der Zug nach Stuttgart; **to leave ~ the USA** in die USA *or* nach Amerika abreisen; **he swam ~ the shore** er schwamm auf die Küste zu, er schwamm in Richtung Küste; **to make ~ home** sich auf den Heimweg machen

b *(indicating suitability)* **it's not ~ you to ask questions** Sie haben kein Recht, Fragen zu stellen; **it's not ~ me to say** es steht mir nicht zu, mich dazu zu äußern; **she's the woman** *or* **the one ~ me** sie ist die (richtige) Frau für mich; **married life is not ~ me** das Eheleben ist nichts für mich

c *(= representing, instead of)* **I'll speak to her ~ you if you like** wenn Sie wollen, rede ich an Ihrer Stelle *or* für Sie mit ihr; **I need someone to make up my mind ~ me** ich brauche jemanden, der die Entscheidung für mich trifft; **to act ~ sb** für jdn handeln; **D ~ Daniel** D wie Daniel; **agent ~ Renault** Vertreter(in) *m(f)* für Renault; **she works ~ a bank** *(in the bank)* sie arbeitet bei *or* in einer Bank; *(outside the bank)* sie arbeitet für eine Bank

d *(= in defence, in favour of)* für; **are you ~ or against it?** sind Sie dafür oder dagegen?; **I'm all ~ it** ich bin ganz *or* sehr dafür; **I'm all ~ helping him** ich bin sehr dafür, ihm zu helfen; **the case ~ nuclear power** die Argumente für die Atomkraft

e *(= with regard to)* **anxious ~ sb** um jdn besorgt; **I'm very happy ~ you** ich freue mich sehr für euch; **~ my part** was mich betrifft; **as ~ him/that** was ihn/das betrifft; **warm/cold ~ the time of year** warm/kalt für die Jahreszeit; **he is tall ~ his age** er ist groß für sein Alter; **what do you want ~ your birthday?** was wünschst du dir zum Geburtstag?; **it's all right** *or* **all very well ~ you (to talk)** Sie haben gut reden; **~ further information see page 77** weitere Informationen finden Sie auf Seite 77

f *(= because of)* aus; **~ this reason** aus diesem Grund; **he did it ~ fear of being left** er tat es aus Angst, zurückgelassen zu werden; **he is famous ~ his jokes/his big nose** er ist für seine Witze bekannt/wegen seiner großen Nase berühmt; **to jump ~ joy** einen Freudensprung machen; **to go to prison ~ theft** wegen Diebstahls ins Gefängnis wandern; **to choose sb ~ his ability** jdn wegen seiner Fähigkeiten wählen; **if it were not ~ him** wenn er nicht wäre; **do it ~ me** tu es für mich

g *(= in spite of)* trotz *(+gen or (inf) +dat)*; **~ all his wealth** trotz all seines Reichtums; **~ all that, you should have warned me** Sie hätten mich trotz allem warnen sollen

h *(= in exchange)* für; **to pay four euros ~ a ticket** vier Euro für eine Fahrkarte zahlen; **he'll do it ~ ten pounds** er macht es für zehn Pfund; **pound ~ pound** Pfund für Pfund

i *(= in contrast)* **~ every job that is created, two are lost** für jede Stelle, die neu geschaffen wird, gehen zwei verloren

j *(in time)* seit; *(with future tense)* für; **I have not seen her ~ two years** ich habe sie seit zwei Jahren nicht gesehen; **he's been here ~ ten days** er ist seit zehn Tagen hier; **I had/have known her ~ years** ich kannte/kenne sie schon seit Jahren; **then I did not see her ~ two years** dann habe ich sie zwei Jahre lang nicht gesehen; **he walked ~ two hours** er ist zwei Stunden lang marschiert; **I am going away ~ a few days** ich werde (für *or* auf) ein paar Tage wegfahren; **I shall be away ~ a month** ich werde einen Monat (lang) weg sein; **he won't be back ~ a week** er wird erst in einer Woche zurück sein; **I'll be back home ~ Christmas** Weihnachten bin ich wieder zu Hause; **can you get it done ~ Monday/this time next week?** können Sie es bis *or* für Montag/bis in einer Woche fertig haben?; **I've got a job ~ you ~ next week** ich habe für nächste Woche Arbeit für dich; **~ a while/time** (für) eine Weile/einige Zeit; **the meeting was scheduled ~ 9 o'clock** die Besprechung sollte um 9 Uhr stattfinden

k *(distance)* **the road is lined with trees ~ two miles** die Straße ist auf *or* über zwei Meilen mit Bäumen gesäumt; **we walked ~ two miles** wir sind zwei Meilen weit gelaufen; **there are roadworks on the M8 ~ two miles** auf der M8 gibt es eine zwei Meilen lange Baustelle; **~ miles** meilenweit; **~ mile upon mile** Meile um Meile

l *(with verbs)* **to pray ~ peace** für den *or* um Frieden beten; **to hope ~ news** auf Nachricht hoffen; **to look ~ sth** (nach) etw suchen → *vbs*

m *(after n: indicating liking, aptitude etc)* für; **a weakness ~ sweet things** eine Schwäche für Süßigkeiten; **his knack ~ saying the wrong thing** sein Talent, das Falsche zu sagen

n *(with infin clauses)* **~ this to be possible** damit dies möglich wird; **it's easy ~ him to do it** für ihn ist es leicht, das zu tun, er kann das leicht tun; **I brought it ~ you to see** ich habe es mitgebracht, damit Sie es sich *(dat)* ansehen können; **the best thing would be ~ you to leave** das Beste wäre, wenn Sie weggingen; **there's still time ~ him to come** er kann immer noch kommen; **their one hope is ~ him to return** ihre einzige Hoffnung ist, dass er zurückkommt

o *(phrases)* **to do sth ~ oneself** etw alleine tun; **~ example** zum Beispiel; **you're (in) ~ it!** *(inf)* jetzt bist du dran! *(inf)*; **oh ~ a cup a tea!** jetzt eine Tasse Tee - das wäre schön!

CONJ denn; **~ it was too late** denn es war zu spät

ADJ *pred (= in favour)* dafür; **17 were ~, 13 against** 17 waren dafür, 13 dagegen

for[2] *abbr of* **free on rail** frei Bahn

forage [ˈfɒrɪdʒ] N **a** *(= fodder)* Futter *nt* **b** *(= search for fodder)* Futtersuche *f*; *(Mil)* Überfall *m* VI nach Futter suchen; *(Mil)* einen Überfall/Überfälle machen; *(fig: = rummage)* herumstöbern *(for* nach)

forage cap N Schiffchen *nt*

foray [ˈfɒreɪ] N (Raub)überfall *m*; *(Mil)* Ausfall *m*; *(fig)* Ausflug *m (into* in *+acc)*; **to make a ~ into the European market** sich auf den europäischen Markt vorwagen VI Raubüberfälle/einen Raubüberfall machen; *(fig)* Ausflüge/einen Ausflug machen

forbad(e) [fəˈbæd] *pret of* **forbid**

forbear[1] [fɔːˈbɛəˈ] *pret* **forbore**, *ptp* **forborne** *(form)* VI **I forbore from expressing my opinion** ich verzichtete darauf *or* nahm Abstand davon, meine Meinung zu äußern; **we begged him to ~** wir baten ihn, darauf zu verzichten VT **he forbore to make any comment** er enthielt sich jeden Kommentars

forbear[2] [ˈfɔːbɛəˈ] N *(form)* Vorfahr(in) *m(f)*, Ahn(e) *m*, Ahne *f*

forbearance [fɔːˈbɛərəns] N Nachsicht *f*

forbearing [fɔːˈbɛərɪŋ] ADJ nachsichtig; *(= patient)* geduldig

forbid [fəˈbɪd] ✪ 9.3, 9.5, 10.4 *pret* **forbad(e)**, *ptp* **forbidden** VT **a** *(= not allow)* verbieten; **to ~ sb to do sth** jdm verbieten, etw zu tun **b** *(= prevent)* verhindern, nicht erlauben; **my health ~s my attending** *or* **me from attending the meeting** meine Gesundheit erlaubt es nicht, dass ich an dem Treffen teilnehme; **God** *or* **Heaven ~!** Gott behüte *or* bewahre!; **Heaven ~ that she should come!** der Himmel bewahre uns davor, dass sie kommt!

forbidden [fəˈbɪdn] ADJ **a** *(= prohibited) love, food, goods* verboten; **~ by law** gesetzlich verboten; **they are ~ to enter** sie dürfen nicht hereinkommen, es ist ihnen verboten, hereinzukommen; **smoking is (strictly) ~** Rauchen ist (streng) verboten; **preaching was ~ to women** Frauen durften nicht predigen, es war Frauen verboten zu predigen; **~ zone** Sperrzone *f*; **~ area** Sperrgebiet *nt*; **some cities and sites are ~ to foreigners** Ausländer dürfen manche Städte und Anlagen nicht betreten

b *(= taboo)* **~ subject/word** Tabuthema *nt*/-wort *nt*; **~ territory** *or* **ground** *(fig)* Tabu(thema) *nt*; **that's ~ territory** *(fig)* das ist tabu; **~ feelings** verbotene Gefühle *pl*

Forbidden City N **the ~** die Verbotene Stadt

forbidden fruit N verbotene Früchte *pl*; **~s are always the sweetest** verbotene Früchte schmecken am süßesten

forbidding [fəˈbɪdɪŋ] ADJ *person, expression* Furcht einflößend; *place, terrain* unwirtlich; *building, rocks, cliffs* bedrohlich; *task (= uninviting)* wenig einladend; *(= overwhelming)* überwältigend; *prospect* düster; **the room was cold and ~** das Zimmer war kalt und unfreundlich

forbiddingly [fəˈbɪdɪŋlɪ] ADV *(= off-puttingly) (+adj)* abstoßend; *long, steep, expensive, difficult* entmutigend; *(+vb) say* unfreundlich; *look* streng, unfreundlich; *loom* bedrohlich; **some find him ~ aloof** einige finden ihn unnahbar in seiner Strenge; **a ~ black cloud** eine bedrohlich schwarze Wolke

forbore [fɔːˈbɔːˈ] *pret of* **forbear**

forborne [fɔːˈbɔːn] *ptp of* **forbear**

force [fɔːs] ✪ 10.3, 26.1 N **a** *no pl (= physical strength, power)* Kraft *f*; *(of blow, impact, collision)* Wucht *f*; *(= physical coercion)* Gewalt *f*; *(Phys)* Kraft *f*; **to resort to ~** Gewalt anwenden; **to settle sth by ~** etw gewaltsam *or* durch Gewalt beilegen; **by sheer ~** durch reine Gewalt; **by** *or* **through sheer ~ of numbers** aufgrund *or* auf Grund zahlenmäßiger Überlegenheit; **there is a ~ 5 wind blowing** es herrscht Windstärke 5; **the ~ of the wind was so great he could hardly stand** der Wind war so stark, dass er kaum stehen konnte; **they were there in ~** sie waren in großer Zahl da; **they came in ~** sie kamen in großer Zahl *or* Stärke

b *no pl (fig) (of argument)* Überzeugungskraft *f*; *(of music, phrase)* Eindringlichkeit *f*; *(of character)* Stärke *f*; *(of words)* Macht *f*; **that was ~ of habit** das war die Macht der Gewohnheit; **by** *or* **from ~ of habit** aus Gewohnheit; **by ~ of will** durch Willensanstrengung *or* Willenskraft; **the ~ of circumstances** der Druck der Verhältnisse; **I see the ~ of what he is saying** ich sehe ein, was er sagt, ist zwingend

c *(= powerful thing, person)* Macht *f*; **Forces of Nature** Naturgewalten *pl*; **there are various ~s at work here** hier sind verschiedene Kräfte am Werk; **he is a powerful ~ in the reform movement** er ist ein einflussreicher Mann in der Reformbewegung → **life force**

d *(= body of men)* **the ~s** *(Mil)* die Streitkräfte *pl*; **the (police) ~** die Polizei; **to join ~s** sich zusammentun → **sales force, workforce**

e to come into/be in ~ in Kraft treten/sein

VT **a** *(= compel)* zwingen; **to ~ sb/oneself to do sth** jdn/sich zwingen, etw zu tun; **he was ~d to resign** er wurde gezwungen zurückzutreten; *(= felt obliged to)* er sah sich gezwungen zurückzutreten; **he was ~d to conclude that …** er sah sich zu der Folgerung gezwungen *or* gedrängt, dass …

b *(= extort, obtain by force)* erzwingen; **he ~d a confession out of** *or* **from me** er erzwang ein Geständnis von mir; **to ~ an error** *(Sport)* einen Fehler erzwingen, den Gegner ausspielen

c to ~ sth (up)on sb *(present, one's company)* jdm etw aufdrängen; *conditions, obedience* jdm etw auferlegen; *conditions, decision, war* jdm etw aufzwingen; **he ~d himself on her** *(sexually)* er

tat ihr Gewalt an
d (= *break open*) aufbrechen; **to ~ (an) entry** sich *(dat)* gewaltsam Zugang *or* Zutritt verschaffen
e (= *push, squeeze*) **to ~ books into a box** Bücher in eine Kiste zwängen; **the liquid is ~d up the tube by a pump** die Flüssigkeit wird von einer Pumpe durch das Rohr nach oben gepresst; **if it won't open/go in, don't ~ it** wenn es nicht aufgeht/passt, wende keine Gewalt an; **to ~ one's way into sth** sich *(dat)* gewaltsam Zugang zu etw *or* in etw *(acc)* verschaffen; **to ~ one's way through** sich *(dat)* gewaltsam einen Weg bahnen; **to ~ a car off the road** ein Auto von der Fahrbahn drängen; **to ~ a bill through parliament** eine Gesetzesvorlage durch das Parlament peitschen
f *plants* treiben
g (= *produce with effort*) **to ~ a smile** gezwungen lächeln; **to ~ the pace** das Tempo forcieren; **don't ~ it** erzwingen Sie es nicht

▶ **force back** VT *sep* zurückdrängen; *tears* unterdrücken

▶ **force down** VT *sep food* sich *(dat)* hinunterquälen; *aeroplane* zur Landung zwingen; *price* drücken; *laugh* unterdrücken; *lid of suitcase etc* mit Gewalt zumachen

▶ **force off** VT *sep lid* mit Gewalt abmachen

▶ **force up** VT *sep prices* hochtreiben

forced [fɔːst] ADJ a (= *imposed*) Zwangs-; *repatriation* gewaltsam; *marriage, resignation, withdrawal* erzwungen; **~ sale** Zwangsverkauf *m;* (= *auction*) Zwangsversteigerung *f* b (= *contrived*) *smile, laughter, conversation, wording* gezwungen; *behaviour* gekünstelt; **to sound ~** sich gezwungen *or* unnatürlich anhören c *plant* getrieben

forced: **forced entry** N (= *break-in*) Einbruch *m;* **forced labour,** *(US)* **forced labor** N Zwangsarbeit *f;* **forced landing** N *(Aviat)* Notlandung *f;* **forced loan** N Zwangsanleihe *f;* **forced march** N *(Mil)* Gewaltmarsch *m;* **forced saving** N Zwangssparen *nt*

force-feed [ˈfɔːsfiːd] *vb: pret, ptp* **force-fed** VT zwangsernähren N *(Tech)* Druckschmierung *f*

forceful [ˈfɔːsfʊl] ADJ a (= *hard*) *blow, kick* kräftig, wuchtig b (= *vigorous*) *person, manner, action* energisch; *character, personality* stark; *rejection, criticism, denial* entschieden; *speech, statement, language, style* eindringlich; *reminder* eindringlich, nachdrücklich; *argument* (= *strong*) eindringlich; (= *convincing*) überzeugend; **he was ~ in his refusal** er weigerte sich entschieden; **she was ~ in her condemnation of the regime** sie verurteilte das Regime aufs schärfste *or* Schärfste

forcefully [ˈfɔːsfəlɪ] ADV a (= *forcibly*) *remove, move* mit Gewalt, gewaltsam; (= *violently*) *push, knock* heftig b (= *vigorously*) *act, intervene* energisch, entschlossen; *argue* eindringlich; *deny, reject, criticize* entschieden; *say, demand, remind* nachdrücklich, eindringlich; **it struck him ~ that ...** es fiel ihm sehr auf, dass ...

forcefulness [ˈfɔːsfʊlnɪs] N a (*of kick, punch*) Wucht *f* b (= *vigour, of person, manner, action, intervention*) energische *or* entschlossene Art; (*of character, personality*) Stärke *f;* (*of rejection, criticism, denial*) Entschiedenheit *f;* (*of speech, statement, language, style*) Eindringlichkeit *f;* (*of argument,* = *strength*) Eindringlichkeit *f;* (= *conviction*) Überzeugungskraft *f*

force majeure [ˌfɔːsmæˈʒɜːˈ] N höhere Gewalt; **to bow to ~** sich höherer Gewalt *(dat)* beugen

forcemeat [ˈfɔːsmiːt] N *(Cook)* Fleischfüllung *f,* Farce *f*

forceps [ˈfɔːseps] PL *(also* **pair of forceps***)* Zange *f;* **~ delivery** Zangengeburt *f*

forcible [ˈfɔːsəbl] ADJ a (= *forced*) *repatriation, removal* gewaltsam; **~ feeding** Zwangsernährung *f* b (= *emphatic*) *speech, declaration, language* eindringlich; *argument* überzeugend; **a ~ reminder of sth** eine eindringliche *or* nachdrückliche Erinnerung an etw *(acc)*

forcible entry N Einbruch *m*

forcibly [ˈfɔːsəblɪ] ADV a (= *by force*) *remove, restrain, separate* gewaltsam, mit Gewalt; **to feed sb ~** jdn zwangsernähren b (= *powerfully*) eindringlich; *argue, express* eindringlich, nachdrücklich; **what struck me most ~ about this incident was ...** was mir an diesem Zwischenfall am meisten auffiel, war ...; **this was brought home to me ~ when ...** das wurde mir in vollem Ausmaß bewusst, als ...

forcing house [ˈfɔːsɪŋhaʊs] N a *(Agr etc)* Gewächshaus *nt* b *(fig:* = *school)* Lernfabrik *f*

ford [fɔːd] N Furt *f* VT durchqueren; *(on foot also)* durchwaten

fore [fɔːˈ] N **to the ~** im Vordergrund; **to come to the ~** ins Blickfeld geraten ADJ *attr* (*Zool, Naut, Aviat:* = *front*) vordere(r, s); **the ~ part of the ship** das Vorschiff; **~ watch** *(Naut)* Vorderwache *f* ADV *(Naut)* vorn; **~ and aft** längsschiffs INTERJ *(Golf)* Achtung!

fore-and-aft [ˌfɔːrəndˈɑːft] ADJ *(Naut)* **~ schooner** Gaffelschoner *m;* **~ sail** Schratsegel *nt*

forearm¹ [ˈfɔːrɑːm] N Unterarm *m*

forearm² [fɔːrˈɑːm] VT vorbereiten; **~ed with this information** mit diesen Informationen gerüstet *or* gewappnet → **forewarn**

forebear¹ [ˈfɔːbɛəˈ] N *(form)* Vorfahr(in) *m(f),* Ahn(e) *m,* Ahne *f*

forebear² [fɔːˈbɛəˈ] VTI = **forbear**

forebode [fɔːˈbəʊd] VT (= *be portent of*) ein Zeichen *or* Omen sein für, ahnen lassen, deuten auf *(+acc)*

foreboding [fɔːˈbəʊdɪŋ] N (= *presentiment*) (Vor)ahnung *f,* Vorgefühl *nt;* (= *feeling of disquiet*) ungutes Gefühl ADJ *look* Unheil verkündend

forebrain [ˈfɔːbreɪn] N Vorderhirn *nt*

forecast [ˈfɔːkɑːst] VT vorhersehen, voraussagen; *(Met)* voraussagen, vorhersagen N Voraussage *f,* Vorhersage *f,* Prognose *f; (Met)* Voraus- *or* Vorhersage *f;* **the ~ is good** der Wetterbericht *or* die Wettervorhersage ist günstig

forecaster [ˈfɔːkɑːstəˈ] N *(Met)* Meteorologe *m,* Meteorologin *f;* **economic ~** Wirtschaftsprognostiker(in) *m(f)*

forecastle [ˈfəʊksl] N *(Naut)* Vorschiff *nt,* Vorderdeck *nt;* (*in Merchant Navy*) Logis *nt*

foreclose [fɔːˈkləʊz] VT *loan, mortgage* kündigen VI **to ~ on a loan/mortgage** ein Darlehen/eine Hypothek kündigen; **to ~ on sb** jds Kredit/Hypothek kündigen

foreclosure [fɔːˈkləʊʒəˈ] N Zwangsvollstreckung *f* (*on* bei)

forecourt [ˈfɔːkɔːt] N Vorhof *m*

foredeck [ˈfɔːdek] N Vor(der)deck *nt*

foredoomed [fɔːˈduːmd] ADJ *(form)* **~ to fail** *or* **to failure** von vorneherein zum Scheitern verurteilt, tot geboren *(fig inf)*

forefather [ˈfɔːˌfɑːðəˈ] N Ahn *m,* Vorfahr *m*

forefinger [ˈfɔːˌfɪŋgəˈ] N Zeigefinger *m*

forefoot [ˈfɔːfʊt] N Vorderfuß *m*

forefront [ˈfɔːfrʌnt] N **in** *or* **at the ~ of** an der Spitze *(+gen)*

foregather [fɔːˈgæðəˈ] VI zusammentreffen, sich versammeln

forego [fɔːˈgəʊ] *pret* **forewent**, *ptp* **foregone** VT verzichten auf *(+acc)*

foregoing [fɔːˈgəʊɪŋ] ADJ vorhergehend, vorangehend; **it can be seen from the ~ that ...** aus dem bisher Gesagten kann entnommen werden, dass ...

foregone [fɔːˈgɒn] *ptp of* **forego** [ˈfɔːgɒn] ADJ **it was a ~ conclusion** es stand von vornherein fest

foreground [ˈfɔːgraʊnd] N *(Art, Phot, Comput)* Vordergrund *m;* **in the ~** im Vordergrund

forehand [ˈfɔːhænd] *(Sport)* N Vorhand *f* ATTR Vorhand-; **~ volley** Vorhandvolley *m*

forehead [ˈfɔːhed, ˈfɒrɪd] N Stirn *f*

foreign [ˈfɒrən] ADJ a *person, product* ausländisch; *food, customs, appearance* fremdländisch; **to be ~** *(person)* Ausländer(in) *m(f)* sein; **a quarter of the population is ~** ein Viertel der Bevölkerung sind Ausländer *or* kommt aus dem Ausland; **~ countries** das Ausland; **he came from a ~ country** er kam aus dem Ausland; **~ travel** Auslandsreisen *pl;* **she was on her first ~ trip** sie machte zum ersten Mal eine Auslandsreise; **~ debt** Auslandsverschuldung *f;* **~ investment** Auslandsinvestition *f;* **~ news** Auslandsnachrichten *pl,* Nachrichten *pl* aus dem Ausland
b (= *alien*) Fremd-; **~ matter** Fremdstoffe *pl;* **~ body** *or* **object** Fremdkörper *m;* **to be ~ to sb** jdm fremd sein; **behaviour that was ~ to his nature** ein Verhalten, das seiner Natur fremd war

foreign: **foreign affairs** PL Außenpolitik *f;* **spokesman on ~** außenpolitischer Sprecher; **foreign agent** N (*in espionage*) ausländischer Agent; *(Comm etc)* Auslandsvertreter(in) *m(f);* **foreign aid** N Entwicklungshilfe *f;* **Foreign and Commonwealth Office** N *(Brit)* Außenministerium *nt;* **foreign-born** ADJ im Ausland geboren; **foreign correspondent** N Auslandskorrespondent(in) *m(f);* **foreign currency** N Devisen *pl*

foreigner [ˈfɒrənəˈ] N *(neg!)* Ausländer(in) *m(f)*

foreign: **foreign exchange** N a (= *currency*) Devisen *pl;* **~ reserves** Devisenreserven *pl* b (= *system, trading*) Devisenmarkt *m,* Devisenhandel *m;* (= *location*) Devisenbörse *f;* **on the ~s** an den Devisenbörsen c (= *stock exchange*) Auslandsbörse *f;* **foreign experience** N Auslandserfahrung *f;* **foreign language** N Fremdsprache *f;* **it was like a ~ to me** *(fig)* das waren böhmische Dörfer für mich *(inf)* ATTR *film* fremdsprachig; **~ assistant** Fremdsprachenassistent(in) *m(f);* **~ skills** Fremdsprachenkenntnisse *pl;* **foreign legion** N Fremdenlegion *f;* **Foreign Minister** N Außenminister(in) *m(f);* **foreign national** N ausländische(r) Staatsangehörige(r) *mf;* **Foreign Office** N *(Brit)* Auswärtiges Amt; **foreign policy** N *(Pol)* Außenpolitik *f;* **foreign relations** PL *(Pol)* Auslandsbeziehungen *pl;* **Foreign Secretary** N *(Brit)* Außenminister(in) *m(f);* **foreign trade** N Außenhandel *m*

foreknowledge [fɔːˈnɒlɪdʒ] N vorherige Kenntnis

foreland [ˈfɔːlənd] N Vorland *nt;* (= *promontory*) Landspitze *f*

foreleg [ˈfɔːleg] N Vorderbein *nt*

forelimb [ˈfɔːlɪm] N Vorderglied *nt*

forelock [ˈfɔːlɒk] N Stirnlocke *f,* Stirnhaar *nt;* **to touch** *or* **tug one's ~ (to sb)** *(Brit)* (jdm) seine Reverenz erweisen

foreman [ˈfɔːmən] N *pl* **-men** [-mən] (*in factory*) Vorarbeiter *m;* (*on building site*) Polier *m;* (*Jur, of jury*) Obmann *m*

foremast [ˈfɔːmɑːst] N *(Naut)* Fockmast *m*

foremost [ˈfɔːməʊst] ADJ a (= *leading*) *authority, writer, scholar etc* führend; **to be ~ in sth/in a field** in etw *(dat)*/auf einem Gebiet führend sein; **to be ~ in doing sth** führend darin sein, etw zu tun; **~ among them was John** John führte mit ihnen; **the thought which is ~ in his mind** der Gedanke, der ihn hauptsächlich beschäftigt b *(Naut)* vorderste(r, s) ADV a (= *above all*) vor allem → **first ADV b** b (= *forwards*) **to jump in feet/head ~** mit den Füßen/dem Kopf zuerst hineinspringen; **hold the spear point ~** halten Sie den Speer mit der Spitze nach vorn

forename [ˈfɔːneɪm] N Vorname *m*

forenoon [ˈfɔːnuːn] N *(form)* Vormittag *m*

forensic [fəˈrensɪk] ADJ a *evidence, test, laboratory* forensisch; *(Med)* gerichtsmedizinisch b *(form) skill* forensisch

forensic: **forensic expert** N *(Police)* Spurensicherungsexperte *m*/-expertin *f;* **forensic medicine** N Gerichtsmedizin *f,* forensische Medizin

forensics [fəˈrensɪks] N *sing* (= *science*) Kriminaltechnik *f;* (= *medicine*) Gerichtsmedizin *f;* (= *police department*) Spurensicherung *f*

forensic: **forensic science** N Kriminaltechnik *f*; ~ **laboratory** kriminaltechnisches Labor; **forensic scientist** N Kriminaltechniker(in) *m(f)*

foreordain [ˌfɔːrɔːˈdeɪn] VT = **preordain**

forepaw N Vorderpfote *f*

foreplay [ˈfɔːpleɪ] N Vorspiel *nt*

forequarters [ˈfɔːˌkwɔːtəz] PL Vorderstücke *pl*

forerib N *(Cook)* Hochrippe *f*

forerunner [ˈfɔːˌrʌnəʳ] N *(= precursor)* Vorläufer *m*; **a ~ of things to come** ein Vorbote *m* der Zukunft

foresaid [ˈfɔːsed] ADJ = **aforesaid**

foresail [ˈfɔːseɪl] N *(Naut)* Focksegel *nt*

foresee [fɔːˈsiː] *pret* **foresaw** [fɔːˈsɔː] *ptp* **foreseen** [fɔːˈsiːn] VT vorhersehen, voraussehen

foreseeable [fɔːˈsiːəbl] ADJ voraussehbar, absehbar; **in the ~ future** in absehbarer Zeit

foreshadow [fɔːˈʃædəʊ] VT ahnen lassen, andeuten

foresheet [ˈfɔːʃiːt] N *(Naut)* Fockschot *f*

foreshore [ˈfɔːʃɔːʳ] N Küstenvorland *nt*; *(= beach)* Strand *m*

foreshorten [fɔːˈʃɔːtn] VT *(Art)* perspektivisch zeichnen; *(Phot)* perspektivisch fotografieren

foreshortening [fɔːˈʃɔːtnɪŋ] N *(Art)* zeichnerische Verkürzung; *(Phot)* fotografische Verkürzung

foresight [ˈfɔːsaɪt] N Weitblick *m*

foreskin [ˈfɔːskɪn] N Vorhaut *f*

forest [ˈfɒrɪst] N Wald *m*; *(for lumber etc)* Forst *m*; *(fig) (of aerials etc)* Wald *m*; *(of ideas etc)* Wust *m*, Menge *f*; **~ deaths** Waldsterben *pl*

forestage [ˈfɔːsteɪdʒ] N Vorbühne *f*

forestall [fɔːˈstɔːl] VT *sb, rival* zuvorkommen *(+dat)*; *accident, eventuality* vorbeugen *(+dat)*; *crisis, danger, disaster* abwenden; *wish, desire* im Keim ersticken; *objection* vorwegnehmen

forestation [fɒrɪˈsteɪʃən] N = **afforestation**

forestay [ˈfɔːsteɪ] N *(Naut)* Fockstag *nt*

Forest Enterprise N *(Brit) Landverwaltungsabteilung der Forstbehörde*

forester [ˈfɒrɪstəʳ] N Förster(in) *m(f)*

forest ranger N *(US)* Förster(in) *m(f)*

forestry [ˈfɒrɪstrɪ] N Forstwirtschaft *f*

Forestry Commission *(Brit)*, **Forestry Service** *(US)* N Forstverwaltung *f*

foretaste [ˈfɔːteɪst] N Vorgeschmack *m*; **to give sb a ~ of sth** jdm einen Vorgeschmack von etw geben

foretell [fɔːˈtel] *pret, ptp* **foretold** [fɔːˈtəʊld] VT vorhersagen

forethought [ˈfɔːθɔːt] N Vorbedacht *m*

forever [fərˈevəʳ] ADV **a** *(= eternally) live, last, be grateful* ewig; *remember, go on* immer; **she is ~ watchful** sie ist ewig wachsam; **Scotland ~!** ein Hoch auf Schottland! **b** *(= irrevocably) go, disappear, change* unwiderruflich; **the old social order was gone ~** das alte Gesellschaftssystem war für immer verschwunden **c** *(inf: = ages)* **it takes ~** es dauert ewig *(inf)*; **these old slate roofs go on** *or* **last ~** diese alten Schieferdächer halten ewig **d** *(inf: = constantly)* **to be ~ doing sth** (an)dauernd *or* ständig etw tun

forevermore [fərˌevəˈmɔːʳ] ADV *(esp US)* = **for evermore**, → **evermore**

forewarn [fɔːˈwɔːn] VT vorher warnen; **that should have ~ed him** das hätte ihm eine Vorwarnung sein sollen; **~ed is forearmed** *(Prov)* Gefahr erkannt, Gefahr gebannt *(Prov)*

forewent [fɔːˈwent] *pret of* **forego**

forewing [ˈfɔːwɪŋ] N Vorderflügel *m*

forewoman [ˈfɔːwʊmən] N *pl* **-women** [-wɪmɪn] Vorarbeiterin *f*; *(Jur, of jury)* Obmännin *f*

foreword [ˈfɔːwɜːd] N Vorwort *nt*

forfeit [ˈfɔːfɪt] VT **a** *(esp Jur) one's rights etc* verwirken **b** *(fig) one's life, health, honour, sb's respect* einbüßen; *chance* verpassen; *right, place* verlieren N *(esp Jur)* Strafe *f*, Buße *f*; *(fig)* Einbuße *f*; *(in game)* Pfand *nt*; **~s** *sing (game)* Pfänderspiel *nt*; **to pay a ~** *(in game)* ein Pfand (ab)geben; **his health was the ~ he paid** er zahlte mit seiner Gesundheit dafür ADJ **to be ~** *(Jur)* verfallen sein; *(fig)* verwirkt sein

forfeiture [ˈfɔːfɪtʃəʳ] N *(Jur, fig)* Verlust *m*, Einbuße *f*; *(of claim)* Verwirkung *f*

forgather [fɔːˈgæðəʳ] VI = **foregather**

forgave [fəˈgeɪv] *pret of* **forgive**

forge [fɔːdʒ] N *(= workshop)* Schmiede *f*; *(= furnace)* Esse *f* VT **a** *metal* schmieden; *(fig) friendship, alliance* schließen; *relationship* aufbauen; *plan* schmieden; **to ~ economic/close links with sb/sth** Wirtschaftsbeziehungen/eine enge Bindung zu jdm/etw aufbauen **b** *(= counterfeit) signature, banknote* fälschen VI **to ~ ahead (with sth)** (mit etw) vorwärtskommen *or* Fortschritte machen; **to ~ ahead** *(in career)* seinen Weg machen; *(Sport)* vorstoßen; **he ~d ahead of the rest of the field** er setzte sich weit vom Rest des Feldes

forger [ˈfɔːdʒəʳ] N Fälscher(in) *m(f)*

forgery [ˈfɔːdʒərɪ] N **a** *(= act)* Fälschen *nt*; **art/cheque** *(Brit) or* **check** *(US)* **~** Kunst-/Scheckfälschung *f*; **to be prosecuted for ~** wegen Fälschung angeklagt sein **b** *(= thing)* Fälschung *f*; **the signature was a ~** die Unterschrift war gefälscht

forgery-proof ADJ fälschungssicher

forget [fəˈget] ✪ 26.3 *pret* **forgot**, *ptp* **forgotten** VT vergessen; *ability, language* verlernen; **never to be forgotten** unvergesslich, unvergessen; **and don't you ~ it!** und dass du das ja nicht vergisst!; **he never lets you ~ it either** er sorgt dafür, dass du auch immer daran denkst; **to ~ to do sth** vergessen, etw zu tun; **I was ~ting you knew him** ich habe ganz vergessen, dass Sie ihn kennen; **I ~ his name** sein Name ist mir entfallen; **I ~ what I wanted to say** es ist mir entfallen, was ich sagen wollte; **to ~ one's differences** seine Meinungsverschiedenheiten ruhen lassen; **not ~ting ...** nicht zu vergessen ...; **~ it!** schon gut!; **you might as well ~ it** *(inf)* das kannst du vergessen *(inf)*
VI es vergessen; **don't ~!** vergiss (es) nicht!; **I never ~** ich vergesse nie etwas; **where has he gone? – I ~** wo ist er hingegangen? – ich habe es vergessen *or* es ist mir entfallen; **she drinks to ~** sie trinkt, um zu vergessen
VR *(= behave improperly)* sich vergessen, aus der Rolle fallen; *(= act unselfishly)* sich selbst vergessen

▶ **forget about** VI *+prep obj* vergessen; **I've forgotten all about what he did** ich habe völlig vergessen, was er getan hat

forgetful [fəˈgetfʊl] ADJ *(= absent-minded)* vergesslich; *(of one's duties etc)* achtlos, nachlässig (*of* gegenüber)

forgetfulness [fəˈgetfʊlnɪs] N *(= absent-mindedness)* Vergesslichkeit *f*; *(of one's duties etc)* Achtlosigkeit *f*, Nachlässigkeit *f* (*of* gegenüber); **in a moment of ~** in einem Augenblick geistiger Abwesenheit

forget-me-not [fəˈgetmɪnɒt] N *(Bot)* Vergissmeinnicht *nt*

forgettable [fəˈgetəbl] ADJ **an eminently ~ second novel** ein zweiter Roman, den man getrost vergessen kann; **it was an instantly ~ game** es war ein Spiel, das man sofort vergessen konnte

forgivable [fəˈgɪvəbl] ADJ verzeihlich, verzeihbar

forgivably [fəˈgɪvəblɪ] ADV verzeihlich; **John was ~ tense** man konnte John seine Nervosität verzeihen; **~, she walked out without answering** sie verließ den Raum ohne zu antworten, was verzeihlich war

forgive [fəˈgɪv] ✪ 18.1, 18.2 *pret* **forgave**, *ptp* **forgiven** [fəˈgɪvn] VT *mistake, clumsiness* verzeihen, vergeben; *person* verzeihen *(+dat)*, vergeben *(+dat)*; *debt* erlassen; *(esp Eccl) sin* vergeben, erlassen; **to ~ sb sth** jdm etw verzeihen *or* vergeben; *(Eccl)* jdm etw vergeben *or* erlassen; **to ~ sb for sth** jdm etw verzeihen *or* vergeben; **to ~ sb for doing sth** jdm verzeihen *or* vergeben, dass er etw getan hat; **you could be ~n for thinking that ...** es ist durchaus verständlich, wenn Sie denken, dass ...; **~ me, but ...** Entschuldigung, aber ...; **I'll never ~ myself if anything happens to him** ich werde es mir nie verzeihen, wenn ihm etwas zustößt; **to ~ and forget** vergeben und vergessen
VI *(person)* verzeihen, vergeben

forgiveness [fəˈgɪvnɪs] N *no pl (quality: = willingness to forgive)* Versöhnlichkeit *f*; **to ask/beg (sb's) ~** (jdn) um Verzeihung *or* Vergebung *(esp Eccl)* bitten; **her complete ~ of them surprised him** es überraschte ihn, dass sie ihnen voll und ganz verzieh; **the ~ of sins** *(Eccl)* die Vergebung der Sünden; **~ of debt** Schuldenerlass *m*; **full of ~** versöhnlich

forgiving [fəˈgɪvɪŋ] ADJ versöhnlich, nicht nachtragend

forgo [fɔːˈgəʊ] *pret* **forwent**, *ptp* **forgone** VT = **forego**

forgot [fəˈgɒt] *pret of* **forget**

forgotten [fəˈgɒtn] *ptp of* **forget**

fork [fɔːk] N **a** *(= implement)* Gabel *f* **b** *(in tree)* Astgabel *f*; *(in road, railway)* Gabelung *f*; **take the left ~** nehmen Sie die linke Abzweigung VT **a** *ground* mit einer Gabel umgraben; *(= turn over) hay* wenden; **to ~ hay onto a cart** Heu mit einer Gabel auf einen Wagen werfen **b** *food* gabeln *(inf)* VI *(roads, branches)* sich gabeln; **to ~ (to the) right** *(road)* nach rechts abzweigen; *(driver)* nach rechts abbiegen

▶ **fork out** *(inf)* VT *sep* blechen *(inf)* VI blechen *(inf)*

▶ **fork over** VT *sep ground* lockern; *hay* wenden

▶ **fork up** VT *sep soil* mit einer Gabel umgraben; *hay* hochheben; *food* gabeln *(inf)*

forked [fɔːkt] ADJ *tail, stick, branch* gegabelt; *tongue* gespalten; **to speak with (a) ~ tongue** *(fig)* mit gespaltener Zunge sprechen *(geh)*

forked lightning N Linienblitz *m*

fork: **fork-lift (truck)** [ˈfɔːklɪft(ˈtrʌk)] *(inf)* N Gabelstapler *m*; **fork luncheon** N *(Brit)* Gabelfrühstück *nt*

forlorn [fəˈlɔːn] ADJ **a** *(= desolate)* verlassen; *(= miserable)* trostlos; **~ appearance** *(of house etc)* desolates *or* trostloses Aussehen; **a ~ figure** eine einsame Gestalt; **her voice sounded ~** ihre Stimme klang einsam und verlassen; **the palaces stood empty and ~** die Paläste standen leer und verlassen da **b** *(= despairing) attempt, effort* verzweifelt; **it is a ~ hope** es ist ziemlich aussichtslos, es ist eine ziemlich aussichtslose Sache; **in the ~ hope of success/of finding a better life** in der verzweifelten Hoffnung auf Erfolg/ein besseres Leben

forlornly [fəˈlɔːnlɪ] ADV **a** *stand, wait* einsam und verlassen; *stare* verloren **b** *hope, try (= desperately)* verzweifelt; *(= vainly)* vergeblich

form [fɔːm] N **a** Form *f*; **~ of government** Regierungsform *f*; **~ of life** Lebensform *f*; **the various ~s of energy** die verschiedenen Energieformen; **~ of address** Anrede *f*; **to choose another ~ of words** es anders formulieren; **~s of worship** Formen *pl* der Gottesverehrung; **a ~ of apology** eine Art der Entschuldigung; **a ~ of punishment** eine Form *or* Art der Bestrafung
b *(= condition, style, guise)* Form *f*, Gestalt *f*; **in the ~ of** in Form von *or +gen*; *(with reference to people)* in Gestalt von *or +gen*; **medicine in tablet ~** Arznei in Tablettenform; **water in the ~ of ice** Wasser in Form von Eis; **the same thing in a new ~** das Gleiche in neuer Form *or* Gestalt; **the first prize will take the ~ of a trip to Rome** der erste Preis ist eine Reise nach Rom; **their discontent took various ~s** ihre Unzufriedenheit äußerte sich in verschiedenen Formen; **her letters are to be published in book ~** ihre Briefe sollen in Buchform *or* als Buch erscheinen
c *(= shape)* Form *f*; *(of person)* Gestalt *f*; **to take ~** *(lit, fig)* Form *or* Gestalt annehmen
d *(Art, Mus, Liter: = structure)* Form *f*; **~ and content** Form und Inhalt

e *(Philos)* Form *f*; **the world of ~s** die Ideenwelt
f *(Gram)* Form *f*; **the plural ~** die Pluralform, der Plural
g *no pl (= etiquette)* (Umgangs)form *f*; **he did it for ~'s sake** er tat es der Form halber; **it's bad ~** so etwas tut man einfach nicht; **what's the ~?** *(inf)* was ist üblich?
h *(= document)* Formular *nt*, Vordruck *m*; **printed ~** vorgedrucktes Formular
i *(= physical condition)* Form *f*, Verfassung *f*; **to be in fine** *or* **good ~** gut in Form sein, in guter Form *or* Verfassung sein; **to be on/off ~** in/nicht in *or* außer Form sein; **to be on top ~** in Höchstform sein; **he was in great ~ that evening** er war an dem Abend in Hochform; **to study (the) ~** *(Horse-racing)* die Form prüfen; **past ~** Papierform *f*; **on past ~** auf dem Papier
j *(esp Brit, = bench)* Bank *f*
k *(Brit Sch)* Klasse *f*
l *no pl (Brit inf: = criminal record)* **to have ~** vorbestraft sein
m *(Tech, = mould)* Form *f*
n *(US, Typ)* = **forme**
o *(of hare)* Nest *nt*, Sasse *f (spec)*
VT **a** *(= shape)* formen, gestalten *(into* zu); *(Gram) plural, negative* bilden; **he ~s his sentences well** er bildet wohlgeformte Sätze
b *(= train, mould) child, sb's character* formen
c *(= develop) liking, desire, idea, habit* entwickeln; *friendship* schließen, anknüpfen; *opinion* sich *(dat)* bilden; *impression* gewinnen; *plan* ausdenken, entwerfen
d *(= set up, organize) government, committee* bilden; *company, society, political party* gründen, ins Leben rufen
e *(= constitute, make up) part, basis* bilden; **the committee is ~ed of ...** der Ausschuss wird von ... gebildet
f *(= take the shape or order of) circle, pattern* bilden; **to ~ a queue** *(Brit) or* **line** *(US)* eine Schlange bilden
VI **a** *(= take shape)* Gestalt annehmen; **an idea ~ed in my mind** eine Idee nahm Gestalt an
b *(esp Mil: also* **form up**) sich aufstellen *or* formieren, antreten; **to ~ into a queue** *(Brit) or* **line** *(US)*/**into two lines** eine Schlange/zwei Reihen bilden; **to ~ into a square** sich im Karree aufstellen; **to ~ into battle order** sich zur Schlachtordnung formieren

formal ['fɔːməl] **ADJ** **a** *person, letter, relationship, behaviour, language* formell, förmlich; *(= official) talks, statement, complaint, agreement, request* formell, offiziell; *(= ceremonial) occasion, reception* feierlich; **he made them a ~ bow** er verbeugte sich formell *or* feierlich vor ihnen; **to make a ~ apology** sich in aller Form entschuldigen; **the dinner was very ~** das Abendessen war sehr formell; **~ affair** *or* **occasion** formeller *or* feierlicher Anlass; **on ~ occasions** bei formellen *or* feierlichen Anlässen; **~ clothes** *or* **dress** *(for smart occasions)* Gesellschaftskleidung *f*; *(for work)* formelle Kleidung; **in ~ dress** formell gekleidet
b *(= ordered) style, approach* formal; *(= severe)* streng; *(in design) garden, borders, square* regelmäßig angelegt; *room* formal eingerichtet; **~ gardens** formal angelegte Gartenanlagen *pl*
c *(= proper) education, training* ordentlich; *qualifications* offiziell
d *(= relating to form) logic, perfection, complexity, defect* formal

formaldehyde [fɔː'mældɪhaɪd] **N** Formaldehyd *m*

formalin(e) ['fɔːməlɪn] **N** Formalin® *nt*

formalism ['fɔːməlɪzəm] **N** Formalismus *m*

formalistic [ˌfɔːmə'lɪstɪk] **ADJ** formalistisch

formality [fɔː'mælɪtɪ] **N** **a** *no pl (of person, dress, greeting, language, ceremony etc)* Förmlichkeit *f*
b *(= matter of form)* Formalität *f*; **it's a mere ~** es ist (eine) reine Formsache *or* Formalität; **let's dispense with the formalities** lassen wir die Formalitäten beiseite

formalize ['fɔːməlaɪz] **VT** *rules, grammar* formalisieren; *agreement, arrangement* formell bekräftigen; *relationship* formell machen

formally ['fɔːməlɪ] **ADV** **a** *speak, behave, dress* formell, förmlich; *(= officially) announce, agree, open, approve* formell, offiziell; *apologize* in aller Form; **~ courteous** förmlich und höflich; **~ dressed** formell gekleidet; **the pact still exists - at least ~** der Pakt besteht immer noch - zumindest der Form nach; **~ charged** *(Jur)* offiziell angeklagt; **~ binding** offiziell verbindlich
b *(in design)* regelmäßig; **~ laid-out gardens** formal angelegte Gartenanlagen; **the chairs were ~ arranged in rows** die Stühle waren streng in Reihen angeordnet
c *(= academically) teach, train* offiziell; *(in an educational establishment)* in einer Bildungsanstalt; **to teach sth ~** etw wissenschaftlich unterrichten; **he is ~ trained** er hat eine ordentliche Ausbildung

format ['fɔːmæt] **N** *(as regards size)* Format *nt*; *(as regards content)* Aufmachung *f*; *(Rad, TV, of programme)* Struktur *f*; *(of computer data, recording)* Format *nt*; **page ~** Seitenformat *nt* **VT** *(Comput) disk, page, paragraph* formatieren

formation [fɔː'meɪʃən] **N** **a** *(= act of forming)* Formung *f*, Gestaltung *f*; *(Gram: of plural etc)* Bildung *f*; *(of character)* Formung *f*; *(of government, committee)* Bildung *f*; *(of company, society)* Gründung *f*; *(of desire, idea, impression, habit etc)* Entwicklung *f*; *(of friendship)* Schließen *nt*, Anknüpfung *f*; *(of opinion)* Bildung *f*; *(of plan)* Entwurf *m* **b** *(of aircraft, dancers, troops)* Formation *f*; **battle ~** Gefechtsaufstellung *f*; **in close ~** *(Aviat)* im geschlossenen Verband; **to dance in ~** in Formation tanzen **c** *(Geol)* Formation *f*

formation: **formation dancing** **N** Formationstanzen *nt*; **formation flying** **N** Formationsflug *m*

formative ['fɔːmətɪv] **ADJ** **a** *influence, experience* prägend; **her ~ years** die charakterbildenden Jahre in ihrem Leben; **the most ~ experience of his life** die Erfahrung, die sein Leben entscheidend geprägt hat; **a ~ period** eine Zeit der Entwicklung **b** *(Gram)* **~ element** Wortbildungselement *nt* **N** *(Gram)* Wortbildungselement *nt*, Formativ *nt*

formatting ['fɔːmætɪŋ] **N** *(Comput)* Formatierung *f*

forme [fɔːm] **N** *(Brit Typ)* (Satz)form *f*

former ['fɔːmə'] ✪ 26.2 **ADJ** **a** *(= previous) president, chairman, employee etc* früher, ehemalig; *home, prison, school, hospital etc* ehemalig; *country, place, strength, authority etc* früher; *times, years, days* vergangen; **~ President Richard Nixon** der frühere *or* ehemalige Präsident Richard Nixon; **his ~ wife** seine Exfrau; **her ~ husband** ihr Exmann *m*; **the radicals of ~ days** die Radikalen der Vergangenheit; **in ~ years** *or* **times** *or* **days** in früheren Zeiten
b *(as opposed to latter)* **the ~ option/alternative** *etc* die erstere Möglichkeit/Alternative *etc*
N **the ~** der/die/das erstere; *(more than one)* die ersteren *pl*; **of these two theories I prefer the ~** von diesen beiden Theorien ziehe ich (die) erstere vor

-former [-ˌfɔːmə'] **N** *suf (Brit Sch)* -klässler(in) *m(f)*; **fifth-former** Fünftklässler(in) *m(f)*

formerly ['fɔːməlɪ] **ADV** früher; **she was more talkative than ~** sie war gesprächiger als sonst *or* vorher; **the ~ communist countries** die ehemals kommunistischen Länder; **the ~ busy office** das früher so geschäftige Büro; **we had ~ agreed that ...** wir hatten uns seinerzeit darauf geeinigt, dass ...

form: **form feed** **N** *(Comput)* Papier- *or* Seitenvorschub *m*; **form-fitting** **ADJ** eng anliegend

Formica® [fɔː'maɪkə] **N** ≈ Resopal® *nt*

formic acid ['fɔːmɪk'æsɪd] **N** Ameisensäure *f*

formidable ['fɔːmɪdəbl] **ADJ** *(= commanding respect) person* Achtung gebietend; *intellect, intelligence* überragend; *(= powerful, impressive) challenge, achievement, task, obstacle, strength, energy, height* gewaltig; *person, reputation* beeindruckend; *opponent* mächtig; *sight* überwältigend; *talents* außerordentlich; *team, combination* außerordentlich stark; **she is small but ~** sie ist klein aber oho *(inf)*; **to be in ~ form** in absoluter Hochform sein

formidably ['fɔːmɪdəblɪ] **ADV** **a** *(= dauntingly)* enorm, außerordentlich; **~ equipped** außerordentlich gut ausgerüstet **b** *(= prodigiously, excellently)* hervorragend; **~ gifted** *or* **talented** außerordentlich begabt *or* talentiert; **~ efficient** überaus *or* außerordentlich effizient

form: **formless** ['fɔːmlɪs] **ADJ** **a** *(= amorphous)* formlos **b** *(pej, = unstructured) book, play, film, music* strukturlos, unstrukturiert; **formlessness** **N** **a** *(= amorphousness)* Formlosigkeit *f* **b** *(pej: = lack of structure)* Strukturlosigkeit *f*; **form letter** **N** *(Comput)* Formbrief *m*, Briefvorlage *f*; *(circular letter)* Serienbrief *m*

formula ['fɔːmjʊlə] **N** *pl* **-s** *or* **-e** ['fɔːmjʊliː] **a** Formel *f (also Sci)*; *(for lotion, medicine, soap powder)* Rezeptur *f*; **winning ~** Erfolgsrezept *nt*; **peace ~** Friedensformel *f*; **there's no sure ~ for success** es gibt kein Patentrezept für Erfolg; **they changed the ~ of the programme** sie änderten die Aufmachung des Programms; **all his books follow the same ~** alle seine Bücher sind nach demselben Rezept geschrieben **b** *no pl (also* **formula milk**) Säuglingsmilch *f*

Formula One **N** *(Motor Racing)* Formel 1

formulate ['fɔːmjʊleɪt] **VT** formulieren

formulation [ˌfɔːmjʊ'leɪʃən] **N** Formulierung *f*

formwork **N** (Ver)schalung *f*

fornicate ['fɔːnɪkeɪt] **VI** Unzucht treiben

fornication [ˌfɔːnɪ'keɪʃən] **N** Unzucht *f*

fornicator ['fɔːnɪkeɪtə'] **N** Hurer *m (inf)*, Hurenbock *m (inf)*; *(woman)* Hure *f (inf)*

forsake [fə'seɪk] *pret* **forsook** [fə'sʊk] *ptp* **forsaken** [fə'seɪkn] **VT** verlassen; *bad habits* aufgeben, entsagen *(+dat) (geh)*; **his charm never ~s him** sein Charme lässt ihn nie im Stich

forswear [fɔː'swɛə'] *pret* **forswore** [fɔː'swɔː'] *ptp* **forsworn** [fɔː'swɔːn] **VT** **a** *(= renounce)* abschwören *(+dat)*; **he has forsworn smoking** er hat hoch und heilig versprochen, nicht mehr zu rauchen **b** *(= deny)* unter Eid verneinen *or* leugnen

forsythia [fɔː'saɪθɪə] **N** Forsythie *f*

fort [fɔːt] **N** *(Mil)* Fort *nt*; **to hold the ~** *(fig)* die Stellung halten

forte[1] ['fɔːteɪ] **N** *(= strong point)* Stärke *f*, starke Seite

forte[2] *(Mus)* **ADV** laut, forte **ADJ** *(= played loudly)* laut *or* forte gespielt; *(= sung loudly)* laut *or* forte gesungen

forth [fɔːθ] **ADV** *(form, dated)* **a** *(= out)* heraus-; *(= forward)* hervor-; **to venture ~** sich hinauswagen; **to come ~** herauskommen; **to pour ~** *(= utter)* von sich *(dat)* geben; **to burst ~** *(person)* herausstürzen; *(sun)* hervorbrechen → **back ADV a**, → *also* **hold forth, put forth, set forth** *etc*
b *(= onwards)* **from this time** *or* **day ~** von jetzt an; **from that day ~** von jenem Tag an; **and so ~** und so weiter

forthcoming [fɔːθ'kʌmɪŋ] **ADJ** *(form)* **a** *attr (= imminent) event, visit* bevorstehend; *album, book* in Kürze erscheinend; *film, play* in Kürze anlaufend; **a leaflet detailing the month's ~ events** eine Broschüre mit einer Programmvorschau für den Monat; **~ books/titles** geplante Neuerscheinungen *pl*; **our ~ titles for next year** Titel, die nächstes Jahr erscheinen; **"forthcoming attractions"** *(outside theatre/cinema)* „demnächst in diesem Theater/Kino"
b *(= available)* **to be ~** *(money, funds)* zur Verfügung gestellt werden; *(evidence)* geliefert werden; *(aid, support)* geleistet werden; *(details)* bekannt werden; **not to be ~** *(evidence, aid, support)* ausbleiben
c *(= communicative) person* mitteilsam; **to be ~ on** *or* **about sth** offen über etw *(acc)* reden; **not to be ~ on** *or* **about sth** sich über etw *(acc)* zurückhalten

forthright [ˈfɔːθraɪt] ADJ *person, manner (= direct)* direkt; *(= frank)* offen; *(= blunt) statement* unverblümt; *language* deutlich; **in ~ terms** unverblümt; **to be ~ in one's response** eine direkte Antwort geben; **to be ~ in saying sth** etw direkt sagen; **to be ~ about sth** sich unverblümt zu etw äußern

forthwith [ˌfɔːθˈwɪθ] ADV *(form)* umgehend, unverzüglich

fortieth [ˈfɔːtɪɪθ] ADJ vierzigste(r, s) N *(= fraction)* Vierzigstel *nt*; *(in series)* Vierzigste(r, s) → *also* **sixth**

fortification [ˌfɔːtɪfɪˈkeɪʃən] N **a** *(= act of fortifying) (of town)* Befestigung *f*; *(of wine)* Vergärung *f*; *(of food)* Anreicherung *f*; *(of person)* Bestärkung *f* **b** **fortifications** PL *(Mil)* Befestigungen *pl*, Festungsanlagen *pl*

fortified wine [ˌfɔːtɪfaɪdˈwaɪn] N weinhaltiges Getränk, Südwein *m*

fortifier [ˈfɔːtɪfaɪəʳ] N Stärkungsmittel *nt*

fortify [ˈfɔːtɪfaɪ] VT *(Mil) town* befestigen; *wine* mit zuckerreichem Most vergären; *food* anreichern; *person* bestärken; *(food, drink)* stärken; **fortified place** befestigte Stellung; **have a drink to ~ you** nehmen Sie einen Schluck zur Stärkung

fortissimo [fɔːˈtɪsɪməʊ] *(Mus)* ADV fortissimo ADJ *(= played very loudly)* fortissimo gespielt; *(= sung very loudly)* fortissimo gesungen

fortitude [ˈfɔːtɪtjuːd] N (innere) Kraft *or* Stärke

Fort Knox [ˌfɔːtˈnɒks] N Fort Knox *nt*; **they've turned their house into ~** sie haben aus ihrem Haus eine Festung gemacht

fortnight [ˈfɔːtnaɪt] N *(esp Brit)* vierzehn Tage, zwei Wochen; **a ~'s holiday** zwei Wochen *or* vierzehn Tage Urlaub

fortnightly [ˈfɔːtnaɪtlɪ] *(esp Brit)* ADJ vierzehntäglich, zweiwöchentlich; *newspaper, magazine also* alle zwei Wochen erscheinend; **~ visits** Besuche *pl* alle zwei Wochen; **a ~ cycle** ein Zyklus *m* von zwei Wochen; **at ~ intervals** in Abständen von zwei Wochen ADV alle vierzehn Tage, alle zwei Wochen

FORTRAN [ˈfɔːtræn] *abbr of* **formula translator** FORTRAN *nt*

fortress [ˈfɔːtrɪs] N Festung *f*

fortuitous ADJ, **fortuitously** ADV [fɔːˈtjuːɪtəs, -lɪ] zufällig

fortuitousness [fɔːˈtjuːɪtəsnɪs], **fortuity** [fɔːˈtjuːɪtɪ] N Zufall *m*

fortunate [ˈfɔːtʃənɪt] ADJ *person, coincidence, choice* glücklich; *circumstances also* günstig; **we are ~ that/because ...** wir können von Glück reden *or* uns glücklich schätzen, dass/weil ...; **it is ~ that ...** es ist ein Glück, dass ...; **it was ~ for him/Mr Fox that...** es war sein Glück/ein Glück für Mr Fox, dass ...; **they were ~ to escape/survive** sie können von Glück sagen *or* sich glücklich schätzen, entkommen zu sein/ überlebt zu haben; **I was ~ enough to go to a good school** ich hatte das Glück, eine gute Schule zu besuchen; **I have been unusually ~ in my parents and teachers** ich habe mit meinen Eltern und Lehrern ungewöhnlich großes Glück gehabt; **how ~!** welch *or* so ein Glück!

fortunately [ˈfɔːtʃənɪtlɪ] ADV glücklicherweise, zum Glück; **~ for me, my friend noticed it** zu meinem Glück hat mein Freund es bemerkt

fortune [ˈfɔːtʃuːn] N **a** *(= fate)* Schicksal *nt*, Geschick *nt*; *(= chance)* Zufall *m*; **she followed his ~s with interest** sie verfolgte sein Geschick mit Interesse; **the ~s of war** das Auf und Ab des Krieges; **he had the good ~ to have rich parents** er hatte das Glück, reiche Eltern zu haben; **by good ~** glücklicherweise, zum Glück; **by sheer good ~** rein zufällig; **~ has favoured** *(Brit) or* **favored** *(US)* **him** das Glück war ihm hold; **~ favours the brave** *or* **bold** *(Brit Prov)* das Glück ist nur dem Tüchtigen hold; **ill ~** Pech *nt*; **to tell sb's ~** jdm wahrsagen

b *(= money)* Reichtum *m*, Vermögen *nt*; **to come into/make a ~** ein Vermögen erben/machen; **to seek/make one's ~** sein Glück versuchen/machen; **to marry a ~** reich heiraten; **it costs a ~** es kostet ein Vermögen; **she spends a (small) ~ on clothes** sie gibt ein (kleines) Vermögen für Kleidung aus

fortune: **fortune-hunter** N Mitgiftjäger(in) *m(f)*; **fortune-teller** N Wahrsager(in) *m(f)*

forty [ˈfɔːtɪ] ADJ vierzig; **to have ~ winks** *(inf)* ein Nickerchen machen *(inf)* N Vierzig *f* → *also* **sixty**

forty-niner [ˌfɔːtɪˈnaɪnəʳ] N *Goldgräber, der im Zuge des Goldrausches von 1849 nach Kalifornien ging*

forum [ˈfɔːrəm] N Forum *nt*

forward [ˈfɔːwəd] ADV **a** *(also* **forwards**, *= onwards, ahead)* vorwärts; *(= to the front, to particular point, out of line)* nach vorn; **please step ~** bitte vortreten; **to take two steps ~** zwei Schritte vortreten; **to rush ~** sich vorstürzen; **to go straight ~** geradeaus gehen; **~!** vorwärts!; **he drove backward(s) and ~(s) between the station and the house** er fuhr zwischen Haus und Bahnhof hin und her

b *(in time)* **from this time ~** *(= from then)* seitdem; *(= from now)* von jetzt an; **if we think ~ to the next stage** wenn wir an die vor uns liegende nächste Stufe denken

c *(= into prominence)* **to come ~** sich melden; **to bring ~ new evidence** neue Beweise *pl* vorlegen

ADJ **a** *(in place)* vordere(r, s); *(in direction)* Vorwärts-; **~ march** Vormarsch *m*; **~ gears** *(Aut)* Vorwärtsgänge *pl*; **this seat is too far ~** dieser Sitz ist zu weit vorn

b *(in time) planning* Voraus-; *(Comm) buying, price* Termin-; *(= well-advanced) season* (weit) fortgeschritten; *plants* früh *pred*; *children* frühreif; **I'd like to be further ~ with my work** ich wollte, ich wäre mit meiner Arbeit schon weiter; **good ~ thinking, Jones** gute Voraussicht, Jones

c *(= presumptuous, pert)* dreist

N *(Sport)* Stürmer(in) *m(f)*

VT **a** *(= advance) plans etc* vorantreiben; *career* voranbringen

b *(= dispatch) goods* befördern, senden; *(= send on) letter, parcel* nachsenden; **please ~** bitte nachsenden

c *(Internet etc) information* weiterleiten; *e-mail* forwarden, weiterleiten; **we'll ~ your suggestions to the committee** wir werden Ihre Vorschläge an den Ausschuss weiterleiten

forwarder [ˈfɔːwədəʳ] N *(= person)* Spediteur(in) *m(f)*; *(= company)* Spedition *f*, Spediteur *m*

forwarding [ˈfɔːwədɪŋ]: **forwarding address** N Nachsendeadresse *f*; **forwarding agent** N *(= person)* Spediteur(in) *m(f)*; *(= company)* Spedition *f*, Spediteur *m*; **forwarding instructions** PL *(for goods)* Lieferanweisungen *pl*; *(for sending on mail)* Nachsendeanweisungen *pl*

forward: **forward line** N *(Sport)* Sturm *m*, Stürmerreihe *f*; **forward-looking** [ˈfɔːwədlʊkɪŋ] ADJ *person, attitude* fortschrittlich, progressiv; *plan, vision* vorausblickend

forwardness [ˈfɔːwədnɪs] N *(= presumption)* Dreistigkeit *f*

forward pass N *(Sport)* Vorwärtspass *m*

forward post N *(Mil)* Vorposten *m*

forwards [ˈfɔːwədz] ADV = **forward ADV a**

forward slash N *(Typ)* Schrägstrich *m*

forwent [fɔːˈwent] *pret of* **forgo**

Fosbury flop [ˈfɒzbrɪˈflɒp] N Fosburyflop *m*

fossil [ˈfɒsl] N *(lit)* Fossil *nt*; **he's an old ~!** *(inf)* er ist so verknöchert ADJ versteinert

fossil fuel N fossiler Brennstoff *m*

fossilization [ˌfɒsɪlaɪˈzeɪʃən] N Versteinerung *f*, Fossilierung *f (spec)*; *(fig: of person)* Verknöcherung *f*

fossilized [ˈfɒsɪlaɪzd] ADJ versteinert; *(fig) person* verknöchert; *customs* verkrustet, starr

foster [ˈfɒstəʳ] ADJ *attr (Admin)* Pflege-; **she was placed in ~ care** sie wurde in Pflege gegeben, sie kam in eine Pflegestelle; **their children are in ~ care** ihre Kinder sind in Pflege VT Kinder/ein Kind in Pflege nehmen VT **a** *child* in Pflege nehmen; **when children are ~ed** wenn Kinder in Pflege *or* bei Pflegeeltern sind; **~ed children** Pflegekinder *pl*, Kinder *pl* in Pflege **b** *(= promote) music, drama, development* fördern; *image, friendship* pflegen; **a popular idea, ~ed by the media** eine populäre Idee, die von den Medien gefördert wird

▶ **foster out** VT *sep* in Pflege geben *(with* bei)

foster: **foster brother** N Pflegebruder *m*; *(fed by same mother)* Milchbruder *m*; **foster child** N Pflegekind *nt*; **foster family** N Pflegefamilie *f*; **foster father** N Pflegevater *m*; **foster home** N Pflegestelle *f*; **she was placed in a ~** sie wurde in Pflege gegeben, sie kam in eine Pflegestelle; **foster mother** N **a** Pflegemutter *f* **b** *(= wet nurse)* Amme *f* **c** *(= apparatus)* Brutkasten *m*; **foster parents** PL Pflegeeltern *pl*; **he was placed with ~** er kam zu Pflegeeltern; **foster sister** N Pflegeschwester *f*

fought [fɔːt] *pret, ptp of* **fight**

foul [faʊl] ADJ **a** *(= disgusting) place, food, taste, breath* ekelhaft, widerlich; *water* faulig; *air* stickig; *smell* übel, ekelhaft

b *(= dreadful) behaviour, crime* abscheulich; *temper* übel; *day* scheußlich *(inf)*; **he was really ~ to her** er war wirklich gemein *or* fies *(inf)* zu ihr; **what a ~ thing (for you) to say about my sister** wie kannst du nur so etwas Gemeines über meine Schwester sagen; **she has a ~ temper** sie ist ein ganz übellauniger Mensch; **to be in a ~ mood** *or* **temper** eine ganz miese Laune haben *(inf)*; **~ weather** scheußliches Wetter; *(Naut)* Sturm *m*; **~ luck** großes Pech; **~ deed** *(liter, hum)* Schandtat *f*

c *(= offensive)* anstößig; **~ language** Schimpfwörter *pl*; **to have a ~ mouth** ein dreckiges Maul haben *(inf)*

d *(= dishonest, unfair)* unredlich; *(Sport: = against the rules) shot* regelwidrig; *tackle* unerlaubt; *(= not valid)* ungültig; **~ ball** *(Baseball)* ungültiger Schlag; **to cry ~** sich über unfaire Behandlung beschweren → **fair ADJ a**

e **to fall** *or* **run ~ of the law/authorities** mit dem Gesetz/den Behörden in Konflikt geraten; **to fall** *or* **run ~ of sb** es sich *(dat)* mit jdm verderben; **to fall ~ of a ship** *(Naut)* mit einem Schiff kollidieren *or* zusammenstoßen

VT **a** *(= dirty, pollute) air* verpesten; *beach* verschmutzen; *(dog) pavement* verunreinigen

b *(= become entangled in) mechanism, device, propeller* sich verfangen in *(+dat)*; *net, fishing line* verheddern; *(= clog) pipe* verstopfen; *chimney, gun barrel* blockieren

c *(Sport)* foulen

d *(Naut, = collide with) ship* rammen

e *(= tarnish) person* entehren; *sb's reputation* beflecken

VI **a** *(= become entangled: rope, line)* sich verheddern *(on, in +dat)*

b *(Sport)* foulen, regelwidrig spielen

N *(Sport)* Foul *nt*, Regelverstoß *m*; **technical/personal ~** *(Basketball)* technisches/persönliches Foul

▶ **foul up** VT *sep (inf)* versauen *(inf)*

fouler [ˈfaʊləʳ] N *(Sport)* Foulspieler(in) *m(f)*

foully [ˈfaʊlɪ] ADV *(= horribly)* übel, schlimm

foul-mouthed [ˈfaʊlmaʊðd] ADJ unflätig, vulgär

foulness [ˈfaʊlnɪs] N **a** *(= disgusting nature, of place, food, taste, smell, breath)* Widerlichkeit *f*; *(of water)* Fauligkeit *f*; *(of air)* Stickigkeit *f* **b** *(= dreadfulness) (of behaviour, crime)* Abscheulichkeit *f*; *(of day, weather)* Scheußlichkeit *f (inf)*; **the ~ of his behaviour** *(Brit) or* **behavior** *(US)* **to her, his ~ to her** sein gemeines Verhalten *or* seine Gemeinheit ihr gegenüber; **the ~ of her mood** ihre ganz üble Laune; **the ~ of her temper** ihre schreckliche Übellaunigkeit **c** *(of language)* Unflätigkeit *f*

foul play N **a** *(Sport)* unfaires *or* regelwidriges Spiel; *(= fouls)* Fouls *pl* **b** *(fig)* Unredlichkeiten *pl*; **the police do not suspect ~** die Polizei hat keinen Verdacht auf einen unnatürlichen *or* gewaltsamen Tod; **there was no evidence of**

~ es gab keine Beweise, die auf Mord *or* einen gewaltsamen Tod schließen ließen

foul shot N *(Basketball)* Freiwurf *m*

foul-smelling [ˌfaʊl'smelɪŋ] ADJ übel riechend *attr*

foul-tempered [ˌfaʊl'tempəd] ADJ sehr übellaunig

found[1] [faʊnd] *pret, ptp of* **find**

found[2] VT **a** *(= set up)* gründen; *town, school, hospital* gründen, errichten **b** **to ~ sth (up)on sth** *(opinion, belief)* etw auf etw *(dat)* gründen *or* stützen; **our society is ~ed on this** darauf beruht *or* basiert unsere Gesellschaft, das ist die Grundlage unserer Gesellschaft; **the novel is ~ed on fact** der Roman beruht *or* basiert auf Tatsachen

found[3] VT *(Metal) metal, glass* schmelzen und in eine Form gießen; *object* gießen

foundation [faʊn'deɪʃən] N **a** *(= act of founding, of business, colony)* Gründung *f*; *(of town, school)* Gründung *f*, Errichtung *f* **b** *(= institution)* Stiftung *f*; **research ~** Forschungsstiftung *f* **c** **~s** *pl (Build, of house etc)* Fundament *nt*; *(of road)* Unterbau *m* **d** *(fig: = basis)* Grundlage *f*; **to be without ~** *(rumours, allegations)* jeder Grundlage entbehren; *(fears)* unbegründet sein; **to rock** *or* **shake sth to its ~s** etw bis in seine Grundfesten erschüttern **e** *(= make-up)* Grundierungscreme *f*

foundation: **foundation cream** N Grundierungscreme *f*; **Foundation Day** N *(Austral) gesetzlicher Feiertag in Australien zur Erinnerung an die Landung der Briten am 26. Januar 1788*; **foundation garment** N Mieder *nt*; **foundation stone** N Grundstein *m*

founder[1] ['faʊndəʳ] N *(of school, colony, organization etc)* Gründer(in) *m(f)*; *(of charity, museum)* Stifter(in) *m(f)*

founder[2] VI **a** *(ship: = sink)* sinken, untergehen **b** *(horse etc: = stumble)* straucheln, stolpern **c** *(fig: = fail, plan, project)* scheitern, fehlschlagen; *(hopes)* auf den Nullpunkt sinken

founder[3] N *(Metal)* Gießer(in) *m(f)*

founder member N Gründungsmitglied *nt*

Founding Fathers ['faʊndɪŋ'fɑːðəz] PL *(US)* Väter *pl*

foundling ['faʊndlɪŋ] N Findling *m*, Findelkind *nt*; **~ hospital** Findelhaus *nt*, Findelheim *nt*

foundry ['faʊndrɪ] N Gießerei *f*

fount [faʊnt] N **a** *(liter: = fountain)* Born *m (poet)*, Quelle *f*; *(fig: = source)* Quelle *f* **b** *(Typ)* Schrift *f*

fountain ['faʊntɪn] N Brunnen *m*; *(with upward jets also)* Springbrunnen *m*; *(= jet, spurt: of water, lava etc)* Fontäne *f*; *(= drinking fountain)* (Trinkwasser)brunnen *m*; *(fig: = source)* Quelle *f*; **~ of youth** Jungbrunnen *m*

fountain: **fountainhead** N *(of river)* Quelle *f*; *(fig)* Quelle *f*, Ursprung *m*; **fountain pen** N Füllfederhalter *m*, Füller *m*

four [fɔːʳ] ADJ vier; **open to the ~ winds** Wind und Wetter ausgesetzt; **scattered to the ~ winds** in alle vier Winde zerstreut; **the Four Hundred** *(US)* die oberen zehntausend N Vier *f*; **on all ~s** auf allen vieren; **will you make up a ~ for bridge?** haben Sie Lust, beim Bridge den vierten Mann zu machen? → *also* **six**

four: **four-ball** N *(Golf)* Vierer *m*; **four-by-four** N Geländewagen *m*; **four-colour**, *(US)* **four-color** ADJ *(Typ)* Vierfarb-; **~ advertisement** Vierfarbanzeige *f*; **~ printing** Vierfarbdruck *m*; **four-cycle** ADJ *(US)* = **four-stroke**; **four-dimensional** ADJ *attr* vierdimensional; **four-eyed** ADJ *attr* vieräugig; **four-eyes** N *sing (hum inf)* Brillenträger(r) *mf (hum inf)*; *(= woman also)* Brillenschlange *f (hum inf)*; **four-figure** ADJ *attr* vierstellig; **fourfold** ADJ vierfach ADV *increase* um das Vierfache; **four-footed** ADJ vierfüßig; **four-four time** N *(Mus)* Viervierteltakt *m*; **four-handed** ADJ *(Mus)* vierhändig, für vier Hände, zu vier Händen; **four-in-hand** N Vierspänner *m*; **four-leaf clover**, **four-leaved clover** N vierblättriges Kleeblatt; **four-legged** ADJ vierbeinig; **four-letter word** N Vulgärausdruck *m*; **four-minute mile** N Vierminutenmeile *f*; **four-part** ADJ *attr series, programme* vierteilig; *plan* aus vier Teilen bestehend; *(Mus)* für vier Stimmen; *harmony, choir* vierstimmig

fourplex (house) ['fɔːplɛks-] N *(US)* Vierfamilienhaus *nt*

four: **four-poster (bed)** N Himmelbett *nt*; **fourscore** ADJ *(obs)* achtzig; **four-seater** ADJ viersitzig N Viersitzer *m*; **foursome** N Quartett *nt*; *(Sport)* Viererspiel *nt*; **to go out in a ~** zu viert ausgehen; **foursquare** ADJ **a** *(lit, = square)* viereckig **b** *(fig: = firm)* unerschütterlich ADV **a** *(lit, = squarely)* fest **b** *(fig: = firmly) stand* fest, entschlossen; **four-star** ADJ Vier-Sterne-; **~ hotel/restaurant** Vier-Sterne-Hotel/-Restaurant *nt*; **four-star general** N *(US)* Vier-Sterne-General *m*; **four-star petrol** N *(Brit)* Super(benzin) *nt*; **four-stroke** ADJ **~ engine** Viertaktmotor *m*

fourteen ['fɔː'tiːn] ADJ vierzehn N Vierzehn *f* → *also* **sixteen**

fourteenth ['fɔː'tiːnθ] ADJ vierzehnte(r, s) N *(= fraction)* Vierzehntel *nt*; *(of series)* Vierzehnte(r, s) → *also* **sixteenth**

fourth [fɔːθ] ADJ vierte(r, s); **the ~ dimension** die vierte Dimension; **the ~ estate** die Presse N *(= fraction)* Viertel *nt*; *(in series)* Vierte(r, s); **to drive in ~** *(Aut)* im vierten Gang fahren; **we need a ~ for our game of bridge** wir brauchen noch einen vierten zum Bridge → *also* **sixth**

> **FOURTH OF JULY**
>
> Der **Fourth of July** (oder auch **Independence Day**) ist der wichtigste Feiertag in den Vereinigten Staaten, an dem der Unterzeichnung der Unabhängigkeitserklärung am 4. Juli 1776 gedacht wird, was als eigentliche Geburtsstunde der USA gilt. Daher sind die Feierlichkeiten recht patriotisch. Viele Bürger hissen die amerikanische Flagge vor ihrem Haus, und im ganzen Land wird mit öffentlichen Veranstaltungen gefeiert: Paraden, Picknicks und nicht zu vergessen das große Feuerwerk am Abend.

fourthly ['fɔːθlɪ] ADV viertens

four: **four-way** ADJ zu viert; **~ valve** Vierwegeventil *nt*; **four-way stop** N *(US Aut) Kreuzung, an der alle Verkehrsteilnehmer Vorfahrt gewähren müssen*; **four-wheel drive**, **4WD** N *(Aut)* Vierradantrieb *m*; *(vehicle)* Geländefahrzeug *nt*

fowl [faʊl] N **a** *(= poultry)* Geflügel *nt*; *(= one bird)* Huhn *nt*/Gans *f*/Truthahn *m etc*; **to keep ~** Hühner *etc* halten; **roast ~** *(Cook)* Brathuhn *nt* **b** **the ~s of the air** *(liter)* die Vögel des Himmels VI *(also* **to go fowling***)* auf Vogeljagd gehen

fowling piece ['faʊlɪŋpiːs] N Schrotflinte *f*

fowl pest N Hühnerpest *f*

fox [fɒks] N **a** *(lit, fig)* Fuchs *m*; **he's a sly ~** *(fig)* er ist ein schlauer Fuchs **b** *(= fox fur)* Fuchs(pelz) *m* **c** *(dated US inf: = sexy woman)* scharfes Weib *(inf)* VT *(= deceive)* täuschen, reinlegen *(inf)*; *(= bewilder)* verblüffen; **that's ~ed you, hasn't it?** da bist du baff, was? *(inf)*

fox: **fox cub** N Fuchsjunge(s) *nt*, Fuchswelpe *m*; **foxglove** N *(Bot)* Fingerhut *m*; **foxhole** N **a** Fuchsbau *m* **b** *(Mil)* Schützengraben *m*, Schützenloch *nt*; **foxhound** N Fuchshund *m*; **fox hunt** N Fuchsjagd *f* VI auf (die) Fuchsjagd gehen; **fox-hunting** N Fuchsjagd *f*; **to go ~** auf die *or* zur Fuchsjagd gehen; **fox terrier** N Foxterrier *m*; **foxtrot** N Foxtrott *m*

foxy ['fɒksɪ] ADJ *(+er)* *(= wily)* listig, pfiffig, verschlagen; **~ lady** *(dated US inf)* scharfes Weib *(inf)*

foyer ['fɔɪeɪ] N *(in theatre)* Foyer *nt*; *(in hotel also)* Empfangshalle *f*; *(esp US, in apartment house)* Diele *f*

Fr *abbr* **a** *of* **Father** **b** *of* **Friar**

fracas ['frækɑː] N Aufruhr *m*, Tumult *m*

fraction ['frækʃən] N **a** *(Math)* Bruch *m* **b** *(fig)* Bruchteil *m*; **a ~ better/shorter** (um) eine Spur besser/kürzer; **move it just a ~** **(of an inch)** verrücke es (um) eine Spur; **for a ~ of a second** einen Augenblick lang; **it missed me by a ~ of an inch** es verfehlte mich um Haaresbreite **c** *(Eccl)* Brechen *nt* des Brotes

fractional ['frækʃənl] ADJ **a** *(Math)* Bruch-; *(fig)* geringfügig; **~ part** Bruchteil *m* **b** *(Chem)* **~ distillation** fraktionierte Destillation

fractionally ['frækʃənəlɪ] ADV *less, slower* geringfügig; *ahead* um eine Nasenlänge; *behind* knapp; *rise, drop* um einen Bruchteil; **the dollar has dropped ~** *or* **is ~ down** der Dollarkurs ist geringfügig gefallen

fraction bar, **fraction line** N *(Math)* Bruchstrich *m*

fractious ['frækʃəs] ADJ verdrießlich; *child* aufsässig

fractiousness ['frækʃəsnɪs] N Verdrießlichkeit *f*; *(of child)* Aufsässigkeit *f*

fracture ['fræktʃəʳ] N Bruch *m*; *(Med also)* Fraktur *f (spec)* VT brechen; **he ~d his shoulder** er hat sich *(dat)* die Schulter gebrochen; **~d skull** Schädelbruch *m* VI *(cheekbone etc)* brechen

fragile ['frædʒaɪl] ADJ *glass, china, object* zerbrechlich; *structure* fragil; *fabric* fein; *beauty, skin, child* zart; *elderly person* gebrechlich; *situation* heikel, unsicher; *confidence* schwach; *ceasefire, peace* brüchig; *health* zart, anfällig; *mental state, ego, economy* labil; *government, democracy* geschwächt; **"fragile (handle) with care"** „Vorsicht, zerbrechlich!"; **the ~ economic/political situation** die labile Wirtschaftslage/politische Situation; **to feel ~** *(inf)* sich angeschlagen fühlen; **to look ~** *(inf)* angeschlagen aussehen

fragility [frə'dʒɪlɪtɪ] N *(of glass, china, object)* Zerbrechlichkeit *f*; *(of beauty, skin, child)* Zartheit *f*; *(of fabric)* Feinheit *f*; *(of elderly person)* Gebrechlichkeit *f*; *(of health)* Zartheit *f*, Anfälligkeit *f*; *(of situation)* Unsicherheit *f*; *(of peace, ceasefire)* Brüchigkeit *f*; *(of mental state, economy)* Labilität *f*; *(of government, democracy)* geschwächter Zustand

fragment ['frægmənt] N **a** Bruchstück *nt*; *(of china, glass)* Scherbe *f*; *(of shell, food)* Stückchen *nt*; *(of paper, letter)* Schnipsel *m*; *(of programme, opera etc)* Bruchteil *m*; **he smashed it to ~s** er schlug es in Stücke; **the window smashed into ~s** das Fenster zersprang in Scherben; **~s of conversation** Gesprächsfetzen *pl* **b** *(esp Liter, Mus, = unfinished work)* Fragment *nt*

VI [fræg'ment] *(rock, glass)* (zer)brechen, in Stücke brechen; *(fig) (hopes)* sich zerschlagen; *(society)* zerfallen

VT [fræg'ment] *rock, glass* in Stücke brechen; *(with hammer etc)* in Stücke schlagen; *(fig) society* zerschlagen; *audience* aufsplittern; *market, industry, work* fragmentieren

fragmentary ['frægməntərɪ] ADJ *(lit, fig)* fragmentarisch, bruchstückhaft

fragmentation [ˌfrægmen'teɪʃən] N *(of rock, glass)* Zerbrechen *nt*; *(fig)* Fragmentierung *f*; *(of society)* Zerfall *m*; *(of hopes)* Zerschlagung *f*

fragmentation bomb N Splitterbombe *f*

fragmented [fræg'mentɪd] ADJ bruchstückhaft; *(= broken up)* unzusammenhängend, ohne Zusammenhang

fragrance ['freɪgrəns] N Duft *m*, Wohlgeruch *m*

fragrant ['freɪgrənt] ADJ duftend, wohlriechend; *(fig liter) memories* köstlich; **~ smell** Duft *m*; **the air was ~ with the scent of roses** der Duft von Rosen hing in der Luft

frail [freɪl] ADJ *(+er)* **a** *(= weak) person* gebrechlich; *health* zart, anfällig; **to be in ~ health** kränklich sein, gesundheitlich angeschlagen sein; **to look ~** schwach aussehen **b** *(= fragile) structure* fragil; *boat, aircraft* leicht gebaut; *(fig) hope* schwach; *ego* labil; **happiness is a ~ commodity** Glück ist eine unsichere Angelegenheit

frailty ['freɪltɪ] N **a** (= *weakness, of person*) Gebrechlichkeit *f*; (*of health*) Zartheit *f*, Anfälligkeit *f* **b** (= *fragility, of structure*) Fragilität *f*; (*of boat, aircraft*) leichte Bauart; (*fig, of hope*) Schwäche *f*; (*of ego*) Labilität *f*; **~, thy name is woman** Schwachheit, dein Name ist Weib

frame [freɪm] **N a** (= *basic structure, border of picture*) Rahmen *m*; (*of building*) (Grund)gerippe *nt*; (*of ship*) Gerippe *nt*; (*Hort*) Mistbeet *nt*, Frühbeet *nt*; (*of spectacles*: *also* **frames**) Gestell *nt*; (*Billiards*: = *single game*) Spiel *nt*; (= *triangle*) Rahmen *m*
b (*of human, animal*) Gestalt *f*; **her ~ was shaken by sobs** ihr Körper wurde von Schluchzen geschüttelt
c ~ of mind (= *mental state*) Verfassung *f*; (= *mood*) Stimmung *f*, Laune *f*; **in a cheerful ~ of mind** in fröhlicher Stimmung *or* Laune; **in a relaxed ~ of mind** entspannt; **I am not in the right ~ of mind for singing** *or* **to sing** ich bin nicht in der (richtigen) Laune *or* Stimmung zum Singen
d (*fig*: = *framework, system*) grundlegende Struktur; **~ of reference** (*lit, fig*) Bezugssystem *nt*; **within the ~ of …** im Rahmen (*+gen*) …; **this proposal is beyond the ~ of the peace agreement** dieser Vorschlag geht über den Rahmen des Friedensvertrags hinaus
e (*Film, Phot, Comput*) (Einzel)bild *nt*; (*in comic strip*) Bild(chen) *nt*
f (*TV*) Abtastbild *nt*, Rasterbild *nt*
g (*Comput: in browser*) Frame *nt*; (= *object frame*) Objektfeld *nt*
VT a *picture* rahmen; (*fig*) *face etc* ein- *or* umrahmen; **he stood ~d in the door** er stand im Türrahmen; **a lake ~d by trees** ein ringsum von Bäumen umgebener See
b (= *draw up, construct*) *constitution, law, plan* entwerfen; *idea* entwickeln; (= *express*) *answer, question* formulieren; *sentence* bilden; *words* bilden, formen; **she ~d the issue rather differently** sie stellte die Sache ganz anders dar
c (*inf*: = *incriminate falsely*) **he said he had been ~d** er sagte, man habe ihm die Sache angehängt (*inf*)
VI (= *develop*) sich entwickeln

▶ **frame up** VT *sep* (*inf* = *manipulate*) manipulieren

frame house N Holzhaus *nt*, Haus *nt* mit Holzrahmen

frameless ['freɪmlɪs] ADJ *spectacles* randlos

framer ['freɪmə'] N (Bilder)rahmer(in) *m(f)*

frame: **frame rucksack** N Rucksack *m* mit Traggestell; **frame saw** N Bügelsäge *f*; **frame story, frame tale** N (*Liter*) Rahmenerzählung *f*; **frame tent** N Steilwandzelt *nt*; **frame-up** N (*inf*) Komplott *nt*; **framework** N (*lit*) Grundgerüst *nt*; (*fig, of essay, novel etc*) Gerüst *nt*, Gerippe *nt*; (*of society, government etc*) grundlegende Struktur; **within the ~ of …** im Rahmen (*+gen*) …; **outside the ~ of …** außerhalb des Rahmens (*+gen*) …

framing ['freɪmɪŋ] N **a** (*action*) (Ein)rahmen *nt* **b** (= *frame*) Rahmen, Einfassung **c** (*TV*) Bildeinstellung *f*

franc [fræŋk] N Franc *m*

France [frɑːns] N Frankreich *nt*

franchise ['fræntʃaɪz] **N a** (*Pol*) Wahlrecht *nt* **b** (*Comm*) Lizenz *f*, Franchise *f* **VT** (*Comm*) *business, name* auf Lizenz vergeben

franchisee [,fræntʃaɪ'ziː] N (*Comm*) Lizenz- *or* Franchisenehmer(in) *m(f)*

franchiser, franchisor ['fræntʃaɪzə'] N (*Comm*) Lizenz- *or* Franchisegeber(in) *m(f)*

Francis ['frɑːnsɪs] N Franz *m*; **St ~ of Assisi** der heilige Franziskus von Assisi

Franciscan [fræn'sɪskən] **N** Franziskaner(in) *m(f)* **ADJ** Franziskaner-; **~ monk/monastery** Franziskanermönch *m*/-kloster *nt*

francization [,frænsaɪ'zeɪʃən] N (*esp in Canada*) Französisierung *f*

francize ['frænsaɪz] VT (*esp in Canada*) französisieren

Franco- ['fræŋkəʊ-] *in cpds* Französisch-, Franko-; **Franco-British** ADJ französisch-britisch; **Franco-Canadian** ADJ frankokanadisch, französisch-kanadisch; **Franco-German** ADJ deutsch-französisch

Franconia [fræŋ'kəʊnɪə] N Franken *nt*

Franconian [fræŋ'kəʊnɪən] **N a** (= *person*) Franke *m*, Fränkin *f* **b** (= *dialect*) Fränkisch *nt* **ADJ** fränkisch

franco: **francophile** N Franzosenfreund(in) *m(f)*; **he is a ~** er ist frankophil; **francophilia** N Frankophilie *f*; **francophobe** N Franzosenfeind(in) *m(f)*; **francophobia** N Frankophobie *f*; **Francophone** **ADJ** frankofon, Französisch sprechend **N** Frankofone(r) *mf*, Französisch sprechende(r) *mf*; **Franco-Prussian** ADJ **the ~ War** der Deutsch-Französische Krieg

frangipane ['frændʒɪpeɪn], **frangipani** [,frændʒɪ'pɑːnɪ] N (= *shrub*) Roter Jasmin(baum); (= *perfume*) Jasminparfüm *nt*

Franglais ['frɑ̃ːŋgleɪ] N Franglais *nt*, Französisch *nt* mit vielen englischen Ausdrücken

frank[1] [fræŋk] ADJ (*+er*) *person* offen; *opinion also* ehrlich; *comment, discussion also* freimütig; **to be ~ with sb** ehrlich *or* offen mit *or* zu jdm sein; **he wasn't very ~ about it** er äußerte sich nicht sehr offen dazu; **to be (perfectly) ~ (with you)** um (ganz) ehrlich zu sein

frank[2] VT *letter* frankieren; (= *postmark*) *letter* stempeln

frank[3] N (*US inf*) → **frankfurter**

Frank [fræŋk] N (*Hist*) Franke *m*, Fränkin *f*

frankfurter ['fræŋk,fɜːtə'] N (= *sausage*) (Frankfurter) Würstchen *nt*

frankincense ['fræŋkɪnsens] N Weihrauch *m*

franking machine ['fræŋkɪŋməʃiːn] N Frankiermaschine *f*

Frankish ['fræŋkɪʃ] **ADJ** fränkisch **N** (*Ling*) Fränkisch *nt*

franklin ['fræŋklɪn] N (*Hist*) Freisasse *m*

frankly ['fræŋklɪ] ADV **a** (= *openly*) *say, talk, admit* offen **b** (= *to be frank*) offen *or* ehrlich gesagt; **quite ~, I don't care** um ganz ehrlich zu sein, es ist mir egal **c** (= *unapologetically*) **~ eccentric/male** unverhohlen exzentrisch/männlich

frankness ['fræŋknɪs] N Offenheit *f*; (*of opinion also*) Ehrlichkeit *f*; (*of discussion also*) Freimütigkeit *f*

frantic ['fræntɪk] ADJ **a** (= *distraught, desperate*) *person, phone call, search* verzweifelt; *shout, yell* erregt; *need, desire* heftig, übersteigert; **I was ~** ich war außer mir; **to become** *or* **get ~** außer sich (*dat*) geraten; (= *worried*) an den Rande der Verzweiflung geraten; **to be ~ with worry** vor Sorge außer sich (*dat*) sein; **to drive sb ~** jdn zur Verzweiflung treiben **b** (= *hectic*) *week, day* hektisch; **~ activity** (*generally*) hektisches Treiben, Hektik *f*; (*particular instance*) fieberhafte Tätigkeit; **~ haste** fieberhafte Eile

frantically ['fræntɪkəlɪ] ADV **a** (= *desperately*) *try, search* verzweifelt **b** (= *hectically*) *work, run around* hektisch; *wave, scribble, scramble, run* wie wild; **she is ~ busy** sie hat wahnsinnig viel zu tun (*inf*)

frappé ['fræpeɪ] N Frappé *nt*

frat [fræt] N (*US Univ inf*) *abbr of* **fraternity**

fraternal [frə'tɜːnl] ADJ brüderlich; **~ twins** zweieiige Zwillinge *pl*

fraternity [frə'tɜːnɪtɪ] N **a** *no pl* Brüderlichkeit *f* **b** (= *community*) Vereinigung *f*, Zunft *f*; (*Eccl*) Bruderschaft *f*; (*US Univ*) Verbindung *f*; **the legal/medical/teaching ~** die Juristen *pl*/Mediziner *pl*/Lehrer *pl*; **the hunting/sailing ~** die Jagd-/Segelfans *pl*; **the criminal ~** die Kriminellen *pl*, die Unterwelt → *also* **sorority**

fraternity pin N (*US Univ*) Mitgliedsabzeichen *nt* (*einer Verbindung*)

fraternization [,frætənaɪ'zeɪʃən] N (freundschaftlicher) Umgang, Verbrüderung *f* (*pej*); (*Mil also*) Fraternisierung *f*

fraternize ['frætənaɪz] VI (freundschaftlichen) Umgang haben, sich verbrüdern (*pej*) (*with* mit); (*Mil also*) fraternisieren (*with* mit)

fratricide ['frætrɪsaɪd] N Brudermord *m*; (= *person*) Brudermörder(in) *m(f)*

fraud [frɔːd] N **a** (*no pl*: = *trickery*) Betrug *m*; (= *trick*) Schwindel *m*, Betrug *m*; **~s** Betrügereien *pl* **b** (= *fraudulent person*) Betrüger(in) *m(f)*, Schwindler(in) *m(f)*; (*feigning illness*) Simulant(in) *m(f)*; (= *fraudulent thing*) (reiner) Schwindel, fauler Zauber (*inf*); **the whole thing was a ~** das ganze war (ein einziger) Schwindel *or* reiner Schwindel

Fraud Squad N (*Brit Police*) Betrugsdezernat *nt*

fraudulence ['frɔːdjʊləns], **fraudulency** ['frɔːdjʊlənsɪ] N Betrügerei *f*; (*of action*) betrügerische Art

fraudulent ['frɔːdjʊlənt] ADJ betrügerisch

fraudulently ['frɔːdjʊləntlɪ] ADV *act* betrügerisch; *obtain* auf betrügerische Weise

fraught [frɔːt] ADJ **a ~ with difficulty** voller Schwierigkeiten; **~ with danger** gefahrvoll, voller Gefahren; **~ with tension** spannungsgeladen, voller Spannung; **~ with meaning** bedeutungsschwer **b** (= *anxious*) *meeting, relationship, situation, atmosphere* gespannt; *person* angespannt; *time* nervenaufreibend

fray[1] [freɪ] N Schlägerei *f*; (*Mil*) Kampf *m*; **ready for the ~** (*lit, fig*) kampfbereit, zum Kampf bereit; **to be eager for the ~** (*lit, fig*) kampflustig sein; **to enter the ~** (*fig*) sich in den Kampf *or* Streit einschalten

fray[2] **VT** *cloth* ausfransen; *cuff, rope* durchscheuern; **this can ~ the nerves** das kann einem ganz schön auf die Nerven gehen **VI** (*cloth*) (aus)fransen; (*cuff, trouser turn-up, rope*) sich durchscheuern; **tempers began to ~** die Gemüter begannen sich zu erhitzen *or* zu erregen; **to be ~ing at** *or* **around the edges** (*inf, alliance, marriage etc*) zu bröckeln beginnen

frayed [freɪd] ADJ *jeans etc* ausgefranst; (*fig*) gereizt, angespannt; **my nerves are quite ~** ich bin mit den Nerven runter *or* am Ende (*inf*); **tempers were ~** die Gemüter waren erhitzt; **I'm a bit ~ at** *or* **around the edges** (*inf*) ich bin ziemlich mit den Nerven runter (*inf*)

frazzle ['fræzl] **N** (*inf*) **burnt to a ~** (*Brit, toast, meat*) völlig verkohlt; (= *sunburnt*) von der Sonne total verbrannt; **worn to a ~** (= *exhausted*) total kaputt (*inf*); **to wear oneself to a ~** sich total kaputtmachen (*inf*) **VT** (*inf*) **a** (*US*: = *fray*) ausfransen **b** (*fig*: = *tire*) völlig erschöpfen *or* ermüden; **his nerves were ~d** er war mit den Nerven völlig am Ende (*inf*)

FRCP (*Brit*) *abbr of* **Fellow of the Royal College of Physicians** Mitglied *nt* des königlichen Ärzteverbands

FRCS (*Brit*) *abbr of* **Fellow of the Royal College of Surgeons** Mitglied *nt* des königlichen Chirurgenverbands

freak [friːk] **N a** (= *abnormal plant*) Missbildung *f*; (= *person, animal*) Missgeburt *f*, Missbildung *f*; **~ of nature** Laune *f* der Natur
b (= *abnormal event*) außergewöhnlicher Zufall; (= *snowstorm etc*) Anomalie *f*
c (*dated sl*: = *hippy*) ausgeflippter Typ (*sl*)
d (*inf*) **jazz/movie ~** Jazz-/Kinofreak *m* (*inf*); **health/fitness ~** Gesundheits-/Fitnessfreak *m* (*inf*)
e (*inf*: = *weird person*) Irre(r) *mf*; **he looked at me as though I were some sort of ~** er sah mich an, als ob ich vom Mond wäre
ADJ *weather, conditions* anormal, abnorm; *wave* ungewöhnlich hoch; *storm* ungewöhnlich stark; *accident, error* verrückt; *victory, goal* überraschend; (*Statistics*) *values* extrem
VI (*inf*) ausflippen (*inf*)

▶ **freak out** (*inf*) **VI** ausflippen (*inf*); (*of society*) aussteigen **VT** *sep* **it freaked me out** dabei bin ich ausgeflippt (*inf*)

freakish ['friːkɪʃ] ADJ **a** → **freak ADJ b** (= *changeable*) *weather* verrückt (*inf*), launisch, unberechenbar; *person* ausgeflippt (*inf*); *hairstyle, idea* verrückt (*inf*), irre (*inf*)

freakishly ['friːkɪʃlɪ] ADV *warm* abnorm; *early also* überraschend; *bounce, deviate* verrückt *(inf)*, unberechenbar, launisch

freak-out N *(sl)* *(dated: = party)* Haschparty *f* *(inf)*; *(= drug trip)* (Wahnsinns)trip *m* *(inf)*

freak show N Monstrositätenshow *f*

freaky ['friːkɪ] ADJ *(+er)* *(inf)* durchgeknallt *(sl)*

freckle ['frekl] N Sommersprosse *f*

freckled ['frekld], **freckly** ['freklɪ] ADJ sommersprossig

Frederick ['fredrɪk] N Friedrich *m*

free [friː] ADJ *(+er)* **a** *(= at liberty, unrestricted) person, animal, state, activity, translation, choice* frei; **as ~ as a bird** *or* **(the) air** frei wie ein Vogel; **to set a prisoner ~** einen Gefangenen freilassen *or* auf freien Fuß setzen; **to go ~** *(= not be imprisoned)* frei ausgehen; *(= be set free)* freigelassen werden; **he is ~ to go** es steht ihm frei zu gehen; **you're ~ to choose** die Wahl steht Ihnen frei; **you're ~ to come too** Sie können ruhig auch kommen; **you're ~ to go now** Sie können jetzt gehen(, wenn Sie wollen); **you're ~ to decide** Sie können das selbst entscheiden; **I'm not ~ to do it** es steht mir nicht frei, es zu tun; **(do) feel ~ to help yourself/ask questions** nehmen Sie sich/fragen Sie ruhig; **feel ~!** *(inf)* bitte, gern(e)!; **to give sb a ~ hand** jdm freie Hand lassen; **he left one end of the rope ~** er ließ ein Ende des Seils lose; **his arms were left ~** *(= not tied)* seine Arme waren frei (gelassen); **~ elections** freie Wahlen *pl* → **rein**
b *(+prep)* **~ from worry** sorgenfrei; **~ from blame/responsibility** frei von Schuld/Verantwortung; **~ of sth** frei von etw; **~ of** *or* **from pain** schmerzfrei; **~ of violence** gewaltlos; **~ of fear** ohne Angst; **a world ~ of nuclear weapons** eine Welt ohne Atomwaffen; **at last I was ~ of her** endlich war ich sie los
c *(= costing nothing)* kostenlos, Gratis-; *(Comm)* gratis; **~ shares** Gratisaktien *pl*; **it's ~** das kostet nichts; **admission ~** Eintritt frei; **to get sth ~** etw umsonst bekommen; **we got in ~** *or* **for ~** *(inf)* wir kamen umsonst rein; **~, gratis and for nothing** gratis und umsonst; **I can tell you that for ~** *(inf)* das kann ich dir gratis sagen; **~ delivery** (porto)freier Versand; **~ alongside ship** *(Comm)* frei Kai; **~ on board** *(Comm)* frei Schiff
d *(= not occupied) room, seat, hour, person* frei; **a few seats are kept ~** einige Plätze werden frei gehalten; **I wasn't ~ earlier** ich hatte nicht eher Zeit; **this leaves our hands ~ for other issues** dadurch haben wir für andere Dinge Zeit; **if you've got a ~ hand could you carry this?** wenn du eine Hand frei hast, kannst du mir das tragen?
e *(= lavish, profuse)* großzügig, freigebig; *(= licentious, improper) language, behaviour* frei, lose; *(= overfamiliar)* plumpvertraulich; **to be ~ with one's money** großzügig mit seinem Geld umgehen; **to be ~ with one's advice** Ratschläge erteilen; **to make ~ with other people's property** sich großzügig anderer Leute Sachen *(gen)* bedienen
VT *prisoner (= release)* freilassen; *(= help escape)* befreien; *caged animal* freilassen; *nation* befreien; *(= untie) person* losbinden; *tangle* (auf)lösen; *pipe* frei machen; *rusty screw, caught fabric* lösen; *(= make available) person* frei machen; **to ~ sb from pain** jdn von seinen Schmerzen befreien; **to ~ oneself from sth** sich von etw frei machen

▶ **free up** VT *(= make available) person, time* frei machen; *money, resources* verfügbar machen

-free ADJ *suf* -frei; **alcohol-/rent-/tax-free** alkohol-/miet-/steuerfrei

free: **free agent** N **to be a ~** frei und ungebunden sein, ein freier Mensch sein; **free-and-easy** ADJ *attr*, **free and easy** ADJ *pred person, lifestyle, atmosphere, relationship* ungezwungen; *(morally)* locker; **free association** N freie Assoziation; **freebase** *(Drugs sl)* N Crack *nt* VT *(= smoke) cocaine* rauchen

freebie, freebee ['friːbiː] N *(inf: = promotional gift)* Werbegeschenk *nt*; **I got it as a ~** ich habe es gratis bekommen; **this is a ~** das ist gratis *or* umsonst

free: **freeboard** N Freibord *nt*; **freebooter** N Freibeuter *m*; **freeborn** ADJ frei geboren; **Free Church** N Freikirche *f*; **free climbing** N Freiklettern *nt*; **free collective bargaining** N Tarifautonomie *f*; **free currency** N *(Fin)* frei konvertierbare Währung

freedman ['friːdmæn] N *pl* **-men** [-men] befreiter *or* freigelassener Sklave

freedom ['friːdəm] N **a** Freiheit *f*; **~ of action/speech/worship** Handlungs-/Rede-/Religionsfreiheit *f*; **~ of association** Vereinsfreiheit *f*; **~ of the press** Pressefreiheit *f*; **~ of the seas** Freiheit *f* der Meere; **to give sb (the) ~ to do sth** jdm (die) Freiheit lassen, etw zu tun; **~ from sth** Freiheit *f* von etw **b** *(= frankness)* Offenheit *f*; *(= overfamiliarity)* plumpe *(inf)* *or* zu große Vertraulichkeit **c** *(= permission to use freely)* **the ~ of the city** die (Ehren)bürgerrechte *pl*; **to give sb the ~ of one's house** jdm sein Haus zur freien Verfügung stellen

FREEDOM OF INFORMATION ACT

Der **Freedom of Information Act** (**FOIA**) ist ein US-Gesetz, das Bundesbehörden dazu verpflichtet, ihnen bekannte Informationen jedem offenzulegen, der danach fragt. Dies ist besonders für Journalisten äußerst wichtig. Das Gesetz verpflichtet die Beamten, die Informationen innerhalb von zehn Werktagen zur Verfügung zu stellen oder aber Gründe anzugeben, weshalb sie die Veröffentlichung verweigern. Material kann zurückgehalten werden, wenn dessen Bekanntgabe die nationale Sicherheit gefährdet, Betriebsgeheimnisse verrät oder jemandes Privatsphäre verletzt. Durch den **Freedom of Information Act** wurde die Veröffentlichung vormals geheimer Informationen zu Angelegenheiten höchster Wichtigkeit, wie zum Beispiel über den Vietnamkrieg sowie über illegale Spionagetätigkeiten des FBI, ermöglicht.

freedom fighter N Freiheitskämpfer(in) *m(f)*

freedwoman ['friːdwʊmən] N *pl* **-women** [-wɪmɪn] befreite *or* freigelassene Sklavin

free: **free enterprise** N freies Unternehmertum; **free fall** N freier Fall; **in ~** *(Space, fig, economy etc)* in freiem Fall; **to go into ~** *(economy etc)* sich auf eine rasante Talfahrt begeben; **free-fall** VI frei fallen; **free-fall parachuting** N Fallschirmspringen *nt* mit freiem Fall; **free fight** N allgemeine Schlägerei

free-floating ADJ nicht gebunden, unabhängig; *currency, exchange rate* frei konvertierbar

Freefone® ['friːfəʊn] N *(Brit)* **call ~ 0800** rufen Sie gebührenfrei unter 0800 an

free: **free-for-all** N Gerangel *nt* *(inf)*; *(= fight)* allgemeine Schlägerei; **to stop the situation becoming a ~** es unterbinden, dass jeder mitmischen kann; **free gift** N (Gratis)geschenk *nt*; **freehand** ADJ **~ drawing** Freihandzeichnung *f*; **~ sketch** Freihandskizze *f* ADV *paint, draw, cut* aus freier Hand; **free-handed** ADJ *(= generous)* großzügig, freigebig; **freehold** N Besitzrecht *nt*; **he bought the ~ of the house** er hat das Haus gekauft ADJ **~ property** freier Grundbesitz; **~ apartment** Eigentumswohnung *f*; **~ house** Eigenheim *nt*; **the house is ~** das Haus ist nicht gepachtet und gehört dem Eigentümer uneingeschränkt ADV **to own sth ~** etw besitzen; **for sale ~** als Eigentumswohnung/Eigenheim zu verkaufen; **free house** N *(Brit)* *Wirtshaus, das nicht an eine bestimmte Brauerei gebunden ist*; **free kick** N *(Sport)* Freistoß *m*; **free labour**, *(US)* **free labor** N *(nonunionized)* nicht organisierte Arbeitnehmer *pl*; **freelance** ADJ *journalist, photographer, writer* frei(schaffend), freiberuflich tätig; *work* freiberuflich; **I do a bit of ~ journalism** ich arbeite gelegentlich als freier Journalist; **most translators are ~** die meisten Übersetzer sind freiberuflich tätig ADV *work* freiberuflich; **she decided to go ~** sie entschloss sich, freiberuflich zu arbeiten N Freiberufler(in) *m(f)*; *(with particular firm)* freier Mitarbeiter, freie Mitarbeiterin VI freiberuflich arbeiten, freiberuflich tätig sein; **free list** N *(Theat)* Liste *f* der Empfänger von Freikarten; **freeload** VI *(inf)* schmarotzen *(on bei)*; **freeloader** N *(inf)* Schmarotzer(in) *m(f)*; **free love** N freie Liebe

freely ['friːlɪ] ADV **a** *spend, give, lend, share (= liberally)* großzügig; *(= willingly)* bereitwillig; *refer* des Öfteren; *perspire* stark; **he was spending very ~** er gab das Geld mit vollen Händen aus; **to use sth ~** reichlich von etw Gebrauch machen; **I ~ admit that ...** ich gebe gern zu, dass ... **b** *(= unrestrictedly) move, operate* frei, ungehindert; *talk, speak, express oneself* frei, offen; *elected, contested* in freien Wahlen; *flow, travel* ungehindert; **to be ~ available** ohne Schwierigkeiten zu haben sein; **the wine was flowing ~** der Wein floss in Strömen

free: **freemail** N *(Internet)* Freemail *f*; **freeman** N **a** *(= not a slave)* Freie(r) *m* **b** *(Brit)* **~ of a city** Ehrenbürger(in) *m(f)* einer Stadt; **free market** N freier Markt; *(St Ex)* Freiverkehr *m*; **free market economy** N freie Marktwirtschaft; **free-marketeer** N Befürworter(in) *m(f)* des freien Marktes; **Freemason** N Freimaurer *m*; **freemasonry** N Freimaurerei *f*; **free port** N Freihafen *m*; **Freepost®** N **"Freepost"** ≈ „Gebühr zahlt Empfänger"; **free-range** ADJ *(Brit) hen* frei laufend; *chicken, pig etc* aus Freilandhaltung; *produce* aus artgerechter Haltung; **~ eggs** Eier *pl* von frei laufenden Hühnern; **free sample** N Gratisprobe *f*; **free sheet** N kostenlose Zeitung

freesia ['friːzɪə] N *(Bot)* Freesie *f*

free: **free speech** N Redefreiheit *f*; **free-spoken** ADJ freimütig; **freestanding** ADJ frei stehend; **it can be ~ or built-in** es kann frei stehen oder eingebaut werden; **freestyle** N *(= freestyle section)* Kür *f*; *(Swimming)* Freistil *m*; **the 200 metres** *(Brit)* *or* **meters** *(US)* **~** die 200 Meter Freistil ATTR **~ swimming/wrestling** Freistilschwimmen/-ringen *nt*; **freethinker** N Freidenker(in) *m(f)*, Freigeist *m*; **freethinking** ADJ *person* freidenkerisch, freigeistig; **free time** N freie Zeit; *(= leisure)* Freizeit *f*; **if you have some ~** wenn Sie etwas Zeit haben; **free trade** N Freihandel *m*; **free-trade area** Freihandelszone *f*; **free-trader** N Freihändler(in) *m(f)*; **free throw** N *(Basketball)* Freiwurf *m*; **free TV** N frei empfangbares Fernsehen; **free verse** N freie Verse *pl*; **Freeview** N *(Brit TV)* *kostenloses digitales Fernsehen mittels einer Zusatzbox*; **Jane has ~** Jane hat eine Freeview-Box; **free vote** N *(esp Brit: Parl)* Abstimmung *f* ohne Fraktionszwang; **freeware** ['friːweəʳ] N *(Comput)* Freeware *f*; **freeway** N *(US)* Autobahn *f*; **freewheel** VI im Freilauf fahren N Freilauf *m*; **freewheeling, free-wheeling** ADJ *lifestyle, style, approach, atmosphere* ungezwungen, zwanglos; *person, community* frei, locker; *discussion* offen; **free will** N *(Philos)* freier Wille; **he did it of his own ~** er hat es aus freien Stücken getan; **Free World** N **the ~** die freie Welt

freezable ['friːzəbl] ADJ gefrierbar, einfrierbar

freeze [friːz] *vb: pret* **froze**, *ptp* **frozen** VI **a** *(Met)* frieren; *(water, liquids)* gefrieren; *(lakes, rivers)* zufrieren; *(pipes)* einfrieren; **it'll ~ hard tonight** es wird heute Nacht starken Frost geben; **to ~ to death** *(lit)* erfrieren; *(fig)* sich zu Tode frieren → **freezing, frozen**
b *(fig)* *(blood)* erstarren, gerinnen; *(heart)* aussetzen; *(smile)* erstarren, gefrieren; **the sound made me ~** das Geräusch ließ mir das Blut in den Adern erstarren *or* gefrieren *or* gerinnen
c *(= keep still)* in der Bewegung verharren *or* erstarren; **he froze in his tracks** er blieb wie angewurzelt stehen; **~!** keine Bewegung!
d *(Cook)* **meat ~s well** Fleisch lässt sich gut einfrieren
e *(Comput)* nicht mehr reagieren, sich aufhängen *(inf)*
VT **a** *water* gefrieren; *(Med, Cook)* einfrieren
b *(Econ) assets* festlegen; *credit, wages, pro-*

gramme, prices, bank account einfrieren; *(= stop) film* anhalten
c *(Med) wound* vereisen
d *(fig)* **to ~ sb with a look** jdm einen eisigen Blick zuwerfen
N a *(Met)* Frost *m*; **the big ~** der harte Frost
b *(Econ)* Stopp *m*; **a wage(s) ~, a ~ on wages** ein Lohnstopp *m*; **a ~ on nuclear weapons testing** ein Atomwaffenteststopp *m*

▸ **freeze off** VT *sep* die kalte Schulter zeigen *(+dat)*

▸ **freeze onto** VI *+prep obj (US inf)* **to freeze onto sb** sich wie eine Klette an jdn hängen *or* heften

▸ **freeze out** VT *sep (inf) person* herausekeln *(inf)*

▸ **freeze over** VI *(lake, river)* überfrieren; *(windscreen, windows)* vereisen

▸ **freeze up** VI **a** zufrieren; *(pipes)* einfrieren; *(windscreen, windows)* vereisen **b** *(Comput inf)* abstürzen VT *sep* **a** *(Comput inf) computer* zum Absturz bringen **b** **we were frozen up last winter** letztes Jahr waren alle unsere Leitungen eingefroren

freeze: **freeze-dry** ['fri:zdraɪ] VT gefriertrocknen; **freeze-frame** N *(Phot)* Standbild *nt*

freezer ['fri:zəʳ] N Tiefkühltruhe *f*; *(upright)* Gefrierschrank *m*; *(Brit: = ice compartment of fridge)* Eisfach *nt*, (Tief)kühlfach *nt*, Gefrierfach *nt*

freeze-up ['fri:zʌp] N **a** *(esp US, of lakes, rivers etc)* **during the ~ a lot of birds perish** während Seen und Flüsse zugefroren sind, kommen viele Vögel ums Leben **b** *(Comput inf)* (Computer)absturz *m*

freezing ['fri:zɪŋ] ADJ **a** *(lit: = below zero) temperature* unter null; **~ conditions** Temperaturen *pl* unter null; **~ weather** Frostwetter *nt*; **~ rain** Eisregen *m*; **in ~ fog** bei Frost und Nebel
b *(= extremely cold)* eiskalt, eisig kalt; *wind* eisig; **in the ~ cold** bei klirrender Kälte; **it's ~ (cold)** es ist eiskalt *or* eisig kalt; **I'm ~** mir ist eiskalt; **my hands/feet are ~** meine Hände/Füße sind eiskalt, ich habe eiskalte Hände/Füße
N a *(Cook)* Einfrieren *nt*
b *(= freezing point)* der Gefrierpunkt; **above/below ~** über/unter null, über/unter dem Gefrierpunkt; **to rise above ~** über null *or* über den Gefrierpunkt steigen; **to fall below ~** unter null *or* unter den Gefrierpunkt fallen

freezing point N Gefrierpunkt *m*; **below ~** unter null, unter dem Gefrierpunkt

freight [freɪt] N **a** *(= cargo)* Fracht *f*, Frachtgut *nt* **b** *(= transport of freight)* Frachtverkehr *m* **c** *(also* **freight charges***)* Fracht *f*, Frachtkosten *pl*; **~ paid** *(Comm)* frachtfrei, Fracht bezahlt; **~ and delivery paid** *(US Comm)* frachtfrei zum Bestimmungsort ADV **to send sth ~/air ~** etw als Frachtgut/per Luftfracht senden VT *goods* verfrachten

freightage ['freɪtɪdʒ] N *(= charge)* Fracht(gebühr) *f*

freight car N *(US Rail)* Güterwagen *m*

freighter ['freɪtəʳ] N *(Naut)* Frachter *m*, Frachtschiff *nt*; *(Aviat)* Frachtflugzeug *nt*

freight: **freight handler** N Frachtverlader(in) *m(f)*; **freight plane** N Frachtflugzeug *nt*; **freight terminal** N Fracht- *or* Güterterminal *nt*; **freight train** N Güterzug *m*

French [frentʃ] ADJ französisch; **~ teacher** *(teaches French)* Französischlehrer(in) *m(f)*; *(comes from France)* französischer Lehrer, französische Lehrerin; **a ~ dictionary** ein Französischwörterbuch *nt*; **he is ~** er ist Franzose; **she is ~** sie ist Französin; **the ~ people** die Franzosen *pl*, das französische Volk **N a** *(Ling)* Französisch *nt*; **in ~** auf französisch; **to speak ~** Französisch sprechen; **excuse my ~** *(hum inf)* entschuldigen Sie die Ausdrucksweise **b** **the ~** *pl* die Franzosen *pl*

French: **French Academy** N **the ~** die Académie Française; **French bean** N grüne Bohne; **French bread** N Baguette *nt*, Stangenbrot *nt*; **French-Canadian** ADJ **a** *person* frankokanadisch; **she is ~** sie ist Frankokanadierin **b** *relations* frankokanadisch, französisch-kanadisch; *(Ling)* frankokanadisch, kanadisch-französisch **N a** Frankokanadier(in) *m(f)* **b** *(Ling)* kanadisches Französisch; **French chalk** N Schneiderkreide *f*; **French cricket** N *dem Kricket ähnliches Kinderspiel*; **French doors** PL = **French windows**; **French dressing** N *(Cook)* **a** *(Brit: = oil and vinegar)* Vinaigrette *f* **b** *(US: = sweet, tomato-flavoured dressing)* French Dressing *nt*; **French Equatorial Africa** N *(Hist)* Französisch-Äquatorialafrika *nt*; **French fried potatoes**, **French fries** PL Pommes frites *pl*; **French Guiana** N Französisch-Guayana *nt*; **French Guianan** [-gaɪ'ænən] **N** Französisch-Guayaner(in) *m(f)* ADJ französisch-guayanisch; **French horn** N *(Mus)* (Wald)horn *nt*

frenchify ['frentʃɪfaɪ] VT französisieren; *clothes, restaurant* auf französisch machen *(inf)*

French: **French kiss** N Zungenkuss *m*; **French knickers** PL French Knickers *pl*; **French leave** N **to take ~** sich französisch *or* auf Französisch empfehlen; **French letter** N *(Brit inf)* Pariser *m (inf)*; **French loaf** N Baguette *f*; **Frenchman** N Franzose *m*; **French marigold** N *(Bot)* Studentenblume *f*, Tagetes *f*; **French pastry** N Blätterteigteilchen *nt* mit Obst und Sahne; **French pleat** N französischer Zopf; **French polish** N Möbelpolitur *f* mit Schellack; **French-polish** VT lackieren; **French Revolution** N **the ~** die Französische Revolution; **French Riviera** N **the ~** die französische Riviera; **French roll** N *Damenfrisur, bei der das Haar seitlich zurückgekämmt und in einer länglichen Rolle aufgesteckt wird*; **French seam** N *(Sew)* französische Naht; **French stick** N Baguette *f*, Stangenbrot *nt*; **French toast** N **a** *nur auf einer Seite gerösteter Toast* **b** *(with egg) in Ei getunktes gebratenes Brot*; **French West Africa** N *(Hist)* Französisch-Westafrika *nt*; **French windows** PL Verandatür *f*; **Frenchwoman** N Französin *f*

frenetic [frə'netɪk] ADJ *activity, pace, period* hektisch; *dancing* wild; *effort* verzweifelt

frenetically [frə'netɪklɪ] ADV *(+vb)* wie wild; *work* fieberhaft; *dance* frenetisch; **she is ~ busy** sie hat wahnsinnig viel zu tun *(inf)*

frenzied ['frenzɪd] ADJ *activity, efforts* hektisch, fieberhaft; *attack, passion, shouts* wild; *atmosphere* überreizt; *applause, crowd, fans, haste* rasend; **the gardens became the scene of ~ activity** in den Gärten herrschte hektische Betriebsamkeit

frenziedly ['frenzɪdlɪ] ADV *dance, shout* wie wild; *work* fieberhaft

frenzy ['frenzɪ] N Raserei *f*; **in a ~** in heller *or* wilder Aufregung; **he worked himself up into a ~** er steigerte sich in eine Raserei (hinein); **he worked the audience up into a ~** er brachte die Menge zur Raserei *or* zum Rasen; **~ of activity** hektische Betriebsamkeit; **~ of excitement** helle *or* wilde Aufregung

frequency ['fri:kwənsɪ] N Häufigkeit *f*; *(Phys)* Frequenz *f*; **high/low ~** Hoch-/Niederfrequenz *f*

frequency: **frequency band** N Frequenzband *nt*; **frequency distribution** N Häufigkeitsverteilung *f*; **frequency modulation** N Frequenzmodulation *f*

frequent ['fri:kwənt] ADJ häufig; *reports* zahlreich; *complaint, criticism* häufig geäußert; **she made ~ visits to Glasgow** sie reiste oft *or* häufig nach Glasgow; **take ~ breaks** machen Sie öfter *or* häufig eine Pause; **he is famous for his ~ changes of mind** er ist bekannt dafür, dass er häufig seine Meinung ändert; **her absences were ~** sie war oft *or* häufig abwesend; **do you suffer from ~ headaches?** haben Sie häufig *or* oft Kopfschmerzen?; **there are ~ trains** es verkehren viele Züge; **violent clashes were a ~ occurrence** es kam häufig *or* oft zu gewalttätigen Zusammenstößen [frɪ'kwent]
VT *(form) place* (oft *or* häufig) besuchen; **he liked to ~ the bars** er hielt sich gern in den Bars auf; **a house which was ~ed by all sorts of famous people** ein Haus, in dem alle möglichen Berühmtheiten verkehrten

frequenter [frɪ'kwentəʳ] N *(of a house)* häufig gesehener Gast; *(of a pub)* Stammgast *m*; *(of a theatre, club)* häufiger Besucher, häufige Besucherin; **he's not a ~ of restaurants** er geht nicht oft ins Restaurant

frequent flyer N Vielflieger(in) *m(f)*

frequent-flyer [,fri:kwənt'flaɪəʳ] ADJ **~ programme** *(Brit) or* **scheme** Vielfliegerprogramm *nt*

frequently ['fri:kwəntlɪ] ADV oft, häufig; **I have ~ said/heard that** das habe ich schon öfter gesagt/gehört; **all too ~, …** es kommt allzu oft *or* häufig vor, dass …; **~ asked questions** *(Comput)* häufig gestellte Fragen *pl*

fresco ['freskəʊ] N *(= technique)* Freskomalerei *f*; *(= painting)* Fresko(gemälde) *nt*

fresh [freʃ] ADJ **a** *(= not stale) food, clothes, taste, smell, breath* frisch
b *(= new, recent) instructions, news, wallpaper* neu; *coat of paint, make-up, memories, scar* frisch; *(= additional, renewed) allegations, reports, inquiries* weitere(r, s); *fighting, attack* erneut; **~ supplies** Nachschub *m*; **a ~ outbreak of violence** erneute Ausschreitungen *pl*; **a ~ pot of tea** eine Kanne frisch aufgegossener Tee; **does your house need a ~ coat of paint?** muss Ihr Haus frisch gestrichen werden?; **we need some ~ faces** wir brauchen neue Gesichter; **to make a ~ start** einen neuen Anfang machen, neu anfangen; **to leave for ~ woods** *or* **fields (and pastures new)** einen Schlussstrich ziehen und anderswo neu anfangen; **to give ~ heart to sb** jdm neuen Mut geben; **the events were still ~ in his mind** *or* **memory** die Ereignisse waren ihm noch frisch im Gedächtnis *or* in Erinnerung
c *(= not dried, processed, frozen) pasta, fruit, herbs, juice* frisch; **~ milk** *(not UHT)* Frischmilch *f*; **~ meat** *(not frozen)* Frischfleisch *nt*; **~ orange juice** frisch gepresster Orangensaft
d *(= refreshed, not tired) person, horse, face, complexion* frisch; **as ~ as a daisy** taufrisch; **to feel ~** sich frisch fühlen
e *(= refreshing, original) approach, style, writing* erfrischend; **he has a ~ approach/~ ideas** er hat einen erfrischend neuen Ansatz/erfrischend neue Ideen
f *(= cool and invigorating) morning, wind, breeze* frisch; **it's a bit ~ today** heute ist es ziemlich frisch; **the air/water is cool and ~** die Luft/das Wasser ist kühl und erfrischend
g *(inf: = cheeky)* frech; *(= disrespectful)* pampig *(inf)*; **to be ~ with sb** frech zu jdm sein; **to get ~** frech werden; **don't get ~ with me!** komm mir bloß nicht frech!
ADV **a** *(= straight)* **young men ~ from** *or* **out of university** junge Männer, die frisch *or* direkt von der Universität kommen; **I was ~ out of Oxford** ich hatte gerade mein Studium in Oxford beendet; **tourists ~ off the plane** Touristen, die gerade erst aus dem Flugzeug gestiegen sind; **milk ~ from the cows** Milch frisch von den Kühen; **cakes ~ from the oven** Kuchen frisch aus dem Backofen, ofenfrische Kuchen; **to come ~ to sth** neu zu etw kommen
b *(inf)* **we're ~ out of cheese** uns ist gerade der Käse ausgegangen; **they are ~ out of ideas** ihnen sind die Ideen ausgegangen, sie haben keine Ideen mehr

▸ **fresh up** VTIR *(US)* = **freshen up**

fresh: **fresh air** N frische Luft; **in the ~** an der frischen Luft; *(= outdoors)* im Freien; **to go out into the ~** an die frische Luft gehen; **to go for a breath of ~** frische Luft schnappen gehen; **I'm dying for a breath of ~** ich muss unbedingt frische Luft schnappen; **to be (like) a breath of ~** *(fig)* wirklich erfrischend sein; **it was a breath of ~ to read the article** es tat richtig gut, den Artikel zu lesen; **he has been a breath of ~ for us** er hat uns neuen Schwung gegeben; **fresh-baked** ADJ frisch gebacken

freshen ['freʃn] VI *(wind)* auffrischen; *(weather, air)* frisch werden VT **can I ~ your drink?** darf ich Ihnen noch nachschenken?; **chewing gum to ~ the breath** Kaugummi, um den Atem zu erfrischen

▶ **freshen up** VI/R *(person)* sich frisch machen VT *sep* a *child, invalid etc* frisch machen; **that will freshen you up** das wird Sie erfrischen b *room etc* frischer aussehen lassen; *team, image* aufmöbeln *(inf)*

fresher [ˈfreʃəˈ] N *(Brit Univ inf)* Erstsemester *nt (inf)*

fresh-faced [ˌfreʃˈfeɪst] ADJ jung aussehend; **a ~ young man** ein junger Mann mit frischem Gesicht

freshly [ˈfreʃlɪ] ADV frisch; **a ~ baked cake** ein frisch gebackener Kuchen; **the ~ dug grave** das frische Grab

freshman [ˈfreʃmən] N *pl* **-men** [-mən] *(US Univ)* Erstsemester *nt (inf)*; *(Sch)* Frischling *m (inf)*

freshness [ˈfreʃnɪs] N a *(of food, fruit, wind, paint, breath, memories etc)* Frische *f*; *(of outlook)* Neuheit *f* b *(inf, = cheekiness)* Frechheit *f*; *(= lack of respect)* Pampigkeit *f (inf)*

freshness date N *(US)* (Mindest)haltbarkeitsdatum *nt*

fresh: **freshwater** ADJ *attr* **~ fish/eel** Süßwasserfisch *m*/-aal *m*; **~ harbour** *(Brit)* or **harbor** *(US)* Binnenhafen *m*; **fresh water** N *(not salty)* Süßwasser *nt*; *(not stale)* frisches Wasser

fret[1] [fret] VI a *(= become anxious)* sich *(dat)* Sorgen machen *(about* um); *(baby)* unruhig sein; **don't ~** beruhige dich; **she ~s over** or **about the slightest thing** sie macht sich wegen jeder Kleinigkeit gleich Sorgen; **the child is ~ting for his mother** das Kind jammert nach seiner Mutter b *(horse)* **to ~ (at the bit)** sich (am Biss) reiben or scheuern VR sich *(dat)* Sorgen machen, sich aufregen N **to be in a ~** sich *(dat)* Sorgen machen, in Sorge sein

fret[2] VT *wood etc* laubsägen

fret[3] N *(on guitar etc)* Bund *m*

fretful [ˈfretfʊl] ADJ *child* quengelig; *adult, behaviour* wehleidig; *(= irritable, on edge)* genervt *(inf)*; *tone* klagend; *(= restless) sleep* unruhig

fretfully [ˈfretfəlɪ] ADV *say* wehleidig; *cry* kläglich

fretfulness [ˈfretfʊlnɪs] N *(of child)* Quengeligkeit *f*; *(of adult)* Wehleidigkeit *f*; *(= irritability)* Nervosität *f*; *(of voice)* klagender Ton

fret: **fret saw** N Laubsäge *f*; **fretwork** N *(in wood)* Laubsägearbeit *f*; *(Archit)* Mäander *m*

Freudian [ˈfrɔɪdɪən] ADJ *(Psych, fig)* Freudsch *attr*, freudianisch; **very ~!** was Freud wohl dazu sagen würde! N Freudianer(in) *m(f)*

Freudian slip N freudsche Fehlleistung; *(spoken)* freudscher Versprecher

FRG *abbr of* **Federal Republic of Germany** BRD *f*

Fri *abbr of* **Friday** Fr.

friable [ˈfraɪəbl] ADJ bröckelig, krümelig

friableness [ˈfraɪəblnɪs] N Bröckeligkeit *f*, Krümeligkeit *f*

friar [ˈfraɪəˈ] N Mönch *m*; **Friar John** Bruder John; **Black Friars** Dominikaner *pl*; **Grey Friars** Franziskaner *pl*; **White Friars** Karmeliter *pl*

friary [ˈfraɪərɪ] N Mönchskloster *nt*

fricassee [ˈfrɪkəsiː] N Frikassee *nt* VT frikassieren

fricative [ˈfrɪkətɪv] ADJ Reibe-; **~ consonant** Reibelaut *m* N Reibelaut *m*

friction [ˈfrɪkʃən] N a Reibung *f*; *(Phys)* Friktion *f*, Reibung *f* b *(fig)* Reibung *f*, Reibereien *pl*; **there is constant ~ between them** sie reiben sich ständig aneinander

friction: **friction clutch** N Friktionskupplung *f*, Reibungskupplung *f*; **friction feed** N *(Comput)* Friktionsvorschub *m*; **friction tape** N *(US)* Isolierband *nt*

Friday [ˈfraɪdɪ] N Freitag *m* → *also* **Tuesday**

fridge [frɪdʒ] N Kühlschrank *m*, Eisschrank *m*

fridge-freezer [ˈfrɪdʒˈfriːzəˈ] N Kühl-Gefrierkombination *f*

fried [fraɪd] *pret, ptp of* **fry**[2] ADJ *food, bread, rice* gebraten; **~ egg** Spiegelei *nt*; **~ potatoes** Bratkartoffeln *pl*; **~ fish** Bratfisch *m*

friend [frend] N a Freund(in) *m(f)*; *(less intimate)* Bekannte(r) *mf*; **to become** or **make ~s with sb** sich mit jdm anfreunden, mit jdm Freundschaft schließen; **to make a ~ of sb** sich *(dat)* jdn zum Freund machen; **he makes ~s easily** er findet leicht Freunde; **she's a ~ of mine** sie ist eine Freundin/eine Bekannte von mir; **he's no ~ of mine** er ist nicht mein Freund; **to be ~s with sb** mit jdm befreundet sein, jds Freund(in) sein; **I'm not ~s with her any more** sie ist nicht mehr meine Freundin; **be a ~** sei so lieb; **we're just (good) ~s** da ist nichts, wir sind nur gut befreundet; **my honourable** *(Brit Parl)***/learned** *(Jur)* **~** mein verehrter (Herr) Kollege, meine verehrte (Frau) Kollegin; **a ~ at court** *(fig)* ein einflussreicher Freund; **a ~ in need is a ~ indeed** *(Prov)* Freunde in der Not gehen tausend auf ein Lot *(Prov)*
b *(= helper, supporter)* Freund(in) *m(f)*; **he's a ~ of the arts** er ist Förderer der schönen Künste; **the Friends of the National Theatre** die Freunde *pl* des Nationaltheaters
c *(Rel)* **Friend** Quäker(in) *m(f)*; **Society of Friends** Quäker *pl*
VT *(Internet)* adden *(hinzufügen)*

friendless [ˈfrendlɪs] ADJ ohne Freunde

friendliness [ˈfrendlɪnɪs] N Freundlichkeit *f*; *(of welcome also)* Wärme *f*; *(of relations, attitude, advice)* Freundschaftlichkeit *f*

friendly [ˈfrendlɪ] ADJ *(+er)* a *(= amiable) person, smile, gesture, welcome, service, place* freundlich; *argument, advice, attitude* freundschaftlich; *cat, dog* zutraulich; **she gave him a ~ smile** sie lächelte ihn freundlich an; **he gave me a ~ pat on the shoulder** er klopfte mir freundlich auf die Schulter; **to get a ~ welcome** freundlich begrüßt werden; **that wasn't a very ~ thing to do** das war nicht gerade sehr freundlich; **to be ~ to sb** freundlich or nett zu jdm sein; **to be ~ (with sb)** *(= to be friends)* (mit jdm) befreundet sein; **we're very/quite ~** wir sind eng befreundet/ganz gute Freunde; **~ relations** freundschaftliche Beziehungen *pl*; **to be on ~ terms with sb** mit jdm auf freundschaftlichem Fuße stehen; **to become** or **get ~ with sb** sich mit jdm anfreunden; **to get ~** *(inf: = intimate)* zärtlich werden → **user-friendly, environmentally**
b *(Pol) country, nation* befreundet; *government, corporation* freundlich gesinnt *(to +dat)*; **countries which are ~ to Libya** Länder, die Libyen freundlich gesinnt sind; **unions ~ to management** unternehmerfreundliche Gewerkschaften *pl*; **~ ports** Häfen *pl* in befreundeten Ländern
N *(Sport: = match)* Freundschaftsspiel *nt*

friendly: **friendly fire** N *(Mil)* Beschuss *m* durch die eigene Seite; **Friendly Islands** PL Freundschaftsinseln *pl*; **friendly match** N *(Sport)* Freundschaftsspiel *nt*; **friendly society** N *(Brit)* Versicherungsverein *m* auf Gegenseitigkeit

friendship [ˈfrendʃɪp] N Freundschaft *f*

fries [fraɪz] PL *(esp US inf)* Fritten *pl (inf)*, Pommes *pl (inf)*

Friesian [ˈfriːʒən] ADJ a friesisch b *cattle* Deutsche(r, s) Schwarzbunte(r, s) N a Friese *m*, Friesin *f* b *(Ling)* Friesisch *nt* c *(= cow)* Deutsche Schwarzbunte *f*

Friesian Islands PL Friesische Inseln *pl*

Friesland [ˈfriːslənd] N Friesland *nt*

frieze[1] [friːz] N *(Archit: = picture)* Fries *m*; *(= thin band)* Zierstreifen *m*

frieze[2] N *(Tex)* Fries *m*

frigate [ˈfrɪgɪt] N *(Naut)* Fregatte *f*

frigging [ˈfrɪgɪŋ] *(sl)* ADJ verdammt *(inf)*, Scheiß- *(inf)*; **that ~ bus** der verdammte Bus *(inf)*, der Scheißbus *(inf)* ADV verdammt *(inf)*

fright [fraɪt] N a Schreck(en) *m*; **to get** or **have a ~** sich erschrecken, einen Schreck bekommen; **to give sb a ~** jdm einen Schreck(en) einjagen, jdn erschrecken; **to take ~** es mit der Angst zu tun bekommen b *(inf: = person)* Vogelscheuche *f (inf)*; **she looks a ~ in that hat** mit dem Hut sieht sie verboten aus *(inf)*

frighten [ˈfraɪtn] VT *(= give a sudden fright)* erschrecken, Angst einjagen *(+dat)*; *(= make scared)* Angst machen *(+dat)*, Angst einjagen *(+dat)*; *(idea, thought)* ängstigen, Angst *or* Furcht einflößen *(+dat)*; **I'm not easily ~ed** ich fürchte mich nicht so schnell, ich habe nicht so schnell Angst; *(with threats etc)* so schnell *or* leicht kann man mir keine Angst machen; **to be ~ed by sth** vor etw *(dat)* erschrecken; **to ~ sb into agreeing to sth** jdm solche Angst machen, dass er/sie einer Sache *(dat)* zustimmt; **to ~ the life out of sb** jdn zu Tode erschrecken
VI **she doesn't ~ easily** so leicht fürchtet sie sich nicht; *(with threats etc)* so schnell *or* leicht kann man ihr keine Angst machen

▶ **frighten away** *or* **off** VT *sep* abschrecken; *(deliberately)* verscheuchen

frightened [ˈfraɪtnd] ADJ *person, animal* ängstlich, verängstigt; *voice, eyes, look* ängstlich, angsterfüllt; **to be ~ (of sb/sth)** (vor jdm/etw) Angst haben; **are you ~ of the dark?** hast du Angst vor der Dunkelheit?; **don't be ~** hab keine Angst; **they were ~ (that) there would be another earthquake** sie hatten Angst (davor), dass es noch ein Erdbeben geben könnte; **to be ~ to do sth** Angst (davor) haben, etw zu tun; **I was too ~ to look** ich hatte zu viel Angst *or* war zu verängstigt, um hinzusehen; **to be ~ about** *or* **of doing sth** Angst davor haben, etw zu tun; **to be ~ to death** *or* **out of one's wits** zu Tode erschrocken sein; **to be ~ to death that...** Todesängste ausstehen, dass ...; **to be ~ to death of sb/sth** eine Todesangst vor jdm/etw haben; **like a ~ rabbit** wie ein verängstigtes Kaninchen

frighteners [ˈfraɪtnəz] PL *(Brit inf)* **to put the ~ on sb** jdm einen Schreck einjagen

frightening [ˈfraɪtnɪŋ] ADJ a *(= alarming) experience, incident* furchterregend; *situation, sight, prospect, feeling, thought, story* erschreckend; **it was a ~ situation** die Situation war zum Fürchten; **the most ~ sight** der entsetzlichste Anblick; **to look ~** zum Fürchten aussehen b *(= scary)* beängstigend; **life was more ~ when I was small** als ich noch klein war, hat das Leben mir mehr Angst gemacht; **it was a ~ place** der Ort war zum Fürchten; **it is ~ to think what could happen** es ist beängstigend, wenn man denkt, was alles passieren könnte

frighteningly [ˈfraɪtnɪŋlɪ] ADV erschreckend; **more ~, one risked one's life** und was noch erschreckender war, es bestand Lebensgefahr

frightful [ˈfraɪtfʊl] ADJ *(inf)* schrecklich, furchtbar; **to look ~** zum Fürchten aussehen

frightfully [ˈfraɪtfəlɪ] ADV *(inf)* schrecklich, furchtbar; **she did ~ well at school** *(dated)* sie war in der Schule unheimlich gut *(inf)*

frightfulness [ˈfraɪtfʊlnɪs] N *(inf)* Schrecklichkeit *f*, Furchtbarkeit *f*

frigid [ˈfrɪdʒɪd] ADJ a *(sexually)* frigide b *(form: = cold) place, air, night, weather* eiskalt; *temperature, silence, stare* eisig; *atmosphere, manner, smile* frostig

frigidity [frɪˈdʒɪdɪtɪ] N a *(sexual)* Frigidität *f* b *(form: = iciness)* eisige Kälte; *(fig, of atmosphere, manner, smile)* Frostigkeit *f*

frill [frɪl] N a *(on dress, shirt etc)* Rüsche *f*; *(on animal, bird)* Kragen *m*; *(round meat, on plant pot etc)* Manschette *f* b **~s** *pl (fig: = ornaments)* Kinkerlitzchen *pl (inf)*, Verzierungen *pl*; **with all the ~s** mit allem Drum und Dran *(inf)*; **a simple meal without ~s** ein schlichtes Essen

frilly [ˈfrɪlɪ] ADJ *(+er)* a *(Tex) apron, cushion, clothing* mit Rüschen; **to be ~** Rüschen haben; **~ dress/blouse/underwear** Rüschenkleid *nt*/-bluse *f*/-unterwäsche *f* b *(fig) speech, style* blumig; *music, decoration* verschnörkelt

fringe [frɪndʒ] N a *(on shawl)* Fransenkante *f*, Fransen *pl* b *(Brit: = hair)* Pony *m* c *(fig: = periphery)* Rand *m*; **on the ~ of the forest** am Waldrand; **to live on the ~(s) of society** am

Rande der Gesellschaft leben; **the ~s of a city** die Randbezirke *pl* einer Stadt **d** *(Pol etc)* Alternativszene *f*; **the Fringe** *(in Edinburgh) alternatives Theaterfestival* → **lunatic fringe** **VT** mit Fransen versehen

fringe: **fringe area** N *(lit, fig)* Randgebiet *nt*; **fringe benefits** PL zusätzliche Leistungen *pl*

fringed [ˈfrɪndʒd] ADJ *skirt, shawl, jacket* mit Fransen; *lampshade* mit Fransenkante; **~ with** *or* **by sth** *(street, beach, lawn, = lined)* von etw gesäumt *(geh)*; *(= surrounded)* von etw umsäumt *(geh)*; **~ with silk** mit Seidenfransen

fringe: **fringe event** N Randveranstaltung *f*; **fringe group** N Randgruppe *f*; **fringe theatre**, *(US)* **fringe theater** N Experimentiertheater *nt*, avantgardistisches Theater

frippery [ˈfrɪpərɪ] N *(pej: = cheap ornament)* Flitter *m*, Kinkerlitzchen *pl (inf)*; *(= trivialities)* belanglose Kleinigkeiten *pl*

Frisbee® [ˈfrɪzbɪ] N Frisbee® *nt*

Frisian [ˈfrɪsɪən] ADJ N = **Friesian ADJ a N a, b**

frisk [frɪsk] **VI** *(= leap about)* umhertollen **VT** *suspect etc* durchsuchen, filzen *(inf)*

friskiness [ˈfrɪskɪnɪs] N Verspieltheit *f*

frisky [ˈfrɪskɪ] ADJ *(+er)* verspielt

frisson [ˈfriːsɒn] N *(= thrill)* Schauer *m*

fritillary [frɪˈtɪlərɪ] N *(= butterfly)* Perlmutterfalter *m*

fritter[1] [ˈfrɪtəʳ] VT *(Brit: also* **fritter away***) money, time* vertun *(inf)*, vergeuden, verplempern *(inf)*

fritter[2] N *(Cook)* Beignet *m*, Schmalzgebackenes *nt no pl* mit Füllung; **apple ~** Apfelbeignet *m*

frivolity [frɪˈvɒlɪtɪ] N Frivolität *f*; *(of appearance, writer)* unseriöse Art

frivolous [ˈfrɪvələs] ADJ *person, attitude, remark* frivol, leichtfertig; *clothes, appearance, writer, scientist* unseriös; *object, activity* albern; **I spend a lot of money on ~ things** ich gebe viel Geld für unwichtige Dinge aus; **the ~ stories of the tabloids** die belanglosen Berichte in den Boulevardzeitungen

frivolously [ˈfrɪvələslɪ] ADV frivol; *remark also* leichtfertig

frizz [frɪz] **VT** *hair* kräuseln **VI** sich kräuseln, kraus werden **N** Kraushaar *nt*

frizzball [ˈfrɪzbɔːl] N *(sl: = hair)* Mähne *f (inf)*

frizzle [ˈfrɪzl] **VI** *(= sizzle)* brutzeln **VT** **a** *bacon etc* knusprig braten **b** *hair* kräuseln; **a man with ~d white hair** ein Mann mit weißem Kraushaar

frizz(l)y [ˈfrɪz(l)ɪ] ADJ *(+er) hair* kraus

fro [frəʊ] ADV → **to, to-ing and fro-ing**

frock [frɒk] N Kleid *nt*; *(of monk)* Kutte *f*

frock coat N Gehrock *m*

frog[1] [frɒg] N **a** Frosch *m*; **to have a ~ in one's throat** einen Frosch im Hals haben; **he's a big ~ in a small pond** *(US)* er ist ein großes Tier am Ort *(inf)* **b** **Frog** *(Brit pej inf: = French person)* Franzmann *m (dated inf)*, Franzose *m*, Französin *f*

frog[2] N *(= fastening)* Paspelverschluss *m*

frogging [ˈfrɒgɪŋ] N *(= fastenings)* Paspelverschlüsse *pl*

Froggy [ˈfrɒgɪ] N *(Brit, pej inf)* Franzose *m*, Französin *f*, Franzmann *m (dated inf)*

frog: **frog kick** N Beinschlag *m* beim Brustschwimmen; **frogman** N Froschmann *m*; **frogmarch** VT *(Brit)* (ab)schleppen *(inf)*, (weg)schleifen; *(= carry)* zu viert wegtragen; **they ~ed him in** sie schleppten ihn herein *(inf)*; **frogs' legs** PL *(Cook)* Froschschenkel *pl*; **frogspawn** N Froschlaich *m*

frolic [ˈfrɒlɪk] *vb: pret, ptp* **frolicked** **VI** *(also* **frolic about** *or* **around***)* herumtollen, herumtoben **N** *(= romp)* Herumtoben *nt*, Herumtollen *nt*; *(= gaiety)* Ausgelassenheit *f*; *(= prank)* Jux *m*, Scherz *m*, Spaß *m*

frolicsome [ˈfrɒlɪksəm] ADJ übermütig, ausgelassen

from [frɒm] PREP **a** *(indicating starting place)* von *(+dat)*; *(indicating place of origin)* aus *(+dat)*; **he/the train has come ~ London** er/der Zug ist von London gekommen; **he/it comes** *or* **is ~ Germany** er/es kommt *or* ist aus Deutschland; **where have you come ~ today?** von wo sind Sie heute gekommen?; **where does he come ~?, where is he ~?** woher kommt *or* stammt er?; **the train ~ Manchester** der Zug aus Manchester; **the train ~ Manchester to London** der Zug von Manchester nach London; **he's on the phone ~ London** er ruft aus London an; **~ house to house** von Haus zu Haus; **a representative ~ the company** ein Vertreter/eine Vertreterin der Firma

b *(indicating time, in past)* seit *(+dat)*; *(in future)* ab *(+dat)*, von *(+dat)* … an; **~ last week until** *or* **to yesterday** von letzter Woche bis gestern; **~ … on** ab …; **~ now on** von jetzt an, ab jetzt; **~ then on** von da an; *(in past also)* seither; **~ his childhood** von Kindheit an, von klein auf; **he comes ~ time to time** er kommt von Zeit zu Zeit; **as ~ the 6th May** vom 6. Mai an, ab (dem) 6. Mai; **5 years ~ now** in 5 Jahren

c *(indicating distance)* von *(+dat)* (… weg); *(from town etc)* von *(+dat)* … (entfernt); **the house is 10 km ~ the coast** das Haus ist 10 km von der Küste entfernt; **to work away ~ home** außer Haus arbeiten

d *(indicating sender, giver)* von *(+dat)*; **tell him ~ me** richten Sie ihm von mir aus; **an invitation ~ the Smiths** eine Einladung von den Smiths; **"from …"** *(on envelope, parcel)* „Absender …", „Abs. …"

e *(indicating removal)* von *(+dat)*; *(= out of: from pocket, cupboard etc)* aus *(+dat)*; **to take/grab** *etc* **sth ~ sb** jdm etw wegnehmen/wegreißen *etc*; **to steal sth ~ sb** jdm etw stehlen; **he took it ~ the top/middle/bottom of the pile** er nahm es oben vom Stapel/aus der Mitte des Stapels/unten vom Stapel weg

f *(indicating source)* von *(+dat)*; *(= out of)* aus *(+dat)*; **where did you get that ~?** wo hast du das her?, woher hast du das?; **I got it ~ the supermarket/the library/Kathy** ich habe es aus dem Supermarkt/aus der Bücherei/von Kathy; **to drink ~ a stream/glass** aus einem Bach/Glas trinken; **quotation ~ "Hamlet"/the Bible/Shakespeare** Zitat *nt* aus „Hamlet"/aus der Bibel/nach Shakespeare; **memories ~ his childhood** Erinnerungen aus seiner Kindheit; **translated ~ the English** aus dem Englischen übersetzt; **made ~ …** aus … hergestellt

g *(= modelled on)* nach *(+dat)*; **painted ~ life** nach dem Leben gemalt

h *(indicating lowest amount)* ab *(+dat)*; **~ £2/the age of 16 (upwards)** ab £ 2/16 Jahren (aufwärts); **dresses (ranging) ~ £60 to £80** Kleider *pl* zwischen £ 60 und £ 80

i *(indicating escape)* **he fled ~ the enemy** er floh vor dem Feind; **he got away ~ his pursuers** er entkam seinen Verfolgern; **he ran away ~ home** er rannte von zu Hause weg; **he escaped ~ prison** er entkam aus dem Gefängnis

j *(indicating change)* **things went ~ bad to worse** es wurde immer schlimmer; **he went ~ office boy to director** er stieg vom Laufjungen zum Direktor auf; **a price increase ~ one euro to two euros** eine Preiserhöhung von einem auf zwei Euro

k *(indicating difference)* **he is quite different ~ the others** er ist ganz anders als die andern; **to tell black ~ white** Schwarz und Weiß auseinanderhalten; **I like all sports, ~ swimming to wrestling** ich mag alle Sportarten, von Schwimmen bis Ringen

l *(= because of, due to)* **to act ~ compassion** aus Mitleid handeln; **to die ~ cancer** an Krebs sterben; **weak ~ hunger** schwach vor Hunger; **weak ~ loss of blood** vom Blutverlust geschwächt

m *(= on the basis of)* **~ experience** aus Erfahrung; **to judge ~ recent reports …** nach neueren Berichten zu urteilen …; **~ your point of view** von Ihrem Standpunkt aus (gesehen); **to conclude ~ the information** aus den Informationen einen Schluss ziehen, von den Informationen schließen; **~ what I heard** nach dem, was ich gehört habe; **~ what I can see …** nach dem, was ich sehen kann …; **~ the look of things …** (so) wie die Sache aussieht …

n *(Math)* **3 ~ 8 leaves 5** 8 weniger 3 ist 5; **take 12 ~ 18** nimm 12 von 18 weg; **£10 will be deducted ~ your account** £ 10 werden von Ihrem Konto abgebucht

o *(in set phrases, see also other element)* **to prevent/stop sb ~ doing sth** jdn daran hindern/davon zurückhalten, etw zu tun; **he prevented me ~ coming** er hielt mich davon ab, zu kommen; **to suffer ~ sth** an etw *(dat)* leiden; **to shelter ~ the rain** sich vor dem Regen unterstellen; **to protect sb ~ sth** jdn vor etw *(dat)* schützen

p *+adv* von; **~ inside/underneath** von innen/unten

q *+prep* **~ above** *or* **over/across sth** über etw *(acc)* hinweg; **~ beneath** *or* **underneath sth** unter etw *(dat)* hervor; **~ out of sth** aus etw heraus; **~ before his mother's death** aus der Zeit vor dem Tod seiner Mutter; **~ among the trees** zwischen den Bäumen hervor; **~ inside/outside the house** von drinnen/draußen; **~ beyond the grave** aus dem Jenseits

frond [frɒnd] N *(of fern)* Farnwedel *m*; *(of palm)* Palmwedel *m*

front [frʌnt] **N** **a** *(= forward side, exterior)* Vorderseite *f*; *(= forward part, including interior)* Vorderteil *nt*; *(of house etc: = façade)* Vorderfront *f*, Stirnseite *f*; *(of shirt, dress)* Vorderteil *nt*; *(= dickey)* Hemdbrust *f*; *(Theat: = auditorium)* Zuschauerraum *m*; **in ~** vorne; *(in line, race etc also)* an der Spitze; **in ~ of sb/sth** vor jdm/etw; **at the ~ of** *(inside)* vorne in *(+dat)*; *(outside)* vor *(+dat)*; *(= at the head of)* an der Spitze *(+gen)*; **to be in ~** vorne sein; *(Sport)* vorn(e) *or* an der Spitze liegen; **look in ~ of you** blicken Sie nach vorne; **in ~ of you you can see …** vor Ihnen können Sie … sehen; **in** *or* **at the ~ of the train/class** vorne im Zug/Klassenzimmer; **he reached the ~ of the queue** *(Brit) or* **line** *(US)* er erreichte die Spitze der Schlange; **she spilled tea down the ~ of her dress** sie verschüttete Tee vorn über ihr Kleid

b *(Mil, Pol, Met)* Front *f*; **he fell at the ~** er ist an der Front gefallen; **they were attacked on all ~s** *(Mil)* sie wurden an allen Fronten angegriffen; *(fig)* sie wurden von allen Seiten angegriffen; **cold ~** *(Met)* Kalt(luft)front *f*; **we must present a common/united ~** wir müssen eine gemeinsame/geschlossene Front bieten; **on the wages ~** was die Löhne betrifft; **on the home** *or* **domestic ~** *(Pol)* im Inland

c *(Brit, of sea)* Strandpromenade *f*; *(of lake)* Uferpromenade *f*

d *(= outward appearance)* Fassade *f*; **to put on a bold ~** eine tapfere Miene zur Schau stellen; **to put on a calm ~** nach außen hin ruhig erscheinen; **it's just a ~** das ist nur Fassade

e *(= cover for illicit activity)* Tarnung *f*, Fassade *f*

f *(US: = figurehead of organization)* Galionsfigur *f*, Aushängeschild *nt*

g *no pl (= effrontery)* Stirn *f*; **to have the ~ to do sth** die Frechheit besitzen *or* die Stirn haben, etw zu tun

h *(poet, = brow, face)* Antlitz *nt (poet)*

ADV **up ~** vorne; **to move up ~** nach vorne rücken; **50% up ~** 50% Vorschuss; **to attack ~ and rear** von vorn und hinten angreifen; **eyes ~!** *(Mil)* Augen geradeaus! → *also* **upfront**

VI **the houses/windows ~ onto the street** die Häuser liegen/die Fenster gehen auf die Straße hinaus

VT **a** **cottages ~ed by well-kept lawns** Häuschen mit gepflegtem Rasen davor

b *organization, band* leiten

ADJ vorderste(r, s), Vorder-; *page* erste(r, s); **~ tooth/wheel/room** Vorderzahn *m*/-rad *nt*/-zimmer *nt*; **~ row** erste *or* vorderste Reihe; **the ~ end of the train** die Spitze des Zuges

frontage [ˈfrʌntɪdʒ] N *(of building)* Front *f*, Vorderseite *f*; *(= ground in front of house)* Grundstück *or* Gelände *nt* vor dem Haus; **the shop has a ~ on two streets** der Laden hat Schaufenster auf *or* zu zwei Straßen hinaus; **because**

of its ~ onto the sea weil es zur See hinaus liegt

frontage road N *(US)* → **service road**

frontal [ˈfrʌntl] ADJ *attr* a *(= direct, head-on)* **~ assault** *or* **attack** Frontalangriff *m*; **~ challenge** direkte Herausforderung; **~ impact** *or* **collision** *(Aut)* Frontalzusammenstoß *m* b **~ nudity** *(TV, Film)* frontale Nacktszenen *pl*; *(Phot)* frontale Nacktaufnahmen *pl*; **(full) ~ nude shots** frontale Nacktaufnahmen *pl* c *(Met)* **~ system** Frontsystem *nt* N a *(Rel)* Altardecke *f* b = **full frontal**

frontal *(Anat, Med)*: **frontal cortex** N Hirnrinde *f*; **frontal lobe** N Stirnlappen *m*; **frontal lobotomy** N Leukotomie *f*

front: **front bench** N *(Parl)* vorderste *or* erste Reihe *(wo die führenden Politiker sitzen)*; **front burner** N **to be sb's ~** *(inf)* für jdn an erster Stelle kommen; **front crawl** N *(Swimming)* Kraulen *nt*, Kraulstil *m*; **front door** N Haustür *f*; **front drive** N *(Aut)* Frontantrieb *m*; **front end** N *(Comput)* Frontende *nt*; **front garden** N Vorgarten *m*

frontier [frʌnˈtɪəˈ] N Grenze *f*, Landesgrenze *f*; *(= boundary area)* Grenzgebiet *nt*; *(fig, of knowledge)* Grenze *f*; **to push back the ~s of science** auf wissenschaftliches Neuland vorstoßen

frontier *in cpds* Grenz-; **frontier dispute** N Grenzstreitigkeiten *pl*; **frontiersman** [frʌnˈtɪəzmən] N *pl* **-men** [-mən] Grenzbewohner *m*; **frontier station** N Grenzposten *m*; **frontierswoman** [frʌnˈtɪəzwʊmən] N *pl* **-women** [-ˈwɪmɪn] Grenzbewohnerin *f*

frontispiece [ˈfrʌntɪspiːs] N zweite Titelseite, Frontispiz *nt (obs)*

front: **front line** N Front(linie) *f*; **frontline** ADJ *(Mil)* Front-; *(fig) employees etc* in vorderster Front; **~ states** Anliegerstaaten *pl (an einen Kriegsschauplatz)*; **~ troops** Fronttruppen *pl*; **front loader** N Frontlader *m*; **front man** N Mann *m* an der Spitze; *(pej)* Strohmann *m*; **front matter** N Titelei *f*; **front money** N *(US, paid upfront)* Vorschuss *m*; **front office** N *(US Comm)* Verwaltung *f*; **front organization** N Tarn- *or* Deckorganisation *f*; **front page** N erste Seite, Titelseite *f*; **to hit the ~** Schlagzeilen machen; **front-page** ADJ *attr news, story, report, headline, coverage* auf der ersten Seite; **~ picture** *or* **photograph** *(of magazine)* Titelbild *nt*; **to be** *or* **make ~ news** Schlagzeilen machen; **it's not exactly ~ news** das wird nicht gerade Schlagzeilen machen; **front rank** N **to be in the ~** *(fig)* zur Spitze zählen; **frontrunner** N a Läufer(in) *m(f)* an der Spitze; **he's by nature a ~** er läuft am liebsten an der Spitze b *(fig)* Spitzenreiter(in) *m(f)*; **front seat** N Platz *m* in der ersten Reihe; *(Aut)* Vordersitz *m*; *(fig)* Logenplatz *m*; **front view** N *(Tech)* Aufriss *m*; **front vowel** N *(Phon)* Vorderzungenvokal *m*; **front-wheel drive** N Vorderradantrieb *m*; **front woman** N Frau *f* an der Spitze; *(pej)* Strohfrau *f*

frosh [frɒʃ] N *(US inf) (Univ)* Erstsemester *nt (inf)*; *(Sch)* Frischling *m (inf)*

frost [frɒst] N a Frost *m*; *(on leaves etc)* Raureif *m*; **late ~s** späte Frostperioden *pl*; **ten degrees of ~** zehn Grad Kälte b *(fig, = cold manner)* Kühle *f*, Kälte *f*, Frostigkeit *f* c *(dated sl, = failure)* Pleite *f (inf)*, Reinfall *m* VT a *glass* mattieren b *(esp US) cake* mit Zuckerguss überziehen, glasieren c *(= quick-freeze)* einfrieren, tiefkühlen

frost: **frostbite** N Frostbeulen *pl*; *(more serious)* Erfrierungen *pl*; **to suffer (from) ~** Frostbeulen/Erfrierungen haben; **frostbitten** ADJ *fingers, toes, person* erfroren; *crops, plants* durch Frost geschädigt; **people with ~ fingers** Leute mit Frostbeulen/Erfrierungen an den Fingern; **he was badly ~** er hatte sehr starke Erfrierungen; **frostbound** ADJ *ground* hart gefroren

frosted [ˈfrɒstɪd] ADJ a *(= frost-covered) grass, trees, roofs* von Raureif bedeckt; *windows, windscreen* vereist b *(fig) eye shadow, nail varnish, lipstick* metallisch c *(esp US: = iced)* mit Zuckerguss überzogen, glasiert; *(= sugared) fruit* mit Zucker bestreut

frosted glass N Mattglas *nt*, Milchglas *nt*; **~ door** Matt- *or* Milchglastür *f*

frostily [ˈfrɒstɪlɪ] ADV *say* frostig; *smile* kühl

frostiness [ˈfrɒstɪnɪs] N *(of weather, fig, of welcome etc)* Frostigkeit *f*

frosting [ˈfrɒstɪŋ] N *(esp US: = icing)* Zuckerguss *m*

frost line N Frostgrenze *f*

frost work N *(on window)* Eisblumen *pl*

frosty [ˈfrɒstɪ] ADJ *(+er)* a *(= cold)* frostig; **~ night** Frostnacht *f*; **a clear and ~ night** eine frostklare Nacht; **~ weather** Frostwetter *nt* b *(= frost-covered) ground, grass* von Raureif bedeckt; *(= frozen) ground* gefroren c *(fig) person, reception, response, atmosphere* frostig, kühl; *look* eisig; *relations* unterkühlt

froth [frɒθ] N a *(on liquids, Med)* Schaum *m* b *(= light conversation, frivolities)* Firlefanz *m*; **the present ~ and commotion over the elections** der ganze Zirkus, der im Moment um die Wahlen gemacht wird VI schäumen; **the beer ~ed over the edge of the glass** der Schaum floss über den Rand des Bierglases; **a cup of ~ing coffee** eine Tasse Kaffee mit Schaum; **the dog was ~ing at the mouth** der Hund hatte Schaum vor dem Maul; **he was ~ing at the mouth (with rage)** er schäumte vor Wut

frothy [ˈfrɒθɪ] ADJ *(+er)* a *(= bubbly) beer, milk shake, coffee, sea etc* schäumend; *mixture, cream* schaumig; **beer with a full ~ head** Bier mit einer großen Schaumkrone b *(= frilly)* duftig und voller Rüschen c *(= superficial) comedy, entertainment* leicht, seicht *(pej)*

frown [fraʊn] N Stirnrunzeln *nt no pl*; **to give a ~** die Stirn(e) runzeln; **... he said with a deep ~** ... sagte er mit einem ausgeprägten Stirnrunzeln; **angry ~** finsterer Blick; **worried/puzzled ~** sorgenvoller/verdutzter Gesichtsausdruck, sorgenvolles/verdutztes Gesicht; **a worried ~ crossed his face** ein sorgenvoller Ausdruck huschte über sein Gesicht VI *(lit, fig)* die Stirn(e) runzeln (*at* über *+acc*)

▶ **frown (up)on** VI *+prep obj (fig) suggestion, idea* missbilligen, mit Stirnrunzeln betrachten; **this practice is frowned (up)on** diese Gewohnheit ist verpönt

frowning [ˈfraʊnɪŋ] ADJ *face, look, glance, expression* finster; **a ~ man** ein finster blickender Mann

frowsy, frowzy [ˈfraʊzɪ] ADJ *(+er) (= unkempt)* schlampig, schlud(e)rig

froze [frəʊz] *pret of* **freeze**

frozen [ˈfrəʊzn] *ptp of* **freeze** ADJ a *ground, land, earth* gefroren; *pipe* eingefroren; *lock* zugefroren; **~ hard** hart gefroren; **~ (over)** *(lake, river)* zugefroren; **~ solid** ganz zugefroren b *(for preservation, Cook) vegetables, meat, meal* tiefgekühlt; *(Med) embryo, sperm* eingefroren; **~ yoghurt** gefrorener Jog(h)urt; **to keep sth ~** etw eingefroren lassen c *(inf: = very cold) person, part of body* eiskalt; **I'm ~** mir ist eiskalt; **to be ~ stiff** *(person, part of body)* steif gefroren sein; **~ to death** *or* **to the bone** völlig durchgefroren → **marrow** d *(= rigid) person, animal* starr; **~ in horror/with fear** starr *or* steif vor Schreck/vor Angst; **I stood** *or* **was ~ to the spot** ich stand wie angewurzelt da; **a village ~ in time** ein Dorf, in dem die Zeit stehen geblieben ist; **he felt as if he was ~ in time** es war ihm, als sei die Zeit stehen geblieben e *(Econ) prices, wages* eingefroren; *(Fin) account* eingefroren

frozen: **frozen assets** PL *(Fin)* festliegendes Kapital, eingefrorene Guthaben *pl*; **frozen food** N Tiefkühlkost *f*; **~ compartment** Tiefkühlfach *nt*, Gefrierfach *nt*; **frozen shoulder** N *(Med)* steife Schulter; **frozen wastes** PL ewiges Eis

FRS *abbr of* **Fellow of the Royal Society**

fructification [ˌfrʌktɪfɪˈkeɪʃən] N *(lit, fig: = making fruitful)* Befruchtung *f*; *(= forming fruit)* Fruchtbildung *f*

fructify [ˈfrʌktɪfaɪ] VT *(lit, fig) seed, writing* befruchten VI Früchte tragen

frugal [ˈfruːgəl] ADJ a *person, life* genügsam; **to be ~ with one's money** sparsam mit seinem Geld umgehen b *meal* karg; *food, diet* frugal *(geh)*, bescheiden

frugality [fruːˈgælɪtɪ] N a *(of person)* Genügsamkeit *f*; *(= thrift)* Sparsamkeit *f*; **a life of great ~** ein sehr genügsames Leben b *(of meal)* Kargheit *f*; *(of food, diet)* Bescheidenheit *f*, Frugalität *f (geh)*

frugally [ˈfruːgəlɪ] ADV *live* genügsam; *use* sparsam; *eat* sehr wenig

fruit [fruːt] N a *(as collective)* Obst *nt*; *(Bot, fig)* Frucht *f*; **is it a ~ or a vegetable?** ist es Obst oder Gemüse?; **what is your favourite** *(Brit) or* **favorite** *(US)* **~?** welches Obst magst du am liebsten?; **would you like some** *or* **a piece of ~?** möchten Sie etwas Obst?; **the ~s of the earth** die Früchte *pl* des Feldes; **to bear ~** *(lit, fig)* Früchte tragen; **the ~(s) of my labour/success** die Früchte *pl* meiner Arbeit/meines Erfolgs; **this project is the first ~ of our cooperation** dieses Projekt ist die erste Frucht unserer Zusammenarbeit *(geh)* b *(dated Brit inf)* **old ~** alter Knabe *(inf)* c *(US pej sl, = homosexual)* Süße(r) *m (inf)*, warmer Bruder *(inf)* VI Früchte tragen

fruit: **fruit bat** N Flughund *m*; **fruit bowl** N Obstschale *f*; **fruitcake** N englischer Kuchen; *(esp Brit inf: = eccentric)* Spinner(in) *m(f) (inf)*; **as nutty as a ~** *(esp Brit inf)* total verrückt; **fruit cocktail** N Obstsalat *m*; **fruit cup** N a *(= drink)* Cocktail *m* mit Früchten b *(US)* Frucht- *or* Früchtebecher *m*; **fruit dish** N Obstteller *m*; **fruit drop** N Drops *m*, Früchtebonbon *m or nt*

fruiterer [ˈfruːtərəˈ] N *(esp Brit)* Obsthändler(in) *m(f)*

fruit: **fruit farmer** N Obstbauer *m*/-bäuerin *f*; **fruit farming** N Obstanbau *m*; **fruit fly** N Fruchtfliege *f*, Taufliege *f*

fruitful [ˈfruːtfʊl] ADJ a *(= profitable) relationship, collaboration, talks, meeting* fruchtbar; *life, career* produktiv; *(= successful) attempt, inquiries* erfolgreich; **it would be more ~ to wait until January** man hätte mehr davon, den Januar abzuwarten; **a ~ source of material** eine ergiebige Materialquelle b *(Agr, Bot) land, plant, growth* fruchtbar, ertragreich

fruitfully [ˈfruːtfəlɪ] ADV *(= usefully)* nutzbringend; *(= advantageously)* vorteilhaft

fruitfulness [ˈfruːtfʊlnɪs] N *(lit, fig)* Fruchtbarkeit *f*

fruition [fruːˈɪʃən] N *(of aims, plans, ideas)* Erfüllung *f*, Verwirklichung *f*; **to come to ~** sich verwirklichen; **to bring sth to ~** etw verwirklichen

fruit jar N Einmachglas *nt*, Einweckglas *nt*

fruit knife N Obstmesser *nt*

fruitless [ˈfruːtlɪs] ADJ a *(= vain) search, talks, effort, morning, hour* fruchtlos, erfolglos; *attempt* vergeblich; **to spend long and ~ hours searching** stundenlang vergeblich suchen; **it's a ~ exercise** es ist verlorene Mühe; **it is ~ to try** es ist zwecklos *or* sinnlos, es zu versuchen; **to prove ~** sich als erfolglos *or* vergeblich erweisen b *(Bot, = infertile)* unfruchtbar

fruit: **fruit machine** N *(Brit)* Spielautomat *m*; **fruit salad** N Obstsalat *m*; *(fig inf)* Lametta *nt*; **fruit sugar** N Fruchtzucker *m*; **fruit tree** N Obstbaum *m*

fruity [ˈfruːtɪ] ADJ *(+er)* a *taste, wine, oil, smell* fruchtig b *(= deep) voice* volltönend c *(inf: = lewd) remark, joke* anzüglich d *(inf, = crazy)* bekloppt *(inf)*; **she's ~** sie spinnt *(inf)* e *(dated US pej sl: = homosexual)* schwul *(inf)*

frump [frʌmp] N *(pej)* Vogelscheuche *f (inf)*; **old ~** alte Schachtel *(inf)*

frumpish [ˈfrʌmpɪʃ] ADJ = **frumpy**

frumpy [ˈfrʌmpɪ] ADJ *(pej)* ohne jeden Schick

frustrate [frʌˈstreɪt] VT *person* frustrieren; *hopes* zunichtemachen; *plans, plot* durchkreuzen, zerstören; **he was ~d in his efforts** seine Anstrengungen waren umsonst *or* vergebens; **rescuers were ~d in their search by bad weather** die Retter wurden durch schlechtes Wetter bei der Suche behindert

frustrated [frʌˈstreɪtɪd] ADJ frustriert; **I get ~ when people criticize my work** es frustriert mich, wenn meine Arbeit kritisiert wird; **he's a ~ poet/intellectual** er wäre gern ein Dichter/Intellektueller

frustrating [frʌˈstreɪtɪŋ] ADJ frustrierend; **it's so ~** das ist alles so frustrierend, so ein Frust *(inf)*

frustratingly [frʌˈstreɪtɪŋlɪ] ADV *slow, complex* frustrierend

frustration [frʌˈstreɪʃən] N Frustration *f no pl*; *(of hopes, plans, plot)* Zerschlagung *f*; **the ~s of city life** die Frustration *or* der Frust *(inf)* des Stadtlebens; **he has had many ~s during the course of this project** er hat im Verlauf dieses Projektes viele Rückschläge erlebt

fry[1] [fraɪ] PL *(= fish)* kleine Fische *pl*

fry[2] VT **a** *meat etc* (in der Pfanne) braten; **to ~ an egg** ein Spiegelei machen, ein Ei in die Pfanne schlagen **b** *(US inf: = electrocute)* auf dem elektrischen Stuhl hinrichten VI **a** *(meat etc)* braten; **we're absolutely ~ing in this heat** *(inf)* wir schmoren (in dieser Hitze) *(inf)* **b** *(US inf)* auf dem elektrischen Stuhl hingerichtet werden N *(US)* Barbecue *nt*

▶ **fry up** VT *sep* (auf)braten, in die Pfanne hauen *(inf)*

frying pan [ˈfraɪɪŋˌpæn] N Bratpfanne *f*; **to jump out of the ~ into the fire** *(Prov)* vom Regen in die Traufe kommen *(Prov)*

fry-up [ˈfraɪʌp] N Pfannengericht *nt*; **to have a ~** sich *(dat)* etwas zusammenbrutzeln *(inf)*

f-stop [ˈefstɒp] N *(Phot)* Blende *f*

FT *abbr of* **Financial Times**

ft **a** *abbr of* **foot** ft **b** *abbr of* **feet** ft

FTC *(US) abbr of* **Federal Trade Commission**

FTP, ftp *(Comput) abbr of* **file transfer protocol** FTP *nt*

fuchsia [ˈfjuːʃə] N Fuchsie *f*

fuck [fʌk] *(vulg)* VT **a** *(lit)* ficken *(vulg)* **b** **you can get ~ed!, ~ you!** leck mich am Arsch *(vulg)*; **~ him/her!** scheiß auf ihn/sie! *(sl)*, der/die kann mich doch am Arsch lecken *(vulg)*; **~ what he thinks!** ich scheiß was auf seine Meinung *(sl)*; **~ this car!** dieses Scheißauto! *(inf)*; **~ me, he didn't say that, did he?** leck mich am Arsch, das hat der wirklich gesagt? *(sl)*

VI ficken *(vulg)*

N **a** *(lit)* Fick *m (vulg)*; **to have a ~** ficken *(vulg)*; **she's a good ~** sie fickt gut *(vulg)* **b** **I don't give a ~** ich kümmere mich einen Scheiß darum *(inf)*; **who/what/where the ~ is that?** wer/was/wo ist denn das, verdammt noch mal? *(inf)*; **it hurts like ~** es tut verdammt weh *(inf)*; **like ~ he will!** das werden wir erst noch sehen, verdammt noch mal! *(inf)*; **shut the ~ up!** halt die Schnauze, verdammt noch mal! *(inf)*

INTERJ (verdammte) Scheiße *(inf)*, Herrgottsack *(S Ger vulg)*

▶ **fuck about** *(Brit vulg)* VI rumgammeln *(inf)*; **to fuck about with sb** jdn verarschen *(inf)*; **someone's been fucking about with the engine** verdammt, da hat irgend so ein Arsch am Motor rumgefummelt *(sl)* VT *sep* verarschen *(inf)*

▶ **fuck around** VI *(vulg)* **a** herumficken *(vulg)* **b** = **fuck about**

▶ **fuck off** VI *(vulg)* sich verpissen *(sl)*; **fuck off!** verpiss dich! *(sl)*, hau ab, du Arsch! *(sl)*

▶ **fuck up** *(vulg)* VT *sep* versauen *(inf)*; *piece of work, life* verpfuschen *(inf)*; **you've really fucked me up** *(= let down, spoiled plans etc)* du hast mir die Sache echt versaut *(inf)*; **she is really fucked up** *(psychologically)* sie ist total verkorkst *(inf)*; **heroin will really fuck you up** Heroin macht dich echt kaputt *(inf)*; **my PC is fucked up** mein PC ist total im Arsch *(inf)* VI Scheiß machen *(inf)*

fuck-all [ˈfʌkɔːl] *(vulg)* N einen Scheiß *(sl)*; **he knows ~ about it** er hat null Ahnung *(inf)*; **it's got ~ to do with him** einen Scheiß hat das mit ihm zu tun *(sl)*; **there was ~ to drink** es gab nichts zum Saufen *(inf)*; **I've done ~ all day** ich hab den ganzen Tag nichts geschafft gekriegt *(inf)* ADJ *attr* **that's ~ use** das ist ja vielleicht ein Scheiß *(inf) or* total beknackt *(sl) or* fürn Arsch *(sl)*; **he's got ~ idea how to do it** er hat null Ahnung, wie er das machen soll *(inf)*

fucker [ˈfʌkəʳ] N *(vulg)* Arsch *m (vulg)*, Arschloch *nt (vulg)*, Saftsack *m (inf)*

fucking [ˈfʌkɪŋ] *(vulg)* ADJ Scheiß- *(inf)*; **this ~ machine** diese Scheißmaschine *(inf)*; **~ idiot** Vollidiot(in) *m(f)*; **~ hell!** verdammte Scheiße! *(inf)* ADV **a** *(intensifying)* **it's ~ cold** es ist arschkalt *(inf)*; **a ~ awful film** ein total beschissener Film *(inf)* **b** *(expressing annoyance)* **I don't ~ believe this** verdammte Scheiße, das darf doch nicht wahr sein! *(inf)*

fuck-up [ˈfʌkʌp] N *(vulg)* **what a ~!** was für eine (totale) Scheiße! *(inf)*; **there's been a ~** da hat einer Scheiße gebaut *(inf)*

fuckwit [ˈfʌkwɪt] N *(Brit vulg)* Vollidiot(in) *m(f) (inf)*, Nullchecker(in) *m(f) (inf)*

fuddled [ˈfʌdld] ADJ *(= muddled)* verwirrt, verdattert *(inf)*; *(= tipsy)* bedüdelt *(inf)*, beschwipst, angesäuselt

fuddy-duddy [ˈfʌdɪˌdʌdɪ] *(inf)* ADJ verknöchert, verkalkt N komischer Kauz *(inf)*; **an old ~** ein alter Kauz

fudge [fʌdʒ] N **a** *(Cook)* Fondant *m* **b** *(Press, = space for stop press)* Spalte *f* für letzte Meldungen; *(= stop press news)* letzte Meldungen *pl* **c** **her answer was a ~** ihre Antwort war ein Ausweichmanöver VT **a** *(= fake up) story, excuse* sich *(dat)* aus den Fingern saugen, (frei) erfinden **b** *(= dodge) question, issue, problem* ausweichen *(+dat)*, aus dem Wege gehen *(+dat)* **c** **to ~ the books** die Bücher frisieren *(inf)*

fuel [fjʊəl] N Brennstoff *m*, Brennmaterial *nt*; *(for vehicle)* Kraftstoff *m*; *(= petrol)* Benzin *nt*; *(Aviat, Space)* Treibstoff *m*; *(fig)* Nahrung *f*; **to add ~ to the flames** *or* **fire** *(fig)* Öl in die Flammen *or* ins Feuer gießen; **what kind of ~ do you use in your central heating?** womit betreiben Sie Ihre Zentralheizung? → **solid fuel**

VT *(= fill) stove, furnace etc* mit Brennstoff versorgen; *ships etc* auftanken, betanken; *(= use for fuel)* betreiben; *(= drive, propel)* antreiben; *(fig) conflict* schüren; *debate* anfachen; *inflation* anheizen; *speculation* Nahrung geben *(+dat)*; **power stations ~led** *(Brit) or* **~ed** *(US)* **by oil** mit Öl befeuerte Kraftwerke; **~led** *(Brit) or* **~ed** *(US)* **by memories** von Erinnerungen angefacht; **~led** *(Brit) or* **~ed** *(US)* **by drink** vom Alkohol angetrieben

VI *(ship, engine, aircraft)* auftanken, Brennstoff/Treibstoff *etc* aufnehmen; **~ling stop** Landung *f* zum Auftanken

fuel: **fuel cell** N Brennstoffzelle *f*; **fuel cock** N Treibstoffhahn *m*; **fuel consumption** N Kraftstoff- *or* Benzinverbauch *m*; **fuel element** N *(of reactor)* Brennelement *nt*; **fuel gauge** N Benzinuhr *f*, Tankuhr *f*

fueling station [ˈfjʊəlɪŋˌsteɪʃən] N *(US)* Tankstelle *f*

fuel: **fuel-injected** ADJ Einspritz-; **~ engine** Einspritzmotor *m*; **fuel injection** N (Benzin)einspritzung *f*; **engine with ~** Einspritzmotor *m*; **fuel oil** N Gasöl *nt*; **fuel pipe** N Benzinleitung *f*; **fuel pump** N Benzinpumpe *f*; **fuel rod** N *(of reactor)* Brennstab *m*; **fuel shortage** N Brennstoffknappheit *f*; **fuel tank** N Öltank *m*

fug [fʌg] N *(esp Brit inf)* Mief *m (inf)*

fuggy [ˈfʌgɪ] ADJ *(+er) (esp Brit inf)* muffig, miefig *(inf)*

fugitive [ˈfjuːdʒɪtɪv] N *(= runaway)* Flüchtling *m (from* vor *+dat)*; **he is a ~ from justice** er ist auf der Flucht vor der Justiz ADJ **a** *(= escaping)* flüchtig; **~ vehicle** Fluchtfahrzeug *nt* **b** *(liter, = fleeting) thought, happiness, hour, visit* flüchtig

fugue [fjuːg] N *(Mus)* Fuge *f*

fulcrum [ˈfʌlkrəm] N Dreh- *or* Stützpunkt *m*; *(fig, of argument, plan, organization)* Angelpunkt *m*

fulfil, *(US)* **fulfill** [fʊlˈfɪl] VT erfüllen; *task, order* ausführen; *ambition* verwirklichen; **the prophecy was ~led** die Prophezeiung erfüllte sich; **being a mother didn't ~ her** sie fand im Muttersein keine Erfüllung; **to be** *or* **feel ~led** Erfüllung finden; **to ~ oneself** sich selbst verwirklichen

fulfilling [fʊlˈfɪlɪŋ] ADJ **a ~ job** ein Beruf, in dem man Erfüllung findet

fulfilment, *(US)* **fulfillment** [fʊlˈfɪlmənt] N Erfüllung *f*; **to bring sth to ~** etw zur Erfüllung bringen; **to come to ~** in Erfüllung gehen; *(life's work)* seine Erfüllung finden; **to lead to the ~ of sth** etw in Erfüllung gehen lassen

full [fʊl] ADJ *(+er)* **a** *(= filled) room, theatre, train* voll; **to be ~ of …** voller *(+gen) or* voll von … sein, voll sein mit …; **he's ~ of good ideas** er steckt voll(er) guter Ideen; **a look ~ of hate** ein hasserfüllter Blick, ein Blick voller Hass; **his heart was ~** *(liter)* das Herz lief ihm über; **don't talk with your mouth ~** sprich nicht mit vollem Mund; **with his arms ~** mit vollgeladenen Armen; **I have a ~ day ahead of me** ich habe einen ausgefüllten Tag vor mir; **I am ~ (up)** *(inf)* ich bin (papp)satt, ich bin voll (bis obenhin) *(inf)*; **we are ~ up for July** wir sind für Juli völlig ausgebucht

b *(= maximum, complete)* voll; *description, report* vollständig; *understanding, sympathy* vollste(r, s); **at ~ speed** in voller Fahrt; **roses in ~ bloom** Rosen in voller Blüte; **to make ~ use of sth** etw voll ausnutzen; **that's a ~ day's work** damit habe ich *etc* den ganzen Tag zu tun; **I need a ~ night's sleep** ich muss mich (ein)mal gründlich ausschlafen; **to be in ~ flight** kopflos fliehen; **battalion at ~ strength** Bataillon in Sollstärke; **I waited two ~ hours** ich habe geschlagene zwei *or* zwei ganze Stunden gewartet; **the ~ details** die genauen *or* alle Einzelheiten; **a ~ colonel** ein Oberst *m*; **to run ~ tilt into sth** mit voller Wucht in etw *(acc) or* auf etw *(acc)* rennen; **to go at ~ tilt** rasen, Volldampf *(inf) or* volle Pulle *(inf)* fahren; **shots of the Rocky Mountains in ~ colour** *(Brit) or* **color** *(US)* schöne Farbaufnahmen von den Rocky Mountains

c *(= preoccupied)* **to be ~ of oneself** von sich (selbst) eingenommen sein, nur sich selbst im Kopf haben; **the papers were ~ of it for weeks** die Zeitungen waren wochenlang voll davon; **she was ~ of it** sie hat gar nicht mehr aufgehört, davon zu reden; **you're ~ of it!** *(inf)* du erzählst lauter Scheiß! *(inf)*; **he's always so ~ of what he's going to do** er ist dauernd von seinen Plänen dran *(inf)*

d *(= rounded) lips, face* voll; *figure, skirt etc* füllig

ADV **a** *(= at least)* **it is a ~ five miles from here** es sind volle *or* gute fünf Meilen von hier

b *(= very, perfectly)* **I know ~ well that …** ich weiß sehr wohl, dass …

c *(= directly)* **to hit sb ~ in the face** jdn voll ins Gesicht schlagen; **to look sb ~ in the face** jdm voll in die Augen sehen; **she kissed him ~ on the mouth** sie küsste ihn voll auf den Mund

d **~ out** *(work)* auf Hochtouren; *drive* mit Vollgas

N **a** **in ~** ganz, vollständig; **to write one's name in ~** seinen Namen ausschreiben; **to pay in ~** den vollen Betrag bezahlen

b **to the ~** vollständig, total

full: **full age** N *(Jur)* Mündigkeit *f*, Volljährigkeit *f*; **of ~** mündig, volljährig; **fullback** N *(Sport)* Verteidiger(in) *m(f)*; **full beam** N *(Brit Aut)* Fernlicht *nt*; **to drive (with one's headlights) on ~** mit Fernlicht fahren; **full-blooded** [fʊlˈblʌdɪd] ADJ *(= vigorous)* kräftig; **he's a ~ German/Scot** er ist Vollblutdeutscher/-schotte; **full-blown** ADJ **a** *(= thoroughgoing) recession,* *crisis, love affair, war* richtiggehend; *scandal* ausgewachsen; *investigation* gründlich; *independence* voll; *heart attack* richtig; *(= fully qualified) doctor* voll qualifiziert; **the ~ disease** die Krankheit im Vollbild; **~ Aids** Vollbild-Aids *nt* **b** *(Bot) flower* voll aufgeblüht; **full-bodied** ['fʊl'bɒdɪd] ADJ *wine* schwer, vollmundig; *woman* füllig; **full-court press** N *(US fig inf)* **to give sb the ~** jdn stark unter Druck setzen; **full-cream milk** N Vollmilch *f*; **full denture** N *(Med)* Vollprothese *f*; **full-dress** ['fʊldres] ADJ **a** *clothes* Gala-; **~ uniform** Galauniform *f* **b** *(fig: = important, ceremonious)* **~ debate** wichtige Debatte; **full employment** N Vollbeschäftigung *f*

fuller's earth [ˌfʊləz'ɜːθ] N Fullererde *f*, Bleicherde *f*

full: **full-face** ADJ *portrait* mit zugewandtem Gesicht; **~ photograph** En-Face-Foto *nt (spec)*; **~ helmet** Integralhelm *m* ADV en face *(spec)*; **she turned ~ to me** sie wandte sich mir voll zu; **she looked ~ at him** sie sah ihm direkt ins Gesicht; **full-faced** ADJ rundgesichtig; **full-flavoured**, *(US)* **full-flavored** ADJ vollmundig; **full-fledged** ADJ *(US)* = **fully fledged**; **full frontal** N Nacktdarstellung *f*; **full-frontal** ADJ Nackt-; *(fig) assault* direkt; **the ~ nudity in this play** die völlig nackten Schauspieler in diesem Stück; **~ photograph** Nacktfoto *nt*; **full-grown** ADJ ausgewachsen; **full house** N *(Theat)* ausverkaufte Vorstellung; *(Cards)* Fullhouse *nt*; *(bei Konzert etc)* volles Haus; **each night they played to a ~** sie spielten jeden Abend vor vollem Haus; **full-length** ADJ **a** *play, film, video* abendfüllend; *novel, album* vollständig **b** *coat, dress, skirt* (boden)lang; *boots* hoch; *curtains* bodenlang; **~ mirror** großer Spiegel(, in dem man sich ganz sehen kann); **~ portrait** Ganzporträt *nt* ADV *lie* (lang) ausgestreckt; **to dive ~** einen Hechtsprung machen; **to stretch oneself ~** sich lang ausstrecken; **to fall ~** der Länge nach hinfallen; **full-lipped** ADJ volllippig; **full member** N Vollmitglied *nt*; **full moon** N Vollmond *m*; **full-mouthed** ['fʊl'maʊðd] ADJ *cattle* mit vollem Gebiss; *(fig) person* lautstark; **full name** N Vor- und Zuname *m*

fullness ['fʊlnɪs] N *(of detail, description)* Vollständigkeit *f*; *(of voice)* Klangfülle *f*; *(of skirt)* Fülle *f*, Weite *f*; *(of flavour)* Vollmundigkeit *f*; *(of skirt)* Fülle *f*, Weite *f*; **out of the ~ of his heart** *(liter)* aus der Fülle seines Herzens *(liter)*; **this cut gives some ~ to the hairstyle** dieser Schnitt gibt der Frisur Fülle; **in the ~ of time** *(= eventually)* zu gegebener Zeit; *(= at predestined time)* da *or* als die Zeit gekommen war, da *or* als die Zeit erfüllt war

full: **full-on** [fʊl'ɒn] ADJ *(inf)* total *(inf)*; **full-page** ADJ *advertisement etc* ganzseitig; **full pay** N **to be suspended on ~** unter Fortzahlung der vollen Bezüge suspendiert sein; **full point** N *(Gram)* → **full stop**; **full professor** N *(Univ)* Ordinarius *m*; **full-scale** ADJ **a** *(= thoroughgoing) war, riot, offensive, invasion* richtiggehend; *investigation, inquiry, review* gründlich; *search* groß angelegt; *production* serienmäßig; *debate, negotiations, report* umfassend; **they are in ~ retreat** *(lit, fig)* sie haben auf der ganzen Linie den Rückzug angetreten **b** *(= life-size) drawing, model* in Originalgröße; **full-size(d)** ADJ *bicycle, violin etc* richtig (groß); **full-sized** ADJ *model, drawing* lebensgroß; **full stop** N *(esp Brit Gram)* Punkt *m*; **to come to a ~** zum völligen Stillstand kommen; **I'm not going, ~!** *(inf)* ich gehe nicht und damit basta *(inf)*; **full term** N *(of pregnancy)* volle Schwangerschaftszeit; **full-term** ADJ *baby* nach der vollen Schwangerschaftszeit geboren; *pregnancy* von voller Länge; *delivery, birth* nach der vollen Schwangerschaftszeit ADV **to be carried ~** *(baby)* nach der vollen Schwangerschaftszeit geboren werden; **to go ~** *(woman)* eine Schwangerschaft von voller Länge haben; **full-text search** N *(Comput)* Volltextsuche *f*; **full time** N *(Sport)* reguläre Spielzeit; **at ~** nach Ablauf der regulären Spielzeit; **the whistle blew for ~** das Spiel wurde abgepfiffen ADV *work* ganztags; *study* voll; **full-time** ADJ **a** *secretary, worker* ganztags angestellt; **~ job** Ganztagsstelle *f*; **it's a ~ job** *(fig inf)* es hält einen ganz schön auf Trab *(inf)*; **~ work** Ganztagsarbeit *f*; **~ student** Vollstudent(in) *m(f)*; **~ mother** Hausfrau *f* und Mutter *f* **b** *(Sport)* **the ~ score** der Schlussstand

fully ['fʊlɪ] ADV **a** *(= completely) fit, aware, conscious* völlig; *developed, operational, qualified* voll; *understand, recover* voll und ganz; *comply, participate* uneingeschränkt; *discuss, describe, answer, brief* ausführlich; **~ automatic** vollautomatisch; **~ pressurized** mit vollem Druckausgleich; **she was ~ aware of my thoughts** sie war sich meiner Gedanken voll (und ganz) bewusst; **~ booked** (ganz *or* völlig) ausgebucht; **~ clothed** (ganz) angezogen; **~ integrated** *(system, service)* voll integriert; *(racially)* ohne jegliche Rassentrennung; **a ~-equipped kitchen** eine komplett ausgestattete Küche; **~ illustrated** vollständig illustriert

b *(= at least)* **~ 200 years** volle *or* gute 200 Jahre; **~ one-quarter of the workers** ein volles *or* gutes Viertel der Arbeiter

fully: **fully fashioned** ['fʊlɪ'fæʃnd] ADJ *stocking, jumper* mit Passform; **fully fledged** ADJ **a** *(fig) member, citizen* richtig; *artist, atheist* richtiggehend; *party* eigenständig; *neurosis* ausgewachsen *(inf)*; *doctor, teacher etc* voll qualifiziert **b** *(Orn) bird* flügge; **fully paid-up** ADJ *member (lit)* ohne Beitragsrückstände; *(fig)* eingeschrieben; **fully qualified** ADJ voll qualifiziert *attr*

fulmar ['fʊlmə'] N Eissturmvogel *m*

fulminate ['fʊlmɪneɪt] VI *(fig)* wettern, donnern

fulmination [ˌfʊlmɪ'neɪʃən] N Attacke *f*

fulsome ['fʊlsəm] ADJ *praise, tribute, compliment, manner, tone (= effusive)* überschwänglich; *(= exaggerated)* übertrieben; *apology, support* uneingeschränkt; **his most ~ praise** sein höchstes Lob; **he paid ~ tribute to her courage** er würdigte ihren Mut uneingeschränkt; **she was ~ in her praise of the children** sie lobte die Kinder überschwänglich

fulsomely ['fʊlsəmlɪ] ADV *praise, thank (= effusively)* überschwänglich; *(= exaggeratedly)* übertrieben; *write, say* in überschwänglichem Ton

fumble ['fʌmbl] VI *(also* **fumble about** *or* **around**) umhertasten *or* -tappen; **to ~ in the dark** im Dunkeln herumtasten *or* -tappen; **to ~ in one's pockets** in seinen Taschen wühlen; **to ~ (about) for sth** nach etw suchen *or* tasten; *(in case, pocket, drawer)* nach etw wühlen; **to ~ with sth** an etw *(dat)* herumfummeln; **to ~ for words** nach Worten suchen *or* ringen VT vermasseln *(inf)*, verpfuschen *(inf)*; **to ~ the ball** den Ball nicht sicher fangen

fumbler ['fʌmblə'] N Stümper(in) *m(f)*

fumbling ADJ, **fumblingly** ADV ['fʌmblɪŋ, -lɪ] ungeschickt

fume [fjuːm] VI **a** *(liquids)* dampfen, rauchen; *(gases)* aufsteigen **b** *(fig inf, person)* wütend sein, kochen *(inf)*

fumes [fjuːmz] PL Dämpfe *pl*; *(of car)* Abgase *pl*; **petrol** *(Brit) or* **gas** *(US)* **~** Benzindämpfe *pl*; **to run on ~** *(fig inf)* auf dem Zahnfleisch gehen *(inf)*

fumigate ['fjuːmɪgeɪt] VT ausräuchern

fun [fʌn] N *(= amusement)* Spaß *m*, *(Aus also)* Spass *m*; **to have great ~ doing sth** viel Spaß daran haben, etw zu tun, viel Spaß an etw *(dat)* haben; **in ~** *(= as a joke)* im *or* als Scherz; **this is ~!** das macht Spaß *or* Freude!; **I'm not doing it for the ~ of it** ich mache das nicht zu meinem Vergnügen; **we just did it for ~** wir haben das nur aus *or* zum Spaß gemacht; **to spoil the ~** den Spaß verderben; **that takes all the ~ out of it** das nimmt einem den Spaß *or* die Freude daran; **it's ~ doing this/being with him** es macht Spaß, das zu tun/mit ihm zusammen zu sein; **it's not much ~ for the others though** es ist allerdings für die anderen nicht gerade ein Vergnügen; **life's not much ~ sometimes** das Leben ist manchmal nicht gerade das reinste Vergnügen; **it's no ~ living on your own/being broke** es macht nicht gerade Spaß, allein zu leben/pleite *(inf)* zu sein; **you're no ~ to be with any more** es macht keinen Spaß mehr, mit dir zusammen zu sein; **he is great ~** man kriegt mit ihm viel Spaß *or* viel zu lachen *(inf)*; **the children thought he was great ~** die Kinder fanden ihn sehr lustig; **the party was good ~** die Party hat viel Spaß gemacht; **what ~!** was für ein Spaß!; **that sounds like ~** das klingt gut; **I wasn't serious, I was just having a bit of ~** das hab ich nicht ernst gemeint, ich hab doch nur Spaß gemacht; **the children had ~ and games at the picnic** die Kinder haben beim Picknick viel Spaß gehabt; **that should be ~ and games** *(iro)* das kann ja (noch) heiter werden *(inf)*; **to make ~ of** *or* **poke ~ at sb/sth** sich über jdn/etw lustig machen; **we had ~ getting the car started** *(inf)* wir hatten ein bisschen Theater, ehe das Auto ansprang *(inf)*; **like ~** *(US inf)* (ja,) Pustekuchen! *(inf)*

ADJ *attr (inf)* **squash is a ~ game** Squash macht Spaß; **he's a real ~ person** er ist wirklich ein lustiger Kerl; **that sounds like a ~ idea** das hört sich prima an *(inf)*

function ['fʌŋkʃən] N **a** *(of heart, tool, word etc)* Funktion *f* **b** *(of person)* Aufgaben *pl*, Pflichten *pl*; **in his ~ as judge** in seiner Eigenschaft als Richter; **his ~ in life** seine Lebensaufgabe **c** *(= meeting)* Veranstaltung *f*; *(= reception)* Empfang *m*; *(= official ceremony)* Feier *f* **d** *(Math)* Funktion *f* VI funktionieren; *(heart, kidney, brain also)* arbeiten; **he can't ~ without his morning coffee** ohne seinen Kaffee am Morgen ist er nicht funktionsfähig; **to ~ as** fungieren als; *(person also)* die Rolle des/der … spielen *or* ausfüllen; *(thing also)* dienen als

functional ['fʌŋkʃənəl] ADJ **a** *(= able to operate)* funktionsfähig **b** *(= utilitarian)* zweckmäßig, funktionell **c** *(Med)* Funktions-; **~ disorder** Funktionsstörung *f*; **~ food** Functional Food *nt*, Funktionsnahrung *f*

functionalism ['fʌŋkʃənəlɪzəm] N Funktionalismus *m*

functionally ['fʌŋkʃnəlɪ] ADV *designed* funktionell; **~ efficient** wirksam funktionierend; **~, they are identical/incompatible** sie sind in ihrer Funktion identisch/in ihren Funktionen unvereinbar; **he is ~ illiterate** er kann nicht gut genug lesen und schreiben, um im täglichen Leben zurechtzukommen

functionary ['fʌŋkʃə nərɪ] N Funktionär(in) *m(f)*

function: **function key** N *(Comput)* Funktionstaste *f*; **function room** N Veranstaltungsraum *m*

fund [fʌnd] N **a** *(Fin)* Fonds *m*; **to start a ~** einen Fonds einrichten *or* gründen

b funds PL Mittel *pl*, Gelder *pl*; **public ~s** öffentliche Mittel *pl*, Staatsgelder *pl*; **no ~s** *(Banking)* keine Deckung; **to be in ~s** zahlungsfähig *or* bei Kasse *(inf)* sein; **to be pressed for ~s, to be short of ~s** knapp bei Kasse sein *(inf)*; **at the moment I haven't the ~s** mir fehlen zurzeit die Mittel *or* Gelder *pl*; **how are we off for ~s at the moment?** wie steht die Kasse zurzeit?

c *(= supply: of wisdom, humour etc)* Schatz *m* (of von *+gen*), Vorrat *m* (of an *+dat*)

d funds PL *(Brit: = government securities)* Staatspapiere *pl*

VT **a** *debt* ausgleichen, bezahlen; *(= put up money for) scheme, project* finanzieren

b *(= invest) money* anlegen, investieren

fundage ['fʌndɪdʒ] N *(US sl: = money)* Knete *f (inf)*

fundament ['fʌndəmənt] N **a** *(lit, fig: = foundation)* Fundament *nt* **b** *(euph, hum: = buttocks)* vier Buchstaben *(inf)*

fundamental [ˌfʌndə'mentl] ✪ 26.1 ADJ **a** *(= essential) issue, question, concept* grundlegend; *reason* eigentlich; *point* zentral; *feature, part* wesentlich; **~ principle/right/beliefs** Grundprinzip *nt*/-recht *nt*/-überzeugungen *pl*; **~ mathematical concepts** Grundbegriffe *pl* der Mathematik; **of ~ importance** von grundlegender Bedeu-

tung; **carbon is ~ to life** Kohlenstoff ist für alles Leben grundlegend; **~ to impressionism was the use of bright colours** die Verwendung von leuchtenden Farben war grundlegend für den Impressionismus
b *(= basic) problem, difference, contradiction* grundsätzlich; *(= basic and deep) change, revolution, shift* grundlegend, umwälzend; *(= elementary) mistake, error, flaw* grundlegend, fundamental; **I don't doubt his ~ goodness** ich zweifle nicht daran, dass er im Grunde ein guter Mensch ist; **his ~ ignorance of this subject** seine fundamentale Unkenntnis auf diesem Gebiet; **~ structure/form** Grundstruktur *f*/-form *f*; **~ research** Grundlagenforschung *f*
c *(Mus)* Grund-; **~ note/frequency** Grundton *m*/-frequenz *f*
PL **~s** *(of subject)* Grundbegriffe *pl*; *(of a problem)* Grundlagen *pl*; **the ~s of physics** die Grundbegriffe *pl* der Physik; **to get down to (the) ~s** bis zu den Grundlagen vordringen

fundamentalism [ˌfʌndəˈmentəlɪzəm] N Fundamentalismus *m*

fundamentalist [ˌfʌndəˈmentəlɪst] ADJ fundamentalistisch N Fundamentalist(in) *m(f)*

fundamentally [ˌfʌndəˈmentəlɪ] ADV a *(= essentially)* im Grunde (genommen); *different, wrong, flawed* grundlegend; **~ different views** grundlegend *or* von Grund auf unterschiedliche Ansichten; **the treaty is ~ flawed** der Vertrag enthält grundlegende Fehler; **~, he is a bully** er ist im Grunde genommen ein Tyrann; **is man ~ good?** ist der Mensch im Grunde gut?; **~ important** von grundlegender Bedeutung b *(= radically) change, affect* grundlegend; *disagree* grundsätzlich; **I am ~ opposed to it** ich bin grundsätzlich dagegen; **we differ quite ~ on this** wir haben dazu grundverschiedene Ansichten

fundamental particle N *(Phys)* Elementarteilchen *nt*

fund: **fundholding** ADJ *(Brit)* **~ doctor** *or* **GP** *Arzt, der die Finanzen seiner Praxis selbst verwaltet*; **fundraiser** N Spendenbeschaffer(in) *m(f)*, Spendensammler(in) *m(f)*; **fundraising** N Geldbeschaffung *f*; **~ campaign** Aktion *f* zur Geldbeschaffung; *(for donations)* Spendenaktion *f*

funeral [ˈfjuːnərəl] N Begräbnis *nt*, Beerdigung *f*, Beisetzung *f (form)*; **were you at his ~?** waren Sie auf seiner Beerdigung?; **well, that's your ~** *(inf)* na ja, das ist dein persönliches Pech *(inf)*, das ist dein Problem *(inf)*

funeral: **funeral director** N Beerdigungsunternehmer(in) *m(f)*; **funeral home** N *(US)* Leichenhalle *f*; **funeral march** N Trauermarsch *m*; **funeral parlour** N *(Brit)* Leichenhalle *f*; **funeral procession** N Leichenzug *m*; **funeral pyre** N Scheiterhaufen *m*; **funeral service** N Trauergottesdienst *m*

funereal [fjuːˈnɪərɪəl] ADJ traurig, trübselig; **~ silence** Grabesstille *f*

funfair [ˈfʌnfɛəʳ] N Kirmes *f*

fungal [ˈfʌŋgəl] ADJ Pilz-; **~ infection** Pilzinfektion *f*

fungi [ˈfʌŋgaɪ] *pl of* **fungus**

fungicide [ˈfʌŋgɪsaɪd] N Fungizid *nt*, pilztötendes Mittel

fungoid [ˈfʌŋgɔɪd], **fungous** [ˈfʌŋgəs] ADJ schwammartig

fungus [ˈfʌŋgəs] N *pl* **fungi** *(Bot, Med)* Pilz *m*

fun house N *(esp US) Rummelplatzattraktion mit Räumen mit beweglichen Böden, Zerrspiegeln etc*

funicular (railway) [fjuːˈnɪkjʊlə(ˈreɪlweɪ)] N Seilbahn *f*

funk [fʌŋk] N a *(esp Brit inf: = fear)* Schiss *m (inf)*, Bammel *m (inf)*; **to be in a (blue) ~** (vor Angst) die Hosen voll haben *(inf)*, mächtig *or* ganz schön Schiss *or* Bammel haben *(inf)*; **to put sb in a (blue) ~** jdm mächtig Bammel einjagen *(inf)* b *(Mus)* Funk *m* VT kneifen vor *(+dat) (inf)*; **he ~ed it** er hat (davor) gekniffen *(inf)*

funky [ˈfʌŋkɪ] ADJ *(+er)* a *(inf) music, person, clothes* geil *(sl)*, funky *(sl)*; **I want something ~** *(when buying clothes)* ich möchte etwas Flippiges *or* Funkiges *(inf)*; **~ beat** *(inf)* Funkrhythmus *m* b *(dated US sl: = terrified)* **to be ~** (fürchterlich) Schiss haben *(sl)* c *(esp Brit, inf, = cowardly)* feige, ängstlich d *(US inf: = smelly)* mufflig *(inf)*; *air* miefig *(inf)*

fun-loving [ˈfʌnlʌvɪŋ] ADJ lebenslustig; **a ~ girl** *(euph)* ein lebenshungriges Mädchen

funnel [ˈfʌnl] N a *(for pouring)* Trichter *m* b *(Naut, Rail)* Schornstein *m*; **two-~led** *(Brit) or* **two-~ed** *(US)* **steamer** Dampfer *m* mit zwei Schornsteinen c *(US: = ventilation shaft etc)* Luftschacht *m* VT *liquid, grain* leiten; *(fig) attention, energies, information, funds* schleusen

funnies [ˈfʌnɪz] PL *(esp US inf: in newspaper)* Comics *pl*, Comic-Teil *m*

funnily [ˈfʌnɪlɪ] ADV a *(= strangely)* komisch, merkwürdig; **~ enough** komischerweise, merkwürdigerweise b *(= amusingly)* amüsant

funny [ˈfʌnɪ] ADJ *(+er)* a *(= comical)* komisch, lustig; *person* witzig; **don't try to be ~** *(inf)* mach keine Witze!; **don't get ~ with me** *(inf)* komm mir bloß nicht komisch; **to see the ~ side of sth** das Lustige an etw *(dat)* sehen; **what's so ~?** was ist denn so komisch *or* lustig?; **it's not ~!** das ist überhaupt nicht komisch *or* zum Lachen!
b *(= bizarre, odd)* komisch; **she gave him a ~ look** sie sah ihn komisch an; **to have ~ ideas about sth** merkwürdige Vorstellungen von etw haben; **there's something ~ about that place** der Ort ist irgendwie merkwürdig *or* seltsam; **I have a ~ feeling I'm going to regret this** ich habe das komische Gefühl, dass mir das noch leidtun wird; **(it's) ~ (that) you should say that** komisch, dass Sie das sagen; **it's ~ but I feel as if I've known you a long time** komisch, ich habe das Gefühl, dass ich dich schon lange kenne; **(that's) ~! I thought he'd left** komisch! ich dachte, er ist schon weg; **the ~ thing is that he was right** das Komische ist, dass er recht hatte; **to go all ~** *(inf: = go wrong)* verrücktspielen *(inf)*; **I just feel a bit ~** *(inf)* mir ist ein bisschen komisch *or* mulmig *(inf)*; **I feel ~ about seeing her again** *(inf)* mir ist komisch dabei zumute *or* zu Mute, sie wiederzusehen; **it's a ~ old world** ganz schön komisch *or* merkwürdig!; **~-peculiar or ~-ha-ha?** *(inf)* komisch im Sinne von seltsam oder lustig?
c *(inf: = mad) person* merkwürdig; **she's a bit ~ (in the head)** sie spinnt ein bisschen *(inf)*
d *(inf: = suspicious)* **~ business** *or* **tricks** faule Sachen *pl or* Tricks *pl (inf)*; **there's something ~ going on here** hier ist doch was faul *(inf)*; **don't try anything ~** keine faulen Tricks! *(inf)*
PL **the funnies** *(US Press inf)* die Cartoons *pl*, die Comicstrips *pl*

funny: **funny bone** N Musikantenknochen *m*; **funny cigarette** N *(inf)* Joint *m (inf)*; **funny farm** N *(inf)* Klapsmühle *f (inf)*; **funny girl** N *(inf: = comedienne)* Komikerin *f*; **funny handshake** N *(inf) besonderer, von Freimaurern verwendeter Händedruck*; **funny man** N *(inf: = comedian)* Komiker *m*; **funny money** N ein Wahnsinnsgeld *nt (inf)*; **funny paper** N *(US)* Witzseiten *pl*

fun run N Volkslauf *m (oft für wohltätige Zwecke durchgeführt)*

fur [fɜːʳ] N a *(on animal)* Fell *nt*, Pelz *m*; *(for clothing)* Pelz *m*; **the cat has beautiful ~** die Katze hat ein wunderschönes Fell; **that will really make the ~ fly** *(inf)* da werden die Fetzen fliegen *(inf)*; **a ~-lined coat** ein pelzgefütterter Mantel b **furs** PL Pelze *pl* c *(in kettle etc)* Kesselstein *m*; *(Med, on tongue)* Belag *m* ATTR Pelz-; **~ coat/collar** Pelzmantel *m*/-kragen *m*; **the ~ trade** der Pelzhandel

▶ **fur up** VI *(washing machine, veins, arteries)* verkalken; *(kettle, boiler)* verkalken, Kesselstein ansetzen; *(tongue)* pelzig werden VT *veins, arteries* verkalken lassen; **to be furred up** *(tongue)* belegt *or* pelzig sein; *(veins, arteries, washing machine, kettle, boiler)* verkalkt sein

furbelow [ˈfɜːbɪləʊ] N a *(old)* Falbel *f*, Faltenbesatz *m* b *usu pl* **~s** *(pej)* Firlefanz *m*

furbish [ˈfɜːbɪʃ] VT a *(= polish)* blank reiben, (auf)polieren b *(= smarten up)* aufpolieren

furious [ˈfjʊərɪəs] ADJ a *(= very angry) person, letter, protest, reaction, row* wütend; *(= violent) argument, debate, attack, battle* heftig; **he was ~ that they had ignored him** er war wütend darüber, dass sie ihn ignoriert hatten; **she was ~ to find that ...** sie war wütend, als sie feststellte, dass ...; **to be ~ about** *or* **at** *or* **over sth** wütend über etw *(acc)* sein; **to be ~ at** *or* **with sb (for doing sth)** wütend auf jdn sein(, weil er/sie etw getan hat); **she was ~ at being disturbed** sie war wütend darüber, dass sie gestört wurde; **I'm ~!** ich bin total sauer! *(inf)*; **he was ~ with himself for getting drunk** er war wütend auf sich, weil er sich betrunken hatte; **they came under ~ attack** sie wurden scharf angegriffen
b *(= tremendous) pace, speed* rasend; **at a ~ pace** in rasendem Tempo; **the car was going at a ~ speed** das Auto fuhr rasend schnell; **the ~ pace of change** die rasend schnellen Veränderungen; **~ activity** wilde Hektik; **fast and ~** rasant; **the jokes came fast and ~** die Witze kamen Schlag auf Schlag; **the punches came fast and ~** es hagelte Schläge

furiously [ˈfjʊərɪəslɪ] ADV a *(= angrily) react, argue, say* wütend; **~ angry** fuchsteufelswild *(inf)* b *(= frantically) work, scribble, beat, search* wie wild; **her heart was beating ~** ihr schlug das Herz bis zum Hals; **to work fast and ~** hektisch arbeiten

furl [fɜːl] VT *sail, flag* einrollen; *umbrella* zusammenrollen

furlong [ˈfɜːlɒŋ] N Achtelmeile *f*

furlough [ˈfɜːləʊ] N *(Mil, Admin)* Urlaub *m*; **to go on ~** in Urlaub gehen

furn *abbr of* **furnished** möbl.

furnace [ˈfɜːnɪs] N Hochofen *m*; *(Metal)* Schmelzofen *m*; **this room is like a ~** dieses Zimmer ist ja das reinste Treibhaus

furnish [ˈfɜːnɪʃ] VT a *house* einrichten; **~ed room** möbliertes Zimmer; **~ed flat** *(esp Brit) or* **apartment** möblierte Wohnung; **to live in ~ed accommodation** zur Miete wohnen *(in einer möblierten Wohnung)*; **~ing fabrics** Dekorationsstoffe *pl* b *information, reason, excuse* liefern, geben; **to ~ sb with sth** jdn mit etw versorgen, jdm etw liefern; *with reason, excuse* jdm etw liefern

furnishings [ˈfɜːnɪʃɪŋz] PL Mobiliar *nt*; *(with carpets etc)* Einrichtung *f*; **with ~ and fittings** voll eingerichtet

furniture [ˈfɜːnɪtʃəʳ] N Möbel *pl*; **a piece of ~** ein Möbelstück *nt*; **I must buy some ~** ich muss Möbel kaufen; **one settee and three chairs were all the ~ we had** unsere Einrichtung bestand nur aus einem Sofa und drei Stühlen; **if I stay here much longer, I'll become a part of the ~** wenn ich noch viel länger hierbleibe, gehöre ich bald zum Inventar

furniture: **furniture depository**, **furniture depot** *(US)* N Möbellager *nt*; **furniture remover** N Möbelspediteur *m*; **furniture van** N *(Brit)* Möbelwagen *m*

furore [fjʊəˈrɔːrɪ], *(US)* **furor** [ˈfjʊrɔːʳ] N Protest(e) *m(pl)*; **to cause a ~** einen Skandal verursachen

furred [fɜːd] ADJ *tongue* belegt, pelzig

furrier [ˈfʌrɪəʳ] N Kürschner(in) *m(f)*

furrow [ˈfʌrəʊ] N *(Agr)* Furche *f*; *(Hort: for flowers etc)* Rinne *f*; *(on brow)* Runzel *f*; *(on sea)* Furche *f* VT *field* pflügen; *brow* runzeln; *(worries etc)* furchen; *(boats) sea* Furchen ziehen in *(+dat)*; **the old man's ~ed brow** die zerfurchte Stirn des alten Mannes

furry [ˈfɜːrɪ] ADJ *(+er)* a *body, belly* haarig; *tail* buschig; **~ animal** Tier *nt* mit Pelz; **~ friend** *(hum)* vierbeiniger Freund *(hum)*; **the kitten is**

so soft and ~ das Kätzchen ist so weich und kuschelig; **the soft ~ skin of the seal** das weiche Fell des Seehundes **b** *(= like fur) hat, slippers, material, lining* flauschig; **~ dice** Plüschwürfel *pl*; **~ toy** Plüschtier *nt* **c** *(= coated) tongue* belegt; *(= scaly) kettle, pipe* verkalkt

further ['fɜːðəʳ] ✪ 19.1, 26.1 ADV *comp of* **far** **a** *(in place, time, fig)* weiter; **~ on** weiter, weiter entfernt; **~ back** *(in place, time)* weiter zurück; *(= in the past)* früher; **nothing could be ~ from the truth** nichts könnte weiter von der Wahrheit entfernt sein; **nothing is ~ from my thoughts** nichts liegt mir ferner; **~ and ~ away** immer weiter weg; **to get ~ and ~ away** sich immer weiter entfernen; **we're no ~ advanced now** viel weiter sind wir jetzt (auch) nicht; **he has decided not to take the matter any ~** er hat beschlossen, die Angelegenheit auf sich beruhen zu lassen; **if we take this line of reasoning ~** wenn wir diese Argumente weiterverfolgen; **to look ~ ahead** *(fig)* weiter in die Zukunft schauen; **in order to make the soup go ~** um die Suppe zu strecken
b *(= more)* **he didn't question me ~** er hat mich nicht weiter *or* mehr gefragt; **and ~ ...** und darüber hinaus ...; **~, I would like to say that ...** darüber hinaus möchte ich sagen, dass ...; **~ to your letter of ...** *(Comm)* Bezug nehmend auf *or* in Bezug auf Ihren Brief vom ... *(form)*
ADJ **a** = **farther**
b *(= additional)* weiter; **to remand a case for ~ inquiry** *(Jur)* einen Fall zurückstellen, bis weitere Nachforschungen angestellt sind; **will there be anything ~?** kann ich sonst noch etwas für Sie tun?; **~ details** nähere *or* weitere Einzelheiten *pl*
VT *one's interests, a cause* fördern; *process* voranbringen; **to ~ one's education** sich weiterbilden; **to ~ one's career** beruflich vorankommen

furtherance ['fɜːðə rə ns] N Förderung *f*; **in ~ of sth** zur Förderung einer Sache *(gen)*

further education N Weiterbildung *f*, Fortbildung *f*

furthermore ['fɜːðəmɔːʳ] ✪ 26.2, 26.3 ADV überdies, außerdem

furthermost ['fɜːðəməʊst] ADJ äußerste(r, s)

furthest ['fɜːðɪst] ADV am weitesten; **these fields are ~ (away) from his farm** diese Felder liegen am weitesten von seinem Hof entfernt; **this is the ~ north you can go** dies ist der nördlichste Punkt, den man erreichen kann; **those who came ~** die, die am weitesten gereist sind; **it was the ~ the Irish team had ever got** so weit war die irische Mannschaft noch nie gekommen; **here prices have fallen ~** hier sind die Preise am meisten *or* stärksten gefallen; **he went the ~ into this question** er drang am tiefsten in diese Frage ein
ADJ am weitesten entfernt; **the ~ of the three villages** das entfernteste von den drei Dörfern; **in the ~ depths of the forest** in den tiefsten Tiefen des Waldes; **5 km at the ~** höchstens 5 km; **the ~ way round** der weiteste Weg herum; **the ~ distance** die größte Entfernung; **taken to the ~ extent** *(fig)* zum Äußersten getrieben; **the ~ limits of endurance** die äußersten Grenzen des Durchhaltevermögens

furtive ['fɜːtɪv] ADJ *action* heimlich; *behaviour, person* heimlichtuerisch; *(= suspicious)* verdächtig; *look* verstohlen; **his ~ eyes** sein ausweichender Blick

furtively ['fɜːtɪvlɪ] ADV *look, glance* verstohlen; *behave* verdächtig

furtiveness ['fɜːtɪvnɪs] N *(of action)* Heimlichkeit *f*; *(of behaviour, person)* Heimlichtuerei *f*; *(of look)* Verstohlenheit *f*

fury ['fjʊərɪ] N **a** *(of person)* Wut *f*; *(of storm also)* Ungestüm *nt*; *(of struggle, wind, passion)* Heftigkeit *f*; **in a ~** wütend; **she flew into a ~** sie kam in Rage; **like ~** *(inf)* wie verrückt *(inf)* **b** *(Myth)* **the Furies** die Furien *pl*

furze [fɜːz] N Stechginster *m*

fuse, *(US)* **fuze** [fjuːz] VT **a** *metals* verschmelzen
b *(Brit Elec)* **to ~ the lights** die Sicherung durchbrennen lassen; **I've ~d the lights** die Sicherung ist durchgebrannt
c *(fig)* vereinigen, verbinden; *(Comm)* fusionieren
VI **a** *(metals)* sich verbinden; *(atoms)* verschmelzen; *(bones)* zusammenwachsen
b *(Brit Elec)* durchbrennen; **the lights ~d** die Sicherung war durchgebrannt
c *(fig: also* **fuse together***)* sich vereinigen
N **a** *(Elec)* Sicherung *f*; **to blow the ~s** die Sicherung durchbrennen lassen; **he'll blow a ~** *(fig inf)* bei dem brennen die Sicherungen durch *(inf)*
b *(Brit, Elec, = act of fusing)* **there's been a ~ somewhere** irgendwo hat es einen Kurzschluss gegeben, da ist irgendwo ein Kurzschluss *or* Kurzer *(inf)*
c *(in bombs etc, Min)* Zündschnur *f*; **to light the ~** die Zündschnur anzünden; **this incident lit the ~ which led to the war** dieser Zwischenfall war der Auslöser des Krieges; **she has got** *or* **is on a short ~** *(fig inf)* sie explodiert schnell *or* leicht

fuse box N Sicherungskasten *m*

fused [fjuːzd] ADJ *plug etc* gesichert

fuselage ['fjuːzəlɑːʒ] N (Flugzeug)rumpf *m*

fuse wire N Schmelzdraht *m*

fusilier [ˌfjuːzɪ'lɪəʳ] N *(Brit)* Füsilier *m*

fusillade [ˌfjuːzɪ'leɪd] N Salve *f*

fusion ['fjuːʒən] N *(of metal, fig)* Verschmelzung *f*, Fusion *f*; *(Phys: also* **nuclear fusion***)* (Kern)fusion *f*, Kernverschmelzung *f*

fusion reactor N Fusionsreaktor *m*

fuss [fʌs] N Theater *nt (inf)*; *(= bother also)* Umstände *pl (inf)*, Aufheben(s) *nt*; *(= lavish attention)* Wirbel *m (inf)*, Getue *nt (inf)*(*of* um); **I don't know what all the ~ is about** ich weiß wirklich nicht, was das ganze Getue *or* der ganze Wirbel soll *(inf)*; **without (any) ~** ohne großes Theater *(inf)*; **to cause a ~** Theater machen *(inf)*; **to make a ~, to kick up a ~** Krach schlagen *(inf)*; **to make a ~ about** *or* **over sth** viel Aufhebens *or* Wirbel *(inf)* um etw machen; **to make a ~ of sb** um jdn viel Wirbel *or* Getue machen *(inf)*; **to be in a ~** Zustände haben *(inf)*; **a lot of ~ about nothing** viel Wirbel *(inf)* *or* Lärm um nichts
VI sich (unnötig) aufregen; *(= get into a fuss)* Umstände *pl* machen; **there's no need to ~ if your son doesn't wear a vest** Sie brauchen nicht gleich Zustände zu kriegen, nur weil Ihr Sohn kein Unterhemd anhat *(inf)*; **don't ~, mother!** ist ja gut, Mutter!; **a mother who ~es unnecessarily** eine übertrieben besorgte Mutter; **with a crowd of attendants ~ing busily around her** mit einer Menge Bediensteter, die eifrig um sie herumhuschten
VT *person* nervös machen; *(= pester)* keine Ruhe lassen *(+dat)*; **don't ~ me** lass mich in Ruhe, lass mir meine Ruhe

▶ **fuss about** *(Brit)* *or* **around** VI herumfuhrwerken *(inf)*

▶ **fuss over** VI *+prep obj details* Theater machen um; *person* bemuttern; *guests, food* sich *(dat)* große Umstände machen mit

fussbudget ['fʌsbʌdʒɪt] N *(US inf)* = **fusspot**

fussed [fʌst] ADJ *(Brit inf)* **I'm not ~ (about it)** es ist mir egal; **he wasn't ~ about getting back to Belfast** es war ihm egal, ob er nach Belfast zurückging

fussily ['fʌsɪlɪ] ADV *(pej)* **a** *(= painstakingly) adjust, check* übertrieben sorgfältig; *accurate* peinlich; *legalistic* übertrieben **b** *(= ornately)* überladen; **~ designed wrought-iron gates** schmiedeeiserne Tore mit verschnörkeltem Muster; **~ dressed** verspielt gekleidet

fussiness ['fʌsɪnɪs] N **a** *(= fastidiousness)* peinliche Genauigkeit; *(= pettiness)* Kleinlichkeit *f*; *(= preciseness)* Genauigkeit *f*; *(= choosiness)* wählerische Art; **because of his incredible ~ about what he eats** weil er so unglaublich wählerisch ist, was das Essen angeht **b** *(pej: = overelaboration, of design, style)* überladene Art; *(of furnishings, dress)* Verspieltheit *f*

fusspot ['fʌspɒt] N *(Brit inf)* Umstandskrämer(in) *m(f) (inf)*; *(= nag)* Nörgler(in) *m(f)*

fussy ['fʌsɪ] ADJ *(+er)* **a** *(= choosy)* wählerisch; *(= petty)* kleinlich; *(= precise)* genau; **to be ~ about cleanliness/punctuality/one's appearance** großen Wert auf Sauberkeit/Pünktlichkeit/sein Äußeres legen; **he was ~ about his toilet paper** er war sehr eigen, was sein Toilettenpapier anging; **she is not ~ about her food** sie ist beim Essen nicht wählerisch; **the child is a ~ eater** das Kind ist beim Essen wählerisch; **I'm not ~** *(inf)* das ist mir egal
b *(pej: = overelaborate) design, style* überladen; *furnishings, dress* verspielt; *food* kompliziert; *details, movements, gestures, acting* übertrieben

fustian ['fʌstɪən] N *(Tex)* Barchent *m* ADJ **a** *(Tex)* aus Barchent **b** *(fig, = pompous)* schwülstig

fusty ['fʌstɪ] ADJ *(+er)* **a** *(pej: = old-fashioned) person, image, establishment* verstaubt **b** *(= musty)* muffig

futile ['fjuːtaɪl] ADJ sinnlos; *plan, idea* nutzlos; *effort, attempt (usu attr: = in vain)* vergeblich; *(usu pred: = pointless)* nutzlos

futility [fjuː'tɪlɪtɪ] N Sinnlosigkeit *f*; *(of plan, idea)* Nutzlosigkeit *f*; *(of effort, attempt)* Vergeblichkeit *f*

futon ['fuːtɒn] N Futon *m*

future ['fjuːtʃəʳ] N **a** Zukunft *f*; **we will have to see what the ~ holds** wir müssen abwarten *or* sehen, was die Zukunft bringt; **they look to the ~ with a certain anxiety** sie blicken mit einer gewissen Angst in die Zukunft; **in ~** in Zukunft; **it won't happen in the foreseeable/near ~** es wird in absehbarer/nächster Zeit nicht passieren; **the strikes will continue into the foreseeable ~** die Streiks werden auf absehbare Zeit anhalten; **in the distant/not too distant ~** in ferner/nicht allzu ferner Zukunft; **that is still very much in the ~** das liegt noch in weiter Ferne; **what plans do you have for the ~?** was für Zukunftspläne haben Sie?; **there is a sound ~ in publishing** das Verlagswesen hat eine sichere Zukunft; **to have a/any ~** eine Zukunft haben; **no one had any faith in its ~** niemand glaubte daran, dass es eine Zukunft hatte; **there is a real ~ for me with this firm** ich habe in dieser Firma glänzende Aussichten; **her ~ lies** *or* **is in politics** ihre Zukunft liegt in der Politik; **there's no ~ in this type of research** diese Art von Forschung hat keine Zukunft
b *(Gram)* **the ~** das Futur, die Zukunft
c *(St Ex)* **futures** PL Termingeschäfte *pl*; **coffee ~s** Terminkontrakte *pl* in Kaffee; **commodity/financial ~s** Waren-/Finanzterminkontrakte *pl*; **~s market** Terminmarkt *m*, Terminbörse *f*
ADJ *attr* **a** *generations, husband, wife, king, queen, role* (zu)künftig; **at a** *or* **some ~ date** zu einem späteren Zeitpunkt; **his ~ prospects/plans** seine Aussichten/Pläne für die Zukunft, seine Zukunftsaussichten/-pläne; **in ~ years** in den kommenden Jahren; **for ~ reference, ...** zu Ihrer Information, ...; **you can keep it for ~ reference** Sie können es behalten, um später darauf Bezug zu nehmen; **~ life** Leben *nt* nach dem Tod
b *(Gram)* **the ~ tense** das Futur, die Zukunft; **the ~ perfect** die vollendete Zukunft

future-proof ADJ zukunftssicher

futurism ['fjuːtʃərɪzəm] N Futurismus *m*

futurist ['fjuːtʃərɪst] N Futurist(in) *m(f)*

futuristic [ˌfjuːtʃə'rɪstɪk] ADJ futuristisch

futurity [fjuː'tjʊərɪtɪ] N *(form: = future time)* Zukunft *f*

futurology [ˌfjuːtʃə'rɒlədʒɪ] N Futurologie *f*

fuze N *(US)* = **fuse**

fuzz [fʌz] N **a** *(on peach, youth's chin etc)* Flaum *m*; *(inf, = bushy beard etc)* Gemüse *nt (inf)*; *(= frizzy hair)* Wuschelkopf *m* **b** *(inf, = blur, blurred sound)* Unschärfen *pl* **c** *(dated esp Brit inf: = police)* **the ~** die Bullen *pl (sl)*

fuzzily [ˈfʌzɪlɪ] ADV verschwommen; **~ worded** unklar formuliert

fuzzy [ˈfʌzɪ] ADJ *(+er)* **a** *(= furry) material, sweater* flauschig; *(= frizzy) hair* kraus; **~ dice** *(US)* Plüschwürfel *pl* **b** *(= unclear) sound, voice, writing* undeutlich; *picture, idea, memory, distinction* verschwommen, unscharf; *details* unklar; **to go ~** *(picture)* verschwimmen; **my brain was ~** ich konnte nicht klar denken; **I'm a little ~ on what happened** ich weiß nicht so genau, was passiert ist; **his head was still ~ from the drink** er war von dem Drink noch benebelt

fuzzy: **fuzzy-headed** [ˈfʌzɪˌhedɪd] ADJ *(inf: = not clear-thinking)* nicht (ganz) klar im Kopf; *(from headache, drugs, drink)* benebelt; **fuzzy logic** N *(Comput)* Fuzzy Logic *f*; **fuzzy-wuzzy** [ˈfʌzɪˌwʌzɪ] N *(dated pej sl)* Krauskopf *m (inf)*

fwd *abbr of* **forward**

FWD, **f.w.d.** **a** *abbr of* **four-wheel drive** **b** *abbr of* **front-wheel drive**

FWH, **f.w.h.** *abbr of* **flexible working hours**

f-word [ˈefˌwɜːd] N *(inf) euphemistischer Bezug auf das Wort „fuck"* **I try not to use the ~ in front of the children** ich versuche, vor den Kindern möglichst keine schlimmen Flüche zu gebrauchen; **the ~ was mentioned 35 times in this short story** in dieser Kurzgeschichte steht 35mal „fuck"

FX [efˈeks] PL *(Film inf)* Spezialeffekte *pl*

FY *(Fin) abbr of* **fiscal year** *(= tax year)* Steuerjahr *nt*; *(= financial year)* Geschäftsjahr *nt*

FYI *abbr of* **for your information** zu Ihrer Information

G

G, g [dʒiː] **N** **a** G *nt*, g *nt* **b** **g's PL** *(= gravitational force)* g *nt* **c** **G** *(US inf: = one thousand dollars)* tausend Dollar *pl* **d** *(Mus)* G *nt*, g *nt*; **G sharp** Gis *nt*, gis *nt*; **G flat** Ges *nt*, ges *nt* → **major, minor**

G *(US) abbr of* **general audience** *(Film)* jugendfrei

g *abbr of* **gram(s), gramme(s)** g

gab [gæb] *(inf)* **N** Gequassel *nt (inf)*, Geschwätz *nt*; **to have a ~** (zusammen) quatschen *(inf)*; **to have a ~ about sth** etw bequatschen *(inf)*; **to have the gift of the ~** *(= talk a lot)* wie ein Wasserfall reden *(inf)*; *(= be persuasive)* reden können, nicht auf den Mund gefallen sein **VI** quatschen *(inf)*, quasseln *(inf)*

gabardine, gaberdine [ˌgæbəˈdiːn] **N** Gabardine *m*

gabble [ˈgæbl] *(Brit)* **VI** *(person)* brabbeln *(inf)*; *(geese)* schnattern **VT** *poem, prayer* herunterrasseln *(inf)*; *excuse, explanation* brabbeln *(inf)*; **he ~d out his story** er rasselte seine Geschichte herunter **N** Gebrabbel *nt (inf)*; *(of geese)* Geschnatter *nt*; **the speaker ended in a ~** der Redner rasselte das Ende herunter *(inf)*

▶ **gabble away** **VI** *(geese, people)* drauflosschnattern *(inf)*

▶ **gabble on** **VI** reden und reden, quasseln und quasseln *(inf)*

gabbler [ˈgæbləˈ] **N** *(pej)* Brabbler *m (pej)*, Schwätzer *m (pej)*

gabby [ˈgæbɪ] **ADJ** *(inf)* geschwätzig, schwatzhaft

gaberdine **N** = **gabardine**

gable [ˈgeɪbl] **N** Giebel *m*

gabled [ˈgeɪbld] **ADJ** Giebel-; **~ house/roof** Giebelhaus/-dach *nt*

gable: **gable end** **N** Giebelwand *or* -seite *f*; **gable window** **N** Giebelfenster *nt*

gad [gæd] **INTERJ** **(by) ~!** *(old)* bei Gott! *(old)*

▶ **gad about** *(Brit) or* **around** **VI** herumziehen *(prep obj* in *+dat)*; **he's always gadding about** er ist ständig auf Achse *(inf)*; **to gad about the country** im Land herumziehen *or* -reisen

gadabout [ˈgædəbaʊt] **N** rastloser Geist; *(who likes travelling)* Reiseonkel *m*/-tante *f*; **she's a real ~, out somewhere every evening** sie ist sehr unternehmungslustig, jeden Abend ist sie irgendwo anders

gadfly [ˈgædflaɪ] **N** (Vieh)bremse *f*

gadget [ˈgædʒɪt] **N** Gerät *nt*, Vorrichtung *f*, Apparat *m*; **with a lot of ~s** mit allen Schikanen *(inf)*

gadgeteer [ˌgædʒɪˈtɪəˈ] **N** Liebhaber(in) *m(f)* von technischen Spielereien

gadgetry [ˈgædʒɪtrɪ] **N** Vorrichtungen *pl*, Geräte *pl*; *(= superfluous equipment)* technische Spielereien *pl*, Kinkerlitzchen *pl (inf)*

gadgety [ˈgædʒɪtɪ] **ADJ** *device* raffiniert, zweckvoll (konstruiert); *person* auf technische Spielereien versessen

gadzooks [gædˈzuːks] **INTERJ** *(old)* Kruzitürken *(old)*

Gael [geɪl] **N** Gäle *m*, Gälin *f*

Gaelic [ˈgeɪlɪk] **ADJ** gälisch **N** *(Ling)* Gälisch *nt*

Gaelic coffee **N** Irish Coffee *m*

gaff[1] [gæf] **N** **a** *(Fishing)* Landungshaken *m*, Gaff *nt* **b** *(Naut)* Gaffel *f* **VT** *(Fishing)* mit dem (Landungs)haken *or* Gaff an Land ziehen

gaff[2] **N** **to blow the ~** *(inf)* nicht dichthalten *(inf)*; **he blew the ~ by saying that** als er das sagte, war alles raus *(inf)*; **to blow the ~ on sth** etw ausquatschen *(inf)*

gaffe [gæf] **N** Fauxpas *m*; *(verbal)* taktlose Bemerkung; **to make a ~** einen Fauxpas begehen; *(by saying sth)* ins Fettnäpfchen treten *(inf)*

gaffer [ˈgæfəˈ] **N** *(Brit inf)* **a** *(= foreman)* Vorarbeiter *m*, Vormann *m*; *(= boss)* Chef *m*, Boss *m (inf)*, Alte(r) *m(f) (inf)* **b** *(= old man)* Alte(r) *m*, Opa *m (inf)*

gag [gæg] **N** **a** Knebel *m*; *(Med)* Mundsperre *f*; **to put a ~ on the press** die Presse mundtot machen **b** *(= joke)* Gag *m* **VT** knebeln; *(Med)* die Mundsperre einlegen *(+dat)*; *(fig) person* zum Schweigen bringen; *press etc* mundtot machen, knebeln **VI** **a** *(= joke)* Witze machen; *(comedian)* Gags machen; **..., he ~ged** ..., witzelte er **b** *(= retch)* würgen (*on* an *+dat*) **c** **to be ~ging for sth** *(inf)* scharf auf etw *(acc)* sein; **to be ~ging for it** *(sl)* geil wie Bock sein *(sl)*

gaga [ˈgɑːgɑː] **ADJ** *(Brit inf)* plemplem *(inf)*, meschugge *(inf)*; *old person* verkalkt *(inf)*; **to go ~** *(= go senile)* verkalken *(inf)*

gage **N VT** *(US)* = **gauge**

gagging order **N** *(lit, fig)* Maulkorberlass *m*

gaggle [ˈgægl] **N** *(of geese)* Herde *f*; *(hum, of people)* Schar *f*, Horde *f* **VI** schnattern

gag law, *(US)* **gag rule** **N** *(inf)* Maulkorbgesetz *nt (inf)*, Maulkorberlass *m (inf)*

gaiety [ˈgeɪɪtɪ] **N** *(= cheerfulness)* Fröhlichkeit *f*, Heiterkeit *f*; *(usu pl: = merrymaking)* Vergnügung *f*

gaily [ˈgeɪlɪ] **ADV** **a** *(= happily)* fröhlich; *(= brightly) painted, dressed* farbenfroh; **~ coloured** *(Brit) or* **colored** *(US)* farbenfroh, farbenprächtig **b** *(= thoughtlessly)* unbekümmert, fröhlich *(inf)*; *spend* ohne Rücksicht auf Verluste

gain [geɪn] **N** **a** *no pl (= advantage)* Vorteil *m*; *(= profit)* Gewinn *m*, Profit *m*; **the love of ~** Profitgier *f (pej)*; **to do sth for ~** etw aus Berechnung *(dat) or* zum eigenen Vorteil tun; *(for money)* etw des Geldes wegen tun; **his loss is our ~** sein Verlust ist unser Gewinn, wir profitieren von seinem Verlust

b **gains** **PL** *(= winnings)* Gewinn *m*; *(= profits)* Gewinne *pl*

c *(= increase)* (*in +gen*) Zunahme *f*; *(in speed)* Erhöhung *f*; *(in wealth)* Steigerung *f*, Zunahme *f*; *(in health)* Besserung *f*; *(in knowledge)* Erweiterung *f*, Vergrößerung *f*; **~ in numbers** zahlenmäßiger Zuwachs; **~ in weight, weight ~** Gewichtszunahme *f*; **~ in sales** Absatzsteigerung *f*; **~ in height** Höhengewinn *m*

VT **a** *(= obtain, win)* gewinnen; *knowledge, wealth* erwerben; *advantage, respect, entry, access* sich *(dat)* verschaffen; *control, the lead* übernehmen; *marks, points* erzielen; *sum of money* verdienen; *liberty* erlangen; *(= achieve) nothing, a little etc* erreichen; **we ~ed something for ourselves** damit haben wir etwas für uns erreicht; **what does he hope to ~ by it?** was verspricht *or* erhofft er sich *(dat)* davon?; **to ~ independence** unabhängig werden; **to ~ sb's goodwill** jdn wohlwollend stimmen; **to ~ sb's confidence** jds Vertrauen erlangen; **to ~ experience** Erfahrungen sammeln; **he ~ed a better view by climbing onto a wall** dadurch, dass er auf eine Mauer kletterte, hatte er einen besseren Ausblick; **they didn't ~ entry to the building** sie kamen nicht in das Gebäude hinein; **we ~ed an advantage over him** wir waren ihm gegenüber im Vorteil; **to ~ ground** (an) Boden gewinnen; *(disease)* um sich greifen, sich verbreiten; *(rumours)* sich verbreiten; **to ~ ground on sb** *(= get further ahead)* den Vorsprung zu jdm vergrößern; *(= catch up)* jdm gegenüber aufholen; **to ~ time** Zeit gewinnen; **how did he ~ such a reputation?** wie ist er zu diesem Ruf gekommen?; **he ~ed a reputation as ...** er hat sich *(dat)* einen Namen als ... gemacht

b *(= reach) other side, shore, summit* erreichen

c *(= increase)* **to ~ height** (an) Höhe gewinnen, höhersteigen; **to ~ speed** schneller werden, beschleunigen; **to ~ strength** stärker werden; **she has ~ed weight/3 kilos** sie hat zugenommen/3 Kilo zugenommen; **as he ~ed confidence** als er sicherer wurde, als seine Selbstsicherheit wuchs *or* zunahm; **to ~ popularity** an Beliebtheit *(dat)* gewinnen; **my watch ~s five minutes each day** meine Uhr geht fünf Minuten pro Tag vor

VI **a** *(watch)* vorgehen

b *(= get further ahead)* den Vorsprung vergrößern; *(= close gap)* aufholen

c *(= profit: person)* profitieren (*by* von); **you can only ~ by it** das kann nur Ihr Vorteil sein, Sie können dabei nur profitieren; **society/the university would ~ from that** das wäre für die Gesellschaft/die Universität von Vorteil; **we stood to ~ from the decision** die Entscheidung war für uns von Vorteil

d **to ~ in confidence** mehr Selbstvertrauen bekommen; **to ~ in popularity** an Beliebtheit *(dat)* gewinnen; **to ~ in speed** schneller werden; **to ~ in height** (an) Höhe gewinnen; **to ~ in weight** zunehmen; **to ~ in prestige** an Ansehen gewinnen, sich *(dat)* größeres Ansehen verschaffen; **to ~ in strength** stärker werden

▶ **gain on** **VI** *+prep obj (= get further ahead)* den Vorsprung zu ... vergrößern; *(= close gap)* einholen; *(= catch up with) work, rust etc* fertig werden mit; **the disease was gaining on him** seine Krankheit schritt fort

gainer [ˈgeɪnəˈ] **N** **I was the ~** ich habe dabei profitiert; **there were more losers than ~s** es gab mehr Verlierer als Gewinner; **the biggest ~ was the government** die Regierung hat am meisten (davon) profitiert

gainful [ˈgeɪnfʊl] **ADJ** *occupation etc* einträglich; **to be in ~ employment** erwerbstätig sein

gainfully [ˈgeɪnfəlɪ] **ADV** *spend time* nutzbringend; **~ employed** erwerbstätig; **there was nothing that could ~ be said** man konnte nichts sagen, was noch etwas genutzt hätte

gainsay [ˌgeɪnˈseɪ] **VT** *pret, ptp* **gainsaid** [ˌgeɪnˈsed] widersprechen *(+dat)*; *fact* (ab)leugnen, bestreiten; *evidence, argument* widerlegen; **it/the facts cannot be gainsaid** es lässt/die Tatsachen lassen sich nicht leugnen; **there is no ~ing his honesty** seine Ehrlichkeit lässt sich nicht leugnen

'gainst [geɪnst] PREP = **against**

gait [geɪt] N Gang *m*; *(of horse)* Gangart *f*; **to have a rolling/shuffling ~** einen schaukelnden/schlurfenden Gang haben; **with an unsteady ~** mit unsicheren Schritten

gaiter ['geɪtəʳ] N Gamasche *f*

gal[1] [gæl] N *(dated inf)* Mädel *nt (dated)*

gal[2] *abbr of* **gallon(s)**

gala ['gɑːlə] N *(= festive occasion)* großes Fest; *(Theat, Film: = ball)* Galaveranstaltung *f*; **swimming/sports ~** großes Schwimm-/Sportfest; **opening/closing ~** Eröffnungs-/Abschlussveranstaltung *f*

galactic [gə'læktɪk] ADJ galaktisch

gala day N Festtag *m*; *(for person)* großer Tag

gala dress N Gala *f*; *(= uniform also)* Galauniform *f or* -anzug *m*

Galahad ['gæləhæd] N Galahad *m*; *(fig)* Kavalier *m*, Ritter *m*

gala night N Galaabend *m*

galantine ['gælənti:n] N *kalt servierte, glasierte Fleisch- oder Geflügelroulade*

gala occasion N festliche Veranstaltung

gala performance N Galavorstellung *f*, Festvorstellung *f*

galaxy ['gæləksɪ] N **a** *(Astron)* Milchstraße *f*, Sternsystem *nt*, Galaxis *f (spec)*; **the Galaxy** die Milchstraße, die Galaxis *(spec)* **b** *(fig)* Schar *f*, Heer *nt*

gale [geɪl] N **a** Sturm *m*; **it was blowing a ~** es stürmte, ein Sturm tobte *or* wütete; **~ force 8** Sturmstärke 8 **b** *(fig)* **~s of laughter** Lachsalven *pl*, stürmisches Gelächter

gale: **gale-force winds** PL orkanartige Winde; **gale warning** N Sturmwarnung *f*

Galicia [gə'lɪsɪə] N **a** *(in Eastern Europe)* Galizien *nt* **b** *(in Spain)* Galicien *nt*

Galician [gə'lɪsɪən] ADJ **a** *(in Eastern Europe)* galizisch **b** *(in Spain)* galicisch N **a** *(in Eastern Europe)* Galizier(in) *m(f)* **b** *(in Spain)* Galicier(in) *m(f)*

Galilean [,gælɪ'li:ən] ADJ galiläisch N Galiläer(in) *m(f)*

Galilee ['gælɪli:] N Galiläa *nt*; **the Sea of ~** der See Genezareth, das Galiläische Meer

gall [gɔːl] N **a** *(Physiol)* Galle(nsaft *m*) *f* **b** *(= sore)* Wundstelle *f*; *(Bot)* Galle *f*; *(nut-shaped)* Gallapfel *m* **c** *(fig liter)* Bitternis *f (geh)* **d** *(inf)* Frechheit *f*; **to have the ~ to do sth** die Frechheit haben *or* besitzen, etw zu tun VT *(= chafe)* wund reiben *or* scheuern; *(fig)* maßlos ärgern; **it ~s me that ...** es ärgert mich maßlos, dass ...

gallant ['gælənt] ADJ **a** *(= courageous) person, effort, attempt, fight* tapfer; **~ conduct** Tapferkeit *f* **b** *(= chivalrous) person, gesture* ritterlich **c** *(liter, = showy)* prächtig N ['gælənt, gə'lænt] *(Hist, = suitor)* Galan *m (old)*

gallantly ['gæləntlɪ] ADV **a** *(= courageously)* tapfer **b** *(= chivalrously)* ritterlich

gallantry ['gæləntrɪ] N **a** *(= bravery)* Tapferkeit *f*; *(= chivalry)* Edelmut *m* **b** *(= attentiveness to women)* Ritterlichkeit *f*, Galanterie *f* **c** *(= compliment)* Galanterie *f*, Artigkeit *f (dated)*

gall bladder N Gallenblase *f*

galleon ['gælɪən] N Galeone *f*

gallery ['gælərɪ] N **a** *(= balcony, corridor)* Galerie *f*; *(in church)* Empore *f*; *(Theat)* oberster Rang, Balkon *m*, Galerie *f*; **to play to the ~** *(fig)* sich in Szene setzen **b** *(Art)* (Kunst)galerie *f* **c** *(underground)* Stollen *m*

galley ['gælɪ] N **a** *(Naut: = ship)* Galeere *f*; *(= kitchen)* Kombüse *f* **b** *(Typ, = tray)* (Setz)schiff *nt*; *(also* **galley proof***)* Fahne *f*, Fahnenabzug *m*

galley slave N Galeerensklave *m*

Gallic ['gælɪk] ADJ gallisch; **the ~ Wars** der Gallische Krieg

Gallicism ['gælɪsɪzəm] N Gallizismus *m*

Gallicize ['gælɪsaɪz] VT französisieren

gallimaufry [,gælɪ'mɔːfrɪ] N *no pl* Durcheinander *nt*, Mischmasch *m (inf)*

galling ['gɔːlɪŋ] ADJ äußerst ärgerlich; *experience* äußerst unangenehm; *person* unausstehlich; **this was especially ~ for him** das hat ihn besonders geärgert

gallivant [,gælɪ'vænt] VI sich amüsieren; **to ~ about** *or* **around** sich herumtreiben, herumstromern *(pej)*; **to ~ off** losziehen *(inf)*; **I was out ~ing last night** ich war gestern Abend bummeln *or* auf Achse *(inf)*

gallon ['gælən] N Gallone *f*

gallop ['gæləp] N Galopp *m*; **at a ~** im Galopp; **at full ~** im gestreckten Galopp; **to go for a ~** ausreiten; **after a quick ~ through Roman history, he ...** nachdem er die römische Geschichte im Galopp abgehandelt hatte, ... VI galoppieren, im Galopp reiten; **to ~ away** davongaloppieren; **we ~ed through our work/the agenda** wir haben die Arbeit im Galopp erledigt *(inf)*/die Tagesordnung im Galopp abgehandelt *(inf)*; **to ~ through a book** ein Buch in rasendem Tempo lesen *(inf)* VT *horse* galoppieren lassen

galloping ['gæləpɪŋ] ADJ *(lit)* galoppierend; **at a ~ pace** *(lit)* im Galopp; *(fig)* in rasendem Tempo; **~ inflation** galoppierende Inflation

gallows ['gæləʊz] N Galgen *m*; **to send/bring sb to the ~** jdn an den Galgen bringen

gallows: **gallows bird** N *(inf)* Galgenvogel *m (inf)*; **gallows humour**, *(US)* **gallows humor** N Galgenhumor *m*

gallstone ['gɔːlstəʊn] N Gallenstein *m*

Gallup poll ['gæləp,pəʊl] N Meinungsumfrage *f*

galore [gə'lɔːʳ] ADV in Hülle und Fülle

galoshes [gə'lɒʃɪz] PL Gummischuhe *pl*, Galoschen *pl*

galumph [gə'lʌmf] VI *(inf)* trapsen *(inf)*

galvanic [gæl'vænɪk] ADJ **a** *(Elec)* galvanisch **b** *(fig) movement* zuckend; *(= stimulating)* mitreißend, elektrisierend

galvanism ['gælvənɪzəm] N Galvanismus *m*

galvanization [,gælvənaɪ'zeɪʃən] N Galvanisierung *f*, Galvanisation *f*

galvanize ['gælvənaɪz] VT **a** *(Elec)* galvanisieren **b** *(fig)* elektrisieren; **to ~ sb into action** jdn plötzlich aktiv werden lassen; **to ~ sb into doing** *or* **to do sth** jdm einen Stoß geben, etw sofort zu tun; **he was ~d into life by the news** die Nachricht hat ihm enormen Auftrieb gegeben

galvanized ['gælvənaɪzd] ADJ *iron, steel* galvanisiert

galvanometer [,gælvə'nɒmɪtəʳ] N Galvanometer *nt*

Gambia ['gæmbɪə] N **(the) ~** Gambia *nt*

Gambian ['gæmbɪən] ADJ gambisch N Gambier(in) *m(f)*

gambit ['gæmbɪt] N **a** *(Chess)* Gambit *nt* **b** *(fig)* (Schach)zug *m*; **his favourite** *(Brit)* *or* **favorite** *(US)* **~ was to ...** was er am liebsten machte, war ...; **his opening ~ is ...** er fängt eine Unterhaltung mit ... an

gamble ['gæmbl] N **a** *(lit)* **I like the occasional ~** ich versuche gern mal mein Glück (im Spiel/bei Pferdewetten/bei Hundewetten *etc*) **to have a ~ on the horses/dogs** auf Pferde/Hunde wetten; **to have a ~ on the stock exchange** an der Börse spekulieren

b *(fig)* Risiko *nt*; **a political ~** ein politisches Wagnis; **it's a ~** es ist riskant *or* eine riskante Sache; **I'll take a ~ on it/him** ich riskiere es/es mit ihm; **he took a ~ in buying the house** beim Kauf des Hauses ist er ein Risiko eingegangen

VI **a** *(lit)* (um Geld) spielen *(with* mit), sich an Glücksspielen beteiligen; *(on horses etc)* wetten; **to ~ on the horses** bei Pferderennen wetten; **to ~ on the stock exchange** an der Börse spekulieren; **he made a lot of money gambling** er hat beim Glückspiel *or (with cards)* beim Kartenspiel viel Geld gewonnen

b *(fig)* **to ~ on sth** sich auf etw *(acc)* verlassen; **she was gambling on his being late** sie hat sich darauf verlassen, dass er sich verspäten würde; **I was gambling on winning their support** ich verließ mich *or* spekulierte *(inf)* darauf, dass sie mich unterstützen würden; **to ~ with sth** mit etw spielen, etw aufs Spiel setzen

VT **a** *money, fortune* einsetzen; **to ~ sth on sth** etw auf etw *(acc)* setzen

b *(fig)* aufs Spiel setzen

▶ **gamble away** VT *sep* verspielen

gambler ['gæmbləʳ] N *(lit, fig)* Spieler(in) *m(f)*; **he's a born ~** er ist eine Spielernatur; **Gamblers Anonymous** Anonyme Spieler *pl*

gambling ['gæmblɪŋ] N Spielen *nt* (um Geld); *(on horses etc)* Wetten *nt*; **to disapprove of ~** gegen das Glücksspiel/Wetten sein

gambling debts PL Spielschulden *pl*

gambling den, **gambling joint** N Spielhölle *f*

gambol ['gæmbəl] N Tollen *nt*, Tollerei *f*; *(of lambs)* Herumspringen *nt*; **to have a ~** herumtollen; herumspringen VI herumtollen; herumspringen

game[1] [geɪm] N **a** Spiel *nt*; *(= sport)* Sport(art *f*) *m*; *(= single game, of team sports, tennis)* Spiel *nt*; *(of table tennis)* Satz *m*; *(of billiards, board games etc, informal tennis match)* Partie *f*; **the wonderful ~ of football** Fußball, das wunderbare Spiel; **to have** *or* **play a ~ of football/tennis/chess** Fußball/Tennis/Schach *etc* spielen; **do you fancy a quick ~ of tennis/chess?** hättest du Lust, ein bisschen Tennis/Schach zu spielen?, hättest du Lust auf eine Partie Tennis/Schach?; **we had a quick ~ of cards after supper** nach dem Essen spielten wir ein bisschen Karten; **shall we play a ~ now?** wollen wir jetzt ein Spiel machen?; **to have a ~ with sb, to give sb a ~** mit jdm spielen; **winning the second set put him back in the ~ again** nachdem er den zweiten Satz gewonnen hatte, hatte er wieder Chancen; **he had a good ~** er spielte gut; **to be off one's ~** nicht in Form sein; **~ of chance** Glücksspiel *nt*; **~ of skill** Geschicklichkeitsspiel *nt*; **~ set and match to X** Satz und Spiel (geht an) X; **~ to X** Spiel X; **one ~ all** eins beide

b *(fig)* Spiel *nt*; *(= scheme, plan)* Absicht *f*, Vorhaben *nt*; **to play the ~** sich an die Spielregeln halten; **to play ~s with sb** mit jdm spielen; **he's just playing (silly) ~s** für ihn ist es nur ein Spiel; **the ~ is up** das Spiel ist aus; **to play sb's ~** jdm in die Hände spielen; **two can play at that ~, that's a ~ (that) two can play** wie du mir, so ich dir *(inf)*; **to beat sb at his own ~** jdn mit den eigenen Waffen schlagen; **to give the ~ away** alles verderben; **to see through sb's ~** jds Spiel durchschauen, jdm auf die Schliche kommen; **to spoil sb's little ~** jdm das Spiel verderben, jdm die Suppe versalzen *(inf)*; **I wonder what his ~ is?** ich frage mich, was er vorhat *or* im Schilde führt; **so that's your ~, is it?** darauf willst du also hinaus!; **to be/keep ahead of the ~** *(fig)* um eine Nasenlänge voraus sein/bleiben; **to be out of the ~** *(inf: = be finished etc)* weg vom Fenster sein *(inf)*; **it's all part of the ~** das gehört alles dazu

c **games** PL *(= sports event)* Spiele *pl*

d **games** SING *(Sch)* Sport *m*; **to be good at ~s** gut in Sport sein

e *(inf: = business, profession)* Branche *f*; **how long have you been in this ~?** wie lange machen Sie das schon?; **the publishing ~** das Verlagswesen; **he's in the second-hand car ~** er macht in Gebrauchtwagen *(inf)*; **to be/go on the ~** *(esp Brit)* auf den Strich gehen *(inf)*

f *(inf, = difficult time)* Theater *nt (inf)*

g *(Hunt, Cook)* Wild *nt*

VI (um Geld) spielen

VT *(also* **game away***)* verspielen

game[2] ADJ *(= brave)* mutig; **to be ~** *(= willing)* mitmachen, dabei sein; **to be ~ for sth** für etw bereit sein; **to be ~ to do sth** bereit sein, etw zu tun; **to be ~ for anything** für alles zu haben sein, zu allen Schandtaten bereit sein *(hum inf)*; **to be ~ for a laugh** jeden Spaß mitmachen

game³ ADJ *(= crippled)* lahm

game: **game bag** N Jagdtasche *f*; **game bird** N Federwild *nt no pl*; **the pheasant is a ~** der Fasan gehört zum Federwild

Gameboy® ['geɪmbɔɪ] N Gameboy® *m*

game: **gamecock** N Kampfhahn *m*; **game console** ['geɪm,kɒnsəʊl] N *(Comput)* Spielekonsole *f*; **game controller** N *(Comput)* Gamecontroller *m*; **game fish** N Sportfisch *m*; **gamekeeper** N Wildhüter(in) *m(f)*; **game laws** PL Jagdgesetz *nt*; **game licence**, *(US)* **game license** N Jagdschein *m*

gamely ['geɪmlɪ] ADV *(= bravely)* mutig

game: **game park** N Wildpark *m*; **game pie** N Wildpastete *f*; **game plan** N *(Sport)* Spielplan *m*; *(fig)* Strategie *f*; **game point** N Spielpunkt *m*; **game port** N *(Comput)* Gameport *nt*, Spieleport *nt*; **game preserve** N Wildhegegebiet *nt*; **game reserve** N Wildschutzgebiet *or* -reservat *nt*

games console ['geɪmz,kɒnsəʊl] N *(Comput)* Spielekonsole *f*

game show N *(TV)* Spielshow *f*

gamesmanship ['geɪmzmənʃɪp] N Ablenkungsmanöver *pl*; **political/diplomatic ~** politische/diplomatische Schläue

games [geɪmz] *(Comput)*: **games master** N Sportlehrer *m*; **games mistress** N Sportlehrerin *f*; **games port** N Spieleport *nt or m*; **games software** N Software *f* für Computerspiele

gamester ['geɪmstə'] N Spieler(in) *m(f)*

game theory N *(in business studies)* Spieltheorie *f*

game warden N Jagdaufseher *m*

gamin ['gæmɛ̃] N Straßenjunge *m*

gamine [gæ'miːn] ADJ jungenhaft, knabenhaft

gaming ['geɪmɪŋ] N = **gambling**; **~ machine** Spielautomat *m*; **~ console** *(Comput)* Spiel(e)konsole *f*

gamma: **gamma radiation** N Gammastrahlung *f*; **gamma ray** ['gæməreɪ] N Gammastrahl *m*

gammon ['gæmən] N *(= bacon)* leicht geräucherter Vorderschinken; *(= ham)* (gekochter) Schinken; **~ steak** *dicke Scheibe Vorderschinken zum Braten oder Grillen*

gammy ['gæmɪ] ADJ *(Brit inf)* lahm

gamp [gæmp] N *(dated hum)* Regenschirm *m*, Musspritze *f (dated hum)*

gamut ['gæmət] N *(Mus)* Noten- *or* Tonskala *f*; *(fig)* Skala *f*; **to run the (whole) ~ of emotions** die ganze Skala der Gefühle durchlaufen; **his facial expressions ran the ~ from pain to terror** sein Gesichtsausdruck durchlief die ganze Skala von Schmerz bis hin zu panischer Angst

gamy ['geɪmɪ] ADJ nach Wild schmeckend; *(= high)* angegangen; **~ taste** Wildgeschmack *m*; *(= high)* Hautgout *m (geh)*, angegangener Geschmack

gander ['gændə'] N **a** Gänserich *m*, Ganter *m (dial)* **b** *(inf)* **to have** *or* **take a ~ at sth** auf etw *(acc)* einen Blick werfen; **let's have a ~!** gucken wir mal! *(inf)*; *(= let me/us look)* lass mal sehen!

G and T, G&T [,dʒiːən'tiː] N *(inf) abbr of* **gin and tonic** Gin Tonic *m*

gang [gæŋ] N Haufen *m*, Schar *f*; *(of workers, prisoners)* Kolonne *f*, Trupp *m*; *(of criminals, youths, terrorists)* Bande *f*, Gang *f*; *(of friends etc: = clique)* Clique *f*, Haufen *m (inf)*; **there was a whole ~ of them** es war ein ganzer Haufen; **do you want to be in our ~?** möchtest du zu unserer Bande/Clique gehören?; **the Gang of Four** die Viererbande

▶ **gang up** VI sich zusammentun; **to gang up against** *or* **on sb** sich gegen jdn verbünden *or* verschwören; *(to fight)* geschlossen auf jdn *or* gegen jdn losgehen

gangbang ['gæŋbæŋ] *(inf)* N **a** *(= rape)* Gruppenvergewaltigung *f* **b** *(voluntary)* **she had six men round for a ~** sie wurde von sechs Männern durchgebumst *(inf)* VT **she was ~ed** *(= raped)* sie wurde Opfer einer Gruppenvergewaltigung; *(voluntarily)* sie wurde von mehreren Männern hintereinander gebumst *(inf)*

gangbanger ['gæŋbæŋə'] N *(US inf)* Mitglied *nt* einer Straßenbande

gang boss N *(inf)* Vorarbeiter *m*, Vormann *m*

ganger ['gæŋə'] N Vorarbeiter *m*, Vormann *m*

Ganges ['gændʒiːz] N Ganges *m*

gangland ['gæŋlænd] N die Unterwelt ADJ Unterwelt-; **a ~ boss** ein Unterweltboss *m*

ganglia ['gæŋglɪə] *pl of* **ganglion**

gangling ['gæŋglɪŋ] ADJ schlaksig, hoch aufgeschossen

ganglion ['gæŋglɪən] N *pl* **ganglia** **a** *(Anat)* Ganglion *nt*; *(Med)* Überbein *nt*, Ganglion *nt* **b** *(fig, of activity)* Zentrum *nt*

gangplank ['gæŋplæŋk] N Laufplanke *f*, Landungssteg *m*

gang rape N Gruppenvergewaltigung *f*

gangrene ['gæŋgriːn] N Brand *m*, Gangrän *f or nt (spec)*

gangrenous ['gæŋgrɪnəs] ADJ brandig, gangränös *(spec)*

gangsta rap ['gæŋstə,ræp] N *(Mus)* Gangsta Rap *m*

gangster ['gæŋstə'] N Gangster(in) *m(f)*, Verbrecher(in) *m(f)*

gangsterism ['gæŋstərɪzəm] N Gangstertum *nt*, Verbrechertum *nt*

gangway ['gæŋweɪ] N **a** *(Naut: = gangplank)* Landungsbrücke *f*, Gangway *f*; *(= ladder)* Fallreep *nt* **b** *(= passage)* Gang *m* INTERJ Platz da

ganja ['gændʒə] N Ganja *nt*

gannet ['gænɪt] N *(Zool)* Tölpel *m*; **she's a real ~** *(inf)* sie ist ein richtiger Vielfraß

gantry ['gæntrɪ] N *(for crane)* Portal *nt*; *(on motorway)* Schilderbrücke *f*; *(Rail)* Signalbrücke *f*; *(for rocket)* Abschussrampe *f*

gaol [dʒeɪl] N VT = **jail**

gaoler ['dʒeɪlə'] N = **jailer**

gap [gæp] N *(lit, fig)* Lücke *f*; *(= chink)* Spalt *m*; *(in surface)* Spalte *f*, Riss *m*; *(Geog)* Spalte *f*; *(Tech: = spark gap)* Abstand *m*; *(fig, in conversation, narrative)* Pause *f*; *(= gulf)* Kluft *f*; **to close the ~** *(in race)* (den Abstand) aufholen; **tax increases to close the ~ between spending and revenue** Steuererhöhungen, um die Lücke zwischen Ausgaben und Einnahmen zu schließen; **to find/spot/fill a ~ in the market** eine Marktlücke finden/erkennen/füllen; **a ~ in one's knowledge** eine Bildungslücke; **a four-year ~, a ~ of four years** ein Abstand *m* von vier Jahren; **she returned to work after a ~ of five years** nach einer Pause von fünf Jahren ging sie wieder arbeiten

gape [geɪp] VI **a** *(= open mouth wide, person)* den Mund aufreißen *or* -sperren; *(bird)* den Schnabel aufsperren; *(chasm etc)* gähnen, klaffen; *(seam, wound)* klaffen **b** *(= stare: person)* starren, gaffen; **to ~ at sb/sth** jdn/etw (mit offenem Mund) anstarren; **the people stood and ~d** die Leute sperrten Mund und Nase auf *(inf)*

gaping ['geɪpɪŋ] ADJ **a** *mouth, beak* weit aufgesperrt; *hole* riesig; *wound* klaffend; *chasm, abyss* klaffend, gähnend **b** *(= staring) person* gaffend; *eyes* weit aufgerissen

gap: **gapless** ADJ lückenlos; **gap-toothed** [gæptuːθt] ADJ mit weiter Zahnstellung; *(= with teeth missing)* mit Zahnlücken

garage ['gærɑːʒ, *(US)* gə'rɑːʒ] N *(for parking)* Garage *f*; *(Brit) (for petrol)* Tankstelle *f*; *(for repairs etc)* (Reparatur)werkstatt *f*; **~ mechanic** *(Brit)* Kraftfahrzeug- *or* Kfz-Mechaniker(in) *m(f)* VT (in einer Garage) ab- *or* unterstellen; *(= drive into garage)* in die Garage fahren; **the car is kept ~d** das Auto wird in einer Garage aufbewahrt

garage: **garage band** N *(Mus)* Amateur-Rockband *f*; **garage sale** N *meist in einer Garage durchgeführter Verkauf von Haushaltsgegenständen und Trödel* → *also* **car-boot sale**

garaging ['gærɑːʒɪŋ, *(US)* gə'rɑːʒɪŋ] N Garagenplätze *pl*

garb [gɑːb] N Gewand *nt* VT kleiden; **~ed all in black** ganz in Schwarz gekleidet

garbage ['gɑːbɪdʒ] N *(lit: esp US)* Abfall *m*, Müll *m*; *(fig: = useless things)* Schund *m*, Mist *m (inf)*; *(= nonsense)* Blödsinn *m*, Quatsch *m (inf)*; *(Comput)* Garbage *m*; **~ in, ~ out** *(Comput)* garbage in, garbage out, Müll rein, Müll raus

garbage: **garbage can** N *(US)* Müll- *or* Abfalleimer *m*; *(outside)* Mülltonne *f*; **garbage collector** N *(US)* Müllarbeiter *m*; **the ~s** die Müllabfuhr; **garbage disposal unit** N *(esp US)* Müllschlucker *m*; **garbage man** N *(US)* = **garbage collector**

garble ['gɑːbl] VT *(deliberately) message* unverständlich machen; **to ~ one's words** sich beim Sprechen überschlagen

garbled ['gɑːbld] ADJ *version, story* entstellt; *message, instructions* konfus; *words, speech, account* wirr; **in a ~ form** völlig entstellt; **the facts got a little ~** die Tatsachen sind etwas durcheinandergeraten

garda ['gɑːrdə] N *pl* **gardaí** ['gɑːrdiː] *(Ir: = police)* Polizei *f*; *(= policeman/-woman)* Polizist(in) *m(f)*

garden ['gɑːdn] N **a** Garten *m*; **the Garden of Eden** der Garten Eden; **everything in the ~ is lovely** *or* **rosy** *(fig)* es ist alles in Butter *(inf)* **b** *(often pl: = park)* Park *m*, Gartenanlagen *pl* VI im Garten arbeiten, Gartenarbeit machen, gärtnern

garden *in cpds* Garten-; **garden apartment** N *(US)* = **garden flat**; **garden burger** N Gemüseburger *m*; **garden centre**, *(US)* **garden center** N Gartencenter *nt*, Gärtnereimarkt *m*

gardener ['gɑːdnə'] N Gärtner(in) *m(f)*

garden: **garden flat** N *(Brit)* Souterrainwohnung *f*; **garden frame** M Frühbeet *nt*; **garden gnome** N Gartenzwerg *m*

gardenia [gɑː'diːnɪə] N Gardenie *f*

gardening ['gɑːdnɪŋ] N Gartenarbeit *f*; **she loves ~** sie arbeitet gerne im Garten, sie gärtnert gerne; **~ tools** Gartengeräte *pl*

garden: **garden party** N Gartenparty *f or* -fest *nt*; **garden path** N **to lead sb up** *(esp Brit) or* **down** *(esp US)* **the ~** *(fig)* jdn an der Nase herumführen *(inf)*; **garden produce** N *(= vegetables)* Gartengemüse *nt*; *(= fruit)* Gartenobst *nt*; **garden shears** PL Heckenschere *f*; **garden-variety** ADJ *(US: = ordinary)* gewöhnlich; *(= standard)* durchschnittlich

gargantuan [gɑː'gæntjʊən] ADJ gewaltig, enorm

gargle ['gɑːgl] VI gurgeln; *(with* mit*)* N *(= liquid)* Gurgelwasser *nt*

gargoyle ['gɑːgɔɪl] N Wasserspeier *m*

garish ['gɛərɪʃ] ADJ *(pej) colours, neon sign* grell, schreiend; *clothes* knallbunt

garishly ['gɛərɪʃlɪ] ADV *(pej) dressed* in grellen Farben; *illuminated* grell; **~ coloured** *(Brit) or* **colored** *(US)* schreiend bunt, knallbunt

garishness ['gɛərɪʃnɪs] N *(pej)* grelle *or* schreiende Farben *pl*; *(of colours, illuminations)* Grellheit *f*

garland ['gɑːlənd] N Kranz *m*; *(= festoon)* Girlande *f*; **a ~ of flowers** eine Blumengirlande VT bekränzen

garlic ['gɑːlɪk] N Knoblauch *m*

garlic: **garlic bread** N Knoblauchbrot *nt*; **garlic clove** N Knoblauchzehe *f*; **garlic crusher** N Knoblauchpresse *f*

garlicky ['gɑːlɪkɪ] ADJ *food* knoblauchhaltig; **~ taste** Knoblauchgeschmack *m*; **she's got ~ breath** ihr Atem riecht nach Knoblauch

garlic: **garlic mushrooms** PL *fritierte Pilze mit Knoblauch*; **garlic press** N Knoblauchpresse *f*; **garlic salt** N Knoblauchsalz *nt*

garment ['gɑːmənt] N Kleidungsstück *nt*; *(= robe)* Gewand *nt (liter)*; **all her ~s** ihre ganzen Kleider; **~ industry** *(US)* Bekleidungsindustrie *f*

garner ['gɑːnə'] VT *(lit, fig) (= gather)* sammeln; *savings* ansammeln; *support* gewinnen; *(= store)* speichern

garnet ['gɑːnɪt] N Granat *m*

garnish ['gɑːnɪʃ] VT garnieren, verzieren; *(fig) story also, style* ausschmücken N Garnierung *f*

garnishing ['gɑːnɪʃɪŋ] N *(Cook)* Garnierung *f*; *(= act also)* Garnieren *nt*; *(fig, of style, story etc)* Ausschmückung *f*

garret ['gærət] N *(= attic room)* Mansarde *f*, Dachkammer *f*; *(= attic)* Dachboden *m*

garrison ['gærɪsən] N Garnison *f* VT *troops* in Garnison legen; **to be ~ed** in Garnison liegen

garrison duty N Garnisonsdienst *m*

garrison town N Garnisonsstadt *f*

garrotte [gə'rɒt] VT *(= execute)* garrottieren, mit der Garrotte hinrichten; *(= strangle)* erdrosseln N Garrotte *f*

garrulity [gə'ruːlɪtɪ] N Geschwätzigkeit *f*, Schwatzhaftigkeit *f*

garrulous ['gærʊləs] ADJ geschwätzig, schwatzhaft

garrulously ['gærʊləslɪ] ADV **to talk/chat** *etc* ~ schwatzen, plappern

garryowen [ˌgærɪ'əʊɪn] N *(Rugby)* hohe Selbstvorlage

garter ['gɑːtə'] N Strumpfband *nt*; *(US: = strap for stocking)* Strumpfhalter *m*; **the (Order of the) Garter** der Hosenbandorden

garter: **garter belt** N *(US)* Strumpf- *or* Hüftgürtel *m*; **garter snake** N Ringelnatter *f*; **garter stitch** N rechts-rechts gestricktes Muster; **5 rows** ~ 5 Reihen rechts-rechts gestrickt

gas [gæs] N **a** Gas *nt*; **to cook with** ~ mit Gas kochen
b *(US: = petrol)* Benzin *nt*; **to step on the** ~ Gas geben
c *(= anaesthetic)* Lachgas *nt*; **to have** *(Brit) or* **get** *(US)* ~ Lachgas bekommen
d *(Mil)* (Gift)gas *nt*
e *(US Med: = wind)* Blähungen *pl*
f *(inf: = talk)* leeres Gefasel *(inf)*; *(boastful)* großspuriges Gerede, Angeberei *f*; **to have a good** ~ einen Schwatz halten
g *(inf)* **it's/he's a** ~ *(= fantastic)* es/er ist klasse *(inf)*; *(= hilarious)* es/er ist zum Schreien *(inf)*
VT vergasen; **they were ~sed during their sleep** *(accidentally)* sie starben im Schlaf an Gasvergiftung; **to ~ oneself** den Gashahn aufdrehen, sich mit Gas vergiften
VI *(inf: = talk)* schwafeln *(inf)*, faseln *(inf)*

gas *in cpds* Gas-; **gasbag** N *(inf)* Quasselstrippe *f (inf)*; **gas bracket** N Gasanschluss(stelle *f*) *m*, Gaszuleitungsrohr *nt*; *(for light)* Wandarm *m*; **gas chamber** N Gaskammer *f*; **gas cooker** N Gasherd *m*; **gas engine** N Gasmaschine *f or* -motor *m*

gaseous ['gæsɪəs] ADJ gasförmig

gas: **gas field** N Erdgasfeld *nt*; **gas fire** N Gasofen *m*; **gas-fired** ADJ Gas-, gasbefeuert *(form)*; ~ **power station** Gaskraftwerk *nt*; **gas fitter** N Gasinstallateur(in) *m(f)*; **gas fittings** PL Gasgeräte *pl*; **gas fixture** N fest installiertes Gasgerät; **gas guzzler** N *(esp US inf)* Säufer *m*, Benzinschlucker *m (inf)*

gash [gæʃ] N *(= wound)* klaffende Wunde; *(in earth, tree)* (klaffende) Spalte; *(= slash)* tiefe Kerbe; *(in upholstery)* tiefer Schlitz VT aufschlitzen; *furniture, wood* tief einkerben; **he fell and ~ed his head/knee** er ist gestürzt und hat sich *(dat)* dabei den Kopf/das Knie aufgeschlagen

gas: **gas heater** N Gasofen *m*; **gasholder** N Gasometer *m*, (Groß)gasbehälter *m*; **gas jet** N Gasdüse *f*

gasket ['gæskɪt] N *(Tech)* Dichtung *f*

gas: **gas lamp** N Gaslampe *f*; *(in streets)* Gaslaterne *f*; **gaslight** N **a** = **gas lamp b** *no pl* Gaslicht *nt or* -beleuchtung *f*; **gas lighter** N **a** Gasanzünder *m* **b** *(for cigarettes etc)* Gasfeuerzeug *nt*; **gas lighting** N Gasbeleuchtung *f*; **gas-lit** ADJ mit Gasbeleuchtung; **gas main** N Gasleitung *f*; **gasman** N Gasmann *m (inf)*; **gas mantle** N (Gas)glühstrumpf *m*; **gas mask** N Gasmaske *f*; **gas meter** N Gaszähler *m or* -uhr *f*

gasoline ['gæsəʊliːn] N *(US)* Benzin *nt*

gasometer [gæ'sɒmɪtə'] N Gasometer *m*, (Groß)gasbehälter *m*

gas oven N Gasherd *m*; *(= gas chamber)* Gaskammer *f*; **to put one's head in the** ~ *(= kill oneself, also hum)* den Gashahn aufdrehen

gasp [gɑːsp] N *(for breath)* tiefer Atemzug; **the ~s of the runner** das Keuchen des Läufers; **to give a** ~ **(of surprise/fear** *etc*) (vor Überraschung/Angst *etc*) die Luft anhalten *or* nach Luft schnappen *(inf)*; **a ~ went up at his audacity** seine Verwegenheit verschlug den Leuten den Atem; **to be at one's last** ~ in den letzten Zügen liegen; *(= exhausted etc)* auf dem letzten Loch pfeifen *(inf)*; **this was the last ~ of the reform movement** das war das letzte Aufbäumen der Reformbewegung
VI *(continually)* keuchen; *(once)* tief einatmen; *(with surprise etc)* nach Luft schnappen *(inf)*; **to make sb** ~ *(lit, fig)* jdm den Atem nehmen; **to ~ for breath** *or* **air** nach Atem ringen, nach Luft schnappen *(inf)*; **he ~ed with astonishment** er war so erstaunt, dass es ihm den Atem verschlug; **heavens, no!, she ~ed** um Himmels willen, nein!, stieß sie hervor; **I'm ~ing for a cup of tea/a cigarette** *(inf)* ich lechze nach einer Tasse Tee/einer Zigarette *(inf)*, ich brauche dringend eine Tasse Tee/eine Zigarette

▶ **gasp out** VT *sep* hervorstoßen

gas pedal N *(esp US)* Gaspedal *nt*

gasper ['gɑːspə'] N *(Brit inf)* Glimmstängel *m (dated inf)*

gas: **gas-permeable** ADJ *lenses* gasdurchlässig; **gas pipe** N Gasrohr *nt or* -leitung *f*; **gas plasma** N Gasplasma *nt*; **gas pump** N *(US)* Zapfsäule *f*; **gas ring** N Gasbrenner *m*; *(portable)* Gaskocher *m*; **gas station** N *(US)* Tankstelle *f*; **gas stove** N Gasherd *m*; *(portable)* Gaskocher *m*

gassy ['gæsɪ] ADJ *(+er)* **a** *(Sci)* gasförmig; **it smells** ~ es riecht nach Gas **b** *drink* kohlensäurehaltig **c** *(inf) person* geschwätzig

gas: **gas tank** N *(US)* Benzintank *m*; **gas tap** N Gashahn *m*; **gastight** ADJ gasdicht

gastric ['gæstrɪk] ADJ Magen-, gastrisch *(spec)*; ~ **acid** Magensäure *f*

gastric: **gastric band** N Magenband *nt*; **gastric flu, gastric influenza** N Darmgrippe *f*; **gastric juices** PL Magensäfte *pl*; **gastric ulcer** N Magengeschwür *nt*

gastritis [gæs'traɪtɪs] N Magenschleimhautentzündung *f*, Gastritis *f*

gastro- ['gæstrəʊ-] PREF Magen-, Gastro- *(spec)*

gastroenteritis [ˌgæstrəʊˌentə'raɪtɪs] N Magen-Darm-Entzündung *f*, Gastroenteritis *f (spec)*

gastroenterologist [ˌgæstrəʊˌentə'rɒlədʒɪst] N Gastroenterologe *m*, Gastroenterologin *f*

gastroenterology [ˌgæstrəʊˌentə'rɒlədʒɪ] N Gastroenterologie *f*

gastronome ['gæstrənəʊm] N Feinschmecker(in) *m(f)*

gastronomic [ˌgæstrə'nɒmɪk] ADJ gastronomisch, kulinarisch

gastronomy [gæs'trɒnəmɪ] N Gastronomie *f*

gastropod ['gæstrəpɒd] N Bauchfüß(l)er *m*, Gastropode *m (spec)*

gastropub ['gæstrəʊpʌb] N **a** *Restaurant mit Kneipenatmosphäre* **b** *Kneipe mit größerer Speisekarte*

gastroscopy [gæ'strɒskəpɪ] N *(Med)* Gastroskopie *f (spec)*, Magenspiegelung *f*

gaswoman ['gæswʊmən] N *pl* **-women** [-wɪmɪn] Frau *f* vom Gaswerk

gasworks ['gæswɜːks] N *sing or pl* Gaswerk *nt*

gate [geɪt] N **a** Tor *nt*; *(small, = garden gate)* Pforte *f*; *(= five-barred gate)* Gatter *nt*; *(in station)* Sperre *f*; *(in airport)* Flugsteig *m*; *(of level crossing)* Schranke *f*; *(Sport: = starting gate)* Startmaschine *f*; *(= sports ground entrance)* Einlass *m*, Eingang *m*; **to open/shut the ~(s)** das Tor *etc* öffnen/schließen; **the ~s of heaven** das Himmelstor, die Himmelstür *or* -pforte **b** *(Sport: = attendance)* Zuschauerzahl *f*; *(= entrance money)* Einnahmen *pl* VT *pupil, student* Ausgangssperre erteilen *(+dat)*

-gate [-geɪt] SUF -Skandal *m*, -Affäre *f*; **Irangate** der Iran(gate)-Skandal, die Iran(gate)-Affäre

gateau ['gætəʊ] N *pl* **gateaux** ['gætəʊz] *(esp Brit)* Torte *f*

gate: **gate-crash** *(inf)* VT **to ~ a party/meeting** in eine Party/Versammlung reinplatzen *(inf)*; *(crowd: = to disrupt it)* eine Party/Versammlung stürmen VI einfach so hingehen *(inf)*; **gatecrasher** N ungeladener Gast; *(at meeting)* Eindringling *m*

gated ['geɪtɪd] ADJ mit einem Tor versehen, durch ein Tor abgeschlossen; ~ **community** bewachtes Wohnviertel, bewachte Wohnanlage

gate: **gatehouse** N Pförtnerhaus *or* -häuschen *nt*; **gatekeeper** N Pförtner(in) *m(f)*; *(Rail)* Schrankenwärter(in) *m(f)*; **gate-leg(ged) table** N Klapptisch *m*; **gate money** N *(Sport)* Einnahmen *pl*; **gatepost** N Torpfosten *m*; **between you, me and the** ~ *(inf)* unter uns gesagt; **gateway** N *(lit, fig)* Tor *nt (to* zu); *(= archway, gate frame)* Torbogen *m*; **gateway drug** N Einstiegsdroge *f*

gather ['gæðə'] VT **a** *(= collect, bring together)* sammeln; *crowd, people* versammeln; *flowers, cultivated fruit* pflücken; *potatoes, corn etc* ernten; *harvest* einbringen; *taxes* einziehen; *support* gewinnen; *(= collect up) broken glass, pins etc* zusammenlegen, aufsammeln; *one's belongings, books, clothes* (zusammen)packen; **to ~ one's strength** Kräfte sammeln; **to ~ one's thoughts** seine Gedanken ordnen, sich sammeln; **velvet curtains ~ dust/dirt** Samtvorhänge sind Staub-/Schmutzfänger; **it just sat there ~ing dust** es stand nur da und verstaubte; **the serial ~ed a huge audience** die Serie gewann ein riesiges Publikum
b *(= increase)* **to ~ speed** schneller werden, an Geschwindigkeit gewinnen; **to ~ strength** stärker werden
c *(= infer)* schließen *(from* aus); **I ~ed that** das dachte ich mir; **I ~ from the papers that he has ...** wie ich aus den Zeitungen ersehe, hat er ...; **from what** *or* **as far as I can** ~ (so) wie ich es sehe; **I ~ his report is very detailed** ich nehme an, dass sein Bericht sehr detailliert ist; **I ~ she won't be coming** ich nehme an, dass sie nicht kommt; **as you will have/might have ~ed ...** wie Sie bestimmt/vielleicht bemerkt haben ...; **as can be ~ed from my report** wie aus meinem Bericht hervorgeht *or* zu ersehen ist
d **to ~ sb into one's arms** jdn in die Arme nehmen *or* schließen; **he ~ed her to him** er zog sie an sich; **she ~ed her mink around her** sie hüllte sich in ihren Nerz
e *(Sew)* kräuseln, raffen; *(at seam)* fassen
f *(Typ)* zusammentragen, kollationieren *(spec)*
VI **a** *(= collect, people)* sich versammeln; *(objects, dust etc)* sich (an)sammeln; *(clouds)* sich zusammenziehen; *(storm)* sich zusammenbrauen; **tears ~ed in her eyes** ihre Augen füllten sich mit Tränen
b *(= increase: darkness, force etc)* zunehmen *(in* an *+dat)*
c *(abscess etc)* sich mit Eiter füllen; *(pus)* sich sammeln
N *(Sew)* Fältchen *nt*; **there were ~s at the waist (of the skirt)** der Rock war in der Taille gekräuselt *or* gerafft *or* gefasst

▶ **gather (a)round** VI zusammenkommen; **come on, children, gather round!** kommt alle her, Kinder! VI *+prep obj* **they gathered (a)round the fire** sie versammelten *or* scharten sich um das Feuer

▶ **gather in** VT *sep* **a** *(= collect)* einsammeln; *crops* einbringen; *taxes* einziehen; *animals* zusammentreiben **b** *(Sew) cloth* fassen

▶ **gather together** VI zusammenkommen, sich versammeln VT *sep* einsammeln; *one's belongings, books* zusammenpacken; *people* versammeln; *team* zusammenstellen; *animals* zusammentreiben; **to gather oneself together** zu sich kommen; *(for jump etc)* sich bereit machen (for zu)

▶ **gather up** VT *sep* aufsammeln; *one's belongings* zusammenpacken; *hair* hochstecken; *skirts* (hoch)raffen; *(fig) pieces* auflesen; **he gathered himself up to his full height** er reckte sich zu voller Größe auf; **to gather up one's courage** seinen ganzen Mut zusammennehmen

gatherer ['gæðərəʳ] N Sammler(in) *m(f)* → **hunter-gatherer**

gathering ['gæðərɪŋ] N **a** *(= group)* Gruppe *f*; *(= assembly)* Versammlung *f*; **family ~** Familientreffen *nt*; **a social ~** ein geselliges Beisammensein **b** *(of people)* Versammeln *nt*; *(of objects)* Sammeln *nt*; *(of fruit)* Pflücken *nt*; *(of crops)* Ernte *f*; *(of speed)* Zunahme *f* **c** *(Sew)* Fältchen *nt* ADJ **a** *(= increasing) dusk, darkness, gloom* zunehmend; *storm, clouds* aufziehend **b** *(= assembling) crowd* zusammenlaufend

gator, 'gator ['geɪtəʳ] N *(US inf)* = **alligator**

GATT [gæt] *(Hist) abbr of* **General Agreement on Tariffs and Trade** GATT *nt*

gauche [gəʊʃ] ADJ *(socially)* unbeholfen, tölpelhaft; *remark* ungeschickt; *(= clumsy)* linkisch, ungeschickt

gauchely ['gəʊʃlɪ] ADV ungeschickt

gaucheness ['gəʊʃnɪs] N *(socially)* Unbeholfenheit *f*, Tölpelhaftigkeit *f*; *(of remark)* Ungeschicktheit *f*

gaucherie ['gəʊʃəriː] N **a** = **gaucheness b** *(= act)* Tölpelei *f*; *(= remark)* ungeschickte Bemerkung

gaucho ['gaʊtʃəʊ] N Gaucho *m*

gaudily ['gɔːdɪlɪ] ADV *painted, decorated, dressed* knallig *(inf)*, knallbunt; **~ coloured** *(Brit) or* **colored** *(US)* knallbunt; **a ~ patterned carpet** ein Teppich *m* mit einem knallbunten Muster

gaudiness ['gɔːdɪnɪs] N *(of colours)* Knalligkeit *f* *(inf)*; *(of clothes, paint etc)* Auffälligkeit *f*

gaudy ['gɔːdɪ] ADJ *(+er) clothes, paint etc* knallig *(inf)*, auffällig bunt; *colours* knallig *(inf)*

gauge [geɪdʒ] N **a** *(= instrument)* Messgerät *or* -instrument *nt*; *(to measure diameter, width etc)* (Mess)lehre *f*; *(for rings)* Ringmaß *nt*; *(to measure water level)* Pegel *m*; **pressure/wind ~** Druck-/Windmesser *m*
b *(= thickness, width, of wire, sheet metal etc)* Stärke *f*; *(of bullet)* Durchmesser *m*, Kaliber *nt*; *(Rail)* Spurweite *f*; **standard/narrow ~** Normal-/ /Schmalspur *f*
c *(fig)* Maßstab *m* (of für)
VT **a** *(Tech: = measure)* messen
b *(fig: = appraise) person's capacities, character, progress* beurteilen; *reaction, course of events* abschätzen; *situation* abwägen; *mood* einschätzen; *(= guess)* schätzen; **I tried to ~ whether she was pleased or not** ich versuchte zu beurteilen, ob sie sich freute oder nicht

Gaul [gɔːl] N *(= country)* Gallien *nt*; *(= person)* Gallier(in) *m(f)*

Gaullism ['gəʊlɪzəm] N Gaullismus *m*

Gaullist ['gəʊlɪst] ADJ gaullistisch N Gaullist(in) *m(f)*

gaunt [gɔːnt] ADJ **a** *(= haggard)* hager; *(= emaciated)* abgezehrt **b** *(liter: = stark) building* trist; *tree* dürr und kahl; *landscape* öde

gauntlet¹ ['gɔːntlɪt] N **a** *(of armour)* Panzerhandschuh *m*; **to throw down/pick up** *or* **take up the ~** *(fig)* den Fehdehandschuh hinwerfen/aufnehmen **b** *(= glove)* (Stulpen)handschuh *m*; *(= part of glove)* Stulpe *f*

gauntlet² N **to run the ~** *(fig)* Spießruten laufen; **to (have to) run the ~ of sth** einer Sache *(dat)* ausgesetzt sein

gauntness ['gɔːntnɪs] N **a** *(= haggardness)* Hagerkeit *f*; *(= emaciation)* Abgezehrtheit *f* **b** *(liter: = starkness, of building)* Tristheit *f*; *(of landscape)* Öde *f*

gauze [gɔːz] N Gaze *f*; *(Med also)* (Verbands)mull *m*

gauzy ['gɔːzɪ] ADJ *(+er)* hauchfein *or* -zart

gave [geɪv] *pret of* **give**

gavel ['gævl] N Hammer *m*

gavotte [gə'vɒt] N Gavotte *f*

gawk [gɔːk] *(inf)* N Schlaks *m (inf)* VI = **gawp**

gawkily ['gɔːkɪlɪ] ADV *move, walk* schlaksig, staksig *(inf)*

gawkiness ['gɔːkɪnɪs] N *(of person, movement)* Schlaksigkeit *f*, Staksigkeit *f (inf)*; *(of appearance)* Unbeholfenheit *f*

gawky ['gɔːkɪ] ADJ *(+er) person, movement* schlaksig, staksig *(inf)*, linkisch; *animal* unbeholfen, staksig *(inf)*; *appearance* unbeholfen

gawp [gɔːp] VI *(Brit inf)* glotzen *(inf)*, gaffen; **to ~ at sb/sth** jdn/etw anglotzen *(inf) or* angaffen; **what are you ~ing at?** was glotzt du da? *(inf)*

gay [geɪ] ADJ *(+er)* **a** *(= homosexual) person* schwul *(inf)*; *(= for homosexuals) rights* für Schwule; *sex* unter Schwulen; **~ men and women** Schwule und Lesben *pl (inf)*; **~ movement** Schwulenbewegung *f*; **~ bar** Schwulenkneipe *f*; **~ marriage** gleichgeschlechtliche Ehe, Homoehe *f (inf)*; **~ group** Schwulengruppe *f*; **the ~ community** die Schwulen *pl*
b *(dated, = happy)* fröhlich; *(= carefree)* sorglos, unbekümmert; *(= merry) party, time, atmosphere* lustig; *music* lebhaft; *(= colourful) paint, costumes* bunt; **with ~ abandon** völlig unbekümmert, ohne Rücksicht auf Verluste *(hum)*
N Schwule(r) *mf*; **~ lib** die Schwulenbewegung

Gaza Strip [gɑːzə'strɪp] N Gazastreifen *m*

gaze [geɪz] N Blick *m*; **in the public ~** im Blickpunkt der Öffentlichkeit VI starren; **to ~ at sb/sth** jdn/etw anstarren; **they ~d into each other's eyes** sie blickten sich tief in die Augen; **to ~ at oneself in the mirror** sich im Spiegel betrachten

▶ **gaze about** *(Brit) or* **around** VI um sich blicken; **he gazed about** *or* **around (him) at the strange scene** er sah sich *(dat)* erstaunt die seltsame Szene an

gazebo [gə'ziːbəʊ] N Gartenlaube *f*

gazelle [gə'zel] N Gazelle *f*

gazette [gə'zet] N *(= magazine)* Zeitung *f*, Gazette *f (dated)*; *(= government publication)* Staatsanzeiger *m*, Amtsblatt *nt* VT im Staatsanzeiger bekannt geben

gazetteer [,gæzɪ'tɪəʳ] N alphabetisches Ortsverzeichnis *(mit Ortsbeschreibung)*

gazump [gə'zʌmp] VT *(Brit) entgegen mündlicher Zusage ein Haus an einen Höherbietenden verkaufen*

GB **a** *abbr of* **Great Britain** GB *nt*, Großbritannien *nt* **b** *abbr of* **gigabyte** GB

gbh *abbr of* **grievous bodily harm**

GC *(Brit) abbr of* **George Cross** *Tapferkeitsmedaille*

GCE *(Brit) abbr of* **General Certificate of Education**

GCH *abbr of* **gas(fired) central heating** Gaszentralheizung *f*

GCHQ *(Brit) abbr of* **Government Communications Headquarters** *Zentralstelle des britischen Nachrichtendienstes*

GCSE *(Brit) abbr of* **General Certificate of Secondary Education**

> **GCSE**
>
> Das **General Certificate of Secondary Education** oder auch **GCSE** ist ein der mittleren Reife vergleichbarer Schulabschluss, den die meisten britischen Oberschüler mit sechzehn Jahren in einer Reihe von Fächern ablegen. Danach steigen sie entweder ins Berufsleben ein oder setzen ihre Schulausbildung bis zum A-Level-Abschluss fort. Die Abschlussnote beim **GCSE** setzt sich normalerweise aus einer Prüfungsnote und der kontinuierlichen Beurteilung der Jahresleistung zusammen, wobei Zensuren von A (die beste Note) bis G vergeben werden. Das schottische Äquivalent ist der **Standard Grade** → A LEVEL

Gdns *abbr of* **Gardens**

GDP *abbr of* **Gross Domestic Product** BIP *nt*

GDR *(Hist) abbr of* **German Democratic Republic** DDR *f*

gear [gɪəʳ] N **a** *(Aut etc)* Gang *m*; **~s** *pl (= mechanism)* Getriebe *nt*; *(on bicycle)* Gangschaltung *f*; **a bicycle with three ~s** ein Fahrrad *nt* mit Dreigangschaltung; **to put the car into ~** einen Gang einlegen; **the car is/you're in ~** der Gang ist drin *(inf) or* eingelegt; **the car is/you're not in ~** das Auto ist im Leerlauf, es ist kein Gang drin *(inf)*; **to leave the car in ~** den Gang eingelegt lassen; **to leave the car out of ~** das Auto im Leerlauf lassen; **to change** *(esp Brit) or* **shift** *(US)* **~** schalten; **to change** *(esp Brit) or* **shift** *(US)* **into third ~** in den dritten Gang schalten, den dritten Gang einlegen; **to move up/down through the ~s** (durch die einzelnen Gänge) herauf-/herunterschalten; **the car jumps out of** *or* **won't stay in ~** der Gang springt heraus; **to move up a ~** *(fig)* einen Gang zulegen *(inf)*; **I am usually in bottom ~ in the mornings** *(fig)* morgens dauert bei mir alles länger; **she lives life in top ~** sie lebt auf Hochtouren; **military production moved into high ~** die Kriegsproduktion wurde auf Hochtouren gebracht; **to get one's brain in(to) ~** *(inf)* seine Gehirnwindungen in Gang setzen → **arse a**
b *(inf: = equipment)* Ausrüstung *f*, Zeug *nt* *(inf)*, Sachen *pl (inf)*; *(= tools)* Gerät *nt*, Zeug *nt (inf)*; *(= belongings)* Sachen *pl (inf)*, Zeug(s) *nt (inf)*; *(= clothing)* Sachen *pl (inf)*
c *(Tech)* Vorrichtung *f* → **landing gear, steering gear**
d *(inf: = drugs)* Stoff *m (inf)*
VT *(fig)* abstellen, ausrichten (to auf +*acc*); **to be ~ed to(wards) sb/sth** auf jdn/etw abgestellt sein; *(person, needs, ambition)* auf jdn/etw ausgerichtet sein; *(= have facilities for)* auf jdn/etw eingerichtet sein; **training is ~ed to make staff more efficient** die Ausbildung ist darauf ausgerichtet, das Personal effizienter zu machen
VI *(Tech)* eingreifen, im Eingriff sein

▶ **gear down** VI *(driver)* herunterschalten, in einen niedrigeren Gang schalten VT *sep engine* niedertouriger auslegen *or* machen; *(fig)* drosseln

▶ **gear up** VI heraufschalten, in einen höheren Gang schalten VT *sep engine* höhertourig auslegen *or* machen; **to gear oneself up for sth** *(fig)* sich auf etw *(acc)* einstellen

gear: gearbox N Getriebe *nt*; **gear change** N Schalten *nt*

gearing ['gɪərɪŋ] N **a** *(Aut)* Auslegung *f* (der Gänge) **b** *(Fin, of company)* Verhältnis *nt* zwischen Eigen- und Fremdkapital

gear: gear lever N Schaltknüppel *m*; *(column-mounted)* Schalthebel *m*; **gear ratio** N Übersetzung(sverhältnis *nt*) *f*; **gearshift** *(US)*, **gear stick** N = **gear lever**; **gearwheel** N Zahnrad *nt*

gecko ['gekəʊ] N *pl* **-os** *or* **-oes** *(Zool)* Gecko *m*

GED *(US Sch) abbr of* **general equivalency diploma** *auf dem zweiten Bildungsweg erworbener Oberschulabschluss*

geddit ['gedɪt] INTERJ **~?** *(inf)* kapiert? *(inf)*

gee [dʒiː] INTERJ **a** *(esp US inf)* Mensch *(inf)*, Mann *(inf)*; **~ whiz!** Mensch Meier! *(inf)* **b** *(to horse)* **~ up!** hü!

gee-gee ['dʒiːdʒiː] N *(baby-talk)* Hottehü *nt* *(inf)*

geek [giːk] N *(esp US inf)* Waschlappen *m (inf)*

geek-speak ['giːkspiːk] N *(esp US inf)* Fachchinesisch *nt (inf)*

geeky ['giːkɪ] ADJ *(+er) (esp US inf)* dämlich *(inf)*

geese [giːs] *pl of* **goose**

geezer ['giːzəʳ] N *(inf)* Typ *m (inf)*, Kerl *m (inf)*; **old ~** Opa *m (inf)*

Geiger counter ['gaɪgə,kaʊntəʳ] N Geigerzähler *m*

geisha (girl) ['geɪʃə(gɜːl)] N Geisha *f*

gel [dʒel] N Gel *nt* VI gelieren; *(jelly etc also)* fest werden; *(fig) (plan, idea)* Gestalt annehmen; *(people)* sich verstehen

gelatin(e) ['dʒelətiːn] N Gelatine *f*

gelatinous [dʒɪ'lætɪnəs] ADJ gelatine- *or* gallertartig

geld [geld] VT kastrieren, verschneiden

gelding ['geldɪŋ] N kastriertes Tier, Kastrat *m (spec)*; *(= horse)* Wallach *m*

gelignite ['dʒelɪgnaɪt] N Plastiksprengstoff *m*

gem [dʒem] N Edelstein *m*; *(cut also)* Juwel *nt (geh)*; *(fig: = person)* Juwel *nt*; *(of collection etc)* Prachtstück *or* -exemplar *nt*; **thanks Pat, you're a ~** danke, Pat, du bist ein Schatz; **that story is a real ~** die Geschichte ist Spitzenklasse *(inf) or* einmalig gut; **every one a ~** *(inf)* einer besser als der andere; **a ~ of a book/painting** *(= splendid)* ein meisterhaftes Buch/Gemälde; **she's a ~ of a girl/writer** sie ist ein reizendes Mädchen/eine hervorragende Schriftstellerin

Gemini ['dʒemɪnaɪ] N Zwillinge *pl*; **he's (a) ~** er ist Zwilling

gemsbok ['gemzbɒk] N *pl* **-boks** *or collectively* **-bok** *(Zool)* Gemsantilope *f*

gemstone ['dʒemstəʊn] N Edelstein *m*

gemstone therapy N Edelsteintherapie *f*

Gen *abbr of* **General** Gen.

gen [dʒen] N *(Brit inf)* Informationen *pl*; **to give sb the ~ on** *or* **about sth** jdn über etw *(acc)* informieren; **to have some ~ on sth** Informationen über etw *(acc)* haben, etwas über etw *(acc)* wissen; **what's the ~ on this?** worum geht es hier?

▶ **gen up** *(Brit inf)* VI **to gen up on sth** sich über etw *(acc)* informieren VT *sep* **to get genned up on sth** sich über etw *(acc)* informieren; **to be genned up on** *or* **about sth** sich in etw *(dat)* (sehr gut) auskennen

gender ['dʒendəʳ] N Geschlecht *nt*; **what ~ is this word?** welches Geschlecht hat dieses Wort?; **the feminine/masculine/neuter ~** das Femininum/Maskulinum/Neutrum

gender: **gender-bender** N *(inf)* **a** *(Comput)* = **gender changer** **b** *(= person)* **to be a ~** *(man)* feminin wirken; *(woman)* maskulin wirken; **gender changer** N *(Comput)* Stecker-Stecker-Adapter *m*; Buchse-Buchse-Adapter *m*; **gender issues** PL geschlechtsspezifische Fragen *pl*; **gender politics** PL Geschlechterpolitik *f*; **gender reassignment** N *(form)* Geschlechtsumwandlung *f*

gene [dʒiːn] N Gen *nt*, Erbfaktor *m*

genealogical [ˌdʒiːnɪə'lɒdʒɪkəl] ADJ genealogisch

genealogical tree N Stammbaum *m*

genealogist [ˌdʒiːnɪ'ælədʒɪst] N Genealoge *m*, Genealogin *f*, Stammbaumforscher(in) *m(f)*

genealogy [ˌdʒiːnɪ'ælədʒɪ] N Genealogie *f*, Stammbaumforschung *f*; *(= ancestry)* Stammbaum *m*

gene: **gene bank** N Genbank *f*; **gene pool** N Erbmasse *f*

genera ['dʒenərə] *pl of* **genus**

general ['dʒenərəl] ADJ allgemein; **to be ~** (= *not detailed or specific: wording, proposals*) allgemein gehalten sein; *(= vague)* unbestimmt *or* vage sein; *(promises, clause)* unverbindlich sein; *(= widespread: custom, weather etc)* weitverbreitet sein; **his ~ appearance** sein Aussehen im Allgemeinen; **this is not the ~ view** diese Ansicht wird nicht allgemein geteilt; **there was ~ agreement among the two groups** die beiden Gruppen waren sich grundsätzlich einig; **it met with ~ approval** es wurde allgemein gebilligt; **the ~ attitude toward(s) the war is optimistic** es herrscht allgemein eine optimistische Einstellung zum Krieg; **to be in ~ use** allgemein verbreitet sein; **fortune tellers are so ~ in their statements** Wahrsager halten ihre Aussagen so allgemein; **the ~ plan** *or* **idea is that ...** wir hatten uns/sie hatten sich *(dat) etc* das so gedacht, dass ...; **the ~ idea of that is to ...** damit soll bezweckt werden, dass ..., es geht dabei darum, dass ...; **that was the ~ idea** so war das gedacht; **the ~ idea is to wait and see** wir/sie *etc* wollen einfach mal abwarten; **I've got the ~ idea (of it)** ich habe eine Vorstellung *or* ich weiß so ungefähr, worum es geht; **to give sb a ~ idea of a subject** jdm eine ungefähre Vorstellung von einem Thema geben; **in ~ terms, in a ~ sense** generell; **she recounted in very ~ terms the events of recent months** sie berichtete in groben Zügen von den Ereignissen der letzten Monate; **I spoke in a ~ way** ich habe ganz allgemein gesprochen; **in the ~ direction of the village** ungefähr in Richtung des Dorfes; **my ~ advice would be to leave them alone** grundsätzlich würde ich Ihnen raten, sie in Ruhe zu lassen; **as a ~ rule** im Allgemeinen; **a ~ ache** ein unbestimmter Schmerz; **~ labourer** ungelernter Arbeiter, ungelernte Arbeiterin; **~ drudge** Mädchen *nt* für alles; **~ reader** Durchschnittsleser(in) *m(f)*

N **a** **in ~** im Allgemeinen; **to go from the ~ to the particular** vom Allgemeinen ins Besondere gehen

b *(Mil)* General(in) *m(f)*

general: **general anaesthetic**, *(US)* **general anesthetic** N Vollnarkose *f*; **General Assembly** N *(of United Nations)* Voll- *or* Generalversammlung *f*; *(Eccl)* Generalsynode *f*; **General Certificate of Education** N *(Brit)* (= *O level*) ≈ mittlere Reife; (= *A level*) ≈ Reifezeugnis *nt*, ≈ Abitur *nt*; **General Certificate of Secondary Education** N *(Brit)* Abschluss *m* der Sekundarstufe, ≈ mittlere Reife; **general confession** N **the ~** *(Rel)* das allgemeine Sündenbekenntnis; **general dealer** N *(US)* = **general store**; **general degree** N *nicht spezialisierter Studienabschluss*; **general delivery** ADV *(US, Canada Post: = poste restante)* postlagernd; **general election** N Parlamentswahlen *pl*; **general factotum** N Mädchen *nt* für alles; **general headquarters** N *sing or pl (Mil)* Generalkommando *nt*; **general holiday** N Feiertag *m* (für alle); **general hospital** N Allgemeinkrankenhaus *nt*

generalissimo [ˌdʒenərə'lɪsɪməʊ] N Generalissimus *m*

generalist ['dʒenərəlɪst] N Generalist(in) *m(f)*

generality [ˌdʒenə'rælɪtɪ] N **a** **to talk in generalities** ganz allgemein sprechen **b** *(= general quality)* Allgemeinheit *f*; *(= general applicability)* Allgemeingültigkeit *f*; **a rule of great ~** eine fast überall anwendbare Regel

generalization [ˌdʒenərəlaɪ'zeɪʃən] N Verallgemeinerung *f*

generalize ['dʒenərəlaɪz] VI verallgemeinern; **to ~ from sth** allgemeine Schlüsse aus etw ziehen; **to ~ about sth** etw verallgemeinern VT verallgemeinern

general: **general knowledge** N Allgemeinwissen *nt or* -bildung *f* ATTR zur Allgemeinbildung; **general linguistics** N *sing* allgemeine Sprachwissenschaft

generally ['dʒenərəlɪ] ADV **a** *(= on the whole, for the most part)* im Großen und Ganzen; **this is ~ true** das trifft im Großen und Ganzen zu **b** *(= usually, as a rule)* im Allgemeinen, meist; **they are ~ cheapest** sie sind meist *or* in der Regel am billigsten **c** *(= widely) accepted, recognized* allgemein; *available* überall, allgemein **d** *(= in general)* im Allgemeinen; **information on things ~** allgemeine Informationen; **a few words on grants ~** ein paar Worte zu Stipendien allgemein *or* im Allgemeinen; **~ speaking** im Allgemeinen

general: **general manager** N Hauptgeschäftsführer(in) *m(f)*; **general medicine** N Allgemeinmedizin *f*; **general meeting** N Generalversammlung *f*, Vollversammlung *f*; *(of shareholders etc)* Hauptversammlung *f*; **General Officer Commanding** N *(Mil)* Oberbefehlshaber(in) *m(f)*; **general pardon** N Generalamnestie *f*; **general partnership** N *(Jur)* offene Handelsgesellschaft; **General Post Office** N *(Brit: = building)* Hauptpost(amt *nt*) *f*; *(dated, = organization)* Post *f*; **general practice** N *(Brit Med)* **a** *(= work)* Allgemeinmedizin *f*; **to be in ~** praktischer Arzt/praktische Ärztin sein **b** *(= place)* allgemeinärztliche Praxis, Allgemeinpraxis *f*; **general practitioner** N Arzt *m*/Ärztin *f* für Allgemeinmedizin, praktischer Arzt, praktische Ärztin; **general public** N Öffentlichkeit *f*, Allgemeinheit *f*; **general-purpose** ADJ Universal-; **~ cleaner** Universalreiniger *m*; **general science** N *(Sch)* Naturwissenschaft *f*; **~ teacher** Naturwissenschaftslehrer(in) *m(f)*; **General Secretary** N Generalsekretär(in) *m(f)*

generalship ['dʒenərəlʃɪp] N *(Mil)* **a** *(= office)* Generalsrang *m*; *(= period of office)* Dienstzeit *f* als General; **under his ~** als er General war **b** *(= skill)* Feldherrnkunst *f*

general: **general staff** N *(Mil)* Generalstab *m*; **general store** N Gemischtwarenhandlung *f*; **general strike** N Generalstreik *m*; **General Studies** PL *(Brit Sch)* *Kurs zur Vermittlung von Allgemeinwissen an spezialisierte Schüler*

generate ['dʒenəreɪt] VT *(lit, fig)* erzeugen; *heat, fumes also* entwickeln; *jobs* schaffen; *income* einbringen; *interest* wecken; *excitement* hervorrufen; *(Ling)* generieren

generating station ['dʒenəreɪtɪŋˌsteɪʃən] Kraftwerk *nt*, Elektrizitätswerk *nt*

generation [ˌdʒenə'reɪʃən] N **a** *(lit, fig)* Generation *f*; **within a ~** in einer Generation **b** *(= act of generating)* Erzeugung *f*; *(of jobs)* Schaffung *f*

generational [ˌdʒenə'reɪʃənl] ADJ *(within particular generation)* der/einer Generation; **~ conflict/divide** Generationskonflikt *m*; **~ differences** Generationsunterschied *m*

generation gap N **the ~** Generationsunterschied *m*; *(as an issue)* Generationskonflikt *m*

generative ['dʒenərətɪv] ADJ *(Biol)* Zeugungs-, generativ *(spec)*; *(Elec)* Erzeugungs-; **~ organs** *(Biol)* Zeugungsorgane *pl*

generative grammar N generative Grammatik, Erzeugungsgrammatik *f*

generator ['dʒenəreɪtəʳ] N Generator *m*

generic [dʒɪ'nerɪk] ADJ artmäßig; **~ name** *or* **term** Oberbegriff *m*; *(Biol)* Gattungsbegriff *or* -name *m*; **~ group** Gattung *f*

generically [dʒɪ'nerɪkəlɪ] ADV *(Biol)* gattungsmäßig; **they could be ~ described as ...** sie könnten unter dem Oberbegriff ... zusammengefasst werden

generic drug N Generikum *nt*

generosity [ˌdʒenə'rɒsɪtɪ] N **a** Großzügigkeit *f*; *(of terms)* Günstigkeit *f* **b** *(= nobleness)* Großmut *m*

generous ['dʒenərəs] ADJ **a** *(= liberal) person, mood* großzügig; **they were in a less ~ mood** sie waren weniger großzügig; **to be ~ in one's praise** mit Lob nicht geizen, voll des Lobes sein *(geh)*; **to be ~ with one's time** großzügig mit seiner Zeit umgehen; **he was ~ in sharing his knowledge** er ließ andere an seinem Wissen großzügig teilhaben

b *(= lavish) gift, hospitality, subsidy, prize, sum, offer* großzügig; *terms* günstig; *(= plentiful) portion, supply* reichlich; **a ~ amount** *or* **helping of ...** eine reichliche Portion ...; **to be a ~ size** großzügig bemessen sein; **a ~ size 14** eine groß ausgefallene Größe 14; **with the ~ support of ...** mit großzügiger Unterstützung von ...; **the car has a ~ boot** *(Brit) or* **trunk** *(US)* der Wagen hat einen großzügigen Kofferraum

c *(= kind) person, gesture, spirit* großmütig; *remarks* wohlwollend; **she was ~ in defeat** sie war eine großmütige Verliererin; **they were ~ enough to overlook the mistake** sie waren so großzügig, den Fehler zu übersehen

generously ['dʒenərəslɪ] ADV **a** *(= liberally) give, donate, provide* großzügigerweise; *reward* großzügig; **to provide ~ for sb** großzügig für jdn sorgen; **please give ~ (to ...)** wir bitten um großzügige Spenden (für ...) **b** *(= kindly) offer, agree* großmütigerweise **c** *(= amply) sized, pro-*

portioned, equipped großzügig; ~ **cut shirts** weit *or* großzügig geschnittene Hemden; **to season** ~ *(Cook)* reichlich würzen; **a ~ illustrated book** ein reich illustriertes Buch

generousness ['dʒenərəsnɪs] N **a** = **generosity** **b** *(of portion, supply)* Reichlichkeit *f*

genesis ['dʒenɪsɪs] N *pl* **geneses** ['dʒenɪsiːz] Entstehung *f*, Genese *f (spec)*; **(the Book of) Genesis** (die) Genesis, das erste Buch Mose

gene therapy N *(Med)* Gentherapie *f*

genetic [dʒɪ'netɪk] ADJ genetisch; **does crime have a ~ cause?** ist Kriminalität erblich bedingt?; ~ **information** Erbinformation *f*; ~ **modification** gentechnische Veränderungen *pl*

genetically [dʒɪ'netɪkəlɪ] ADV genetisch; ~ **engineered** genmanipuliert; ~ **modified** gentechnisch verändert

genetic: **genetic code** N genetischer Code; **genetic counselling**, *(US)* **genetic counseling** N genetische Beratung; **genetic engineer** N Gentechniker(in) *m(f)*; **genetic engineering** N Gentechnologie *f*; *(= manipulation)* Genmanipulation *f*; **genetic fingerprint** N genetischer Fingerabdruck; **genetic fingerprinting** N genetische Fingerabdrücke *pl*

geneticist [dʒɪ'netɪsɪst] N Vererbungsforscher(in) *m(f)*, Genetiker(in) *m(f)*

genetics [dʒɪ'netɪks] N *sing* Vererbungslehre *f*, Genetik *f*

Geneva [dʒɪ'niːvə] N Genf *nt*; **Lake ~** der Genfer See

Geneva Convention N Genfer Konvention *f*

genial ['dʒiːnɪəl] ADJ *person (= affable, cordial)* herzlich; *(= jovial)* leutselig; *(= sociable)* gesellig; *smile* freundlich; *company, atmosphere* angenehm; *warmth* wohltuend; **a ~ host** ein warmherziger Gastgeber; **a kind ~ face** ein freundlich lächelndes Gesicht; **in a ~ mood** gut aufgelegt

geniality [,dʒiːnɪ'ælɪtɪ] N *(of person)* Herzlichkeit *f*; *(= good humour also)* gute Laune; *(= joviality)* Leutseligkeit *f*; *(= sociableness)* Geselligkeit *f*; *(of smile)* Freundlichkeit *f*

genially ['dʒiːnɪəlɪ] ADV *smile, wave* freundlich; *laugh* herzlich; *(= jovially)* leutselig

genie ['dʒiːnɪ] N dienstbarer Geist; **the ~ is out of the bottle** *(fig)* der Geist ist aus der Flasche; **to let the ~ out of the bottle** *(fig)* den Geist aus der Flasche lassen; **to put the ~ back in the bottle** *(fig)* den Geist wieder in die Flasche bannen

genii ['dʒiːnɪaɪ] *pl of* **genius**

genital ['dʒenɪtl] ADJ Geschlechts-, Genital-, genital; ~ **organs** Geschlechts- *or* Genitalorgane *pl*

genital herpes N Herpes genitalis *m*

genitalia [,dʒenɪ'teɪlɪə] PL *(form)* Genitalien *pl*

genitals ['dʒenɪtlz] PL Geschlechtsteile *pl*, Genitalien *pl*

genital warts PL Feigwarzen *pl*

genitive ['dʒenɪtɪv] **N** *(Gram)* Genitiv *m*; **in the ~** im Genitiv **ADJ** Genitiv-; ~ **object** Genitivobjekt *nt*; ~ **case** Genitiv *m*

genitor ['dʒenɪtəʳ] N *(Biol)* Erzeuger *m*

genius ['dʒiːnɪəs] N *pl* **-es** *or* **genii** **a** Genie *nt*; *(= mental or creative capacity)* Genius *m*, Schöpferkraft *f*; **her real ~ as a designer** ihre Genialität als Designerin; **a man of ~** ein genialer Mensch, ein Genie *nt*; **to have a ~ for sth/doing sth** *(= talent)* eine besondere Gabe für etw haben/dafür haben, etw zu tun; **her ~ for languages** ihre hohe Sprachbegabung; **she has a ~ for controversy** sie hat ein Talent dafür, Streit anzufangen; **a flash of ~** eine geniale Eingebung **b** *(= spirit: of period, country etc)* (Zeit)geist *m* **c** *(= bad influence)* **evil ~** böser Geist

Genoa ['dʒenəʊə] N Genua *nt*

Genoa cake N *mandelverzierter Früchtekuchen*

genocidal [,dʒenəʊ'saɪdl] ADJ *war, campaign* völkermordähnlich; ~ **crime** Völkermord- *or* Genozidverbrechen *nt*

genocide ['dʒenəʊsaɪd] N Völkermord *m*, Genozid *nt (geh)*

Genoese [,dʒenəʊ'iːz] **ADJ** genuesisch **N** Genuese *m*, Genuesin *f*

genome ['dʒiːnəʊm] N *(Biol)* Genom *nt*

genotype ['dʒenəʊtaɪp] N Genotyp(us) *m*, Erbgut *nt*

genre ['ʒɑ̃ːŋrə] N Genre *nt (geh)*, Gattung *f*; *(Art: also* **genre painting***)* Genremalerei *f*

gent [dʒent] N *(inf) abbr of* **gentleman** Herr *m*; **~s' shoes/outfitter** *(Comm)* Herrenschuhe *pl*/-ausstatter *m*; **"Gents"** *(Brit: = lavatory)* „Herren"; **where is the ~s?** wo ist die Herrentoilette?

genteel [dʒen'tiːl] **ADJ** **a** *(= refined) person, institution, atmosphere, place* vornehm; *family, manners* vornehm, fein; **to live in ~ poverty** arm, aber vornehm leben → **shabby** **b** *(= overpolite)* geziert; *(= euphemistic) term, language* beschönigend **N** **the genteel** **PL** *(form)* die Vornehmen *pl*

genteelly [dʒen'tiːlɪ] ADV vornehm; *(= overpolitely)* geziert

gentian ['dʒenʃɪən] N Enzian *m*

Gentile ['dʒentaɪl] **N** Nichtjude *m*, Nichtjüdin *f* **ADJ** nichtjüdisch, nicht jüdisch

gentility [dʒen'tɪlɪtɪ] N Vornehmheit *f*

gentle ['dʒentl] ADJ *(+er)* **a** *person, disposition* sanft(mütig); *animal* zahm; *voice, eyes, manner, smile* sanft; *treatment* schonend; **to be ~ with sb** *(physically)* sanft *or* behutsam mit jdm umgehen; *(mentally)* sanft *or* einfühlsam mit jdm umgehen; **to be ~ with** etw vorsichtig *or* behutsam mit etw umgehen; **as ~ as a lamb** sanft wie ein Lamm; **she needs ~ treatment** sie muss behutsam behandelt werden; **the ~** *or* **~r sex** *(dated)* das zarte Geschlecht

b *(= light, soft) touch, caress* sanft, zart; *hand* sanft, behutsam; *movement, pressure, breeze, wind, rain* sanft, leicht; *(= low) heat* mäßig; *(= not severe) hill, slope, curve, landscape* sanft; *colour* sanft, zart; *sound* leise; *pace, stroll, exercise* gemächlich; **cook over a ~ heat** bei geringer Hitze kochen; **we made ~ progress** wir machten langsame, aber stetige Fortschritte

c *(= mild) detergent, lotion, cream* mild; **this detergent is ~ on the skin** dieses Putzmittel schont die Haut

d *(= subtle, discreet)* mild; *rebuke* sanft, mild; *persuasion* freundlich, sanft; **a ~ hint** eine zarte Andeutung; **a ~ reminder** ein zarter Wink, ein sanfter Hinweis; **to poke ~ fun at sb, to have a ~ dig at sb** jdn freundlich necken

e *(= wellborn)* **of ~ birth** *(dated form)* von edler *or* hoher Geburt

gentlefolk ['dʒentlfəʊk] PL *(dated)* vornehme *or* feine Leute *pl*

gentleman ['dʒentlmən] N *pl* **-men** [-mən] **a** *(well-mannered, well-born)* Gentleman *m*, Herr *m*; *(trustworthy)* Ehrenmann *m*, Gentleman *m*; **he's a real ~** er ist ein richtiger Gentleman; **be a ~ and take her home** sei ein richtiger Gentleman und bringe sie nach Hause **b** *(= man)* Herr *m*; **gentlemen!** meine Herren!; *(in business letter)* sehr geehrte Herren!; **gentlemen of the jury/press!** meine Herren Geschworenen/von der Presse! **c** *(dated: with private income)* Privatier *m*; *(Hist, rank)* Mann *m* von Stand; *(at court)* Höfling *m*; **~-farmer** Gutsbesitzer *m*

gentlemanly ['dʒentlmənlɪ] ADJ *man, manner, behaviour* ritterlich, gentlemanlike *pred*; **of ~ appearance** vornehm aussehend; **in an orderly and ~ way** ordentlich und wie Gentlemen/ein Gentleman; **in a ~ manner** in der Art von Gentlemen/eines Gentlemans; **that is hardly ~ conduct** dieses Verhalten gehört sich nicht für einen Gentleman

gentlemen's agreement ['dʒentlmənzə'griːmənt] N Gentlemen's Agreement *nt*; *(esp in business)* Vereinbarung *f* auf Treu und Glauben

gentlemen's club N ['dʒentlmənz'klʌb] *(esp Brit) Klub, zu dem nur Männer bestimmter Gesellschaftsschichten zugelassen sind*

gentleness ['dʒentlnɪs] N **a** Sanftheit *f*; *(of animal)* Zahmheit *f*; *(of treatment)* Behutsamkeit *f*; *(of touch, colour)* Zartheit *f*, Sanftheit *f*; *(of pace, exercise)* Gemächlichkeit *f* **b** *(= mildness: of detergent, lotion, cream)* Milde *f* **c** *(= subtlety)* Milde *f*

gentlewoman ['dʒentlwʊmən] N *pl* **-women** [-wɪmɪn] *(dated)* Dame *f* (von Stand); *(at court)* Hofdame *f*; *(Hist, = attendant)* Zofe *f*

gently ['dʒentlɪ] ADV *say, smile, slope, fall* sanft; *move, shake, touch, caress, handle, press* sanft, behutsam; *knock* leise; *stroll* gemächlich; *climb* leicht; *simmer, cook* langsam; *treat* schonend; **you must tell him ~** du musst es ihm schonend beibringen; **it/she needs to be handled ~** damit/mit ihr muss man behutsam umgehen; **~ does it!** sachte, sachte!; **the doctor told me to take things ~** der Arzt sagte mir, dass ich es langsam angehen lassen soll *(inf)*; **to simmer ~** auf kleiner Flamme langsam kochen (lassen)

gentrification [,dʒentrɪfɪ'keɪʃən] N Aufwertung *f (durch Renovierungsarbeiten, Zuzug von sozial Bessergestellten etc)*

gentrify ['dʒentrɪfaɪ] VT *area* aufwerten *(durch Renovierungsarbeiten, Zuzug von sozial Bessergestellten etc)*

gentry ['dʒentrɪ] PL **a** Gentry *f*, niederer Adel **b** *(dated pej: = people)* Leute *pl*

genuflect ['dʒenjʊflekt] VI *(Rel)* eine Kniebeuge machen

genuflection, **genuflexion** [,dʒenjʊ'flekʃən] N *(Rel)* Kniebeuge *f*

genuine ['dʒenjʊɪn] ADJ **a** *(= authentic, not fake) picture, antique, coin, leather, refugee, democracy* echt; **the picture is ~** *or* **the ~ article** das Bild ist echt *or* ein Original; **this is the ~ article!** *(inf: beer, food etc)* das ist das Wahre!; **she's the ~ article, a cook who loves cooking** *(inf)* sie ist eine richtige Köchin, die das Kochen wirklich liebt

b *(= sincere) person, commitment, disbelief, astonishment, feeling* aufrichtig; *concern, interest, buyer* ernsthaft; *offer, friendship, relationship* ernst gemeint, ernsthaft; *Christian, Communist etc* überzeugt; *love, enthusiasm, difficulty* echt; *mistake* wirklich; **she looked at me in ~ astonishment** sie sah mich aufrichtig erstaunt an

c *(= natural, not affected) person* natürlich, ungekünstelt

genuinely ['dʒenjʊɪnlɪ] ADV wirklich; **he is ~ interested in making it work** er ist wirklich *or* ernsthaft daran interessiert, dass es klappt; **they are ~ concerned** sie machen sich ernsthafte Sorgen; **I'm ~ sorry that Peter has gone** es tut mir wirklich leid, dass Peter gegangen ist

genuineness ['dʒenjʊɪnnɪs] N **a** *(= authenticity)* Echtheit *f* **b** *(= honesty, sincerity)* Aufrichtigkeit *f*; *(of concern, interest, offer, relationship)* Ernsthaftigkeit *f*; *(of love, enthusiasm)* Echtheit *f* **c** *(= naturalness)* Natürlichkeit *f*, Ungekünsteltheit *f*

genus ['dʒenəs] N *pl* **genera** *(Biol)* Gattung *f*

geocentric [,dʒiːəʊ'sentrɪk] ADJ geozentrisch

geochemistry [,dʒiːəʊ'kemɪstrɪ] N Geochemie *f*

geodesic [,dʒiːəʊ'desɪk] ADJ geodätisch

geodesic dome N Traglufthalle *f*

geodesy [dʒiː'ɒdɪsɪ] N Geodäsie *f*

geographer [dʒɪ'ɒgrəfəʳ] N Geograf(in) *m(f)*

geographic(al) [dʒɪə'græfɪk(əl)] ADJ geografisch

geographically [dʒɪə'græfɪkəlɪ] ADV *isolated* geografisch; *(introducing sentence)* geografisch gesehen

geography [dʒɪ'ɒgrəfɪ] N Geografie *f*; *(Sch also)* Erdkunde *f*; **policemen who knew the local ~** Polizisten, die sich vor Ort auskannten

geological ADJ, **geologically** ADV [dʒɪəʊ'lɒdʒɪkəl, -ɪ] geologisch

geologist [dʒɪ'ɒlədʒɪst] N Geologe *m*, Geologin *f*

geology [dʒɪ'ɒlədʒɪ] N Geologie *f*

geomancy ['dʒiːəʊmænsɪ] N Geomantie *f*

geometric(al) [ˌdʒɪəʊˈmetrɪk(əl)] ADJ geometrisch

geometrically [ˌdʒɪəʊˈmetrɪkəlɪ] ADV geometrisch

geometrician [ˌdʒɪəməˈtrɪʃən] N Fachmann *m*/-frau *f* für Geometrie, Geometer *m (old)*

geometry [dʒɪˈɒmɪtrɪ] N *(Math)* Geometrie *f*; **~ set** (Zirkelkasten *m* mit) Zeichengarnitur *f*

geophysics [ˌdʒiːəʊˈfɪzɪks] N *sing* Geophysik *f*

geopolitics [ˌdʒiːəʊˈpɒlɪtɪks] N *sing* Geopolitik *f*

Geordie [ˈdʒɔːdɪ] N *(inf) Bewohner(in)/Dialekt von Newcastle upon Tyne und Umgebung*

George [dʒɔːdʒ] N Georg *m*; **by ~!** *(dated Brit)* potz Blitz! *(dated inf)*; *(indicating determination)* bei Gott! *(dated)*

georgette [dʒɔːˈdʒet] N Georgette *f or m*

Georgia [ˈdʒɔːdʒɪə] N *(US)* Georgia *nt*; *(in Europe)* Georgien *nt*, Grusinien *nt*

Georgian [ˈdʒɔːdʒɪən] ADJ **a** *(Brit) architecture, house, style, period* georgianisch; **the ~-style library** die Bibliothek im georgianischen Stil **b** *(Geog, in Europe)* georgisch; *(in USA) capital, people, state boundary etc* von Georgia; *person* aus Georgia N **a** *(= person) (in USA)* Einwohner(in) *m(f)* von Georgia; *(in Europe)* Georgier(in) *m(f)* **b** *(Ling)* Georgisch *nt*, Grusinisch *nt*

geostationary [ˌdʒiːəʊˈsteɪʃənərɪ] ADJ geostationär

geothermal [ˌdʒiːəʊˈθɜːməl] ADJ geothermal

geranium [dʒɪˈreɪnɪəm] N Geranie *f*

gerbil [ˈdʒɜːbɪl] N Wüstenspringmaus *f*

geriatric [ˌdʒerɪˈætrɪk] ADJ **a** *(Med) patient* geriatrisch; **~ nurse** Altenpfleger(in) *m(f)* **b** *(pej inf)* altersschwach N **a** *(Med)* alter Mensch **b** *(pej inf: = senile person)* Tattergreis(in) *m(f) (pej inf)*

geriatric: **geriatric care** N Altenpflege *f*; **geriatric hospital** N geriatrische Klinik

geriatrician [ˌdʒerɪəˈtrɪʃən] N Facharzt *m*/-ärztin *f* für Geriatrie, Geriater(in) *m(f)*

geriatric medicine N Geratrie *f*, Altersheilkunde *f*

geriatrics [ˌdʒerɪˈætrɪks] N *sing* Geriatrie *f*, Altersheilkunde *f*

geriatric ward N Pflegestation *f (für alte Menschen)*, Geriatriestation *f*

germ [dʒɜːm] N *(lit, fig)* Keim *m*; *(of particular illness also)* Krankheitserreger *m*; *(esp of cold)* Bazillus *m*; **don't spread your ~s around** behalte deine Bazillen für dich

German [ˈdʒɜːmən] ADJ deutsch; **he is ~** er ist Deutscher; **she is ~** sie ist Deutsche N **a** *(= person)* Deutsche(r) *mf*; **the ~s** die Deutschen **b** *(Ling)* Deutsch *nt*; **~ lessons** Deutschunterricht *m*; **in ~** auf Deutsch; **to speak ~** Deutsch sprechen

German Democratic Republic N *(Hist)* Deutsche Demokratische Republik

germane [dʒɜːˈmeɪn] ADJ *(form)* von Belang *(geh)* (to für)

Germanic [dʒɜːˈmænɪk] ADJ **a** *(= German in character) voice, accent* deutsch klingend; *(= typically German) trait, style* (typisch) deutsch **b** *(Hist, Ling) language, people, tribe, society* germanisch

germanium [dʒɜːˈmeɪnɪəm] N *(Chem)* Germanium *nt*

Germanize [ˈdʒɜːmənaɪz] VT germanisieren; *word* eindeutschen

German: **German measles** N *sing* Röteln *pl*; **German shepherd (dog)**, *(US)* **German sheep dog** N Deutscher Schäferhund; **German-speaking** ADJ deutschsprachig; **~ Switzerland** die deutschsprachige Schweiz, die Deutschschweiz; **German text**, **German type** N *(Typ)* Fraktur *f*, Frakturschrift *f*

Germany [ˈdʒɜːmənɪ] N Deutschland *nt*

germ: **germ carrier** N Bazillenträger *m*; **germ cell** N *(Biol)* Keimzelle *f*; **germ-free** [ˈdʒɜːmfriː] ADJ keimfrei

germicidal [ˌdʒɜːmɪˈsaɪdl] ADJ keimtötend

germicide [ˈdʒɜːmɪsaɪd] N keimtötendes Mittel

germinal [ˈdʒɜːmɪnəl] ADJ *(fig)* aufkeimend *(geh)*

germinal disc N *(Biol)* Keimscheibe *f*

germinate [ˈdʒɜːmɪneɪt] VI keimen; *(fig)* aufkeimen *(geh)*; **he let the idea ~ in his mind** er ließ die Idee in sich *(dat)* keimen VT *(lit, fig)* keimen lassen

germination [ˌdʒɜːmɪˈneɪʃən] N *(lit)* Keimung *f*; *(fig)* Aufkeimen *nt (geh)*

germ: **germ-killer** N keimtötendes Mittel; **germ layer** N *(Biol)* Keimblatt *nt*; **germproof** ADJ keimsicher, keimfrei; **germ warfare** N bakteriologische Kriegsführung, Bakterienkrieg *m*

gerontocracy [ˌdʒerɒnˈtɒkrəsɪ] N Gerontokratie *f*

gerontologist [ˌdʒerɒnˈtɒlədʒɪst] N Gerontologe *m*, Gerontologin *f*

gerontology [ˌdʒerɒnˈtɒlədʒɪ] N Gerontologie *f*

gerrymander [ˈdʒerɪmændəˈ] *(Pol)* VT **to ~ constituency boundaries** Wahlkreisschiebungen vornehmen N Wahlkreisschiebung *f*

gerrymandering [ˈdʒerɪmændərɪŋ] N *(Pol)* Wahlkreisschiebungen *pl*

gerund [ˈdʒerənd] N Gerundium *nt*

gerundive [dʒɪˈrʌndɪv] N Gerundivum *nt*

Gestalt psychology [gəˈʃtæltsaɪˈkɒlədʒɪ] N Gestaltpsychologie *f*

Gestapo [geˈstɑːpəʊ] N Gestapo *f*

gestate [dʒeˈsteɪt] VI *(lit form, animal)* trächtig sein, tragen *(form)*; *(human)* schwanger sein; *(fig)* reifen VT tragen; *(fig)* in sich *(dat)* reifen lassen; *plan, idea* sich tragen mit *(geh)*

gestation [dʒeˈsteɪʃən] N *(lit, of animals)* Trächtigkeit *f*; *(of humans)* Schwangerschaft *f*; *(fig)* Reifwerden *nt*; **his book was 10 years in ~** der Reifungsprozess seines Buches dauerte 10 Jahre

gesticulate [dʒeˈstɪkjʊleɪt] VI gestikulieren; **to ~ at sb/sth** auf jdn/etw deuten

gesticulation [dʒeˌstɪkjʊˈleɪʃən] N *(= act)* Gestikulieren *nt*; *(= instance)* Gebärde *f (geh)*, Geste *f*; **all his ~s** all sein Gestikulieren

gesture [ˈdʒestʃəˈ] N *(lit, fig)* Geste *f*; **to make a ~** eine Geste machen; **a ~ of defiance/approval** eine herausfordernde/zustimmende Geste; **as a ~ of support/goodwill** als Zeichen der Unterstützung/des guten Willens; **his use of ~** seine Gestik VI gestikulieren; **to ~ at sb/sth** auf jdn/etw deuten; **he ~d with his head toward(s) the safe** er deutete mit dem Kopf auf den Safe VT **to ~ sb to do sth** jdm bedeuten *or* zu verstehen geben, etw zu tun

get [get]
pret **got**, *ptp* **got** *or (US)* **gotten**

1 TRANSITIVE VERB	3 REFLEXIVE VERB
2 INTRANSITIVE VERB	4 PHRASAL VERBS

1 – TRANSITIVE VERB

When *get* is part of a set combination, eg. *get the sack, get hold of, get it right*, look up the other word.

a [= receive] bekommen, kriegen *(inf)*; *sun, light, full force of blow* abbekommen, abkriegen *(inf)*; *wound* sich *(dat)* zuziehen; *wealth, glory* kommen zu; *time, personal characteristics* haben (*from* von); **where did you get it (from)?** woher hast du das?; **this country gets very little rain** in diesem Land regnet es sehr wenig; **he wanted to get all the glory** er wollte all den Ruhm (haben); **he got the idea for his book while he was abroad/from an old document** die Idee zu dem Buch kam ihm, als er im Ausland war/hatte er von einem alten Dokument; **where did you get that idea?** wie kommst du denn auf die Idee?; **I got quite a surprise** ich war ziemlich überrascht; **I got quite a shock** ich habe einen ziemlichen Schock gekriegt *(inf)* *or* bekommen; **I get the feeling that …** ich habe das Gefühl, dass …

b [= obtain by one's own efforts] *object* sich *(dat)* besorgen; *visa, money* sich *(dat)* beschaffen *or* besorgen; *(= find) staff, finance, partner, job* finden; *(= buy)* kaufen; *(= buy and keep) large item, car, cat* sich *(dat)* anschaffen; **not to be able to get sth** etw nicht bekommen *or* kriegen *(inf)* können; **to get sb/oneself sth, to get sth for sb/oneself** jdm/sich etw besorgen; *job* jdm/sich etw verschaffen; **to need to get sth** etw brauchen; **I've still three to get** ich brauche noch drei; **to get a glimpse of sb/sth** jdn/etw kurz zu sehen bekommen; **you'll have to get a job/more staff** Sie müssen zusehen, dass Sie eine Stelle/mehr Personal bekommen *or* finden; **he's been trying to get a house/job** er hat versucht, ein Haus/eine Stelle zu bekommen; **why don't you get a place of your own?** *(= buy)* warum schaffen Sie sich *(dat)* nicht eine eigene Wohnung an?; *(= rent)* warum nehmen Sie sich *(dat)* nicht eine eigene Wohnung?; **he got himself a wife/a good job** er hat sich *(dat)* eine Frau zugelegt *(inf)*/einen guten Job verschafft; **what are you getting her for Christmas?** was schenkst du ihr zu Weihnachten?; **I got her a doll for Christmas** ich habe für sie eine Puppe zu Weihnachten besorgt; **we could get a taxi** wir könnten (uns *dat*) ein Taxi nehmen; **could you get me a taxi?** könnten Sie mir ein Taxi rufen *or* besorgen?; **we don't get a paper** wir haben keine Zeitung abonniert

c [= fetch] *person, doctor, object* holen; **to get sb from the station** jdn vom Bahnhof abholen; **can I get you a drink?** möchten Sie etwas zu trinken?; **I got him/myself a drink** ich habe ihm/mir etwas zu trinken geholt; **why don't you get a dictionary and look it up?** warum sehen Sie nicht in einem Wörterbuch nach?

d [= catch] bekommen, kriegen *(inf)*; *(in children's game)* fangen; *(= take) train, bus* fahren mit; **to get sb by the arm/leg** jdn am Arm/Bein packen; **he's got it bad** *(inf)* den hats übel erwischt *(inf)*; **get him/it!** *(to dog)* fass!; **(I've) got him!** *(inf)* ich hab ihn! *(inf)*; **(I've) got it!** *(inf)* ich habs! *(inf)*; **got you!** *(inf)* hab dich (erwischt)! *(inf)*; **ha, ha, can't get me!** ha, ha, mich kriegst du nicht! *(inf)*; **my big brother will get you!** *(inf)* mein großer Bruder, der zeigts dir *or* der macht dich fertig! *(inf)*; **he's out to get you** *(inf)* er hats auf dich abgesehen *(inf)*; **we'll get them yet!** *(inf)* die werden wir schon noch kriegen! *(inf)*; **I'll get you for that!** *(inf)* das wirst du mir büßen!; **you've got me there!** *(inf)* da bin ich überfragt

e [= hit] treffen, erwischen *(inf)*

f [Rad, TV] bekommen, kriegen *(inf)*

g [Telec] *= contact* erreichen; *number* bekommen; *(= put through to, get for sb)* geben; **I'll get the number (for you)** *(switchboard)* ich verbinde Sie mit der Nummer; **get me 339/Mr Johnston please** *(to secretary)* geben Sie mir bitte 339/Herrn Johnston; *(to switchboard)* verbinden Sie mich bitte mit 339/Herrn Johnston; **you've got the wrong number** Sie sind falsch verbunden

h [= prepare] *meal* machen; **I'll get you/myself some breakfast** ich mache dir/mir etwas zum Frühstück

i [= eat] essen; **to get breakfast** frühstücken; **to get lunch** zu Mittag essen; **to get a snack** eine Kleinigkeit essen; **let's get Italian/Chinese/Indian** *etc* gehen wir zum Italiener/Chinesen/Inder (essen)

j [= send, take] bringen; **to get sb to hospital** jdn ins Krankenhaus bringen; **get the children to bed** bring die Kinder ins Bett; **they managed to get him home** sie schafften ihn nach Hause; **we'll get you there somehow** irgendwie kriegen wir dich schon dahin *(inf)*; **where does that get us?** *(inf)* was bringt uns *(dat)* das? *(inf)*; **this discussion isn't getting us anywhere** diese Diskussion führt zu nichts; **get the cat out of the room** tu die Katze aus dem Zimmer *(inf)*; **to get sth to sb** jdm etw zukommen lassen; *(= take it oneself)* jdm etw bringen; **tell him to get it there as quickly as pos-**

sible er soll zusehen, dass das so schnell wie möglich dorthin gebracht wird

k = manage to move bekommen, kriegen *(inf)*; **he couldn't get her up the stairs** er bekam *or* kriegte *(inf)* sie nicht die Treppe rauf; **he couldn't get himself out of bed** er kam nicht aus dem Bett

l = understand kapieren *(inf)*, mitbekommen; *(= hear)* mitbekommen, mitkriegen *(inf)*; *(= make a note of)* notieren; **I don't get it** *(inf)* da komme ich nicht mit *(inf)*; **I don't get you** *or* **your meaning** ich verstehe nicht, was du meinst; **get it?** *(inf)* kapiert? *(inf)*

m = profit, benefit **what do you get from it?** was hast du davon?, was bringt es dir? *(inf)*; **I don't get much from his lectures** seine Vorlesungen geben mir nicht viel; **he's only in it for what he can get** er will nur dabei profitieren

n in exclamations *iro inf* **get (a load of) that!** was sagst du dazu! *(inf)*, hat man Töne! *(inf)*; **get her!** *(regarding looks)* was sagst du zu der da? *(inf)*; *(iro)* sieh dir bloß die mal an! *(inf)*

o person *inf: = annoy* ärgern, aufregen; *(= upset)* an die Nieren gehen *(+dat)* *(inf)*; *(= thrill)* packen *(inf)*; *(= amuse)* amüsieren

p to form passive *inf* werden; **when did it last get painted?** wann ist es zuletzt gestrichen worden?; **I got paid** ich wurde bezahlt

q set structures

♦ **to get sb to do sth** *(= have sth done by sb)* etw von jdm machen lassen; *(= persuade sb)* jdn dazu bringen, etw zu tun; **I'll get him to phone you back** ich sage ihm, er soll zurückrufen; *(= make him)* ich werde zusehen, dass er zurückruft; **you'll never get him to understand** du wirst es nie schaffen, dass er das versteht

♦ **to get sb + participle** **you'll get me/yourself thrown out** du bringst es so weit, dass ich hinausgeworfen werde/du hinausgeworfen wirst; **that'll get him disqualified** damit wird er disqualifiziert; **has she got the baby dressed yet?** hat sie das Baby schon angezogen?

♦ **to get sth done/made** *etc* **to get sth done** etw gemacht kriegen *(inf)*; **to get the washing done** die Wäsche waschen; **to get some work done** Arbeit erledigen; **I'm not going to get much done** ich werde nicht viel geschafft kriegen *(inf)* *or* bekommen; **we ought to get it done soon** das müsste bald gemacht werden; **to get things done** was fertig kriegen *(inf)*; **to get sth made for sb/oneself** jdm/sich etw machen lassen; **to get one's hair cut** sich *(dat)* die Haare schneiden lassen; **I got the bathroom cleaned this morning** ich habe heute Morgen das Bad geputzt; **I'll get the grass cut/the house painted soon** *(by sb else)* ich lasse bald den Rasen mähen/das Haus streichen; **did you get your expenses paid/your question answered?** haben Sie Ihre Spesen erstattet/eine Antwort auf Ihre Frage bekommen?

♦ **to get sth/sb + adjective** *(= cause to be)* **to get sb/sth/oneself ready** jdn/etw/sich fertig machen; **to get sth clean/open/shut** *(person)* etw sauber kriegen/aufkriegen/zukriegen *(inf)*; **that'll get it clean** damit wird es sauber; **that'll get it open/shut** damit geht es auf/zu; **to get sb drunk** jdn betrunken machen *or (inf)* kriegen; **to get one's arm broken** sich *(dat)* den Arm brechen; **to get one's hands dirty** *(lit, fig)* sich *(dat)* die Hände schmutzig machen; **to get one's things packed** seine Sachen packen

♦ **to get sth to do sth** **I can't get the car to start** ich kriege das Auto nicht an *(inf)*; **he can't get the sum to work out/the lid to stay open** er kriegt es nicht hin, dass die Rechnung aufgeht/dass der Deckel aufbleibt *(inf)*; **can you get these two pieces to fit together?** kriegen Sie die beiden Teile zusammen; **can you get the wound to stop bleeding?** können Sie etwas machen, dass die Wunde nicht mehr blutet?; **once I've got this machine to work** wenn ich die Maschine erst einmal zum Laufen gebracht habe

♦ **to get sth/sb doing sth** **to get sth going** *(car, machine)* etw in Gang bringen; *party* etw in Fahrt bringen; **to get sb talking** jdn zum Sprechen bringen

♦ **to have got sth** *(Brit: = have)* etw haben

2 – INTRANSITIVE VERB

a = arrive kommen; **to get home** nach Hause kommen; **to get here** hier ankommen; **can you get to work by bus?** kannst du mit dem Bus zur Arbeit fahren?; **I've got as far as page 16** ich bin auf Seite 16

♦ **to get there** *(fig inf: = succeed)* es schaffen *(inf)*; **now we're getting there** *(to the truth)* jetzt kommts raus! *(inf)*; **how's the work going? – we're getting there!** wie geht die Arbeit voran? – langsam wirds was! *(inf)*

♦ **to get somewhere/nowhere** *(in job, career etc)* es zu etwas/nichts bringen; *(with work, in discussion etc)* weiterkommen/nicht weiterkommen; **to get somewhere/nowhere (with sb)** (bei jdm) etwas/nichts erreichen; **we're not getting anywhere by arguing like this** wir erreichen doch gar nichts, wenn wir uns streiten; **now we're getting somewhere** *(in project etc)* jetzt wird die Sache *(inf)*; *(in interrogation, discussion etc)* jetzt kommen wir der Sache schon näher; **to get nowhere fast** *(inf)* absolut nichts erreichen

♦ **to get far** *(lit)* weit kommen; *(fig)* es weit bringen; **you won't get far on £10** mit £ 10 kommst du nicht weit

b = become werden; **to get old/tired** *etc* alt/müde *etc* werden; **I'm getting cold/warm** mir wird es kalt/warm; **the weather is getting cold/warm** es wird kalt/warm; **to get dressed/shaved/washed** *etc* sich anziehen/rasieren/waschen *etc*; **to get married** heiraten; **to get free** sich befreien; **I'm getting bored** ich langweile mich langsam; **things can only get better** es kann nur besser werden; **to get lucky** *(inf)* Schwein haben *(inf)*; **how lucky can you get?** so ein Glück!; **how stupid can you get?** wie kann man nur so dumm sein?

♦ **to get started** anfangen; **let's get started** fangen wir an!

♦ **to get + infinitive** **to get to know sb/sth** jdn/etw kennenlernen; **how did you get to know about that?** wie hast du davon erfahren?; **to get to like sb** jdn sympathisch finden; **to get to like sth** an etw *(dat)* Gefallen finden; **after a time you get to realize ...** nach einiger Zeit merkt man ...; **to get to do sth** *(= get chance to)* die Möglichkeit haben, etw zu tun; **to get to be ...** (mit der Zeit) ... werden; **to get to see sb/sth** jdn/etw zu sehen bekommen; **to get to work** sich an die Arbeit machen

♦ **to get + -ing** **to get working/scrubbing** *etc* anfangen zu arbeiten/schrubben *etc*; **you lot, get cleaning/working!** ihr da, ans Putzen/an die Arbeit!; **I got talking to him** ich kam mit ihm ins Gespräch; **to get going** *(person, = leave)* aufbrechen; *(= start working)* sich daranmachen; *(= start talking)* loslegen *(inf)*; *(party etc)* in Schwung kommen; *(machine, fire etc)* in Gang kommen; **get going!** fang an!; *(= leave)* geh schon!

♦ **to have got to do sth** *(= be obliged to)* etw tun müssen; **I've got to** ich muss

3 – REFLEXIVE VERB

♦ **to get oneself ...**

= convey oneself gehen; *(= come)* kommen; **I had to get myself to the hospital** ich musste ins Krankenhaus (gehen); **how did you get yourself home?** wie bist du nach Hause gekommen?; **get yourself over here** komm hier rüber *(inf)*

with adjective sich ... machen; **to get oneself dirty/wet** sich schmutzig/nass machen; **to get oneself pregnant/fit** schwanger/fit werden

+ past participle **to get oneself washed/dressed** sich waschen/anziehen; **he managed to get himself promoted** er hat es geschafft, dass er befördert wurde; **he got himself hit in the leg** er wurde am Bein getroffen; **in order to get oneself elected** um gewählt zu werden; **you'll get yourself killed if you go on driving like that** du bringst dich noch um, wenn du weiter so fährst

4 – PHRASAL VERBS

► **get about** VI *(Brit)* *(prep obj* in *+dat)* **a** *(person)* sich bewegen können; *(to different places)* herumkommen **b** *(news)* sich herumsprechen; *(rumour)* sich verbreiten

► **get across** VI **a** *(= cross)* hinüberkommen; *(+prep obj) road, river* kommen über *(+acc)*; **to get across to the other side** auf die andere Seite kommen *or* gelangen

b *(= communicate, play, joke, comedian etc)* ankommen (*to* bei); *(teacher etc)* sich mitteilen (*to +dat*); *(idea, meaning)* klar werden, verständlich werden (*to +dat*)

VT *always separate* **a** *(= transport)* herüberbringen; *(= manage to get across)* herüberbekommen; *(+prep obj)* (herüber)bringen/-bekommen über *(+acc)*

b *(= communicate) play, joke* ankommen mit (*to* bei); *one's ideas, concepts* verständlich machen, mitteilen (*to sb* jdm); **he got his message across (to them)** er machte es ihnen klar *or* verständlich

► **get ahead** VI *(= make progress)* vorankommen (*in* in *+dat*); *(in race)* sich *(dat)* einen Vorsprung verschaffen; *(from behind)* nach vorn kommen; **to get ahead of sb** jdn überflügeln; *(in race)* einen Vorsprung zu jdm gewinnen; *(= overtake)* jdn überholen; **if he gets too far ahead in his reading** wenn er im Lesen den anderen zu weit voraus ist; **to get ahead of schedule** schneller als geplant vorankommen

► **get along** VI **a** *(= go)* gehen; **I must be getting along** ich muss jetzt gehen, ich muss mich auf den Weg machen; **get along now!** nun geh/geht schon!; **get along with you!** *(inf)* jetzt hör aber auf! *(inf)* **b** *(= manage)* zurechtkommen; **to get along without sb/sth** ohne jdn/etw auskommen *or* zurechtkommen **c** *(= progress)* vorankommen; *(work, patient etc)* sich machen **d** *(= be on good terms)* auskommen (*with* mit); **they get along quite well** sie kommen ganz gut miteinander aus

► **get around** VI **a** = **get about** **b** *(inf: = be promiscuous)* **he/she gets around** er/sie schläft mit jeder/jedem VTI *+prep obj* = **get round VI b VT c, d**

► **get around to** VI *+prep obj* = **get round to**

► **get at** VI *+prep obj* **a** *(= gain access to, reach)* herankommen an *(+acc)*; *town, house* erreichen, (hin)kommen zu; *(= take, eat etc) food, money* gehen an *(+acc)*; **put it where the dog won't get at it** stellen Sie es irgendwohin, wo der Hund nicht drankommt *(inf)*; **don't let him get at the whisky** lass ihn nicht an den Whisky (ran); **let me get at him!** *(inf)* na, wenn ich den erwische! *(inf)*; **the moths had got at the carpets** die Motten hatten sich an den Teppichen zu schaffen gemacht

b *(= discover, ascertain) truth* herausbekommen *or* -finden; *facts* kommen an *(+acc)*

c *(inf: = mean)* hinauswollen auf *(+acc)*; **what are you getting at?** worauf willst du hinaus?

d **to get at sb** *(inf: = criticize)* an jdm etwas auszusetzen haben *(inf)*; *(= nag)* an jdm herumnörgeln *(inf)*; **he had the feeling that he was being got at** *(inf)* er hatte den Eindruck, dass ihm das galt *or* dass man ihm was am Zeug flicken wollte *(inf)*; **are you trying to get at me?** hast du was an mir auszusetzen? *(inf)*

e *(inf: = corrupt)* beeinflussen; *(by threats)* unter Druck setzen *(inf)*; *(by bribes)* schmieren *(inf)*

f *(inf, = start work on)* sich machen an *(+acc)*

► **get away** VI *(= leave)* wegkommen; *(prisoner, thief)* entkommen, entwischen (*from sb* jdm); *(sportsman: from start)* loskommen *(inf)*; *(fig: = break away)* wegkommen *(inf)*; (*from* von) **I must get away from here** ich muss hier weg *(inf)*; **I'm looking forward to getting away** ich freue mich darauf, mal von hier wegzukommen; **I'd like to get away early today** ich würde heute gern früher gehen; **I just can't get away from him/my work** ich kann ihm/der Arbeit einfach nicht entrinnen; **you can't get away** *or* **there's no getting away from the fact**

that ... man kommt nicht um die Tatsache herum, dass ...; **to get away from it all** sich von allem frei machen *or* losmachen; **get away (with you)!** *(inf)* ach, hör auf! *(inf)*
VT *always separate (= remove)* wegbekommen; *(= move physically) person* weg- *or* fortbringen; *objects* wegschaffen; **get her away from here/him** sehen Sie zu, dass sie hier/von ihm wegkommt; **get them away from danger** bringen Sie sie außer Gefahr; **get him away from the propeller** sehen Sie zu, dass er von dem Propeller weggeht; **get him/that dog away from me** schaff ihn mir/schaff mir den Hund vom Leib; **to get sth away from sb** *(= take away)* jdm etw weg- *or* abnehmen

▶ **get away with** VI *+prep obj* **a** *(= abscond with)* entkommen mit **b** *(inf: = escape punishment for)* **you'll/he'll** *etc* **never get away with that** das wird nicht gut gehen; **he got away with it** er ist ungestraft *or* ungeschoren *(inf)* davongekommen, es ist gut gegangen; **the things he gets away with!** was er sich *(dat)* alles erlauben kann!; **to let sb get away with sth** jdm etw durchgehen lassen; **to let sb get away with doing sth** es jdm durchgehen lassen, dass er etw tut **c** *(= be let off with)* davonkommen mit

▶ **get back** **VI** **a** *(= come back)* zurückkommen; *(= go back)* zurückgehen; **to get back (home)** nach Hause kommen; **to get back to bed/sleep** wieder ins Bett gehen/einschlafen; **to get back to work** *(after interruption etc)* wieder arbeiten können; *(after break)* wieder arbeiten gehen; **I ought to be getting back (home/to the office)** ich sollte (nach Hause/ins Büro) zurück(gehen); **I must be getting back (home)** ich muss nach Hause; **we soon got back to the subject of money** wir kamen bald auf das Thema Geld zurück
b *(= move backwards)* zurückgehen; **get back!** zurück(treten)!
VT *sep* **a** *(= recover) money, possessions, person* zurückbekommen; *strength* zurückgewinnen; **now that I've got you/it back** jetzt, wo ich dich/es wiederhabe
b *(= bring back)* zurückbringen; *(= put back in place)* zurücktun; **he took it out and can't get it back in** er hat es herausgenommen und kriegt es nicht wieder hinein
c *(= pay back)* **I'll get you back for that** das werde ich dir heimzahlen

▶ **get back at** VI *+prep obj (inf)* sich rächen an *(+dat)*; **to get back at sb for sth** jdm etw heimzahlen *(inf)*

▶ **get back to** VI *+prep obj (esp Comm: = contact again)* sich wieder in Verbindung setzen mit; **I'll get back to you on that** ich werde darauf zurückkommen

▶ **get behind** VI **a** *(+prep obj) tree, person* sich stellen hinter *(+acc)*; *desk* sich setzen an *(+acc)*; **to get behind the wheel** sich ans *or* hinter das Steuer setzen **b** *(fig)* zurückbleiben; *(person)* ins Hintertreffen geraten; *(+prep obj)* zurückbleiben hinter *(+dat)*; *(with schedule)* in Rückstand kommen; **to get behind with one's work/payments** mit seiner Arbeit/den Zahlungen in Rückstand kommen **c** **the supporters got behind their team in the second half** in der zweiten Halbzeit fingen die Fans an, ihre Mannschaft anzufeuern

▶ **get by** VI **a** *(= move past)* vorbeikommen *(prep obj* an *+dat)*; **to let sb/a vehicle get by** jdn/ein Fahrzeug vorbeilassen **b** *(fig: = pass unnoticed)* durchrutschen *(inf)*; **how did that film get by the censors?** wie ist der Film nur durch die Zensur gekommen? **c** *(inf: = pass muster, work, worker)* gerade noch annehmbar *or* passabel *(inf)* sein; *(knowledge)* gerade ausreichen; **she could just about get by in German** mit ihren Deutschkenntnissen könnte sie gerade so durchkommen *(inf)* **d** *(inf: = manage)* durchkommen *(inf)*; **she gets by on very little money** sie kommt mit sehr wenig Geld aus

▶ **get down** **VI** **a** *(= descend)* heruntersteigen *(prep obj, from* von); *(= manage to get down, in commands)* herunterkommen *(prep obj, from +acc)*; *(from horse, bicycle)* absteigen *(from* von); *(from bus)* aussteigen *(from* aus); **to get down the stairs** die Treppe hinuntergehen; **get down!** runter! *(inf)*
b *(= leave table)* aufstehen
c *(= bend down)* sich bücken; *(to hide)* sich ducken; **to get down on one's knees** auf die Knie fallen; **to get down on all fours** sich auf alle Viere begeben; **get down, somebody's shooting!** runter, da schießt jemand!
VT *sep* **a** *(= take down)* herunternehmen; *trousers etc* herunterziehen; *(= lift down)* herunterholen; *(= carry down)* herunterbringen; *(= manage to get down)* herunterbringen *or* -kriegen *(inf)*
b *(= reduce) (to* auf *+acc)* beschränken; *(as regards length)* verkürzen; *temperature* herunterbekommen; *seller, price* herunterhandeln
c *(= swallow) food* hinunterbringen; **get this down (you)!** *(inf: = eat/drink)* iss/trink das!
d *(= make a note of)* aufschreiben, notieren
e *(inf: = depress)* fertigmachen *(inf)*; **don't let it get you down** lass dich davon nicht unterkriegen *(inf)*

▶ **get down to** VI *+prep obj (= start)* sich machen an *(+acc)*, in Angriff nehmen; *negotiations, consideration* beginnen; *(= find time to do)* kommen zu; **to get down to business** zur Sache kommen

▶ **get in** **VI** **a** *(= enter)* hereinkommen *(prep obj, -to* in *+acc)*; *(into car, train etc)* einsteigen *(prep obj, -to* in *+acc)*; *(into bath)* hineinsteigen; *(into bed)* sich hineinlegen; **to get in(to) the bath** in die Badewanne steigen; **to get into bed** sich ins Bett legen; **the smoke got in(to) my eyes** ich habe Rauch in die Augen gekriegt *(inf) or* bekommen; **he can't get in** er kann *(inf) or* kommt nicht hinein; **he got in between them** *(in bed)* er legte sich zwischen sie
b *(= arrive, train, bus)* ankommen *(-to* in *+dat)*; *(plane)* landen
c *(= be admitted)* hineinkommen *(-to* in *+acc)*; *(into school, profession)* ankommen, angenommen werden *(-to* in *+dat)*
d *(Pol: = be elected)* gewählt werden *(-to* in *+acc)*, es schaffen *(inf)*
e *(= get home)* nach Hause kommen
f *(inf: = manage)* **to get in with a request** ein Gesuch anbringen; **he got in first/before me** er ist mir zuvorgekommen
VT **a** *sep (= bring in)* hereinbringen *(prep obj, -to* in *+acc)*; *crops, harvest* einbringen; *taxes* eintreiben; *(= fetch)* hereinholen *(-to* in *+acc)*; *(= help enter)* hineinhelfen *(+dat) (prep obj, -to* in *+acc)*
b *sep (= receive) forms etc* bekommen; *(= submit) forms* einreichen; *homework* abgeben
c *sep (= plant) (prep obj, -to* in *+acc) bulbs etc* einpflanzen; *seeds* säen
d *always separate (= get admitted to, into club etc) (prep obj, to* in *+acc) (as member)* zur Aufnahme verhelfen *(+dat)*; *(as guest)* mitnehmen; **how did his parents get him in?** wie haben es seine Eltern geschafft, dass er angenommen wurde?
e *always separate (= get elected) candidate* zu einem Sitz verhelfen *(+dat) (-to* in *+dat)*; *party* zu einem Wahlsieg verhelfen *(+dat)*
f *sep (= fit, insert into, find room for)* hineinbringen *or* -kriegen *(inf) or* -bekommen *(-to* in *+acc)*; *(fig) blow, punch, request, words* anbringen; **it was hard to get a word in** es war schwer, auch nur ein Wort dazwischen zu kriegen *(inf) or* bekommen
g *sep (= get a supply) groceries, coal* holen, ins Haus bringen; **to get in supplies** sich *(dat)* Vorräte zulegen
h *sep (= send for) doctor, plumber* holen, kommen lassen; *specialist, consultant etc* zuziehen
i *always separate* **to get one's eye/hand in** in Übung kommen

▶ **get in on** VI *+prep obj (inf)* mitmachen bei *(inf)*, sich beteiligen an *(+dat)*; **to get in on the act** mitmachen, mitmischen *(inf)* **VT** *sep +prep obj* beteiligen an *(+dat)*; *(= let take part in)* mitmachen lassen bei

▶ **get into** **VI** *+prep obj* → *also* **get in VI a-d**
a *rage, panic, debt, situation, company etc* geraten in *(+acc)*; *fight* verwickelt werden in *(+acc)*; *trouble, difficulties* kommen *or* geraten in *(+acc)*; *(inf: = upset)* fahren in *(+acc) (inf)*; **what's got into him?** *(inf)* was ist bloß in ihn gefahren? *(inf)*
b *bad habits* sich *(dat)* angewöhnen; **to get into the habit** *or* **way of doing sth** sich *(dat)* angewöhnen, etw zu tun; **it's easy once you've got into the swing** *or* **way of it** es ist leicht, wenn Sie erst mal ein bisschen Übung darin haben
c *(= get involved in) book* sich einlesen bei; *work* sich einarbeiten in *(+acc)*; **I just can't get into it** *(job)* ich kann mich einfach nicht einarbeiten
d *(= put on)* anziehen, schlüpfen in *(+acc)*; *(= fit into)* hineinkommen *or* -passen in *(+acc)*
VT *+prep obj always separate* **a** **I got the kids into bed** ich habe die Kinder ins Bett gebracht;**those results should get him into any university** mit den Zeugnissen müsste er auf jeder Universität angenommen werden *or* ankommen; **his parents wanted to get him into a good school** seine Eltern wollten ihn auf eine gute Schule schicken; **that got the Liberals into Parliament** dadurch kamen die Liberalen ins Parlament; **he always tries to get it into the conversation that ...** er versucht immer, (es) in die Unterhaltung einfließen zu lassen, dass ...
b *rage, debt, situation etc* bringen in *(+acc)*; **to get sb/oneself into trouble** jdn/sich in Schwierigkeiten *(acc)* bringen *(also euph)*
c **to get sb into bad habits** jdm schlechte Gewohnheiten beibringen; **who/what got you into the habit of getting up early?** wer hat Ihnen das angewöhnt/wieso haben Sie es sich angewöhnt, früh aufzustehen?
d **to get sb into a dress** jdm ein Kleid anziehen; *(= manage to put on)* jdn in ein Kleid hineinbekommen *or* -kriegen *(inf)*

▶ **get in with** VI *+prep obj (= associate with)* Anschluss finden an *(+acc)*; *bad company* geraten in *(+acc)*; *(= ingratiate oneself with)* sich gut stellen mit

▶ **get off** **VI** **a** *(= descend, from bus, train etc)* aussteigen *(prep obj* aus); *(from bicycle, horse)* absteigen *(prep obj* von); **to tell sb where to get off** *(inf)* jdm gründlich die Meinung sagen *(inf)*; **he knows where he can get off!** *(inf)* der kann mich mal! *(inf)*
b *(= remove oneself) (prep obj* von) *(from premises)* weggehen, verschwinden; *(from lawn, ladder, sb's toes, furniture)* heruntergehen; *(= stand up: from chair)* aufstehen; **get off!** *(= let me go)* lass (mich) los!; **let's get off this subject** lassen wir das Thema! *(inf)*; **he needs to get off his backside and find a job** *(inf)* er muss mal seinen Hintern heben *(inf)* und sich *(dat)* eine Stelle suchen
c *(= leave)* weg- *or* loskommen; **I must be getting off** ich muss los; **it's time you got off to school** es ist Zeit, dass ihr in die Schule geht; **to get off to an early start** früh wegkommen; **to get off to a good/bad start** *(Sport)* einen guten/schlechten Start haben; *(fig, person)* einen guten/schlechten Anfang machen; *(campaign etc)* sich gut/schlecht anlassen; **to get off on the right/wrong foot** einen guten/schlechten Start haben
d *+prep obj (= be excused) homework, task etc* nicht machen müssen; **to get off work/school** nicht zur Arbeit/Schule gehen müssen; **he got off tidying up his room** er kam darum herum, sein Zimmer aufräumen zu müssen *(inf)*
e *(fig: = escape, be let off)* davonkommen *(inf)*; **to get off lightly/with a fine** billig/mit einer Geldstrafe davonkommen *(inf)*
f *(= fall asleep)* **to get off (to sleep)** einschlafen
g *(from work etc)* gehen können *(prep obj* in *+dat)*; **I'll see if I can get off (work) early** ich werde mal sehen, ob ich früher (von der Arbeit) wegkann *(inf)*; **what time do you get off work?** wann hören Sie mit der Arbeit auf?
VT **a** *sep (= remove)* wegbekommen *or* -bringen *or* -kriegen *(inf) (prep obj* von); *clothes,*

shoes ausziehen; *(= manage to get off)* herunterbekommen *or* -kriegen *(inf)* *(prep obj* von); *cover, lid* heruntertun *(prep obj* von); *(= manage to get off)* abbekommen *(prep obj* von); *stains* herausmachen *(prep obj* aus); *(= manage to get off)* herausbekommen *or* -kriegen *(inf) or* -bringen *(prep obj* aus); *(= take away from)* abnehmen *(prep obj +dat)*; **I want to get all these books off my desk** ich möchte diese ganzen Bücher vom Tisch kriegen *(inf)*; **get your dirty hands off my clean shirt** nimm deine schmutzigen Hände von meinem sauberen Hemd; **get your shoes off!** zieh die Schuhe aus!; **get him off me!** schaff ihn mir vom Leib! *(inf)*; **get him off my property!** schaffen Sie ihn von meinem Grundstück!; **we need to get the homeless off the streets** wir müssen dafür sorgen, dass die Obdachlosen von der Straße kommen; **can't you get him off that subject?** können Sie ihn nicht von dem Thema abbringen?

b *always separate (from bus etc)* aussteigen lassen *(prep obj* aus); *(= manage to get off)* herausbekommen *or* -bringen *(prep obj* aus); *(from boat, roof, ladder etc)* herunterholen *(prep obj* von); *(= manage to get off)* herunterbringen *or* -kriegen *(inf) or* -bekommen *(prep obj* von)

c *+prep obj always separate (inf: = obtain)* bekommen, kriegen *(inf)* *(prep obj* von); **I got that idea/pencil off John** ich habe die Idee/den Bleistift von John

d *sep (= send away) mail, children* losschicken; **to get sb/sth off to a good start** jdm/einer Sache zu einem guten Start verhelfen; **to get sb/sth off to a bad start** jdn/etw schon schlecht anfangen lassen; **to get sb off to school** jdn für die Schule fertig machen

e *always separate (= let off)* **that got him off school for the afternoon** dadurch musste er am Nachmittag nicht in die Schule; **that got her off doing the dishes** dadurch ist sie um den Abwasch herumgekommen

f *sep (= save from punishment) accused (lawyer)* freibekommen *or* -kriegen *(inf)*; *(evidence etc)* entlasten; **only his good manners got him off** er ist nur wegen seines guten Benehmens davongekommen

g *always separate* **to get sb off (to sleep)** jdn zum Schlafen bringen

h *sep (from work etc) day, afternoon* freibekommen

▶ **get off on** VI *+prep obj (inf)* einen Kick bekommen von *(inf)*

▶ **get off with** VI *+prep obj (inf)* **a** *(= start a relationship with)* aufreißen *(inf)*; *(= have sex with)* bumsen mit *(inf)* **b** = **get away with c**

▶ **get on** VI **a** *(= climb on)* hinaufsteigen; *(+prep obj)* (hinauf)steigen auf *(+acc)*; *(on bus, train etc)* einsteigen *(prep obj, -to* in *+acc)*; *(on bicycle, horse etc)* aufsteigen *(prep obj, -to* auf *+acc)*; **get on the back and I'll give you a lift** steigen Sie hinten auf, dann nehme ich Sie mit

b *(= continue: with work etc)* weitermachen; *(= manage to get on)* weiterkommen

c *(= get late, old)* **time is getting on** es wird langsam spät; **he is getting on (in years)** er wird langsam alt

d → **get along a**

e *(= progress)* vorankommen; *(work, patient, pupil)* Fortschritte machen; *(= succeed)* Erfolg haben; **to get on in the world** es zu etwas bringen

f *(= fare, cope: in exam etc)* zurechtkommen; **how did you get on in the exam?** wie gings (dir) in der Prüfung?; **how are you getting on?** wie gehts?; **to get on without sb/sth** ohne jdn/etw zurechtkommen

g *(= have a good relationship)* sich verstehen, auskommen *(with* mit); **they don't get on (with each other)** sie kommen nicht miteinander aus, sie verstehen sich nicht

VT **a** *sep (prep obj* auf *+acc) clothes, shoes* anziehen; *hat, kettle* aufsetzen; *lid, cover* drauftun; *load (onto cart etc)* hinauftun; *(= manage to get on)* draufbekommen *or* -kriegen *(inf)*

b *always separate (on train, bus etc)* hineinsetzen; *(+prep obj, -to)* setzen in *(+acc)*; *(= manage to get on)* hineinbekommen *or* -kriegen *(inf)* *(prep obj, -to* in *+acc)*; *(on bicycle, horse)* hinaufsetzen; *(prep obj, -to)* setzen auf *(+acc)*; **to get it on** *(= start)* anfangen; *(US inf: = have sex)* bumsen *(inf)* *(with sb* mit jdm)

▶ **get on for** VI *+prep obj (time, person in age)* zugehen auf *(+acc)*; **he's getting on for 40** er geht auf die 40 zu; **there were getting on for 60 people there** es waren fast 60 Leute da

▶ **get on to** VI *+prep obj (inf)* **a** *(= get on track of) person* auf die Spur *or* Schliche kommen *(+dat)* *(inf)*; *dubious activity, double-dealing* aufdecken, herausfinden; **they got on to her trail** sie kamen ihr auf die Spur **b** *(= move on to) next item, new subject* übergehen zu **c** *(= contact)* sich in Verbindung setzen mit; **I'll get on to him about it** ich werde ihn daraufhin ansprechen

▶ **get onto** VTI *+prep obj* = **get on VI a VT a, b**

▶ **get on with** VI *+prep obj (= continue)* weitermachen mit; *(= manage to get on with)* weiterkommen mit; **get on with it!** nun mach schon! *(inf)*; **get on with what you're doing** mach weiter; **get on with your work, will you?** nun mach schon deine Arbeit!; **to let sb get on with sth** jdn etw machen lassen; **to leave sb to get on with it** jdn einfach machen lassen; **this will do to be getting on with** das tuts wohl für den Anfang *(inf)*

▶ **get out** VI **a** *(= leave)* herauskommen *(of* aus); *(= walk out)* hinausgehen *(of* aus); *(= drive out)* hinausfahren *(of* aus); *(= climb out)* herausklettern *or* -steigen *(of* aus); *(of bus, train, car)* aussteigen *(of* aus); *(= leave)* weggehen *(of* aus); *(fig) (of business, scheme, contract)* aussteigen *(inf)* *(of* aus); *(of job)* wegkommen *(of* von); **he has to get out of the country/city** er muss das Land/die Stadt verlassen; **I just need to get out of the house for a while** ich muss nur mal eine Zeit lang aus dem Haus; **let's get out (of here)!** bloß weg hier! *(inf)*; **get out!** raus! *(inf)*; **get the hell out of here!** *(esp US inf)* verpiss dich! *(sl)*; **get outta here!** *(inf)* verarsch mich nicht! *(inf)*, das ist ja wohl nicht dein Ernst! *(inf)*; **get out of my house/room!** verlassen Sie mein Haus/Zimmer!, raus aus meinem Haus/Zimmer! *(inf)*; **get out of my life!** ich will nichts mehr mit dir zu tun haben!; **the dog couldn't get out (of the hole)** der Hund kam (aus dem Loch) nicht mehr heraus; **I might need to get out in a hurry** es kann sein, dass ich schnell raus- *(inf) or* hinausmuss; **to get out of bed** aufstehen; **to get out while the going's good** gehen *or (of contract, affair etc)* aussteigen *(inf)*, solange man das noch kann

b *(= go walking, shopping etc)* weggehen; **you ought to get out (of the house) more** Sie müssten mehr rauskommen *(inf)*; **I'd like to get out into the countryside** ich würde gern irgendwo ins Grüne kommen; **to get out and about** herumkommen

c *(lit, fig: = escape, leak out)* *(of* aus) herauskommen; *(animal, prisoner)* entkommen; *(poisonous liquid, gas)* entweichen; *(news)* an die Öffentlichkeit dringen; **wait till the news gets out** warte, bis das herauskommt

VT *sep* **a** *(= remove)* *(of* aus) *cork, tooth, splinter, stain etc* herausmachen; *people* hinausbringen; *(= send out)* hinausschicken; *(= manage to get out)* hinausbekommen *or* -kriegen *(inf)*; **I couldn't get him/it out of my head** *or* **mind** ich konnte ihn/es nicht vergessen; **get him out of my house/sight** schaff mir ihn aus dem Haus/aus den Augen!; **cold water will get the stain out** mit kaltem Wasser bekommen Sie *etc* den Fleck heraus

b *(= bring, take out)* herausholen *or* -nehmen *(of* aus); *car, boat, horse* herausholen *(of* aus)

c *(= withdraw) money* abheben *(of* von)

d *(= produce) words, apology* herausbekommen *or* -kriegen *(inf) or* -bringen

e *(= publish, present) book, list etc* herausbringen

f *(= borrow from library)* ausleihen *(of* aus)

g *(Sport) batsman* ausschlagen

h *(= derive)* **you only get out what you put in** Sie bekommen nur das zurück, was Sie hineinstecken

▶ **get out of** VI *+prep obj* → *also* **get out VI a, c**

a *(= avoid, escape) obligation, punishment* herumkommen um; *difficulty* herauskommen aus; **you can't get out of it now** jetzt kannst du nicht mehr anders; **there's no getting out of paying tax** man kommt nicht darum herum, Steuern zu zahlen; **I have signed the contract and now I can't get out of it** ich habe den Vertrag unterschrieben, jetzt gibt es kein Zurück

b *(= become unaccustomed to)* **I've got out of the way of playing tennis** ich habe das Tennisspielen verlernt; **I'll get out of practice** ich verlerne es; **to get out of the habit of doing sth** sich *(dat)* abgewöhnen, etw zu tun; **it's hard to get out of the habit of waking up early** es ist schwer sich abzugewöhnen, früh aufzuwachen

VT *+prep obj always separate* → *also* **get out VT a-c** **a** *(= extract) words, confession, truth* herausbekommen *or* -bringen *or* -kriegen *(inf)* aus; **we could get nothing out of him** wir konnten nichts aus ihm herausbekommen

b *(= gain from) profit* machen bei; *money* herausholen aus; *benefit, knowledge, wisdom, much, little, nothing* haben von; *pleasure* haben an *(+dat)*; *happiness etc* finden in *(+dat)*; **there's nothing to be got out of his lectures** von seinen Vorlesungen hat man nichts; **to get the best/most out of sb/sth** das Beste aus jdm herausholen/etw machen; **what can we get out of them/it?** wie können wir von ihnen/davon profitieren?

c **to get sb out of a habit** jdm eine Unsitte abgewöhnen; **to get sb out of (the habit of) doing sth** es jdm abgewöhnen, etw zu tun

▶ **get over** VI **a** *(= cross)* hinübergehen *(prep obj* über *+acc)*; *(= climb over)* hinübersteigen *or* -klettern; *(+prep obj)* steigen *or* klettern über *(+acc)*; *(= manage to get over)* hinüberkommen; *(+prep obj)* kommen über *(+acc)*; **they got over to the other side** sie kamen *or* gelangten auf die andere Seite

b *+prep obj (lit, fig: = recover from) disappointment, loss, sb's cheek, fact, experience* (hin)wegkommen über *(+acc)*; *shock, surprise, illness* sich erholen von; **I can't get over the fact that ...** ich komme gar nicht darüber hinweg, dass ...; **I can't get over it** *(inf)* da komm ich nicht drüber weg *(inf)*

c *+prep obj (= overcome) problem, nervousness, fear, handicap, obstacle* überwinden

d *(= communicate, play, actor)* ankommen *(to* bei); *(speaker)* sich verständlich machen *(to +dat)*

VT **a** *always separate (= transport across) person, animal, vehicle* hinüberbringen *(prep obj* über *+acc)*; *(= manage to get over)* hinüberbekommen *(prep obj* über *+acc)*; *(= send)* hinüberschicken; *(= fetch)* holen; *(= help sb to cross, climb)* hinüberhelfen *(sb* jdm) *(prep obj* über *+acc)*

b *sep (= make comprehensible) information, ideas etc* verständlich machen *(to dat)*; *(= impress upon)* klarmachen *(to dat)*; **she gets her songs over well** sie kommt mit ihren Liedern gut an; **she got the news over (to them)** es gelang ihr, (ihnen) die Nachricht zu übermitteln

c = **get over with**

▶ **get over with** VT *always separate* hinter sich *(acc)* bringen; **let's get it over with** bringen wirs hinter uns; **to get sth over and done with** etw ein für alle Mal erledigen *or* hinter sich bringen

▶ **get past** VI = **get by a, b** VT *sep* vorbeibringen *(prep obj* an *+dat)*

▶ **get round** *(esp Brit)* VI **a** *(= drive, walk etc round)* herumkommen *(prep obj* um); **it's difficult to get round the shops in a wheelchair** es ist schwierig, im Rollstuhl durch die Geschäfte zu kommen

b *+prep obj (= evade, circumvent)* herumkommen um; *difficulty, law, regulations* umgehen

c *+prep obj (= persuade)* herumkriegen *(inf)*

d *+prep obj* **to get round the conference table** sich an einen Tisch setzen

VT *always separate* **a** *(= restore to consciousness)* zu Bewusstsein *or* zu sich bringen

b *(= make agree)* herumbringen *or* -kriegen *(inf)*; **I'm sure I can get her round to my way of thinking** ich bin sicher, dass ich sie überzeugen kann

c *+prep obj* **to get one's tongue round a word** ein Wort aussprechen können; **I still can't get my head round it** *(inf)* ich kann es immer noch nicht begreifen

d *+prep obj* **to get people (together) round the conference table** Leute an einem Tisch zusammenbringen

▶ **get round to** VI *+prep obj (esp Brit inf)* **to get round to sth** zu etw kommen; **to get round to doing sth** dazu kommen, etw zu tun

▶ **get through** **VI** **a** *(through gap, snow etc)* durchkommen *(prep obj* durch); **we only just got through with the car** wir kamen mit dem Auto gerade noch durch; **the news got through (to us)** die Nachricht kam (zu uns) durch

b *(= be accepted, pass)* durchkommen *(prep obj* bei); **to get through to the final** in die Endrunde kommen

c *(Telec)* durchkommen *(inf) (to sb* zu jdm, *to London/Germany* nach London/Deutschland)

d *(= communicate, be understood, person)* durchdringen *(to* zu); *(idea etc)* klar werden *(to +dat)*; **he has finally got through to her** endlich hat er es geschafft, dass sie es begreift

e *+prep obj (= finish) work* fertig machen, erledigen; *(= manage to get through)* schaffen *(inf)*; *book* fertig lesen*or* auslesen; *bottle* leer machen; **to get through doing sth** etw fertig machen; **when I've got through this** wenn ich damit fertig bin

f *+prep obj (= survive) days, time* herumbekommen *or* -kriegen *(inf)*

g *+prep obj (= consume, use up)* verbrauchen; *clothes, shoes* abnutzen; *food* aufessen, verputzen *(inf)*; *fortune* durchbringen *(inf)*

VT *always separate* **a** *person, vehicle, object* durchbekommen *or* -kriegen *(inf) or* -bringen *(prep obj* durch); **to get a comb through one's hair** mit dem Kamm durchkommen

b *(= cause to succeed) candidate, proposal, bill* durchbekommen *or* -bringen *(prep obj* durch); **to get sb through an exam** *(teacher)* jdn durchs Examen bringen; **it was his spoken English that got him through** er hat das nur geschafft, weil er so gut Englisch spricht *(inf)*; **he got the team through to the finals** er hat die Mannschaft in die Endrunde gebracht

c *(= send) message* durchgeben *(to +dat)*; *supplies* durchbringen; **they couldn't get the ammunition through to the men** es ist ihnen nicht gelungen, Munition zu den Leuten zu bringen; **we eventually got supplies/a message through to them** wir konnten ihnen schließlich Vorräte/eine Nachricht zukommen lassen

d *(= make understand)* **to get sth through (to sb)** (jdm) etw klarmachen

▶ **get through with** VI *+prep obj (inf: = finish)* hinter sich bringen; *job, formalities, subject* erledigen; *book* auslesen *(inf)*, durchbekommen *(inf)*; **by the time I've got through with him** wenn ich mit ihm fertig bin; **I'll never get through with that** ich werde das nie schaffen

▶ **get to** VI *+prep obj* **a** *(lit, fig: = arrive at)* kommen zu; *hotel, town etc* ankommen in *(+dat)*; **where did you get to last night?** *(= where were you)* wo bist du gestern Abend abgeblieben? *(inf)*; **where have you got to in French/with that book?** wie weit seid ihr in Französisch/mit dem Buch?; **to get to a high position** auf einen hohen Posten kommen *or* gelangen

b *(inf)* **I got to thinking/wondering** ich hab mir überlegt/mich gefragt; **we got to talking about it** wir sind darauf zu sprechen gekommen

c *(inf: = annoy, upset)* aufregen; **don't let them/their comments get to you** ärgere dich nicht über sie/ihre Kommentare; **don't let them get to you with their sarcasm** lass dich von ihrem Sarkasmus nicht rausbringen *(inf)*

▶ **get together** **VI** zusammenkommen; *(estranged couple)* sich versöhnen; *(= combine forces)* sich zusammenschließen; **to get together about sth** zusammenkommen *or* sich zusammensetzen und etw beraten; **she has got together with John** sie ist jetzt mit John zusammen; **let's get together and decide ...** wir sollten uns zusammensetzen und entscheiden ...; **why don't we get together later and have a drink?** warum treffen wir uns nicht später und trinken einen?

VT *sep people, collection* zusammenbringen; *documents, papers* zusammentun *or* -suchen; *thoughts, ideas* sammeln; *band* gründen; *money* zusammenbekommen; **to get one's things together** seine Sachen zusammenpacken; **once I've got my thoughts** *or* **head** *(inf)* **together** wenn ich meine Gedanken beisammenhabe *(inf)*; **to get it together** *(inf)* es bringen *(sl)*; **that's no good, come on, get it together** *(inf)* das taugt doch nichts, nun reiß dich mal am Riemen *(inf)*

▶ **get under** **VI** darunterkriechen; *(under umbrella etc)* darunterkommen; *(+prep obj)* kriechen/kommen unter *(+acc)*; *(= manage to get under)* darunterkommen; *(+prep obj)* kommen unter *(+acc)* **VT** *+prep obj always separate* bringen unter *(+acc)*

▶ **get up** **VI** **a** *(= stand up, get out of bed)* aufstehen

b *(= climb up)* hinaufsteigen *or* -klettern *(prep obj* auf *+acc)*; *(on horse)* aufsteigen *(prep obj,* on auf *+acc)*; *(= manage to get up)* hinaufkommen *(prep obj,* on auf *+acc)*; *(vehicle)* hinaufkommen *(prep obj +acc)*; **to get up behind sb** hinter jdm aufsitzen; **he couldn't get up the stairs** er kam nicht die Treppe hinauf; **getting up is all right, coming down is much harder** hinauf *or* rauf *(inf)* kommt man leicht, nur hinunterzukommen ist schwieriger

c *(= get stronger, wind)* aufkommen; *(sea)* stürmisch werden

VT **a** *always separate (= get out of bed)* aus dem Bett holen; *(= help to stand up)* aufhelfen *(+dat)*; *(= manage to get up)* hochbringen; **he couldn't get it up** *(inf)* er hat ihn nicht hochgekriegt *(inf)*; **I'll get myself up in the morning** ich stehe morgen früh allein auf

b *always separate (= carry up)* hinaufbringen *(prep obj +acc)*; *(= manage to get up)* hinaufbekommen *or* -kriegen *(inf) (prep obj +acc)*; *(= help climb up)* hinaufhelfen *(+dat) (prep obj* auf *+acc)*; *(= fetch)* heraufholen

c *sep (= gather) steam* aufbauen; **to get up speed** sich beschleunigen; **to get one's strength up, to get up one's strength** sich erholen, wieder neue Kräfte sammeln; **to get up an appetite** *(inf)* Hunger kriegen *(inf) or* bekommen

d *sep (= organize)* organisieren

e *always separate (= dress up, make attractive) person, oneself* zurechtmachen; *article for sale* aufmachen, herrichten; **to get oneself up as sb/sth** sich als jd/etw verkleiden; **to get sth up as sth** *or* **to look like sth** etw als etw aufmachen

f *always separate* **to get one up on sb** *(Sport inf)* jdm eins reinsemmeln *(inf)*

▶ **get up against** VI *+prep obj (inf: = come in conflict with)* sich anlegen mit *(inf)*

▶ **get up to** **VI** *+prep obj* **a** *(lit, fig: = reach)* erreichen; *standard* herankommen an *(+acc)*, kommen auf *(+acc)*; *page* kommen bis; **as soon as he got up to me** sobald er neben mir stand **b** *(= be involved in)* anstellen *(inf)*; **to get up to mischief/all sorts** etwas/alles Mögliche anstellen; **what have you been getting up to?** was hast du getrieben? *(inf)* **VT** *+prep obj always separate (= bring up to) top of mountain* hinaufbringen auf *(+acc)*; *standard* bringen auf *(+acc)*

get: **get-at-able** [ˌget'ætəbl] ADJ *(inf)* leicht erreichbar *or* zu erreichen *pred*; *house, person also* zugänglich; **it's not very ~** es ist schwer zu erreichen; **getaway** **N** Flucht *f*; **to make one's ~** sich davonmachen *(inf)*; **to make a quick ~** schnell abhauen *(inf)* **ADJ** *attr* Flucht-; **~ car/plans** Fluchtauto *nt*/-pläne *pl*; **the ~ driver** der Fahrer/die Fahrerin des Fluchtautos; **get-go** N *(US inf)* Anfang *m*, Beginn *m*; **from the ~** von Anfang an; **to learn sth from the ~** etw als Allererstes lernen

Gethsemane [geθ'seməni] N Gethsemane *no art*, Gethsemani *no art*

get: **get-together** N *(inf)* Treffen *nt*; **family ~** Familientreffen *nt*; **we have a ~ once a year** wir treffen uns einmal im Jahr; **get-tough** ADJ *politics* aggressiv, entschlossen; **get-up** N *(inf)* Aufzug *m (inf)*, Aufmachung *f (inf)*; **get-up-and-go** N *(inf)* Elan *m*; **get-well card** N Karte *f* mit Genesungswünschen

gewgaw ['gju:gɔ:] N protziges, wertloses Schmuckstück; *(fig)* Lappalie *f*, Kleinigkeit *f*

geyser ['gi:zə'] N **a** *(Geol)* Geiser *m*, Geysir *m* **b** *(= domestic geyser)* Durchlauferhitzer *m*

G-force ['dʒi:fɔ:s] N g-Druck *m*, Andruck *m*

Ghana ['gɑ:nə] N Ghana *nt*

Ghanaian [gɑ:'neɪən] **ADJ** ghanaisch **N** *(= person)* Ghanaer(in) *m(f)*

ghastliness ['gɑ:stlɪnɪs] N Grässlichkeit *f*; *(= appearance)* grässliches Aussehen; *(= pallor)* Totenblässe *f*

ghastly ['gɑ:stlɪ] ADJ *(+er)* **a** *(inf: = dreadful) person* grässlich *(inf)*; *object* scheußlich *(inf)*; *situation, experience, mistake* schrecklich, furchtbar; *pain* entsetzlich; **to look ~** entsetzlich aussehen; **I feel ~** mir gehts scheußlich *(inf)* **b** *(= frightening, spectral) pallor* gespenstisch; *(= grim, gruesome) accident, injuries, war, battle, news* schrecklich, entsetzlich; *crime, murder* grausig

ghat [gɑ:t] N *(Indian)* **a** *(= mountain pass)* Gebirgspass *m* **b** *(at river)* Lande- und Badeplatz *m* mit Ufertreppe; **burning ~** Totenverbrennungsplatz *m* an einer Ufertreppe

Ghent [gent] N Gent *nt*

gherkin ['gɜ:kɪn] N Gewürz- *or* Essiggurke *f*

ghetto ['getəʊ] N *(lit, fig)* G(h)etto *nt*

ghetto blaster ['getəʊblɑ:stə'] N *(inf)* G(h)ettoblaster *m (inf)*, großes Kofferradio

ghettoization [ˌgetəʊaɪ'zeɪʃən] N **the ~ of this district** die G(h)ettobildung in diesem Viertel

ghettoize ['getəʊaɪz] VT zum G(h)etto machen

ghillie N = **gillie**

ghost [gəʊst] **N** **a** *(= apparition)* Geist *m*, Gespenst *nt*; *(of sb)* Geist *m*

b *(fig)* **with the ~ of a smile** mit dem Anflug eines Lächelns; **she gave the ~ of a smile** sie lächelte zaghaft; **I don't have** *or* **stand the ~ of a chance** ich habe nicht die geringste Chance

c **to give up the ~** *(dated inf)* seinen *or* den Geist aufgeben

d *(TV: also* **ghost image)** Geisterbild *nt*

e *(= writer)* Ghostwriter *m*

VI **to ~ for sb** jds Ghostwriter sein

VT **to be ~ed** von einem Ghostwriter geschrieben sein; **to have sth ~ed** sich *(dat)* etw von einem Ghostwriter schreiben lassen; **to ~ sb's books/speeches** für jdn Bücher/Reden (als Ghostwriter) schreiben

ghost driver N *(US inf)* Geisterfahrer(in) *m(f) (inf)*

ghosting ['gəʊstɪŋ] N *(TV)* Geisterbilder *pl*

ghostly ['gəʊstlɪ] ADJ *(+er)* geisterhaft, gespenstisch; **a ~ presence** die Gegenwart eines Geistes

ghost *in cpds* Geister-; **ghost story** N Geister- *or* Gespenstergeschichte *f*; **ghost town** N Geisterstadt *f*; **ghost train** N *(Brit, at funfair)* Geisterbahn *f*; **ghostwriter** N Ghostwriter *m*

ghoul [gu:l] N *(= evil spirit)* Ghul *m*; *(fig)* Mensch *m* mit schaurigen Gelüsten

ghoulish ['gu:lɪʃ] ADJ makaber; *description* schaurig

ghoulishly ['gu:lɪʃlɪ] ADV auf makabre Art

GHQ *abbr of* **General Headquarters**

GI *(US) abbr of* **government issue** N GI *m*, US-Soldat *m* ADJ *attr* GI-; **GI uniform** GI-Uniform *f*

giant [ˈdʒaɪənt] N Riese *m*; *(= star also)* Riesenstern *m*; *(fig)* (führende) Größe; *(= company)* Gigant *m*; **a ~ of a man** ein Riese (von einem Mann); **football ~** Fußballass *nt*, (führende) Größe im Fußball; **insurance/publishing ~** Großversicherung *f*/-verlag *m*; **one of the ~s in his field** einer der Großen auf seinem Gebiet; **the ~ of opera, Luciano Pavarotti** der Gigant der Oper, Luciano Pavarotti ADJ *(= huge)* riesig, riesenhaft, Riesen-; *hill* enorm; *(in animal names)* Riesen-; **~(-size) packet** Riesenpackung *f*; **~ tortoise** Riesenschildkröte *f*

giantess [ˈdʒaɪəntes] N Riesin *f*

giant: **giant killer** N *(fig)* Goliathbezwinger(in) *m(f)*; **giant-killing** *(fig)* N Goliathbezwingung *f* ADJ *attr* **Spain's ~ French Open champion** der spanische Favoritenschreck und French-Open-Gewinner; **giant panda** N Großer Panda, Riesenpanda *m*

Gib [dʒɪb] N *abbr of* **Gibraltar**

gibber [ˈdʒɪbəʳ] VI *(ape)* schnattern; *(foreigner)* plappern; **he ~ed at me** er plapperte *or* schnatterte drauflos *(inf)*; **to ~ with rage/fear** vor Wut/Angst stammeln; **a ~ing idiot** ein daherplappernder Idiot; **I was a ~ing wreck by this stage** da war ich schon so nervös, dass ich nur noch Kauderwelsch herausbrachte

gibberish [ˈdʒɪbərɪʃ] N Quatsch *m (inf)*; *(= foreign language, baby's gibberish)* Kauderwelsch *nt*

gibbet [ˈdʒɪbɪt] N Galgen *m*

gibbon [ˈgɪbən] N Gibbon *m*

gibbous [ˈgɪbəs] ADJ *moon* Dreiviertel-

gibe [dʒaɪb] N Spöttelei *f*, Stichelei *f* VI spotten, sticheln; **to ~ at sb/sth** sich über jdn/etw lustig machen, spöttische Bemerkungen über jdn/etw machen

giblets [ˈdʒɪblɪts] PL Geflügelinnereien *pl*

Gibraltar [dʒɪˈbrɔːltəʳ] N Gibraltar *nt*

giddily [ˈgɪdɪlɪ] ADV **a** benommen **b** *climb etc* schwindelerregend; *spin* in schwindelerregendem Tempo **c** *(fig)* leichtfertig, unbesonnen

giddiness [ˈgɪdɪnɪs] N **a** *(= dizziness)* Schwindelgefühl *nt*; **wave of ~** Schwindelanfall *m* **b** *(fig)* Leichtfertigkeit *f*, Unbesonnenheit *f*

giddy [ˈgɪdɪ] ADJ *(+er)* **a** *(lit: = dizzy)* schwind(e)lig; **~ spells** Schwindelanfälle *pl*; **I feel ~** mir ist schwind(e)lig; **it makes me feel ~** mir wird (davon) schwind(e)lig; **heights always make me ~** ich bin nicht schwindelfrei **b** *(= causing dizziness) climb, speed* schwindelerregend; *heights* schwindelerregend, schwindelnd *(also fig)*; *spin* rasend schnell **c** *(fig: = heedless, not serious)* leichtfertig, flatterhaft; *(= excited)* ausgelassen; **their life was one ~ round of pleasure** ihr Leben bestand nur aus Jubel, Trubel, Heiterkeit; **she was ~ with excitement** sie war vor Aufregung ganz aus dem Häuschen *(inf)*; **that's the ~ limit!** *(dated inf)* das ist wirklich der Gipfel *or* die Höhe!

gift [gɪft] ✪ 16.4, 24.3 N **a** *(= thing given)* Geschenk *nt*, Gabe *f (liter)*; *(= donation to charity)* Spende *f*; *(Jur)* Schenkung *f*; **to make a ~ of sth to sb, to make sb a ~ of sth** jdm etw zum Geschenk machen *(form)*; **there is a free ~ with every purchase over £10** bei jedem Kauf im Wert von über £ 10 erhalten Sie ein Geschenk; **a free ~ of a tin of soup** eine Dose Suppe umsonst; **I wouldn't have it as a ~** ich möchte es nicht geschenkt haben; **that question/goal was a ~** *(inf)* die Frage/das Tor war ja geschenkt *(inf)*; **he thinks he's God's ~ (to women)** *(inf)* er denkt, er ist der Traum aller Frauen **b** *(form: = right to give)* **this is in the ~ of the government** das liegt im Ermessen der Regierung **c** *(= talent)* Gabe *f*; **to have a ~ for sth** ein Talent *nt* für etw haben; **she has a ~ for teaching** sie hat eine Begabung zur Lehrerin; **he has a ~ for languages/music** er ist sprachbegabt/musikalisch begabt → **gab** VT als Schenkung überlassen

gift card N *(US)* Gift Card *f*; *(= voucher also)* elektronische Guthabenkarte; *(= greeting card also)* elektronische Glückwunschkarte

gifted [ˈgɪftɪd] ADJ begabt *(in* für); **he is very ~ in languages/music** er ist sehr sprachbegabt/musikalisch sehr begabt

gift: **gift horse** N **don't look a ~ in the mouth** *(Prov)* einem geschenkten Gaul schaut man nicht ins Maul *(Prov)*; **gift tax** N Schenkungssteuer *f*; **gift token, gift voucher** N Geschenkgutschein *m*; **giftwrap** VT in *or* mit Geschenkpapier einwickeln N Geschenkpapier *nt*; **gift-wrapping** N Geschenkpapier *nt*

gig [gɪg] N **a** *(= carriage, boat)* Gig *nt* **b** *(inf: = concert)* Konzert *nt*, Gig *m (inf)*; *(of comedian, singer, group)* Auftritt *m*; **to do a ~** ein Konzert geben, auftreten **c** *(US: = temporary job)* Job *m* VI auftreten

giga- [ˈdʒɪgə-] PREF Giga-

gigabyte [ˈdʒɪgəbaɪt] N *(Comput)* Gigabyte *nt*

gigahertz [ˈdʒɪgəhɜːts] N Gigahertz *nt*

gigantic [dʒaɪˈgæntɪk] ADJ riesig, riesengroß; *building, man, task also* gigantisch; *appetite, mistake* riesig, gewaltig; *amount* riesenhaft, enorm; **of ~ proportions** von riesigen Ausmaßen

gigantically [dʒaɪˈgæntɪkəlɪ] ADV enorm

gigawatt [ˈdʒɪgəˌwɒt] N Gigawatt *nt*

giggle [ˈgɪgl] N Gekicher *nt no pl*, Kichern *nt no pl*; **..., he said with a ~** ..., sagte er kichernd; **we had a good ~ about it** *(inf)* wir haben uns darüber gekringelt *(inf)*; **it was a bit of a ~** *(inf)* es war ganz lustig; **a fit of the ~s** ein Kicheranfall *m*; **to get the ~s** anfangen herumzukichern; **to do sth as a ~** etw aus Spaß tun VI kichern, gickeln *(inf)*

giggler [ˈgɪgləʳ] N Kichernde(r) *mf*; **she's a ~** sie kichert viel

giggly [ˈgɪglɪ] ADJ *(+er)* albern, gickelig *(inf)*

GIGO [ˈgaɪgəʊ] *(Comput) abbr of* **garbage in, garbage out**

gigolo [ˈʒɪgələʊ] N Gigolo *m*

gigot [ˈdʒɪgət] N *(old)* Hammelkeule *f*; **~ chop** *(Scot)* Hammelkotelett *nt (mit Mark im Knochen)*

GI Joe [ˌdʒiːaɪˈdʒəʊ] N *(inf)* GI *m*

gild [gɪld] *pret* **gilded**, *ptp* **gilded** *or* **gilt** VT vergolden; **to ~ the lily** des Guten zu viel tun

gilder [ˈgɪldəʳ] N Vergolder(in) *m(f)*

gilding [ˈgɪldɪŋ] N Vergoldung *f*

gill[1] [gɪl] N *(of fish)* Kieme *f*; **green about the ~s** *(inf)* blass um die Nase *(inf)*

gill[2] [dʒɪl] N *(= measure)* Gill *nt (0,148 l)*

gillie [ˈgɪlɪ] N *(Scot)* Jagdaufseher(in) *m(f)*

gilt [gɪlt] *ptp of* **gild** N **a** *(= material)* Vergoldung *f*; **to take the ~ off the gingerbread** *(fig)* jdm die Freude verderben **b** *(Fin)* **~s** mündelsichere Wertpapiere *pl* ADJ vergoldet

gilt-edged [ˌgɪltˈedʒd] ADJ mit Goldrand, goldumrandet; *(Fin) securities, stocks* mündelsicher; *(fig)* solide

gimcrack [ˈdʒɪmkræk] ADJ billig; *furniture, toys also* minderwertig

gimcrackery [ˈdʒɪmˌkrækərɪ] N Plunder *m*, Firlefanz *m (both pej inf)*

gimlet [ˈgɪmlɪt] N Hand- *or* Vorbohrer *m*; **her ~ eyes** ihre Luchsaugen; **to have eyes like ~s** Augen wie ein Luchs haben; **~-eyed** luchsäugig

gimme [ˈgɪmɪ] *(inf)* = **give me**

gimmick [ˈgɪmɪk] N Gag *m (inf)*; *(in film etc)* effekthaschender Gag, Spielerei *f*; *(= gadget)* Spielerei *f*; **an election ~** ein Wahltrick *m*; **changing the name and not the product is just a (sales) ~** den Namen, aber nicht das Produkt zu ändern, ist nur ein (Verkaufs)trick

gimmickry [ˈgɪmɪkrɪ] N Effekthascherei *f*; *(in advertising, sales)* Gags *pl*; *(= gadgetry)* Spielereien *pl*

gimmicky [ˈgɪmɪkɪ] ADJ effekthascherisch

gimp [gɪmp] *(US inf)* N **a** *(= limp)* Hinken *nt*, Humpeln *nt* **b** *(pej) (= cripple)* Krüppel *m*; *(= weakling)* Schwächling *m*, Waschlappen *m (inf)*; *(= rustic, uncouth person)* Provinzler(in) *m(f) (inf)*, Hinterwäldler(in) *m(f) (inf)*; *(= simpleton)* Einfaltspinsel *m (inf)* VI *(= limp)* hinken, humpeln

gimpy [ˈgɪmpɪ] *(US inf)* ADJ *(= limping)* hinkend, humpelnd N Hinkebein *nt (inf)*

gin[1] [dʒɪn] N *(= drink)* Gin *m*, Wacholder(-schnaps) *m*; **~ and tonic** Gin Tonic *m*; **~ and it** *Gin und (italienischer) Wermut*

gin[2] N **a** *(Hunt)* Falle *f*; *(= snare)* Schlinge *f* **b** *(Tex: = cotton gin)* (Baumwoll)entkernungsmaschine *f*

ginger [ˈdʒɪndʒəʳ] N **a** Ingwer *m* **b** *(pej inf, address for person)* Rotkopf *or* -schopf *m* ADJ **a** *(Cook)* Ingwer-; **~ biscuits/wine** Ingwerplätzchen *pl*/-wein *m* **b** *hair* kupferrot; *cat* rötlich gelb

► **ginger up** VT *sep (inf)* in Schwung bringen; *person also* aufmöbeln *(inf)*; *book* würzen

ginger: **ginger ale** N Gingerale *nt*; **ginger beer** N Ingwerlimonade *f*; *(alcoholic)* Ingwerbier *nt*; **gingerbread** N Lebkuchen *m*, Pfefferkuchen *m (mit Ingwergeschmack)* ADJ *attr* Lebkuchen-; **~ man/house** Lebkuchenmann *m*/-haus *nt*; **ginger group** N *(Parl)* Aktionsgruppe *f*

gingerly [ˈdʒɪndʒəlɪ] ADV *(= carefully) step, walk, touch* vorsichtig, behutsam; *pick up, handle (sth dirty)* mit spitzen Fingern; *(sth cold or hot)* zaghaft

ginger: **ginger nut** N Ingwerplätzchen *nt*; **ginger snap** N Ingwerwaffel *f*

gingery [ˈdʒɪndʒərɪ] ADJ *hair, colour* rötlich

gingham [ˈgɪŋəm] N Gingan *m*, Gingham *m*

gingivitis [ˌdʒɪndʒɪˈvaɪtɪs] N Zahnfleischentzündung *f*

gin mill N *(US inf)* (billige *or* verrufene) Kneipe

ginormous [dʒaɪˈnɔːməs] ADJ *(inf: = enormous)* riesig *(inf)*

gin: **gin rummy** N Rommé *nt or* Rommee *nt* mit Zehn; **gin sling** N Gin-Fizz *m*

gippy tummy [ˈdʒɪpɪˈtʌmɪ] N *(inf)* Durchfall *m*

gipsy, gypsy [ˈdʒɪpsɪ] N Zigeuner(in) *m(f) (neg!)* ADJ *attr* Zigeuner-; **~ music** Zigeunermusik *f*

gipsy moth N Schwammspinner *m*

giraffe [dʒɪˈrɑːf] N Giraffe *f*

gird [gɜːd] *pret, ptp* **girded** *or (rare)* **girt** VT *(old)* gürten *(old)*; *(fig)* umgeben; **to ~ oneself** sich gürten *(with* mit); *(fig: = prepare)* sich wappnen; *(for* für)

gird up [ˈgɜːdˈʌp] VT *sep (old) robe* gürten; **to gird (up) one's loins** *(esp Bibl)* seine Lenden gürten *(Bibl)*; **to gird oneself up** *(fig)* sich wappnen; **he girded himself up for action** er machte sich bereit (zum Handeln)

girder [ˈgɜːdəʳ] N Träger *m*

girdle[1] [ˈgɜːdl] N **a** *(= belt, also fig)* Gürtel *m* **b** *(= corset)* Hüftgürtel *or* -halter *m* VT *(lit)* gürten; *(fig)* umgeben

girdle[2] N *(Scot)* = **griddle**

girl [gɜːl] N **a** Mädchen *nt*; *(= daughter)* Tochter *f*; *(= girlfriend)* Freundin *f*; **an English ~** eine Engländerin; **they are hoping for a little ~** sie wünschen sich *(dat)* ein Töchterchen; **the Smith ~s** die Smith-Mädchen, die Mädchen von den Smiths; **my eldest ~** meine älteste Tochter, meine Älteste; **the ~s** *(= colleagues)* die Damen; **~s' night out** Damengesellschaft *f*; **I'm going out with the ~s tonight** ich gehe heute Abend mit meinen Freundinnen aus; **thank you, ~s** vielen Dank; **the old ~** die Alte *(inf) or* alte Frau; *(inf, = wife, mother)* meine/seine *etc* Alte *(inf)* → **big** **b** *(= employee)* Mädchen *nt*; *(in shop)* Verkäuferin *f*; *(in factory)* Arbeiterin *f* → **blouse**

girl: **girl band** N *(Mus)* Girlband *f*; **girl Friday** N Allroundsekretärin *f*; **girlfriend** N Freundin *f*; **Girl Guide** N *(Brit)* Pfadfinderin *f*; **girlhood**

N Mädchenzeit *f*, Jugend *f*; **in her ~** in ihrer Jugend

girlie [ˈgɜːlɪ] **N** *(inf)* Mädchen *nt* **ADJ** *attr magazine* mit nackten Mädchen; *photos* von nackten Mädchen

girlish [ˈgɜːlɪʃ] ADJ mädchenhaft; **she still looked ~** sie sah immer noch wie ein Mädchen aus

girlishly [ˈgɜːlɪʃlɪ] ADV mädchenhaft

girlishness [ˈgɜːlɪʃnɪs] N Mädchenhaftigkeit *f*

Girl Scout N *(US)* Pfadfinderin *f*

giro [ˈdʒaɪrəʊ] N *(Brit)* *(= bank giro)* Giro(verkehr *m*) *nt*; *(= post-office giro)* Postscheckverkehr *or* -dienst *m*; **~ (cheque)** *(Social Security)* Sozialhilfeüberweisung *f*; **~ cheque** *(for paying)* Postscheck *m*; **to pay a bill by ~** eine Rechnung durch Überweisung bezahlen

Girobank [ˈdʒaɪrəʊbæŋk] N *(Brit)* Postbank *f*; **~ transfer** Postüberweisung *f*

girt [gɜːt] *(rare) pret, ptp of* **gird**

girth [gɜːθ] N **a** *(= circumference)* Umfang *m*; **in ~** im Umfang; **a man of ample ~** ein Mann mit beträchtlichem Umfang **b** *(= harness)* (Sattel)gurt *m*

gismo N *(inf)* = **gizmo**

gist [dʒɪst] N *no pl (of report, conversation, argument)* Wesentliche(s) *nt*; **that was the ~ of what he said** das war im Wesentlichen, was er gesagt hat; **to give sb the ~ of sth** jdm sagen, worum es bei etw geht; **to get the ~ of sth/the conversation** im Wesentlichen verstehen, worum es sich bei etw handelt/wovon geredet wird; **I got the ~ of it** das Wesentliche habe ich verstanden

git [gɪt] N *(inf: = stupid person)* Schwachkopf *m*, Depp *m (dial)*; **a miserable old ~** ein alter Miesepeter *(inf)*

give [gɪv]
vb: pret **gave**, *ptp* **given**

1 TRANSITIVE VERB	3 NOUN
2 INTRANSITIVE VERB	4 PHRASAL VERBS

1 – TRANSITIVE VERB

When *give* is part of a set combination, eg. *give evidence, give chase*, look up the other word.

a geben; **to give sb sth** *or* **sth to sb** jdm etw geben; **they gave us food and drink** sie gaben uns zu essen und zu trinken; **the teacher gave us three exercises** der Lehrer hat uns drei Übungen gegeben *or (as homework)* aufgegeben; **we were given three exercises** wir haben drei Übungen bekommen *or (as homework)* aufbekommen; **she was given a sedative** man hat ihr *or* ihr wurde ein Beruhigungsmittel gegeben; **they gave us roast beef for lunch** sie servierten uns Roastbeef zum (Mittag)essen; **I'd give a lot/the world/anything to know ...** ich würde viel/sehr viel/alles darum geben, wenn ich wüsste, ...; **what wouldn't I give to be like you** was würde ich nicht darum geben, so wie du zu sein; **to give sb one's cold** *(inf)* jdn mit seiner Erkältung anstecken; **to give as good as one gets** sich kräftig wehren; **he gave everything he had** *(fig)* er holte das Letzte aus sich heraus

♦ **to give sth for sth** *(= pay)* etw für etw ausgeben; *(= sacrifice)* etw für etw (her)geben; *(= exchange)* etw gegen etw tauschen; **what will you give me for it?** was gibst du mir dafür?; **how much did you give for it?** wie viel hast du dafür bezahlt?

♦ **give or take 11 o'clock, give or take a few minutes** so gegen 11 Uhr; **six foot, give or take a few inches** ungefähr sechs Fuß

b [as present] schenken; *(= donate)* spenden, geben; **to give sb sth** *or* **sth to sb** jdm etw schenken; **it was given to me by my uncle, I was given it by my uncle** ich habe es von meinem Onkel bekommen *or* geschenkt bekommen; **he gave me a book as a present** er schenkte mir ein Buch, er machte mir ein Buch zum Geschenk

c [with abstract nouns] *trouble* machen; *one's love, attention* schenken; *hospitality* gewähren; **he gave the impression he didn't care** er machte den Eindruck, als ob es ihm egal wäre; **to give sb help** jdm helfen *or* Hilfe leisten; **to give sb support** jdn unterstützen; **(God) give me strength to do it** Gott gebe mir die Kraft, es zu tun!; **give me strength/patience!** großer Gott! *(inf)*; **to be given a choice** die Wahl haben; **to give sb a look/smile** jdn ansehen/anlächeln; **to give sb a blow** jdn schlagen, jdm einen Schlag versetzen; **to give sb a push/kick** jdm einen Stoß/Tritt geben, jdn stoßen/treten; **to give sb's hand a squeeze** jdm die Hand drücken; **to give one's hair a brush/wash** sich *(dat)* die Haare bürsten/waschen; **this incident gave him the basic plot of the story** durch dieses Ereignis bekam er die Grundidee für die Handlung der Geschichte; **who gave you that idea?** wer hat dich denn auf die Idee gebracht?; **what gives you that idea?** wie kommst du denn auf die Idee?; **that will give you something to think about** da hast du etwas, worüber du nachdenken kannst; **I'll give you something to cry about** ich werde schon zusehen, dass du weißt, warum du weinst; **give me Shakespeare/Spain (every time)!** *(inf)* es geht doch nichts über Shakespeare/Spanien!; **give me Renoir and Rembrandt, not these surrealist artists** mir sind Renoir und Rembrandt viel lieber als diese Surrealisten

♦ **to give way**
[= yield] nachgeben *(to +dat)*; **I'm not going to give way on this** ich werde in dieser Sache nicht nachgeben; **to give way to pressure** unter Druck nachgeben; **don't give way to despair** überlass dich nicht der Verzweiflung; **she gave way to tears** sie ließ den Tränen freien Lauf
[= be superseded] **to give way to sth** von etw abgelöst werden; **tears gave way to smiles** die Tränen machten einem Lächeln Platz; **radio has almost given way to television** das Radio ist vom Fernsehen fast verdrängt worden
[on road] *(Brit)* **give way to oncoming traffic** der Gegenverkehr hat Vorfahrt; **who has to give way here?** wer hat hier Vorfahrt?; **I was expecting him to give way** ich nahm an, er würde mir die Vorfahrt lassen; **"give way"** „Vorfahrt (gewähren)“

d [= cause, cause to feel] *pleasure, joy* machen, bereiten; *pain* bereiten; **to give sb pain** jdm wehtun *(also fig)*, jdm Schmerzen bereiten; **it gives me great pleasure to ...** es ist mir eine große Freude ...; **to give sb a shock** jdm einen Schock versetzen

♦ **to give sb to understand that ...** jdm zu verstehen geben, dass ...; **I was given to understand/believe that ...** mir wurde zu verstehen gegeben, dass ...

e [= punish with] erteilen; **he gave the child a smack** er gab dem Kind einen Klaps; **he gave her 100 lines** *(Brit)* *or* **sentences** *(US)* er gab ihr 100 Zeilen als Strafarbeit auf; **to give sb five years** jdn zu fünf Jahren verurteilen, jdm fünf Jahre aufbrummen *(inf)*; **he was given a thrashing/five years** er hat eine Tracht Prügel/fünf Jahre bekommen

♦ **to give sb what for** *(inf)* jdm Saures geben *(inf)*, es jdm geben *(inf)*

f [= utter] **to give a cry/groan/laugh/sigh** aufschreien/-stöhnen/-lachen/-seufzen

g [= yield, produce] *milk, warmth, light etc* geben; *results* (er)bringen; *answer* liefern; **our satellite dish gives a very good picture** unsere Parabolantenne gibt ein sehr gutes Bild

h [= allow] *time* geben; **they gave me a week to do it** sie gaben *or* ließen mir eine Woche Zeit, um es zu machen; **give yourself time to recover** lassen Sie sich Zeit, um sich zu erholen; **give yourself half an hour** rechnen Sie mit einer halben Stunde; **I always give myself an extra hour in bed** ich genehmige mir eine Extrastunde im Bett; **how long do you give that marriage?** *(inf)* wie lange gibst du dieser Ehe? *(inf)*

♦ **I'll give you that** *(= concede)* **it's an improvement, I'll give you that** es ist eine Verbesserung, das gestehe ich (dir) ein; **he's a good worker, I'll give him that** eines muss man ihm lassen, er arbeitet gut

i [= report, tell] *information, details, description, answer, advice* geben; *one's name, particulars* angeben; *suggestion* machen; *(= let sb know by letter, phone etc) decision, opinion, results* mitteilen; **the court hasn't given a decision yet** das Gericht hat noch kein Urteil gefällt; **he wouldn't give me his decision/opinion** er wollte mir seine Entscheidung/Meinung nicht sagen; **they interrupted the film to give the football results** sie unterbrachen den Film, um die Fußballergebnisse zu bringen; **give him my regards** bestellen Sie ihm (schöne) Grüße, richten Sie ihm (schöne) Grüße von mir aus; **give her my thanks** richten Sie ihr meinen Dank aus; **to give no/the right answer** nicht/richtig antworten; **to give sb a warning** jdn warnen; **his letter gave us the latest news** in seinem Brief stand das Neueste; **she was given the news by John** John hat ihr das mitgeteilt; **he forgot to give us the date** er hat vergessen, uns das Datum anzugeben *or (verbally also)* zu sagen *or (by letter, phone etc also)* mitzuteilen; **who gave you that information?** wer hat Ihnen das gesagt *or* die Auskunft gegeben *or* erteilt?

j [= hold, perform] *party, dinner, play* geben; *speech* halten; *song* singen; *toast* ausbringen *(to sb* auf jdn); **give us a song** sing uns was vor; **I give you Mary** *(as toast)* auf Mary!, auf Marys Wohl!; *(as speaker)* ich gebe Mary das Wort

k [= do] **the child gave a little jump of excitement** das Kind machte vor Aufregung einen kleinen Luftsprung; **he gave a shrug of his shoulders** er zuckte mit den Schultern

l [= devote] widmen *(to +dat)*; **he has given himself entirely to medicine** er hat sich ganz der Medizin verschrieben; **he gave himself/his life to God** er weihte sich/sein Leben Gott

2 – INTRANSITIVE VERB

a [= give way] *lit, fig: = collapse, yield* nachgeben; *(strength, health, nerve, voice)* versagen; *(= break, rope, cable)* reißen; *(cold weather)* nachlassen; **when you're under as much strain as that, something is bound to give** *(inf)* wenn man unter so viel Druck steht, muss es ja irgendwo aushaken *(inf)*

b [= bend, be flexible] nachgeben; *(bed)* federn; *(dress)* sich dehnen *or* weiten

c [= give money etc] geben, spenden; **it is more blessed to give than to receive** *(Bibl)* Geben ist seliger denn Nehmen; **you have to be prepared to give and take** *(fig)* man muss zu Kompromissen bereit sein, man muss auch mal zurückstecken können

d [= be the matter] *esp US inf* **what gives?** was gibts? *(inf)*, was ist los? *(inf)*; **what gives with him?** was ist los mit ihm? *(inf)*; **what gives in this town?** was ist hier (in der Stadt) los? *(inf)*

e [= tell] *US inf* **OK, now give!** also, raus mit der Sprache! *(inf)*

3 – NOUN

Nachgiebigkeit *f*, Elastizität *f*; *(of floor, bed, chair)* Federung *f*; **this elastic hasn't got much give left** dieses Gummiband ist nicht mehr sehr elastisch; **it has a lot of give** es gibt sehr stark nach

4 – PHRASAL VERBS

▸ **give away** VT *sep* **a** *(= give without charge)* weggeben; *(as present)* verschenken; **at £5 I'm practically giving it away** ich will £ 5 dafür, das ist fast geschenkt **b** *advantage, goal* verschenken **c** *bride* zum Altar führen *(als Brautvater etc)* **d** *(= hand out) prizes etc* vergeben, verteilen **e** *(fig: = betray)* verraten *(to sb* an jdn); **to give the game** *or* **show away** *(inf)* alles verraten; **to give oneself away** sich verraten

▸ **give back** VT *sep* zurück- *or* wiedergeben; *(mirror) image* reflektieren

▶ **give in** VI (= *surrender*) sich ergeben (*to sb* jdm); (*in guessing game etc*) aufgeben; (= *accede, back down*) nachgeben (*to +dat*); **to give in to the majority** sich der Mehrheit beugen; **to give in to blackmail** auf Erpressung eingehen; **to give in to temptation** der Versuchung erliegen *or* nicht widerstehen VT *sep document, essay* einreichen; **to give in sb's/one's name** jdn/sich anmelden

▶ **give off** VT *insep heat, gas* abgeben; *smell* verbreiten, ausströmen; *rays* ausstrahlen

▶ **give on to** VI *+prep obj (window)* hinausgehen auf (*+acc*); (*door*) hinausführen auf (*+acc*); *garden* hinausführen in (*+acc*)

▶ **give out** VI (*supplies, patience, strength*) zu Ende gehen *or* (*in past tense*) sein; (*engine, feet*) versagen; (*inspiration*) versiegen; **my voice gave out** mir versagte die Stimme VT *sep* **a** (= *distribute*) aus- *or* verteilen **b** (= *announce*) bekannt geben; **to give oneself out as sth** *or* **to be sth** sich als etw ausgeben VT *insep* = **give off**

▶ **give over** VT *sep* **a** (= *hand over*) übergeben (*to +dat*) **b** (= *set aside, use for*) **to be given over to sth** für etw beansprucht werden **c to give oneself over to pleasure/despair** *etc* sich ganz dem Vergnügen/der Verzweiflung *etc* hingeben; **to be given over to pleasure** (*life*) ganz dem Vergnügen gewidmet sein VI (*dial inf*: = *stop*) aufhören; **give over!** hör auf! VI *+prep obj* aufhören; **give over tickling me!** hör auf, mich zu kitzeln!

▶ **give up** VI aufgeben; **I give up** ich gebe auf, ich gebs auf (*inf*)
VT *sep* **a** *habit, job, idea, hope* aufgeben; *claim* verzichten auf (*+acc*), aufgeben; **to give up doing sth** aufhören *or* es aufgeben, etw zu tun; **I'm trying to give up smoking** ich versuche, das Rauchen aufzugeben; **I gave it/him up as a bad job** (*inf*) das/ihn habe ich abgeschrieben; **to give sb/sth up as lost** jdn/etw verloren geben; **to give sb up for dead** jdn für tot halten
b (= *surrender*) *land, territory* abgeben, abtreten (*to +dat*); *authority* abgeben, abtreten (*to* an *+acc*); *seat, place* frei machen (*to* für), abtreten (*to +dat*); *ticket* abgeben (*to* bei); **to give up one's life for one's country** sein Leben für sein Land opfern
c (= *hand over to authorities*) übergeben (*to dat*); **to give oneself up** sich stellen; (*after siege etc*) sich ergeben
d (= *devote*) widmen; **to give one's life up to music** sein Leben der Musik widmen *or* verschreiben
e (= *disclose, yield up*) *secret, treasure* enthüllen (*geh*)

▶ **give up on** VI *+prep obj person, project* abschreiben; **to give up on life** am Leben verzweifeln

give: **give-and-take** N Entgegenkommen *nt*; (*in personal relationships*) (gegenseitiges) Geben und Nehmen; **giveaway** N **a the expression on her face was a (dead) ~** ihr Gesichtsausdruck verriet (wirklich) alles; **it was a real ~ when he said ...** er verriet sich, als er sagte ... **b** (*inf*) **that exam question was a ~** diese Prüfungsfrage war geschenkt (*inf*) **c** (*US Comm*: = *gift*) Geschenk *nt* **d** (*US*: *Rad, TV*) Preisraten *nt*; **giveaway price** N Schleuderpreis *m*

given [ˈgɪvn] *ptp of* **give** ADJ **a** (*with indef art*) bestimmt; (*with def art*) angegeben; **in a ~ period** in einem bestimmten Zeitraum; **within the ~ period** im angegebenen Zeitraum
b ~ name (*esp US*) Vorname *m*
c (= *having inclination*) **to be ~ to sth** zu etw neigen; **I'm ~ to doing that** ich tue das gern; **I'm not ~ to doing that** es ist nicht meine Art, das zu tun; **I'm not ~ to drinking on my own** ich habe nicht die Angewohnheit, allein zu trinken
CONJ **~ sth** (= *with*) vorausgesetzt, man/er *etc* hat etw, wenn man/er *etc* etw hat; (= *in view of*) angesichts einer Sache (*gen*); **~ that he ...** (= *in view of the fact*) angesichts der Tatsache, dass er ...; (= *assuming*) vorausgesetzt *or* angenommen, (dass) er ...; **~ time, we can do it** vorausgesetzt, wir haben genug Zeit *or* wenn wir genug Zeit haben, können wir es schaffen; **~ the chance, I would ...** wenn ich die Gelegenheit hätte, würde ich ...; **~ these circumstances/conditions** unter diesen Umständen/Voraussetzungen; **~ these premises you can work out the answer** anhand dieser Voraussetzungen kannst du die Lösung finden; **~ the triangle ABC** (*Math*) gegeben ist *or* sei das Dreieck ABC

giver [ˈgɪvəʳ] N Spender(in) *m(f)*; **he was a generous ~ to church funds** er hat großzügig für die Kirche gespendet

give-way sign [gɪvˈweɪˌsaɪn] N (*Brit*) Vorfahrtsschild *nt*

giving [ˈgɪvɪŋ] ADJ großzügig

gizmo [ˈgɪzməʊ] N (*inf*) Ding *nt* (*inf*)

gizzard [ˈgɪzəd] N Muskelmagen *m*

Gk *abbr of* **Greek** griech.

glabrous [ˈglæbrəs] ADJ (*Zool*) unbehaart; (*liter*) *youth* bartlos

glacé [ˈglæseɪ] ADJ *bun* mit Zuckerguss, glasiert; *cherry, fruit* kandiert; **~ icing** Zuckerguss *m*; **~ leather** Glacee- *or* Glacéleder *nt*

glacial [ˈgleɪsɪəl] ADJ **a** (*Geol*) Gletscher-, glazial (*spec*); **~ landscape** Gletscherlandschaft *f*; **at a ~ pace** (*fig*) im Schneckentempo **b** (= *cold*) *look, wind* eisig; (*fig*) *person, atmosphere, smile* frostig

glacial period N Eiszeit *f*, Glazial *nt* (*form*)

glaciated [ˈgleɪsɪeɪtɪd] ADJ (= *covered with glaciers*) gletscherbedeckt, vergletschert; (= *eroded by glaciers*) durch Gletschertätigkeit entstanden

glacier [ˈglæsɪəʳ] N Gletscher *m*

glaciology [ˌgleɪsɪˈɒlədʒɪ] N Gletscherkunde *f*, Glaziologie *f* (*form*)

glad [glæd] ✪ 3.1, 25.2 ADJ (*+er*) **a** *pred* (= *pleased*) froh; **to be ~ about sth** sich über etw (*acc*) freuen; **I'm ~ (about that)** das freut mich, da bin ich froh; **to be ~ of sth** froh über etw (*acc*) sein; **he was ~ of a chance to change the subject** er freute sich über die Gelegenheit, das Thema zu wechseln; **I'd be ~ of an opportunity to show you the house** ich würde dir gerne das Haus zeigen; **you'll be ~ of an umbrella** du wirst einen Schirm gut gebrauchen können; **we'd be ~ of your help** wir wären froh, wenn Sie uns helfen könnten; **I'd be ~ of your opinion on this** ich würde gerne Ihre Meinung dazu hören; **to be ~ (that)...** sich freuen, dass ...; (= *relieved*) froh sein, dass ...; **I'm ~ you like it** ich freue mich, dass es Ihnen gefällt; **I'm ~ I relented in the end** ich bin froh, dass ich schließlich nachgegeben habe; **to be ~ to do sth** sich freuen, etw zu tun; (= *relieved*) froh sein, etw zu tun; **~ to be of service** gern geschehen; **he is always ~ to come with us** er kommt immer gern mit (uns mit); **we should be ~ to answer any questions** eventuelle Fragen beantworten wir gerne; **I'll be ~ to show you everything** ich zeige Ihnen gerne alles; **to be only too ~ to do sth** etw sehr gern tun; **I was only too ~ to get away** ich war heilfroh, da wegzukommen (*inf*)
b *attr* **the ~ tidings** die frohe Botschaft (*geh*), die gute *or* freudige Nachricht; **to give sb the ~ tidings** jdm die frohe Botschaft (*geh*) *or* freudige Nachricht überbringen → **glad eye, glad hand, glad rags**

gladden [ˈglædn] VT *person, heart* erfreuen

glade [gleɪd] N Lichtung *f*

glad: **glad eye** N **to give sb the ~** jdm schöne Augen machen (*inf*); **glad hand** N **to give sb the ~** jdn überschwänglich begrüßen

gladiator [ˈglædɪeɪtəʳ] N Gladiator *m*

gladiatorial [ˌglædɪəˈtɔːrɪəl] ADJ Gladiatoren-; **~ combat** Gladiatorenkampf *m*

gladiolus [ˌglædɪˈəʊləs] N *pl* **gladioli** [ˌglædɪˈəʊlaɪ] Gladiole *f*

gladly [ˈglædlɪ] ADV (= *willingly, happily*) gern(e); **I'd ~ give her £5 to go away** ich gäbe ihr gern(e) £ 5, wenn sie nur wegginge

gladness [ˈglædnɪs] N (= *joy*) Freude *f*; (= *relief*) Erleichterung *f*; **an occasion of great ~** ein sehr freudiger Anlass

glad rags PL (*inf*) beste Klamotten *pl* (*inf*), Sonntagsstaat *m* (*inf*); **go and put your ~ on!** wirf dich in Schale! (*inf*)

gladsome [ˈglædsəm] ADJ (*old*) freudenreich (*liter*)

glam [glæm] ADJ (*inf*) schick

glamor N (*US*) = **glamour**

glamorize [ˈglæməraɪz] VT idealisieren, einen glamourösen Anstrich geben (*+dat*); *job, lifestyle also* einen besonderen Glanz *or* Reiz verleihen (*+dat*); (*author*) *war, violence* glorifizieren, verherrlichen

glamorous [ˈglæmərəs] ADJ (= *attractive*) *person, job, life* glamourös; *place, clothes* mondän, schick; *occasion* glanzvoll; **there's nothing ~ about the job** der Job ist überhaupt nicht reizvoll

glamorously [ˈglæmərəslɪ] ADV glamourös; **a ~ exciting life** ein fabelhaft aufregendes Leben

glamour, (*US*) **glamor** [ˈglæməʳ] N Glamour *m*; (*of occasion, situation*) Glanz *m*; **she/the job doesn't have much ~** sie/dieser Beruf hat keinen besonderen Reiz; **she has ~ as well as prettiness** sie ist nicht nur hübsch, sondern besitzt auch noch einen besonderen Reiz

glamour, (*US*) **glamor**: **glamour boy** N (*inf*) Schönling *m* (*inf*); **glamour girl** N (*inf*) Glamourgirl *nt*; **glamour model** N Pin-up-Girl *nt*; **glamourpuss** N (*esp Brit inf*: = *female*) Glamourkätzchen *nt* (*inf*); (= *male*) Schönling *m* (*inf*)

glam rock N (*Mus inf*) Glam-Rock *m*

glance [glɑːns] N Blick *m*; **at a ~** auf einen Blick; **at first ~** auf den ersten Blick; **she gave him a warning/quick ~** sie warf ihm einen warnenden/kurzen Blick zu; **to take a quick ~ at sth** einen kurzen Blick auf etw (*acc*) werfen; **he cast** *or* **had a quick ~ round the room** er sah sich kurz im Zimmer um; **we exchanged ~s** wir sahen uns kurz an
VI sehen, blicken, schauen (*esp S Ger*); **to ~ at sb/sth** jdn/etw kurz ansehen, einen kurzen Blick auf etw (*acc*) werfen; **to ~ at** *or* **through a newspaper/report** einen kurzen Blick in eine Zeitung/einen Bericht werfen, eine Zeitung/einen Bericht überfliegen *or* kurz durchsehen; **to ~ over sth** etw überfliegen; **to ~ across to sb** jdm einen Blick zuwerfen; **to ~ down/in** einen Blick hinunter-/hineinwerfen, kurz hinunter-/hineinsehen; **to ~ up** aufsehen *or* -blicken (*from* von); **to ~ round** sich umblicken; **he ~d round the room** er sah sich im Zimmer um

▶ **glance off** VI (*prep obj* von) (*bullet etc*) abprallen; (*sword*) abgleiten; (*light*) reflektiert werden

glancing [ˈglɑːnsɪŋ] ADJ **to strike sth a ~ blow** etw streifen; **she struck him a ~ blow** ihr Schlag streifte ihn; **it was only a ~ blow** ich/er *etc* wurde nur gestreift

gland [glænd] N Drüse *f*; (= *lymph gland*) Lymphdrüse *f or* -knoten *m*

glandular [ˈglændjʊləʳ] ADJ **~ fever** Drüsenfieber *nt*

glans penis [ˈglænzˈpiːnɪs] N Glans *f*, Eichel *f*

glare [glɛəʳ] N **a** greller Schein; (*from sun, bulb, lamp*) grelles Licht, greller Schein; **the ~ of the sun** das grelle Sonnenlicht; **to escape the ~ of publicity** dem grellen Licht der Öffentlichkeit entkommen **b** (= *stare*) wütender *or* stechender Blick; **a ~ of hatred/anger** ein hasserfüllter/zorniger Blick VI **a** (*light, sun*) grell scheinen; (*headlights*) grell leuchten; (*bulb*) grell brennen **b** (= *stare*) (zornig) starren; **to ~ at sb/sth** jdn/etw zornig anstarren VT **to ~ defiance/hatred at sb** jdn trotzig *or* voller Trotz/hasserfüllt *or* voll von Hass anstarren

glaring [ˈglɛərɪŋ] ADJ **a** *look* stechend; (= *furious*) wütend; **her ~ eyes** ihr stechender Blick **b** *sun, light* grell, gleißend (*geh*) **c** (= *blatant*) *example, omission* eklatant; *error* offensichtlich, grob; *weakness* offensichtlich; *contradiction, inconsistency* krass; *injustice* (himmel)schreiend

glaringly [ˈglɛərɪŋlɪ] ADV **a** *shine* grell; **~ bright** grell **b** *(= blatantly)* **~ obvious** *(fact, statement)* überdeutlich; **it was ~ obvious that he had no idea** es war nur zu ersichtlich, dass er keine Ahnung hatte; **a ~ obvious error** ein Fehler, der einem geradezu ins Auge springt; **it's ~ wrong** das ist ein eklatanter Fehler

glasnost [ˈglæznɒst] N Glasnost *f*

glass [glɑːs] N **a** *(= substance)* Glas *nt*; **a pane of ~** eine Glasscheibe; **to be grown under ~** *(Hort)* unter Glas gezogen werden
b *(= object, vessel, contents, glassware)* Glas *nt*; *(dated, = mirror)* Spiegel *m*; **a ~ of wine** ein Glas Wein; **he's quite friendly when he's had a ~** *(inf)* er ist recht freundlich, wenn er ein Gläschen getrunken hat
c *(= spectacles)* **~es** *pl*, **pair of ~es** Brille *f*; **he wears thick ~es** er trägt eine starke Brille *or* starke Gläser
d *(= instrument) (= magnifying glass)* (Vergrößerungs)glas *nt*, Lupe *f*; *(= telescope)* Teleskop *nt*, Fernrohr *nt*; *(= barometer)* Barometer *nt*; **~es** *pl (= binoculars)* (Fern)glas *nt*
VT verglasen
ADJ *attr* Glas-; **~ bottle** Glasflasche *f*; **people who live in ~ houses shouldn't throw stones** *(Prov)* wer im Glashaus sitzt, soll nicht mit Steinen werfen *(Prov)*

glass *in cpds* Glas-; **glass block** N Glasbaustein *m*; **glass-blower** N Glasbläser(in) *m(f)*; **glass-blowing** N Glasbläserei *f*; **glass brick** N Glasziegel *m*; **glass case** N Glaskasten *m*, Vitrine *f*; **glass ceiling** N *(fig)* gläserne Decke; **she hit the ~** sie kam als Frau beruflich nicht mehr weiter; **glass cloth** N Gläsertuch *nt*; **glass-cutter** N *(= tool)* Glasschneider *m*; *(= person)* Glasschleifer(in) *m(f)*

glassed-in [ˈglɑːstˈɪn] ADJ verglast

glass: **glass eye** N Glasauge *nt*; **glass fibre**, *(US)* **glass fiber** N Glasfaser *f*; **glassful** N = **glass N b**; **glasshouse** N *(Brit)* **a** *(Hort)* Gewächshaus *nt* **b** *(Mil sl)* Bau *m*, Bunker *m (sl)*; **glasspaper** N Glaspapier *nt*; **glassware** N Glaswaren *pl*; **glass wool** N Glaswolle *f*; **glassworks** N *sing or pl* Glashütte *f*

glassy [ˈglɑːsɪ] ADJ *(+er) surface, sea etc* spiegelglatt; *eye, look* glasig; **~-eyed** *(look)* glasig; **to be ~-eyed** einen glasigen Blick haben; **to stare at sb ~-eyed** jdn mit glasigem Blick anstarren

Glaswegian [glæzˈwiːdʒən] N **a** Glasgower(in) *m(f)* **b** *(= dialect)* Glasgower Dialekt *m*
ADJ Glasgower, von Glasgow

glaucoma [glɔːˈkəʊmə] N grüner Star, Glaukom *nt (form)*

glaucous [ˈglɔːkəs] ADJ *leaves* mit einer weißlichen Schicht überzogen; **~ blue/green** gräulich blau/grün

glaze [gleɪz] N *(on pottery, tiles, Cook)* Glasur *f*; *(on paper, fabric)* Appretur *f*; *(on painting)* Lasur *f* VT **a** *door, window* verglasen **b** *pottery, tiles* glasieren; *fabric, paper* appretieren; *painting* lasieren; **~d tile** Kachel *f* **c** *(Cook) cake* glasieren; *meat* mit Gelee überziehen; *fruit* kandieren; **~d ham** Schinken *m* in Aspik VI *(eyes: also* **glaze over***)* glasig werden; **she had a ~d look in her eyes** sie hatte einen glasigen Blick

glazier [ˈgleɪzɪəʳ] N Glaser(in) *m(f)*

glazing [ˈgleɪzɪŋ] N **a** *(= act)* Verglasen *nt*; *(= glass)* Verglasung *f*; *(= trade)* Glaserei *f* **b** = **glaze N**

GLC *abbr of* **Greater London Council**

gleam [gliːm] N **a** Schein *m*, Schimmer *m*; *(of metal, water)* Schimmern *nt*; **a ~ of light** ein Lichtschimmer *m*; **a ~ of white** ein weißer Schimmer; **the ~ from his torch** der Schein seiner Taschenlampe; **~s of moonlight came through the curtains** das Mondlicht schimmerte durch die Vorhänge
b *(fig)* **a ~ of hope** ein Hoffnungsschimmer *m*; **a ~ of pride/curiosity** ein Funke *m* von Stolz/Neugier; **a ~ of sense** ein Hauch *m* von Vernunft; **not a ~ of hope/pride** kein Funke *m* Hoffnung/Stolz; **he had a (dangerous) ~ in his eye** seine Augen funkelten (gefährlich)
VI schimmern; *(hair, skin also)* glänzen; *(eyes)* funkeln

gleaming [ˈgliːmɪŋ] ADJ schimmernd; *car, hair, silver, water also* glänzend; *smile* strahlend; *eyes* funkelnd; **~ white teeth** blendend weiße Zähne

glean [gliːn] VT *(lit) corn, field* nachlesen; *(fig) facts, news* herausbekommen, ausfindig machen, erkunden *(geh)*; **to ~ sth from sb/sth** etw von jdm erfahren/einer Sache *(dat)* entnehmen

gleaner [ˈgliːnəʳ] N Ährenleser(in) *m(f)*

gleanings [ˈgliːnɪŋz] PL *(lit)* Nachlese *f*, aufgelesene Ähren *pl*; **the ~ of twenty years of study** die Ausbeute eines zwanzigjährigen Studiums; **a few ~ from the press conference** ein paar Informationen von der Pressekonferenz

glebe [gliːb] N *(Eccl)* Pfarrland *nt*; **~ house** pfarreieigenes Haus; *(= vicarage)* Pfarrhaus *nt*

glee [gliː] N **a** Freude *f*; *(malicious)* Schadenfreude *f*; **he shouted with ~** er stieß einen Freudenschrei aus; **he told the story with great ~** er erzählte die Geschichte mit großem Vergnügen; **his victory was greeted with ~** sein Sieg löste Begeisterung aus; **they were full of ~** sie waren (hell) begeistert; **they were full of malicious ~** sie freuten sich hämisch *or* diebisch; **they were rubbing their hands in ~** *(also fig)* sie rieben sich *(dat)* schadenfroh die Hände; **his defeat caused great ~ among his enemies** seine Feinde freuten sich diebisch *or* hämisch über seine Niederlage
b *(Mus)* mehrstimmiges Lied

glee club N *(esp US)* Chor *m*

gleeful [ˈgliːfʊl] ADJ fröhlich, vergnügt; *(maliciously)* hämisch, schadenfroh; **they were all ~ about his failure** sie freuten sich alle diebisch über sein Versagen

gleefully [ˈgliːfəlɪ] ADV *(= exultantly)* fröhlich, vergnügt; *(= maliciously)* hämisch, schadenfroh

glen [glen] N Tal *nt*

glib [glɪb] ADJ *(+er) person* zungenfertig; *excuse, reply* glatt, leichtzüngig; *attitude, ideas* leichtfertig; *promise, generalization* vorschnell; **~ talk** leichtfertiges Gerede; **~ phrases** schön klingende Phrasen *pl*; **I don't want to sound ~** ich möchte nicht den Eindruck erwecken, das so leichthin zu sagen; **to have a ~ tongue** zungenfertig sein, eine glatte Zunge haben

glibly [ˈglɪblɪ] ADV *talk* leichthin; *promise, generalize* vorschnell; *reply* glatt; *lie* geschickt; **he ~ produced a couple of excuses** er war schnell mit ein paar glatten Ausreden bei der Hand

glibness [ˈglɪbnɪs] N *(of person)* Zungenfertigkeit *f*; *(of reply, excuse, lie)* Leichtzüngigkeit *f*; **a remark of such ~** eine so leichtzüngige Bemerkung

glide [glaɪd] VI **a** *(person)* gleiten; *(through the air)* schweben, gleiten; **to ~ into a room** in ein Zimmer schweben; **to ~ in** hereinschweben; **to ~ off** *or* **away** davongleiten; *(person, ghost)* davonschweben **b** *(bird)* gleiten; *(plane)* im Gleitflug fliegen; *(glider)* gleiten, schweben; *(= fly in a glider)* segelfliegen; **I would like to learn to ~** ich möchte Segelfliegen lernen; **to ~ down to land** zur Landung ansetzen VT gleiten lassen; *plane* im Gleitflug fliegen (lassen) N **a** *(Dancing)* Gleit- *or* Schleifschritt *m* **b** *(Mus)* Portamento *nt*; *(Phon)* Gleitlaut *m* **c** *(Aviat)* Gleitflug *m*

glider [ˈglaɪdəʳ] N *(Aviat)* Segelflugzeug *nt*; **~ pilot** Segelflieger(in) *m(f)*

gliding [ˈglaɪdɪŋ] N *(Aviat)* Segelfliegen *nt*; **~ club** Segelfliegerklub *m*

glimmer [ˈglɪməʳ] N **a** *(of light, candle etc)* Schimmer *m*; *(of fire)* Glimmen *nt*; **the ~ of the distant river** das Schimmern des Flusses in der Ferne; **the faint ~ of dawn** der schwache Schein der Morgendämmerung **b** *(fig: also* **glimmering***)* = **gleam N b** VI *(light, water)* schimmern; *(flame, fire)* glimmen

glimpse [glɪmps] N Blick *m*; **it was our last ~ of home** das war der letzte Blick auf unser Zuhause; **a ~ of life in 18th-century London** ein (Ein)blick in das Leben im London des 18. Jahrhunderts; **to catch a ~ of sb/sth** einen flüchtigen Blick auf jdn/etw werfen können *or* von jdm/etw erhaschen; *(fig)* eine Ahnung von etw bekommen; **a ~ into the future** ein Blick *m* in die Zukunft VT kurz sehen, einen Blick erhaschen von VI **to ~ at sth** einen Blick auf etw *(acc)* werfen; **to ~ through a window** einen Blick durch ein Fenster werfen

glint [glɪnt] N *(of light, metal)* Glitzern *nt no pl*, Blinken *nt no pl*; *(of eyes)* Funkeln *nt no pl*; **a ~ of light** ein glitzernder Lichtstrahl; **brown hair with golden ~s in it** braunes Haar mit einem goldenen Schimmer; **he has a wicked/merry ~ in his eyes** seine Augen funkeln böse/lustig; **a ~ of triumph/amusement** ein triumphierendes/amüsiertes Augenfunkeln VI glitzern, blinken; *(eyes)* funkeln

glissade [glɪˈseɪd] N *(in dancing)* Glissade *f*

glisten [ˈglɪsn] VI glänzen; *(dewdrops, tears)* glitzern N Glänzen *nt*, Glitzern *nt*

glister [ˈglɪstəʳ] N, VI *(old)* = **glitter**

glitch [glɪtʃ] N *(Comput)* Funktionsstörung *f*; **a technical ~** eine technische Panne

glitter [ˈglɪtəʳ] N Glitzern *nt*; *(of eyes, diamonds)* Funkeln *nt*; *(for decoration)* Glitzerstaub *m*; *(fig)* Glanz *m*, Prunk *m*; **the ~ of life in London** das glanzvolle Leben in London VI glitzern; *(eyes, diamonds)* funkeln; **all that ~s is not gold** *(Prov)* es ist nicht alles Gold, was glänzt *(Prov)*

glitterati [ˌglɪtəˈrɑːtɪ] PL *(inf)* Hautevolee *f*

glitter gel N *(Fashion)* Glitzergel *nt*

glittering [ˈglɪtərɪŋ] ADJ glitzernd; *eyes, diamonds* funkelnd; *occasion* glanzvoll; *career* glänzend; *prizes* verlockend; **a ~ array of celebrities** ein glanzvolles Aufgebot an Stars

glitter powder N *(Fashion)* Glitterpuder *m or* -pulver *nt*

glittery [ˈglɪtərɪ] ADJ *(inf)* glitzernd

glitz [glɪts] N *(inf)* Glanz *m*

glitzy [ˈglɪtsɪ] ADJ *(+er) (inf) occasion* glanzvoll, schillernd; *dress* schick

gloaming [ˈgləʊmɪŋ] N *(liter)* Dämmer- *or* Zwielicht *nt (geh)*

gloat [gləʊt] VI *(with pride at oneself)* sich großtun *(over, about* mit); *(verbally also)* sich brüsten *(over, about* mit); *(over sb's misfortune or failure)* sich hämisch freuen *(over, about* über *+acc)*; **to ~ over sb's misfortune** sich an jds Unglück weiden; **to ~ over one's successes** sich in seinen Erfolgen sonnen; **there's no need to ~ (over me)!** das ist kein Grund zur Schadenfreude!

gloating [ˈgləʊtɪŋ] N Selbstgefälligkeit *f*; *(over sb's misfortune or failure)* Schadenfreude *f*; **it wasn't pleasant to listen to their ~** es war kein Vergnügen, ihren selbstgefälligen Reden/schadenfrohen Bemerkungen zuzuhören; **their ~ over their own success** ihre selbstgefällige Freude über ihren Erfolg ADJ *(= self-satisfied)* selbstgefällig; *(= malicious)* hämisch, schadenfroh; **he cast a ~ look at the money** er weidete sich genüsslich am Anblick des Geldes

gloatingly [ˈgləʊtɪŋlɪ] ADV *say, smile, laugh* selbstgefällig

glob [glɒb] N *(inf)* Klacks *m (inf)*; *(of mud)* Klümpchen *nt*

global [ˈgləʊbl] ADJ global; *recession, problem* weltweit; **taking a ~ view of the matter …** global gesehen …; **a ~ figure of £2 million** eine Gesamtsumme von £ 2 Millionen; **~ peace/war** Weltfrieden/-krieg *m*

global: **global climate** N Erdklima *nt*, Weltklima *nt*; **global economy** N Weltwirtschaft *f*

globalization [ˌgləʊbəlaɪˈzeɪʃən] N Globalisierung *f*

globalize [ˈgləʊbəlaɪz] VI globalisieren, weltweit zusammenarbeiten *or* tätig werden VT *economy* globalisieren

globally ['gləʊbəlɪ] ADV **a** *(= worldwide)* global, weltweit; *think* global; **~, the risks are huge** global gesehen sind die Risiken enorm **b** *(= universally) accepted, recognized* allgemein

global: **global navigation system** N globales Navigationssystem; **global player** N *(= company)* Weltfirma *f*, Global Player *m*; **global positioning system** N globales Positionsbestimmungssystem, GPS *nt*; **global trade** N Welthandel *m*; **global village** N Weltdorf *nt*; **the world is considered as a ~** die Welt wird als Dorf angesehen; **global warming** N Erwärmung *f* der Erdatmosphäre

globe [gləʊb] N *(= sphere)* Kugel *f*; *(= map)* Globus *m*; *(= fish bowl)* Glaskugel *f*; **the ~** *(= the world)* der Globus, der Erdball; **all over the ~** auf der ganzen Erde *or* Welt; **terrestrial/celestial ~** Erd-/Himmelskugel *f*

globe: **globe artichoke** N Artischocke *f*; **globefish** N Kugelfisch *m*; **globeflower** N *(Bot)* Trollblume *f*; **globe lightning** N Kugelblitz *m*; **globetrotter** N Globetrotter(in) *m(f)*, Weltenbummler(in) *m(f)*; **globetrotting** N Globetrotten *nt* ATTR *reporter etc* globetrottend

globular ['glɒbjʊlə'] ADJ kugelförmig

globule ['glɒbju:l] N Klümpchen *nt*, Kügelchen *nt*; *(of oil, water)* Tröpfchen *nt*; **~s of grease floating on the soup** Fettaugen *pl* auf der Suppe

glockenspiel ['glɒkənʃpi:l] N Glockenspiel *nt*

gloom [glu:m] N **a** *(= darkness)* Düsterkeit *f* **b** *(= sadness)* düstere *or* gedrückte Stimmung; **economic ~** depressive Wirtschaftslage; **an air** *or* **atmosphere of ~** eine düstere *or* gedrückte Atmosphäre; **to cast a ~ over sth** einen Schatten auf etw *(acc)* werfen; **a ~ descended on us** eine düstere Stimmung überkam uns; **he was filled with ~** er war sehr bedrückt *or* niedergeschlagen

gloomily ['glu:mɪlɪ] ADV **a ~ lit** schlecht beleuchtet **b** *ask, think, say* niedergeschlagen, bedrückt; *(= pessimistically) view, predict* pessimistisch

gloominess ['glu:mɪnɪs] N **a** *(= darkness, of place, sky)* Düsterkeit *f*; *(of day, weather, light)* Trübheit *f* **b** *(= despondency: of person)* Niedergeschlagenheit *f*, Bedrücktheit *f*; *(= melancholy)* Trübsinn *m*; *(= pessimism)* Pessimismus *m*; *(of thoughts, expression)* Düsterkeit *f*; *(of forecast, future, news)* bedrückende Art; *(of outlook)* Trübheit *f*; *(of assessment, view)* pessimistische Art

gloomster ['glu:mstə'] N *(inf)* Pessimist(in) *m(f)*, Schwarzmaler(in) *m(f) (inf)*

gloomy ['glu:mɪ] ADJ *(+er)* **a** *(= dark) place, sky* düster; *day, weather, light* trüb **b** *(= dismal, despondent) person, mood* niedergeschlagen, bedrückt; *voice* traurig; *(= pessimistic)* pessimistisch (*about* über *+acc*); *thought, expression* düster; *(= dispiriting) picture, forecast, future* düster, bedrückend; *news* bedrückend; *outlook, prospects* trübe; *assessment, view* pessimistisch; **there is a ~ future ahead** die Zukunft sieht düster aus; **to feel/look ~** niedergeschlagen *or* bedrückt sein/aussehen; **to take a ~ view of things** schwarzsehen; **just thinking about the situation makes me feel ~** es bedrückt mich, wenn ich nur über die Lage nachdenke; **he is very ~ about his chances of success** er beurteilt seine Erfolgschancen sehr pessimistisch

gloop [glu:p] N *(inf)* Schmiere*f (inf)*, Pampe*f (inf)*

gloopy ['glu:pɪ] ADJ *(inf)* schmierig*f*, pampig*f (inf)*

glorification [ˌglɔ:rɪfɪ'keɪʃən] N Verherrlichung *f*; *(of God also)* Lobpreis *m*; *(= beautification)* Verschönerung *f*

glorified ['glɔ:rɪfaɪd] ADJ **this restaurant is just a ~ snack bar** dieses Restaurant ist nur eine bessere Imbissstube; **I'm just a ~ secretary** ich bin nur eine bessere Sekretärin

glorify ['glɔ:rɪfaɪ] VT verherrlichen; *(= praise) God* lobpreisen

gloriole ['glɔ:rɪəʊl] N Gloriole *f*, Heiligenschein *m*

glorious ['glɔ:rɪəs] ADJ **a** *(= splendid)* herrlich, wunderbar; **a ~ mess** *(iro)* ein schönes *or* herrliches Durcheinander **b** *(= illustrious) career, future* glanzvoll; *years, days, era, victory, history* ruhmreich

gloriously ['glɔ:rɪəslɪ] ADV **a** *(= marvellously)* herrlich; **~ happy** überglücklich **b** *(= illustriously)* glanzvoll; *die* ruhmreich

glory ['glɔ:rɪ] N **a** *(= honour, fame)* Ruhm *m*; **moment of ~** Ruhmesstunde *f*; **covered in ~** ruhmbedeckt; **she led her team to Olympic ~** sie führte ihre Mannschaft zu olympischen Ehren
b *(= praise)* Ehre *f*; **~ to God in the highest** Ehre sei Gott in der Höhe; **~ be!** *(dated inf)* du lieber Himmel! *(inf)*
c *(= beauty, magnificence)* Herrlichkeit *f*; **the glories of the past, past glories** vergangene Herrlichkeiten *pl*; **the glories of the desert** die Schönheiten *pl* der Wüste; **the rose in all its ~** die Rose in ihrer ganzen Pracht *or* Herrlichkeit; **Rome at the height of its ~** Rom in seiner Blütezeit; **they restored the car to its former ~** sie restaurierten das Auto, bis es seine frühere Schönheit wiedererlangt hatte
d *(= source of pride)* Stolz *m*
e *(= celestial bliss)* **the saints in ~** die Heiligen in der himmlischen Herrlichkeit; **Christ in ~** Christus in seiner Herrlichkeit; **to go to ~** *(euph liter)* ins ewige Leben *or* in die Ewigkeit eingehen *(euph liter)*
VI **to ~ in sb's attention** jds Aufmerksamkeit genießen; **to ~ in one's/sb's success** sich in seinem/jds Erfolg sonnen; **to ~ in the knowledge/fact that ...** das Wissen/die Tatsache, dass …, voll auskosten; **they gloried in showing me my mistakes** sie genossen es *or* kosteten es voll aus, mir meine Fehler zu zeigen; **to ~ in the name/title of ...** den stolzen Namen/Titel … führen

glory hole N **a** *(inf)* Rumpel- *or* Kramecke *f*; *(= room)* Rumpelkammer *f*; *(= box)* Rumpelkiste *f*; *(= drawer)* Kramschublade *f* **b** *(Naut)* Logis *nt*

gloss[1] [glɒs] N *(= shine, lip gloss)* Glanz *m*; *(fig, of respectability etc)* Schein *m*; **to take the ~ off sth** *(lit)* etw stumpf werden lassen; *(fig)* einer Sache *(dat)* den Glanz nehmen; **to lose its ~** *(lit, fig)* seinen Glanz verlieren; **~ finish** *(Phot: on paper)* Glanz(beschichtung *f*) *m*; *(of paint)* Lackanstrich *m*; **the photos had a ~ finish** es waren Glanzabzüge → *also* **gloss (paint)**

▶ **gloss over** VT *sep* *(= try to conceal)* vertuschen; *(= make light of)* beschönigen; **he glossed over the various points raised by the critics** er hat die verschiedenen Punkte der Kritiker einfach vom Tisch gewischt

gloss[2] N *(= explanation)* Erläuterung *f*; *(= note also)* Anmerkung *f*, Glosse *f (geh)*; **to put a ~ on sth** etw interpretieren VT erläutern

glossary ['glɒsərɪ] N Glossar *nt*

glossily ['glɒsɪlɪ] ADV effektvoll

glossiness ['glɒsɪnɪs] N Glanz *m*

gloss (paint) N Glanzlack(farbe *f*) *m*; **high ~** Hochglanzlackfarbe *f*

glossy ['glɒsɪ] ADJ *(+er)* glänzend; **to be ~** glänzen; **~ brochure** Hochglanzbroschüre *f*; **~ magazine** (Hochglanz)magazin *nt*; **~ paper/paint** Glanzpapier *nt*/-lack *m*; **~ print** *(Phot)* Hochglanzbild *or* -foto *nt* N *(inf)* (Hochglanz)magazin *nt*

glottal ['glɒtl] ADJ *sound* in der Stimmritze gebildet, glottal *(spec)*

glottal stop N *(Phon)* Knacklaut *m*, Stimmritzenverschlusslaut *m*

glottis ['glɒtɪs] N Stimmritze *f*, Glottis *f (spec)*

Gloucs *(Brit) abbr of* **Gloucestershire**

glove [glʌv] N (Finger)handschuh *m*; *(Sport)* Handschuh *m*; **to fit (sb) like a ~** (jdm) wie angegossen passen; **with the ~s off** *(fig)* schonungslos, ohne Rücksicht auf Verluste *(inf)*; **the ~s are off** *(fig)* mit der Rücksichtnahme ist es vorbei, die Schonzeit ist vorbei

glove box N **a** *(Tech)* Handschuhschutzkasten *m* **b** *(Aut: also* **glove compartment***)* Handschuhfach *nt*

gloved [glʌvd] ADJ behandschuht

glove puppet N *(Brit)* Handpuppe *f*

glover ['glʌvə'] N Handschuhmacher(in) *m(f)*

glow [gləʊ] VI glühen; *(colour, hands of clock)* leuchten; *(lamp, candle)* scheinen; **her cheeks ~ed** ihre Wangen glühten; **she/her cheeks ~ed with health** sie hatte ein blühendes Aussehen; **to ~ with pride** vor Stolz glühen; **to ~ with pleasure** vor Freude strahlen; **she ~ed with confidence** sie strahlte Selbstvertrauen vor; **to ~ red** rot leuchten
N Glühen *nt*; *(of colour, clock hands)* Leuchten *nt*; *(of lamp, candle)* Schein *m*; *(of fire, sunset, passion)* Glut *f*; **her face had a healthy ~** ihr Gesicht hatte eine blühende Farbe; **she felt a ~ of satisfaction/affection** sie empfand eine tiefe Befriedigung/Zuneigung; **there was a ~ about her** sie strahlte

glower ['glaʊə'] VI ein finsteres Gesicht machen; **to ~ at sb** jdn finster ansehen N finsterer Blick; **surly ~** mürrischer Blick; **there was a ~ on his face** ein finsterer Ausdruck lag auf seinem Gesicht

glowering ['glaʊərɪŋ] ADJ finster

gloweringly ['glaʊərɪŋlɪ] ADV finster

glowing ['gləʊɪŋ] ADJ **a** glühend; *candle, colour, eyes* leuchtend; *cheeks, complexion* blühend; **to be ~ with health** blühend aussehen **b** *(fig: = enthusiastic) account, description* begeistert; *words* leidenschaftlich, begeistert; *praise, report* überschwänglich; *pride, admiration, enthusiasm* glühend; **to speak of sb/sth in ~ terms** voller Begeisterung von jdm/etw sprechen; **to paint sth in ~ colours** *(fig)* etw in den leuchtendsten Farben schildern

glowingly ['gləʊɪŋlɪ] ADV *(fig)* begeistert; *describe* in glühenden Farben; *praise* überschwänglich

glow-worm ['gləʊˌwɜ:m] N Glühwürmchen *nt*

glucose ['glu:kəʊs] N Glucose *f*, Glukose *f*, Traubenzucker *m*

glue [glu:] N Klebstoff *m*, Leim *m*; **to stick to sb/sth like ~** an jdm/etw kleben *(inf)*
VT kleben, leimen; **to ~ sth together** etw zusammenkleben *or* -leimen; **to ~ sth down/on** etw fest-/ankleben; **to ~ sth to sth** etw an etw *(acc)* kleben, etw an etw *(dat)* festkleben; **her ear was ~d to the keyhole** ihr Ohr klebte am Schlüsselloch; **to keep one's eyes ~d to sb/sth** jdn/etw nicht aus den Augen lassen; **his eyes were ~d to the screen** seine Augen hingen an der Leinwand; **he's been ~d to the TV all evening** er hängt schon den ganzen Abend vorm Fernseher *(inf)*; **he stood there as if ~d to the spot** er stand wie angewurzelt da; **we were ~d to our seats** wir saßen wie gebannt auf unseren Plätzen

glue: **glue pot** N Leimtopf *m*; **glue-sniffer** ['glu:snɪfə'] N (Klebstoff)schnüffler(in) *m(f)*; **glue-sniffing** ['glu:snɪfɪŋ] N (Klebstoff)schnüffeln *nt*

gluey ['glu:ɪ] ADJ klebrig

glum [glʌm] ADJ *(+er)* niedergeschlagen, bedrückt; *atmosphere* gedrückt; *thoughts* schwarz; **to feel/look ~** bedrückt sein/aussehen

glumly ['glʌmlɪ] ADV niedergeschlagen, bedrückt

glumness ['glʌmnɪs] N Bedrücktheit *f*, Niedergeschlagenheit *f*

glut [glʌt] VT **a** *(Comm) market (manufacturer etc)* überschwemmen; **sugar is ~ting the world market** der Weltmarkt wird mit Zucker überschwemmt **b to ~ oneself** *(with food)* schlemmen; **to be ~ted with sth** mit etw vollgestopft sein N Schwemme *f*; *(of manufactured goods also)* Überangebot *nt* (*of* an *+dat*); **a ~ of oil** ein Überangebot an Öl

glutamate ['glu:təmeɪt] N = **monosodium glutamate**

glute ['glu:t] N *usu pl* (*inf:* = *gluteus*) Hintern *m* (*inf*), Gesäß *nt*, Gesäßmuskel *m*

gluteal ['glu:tɪəl] ADJ Gesäß-; **~ muscles** Gesäßmuskeln *pl*

gluten ['glu:tən] N Gluten *nt*; (*glue in flour*) Kleber *m*

gluten intolerance ['glu:tən-] N (*Med*) Glutenunverträglichkeit *f*

glutinous ['glu:tɪnəs] ADJ klebrig

glutton ['glʌtn] N Vielfraß *m* (*also Zool*); **to be a ~ for work** ein Arbeitstier *nt* sein (*inf*); **she's a ~ for punishment** sie ist die reinste Masochistin (*inf*)

gluttonous ['glʌtənəs] ADJ (*lit, fig*) unersättlich; *person* gefräßig

gluttony ['glʌtənɪ] N Völlerei *f*, Fresserei *f* (*inf*)

glycerin(e) ['glɪsəri:n] N Glyzerin *nt*, Glycerin *nt* (*spec*)

glycerol ['glɪsərɒl] N Glyzerin *nt*

glycol ['glaɪkɒl] N Glykol *nt*

GM **a** *abbr of* **genetically modified**; **GM crops** gentechnisch verändertes Getreide; **GM foods/potatoes/tomatoes** gentechnisch veränderte Lebensmittel/Kartoffeln/Tomaten; **GM maize/rapeseed** Genmais *m*/-raps *m* **b** (*Brit*) *abbr of* **George Medal** *Tapferkeitsmedaille*

gm *abbr of* **gram(s), gramme(s)** g

G-man ['dʒi:mæn] N *pl* **-men** [-men] (*US inf*) FBI-Mann *m*

GMAT (*US Univ*) *abbr of* **Graduate Management Admission Test** *Zulassungstest für das postgraduale Studium der Betriebswirtschaft*

GMC (*Brit*) *abbr of* **General Medical Council**

GMO N ABBR *of* **genetically modified organism**

gms *abbr of* **gram(me)s** g

GMT *abbr of* **Greenwich Mean Time** WEZ

gnarled [nɑ:ld] ADJ *tree, roots, branch, trunk* knorrig; *hands, fingers* knotig; *person* verhutzelt; (= *bent*) krumm

gnash [næʃ] VT **to ~ one's teeth** mit den Zähnen knirschen

gnat [næt] N (Stech)mücke *f*

gnat's piss ['nætspɪs] N (*sl*) Gesöff *nt* (*inf*)

gnaw [nɔ:] **VT** nagen an (*+dat*); *fingernails also* kauen an (*+dat*); (*rust, disease*) fressen an (*+dat*); *hole* nagen; (*fig*) (*person*) (*hunger, anxiety*) quälen; (*remorse*) verzehren; **to ~ sth off** etw abnagen; **the box had been ~ed by the rats** die Ratten hatten die Kiste angenagt **VI** nagen; **to ~ at sth** an etw (*dat*) nagen; (*rust, disease*) sich durch etw fressen; **to ~ at sb** (*fig*) jdn quälen; **to ~ on sth** an etw (*dat*) nagen; **to ~ through sth** etw durchnagen

▶ **gnaw away** **VI** nagen (*at, on* an *+dat*) **VT** *sep* wegnagen

gnawer ['nɔ:ə'] N (*Zool*) Nager *m*, Nagetier *nt*

gnawing ['nɔ:ɪŋ] ADJ *doubt, hunger, pain* nagend; *fear, guilt, remorse, anxiety* quälend

gneiss [naɪs] N Gneis *m*

gnocchi ['nɒkɪ] PL Gnocchi *pl*

gnome [nəʊm] N Gnom *m*; (*in garden*) Gartenzwerg *m*; **the ~s of Zurich** die Zürcher Gnome *pl*

GNP *abbr of* **gross national product**

gnu [nu:] N Gnu *nt*

GNVQ (*Brit Sch*) *abbr of* **General National Vocational Qualification** ≈ Berufsschulabschluss *m*

go [gəʊ]
vb: pret **went**, *ptp* **gone**

1 INTRANSITIVE VERB	4 NOUN
2 AUXILIARY VERB	5 ADJECTIVE
3 TRANSITIVE VERB	6 PHRASAL VERBS

When *go* is part of a set combination, eg. *go crazy, go unheard, go ballistic, going cheap,* look up the other word.

1 – INTRANSITIVE VERB

a [= proceed = move] gehen; (*vehicle, person in vehicle*) fahren; (*plane*) fliegen; (= *travel*) reisen; (*road*) führen; **we can talk as we go** wir können uns unterwegs unterhalten; **the doll goes everywhere with her** sie nimmt die Puppe überallhin mit; **Sunny Boy is going well** Sunny Boy liegt gut im Rennen; **you go first** geh du zuerst!; **you go next** du bist der Nächste; **to go and** *or* **to get sth** (*esp Brit*) **to go get sth** (*US*) etw holen gehen; **who goes there?** (*guard*) wer da?; **there he goes!** da ist er ja!; **there you go** (*giving sth*) bitte; (= *I told you so*) na bitte; **there you go again!** (*inf*) du fängst ja schon wieder an!; **here we go again!** (*inf*) jetzt geht das schon wieder los! (*inf*); **where do we go from here?** (*lit*) wo gehen wir anschließend hin?; (*fig*) und was (wird) jetzt?; **you're going too fast for me** (*lit, fig*) du bist mir zu schnell

♦ **to go to ... to go to France** nach Frankreich fahren; **I have to go to the doctor/to London** ich muss zum Arzt (gehen)/nach London; **to go to sb for sth** (= *ask sb*) jdn wegen etw fragen; (= *fetch from sb*) bei jdm etw holen

♦ **to go on ... to go on a journey** verreisen, eine Reise machen; **to go on a course** einen Kurs machen; **to go on holiday** (*Brit*) *or* **vacation** (*US*) in Urlaub gehen

♦ **to go for ... to go for a walk/swim** spazieren/schwimmen gehen; **to go for a doctor/newspaper** einen Arzt/eine Zeitung holen (gehen)

♦ **to go and ... go and shut the door** mach mal die Tür zu; **go and tell him** sags ihm; **he's gone and lost his new watch** (*inf*) er hat seine neue Uhr verloren; **now you've gone and done it!** (*inf*) na, jetzt hast du es geschafft!; **don't go and tell him** geh jetzt bitte nicht hin und erzähl ihm das (*inf*)

♦ **to go + -ing to go fishing/shopping/shooting** angeln/einkaufen/auf die Jagd gehen; **to go looking for sb/sth** nach jdm/etw suchen; **don't go telling him** geh jetzt bitte nicht hin und erzähl ihm das (*inf*); **don't go doing that!** mach das bloß nicht!

b [= attend] gehen; **to go to church** in die Kirche gehen; **to go to evening classes** Abendkurse besuchen; **to go to work** zur Arbeit gehen; **he's going as a pirate** er geht als Pirat; **what shall I go as?** wie soll ich mich verkleiden?; **what shall I go in?** was soll ich anziehen?

c [= depart] gehen; (*vehicle, person in vehicle*) (ab)fahren; (*plane, person in plane*) (ab)fliegen; (= *die*) sterben; **has he gone yet?** ist er schon weg?; **I must go now** ich muss jetzt gehen *or* weg; **when I go** *or* **have gone** *or* **am gone** (= *leave*) wenn ich weg bin; (= *die*) wenn ich (einmal) nicht mehr (da) bin; **we must go** *or* **be going** *or* **get going** (*inf*) wir müssen gehen *or* uns langsam auf den Weg machen (*inf*); **time I was going** Zeit, dass ich gehe; **be gone!** (*old*) hinweg mit dir (*old*); **go!** (*Sport*) los!; **here goes!** jetzt gehts los! (*inf*)

d [= no longer exist = disappear, vanish] verschwinden; (= *be used up*) aufgebraucht werden; (*time*) vergehen; **it is** *or* **has gone** (= *disappeared*) es ist weg; (= *used up, eaten etc*) es ist alle (*inf*); **where has it gone?** wo ist es hin *or* geblieben?; **the trees have been gone for years** die Bäume sind schon seit Jahren nicht mehr da; **gone are the days when ...** die Zeiten sind vorbei, wo ...; **I don't know where the money goes** ich weiß nicht, wo all das Geld bleibt; **all his money goes on computer games** er gibt sein ganzes Geld für Computerspiele aus, sein ganzes Geld geht für Computerspiele drauf (*inf*); **£75 a week goes in** *or* **on rent** £ 75 die Woche sind für die Miete (weg); **how is the time going?** wie stehts mit der Zeit?; **it's just gone three** es ist gerade drei vorbei, es ist kurz nach drei; **there goes another one!** und noch eine(r, s) weniger!

♦ **... to go two days to go till ...** noch zwei Tage bis ...; **only two more exams to go** nur noch zwei Prüfungen; **two exams down and one to go** zwei Prüfungen geschafft und eine kommt noch

e [= be discarded = be dismissed] gehen; (= *be got rid of*) verschwinden; (= *be abolished*) abgeschafft werden; **that minister will have to go** der Minister wird gehen müssen; **that old settee will have to go** das alte Sofa muss weg; **once that table has gone** wenn der Tisch erst einmal weg ist; **racial discrimination must go!** weg mit der Rassendiskriminierung!; **hundreds of jobs will go** hunderte *or* Hunderte von Stellen werden verloren gehen

f [= be sold] **the hats aren't going very well** die Hüte gehen nicht sehr gut (weg); **to go for next to nothing** so gut wie umsonst sein; **it went for £5** es ging für £ 5 weg; **they are going at 20p each** sie werden zu 20 Pence das Stück verkauft; **I won't let it go for less than that** billiger gebe ich es nicht her; **how much did the house go for?** für wie viel wurde das Haus verkauft?; **going, going, gone!** zum Ersten, zum Zweiten, und zum Dritten!

g [= have recourse to] gehen; **to go to the country** (*Brit Parl*) Wahlen ausrufen; **to go to law** vor Gericht gehen (*over* wegen); **to go to war** Krieg führen (*over* wegen); **he has gone so far as to accuse me** er ist so weit gegangen, mich zu beschuldigen

h [= be awarded] *prize, first place etc* gehen (*to* an *+acc*); (*inheritance*) zufallen (*to sb* jdm)

i [= extend] gehen; **the garden goes down to the river** der Garten geht bis zum Fluss hinunter; **the difference between them goes deep** der Unterschied zwischen ihnen geht tief; **I'll go to £100** ich gehe bis £ 100

j [= function] *watch* gehen; (*car, machine*) laufen, gehen; (*workers*) arbeiten; **to make sth go** etw in Gang bringen; **to go slow** (*workers*) im Bummelstreik sein; (*watch*) nachgehen

♦ **to get going** in Schwung *or* Fahrt kommen

♦ **to get going on** *or* **with sth** etw in Angriff nehmen; **once you get going on it** wenn man erst mal damit angefangen hat

♦ **to get sth going** etw in Gang bringen; *party* etw in Fahrt bringen; *business* etw auf Vordermann bringen

♦ **to get sb going** jdn in Fahrt bringen

♦ **to keep going** (*person*) weitermachen; (*business, machine, engine etc*) weiterlaufen; (*car*) weiterfahren; **keep going!** weiter!

♦ **to keep sth/sb going to keep a factory going** eine Fabrik in Betrieb halten; **to keep the fire going** das Feuer anbehalten; **she needs these pills/his friendship to keep her going** sie braucht diese Pillen/seine Freundschaft, um durchzuhalten; **this medicine/prospect kept her going** dieses Medikament/diese Aussicht hat sie durchhalten lassen; **here's £50/some work to keep you going** hier hast du erst mal £ 50/etwas Arbeit; **to keep sb going in food** jdn mit Essen versorgen

k [= turn out] *project, things* gehen; (*event, evening*) verlaufen; (*voting, election*) ausgehen; **I've forgotten how the words go** ich habe den Text vergessen; **how does the story/tune go?** wie war die Geschichte/Melodie noch mal?; **how does his theory go?** welche Theorie hat er?, was ist seine Theorie?; **the story goes that ...** es geht das Gerücht, dass ...; **the election/decision went in his favour** (*Brit*) *or* **favor** (*US*) die Wahl/Entscheidung fiel zu seinen Gunsten aus; **we'll see how things go** (*inf*) wir werden sehen, wie es läuft (*inf*) *or* geht; **you know the way things go** Sie wissen ja, wie das so ist *or* geht; **the way things are going I'll ...** so wie es aussieht, werde ich ...; **nothing went unnoticed** nichts blieb unbemerkt; **she has a lot going for her** sie ist gut dran; **how's it going?, how goes it?** (*inf*) wie gehts (denn so)? (*inf*); **how did it go?** wie wars?; **how did the exam go?** wie gings in der Prüfung?; **how did your holiday go?** wie war der Urlaub?; **how's the essay going?** was macht der Aufsatz?

♦ **to go well/badly things have gone well/badly** es ist gut/schlecht gelaufen; **everything is going well (with us)** alles läuft gut, bei uns läuft alles gut; **if everything goes well** wenn alles gut geht; **all went well for him until ...** alles ging gut bei ihm, bis ...

l [= fail, wear out] *material, mechanism, bulb, zip etc* kaputtgehen; (*health, strength, eyesight etc*) nachlassen; *(brakes, steering)* versagen; *(button)* abgehen; **the sweater has gone at the elbows** der Pullover ist an den Ärmeln durch *(inf)*; **his mind is going** er lässt geistig sehr nach

m = be accepted *behaviour, dress etc* gehen *(inf)*; **anything goes!** alles ist erlaubt; **what I say goes!** was ich sage, gilt *or* wird gemacht!; **that goes for me too** *(= that applies to me)* das gilt auch für mich; *(= I agree with that)* das meine ich auch

n = be available **there are several houses/jobs going** es sind mehrere Häuser/Stellen zu haben; **is there any tea going?** gibt es Tee?; **I'll have whatever is going** ich nehme, was es gibt; **what do you want? – anything that's going** was möchtest du? – was da ist; **the best beer going** das beste Bier, das es gibt

o = become werden; **to go deaf/mad/grey** *(Brit) or* **gray** *(US)* taub/verrückt/grau werden; **to go hungry** hungern; **I went cold** mir wurde kalt; **to go to sleep** einschlafen; **to go to ruin** zerfallen; **to go Japanese/ethnic** auf japanisch/auf Folklore machen *(inf)*; **to go Labour** Labour wählen

p = be placed = be contained, fit gehen, passen; *(= belong)* hingehören; *(in drawer, cupboard etc)* (hin)kommen; **it won't go in the box** es geht *or* passt nicht in die Kiste; **the books go in that cupboard** die Bücher kommen *or* gehören in den Schrank dort; **4 into 12 goes 3** 4 geht in 12 dreimal; **4 into 3 won't go** 3 durch 4 geht nicht

q = match dazu passen; **to go with sth** zu etw passen; **these earrings don't go with that sweater** diese Ohrringe passen nicht zu dem Pullover

r = contribute **the money goes to help the poor** das Geld soll den Armen helfen; **the money will go toward(s) a new car** das ist Geld für ein neues Auto; **the qualities that go to make a great man** die Eigenschaften, die einen großen Mann ausmachen

s = make a sound or movement machen; **to go bang/shh/ticktock** peng/pst/ticktack machen; **how does a dog go?** wie macht der Hund?; **go like that (with your left foot)** mach so (mit deinem linken Fuß); **there goes the bell** es klingelt

t = take away *US* **large fries to go** eine große Portion Fritten zum Mitnehmen

u comparison

♦ **as … go as things go today that's not very expensive** für heutige Verhältnisse ist das nicht teuer; **he's not bad as boys/bosses go** verglichen mit anderen Jungen/Chefs ist er nicht übel

2 – AUXILIARY VERB

forming future tense

♦ **to be going to … I'm/I was going to do it** ich werde/wollte es tun; **I had been going to do it** ich habe es tun wollen; **I wasn't going to do it (anyway)** ich hätte es sowieso nicht gemacht; **it's going to rain** es wird wohl regnen; **he knew that he wasn't going to see her again** er wusste, dass er sie nicht wiedersehen würde; **there's going to be trouble** es wird Ärger geben

3 – TRANSITIVE VERB

a route, way gehen; *(vehicle, person in vehicle)* fahren

♦ **to go it** *(inf: = go fast)* ein tolles Tempo draufhaben *(inf)*; *(= live hard)* es toll treiben *(inf)*; *(= work hard)* sich hineinknien *(inf)*; **to go it alone** sich selbstständig machen

b Cards, Gambling setzen; **he went £50 on the red** er setzte £ 50 auf Rot

c = become **my mind went a complete blank** ich hatte ein Brett vor dem Kopf *(inf)*

d = say *inf* sagen; **he goes to me: "what do you want?"** er sagt zu mir: „was willst du?"

e = fancy *inf* **I could go a beer** ich könnte ein Bier vertragen

4 – NOUN *pl* goes

a = energy *inf* Schwung *m*; **to be full of go** unternehmungslustig sein

♦ **on the go to be on the go** auf Trab sein *(inf)*; **to keep sb on the go** jdn auf Trab halten; **he's got two women/books on the go** er hat zwei Frauen/schreibt an zwei Büchern gleichzeitig

♦ **it's all go** es ist immer was los *(inf)*

b = attempt Versuch *m*; **at the first go** auf Anhieb *(inf)*; **at the second go** beim zweiten Mal *or* Versuch

♦ **at** *or* **in one go** auf einen Schlag *(inf)*; *(drink)* in einem Zug *(inf)*

♦ **to have a go** *(Brit)* es versuchen, es probieren; **to have a go at doing sth** versuchen *or* probieren, etw zu tun; **have a go!** versuchs *or* probiers *(inf)* doch mal!; **he's had several goes at the exam** er hat schon mehrere Anläufe auf das Examen genommen

♦ **to have a go at sb** *(inf: = criticize)* jdn runterputzen *(inf)*; *(= fight)* es mit jdm aufnehmen; **the public were warned not to have a go** *(Brit)* die Öffentlichkeit wurde gewarnt, nichts zu unternehmen

c = turn **it's your go** du bist dran *(inf) or* an der Reihe; **you've had your go** du warst schon dran *(inf) or* an der Reihe; **miss one go** *(Brit)* einmal aussetzen; **can I have a go?** darf ich mal?; **she asked for a go on his bike** sie wollte mal sein Fahrrad ausprobieren

d = bout *(of illness etc)* Anfall *m*

e other set structures

♦ **(it's) no go** *(inf)* das ist nicht drin *(inf)*, da ist nichts zu machen

♦ **to make a go of sth** in etw *(dat)* Erfolg haben

♦ **from the word go** von Anfang an

5 – ADJECTIVE

(esp Space) **you are go for takeoff/landing** alles klar zum Start/zur Landung; **all systems (are) go** (es ist) alles klar

6 – PHRASAL VERBS

▶ **go about** VI **a** *(Brit: = move from place to place)* herumgehen, herumlaufen *(inf)*; *(by vehicle)* herumfahren; *(in old clothes etc)* herumlaufen; **to go about in gangs** in Banden durch die Gegend ziehen; **to go about with sb** mit jdm zusammen sein *or* herumziehen *(pej inf)*; **she's going about with John** sie geht mit John *(inf)*; **you shouldn't go about doing that kind of thing** solche Sachen solltest du nicht machen
b *(Brit)* *(= be current: rumour, flu etc)* umgehen
c *(Naut, = change direction)* wenden
VI *+prep obj* **a** *(= set to work at) task, problem* anpacken; **we must go about it carefully** wir müssen vorsichtig vorgehen; **how does one go about getting seats/finding a job?** wie bekommt man Plätze/eine Stelle?
b *(= be occupied with) work, jobs* erledigen; **to go about one's business** sich um seine eigenen Geschäfte kümmern

▶ **go across** VI *+prep obj* überqueren; *street etc also* gehen über *(+acc)*; *river also* fahren über *(+acc)*; **to go across the sea to Ireland** übers Meer nach Irland fahren VI hinübergehen; *(by vehicle)* hinüberfahren; *(by plane)* hinüberfliegen; *(to the enemy etc)* überlaufen *(to* zu); **to go across to the other side** auf die andere Seite hinübergehen/-fahren; *(to the enemy etc)* zur anderen Seite überlaufen *or* -wechseln; **to go across to one's neighbour/the pub** zum Nachbarn/in die Kneipe hinübergehen

▶ **go after** VI *+prep obj* **a** *(= follow)* nachgehen *(+dat)*, nachlaufen *(+dat)*; *(in vehicle)* nachfahren *(+dat)*; **the police went after the escaped criminal** die Polizei hat den entkommenen Verbrecher gejagt **b** *(= try to win or obtain)* anstreben, es abgesehen haben auf *(+acc) (inf)*; *job* sich bemühen um, aus sein auf *(+acc) (inf)*; *goal* verfolgen, anstreben; *(Sport) record* einstellen wollen; *personal best* anstreben; *girl* sich bemühen um, nachstellen *(+dat) (pej)*; **when he decides what he wants he really goes after it** wenn er weiß, was er will, tut er alles, um es zu bekommen

▶ **go against** VI *+prep obj* **a** *(= be unfavourable to, luck)* sein gegen; *(events)* ungünstig verlaufen für; *(evidence, appearance)* sprechen gegen; **the verdict/decision went against her** das Urteil/die Entscheidung fiel zu ihren Ungunsten aus; **the vote went against her** sie verlor die Abstimmung; **the first round went against him** er hat die erste Runde verloren **b** *(= be contrary to)* im Widerspruch stehen zu; *principles, conscience, trend* gehen gegen; *(= oppose) person* handeln gegen, sich widersetzen *(+dat)*; *wishes, orders* zuwiderhandeln *(+dat)*

▶ **go ahead** VI **a** *(= go in front)* vorangehen; *(in race)* sich an die Spitze setzen; *(= go earlier)* vorausgehen; *(in vehicle)* vorausfahren; **to go ahead of sb** vor jdm gehen; sich vor jdn setzen; jdm vorausgehen/-fahren **b** *(= proceed, person)* es machen; *(work, project)* vorangehen; *(event)* stattfinden; **he just went ahead and did it** er hat es einfach gemacht; **go ahead!** nur zu!; **to go ahead with sth** etw durchführen

▶ **go along** VI **a** *(= walk along)* entlanggehen, entlangspazieren *(inf)*; *(to an event)* hingehen; **to go along to sth** zu etw gehen; **as one goes along** *(= while walking)* unterwegs; *(= bit by bit)* nach und nach; *(= at the same time)* nebenbei, nebenher; **I made the story up as I went along** ich habe mir die Geschichte beim Erzählen ausgedacht; **go along with you!** *(inf)* jetzt hör aber auf! *(inf)*
b *(= accompany)* mitgehen, mitkommen *(with* mit); **the furniture goes along with the apartment** die Möbel gehören zur Wohnung
c *(= agree)* zustimmen *(with +dat)*; *(= not object)* sich anschließen *(with +dat)*; **he went along with all my suggestions** er schloss sich allen meinen Vorschlägen an
d *(= proceed)* **things are going along very smoothly** es läuft alles sehr gut

▶ **go around** VI = **go about VI a, b, go round**

▶ **go at** VI *+prep obj (inf: = attack) person* losgehen auf *(+acc) (inf)*; *task* sich machen an *(+acc)*; **to go at it** loslegen *(inf)*

▶ **go away** VI (weg)gehen; *(for a holiday)* wegfahren; *(from wedding)* abreisen, wegfahren; **they went away together** *(illicitly)* sie sind miteinander durchgebrannt *(inf)*; **"gone away"** *(on letter)* „verzogen"; **the smell still hasn't gone away** der Geruch ist immer noch nicht weg

▶ **go back** VI **a** *(= return)* zurückgehen; *(to a subject)* zurückkommen *(to* auf *+acc)*; *(= revert: to habits, methods etc)* zurückkehren *(to* zu); **they have to go back to Germany/school next week** nächste Woche müssen sie wieder nach Deutschland zurück/wieder zur Schule; **when do the schools go back?** wann fängt die Schule wieder an?; **to go back to the beginning** wieder von vorn anfangen; **you can't go back now** du kannst jetzt nicht zurück; **there's no going back now** jetzt gibt es kein Zurück mehr; **I'll go back there next year** da gehe *or* fahre ich nächstes Jahr wieder hin
b *(= be returned, faulty goods)* zurückgehen; *(library books)* zurückgebracht werden
c *(= date back)* zurückgehen, zurückreichen *(to* bis zu); **we go back a long way** wir kennen uns schon ewig; **our friendship goes back to our student days** wir sind schon seit unserer Studienzeit befreundet; **this practice goes back to medieval times** dieser Brauch geht auf das Mittelalter zurück
d *(clock: = be put back)* zurückgestellt werden
e *(= extend back: cave, garden etc)* zurückgehen, zurückreichen *(to* bis zu)

▶ **go back on** VI *+prep obj* zurücknehmen; *decision* rückgängig machen; **I never go back on my word** was ich versprochen habe, halte ich auch

▶ **go before** VI *(= live before)* in früheren Zeiten leben; *(= happen before)* vorangehen; **those who have gone before (us)** unsere Vorfahren; **everything that had gone before** alles Vorhergehende VI *+prep obj* **to go before the court** vor Gericht erscheinen; **to go before the headmaster/committee** zum Rektor/vor den Ausschuss kommen

▶ **go below** VI *(Naut)* unter Deck gehen

▶**go beyond** VI *+prep obj (= exceed)* hinausgehen über *(+acc)*; *orders, instructions also* überschreiten; *hopes, expectations also* übertreffen; **he went beyond the bounds of decency** er hat den Anstand nicht gewahrt

▶**go by** **VI** *(person, opportunity)* vorbeigehen *(prep obj* an *+dat)*; *(procession)* vorbeiziehen *(prep obj* an *+dat)*; *(vehicle)* vorbeifahren *(prep obj* an *+dat)*; *(time)* vergehen; **as time went by** mit der Zeit; **in days gone by** in längst vergangenen Tagen

VI *+prep obj* **a** *(= base judgement or decision on)* gehen nach; *(= be guided by) compass, stars, watch etc, sb's example* sich richten nach; *(= stick to) rules* sich halten an *(+acc)*; **if that's anything to go by** wenn man danach gehen kann; **going by what he said** nach dem, was er sagte; **that's not much to go by** das will nicht viel heißen

b **to go by the name of Smith** Smith heißen

▶**go down** VI **a** *(= descend)* hinuntergehen *(prep obj +acc)*; *(by vehicle, lift)* hinunterfahren *(prep obj +acc)*; *(sun, moon: = set)* untergehen; *(Theat: curtain)* fallen; *(= fall, boxer etc)* zu Boden gehen; *(horse)* stürzen; **to go down on one's knees** sich hinknien; *(to apologize)* auf die Knie fallen; **to go down on one knee** *(to propose)* auf die Knie fallen; **this wine/cake goes down rather well** dieser Wein/der Kuchen schmeckt gut; **it will help the tablet go down** dann rutscht die Tablette besser (hinunter); **to go down on sb** *(sl: = have oral sex with)* es jdm mit dem Mund machen *(inf)*

b *(ship, person: = sink)* untergehen; *(plane)* abstürzen; *(= be defeated)* geschlagen werden (*to* von); *(= fail examination)* durchfallen → **fight VI**

c *(Brit Univ)* die Universität verlassen; *(for vacation)* in die Semesterferien gehen

d *(inf: = go to prison)* eingelocht werden *(inf)*

e *(= be accepted, approved)* ankommen (*with* bei); **that won't go down well with him** das wird er nicht gut finden; **he went down big in the States** *(inf)* in den Staaten kam er ganz groß heraus *(inf)*

f *(= be reduced, lessen, floods, temperature, fever, supplies, swelling)* zurückgehen; *(taxes, value)* sich verringern, weniger werden; *(prices)* sinken, runtergehen *(inf)*; *(barometer)* fallen; *(wind)* nachlassen; *(sea)* sich beruhigen; *(balloon, tyre)* Luft verlieren; *(= deteriorate: neighbourhood)* herunterkommen; **he has gone down in my estimation** er ist in meiner Achtung gesunken → **world**

g *(= go as far as)* gehen (*to* bis); **I'll go down to the bottom of the page** ich werde die Seite noch fertig machen

h *(= be noted, remembered)* vermerkt werden; **to go down to posterity** der Nachwelt überliefert werden; **to go down in history** in die Geschichte eingehen; **it went down as a significant event in British history** es ging als ein bedeutendes Ereignis in die britische Geschichte ein

i *(Bridge)* den Kontrakt nicht erfüllen; **she went five down** sie blieb fünf unter dem gebotenen Kontrakt

j *(= become ill)* **to go down with a cold** eine Erkältung bekommen

k *(Mus inf, = lower pitch)* heruntergehen *(inf)*, tiefer singen/spielen

l *(Comput)* ausfallen

m *(Sport) (= be relegated)* absteigen; *(= be defeated)* verlieren; **they went down 2-1 to Rangers** sie verloren 2:1 gegen Rangers

▶**go for** VI *+prep obj* **a** *(inf: = attack) person* losgehen auf *(+acc) (inf)*; *(verbally)* herziehen über *(+acc)*; **the fumes went for my throat** ich habe die Abgase im Hals gespürt; **go for him!** *(to dog)* fass! **b** *(inf: = admire, like)* gut finden, stehen auf *(+acc) (inf)*; *(= choose)* nehmen

c *(= aim at)* zielen auf *(+acc)*; *(fig)* aus sein auf *(+acc) (inf)*; *(in claim etc)* fordern; **go for it!** nichts wie ran! *(inf)*; **if I were you I'd go for it** an deiner Stelle würde ich zugreifen; **he was obviously going for the ball** er hatte es offensichtlich auf den Ball abgesehen

▶**go forth** VI *(old, liter, person)* hingehen; *(order)* ergehen *(liter)*; **to go forth into battle** in den Kampf ziehen

▶**go forward** VI **a** *(= make progress: work etc)* vorangehen **b** *(= proceed, go ahead)* **to go forward with sth** etw durchführen, etw in die Tat umsetzen **c** *(= be put forward: suggestion etc)* vorgelegt werden (*to dat*)

▶**go in** VI **a** *(= enter)* hineingehen; **I must go in now** ich muss jetzt hinein(gehen) **b** *(sun, moon: = go behind clouds)* weggehen, verschwinden **c** *(= fit in)* hineingehen, hineinpassen **d** *(= sink in, be assimilated)* jdm eingehen

▶**go in for** VI *+prep obj* **a** *(= enter for)* teilnehmen an *(+dat)* **b** *(= approve of, be interested in, practise)* zu haben sein für; *(as career)* sich entschieden haben für, gewählt haben; **to go in for sports/tennis** *(= play oneself)* Sport treiben/Tennis spielen; *(= be interested in)* sich für Sport/Tennis interessieren; **he's gone in for growing vegetables/breeding rabbits** *etc* er hat sich auf den Gemüseanbau/die Kaninchenzucht *etc* verlegt; **he goes in for big words** große Worte haben es ihm angetan

▶**go into** VI *+prep obj* **a** *drawer, desk etc* kramen in *(+dat)*; *a house, hospital, politics, the grocery trade* gehen in *(+acc)*; *the army, navy etc* gehen zu; **to go into publishing** ins Verlagswesen gehen; **to go into teaching/parliament/the Church** Lehrer(in)/Abgeordnete(r)/Geistliche(r) werden; **it's going into its second year** das geht jetzt schon ins zweite Jahr

b *(= crash into) car* (hinein)fahren in *(+acc)*; *wall* fahren gegen

c *(= embark on) explanation, description etc* von sich *(dat)* geben, vom Stapel lassen *(inf)*; *routine* verfallen in *(+acc)*

d *trance, coma* fallen in *(+acc)*; *convulsions, fit* bekommen; **to go into hysterics** hysterisch werden; **to go into fits of laughter** einen Lachanfall bekommen; **to go into mourning** *(emotionally)* trauern

e *(= start to wear) long trousers etc* tragen

f *(= look into)* sich befassen mit; *(= treat, explain at length)* abhandeln; **I don't want to go into that now** darauf möchte ich jetzt nicht (näher) eingehen; **this matter is being gone into** man befasst sich im Moment mit dieser Angelegenheit; **to go into detail** auf Einzelheiten eingehen

g *(= be invested)* **a lot of time/money/effort has gone into it** da steckt viel Zeit/Geld/Mühe drin

▶**go in with** VI *+prep obj* sich zusammentun *or* zusammenschließen mit

▶**go off** **VI** **a** *(= leave)* weggehen; *(by vehicle)* abfahren, wegfahren (*on* mit); *(Theat)* abgehen; **he went off to the States** er fuhr in die Staaten; **to go off with sb/sth** *(illicitly)* mit jdm/etw auf und davon gehen *(inf)*

b *(= stop operating, light)* ausgehen; *(water, electricity, gas)* wegbleiben; *(telephones)* nicht funktionieren

c *(gun, bomb, alarm)* losgehen; *(alarm clock)* klingeln

d **to go off into fits of laughter** einen Lachanfall bekommen

e *(Brit: = go bad, food)* schlecht werden; *(milk)* sauer *or* schlecht werden; *(butter)* ranzig *or* schlecht werden; *(fig, person, work, performance)* nachlassen, sich verschlechtern; *(sportsman, writer, actor)* abbauen *(inf)*, schlechter werden

f *(inf: = go to sleep)* einschlafen; *(into trance)* in Trance verfallen

g *(= take place)* verlaufen; **to go off well/badly** gut/schlecht gehen

VI *+prep obj* **a** *(Brit: = lose liking for)* nicht mehr mögen; *hobby* das Interesse verlieren an *(+dat)*; **I've gone off him/that** ich mache mir nichts mehr aus ihm/daraus, ich mag ihn/es nicht mehr; **it's funny how you go off people** so schnell kann einem jemand unsympathisch werden

b **to go off the gold standard** vom Goldstandard abgehen

▶**go on** **VI** **a** *(= fit)* passen *(prep obj* auf *+acc)*

b *(= begin to operate: light, power)* angehen

c *(= walk on etc)* weitergehen; *(by vehicle)* weiterfahren; *(ahead of others)* vorausgehen

d *(= carry on, continue, talks, problems, war etc)* weitergehen; *(person)* weitermachen; **it goes on and on** es hört nicht mehr auf; **to go on with sth** etw fortsetzen, mit etw weitermachen; **to go on working/coughing** weiterarbeiten/-husten; **to go on hoping** weiter hoffen; **to go on trying** es weiter(hin) versuchen; **go on with your work** arbeitet *or* macht weiter; **I want to go on being a teacher** *etc* ich möchte Lehrer *etc* bleiben; **to go on speaking** weitersprechen; *(after a pause)* fortfahren; **go on, tell me!** na, sag schon!; **go on, give it a try!** na, versuchs doch!; **go on (with you)!** *(iro inf)* na komm, komm! *(iro inf)*; **to have enough/something to be going on with** fürs Erste genug haben/schon mal etwas haben; **to go on to another matter** zu einer anderen Sache übergehen; **he went on to say that ...** dann sagte er, dass ...; **she went on to become a doctor** sie wurde später Ärztin; **I can't go on** ich kann nicht mehr; *(= I'm stuck)* ich weiß nicht mehr weiter

e *(= talk incessantly)* wie ein Buch *(inf) or* unaufhörlich reden; *(= nag, harp on)* darauf herumhacken *(inf)*; **she just goes on and on** sie redet und redet; **don't go on (about it)** nun hör aber (damit) auf; **you do go on a bit** du weißt manchmal nicht, wann du aufhören solltest; **to go on about sb/sth** *(= talk a lot)* stundenlang von jdm/etw erzählen; *(= complain)* dauernd über jdn/etw klagen; **to go on at sb** an jdm herumnörgeln, auf jdm herumhacken *(inf)*

f *(= happen)* passieren, vor sich gehen; *(party, argument etc)* im Gange sein; **this has been going on for a long time** das geht schon lange so; **what's going on here?** was geht hier vor?

g *(time: = pass)* vergehen; **as time goes on** im Laufe der Zeit

h *(pej: = behave)* sich aufführen; **what a way to go on!** wie kann man sich nur so aufführen!

i *(= appear, Theat)* auftreten; *(Sport)* dran sein *(inf)*, an der Reihe sein

j *(US sl)* **he's/she's got it going on** er/sie ist ein total scharfer Typ *(inf)*

VI *+prep obj* **a** *(= ride on) bus, bike, roundabout etc* fahren mit; *tour* machen; *horse, donkey etc* reiten auf *(+dat)*; **to go on the swings/slide** auf die Schaukel/Rutschbahn gehen

b *(= be guided by)* gehen nach, sich verlassen auf *(+acc)*; *evidence* sich stützen auf *(+acc)*; **what have you got to go on?** worauf stützt du dich dabei?, wovon gehst du dabei aus?; **we've got nothing to go on** wir haben keine Anhaltspunkte

c **to go on short time** kurzarbeiten; **to go on the dole** *(Brit)* stempeln gehen *(inf)*; **to go on a diet** eine Schlankheitskur machen; **to go on the pill** die Pille nehmen

d *(inf, = like)* stehen auf *(+acc) (inf)* → **gone**

e *(= approach) fifty etc* zugehen auf *(+acc)*

f *(= appear on)* **to go on television** im Fernsehen auftreten

▶**go on for** VI *+prep obj fifty, one o'clock* zugehen auf *(+acc)*; **there were going on for twenty people there** es waren fast zwanzig Leute da

▶**go out** VI **a** *(= leave)* hinausgehen; **to go out of a room** aus einem Zimmer gehen

b *(shopping etc)* weggehen; *(socially, to theatre etc)* ausgehen; *(with girl-/boyfriend)* gehen; **to go out riding** ausreiten; **to go out for a meal** essen gehen; **John has been going out with Susan for months** John geht schon seit Monaten mit Susan

c *(= be extinguished: fire, light)* ausgehen

d *(= become unconscious)* das Bewusstsein verlieren, weg sein *(inf)*; *(= fall asleep)* einschlafen, weg sein *(inf)*

e *(= become outmoded, fashion)* unmodern werden; *(custom)* überholt sein

f **to go out to work** arbeiten gehen

g *(Pol, = leave office)* abgelöst werden

h *(Brit: = emigrate, go overseas)* **the family went out to Australia** die Familie ging nach Australien

i *(= strike)* streiken; **to go out on strike** in den Streik treten
j *(tide)* zurückgehen
k my heart went out to him ich fühlte mit ihm mit; **all our sympathy goes out to you** wir teilen Ihr Leid
l *(Sport: = be defeated)* ausscheiden, herausfliegen *(inf)*
m *(= strive)* **to go all out** sich ins Zeug legen *(for* für)
n *(= be issued: pamphlet, circular)* (hinaus)gehen; *(Rad, TV: programme)* ausgestrahlt werden; *(message)* verbreitet werden
o *(year, month: = end)* enden, zu Ende gehen
p to go out for *(US: = be a candidate for)* antreten für; *(Ftbl etc also)* spielen für
q *(= disappear, be lost)* **the fun had gone out of it** es machte keinen Spaß mehr; **the love had gone out of their marriage** ihre Ehe war lieblos geworden; **all the fight had gone out of him** sein Kampfgeist war erloschen

▶ **go over** VI **a** *(= cross)* hinübergehen, rübergehen *(inf)*; *(by vehicle)* hinüberfahren, rüberfahren *(inf)*
b *(= change allegiance, habit, diet etc)* übergehen *(to* zu); *(to another party)* überwechseln *(to* zu); **to go over to the other side** zur anderen Seite überwechseln
c *(TV, Rad, to news desk, another studio)* umschalten
d *(vehicle etc: = be overturned)* umkippen
e *(= be received: play, remarks etc)* ankommen
VI +prep obj **a** *(= examine, check over) accounts, report* durchgehen; *house, luggage* durchsuchen; *person, car* untersuchen; *(= see over) house etc* sich *(dat)* ansehen, besichtigen
b *(= repeat, rehearse, review) lesson, role, facts* durchgehen; **to go over sth in one's mind** etw durchdenken *or* überdenken; **to go over the ground** es durchsprechen
c *(= wash, dust etc) windows, room* schnell sauber machen
d *(= redraw) outlines etc* nachzeichnen

▶ **go past** VI vorbeigehen *(prep obj* an *+dat)*; *(vehicle)* vorbeifahren *(prep obj* an *+dat)*; *(procession)* vorbeiziehen *(prep obj* an *+dat)*; *(time)* vergehen, verfließen

▶ **go round** VI *(esp Brit)* **a** *(= turn, spin)* sich drehen; **my head is going round** mir dreht sich alles
b *(= make a detour)* außen herumgehen; *(by vehicle)* außen herumfahren; **to go round sth** um etw herumgehen/-fahren; **to go round the long way** ganz außen herumgehen/-fahren; **we went round by Winchester** wir fuhren bei Winchester herum
c *(= visit, call round)* vorbeigehen *(to* bei)
d *(= tour: round museum etc)* herumgehen *(prep obj* in *+dat)*
e *(= be sufficient)* langen, (aus)reichen; **there's enough food to go round (all these people)** es ist (für all diese Leute) genügend zu essen da; **to make the money go round** mit dem Geld auskommen
f *+prep obj (= encircle, reach round)* herumgehen um
g = **go about VI a, b**

▶ **go through** VI *(lit, fig)* durchgehen; *(business deal)* abgeschlossen werden; *(divorce, law, bill)* durchkommen
VI *+prep obj* **a** *hole, door, customs etc* gehen durch
b *(= suffer, endure)* durchmachen
c *(= examine, discuss, rehearse) list, subject, play, mail, lesson* durchgehen
d *(= search) pocket, suitcase* durchsuchen
e *(= use up)* aufbrauchen; *money* ausgeben, durchbringen *(inf)*; *shoes* durchlaufen *(inf)*; *food* aufessen; **he has gone through the seat of his trousers** *(Brit) or* **pants** *(esp US)* er hat seine Hose durchgesessen; **this book has already gone through 13 editions** das Buch hat schon 13 Auflagen erlebt
f *formalities, apprenticeship, initiation* durchmachen; *course* absolvieren; *funeral, matriculation* mitmachen; *routine* abziehen *(inf)*; **they went through the agenda very quickly** sie haben die Tagesordnung sehr schnell abgearbeitet; **to go through the marriage ceremony** sich trauen lassen
g *(= ignore)* **to go through a stop sign/a red light** ein Stoppschild/eine rote Ampel überfahren

▶ **go through with** VI *+prep obj plan* durchziehen *(inf)*; *crime* ausführen; **she realized that she had to go through with it** sie sah, dass es kein Zurück gab *or* dass sich das nicht mehr vermeiden ließ; **she couldn't go through with it** sie brachte es nicht fertig

▶ **go to** VI *+prep obj* **a to go to sb** *(credit, job)* an jdn gehen **b** *(= make an effort)* **to go to it** sich ranhalten *(inf)*; **go to it!** los, ran! *(inf)*, auf gehts! *(inf)*

▶ **go together** VI **a** *(= harmonize: colours, ideas, people)* zusammenpassen **b** *(= go hand in hand: events, conditions)* zusammen auftreten **c** *(= go out together)* miteinander gehen

▶ **go under** VI *(= sink: ship, person)* untergehen; *(= fail, businessman)* scheitern *(because of* an *+dat)*; *(company)* eingehen *(inf)* VI *+prep obj* **a** *(= pass under)* durchgehen unter *(+dat)*; *(= fit under)* gehen *or* passen unter *(+acc)* **b to go under the name of Jones** als Jones bekannt sein

▶ **go up** VI **a** *(= rise: price, temperature etc)* steigen; **to go up (and up) in price** (immer) teurer werden
b *(= climb, up stairs, hill)* hinaufgehen, hinaufsteigen *(prep obj +acc)*; *(up ladder)* hinaufsteigen *(prep obj +acc)*; *(up tree)* hinaufklettern *(prep obj* auf *+acc)*; **to go up to bed** nach oben gehen
c *(lift)* hochfahren; *(balloon)* aufsteigen; *(Theat: curtain)* hochgehen; *(= be built: new flats etc)* gebaut werden
d *(= travel, to the north)* hochfahren; *(to London)* fahren; **to go up (to university)** *(Brit)* auf die Universität gehen
e *(= explode, be destroyed)* hochgehen *(inf)*, in die Luft gehen; **to go up in flames** in Flammen aufgehen
f *(cheer, shout)* ertönen
g *(Sport: = be promoted)* aufsteigen

▶ **go with** VI *+prep obj* **a** *sb* gehen mit **b** *(= go hand in hand with)* Hand in Hand gehen mit **c** *(= be included or sold with)* gehören zu **d** *(= harmonize with)* passen zu

▶ **go without** VI *+prep obj* nicht haben; **to go without food** nichts essen; **to go without breakfast** nicht frühstücken; **to have to go without sth** ohne etw auskommen müssen, auf etw *(acc)* verzichten müssen; **to manage to go without sth** ohne etw auskommen; **he doesn't like to go without the luxuries of life** er verzichtet nicht gern auf den Luxus im Leben VI darauf verzichten

---

goad [gəʊd] **N** *(= stick)* Stachelstock *m*; *(fig: = spur)* Ansporn *m*; *(= taunt)* aufstachelnde Bemerkung **VT** *(= taunt)* aufreizen; **to ~ sb into sth** jdn zu etw anstacheln *or* treiben

▶ **goad on** VT *sep cattle* antreiben; *(fig)* anstacheln, aufstacheln

go-ahead [ˈgəʊəhed] **ADJ** fortschrittlich, progressiv **N to give sb/sth the ~** jdm/für etw grünes Licht *or* freie Fahrt geben

goal [gəʊl] N **a** *(Sport)* Tor *nt*; **to keep ~, to play in ~** im Tor stehen, im Tor spielen, das Tor hüten; **to score/kick a ~** ein Tor erzielen/schießen **b** *(= aim, objective)* Ziel *nt*; **to set (oneself) a ~** (sich *dat*) ein Ziel setzen

goal: **goal area** N Torraum *m*; **goal average** N *(Brit Ftbl)* Tordifferenz *f*, Torverhältnis *nt*; **goal crease** N *(Ice hockey)* Torraum *m*; **goalgetter** [ˈgəʊl,getəʳ] N *(Sport)* Torjäger(in) *m(f)*

goalie [ˈgəʊlɪ] N *(inf)* Tormann *m*/-frau *f*, Goalie *m (inf)*

goal: **goal judge** N *(Ice hockey)* Torrichter(in) *m(f)*; **goalkeeper** N Torwart *m*, Torhüter(in) *m(f)*; **goalkeeping** N Torhüten *nt*; **his excellent ~ saved the game** seine hervorragende Leistung als Torwart rettete das Spiel; **goal kick** N Abstoß *m* (vom Tor); **goalless** [ˈgəʊllɪs] ADJ *draw, half* torlos; **goal line** N Torlinie *f*; **goalmouth** N unmittelbarer Torbereich; **goal poacher** N *(Sport)* Abstauber(in) *m(f)*; **goalpost** N Torpfosten *m*; **to move the ~s** *(fig inf)* die Spielregeln (ver)ändern

goanna [gəʊˈænə] N *(Zool)* Waran *m*

go-as-you-please ADJ ungezwungen, ungebunden; **~ ticket** *or* **pass** *(Rail)* Netzkarte *f*

goat [gəʊt] N Ziege *f*; *(inf: = silly person) (= man)* Esel *m (inf)*; *(= woman)* Ziege *f (inf)*; *(= lecher)* Bock *m (inf)*; **to act the ~** *(inf)* herumalbern; **to get sb's ~** *(inf)* jdn auf die Palme bringen *(inf)*

goat cheese N Ziegenkäse *m*

goatee (beard) [gəʊˈtiː(,bɪəd)] N Spitzbart *m*

goat: **goatfish** N *(US)* Meerbarbe *f*; **goatherd** N Ziegenhirt(in) *m(f)*; **goat's cheese** N = **goat cheese**; **goatskin** N Ziegenleder *nt*; **goat's milk** N Ziegenmilch *f*; **~ yoghurt** Jog(h)urt *m or nt* aus Ziegenmilch; **goatsucker** N *(US Orn)* Ziegenmelker *m*, Nachtschwalbe *f*

gob[1] [gɒb] **N** *(= lump)* Klumpen *m*; **a ~ of spit** *(inf)* eine Ladung Spucke *(inf)* **VI** *(Brit inf)* spucken; **to ~ at sb** jdn anspucken

gob[2] N *(Brit inf: = mouth)* Schnauze *f (inf)*; **shut your ~!** halt die Schnauze! *(inf)*

gob[3] N *(dated US, sl, = sailor)* blauer Junge *(inf)*, Blaujacke *f (inf)*

gobbet [ˈgɒbɪt] N Brocken *m*

gobble [ˈgɒbl] **VT** verschlingen **VI a** *(= eat noisily)* schmatzen **b** *(turkey)* kollern **N** *(of turkey)* Kollern *nt*

▶ **gobble down** VT *sep* hinunterschlingen

▶ **gobble up** VT *sep (lit, fig)* verschlingen; *(company)* schlucken

gobbledegook, gobbledygook [ˈgɒbldɪ,guːk] N *(inf)* Kauderwelsch *nt*

gobbler [ˈgɒbləʳ] N Truthahn *m*

go-between [ˈgəʊbɪ,twiːn] N *pl* **-s** Vermittler(in) *m(f)*, Mittelsmann *m*

Gobi Desert [ˈgəʊbɪˈdezət] N Wüste *f* Gobi

goblet [ˈgɒblɪt] N Pokal *m*; *(esp of glass)* Kelchglas *nt*

goblin [ˈgɒblɪn] N Kobold *m*

gobo [ˈgəʊbəʊ] N *pl* **gobos** *or* **goboes** *(TV, Film)* Linsenschirm *m*; *(for microphones)* Schallschirm *m*

gobsmacked [ˈgɒbsmækt] ADJ *(inf: = amazed)* platt *(inf)*; **I was ~** mir blieb die Spucke weg *(inf)*

gobstopper [ˈgɒb,stɒpəʳ] N Riesenbonbon *m or nt (mit verschiedenen Farbschichten)*

goby [ˈgəʊbɪ] N *(= fish)* Meergrundel *f*

go-by [ˈgəʊbaɪ] N *(inf)* **to give sb the ~** jdn schneiden, jdn links liegen lassen *(inf)*

GOC *abbr of* **General Officer Commanding**

go-cart [ˈgəʊkaːt] N *(= child's cart)* Seifenkiste *f*; *(Sport: = kart)* Gokart *m*; *(US: = walker)* Laufstuhl *m*; *(= pushchair)* Sportwagen *m*

god [gɒd] N **a God** Gott *m*; **now he lies in God's (green) acre** *(euph)* nun deckt ihn der grüne Rasen *(euph)*, nun liegt er auf dem Gottesacker *(old)*; **God willing** so Gott will; **God forbid** *(inf)* Gott behüte *or* bewahre; **please God, let him be all right** lieber Gott, bitte mach, dass er durchkommt; **would to God that** *(form)* ich hoffe zu Gott, dass *(geh)*; **I wish to God I hadn't told him** ich wünschte (bei Gott), ich hätte es ihm nicht gesagt; **God (only) knows** *(inf)* wer weiß; **do you think he'll succeed? – God knows!** glaubst du, dass er Erfolg haben wird? – das wissen die Götter!; **(my) God!, good God!, God almighty!** *(all inf)* O Gott! *(inf)*, großer Gott! *(inf)*; **be quiet, for God's sake!** sei still, verdammt noch mal *or* Herrgott noch mal! *(inf)*; **for God's sake!** *(inf)* um Gottes *or* Himmels willen *(inf)*; **what/why in God's name ...?** um Himmels willen, was/warum ...?; **God help you if ...** der Himmel steh euch bei, wenn ...; **he thinks he's God** er hält sich für Gott *or* den Herrgott; **to play God**

Gott *or* den Herrgott spielen
b *(non-Christian)* Gott *m*; **Mars, the ~ of war** Mars, der Gott des Krieges; **the commander was a ~ to his men** der Kommandant wurde von seinen Leuten wie ein (Ab)gott verehrt; **money is his ~** das Geld ist sein Gott *or* Götze
c *(Brit Theat inf)* **the ~s** die Galerie, der Olymp *(inf)*

god: **god-awful** ADJ *(inf)* beschissen *(inf)*; **god-botherer** ['gɒd,bɒðərəʳ] N *(pej)* Religionsfanatiker(in) *m(f) (inf)*, Proselytenmacher(in) *m(f) (pej geh)*; **godchild** N Patenkind *nt*; **goddammit, goddamnit** [gɒd'dæmɪt] INTERJ *(US inf)* verdammt noch mal! *(inf)*; **goddamn, goddam** *(esp US inf)* INTERJ verdammt! *(inf)*; **I don't give a ~!** es ist mir scheißegal! *(inf)* ADJ *(emph)* gottverdammt *(inf)*; **it's no ~ use!** es hat überhaupt keinen Zweck, verdammt noch mal! *(inf)* ADV *(emph)* verdammt *(inf)*; **you're ~ right** du hast, verdammt noch mal, recht *(inf)*; **you don't belong here and you ~ well know it** du gehörst nicht hierher und du weißt es auch, verdammt noch mal *(inf)*; **goddamned** ADJ ADV = **goddamn**; **goddamnit** INTERJ = **goddammit**; **goddaughter** N Patentochter *f*

goddess ['gɒdɪs] N Göttin *f*

god: **godfather** N *(lit, fig)* Pate *m*; **my ~** mein Patenonkel *m*; **God-fearing** ['gɒdfɪərɪŋ] ADJ gottesfürchtig; **godforsaken** ADJ *(inf)* gottverlassen; **godhead** N Gottheit *f*; **the Godhead** Gott *m*; **godless** ADJ gottlos; **godlessness** ['gɒdlɪsnɪs] N Gottlosigkeit *f*; **godlike** ADJ göttergleich; *characteristics* gottähnlich

godliness ['gɒdlɪnɪs] N Frömmigkeit *f*, Gottesfürchtigkeit *f*

godly ['gɒdlɪ] ADJ *(+er)* fromm, gottesfürchtig

god: **godmother** N Patin *f*; **my ~** meine Patentante *f* → **fairy godmother**; **godparent** N Pate *m*, Patin *f*; **godsend** N Geschenk *nt* des Himmels; **God slot** N *(Brit TV inf)* religiöse Sendungen *pl*, ≈ Wort *nt* zum Sonntag; **godson** N Patensohn *m*; **Godspeed** INTERJ *(old)* behüt dich/euch Gott *(old)*, geh/geht mit Gott *(old)*; **to wish sb ~** jdn mit den besten Segenswünschen auf die Reise schicken

goer ['gəʊəʳ] N **a to be a good ~** gut laufen **b** *(Austral, inf, = good idea)* **to be a ~** was taugen *(inf)*

-goer N *suf* -besucher(in), -gänger(in) *m(f)*; **cinemagoer** Kinogänger(in) *or* -besucher(in) *m(f)*

goes [gəʊz] *3rd pers sing present of* **go**

gofer ['gəʊfəʳ] N *(inf)* Mädchen *nt* für alles *(inf)*

go-getter ['gəʊgetəʳ] N *(inf)* Tatmensch *m*, Ellbogentyp *m (pej inf)*

go-getting ['gəʊgetɪŋ] ADJ *(inf) person* aufstrebend

goggle ['gɒgl] VI *(person)* staunen, starren, glotzen *(pej inf)*; *(eyes)* weit aufgerissen sein; **to ~ at sb/sth** jdn/etw anglotzen *(pej inf) or* anstarren, auf jdn/etw glotzen *(pej inf) or* starren

goggle: **gogglebox** N *(Brit inf)* Glotzkiste *f (inf)*, Glotze *f (inf)*; **goggle-eyed** ADJ mit Kulleraugen, kulleräugig; **he stared at him/it ~** er starrte *or* glotzte *(pej inf)* ihn/es an; **they were ~ from watching TV** sie hatten Glotzaugen vom Fernsehen *(inf)*

goggles ['gɒglz] PL Schutzbrille *f*; *(inf: = glasses)* Brille *f*

go-go ['gəʊgəʊ] ADJ **a** Go-go-Girl *nt*; **~ girl** Go-go-Girl *nt* **b** *(US Comm inf)* **~ years** Hochkonjunktur- *or* Boomjahre *pl*; **the ~ days of the late 1960s** die Zeit der Hochkonjunktur Ende der 60er Jahre; **the ~ 1980s** die vom Boom geprägten 80er Jahre

go-go: **go-go dancer** N Go-go-Tänzerin *f*; **go-go dancing** N Go-go *nt*

going ['gəʊɪŋ] *prp of* **go** N **a** *(= departure)* Weggang *m*, (Weg)gehen *nt*
b *(= pace, conditions)* **it's slow ~** es geht nur langsam voran; **that's good ~** das ist ein flottes Tempo; **that's not bad ~ for you** das ist gar nicht schlecht für deine Verhältnisse; **the ~ is good/soft/hard** *(Horse-racing)* die Bahn ist gut/weich/hart; **the road was rough ~** man kam auf der Straße nur mit Mühe voran; **it's heavy ~ talking to him** es ist sehr mühsam, sich mit ihm zu unterhalten; **to get out while the ~ is good** sich rechtzeitig absetzen; **when the ~ gets tough** wenn es hart auf hart kommt; **when the ~ gets tough, the tough get ~** wenn es hart auf hart kommt zeigt sich, wer wirklich was kann
ADJ **a** *(= customary) rate, price* gängig, üblich
b *(after superl: inf)* **the best thing ~** das Beste überhaupt; **the biggest fool ~** der allergrößte Idiot
c a ~ concern *(Comm)* ein gut gehendes Unternehmen; **to sell a business as a ~ concern** ein bestehendes Unternehmen verkaufen; **to be a ~ concern** *(fig: = successful)* ein Erfolg *m* sein; *(= working)* in Betrieb sein; *(= in existence)* bestehen; **he sold me the car as a ~ concern** *(hum)* als er mir das Auto verkaufte, lief es angeblich noch

going-away outfit [,gəʊɪŋə'weɪ,aʊtfɪt] N *Kleidung, die die Braut trägt, wenn sie den Hochzeitsempfang verlässt*

going-over [,gəʊɪŋ'əʊvəʳ] N **a** *(= examination)* Untersuchung *f*; **to give sth a good ~** *(contract)* etw gründlich prüfen; *house* etw gründlich durchsuchen; **she gave the patient a good ~** sie untersuchte den Patienten gründlich **b** *(inf: = beating-up)* Abreibung *f (inf)*; **to give sb a good ~** jdm eine tüchtige Abreibung verpassen *(inf)*

goings-on [,gəʊɪŋ'zɒn] PL *(inf: = happenings)* Dinge *pl*; **there have been strange ~** da sind seltsame Dinge passiert; **the ~ in parliament** die Sachen, die im Parlament passieren

goitre, ** *(US)* **goiter ['gɔɪtəʳ] N Kropf *m*

go-kart ['gəʊ,kɑːt] N Gokart *m*

gold [gəʊld] N **a** *(= metal, currency, objects)* Gold *nt* → *also* **glitter VI, heart b, weight N a**
b *(Sport inf: = gold medal)* Goldmedaille *f*; **four swimming ~s** vier Goldmedaillen im Schwimmen; **she won (the) ~ at 100 and 200 metres** sie gewann die Goldmedaille im 100- und 200--Meter-Lauf
c *(= colour)* Gold *nt*
ADJ **a** *(= made of gold) bracelet, chain, ring, earring etc* golden; **~ jewellery** *(Brit) or* **jewelry** *(US)* Goldschmuck *m*; **~ coin** Goldmünze *f*; **~ bullion** *or* **bars** Goldbarren *pl*; **~ tooth** Goldzahn *m*
b *(= gold-coloured) fabric, paint, frame, lettering etc* golden; **~ braid** Goldtressen *pl*; **a green--and-~ flag** eine grün-goldene Fahne

gold: **goldbrick** *(US)* N **a** *(inf: = gilded metal bar)* falscher Goldbarren; *(= worthless object)* schöner Schund; **to sell sb a ~** jdm etwas andrehen *(inf)* **b** *(sl: = shirker)* Drückeberger *m (inf)* VI *(sl)* sich drücken *(inf)*; **goldbricker** ['gəʊldbrɪkəʳ] N *(US sl)* = **goldbrick N b**; **Gold Card®** N Goldkarte *f*; **Gold Coast** N Goldküste *f*; **gold-coloured,** *(US)* **gold-colored** ADJ goldfarben; **goldcrest** N Goldhähnchen *nt*; **gold-digger** N Goldgräber(in) *m(f)*; **she's really just a ~** *(inf)* sie ist eigentlich nur aufs Geld aus *(inf)*; **gold disc** N goldene Schallplatte; **gold dust** N Goldstaub *m*; **to be (like) ~** *(fig)* sehr schwer zu finden sein, (selten wie) ein weißer Rabe sein

golden ['gəʊldən] ADJ **a** *(in colour)* golden; *hair* golden, goldblond; *suntan* goldbraun; *sand* goldgelb; *(Cook)* goldbraun; **fry until ~** anbräunen; **~ yellow/brown** goldgelb/-braun **b** *(liter: = made of gold)* golden → *also* **goose c** *(fig: = excellent) future, years, era* golden; **a ~ opportunity/chance** eine einmalige Gelegenheit/Chance

golden: **golden age** N *(Myth)* goldenes Zeitalter; *(fig)* Blütezeit *f*; **golden boy** N *(inf)* Goldjunge *m*; **golden buck** N *(US Cook) überbackene Käseschnitte mit pochiertem Ei*; **golden calf** N **the ~** das Goldene Kalb; **golden chain** N Goldkette *f*; **Golden Delicious** N Golden Delicious *m*; **golden eagle** N Steinadler *m*; **Golden Fleece** N **the ~** das Goldene Vlies; **Golden Gate** N **the ~ (Bridge)** die Golden-Gate-Brücke; **golden girl** N *(inf)* Goldmädchen *nt*; **golden goal** N *(Ftbl)* Golden Goal *nt*; **golden goose** N *(fig)* Huhn, das goldene Eier legt, Goldgrube *f*; **golden hamster** N *(Zool)* Goldhamster *m*; **golden handcuffs** PL *(inf)* Vergünstigungen *pl (für leitende Angestellte, um diese längerfristig an ein Unternehmen zu binden)*; **golden handshake** N *(inf)* goldener Handschlag *(inf)*, Abstandssumme *f*; **the director got a ~ of £50,000** der Direktor hat bei seinem Ausscheiden £ 50.000 bekommen; **golden hello** N *(inf)* Einstellungsprämie *f*; **golden jubilee** N goldenes Jubiläum; **golden labrador** N Goldener Labrador; **golden mean** N **the ~** *(form)* der goldene Mittelweg; **to follow** *or* **pursue the ~** die goldene Mitte wählen; **golden oldie** N *(inf: = tune, record)* (Golden) Oldie *m (inf)*; **golden oriole** N Pirol *m*; **golden parachute** N *(inf) Schutzklausel für leitende Angestellte für den Fall einer Übernahme oder Fusion*, goldener Fallschirm *(inf)*; **golden pheasant** N Goldfasan *m*; **golden retriever** N Golden Retriever *m*; **goldenrod** N Goldrute *f*; **golden rule** N goldene Regel; **my ~ is never to ...** ich mache es mir zu Regel, niemals zu ...; **golden section** N *(Math, Phot)* goldener Schnitt; **golden syrup** N *(Brit)* (gelber) Sirup; **Golden Temple** N **the ~** *(Rel)* der goldene Tempel; **golden thread** N *(fig liter)* roter Faden; **Golden Triangle** N **the ~** *(Geog)* das goldene Dreieck; **golden wedding (anniversary)** N goldene Hochzeit

gold: **gold fever** N Goldfieber *nt*; **gold field** N Goldfeld *nt*; **goldfinch** N *(European)* Stieglitz *m*, Distelfink *m*; *(US)* Amerikanischer Fink; **goldfish** N Goldfisch *m*; **goldfish bowl** N Goldfischglas *nt*; **it's like living in a ~** da ist man wie auf dem Präsentierteller; **gold foil** N Goldfolie *f*; **gold leaf** N Blattgold *nt*; **gold medal** N Goldmedaille *f*; **gold medallist,** *(US)* **gold medalist** N *(Sport)* Goldmedaillengewinner(in) *m(f)*; **gold mine** N Goldbergwerk *nt*, Goldgrube *f (also fig)*; **gold plate** N *(= plating)* Goldüberzug *m*; *(= plated articles)* vergoldetes Gerät; *(= gold articles)* goldenes Gerät; **gold-plate** VT vergolden; **gold record** N = **gold disc**; **gold reserves** PL Goldreserven *pl*; **gold rush** N Goldrausch *m*; **goldsmith** N Goldschmied(in) *m(f)*; **gold standard** N Goldstandard *m*

golf [gɒlf] N Golf *nt* VI Golf spielen

golf: **golf bag** N Golftasche *f*; **golf ball** N **a** Golfball *m* **b** *(on typewriter)* Kugelkopf *m*; **golf-ball printer** Kugelkopfdrucker *m*; **golf club** N *(= instrument)* Golfschläger *m*; *(= association)* Golfklub *m*; **golf course** N Golfplatz *m*

golfer ['gɒlfəʳ] N Golfer(in) *m(f)*, Golfspieler(in) *m(f)*

golf links PL Golfplatz *m*

golf pro N *(inf)* Golfprofi *m*

Goliath [gəʊ'laɪəθ] N *(lit, fig)* Goliath *m*

golliwog ['gɒlɪwɒg] N Negerpuppe *f (neg!)*; **to look like a ~** eine Negerkrause haben *(neg!)*

golly[1] ['gɒlɪ] N *(Brit inf)* = **golliwog**

golly[2] INTERJ *(inf)* Menschenskind *(inf)*

goloshes [gə'lɒʃəz] PL = **galoshes**

Gomorrah, Gomorrha [gə'mɒrə] N Gomor(h)a *nt*

gonad ['gəʊnæd] N Gonade *f*

gondola ['gɒndələ] N **a** *(in Venice, of balloon, cable car etc)* Gondel *f* **b** *(US Rail: also* **gondola car***)* offener Güterwagen **c** *(in supermarket)* Gondel *f*

gondolier [,gɒndə'lɪəʳ] N Gondoliere *m*

gone [gɒn] *ptp of* **go** ADJ *pred* **a** *(inf: = enthusiastic)* **to be ~ on sb/sth** von jdm/etw (ganz) weg sein *(inf)*; **I'm not ~ on ...** ich bin nicht verrückt auf *(+acc)*... *(inf)* **b** *(inf: = pregnant)* **she was 6 months ~** sie war im 7. Monat **c** → **far ADV d** PREP **it's just ~ three** es ist gerade drei Uhr vorbei

goner ['gɒnəʳ] N *(inf)* **to be a ~** *(patient)* es nicht mehr lange machen; *(socially, professionally: person, company)* weg vom Fenster sein *(inf)*; **if you pull out the whole plan's a ~** wenn du nicht mitmachst, wird aus der ganzen Sache nichts

gong [gɒŋ] N **a** Gong *m* **b** *(Brit inf: = medal)* Blech *nt (inf)*; **~s** Lametta *nt (inf)*

gonk [gɒŋk] N *(= toy)* Stoffpuppe *f*

gonna ['gɒnə] *(incorrect)* = **going to**; **I'm not ~ tell you** das sage ich dir nicht

gonorrhoea, *(US)* **gonorrhea** [,gɒnə'rɪə] N Gonorrhö(e) *f*, Tripper *m*

goo [gu:] N *(inf: = sticky stuff)* Papp *m (inf)*, Schmiere *f (inf)*; *(fig, = sentimentality)* Schmalz *m (inf)*

goober ['gu:bəʳ] N *(US inf)* *(= peanut)* Erdnuss *f*; *(= idiot)* Blödmann *m (inf)*

good [gʊd]

11.2, 16.4, 23.5, 24.3

1 ADJECTIVE 3 NOUN
2 ADVERB

1 – ADJECTIVE

comp **better**, *superl* **best**

a gut; **good weather** gutes Wetter; **that's a good one!** *(joke)* das ist ein guter Witz; *(usu iro: excuse)* wers glaubt, wird selig! *(inf)*; **you've done a good day's work** du hast gute Arbeit (für einen Tag) geleistet; **all I need is a good meal** ich brauche nur eine ordentliche *or* anständige Mahlzeit; **this is a good firm to work for** in dieser Firma lässt es sich gut arbeiten; **he tells a good story** er erzählt gut; **it must be good for something** das muss doch zu *or* für etwas gut sein; **she looks good enough to eat** sie sieht zum Anbeißen aus *(inf)*; **to be good with people** gut mit Menschen umgehen können; **good fortune** Glück *nt*; **you've never had it so good!** es ist euch noch nie so gut gegangen, ihr habt es noch nie so gut gehabt; **it's too good to be true** es ist zu schön, um wahr zu sein; **to come in a good third** einen guten dritten Platz belegen; **this is as good as it gets** besser wirds nicht mehr

♦ **to be good at sth** gut in etw *(dat)* sein; **to be good at sport/languages** gut im Sport/in Sprachen sein; **to be good at sewing/typing** gut nähen/tippen können; **I'm not very good at it** ich kann es nicht besonders gut; **he's good at telling stories** er kann gut Geschichten erzählen

♦ **good enough that's (not) good enough** das reicht (nicht); **that's not good enough, you'll have to do better than that** das geht so nicht, du musst dich schon etwas mehr anstrengen; **if he gives his word, that's good enough for me** wenn er sein Wort gibt, reicht mir das; **it's just not good enough!** so geht das nicht!; **his attitude is just not good enough** er hat einfach nicht die richtige Einstellung; **her work/conduct is just not good enough** ihre Arbeit/ihr Benehmen ist einfach nicht gut genug *or* nicht akzeptabel; **they felt he wasn't good enough for her** sie waren der Meinung, dass er nicht gut genug für sie war

♦ **to feel good** sich wohlfühlen; **I don't feel too good** mir ist nicht gut, ich fühle mich nicht wohl; **I don't feel too good about it** mir ist nicht ganz wohl dabei

♦ **to look good you look good in that** du siehst gut darin aus, das steht dir gut

♦ **to make good** *mistake, damage* wiedergutmachen; *threat* wahr machen; *promise* erfüllen; **to make good one's losses** seine Verluste wettmachen; **to make good sb's losses** jdm seine Verluste ausgleichen *or* ersetzen

♦ **as good as** *(= practically)* so gut wie; **as good as new** so gut wie neu; **as good as dead** so gut wie tot; **he was as good as his word** er hat sein Wort gehalten; **he as good as called me a liar/invited me to come** er nannte mich praktisch einen Lügner/hat mich praktisch eingeladen

b [= beneficial] gut; **to be good for sb** gut für jdn sein; *(= be healthy)* gesund für jdn sein; **milk is good for children** Milch ist gut *or* gesund für Kinder; **to be good for toothache/one's health** gut gegen Zahnschmerzen/für die Gesundheit sein; **to drink more than is good for one** mehr trinken, als einem guttut

♦ **what's good for what's good for consumers isn't always good for the economy** was gut für den Verbraucher ist, ist nicht immer gut für die Wirtschaft

c [= favourable] *moment, chance, opportunity* günstig, gut; **a good day for a picnic** ein günstiger *or* guter Tag für ein Picknick; **it's a good thing or job I was there** (nur) gut, dass ich dort war

d [= enjoyable] *holiday, evening* schön; **the good life** das süße Leben; **did you have a good day?** wie wars heute?, wie gings (dir) heute?

♦ **a good time to have a good time** sich gut amüsieren; **have a good time!** viel Spaß *or* Vergnügen!

e [= kind] gut, lieb; **good nature** Gutmütigkeit *f*; **to be good to sb** gut zu jdm sein; **that's very good of you** das ist sehr lieb *or* nett von Ihnen; **(it was) good of you to come** nett, dass Sie gekommen sind; **would you be good enough to tell me ...** wären Sie so nett, mir zu sagen ... *(also iro)*; **with every good wish** mit den besten Wünschen

f [= virtuous] *name, manners, behaviour* gut; **the Good Shepherd** der Gute Hirte; **all good men and true** alle wackeren und aufrechten Männer *(old)*; **if you can't be good, be careful** wenn du es schon tun musst, sei wenigstens vorsichtig

g [= well-behaved] artig, brav *(inf)*; **(as) good as gold** mustergültig; **be a good girl/boy** sei artig *or* lieb *or* brav *(inf)*; **be a good girl/boy and ...** sei so lieb und ...; **good girl/boy!** *(= well done)* gut!; **that's a good dog!** guter Hund!

h [= admirable] **your good lady** *(dated)* Ihre werte Gemahlin *(geh)*; **my good man** *(dated)* mein Guter *(old)*; **good man!** sehr löblich!, gut gemacht!; **good old Charles!** der gute alte Charles!; **the Good Book** das Buch der Bücher; **the good ship Santa Maria** die Santa Maria

i [= valid] *advice, excuse* gut; *reason* gut, triftig; *ticket* gültig; **is his credit good?** ist er kreditfähig?

♦ **good for he's good for £10,000** *(= will give us)* bei ihm kannst du mit £ 10.000 rechnen; *(= has got)* er hat gut und gern £ 10.000; **he is good for another few years** mit ihm kann man noch ein paar Jahre rechnen; **the car is good for another few years** das Auto hält *or* tuts *(inf)* noch ein paar Jahre; **she's good for nothing** sie ist ein Nichtsnutz *or* Taugenichts; **that's always good for a laugh** darüber kann man immer lachen

j [= handsome] *looks, figure, features* gut; *legs, body* schön; **a good appearance** *(of person)* ein gepflegtes Äußeres

k [= uninjured] *eye, leg* gesund

l [= thorough] gut, gründlich, tüchtig *(inf)*; **to give sb a good scolding** jdn gründlich *or* tüchtig *(inf)* ausschimpfen; **to give sth a good clean** etw gut *or* gründlich reinigen; **to have a good cry** sich ausweinen; **to have a good laugh** ordentlich *or* so richtig lachen *(inf)*; **to take a good look at sth** sich *(dat)* etw gut ansehen; **to have a good grounding in sth** gute Grundkenntnisse in etw *(dat)* haben

m [= considerable] *hour, while* gut; *amount, distance, way* gut, schön; **it's a good distance** es ist eine ganz schöne Strecke; **it's a good 8 km** es sind gute 8 km; **he ate a good half of the cake** er hat gut und gern den halben Kuchen gegessen; **a good many/few people** ziemlich viele/nicht gerade wenig Leute

n [in greetings] gut; **good morning** guten Morgen

o [in exclamations] gut, prima; **that's good!** gut!, prima!; **(it's) good to see you/to be here** (es ist) schön, dich zu sehen/hier zu sein; **good enough!** *(= OK)* schön!; **good heavens** *or* **Lord** *or* **God!** um Himmels willen! *(inf)*; **good grief** *or* **gracious!** ach du liebe *or* meine Güte! *(inf)*; **very good, sir** sehr wohl *(old)*; **good for** *or (esp Austral)* **on you/him** *etc*! gut!, prima!; *(iro also)* das ist ja toll!

p [emphatic use] schön; **a good strong stick** ein schön(er) starker Stock; **a good old age** ein schön(es) hohes Alter

♦ **good and ...** ganz; **good and hard/strong** *(inf)* ganz schön fest/stark *(inf)*; **good and proper** *(inf)* ganz anständig *(inf)*

2 – ADVERB

a [= fine] gut; **how are you? – good!** wie gehts? – gut!

b [= well] *strictly incorrect* gut

3 – NOUN

a [= what is morally right] Gute(s) *nt*; **good and evil** Gut und Böse; **to do good** Gutes tun; **there's some good in everybody** in jedem steckt etwas Gutes; **to be up to no good** *(inf)* nichts Gutes im Schilde führen *(inf)*

b [= advantage, benefit] Wohl *nt*; **the common good** das Gemeinwohl; **for the good of the nation** zum Wohl(e) der Nation; **this affects us, for good or ill** das wirkt sich auf uns aus, positiv oder negativ; **it's done now, for good or ill** es ist nun einmal geschehen; **I did it for your own good** ich meine es nur gut mit dir, es war nur zu deinem Besten; **for the good of one's health** *etc* seiner Gesundheit *etc* zuliebe; **he'll come to no good** mit ihm wird es noch ein böses Ende nehmen

♦ **to do good to do (some) good** (etwas) helfen *or* nützen; **to do sb good** jdm helfen; *(rest, drink, medicine etc)* jdm guttun; **what good will that do you?** was hast du davon?; **much good may it do you** *(iro inf)* na, dann viel Vergnügen! *(iro inf)*; **that won't do much/any good** das hilft auch nicht viel/auch nichts; **that won't do you much/any good** das hilft dir auch nicht viel/auch nichts; *(= will be unhealthy etc)* das ist nicht gut für dich; **a (fat) lot of good that will do!** *(iro inf)* als ob das viel helfen würde! *(iro)*; **a (fat) lot of good that will do you!** *(iro inf)* und wie dir das guttun wird! *(iro inf)*

c [= use] **what's the good of hurrying?** wozu eigentlich die Eile?; **it would be some good** es wäre ganz nützlich; **if that is any good to you** wenn es dir hilft

♦ **no/not any good that's no good** das ist nichts; **he's no good to us** er nützt uns *(dat)* nichts; **it's no good complaining to me** es ist sinnlos *or* es nützt nichts, sich bei mir zu beklagen; **it's no good doing it like that** es hat keinen Sinn, das so zu machen; **he's no good at it** er kann es nicht; **I'm no good at things like that** ich bin nicht gut in solchen Dingen; **the applicant was no good** der Bewerber war nicht gut; **he wasn't any good for the job** er eignete sich nicht für die Arbeit; **he wasn't any good at the job** er machte die Arbeit nicht gut

d [set structures]

♦ **for good** *(= for ever)* **for good (and all)** für immer (und ewig)

♦ **to the good we were 5 points/£5 to the good** wir hatten 5 Punkte zu viel/£ 5 plus; **that's all to the good** auch gut!

goodbye [gʊd'baɪ] N Abschied *m*, Lebewohl *nt (geh)*; **to say ~, to say** *or* **make one's ~s** sich verabschieden, Lebewohl sagen *(geh)*; **to wish sb ~, to say ~ to sb** sich von jdm verabschieden, von jdm Abschied nehmen; **to say ~ to sth** einer Sache *(dat)* Lebewohl sagen; **well, it's ~ to all that** damit ist es jetzt vorbei; **when all the ~s were over** als das Abschiednehmen vorbei war INTERJ auf Wiedersehen, lebe wohl *(geh)* ADJ *attr* Abschieds-; **~ party** Abschiedsparty *f*

good: **good-for-nothing** N Nichtsnutz *m*, Taugenichts *m* ADJ nichtsnutzig; **his ~ brother** sein Nichtsnutz von Bruder; **Good Friday** N Karfreitag *m*; **good-hearted** ADJ gutherzig; **good-humoured**, *(US)* **good-humored** ADJ *person (by nature)* gutmütig; *(on a certain occasion)* gut gelaunt; *crowd* gut gelaunt; *atmosphere* freundlich; *rivalry* gutmütig; *event, demonstration* friedlich; **it was a ~ conference** bei der Konferenz herrschte eine freundliche Atmosphäre

goodish ['gʊdɪʃ] **ADJ** *(= quite good)* ganz gut, anständig *(inf)*; *(= considerable)* ganz schön

good: **good-looker** **N** *(inf)* **to be a real ~** wirklich gut *or* klasse *(inf)* aussehen; **good-looking** **ADJ** gut aussehend

goodly ['gʊdlɪ] **ADJ** ansehnlich, stattlich *(geh)*

good: **good-natured** **ADJ** *person (by nature)* gutmütig; *(on a certain occasion)* gut gelaunt; *face, smile, attitude* gutmütig; *crowd, demonstration* friedlich; *atmosphere, conversation, laughter* freundlich; *fun* harmlos; **good-naturedly** **ADV** gutmütig

goodness ['gʊdnɪs] **N** **a** Güte *f*; *(of food)* Güte *f*, Nährgehalt *m*; **out of the ~ of his/her heart** aus reiner Herzensgüte; **would you have the ~ to ...** *(form)* hätten Sie bitte die Güte, zu ... *(geh)* **b** *(in exclamations etc)* **~ knows** weiß der Himmel *(inf)*; **for ~' sake** um Himmels willen *(inf)*; **I wish to ~ I had never met him** wenn ich ihn doch bloß nie begegnet wäre!; **(my) ~!** meine Güte! *(inf)*; **~ gracious** *or* **me!** ach du liebe *or* meine Güte! *(inf)*

goodnight [gʊd'naɪt] **ADJ** *attr* Gutenacht-; **~ kiss** Gutenachtkuss *m*

goods [gʊdz] ✪ 20.5 **PL** Güter *pl (also Comm)*; *(= merchandise also)* Waren *pl*; *(= possessions also)* Gut *nt (geh)*, Habe *f (geh, liter)*; **leather/manufactured ~** Leder-/Fertigwaren *pl*; **canned ~** Konserven *pl*; **stolen ~** gestohlene Waren *pl*, Diebesgut *nt*; **~ depot/train/yard** Güterdepot *nt*/-zug *m*/-bahnhof *m*; **one's ~ and chattels** *(Brit)* sein Hab und Gut *(also Jur)*, seine Siebensachen *(inf)*; **to send sth ~** etw als Frachtgut schicken; **it's the ~** *(esp US inf)* das ist große Klasse *(inf)*; **to get/have the ~ on sb** *(esp US inf)* gegen jdn etwas in die Hand bekommen/in der Hand haben; **if we don't come up with the ~ on time** *(inf)* wenn wir es nicht rechtzeitig schaffen

good: **good-sized** **ADJ** ziemlich groß; *building, room also* geräumig; **good-tempered** **ADJ** *person* verträglich; *animal* gutartig; *behaviour* gutmütig; **good-time Charlie** **N** *(US inf)* Luftikus *m*, (Bruder) Leichtfuß *m*; **good-time girl** **N** Playgirl *nt*; *(= prostitute)* Freudenmädchen *nt*; **goodwill** **N** Wohlwollen *nt*; *(between nations, Comm)* Goodwill *m*; **a gesture of ~** ein Zeichen seines/ihres *etc* guten Willens; **to gain sb's ~** jds Gunst gewinnen; **~ ambassador** *(for UNICEF etc)* Botschafter(in) *m(f)* des guten Willens; **~ mission/tour** Goodwillreise *f*/-tour *f*

goody ['gʊdɪ] *(inf)* **INTERJ** toll, prima; **~, ~ gumdrops!** *(hum)* juchhei, juchhe! **N** **a** *(= person)* Gute(r) *m* **b** *(= delicacy)* gute Sache *(inf)*, Leckerbissen *m*; *(= sweet)* Süßigkeit *f* **c** *(inf, = good joke, story etc)* guter Witz/gute Geschichte *etc*

goody: **goody bag** **N** *(inf)* Tüte *f* mit Leckereien; *(Comm) (with gifts)* Tüte *f* mit Geschenken; *(with free samples)* Tüte *f* mit Probepackungen; **goody-goody** *(inf)* **N** Tugendlamm *nt*, Musterkind *nt (inf)* **ADJ** tugendhaft, superbrav *(pej inf)*; *attitude, behaviour also* musterhaft; *(pretending)* scheinheilig; **goody two-shoes** **N** *(pej inf)* Tugendlamm *nt (pej)*

gooey ['gu:ɪ] **ADJ** *(+er) (inf)* **a** *(= sticky)* klebrig; *(= slushy)* breiig **b** *(pej) behaviour, song, letter* rührselig, schnulzig *(pej inf)*; **to go (all) ~** vor Rührung zerfließen; **he makes her go all ~** bei seinem Anblick gerät sie ins Schwärmen; **to go ~ over sb** für jdn schwärmen

goof [gu:f] *(inf)* **N** **a** *(esp US: = idiot)* Dussel *m (inf)*, Doofie *m (inf)* **b** *(= mistake)* Schnitzer *m (inf)*, dicker Hund *(dated inf)* **VI** **a** *(= blunder)* sich *(dat)* etwas leisten *(inf)*, danebenhauen *(inf)* **b** *(US: = loiter: also* **goof around**) (herum)trödeln, bummeln; **to ~ off** abzwitschern *(inf)*

▶ **goof up** **VT** *sep (inf)* vermasseln *(inf)*, vermurksen *(inf)*

goofball ['gu:fbɔ:l] **N** *(esp US inf)* Doofkopp *m (sl)*

go-off **N** *(inf)* Anfang *m*, Start *m*; **at the first ~** (gleich) beim ersten Mal, auf Anhieb

goofy ['gu:fɪ] **ADJ** *(+er) (inf)* dämlich *(inf)*, doof *(inf)*

google ['gu:gl] **VI** *(Internet) im Internet mit der Suchmaschine Google® nach Informationen suchen*

googler ['gu:glə] **N** *(Internet) jd, der im Internet mit der Suchmaschine Google® nach Informationen sucht*

googly ['gu:glɪ] **N** *(Cricket)* gedrehter Ball

goo-goo eyes [,gu:gu:'aɪz] **N** *(hum inf)* **to make ~ at sb** jdn anhimmeln *(inf)*

goolies ['gu:lɪz] **N** *(Brit vulg sl: = testicles)* Eier *pl (vulg)*

goon [gu:n] **N** **a** *(inf: = idiot)* Idiot *m*, Dussel *m (inf)* **b** *(US inf: = hired thug)* Schlägertyp *m (inf)*

goop [gu:p] **N** *(esp US inf)* klebriger Schleim

goose [gu:s] **N** *pl* **geese** *(lit, inf)* Gans *f*; **silly little ~!** *(inf)* dummes Gänschen! *(inf)*; **all his geese are swans** bei ihm ist immer alles besser; **to kill the ~ that lays the golden eggs** das Huhn schlachten, das die goldenen Eier legt **VT** *(inf)* einen Klaps auf den Hintern geben *(+dat) (inf)*

gooseberry ['gʊzbərɪ] **N** *(= plant, fruit)* Stachelbeere *f*; **~ bush** Stachelbeerstrauch *m*; **to play ~** *(Brit inf)* Anstandswauwau spielen *(inf)*, das fünfte Rad am Wagen sein

goose: **goose bumps** **PL**, **goose flesh** **N** Gänsehaut *f*; **gooseneck lamp** **N** Bogenleuchte *f*; **goose pimples** **PL** *(Brit)* Gänsehaut *f*; **goose step** **N** Stechschritt *m*; **goose-step** **VI** im Stechschritt marschieren

goosey ['gu:sɪ] **ADJ** *(+er) (inf) (= foolish)* dumm; *(US: = ticklish)* kitz(e)lig; *(= nervous)* nervös; **to get ~** eine Gänsehaut bekommen

GOP *(US Pol) abbr of* **Grand Old Party**

Gopher ['gəʊfə'] **N** *(Comput)* Gopher *m*

gopher ['gəʊfə'] **N** Taschenratte *f*; *(= squirrel)* Ziesel *m*

gorblimey [,gɔ:'blaɪmɪ] **INTERJ** *(Brit inf)* ach du grüne Neune *(inf)*, ich denk mich laust der Affe *(inf)*

Gordian ['gɔ:dɪən] **ADJ** gordisch; **to cut the ~ knot** den gordischen Knoten durchhauen

gore[1] [gɔ:'] **N** *(liter: = blood)* Blut *nt*

gore[2] **VT** aufspießen, durchbohren; **~d to death by a bull** durch die Hörner eines Stiers tödlich verletzt

gore[3] **N** *(= panel)* Bahn *f*; *(in sail)* Gehren *m*

gored [gɔ:d] **ADJ** mit Bahnen; **~ skirt** Bahnenrock *m*

gorge [gɔ:dʒ] **N** **a** *(Geog)* Schlucht *f* **b** *(old: = gullet)* Schlund *m*; **it stuck in my ~ to ...** *(fig)* es war mir zuwider, zu ...; **it makes my ~ rise** *(fig: = makes me angry)* dabei kommt mir die Galle hoch **VR** schlemmen, sich vollessen; *(animal)* gierig fressen, schlingen; **to ~ (oneself) on sth** *(also fig)* etw in sich *(acc)* hineinschlingen, etw verschlingen **VT** **they were ~d** sie hatten sich reichlich gesättigt *(on* an *+dat)*; *(animals)* sie hatten sich vollgefressen *(on* an *+dat)*

gorgeous ['gɔ:dʒəs] **ADJ** **a** *(= lovely) weather, scenery, sunset, colours, food, wine, melody* herrlich, fantastisch, phantastisch; **to look ~** fantastisch *or* phantastisch aussehen; **to taste/smell ~** herrlich schmecken/duften **b** *(inf: = beautiful) woman, man, eyes, hair* hinreißend; *clothes* hinreißend, toll *(inf)*; *present* toll *(inf)*; **a ~ blonde** eine sagenhafte Blondine *(inf)*; **a ~ hunk** ein toller Typ *(inf)*; **hi, ~!** hallo, Süßer/Süße! **c** *(= sumptuous, magnificent) clothes, fabric, jewellery, flowers, building* prächtig

gorgeously ['gɔ:dʒəslɪ] **ADV** herrlich; **~ dressed women** hinreißend angezogene Frauen; **~ embroidered clothing** prächtig bestickte Kleidung

gorgeousness ['gɔ:dʒəsnɪs] **N** Herrlichkeit *f*; *(= splendour)* Pracht *f*; *(= beauty)* hinreißende Schönheit

Gorgon ['gɔ:gən] **N** *(Myth)* Gorgo *f*; *(inf)* Drachen *m (inf)*

Gorgonzola [,gɔ:gən'zəʊlə] **N** Gorgonzola *m*

gorilla [gə'rɪlə] **N** Gorilla *m*

gormless ['gɔ:mlɪs] **ADJ** *(Brit inf)* doof *(inf)*

gorse [gɔ:s] **N** Stechginster *m*; **~ bush** Stechginsterstrauch *m*

gory ['gɔ:rɪ] **ADJ** *scene, story, violence* blutrünstig; *murder, detail* blutig

gosh [gɒʃ] **INTERJ** Mensch *(inf)*, Mann *(inf)*

goshawk ['gɒshɔ:k] **N** (Hühner)habicht *m*

gosling ['gɒzlɪŋ] **N** junge Gans, Gänschen *nt*

go-slow ['gəʊsləʊ] **N** *(Brit)* Bummelstreik *m*

gospel ['gɒspəl] **N** **a** *(Bibl)* Evangelium *nt*; **the Gospels** das Evangelium, die Evangelien *pl*; **the Gospel according to St John** das Evangelium nach Johannes; **St John's Gospel** das Johannesevangelium; **the Gospel for today** das heutige Evangelium **b** *(fig: = doctrine)* Grundsätze *pl*, Prinzipien *pl*; *(of ideology, religion)* Lehre *f*; **to preach the ~ of abstinence** Abstinenz predigen; **she's a firm believer in the ~ of free enterprise** sie ist eine überzeugte Anhängerin des freien Unternehmertums; **to take sth for** *or* **as ~** etw für bare Münze nehmen *(inf)*; **whatever he said was ~ to her** alles, was er auch sagte, war für sie (ein) Evangelium **c** *(Mus)* Gospel *m*

gospeller ['gɒspələ'] **N** → **hot gospeller**

gospel: **gospel song** **N** Gospel(lied) *nt*; **gospel truth** **N** *(inf)* reine Wahrheit

goss [gɒs] **N** *(Brit inf: = gossip)* Klatsch *m (inf)*; **have you heard the latest ~?** weißt du schon das Neueste?

gossamer ['gɒsəmə'] **N** **a** Spinnfäden *pl*, Marienfäden *pl* **b** *(Tex)* hauchdünne Gaze **ADJ** hauchdünn

gossip ['gɒsɪp] **N** **a** Klatsch *m*, Tratsch *m (inf)*; *(= chat)* Schwatz *m*; **to have a ~ with sb** mit jdm schwatzen *or* plauschen *(inf) or* klönen *(N Ger)*; **it started a lot of ~** es gab Anlass zu vielem Gerede *or* Tratsch *(inf) or* Klatsch; **office ~** Bürotratsch *m (inf)* **b** *(= person)* Klatschbase *f* **VI** schwatzen, plauschen *(inf)*, klönen *(N Ger)*; *(maliciously)* klatschen, tratschen *(inf)*

gossip: **gossip column** **N** Klatschkolumne *or* -spalte *f*; **gossip columnist** **N** Klatschkolumnist(in) *m(f)*

gossiping ['gɒsɪpɪŋ] **ADJ** geschwätzig, schwatzhaft; *(malicious)* klatschsüchtig; **to have a ~ tongue** ein Klatschmaul sein *(inf)*; **her ~ tongue will get her into trouble** ihre Klatschsucht wird ihr noch einmal Unannehmlichkeiten einbringen **N** Geschwätz *nt*; *(malicious)* Geklatsche *nt*, Getratsche *nt (inf)*; **there's too much ~ and not enough work done in this office** in diesem Büro wird zu viel geschwatzt und zu wenig gearbeitet

gossip: **gossipmonger** ['gɒsɪp,mʌŋgə'] **N** Klatschmaul *nt (inf)*; **gossipmongering** ['gɒsɪp,mʌŋgərɪŋ] **N** Klatscherei *f*, Tratscherei *f (inf)*

gossipy ['gɒsɪpɪ] **ADJ** *person* geschwätzig; *book, letter* im Plauderton geschrieben; **the ~ world of publishing** die klatschsüchtige Welt des Verlagswesens; **a long ~ phone call** ein langer Schwatz *or* Tratsch am Telefon *(inf)*; **~ style** Plauderton *m*

got [gɒt] *pret, ptp of* **get**

gotcha ['gɒtʃə] **INTERJ** *(inf)* **a** *(= I see)* kapiert! *(inf)* **b** *(when catching, hitting, killing sb)* erwischt! *(inf)*

Goth [gɒθ] **N** **a** *(Hist)* Gote *m*, Gotin *f* **b** *(Mus, Fashion)* = **goth** **ADJ** *(Mus, Fashion)* = **goth**

goth [gɒθ] *(esp Brit)* **N** **a** *(= person)* Grufti *m* **b** *(Mus)* Gruftimusik *f* **c** *(= fashion)* Gruftistil *m* **ADJ** *(Mus, Fashion)* Grufti-; **~ band** Gruftiband *f*

Gothic ['gɒθɪk] **ADJ** **a** *people, language, script, lettering* gotisch **b** *(Art)* gotisch; **the ~ age** das

Zeitalter der Gotik; ~ **Revival** *(Archit)* Neugotik *f*; ~ **Revival architecture** neugotische Architektur **c** *(Liter. = horror)* schaurig; **a ~ story** eine Schauergeschichte; ~ **(horror) novel** Schauerroman *m* **N a** *(Archit)* Gotik *f* **b** *(= language)* Gotisch *nt* **c** *(Typ)* Gotisch *nt*; *(US)* Grotesk *f*

gotten [ˈgɒtn] *(esp US) ptp of* **get**

gouache [gʊˈɑːʃ] N Guasch *f*, Gouache *f*

gouge [gaʊdʒ] **N** *(= tool)* Hohlmeißel *or* -beitel *m*; *(= groove)* Rille *f*, Furche *f* **VT** bohren; **the river ~d a channel in the mountainside** der Fluss grub sich *(dat)* sein Bett in den Berg

▶ **gouge out** VT *sep* herausbohren; **to gouge sb's eyes out** jdm die Augen ausstechen

goulash [ˈguːlæʃ] N Gulasch *nt*

gourd [gʊəd] N Flaschenkürbis *m*; *(dried)* Kürbisflasche *f*

gourmand [ˈgʊəmənd] N Schlemmer *m*, Gourmand *m*

gourmet [ˈgʊəmeɪ] N Feinschmecker(in) *m(f)*, Gourmet *m*

gout [gaʊt] N *(Med)* Gicht *f*

gouty [ˈgaʊtɪ] ADJ *(+er) person* gichtkrank; *limb, joint also* gichtisch; ~ **condition** Gichtleiden *nt*

gov *abbr of* **government**

Gov *abbr of* **governor**

govern [ˈgʌvən] **VT a** *(= rule) country* regieren; *province, colony, school etc* verwalten **b** *(= control: rules, laws etc)* bestimmen; *(legislation)* regeln; *(= determine, influence) choice, decision* bestimmen, beeinflussen; *development, person, actions* beeinflussen; *life* beherrschen; **regulations ~ing the sale of spirits** Bestimmungen über den Verkauf von Spirituosen; **strict rules ~ing how much they can earn** strenge Vorschriften darüber, wie viel sie verdienen dürfen; **to be ~ed by sb's wishes** sich nach jds Wünschen richten **c** *(= hold in check) passions etc* beherrschen; *(Mech) speed, engine* regulieren; **to ~ one's temper** sich beherrschen **d** *(Gram) case* regieren; **the number of the verb is ~ed by the subject** das Verb richtet sich in der Zahl nach dem Subjekt **VI** *(Pol)* regieren, an der Regierung sein

governable [ˈgʌvənəbl] ADJ regierbar

governance [ˈgʌvənəns] N *(action)* Regierungsgewalt *f*; *(manner)* Regierungsform *f*; *(fig: = control)* Gewalt *f*, Kontrolle *f* *(of* über)

governess [ˈgʌvənɪs] N Gouvernante *f*, Hauslehrerin *f*

governing [ˈgʌvənɪŋ] **N** *(of country)* Regierung *f*; *(of town, province etc)* Verwaltung *f* **ADJ a** *(Pol) coalition* regierend **b** *(Admin) committee* leitend; ~ **authority** Regierungsbehörde *f*; **the ~ class** die herrschende Klasse; ~ **council/board** Vorstand *m*; **the ~ party** die Regierungspartei

governing body N *(of sport, professional association)* leitendes Gremium; *(of school)* ≈ Schulbeirat *m*; *(of university)* Senat *m*

government [ˈgʌvənmənt] N **a** *(= action of governing, body of administrators)* Regierung *f*; **strong ~ is difficult in a democracy** es ist schwierig, in einer Demokratie mit fester Hand zu regieren; **to form a ~** eine Regierung bilden **b** *(= system)* Regierungsform *f* *attr* Regierungs-, der Regierung; *agency* staatlich; ~ **official** Regierungsbeamter *m*/-beamtin *f*; ~ **action** Maßnahmen *pl* der Regierung; *(= intervention)* staatlicher Eingriff; ~ **backing** staatliche Unterstützung; ~ **intervention** staatlicher Eingriff

governmental [ˌgʌvənˈmentl] ADJ Regierungs-; ~ **system/crisis/policy** Regierungssystem *nt*/-krise *f*/-politik *f*

government: **government department** N Ministerium *nt*; **government grant** N (staatliche) Subvention; **Government House** N Gouverneursresidenz *f*; **government loan** N Staatsanleihe *f*; **government monopoly** N Staatsmonopol *nt*, staatliches Monopol; **government-run** ADJ *television, newspaper etc* staatlich; **government securities** PL Staatsanleihen *pl*; **government spending** N öffentliche Ausgaben *pl*; **government stocks** PL *(Fin)* Staatspapiere *or* -anleihen *pl*

governor [ˈgʌvənəˈ] N **a** *(of colony, state etc)* Gouverneur(in) *m(f)* **b** *(esp Brit, of bank, prison)* Direktor(in) *m(f)*; *(of school)* ≈ Mitglied *nt* des Schulbeirats; **the (board of) ~s** der Vorstand; *(of bank also)* das Direktorium; *(of school)* ≈ der Schulbeirat **c** *(Brit inf: = boss)* Chef *m* *(inf)*; *(= father)* alter Herr *(inf)* **d** *(Mech)* Regler *m*

governor general N Generalgouverneur(in) *m(f)*

governorship [ˈgʌvənəʃɪp] N *(= office)* Gouverneursamt *nt*; *(= period)* Amtszeit *f* als Gouverneur

govt *abbr of* **government** Reg.

gown [gaʊn] **N a** Kleid *nt*; *(= evening gown)* Robe *f*, Abendkleid *nt*; *(= dressing gown)* Morgenmantel *m*; *(in hospital)* Kittel *m*; **wedding ~** Hochzeitskleid *nt* **b** *(= academic gown)* Robe *f*; *(of clergyman, judge)* Talar *m* → **town VT** kleiden

GP *(Brit) abbr of* **general practitioner** praktischer Arzt, praktische Ärztin; **to go to one's GP** zu seinem Hausarzt/seiner Hausärztin gehen

GPMU *(Brit) abbr of* **Graphical, Paper and Media Union** ≈ IG Medien

GPO *abbr of* **General Post Office**

GPS *abbr of* **Global Positioning System** GPS *nt*

gr N *abbr of* **gross**[1] Gr **ADJ** *abbr of* **gross**[2] btto.

grab [græb] **N a** Griff *m*; **to make a ~ at** *or* **for sth** nach etw greifen *or* schnappen *(inf)* **b** *(Mech)* Greifer *m* **c** *(inf)* **to be up for ~s** zu haben sein *(inf)*; **there are big prizes up for ~s** es gibt tolle Preise zu gewinnen; ~ **bag** *(US)* Glücksbeutel *m*, Grabbelsack *m* **VT a** *(= seize)* packen; *(greedily)* packen, sich *(dat)* schnappen *(inf)*; *(= take, obtain)* wegschnappen *(inf)*; *money* raffen; *(inf: = catch) person* schnappen *(inf)*; *chance* beim Schopf ergreifen *(inf)*; *attention* auf sich *(acc)* ziehen; **he ~bed (hold of) my sleeve** er packte mich am Ärmel; **to ~ sth away from sb** jdm etw wegreißen; **to ~ something to eat** *(inf)* **to ~ a bite** *(inf)* schnell was essen; **I'll just ~ a sandwich** *(inf)* ich esse nur schnell ein Sandwich; **I'll just ~ a nap** *(inf)* ich mache nur schnell ein Nickerchen *(inf)*; **to ~ the headlines** Schlagzeilen machen **b** *(inf: = appeal to)* anmachen *(inf)*; **it didn't ~ me** das hat mich nicht angemacht *(inf)*; **how does that ~ you?** wie findest du das?, was meinst du dazu? **VI** (hastig) zugreifen *or* zupacken; **to ~ at** greifen *or* grapschen *(inf)* nach, packen *(+acc)*; **he ~bed at the chance of promotion** er ließ sich die Chance, befördert zu werden, nicht entgehen; **help yourselves, children, but don't ~** greift zu, Kinder, aber nicht so hastig

grabby [ˈgræbɪ] ADJ *(inf: = wanting possessions)* raffgierig, raffsüchtig; *(= wanting more)* gierig

grace [greɪs] **N a** *no pl (= gracefulness, graciousness)* Anmut *f*; *(of movement)* Anmut *f*, Grazie *f*; *(of monarch etc)* Würde *f*; **with ~** anmutig; **he performs his office with ~ and charm** er übt sein Amt würdevoll und charmant aus; **to do sth with (a) good/bad ~** etw anstandslos/widerwillig *or* unwillig tun; **he bore his defeat with good ~** er nahm seine Niederlage mit Fassung *or* anstandslos hin; **he took it with good ~** er machte gute Miene zum bösen Spiel; **he took it with bad ~** er war sehr ungehalten darüber; **he had/didn't even have the (good) ~ to apologize** er war so anständig/brachte es nicht einmal fertig, sich zu entschuldigen **b** *(= pleasing quality)* (angenehme) Eigenschaft; **social ~s** (gesellschaftliche) Umgangsformen *pl*; **a young woman with many ~s** eine sehr kultivierte junge Dame **c** *(= favour)* **to be in sb's good ~s** bei jdm gut angeschrieben sein **d** *(= respite: for payment)* Zahlungsfrist *f*; **a day's ~** ein Tag *m* Aufschub; **to give sb a few days' ~** jdm ein paar Tage Zeit lassen; **days of ~** *(Comm)* Respekttage *pl* **e** *(= prayer)* Tischgebet *nt*; **to say ~** das Tischgebet sprechen **f** *(= mercy)* Gnade *f*; **act of ~** Gnadenakt *m*; **by the ~ of God** durch die Gnade Gottes; **by the ~ of God Queen …** Königin … von Gottes Gnaden; **there but for the ~ of God go I** es hätte genauso gut auch mich treffen können; **in this year of ~ 1998** im Jahre des Heils 1998; **in a state of ~** *(Eccl)* im Zustand der Gnade; **to fall from ~** in Ungnade fallen **g** *(= title) (duke, duchess)* Hoheit *f*; *(archbishop)* Exzellenz *f*; **Your Grace** Euer Gnaden **h** *(Myth)* **the Graces** die Grazien *pl* **i** *(Mus)* Verzierung *f*, Ornament *nt*; ~ **note** Verzierung *f* **VT a** *(= adorn)* zieren *(geh)* **b** *(= honour)* beehren *(with* mit); *event etc* zieren *(geh)*, sich *(dat)* die Ehre geben bei *(+dat)*; **to ~ the occasion with one's presence** sich *(dat)* die Ehre geben

graceful [ˈgreɪsfʊl] ADJ *person, animal, movement* anmutig, graziös; *appearance, outline, shape* anmutig, elegant; *building, bow, manner, way of doing sth* elegant

gracefully [ˈgreɪsfəlɪ] ADV **a** *move, dance* anmutig, graziös; *curved, shaped* anmutig, elegant **b** *(= without a fuss) retire, accept, withdraw* anstandslos; **he gave in ~** er gab großzügig(erweise) nach; **to grow old ~** in Würde alt werden

gracefulness [ˈgreɪsfʊlnɪs] N Anmut(igkeit) *f*; *(of movement also)* Grazie *f*; *(of building, handwriting, bow, manner)* Eleganz *f*

graceless [ˈgreɪslɪs] ADJ **a** *(Eccl)* ruchlos, gottlos **b** *(= unattractive) building* reizlos **c** *(= rude)* schroff; *person, behaviour* ungehobelt, schroff; *(= lacking charm) teenager* linkisch

gracious [ˈgreɪʃəs] **ADJ a** *(form) person, manner, character (= courteous, kind)* liebenswürdig; *(condescendingly)* gnädig; **by ~ permission of …** mit der gütigen Erlaubnis *(+gen)*; **she was so ~ as to give her blessing** sie war so gnädig *or* gütig, ihren Segen dazu zu geben; **to be ~ to sb** jdn liebenswürdig behandeln **b** *(= elegant) lifestyle, era* kultiviert, elegant; *district* vornehm, elegant; ~ **living** ein kultivierter Lebensstil **INTERJ** *(dated)* **good** *or* **goodness ~ (me)!** *(expressing surprise or interest)* ach du meine Güte!; *(expressing annoyance)* um Gottes willen!; **good ~ yes/no** aber natürlich/nein

graciously [ˈgreɪʃəslɪ] ADV liebenswürdig; *(= condescendingly)* gnädigerweise

graciousness [ˈgreɪʃəsnɪs] N **a** Liebenswürdigkeit *f* *(towards* gegenüber); *(condescending)* Gnädigkeit *f* **b** *(= elegance: of lifestyle)* Kultiviertheit *f*

grad N *(inf) abbr of* **graduate**[1]

gradate [grəˈdeɪt] VT abstufen

gradation [grəˈdeɪʃən] N **a** *(= step, degree)* Abstufung *f*; *(= mark on thermometer etc)* Gradeinteilung *f*; **the ~s of public opinion ran from sympathy to anger** die Skala der öffentlichen Meinung reichte von Sympathie bis zu Zorn **b** *(= gradual change)* Abstufung *f*

grade [greɪd] **N a** *(= level, standard)* Niveau *nt*; *(of goods)* (Güte)klasse *f*; **high-/low-~ goods** hoch-/minderwertige Ware; **small-/large-~ eggs** kleine/große Eier; **this is ~ A** *(inf)* das ist I a *(inf)*; **to make the ~** *(fig inf)* es schaffen *(inf)* **b** *(= job grade)* Position *f*, Stellung *f*; *(Mil)* Rang *m*, (Dienst)grad *m* *(auch von Beamten)*; *(= salary grade)* Gehaltsgruppe *f*, Gehaltsstufe *f*; **she's on (salary) ~ 3** sie ist in Gehaltsgruppe 3; **to go up a ~** *(in salary)* in die nächste Gehaltsgruppe *or* Gehaltsstufe vorrücken **c** *(Sch: = mark)* Note *f*; *(esp US: = class)* Klasse *f*; **to get good/poor ~s** gute/schlechte Noten bekommen **d** *(esp US)* = **gradient** **e** *(US)* **at ~** auf gleicher Ebene; **an apartment at ~ (level)** eine Wohnung zu ebener Erde **VT a** *goods, animals* klassifizieren; *colours* abstufen; *students etc* einstufen

b (*US Sch: = mark*) benoten
c (*= level*) *road, slope* ebnen

▸ **grade down** VT *sep* (*= put in lower grade*) niedriger einstufen; *exam paper* schlechter benoten

▸ **grade up** VT *sep* höher einstufen; *exam paper* höher benoten

> **GRADE**
>
> In den USA und Kanada werden die Schuljahre als **grades** bezeichnet, beginnend mit dem **first grade** in der Grundschule bis hin zum **twelfth grade** in der Highschool. In den Highschools der USA werden die Schüler der 9. bis 12. Klasse mit folgenden Spitznamen belegt: **freshmen (ninth grade), sophomores (tenth grade), juniors (eleventh grade)** und **seniors (twelfth grade).**

grade crossing N (*US*) Bahnübergang *m*

-grader [-greɪdəʳ] N *suf* (*US Sch*) -klässler(in) *m(f)*; **sixth-grader** Sechstklässler(in) *m(f)*

grade school N (*US*) ≈ Grundschule *f*

gradient [ˈgreɪdɪənt] N (*esp Brit*) Neigung *f*; (*upward also*) Steigung *f*; (*downward also*) Gefälle *nt*; **a ~ of 1 in 10** eine Steigung/ein Gefälle von 10%; **what is the ~?** wie groß ist die Steigung/das Gefälle?; **what is the ~ of the hill?** welche Steigung/welches Gefälle hat der Berg?

gradual [ˈgrædjʊəl] ADJ allmählich; *decline, recovery, progress* langsam; *slope* sanft

gradually [ˈgrædjʊəlɪ] ADV nach und nach, allmählich; *slope* sanft

graduate¹ [ˈgrædjʊɪt] N (*Brit Univ*) (Hochschul)absolvent(in) *m(f)*; (*= person with degree*) Akademiker(in) *m(f)*; (*US Sch*) Schulabgänger(in) *m(f)*; **high-school ~** (*US*) ≈ Abiturient(in) *m(f)*

graduate² [ˈgrædjʊeɪt] **VT** **a** (*= mark*) einteilen, graduieren (*form*) **b** (*US: Sch, Univ*) als Absolventen haben **VI** **a** (*Univ*) graduieren; (*US Sch*) die Abschlussprüfung bestehen (*from* an *+dat*); **to ~ in English** einen Hochschulabschluss in Englisch machen; **she ~d to television from radio** sie arbeitete sich vom Radio zum Fernsehen hoch; **to ~ from the school of hard knocks** (*fig*) eine harte Lehre durchmachen **b** (*= change by degrees*) allmählich übergehen

graduate [ˈgrædʊɪt-] *in cpds* (*Brit*) für Akademiker; *unemployment* unter den Akademikern; **graduate course** N *Kurs für Studenten mit abgeschlossenem Studium*

graduated [ˈgrædjʊeɪtɪd] ADJ **a** (*= rising*) stufenweise zunehmend; *increase* stufenweise; (*Fin*) gestaffelt **b** (*= calibrated*) mit Maßeinteilung, graduiert (*form*); **~ tube/measure/flask** Messglas *nt*

graduate [ˈgrædʊɪt]: **graduate school** N (*US*) *Hochschulabteilung für Studenten mit abgeschlossenem Studium*; **graduate student** N (*US*) *Student(in) mit abgeschlossenem Studium*, Jungakademiker(in) *m(f)*

graduation [ˌgrædjʊˈeɪʃən] N **a** (*= mark*) (Maß)einteilung *f* **b** (*Univ, US Sch: = ceremony*) (Ab)schlussfeier *f* (*mit feierlicher Überreichung der Zeugnisse*); **his ~ was delayed by illness** wegen Krankheit wurde ihm sein Zeugnis erst später überreicht

> **GRADUATION**
>
> Der erfolgreiche Studienabschluss wird traditionell in Form einer offiziellen Zeremonie, der **graduation**, gefeiert. Dabei bekommen die Absolventen ihre Diplome oder Zeugnisse öffentlich vor den versammelten Angehörigen und Gästen vom Leiter des jeweiligen Instituts überreicht. Doktorhüte und -roben werden auch heute noch mit Stolz getragen, und das offizielle Foto des Absolventen in komplettem Outfit bekommt häufig einen Ehrenplatz auf dem Kaminsims der Eltern und Großeltern.
>
> In den USA versteht man unter **graduation** auch eine ähnliche Feier zum Abschluss der Highschool.

graduation day N Tag *m* der Abschlussfeier (und Überreichung der Zeugnisse)

Graeco- (*Brit*), **Greco-** (*esp US*) [ˈgriːkəʊ-] PREF griechisch-

Graeco-Roman (*Brit*), **Greco-Roman** (*esp US*) [ˌgriːkəʊˈrəʊmən] ADJ *art, sculpture* griechisch-römisch; **~ wrestling** Ringen *nt* im griechisch-römischen Stil

graffiti [grəˈfiːtɪ] PL Graffiti *pl*, Wandschmierereien *pl* (*pej*); **a piece of ~** eine Wandschmiererei, ein Graffito *nt*

graffiti artist N Graffitikünstler(in) *m(f)*

graft [grɑːft] **N** **a** (*Bot*) (Pfropf)reis *nt*; (*Med*) Transplantat *nt* **b** (*esp US inf: = corruption*) Mauschelei *f* (*inf*), Schiebung *f* **c** (*Brit inf: = hard work*) Schufterei *f* (*inf*), Plackerei *f* (*inf*) **VT** (*Bot*) (auf)pfropfen (*on* auf *+acc*), (ein)pfropfen (*in* in *+acc*); (*Med*) übertragen (*on* auf *+acc*), einpflanzen (*in* in *+acc*); (*fig: = incorporate*) einbauen (*onto* in *+acc*); (*artificially*) aufpfropfen (*onto +dat*) **VI** (*inf: = work hard*) schuften (*at* an *+dat*) (*inf*)

▸ **graft on** VT *sep* = **graft VT**

grafter [ˈgrɑːftəʳ] N (*inf*) **a** (*Brit = hard worker*) Arbeitstier *nt* (*inf*), Malocher(in) *m(f)* (*inf*) **b** (*esp US*) Gauner(in) *m(f)*

graham [ˈgreɪəm] ADJ (*US*) **~ flour** Weizenschrot(mehl) *nt*

grail [greɪl] N Gral *m*

grain [greɪn] **N** **a** *no pl* Getreide *nt*, Korn *nt* **b** (*of corn, salt, sand etc*) Korn *nt*; (*fig, of sense, malice*) Spur *f*; (*of truth*) Körnchen *nt*; (*of hope*) Funke *m*; **that's a ~ of comfort** das ist wenigstens ein kleiner Trost **c** (*of leather*) Narben *m*; (*of cloth*) Strich *m*; (*of meat*) Faser *f*; (*of wood, marble*) Maserung *f*; (*of stone*) Korn *nt*, Gefüge *nt*; (*Phot*) Korn *nt*; **it goes against the** (*Brit*) *or* **my** (*US*) **~** (*fig*) es geht einem gegen den Strich **d** (*= weight*) Gran *nt* **VT** *wood* masern; *leather, paper* narben

grain: **grain alcohol** N Äthylalkohol *m*; **grain elevator** N Getreideheber *m*

grainy [ˈgreɪnɪ] ADJ (*+er*) **a** (*= granular*) *texture* körnig; *surface* gekörnt **b** *leather* genarbt; *wood* maserig, gemasert **c** *photograph, video* unscharf

gram, gramme [græm] N Gramm *nt*

gram flour N Kichererbsenmehl *nt*

grammar [ˈgræməʳ] N **a** (*= subject, book*) Grammatik *f*, Sprachlehre *f*; **your ~ is terrible** von Grammatik hast du keine Ahnung; **his ~ is excellent** seine Grammatik ist fehlerfrei; **that is bad ~** das ist grammat(ikal)isch falsch **b** (*inf*) = **grammar school**

grammar book N Grammatik(buch *nt*) *f*, Sprachlehrbuch *nt*

grammarian [grəˈmɛərɪən] N Grammatiker(in) *m(f)*

grammar school N (*Brit*) ≈ Gymnasium *nt*; (*US*) ≈ Mittelschule *f* (*Stufe zwischen Grundschule und Höherer Schule*)

grammatical [grəˈmætɪkəl] ADJ **a** (*= relating to grammar*) grammatisch; **~ error/rule** Grammatikfehler *m*/-regel *f* **b** (*= correct*) grammat(ikal)isch richtig *or* korrekt; **his English is not ~** sein Englisch ist grammatikalisch falsch

grammaticality [grəˌmætɪˈkælɪtɪ] N Grammatikalität *f*

grammatically [grəˈmætɪkəlɪ] ADV *write, speak* grammat(ikal)isch richtig *or* korrekt; **~ correct** grammat(ikal)isch richtig; **~, this sentence is wrong** dieser Satz ist grammat(ikal)isch falsch; **~, his work is poor** von der Grammatik her ist seine Arbeit schlecht

gramme N = **gram**

Grammy [ˈgræmɪ] N (*= award*) Grammy *m* (*Schallplattenpreis*)

gramophone [ˈgræməfəʊn] N (*Brit old*) Grammophon® *nt* (*dated*), Grammofon *nt*; **~ record** Schallplatte *f*

gramps [græmps] N (*US inf*) Opa *m* (*inf*), Opapa *m* (*inf*)

grampus [ˈgræmpəs] N Rundkopf- *or* Rissosdelfin *m or* -delphin *m*, Grampus *m* (*spec*); **to puff/snort like a ~** (*inf*) wie eine Lokomotive schnaufen (*inf*)

gran [græn] N (*inf*) Oma *f* (*inf*), Omi *f* (*inf*)

granary [ˈgrænərɪ] N Kornkammer *f* (*also fig*), Kornspeicher *m*

grand [grænd] **ADJ** (*+er*) **a** (*= imposing*) grandios; *architecture, building* prachtvoll, grandios; *scheme, strategy* groß angelegt; *gesture* großartig; *ideas* hochfliegend; *person, clothes, manner* vornehm; *job* bedeutend; **~ design** groß angelegter (Gesamt)plan; **on a ~ scale** im großen Rahmen; **to make a ~ entrance** einen großen Auftritt inszenieren; **to do sth in the ~ manner** etw im großen Stil tun; **to give oneself ~ airs** den großen Herrn/die große Dame spielen; **~ occasion** großer *or* feierlicher Anlass; **the ~ opening** die große Eröffnung; **the ~ old man of English politics** der große Alte *or* der Grand Old Man der englischen Politik
b (*dated: = great, wonderful, inf*) *activity, experience, success, idea* fabelhaft, großartig; *person* fantastisch (*inf*), phantastisch (*inf*), toll (*inf*); **to have a ~ (old) time** sich glänzend *or* großartig amüsieren
N **a** (*Fin inf: = thousand pounds or dollars*) Riese *m* (*inf*); **ten ~** zehn Riesen (*inf*)
b (*Mus inf: = grand piano*) Flügel *m* → *also* **baby grand (piano)**

grand: **grandaunt** N Großtante *f*; **Grand Canary** N Gran Canaria *nt*; **Grand Canyon** N Grand Canyon *m*; **grandchild** N Enkel(kind *nt*) *m*; **grand(d)ad** N (*inf*) Opa *m* (*inf*), Opi *m* (*inf*); **granddaughter** N Enkelin *f*; **grand duchess** N Großherzogin *f*; **grand duchy** N Großherzogtum *nt*; **grand duke** N Großherzog *m*

grandee [grænˈdiː] N (*of Spain*) Grande *m*; (*fig*) Fürst *m* (*inf*); **the ~s of broadcasting/business** die Größen des Fernsehens/der Geschäftswelt

grandeur [ˈgrændjəʳ] N Größe *f*; (*of scenery, music also*) Erhabenheit *f*; (*of manner also*) Würde *f*, Vornehmheit *f*

grandfather [ˈgrændfɑːðəʳ] N Großvater *m*

grandfather clock N Standuhr *f*, Großvateruhr *f*

grandfatherly ADJ großväterlich

grand finale N großes Finale

grandiloquence [grænˈdɪləkwəns] N (*form, of language, speech, style*) hochtrabende Art; **his ~** seine hochtrabende Art; (*= words*) seine großtönenden Worte

grandiloquent [grænˈdɪləkwənt] ADJ (*form*) *language, style, speech* hochtrabend; *gesture* übertrieben; *description* grandios

grandiloquently [grænˈdɪləkwəntlɪ] ADV *speak* hochtrabend; *announce* großspurig; *expressed, phrased, described* hochtrabend, grandios

grandiose [ˈgrændɪəʊz] ADJ (*= impressive*) *house, speech, ambition* grandios (*also pej*), großartig; (*pej: = pompous*) *person, style* schwülstig, bombastisch (*inf*); *idea, plan* grandios, hochfliegend; *claim* großspurig

grandiosely [ˈgrændɪəʊzlɪ] ADV *remark* grandios (*also pej*); *name* schwülstig

grand jury N (*US Jur*) Großes Geschworenengericht

> **GRAND JURY**
>
> Im US-Rechtssystem entscheidet die **grand jury** darüber, ob jemand wegen einer Straftat angeklagt und der Fall vor Gericht behandelt werden soll. Eine **grand jury** setzt sich aus zwölf bis dreiundzwanzig Personen zusammen. Das Verfahren findet normalerweise nicht öffentlich statt. Die **grand jury** ist ermächtigt, Zeugen vorzuladen und sie zu ei-

ner Aussage zu zwingen. Die Jury aus zwölf Geschworenen, die bei einer Gerichtsverhandlung über die Schuld oder Unschuld eines Angeklagten zu entscheiden hat, wird **trial jury** oder **petit jury** genannt.

grand larceny N schwerer Diebstahl

grandly ['grændlɪ] ADV **a** (= *impressively*) eindrucksvoll; *named* grandios; *situated, built* prachtvoll; **it is ~ described as/called/titled ...** es trägt die grandiose Bezeichnung ... **b** (= *pompously*) *announce, proclaim, declare* großspurig; *say* hochtrabend

grand: **grandma** N (*inf*) Oma *f* (*inf*), Omi *f* (*inf*); **grand mal** [ˌgrɒn'mæl] N (*Med*) Grand Mal *nt*; **grand master, grandmaster** N (*Chess*) Großmeister(in) *m(f)*; **grandmother** N Großmutter *f*; **grandmotherly** ADJ großmütterlich; **Grand National** N Grand National *nt (bedeutendes Pferderennen in Großbritannien)*

grandness ['grændnɪs] N grandiose Art; (*of architecture, building also*) Pracht *f*; (*of scheme*) groß angelegte Art; (*of person, clothes, manner*) Vornehmheit *f*; (*of occasion*) Größe *f*; (*of gesture*) Großartigkeit *f*

grand: **Grand Old Party** N **the ~** (*US Pol*) die Republikanische Partei; **grand opera** N große Oper; **grandpa** N (*inf*) Opa *m* (*inf*), Opi *m* (*inf*); **grandparent** N Großelternteil *m* (*form*), Großvater *m*/-mutter *f*; **grandparents** PL Großeltern *pl*; **grand piano** N Flügel *m*; **Grand Prix** N Grand Prix *m*; **grand slam** N (*Bridge*) Großschlemm *m*; **to win the ~** (*Sport*) alle Wettbewerbe gewinnen; **grandson** N Enkel(sohn) *m*; **grandstand** N Haupttribüne *f*; **a ~ finish** eine Entscheidung auf den letzten Metern; **to have a ~ view of sth** (direkten) Blick auf etw (*acc*) haben; **grand total** N Gesamtsumme *f*; **a ~ of £50** insgesamt £ 50; **grand tour** N **a the Grand Tour** (*Hist*) die Kavalierstour **b** (*fig, of a place*) große Besichtigungstour; **to give sb a ~ of sth** jdm etw in allen Einzelheiten zeigen; **grand vizier** N (*Hist*) Großwesir *m*

grange [greɪndʒ] N Bauernhof *m*, (kleiner) Gutshof

granger [greɪndʒəʳ] Bauer *m*, Farmer *m*

granite ['grænɪt] N Granit *m*

granny, grannie ['grænɪ] N **a** (*inf*) Oma *f* (*inf*), Omi *f* (*inf*) **b** (*also* **granny knot**) Altweiberknoten *m*

granny: **granny bonds** PL (*Brit Fin inf*) *indexgebundene staatliche Sparbriefe*; **granny flat** N (*Brit*) Einliegerwohnung *f*; **granny glasses** PL randlose Brille; **Granny Smith** N (= *apple*) Granny Smith *m*

grant [grɑːnt] VT **a** (= *accord*) gewähren (*sb* jdm); *period of grace, privilege, right* gewähren, zugestehen (*sb* jdm); *prayer* erhören; *honour* erweisen (*sb* jdm); *permission, licence, visa* erteilen (*sb* jdm); *request* stattgeben (*+dat*) (*form*); *land, pension* zusprechen, bewilligen (*sb* jdm); *wish* (= *give*) gewähren, freistellen (*sb* jdm); (= *fulfil*) erfüllen; **to ~ recognition to sb/sth** jdn/etw anerkennen; **to ~ an amnesty to sb** jdn amnestieren; **I beg your pardon – ~ed** ich bitte (vielmals) um Entschuldigung – sie sei dir gewährt (*hum, form*)
b (= *admit, agree*) zugeben, zugestehen; **~ed that this is true ...** angenommen, das ist wahr ...; **~ed, he looks good for his age** man muss zugeben, dass er für sein Alter gut aussieht; **I ~ you that** da gebe ich dir recht, das gebe ich zu; **to take sb/sth for ~ed** jdn/etw als selbstverständlich hinnehmen; **to take it for ~ed that ...** es selbstverständlich finden *or* als selbstverständlich betrachten, dass ...; **you take too much for ~ed** für dich ist (zu) vieles (einfach) selbstverständlich
N (*of money*) Subvention *f*; (*for studying etc*) Stipendium *nt*

grantable ['grɑːntəbl] ADJ **a** (= *transferable*) verleihbar (*to dat*), übertragbar (*to* auf *+acc*) **b** (= *approvable*) zu bewilligen(d)

grant-aided ADJ *student* gefördert; *group, school, programme* subventioniert

grantee [grɑːn'tiː] N Begünstigte(r) *mf*; (*Jur*) Zessionar(in) *m(f)*, Rechtsnachfolger(in) *m(f)*

grant: **grant-in-aid** N Zuschuss *m*, Beihilfe *f*; **grant-maintained** ADJ *school* staatlich finanziert; **to have ~ status** staatlich finanziert sein

GRANT-MAINTAINED SCHOOL

Eine **grant-maintained school** ist eine staatliche Schule in Großbritannien, die nicht von einer lokalen Schulbehörde, sondern durch Subventionen, **grants**, der Zentralregierung finanziert wird. Das System wurde ins Leben gerufen, um einzelnen Schulen größere Autonomie zu gewähren und den Einfluss der kommunalen Behörden auf das Bildungswesen zu begrenzen, auch wenn es viele Schulen vorgezogen haben, weiterhin der lokalen Schulbehörde zu unterstehen. Jede Schule, die sich für den Status einer **grant-maintained school** entscheidet, wird von einem eigenen Verwaltungsausschuss geleitet, in dem Vertreter des Personals, der Eltern und andere gewählte Mitglieder viele der schulischen Entscheidungen übernehmen, die sonst der Schulbehörde vorbehalten waren, wie die Einstellung neuen Personals, die Zuteilung des Schulbudgets und der Unterhalt des Schulgebäudes.

grantor [grɑːn'tɔː, 'grɑːntəʳ] N Verleiher(in) *m(f)*, Erteiler(in) *m(f)*; (*Jur*) Zedent(in) *m(f)*

granular ['grænjʊləʳ] ADJ körnig, gekörnt, granular (*spec*); *leather* genarbt, narbig

granulate ['grænjʊleɪt] VT granulieren, körnen; *leather* rauen VI körnig werden

granulated sugar ['grænjʊleɪtɪd'ʃʊgəʳ] N Zuckerraffinade *f*

granule ['grænjuːl] N Körnchen *nt*

grape [greɪp] N (Wein)traube *f*, Weinbeere *f*; **a pound of ~s** ein Pfund (Wein)trauben; **a bunch of ~s** eine (ganze) Weintraube

grape: **grapefruit** N Grapefruit *f*, Pampelmuse *f*; **grapefruit juice** N Grapefruitsaft *m*; **grape harvest** N Weinlese *f*; **grape hyacinth** N Traubenhyazinthe *f*; **grape juice** N Traubensaft *m*; **grapeshot** N (*Hist*) Kartätsche *f*; **grapestone** N Traubenkern *m*; **grape sugar** N Traubenzucker *m*; **grape type** N Rebsorte *f*; **grapevine** N Weinstock *m*; (*inf*) Nachrichtendienst *m* (*inf*); **I heard it on** *or* **through the ~** es ist mir zu Ohren gekommen

graph [grɑːf] N Diagramm *nt*, Schaubild *nt*; (*Math, of a function*) Graph *m*, Schaubild *nt*

grapheme ['græfiːm] N Graphem *nt*

graphic ['græfɪk] ADJ **a** (= *vivid*) *account, description* anschaulich; (= *unpleasantly realistic*) drastisch; **to describe sth in ~ detail** etw in allen Einzelheiten anschaulich darstellen **b** (*Art*) grafisch; **~ work** Grafiken *pl* → *also* **graphics**

graphical ['græfɪkəl] ADJ grafisch

graphically ['græfɪkəlɪ] ADV **a** (= *clearly*) *describe, portray* anschaulich, in allen Einzelheiten; (= *in unpleasantly realistic way*) *illustrate, demonstrate, display* auf drastische Art; **~ clear** sonnenklar (*inf*) **b** (= *using illustrations*) *display, illustrate* grafisch

graphical user interface N (*Comput*) grafische Benutzeroberfläche

graphic: **graphic artist** N Grafiker(in) *m(f)*; **graphic arts** PL, **graphic design** N Grafik *f*; **graphic designer** N Grafiker(in) *m(f)*; **graphic display** N (*Comput*) grafische Anzeige; **graphic equalizer** N (Graphic) Equalizer *m*; **graphic novel** N *Roman in Cartoonform*, Comicheft *nt*

graphics ['græfɪks] N **a** *sing* (= *subject*) Zeichnen *nt*, zeichnerische *or* grafische Darstellung **b** *pl* (= *drawings*) Zeichnungen *pl*, (grafische) Darstellungen *pl* **c** *pl* (*Comput*) Grafik *f*; **can your computer do ~?** ist Ihr Computer grafikfähig? ADJ *attr* (*Comput*) Grafik-; **~ card** Grafikkarte *f*; **~ mode** Grafikmodus *m*; **~ printer** Grafikdrucker *m*; **~ software** Grafiksoftware *f*

graphite ['græfaɪt] N Grafit *m*, Graphit *m*

graphologist [græ'fɒlədʒɪst] N Grafologe *m*, Grafologin *f*

graphology [græ'fɒlədʒɪ] N Grafologie *f*, Handschriftendeutung *f*

graph paper N Millimeterpapier *nt*

-graphy [-grəfɪ] N *suf* -grafie *f*

grapnel ['græpnəl] N **a** (= *anchor*) (Dregg)anker *m*, Draggen *m* (*spec*) **b** = **grappling iron**

grapple ['græpl] N = **grappling iron** VI (*lit*) ringen, kämpfen; **to ~ with a problem/situation** sich mit einem Problem/einer Situation herumschlagen; **the wrestlers ~d with each other** die Ringer hielten sich in enger Umklammerung VT festhaken; *enemy boat* die Enterhaken verwenden bei; **the boats were ~d together** die Boote waren durch Haken verbunden

grappling ['græplɪŋ] N (*Sport inf*) Ringen *nt*

grappling hook, grappling iron N Haken *m*, Greifer *m*; (*Naut*) Enterhaken *m*

grasp [grɑːsp] N **a** (= *hold*) Griff *m*; **he held my arm firmly in his ~** er hielt meinen Arm mit festem Griff; **the knife slipped from her ~** das Messer rutschte ihr aus der Hand; **just when peace/fame was within their ~** gerade als Frieden/Ruhm greifbar nahe war *or* in greifbare Nähe gerückt war
b (*fig*: = *understanding*) Verständnis *nt*; **to have a good ~ of sth** etw gut beherrschen; **her ~ of the language/subject is not very good** sie beherrscht die Sprache/das Gebiet nicht sehr gut; **it is beyond his ~** das geht über seinen Verstand; **it's within his ~** das kann er verstehen *or* begreifen
VT **a** (= *catch hold of*) ergreifen, greifen nach; (= *hold tightly*) festhalten; **he ~ed the bundle in his arms** er hielt das Bündel in den Armen; **to ~ a chance** eine Gelegenheit ergreifen; **to ~ sb's hand** nach jds Hand greifen
b (*fig*: = *understand*) begreifen, erfassen
VI **to ~ at sth** (*lit*) nach etw greifen; (*fig*) sich auf etw (*acc*) stürzen; *hope* sich klammern an (*+dat*); **to ~ at an opportunity** eine Gelegenheit ergreifen *or* beim Schopfe packen → *also* **straw**

grasping ['grɑːspɪŋ] ADJ (*fig*) habgierig

grass [grɑːs] N **a** (= *plant*) Gras *nt*; **wheat is a ~** der Weizen gehört zu den Gräsern; **blade of ~** Grashalm *m*; **~ seed** Grassamen *m*; **to let the ~ grow under one's feet** die Sache auf die lange Bank schieben; **the ~ is always greener (on the other side of the fence** *or* **hill)** (*Prov*) auf des Nachbars Feld steht das Korn immer besser (*Prov*), die Kirschen in Nachbars Garten ... (*Prov*)
b *no pl* (= *lawn*) Rasen *m*; (= *pasture*) Weide(-land *nt*) *f*; **to play on ~** (*Sport*) auf (dem) Rasen spielen; **the cattle are out at ~** (*Brit*) das Vieh ist auf der Weide; **to put** *or* **turn out to ~** (*Brit, cattle*) auf die Weide führen *or* treiben; *old horses* das Gnadenbrot geben (*+dat*); (*inf*) *employee* aufs Abstellgleis schieben (*inf*)
c (*inf*: = *marijuana*) Gras(s) *nt* (*inf*)
d (*Brit inf*: = *informer*) Spitzel *m* (*sl*)
VT (*also* **grass over**) *ground* mit Gras bepflanzen
VI (*Brit inf*) singen (*inf*) (*to* bei); **to ~ on sb** jdn verpfeifen (*inf*)

grass: **grass blade** N Grashalm *m*; **grass box** N Grasfangkorb *m*; **grass-green** ADJ grasgrün; **grass-grown** ADJ mit Gras bewachsen; **grasshopper** N Heuschrecke *f*, Grashüpfer *m* (*inf*); **grassland** N Grasland *nt*; **grass plot** N Rasenfläche *f*; **grass roots** PL Volk *nt*; (*of a party*) Basis *f*, Fußvolk *nt* (*hum inf*); **grass-roots** ADJ *attr* Basis-, an der Basis; **~ democracy** Basisdemokratie *f*; **at ~ level** an der Basis; **a ~ movement** eine Bürgerinitiative; **grass skirt** N Bastrock *m*; **grass snake** N Ringelnatter *f*; **grass widow** N Strohwitwe *f*; (*dated US, divorced*) geschiedene Frau; (*separated*) (von ihrem Mann) getrennt lebende Frau; **grass widower** N Strohwitwer *m*; *(dated US, divorced)* geschiedener Mann; *(separated)* (von seiner Frau) getrennt lebender Mann

grassy ['grɑːsɪ] ADJ *(+er)* grasig; **~ slope** Grashang *m*

grate¹ [greɪt] N *(= grid)* Gitter *nt*; *(in fire)* (Feuer)rost *m*; *(= fireplace)* Kamin *m*

grate² VT **a** *(Cook)* reiben; *vegetables* raspeln, reiben **b** *(bottom of car, boat etc: = scrape)* streifen; *(person: = make a grating noise with)* kratzen mit; *one's teeth* knirschen mit VI *(= scrape)* streifen *(against +acc)*; *(= make a noise)* kratzen; *(rusty door)* quietschen; *(feet on gravel)* knirschen; *(fig)* wehtun *(on sb* jdm), krank machen *(on sb* jdn); **to ~ on sb's nerves** jdm auf die Nerven gehen; **this phrase ~s on the ear** dieser Ausdruck hört sich schlimm an

grateful ['greɪtfʊl] ✪ 2.1, 4, 20.1, 22 ADJ dankbar; **he was ~ for her support** er war dankbar für ihre Unterstützung; **I'm ~ to you for believing me** ich bin dir dankbar (dafür), dass du mir glaubst; **I'm ~ to you for buying** *or* **having bought the tickets** ich bin dir dankbar (dafür), dass du die Karten gekauft hast; **he was ~ to be home/that he was still alive** er war froh *or* dankbar, zu Hause zu sein/noch am Leben zu sein; **to express one's ~ thanks (to sb)** (jdm) seine aufrichtige Dankbarkeit aussprechen

gratefully ['greɪtfəlɪ] ADV dankbar; *acknowledged also* in Dankbarkeit

grater ['greɪtəʳ] N Reibe *f*

gratification [,grætɪfɪ'keɪʃən] N **a** *(= pleasure)* Genugtuung *f*; **it is a source of great ~ to me** ich empfinde große Genugtuung darüber **b** *(= satisfying: of desires etc)* Befriedigung *f*

gratify ['grætɪfaɪ] VT **a** *(= give pleasure)* erfreuen; **to be gratified at** *or* **by** *or* **with sth** über etw *(acc)* hocherfreut sein; **I was gratified to hear that ...** ich habe mit Genugtuung gehört, dass ... **b** *(= satisfy)* befriedigen, zufriedenstellen

gratifying ['grætɪfaɪɪŋ] ADJ (sehr) erfreulich; **it is ~ to learn that ...** es ist erfreulich zu erfahren, dass ...

gratifyingly ['grætɪfaɪɪŋlɪ] ADV erfreulich; **he was ~ pleased** es war erfreulich zu sehen, wie er sich freute

grating¹ ['greɪtɪŋ] N Gitter *nt*

grating² ADJ kratzend; *sound* quietschend; *(= rasping)* knirschend; *(on nerves)* auf die Nerven gehend; *voice* schrill N Kratzen *nt*; *(of rusty door)* Quietschen *nt*; *(of teeth, feet on gravel)* Knirschen *nt*

gratis ['grætɪs] ADJ ADV gratis, umsonst

gratitude ['grætɪtjuːd] ✪ 22, 24.4 N Dankbarkeit *f* *(to* gegenüber)

gratuitous [grə'tjuːɪtəs] ADJ überflüssig, unnötig; *(= unasked-for)* unerwünscht

gratuitously [grə'tjuːɪtəslɪ] ADV unnötigerweise

gratuity [grə'tjuːɪtɪ] N Gratifikation *f*, (Sonder)zuwendung *f*; *(form: = tip)* Trinkgeld *nt*

grave¹ [greɪv] N *(lit, fig)* Grab *nt*; **silent as the ~** totenstill; **the house was like the ~** es herrschte Totenstille im Haus; **to turn in one's ~** sich im Grabe herumdrehen; **from beyond the ~** aus dem Jenseits; **to go to an early ~** einen frühen Tod finden; **to rise from the ~** von den Toten auferstehen; **to dig one's own ~** *(fig)* sein eigenes Grab graben *or* schaufeln

grave² ADJ *(+er)* **a** *(= serious, considerable) concern, danger, problem, difficulty* groß; *consequences* schwerwiegend; *threat, situation, matter* ernst; *mistake* schwer, gravierend; *illness, crime* schwer; *news* schlimm; *suspicion, doubt* stark **b** *(= solemn) person, face, expression* ernst

grave³ [grɑːv] ADJ **~ accent** Gravis *m*, Accent grave *m*; *(in Greek)* Gravis *m*; **e ~, ~ e** e Accent grave N Gravis *m*

grave: **graveclothes** PL Totengewand *nt*; **grave digger** N Totengräber(in) *m(f)*; **grave goods** PL *(Archeol)* Grabbeigaben *pl*

gravel ['grævəl] N **a** Kies *m*; *(= large chippings)* Schotter *m* **b** *(Med)* Nierensand *or* -grieß *m*; *(in bladder)* Harngrieß *m* ADJ *attr* Kies-; *road, drive* mit Kies bedeckt; **~ path** Kiesweg *m*; **~ pit** Kiesgrube *f* VT *path, lane* mit Kies bestreuen, schottern

gravelled, *(US)* **graveled** ['grævəld] ADJ mit Kies bedeckt; **~ path** Kiesweg *m*

gravelly ['grævəlɪ] ADJ **a** *(liter: = stony) shore, drive* kiesbedeckt; *soil* steinig **b** *(fig) voice* tief und rau; *(= hoarse)* heiser

gravely ['greɪvlɪ] ADV **a** *(= severely, seriously) ill, wounded* schwer; **~ ill patients** schwer kranke Patienten; **~ concerned** ernstlich besorgt **b** *(= solemnly) say, nod* ernst

grave mound N Grabhügel *m*

graven ['greɪvən] ADJ *(old, liter)* gehauen *(on, in* in *+acc)*; **~ image** Götzenbild *nt*; **to be ~ in one's heart** *or* **on one's memory** sich in jds Gedächtnis *(acc)* eingegraben haben *(geh)*

grave: **grave robber** N Grabräuber(in) *m(f)*; **graveside** N **at the ~** am Grabe; **a ~ service** ein Gottesdienst am Grabe; **gravestone** N Grabstein *m*; **graveyard** N Friedhof *m*; **that ministry is a ~ of political careers** in diesem Ministerium hat schon manche politische Laufbahn ein vorzeitiges Ende genommen; **graveyard shift** N *(esp US)* Nachtschicht *f*

graving dock ['greɪvɪŋ,dɒk] N Trockendock *nt*

gravitate ['grævɪteɪt] VI *(lit)* gravitieren *(form)* *(to(wards)* zu, auf *+acc)*, angezogen werden *(to(wards)* von); *(fig)* hingezogen werden *(to(wards)* zu), angezogen werden *(to(wards)* von)

gravitation [,grævɪ'teɪʃən] N *(Phys)* Gravitation *f*, Schwerkraft *f*; *(fig)* Hinneigung *f* *(to* zu); **the hippies' ~ to San Francisco** die Anziehungskraft, die San Francisco auf die Hippies ausübt

gravitational [,grævɪ'teɪʃənl] ADJ Gravitations-

gravitational: **gravitational field** N Gravitations- *or* Schwerefeld *nt*; **gravitational force** N Schwerkraft *f*; *(Space)* Andruck *m*; **gravitational pull** N Anziehungskraft *f*

gravity ['grævɪtɪ] N **a** *(Phys)* Schwere *f*, Schwerkraft *f*; **the law(s) of ~** das Gravitationsgesetz; **centre** *(Brit)* *or* **center** *(US)* **of ~** Schwerpunkt *m*; **force of ~** Schwerkraft *f*; **~ feed** Fall- *or* Schwerkraftspeisung *f* **b** *(= seriousness, of person, expression, situation, matter, threat)* Ernst *m*; *(of mistake, illness, crime)* Schwere *f*; *(of danger, problem, difficulty)* Größe *f*; *(of consequences)* schwerwiegende Art; **the ~ of the news** die schlimmen Nachrichten

gravlax ['grævlæks] N *Art Räucherlachs*

gravy ['greɪvɪ] N **a** *(Cook: = juice)* Fleisch- *or* Bratensaft *m*; *(= sauce)* Soße *f* **b** *(inf: = perks)* Spesen *pl*; *(= corrupt money)* Schmiergelder *pl* *(inf)*; **to get on the ~ train** auch ein Stück vom Kuchen abbekommen *(inf)*; **to ride on the ~ train** locker Geld machen *(inf)*

gravy: **gravy boat** N Sauciere *f*, Soßenschüssel *f*; **gravy train** N *(inf)* **to climb** *or* **get on the ~** leicht ans große Geld kommen

gray N ADJ VI *(US)* = **grey**

grayscale ['greɪskeɪl] N *(US) (Comput)* Graustufen *pl*

graze¹ [greɪz] VI *(cattle etc)* grasen, weiden VT *meadow, field* abgrasen, abweiden; *cattle* weiden lassen

graze² VT *(= touch lightly)* streifen; *(= scrape skin off)* aufschürfen; **to ~ one's knees** sich *(dat)* die Knie aufschürfen; **to ~ oneself** sich *(dat)* die Haut aufschürfen, sich aufschürfen VI streifen; **the car ~d along the wall** das Auto ist an der Mauer entlanggestreift N Abschürfung *f*, Schürfwunde *f*

grazier ['greɪzɪəʳ] N *(esp Brit)* Viehzüchter(in) *m(f)*

grazing ['greɪzɪŋ] N Weideland *nt*; **this land offers good ~** dies ist gutes Weideland; **~ land** Weideland *nt*; **~ rights** Weiderechte *pl*

GRE *(US Univ) abbr of* **Graduate Record Examination** *Zulassungsprüfung für ein weiterführendes Studium*

grease [griːs] N **a** Fett *nt*; *(= lubricant)* (Schmier)fett *nt*, Schmiere *f*; **his hair was thick with ~** seine Haare starrten vor Fett **b** *(also* **grease wool)** Schweißwolle *f* VT fetten; *skin* einfetten, einschmieren *(inf)*; *(Aut, Tech)* schmieren; **to ~ back one's hair** sich *(dat)* die Haare mit Pomade nach hinten frisieren; **to ~ sb's palm** *(inf)* jdm etwas zustecken *(inf)*, jdn schmieren *(inf)*; **like ~d lightning** *(inf)* wie ein geölter Blitz

grease: **grease gun** N Fettspritze *or* -presse *f*; **grease mark** N Fettfleck *m*; **grease monkey** N *(inf)* Mechanikerlehrling *m*; **grease nipple** N Schmiernippel *m*; **greasepaint** N *(Theat)* (Fett)schminke *f*; **greaseproof** ADJ fettdicht; **~ paper** Pergamentpapier *nt*

greaser ['griːsəʳ] N **a** *(inf, = motorcyclist)* Motorradfahrer(in) *m(f)*; *(= gang member)* Rocker *m* *(inf)* **b** *(US pej: = Latin American)* Latino *m* *(inf)* **c** *(inf, = motor mechanic)* Automechaniker(in) *m(f)*

grease remover N Fettlösungsmittel *nt*, Entfetter *m*

greasiness ['griːsɪnɪs] N **a** *(= oiliness)* Fettigkeit *f* **b** *(= dirtiness: of hands, clothes etc)* Schmierigkeit *f*; *(= slipperiness)* Glätte *f* **c** *(pej: = smarminess)* Schmierigkeit *f* *(pej inf)*

greasy ['griːsɪ] ADJ *(+er)* **a** *(= oily) food* fett; *hair, skin, complexion* fettig **b** *(= dirty) clothes* schmierig; *(= slippery) surface* rutschig, glatt **c** *(pej: = smarmy)* schmierig *(pej inf)*

greasy spoon (café) N *(pej inf)* billiges Fresslokal *(pej inf)*

great [greɪt] ✪ 3.2, 13, 24.4, 26.1 ADJ *(+er)* **a** *(in size)* groß; *(= very large)* sehr groß; *(= huge)* riesig; *(in extent) effort, variety, shock, need, success, help etc* groß; **with a ~ effort** mit großer Mühe *or* Anstrengung; **a ~ variety of opinions** viele ganz unterschiedliche Ansichten; **there is a ~ need for economic development** wirtschaftliche Entwicklung ist dringend nötig; **of no ~ importance** ziemlich unwichtig; **at a ~ pace** in *or* mit schnellem Tempo; **x is ~er/not ~er than 10** *(Math)* x ist größer/kleiner (oder) gleich 10; **~ good fortune** großes Glück; **with ~ good humour** sehr gut gelaunt; **in ~ detail** ganz ausführlich; **with ~ care** mit großer Vorsicht; **I'll take ~ care of it** ich werde sehr gut darauf aufpassen; **to take a ~ interest in sth** sich sehr für etw interessieren; **he did not live to a ~ age** er erreichte kein hohes Alter; **with ~ difficulty** mit großen Schwierigkeiten; **a player of ~ ability** ein sehr *or* ausgesprochen fähiger Spieler; **to a ~ extent** in hohem Maße; **it was ~ fun** es hat großen Spaß gemacht; **a ~ many, a ~ number of** sehr viele; **a ~ many people** sehr viele *or* eine Menge *(inf)* Leute → *also* **deal**

b *(= important, famous) person, achievement, work, event, city etc* groß; **his ~est work** sein Hauptwerk *nt*; **to think ~ thoughts** geniale Gedanken haben; **the ~ thing is to ...** das Wichtigste ist zu ...; **~ minds think alike** große Geister denken gleich; **Alexander the Great** Alexander der Große

c *(= strong, enthusiastic)* **he was a ~ friend of my father** er war mit meinem Vater sehr gut befreundet; **he is a ~ admirer of British orchestras** er bewundert britische Orchester sehr; **I'm a ~ lover of** *or* **a ~ one for cakes** ich esse für mein Leben gern Kuchen; **she's a ~ one for punctuality** sie legt großen Wert auf Pünktlichkeit; **he's a ~ one for criticizing others** im Kritisieren anderer ist er (ganz) groß; **to be a ~ believer in sth** sehr viel von etw halten; **to be a ~ believer in doing sth** grundsätzlich dafür sein, etw zu tun; **he was a ~ womanizer** er stellte ständig den Frauen nach

d *(inf: = terrific) person, idea* toll *(inf)*, prima *(inf)*; **I think she's ~** ich finde sie toll *(inf)* *or* prima *(inf)*; **this cookbook is ~ for desserts** in diesem Kochbuch findet man besonders gute Nachspeisen; **this whisk is ~ for sauces** dieser Schneebesen eignet sich besonders gut für Soßen; **to be ~ at football/at singing** ein großer Fußballspieler/Sänger sein; **to be ~ on jazz** ein

großer Jazzkenner sein; **to feel ~** sich toll *or* prima fühlen *(inf)*; **my wife isn't feeling so ~** meiner Frau geht es nicht besonders gut; **Great Scott** *or* **Heavens!** *(dated)* (ach du) großer Gott *or* lieber Himmel!
c *(= excellent, outstanding)* ausgezeichnet, großartig; **one of the ~ footballers of our generation** einer der großen Fußballspieler unserer Generation
INTERJ *(inf)* toll *(inf)*, super *(inf)*; **oh ~** *(iro)* na wunderbar; **if that's what they want to believe, ~** wenn sie das glauben wollen, dann sollen sie doch
ADV **a** *(inf: = well)* **she's doing ~** *(in job)* sie macht sich hervorragend; *(healthwise)* sie macht große Fortschritte; **everything's going ~** alles läuft nach Plan
b **~ big** *(emph inf)* riesengroß; **I want to give you a ~ big kiss** ich möchte dir einen ganz dicken Kuss geben; **a ~ big wedding** eine Hochzeit im großen Stil; **he's a ~ big softie** er ist ein ganz großer Softie
N **a** *pl* **the ~** die Großen *pl*; **the ~ and the good** die Prominenz
b *usu pl (= person)* Größe *f*; **the ~s** *(= stars)* die Größen *pl*; **one of the all-time ~s** einer der Größten aller Zeiten; **the golfing/literary ~s** die Golfgrößen/literarischen Größen

great: **great ape** N Menschenaffe *m*; **great assize** [ˌgreɪtəˈsaɪz] N *(Rel)* Jüngstes Gericht; **great auk** N Toralk *m*; **great-aunt** N Großtante *f*; **Great Australian Bight** N **the ~** die Große Australische Bucht; **Great Barrier Reef** N **the ~** das Große Barriereriff; **Great Bear** N **the ~** der Große Bär; **Great Britain** N Großbritannien *nt*; **great calorie** N Kilokalorie *f*; **greatcoat** N Überzieher *m*, Paletot *m*; **Great Dane** N Deutsche Dogge; **Great Depression** N *(Hist)* Weltwirtschaftskrise *f*; **Great Divide** N *(US)* **the ~** die Rocky Mountains *pl*; *(fig: = death)* die Schwelle des Todes *(liter)*; **the great divide between ...** der Abgrund zwischen ... *(dat)*; **Great Dividing Range** N **the ~** die Ostaustralischen Kordilleren *pl*

greater [ˈgreɪtəʳ] ADJ *comp of* **great** größer; **to pay ~ attention** besser aufpassen; **of ~ importance is ...** noch wichtiger ist ...; **one of the ~ painters** einer der bedeutenderen Maler; **~ and ~** immer größer

Greater London N Groß-London *nt*

greatest [ˈgreɪtɪst] **ADJ** *superl of* **great** größte(r, s); **with the ~ (of) pleasure** mit dem größten Vergnügen **N** **he's the ~** *(inf)* er ist der Größte; **it's the ~** *(inf)* das ist das Größte *(sl)*, das ist einsame Klasse *(inf)*

great: **great-grandchild** N Urenkel(in) *m(f)*; **great-grandparents** PL Urgroßeltern *pl*; **great-great-grandchild** N Ururenkel(in) *m(f)*; **great-great-grandparents** PL Ururgroßeltern *pl*; **great-hearted** ADJ *(= brave)* beherzt; *(= generous)* hochherzig; **Great Lakes** PL **the ~** die Großen Seen *pl*

greatly [ˈgreɪtlɪ] ADV *increase, influence, exaggerated, diminished* stark; *admire, surprise* sehr; **he was not ~ surprised** er war nicht besonders überrascht

great-nephew [ˈgreɪtˌnefjuː] N Großneffe *m*

greatness [ˈgreɪtnɪs] N Größe *f*; *(of size, height, degree etc also)* Ausmaß *nt*; *(= importance also)* Bedeutung *f*; **~ of heart** Hochherzigkeit *f*, Großmut *f*; **~ of mind** Geistesgröße *f*

great: **great-niece** N Großnichte *f*; **Great Plains** PL **the ~** die Great Plains *pl*, die Großen Ebenen *pl*; **Great Powers** PL *(Pol)* **the ~** die Großmächte *pl*; **great tit** N Kohlmeise *f*; **great-uncle** N Großonkel *m*; **Great Wall of China** N Chinesische Mauer; **Great War** N **the ~** der Erste Weltkrieg; **Great Week** N *(Rel)* Karwoche *f*; **Great White Way** N **the ~** *(esp US inf)* das Theaterviertel am Broadway

greaves [griːvz] PL *(Cook)* Grieben *pl*

grebe [griːb] N (See)taucher *m*

Grecian [ˈgriːʃən] ADJ griechisch

Greco- [ˈgriːkəʊ-] PREF *(esp US)* = **Graeco-**

Greece [griːs] N Griechenland *nt*

greed [griːd] N Gier *f (for* nach *+dat)*; *(for material wealth also)* Habsucht *f*, Habgier *f*; *(= gluttony)* Gefräßigkeit *f*; **~ for money/power** Geld-/Machtgier *f*

greedily [ˈgriːdɪlɪ] ADV gierig

greediness [ˈgriːdɪnɪs] N Gierigkeit *f*; *(= gluttony)* Gefräßigkeit *f*

greedy [ˈgriːdɪ] ADJ *(+er)* gierig *(for* auf *+acc,* nach); *(for material wealth also)* habgierig; *(= gluttonous)* gefräßig; **~ for power/money** macht-/geldgierig; **to be ~ for approval** nach Anerkennung gieren; **don't be so ~!** sei nicht so unbescheiden; **you ~ thing!** du Nimmersatt! *(inf)*

greedy guts [ˈgriːdɪgʌts] N *sing (Brit inf)* Fresssack *m (inf)*

Greek [griːk] **ADJ** griechisch; **he is ~** er ist Grieche; **~ letter society** *(US Univ)* *Studentenverbindung, deren Name aus drei griechischen Buchstaben besteht*; **the ~ Orthodox Church** die griechisch-orthodoxe Kirche **N** **a** *(Ling)* Griechisch *nt*; **Modern ~** Neugriechisch *nt*; **Ancient ~** Altgriechisch *nt*; **it's all ~ to me** *(inf)* das sind böhmische Dörfer für mich *(inf)* **b** *(= person)* Grieche *m*, Griechin *f*

Greek gift N *(fig)* Danaergeschenk *nt*

Greek tragedy N *(Theat) (= genre)* die griechische Tragödie; *(= play)* griechische Tragödie

green [griːn] **ADJ** *(+er)* **a** grün; **~ space** Grünfläche *f*; **to go ~** *(person)* grün im Gesicht werden; **to be/turn ~ with envy** blass *or* grün *or* gelb vor Neid sein/werden; **to make sb ~ with envy** jdn vor Neid erblassen lassen; **the ~ shoots of recovery** die ersten Anzeichen für einen Aufschwung; **~ salad** grüner Salat
b *(Pol) movement, party, issues* grün; *person, company* grün, umweltbewusst; *policy, measures, product, technology* grün, umweltfreundlich; **he stressed his ~ credentials** er betonte, was er alles schon für die Umwelt getan habe; **~ eggs** grüne Eier *pl*
c *(= unripe) fruit, tomatoes* grün
d *(= inexperienced)* grün; *(= naive)* naiv; **I'm not as ~ as I look** *(inf)* ich bin nicht so dumm, wie ich aussehe *(inf)*
N **a** *(= colour)* Grün *nt*
b *(= area of grass)* Grünfläche *f*; *(Golf)* Grün *nt*; **(village) ~** Dorfwiese *f*, Dorfanger *m* *(dated)* → *also* **bowling green**
c **greens** **PL** *(= vegetables)* Grüngemüse *nt*
d *(Pol)* **the Greens** die Grünen *pl*
ADV *(Pol) vote, think* grün

green: **green algae** PL *(Bot)* Grünalgen *pl*; **greenback** N *(US inf)* Lappen *m (sl)*, Geldschein *m*; **green bean** N grüne Bohne; **green belt** N Grüngürtel *m*; **Green Berets** PL *(US Mil)* Kommandotruppe *f* der US-Streitkräfte; **green card** N **a** *(US: = residence permit)* Aufenthaltsgenehmigung *f* **b** *(Brit Insur)* grüne Versicherungskarte; **green cloth** N *(esp US) (for gambling)* Spieltisch *m*; *(for billiards)* Billardtisch *m*; **Green Cross Code** N *(Brit)* *Regeln für Kinder zur Sicherheit im Straßenverkehr*

greenery [ˈgriːnərɪ] N Grün *nt*; *(= foliage)* grünes Laub, grüne Zweige *pl*

green: **green-eyed** ADJ *(lit)* grünäugig; *(fig)* scheel(äugig), missgünstig; **the ~ monster** *(fig)* der blasse Neid; **greenfield** ADJ *land etc* unerschlossen; **~ site** Bauplatz *m* im Grünen; **many universities are on ~ sites** viele Universitäten befinden sich im Grünen; **greenfinch** N Grünfink *m*; **green fingers** PL *(Brit)* gärtnerisches Geschick; **to have ~** eine Hand für Pflanzen haben; **greenfly** N Blattlaus *f*; **greengage** N Reneklode *f*, Reineclaude *f*; **green goddess** N *(Brit inf)* *meist vom Militär eingesetztes Feuerwehrauto*; **greengrocer** N *(esp Brit)* (Obst- und) Gemüsehändler(in) *m(f)*; **at the ~'s (shop)** im Gemüseladen; **greengrocery** N *(esp Brit: = shop)* Obst- und Gemüsehandlung *f*; *(= trade)* Obst- und Gemüsehandel *m*; *(= articles)* Obst und Gemüse *nt*; **greenhorn** N *(inf, inexperienced)* Greenhorn *nt*; *(gullible)* Einfaltspinsel *m*; **greenhouse** N Gewächshaus *nt*, Treibhaus *nt*; **greenhouse effect** N Treibhauseffekt *m*; **greenhouse gas** N Treibhausgas *nt*

greening [ˈgriːnɪŋ] N *(Pol)* **the ~ of Japan/politics** das zunehmende Umweltbewusstsein in Japan/in der Politik

greenish [ˈgriːnɪʃ] ADJ grünlich

green keeper N *(Sport)* Platzwart(in) *m(f)*

Greenland [ˈgriːnlənd] N Grönland *nt*

Greenlander [ˈgriːnləndəʳ] N Grönländer(in) *m(f)*

Greenlandic [griːnˈlændɪk] **ADJ** grönländisch **N** *(Ling)* Grönländisch *nt*

green: **green light** N grünes Licht; **to give sb/sth the ~** jdm/einer Sache grünes Licht *or* freie Fahrt geben; **green lung** N *(fig)* grüne Lunge, Grünfläche *f*; **green man** N *(at street crossing)* grünes Licht; *(as said to children)* grünes Männchen; **little green men** kleine grüne Männchen; **green monkey disease** N *(Med)* Marburg-Krankheit *f*; **Green Mountain State** N **the ~** *der US-Bundesstaat Vermont*

greenness [ˈgriːnnɪs] N **a** *(= colour)* Grün *nt* **b** *(Pol, of policies)* Umweltfreundlichkeit *f*; *(of person)* Umweltbewusstsein *nt* **c** *(= unripeness)* Grünheit *f*, Unreife *f* **d** *(= lack of experience)* Grünheit *f*; *(= naivety)* Naivität

green: **green onion** N *(US)* Frühlingszwiebel *f*; **Green Paper** N *(Brit Pol)* Vorlage *f* für eine Parlamentsdebatte; **Green Party** N **the ~** die Grünen *pl*; **green pea** N (grüne) Erbse *f*; **Greenpeace** N Greenpeace *nt*; **green pepper** N (grüne) Paprikaschote; **green pound** N *(Econ)* **the ~** das grüne Pfund; **green revolution** N *(Econ, Agr)* **the ~** die grüne Revolution; **greenroom** N *(Theat)* ≈ Garderobe *f*; **greenstick fracture** N Grünholzbruch *m*; **greenstuff** N **a** *(for cattle)* Grünfutter *nt* **b** *(= vegetable)* grünes Gemüse; **green table** N Sitzungstisch *m*; **green tax** N Ökosteuer *f*; **green tea** N grüner Tee; **green thumb** N *(US)* = **green fingers**; **green vegetables** PL Grüngemüse *nt*; **greenwash** N *(Pol inf)* grüne PR, Greenwash *m or nt*

> **GREEN-WELLIE BRIGADE**
>
> **Green wellingtons**, grüne Gummistiefel von hoher Qualität, werden in Großbritannien von all jenen getragen, die auf dem Land ausreiten, zum Jagen oder Angeln gehen, also den „klassischen" Freizeitaktivitäten der reichen Oberschicht nachgehen. Daher werden die **green wellingtons** zwangsläufig mit der gesellschaftlichen Oberschicht assoziert. Der Ausdruck **green-wellie brigade** wird als Verallgemeinerung für all die Reichen und Adeligen benutzt, die manchmal ein recht elitäres Gruppenverhalten an den Tag legen.

Greenwich (Mean) Time [ˈgrenɪtʃ(ˈmiːn),taɪm] N westeuropäische Zeit, Greenwicher Zeit *f*

greenwood [ˈgriːnwʊd] N grüner Wald

green woodpecker N *(Orn)* Grünspecht *m*

greet [griːt] VT *(= welcome)* begrüßen; *(= receive, meet)* empfangen; *(= say hallo to)* grüßen; *news, decision* aufnehmen; **a terrible sight ~ed him** ihm bot sich ein fürchterlicher Anblick

greeting [ˈgriːtɪŋ] N Gruß *m*; *(act, = welcoming)* Begrüßung *f*; *(= receiving, meeting)* Empfang *m*; **we received a friendly ~ from the crowd** die Menge bereitete uns einen freundlichen Empfang; **~s** Grüße *pl*; *(= congratulations)* Glückwünsche *pl*; **to send ~s to sb** Grüße an jdn senden; *(through sb else)* jdn grüßen lassen; **please give my ~s to them** bitte grüße sie von mir

greetings card N Grußkarte *f*

gregarious [grɪˈgɛərɪəs] ADJ *person* gesellig; **~ animal/instinct** Herdentier *nt*/-trieb *or* -instinkt *m*

Gregorian [grɪˈgɔːrɪən] ADJ gregorianisch

Gregorian calendar N gregorianischer Kalender

Gregorian chant N gregorianischer Choral *or* Gesang

greige [greɪʒ] ADJ *textiles* naturfarben

gremlin ['gremlɪn] N *(hum)* böser Geist, Maschinenteufel *m (hum)*

Grenada [gre'neɪdə] N Grenada *nt*

grenade [grɪ'neɪd] N Granate *f*

Grenadian [gre'neɪdɪən] ADJ grenadisch N Grenader(in) *m(f)*

grenadier [,grenə'dɪə'] N Grenadier *m*

grenadine ['grenədi:n] N Grenadine *f*

grew [gru:] *pret of* **grow**

grey, *(US)* **gray** [greɪ] ADJ (+er) **a** *(in colour)* grau; *(= ashen) person, face* grau, fahl; *weather, sky, day* grau, trüb; **to go** *or* **turn ~** *(person, hair)* grau werden, ergrauen *(geh)*; **their faces were ~ with fatigue** sie *or* ihre Gesichter waren ganz blass vor Müdigkeit; **men in ~ suits** *anonyme, aber mächtige Hintermänner*
b *(= bleak) world, year, days, outlook* grau, trostlos, öde
c *(= anonymous) person* grau, gesichtslos; *place* grau, anonym
N *(= colour)* Grau *nt*; **subtle ~s** zarte Grautöne *pl*
VI *(person, hair)* grau werden, ergrauen *(geh)*; **he was ~ing at the temples** seine Schläfen wurden grau, seine Schläfen ergrauten
VT *(Comput) button, function* ab- *or* ausgeblenden, deaktivieren; **~ed (out)** deaktiviert

grey, *(US)* **gray**: **grey area** N *(fig)* Grauzone *f*; **greybeard**, *(US)* **graybeard** N Graubart *m*; **grey cells** PL *(inf)* **(little) ~** (kleine) graue Zellen *pl (inf)*; **grey eminence** N graue Eminenz; **grey-haired** ADJ grauhaarig

greyhound ['greɪhaʊnd] N Windhund *m*, Windspiel *nt*

> **GREYHOUND**
>
> Die Greyhound-Gesellschaft betreibt ein Netz von Langstreckenbussen in den gesamten Vereinigten Staaten. Auch wenn eine Reise mit dem Greyhound wesentlich länger dauert als ein Flug, bietet sie doch einige Vorteile: Busse sind billig und zuverlässig und sind nun einmal für Touristen der beste Weg, Amerika mit einem schmalen Geldbeutel zu bereisen und dabei viele interessante Menschen kennenzulernen. Die Gesellschaft bietet auch ein Ticket an, mit dem man unbegrenzt durch die USA reisen kann, den sogenannten „Ameripass".
> Die Amerikaner betrachten die Greyhound-Busse als einen nostalgischen Teil ihrer Tradition, immer unterwegs zu sein, der auch ins Liedgut Eingang gefunden hat: so gibt es einen Song mit dem Titel „Thank God and Greyhound she's gone".

greyhound racing N Windhundrennen *nt*

greyish, *(US)* **grayish** ['greɪɪʃ] ADJ gräulich

grey, *(US)* **gray**: **greylag (goose)** N Graugans *f*, Wildgans *f*; **grey market**, *(US)* **gray market** N *(Comm)* grauer Markt; **grey matter**, *(US)* **gray matter** N *(Med inf)* graue Zellen *pl*; **grey mullet** N Meeräsche *f*

greyness, *(US)* **grayness** ['greɪnɪs] N **a** *(= colour)* Grau *nt*; *(of face)* Fahlheit *f*; *(of weather, day)* Trübheit *f* **b** *(= bleakness: of life, world, outlook)* Trostlosigkeit *f*, Öde *f* **c** *(= anonymity, of person)* Gesichtslosigkeit *f*; *(of place)* Anonymität *f*

grey, *(US)* **gray**: **grey parrot** N Graupapagei *m*; **grey seal** N Kegelrobbe *f*; **grey squirrel** N Grauhörnchen *nt*; **grey vote** N Seniorenstimmen *pl*, *Kollektivbegriff für die Wahlstimmen älterer Wahlberechtigter*; **grey wolf** N Timberwolf *f*

grid [grɪd] N **a** *(= grating)* Gitter *nt*; *(in fireplace, on barbecue)* Rost *m*; **~ system** *(in road-building)* Rechteckschema *nt* **b** *(on map)* Gitter *nt*, Netz *nt* **c** *(= electricity, gas network)* Verteilernetz *nt*; **the (national) ~** *(Elec)* das Überland(leitungs)netz **d** *(Motor-racing: = starting grid)* Start(platz) *m*; *(US Ftbl)* Spielfeld *nt*; **they're on the ~** sie sind auf den Startplätzen **e** *(Elec: = electrode)* Gitter *nt* **f** *(Theat)* Schnürboden *m* **g** *(Comput)* Raster *nt*

griddle ['grɪdl] N *(Cook) gusseiserne Platte zum Pfannkuchenbacken*

griddlecake ['grɪdlkeɪk] N kleiner Pfannkuchen

gridiron ['grɪd,aɪən] N **a** *(Cook)* (Brat)rost *m* **b** *(US Ftbl)* Spielfeld *nt*

grid line ['grɪdlaɪn] N *(Comput etc)* Rasterlinie *f*; **~s** *(in table etc)* Gitternetz *nt*

gridlock ['grɪdlɒk] N *(Mot)* totaler Stau, Verkehrsinfarkt *m*; *(fig)* festgefahrene Situation; **total ~** *(Mot)* Verkehrskollaps *m*

gridlocked ['grɪdlɒkt] ADJ **a** *road* völlig verstopft; **traffic is ~ in the cities** der Verkehr in den Städten ist zum völligen Stillstand gekommen **b** *(fig) talks, negotiations* festgefahren

grid: **grid reference** N Planquadratangabe *f*; **grid square** N Planquadrat *nt*

grief [gri:f] N Leid *nt*, Kummer *m*, Gram *m (geh)*; *(because of loss)* große Trauer, Schmerz *m*, Gram *m (geh)*; **to cause ~ to sb** jdn zutiefst betrüben; *(death, loss also)* jdm großen Schmerz bereiten; *(failure, sb's behaviour also)* jdm großen Kummer bereiten; **to come to ~** Schaden erleiden; *(= be hurt, damaged)* zu Schaden kommen; *(= fail)* scheitern

grief-stricken ['gri:f,strɪkən] ADJ untröstlich, tieftraurig; *look, voice* schmerzerfüllt, gramgebeugt *(geh)*

grievance ['gri:vəns] N Klage *f*; *(= resentment)* Groll *m*; **~ procedure** Beschwerdeweg *m*; **I've no ~ against him** *(= no cause for complaint)* ich habe an ihm nichts auszusetzen; *(= no resentment)* ich nehme ihm nichts übel; **to have a ~ against sb for sth** jdm etw übel nehmen; **to air one's ~s** seine Beschwerden vorbringen, sich offen beschweren, sich beklagen

grieve [gri:v] VT Kummer bereiten *(+dat)*, betrüben; **it ~s me to see that ...** ich sehe mit Schmerz *or* Kummer, dass ...; **I was deeply ~d to hear of his death** die Nachricht von seinem Tod hat mich tief betrübt
VI sich grämen *(geh)*, trauern *(at, about* über *+acc)*; **to ~ for sb/sth** um jdn/etw trauern; **to ~ for sb** *(= sympathize with)* zutiefst mit jdm mitfühlen, jds Schmerz teilen; **my heart ~s for you** mir blutet das Herz; **to ~ over sb/sth** sich über jdn/etw grämen *(geh)*, über jdn/etw zutiefst bekümmert sein; **I didn't have any time to ~** ich hatte keine Zeit zum Trauern; **the grieving process** das Trauern

grievous ['gri:vəs] ADJ *(form) damage, injury, suffering, blow, setback, crime, neglect* schwer; *news* schmerzlich; *error* schwerwiegend, schwer wiegend; *injustice, wrong* schreiend; **his death is a ~ loss** sein Tod ist ein schwerer *or* schmerzlicher Verlust; **~ bodily harm** *(Jur)* schwere Körperverletzung

grievously ['gri:vəslɪ] ADV *(form) injure, wound, disappoint, offend, neglect* schwer; **he had been ~ wronged** man hatte ihm sehr großes Unrecht zugefügt

griffin ['grɪfɪn] N *(Myth)* (Vogel) Greif *m*

griffon ['grɪfən] N **a** *(= bird)* (Gänse)geier *m* **b** *(= dog)* Griffon *m*, Affenpinscher *m* **c** *(Myth)* = **griffin**

grift [grɪft] *(dated US, sl)* N *(= money)* ergaunertes *or* erschwindeltes Geld VI krumme Dinger drehen *(sl)*

grifter ['grɪftə'] N *(dated US sl: = swindler)* Gauner(in) *m(f)*, Schwindler(in) *m(f)*

grill [grɪl] N **a** *(Cook, on cooker etc)* Grill *m*; *(= gridiron)* Grill *m*, (Brat)rost *m*; *(= food)* Grillgericht *nt*, Grillade *f*; *(= restaurant)* Grill(room) *m* **b** = **grille** VT **a** *(Cook)* grillen **b** *(inf: = interrogate)* in die Zange nehmen *(inf)*; **to ~ sb about sth** jdn über etw *(acc)* ausquetschen *(inf)* *or* ins Verhör nehmen VI **a** *(food)* auf dem Grill liegen, gegrillt werden **b** *(inf, in sun)* schmoren *(inf)*

grille [grɪl] N Gitter *nt*; *(on window)* Fenstergitter *nt*; *(to speak through)* Sprechgitter *nt*; *(Aut)* Kühlergrill *m*

grilling ['grɪlɪŋ] N **a** *(Cook)* Grillen *nt* **b** *(= interrogation)* strenges Verhör; **to give sb a ~** jdn in die Zange nehmen *(inf)*; **to give sb a ~ about sth** jdn über etw *(acc)* ausquetschen *(inf) or* ins Verhör nehmen

grill: **grill pan** N *(Brit)* Grillpfanne *f*; **grillroom** N Grillroom *m*

grilse [grɪls] N junger Lachs

grim [grɪm] ADJ (+er) **a** *(= terrible) discovery, scene, task, news, story* grauenvoll; *joke, warning, reminder* grauenhaft; *situation* ernst, trostlos; *necessity, truth* bitter; *(= depressing) building, place, news, story* trostlos; *prospect* trübe, düster; *(= stern) person, face, smile, humour, silence, determination* grimmig; *voice* ernst; *battle, struggle* verbissen, unerbittlich; **the ~ reality of hospital work** die harte Realität der Arbeit in einem Krankenhaus; **a ~ picture of life in the war zone** ein trostloses Bild vom Leben im Kriegsgebiet; **to paint a ~ picture of sth** etw in düsteren Farben schildern; **to look ~** *(situation, future)* trostlos aussehen; *(person)* ein grimmiges Gesicht machen; **~ (sense of) humour** *(Brit) or* **humor** *(US)* Galgenhumor *m*; **to cling** *or* **hang on to sth like ~ death** sich verzweifelt an etw *(dat)* festklammern; **the Grim Reaper** der Sensenmann
b *(inf: = lousy)* fürchterlich *(inf)*; **the side effects are pretty ~** die Nebenwirkungen sind ziemlich schlimm; **to feel ~** *(= unwell)* sich elend *or* mies *(inf)* fühlen; **you're looking pretty ~** du siehst ziemlich elend *or* schlecht aus

grimace ['grɪməs] N Grimasse *f*; **to make a ~** eine Grimasse machen *or* schneiden; *(with disgust, pain also)* das Gesicht verziehen VI Grimassen machen *or* schneiden; *(with disgust, pain etc also)* das Gesicht verziehen

grime [graɪm] N Dreck *m*, Schmutz *m*; *(sooty)* Ruß *m*

grimly ['grɪmlɪ] ADV *fight, struggle, hold on* verbissen; *(= sternly) look, nod, say* mit grimmiger Miene; *smile, silent* grimmig; *bleak, barren* trostlos; *depressing* grauenhaft; **~ determined** verbissen

Grimm's law [,grɪmz'lɔ:] N *(Ling)* Lautverschiebungsgesetz *nt*, erste Lautverschiebung

grimness ['grɪmnɪs] N *(= terribleness)* Grauenhaftigkeit *f*; *(of situation)* Ernst *m*; *(= depressing nature, of building, place, news, story)* Trostlosigkeit *f*; *(of prospects)* Trübheit *f*; *(= sternness, of person, face, expression, smile, humour, determination)* Grimmigkeit *f*; *(of voice)* Ernst *m*; *(of battle, struggle)* Verbissenheit *f*, Unerbittlichkeit *f*

grimy ['graɪmɪ] ADJ schmutzig, dreckig; *clothes also* verdreckt; *(= greasy)* schmierig; *(= blackened with soot) city, building* verrußt

grin [grɪn] N *(showing pleasure)* Lächeln *nt*, Strahlen *nt*; *(showing scorn, stupidity, impudence)* Grinsen *nt*; **to give a huge ~** *(with pleasure)* über das ganze Gesicht strahlen; *(in scorn etc)* breit grinsen; **to give a wry ~** ironisch lächeln VI *(with pleasure)* lächeln, strahlen; *(in scorn, stupidly, cheekily)* grinsen; **to ~ and bear it** gute Miene zum bösen Spiel machen; *(= tolerate pain)* die Zähne zusammenbeißen; **to ~ at sb** jdn anlächeln/angrinsen; **to ~ from ear to ear** über das ganze Gesicht strahlen; **to ~ like a Cheshire cat** wie ein Honigkuchenpferd grinsen

grind [graɪnd] *vb: pret, ptp* **ground** VT **a** *(= crush)* zerkleinern, zermahlen; *corn, coffee, pepper, flour* mahlen; *(in mortar)* zerstoßen; **to ~ sth to a powder** etw fein zermahlen/zerstoßen; **to ~ one's teeth** mit den Zähnen knirschen
b *(= polish, sharpen) gem, lens, knife* schleifen
c *(= turn) handle, barrel organ* drehen; **to ~ one's heel into the earth** den Absatz in die Erde bohren
d **the tyrant ground the people into the dust** der Tyrann hat das Volk zu Tode geschunden

VI a *(mill)* mahlen; *(brakes, teeth, gears)* knirschen; **the metal ground against the stone** das Metall knirschte auf dem Stein; **the ship ground against the rocks** das Schiff lief knirschend auf die Felsen auf; **to ~ to a halt** *or* **standstill** *(lit)* quietschend zum Stehen kommen; *(fig)* stocken; *(production etc)* zum Erliegen kommen; *(negotiations)* sich festfahren; **the tanks were ~ing south** die Panzer rollten langsam nach Süden
b *(inf, = study)* büffeln *(inf)*
N a *(= sound)* Knirschen *nt* → **bump**
b *(fig inf: = drudgery)* Schufterei *f (inf)*; *(US inf: = swot)* Streber(in) *m(f) (inf)*; **the daily ~** der tägliche Trott; **it's a real ~** das ist ganz schön mühsam *(inf)*; **she found housework a ~** sie empfand Hausarbeit als Plackerei *(inf)*

▶ **grind away** VI schuften *(inf)*; **to grind away at sth** an etw *(dat)* schuften *(inf)*

▶ **grind down** VT *sep (lit) (mill) pepper etc* zermahlen; *(sea) rocks* abschleifen; *(fig) people, resistance* zermürben; **ground down by poverty** von Armut niedergedrückt

▶ **grind on** VI *(enemy, invasion)* unaufhaltsam vorrücken; *(fig, bureaucracy etc)* unaufhaltsam sein; **to grind on toward(s) sth** einer Sache *(dat)* unaufhaltsam entgegengehen; **the process grinds slowly on** das Verfahren schleppt sich hin

▶ **grind out** VT *sep* a *article, essay* sich *(dat)* abquälen; *propaganda* ausspucken *(inf)*; *victory* sich *(dat)* mühsam erkämpfen; *tune* orgeln *(inf)* b *(= extinguish by crushing) cigarette (with hand)* ausdrücken; *(with foot)* austreten

▶ **grind up** VT *sep* zermahlen

grinder ['graɪndəʳ] N a *(= meat grinder)* Fleischwolf *m*; *(= coffee grinder)* Kaffeemühle *f*; *(for sharpening)* Schleifmaschine *f*; *(= stone)* Schleifstein *m* b *(= person)* Schleifer(in) *m(f)* c *(= tooth)* Backenzahn *m*; *(of animals)* Mahlzahn *m*

grinding ['graɪndɪŋ] ADJ a *(= grating) noise* knirschend; **to come to a ~ halt** *(lit, fig)* völlig zum Stillstand kommen; *(vehicle)* plötzlich stehen bleiben; **to bring sth to a ~ halt** *(lit, fig)* etw völlig zum Stillstand bringen b *(= relentless) poverty* (er)drückend; *tedium, work* zermürbend

grindingly ['graɪndɪŋlɪ] ADV erdrückend; **~ hard work** zermürbende Knochenarbeit; **~ slow** zermürbend langsam

grinding wheel N Schleifscheibe *f*, Schleifstein *m*

grindstone ['graɪndstəʊn] N **to keep one's nose to the ~** hart arbeiten; **to keep sb's nose to the ~** jdn hart arbeiten lassen; **back to the ~** wieder in die Tretmühle *(hum)*

gringo ['grɪŋgəʊ] N *(esp US pej)* Gringo *m*

grip [grɪp] N a Griff *m*; *(on rope, on road)* Halt *m*; **to get a ~ on the road/rope** auf der Straße/am Seil Halt finden; **these shoes/tyres** *(Brit) or* **tires** *(US)* **have got a good ~** diese Schuhe/Reifen greifen gut; **I can't get a ~ with these shoes** ich finde mit diesen Schuhen keinen Halt; **cold weather had a firm ~ on the capital** das kalte Wetter hatte die Hauptstadt fest im Griff; **to get a ~ on sth** *(on situation, inflation etc)* etw in den Griff bekommen; **to get a ~ on oneself** *(inf)* sich zusammenreißen *(inf)*; **he had a good ~ on himself** er hatte sich gut im Griff *or* in der Gewalt; **to have a good ~ of a subject** ein Thema im Griff haben; **to let go** *or* **release one's ~** loslassen *(on sth* etw); **to lose one's ~** *(lit)* den Halt verlieren; *(fig)* nachlassen; **the chairman is losing his ~ (on the company)** der Vorsitzende hat die Firma nicht mehr richtig im Griff; **the President was losing his ~ on power** dem Präsidenten entglitt die Macht; **I must be losing my ~** mit mir gehts bergab; **to lose one's ~ on reality** den Bezug zur Wirklichkeit verlieren; **to lose one's ~ on a situation** eine Situation nicht mehr im Griff haben; **to have sb in one's ~** jdn in seiner Gewalt haben; **to be in the ~ of fear/passion** von Angst/Leidenschaft erfasst sein; **the country is in the ~ of a general strike** das Land ist von einem Generalstreik lahmgelegt; **the country is in the ~ of winter** der Winter hat im Land seinen Einzug gehalten; **to get** *or* **come to ~s with sth** mit etw klarkommen *(inf)*, etw in den Griff bekommen; **to get** *or* **come to ~s with sb** jdm zu Leibe rücken, zum Angriff gegen jdn übergehen
b *(= handle)* Griff *m*
c *(esp Brit: = hair grip)* Klemmchen *nt*
d *(= travelling-bag)* Reisetasche *f*
VT packen; *hand also* ergreifen; *(fig, fear etc also)* ergreifen; *(film, story etc also)* fesseln; **the car ~s the road well** der Wagen liegt gut auf der Straße; **the tyre** *(Brit) or* **tire** *(US)* **~s the road well** der Reifen greift gut; **fear ~ped his heart** Furcht ergriff *or* packte ihn
VI greifen

gripe [graɪp] VT *(US, inf, = annoy)* aufregen, fuchsen *(inf)* VI *(inf: = grumble)* meckern *(inf)*, nörgeln; **to ~ at sb** jdn anmeckern *(inf)*, jdn anmotzen *(inf)* N a **the gripes** PL Kolik *f*, Bauchschmerzen *pl*; **~ water** Kolikmittel *nt* b *(inf: = complaint)* Meckerei *f (inf)*; **have you any more ~s?** sonst hast du nichts zu meckern? *(inf)*

grippe [grɪp] N *(dated US)* Grippe *f*

gripping ['grɪpɪŋ] ADJ *story, book, film* packend, fesselnd; **the Olympics have made ~ television** die Olympiade war ein fesselndes Fernseherlebnis; **it's ~ stuff** *(inf)* es packt *or* fesselt einen total *(inf)*

gripsack N *(US)* Reisetasche *f*

grisly ['grɪzlɪ] ADJ *(+er)* grausig, grässlich

grist [grɪst] N **it's all ~ to his/the mill** das kann er/man alles verwerten; *(for complaint)* das ist Wasser auf seine Mühle

gristle ['grɪsl] N Knorpel *m*

gristly ['grɪslɪ] ADJ *(+er)* knorpelig

grit [grɪt] N a *(= dust, in eye)* Staub *m*; *(= gravel)* Splitt *m*, feiner Schotter; *(for roads in winter)* Streusand *m* b *(= courage)* Mut *m*, Mumm *m (inf)* c **grits** PL *(US)* Grütze *f* VT a *road etc* streuen b **to ~ one's teeth** *(lit, fig)* die Zähne zusammenbeißen

gritter ['grɪtəʳ] N Streuwagen *m*

gritty ['grɪtɪ] ADJ *(+er)* a *(lit) (= sandy) soil, path* sandig; *(= grainy) texture, food* körnig b *(fig: = courageous) person* mutig, tapfer; *determination* zäh; **the team's ~ display** das tapfere Spiel der Mannschaft c *(fig: = unsentimental) realism* hart; *drama, film* wirklichkeitsnah; *portrayal, account* ungeschminkt

grizzle ['grɪzl] VI *(Brit inf)* quengeln

grizzled ['grɪzld] ADJ *person* grauhaarig; *hair, beard (= grey)* grau; *(= streaked with grey)* grau meliert

grizzly ['grɪzlɪ] N *(also* **grizzly bear***)* Grisli(-bär) *m*, Grizzly(bär) *m* ADJ *(Brit inf) baby* quengelig

groan [grəʊn] N Stöhnen *nt no pl*; *(of gate, planks etc)* Ächzen *nt no pl*; **to let out** *or* **give a ~** (auf)stöhnen; **moans and ~s** Jammern und Stöhnen *nt* VI stöhnen *(with* vor *+dat)*; *(gate, planks)* ächzen *(with* vor *+dat)*; **the table ~ed under the weight** der Tisch ächzte unter der Last; **the country ~ed under** *or* **beneath its burdens** das Land ächzte unter seiner Last; **to ~ about sb/sth** über jdn/etw stöhnen

groat [grəʊt] N *(Brit Hist) Silbermünze im Wert von 4 alten Pence*

groats [grəʊts] PL Schrot *nt or m*; *(= porridge)* Grütze *f*

grocer ['grəʊsəʳ] N Lebensmittelhändler(in) *m(f)*, Kaufmann *m/*-frau *f*; **at the ~'s** im Lebensmittelladen, beim Kaufmann

grocery ['grəʊsərɪ] N a *(= business, shop)* Lebensmittelgeschäft *nt* b **groceries** PL *(= goods)* Lebensmittel *pl*

grody ['grəʊdɪ] ADJ *(US sl: = disgusting)* eklig, asslig *(sl)*

grog [grɒg] N Grog *m*

groggily ['grɒgɪlɪ] ADV *(inf)* groggy *(inf)*; *shake one's head, answer* schwach; *move* benommen

groggy ['grɒgɪ] ADJ *(+er) (inf)* angeschlagen *(inf)*, groggy *pred inv (inf)*

groin [grɔɪn] N a *(Anat)* Leiste *f*; **to kick sb in the ~** jdn in den Unterleib *or* die Leistengegend treten b *(Archit)* Grat *m* c = **groyne**

grommet ['grɒmɪt] N Öse *f*; *(Naut)* Taukranz *m*

groom [gru:m] N a *(in stables)* Stallbursche *m*, Pferde- *or* Reitknecht *m* b *(= bridegroom)* Bräutigam *m* VT a *horse* striegeln, putzen; **to ~ oneself** *(birds, animals)* sich putzen; *(people)* sich pflegen; **well ~ed** gepflegt; **badly ~ed** ungepflegt b *(= prepare)* **he's being ~ed for the job of chairman/for the Presidency** er wird als zukünftiger Vorsitzender/Präsidentschaftskandidat aufgebaut; **to ~ sb for stardom** jdn als Star lancieren; **he is ~ing him as his successor** er zieht sich *(dat)* ihn als Nachfolger heran

grooming ['gru:mɪŋ] N ein gepflegtes Äußeres

groove [gru:v] N Rille *f*; *(in rock also)* Rinne *f*, Furche *f*; *(in face)* Furche *f*; *(fig)* altes Gleis; **to get into the ~** *(inf)* in Fahrt kommen; **he's (stuck) in a ~** *(inf)* er kommt aus seinem alten Trott nicht heraus VT Rillen machen in *(+acc)*, rillen; *(water) stone* aushöhlen, Rinnen *or* Furchen machen in *(+acc)*; *face* furchen VI *(dated sl)* einen losmachen *(dated sl)*; **to ~ to the music** mit der Musik mitgehen

groover ['gru:vəʳ] N *(dated sl, = man)* irrer *or* starker Typ *(sl)*; *(= woman)* irre *or* starke Frau *(sl)*

groovy ['gru:vɪ] ADJ *(+er) (inf)* irr *(sl)*, stark *(sl)*

grope [grəʊp] VI *(also* **grope around** *or* **about***)* (herum)tasten *(for* nach); *(for words, solution)* suchen *(for* nach); **to be groping in the dark** im Dunkeln tappen; *(= try things at random)* vor sich *(acc)* hin wursteln *(inf)*; **groping hands** tastende Hände *pl* VT tasten nach; *(inf) girlfriend* befummeln *(inf)*; **to ~ one's way** sich vorwärtstasten; **to ~ (one's way) in/out** sich hinein-/hinaustasten; **they are groping (their way) toward(s) a cure** sie bemühen sich darum, ein Heilmittel zu finden N *(inf)* **to have a ~** fummeln *(inf)*; **a quick ~** eine schnelle Fummelei *(inf)*

gropingly ['grəʊpɪŋlɪ] ADV tastend

grosgrain ['grəʊgreɪn] N grob gerippter Seidentuch

gross[1] [grəʊs] N *no pl* Gros *nt*

gross[2] ADJ *(+er)* a *(= serious) mismanagement, exaggeration, simplification, error, insult* grob; *inequality, violation* krass; *injustice* schreiend; **that is a ~ understatement** das ist stark untertrieben
b *(= fat)* fett
c *(inf) person, remarks, jokes (= disgusting)* abstoßend; *(= tasteless)* ordinär; **he is the ~est thing alive** er ist total ekelhaft
d *(= total)* Gesamt-; *(= before deductions)* Brutto-; **~ amount** Gesamtbetrag *m*, Gesamtsumme *f*; **~ income** Bruttoeinkommen *nt*; **~ output** Gesamtproduktion *f*; **~ register(ed) ton** *(Naut)* Bruttoregistertonne *f*
ADV *earn, pay, weigh* brutto; **she earns £30,000 ~ per annum** sie verdient £ 30 000 brutto im Jahr, ihr Bruttoverdienst ist £ 30 000 im Jahr; **the yield is 10% ~** der Bruttoertrag ist 10%
VT *(= earn)* brutto verdienen
N **the ~** *(= amount)* die Gesamtsumme

gross: **gross domestic product** N *(Econ)* Bruttoinlandsprodukt *nt*; **gross indecency** N *(Jur)* grob unsittliches Verhalten

grossly ['grəʊslɪ] ADV a *(= very) unfair, misleading, inadequate, inaccurate, inefficient, irresponsible* äußerst; *overweight, exaggerate, underestimate, overestimate* stark; *mislead* grob; *underpaid, underfunded, overpaid* extrem; **to be ~ negligent** grob fahrlässig handeln b *(= crassly) express, put* krass; *classify* grob; **~ comic** urkomisch c *(inf: = coarsely) behave, talk* derb, rüde; **to eat ~** essen wie ein Schwein

gross: **gross margin** N *(Econ)* Bruttomarge *f*; **gross misconduct** N *(Jur)* grobes Fehlverhalten; **gross national product** N *(Econ)* Bruttosozialprodukt *nt*; **gross negligence** N grobe Fahrlässigkeit

grossness ['grəʊsnɪs] N **a** (= *seriousness, of error, insult, exaggeration, simplification*) Grobheit *f*; (*of inequality, violation*) Krassheit *f*; (*of negligence, injustice*) ungeheures Ausmaß **b** (= *fatness*) Körperfülle *f*, Fettheit *f* **c** (*inf*) (= *disgusting nature*) abstoßende Art; (= *tastelessness*) ordinäre Art

gross: **gross profit** N Gesamtgewinn *m*; (*before deductions*) Bruttogewinn *m*; **gross salary** N Bruttogehalt *nt*; **gross turnover** N Gesamtumsatz *m*; **gross weight** N Bruttogewicht *nt*; **gross yield** N Gesamt-/Bruttoertrag *m*

grotesque [grəʊ'tesk] ADJ **a** (= *outlandish, ridiculous*) *sight, spectacle, shape* grotesk; *idea, proposal, allegation* absurd **b** (= *distorted*) *grimace* verzerrt; **the body was in a ~ position** der Körper lag völlig verzerrt da; **he was rather ~ to look at** seine Erscheinung wirkte grotesk **c** (*Art*) grotesk N **a** (*Art*) **the ~** die Groteske **b** (*Typ*) Grotesk *f*

grotesquely [grəʊ'tesklɪ] ADV auf groteske Art; *swollen, deformed* grauenhaft; **~ exaggerated** bis ins Groteske übertrieben; **the image in the mirror was ~ distorted** das Spiegelbild war so verzerrt, dass es schon grotesk war

grotesqueness [grəʊ'tesknɪs] N **a** (= *outlandishness: of idea, proposal, allegation*) Absurdität *f*; **the ~ of the shape/this answer/his appearance** das Groteske an der Form/dieser Antwort/seiner Erscheinung **b** (= *distortion*) Verzerrtheit *f*

grotto ['grɒtəʊ] N *pl* **-(e)s** Grotte *f*, Höhle *f*; **fairy ~** Märchenhöhle *f*; **Santa's ~** *Raum, in dem der Weihnachtsmann in Kaufhäusern etc auftritt*

grotty ['grɒtɪ] ADJ (+*er*) (*inf*) **a** (= *foul*) grausig (*inf*); (= *filthy*) dreckig, verdreckt (*inf*) **b** (= *awful, lousy*) mies (*inf*); (= *dilapidated*) heruntergekommen; (= *tacky*) geschmacklos; **to feel ~** sich mies fühlen (*inf*)

grouch [graʊtʃ] N **a** (= *complaint*) Klage *f*; **to have a ~** (= *grumble*) schimpfen (*about* über +*acc*) **b** (*inf*: = *person*) Miesepeter *m* (*inf*), Muffel *m* (*inf*) VI schimpfen, meckern (*inf*)

grouchiness ['graʊtʃɪnɪs] N schlechte Laune, Miesepetrigkeit (*inf*) *f*

grouchy ['graʊtʃɪ] ADJ (+*er*) griesgrämig, miesepetrig (*inf*)

ground[1] [graʊnd] ✪ 15.2, 26.1 N **a** (= *soil, terrain, fig*) Boden *m*; **snow on high ~** Schnee in höheren Lagen; **hilly ~** hügeliges Gelände; **how much ~ do you own?** wie viel Grund und Boden *or* wie viel Land besitzen Sie?; **the middle ~ of politics** die politische Mitte; **there is common ~ between us** uns verbindet einiges; **they found common ~ in the fact that ...** die Tatsache, dass ..., verband sie; **to be on dangerous ~** (*fig*) sich auf gefährlichem Boden bewegen; **to be on firm** *or* **sure ~** festen *or* sicheren Boden unter den Füßen haben; (*fig*) sich auf sicherem Boden bewegen; **on familiar ~** auf vertrautem Boden; **to meet sb on his own ~** zu jdm kommen; **to be beaten on one's own ~** auf dem eigenen Gebiet geschlagen werden; **to cut the ~ from under sb** *or* **sb's feet** jdm den Boden unter den Füßen wegziehen; **to gain/lose ~** Boden gewinnen/verlieren; (*disease, rumour*) um sich greifen/im Schwinden begriffen sein; **to lose ~ to sb/sth** gegenüber jdm/etw an Boden verlieren; **to give ~ to sb/sth** vor jdm/etw zurückweichen; **to regain the ~ lost to sb** seine Position jdm gegenüber zurückerobern; **to break new ~** (*lit, fig*) neue Gebiete erschließen; (*person*) sich auf ein neues *or* unbekanntes Gebiet begeben; **to prepare the ~ for sth** den Boden für etw vorbereiten; **to go over the ~** (*fig*) alles durchgehen; **to cover the/a lot of ~** (*lit*) die Strecke/eine weite Strecke zurücklegen; (*fig*) das Thema/eine Menge Dinge behandeln; **that covers the ~** das umreißt das Thema; **to hold** *or* **stand one's ~** (*lit*) nicht von der Stelle weichen; (*fig*) seinen Mann stehen, sich nicht unterkriegen lassen; **to shift** *or* **change one's ~** (*fig*) seine Haltung ändern → **foot N b**

b (= *surface*) Boden *m*; **above/below ~** über/unter der Erde; (*Min*) über/unter Tage; (*fig*) unter den Lebenden/unter der Erde; **to fall to the ~** (*lit*) zu Boden fallen; (*fig, plans*) ins Wasser fallen, sich zerschlagen; **to sit on the ~** auf der Erde *or* dem Boden sitzen; **our hopes were dashed to the ~** unsere Hoffnungen wurden am Boden zerstört; **to burn sth to the ~** etw niederbrennen; **to raze sth to the ~** etw dem Erdboden gleichmachen; **it suits me down to the ~** das ist ideal für mich; **to get off the ~** (*plane etc*) abheben; (*fig: plans, project etc*) sich realisieren; **to go to ~** (*fox*) im Bau verschwinden; (*person*) untertauchen (*inf*); **to run a fox to ~** einen Fuchs aufstöbern; **to run sb/sth to ~** jdn/etw aufstöbern, jdn/etw ausfindig machen; **to run sb/oneself into the ~** (*inf*) jdn/sich selbst fertigmachen (*inf*); **to run a car into the ~** (*inf*) ein Auto schrottreif fahren

c (= *pitch*) Feld *nt*, Platz *m*; (= *parade ground, drill ground*) Platz *m*; **hunting ~s** Jagdgebiete *pl*; **fishing ~s** Fischgründe *pl*

d **grounds** PL (= *premises, land*) Gelände *nt*; (= *gardens*) Anlagen *pl*; **a house standing in its own ~s** ein von Anlagen umgebenes Haus

e **grounds** PL (= *sediment*) Satz *m*; **let the coffee ~s settle** warten Sie, bis sich der Kaffee gesetzt hat

f (= *background*) Grund *m*; **on a blue ~** auf blauem Grund

g (*US Elec*) Erde *f*

h (= *sea-bed*) Grund *m*

i (= *reason*) Grund *m*; **to have ~(s) for sth** Grund zu etw haben; **to be ~(s) for sth** Grund für *or* zu etw sein; **to give sb ~(s) for sth** jdm Grund zu etw geben; **~s for divorce** Scheidungsgrund *m*; **~s for dismissal** Entlassungsgrund *m*/-gründe *pl*; **~s for suspicion** Verdachtsmomente *pl*; **on the ~s of...** aufgrund ... (*gen*), auf Grund ... (*gen*), aufgrund *or* auf Grund von ...; **on the ~s that ...** mit der Begründung, dass ...; **on health ~s** aus gesundheitlichen Gründen

VT **a** *ship* auflaufen lassen, auf Grund setzen; **to be ~ed** aufgelaufen sein

b (*Aviat*) *plane* (*for mechanical reasons*) aus dem Verkehr ziehen; *pilot* sperren, nicht fliegen lassen; **to be ~ed by bad weather/a strike** wegen schlechten Wetters/eines Streiks nicht starten *or* fliegen können

c (= *punish*) *child* Hausarrest erteilen (+*dat*); **she was ~ed for a week** sie hatte eine Woche Hausarrest

d (*US Elec*) erden

e (= *base*) **to be ~ed on sth** sich auf etw (*acc*) gründen, auf etw (*dat*) basieren; **the story wasn't ~ed in reality** die Geschichte hatte keinen Bezug zur Wirklichkeit

f **to ~ sb in a subject** jdm die Grundlagen eines Faches beibringen; **to be well ~ed in English** gute Grundkenntnisse im Englischen haben

VI (*Naut*) auflaufen

ground[2] *pret, ptp of* **grind** ADJ *glass* matt; *coffee* gemahlen; **~ rice** Reismehl *nt*; **freshly ~ black pepper** frisch gemahlener schwarzer Pfeffer; **~ meat** (*US*) Hackfleisch *nt*

ground: **ground advantage** N (*Sport*) Platzvorteil *m*; **ground alert** N (*Mil*) Alarmbereitschaft *f*; (*Aviat*) Startbereitschaft *f*; **ground attack** N Bodenangriff *m*; **groundbait** N Grundköder *m*; **ground bass** N Grundbass *m*; **ground-breaking** ADJ umwälzend; *research etc* bahnbrechend; **ground coat** N Grundanstrich *m*; **ground colour**, (*US*) **ground color** N Untergrund *m*; (= *undercoat*) Grundierfarbe *f*; **ground conditions** PL (*Sport*) Platzverhältnisse *pl*; **ground control** N (*Aviat*) Bodenkontrolle *f*; **ground cover** N (*Hort*) Bodenvegetation *f*; **ground crew** N Bodenpersonal *nt*

grounder ['graʊndə'] N (*US Sport*) Bodenball *m*

ground: **ground floor** N Erdgeschoss *nt*, Erdgeschoß *nt* (*Aus*); **to get in on the ~** (*fig*) gleich zu Anfang einsteigen (*inf*); **ground fog** N Bodennebel *m*; **ground forces** PL (*Mil*) Bodentruppen *pl*, Landstreitkräfte *pl*; **ground frost** N Bodenfrost *m*; **groundhog** N (*US*) Waldmurmeltier *nt*

> **GROUNDHOG DAY**
>
> Am **Groundhog Day** wird in den USA ein nicht ganz ernst gemeinter Brauch gepflegt, den Frühlingsbeginn vorherzusagen. Am 2. Februar, dem **Groundhog Day**, soll der **groundhog**, auch bekannt als **woodchuck**, eine Art Murmeltier, aus seinem Winterschlaf erwachen und aus seinem Bau hervorkommen. Wenn nun die Sonne scheint und das Tier seinen eigenen Schatten erblickt, erschrickt es so sehr, dass es wieder in seinen Bau zurückkehrt und weitere sechs Wochen Winterschlaf einlegt – es wird also weitere sechs Wochen Winter geben. Das Ereignis wird landesweit aus Punxsutawney, Pennsylvania, übertragen, wo sich der bekannteste Groundhog-Bau befindet, dessen Bewohner immer Phil genannt wird. Manchmal weigert sich das Tier jedoch aufzutauchen. 1993 wurde eine Komödie über einen Meteorologen gedreht, der auf das Punxsutawney-Fest wartet: „Groundhog Day - Und täglich grüßt das Murmeltier".

grounding ['graʊndɪŋ] N **a** (= *basic knowledge*) Grundwissen *nt*; **to give sb a ~ in English** jdm die Grundlagen *pl* des Englischen beibringen **b** (*Aviat, of plane*) Startverbot *nt* (*of* für); (*due to strike, bad weather*) Hinderung *f* am Start; (*of pilot*) Sperren *nt*

ground: **ground ivy** N Gundelrebe *f*, Gundermann *m*; **groundkeeper** N (*US*) = **groundsman**; **ground-launched** ADJ *missile* bodengestützt; **groundless** ADJ grundlos, unbegründet; **ground level** N Boden *m*; **below ~** unter dem Boden; **ground note** N (*Mus*) Grundton *m*; **groundnut** N Erdnuss *f*; **ground pass** N (*Sport*) Flachpass *m*; **ground plan** N Grundriss *m*; **ground rent** N Grundrente *f*; **ground rules** PL Grundregeln *pl*

groundsel ['graʊnsl] N Kreuzkraut *nt*

groundsheet N Zeltboden(plane *f*) *m*

groundsman ['graʊndzmən] N *pl* **-men** [-mən] (*esp Brit*) Platzwart *m*

ground: **groundspeed** N Bodengeschwindigkeit *f*; **ground squirrel** N Erdhörnchen *nt*; **ground staff** N (*Aviat*) Bodenpersonal *nt*; (*Sport*) Platzwarte *pl*; **ground stroke** N (*Tennis*) nicht aus der Luft gespielter Ball; **groundswell** N Dünung *f*; (*fig*) Anschwellen *nt*, Zunahme *f*; **there was a growing ~ of public opinion against him** die Öffentlichkeit wandte sich zunehmend gegen ihn; **ground-to-air missile** N Boden-Luft-Rakete *f*; **ground-to-ground missile** N Boden-Boden-Flugkörper *m*; **ground troops** PL (*Mil*) Bodentruppen *pl*; **ground water** N Grundwasser *nt*; **groundwire** N (*US Elec*) Erdleitung *f*; **groundwork** N Vorarbeit *f*; **to do the ~ for sth** die Vorarbeit für etw leisten; **ground zero** N **a** (*of atomic bomb*) Bodennullpunkt *m* **b** (*fig*) absoluter Nullpunkt; **to start at ~** bei null anfangen **c** (*Hist*) **Ground Zero** *Gelände, auf dem am 11. September 2001 das World Trade Center in New York City einstürzte*

group [gru:p] N Gruppe *f*; (*Comm also*) Konzern *m*; (= *theatre group also*) Ensemble *nt*; **a ~ of people** eine Gruppe Menschen; **a ~ of houses/trees** eine Häuser-/Baumgruppe; **to form a ~ around sb/sth** sich um jdn/etw gruppieren

ATTR Gruppen-; *living, activities* in der Gruppe *or* Gemeinschaft; **~ discussion** Gruppendiskussion *f*

VT gruppieren; **to ~ together** (*in one group*) zusammentun; (*in several groups*) in Gruppen einteilen *or* anordnen; **pupils are ~ed according to age and ability** die Schüler werden nach Alter und Fähigkeiten in Gruppen eingeteilt; **it's wrong to ~ all criminals together** es ist nicht richtig, alle Verbrecher über einen Kamm zu scheren *or* in einen Topf zu werfen (*inf*); **~ the**

blue ones with the red ones ordnen Sie die Blauen bei den Roten ein, tun Sie die Blauen mit den Roten zusammen; **they ~ed themselves round him** sie stellten sich um ihn (herum) auf, sie gruppierten sich um ihn; **the books were ~ed on the shelf according to subject** die Bücher standen nach Sachgruppen geordnet im Regal

group: **group booking** N Gruppenbuchung *or* -reservierung *f*; **group captain** N *(Aviat)* Oberst *m*; **group dynamics** N **a** *pl (= relationships)* Gruppendynamik *f* **b** *sing (= subject)* Gruppendynamik *f*

groupie ['gru:pɪ] N Groupie *nt*

grouping ['gru:pɪŋ] N Gruppierung *f*; *(= group of things also)* Anordnung *f*

group: **group insurance** N Gruppenversicherung *f*; **Group of Eight** N G-8(-Staaten *pl*) *f*; **group practice** N Gemeinschaftspraxis *f*; **to be in a ~** in einem Ärztekollektiv arbeiten; **group therapy** N Gruppentherapie *f*; **groupware** N *(Comput)* Groupware *f*

grouse[1] [graʊs] N *pl* - Waldhuhn *nt*, Raufußhuhn *nt*; *(= red grouse)* Schottisches Moor(schnee)huhn; **~ shooting** Moorhuhnjagd *f*

grouse[2] *(Brit inf)* N *(= complaint)* Klage *f*; **to have a good ~** sich ausschimpfen *(inf)* VI schimpfen, meckern *(inf)* *(about* über *+acc)*

grouser ['graʊsəʳ] N *(inf)* Meckerfritze *m*/-liese *f* *(inf)*

grout [graʊt] VT *tiles* verfugen, verkitten; *bricks* mit Mörtel ausgießen N Vergussmaterial *nt*, Fugenkitt *m*; *(for bricks)* Mörtel *m*

grove [grəʊv] N Hain *m*, Wäldchen *nt*

grovel ['grɒvl] VI kriechen; **to ~ at sb's feet** vor jdm kriechen; *(dog)* sich um jdn herumdrücken; **to ~ to** *or* **before sb** *(fig)* vor jdm kriechen; *(in apology)* vor jdm zu Kreuze kriechen

groveller ['grɒvləʳ] N Kriecher(in) *m(f)* *(inf)*, Speichellecker(in) *m(f)* *(inf)*

grovelling, *(US)* **groveling** ['grɒvlɪŋ] ADJ kriecherisch *(inf)*, unterwürfig N Kriecherei *f* *(inf)*, Speichelleckerei *f* *(inf)*

grow [grəʊ] *pret* **grew**, *ptp* **grown** VT **a** *plants* ziehen; *(commercially) potatoes, wheat, tea etc* anbauen, anpflanzen; *(= cultivate) flowers* züchten
b **to ~ a beard/one's hair** sich *(dat)* einen Bart/die Haare wachsen lassen
VI **a** *(= get bigger, longer etc)* wachsen; *(person, baby)* wachsen, größer werden; *(hair)* wachsen, länger werden; *(in numbers)* zunehmen; *(in size)* sich vergrößern; *(fig: = become more mature)* sich weiterentwickeln; **to ~ in stature/wisdom** an Ansehen/Weisheit zunehmen; **to ~ in popularity** immer beliebter werden; **to ~ in beauty** schöner werden; **my, how you've** *or* **haven't you ~n!** du bist aber groß geworden!; **fears were ~ing for her safety** man machte sich zunehmend Sorgen um ihre Sicherheit; **the economy/market/population is ~ing by 2% a year** die Wirtschaft/der Markt/die Bevölkerung wächst um 2% pro Jahr; **pressure is ~ing for him to resign** er gerät zunehmend unter Druck zurückzutreten
b *(= become)* werden; **to ~ to do/be sth** allmählich etw tun/sein; **to ~ to hate/love sb** jdn hassen/lieben lernen; **to ~ to enjoy sth** langsam Gefallen an etw *(dat)* finden; **I've ~n to like him** ich habe ihn mit der Zeit lieb gewonnen; **to ~ used to sth** sich an etw *(acc)* gewöhnen; **to ~ like sb** jdm immer ähnlicher werden

▶ **grow apart** VI *(fig)* sich auseinanderentwickeln

▶ **grow away** VI *(fig)* **to grow away from sb** sich jdm entfremden

▶ **grow from** VI *+prep obj* = **grow out of b**

▶ **grow in** VI *(hair)* nachwachsen; *(teeth)* kommen; *(toenail)* einwachsen

▶ **grow into** VI *+prep obj* **a** *clothes, job* hineinwachsen in *(+acc)* **b** *(= become)* sich entwickeln zu, werden zu; **to grow into a man/woman** zum Mann/zur Frau heranwachsen; **to grow into a crisis** sich zur Krise auswachsen *or* entwickeln

▶ **grow on** VI *+prep obj* **it'll grow on you** das wird dir mit der Zeit gefallen, du wirst schon noch Geschmack daran finden

▶ **grow out** VI *(perm, colour)* herauswachsen

▶ **grow out of** VI *+prep obj* **a** *clothes* herauswachsen aus; **to grow out of a habit** eine Angewohnheit ablegen; **to grow out of one's friends** seinen Freunden entwachsen *(geh)*, sich von seinen Freunden entfernen **b** *(= arise from)* entstehen aus, erwachsen aus *(geh)*

▶ **grow together** VI *(lit, fig)* zusammenwachsen

▶ **grow up** VI *(= spend childhood)* aufwachsen; *(= become adult)* erwachsen werden; *(fig, custom, hatred)* aufkommen; *(city)* entstehen; **what are you going to do when you grow up?** was willst du mal werden, wenn du groß bist?; **she's grown up into an attractive young woman/an alcoholic** sie hat sich zu einer attraktiven jungen Frau/Alkoholikerin entwickelt; **grow up!, when are you going to grow up?** werde endlich erwachsen!

grow bag N Tüte *f* mit Komposterde

grower ['grəʊəʳ] N **a** *(= plant)* **to be a fast ~** schnell wachsen **b** *(= person, of fruit, vegetables)* Anbauer(in) *m(f)*; *(of flowers)* Züchter(in) *m(f)*; *(of tobacco, tea)* Pflanzer(in) *m(f)*

growing ['grəʊɪŋ] ADJ *(lit, fig)* wachsend; *child* heranwachsend, im Wachstum befindlich *(form)*; *importance, interest, number etc* wachsend, zunehmend; **he's still a ~ boy** er steckt noch *(inf)* *or* befindet sich noch im Wachstum N Wachstum *nt*, Wachsen *nt*

growing pains PL *(Med)* Wachstumsschmerzen *pl*; *(fig)* Kinderkrankheiten *pl*, Anfangsschwierigkeiten *pl*

growing season N Zeit *f* des Wachstums, Vegetationszeit *f* *(spec)*

growl [graʊl] N Knurren *nt no pl*; *(of bear)* (böses) Brummen *no pl* VI knurren; *(bear)* böse brummen; **to ~ at sb** jdn anknurren/anbrummen VT *answer* knurren

grown [grəʊn] *ptp of* **grow** ADJ erwachsen; **fully ~** ausgewachsen

grown: **grown-over** ADJ überwachsen; *garden also* überwuchert; **grown-up** ['grəʊnʌp] ADJ erwachsen; *clothes, book* für Erwachsene, für Große *(inf)*; **they have a ~ family** sie haben schon erwachsene Kinder N Erwachsene(r) *mf*

growth [grəʊθ] N **a** Wachstum *nt*; *(= increase in quantity, fig: of love, interest etc)* Zunahme *f*, Anwachsen *nt*; *(= increase in size)* Vergrößerung *f*, Wachstum *nt*; *(of capital etc)* Zuwachs *m*; **to reach full ~** seine/ihre volle Größe erreichen; **~ industry/stock** Wachstumsindustrie *f*/-aktien *pl*; **rate of export ~** Wachstums- *or* Zuwachsrate *f* im Export
b *(= plants)* Vegetation *f*; *(of one plant)* Triebe *pl*; **~ ring** *(of tree)* Jahresring *m*; **covered with a thick ~ of ivy** von Efeu überwuchert *or* überwachsen; **cut away the old ~** schneiden Sie die alten Blätter und Zweige aus; **with two days' ~ (of beard) on his face** mit zwei Tage alten Bartstoppeln
c *(Med)* Gewächs *nt*, Wucherung *f*

growth industry N Wachstumsbranche *f*

groyne [grɔɪn] N Buhne *f*

grub [grʌb] N **a** *(= larva)* Larve *f* **b** *(inf: = food)* Fressalien *pl* *(hum inf)*, Futterage *f* *(inf)*; **~('s) up!** antreten zum Essenfassen *(inf)* VT *(animal) ground, soil* aufwühlen, wühlen in *(+dat)* VI *(also* **grub about** *or* **around**, *pig)* wühlen *(in* in *+dat)*; *(person)* (herum)kramen, (herum)wühlen *(in* in *+dat, for* nach)

▶ **grub out** VT *sep* ausgraben

▶ **grub up** VT *sep weeds* jäten; *potatoes, bush etc* ausgraben; *soil* wühlen in *(+dat)*; *(bird) worms* aus dem Boden ziehen; *(fig) information, people* auftreiben, zusammensammeln

grubbily ['grʌbɪlɪ] ADV schmuddelig *(inf)*

grubbiness ['grʌbɪnɪs] N **a** *(= dirtiness)* Dreckigkeit *f*; *(of person, clothes, house)* Schmuddeligkeit *f* *(inf)* **b** *(fig: = sordidness)* Schmutzigkeit *f*

grubby ['grʌbɪ] ADJ *(+er)* **a** *(= dirty)* dreckig; *person, clothes, house* schmuddelig *(inf)* **b** *(fig: = sordid) business, corruption, politics* schmutzig; *aspect* zwielichtig

grudge [grʌdʒ] N Groll *m* *(against* gegen); **to bear sb a ~, to have a ~ against sb** jdm böse sein, jdm grollen, einen Groll gegen jdn hegen *(geh)*; **I bear him no ~** ich trage ihm das nicht nach, ich nehme ihm das nicht übel; **to bear ~s** nachtragend sein; **to settle a ~** eine alte Rechnung begleichen
VT **to ~ sb sth** jdm etw nicht gönnen, jdm etw neiden *(geh)*; **I don't ~ you your success** ich gönne Ihnen Ihren Erfolg; **to ~ doing sth** etw äußerst ungern tun, etw mit Widerwillen tun; **I don't ~ doing it** es macht mir nichts aus, das zu tun; **I ~ spending money/time on it** es widerstrebt mir *or* es geht mir gegen den Strich, dafür Geld auszugeben/Zeit aufzuwenden; **I don't ~ the money/time** es geht mir nichts ums Geld/um die Zeit; **I do ~ the money/time for things like that** das Geld/meine Zeit für solche Dinge tut mir leid

grudge match N *(inf: Sport, fig)* erbitterter Zweikampf *(von Mannschaften oder Persönlichkeiten, zwischen denen eine offene Feindschaft besteht)*

grudging ['grʌdʒɪŋ] ADJ *respect, admiration, consent, approval, support* widerwillig; *attitude* unwillig; *applause* sparsam; *apology* widerwillig gegeben; **we have a ~ attitude to spending money** es widerstrebt uns, Geld auszugeben; **to do sth in a ~ way** etw nur widerwillig tun; **he was ~ about her talent** er nahm ihr Talent nur widerwillig zur Kenntnis; **to be ~ in one's support for sth** etw nur widerwillig unterstützen

grudgingly ['grʌdʒɪŋlɪ] ADV widerwillig; **albeit ~** wenn auch nur widerwillig; **he ~ accepted the offer** er nahm das Angebot widerwillig an

gruel [grʊəl] N Haferschleim *m*, Schleimsuppe *f*

gruelling, *(US)* **grueling** ['grʊəlɪŋ] ADJ *schedule, journey, day, week* (äußerst) anstrengend; *pace, conditions* mörderisch *(inf)*; *race, match, event* (äußerst) strapaziös; *talks, negotiations* aufreibend; **200 ~ miles** 200 mörderische Meilen *(inf)*; **the most ~ part of my trip** der anstrengendste Teil meiner Reise

gruesome ['gru:səm] ADJ grausig, schauerlich, schaurig; *laugh* schaurig, makaber

gruesomely ['gru:səmlɪ] ADV *(+vb)* auf grausame Weise; *(+adj)* grausam, schauerlich

gruff [grʌf] ADJ *voice* barsch, schroff; *(= brusque) person, manner* barsch, schroff; *exterior* bärbeißig

gruffly ['grʌflɪ] ADV barsch, schroff

gruffness ['grʌfnɪs] N *(of voice)* Barschheit *f*; *(of person, manner)* Barschheit *f*, Schroffheit *f*

grumble ['grʌmbl] N *(= complaint)* Murren *nt no pl*, Schimpfen *nt no pl*; *(= noise: of thunder, guns)* Grollen *nt*; **his only ~ is that ...** das Einzige, was er auszusetzen hat, ist, dass ...; **all his ~s** sein ständiges Schimpfen *or* Gemecker *(inf)* VI murren, schimpfen *(about, over* über *+acc)*; *(thunder, gunfire)* grollen; **to ~ at sb** jdm gegenüber schimpfen *or* klagen; **grumbling appendix** *(inf)* gereizter Blinddarm

grumbler ['grʌmbləʳ] N Nörgler(in) *m(f)*, Brummbär *m* *(inf)*

grummet ['grʌmɪt] N = **grommet**

grump [grʌmp] N **a** *(inf) (= person)* **to be a ~** ein alter Brummbär sein *(inf)* **b** *(= bad mood)* **to have the ~s** brummig sein *(inf)*

grumpily ['grʌmpɪlɪ] ADV *(inf)* brummig *(inf)*, mürrisch

grumpy ['grʌmpɪ] ADJ *(+er)* *(inf)* brummig *(inf)*, mürrisch, grantig; *child* quengelig *(inf)*

grunge [grʌndʒ] N Grunge *nt*

grungy ['grʌndʒɪ] ADJ *(inf)* mies *(inf)*

grunt [grʌnt] N **a** *(of animal, person)* Grunzen *nt no pl*; *(of pain, in exertion)* Ächzen *nt no pl*,

Ächzer *m (inf)*; **to give a ~** grunzen (*of* vor *+dat*), ächzen (*of* vor *+dat*) **b** (*US inf*) kleiner Angestellter, kleine Angestellte; *(= dogsbody)* Mädchen *nt* für alles *(inf)* **VI** *(animal, person)* grunzen; *(with pain, exertion)* ächzen, aufseufzen; *(in irritation)* knurren **VT** *reply* brummen, knurren

grunt work N (*US inf*) Knochenarbeit *f*

gryphon [ˈɡrɪfən] N = **griffin**

GS *abbr of* **General Staff**

GSM *abbr* **a** *(Telec) of* **Global System for Mobile Communications** GSM; **~ standard** GSM-Standard *m* **b** *abbr of* **general sales manager** Verkaufsleiter(in) *m(f)*

gsm *abbr of* **gram(me)s per square metre** g/m^2

GSOH *(inf) abbr of* **good sense of humour** guter Sinn für Humor

g-spot [ˈdʒiːspɒt] N G-Punkt *m*

G-string [ˈdʒiːstrɪŋ] N **a** *(Mus)* G-Saite *f*; **Bach's Air on a ~** Bachs Air *nt* **b** *(= clothing)* Minislip *m*, Tangahöschen *nt*

GT *abbr of* **gran turismo** GT

Gt *abbr of* **Great**

Guadeloupe [ˌɡwɑːdəˈluːp] N Guadalupe *nt*, Guadelupe *nt*

guano [ˈɡwɑːnəʊ] N Guano *m*

guarantee [ˌɡærənˈtiː] **N** **a** *(Comm)* Garantie *f*; *(= guarantee slip)* Garantie(schein *m*) *f*; **to have** *or* **carry a 6-month ~** 6 Monate Garantie haben; **there is a year's ~ on this watch** auf der Uhr ist ein Jahr Garantie; **while it is still under ~** solange noch Garantie darauf ist; **to sell sth with a money-back ~** volles Rückgaberecht beim Verkauf von etw garantieren
b *(= promise)* Garantie *f* (*of* für); **that's no ~ that ...** das heißt noch lange nicht, dass ...; **it will be sent today, I give you my ~** *or* **you have my ~** es wird heute noch abgeschickt, das garantiere ich Ihnen
c *(Jur)* = **guaranty**
VT **a** *(Comm)* garantieren
b *(= promise, ensure)* garantieren (*sb sth* jdm etw); *(= take responsibility for)* garantieren für; **I can't ~ (that) he will be any good** ich kann nicht dafür garantieren, dass er gut ist; **I ~ to come tomorrow** ich komme garantiert morgen
c *(Jur)* garantieren, gewährleisten; *loan, debt* bürgen für

guaranteed [ˌɡærənˈtiːd] ADJ garantiert; **to be ~ for three months** *(goods)* drei Monate Garantie haben; *(prices)* für drei Monate garantiert sein; **to be ~ not to rust** garantiert nicht rostend sein; **~ price** Garantiepreis *m*; **that's a ~ success** das wird garantiert ein Erfolg; **such reports are ~ to cause anxiety** solche Berichte machen den Leuten garantiert Angst

guarantor [ˌɡærənˈtɔː] N Garant(in) *m(f)*; *(Jur also)* Bürge *m*, Bürgin *f*; **to stand ~ for sb** für jdn eine Bürgschaft übernehmen

guaranty [ˈɡærəntɪ] N *(Jur)* Garantie *f*; *(= pledge of obligation)* Bürgschaft *f*; *(= security)* Sicherheit *f*

guard [ɡɑːd] **N** **a** *(Mil)* Wache *f*; *(= single soldier)* Wachtposten *m*, Wache *f*; *(no pl: = squad)* Wachmannschaft *f*; **the Guards** *(Brit)* die Garde, das Garderegiment; **~ of honour** *(Brit)* **honor ~** *(US)* Ehrenwache *f*; **to change ~** Wachablösung machen
b *(= security guard)* Sicherheitsbeamte(r) *m*/-beamtin *f*; *(at factory gates, in park etc)* Wächter(in) *m(f)*; *(esp US: = prison guard)* Gefängniswärter(in) *m(f)*; *(Brit Rail)* Schaffner(in) *m(f)*, Zugbegleiter(in) *m(f)*
c *(= watch: also Mil)* Wache *f*; **under ~** unter Bewachung; **to be under ~** bewacht werden; *(person also)* unter Bewachung *or* Aufsicht stehen; **to keep sb/sth under ~** jdn/etw bewachen; **to be on ~, to stand** *or* **keep ~** Wache halten *or* stehen; **to keep** *or* **stand ~ over sth** etw bewachen; **to put a ~ on sb/sth** jdn/etw bewachen lassen
d *(Boxing, Fencing)* Deckung *f*; **on ~!** *(Fencing)* en garde!; **to take ~** in Verteidigungsstellung gehen; *(Cricket)* in Schlagstellung gehen; **to drop** *or* **lower one's ~** *(lit)* seine Deckung vernachlässigen; *(fig)* seine Reserve aufgeben; **to have one's ~ down** *(lit)* nicht gedeckt sein; *(fig)* nicht auf der Hut sein; **he caught his opponent off (his) ~** er hat seinen Gegner mit einem Schlag erwischt, auf den er nicht vorbereitet *or* gefasst war; **the invitation caught me off ~** ich war auf die Einladung nicht vorbereitet; **I was off (my) ~ when he mentioned that** ich war nicht darauf gefasst *or* vorbereitet, dass er das erwähnen würde; **to be on/off one's ~ (against sth)** *(fig)* (vor etw *dat*) auf der/nicht auf der Hut sein; **to put sb on his ~ (against sth)** jdn (vor etw *dat*) warnen; **to throw** *or* **put sb off his ~** *(lit)* jdn seine Deckung vernachlässigen lassen; *(fig)* jdn einlullen
e *(= safety device, for protection)* Schutz *m* (*against* gegen); *(on machinery)* Schutz(vorrichtung *f*) *m*; *(= fire guard)* Schutzgitter *nt*; *(on foil)* Glocke *f*; *(on sword etc)* Korb *m*
f *(in basketball)* Verteidigungsspieler(in) *m(f)*
VT *prisoner, place, valuables* bewachen; *treasure, secret, tongue* hüten; *machinery* beaufsichtigen; *luggage* aufpassen auf *(+acc)*; *(= protect) (lit) person, place* schützen (*from, against* vor *+dat*), abschirmen (*from, against* gegen); *one's life* schützen; *one's reputation* achten auf *(+acc)*; *(fig) child etc* behüten, beschützen (*from, against* vor *+dat*); **a closely ~ed secret** ein gut *or* streng gehütetes Geheimnis

▶ **guard against** VI *+prep obj (= take care to avoid) suspicion, being cheated etc* sich in Acht nehmen vor *(+dat)*; *hasty reaction, bad habit, scandal also* sich hüten vor *(+dat)*; *(= take precautions against) illness, attack, danger, misunderstandings* vorbeugen *(+dat)*; *accidents* verhüten; **you must guard against catching cold** Sie müssen aufpassen *or* sich in Acht nehmen, dass Sie sich nicht erkälten; **in order to guard against this** um (dem) vorzubeugen

guard: **guard chain** N Sicherheitskette *f*; **guard dog** N Wachhund *m*; **guard duty** N Wachdienst *m*; **to be on ~** auf Wache sein, Wache haben *(inf)*

guarded [ˈɡɑːdɪd] ADJ *person, smile* zurückhaltend, reserviert; *response, support, optimism* vorsichtig; **I'm being a bit ~, I suppose** ich bin wohl ein bisschen zu vorsichtig; **to give sth a ~ welcome** etw vorsichtig begrüßen; **to be ~ about sth** sich über etw *(acc)* zurückhalten; **he is ~ about his intentions** er hält sich mit seinen Absichten zurück

guardedly [ˈɡɑːdɪdlɪ] ADV vorsichtig; *smile* zurückhaltend; **~ optimistic** vorsichtig optimistisch

guardedness [ˈɡɑːdɪdnɪs] N Vorsichtigkeit *f*; *(of smile)* Reserviertheit *f*

guardhouse [ˈɡɑːdhaʊs] N *(Mil, for soldiers)* Wachlokal *nt*, Wachstube *f*; *(for prisoners)* Arrestlokal *nt*, Bunker *m (sl)*

guardian [ˈɡɑːdɪən] N Hüter(in), Wächter(in) *m(f)*; *(Jur)* Vormund *m*; **~ of tradition** Hüter(in) *m(f)* der Tradition

guardian angel N Schutzengel *m*

> **GUARDIAN READER**
>
> „Sage mir, welche Zeitung du liest und ich sage dir, wer du bist!" Dieser Spruch hat nirgendwo mehr Gültigkeit als in Großbritannien, wo sich recht ausgeprägte Klischees vom typischen Leser der größten und bekanntesten Tageszeitungen entwickelt haben. Der **Guardian reader** ist demnach linksorientiert, bürgerlich, sieht sich Politmagazine an und interessiert sich für ausländische Kunst und Filme. Lehrer und Sozialarbeiter gelten als typische Vertreter dieses Leserkreises. Ihnen gegenübergestellt werden die **Sun readers**. Die **Sun** ist ein Boulevardblatt, dessen Leser als sexistische Proletarier eingestuft werden, die Ausländer und Homosexuelle hassen.

guardianship [ˈɡɑːdɪənʃɪp] N Wachen *nt* (*of* über *+acc*); *(Jur)* Vormundschaft *f* (*of* über *+acc*)

guard: **guardrail** [ˈɡɑːdreɪl] N Schutzgeländer *nt*; *(around machinery)* Schutzleiste *f*; *(Rail)* Schutzschiene *f*, Zwangsschiene *f*; (= *US*: *Mot*) Leitplanke *f*; **guardroom** N *(used by guard)* Wachstube *f*; **guard rope** N Absperrseil *nt*

guardsman [ˈɡɑːdzmən] N *pl* **-men** [-mən] Wache *f*, Wachtposten *m*; *(= member of guards regiment)* Gardist *m*; *(US, in National Guard)* Nationalgardist *m*

guard's van [ˈɡɑːdzvæn] N *(Brit Rail)* Schaffnerabteil *nt*, Dienstwagen *m*

Guatemala [ˌɡwɑːtɪˈmɑːlə] N Guatemala *nt*

Guatemalan [ˌɡwɑːtɪˈmɑːlən] **ADJ** guatemaltekisch, aus Guatemala **N** Guatemalteke *m*, Guatemaltekin *f*

guava [ˈɡwɑːvə] N Guave *f*; *(= tree also)* Guavenbaum *m*

gubbins [ˈɡʌbɪnz] N *(Brit dated inf, things)* Zeug *nt (inf)*; *(person)* Dussel *m (inf)*

gubernatorial [ˌɡuːbənəˈtɔːrɪəl] ADJ *(esp US Pol)* Gouverneurs-; *candidate, campaign* für das Gouverneursamt; **~ election** Gouverneurswahl *f*

guddle [ˈɡʌdl] *(Scot)* **VT** *fish* mit den Händen fangen **N** (*inf*: = *mess*) Durcheinander *nt*; **this room's (in) a ~** in diesem Zimmer herrscht das reinste Durcheinander *(inf)*

gudgeon [ˈɡʌdʒən] N Gründling *m*

guelder-rose [ˈɡeldəˌrəʊz] N *(Bot)* Schneeball *m*

Guernsey [ˈɡɜːnzɪ] N **a** Guernsey *nt* **b** *(= sweater)* dicker Pullover *(von Fischern getragen)*

guer(r)illa [ɡəˈrɪlə] **N** Guerillero *m*, Guerillera *f*, Guerillakämpfer(in) *m(f)*; **Palestinian ~s** palästinensische Freischärler *or* Guerillas *pl* **ATTR** Guerilla-

guer(r)illa fighter N Guerillakämpfer(in) *m(f)*

guer(r)illa war, guer(r)illa warfare N Guerillakrieg *m*

guess [ges] **N** Vermutung *f*, Annahme *f*; *(= estimate)* Schätzung *f*; **to have** *or* **make a ~ (at sth)** (etw) raten; *(= estimate)* (etw) schätzen; **his ~ was nearly right** er hat es fast erraten/hat es gut geschätzt; **it's a good ~** gut geraten *or* geschätzt *or* getippt; **it was just a lucky ~** das war nur gut geraten, das war ein Zufallstreffer *m*; **I'll give you three ~es** dreimal darfst du raten; **50 people, at a ~** schätzungsweise 50 Leute; **at a rough ~** grob geschätzt, über den Daumen gepeilt *(inf)*; **my ~ is that ...** ich tippe darauf *(inf) or* schätze *or* vermute, dass ...; **your ~ is as good as mine!** *(inf)* da kann ich auch nur raten!; **it's anybody's ~** *(inf)* das wissen die Götter *(inf)*
VI **a** *(= surmise)* raten; **how did you ~?** wie hast du das bloß erraten?; *(iro)* du merkst auch alles!; **to keep sb ~ing** jdn im Ungewissen lassen; **he's only ~ing when he says they'll come** das ist eine reine Vermutung von ihm, dass sie kommen; **you'll never ~!** das wirst du nie erraten!; **you'll never ~ what!** darauf kommst du nie!; **to ~ at sth** etw raten
b *(esp US: = suppose)* **I ~ not** wohl nicht; **he's right, I ~** er hat wohl recht; **I think he's right – I ~ so** ich glaube, er hat recht – ja, das hat er wohl; **shall we go? – I ~ (so)** sollen wir gehen? – na gut *or* (ich) schätze ja *(inf)*; **that's all, I ~** das ist wohl alles, (ich) schätze, das ist alles *(inf)*
VT **a** *(= surmise)* raten; *(= surmise correctly)* erraten; *(= estimate) weight, numbers, amount* schätzen; **I ~ed as much** das habe ich mir schon gedacht; **to ~ sb to be 20 years old/sth to be 10 lbs** jdn auf 20 Jahre/etw auf 10 Pfund schätzen; **I ~ed (that) she was about 40** ich schätzte sie auf etwa 40; **you'll never ~ who/what ...** das errätst du nie, wer/was ...; **~ who!** *(inf)* rat mal, wer!; **~ what!** *(inf)* stell dir vor! *(inf)*, denk nur! *(inf)*
b *(esp US: = suppose)* **I ~ we'll just have to wait**

and see wir werden wohl abwarten müssen, ich schätze, wir werden abwarten müssen

guessable ['gesəbl] ADJ *answer* erratbar, zu erraten *pred*; *number* schätzbar, zu schätzen *pred*

guesser ['gesəʳ] N **to be a good ~** gut schätzen können

guessing game ['gesɪŋ,geɪm] N *(lit, fig)* Ratespiel *nt*

guesstimate ['gestɪmɪt] N grobe Schätzung

guesswork ['geswɜːk] N (reine) Vermutung; **there's too much ~ in historical essays** in historischen Aufsätzen wird zu viel vermutet; **they did it by ~** sie haben nur geraten; **it's all ~** das sind doch nur Vermutungen, das ist doch alles nur geraten

guest [gest] **N** Gast *m*; **~ of honour** *(Brit)* or **honor** *(US)* Ehrengast *m*; **be my ~** *(inf)* nur zu! *(inf)* **VI to ~ on sth** einen Gastauftritt in etw *(dat)* haben; **he ~ed for several clubs** er hatte in mehreren Klubs Gastauftritte

guest *in cpds* Gast-; **guest appearance** N Gastauftritt *m*; **to make a ~** als Gast auftreten; **guest artist** N Gast(star) *m*, Gastkünstler(in) *m(f)*; *(Theat)* Gastspieler(in) *m(f)*; **guesthouse** N Gästehaus *nt*; *(= boarding house)* (Fremden)pension *f*; **guest list** N Gästeliste *f*; **guest night** N Gästeabend *m*; **guest room** N Gästezimmer *nt*; **guest speaker** N Gastredner(in) *m(f)*

guff [gʌf] N *(inf)* Quark *m (inf)*, Käse *m (inf)*

guffaw [gʌ'fɔː] **N** schallendes Lachen *no pl*; **~s of laughter** Lachsalven *pl*; **to let out a ~** schallend lachen **VI** schallend (los)lachen

GUI *(Comput) abbr of* **graphical user interface** GUI *nt*

Guiana [gaɪ'ænə] N Guayana *nt*

guidance ['gaɪdəns] N *(= direction)* Führung *f*, Leitung *f*; *(= counselling)* Beratung *f* (*on* über *+acc*); *(from superior, parents, teacher etc)* Anleitung *f*; **spiritual ~** geistiger Rat; **for your ~** zu Ihrer Orientierung *or* Hilfe; **to give sb ~ on sth** jdn bei etw beraten; **to pray for ~** um Erleuchtung bitten

guidance: **guidance system** N *(on rocket)* Steuerungssystem *nt*; **guidance teacher** N *(Scot)* Verbindungslehrer(in) *m(f)*

guide [gaɪd] **N a** *(= person)* Führer(in) *m(f)*; *(fig: = indication, pointer)* Anhaltspunkt *m* (*to* für); *(= model)* Leitbild *nt*; **let reason/your conscience be your ~** lassen Sie sich von der Vernunft/Ihrem Gewissen leiten; **they used the star as their ~** sie ließen sich von dem Stern leiten; **he is my spiritual ~** er ist mein geistiger Berater

b *(Tech)* Leitvorrichtung *f*

c *(Brit: = Girl Guide)* Pfadfinderin *f*

d *(= instructions)* Anleitung *f*; *(= manual)* Leitfaden *m*, Handbuch *nt* (*to* +*gen*); *(= travel guide)* Führer *m*; **let this piece of work be your ~** orientieren Sie sich an dieser Arbeit; **as a rough ~** als Faustregel

VT *people, blind man etc* führen; *discussion also* leiten; *missile, rocket, sb's behaviour, studies, reading* lenken; **to ~ a plane in** ein Flugzeug einweisen; **to be ~d by sb/sth** *(person)* sich von jdm/etw leiten lassen; **to ~ sb to victory** jdn zum Sieg führen; **this will ~ you through difficult times** das wird dich in schweren Zeiten begleiten; **his life was ~d by his beliefs** sein Leben war von seinen Überzeugungen bestimmt; **to ~ sb on his way** jdm den Weg zeigen *or* weisen

guidebook ['gaɪdbʊk] N (Reise)führer *m* (*to* von)

guided missile [,gaɪdɪd'mɪsaɪl] N ferngelenktes Geschoss, Lenkwaffe *f*

guide dog N Blindenhund *m*

guided tour [,gaɪdɪd'tʊəʳ] N Führung *f* (*of* durch); **to give sb a ~** jdn herumführen

guide: **guideline** ['gaɪdlaɪn] N Richtlinie *f*, Richtschnur *f no pl*; *(Typ, for writing)* Leitlinie *f*; **safety ~s** Sicherheitshinweise *pl*; **I gave her a few ~s on looking after a kitten** ich gab ihr ein paar Hinweise, wie man eine junge Katze versorgt; **guide price** N *(Comm)* Richtpreis *m*; **guidepost** N Wegweiser *m*

Guider ['gaɪdəʳ] N *(Brit)* Pfadfinderinnenführerin *f*

guide rope N Schlepptau *nt*

guiding ['gaɪdɪŋ] ATTR **he took on a ~ role in his nephew's life** er wurde ein Leitbild im Leben seines Neffen; **~ force** leitende Kraft; **~ hand** leitende Hand; **~ principle** Leitmotiv *nt*; **~ star** Leitstern *m*

guild [gɪld] N *(Hist)* Zunft *f*, Gilde *f*; *(= association)* Verein *m*

guilder ['gɪldəʳ] N Gulden *m*

guildhall ['gɪldhɔːl] N **a** *(Hist)* Zunfthaus *nt* **b** *(Brit)* Rathaus *nt*; **the Guildhall** *das Rathaus der City of London*

guile [gaɪl] N Tücke *f*, (Arg)list *f*; **to have ~** sehr tückisch *or* arglistig sein; **without ~** ohne Arg, ohne Falsch *(liter)*

guileful ['gaɪlfʊl] ADJ hinterhältig, tückisch, arglistig

guileless ['gaɪllɪs] ADJ arglos, harmlos, unschuldsvoll

guillemot ['gɪlɪmɒt] N Lumme *f*

guillotine [,gɪlə'tiːn] **N a** Guillotine *f*, Fallbeil *nt* **b** *(for paper)* (Papier)schneidemaschine *f* **c** *(Parl)* Beschränkung *f* der Diskussionszeit **VT a** *person* mit der Guillotine *or* dem Fallbeil hinrichten **b** *paper* schneiden **c** *(Parl) bill* die Diskussionszeit einschränken für

guilt [gɪlt] N Schuld *f* (*for, of* an +*dat*); **to feel ~ (about sth)** sich (wegen etw) schuldig fühlen, (wegen etw) Schuldgefühle haben; **feelings of ~** Schuldgefühle *pl*; **~ complex** Schuldkomplex *m*

guiltily ['gɪltɪlɪ] ADV schuldbewusst

guiltiness ['gɪltɪnɪs] N Schuld *f*; *(of look, smile, silence)* Schuldbewusstsein *nt*

guiltless ['gɪltlɪs] ADJ schuldlos, unschuldig (*of* an *+dat*); **he is ~ of any crime** er ist keines Verbrechens schuldig

guilty ['gɪltɪ] ADJ (+er) **a** *smile, look, silence* schuldbewusst; *secret, pleasure* mit Schuldgefühlen verbunden; **~ conscience** schlechtes Gewissen; **~ feelings** Schuldgefühle *pl*; **to feel ~ (about doing sth)** ein schlechtes Gewissen haben(, weil man etw tut/getan hat); **she felt ~ about** *or* **because of her rudeness** sie hatte wegen ihrer Unhöflichkeit ein schlechtes Gewissen; **I never stop feeling ~ about having let you down** ich habe immer ein schlechtes Gewissen, weil ich dich im Stich gelassen habe; **to make sb feel ~** jdm ein schlechtes Gewissen einreden; **to look ~** schuldbewusst aussehen

b *(= to blame) person* schuldig (*of sth* einer Sache *gen*); **the ~ person** der/die Schuldige; **the ~ party** die schuldige Partei; **to find sb ~/not ~ (of sth)** jdn (einer Sache *gen*) für schuldig/nicht schuldig befinden; **they were found not ~ of murder** sie wurden des Mordes für nicht schuldig befunden; **they were found not ~ of killing him** sie wurden für nicht schuldig befunden, ihn getötet zu haben; **to plead (not) ~ to a crime** sich eines Verbrechens (nicht) schuldig bekennen; **do you plead ~ or not ~?** plädieren Sie auf schuldig oder nicht schuldig?; **a ~ verdict, a verdict of ~** ein Schuldspruch *m*; **a not ~ verdict, a verdict of not ~** ein Freispruch *m*; **they returned a verdict of not ~ on him** sie sprachen ihn frei; **a ~ plea, a plea of ~** ein Geständnis *nt*; **a not ~ plea, a plea of not ~** ein Unschuldsbekenntnis *nt*; **their parents are ~ of gross neglect** ihre Eltern haben sich grobe Fahrlässigkeit zuschulden *or* zu Schulden kommen lassen; **we're all ~ of neglecting the problem** uns trifft alle die Schuld, dass das Problem vernachlässigt wurde; **I've been ~ of that too** ich muss zugeben, dass ich das auch schon gemacht habe

Guinea ['gɪnɪ] N Guinea *nt*

guinea ['gɪnɪ] N *(Brit old)* Guinee *f*, Guinea *f (21 Shilling)*

guinea: **guinea fowl** N Perlhuhn *nt*; **guinea pig** N Meerschweinchen *nt*; *(fig)* Versuchskaninchen *nt*

guise [gaɪz] N *(= disguise)* Gestalt *f*; *(= pretence)* Vorwand *m*; **in the ~ of a clown** als Clown verkleidet; **under the ~ of friendship/scientific research** unter dem Deckmantel der Freundschaft/der wissenschaftlichen Forschung; **under the ~ of doing sth** unter dem Vorwand, etw zu tun

guitar [gɪ'tɑːʳ] N Gitarre *f*

guitarist [gɪ'tɑːrɪst] N Gitarrist(in) *m(f)*

gulch [gʌlʃ] N *(US)* Schlucht *f*

gulf [gʌlf] N **a** *(= bay)* Golf *m*, Meerbusen *m*; **the Gulf of Mexico** der Golf von Mexiko; **the Gulf of Bothnia** der Bottnische Meerbusen; **the (Persian) Gulf** der (Persische) Golf **b** *(lit, fig: = chasm)* tiefe Kluft

Gulf: **Gulf States** PL **the ~** die Golfstaaten *pl*; **Gulf Stream** N Golfstrom *m*; **Gulf War** N Golfkrieg *m*

gull[1] [gʌl] N *(= seagull)* Möwe *f*

gull[2] *(liter)* **N** Spielball *m (of +gen)* **VT** übertölpeln; **to ~ sb out of his money** jdm sein Geld ablisten; **to be ~ed into sth** durch eine üble List dazu gebracht werden, etw zu tun

gullet ['gʌlɪt] N Speiseröhre *f*, Kehle *f*; **that really stuck in my ~** *(fig)* das ging mir sehr gegen den Strich *(inf)*

gullibility [,gʌlɪ'bɪlɪtɪ] N Leichtgläubigkeit *f*

gullible ADJ, **gullibly** ADV ['gʌlɪbl, -ɪ] leichtgläubig

gull: **gull wing door** N *(Aut)* Flügeltür *f*; **gull-winged** ADJ *car* mit Flügeltüren

gully ['gʌlɪ] N *(= ravine)* Schlucht *f*; *(= narrow channel)* Rinne *f*

gulp [gʌlp] **N** Schluck *m*; **at a ~, in one ~** auf einen Schluck; **..., he said with a ~** ..., sagte er und schluckte **VT** *(also* **gulp down**) *drink* runterstürzen; *food* runterschlingen; *medicine* hinunterschlucken; **to ~ back one's tears** die Tränen hinunterschlucken; **to ~ back a sob** einen Schluchzer unterdrücken; **what?, he ~ed** was?, presste er hervor **VI** *(= try to swallow)* würgen; *(= eat fast)* schlingen; *(= drink fast)* hastig trinken; *(from emotion)* trocken schlucken; **to make loud ~ing noises** gluckernd trinken

gum[1] [gʌm] N *(Anat)* Zahnfleisch *nt no pl*

gum[2] **N a** Gummi *nt*; *(= gumtree)* Gummibaum *m*; *(= glue)* Klebstoff *m* **b** *(= chewing gum)* Kaugummi *m*; *(= sweet)* Weingummi *m* **c** *(US inf)* = **gumshoe VT** *(= stick together)* kleben; *(= spread gum on)* gummieren

▶ **gum down** VT *sep label* aufkleben; *envelope* zukleben

▶ **gum up** VT *sep* verkleben; **to gum up the works** *(inf)* alles verkleben; *(fig)* die Sache vermasseln *(inf)*; **to get gummed up** verkleben

gum[3] N *(dated inf)* **by ~!** Teufel noch mal! *(dated sl)*

gum arabic N Gummiarabikum *nt*

gumbo ['gʌmbəʊ] N Gumbo *m*

gum: **gumboil** N Zahnfleischabszess *m*; **gumboot** N Gummistiefel *m*; **gumdrop** N Weingummi *m*

gummy ['gʌmɪ] ADJ (+er) *substance, surface, food* klebrig; *eyes* verklebt

gumption ['gʌmpʃən] N *(inf)* Grips *m (inf)*; **to have the ~ to do sth** geistesgegenwärtig genug sein, etw zu tun

gum: **gumshield** N Zahnschutz *m*; **gumshoe** *(US)* **N a** *(= overshoe)* Überschuh *m*, Galosche *f*; *(= gym shoe)* Turnschuh *m* **b** *(sl: = detective)* Schnüffler(in) *m(f) (inf)* **VI** *(sl: = move stealthily)* schleichen; **gumtree** N Gummibaum *m*; *(Austral)* Eukalyptusbaum *m*, Eukalyptus *m*; **to be up a ~** *(Brit inf)* aufgeschmissen sein *(inf)*

gun [gʌn] **N a** *(= cannon etc)* Kanone *f*, Geschütz *nt*; *(= rifle)* Gewehr *nt*; *(= pistol etc)* Pistole *f*, Kanone *f (sl)*, Schießeisen *nt (hum inf)*; **to carry a ~** (mit einer Schusswaffe) bewaffnet sein, eine Schusswaffe tragen *(form)*; **to draw a**

~ eine (Schuss)waffe ziehen; **to draw a ~ on sb** jdn mit einer Schusswaffe bedrohen; **to fire a 21-~ salute** 21 Salutschüsse abgeben; **the big ~s** die schweren Geschütze; **big ~** *(fig inf)* hohes *or* großes Tier *(inf)* *(in* in *+dat)*; **to hold** *or* **put a ~ to sb's head** *(fig)* jdm die Pistole auf die Brust setzen; **to stick to one's ~s** nicht nachgeben, festbleiben; **to jump the ~** *(Sport)* Frühstart machen; *(fig)* voreilig sein *or* handeln; **to be going great ~s** *(Brit inf, team, person)* toll in Schwung *or* Fahrt sein *(inf)*; *(car)* wie geschmiert laufen *(inf)*; *(business)* gut in Schuss sein *(inf)*
b *(= spray gun)* Pistole *f*
c *(= person)* Schütze *m*, Schützin *f*; *(Hunt)* Jäger(in) *m(f)*; *(esp US inf: = gunman)* Pistolenheld *m (inf)*; **he's the fastest ~ in the West** *(inf)* er zieht am schnellsten im ganzen Westen *(inf)*
VT a *(= kill: also* **gun down***) person* erschießen, zusammenschießen; *pilot, plane* abschießen
b *(inf: = rev) engine* aufheulen lassen
VI a *(inf)* **to be ~ning for sb** *(lit)* Jagd auf jdn machen; *(fig)* jdn auf dem Kieker haben *(inf)*; *for opponent* jdn auf die Abschussliste gesetzt haben
b *(inf, = speed)* schießen *(inf)*

gun: **gun barrel** N *(on cannon)* Kanonen- *or* Geschützrohr *nt*; *(on rifle)* Gewehrlauf *m*; *(on pistol)* Pistolenlauf *m*; **gunboat** N Kanonenboot *nt*; **gunboat diplomacy** N Kanonenbootdiplomatie *f*; **gun carriage** N Lafette *f*

GUN CONTROL

In den USA ist **gun control**, also die Frage, ob und wie der Schusswaffenverkauf kontrolliert werden soll, ein kontrovers diskutiertes Thema. Das Recht aller Bürger, eine Waffe zu tragen, ist in der US-Verfassung festgeschrieben, und die Lobbyisten der Schusswaffenbefürworter, wie zum Beispiel die mächtige **National Rifle Association**, drängen die Bürger weiterhin, sich zur Selbstverteidigung legal zu bewaffnen. Dennoch ist man besorgt über eine alarmierend hohe Zahl von Unfällen mit Schusswaffen und – vor allen Dingen in den Großstädten – über den weitverbreiteten illegalen Waffengebrauch sowie eine ständig steigende Zahl von Verletzten und Todesopfern. Durch eine strengere Gesetzgebung wurden daher Verkauf und Besitz von Schusswaffen eingeschränkt und viele Typen halb automatischer Waffen wurden verboten.

gun: **guncotton** N Schießbaumwolle *f*; **gun crew** N Geschützbedienung *f*; **gun dog** N Jagdhund *m*; **gunfight** N Schießerei *f*; *(Mil)* Feuergefecht *nt*, Schusswechsel *m*; **gunfighter** N Revolverheld *m*; **gunfire** N Schießerei *f*, Schüsse *pl*; *(Mil)* Geschützfeuer *nt*, Artilleriefeuer *nt*

gunge [gʌndʒ] N *(Brit inf)* klebriges *or* schmieriges Zeug *(inf)*

gung ho ['gʌŋ'həʊ] ADJ *(inf)* übereifrig

gungy ['gʌndʒɪ] ADJ *(+er) (inf)* schmierig

gunk [gʌŋk] N *(esp US inf)* klebriges *or* schmieriges Zeug *(inf)*; **you've got some ~** du hast noch Schlaf in den Augen *(inf)*

gun: **gunmaker** N Waffenhersteller(in) *m(f)*; **gunman** N (mit einer Schusswaffe) Bewaffnete(r) *m*; **they saw the ~** sie haben den Schützen gesehen; **gunmetal** N Geschützmetall *nt*, Geschützbronze *f*; *(= colour)* metallisches Blaugrau **ADJ** *attr* aus Geschützmetall *or* -bronze; *grey, colour* metallisch; **gun permit** N Waffenschein *m*

gunnel ['gʌnəl] N = **gunwale**

gunner ['gʌnəʳ] N *(Mil)* Artillerist *m*; *(= title)* Kanonier *m*; *(Naut)* Geschützführer *m*; *(in plane)* Bordschütze *m*; **to be in the ~s** *(Mil)* bei der Artillerie sein

gunnery ['gʌnərɪ] N Schießkunst *f*; **~ officer** Artillerieoffizier *m*

gunny ['gʌnɪ] N Sackleinen *nt*

gun: **gunpoint** N **to hold sb at ~** jdn mit einer Schusswaffe bedrohen; **to force sb to do sth at ~** jdn mit vorgehaltener Waffe zwingen, etw zu tun; **to kidnap sb at ~** jdn mit Waffengewalt entführen; **gunpowder** N Schießpulver *nt*; **Gunpowder Plot** N *(Brit Hist)* Pulververschwörung *f*; **gun room** N Waffenkammer *f*; *(Naut)* Kadettenmesse *f*; **gunrunner** N Waffenschmuggler(in) *or* -schieber(in) *m(f)*; **gunrunning** N Waffenschmuggel *m*, Waffenschieberei *f (inf)*; **gunshot** N Schuss *m*; *(= range)* Schussweite *f*; **~ wound** Schusswunde *f*; **gunslinger** ['gʌnslɪŋəʳ] N *(inf)* Pistolenheld *m (inf)*; **gunsmith** N Büchsenmacher(in) *m(f)*; **gun turret** N Geschützturm *m*; **gunwale** ['gʌnl] N Dollbord *nt*

guppy ['gʌpɪ] N Guppy *m*, Millionenfisch *m*

gurgle ['gɜːgl] **N** *(of liquid)* Gluckern *nt no pl*; *(of brook also)* Plätschern *nt no pl*; *(of baby)* Glucksen *nt no pl*; **to give a ~ of pleasure/laughter** vor Vergnügen/Lachen glucksen **VI** *(liquid)* gluckern; *(brook also)* plätschern; *(person)* glucksen *(with* vor *+dat)*

Gurkha ['gɜːkə] N Gurkha *mf*

gurney ['gɜːnɪ] N *(US)* (Trag)bahre *f*

guru ['gʊruː] N *(lit, fig)* Guru *m*

gush [gʌʃ] **N a** *(of liquid)* Strahl *m*, Schwall *m*; *(of words)* Schwall *m*; *(of emotion, enthusiasm)* Ausbruch *m* **b** *(inf: = gushing talk)* Geschwärme *nt (inf)* **VI a** *(also* **gush out***, water)* herausschießen, heraussprudeln; *(smoke, blood, tears)* hervorquellen; *(flames)* herausschlagen **b** *(inf: = talk)* schwärmen *(inf)* *(about, over* von); *(insincerely)* sich ergehen *(about, over* über *+acc)* **VT** *(liter, volcano)* ausstoßen; **the wound ~ed blood** aus der Wunde schoss *or* quoll Blut; **what a delightful hat, she ~ed** welch entzückender Hut, sagte sie überschwänglich

gusher ['gʌʃəʳ] N*(= oil well)* (natürlich sprudelnde) Ölquelle

gushing ['gʌʃɪŋ] ADJ **a** *water* sprudelnd, (heraus)schießend **b** *(fig)* überschwänglich; *talk* schwärmerisch, überschwänglich

gushingly ['gʌʃɪŋlɪ] ADV überschwänglich

gushy ['gʌʃɪ] ADJ *(pej inf)* schwärmerisch

gusset ['gʌsɪt] N *(in garment)* Keil *m*, Zwickel *m*

gust [gʌst] **N** *(of wind)* Stoß *m*, Bö(e) *f*; *(of rain)* Böe *f*; *(fig, of emotion)* Anfall *m*; **a ~ of cold/hot air** ein Schwall *m* kalte/heiße Luft; **a ~ of laughter** eine Lachsalve; **~s of up to 100 km/h** Böen von bis zu 100 km/h; **the wind was blowing in ~s** der Wind wehte böig *or* stürmisch **VI** böig *or* stürmisch wehen

gustatory ['gʌstətərɪ] ADJ*(form)* **~ sense** Geschmackssinn *m*

gustily ['gʌstɪlɪ] ADV böig, stürmisch

gusto ['gʌstəʊ] N Begeisterung *f*; **to do sth with ~** etw mit Genuss tun

gusty ['gʌstɪ] ADJ *(+er) wind, day, rain* böig, stürmisch

gut [gʌt] **N a** *(= alimentary canal)* Darm *m*; *(= stomach, paunch)* Bauch *m*
b *usu pl (inf: = stomach)* Eingeweide *nt*; *(fig) (= essence: of problem, matter)* Kern *m*; *(= contents)* Substanz *f*; **to slog** *or* **work one's ~s out** *(inf)* wie blöd schuften *(inf)*; **to spill one's ~s (to sb)** *(inf)* (jdm) sein Herz ausschütten; **to hate sb's ~s** *(inf)* jdn auf den Tod nicht ausstehen können *(inf)*; **I'll have his ~s for garters!** *(Brit inf)* den mache ich zur Minna *(inf)* *or* zur Schnecke *(inf)*; **~ reaction** Bauchentscheidung *f (inf)*; **my ~ feeling is that ...** rein gefühlsmäßig *or* so aus dem Bauch heraus *(inf)* würde ich sagen, dass ...; **to know sth at ~ level** etw instinktiv wissen
c guts PL *(inf: = courage)* Mumm *m (inf)*, Schneid *m (inf)*
d *(= catgut)* Darm *m*; *(for racket, violin)* Darmsaiten *pl*
VT a *animal, chicken, fish* ausnehmen
b *(fire)* ausbrennen; *(= remove contents)* ausräumen; **it was completely ~ted by the fire** es war völlig ausgebrannt → *also* **gutted**

gutless ['gʌtlɪs] ADJ *(fig inf)* feige

gutsy ['gʌtsɪ] ADJ *(inf)* **a** *(= plucky) person, action, effort* mutig, tapfer; *performance, approach* kämpferisch; **he is a ~ performer** er ist eine richtige Kämpfernatur **b** *(= powerful) food, wine* kräftig; *music* feurig; *lyrics* kraftvoll; *car, engine* kraftstrotzend

gutta-percha [ˌgʌtə'pɜːtʃə] N Guttapercha *f or nt*

gutted ['gʌtɪd] ADJ *(esp Brit inf: = disappointed)* am Boden (zerstört) *(inf)*; **I was ~** ich war total am Boden *(inf)*; **he was ~ by the news** die Nachricht machte ihn völlig fertig *(inf)*

gutter ['gʌtəʳ] **N** *(on roof)* Dachrinne *f*; *(in street)* Gosse *f (also fig)*, Rinnstein *m*; **to be born in the ~** aus der Gosse kommen; **the language of the ~** die Gassensprache **VI** *(candle, flame)* flackern

guttering ['gʌtərɪŋ] **N** Regenrinnen *pl* **ADJ** flackernd

gutter: **gutter press** N *(Brit pej)* Boulevardpresse *f*; **guttersnipe** N Gassenkind *nt*

guttural ['gʌtərəl] **N** Guttural(laut) *m*, Kehllaut *m* **ADJ** *voice, accent* guttural, kehlig; *(Phon) sound* guttural

guv [gʌv], **guv'nor** ['gʌvnəʳ] N *(Brit inf)* Chef *m (inf)*

guy[1] [gaɪ] **N a** *(inf: = man)* Typ *m (inf)*, Kerl *m (inf)*; **hey, you ~s** he Leute *(inf)*; **great ~s** dufte Typen *pl (inf)*; **I'll ask the ~ next door** ich werde (den Typ von) nebenan fragen *(inf)*; **are you ~s ready?** seid ihr fertig? **b** *(Brit: = effigy)* (Guy-Fawkes-)Puppe *f*; *(inf: = sight)* Schießbudenfigur *f (inf)*; **a penny for the ~** Geld *nt* für das (Guy Fawkes) Feuerwerk **VT** *(= ridicule)* sich lustig machen über *(+acc)*

guy[2] N *(also* **guy-rope***)* Haltetau *or* -seil *nt*; *(for tent)* Zeltschnur *f*

Guyana [gaɪ'ænə] N Guyana *nt (form)*, Guayana *nt*

Guyanese [ˌgaɪə'niːz] N Guayaner(in) *m(f)*

GUY FAWKES' NIGHT

In Großbritannien wird in der **Guy Fawkes' Night**, auch **Firework Night** oder **Bonfire Night** genannt, am 5. November an den **Gunpowder Plot** erinnert, einen misslungenen Attentatsversuch auf König James I. und das Parlament im Jahre 1605. Der Kopf der Verschwörer, Guy Fawkes, wurde damals auf frischer Tat ertappt, als er das Parlamentsgebäude in die Luft sprengen wollte, und später hingerichtet. In der **Guy Fawkes' Night** werden überall Feuerwerke und Freudenfeuer abgebrannt. Vor der **Guy Fawkes' Night** basteln Kinder eine Puppe, den **guy**, der dann im Freudenfeuer verbrannt wird. Wegen der Verletzungsgefahr bei privaten Feuerwerken erfreuen sich die spektakulären öffentlichen Veranstaltungen immer größerer Beliebtheit.

guzzle ['gʌzl] *(inf)* **VI** *(= eat)* futtern *(inf)*; *(= drink)* schlürfen **VT** *(= eat)* futtern *(inf)*; *(= drink)* schlürfen; *fuel* saufen *(inf)*

guzzler ['gʌzləʳ] N *(inf: = eater)* Fresser(in) *m(f) (inf pej)*; *(= drinker)* Säufer(in) *m(f) (inf pej)*

gym [dʒɪm] N **a** *(= gymnasium)* Turnhalle *f*; *(for working out)* Fitnesscenter *nt or* -studio *nt*; **to work out in the ~** Fitnesstraining machen **b** *(= gymnastics)* Turnen *nt*

gymkhana [dʒɪm'kɑːnə] N Reiterfest *nt*

gymnasium [dʒɪm'neɪzɪəm] N *pl* **-s** *or (form)* **gymnasia** [dʒɪm'neɪzɪə] Turnhalle *f*

gymnast ['dʒɪmnæst] N Turner(in) *m(f)*

gymnastic [dʒɪm'næstɪk] ADJ *ability, training* turnerisch; **~ exercises** Turnübungen

gymnastics [dʒɪm'næstɪks] N **a** *sing (= discipline)* Gymnastik *f no pl*; *(with apparatus)* Turnen *nt no pl* **b** *pl (= exercises)* Übungen *pl*; **verbal ~** Wortakrobatik *f*

gym: **gym shoe** N *(Brit)* Turnschuh *m*; **gymslip** N *(Brit)* Schulträgerrock *m*; **gym teacher** N Turnlehrer(in) *m(f)*

gynaecological, *(US)* **gynecological** [ˌgaɪnɪkəˈlɒdʒɪkəl] ADJ gynäkologisch; ~ **illness** Frauenleiden *nt*, gynäkologisches Leiden

gynaecologist, *(US)* **gynecologist** [ˌgaɪnɪˈkɒlədʒɪst] N Gynäkologe *m*, Gynäkologin *f*, Frauenarzt *m*/-ärztin *f*

gynaecology, *(US)* **gynecology** [ˌgaɪnɪˈkɒlədʒɪ] N Gynäkologie *f*, Frauenheilkunde *f*

gyp [dʒɪp] N **a** *(Brit inf, = swindle)* Gaunerei *f* *(inf)* **b** *(inf, = swindler)* Gauner(in) *m(f)* **c** *(Brit Univ inf)* Putzfrau *f* **d** *(Brit inf)* **to give sb** ~ jdn plagen *(inf)*

gyppo [ˈdʒɪpəʊ] N *(pej inf)* Zigeuner *m* *(neg!)*, Zigeunerin *f* *(neg!)*

gypsum [ˈdʒɪpsəm] N Gips *m*

gypsy [ˈdʒɪpsɪ] **N** Zigeuner(in) *m(f)* *(neg!)* **ADJ** **a** *(= Romany)* Zigeuner- *(neg!)*, Roma-; ~ **child** Zigeunerkind *nt* *(neg!)*; ~ **woman** Zigeunerin *f* *(neg!)*; ~ **camp** Zigeunerlager *nt* *(neg!)*; ~ **music** Zigeunermusik *f* **b** *(US, pej, = unofficial)* cab, *driver* illegal

gyrate [ˌdʒaɪəˈreɪt] VI *(= whirl)* (herum)wirbeln; *(= rotate)* sich drehen, kreisen; *(dancer)* sich drehen und winden

gyration [ˌdʒaɪəˈreɪʃən] N *(= whirling)* Wirbeln *nt no pl*; *(= rotation)* Drehung *f*, Kreisen *nt no pl*; *(of dancer)* Drehung und Windung *f usu pl*

gyratory [ˌdʒaɪəˈreɪtərɪ] ADJ *(= whirling)* wirbelnd; *(= revolving)* kreisend

gyrocompass [ˈdʒaɪərəʊˈkʌmpəs] N Kreiselmagnetkompass *m*

gyroscope [ˈdʒaɪərəˌskəʊp] N Gyroskop *nt*

gyroscopic [ˌdʒaɪərəʊˈskɒpɪk] ADJ gyroskopisch

H, **h** [eɪtʃ] N H *nt*, h *nt* → **drop**

H *abbr of* **hard** *(on pencil)* H

h *abbr of* **hour(s)** h

ha [hɑː] INTERJ ha

habeas corpus ['heɪbɪəs'kɔːpəs] N *(Jur)* Habeaskorpusakte *f*; **to file a writ of ~** einen Vorführungsbefehl erteilen; **the lawyer applied for a writ of ~** der Rechtsanwalt verlangte, dass sein Klient einem Untersuchungsrichter vorgeführt wurde

haberdasher ['hæbədæʃəʳ] N *(Brit)* Kurzwarenhändler(in) *m(f)*; *(US)* Herrenausstatter *m*; **to go to the ~'s** *(Brit)* zum Kurzwarengeschäft gehen; *(US)* zum Herrenmodengeschäft gehen

haberdashery [,hæbə'dæʃərɪ] N *(Brit: = articles)* Kurzwaren *pl*; *(= shop)* Kurzwarengeschäft *nt or* -handlung *f*; *(US: = articles)* Herrenbekleidung *f*, Herrenartikel *pl*; *(= shop)* Herrenmodengeschäft *nt*

habiliments [hə'bɪlɪmənts] PL *(form)* Ornat *nt (form)*

habit ['hæbɪt] N **a** Gewohnheit *f*; *(esp undesirable)* (An)gewohnheit *f*; **~ of mind** Denkweise *f*; **to be in the ~ of doing sth** die Angewohnheit haben, etw zu tun, etw gewöhnlich tun; **... as was his ~** ... wie es seine Gewohnheit war; **it became a ~** es wurde zur Gewohnheit; **out of (sheer) ~** aus (reiner) Gewohnheit, (rein) gewohnheitsmäßig; **his life was ruled by ~** sein Leben war von seinen Gewohnheiten bestimmt; **from (force of) ~** aus Gewohnheit; **she was a creature of ~** sie war ein Gewohnheitstier *(inf) or* Gewohnheitsmensch; **I don't make a ~ of inviting strangers in** (für) gewöhnlich bitte ich Fremde nicht herein; **don't make a ~ of it** lassen Sie (sich *dat*) das nicht zur Gewohnheit werden; **to get into/to get sb into the ~ of doing sth** sich/jdm angewöhnen, etw zu tun; **to get** *or* **fall into bad ~s** in schlechte Gewohnheiten verfallen; **to get out of/to get sb out of the ~ of doing sth** sich/jdm abgewöhnen, etw zu tun; **you must get out of the ~ of biting your nails** du musst dir das Nägelkauen abgewöhnen; **to have a ~ of doing sth** die Angewohnheit haben, etw zu tun; **he has a strange ~ of staring at you** er hat die merkwürdige Art, einen anzustarren; **history has a ~ of repeating itself** es kommt oft vor, dass die Geschichte sich wiederholt
b *(= addiction)* Sucht *f*; **to have a cocaine ~** kokainsüchtig sein
c *(= costume)* Gewand *nt*; *(esp monk's)* Habit *nt or m*; **(riding) ~** Reitkleid *nt*

habitable ['hæbɪtəbl] ADJ bewohnbar

habitat ['hæbɪtæt] N Heimat *f*; *(of animals also)* Lebensraum *m*

habitation [,hæbɪ'teɪʃən] N (Be)wohnen *nt*; *(= place)* Wohnstätte *f*, Behausung *f*; **to show signs of ~** bewohnt aussehen; **unfit for human ~** menschenunwürdig, für Wohnzwecke nicht geeignet

habit-forming ['hæbɪt,fɔːmɪŋ] ADJ **to be ~** zur Gewohnheit werden; **are those ~ drugs?** wird man davon abhängig?

habitual [hə'bɪtjʊəl] ADJ **a** *(= customary) smile, expression, behaviour, way, position* gewohnt; **he was smiling his ~ smile** er lächelte wie üblich; **his ~ guilty grin** das schuldbewusste Grinsen, das er sich angewöhnt hatte; **to become ~** zur Gewohnheit werden **b** *(= regular) smoker, drug user, drug use* gewohnheitsmäßig; *liar* notorisch; *joker, gossip* ewig; **~ criminal** Gewohnheitsverbrecher(in) *m(f)*; **~ offender** Gewohnheitstäter(in) *m(f)*; **~ drinker** Gewohnheitstrinker(in) *m(f)*

habitually [hə'bɪtjʊəlɪ] ADV ständig; *(= regularly)* regelmäßig; *drink, smoke* gewohnheitsmäßig

habituate [hə'bɪtjʊeɪt] VT gewöhnen *(sb to sth* jdn an etw *(acc)*, *sb to doing sth* jdn daran, etw *(acc)* zu tun); **to be ~d to sth** an etw *(acc)* gewöhnt sein

habitué [hə'bɪtjʊeɪ] N regelmäßiger Besucher, regelmäßige Besucherin, Habitué *m (geh, Aus)*; *(in pubs etc)* Stammgast *m*

hacienda [,hæsɪ'endə] N Hazienda *f*

hack¹ [hæk] **N** **a** *(= cut)* (Ein)schnitt *m*, Kerbe *f*; *(= action)* Hieb *m*; **to take a ~ at sth** mit der Axt *etc* auf etw *(acc)* schlagen; *(in rage)* auf etw *(acc)* einhacken
b *(= kick)* Tritt *m*; **he had a ~ at his opponent's ankle** er versetzte seinem Gegner einen Tritt gegen den Knöchel
c *(= cough)* trockener Husten
VT **a** *(= cut)* schlagen, hacken; **don't ~ your meat, cut it** du musst das Fleisch nicht hacken, sondern schneiden; **to ~ sb/sth to pieces** *(lit)* jdn/etw zerstückeln; *(fig)* jdn/etw zerfetzen; **he was brutally ~ed to death** er ist brutal (mit einem Beil *etc*) erschlagen worden; **to ~ one's way out** sich einen Weg frei schlagen; **to ~ one's way through (sth)** sich *(dat)* einen Weg (durch etw) schlagen, sich (durch etw) durchhauen
b *(Sport) ball* treten gegen, einen Tritt versetzen *(+dat)*; **to ~ sb on the shin** jdn vors *or* gegen das Schienbein treten
c *(inf: = cope)* **to ~ it** es bringen *(sl)*
VI **a** *(= chop)* hacken; **he ~ed (away) at the branch** er schlug auf den Ast; **don't ~ at it** hack nicht daran herum
b *(= cough)* trocken husten
c *(Sport)* **he was booked for ~ing** er wurde wegen Holzerei verwarnt
d *(Comput)* hacken; **to ~ into the system** in das System eindringen

▶ **hack about** VT *sep (esp Brit fig) text etc* zerstückeln

▶ **hack down** VT *sep bushes etc* abhacken; *people also* niedermetzeln; *tree* umhauen

▶ **hack off** VT *sep* **a** abhacken, abschlagen; **to hack sth off sth** etw von etw abhacken *or* abschlagen **b** *(inf: = annoy)* ankotzen *(sl)*; **I'm really hacked off with her** sie kotzt mich echt an *(sl)*

▶ **hack out** VT *sep clearing* schlagen; *hole* heraushacken

▶ **hack up** VT *sep* zerhacken; *meat, wood, furniture also* klein hacken; *bodies* zerstückeln

hack² **N** **a** *(= hired horse)* Mietpferd *nt*; *(= ride)* Ritt *m* **b** *(pej: = literary hack)* Schreiberling *m*; **the newspaper ~s** die Zeitungsschreiber *pl*; **paid ~** Lohn- *or* Soldschreiber(in) *m(f)* **c** *(pej inf)* **(party) ~** (Partei)heini *m (inf) or* -typ *m (inf)* **d** *(US: = taxi)* Taxi *nt* **ADJ** *attr (pej) writing* stumpfsinnig; **~ writer** Schreiberling *m* **VI** einen Spazierritt machen; **to go ~ing** ausreiten

hacker ['hækəʳ] N *(Comput)* Hacker(in) *m(f)*

hackie ['hækɪ] N *(US inf)* Taxifahrer(in) *m(f)*

hacking ['hækɪŋ] **ADJ** **~ cough** trockener Husten **N** *(Comput)* Hacken *nt*

hacking jacket N Sportsakko *m or nt*; *(for riding)* Reitjacke *f*

hackle ['hækl] N *(Orn)* lange Nackenfeder; *(= plumage also)* Nackengefieder *nt*; *(pl: of dog etc)* Fell *nt* im Nacken; **the dog's ~s rose** dem Hund sträubte sich das Fell; **his ~s rose at the very idea** bei dem bloßen Gedanken sträubte sich alles in ihm; **to get sb's ~s up, to raise sb's ~s** jdn reizen, jdn auf die Palme bringen *(inf)*

hackney carriage ['hæknɪ,kærɪdʒ] N *(horse-drawn)* (Pferde)droschke *f*; *(form: = taxi)* (Kraft)droschke *f (form)*

hackneyed ['hæknɪd] ADJ *(Brit) phrase, word, metaphor, theme* abgenutzt, abgedroschen *(inf)*; *photograph, image* stereotyp; **~ idea** Klischee *nt*, Klischeevorstellung *f*

hack: **hack pack** ['hækpæk] N *(pej)* Journalistenzunft *f*; **hacksaw** ['hæksɔː] N Metallsäge *f*; **hackwork** N *(= trivial writing)* Schmiererei *f (inf)*; *(= mindless editing)* Routinearbeit *f*

had [hæd] *pret, ptp of* **have**

haddock ['hædək] N Schellfisch *m*

Hades ['heɪdiːz] N *(Myth)* Hades *m*

hadn't ['hædnt] *contr of* **had not**

Hadrian ['heɪdrɪən] N **~'s Wall** Hadrianswall *m*

haematologist, *(US)* **hematologist** [,hiːmə'tɒlədʒɪst] N Hämatologe *m*, Hämatologin *f*

haematology, *(US)* **hematology** [,hiːmə'tɒlədʒɪ] N Hämatologie *f*

haematoma, *(US)* **hematoma** [,hiːmə'təʊmə] N *pl* **-mas** *or* **-mata** Hämatom *nt (spec)*, Bluterguss *m*

haemoglobin, *(US)* **hemoglobin** [,hiːməʊ'gləʊbɪn] N Hämoglobin *nt*, roter Blutfarbstoff

haemophilia, *(US)* **hemophilia** [,hiːməʊ'fɪlɪə] N Bluterkrankheit *f*, Hämophilie *f (spec)*

haemophiliac, *(US)* **hemophiliac** [,hiːməʊ'fɪlɪæk] N Bluter *m*

haemorrhage, *(US)* **hemorrhage** ['hemərɪdʒ] **N** Blutung *f*, Hämorrhagie *f (spec)*; *(fig, of talent, young people etc)* Exodus *m*, Abwanderung *f* **VI** bluten

haemorrhoids, *(US)* **hemorrhoids** ['hemərɔɪdz] PL Hämorr(ho)iden *pl*

hafnium ['hæfnɪəm] N *(Chem)* Hafnium *nt*

haft [hɑːft] N *(of knife)* Heft *nt*; *(of sword)* Griff *m*

hag [hæg] N Hexe *f*

haggard ['hægəd] ADJ ausgezehrt; *(from tiredness)* abgespannt; *(from worry)* abgehärmt, verhärmt; **he had a very ~ expression throughout the trial** er wirkte während der ganzen Verhandlung sehr mitgenommen

haggis ['hægɪs] N *schottisches Gericht aus gehackten Schafsinnereien und Hafer im Schafsmagen*

haggish ['hægɪʃ] ADJ zänkisch, garstig

haggle ['hægl] VI *(= bargain)* feilschen *(about or over* um); *(= argue also)* sich (herum)streiten (o-

ver um *or* wegen); **let's stop haggling over who's going to pay** hören wir doch auf mit dem Hin und Her (darüber), wer nun bezahlt

haggling [ˈhæglɪŋ] N Feilschen *nt*, Gefeilsche *nt*, Feilscherei *f*

hagiographer [ˌhægɪˈɒgrəfəˈ] N *(lit, fig)* Hagiograf(in) *m(f)*

hagiography [ˌhægɪˈɒgrəfɪ] N *(lit, fig)* Hagiografie *f*; *(lit also)* Heiligengeschichte *f*

hagiology [ˌhægɪˈɒlədʒɪ] N *(form)* Hagiologie *f* *(spec)*

hag-ridden [ˈhægrɪdn] ADJ *(= worried)* vergrämt, verhärmt; **to be ~** *(hum: = tormented by women)* unter Weiberherrschaft stehen

Hague [heɪg] N **the ~** Den Haag *nt*; **in the ~** in Den Haag; **the ~ Conventions** *(Pol)* die Haager Abkommen; **the ~ Tribunal** *(Pol)* der Internationale Gerichtshof

ha-ha [ˈhɑːˈhɑː] INTERJ ha, ha N *(= fence)* versenkter Grenzzaun

hail[1] [heɪl] N Hagel *m*; **a ~ of stones** ein Steinhagel *m*, ein Hagel von Steinen; **a ~ of blows** ein Hagel von Schlägen; **in a ~ of bullets** im Kugel- *or* Geschosshagel VI hageln

▸ **hail down** VI *(stones etc)* niederprasseln, niederhageln *(on sb/sth* auf jdn/etw); **blows hailed down (on him)** es hagelte Schläge (auf ihn nieder) VT *sep blows* niederprasseln lassen

hail[2] VT **a** *(= acclaim)* zujubeln *(+dat)*, bejubeln; **to ~ sb/sth as sth** jdn/etw als etw feiern
b *(= call loudly)* zurufen *(+dat)*; *ship* anrufen, preien *(spec)*; *taxi (by calling)* rufen; *(by making sign)* anhalten, (herbei)winken; **within ~ing distance** in Rufweite
VI **a ship ~ing from London** ein Schiff *nt* mit (dem) Heimathafen London; **where does that boat ~ from?** was ist der Heimathafen dieses Schiffs?; **they ~ from all parts of the world** sie kommen *or* stammen aus allen Teilen der Welt; **where do you ~ from?** wo stammen Sie her?
INTERJ *(obs, liter)* **~ (to) ...** sei gegrüßt, ... *(liter)*; **~ Caesar** heil dir Cäsar; **the Hail Mary** das Ave Maria
N (Zu)ruf *m*; **within ~** in Rufweite

hail-fellow-well-met [ˈheɪlfeləʊˌwelˈmet] ADJ plumpvertraulich; **he tries to be ~ with everyone** er versucht, sich bei allen anzubiedern

hail: **hailstone** N Hagelkorn *nt*; **hailstorm** N Hagel(schauer) *m*

hair [hɛəˈ] N **a** *(collective: on head)* Haare *pl*, Haar *nt*; **a fine head of ~** schönes volles Haar, schöne volle Haare; **to do one's ~** sich frisieren, sich *(dat)* die Haare (zurecht)machen *(inf)*; **to have one's ~ cut/done** sich *(dat)* die Haare schneiden/frisieren lassen; **her ~ always looks nice** sie ist immer sehr gut frisiert; **she usually wears her ~ up** *(in pony tail/bun)* sie trägt ihr Haar normalerweise in einem Pferdeschwanz/Knoten; **to let one's ~ down** *(lit)* sein Haar aufmachen *or* lösen *(geh)*; *(fig)* aus sich *(dat)* herausgehen; **keep your ~ on!** *(Brit inf)* ruhig Blut!; **to get in sb's ~** *(inf)* jdm auf den Wecker *or* auf die Nerven gehen *(inf)*; **I wish you'd get out of my ~ while I'm working** *(inf)* kannst du mich vielleicht in Ruhe lassen, während ich arbeite; **that film really made my ~ stand on end** bei dem Film lief es mir eiskalt den Rücken herunter
b *(= single hair)* Haar *nt*; **not a ~ on his head was harmed** *(fig)* ihm wurde kein Haar gekrümmt; **not a ~ out of place** *(fig)* wie aus dem Ei gepellt; **to win/lose by a ~** ganz knapp gewinnen/verlieren → **turn, split**
c *(= on body)* Haar *nt*, Haare *pl*; *(= total body hair)* Behaarung *f*; **body ~** Körperbehaarung *f*
d *(of animal, plant)* Haar *nt*; *(of pig)* Borste *f*; **I'm allergic to cat ~** ich bin gegen Katzenhaare allergisch; **the best cure for a hangover is the ~ of the dog (that bit you)** einen Kater kuriert man am besten, wenn man mit dem anfängt, womit man aufgehört hat
ATTR Haar-; *(= horsehair)* Rosshaar-; **~ growth** Haarwuchs *m*

hair: **hairball** N Haarknäuel *nt*; **hairband** N Haarband *nt*; **hairbrush** N Haarbürste *f*; **hair care** N Haarpflege *f*; **hair clip** N Clip *m*, Klipp *m*; *(for ponytail etc)* Haarspange *f*; **hair clippers** PL elektrische Haarschneidemaschine; **hair conditioner** N Pflegespülung *f*; **hair cream** N Haarcreme *f*, Pomade *f*; **hair curler** N Lockenwickler *m*; **haircut** N Haarschnitt *m*; *(= act also)* Haarschneiden *nt*; *(= hairdo)* Frisur *f*; **to have** *or* **get a ~** sich *(dat)* die Haare schneiden lassen; **I need a ~** ich muss zum Friseur, ich muss mir die Haare schneiden lassen; **hairdo** N *(inf)* Frisur *f*; **hairdresser** N Friseur *m*, Friseuse *f*; **the ~'s** der Friseur; **hairdressing** N Frisieren *nt*; *(= tonic)* Haarwasser *nt*; **hairdressing salon** N Friseursalon *m*; **hairdrier** N Haartrockner *m*; *(hand-held also)* Fön® *m*, Föhn *m*; *(over head also)* Trockenhaube *f*

-haired [ˈhɛəd] ADJ *suf* -haarig; **dark-/long-haired** dunkel-/langhaarig

hair: **hair extension** N Haarverlängerung *f*; **hair follicle** N Haarfollikel *nt*, Haarbalg *m*; **hair gel** N (Haar)gel *nt*; **hairgrip** N *(Brit)* Haarklemme *f*, Klemmchen *nt*

hairiness [ˈhɛərɪnɪs] N Behaartheit *f*; **is ~ a sign of virility?** ist starker Haarwuchs ein Zeichen von Männlichkeit?

hair: **hair lacquer** N Haarspray *m or nt*; **hairless** ADJ unbehaart; *plant* haarlos; **hairline** N **a** Haaransatz *m* **b** *(= thin line)* haarfeine Linie; *(in telescope, on sight)* Faden *m*; *(Typ)* senkrechter Strich; **~s** Fadenkreuz *nt*; **hairline crack** N Haarriss *m*; **hairline fracture** N Haarriss *m*; **hair loss** N Haarausfall *m*; **hairnet** N Haarnetz *nt*; **hair oil** N Haaröl *nt*; **hairpiece** N Haarteil *nt*; *(for men)* Toupet *nt*; **hairpin** N Haarnadel *f*; **hairpin (bend)** N Haarnadelkurve *f*; **hair-raiser** N *(inf: = experience)* haarsträubendes *or* entsetzliches Erlebnis; *(= film)* Horror- *or* Gruselfilm *m*, Schocker *m* *(inf)*; *(= story)* Grusel- *or* Horrorgeschichte *f*; **hair-raising** ADJ haarsträubend; **hair remover** N Haarentferner *m*, Haarentfernungsmittel *nt*; **hair restorer** N Haarwuchsmittel *nt*; **hair roller** N Lockenwickler *m*; **hair's breadth** N Haaresbreite *f*; **by a ~** um Haaresbreite; **to be within a ~ of ruin** am Rande des Ruins stehen; **he was within a ~ of winning** er hätte um ein Haar gewonnen; **to escape by a ~** mit knapper Not entkommen; **hair shirt** N härenes Gewand *(old, liter)*; *(fig)* Büßerhemd *nt*; **hair slide** N *(Brit)* Haarspange *f*; **hair space** N *(Typ)* Haarspatium *nt*; **hairsplitter** N Haarspalter *m*; **hairsplitting** N Haarspalterei *f* ADJ haarspalterisch; **hairspray** N Haarspray *m or nt*; **hairspring** N Spiralfeder *f*; **hairstyle** N Frisur *f*; **hair stylist** N Coiffeur *m*, Coiffeuse *f*, Haarkünstler(in) *m(f)*; **hair transplant** N Haartransplantation *f*; **hair trigger** N Stecher *m*

hairy [ˈhɛərɪ] ADJ *(+er)* **a** *person, body, plant, spider* behaart; *leg, arm, chest, armpits* haarig, behaart; *animal, coat* haarig; **she has very ~ armpits** sie hat viele Achselhaare **b** *(inf: = scary, risky)* haarig *(inf)*; *situation* brenzlig *(inf)*; *adventure* riskant; *driving* rasant *(inf)*

Haiti [ˈheɪtɪ] N Haiti *nt*

Haitian [ˈheɪʃɪən] ADJ haitianisch, haitisch N **a** Haitianer(in) *m(f)* **b** *(Ling)* Haitisch *nt*

hake [heɪk] N See- *or* Meerhecht *m*, Hechtdorsch *m*

halberd [ˈhælbəd] N Hellebarde *f*

halberdier [ˌhælbəˈdɪəˈ] N Hellebardier *m*

halcyon [ˈhælsɪən] ADJ **~ days** glückliche Tage *pl*

hale [heɪl] ADJ *(+er)* kräftig; *old man* rüstig; **~ and hearty** gesund und munter

half [hɑːf] N *pl* **halves** **a** Hälfte *f*; **two halves make a whole** zwei Halbe machen ein Ganzes; **the first ~ of the year** die erste Jahreshälfte; **to cut sth in ~** etw halbieren; *(with knife also)* etw in zwei Hälften *or* Teile schneiden; *salary etc* etw um *or* auf die Hälfte kürzen; **to break/tear sth in ~** etw durchbrechen/durchreißen; **~ of it/them** die Hälfte davon/von ihnen; **~ the book/money** die Hälfte des Buches/Geldes, das halbe Buch/Geld; **~ my life** die Hälfte meines Lebens, mein halbes Leben; **~ a million dollars** eine halbe Million Dollar; **he gave me ~** er gab mir die Hälfte; **~ a cup/an hour** eine halbe Tasse/Stunde; **~ a lifetime** ein halbes Leben; **he's not ~ the man he used to be** er ist längst nicht mehr das, was er einmal war; **~ a second!** (einen) Augenblick mal!; **I'll be round in ~ a second** *(inf)* ich komme gleich (mal) hin; **to listen with ~ an ear** nur mit halbem Ohr zuhören; **to take ~ of sth** die Hälfte von etw nehmen; **to go halves (with sb on sth)** (mit jdm mit etw) halbe-halbe machen *(inf)*; **that's only ~ the story** das ist nur die halbe Geschichte; **have ~ of my apple** willst du einen halben Apfel von mir haben?; **bigger by ~** anderthalbmal so groß; **to increase sth by ~** etw um die Hälfte vergrößern; **he is too clever by ~** *(Brit inf)* das ist ein richtiger Schlaumeier; **he's too cocky by ~** *(Brit inf)* er hält sich für wer weiß was *(inf)*; **one and a ~** eineinhalb, anderthalb; **an hour and a ~** eineinhalb *or* anderthalb Stunden; **he's two and a ~** er ist zweieinhalb; **he doesn't do things by halves** er macht keine halben Sachen; **~ and ~** halb und halb; **that's a hill and a ~!** *(inf)* das ist vielleicht ein Berg!; **that's not the ~ of it** *(inf)* **I haven't told you the ~ of it yet** *(inf)* und das ist noch nicht einmal die Hälfte *(inf)*
b *(Sport, of match)* (Spiel)hälfte *f*, Halbzeit *f*; *(= player)* Läufer(in) *m(f)*
c *(of ticket)* Abschnitt *m* der Fahrkarte; *(= travel, admission fee)* halbe Karte *(inf)*; **return ~** *(Brit)* Abschnitt *m* für die Rückfahrt; **two adults and one ~, please** zwei Erwachsene und ein Kind, bitte; **two and a ~ (to London)** zweieinhalb(mal London)
d *(= beer)* kleines Bier, Halbe *f (dial)*, Halbe(s) *nt*, Kleine(s) *nt*; *(Scot, = whisky)* einfacher Whisky, Einfache(r) *m*
e *(= husband etc)* **my better** *(hum) or* **other ~** meine bessere Hälfte
ADJ halb; **a ~ cup** eine halbe Tasse; **with ~ his usual strength** nur mit halber Kraft; **at** *or* **for ~ price** zum halben Preis; **~ one thing ~ another** halb und halb, halb das eine und halb das andere; **~ man ~ beast** halb Mensch, halb Tier; **it's neither opera nor operetta but sort of ~ and ~** es ist so ein Zwischending *nt* zwischen Oper und Operette
ADV **a** halb; **I ~ thought ...** ich hätte fast gedacht ...; **I was ~ afraid that ...** ich habe fast befürchtet, dass ...; **~ melted** halb geschmolzen; **the work is only ~ done** die Arbeit ist erst halb *or* zur Hälfte erledigt; **that's ~ right** das ist zur Hälfte richtig; **to be ~ asleep** *(= almost asleep)* schon fast schlafen; *(= very tired)* todmüde sein *(inf)*; **to be ~ awake** halb wach sein; **~ laughing, ~ crying** halb lachend, halb weinend; **~ laughing, ~ crying he told me ...** mit einem lachenden und einem weinenden Auge erzählte er mir ...; **he ~ rose to his feet** er erhob sich halb; **I ~ think that ...** ich habe beinahe den Eindruck, dass ...; **he only ~ understands** er begreift *or* versteht nur die Hälfte; **the book was ~ in German, ~ in English** das Buch war zur Hälfte auf Deutsch und zur Hälfte auf Englisch; **she's ~ German and ~ Russian** sie ist zur Hälfte Deutsche und zur Hälfte Russin
b *(Brit inf)* **he's not ~ stupid/rich** *etc* er ist vielleicht *or* unheimlich dumm/reich *etc*; **it didn't ~ rain** es HAT vielleicht geregnet; **not ~ bad** gar nicht schlecht; **not ~!** und wie! und ob!
c it's ~ past three *or* **~ three** es ist halb vier
d he is ~ as big as his sister er ist halb so groß wie seine Schwester; **~ as big again** anderthalbmal so groß; **he earns ~ as much as you** er verdient halb so viel wie Sie; **he earns ~ as much again as you** er verdient die Hälfte mehr als du *or* anderthalbmal so viel wie du; **give me ~ as much again** gib mir noch die Hälfte dazu

half: **half-a-crown** N = **half-crown**; **half-a-dozen** N = **half-dozen**; **half-arsed**, *(US)*

half-assed ADJ *(vulgar)* bescheuert *(inf)*; *(= incompetent)* unfähig; **halfback** N *(Sport)* Läufer(in) *m(f)*; **half-baked** ADJ *(fig) person, plan, idea* unausgegoren; **half-binding** N *(of book)* Halbband *m*; **half board** N Halbpension *f*; **half bottle** N kleine Flasche; **a ~ of wine** eine kleine Flasche Wein; **half-bred** ADJ = **half-breed** ADJ; **half-breed** N **a** *(dated: = person)* Mischling *m*; *(esp Native American)* Halbblut *nt* **b** *(= animal)* Rassenmischung *f*; *(= horse)* Halbblut *nt*, Halbblüter *m* ADJ **a** *animal* gekreuzt; **~ horse** Halbblut *nt*; **a ~ dog** eine Mischrasse, eine Rassenmischung **b** **a ~ child** *(dated)* ein Mischlingskind *nt*; **a ~ Indian** *(dated)* ein Halbblutindianer *m*; **half-brother** N Halbbruder *m*; **half-caste** *(dated)* N Mischling *m*; *(esp Native American)* Halbblut *nt* ADJ Mischlings-; *(esp Native American)* Halbblut-; **a ~ child** ein Mischlingskind *nt*; *(Native American)* ein Halbblut *nt*; **a ~ American** ein amerikanischer Mischling; **half-circle** N Halbkreis *m*; **half-closed** ADJ halb geschlossen; **half-cock** N **to go off at ~** *(inf)* ein Reinfall sein *(inf)*, ein Schuss in den Ofen sein *(inf)*; **half-cocked** ADJ *pistol* in Vorderraststellung; **to go off ~** *(fig inf: person)* voreilig handeln, einfach drauflosmachen *(inf)*; **half-cooked** ADJ halb gar; **half-cracked** ADJ *(esp Brit inf: = crazy)* beknackt *(sl)*, bescheuert *(inf)*; **half-crown** N *(in old Brit system)* Half Crown *f*, Zweieinhalbschillingstück *nt*; **half-cup brassière** N Büstenhalter *m* mit Halbschalen; **half-cut** ADJ *(Brit inf: = drunk)* besoffen *(inf)*; **half-day** N *(= holiday)* halber freier Tag; **we've got a ~** wir haben einen halben Tag frei; **half-dead** ADJ *(lit, fig)* halb tot *(with* vor *+dat)*; **half-dollar** N halber Dollar; **half-dozen** N halbes Dutzend; **half-dressed** ADJ halb bekleidet; **half-empty** ADJ halb leer VT zur Hälfte leeren *or* leer machen; **half face** N *(in painting, photography)* Profil *nt*; **half-fare** N halber Fahrpreis ADV zum halben Preis; **half-fill** VT halb füllen; **half-forgotten** ADJ fast vergessen; **half-frame camera** N Halbformatkamera *f*; **half-full** ADJ halb voll; **half-hearted** ADJ halbherzig; *attempt also* lustlos; *manner* lustlos, lau; **he was rather ~ about accepting** er nahm ohne rechte Lust an; **he seems ~ about it** er scheint sich dafür nicht so recht begeistern zu können; **half-heartedly** ADV *agree* halben Herzens, mit halbem Herzen; **to do sth ~** etw ohne rechte Überzeugung *or* Lust tun; **half-heartedness** N Halbherzigkeit *f*, Lustlosigkeit *f*; **the ~ of his attempts** seine halbherzigen *or* lustlosen Versuche *pl*; **half holiday** N *(Brit)* halber Urlaubstag; *(= public holiday)* halber Feiertag; **we've got a ~ tomorrow morning** wir haben morgen Vormittag frei; **half-hour** N halbe Stunde; **half-an-hour's** *or* **a ~ interval** eine halbstündige Pause, eine halbe Stunde Pause; **it strikes (on) the ~** sie schlägt die halben Stunden; **half-hourly** ADV jede *or* alle halbe Stunde, halbstündlich ADJ halbstündlich; **half landing** N Treppenabsatz *m*; **half-length** ADJ **~ portrait** Brustbild *nt*; **half-life** N *(Phys)* Halbwertszeit *f*; **half-light** N Dämmerlicht *nt*, Halbdunkel *nt*; **half-mast** N **at ~** *(also hum)* (auf) halbmast; **with his trousers at ~** *(Brit: = too short)* mit Hochwasserhosen; **half measure** N halbe Maßnahme, Stehenbleiben *nt no pl* auf halbem Weg; **we don't do things by ~s** wir machen keine halben Sachen, wir begnügen uns nicht mit Halbheiten; **half-monthly** ADJ zweiwöchentlich, vierzehntäglich; *publication* zweimal im Monat erscheinend ADV zweimal im Monat; **half-moon** N **a** Halbmond *m* **b** *(of fingernails)* Mond *m*; **half-naked** ADJ halb nackt; **half nelson** N *(Wrestling)* Nelson *m*, einfacher Nackenheber; **to have sb in a ~** einen Nelson bei jdm ansetzen; **half-note** N *(US Mus)* halbe Note; **half-open** ADJ halb offen VT halb öffnen *or* aufmachen; **half-pay** N halber Lohn; *(of salaried employee)* halbes Gehalt; **to be on ~** den halben Lohn/das halbe Gehalt bekommen; **to go on ~** auf halben Lohn/halbes Gehalt gesetzt werden; **halfpence** ['hɑːfpens] N halber Penny; **halfpenny** ['heɪpnɪ] *(Brit old)* N halber Penny, Halfpenny *m* ATTR Halfpenny-; **~ stamp/coin** Halfpennymarke/-münze *f*; **half-pint** N **a** ≈ Viertelliter *m or nt*; *(of beer)* kleines Bier **b** *(inf, = person)* halbe Portion *(inf)*, Knirps *m (inf)*; **half-pipe** N *(Sport)* Halfpipe *f*; **half-price** ADJ zum halben Preis; **to be ~** die Hälfte kosten, um die Hälfte reduziert sein; **~ electricity** Strom *m* zum halben Preis ADV *drink, stay* zum halben Preis; **half-rest** N *(US Mus)* halbe Pause; **half seas over** ADJ *(dated inf)* bezecht, leicht hinüber *(inf)*; **half-serious** ADJ **I was only ~ about it** ich habe das nicht ganz ernst gemeint; **actually, I was ~ about it** ich habe das nicht nur im Scherz gesagt; **half-sister** N Halbschwester *f*; **half-size** N Zwischengröße *f* ADJ halb so groß; **~ desk** kleiner Schreibtisch; **a ~ model of sth** ein Modell *nt* von etw in halber Größe; **half term** N *(Brit)* Ferien *pl* in der Mitte des Trimesters; **we get three days at ~** wir haben drei Tage Ferien in der Mitte des Trimesters; **half-timbered** ADJ Fachwerk-; **~ building/house** Fachwerkbau *m*/-haus *nt*; **half-timbering** N Fachwerkbauweise *f*; **half-time** N **a** *(Sport)* Halbzeit *f*; **at ~** bei *or* zur Halbzeit **b** *(Ind)* **to be on/to be put on ~** auf Kurzarbeit sein/gesetzt werden ATTR Halbzeit-, zur Halbzeit; **~ whistle/score** Halbzeitpfiff *m*/-stand *m* ADV **to work ~** halbtags arbeiten *or* beschäftigt sein; **half-title** N Schmutztitel *m*; **halftone** N *(Art, Phot, US Mus)* Halbton *m*; *(Phot: = process)* Halbtonverfahren *nt*; *(= picture)* Halbtonbild *nt*; **halftone screen** N *(Typ)* Raster *m*; **half-track** N *(= vehicle)* Halbkettenfahrzeug *nt*; **half-truth** N Halbwahrheit *f*; **half volley** N *(Tennis)* Halfvolley *m*, Halbflugball *m*; **half-volley** VT *(Tennis) ball* als Halfvolley schlagen

halfway ['hɑːfweɪ] ADJ *attr measures* halb; **at the ~ stage of the Tour de France** in der Mitte der Tour de France; **when we reached the ~ stage** *or* **point on our journey** als wir die Hälfte der Reise hinter uns *(dat)* hatten; **he was at the ~ stage in his musical career** er befand sich in der Mitte seiner musikalischen Karriere; **we're past the ~ stage** wir haben die Hälfte geschafft ADV **her hair reached ~ down her back** die Haare gingen ihr bis weit über die Schultern; **~ to** auf halbem Weg nach; **we drove ~ to London** wir fuhren die halbe Strecke *or* den halben Weg nach London; **~ between two points** (in der Mitte *or* genau) zwischen zwei Punkten; **I live ~ up the hill** ich wohne auf halber Höhe des Berges; **we went ~ up the hill** wir gingen den Berg halb hinauf; **~ through a book** halb durch ein Buch (durch); **she dropped out ~ through the race** nach der Hälfte des Rennens gab sie auf; **to go ~** *(lit)* die halbe Strecke *or* die Hälfte des Weges zurücklegen; **he went ~ round the world to find her** er reiste um die halbe Welt, um sie zu finden; **this money will go ~ toward(s) the cost of the car** diese Summe wird die Hälfte der Kosten für das Auto decken; **to meet sb ~** *(lit, fig)* jdm (auf halbem Weg) entgegenkommen; **~ decent** halbwegs anständig

halfway house N Gasthaus *nt* auf halbem Weg; *(= hostel)* offene Anstalt; *(fig)* Zwischending *nt*; **we could stop off at the King's Head, that's a ~** wir können im „King's Head" einkehren, das liegt auf halbem Wege; **it is a ~ between democracy and …** das ist ein Zwischending zwischen Demokratie und …; *(non-temporal)* es nimmt eine Zwischenstellung zwischen Demokratie und … ein

half: **halfwit** N Schwachsinnige(r) *mf*; *(fig)* Schwachkopf *m*; **halfwitted** ADJ schwachsinnig; **half-year** N Halbjahr *nt*; **half-yearly** ADJ halbjährlich ADV halbjährlich, jedes halbe Jahr

halibut ['hælɪbət] N Heilbutt *m*

halitosis [ˌhælɪ'təʊsɪs] N schlechter Mundgeruch

hall [hɔːl] N **a** *(= entrance hall of house)* Diele *f*, Korridor *m* **b** *(= large building)* Halle *f*; *(= large room)* Saal *m*; *(Brit: of college)* Speisesaal *m*; *(Brit: = college mealtime)* Essen *nt*; *(= dance hall)* Tanzdiele *f*; *(= village hall)* Gemeindehalle *f*, Gemeindehaus *nt*; *(= school assembly hall)* Aula *f*; **he will join the ~ of fame of …** *(fig)* er wird in die Geschichte des … eingehen, er wird in die Ruhmeshalle des … aufgenommen *(liter)* **c** *(= mansion)* Herrensitz *m*, Herrenhaus *nt*; *(Brit: = students' residence: also* **hall of residence***)* Studenten(wohn)heim *nt*; **to live** *or* **be in ~** *(Brit)* im Wohnheim wohnen; **Ruskin ~** Haus Ruskin *nt* **d** *(US: = corridor)* Korridor *m*, Gang *m*

hallelujah [ˌhælɪ'luːjə] INTERJ halleluja N Halleluja *nt*

hallmark ['hɔːlmɑːk] N **a** *(on gold, silver)* (Feingehalts)stempel *m*, Repunze *f* **b** *(fig)* Kennzeichen *nt (of +gen*, für); **a ~ of good quality** ein Gütesiegel *nt*; **this is the ~ of a true genius** daran erkennt man das wahre Genie VT *gold, silver* stempeln; **to be ~ed by sth** *(fig)* durch etw gekennzeichnet sein

hallo [hə'ləʊ] INTERJ, N = **hello**

halloo [hə'luː] INTERJ hallo; *(Hunt)* horrido, hallo N Halloruf *m*; *(Hunt)* Horrido *nt*, Hallo *nt* VI (hallo) rufen; *(Hunt)* die Hunde hetzen

hallow ['hæləʊ] VT heiligen; *(= consecrate)* weihen

hallowed ['hæləʊd] ADJ geheiligt; **~ traditions** geheiligte Traditionen *pl*; **on ~ ground** auf heiligem Boden; **~ be Thy name** *(Bibl)* geheiligt werde Dein Name

Halloween, **Hallowe'en** [ˌhæləʊ'iːn] N der Tag vor Allerheiligen, Halloween *nt*

> **HALLOWEEN**
>
> **Halloween** wird in der Nacht vor Allerheiligen, am 31. Oktober, gefeiert. Früher glaubte man, dass in dieser Nacht die Seelen der Toten in ihre ehemaligen Häuser zurückkehrten, doch heutzutage ist **Halloween** ein willkommener Anlass zu feiern und Schabernack zu treiben. Kinder verkleiden sich (traditionellerweise als Hexen und Gespenster) und basteln sich Laternen aus ausgehöhlten Rüben und Kürbissen, in die Kerzen gestellt werden. Sie ziehen dann von Tür zu Tür und sammeln bei Freunden und Nachbarn Süßigkeiten und Geld ein. Der Spruch dabei ist **trick or treat**, d. h., die Kinder drohen damit, dem Hausbesitzer einen Streich **(trick)** zu spielen, wenn sie kein Geschenk **(treat)**, normalerweise Süßigkeiten, bekommen. Außerdem werden jede Menge Halloween-Partys – auch für Erwachsene – veranstaltet, bei denen man kostümiert erscheint.

hall: **hall porter** N Portier *m*; **hall stand** N (Flur)garderobe *f*; *(tree-like)* Garderobenständer *m*

hallucinate [hə'luːsɪneɪt] VI halluzinieren, Wahnvorstellungen haben

hallucination [həˌluːsɪ'neɪʃən] N **a** Halluzination *f*, Wahnvorstellung *f* **b** *(inf: = false idea)* Wahnvorstellung *f*

hallucinatory [hə'luːsɪnətərɪ] ADJ *drug* Halluzinationen hervorrufend *attr*, halluzinogen *(spec)*; *state, effect, vision, experience* halluzinatorisch

hallucinogenic [həˌluːsɪnə'dʒenɪk] ADJ Halluzinationen hervorrufend *attr*, halluzinogen *(spec)*; **LSD is ~** LSD ist ein Halluzinogen *nt*

hallway ['hɔːlweɪ] N Flur *m*, Korridor *m*

halo ['heɪləʊ] N *pl* **-(e)s** *(of saint, fig iro)* Heiligenschein *m*; *(Astron)* Hof *m*, Halo *m (spec)*; **his ~ slipped** er büßte seinen Heiligenschein ein VT *(fig)* umrahmen

halogen ['hæləʊdʒɪn] N Halogen *nt*

halogen lamp N Halogenlampe *f*; *(Aut)* Halogenscheinwerfer *m*

halt[1] [hɔːlt] N **a** *(= stop)* Pause *f*; *(Mil)* Halt *m*; *(in production)* Stopp *m*; **to come to a ~** zum Stillstand kommen; **to bring sth to a ~** etw

zum Stillstand bringen; **the officer called a ~** der Offizier ließ haltmachen; **the referee called a ~** der Schiedsrichter pfiff ab; **shall we call a ~ now, gentlemen?** wollen wir jetzt Schluss machen, meine Herren?; **to call a ~ to sth** einer Sache *(dat)* ein Ende machen *or* bereiten; **he called a ~ to the discussion** er beendete die Diskussion; **the government called for a ~ to the fighting** die Regierung verlangte die Einstellung der Kämpfe
b *(= small station)* Haltepunkt *m*
VI zum Stillstand kommen; *(person)* anhalten, stehen bleiben; *(Mil)* haltmachen; **he was going to call her back but then ~ed** er wollte sie zurückrufen, aber hielt dann inne; **we ~ed briefly before attempting the summit** wir hielten kurz an *or* machten kurz halt, bevor wir den Gipfel in Angriff nahmen
VT zum Stillstand bringen; *fighting* einstellen; *arms race, war* beenden; *troops* haltmachen lassen; **bad light ~ed play** das Spiel wurde wegen der schlechten Lichtverhältnisse abgebrochen
INTERJ halt; *(traffic sign)* stop

halt² **VI** *(obs)* hinken; *(in speech)* stockend sprechen **N** *(Bibl)* **the ~ and the lame** die Krummen und die Lahmen

halter¹ [ˈhɔːltəˈ] **N** **a** *(horse's)* Halfter *nt* **b** *(for hanging)* Schlinge *f*

halter² **N** *(esp US Tex, also* **halter top***)* Neckholder-Top *nt*

halterneck [ˈhɒltənek] **N** = **halter²** **ADJ** rückenfrei mit Nackenverschluss

halting [ˈhɔːltɪŋ] **ADJ** *voice, efforts, steps, answer* zögernd; *speech, performance, progress* stockend; *French, German, verse* holprig; **their steps toward(s) reform are ~** sie machen nur zögernde Schritte zur Reform

haltingly [ˈhɔːltɪŋlɪ] **ADV** zögernd; *speak, progress* stockend

halt sign **N** *(Aut)* Stoppschild *nt*

halve [hɑːv] **VT** **a** *(= separate in two)* halbieren **b** *(= reduce by one half)* auf die Hälfte reduzieren, halbieren

halves [hɑːvz] *pl of* **half**

halyard [ˈhæljəd] **N** *(Naut)* Fall *nt*; *(for flag)* Flaggleine *f*

ham [hæm] **N** **a** *(Cook)* Schinken *m*; **~ sandwich** Schinkenbrot *nt* **b** *(Anat)* **~s** (hintere) Oberschenkel *pl*; *(of animal)* (Hinter)keulen *pl*; **to squat on one's ~s** hocken, in der Hocke sitzen **c** *(Theat)* Schmierenkomödiant(in) *m(f)* **d** *(Rad inf)* Funkamateur(in) *m(f)* **ADJ** *attr acting* übertrieben, zu dick aufgetragen; **~ actor** Schmierenkomödiant(in) *m(f)* **VI** *(Theat)* chargieren, übertrieben spielen

▶ **ham up** **VT** *sep (inf)* übertreiben; **to ham it up** zu dick auftragen

hamburger [ˈhæm,bɜːgəˈ] **N** Hamburger *m*

ham-fisted [,hæmˈfɪstɪd], **ham-handed** [,hæmˈhændɪd] **ADJ** ungeschickt; *efforts, person also* tollpatschig *(inf)*

Hamitic [hæˈmɪtɪk] **ADJ** hamitisch

hamlet [ˈhæmlɪt] **N** Weiler *m*, kleines Dorf

hammer [ˈhæməˈ] **N** *(generally)* Hammer *m*; *(of gun)* Hahn *m*; **to go at it ~ and tongs** *(inf)* sich ins Zeug legen *(inf)*, sich reinhängen *(sl)*; *(= work also)* schuften, dass die Fetzen fliegen *(inf)*; *(= quarrel)* sich in die Wolle kriegen *(inf)*, sich streiten, dass die Fetzen fliegen; *(= have sex)* es miteinander machen *(inf)*; **to go/come under the ~** *(at auction)* unter den Hammer kommen; **throwing the ~** *(Sport)* Hammerwerfen *nt*; **in the ~** *(Sport)* im Hammerwurf
VT **a** *nail, metal* hämmern; **to ~ a nail into a wall** einen Nagel in die Wand schlagen; **to ~ sth into shape** *(metal)* etw zurechthämmern; *(fig) agreement* etw ausarbeiten; **to ~ sth into sb** *or* **into sb's head** *(inf)* jdm etw einbläuen *(inf)*
b *(inf: = defeat badly)* eine Schlappe beibringen *+dat (inf)*; **Chelsea were ~ed 6-1** Chelsea musste eine 6:1-Schlappe einstecken *(inf)*
c *(St Ex sl) stockbroker* für zahlungsunfähig erklären
d *(inf: = criticize)* kritisieren, attackieren
e *(inf: = harm)* **small businesses have been ~ed by the recession** kleine Firmen sind von der Rezession schwer in Mitleidenschaft gezogen worden
VI hämmern; **to ~ on the door** an die Tür hämmern; **my heart was ~ing** mein Herz pochte wild

▶ **hammer away** **VI** (darauflos)hämmern; **to hammer away at an issue** sich *(dat)* über eine Frage den Kopf zerbrechen; **the politicians were hammering away at each other** die Politiker hackten aufeinander herum; **his heart was hammering away** sein Herz pochte wild; **the pianist hammered away at the keys** der Pianist hämmerte auf die Tasten

▶ **hammer down** **VT** *sep* festhämmern; *nail, door* einschlagen; *bump* flach hämmern

▶ **hammer home** **VT** *sep* **a** *nail* fest hineinschlagen **b** *argument, point etc* Nachdruck verleihen *(+dat)*, untermauern; **he tried to hammer it home to the pupils that ...** er versuchte, den Schülern einzubläuen *or* einzuhämmern, dass...

▶ **hammer in** **VT** *sep* **a** *nail etc* einschlagen, einhämmern **b** *(fig) fact* einhämmern, einbläuen *(inf)*

▶ **hammer out** **VT** *sep* **a** *metal* hämmern; *nail, bricks* (her)ausschlagen *or* -klopfen; *dent* ausbeulen **b** *(fig) plan, agreement, solution* ausarbeiten, aushandeln; *difficulties* beseitigen, bereinigen; *verse* schmieden; *tune* hämmern

hammer and sickle **N** *sing* Hammer und Sichel *pl*

hammer: **hammer beam** **N** Stichbalken *m*; **hammer drill** **N** Schlagbohrmaschine *f*

hammered **ADJ** *(Brit inf: = drunk)* besoffen *(inf)*, hacke *(inf)*

hammerhead [ˈhæməhed] **N** *(= shark)* Hammerhai *m*; *(of hammer)* Hammerkopf *m*

hammering [ˈhæmərɪŋ] **N** *(esp Brit)* **a** Hämmern *nt*, Klopfen *nt* **b** *(inf: = defeat)* Schlappe *f (inf)*; **our team took a ~** unsere Mannschaft musste eine Schlappe einstecken *(inf)* **c** *(inf: = criticism)* scharfe Kritik; **doctors took a terrible ~ in the report** die Ärzteschaft wurden in dem Bericht scharf unter Beschuss genommen *(inf)*

hammertoe [ˈhæmə,təʊ] **N** Hammerzehe *f or* -zeh *m*

hammock [ˈhæmək] **N** Hängematte *f*

hammy [ˈhæmɪ] **ADJ** *(+er) (inf) actor* übertrieben spielend; *acting* übertrieben

hamper¹ [ˈhæmpəˈ] **N** *(esp Brit) (= basket)* Korb *m*; *(as present)* Geschenkkorb *m*

hamper² **VT** behindern; *movement also* erschweren; *person also* Schwierigkeiten bereiten *(+dat)*; **to be ~ed (by sth)** (durch etw) gehandikapt sein; **the police were ~ed in their search by the shortage of clues** der Mangel an Hinweisen erschwerte der Polizei die Suche

hamster [ˈhæmstəˈ] **N** Hamster *m*

hamstring [ˈhæmstrɪŋ] *vb: pret, ptp* **hamstrung** [ˈhæmstrʌŋ] **N** *(Anat)* Kniesehne *f*; *(of animal)* Achillessehne *f* **VT** **a** *(lit) person, animal* die Kniesehne/Achillessehne durchschneiden *(+dat)* **b** *(fig) attempt etc* vereiteln, unterbinden; *person* handlungsunfähig machen; **to be hamstrung** aufgeschmissen sein *(inf)*; *(project)* lahmgelegt sein, lahmliegen

hand [hænd]

⊙ 26.2, 26.3

1 NOUN	3 PHRASAL VERBS
2 TRANSITIVE VERB	

1 – NOUN

a Hand *f*; *(of clock)* Zeiger *m*; **on (one's) hands and knees** auf allen vieren; **to take/lead sb by the hand** jdn an die *or* bei der Hand nehmen/an der Hand führen; **hand in hand** Hand in Hand; **to go hand in hand with sth** mit etw einhergehen *or* Hand in Hand gehen; **these symptoms often go hand in hand** diese Symptome treten oft gleichzeitig auf; **hands up!** Hände hoch!; *(Sch)* meldet euch!; **hands up who knows the answer/who wants to go** Hand hoch, wer es weiß/wer gehen will; **hands off!** *(inf)* Hände weg!; **keep your hands off my wife** lass die Finger *or* Pfoten *(inf)* von meiner Frau!; **done** *or* **made by hand** handgearbeitet; **this sweater was knitted by hand** dieser Pullover ist handgestrickt; **to deliver a letter by hand** einen Brief persönlich überbringen; **"by hand"** „durch Boten"; **to raise an animal by hand** ein Tier von Hand *or* mit der Flasche aufziehen; **pistol in hand** mit vorgehaltener Pistole, mit der Pistole in der Hand; **to climb hand over hand** Hand über Hand klettern; **to live (from) hand to mouth** von der Hand in den Mund leben; **with a heavy/firm hand** *(fig)* mit harter/fester *or* starker Hand; **to get one's hands dirty** *(fig)* sich *(dat)* die Hände schmutzig machen; **to give with one hand and take away with the other** mit einer Hand geben, mit der anderen nehmen; **it's a case of the right hand not knowing what the left hand's doing** das ist so ein Fall, wo die rechte Hand nicht weiß, was die linke tut; **we're forced to do it with one hand** *or* **both hands** *or* **our hands tied behind our back** *(fig)* wir sind gezwungen, es zu tun, während uns die Hände gebunden sind → **hold, shake**

b = side Seite *f*; **on the right hand** auf der rechten Seite, rechts, rechter Hand; **on my right hand** rechts von mir, zu meiner Rechten *(geh)*; **on every hand, on all hands** auf allen Seiten, ringsum(her); **on the one hand ... on the other hand ...** einerseits *or* auf der einen Seite ..., andererseits *or* auf der anderen Seite ...

c = agency, possession **it's the hand of God/fate** das ist die Hand Gottes/des Schicksals; **your future is in your own hands** Sie haben Ihre Zukunft (selbst) in der Hand; **to take one's life in one's hands** sein Leben selbst in die Hand nehmen; **to put sth into sb's hands** jdm etw in die Hand geben, etw in jds Hände legen; **he put the matter in the hands of his lawyer** er übergab die Sache seinem Anwalt; **to leave sb in sb's hands** jdn in jds Obhut lassen; **to leave sth in sb's hands** jdm etw überlassen; **to put oneself in(to) sb's hands** sich jdm anvertrauen, sich in jds Hände begeben *(geh)*; **my life is in your hands** mein Leben ist *or* liegt in Ihren Händen; **to fall into the hands of sb** jdm in die Hände fallen; **to fall into the wrong hands** in die falschen Hände geraten; **to be in good hands** in guten Händen sein; **to change hands** den Besitzer wechseln; **I received some pretty rough treatment at her hands** ich bin von ihr ganz schön grob behandelt worden; **he suffered terribly at the hands of the enemy** er machte in den Händen des Feindes Schreckliches durch; **he has too much time on his hands** er hat zu viel Zeit zur Verfügung; **he has a problem/five children on his hands** er hat ein Problem/fünf Kinder am Hals *(inf)*; **it's no fun having three noisy children on your hands** es macht keinen Spaß, drei laute Kinder am Hals zu haben *(inf)*; **we've got a fight on our hands** wir haben einen harten Kampf vor uns; **I've got enough on my hands already** ich habe ohnehin schon alle Hände voll zu tun, ich habe schon genug um die Ohren *(inf) or* am Hals *(inf)*; **she read everything she could get her hands on** sie las alles, was sie in die Finger bekommen konnte; **just wait till I get my hands on him!** warte nur, bis ich ihn zwischen die Finger kriege! *(inf)*; **to get sb/sth off one's hands** jdn/etw loswerden; **to take sb/sth off sb's hands** jdm jdn/etw abnehmen; **goods left on our hands** *(Comm)* nicht abgesetzte Waren → **die¹ VI a, change VT a, free ADJ a**

d = applause Applaus *m*, Beifall *m*; **they gave him a big hand** sie gaben ihm großen Applaus, sie klatschten ihm großen Beifall; **let's give our guest a big hand** und nun großen Beifall für unseren Gast

c [= worker] Arbeitskraft *f*, Arbeiter(in) *m(f)*; *(Naut)* Besatzungsmitglied *nt*; **to take on hands** Leute einstellen; *(Naut)* Leute anheuern; **hands** Leute *pl*, Belegschaft *f*; **(ship's) hands** Besatzung *f*, Mannschaft *f*; **all hands on deck!** alle Mann an Deck!; **lost with all hands** mit der ganzen Besatzung untergegangen

f [= expert] **to be an old hand (at sth)** ein alter Hase (in etw *dat*) sein; **he is an experienced hand at that** er hat viel Erfahrung darin → **dab[2]**

g [= handwriting] Handschrift *f*; **it is written in his own hand** es ist in seiner Handschrift geschrieben

h [= measure] *of horse* ≈ 10 cm

i [Cards] Blatt *nt*; *(= person)* Mann *m*; *(= game)* Runde *f*; **3 hands** *(= people)* 3 Mann; **a hand of bridge** eine Runde Bridge; **to show one's hand** seine Karten aufdecken; *(fig)* sich *(dat)* in die Karten sehen lassen

j [other phrases] **to ask for a lady's hand (in marriage)** um die Hand einer Dame anhalten; **to have one's hands full with sb/sth** mit jdm/etw alle Hände voll zu tun haben; **to wait on sb hand and foot** jdn von vorne und hinten bedienen; **to have a hand in sth** *(in decision)* an etw *(dat)* beteiligt sein; *in crime* die Hand bei etw im Spiel haben; **I had no hand in it** ich hatte damit nichts zu tun; **to take a hand in sth** an etw *(dat)* teilnehmen, sich an etw *(dat)* beteiligen; **to keep one's hand in** in Übung bleiben; **to lend** *or* **give sb a hand** jdm behilflich sein, jdm zur Hand gehen; **give me a hand!** hilf mir mal!; **to give sb a hand up** jdm hochhelfen; **give me a hand down** helfen Sie mir mal herunter; **to force sb's hand** jdn zwingen, auf jdn Druck ausüben; **he never does a hand's turn** er rührt keinen Finger, er macht keinen Finger krumm; **to be hand in glove with sb** mit jdm unter einer Decke stecken, mit jdm gemeinsame Sache machen; **to win hands down** mühelos *or* spielend gewinnen; **to stay one's hand** abwarten; **to have the upper hand** die Oberhand behalten; **to get** *or* **gain the upper hand (of sb)** (über jdn) die Oberhand gewinnen; **he is making money hand over fist** er scheffelt das Geld nur so; **we're losing money hand over fist** wir verlieren massenweise Geld; **the inflation rate is rising hand over fist** die Inflationsrate steigt rasend schnell

♦ **at + hand** **to keep sth at hand** etw in Reichweite haben; **according to the information at hand** gemäß *or* laut der vorhandenen *or* vorliegenden Informationen; **it's quite close at hand** es ist ganz in der Nähe; **summer/Christmas is (close) at hand** der Sommer/Weihnachten steht vor der Tür, es ist bald Sommer/Weihnachten; **at first/second hand** aus erster/zweiter Hand → *also* **(c)**

♦ **in + hand** **he had the situation well in hand** er hatte die Situation im Griff; **she took the child in hand** sie nahm die Erziehung des Kindes in die Hand; **to take sb in hand** *(= discipline)* jdn in die Hand nehmen; *(= look after)* jdn in Obhut nehmen, nach jdm sehen; **stock in hand** *(Comm)* Warenlager *nt*; **what stock have you in hand?** welche Waren haben Sie am Lager?; **he still had £600/a couple of hours in hand** er hatte £ 600 übrig/noch zwei Stunden Zeit; **the matter in hand** die vorliegende *or* *(in discussion)* die zur Debatte stehende Angelegenheit; **work in hand** Arbeit, die zurzeit erledigt wird; **we've got a lot of work in hand** wir haben viel Arbeit anstehen *or* zu erledigen; **a matter/project is in hand** eine Sache/ein Projekt ist in Bearbeitung; **we still have a game in hand** wir haben noch ein Spiel ausstehen; **to put sth in hand** zusehen, dass etw erledigt wird → *also* **(a, c, g)**

♦ **on + hand** **according to the information on hand** gemäß *or* laut der vorhandenen *or* vorliegenden Informationen; **we have little information on hand** wir haben kaum Informationen *pl* (zur Verfügung) → *also* **(a, b, c)**

♦ **out + hand** **to eat out of sb's hand** *(lit, fig)* jdm aus der Hand fressen; **the children got out of hand** die Kinder waren nicht mehr zu bändigen *or* gerieten außer Rand und Band; **the horse got out of hand** er hat/ich habe *etc* die Kontrolle über das Pferd verloren; **the party got out of hand** die Party ist ausgeartet; **things got out of hand** die Dinge sind außer Kontrolle geraten; **I dismissed the idea out of hand** ich verwarf die Idee sofort

♦ **to + hand** **I don't have the letter to hand** ich habe den Brief gerade nicht zur Hand; **your letter has come to hand** *(Comm)* wir haben Ihren Brief erhalten; **he seized the first weapon to hand** er ergriff die erstbeste Waffe; **we have little information to hand** wir haben kaum Informationen *pl* (zur Verfügung) → **palm[2]**, **cash**

2 – TRANSITIVE VERB

(= give) reichen, geben *(sth to sb, sb sth* jdm etw); **he handed the lady into/out of the carriage** er half der Dame in die/aus der Kutsche; **you've got to hand it to him** *(fig inf)* das muss man ihm lassen *(inf)*

3 – PHRASAL VERBS

► **hand (a)round** VT *sep* herumreichen; *bottle also* herumgehen lassen; *(= distribute) papers* austeilen, verteilen

► **hand back** VT *sep* zurückgeben

► **hand down** VT *sep* **a** *(lit)* herunterreichen *or* -geben (*to sb* jdm) **b** *(fig)* weitergeben; *tradition, belief* überliefern, weitergeben; *heirloom etc* vererben (*to* +*dat*); *clothes* vererben *(inf)* (*to* +*dat*); *story (from sb to sb)* überliefern (*to* an +*acc*), weitergeben (*to* an +*acc*); **the farm's been handed down from generation to generation** der Hof ist durch die Generationen weitervererbt worden; **all his clothes were handed down from his elder brothers** er musste die Kleidung seiner älteren Brüder auftragen **c** *(Jur) sentence* fällen

► **hand in** VT *sep* abgeben; *forms, thesis also, resignation* einreichen

► **hand off** VT *sep (Rugby)* (mit der Hand) wegstoßen

► **hand on** VT *sep* weitergeben (*to* an +*acc*)

► **hand out** VT *sep* austeilen, verteilen (*to sb* an jdn); *advice* geben, erteilen (*to sb* jdm); *heavy sentence* verhängen, austeilen; **the Spanish boxer was really handing it out** *(inf)* der spanische Boxer hat wirklich ganz schön zugeschlagen *or* ausgeteilt *(inf)*

► **hand over** VT *sep (= pass over)* (herüber)reichen (*to dat*); *(= hand on)* weitergeben (*to* an +*acc*); *(= give up)* (her)geben (*to dat*); *(to third party)* (ab)geben (*to dat*); *criminal, prisoner* übergeben (*to dat*); *(from one state to another)* ausliefern; *leadership, authority, powers* abgeben, abtreten (*to* an +*acc*); *the controls, property, business* übergeben (*to dat*, an +*acc*); **hand over that gun!** Waffe her!; **I now hand you over to our political correspondent** ich gebe nun weiter *or* übergebe nun an unseren (politischen) Korrespondenten; **to hand oneself over to the police/authorities** sich der Polizei/den Behörden ergeben
VI **when the Conservatives handed over to Labour** als die Konservativen die Regierung an Labour abgaben; **when the chairman handed over to his successor** als der Vorsitzende das Amt an seinen Nachfolger abgab; **I now hand over to our sports correspondent** ich übergebe nun an unseren Sportberichterstatter; **he handed over to the co-pilot** er übergab an den Kopiloten

► **hand up** VT *sep* hinaufreichen

---

hand: **handbag** N Handtasche *f*; **hand baggage** N Handgepäck *nt*; **handball** N **a** *(= game)* Handball *m* **b** *(Ftbl: = foul)* Handspiel *nt*, Hand *f* INTERJ *(Ftbl)* Hand; **handbarrow** N Schubkarre *f*; **hand basin** N Handwaschbecken *nt*; **handbell** N Schelle *f*, Glocke *f* (mit Stiel); **handbill** N Flugblatt *nt*, Handzettel *m*; **handbook** N Handbuch *nt*; *(tourist's)* Reiseführer *m*; **handbrake** N *(esp Brit)* Handbremse *f*; **handbrake turn** N *(Aut)* **to do a ~** durch Anziehen der Handbremse wenden; **handbreadth** N Handbreit *f*

h & c *abbr of* **hot and cold (water)** k.u.w., kalt und warm

hand: **handcar** N *(Rail)* Draisine *f*, Dräsine *f*; **handcart** N Handwagen *m*; **handclasp** N *(US)* Händedruck *m*; **hand controls** PL *(Aut)* Handbedienung *f*; **handcuff** VT Handschellen anlegen (+*dat*); **he ~ed himself to the railings** er machte sich mit Handschellen am Geländer fest; **to be ~ed** Handschellen angelegt bekommen; **the accused was ~ed to a police officer** der Angeklagte war (mit Handschellen) an einen Polizisten gefesselt; **handcuffs** PL Handschellen *pl*; **handdrier** N Händetrockner *m*

-hander [-hændəʳ] SUFF *(esp Brit: Theat, TV)* **a two-/three-hander** ein Zwei-/Dreipersonenstück *nt*

hand-eye coordination [ˈhændaɪkəʊˌɔːdɪˈneɪʃən] N visuell-motorische Koordination *f*

handfeed [ˈhændˌfiːd] *pret, ptp* **handfed** [ˈhændˌfed] VT *animal* mit der Flasche aufziehen

handful [ˈhændfʊl] N **a** Hand *f* voll; *(of hair, fur)* Büschel *nt*; **a ~ of soil** eine Handvoll Erde; **by the ~, in ~s** händeweise; *(hair, fur)* büschelweise **b** *(= small number)* Hand *f* voll **c** *(fig)* **those children are a ~** die Kinder können einen ganz schön in Trab halten; **his new girl's quite a ~** *(hum)* an seiner neuen Freundin ist ganz hübsch was dran *(inf)*

hand: **hand grenade** N Handgranate *f*; **handgrip** N (Hand)griff *m*; *(= handshake)* Händedruck *m*; **handgun** N Handfeuerwaffe *f*; **hand-held** ADJ *device, computer* im Taschenformat; **taken with a ~ camera** aus der (freien) Hand aufgenommen Handheld *nt*; **handhold** N Halt *m*

handicap [ˈhændɪkæp] N **a** *(Sport)* Handicap *nt*, Handikap *nt*, Vorgabe *f*; *(= race)* Handicaprennen *nt*; **a ~ of 5lbs** eine (Gewichts)vorgabe *or* ein Handicap von 5 Pfund **b** *(= disadvantage)* Handicap *nt*; *(physical, mental)* Behinderung *f*; **to be under a great ~** sehr im Nachteil sein, stark gehandicapt sein VT ein Handicap *nt* darstellen für; *chances* beeinträchtigen; *(fig) person* benachteiligen; **he has always been ~ped by his accent** sein Akzent war immer ein Nachteil *m* für ihn; **to be (physically/mentally) ~ped** (körperlich/geistig) behindert sein; **~ped children** behinderte Kinder *pl*

handicraft [ˈhændɪkrɑːft] N **a** *(= work)* Kunsthandwerk *nt*; *(= needlework etc)* Handarbeit *f*; *(= woodwork, modelling etc)* Werken *nt*, Bastelarbeit *f*; **~s** *(= products)* Kunstgewerbe *nt* **b** *(= skill)* Geschick *nt*, Handfertigkeit *f*, Geschicklichkeit *f*

handily [ˈhændɪlɪ] ADV **a** *situated* günstig **b** *(US: = easily) win* mit Leichtigkeit

handiness [ˈhændɪnɪs] N **a** *(= skill)* Geschick *nt*, Geschicklichkeit *f* **b** *(= nearness, accessibility: of shops etc)* günstige Lage **c** *(= convenience, usefulness: of tool, car etc)* Nützlichkeit *f*; *(= easiness to handle)* Handlichkeit *f*

handiwork [ˈhændɪwɜːk] N *no pl* **a** *(lit)* Arbeit *f*; *(Sch: = subject)* Werken *nt*; *(= needlework etc)* Handarbeit *f*; **examples of the children's ~** Werkarbeiten/Handarbeiten *pl* der Kinder; **to do ~** werken, handarbeiten; *(at home)* basteln **b** *(fig)* Werk *nt*; *(pej)* Machwerk *nt*; **that looks like the ~ of the Gillies gang** das sieht ganz nach der Gillies-Bande aus

handjob N *(vulg sl)* **to give sb a ~** jdm einen runterholen *(vulg sl)*

handkerchief [ˈhæŋkətʃɪf] N Taschentuch *nt*

hand-knitted [ˈhændˌnɪtɪd] ADJ handgestrickt

handle [ˈhændl] N **a** Griff *m*; *(of door)* Klinke *f*, Griff *m*; *(esp of broom, saucepan)* Stiel *m*; *(esp of basket, bucket, casserole, cup, jug etc)* Henkel *m*; *(of handbag)* Griff *m*, Bügel *m*; *(of pump)* Schwengel *m*; *(of car: = starting handle)* (Anlass- *or* Start)kurbel *f*; **to fly off the ~** *(inf)* an die Decke gehen *(inf)*; **to have/get a ~ on sth** *(inf)* etw im Griff haben/in den Griff bekommen **b** *(fig, = pretext)* Handhabe *f*

c *(inf)* Titel *m*; **to have a ~ to one's name** ein „von und zu" sein *(inf)*

VT a *(= touch, use hands on)* anfassen, berühren; *(Ftbl) ball* mit der Hand berühren; **be careful how you ~ that** gehen Sie vorsichtig damit um; **please do not ~ the goods** Waren bitte nicht berühren; **"handle with care"** „Vorsicht - zerbrechlich"; „Vorsicht Glas/Blumen" *etc*

b *(= deal with) person, animal, plant, tool, weapon, machine, words, numbers, money etc* umgehen mit; *economy* handhaben; *legal or financial matters* erledigen; *legal case* handhaben, bearbeiten; *applicant, matter, problem* sich befassen mit; *material for essay etc* bearbeiten, verarbeiten; *(= tackle) problem, interview etc* anfassen, anpacken; *(= succeed in coping with) child, drunk, situation, problem, emergency* fertig werden mit; *(= resolve) matter* erledigen; *(= control) vehicle, plane, ship* steuern; **how would you ~ the situation?** wie würden Sie sich in der Situation verhalten?; **you have to ~ this situation very carefully** in dieser Situation müssen Sie sehr behutsam vorgehen; **you didn't ~ the situation very well** du bist mit der Situation nicht gut fertig geworden; **you have to ~ these people very carefully** Sie müssen mit diesen Leuten sehr vorsichtig umgehen; **a car that is easy to ~** ein Auto, das leicht zu fahren *or* zu steuern ist; **I can't ~ pressure** ich komme unter Druck nicht zurecht; **six children are too much for one woman to ~** mit sechs Kindern kann eine Frau allein nicht fertig werden; **there's a salesman at the door – I'll ~ him** ein Vertreter ist an der Tür – ich werde ihn abfertigen; **you keep quiet, I'll ~ this** sei still, lass mich mal machen; **the accused decided to ~ his own defence** *(Brit) or* **defense** *(US)* der Angeklagte beschloss, seine eigene Verteidigung zu übernehmen; **who's handling the publicity for this?** wer macht die Öffentlichkeitsarbeit dafür?; **could you ~ these interviews for me?** könnten Sie diese Interviews für mich machen?

c *(Comm) types of goods, items* handeln mit *or* in *(+dat)*; *orders* bearbeiten; *prescriptions* ausführen; *shares, securities* handeln; *financial affairs* besorgen; **airport workers refused to ~ goods for Uganda** die Flughafenarbeiter weigerten sich, Waren nach Uganda abzufertigen; **we ~ tax problems for several big companies** wir bearbeiten die Steuerangelegenheiten mehrerer großer Firmen; **the millionaire has several secretaries to ~ his business** der Millionär hat mehrere Sekretäre, die seine Geschäfte für ihn führen; **this department ~s all the export business** diese Abteilung bearbeitet den gesamten Export

VI *(ship, plane)* sich steuern lassen; *(car, motorbike)* sich fahren *or* lenken lassen; *(gun)* sich handhaben lassen; **how does the car ~?** wie fährt sich der Wagen?

VR he ~s himself well in a fight er kann sich in einer Schlägerei behaupten; **they observed how the applicant ~d himself** sie beobachteten, wie der Bewerber sich verhielt

handlebar moustache N Schnauzbart *m*, Schnäuzer *m (inf)*

handlebar(s) ['hændlbɑː', -bɑːz] N(PL) Lenkstange *f*

handler ['hændlə'] N *(= dog-handler)* Hundeführer(in) *m(f)*; **baggage ~** Gepäckmann *m*

handling ['hændlɪŋ] N **a** *(= touching)* Berühren *nt*

b *(of plant, animal, matter, problem)* Behandlung *f* (of +*gen*); *(of person, patient etc)* Umgang *m* (of mit), Behandlung *f* (of +*gen*); *(of vehicle, plane, ship, drug, explosive)* Umgang *m* (of mit); *(of tool, weapon, machine)* Umgang *m* (of mit), Handhabung *f*; *(of writer's material)* Verarbeitung *f*, Bearbeitung *f*; *(of legal or financial matters)* Erledigung *f*; *(= official handling of matters, of legal case)* Bearbeitung *f*; **his adroit ~ of the car/troops** sein geschickter Umgang mit dem Auto/den Truppen; **her adroit ~ of the economy** ihre geschickte Handhabung der Wirtschaft; **the policeman's tactful ~ of the drunk/crowd** das taktvolle Verhalten des Polizisten gegenüber dem Betrunkenen/der Menge; **his ~ of the matter/situation** die Art, wie er die Angelegenheit/die Situation angefasst hat; **his successful ~ of the crisis/task** seine Bewältigung der Krise/der Aufgabe; **his expert ~ of the deal** sein Geschick beim Abschluss des Geschäfts; **toxic waste requires very careful ~** mit Giftmüll muss sehr vorsichtig umgegangen werden; **this package needs careful ~** dieses Paket muss vorsichtig behandelt werden; **these goods were damaged in ~** *(Comm)* diese Waren wurden beschädigt

c *(of vehicle)* **what's its ~ like?** wie fährt es sich?; **a car not renowned for its easy ~** ein Auto, das sich nicht gerade durch leichte Lenkung auszeichnet

handling charge N *(= management fee)* Bearbeitungsgebühr *f*; *(in warehouse)* Umladekosten *pl*; *(in banking)* Kontoführungsgebühren *pl*

hand: **hand loom** N Handwebstuhl *m*; **hand-loom weaver** Handweber(in) *m(f)*; **hand-loom weaving** Handweben *nt*; **hand lotion** N Handlotion *f*; **hand luggage** N *(Brit)* Handgepäck *nt*; **handmade** ADJ handgearbeitet; **this is ~** das ist Handarbeit; **handmaid** N *(obs)* Zofe *f (old)*; *(Bibl)* Magd *f*; **hand-me-down** *(inf)* **N** abgelegtes Kleidungsstück **ADJ** *clothes* abgelegt; *piano, books* geerbt *(hum)*; **hand mirror** N Handspiegel *m*; **hand-off** N *(Rugby)* Wegstoß(en *nt*) *m* (mit der Hand); **hand-operated** ADJ von Hand bedient *or* betätigt, handbedient, handbetrieben; **hand-out** N *(= money)* Unterstützung *f*, (Geld)zuwendung *f*; *(= food)* Essensspende *f*; *(= leaflet)* Flugblatt *nt*; *(with several pages)* Broschüre *f*; *(in school)* Arbeitsblatt *nt*; *(= publicity hand-out)* Reklamezettel *m*; **budget ~** Zuwendung *f or* Geschenk *nt* aus dem Etat; **handover** N *(Pol)* Übergabe *f*; **~ of power** Machtübergabe *f*; **hand-picked** ADJ *(lit)* von Hand geerntet, handverlesen; *(fig) successor, team, staff* sorgfältig ausgewählt, handverlesen *(hum)*; **hand puppet** N *(US)* = **glove puppet**; **handrail** N *(of stairs etc)* Geländer *nt*; *(of ship)* Reling *f*; *(for bath etc)* Haltegriff *m*; **handsaw** N Handsäge *f*, Fuchsschwanz *m*; **handset** **N** *(Telec)* Hörer *m* **VT** *(Typ)* (von Hand) setzen

hands-free ['hændz'friː] ADJ *car phone etc* Freisprech-; **~ phone** Freisprecheinrichtung *f*; **~ kit** Freisprechset *nt or* -anlage *f*

handshake ['hændʃeɪk] N **a** Händedruck *m* **b** *(Comput)* Handshake *m*, Quittungsaustausch *m*

handshaking ['hændʃeɪkɪŋ] N Händeschütteln *nt*

hands-off ['hændz'ɒf] ADJ *approach etc* passiv; **a ~ manager** ein Geschäftsführer, der die Zügel gern locker lässt; **they have a ~ policy/attitude** sie lassen die Zügel gern locker

handsome ['hænsəm] ADJ **a** *(= good-looking) man, woman* gut aussehend; *(= well-built)* stattlich; *face, features* attraktiv; *animal, building, place, furniture* schön; *(= elegant)* elegant; *(= imposing)* stattlich, imposant; **he is ~/has a ~ face** er sieht gut aus; **~ is as ~ does** *(Prov)* edel ist, wer edel handelt **b** *(= large) profit, return, increase, salary* ansehnlich; *reward* großzügig; *sum* stolz, stattlich; *win, victory* deutlich, entscheidend; **a ~ 57 per cent** ansehnliche 57 Prozent; **to win a ~ victory** überlegen gewinnen

handsomely ['hænsəmlɪ] ADV **a** *(= attractively) produced, bound, printed, dressed* schön **b** *(= generously) pay* großzügig; *reward, profit* reichlich; *(= convincingly) win* überlegen; **this strategy has paid off ~** diese Strategie hat sich voll ausgezahlt

handsomeness ['hænsəmnɪs] N **a** *(= good looks)* gutes Aussehen; *(of animal, thing)* Schönheit *f*; *(= elegance)* Eleganz *f*; *(= imposing nature)* Stattlichkeit *f* **b** *(= generosity, of profit, return, increase, salary)* Ansehnlichkeit *f*; *(of reward)* Großzügigkeit *f*

hands-on ['hændz'ɒn] ADJ *experience, approach etc* aktiv; *exhibit* interaktiv; **a ~ manager** ein Geschäftsführer, der die Zügel gern fest in der Hand hält; **they have a ~ policy/attitude** sie halten die Zügel fest in der Hand

hand: **handspring** N (Handstand)überschlag *m*; **handstand** N Handstand *m*; **to do a ~** (einen) Handstand machen; **hand-stitched** ADJ handgenäht; **hand-to-hand** **ADV** im Nahkampf, Mann gegen Mann **ADJ** **~ fight/fighting** Nahkampf *m*; **hand-to-mouth** ADJ *existence* kümmerlich, armselig; **to lead a ~ existence, to exist on a ~ basis** von der Hand in den Mund leben; **hand towel** N Händehandtuch *nt*; **handwork** N Handarbeit *f*; **hand-woven** ADJ handgewebt; **handwriting** N Handschrift *f*; **handwritten** ADJ handgeschrieben, von Hand geschrieben

handy ['hændɪ] ADJ *(+er)* **a** *(= useful, convenient) tool, device* praktisch; *hint, tip* nützlich, praktisch; *car, size* handlich; **to come in ~** sich als nützlich erweisen; **that key will come in ~** den Schlüssel wirst du noch gut gebrauchen können; **the salary increase comes in ~** die Gehaltserhöhung kommt sehr gelegen; **my experience as a teacher comes in ~** meine Lehrerfahrung kommt mir zugute; **a ~ way to do sth** eine praktische Art, etw zu tun; **this is a ~ way to take notes** auf diese Art kann man leicht *or* gut Notizen machen

b *(= skilful)* geschickt; **he's ~ around the home** *or* **house** er ist ein geschickter Heimwerker; **to be ~ with a tool** mit einem Werkzeug gut umgehen können

c *(= conveniently close)* in der Nähe; **the house is (very) ~ for the shops** das Haus liegt (ganz) in der Nähe der Geschäfte; **to keep** *or* **have sth ~** etw griffbereit *or* zur Hand haben

handyman ['hændɪmæn] N *pl* **-men** [-mən] *(= servant)* Faktotum *nt*, Mädchen *nt* für alles *(inf)*; *(= in DIY)* Bastler *m*, Heimwerker *m*; *(as job)* Hilfskraft *f*; **I'm not much of a ~** ich bin kein großer Bastler, Basteln ist nicht gerade meine Stärke

handywoman ['hændɪwʊmən] N *pl* **-women** [-wɪmɪn] *(in DIY)* Bastlerin *f*, Heimwerkerin *f*; *(as job)* Hilfskraft *f*

hang [hæŋ] *vb: pret, ptp* **hung** **VT a** hängen; *painting, curtains, decorations, clothes* aufhängen; *door, gate* einhängen; *(Cook) game* abhängen lassen; **to ~ wallpaper** tapezieren; **to ~ sth from sth** etw an etw *(dat)* aufhängen; **to ~ sth on a hook** etw an einen Haken hängen; **to ~ clothes on the line** Wäsche auf die Leine hängen

b the rooms of the castle were hung with priceless pictures kostbare Gemälde hingen in den Räumen des Schlosses; **the walls were hung with tapestries** die Wände waren mit Gobelins behängt; **they hung the windows/streets with bunting** sie schmückten die Fenster/Straßen mit Fahnen

c to ~ one's head den Kopf hängen lassen

d to ~ fire *(lit: guns)* das Feuer einstellen; *(fig, people)* zögern; **I think we should ~ fire a little longer** *(fig)* ich glaube, wir sollten noch etwas (zu)warten

e *pret, ptp* **hanged** *criminal* hängen, aufhängen, henken *(form)*; **hung, drawn and quartered** gehängt, gestreckt und gevierteilt; **to ~ oneself** sich erhängen *or* aufhängen *(inf)*

f *(inf)* **~ him!** zum Kuckuck mit ihm *(inf)*; **(I'm) ~ed if I will ...** den Teufel werd ich ... *(inf)*; **(I'm) ~ed if I know** weiß der Henker *(inf)*; **~ it!** so ein Mist *(inf)*, verflixt (noch mal) *(inf)*; **~ the cost!** ist doch piepegal, was es kostet *(inf)*

VI a *(curtains, painting)* hängen (on an +*dat*, from von); *(drapery, clothes, hair)* fallen; *(inelegantly)* (herunter)hängen; *(pheasant etc)* abhängen

b *(gloom, fog etc)* hängen (over über +*dat*); **to ~ in the air** *(fig)* in der Schwebe sein; **the question was left ~ing in the air** die Frage blieb im Raum stehen; **the hawk hung motionless in the sky** der Falke stand bewegungslos in der Luft; **time ~s heavy on my hands** die Zeit wird mir sehr lang; **the constant threat of unemployment ~s over us** *or* **our heads** über uns hängt die ständige Angst vor der Arbeitslosigkeit → *also* **balance N a**

c *(criminal)* gehängt werden, hängen; **to be sentenced to ~** zum Tod durch Erhängen verurteilt werden

d **it/he can go ~!** *(inf)* es/er kann mir gestohlen bleiben *(inf)*; **how's it ~ing?** *(US sl)* wie gehts, wie stehts?

N a *(of drapery)* Fall *m*; *(of suit)* Sitz *m*

b *no pl (inf)* **to get the ~ of sth** den (richtigen) Dreh bei etw herauskriegen *or* -finden *(inf)*; **to get the ~ of doing sth** den Dreh herausbekommen, wie man etw macht *(inf)*

▶ **hang about** *(Brit) or* **around VI a** *(inf: = wait)* warten; *(= loiter)* sich herumtreiben *(inf)*, herumlungern; **to keep sb hanging around** jdn warten lassen; **to hang around with sb** sich mit jdm herumtreiben *(inf)*; **he got sick of hanging around waiting for me** er hatte die Nase voll davon, auf mich zu warten *(inf)*; **we just hung around together** *(Brit)* wir haben einfach nur zusammen rumgegammelt *(inf) or* gechillt *(sl)*

b *(Brit inf: = hold on)* warten; **hang about, I'm just coming** wart mal, ich komm ja schon; **now hang about, I didn't say that** Moment mal, das habe ich nicht gesagt *(inf)*

c *(inf)* **this car doesn't hang around** das Auto zieht ganz schön ab *(inf)*; **he doesn't hang around** *(= move quickly)* er ist einer von der schnellen Truppe *(inf)*

VI *+prep obj* **to hang around sb** um jdn herumstreichen; **to hang around a place** sich an einem Ort herumtreiben *(inf)*, an einem Ort herumlungern

▶ **hang back VI** *(lit)* sich zurückhalten; *(fig: = hesitate)* zögern; **one little boy was hanging back** ein kleiner Junge hielt sich immer im Hintergrund; **don't hang back, go and ask her** worauf wartest du denn, frag sie doch; **they hung back on closing the deal** sie zögerten, das Geschäft abzuschließen

▶ **hang behind VI** zurückbleiben; *(= dawdle)* (hinterher)bummeln *or* -trödeln

▶ **hang down VI** herunterhängen **VT** *sep* herunterhängen lassen

▶ **hang in VI** *(inf)* **just hang in there!** bleib am Ball *(inf)*

▶ **hang on VI a** *(= hold)* sich festhalten, sich festklammern *(to sth* an etw *dat)*; **to hang on by one's fingernails** *or* **fingertips (to sth)** sich (an etw *dat*) festkrallen

b *(= hold out)* durchhalten; *(Telec)* am Apparat bleiben; *(inf: = wait)* warten; **hang on (a minute)** wart mal, einen Augenblick (mal); **hang on tight, we're off!** festhalten, es geht los!; **Liverpool hung on to win the match** Liverpool konnte seine Führung verteidigen und gewann das Spiel

VI *+prep obj* **a to hang on sb's arm** an jds Arm *(dat)* hängen; **he hangs on her every word** er hängt an ihren Lippen

b *(= depend on)* **everything hangs on his decision/getting the cash** alles hängt von seiner Entscheidung ab/davon ab, ob man das Geld bekommt

▶ **hang on to VI** *+prep obj* **a** *(lit: = hold on to)* festhalten; *(fig) hope* sich klammern an *(+acc)*; *ideas* festhalten an *(+dat)* **b** *(= keep)* behalten; **to hang on to power** sich an die Macht klammern; **to hang on to one's lead** seine Führung verteidigen; **could you hang on to my seat until I get back?** können Sie mir den Platz so lange frei halten, bis ich zurück bin?

▶ **hang out VI a** *(tongue, shirt tails etc)* heraushängen **b** *(inf)* sich aufhalten; *(= live)* hausen, wohnen; *(= usually be found also)* sich herumtreiben *(inf)*, zu finden sein; **let's just hang out tonight** lass(t) uns heute Abend einfach mal chillen*(inf)* **c** *(= resist, endure)* nicht aufgeben; **they hung out for more pay** sie hielten an ihrer Lohnforderung fest **d** *(inf)* **to let it all hang out** die Sau rauslassen *(inf)*; **come on now, let it all hang out** lass jucken *(sl)*, und ab geht die Post *(inf)* **VT** *sep* hinaushängen; *washing also* (draußen) aufhängen; **to hang sb out to dry** *(inf)* jdn seinem Schicksal überlassen

▶ **hang over VI** *(= continue)* andauern

▶ **hang together VI** *(people)* zusammenhalten; *(argument, ideas)* folgerichtig *or* zusammenhängend sein; *(alibi)* keinen Widerspruch aufweisen *or* enthalten; *(story, report etc)* zusammenhängen; *(statements)* zusammenpassen, keine Widersprüche *pl* aufweisen

▶ **hang up VI** *(Telec)* auflegen, aufhängen; **he hung up on me** er legte einfach auf **VT** *sep hat, picture* aufhängen; *telephone receiver* auflegen, aufhängen; **Keegan announced he was hanging up his boots for good** Keegan erklärte, dass er die Fußballschuhe an den Nagel hängen würde → **hung up**

▶ **hang upon VI** *+prep obj* = **hang on VI** *+prep obj* **b**

hangar [ˈhæŋəˈ] **N** Hangar *m*, Flugzeughalle *f*

hangdog [ˈhæŋdɒg] **ADJ** *look, expression (= abject)* niedergeschlagen, trübsinnig; *(= ashamed)* zerknirscht

hanger [ˈhæŋəˈ] **N** *(for clothes)* (Kleider)bügel *m*; *(= loop on garment)* Aufhänger *m*

hanger-on [ˌhæŋərˈɒn] **N** *pl* **hangers-on** *(to celebrity)* Trabant *m*, Satellit *m*; **the film crew turned up with all its hangers-on** die Filmmannschaft erschien mit ihrem ganzen Anhang; **the celebrity was accompanied by his usual crowd of hangers-on** die Berühmtheit kam mit dem üblichen Schwarm von Gefolgsleuten

hang: **hang-glide VI** Drachen fliegen; **hang-glider N** *(= device)* Drachen *m*; *(= person)* Drachenflieger(in) *m(f)*; **hang-gliding N** Drachenfliegen *nt*

hanging [ˈhæŋɪŋ] **N a** *(of criminal)* Tod *m* durch den Strang, Erhängen *nt*; *(= event)* Hinrichtung *f* (durch den Strang); **he deserves ~** er sollte aufgehängt werden; **to bring back ~** die Todesstrafe wieder einführen **b** *(of wallpaper)* Anbringen *nt*, Kleben *nt*; *(of door)* Einhängen *nt*; *(of pictures)* (Auf)hängen *nt*; **wallpaper ~** Tapezieren *nt* **c hangings PL** *(= curtains etc)* Vorhänge *pl*; *(on wall)* Tapete *f*; *(= tapestry)* Wandbehang *m or* -behänge *pl*; **bed ~s** Vorhänge *pl* des Himmelbetts **ADJ** *attr* **a** hängend; **the ~ gardens of Babylon** die Hängenden Gärten der Semiramis **b it's a ~ matter** darauf steht der Galgen

hanging: **hanging basket N** Blumen- *or* Hängeampel *f*; **hanging bridge N** Hängebrücke *f*; **hanging committee N** *(Art)* Hängekommission *f*; **hanging judge N** Richter, der (zu) leicht das Todesurteil fällt

hang: **hangman N** Henker *m*; *(= game)* Galgen *m*; **hangnail N** Niednagel *m*; **hang-out N** *(inf, = place where one lives)* Bude *f (inf)*; *(inf: = pub, café etc)* Stammlokal *nt*; *(of group)* Treff *m (inf)*; **this club is his usual ~** er hängt für gewöhnlich in diesem Klub herum *(inf)*; **hangover N a** Kater *m (inf)* **b** *(= sth left over)* Überbleibsel *nt*

Hang Seng Index [ˌhæŋseŋˈɪndeks] **N** Hang-Seng-Index *m*

hang-up [ˈhæŋʌp] **N** *(inf)* Komplex *m (about* wegen); *(= obsession)* Fimmel *m (inf)*; **he has a ~ about people smoking** er stellt sich furchtbar an, wenn Leute rauchen *(inf)*

hank [hæŋk] **N** *(of wool etc)* Strang *m*; *(of hair, fur)* Büschel *nt*

hanker [ˈhæŋkəˈ] **VI** sich sehnen, Verlangen haben *(for or after sth* nach etw)

hankering [ˈhæŋkərɪŋ] **N** Verlangen *nt*, Sehnsucht *f*; **to have a ~ for sth** Verlangen *or* Sehnsucht nach etw haben; **I've always had a ~ to be an actress** ich wollte schon immer Schauspielerin werden

hankie, hanky [ˈhæŋkɪ] **N** *(inf)* Taschentuch *nt*

hanky-panky [ˈhæŋkɪˈpæŋkɪ] **N** *(inf)* **a** *(esp US: = dishonest dealings)* Mauscheleien *pl (inf)*, Tricks *pl (inf)*; **there's some ~ going on** hier ist was faul *(inf)* **b** *(= love affair)* Techtelmechtel *nt (inf)* **c** *(esp Brit: = intimate behaviour)* Gefummel *nt (inf)*; **they were having a bit of ~ on the settee** sie haben auf dem Sofa ein bisschen gefummelt *(inf)*

Hanover [ˈhænəʊvəˈ] **N** Hannover *nt*

Hanoverian [ˌhænəʊˈvɪərɪən] **ADJ** hannover(i)sch; **the ~ dynasty** das Haus Hannover **N** Hannoveraner(in) *m(f)*

Hansard [ˈhænsɑːd] **N** der Hansard, die britischen Parlamentsberichte

Hanseatic [ˌhænzɪˈætɪk] **ADJ** hanseatisch; **~ town/port** Hansestadt *f*

Hanseatic League N Hanse *f*, Hansebund *m*

hansom [ˈhænsəm] **N** (zweirädriger) Einspänner, Hansom *m*

Hants [hænts] *abbr of* **Hampshire**

hap [hæp] **VI** *(obs)* = **happen**[1]

ha'pence [ˈheɪpəns] **N** *(Brit old)* halber Penny

haphazard [ˌhæpˈhæzəd] **ADJ** willkürlich, planlos; **the whole thing was very ~** das Ganze war ziemlich zufällig *or* planlos; **nothing is ~ in the universe** im Universum bleibt nichts dem Zufall überlassen; **in a ~ way** *or* **fashion** planlos, wahllos

haphazardly [ˌhæpˈhæzədlɪ] **ADV** wahllos, (ganz) willkürlich, planlos; **decisions are made ~** Entscheidungen werden willkürlich *or* aufs Geratewohl *or* auf gut Glück getroffen; **a ~ organized reception** ein völlig ungeplanter Empfang

hapless [ˈhæplɪs] **ADJ** glücklos; **yet another misfortune in the life of this ~ man** noch ein Unglück im Leben dieses vom Pech verfolgten Menschen

ha'p'orth [ˈheɪpəθ] **N** *contr of* **halfpennyworth**; **a ~ of sweets** Bonbons für einen halben Penny; **to spoil the ship for a ~ of tar** *(Prov)* am falschen Ende sparen

happen[1] [ˈhæpən] **VI a** *(= occur)* geschehen; *(somewhat special or important event)* sich ereignen; *(esp unexpected, unintentional or unpleasant event)* passieren, geschehen; *(process also)* vor sich gehen, geschehen; **it ~ed like this ...** es geschah *or* war so ...; **nothing ever ~s here** hier ereignet sich *or* geschieht *or* passiert (doch) überhaupt nie etwas; **this interview/conversation never ~ed** dieses Interview/Gespräch hat nicht stattgefunden; **it's all ~ing here today** heute ist hier ganz schön was los *(inf)*; **what's ~ing?** was läuft? *(inf)*, was ist los?; **you can't just let things ~** du kannst die Dinge nicht einfach laufen lassen; **it's broken, how did it ~?** es ist kaputt, wie ist denn das passiert?; **it just ~ed** es ist (ganz) von allein passiert *or* gekommen; **as if nothing had ~ed** als ob nichts geschehen *or* gewesen wäre; **worse things have ~ed** es ist schon Schlimmeres passiert *or* vorgekommen; **don't let it ~ again** dass das nicht noch mal vorkommt *or* passiert!; **these things ~** so was kommt (schon mal) vor; **what has ~ed to him?** was ist ihm passiert *or* geschehen?; *(= what have they done to him)* was ist mit ihm passiert?; *(= what's wrong with him)* was ist mit ihm los?; *(= what has become of him)* was ist aus ihm geworden?; **what's ~ed to your leg?** was ist mit deinem Bein los *or* passiert?; **if anything should ~ to me** wenn mir etwas zustoßen *or* passieren sollte; **you're the best thing that's ever ~ed to me** du bist der größte Glücksfall in meinem Leben; **it all ~ed so quickly** es ging alles so schnell

b *(= chance)* **how does it ~ that ...?** *(cause)* wie kommt es, dass ...?; *(possibility)* wie ist es möglich, dass ...?; **it might ~ that you will be asked such a question** es könnte passieren *or* sein, dass Ihnen solch eine Frage gestellt wird; **to ~ to do sth** zufällig(erweise) etw tun; **we ~ed to discover we had a friend in common** wir stellten durch Zufall fest, dass wir einen gemeinsamen Bekannten hatten; **do you ~ to know whether ...?** wissen Sie vielleicht *or* zufällig, ob ...?; **I ~ to know it's true** ich weiß zufällig(erweise), dass es stimmt; **I just ~ed to come along when ...** ich kam zufällig (gerade) vorbei, als ...; **he ~ed to see me just as I ...** muss er mich doch gerade in dem Augenblick sehen, als ich ...; **I picked up the nearest paper, which ~ed to be the Daily Mail** ich nahm die erstbeste Zeitung zur Hand, es war zufällig die Daily Mail; **it so ~s** *or* **as it ~s I (don't) like that kind of thing** so etwas mag ich nun einmal (nicht); **as it ~s I've been there too/I'm going there today** zufällig(erweise) bin ich auch dort gewesen/gehe ich heute (dort)hin; **you don't want to come, do you? – it so ~s, I do** du möchtest doch sicher nicht kommen, oder? – doch, natürlich

▶ **happen along** VI zufällig (an)kommen

▶ **happen (up)on** VI *+prep obj* zufällig stoßen auf *(+acc)*; *person* zufällig treffen *or* sehen

happen² ['æpn] ADV *(N Engl inf: = perhaps)* vielleicht

happening ['hæpnɪŋ] **N** **a** Ereignis *nt*; *(not planned)* Vorfall *m*; **there have been some strange ~s in that house** in dem Haus sind sonderbare Dinge vorgegangen **b** *(Theat)* Happening *nt* **ADJ** *(inf: = exciting)* toll *(inf)*, geil *(inf)*; **the concert last night was really ~** das Konzert gestern Abend war echt geil *(sl)*

happenstance ['hæpənstæns] N *(inf)* Zufall *m*; **by ~** durch Zufall, zufällig

happily ['hæpɪlɪ] ADV **a** glücklich; *say, play* vergnügt, fröhlich; **it all ended ~** es ging alles gut *or* glücklich aus; **a ~ married man** ein glücklich verheirateter Mann; **they lived ~ ever after** *(in fairy tales)* und wenn sie nicht gestorben sind, dann leben sie noch heute; **his dream was to get married and live ~ ever after** sein Wunschtraum war, zu heiraten und dann glücklich und zufrieden zu leben

b *(= harmoniously) live together, combine* harmonisch; **these plants grow ~ in any good soil** diese Pflanzen wachsen gut *or* problemlos in allen guten Böden

c *(= gladly)* gern; **I would ~ have lent her the money** ich hätte ihr das Geld ohne Weiteres geliehen

d *(= fortunately)* glücklicherweise, zum Glück; **~ for him, he can afford it** zu seinem Glück kann er es sich leisten

e *(= felicitously)* glücklich, treffend; **~ worded/chosen** glücklich formuliert/gewählt

happiness ['hæpɪnɪs] N Glück *nt*; *(= feeling of contentment)* Zufriedenheit *f*; *(= cheerfulness)* Heiterkeit *f*, Fröhlichkeit *f*; **the ~ of his expression** sein glücklicher *or* freudiger Gesichtsausdruck

happy ['hæpɪ] ✪ 3.1, 3.2, 14, 23.2, 23.3, 24.1, 24.2, 24.3, 25.2 ADJ *(+er)* **a** *(= joyful, glad) person, smile, expression, time, life, home, marriage* glücklich; *atmosphere* harmonisch; **the ~ couple** *(= newlyweds)* das Brautpaar; **a ~ feeling** ein Glücksgefühl *nt*; **that gives me a ~ feeling** das macht mich glücklich; **to make sb ~** jdn glücklich machen; **they were having such a ~ time** sie hatten so viel Spaß; **the school is a ~ place, it's a ~ school** an der Schule sind die Kinder glücklich; **a ~ atmosphere for their children** eine glückliche Umgebung für ihre Kinder; **a ~ ending** ein guter *or* glücklicher Ausgang, ein Happy End *nt*, ein Happyend *nt*; **~ birthday (to you)** herzlichen Glückwunsch zum Geburtstag; **Happy Easter/Christmas** frohe Ostern/Weihnachten → **return N a**

b *(= content, satisfied)* **(not) to be ~ about** *or* **with sth** mit etw (nicht) zufrieden sein; **to be ~ to do sth** *(= willing)* etw gern tun; *(= pleased)* sich freuen, etw zu tun; *(= relieved)* froh sein, etw zu tun; **that's a risk I'm ~ to take** dieses Risiko gehe ich gern ein; **I was ~ to hear that you passed your exam** es hat mich gefreut zu hören, dass du die Prüfung bestanden hast; **I'm just ~ to be back** ich bin einfach nur froh, wieder da zu sein; **to be ~ to let sb do sth** damit einverstanden sein, dass jd etw tut; **he's ~ to leave it to me** er überlässt es mir gern

c *(= fortunate, felicitous) chance, coincidence, solution, choice* glücklich; **by ~ chance** durch einen glücklichen Zufall

d *(inf: = tipsy)* angeheitert, beschwipst *(inf)*

-happy ADJ *suf (inf)* **trigger-/strike-happy** schieß-/streikfreudig *(inf)*; **snap-happy** fotowütig *(inf)*

happy: **happy camper** N *(inf)* zufriedener *or* glücklicher Mensch; **I'm not a ~** ich bin (überhaupt) nicht gut drauf *(inf)*; **happy-clappy** ['hæpɪ'klæpɪ] ADJ *(pej inf Rel) service* mit Händeklatschen und moderner Musik; **happy event** N *(inf)* frohes *or* freudiges Ereignis; **happy families** N *sing (Cards)* ≈ Quartett *nt*; **happy-go-lucky** ADJ unbekümmert, sorglos; **I wish you wouldn't be so ~ about things** ich wollte, du wärest nicht bei allem so sorglos *or* würdest nicht alles so lässig nehmen *(inf)*; **happy hour** N *(in pubs etc) Zeit, in der Getränke zu ermäßigten Preisen angeboten werden*; **happy hunting ground** N **a** *(Myth)* ewige Jagdgründe *pl* **b** *(fig)* Paradies *nt*; **happy medium** N goldener Mittelweg; **to strike a ~** den goldenen Mittelweg finden

hara-kiri [ˌhærə'kɪrɪ] N Harakiri *nt*

harangue [hə'ræŋ] **N** *(= scolding)* (Straf)predigt *f*, Sermon *m*; *(lengthy also)* Tirade *f*; **to give sb a ~** jdm eine (Straf)predigt *etc* halten **VT** *person* eine (Straf)predigt *or* einen Sermon halten *(+dat)*; *(at length also)* eine Tirade loslassen auf *(+acc) (inf)*; **I don't like being ~d** ich kann es nicht leiden, wenn mir jemand lange Reden hält; **stop haranguing me about how lucky other men's wives are** hör auf, mir dauernd vorzuhalten *or* mir damit in den Ohren zu liegen *(inf)*, wie gut es die Frauen anderer Männer haben; **he tried to ~ the mob into direct action** er versuchte, den Mob zum direkten Handeln aufzustacheln

harass ['hærəs] VT belästigen; *(= mess around)* schikanieren; *(Mil) the enemy* Anschläge verüben auf *(+acc)*, immer wieder überfallen; **don't ~ me** dräng *or* hetz *(inf)* mich doch nicht so!; **he sexually ~ed her** er belästigte sie (sexuell); **they eventually ~ed him into resigning** sie setzten ihm so lange zu, bis er schließlich zurücktrat; **the landlord was ~ing me about the rent** der Hauswirt belästigte mich ständig wegen der Miete; **a lot of these people are ~ed by the police** viele dieser Leute werden ständig von der Polizei schikaniert; **a salesman should never seem to ~ a potential customer** ein Vertreter sollte einem potenziellen *or* potentiellen Kunden gegenüber niemals aufdringlich werden

harassed ['hærəst] ADJ abgespannt, angegriffen, mitgenommen; *(= worried)* von Sorgen gequält; **a ~ father** ein (viel) geplagter Vater; **she was very ~ that day** an dem Tag wusste sie nicht, wo ihr der Kopf stand; **he wiped his brow in a ~ manner** er wischte sich *(dat)* gequält die Stirn

harassment ['hærəsmənt] N *(= act)* Belästigung *f*, Bedrängung *f*; *(= messing around)* Schikanierung *f*; *(= state)* Bedrängnis *f*; *(Mil)* Kleinkrieg *m*; **constant ~ of the enemy** ständiger Kleinkrieg gegen den Feind; **police ~** Schikane *f* vonseiten *or* von Seiten der Polizei; **racial ~** rassistisch motivierte Schikanierung; **sexual ~** sexuelle Belästigung

harbinger ['hɑːbɪndʒə'] N *(liter)* Herold *m (liter)*, (Vor)bote *m/-botin f*

harbour, *(US)* **harbor** ['hɑːbə'] **N** Hafen *m* **VT** **a** *criminal etc* beherbergen, Unterschlupf gewähren *(+dat)*; *goods* (bei sich) aufbewahren **b** *suspicions, grudge, doubts, resentment* hegen; *ambitions, feelings* haben; *regrets* empfinden; **to ~ thoughts of revenge** Rachegedanken hegen **c** *(= conceal, contain)* **dirt ~s germs** Schmutz ist eine Brutstätte für Krankheitserreger; **some sufferers continue to ~ the virus** in manchen Kranken lebt der Virus weiter

harbour, *(US)* **harbor**: **harbour bar** N Sandbank *f* vor dem Hafen; **harbour dues** PL Hafengebühr(en) *f(pl)*; **harbour master** N Hafenmeister(in) *m(f)*

hard [hɑːd] **ADJ** *(+er)* **a** *(= not soft)* hart; **as ~ as rocks** *or* **iron** steinhart; **the ground was baked ~** der Boden war völlig ausgedörrt

b *(= difficult)* schwer, schwierig; **this is ~ to do, it is ~ to do** es ist schwer, das zu tun; **stories that are ~ to understand** Geschichten, die schwer verständlich sind; **that is a very ~ question to answer** diese Frage lässt sich nur schwer beantworten; **their prices are ~ to beat** ihre Preise sind kaum zu unterbieten; **she is ~ to please** man kann ihr kaum etwas recht machen; **it's ~ to tell** es lässt sich schwer sagen, es ist schwer zu sagen; **it was ~ to believe** es war kaum zu glauben; **I find it ~ to believe** ich kann es kaum glauben; **she found it ~ to make friends** es fiel ihr schwer, Freunde zu finden; **to do sth the ~ way** etw auf die schwere Art machen; **I don't see the point in doing it the ~ way** warum soll man es sich schwer machen?; **to play ~ to get** so tun, als sei man nicht interessiert

c *(= strenuous, demanding) work, day, week* hart, anstrengend; **he leaves all the ~ work to me** die ganze Schwerarbeit überlässt er mir; **it was very ~ work in the shop** die Arbeit in dem Geschäft war sehr anstrengend; **he's ~ work** *(inf)* er ist ziemlich anstrengend *(inf)*; *(= difficult to know or persuade)* er ist ein harter Brocken *(inf)*; **getting on with him is ~ work** *(inf)* es gehört schon etwas dazu, mit ihm auszukommen *(inf)*; **it was ~ work for me not to swear at him** es hat mich große Mühe gekostet, ihn nicht zu beschimpfen; **a ~ worker** ein fleißiger Arbeiter; **to be a ~ worker** sehr fleißig sein; **it was ~ going** man kam nur mühsam voran; **learning Japanese is ~ going** Japanisch zu lernen ist sehr schwierig; **this novel is ~ going** durch dieses Roman muss man sich mühsam durchbeißen; **chatting her up is ~ going** *(inf)* es ist gar nicht so einfach, sie anzumachen *(inf)*

d *(= forceful) pull, tug, kick* kräftig; *blow, punch* heftig; **to give sb/sth a ~ push** jdm/etw einen harten Stoß versetzen; **to give sth a ~ pull** *or* **tug** kräftig an etw *(dat)* ziehen; **it was a ~ blow** *or* **knock (for** *or* **to them)** *(fig)* es war ein schwerer Schlag (für sie); **to take a ~ knock** *(fig)* schwer angeschlagen werden; **he took a ~ knock** *(fig)* er musste einen schweren Schlag einstecken

e *(= severe, tough) person, look, eyes, smile, voice, life* hart; *winter, frost* streng, hart; **to be ~ on sb** *(= cause strain or wear)* jdn strapazieren; *(person)* hart zu *or* streng mit jdm sein; **to be ~ on sth** *(= cause strain or wear)* etw strapazieren; *(person)* etw kritisieren; **the job's a bit ~ on the nerves** die Arbeit ist ziemlich nervenaufreibend; **don't be so ~ on the children** sei nicht so streng mit den Kindern; **to have a ~ time** es schwer *or* nicht leicht haben; **I had a ~ time finding a job** ich hatte Schwierigkeiten, eine Stelle zu finden; **he had a ~ time of it** er hat es nicht leicht gehabt; *(in negotiations, boxing match etc)* es hat ihn einen harten Kampf gekostet; *(with illness, operation etc)* es war eine schwere Zeit für ihn; **to give sb a ~ time** jdm das Leben schwer machen; **~ times** schwere Zeiten *pl*; **to fall on ~ times** in finanzielle Schwierigkeiten geraten; **there are no ~ feelings between them** sie sind einander nicht böse; **no ~ feelings?** nimm es mir nicht übel; **to be as ~ as nails** knallhart sein *(inf)* → *also* **nut a, bargain N a**

f *(= harsh) light* grell; *sound* hart

g *(= real, unquestionable) facts, information* gesichert; **~ evidence** sichere Beweise *pl*

h *(Typ, Comput)* → **hard hyphen, hard return**

ADV **a** *(= with effort) work* hart, schwer; *run, drive* sehr schnell; *breathe* schwer; *study, play* eifrig; *(= carefully) listen, look* genau, gut; *think* scharf, angestrengt; *(= strongly, forcefully) push, pull* kräftig, fest; *laugh, scream, cry, beg* sehr; *rain, snow* stark; *blow* kräftig; **I've been ~ at work** *or* **(going) ~ at it** *(inf)* **since 7 this morning** ich bin seit heute Morgen um 7 schwer am Werk *or* schwer dabei *(inf)*; **she works ~ at keeping herself fit** sie gibt sich viel Mühe, sich fit zu halten; **to try ~** sich wirklich Mühe geben; **no matter how ~ I try ...** wie sehr ich mich auch anstrenge, ...; **if you try ~ you can do it** wenn du dich richtig bemühst *or* anstrengst, kannst du es tun; **you're not trying ~ enough** du strengst dich nicht genügend an; **he tried as ~ as he could** er hat sein Bestes getan *or* sich nach Kräften bemüht; **he listened ~** *(straining to hear)* er horchte angestrengt; **you're not thinking ~ enough** du denkst nicht angestrengt genug nach; **think ~er** denk mal ein bisschen besser nach; **she slammed the door ~ behind us** sie knallte die Tür fest hinter uns zu; **it was freezing ~** es herrschte strenger Frost

b *(= severely)* **to be ~ pushed** *or* **put to do sth** es sehr schwer finden, etw zu tun; **to clamp down ~** hart durchgreifen; **it'll go ~ for** *or* **with him if ...** er wird Schwierigkeiten bekommen, wenn ...; *(= it will cost him dear)* es kann ihn teuer zu stehen kommen, wenn ...; **to be ~ done by** übel dran sein; *(= unfairly treated)* ungerecht behandelt sein; **he reckons he's ~ done by having to work on Saturdays** er findet es ungerecht, dass er samstags arbeiten muss; **they are ~ hit by the cuts** sie sind von den Kürzungen schwer getroffen; **she took it very ~** es traf sie sehr *or* schwer, es ging ihr sehr nahe → *also* **hard-pressed**

c *(= as far as possible)* **~ right/left** scharf rechts/links; **to turn/go ~ round** eine scharfe Kehrtwendung machen; **bear ~ round to your left** halten Sie sich scharf links; **to lock ~ over** voll einschlagen; **~ a-port/a-starboard/astern** *etc (Naut)* hart backbord/steuerbord/nach achtern *etc*

d *(= close)* **to follow ~ behind/upon sth** unmittelbar auf etw *(acc)* folgen; **my sister was ~ behind me** meine Schwester war direkt hinter mir; **following ~ upon the opening of the new cinema** kurz nach der Öffnung des neuen Kinos; **~ by (sth)** *(dated)* ganz in der Nähe (von etw) → *also* **heel¹ N a**

hard: **hard and fast** ADJ fest; *rules also* bindend, verbindlich; **hardback** ADJ *(also* **hard-backed)** **a** *book* gebunden **b** *chair* mit einer harten Rückenlehne **N** gebundene Ausgabe; **hardball** N *(US)* **a** *(Baseball)* Hardball *m* **b** *(fig)* **to play ~** rücksichtslos sein *or* vorgehen; **hard-bitten** ADJ *person* abgebrüht; *manager* knallhart *(inf)*; **hardboard** N Hartfaser- *or* Pressspanplatte *f*; **hard-boiled** ADJ **a** *egg* hart gekocht **b** *(fig: = shrewd)* gerissen, ausgekocht *(inf)*, mit allen Wassern gewaschen *(inf)* **c** *(fig: = unsentimental)* kaltschnäuzig *(inf)* **d** *(fig: = realistic) approach, appraisal etc* nüchtern, sachlich; **hardboot** N *(Sport)* Hardboot *m*, *Stiefel mit harter Plastikoberfläche*; **hard case** N *(inf)* **a** *(= difficult person)* schwieriger Mensch **b** *(= criminal)* Gewohnheitsverbrecher(in) *m(f)* **c** *(= hardship)* Härtefall *m*; **hard cash** N Bargeld *nt*, Bare(s) *nt (inf)*; **hard cheese** INTERJ *(Brit inf)* = **hard lines**; **hard copy** N Ausdruck *m*, Hardcopy *f*; **hard core** N **a** *(for road)* Schotter *m* **b** *(fig)* harter Kern; *(= pornography)* harter Porno *(inf)*; **hard-core** ADJ **a** *pornography* hart; **~ film** harter Pornofilm, Hardcoreporno *m* **b** *(= committed) members* zum harten Kern gehörend; *support* des harten Kerns; **he's a ~ heroin addict** er kommt vom Heroin nicht mehr los; **hardcore** N *(Mus)* Hardcore *m*; **hard court** N Hartplatz *m*; **hardcover** ADJ N *(US)* = **hardback ADJ a N**; **hard currency** N harte Währung; **hard disk** N *(Comput)* Festplatte *f*; **hard disk computer** N Festplattencomputer *m*; **hard disk drive** N Festplattenlaufwerk *nt*; **hard drink** N hartes Getränk; **hard-drinking** ADJ stark trinkend; **hard drug** N harte Droge; **hard-earned** ADJ *wages, cash* sauer verdient; *savings* mühsam erspart; *reward* redlich verdient; *victory* hart erkämpft; **hard-edged** ADJ *(fig)* hart, kompromisslos; *reality* hart

harden [ˈhɑːdn] VT *steel* härten; *body, muscles* kräftigen, stählen *(geh)*; *person (physically)* abhärten; *(emotionally)* verhärten *(pej)*, abstumpfen *(pej)*; *clay* hart werden lassen; **this ~ed his attitude** dadurch hat sich seine Haltung verhärtet; **to ~ oneself to sth** *(physically)* sich gegen etw abhärten; *(emotionally)* gegen etw unempfindlich werden; **war had ~ed the soldiers to death and killing** der Krieg hatte die Soldaten gegen den Tod und das Töten abgestumpft; **to ~ one's heart against sb** sein Herz gegen jdn verhärten *(geh)* → **hardened**

VI *(substance)* hart werden; *(fig, attitude)* sich verhärten; *(St Ex: = cease to fluctuate)* sich festigen, sich stabilisieren; *(= rise)* anziehen; **his voice ~ed** seine Stimme wurde hart *or* bekam einen harten Klang; **his eyes/face ~ed** seine Augen bekamen/sein Gesicht bekam einen harten Ausdruck

▶ **harden off** VT *sep plants* widerstandsfähig machen

▶ **harden up** VI *(concrete, glue etc)* hart werden VT *sep (= make hard)* härten, hart machen; *(fig: = toughen)* abhärten

hardened [ˈhɑːdnd] ADJ *steel* gehärtet; *troops* zäh, abgehärtet; *sinner* verstockt; *attitude* verhärtet; *arteries* verkalkt; **~ criminal** Gewohnheitsverbrecher(in) *m(f)*; **to be ~ to the cold/the climate** gegen die Kälte/das Klima abgehärtet sein; **to be ~ to sb's charms** unempfänglich für jds Charme sein; **to be ~ to death** an den Tod gewöhnt sein; **you become ~ to it after a while** daran gewöhnt man sich mit der Zeit

hardening [ˈhɑːdnɪŋ] N *(of steel)* (Er)härten *nt*, Härtung *f*; *(fig)* Verhärten *nt*, Verhärtung *f*; *(St Ex)* Versteifung *f*, Festigung *f*; *(= rise)* Anziehen *nt*; **I noticed a ~ of his attitude** ich habe bemerkt, dass sich seine Einstellung verhärtet; **~ of the arteries** Arterienverkalkung *f*

hard: **hard-featured** ADJ *person* mit harten Gesichtszügen; **hard-fought** ADJ *battle, campaign* erbittert; *victory* hart erkämpft; *boxing match, competition, game* hart; **a ~ election** eine (erbitterte) Wahlschlacht; **hard hat** N Schutzhelm *m*; *(= construction worker)* Bauarbeiter(in) *m(f)*; **hard-headed** ADJ nüchtern; **hardhearted** ADJ hartherzig *(towards sb* jdm gegenüber); **hardheartedness** N Hartherzigkeit *f*; **hard-hitting** ADJ *speech, report* äußerst kritisch; **hard hyphen** N *(Typ, Comput)* fester Bindestrich

hardihood [ˈhɑːdɪhʊd] N Kühnheit *f*; *(= courage also)* Mut *m*; *(= audacity also)* Dreistigkeit *f*

hardiness [ˈhɑːdɪnɪs] N **a** *(= toughness)* Zähigkeit *f*; *(= hardened nature)* Abgehärtetsein *nt*; *(Bot)* Winterhärte *f* **b** *(= courage)* Unerschrockenheit *f*

hard: **hard labour**, *(US)* **hard labor** N Zwangsarbeit *f*; **hard left** N *(Pol)* **the ~** die extreme Linke; **hard lens** N *(Opt)* harte Kontaktlinse; **hard line** N harte Haltung, harte Linie; **to take a ~** eine harte Haltung einnehmen, eine harte Linie verfolgen; **hardline** ADJ kompromisslos; **hardliner** N Vertreter(in) *m(f)* der harten Linie, Hardliner(in) *m(f) (esp Pol)*; **hard lines** INTERJ *(Brit inf)* Pech (gehabt)!; **hard liquor** N Schnaps *m*; **hard luck** N *(inf)* Pech *nt (on* für); **~!** Pech gehabt!; **it was very ~ on him** da hat er aber wirklich Pech gehabt; **that's just his ~** das ist sein Pech; **hard-luck story** N Leidensgeschichte *f*

hardly [ˈhɑːdlɪ] ADV **a** *(= barely)* kaum; **I ~ knew him** ich kannte ihn kaum; **the boy was ~ seventeen** der Junge war kaum *or* keine siebzehn; **I could understand ~ a word** ich konnte kaum ein Wort *or* fast kein Wort verstehen; **~ ever** fast nie; **~ any money** fast kein Geld; **it's worth ~ anything** es ist fast nichts wert; **you've ~ eaten anything** du hast (ja) kaum etwas gegessen; **I ~ know any French** ich kann kaum Französisch *or* fast kein Französisch; **there was ~ anywhere to go** man konnte fast nirgends hingehen; **~ a day goes by when we don't read about murder in the newspaper** es vergeht kaum ein Tag, an dem wir nicht von Mordfällen in der Zeitung lesen; **I can still ~ believe it** ich kann es immer noch kaum glauben; **~ had he uttered the words when he began laughing** er hatte die Worte kaum ausgesprochen, als er anfing zu lachen

b *(= certainly not)* wohl kaum; **I will ~ need to remind you to be polite to your grandmother** ich muss euch wohl kaum daran erinnern, höflich zu eurer Großmutter zu sein; **will she remember? – ~!** wird sie daran denken? – bestimmt nicht!

hardness [ˈhɑːdnɪs] N **a** Härte *f* **b** *(= difficulty)* Schwere *f*, Schwierigkeit *f*; **~ of hearing** Schwerhörigkeit *f* **c** *(= severity)* Härte *f*; *(of winter, frost)* Strenge *f*; *(of light)* Grelle *f*, Grellheit *f*; **the ~ of his heart** seine Hartherzigkeit

hard: **hard-nosed** ADJ *(inf: = down-to-earth)* nüchtern; *(= tough) person, government* abgebrüht *(inf)*; *approach, attitude, leadership* rücksichtslos; **hard on** N *(sl)* Ständer *m (inf)*; **to have a ~** einen stehen *or* einen Ständer haben *(inf)*; **hard-packed** ADJ *snow* festgetreten; *sand, earth* festgedrückt; **hardpad** N *(Vet)* Hartballenkrankheit *f*; **hard palate** N *(Anat)* harter Gaumen, Vordergaumen *m*; **hardpan** N *(Geol)* Ortstein *nt*; **hard-pressed** ADJ *consumer, firm, family, troops etc* hart bedrängt;; *(with work)* stark beansprucht; **to be ~ to do sth** es sehr schwer finden, etw zu tun; **to be ~ (for money)** in Geldnot sein, knapp bei Kasse sein *(inf)*; **hard return** N *(Comput)* harte Zeilenschaltung; Absatzmarke *f*; **hard right** N *(Pol)* **the ~** die extreme Rechte; **hardrock** N *(Mus)* Hardrock *m*; **hardscrabble** ADJ **a** *circumstances, situation* ärmlich, bescheiden **b** *soil* karg; **hard sell** **N** aggressive Verkaufstaktik, Hardselling *nt* **ATTR** aggressiv

hardship [ˈhɑːdʃɪp] N *(= condition)* Not *f*, Elend *nt*; *(= instance)* Härte *f*; *(= deprivation)* Entbehrung *f*; **economic/financial ~** wirtschaftliche/finanzielle Not; **to suffer great ~s** große Not leiden; **the ~s of war** das Elend/die Entbehrungen des Kriegs; **is that such a great ~?** ist das wirklich ein solches Unglück?; **it was no ~ at all** es hat überhaupt keine Mühe gemacht; **if it's not too much (of a) ~ for you ...** *(also iro)* wenn es dir nichts ausmacht *or* nicht zu viel Mühe macht ...; **the ~(s) of life in the country** die Entbehrungen *pl* des Landlebens

hard: **hard shoulder** N *(Brit)* Seitenstreifen *m*; **hardstanding** N *(Brit: for vehicle)* befestigter Abstellplatz; **hardtack** N Schiffszwieback *m*; **hardtop** N Hardtop *nt or m*

hardware [ˈhɑːdweəʳ] **N** **a** Eisenwaren *pl*; *(= household goods)* Haushaltswaren *pl* **b** *(Comput)* Hardware *f* **c** *(Mil)* (Wehr)material *nt* **d** *(US inf: = gun)* Schießeisen *nt (hum inf)*, Kanone *f (sl)* **ATTR** **a** **~ dealer** Eisenwarenhändler(in) *m(f)*; *(including household goods)* Haushalts- und Eisenwarenhändler(in) *m(f)*; **~ shop** *or* **store** Eisenwarenhandlung *f*; *(including household goods)* Haushalts- und Eisenwarengeschäft *nt* **b** *(Comput)* Hardware-; **~ detection** Hardwareerkennung *f*; **~ manufacturer** Hardwarehersteller *m*

hard: **hard-wearing** ADJ widerstandsfähig; *cloth, clothes* strapazierfähig; **hard-wired** ADJ *(Comput)* fest verdrahtet; **hard-won** ADJ hart *or* schwer erkämpft; *expertise* schwer erarbeitet; **hardwood** N Hartholz *nt*; **hard-working** ADJ *person* fleißig; *engine* leistungsfähig

hardy [ˈhɑːdɪ] ADJ *(+er)* **a** *(= tough, robust) person, animal* robust, zäh; *(= hardened)* abgehärtet; *(Bot) plant* winterhart **b** *(= bold) person* unerschrocken

hardy annual N einjährige winterharte Pflanze

hardy perennial N mehrjährige winterharte Pflanze

hare [heəʳ] **N** (Feld)hase *m*; **~ and hounds** *(= game)* Schnitzeljagd *f*; **to run with the ~ and hunt with the hounds** *(prov)* es mit niemandem verderben wollen; **to start a ~** *(fig)* vom Thema ablenken → **mad** VI *(Brit inf)* sausen, flitzen *(inf)*; **to ~ off** lossausen *or* -flitzen *(inf)*

hare: **harebell** N Glockenblume *f*; **hare-brained** [ˈheəbreɪnd] ADJ *person, plan* verrückt, behämmert *(inf)*; **harelip** N Hasenscharte *f*

harem [hɑːˈriːm] N Harem *m*

haricot [ˈhærɪkəʊ] N **~ (bean)** Gartenbohne *f*

hark [hɑːk] VI **to ~ to sth** *(liter)* einer Sache *(dat)* lauschen *(liter)*; **~!** *(liter)* horch(t)! *(liter)*, höret!; ~ **at him!** *(inf)* hör ihn dir nur an!, hör sich einer den an! *(inf)*

▶ **hark back to** VI *+prep obj* zurückkommen; **this custom harks back to the days when ...** dieser Brauch geht auf die Zeit zurück, als ...; **he's always harking back to the good old days** er fängt immer wieder von der guten alten Zeit an; **the author is harking back to former times** der Autor geht auf vergangene Zeiten zurück

Harlequin ['hɑːlɪkwɪn] **N** *(Theat)* Harlekin *m*, Hanswurst *m* **ADJ** Harlekin(s)-; ~ **costume** Harlekin(s)kostüm *nt*

harlequin ['hɑːlɪkwɪn] N *(= colourful)* bunt; ~ **glasses** buntes Brillengestell

harlot ['hɑːlət] N *(old)* Metze *f (old)*, Hure *f*

harm [hɑːm] **N** *(bodily)* Verletzung *f*; *(= material damage, to relations, psychological)* Schaden *m*; **to do ~ to sb** jdm eine Verletzung/jdm Schaden zufügen; **to do ~ to sth** einer Sache *(dat)* schaden; **you could do somebody/yourself ~ with that knife** mit dem Messer können Sie jemanden/sich verletzen; **the blow didn't do him any ~** der Schlag hat ihm nichts getan *or* ihn nicht verletzt; **a bit of exercise never did anyone any ~** ein bisschen Sport hat noch niemandem geschadet; **he never did anyone any ~** er hat keiner Fliege jemals etwas zuleide *or* zu Leide getan; **he did his reputation quite a lot of ~ with his TV appearance** er hat seinem Ruf mit diesem Fernsehauftritt ziemlich geschadet; **you will come to no ~** es wird Ihnen nichts geschehen; **I'll make sure no ~ comes to him** ich werde dafür sorgen, dass ihm nichts passiert *or* geschieht; **it will do more ~ than good** es wird mehr schaden als nützen; **it won't do you any ~** es wird dir nicht schaden; **I see no ~ in the odd cigarette** ich finde nichts dabei, wenn man ab und zu eine Zigarette raucht; **to mean no ~** es nicht böse meinen; **I don't mean him any ~** ich meine es nicht böse mit ihm; *(bodily, = not offend)* ich will ihm nicht wehtun; **no ~ done** es ist nichts Schlimmes passiert; **there's no ~ in asking/trying** es kann nicht schaden, zu fragen/es zu versuchen; **there's no ~ in me putting a word in for him, is there?** es kann doch nichts schaden, wenn ich ein gutes Wort für ihn einlege, oder?; **where's** *or* **what's the ~ in that?** was kann denn das schaden?; **to keep** *or* **stay out of ~'s way** die Gefahr meiden, der Gefahr *(dat)* aus dem Weg gehen; **you stay here out of ~'s way** du bleibst schön hier, in Sicherheit; **I've put those tablets in the cupboard out of ~'s way** ich habe die Tabletten im Schrank in Sicherheit gebracht
VT *person* verletzen; *thing, environment* schaden *(+dat)*; *sb's interests, relations, reputation etc* schaden *(+dat)*, abträglich sein *(+dat)*; **don't ~ the children** tu den Kindern nichts (an); **it wouldn't ~ you to be a little more polite** es würde nicht(s) schaden, wenn du ein bisschen höflicher wärest

harmful ['hɑːmfʊl] ADJ schädlich *(to* für); *remarks* verletzend; ~ **to one's health** gesundheitsschädlich

harmless ['hɑːmlɪs] ADJ *(= safe) substance, animal* harmlos, ungefährlich; *(fig: = inoffensive) person, pleasure, question* harmlos; **the bomb was rendered ~** die Bombe wurde entschärft; **this experiment was ~ to the animals** dieses Experiment war für die Tiere ungefährlich; **it's just a bit of ~ fun** es ist nur ein harmloser Spaß

harmlessly ['hɑːmlɪslɪ] ADV **a** *(= without causing damage)* harmlos; **the missile exploded ~ outside the town** die Rakete explodierte außerhalb der Stadt, ohne Schaden anzurichten **b** *(= inoffensively)* harmlos, arglos; **they lived ~ in their seaside paradise** sie lebten arglos in ihrem Paradies am Meer

harmlessness ['hɑːmlɪsnɪs] N *(lit, fig)* Harmlosigkeit *f*; *(of substance, animal also)* Ungefährlichkeit *f*

harmonic [hɑː'mɒnɪk] **N** *(Mus)* Oberton *m* **ADJ** *(Mus, Phys)* harmonisch

harmonica [hɑː'mɒnɪkə] N Harmonika *f*

harmonics [hɑː'mɒnɪks] N *sing* Harmonik *f*

harmonious ADJ, **harmoniously** ADV [hɑː'məʊnɪəs, -lɪ] *(Mus, fig)* harmonisch

harmonium [hɑː'məʊnɪəm] N Harmonium *nt*

harmonization [ˌhɑːmənaɪ'zeɪʃən] N *(Mus, fig)* Harmonisierung *f*

harmonize ['hɑːmənaɪz] **VT** *(Mus, fig)* harmonisieren; *ideas etc* miteinander in Einklang bringen; *plans, colours* aufeinander abstimmen *(sth with sth* etw auf etw *acc)* **VI** **a** *(notes, colours, people etc)* harmonieren; *(facts)* übereinstimmen **b** *(= sing in harmony)* mehrstimmig singen

harmony ['hɑːmənɪ] N Harmonie *f*; *(of colours also)* harmonisches Zusammenspiel; *(fig: = harmonious relations)* Eintracht *f*; **to live/work in perfect ~ with sb** in Harmonie *or* Eintracht mit jdm leben/zusammenarbeiten; **to be in/out of ~ with** *(lit)* harmonieren/nicht harmonieren mit; *(fig also)* in Einklang/nicht in Einklang stehen *or* sein mit; **to live in ~ with nature** im Einklang mit der Natur leben; **to sing in ~** mehrstimmig singen; *(= in tune)* rein singen; **his ideas are out of ~ with the age** seine Vorstellungen sind nicht zeitgemäß *or* passen nicht in die Zeit

harness ['hɑːnɪs] **N** **a** Geschirr *nt*; **to be back in ~** *(fig)* wieder bei der Arbeit *or* im gewohnten Trott sein; **to work in ~** *(fig)* zusammenarbeiten; **to die in ~** *(fig: often hum)* in den Sielen sterben **b** *(of parachute)* Gurtwerk *nt*; *(for baby)* Laufgurt *m* **c** *(Elec)* Kabelbaum *m* **VT** **a** *horse* anschirren, aufzäumen; **a horse that has never been ~ed** ein Pferd, das nie im Geschirr gegangen ist; **to ~ a horse to a carriage** ein Pferd vor einen Wagen spannen **b** *(= utilize)* nutzen; *river etc also* nutzbar machen; *anger etc* nutzen, sich *(dat)* zunutze *or* zu Nutze machen

harp [hɑːp] N Harfe *f*

▶ **harp on** VI *(inf)* **to harp on sth** auf etw *(dat)* herumreiten; **he's always harping on about the need for ...** er spricht ständig von der Notwendigkeit *+gen* ...; **she's always harping on about her problems** sie lamentiert ständig über ihre Probleme, sie jammert einem dauernd die Ohren voll mit ihren Problemen *(inf)*; **she is always harping on the same theme** es ist immer die alte Leier *or* das alte Lied bei ihr

harpist ['hɑːpɪst] N Harfenspieler(in) *m(f)*, Harfenist(in) *m(f)*

harpoon [hɑː'puːn] **N** Harpune *f*; ~ **gun** Harpunenkanone *f* **VT** harpunieren

harpsichord ['hɑːpsɪkɔːd] N Cembalo *nt*

harpy ['hɑːpɪ] N Harpyie *f*; *(= shrewish woman)* Hexe *f*; *(= grasping person)* Hyäne *f*

harpy eagle N Harpyie *f*

harridan ['hærɪdən] N Vettel *f*, Drache *m*

harrier ['hærɪə'] N **a** *(Sport)* Querfeldeinläufer(in) *m(f)*, Geländeläufer(in) *m(f)* **b** *(Orn)* Weih *m* **c** *(= dog) Hund für die Hasenjagd*

harrow ['hærəʊ] *(Agr)* **N** Egge *f* **VT** **a** *(Agr)* eggen **b** *(fig, usu pass)* **to ~ sb** jdn quälen *or* peinigen *(geh)*

harrowed ['hærəʊd] ADJ *look* gequält

harrowing ['hærəʊɪŋ] ADJ *story, picture etc* entsetzlich, erschütternd, grauenhaft; *experience* qualvoll, grauenhaft; *time* entsetzlich

harrumph [hə'rʌmf] VI sich (laut) räuspern

Harry ['hærɪ] N *dim of* **Henry**

harry ['hærɪ] VT **a** *(= hassle) sb, government* bedrängen, zusetzen *(+dat)* **b** *(old) country* plündern

harsh [hɑːʃ] ADJ *(+er)* **a** *(= inclement) winter* hart, streng; *weather, climate, environment* rau, unwirtlich; *conditions* hart
b *(= severe) words, remarks, criticism* scharf; *verdict, punishment, treatment* hart; *discipline* streng; **~ justice** ein strenges Urteil; **to be ~ with** *or* **on sb** jdn hart anfassen; **don't be too ~ with him** sei nicht zu streng mit *or* hart zu ihm
c *(= abrasive, grating) sound, voice* rau, kratzig; *breathing* rasselnd; *cleaner, detergent* scharf; *wool, fabric* rau; *taste, wine, whisky* herb; *light, glare, colours* grell; **the ~ glare of the sun** das grelle Sonnenlicht; **the ~ cries of the seagulls** das Kreischen der Möwen
d *(= unpleasant, unwelcome) reality, facts, truth* bitter

harshly ['hɑːʃlɪ] ADV **a** *(= severely) judge, treat* streng; *criticize* scharf; **he was ~ treated by the referee** *(= too severely)* der Schiedsrichter behandelte ihn streng; **to be ~ critical of sth** etw scharf kritisieren; **a ~ worded attack** ein scharf formulierter Angriff **b** *(= in a harsh voice) say* scharf, schroff; *laugh* kratzig; **he never once spoke ~ to her** *(= unkindly)* er sprach sie nie in einem scharfen Ton an

harshness ['hɑːʃnɪs] N **a** *(of winter, conditions)* Härte *f*; *(of weather, climate, environment)* Rauheit *f*, Unwirtlichkeit *f* **b** *(= severity, of words, remarks, criticism)* Schärfe *f*; *(of verdict, sentence, punishment, treatment)* Härte *f*; *(of discipline)* Strenge *f* **c** *(= roughness, of sound, voice, wool, fabric)* Rauheit *f*; *(of breathing)* rasselnde Art; *(of cleaner, detergent)* Schärfe *f*; *(of taste, wine, whisky)* Herbheit *f*; *(of light, colours)* Grelle *f*

hart [hɑːt] N Hirsch *m*

harum-scarum ['hɛərəm'skɛərəm] **ADJ** unbesonnen, unbedacht **N** unbedachter Tollkopf

harvest ['hɑːvɪst] **N** Ernte *f*; *(of wines, berries also)* Lese *f*; *(of the sea)* Ausbeute *f*, Ertrag *m*; *(fig)* Frucht *f*, Ertrag *m*; **the ~ of ideas** die Ausbeute an Ideen; **a bumper potato ~** eine Rekordkartoffelernte; **to reap the ~ of sth** *(= benefit)* die Früchte einer Sache *(gen)* ernten; *(= suffer)* die Konsequenzen einer Sache *(gen)* tragen **VT** *(= reap: also fig)* ernten; *vines also* lesen; *trees, timber* schlagen; *fish* fangen; *(= bring in)* einbringen **VI** ernten

harvester ['hɑːvɪstə'] N *(= person)* Erntearbeiter(in) *m(f)*; *(= machine)* Mähmaschine *f*; *(cuts and binds)* Mähbinder *m*, Bindemäher *m*; *(= combine harvester)* Mähdrescher *m*

harvest: **harvest festival** N Erntedankfest *nt*; **harvest fly** N *(Zool)* Zikade *f*; **harvest home** N (Einbringen *nt* der) Ernte *f*; *(= festival)* Erntedankfest *nt*; **harvest moon** N Herbstmond *m*, *heller Vollmond im September*; **harvest time** N Erntezeit *f*

has [hæz] *3rd pers sing present of* **have**

has-been ['hæzbiːn] N *(pej)* vergangene *or* vergessene Größe; **every comedian must dread becoming a ~** jeder Komiker hat Angst davor, in Vergessenheit zu geraten

hash [hæʃ] **N** **a** *(Cook)* Haschee *nt* **b** *(fig: = mess)* Durcheinander *nt*, Kuddelmuddel *m (inf)*; *(= bad work)* Pfusch *m (inf)*, Pfuscherei *f (inf)*; **to make a ~ of sth** etw verpfuschen *or* vermasseln *(inf)* **c** *(inf: = hashish)* Hasch *nt (inf)* **VT** *(Cook)* hacken

▶ **hash over** VI *+prep obj strategy etc* ändern

▶ **hash up** VT *sep* **a** *(Cook)* hacken, zerkleinern **b** *(inf: = mess up)* verpfuschen, vermasseln *(inf)*

hash: **hash brown potatoes** PL *(esp US)* = **hash browns**; **hash browns** [ˌhæʃ'braʊnz] PL *(esp US)* ≈ *Rösti mit Zwiebeln*, ≈ Kartoffelpuffer *pl*; **hash head** N *(inf)* Kiffer(in) *m(f)*, Hascher(in) *m(f)*; **hash house** N *(esp US inf)* billiges Lokal

hashish ['hæʃɪʃ] N Haschisch *nt*

hashtag N *(Internet)* Hashtag *m*

hasn't ['hæznt] *contr of* **has not**

hasp [hɑːsp] N *(for chest, door etc)* Überfall *m*; *(for book covers)* (Verschluss)spange *f*, Schließe *f*

Hassidic [hæ'sɪdɪk] ADJ chassidisch; ~ **Jews** Hassidim *pl*, Chassidim *pl*

hassle ['hæsl] *(inf)* **N** Auseinandersetzung *f*; *(= bother, trouble)* Mühe *f*, Theater *nt (inf)*; **we had a real ~ getting these tickets for tonight** es war ein richtiges Theater *(inf)* or es hat uns *(dat)* viel Mühe gemacht, diese Karten für heute Abend zu bekommen; **getting there is such a ~** es ist so umständlich, dorthin zu kommen; **commuting is a bit of a ~** Pendeln ist

etwas lästig; **it's too much ~ cooking for myself** es ist mir zu umständlich *or* mühsam, für mich allein zu kochen; **don't worry, it's no ~!** keine Sorge, es macht keine Mühe *or* Umstände!; **legal ~s** Anwaltskram *m (inf)*; **don't give me any ~** mach kein Theater *(inf)*; **it's not worth the ~** es ist die ganze Mühe *or* das ganze Theater *(inf)* nicht wert
VT **a** *(= mess around)* schikanieren
b *(= keep on at)* bedrängen; **keep hassling them till they pay** bleib ihnen auf den Fersen, bis sie bezahlen; **stop hassling me** lass mich in Ruhe!; **I'm feeling a bit ~d** ich fühle mich etwas im Stress *(inf) or* unter Druck; **she gets easily ~d** sie lässt sich leicht unter Druck setzen; **he was always being ~d for money** man wollte ständig Geld von ihm
VI **keep hassling** bleib ihm/ihnen *etc* auf den Fersen; **in a job like this you have to be prepared to ~** in diesem Job muss man (anderen) Dampf machen können

hassler [ˈhæslə'] **N** aufdringlicher Typ; **we need someone who is a bit of a ~** wir brauchen einen, der Dampf machen kann

hassock [ˈhæsək] **N** Betkissen *nt*, Kniekissen *nt*

hast [hæst] *(obs) 2nd pers sing present of* **have**

haste [heɪst] **N** Eile *f*; *(nervous)* Hast *f*; **to do sth in ~** etw in Eile tun; **in great ~** in großer Eile; **to make ~ to do sth** sich beeilen, etw zu tun; **make ~!** *(old)* spute dich *(old)*; **more ~ less speed** *(Prov)* eile mit Weile *(Prov)*

hasten [ˈheɪsn] **VI** sich beeilen; **he ~ed to add that ...** er fügte schnell hinzu dass ..., er beeilte sich hinzuzufügen, dass ...; **I ~ to add that ...** ich muss allerdings hinzufügen, dass ...; **she ~ed down the stairs** sie eilte *or* hastete die Treppe hinunter **VT** beschleunigen; **the strain of office ~ed his death** die Belastung seines Amtes trug zu seinem vorzeitigen Tod bei; **to ~ sb's departure** jdn zum Aufbruch drängen

▸ **hasten away** **VI** forteilen *or* -hasten, eilig weggehen

▸ **hasten back** **VI** eilig *or* schnell zurückkehren, zurückeilen

▸ **hasten off** **VI** weg- *or* forteilen

hastily [ˈheɪstɪlɪ] **ADV** **a** *(= hurriedly) arranged* eilig; *examine, glance* flüchtig; *dress, dash, eat, drink* hastig; *(= quickly) say, add* schnell, eilig **b** *(= too quickly) act, decide, thought out* überstürzt, übereilt; *judge, speak* vorschnell; **the decision was ~ made** die Entscheidung war übereilt

hastiness [ˈheɪstɪnɪs] **N** **a** *(= hurriedness)* Eile *f*; *(of meal, movement, goodbye)* Hastigkeit *f*; *(of glance, examination, kiss)* Flüchtigkeit *f*; *(of departure)* Plötzlichkeit *f* **b** *(= rashness, excessive haste)* Übereile *f*; *(of marriage, decision, reaction)* Überstürzung *f*; *(of action, judgement)* Voreiligkeit *f*; **he regretted his ~ in resorting to violence** er bedauerte, dass er so schnell gewalttätig geworden war

hasty [ˈheɪstɪ] **ADJ** *(+er)* **a** *(= hurried) meal, movement, goodbye* hastig; *kiss, glance, examination* flüchtig; *departure* plötzlich; **to beat a ~ retreat, to make a ~ escape** sich schnellstens aus dem Staub machen *(inf)*; **we ate a ~ breakfast** wir frühstückten hastig *or* in aller Eile; **I bade a ~ goodbye** *(dated)* ich verabschiedete mich hastig *or* in aller Eile
b *(= rash, too quick) marriage, decision, reaction* überstürzt, übereilt; *action* voreilig; *judgement* vorschnell; **don't be ~!** nicht so schnell *or* hastig!; **I had been too ~** ich hatte voreilig gehandelt; **to take a ~ decision** eine Entscheidung überstürzen

hasty pudding **N** *(US)* Maismehlbrei *m*

hat [hæt] **N** **a** Hut *m*; *(of cook)* Mütze *f*; **to put on one's ~** den *or* seinen Hut aufsetzen; **to take one's ~ off** den Hut abnehmen; *(for greeting also)* den Hut ziehen (*to sb* vor jdm); **~s off!** Hut ab!; **my ~!** *(dated inf)* dass ich nicht lache! *(inf)*
b *(fig)* **he's a bad ~** *(dated inf)* er ist ein übler Patron *(dated inf)*; **I'll eat my ~ if ...** ich fresse einen Besen, wenn ... *(inf)*; **I take my ~ off to him** Hut ab vor ihm!; **~s off to them for supporting us** Hut ab vor ihnen, dass sie uns unterstützt haben; **to talk through one's ~** *(inf)* dummes Zeug reden; **to keep sth under one's ~** *(inf)* etw für sich behalten; **at the drop of a ~** auf der Stelle, ohne Weiteres; **to toss one's ~ in the ring** sich am politischen Reigen beteiligen; *(non-political)* sich einschalten; **that's old ~** *(inf)* das ist ein alter Hut *(inf)*; **they're all pretty old ~** *(inf)* das sind doch alles olle Kamellen *(inf)*; **to pass round the ~ for sb** für jdn sammeln *or* den Hut rumgehen lassen *(inf)*; **with my accountant's ~ on I would say ...** *(inf)* als Buchhalter würde ich sagen ...; **he wears several different ~s** *(inf)* er übt mehrere Funktionen aus

hatable [ˈheɪtəbl] **ADJ** hassenswert, abscheulich

hat: **hatband** **N** Hutband *nt*; **hatbox** **N** Hutschachtel *f*

hatch[1] [hætʃ] **VT** *(also* **hatch out**) ausbrüten; *(fig) plot, scheme also* aushecken; *compromise* aushandeln **VI** *(also* **hatch out**: *bird)* ausschlüpfen; **when will the eggs ~?** wann schlüpfen die Jungen aus? **N** *(= brood)* Brut *f*

hatch[2] **N** **a** *(Naut)* Luke *f*; *(in floor, ceiling)* Bodenluke *f*; *(= half-door)* Halbtür *f*, Niedertür *f* → **batten down** **b** **(service)** ~ Durchreiche *f* **c** **down the ~!** *(inf)* hoch die Tassen! *(inf)*

hatch[3] **VT** *(Art)* schraffieren

hatchback [ˈhætʃbæk] **N** Hecktürmodell *nt*; *(= door)* Hecktür *f*

hatchery [ˈhætʃərɪ] **N** Brutplatz *m or* -stätte *f*

hatchet [ˈhætʃɪt] **N** Beil *nt*; *(= tomahawk)* Kriegsbeil *nt*; **to bury the ~** *(fig)* das Kriegsbeil begraben

hatchet: **hatchet face** **N** scharf geschnittenes Gesicht; *(inf: = person)* Raubvogelgesicht *nt*; **hatchet-faced** **ADJ** mit scharfen Gesichtszügen; **hatchet job** **N** *(inf)* **to do a ~ on sb** jdn fertigmachen *(inf)*; **hatchet man** **N** *(= hired killer)* gedungener Mörder; *(fig)* Vollstreckungsbeamte(r) *m*

hatching [ˈhætʃɪŋ] **N** *(Art)* Schraffur *f*, Schraffierung *f*

hatchway [ˈhætʃweɪ] **N** = **hatch**[2] **a**

hate [heɪt] ✪ 7.3 **VT** hassen; *(= detest also)* verabscheuen, nicht ausstehen können; *(= dislike also)* nicht leiden können; **to ~ the sound of sth** etw nicht hören können; **to ~ to do sth** *or* **doing sth** es hassen, etw zu tun; *(weaker)* etw äußerst ungern tun; **I ~ being late** ich hasse es, zu spät zu kommen, ich komme äußerst ungern zu spät; **I ~ seeing** *or* **to see her in pain** ich kann es nicht ertragen, sie leiden zu sehen; **I ~ the idea of leaving** der Gedanke, wegzumüssen, ist mir äußerst zuwider; **I ~ it when people accuse me of lying** ich kann es nicht ausstehen, wenn man mich als Lügner bezeichnet; **I ~ to bother/rush you** es ist mir sehr unangenehm, dass ich Sie belästigen/zur Eile drängen muss; **I ~ to say/admit it but ...** es fällt mir sehr schwer, das sagen/zugeben zu müssen, aber ...; **I ~d myself for writing that letter** ich konnte es mir nicht verzeihen, dass ich diesen Brief geschrieben hatte; **she ~s me having any fun** sie kann es nicht haben, wenn ich Spaß habe; **you'll ~ me for this but ...** du wirst es mir vielleicht übel nehmen, aber ...; **don't ~ me for telling you the truth** nimm es mir nicht übel *or* sei mir nicht böse, dass ich dir die Wahrheit sage; **I should ~ to keep you waiting** ich möchte Sie auf keinen Fall warten lassen; **I'd ~ to think I'd never see him again** ich könnte den Gedanken, ihn nie wiederzusehen, nicht ertragen
N **a** *(= hatred)* Hass *m* (*for, of* auf *+acc*)
b *(= object of hatred)* **one of his pet ~s is plastic cutlery/having to wait** Plastikbesteck/Warten ist ihm ein Gräuel, Plastikbesteck/Warten gehört zu den Dingen, die er am meisten hasst *or* verabscheut; **celery is/spiders are my pet ~** ich kann Sellerie/Spinnen auf den Tod nicht ausstehen *or* leiden *(inf)*

hate campaign **N** Hasskampagne *f*

hated [ˈheɪtɪd] **ADJ** verhasst

hateful [ˈheɪtfʊl] **ADJ** **a** abscheulich; *remarks also* hässlich; *person* unausstehlich; **sth is ~ to sb** etw ist jdm verhasst; **it was a ~ thing to say/do** das war abscheulich **b** *(= full of hate)* hasserfüllt

hatefully [ˈheɪtfəlɪ] **ADV** abscheulich

hate mail **N** beleidigende Briefe *pl*

hatemonger [ˈheɪt,mʌŋgə'] **N** Aufhetzer(in) *m(f)*, Aufwiegler(in) *m(f)*

hath [hæθ] *(obs)* = **has**

hat: **hatless** **ADJ** ohne Hut; **hatpin** **N** Hutnadel *f*; **hat rack** **N** Hutablage *f*

hatred [ˈheɪtrɪd] **N** Hass *m* (*for, of* auf *+acc*); *(of spinach, spiders etc)* Abscheu *m* (*of* vor *+dat*); **racial ~** Rassenhass *m*

hat stand, *(US)* **hat tree** **N** Garderobenständer *m*; *(for hats only)* Hutständer *m*

hatter [ˈhætə'] **N** Hutmacher(in) *m(f)*; *(= seller)* Hutverkäufer(in) *m(f)* → **mad**

hat trick **N** Hattrick *m*; **to score a ~** einen Hattrick erzielen; **with two husbands already behind her she looks like making it a ~** nachdem sie nun schon zweimal geschieden ist, denkt sie wohl, aller guten Dinge sind drei

haughtily [ˈhɔːtɪlɪ] **ADV** *say* hochmütig, überheblich; *dismiss, ignore* arrogant; *look* geringschätzig

haughtiness [ˈhɔːtɪnɪs] **N** Hochmut *m*, Überheblichkeit *f*; *(of look)* Geringschätzigkeit *f*

haughty [ˈhɔːtɪ] **ADJ** *(+er) manner, attitude, voice, expression* hochmütig, überheblich; *disdain, person also* arrogant; *look* geringschätzig

haul [hɔːl] **N** **a** *(= hauling)* **a truck gave us a ~** ein Lastwagen schleppte uns ab *or (out of mud etc)* zog uns heraus
b *(= journey)* Strecke *f*; **it's a long ~ to recovery** es ist ein weiter Weg bis zum Aufschwung; **short/long/medium ~ aircraft** Kurz-/Lang-/Mittelstreckenflugzeug *nt*; **the project has been a long ~** das Projekt hat sich lang hingezogen; **the long ~ through the courts** der lange Weg durch die Instanzen; **revitalizing the economy will be a long ~** es wird lange dauern, die Wirtschaft wieder anzukurbeln; **over the long ~** *(esp US)* langfristig
c *(Fishing)* (Fisch)fang *m*; *(fig: = booty: from robbery)* Beute *f*; *(of cocaine etc)* Fund *m*; *(inf, of presents)* Ausbeute *f (inf)*; **our ~ on the last trawl was 500 kg of herring** bei unserer letzten Fahrt hatten wir eine Ausbeute von 500 kg Hering; **drugs ~** Drogenfund *m*
VT **a** *(= pull)* ziehen; *heavy objects* ziehen, schleppen; **he ~ed himself/Paul to his feet** er wuchtete sich/Paul wieder auf die Beine → **coal**
b *(= transport)* befördern, transportieren
c *(Naut)* den Kurs (*+gen*) ändern; **to ~ a boat into the wind** an den Wind segeln
VI *(Naut: also* **haul round**) den Kurs ändern; **the yacht ~ed into the wind** die Jacht segelte an den Wind

▸ **haul away** **VI** *(= pull)* mit aller Kraft ziehen (*at, on* an *+dat*); *(rowers)* sich in die Riemen legen; **haul away!** hau ruck!

▸ **haul down** **VT** *sep* **a** *flag, sail* einholen, niederholen **b** *(with effort)* herunterschleppen; *(= pull down)* herunterzerren

▸ **haul in** **VT** *sep* einholen; *rope* einziehen; *(police)* festnehmen

▸ **haul off** **VI** *(Naut)* (ab)drehen, den Kurs ändern

▸ **haul round** **VI** *(Naut, ship)* den Kurs ändern; *(wind)* drehen

▸ **haul up** **VT** *sep* **a** *(= carry)* hinauf- *or* hochschleppen; *flag, sail* hissen; *(aboard ship)* (an Bord) hieven, hochziehen; *(onto beach)* schleppen, ziehen; *(= pull up)* hochzerren, hochziehen; **the dinghies were lying hauled up on the beach for the winter** man hatte die Jollen für den Winter an Land gezogen
b *(fig inf)* **to haul sb up before the magis-**

trate/headmaster jdn vor den Kadi/Schulleiter schleppen *(inf)*; **he's been hauled up on a drugs charge** er wurde wegen einer Rauschgiftsache vor den Kadi gebracht *(inf)*; **he was hauled up for speeding** er wurde wegen Geschwindigkeitsüberschreitung vor Gericht gebracht

haulage ['hɔːlɪdʒ] N *(Brit)* **a** *(= road transport)* Transport *m* **b** *(= transport charges)* Speditions- *or* Transportkosten *pl*

haulage business N *(esp Brit) (= firm)* Transport- *or* Fuhrunternehmen *nt*, Spedition(sfirma) *f*; *(= trade)* Speditionsbranche *f*, Fuhrwesen *nt*

haulage contractor N *(esp Brit) (= firm)* Transportunternehmen *nt*, Spedition(sfirma) *f*; *(= person)* Transport- *or* Fuhrunternehmer(in) *m(f)*, Spediteur(in) *m(f)*

haulier ['hɔːlɪəʳ], *(US)* **hauler** ['hɔːləʳ] N Spediteur(in) *m(f)*, Fuhrunternehmer(in) *m(f)*; *(= company)* Spedition *f*; **firm of ~s** Spedition(sfirma) *f*, Transportunternehmen *nt*

haulm [hɔːm] N *(single)* Stängel *m*; *(grain, grass also)* Halm *m*; *(collectively)* Stroh *nt*

haunch [hɔːntʃ] N *(of person)* Hüfte *f*; *(= hip area)* Hüftpartie *f*; *(of animal, = hindquarters)* Hinterbacke *f*; *(= top of leg)* Keule *f*; *(Cook)* Keule *f*, Lendenstück *nt*; **~es** Gesäß *nt*; *(of animal)* Hinterbacken *pl*; **to go down on one's ~es** in die Hocke gehen; **to squat on one's ~es** in der Hocke sitzen; **the dog was sitting on its ~es** der Hund saß auf den Hinterbeinen; **~ of venison** *(Cook)* Rehkeule *f*

haunt [hɔːnt] **VT** **a** *(ghost) house, place* spuken in *(+dat)*, umgehen in *(+dat)*
b *person* verfolgen; *(memory)* nicht loslassen, verfolgen; *(fear, decision)* quälen; **the nightmares which ~ed him** die Albträume *or* Alpträume, die ihn heimsuchten; **lack of money ~ed successive projects** mehrere aufeinanderfolgende Projekte waren vom Geldmangel verfolgt
c *(= frequent)* verkehren in *(+dat)*, frequentieren, häufig besuchen; *(animal)* vorkommen, auftreten
N *(of person, = pub etc)* Stammlokal *nt*; *(= favourite resort)* Lieblingsort *or* -platz *m*; *(of criminals)* Treff(punkt) *m*; *(of animal)* Heimat *f*; **the riverbank is the ~ of a variety of animals** eine Vielzahl von Tieren lebt an Flussufern; **to revisit the ~s of one's youth** die Stätten seiner Jugend wieder aufsuchen; **her usual childhood ~s** Stätten, die sie in ihrer Kindheit oft aufsuchte; **a ~ of literary exiles** ein Treffpunkt *m* für Exilliteraten

haunted ['hɔːntɪd] ADJ **a** Spuk-; **~ castle** Spukschloss *nt*; **a ~ house** ein Spukhaus *nt*, ein Haus *nt*, in dem es spukt; **this place is ~** hier spukt es; **is it ~?** spukt es da? **b** *look* gehetzt, gequält; *person* ruhelos

haunting ['hɔːntɪŋ] ADJ *doubt* quälend, nagend; *tune, visions, poetry, cry, eyes* eindringlich; *memory* lastend; *music* schwermütig; **these ~ final chords** diese Schlussakkorde, die einen nicht loslassen

hauntingly ['hɔːntɪŋlɪ] ADV ergreifend; *melodious, tuneful* eindringlich

haute couture [ˌəʊtkuːˈtʊəʳ] **N** Haute Couture *f* **ADJ** *attr* der Haute Couture

hauteur [əʊ'tɜːʳ] N *(liter)* Hochmütigkeit *f*

Havana [hə'vænə] N **a** Havanna *nt* **b** *(= cigar)* Havanna(zigarre) *f*

have [hæv]
pret, ptp **had**, *3rd pers sing present* **has**
✪ 10.2, 10.3

1 AUXILIARY VERB	3 TRANSITIVE VERB
2 MODAL AUXILIARY VERB	4 PHRASAL VERBS

When *have* is part of a set combination, eg *have a look, have a dream, have a good time*, look up the noun.

1 – AUXILIARY VERB

a haben

The verb *haben* is the auxiliary used with most verbs to form past tenses in German. For important exceptions see *(b)*.

to have seen/heard/eaten gesehen/gehört/gegessen haben; **I have/had seen** ich habe/hatte gesehen; **I have not/had not** *or* **I haven't/I hadn't seen him** ich habe/hatte ihn nicht gesehen; **had I seen him, if I had seen him** hätte ich ihn gesehen, wenn ich ihn gesehen hätte; **having seen him** *(= after I had)* als ich ihn gesehen hatte; **having realized this** *(= since I had)* nachdem ich das erkannt hatte; **having said that he left** nachdem *or* als er das gesagt hatte, ging er

Note the tenses used in the following:

I have lived *or* **have been living here for 10 years/since January** ich wohne *or* lebe schon 10 Jahre/seit Januar hier

b sein

The verb *sein* is used with verbs of motion, eg. *gehen, fahren*, or verbs implying development, eg. *wachsen*, and to form past tenses.

to have gone/run gegangen/gelaufen sein; **you HAVE grown!** du bist aber gewachsen!; **to have been** gewesen sein; **I have been to London** ich bin in London gewesen; **I have been against this for years** ich bin schon seit Jahren dagegen

c *in tag questions etc* **you've seen her, haven't you?** du hast sie gesehen, oder nicht?; **you haven't seen her, have you?** du hast sie nicht gesehen, oder?; **you haven't seen her – yes, I have** du hast sie nicht gesehen – doch *or* wohl *(inf)*; **you've made a mistake – no, I haven't** du hast einen Fehler gemacht – nein(, hab ich nicht); **you've dropped your book – so I have** dir ist dein Buch hingefallen – stimmt *or* tatsächlich; **have you been there? if you have/haven't ...** sind Sie schon mal da gewesen? wenn ja/nein *or* nicht, ...; **I have seen a ghost – have you?** ich habe ein Gespenst gesehen – wahrhaftig *or* tatsächlich?; **I've lost it – you haven't!** *(disbelieving)* ich habe es verloren – nein!

2 – MODAL AUXILIARY VERB

♦ **to have to do sth** *(= to be obliged)* etw tun müssen; **I have (got** *esp Brit*) **to do it** ich muss es tun *or* machen; **have you got to go now?** *(Brit)* **do you have to go now?** müssen Sie jetzt (wirklich) unbedingt gehen?; **do you have to make such a noise?** müssen Sie (unbedingt) so viel Lärm machen?; **she was having to get up at 6 o'clock each morning** sie musste jeden Morgen um 6 Uhr aufstehen; **we've had to go and see her twice this week** wir mussten diese Woche schon zweimal zu ihr (hin); **the letter will have to be written tomorrow** der Brief muss morgen unbedingt geschrieben werden; **I'm afraid it has to be** das muss leider sein; **it's got to be** *or* **it has to be the biggest scandal this year** das ist todsicher der (größte) Skandal des Jahres

♦ **don't/doesn't have to** *or (esp Brit)* **haven't/hasn't got to I haven't got to do it** *(esp Brit)* **I don't have to do it** ich muss es nicht tun, ich brauche es nicht zu tun; **you didn't have to tell her** das mussten Sie ihr nicht unbedingt sagen, das hätten Sie ihr nicht unbedingt sagen müssen *or* brauchen; **he hasn't got to work** *(esp Brit)* **he doesn't have to work** er braucht nicht zu arbeiten, er muss nicht arbeiten

3 – TRANSITIVE VERB

a *= possess* haben; **have you (got** *esp Brit*) *or* **do you have a car?** hast du ein Auto?; **I haven't (got** *esp Brit*) *or* **I don't have a pen** ich habe keinen Kugelschreiber; **to have something/nothing to do** etwas/nichts zu tun haben; **I have (got** *esp Brit*) **work/a translation to do** ich habe zu arbeiten/eine Übersetzung zu erledigen; **I must have more time** ich brauche mehr Zeit; **have you (got** *esp Brit*) *or* **do you have a cigarette?** hast du (mal) eine Zigarette?; **I don't have any German** *(Brit)* ich kann kein (Wort) Deutsch; **she has (got** *esp Brit*) **blue eyes** sie hat blaue Augen; **I have it!** ich habs!; **what time do you have?** *(US)* wie viel Uhr hast du? *(inf)*, wie spät hast du es?

b *= receive, obtain, get* haben; **to have news from sb** von jdm hören; **I have it on good authority that ...** ich habe aus zuverlässiger Quelle gehört *or* erfahren, dass ...; **I must have something to eat** ich brauche etwas zu essen, ich muss dringend etwas zu essen haben; **there are no newspapers to be had** es sind keine Zeitungen zu haben; **it's nowhere to be had** es ist nirgends zu haben *or* kriegen *(inf)*; **there are some great bargains to be had in the shops** in den Geschäften gibt es tolle Angebote; **I'll have the bed in this room** das Bett möchte *or* werde ich in dieses Zimmer stellen; **thanks for having me** vielen Dank für Ihre Gastfreundschaft

♦ **to let sb have sth** jdm etw geben; **please let me have your address** geben Sie mir bitte Ihre Adresse; **I'll let you have it for £50** ich gebe es dir für £ 50

c *= eat, drink, take* **to have breakfast** frühstücken; **to have lunch/dinner** zu Mittag/Abend essen; **to have tea with sb** mit jdm (zusammen) Tee trinken; **will you have tea or coffee?** möchten Sie lieber Tee oder Kaffee?; **will you have a drink/cigarette?** möchten Sie etwas zu trinken/eine Zigarette?; **what will you have? – I'll have the steak** was möchten *or* hätten Sie gern(e)? – ich hätte *or* möchte gern das Steak; **he had a cigarette/drink/steak** er rauchte eine Zigarette/trank etwas/aß ein Steak; **will you have some more?** möchten Sie *or* hätten Sie gern(e) (noch etwas) mehr?; **have another one** nimm noch eine/einen/eines; *(drink)* trink noch einen; *(cigarette)* rauch noch eine

d *= catch, hold* (gepackt) haben; **he had (got** *(esp Brit)*) **me by the throat/the hair** er hatte *or* hielt mich am Hals/bei den Haaren gepackt; **I have (got** *(esp Brit)*) **him where I want him** ich habe ihn endlich so weit, ich habe ihn endlich (da), wo ich ihn will; **the champion had him now** der Meister hatte ihn jetzt fest im Griff *or* in der Tasche *(inf)*; **I'll have you** *(inf)* dich krieg ich (beim Kragen); **you have me there** da bin ich überfragt

e *= suffer from* **he has diabetes** er ist zuckerkrank, er hat Zucker *(inf)*; **to have a heart attack** einen Herzinfarkt bekommen; **I've (got** *(esp Brit)*) **a headache** ich habe Kopfschmerzen

f *= experience* **to have a pleasant evening** einen netten Abend verbringen; **to have a good time** Spaß haben, sich amüsieren; **have a good time!** viel Spaß!

g *= hold, organize* *party* geben, machen; *meeting* abhalten; **are you having a reception?** gibt es einen Empfang?; **we decided not to have a reception** wir haben uns gegen einen Empfang entschieden

h *= go for* **to have a walk** einen Spaziergang machen, spazieren gehen; **to have a swim** schwimmen gehen

i *= give birth to* **to have a child** *or* **baby** ein Kind *or* Baby bekommen; **she is having a baby in April** sie bekommt *or* kriegt *(inf)* im April ein Kind; **she had twins** sie hat Zwillinge bekommen *or* geboren *or* gekriegt *(inf)*; **our cat has had kittens** unsere Katze hat Junge gekriegt *(inf) or* bekommen

j *= cause to be* **I had him in such a state that ...** er war in einer solchen Verfassung, dass ...; **he had the audience in hysterics** das Publikum kugelte sich vor Lachen; **he had the police baffled** die Polizei stand vor einem Rätsel; **she nearly had the table over** *(Brit)* sie hätte den Tisch beinahe umgekippt *or* zum Umkippen gebracht

k *= maintain, insist* **he will have it that Paul is guilty** *(Brit)* **as he has it, Paul is guilty** er besteht darauf, dass Paul schuldig ist; **he wouldn't have it that Paul is guilty** *(Brit)* **as he had it, Paul isn't guilty** er wollte nichts davon hören, dass Paul schuldig ist; **as rumour** *(Brit) or* **rumor** *(US)* **has it** Gerüchten zufolge; **as the**

Bible/Shakespeare has it wie es in der Bibel/bei Shakespeare steht

l = refuse to allow *in negative sentences* **I won't have this nonsense** dieser Unsinn kommt (mir) nicht infrage *or* in Frage!; **I won't have this sort of rudeness!** diese Unhöflichkeit lasse ich mir ganz einfach nicht bieten; **I won't have it!** das lasse ich mir nicht bieten!; **I won't have him insulted** ich lasse es nicht zu *or* dulde es nicht, dass man ihn beleidigt; **I won't have him insult his mother** ich lasse es nicht zu, dass er seine Mutter beleidigt; **we won't have women in our club** in unserem Klub sind Frauen nicht zugelassen; **I'm not having any of that!** *(inf)* mit mir nicht! *(inf)*; **but she wasn't having any** *(inf)* aber sie wollte nichts davon wissen

m = wish mögen; **which one will you have?** welche(n, s) möchten Sie haben *or* hätten Sie gern?; **as fate would have it, …** wie es das Schicksal so wollte, …; **what would you have me do?** was wollen Sie, dass ich mache?

n set structures

♦ **to have sth done**

= request, order etw tun lassen; **to have one's hair cut** sich *(dat)* die Haare schneiden lassen; **to have a suit made** sich *(dat)* einen Anzug machen lassen; **I had my cases brought up** ich habe (mir) meine Koffer nach oben bringen lassen; **have it mended** geben Sie es in Reparatur, lassen Sie es reparieren; **they had him shot** sie ließen ihn erschießen

= suffer, experience **he had his car stolen** man hat ihm sein Auto gestohlen; **he had his arm broken** er hat/hatte einen gebrochenen Arm; **I've had three windows broken** (bei) mir sind drei Fenster eingeworfen worden

♦ **to have sb do sth**

= make them do jdn etw tun lassen; **I had him wash the car** ich ließ ihn den Wagen waschen; **I'll have you know …** Sie müssen nämlich wissen …

= experience **I had my friends turn against me** ich musste es erleben, wie *or* dass sich meine Freunde gegen mich wandten

♦ **to have sb doing sth she had us all helping with the dinner** nach ihrer Ermunterung halfen wir alle mit dem Abendessen; **she soon had them all reading and writing** dank ihres Engagements konnten alle schon bald lesen und schreiben

♦ **to have had it** *(inf)* **he has had it with politics** er hat von der Politik die Nase voll *(inf)*; **that coat has had it** der Mantel ist im Eimer *(inf)*; **if I miss the last bus, I've had it** wenn ich den letzten Bus verpasse, bin ich geliefert *(inf)* *or* ist der Ofen aus *(inf)*

♦ **let him have it!** *(inf)* gibs ihm! *(inf)*

♦ **have it your own way** machen Sie es *or* halten Sie es, wie Sie wollen

♦ **to be had** *(inf: = tricked)* **you've been had!** da hat man dich übers Ohr gehauen *(inf)*

4 – PHRASAL VERBS

▸ **have around** VT *always separate* **a** (bei sich) zu Besuch haben; *(= invite)* einladen **b he's a useful man to have around** es ist ganz praktisch, ihn zur Hand zu haben

▸ **have at** VI *+prep obj (old)* angreifen; **she had at me with her umbrella** sie ging mit ihrem Regenschirm auf mich los

▸ **have away** VT *always separate* **to have it away with sb** *(inf)* es mit jdm treiben *(inf)*

▸ **have back** VT *sep* zurückhaben

▸ **have down** VT **a** *sep people, guests* (bei sich) zu Besuch haben **b** *always separate (= take down) scaffolding* abbauen; *(= knock down) buildings* abreißen; *vase* herunterwerfen; *(= put down) carpets* verlegen

▸ **have in** VT *always separate* **a** *(in the house)* im Haus haben; **we've (got** *esp Brit*) **the decorators in all week** wir haben die ganze Woche (über) die Anstreicher im Haus **b to have it in for sb** *(inf)* jdn auf dem Kieker haben *(inf)* **c** *(= make come in)* hereinrufen; **can we have the next interviewee in?** können wir den nächsten Kandidaten haben? **d** *(= put in)* **he had the new engine in by lunchtime** er hatte den neuen Motor bis mittags drin *(inf)* **e I didn't know he had it in him** ich hätte ihm das nicht zugetraut; **he's got it in him to succeed** er hat das Zeug dazu, erfolgreich zu sein

▸ **have off** VT *always separate* **a to have it off with sb** *(Brit inf)* es mit jdm treiben *(inf)* **b** *(= take off)* **he had the top off in a second** er hatte den Deckel in Sekundenschnelle (he)runter; **he had to have his leg off** ihm musste das Bein abgenommen werden

▸ **have on** VT **a** *sep (= wear)* anhaben; *radio, TV* anhaben

VT *always separate* **a** *(= have arranged)* vorhaben; *(= be busy with)* zu tun haben; **we've (got** *esp Brit*) **a big job on** wir haben ein großes Projekt in Arbeit

b *(inf: = deceive, trick)* übers Ohr hauen *(inf)*; *(= tease)* auf den Arm nehmen *(inf)*; **you're having me on** do willst mich wohl auf den Arm nehmen *(inf)*

c to have nothing on sb nichts gegen jdn in der Hand haben; **they've got nothing on me!** mir kann keiner! *(inf)*

d *(= put on)* **they had new tyres** *(Brit)* *or* **tires** *(US)* **on in no time** sie hatten die neuen Reifen im Nu drauf *(inf)*; **they still haven't got the roof on** das Dach ist immer noch nicht drauf

▸ **have out** VT *always separate* **a** *(= have taken out)* herausgenommen bekommen; **he had his tonsils/appendix out** ihm wurden die Mandeln/wurde der Blinddarm herausgenommen **b** *(= discuss)* ausdiskutieren; **to have it out with sb** etw mit jdm ausdiskutieren; **I'll have it out with him** ich werde mit ihm reden, ich werde mich mit ihm aussprechen

▸ **have over** *or (esp Brit)* **round** VT *always separate* (bei sich) zu Besuch haben; *(= invite)* (zu sich) einladen

▸ **have up** VT *always separate* **a** *(inf: = cause to appear in court)* drankriegen *(inf)*; **that's the second time he's been had up for drunken driving** jetzt haben sie ihn schon zum zweiten Mal wegen Trunkenheit am Steuer drangekriegt *(inf)*; **he's been had up again** er war schon wieder vor dem Kadi *(inf)* **b** *(= put up)* **as soon as we had the tent/shelves up** sobald wir das Zelt aufgestellt/die Regale an der Wand hatten

---

have-a-go [ˌhævəˈgəʊ] ADJ ATTR *(Brit inf)* **~-hero** heldenmütiger Kämpfer

haven [ˈheɪvən] N *(fig)* Zufluchtsstätte *f*

haven't [ˈhævnt] *contr of* **have not**

haves [hævz] PL *(inf)* **the ~** die Betuchten *pl (inf)*, die Begüterten *pl*; **the ~ and the have-nots** die Betuchten und die Habenichtse

havoc [ˈhævək] N verheerender Schaden; *(= devastation also)* Verwüstung *f*; *(= chaos)* Chaos *nt*; **to cause** *or* **create ~** ein Chaos verursachen; **to wreak ~ in** *or* **on** *or* **with sth, to play ~ with sth** bei etw verheerenden Schaden anrichten; *(physical damage also)* etw verwüsten, etw verheerend zurichten; *with health, part of the body* für etw üble *or* schlimme Folgen haben, sich übel auf etw *(acc)* auswirken; *with life, career* etw ruinieren; **the tornado wreaked ~ all along the coast** der Tornado richtete entlang der ganzen Küste große Verwüstungen an; **this wreaked ~ with their plans** das brachte ihre Pläne völlig durcheinander; **the sudden rise in oil prices played ~ with India's five-year plan** der plötzliche Anstieg der Ölpreise hat Indiens Fünfjahresplan vollständig über den Haufen geworfen *(inf)*

haw[1] [hɔː] N *(Bot)* Mehlfässchen *nt*, Mehlbeere *f*

haw[2] → **hum**

Hawaii [həˈwaɪː] N Hawaii *nt*

Hawaiian [həˈwaɪjən] ADJ hawaii(ani)sch, Hawaii-; **~ island** Hawaii-Insel *f*; **~ Standard Time** *(US)* hawaiische Zeit N **a** Hawaiianer(in) *m(f)* **b** *(Ling)* Hawaiisch *nt*

Hawaiian guitar N Hawaiigitarre *f*

Hawaiian shirt N grellbuntes Hemd

hawfinch [ˈhɔːfɪntʃ] N *(Orn)* Kernbeißer *m*

hawk[1] [hɔːk] N **a** *(Orn)* Habicht *m*; *(= sparrow hawk)* Sperber *m*; *(= falcon)* Falke *m*; **to watch sb like a ~** jdn ganz genau beobachten **b** *(fig: = politician)* Falke *m*; **the ~s and the doves** die Falken und die Tauben VI mit Falken jagen

hawk[2] VI *(with phlegm)* sich räuspern

hawk[3] VT hausieren (gehen) mit; *(in street)* verkaufen, feilhalten, feilbieten; *(by shouting out)* ausschreien

▸ **hawk about** VT *sep (Brit) term etc* benutzen

▸ **hawk around** VT *sep (lit, fig)* hausieren (gehen) mit

▸ **hawk up** VT *sep phlegm* aushusten

hawker [ˈhɔːkəˈ] N **a** *(= hunter)* Falkner(in) *m(f)* **b** *(= pedlar, door-to-door)* Hausierer(in) *m(f)*; *(in street)* Straßenhändler(in) *m(f)*; *(at market)* Marktschreier(in) *m(f)*

hawk-eyed [ˈhɔːkaɪd] ADJ scharfsichtig, adleräugig; **to be ~** Adleraugen haben

hawking [ˈhɔːkɪŋ] N (Falken)beize *f*, Falkenjagd *f*

hawk moth N Schwärmer *m*

hawser [ˈhɔːzəˈ] N *(Naut)* Trosse *f*

hawthorn [ˈhɔːθɔːn] N *(also* **hawthorn bush/tree**) Weiß- *or* Rot- *or* Hagedorn *m*; **~ hedge** Weiß- *or* Rotdornhecke *f*

hay [heɪ] N Heu *nt*; **to make ~** Heu machen, heuen; *(fig)* profitieren; **to hit the ~** *(inf)* sich aufs Ohr hauen *(inf)*; **to make ~ while the sun shines** *(Prov)* das Eisen schmieden, solange es heiß ist *(Prov)*

hay: **haycock** N Heuhaufen *m*; **hay fever** N Heuschnupfen *m*; **hayfork** N Heugabel *f*; *(motor-driven)* Heuwender *m*; **hayloft** N Heuboden *m*; **haymaker** N **a** Heumacher(in) *m(f)* **b** *(Boxing inf)* knallharter Schlag, Schwinger *m*; **haymaking** N Heuen *nt*, Heuernte *f*; **hayrack** N *(for fodder)* (Heu)raufe *f*; *(US, on wagon)* Heuwagenaufbau *m*; **hayrick, haystack** N Heuhaufen *m*

haywire [ˈheɪwaɪəˈ] ADJ *pred (inf)* **to be (all) ~** (vollständig) durcheinander *or* ein Wirrwarr *(inf)* sein; **the local economy is all ~ again** die örtliche Wirtschaft ist wieder im Chaos versunken *(inf)*; **to go ~** *(= go crazy)* durchdrehen *(inf)*; *(plans, arrangements)* durcheinandergeraten, über den Haufen geworfen werden *(inf)*; *(machinery)* verrücktspielen *(inf)*

hazard [ˈhæzəd] N **a** *(= danger)* Gefahr *f*; *(= risk)* Risiko *nt*; **the ~s of war** die Gefahren des Krieges; **a safety ~** ein Sicherheitsrisiko *nt*; **it's a fire ~** es ist feuergefährlich, es stellt eine Feuergefahr dar; **to pose a ~ (to sb/sth)** eine Gefahr (für jdn/etw) darstellen

b *(= chance)* **by ~** durch Zufall

c *(Sport, Golf, Showjumping)* Hindernis *nt*

d hazards PL *(Aut: also* **hazard (warning) lights**) Warnblinklicht *nt*

VT **a** *(= risk) life, health, reputation* riskieren, aufs Spiel setzen; *(= endanger) person* in Gefahr bringen

b *(= venture to make)* wagen, riskieren; **if I might ~ a remark/suggestion** wenn ich mir eine Bemerkung/einen Vorschlag erlauben darf; **to ~ a guess** (es) wagen, eine Vermutung anzustellen; **to ~ a guess that …** zu vermuten wagen, dass …

hazardous [ˈhæzədəs] ADJ *(= dangerous)* gefährlich; *(= risky)* riskant; **~ to health** gesundheitsgefährdend; **bungee jumping is a ~ business** Bungeespringen ist eine gefährliche *or* riskante Angelegenheit; **such jobs are ~ to one's health** solche Arbeiten gefährden die Gesundheit

hazardous: **hazardous material** N Gefahrstoff *m*; *(Mot)* Gefahrgut *nt*; **hazardous waste** N Sondermüll *m*

haze [heɪz] N **a** Dunst *m*; **a ~ of exhaust fumes** ein Dunstschleier *m* von Abgasen **b** *(fig)* **he/his mind was in a ~** *(= confused)* er war vollkommen verwirrt; **in a ~ of alcohol** vom Alkohol benebelt *(inf)*

hazel [ˈheɪzl] N *(Bot)* Haselnussstrauch *m*, Haselbusch *m* ADJ *(colour)* haselnuss- *or* hellbraun

hazelnut ['heɪzlnʌt] N Haselnuss *f*

hazily ['heɪzɪlɪ] ADV **a** **the island/hills loomed ~ through the mist** die Insel zeichnete/die Berge zeichneten sich verschwommen im Dunst ab **b** *(= vaguely) remember, say* vage

haziness ['heɪzɪnɪs] N **a** *(of sunshine)* Trübheit *f*; *(of view, outline, vision, surroundings)* Verschwommenheit *f*; **due to the ~ of the weather** wegen des dunstigen *or* diesigen Wetters **b** *(of ideas, memory, details)* Unklarheit *f*, Vagheit *f*

HAZMAT ['hæz,mæt] N *(inf) of* **hazardous material** Gefahrstoff *m*; *(Mot)* Gefahrgut *nt*

hazy ['heɪzɪ] ADJ *(+er)* **a** *day, morning, weather* dunstig, diesig; *sunshine, sky* trübe; *view* verschwommen; **the ~ horizon** der im Dunst liegende Horizont; **~ blue** blassblau **b** *(= blurred) outline, vision, surroundings* verschwommen **c** *(= confused) notion, details, memory* unklar, vage; **to have only a ~ notion/idea of sth** nur unklare *or* vage Vorstellungen von etw haben; **I have only a ~ memory of her** ich erinnere mich nur dunkel *or* vage an sie; **I'm a bit ~ about that** ich bin mir nicht ganz im Klaren darüber; **I'm ~ about what really happened** ich weiß nicht so genau, was wirklich passiert ist; **my memory's a little ~ on this** ich kann mich nur dunkel *or* vage daran erinnern; **she's still (feeling) ~ (from the anaesthetic** *(Brit) or* **anesthetic** *(US)*) sie ist (von der Narkose) noch benommen

HB ADJ *(on pencil)* HB

H-bomb ['eɪtʃbɒm] N H-Bombe *f*

HDD *(Comput) abbr of* **hard disk drive** Festplattenlaufwerk *nt*

HDTV *abbr of* **high-definition television** HDTV *nt*

HE *abbr of* **His Excellency, His Eminence** S. E.

he [hi:] PERS PRON **a** er; **it is he** *(form)* er ist es, es ist er; **if I were he** *(form)* wenn ich er wäre; **he didn't do it, I did it** nicht er hat das getan, sondern ich; **so he's the one** der *(inf) or* er ist es also!; **Harry Rigg? who's he?** Harry Rigg? wer ist das denn? **b** **he who** *or* **that ...** *(liter)* derjenige, der ...; *(in proverbs)* wer ... N *(of animal)* Männchen *nt*; **it's a he** *(inf: of newborn baby)* es ist ein Er PREF männlich

head [hed]

1 NOUN	3 INTRANSITIVE VERB
2 TRANSITIVE VERB	4 PHRASAL VERBS

1 – NOUN

a [Anat] Kopf *m*, Haupt *nt (geh)*; **from head to foot** von Kopf bis Fuß; **covered from head to foot** *or* **toe in mud** von oben bis unten mit Schlamm bedeckt; **head down(wards)** mit dem Kopf nach unten; **he can hold his head high in any company** er kann sich in jeder Gesellschaft sehen lassen; **the condemned man held his head high as he went to the scaffold** der Verurteilte ging erhobenen Hauptes zum Schafott; **to keep one's head above water** *(lit)* den Kopf über Wasser halten; *(fig)* sich über Wasser halten; **I've got a really bad head this morning** *(inf)* ich habe einen ziemlichen Brummschädel heute Morgen *(inf)*; **to give a horse its head** einem Pferd die Zügel schießen lassen; **to give sb his head** jdn machen lassen; **to go to one's head** *(whisky, power)* einem in den *or* zu Kopf steigen; **I can't make head nor tail of it** daraus werde ich nicht schlau

♦ **a** *or* **per head** pro Kopf; **to pay 10 euros a** *or* **per head** 10 Euro pro Kopf bezahlen

♦ **head and shoulders to stand** *or* **be head and shoulders above sb** *(lit)* jdn um Haupteslänge überragen; *(fig)* jdm haushoch überlegen sein

♦ **head over heels to fall head over heels in love with sb** sich bis über beide Ohren in jdn verlieben; **to fall head over heels down the stairs** kopfüber die Treppe herunterfallen

♦ **on one's/its head to stand on one's head** auf dem Kopf stehen; **to stand** *or* **turn sth on its head** etw auf den Kopf stellen; *(fig)* etw umkehren; **you could do it standing on your head** *(inf)* das kann man ja im Schlaf machen

♦ **on one's (own) head on your (own) head be it** auf Ihre eigene Kappe *(inf) or* Verantwortung

♦ **over sb's head to go over sb's head** über jds Kopf hinweg handeln; **he gave orders over my head** er hat über meinen Kopf (hin)weg Anordnungen gegeben; **to be promoted over sb's head** vor jdm bevorzugt befördert werden

♦ **one's head off to talk one's head off** *(inf)* reden wie ein Wasserfall *(inf) or* wie ein Buch *(inf)*; **to laugh one's head off** *(inf)* sich fast totlachen *(inf)*; **to shout one's head off** *(inf)* sich *(dat)* die Lunge aus dem Leib schreien *(inf)*; **to scream one's head off** *(inf)* aus vollem Halse schreien

b [= measure of length] Kopf *m*; **taller by a head** (um) einen Kopf größer; **by a short head** *(Horse Racing, fig)* um Nasenlänge

c [= intellect] Kopf *m*, Verstand *m*; **use your head** streng deinen Kopf an; **it never entered his head that ...** es kam ihm nie in den Sinn, dass ...; **we put our heads together** wir haben unsere Köpfe zusammengesteckt; **he has an old head on young shoulders** er ist sehr reif für sein Alter; **two heads are better than one** *(prov)* besser zwei als einer allein; **to be above** *or* **over sb's head** über jds Horizont *(acc)* gehen; **the joke went** *or* **was over his head** er verstand *or* kapierte *(inf)* den Witz nicht; **he talked over their heads** er hat über ihre Köpfe hinweg geredet; **to keep one's head** den Kopf nicht verlieren; **to lose one's head** den Kopf verlieren; **to be weak** *or* **soft in the head** *(inf)* einen (kleinen) Dachschaden haben *(inf)*

♦ **into one's/sb's head to get sth into one's head** etw begreifen; **he can't get it into his head that ...** es will ihm nicht in den Kopf, dass ...; **I can't get it into his head that ...** ich kann es ihm nicht begreiflich machen, dass ...; **to take it into one's head to do sth** sich *(dat)* in den Kopf setzen, etw zu tun; **don't put ideas into his head** bring ihn bloß nicht auf dumme Gedanken!; *(= unrealistic wish)* setz ihm bloß keinen Floh ins Ohr! *(inf)*; **what/who put that idea into his head?** wie kommt er denn darauf?

♦ **out of one's head to put** *or* **get sb/sth out of one's head** sich *(dat)* jdn/etw aus dem Kopf schlagen; **he couldn't get her out of his head** er konnte sie sich nicht aus dem Kopf schlagen

♦ **off one's head he is off his head** *(Brit inf)* er ist (ja) nicht (ganz) bei Trost *(inf)*, er hat ja den Verstand verloren; *(with drugs)* er ist auf dem Trip *(inf)*

♦ **a (good) head (for) he has a good head for figures** er ist ein guter Rechner; **you need a good head for heights** Sie müssen schwindelfrei sein; **he has a good business head** er hat einen ausgeprägten Geschäftssinn; **he has a good head on his shoulders** er ist ein heller *or* kluger Kopf

d [of cattle] **twenty head of cattle** zwanzig Stück Vieh

e [of vegetable: of lettuce, cabbage, asparagus] Kopf *m*; *(of celery)* Staude *f*

f [= top part] *of flower, hammer, nail, page, pier* Kopf *m*; *(of arrow, spear)* Spitze *f*; *(of bed)* Kopf(ende *nt*) *m*; *(on beer)* Blume *f*; *(of cane)* Knauf *m*, Griff *m*; *(of corn)* Ähre *f*; *(Archit: of column)* Kapitell *nt*; *(of stream, = upper area)* Oberlauf *m*; *(= source)* Ursprung *m*; *(of abscess etc)* Eiterpfropf *m*; **head of steam/water** *(= pressure)* Dampf-/Wasserdruck *m*; **at the head of the lake** am Zufluss des Sees; **at the head of the page/stairs** oben auf der Seite/an der Treppe; **at the head of the list** oben auf der Liste; **at the head of the table** oben am Tisch, am Kopf(ende) des Tisches; **at the head of the queue** *(Brit)***/army** an der Spitze der Schlange/des Heeres; **at the head of the field** *(in race)* an der Spitze des Feldes

g [= crisis]

♦ **to a head to come to a head** sich zuspitzen; **the problem has come to a head** das Problem hat sich zugespitzt; **if things come to a head** wenn sich die Sache zuspitzt; **to bring matters to a head** die Sache auf die Spitze treiben

h [= leader] *of family* Oberhaupt *nt*; *(of business, organization)* Chef(in) *m(f)*, Boss *m (inf)*; *(of department)* Leiter(in) *m(f)*; *(of office, sub-department)* Vorsteher(in) *m(f)*; *(Sch)* Schulleiter(in) *m(f)*; **head of department** *(in business)* Abteilungsleiter(in) *m(f)*; *(Sch, Univ)* Fachbereichsleiter(in) *m(f)*; **head of state** Staatsoberhaupt *nt*

i [= heading] Rubrik *f*; **listed under three main heads** in drei Rubriken eingetragen

j [of coin] Kopfseite *f*; **heads or tails?** Kopf oder Zahl?; **heads you win** bei Kopf gewinnst du

k [Naut] *(= bow)* Bug *m*; *(of mast)* Topp *m*; *(= toilet)* Pütz *f*

l [Tech] *on tape recorder* Tonkopf *m*; *(Comput: = read/write head)* Kopf *m*

m [Drugs] *(inf)* Junkie *m (inf)*

2 – TRANSITIVE VERB

a [= lead = be at the head of] anführen; *(= be in charge of)* führen; *team* leiten; **they headed the procession/list** sie führten den Umzug/die Liste an; **a coalition government headed by Mr Schröder** eine Koalitionsregierung unter der Führung von Herrn Schröder

b [= direct] steuern, lenken *(towards, for* in Richtung *+gen)*

c [= give a heading] überschreiben, eine Überschrift geben *(+dat)*; **in the chapter headed ...** in dem Kapitel mit der Überschrift ...; **he heads each chapter with a quotation** er stellt jedem Kapitel ein Zitat voran

d [Ftbl] köpfen

3 – INTRANSITIVE VERB

gehen; *(vehicle)* fahren; **where are you heading** *or* **headed?** *(inf)* wo gehen/fahren Sie hin?; **are you heading my way?** gehen/fahren Sie in der gleichen Richtung wie ich?; **and the tornado was heading our way** und der Tornado kam auf uns zu

4 – PHRASAL VERBS

▶ **head back** VI zurückgehen/-fahren; **to be heading back** auf dem Rückweg sein; **it's time we were heading back now** es ist Zeit, umzukehren *or* sich auf den Rückweg zu machen

▶ **head for** VI *+prep obj* **a** *place, person* zugehen/zufahren auf *(+acc)*; *town, country, direction* gehen/fahren in Richtung *(+gen)*; *door, pub, bargain counter, prettiest girl* zusteuern auf *(+acc) (inf)*; *(ship)* zufahren *or* Kurs halten auf *(+acc)*; **where are you heading** *or* **headed for?** wo gehen/fahren *or* steuern *(inf)* Sie hin?; **to head for home** sich auf den Heimweg machen **b** *(fig)* zusteuern auf *(+acc)*, auf dem Weg sein zu; **you're heading for trouble** du bist auf dem besten Weg, Ärger zu bekommen; **he is heading for a fall/the rocks** er rennt in sein Verderben; **to head for victory/defeat** auf einen Sieg/eine Niederlage zusteuern

▶ **head in** VT *sep ball* hineinköpfen; **to head the ball into the net** den Ball ins Netz köpfen VI köpfen

▶ **head off** VT *sep* **a** *(= divert)* umdirigieren **b** *(= avert) quarrel, war, strike* abwenden; *person* ablenken; *questions* abbiegen VI *(= set off)* sich aufmachen

▶ **head up** VT *sep committee, delegation* führen, leiten

---

head *in cpds (= top, senior)* Ober-; **headache** N Kopfweh *nt*, Kopfschmerzen *pl*; *(inf: = problem)* Problem *nt*; **to have a ~** Kopfschmerzen haben; **this is a bit of a ~ (for us)** das macht *or* bereitet uns ziemliches Kopfzerbrechen; **his teenage daughter was a real ~** mit seiner heranwachsenden Tochter hatte er große Schwierigkeiten; **headachy** ['hedeɪkɪ] ADJ *(inf)* **to be ~** *(= to suffer from headache)* an (leichten) Kopfschmerzen leiden; *(= to cause a headache)* Kopfschmerzen verursachen; **headband** N Stirnband *nt*; **head-banger** N *(inf: = crazy person)* Bekloppte(r) *mf (inf)*; **headboard** N Kopfteil *nt*; **head boy** N *vom Schulleiter bestimmter Schulsprecher*; **headbutt** N Kopfstoß *m* VT mit dem Kopf stoßen; **headcase** N *(inf)* Spinner(in) *m(f) (inf)*; **headcheese** N *(US)* Schweinskopfsülze *f*; **head clerk** N *(Comm)* Bürovorsteher(in) *m(f)*; *(Jur)* Kanzleivorsteher(in) *m(f)*; **head cold** N Kopfgrippe *f*; **head count** N **to have** *or* **take a ~** abzählen; **headcrash** N *(Comput)* Headcrash *m*, Festplattendefekt *m*; **headdress** N Kopfschmuck *m*

-headed [-hedɪd] ADJ *suf* -köpfig; **bald-headed** kahlköpfig; **a curly-headed child** ein lockiges Kind, ein Kind *nt* mit lockigen Haaren

headed notepaper N Schreibpapier *nt* mit Briefkopf

header [ˈhedəˈ] N **a** *(Brit: = dive)* Kopfsprung *m*, Köpfer *m (inf)*; **to take a ~ into the water** einen Kopfsprung ins Wasser machen; *(= fall)* kopfüber ins Wasser fallen; **the dollar took a ~** der Dollarkurs fiel, der Dollar machte eine Talfahrt *(inf)* **b** *(Ftbl)* Kopfstoß *m*, Kopfball *m*; **he's a good ~ of the ball** er köpft gut **c** *(Typ)* Kopfzeile *f*

head: **headfirst** ADV *(lit, fig)* kopfüber; **head gate** N (oberes) Schleusentor; **headgear** N Kopfbedeckung *f*; *(of horse: = bridle)* Zaumzeug *nt*; **head girl** N *vom Schulleiter bestimmte Schulsprecherin*; **headguard** N Kopfschutz *m*; **head-hunt** VT abwerben; **I've been ~ed** ich bin abgeworben worden; *(= have been approached)* man hat versucht, mich abzuwerben VI **we'll have to go out and ~** wir werden Mitarbeiter von anderen Firmen abwerben müssen; **head-hunter** N *(lit)* Kopfjäger *m*; *(fig)* Kopfjäger(in) *m(f)*, Headhunter(in) *m(f)*; **head-hunting** N *(fig)* Abwerbeversuch(e *pl*) *m*

headiness [ˈhedɪnɪs] N **a** berauschende Art; *(of experience)* Aufregung *f*; **the ~ of success** der Erfolgsrausch; **this wine is known for its ~** dieser Wein ist dafür bekannt, dass er schnell zu Kopf(e) steigt; **the ~ of this intellectual atmosphere** das Berauschende dieser geistesgeladenen Atmosphäre **b** *(= impetuosity)* Unbesonnenheit *f*

heading [ˈhedɪŋ] N **a** Überschrift *f*; *(on letter, document)* Kopf *m*; *(in encyclopedia)* Stichwort *nt*; **under the ~ of anthropology** unter dem Stichwort Anthropologie **b** *(Ftbl)* Köpfen *nt*

head: **head lad** N *(Horse Racing)* erster Stallbursche; **headlamp**, **headlight** N Scheinwerfer *m*; **headland** N Landspitze *f*; **headless** ADJ ohne Kopf; *(fig old)* kopflos; **to run around like a ~ chicken** *(Brit)* *or* **like a chicken with its head cut off** *(US)* wie ein aufgescheuchtes *or* kopfloses Huhn herumlaufen *(inf)*; **headlight** N = **headlamp**; **headline** N *(Press)* Schlagzeile *f*; **he is always in the ~s** er macht immer Schlagzeilen; **the ~s were full of the story** die Geschichte beherrschte die Schlagzeilen; **to grab** *or* **hit** *or* **make the ~s** Schlagzeilen machen; **the news ~s** Kurznachrichten *pl*, das Wichtigste in Kürze VT **to be ~d ...** die Überschrift ... haben; **an article ~d ...** ein Artikel mit der Überschrift ...; **headline news** N *no pl* **to be ~** in den Schlagzeilen sein; **headliner** N *(US Mus, Theat inf)* Headliner(in) *m(f)*; **headline rate** N *(Brit Econ)* **~ of inflation** Inflationsrate *f (unter Einbeziehung von Variablen wie Hypothekenzinssätzen etc)*; **headlock** N **to get/have sb in a ~** jdn in den Schwitzkasten nehmen/im Schwitzkasten haben; **headlong** ADV **a** *(= very fast) flee, run* überstürzt, Hals über Kopf *(inf)*; *(= with head forward) fall* vornüber; **he ran ~ down the stairs** er rannte in Windeseile die Treppe hinunter **b** *(fig, without careful thought) rush, plunge* überstürzt, Hals über Kopf *(inf)*; **to rush** *or* **plunge ~ into sth** sich Hals über Kopf in etw *(acc)* stürzen *(inf)* ADJ *flight, dash, rush* überstürzt; **the army was in ~ flight** die Armee hatte Hals über Kopf die Flucht ergriffen *(inf)*; **they made a ~ dash for the door** sie stürzten blindlings auf die Tür zu; **the dollar's ~ fall** der unaufhaltsame Sturz des Dollars; **headman** N *(of tribe)* Häuptling *m*, Stammesoberhaupt *nt*; **headmaster** N *(esp Brit)* Schulleiter *m*; *(of secondary school also)* Direktor *m*; *(of primary school also)* Rektor *m*; **headmistress** N *(esp Brit)* Schulleiterin *f*; *(of secondary school also)* Direktorin *f*; *(of primary school also)* Rektorin *f*; **headnote** N *(at the beginning of chapter, article)* kurze (Inhalts)angabe; **head office** N Zentrale *f*; **head-on** ADV **a** *collide, crash* frontal **b** *(fig: = directly) meet, confront, tackle* direkt; **to meet tough issues ~** schwierige Fragen direkt angehen; **to confront sb/sth ~** jdm/einer Sache ohne Umschweife entgegentreten ADJ **a ~ collision** *or* **smash** Frontalzusammenstoß *m* **b** *(fig) conflict, confrontation* offen, direkt; **headphones** PL Kopfhörer *pl*; **head post office** N Hauptpostamt *nt*; **headquarter** VT **to be ~ed in** *(Mil)* sein Hauptquartier haben in *(+dat)*; *(business)* seine Hauptstelle *or* Zentrale haben in *(+dat)*; *(political party)* seine Parteizentrale haben in *(+dat)*; **headquarters** N *sing or pl (Mil)* Hauptquartier *nt*; *(of business)* Hauptstelle *f*, Zentrale *f*; *(of political party)* Parteizentrale *f*, Hauptquartier *nt*; **headrace** N Gerinne *nt*; **headrest** N Kopfstütze *f*; **head restraint** N Kopfstütze *f*; **headroom** N lichte Höhe; *(in car)* Kopfraum *m*; **15 ft ~** (lichte) Höhe 15 Fuß; **headscarf** N Kopftuch *nt*; **headset** N Kopfhörer *pl*; **headship** N Schulleiterstelle *f*, Direktoren-/ /Rektorenstelle *f*; **headshrinker** [ˈhedʃrɪŋkəˈ] N *(lit)* Schrumpfkopfindianer *m*; *(inf: = psychiatrist)* Seelenklempner(in) *m(f) (inf)*; **headsquare** N Kopftuch *nt*; **head start** N Vorsprung *m (on sb* jdm gegenüber); **headstone** N *(on grave)* Grabstein *m*; **headstrong** ADJ eigensinnig, dickköpfig

heads-up [ˈhedzʌp] N *(esp US inf)* **to give sb a ~** jdn vorwarnen

head: **head teacher** N *(Brit)* = **headmaster, headmistress**; **head-to-head** ADV **to compete ~ with sb** sich direkt mit jdm messen ADJ *contest, competition* direkt; *(with* mit); **head voice** N *(Mus)* Kopfstimme *f*; **head waiter** N Oberkellner *m*; **head waitress** N Oberkellnerin *f*; **headwaters** PL Quellflüsse *pl*; **headway** N **to make ~** *(lit, fig)* vorankommen; **did you make any ~ with the unions?** haben Sie bei den Gewerkschaften etwas erreicht?; **headwind** N Gegenwind *m*; **headword** N Anfangswort *nt*; *(in dictionary)* Stichwort *nt*; **headwork** N **a** *(= mental work)* Kopfarbeit *f*, geistige Arbeit **b** *(Ftbl)* Kopfballspiel *nt* **c** *(Tech)* Wasserkontrollanlage

heady [ˈhedɪ] ADJ *(+er)* **a** *wine, scent, mixture, speed, atmosphere, sensation, success* berauschend; *experience* aufregend; **the air is ~ with scent/spices** ein berauschender Duft/der berauschende Duft von Gewürzen hängt in der Luft; **to feel ~** berauscht sein; **the ~ heights of the Premier League** die schwindelerregenden Höhen der Bundesliga; **to be ~ with success** im Erfolgsrausch sein; **~ with victory** siegestrunken; **~ stuff** *(fig inf)* eine aufregende Sache **b** *(= impetuous)* unbesonnen, impulsiv

heal [hiːl] VI *(Med, fig)* heilen VT **a** *(Med)* heilen; **time ~s all wounds** *(Prov)* die Zeit heilt alle Wunden *(Prov)* **b** *(fig) differences etc* beilegen; *(third party)* schlichten; **they succeeded in ~ing the rift between them** es gelang ihnen, die Kluft zwischen ihnen zu überbrücken

▶ **heal over** VI zuheilen

▶ **heal up** VI zuheilen VT *sep* zuheilen lassen

healer [ˈhiːləˈ] N Heiler(in) *m(f) (geh)*; *(= herb etc)* Heilmittel *nt*; **time is a great ~** *(prov)* die Zeit heilt alle Wunden *(Prov)*

healing [ˈhiːlɪŋ] N Heilung *f*; *(of wound)* (Zu)heilen *nt* ADJ *(Med)* Heil-, heilend; *(fig)* besänftigend; **~ process** Heilprozess *m*; **~ powers** Heilkräfte *pl*, heilende Kräfte *pl*

health [helθ] N **a** Gesundheit *f*; *(= state of health)* Gesundheitszustand *m*; **in good ~** gesund, bei guter Gesundheit; **in poor ~** nicht gesund, bei schlechter Gesundheit; **state of ~** Gesundheitszustand *m*, Befinden *nt*; **how is his ~?** wie geht es ihm gesundheitlich?; **to regain one's ~** wieder gesund werden; **at least we still have our ~** wenigstens sind wir immer noch gesund; **to enjoy good ~** sich guter Gesundheit *(gen)* erfreuen; **to suffer from poor** *or* **bad ~** kränklich sein; **to be good/bad for one's ~** gesund/ungesund *or* gesundheitsschädlich sein, der Gesundheit *(dat)* zuträglich/nicht zuträglich sein; **poverty can cause poor ~** Armut kann zu schlechter Gesundheit führen; **~ and safety regulations** Arbeitsschutzvorschriften *pl*; **Ministry of Health** Gesundheitsministerium *nt*; **I'm not just doing it for the good of my ~** *(inf)* ich mache das doch nicht bloß aus Spaß *(inf)*; **he stressed the ~ benefits of regular exercise** er betonte, wie gut regelmäßige Bewegung für die Gesundheit sei **b** *(fig)* Gesundheit *f* **c to drink (to) sb's ~** auf jds Wohl *(acc)* or Gesundheit *(acc)* trinken; **your ~!, good ~!** zum Wohl!, auf Ihre Gesundheit!

health: **Health and Safety Executive** N *(Brit)* Arbeitsschutzbehörde *f*; **Health and Social Services** PL *(US) das amerikanische Gesundheits- und Sozialministerium*; **health authority** N Gesundheitsbehörde *f*; **health care** N Gesundheitsfürsorge *f*; **home ~ aid** (mobiler) Helfer/(mobile) Helferin für häusliche Pflege; **health centre** *(Brit)* N **a** *(Med)* Ärztezentrum *nt* **b** *(keep-fit)* Fitnesscenter *nt*; **health certificate** N Gesundheitszeugnis *nt*; **health check** N Check-up *m*; **health club** N *(= place)* Fitnesscenter *nt*; **health education** N Hygiene *f*; **health farm** N Gesundheitsfarm *f*; **health food** N Reformkost *f*; **health food shop** *(Brit)*, **health food store** *(esp US)* N Reformhaus *nt*, Bioladen *m*, Naturkostladen *m*

healthful [ˈhelθfʊl], **healthgiving** [ˈhelθgɪvɪŋ] ADJ gesund

health hazard N Gefahr *f* für die Gesundheit

healthily [ˈhelθɪlɪ] ADV **a** *(= sensibly) eat, live* gesund; *(= robustly) grow* kräftig; **the recipe is ~ low in fat** das Rezept ist fettarm und daher gesund; **we felt ~ tired** wir fühlten eine gesunde Müdigkeit; **her face was glowing ~** ihr Gesicht hatte eine blühende Farbe **b** *(fig: = refreshingly)* **~ cynical/irreverent/independent** erfrischend zynisch/respektlos/unabhängig

healthiness [ˈhelθɪnɪs] N *(lit, fig)* Gesundheit *f*; *(of bank balance)* gesunder Zustand

health: **health inspector** N Hygieneinspektor(in) *m(f)*; **health insurance** N Krankenversicherung *f*

> **HEALTH MAINTENANCE ORGANIZATION**
>
> Eine **health maintenance organization** (oder auch **HMO**) ist eine Gesellschaft, die in den Vereinigten Staaten ihren Mitgliedern medizinische Dienste anbietet. Die Mitglieder müssen einen monatlichen oder jährlichen Beitrag entrichten, im Gegenzug stellt die Gesellschaft medizinisches Personal an, das sich um alle gesundheitlichen Belange kümmert, auch bei stationären Krankenhausaufenthalten. Obwohl **HMOs** ähnlich eingestuft werden wie private Krankenversicherungen, gibt es doch einige wichtige Unterschiede. So haben die Mitglieder keine freie Arztwahl. Aus Kostendämpfungsgründen wird besonderer Wert auf Prävention gelegt, und unnötige Untersuchungen und Operationen werden nach Möglichkeit vermieden.

health: **health problem** N **to have ~s** gesundheitliche Probleme haben; **he retired because of ~s** er trat aus gesundheitlichen Gründen in den Ruhestand; **health resort** N Kurort *m*; *(= spa also)* Kurbad *nt*, Heilbad *nt*; **Health Service** N *(Brit)* **the ~** das Gesundheitswesen; **~ doctor** Kassenarzt *m*/-ärztin *f*; **health studio** N Fitnessstudio *nt*; **health visitor** N *(Brit)* Sozialarbeiter(in) *m(f) (in der Gesundheitsfürsorge)*; **health warning** N *(on cigarette packet)* (gesundheitlicher) Warnhinweis

healthy ['helθɪ] ADJ *(+er) (lit, fig)* gesund; **a ~ mind in a ~ body** ein gesunder Geist in einem gesunden Körper; **to earn a ~ profit** einen ansehnlichen Gewinn machen; **he has a ~ bank balance** sein Kontostand ist gesund; **a ~ dose of sth** ein gesundes Maß an etw *(dat)*; **that's not a ~ idea/attitude** das ist keine vernünftige Idee/gesunde Haltung; **to have a ~ respect for sb/sth** einen gesunden Respekt vor jdm/etw haben; **a ~ interest in sth** ein gesundes Interesse an etw *(dat)*

heap [hi:p] **N** **a** Haufen *m*; *(inf: = old car)* Klapperkiste *f (inf)*; **(to leave sth) in a ~** (etw) auf einem Haufen (liegen lassen); **the building was reduced to a ~ of rubble** das Haus sank in Schutt und Asche; **he fell in a ~ on the floor** er sackte zu Boden; **at the bottom/top of the ~** *(fig)* ganz unten/oben

b **~s of** *(inf)* ein(en) Haufen *(inf)*; **it's happened ~s of times** es ist schon zigmal vorgekommen *(inf)*; **do you have any glasses? – yes, ~s** haben Sie Gläser? – (ja,) jede Menge *(inf)*; **she has ~s of enthusiasm/time** sie hat jede Menge Enthusiasmus/Zeit *(inf)*; **to be in a whole ~ of trouble** tief in Schwierigkeiten stecken; **they got ~s of criticism** sie wurden massiv kritisiert

ADV **~s** *(inf)* (unheimlich) viel

VT häufen; **he ~ed his clothes together** er warf seine Kleider auf einen Haufen; **to ~ praise on sb/sth** über jdn/etw voll des Lobes sein *(geh)*, jdn/etw über den grünen Klee loben *(inf)*; *(in addressing)* jdn mit Lob überschütten; **to ~ scorn on sb/sth** jdn/etw mit Spott übergießen; **to ~ abuse on sb** jdm Beleidigungen an den Kopf werfen; *(cursing)* jdn mit einer Flut von Schimpfwörtern überschütten; **a ~ed spoonful** ein gehäufter Löffel; **an armchair ~ed with cushions** ein Sessel, auf dem sich Kissen türmen

▸ **heap up** **VT** *sep* aufhäufen; **he heaped up the litter into piles/a pile** er machte aus dem Abfall Haufen/einen Haufen **VI** sich häufen

hear [hɪə'] ✪ 11.1, 12.2, 21.1, 24.3, 26.1 *pret, ptp* **heard** **VT** **a** *(= also learn)* hören; **I ~d him say that ...** ich habe ihn sagen hören, dass ...; **I ~d somebody come in** ich habe jemanden (herein)kommen hören; **there wasn't a sound to be ~d** es war kein Laut zu hören, man hörte keinen Laut; **he was ~d to say that ...** man hat ihn sagen hören, dass ...; **to make oneself ~d** sich *(dat)* Gehör verschaffen; **you're not going, do you ~ me!** du gehst nicht, hörst du (mich)!; **to ~ him speak you'd think ...** wenn man ihn so reden hört, könnte man meinen, ...; **I've often ~d say** *or* **it said that ...** ich habe oft gehört *or* sagen hören, dass ...; **I ~ you play chess** ich höre, Sie spielen Schach; **have you ~d the one about ...?** (haben Sie) den schon gehört von ...?; **I ~ tell you're going away** ich höre, Sie gehen weg; **I've ~d tell of a monster in the lake** ich habe von einem Ungeheuer in dem See gehört; **I've ~d it all before** ich habe das schon hundertmal gehört; **I've been ~ing things about you** von dir hört man ja schöne Dinge; **I must be ~ing things** ich glaube, ich höre nicht richtig

b *(= listen to) lecture, programme etc* hören; **to ~ a case** *(Jur)* einen Fall verhandeln; **to ~ evidence** *(Jur)* Zeugen vernehmen; **Lord, ~ our prayer** Herr, (er)höre unser Gebet; **Lord, ~ us** Herr, erhöre uns; **let's ~ your prayers before you go to sleep** wir wollen beten, bevor du schläfst

VI **a** *(physically)* hören; **he does not** *or* **cannot ~ very well** er hört nicht sehr gut; **~, ~!** (sehr) richtig!; *(Parl)* hört!, hört!

b *(= get news)* hören; **he's left his wife – yes, so I ~** er hat seine Frau verlassen – ja, ich habe es gehört; **I ~ from my daughter every week** ich höre jede Woche von meiner Tochter; **you'll be ~ing from me!** *(threatening)* Sie werden noch von mir hören!; **to ~ about sth** von etw hören *or* erfahren; **have you ~d about John? he's getting married** haben Sie gehört? John heiratet; **I've ~d a lot about you** ich habe schon viel von Ihnen gehört; **never ~d of him/it** nie (von ihm/davon) gehört; **I've ~d of him** ich habe schon von ihm gehört; **he wasn't ~d of for a long time** man hat lange Zeit nichts von ihm gehört; **he was never ~d of again** man hat nie wieder etwas von ihm gehört; **I've never ~d of such a thing!** das ist ja unerhört!; **I ~ about nothing else (but that)!** ich höre überhaupt nichts anderes mehr!

▸ **hear of** **VI** *+prep obj (fig: = allow)* hören wollen von; **I won't hear of it** ich will davon (gar) nichts hören

▸ **hear out** **VT** *sep person* ausreden lassen; *story* zu Ende hören

heard [hɜ:d] *pret, ptp of* **hear**

hearer ['hɪərə'] N Hörer(in) *m(f)*

hearing ['hɪərɪŋ] N **a** Gehör *nt*; **to have a keen sense of ~** ein gutes Gehör haben

b **within/out of ~ (distance)** in/außer Hörweite; **he said that in/out of my ~** ich war in Hörweite/nicht in Hörweite, als er das sagte

c *(Pol)* Hearing *nt*, Anhörung *f*; *(Jur)* Verhandlung *f*; **disciplinary ~** Disziplinarverfahren *nt*; **~ of witnesses** *(Jur)* Zeugenvernehmung *f*; **he was refused a ~** er wurde nicht angehört; **he didn't get a fair ~** man hörte ihn nicht richtig an; *(Jur)* er bekam keinen fairen Prozess; **he got a sympathetic ~** er wurde wohlwollend angehört; **the Minister gave the petitioners a ~** der Minister hörte die Überbringer der Petition an; **to condemn sb without a ~** jdn verurteilen, ohne ihn (an)gehört zu haben; *(Jur)* jdn ohne Anhörung verurteilen

hearing: **hearing aid** N Hörgerät *nt*, Hörhilfe *f*; **hearing-impaired** ['hɪərɪŋɪm,pɛəd] **ADJ** *(= deaf)* gehörlos; *(= partially deaf)* hörgeschädigt **N** **the ~** *(= deaf)* Gehörlose *pl*; *(= partially deaf)* Hörgeschädigte *pl*

hearken ['hɑ:kn] VI *(old, liter)* horchen *(to* auf *+acc)*

hearsay ['hɪəseɪ] N Gerüchte *pl*; **to know sth from** *or* **by ~** etw vom Hörensagen wissen *or* haben; **~ rule** *(Jur) Regel über den grundsätzlichen Ausschluss aller Beweise vom Hörensagen*

hearsay: **hearsay account** N Bericht *m* aus zweiter Hand; **hearsay evidence** N Zeugenaussage, die auf Hörensagen beruht

hearse [hɜ:s] N Leichenwagen *m*

heart [hɑ:t] N **a** *(Anat)* Herz *nt*

b *(fig, for emotion, courage etc)* Herz *nt*; **to break sb's ~** jdm das Herz brechen; **it breaks my ~ to see her so upset** es bricht mir das Herz, sie so betrübt zu sehen; **it breaks my ~ to think that ...** mir bricht das Herz, wenn ich daran denke, dass ...; **she thought her ~ would break** sie meinte, ihr würde das Herz brechen; **you're breaking my ~** *(iro)* ich fang gleich an zu weinen *(iro)*; **a man after my own ~** ein Mann ganz nach meinem Herzen; **to have a change of ~** sich anders besinnen, seine Meinung ändern; **to be close** *or* **dear to one's ~** *(cause, subject)* jdm am Herzen liegen; **to learn/know/recite sth (off) by ~** etw auswendig lernen/kennen/aufsagen; **I know the route by ~** ich kenne die Strecke (in- und) auswendig; **he knew in his ~ she was right** er wusste im Grunde seines Herzens, dass sie recht hatte; **in my ~ of ~s** im Grunde meines Herzens; **with all my ~** von ganzem Herzen; **from the bottom of one's ~** aus tiefstem Herzen; **to be the ~ and soul of sth** das Herz und die Seele einer Sache *(gen)* sein; **to put (one's) ~ and soul into sth** sich mit Leib und Seele einer Sache *(dat)* widmen; **to take sth to ~** sich *(dat)* etw zu Herzen nehmen; **we (only) have your interests at ~** uns liegen doch nur Ihre Interessen am Herzen; **to set one's ~ on sth** sein Herz an etw *(acc)* hängen *(geh)*; **it did my ~ good** es wurde mir warm ums Herz; **to one's ~'s content** nach Herzenslust; **most men are boys at ~** die meisten Männer sind im Grunde (ihres Herzens) noch richtige Kinder; **I couldn't find it in my ~ to forgive him** ich konnte es nicht über mich bringen, ihm zu verzeihen; **his ~ isn't in his work/in it** er ist nicht mit dem Herzen bei der Sache/dabei; **he's putting/not putting his ~ into his work** er ist mit ganzem Herzen/nur mit halbem Herzen bei seiner Arbeit; **to give sb ~** jdm Mut machen; **to lose ~** den Mut verlieren; **to lose one's ~ (to sb/sth)** sein Herz (an jdn/etw) verlieren; **to take ~** Mut fassen; **he took ~ from his brother's example** das Beispiel seines Bruders machte ihm Mut; **they've taken him to their ~s** sie haben ihn ins Herz geschlossen; **to put new** *or* **fresh ~ into sb** jdn mit neuem Mut erfüllen; **to put new ~ into sth** etw mit neuem Leben erfüllen; **to be in good ~** *(liter)* guten Mutes sein *(geh)*; **her ~ is in the right place** *(inf)* sie hat das Herz auf dem rechten Fleck *(inf)*; **to have a ~ of stone** ein Herz aus Stein haben; **to wear one's ~ on one's sleeve** *(prov)* das Herz auf der Zunge tragen *(prov)*; **my ~ was in my mouth** *(inf)* mir schlug das Herz bis zum Hals; **his ~ was in his boots** *(inf)* ihm ist das Herz in die Hose(n) gerutscht *(inf)*; **have a ~!** *(inf)* gib deinem Herzen einen Stoß! *(inf)*; **I didn't have the ~ to say no** ich brachte es nicht übers Herz, nein *or* Nein zu sagen; **she has a ~ of gold** sie hat ein goldenes Herz; **my ~ sank** *(with apprehension)* mir wurde bang ums Herz *(liter)*, mir rutschte das Herz in die Hose(n) *(inf)*; *(with sadness)* das Herz wurde mir schwer; *(= I was discouraged)* mein Mut sank

c *(= centre: of town, country, cabbage etc)* Herz *nt*; **in the ~ of the forest** im tiefsten *or* mitten im Wald; **the ~ of the matter** der Kern der Sache; **the ~ of the tree** das Mark des Baumes; **artichoke ~** Artischockenherz *nt*

d **yes, my ~** *(liter)* ja, mein Herz *(liter)*; **dear ~** *(old, liter)* liebes Herz *(liter)*

e **hearts** PL *(Cards)* Herz *nt*; *(Bridge)* Coeur *nt*; **queen of ~s** Herz-/Coeurdame *f*

heart: **heartache** N Kummer *m*, Herzeleid *nt (old liter)*, Herzweh *nt (geh)*; **heart attack** N Herzanfall *m*; *(= thrombosis)* Herzinfarkt *m*; **I nearly had a ~** *(fig inf, from shock)* ich habe fast einen Herzschlag gekriegt *(inf)*; *(from surprise also)* da hat mich doch fast der Schlag getroffen *(inf)*; **heartbeat** N Herzschlag *m*; **heartbreak** N großer Kummer, Leid *nt*; **I've had my share of ~s** ich habe meinen Teil an Kummer gehabt; **it caused ~ for him** es brach ihm (beinahe) das Herz; **heartbreaker** N Herzensbrecher *m*; **heartbreaking** ADJ herzzerreißend; **it was ~ to see him with crutches** es brach einem das Herz, ihn an Krücken zu sehen; **it's a ~ situation** es bricht einem das Herz; **heartbroken** ADJ untröstlich, todunglücklich; **she was ~ about it** sie war darüber todunglücklich; *(because of love, death etc also)* es hat ihr das Herz gebrochen; **don't look so ~** schau (doch) nicht so unglücklich drein; **heartburn** N Sodbrennen *nt*; **heart case** N Herzpatient(in) *m(f)*; **heart complaint** N Herzbeschwerden *pl*; **heart condition** N Herzleiden *nt*; **he has a ~** er ist herzleidend, er hats am Herzen *(inf)*; **heart disease** N Herzkrankheit *f*

-hearted [-hɑ:tɪd] ADJ *suf* -herzig; **kind-/cold--hearted** gut-/kaltherzig

hearten ['hɑ:tn] VT ermutigen

heartening ['hɑ:tnɪŋ] ADJ *news* ermutigend

heart: **heart failure** N Herzversagen *nt*; **he suffered ~** sein Herz hat versagt; **heartfelt** ADJ *thanks, apology* aufrichtig; *sympathy, tribute, appeal, plea* tief empfunden; **~ thanks to you all** Ihnen allen danke ich von ganzem Herzen; **her apology did not seem to be ~** ihre Entschuldigung schien nicht von Herzen zu kommen; **my ~ sympathy** *or* **condolences** mein tief empfundenes *or* herzliches Beileid

hearth [hɑ:θ] N Feuerstelle *f*; *(= whole fireplace)* Kamin *m*; *(fig: = home)* (häuslicher) Herd; **the kettle was keeping warm on the ~** der Kessel wurde auf dem Herd warm gehalten; **~ and home** Haus und Herd

hearth: **hearth brush** N Kaminbesen *m*; **hearthrug** ['hɑːθrʌg] N Kaminvorleger *m*

heartily ['hɑːtɪlɪ] ADV **a** (= *enthusiastically*) *laugh, say* herzlich; *sing* aus voller Kehle; *eat* tüchtig **b** (= *thoroughly*) *recommend* uneingeschränkt; *agree* voll und ganz; *endorse, welcome* von Herzen; **to ~ dislike doing sth** etw äußerst ungern tun; **to be ~ sick of sth** etw herzlich leid sein; **to be ~ fed up with sth** (*inf*) die Nase von etw gestrichen voll haben (*inf*); **I'm ~ glad he isn't coming** ich bin ausgesprochen froh, dass er nicht kommt

heartland ['hɑːtlænd] N Herzland *nt*, Herz *nt* des Landes; **in the Tory ~s** in den Hochburgen der Konservativen

heart: **heartless** ADJ herzlos; (= *cruel also*) grausam; **heartlessly** ADV grausam; **she ~ abandoned the child** sie verließ das Kind auf herzlose Weise; **how can you be so ~ cruel?** wie kannst du nur so schrecklich grausam sein?; **heartlessness** N Herzlosigkeit *f*; (= *cruelty*) Grausamkeit *f*; **heart-lung machine** N Herz-Lungen-Maschine *f*; **heart murmur** N Herzgeräusche *pl*; **heart-rending** ADJ herzzerreißend; **heart-searching** N Selbstprüfung *f*; **heart-shaped** ADJ herzförmig; **heartsick** ADJ (*liter*) **to be ~** Herzeleid haben (*old liter*); **heartstrings** PL **to pull** *or* **tug at sb's ~** jdn zu Tränen rühren, bei jdm auf die Tränendrüsen drücken (*inf*); **he plucked the ~ of rich old women** er nutzte die Gefühle von reichen alten Frauen aus; **heart-throb** N (*inf*) Schwarm *m* (*inf*); **heart-to-heart** ADJ ganz offen; **to have a ~ talk with sb** sich mit jdm ganz offen aussprechen N offene Aussprache; **it's time we had a ~** es ist Zeit, dass wir uns einmal offen aussprechen; **heart transplant** N Herztransplantation *f*, Herzverpflanzung *f*; **heart trouble** N Herzbeschwerden *pl*; **heart-warming** ADJ herzerfreuend

hearty ['hɑːtɪ] ADJ (+*er*) **a** (= *loud and friendly*) *laugh, voice, greeting* herzlich; *person, manner* (= *boisterous*) raubeinig; (= *over-familiar*) plumpvertraulich; **he gave a ~ laugh** er lachte herzlich *or* herzhaft
b *slap, blow* kräftig
c (= *wholehearted*) *endorsement, condemnation* uneingeschränkt; *agreement* ungeteilt; *hatred, dislike* tief; **~ congratulations** herzliche Glückwünsche *pl*; **~ welcome** herzlicher Empfang; **we bid you a ~ welcome** wir heißen Sie herzlich willkommen
d *food* herzhaft, kräftig; *meal* herzhaft, deftig (*inf*); *appetite* gesund; *helping* kräftig, ordentlich; **to be a ~ eater** einen gesunden Appetit haben, kräftig zulangen (*inf*) → *also* **hale**
N **a** (*Naut inf*) **me hearties!** Jungs! (*inf*), Leute!
b (*inf*, = *sporting man/woman*) Sportfreund(in) *m(f)*; **a rugby ~** ein Rugbyfan *m*

heat [hiːt] N **a** Hitze *f*; (*pleasant, Phys*) Wärme *f*; (*of curry etc*) Schärfe *f*; (= *heating*) Heizung *f*; **I don't mind the ~** mir macht (die) Hitze nichts aus; **in the ~ of the day** wenn es heiß ist; **on** *or* **over (a) low ~** bei schwacher Hitze; **to regulate the ~** (*in oven*) die Hitze regulieren; (*on fire*) die Wärme regulieren
b (*fig, of argument, discussion*) Hitze *f*; **in the ~ of the moment** in der Hitze des Gefechts; (*when upset*) in der Erregung; **the discussion generated quite a lot of ~** die Diskussion erhitzte die Gemüter; **to take the ~ out of the situation/an argument** die Situation/Diskussion entschärfen; **with some ~** (*say, debate*) hitzig; **in the ~ of the election campaign** in der Aufregung des Wahlkampfs
c (*inf*: = *pressure*) Druck *m*; **to put the ~ on** Druck machen (*inf*); **to turn up the ~ on sb** jdm die Hölle heißmachen (*inf*); **the ~ is on now** wir/sie *etc* stehen jetzt unter enormem Druck; **the ~ is off** der Druck ist weg (*inf*); (= *danger is past*) die Gefahr ist vorbei
d (*Sport*) Vorlauf *m*; (*Boxing etc*) Vorkampf *m*; **final ~** Finale *nt*
e (*Zool*) Brunst *f*; (*Hunt*) Brunft *f*; (*of dogs, cats*) Läufigkeit *f*; **on** (*Brit*) *or* **in** (*esp US*) ~ brünstig; (*Hunt*) brunftig; (*dog, cat*) läufig, heiß; (*inf*: *person*) heiß (*inf*)
VT erhitzen; *food also* aufwärmen, heiß *or* warm machen; *house, room* heizen; *pool* beheizen; (= *provide with heat*) *house, town* beheizen
VI (*room etc*) sich erwärmen, warm werden; (*get very hot*) sich erhitzen, heiß werden; **your dinner is ~ing in the oven** dein Essen steht (im Backofen) warm

▶ **heat up** VI sich erwärmen, warm werden; (= *get very hot*) sich erhitzen; (*engine*) heiß laufen; (*fig, situation*) sich zuspitzen VT *sep* erwärmen; *food* aufwärmen, warm *or* heiß machen; (*fig*) *discussion* anheizen

heat death N Wärmetod *m*

heated ['hiːtɪd] ADJ **a** (*lit*) *swimming pool, greenhouse etc* beheizt; *room* geheizt; *rear window, towel rail* heizbar; **~ air** Warmluft *f* **b** (*fig*: = *angry*) *debate, discussion, dispute, meeting* hitzig, erregt; *argument, exchange, row* heftig; *words* erregt; **to grow** *or* **become ~** (*person*) sich aufregen; (*debate*) hitzig *or* erregt werden; **things got very ~** die Gemüter erhitzten sich

heatedly ['hiːtɪdlɪ] ADV hitzig; *argue* heftig

heater ['hiːtəʳ] N Ofen *m*; (*electrical also*) Heizgerät *nt*; (*in car*) Heizung *f*; (*for fondue*) Rechaud *m*; **what sort of ~s do you have?** was für eine Heizung haben Sie?; **turn the ~ on** stell die Heizung an

heat: **heat exchanger** N Wärme(aus)tauscher *m*; **heat exhaustion** N Hitzeschäden *pl*; **heat flash** N Hitzeblitz *m*

heath [hiːθ] N **a** (= *moorland*) Heide *f*; (= *type of country*) Heide *f*, Heideland *nt* **b** (= *plant*) Heidekraut *nt*, Erika *f*

heat haze N Hitzeflimmern *nt*

heathen ['hiːðən] ADJ heidnisch; (*fig*) unkultiviert, unzivilisiert N Heide *m*, Heidin *f*; (*fig*) unkultivierter *or* unzivilisierter Mensch; **the ~** (*collectively, lit*) die Heiden; (*fig*) die Barbaren

heathenism ['hiːðənɪzəm] N Heidentum *nt*

heather ['heðəʳ] N Heidekraut *nt*, Erika *f*, Heide *f*

Heath Robinson [ˌhiːθ'rɒbɪnsən] ADJ (*inf*) *device, machine* wunderlich

heating ['hiːtɪŋ] N Heizung *f*; (= *act, of room, house*) (Be)heizen *nt*; (*of substances*) Erwärmen *nt*, Erhitzen *nt*; **what sort of ~ do you have?** was für eine Heizung haben Sie?

heating: **heating apparatus** N Heizapparat *m*; **heating element** N Heizelement *nt*; **heating engineer** N Heizungsinstallateur(in) *m(f)*; **heating pad** N Heizkissen *nt*; **heating system** N Heizungssystem *nt*; (= *apparatus*) Heizungsanlage *f*

heat: **heat lightning** N Wetterleuchten *nt*; **heat loss** N Wärmeverlust *m*; **heatproof** ADJ hitzebeständig; **heat pump** N Wärmepumpe *f*; **heat rash** N Hitzeausschlag *m*, Hitzepocken *pl*; **heat recovery** N Wärmerückgewinnung *f*; **heat-resistant** ADJ hitzebeständig; **heat-seeking** ADJ Wärme suchend; **heat-sensitive** ADJ wärmeempfindlich; **heat shield** N (*for protection*) Hitzeschild *m*; (*to retain heat*) Wärmeschutz *m*; **heat spot** N (*Brit*) Hitzebläschen *nt*; **heatstroke** N Hitzschlag *m*; **heat treatment** N (*Metal, Med*) Wärmebehandlung *f*; **heat wave** N Hitzewelle *f*

heave [hiːv] VT **a** (= *lift*) (hoch)hieven, (hoch)heben, wuchten (*onto* auf +*acc*); (= *drag*) schleppen; **he ~d himself out of bed** er hievte sich aus dem Bett (*inf*); **she ~d him to his feet** sie wuchtete ihn auf die Beine
b (= *throw*) werfen, schmeißen (*inf*)
c *sigh, sob* ausstoßen
d *pret, ptp* **hove** (*Naut*) wenden; **to ~ anchor** den Anker lichten
VI **a** (= *pull*) ziehen, hieven
b (= *move*: *ground*) sich heben und senken; (*sea, waves, bosom*) wogen (*geh*); (*stomach*) sich umdrehen; (*body*) sich krümmen; **the earthquake made the ground ~** bei dem Beben hob sich die Erde
c *pret, ptp* **hove** (*Naut*) **to ~ into sight** *or* **view** in Sicht kommen; **to ~ alongside** längsseits gehen
N (*of sea, waves*) Auf und Ab *nt*, Wogen *nt* (*geh*); (*of bosom, chest*) Wogen *nt* (*geh*); **to lift/throw sth with a great ~** etw mit großer Anstrengung hochhieven *or* hochwuchten/mit großer Wucht werfen

▶ **heave to** (*Naut*) VI beidrehen VT *sep ship* stoppen

▶ **heave up** VI (*inf*, = *vomit*) brechen VT *sep* **a** (= *pull up*) hochhieven, hochwuchten; (= *push up*) hochstemmen **b** (*inf*, = *vomit*) ausbrechen, von sich geben (*inf*)

heave ho INTERJ hau ruck

heaven ['hevn] N **a** (*lit, fig inf*) Himmel *m*; **the ~s** (*liter*) der Himmel; **in ~** im Himmel; **to go to ~** in den Himmel kommen; **he is in (seventh) ~** er ist im siebten Himmel; **to move ~ and earth** Himmel und Hölle in Bewegung setzen; **it was ~** es war einfach himmlisch; **the shop was a chocolate lover's ~!** das Geschäft war ein Paradies für Schokoladenfans!; **the ~s opened** der Himmel öffnete seine Schleusen
b (*inf*) **(good) ~s!** (du) lieber Himmel! (*inf*), du liebe Zeit! (*inf*); **would you like to? – (good) ~s no!** möchten Sie? – um Gottes *or* Himmels willen, bloß nicht!; **I wish to ~ (that) ...** ich wünschte mir wirklich, dass ...; **~ knows what ...** weiß Gott *or* der Himmel, was ... (*inf*); **~ knows I need some good luck** ich brauche weiß Gott ein bisschen Glück; **~ forbid!** bloß nicht, um Himmels willen! (*inf*); **~ forbid that I should end up like him** dass ich um Himmels willen nicht auch so wie er werde! (*inf*); **~ help the man she marries** der arme Mann, den sie mal heiratet (*inf*); **for ~'s sake!** um Himmels *or* Gottes willen!; **what in ~'s name ...?** was um Himmels *or* Gottes willen ...?

heavenly ['hevnlɪ] ADJ **a** himmlisch, Himmels-; **~ body** Himmelskörper *m*; **~ host** himmlische Heerscharen *pl*; **~ peace** himmlischer Frieden **b** (*inf*: = *delightful*) himmlisch, traumhaft

heaven-sent ['hevnˌsent] ADJ *opportunity* ideal; **it was ~** das kam wie gerufen

heavenward(s) ['hevnwəd(z)] ADV zum Himmel, gen Himmel (*liter*); **to raise one's eyes heavenward** die Augen zum Himmel erheben

heaves [hiːvz] N *sing* (*Vet*) Dämpfigkeit *f*; **to have the ~** dämpfig sein; (*sl*: = *vomit*) reihern (*sl*)

heavily ['hevɪlɪ] ADV **a** (= *a lot*) stark; *populated, wooded* dicht; *armed, fortified* schwer; *guarded* streng; **~ underlined** (*word, passage*) dick unterstrichen; **~ accented** (*English, German etc*) mit starkem Akzent; **to borrow ~** hohe Kredite aufnehmen; (*fig*) viele Anleihen machen (*from* bei); **to gamble ~** ein leidenschaftlicher Spieler sein; **to gamble ~ on sth** viel Geld auf etw (*acc*) wetten; (*fig*) sehr auf etw (*acc*) bauen; **his face was ~ bruised** sein Gesicht war voller blauer Flecken; **their feet are ~ bandaged** ihre Füße sind dick verbunden; **~ disguised** (*lit, fig*) völlig unkenntlich gemacht; **to lose ~** (*in gambling, sport, election*) hoch verlieren; **to be ~ reliant on sb/sth** stark auf jdn/etw angewiesen sein; **to depend** *or* **rely ~ on sb/sth** stark von jdm/etw abhängen; **to draw ~ on sth** sich zum großen Teil auf etw (*acc*) stützen; **to be ~ involved in** *or* **with sth** sehr viel mit etw zu tun haben; **to be ~ involved in a party/movement** in einer Partei/Bewegung stark engagiert sein; **to be ~ into sth** (*inf*) voll auf etw (*acc*) abfahren (*inf*); **to be ~ in debt** stark verschuldet sein; **to be ~ weighted in sb's favour** (*Brit*) *or* **favor** (*US*)**/against sb** jdn stark begünstigen/benachteiligen; **to be ~ fined** zu einer hohen Geldstrafe verurteilt werden; **to be ~ outnumbered** zahlenmäßig stark unterlegen sein; **to be ~ defeated** eine schwere Niederlage erleiden; **to be ~ booked** fast ganz ausgebucht sein; **~ pregnant** hochschwanger
b (= *deeply*) *breathe* schwer; *sigh* tief; *pant* stark
c (*lit*) *land, lean, fall* schwer; (= *clumsily*) *move,*

walk schwerfällig; **~ laden** schwer beladen; **~ built** kräftig gebaut; **she sat down ~ on the bed** sie setzte sich schwerfällig aufs Bett
d *(= slowly) say* schleppend
e *(= richly) carved, encrusted, embroidered, gilded* reich

heaviness ['hevɪnɪs] N **a** *(of person, object, load)* Schwere *f*; *(of features)* Grobheit *f*; **~ of heart** schweres Herz; **~ of spirit** gedrückte Stimmung, Niedergeschlagenheit *f* **b** *(of tread, blow, gunfire, casualties etc)* Schwere *f*; *(of traffic)* Stärke *f*; *(of defeat, losses, taxes)* Höhe *f*; *(of buying)* Umfang *m*; *(of line)* Dicke *f*; *(of sleep)* Tiefe *f* **c** *(= heavy-handedness: of manner, style)* Schwerfälligkeit *f* **d** *(= oppressiveness, of air)* Schwüle *f*; *(of sky)* Bedecktheit *f*

heavy ['hevɪ] ADJ *(+er)* **a** *(= of great weight, Phys, fig)* schwer; *features* grob; **with a ~ heart** schweren Herzens, mit schwerem Herzen; **~ with pollen** mit Pollen geschwängert *(geh)*; **~ with sleep** *(person)* schläfrig; *eyes also* schwer; **the air was ~ with smoke/the smell of cooking** der Rauch/Essensgeruch hing schwer in der Luft; **his voice was ~ with sarcasm** seine Stimme triefte von *or* vor Sarkasmus
b *blow, gunfire, casualties, fog, book, meal, defeat, losses* schwer; *rain, traffic, drinker, smoker, period* stark; *expenses, taxes* hoch; *buying* groß; *line* dick; *sleep* tief; *landing, fall* hart; **~ buyer** Großabnehmer *m*; **~ type** *(Typ)* Fettdruck *m*; **~ breathing** schweres Atmen; **to be ~ on petrol** *(Brit) or* **gas** *(US)* viel Benzin brauchen; **to be ~ on the stomach** schwer im Magen liegen; **to be ~ with child** *(liter)* schweren Leibes sein *(geh)*
c *(= heavy-handed) manner, style, sense of humour* schwerfällig
d *(= oppressive) silence* bedrückend; *weather, air* drückend, schwül; *sky* bedeckt
e *(= difficult) task, work, day* schwer; **the going was ~** wir kamen nur schwer voran; **she can be ~ going** sie kann ziemlich anstrengend sein; **the conversation was ~ going** die Unterhaltung war mühsam; **this book is very ~ going** das Buch liest sich schwer
f *(Theat) part* schwer, ernst
g *(inf: = strict)* streng *(on* mit*)*; **to play the ~ father/husband** den gestrengen Vater/Ehemann spielen
h *(dated US sl)* prima *(inf)*, dufte *(dated inf)*
ADV schwer; **his guilt weighs** *or* **lies ~ on him** seine Schuld lastet schwer auf ihm
N **a** *(Brit inf: = thug)* Schlägertyp *m*
b *(Theat, = villain)* Schurke *m*
c *(Scot: = beer)* *dunkleres, obergäriges Bier*

heavy: **heavy artillery** N *(Mil)* schwere Artillerie; **heavy-duty** ADJ *clothes, tyres etc* strapazierfähig; *plastic, flex* dick; **~ machine** Hochleistungsmaschine *f*; **heavy-footed** ADJ schwerfällig; **heavy goods vehicle** N Lastkraftwagen *m*; **heavy-handed** ADJ schwerfällig, ungeschickt; **heavy-hearted** ADJ mit schwerem Herzen, bedrückt; **heavy hitter** N *(US)* sehr wichtige *or* einflussreiche Persönlichkeit; **heavy industry** N Schwerindustrie *f*; **heavy-laden** ADJ schwer beladen *(also Bibl)*; **heavy metal** N **a** Schwermetall *nt* **b** *(Mus)* Heavymetal *m*; **heavy water** N schweres Wasser; **heavy water reactor** N Schwerwasserreaktor *m*

heavyweight ['hevɪweɪt] N **a** *(Sport)* Schwergewicht *nt*, Schwergewichtler(in) *m(f)* **b** *(fig inf: = influential person)* großes Tier *(inf)*; **the literary ~s** die literarischen Größen *pl* ADJ **a** *(Sport)* **~ champion** Meister(in) *m(f)* im Schwergewicht; **~ boxer** (Boxer(in) *m(f)* im) Schwergewicht *nt*, Schwergewichtler(in) *m(f)*; **~ class** Schwergewicht *nt* **b** *(fig inf: = serious) issue, subject* gewichtig; *writer, commentator, interviewer* ernst zu nehmend; *position* bedeutend; *newspaper* seriös **c** *(= thick, heavy) cloth, plastic, paper* schwer

hebdomadal [heb'dɒmədl] ADJ *(form)* wöchentlich

Hebrew ['hi:bru:] ADJ hebräisch N **a** Hebräer(in) *m(f)* **b** *(Ling)* Hebräisch *nt* → *also* **English**

Hebridean [ˌhebrɪ'di:ən] ADJ Hebriden-, der Hebriden; **~ island** Hebrideninsel *f*

Hebrides ['hebrɪdi:z] PL Hebriden *pl*

heck [hek] INTERJ *(inf)* **oh ~!** zum Kuckuck! *(inf)*; **ah, what the ~!** ach, was solls! *(inf)*; **what the ~ do you mean?** was zum Kuckuck soll das heißen? *(inf)*; **I've a ~ of a lot to do** ich habe irrsinnig viel zu tun *(inf)*; **I'm in one ~ of a mess** ich stecke bis zum Hals im Schlamassel *(inf)*

heckle ['hekl] VT *speaker* (durch Zwischenrufe) stören VI stören, Zwischenrufe machen

heckler ['heklə'] N Zwischenrufer(in) *m(f)*, Störer(in) *m(f)* *(pej)*

heckling ['heklɪŋ] N Zwischenrufe *pl*

hectare ['hektɑ:'] N Hektar *m or nt*

hectic ['hektɪk] ADJ *(also Med)* hektisch; **~ colour** *(Med)* hektische Röte

hectogramme, *(US)* **hectogram** ['hektəʊgræm] N Hektogramm *nt*

hectolitre, *(US)* **hectoliter** ['hektəʊˌli:tə'] N Hektoliter *m*

hector ['hektə'] VT *(liter: = bully)* tyrannisieren

hectoring ['hektərɪŋ] ADJ herrisch, tyrannisch

he'd [hi:d] *contr of* **he would, he had**

hedge [hedʒ] N Hecke *f*; *(fig: = protection)* Schutz *m*; **to be a ~ against sth** ein Schutz (-wall) *m* gegen etw sein
VI ausweichen, kneifen *(inf)* *(at* bei*)*; **to ~ on a question** einer Frage ausweichen; **to ~ on a promise** nichts versprechen wollen; **the president continues to ~ on whether to ...** der Präsident lässt es weiterhin offen, ob ...; **stop hedging and say what you think** weich nicht immer aus, sag, was du denkst!; **to ~ against sth** sich vor etw *(dat)* schützen
VT **a** *investment* absichern; **to ~ one's bets** *(lit, fig)* sich absichern, auf Nummer sicher gehen *(inf)*
b *field, garden* (mit einer Hecke) umgeben

▶ **hedge about** *(Brit) or* **around** VT *sep* **a** *(with restrictions etc) procedure* erschweren, behindern; *offer, reform* einschränken *(with* durch*)* **b** *(rare: lit)* (mit einer Hecke) einfassen

▶ **hedge in** *or (esp Brit)* **round** VT *sep* **a** *field* mit einer Hecke umgeben *or* einfassen **b** *(fig) procedure* behindern, erschweren; **to hedge sb in** jdn in seiner Freiheit einengen *or* beschränken

▶ **hedge off** VT *sep* mit einer Hecke abgrenzen *or* abtrennen

hedgehog ['hedʒhɒg] N Igel *m*

hedge: **hedgehop** VI tief fliegen; **hedgerow** N Hecke *f*, Knick *m* *(N Ger)*; **hedge sparrow** N Heckenbraunelle *f*; **hedge trimmer** N Elektroheckenschere *f*

hedonism ['hi:dənɪzəm] N Hedonismus *m*

hedonist ['hi:dənɪst] N Hedonist(in) *m(f)* ADJ hedonistisch

hedonistic [ˌhi:də'nɪstɪk] ADJ hedonistisch

heebie-jeebies ['hi:bɪ'dʒi:bɪz] PL *(inf)* Gänsehaut *f* *(inf)*; **it/he gives me the ~** dabei/wenn ich ihn sehe, bekomm ich eine Gänsehaut *(inf)*

heed [hi:d] N Beachtung *f*; **to take ~** achtgeben, aufpassen; **to pay ~ to sb/sth, to take ~ of sb/sth** jdn/etw beachten, jdm/einer Sache Beachtung schenken; **to pay no ~ to sb/sth, to take no ~ of sb/sth** jdn/etw nicht beachten, jdm/einer Sache keine Beachtung schenken; **to take ~ to do sth** darauf achten, etw zu tun
VT beachten, Beachtung schenken *(+dat)*; **just ~ what your father says** hör auf deinen Vater; **he never ~s my advice** er hört nie auf meinen Rat

heedful ['hi:dfʊl] ADJ **to be ~ of sb's warning/advice** auf jds Warnung *(acc)*/Rat *(acc)* hören

heedless ['hi:dlɪs] ADJ rücksichtslos; *extravagance* leichtsinnig; **to be ~ of sth** etw nicht beachten, auf etw *(acc)* nicht achten; **~ of their complaints** ohne sich um ihre Beschwerden zu kümmern, ohne Rücksicht auf ihre Beschwerden

heedlessly ['hi:dlɪslɪ] ADV rücksichtslos

heehaw ['hi:hɔ:] N Iah *nt* VI iahen

heel[1] [hi:l] N **a** Ferse *f*; *(of shoe)* Absatz *m*; **the ~ of the hand** der Handballen; **I like to wear ~s** ich trage gerne Schuhe mit hohen Absätzen; **with his dog/the children at his ~s** gefolgt von seinem Hund/den Kindern; **to be right on sb's ~s** jdm auf den Fersen folgen; *(fig: = chase)* jdm auf den Fersen sein; **to follow hard upon sb's ~s** jdm dicht auf den Fersen sein, sich an jds Fersen *(acc)* heften *(geh)*; **panic buying came hard on the ~s of the government's announcement** Hamsterkäufe folgten der Erklärung der Regierung auf dem Fuße; **the police were hot on our ~s** die Polizei war uns dicht auf den Fersen; **to be snapping at sb's ~s** *(fig inf)* jdm dicht auf den Fersen sein; **to be down at ~** *(person)* abgerissen *or* heruntergekommen sein; *(building)* heruntergekommen sein; **to take to one's ~s** sich aus dem Staub(e) machen, Fersengeld geben *(dated, hum)*; **to show sb a clean pair of ~s** *(= escape)* vor jdm davonlaufen, jdm die Fersen zeigen *(geh)*; *(= leave behind)* jdm weit voraus sein, jdn weit hinter sich lassen; **~!** *(to dog)* (bei) Fuß!; **he brought the dog to ~** er befahl dem Hund, bei Fuß zu gehen; **to bring sb to ~** jdn an die Kandare nehmen *(inf)*; **to turn** *or* **spin on one's ~** auf dem Absatz kehrtmachen; **to cool** *or* **kick one's ~s** *(inf: = wait)* warten; *(= do nothing)* Däumchen drehen; **to set** *or* **rock sb back on his/her** *etc* **~s** *(fig inf)* jdm einen Schock versetzen
b *(of golf club)* Ferse *f*; *(of loaf)* Kanten *m*; *(of mast)* Fuß *m*
c *(dated pej sl, = person)* Saukerl *m* *(sl)*
VT **a** **to ~ shoes** auf Schuhe neue Absätze machen; **these shoes need ~ing** diese Schuhe brauchen neue Absätze
b *(Rugby) ball* hakeln

heel[2] *(Naut)* VI *(ship: also* **heel over***)* krängen *(spec)*, sich (auf die Seite) legen *or* neigen; **to ~ hard over** sich stark auf die Seite legen, stark krängen *(spec)* VT krängen lassen *(spec)*, sich seitlich überlegen lassen N (seitliches) Überlegen, Seitenneigung *f*

heel bar N Absatzbar *f*

heft [heft] VT *(US inf)* *(= lift)* (hoch)heben; *(= assess weight)* abwägen, das Gewicht (ab)schätzen von N Gewicht *nt*; *(= strength)* (Muskel)-kraft *f*

hefty ['heftɪ] ADJ *(+er)* *(inf)* **a** *(= large) person* kräftig (gebaut); *object* massiv; *meal* kräftig, deftig *(inf)*; *fine, bill, increase, fees, payment* saftig *(inf)*; *profit* anständig *(inf)*; *debt* hoch; **a ~ tome** ein Schmöker *m* *(inf)* **b** *(= powerful) kick, punch, slap* kräftig, saftig *(inf)*

Hegelian [heɪ'geɪlɪən] ADJ Hegelsch; *(= in Hegelian tradition)* hegelianisch N Hegelianer(in) *m(f)*

hegemony [hɪ'gemənɪ] N Hegemonie *f*

hegira [he'dʒaɪərə] N Hedschra *f*

Heidelberg man ['haɪdlbɜ:g'mæn] N Homo heidelbergensis *m*

heifer ['hefə'] N Färse *f*

heigh [heɪ] INTERJ **~-ho!** nun ja!

height [haɪt] N **a** *(of building, mountain etc, = altitude)* Höhe *f*; *(of person)* Größe *f*; **to be six feet in ~** sechs Fuß groß *or (wall etc)* hoch sein; **what ~ are you?** wie groß sind Sie?; **he pulled himself up to his full ~** er richtete sich zu voller Größe auf; **you can raise the ~ of the saddle** du kannst den Sattel höherstellen; **at shoulder/head ~** in Schulter-/Kopfhöhe
b **heights** PL *(= high place)* Höhen *pl*; **to scale the ~s of Everest** den Mount Everest besteigen; **fear of ~s** Höhenangst *f*; **to be afraid of ~s** nicht schwindelfrei sein **c** *(fig)* Höhe *f*; *(of stupidity)* Gipfel *m*; **at the ~ of his power** auf der Höhe seiner Macht; **the speculation has**

reached new ~s die Spekulationen haben einen neuen Höhepunkt erreicht; **the ~ of luxury** das Nonplusultra an Luxus; **that is the ~ of arrogance/folly** das ist der Gipfel der Arroganz/der Torheit; **that is the ~ of bad manners!** das ist doch die Höhe!, das ist der Gipfel der Unverschämtheit!; **it is the ~ of bad manners to ...** es verstößt gegen jede Etikette, zu ...; **at the ~ of the season** in der Hauptsaison; **at the ~ of the storm** als der Sturm am heftigsten war; **at the ~ of summer** im Hochsommer; **at its ~ the company employed 12,000 people** in ihrer Glanzzeit hatte die Firma 12.000 Angestellte; **during the war emigration was at its ~** im Krieg erreichte die Auswanderungswelle ihren Höhepunkt; **to be the ~ of fashion** große Mode *or* der letzte Schrei sein

height-adjustable ADJ höhenverstellbar

heighten ['haɪtn] VT *(= raise)* höherstellen *or* -machen; *(= emphasize) colour etc* hervorheben; *(Med) fever* steigen lassen, erhöhen; *intensity* steigern; *colour, feelings, anger, love, ambition* verstärken; *passions, fear, fitness, effect, tension* verstärken, erhöhen; **with ~ed colour** *(Brit) or* **color** *(US)* mit (hoch)rotem Gesicht; **~ed awareness** erhöhte Aufmerksamkeit VI *(fig: = increase)* wachsen, größer *or* stärker werden

heinous ['heɪnəs] ADJ abscheulich, verabscheuungswürdig

heinously ['heɪnəslɪ] ADV auf abscheuliche Weise

heinousness ['heɪnəsnɪs] N Abscheulichkeit *f*

heir [ɛə'] N Erbe *m*, Erbin *f* (*to +gen*); **~ to the throne** Thronfolger(in) *m(f)*

heir apparent N gesetzlicher Erbe, gesetzliche Erbin

heiress ['ɛəres] N Erbin *f*

heirloom ['ɛəlu:m] N Erbstück *nt*

heist [haɪst] *(esp US inf)* N Raubüberfall *m* VT rauben

held [held] *pret, ptp of* **hold**

Helen ['helɪn] N Helene *f*; *(Myth)* Helena *f*; **~ of Troy** die Schöne Helena

helical ['helɪkəl] ADJ spiralförmig, helikal *(spec)*; *gear* schräg verzahnt

helicopter ['helɪkɒptə'] N Hubschrauber *m* VT **he was ~ed out of the area** er wurde per Hubschrauber aus dem Gebiet abtransportiert

helicopter gunship N Kampfhubschrauber *m*

Heligoland ['helɪgəʊlænd] N Helgoland *nt*

heliocentric [ˌhi:lɪəʊ'sentrɪk] ADJ heliozentrisch

heliograph ['hi:lɪəʊgrɑ:f] N Heliograf *m* VT heliografisch übermitteln

heliotrope ['hi:lɪətrəʊp] N *(Bot: = colour)* Heliotrop *nt* ADJ heliotrop(isch)

heliotropic [ˌhi:lɪəʊ'trəʊpɪk] ADJ heliotrop(isch)

helipad ['helɪpæd] N Hubschrauberlandeplatz *m*

heliport ['helɪpɔ:t] N Heliport *m*, Hubschrauberflugplatz *m*

heliskiing ['helɪˌski:ɪŋ] N Heliskiing *nt (Skifahren mit einem Hubschrauber, der den Skifahrer auf den Gipfel fliegt)*

helispot ['helɪspɒt] N provisorischer Hubschrauberlandeplatz

helium ['hi:lɪəm] N Helium *nt*

helix ['hi:lɪks] N (räumliche) Spirale, Helix *f*

hell [hel] N **a** Hölle *f*; **to go to ~** *(lit)* in die Hölle kommen, zur Hölle fahren *(liter)*; **the road to Hell is paved with good intentions** *(prov)* der Weg zur Hölle ist mit guten Vorsätzen gepflastert *(Prov)*; **~ hath no fury like a woman scorned** *(liter)* es gibt nichts Schlimmeres als die Rache einer geschmähten Frau
b *(fig uses)* **all ~ broke loose** die Hölle war los; **it's ~ working there** es ist die reine Hölle, dort zu arbeiten; **it was ~ in the trenches** es war die reine Hölle in den Schützengräben; **their life together was ~ on earth** ihr gemeinsames Leben war die reinste Hölle *or* die Hölle auf Erden; **a living ~** die Hölle auf Erden; **life became ~** das Leben wurde zur Hölle; **to go through ~** Höllenqualen ausstehen; **I put her through ~** ich machte ihr das Leben zur Hölle; **she made his life ~** sie machte ihm das Leben zur Hölle; **we've been to ~ and back** *(inf)* es war die reinste Hölle; **to give sb ~** *(inf: = tell off)* jdm die Hölle heißmachen; *(= make life unpleasant)* jdm das Leben zur Hölle machen; **you'll get ~ if he finds out** *(inf)* der macht dich zur Schnecke *or* Sau, wenn er das erfährt *(inf)*; **there'll be ~ to pay when he finds out** wenn er das erfährt, ist der Teufel los *(inf)*; **to play ~ with sth** etw total durcheinanderbringen; **I did it (just) for the ~ of it** *(inf)* ich habe es nur zum Spaß *or* aus Jux gemacht; **come ~ or high water** egal, was passiert; **you can wait until ~ freezes over** da kannst du warten, bis du schwarz wirst; **~ for leather** was das Zeug hält; *run also* was die Beine hergeben; **the mother-in-law from ~** die böse Schwiegermutter, wie sie im Buche steht; **the holiday from ~** der absolut katastrophale Urlaub
c *(inf, intensifier)* **a ~ of a noise** ein Höllen- *or* Heidenlärm *m (inf)*; **it's (as) hot as ~** es ist höllisch heiß *(inf)*; **I was angry as ~** ich war stinksauer *(inf)*; **to work like ~** arbeiten, was das Zeug hält, wie wild arbeiten *(inf)*; **to run like ~** laufen, was die Beine hergeben; **it hurts like ~** es tut wahnsinnig weh *(inf)*; **we had a** *or* **one ~ of a time** *(= bad, difficult)* es war grauenhaft; *(= good)* wir haben uns prima amüsiert *(inf)*; **a ~ of a lot** verdammt viel *(inf)*; **she's a** *or* **one ~ of a girl** die ist schwer in Ordnung *(inf)*, das ist ein klasse Mädchen *(inf)*; **that's one** *or* **a ~ of a problem/difference/climb** das ist ein verdammt *or* wahnsinnig schwieriges Problem *(inf)*/ein wahnsinniger Unterschied *(inf)*/eine wahnsinnige Kletterei *(inf)*; **I hope to ~ he's right** ich hoffe ja nur, dass er recht hat; **to ~ with you/him** hol dich/ihn der Teufel *(inf)*, du kannst/der kann mich mal *(inf)*; **to ~ with it!** verdammt noch mal *(inf)*; **to ~ with your problems!** deine Probleme können mir gestohlen bleiben *(inf)*; **get the ~ out of my house!** mach, dass du aus meinem Haus kommst!; **go to ~!** scher dich *or* geh zum Teufel! *(inf)*; **he can go to ~ for all I care** meinetwegen soll er sich zum Teufel scheren *(inf)*; **what the ~ do you want?** was willst du denn, verdammt noch mal? *(inf)*; **where the ~ is it?** wo ist es denn, verdammt noch mal? *(inf)*; **you scared the ~ out of me** du hast mich zu Tode erschreckt; **like ~ he will!** den Teufel wird er tun *(inf)*; **pay that much for a meal? like ~** so viel für ein Essen bezahlen? ich bin doch nicht verrückt!; **he knows the Queen? – like ~!** er und die Königin kennen? – wers glaubt!; **~!** so'n Mist! *(inf)*, verdammt noch mal! *(inf)*; **~'s bells!, ~'s teeth!** *(euph, expressing surprise)* heiliger Strohsack *or* Bimbam! *(inf)*; *(expressing anger)* zum Kuckuck noch mal! *(inf)*; **what the ~, I've nothing to lose** zum Teufel, ich habe nichts zu verlieren *(inf)*

he'll [hi:l] *contr of* **he shall, he will**

hellacious [he'leɪʃəs] ADJ *(US inf)* **a** *(= terrible) fighting, car crash* höllisch *(inf)* **b** *(= wild) party* wild **c** *(= excellent) vacation* fantastisch, phantastisch

hell: **hellbender** N *(US)* **a** *(Zool)* Schlammteufel *m*, Riesensalamander *m* **b** *(inf: = hell-raiser)* ausschweifender Mensch; **hellbent** ADJ versessen (*on* auf *+acc*); **to be ~ on vengeance** unerbittlich auf Rache sinnen; **hellcat** N Giftziege *f (inf)*

hellebore ['helɪbɔ:] N *(Bot)* Nieswurz *f*

Hellenic [he'li:nɪk] ADJ hellenisch; **a ~ cruise** eine Hellas-Kreuzfahrt

hell: **hellfire** N Höllenfeuer *nt*; *(= punishment)* Höllenqualen *pl*; **hellhole** N grässliches Loch; **the trenches were a real ~** die (Schützen)gräben waren die reine Hölle; **hellhound** N Höllenhund *m*; *(fig)* Teufel *m*

hellish ['helɪʃ] *(inf)* ADJ **a** *(fig: = diabolical)* höllisch *(inf)*; *traffic, heat, cold* mörderisch *(inf)*; **it's ~** es ist die reinste Hölle *(inf)*; **the exams were ~** die Prüfungen waren verteufelt schwer *(inf)* **b** *(= wicked) plan, actions* höllisch, teuflisch ADV *(= awfully)* höllisch *(inf)*, mörderisch *(inf)*; **he felt ~ guilty** er hatte schreckliche Schuldgefühle

hellishly ['helɪʃlɪ] ADV *(inf) hot, cold* höllisch *(inf)*, mörderisch *(inf)*; *difficult, complicated* verteufelt *(inf)*; *busy, tired* fürchterlich

hello [hə'ləʊ] ✪ 21.2 INTERJ hallo; **say ~ to your aunt** sag deiner Tante mal schön „Guten *or* guten Tag!"; **say ~ to your parents (from me)** grüß deine Eltern (von mir); **~, ~, ~! what's going on here?** nanu *or* he! was ist denn hier los? N Hallo *nt*

hell-raiser ['helreɪzə'] N *(inf)* ausschweifender Mensch

Hell's Angels [ˌhelz'eɪndʒəlz] PL Hell's Angels *pl*

helluva ['heləvə] ADJ, ADV *(inf)* = **hell of a**, → **hell c**

hell week N *(US Univ inf) Woche, in der angehende Mitglieder einer Studentenverbindung durch Demütigungen „getestet" werden*

helm [helm] N **a** *(Naut)* Ruder *nt*, Steuer *nt*; **to be at the ~** *(lit, fig)* am Ruder sein **b** *(obs, = helmet)* Helm *m*

helmet ['helmɪt] N Helm *m*; *(Fencing)* Maske *f*

helmeted ['helmɪtɪd] ADJ behelmt

helmsman ['helmzmən] N *pl* **-men** [-mən] Steuermann *m*

helo ['heləʊ] N *(inf: = helicopter)* Hubschrauber *m*

help [help] ✪ 6.2 N *no pl* Hilfe *f*; *(= person: with pl)* Hilfe *f*; **with his brother's ~** mithilfe *or* mit (der) Hilfe seines Bruders; **his ~ with the project** seine Mithilfe an dem Projekt; **with the ~ of a knife** mithilfe *or* mit Hilfe eines Messers; **we need all the ~ we can get** wir brauchen jede nur mögliche Hilfe; **~ was at hand** Hilfe war zur Stelle; **he is beyond ~** ihm ist nicht mehr zu helfen; **he is beyond medical ~** ihm kann kein Arzt mehr helfen; **to ask sb for ~** jdn um Hilfe bitten; **to give ~** Hilfe leisten; **to come to sb's ~** jdm zu Hilfe kommen; **to be of ~ to sb** jdm helfen; *(person also)* jdm behilflich sein; *(thing also)* jdm nützen; **he isn't much ~ to me** er ist mir keine große Hilfe; **you're a great ~!** *(iro)* du bist mir eine schöne Hilfe!; **we are short of ~ in the shop** wir haben nicht genügend (Hilfs)kräfte im Geschäft; **there's no ~ for it** da ist nichts zu machen
VT **a** helfen *(+dat)*; **to ~ sb (to) do sth** jdm (dabei) helfen, etw zu tun; **to ~ sb with the cooking/his bags** jdm beim Kochen/mit seinen Taschen helfen; **~!** Hilfe!, zu Hilfe! *(old)*; **so ~ me God!** so wahr mir Gott helfe!; **can I ~ you?** kann ich (Ihnen) helfen *or* behilflich sein?; **that won't ~ you** das wird Ihnen nichts nützen; **this will ~ the pain/your headache** das wird gegen die Schmerzen/gegen Ihr Kopfweh helfen; **it will ~ the wound to heal** das wird die Heilung (der Wunde) fördern; **it will ~ the crops to grow** es wird das Wachstum des Getreides fördern; **God ~s those who ~ themselves** *(Prov)* hilf dir selbst, so hilft dir Gott *(Prov)*; **a man is ~ing the police with their inquiries** *(form euph)* ein Mann wird zurzeit von der Polizei vernommen
b *(with particle)* **to ~ sb down** jdm hinunterhelfen; **take some water to ~ the pill down** trinken Sie etwas Wasser, damit die Tablette besser rutscht; **to ~ sb on/off with his/her** *etc* **coat** jdm in den/aus dem Mantel helfen; **he ~ed her out of the car** er half ihr aus dem Auto; **to ~ sb over the street** jdm über die Straße helfen; **to ~ sb through a difficult time** *(belief, hope, pills etc)* jdm in einer schwierigen Zeit durchhelfen; *(person also)* jdm in einer schwierigen Zeit beistehen; **to ~ sb up** *(from floor, chair etc)* jdm aufhelfen *or (up stairs etc)* hinaufhelfen; **I ~ed him in with his cases** ich half ihm mit seinem Gepäck
c **she ~ed him to potatoes/meat** sie gab ihm

Kartoffeln/Fleisch; **to ~ oneself to sth** sich *(dat)* etw nehmen; *(inf: = steal)* etw mitgehen lassen; **~ yourself!** nehmen Sie sich doch!; **I'll ~ the children first** *(inf)* ich gebe den Kindern zuerst
d *(with can or cannot)* **he can't ~ it, he's only a baby** er kann nichts dafür, er ist doch noch ein Baby; **he can't ~ it!** *(hum inf: = he's stupid)* (d)er ist nun mal so (doof); **I can't ~ being clever** (ich kann nichts dafür,) ich bin nun mal ein Genie *or* so schlau *(inf)*; **he can't ~ the way he is** das ist nun mal (so) seine Art; **don't say more than you can ~** sagen Sie nicht mehr als unbedingt nötig; **not if I can ~ it** nicht, wenn es nach mir geht; **I couldn't ~ laughing** ich konnte mir nicht helfen, ich musste (einfach) lachen; **I had to do it, I couldn't ~ it** *or* **myself** ich konnte mir nicht helfen, ich musste es einfach tun; **I couldn't ~ thinking** *or* **but think ...** ich konnte nicht umhin zu denken ...; **one cannot ~ wondering whether ...** man muss sich wirklich fragen, ob ...; **it can't be ~ed** das lässt sich nicht ändern, das ist nun mal so; **I can't ~ it if he's always late** ich kann nichts dafür, dass er immer zu spät kommt
VI helfen; **and your attitude didn't ~ either** und Ihre Einstellung war auch nicht gerade hilfreich; **it ~s (to) fight pollution** es trägt zur Bekämpfung der Umweltverschmutzung bei

▶ **help out** ✪ 2.1 **VI** aushelfen *(with* bei) **VT** *sep* helfen *(+dat)* *(with* mit); *(in crisis also)* aufhelfen *(+dat)* *(with* bei); **will £3 help you out?** helfen Ihnen £ 3 weiter?

help desk N *telefonischer Informationsdienst*, Helpdesk *nt*

helper ['helpə'] N Helfer(in) *m(f)*; *(= assistant)* Gehilfe *m*, Gehilfin *f*

help file N *(Comput)* Hilfedatei *f*

helpful ['helpfʊl] ✪ 4 ADJ **a** *person (= willing to help)* hilfsbereit; *(= giving help)* hilfreich; **to be ~ to sb** jdm helfen *or* behilflich sein; **they were very ~ with the move** sie haben beim Umzug viel geholfen **b** *(= useful) advice, information, theory, book, tool* nützlich; *remedy* hilfreich; **meditation is often ~ at these times** in solchen Zeiten hilft es oft zu meditieren; **you'll find these tablets most ~** diese Tabletten werden Ihnen sehr helfen *or* guttun; **she finds it ~ to pray** sie findet, es hilft ihr zu beten

helpfully ['helpfəlɪ] ADV *(= willing to help)* hilfsbereit; *(= giving help)* hilfreich; *(= thoughtfully) provide, include* liebenswürdigerweise; **he ~ showed us the best beach** er war so hilfsbereit, uns den besten Strand zu zeigen

helpfulness ['helpfʊlnɪs] N **a** *(of person)* Hilfsbereitschaft *f* **b** *(= usefulness: of suggestion, advice, information, theory, book, tool)* Nützlichkeit *f*

help function N *(Comput)* Hilfefunktion *f*

helping ['helpɪŋ] **N** *(at table, fig)* Portion *f*; **to take a second ~ of sth** sich *(dat)* noch einmal von etw nehmen; **he even had a third ~** er nahm sich *(dat)* sogar noch eine dritte Portion; **the public appetite for huge ~s of nostalgia** das Bedürfnis der Öffentlichkeit nach großen Portionen Nostalgie **ADJ** *attr* **to give** *or* **lend a ~ hand to sb** jdm helfen, jdm behilflich sein; **if you want a ~ hand ...** wenn Sie Hilfe brauchen, ...

helpless ['helplɪs] ADJ *(= powerless) person* machtlos *(against* gegen); *(= vulnerable) child, victim, invalid, gesture* hilflos; **a ~ feeling** ein Gefühl *nt* der Hilflosigkeit; **he was ~ to prevent it** er konnte es nicht verhindern; **he was ~ to resist** er konnte nicht widerstehen; **to feel ~** sich hilflos fühlen; **she was ~ with laughter** sie konnte sich vor Lachen kaum halten; **~ state** Hilflosigkeit *f*; **he is reduced to a ~ state** er ist zur Hilflosigkeit verurteilt

helplessly ['helplɪslɪ] ADV *look, stand, shrug, sob, drift, lie* hilflos; *(lit, fig: = impotently) watch* machtlos; **~ confused** völlig verwirrt; **~ drunk** sinnlos betrunken

helplessness ['helplɪsnɪs] N Hilflosigkeit *f*; *(= powerlessness)* Machtlosigkeit *f*

help: **helpline** N *(for emergencies)* Notruf *m*; *(for information)* Informationsdienst *m*; **helpmate** *(old)*, **helpmeet** *(obs)* N Gefährte *m (geh)*, Gefährtin *f (geh)*; *(= helper)* Gehilfe *m (old)*, Gehilfin *f (old)*; **help screen** N *(Comput)* Hilfebildschirm *m*

helter-skelter ['heltə'skeltə'] **ADJ** wild; *account* chaotisch; **the last minute ~ rush for the bus** die wilde Hetze in letzter Minute, um den Bus zu erwischen **ADV** *run, rush* Hals über Kopf *(inf)* **N** **a** *(Brit, in fairground)* spiralförmige Rutschbahn **b** *(= disorder)* wildes Durcheinander; *(= haste)* wilde Hetze

hem[1] [hem] INTERJ = **hum VI c**

hem[2] **N** Saum *m* **VT** säumen

▶ **hem about** *(Brit) or* **around** VT *sep* umgeben

▶ **hem in** VT *sep troops etc* einschließen, umgeben; *(fig)* einengen

he-man ['hi:mæn] N *pl* **-men** [-men] *(inf)* sehr männlicher Typ, echter *or* richtiger Mann; **he fancies himself as a ~** er kommt sich unheimlich männlich vor *(inf)*

hematite ['hi:mətaɪt] N Hämatit *m*

hematology N *(US)* = **haematology**

hemidemisemiquaver [,hemɪdemɪ'semɪ,kweɪvə'] N *(Mus)* Vierundsechzigstel(note *f*) *nt*

hemiplegia [,hemɪ'pli:dʒɪə] N halbseitige Lähmung

hemiplegic [,hemɪ'pli:dʒɪk] ADJ halbseitig gelähmt

hemisphere ['hemɪsfɪə'] N Halbkugel *f*, Hemisphäre *f*; *(of brain)* Hemisphäre *f*, Gehirnhälfte *f*; **in the northern ~** auf der nördlichen Halbkugel, in der nördlichen Hemisphäre

hemispheric [,hemɪ'sferɪk] ADJ **a** *(Geog)* **Northern ~ summers** die Sommer in der nördlichen Hemisphäre *or* auf der nördlichen Halbkugel **b** *(Med, Psych) asymmetry, specialization, activity* hemisphärisch **c** *(Pol)* **Western ~ nations** die Länder *pl* der westlichen Hemisphäre **d** *(US Pol) relations, solidarity* zwischen den Nord- und Südstaaten der USA; **a sense of ~ identity** ein Gefühl der Identität in den Nord- und Südstaaten der USA

hemline ['hemlaɪn] N Saum *m*; **~s are lower this year** der Rocksaum ist dieses Jahr etwas tiefer gerutscht

hemlock ['hemlɒk] N *(Bot: = poisonous plant)* Schierling *m*; *(= tree)* Schierlings- *or* Hemlocktanne *f*; *(= poison)* Schierling(saft) *m*; **Socrates drank the ~** Sokrates trank den Schierlingsbecher

hemo- *in cpds (US)* = **haemo-**

hemp [hemp] N **a** *(Bot)* Hanf *m*; **~ seed** Hanfsamen *pl* **b** *(= drug)* Hanf *m* **c** *(= fibre)* Hanf(faser *f*) *m*

hemstitch ['hemstɪtʃ] **VT** in Hohlsaum nähen **N** Hohlsaum *m*

hen [hen] N **a** Huhn *nt*, Henne *f*; **as scarce** *or* **rare as ~'s teeth** *(dated inf)* so selten wie ein weißer Rabe **b** *(= female bird, lobster)* Weibchen *nt* **c** *(inf: also* **mother hen**) Glucke *f* *(inf)*

hen: **henbane** N Bilsenkraut *nt*; **hen bird** N (Vogel)weibchen *nt*

hence [hens] ADV **a** *(= for this reason)* also; **~ the name** daher der Name **b** *(= from now)* **two years ~** in zwei Jahren **c** *(obs, liter, = from here)* von hier; **(get thee) ~!** hinweg (mit dir)! *(liter)*; **get thee ~, Satan!** weiche, Satan! *(liter)*

henceforth [,hens'fɔ:θ], **henceforward** [,hens'fɔ:wəd] ADV *(= from that time on)* von da an, fortan *(liter)*; *(= from this time on)* von nun an, künftig

henchman ['hentʃmən] N *pl* **-men** [-mən] *(pej)* Spießgeselle *m*, Kumpan *m*

hencoop ['henku:p] N Hühnerstall *m*

henhouse ['henhaʊs] N Hühnerhaus *nt*, Hühnerstall *m*

henna ['henə] **N** Henna *f* **VT** mit Henna färben

hen: **hen night** N *für die Braut vor der Hochzeit arrangierte Damengesellschaft*; **hen party** N *(inf)* Damenkränzchen *nt*, ≈ Kaffeeklatsch *m (inf)*, reine Weibergesellschaft *(pej, inf)*; *(before wedding) für die Braut vor der Hochzeit arrangierte Damengesellschaft*; **henpeck** VT unterm Pantoffel haben *(inf)*; **a ~ed husband** ein Pantoffelheld *m (inf)*; **he is ~ed** er steht unterm Pantoffel *(inf)*; **hen run** N Hühnerhof *m*

Henry ['henrɪ] N Heinrich *m*

hep [hep] ADJ *(dated US sl)* = **hip**[3]

hepatitis [,hepə'taɪtɪs] N Hepatitis *f*

heptagon ['heptəgən] N Siebeneck *nt*, Heptagon *nt*

heptathlon [hep'tæθlɒn] N Siebenkampf *m*

her [hɜ:'] **PERS PRON** **a** *(dir obj, with prep +acc)* sie; *(indir obj, with prep +dat)* ihr; *(when she is previously mentioned in clause)* sich; **with ~ books about ~** mit ihren Büchern um sich **b** *(emph)* sie; **it's ~** sie ists; **who, ~?** wer, sie? **POSS ADJ** ihr → *also* **my**

Heraclitean [,herə'klaɪtɪən] ADJ heraklitisch

Heraclitus [,herə'klaɪtəs] N Heraklit *m*

herald ['herəld] **N** **a** *(Hist)* Herold *m*; *(in newspaper titles)* Bote *m* **b** *(fig)* (Vor)bote *m (geh)*; **~ of spring** Frühlingsbote *m* **c** *(Her)* **College of Heralds** Heroldsamt *nt* **VT** *arrival of summer* ankündigen, Vorbote(n) sein für; **to ~ (in) a new age** den Beginn eines neuen Zeitalters ankündigen; **tonight's game is being ~ed as the match of the season** das Spiel heute Abend wird als die Begegnung der Saison groß herausgebracht

heraldic [he'rældɪk] ADJ heraldisch; **~ arms** Wappen *pl*

heraldry ['herəldrɪ] N **a** *(= science)* Wappenkunde *f*, Heraldik *f* **b** *(= heraldic signs)* Wappen *pl* **c** *(= ceremonial)* traditioneller höfischer Prunk

herb [hɜ:b] N Kraut *nt*

herbaceous [hɜ:'beɪʃəs] ADJ krautig

herbaceous border N Staudenrabatte *f*

herbage ['hɜ:bɪdʒ] N Grünpflanzen *pl*; *(= leaves and stems)* Grünzeug *nt*; *(= pasturage)* Weide (-land *nt*) *f*

herbal ['hɜ:bəl] **ADJ** Kräuter-; **~ tea** Kräutertee *m*; **~ remedies** Kräuterheilmittel *pl* **N** Kräuterbuch *nt*

herbalism ['hɜ:bəlɪzəm] N Kräuterheilkunde *f*

herbalist ['hɜ:bəlɪst] N Kräutersammler(in) *m(f)*; *(= healer)* Naturheilkundige(r) *mf*

herbarium [hɜ:'beərɪəm] N Herbarium *nt*

herb garden N Kräutergarten *m*

herbicide ['hɜ:bɪsaɪd] N Herbizid *nt*

herbivore ['hɜ:bɪvɔ:] N *(Zool)* Pflanzenfresser *m*, Herbivore *m (spec)*

herbivorous [hɜ:'bɪvərəs] ADJ *(form)* pflanzenfressend

herculean [,hɜ:kjʊ'li:ən] ADJ herkulisch; *proportions* riesenhaft; *effort* übermenschlich; **~ strength** Bären- *or* Riesenkräfte *pl*; **a ~ task** eine Herkulesarbeit

Hercules ['hɜ:kjʊli:z] N *(lit, fig)* Herkules *m*

herd [hɜ:d] **N** *(of cattle etc)* Herde *f*; *(of deer)* Rudel *nt*; *(fig pej: of people)* Herde *f*, Schar *f*; **the common ~** die breite Masse; **to follow the ~** *(fig)* der Herde folgen, mit der Herde laufen **VT** **a** *(= drive) sheep, cattle, prisoners* treiben **b** *(= tend) cattle* hüten

▶ **herd together** **VI** sich zusammendrängen **VT** *sep* zusammentreiben

herd instinct N Herdentrieb *m*

herdsman ['hɜ:dzmən] N Hirt *m*, Hirte *m*

here [hɪə'] **ADV** **a** hier; *(with motion)* hierher, hierhin; **~!** *(at roll call)* hier!; *(to dog)* hierher!; **come ~!** komm her!; **~ I am** da *or* hier bin ich; **~'s the taxi** das Taxi ist da; **~ he comes** da kommt *or* ist er ja; **spring is ~** der Frühling ist da; **this one ~** der/die/das hier *or* da; **this man ~** dieser Mann (hier) ...; **John ~ reckons ...**

John hier meint ...; **this ~ notice** *(incorrect)* dieser Anschlag da *(inf)*; **~ and now** auf der Stelle, jetzt sofort; **I won't be ~ for lunch** ich bin zum Mittagessen nicht da; **she's not ~ yet** sie ist noch nicht da; **shall we wait till he gets ~?** sollen wir warten, bis er hier *or* da ist?; **~ and there** hier und da; **~, there and everywhere** überall; **around/about ~** hierherum, ungefähr hier; **near ~** (hier) in der Nähe; **I've read down to ~** ich habe bis hierher *or* hierhin gelesen; **it's in/over ~** es ist hier (drin)/hier drüben; **put it in/over ~** stellen Sie es hierherein/hierherüber *or* hierher; **come in/over ~** kommen Sie hierherein/hierherüber *or* hierher; **from ~ on in** *(esp US)* von jetzt *or* nun an; **~ I would like to draw your attention to ...** an dieser Stelle möchte ich Sie auf ... aufmerksam machen
b *(in phrases)* **~ you are** *(giving sb sth)* hier(, bitte); *(on finding sb)* da bist du ja!, ach, hier bist du!; *(on finding sth)* da *or* hier ist es ja; **~ we are, home again** so, da wären wir also wieder zu Hause; **~ we go again, another crisis** da hätten wir also wieder eine Krise; **look out, ~ he comes** Vorsicht, er kommt!; **~ comes trouble** jetzt gehts los *(inf)*; **~ goes!** *(before attempting sth)* dann mal los; **~, try this one** hier, versuchs mal damit; **~, let me do that** komm, lass mich das mal machen; **~!** he!; **~'s to you!** *(in toast)* auf Ihr Wohl!; **~'s to the success of the venture!** auf den Erfolg des Vorhabens!; **it's neither ~ nor there** es spielt keine Rolle, tut nichts zur Sache; **I've had it up to ~ (with him/it)** *(inf)* ich habe die Nase voll (von ihm/davon) *(inf)*; **I'm up to ~ with paperwork** *(inf)* der Papierkram steht mir bis zum Hals *(inf)*
N **the ~ and now** das Hier und Heute; *(Rel, Philos)* das Diesseits

here: **hereabouts** ['hɪərəbaʊts] ADV hier (in der Gegend), in dieser Gegend; **hereafter** *(form)* **N** **the/a ~** das/ein Jenseits **ADV** **a** *(Jur etc)* im Folgenden **b** *(= from now on)* künftig, in Zukunft **c** *(= later)* **I shall say more of this ~** ich werde später darauf zurückkommen; **hereby** ADV *(form)* hiermit

hereditable [hə'redɪtəbl] ADJ *(Jur)* vererbbar; *(Med also)* (ver)erblich

hereditary [hɪ'redɪtərɪ] ADJ *factor, characteristic* erblich, angeboren; *ruler, title, position, right* erblich; **~ disease** *or* **illness** Erbkrankheit *f*, erbliche Krankheit; **~ peer** *Peer, der seine Peerswürde geerbt hat*; **~ monarch** Erbmonarch(in) *m(f)*

heredity [hɪ'redɪtɪ] N Vererbung *f*; **the title is his by ~** er hat den Titel geerbt/wird den Titel erben

here: **herein** ADV *(form)* hierin; **and ~ lies the problem** und das ist *or* hier liegt das Problem; **hereinafter** ADV *(form)* im Folgenden; **hereof** ADV *(form)* hiervon *(form)*; **the house and the inhabitants ~** das Haus und die Bewohner desselben *(form)*

heresy ['herəsɪ] N Ketzerei *f*, Häresie *f (spec)*; **heresies** Ketzereien *pl*, ketzerische Lehren *pl*

heretic ['herətɪk] N Ketzer(in) *m(f)*, Häretiker(in) *m(f) (spec)*

heretical [hɪ'retɪkəl] ADJ ketzerisch, häretisch *(spec)*

here: **hereto** ADV *(form)* **the documents attached ~** die beigefügten Dokumente; **additions ~ can only be made with his permission** Zusätze können hierzu nur mit seiner Erlaubnis gemacht werden; **he gave his signature ~** er setzte seine Unterschrift hinzu; **heretofore** ADV *(form: = up to this time)* bisher; *(= up to that time)* bis dahin; **hereunto** ADV *(form)* = **hereto**; **hereupon** ADV daraufhin; **herewith** ADV *(form)* hiermit

heritable ['herɪtəbl] ADJ **a** erblich **b** *(Jur) person* erbfähig

heritage ['herɪtɪdʒ] N *(lit, fig)* Erbe *nt*, Erbschaft *f*

heritage centre N *(Brit) auf ein bestimmtes Gebiet spezialisiertes (Heimat)museum*

hermaphrodite [hɜː'mæfrədaɪt] **N** Zwitter *m*, Hermaphrodit *m (geh)* **ADJ** zwittrig, hermaphroditisch *(geh)*; *plants also* gemischtgeschlechtig

hermaphroditic [hɜːmæfrə'dɪtɪk] ADJ hermaphroditisch

hermetic [hɜː'metɪk] ADJ hermetisch

hermetically [hɜː'metɪkəlɪ] ADV hermetisch; **~ sealed** *(jar, container)* hermetisch verschlossen; *(fig) world, existence* hermetisch abgeriegelt

hermit ['hɜːmɪt] N Einsiedler(in) *m(f) (also fig)*, Eremit(in) *m(f)*

hermitage ['hɜːmɪtɪdʒ] N *(lit, fig)* Einsiedelei *f*, Klause *f*

hermit crab N Einsiedlerkrebs *m*

hernia ['hɜːnɪə] N (Eingeweide)bruch *m*, Hernie *f (spec)*

hero ['hɪərəʊ] N *pl* **-es** Held *m*, Heros *m (geh)*; *(fig: = object of hero-worship also)* Idol *nt*; *(Liter, of novel etc)* Held *m*; **the ~ of the hour** der Held des Tages

Herod ['herəd] N Herodes *m*

heroic [hɪ'rəʊɪk] **ADJ** **a** *person* heldenhaft; *(= brave)* mutig; *behaviour, action* heroisch; *struggle, resistance, match* heldenhaft, heroisch; **~ action** *or* **deed** Heldentat *f*; **~ efforts** gewaltige Anstrengungen *pl*; **~ attempt** tapferer Versuch
b *(Liter)* Helden-; **~ poem/epic** Heldengedicht *nt*/-epos *nt*; **~ character** *or* **figure** heroische Gestalt, Heldengestalt *f*; *(= hero/heroine)* Held *m*, Heldin *f*; **a novel of ~ proportions** ein groß angelegter Roman
N **heroics** *pl (= heroic deeds)* Heldentaten *pl*; **the actor's ~s** das übertriebene Pathos des Schauspielers; **it is recorded without ~s** es wird ohne hochtrabende *or* große Worte beschrieben

heroic age N Heldenzeitalter *nt*

heroically [hɪ'rəʊɪkəlɪ] ADV **a** heldenhaft; *(= bravely)* mutig **b** *(= with great effort) work, struggle, play* mit heroischem *or* heldenhaftem Einsatz; *sacrifice, try* heldenhafterweise **c** *(= grandly)* **his brow furrows ~** er runzelt dramatisch *or* pathetisch die Stirn; **a ~ delivered speech** eine mit viel Pathos vorgetragene Rede

heroic couplet N *(Poet)* Heroic Couplet *nt*, *Reimpaar aus fünffüßigen Jamben*

heroic verse N *(Poet)* heroischer Vers

heroin ['herəʊɪn] N Heroin *nt*; **~ addict** Heroinsüchtige(r) *mf*

heroine ['herəʊɪn] N Heldin *f*; *(esp Theat also)* Heroine *f*

heroism ['herəʊɪzəm] N Heldentum *nt*, Heroismus *m*; *(= daring)* Kühnheit *f*; **I'm not one for ~** ich bin kein Held

heroize ['hɪərəʊaɪz] VT heroisieren, zum Helden/zur Heldin machen

heron ['herən] N Reiher *m*

hero worship N Verehrung *f* (*of* +*gen*); *(in ancient tribe etc)* Heldenverehrung *f*; *(of pop star etc)* Schwärmerei *f* (*of* für); **the ~ of a boy for his older brother** die blinde Bewunderung eines Jungen für seinen älteren Bruder

hero-worship ['hɪːrəʊˌwɜːʃɪp] VT anbeten, verehren; *popstar etc* schwärmen für

herpes ['hɜːpiːz] N *(Med)* Herpes *m*; **~ labialis** Herpes *m* labialis, Lippen-/Gesichtsherpes *m*

herring ['herɪŋ] N Hering *m* → **red herring**

herring: **herringbone** **N** **a** *(= pattern)* Fischgrät *m* **b** *(Ski)* Grätenschritt *m* **ADJ** *attr* **~ pattern** Fischgrät(en)muster *nt*; **~ suit** Anzug *m* mit Fischgrätmuster; **herringbone stitch** N Hexenstich *m*; **herring gull** N Silbermöwe *f*; **herring pond** N *(hum inf)* großer Teich *(hum)*

hers [hɜːz] POSS PRON ihre(r, s); **~** *(on towels etc)* sie → *also* **mine**[1]

herself [hɜː'self] **PERS PRON** **a** *(dir and indir obj, with prep)* sich → *also* **myself** **b** *(emph)* (sie) selbst **N** *(Ir inf)* **it was ~ who told me** sie selbst hat es mir gesagt

herstory ['hɜːstərɪ] N *(inf) feministische Geschichtsbetrachtung*

Herts [hɑːts] *abbr of* **Hertfordshire**

he's [hiːz] *contr of* **he is, he has**

hesitancy ['hezɪtənsɪ] N Zögern *nt*; *(= indecision)* Unschlüssigkeit *f*; *(of voice)* Unsicherheit *f*

hesitant ['hezɪtənt] ADJ zögernd; *person (= undecided)* unschlüssig, unsicher; *voice* unsicher; **to be ~ to do sth** *or* **about doing sth** zögern, etw zu tun; *(= reluctant)* etw nicht tun wollen; *(= doubtful)* Bedenken haben, etw zu tun

hesitantly ['hezɪtəntlɪ] ADV zögernd

hesitate ['hezɪteɪt] VI zögern, zaudern *(geh)*; *(in speech)* stocken; **he who ~s is lost** *(Prov)* dem Feigen kehrt das Glück den Rücken *(Prov)*; **I ~ to ask him round** ich bin mir nicht schlüssig, ob ich ihn einladen soll; **I'd ~ to take** *or* **at taking on such a task** ich würde es mir gut überlegen, ob ich so eine Aufgabe übernehmen würde; **I ~d about having another baby** ich hatte Bedenken, noch ein Kind zu bekommen; **he didn't ~ at the idea of leaving home** er zögerte keinen Augenblick, von zu Hause wegzugehen; **even he would ~ at murder** selbst er hätte bei einem Mord Bedenken; **he ~s at nothing** er macht vor nichts halt, er schreckt vor nichts zurück; **the President is hesitating over whether to attend the conference** der Präsident ist sich unschlüssig, ob er an der Konferenz teilnehmen soll; **I am still hesitating about what I should do** ich bin mir immer noch nicht schlüssig, was ich tun soll; **I ~ to say it, but ...** es widerstrebt mir, das zu sagen, aber ...; **if I did think that, I wouldn't ~ to say so** wenn ich wirklich der Meinung *(gen)* wäre, hätte ich keine Hemmungen, es zu sagen; **don't ~ to ask/contact me** fragen Sie mich ruhig/wenden Sie sich ruhig an mich; *(more formally)* zögern Sie nicht, mich zu fragen/sich an mich zu wenden

hesitation [ˌhezɪ'teɪʃən] N Zögern *nt*, Zaudern *nt (geh)*; **after some/a moment's ~** nach einigem/kurzem Zögern; **without the slightest ~** ohne auch nur einen Augenblick zu zögern; **I have no ~ in saying that ...** ich kann ohne Weiteres sagen, dass ...; **I had no ~ about taking the job** ich zögerte keinen Augenblick, die Stelle anzunehmen

hessian ['hesɪən] **N** Sackleinen *nt*, Rupfen *m* **ATTR** sackleinen, aus Sackleinen *or* Rupfen

hetaera [hɪ'taɪərə] N *pl* **-rae** *or* **-ras** Hetäre *f*

hetero ['hetərəʊ] N *(inf)* Hetero *m (inf)*, Heterosexuelle(r) *mf*

heterodox ['hetərədɒks] ADJ heterodox, andersgläubig

heterodoxy ['hetərədɒksɪ] N Heterodoxie *f*, Andersgläubigkeit *f*

heterogeneity [ˌhetərəʊdʒɪ'neɪɪtɪ] N Heterogenität *f*

heterogeneous [ˌhetərəʊ'dʒiːnɪəs] ADJ heterogen

heterosexism ['hetərəʊ'seksɪzm] N Heterosexismus *m*

heterosexual [ˌhetərəʊ'seksjʊəl] **ADJ** heterosexuell **N** Heterosexuelle(r) *mf*

heterosexuality [ˌhetərəʊˌseksjʊ'ælɪtɪ] N Heterosexualität *f*

het up [ˌhet'ʌp] ADJ *(Brit inf)* aufgeregt; **to get ~ about/over sth** sich über etw *(acc)*/wegen einer Sache *(gen)* aufregen

heuristic [hjʊə'rɪstɪk] **ADJ** heuristisch **N** **~s** *sing* Heuristik *f*

hew [hjuː] *pret* **hewed**, *ptp* **hewn** *or* **hewed** VT hauen; *(= shape)* behauen; **to ~ sth (in)to pieces** etw in Stücke hauen; **to be ~n into logs** zu Klötzen gehackt werden; **they ~ed their captives to pieces** sie zerstückelten ihre Gefangenen

► **hew down** VT *sep trees* fällen, umhauen; *persons* niederhauen; *(with machine gun)* niedermähen

► **hew off** VT *sep* abhauen, abhacken, abschlagen

▸ **hew out** VT *sep* heraushauen, herausschlagen (*of* aus); **he's hewn out a career for himself** er hat sich *(dat)* seine Karriere erkämpft

▸ **hew up** VT *sep* zerstückeln; *wood* zerhacken

hewer ['hju:əʳ] N *(Min)* Hauer *m*

hex [heks] *(esp US inf)* N Fluch *m*; **there must be a ~ on this project** dieses Projekt muss verhext sein *(inf)*; *(more serious)* auf dem Projekt muss ein Fluch liegen; **to put a ~ on sb/sth** jdn/etw verhexen VT verhexen

hexadecimal [ˌheksə'desɪməl] ADJ hexadezimal

hexagon ['heksəgən] N Sechseck *nt*, Hexagon *nt*

hexagonal [hek'sægənəl] ADJ sechseckig, hexagonal

hexameter [hek'sæmɪtəʳ] N Hexameter *m*

hex code N *(Comput)* Hexadezimalcode *m*

hey [heɪ] INTERJ *(to attract attention)* he (Sie/du); *(in surprise)* he, Mensch *(inf)*; **~ presto** Hokuspokus (Fidibus)

heyday ['heɪdeɪ] N Glanzzeit *f*, Blütezeit *f*; **in the ~ of his power** auf dem Höhepunkt seiner Macht; **in the ~ of glam rock** als Glam-Rock groß in Mode war; **in his ~** in seiner Glanzzeit

Hezbollah ['hezbə'lɑ:] N = **Hizbollah**

HGV *(Brit) abbr of* **heavy goods vehicle** LKW *m*

HH ADJ *(on pencil)* HH, 2H

H-hour N *(Mil)* Stunde *f* X *(für militärische Operationen)*

hi [haɪ] INTERJ hallo

hiatus [haɪ'eɪtəs] N Lücke *f*; *(Gram, Poet)* Hiatus *m*; **after a two-week ~** nach einer Unterbrechung von zwei Wochen

hibernate ['haɪbəneɪt] VI Winterschlaf halten *or* machen

hibernation [ˌhaɪbə'neɪʃən] N *(lit, fig)* Winterschlaf *m*

hibernator ['haɪbəneɪtəʳ] N *Tier, das Winterschlaf hält*

Hibernian [hɪ'bɜ:nɪən] *(poet)* ADJ hibernisch N Hibernier(in) *m(f)*

hibiscus [hɪ'bɪskəs] N Hibiskus *m*, Eibisch *m*

hic [hɪk] INTERJ hick

hiccough, hiccup ['hɪkʌp] N Schluckauf *m*; *(fig inf: = problem)* Problemchen *nt (inf)*; **to have the ~s** den Schluckauf haben; **to give a ~** hick machen *(inf)*, hicksen *(dial)*; **without any ~s** ohne Störungen; **the recent sales ~** die jüngsten Verkaufsprobleme VI hicksen *(dial)*; **he started ~ing** er bekam den Schluckauf

hick [hɪk] N *(US inf)* Hinterwäldler(in) *m(f) (inf)*; *(female also)* Landpomeranze *f (inf)*

hickey ['hɪkɪ] N *(inf)* **a** *(= thingummy)* Dingsbums *nt (inf)* **b** *(= love bite)* Knutschfleck *m (inf)*

hickory ['hɪkərɪ] N *(= tree)* Hickory(nussbaum) *m*; *(= wood)* Hickory(holz) *nt*

Hicksville [ˌhɪks'vɪl] N *(US inf)* Posemuckel *nt (inf)*, Hintertupfing *nt (inf)*; **to live out in ~** am Arsch der Welt wohnen *(inf)*

hidden ['hɪdn] ADJ versteckt, verborgen *(also computer file)*

hide¹ [haɪd] *vb: pret* **hid** [hɪd] *ptp* **hid** *or* **hidden** ['hɪdn] VT verstecken *(from* vor *+dat)*; *truth, tears, grief, feelings, face* verbergen *(from* vor *+dat)*; *(= obstruct from view) moon, rust* verdecken; *(Comput) tagging, comments etc* ausblenden; **hidden from view** nicht zu sehen, dem Blick *or* den Blicken entzogen; **the building was hidden by trees** das Gebäude war hinter Bäumen versteckt; **he's hiding something in his pocket** er hat etwas in seiner Tasche versteckt; **I have nothing to ~** ich habe nichts zu verbergen; **his words had a hidden meaning** seine Worte hatten eine verborgene *or* versteckte Bedeutung; **they have a hidden agenda** sie führen etwas im Schilde; **there is a hidden agenda** da steckt noch etwas anderes dahinter; **hidden earnings** *(of politician etc)* Schatteneinkommen *nt*; **you're hiding something from me** *(truth etc)* Sie verheimlichen mir etwas, Sie verbergen etwas vor mir; **he tried to ~ his excitement** er versuchte, seine Aufregung nicht zu zeigen VI sich verstecken, sich verbergen *(from sb* vor jdm); **quick! ~ in the cupboard** schnell, versteck dich im Schrank!; **he was hiding in the cupboard** er hielt sich im Schrank versteckt *or* verborgen; **he's hiding behind a pseudonym** er verbirgt sich hinter einem Pseudonym; **he's hiding behind his office** *(fig)* er benutzt sein Amt als Vorwand N Versteck *nt*

▸ **hide away** VI sich verstecken, sich verbergen VT *sep* verstecken

▸ **hide out** *or* **up** VI sich verstecken; *(= to be hiding also)* sich versteckt *or* verborgen halten

hide² N *(of animal)* Haut *f*; *(on furry animal)* Fell *nt*; *(processed)* Leder *nt*; *(fig, of person)* Haut *f*, Fell *nt*; **the bags are made out of rhino ~** die Taschen sind aus Nashornleder; **to save one's own ~** die eigene Haut retten; **I haven't seen ~ nor hair of him for weeks** *(inf)* den habe ich in den letzten Wochen nicht mal von Weitem gesehen

hide: **hide-and-seek**, *(US)* **hide-and-go-seek** N Versteckspiel *nt*; **to play ~** Verstecken spielen; **hideaway** N Versteck *nt*; *(= refuge)* Zufluchtsort *m*; **hidebound** ADJ *person, views* engstirnig; **an officer of the old school, ~ by convention** ein Offizier der alten Schule, der den Konventionen verhaftet ist

hideous ['hɪdɪəs] ADJ **a** *(= very ugly)* grauenhaft, scheußlich; *colour* scheußlich, schrecklich **b** *(= appalling) embarrassment, disappointment, expense, price* fürchterlich

hideously ['hɪdɪəslɪ] ADV **a** *painted, designed, deformed, scream* grauenhaft; **~ ugly** potthässlich *(inf)*; **to grimace ~** scheußliche Grimassen ziehen **b** *(emph) expensive, slow, loud* schrecklich, fürchterlich; **she'd probably be ~ embarrassed** es wäre ihr sicher schrecklich *or* fürchterlich peinlich

hideousness ['hɪdɪəsnɪs] N Grauenhaftigkeit *f*, Scheußlichkeit *f*

hideout ['haɪdaʊt] N Versteck *nt*

hidey-hole ['haɪdɪhəʊl] N *(inf)* Versteck *nt*

hiding¹ ['haɪdɪŋ] N **to be in ~** sich versteckt halten; **to go into ~** untertauchen, sich verstecken; **he came out of ~** er tauchte wieder auf, er kam aus seinem Versteck

hiding² N **a** *(= beating)* Tracht *f* Prügel; **to give sb a good ~** jdm eine Tracht Prügel geben **b** *(inf: = defeat)* Schlappe *f (inf)*; **the team took** *or* **got a real ~** die Mannschaft musste eine schwere Schlappe einstecken *(inf)*; **to be on a ~ to nothing** keine Aussicht auf Erfolg haben

hiding place N Versteck *nt*

hidy-hole ['haɪdɪhəʊl] N *(inf)* Versteck *nt*

hie [haɪ] VR *(old, hum)* eilends laufen; **~ thee hence!** hebe dich hinweg *(old, hum)*

hierarchic(al) [ˌhaɪə'rɑ:kɪk(əl)] ADJ, **hierarchically** [ˌhaɪə'rɑ:kɪkəlɪ] ADV hierarchisch

hierarchy ['haɪərɑ:kɪ] N Hierarchie *f*

hieratic [haɪə'rætɪk] ADJ *(Rel)* hieratisch

hieroglyph ['haɪərəglɪf] N Hieroglyphe *f*

hieroglyphic [ˌhaɪərə'glɪfɪk] ADJ hieroglyphisch N, **hieroglyphics** PL Hieroglyphen *pl*, Hieroglyphenschrift *f*

hi-fi ['haɪˌfaɪ] N **a** Hi-Fi *nt* **b** *(= system)* Hi-Fi-Anlage *f* ADJ Hi-Fi-; **~ equipment** Hi-Fi-Geräte *pl*

higgledy-piggledy ['hɪgldɪ'pɪgldɪ] ADV durcheinander, wie Kraut und Rüben *(inf)* ADJ durcheinander; *(= confused)* wirr

high [haɪ] ADJ *(+er)* **a** *mountain, wall, forehead, building* hoch *pred*, hohe(r, s) *attr*; **a building 80 metres** *(Brit) or* **meters** *(US)* **~, an 80-metre** *(Brit) or* **80-meter** *(US)* **~ building** ein 80 Meter hohes Gebäude; **the building is 80 metres** *(Brit) or* **meters** *(US)* **~** das Gebäude ist 80 Meter hoch; **a ~ dive** ein Kopfsprung *m* aus großer Höhe; **on one of the ~er floors** in einem der oberen Stockwerke; **he lives on a ~er floor** er wohnt weiter oben; **the ~est floor** die oberste Etage; **at ~ tide** *or* **water** bei Flut *or* Hochwasser; **the river is quite ~** der Fluss führt ziemlich viel Wasser; **~ and dry** *(boat)* auf dem Trockenen; **to be left ~ and dry** auf dem Trockenen sitzen *(inf)*; **he left her ~ and dry with four young children** er hat sie mit vier kleinen Kindern sitzen lassen; **I knew him when he was only so ~** ich kannte ihn, als er nur SO groß war *or* noch so klein war → *also* **high ground**

b *(= important, superior)* hoch *pred*, hohe(r, s) *attr*; **~ office** hohes Amt; **on the ~est authority** von höchster Stelle; **to be ~ and mighty** erhaben tun; **to be on one's ~ horse** *(fig)* auf dem hohen Ross sitzen; **O Lord most ~** *(Bibl)* erhabener Gott

c *(= considerable, extreme, great) opinion, speed, temperature, fever, pressure, salary, price, rate, density, sea* hoch *pred*, hohe(r, s) *attr*; *reputation* ausgezeichnet, hervorragend; *altitude* groß; *wind* stark; *complexion, colour* (hoch)rot; **of the ~est calibre** *(Brit) or* **caliber** *(US)***/quality** von bestem Format/bester Qualität; **casualties were ~** es gab viele Opfer; *(Mil)* es gab hohe Verluste; **the temperature was in the ~ twenties** die Temperatur lag bei fast 30 Grad; **to pay a ~ price for sth** *(lit, fig)* etw teuer bezahlen; **to put a ~ value on sth** etw hoch einschätzen; **the ~est common factor** der größte gemeinsame Teiler; **to the ~est degree** im höchsten Grad *or* Maß; **to have ~ expectations of sb/sth** hohe Erwartungen an jdn/etw stellen; **in (very) ~ spirits** in Hochstimmung, in äußerst guter Laune; **~ in fat** fettreich; **to have a ~ old time** *(inf)* sich prächtig amüsieren, mächtig Spaß haben *(inf)*; **it was ~ drama** es war hochdramatisch

d *(= good, admirable) ideals, principles* hoch; **a man of ~ character** ein Mann von Charakter

e *(of time)* **~ noon** zwölf Uhr mittags; **it's ~ time you went home** es ist *or* wird höchste Zeit, dass du nach Hause gehst

f *sound, note* hoch; *(= shrill)* schrill

g *(inf, on drugs)* high *(inf)*; *(on drink)* blau *(inf)*; **to get ~ on alcohol** sich (mit Alkohol) besaufen *(inf)*; **to get ~ on cocaine** sich mit Kokain anturnen *(sl)*

h *meat* angegangen

i *(Cards)* hoch *pred*, hohe(r, s) *attr*; **aces ~** Ass ist die höchste (Stich)karte

ADV *(+er)* **a** hoch; **~ up** *(position)* hoch oben; *(motion)* hoch hinauf; **birds circling very ~ up** Vögel, die ganz weit oben kreisen; **~er up the hill was a small farm** etwas weiter oben am Berg lag ein kleiner Bauernhof; **~ (up) on the agenda** ganz oben auf der Tagesordnung; **~ up in the organization** weit oben in der Organisationsstruktur; **one floor ~er** ein Stockwerk höher; **to throw sth ~ in(to) the air** etw hoch in die Luft werfen

b to go as ~ as £200 bis zu £ 200 (hoch) gehen; **inflation is climbing ~er and ~er** die Inflationsrate steigt immer mehr *or* wird immer höher; **the sea is running ~** das Meer ist sehr stürmisch; **feelings ran ~** die Gemüter erhitzten sich; **to search ~ and low** überall suchen

N **a God on ~** Gott in der Höhe *or* im Himmel; **the orders have come from on ~** *(hum inf)* der Befehl kommt von oben

b unemployment/the pound has reached a new ~ die Arbeitslosenzahlen haben/das Pfund hat einen neuen Höchststand erreicht; **sales have reached an all-time ~** die Verkaufszahlen sind so hoch wie nie zuvor; **the ~s and lows of my career** die Höhen und Tiefen *pl* meiner Laufbahn

c *(Met)* Hoch *nt*

d he's still on a ~ *(inf: = on drugs)* er ist immer noch high *(inf)*; **I was on a ~ after the concert** *(inf: = excited)* nach dem Konzert war ich ganz high *(inf)*

e *(US Aut: = top gear)* **in ~** im höchsten Gang; **he moved into ~** er schaltete hoch *or* in den höchsten Gang

f *(US inf: = high school)* Penne *f (inf)*

high: **high altar** N Hochaltar *m*; **highball** N *(US)* Highball *m*; **high beam** N *(Aut)* Fernlicht *nt*; **highboard** N *(for diving)* Turm *m*; **highborn** ADJ von hoher Geburt, von edler Abkunft *(liter)*; **highboy** N *(US)* hohe Kommode; **highbrow** N Intellektuelle(r) *mf* ADJ *interests* intellektuell, hochgestochen *(pej)*; *tastes, music, author* anspruchsvoll; **high-calorie** ADJ kalorienreich; **highchair** N Hochstuhl *m*; **High Church** N Hochkirche *f* ADJ der Hochkirche; **to be very ~** streng hochkirchlich eingestellt sein; **high-circulation** ADJ *newspaper* auflagenstark; **high-class** ADJ erstklassig; **~ prostitute** Edelnutte *f (inf)*; **high-coloured**, *(US)* **high-colored** ADJ *complexion, skin* rot; **high comedy** N Gesellschaftskomödie *f*; **high commission** N Hochkommissariat *nt*; **high commissioner** N Hochkommissar(in) *m(f)*; **high court** N oberstes *or* höchstes Gericht; *(= institution also)* oberster Gerichtshof; **high court judge** N Richter(in) *m(f)* am obersten Gerichtshof; **high day** N *(Brit)* Festtag *m*; **~s and holidays** Fest- und Feiertage; **high-density** ADJ **a** *housing, population* dicht **b** *(Comput) disk* mit hoher Schreibdichte; **high diving** N Turmspringen *nt*; **high-energy** ADJ *particle, food* energiereich

higher [ˈhaɪəˈ] ADJ **a** *comp of* **high** **b** *mathematics* höher; *animals, life-forms* höher (entwickelt) N **Higher** *(Scot)* ≈ Abiturabschluss *m*; **to take one's Highers** ≈ das Abitur machen; **three Highers** ≈ das Abitur in drei Fächern

higher: **higher education** N Hochschulbildung *f*; **Higher National Certificate** N *(Brit)* ≈ Berufsschulabschluss *m*; **Higher National Diploma** N *(Brit) Qualifikationsnachweis in technischen Fächern*; **higher-up** N *(inf)* höheres Tier *(inf)*

high: **high explosive** N hochexplosiver Sprengstoff; **high-explosive shell** N Sprenggranate *f*, Brisanzgeschoss *nt*; **highfalutin** [ˌhaɪfəˈluːtɪn], **highfaluting** [ˌhaɪfəˈluːtɪŋ] ADJ *(inf) language, behaviour* hochtrabend, geschwollen; *scheme* großkotzig *(inf)*; *idea* hochgestochen; *people* aufgeblasen, hochgestochen; **high farming** N *(Agr)* intensive Bodenbewirtschaftung; **high-fibre**, *(US)* **high-fiber** ADJ *diet* ballaststoffreich; **high fidelity** N High Fidelity *f*, Tontreue *f*; **high-fidelity** ADJ Hi-Fi-; **~ sound** Hi-Fi-Sound *m*; **high-five** N *(inf)* Highfive *nt*; **to give sb a ~** jdn mit Highfive begrüßen; **high-flier** N *(inf: = successful person)* Senkrechtstarter(in) *m(f)*; *(= ambitious person)* Ehrgeizling *m (pej)*; **he's a ~** er ist ein Erfolgstyp *(inf)*; **high-flown** ADJ *style, speech* hochtrabend, geschwollen; *ambitions* hochgesteckt; *ideas, plans* hochfliegend; **high-flyer** N = **high-flier**; **high-flying** ADJ *aircraft* mit großer Flughöhe; *(fig) businessman etc* erfolgreich; *lifestyle* exklusiv; **high frequency** N Hochfrequenz *f* ADJ hochfrequent, Hochfrequenz-; **~ signal** Hochfrequenzsignal *nt*; **High German** N Hochdeutsch *nt*; **high-grade** ADJ hochwertig; *ore* gediegen; **high ground** N **a** hoch liegendes Land; **snow on ~** Schnee in hoch liegenden Gebieten **b** *(fig)* **to regain the ~** seine überlegene Position zurückerobern; **to take the political/intellectual ~** sich politisch/intellektuell aufs hohe Ross setzen; **to lose/claim the moral ~** die moralische Überlegenheit verlieren/für sich beanspruchen; **high-handed** ADJ *character* überheblich; *manner, behaviour, attitude* selbstherrlich; *treatment* arrogant; **high hat** N *(US inf)* hochnäsiger Typ *(inf)*; **high-hat** *(US inf)* ADJ hochnäsig *(inf)* VT herablassend behandeln, von oben herab behandeln; **high-heeled** ADJ mit hohen Absätzen, hochhackig; **high heels** PL hohe Absätze *pl*; **high-income** ADJ einkommensstark; **high-interest** ADJ *(Fin) shares, account* hochverzinslich; *loan* hochverzinst; *purchase* mit hohen Zinsen; **highjack** VT, N = **hijack**; **highjacker** N = **hijacker**; **high jinks** PL *(inf)* ausgelassene Späße *pl*; **the ~ over this bill** das Theater um diesen Gesetzesentwurf *(inf)*; **there wasn't much substance behind the verbal ~** hinter den Worten steckte nicht viel; **high jump** N *(Sport)* Hochsprung *m*; **to be for the ~** *(fig inf)* dran sein *(inf)*; **high jumper** N *(Sport)* Hochspringer(in) *m(f)*; **highland** ADJ hochländisch; *area, town also* im Hochland; **Highlander** N Bewohner(in) *m(f)* des schottischen Hochlands *or* der schottischen Highlands; **Highland fling** N *schottischer Volkstanz*; **Highland Games** PL *schottisches Volksfest mit traditionellen Wettkämpfen*; **Highlands** PL schottisches Hochland, (schottische) Highlands *pl*; *(generally)* Berg- *or* Hochland *nt*; **high-level** ADJ *talks, discussion* auf höchster Ebene; *(Comput) language* höher; **~ official** Spitzenfunktionär(in) *m(f)*; **high life** N Highlife *nt*, Leben *nt* in großem Stil; **highlight** ✪ 26.3 N **a** *(Art, Phot)* Glanzlicht *nt*; *(in hair)* Strähne *f*; **~s** *(in hair)* Strähnchen *pl* **b** *(fig)* Höhepunkt *m*; **I watched the ~s of the match** ich sah mir die Höhepunkte des Spiels an VT **a** *need, issue, problem, dangers* ein Schlaglicht werfen auf *(+acc)*; **this ~s the fact that ...** das verdeutlicht die Tatsache, dass ... **b** *text (with highlighter)* hervorheben, markieren; *(on computer screen)* markieren; *hair* Strähnen machen in *(+acc)*; **highlighter** N **a** *(= pen)* Leuchtstift *m*, Textmarker *m* **b** *(for hair)* Aufheller *m*; *(= cosmetic)* Töner *m*; **high living** N flottes *or (pej)* ausschweifendes Leben

highly [ˈhaɪlɪ] ADV **a** *(emph: = extremely) successful, sensitive, competitive, controversial, critical* äußerst; *inflammable* leicht; *spiced* stark; *individual, unusual, significant, efficient* äußerst, höchst; **~ charged** *(atmosphere)* aufgeladen; *debate* hitzig; **~ coloured** *(Brit) or* **colored** *(US) (lit)* farbenfroh, sehr bunt; *(fig) report, description (= one-sided)* stark gefärbt; *(= detailed)* ausgeschmückt; **to be ~ critical of sb/sth** jdn/etw scharf kritisieren; **~ trained** äußerst gut ausgebildet; *skilled worker* hoch qualifiziert; *sportsperson* durchtrainiert; **~ skilled** äußerst geschickt; *worker, workforce* hoch qualifiziert; **~ placed** *(in organization, society)* hochgestellt; *(Sport, in league)* führend; **~ respected/gifted/educated/paid/developed** hoch geachtet/bezahlt/entwickelt, hochbegabt, hochgebildet; **~ intelligent/topical** hochintelligent/-aktuell; **~ polished** *(= shiny)* auf Hochglanz poliert; *shoes, brass* blank geputzt; *(= accomplished) performance, style, manners, language* perfekt ausgefeilt; **~ sophisticated** *(person, audience)* höchst anspruchsvoll; *technology, equipment* hoch entwickelt; **~ toxic** hochgiftig; **~ unlikely** *or* **improbable** äußerst *or* höchst unwahrscheinlich
b *regard, rate, prize* hoch; **he is a ~ regarded writer** er ist ein hoch angesehener Autor; **they were ~ praised** sie wurden hoch gelobt; **I don't rate him very ~ at all** ich halte überhaupt nicht viel von ihm; **she rates ~ among world class athletes** sie zählt zu den Weltklassesportlern; **to be ~ prized for its flavour** wegen seines Geschmacks hoch geschätzt werden; **to speak ~ of sb/sth** sich sehr positiv über jdn/etw äußern; **to think ~ of sb/sth** eine hohe Meinung von jdm/etw haben; **~ recommended** sehr empfehlenswert; **I can ~ recommend it** ich kann es sehr empfehlen; **she came ~ recommended** sie kam mit einer sehr guten Empfehlung

highly strung ADJ *(Brit)* nervös

high: **high-maintenance** ADJ **a** *patient, baby* pflegebedürftig **b** *machine* wartungsintensiv **c** *(inf) girlfriend etc* anspruchsvoll; *relationship* zeitintensiv; **a ~ author** ein nicht gerade pflegeleichter Autor *(inf)*; **High Mass** N Hochamt *nt*; **high-minded** ADJ *ideals* hoch; *intentions* hochgesinnt; *critics* anspruchsvoll; **high muck-a-muck** [ˌhaɪˈmʌkəmʌk] N *(sl)* arrogantes, hohes Tier *(pej)*; **high-necked** ADJ hochgeschlossen

highness [ˈhaɪnɪs] N **a** Höhe *f*; **~ of ideals** hohe Ideale *pl* **b** **Her/Your Highness** Ihre/Eure Hoheit; **yes, Your Highness** ja, Hoheit

high: **high-octane** ADJ mit einer hohen Oktanzahl; **high-performance** ADJ Hochleistungs-; **~ computer** Hochleistungscomputer *m*; **high-pitched** ADJ **a** *sound, voice* hoch; *scream, squeak* schrill **b** *(Archit) roof* steil; **high point** N Höhepunkt *m*; **high-powered** ADJ **a** *(= powerful) machine, engine, computer* leistungsfähig; *rifle, gun* leistungsstark; *car* stark (-motorig); *laser* stark **b** *person* hochgestellt, hochkarätig *(inf)*; *(= dynamic)* dynamisch; *academic etc* äußerst fähig; *job, career, course* anspruchsvoll; *conversation* hochintellektuell; *delegation* hochkarätig *(inf)*; **high-pressure** ADJ **a** *(using air or liquid)* Hochdruck-; **~ pump** Hochdruckpumpe *f*; **~ cylinder** Hochdruckzylinder *m*; **~ air** Druckluft *f*; **~ hose** Druckleitung *f* **b** *(Met)* **~ area** Hochdruckgebiet *nt*; **a ~ area over the Atlantic** ein Hoch(druckgebiet) *nt* über dem Atlantik, ein atlantisches Hoch **c** *(fig) sales technique* aggressiv; *salesman also* aufdringlich **d** *(= stressful) job* sehr stressig; *atmosphere* sehr (an)gespannt VT *(US)* **to ~ sb into doing sth** jdn so unter Druck setzen, dass er etw tut; **high-priced** ADJ teuer; **high priest** N *(lit, fig)* Hohepriester *m*; **a ~** ein Hoher Priester *m*; **of the ~** des Hohen Priesters; **high priestess** N *(lit, fig)* Hohepriesterin *f*; **of the ~** der Hohen Priesterin; **high-principled** ADJ mit strengen Grundsätzen; **high-profile** ADJ profiliert; **high-protein** ADJ eiweißreich; **high-ranking** ADJ hoch(rangig), von hohem Rang; **high relief** N Hochrelief *nt*; **high-resolution** ADJ *screen, graphics* hochauflösend; **high-rise** ADJ **~ building** Hochhaus *nt*; **~ office (block)** Bürohochhaus *nt*; **~ flats** *(Brit)* (Wohn)hochhaus *nt*; **high-risk** ADJ risikoreich; **~ group** Risikogruppe *f*; **~ victim** einer Risikogruppe angehörendes Opfer; **highroad** N *(old)* Landstraße *f*; **the ~ to success** der sichere Weg zum Erfolg; **high school** N *(Brit)* ≈ Oberschule *f (für 11 bis 18-Jährige)*; *(US)* ≈ Oberschule *f (für 15 bis 18-Jährige)*

> **HIGH SCHOOLS**
>
> In den USA sind **high schools** weiterführende Bildungseinrichtungen für alle Jugendlichen im Alter von 15 bis 18 Jahren (neunte bis zwölfte Klasse), **Junior high schools** beginnen bereits mit der siebten Klasse. Wenn die Schüler die zwölfte Klasse mindestens mit dem Prädikat „zufriedenstellend" abschließen, erhalten sie auf einer feierlichen Zeremonie ihr Highschool-Diplom. Zu diesem Anlass kaufen sie sich auch häufig einen besonderen Jahrgangsring. Viele amerikanische Teenieserien und -filme beschäftigen sich mit der **high school** und mit allem, was dazugehört. Besonderes Augenmerk gilt dabei dem Sport, vor allem Football und Basketball, und dem **senior prom**, dem Abschlussball. Über jedes Schuljahr wird ein Jahrbuch angelegt, das die Schüler erwerben können → PROM

high: **high-scoring** ADJ *game (Ftbl, Hockey, Handball)* torreich; *(Basketball)* punktreich; **high seas** PL **the ~** die Meere *pl*; **on the ~** auf hoher See, auf offenem Meer; **high season** N Hochsaison *f*; **during (the) ~** während der Hochsaison; **high seat** N *(Hunt)* Hochsitz *m*; **high-security** ADJ **~ prison** Hochsicherheitsgefängnis *nt*; **~ wing** Hochsicherheitstrakt *m*; **high-sided** ADJ **~ vehicle** hohes Fahrzeug; **high sign** N *(US inf)* vereinbartes Signal; **to give sb a ~** jdm ein vereinbartes Signal geben; **high society** N High Society *f*; **high-sounding** ADJ klangvoll; **high-speed** ADJ schnell; *drill* mit hoher Umdrehungszahl; **~ car chase** wilde Verfolgungsjagd im Auto; **~ crash** Zusammenstoß *m* bei hoher Geschwindigkeit; **~ train** Hochgeschwindigkeitszug *m*; **~ rail link** Hochgeschwindigkeitszugverbindung *f*; **~ printer** Schnelldrucker *m*; **~ lens** hoch lichtstarkes Objektiv, lichtstarke Linse; **~ film** hoch lichtempfindlicher Film, hochempfindlicher Film; **high-spirited** ADJ temperamentvoll, lebhaft; **high spirits** PL Hochstimmung *f*; **youthful ~** jugendlicher Übermut; **high spot** N Höhepunkt *m*; **to hit the ~s** *(inf)* auf den Putz hauen *(inf)*; **high street** N *(Brit)* Hauptstraße *f*; **~ banks** Geschäftsbanken *pl*; **~ shops** Geschäfte *pl* in der Innenstadt; **high-strung**

ADJ *(US)* nervös; **high summer** N Hochsommer *m*; **high table** N *(Sch)* Lehrertisch *m*; *(Univ)* Tisch *m* für Professoren und Dozenten

hightail [ˈhaɪteɪl] VI *(US inf)* **to ~ (it) out of a place** (aus einem Ort) abhauen *(inf)*, (von *or* aus einem Ort) verduften *(inf)*

high: **high tea** N (frühes) Abendessen; **high-tech** N, ADJ = **hi-tech**; **high technology** N Hochtechnologie *f*, Spitzentechnologie *f*; **high-tension** ADJ *(Elec)* Hochspannungs-; **~ cable** Hochspannungskabel *nt*; **high treason** N Hochverrat *m*; **high-up** ADJ *person* hochgestellt N *(inf)* hohes Tier *(inf)*; **high-velocity** ADJ Hochgeschwindigkeits-; **~ rifle** Hochgeschwindigkeitsgewehr *nt*; **high-water mark** N *(lit)* Hochwasserstandsmarke *f*; *(fig)* höchster Stand; **highway** N **a** *(US)* Highway *m*, ≈ Autobahn *f* **b** *(Brit)* Landstraße *f*; **public ~** öffentliche Straße; **the ~s and byways** die Straßen und Wege *pl*; *(fig, of life, music)* alle Aspekte; **he knows all the ~s and byways of Dorset** er kennt Weg und Steg in Dorset; **Highway Code** N *(Brit)* Straßenverkehrsordnung *f*; **highwayman** N Räuber *m*, Wegelagerer *m*, Strauchdieb *m*; **highway robbery** N Straßenraub *m*; *(fig inf)* Nepp *m (inf)*; **Highways Department** N Tiefbauamt *nt*; **high wire** N Drahtseil *nt*; **high-yield** ADJ *(Agr)* ertragsreich; *(Fin) investment, bond* ertragsstark

hijack [ˈhaɪdʒæk] VT *aircraft etc* entführen; *(fig)* für sich beanspruchen N *(of aircraft etc)* Entführung *f*

hijacker [ˈhaɪdʒækəʳ] N Entführer(in) *m(f)*, Hijacker(in) *m(f)*

hike [haɪk] VI wandern VT *prices, rates* erhöhen N **a** *(lit)* Wanderung *f* **b** *(fig: in interest rates)* Erhöhung *f*

▶ **hike up** VT *sep* **a** *trousers, skirt* hochziehen **b** *prices, rates* erhöhen

hiker [ˈhaɪkəʳ] N Wanderer *m*, Wanderin *f*

hiking [ˈhaɪkɪŋ] N Wandern *nt*

hiking boots PL Wanderstiefel *pl*

hilarious [hɪˈlɛərɪəs] ADJ irrsinnig komisch *(inf)*, urkomisch *(inf)*; *(= loud and happy) mood* ausgelassen, übermütig

hilariously [hɪˈlɛərɪəslɪ] ADV *talk* sehr amüsant; *juxtaposed, mixed up* auf komische Weise; *disguised, dressed up* urkomisch *(inf)*; **~ funny** zum Schreien *(inf)*, irrsinnig komisch *(inf)*; **~ old-fashioned** so altmodisch, dass es zum Schreien ist

hilarity [hɪˈlærɪtɪ] N Heiterkeit *f*; *(= gaiety)* Fröhlichkeit *f*; *(= laughter)* Gelächter *nt*; **his statement caused some ~** seine Behauptung löste einige Heiterkeit aus

Hilary [ˈhɪlərɪ] N *(Oxford Univ)* Frühjahrstrimester *nt*; *(Jur)* Frühjahrssitzungsperiode *f*

hill [hɪl] N **a** Hügel *m*; *(higher)* Berg *m*; *(= incline)* Hang *m*; **the castle stands on a ~** das Schloss steht auf einem Berg; **the houses on the ~ beneath the castle** die Häuser am Schlossberg; **these flats are built on a ~** diese Wohnungen sind am Hang *or* Berg gebaut; **to park on a ~** am Berg parken; **you hardly feel the ~s in this car** in diesem Auto spürt man die Steigungen kaum; **up ~ and down dale** bergauf und bergab; **as old as the ~s** steinalt, uralt; **that joke's as old as the ~s** der Witz hat ja so einen langen Bart; **to take to the ~s** sich in die Berge flüchten; **to be over the ~** *(fig inf)* seine beste Zeit *or* die besten Jahre hinter sich *(dat)* haben **b** → **ant hill, molehill** *etc*

hillbilly [ˈhɪlbɪlɪ] *(US inf)* N Hinterwäldler(in) *m(f) (pej)*; *(female also)* Landpomeranze *f (inf)* ADJ hinterwäldlerisch *(pej)*; **~ music** Hillbilly *no art*, Hillbillymusik *f*

hill farmer N Bergbauer *m*, Bergbäuerin *f*

hilliness [ˈhɪlɪnɪs] N Hügeligkeit *f*; *(higher)* Bergigkeit *f*; **the ~ of the terrain** das hügelige *or (higher)* bergige Gelände

hillock [ˈhɪlək] N Hügel *m*, Anhöhe *f*

hill: **hillside** N Hang *m*; **hilltop** N Gipfel *m*; **hill-walker** N Bergwanderer *m*, Bergwanderin *f*; **hill-walking** N Bergwandern *nt*

hilly [ˈhɪlɪ] ADJ *(+er)* hüg(e)lig; *(higher)* bergig

hilt [hɪlt] N Heft *nt*; *(of dagger)* Griff *m*; **(up) to the ~** *(fig)* voll und ganz; *(involved, in debt also)* bis über beide Ohren *(inf)*; **I'll back you (up) to the ~** ich stehe voll und ganz hinter Ihnen

him [hɪm] PERS PRON **a** *(dir obj, with prep +acc)* ihn; *(indir obj, with prep +dat)* ihm; *(when he is previously mentioned in clause)* sich; **with his things around ~** mit seinen Sachen um sich **b** *(emph)* er; **it's ~** er ists; **who, ~?** wer, er?

Himalayan [ˌhɪməˈleɪən] ADJ Himalaya-, des Himalaya; **~ state** Himalayastaat *m*

Himalayas [ˌhɪməˈleɪəz] PL Himalaya *m*

himbo [ˈhɪmbəʊ] N *(inf pej) gut aussehender aber wenig intelligenter Mann*

himself [hɪmˈself] PERS PRON **a** *(dir and indir obj, with prep)* sich → *also* **myself** **b** *(emph)* (er) selbst N *(Ir inf)* **it was ~ who told me** er selbst hat es mir gesagt

hind[1] [haɪnd] N *(Zool)* Hirschkuh *f*, Hindin *f (poet)*

hind[2] ADJ Hinter-; **~ legs** Hinterbeine *pl*; **~ feet** Hinterfüße *pl*; **~ paws** Hinterpfoten *pl*; **the horse reared up on its ~ legs** das Pferd bäumte sich auf; **he can** *or* **could talk the ~ leg(s) off a donkey** *(inf)* er kann einem ein Ohr *or* die Ohren abreden *(inf)*

hinder [ˈhɪndəʳ] VT **a** *(= obstruct, impede)* behindern; *(= delay) person* aufhalten; *arrival* verzögern **b** *(= stop, prevent from happening)* verhindern; **to ~ sb from doing sth** jdn daran hindern *or* davon abhalten, etw zu tun; **he doesn't let his disability ~ him** er lässt sich nicht durch seine Behinderung abhalten

Hindi [ˈhɪndiː] N Hindi *nt*

hind: **hindmost** ADJ *superl of* **hind**[2] hinterste(r, s); **hindquarters** PL Hinterteil *nt*; *(of carcass)* Hinterviertel *nt*; *(of horse)* Hinterhand *f*

hindrance [ˈhɪndrəns] N Behinderung *f*; *(= obstacle)* Hindernis *nt* (*to* für); **the rules/children are a ~** die Regeln/Kinder sind hinderlich; **it was a serious ~ to progress** es behinderte den Fortschritt sehr; **he/it is more of a ~ than a help** er/es hindert mehr, als dass er/es hilft; **without ~** unbehindert

hindsight [ˈhaɪndsaɪt] N **now with the benefit** *or* **wisdom of ~** hinterher *or* im Nachhinein ist man ja immer schlauer; **with ~ it's easy to criticize** hinterher *or* im Nachhinein ist es leicht zu kritisieren; **it was, in ~, a mistaken judgement** es war, rückblickend betrachtet, ein Fehlurteil

Hindu [ˈhɪnduː] ADJ hinduistisch; **~ people** Hindu(s) *pl* N Hindu *m*

Hinduism [ˈhɪnduːɪzəm] N Hinduismus *m*

Hindustan [ˌhɪndʊˈstɑːn] N Hindustan *nt*, Hindostan *nt*

Hindustani [ˌhɪndʊˈstɑːnɪ] ADJ hindustanisch N **a** Bewohner(in) *m(f)* Hindustans **b** *(Ling)* Hindustani *nt*

hinge [hɪndʒ] N **a** *(of door)* Angel *f*; *(of box etc)* Scharnier *nt*; *(of limb, shell)* Gelenk *nt*; *(fig)* Angelpunkt *m*; **the door is off its ~s** die Tür ist aus den Angeln; **the lid is off its ~s** das Scharnier des Deckels ist ab; **take the door off its ~s** häng die Tür aus! **b** (*also* **stamp hinge**) (Klebe)falz *m* VT **to ~ sth (to sth)** etw mit einem Scharnier/mit Scharnieren (an etw *dat*) befestigen VI *(fig)* abhängen (*on* von), ankommen (*on* auf *+acc*)

hinged [hɪndʒd] ADJ mit Scharnier/mit Scharnieren (versehen); *door* eingehängt; **~ lid** Klappdeckel *m*

hint [hɪnt] N **a** *(= intimation, suggestion)* Andeutung *f*, Hinweis *m*; **a strong ~** ein deutlicher Hinweis; **a subtle ~** ein zarter Wink; **to give a/no ~ of sth** etw ahnen lassen *or* andeuten/nicht ahnen lassen *or* andeuten; **to give** *or* **drop sb a ~** jdm einen Wink geben, jdm gegenüber eine Andeutung machen; **he was given a gentle ~ about attention to detail** man hat ihm leise angedeutet *or* den leisen Wink gegeben, auf Details zu achten; **to throw out** *or* **drop a ~** eine Andeutung machen, eine Bemerkung fallen lassen; **to know how to take a ~** einen Wink verstehen; **OK, I can take a ~** schon recht, ich verstehe *or* ich habe den Wink mit dem Zaunpfahl verstanden *(inf)*; **I've almost run out of this perfume, ~, ~** ich habe fast nichts mehr von dem Parfüm, hörst du? **b** *(= trace)* Spur *f*; **a ~ of garlic** eine Spur Knoblauch; **a ~ of irony** ein Hauch *m* von Spott; **with just a ~ of sadness in his smile** mit einem leichten Anflug von Traurigkeit in seinem Lächeln; **with the ~ of a smile** mit dem Anflug eines Lächelns; **not a ~ of emotion** keinerlei Gefühl; **a ~ of desperation** ein Anflug *m* von Verzweiflung; **at the first ~ of trouble** beim ersten Zeichen von Ärger; **there was no ~ of apology in his voice** seine Stimme klang überhaupt nicht entschuldigend **c** *(= tip, piece of advice)* Tipp *m*; **~s for travellers** *(Brit) or* **travelers** *(US)* Reisetipps *pl*; **I'll give you a ~, the answer has two words** ich gebe dir einen Tipp *or* Hinweis, die Antwort besteht aus zwei Wörtern VT andeuten (*to* gegenüber); **what are you ~ing?** was wollen Sie damit sagen *or* andeuten?; **he ~ed strongly that …** er gab deutlich zu verstehen, dass …

▶ **hint at** VI *+prep obj* **he hinted at changes in the cabinet** er deutete an, dass es Umbesetzungen im Kabinett geben würde; **he hinted at my involvement in the affair** er spielte auf meine Rolle in der Affäre an

hinterland [ˈhɪntəlænd] N Hinterland *nt*

hip[1] [hɪp] N Hüfte *f*; **with one's hands on one's ~s** die Arme in die Hüften gestemmt → **shoot**

hip[2] N *(Bot)* Hagebutte *f*

hip[3] INTERJ **~! ~!, hurrah!** hipp hipp, hurra!

hip[4] ADJ *(inf)* hip *(inf)*; **to be ~ to sth** in etw *(dat)* voll drin sein *(inf)*; **to get ~ to sth** sich in etw *(acc)* voll reinhängen *(sl)*

hip *in cpds* Hüft-; **hip bath** N Sitzbad *nt*; **hipbone** N *(Anat)* Hüftbein *nt*, Hüftknochen *m*; **hip flask** N Taschenflasche *f*, Flachmann *m (inf)*; **hip-hop** [ˈhɪphɒp] N *(Mus)* Hip-Hop *n*; **hip-huggers** [ˈhɪphʌgəz] PL *(US)* Hüfthose(n) *f(pl)*; **hip joint** N *(Anat)* Hüftgelenk *nt*; **hip measurement** N Hüftweite *f*, Hüftumfang *m*

hi-pot [ˈhaɪpɒt] N *abbr of* **high potential** Führungsnachwuchskraft *f*

-hipped [-hɪpt] ADJ *suf* mit … Hüften; **a big-hipped woman** eine Frau mit breiten Hüften, eine breithüftige Frau

hippie N = **hippy**

hippo [ˈhɪpəʊ] N *(inf)* Nilpferd *nt*

hip pocket N Gesäßtasche *f*

Hippocratic oath [ˌhɪpəʊˌkrætɪkˈəʊθ] N hippokratischer Eid, Eid *m* des Hippokrates

hippodrome [ˈhɪpədrəʊm] N Hippodrom *m or nt*; *(dated: = music hall)* Varieté- *or* Varietee(-theater) *nt*

hippopotamus [ˌhɪpəˈpɒtəməs] N *pl* **-es** *or* **hippopotami** [ˌhɪpəˈpɒtəmaɪ] Nilpferd *nt*, Flusspferd *nt*

hippy, hippie [ˈhɪpɪ] N Hippie *m*

hip replacement N Hüftoperation *f*; *(= device)* Hüftprothese *f*

hip roof N *(Archit)* Walmdach *nt*

hipster [ˈhɪpstəʳ] N **a** *(dated inf: = one who is hip)* hipper Typ *(sl)* **b** **hipsters** PL *(= trousers)* Hüfthose(n) *f(pl)* ADJ Hüft-; **~ pants** Hüfthose(n) *f(pl)*

hire [haɪəʳ] *(esp Brit)* N **a** *(= rental)* Mieten *nt*; *(of car also, of suit)* Leihen *nt*; *(= employment: of servant)* Einstellen *nt*; **to have sth for ~** etw vermieten/verleihen; **the hall is available for ~** man kann den Saal mieten; **for ~** *(taxi)* frei; **it's on ~** *(= is a hired item)* es ist gemietet/geliehen; **to be (out) on ~** vermietet sein **b** *(= wages)* Lohn *m*; *(of sailor)* Heuer *f* VT **a** *(= rent)* mieten; *car* mieten, leihen; *suit* leihen; **~d car** Mietwagen *m*, Leihwagen *m* **b** *(= employ) staff,* *person* einstellen; **~d assassin** gedungener Mörder **c** = **hire out VT**

▶**hire out** VT *sep (esp Brit)* vermieten, verleihen VI *(US)* sich verdingen

hired gun [ˌhaɪəd'gʌn] N gedungener Mörder, bezahlter Killer *(inf)*

hired hand [ˌhaɪəd'hænd] N Lohnarbeiter(in) *m(f)*

hireling ['haɪəlɪŋ] N *(pej)* Mietling *m (old pej)*

hire-purchase [ˌhaɪə'pɜːtʃəs] N *(Brit)* Ratenkauf *m*, Teilzahlungskauf *m*; **on ~** auf Raten *or* Teilzahlung; **~ agreement** Teilzahlungs(kauf)vertrag *m*

hirsute ['hɜːsjuːt] ADJ stark behaart

his [hɪz] POSS ADJ sein → *also* **my** POSS PRON seine(r, s); **~** *(on towels etc)* er → *also* **mine**[1]

Hispanic [hɪs'pænɪk] ADJ hispanisch; *community* spanisch N Hispanoamerikaner(in) *m(f)*

hiss [hɪs] VI zischen; *(cat)* fauchen VT **a** zischen; **come here, he ~ed** komm her, zischte er **b** *actor, speaker* auszischen N Zischen *nt*; *(of cat)* Fauchen *nt*

histamine ['hɪstəmiːn] N *(Med)* Histamin *nt*

histology [hɪs'tɒlədʒɪ] N Histologie *f*

historian [hɪs'tɔːrɪən] N Historiker(in) *m(f)*; *(in ancient times)* Geschichtsschreiber(in) *m(f)*

historic [hɪs'tɒrɪk] ADJ *(also Gram)* historisch

historical [hɪs'tɒrɪkəl] ADJ historisch; *studies, background, investigation, method also* geschichtlich; **~ research** Geschichtsforschung *f*; **places of ~ interest** historisch *or* geschichtlich interessante Stätten *pl*

historically [hɪs'tɒrɪkəlɪ] ADV **a** *(= traditionally)* traditionellerweise; **the country has ~ been very dependent on agriculture** das Land war immer schon stark von der Landwirtschaft abhängig **b** *(= relating to history) important, accurate, consider* historisch; **~ unique** einmalig in der Geschichte; **as ~ significant as ...** von gleicher historischer Bedeutung wie ...; **~ (speaking)** historisch gesehen, aus historischer Sicht **c** *(= uniquely) important, high etc* einmalig, beispiellos

historicism [hɪs'tɒrɪsɪzəm] N Historizismus *m*

historicity [hɪstə'rɪsɪtɪ] N Geschichtlichkeit *f*, Historizität *f*

historiography [ˌhɪstɒrɪ'ɒgrəfɪ] N Geschichtsschreibung *f*, Historiografie *f*

history ['hɪstərɪ] N **a** Geschichte *f*; *(= study of history)* Geschichte *f*, Geschichtswissenschaft *f*; **~ will judge** die Geschichte wird ihr Urteil fällen; **~ has taught us that ...** die Geschichte lehrt uns, dass ...; **the highest salary in television ~** das höchste Gehalt in der Geschichte des Fernsehens; **to make ~** Geschichte machen; **... and the rest is ~** ... und der Rest ist Geschichte; **that's all ~ now** *(fig)* das gehört jetzt alles der Vergangenheit an; **he's ~** er ist schon lange vergessen *or* passé *(inf)*
b *(= personal record)* Geschichte *f*; **he has a ~ of violence** er hat eine Vorgeschichte als Gewalttäter; **the family has a ~ of heart disease** Herzleiden liegen in der Familie; **he has a ~ of heart disease** er hat schon lange ein Herzleiden
c *(= background)* Vorgeschichte *f*; **to know the ~ of an affair** den Hintergrund einer Affäre kennen
d *(Comput)* Verlauf *m*, Protokoll *nt*

histrionic [ˌhɪstrɪ'ɒnɪk] ADJ **a** *(= overdone, affected)* theatralisch **b** *(= relating to acting)* schauspielerisch

histrionically [ˌhɪstrɪ'ɒnɪkəlɪ] ADV theatralisch

histrionics [ˌhɪstrɪ'ɒnɪks] PL **a** theatralisches Getue; **to put on a display of ~** sich theatralisch aufführen **b** *(Theat)* Schauspielkunst *f*

hit [hɪt] *vb: pret, ptp* **hit** N **a** *(= blow)* Schlag *m*; *(on target, Fencing)* Treffer *m*; *(Baseball)* Schlag *m* → **score**
b *(= success, also Theat)* Erfolg *m*, Knüller *m (inf)*; *(= song)* Hit *m*; **to be** *or* **make a (big) ~ with sb** bei jdm (ausgesprochen) gut ankommen
c *(of sarcasm etc)* Spitze *f*; **that's a ~ at me** das ist eine Spitze gegen mich; *(indirect also)* das ist auf mich gemünzt
d *(Internet)* Hit *m*; *(on home page etc)* Abrufzahlen *pl*; **~s counter** Zugriffs- *or* Besucherzähler *m*, Counter *m*
e *(Drugs inf) (= injection)* Schuss *m*; *(= drag)* Zug *m*
f *(inf, = murder)* Mord *m*
VT **a** *(= strike)* schlagen; *(Comput) key* drücken; **to ~ sb a blow** jdm einen Schlag versetzen; **he ~ him a blow over the head** er gab ihm einen Schlag auf den Kopf; **to ~ one's head against sth** sich *(dat)* den Kopf an etw *(dat)* stoßen; **he ~ his head on the table** er schlug mit dem Kopf auf den Tisch auf; **the car ~ a tree** das Auto fuhr gegen einen Baum; **he was ~ by a stone** er wurde von einem Stein getroffen, ihn traf ein Stein; **the house was ~ by a shell** das Haus wurde von einer Granate getroffen; **the tree was ~ by lightning** der Baum wurde vom Blitz getroffen; **to ~ one's way out of trouble** sich freischlagen; *(Tennis)* sich freispielen; *(Boxing)* sich freiboxen; **we're going to ~ the enemy as hard as we can** wir werden so hart wie möglich gegen den Feind vorgehen; **the commandos ~ the town at dawn** die Kommandos griffen die Stadt im Morgengrauen an; **the hurricane ~ Miami last night** der Hurrikan erreichte gestern Abend Miami; **the courts will ~ drug pushers hard** die Gerichte werden hart gegen Dealer vorgehen; **the smell ~ me as I entered the room** der Geruch schlug mir entgegen, als ich ins Zimmer kam; **he didn't know what had ~ him** *(inf)* er wusste nicht, wie ihm geschah; **you won't know what has ~ you** *(inf)* du wirst dein blaues Wunder erleben *(inf)*
b *(= wound)* treffen; **he's been ~ in the leg** es hat ihn am Bein getroffen, er ist am Bein getroffen worden; **I've been ~!** ich bin getroffen worden, mich hats erwischt *(inf)*
c *mark, target* treffen; **that ~ home** *(fig)* das hat getroffen, das saß *(inf)*; **you've ~ it (on the head)** *(fig)* du hast es (genau) getroffen
d *(= affect adversely)* betreffen; **the crops were ~ by the rain** der Regen hat der Ernte geschadet; **to be hard ~ by sth** von etw schwer getroffen werden; **how will this tax ~ you?** wie wird sich diese Steuer auf Sie auswirken?
e *(= achieve, reach) likeness, top C* treffen; *speed, level, top form etc* erreichen
f *(news, story)* **to ~ the papers** in die Zeitungen kommen; **the news ~ us/Wall Street like a bombshell** die Nachricht schlug bei uns/in Wall Street wie eine Bombe ein
g *(= occur to)* **to ~ sb** jdm aufgehen; **has it ever ~ you how alike they are?** ist dir schon mal aufgefallen, wie ähnlich sie sich sind?
h *(= come to, arrive at) beaches etc* erreichen; **to ~ town** *(inf)* die Stadt erreichen; **we eventually ~ the right road** schließlich haben wir den richtigen Weg gefunden *or* erwischt *(inf)*; **we're going to ~ the rush hour** wir geraten *or* kommen direkt in den Stoßverkehr; **the driver ~ a patch of ice** der Fahrer geriet auf eine vereiste Stelle; **to ~ trouble/a problem** auf Schwierigkeiten/ein Problem stoßen
i *(= score)* schlagen; **to ~ a century** hundert Läufe machen
j *(inf, = murder)* killen *(inf)*, umlegen *(inf)*
k *(US inf)* **to ~ sb for 50 dollars** jdn um 50 Dollar anhauen *(inf)*
l *(fig inf phrases)* **to ~ the bottle** zur Flasche greifen; **to ~ the roof** an die Decke *or* in die Luft gehen *(inf)*; **to ~ the deck** sich zu Boden werfen, sich hinwerfen; **the vase ~ the deck and shattered** die Vase schlug *or* knallte *(inf)* auf den Boden und zerschellte; **to ~ the dance floor** tanzen; **let's ~ the floor** lass uns tanzen; **to ~ the road** sich auf den Weg *or* die Socken *(inf)* machen; **in April the candidates will ~ the campaign trail** im April werden sich die Kandidaten in den Wahlkampf stürzen; **to ~ the ground running** *(person)* sofort alles im Griff haben
VI **a** *(= strike)* schlagen; **he ~s hard** er schlägt hart zu
b *(= collide)* zusammenstoßen
c *(= attack, go in)* losschlagen

▶**hit back** VI *(lit, fig)* zurückschlagen; **to hit back at the enemy** zurückschlagen; **he hit back at his critics** er gab seinen Kritikern Kontra; **he hit back at the accusations** er wehrte sich gegen die Anschuldigungen VT *sep* zurückschlagen

▶**hit off** VT *sep* **a he hit him off beautifully** er hat ihn ausgezeichnet getroffen **b to hit it off with sb** *(inf)* sich gut mit jdm verstehen, prima mit jdm auskommen *(inf)*; **they hit it off straight away** sie haben sich von Anfang an gut verstanden

▶**hit on** VI *+prep obj* **a** stoßen auf *(+acc)*, finden **b** *(esp US inf: = chat up)* anmachen *(inf)*

▶**hit out** VI **a** *(lit)* einschlagen, losschlagen *(at sb* auf jdn) **b** *(fig)* **to hit out at** *or* **against sb/sth** jdn/etw attackieren *or* scharf angreifen; **he hit out angrily when I suggested it was his fault** er griff mich scharf an, als ich ihm die Schuld geben wollte

▶**hit up** VT *sep (US inf)* **to hit sb up for 50 dollars** jdn um 50 Dollar anhauen *(inf)*

▶**hit upon** VI *+prep obj* = **hit on a**

hit-and-run ['hɪtən'rʌn] N **there was a ~ here last night** hier hat heute Nacht jemand einen Unfall gebaut und Fahrerflucht begangen ADJ **~ raid** *(Mil)* Blitzüberfall *m*; **~ accident/incident** Unfall *m* mit Fahrerflucht; **~ cases** Fälle *pl* von Fahrerflucht; **~ driver** unfallflüchtiger Fahrer, unfallflüchtige Fahrerin, Unfallflüchtige(r) *mf*

hitch [hɪtʃ] N **a** *(= snag)* Haken *m*; *(in plan, proceedings, programme)* Schwierigkeit *f*, Problem *nt*; **a technical ~** eine technische Panne; **without a ~** reibungslos, ohne Schwierigkeiten; **but there is a ~** aber die Sache hat einen Haken; **there's been a ~** es haben sich Schwierigkeiten ergeben, da ist ein Problem aufgetaucht
b *(= quick pull)* Ruck *m*; **she gave her skirt a quick ~** sie zog schnell ihren Rock am Bund zurecht
c *(= knot)* Knoten *m*; *(Naut)* Stek *m*
d *(inf, = lift)* **I got a ~ all the way to London** ich bin in einem Rutsch bis London (durch)getrampt *(inf)*
VT **a** *(= fasten)* festmachen, anbinden *(sth to sth* etw an etw *dat)*; **to ~ one's wagon to a star** *(dated US)* sich *(dat)* ein hohes Ziel setzen, nach den Sternen greifen *(geh)*; **to ~ one's wagon to sb** *(dated US)* sich mit jdm zusammentun
b *(inf)* **to get ~ed** heiraten, vor Anker gehen *(hum)*; **why don't we get ~ed?** warum heiraten wir (eigentlich) nicht?
c to ~ a lift *or* **ride** trampen, per Anhalter fahren; **she ~ed a lift** *or* **ride with a truck driver** ein Lastwagenfahrer nahm sie mit
VI *(esp Brit)* trampen, per Anhalter fahren → *also* **hitchhike**

▶**hitch up** VT *sep* **a** *horses, oxen* anschirren, anspannen; *trailer etc* anhängen; **we hitched up the horses to the wagon** wir spannten die Pferde vor den Wagen **b** *trousers, skirt* hochziehen

hitcher ['hɪtʃə'] N *(esp Brit inf)* Anhalter(in) *m(f)*, Tramper(in) *m(f)*

hitch: **hitchhike** VI per Anhalter fahren, trampen; **he's been away hitchhiking around Europe** er ist durch Europa getrampt; **hitchhiker** N Anhalter(in) *m(f)*, Tramper(in) *m(f)*; **hitchhiking** N Trampen *nt*

hitching post ['hɪtʃɪŋpəʊst] N Pfosten *m (zum Anbinden von Pferden)*

hi tech ['haɪˌtek] N Spitzentechnologie *f*, Hitech *nt*, Computertechnik *f*

hi-tech ['haɪˌtek] ADJ Hitech-; **~ equipment** Hitechgeräte *pl*

hither ['hɪðə'] ADV **a** *(old, = to this place)* hierher → *also* **come-hither b ~ and thither** *(liter. = to and fro)* hierhin und dorthin

hitherto [ˌhɪðə'tuː] ADV bisher, bis jetzt

hit: **hit list** N *(lit, fig)* Abschussliste *f*; **hitman** N *(inf)* Killer *m (inf)*; **hit-or-miss** ADJ auf gut Glück *pred*, aufs Geratewohl *pred*; *methods, planning* schlampig, schludrig *(inf)*; **it was a rather ~ affair** das ging alles aufs Geratewohl; **hit parade** N Hitparade *f*; **hit record** N Hit *m*; **hit show** N erfolgreiche Show, Publikumserfolg *m*; **hit single** N Hitsingle *f*; **hit song** N Hit *m*; **hit squad**, **hit team** N Killerkommando *nt*

hitter ['hɪtəʳ] N *(Boxing, inf)* Schlager *m*, Puncher *m*

hit: **hit tune** N Schlagermelodie *f*; **hitwoman** N *(inf)* Killerin *f (inf)*

HIV *abbr of* **human immunodeficiency virus** HIV *nt*; **~ positive/negative** HIV-positiv/-negativ

hive [haɪv] N **a** *(= beehive)* Bienenkorb *m*, Bienenstock *m*; *(= bees in a hive)* (Bienen)schwarm *m*, (Bienen)volk *nt* **b** *(fig)* **to be a ~ of industry** das reinste Bienenhaus sein; **the office was a ~ of activity** das Büro glich einem Bienenhaus VT *bees, swarm* einfangen, in den Stock bringen VI *(= swarm)* in den (Bienen)stock (ein)fliegen, einen Stock beziehen

▶ **hive off** VT *sep department, company* ausgliedern; *staff* abbauen; *work* vergeben *(to* an *+acc)*; **the branch could be hived off into a separate company** die Filiale könnte als eigene Firma verselbstständigt werden VI **a** *(= branch out)* sich absetzen **b** *(inf, = slip away)* abschwirren *(inf)*

hives [haɪvz] PL *(Med)* Nesselausschlag *m*, Nesselsucht *f*; **oranges give me ~** von Orangen krieg ich Auschlag *(inf)*

hiya ['haɪjə] INTERJ hallo

Hizbollah ['hɪzbə'lɑː] N Hisb Allah *f*, Hisbollah *f*

HM *abbr of* **His/Her Majesty** S. M./I. M.

HMG *abbr of* **His/Her Majesty's Government**

HMI *(Brit) abbr of* **His/Her Majesty's Inspector** ≈ Schulrat *m*, Schulrätin *f*

HMS *(Brit) abbr of* **His/Her Majesty's Ship** HMS *f*

HMSO *(Brit) abbr of* **His/Her Majesty's Stationery Office** *Druckerei für staatliche Drucksachen*

HNC *(Brit) abbr of* **Higher National Certificate**

HND *(Brit) abbr of* **Higher National Diploma**

ho [həʊ] N *(sl)* Schlampe *f (inf)*

hoagie, **hoagy** ['həʊgɪ] N *(US) großes, reichlich belegtes Sandwich*, Jumbo-Sandwich *nt (inf)*

hoar [hɔːʳ] N Reif *m*

hoard [hɔːd] N Vorrat *m*; *(= treasure)* Schatz *m*; **a ~ of weapons** ein Waffenlager *nt*; **~ of money** Schatz *m*, gehortetes Geld VT *(also* **hoard up***) food etc* hamstern; *money, supplies, weapons* horten; *information* zusammentragen; **a squirrel ~s nuts for the winter** ein Eichhörnchen hortet Nüsse für den Winter

hoarder ['hɔːdəʳ] N *(= animal) Tier, das Vorräte anlegt (= person)* Hamsterer *m*, Hamsterin *f*

hoarding¹ ['hɔːdɪŋ] N *(of food etc)* Hamstern *nt*; *(of capital)* Anhäufen *nt*, Anhäufung *f*

hoarding² N *(Brit: = fence, board)* Bretterzaun *m*; *(at building sites also)* Bauzaun *m*; **(advertising) ~** Plakatwand *f*

hoarfrost ['hɔː'frɒst] N (Rau)reif *m*

hoarse [hɔːs] ADJ *(+er)* heiser; **he shouted himself ~** er schrie sich heiser; **you sound rather ~** deine Stimme klingt heiser

hoarsely ['hɔːslɪ] ADV heiser, mit heiserer Stimme

hoarseness ['hɔːsnɪs] N *(of person)* Heiserkeit *f*; **the ~ of his voice** seine heisere Stimme

hoary ['hɔːrɪ] ADJ *(+er)* **a** *hair, old man etc* ergraut **b** *(fig: = old)* uralt, altehrwürdig; **a ~ old joke** ein alter Hut, ein Witz mit (einem langen) Bart

hoax [həʊks] N *(= practical joke)* Streich *m*; *(= trick etc)* Trick *m*; *(= false alarm)* blinder Alarm; **to play a ~ on sb** jdm einen Streich spielen VT anführen, hereinlegen *(inf)*; **to ~ sb into believing sth** jdm etw weismachen; **we were completely ~ed** wir ließen uns anführen, wir fielen darauf herein ADJ *(Internet)* **~ e-mail** Hoax *m*; **~ virus warning** Hoax *m*

hoax: **hoax call** N **a ~** ein blinder Alarm; **hoax caller**, **hoaxer** ['həʊksəʳ] N *(in bomb scares etc) jd, der einen blinden Alarm auslöst*; **hoax story** N Zeitungsente *f*

hob [hɒb] N Kamineinsatz *m* (zum Warmhalten); *(on modern cooker)* Kochfeld *nt*

hobble ['hɒbl] VI humpeln, hinken; **to ~ in/out** herein-/hinaushumpeln VT **a** *horse* Fußfesseln anlegen *(+dat)*, die Vorderbeine fesseln *(+dat)* **b** *(fig) person, company* einschränken, behindern; *economy* lahmlegen N *(for horses)* Fußfessel *f*

hobbledehoy ['hɒbldɪ'hɔɪ] N *(old)* Tollpatsch *m*

hobby ['hɒbɪ] N Hobby *nt*, Steckenpferd *nt (dated)*

hobbyhorse ['hɒbɪhɔːs] N *(lit, fig)* Steckenpferd *nt*; *(lit: = rocking horse)* Schaukelpferd *nt*; **this is my personal ~** *(fig)* das ist mein Lieblingsthema

hobgoblin ['hɒb,gɒblɪn] N Kobold *m*, Butzemann *m*; *(= bogey)* schwarzer Mann, Butzemann *m*

hobnail ['hɒbneɪl] N Schuhnagel *m*, Schuhzwecke *f*

hobnailed ['hɒbneɪld] ADJ genagelt; **~ boots** genagelte Schuhe *pl*, Nagelschuhe *pl*; **~ liver** Säuferleber *f (inf)*, Alkoholleber *f*

hobnob ['hɒbnɒb] VI **of course I'm not used to ~bing with the aristocracy** ich stehe *or* bin natürlich nicht mit dem Adel auf Du und Du; **she's been seen ~bing with the chairman and his wife** sie ist viel mit dem Vorsitzenden und seiner Frau zusammen gesehen worden; **who was that you were ~bing with last night?** mit wem hast du da gestern zusammengesessen?

hobo ['həʊbəʊ] N *(US)* **a** *(= tramp)* Penner *m (inf)* **b** *(= worker)* Wanderarbeiter *m*

Hobson's choice ['hɒbsəns'tʃɔɪs] N **it's ~** da habe ich (wohl) keine andere Wahl

hock¹ [hɒk] N *(Anat, of animal)* Sprunggelenk *nt*

hock² N *(= wine)* weißer Rheinwein

hock³ *(inf)* VT *(= pawn)* versetzen, verpfänden N **in ~** verpfändet, versetzt, im Leihhaus; **to be in ~ to sb** in jds Schuld stehen

hockey ['hɒkɪ] N Hockey *nt*; *(US)* Eishockey *nt*

hockey: **hockey pitch** N Hockeyfeld *nt*; **hockey player** N Hockeyspieler(in) *m(f)*; *(US)* Eishockeyspieler(in) *m(f)*; **hockey stick** N Hockeyschläger *m*

hocus-pocus ['həʊkəs'pəʊkəs] N **a** *(inf: = trickery)* faule Tricks *pl (inf)*, Hokuspokus *m* **b** *(= formula)* Hokuspokus *m*

hod [hɒd] N **a** *(for bricks, mortar etc)* Tragmulde *f* **b** *(= also coal hod)* Kohlenschütte(r *m*) *f*

hodgepodge ['hɒdʒpɒdʒ] N *(US)* = **hotchpotch**

hoe [həʊ] N Hacke *f* VTI hacken

hoebag ['həʊbæg] N *(sl)* Schlampe *f*

hoedown ['həʊdaʊn] N *(US)* Schwof *m (inf)*

hog [hɒg] N **a** (Mast)schwein *nt*; *(US: = pig)* Schwein *nt* **b** *(pej inf: = person)* Schwein *nt (inf)*; *(greedy)* Vielfraß *m (inf)*; *(selfish)* Sau *f (inf)*; *(dirty)* Sau *f (inf)*, Ferkel *nt (inf)* → **road hog, whole hog** VT *(inf)* sich *(dat)* aneignen, in Beschlag nehmen; **he always ~s the bathroom** er nimmt immer das Badezimmer in Beschlag; **she ~ged his attention all evening** sie belegte ihn den ganzen Abend lang mit Beschlag; **a lot of drivers ~ the middle of the road** viele Fahrer meinen, sie hätten die Straßenmitte gepachtet *(inf)*; **stop ~ging the ball!** *(Ftbl etc)* gib endlich (den Ball) ab!; **to ~ the limelight** alle Aufmerksamkeit für sich beanspruchen

Hogmanay [,hɒgmə'neɪ] N *(Scot)* Silvester *nt*

> **HOGMANAY**
>
> **Hogmanay** ist der schottische Name für den Silvesterabend, der dort ein wichtiger Feiertag ist. Der Silvesterabend wird mit Partys gefeiert. Um Mitternacht stoßen die Menschen dann auf das neue Jahr an und singen das traditionsreiche Lied „Auld Lang Syne", was so viel wie „Längst vergangene Zeiten" heißt und auf sentimentale Weise an die Vergangenheit erinnern soll. Dann wird zum **first footing** aufgebrochen: man besucht Freunde, um zusammen mit ihnen das neue Jahr mit einem Drink willkommen zu heißen. Nach alter Tradition bringt es besonders viel Glück, wenn der Erste, der nach Mitternacht die Schwelle überschreitet, ein dunkelhaariger Mann ist, der etwas zu essen, zu trinken oder zum Verbrennen (normalerweise einen Brocken Kohle) mitbringt, was als Zeichen für Wohlstand im neuen Jahr gilt.

hogshead ['hɒgzhed] N großes Fass; *(= measure)* Oxhoft *nt (obs)*, *Flüssigkeitsmaß zwischen 200-250 l*

hog: **hogtie** VT *(US)* an allen vieren fesseln; *(fig inf)* handlungsunfähig machen; **we're ~d** uns *(dat)* sind Hände und Füße gebunden; **hogwash** N **a** *(= swill)* Schweinefutter *nt* **b** *(inf: = nonsense)* Quatsch *m*, Quark *m (inf)*, blödes Zeug *(inf)*; **hog wild** ADJ *(US inf)* **to go ~** total ausflippen *(inf)*

ho hum ['həʊ'hʌm] INTERJ *(hum)* na und?

hoick [hɔɪk] VT *(Brit, inf)* **a** *(= lift)* **to ~ one's trousers up** sich *(dat)* schnell die Hose hochziehen; **to ~ sb out of bed** jdn aus dem Bett reißen **b** *(Sport, = hit) shot, ball* schießen

hoi polloi [,hɔɪpə'lɔɪ] N *(pej)* Volk *nt*, Pöbel *m*, Plebs *m*

hoist [hɔɪst] VT hochheben, hieven *(inf)*; *(= pull up)* hochziehen, hieven *(inf)*; *flag* hissen; *sails* aufziehen, hissen; **to be ~ with** *or* **by** *or* **on** *(US)* **one's own petard** *(prov)* in die eigene Falle gehen N Hebezeug *nt*, Hebevorrichtung *f*; *(in ships)* Hebewerk *nt*; *(= lift)* (Lasten)aufzug *m*; *(= block and tackle)* Flaschenzug *m*; *(= winch)* Winde *f*; *(= crane)* Kran *m*

hoity-toity ['hɔɪtɪ'tɔɪtɪ] *(inf)* ADJ hochnäsig, eingebildet; **she's gone all ~** sie markiert die feine Dame *(inf)*; **oh ~, are we?** wohl zu fein für unsereins? INTERJ sieh mal einer an *(inf)*

hokey ['həʊkɪ] ADJ *(US inf)* **a** *(= phoney)* künstlich; *excuse* faul *(inf)*; **it's ~** das ist Quatsch **b** *(= corny) excuse* abgedroschen; *story, song* kitschig

hokum ['həʊkəm] N *(US inf)* **a** *(= nonsense)* Quatsch *m (inf)*, Mumpitz *m* **b** *(= cheap sentiment)* Gefühlsduselei *f (inf)*

hold [həʊld]
vb: pret, ptp **held**
✪ 5.3, 27.3

1 NOUN	3 INTRANSITIVE VERB
2 TRANSITIVE VERB	4 PHRASAL VERBS

1 – NOUN

a [= grip, clutch] Griff *m*; *(Mountaineering)* Halt *m no pl*; *(Wrestling)* Griff *m*; **I tried to break free from his hold** ich versuchte, mich aus seinem Griff zu befreien; **the rock face offers few holds to climbers** die Felswand bietet dem Bergsteiger wenig Halt; **to release/loosen one's hold on sb/sth** jdn/etw loslassen; **to have a firm hold on sb** *(lit)* jdn festhalten

♦ **to have/get/keep etc (a) hold of to have/catch hold of sth** *(lit)* etw festhalten/fassen *or* packen; **to keep hold of sth** etw nicht loslassen; *(= keep)* etw behalten; **to seize** *or* **grab hold of sb/sth** jdn/etw fassen *or* packen; **grab hold of my hand** fass mich bei der Hand; **to get** *or* **take (a) hold of sth** sich an etw *(dat)* festhalten; **to get** *or* **lay hold of sth** *(fig: = obtain)* etw finden *or* auftreiben *(inf)*; *guns, drugs* etw in die Finger bekommen; *information, story,* *facts* etw in Erfahrung bringen; **where did you get hold of that idea?** wie kommst du denn auf die Idee?; **to get hold of sb** *(fig)* jdn finden *or* auftreiben *(inf)*; *(on phone etc)* jdn erreichen; **to get (a) hold of oneself** *(fig)* sich in den Griff bekommen; **get (a) hold of yourself!** reiß dich zusammen!

♦ **to lose one's hold** den Halt verlieren; **he lost his hold and fell** er verlor den Halt und stürzte ab; **to lose one's hold on life** mit dem Leben nicht mehr fertig werden; **he's lost his hold on reality** er hat den Sinn für die Realität verloren

♦ **to take hold** *(person: of rope, support)* sich festhalten; *(fig, custom, practice, fashion, idea)* sich durchsetzen; *(fire, epidemic)* sich ausbreiten; *(disease)* sich verschlimmern; *(recession)* sich breitmachen; *(truce, ceasefire)* andauern

♦ **on hold** **to be on hold** warten; *(fig)* auf Eis liegen; **to put sb on hold** *(Telec)* jdn auf Wartestellung schalten; *(in larger organizations)* jdn auf die Warteschlange legen; **to put sth on hold** *(fig, decision, plan, career)* etw auf Eis legen; **can we put this discussion on hold?** können wir diese Diskussion unterbrechen?

♦ **no holds barred** **when those two have a row, there are no holds barred** *(fig)* wenn die beiden sich streiten, dann kennen sie nichts mehr *(inf) or* kein Pardon *(inf)*

b = influence Einfluss *m* *(over* auf *+acc)*

♦ **hold on** *or* **over sb/sth** **to have a hold over** *or* **on sb** (großen) Einfluss auf jdn ausüben; *audience, followers* jdn in seiner Gewalt haben; **to have a firm hold on sb** *(fig)* jdn fest im Griff haben; **he hasn't got any hold on** *or* **over me** er kann mir nichts anhaben; **she still has a hold on him** sie hat ihn immer noch in der Hand; **the president has consolidated his hold on power** der Präsident hat seine Macht gefestigt

c of hairspray, mousse Halt *m*; **firm/extra hold** fester/zusätzlicher Halt

d Naut, Aviat Laderaum *m*, Frachtraum *m*

2 – TRANSITIVE VERB

a = grasp, grip halten; **to hold one's sides with laughter** sich *(dat)* den Bauch vor Lachen halten; **to hold sb/sth tight** jdn/etw (ganz) festhalten; **the frightened children held each other tight** die verängstigten Kinder klammerten sich aneinander; **this car holds the road well** dieses Auto hat eine gute Straßenlage; **to hold sth in place** etw (fest)halten

♦ **to hold hands** sich an der Hand halten, sich anfassen; *(lovers, children etc)* Händchen halten; **to walk along holding hands** angefasst gehen

b = carry, maintain halten; **to hold oneself upright** sich gerade *or* aufrecht halten; **to hold oneself/sth ready** *or* **in readiness** sich/etw bereithalten

c = contain enthalten; *(= have capacity etc of: bottle, tank etc)* fassen; *(= have room for: bus, plane, hall etc)* Platz haben für; **this room holds twenty people** in diesem Raum haben zwanzig Personen Platz; **this CD rack holds 20 CDs** in diesem CD-Ständer haben 20 CDs Platz; **this holds the radar equipment** dies enthält die Radarausrüstung; **my brain can't hold so much information at one time** so viel kann ich nicht auf einmal behalten; **what does the future hold (for us)?** was bringt *or* birgt *(geh)* (uns) die Zukunft?; **death holds no fears for them** der Tod hat *or* birgt *(geh)* nichts Beängstigendes für sie

d = believe meinen; *(= maintain)* behaupten; **it was universally held that Andy was an excellent teacher** alle meinten, dass Andy ein hervorragender Lehrer sei; **I have always held that ...** ich habe schon immer behauptet, dass ...; **to hold sth to be true/false/immoral** *etc* etw für wahr/falsch/unmoralisch *etc* halten; **to hold the belief that ...** glauben, dass ...; **to hold the view** *or* **opinion that ...** die Meinung vertreten, dass ...; **the court held that ...** das Gericht entschied, dass...

e = consider **to hold sb responsible (for sth)** jdn (für etw) verantwortlich machen; **she held the memory of her late husband dear** sie hielt das Andenken an ihren verstorbenen Mann hoch; **she held her youngest grandchild dear** ihr jüngstes Enkelkind bedeutete ihr sehr viel *or* war ihr teuer *(liter)*

f = restrain, retain, keep back *train* aufhalten; *one's breath* anhalten; *suspect, hostages etc* festhalten; *parcel, confiscated goods etc* zurückhalten; **to hold sb (prisoner)** jdn gefangen halten; **to hold sb hostage** jdn als Geisel festhalten; **there's no holding him** er ist nicht zu bremsen *(inf)*; **hold everything!** *(inf)* stop!; **hold the line!** bleiben Sie am Apparat!; **hold hard, hold your horses** *(inf)* immer mit der Ruhe, immer sachte mit den jungen Pferden! *(inf)*

♦ **to hold one's fire** *(= not shoot)* nicht schießen; *(fig: = delay action)* sich zurückhalten

♦ **to hold one's breath** *(lit)* den Atem anhalten; **don't hold your breath!** *(iro)* erwarte nicht zu viel!

♦ **hold it!** *(inf)* Momentchen *(inf)*, Moment mal *(inf)*; **hold it there!** *(when taking photograph)* so ist gut; **hold it right there, buster** *(inf)* keine Bewegung, Freundchen *(inf)*

g = possess, occupy *post, position* innehaben, bekleiden *(form)*; *passport, permit, degree* haben; *power* haben, besitzen; *(Fin) shares* besitzen; *(= have) records* führen; *file* haben; *(= store: on computer, disk)* speichern; *(Sport) record* halten; *(Mil) position* halten; *(against attack)* behaupten, halten; **the family holds most of the shares** die meisten Aktien sind *or* befinden sich in den Händen *or* im Besitz der Familie; **when Spain held vast territories in South America** als Spanien riesige Besitzungen in Südamerika hatte; **she holds the key to the mystery** sie hat den Schlüssel zu dem Geheimnis; **to hold office** im Amt sein

h = keep, not let go **to hold its value** seinen Wert behalten; **to hold one's own** sich behaupten (können); **to hold course for** *(Naut)* Kurs halten auf *(+acc)*; **to hold one's course** die Richtung beibehalten; **to hold one's serve** *(Tennis)* den Aufschlag behalten; **to hold sb's attention** jds Aufmerksamkeit fesseln; **to hold sb's interest** jds Interesse wachhalten; **to hold a note** *(Mus)* einen Ton halten

♦ **to hold sb to sth** **I'll hold you to your promise** *or* **to that!** ich werde Sie beim Wort nehmen

i = organize, have *meeting, session, debate, election* abhalten; *talks* führen; *party* geben; *(Eccl) service* (ab)halten; **services are held every Sunday at 11 am** Gottesdienst findet jeden Sonntag um 11 Uhr statt; **to hold a check on sb/sth** jdn/etw kontrollieren; **to hold a conversation** eine Unterhaltung führen *or* haben, sich unterhalten

j = cope with **he can't hold his liquor** er verträgt nichts; **she can hold her drink** *(esp Brit)* sie verträgt was

3 – INTRANSITIVE VERB

a rope, nail, roof etc halten; **to hold firm** *or* **fast** halten

b person **to hold still** still halten; **to hold tight** festhalten; **he held tight to his assertion** er hielt an seiner Behauptung fest

c Telec **please hold!** bitte bleiben Sie am Apparat!; **I've been holding for five minutes** ich warte schon fünf Minuten

d = continue **will the weather hold?** wird sich das Wetter wohl halten?; **if his luck holds** wenn ihm das Glück treu bleibt

e = be valid, apply to gelten; *theory* stimmen; **to hold good** *(rule, promise etc)* gelten; **it holds for all these cases** es gilt in allen diesen Fällen *or* für alle diese Fälle

4 – PHRASAL VERBS

▶ **hold against** VT *always separate* **to hold sth against sb** jdm etw übel nehmen *or* verübeln; *criminal record, past failings* jdm etw anlasten *or* zur Last legen

▶ **hold back** VI *(= stay back, hesitate, not perform fully)* sich zurückhalten; *(= fail to act)* zögern; **I think he's holding back, he knows more** ich glaube, er weiß mehr und rückt nur nicht mit der Sprache heraus; **I held back from telling him just what I thought of him** ich unterließ es, ihm meine Meinung zu sagen

VT *sep* **a** *crowd* zurückhalten; *river, floods* (auf)stauen; *tears* zurückhalten, unterdrücken; *emotions* verbergen, unterdrücken; **to hold sb back from doing sth** jdn daran hindern, etw zu tun

b *(= prevent from making progress)* daran hindern, voranzukommen; **he would let nothing hold him back from getting his way** nichts kann ihn daran hindern, seinen Willen durchzusetzen; **nothing can hold him back now** jetzt ist er nicht mehr aufzuhalten

c *(= withhold)* verheimlichen, verbergen; *information, report* geheim halten; *pay increase* verzögern; **he was holding something back from me** er verheimlichte *or* verbarg mir etwas

▶ **hold down** VT *sep* **a** *(= keep on the ground)* niederhalten, unten halten; *(= keep in its place)* (fest)halten; *(= oppress) country, people* unterdrücken; *(= keep in check)* unter Kontrolle haben; *(= keep low) prices, costs, numbers, pressure* niedrig halten; **to hold one's head down** den Kopf senken **b** *job* haben; **he can't hold any job down for long** er kann sich in keiner Stellung lange halten

▶ **hold forth** VI sich ergehen *(geh)*, sich auslassen *(on* über *+acc)* VT *sep (form, = offer)* bieten

▶ **hold in** VT *sep stomach* einziehen; *emotions* zurückhalten; *horse* zurückhalten, zügeln; **to hold in one's anger** seinen Ärger unterdrücken; **to hold oneself in** *(emotionally)* sich beherrschen, an sich halten

▶ **hold off** VI **a** *(= keep away)* sich fernhalten *(from* von*)*; *(= not act)* warten; *(enemy)* nicht angreifen; **they held off where they should have intervened** sie hätten eingreifen sollen, haben sich aber zurückgehalten; **they held off eating until she arrived** sie warteten mit dem Essen, bis sie kam **b** *(rain, storm)* ausbleiben; **I hope the rain holds off** ich hoffe, dass es nicht regnet VT *sep (= keep back, resist) enemy, attack, challenge* abwehren; *inflation* eindämmen; **how much longer can she go on holding him off?** wie lange kann sie ihn wohl noch hinhalten?

▶ **hold on** VI *(lit: = maintain grip)* sich festhalten; *(= endure, resist)* durchhalten, aushalten; *(= wait)* warten; **hold on (a minute)!** Moment!; *(Telec)* einen Moment bitte!; **now hold on a minute!** Moment mal! VT *sep* (fest)halten; **to be held on by sth** mit etw befestigt sein; **this Sellotape won't hold it on** mit dem Tesafilm hält das nicht

▶ **hold on to** VI *+prep obj* **a** *(lit)* festhalten; **here, hold on to this!** halt das mal (fest)!; **he was holding on to the ledge** er hielt *or* klammerte sich am Felsvorsprung fest; **they held on to each other** sie hielten sich aneinander fest, sie klammerten sich aneinander **b** *(fig) hope* nicht aufgeben; *idea, belief* festhalten an *(+dat)* **c** *(= keep)* behalten; *position* beibehalten; *staff* halten; **to hold on to the lead** in Führung bleiben; **to hold on to power** sich an der Macht halten

▶ **hold out** VI **a** *(supplies etc)* reichen **b** *(= endure, resist)* aushalten, durchhalten; *(= refuse to yield)* nicht nachgeben; **to hold out against sb/sth** sich gegen jdn/etw behaupten; **to hold out for sth** auf etw *(dat)* bestehen VT *sep* **a** *(lit)* vorstrecken, ausstrecken; **to hold out sth to sb** jdm etw hinhalten; **to hold out one's hand** die Hand ausstrecken; **hold your hand out** halt die Hand auf; **she held out her arms** sie breitete die Arme aus **b** *(fig) prospects* bieten; *offer* machen; **I held out little hope of seeing him again** ich machte mir nur wenig Hoffnung, ihn wiederzusehen

▶ **hold out on** VI *+prep obj (inf)* **you've been holding out on me** du verheimlichst mir doch was *(inf)*

▶ **hold over** VT *sep* **a** *question, matter* vertagen; *meeting also, decision* verschieben *(until* auf *+acc)* **b** **to hold sth over sb** *(= threaten)* jdn etw nicht vergessen lassen; **he held it over me as a threat** er bedrohte mich damit

▶ **hold to** VI *+prep obj* festhalten an *(+dat)*, bleiben bei; **I hold to my belief that …** ich bleibe dabei, dass …; **you should hold to the assurance you gave them** Sie sollten Ihr Wort ihnen gegenüber einhalten

▶ **hold together** VT *sep* zusammenhalten VI zusammenhalten

▶ **hold under** VT *sep country, race* unterdrücken, knechten

▶ **hold up** VI **a** *(tent, wall etc)* stehen bleiben; *(light fitting, tile etc)* halten
b *(belief)* standhalten; *(theory)* sich halten lassen; **their support held up well in the election** ihre Anhänger blieben ihnen bei der Wahl treu
VT *sep* **a** *(= raise)* hochheben, hochhalten; *face* nach oben wenden; **hold up your hand** heb die Hand; **to hold sth up to the light** etw gegen das Licht halten
b *(= support, from above)* halten; *(from the side)* stützen; *(from beneath)* tragen
c to hold sb/sth up to ridicule/scorn jdn/etw lächerlich/verächtlich machen; **to hold sb up as an example** jdn als Beispiel hinstellen; **I don't want to hold him up as the perfect statesman/goalkeeper** *etc* **but …** ich möchte ihn nicht als den perfekten Politiker/Torwart *etc* hinstellen, aber …
d *(= stop)* anhalten; *(= delay) people* aufhalten; *traffic, production* ins Stocken bringen; *talks, delivery* verzögern; **my application was held up by the postal strike** durch den Poststreik hat sich meine Bewerbung verspätet
e *(robbers) bank, person, vehicle* überfallen

▶ **hold with** VI *+prep obj (inf)* **I don't hold with that** ich bin gegen so was *(inf)*

holdall [ˈhəʊldɔːl] N Reisetasche *f*

holdback [ˈhəʊldbæk] N **a** *(= obstacle)* Hindernis *nt* **b** *(= thing held back)* Einbehaltung *f (form)*; **~ pay** einbehaltener Lohn

holder [ˈhəʊldəˈ] N **a** *(= person)* Besitzer(in) *m(f)*, Inhaber(in) *m(f)*; *(of title, office, record, passport)* Inhaber(in) *m(f)*; *(of farm)* Pächter(in) *m(f)* **b** *(= object)* Halter *m*; *(= cigarette-holder)* Spitze *f*; *(= flowerpot-holder)* Übertopf *m*

holding [ˈhəʊldɪŋ] N **a** *(Fin, of shares)* Anteil *m* (in an *+dat*); **the maximum ~** der maximal zulässige Anteil **b** *(of books, paintings)* Sammlung *f* (of von) **c** *(of land)* Landgut *nt*; **a ~ of 10 hectares** ein Landgut von 10 Hektar

holding: **holding company** N Holding(gesellschaft) *f*; **holding operation** N provisorische Maßnahme; *(= damage limitation)* Schadensbegrenzungsaktion *f*; **holding pattern** N *(Aviat)* Warteschleife *f*; *(fig)* Warteposition *f*

hold: **holdout** N *(US)* Verweigerer *m*; **Britain was the only ~ on this agreement** Großbritannien war das einzige Land, das sich dieser Vereinbarung widersetzte; **hold-up** N **a** *(= delay)* Verzögerung *f*; *(of traffic)* Stockung *f*; **what's the ~?** warum dauert das so lange?; **the strike caused a two-week ~ in production** der Streik brachte die Produktion zwei Wochen lang ins Stocken **b** *(= armed robbery)* bewaffneter Raubüberfall; **(hands up,) this is a ~!** Hände hoch, das ist ein Überfall!

hole [həʊl] N **a** *(in clothes, bucket, ground etc)* Loch *nt*; **to make** *or* **blow a ~ in sb's savings** ein Loch in jds Ersparnisse reißen; **to blow a ~ in sb's plans** jds Pläne über den Haufen werfen *(inf)*; **to be full of ~s** *(fig, plot, story)* viele Schwächen aufweisen; *(argument, theory)* unhaltbar sein; **I need that like I need a ~ in the head** *(inf)* das ist das Letzte, was ich gebrauchen kann
b *(inf: = awkward situation)* Klemme *f (inf)*, Patsche *f (inf)*; **to be in a ~** in der Patsche *or* Klemme sitzen *(inf)*; **to get sb out of a ~** jdm aus der Patsche *or* Klemme helfen *(inf)*
c *(rabbit's, fox's)* Bau *m*, Höhle *f*; *(mouse's)* Loch *nt*
d *(pej inf)* Loch *nt (inf)*; *(= town)* Kaff *nt (inf)*, Nest *nt (inf)*
e *(Golf)* Loch *nt*; **an 18-~ course** ein 18-Loch-Platz *m*
f *(vulg: = vagina)* Loch *nt (vulg)*
VT **a** *(= make a hole in)* ein Loch machen in *(+acc)*; **to be ~d** ein Loch bekommen; **the ship was ~d by an iceberg** der Eisberg schlug das Schiff leck
b *ball (Golf)* einlochen, versenken; *(Billiards)* versenken; **to ~ a putt** einen Putt einlochen
VI **a** *(socks etc)* Löcher bekommen
b *(Golf)* einlochen

▶ **hole out** VI *(Golf)* ein Loch spielen; **to hole out in one** ein Hole-in-One spielen

▶ **hole up** VI *(animal)* sich verkriechen; *(inf: gang etc, = hide)* sich verkriechen *(inf) or* verstecken; *(= barricade themselves in)* sich verschanzen

hole: **hole-and-corner** ADJ obskur, zwielichtig; **hole in one** N *(Golf)* Hole-in-One *nt*; **hole in the heart** N Loch *nt* in der Herzscheidewand; **hole-in-the-heart** ADJ *attr* **~ baby** Baby *nt* mit (angeborenem) Herzfehler; **hole-in-the-wall** N (in die Wand eingebauter) Geldautomat *m* ATTR *machine* in die Wand eingebaut

holey [ˈhəʊlɪ] ADJ *(inf)* löchrig

holiday [ˈhɒlədɪ] N **a** *(= day off)* freier Tag; *(= public holiday)* Feiertag *m*; **to take a ~** einen Tag freinehmen
b *(esp Brit: = period) often pl* Ferien *pl*, Urlaub *m*; *(Sch)* Ferien *pl*; **the school/Christmas ~s** die Schul-/Weihnachtsferien *pl*; **on ~** in den Ferien, auf *or* im Urlaub; **to go on ~** Ferien/Urlaub machen; **where are you going for your ~(s)?** wo fahren Sie in den Ferien/im Urlaub hin?, wo machen Sie Ferien/Urlaub?; **to take a ~** Urlaub nehmen *or* machen; **to take one's ~s** seinen Urlaub nehmen; **I need a ~** ich bin ferienreif; **to take a month's ~** einen Monat Urlaub nehmen; **~ with pay, paid ~s** bezahlter Urlaub; **it was no ~, I can tell you** ich kann dir sagen, das war alles andere als eine Erholung
VI *(esp Brit)* Ferien *or* Urlaub machen

holiday *in cpds (esp Brit)* Ferien-, Urlaubs-; **holiday apartment** N Ferienwohnung *f*; **holiday camp** N Feriendorf *nt*; **holiday clothes** PL Urlaubskleidung *f*; **holiday destination** N Urlaubs- or Ferienziel *nt*; **holiday entitlement** N Urlaubsanspruch *m*; **holiday feeling** N Urlaubsstimmung *f*; **holiday guest** N *(esp Brit)* Feriengast *m*; **holiday home** N Ferienhaus *nt*/-wohnung *f*; **holiday job** N Ferienjob *m*; **holiday-maker** N Urlauber(in) *m(f)*; **holiday mood** N Urlaubsstimmung *f*; **holiday resort** N Ferienort *m*; **holiday season** N Urlaubszeit *f*; **holiday traffic** N Reiseverkehr *m*; **holiday trip** N Urlaubsreise *f*

holier-than-thou [ˈhəʊlɪəðənˈðaʊ] ADJ *attitude, person* selbstgerecht, selbstgefällig

holiness [ˈhəʊlɪnɪs] N Heiligkeit *f*; **His/Your Holiness** *(Eccl)* Seine/Eure Heiligkeit

holism [ˈhəʊlɪzəm] N Holismus *m*

holistic [həʊˈlɪstɪk] ADJ holistisch

Holland [ˈhɒlənd] N Holland *nt*

Hollander [ˈhɒləndəˈ] N *(Typ)* Holländer *m*

holler [ˈhɒləˈ] *(inf)* N Schrei *m* VTI *(also* **holler out**) brüllen

hollow [ˈhɒləʊ] ADJ **a** hohl; *(= concave) surface, cheeks* hohl, eingefallen; *eyes* tief liegend; *(= empty) feeling* hohl, leer; **I feel ~ (inside)** *(= hungry)* ich habe ein Loch im Bauch *(inf)*; *(after a bad shock)* ich fühle mich innerlich leer
b *(= meaningless) gesture, threat, sham, words, promise* leer; *victory* geschenkt; *(= insincere) person* unaufrichtig; *laugh* hohl; *(= forced)* gequält; **to sound ~, to have a ~ ring (to it)** *(fig)* hohl klingen; **this claim rings ~** diese Behauptung klingt hohl *or* falsch
c *sound* hohl, dumpf; *voice* hohl; **with a (deep,) ~ voice** mit Grabesstimme
N **a** *(= cavity)* Höhlung *f*; *(in larger structure)* Hohlraum *m*; **the ~ in the tree's trunk** die Höhlung im Baum
b *(= depression)* Vertiefung *f*; *(= small valley)* (Boden)senke *f*; **a wooded ~** eine bewaldete Niederung; **in the ~ between two waves** im Wellental; **to hold sth in the ~ of one's hand** etw in der hohlen Hand halten; **the ~ of the back** das Kreuz
ADV *(Brit)* **to beat sb ~** *(inf)* jdn haushoch schlagen, jdn fertigmachen *(inf)*

▶ **hollow out** VT *sep* aushöhlen

hollow-eyed [ˈhɒləʊaɪd] ADJ hohläugig

hollowly [ˈhɒləʊlɪ] ADV hohl; *laugh also* gequält; *say also* mit hohler Stimme; *sound, echo* hohl, dumpf

hollowness [ˈhɒləʊnɪs] N *(fig: of promise)* Leere *f*; *(of guarantee)* Wertlosigkeit *f*

holly [ˈhɒlɪ] N **a** *(= tree)* Stechpalme *f*, Ilex *m*; **~ berry** Stechpalmenfrucht *f* **b** *(= foliage)* Stechpalme(nzweige *pl*) *f*

hollyhock [ˈhɒlɪhɒk] N Malve *f*

Hollywood [ˈhɒlɪwʊd] N Hollywood *nt*

holmium [ˈhɒlmɪəm] N *(Chem)* Holmium *nt*

holm oak [ˈhəʊmˈəʊk] N Steineiche *f*

holocaust [ˈhɒləkɔːst] N **a** Inferno *nt*; **nuclear ~** Atominferno *nt* **b** *(= mass extermination)* Massenvernichtung *f*; *(in Third Reich)* Holocaust *m*

hologram [ˈhɒləgræm] N Hologramm *nt*

holograph [ˈhɒləgrɑːf] N handschriftliches Dokument ADJ eigenhändig geschrieben, holografisch *(form)*

holography [hɒˈlɒgrəfɪ] N Holografie *f*

hols [hɒlz] *(Brit inf) abbr of* **holidays**

holster [ˈhəʊlstəˈ] N (Pistolen)halfter *nt or f*

holy [ˈhəʊlɪ] ADJ **a** *(Rel)* heilig; *oil, bread, ground* geweiht **b ~ cow** *or* **mackerel!** *(inf)* (ach du) heiliger Strohsack *or* Bimbam! *(inf)*; **~ smoke!** *(inf)* großer Gott! *(inf)*; **~ shit!** *(sl)* du liebe Scheiße! *(inf)*; **~ terror** Nervensäge *f (inf)*, Landplage *f (hum)* N **the Holy of Holies** *(lit)* das Allerheiligste; *(fig)* ein Heiligtum *nt*

holy: **Holy Ark** N *(Eccl)* Thoraschrein *m*; **Holy Bible** N **the ~** die Bibel, die Heilige Schrift; **Holy City** N **the ~** die Heilige Stadt; **Holy Communion** N die heilige Kommunion, das heilige Abendmahl; **Holy Father** N **the ~** *(= the Pope)* der Heilige Vater; **Holy Ghost** N = **Holy Spirit**; **Holy Grail** N **the ~** der Heilige Gral; **Holy Land** N **the ~** das Heilige Land; **holy orders** PL Priesterweihe *f*; **to be in ~** dem geistlichen Stand angehören; **to take ~** die Priesterweihe empfangen; **Holy Roman Empire** N **the ~** *(Hist)* das Heilige Römische Reich; **Holy Rood** N (heiliges) Kruzifix *nt*; **Holy Saturday** N Karsamstag *m*; **Holy Scripture** N die Heilige Schrift; **Holy See** N **the ~** der Heilige Stuhl; **Holy Sepulchre** N **the ~** das Heilige Grab; **Holy Spirit** N **the ~** der Heilige Geist; **Holy Thursday** N **a** *(in Roman Catholic Church)* Gründonnerstag *m* **b** *(in Anglican Church)* Himmelfahrtstag *m*; **Holy Trinity** N **the ~** die Heilige Dreifaltigkeit *or* Dreieinigkeit; **holy war** N Heiliger Krieg; **holy water** N heiliges Wasser; *(in Catholic Church)* Weihwasser *nt*; **Holy Week** N Karwoche *f*; **Holy Writ** N *(dated)* **the ~** die Heilige Schrift

homage [ˈhɒmɪdʒ] N Huldigung *f*; *(for elders)* Ehrerbietung *f*; **to pay** *or* **do ~ to sb** jdm huldigen; jdm seine Ehrerbietung erweisen; **in order to pay ~ to the dead king** um dem König die letzte Ehre zu erweisen; **a speech in ~ to the president/the victims of the disaster** eine Rede als Hommage für den Präsidenten/als Ehrerbietung für die Opfer der Katastrophe; **they stood there in silent ~** sie standen in stummer Ehrerbietung da

homburg [ˈhɒmbɜːg] N Homburg *m*

home [həʊm] N **a** *(= where one lives)* Zuhause *nt*, Heim *nt*; *(= house)* Haus *nt*; *(= country, area etc)* Heimat *f*; **a loving/good ~** ein liebevolles/gutes Zuhause; **gifts for the ~** Geschenke *pl* für das Haus *or* die Wohnung; **a useful gadget to have in your ~** ein sehr praktisches Gerät für den Haushalt; **his ~ is in Brussels** er ist in Brüssel zu Hause; **Bournemouth is his second**

~ Bournemouth ist seine zweite Heimat (geworden); **haven't you got a ~ to go to?** hast du kein Zuhause?; **he invited us round to his ~** er hat uns zu sich (nach Hause) eingeladen; **away from ~** von zu Hause weg; **a long way from ~** weit von zu Hause weg *or* entfernt; *(in different country also)* weit von der Heimat entfernt; **to live away from ~** nicht zu Hause wohnen; **he worked away from ~** er hat auswärts gearbeitet; **let's concentrate on problems closer to ~** wir sollten uns auf unsere eigenen Probleme konzentrieren; **to have a ~ of one's own** ein eigenes Heim *or* Zuhause haben; **to find a ~ for sb/an animal** ein Zuhause für jdn/ein Tier finden; **does this hammer have a ~?** *(hum)* gehört dieser Hammer an einen bestimmten Platz?; **I'll give that picture a ~** bei mir wird das Bild einen guten Platz finden *or* haben; **it's a ~ from ~** es ist wie zu Hause; **at ~** zu Hause; *(Comm)* im Inland; *(Sport)* auf eigenem Platz; **the next match will be at ~** das nächste Spiel ist ein Heimspiel; **Miss Hooper is not at ~ today** Frau Hooper ist heute nicht zu Hause *or* nicht da; **Miss Hooper is not at ~ to anyone today** Frau Hooper ist heute für niemanden zu Hause *or* zu sprechen; **who's he when he's at ~?** *(inf)* wer in aller Welt ist er?; **to be** *or* **feel at ~ with sb** sich in jds Gegenwart *(dat)* wohlfühlen; **he doesn't feel at ~ with English** er fühlt sich im Englischen nicht sicher *or* zu Hause; **I don't feel at ~ with this new theory yet** ich komme mit dieser neuen Theorie noch nicht ganz zurecht; **to make oneself at ~** es sich *(dat)* gemütlich *or* bequem machen; **to make sb feel at ~** es jdm gemütlich machen; **to leave ~** von zu Hause weggehen; **Scotland is the ~ of the haggis** Schottland ist die Heimat des Haggis, das Haggis ist in Schottland zu Hause; **the city/this building is ~ to some 1,500 students** in dieser Stadt/diesem Gebäude wohnen etwa 1.500 Studenten *or* sind etwa 1.500 Studenten zu Hause; **there's no place like ~** *(Prov)* daheim ist daheim *(prov)*, eigener Herd ist Goldes wert *(Prov)*; **~ sweet ~** *(Prov)* trautes Heim, Glück allein *(Prov)*

b *(= institution)* Heim *nt*; *(for orphans)* Waisenhaus *nt*, Heim *nt*; *(for blind)* Heim *nt*, Anstalt *f* → **nursing home**

c *(Zool, Bot)* Heimat *f*

d *(Sport) (= base)* Mal *nt*; *(Racing)* Ziel *nt*

ADV **a** *(position)* zu Hause, zuhause *(Aus, Sw)*, daheim; *(with verb of motion)* nach Hause, nachhause *(Aus, Sw)*, heim; **to go ~** *(to house)* nach Hause *or (Aus, Sw)* nachhause gehen/fahren; *(to country)* heimfahren; **on the way ~** auf dem Heim- *or* Nachhauseweg; **the first runner ~** der Erste, der durchs Ziel geht; **the first runner ~ was Fred** Fred ging als Erster durchs Ziel; **to get ~** nach Hause *or (Aus, Sw)* nachhause kommen, heimkommen; *(in race)* durchs Ziel gehen; **I have to get ~ before ten** ich muss vor zehn zu Hause *or (Aus, Sw)* zuhause *or* daheim sein; **to return ~ from abroad** aus dem Ausland zurückkommen

b *(= to the mark)* **to drive a nail ~** einen Nagel einschlagen; **he nudged the ball ~** *(Ftbl)* er schob den Ball ins Tor; **to bring** *or* **get sth ~ to sb** jdm etw klarmachen *or* beibringen; **it came ~ to him that ...** es wurde ihm klar, dass ...; **to strike ~** *(torpedo etc)* treffen; *(fig: remark)* ins Schwarze treffen, sitzen *(inf)* → **drive home, hammer home, hit, press, push**

VI *(pigeons)* heimkehren

▶ **home in** VI *(missiles)* sich ausrichten (*on sth* auf etw *acc*); **the missile will home in** das Geschoss findet sein Ziel; **to home in on a target** ein Ziel finden *or* selbstständig ansteuern; **he immediately homed in on the essential point** er hat sofort den wichtigsten Punkt herausgegriffen

home: **home address** N Heimatadresse *or* -anschrift *f*; *(as opposed to business address)* Privatanschrift *f*; **home-baked** ADJ selbst gebacken; **home banking** N Homebanking *nt*; **home base** N *(Baseball)* Homebase *nt*, Schlagmal *nt*; **home birth** N Hausgeburt *f*; **homebody** N *(inf)* Heimchen *nt*; **homeboy** N *(dated US inf)* Einheimische(r) *m*; *(US sl: = close friend)* Kumpel *m*; **homebred** ADJ *(= indigenous)* einheimisch; **home-brew** N selbst gebrautes Bier, Selbstgebraute(s) *nt*; **home-brewed** ADJ selbst gebraut; **home comforts** PL häuslicher Komfort; **homecoming** N Heimkehr *f*; **home computer** N Homecomputer *m*, Heimcomputer *m*; **home computing** N Computern *nt*; **home contents** PL Hausrat *m*; **~ insurance** Hausratsversicherung *f*; **home cooking** N häusliche Küche, Hausmannskost *f*; **Home Counties** PL *Grafschaften, die an London angrenzen*; **home-cured** ADJ selbst gebeizt; **home economics** N *sing* Hauswirtschaft(slehre) *f*; **home entertainment system** N Home-Entertainment-System *nt*; **home exercise machine** N Hometrainer *m*; **home front** N **on the ~** *(Mil, Pol)* im eigenen Land; *(in business contexts)* im eigenen Betrieb; *(in personal, family contexts)* zu Hause; **home game** N *(Sport)* Heimspiel *nt*; **homegirl** N *(dated US inf)* Einheimische *f*; *(US sl: = close friend)* Kumpel *m*; **home ground** N *(Sport)* eigener Platz; **to be on ~** *(fig)* sich auf vertrautem Terrain bewegen; **home-grown** ADJ *vegetables* selbst gezogen; *(= not imported)* einheimisch; *(fig) talent, player* heimisch; **Home Guard** N Bürgerwehr *f*; **home help** N Haushaltshilfe *f*; **home improvements** N Renovierungsarbeiten *pl (am Haus oder in der Wohnung)*; **home improvements loan** N Modernisierungsdarlehen *nt*; **home key** N *(Comput)* Pos-1-Taste *f*, Home-Taste *f*; **homeland** N Heimat(land *nt*) *f*, Vaterland *nt*; **homeless** **ADJ** obdachlos **PL** **the ~** die Obdachlosen *pl*; **homelessness** N Obdachlosigkeit *f*; **home life** N Familienleben *nt*; **homelike** ADJ heimelig, wie daheim; **home loan** N Hypothek *f*; **home-loving** ADJ häuslich

homely ['həʊmlɪ] ADJ *(+er)* **a** *person (Brit: = home-loving)* häuslich, hausbacken *(pej)*; *atmosphere, restaurant* heimelig, gemütlich, behaglich; *style* anspruchslos, hausbacken *(pej)*; *advice* einfach **b** *food* bürgerlich **c** *(US: = plain) person* unscheinbar; *face* reizlos

home: **home-made** ADJ selbst gemacht; *(pej)* selbst gestrickt; **homemaker** N *(US: = housewife)* Hausfrau *f*, Hausmutter *f*; *(= social worker)* Familienfürsorger(in) *m(f)*; **home market** N Inlandsmarkt *m*, inländischer Markt; **home match** N *(Sport)* Heimspiel *nt*; **home movie** N Amateurfilm *m*; **home news** N Meldungen *pl* aus dem Inland; **Home Office** N *(Brit)* Innenministerium *nt*; *(with relation to aliens)* Einwanderungsbehörde *f*

homeopath *etc (US)* = **homoeopath** *etc*

home: **homeowner** N *(of house)* Hauseigentümer(in) *m(f)*; *(of flat)* Wohnungseigentümer(in) *m(f)*; **homeownership** N Eigenbesitz *m* von Häusern/Wohnungen; **home page** N *(Comput)* Homepage *f*; **home plate** N *(Baseball)* Ausgangsbase *nt*; **home port** N Heimathafen *m*

Homer ['həʊmə'] N Homer *m*

homer ['həʊmə'] N **a** *(= homing pigeon)* Brieftaube *f* **b** *(Brit inf: = job)* Nebenjob *m (inf)*; **to do sth as a ~** etw privat *or* nebenher machen

Homeric [həʊ'merɪk] ADJ homerisch

home: **home rule** N Selbstbestimmung *f*, Selbstverwaltung *f*; **home run** N *(Baseball)* Homerun *m*; **to hit a ~** um alle vier Male laufen; *(US fig)* das große Los ziehen; **home sales** PL Inlandsumsatz *m*; **Home Secretary** N *(Brit)* Innenminister(in) *m(f)*; **home shopping** N Homeshopping *nt*; *(on TV also)* Teleshopping *nt*; **homesick** ADJ heimwehkrank; **to be ~** Heimweh haben (*for* nach); **homesickness** N Heimweh *nt* (*for* nach); **home side** N *(Sport)* Gastgeber *pl*, Heimmannschaft *f*; **homespun** **ADJ** **a** *cloth* selbst gesponnen, handgesponnen **b** *(fig: = simple)* einfach; *(pej)* hausbacken; **~ philosophy** Lebensweisheiten *pl*; **~ advice** altbewährter Rat **N** *(= cloth)* Homespun *nt (grober, genoppter Wollstoff)*; **homestead** N **a** Heimstätte *f* **b** *(US)* Heimstätte *f* für Siedler; **homesteader** ['həʊmstedə'] N **a** Heimstättenbesitzer(in) *m(f)* **b** *(US)* Heimstättensiedler(in) *m(f)*; **home straight, home stretch** N *(Sport)* Zielgerade *f*; **we're in the ~ now** *(fig inf)* das Ende ist in Sicht; **home team** N *(Sport)* Gastgeber *pl*, Heimmannschaft *f*, Platzherren *pl (inf)*; **home town**, *(US)* **hometown** N Heimatstadt *f*; **home truth** N *(Brit)* bittere Wahrheit; **to tell sb a few ~s** jdm die Augen öffnen; **home video** N Amateurvideo *nt*

homeward ['həʊmwəd] ADJ **~ journey/flight** Heimreise *f*/-flug *m*; **to be on the ~ stretch** bald zu Hause sein; **we are ~ bound** es geht Richtung Heimat

homeward(s) ['həʊmwəd(z)] ADV nach Hause *or (Aus, Sw)* nachhause, heim; *(= to country also)* in Richtung Heimat

home: **home waters** PL *(Naut)* heimatliche Gewässer *pl*; **homework** N *(Sch)* Hausaufgaben *pl*, Schulaufgaben *pl*; **to give sb sth as ~** jdm etw aufgeben; **what ~ have you got?** was hast du auf?; **the minister had not done his ~** *(inf)* der Minister hatte sich mit der Materie nicht vertraut gemacht; **homeworker** N Heimarbeiter(in) *m(f)*; **homeworking** N Heimarbeit *f*

homey ['həʊmɪ] ADJ *(+er)* *(US inf)* gemütlich; *atmosphere also* heimelig, behaglich

homicidal [,hɒmɪ'saɪdl] ADJ *(= murderous) person* gemeingefährlich; **that man is a ~ maniac** dieser Mann ist ein mordgieriger Verrückter; **he is potentially ~, he has ~ tendencies** er könnte zum Mörder werden; **~ fury** *or* **rage** Mordrausch *m*

homicide ['hɒmɪsaɪd] N **a** Totschlag *m*; **~ (squad)** Mordkommission *f* **b** *(= person)* Mörder(in) *m(f)*; Totschläger(in) *m(f)*

homie ['həʊmi:] N *(US inf)* Homie *m*

homily ['hɒmɪlɪ] N Predigt *f*; *(fig also)* Sermon *m (pej)*

homing ['həʊmɪŋ] ADJ *missile* mit Zielsucheinrichtung; **~ device** Zielfluggerät *nt*, Zielsucheinrichtung *f*

homing instinct N Heimfindevermögen *nt*

homing pigeon N Brieftaube *f*

homo ['həʊməʊ] N *(pej inf)* Homo *m (dated inf)*

homoeopath, *(US)* **homeopath** ['həʊmɪəʊpæθ] N Homöopath(in) *m(f)*

homoeopathic, *(US)* **homeopathic** [,həʊmɪəʊ'pæθɪk] ADJ homöopathisch

homoeopathy, *(US)* **homeopathy** [,həʊmɪ'ɒpəθɪ] N Homöopathie *f*

homoerotic [,həʊməʊɪ'rɒtɪk] ADJ *image, fantasy, subtext* homoerotisch

homogeneity [,hɒməʊdʒə'ni:ɪtɪ] N Homogenität *f*

homogeneous [,hɒmə'dʒi:nɪəs] ADJ homogen

homogenize [hə'mɒdʒənaɪz] VT homogenisieren; **~d milk** homogenisierte Milch

homogenous [hə'mɒdʒɪnəs] ADJ homogen

homograph ['hɒməʊgrɑ:f] N Homograf *nt*

homologous [hə'mɒləgəs] ADJ homolog

homonym ['hɒmənɪm] N Homonym *nt*

homonymous [hə'mɒnɪməs] ADJ homonym

homophobe ['həʊməʊ,fəʊb] N Homophobe(r) *mf*

homophobia [,həʊməʊ'fəʊbɪə] N Homophobie *f*

homophobic [,həʊməʊ'fəʊbɪk] ADJ homophob

homophone ['hɒməfəʊn] N Homofon *nt*

Homo sapiens [,həʊməʊ'sæpɪenz] N Homo sapiens *m*

homosexual [,hɒməʊ'seksjʊəl] **ADJ** homosexuell **N** Homosexuelle(r) *mf*

homosexuality [,hɒməʊseksjʊ'ælɪtɪ] N Homosexualität *f*

homunculus [hɒ'mʌŋkjʊləs] N Homunkulus *m*

homy ADJ *(+er)* *(US inf)* = **homey**

Hon **a** *abbr of* **honorary** **b** *abbr of* **Honourable**

hon [hʌn] *(US inf) abbr of* **honey**; **hi, ~!** hallo, Schatz!

honcho ['hɒntʃəʊ] N *(inf)* Boss *m (inf)*; **head ~** Oberboss *m (inf)*

Honduran [hɒn'djʊərən] **ADJ** honduranisch **N** Honduraner(in) *m(f)*

Honduras [hɒn'djʊərəs] N Honduras *nt*

hone [həʊn] **N** Schleifstein *m*, Wetzstein *m* **VT** *blade* schleifen; *(fig) person* aufbauen; *(as a successor)* heranziehen; *skills* vervollkommnen

▸ **hone down** VT *sep (fig)* (zurecht)feilen *(to* auf *+acc)*

honest ['ɒnɪst] **ADJ** **a** *(= truthful)* ehrlich; **to be ~ with sb** jdm die Wahrheit sagen, jdm nichts vormachen *(inf)*; **you must be brutally ~ with yourself** du darfst dir absolut nichts vormachen *(inf)*; **I don't think you've been quite ~ with us** ich glaube, du hast uns nicht die ganze Wahrheit gesagt; **to be ~ about sth** etw ehrlich darstellen; **to be perfectly ~ (with you), I don't really know** um (ganz) ehrlich zu sein, ich weiß es nicht genau, (ganz) offen *or* ehrlich gesagt, ich weiß es nicht genau; **I'd like your ~ opinion of it** ich möchte wissen, was Sie wirklich davon halten; **what do you think of the school, in your ~ opinion?** was hältst du von der Schule, ganz ehrlich gesagt?; **the ~ truth** die reine Wahrheit
b *(= law-abiding, decent) person* redlich; *money, profit* ehrlich *or* redlich erworben; **they are good ~ people** sie sind gute, rechtschaffene Leute; **to make an ~ living** *or* **penny** sein Geld ehrlich *or* redlich verdienen; **he made an ~ woman of her** *(dated hum)* er machte sie zu seiner Angetrauten *(hum)*; **after an ~ day's work** nach einem ordentlichen Tagewerk; **he's never done an ~ day's work in his life** er ist in seinem ganzen Leben noch keiner ordentlichen Arbeit nachgegangen; **(as) ~ as the day is long** grundehrlich
c *(= straightforward, real) material, cooking* einfach, echt; *mistake* echt; **good ~ cooking** gutbürgerliche Küche
ADV *(inf)* **I didn't know about it, ~** ich wusste nichts davon, ehrlich *or* Ehrenwort!; **it's true, ~ it is** es stimmt, ganz ehrlich; **~ to God** *or* **goodness** *(emph)* ehrlich; **~ injun** *(emph inf)* ganz ehrlich

honest broker N *(esp Pol)* Vermittler(in) *m(f)*

honestly ['ɒnɪstlɪ] ADV **a** *(= truthfully) answer* ehrlich, aufrichtig; *(= legally) earn money* ehrlich, auf ehrliche *or* redliche Weise; **to talk about** *or* **discuss sth openly and ~** offen und ehrlich über etw *(acc)* reden
b *(emph) say, believe* ehrlich, wirklich; *call, think, expect* wirklich; **I ~ thought you'd be pleased** ich dachte wirklich, dass du dich freuen würdest; **no, ~, I'm fine** nein, wirklich *or* (ganz) ehrlich, mir gehts gut; **I don't mind, ~** es ist mir wirklich *or* ehrlich egal; **~, it's terrible** das ist wirklich furchtbar; **quite ~ I don't remember it** ehrlich gesagt *or* um ehrlich zu sein, ich kann mich daran nicht erinnern; **~!** *(showing exasperation)* also ehrlich *or* wirklich!

honest-to-goodness ['ɒnɪstə'gʊdnɪs] ADJ *(inf: = genuine)* echt; *person, expression* waschecht

honesty ['ɒnɪstɪ] N **a** *(= truthfulness)* Ehrlichkeit *f*; *(= being law-abiding, decent)* Redlichkeit *f*; **in all ~** ganz ehrlich; **one must admit, in all ~, ...** man muss ehrlicherweise zugeben, ...; **~ is the best policy** *(Prov)* ehrlich währt am längsten *(Prov)* **b** *(Bot)* Mondviole *f*, Silberblatt *nt*, Judassilberling *m (inf)*

honesty box N *Büchse, in der man Geld hinterlässt, wenn niemand da ist, um es zu kassieren*, Kasse *f* des Vertrauens *(esp E Ger)*

honey ['hʌnɪ] N **a** Honig *m* **b** *(inf: = dear)* Schätzchen *nt*; **she is an absolute ~** *(= she's gorgeous)* sie ist einfach süß *(inf)*; **my mum's a real ~** meine Mutter ist ein (Gold)schatz *(inf)*

honey: **honeybee** N (Honig)biene *f*; **honeybunch** N *(inf)* Schätzchen *nt*; **honeycomb** **N** (Bienen)wabe *f*; *(filled with honey also)* Honigwabe *f* **VT** *usu pass* durchlöchern; **the mountain was ~ed with caves** der Berg war von Höhlen durchsetzt; **honeydew** N Honigtau *m*; **honeydew melon** N Honigmelone *f*; **honey eater** N *(Orn)* Honigfresser *m*

honeyed ['hʌnɪd] ADJ *words, voice* honigsüß

honey extractor N Honigschleuder *f*

honeymoon ['hʌnɪmu:n] **N** Flitterwochen *pl*; *(= trip)* Hochzeitsreise *f*; **to be on one's ~** in den Flitterwochen/auf Hochzeitsreise sein; **where did you go for your ~?** wo habt ihr eure Flitterwochen verbracht?, wohin habt ihr eure Hochzeitsreise gemacht?; **the ~ is over** *(fig inf)* jetzt werden andere Saiten aufgezogen *(inf)*, die Schonzeit ist vorbei **VI** seine Hochzeitsreise machen; **they are ~ing in Spain** sie sind in Spanien auf Hochzeitsreise

honeymoon couple N Flitterwöchner *pl*

honeymooner ['hʌnɪmu:nə'] N Hochzeitsreisende(r) *mf*, Flitterwöchner(in) *m(f)*

honeymoon period N *(fig)* Schonzeit *f*

honeymoon suite N Suite *f* für Hochzeitsreisende

honeysuckle ['hʌnɪsʌkəl] N Geißblatt *nt*

Hong Kong ['hɒŋ'kɒŋ] N Hongkong *nt*

honk [hɒŋk] **N** *(of car)* Hupen *nt*; *(of goose etc)* Schrei *m* **INTERJ** **~ ~** tut, tut, tüt, tüt **VI** **a** *(car)* hupen, tuten **b** *(geese)* schreien **c** *(inf: = stink)* stinken **VT** *horn* drücken auf *(+acc)*

honky ['hɒŋkɪ] N *(pej inf)* Weiße(r) *mf*

honky-tonk [,hɒŋkɪ'tɒŋk] **N** *(US inf: = country-music bar)* Schuppen *m (inf)* **ADJ** *music, piano* schräg; **~ bar** Schuppen *m (inf)*

Honolulu [,hɒnə'lu:lu:] N Honolulu *nt*

honor *etc (US)* = **honour** *etc*

honorarium [,ɒnə'reərɪəm] N *pl* **honoraria** [,ɒnə'reərɪə] Honorar *nt*

honorary ['ɒnərərɪ] ADJ Ehren-; **~ member/president/title/citizen** Ehrenmitglied *nt*/-präsident/-titel/-bürger *m*

honorary degree N *ehrenhalber verliehener akademischer Grad*

Honorary Secretary N ehrenamtlicher Sekretär, ehrenamtliche Sekretärin

honor guard N *(US)* Ehrenwache *f*

honour, *(US)* **honor** ['ɒnə'] **N** **a** Ehre *f*; **sense of ~** Ehrgefühl *nt*; **he made it a point of ~** er betrachtete es als Ehrensache; **he decided to make it a point of ~, never to ...** er schwor sich *(dat)*, nie zu ...; **there is ~ among thieves** es gibt so etwas wie Ganovenehre; **~ where ~ is due** Ehre, wem Ehre gebührt; **on my ~!** *(old)* bei meiner Ehre *(old)*; **I promise on my ~** ich gebe mein Ehrenwort; **you're on your ~ not to leave** Sie haben Ihr Ehrenwort gegeben, dass Sie bleiben; **to put sb on his ~** jdm vertrauen; **he's put me on my ~ not to tell** ich habe ihm mein Ehrenwort gegeben, dass ich nichts sage; **man of ~** Ehrenmann *m*; **to lose one's ~** *(old)* seine Ehre verlieren *(old)*; **to do ~ to sb** *(at funeral)* jdm die letzte Ehre erweisen; *(action, thought etc)* jdm zur Ehre gereichen; **to do ~ to sth** einer Sache *(dat)* Ehre machen; **in ~ of sb** zu Ehren von jdm, zu jds Ehren; *of dead person* in ehrendem Andenken an jdn; **in ~ of sth** zu Ehren von etw; *of past thing* in ehrendem Andenken an etw; **may I have the ~ of accompanying you?** *(form)* ich bitte um die Ehre, Sie begleiten zu dürfen *(geh)*; **may I have the ~ (of the next dance)?** *(form)* darf ich (um den nächsten Tanz) bitten?; **if you would do me the ~ of accepting** *(form)* wenn Sie mir die Ehre erweisen würden anzunehmen *(geh)*; **to whom do I have the ~ of speaking?** *(form, hum)* mit wem habe ich die Ehre? *(geh, hum)*; **he is ~ bound to do it** es ist Ehrensache für ihn, das zu tun
b *(= title)* **Your Honour** Hohes Gericht; **His Honour** das Gericht; **the case was up before His Honour, Sir Charles** der Fall wurde unter dem Vorsitz des vorsitzenden Richters Sir Charles verhandelt
c *(= distinction, award)* **~s** Ehren *pl*, Auszeichnung(en) *f(pl)*; **with full military ~s** mit militärischen Ehren; **New Year's Honour** Titelverleihung *f* am Neujahrstag
d **to do the ~s** *(inf)* die Honneurs machen; *(on private occasions)* den Gastgeber spielen
e *(Univ)* **~s** *(also* **honours degree***)* *akademischer Grad mit Prüfung im Spezialfach*; **to do** *or* **take ~s in English** Englisch belegen, um den „Honours Degree" zu erwerben; **to get first-class ~s** das Examen mit Auszeichnung *or* „sehr gut" bestehen
f *(Golf)* **it's his ~** er hat die Ehre
g *(Cards) eine der (beim Bridge) 5 bzw. (beim Whist) 4 höchsten Karten einer Farbe* **the ~s** die Honneurs *pl*
VT **a** *person* ehren; **to ~ sb with a title** jdm einen Titel verleihen; **I would be ~ed** es wäre mir eine Ehre; **I should be (deeply) ~ed if you ...** ich würde mich (zutiefst) geehrt fühlen, wenn Sie ...; **we are ~ed by your visit** *(also iro)* wir fühlen uns durch Ihren Besuch geehrt; **he ~ed us with his presence** *(also iro)* er beehrte uns mit seiner Gegenwart; **it's Angelika, we ARE ~ed** *(iro)* es ist Angelika, welche Ehre; **would you ~ me by dining with me tonight?** würden Sie mir die Ehre erweisen, heute Abend mit mir zu speisen? *(geh)*
b *cheque* annehmen, einlösen; *debt* begleichen; *bill of exchange* respektieren; *obligation* nachkommen *(+dat)*; *commitment* stehen zu; *credit card* anerkennen; *pledge, promise* halten, einlösen; *agreement, contract* sich halten an *(+acc)*, erfüllen

honourable, *(US)* **honorable** ['ɒnərəbl] ADJ **a** ehrenhaft; *person* ehrenhaft, ehrenwert; *peace, discharge* ehrenvoll; *exception* rühmlich; **to get an ~ mention** rühmend *or* lobend erwähnt werden
b *(Brit Parl) Anrede von Abgeordneten innerhalb des Parlaments* **the Honourable member for X** der (Herr)/die (Frau) Abgeordnete für X; **the Honourable member** *or* **gentleman is wrong** der geschätzte *or* ehrenwerte (Herr) Kollege täuscht sich; **I agree with my right ~ friend** ich stimme meinem geschätzten Herrn Kollegen/meiner geschätzten Frau Kollegin zu
c *(= title) Titel der jüngeren Söhne von Grafen und der Kinder von Freiherren und Baronen* **I didn't know he was an Honourable** ich wusste nicht, dass er adlig *or* ein „von" *(inf)* ist

honourably, *(US)* **honorably** ['ɒnərəblɪ] ADV in Ehren; *behave, act* ehrenhaft, wie ein Ehrenmann; *settle peace* ehrenvoll; *mention* rühmend, lobend

honours, *(US)* **honors** ['ɒnəz-]: **honours board** N Ehrentafel *f*; **honours degree** N = **honour N e**; **honours list** N *(Brit)* Liste *f* der Titel- und Rangverleihungen *(die zweimal im Jahr veröffentlicht wird)*; *(Univ) Liste der Kandidaten, die den „Honours Degree" verliehen bekommen*

> **HONOURS LIST**
>
> Die **honours list** ist eine vom britischen Premierminister aufgestellte und vom Monarchen gebilligte Liste, auf der Personen aufgeführt werden, die eine besondere Auszeichnung erhalten sollen und daher mit einem bestimmten Titel geehrt werden. Ein Großteil der Auszeichnungen geht an herausragende Persönlichkeiten des öffentlichen Lebens, aber auch an Leute, die einen bedeutenden Beitrag zum Gemeinwohl geleistet haben. Zweimal im Jahr wird eine solche Liste veröffentlicht, die **New Year's Honours List** im Januar und die **Queen's Birthday Honours List** im Juni. Die meisten der vergebenen Auszeichnungen sind **MBE (Member of the British Empire)** oder **OBE (Order of the British Empire)**.

Hon. Sec. *abbr of* **Honorary Secretary**

hooch [hu:tʃ] N *(esp US inf)* Stoff *m (sl)*

hoochie ['hu:tʃɪ] N *(US inf)* Schlampe *f*

hood [hʊd] N a Kapuze *f*; *(thief's)* Maske *f*; *(hawk's)* Kappe *f* b *(Aut) (= roof)* Verdeck *nt*; *(US: = bonnet)* (Motor)haube *f*; *(on fireplace etc)* Abzug *m*; *(on cooker)* Abzugshaube *f* c *(of cobra)* Brillenzeichnung *f* d *(esp US inf) (= gangster)* Gangster *m (inf)*, Ganove *m (inf)*; *(= young ruffian)* Rowdy *m*, Rüpel *m* e *(esp US inf: = neighbourhood)* Gegend *f*, Viertel *nt* f *(esp US sl: = ghetto)* G(h)etto *nt* VT eine Kapuze aufsetzen *(+dat)*; *hawk* eine Kappe aufsetzen *(+dat)*

hooded ['hʊdɪd] ADJ **the ~ executioner/monk** der Scharfrichter/Mönch mit seiner Kapuze; **the ~ robber/gunman** der maskierte Räuber/Schütze; **~ anorak/sweatshirt** Anorak *m*/Sweatshirt *nt* mit Kapuze; **~ eyes** Augen mit schweren Lidern

hoodie ['hu:dɪ] N a Kapuzenjacke*f*, Kapuzenpullover *m* b *jemand, der eine Kapuzenjacke oder einen Kapuzenpullover trägt*

hoodlum ['hu:dləm] N Rowdy *m*; *(= member of gang)* Ganove *m (inf)*, Gangster *m (inf)*; **you young ~** du Rowdy, du Rüpel

hoodoo ['hu:du:] N Unglück *nt*; *(= person, thing)* Unglücksbote *m*

hoodwink ['hʊdwɪŋk] VT *(inf)* (he)reinlegen *(inf)*; **to ~ sb into doing sth** jdn dazu verleiten, etw zu tun; **they ~ed him into signing the contract** er ließ sich von ihnen (dazu) verleiten, den Vertrag zu unterschreiben; **I was ~ed into buying an imitation** man hat mir eine Imitation angedreht *(inf)*

hooey ['hu:ɪ] N *(dated inf)* Gelabere *nt (inf)*, Quatsch *m (inf)*

hoof [hu:f] N *pl* **-s** *or* **hooves** Huf *m*; **hooves** *(hum inf: = feet)* Quadratlatschen *pl (inf)*; **cattle on the ~** Vieh *nt*; **to eat on the ~** *(inf)* unterwegs essen; **they tend to make policy on the ~** *(inf)* sie legen ihre Politik oft aus dem Stegreif fest VT **to ~ it** *(inf: = go on foot)* latschen *(inf)*; *(= dance on stage)* tingeln *(inf)*

hoofbeat ['hu:fbi:t] N Hufschlag *m*

hoofed [hu:ft] ADJ Huf-; **~ animal** Huftier *nt*

hook [hʊk] N a Haken *m*
b *(Boxing)* Haken *m*; *(Golf)* Kurvball *m (nach links)*
c *(Geog)* (gekrümmte) Landzunge
d *(fig uses)* **he swallowed the story ~, line and sinker** er hat die Geschichte tatsächlich mit Stumpf und Stiel geschluckt *(inf)*; **he fell for it ~, line and sinker** er ging auf den Leim; **he fell for her ~, line and sinker** er war ihr mit Haut und Haaren verfallen; **by ~ or by crook** auf Biegen und Brechen; **to get sb off the ~** *(inf)* jdn herausreißen *(inf)*; *(= out of trouble also)* jdn herauspauken *(inf)*; **it gets him off the ~ every time** damit kommt er jedes Mal wieder davon; **that lets me off the ~** *(inf)* damit bin ich aus dem Schneider *(inf)*; **to leave the phone off the ~** den Hörer neben das Telefon legen; *(unintentionally)* nicht auflegen; **the phone was ringing off the ~** *(US inf)* das Telefon klingelte pausenlos; **to do sth on one's own ~** *(US inf)* etw auf eigene Faust machen; **to get one's ~s into sb/sth** *(pej inf)* jdn/etw in die Finger kriegen *(inf)*
VT a *(= fasten with hook)* **he ~ed the door back** er hakte die Tür fest; **the old man ~s the rowing boats and pulls them in** der alte Mann zieht die Ruderboote mit einem Haken ans Ufer; **to ~ a trailer to a car** einen Anhänger an ein Auto hängen
b **to ~ one's arm/feet around sth** seinen Arm/seine Füße um etw schlingen; **the trapeze artist ~s his legs over the bar** der Trapezkünstler hängt sich mit den Beinen an der Stange ein
c *fish* an die Angel bekommen; *(fig) husband, wife* sich *(dat)* angeln; **to be ~ed** an der Angel hängen; **the helicopter ~ed him out of the water** der Hubschrauber zog *or* angelte *(inf)* ihn aus dem Wasser
d *(Boxing)* einen Haken versetzen *(+dat) or* geben *(+dat)*
e **to be/get ~ed on sth** *(inf: = addicted, on drugs)* von etw abhängig sein/werden; *on film, food, place etc* auf etw *(acc)* stehen *(inf)*; **he's ~ed on the idea** er ist von der Idee besessen; **he's become ~ed on power and money** er ist jetzt auf Macht und Geld versessen
f *(Rugby)* hakeln
g *(Sport) ball* einen Linksdrall geben *(+dat)*
h *(inf: = clear off)* **to ~ it** die Fliege machen *(sl)*
VI *(dress etc)* zugehakt werden

▸ **hook on** VI (an)gehakt werden (*to* an *+acc*); *(with towbar)* angekoppelt *or* angehängt werden (*to* an *+acc*); *(burrs etc)* sich festhaken (*to* an *+dat*) VT *sep* anhaken (*to* an *+acc*), mit einem Haken befestigen (*to* an *+dat*); *(with towbar)* ankoppeln, anhängen; **to hook sth onto sth** etw an etw *(acc)* (an)haken; **the gliders were hooked on behind the towplane** die Segelflugzeuge waren hinten an das Schleppflugzeug angehängt *or* angekoppelt

▸ **hook up** VI a *(Rad, TV)* gemeinsam ausstrahlen; **to hook up with sb** sich jdm anschließen b *(US inf: = meet)* sich treffen VT *sep* a *dress etc* zuhaken; **hook me** *or* **the dress up, please** mach mir bitte die Haken zu, mach an dem Kleid bitte die Haken zu b *trailer, caravan* ankoppeln, anhängen; *broken-down car* abschleppen; *(recovery vehicle)* auf den Haken nehmen c *(= connect) computer etc* anschließen (*to* an *+acc*); *(Rad, TV)* anschließen (*with* an *+acc*); **the doctor hooked her up to a drip** der Arzt hängte sie an den Tropf *(inf)*

hookah ['hʊkə] N *(Brit)* Wasserpfeife *f*, Huka *f*

hook and eye N Haken und Öse *no art, pl vb*

hooked [hʊkt] ADJ a *(= hook-shaped)* gebogen; **~ beak/nose** Hakenschnabel *m*/-nase *f* b *(= equipped with hooks)* mit Haken versehen

hooker[1] ['hʊkə'] N *(esp US inf)* Nutte *f (inf)*

hooker[2] N *(Rugby)* Hakler *m*

hook: **hooknosed** ADJ mit einer Hakennase, hakennasig; **hook-up** ['hʊkʌp] N a *(Rad, TV)* gemeinsame Ausstrahlung; **a telephone ~** eine Konferenzschaltung b *(= connection)* Anschluss *m*; **hookworm** N Hakenwurm *m*; *(= disease)* Hakenwurmkrankheit *f*

hooky ['hʊkɪ] N *(US, inf)* Schuleschwänzen *nt (inf)*; **to play ~** (die) Schule schwänzen *(inf)*

hooligan ['hu:lɪgən] N Rowdy *m*

hooliganism ['hu:lɪgənɪzəm] N Rowdytum *nt*

hoop [hu:p] N Reifen *m*; *(in croquet)* Tor *nt*; *(in basketball)* Korb *m*; *(on bird's plumage)* Kranz *m*; *(on animal)* Ring *m*; *(= earring)* Creole *f*; **to jump through ~s** *(fig inf)* sich *(dat)* ein Bein ausreißen *(inf)*; **they put him through** *or* **made him jump through ~s** *(fig)* sie haben ihn auf Herz und Nieren geprüft VT *barrel* bereifen

hoop(ed) skirt ['hu:p(t)skɜ:t] N Reifrock *m*

hoopla ['hu:plɑ:] N Ringwerfen *nt*

hoopoe ['hu:pu:] N Wiedehopf *m*

hooray [hu:'reɪ] INTERJ = **hurrah**

Hooray Henry N *junger Angehöriger der Oberschicht mit auffälligem Gehabe*

hoosegow ['hu:sgaʊ] N *(dated US sl: = jail)* Knast *m (inf)*

hoot [hu:t] N a *(of owl)* Ruf *m*, Schrei *m*; **~s of derision** verächtliches Gejohle; **~s of laughter** johlendes Gelächter; **I don't care** *or* **give a ~** *or* **two ~s** *(inf)* das ist mir piepegal *(inf) or* völlig schnuppe *(inf)*; **to be a ~** *(inf, person)* zum Schreien (komisch) sein, zum Schießen sein *(inf)*; *(event also)* ein Brüller sein *(inf)*
b *(Aut)* Hupen *nt no pl*; *(of train, hooter)* Pfeifen *nt no pl*
VI a *(owl)* schreien, rufen; *(person: derisively)* johlen, buhen; **to ~ with derision/delight** verächtlich/begeistert johlen; **to ~ with laughter** in johlendes Gelächter ausbrechen
b *(Aut)* hupen; *(train, factory hooter)* pfeifen
VT a *actor, speaker* auspfeifen, ausbuhen; **he was ~ed off the stage** er wurde mit Buhrufen von der Bühne verjagt
b *(esp Brit Aut)* **to ~ one's/the horn** hupen, auf die Hupe drücken *(inf)*

▸ **hoot down** VT *sep* niederschreien

hootchy-kootchy ['hu:tʃɪ'ku:tʃɪ] N *(dated US, inf)* Bauchtanz *m*

hootenanny ['hu:tə'nænɪ] N Hootenanny *f*

hooter ['hu:tə'] N *(Brit)* a *(Aut)* Hupe *f*; *(at factory)* Sirene *f* b *(inf: = nose)* Zinken *m (inf)*

Hoover® ['hu:və'] N *(Brit)* ≈ Staubsauger *m*

hoover ['hu:və'] *(Brit)* VT (staub)saugen, Staub saugen; *carpet also* absaugen VI *(also* **hoover up**) (staub)saugen

▸ **hoover up** VI *+prep obj* (staub)saugen; *(fig) food* verputzen *(inf)*

hoovering ['hu:vərɪŋ] N **to do the ~** (staub)saugen, Staub saugen

hooves [hu:vz] *pl of* **hoof**

hop[1] [hɒp] N a (kleiner) Sprung; *(of deer, rabbit)* Satz *m*, Sprung *m*; **to catch sb on the ~** *(fig inf)* jdn überraschen *or* überrumpeln; **to keep sb on the ~** *(fig inf)* jdn in Trab halten
b *(inf, = dance)* Tanz *m*, Hopserei *f (pej inf)*
c *(Aviat inf)* Sprung *m*, Satz *m (inf)*; **a short ~** ein kleiner Satz *(inf)*, ein Katzensprung *m (inf)*
VI *(animal)* hüpfen, springen; *(rabbit)* hoppeln; *(person)* (auf einem Bein) hüpfen, hopsen *(inf)*; **~ in, said the driver** steigen Sie ein, sagte der Fahrer; **he'd ~ into bed with anyone** der steigt mit jeder ins Bett *(inf)*; **to ~ off (the train)** (aus dem Zug) aussteigen; *(while moving)* (vom Zug) abspringen; **he ~ped off his bicycle** er sprang vom Fahrrad; **to ~ on** aufsteigen; **to ~ on a train** in einen Zug einsteigen; *(while moving)* auf einen Zug aufspringen; **he ~ped on his bicycle** er schwang sich auf sein Fahrrad; **to ~ out** heraushüpfen; **he ~ped over the wall** er sprang über die Mauer
VT a *ditch* springen über *(+acc)*; *bus etc* schwarzfahren in *(+dat) or* mit
b *(Brit inf)* **~ it!** verschwinde, zieh Leine *(inf)*; **I ~ped it quick** ich habe mich schnell aus dem Staub gemacht *(inf)*

▸ **hop off** VI *(inf)* sich verdrücken *(inf)*, sich aus dem Staub machen *(inf)* (*with sth* mit etw)

hop[2] N *(Bot)* Hopfen *m*

hope [həʊp] ✪ 8.4 N *(also person)* Hoffnung *f*; **she is our best ~** sie ist unsere größte Hoffnung; **past** *or* **beyond ~** hoffnungslos, aussichtslos; **the patient is beyond ~** für den Patienten besteht keine Hoffnung mehr; **to be full of ~** hoffnungsvoll *or* voller Hoffnung sein; **my ~ is that ...** ich hoffe nur, dass ...; **in the ~ that ...** in der Hoffnung, dass ...; **in the ~ of doing sth** in der Hoffnung, etw zu tun; **to have (high** *or* **great) ~s of doing sth** hoffen, etw zu tun; **her family has high** *or* **great ~s of her** ihre Familie setzt große Hoffnungen in sie; **to live in ~ of sth** in der Hoffnung auf etw *(acc)* leben; **well, we live in ~** nun, wir hoffen eben (weiter); **to place one's ~ in sb/sth** seine Hoffnungen in *or* auf jdn/etw setzen; **don't get** *or* **build your ~s up too much** mach dir keine allzu großen Hoffnungen; **there is no ~ of him having survived** es besteht keine Hoffnung, dass er überlebt hat; **we have some ~ of success** es besteht die Hoffnung, dass wir Erfolg haben; **there's no ~ of that** da braucht man sich gar keine Hoffnungen zu machen; **where there's life there's ~** es ist noch nicht aller Tage Abend; *(said of invalid)* solange er/sie sich noch regt, besteht auch noch Hoffnung; **to give up/lose ~ of doing sth** die Hoffnung aufgeben, etw zu tun; **what a ~!** *(inf)* **some ~(s)!** *(inf)* schön wärs! *(inf)*; **she hasn't got a ~ in hell of passing her exams** *(inf)* es besteht nicht die geringste Chance, dass sie ihre Prüfung besteht; **~ springs eternal** *(prov)* wenn die Hoffnung nicht wäre!
VI hoffen (*for* auf *+acc*); **to ~ for the best** das Beste hoffen; **you can't ~ for anything else from him** man kann sich doch von ihm nichts anderes erhoffen; **one might have ~d for something better** man hätte (eigentlich) auf etwas

Besseres hoffen dürfen, man hätte sich eigentlich Besseres erhoffen dürfen; **a pay rise would be too much to ~ for** auf eine Gehaltserhöhung braucht man sich *(dat)* gar keine Hoffnungen zu machen; **I ~ so** hoffentlich, ich hoffe es; **I ~ not** hoffentlich nicht, ich hoffe nicht **VT** hoffen; **I ~ to see you** hoffentlich sehe ich Sie, ich hoffe, dass ich Sie sehe; **the party cannot ~ to win** für die Partei besteht keine Hoffnung zu gewinnen; **I ~ I'm not disturbing you** ich hoffe, dass ich Sie nicht störe; **to ~ against ~ that …** trotz allem die Hoffnung nicht aufgeben, dass …, wider alle Hoffnung hoffen, dass …; **hoping to hear from you** ich hoffe, von Ihnen zu hören, in der Hoffnung *(form)*, von Ihnen zu hören

hope chest N *(US)* Aussteuertruhe *f*

hoped-for ['həʊptfɔː'] ADJ erhofft

hopeful ['həʊpfʊl] **ADJ** **a** *person, face, action* hoffnungsvoll; **he was still ~ (that …)** er machte sich *(dat)* immer noch Hoffnungen(, dass …); **I am ~ (that) this misunderstanding will be rectified** ich habe die Hoffnung, dass dieses Missverständnis aufgeklärt wird; **people ~ of obtaining the few tickets available were all disappointed** Leute, die sich auf die wenigen erhältlichen Karten Hoffnungen machten, wurden alle enttäuscht; **they weren't very ~** sie hatten keine große Hoffnung; **the doctor was not very ~** der Arzt war nicht sehr zuversichtlich; **they are ~ about the negotiations** sie setzen Hoffnungen in die Verhandlungen; **he was feeling more ~** er war optimistischer; **don't be too ~** machen Sie sich *(dat)* keine zu großen Hoffnungen; **they continue to be ~** sie hoffen weiter, sie geben die Hoffnung nicht auf; **you're (being) ~!** *(iro)* du bist vielleicht ein Optimist! *(inf)*
b *(= promising) future* vielversprechend; *news* positiv; *forecast* optimistisch; **it is not a ~ sign for the future** es ist kein gutes Zeichen für die Zukunft
N *(= aspirant)* Anwärter(in) *m(f)*; *(= applicant)* Bewerber(in) *m(f)*; *(= candidate)* Kandidat(in) *m(f)*; **presidential ~s** Anwärter *pl* auf die Präsidentschaft; **our Olympic ~s** unsere olympischen Hoffnungen; **a young ~** *(seems likely to succeed)* eine junge Hoffnung; *(hopes to succeed)* ein hoffnungsvoller junger Mensch

hopefully ['həʊpfəlɪ] ADV **a** *ask, look, say* hoffnungsvoll; **I looked ~ around for a glimpse of my luggage** ich sah mich um, in der Hoffnung, mein Gepäck zu erspähen **b** *(inf: introducing sentence or as answer: = with any luck)* hoffentlich

hopeless ['həʊplɪs] ADJ **a** *(= impossible) love, attempt, task, cause* aussichtslos; *situation, case* hoffnungslos; *(= despairing) person, cry, sigh, gesture, look* verzweifelt; **to feel ~** keine Hoffnung haben; **pupils feel ~ about job prospects** Schüler haben keine Hoffnung auf eine Stelle
b *(inf) (= useless, terrible)* hoffnungslos; *(= incorrigible) drunk, liar, romantic* unverbesserlich; **she's a ~ manager/organizer** als Managerin/im Organisieren ist sie ein hoffnungsloser Fall; **I'm ~ at maths/sport** in Mathe/Sport bin ich hoffnungslos *or* ein hoffnungsloser Fall; **to be ~ at doing sth** etw absolut *or* überhaupt nicht können; **her room is in a ~ muddle** *or* **mess** in ihrem Zimmer herrscht ein hoffnungsloses *or* heilloses Durcheinander; **the buses are quite ~** die Busse kann man vergessen *(inf)*; **the weather/food was ~** das Wetter/Essen war unmöglich

hopelessly ['həʊplɪslɪ] ADV **a** *(= despairingly) sigh, shrug, cry* verzweifelt **b** *(emph: = utterly)* **~ confused** völlig verwirrt; **the service was ~ inadequate** der Service war völlig unmöglich; **I feel ~ inadequate** ich komme mir völlig minderwertig vor; **he got ~ lost in the fog** er hat sich im Nebel hoffnungslos verirrt; **I was ~ in love with Louise** ich hatte mich rettungslos in Louise verliebt; **I'm ~ bad at maths** in Mathe bin ich ein hoffnungsloser Fall

hopelessness ['həʊplɪsnɪs] N *(of love, attempt, cause, task)* Aussichtslosigkeit *f*; *(of situation)* Hoffnungslosigkeit *f*; **a sense of ~** ein Gefühl *nt* der Verzweiflung *or* Hoffnungslosigkeit

hop garden N Hopfengarten *m*

hophead ['hɒphed] N *(US pej inf)* Junkie *m (inf)*

hoplite ['hɒplaɪt] N Hoplit *m*

hop-o'-my-thumb ['hɒpəmaɪ'θʌm] N Knirps *m*, Stöpsel *m (inf)*

hopper ['hɒpə'] N **a** *(Tech)* Einfülltrichter *m*; *(for coal)* Einfüll- *or* Speisetrichter *m* **b** *(= young locust)* junge Heuschrecke

hop-picker ['hɒppɪkə'] N Hopfenpflücker(in) *m(f)*

hop-picking ['hɒppɪkɪŋ] N Hopfenernte *f*, Hopfenpflücken *nt*; **~ season** Hopfenernte *f*

hopping mad ['hɒpɪŋ'mæd] ADJ *(inf)* fuchsteufelswild *(inf)*

hop: **hopscotch** N Himmel-und-Hölle(-Spiel) *nt*, Hopse *f (inf)*; **hop, skip and jump**, N, **hop, step and jump** N Dreisprung *m*; **it's a ~ from here** es ist nur ein Katzensprung von hier

hopvine ['hɒpvaɪn] N *(= vine)* Hopfenranke *f*; *(= plant)* Hopfenpflanze *f*

Horace ['hɒrɪs] N Horaz *m*

Horatian [hə'reɪʃən] ADJ horazisch

horde [hɔːd] N **a** *(of wild animals)* Horde *f*; *(of insects)* Schwarm *m* **b** *(inf)* Masse *f*; *(of football fans, children etc)* Horde *f (pej)*

horizon [hə'raɪzn] N Horizont *m*; *(fig also)* Gesichtskreis *m no pl*; **new ~s** neue Horizonte; **a limited ~** ein enger *or* begrenzter Horizont; **on the ~** am Horizont; *(fig)* in Sicht; **the ship went over the ~** das Schiff verschwand am Horizont; **the sun was below the ~** die Sonne war hinter dem Horizont

horizontal [,hɒrɪ'zɒntl] ADJ waag(e)recht, horizontal; **~ line** Waag(e)rechte *f*, Horizontale *f*

horizontal: **horizontal bar** N Reck *nt*; **horizontal hold** N *(TV)* Zeilenfang *m*, Bildfang *m*

horizontally [,hɒrɪ'zɒntəlɪ] ADV horizontal

hormonal [hɔː'məʊnəl] ADJ hormonal, hormonell

hormone ['hɔːməʊn] N Hormon *nt*

hormone replacement therapy N Hormonersatztherapie *f*

hormone treatment N Hormonbehandlung *f*

horn [hɔːn] **N** **a** *(of cattle, substance, container, Mus)* Horn *nt*; *(inf, = trumpet, saxophone etc)* Kanne *(sl)*, Tüte *(sl) f*; **~s** *(of deer)* Geweih *nt*; *(fig, of cuckold)* Hörner *pl*; **caught on the ~s of a dilemma** in einer Zwickmühle; **~ of plenty** Füllhorn *nt*; **to lock ~s** *(lit)* beim Kampf die Geweihe verhaken; *(fig)* die Klingen kreuzen
b *(Aut)* Hupe *f*; *(Naut)* (Signal)horn *nt*; **to sound** *or* **blow the ~** *(Aut)* hupen, auf die Hupe drücken *(inf)*; *(Naut)* tuten, das Horn ertönen lassen
c *(of snail, insect)* Fühler *m*; **to draw** *or* **pull in one's ~s** *(fig)* einen Rückzieher machen; *(= spend less)* den Gürtel enger schnallen
d *(of crescent moon)* Spitze *f* (der Mondsichel)
VT *(= gore)* mit den Hörnern aufspießen; *(= butt)* auf die Hörner nehmen

▶ **horn in** VI *(inf) (= interfere)* mitmischen *(inf)* *(on* bei); *(= muscle in)* sich hineindrängen *(on* in *+acc)*; **dozens of entrepreneurs started horning in** zig Unternehmer versuchten, auch ein Stück vom Kuchen zu bekommen *(inf)*

horn *in cpds* Horn-; **hornbeam** N *(Bot)* Hain- *or* Weißbuche *f*; **hornbill** N *(Orn)* (Nas)hornvogel *m*; **horn bug** N *(Zool)* Hirschkäfer *m*

horned [hɔːnd] ADJ gehörnt, mit Hörnern

horned owl N Ohreule *f*

horned toad N Krötenechse *f*

hornet ['hɔːnɪt] N Hornisse *f*; **to stir up a ~'s nest** *(fig)* in ein Wespennest stechen

hornist ['hɔːnɪst] N *(Mus)* Hornist (in)*m(f)*

hornless ['hɔːnlɪs] ADJ ohne Hörner, hornlos

horn: **hornpipe** N *englischer Seemannstanz*; **horn-rimmed** ['hɔːnrɪmd] ADJ **~ glasses** *or* **spectacles** Hornbrille *f*

horny ['hɔːnɪ] ADJ *(+er)* **a** *(= like horn)* hornartig; *hands etc* schwielig; *soles* hornig **b** *(inf) (= sexually aroused)* scharf *(inf)*, geil *(inf)*; *(Brit: = sexually attractive)* scharf *(inf)*

horology [hɔː'rɒlədʒɪ] N *(measuring time)* Zeitmessung *f*; *(= watchmaking)* Uhrmacherkunst *f*

horoscope ['hɒrəskəʊp] N Horoskop *nt*

horrendous [hɒ'rendəs] ADJ **a** *(= horrific) accident, injury, war, experience* entsetzlich, grauenhaft; *crime, attack, violence* entsetzlich, abscheulich **b** *(inf: = dreadful) conditions, traffic* fürchterlich *(inf)*; *loss, cost, price, stupidity* horrend; **children's shoes are a ~ price** Kinderschuhe sind horrend teuer

horrendously [hɒ'rendəslɪ] ADV **a** *(= horrifically)* entsetzlich **b** *(inf: = dreadfully)* fürchterlich *(inf)*; *expensive* horrend

horrible ['hɒrɪbl] ADJ **a** *(inf: = awful)* schrecklich *(inf)*; *(= ghastly) food* grauenhaft *(inf)*; *clothes, colour, sight, smell, taste* scheußlich, abscheulich; *person* gemein, fies *(inf)*; **what a ~ thought!** was für eine schreckliche Vorstellung!; **to look ~** scheußlich aussehen; **that jumper looks ~ on you** in dem Pullover siehst du schrecklich aus; **to be ~ to sb** fies *(inf) or* gemein zu jdm sein **b** *(= horrific) death, crime, sound, war, accident, injury* grauenhaft

horribly ['hɒrɪblɪ] ADV **a** *(= in a horrible manner)* grauenhaft; *murdered* auf grauenhafte Art; **they died ~** sie starben einen grauenhaften Tod; **the man had been ~ injured** der Mann hatte grauenhafte Verletzungen davongetragen **b** *(inf: = dreadfully) drunk, expensive, embarrassed* schrecklich *(inf)*, fürchterlich *(inf)*

horrid ['hɒrɪd] ADJ entsetzlich, fürchterlich, schrecklich; **don't be so ~** sei nicht so gemein *(inf)*

horridly ['hɒrɪdlɪ] ADV *behave* schrecklich

horrific [hɒ'rɪfɪk] ADJ entsetzlich, schrecklich; *documentary* erschreckend; *price increase* horrend

horrifically [hɒ'rɪfɪkəlɪ] ADV grauenhaft; **he was ~ injured in the crash** bei dem Unfall trug er grauenhafte Verletzungen davon; **~ expensive** horrend teuer

horrify ['hɒrɪfaɪ] VT entsetzen; **he was horrified by** *or* **at the suggestion** er war über den Vorschlag entsetzt; **it horrifies me to think what …** ich denke (nur) mit Entsetzen daran, was …

horrifying ['hɒrɪfaɪɪŋ] ADJ schrecklich, fürchterlich, entsetzlich; *mutilation* grauenhaft; *crash* entsetzlich

horrifyingly ['hɒrɪfaɪɪŋlɪ] ADV *high, low, violent, fast* entsetzlich, fürchterlich; *mutilated, disfigured* grauenhaft; *crash, die* auf entsetzliche Weise; **and, perhaps most ~, this is only the beginning** und, was vielleicht am erschreckendsten ist, dies ist nur der Anfang

horror ['hɒrə'] **N** **a** Entsetzen *nt*, Grauen *nt*; *(= strong dislike)* Horror *m* (of vor *+dat)*; **to have a ~ of sth** einen Horror vor etw *(dat)* haben; **to have a ~ of doing sth** einen Horror davor haben, etw zu tun; **he has a ~ of growing old** er hat eine panische Angst vor dem Altwerden, ihm graut vor dem Altwerden; **she shrank back in ~** sie fuhr entsetzt zurück; **they watched in ~** sie sahen entsetzt zu; **a scene of ~** ein Bild *nt* des Grauens
b *usu pl (= horrifying thing, of war etc)* Schrecken *m*, Gräuel *m*
c *(inf)* **to be a real ~** furchtbar sein *(inf)*; **you little ~!** du kleines Ungeheuer! *(inf)*
d *(inf usages)* **to have the ~s** *(in delirium tremens)* weiße Mäuse sehen *(inf)*; **~ of ~s** *(referring to an actual event)* oh Schreck *(inf)*; **if, ~ of ~s, …** wenn, Gott behüte, …
ATTR Horror-; **~ film** *or* **movie** *(esp US)* Horrorfilm *m*; **~ story** Horrorgeschichte *f*; **most people have a ~ story about holidays** fast jeder kann eine Horrorgeschichte aus dem Urlaub erzählen; **~ scenario** Horrorszenario *nt*; **~ trip** *(inf)* Horrortrip *m*

horror-stricken ['hɒrə,strɪkən], **horror-struck** ['hɒrə,strʌk] ADJ von Entsetzen *or* Grauen gepackt; **I was ~ when he told me** mir grauste es *or* ich war hell entsetzt, als er es mir erzählte

hors de combat [ɔːdəˈkɒmbɑː] ADJ *(lit, fig)* außer Gefecht gesetzt, kampfunfähig

hors d'oeuvre [ɔːˈdɜːv] N Hors d'oeuvre *nt*, Vorspeise *f*

horse [hɔːs] N **a** Pferd *nt*, Ross *nt (liter, pej)*; **he lost a lot of money on the ~s** *(betting)* er hat beim Pferderennen *or* bei der Pferdewette viel Geld verloren
b *(fig usages)* **wild ~s would not drag me there** keine zehn Pferde würden mich dahin bringen; **to eat like a ~** wie ein Scheunendrescher *m* essen *or* fressen *(inf)*; **I could eat a ~** ich könnte ein ganzes Pferd essen; **to work like a ~** wie ein Pferd arbeiten; **information straight from the ~'s mouth** Informationen *pl* aus erster Hand; **to back the wrong ~** aufs falsche Pferd setzen; **to change** *or* **switch ~s in midstream** mitten im Strom die Pferde wechseln; **it's a case of ~s for courses** *(Brit)* man muss den Richtigen/die Richtige/das Richtige dafür finden
c *(Gymnastics)* Pferd *nt*; *(= sawhorse)* Sägebock *m*
d *(Mil) collective sing* Reiterei *f*, Kavallerie *f*; **light ~** leichte Kavallerie; **a thousand ~** tausend Reiter *or* Berittene

▶ **horse about** *(Brit) or* **around** VI *(inf)* herumalbern *(inf)*

horse: **horse-and-buggy** ADJ *(US) approach, system* vorsintflutlich *(inf)*; **horse artillery** N berittene Artillerie; **horseback** ADV **to ride ~** (zu Pferd) reiten N **on ~** zu Pferd; **to travel by** *or* **on ~** zu Pferd reisen; **to go/set off on ~** (zu Pferd) reiten/wegreiten; **policemen on ~** berittene Polizisten; **horsebean** N Saubohne *f*; **horsebox** N *(= van)* Pferdetransporter *m*; *(= trailer)* Pferdetransportwagen *m*; *(in stable)* Box *f*; **horse brass** N Zaumzeugbeschlag *m*; **horse breeder** N Pferdezüchter(in) *m(f)*; **horse chestnut** N *(= tree, fruit)* Rosskastanie *f*; **horse doctor** N *(inf)* Viehdoktor(in) *m(f) (inf)*; **horse-drawn** ADJ von Pferden gezogen; *hearse, milk cart* pferdebespannt *attr*; **~ cart** Pferdewagen *m*; **~ carriage** Kutsche *f*; **horseflesh** N *(= meat of horse)* Pferdefleisch *nt*; *(= horses collectively)* Pferde *pl*; **a good judge of ~** ein guter Pferdekenner; **horsefly** N (Pferde)bremse *f*; **Horse Guards** PL berittene Garde, Gardekavallerie *f*; **horsehair** N Rosshaar *nt* ADJ *attr* Rosshaar-; **~ mattress** Rosshaarmatratze *f*; **horse latitudes** PL Rossbreiten *pl*; **horse laugh** N wieherndes Lachen *or* Gelächter; **horseless** ADJ ohne Pferd; **~ carriage** *(old: = motorcar)* selbstfahrender Wagen; **horseman** N Reiter *m*; **horsemanship** N Reitkunst *f*; **horse meat** N Pferdefleisch *nt*; **horse opera** N *(hum inf: Film)* Western *m*; **horseplay** N Alberei *f*, Balgerei *f*; **horse pond** N Pferdeschwemme *f*; **horsepower** N Pferdestärke *f*; **a 200 ~ car/engine** ein Auto/Motor mit 200 PS *or* Pferdestärken; **horse race** N Pferderennen *nt*; **horse racing** N Pferderennsport *m*; *(= races)* Pferderennen *pl*; **horseradish** N Meerrettich *m*; **horse-riding** N Reiten *nt*; **horse sense** N gesunder Menschenverstand; **horseshit** N *(fig sl: = nonsense)* Scheiß *m (inf)*; **horseshoe** N Hufeisen *nt* ATTR hufeisenförmig, Hufeisen-; **~ shape** Hufeisenform *f*; **~ throwing** Hufeisenwerfen *nt*; **horse show** N Pferdeschau *f*; **horse trading** N *(fig)* Kuhhandel *m*; **horsewhip** N Reitpeitsche *f* VT auspeitschen; **horsewoman** N Reiterin *f*

horsey, horsy [ˈhɔːsɪ] ADJ *(+er)* **a** *(= keen on horses) person, family* pferdenärrisch; **~ people** Pferdenarren *pl*; **she's a bit ~** sie ist ein ziemlicher Pferdenarr *or* -fan **b** *(pej: = horse-like) person* pferdeähnlich; **~ face** Pferdegesicht *nt*

hortative [ˈhɔːtətɪv] ADJ anspornend

horticultural [ˌhɔːtɪˈkʌltʃərəl] ADJ Garten(bau)-; **~ show** Gartenschau *f*, Gartenbauausstellung *f*

horticulturalist [ˌhɔːtɪˈkʌltʃərəlɪst] N Gärtner(in) *m(f)*

horticulture [ˈhɔːtɪkʌltʃəˈ] N Gartenbau(kunst *f*) *m*

horticulturist [ˌhɔːtɪˈkʌltʃərɪst] N Gärtner(in) *m(f)*

hosanna [həʊˈzænə] INTERJ hos(i)anna N Hos(i)anna *nt*

hose¹ [həʊz] N Schlauch *m* VT *(also* **hose down***)* abspritzen

▶ **hose out** VT *sep* ausspritzen

hose² N *no pl* **a** *(Comm: = stockings)* Strümpfe *pl*, Strumpfwaren *pl* **b** *(Hist, for men)* (Knie)hose *f*

hosepipe [ˈhəʊzpaɪp] N *(esp Brit)* Schlauch *m*

hosepipe ban N *durch Wasserknappheit bedingtes Verbot, den Rasen zu sprengen oder das Auto mit dem Gartenschlauch zu waschen*

hosier [ˈhəʊʒəˈ] N Strumpfwarenhändler(in) *m(f)*

hosiery [ˈhəʊʒərɪ] N Strumpfwaren *pl*

hosp *abbr of* **hospital**

hospice [ˈhɒspɪs] N **a** *(for terminally ill)* Pflegeheim *nt (für unheilbar Kranke)* **b** *(for travellers)* Hospiz *nt*

hospitable [hɒsˈpɪtəbl] ADJ **a** *(= friendly, sociable) person* gastfreundlich, gastlich; *welcome* gastlich; **to be ~ to sb** jdn gastfreundlich *or* gastlich aufnehmen **b** *(= favourable) place, climate* gastlich; *environment* freundlich; **~ to sth** *(soil, environment)* günstig für etw

hospitably [hɒsˈpɪtəblɪ] ADV gastfreundlich, gastlich

hospital [ˈhɒspɪtl] N Krankenhaus *nt*, Klinik *f*, Hospital *nt (old, Sw)*; **in** *or (US)* **in the ~** im Krankenhaus; **he's got to go (in)to ~** *or (US)* **(in)to the ~** er muss ins Krankenhaus (gehen)

hospital *in cpds* Krankenhaus-; **hospital administration** N Krankenhausverwaltung *f*; **hospital administrator** N Krankenhausverwalter(in) *m(f)*; **hospital bed** N Krankenhausbett *nt*; **hospital case** N Fall, der im Krankenhaus behandelt werden muss; **hospital facilities** PL *(= equipment)* Krankenhauseinrichtung(en) *f(pl)*; *(= hospitals)* Kranken(heil)anstalnten *pl*

hospitalism [ˈhɒspɪtlɪzəm] N *(Med)* Hospitalismus *m*

hospitality [ˌhɒspɪˈtælɪtɪ] N Gastfreundschaft *f*, Gastlichkeit *f*; *(Comm: = refreshments etc for clients)* Bewirtung *f*

hospitalization [ˌhɒspɪtəlaɪˈzeɪʃən] N **a** Einweisung *f* ins Krankenhaus; *(= stay in hospital)* Krankenhausaufenthalt *m* **b** *(US: = hospitalization insurance)* Versicherung *f* für Krankenhauspflege

hospitalize [ˈhɒspɪtəlaɪz] VT ins Krankenhaus einweisen; **he was ~d for three months** er lag drei Monate lang im Krankenhaus

hospital: **hospital nurse** N Krankenschwester *f* (im Krankenhaus); **hospital porter** N Pfleger(in) *m(f)*; *(= doorman)* Pförtner(in) *m(f)* (im Krankenhaus); **hospital ship** N Lazarett- *or* Krankenschiff *nt*; **hospital train** N Lazarettzug *m*

Host [həʊst] N *(Eccl)* Hostie *f*

host¹ [həʊst] N **a** Gastgeber(in) *m(f)*; *(in own home)* Hausherr(in) *m(f)*, Gastgeber(in) *m(f)*; **to be** *or* **play ~ to sb** jds Gastgeber(in) *m(f)* sein; *(in own home also)* jdn zu Besuch *or* Gast haben; **to play ~ to an event** eine Veranstaltung ausrichten
b *(in hotel etc)* Wirt(in) *m(f)*; **your ~s are Mr and Mrs X** Ihre Wirtsleute sind Herr und Frau X; **mine ~** *(obs, hum)* der Herr Wirt
c *(Bot)* Wirt(spflanze *f*) *m*; *(Zool)* Wirt(stier *nt*) *m*
d *(on TV programme etc)* Gastgeber(in) *m(f)*
e *(also* **host computer***)* Host(-Rechner) *m*
VT *banquet, ball, TV programme* Gastgeber(in) sein bei; *(country, city) event, conference, Olympics* ausrichten

host² N **a** Menge *f*, Masse *f (inf)*; **he has a ~ of friends** er hat massenweise *(inf) or* eine Menge Freunde; **a whole ~ of reasons** eine ganze Menge *or* Anzahl von Gründen **b** *(obs, liter)* Heerschar *f (obs, liter)*; **a ~ of angels** eine Engelschar; **the Lord of Hosts** der Herr der Heerscharen

hostage [ˈhɒstɪdʒ] N Geisel *f*; **to take/hold sb ~** jdn als Geisel nehmen/halten; **to take ~s** Geiseln nehmen

hostage: **hostage-taker** N Geiselnehmer(in) *m(f)*; **hostage-taking** N Geiselnahme *f*

host country N Gastland *nt*

host drive N *(Comput)* Hostlaufwerk *nt*

hostel [ˈhɒstəl] N *(for students, workers etc)* (Wohn)heim *nt* VI **to go ~ling** in Jugendherbergen übernachten

hosteller, hosteler *(US)* [ˈhɒstələˈ] N Heimbewohner(in) *m(f)*; *(in youth hostel)* Herbergsgast *m*

hostelry [ˈhɒstəlrɪ] N *(obs)* Herberge *f (liter)*

hostess [ˈhəʊstes] N **a** *(person)* Gastgeberin *f*; *(in own home)* Hausherrin *f*, Gastgeberin *f*; **to be** *or* **play ~ to sb** jds Gastgeberin sein; *(in own home also)* jdn zu Besuch *or* Gast haben **b** *(in hotel etc)* Wirtin *f* **c** *(in nightclub)* Hostess *f* **d** *(= air hostess)* Stewardess *f*; *(at exhibition etc)* Hostess *f* **e** *(on TV programme etc)* Gastgeberin *f*

hostess trolley N Servierwagen *m*

hostile [ˈhɒstaɪl] ADJ **a** *(= antagonistic) person (in attitude, feelings)* feindselig; *(= opposed in principle) person, society, press, government* feindlich (gesinnt); *question, attitude, reception, atmosphere* feindselig; *(Mil) fire, forces, aircraft* feindlich; **to feel ~** feindselig (gesinnt) sein; **to be ~ to sb** sich jdm gegenüber feindselig verhalten; **to be ~ to** *or* **toward(s) sth** einer Sache *(dat)* feindlich gegenüberstehen; **a church ~ to any form of birth control** eine Kirche, die jede Art von Geburtenkontrolle ablehnt
b *(= unfavourable) conditions, environment, weather* unwirtlich
c *(Econ, Fin) bid, takeover, bidder* feindlich

hostility [hɒsˈtɪlɪtɪ] N **a** Feindseligkeit *f*; *(between people)* Feindschaft *f*; **to show ~ to sb** sich jdm gegenüber feindselig verhalten; **to show ~ to sth** einer Sache *(dat)* feindlich gegenüberstehen; **feelings of ~** feindselige Gefühle *pl*; **he feels no ~ toward(s) anybody** er ist niemandem feindlich gesinnt; **there is some ~ among them to the idea** sie sind teilweise gegen den Gedanken; **~ to foreigners** Ausländerfeindlichkeit *f* **b** **hostilities** PL *(= warfare)* Feindseligkeiten *pl*

hostler [ˈɒsləˈ] N = **ostler**

hot [hɒt] ADJ *(+er)* **a** heiß; *meal, tap, drink* warm; **I am** *or* **feel ~** mir ist (es) heiß; **with ~ and cold water** mit warm und kalt Wasser; **it was a ~ and tiring climb** der Aufstieg machte warm und müde; **the weather is ~** es ist heißes Wetter; **in the ~ weather** bei dem heißen Wetter, wenn es so heiß ist; **the room was ~** in dem Zimmer war es heiß; **Africa is a ~ country** in Afrika ist es heiß; **to get ~** *(things)* heiß werden; **I'm getting ~** mir wird (es) warm
b *(to taste) curry, spices etc* scharf
c *(inf) radioactive material* radioaktiv, heiß *(inf)*
d *(inf) stolen goods* heiß *(inf)*; **it's too ~ to sell** so heiße Ware lässt sich nicht verkaufen *(inf)*
e *(inf: = in demand) product* zugkräftig; **she's the ~test property in show business** sie ist die heißeste Nummer im Showbusiness; **... are totally ~ this season** ... sind momentan total in *(inf)*
f *(inf: = good, competent)* stark *(inf)*; **the ~test show in town** die stärkste Show in der Stadt *(inf)*; **he's pretty ~ at maths** in Mathe ist er ganz schön stark *(inf)*; **I'm not feeling too ~** mir gehts nicht besonders *(inf)*; **she's so ~** *(inf)* sie ist eine starke Frau *(inf)*
g *(fig)* **to be (a) ~ favourite** *(Brit) or* **favorite** *(US)* hoch favorisiert sein, der große Favorit sein; **~ tip** heißer Tipp; **a ~ issue** eine umstrit-

tene Frage; **a ~ topic of conversation** ein kontroverses Gesprächsthema; **~ news** das Neuste vom Neuen; **~ off the press** gerade erschienen; **the latest designs ~ from Milan** die neuesten Entwürfe, gerade aus Mailand eingetroffen; **the competition was very ~** der Wettbewerb war äußerst scharf; **she has a ~ temper** sie braust leicht auf, sie hat ein hitziges Wesen; **she's too ~ to handle** *(inf)* mit der wird keiner fertig *(inf)*; **it's too ~ to handle** *(political issue, in journalism)* das ist ein heißes Eisen; **that's a ~ button, that hits a ~ button** *(US)* das ist ein heißes Eisen; **to get into ~ water** in Schwulitäten kommen *(inf)*, in (des) Teufels Küche kommen *(inf)*; **to be/get (all) ~ and bothered** *(inf)* ganz aufgeregt sein/werden (*about* wegen); **to feel ~ and bothered** *(inf)* ins Schwitzen kommen *(inf)*; **to get ~ under the collar about sth** wegen etw in Rage geraten; *(= embarrassed)* wegen etw verlegen werden; **I went ~ and cold all over** (*inf, with emotion*) mir wurde es ganz anders *(inf)*; **things started getting ~ in the tenth round** *(inf)* in der zehnten Runde wurde es langsam spannend *or* gings los *(inf)*; **to make things too ~ for sb** *(inf)* jdm die Hölle heißmachen *(inf)*, jdm einheizen *(inf)*; **it's getting too ~ for me here** *(inf)* hier wird mir der Boden unter den Füßen zu heiß; **that girl's smoking ~** (*US sl*) die Frau ist voll scharf *(inf)* → **trail N b**

ADV *(+er)* **the engine's running ~** der Motor läuft heiß; **he keeps blowing ~ and cold** er sagt einmal hü und einmal hott

N to have the ~s for sb *(inf)* auf jdn scharf sein *(inf)*

▶ **hot up VI** *(inf)* **the pace is hotting up** das Tempo wird schneller; **things are hotting up in the Middle East** die Lage im Nahen Osten spitzt sich zu *or* verschärft sich; **things are hotting up** es geht langsam los; *(party also)* die Sache kommt in Schwung; **the bars rarely hot up before midnight** in den Bars geht es selten vor Mitternacht richtig los **VT** *sep (fig) music* verpoppen *(inf)*; *pace* steigern; *surveillance* verschärfen; *engine* frisieren

hot: **hot air N** *(fig)* leeres Gerede, Gewäsch *nt*; **hot-air balloon N** Heißluftballon *m*; **hot-air drier N** Heißlufttrockner *m*; **hotbed N a** *(fig)* Brutstätte *f*, Nährboden *m* (*of* für) **b** *(Hort)* Mist- *or* Frühbeet *nt*; **hot-blooded ADJ** heißblütig; **hotcake N** *(US)* = **pancake**

hotchpotch ['hɒtʃpɒtʃ] **N** *(Brit)* Durcheinander *nt*, Mischmasch *m*

hot: **hot cross bun N** *Rosinenbrötchen mit kleinem Teigkreuz, wird in der Karwoche gegessen*; **hot-desking N** Desksharing *nt*; **hot dog N** Hotdog *m or nt*; **hot-dogging N** *(Ski)* Freestyle *nt*

hotel [həʊ'tel] **N** Hotel *nt*

hotelier [həʊ'teliə'] **N** Hotelier *m*

hotel: **hotel industry N** Hotelgewerbe *nt*, Hotellerie *f*; **hotel keeper N** Hotelier *m*, Hotelbesitzer(in) *m(f)*; **hotel manager N** Hoteldirektor(in) *m(f)*; **hotel porter N** Haus- *or* Hoteldiener(in) *m(f)*; **hotel room N** Hotelzimmer *nt*

hot: **hot flushes PL** *(Med)* fliegende Hitze; **hotfoot** *(inf)* **ADV** *arrive* stehenden Fußes **VT he ~ed it back home/out of town** er ging schleunigst nach Hause/verließ schleunigst die Stadt; **hot gospeller N** Erweckungsprediger(in) *m(f)*; **hothead N** Hitzkopf *m*; **hot-headed ADJ** hitzköpfig, unbeherrscht; **hothouse N** *(lit, fig)* Treibhaus *nt* **ADJ** *attr (lit)* Treibhaus-; *(fig) atmosphere* spannungsgeladen, angespannt; **~ plant/vegetables** Treibhauspflanze *f*/-gemüse *nt*; **hot-housing N** *Intensivunterricht für besonders begabte Kleinkinder*; **hot jazz N** Hot Jazz *m*; **hot key N** *(Comput)* Hotkey *m*, Abkürzungstaste *f*; **hot line N** *(Pol)* heißer Draht; *(TV etc)* Hotline *f*; **to get on the ~** *(Pol)* sich an den heißen Draht hängen *(inf)*

hotly ['hɒtlɪ] **ADV a** *(= fiercely) debate, deny, say, protest* heftig; *contest, dispute* heiß; **a ~ contested final** ein heiß umkämpftes Finale; **a ~ contested** *or* **disputed move** eine heiß umstrittene Maßnahme; **this claim is ~ disputed** diese Behauptung ist heiß umstritten *or* wird heftig bestritten **b he was ~ pursued by two policemen** zwei Polizisten waren ihm dicht auf den Fersen *(inf)*; **he has been ~ pursued by the media** die Medien haben ihn auf Schritt und Tritt verfolgt **c to be ~ tipped for sth** als heißer Favorit für etw gelten; **the ~ tipped new band** die neue Band, der eine große Zukunft vorausgesagt wird

hot: **hot metal** *(Typ)* **N** Blei *nt*; *(= setting)* Bleisatz *m*; **hot-metal ADJ** *attr* **~ setting** Bleisatz *m*; **hot pants PL** heiße Höschen, Hotpants *pl*, Hot Pants *pl*; **hot pepper N** Peperoni *f*; **hotplate N a** *(of stove)* Koch- *or* Heizplatte *f* **b** *(= plate warmer)* Warmhalteplatte *f*, Wärmplatte *f*; **hotpot N** (*esp Brit Cook*) Fleischeintopf *m* mit Kartoffeleinlage; **hot potato N** *(fig inf)* heißes Eisen; **hot rod N** *(Aut)* hochfrisiertes Auto; **hot seat N** Schleudersitz *m*; (*US inf: = electric chair*) elektrischer Stuhl; **to be in the ~** auf dem Schleudersitz sein; *(in quiz etc)* auf dem Armsünderbänkchen sitzen *(hum)*; **to step into the ~** auf den Schleudersitz kommen; **hot shoe N** *(Phot)* Steckschuh *m*; **hotshot** *(inf)* **N** Kanone *f (inf)*, Ass *nt (inf)* **ADJ** *attr* Spitzen- *(inf)*, erstklassig; **hot spot N** *(Pol)* Krisenherd *m*; (*inf: = club etc*) heißer Schuppen *(inf)*; **hot spring N** heiße Quelle, Thermalquelle *f*; **hot stuff N** *(inf)* **this is ~** *(= very good)* das ist große Klasse *(inf)*; *(= provocative)* das ist Zündstoff; **she's/he's ~** *(= very good)* sie/er ist große Klasse *(inf)* *or* eine Kanone *(inf)*; *(= very sexy)* das ist eine Klassefrau *(inf)* *or* scharfer Braut *(sl)*/ein scharfer Typ *(inf)*; **hot-tempered ADJ** leicht aufbrausend, jähzornig

Hottentot ['hɒtəntɒt] **N a** Hottentotte *m*, Hottentottin *f* **b** *(Ling)* Hottentottisch *nt* **ADJ** hottentottisch

hottie ['hɒtɪ] **N a** (*Austral inf*) Wärmflasche *f* **b** (*US sl: = sexy person*) total scharfer Typ *(inf)*

hot-water bottle [ˌhɒt'wɔːtəˌbɒtl] **N** Wärmflasche *f*

hotwire ['hɒtwaɪə'] **VT** (*Aut inf*) *car* kurzschließen

hoummos, houm(o)us ['huːməs] **N** *orientalische Creme aus Kichererbsen, Sesam und Knoblauch*

hound [haʊnd] **N a** *(Hunt)* (Jagd)hund *m*; **the ~s lost the scent** die Meute verlor die Spur; **to ride to ~s** *(person)* mit der Meute jagen **b** *(any dog)* Hund *m*, Tier *nt* **VT** hetzen, jagen; **to be ~ed** gehetzt sein; **to be ~ed by the press** von der Presse verfolgt werden

▶ **hound down VT** *sep* Jagd machen auf *(+acc)*, niederhetzen *(form)*; *criminal also* zur Strecke bringen

▶ **hound out VT** *sep* verjagen, vertreiben (*of* aus)

hound's-tooth (check) ['haʊndztuːθ(ˌtʃek)] **N** Hahnentritt(muster *nt*) *m*

hour ['aʊə'] **N a** Stunde *f*; *(= time of day)* Zeit *f*; **half an ~, a half ~** eine halbe Stunde; **three-quarters of an ~** eine Dreiviertelstunde, drei viertel Stunden; **a quarter of an ~** eine Viertelstunde, eine viertel Stunde; **an ~ and a half** anderthalb *or* eineinhalb Stunden; **it's two ~s' walk from here** von hier geht man zwei Stunden, von hier sind es zu Fuß zwei Stunden; **two ~s' walk from here there is an old castle** nach einem Weg von zwei Stunden kommt man an ein altes Schloss *or* zu einem alten Schloss; **at 1500/1530 ~s** um 15.00/15.30 Uhr; **at fifteen hundred/fifteen thirty ~s** *(spoken)* um fünfzehn Uhr/fünfzehn Uhr dreißig; **~ by ~** mit jeder Stunde, stündlich; **~ after ~** Stunde um Stunde; **on the ~** zur vollen Stunde; **every ~ on the ~** jede volle Stunde; **20 minutes past the ~** 20 Minuten nach; **at the ~ of his death** in der Stunde seines Todes, in seiner Todesstunde; **at an early ~** früh, zu früher Stunde *(geh)*; **at a late ~** spät, zu später Stunde *(geh)*; **at all ~s (of the day and night)** zu jeder (Tages- und Nacht)zeit; **what! at this ~ of the night!** was! zu dieser nachtschlafenden Zeit!; **what is the ~?** *(old)* wie viel Uhr ist es?; **to drive at 50 kilometres an ~** 50 Kilometer in der Stunde *or* 50 Stundenkilometer fahren; **a 30 mile(s) an** *or* **per ~ limit** eine Geschwindigkeitsbegrenzung von 30 Meilen in der Stunde; **to be paid by the ~** stundenweise bezahlt werden; **she is paid £6 an ~** sie bekommt £6 pro Stunde

b hours PL (*inf: = a long time*) Stunden *pl*; **for ~s** stundenlang; **~s and ~s** Stunden und aber Stunden; **I was ~s late** ich war sehr spät dran *(inf)*, ich hatte mich um Stunden verspätet; **the train was ~s late** der Zug hatte Stunden Verspätung; **he took ~s to do it** er brauchte ewig lang *(inf)* *or* stundenlang dazu **c hours PL** *(of banks, shops etc)* Geschäftszeit(en) *f(pl)*; *(of pubs, park etc)* Öffnungszeiten *pl*; *(of post office)* Schalterstunden *pl*; *(= office hours)* Dienststunden *pl*; *(= working hours etc)* Arbeitszeit *f*; *(of doctor etc)* Sprechstunde *f*; **out of/after ~s** *(in pubs)* außerhalb der gesetzlich erlaubten Zeit/nach der Polizeistunde; *(of school)* außerhalb der Unterrichtszeit/nach Schulschluss; *(in shops etc)* außerhalb der Geschäftszeit(en)/nach Laden- *or* Geschäftsschluss; *(in office etc)* außerhalb der Arbeitszeit/nach Dienstschluss; *(of doctor etc)* außerhalb/nach der Sprechstunde; **what are your ~s?** *(shops, pubs etc)* wann haben Sie geöffnet *or* offen?; *(employee)* wie ist Ihre Arbeitszeit?; **the ~s are good** die Arbeitszeit ist günstig; **to work long ~s** einen langen Arbeitstag haben; *(doctors, nurse, policeman etc)* lange Dienststunden haben **d** *(fig)* **his ~ has come** seine Stunde ist gekommen; *(= death also)* sein (letztes) Stündchen hat geschlagen; **in the ~ of danger** in der Stunde der Gefahr; **the man/hero of the ~** der Mann/Held der Stunde; **the issue of the ~** die aktuelle Frage

hour: **hourglass N** Sanduhr *f*, Stundenglas *nt (old)* **ADJ** *figure* kurvenreich; **hour hand N** Stundenzeiger *m*, kleiner Zeiger

houri ['huːrɪ] **N** *(Rel)* Huri *f*; *(fig)* orientalische Schönheit

hourly ['aʊəlɪ] **ADJ a** *(= every hour)* stündlich; **an ~ bus service** ein stündlich verkehrender Bus; **at ~ intervals** stündlich, jede Stunde; **at two-~ intervals** alle zwei Stunden **b** *(= per hour) earnings* pro Stunde; *worker, job* stundenweise bezahlt; **~ wage** *or* **pay** Stundenlohn *m*; **~ rate** Stundensatz *m*; **they are engaged on an ~ rate** sie werden stundenweise engagiert; **an ~ fee** stundenweise Bezahlung; **on an ~ basis** stundenweise

ADV a (*lit: = every hour*) stündlich, jede Stunde; *(fig) (= constantly)* ständig; *diminish, grow* mit jeder Stunde; *(= at any moment) expect* stündlich, jeden Augenblick **b** *pay* stundenweise; **~ paid work/worker** stundenweise bezahlte Arbeit/Arbeitskraft

house [haʊs] **N** *pl* **houses** ['haʊzɪz] **a** Haus *nt*; *(= household)* Haushalt *m*; **at my ~** bei mir (zu Hause *or* zuhause (*Aus, Sw*)); **to my ~** zu mir (nach Hause *or* nachhause (*Aus, Sw*)); **to keep ~ (for sb)** (jdm) den Haushalt führen; **to set up ~** einen eigenen Hausstand gründen; *(in particular area)* sich niederlassen; **they set up ~ together** sie gründeten einen gemeinsamen Hausstand; **to play at ~s** Vater und Mutter spielen; **to put** *or* **set one's ~ in order** *(fig)* seine Angelegenheiten in Ordnung bringen; **he gets on like a ~ on fire with her** *(inf)* er kommt ausgezeichnet *or* prima *(inf)* mit ihr aus; **they get on like a ~ on fire** *(inf)* sie kommen ausgezeichnet miteinander aus; **as safe as ~s** *(Brit)* bombensicher *(inf)*; **a steak ~** ein Steakhaus *nt*; **a coffee ~** ein Café *nt*; **House of God** *or* **the Lord** Haus *nt* Gottes, Gotteshaus *nt*; **a ~ of worship** ein Ort *m* des Gebets, ein Haus *nt* der Andacht

b *(Pol)* **the upper/lower ~** das Ober-/Unterhaus; **House of Commons/Lords** *(Brit)* (britisches) Unter-/Oberhaus; **the House** *(Brit inf)* das Parlament; *(as address also)* das Hohe Haus; **House of Representatives** *(US)* Repräsentanten-

haus *nt;* **the Houses of Parliament** das Parlament(sgebäude)
c *(= family, line)* Haus *nt,* Geschlecht *nt;* **the House of Bourbon** das Haus Bourbon, das Geschlecht der Bourbonen
d *(= firm)* Haus *nt;* **on the ~** auf Kosten des Hauses; *(on the company)* auf Kosten der Firma; **we ordered a bottle of ~ red** wir bestellten eine Flasche von dem roten Hauswein
e *(Theat)* Haus *nt;* *(= performance)* Vorstellung *f;* **to bring the ~ down** *(inf)* ein Bombenerfolg (beim Publikum) sein *(inf)*
f *(in boarding school)* Gruppenhaus *nt;* *(in day school) eine von mehreren Gruppen verschiedenaltriger Schüler, die z. B. in Wettkämpfen gegeneinander antreten*
g *(in debate)* **House** Versammlung *f;* **the motion before the House** das Diskussionsthema, das zur Debatte *or* Diskussion stehende Thema; **this House believes capital punishment should be reintroduced** wir stellen die Frage zur Diskussion, ob die Todesstrafe wieder eingeführt werden sollte; *(in conclusion)* die Anwesenden sind der Meinung, dass die Todesstrafe wieder eingeführt werden sollte
h **full ~** *(Cards)* Full House *nt;* *(= bingo)* volle Karte
i *(Mus)* House *m* [hauz]
VT *people, goods, collection* unterbringen; *(Tech also)* einbauen; **this building ~s three offices/ten families** in diesem Gebäude sind drei Büros/zehn Familien untergebracht, dieses Gebäude beherbergt drei Büros/zehn Familien; **the sauna is ~d in their garage** die Sauna befindet sich in ihrer Garage

HOUSE

Britisches und amerikanisches Englisch haben für Häuser und Wohnungen häufig verschiedene Ausdrücke. Mit **flat** (Brit) oder **apartment** (US) wird allgemein eine Wohnung innerhalb eines größeren Gebäudes bezeichnet. Bei einem **condominium** (US) handelt es sich um einen Wohnblock mit Eigentumswohnungen, dessen Gemeinschaftseinrichtungen allen Bewohnern gemeinsam gehören. **Terraced** (Brit) oder **row** (US) **houses** heißen die Reihenhäuser. Doppelhäuser heißen **semi-detached** (Brit) oder **duplex** (US) **houses**. **Detached houses** (Brit) sind frei stehende Eigenheime, die normalerweise von einem Garten umgeben sind. Für die USA typisch sind die **ranch houses** (US), lang gezogene, einstöckige Gebäude, und **colonials** (US), zweigeschossige Schindel- oder Backsteinhäuser im traditionellen Stil, denen eine überdachte Veranda vorgebaut ist.

house *in cpds* Haus-; **house arrest** N Hausarrest *m;* **houseboat** N Hausboot *nt;* **housebound** ADJ ans Haus gefesselt; **houseboy** N *(dated)* Hausdiener *m;* **housebreaker** N Einbrecher(in) *m(f);* **housebreaking** N Einbruch(sdiebstahl) *m;* **house-broken** ADJ *(US: = house-trained)* stubenrein; **house call** N *(of doctor)* Hausbesuch *m;* **house captain** N *(Brit Sch) (in boarding school)* Haussprecher(in) *m(f),* Hausälteste(r) *mf;* *(in day school)* Gruppensprecher(in) *m(f),* Gruppenälteste(r) *mf;* **house cleaning** N **a** *(= cleaning)* Hausputz *m,* Großreinemachen *nt* **b** *(fig)* Säuberungsaktion *f;* **housecoat** N Morgenrock *or* -mantel *m;* **house detective** N *(in hotel, shop etc)* Hausdetektiv *m;* **house dog** N Haushund *m;* **housedress** N *(US)* Schürzenkleid *nt;* **house dust mite** N *(Zool)* Haisstaubmilbe *f;* **~ allergy** Hausstaubmilbenallergie *f;* **housefly** N Stubenfliege *f;* **houseguest** N (Haus)gast *m*

household ['haʊshəʊld] **N** Haushalt *m;* **a male-only ~** ein Haushalt, der nur aus Männern besteht **ATTR** Haushalts-; **~ appliance** Haushaltsgerät *nt;* **~ furniture** Wohnmöbel *pl;* **~ chores** häusliche Pflichten *pl,* Hausarbeit *f;* **~ commodities** Haushaltswaren *pl;* **~ goods** Hausrat *m,* Haushaltswaren *pl*

Household Cavalry N *(Brit)* Gardekavallerie *f*

householder ['haʊsˌhəʊldə'] N Haus-/Wohnungsinhaber(in) *m(f)*

household: **household god** N Hausgott *m;* **the telly has become the ~ in many homes** der Fernseher ist in vielen Familien zum Götzen geworden; **household insurance** N Hausratversicherung *f;* **household linen** N Tisch- und Bettwäsche *f,* Weißwäsche *f (dated);* **household name** N **to be a ~** ein Begriff sein; **to become a ~** zu einem Begriff werden; **household word** N Begriff *m;* **to become a ~** zu einem Begriff werden

house: **house-hunt** VI auf Haussuche sein; **they have started ~ing** sie haben angefangen, nach einem Haus zu suchen; **house-hunting** N Haussuche *f;* **househusband** N Hausmann *m;* **house journal** N Hausnachrichten *pl;* **housekeeper** N Haushälterin *f,* Wirtschafterin *f;* *(in institution also)* Wirtschaftsleiterin *f;* **his wife is a good ~** seine Frau ist eine gute Hausfrau; **housekeeping** N **a** Haushalten *nt* **b** *(Brit: also* **housekeeping money***)* Haushalts- *or* Wirtschaftsgeld *nt;* **houseless** ['haʊslɪs] ADJ *person* obdachlos; *area* ohne Häuser, unbebaut; **house lights** PL Lichter *pl* im Saal; **house magazine** N = **house journal**; **housemaid** N Dienstmädchen *nt;* **housemaid's knee** N Schleimbeutelentzündung *f;* **houseman** N *(Brit)* Assistenzarzt *m;* **house martin** N Mehlschwalbe *f;* **housemaster** N *(Brit)* Erzieher *m;* *(on teaching staff)* Lehrer *m,* der für ein Gruppenhaus zuständig ist; **housemate** N **my ~s** meine Mitbewohner; **four young ~s** vier junge Mieter in einer Wohngemeinschaft; **housemistress** N *(Brit)* Erzieherin *f;* *(on teaching staff)* Lehrerin *f,* die für ein Gruppenhaus zuständig ist; **House music** N House *m;* **house parent** N Hausvater *m*/-mutter *f;* **~s** Hauseltern *pl;* **house party** N mehrtägige Einladung; *(= group invited)* Gesellschaft *f;* **house physician** N im (Kranken)haus wohnender Arzt; *(in private clinic etc)* Haus- *or* Anstaltsarzt *m*/-ärztin *f;* **house plant** N Zimmerpflanze *f;* **house-proud** ADJ **she is ~** sie ist eine penible Hausfrau; **houseroom** N **I wouldn't give it ~** das wollte ich nicht geschenkt haben; **I wouldn't give him ~** *(fig)* mit ihm möchte ich nichts zu tun haben; **house rule** N (Bestimmung der) Hausordnung *f;* **house-sit** VI **to ~ for sb** *während jds Abwesenheit in dessen Haus/Wohnung einziehen, um darauf aufzupassen;* **house-sitter** N Housesitter(in) *m(f) (jd, der während der Abwesenheit der Bewohner in ein Haus/eine Wohnung zieht, um darauf aufzupassen);* **house sparrow** N Haussperling *m;* **house style** N Stil *m* des Hauses; **house surgeon** N Chirurg(in) *m(f) (der/die im Krankenhaus selbst wohnt);* *(in private clinic)* Haus- *or* Anstaltschirurg(in) *m(f);* **house-to-house** ADJ von Haus zu Haus; **a ~ search** eine Suche *or* Fahndung von Haus zu Haus; **to conduct ~ inquiries** von Haus zu Haus gehen und fragen; **~ collection** Haussammlung *f;* **housetop** N (Haus)dach *nt;* **house-train** VT stubenrein machen; **house-trained** ADJ stubenrein; **House Un-American Activities Committee** N *(US Hist)* Senatsausschuss *m* zur Untersuchung unamerikanischer Umtriebe; **house-warming (party)** N Einzugsparty *f;* **to have a ~** Einzug feiern; **housewife** N **a** *(= person)* Hausfrau *f* **b** ['hʌzɪf] *(dated: = sewing case)* Nähetui *nt,* Nähzeug *nt;* **housewifely** ADJ hausfraulich; **house wine** N Hauswein *m;* **housework** N Hausarbeit *f*

housey-housey ['haʊsɪ'haʊsɪ] N *(dated)* Lotto *nt*

housing ['haʊzɪŋ] N **a** *(act)* Unterbringung *f* **b** *(= houses)* Wohnungen *pl;* *(temporary)* Unterkunft *f* **c** *(= provision of houses)* Wohnungsbeschaffung *f;* *(= building of houses)* Wohnungsbau *m* **d** *(Tech)* Gehäuse *nt*

housing *in cpds* Wohnungs-; **housing association** N Wohnungsbaugesellschaft *f;* **housing benefit** N *(Brit)* Wohngeld *nt;* **housing complex** N Wohnungskomplex *m;* **housing conditions** PL Wohnbedingungen *or* -verhältnisse *pl;* **housing development,** *(Brit also)* **housing estate** N Wohnsiedlung *f;* **housing list** N Warteliste *f* für Sozialwohnungen; **housing market** N Wohnungsmarkt *m;* **housing programme,** *(US)* **housing program** N Wohnungsbeschaffungsprogramm *nt;* **housing scheme** N *(= estate)* Siedlung *f;* *(= project)* Siedlungsbauvorhaben *nt;* **housing stock** N Bestand *m* an Häusern und Wohnungen

hove [həʊv] *pret, ptp of* **heave VT d VI c**

hovel ['hɒvəl] N armselige Hütte; *(fig pej)* Bruchbude *f,* Loch *nt (inf)*

hover ['hɒvə'] VI **a** *(helicopter, insect)* schweben; *(bird)* schweben, stehen
b *(fig)* **a smile ~ed on her lips** ein Lächeln lag auf ihren Lippen; **she ~ed on the verge of death** sie war dem Tode nahe; **to ~ on the brink of disaster** am Rande des Ruins stehen; **danger was ~ing all around them** ringsum lauerte Gefahr; **he ~ed between two alternatives** er schwankte zwischen zwei Alternativen; **he was ~ing between life and death** er schwebte zwischen Leben und Tod; **the exchange rate is ~ing around 110 yen to the dollar** der Wechselkurs bewegt sich um die 110 Yen für den Dollar
c *(fig: = stand around)* herumstehen; **to ~ over sb** jdm nicht von der Seite weichen; **don't ~ over me** geh endlich weg; **a waiter ~ed at his elbow, waiting to refill his glass** ein Kellner schwebte herum und wartete nur darauf, nachzuschenken

▶ **hover about** *(Brit) or* **around** **VI** *(person)* herumlungern, herumhängen; *(helicopter, bird etc)* (in der Luft) kreisen; **he was hovering around, waiting to speak to us** er strich um uns herum und wartete auf eine Gelegenheit, mit uns zu sprechen **VI** *+prep obj* **to hover around sb/sth** um jdn/etw herumschleichen *or* -streichen, sich um jdn/etw herumdrücken; **the hostess hovered around her guests** die Gastgeberin umsorgte ihre Gäste mit (über)großer Aufmerksamkeit

hover: **hovercraft** N Luftkissenboot *nt;* **hoverport** N Anlegestelle *f* für Luftkissenboote; **hovertrain** N Luftkissenzug *m*

how[1] [haʊ] ADV **a** *(= in what way)* wie; **~ will we ever survive?** wie sollen wir nur *or* bloß überleben?; **~ so?, ~'s that?, ~ come?** *(all inf)* wieso (denn das)?, wie kommt (denn) das?; **~ do you mean?** *(inf)* wie meinst du das?; **~ is it that we** *or* **~ come** *(inf)* **we earn less?** wieso *or* warum verdienen wir denn weniger?; **~ is it that ...?** wie kommt es, dass ...?; **I see ~ it is** ich verstehe (schon); **~'s that for luck?** ist das nicht ein Glück?; **~ do you know that?** woher wissen Sie das?; **to learn/know ~ to do sth** lernen/wissen, wie man etw macht; **I'd like to learn ~ to swim/drive** *etc* ich würde gerne schwimmen/Auto fahren *etc* lernen
b *(in degree, quantity etc)* wie; **~ nice!** wie nett!; **~ much** *(+n, adj, adv)* wie viel; *(+vb)* wie sehr; *(+vbs of physical action)* wie viel; **~ often do you visit them/go out?** wie oft besuchen Sie sie/gehen Sie aus?; **~ many** wie viel, wie viele; **I can't tell you ~ glad I was to leave** ich kann Ihnen gar nicht sagen, wie froh ich war, dort wegzukommen; **~ would you like to ...?** hätten Sie Lust, ... zu ...?
c *(regarding health, general situation etc)* **~ do you do?** *(on introduction)* Guten Tag/Abend!, angenehm! *(form);* **~ are you?** wie geht es Ihnen?; **~'s you?** *(Brit sl)* wie gehts? *(inf);* **~'s life?** wie gehts?; **~'s work/the new job?** *etc* was macht die Arbeit/die neue Stelle? *etc (inf);* **~ are things at school/in the office?** *etc* wie gehts in der Schule/im Büro? *etc;* **~ did the job interview go?** wie ist das Bewerbungsgespräch gelaufen?
d **~ about ...?** wie wäre es mit ...?; **~ about it?** *(about suggestion)* wie wäre es damit?; **~ about going for a walk?** wie wärs mit einem Spaziergang?; **~ about we meet for lunch to-**

morrow? wie wäre es, wenn wir uns morgen zum Mittagessen treffen?; **I've had enough, ~ about you?** mir reichts, wie siehts bei dir aus? e **and ~!** und ob *or* wie!; **~ he's grown!** er ist aber *or* vielleicht groß geworden; **look ~ he's grown!** sieh mal, wie groß er geworden ist
f *(= that)* dass; **she told me ~ she had seen him there** sie sagte mir, dass sie ihn dort gesehen hat

how² INTERJ *(American Indian greeting)* hugh

howdah [ˈhaʊdə] N Sänfte *f (auf Elefanten)*

howdy [ˈhaʊdɪ] INTERJ *(US inf)* Tag *(inf)*

how-d'ye-do [ˈhaʊdjədu:] *(inf)* INTERJ Tag *(inf)*, Tagchen *(inf)* N *(= palaver, fuss)* Theater *nt*; *(= argument also)* Krach *m*; **a fine** *or* **pretty ~** eine schöne Bescherung *(inf)*

howe'er [haʊˈɛəˈ] CONJ, ADV *(poet) contr of* **however**

however [haʊˈevəˈ] ✪ 26.1, 26.2, 26.3 CONJ a jedoch, aber; **~, we finally succeeded** wir haben es schließlich doch noch geschafft
b *(inf: = oh well)* na ja *(inf)*, nun ja *(inf)*
ADV a *(= no matter how)* wie ... auch, egal wie *(inf)*; *(= in whatever way)* wie; **~ strong he is** wie stark er auch ist, egal wie stark er ist *(inf)*; **~ you do it** wie immer du es machst, wie du es auch machst; **do it ~ you like** machs, wie du willst; **buy it ~ expensive it is** kaufen Sie es, egal, was es kostet; **~ much you cry** und wenn du noch so weinst, wie sehr du auch weinst; **wait 30 minutes or ~ long it takes** warte eine halbe Stunde oder so lange, wie es dauert; **~ that may be** wie dem auch sei
b *(in question)* wie ... bloß *or* nur; **~ did you manage it?** wie hast du das bloß *or* nur geschafft?

howitzer [ˈhaʊɪtsəˈ] N Haubitze *f*

howl [haʊl] N a Schrei *m*; *(of animal, wind)* Heulen *nt no pl*; **the dog let out a ~** der Hund heulte auf *or* jaulte; **a ~ of pain** ein Schmerzensschrei *m*; **~s of derision/rage** höhnisches/wütendes Geschrei *or* Gebrüll; **~s of laughter** brüllendes Gelächter; **~s (of protest)** Protestgeschrei *nt*
b *(from loudspeaker)* Pfeifen *nt no pl*, Rückkopp(e)lung *f*
VI a *(person)* brüllen, schreien; *(animal)* heulen, jaulen; *(wind)* heulen; **to ~ with laughter** in brüllendes Gelächter ausbrechen; **to ~ with delight** vor Freude schreien
b *(= weep noisily)* heulen; *(baby)* schreien, brüllen *(inf)*
c *(Elec, loudspeaker etc)* rückkoppeln, pfeifen
VT hinausbrüllen, hinausschreien; **they ~ed their disapproval** sie äußerten lautstark ihr Missfallen

▶ **howl down** VT *sep* niederbrüllen, niederschreien

howler [ˈhaʊləˈ] N *(Brit inf)* Hammer *m (inf)*, Schnitzer *m (inf)*; **he made a real ~** da hat er sich *(dat)* einen Hammer geleistet *(inf)*; **stylistic ~** Stilblüte *f (hum)*

howling [ˈhaʊlɪŋ] N *(of person)* Gebrüll *nt*, Geschrei *nt*; *(= noisy crying, of animal)* Heulen *nt*, Geheul *nt*; *(of wind)* Heulen *nt*; **stop that child's ~!** bring das Kind zum Schweigen! ADJ a *(lit)* heulend b *(inf: = tremendous)* enorm; **a ~ success** ein Riesenerfolg *m*

howsoever [ˌhaʊsəʊˈevəˈ] *(old, form)* ADV wie auch (immer); **~ bad the situation may seem** wie schlecht die Lage auch (immer) aussehen mag CONJ **~ that may be** wie dem auch sei

hoy [hɔɪ] INTERJ he

hoyden [ˈhɔɪdn] N wilde Range *(dated)*, Wildfang *m (dated)*

hoydenish [ˈhɔɪdənɪʃ] ADJ rangenhaft *(dated)*, wild, ungestüm

HP, hp a *abbr of* **hire purchase** b *abbr of* **horse power** PS

HQ *abbr of* **headquarters**

hr *abbr of* **hour** Std.

HR *abbr of* **human resources**

HRH *abbr of* **His/Her Royal Highness** S. M./I. M.

HRT *abbr of* **hormone replacement therapy**

HSS *(US) abbr of* **Health and Social Services** *das amerikanische Gesundheits- und Sozialministerium*

HST a *(Brit) abbr of* **high speed train** Hochgeschwindigkeitszug *m* b *(US) abbr of* **Hawaiian Standard Time** hawaiische Zeit

ht *abbr of* **height**

HTML *(Comput) abbr of* **hypertext mark-up language** HTML

HTTP, http *(Comput) abbr of* **hypertext transfer protocol** http

HUAC *(US Hist) abbr of* **House Un-American Activities Committee**

hub [hʌb] N a *(of wheel)* (Rad)nabe *f* b *(fig)* Zentrum *nt*, Mittelpunkt *m*; **a ~ of finance** ein finanzielles Zentrum; **the ~ of the universe** der Nabel der Welt; **a ~ of activity** das reinste Bienenhaus; **the island's social ~** der gesellschaftliche Mittelpunkt der Insel

hub airport N *(US)* Großflughafen *m*

hubble-bubble [ˈhʌblˈbʌbl] N a *(Brit: = pipe)* Wasserpfeife *f* b *(= noise)* Brodeln *nt*

hubbub [ˈhʌbʌb] N Tumult *m*; **a ~ (of noise)** ein Radau *m*; **a ~ of voices** ein Stimmengewirr *nt*

hubby [ˈhʌbɪ] N *(inf)* Mann *m*

hubcap [ˈhʌbkæp] N Radkappe *f*

hubris [ˈhju:brɪs] N *(liter)* Anmaßung *f*; *(esp in Greek drama)* Hybris *f*

huckleberry [ˈhʌklbərɪ] N amerikanische Heidelbeere

huckster [ˈhʌkstəˈ] N a *(= hawker)* Straßenhändler(in) *m(f)* b *(US inf)* Reklamefritze *m (inf)*

huddle [ˈhʌdl] N (wirrer) Haufen *m*; *(of people)* Gruppe *f*; **in a ~** dicht zusammengedrängt; **to go into a ~** *(inf)* die Köpfe zusammenstecken VI *(also* **to be huddled***)* (sich) kauern; **they ~d under the umbrella** sie drängten sich unter dem Schirm zusammen; **we ~d around the fire** wir saßen eng zusammengedrängt um das Feuer herum; **small sheds, ~d under the trees** kleine Hütten, die sich unter die Bäume kauerten; **the president was ~d with his aides** der Präsident und seine Berater steckten die Köpfe zusammen

▶ **huddle down** VI sich kuscheln

▶ **huddle together** VI sich aneinanderkauern; **to be huddled together** aneinanderkauern

▶ **huddle up** VI sich zusammenkauern; **to be huddled up** zusammenkauern; **to huddle up against sb/sth** sich an jdn/etw kauern

hue¹ [hju:] N *(= colour)* Farbe *f*; *(= shade)* Schattierung *f*; *(fig: = political leaning)* Schattierung *f*, Färbung *f*, Couleur *f (geh)*

hue² N **~ and cry** Zeter und Mordio *(against* gegen); **to set up** *or* **raise a ~ and cry** Zeter und Mordio schreien

huff [hʌf] N **to be/go off in a ~** beleidigt *or* eingeschnappt sein/abziehen *(inf)*; **to get into a ~** einschnappen *(inf)*, den Beleidigten spielen VI **to ~ and puff** *(inf)* schnaufen und keuchen

huffily [ˈhʌfɪlɪ] ADV beleidigt

huffiness [ˈhʌfɪnɪs] N Beleidigtsein *nt*; *(= touchiness)* Empfindlichkeit *f*; **the ~ in his voice** sein beleidigter Ton

huffy [ˈhʌfɪ] ADJ *(+er) (= in a huff)* beleidigt; *(= touchy)* empfindlich; **to get/be ~ about sth** wegen etw eingeschnappt *(inf) or* beleidigt sein; **he's quite a ~ person** er ist leicht beleidigt *or* eingeschnappt *(inf)*

hug [hʌg] N Umarmung *f*; **to give sb a ~** jdn umarmen
VT a *(= hold close)* umarmen; *(bear etc)* umklammern; *(fig) hope, belief* sich klammern an *(+acc)*; **to ~ sb/sth to oneself** jdn/etw an sich *(acc)* pressen *or* drücken; **she ~ged her legs tight to her** sie schlang die Arme eng um die Beine
b *(= keep close to)* sich dicht halten an *(+acc)*; *(car, ship etc also)* dicht entlangfahren an *(+dat)*
VI sich umarmen; **we ~ged and kissed** wir umarmten und küssten uns
VR a **to ~ oneself to keep warm** die Arme verschränken, damit einem warm ist; **she stood ~ging herself** sie stand mit verschränkten Armen da
b **he ~ged himself with pleasure** er war sehr zufrieden mit sich selbst

huge [hju:dʒ] ADJ *(+er)* riesig; *appetite, thirst, disappointment, deficit, selection* Riesen- *(inf)*; *effort* gewaltig; *problem, difference, increase* riesig, enorm; **a ~ success** ein Riesenerfolg *(inf)*; **a ~ city** eine Riesenstadt *(inf)*; **a ~ job** eine Riesenarbeit *(inf)*; **~ numbers of these children** ungeheuer viele von diesen Kindern; **human suffering on a ~ scale** unermessliches menschliches Leiden

hugely [ˈhju:dʒlɪ] ADV *(emph) successful, expensive, important, entertaining, talented* außerordentlich, ungeheuer; *enjoy oneself* riesig; *vary, increase* ungemein; **the whole thing is ~ enjoyable** das Ganze macht ungeheuer viel Spaß; **I enjoyed the play ~** das Stück hat mir ausgesprochen gut gefallen

hugeness [ˈhju:dʒnɪs] N gewaltiges *or* riesiges Ausmaß

Huguenot [ˈhju:gənəʊ] ADJ hugenottisch N Hugenotte *m*, Hugenottin *f*

huh [hʌ] INTERJ was; *(derision)* haha

hula [ˈhu:lə] N Hula(-Hula) *m or f*; **to do the ~(--)** Hula(-Hula) tanzen

Hula Hoop® N Hula-Hoop-Reifen *m*

hula skirt N Bastrock *m*

hulk [hʌlk] N a *(Naut: = body of ship)* (Schiffs)-rumpf *m* b *(inf: = person)* Hüne *m (inf)*; **I followed his big ~ into the room** ich folgte seiner hünenhaften Gestalt ins Zimmer c *(= wrecked vehicle)* Wrack *nt*; *(= wrecked building etc)* Ruine *f*

hulking [ˈhʌlkɪŋ] ADJ **~ great, great ~** massig; **a great ~ wardrobe** ein Ungetüm *nt* von einem Kleiderschrank; **a ~ great brute of a man** ein grobschlächtiger, brutaler Kerl; **a ~ great brute of a dog** ein scheußliches Ungetüm von einem Hund

hull¹ [hʌl] N *(Naut)* Schiffskörper *m*; *(Aviat)* Rumpf *m*; **ship ~ down on the horizon** Schiff in Sicht am Horizont

hull² N Hülse *f*; *(of strawberries etc)* Blättchen *nt* VT schälen; *strawberries etc* entstielen

hullabaloo [ˌhʌləbəˈlu:] N *(Brit inf)* Spektakel *m*; *(= noise also)* Radau *m*; **I don't know what all the ~ is about** ich verstehe nicht, was das ganze Theater eigentlich soll *(inf)*

hullo [hʌˈləʊ] INTERJ *(Brit)* = **hello**

hum [hʌm] N a *(of insect, person)* Summen *nt*; *(of traffic)* Brausen *nt*; *(of engine, electric tool, radio, top etc)* Brummen *nt*; *(of small machine, camera etc)* Surren *nt*; *(of voices)* Gemurmel *nt*
b *(inf: = smell)* Gestank *m (inf)*
VI a *(insect, person)* summen; *(traffic)* brausen; *(engine, electric tool, radio, top etc)* brummen; *(small machine, camera etc)* surren; **the lines were ~ming with the news** *(fig)* die Drähte liefen heiß
b *(fig inf: party, concert etc)* in Schwung kommen; **to make things/the party ~** die Sache/die Party in Schwung bringen; **the headquarters was ~ming with activity** im Hauptquartier ging es zu wie in einem Bienenstock
c **to ~ and haw** *(inf)* herumdrucksen *(inf) (over, about* um)
d *(inf: = smell)* stinken *(inf)*
VT *music, tune* summen
INTERJ hm

human [ˈhju:mən] ADJ menschlich; *health, brain, part of the body* des Menschen; **~ dignity** die Menschenwürde; **~ sacrifice** Menschenopfer *nt*; **not fit for ~ consumption** zum Verzehr (durch den Menschen) ungeeignet; **~ error** menschliches Versagen; **~ capital** Menschenkapital *nt*; **~ chain** Menschenkette *f*; **~ shield** menschlicher Schutzschild; **I'm only ~** ich bin auch nur ein Mensch; **that's only ~** das ist doch nur menschlich; **these footprints certainly aren't ~** diese Fußspuren sind *or* stammen sicher nicht von Menschen **N** Mensch *m*

human being N Mensch *m*

humane [hjuːˈmeɪn] ADJ **a** *(= considerate) person, society, decision, treatment, prison* human; *treatment of people* menschenwürdig, human; *rearing of animals* unter humanen Bedingungen; **a ~ method of killing animals** eine möglichst schmerzlose Methode, Tiere zu töten **b** *(form: = civilizing) education* humanistisch

humanely [hjuːˈmeɪnlɪ] ADV *treat* human; *treat people also* menschenwürdig; *rear animals* unter humanen Bedingungen; *destroy, slaughter, kill* (möglichst) schmerzlos; **to destroy an animal ~** *(= put to sleep)* ein Tier einschläfern

human interest N *(in newspaper story etc)* Emotionalität *f*; **a ~ story** eine ergreifende Story; **the film's main ~ is centred on this relationship** auf der menschlichen Ebene dreht sich der Film hauptsächlich um diese Beziehung

humanism [ˈhjuːmənɪzəm] N Humanismus *m*

humanist [ˈhjuːmənɪst] **N** Humanist(in) *m(f)* **ADJ** humanistisch

humanistic [ˌhjuːməˈnɪstɪk] ADJ humanistisch

humanitarian [hjuːˌmænɪˈtɛərɪən] **N** Vertreter(in) *m(f)* des Humanitätsgedankens **ADJ** humanitär

humanitarianism [ˌhjuːmænɪˈtɛərɪənɪzəm] N Humanitarismus *m*; *(of individual)* humanitäre Gesinnung

humanity [hjuːˈmænɪtɪ] N **a** *(= mankind)* die Menschheit **b** *(= human nature)* Menschlichkeit *f*, Menschenhaftigkeit *f* **c** *(= humaneness)* Humanität *f*, Menschlichkeit *f*; **to treat sb with ~** jdn human behandeln **d humanities** PL Geisteswissenschaften *pl*; *(= Latin and Greek)* Altphilologie *f*

humanize [ˈhjuːmənaɪz] VT humanisieren

humankind [ˌhjuːmənˈkaɪnd] N die Menschheit

humanly [ˈhjuːmənlɪ] ADV menschlich; **~ comprehensible** für den Menschen verständlich; **the ~ constructed world** die vom Menschen gebaute Welt; **as far as ~ possible** soweit es überhaupt möglich ist, soweit überhaupt möglich; **as safe as ~ possible** so sicher wie überhaupt möglich; **to do all that is** *or* **everything ~ possible** alles Menschenmögliche tun

human nature N die menschliche Natur; **it's ~ to do that** es liegt (nun einmal) in der Natur des Menschen, das zu tun

humanoid [ˈhjuːmənɔɪd] **ADJ** menschenähnlich **N** *(esp in science fiction) (= robot)* menschenähnlicher Roboter; *(= creature)* menschenähnliches Lebewesen

human: **human race** N **the ~** die Menschheit, das Menschengeschlecht *(geh)*; **human resources** PL *(= people)* Personal *nt*, Arbeitskräfte *pl*; **human-resources** ADJ ATTR Personal-; **~ department** Personalabteilung *f*; **~ manager** Personalleiter(in) *m(f)*; **human rights** PL Menschenrechte *pl*; **~ organization** Menschenrechtsorganisation *f*; **~ activist** Menschenrechtler(in) *m(f)*; **human touch** N **the ~** die menschliche Wärme; **to lack the ~** nichts Menschliches haben; **human trial** N *(Med)* Menschenversuch *m*

humble [ˈhʌmbl] **ADJ** *(+er)* **a** *(= modest) person* bescheiden, demütig *(esp Rel)*; *apology* demütig; **my ~ apologies!** ich bitte inständig um Verzeihung!; **to be ~ about one's origins** mit seiner Herkunft nicht angeben; **to eat ~ pie** klein beigeben; **in my ~ opinion** meiner bescheidenen Meinung nach → **servant**
b *(= lowly) curate, clerk, beginner* einfach; *origins* niedrig, einfach; *background, beginnings* bescheiden; **of ~ origins/birth** von niedriger Herkunft/Geburt
c *(= insignificant) abode, restaurant, potato, maggot* bescheiden
VT *(= crush)* demütigen; **to ~ oneself** sich demütigen *or* erniedrigen; **to be/feel ~d** sich *(dat)* klein vorkommen, sich gedemütigt fühlen

humblebee [ˈhʌmblˌbiː] N Hummel *f*

humbleness [ˈhʌmblnɪs] N *(= modesty, insignificance)* Bescheidenheit *f*; *(= lowliness)* Einfachheit *f*; *(esp Rel: = meekness, humility)* Demut *f*

humbly [ˈhʌmblɪ] ADV *(= unassumingly, with deference)* bescheiden, demütig *(esp Rel)*; *(= in a lowly way)* einfach, bescheiden; **~ born** von niedriger Geburt; **I ~ submit this little work** in aller Bescheidenheit überreiche ich diese kleine Arbeit; **she ~ apologized** sie entschuldigte sich kleinlaut *or* zerknirscht; **he ~ agreed that he was wrong** er gab kleinlaut zu, dass er unrecht hatte; **I most ~ beg your pardon** ich bitte ergebenst um Verzeihung

humbug [ˈhʌmbʌg] N **a** *(Brit: = sweet)* Pfefferminzbonbon *m or nt* **b** *(inf: = talk)* Humbug *m*, Mumpitz *m (inf)* **c** *(inf: = person)* Halunke *m*, Gauner(in) *m(f)*

humdinger [ˈhʌmdɪŋəʳ] N *(inf: = person, thing)* **to be a ~** Spitze *or* große Klasse sein *(inf)*; **a ~ of a job/girl** *etc* ein klasse Job/Mädchen *etc (inf)*; **a ~ of a hangover** ein Kater, der sich gewaschen hat *(inf)*; **he hit him with a real ~ of a left hook** er landete einen erstklassigen linken Haken bei ihm *(inf)*

humdrum [ˈhʌmdrʌm] ADJ stumpfsinnig

humerus [ˈhjuːmərəs] N Oberarmknochen *m*

humid [ˈhjuːmɪd] ADJ feucht; **it's (hot and) ~ today** es ist schwül heute

humidifier [hjuːˈmɪdɪfaɪəʳ] N Luftbefeuchter *m*; *(= humidification system)* Luftbefeuchtungsanlage *f*

humidify [hjuːˈmɪdɪfaɪ] VT *air* befeuchten; **to ~ a room** die Luft in einem Zimmer befeuchten

humidity [hjuːˈmɪdɪtɪ] N (Luft)feuchtigkeit *f*

humidor [ˈhjuːmɪdɔːʳ] N Feuchtraum *m*

humiliate [hjuːˈmɪlɪeɪt] VT demütigen, erniedrigen; **to ~ oneself** sich beschämen

humiliating [hjuːˈmɪlɪeɪtɪŋ] ADJ *defeat, experience* demütigend; *blow, conditions* beschämend

humiliatingly [hjuːˈmɪlɪeɪtɪŋlɪ] ADV beschämend; *lose, be defeated, concede* beschämenderweise; *(introducing sentence)* zu seiner/ihrer *etc* Beschämung

humiliation [hjuːˌmɪlɪˈeɪʃən] N Demütigung *f*, Erniedrigung *f*; *(because of one's own actions)* Beschämung *f no pl*; **much to my ~** sehr zu meiner Schande *or* Beschämung; **she couldn't hide her ~** sie konnte das Gefühl der Demütigung/Beschämung nicht verbergen; **the result is a ~ for the prime minister** das Ergebnis ist eine demütigende Niederlage für den Premierminister

humility [hjuːˈmɪlɪtɪ] N Demut *f*; *(= unassumingness)* Bescheidenheit *f*

humming [ˈhʌmɪŋ] N *(of insect, person)* Summen *nt*; *(of traffic)* Brausen *nt*; *(of engine, electric tool, radio, top etc)* Brummen *nt*; *(of small machine, camera etc)* Surren *nt*; *(of voices)* Murmeln *nt*, Gemurmel *nt*

humming: **hummingbird** [ˈhʌmɪŋbɜːd] N Kolibri *m*; **humming top** N Brummkreisel *m*

hummock [ˈhʌmək] N (kleiner) Hügel

hummus [ˈhʊməs] N = **hoummos**

humongous [hjuːˈmɒŋgəs] ADJ *(inf)* wahnsinnig groß *(inf)*, Riesen- *(inf)*; **she's a ~ star** sie ist ein Riesenstar *(inf)*; **we had a ~ row** wir hatten einen Riesenkrach *(inf)*

humor *etc (US)* = **humour** *etc*

humorist [ˈhjuːmərɪst] N Humorist(in) *m(f)*

humorous [ˈhjuːmərəs] ADJ *person, speech, comment* humorvoll; *book, story etc also, situation* lustig, komisch; *idea, thought* witzig; *smile, programme* lustig, heiter; **to see the ~ side of sth** die lustige *or* komische Seite an etw *(dat)* sehen

humorously [ˈhjuːmərəslɪ] ADV humorvoll, witzig; *reflect, smile, say* heiter

humour, *(US)* **humor** [ˈhjuːməʳ] **N** **a** Humor *m*; **a sense of ~** (Sinn *m* für) Humor *m*; **their own inimitable brand of ~** ihre eigene unnachahmliche Art von Humor; **a story full of ~** eine humorvolle Geschichte; **I don't see the ~ in that** ich finde das gar nicht komisch; **there was little room for ~** es war nicht die Zeit für Witze
b *(= mood)* Stimmung *f*, Laune *f*; **to be in a good ~** in guter Stimmung sein, gute Laune haben; **with good ~** gut gelaunt; **to be out of ~, to be in a bad ~** schlechte Laune haben, schlecht gelaunt sein
c *(old Med)* Körpersaft *m*
VT **to ~ sb** jdm seinen Willen lassen *or* tun; **do it just to ~ him** tus doch, damit er seinen Willen hat

-humoured, *(US)* **-humored** [ˈhjuːməd] ADJ *suf* gelaunt; **good-/ill-humoured** gut/schlecht gelaunt

humourless, *(US)* **humorless** [ˈhjuːməlɪs] ADJ humorlos, ohne jeden Humor; *speech, laugh, book etc also* trocken

humourlessly, *(US)* **humorlessly** [ˈhjuːməlɪslɪ] ADV humorlos, ohne jeden Humor

hump [hʌmp] **N** **a** *(Anat)* Buckel *m*; *(of camel)* Höcker *m* **b** *(= hillock)* Hügel *m*, Buckel *m (esp S Ger)*; **we're over the ~ now** *(fig)* wir sind jetzt über den Berg **c** *(Brit inf)* **he's got the ~** er ist sauer *(inf)*; **he/that gives me the ~** er/das fällt mir auf den Wecker *(inf)* **VT** **a** **to ~ one's back** einen Buckel machen **b** *(inf: = carry)* schleppen; *(on back, shoulders)* auf dem Rücken/den Schultern tragen *or* schleppen **c** *(inf: = have sex with)* bumsen *(inf)*

humpback [ˈhʌmpbæk] N *(= person)* Buck(e)lige(r) *mf*; *(= back)* Buckel *m*

humpbacked [ˈhʌmpbækt] ADJ *person* buck(e)lig; *bridge* gewölbt

humpbacked whale N Buckelwal *m*

humped [hʌmpt] ADJ buck(e)lig

humph [mm] INTERJ hm

humpy [ˈhʌmpɪ] ADJ *(+er) country* hügelig, buckelig *(esp S Ger)*

humungous [hjuːˈmʌŋgəs] ADJ *(inf)* = **humongous**

humus [ˈhjuːməs] N Humus *m*

Hun [hʌn] N **a** *(Hist)* Hunne *m*, Hunnin *f* **b** *(pej inf)* Teutone *m (pej)*, Teutonin *f (pej)*, Boche *m (pej)*

hunch [hʌntʃ] **N** **a** *(= hump on sb's back)* Buckel *m* **b** *(= premonition)* Gefühl *nt*, Ahnung *f*; **to act on a ~** einem inneren Gefühl zufolge handeln; **to have a ~ that …** den (leisen *(inf)*) Verdacht *or* das (leise) Gefühl haben, dass …; **your ~ paid off** du hattest die richtige Ahnung, es hat sich gelohnt **VT** *(also* **hunch up)** **to ~ one's back** einen Buckel machen, den Rücken krümmen; **to ~ one's shoulders** die Schultern hochziehen; **to ~ oneself over sth** sich über etw *(acc)* beugen; **he was ~ed over his desk** er saß über seinen Schreibtisch gebeugt; **~ed up in pain** vor Schmerzen gekrümmt

hunch: **hunchback** N *(= person)* Buck(e)lige(r) *mf*; *(= back)* Buckel *m*; **The Hunchback of Notre Dame** der Glöckner von Notre-Dame; **hunchbacked** ADJ buck(e)lig

hundred [ˈhʌndrɪd] **ADJ** hundert; **a** *or* **one ~ years** (ein)hundert Jahre; **two/several ~ years** zweihundert/mehrere hundert *or* Hundert Jahre; **a** *or* **one ~ and one** *(lit)* (ein)hundert(und)eins; *(fig)* tausend; **a** *or* **one ~ and two/ten** (ein)hundert(und)zwei/-zehn; **(one) ~ and first/second** *etc* hundert(und)erste(r, s)/-zweite(r, s) *etc*; **a** *or* **one ~ thousand** (ein)hunderttausend; **a ~-mile walk** ein Hundertmeilenmarsch; **a** *or* **one ~ per cent** hundert Prozent; **a (one) ~ per cent increase** eine hundertprozentige Erhöhung, eine Erhöhung von *or* um hundert Prozent; **a** *or* **one ~ per cent inflation** eine Inflationsrate von hundert Prozent; **I'm not a** *or* **one ~ per cent fit/sure** ich bin nicht hundertprozentig fit/sicher; **I agree with you one ~ per cent** ich stimme hundertprozentig mit Ihnen überein; **the Hundred Years' War** *(Hist)* der Hundertjährige Krieg; **never in a ~ years!** nie im Leben!

N hundert *num*; *(written figure)* Hundert *f*; **~s** *(lit, fig)* hunderte *or* Hunderte *pl*; *(Math: figures in column)* Hunderter *pl*; **to count in ~s** in hunderten *or* Hunderten zählen; **to count up to a** *or* **one ~** bis hundert zählen; **the ~s column** *(Math)* die Hunderterspalte; **one in a ~** einer unter hundert; **eighty out of a ~** achtzig von hundert; **an audience of a** *or* **one/two ~** hundert/zweihundert Zuschauer; **~s of times** hundertmal, hunderte *or* Hunderte von Malen; **~s and ~s** Hunderte und Aberhunderte, hunderte und aberhunderte; **~s of** *or* **and thousands** hunderttausende *or* Hunderttausende *pl*; **~s and thousands** *(Cook)* Liebesperlen *pl*; **he earns nine ~ a month** er verdient neunhundert im Monat; **I'll lay (you) a ~ to one** ich wette hundert gegen eins; **to sell sth by the ~** *(lit, fig)* etw im Hundert verkaufen; **it'll cost you a ~** das wird dich einen Hunderter kosten; **to live to be a ~** hundert Jahre alt werden; **they came in (their) ~s** *or* **by the ~** sie kamen zu hunderten *or* Hunderten

hundredfold ['hʌndrɪdfəʊld] **ADJ, ADV** hundertfach; **to increase a ~** um das Hundertfache steigern

hundredth ['hʌndrɪdθ] **ADJ** *(in series)* hundertste(r, s); *(of fraction)* hundertstel **N** Hundertste(r, s) *decl as adj*; *(= fraction)* Hundertstel *nt* → *also* **sixth**

hundredweight ['hʌndrɪdweɪt] **N** Zentner *m*; *(Brit)* 50,8 kg; *(US)* 45,4 kg

hung [hʌŋ] *pret, ptp of* **hang** **ADJ** *(inf: sexually)* **the way he's ~** wie er ausgestattet ist *(inf)*; **to be ~ like a mule** ein Riesengehänge haben *(inf)*

Hungarian [hʌŋ'gɛərɪən] **ADJ** ungarisch **N** **a** *(= person)* Ungar(in) *m(f)* **b** *(Ling)* Ungarisch *nt*

Hungary ['hʌŋgərɪ] **N** Ungarn *nt*

hunger ['hʌŋgəʳ] **N** **a** *(lit)* Hunger *m*; **to die of ~** verhungern **b** *(fig)* Hunger *m* *(for* nach) **VI** *(old, liter)* hungern; **to ~ to do sth** danach hungern, etw zu tun

▶ **hunger after** *or* **for** **VI** *+prep obj (liter)* hungern nach; *news* sehnsüchtig warten auf *(+acc)*

hunger march **N** Hungermarsch *m*

hunger strike **N** **to be on (a) ~** sich im Hungerstreik befinden; **to go on (a) ~** in (den) Hungerstreik treten

hung over **ADJ** **to be ~** einen Kater haben *(inf)*; **to look ~** verkatert aussehen *(inf)*

hung parliament **N** Parlament *nt* ohne klare Mehrheitsverhältnisse; **the election resulted in a ~** die Wahl führte zu einem parlamentarischen Patt

hungrily ['hʌŋgrɪlɪ] **ADV** *(lit, fig)* hungrig

hungry ['hʌŋgrɪ] **ADJ** *(+er)* **a** *(lit)* hungrig; **to be** *or* **feel/get ~** Hunger haben/bekommen; **to go ~** hungern **b** *(fig)* hungrig; **~ for knowledge/love/power** bildungs-/liebes-/machthungrig; **to be ~ for news** sehnsüchtig auf Nachricht warten; **to be ~ for fame/riches/company** sich nach Ruhm/Reichtum/Gesellschaft sehnen; **this is ~ work** das macht hungrig

hung up **ADJ** *(inf)* **to be/get ~ about sth** *(= be neurotic)* wegen etw einen Knacks weghaben *(inf)*/durchdrehen *(inf)*; *(= have complex)* Komplexe wegen etw haben/kriegen; **he's really ~ about things like that** wenn es darum geht, hat er einen richtigen Knacks weg *(inf)*; **to be ~ about being old/single** *etc* einen Komplex haben, weil man alt/nicht verheiratet *etc* ist; **he's ~ on her** *(inf)* er steht auf sie *(sl)*

hunk [hʌŋk] **N** **a** Stück *nt* **b** *(fig inf: = man)* **a gorgeous ~ (of a man)** ein *Mann! (inf)*

hunky-dory ['hʌŋkɪ'dɔːrɪ] **ADJ** *(inf)* **that's ~** das ist in Ordnung

hunt [hʌnt] **N** Jagd *f*; *(= huntsmen)* Jagd(gesellschaft) *f*; *(fig: = search)* Suche *f*; **tiger ~** Tigerjagd *f*; **the ~ is on** die Suche hat begonnen; **to have a ~ for sth** nach etw fahnden *(inf)*, eine Suche nach etw veranstalten; **to be on the ~ for sth** *(for animal)* etw jagen, auf etw *(acc)* Jagd machen; *(fig)* auf der Suche *or* Jagd nach etw sein *(inf)*

VT **a** *(Hunt)* jagen; *(= search for) criminal* jagen, fahnden nach; *missing article etc* suchen; *missing person* suchen, fahnden nach; **~ the slipper/thimble** Pantoffel-/Fingerhutverstecken *nt* **b** **to ~ a horse/hounds** zu Pferd/mit Hunden jagen

VI **a** *(Hunt)* jagen; **to go ~ing** jagen, auf die Jagd gehen **b** *(= search)* suchen *(for, after* nach); **to ~ for an animal** auf ein Tier Jagd machen; **he is ~ing for a job** er sucht eine Stelle

▶ **hunt about** *(Brit) or* **around** **VI** herumsuchen *or* -kramen *(for* nach)

▶ **hunt down** **VT** *sep animal, person* (unerbittlich) Jagd machen auf *(+acc)*; *(= capture)* zur Strecke bringen

▶ **hunt out** **VT** *sep* heraussuchen, hervorkramen *(inf)*; *person, facts* ausfindig machen, aufstöbern *(inf)*

▶ **hunt up** **VT** *sep person* Nachforschungen anstellen über *(+acc)*; *facts* ausfindig machen; *old clothes, records etc* kramen nach *(+dat)*, hervorkramen; **hunt him up for me, would you?** sieh mal bitte nach, ob du ihn irgendwo auftreiben kannst

hunt-and-peck method **N** *(inf hum: typing)* Adlersuchsystem *nt*, Zweifingersystem *nt*

hunt ball **N** Jagdball *m*

hunter ['hʌntəʳ] **N** **a** *(= person)* Jäger(in) *m(f)*; *(= horse)* Jagdpferd *nt*; *(= dog)* Jagdhund *m* **b** *(= watch)* Sprungdeckeluhr *f* **c** *(Astron)* **the Hunter** Orion *m*

hunter-gatherer [,hʌntə'gæðərəʳ] **N** Jäger und Sammler *m*; **they were hunters-gatherers** sie waren Jäger und Sammler

hunter-killer [,hʌntə'kɪləʳ] **N** Jagd-U-Boot *nt*

hunting ['hʌntɪŋ] **N** **a** die Jagd, das Jagen; **the ~ in these woods is excellent** diese Wälder sind ein gutes Jagdgebiet **b** *(fig: = search)* Suche *f* *(for* nach); **after a lot of ~ ...** nach langer Suche ...

hunting *in cpds* Jagd-; **hunting box** **N** Jagdhütte *f*; **hunting ground** **N** *(lit, fig)* Jagdrevier *nt*, Jagdgebiet *nt*; **to go to the happy ~s** in die ewigen Jagdgründe eingehen; **a happy ~** *(fig)* ein beliebtes *or* einträgliches Jagdrevier *(for* für); **hunting horn** **N** Jagdhorn *nt*; **hunting licence**, *(US)* **hunting license** **N** Jagdschein *m*; **hunting lodge** **N** Jagdhütte *f*; *(larger)* Jagdschloss *nt*; **hunting pink** **N** *(= colour)* Rot *nt* *(des Reitrockes)*; *(= clothes)* roter (Jagd)rock

Huntington's chorea [,hʌntɪŋtənzkɔː'rɪə], **Huntington's disease** [,hʌntɪŋtənzdɪ'ziːz] **N** Chorea Huntington *f (spec)*, huntingtonsche Krankheit

huntress ['hʌntrɪs] **N** Jägerin *f*

hunt saboteur **N** *(Brit) jd, der versucht, die Fuchsjagd durch Sabotageakte zu verhindern*, Jagdsaboteur(in) *m(f)*

huntsman ['hʌntsmən] **N** *pl* **-men** [-mən] Jagdreiter *m*

huntswoman ['hʌntswʊmən] **N** *pl* **-women** [-wɪmɪn] Jagdreiterin *f*

hurdle ['hɜːdl] **N** *(Sport, fig)* Hürde *f*; **~s** *sing (= race)* Hürdenlauf *m*; *(Horse Racing)* Hürdenrennen *nt*; **the 100m ~s** (die) 100 m Hürden, (der) 100-m-Hürdenlauf; **to fall at the first ~** *(fig)* (schon) über die erste *or* bei der ersten Hürde stolpern **VT** *fence* nehmen **VI** Hürdenlauf machen; **hurdling** der Hürdenlauf

hurdler ['hɜːdləʳ] **N** *(Sport)* Hürdenläufer(in) *m(f)*

hurdle race **N** Hindernislauf *m*; *(Sport)* Hürdenlauf *m*; *(for horses)* Hindernisrennen *nt*

hurdy-gurdy ['hɜːdɪ,gɜːdɪ] **N** Leierkasten *m*, Drehorgel *f*

hurl [hɜːl] **VT** schleudern; **to ~ oneself at sb/into a chair** sich auf jdn stürzen/in einen Sessel werfen; **she ~ed herself from the roof** sie stürzte sich vom Dach; **they ~ed back their attackers** sie warfen ihre Angreifer zurück; **to ~ insults at sb** jdm Beleidigungen entgegenschleudern **VI** *(inf: = vomit)* sich erbrechen, kotzen *(inf)*

hurly-burly ['hɜːlɪ'bɜːlɪ] **N** Getümmel *nt*, Rummel *m (inf)*; **the ~ of politics** der Rummel der Politik

hurrah [hə'rɑː], **hurray** [hə'reɪ] **INTERJ** hurra; **~ for the king!** ein Hoch dem König!

hurricane ['hʌrɪkən] **N** Orkan *m*; *(tropical)* Hurrikan *m*; **~ force** Orkanstärke *f*

hurricane-force ['hʌrɪkən,fɔːs] **ADJ** **~ wind** Wind *m* von Orkanstärke

hurricane lamp **N** Sturmlaterne *f*

hurried ['hʌrɪd] **ADJ** eilig; *letter, essay* eilig *or* hastig geschrieben; *ceremony, meeting* hastig durchgeführt; *work* in Eile gemacht; *(= with little preparation) departure, wedding etc* überstürzt; **to have a ~ breakfast** hastig frühstücken; **a ~ goodbye** ein hastiger Abschied; **to pay sb a ~ visit** jdm einen hastigen Besuch abstatten

hurriedly ['hʌrɪdlɪ] **ADV** *(= rapidly)* eilig, hastig; *say* hastig; *leave* in großer Eile; **a ~ arranged press conference** eine hastig einberufene Pressekonferenz

hurry ['hʌrɪ] **N** Eile *f*; **in my ~ to get it finished ...** vor lauter Eile, damit fertig zu werden ...; **to do sth in a ~** etw schnell *or (too fast)* hastig tun; **I need it in a ~** ich brauche es schnell *or* eilig *or* dringend; **to be in a ~** es eilig haben, in Eile sein; **I'm in no particular ~** ich habe es nicht besonders eilig; **I'm in no ~ to leave home** ich will nicht so schnell von zu Hause ausziehen; **I won't do that again in a ~!** *(inf)* das mache ich so schnell nicht wieder!; **what's the ~?** was soll die Eile *or* Hast?; **what's your ~?** warum (hast dus) so eilig?; **is there any ~ for it?** eilt es damit?, eilt das?; **there's no ~** es eilt nicht, es hat Zeit

VI sich beeilen; *(= run/go quickly)* laufen, eilen *(geh)*; **there's no need to ~** kein Grund zur Eile; **can't you make her ~?** kannst du sie nicht zur Eile antreiben?; **don't ~!** lass dir Zeit!, immer mit der Ruhe! *(inf)*; **I must ~ back** ich muss schnell zurück

VT *person (= make act quickly)* (zur Eile) antreiben; *(= make move quickly)* scheuchen *(inf)*; *work etc* beschleunigen, schneller machen; *(= do too quickly)* überstürzen; **troops were hurried to the spot** es wurden schleunigst Truppen dorthin gebracht; **don't ~ me** hetz mich nicht so!; **don't ~ your meals** schling das Essen nicht so runter!; **I won't be hurried into a decision** ich lasse mich nicht zu einer schnellen Entscheidung drängen

▶ **hurry along** **VI** sich beeilen; **hurry along there, please!** schnell weitergehen, bitte!; **she hurried along to where her friend was waiting** sie lief schnell zu ihrer wartenden Freundin; **to hurry along the road** die Straße entlanglaufen **VT** *sep person* weiterdrängen; *(with work etc)* zur Eile antreiben; *things, work etc* vorantreiben, beschleunigen

▶ **hurry away** *or* **off** **VI** schnell weggehen, forteilen *(geh)* **VT** *sep* schnell wegbringen; **they hurried him off to the waiting car** sie brachten ihn schnell zu dem wartenden Wagen

▶ **hurry on** **VI** weiterlaufen; *(verbally, with work)* weitermachen; **she hurried on ahead** sie lief *or* eilte *(geh)* voraus **VT** *sep person* weitertreiben; *(with work)* antreiben

▶ **hurry out** **VI** hinauslaufen *or* -eilen **VT** *sep* schnell hinausbringen *or* -treiben

▶ **hurry up** **VI** sich beeilen; **hurry up!** Beeilung!, beeil dich!; **hurry up and put your coat on!** jetzt zieh dir schnell deinen Mantel an!, mach schon und zieh dir deinen Mantel an!; **can't you make him hurry up?** kannst du nicht dafür sorgen, dass er sich beeilt?; **hurry up with that coffee, will you!** beeilen Sie sich mit dem Kaffee! **VT** *sep person* zur Eile antreiben; *work, process etc* vorantreiben, beschleunigen; **hurry it up!** Beeilung!

hurry-scurry ['hʌrɪ'skʌrɪ] **N** Gewühl *nt*, Gewimmel *nt* **VI** (hin und her) hasten, herumschwirren; *(children, insects)* wuseln

hurt [hɜːt] *vb: pret, ptp* **hurt** VT **a** *(lit, fig) (= cause pain) person, animal* wehtun *(+dat); (= injure)* verletzen; **to ~ oneself** sich *(dat)* wehtun; **to ~ one's arm** sich *(dat)* am Arm wehtun; *(= injure)* sich *(dat)* den Arm verletzen; **my arm is ~ing me** mein Arm tut mir weh, mir tut der Arm weh; **if you go on like that someone is bound to get ~** wenn ihr so weitermacht, verletzt sich bestimmt noch jemand
b *(= harm)* schaden *(+dat)*; **it won't ~ him to wait** es schadet ihm gar nicht(s), wenn er etwas wartet *or* warten muss; **it never ~s to talk to somebody** es kann nie schaden, mit jemandem zu sprechen; **walking on the grass doesn't ~ it** es schadet dem Gras nicht, wenn man darauf (herum)läuft; **those most ~ by this measure** die von dieser Maßnahme am stärksten Betroffenen
VI **a** *(= be painful)* wehtun; *(fig)* wehtun, verletzend sein; **that ~s!** *(lit, fig)* das tut weh!; **nothing ~s like the truth** nichts schmerzt mehr *or* tut mehr weh als die Wahrheit; **I love him so much it ~s** ich liebe ihn so sehr, dass es wehtut
b *(= do harm)* schaden; **but surely one drink won't ~** aber ein Gläschen kann doch wohl nicht schaden
N Schmerz *m*; *(baby-talk)* Wehweh *nt*; *(to feelings)* Verletzung *f (to +gen)*; *(to reputation etc)* Schädigung *f (to +gen)*
ADJ *limb, feelings* verletzt; *tone, look* gekränkt

hurtful [ˈhɜːtfʊl] ADJ *words, action* verletzend; **it was very ~ to him** es verletzte ihn sehr; **to say/do ~ things** Verletzendes sagen/tun

hurtfully [ˈhɜːtfəlɪ] ADV verletzend; *say* in verletzendem Ton

hurtle [ˈhɜːtl] VI rasen; **the car was hurtling along** das Auto sauste *or* brauste dahin; **it ~d into the wall** es sauste gegen die Mauer; **he came hurtling round the corner** er kam um die Ecke gerast

husband [ˈhʌzbənd] N Ehemann *m*; **my/her** *etc* **~** mein/ihr *etc* Mann; **give my best wishes to your ~** grüßen Sie Ihren Mann *or* Gatten *(form)* von mir; **~ and wife** Mann und Frau; **they are ~ and wife** sie sind Eheleute *or* verheiratet VT *strength, resources* haushalten *or* Haus halten mit, sparsam umgehen mit

husbandry [ˈhʌzbəndrɪ] N **a** *(= management)* Haushalten *nt*, Wirtschaften *nt* **b** *(= farming)* Landwirtschaft *f*

husband-to-be N *pl* **husbands-to-be her ~** ihr zukünftiger Mann

hush [hʌʃ] VT *person* zum Schweigen bringen; *(= soothe) fears etc* beschwichtigen VI still sein N Stille *f*; **a ~ fell over the crowd** die Menge verstummte plötzlich INTERJ pst; **~, ~, it's all right** sch, sch, es ist ja gut
▶ **hush up** VT *sep* vertuschen

hushed [hʌʃt] ADJ *voices* gedämpft; *words* leise; *crowd* schweigend; *courtroom* still; **in ~ tones** mit gedämpfter Stimme, in gedämpftem Ton; **in ~ whispers** im gedämpften Flüsterton

hush-hush [ˈhʌʃˈhʌʃ] ADJ *(inf)* streng geheim

hush money [ˈhʌʃmʌnɪ] N Schweigegeld *nt*

husk [hʌsk] N Schale *f*; *(of wheat, rice)* Spelze *f*; *(of maize)* Hüllblatt *nt* VT schälen

huskily [ˈhʌskɪlɪ] ADV mit rauer Stimme; *(= hoarsely)* heiser, mit heiserer Stimme

huskiness [ˈhʌskɪnɪs] N Rauheit *f*; *(= hoarseness)* Heiserkeit *f*

husky[1] [ˈhʌskɪ] ADJ *(+er)* **a** rau, belegt; *singer's voice* rauh, rauchig; *(= hoarse)* heiser; **his voice was ~ with emotion** seine Stimme war heiser vor Erregung **b** *(= sturdy) person* stämmig

husky[2] N *(= dog)* Schlittenhund *m*

hussar [hʊˈzɑː] N Husar *m*

hussy [ˈhʌsɪ] N *(= pert girl)* Fratz *m (inf)*, (freche) Göre *(inf)*; *(= whorish woman)* Flittchen *nt (pej)*; **a brazen** *or* **wanton ~** ein schamloses Flittchen

hustings [ˈhʌstɪŋz] PL *(Brit) (= campaign)* Wahlkampf *m*; *(= meeting)* Wahlveranstaltung *f*; **on the ~** im Wahlkampf; *(= at election meeting)* in *or* bei einer Wahlveranstaltung

hustle [ˈhʌsl] N *(= jostling)* Gedränge *nt*; *(= hurry)* Hetze *f*, Eile *f*; **the ~ (and bustle) of the city centre** das geschäftige Treiben *or* das Gewühl *(inf)* in der Innenstadt
VT **a** *(= hurry)* **to ~ sb into a room/out of a building** jdn schnell in einen Raum/aus einem Gebäude bringen *or* befördern *(inf)*; **she ~d her way through the crowd** sie drängelte sich durch die Menge
b *(fig inf)* drängen; **I won't be ~d into a decision** ich lasse mich nicht zu einer Entscheidung drängen; **I won't be ~d into selling my shares** ich lasse mich nicht dazu drängen, meine Aktien zu verkaufen; **to ~ things (on** *or* **along)** die Dinge vorantreiben *or* beschleunigen
VI **a** hasten, eilen; *(through crowd etc)* sich (durch)drängeln
b *(= solicit)* auf den Strich gehen *(inf)*; **to ~ for business** *(entrepreneur etc)* Aufträgen nachjagen
c *(US inf: = work quickly)* sich ins Zeug legen *(inf)*

hustler [ˈhʌsləˈ] N **a** *(male)* Strichjunge *m (inf)* **b** *(US inf: = hard worker)* Arbeitstier *nt (inf)*

hustling [ˈhʌslɪŋ] N (Straßen)prostitution *f*, der Strich *(inf)*

hut [hʌt] N Hütte *f*; *(Mil)* Baracke *f*

hutch [hʌtʃ] N Verschlag *m*, Stall *m*

HWM *abbr of* **high-water mark**

hyacinth [ˈhaɪəsɪnθ] N Hyazinthe *f*

hyaena, hyena [haɪˈiːnə] N Hyäne *f*; **to laugh like a ~** wiehernd lachen

hybrid [ˈhaɪbrɪd] N *(Ling)* hybride Bildung *or* Form; *(Bot, Zool)* Kreuzung *f*, Hybride *mf (form)*; *(fig)* Mischform *f* ADJ *(Ling)* hybrid *(spec)*; *(Bot, Zool)* Misch-; **~ plant** Mischpflanze *f*; **~ car** *or* **vehicle** Hybridauto *nt*, Hybridfahrzeug *nt*

hybridism [ˈhaɪbrɪdɪzəm] N *(lit, fig)* Hybridismus *m*

hybridization [ˌhaɪbrɪdaɪˈzeɪʃən] N *(Ling)* Hybridisation *f (spec)*; *(Bot, Zool also)* Kreuzung *f*; *(fig)* Mischung *f*, Zwitter *m*

hybridize [ˈhaɪbrɪdaɪz] VT *(Ling)* hybridisieren *(spec)*; *(Bot, Zool also)* kreuzen; *(fig)* mischen, kreuzen

hydra [ˈhaɪdrə] N *(Zool, Myth)* Hydra *f*

hydrangea [haɪˈdreɪndʒə] N Hortensie *f*

hydrant [ˈhaɪdrənt] N Hydrant *m*

hydrate N [ˈhaɪdreɪt] Hydrat *nt* VT [haɪˈdreɪt] hydratisieren

hydrated [haɪˈdreɪtɪd] ADJ wasserhaltig

hydraulic [haɪˈdrɒlɪk] ADJ hydraulisch; **~ dock** *(Naut)* Schwimmdock *nt*

hydraulics [haɪˈdrɒlɪks] N *sing* Hydraulik *f*

hydro [ˈhaɪdrəʊ] N Kurhotel *nt (mit Hydrotherapie)*

hydro- [ˈhaɪdrəʊ-] PREF *(= concerning water)* Hydro-, hydro-, Wasser-, wasser-; *(Chem, +n)* -wasserstoff *m*; **hydrocarbon** N Kohlenwasserstoff *m*; **hydrocephalic** [ˌhaɪdrəʊseˈfælɪk] ADJ wasserköpfig, mit einem Wasserkopf; **hydrocephalus** [ˌhaɪdrəʊˈsefələs] N Wasserkopf *m*; **hydrochloric acid** N Salzsäure *f*; **hydrodynamics** N *sing or pl* Hydrodynamik *f*; **hydroelectric** ADJ hydroelektrisch; **hydroelectricity** N durch Wasserkraft erzeugte Energie; **hydroelectric power** N durch Wasserkraft erzeugte Energie; **hydroelectric power station** N Wasserkraftwerk *nt*; **hydrofoil** N *(= boat)* Tragflächen- *or* Tragflügelboot *nt*; *(= fin)* Tragfläche *f or* -flügel *m*

hydrogen [ˈhaɪdrɪdʒən] N Wasserstoff *m*, Hydrogenium *nt (spec)*

hydrogen: **hydrogen bomb** N Wasserstoffbombe *f*; **hydrogen bond** N Wasserstoffbrücke(nbindung) *f*; **hydrogen sulphide** N *(= gas)* Schwefelwasserstoff *m*

hydrography [haɪˈdrɒgrəfɪ] N Gewässerkunde *f*

hydrology [haɪˈdrɒlədʒɪ] N Hydrologie *f*

hydrolysis [haɪˈdrɒlɪsɪs] N Hydrolyse *f*

hydrometer [haɪˈdrɒmɪtəˈ] N Hydrometer *nt*

hydro-: **hydropathic** [ˌhaɪdrəʊˈpæθɪk] ADJ hydrotherapeutisch; **hydrophobia** N Hydrophobie *f (spec)*, Wasserscheu *f*; *(= rabies)* Tollwut *f*; **hydrophobic** ADJ hydrophob *(spec)*, wasserscheu; **hydroplane** N **a** *(Aviat) (= aircraft)* Wasserflugzeug *nt*, Flugboot *nt*; *(= float)* Schwimmer *m* **b** *(Naut) (= boat)* Gleitboot *nt*; *(of submarine)* Tiefenruder *nt*; **hydroponics** [ˌhaɪdrəʊˈpɒnɪks] N *sing* Hydrokultur *f*; **hydropower** N Wasserkraft *f*; **hydrotherapeutics** N *sing* Wasserheilkunde *f*, Hydrotherapeutik *f (spec)*; **hydrotherapy** N Wasserbehandlung *f*, Hydrotherapie *f (spec)*

hydroxide [haɪˈdrɒksaɪd] N Hydroxid *nt*

hyena [haɪˈiːnə] N = **hyaena**

hygiene [ˈhaɪdʒiːn] N Hygiene *f*; **personal ~** Körperpflege *f*

hygienic [haɪˈdʒiːnɪk] ADJ hygienisch

hygienically [haɪˈdʒiːnɪkəlɪ] ADV hygienisch

hygienics [haɪˈdʒiːnɪks] N *sing* Hygiene *f*, Gesundheitslehre *f*

hygro- [ˈhaɪgrəʊ-] PREF Hygro-, hygro-, (Luft)feuchtigkeits-; **hygrometer** [ˈhaɪˈgrɒmɪtəˈ] N Hygrometer *nt*, (Luft)feuchtigkeitsmesser *m*

hymen [ˈhaɪmen] N Hymen *nt (spec)*, Jungfernhäutchen *nt*

hymenopterous [ˌhaɪməˈnɒptərəs] ADJ **~ insect** Hautflügler *m*

hymn [hɪm] N Kirchenlied *nt*; **~ of praise** *(fig)* Lobeshymne *f* VT *(old)* besingen; *(Eccl)* (lob)preisen

hymnal [ˈhɪmnəl] N Gesangbuch *nt*

hymn book N Gesangbuch *nt*

hymnic [ˈhɪmnɪk] ADJ hymnenartig, hymnisch

hymn-singing [ˈhɪmˌsɪŋɪŋ] N Singen *nt* (von Chorälen); **we had ~ once a week** wir hatten einmal in der Woche Choralsingen

hype [haɪp] *(inf)* N Publicity *f*; **media ~** Medienrummel *m (inf)*; **the concept is mainly ~** das Konzept beruht hauptsächlich auf Publicity; **all this ~ about ...** dieser ganze Rummel um ... *(inf)* VT *(also* **hype up**) *product etc* Publicity machen für; **the film was ~d up too much** um den Film wurde zu viel Rummel gemacht *(inf)*

hyped up [ˈhaɪptˈʌp] ADJ *(inf) product* übertrieben hochgeputscht *or* hochgejubelt; *subject etc* hochgespielt; *person* überdreht *(inf)*, überspannt; *(= excited)* aufgedreht *(inf)*; **to get ~** aus dem Häuschen geraten *(about* wegen *(inf)*, ausflippen *(inf)*; **to be ~ for sth** total scharf auf etw sein *(inf)*

hyper- [ˈhaɪpəˈ] PREF Hyper-, hyper-, Über-, über-; **hyperacidity** N Übersäuerung *f*, Hyperazidität *f (spec)*; **hyperactive** ADJ überaktiv, sehr *or* äußerst aktiv; **a ~ thyroid** eine Überfunktion der Schilddrüse

hyperbola [haɪˈpɜːbələ] N *(Math)* Hyperbel *f*

hyperbole [haɪˈpɜːbəlɪ] N *(Liter)* Hyperbel *f*

hyperbolic(al) [ˌhaɪpəˈbɒlɪk(əl)] ADJ *(Liter, Math)* hyperbolisch; *(Math also)* Hyperbel-; **hyperbolic function** Hyperbelfunktion *f*

hyper-: **hypercard** N *(Comput)* Hypercard *f*; **hypercritical** ADJ übertrieben kritisch

hyperglycaemia, *(US)* **hyperglycemia** [ˌhaɪpəglaɪˈsiːmɪə] N Hyperglykämie *f (spec)*, Überzuckerung *f*

hyperglycaemic, *(US)* **hyperglycemic** [ˌhaɪpəglaɪˈsiːmɪk] ADJ *symptoms* hyperglykämisch *(spec)*; *person* hyperglykämisch *(spec)*, an Überzuckerung leidend

hyper-: **hyperlink** N *(Comput, Internet)* Hyperlink *f*; **hypermarket** N *(Brit)* Verbrauchermarkt *m*, Hypermarkt *m*; **hypersensitive** ADJ überempfindlich; **hypertension** N Hypertonie *f*, erhöhter Blutdruck; **hypertext** N *(Comput)* Hypertext *m*; **hyperthyroidism** [ˌhaɪpəˈθaɪrɔɪdɪzəm] N Überfunktion *f* der Schilddrüse; **hypertrophy** [haɪˈpɜːtrəfɪ] N Hypertrophie *f*; **hyperventilate** [ˌhaɪpəˈventɪleɪt] VI hyperventilieren; **hyperventilation** [ˈhaɪpəˌventɪˈleɪʃən] N Hyperventilation *f*

hyphen [ˈhaɪfən] N Bindestrich *m*; *(at end of line)* Trenn(ungs)strich *m*; *(Typ)* Divis *nt*

hyphenate [ˈhaɪfəneɪt] VT mit Bindestrich schreiben; *(Typ)* koppeln *(spec)*; **~d word** Bindestrich- *or (Typ)* Koppelwort *nt*

hyphenation [ˌhaɪfəˈneɪʃən] N Silbentrennung *f*; **~ program** *(Comput)* Silbentrennprogramm *nt*

hypnosis [hɪpˈnəʊsɪs] N Hypnose *f*; **under ~** unter *or* in Hypnose, in hypnotisiertem Zustand

hypnotherapist [ˌhɪpnəʊˈθerəpɪst] N Hypnotherapeut(in) *m(f)*

hypnotherapy [ˌhɪpnəʊˈθerəpɪ] N Hypnotherapie *f*

hypnotic [hɪpˈnɒtɪk] ADJ **a** *(= hypnotized) regression, trance* hypnotisch; **~ state** Hypnose *f*, Hypnosezustand *m* **b** *(= mesmerizing) effect, rhythm, music, power, voice, eyes* hypnotisch, hypnotisierend N **a** *(= drug)* Hypnotikum *nt* *(spec)*, Schlafmittel *nt* **b** *(= person) (easily hypnotized)* leicht hypnotisierbarer Mensch; *(under hypnosis)* Hypnotisierte(r) *mf*

hypnotism [ˈhɪpnətɪzəm] N Hypnotismus *m*; *(= act)* Hypnotisierung *f*

hypnotist [ˈhɪpnətɪst] N Hypnotiseur(in) *m(f)*

hypnotize [ˈhɪpnətaɪz] VT hypnotisieren; **to be ~d by sb/sth** *(= fascinated)* von jdm/etw wie hypnotisiert sein

hypo [ˈhaɪpəʊ] N *(Med inf)* Hypo *m (inf)*

hypo- [haɪpəʊ-] PREF Hypo-, hypo-; **hypoallergenic** hypoallergen

hypochondria [ˌhaɪpəʊˈkɒndrɪə] N Hypochondrie *f*

hypochondriac [ˌhaɪpəʊˈkɒndrɪæk] N Hypochonder *m* ADJ *(also* **hypochondriacal***)* [ˌhaɪpəʊkɒnˈdraɪəkəl] hypochondrisch

hypocrisy [hɪˈpɒkrɪsɪ] N *(= hypocritical behaviour)* Heuchelei *f*; *(= sanctimony)* Scheinheiligkeit *f*

hypocrite [ˈhɪpəkrɪt] N Heuchler(in) *m(f)*, Scheinheilige(r) *mf*

hypocritical ADJ, **hypocritically** ADV [ˌhɪpəˈkrɪtɪkəl, -ɪ] heuchlerisch, scheinheilig

hypodermic [ˌhaɪpəˈdɜːmɪk] ADJ *injection* subkutan N **a** *(= syringe)* subkutane Spritze **b** *(= injection)* subkutane Injektion

hypodermic needle N (Injektions)nadel *f*

hypodermic syringe N (Injektions)spritze *f*

hypoglycaemia, *(US)* **hypoglycemia** [ˌhaɪpəʊglaɪˈsiːmɪə] N *(Med)* Hypoglykämie *f* *(spec)*, Unterzuckerung *f*

hypoglycaemic, *(US)* **hypoglycemic** [ˌhaɪpəʊglaɪˈsiːmɪk] ADJ *(Med) symptoms* hypoglykämisch *(spec)*, Unterzuckerungs-; *person* hypoglykämisch *(spec)*, an Unterzuckerung leidend

hypotenuse [haɪˈpɒtɪnjuːz] N Hypotenuse *f*; **the square on the ~** das Quadrat über der Hypotenuse

hypothalamus [ˌhaɪpəˈθæləməs] N *pl* **-mi** [-maɪ] *(Anat)* Hypothalamus *m*

hypothermia [ˌhaɪpəʊˈθɜːmɪə] N Unterkühlung *f*, Kältetod *m*

hypothesis [haɪˈpɒθɪsɪs] N *pl* **hypotheses** [haɪˈpɒθɪsiːz] Hypothese *f*, Annahme *f*; **working ~** Arbeitshypothese *f*

hypothesize [haɪˈpɒθɪsaɪz] VI Hypothesen aufstellen VT annehmen

hypothetical [ˌhaɪpəʊˈθetɪkəl] ADJ hypothetisch, angenommen; **purely ~** reine Hypothese

hypothetically [ˌhaɪpəʊˈθetɪkəlɪ] ADV **a** *(= as a hypothesis)* hypothetisch, als Hypothese **b** *(= in theory)* theoretisch

hysterectomy [ˌhɪstəˈrektəmɪ] N Hysterektomie *f (spec)*, Totaloperation *f*

hysteria [hɪˈstɪərɪə] N Hysterie *f*; **completely overcome with ~** völlig hysterisch

hysterical [hɪˈsterɪkəl] ADJ **a** *(also Psych)* hysterisch; **I was nearly ~** ich war der Hysterie nahe **b** *(inf: = hilarious)* wahnsinnig komisch *(inf)*

hysterically [hɪˈsterɪkəlɪ] ADV **a** *scream, cry, sob, laugh* hysterisch **b** *(inf)* **~ funny** wahnsinnig komisch *(inf)* **c** *(= frantically)* wie wahnsinnig *(inf)*

hysterics [hɪˈsterɪks] PL Hysterie *f*, hysterischer Anfall; **to go into** *or* **have ~** hysterisch werden, einen hysterischen Anfall bekommen; *(fig inf: = laugh)* sich totlachen, sich nicht mehr halten können vor Lachen; **to be in ~** hysterisch sein, einen hysterischen Anfall haben; *(fig inf: = be laughing)* sich (halb) totlachen *(inf)*; **we were in ~ about it** *(fig inf)* wir haben uns darüber (halb) totgelacht *(inf)*; **he had us all in ~** *(fig inf)* wir haben uns über ihn (halb) totgelacht *(inf)*

Hz *abbr of* **hertz** Hz

I

I[1], **i** [aɪ] N I *nt*, i *nt* → **dot**

I[2] *abbr of* **Island, Isle**

I[3] PERS PRON ich; **it is I** *(form)* ich bin es

IAAF *abbr of* **International Amateur Athletic Federation** IAAF *f*, Leichtathletik-Weltverband *m*

IAEA *abbr of* **International Atomic Energy Agency**

iambic [aɪˈæmbɪk] ADJ jambisch; **~ pentameter** fünffüßiger Jambus N Jambus *m*

IATA [aɪˈɑːtə] *abbr of* **International Air Transport Association** IATA *f*

iatrogenic [ˌjætrəʊˈdʒenɪk, aɪˌætrəʊ-] ADJ iatrogen

IBA *(Brit) abbr of* **Independent Broadcasting Authority** *Aufsichtsgremium der Fernsehanstalt ITV*

Iberia [aɪˈbɪərɪə] N Iberien *nt*

Iberian [aɪˈbɪərɪən] ADJ iberisch N **a** Iberer(in) *m(f)* **b** *(Ling)* Iberisch *nt*

Iberian Peninsula N Iberische Halbinsel

ibex [ˈaɪbeks] N Steinbock *m*

ib(id) *abbr of* **ibidem** ib., ibd

ibis [ˈaɪbɪs] N Ibis *m*

IBRD *abbr of* **International Bank of Reconstruction and Development**

IBS *abbr of* **irritable bowel syndrome** Reizdarm *m*

IC *abbr of* **intellectual capital** geistiges Kapital

i/c, I/C *abbr of* **in charge** v. D., vom Dienst

ICBM *abbr of* **intercontinental ballistic missile** Interkontinentalrakete *f*

ice [aɪs] N **a** Eis *nt*; *(on roads)* (Glatt)eis *nt*; **to be as cold as ~** eiskalt sein; **my hands are like ~** ich habe eiskalte Hände; **"Cinderella on Ice"** „Aschenputtel auf dem Eis"; **to keep** *or* **put sth on ~** *(lit)* etw kalt stellen; *(fig)* etw auf Eis legen; **to break the ~** *(fig)* das Eis brechen; **to be** *or* **be treading** *or* **be skating on thin ~** *(fig)* sich aufs Glatteis begeben/begeben haben; **you are (skating) on thin ~ there** *(fig)* da begibst du dich aufs Glatteis; **to cut no ~ with sb** *(inf)* auf jdn keinen Eindruck machen; **that cuts no ~ with me** *(inf)* das kommt bei mir nicht an
b *(Brit: = ice cream)* (Speise)eis *nt*, Eiskrem *f*
c *no pl (US sl: = diamond)* Klunker *m (inf)*
VT **a** *(= make cold)* (mit Eis) kühlen; *(= freeze)* tiefkühlen
b *cake* glasieren, mit Zuckerguss überziehen

▶ **ice over** VI zufrieren; *(windscreen)* vereisen

▶ **ice up** VI *(aircraft wings, rail points, windscreen)* vereisen; *(pipes etc)* einfrieren

ice *in cpds* Eis-; **ice age** N Eiszeit *f*; **ice axe,** *(US)* **ice ax** N Eispickel *m*; **ice bag** N Eisbeutel *m*; **iceberg** N *(lit, fig)* Eisberg *m*; **ice-blue** ADJ eisblau; **iceboat** N **a** *(Sport)* Segelschlitten *m* **b** = **icebreaker**; **icebound** ADJ *port, lake* zugefroren, vereist; *ship, place* vom Eis eingeschlossen; *road* vereist; *ground* zu Eis gefroren; **icebox** N *(Brit: in refrigerator)* Eisfach *nt*; *(US)* Eisschrank *m*; *(= insulated box)* Eisbox *f*, Kühltasche *f*; **this room is like an ~** dieses Zimmer ist der reinste Eiskeller; **icebreaker** N Eisbrecher *m*; **ice bucket** N Eiskühler *m*; **icecap** N Eisdecke *f*, Eisschicht *f*; *(polar)* Eiskappe *f*; **ice-cold** ADJ eiskalt; **ice cream** N Eis *nt*, Eiskrem *f*; **ice-cream cone, ice-cream cornet** N Eistüte *f*; **ice-cream parlour,** *(US)* **ice-cream parlor** N Eisdiele *f*; **ice-cream soda** N *Eisbecher mit Sirup, Marmelade, Früchten, Milch und Ingwerlimonade*; **ice-cream van** N *(Brit)* Eiswagen *m*; **ice crusher** N Eiszerkleinerer *m*; **ice cube** N Eiswürfel *m*

iced [aɪst] ADJ **a** *(= cooled) drink* eisgekühlt; **~ tea** Eistee *m*; **~ coffee** Eiskaffee *m* **b** *(= covered in icing) cake, bun* glasiert, mit Zuckerguss überzogen

ice: **ice dancing** N Eistanz *m*; **ice floe** N Eisscholle *f*; **ice hockey** N Eishockey *nt*; **ice house** N Eiskeller *m*

Iceland [ˈaɪslənd] N Island *nt*

Icelander [ˈaɪsləndəʳ] N Isländer(in) *m(f)*

Icelandic [aɪsˈlændɪk] ADJ isländisch N *(Ling)* Isländisch *nt*

ice: **ice lolly** N *(Brit)* Eis *nt* am Stiel; **ice maiden** N *(inf)* eiskalte Schönheit; **ice man** N *(US)* Eisverkäufer *m*; **ice pack** N Packeis *nt*; *(on head)* Eisbeutel *m*; **ice pick** N Eispickel *m*; **ice point** N *(Phys)* Gefrierpunkt *m*; **ice rink** N (Kunst)eisbahn *f*, Schlittschuhbahn *f*; **ice sheet** N Eisschicht *f*; **ice-skate** VI Schlittschuh laufen *or* fahren; **ice skate** N Schlittschuh *m*; **ice-skater** N Schlittschuhläufer(in) *m(f)*; *(= figure-skater)* Eiskunstläufer(in) *m(f)*; **ice-skating** N Eislauf *m*, Schlittschuhlaufen *nt*; *(= figure-skating)* Eiskunstlauf *m*; **ice storm** N *(US)* Eissturm *m*; **ice tea** N Eistee *m*; **ice tray** N Eisschale *f*; **ice water** N Eiswasser *nt*

ichneumon fly [ɪkˈnjuːmənˌflaɪ] N Schlupfwespe *f*

ichthyology [ˌɪkθɪˈɒlədʒɪ] N Fischkunde *f*, Ichthyologie *f (spec)*

icicle [ˈaɪsɪkl] N Eiszapfen *m*

icily [ˈaɪsɪlɪ] ADV **a** *blow* eisig; **a north-east wind blew ~** es wehte ein eisiger Nordostwind; **~ cold** eisig kalt, eiskalt **b** *(fig) say, stare* eisig, frostig; *smile* kalt; *calm, polite, cold* eisig; **to look ~ at sb** jdm einen eisigen Blick zuwerfen

iciness [ˈaɪsɪnɪs] N **a** *(of windows etc)* Vereisung *f*; **the ~ of the roads** das Glatteis auf den Straßen **b** *(= freezing cold)* Eiseskälte *f*, eisige Kälte **c** *(fig) (of stare)* eisige Kälte; *(of tone, reception, silence)* Frostigkeit *f*

icing [ˈaɪsɪŋ] N **a** *(Cook)* Zuckerguss *m*; **this is the ~ on the cake** *(fig)* das ist die Krönung des Ganzen **b** *(on aircraft, rail points)* Eisbildung *f*, Vereisung *f*

icing sugar N *(Brit)* Puderzucker *m*

icky [ˈɪkɪ] ADJ *(inf)* **a** *(= yucky)* ekelhaft, eklig *(inf)* **b** *(= sentimental)* kitschig *(pej)*

icon [ˈaɪkɒn] N **a** *(Art)* Ikone *f* **b** *(= cultural symbol)* Ikone *f* **c** *(Comput)* Icon *nt*, ikonisches Zeichen

iconic [aɪˈkɒnɪk] ADJ **a** *(Ling, Comput, Psych)* ikonisch **b** *(Art) portrait* ikonisch **c** *(culturally)* **an ~ figure** eine Ikone; **to achieve ~ status** zur Ikone werden

iconoclasm [aɪˈkɒnəklæzəm] N *(lit, fig)* Bilderstürmerei *f*

iconoclast [aɪˈkɒnəklæst] N *(lit)* Bilderstürmer *m*, Ikonoklast *m (liter)*; *(fig)* Bilderstürmer(in) *m(f)*

iconoclastic [aɪˌkɒnəˈklæstɪk] ADJ *(fig)* bilderstürmerisch

iconographic [aɪˌkɒnəˈgræfɪk] ADJ ikonografisch

ictus [ˈɪktəs] N *pl* **ictuses** *or* **ictus** *(Liter)* Iktus *m*, Versakzent *m*

ICU *(US) abbr of* **intensive care unit**; **to be in ~** auf der Intensivstation liegen

icy [ˈaɪsɪ] ADJ *(+er)* **a** *(= ice-covered) road, pavement* vereist; **the ~ conditions on the roads** das Glatteis auf den Straßen; **when it's ~** bei Glatteis **b** *(= freezing cold) air, wind, river, hands, feet* eiskalt, eisig; **~ cold** *(water, weather)* eiskalt, eisig; *drink* eiskalt, eisgekühlt **c** *(fig) stare* eisig; *tone, reception, silence* frostig

ID N *abbr of* **identification, identity I don't have any ID on me** ich habe keinen Ausweis dabei; **he showed them his ID** er zeigte ihnen seinen Ausweis; **you need ID to get in** man braucht einen Ausweis, um hineinzukommen; **can I see some ID?** kann ich Ihren Ausweis sehen? VT *person* identifizieren; **we've ID'd the girl** wir haben das Mädchen identifiziert; **Molly got ID'd** sie haben Mollys Ausweis kontrolliert

I'd [aɪd] *contr of* **I would, I had**

id [ɪd] N *(Psych)* Es *nt*

ID card [aɪˈdiːkɑːd] N Ausweis *m*; *(state-issued)* Personalausweis *m*

idea [aɪˈdɪə] ✪ 1.1, 6.2, 6.3, 8.2, 8.3, 26.2 N **a** Idee *f (also Philos)*; *(esp sudden)* Einfall *m*; **good ~!** gute Idee!; **that's not a bad ~** das ist keine schlechte Idee; **what an ~!** so eine *or* was für eine Idee!; **who thought of that ~?** wer hat sich *(dat)* denn das einfallen lassen?; **whose bright ~ was that?** *(iro)* wer hat denn diese glänzende Idee gehabt?; **he's our new ~s man** *(inf)* er ist hier der Mann mit den neuen Ideen; **history of ~s** Geistesgeschichte *f*; **man of ~s** Denker *m*; **the very ~!** (nein,) so was!; **the very ~ of eating horse meat revolts me** der bloße Gedanke an Pferdefleisch ekelt mich; **the ~ never entered my head!** auf den Gedanken bin ich überhaupt nicht gekommen; **he is full of (bright) ~s** ihm fehlt es nie an (guten) Ideen; **to hit upon the ~ of doing sth** den plötzlichen Einfall haben, etw zu tun; **that gives me an ~, we could ...** da fällt mir ein, wir könnten ...; **he got the ~ for his novel while he was having a bath** die Idee zu seinem Roman kam ihm in der Badewanne; **to lack ~s** fantasielos *or* phantasielos *or* einfallslos sein; **somehow he's got the ~ into his head that ...** er bildet sich *(dat)* irgendwie ein, dass ...; **where did you get the ~ that I was ill?** wie kommst du auf den Gedanken, dass ich krank war?; **don't get ~s** *or* **don't you go getting ~s about promotion** machen Sie sich *(dat)* nur keine falschen Hoffnungen auf eine Beförderung; **don't get** *or* **go getting any ~s about that fur coat** bilde dir nur nicht ein, du würdest den Pelzmantel bekommen; **to put ~s into sb's head** jdm einen Floh ins Ohr setzen, jdn auf dumme Gedanken bringen
b *(= purpose)* **the ~ was to meet at 6** wir wollten uns um 6 treffen; **what's the ~ of keeping him waiting?** was soll denn das, ihn warten zu lassen?; **what's the big ~?** *(inf)* was soll das denn?; **the ~ is to reduce expenditure** es geht

darum, die Ausgaben zu senken; **he sat down with the ~ of writing a letter** er setzte sich mit der Absicht, einen Brief zu schreiben; **that's the ~** so ist es richtig, genau (das ists)!; **you're getting the ~** Sie verstehen langsam, worum es geht
c *(= opinion)* Meinung *f*, Ansicht *f*; *(= conception)* Vorstellung *f*; **if that's your ~ of fun** wenn Sie das lustig finden, wenn das Ihre Vorstellung von Spaß ist; **this isn't my ~ of a holiday** so stelle ich mir den Urlaub nicht vor; **he has some very strange ~s** er hat manchmal merkwürdige Vorstellungen; **according to his ~** seiner Meinung *or* Ansicht nach; **he has no ~ of right and wrong** er kann zwischen Gut und Böse nicht unterscheiden; **his ~ of a pleasant evening is ...** seine Vorstellung von einem angenehmen Abend ist ...
d *(= knowledge)* Ahnung *f*; **you've no ~ how worried I've been** du kannst dir nicht vorstellen, welche Sorgen ich mir gemacht habe; **(I've) no ~** (ich habe) keine Ahnung; **I've got some ~ (of) what this is all about** ich weiß so ungefähr, worum es hier geht; **I haven't the least** *or* **slightest** *or* **faintest ~** ich habe nicht die leiseste *or* geringste Ahnung; **I have an ~ that ...** ich habe so das Gefühl, dass ...; **I had no ~ that ...** ich hatte ja keine Ahnung, dass ...; **just to give me an ~ of how long it will take** damit ich so ungefähr weiß, wie lange es dauert; **could you give me an ~ of how long ...?** könnten Sie mir ungefähr sagen, wie lange ...?; **to give you an ~ of how difficult it is** um Ihnen eine Vorstellung davon zu vermitteln, wie schwierig es ist

ideal [aɪˈdɪəl] **N** Ideal *nt (of +gen)*; *(= model)* Ideal(bild) *nt (of +gen)* **ADJ** ideal; **~ solution** Ideallösung *f*; **~ weight** Idealgewicht *nt*; **he is ~** *or* **the ~ person for the job** er ist für den Job ideal geeignet; **the plants are ~ for growing in the home** die Pflanzen eignen sich ideal als Zimmerpflanzen; **in an ~ world** im Idealfall; *(philosophical statement)* in einer vollkommenen *or* idealen Welt

idealism [aɪˈdɪəlɪzəm] **N** Idealismus *m*

idealist [aɪˈdɪəlɪst] **N** Idealist(in) *m(f)*

idealistic [aɪˌdɪəˈlɪstɪk] **ADJ** idealistisch

idealize [aɪˈdɪəlaɪz] **VT** idealisieren

idealized [aɪˈdɪəlaɪzd] **ADJ** *person, version, landscape* idealisiert; *image, view* idealisierend

ideally [aɪˈdɪəlɪ] **ADV** **a** *(introducing sentence)* idealerweise, im Idealfall **b** *(= perfectly) suited, placed, situated, located* ideal; **they were ~ suited** sie passten ideal zusammen; **I'm not ~ placed to give you advice** ich bin nicht gerade der Richtige/die Richtige, um dir Ratschläge zu geben; **the hotel is ~ located** das Hotel liegt ideal; **I'm ~ situated in this neighbourhood** diese Gegend liegt für mich ideal

ideation [ˌaɪdɪˈeɪʃən] **N** Ideenbildung *f*; *(= imagination)* Vorstellungsvermögen *nt*

idée fixe [ˌiːdeɪˈfiːks] **N** *pl* **idées fixes** fixe Idee

idem [ˈɪdem] **PRON, ADJ** idem, derselbe

ident [aɪˈdent] **N** *(TV inf: also* **station ident***)* Logo *nt* des Senders; **the MTV station ~s** die Logos des Senders MTV

identical [aɪˈdentɪkəl] **ADJ** *(= exactly alike)* identisch, (völlig) gleich; *(= same)* der-/die-/dasselbe; **~ twins** eineiige Zwillinge *pl*; **we have ~ views** wir haben die gleichen Ansichten

identically [aɪˈdentɪkəlɪ] **ADV** identisch, gleich

identifiable [aɪˈdentɪˌfaɪəbl] **ADJ** erkennbar; *(esp in scientific contexts)* identifizierbar; **he is ~ by his red hair** er ist an seinem roten Haar zu erkennen; **that makes him/it ~** daran kann man ihn/es erkennen

identification [aɪˌdentɪfɪˈkeɪʃən] **N** **a** *(of criminal, dead person etc)* Identifizierung *f*, Feststellung *f* der Identität; *(of genes)* Identifizierung *f*; *(fig) (of goals)* Setzen *nt*; *(of problems)* Erkennen *nt*; **a system of ~ using fingerprints** ein erkennungsdienstliches System auf der Basis von Fingerabdrücken
b *(= papers)* Ausweispapiere *pl*, Legitimation *f*; **because he had no (means of) ~** weil er sich nicht ausweisen konnte
c *(= considering as identical, equation)* Gleichsetzung *f*, Identifizierung *f*
d *(= association)* Identifikation *f*; **a politician who has a strong ~ with a criminal group** ein Politiker, der mit einer kriminellen Gruppe in Verbindung gebracht wird
e *(= sympathy, support)* Identifikation *f*

identification: **identification parade** **N** Gegenüberstellung *f* (zur Identifikation des Täters); **identification tag** **N** *(US)* Erkennungsmarke *f*

identifier [aɪˈdentɪfaɪəʳ] **N** *(Comput)* Bezeichner *m*

identify [aɪˈdentɪfaɪ] **VT** **a** *(= establish identity of)* identifizieren, die Identität *(+gen)* feststellen; *gene, virus etc* identifizieren; *plant, species etc* bestimmen; *(= mark identity of)* kennzeichnen; *(= recognize, pick out)* erkennen; **to ~ one's goals** sich *(dat)* Ziele setzen; **to ~ sb/sth by sth** jdn/etw an etw *(dat)* erkennen **b** *(= consider as the same)* gleichsetzen *(with* mit) **c** *(= associate with)* assoziieren *(with* mit) **VR** **a** **to ~ oneself** sich ausweisen **b** **to ~ oneself with sb/sth** sich mit jdm/etw identifizieren **VI** *(with film hero etc)* sich identifizieren *(with* mit)

Identikit® [aɪˈdentɪkɪt] **N** ~ **(picture)** Phantombild *nt*

identity [aɪˈdentɪtɪ] **N** **a** Identität *f*; **to prove one's ~** sich ausweisen; **a driving licence will be accepted as proof of ~** ein Führerschein genügt, um sich auszuweisen; **proof of ~** *(= permit)* Legitimation *f*; **a sense of ~** ein Bewusstsein *nt* der eigenen Identität → **mistaken**
b *(= identicalness)* Gleichheit *f*, Übereinstimmung *f*, Identität *f*; **~ of interest** Interessengleichheit *f*

identity: **identity bracelet** **N** Identitätsarmband *nt*; **identity card** **N** Ausweis *m*; *(state-issued)* Personalausweis *m*; **identity crisis** **N** Identitätskrise *f*; **identity disc** **N** *(Brit Mil)* Erkennungsmarke *f*; *(for dogs)* Hundemarke *f*; **identity papers** **PL** Ausweispapiere *pl*; **identity parade** **N** Gegenüberstellung *f*; **identity theft** **N** *(Internet)* Identitätsraub *m (Straftat, bei der die Identität einer anderen Person vorgegeben wird, auf deren Kosten im Internet eingekauft wird)*

ideogram [ˈɪdɪəʊgræm], **ideograph** [ˈɪdɪəʊgrɑːf] **N** Ideogramm *nt*

ideological [ˌaɪdɪəˈlɒdʒɪkəl] **ADJ** ideologisch

ideologically [ˌaɪdɪəˈlɒdʒɪkəlɪ] **ADV** ideologisch; **to be ~ opposed to sth** etw vom ideologischen Standpunkt aus ablehnen; **~, there was nothing in common between them** in ideologischer Hinsicht hatten sie nichts gemeinsam

ideologist [ˌaɪdɪˈɒlədʒɪst] **N** Ideologe *m*, Ideologin *f*

ideologue [ˈaɪdɪəlɒg] **N** *(form)* = **ideologist**

ideology [ˌaɪdɪˈɒlədʒɪ] **N** Weltanschauung *f*, Ideologie *f*

ides [aɪdz] **PL** Iden *pl*; **the ~ of March** die Iden *pl* des März

idiocy [ˈɪdɪəsɪ] **N** **a** *no pl* Idiotie *f*, Schwachsinn *m* **b** *(= stupid act, words)* Dummheit *f*, Blödheit *f*

idiolect [ˈɪdɪəʊlekt] **N** Idiolekt *m*

idiom [ˈɪdɪəm] **N** **a** *(= special phrase, group of words)* idiomatische Wendung, Redewendung *f*
b *(= language)* Sprache *f*, Idiom *nt*; *(of region)* Mundart *f*, Dialekt *m*; *(of author)* Ausdrucksweise *f*, Diktion *f*; **... to use the modern ~** ... um es modern auszudrücken **c** *(in music, art)* Ausdrucksform *f*

idiomatic [ˌɪdɪəˈmætɪk] **ADJ** idiomatisch; **to speak ~ German** idiomatisch richtiges Deutsch sprechen; **an ~ expression** eine Redensart, eine idiomatische Redewendung

idiomatically [ˌɪdɪəˈmætɪkəlɪ] **ADV** idiomatisch

idiomaticity [ˌɪdɪəʊməˈtɪsɪtɪ] **N** Idiomatik *f*; **his language lacked ~** er drückte sich nicht sehr idiomatisch aus

idiosyncrasy [ˌɪdɪəˈsɪŋkrəsɪ] **N** Eigenheit *f*, Eigenart *f*, Besonderheit *f*; *(Ling, Med)* Idiosynkrasie *f*

idiosyncratic [ˌɪdɪəsɪŋˈkrætɪk] **ADJ** eigenartig; *(Ling, Med)* idiosynkratisch; **in his own ~ way** in der ihm eigenen Art

idiot [ˈɪdɪət] **N** Idiot *m*, Dummkopf *m*, Schwachkopf *m*; *(old Med)* Idiot(in) *m(f)*, Schwachsinnige(r) *mf*; **what an ~!** so ein Idiot *or* Dummkopf!; **you (stupid) ~!** du Idiot!; **where's that ~ waiter?** wo ist dieser blöde Ober?, wo ist dieser Idiot von Ober?; **this ~ brother of mine** dieser Schwachkopf *or* Dummkopf *or* Idiot von meinem Bruder; **what an ~ I am/was!** ich Idiot!; **to feel like an ~** sich dumm vorkommen; **to look like an ~** dumm aussehen

idiot: **idiot board** **N** *(inf)* Teleprompter *m*; **idiot box** **N** *(inf)* Glotze *f (inf)*; **idiot card** **N** *(TV)* Neger *m (spec)*

idiotic [ˌɪdɪˈɒtɪk] **ADJ** blöd(sinnig), idiotisch; **don't be ~!** sei nicht so blöd!; **what an ~ mistake to make!** so ein blöder Fehler!

idiotically [ˌɪdɪˈɒtɪkəlɪ] **ADV** blödsinnig, idiotisch; *fast* schwachsinnig; **~, I had/said ...** blödsinniger- *or* idiotischerweise hatte/sagte ich ...

idiot-proof [ˈɪdɪətˌpruːf] **ADJ** *(inf)* idiotensicher *(inf)*

idle [ˈaɪdl] **ADJ** **a** *(= not working) person* müßig, untätig; *moment* ruhig; **the ~ rich** die reichen Müßiggänger; **in my ~ moments** in ruhigen *or* stillen Augenblicken; **~ life** faules Leben; **~ money, money lying ~** totes *or* brachliegendes Kapital; **we don't want to let the money lie ~** wir wollen das Geld nicht ungenutzt liegen lassen; **his car was lying ~ most of the time** sein Auto stand meistens unbenutzt herum
b *(= lazy)* faul, träge
c *(in industry) person* unbeschäftigt; *machine* stillstehend *attr*, stillliegend *attr*, außer Betrieb; **500 men have been made ~ by the strike** durch den Streik mussten 500 Leute ihre Arbeit einstellen; **the whole factory stood ~** die ganze Fabrik hatte die Arbeit eingestellt; **the machine stood ~** die Maschine stand still *or* arbeitete nicht *or* war außer Betrieb; **~ capacity** freie *or* brachliegende Kapazität
d *promise, threat, words* leer; *speculation, talk* müßig; *remark* beiläufig; **~ boast** bloße Angeberei; **~ curiosity** pure *or* bloße Neugier; **~ fear** grundlose *or* unbegründete Angst; **~ wish** Wunschtraum *m*; **the ~ pleasures of this worldly life** die eitlen Vergnügungen dieses Erdenlebens
e *(= useless)* **it would be ~ to go on trying** es wäre nutzlos *or* zwecklos, (es) weiter zu versuchen
VI **a** *(person)* untätig sein, faulenzen, nichts tun; **a day spent idling on the river** ein Tag, den man untätig auf dem Wasser verbringt
b *(engine)* leerlaufen; **when the engine is idling** wenn der Motor im Leerlauf ist

▶ **idle about** *(Brit) or* **around** **VI** herumtrödeln, bummeln; *(= loiter)* herumlungern; **we were idling about** *or* **around on the beach** wir faulenzten am Strand herum; **don't idle about** *or* **around** trödle nicht herum!, bummle nicht!

▶ **idle away** **VT** *sep one's time etc* vertrödeln, verbummeln

idleness [ˈaɪdlnɪs] **N** **a** *(= state of not working)* Untätigkeit *f*; *(pleasurable)* Muße *f*, Müßiggang *(liter) m*; **to live in ~** ein untätiges Leben führen, ein Leben der Muße führen *(liter)*; **a life of blissful ~** ein Leben voller köstlicher Muße
b *(= laziness)* Faulheit *f*, Trägheit *f* **c** *(of promise, threat, words)* Leere *f*; *(of speculation, talk)* Müßigkeit *f*; *(of remark)* Beiläufigkeit *f*; *(= uselessness)* Nutzlosigkeit *f*, Vergeblichkeit *f*, Eitelkeit *f (old)*

idler [ˈaɪdləʳ] **N** **a** *(Brit: = person not working)* Müßiggänger(in) *m(f)*; *(= lazy person)* Faulenzer(in) *m(f)*, Faulpelz *m* **b** *(Tech, = wheel)* Zwischenrad *nt*; *(= pulley)* Spannrolle *f*

idle time **N** Brachzeit *f*, Leerzeit *f*

idly [ˈaɪdlɪ] ADV **a** *(= without working)* untätig; *(= pleasurably)* müßig; **to stand ~ by** untätig herumstehen **b** *(= lazily)* faul, träge **c** *(= abstractedly) watch, toy with sth* gedankenverloren; *(= without thinking) say, suggest* ohne sich/mir *etc* etwas dabei zu denken; **I was ~ curious** ich war irgendwie neugierig **d** *(= vainly) speculate* müßig

idol [ˈaɪdl] N *(lit)* Götze *m*, Götzenbild *nt*; *(fig)* Idol *nt*, Abgott *m*; *(Film, TV etc)* Idol *nt*; **a teen ~** ein Teenageridol *nt*; **a fallen ~** ein gefallenes Idol

idolater [aɪˈdɒlətəʳ] N Götzendiener *m*

idolatress [aɪˈdɒlətrɪs] N Götzendienerin *f*

idolatrous [aɪˈdɒlətrəs] ADJ *(lit)* Götzen-; *(fig)* abgöttisch

idolatry [aɪˈdɒlətrɪ] N *(lit)* Götzendienst *m*, Götzenverehrung *f*; *(fig)* Vergötterung *f*, abgöttische Verehrung

idolize [ˈaɪdəlaɪz] VT abgöttisch lieben *or* verehren, vergöttern; **to ~ sth** etw anbeten

I'd've [ˈaɪdəv] *contr of* **I would have**

idyll [ˈɪdɪl] N **a** *(Liter)* Idylle *f* **b** *(fig)* Idyll *nt*

idyllic ADJ, **idyllically** ADV [ɪˈdɪlɪk, -lɪ] idyllisch

i.e. *abbr of* **id est** i.e., d.h.

if [ɪf] ✪ 1.1, 2.2, 17.1 CONJ wenn; *(= in case also)* falls, für den Fall, dass ...; *(= whether, in direct clause)* ob; **I would be really pleased if you could do it** wenn Sie das tun könnten, wäre ich sehr froh; **if it rains tomorrow** wenn es *or* falls es morgen regnet; **if I may say so** wenn ich das sagen darf; **I wonder if he'll come** ich bin gespannt, ob er kommt; **do you know if they have gone?** wissen Sie, ob sie gegangen sind?; **what if something happens to him?** was ist, wenn ihm etwas passiert?; **I'll let you know if and when I come to a decision** ich werde Ihnen mitteilen, ob und wenn ich mich entschieden habe; **where will you live when you get married? – if we get married!** wo wollt ihr wohnen, wenn ihr heiratet? – wenn wir überhaupt heiraten!; **if I ask him he does help me** wenn ich ihn darum bitte, hilft er mir auch; **(even) if** auch wenn; **it's a good film (even) if rather long** es ist ein guter Film, auch wenn er etwas lang ist; **even if they are poor, at least they are happy** sie sind zwar arm, aber wenigstens glücklich; **if only** wenn (doch) nur; **if only I had known!** wenn ich das nur gewusst hätte!; **I would like to see him, if only for a few hours** ich würde ihn gerne sehen, wenn auch nur für ein paar Stunden; **as if** als ob; **he acts as if he were** *or* **was** *(inf)* **rich** er tut so, als ob er reich wäre; **it's not as if I meant to hurt her** es ist nicht so, dass ich ihr hätte wehtun wollen; **as if by chance** wie zufällig; **he stood there as if he were dumb** er stand wie stumm da; **meat was available once a week, if at all** Fleisch gab es einmal in der Woche, wenn überhaupt; **if necessary** falls nötig, im Bedarfsfall; **if so** wenn ja; **if not** falls nicht; **if not, why not?** falls nicht, warum?; **this is difficult, if not impossible, to do** das ist schwer, wenn nicht sogar unmöglich; **if I were you/him** wenn ich Sie/er wäre, an Ihrer/seiner Stelle; **if anything this one is bigger** wenn überhaupt, dann ist dieses hier größer; **if I know Pete, he'll ...** so wie ich Pete kenne, wird er ...; **well, if he didn't try to steal my bag!** *(inf)* wollte der doch tatsächlich meine Tasche klauen *(inf)*; **well, if it isn't old Jim!** *(inf)* ich werd verrückt, das ist doch der Jim *(inf)*
N Wenn *nt*; **it's a big if** das ist noch sehr fraglich, das ist die große Frage; **ifs and buts** Wenn und Aber *nt*

iffy [ˈɪfɪ] ADJ *(+er) (inf)* strittig, fraglich; *neighbourhood etc* zweifelhaft; **he was a bit ~** er hat sich sehr vage ausgedrückt; **I was feeling a bit ~** ich fühlte mich nicht wohl

igloo [ˈɪgluː] N Iglu *m or nt*

igneous [ˈɪgnɪəs] ADJ *(Geol)* **~ rock** Eruptivgestein *nt*

ignite [ɪgˈnaɪt] VT entzünden, anzünden; *(Aut)* zünden; *(fig) passions, interest* erwecken VI sich entzünden, Feuer fangen; *(Aut)* zünden

ignition [ɪgˈnɪʃən] N **a** Entzünden *nt*, Anzünden *nt* **b** *(Aut)* Zündung *f*; **we have ~** *(of rocket)* „Zündung"

ignition *(Aut) in cpds* Zünd-; **ignition coil** N Zündspule *f*; **ignition key** N Zündschlüssel *m*; **ignition lock** N Zündschloss *nt*; **ignition switch** N Zündschalter *m*

ignoble [ɪgˈnəʊbl] ADJ schändlich, unwürdig, unehrenhaft

ignominious [ˌɪgnəˈmɪnɪəs] ADJ schmachvoll; *(= humiliating)* entwürdigend; *defeat* schmachvoll, schmählich; *behaviour* schändlich, unehrenhaft; **to come to an ~ end** ein schmachvolles Ende finden

ignominiously [ˌɪgnəˈmɪnɪəslɪ] ADV schmachvoll; *(= humiliatingly)* entwürdigend

ignominy [ˈɪgnəmɪnɪ] N Schmach *f*, Schande *f*, Schimpf *m (old)*

ignoramus [ˌɪgnəˈreɪməs] N Nichtswisser(in) *m(f)*, Ignorant(in) *m(f)*

ignorance [ˈɪgnərəns] N *(= general lack of knowledge, education)* Unwissenheit *f*, Mangel *m* an Bildung, Ignoranz *f*; *(of particular subject, language, plan etc)* Unkenntnis *f*; **to keep sb in ~ of sth** jdn in Unkenntnis über etw *(acc)* lassen, jdn etw nicht wissen lassen; **to be in ~ of sth** etw nicht wissen; **~ (of the law) is no excuse** Unkenntnis schützt vor Strafe nicht

ignorant [ˈɪgnərənt] ADJ **a** *(= generally uneducated)* unwissend, ungebildet, ignorant; *(of particular subject)* unwissend; *(of plan, requirements etc)* nicht informiert (of über *+acc*); **to be ~ of geography** sich in Geografie nicht auskennen; **to be ~ of the facts** die Tatsachen nicht kennen; **I am not exactly ~ of what has been going on** es ist nicht so, als wüsste ich nicht, was los ist; **they are ~ of** *or* **about what happened** sie wissen nicht, was geschehen ist **b** *(= ill-mannered)* unhöflich, ungeschliffen, ungehobelt; **you ~ fool** du ungehobelter Patron

ignorantly [ˈɪgnərəntlɪ] ADV unwissentlich; *behave* unhöflich, ungeschliffen, ungehobelt

ignore [ɪgˈnɔːʳ] VT ignorieren; *(= deliberately overlook also)* hinwegsehen über *(+acc)*; *(= pass over, pay no attention to)* nicht beachten, unbeachtet lassen; *remark* überhören, übergehen; *person* übersehen, nicht beachten; **I'll ~ that** *(remark)* ich habe nichts gehört; **but I can't ~ the fact that ...** aber ich kann mich der Tatsache nicht verschließen, dass ...

iguana [ɪˈgwɑːnə] N Leguan *m*

ikon [ˈaɪkɒn] N = **icon**

ILEA [ˈɪlɪə] *abbr of* **Inner London Education Authority** *Londoner Schulaufsichtsbehörde*

ilex [ˈaɪleks] N **a** *(= holm oak)* Steineiche *f*, Immergrüneiche *f* **b** *(= holly)* Ilex *f*, Stechpalme *f*

Iliad [ˈɪlɪæd] N Ilias *f*, Iliade *f*

ilk [ɪlk] N **people of that ~** solche Leute; **all things of that ~** dergleichen Dinge; **and others of that ~** und dergleichen, und ihresgleichen

ill [ɪl] ADJ **a** *pred (= sick)* krank; **to fall** *or* **take** *(inf) or* **be taken ~** erkranken (*with sth* an etw *dat*), krank werden; **to feel ~** sich unwohl *or* krank fühlen; **I feel (terribly) ~** mir ist (ganz und gar) nicht gut; **he is ~ with fever/a cold** er hat Fieber/eine Erkältung; **to be ~ with chicken pox** an Windpocken erkrankt sein; **~ with anxiety/jealousy** krank vor Angst/Eifersucht; **she is making herself ~ with worry** sie macht sich ganz krank vor lauter Sorgen
b *comp* **worse**, *superl* **worst** *(= bad)* schlecht, übel; *(= adverse) effects* unerwünscht; **~ will** böses Blut; **I don't bear them any ~ will** ich trage ihnen nichts nach; **~ health** schlechter Gesundheitszustand; **to suffer ~ health** gesundheitlich angeschlagen sein; **due to ~ health** aus Gesundheitsgründen; **~ humour** *or (US)* **humor** schlechte Laune; **~ luck** Pech *nt*; **as ~ luck would have it** wie es der Teufel so will; **~ nature** Übellaunigkeit *f*; **it's an ~ wind (that blows nobody any good)** *(Prov)* so hat alles seine guten Seiten
N **a** *(liter. = evil)* **to bode** *or* **augur ~** Böses ahnen lassen; **to think ~ of sb** schlecht *or* Schlechtes von jdm *or* über jdn denken; **to speak ~ of sb** schlecht über jdn reden
b **ills** PL *(= misfortunes)* Missstände *pl*, Übel *pl*; **to do ~** *(old)* Böses *or* Unrecht tun
ADV schlecht; **to take sth ~** *(liter)* etw übel nehmen; **things went ~ with him** *(liter)* es erging ihm nicht gut, es ward ihm kein Glück beschieden *(liter)*; **he can ~ afford to refuse** er kann es sich *(dat)* schlecht leisten abzulehnen; **it ~ becomes you** *(form)* es steht Ihnen nicht an *(form)*

ill. *abbr of* **illustrated, illustration** Abb., Abbildung *f*

I'll [aɪl] *contr of* **I will, I shall**

ill: **ill-advised** ADJ *person, attempt* unklug; *action also* unratsam; **you would be ~ to trust her** Sie wären schlecht beraten, wenn Sie ihr trauten; **ill-assorted** ADJ *group, bunch* schlecht zusammenpassend; **ill-at-ease** ADJ unbehaglich; **I always felt ~ in his presence** ich habe mich in seiner Gegenwart nie wohlgefühlt; **ill-bred** ADJ ungezogen, schlecht erzogen; **ill-breeding** N schlechte Erziehung, Unerzogenheit *f*; **it's a sign of ~ to ...** es ist ein Zeichen für eine schlechte Kinderstube, wenn man ...; **ill-conceived** ADJ *plan, policy* schlecht durchdacht; **ill-conditioned** ADJ übellaunig; **ill-considered** ADJ *action, words* unüberlegt, unbedacht; **ill-defined** ADJ *goals, task, powers* unklar definiert; **ill-disposed** ADJ **to be ~ to(wards) sb** jdm übel gesinnt sein

illegal [ɪˈliːgəl] ADJ unrechtmäßig, ungesetzlich; *(= against a specific law)* gesetzwidrig; *trade, immigration, possession, drugs, profits* illegal; *(= prohibited) substance, organization* verboten, illegal; *(Sport)* regelwidrig

illegality [ˌɪliːˈgælɪtɪ] N Unrechtmäßigkeit *f*, Ungesetzlichkeit *f*; *(against a specific law)* Gesetzwidrigkeit *f*; *(of trade, possession, drug, organization, profits)* Illegalität *f*; *(Sport)* Regelwidrigkeit *f*

illegally [ɪˈliːgəlɪ] ADV *(= against the law)* unrechtmäßig, ungesetzlich; *(= against a specific law)* gesetzwidrig; **~ imported** illegal eingeführt; **you're ~ parked** Sie stehen im Parkverbot; **to act ~** sich gesetzwidrig verhalten; *(against international law)* gegen das Völkerrecht verstoßen; **they were convicted of ~ possessing a handgun** sie wurden wegen unerlaubten Besitzes einer Handfeuerwaffe verurteilt

illegibility [ɪˌledʒɪˈbɪlɪtɪ] N Unleserlichkeit *f*

illegible ADJ, **illegibly** ADV [ɪˈledʒəbl, -ɪ] unleserlich

illegitimacy [ˌɪlɪˈdʒɪtɪməsɪ] N **a** *(of child)* Unehelichkeit *f* **b** *(= unlawfulness)* Unzulässigkeit *f*; *(of government)* Unrechtmäßigkeit *f* **c** *(of argument, conclusion)* Unzulässigkeit *f*

illegitimate [ˌɪlɪˈdʒɪtɪmɪt] ADJ **a** *child, birth* unehelich **b** *(= contrary to law)* unzulässig, unerlaubt; *government* unrechtmäßig; **the ~ use of drugs** (der) Drogenmissbrauch **c** *argument, conclusion, inference* unzulässig, nicht folgerichtig, illegitim

illegitimately [ˌɪlɪˈdʒɪtɪmɪtlɪ] ADV **a** *born* unehelich **b** *(= contrary to law)* unzulässig, unerlaubt; *use* unrechtmäßigerweise, unzulässigerweise **c** *argue, conclude* unzulässig, nicht folgerichtig

ill: **ill-fated** ADJ **a** *(= unfortunate, unlucky) person* vom Unglück verfolgt, unglücklich **b** *(= doomed, destined to fail)* unglückselig, verhängnisvoll; **the ~ Titanic** die unglückselige Titanic; **ill-favoured** ADJ *(liter. = ugly)* ungestalt *(liter)*, hässlich, unschön; **ill feeling** N böses Blut; **no ~?** ist es wieder gut?; **no ~!** ist schon vergessen; **ill-fitting** ADJ *clothes, dentures* schlecht sitzend; *shoes* schlecht passend; **ill-founded** ADJ unbegründet, unerwiesen, fragwürdig; **ill-gotten gains** PL unrechtmäßiger Gewinn, Sündengeld *nt (hum)*; **ill-humoured**, *(US)* **ill-humored** ADJ schlecht *or* übel gelaunt, schlecht aufgelegt, verstimmt

illiberal [ɪˈlɪbərəl] ADJ **a** *(= narrow-minded)* engstirnig, intolerant, engherzig; *(= reactionary)* reaktionär; *(Pol, Jur. = strict, repressive) law* restriktiv; *rule* antiliberal; *system, regime* autoritär **b** *(= niggardly)* knauserig, geizig

illicit [ɪˈlɪsɪt] ADJ illegal; *affair, relationship* verboten; *spirits* schwarz hergestellt *or* gebrannt; **~ trade** *or* **sale** Schwarzhandel *m*

illicitly [ɪˈlɪsɪtlɪ] ADV verbotenerweise; *(= illegally)* illegal(erweise); **~ acquired** unrechtmäßig erworben

illimitable [ɪˈlɪmɪtəbl] ADJ grenzenlos, unbegrenzt; **the ~ ocean** der unendliche Ozean

ill-informed [ˈɪlɪn,fɔːmd] ADJ *person* schlecht informiert *or* unterrichtet *(about* über); *attack, criticism, speech* wenig sachkundig

illiteracy [ɪˈlɪtərəsɪ] N Analphabetentum *nt*; **~ rate** Analphabetismus *m*

illiterate [ɪˈlɪtərət] ADJ des Schreibens und Lesens unkundig; *country, population* analphabetisch; *(= badly-educated, uncultured) person* ungebildet, unwissend; *letter* voller Fehler; **he's ~** er ist Analphabet; **to be functionally ~** praktisch nicht lesen und schreiben können; **economically/musically ~** völlig unwissend, wenn es um Wirtschaft/Musik geht; **many people are computer-~** viele Menschen kennen sich nicht mit Computern aus N Analphabet(in) *m(f)*

ill: **ill-judged** ADJ unklug, wenig bedacht; **ill-mannered** ADJ unhöflich; **ill-matched** ADJ nicht zusammenpassend; **they're ~** sie passen nicht zueinander; **ill-natured** ADJ, **ill-naturedly** ADV bösartig

illness [ˈɪlnɪs] N Krankheit *f*

illogical [ɪˈlɒdʒɪkəl] ADJ unlogisch

illogicality [ɪ,lɒdʒɪˈkælɪtɪ] N mangelnde Logik, Unlogik *f*; **the illogicalities in his argument** die logischen Fehler in seiner Argumentation

illogically [ɪˈlɒdʒɪkəlɪ] ADV *behave, argue* unlogisch; **~, I felt guilty** entgegen jeder Logik hatte ich Schuldgefühle

ill: **ill-omened** ADJ unter einem unglücklichen Stern *or* unter einem Unstern stehend; **ill-prepared** ADJ schlecht vorbereitet; **ill-starred** ADJ *person* vom Unglück *or* Pech verfolgt; *undertaking etc* unter einem ungünstigen Stern (stehend); **~ day** Unglückstag *m*; **ill-suited** ADJ *(to one another)* nicht zusammenpassend; *(to sth)* ungeeignet *(to* für); **they are ~** sie passen nicht zueinander; **ill-tempered** ADJ *(habitually)* missmutig, übellaunig; *(on particular occasion)* schlecht gelaunt *pred*; *(violently)* schlecht gelaunt *attr*; **ill-timed** ADJ ungelegen, unpassend; *move, speech* zeitlich schlecht abgestimmt; **ill-treat** VT schlecht behandeln, misshandeln; **ill-treatment** N Misshandlung *f*, schlechte Behandlung

illuminate [ɪˈluːmɪneɪt] VT **a** *(= light up) room, building* erhellen, erleuchten, beleuchten; *sky* erleuchten; *(spotlight etc)* anstrahlen; *(= decorate with lights)* festlich beleuchten, illuminieren; **~d sign** Leuchtzeichen *nt* **b** *(Art) manuscript* illuminieren; **~d letters** (verzierte) Initialen *pl* **c** *(fig) subject* erhellen, erläutern

illuminating [ɪˈluːmɪneɪtɪŋ] ADJ *(= instructive)* aufschlussreich

illumination [ɪ,luːmɪˈneɪʃən] N **a** *(of street, room, building)* Beleuchtung *f*; **source of ~** Lichtquelle *f* **b** **illuminations** PL *(= decorative lights)* festliche Beleuchtung, Illumination *f* **c** *(Art) (of manuscript)* Illumination *f*; *(subject)* Buchmalerei *f* **d** *(fig)* Erläuterung *f*

illuminator [ɪˈluːmɪneɪtəʳ] N *(Art, of manuscript)* Buchmaler(in) *m(f)*, Illuminator(in) *m(f)*

illumine [ɪˈluːmɪn] VT *(liter fig)* erhellen

illus. *abbr of* **illustrated, illustration** Abb., Abbildung *f*

ill-use [,ɪlˈjuːz] VT schlecht behandeln, schlecht umgehen mit; *(physically)* misshandeln

illusion [ɪˈluːʒən] N Illusion *f*; *(= hope also)* trügerische Hoffnung; *(= misperception)* Täuschung *f*; **to be under an ~** einer Täuschung *(dat)* unterliegen, sich *(dat)* Illusionen machen; **to be under the ~ that ...** sich *(dat)* einbilden, dass ...; **to be under** *or* **have no ~s** sich *(dat)* keine Illusionen machen, sich *(dat)* nichts vormachen *(about* über *+acc)*; **no one has any ~s about winning the war** niemand macht sich Illusionen, dass der Krieg gewonnen werden kann; **it gives the ~ of space** es vermittelt die Illusion von räumlicher Weite; **a tan can give the ~ of being slimmer** wenn man braun ist, kann das den Eindruck erwecken, dass man schlanker ist → **optical illusion**

illusionary [ɪˈluːʒənərɪ] ADJ illusorisch

illusionist [ɪˈluːʒənɪst] N Illusionist(in) *m(f)*

illusive [ɪˈluːsɪv], **illusory** [ɪˈluːsərɪ] ADJ illusorisch, trügerisch

illustrate [ˈɪləstreɪt] ✪ 26.2 VT **a** *book, story* illustrieren, bebildern; **his lecture was ~d by coloured slides** er veranschaulichte seinen Vortrag mit Farbdias; **~d (magazine)** Illustrierte *f* **b** *(fig)* veranschaulichen, illustrieren

illustration [,ɪləsˈtreɪʃən] N **a** *(= picture)* Abbildung *f*, Bild *nt*, Illustration *f* **b** *(fig) (of problem, subject)* Erklärung *f*, Erläuterung *f*; *(of rule) (= act)* Veranschaulichung *f*; *(= thing)* Beispiel *nt*; **by way of ~** als Beispiel

illustrative [ˈɪləstrətɪv] ADJ veranschaulichend, verdeutlichend; **~ of** bezeichnend *or* beispielhaft für; **for ~ purposes** zur Veranschaulichung

illustrator [ˈɪləstreɪtəʳ] N Illustrator(in) *m(f)*

illustrious [ɪˈlʌstrɪəs] ADJ glanzvoll; *person* berühmt; *deeds, past* glorreich

ILO *abbr of* **International Labour Organization**

IM *(Internet) abbr of* **Instant Messenger**

I'm [aɪm] *contr of* **I am**

image [ˈɪmɪdʒ] N **a** *(= carved, sculpted figure)* Standbild *nt*, Figur *f*; *(= painted figure)* Bild *nt*, Bildnis *nt (geh)*
b *(= likeness)* Ebenbild *nt*, Abbild *nt*; **he is the (spitting** *(inf)* *or* **living) ~ of his father** er ist sein Vater, wie er leibt und lebt, er ist seinem Vater wie aus dem Gesicht geschnitten; **God created man in his own ~** Gott (er)schuf den Menschen nach seinem Bilde
c *(Opt)* Bild *nt*; **~ processing** Bildverarbeitung *f*
d *(= mental picture)* Vorstellung *f*, Bild *nt*
e *(= public face)* Image *nt*; **brand ~** Markenimage *nt*; **~ maker** Imagemacher(in) *m(f)*
f *(Liter)* **to think in ~s** in Bildern *or* Metaphern denken

image-building N Imagepflege *f*; **~ campaign** Imagekampagne *f*

image converter [ˈɪmɪdʒkən,vɜːtəʳ] N *(Elec)* Bildwandler *m*

image enhancement [ˈɪmɪdʒɪn,hɑːnsmənt] N Bildoptimierung *f*

imagery [ˈɪmɪdʒərɪ] N Metaphorik *f*; **visual ~** Bildersymbolik *f*

imaginable [ɪˈmædʒɪnəbl] ADJ vorstellbar, denkbar, erdenklich; **the best excuse ~** die beste Ausrede, die man sich vorstellen kann; **the easiest/fastest way ~** der denkbar einfachste/schnellste Weg; **parents encourage every activity ~** Eltern fördern alle erdenklichen Aktivitäten; **this is of no ~ value** das hat keinen erdenklichen Wert

imaginary [ɪˈmædʒɪnərɪ] ADJ *danger* eingebildet, imaginär; *characters* frei ersonnen, erfunden; *friend* erfunden; *line* vorgestellt; **~ world** Fantasiewelt *f*; **an ~ case** ein konstruierter Fall

imagination [ɪ,mædʒɪˈneɪʃən] N *(creative)* Fantasie *f*, Phantasie *f*, Vorstellungskraft *f*, Einbildungskraft *f*; *(self-deceptive)* Einbildung *f*; **to have (a lively** *or* **vivid) ~** (eine lebhafte *or* rege) Fantasie haben; **he has little ~** er hat wenig Fantasie; **use your ~** lassen Sie Ihre Fantasie spielen; **in order to encourage children to use their ~(s)** um die Fantasie von Kindern anzuregen; **to lack ~** fantasielos *or* einfallslos sein; **it's just your ~!** das bilden Sie sich *(dat)* nur ein!; **it's all in your ~** das ist alles Einbildung; **to capture** *or* **catch sb's ~** jdn in seinen Bann ziehen; **it captures the ~** es ist faszinierend; **to stretch the ~** große Vorstellungskraft erfordern

imaginative ADJ, **imaginatively** ADV [ɪˈmædʒɪnətɪv, -lɪ] fantasievoll

imaginativeness [ɪˈmædʒɪnətɪvnɪs] N Fantasiereichtum *m*, Phantasiereichtum *m*; *(of person also)* Fantasie *f*, Phantasie *f*

imagine [ɪˈmædʒɪn] VT **a** *(= picture to oneself)* sich *(dat)* vorstellen, sich *(dat)* denken; **~ you're rich/lying on a beach** stellen Sie sich mal vor, Sie wären reich/lägen am Strand; **he ~d himself kissing her** er stellte sich vor, sie zu küssen; **you can ~ how I felt** Sie können sich vorstellen, wie mir zumute *or* zu Mute war; **you can't ~ how ...** Sie machen sich kein Bild *or* Sie können sich nicht vorstellen wie ...; **I can't ~ living there** ich kann mir nicht vorstellen, dort zu leben; **just ~ my surprise** stellen Sie sich nur meine Überraschung vor; **you can't ~ it!** Sie machen sich keine Vorstellungen!; **as may (well) be ~d** wie man sich (leicht) denken *or* vorstellen kann
b *(= be under the illusion that)* sich *(dat)* einbilden; **don't ~ that ...** bilden Sie sich nur nicht ein, dass ..., denken Sie nur nicht, dass ...; **he is always imagining things** *(inf)* er leidet ständig an Einbildungen; **you're (just) imagining things** *(inf)* Sie bilden sich das alles nur ein
c *(= suppose, conjecture)* annehmen, vermuten; **is that her father? – I would ~ so** ist das ihr Vater? – ich denke schon; **I would never have ~d he could have done that** ich hätte nie gedacht, dass er das tun würde; **I ~d her to be dark-haired** ich habe sie mir dunkelhaarig vorgestellt

imaging [ˈɪmɪdʒɪŋ] N *(Comput)* Imaging *nt*

imbalance [ɪmˈbæləns] N Unausgeglichenheit *f*

imbalanced [ɪmˈbælənst] ADJ *distribution* ungleichmäßig; *structure* unausgewogen

imbecile [ˈɪmbəsiːl] N **a** Dummkopf *m*, Idiot *m*, Schwachkopf *m*; **to behave like an ~** sich völlig blödsinnig *or* wie ein Idiot benehmen **b** *(Med)* Schwachsinnige(r) *mf* ADJ **a** *person* beschränkt, schwachsinnig, geistig minderbemittelt *(inf)*; *laugh* schwachsinnig, dumm, blöd(e); *idea* dumm, töricht **b** *(Med)* schwachsinnig, geistesschwach, imbezil *(spec)*

imbecilic [,ɪmbəˈsɪlɪk] ADJ = **imbecile ADJ**

imbecility [,ɪmbəˈsɪlɪtɪ] N **a** Beschränktheit *f*, Idiotie *f*, Schwachsinn *m* **b** *(Med)* Schwachsinn *m*

imbed [ɪmˈbed] VT = **embed**

imbibe [ɪmˈbaɪb] VT **a** *(form, hum)* trinken, bechern *(hum)* **b** *(fig) ideas, information* in sich *(acc)* aufnehmen VI *(hum: = drink)* viel trinken

imbroglio [ɪmˈbrəʊlɪəʊ] N *(liter)* verwickelte Lage, Verwirrung *f*

imbue [ɪmˈbjuː] VT *(fig)* durchdringen, erfüllen *(with* mit)

IMF *abbr of* **International Monetary Fund** IWF *m*

imitable [ˈɪmɪtəbl] ADJ nachahmbar, imitierbar

imitate [ˈɪmɪteɪt] VT **a** *(= copy) person, accent etc* imitieren, nachmachen, nachahmen; **children learn by imitating their parents** Kinder lernen dadurch, dass sie ihre Eltern nachahmen **b** *(= counterfeit)* nachmachen, imitieren

imitation [,ɪmɪˈteɪʃən] N Imitation *f*, Nachahmung *f*; **to do an ~ of sb** jdn imitieren *or* nachmachen *or* nachahmen; **~ is the sincerest form of flattery** *(prov)* Nachahmung ist das beste Kompliment ADJ unecht, künstlich, falsch; **~ gold/pearl** Gold-/Perlenimitation *f*; **~ leather** Lederimitation *f*, Kunstleder *nt*; **~ jewellery** unechter Schmuck; **~ fur** Webpelz *m*

imitative [ˈɪmɪtətɪv] ADJ nachahmend, imitierend; **children are naturally ~** Kinder machen von Natur aus alles nach

imitator [ˈɪmɪteɪtəʳ] N Nachahmer(in) *m(f)*, Imitator(in) *m(f)*

immaculate [ɪˈmækjʊlɪt] ADJ **a** untadelig, tadellos, picobello *inv (inf)*; *behaviour* tadellos, mustergültig; *manuscript etc* fehlerfrei, einwandfrei **b** *(Eccl)* **the Immaculate Conception** die Unbefleckte Empfängnis

immaculately [ɪˈmækjʊlɪtlɪ] ADV tadellos; *behave also* untadelig

immanence [ˈɪmənəns] N Immanenz *f*

immanent [ˈɪmənənt] ADJ innewohnend, immanent *(also Philos)*; **to be ~ in sth** einer Sache *(dat)* eigen sein *or* innewohnen

immaterial [ˌɪməˈtɪərɪəl] ADJ **a** *(= unimportant) objection, question* nebensächlich, unwesentlich, bedeutungslos; **it is quite ~ to me (whether) …** es ist für mich ohne Bedeutung *or* unwichtig, (ob) …; **that's (quite) ~** das spielt keine Rolle, das ist egal **b** *(Philos etc)* immateriell

immature [ˌɪməˈtjʊəˈ] ADJ *(lit, fig)* unreif; *plans, ideas etc also* unausgegoren; *wine* nicht ausreichend gelagert; **don't be so ~** sei nicht so kindisch!

immaturely [ˌɪməˈtjʊəlɪ] ADV *react, behave* unreif

immaturity [ˌɪməˈtjʊərɪtɪ] N Unreife *f*

immeasurable [ɪˈmeʒərəbl] ADJ unermesslich, grenzenlos; *amount, distances* unmessbar, riesig

immeasurably [ɪˈmeʒərəblɪ] ADV unermesslich, grenzenlos; **it has helped ~ that …** es hat ungeheuer geholfen, dass …

immediacy [ɪˈmiːdɪəsɪ] N Unmittelbarkeit *f*, Direktheit *f*; *(= urgency)* Dringlichkeit *f*

immediate [ɪˈmiːdɪət] ADJ **a** *knowledge, future, object, danger, threat, need, neighbour* unmittelbar; *vicinity, neighbourhood* unmittelbar, nächste(r, s); *cause, impact, successor* direkt, unmittelbar; **only the ~ family were invited** nur die engste Familie wurde eingeladen; **in the ~ aftermath of the war** unmittelbar nach dem Krieg; **our ~ plan is to go to France** wir fahren zuerst einmal nach Frankreich; **he has no ~ plans to retire** er hat derzeit *or* im Moment nicht die Absicht, sich zur Ruhe zu setzen
b *(= instant) reply, reaction* sofortig, umgehend, prompt; *thought, conclusion* unmittelbar; *access* direkt; **to take ~ action** sofort handeln; **with ~ effect** mit sofortiger Wirkung; **to come into ~ effect** sofort in Kraft treten; **this had the ~ effect of …** das hatte prompt zur Folge, dass …; **for ~ delivery** zur sofortigen Lieferung; **the matter requires your ~ attention** die Sache bedarf sofort Ihrer Aufmerksamkeit
c *(= most urgent) problem, concern* dringendste(r, s); **my ~ concern was for the children** mein erster Gedanke galt den Kindern

immediately [ɪˈmiːdɪətlɪ] ADV **a** *(= at once)* sofort, gleich; *reply, return, depart* umgehend, sofort; **~ after/before that** unmittelbar danach/davor; **that's not ~ obvious** das ist nicht sofort *or* unmittelbar klar **b** *(= directly)* direkt, unmittelbar; **~ below/above sth** direkt unter/über etw *(dat)* CONJ *(Brit)* sobald, sofort als …

immemorial [ˌɪmɪˈmɔːrɪəl] ADJ uralt; **from time ~** seit undenklichen Zeiten, seit Urzeiten

immense [ɪˈmens] ADJ *difficulty, fortune, sum of money, possibilities* riesig, enorm, immens; *problem, difference also, ocean, heat* gewaltig; *self-confidence, success* ungeheuer, enorm; *achievement* großartig

immensely [ɪˈmenslɪ] ADV unheimlich *(inf)*, enorm; **to enjoy oneself ~** sich ausgezeichnet *or* unheimlich *(inf)* or köstlich amüsieren; **~ grateful** äußerst dankbar

immensity [ɪˈmensɪtɪ] N ungeheure Größe, Unermesslichkeit *f*; **the ~ of this task** das gewaltige Ausmaß dieser Aufgabe; **the ~ of space** die Unendlichkeit des (Welt)alls

immerse [ɪˈmɜːs] VT **a** *(lit)* eintauchen *(in* in *+acc)*; **to ~ sth in water** etw in Wasser tauchen; **to be ~d in water** unter Wasser sein **b** *(fig)* **to ~ oneself in one's work** sich in seine Arbeit vertiefen *or* stürzen *(inf)*; **to ~ oneself in a language** sich vollkommen in eine Sprache vertiefen; **to be ~d in one's work** in seine Arbeit vertieft sein **c** *(Eccl)* untertauchen

immerser [ɪˈmɜːsəˈ] N Boiler *m*, Heißwasserbereiter *m*

immersion [ɪˈmɜːʃən] N **a** *(lit)* Eintauchen *nt*, Untertauchen *nt*; **after two hours' ~ in this solution** nach zwei Stunden in dieser Flüssigkeit **b** *(fig)* Vertieftsein *nt*, Versunkensein *nt* **c** *(Eccl)* Taufe *f* durch Untertauchen

immersion course N Intensivkurs *m*

immersion heater N *(Brit)* Boiler *m*, Heißwasserbereiter *m*; *(for jug etc)* Tauchsieder *m*

immigrant [ˈɪmɪgrənt] N Einwanderer *m*, Einwanderin *f*, Immigrant(in) *m(f)* ATTR **the ~ population/community** die Einwanderer *pl*; **… has an ~ population of 50,000** … hat einen ausländischen Bevölkerungsanteil von 50.000

immigrant labour N, **immigrant workers** PL ausländische Arbeitnehmer *pl*; *(esp in Germany)* Gastarbeiter *pl (neg!)*; *(in Switzerland)* Fremdarbeiter *pl (neg!)*

immigrate [ˈɪmɪgreɪt] VI einwandern, immigrieren *(to* in *+dat)*

immigration [ˌɪmɪˈgreɪʃən] N Einwanderung *f*, Immigration *f*; *(also* **immigration control**: *at airport etc)* Einwanderungsstelle *f*

immigration authorities PL, **immigration department** N Einwanderungsbehörde *f*

immigration officer N Beamte(r) *m*/Beamtin *f* der Einwanderungsbehörde; *(at customs)* Grenzbeamte(r) *m*/-beamtin *f*

imminence [ˈɪmɪnəns] N nahes Bevorstehen; **he hadn't appreciated the ~ of the danger/of war** er war sich *(dat)* nicht bewusst, dass die Gefahr/der Krieg so unmittelbar bevorstand

imminent [ˈɪmɪnənt] ADJ nahe bevorstehend; **to be ~** nahe bevorstehen; **I think an announcement is ~** ich glaube, es steht eine Ankündigung bevor

immobile [ɪˈməʊbaɪl] ADJ *(= not moving)* unbeweglich; *(= not able to move) person (through injury etc)* bewegungslos; *(through lack of transport)* unbeweglich, immobil; **to render sb ~** jdn bewegungsunfähig machen

immobiliser [ɪˈməʊbɪlaɪzəˈ] N *(Aut)* Wegfahrsperre *f*

immobility [ˌɪməʊˈbɪlɪtɪ] N *(= inability to move) (through injury etc)* Unbeweglichkeit *f*, Bewegungslosigkeit *f*; *(through lack of transport)* Immobilität *f*

immobilize [ɪˈməʊbɪlaɪz] VT *car, broken limb* stilllegen; *army* bewegungsunfähig machen; *enemy tanks* außer Gefecht setzen; *(Fin) capital* festlegen; **to be ~d by fear/pain** sich vor Angst/Schmerzen nicht bewegen können

immoderate [ɪˈmɒdərɪt] ADJ *desire* übermäßig, unmäßig; *views* übertrieben, extrem; *person* extrem

immoderately [ɪˈmɒdərɪtlɪ] ADV *eat, drink* unmäßig; *hate* maßlos

immodest [ɪˈmɒdɪst] ADJ unbescheiden; *(= indecent)* unanständig

immodestly [ɪˈmɒdɪstlɪ] ADV *say, claim* unbescheiden; *(= indecently)* unanständig

immodesty [ɪˈmɒdɪstɪ] N Unbescheidenheit *f*; *(= indecency)* Unanständigkeit *f*

immolate [ˈɪməʊleɪt] VT *(liter)* opfern, zum Opfer bringen

immolation [ˌɪməʊˈleɪʃən] N *(liter)* **a** *(= sacrifice)* Opfer *nt* **b** *(action)* Opfern *nt*, Opferung *f*

immoral [ɪˈmɒrəl] ADJ *action, life* unmoralisch; *behaviour also* unsittlich; *person also* sittenlos; **~ earnings** *(Jur)* Einkünfte *pl* aus gewerbsmäßiger Unzucht

immorality [ˌɪməˈrælɪtɪ] N Unmoral *f*; *(of behaviour also)* Unsittlichkeit *f*; *(of person also)* Sittenlosigkeit *f*; *(= immoral act)* Unsittlichkeit *f*

immorally [ɪˈmɒrəlɪ] ADV *act, live* unmoralisch; *behave also* unsittlich

immortal [ɪˈmɔːtl] ADJ *person, soul, God, phrase* unsterblich; *fame also* unvergänglich, ewig; *life* ewig; **in the ~ words of …** in den unsterblichen Worten *+gen* … N Unsterbliche(r) *mf*

immortality [ˌɪmɔːˈtælɪtɪ] N *(of person, God)* Unsterblichkeit *f*; *(of fame)* Unvergänglichkeit *f*; *(of life)* Ewigkeit *f*

immortalize [ɪˈmɔːtəlaɪz] VT verewigen; **the film which ~d her** der Film, der sie unsterblich machte

immovable [ɪˈmuːvəbl] ADJ **a** *(lit)* unbeweglich; *(fig) obstacle* unüberwindlich, unbezwinglich **b** *(fig: = steadfast)* fest; **John was ~ in his decision** John war von seiner Entscheidung nicht abzubringen

immovably [ɪˈmuːvəblɪ] ADV unbeweglich; **each picture was nailed ~ in place** alle Bilder waren fest angenagelt

immune [ɪˈmjuːn] ADJ **a** *(Med)* immun *(from, to* gegen); **~ deficiency syndrome** Immunschwächekrankheit *f* **b** *(fig)* sicher *(from, to* vor *+dat)*; *(from temptation etc)* geschützt, gefeit *(from, to* gegen); *(= not susceptible: to criticism etc)* unempfindlich, immun *(to* gegen); **~ from prosecution** vor Strafverfolgung geschützt, immun *(spec)*

immune system N Immunsystem *nt*

immunity [ɪˈmjuːnɪtɪ] N **a** *(Med)* Immunität *f* *(to, against* gegen) **b** *(fig)* Sicherheit *f (from* vor *+dat)*; *(diplomatic)* Immunität *f*; *(to temptation etc)* Geschütztheit *f*, Gefeitheit *f (to* gegen); *(= imperviousness to criticism etc)* Unempfindlichkeit *f*, Immunität *f (to* gegen); **~ from prosecution** Schutz *m* vor Strafverfolgung

immunization [ˌɪmjʊnaɪˈzeɪʃən] N Immunisierung *f*

immunize [ˈɪmjʊnaɪz] VT immunisieren, immun machen

immunocompromised [ɪˌmjuːnəʊˈkɒmprəmaɪzd] ADJ *(Med)* immungeschwächt

immunodeficiency [ˌɪmjʊnəʊdɪˈfɪʃənsɪ] N *(Med)* Immunschwäche *f*

immunoglobulin [ˌɪmjʊnəʊˈglɒbjʊlɪn] N Immunglobulin *nt*

immunological [ˌɪmjʊnəʊˈlɒdʒɪkəl] ADJ *(Med)* immunologisch

immunologist [ˌɪmjʊˈnɒlədʒɪst] N *(Med)* Immunologe *m*, Immunologin *f*

immunology [ˌɪmjʊˈnɒlədʒɪ] N *(Med)* Immunologie *f*

immunosuppressive [ˌɪmjʊnəʊsʌˈpresɪv] ADJ immunosuppressiv, das Immunsystem unterdrückend

immure [ɪˈmjʊəˈ] VT einkerkern

immutability [ɪˌmjuːtəˈbɪlɪtɪ] N Unveränderlichkeit *f*, Unwandelbarkeit *f*

immutable [ɪˈmjuːtəbl] ADJ unveränderlich, unwandelbar

imp [ɪmp] N Kobold *m*; *(inf: = child)* Racker *m (inf)*

impact [ˈɪmpækt] N Aufprall *m (on, against* auf *+acc)*; *(of two moving objects)* Zusammenprall *m*, Aufeinanderprallen *nt*; *(of bomb) (on house, factory)* Einschlag *m (on* in *+acc)*; *(on roof, ground)* Aufschlag *m (on* auf *+dat)*; *(of light, rays)* Auftreffen *nt (on* auf *+acc)*; *(= force)* Wucht *f*; *(fig)* (Aus)wirkung *f (on* auf *+acc)*; **on ~ (with)** beim Aufprall (auf *+acc*)/Zusammenprall (mit) *etc*; **he staggered under the ~ of the blow** er taumelte unter der Wucht des Schlages; **his speech had a great ~ on his audience** seine Rede machte großen Eindruck auf seine Zuhörer; **you can imagine the ~ of this on a four-year-old** Sie können sich vorstellen, wie sich das auf einen Vierjährigen auswirkt
VI **to ~ on sb/sth** *(fig)* auf jdn/etw einwirken
VT aufschlagen auf *(+acc)*; *two things* zusammendrücken; *(fig: = have an effect on)* einwirken auf *(+acc)*

impacted [ɪmˈpæktɪd] ADJ eingeklemmt, eingekeilt; *tooth also* impaktiert *(spec)*; **to be ~ by sth** *(fig)* von etw getroffen werden

impact printer N Impactdrucker *m*

impair [ɪmˈpeəˈ] VT beeinträchtigen; *hearing, sight also* verschlechtern; *relations also, health* schaden *(+dat)*

impairment [ɪm'pɛəmənt] N **a** *no pl (= weakening: of judgement, mental functions)* Beeinträchtigung *f* **b** *(= defect)* Schaden *m*; **hearing/visual ~** Hör-/Sehschaden *m*; **speech** *or* **language ~** Sprachfehler *m*

impala [ɪm'pɑːlə] N Impala *f*

impale [ɪm'peɪl] VT aufspießen *(on* auf *+dat)*

impalpable [ɪm'pælpəbl] ADJ *(lit)* nicht fühlbar; *(fig)* nicht greifbar, vage

impanel [ɪm'pænl] VT als Geschworenen einsetzen

imparity [ɪm'pærɪtɪ] N Ungleichheit *f*

impart [ɪm'pɑːt] VT **a** *(= make known) information, news* mitteilen, übermitteln; *knowledge* vermitteln; *secret* preisgeben **b** *(= bestow)* verleihen, geben *(to +dat)*

impartial [ɪm'pɑːʃəl] ADJ unparteiisch, unvoreingenommen

impartiality [ɪm,pɑːʃɪ'ælɪtɪ] N Unparteilichkeit *f*, Unvoreingenommenheit *f*

impartially [ɪm'pɑːʃəlɪ] ADV *act* unparteiisch; *judge* unvoreingenommen

impassable [ɪm'pɑːsəbl] ADJ unpassierbar

impasse [ɪm'pɑːs] N *(fig)* Sackgasse *f*; **to have reached an ~** sich festgefahren haben, einen toten Punkt erreicht haben

impassioned [ɪm'pæʃnd] ADJ leidenschaftlich

impassive ADJ, **impassively** ADV [ɪm'pæsɪv, -lɪ] gelassen

impassiveness [ɪm'pæsɪvnɪs], **impassivity** [ɪmpæ'sɪvɪtɪ] N Gelassenheit *f*

impatience [ɪm'peɪʃəns] N Ungeduld *f*; *(= intolerance)* Unduldsamkeit *f*

impatient [ɪm'peɪʃənt] ADJ ungeduldig; *(= intolerant)* unduldsam *(of* gegenüber*)*; **to be ~ to do sth** unbedingt etw tun wollen

impatiently [ɪm'peɪʃəntlɪ] ADV ungeduldig; **he looked forward ~ to her next visit** er konnte ihren nächsten Besuch kaum erwarten

impeach [ɪm'piːtʃ] VT **a** *(Jur: = accuse) public official* (eines Amtsvergehens) anklagen; *(US) president* ein Amtsenthebungsverfahren *or* Impeachment einleiten gegen; **to ~ sb for sth** jdn wegen einer Sache anklagen; **to ~ sb for doing sth** jdn anklagen, etw getan zu haben **b** *(= challenge) sb's character, motives* infrage *or* in Frage stellen, anzweifeln; *witness's testimony also* anfechten; **to ~ a witness** die Glaubwürdigkeit eines Zeugen anzweifeln *or* anfechten

impeachable [ɪm'piːtʃəbl] ADJ *person* (eines Amtsvergehens) anzuklagen; *action* als Amtsvergehen verfolgbar

impeachment [ɪm'piːtʃmənt] N **a** *(Jur: = accusation)* Anklage *f (wegen eines Amtsvergehens)*; *(US: of president)* Amtsenthebungsverfahren *nt*, Impeachment *nt* **b** *(= questioning) (of sb's character, motives)* Infragestellung *f*, Anzweiflung *f*; *(of testimony also)* Anfechtung *f*

impeccable [ɪm'pekəbl] ADJ untadelig, tadellos

impeccably [ɪm'pekəblɪ] ADV tadellos; **~ high standards** kompromisslos hohe Ansprüche

impecunious [,ɪmpɪ'kjuːnɪəs] ADJ mittellos, unbemittelt

impede [ɪm'piːd] VT *person* hindern; *action, progress, work* behindern, erschweren; *movement, traffic, process* behindern

impediment [ɪm'pedɪmənt] N **a** Hindernis *nt* **b** *(Med)* Behinderung *f*; **speech ~** Sprachfehler *m*, Sprachstörung *f*

impedimenta [ɪm,pedɪ'mentə] PL **a** *(inf)* (unnötiges) Gepäck **b** *(Mil)* Tross *m*

impel [ɪm'pel] VT **a** *(= force)* nötigen; **to ~ sb to do sth** jdn (dazu) nötigen, etw zu tun; **to ~ sb (in)to action** jdn zum Handeln nötigen **b** *(= drive on)* (voran)treiben

impend [ɪm'pend] VI bevorstehen; *(= threaten)* drohen

impending [ɪm'pendɪŋ] ADJ bevorstehend; *death, disaster also* nahe; *storm also* heraufziehend; *(= threatening)* drohend; **a sense of ~ doom** eine Ahnung von unmittelbar drohendem Unheil

impenetrability [ɪm,penɪtrə'bɪlɪtɪ] N Undurchdringlichkeit *f*; *(of fortress)* Uneinnehmbarkeit *f*; *(of enemy lines)* Undurchlässigkeit *f*; *(of mind, character, mystery)* Unergründlichkeit *f*; *(of theory)* Undurchschaubarkeit *f*, Undurchsichtigkeit *f*

impenetrable [ɪm'penɪtrəbl] ADJ undurchdringlich; *fortress* uneinnehmbar; *enemy lines* undurchlässig; *mind, character, mystery* unergründlich; *theory* undurchschaubar, undurchsichtig; *accent* völlig unverständlich *(to sb* für jdn*)*

impenetrably [ɪm'penɪtrəblɪ] ADV **a** *thick, dark* undurchdringlich **b** *(= incomprehensibly)* unergründlich, undurchschaubar; **his pictures can appear, at first sight, ~ obscure** auf den ersten Blick kann die Obskurität seiner Bilder unverständlich erscheinen

impenitence [ɪm'penɪtəns] N Reuelosigkeit *f*

impenitent [ɪm'penɪtənt] ADJ reuelos; **he remained quite ~** er zeigte keine Reue, er bereute es gar nicht; **to die ~** sterben, ohne bereut zu haben

impenitently [ɪm'penɪtəntlɪ] ADV ohne Reue

imperative [ɪm'perətɪv] ADJ **a** *need, desire* dringend; **immediate action is ~** sofortiges Handeln ist dringend geboten **b** *manner* gebieterisch, befehlend, herrisch; *order* strikt **c** *(Gram)* imperativisch, Imperativ-, befehlend, Befehls-; **~ form** Imperativ- *or* Befehlsform *f* N **a the political/moral/economic ~** die politische/moralische/wirtschaftliche Notwendigkeit; **there is a moral ~ to help the poor** es ist moralisch geboten, den Armen zu helfen **b** *(Gram)* Imperativ *m*; **in the ~** im Imperativ, in der Befehlsform

imperceptible [,ɪmpə'septəbl] ADJ *(to sb* für jdn*)* nicht wahrnehmbar; *difference, movement also* unmerklich; *sight also* unsichtbar; *sound also* unhörbar

imperceptibly [,ɪmpə'septəblɪ] ADV kaum wahrnehmbar; *move, differ also* unmerklich; *(= invisibly)* unsichtbar; *(= inaudibly)* unhörbar

imperfect [ɪm'pɜːfɪkt] ADJ **a** *(= faulty)* unvollkommen, mangelhaft; *(Comm) goods* fehlerhaft **b** *(= incomplete)* unvollständig, unvollkommen **c** *(Gram)* Imperfekt-, Vergangenheits-; **~ form** Imperfekt- *or* Vergangenheitsform *f* N *(Gram)* Imperfekt *nt*, Vergangenheit *f*

imperfect competition N *(Econ)* unvollständige Konkurrenz

imperfection [,ɪmpə'fekʃən] N **a** *no pl (= faultiness)* Unvollkommenheit *f*, Mangelhaftigkeit *f*; *(= incompleteness)* Unvollständigkeit *f* **b** *(= fault, defect)* Mangel *m*

imperfectly [ɪm'pɜːfɪktlɪ] ADV unvollkommen; *(= incompletely)* unvollständig

imperfect market N *(Econ)* unvollkommener Markt

imperial [ɪm'pɪərɪəl] ADJ **a** *(= of empire)* Reichs-; *(= of emperor)* kaiserlich, Kaiser-; **~ Rome** das Rom der Kaiserzeit; **His Imperial Highness** Seine Kaiserliche Majestät; **~ eagle** Kaiseradler *m* **b** *(= of British Empire)* Empire-, des Empire **c** *(= lordly, majestic)* majestätisch, gebieterisch **d** *weights, measures* englisch

> **IMPERIAL SYSTEM**
>
> In Großbritannien ist für Maß- und Gewichtsangaben zum Teil noch das **imperial system** in Gebrauch, auch wenn das metrische System offiziell bereits 1971 eingeführt wurde. Die Kinder rechnen in der Schule im metrischen Dezimalsystem, doch Lebensmittel werden oft immer noch in **pounds** verkauft, Bier wird nach **pints** abgezapft und viele Leute denken noch in **stones** und **pounds**, wenn es um das eigene Gewicht, bzw. in **feet** und **inches**, wenn es um die persönliche Größe geht. Entfernungen werden in **miles** angegeben. In den USA ist das **imperial system** sowieso noch für alle Gewichts- und Maßangaben gültig, wobei es bei den Flüssigkeiten einen kleinen Unterschied zu den britischen Maßen gibt: die amerikanischen Mengen von **liquid ounce**, **pint** und **gallon** sind etwas kleiner als die britischen Entsprechungen. Und über ihr persönliches Gewicht sprechen die Amerikaner nur in **pounds**.

imperialism [ɪm'pɪərɪəlɪzəm] N Imperialismus *m (often pej)*, Weltmachtpolitik *f*

imperialist [ɪm'pɪərɪəlɪst] N Imperialist(in) *m(f)*

imperialistic [ɪm,pɪərɪə'lɪstɪk] ADJ imperialistisch

imperially [ɪm'pɪərɪəlɪ] ADV majestätisch, gebieterisch

imperil [ɪm'perɪl] VT gefährden, in Gefahr bringen

imperious ADJ, **imperiously** ADV [ɪm'pɪərɪəs, -lɪ] herrisch, gebieterisch

imperishable [ɪm'perɪʃəbl] ADJ *(lit)* unverderblich; *(fig)* unvergänglich

impermanence [ɪm'pɜːmənəns] N Unbeständigkeit *f*

impermanent [ɪm'pɜːmənənt] ADJ unbeständig

impermeable [ɪm'pɜːmɪəbl] ADJ undurchlässig, impermeabel *(spec)*

impermissible [,ɪmpə'mɪsɪbl] ADJ unzulässig, unstatthaft

impers. *abbr of* **impersonal**

impersonal [ɪm'pɜːsənl] ADJ unpersönlich *(also Gram)*

impersonality [ɪm,pɜːsə'nælɪtɪ] N Unpersönlichkeit *f*

impersonally [ɪm'pɜːsənəlɪ] ADV unpersönlich

impersonate [ɪm'pɜːsəneɪt] VT **a** *(= pretend to be)* sich ausgeben als **b** *(= take off)* imitieren, nachahmen

impersonation [ɪm,pɜːsə'neɪʃən] N **a** *(= passing oneself off)* Verkörperung *f*; **his ~ of an officer** sein Auftreten *nt* als Offizier **b** *(= impression, takeoff)* Imitation *f*, Nachahmung *f*; **he does ~s of politicians** er imitiert Politiker; **his Elvis ~** seine Elvis-Imitation

impersonator [ɪm'pɜːsəneɪtə'] N *(Theat)* Imitator(in) *m(f)*

impertinence [ɪm'pɜːtɪnəns] N Unverschämtheit *f*, Impertinenz *f (dated)*; **what ~!, the ~ of it!** so eine Unverschämtheit!; **to ask would be an ~** es wäre unverschämt zu fragen

impertinent [ɪm'pɜːtɪnənt] ADJ **a** *(= impudent)* unverschämt *(to* zu, gegenüber*)*, impertinent *(dated) (to* gegenüber*)* **b** *(form: = irrelevant)* irrelevant

impertinently [ɪm'pɜːtɪnəntlɪ] ADV unverschämt

imperturbability ['ɪmpə,tɜːbə'bɪlɪtɪ] N Unerschütterlichkeit *f*

imperturbable [,ɪmpə'tɜːbəbl] ADJ unerschütterlich; **he is completely ~** er ist durch nichts zu erschüttern

impervious [ɪm'pɜːvɪəs] ADJ **a** *substance, rock* undurchlässig; **~ to rain/water** regen-/wasserundurchlässig; *coat, material* regen-/wasserdicht **b** *(fig)* unzugänglich *(to* für*)*; *(to criticism)* unberührt *(to* von*)*; **he is ~ to logic** ihm ist mit Logik nicht beizukommen; **she is ~ to pressure** sie lässt sich nicht unter Druck setzen

impetigo [,ɪmpɪ'taɪgəʊ] N *(Med)* Eiterflechte *f*, Impetigo *f*

impetuosity [ɪm,petjʊ'ɒsɪtɪ] N **a** *(of action, person)* Ungestüm *nt*; *(of decision)* Impulsivität *f*; *(of attack)* Stürmische(s) *nt* **b** *(= impetuous behaviour)* ungestümes Handeln

impetuous [ɪm'petjʊəs] ADJ *act, person* ungestüm, stürmisch; *decision* impulsiv; *(liter) attack, wind* stürmisch

impetuously [ɪm'petjʊəslɪ] ADV ungestüm

impetuousness [ɪm'petjʊəsnɪs] N = **impetuosity**

impetus [ˈɪmpɪtəs] N *(lit, fig)* Impuls *m*; *(= force)* Kraft *f*; *(= momentum)* Schwung *m*, Impetus *m* *(geh)*; **the ~ behind this increase in activity** die treibende Kraft hinter dieser zunehmenden Aktivität; **to give (an) ~ to sth** *(fig)* einer Sache *(dat)* Impulse geben

impiety [ɪmˈpaɪətɪ] N **a** Gottlosigkeit *f*, Ungläubigkeit *f*; *(= irreverence)* Pietätlosigkeit *f*; *(to God)* Ehrfurchtslosigkeit *f*; *(to superior etc)* Respektlosigkeit *f* **b** *(= act)* Pietätlosigkeit *f*; *(= irreverence)* Respektlosigkeit *f*

impinge [ɪmˈpɪndʒ] VI **a** *(= have effect: on sb's life, habits)* sich auswirken *(on* auf *+acc)*, beeinflussen *(on +acc)*; *(= infringe: on sb's rights etc)* einschränken *(on +acc)*; **to ~ on sb/sb's consciousness** jdm zu Bewusstsein kommen **b** *(= strike)* (auf)treffen, fallen *(on* auf *+acc)*

impingement [ɪmˈpɪndʒmənt] N **a** Auswirkung *f*, Einfluss *m* *(on* auf *+acc)* **b** *(= striking)* Auftreffen *nt* *(on* auf *+dat)*

impious [ˈɪmpɪəs] ADJ *(= not pious)* gottlos, ungläubig; *(= irreverent)* pietätlos; *(to God)* ehrfurchtslos; *(to superior etc)* respektlos

impish [ˈɪmpɪʃ] ADJ *remark* schelmisch; *smile, look also* verschmitzt; *child also* lausbübisch

impishly [ˈɪmpɪʃlɪ] ADV schelmisch; *smile, look also* verschmitzt

impishness [ˈɪmpɪʃnɪs] N *(of remark)* Schelmische(s) *nt*; *(of smile, look also)* Verschmitztheit *f*; *(of child also)* Lausbubenhaftigkeit *f*

implacable [ɪmˈplækəbl] ADJ *opponent, enemy, hatred, logic* unerbittlich; *fate* unausweichlich; *face* unnachgiebig

implacably [ɪmˈplækəblɪ] ADV unerbittlich; **he was ~ opposed to capital punishment** er war ein unerbittlicher Gegner der Todesstrafe

implant [ɪmˈplɑːnt] VT **a** *(fig)* einimpfen *(in sb* jdm); **to be deeply ~ed in sb** (tief) in jdm verwurzelt sein **b** *(Med)* implantieren, einpflanzen VI *(Med: in womb)* sich einnisten N [ˈɪmplɑːnt] *(Med)* Implantat *nt*; **breast ~** Brustimplantat *nt*

implantation [ˌɪmplɑːnˈteɪʃən] N **a** *(fig)* Einimpfung *f* *(in sb* jdm) **b** *(Med)* Implantation *f*, Einpflanzung *f*; *(in womb)* Einnisten *nt*

implausibility [ɪmˌplɔːzəˈbɪlɪtɪ] N mangelnde Plausibilität *f*; *(of story, tale, excuse also)* Unglaubhaftigkeit *f*, Unglaubwürdigkeit *f*; *(of lie)* Ungeschicktheit *f*

implausible [ɪmˈplɔːzəbl] ADJ nicht plausibel; *story, tale, excuse also* unglaubhaft, unglaubwürdig; *lie* wenig überzeugend, ungeschickt; *combination* unwahrscheinlich

implement [ˈɪmplɪmənt] N **a** Gerät *nt*; *(= tool)* Werkzeug *nt* **b** *(fig: = agent)* Werkzeug *nt* [ˈɪmplɪment] VT *law* vollziehen; *contract, promise* erfüllen; *(= carry out, put into effect) plan, reform, measure etc* durchführen, ausführen; *decisions, ceasefire* in die Tat umsetzen, durchführen

implementary [ˈɪmplɪmentərɪ], **implementing** [ˈɪmplɪmentɪŋ] ADJ ausführend; **~ regulations** *pl* Ausführungsbestimmungen *pl*

implementation [ˌɪmplɪmenˈteɪʃən] N *(of law)* Vollzug *m*; *(of contract, promise)* Erfüllung *f*; *(= carrying out) (of plan etc)* Ausführung *f*, Durchführung *f*; *(of decisions, ceasefire)* Durchführung *f*

implicate [ˈɪmplɪkeɪt] VT **to ~ sb in sth** jdn in etw verwickeln

implication [ˌɪmplɪˈkeɪʃən] N **a** *(of statement, situation)* Implikation *f*; *(of law, agreement etc)* Auswirkung *f*; *(of events)* Bedeutung *f no pl*, Implikation *f*; **the ~ of your statement is that ...** Ihre Behauptung impliziert, dass ...; **the possible ~s of his decision** die ganze Tragweite seiner Entscheidung; **by ~** implizit; **what are the political ~s?** was sind die politischen Auswirkungen?, was bedeutet das politisch gesehen? **b** *(in crime)* Verwicklung *f* *(in* in *+acc)*

implicit [ɪmˈplɪsɪt] ADJ **a** *(= implied)* implizit; *threat* indirekt, implizit; *agreement, recognition* stillschweigend; **to be ~ in sth** durch etw impliziert werden; *in contract etc* in etw *(dat)* impliziert sein; **a threat was ~ in his action** in seiner Handlungsweise lag eine indirekte Drohung **b** *(= unquestioning) belief, confidence* absolut, unbedingt

implicitly [ɪmˈplɪsɪtlɪ] ADV **a** *(= by implication)* implizit; *accept, recognize* stillschweigend; *criticize* indirekt **b** *(= unquestioningly)* **to trust/believe sb ~** jdm blind vertrauen/vorbehaltlos glauben

implied [ɪmˈplaɪd] ADJ impliziert; *threat also* indirekt

implied reader N *(Liter)* fiktiver Leser *(als Bestandteil der literarischen Fiktion)*

implied warranty N *(US Jur)* konkludente Zusicherung *(spec) (stillschweigende Zusage der Freiheit von Mängeln)*

implode [ɪmˈpləʊd] VI implodieren VT *(Ling)* als Verschlusslaut *or* Explosivlaut sprechen

implore [ɪmˈplɔːʳ] VT *person* anflehen, inständig bitten; *forgiveness etc* erbitten, erflehen; **do it, I ~ you!** ich flehe Sie an, tun Sie es!

imploring ADJ, **imploringly** ADV [ɪmˈplɔːrɪŋ, -lɪ] flehentlich, flehend

implosion [ɪmˈpləʊʒən] N Implosion *f*

imply [ɪmˈplaɪ] VT **a** *(= suggest)* andeuten, implizieren; **are you ~ing or do you mean to ~ that ...?** wollen Sie damit vielleicht sagen *or* andeuten, dass ...?; **this implies that he has changed his mind** das deutet darauf hin, dass er es sich *(dat)* anders überlegt hat **b** *(= indicate, lead to conclusion)* schließen lassen auf *(+acc)* **c** *(= involve)* bedeuten

impolite [ˌɪmpəˈlaɪt] ADJ unhöflich *(to sb* jdm gegenüber)

impolitely [ˌɪmpəˈlaɪtlɪ] ADV unhöflich

impoliteness [ˌɪmpəˈlaɪtnɪs] N Unhöflichkeit *f*

impolitic [ɪmˈpɒlɪtɪk] ADJ unklug

imponderable [ɪmˈpɒndərəbl] ADJ unberechenbar, unwägbar N unberechenbare *or* unwägbare Größe; **~s** Unwägbarkeiten *pl*, Imponderabilien *pl (geh)*

import [ˈɪmpɔːt] N **a** *(Comm)* Import *m*, Einfuhr *f* **b** *(of speech, document etc) (= meaning)* Bedeutung *f*; *(= significance)* Wichtigkeit *f*, Bedeutung *f*; **to be of (great) ~ to sb** für jdn von (großer) Bedeutung sein VT [ɪmˈpɔːt] **a** *(Comm) goods* einführen, importieren; *population, workforce* importieren **b** *(= mean, imply)* bedeuten, beinhalten **c** *(Comput)* importieren

importable [ɪmˈpɔːtəbl] ADJ einführbar

importance [ɪmˈpɔːtəns] ✪ 7.5 N Wichtigkeit *f*; *(= significance also)* Bedeutung *f*; *(= influence also)* Einfluss *m*; **I don't see the ~ of this** ich verstehe nicht, warum das wichtig sein soll; **to be of great ~** äußerst wichtig sein; **to be of no (great) ~** nicht (besonders) wichtig sein; **to be without ~** unwichtig sein; **to attach the greatest ~ to sth** einer Sache *(dat)* größten Wert *or* größte Wichtigkeit beimessen; **a man of ~** ein wichtiger *or* einflussreicher Mann; **to be full of one's own ~** ganz von seiner eigenen Wichtigkeit erfüllt sein

important [ɪmˈpɔːtənt] ADJ wichtig; *(= significant also)* bedeutend; *(= influential)* einflussreich, bedeutend; **that's not ~** das ist unwichtig; **it's not ~** *(= doesn't matter)* das macht nichts; **the (most) ~ thing is to stay fit** das Wichtigste *or* die Hauptsache ist, fit zu bleiben; **to try to look ~** sich *(dat)* ein gewichtiges Aussehen geben; **that letter looks ~** dieser Brief scheint wichtig zu sein; **it sounds ~** es hört sich an, als ob es wichtig sei; **he's trying to sound ~** er spielt sich auf; **to make sb feel ~** jdm das Gefühl geben, er/sie sei wichtig ADV = **importantly c**

importantly [ɪmˈpɔːtəntlɪ] ADV **a** *(usu pej: = self-importantly)* wichtigtuerisch *(pej)* **b** *(= significantly)* bedeutend, wesentlich; **to figure ~ in sth** eine bedeutende Rolle in etw *(dat)* spielen; **it is ~ different** das ist entscheidend anders **c** *(qualifying sentence)* **I was hungry and, more/most ~, my children were hungry** ich hatte Hunger, und was noch wichtiger/am allerwichtigsten war, meine Kinder hatten Hunger

importation [ˌɪmpɔːˈteɪʃən] N Einfuhr *f*, Import *m*

import duty N Einfuhrzoll *m*, Importzoll *m*

imported [ɪmˈpɔːtɪd] ADJ importiert, eingeführt, Import-; **~ goods/cars** importierte Waren/Autos, Importwaren/-autos *pl*

importer [ɪmˈpɔːtəʳ] N Importeur(in) *m(f)* *(of* von); *(= country also)* Importland *nt* *(of* für)

import: **import-export trade** N Import-Export-Handel *m*, Ein- und Ausfuhr *f*; **import licence** N Einfuhrlizenz *f*, Importlizenz *f*; **import permit** N Einfuhr- *or* Importerlaubnis *f*

importunate [ɪmˈpɔːtjʊnɪt] ADJ aufdringlich; *salesman also, creditor, demand* hartnäckig, beharrlich

importunately [ɪmˈpɔːtjʊnɪtlɪ] ADV aufdringlich

importunateness [ɪmˈpɔːtjʊnɪtnɪs] N Aufdringlichkeit *f*; *(of salesman also, creditor, demand)* Hartnäckigkeit *f*, Beharrlichkeit *f*

importune [ˌɪmpɔːˈtjuːn] VT belästigen; *(creditor, with questions)* zusetzen *(+dat)*; *(visitor)* zur Last fallen *(+dat)*

importunity [ˌɪmpɔːˈtjuːnɪtɪ] N **a** = **importunateness b** *(= demand, request)* unverschämte Bitte

impose [ɪmˈpəʊz] VT **a** *task, conditions* aufzwingen, auferlegen *(on sb* jdm); *sanctions, fine, sentence* verhängen *(on* gegen); *tax* erheben; *opinions, taste* aufzwingen *(on sb* jdm); **to ~ a tax on sth** etw mit einer Steuer belegen, etw besteuern; **the pressures ~d upon teachers** der Druck, dem Lehrer ausgesetzt sind **b to ~ oneself** *or* **one's presence on sb** sich jdm aufdrängen; **he ~d himself on them for three months** er ließ sich einfach drei Monate bei ihnen nieder VI zur Last fallen *(on sb* jdm); **I don't wish to ~** ich möchte Ihnen nicht zur Last fallen

imposing [ɪmˈpəʊzɪŋ] ADJ beeindruckend, imponierend; *person, appearance, building also* stattlich, imposant

imposition [ˌɪmpəˈzɪʃən] N **a** *no pl (of task, conditions)* Aufzwingen *nt*, Auferlegung *f* *(on sb* jdm); *(of sanctions, fine, sentence)* Verhängung *f* *(on* gegen); *(of tax)* Erhebung *f* **b** *(= tax)* Steuer *f* *(on* für, auf *+dat)* **c** *(= taking advantage)* Zumutung *f* *(on* für); **I'd love to stay if it's not too much of an ~ (on you)** ich würde liebend gern bleiben, wenn ich Ihnen nicht zur Last falle

impossibility [ɪmˌpɒsəˈbɪlɪtɪ] N Unmöglichkeit *f*; **that's an ~** das ist unmöglich *or* ein Ding der Unmöglichkeit

impossible [ɪmˈpɒsəbl] ✪ 16.1 ADJ **a** unmöglich; *dream* unerfüllbar; **~!** ausgeschlossen!, unmöglich!; **it is ~ for him to leave/do that** er kann unmöglich gehen/das unmöglich tun; **this cooker is ~ to clean** es ist unmöglich, diesen Herd sauber zu kriegen; **I find it ~ to understand why she resigned** ich finde es unverständlich *or* unbegreiflich *or* ich kann nicht begreifen, warum sie gekündigt hat; **to make it ~ for sb to do sth** es jdm unmöglich machen, etw zu tun

b *(= hopeless) situation, position* aussichtslos; **I am faced with an ~ choice/decision** ich stehe vor einer unmöglichen Wahl/Entscheidung; **you put me in an ~ position** du bringst mich in eine unmögliche Lage

c *(inf: = intolerable) person* unerträglich, unmöglich *(inf)*; **you're ~!** du bist unmöglich! *(inf)*

N Unmögliche(s) *nt*; **to ask for the ~** Unmögliches verlangen; **to do the ~** *(in general)* Unmögliches tun; *(in particular case)* das Unmögliche tun

impossibly [ɪmˈpɒsəblɪ] ADV unmöglich; **an ~ high standard** ein unerreichbar hohes Niveau

impostor [ɪmˈpɒstəʳ] N Betrüger(in) *m(f)*, Schwindler(in) *m(f)*; *(assuming higher position also)* Hochstapler(in) *m(f)*

imposture [ɪm'pɒstʃə'] N Betrug *m*, Schwindelei *f*

impotence ['ɪmpətəns] N **a** *(sexual)* Impotenz *f* **b** *(fig)* Schwäche *f*, Machtlosigkeit *f* **c** *(physical)* Schwäche *f*, Kraftlosigkeit *f*

impotent ['ɪmpətənt] ADJ **a** *(sexually)* impotent **b** *(fig)* schwach, machtlos; *grief, rage* ohnmächtig **c** *(physically)* schwach, kraftlos

impound [ɪm'paʊnd] VT **a** *(= seize) goods, assets, contraband* beschlagnahmen **b** *cattle* einsperren; *car* abschleppen (lassen)

impoverish [ɪm'pɒvərɪʃ] VT *person, country* in Armut bringen, verarmen lassen; *soil* auslaugen, erschöpfen; *(fig) culture* verkümmern *or* verarmen lassen

impoverished [ɪm'pɒvərɪʃt] ADJ arm; *person, conditions also* ärmlich; *(= having become poor)* verarmt; *soil* ausgelaugt, erschöpft; *supplies* erschöpft; *(fig)* dürftig

impoverishment [ɪm'pɒvərɪʃmənt] N Verarmung *f*; *(of soil)* Auslaugung *f*, Erschöpfung *f*; *(fig: of culture)* Verkümmerung *f*

impracticability [ɪm,præktɪkə'bɪlɪtɪ] N Impraktikabilität *f*; *(of design, size)* Unbrauchbarkeit *f*; *(of road)* schlechte Befahrbarkeit

impracticable [ɪm'præktɪkəbl] ADJ impraktikabel; *plan also* in der Praxis nicht anwendbar, praktisch unmöglich; *design, size* unbrauchbar; *road* schwer befahrbar

impractical [ɪm'præktɪkəl] ADJ unpraktisch; *scheme also* unbrauchbar

impracticality [ɪm,præktɪ'kælɪtɪ] N *(of person)* unpraktische Art; *(of scheme, idea)* Unbrauchbarkeit *f*

imprecate ['ɪmprɪkeɪt] VT verfluchen, verwünschen; **to ~ curses on sb** jdn verfluchen

imprecation [,ɪmprɪ'keɪʃən] N Verwünschung *f*, Fluch *m*

imprecise ADJ, **imprecisely** ADV [,ɪmprɪ'saɪs, -lɪ] ungenau, unpräzis(e)

imprecision [,ɪmprɪ'sɪʒən] N Ungenauigkeit *f*

impregnable [ɪm'pregnəbl] ADJ *(Mil) fortress, defences* uneinnehmbar; *(fig) position* unerschütterlich; *argument* unwiderlegbar, unumstößlich

impregnate ['ɪmpregneɪt] VT **a** *(= saturate)* tränken **b** *(fig)* erfüllen; *person* durchdringen, erfüllen **c** *(Biol: = fertilize)* befruchten; *humans also* schwängern

impregnation [,ɪmpreg'neɪʃən] N **a** *(= saturation)* Tränkung *f* **b** *(fig)* Erfüllung *f* **c** *(Biol: = fertilization)* Befruchtung *f*; *(of humans also)* Schwängerung *f*

impresario [,ɪmpre'sɑːrɪəʊ] N Impresario *m*, Theater-/Operndirektor(in) *m(f)*

impress [ɪm'pres] ✪ 13 VT **a** *person* beeindrucken; *(= arouse admiration in)* imponieren *(+dat)*; **how did it/he ~ you?** wie fanden Sie das/ihn?; **he/it ~ed me favourably** er/das hat einen guten *or* günstigen Eindruck auf mich gemacht; **I am not ~ed** das beeindruckt mich nicht, das imponiert mir gar nicht; **she is not easily ~ed** sie lässt sich nicht so leicht beeindrucken; **he doesn't ~ me as a politician** als Politiker macht er keinen Eindruck auf mich
b *(= fix in mind)* einschärfen *(on sb* jdm); *idea, danger, possibility* (deutlich) klarmachen *(on sb* jdm)
c *(= press to make mark)* **to ~ sth onto/into sth** etw auf etw *(acc)* aufdrücken *or* aufprägen/in etw *(acc)* eindrücken *or* einprägen; **his parting words ~ed themselves on my mind** seine Abschiedsworte haben sich mir eingeprägt; **that day has remained ~ed in my memory** diesen Tag werde ich nie vergessen
VI Eindruck machen; *(person: deliberately)* Eindruck schinden *(inf)*
N ['ɪmpres] Abdruck *m*

impressible [ɪm'presɪbl] ADJ beeinflussbar, leicht zu beeindrucken *(to* durch), empfänglich *(to* für)

impression [ɪm'preʃən] ✪ 6.2 N **a** Eindruck *m*; **to make a good/bad ~ on sb** einen guten/schlechten Eindruck auf jdn machen; **the theatre made a lasting ~ on me** das Theater beeindruckte mich tief; **his words made an ~** seine Worte machten Eindruck; **I haven't made any ~ on this job** ich bin mit dieser Arbeit noch nicht weit gekommen; **he made quite an ~ on the pile of ironing** er hat den Stapel Bügelwäsche fast ganz weggebügelt; **he created an ~ of power** er erweckte den Eindruck von Macht; **first ~s are usually right** der erste Eindruck ist gewöhnlich richtig
b *(= idea)* Eindruck *m*; *(= feeling)* Gefühl *nt*; **to give sb the ~ that ...** jdm den Eindruck vermitteln, dass ...; **he gave the ~ of being unhappy/self-confident** er wirkte unglücklich/selbstsicher; **I was under the ~ that ...** ich hatte den Eindruck, dass ...; **that gives an ~ of light** das vermittelt den Eindruck von Licht; **he had the ~ of falling** er hatte das Gefühl, zu fallen
c *(on wax etc)* Abdruck *m*; *(of engraving)* Prägung *f*
d *(of book etc)* Nachdruck *m*; **first ~** Erstdruck *m*
e *(= take-off)* Nachahmung *f*, Imitation *f*; **to do an ~ of sb** jdn imitieren *or* nachahmen

impressionable [ɪm'preʃnəbl] ADJ für Eindrücke empfänglich, leicht zu beeindrucken *pred (pej)*; **at an ~ age** in einem Alter, in dem man für Eindrücke besonders empfänglich ist

impressionism [ɪm'preʃənɪzəm] N Impressionismus *m*

impressionist [ɪm'preʃənɪst] N Impressionist(in) *m(f)*

impressionistic [ɪm,preʃə'nɪstɪk] ADJ impressionistisch; *(fig) story, account also* in groben Zügen (geschildert)

impressive [ɪm'presɪv] ADJ beeindruckend; *performance, speech, ceremony, personality also* eindrucksvoll; *(in size) building, person also* imposant

impressively [ɪm'presɪvlɪ] ADV eindrucksvoll; **he was ~ brave** sein Mut war beeindruckend; **she won both tournaments ~** sie gewann beide Turniere auf eindrucksvolle Weise

imprimatur [,ɪmprɪ'mɑːtə'] N *(form)* Imprimatur *nt*

imprint [ɪm'prɪnt] VT **a** *(= mark) leather* prägen; *paper* bedrucken; *seal etc* aufprägen *(on* auf *+acc)*; *(on paper)* aufdrucken *(on* auf *+acc)* **b** *(fig)* einprägen *(on sb* jdm); **to be ~ed on sb's mind** sich jdm eingeprägt haben; **to be ~ed on sb's memory** sich in jds Gedächtnis *(acc)* eingeprägt haben N ['ɪmprɪnt] **a** *(lit) (on leather, wax etc)* Abdruck *m*; *(on paper)* (Auf)druck *m*; *(fig)* Spuren *pl*, Zeichen *pl*, bleibender Eindruck **b** *(Typ)* Impressum *nt*; **under the Collins ~** mit dem Collins-Impressum

imprison [ɪm'prɪzn] VT *(lit)* inhaftieren, einsperren *(inf)*; *(fig)* gefangen halten; **to be ~ed** *(lit, fig)* gefangen sein; **to keep sb ~ed** jdn gefangen halten

imprisonment [ɪm'prɪznmənt] N *(= action)* Einsperren *nt (inf)*, Inhaftierung *f*; *(= state)* Gefangenschaft *f*; **the prospect of ~** die Aussicht auf eine Freiheitsstrafe; **to sentence sb to one month's/life ~** jdn zu einem Monat Gefängnis *or* Freiheitsstrafe/zu lebenslänglicher Freiheitsstrafe verurteilen; **to serve a term of ~** eine Freiheitsstrafe verbüßen

impro ['ɪmprəʊ] N *(inf)* Impro *f (inf)*, Improvisation *f*

improbability [ɪm,prɒbə'bɪlɪtɪ] N Unwahrscheinlichkeit *f*

improbable [ɪm'prɒbəbl] ADJ unwahrscheinlich

improbably [ɪm'prɒbəblɪ] ADV unwahrscheinlich; **he works, ~, for the World Bank** er arbeitet, kaum zu glauben, für die Weltbank

impromptu [ɪm'prɒmptjuː] ADJ improvisiert; **an ~ speech** eine Stegreifrede ADV improvisiert; *perform* aus dem Stegreif; **to speak/sing ~** improvisieren N *(Mus)* Impromptu *nt*

improper [ɪm'prɒpə'] ADJ *(= unsuitable)* unpassend, unangebracht; *(= unseemly)* unschicklich; *(= indecent)* unanständig; *(= wrong) diagnosis, interpretation* unzutreffend; *use* unsachgemäß; *(= dishonest) practice* unlauter; *(= not professional) conduct* unehrenhaft; **it is ~ to do that** es gehört sich nicht, das zu tun; **~ use of tools** Zweckentfremdung *f* von Geräten; **~ use of drugs/one's position** Drogen-/Amtsmissbrauch *m*

improperly [ɪm'prɒpəlɪ] ADV *act, dress* unpassend; *use, install* unsachgemäß; *diagnose* unzutreffend; *behave* unangemessen; *(= indecently)* unanständig

impropriety [,ɪmprə'praɪətɪ] N Unschicklichkeit *f*; *(of behaviour etc, language, remark)* Ungehörigkeit *f*; *(= indecency: of jokes etc)* Unanständigkeit *f*; **sexual/financial ~** sexuelles/finanzielles Fehlverhalten

improv ['ɪmprɒv] N *(inf)* improvisierter Sketch

improve [ɪm'pruːv] VT **a** *(= make better)* verbessern; *knowledge* erweitern; *salaries* aufbessern; *area, appearance* verschönern; *sauce, food etc* verfeinern; *production, value* erhöhen, steigern; **to ~ one's mind** sich weiterbilden
b **to ~ the shining hour** *(liter)* die Gelegenheit beim Schopfe packen
VI sich verbessern, sich bessern; *(area, appearance)* schöner werden; *(production, value)* sich erhöhen, steigen; **he has ~d in maths** er hat sich in Mathematik gebessert; **to ~ with practice** durch Übung besser werden; **wine ~s with age** je älter der Wein desto besser; **the invalid is improving** dem Kranken geht es besser; **I'll try to ~** ich werde versuchen, mich zu bessern; **things are improving** es sieht schon besser aus, die Lage bessert sich
VR **to ~ oneself** an sich *(dat)* arbeiten

▸ **improve (up)on** VI *+prep obj* **a** *(= improve)* übertreffen, besser machen; *nature, performance* verbessern; **that can't be improved upon** das kann man nicht übertreffen **b** *(Comm, Fin) offer* überbieten, gehen über *(+acc)*

improved [ɪm'pruːvd] ADJ besser, verbessert; *offer also* höher

improvement [ɪm'pruːvmənt] N Verbesserung *f*, Besserung *f*; *(of area, appearance)* Verschönerung *f*; *(of sauce, food etc)* Verfeinerung *f*; *(= increase) (in production, value)* Erhöhung *f*, Steigerung *f*; *(of knowledge)* Erweiterung *f*; *(of salaries)* Aufbesserung *f*; *(in health)* Besserung *f*; *(in studies)* Verbesserung *f*, Fortschritte *pl*; **an ~ in performance** eine Leistungssteigerung; **to be open to ~** verbesserungsfähig sein; **an ~ on the previous one** eine Verbesserung gegenüber dem Früheren; **to make ~s** Verbesserungen machen *or* durchführen *(to* an *+dat)*; **to carry out ~s to a house** Ausbesserungs- *or (to appearance)* Verschönerungsarbeiten an einem Haus vornehmen

improvidence [ɪm'prɒvɪdəns] N mangelnde Vorsorge *(of* für), Sorglosigkeit *f (of* in Bezug auf *+acc)*

improvident [ɪm'prɒvɪdənt] ADJ sorglos

improving [ɪm'pruːvɪŋ] ADJ informativ, lehrreich; *book also* bildend; *(= morally improving)* erbaulich

improvisation [,ɪmprəvaɪ'zeɪʃən] N Improvisation *f*, Improvisierung *f*; *(object improvised)* Provisorium *nt*

improvise ['ɪmprəvaɪz] VTI improvisieren VI improvisieren; **to ~ on a tune** *(Mus)* über eine Melodie improvisieren; **to ~ on a story** eine Geschichte abändern

imprudence [ɪm'pruːdəns] N Unklugheit *f*

imprudent ADJ, **imprudently** ADV [ɪm'pruːdənt, -lɪ] unklug

impudence ['ɪmpjʊdəns] N Unverschämtheit *f*, Frechheit *f*; **what ~!** so eine Unverschämtheit *or* Frechheit!; **he had the ~ to ask me** er hatte die Stirn *or* er besaß die Frechheit, mich zu fragen

impudent ADJ, **impudently** ADV ['ɪmpjʊdənt, -lɪ] unverschämt, dreist

impugn [ɪm'pjuːn] VT *person* angreifen; *sb's behaviour etc also* scharfe Kritik üben an *(+dat)*; *sb's* *honesty, motives* in Zweifel ziehen, Zweifel hegen an *(+dat)*; *statement, evidence, veracity of witness* bestreiten, anfechten

impulse [ˈɪmpʌls] N Impuls *m*; *(= driving force)* (Stoß- *or* Trieb)kraft *f*; **nerve ~** nervöser Reiz *or* Impuls; **to give a new ~ to the peace process** dem Friedensprozess einen neuen Impuls geben; **man of ~** impulsiver Mensch; **she resisted an ~ to smile** sie widerstand dem Impuls zu lächeln; **to yield to a sudden ~** einem Impuls nachgeben *or* folgen; **on ~** aus einem Impuls heraus, impulsiv; **I had an ~ to hit him** ich hatte den unwiderstehlichen Drang *or* das plötzliche Verlangen, ihn zu schlagen; **he is ruled by his ~s** er lässt sich von seinen spontanen Regungen leiten

impulse buying [ˌɪmpʌlsˈbaɪɪŋ] N impulsives *or* spontanes Kaufen; **an impulse buy** *or* **purchase** ein Impulsivkauf *m*

impulsion [ɪmˈpʌlʃən] N *(lit: = act of impelling)* Antrieb *m*; *(lit, fig: = driving force also)* Antriebskraft *f*; *(fig) (= impetus)* Impuls *m*; *(= compulsion)* Trieb *m*, Drang *m*

impulsive [ɪmˈpʌlsɪv] ADJ **a** impulsiv; *(= spontaneous)* spontan **b** *(Phys, Tech)* (an)treibend; **~ force** Triebkraft *f*

impulsively [ɪmˈpʌlsɪvlɪ] ADV impulsiv; *(= spontaneously)* spontan

impulsiveness [ɪmˈpʌlsɪvnɪs] N Impulsivität *f*; *(= spontaneity)* Spontaneität *f*

impunity [ɪmˈpjuːnɪtɪ] N Straflosigkeit *f*; **with ~** ungestraft

impure [ɪmˈpjʊəˈ] ADJ *water, drugs, thoughts, mind* unrein; *food* verunreinigt; *motives* unsauber

impurity [ɪmˈpjʊərɪtɪ] N Unreinheit *f*; *(of food)* Verunreinigung *f*; *(of motives)* Unsauberkeit *f*; **the impurities in the liquid** die Verunreinigungen in der Flüssigkeit

imputation [ˌɪmpjʊˈteɪʃən] N *(of crime)* Bezichtigung *f*; *(of lie also)* Unterstellung *f*

impute [ɪmˈpjuːt] VT zuschreiben (*to sb/sth* jdm/einer Sache); **to ~ a crime to sb** jdn eines Verbrechens bezichtigen

in [ɪn]

1 PREPOSITION	3 ADJECTIVE
2 ADVERB	4 PLURAL NOUN

1 – PREPOSITION

When *in* is the second element of a phrasal verb, eg *ask in, fill in, hand in,* look up the verb. When it is part of a set combination, eg *in danger, in the end, weak in, wrapped in,* look up the other word.

a [position] in *(+dat)*; *(with motion)* in *(+acc)*; **it was in the lorry/bag/car** es war auf dem Lastwagen/in der Tasche/im Auto; **he put it in the lorry/car/bag** er legte es auf den Lastwagen/ins Auto/steckte es in die Tasche; **in here/there** hierin/darin, hier/da drin *(inf)*; *(with motion)* hier/da hinein *or* rein *(inf)*; **go in that direction** gehen Sie in diese *or* dieser Richtung; **in the street** auf der/die Straße; **in Thompson Street** in der Thompsonstraße; **he lives in a little village** er wohnt auf *or* in einem kleinen Dorf; **sitting in the window** am Fenster sitzend; **a flag hung in the window** eine Flagge hing im Fenster; **in (the) church** in der Kirche; **to stay in the house** im Haus *or (at home)* zu Hause *or* zuhause *(Aus, Sw)* bleiben; **in bed/prison** im Bett/Gefängnis; **in Germany/Switzerland/the United States** in Deutschland/der Schweiz/den Vereinigten Staaten

after the superlative, *in* is sometimes untranslated and the genitive case used instead.

the highest mountain in Scotland der höchste Berg Schottlands *or* in Schottland; **the best in the class** der Beste der Klasse, der Klassenbeste

b [people] bei; **you can find examples of this in Dickens** man findet Beispiele dafür bei Dickens *or* in Dickens' Werken; **rare in a child of that age** selten bei einem Kind in diesem Alter; **you have a great leader in him** in ihm habt ihr einen großen Führer; **he hasn't got it in him** er hat nicht das Zeug dazu; **he doesn't have it in him to …** er bringt es nicht fertig, … zu …

c [dates, seasons, time of day] in *(+dat)*; **in 1999** (im Jahre) 1999; **in May 1999** im Mai 1999; **in the sixties** in den sechziger Jahren *or* Sechzigerjahren; **in June** im Juni; **in (the) spring** im Frühling; **in the morning(s)** morgens, am Morgen, am Vormittag; **in the afternoon** nachmittags, am Nachmittag; **in the daytime** tagsüber, während des Tages; **in the evening** abends, am Abend; **three o'clock in the afternoon** drei Uhr nachmittags; **in those days** damals, zu jener Zeit

d [time of life] in *(+dat)*; **she is in her thirties** sie ist in den Dreißigern; **in middle age** im mittleren Alter; **in old age** im Alter; **in childhood** in der Kindheit, im Kindesalter; **in my childhood** in meiner Kindheit

e [interval of time] in *(+dat)*; **she did it in three hours** sie machte es in drei Stunden *or* innerhalb von drei Stunden; **in a short time** in kurzer Zeit; **in a week('s time)** in einer Woche; **I haven't seen him in years** ich habe ihn jahrelang *or* seit Jahren nicht mehr gesehen; **in a moment** *or* **minute** sofort, gleich

f [numbers, quantities] zu; **packed in hundreds** zu Hunderten abgepackt; **to walk in twos** zu zweit gehen; **to count in fives** in Fünfern zählen; **to die in hundreds** zu hunderten *or* Hunderten sterben; **in large/small quantities** in großen/kleinen Mengen; **in some measure** in gewisser Weise, zu einem gewissen Grad; **in part** teilweise, zum Teil

g [ratios] **he has a one in 500 chance of winning** er hat eine Gewinnchance von eins zu 500; **one (man) in ten** einer von zehn, jeder Zehnte; **one book/child in ten** jedes zehnte Buch/Kind, ein Buch/Kind von zehn; **one in five children** ein Kind von fünf; **a tax of twenty pence in the pound** ein Steuersatz von zwanzig Prozent; **there are 12 inches in a foot** ein Fuß hat 12 Zoll

h [manner, state, condition] **to speak in a loud/soft voice** mit lauter/leiser Stimme sprechen, laut/leise sprechen; **to speak in a whisper** flüstern, flüsternd sprechen; **to speak in German** Deutsch reden; **the background is painted in red** der Hintergrund ist rot (gemalt) *or* in Rot gehalten; **to pay in dollars** mit *or* in Dollar bezahlen; **to stand in a row/in groups** in einer Reihe/in Gruppen stehen; **in this way** so, auf diese Weise; **she squealed in delight** sie quietschte vor Vergnügen; **in anger** im Zorn; **in surprise** überrascht; **to be in a rage** wütend *or* zornig sein; **in good condition** in gutem Zustand; **to live in luxury/poverty** im Luxus/in Armut leben

i [clothes] in *(+dat)*; **in one's best clothes** in Sonntagskleidung; **in his shirt** im Hemd; **in his shirt sleeves** in Hemdsärmeln, hemdsärmelig; **in his slippers** in Hausschuhen; **dressed in white** weiß gekleidet; **she was dressed in silk** sie war in Seide gekleidet; **the lady in green** die Dame in Grün

j [substance, material] **upholstered in silk** mit Seide bezogen; **to paint in oils** in Öl malen; **to write in ink/pencil** mit Tinte/Bleistift schreiben; **in marble** in Marmor, marmorn; **a sculptor who works in marble** ein Bildhauer, der mit Marmor arbeitet

k [in respect of] **blind in the left eye** auf dem linken Auge blind, links blind; **a rise in prices** ein Preisanstieg *m*, ein Anstieg *m* der Preise; **ten feet in height by thirty in length** zehn Fuß hoch auf dreißig Fuß lang; **the trousers are too long in the leg** die (Hosen)beine sind zu lang; **five in number** fünf an der Zahl; **the latest thing in hats** der letzte Schrei bei Hüten

l [occupation, activity] **he is in the army** er ist beim Militär; **he is in banking/the motor business** er ist im Bankwesen/in der Autobranche (tätig)

m [set structures]

♦ **in** + *-ing* **in saying this, I …** wenn ich das sage, … ich; **in trying to escape** beim Versuch zu fliehen, beim Fluchtversuch; **in trying to save him she fell into the water herself** beim Versuch *or* als sie versuchte, ihn zu retten, fiel sie selbst ins Wasser; **but in saying this** aber indem ich dies sage; **he made a mistake in saying that** es war ein Fehler von ihm, das zu sagen

♦ **in that** *(= seeing that)* insofern als; **the plan was unrealistic in that it didn't take account of the fact that …** der Plan war unrealistisch, da *or* weil er nicht berücksichtigte, dass …

2 – ADVERB

When *in* is the second element in a phrasal verb, eg *come in, live in, sleep in,* look up the verb.

da; *(at home also)* zu Hause, zuhause *(Aus, Sw)*; **there is nobody in** es ist niemand da/zu Hause

to be in may require a more specific translation.

the train is in der Zug ist da *or* angekommen; **the harvest is in** die Ernte ist eingebracht; **the tide is in** es ist Flut; **our team is in** *(Cricket)* unsere Mannschaft ist am Schlag; **the Socialists are in** *(= in power)* die Sozialisten sind an der Regierung; **our candidate is in** unser Kandidat wurde gewählt *or* ist reingekommen *(inf)*; **my luck is in** ich habe einen Glückstag

♦ **to be in for sth he's in for a surprise/disappointment** ihm steht eine Überraschung/Enttäuschung bevor, er kann sich auf eine Überraschung/Enttäuschung gefasst machen; **we are in for rain/a cold spell** uns *(dat)* steht Regen/eine Kältewelle bevor; **he is in for the job of manager** *(= applying for)* er hat sich um die Stelle des Managers beworben; **he's in for it!** der kann sich auf was gefasst machen *(inf)*, der kann sich freuen *(iro)*

♦ **to have it in for sb** *(inf)* es auf jdn abgesehen haben *(inf)*

♦ **to be in on sth** an einer Sache beteiligt sein; *on secret etc* über etw *(acc)* Bescheid wissen; **he likes to be in on things** er mischt gern (überall) mit *(inf)*

♦ **to be (well) in with sb** sich gut mit jdm verstehen

3 – ADJECTIVE

(inf) in *inv (inf)*; **long skirts are in** lange Röcke sind in *(inf) or* sind in Mode; **the in thing** das, was zurzeit in ist *(inf) or* Mode ist; **the in thing is to …** es ist zurzeit in *(inf) or* Mode, zu …; **it's the in place to go** da gehen jetzt alle hin; **the in thing to do** groß in Mode

4 – the ins PLURAL NOUN

a [= details]

♦ **the ins and outs** die Einzelheiten *pl*; **to know the ins and outs of sth** bei einer Sache genau Bescheid wissen; **I don't know the ins and outs of the situation** über die Einzelheiten der Sache weiß ich nicht Bescheid

b [Pol] *US* **the ins** die Regierungspartei

inability [ˌɪnəˈbɪlɪtɪ] N Unfähigkeit *f*, Unvermögen *nt*; **~ to pay** Zahlungsunfähigkeit *f*

inaccessibility [ˈɪnækˌsesəˈbɪlɪtɪ] N Unzugänglichkeit *f*; *(of place also)* Unerreichbarkeit *f*; *(fig: of idea, music, painting, novel)* Unverständlichkeit *f*

inaccessible [ˌɪnækˈsesəbl] ADJ **a** *(= impossible to reach)* unzugänglich (*to sb/sth* für jdn/etw); *place also* unerreichbar; **to be ~ by land/sea** auf dem Landweg/Seeweg nicht erreichbar sein **b** *(fig: = difficult to understand) idea, music, painting, novel* unverständlich

inaccuracy [ɪnˈækjʊrəsɪ] N Ungenauigkeit *f*; *(= incorrectness)* Unrichtigkeit *f*

inaccurate [ɪnˈækjʊrɪt] ADJ *(= lacking accuracy)* ungenau; *(= not correct)* unrichtig; **she was ~ in her judgement of the situation** ihre Beurteilung der Lage traf nicht zu; **it is ~ to say that …** es ist nicht richtig zu sagen, dass …

inaccurately [ɪnˈækjʊrɪtlɪ] ADV ungenau; *(= incorrectly)* unrichtig

inaction [ɪnˈækʃən] N Untätigkeit *f*, Tatenlosigkeit *f*

inactive [ɪnˈæktɪv] ADJ untätig; *person, life, hands also* müßig *(geh)*; *mind* träge, müßig *(geh)*; *volcano* erloschen, untätig; *(Fin) account* umsatzlos; **don't have money lying ~ in the bank** lassen Sie (Ihr) Geld nicht auf der Bank brachliegen

inactivity [ˌɪnækˈtɪvɪtɪ] N Untätigkeit *f*; *(of mind)* Trägheit *f*; *(Comm)* Stille *f*, Flaute *f*

inadequacy [ɪnˈædɪkwəsɪ] N Unzulänglichkeit *f*; *(of measures)* Unangemessenheit *f*

inadequate [ɪnˈædɪkwɪt] ADJ unzulänglich, inadäquat *(geh)*; *supplies, resources, punishment, reasons, proposals also* unzureichend; *measures* unangemessen; **he is ~ for such a job/responsibility** er ist für eine solche Stelle nicht geeignet/einer solchen Verantwortung nicht gewachsen; **she makes him feel ~** sie gibt ihm das Gefühl der Unzulänglichkeit

inadequately [ɪnˈædɪkwɪtlɪ] ADV unzulänglich, inadäquat *(geh)*; *equipped, explained, documented also* unzureichend

inadmissibility [ˈɪnədˌmɪsəˈbɪlɪtɪ] N Unzulässigkeit *f*

inadmissible [ˌɪnədˈmɪsəbl] ADJ unzulässig

inadvertence [ˌɪnədˈvɜːtəns] N Ungewolltheit *f*; **it resulted from ~** es geschah versehentlich *or* aus Versehen

inadvertent [ˌɪnədˈvɜːtənt] ADJ unbeabsichtigt, ungewollt

inadvertently [ˌɪnədˈvɜːtəntlɪ] ADV versehentlich

inadvisability [ˈɪnədˌvaɪzəˈbɪlɪtɪ] N Unratsamkeit *f* (*of doing sth* etw zu tun)

inadvisable [ˌɪnədˈvaɪzəbl] ✪ 2.2 ADJ unratsam, nicht zu empfehlen *pred*, nicht zu empfehlend *attr*

inalienable [ɪnˈeɪlɪənəbl] ADJ *rights* unveräußerlich

inalterable [ɪnˈɔːltərəbl] ADJ unveränderlich, unabänderlich; **it is ~** es lässt sich nicht ändern

inane [ɪˈneɪn] ADJ dumm; *suggestion also* hirnverbrannt

inanely [ɪˈneɪnlɪ] ADV dumm; **they chatted on ~** sie plauderten albern weiter; **he suggested ~ that ...** er machte den hirnverbrannten Vorschlag, zu ...

inanimate [ɪnˈænɪmɪt] ADJ leblos, tot; *nature, world* unbelebt

inanition [ˌɪnəˈnɪʃən] N Auszehrung *f*

inanity [ɪˈnænɪtɪ] N Dummheit *f*; *(of suggestion also)* Hirnverbranntheit *f*

inappetency [ɪnˈæpɪtənsɪ] N *(fig liter)* Lustlosigkeit *f*, Unlust *f*

inapplicable [ɪnˈæplɪkəbl] ADJ *answer* unzutreffend; *laws, rules* nicht anwendbar (*to sb* auf jdn)

inapposite [ɪnˈæpəzɪt] ADJ unpassend, unangebracht

inappropriate [ˌɪnəˈprəʊprɪɪt] ADJ unpassend, unangebracht; *action also* unangemessen; *time* unpassend, ungelegen, ungünstig; **this translation is rather ~** das ist keine angemessene Übersetzung; **you have come at a most ~ time** Sie kommen sehr ungelegen

inappropriately [ˌɪnəˈprəʊprɪɪtlɪ] ADV unpassend; **she was ~ treated** sie wurde nicht richtig behandelt

inappropriateness [ˌɪnəˈprəʊprɪɪtnɪs] N Unpassende(s) *nt*, Unangebrachtheit *f*; *(of action also)* Unangemessenheit *f*; *(of time)* Ungünstigkeit *f*

inapt [ɪnˈæpt] ADJ ungeschickt; *comparison* unpassend

inaptitude [ɪnˈæptɪtjuːd] N *(of person)* Unfähigkeit *f*; *(for work etc)* Untauglichkeit *f*; *(of remark)* Ungeschicktheit *f*

inarticulacy [ˌɪnɑːˈtɪkjʊləsɪ] N *(form)* Inartikuliertheit *f (geh)*, mangelnde Wortgewandtheit *f*; **he was reduced to ~** er konnte keine Worte mehr finden

inarticulate [ˌɪnɑːˈtɪkjʊlɪt] ADJ **a** *essay* schlecht *or* unklar ausgedrückt, inartikuliert *(geh)*; *speech also* schwerfällig; **she's very ~** sie kann sich kaum *or* nur schlecht ausdrücken; **a brilliant but ~ scientist** ein glänzender, aber wenig wortgewandter Wissenschaftler; **~ with rage** sprachlos vor Zorn; **just a string of ~ grunts** nur eine Reihe unverständlicher Grunzlaute **b** *(Zool)* nicht gegliedert

inarticulately [ˌɪnɑːˈtɪkjʊlɪtlɪ] ADV *(= incomprehensibly)* unverständlich

inartistic ADJ, **inartistically** ADV [ˌɪnɑːˈtɪstɪk, -əlɪ] unkünstlerisch; *work also* kunstlos

inasmuch [ɪnəzˈmʌtʃ] ADV **~ as** da, weil; *(= to the extent that)* insofern als

inattention [ˌɪnəˈtenʃən] N Unaufmerksamkeit *f*; **~ to detail** Ungenauigkeit *f* im Detail

inattentive [ˌɪnəˈtentɪv] ADJ unaufmerksam; **he was ~ to her requests** er beachtete ihre Wünsche nicht

inattentively [ˌɪnəˈtentɪvlɪ] ADV unaufmerksam

inattentiveness [ˌɪnəˈtentɪvnɪs] N Unaufmerksamkeit *f*

inaudibility [ɪnˌɔːdəˈbɪlɪtɪ] N Unhörbarkeit *f*

inaudible ADJ, **inaudibly** ADV [ɪnˈɔːdəbl, -ɪ] unhörbar (*to* für)

inaugural [ɪˈnɔːgjʊrəl] ADJ *lecture* Antritts-; *meeting, address, speech* Eröffnungs- N *(= speech)* Antritts-/Eröffnungsrede *f*

inaugurate [ɪˈnɔːgjʊreɪt] VT **a** *president, pope, king, official etc* (feierlich) in sein/ihr Amt einsetzen *or* einführen, inaugurieren *(geh)* **b** *policy* einführen; *building* einweihen; *exhibition* eröffnen; *era* einleiten

inauguration [ɪˌnɔːgjʊˈreɪʃən] N **a** *(of president, pope, king, official etc)* Amtseinführung *f*, Inauguration *f (geh)* **b** *(of policy)* Einführung *f*; *(of building)* Einweihung *f*; *(of exhibition)* Eröffnung *f*; *(of era)* Beginn *m*, Anfang *m*

INAUGURATION DAY

Inauguration Day ist der Tag der feierlichen Amtseinführung des frisch gewählten Präsidenten der Vereinigten Staaten von Amerika. Die Zeremonie wird am 20. Januar abgehalten, auch wenn die Präsidentschaftswahlen schon im vorhergehenden November stattgefunden haben. Gewöhnlich wird in der Hauptstadt Washington DC eine Parade abgehalten, und der Präsident erklärt in einer Ansprache die Ziele und Pläne für seine Amtszeit. Bei dieser Zeremonie wird auch der Vizepräsident in sein Amt eingeführt.

inauspicious [ˌɪnɔːsˈpɪʃəs] ADJ Unheil verheißend; *circumstances, omen also* unheilträchtig; **to get off to an ~ start** *(career, campaign)* sich nicht gerade vielversprechend anlassen; *(person)* keinen vielversprechenden Anfang machen

inauspiciously [ˌɪnɔːsˈpɪʃəslɪ] ADV Unheil verheißend

in-between [ɪnbɪˈtwiːn] *(inf)* N **the ~s** wer/was dazwischenliegt *or* -kommt ADJ Mittel-, Zwischen-; **it is sort of ~** es ist so ein Mittelding; **~ stage** Zwischenstadium *nt*; **~ times** *adv* zwischendurch, dazwischen

inboard [ˈɪnbɔːd] *(Naut)* ADJ Innenbord-; **~ motor** Innenbordmotor *m* ADV binnenbords N Innenbordmotor *m*

inborn [ˈɪnˈbɔːn] ADJ angeboren

inbound [ˈɪnˌbaʊnd] ADJ *flight* ankommend; **a special ~ flight from Honduras** eine ankommende Sondermaschine aus Honduras

inbox N *(= E-mail)* Posteingang *m*

inbred [ˈɪnˈbred] ADJ **a an ~ family** eine Familie, in der Inzucht herrscht; **they look very ~** sie sehen nach Inzucht aus; **to stop them becoming ~** um die Inzucht bei ihnen aufzuhalten; **the royal family became very ~** in der Königsfamilie herrschte Inzucht **b** *quality* angeboren (*in sb* jdm)

inbreed [ˈɪnˈbriːd] VT *animals* durch Inzucht züchten

inbreeding [ˈɪnˈbriːdɪŋ] N Inzucht *f*

inbuilt [ˈɪnbɪlt] ADJ *safety features, error detection etc* integriert; *dislike, fear, awareness* angeboren, instinktiv; *majority* automatisch; *predisposition, fondness, resistance* natürlich

Inc *(US) abbr of* **Incorporated**

Inca [ˈɪŋkə] N Inka *mf* ADJ *(also* **Incan***)* Inka-, inkaisch; **~(n) empire** Inkareich *nt*

incalculable [ɪnˈkælkjʊləbl] ADJ **a** *amount* unschätzbar, unermesslich; *damage, harm* unermesslich, unabsehbar; *consequences* unabsehbar **b** *(Math)* nicht berechenbar **c** *character, mood* unberechenbar, unvorhersehbar

incandescence [ˌɪnkænˈdesns] N (Weiß)glühen *nt*, (Weiß)glut *f*; *(fig)* Leuchten *nt*, Strahlen *nt*

incandescent [ˌɪnkænˈdesnt] ADJ *(lit)* (weiß) glühend; *(fig liter)* hell leuchtend, strahlend; **~ light** Glühlampe *f*, Glühbirne *f*; **~ with rage** *or* **fury** bis zur Weißglut gereizt

incantation [ˌɪnkænˈteɪʃən] N Zauber(spruch) *m*, Zauberformel *f*; *(= act)* Beschwörung *f*

incapability [ɪnˌkeɪpəˈbɪlɪtɪ] N Unfähigkeit *f*, Unvermögen *nt* (*of doing sth* etw zu tun)

incapable [ɪnˈkeɪpəbl] ✪ 16.4 ADJ **a** *person* unfähig; *(physically)* hilflos; **to be ~ of doing sth** unfähig *or* nicht imstande *or* nicht im Stande sein, etw zu tun, etw nicht tun können; **she is physically ~ of lifting it** sie ist körperlich nicht in der Lage, es zu heben; **drunk and ~** volltrunken; **he was completely ~** *(because drunk)* er war volltrunken; **~ of working** arbeitsunfähig; **~ of tenderness** zu Zärtlichkeit nicht fähig; **do it yourself, you're not ~** *(inf)* mach es doch selbst, du bist nicht so hilflos
b *(form)* **~ of proof** nicht beweisbar; **~ of measurement** nicht messbar; **~ of improvement** nicht verbesserungsfähig; **~ of solution** unlösbar

incapacitate [ˌɪnkəˈpæsɪteɪt] VT **a** *(= immobilize)* unfähig machen (*for* für, *from doing sth* etw zu tun); **to ~ sb for work** jdn arbeitsunfähig machen; **physically ~d** körperlich behindert; **somewhat ~d by his broken ankle** durch seinen gebrochenen Knöchel ziemlich behindert **b** *(Jur)* entmündigen

incapacity [ˌɪnkəˈpæsɪtɪ] N **a** Unfähigkeit *f* (*for* für); **~ for work** Arbeitsunfähigkeit *f* **b** *(Jur)* mangelnde Berechtigung (*for* zu); **~ to inherit** Erbunfähigkeit *f*; **~ of a minor** Geschäftsunfähigkeit *f* eines Minderjährigen

in-car [ˈɪnkɑːˈ] ADJ *attr* Auto-; *entertainment, stereo* im Auto; **~ computer** Autocomputer *m*

incarcerate [ɪnˈkɑːsəreɪt] VT einkerkern

incarceration [ˌɪnkɑːsəˈreɪʃən] N *(= act)* Einkerkerung *f*; *(= period)* Kerkerhaft *f*

incarnate [ɪnˈkɑːnɪt] ADJ *(Rel)* fleischgeworden, Mensch geworden; *(= personified)* leibhaftig *attr*, in Person; **to become ~** Fleisch werden, Mensch werden; **the word Incarnate** das fleischgewordene Wort; **he's the devil ~** er ist der leibhaftige Teufel *or* der Teufel in Person; **she is cynicism ~** sie ist der Zynismus in Person VT [ˈɪnkɑːneɪt] *(= make real)* Gestalt *or* Form geben *(+dat)*; *(= be embodiment of)* verkörpern

incarnation [ˌɪnkɑːˈneɪʃən] N *(Rel)* Inkarnation *f (geh)*, Menschwerdung *f*, Fleischwerdung *f*; *(fig)* Inbegriff *m*, Verkörperung *f*, Inkarnation *f (geh)*

incautious ADJ, **incautiously** ADV [ɪnˈkɔːʃəs, -lɪ] unvorsichtig, unbedacht

incendiary [ɪnˈsendɪərɪ] ADJ **a** *(lit)* Brand-; **~ attack** Brandanschlag *m*; **~ bomb** Brandbombe *f* **b** *(fig) speech* aufwiegelnd, aufhetzend N **a** *(= bomb)* Brandbombe *f* **b** *(= person) (lit)* Brandstifter(in) *m(f)*; *(fig)* Aufrührer(in) *m(f)*, Unruhestifter(in) *m(f)*

incendiary device N Brandsatz *m*

incense[1] [ɪn'sens] VT wütend machen, erbosen, erzürnen; **~d** wütend, erbost *(at, by* über *+acc)*

incense[2] ['ɪnsens] N *(Eccl)* Weihrauch *m*; *(fig)* Duft *m*

incense: **incense bearer** N Weihrauchschwenker *m or* -träger *m*; **incense burner** N Weihrauchschwenker *m*, Räucherpfanne *f*

incentive [ɪn'sentɪv] N Anreiz *m*; **this will give them a bit of an ~** das wird ihnen einen gewissen Anreiz *or* Ansporn geben; **they have little ~ to keep going** ihnen fehlt der Anreiz durchzuhalten; **financial/economic ~s** finanzielle/wirtschaftliche Anreize *pl*; **~ bonus payment** Leistungszulage *f*; **~ scheme** *(Ind)* Anreizsystem *nt*

inception [ɪn'sepʃən] N Beginn *m*, Anfang *m*; **from its ~** von Anbeginn an; **at its ~** zu Anbeginn

incertitude [ɪn'sɜːtɪtjuːd] N Ungewissheit *f*, Unsicherheit *f*

incessant [ɪn'sesnt] ADJ unaufhörlich, unablässig; *complaints also* nicht abreißend; *noise* ununterbrochen

incessantly [ɪn'sesntlɪ] ADV unaufhörlich

incest ['ɪnsest] N Inzest *m*, Blutschande *f*

incestuous [ɪn'sestjʊəs] ADJ blutschänderisch, inzestuös *(geh)*

inch [ɪntʃ] **N** Zoll *m*, Inch *m*; **3.5 ~ disk** 3,5-Zoll-Diskette *f*; **because of his lack of ~es** weil er ein bisschen klein ist; **she's grown a few ~es** sie ist ein paar Zentimeter gewachsen; **~ by ~** Zentimeter um Zentimeter; **an ~-by-~ search** eine gründliche Durchsuchung; **he came within an ~ of winning/victory** er hätte um ein Haar *or* beinahe gewonnen; **he came within an ~ of being killed** er ist dem Tod um Haaresbreite entgangen; **they beat/thrashed him (to) within an ~ of his life** sie haben ihn so geschlagen/verprügelt, dass er fast gestorben wäre; **the lorry missed me by ~es** der Lastwagen hat mich um Haaresbreite verfehlt; **he knows every ~ of the area** er kennt die Gegend wie seine Westentasche; **he is every ~ a soldier** er ist jeder Zoll ein Soldat; **we will not surrender one ~ of our territory** wir werden keinen Zentimeter unseres Gebiets abtreten; **they searched every ~ of the room** sie durchsuchten das Zimmer Zentimeter für Zentimeter; **he couldn't see an ~ in front of him** er konnte die Hand nicht vor den Augen sehen; **give him an ~ and he'll take a mile** *(prov)* wenn man ihm den kleinen Finger gibt, nimmt er die ganze Hand *(prov)*
VI to ~ forward/out/in sich millimeterweise *or* stückchenweise vorwärtsschieben/hinausschieben/hineinschieben; **because prices are ~ing up** weil die Preise allmählich ansteigen; **the Dutch swimmer is ~ing ahead** der holländische Schwimmer schiebt sich langsam an die Spitze
VT langsam manövrieren; **he ~ed his way forward/through** er schob sich langsam vorwärts/durch

inchoate ['ɪnkəʊeɪt] ADJ *(liter)* unausgeformt

incidence ['ɪnsɪdəns] N **a** *(Opt)* Einfall *m*; **angle of ~** Einfallswinkel *m* **b** *(of crime, disease)* Häufigkeit *f*; **a high ~ of crime** eine hohe Verbrechensquote *(= occurrence)* Vorkommen *nt* **c** *(= occurrence)* Vorkommen *nt*; **isolated ~s** vereinzelte Fälle *pl*

incident ['ɪnsɪdənt] **N a** *(= event)* Ereignis *nt*, Begebenheit *f*, Vorfall *m*; **a day/book full of ~** ein ereignisreicher Tag/ereignisreiches Buch; **an ~ from his childhood** ein Kindheitserlebnis *nt* **b** *(diplomatic etc)* Zwischenfall *m*; *(= disturbance in bar etc)* Vorfall *m*; **without ~** ohne Zwischenfälle; **there were several ~s of violence** es kam mehrmals zu Gewalttätigkeiten; *(during demonstration etc)* es kam mehrmals zu gewalttätigen Ausschreitungen **c** *(in book, play)* Episode *f* **ADJ a ~ to** *(form)* verbunden mit **b** *(Opt) ray* einfallend

incidental [ˌɪnsɪ'dentl] **ADJ a dangers ~ to foreign travel** *(liter)* mit Auslandsreisen verbundene Gefahren **b** *(= unplanned) event* zufällig **c** *(= secondary etc)* nebensächlich; *remark* beiläufig **N** Nebensächlichkeit *f*, Nebensache *f*; **~s** *(= expenses)* Nebenausgaben *pl*

incidental expenses PL Nebenkosten *pl*

incidentally [ˌɪnsɪ'dentəlɪ] ✪ 26.2 ADV **a** *(= by the way)* übrigens **b** *(= casually)* **to mention sth ~** etw beiläufig erwähnen **c** *(= secondarily)* **it's only ~ important** das ist nur von nebensächlicher Bedeutung

incidental music N Begleitmusik *f*

incident room N *(Police)* Einsatzzentrale *f*

incinerate [ɪn'sɪnəreɪt] VT verbrennen; *(= cremate)* einäschern

incineration [ɪnsɪnə'reɪʃən] N Verbrennung *f*; *(= cremation)* Einäscherung *f*

incinerator [ɪn'sɪnəreɪtə'] N (Müll)verbrennungsanlage *f*; *(= garden incinerator)* Verbrennungsofen *m*; *(in crematorium)* Feuerbestattungsofen *m*, Verbrennungsofen *m*

incipience [ɪn'sɪpɪəns] N Anfang *m*, Beginn *m*

incipient [ɪn'sɪpɪənt] ADJ anfangend, beginnend; *disease, difficulties also* einsetzend; *panic* aufkommend; *democracy* jung

incise [ɪn'saɪz] VT **a** *(= cut)* (ein)schneiden *(into* in *+acc)* **b** *(Art, in wood)* (ein)schnitzen; *(in metal, stone)* eingravieren, einritzen

incision [ɪn'sɪʒən] N Schnitt *m*; *(Med)* Einschnitt *m*

incisive [ɪn'saɪsɪv] ADJ *style, tone, words* prägnant; *criticism* treffend, scharfsinnig; *mind* scharf; *person* scharfsinnig

incisively [ɪn'saɪsɪvlɪ] ADV *speak, formulate, put* prägnant; *argue, criticize, reason* treffend, scharfsinnig

incisiveness [ɪn'saɪsɪvnɪs] N *(of style, tone, words)* Prägnanz *f*; *(of criticism)* Scharfsinnigkeit *f*; *(of mind)* Schärfe *f*; *(of person)* Scharfsinn *m*

incisor [ɪn'saɪzə'] N Schneidezahn *m*

incite [ɪn'saɪt] VT aufhetzen; *masses also* aufwiegeln; *racial hatred, violence, riot* aufhetzen zu; **to ~ the masses/sb to violence** die Massen/jdn zu Gewalttätigkeiten aufhetzen

incitement [ɪn'saɪtmənt] N **a** *no pl* Aufhetzung *f*; *(of masses also)* Aufwieg(e)lung *f (to* zu*)* **b** *(= incentive)* Anreiz *m (to* zu*)*, Ansporn *m (to* zu*)*

incivility [ˌɪnsɪ'vɪlɪtɪ] N Unhöflichkeit *f*

incl *abbr of* **inclusive(ly), including** incl., inkl.

inclemency [ɪn'klemənsɪ] N *(of weather)* Rauheit *f*, Unfreundlichkeit *f*

inclement [ɪn'klemənt] ADJ *weather* rau, unfreundlich

inclinable [ɪn'klaɪnəbl] ADJ **a** *(= with a tendency to)* tendierend, (hin)neigend; **to be ~ to** tendieren zu, neigen zu **b** *(= in favour of)* wohlwollend gegenüberstehend *(geh) dat*, günstig gesinnt *(geh) dat*

inclination [ˌɪnklɪ'neɪʃən] N **a** *(= tendency, wish etc)* Neigung *f*; **he follows his (own) ~s** er tut das, wozu er Lust hat; **what are his natural ~s?** welches sind seine Neigungen?; **my (natural) ~ is to carry on** ich neige dazu, weiterzumachen; **~ to stoutness** Anlage *f or* Neigung *f* zu Korpulenz; **to have an ~ toward(s) rudeness** zur Unhöflichkeit neigen; **I have no ~ to see him again** ich habe keinerlei Bedürfnis, ihn wiederzusehen; **my immediate ~ was to refuse** mein erster Gedanke war abzulehnen; **he showed no ~ to leave** er schien nicht gehen zu wollen
b *(of head, body)* Neigung *f*
c *(of hill, slope etc)* Neigung *f*, Gefälle *nt*

incline [ɪn'klaɪn] **VT a** *head, body, roof* neigen **b** *(= dispose)* veranlassen, bewegen; **this ~s me to think that he must be lying** das lässt mich vermuten, dass er lügt; **the news ~s me to stay** aufgrund *or* auf Grund der Nachricht würde ich gern bleiben → **inclined VI a** *(= slope)* sich neigen; *(ground)* abfallen **b** *(= be disposed, tend towards)* neigen; **to ~ to a point of view** zu einer Ansicht neigen *or* tendieren; **he's beginning to ~ toward(s) our point of view** er beginnt unserer Ansicht zuzuneigen **N** ['ɪnklaɪn] Neigung *f*; *(of hill)* Abhang *m*; *(= gradient: Rail etc)* Gefälle *nt*

incline bench ['ɪnklaɪn-] N *(in fitness centre)* Schrägbank *f*

inclined [ɪn'klaɪnd] ADJ **a to be ~ to do sth** *(= feel that one wishes to)* Lust haben, etw zu tun, etw tun wollen; *(= have tendency to)* dazu neigen, etw zu tun; **they are ~ to be late** sie kommen gern zu spät, sie neigen zum Zuspätkommen; **I am ~ to think that ...** ich neige zu der Ansicht, dass ...; **I'm ~ to disagree** ich möchte da doch widersprechen; **I am not ~ to approve of this** ich bin nicht geneigt, das gutzuheißen; **I'm ~ to believe you** ich möchte Ihnen gern glauben; **it's ~ to break** das bricht leicht; **if you feel ~** wenn Sie Lust haben *or* dazu aufgelegt sind; **to be well** *or* **favourably** *(Brit) or* **favorably** *(US)* **~ toward(s) sb** jdm geneigt *or* gewogen sein; **he is ~ towards our viewpoint** er ist unserer Ansicht zugeneigt; **if you're that way ~** wenn Ihnen so etwas liegt; **mathematically/artistically ~** mathematisch/künstlerisch veranlagt; **to be romantically ~** eine romantische Ader haben
b *(= at an angle)* geneigt; *plane* geneigt, schräg; **~ towards the sun** *(hemisphere)* der Sonne zugewandt

inclose [ɪn'kləʊz] VT = **enclose**

include [ɪn'kluːd] VT einschließen, enthalten; *(on list, in group etc)* aufnehmen, einbeziehen; **your name is not ~d on the list** Ihr Name ist nicht auf der Liste; **service not ~d** Bedienung nicht inbegriffen; **all ~d** alles inklusive *or* inbegriffen; **everyone, children ~d** alle einschließlich der Kinder; **the invitation ~s everybody** die Einladung betrifft alle; **the hostages ~d three Britons** unter den Geiseln befanden sich drei Briten; **does that ~ me?** gilt das auch für mich?; **shut up! you ~d** *or* **that ~s you** Ruhe! Sie sind auch gemeint; **to ~ sb in one's prayers** jdn in sein Gebet einschließen; **I worked hard to be ~d in the project** ich habe mich sehr angestrengt, um an dem Projekt teilnehmen zu können; **in which category would you ~ this?** in welche Kategorie würden Sie das aufnehmen?; **I think we should ~ a chapter on ...** ich finde, wir sollten auch ein Kapitel über ... dazunehmen; **the book ~s two chapters on grammar** das Buch enthält auch zwei Grammatikkapitel

► **include out** VT *sep (hum inf)* auslassen; **include me out** ohne mich

including [ɪn'kluːdɪŋ] PREP einschließlich, inklusive, inbegriffen, mit; **that makes seven ~ you** mit Ihnen sind das sieben; **that comes to 100 euros ~ postage and packing** das kommt auf 100 EUR inklusive *or* einschließlich Porto und Verpackung; **there were six rooms ~ kitchen** mit Küche waren es sechs Zimmer, es waren sechs Zimmer einschließlich Küche; **many people, ~ my father, had been invited** viele Leute, darunter mein Vater, waren eingeladen; **~ the service charge, ~ service** inklusive Bedienung, Bedienung (mit) inbegriffen; **up to and ~ chapter V** bis inklusive *or* einschließlich Kapitel V; **up to and ~ March 4th** bis einschließlich 4. März

inclusion [ɪn'kluːʒən] N Aufnahme *f*; **the team was revamped with the ~ of John** das Team wurde neu zusammengestellt und John gehörte dazu

inclusive [ɪn'kluːsɪv] ADJ inklusive, einschließlich; **~ price** Inklusiv- *or* Pauschalpreis *m*; **~ sum** Pauschale *f*, Pauschalsumme *f*; **~ terms** Pauschalpreis *m*; **it's a fully ~ price** im Preis ist alles inbegriffen; **to be ~ of all charges** alle Gebühren einschließen, einschließlich aller Gebühren *(gen)* sein; **the course fee is fully ~ of all costs** in den Kursgebühren sind alle Kosten enthalten; **to the fifth page ~** bis einschließlich der fünften Seite, bis Seite fünf einschließlich; **from 1st to 6th May ~** vom 1. bis einschließlich *or* inklusive 6. Mai, vom 1. bis 6. Mai inklusive

inclusively [ɪn'kluːsɪvlɪ] ADV inklusive, einschließlich; **from 7 to 10 ~** von 7 bis einschließlich *or* inklusive 10

incognito [ˌɪnkɒgˈniːtəʊ] ADV inkognito N Inkognito *nt* ADJ *traveller* unter fremdem Namen; **to remain ~** inkognito bleiben

incoherence [ˌɪnkəʊˈhɪərəns] N *(of style, prose)* Zusammenhanglosigkeit *f*, mangelnder Zusammenhang; **with each drink his ~ grew** seine Worte wurden mit jedem Glas wirrer *or* zusammenhangloser

incoherent [ˌɪnkəʊˈhɪərənt] ADJ *style, argument, speech* zusammenhanglos, unzusammenhängend, inkohärent *(geh)*; *person* sich unklar *or* undeutlich ausdrückend; *drunk etc* schwer verständlich; **he was ~ with rage** seine wütenden Worte waren kaum zu verstehen; **the patient is still ~** der Kranke ist noch nicht ansprechbar; **an ~ set of objectives** in sich widersprüchliche Ziele *pl*

incoherently [ˌɪnkəʊˈhɪərəntlɪ] ADV *talk, write* zusammenhanglos, unzusammenhängend, wirr

incombustible [ˌɪnkəmˈbʌstəbl] ADJ unbrennbar

income [ˈɪnkʌm] N Einkommen *nt*; *(= receipts)* Einkünfte *pl*; **an annual ~ of £45,000** ein Jahreseinkommen von £ 45.000; **families on low ~s, low-~ families** einkommensschwache Familien *pl*; **to live within one's ~** seinen Verhältnissen entsprechend leben

income: **income account** N Ertragskonto *nt*; **income bond** N Schuldverschreibung *f (mit vom Gewinn der Gesellschaft abgängiger Verzinsung)*; **income bracket** N Einkommensklasse *f*; **income group** N Einkommensgruppe *f*

incomer [ˈɪnˌkʌməʳ] N *(= new arrival)* Neuankömmling *m*; *(= successor)* Nachfolger(in) *m(f)*

income: **incomes policy** N Lohnpolitik *f*; **income statement** N *(US)* Gewinn- und Verlustrechnung *f*; **income support** N *(Brit)* ≈ Sozialhilfe *f*; **income tax** N Lohnsteuer *f*; *(on private income)* Einkommensteuer *f*; **income tax return** N Steuererklärung *f*

incoming [ˈɪnˌkʌmɪŋ] ADJ **a** ankommend; *train also* einfahrend; *ship also* einlaufend; *missile* anfliegend; *mail, orders* eingehend; *(Phys) light, radiation* einfallend; **~ tide** Flut *f*; **to receive ~ (phone) calls** (Telefon)anrufe entgegennehmen **b** *(= succeeding) president etc* nachfolgend, neu

incomings [ˈɪnˌkʌmɪŋz] PL Einkünfte *pl*, Einnahmen *pl*

incommensurable [ˌɪnkəˈmenʃərəbl] ADJ nicht zu vergleichend *attr*, nicht vergleichbar; *(Math)* inkommensurabel

incommensurate [ˌɪnkəˈmenʃərɪt] ADJ **a to be ~ with sth** in keinem Verhältnis zu etw stehen **b** *(= inadequate)* unzureichend (*to* für)

incommode [ˌɪnkəˈməʊd] VT *(form)* lästig sein *(+dat)*; **I don't wish to ~ you but could you …** ich möchte Sie nicht behelligen, aber könnten Sie vielleicht …

incommodious [ˌɪnkəˈməʊdɪəs] ADJ *(form)* lästig, unbequem; *(= cramped)* beengt

incommunicado [ˌɪnkəmjʊnɪˈkɑːdəʊ] ADJ *pred* ohne jede Verbindung zur Außenwelt, abgesondert; **he was held ~** er hatte keinerlei Verbindung zur Außenwelt; **to be ~** *(fig)* für niemanden zu sprechen sein

in-company ADJ firmenintern

incomparable [ɪnˈkɒmpərəbl] ADJ nicht vergleichbar (*with* mit); *beauty, skill* unvergleichlich

incomparably [ɪnˈkɒmpərəblɪ] ADV unvergleichlich

incompatibility [ˈɪnkəmˌpætəˈbɪlɪtɪ] N *(of characters, temperaments, ideas, propositions)* Unvereinbarkeit *f*; *(of drugs, blood groups, colours)* Unverträglichkeit *f*; *(of technical systems)* Inkompatibilität *f*; **divorce on grounds of ~** Scheidung aufgrund *or* auf Grund der Unvereinbarkeit der Charaktere der Ehepartner

incompatible [ˌɪnkəmˈpætəbl] ADJ *characters, ideas, propositions, temperaments* unvereinbar; *technical systems* nicht kompatibel; *drugs, blood groups, colours* nicht miteinander verträglich; **the drugs are ~** die Arzneimittel vertragen sich nicht miteinander; **we are ~, she said** wir passen überhaupt nicht zusammen *or* zueinander, sagte sie; **to be ~ with sb/sth** sich nicht mit jdm/etw vertragen; *(= not suit)* nicht zu jdm/etw passen; **the possession of great wealth is surely ~ with genuine Marxist beliefs** der Besitz großer Reichtümer lässt sich wohl kaum mit echtem Marxismus vereinbaren

incompetence [ɪnˈkɒmpɪtəns], **incompetency** [ɪnˈkɒmpɪtənsɪ] N **a** Unfähigkeit *f*; *(for job)* Untauglichkeit *f* **b** *(Jur)* Unzuständigkeit *f*, Inkompetenz *f*

incompetent [ɪnˈkɒmpɪtənt] ADJ **a** *person, institution* unfähig; *(for sth)* untauglich; *management* stümperhaft, inkompetent; *piece of work* stümperhaft, unzulänglich; **to be ~ in business** nicht geschäftstüchtig sein; **to be ~ to teach music** unfähig sein, Musik zu unterrichten, zum Musiklehrer untauglich sein; **I was ~ at playing the piano** *or* **an ~ pianist** ich konnte nur sehr schlecht Klavier spielen **b** *(Jur) court, authority etc* unzuständig, nicht zuständig; **(legally/mentally) ~** *(= not capable of contracting)* geschäftsunfähig **c** *(Med)* **~ cervix** isthmozervikale Insuffizienz, Zervixinsuffizienz *f* N Nichtskönner(in) *m(f)*

incompetently [ɪnˈkɒmpɪtəntlɪ] ADV schlecht, stümperhaft

incomplete [ˌɪnkəmˈpliːt] ADJ *collection, series* unvollkommen, unvollständig; *knowledge, information* lückenhaft; *(= not finished also) painting, novel* unfertig; *(referring to numbers)* unvollständig, nicht vollzählig

incompletely [ˌɪnkəmˈpliːtlɪ] ADV unvollständig

incompleteness [ˌɪnkəmˈpliːtnɪs] N *(of collection, series)* Unvollkommenheit *f*, Unvollständigkeit *f*; *(of knowledge, information)* Lückenhaftigkeit *f*; *(= unfinished state: of painting, novel)* Unfertigkeit *f*

incomprehensible [ɪnˌkɒmprɪˈhensəbl] ADJ unverständlich (*to sb* jdm); *act also* unbegreiflich, unfassbar (*to sb* jdm); **people like that are just ~** solche Leute kann ich einfach nicht begreifen

incomprehensibly [ɪnˌkɒmprɪˈhensəblɪ] ADV unverständlich; **~, their offer was turned down** unverständlicherweise wurde ihr Angebot abgelehnt

inconceivable [ˌɪnkənˈsiːvəbl] ADJ unvorstellbar, undenkbar; *(= hard to believe also)* unfassbar, unbegreiflich; **it was ~ to her that …** sie konnte sich *(dat)* nicht vorstellen, dass …

inconceivably [ˌɪnkənˈsiːvəblɪ] ADV unvorstellbar; **almost ~, she …** es war fast nicht zu fassen, aber sie …

inconclusive [ˌɪnkənˈkluːsɪv] ADJ *(= not decisive) result* unbestimmt, zu keiner Entscheidung führend; *election* ohne eindeutiges Ergebnis; *action, discussion, investigation* ohne (schlüssiges) Ergebnis, ergebnislos; *war* erfolglos; *(= not convincing) evidence, argument* nicht überzeugend, nicht schlüssig, nicht zwingend

inconclusively [ˌɪnkənˈkluːsɪvlɪ] ADV *(= without result)* ergebnislos; *argue* nicht überzeugend, nicht schlüssig, nicht zwingend; **his speech ended rather ~** seine Rede kam zu keinem überzeugenden Schluss

incongruent [ɪnˈkɒŋgrʊənt] ADJ *(= incompatible)* nicht übereinstimmend (*to, with* mit); *(= incongruous)* unpassend, unangebracht; *(Math, Ling)* inkongruent; *(fig) story* ungereimt, widersinnig

incongruity [ˌɪnkɒŋˈgruːɪtɪ] N **a** *no pl (of remark, sb's presence)* Unpassende(s), Unangebrachtsein *nt*; *(of juxtaposition, mixture)* Missklang *m*; *(of situation)* Absurdität *f*; *(of behaviour)* Unangebrachtheit *f*; **such was the ~ of his remark** seine Bemerkung war so unangebracht *or* unpassend; **the ~ between what is said and what is left unsaid** das Missverhältnis zwischen dem, was gesagt wird, und dem, was ungesagt bleibt; **the film relies on the ~ of these images** der Film lebt von der inneren Widersprüchlichkeit dieser Bilder; **he commented on the ~ of it all** er bemerkte, wie absurd das alles war **b** *(= incongruous thing)* Unstimmigkeit *f*

incongruous [ɪnˈkɒŋgrʊəs] ADJ *couple, juxtaposition, mixture* wenig zusammenpassend *attr*; *thing to do, remark* unpassend; *behaviour* unangebracht; **he uses these ~ images** er benutzt diese unstimmigen Bilder; **it seems ~ that …** es scheint abwegig *or* widersinnig, dass …; **how ~ it seemed that he should have been chosen** es schien eigenartig, dass ausgerechnet er ausgewählt wurde; **he was an ~ figure among the tourists** unter den Touristen wirkte er fehl am Platz

incongruously [ɪnˈkɒŋgrʊəslɪ] ADV unpassend

inconsequence [ɪnˈkɒnsɪkwəns] N *(in logic)* Inkonsequenz *f*, Unlogik *f*; *(irrelevance)* Belanglosigkeit *f*

inconsequent [ɪnˈkɒnsɪkwənt] ADJ unlogisch, nicht folgerichtig; *remark* nicht zur Sache gehörend *attr*, beziehungslos

inconsequential [ɪnˌkɒnsɪˈkwenʃəl] ADJ beziehungslos, irrelevant; *(= not logical)* unlogisch, nicht folgerichtig; *(= unimportant)* unbedeutend, unwichtig

inconsequentially [ɪnˌkɒnsɪˈkwenʃəlɪ] ADV unlogisch

inconsiderable [ˌɪnkənˈsɪdərəbl] ADJ unbedeutend, unerheblich; **a not ~ amount** ein nicht unbedeutender Betrag

inconsiderate [ˌɪnkənˈsɪdərɪt] ADJ rücksichtslos; *(in less critical sense: = not thinking)* unaufmerksam

inconsiderately [ˌɪnkənˈsɪdərɪtlɪ] ADV rücksichtslos

inconsiderateness [ˌɪnkənˈsɪdərɪtnɪs]

inconsideration [ˈɪnkənˌsɪdəˈreɪʃən] N Rücksichtslosigkeit *f*

inconsistency [ˌɪnkənˈsɪstənsɪ] N **a** *(= contradictoriness)* Widersprüchlichkeit *f*, Ungereimtheit *f*; **the inconsistencies in his evidence** die Widersprüche in seiner Aussage **b** *(= unevenness: of work, in quality etc)* Unbeständigkeit *f*

inconsistent [ˌɪnkənˈsɪstənt] ADJ **a** *(= contradictory) action, speech* widersprüchlich, ungereimt; **to be ~ with sth** zu etw im Widerspruch stehen, mit etw nicht übereinstimmen **b** *(= uneven, irregular) work* unbeständig, ungleich; *person* inkonsequent; **but you're ~, sometimes you say …** aber da sind Sie nicht konsequent, manchmal sagen Sie …; **recently we** *or* **our performances have been ~** in letzter Zeit schwanken unsere Leistungen

inconsistently [ˌɪnkənˈsɪstəntlɪ] ADV **a** *argue, behave* widersprüchlich; **he is behaving ~ with his beliefs** sein Verhalten steht im Widerspruch zu seinen Auffassungen **b** *work, perform* unbeständig, ungleichmäßig

inconsolable [ˌɪnkənˈsəʊləbl] ADJ untröstlich

inconsolably [ˌɪnkənˈsəʊləblɪ] ADV untröstlich; **she wept ~** sie weinte und war nicht zu trösten

inconspicuous [ˌɪnkənˈspɪkjʊəs] ADJ unauffällig; **to make oneself ~** so wenig Aufsehen wie möglich erregen, sich kleinmachen *(inf)*

inconspicuously [ˌɪnkənˈspɪkjʊəslɪ] ADV unauffällig

inconstancy [ɪnˈkɒnstənsɪ] N *(of friend)* Unbeständigkeit *f*, Wankelmut *m*; *(of lover)* Unstetigkeit *f*, Wankelmut *m*; *(of weather, quality)* Veränderlichkeit *f*

inconstant [ɪnˈkɒnstənt] ADJ *person (in friendship)* unbeständig, wankelmütig; *(in love)* unstet, wankelmütig; *(= variable) weather, quality* veränderlich, unbeständig

incontestable [ˌɪnkənˈtestəbl] ADJ unbestreitbar, unanfechtbar; **it is ~ that …** es ist unbestritten, dass …

incontestably [ˌɪnkənˈtestəblɪ] ADV unbestreitbar

incontinence [ɪnˈkɒntɪnəns] N *(Med)* Inkontinenz *f*; *(of desires)* Zügellosigkeit *f*, Hemmungslosigkeit *f*

incontinence: **incontinence pad** N Einlage *f* für Inkontinente; **incontinence sheet** N Unterlage *f* für Inkontinente

incontinent [ɪnˈkɒntɪnənt] ADJ *(Med)* inkontinent; *desires* zügellos, hemmungslos

incontrovertible [ɪnˌkɒntrəˈvɜːtəbl] ADJ unbestreitbar, unwiderlegbar; *evidence* unwiderlegbar; *argument* unanfechtbar

incontrovertibly [ɪnˌkɒntrəˈvɜːtəblɪ] ADV unbestreitbar

inconvenience [ˌɪnkənˈviːnɪəns] N **a** *(= inconvenient thing)* Unannehmlichkeit *f*; **it's one of the ~s of getting old** es ist einer der Nachteile, wenn man älter wird; **it was something of an ~ not having a car** es war eine ziemlich lästige *or* leidige Angelegenheit, kein Auto zu haben
b *no pl (= trouble, awkwardness)* Unannehmlichkeit(en) *f(pl)* *(to sb* für jdn); **the ~ of a delayed flight** die Unannehmlichkeiten, die durch einen verspäteten Flug verursacht werden; **she complained about the ~ of having no shops nearby** sie beklagte sich darüber, wie unbequem *or* beschwerlich es sei, keine Geschäfte in der Nähe zu haben; **I don't want to cause you any ~** ich möchte Ihnen keine Umstände bereiten *or* machen; **to put sb to great ~** jdm große Umstände bereiten; **he went to a great deal of ~ to help** er machte sich viele Unannehmlichkeiten, um zu helfen; **at considerable personal ~** trotz beträchtlicher persönlicher Unannehmlichkeiten; **because of the ~ of the time/date** weil die Uhrzeit/der Termin ungelegen war
VT Unannehmlichkeiten *or* Umstände bereiten *(+dat)*; *(with reference to time)* ungelegen kommen *(+dat)*; **don't ~ yourself** machen Sie keine Umstände

inconvenient [ˌɪnkənˈviːnɪənt] ✪ 14 ADJ **a** *time* ungelegen, ungünstig; *house, design* unbequem, unpraktisch; *location* ungünstig; *shops* ungünstig *or* ungeschickt gelegen; *journey* beschwerlich, lästig; **3 o'clock is very ~ for me** 3 Uhr kommt mir sehr ungelegen *or* ist sehr ungünstig für mich; **if it's ~, I can come later** wenn es Ihnen ungelegen ist, kann ich später kommen; **you couldn't have chosen a more ~ time** einen ungünstigeren Zeitpunkt hätten Sie kaum wählen können; **it's very ~ of you to come so early** es kommt mir wirklich sehr ungelegen, dass Sie so früh kommen; **it's very ~ of you to live so far out** es ist wenig rücksichtsvoll von Ihnen, so weit außerhalb zu wohnen; **it is ~ to have to wait** es ist lästig, warten zu müssen
b *(= embarrassing) fact, information* unbequem

inconveniently [ˌɪnkənˈviːnɪəntlɪ] ADV *situated* ungünstig; *laid out, designed* unpraktisch; **it was ~ timed** es fand zu einer ungünstigen Zeit statt; **he ~ decided to leave** er beschloss zu gehen, was sehr ungünstig war *or* was sehr ungelegen kam

inconvertibility [ˈɪnkənˌvɜːtɪˈbɪlɪtɪ] N *(Fin)* Uneinlösbarkeit *f*, Inkonvertibilität *f*

inconvertible [ˌɪnkənˈvɜːtəbl] ADJ *(Fin)* uneinlösbar, inkonvertibel

incorporate [ɪnˈkɔːpəreɪt] VT **a** *(= integrate)* aufnehmen, einbauen, integrieren *(into* in *+acc)*; **her proposals were ~d into the project** ihre Vorschläge gingen in das Projekt ein; **Hanover was ~d into Prussia in 1886** Hannover wurde 1886 Preußen angegliedert *or* mit Preußen vereinigt
b *(= contain)* (in sich *dat*) vereinigen, enthalten; **the tax is ~d in the price** (die) Steuer ist im Preis enthalten; **a new James Bond film incorporating all the standard ingredients** ein neuer James-Bond-Film, der alle Standardelemente enthält; **all the tribes are now ~d in one state** alle Stämme sind jetzt zu einem Staat zusammengeschlossen
c *(Jur, Comm)* gesellschaftlich organisieren; *(US)* (amtlich) als Aktiengesellschaft eintragen, registrieren; **to ~ a company** eine Gesellschaft gründen; **~d company** *(US)* (als Kapitalgesellschaft) eingetragenes Unternehmen

incorporation [ɪnˌkɔːpəˈreɪʃən] N **a** *(= integration)* Aufnahme *f*, Integration *f* *(into, in* in *+acc)* **b** *(= containing)* Verbindung *f*, Vereinigung *f* **c** *(Jur, Comm: of company)* Gründung *f*

incorporeal [ˌɪnkɔːˈpɔːrɪəl] ADJ nicht körperlich, körperlos

incorrect [ˌɪnkəˈrekt] ADJ **a** *(= wrong)* falsch; *calculation* falsch, fehlerhaft; *statement, assessment* falsch, unzutreffend, unrichtig; *opinion* falsch, irrig; *text* ungenau, fehlerhaft; **~ diet** Fehlernährung *f*, falsche Ernährung; **that is ~** das stimmt nicht, das ist nicht richtig *or* wahr; **you are ~** Sie irren sich, Sie haben unrecht; **you are ~ in your assumption** Sie irren sich in Ihrer Annahme; **you are ~ in thinking that …** Sie haben unrecht, wenn Sie denken, dass …
b *(= improper) behaviour* inkorrekt, nicht einwandfrei; *dress* inkorrekt, falsch; **it is ~ to …** es ist nicht korrekt, zu …

incorrectly [ˌɪnkəˈrektlɪ] ADV *(= wrongly)* falsch; *state also* unzutreffend; *(= improperly)* inkorrekt, nicht korrekt; **I had ~ assumed that …** ich hatte fälschlich(erweise) angenommen, dass …

incorrigible [ɪnˈkɒrɪdʒəbl] ADJ unverbesserlich

incorrigibly [ɪnˈkɒrɪdʒəblɪ] ADV unverbesserlich; **to be ~ romantic/optimistic** ein unverbesserlicher Romantiker/Optimist sein

incorruptible [ˌɪnkəˈrʌptəbl] ADJ **a** *person* charakterstark; *(= not bribable)* unbestechlich; **she's ~** man kann sie nicht verderben **b** *material, substance* unzerstörbar

increase [ɪnˈkriːs] VI zunehmen; *(taxes)* erhöht werden; *(pain also)* stärker werden; *(amount, number, noise, population also)* anwachsen; *(possessions, trade, riches also)* sich vermehren, (an)wachsen; *(pride also, strength)* wachsen; *(price, sales, demand)* steigen; *(supply, joy, rage)* sich vergrößern, größer werden; *(business, institution, town)* sich vergrößern, wachsen; *(rain, wind)* stärker werden; **to ~ in volume/weight** umfangreicher/schwerer werden, an Umfang/Gewicht zunehmen; **to ~ in breadth/size/number** sich verbreitern/vergrößern/vermehren, breiter/größer/mehr werden; **to ~ in height** höher werden; **industrial output ~d by 2% last year** die Industrieproduktion wuchs im letzten Jahr um 2%
VT vergrößern; *rage, sorrow, joy, possessions, riches also* vermehren; *darkness, noise, love, resentment also, effort* verstärken; *trade, sales* erweitern; *numbers, taxes, price, speed, demand, tension* erhöhen; *chances* verbessern; **he ~d his efforts** er strengte sich mehr an, er machte größere Anstrengungen; **then to ~ our difficulties** was die Dinge noch schwieriger machte, was unsere Schwierigkeiten noch vergrößerte; **~d demand** erhöhte *or* verstärkte Nachfrage; **~d efficiency** Leistungssteigerung *f*; **his hours were ~d to 25 per week** seine Stundenzahl wurde auf 25 Wochenstunden erhöht; **we ~d output to …** wir erhöhten den Ausstoß auf …; **they ~d her salary by £2,000 to £20,000 a year** sie erhöhten ihr Jahresgehalt um £ 2.000 auf £ 20.000
N [ˈɪnkriːs] Zunahme *f*, Erhöhung *f*, Steigerung *f*; *(in size)* Vergrößerung *f*, Erweiterung *f*; *(in number)* Vermehrung *f*, Zuwachs *m*, Zunahme *f*; *(in speed, spending)* Erhöhung *f* *(in +gen)*, Steigerung *f* *(in +gen)*; *(of business)* Erweiterung *f*, Vergrößerung *f*; *(in sales)* Zuwachs *m*; *(in expenses)* Vermehrung *f* *(in +gen)*, Steigerung *f* *(in +gen)*; *(of effort etc)* Vermehrung *f*, Steigerung *f*, Verstärkung *f*; *(of demand)* Verstärkung *f*, Steigen *nt*; *(of work)* Mehr *nt* (of an *+dat*), Zunahme *f*; *(of violence)* Zunahme *f*, Anwachsen *nt*; *(of salary)* Gehaltserhöhung *f* *or* -aufbesserung *f*; *(of noise)* Zunahme *f*, Verstärkung *f*; **an ~ in the population of 10% per year** eine jährliche Bevölkerungszunahme *or* ein jährlicher Bevölkerungszuwachs von 10%; **to get an ~ of £5 per week** £ 5 pro Woche mehr bekommen, eine Lohnerhöhung von £ 5 pro Woche bekommen; **to be on the ~** ständig zunehmen; **~ in value** Wertzuwachs *m*, Wertsteigerung *f*; **rent ~** Mieterhöhung *f*

increasing [ɪnˈkriːsɪŋ] ADJ zunehmend, steigend, (an)wachsend; **an ~ number of people are changing to …** mehr und mehr Leute steigen auf *(+acc)* … um; **there is ~ pressure on her to resign** sie gerät zunehmend unter Druck zurückzutreten; **there are ~ signs that …** es gibt immer mehr Anzeichen dafür, dass …

increasingly [ɪnˈkriːsɪŋlɪ] ADV zunehmend, immer mehr; **he became ~ angry** er wurde immer *or* zunehmend ärgerlicher; **~, people are finding that …** man findet in zunehmendem Maße, dass …; **this is ~ the case** dies ist immer häufiger der Fall

incredible [ɪnˈkredəbl] ADJ unglaublich; *(inf: = amazing also)* unwahrscheinlich *(inf)*; *scenery* sagenhaft; **it seems ~ to me that …** ich kann es nicht fassen, dass …; **~ though it may seem, …** so unglaublich es auch scheinen mag, …; **this music is ~** *(inf)* diese Musik ist sagenhaft *(inf)*; **you're ~** *(inf)* du bist wirklich unschlagbar

incredibly [ɪnˈkredəblɪ] ADV unglaublich, unwahrscheinlich; **~, he wasn't there** unglaublicherweise war er nicht da

incredulity [ˌɪnkrɪˈdjuːlɪtɪ] N Ungläubigkeit *f*, Skepsis *f*

incredulous [ɪnˈkredjʊləs] ADJ ungläubig, skeptisch; *look also* zweifelnd; **his voice was ~** seine Stimme klang ungläubig

incredulously [ɪnˈkredjʊləslɪ] ADV ungläubig, skeptisch; *look also* zweifelnd

increment [ˈɪnkrɪmənt] N Zuwachs *m*, Steigerung *f*; *(in salary)* Gehaltserhöhung *f* *or* -zulage *f*; *(on scale)* Stufe *f*

incriminate [ɪnˈkrɪmɪneɪt] VT belasten; **he is afraid of incriminating himself** er hat Angst, dass er sich belasten könnte

incriminating [ɪnˈkrɪmɪneɪtɪŋ], **incriminatory** [ɪnˈkrɪmɪneɪtərɪ] ADJ belastend

incrimination [ɪnˌkrɪmɪˈneɪʃən] N Belastung *f*

incriminator [ɪnˈkrɪmɪneɪtəʳ] N Beschuldiger(in) *m(f)*

in-crowd [ˈɪnkraʊd] N *(inf)* Schickeria *f* *(inf)*; **to be in with the ~** zur Schickeria gehören *(inf)*

incrust [ɪnˈkrʌst] VT = **encrust**

incubate [ˈɪnkjʊbeɪt] VT *egg* ausbrüten; *bacteria* züchten; *plan, idea* ausbrüten *(inf)*, ausreifen lassen VI *(lit)* ausgebrütet *or* bebrütet werden; *(fig)* (aus)reifen, sich formen; **the virus can ~ for up to 10 days** das Virus hat eine Inkubationszeit von bis zu 10 Tagen

incubation [ˌɪnkjʊˈbeɪʃən] N *(of egg, fig: of plan)* Ausbrüten *nt*; *(of bacteria)* Züchten *nt*

incubation period N *(Med)* Inkubationszeit *f*

incubator [ˈɪnkjʊbeɪtəʳ] N *(for babies)* Brutkasten *m*, Inkubator *m*; *(for chicks)* Brutapparat *m*; *(for bacteria)* Brutschrank *m*

incubus [ˈɪŋkjʊbəs] N **a** *(= demon)* Alp *m* **b** *(= burden)* Albtraum *m*, Alptraum *m*, drückende Last

inculcate [ˈɪnkʌlkeɪt] VT einimpfen, einprägen *(in sb* jdm)

inculcation [ˌɪnkʌlˈkeɪʃən] N Einimpfen *nt*, Einimpfung *f*

incumbency [ɪnˈkʌmbənsɪ] N **a** *(Eccl)* Pfründe *f* **b** *(form: = tenure of office)* Amtszeit *f* **c** *(form, = obligation)* Obliegenheit *f* *(form)*, Verpflichtung *f*

incumbent [ɪnˈkʌmbənt] *(form)* ADJ **a** **to be ~ upon sb** jdm obliegen *(form)*, jds Pflicht sein *(to do sth* etw zu tun) **b** **the ~ mayor** der amtierende Bürgermeister, die amtierende Bürgermeisterin N Amtsinhaber(in) *m(f)*; *(Eccl)* Inhaber(in) *m(f)* einer Pfarrstelle

incunabula [ˌɪnkjʊˈnæbjʊlə] PL Inkunabeln *pl*, Wiegendrucke *pl*

incur [ɪnˈkɜːʳ] VT **a** *anger, injury, displeasure* sich *(dat)* zuziehen, auf sich *(acc)* ziehen; *penalty* belegt werden mit; *risk* eingehen, laufen; **to ~ the wrath of sb** jds Zorn auf sich *(acc)* ziehen

b *(Fin) loss* erleiden; *debts, expenses* machen; *costs* haben; **other expenses ~red** weitere Auslagen *or* Ausgaben *pl*

incurable ADJ, **incurably** ADV [ɪn'kjʊərəbl, -ɪ] unheilbar; *(fig)* unverbesserlich **N** *(Med)* unheilbar Kranke(r) *mf*

incurious [ɪn'kjʊərɪəs] ADJ *(= not curious)* nicht wissbegierig, nicht neugierig; *(= uninterested)* gleichgültig, uninteressiert

incuriously [ɪn'kjʊərɪəslɪ] ADV *(= uninterestedly)* gleichgültig

incursion [ɪn'kɜːʃən] N Einfall *m*, Eindringen *nt* *(into* in *+acc)*; *(fig)* Ausflug *m* *(into* in *+acc)*

indebted [ɪn'detɪd] ADJ **a** *(fig)* verpflichtet; **to be ~ to sb for sth** jdm für etw (zu Dank) verpflichtet sein, für etw in jds Schuld *(dat)* stehen; **he's obviously greatly ~ to Matisse/Steinbeck** er hat offensichtlich Matisse/Steinbeck viel zu verdanken; **thank you very much, I am most ~ to you** vielen Dank, ich stehe zutiefst in Ihrer Schuld *(geh)* **b** *(Fin)* verschuldet *(to sb* bei jdm); **I was ~ to them for £3,000** ich schuldete ihnen £ 3000, ich war bei ihnen mit £ 3000 verschuldet

indebtedness [ɪn'detɪdnɪs] N *(fig)* Verpflichtung *f* *(to* gegenüber); *(Fin)* Verschuldung *f*; **we can see his obvious ~ to Matisse** wir können sehen, dass er Matisse viel zu verdanken hat

indecency [ɪn'diːsnsɪ] N Unanständigkeit *f*, Anstößigkeit *f*; **act of ~** *(Jur)* unsittliches Verhalten

indecent [ɪn'diːsnt] ADJ unanständig, anstößig; *(Jur) act* unsittlich, unzüchtig; *joke* schmutzig, unanständig, zotig; *(= excessive) amount* unerhört; **with ~ haste** mit ungebührlicher Eile *or* Hast

indecent assault N Notzucht *f*

indecent exposure N Erregung *f* öffentlichen Ärgernisses

indecently [ɪn'diːsntlɪ] ADV unanständig; **to be ~ assaulted** sexuell missbraucht werden

indecipherable [ˌɪndɪ'saɪfərəbl] ADJ nicht zu entziffern *pred*, nicht zu entziffernd *attr*; *handwriting* unleserlich

indecision [ˌɪndɪ'sɪʒən] N Unentschlossenheit *f*, Unschlüssigkeit *f*

indecisive [ˌɪndɪ'saɪsɪv] ADJ **a** *person, manner* unschlüssig, unentschlossen *(in or about or over sth* in Bezug auf etw *acc)* **b** *(= inconclusive) discussion, vote* ergebnislos; *argument, battle* nicht(s) entscheidend *attr*; *result* nicht eindeutig

indecisively [ˌɪndɪ'saɪsɪvlɪ] ADV unentschlossen; *(= inconclusively)* unentschieden, ergebnislos

indeclinable [ˌɪndɪ'klaɪnəbl] ADJ *(Gram)* nicht deklinierbar, unbeugbar, beugungsunfähig

indecorous [ɪn'dekərəs] ADJ unschicklich, ungehörig

indecorously [ɪn'dekərəslɪ] ADV unschicklich, ungehörig

indecorum [ˌɪndɪ'kɔːrəm] N Unschicklichkeit *f*, Ungehörigkeit *f*

indeed [ɪn'diːd] ADV **a** *(= really, in reality, in fact)* tatsächlich, wirklich, in der Tat; **I am ~ quite tired** ich bin wirklich *or* tatsächlich *or* in der Tat recht müde; **I feel, ~ I know he is right** ich habe das Gefühl, ja ich weiß (sogar), dass er recht hat; **who else? – ~, who else?** wer sonst? – in der Tat *or* ganz recht, wer sonst?
b *(confirming)* **isn't that strange? – ~ (it is)** ist das nicht seltsam? – allerdings; **are you coming? – ~ I am!** kommst du? – aber sicher *or* natürlich; **may I open the window? – you may ~/~ you may not** darf ich das Fenster öffnen? – ja bitte, aber gern doch!/nein, das dürfen Sie nicht!; **are you pleased? – yes, ~** *or* **~, yes!** bist du zufrieden? – oh ja, das kann man wohl sagen!; **is that Charles? – ~** ist das Charles? – ganz recht
c *(as intensifier)* wirklich; **very ... ~** wirklich sehr ...; **thank you very much ~** vielen herzlichen Dank
d *(showing interest, irony, surprise)* wirklich, tatsächlich; **did you/is it/has she** *etc* **~?** nein wirklich?, tatsächlich?; **his wife, ~!** seine Frau ..., dass ich nicht lache!; **who is she ~?** na, wer wohl *or* wer schon!; **what ~!** was wohl!; **~?** ach so?, ach wirklich?; **where ~?** ja, wo?; **what ~?** ja, was?
e *(= admittedly)* zwar; **there are ~ mistakes in it, but ...** es sind zwar Fehler darin, aber ...
f *(expressing possibility)* **if ~ ...** falls ... wirklich; **if ~ he were wrong** falls er wirklich unrecht haben sollte; **I may ~ come** es kann gut sein, dass ich komme

indefatigable ADJ, **indefatigably** ADV [ˌɪndɪ'fætɪgəbl, -ɪ] unermüdlich, rastlos

indefensible [ˌɪndɪ'fensəbl] ADJ **a** *behaviour, remark etc* unentschuldbar, nicht zu rechtfertigend *attr or* rechtfertigen *pred*; *cause, theory* unhaltbar, unvertretbar; *policy* unhaltbar; **morally ~** moralisch nicht vertretbar **b** *town etc* nicht zu verteidigend *attr or* verteidigen *pred*, unhaltbar

indefinable [ˌɪndɪ'faɪnəbl] ADJ *word, colour, charm* unbestimmbar, undefinierbar; *feeling, impression* unbestimmt; **she has a certain ~ something** sie hat das gewisse Etwas

indefinably [ˌɪndɪ'faɪnəblɪ] ADV undefinierbar

indefinite [ɪn'defɪnɪt] ADJ **a** *number, length* unbestimmt; *(Gram) article, pronoun* unbestimmt; **for the ~ future** auf unbestimmte Zeit; **at some ~ time** irgendwann einmal; **~ leave** unbeschränkter *or* unbegrenzter Urlaub, Urlaub *m* auf unbestimmte Zeit **b** *(= vague)* unklar, undeutlich; **he was very ~ about it** er war sehr unbestimmt *or* vage in dieser Sache

indefinite article N *(Gram)* unbestimmter Artikel

indefinitely [ɪn'defɪnɪtlɪ] ADV **a** *wait etc* unbegrenzt (lange), unendlich lange, endlos; *postpone, continue, close* auf unbestimmte Zeit; **we can't go on like this ~** wir können nicht endlos so weitermachen; **to be extended ~** auf unbestimmte Zeit verlängert werden **b** *(= vaguely)* unklar, undeutlich

indeliberate [ˌɪndɪ'lɪbərɪt] ADJ *(form: = inconsiderate)* unüberlegt; *(= unintentional)* unabsichtlich

indelible [ɪn'deləbl] ADJ *stain* nicht zu entfernen; *ink also* wasserunlöslich; *(fig) impression* unauslöschlich; **~ pencil** Kopierstift *m*, Tintenstift *m*; **to leave an ~ mark on sb/sth** *(fig)* jdn/etw für immer zeichnen

indelibly [ɪn'delɪblɪ] ADV *(fig)* unauslöschlich

indelicacy [ɪn'delɪkəsɪ] N Taktlosigkeit *f*, Ungehörigkeit *f*; *(of person)* Mangel *m* an Feingefühl, Taktlosigkeit *f*; *(= crudity)* Geschmacklosigkeit *f*

indelicate [ɪn'delɪkət] ADJ *person* taktlos; *act, remark also* ungehörig; *subject* peinlich; *(= crude)* geschmacklos

indelicately [ɪn'delɪkətlɪ] ADV *(= tactlessly)* taktlos; *(= rudely)* ungehörig; *(= crudely)* geschmacklos

indemnification [ɪnˌdemnɪfɪ'keɪʃən] N **a** *(= compensation)* Schadensersatz *m*, Entschädigung *f* *(for* für); *(= sum received)* Schadensersatz(summe *f*) *m*, Entschädigung(ssumme) *f*; *(for expenses)* Erstattung *f* *(for +gen)* **b** *(for, against* gegen) *(= safeguard)* Absicherung *f*; *(= insurance)* Versicherung *f*

indemnify [ɪn'demnɪfaɪ] VT **a** *(= compensate)* entschädigen *(for* für); *(for expenses)* erstatten *(sb for sth* jdm etw) **b** *(= safeguard)* absichern *(from, against* gegen); *(= insure)* versichern *(against, from* gegen)

indemnitee [ɪnˌdemnɪ'tiː] N Entschädigungsberechtigte(r) *mf*

indemnity [ɪn'demnɪtɪ] N **a** *(= compensation) (for damage, loss etc)* Schadensersatz *m*, Entschädigung *f*, Abfindung *f*; *(after war)* Wiedergutmachung *f* **b** *(= insurance)* Versicherung(sschutz *m*) *f*; **deed of ~** *(Jur)* ≈ Versicherungspolice *f*

indent [ɪn'dent] VT *border, edge* einkerben; *coast* zerklüften, einbuchten; *(Typ) word, line* einrücken, einziehen; *(= leave dent in) metal etc* einbeulen VI **to ~ on sb for sth** *(Brit Comm)* etw bei jdm ordern **N** ['ɪndent] *(in border etc)* Einkerbung *f*, Kerbe *f*; *(in coast)* Einbuchtung *f*; *(Typ, of line)* Einrückung *f*, Einzug *m*; *(= dent: in metal etc)* Beule *f*, Delle *f*

indentation [ˌɪnden'teɪʃən] N *(= notch, dent) (in border, edge)* Kerbe *f*, Einschnitt *m*; *(in coast)* Einbuchtung *f*; *(Typ)* Einrückung *f*, Einzug *m*; *(in metal etc)* Delle *f*, Vertiefung *f*; *(= print: of foot, shoe)* Abdruck *m*

indenture [ɪn'dentʃə'] N **a** **indentures** PL *(of apprentice)* Ausbildungs- *or* Lehrvertrag *m* **b** *(Jur) Vertrag in zwei oder mehreren Ausführungen mit bestimmter Kanteneinkerbung zur Identifizierung* VT *apprentice* in die Lehre nehmen

independence [ˌɪndɪ'pendəns] N Unabhängigkeit *f* *(of* von); *(of person: in attitude, spirit also)* Selbstständigkeit *f*; **to gain** *or* **achieve/declare ~** die Unabhängigkeit erlangen/erklären

Independence Day N *(US)* der Unabhängigkeitstag

independent [ˌɪndɪ'pendənt] ADJ **a** *(= autonomous)* unabhängig *(of sb/sth* von jdm/etw) *(also Pol: country)*; *person (in attitude, spirit)* selbstständig, unabhängig; *income* eigen, privat; **she is a very ~ young lady** sie ist eine sehr selbstständige junge Dame; **a man of ~ means** eine Person mit Privateinkommen, ein Privatmann *m*; **to become ~** *(country)* die Unabhängigkeit erlangen
b *(= unconnected) report, research, thinker etc* unabhängig; **~ confirmation** Bestätigung *f* aus unabhängiger Quelle; **they reached the summit by ~ routes** sie erreichten den Gipfel auf getrennten *or* gesonderten Wegen; **the two explosions were ~ of each other** die beiden Explosionen hatten nichts miteinander zu tun *or* hatten keine gemeinsame Ursache
N *(Pol)* Unabhängige(r) *mf*

independent clause N *(Gram)* übergeordneter Satz, Hauptsatz *m*

independently [ˌɪndɪ'pendəntlɪ] ADV unabhängig *(of sb/sth* von jdm/etw); *(in attitude, spirit also)* selbstständig; *(on own initiative also)* von allein(e); *live* ohne fremde Hilfe; *work* selbstständig; **quite ~ he offered to help** er bot von sich aus seine Hilfe an; **they each came ~ to the same conclusion** sie kamen unabhängig voneinander zur gleichen Schlussfolgerung; **she is ~ wealthy** sie hat ein Privatvermögen

independent school N freie *or* unabhängige Schule

independent suspension N *(Aut)* Einzel(rad)aufhängung *f*

in-depth ['ɪndepθ] ADJ eingehend, gründlich; *interview* ausführlich

indescribable [ˌɪndɪ'skraɪbəbl] ADJ unbeschreiblich; *(inf: = terrible)* fürchterlich, schrecklich

indescribably [ˌɪndɪ'skraɪbəblɪ] ADV unbeschreiblich; *(inf: = terribly also)* schrecklich, fürchterlich

indestructibility ['ɪndɪˌstrʌktə'bɪlɪtɪ] N Unzerstörbarkeit *f*

indestructible ADJ, **indestructibly** ADV [ˌɪndɪ'strʌktəbl, -ɪ] unzerstörbar

indeterminable [ˌɪndɪ'tɜːmɪnəbl] ADJ unbestimmbar, nicht zu bestimmend *attr or* bestimmen *pred*

indeterminate [ˌɪndɪ'tɜːmɪnɪt] ADJ *amount, length* unbestimmt; *duration also* ungewiss; *meaning, concept* unklar, vage; **of ~ sex/age** von unbestimmbarem *or* nicht bestimmbarem Geschlecht/Alter

indeterminately [ˌɪndɪ'tɜːmɪnɪtlɪ] ADV unbestimmt; **it continued ~** es ging auf unbestimmte Zeit weiter

indetermination ['ɪndɪˌtɜːmɪ'neɪʃən] N *(= indecisiveness)* Entschlusslosigkeit *f*, Unschlüssigkeit *f*, Unentschiedenheit *f*

index ['ɪndeks] N **a** *pl* **-es** *(in book)* Register *nt*, Index *m*; *(of sources)* Quellenverzeichnis *nt*; *(in*

library) (of topics) (Schlagwort)katalog *m*; *(of authors)* (Verfasser)katalog *m*; *(= card index)* Kartei *f*; **Index** *(Eccl)* Index *m*
b *pl* **indices** *(= pointer, = Typ)* Hinweiszeichen *nt*, Handzeichen *nt*; *(on scale)* (An)zeiger *m*, Zunge *f*; **this is a good ~ of his character** das zeigt deutlich seinen Charakter, das lässt deutlich auf seinen Charakter schließen; **to provide a reliable ~ to** *or* **of the true state of affairs** zuverlässigen Aufschluss über den wahren Stand der Dinge geben
c *pl* **-es** *or* **indices** *(= number showing ratio)* Index *m*, Messzahl *f*, Indexziffer *f*; **cost-of-living ~** Lebenshaltungskostenindex *m*
d *pl* **indices** *(Math)* Index *m*; *(= exponent)* Wurzelexponent *m*
VT **a** mit einem Register *or* Index versehen; *word* in das Register *or* in den Index aufnehmen; *(Comput)* indexieren, indizieren; **the book is clearly ~ed** das Buch hat ein klares Register *or* einen klaren Index
b **to ~ sth to inflation** etw an den Index binden, etw indexieren; *pension* etw dynamisieren

index card N Karteikarte *f*

indexed [ˈɪndekst] ADJ *(Econ)* dynamisch

index: **index finger** N Zeigefinger *m*; **index-linked** ADJ *rate, salaries, trading, gilts* indexgebunden; *pensions* dynamisch; **index-tracker (fund)**, **index-tracking fund** N *(Fin)* indexorientierter Fonds

India [ˈɪndɪə] N Indien *nt*; **~man** Indienfahrer *m*

India ink N *(US)* Tusche *f*

Indian [ˈɪndɪən] **ADJ** **a** indisch; **the ~ rope-trick** der indische Seiltrick **b** *(= American Indian) (neg!)* indianisch, Indianer- **N** **a** Inder(in) *m(f)* **b** *(= American Indian) (neg!)* Indianer(in) *m(f)*; **too many chiefs and not enough ~s** *(fig)* zu viele Köpfe und nicht genug Hände

Indian: **Indian-British** ADJ indisch-britisch *(britisch mit indischer Herkunft)*; **Indian club** N Keule *f*; **Indian corn** N Mais *m*; **Indian cress** N *(Bot)* Kapuzinerkresse *f*; **Indian elephant** N Indischer Elefant; **Indian file** N Gänsemarsch *m*; **in ~** im Gänsemarsch; **Indian giver** N *(US inf) jd, der etwas Geschenktes zurückfordert*; **Indian ink** N Tusche *f*; **Indian meal** N **a** *(US, of corn)* Maismehl *nt* **b** *(Cook: = dish)* indisches Gericht; **Indian Ocean** N Indischer Ozean; **Indian reservation** N *(neg!)* Indianerreservat *nt*; **Indian sign** N *(US)* Zauber *m*; **to put an ~ on sb** jdn verzaubern *or* verhexen; **Indian summer** N Altweibersommer *m*, Spät- *or* Nachsommer *m*; *(esp Brit fig: = success late in life)* späte Blüte; **Indian wrestling** N Armdrücken *nt*

India: **India paper** N Dünndruckpapier *nt*; **India rubber** **N** Gummi *m*, Kautschuk *m*; *(= eraser)* Radiergummi *m* **ATTR** Gummi-; **~ ball** Gummiball *m*

indicate [ˈɪndɪkeɪt] **VT** **a** *(= point out, mark)* zeigen, deuten auf *(+acc)*; *(= point to)* zeigen *or* deuten auf *(+acc)*; **large towns are ~d in red** Großstädte sind rot eingezeichnet *or* gekennzeichnet; **sit down, he said, indicating a chair** setzen Sie sich, sagte er und zeigte *or* deutete auf einen Stuhl
b *(person: = gesture, express)* andeuten, zeigen, zu verstehen geben; **to ~ one's feelings** seine Gefühle zeigen *or* zum Ausdruck bringen; **to ~ one's intention to do sth** seine Absicht anzeigen, etw zu tun
c *(= be a sign of, suggest)* erkennen lassen, schließen lassen auf *(+acc)*, (hin)deuten auf *(+acc)*; **what does it ~ to you?** was erkennen Sie daraus?, welche Schlüsse ziehen Sie daraus?; **opinion polls ~ that …** die Meinungsumfragen deuten darauf hin, dass …
d *(= register and display) temperature, speed* (an)zeigen
e *(Med) treatment* indizieren; *illness* Anzeichen sein für, anzeigen
VI *(esp Brit Aut)* (Richtungswechsel) anzeigen *(form)*, blinken, den Blinker setzen; **to ~ right** rechts blinken, Richtungswechsel nach rechts anzeigen *(form)*

indication [ˌɪndɪˈkeɪʃən] ✪ 26.3 N **a** *(= sign)* (An)zeichen *nt (also Med) (of* für), Hinweis *m (of* auf *+acc)*; **there is every/no ~ that he is right** alles/nichts weist darauf hin *or* lässt darauf schließen, dass er recht hat; **there are few ~s that they are ready to come to an agreement** es gibt kaum Anzeichen dafür, dass sie zu einer Einigung bereit sind; **he gave a clear ~ of his intentions** er zeigte seine Absichten deutlich, er ließ seine Absichten deutlich erkennen; **he gave no ~ that he was ready to compromise** nichts wies darauf hin, dass er zu einem Kompromiss bereit war; **what are the ~s that it will happen?** was deutet darauf hin *or* spricht dafür *or* welchen Hinweis gibt es dafür, dass es geschieht?; **we had no ~ that …** es gab kein Anzeichen dafür, dass …; **that is some ~ of what we can expect** das gibt uns einen Vorgeschmack auf das, was wir zu erwarten haben; **if you could give me a rough ~ of …** wenn Sie mir eine ungefähre Vorstellung davon geben könnten …
b *(= showing, marking) (by gesturing, facial expression)* Anzeigen *nt*, Erkennenlassen *nt*; *(by pointing, drawing)* Anzeigen *nt*, Bezeichnen *nt*; **~ of the boundaries on this map is very poor** die Grenzen sind auf dieser Karte sehr undeutlich bezeichnet
c *(on gauge)* Anzeige *f*

indicative [ɪnˈdɪkətɪv] **ADJ** **a** bezeichnend *(of* für); **to be ~ of sth** auf etw *(acc)* schließen lassen, auf etw *(acc)* hindeuten; *of sb's character* für etw bezeichnend sein **b** *(Gram)* indikativisch; **~ mood** Indikativ *m*, Wirklichkeitsform *f* **N** *(Gram)* Indikativ *m*, Wirklichkeitsform *f*; **in the ~** im Indikativ, in der Wirklichkeitsform

indicator [ˈɪndɪkeɪtəʳ] N *(= instrument, gauge)* Anzeiger *m*; *(= needle)* Zeiger *m*; *(esp Brit Aut)* Richtungsanzeiger *m (form)*; *(flashing)* Blinker *m*; *(Chem)* Indikator *m*; *(fig: of economic position etc)* Messlatte *f*; **altitude/pressure ~** Höhen-/ /Druckmesser *m*; **~ board** Anzeigetafel *f*; **arrival/ departure ~ board** *(Rail)* Ankunfts-/Abfahrts(anzeige)tafel *f*; *(Aviat)* Anzeige(tafel) *f* für Ankünfte/Abflüge, Fluginformationsanzeige *f*; **this is an ~ of economic recovery** dies ist ein Indikator für den Aufschwung

indices [ˈɪndɪsiːz] *pl of* **index**

indict [ɪnˈdaɪt] VT *(= charge)* anklagen, beschuldigen *(on a charge of sth* einer Sache *gen)*, unter Anklage stellen; *(US Jur)* Anklage erheben gegen *(for* wegen *+gen)*; **to ~ sb as a murderer** jdn unter Mordanklage stellen, jdn des Mordes anklagen

indictable [ɪnˈdaɪtəbl] ADJ *offence* strafbar; *person* strafrechtlich verfolgbar

indictment [ɪnˈdaɪtmənt] N *(of person) (= accusation)* Beschuldigung *f*, Anschuldigung *f*; *(= charge sheet)* Anklage *f (for, on a charge of* wegen); *(US: by grand jury)* Anklageerhebung *f*; **to bring an ~ against sb** gegen jdn Anklage erheben, jdn unter Anklage stellen; **bill of ~** Anklageschrift *f*; **to be an ~ of sth** *(fig)* ein Armutszeugnis *nt* für etw sein; **the speech was a damning ~ of government policy** die Rede war eine vernichtende Anklage gegen die Regierungspolitik

indie [ˈɪndɪ], **indie rock** N *(Mus)* Indie *m*

indifference [ɪnˈdɪfrəns] N Gleichgültigkeit *f (to, towards* gegenüber), Indifferenz *f (geh) (to, towards* gegenüber); **it's a matter of complete ~ to me** das ist mir völlig egal *or* gleichgültig

indifferent [ɪnˈdɪfrənt] ADJ **a** *(= lacking interest)* gleichgültig, indifferent *(geh) (to, towards* gegenüber); **he is quite ~ about it/to her** es/sie ist ihm ziemlich gleichgültig; **~ to her despair** ungerührt von ihrer Verzweiflung; **his ~ attitude to the killings** seine Gleichgültigkeit gegenüber den Morden **b** *(= mediocre)* mittelmäßig, durchschnittlich

indifferently [ɪnˈdɪfrəntlɪ] ADV **a** *(= without interest)* gleichgültig **b** *(= poorly)* (mittel)mäßig (gut), nicht besonders (gut)

indigence [ˈɪndɪdʒəns] N Bedürftigkeit *f*, Armut *f*

indigenous [ɪnˈdɪdʒɪnəs] ADJ einheimisch *(to* in *+dat)*; *customs* landeseigen; **~ language** Landessprache *f*; **plants ~ to Canada** in Kanada heimische *or* beheimatete Pflanzen; **~ tribes** einheimische *or* eingeborene Volksstämme

indigent [ˈɪndɪdʒənt] ADJ bedürftig, arm, ärmlich

indigestible [ˌɪndɪˈdʒestəbl] ADJ *(Med)* unverdaulich; *(fig)* schwer verdaulich, schwer zu ertragend *attr or* ertragen *pred*; **fried food is very ~** Gebratenes ist sehr schwer verdaulich

indigestion [ˌɪndɪˈdʒestʃən] N Verdauungsbeschwerden *pl*; **acid ~** Sodbrennen *nt*

indignant [ɪnˈdɪgnənt] ADJ entrüstet, empört *(at, about, with* über *+acc)*, unwillig *(at, about* wegen); **to be ~ with sb** über jdn empört sein; **to become ~** ungehalten werden, sich aufregen; **to make sb ~** jds Unwillen *or* Entrüstung erregen; **it's no good getting ~** es hat keinen Zweck, sich zu entrüsten *or* sich aufzuregen

indignantly [ɪnˈdɪgnəntlɪ] ADV entrüstet, empört

indignation [ˌɪndɪgˈneɪʃən] N Entrüstung *f (at, about, with* über *+acc)*, Unwillen *m (at, about* wegen); **to fill sb with ~** jdn empören *or* aufbringen

indignity [ɪnˈdɪgnɪtɪ] N Demütigung *f*, Schmach *f (liter)*; **oh, the ~ of it!** also, das ist doch der Gipfel!

indigo [ˈɪndɪgəʊ] **N** Indigo *nt or m* **ADJ** indigofarben

indigo blue ADJ indigoblau

indirect [ˌɪndɪˈrekt] ADJ **a** indirekt; *consequence, result* indirekt, mittelbar; **in an ~ way, by ~ means** auf indirekte Weise, auf Umwegen; **by an ~ route/path/road** auf Umwegen *or* einem Umweg; **to make an ~ reference to sb/sth** auf jdn/etw anspielen *or* indirekt Bezug nehmen **b** *(Gram)* indirekt

indirect discourse *(US)* N *(Gram)* indirekte Rede

indirectly [ˌɪndɪˈrektlɪ] ADV indirekt

indirectness [ˌɪndɪˈrektnɪs] N Indirektheit *f*

indirect object N *(Gram)* Dativobjekt *nt*

indirect speech N *(Gram)* indirekte Rede

indiscernible [ˌɪndɪˈsɜːnəbl] ADJ nicht erkennbar *or* sichtbar; *improvement, change etc also* unmerklich; *noise* nicht wahrnehmbar; **to be almost ~** kaum zu erkennen sein; *(noise)* kaum wahrzunehmen sein

indiscipline [ɪnˈdɪsɪplɪn] N Mangel *m* an Disziplin, Undiszipliniertheit *f*, Disziplinlosigkeit *f*

indiscreet [ˌɪndɪˈskriːt] ADJ indiskret; *(= tactless)* taktlos, ohne Feingefühl; **to be ~ about sth** in Bezug auf etw *(acc)* indiskret sein; **he is too ~ ever to be a successful diplomat** wegen seiner Neigung zu Indiskretionen wird er nie ein erfolgreicher Diplomat werden

indiscreetly [ˌɪndɪˈskriːtlɪ] ADV indiskret; *(= tactlessly)* taktlos

indiscreetness [ˌɪndɪˈskriːtnɪs] N = **indiscretion**

indiscrete [ˌɪndɪˈskriːt] ADJ kompakt, zusammenhängend, homogen

indiscretion [ˌɪndɪˈskreʃən] N Indiskretion *f*; *(= tactlessness)* Taktlosigkeit *f*, Mangel *m* an Feingefühl; *(= affair)* Abenteuer *nt*, Affäre *f*; **his youthful ~s** seine jugendliche Unvernunft, sein jugendlicher Leichtsinn

indiscriminate [ˌɪndɪˈskrɪmɪnɪt] ADJ wahllos; *spending also* unüberlegt; *reading also* kritiklos, unkritisch; *mixture also* kunterbunt; *choice* willkürlich; *reader, shopper* kritiklos, unkritisch; *tastes* unausgeprägt; **you shouldn't be so ~ in the friends you make** du solltest dir deine Freunde etwas sorgfältiger aussuchen; **he was completely ~ in whom he punished** er verteilte seine Strafen völlig wahllos *or* willkürlich

indiscriminately [ˌɪndɪˈskrɪmɪnɪtlɪ] ADV wahllos; *choose* willkürlich

indiscriminating [ˌɪndɪˈskrɪmɪneɪtɪŋ] ADJ unkritisch, kritiklos

indispensability [ˈɪndɪˌspensɪˈbɪlɪtɪ] N Unentbehrlichkeit *f*, unbedingte Notwendigkeit (*to* für)

indispensable [ˌɪndɪˈspensəbl] ADJ unentbehrlich, unbedingt notwendig *or* erforderlich (*to* für); **nobody's ~** niemand ist unentbehrlich; **to make oneself ~ to sb** sich für jdn unentbehrlich machen

indispensably [ˌɪndɪˈspensəblɪ] ADV **it is ~ necessary to them** es ist unbedingt notwendig *or* erforderlich für sie; **that is necessarily and ~ a part of our system** das ist notwendiger und unverzichtbarer Bestandteil unseres Systems

indisposed [ˌɪndɪˈspəʊzd] ADJ **a** *(= unwell)* unwohl, indisponiert *(geh)*, unpässlich *(geh)* **b** *(= disinclined)* **to be ~ to do sth** nicht gewillt *or* geneigt sein, etw zu tun

indisposition [ˌɪndɪspəˈzɪʃən] N **a** *(= illness)* Unwohlsein *nt*, Indisposition *f (geh)*, Unpässlichkeit *f (geh)* **b** *(= disinclination)* Unwilligkeit *f*

indisputability [ˈɪndɪˌspjuːtəˈbɪlɪtɪ] N Unbestreitbarkeit *f*, Unstrittigkeit *f*

indisputable [ˌɪndɪˈspjuːtəbl] ADJ unbestreitbar; *evidence* unanfechtbar

indisputably [ˌɪndɪˈspjuːtəblɪ] ✪ 26.3 ADV unbestreitbar

indissolubility [ˈɪndɪˌsɒljʊˈbɪlɪtɪ] N *(Chem)* Unlöslichkeit *f*, Unlösbarkeit *f*; *(fig)* Unauflöslichkeit *f*, Unauflösbarkeit *f*

indissoluble ADJ, **indissolubly** ADV [ˌɪndɪˈsɒljʊbl, -ɪ] *(Chem)* unlöslich, unlösbar; *(fig)* unauflöslich, unauflösbar, unlöslich

indistinct [ˌɪndɪˈstɪŋkt] ADJ *object, shape, words* verschwommen, unklar, undeutlich; *noise* schwach, unklar; *memory* undeutlich; *voice* undeutlich, unklar; *line* unscharf

indistinctly [ˌɪndɪˈstɪŋktlɪ] ADV *see* nicht deutlich, verschwommen; *speak* undeutlich; *remember* schwach, dunkel

indistinguishable [ˌɪndɪˈstɪŋgwɪʃəbl] ADJ **a** nicht unterscheidbar, nicht zu unterscheidend *attr or* unterscheiden *pred* (*from* von); **the twins are ~ (from one another)** man kann die Zwillinge nicht (voneinander) unterscheiden **b** *(= indiscernible)* nicht erkennbar *or* sichtbar; *improvement, change, difference etc* unmerklich, nicht erkennbar; *noise* nicht wahrnehmbar

individual [ˌɪndɪˈvɪdjʊəl] ADJ **a** *(= separate)* einzeln; **~ cases** Einzelfälle *pl*; **to give ~ help** jedem Einzeln helfen, Einzelhilfe leisten; **~ tastes differ** jeder hat einen eigenen *or* individuellen Geschmack, die Geschmäcker sind verschieden
b *(= own)* eigen; *(= for one person)* einzeln; **serve on ~ plates** auf einzelnen Tellern servieren; **~ portions cost 95p** eine Einzelportion kostet 95 Pence
c *(= distinctive, characteristic)* eigen, individuell
N Individuum *nt*, Einzelne(r) *mf*, Einzelperson *f*; *(inf)* Individuum *nt*, Mensch *m*, Person *f*; **the freedom of the ~** die Freiheit des Einzelnen, die individuelle Freiheit → **private**

individualism [ˌɪndɪˈvɪdjʊəlɪzəm] N Individualismus *m*

individualist [ˌɪndɪˈvɪdjʊəlɪst] N Individualist(in) *m(f)* ADJ individualistisch

individualistic [ˌɪndɪˈvɪdjʊəlɪstɪk] ADJ individualistisch

individuality [ˈɪndɪˌvɪdjʊˈælɪtɪ] N Individualität *f*, (eigene) Persönlichkeit

individualize [ˌɪndɪˈvɪdjʊəlaɪz] VT individualisieren; *(= treat separately)* einzeln behandeln; *(= give individuality to) book, author's style, performance* eine persönliche *or* individuelle *or* eigene Note verleihen *(+dat)*; **each patient has ~d treatment/an ~d exercise plan** jeder Patient bekommt eine individuelle Behandlung/seinen eigenen Trainingsplan

individually [ˌɪndɪˈvɪdjʊəlɪ] ADV individuell; *(= separately) numbered, wrapped* einzeln; **~ styled suit** Modellanzug *m*; **to be ~ responsible for sth** persönlich für etw verantwortlich sein

indivisible ADJ, **indivisibly** ADV [ˌɪndɪˈvɪzəbl, -ɪ] unteilbar *(also Math)*, untrennbar

Indo- [ˈɪndəʊ-] PREF Indo-; **Indo-China** N Indochina *nt*

indocile [ɪnˈdəʊsaɪl] ADJ *(form) (difficult to teach)* ungelehrig; *(= insubordinate)* unfügsam

indoctrinate [ɪnˈdɒktrɪneɪt] VT indoktrinieren

indoctrination [ɪnˌdɒktrɪˈneɪʃən] N Indoktrination *f*

Indo: **Indo-European** ADJ indogermanisch, indoeuropäisch N **a** Indogermane *m*, Indogermanin *f*, Indoeuropäer(in) *m(f)* **b** *(Ling)* Indogermanisch *nt*, Indoeuropäisch *nt*; **Indo-Germanic** *(old)* ADJ, N = **Indo-European ADJ, N b**

indolence [ˈɪndələns] N Trägheit *f*, Indolenz *f (rare)*

indolent ADJ, **indolently** ADV [ˈɪndələnt, -lɪ] träge, indolent *(rare)*

indomitable [ɪnˈdɒmɪtəbl] ADJ *person, courage* unbezähmbar, unbezwingbar; *will* unbeugsam, eisern, unerschütterlich; **his ~ pride** sein nicht zu brechender Stolz

Indonesia [ˌɪndəʊˈniːzɪə] N Indonesien *nt*

Indonesian [ˌɪndəʊˈniːzɪən] ADJ indonesisch N **a** Indonesier(in) *m(f)* **b** *(Ling)* Indonesisch *nt*

indoor [ˈɪndɔː] ADJ Innen-; *clothes* für zu Hause *or* zuhause *(Aus, Sw)*; **~ activity** Beschäftigung *f* für drinnen; **~ aerial** Zimmerantenne *f*; **~ cycle track** Radsporthalle *f*; **~ market** überdachter Markt; **~ plant** Zimmerpflanze *f*; **~ sport** Hallensport *m*; **~ swimming pool** *(public)* Hallenbad *nt*; *(private)* überdachter Swimmingpool; **~ tennis court** Tennishalle *f*; **~ tournament** *(Sport)* Hallenturnier *nt*; **~ work** Arbeit, die nicht im Freien ausgeführt wird; **~ air pollution** Innenraumluftverschmutzung *f*; **~ games** Spiele *pl* fürs Haus, Haus- *or* Zimmerspiele *pl*; *(Sport)* Hallenspiele *pl*

indoors [ɪnˈdɔːz] ADV drin(nen) *(inf)*, innen; *(= at home)* zu Hause, zuhause *(Aus, Sw)*; *(= into house)* ins Haus; **what's the house like ~?** wie sieht das Haus innen aus?; **to stay ~** im Haus bleiben, drinbleiben *(inf)*; **go and play ~** geh ins Haus *or* nach drinnen spielen; **to go ~** ins Haus gehen, nach drinnen gehen; **~ and outdoors** im und außer Haus, drinnen und draußen, im Haus und im Freien

indrawn [ˈɪnˈdrɔːn] ADJ **a** *breath* eingezogen **b** *(form) person* zurückhaltend

indubitable ADJ, **indubitably** ADV [ɪnˈdjuːbɪtəbl, -ɪ] zweifellos, unzweifelhaft

induce [ɪnˈdjuːs] VT **a** *(= persuade)* **to ~ sb to do sth** jdn dazu bewegen *or* bringen *or* veranlassen, etw zu tun
b *reaction, change, hypnosis* herbeiführen; *relaxation* bewirken; *sleep* herbeiführen; *illness, vomiting* verursachen, führen zu; *labour, birth* einleiten; **this drug ~s sleep** dieses Mittel hat eine einschläfernde Wirkung; **she had to be ~d** die Geburt musste eingeleitet werden; **(artificially) ~d sleep** künstlicher Schlaf; **a stress-/drug-~d condition** ein durch Stress/Drogen ausgelöstes Leiden
c *(Philos)* induktiv *or* durch Induktion erarbeiten
d *(Elec) current, magnetic effect* induzieren

inducement [ɪnˈdjuːsmənt] N **a** *(no pl: = persuasion)* Überredung *f*; *(= motive, incentive)* Anreiz *m*, Ansporn *m no pl*; **to offer ~s** Anreize bieten; **cash/financial ~s** finanzielle Anreize *pl* **b** = **induction b**

induct [ɪnˈdʌkt] VT **a** *bishop, president etc* in sein Amt einsetzen *or* einführen **b** *(US Mil)* einziehen, einberufen

inductee [ɪndʌkˈtiː] N *(US Mil)* (zum Wehrdienst) Eingezogene(r) *or* Einberufene(r) *mf*

induction [ɪnˈdʌkʃən] N **a** *(of bishop, president etc)* Amtseinführung *f*; *(US Mil)* Einberufung *f*, Einziehung *f* **b** *(of sleep, reaction etc)* Herbeiführen *nt*; *(of labour, birth)* Einleitung *f* **c** *(Philos, Math, Elec)* Induktion *f*

induction: **induction coil** N *(Elec)* Induktionsspule *f*; **induction course** N Einführungskurs *m*; **induction loop** N *(Elec)* Induktionsschleife *f*

inductive ADJ, **inductively** ADV [ɪnˈdʌktɪv, -lɪ] induktiv

indulge [ɪnˈdʌldʒ] VT **a** *appetite, desires etc, person* nachgeben *(+dat)*; *(= overindulge) children* verwöhnen, verhätscheln; *one's imagination* frönen *(+dat)*; **he ~s her every whim** er erfüllt ihr jeden Wunsch; **to ~ oneself in sth** sich *(dat)* etw gönnen, in etw *(dat)* schwelgen; **she ~d herself with a glass of wine** sie gönnte sich *(dat)* ein Glas Wein; **go on, ~ yourself!** nun komm schon, gönn dir mal was *(inf)*
b *debtor* Zahlungsaufschub gewähren *(+dat)*
VI **to ~ in sth** sich *(dat)* etw gönnen *or* genehmigen *(inf)*; *in vice, drink, daydreams* einer Sache *(dat)* frönen, sich einer Sache *(dat)* hingeben; **to ~ in sth to excess** etw bis zum Exzess treiben; **dessert came, but I didn't ~** *(inf)* der Nachtisch kam, aber ich konnte mich beherrschen; **I don't ~** ich trinke/rauche *etc* nicht; **we don't ~ in such underhand tactics** wir geben uns mit solchen hinterhältigen Taktiken nicht ab

indulgence [ɪnˈdʌldʒəns] N **a** Nachsicht *f*; *(of appetite etc)* Nachgiebigkeit *f* (*of* gegenüber); *(= overindulgence)* Verwöhnung *f*, Verhätschelung *f*
b *(in activity, drink etc)* **~ in drink/food/sport** übermäßiges Trinken/Essen/Sporttreiben
c *(= thing indulged in)* Luxus *m*; *(= food, drink, pleasure)* Genuss *m*; **he allowed himself the ~ of a day off work** er gönnte sich *(dat)* den Luxus eines freien Tages; **smoking/the car is one of my few ~s** Rauchen/das Auto ist fast das Einzige, was ich mir gönne
d (*form*: *= permission*) Einwilligung *f*, Zustimmung *f*
e *(Eccl)* Ablass *m*

indulgent [ɪnˈdʌldʒənt] ADJ nachsichtig (*to* gegenüber); *mother etc also* nachgiebig; *(to one's own desires etc)* zu nachgiebig

indulgently [ɪnˈdʌldʒəntlɪ] ADV nachsichtig

industrial [ɪnˈdʌstrɪəl] ADJ industriell, Industrie-; **~ country** Industriestaat *m*; **~ fabric** Industriefasern *pl*; **~ growth** Industriewachstum *nt*; **~ nation** Industriestaat *m*; **~ production** Industrieproduktion *f*; **~ research** Arbeits- *or* Betriebsforschung *f*; **the Industrial Revolution** die industrielle Revolution; **~ robot** Industrieroboter *m*; **~ state** Industriestaat *m*; **~ training** betriebliche Ausbildung *f* N **industrials** PL *(St Ex)* Industrieaktien *pl*

industrial: **industrial accident** N Betriebs- *or* Arbeitsunfall *m*; **industrial action** N Arbeitskampfmaßnahmen *pl*; **to take ~** in den Ausstand treten; **industrial archaeology**, *(US)* **industrial archeology** N Industriearchäologie *f*; **industrial democracy** N Demokratie *f* im Betrieb; **industrial design** N Konstruktionslehre *f*; **industrial designer** N Industriedesigner(in) *m(f)*; **industrial diamond** N Industriediamant *m*; **industrial disease** N Berufskrankheit *f*; **industrial dispute** N Auseinandersetzungen *pl* zwischen Arbeitgebern und Arbeitnehmern; *(about pay also)* Tarifkonflikt *m*; *(= strike)* Streik *m*; **industrial engineering** N Fertigungstechnik *f*; **industrial espionage** N Industriespionage *f*; **industrial estate** N *(Brit)* Industriegebiet *nt*; **industrial injury** N Arbeitsunfall *m*; **industrial insurance** N Unfallversicherung *f*

industrialism [ɪnˈdʌstrɪəlɪzəm] N Industrie *f*

industrialist [ɪnˈdʌstrɪəlɪst] N Industrielle(r) *mf*

industrialization [ɪnˌdʌstrɪəlaɪˈzeɪʃən] N Industrialisierung *f*

industrialize [ɪnˈdʌstrɪəlaɪz] VTI industrialisieren

industrial: **industrial medicine** N Arbeits- *or* Betriebsmedizin *f*; **industrial park** N *(US)* Industriegelände *nt*; **industrial psychology** N Arbeits- *or* Betriebspsychologie *f*; **industrial relations** PL Beziehungen *pl* zwischen Arbeitgebern und Gewerkschaften; **industrial-strength** ADJ *(usu hum)* extrastark; ~ **claret** vollmundiger Bordeaux; **industrial tribunal** N Arbeitsgericht *nt*; **industrial trouble, industrial unrest** N Arbeitsunruhen *pl*; **industrial waste** N Industrieabfälle *pl*, Industriemüll *m*; **industrial worker** N Industriearbeiter(in) *m(f)*

industrious ADJ, **industriously** ADV [ɪnˈdʌstrɪəs, -lɪ] arbeitsam, fleißig

industriousness [ɪnˈdʌstrɪəsnɪs] N Arbeitsamkeit *f*, Fleiß *m*

industry [ˈɪndəstrɪ] N **a** *(= trade, branch of industry)* Industrie *f*; **heavy/light** ~ Schwer-/ /Leichtindustrie *f*; **hotel** ~ Hotelgewerbe *nt*; **tourist** ~ Tourismusbranche *or* -industrie *f*; **in certain industries** in einigen Branchen **b** *(= industriousness)* Fleiß *m*

industry standard N Industrienorm *f* ADJ **industry-standard** der Industrienorm entsprechend

inebriate [ɪˈniːbrɪɪt] N *(form)* Trinker(in) *m(f)* ADJ = **inebriated a** VT [ɪˈniːbrɪeɪt] *(lit)* betrunken machen; *(fig)* trunken machen; *(success, popularity etc)* berauschen

inebriated [ɪˈniːbrɪeɪtɪd] ADJ **a** *(form)* betrunken, unter Alkoholeinfluss *(form)* **b** *(fig)* berauscht, trunken *(liter)*

inebriation [ɪˌniːbrɪˈeɪʃən] N *(form)* betrunkener Zustand

inedible [ɪnˈedɪbl] ADJ nicht essbar; *(= unpleasant) meal etc* ungenießbar

ineducable [ɪnˈedjʊkəbl] ADJ bildungsunfähig

ineffable [ɪnˈefəbl] ADJ *(form)* unsäglich *(geh)*, unsagbar, unaussprechlich

ineffably [ɪnˈefəblɪ] ADV *(form: = indescribably)* unsäglich *(geh)*, unaussprechlich; **Walters is ~ entertaining** Walters ist unbeschreiblich unterhaltsam

ineffective [ˌɪnɪˈfektɪv] ADJ unwirksam, ineffektiv; *attempt also* fruchtlos, nutzlos; *person* unfähig, untauglich; *government, management* unfähig; **to be ~ against sth** nicht wirksam gegen etw sein; **to render sth ~** etw unwirksam machen

ineffectively [ˌɪnɪˈfektɪvlɪ] ADV ineffektiv

ineffectiveness [ˌɪnɪˈfektɪvnɪs] N Unwirksamkeit *f*, Ineffektivität *f*; *(of attempt)* Fruchtlosigkeit *f*, Nutzlosigkeit *f*; *(of person)* Unfähigkeit *f*

ineffectual [ˌɪnɪˈfektjʊəl] ADJ ineffektiv; *(= half-hearted)* halbherzig

ineffectually [ˌɪnɪˈfektjʊəlɪ] ADV ohne Wirkung; *(= half-heartedly)* halbherzig

inefficacious [ˌɪnefɪˈkeɪʃəs] ADJ unwirksam, wirkungslos, ohne Wirkung; *policy* erfolglos, fruchtlos

inefficacy [ɪnˈefɪkəsɪ] N Unwirksamkeit *f*, Wirkungslosigkeit *f*; *(of policy)* Erfolglosigkeit *f*, Fruchtlosigkeit *f*

inefficiency [ˌɪnɪˈfɪʃənsɪ] N *(of person)* Unfähigkeit *f*, Ineffizienz *f (geh)*; *(of machine, engine)* geringe Leistung; *(of factory, company)* Unproduktivität *f*; **the ~ of this method** diese unrationelle Methode

inefficient [ˌɪnɪˈfɪʃənt] ADJ *person* unfähig, ineffizient *(geh)*; *machine, engine* leistungsschwach; *method* unrationell; *use* unwirtschaftlich; *factory, company* unproduktiv, ineffizient *(geh)*; **to be ~ at doing sth** etw schlechtmachen; **the ~ working of a mechanism** das schlechte Funktionieren eines Mechanismus; **~ combustion of fuel** unwirtschaftliche Verbrennung des Treibstoffs

inefficiently [ˌɪnɪˈfɪʃəntlɪ] ADV schlecht; **to work ~** *(person)* unrationell arbeiten; *(machine)* unwirtschaftlich arbeiten

inelastic [ˌɪnɪˈlæstɪk] ADJ *(lit)* unelastisch; *(fig)* starr, nicht flexibel

inelasticity [ˌɪnɪlæsˈtɪsɪtɪ] N *(lit)* Mangel *m* an Elastizität; *(fig)* Mangel *m* an Flexibilität, Starrheit *f*

inelegance [ɪnˈelɪgəns] N Uneleganz *f*; *(of clothes, person also)* Mangel *m* an Schick *or* Eleganz; *(of style also)* Schwerfälligkeit *f*, Unausgewogenheit *f*; *(of prose, phrase also)* Ungeschliffenheit *f*, Plumpheit *f*, Schwerfälligkeit *f*; *(of dialect)* Derbheit *f*, Schwerfälligkeit *f*

inelegant [ɪnˈelɪgənt] ADJ unelegant; *clothes, person also* ohne Schick *or* Eleganz; *style also* schwerfällig, unausgewogen; *prose, phrase also* ungeschliffen, plump, schwerfällig; *dialect* derb, schwerfällig

inelegantly [ɪnˈelɪgəntlɪ] ADV unelegant; **she walks very ~** ihr Gang ist ohne Eleganz, sie hat einen wenig eleganten Gang

ineligibility [ɪnˌelɪdʒəˈbɪlɪtɪ] N *(for benefits, grant)* Nichtberechtigtsein *nt*; *(for election)* Unwählbarkeit *f*; *(for job, office, as husband)* mangelnde Eignung, Untauglichkeit *f*

ineligible [ɪnˈelɪdʒəbl] ADJ *(for benefits, grant)* nicht berechtigt *(for* zu Leistungen *+gen)*; *(for election)* nicht wählbar; *(for job, office, as husband)* ungeeignet, untauglich; **~ for military service** wehruntauglich; **you are ~ for social security benefits** Sie sind nicht zu Leistungen der Sozialversicherung berechtigt; **to be ~ for a pension** nicht pensionsberechtigt sein

ineloquent [ɪnˈeləkwənt] ADJ nicht wortgewandt

ineluctable [ˌɪnɪˈlʌktəbl] ADJ *(liter)* unausweichlich, unabwendbar *(liter)*

inept [ɪˈnept] ADJ *behaviour* ungeschickt, linkisch, unbeholfen; *remark* unpassend, unangebracht, ungeschickt; *performance, display* ungeschickt, stümperhaft *(pej)*; *compliment, refusal, attempt* plump; *comparison* ungeeignet, unpassend; *person (= clumsy)* ungeschickt, unbeholfen; *(= slow at learning)* begriffsstutzig, ungelehrig, unverständig

ineptitude [ɪˈneptɪtjuːd], **ineptness** [ɪˈneptnɪs] N *(of behaviour)* Ungeschicktheit *f*, Unbeholfenheit *f*; *(of remark)* Unangebrachtheit *f*, Ungeschicktheit *f*; *(of performance, display)* Ungeschicklichkeit *f*, Stümperhaftigkeit *f (pej)*; *(of compliment, refusal, attempt)* Plumpheit *f*; *(of comparison)* Ungeeignetheit *f*; *(of person) (= clumsiness)* Ungeschick *nt*, Unbeholfenheit *f*; *(= slowness at learning)* Begriffsstutzigkeit *f*, Ungelehrigkeit *f*

inequality [ˌɪnɪˈkwɒlɪtɪ] N *(= lack of equality)* Ungleichheit *f*; *(= instance of inequality)* Unterschied *m*; **great inequalities in wealth** große Unterschiede *pl* in der Verteilung von Reichtum; **~ of opportunity** Chancenungleichheit *f*; **~ of opportunity in education** Ungleichheit *f* der Bildungschancen

inequitable [ɪnˈekwɪtəbl] ADJ ungerecht

inequity [ɪnˈekwɪtɪ] N Ungerechtigkeit *f*

ineradicable [ˌɪnɪˈrædɪkəbl] ADJ *mistake, failing* unabänderlich, unwiderruflich; *feeling of guilt, hatred* tief sitzend, unauslöschlich; *disease, prejudice* unausrottbar

inerrancy [ɪnˈerənsɪ] N *(form: of scriptures)* Unfehlbarkeit *f*

inert [ɪˈnɜːt] ADJ unbeweglich; *(Phys) matter* träge; *(Chem) substance* inaktiv

inert gas N *(Chem)* Edelgas *nt*

inertia [ɪˈnɜːʃə] N *(lit, fig)* Trägheit *f*; **~-reel seat belt** Automatikgurt *m*

inescapable [ˌɪnɪsˈkeɪpəbl] ADJ unvermeidlich; *fact, reality* unausweichlich; *consequence, logic, conclusion* zwangsläufig, unausweichlich

inescapably [ˌɪnɪsˈkeɪpəblɪ] ADV unvermeidlich; **~, this means that ...** dies bedeutet unvermeidlicherweise, dass ...

inessential [ˌɪnɪˈsenʃəl] ADJ unwesentlich, unerheblich, unwichtig N Unwesentliche(s) *nt no pl*, Nebensächlichkeit *f*

inestimable [ɪnˈestɪməbl] ADJ unschätzbar

inevitability [ɪnˌevɪtəˈbɪlɪtɪ] N Unvermeidlichkeit *f*

inevitable [ɪnˈevɪtəbl] ✪ 15.1 ADJ unvermeidlich, unvermeidbar; *result also* zwangsläufig; **victory/defeat seemed ~** der Sieg/die Niederlage schien unabwendbar; **a tourist with his ~ camera** ein Tourist mit dem unvermeidlichen Fotoapparat N **the ~** das Unvermeidliche

inevitably [ɪnˈevɪtəblɪ] ADV zwangsläufig; **if it's ~ the case that ...** wenn es notgedrungenerweise *or* zwangsläufig so sein muss, dass ...; **~ rising prices** zwangsläufig steigende Preise; **one question ~ leads to another** eine Frage zieht unweigerlich weitere nach sich; **talk ~ turned to politics** das Gespräch kam unweigerlich *or* zwangsläufig auf Politik; **~, he got drunk/was late** es konnte ja nicht ausbleiben, dass er sich betrank/zu spät kam; **as ~ happens on these occasions** wie es bei solchen Anlässen immer ist

inexact ADJ, **inexactly** ADV [ˌɪnɪgˈzækt, -lɪ] ungenau

inexactitude [ˌɪnɪgˌzæktɪtjuːd] N Ungenauigkeit *f*

inexcusable [ˌɪnɪksˈkjuːzəbl] ADJ unverzeihlich, unverzeihbar, unentschuldbar; *failure* unverzeihlich; **it would be ~ for him to leave now** es wäre unverzeihlich, wenn er jetzt gehen würde

inexcusably [ˌɪnɪksˈkjuːzəblɪ] ADV unverzeihlich; **she had been ~ careless/lazy** ihre Nachlässigkeit/Faulheit war unverzeihlich gewesen

inexhaustible [ˌɪnɪgˈzɔːstəbl] ADJ unerschöpflich; *source, spring also* nie versiegend; *curiosity* unstillbar, unendlich; *person, talker* unermüdlich

inexorable [ɪnˈeksərəbl] ADJ *(= relentless)* erbarmungslos, unerbittlich; *(= not to be stopped)* unaufhaltsam; *truth, facts* unumstößlich

inexorably [ɪnˈeksərəblɪ] ADV erbarmungslos, unerbittlich; *(= unstoppably)* unaufhaltsam

inexpediency [ˌɪnɪkˈspiːdɪənsɪ] N *(of plan, measures, action, decision)* Ungeeignetheit *f*, Unzweckmäßigkeit *f*; *(of policy)* Unratsamkeit *f*, Unklugheit *f*

inexpedient [ˌɪnɪkˈspiːdɪənt] ADJ *plan, measures, action, decision* ungeeignet, unzweckmäßig; *policy* unratsam, unklug; **it would be ~ to do that** es wäre unklug, das zu tun

inexpensive [ˌɪnɪkˈspensɪv] ADJ billig, preisgünstig

inexpensively [ˌɪnɪkˈspensɪvlɪ] ADV billig; *live also* ohne große Kosten; *buy also* günstig

inexperience [ˌɪnɪkˈspɪərɪəns] N Unerfahrenheit *f*, Mangel *m* an Erfahrung; **his ~ with our system** seine mangelnde Vertrautheit mit unserem System

inexperienced [ˌɪnɪkˈspɪərɪənst] ADJ unerfahren; *woodworker, skier etc* ungeübt, nicht so versiert; **to be ~ in doing sth** wenig Erfahrung darin haben, etw zu tun

inexpert [ɪnˈekspɜːt] ADJ unfachmännisch, laienhaft; *treatment also* unsachgemäß; *(= untrained)* ungeübt; **to be ~ in sth** in etw *(dat)* ungeübt sein

inexpertly [ɪnˈekspɜːtlɪ] ADV unfachmännisch, laienhaft

inexpertness [ɪnˈekspɜːtnɪs] N Laienhaftigkeit *f*; *(of treatment also)* Unsachgemäßheit *f*; *(= lack of training)* Ungeübtheit *f*

inexplicability [ˌɪnɪksplɪkəˈbɪlɪtɪ] N Unerklärlichkeit *f*, Unerklärbarkeit *f*

inexplicable [ˌɪnɪkˈsplɪkəbl] ADJ unerklärlich, unerklärbar

inexplicably [ˌɪnɪkˈsplɪkəblɪ] ADV *(+adj)* unerklärlich; *(+vb)* unerklärlicherweise

inexplicit [ɪnɪkˈsplɪsɪt] ADJ unklar, ungenau

inexpressible [ˌɪnɪkˈspresəbl] ADJ *thoughts, feelings* unbeschreiblich, unbeschreibbar; *pain, joy also* unsagbar

inexpressive [ˌɪnɪkˈspresɪv] ADJ *face* ausdruckslos; *word* blass, nichtssagend; *style* blass, ohne Ausdruckskraft

in extenso [ˌɪnɪkˈstensəʊ] ADV in extenso; *(= at length)* ausführlich; *(= in full)* vollständig, ungekürzt

inextinguishable [ˌɪnɪkˈstɪŋgwɪʃəbl] ADJ *fire* unlöschbar; *love, hope* unerschütterlich, beständig; *passion* unbezwinglich

in extremis [ˌɪnekˈstriːmɪs] ADV **to be ~** *(= dying)* im Sterben liegen; *(= in difficulties)* sich in äußerster Not befinden; **to help a friend ~** einem Freund in der Not helfen

inextricable [ˌɪnɪkˈstrɪkəbl] ADJ *tangle* unentwirrbar; *confusion* unüberschaubar; *link, relationship* untrennbar

inextricably [ˌɪnɪkˈstrɪkəblɪ] ADV *entangled* unentwirrbar; *linked* untrennbar; **he has become ~ involved with her** er kommt nicht mehr von ihr los

infallibility [ɪnˌfæləˈbɪlɪtɪ] N Unfehlbarkeit *f (also Eccl)*

infallible [ɪnˈfæləbl] ADJ unfehlbar *(also Eccl)*

infallibly [ɪnˈfæləblɪ] ADV unfehlbar; *work* fehlerfrei

infamous [ˈɪnfəməs] ADJ *(= notorious)* berüchtigt *(for* wegen); *area, bar* berüchtigt, verrufen; *(= shameful) person* niederträchtig, gemein, ruchlos *(old, liter)*; *deed, conduct* niederträchtig, infam, schändlich *(geh)*

infamy [ˈɪnfəmɪ] N a *(= notoriousness)* Verrufenheit *f*; *(= shamefulness)* Niedertracht *f*, Gemeinheit *f*; *(of deed, conduct)* Niedertracht *f*, Infamie *f*, Schändlichkeit *f (geh)* b *(= public disgrace)* Schande *f*

infancy [ˈɪnfənsɪ] N frühe Kindheit, Kindesalter *nt*; *(Jur)* Minderjährigkeit *f*; *(fig)* Anfangsstadium *nt*; **in early ~** in frühester Kindheit; **when radio was still in its ~** als das Radio noch in den Kinderschuhen steckte; **data processing is no longer in its ~** die Datenverarbeitung steckt nicht mehr in den Kinderschuhen *or* ist den Kinderschuhen entwachsen

infant [ˈɪnfənt] N *(= baby)* Säugling *m*; *(= young child)* Kleinkind *nt*; *(Jur)* Minderjährige(r) *mf*; **she teaches ~s** sie unterrichtet Grundschulkinder; **~ care** Säuglingspflege *f*; **~ class** *(Brit) erste und zweite Grundschulklasse*; **~ death** Säuglingstod *m*, Tod *m* im ersten Lebensjahr; **~ formula** Säuglingsnahrung *f*; **~ seat** Kindersitz *m* ADJ *(= new) democracy, industry etc* jung

infanta [ɪnˈfæntə] N Infantin *f*

infante [ɪnˈfæntɪ] N Infant *m*

infanticide [ɪnˈfæntɪsaɪd] N Kindesmord *m*, Kindestötung *f*; *(= person)* Kindesmörder(in) *m(f)*

infantile [ˈɪnfəntaɪl] ADJ a *(= childish)* kindisch, infantil b *(Med)* Kinder-

infantile paralysis N *(dated Med)* Kinderlähmung *f*

infantilize [ɪnˈfæntɪˌlaɪz] VT infantilisieren; *(= decide for)* bevormunden

infant mortality N Säuglingssterblichkeit *f*

infantry [ˈɪnfəntrɪ] N *(Mil)* Infanterie *f*, Fußtruppe *f (Hist)*

infantryman [ˈɪnfəntrɪmən] N *pl* **-men** [-mən] Infanterist *m*, Fußsoldat *m (Hist)*

infant school N *(Brit) Grundschule für die ersten beiden Jahrgänge*

infarct [ˈɪnfɑːkt] N *(Med)* Infarkt *m*

infarction [ɪnˈfɑːkʃən] N *(Med)* a *(= dead tissue)* Infarkt *m* b *(= forming of dead tissue)* Infarktbildung *f*

infatuated [ɪnˈfætjʊeɪtɪd] ADJ vernarrt, verknallt *(inf)* *(with* in *+acc)*; **to become ~ with sb** sich in jdn vernarren; **he's ~ with himself** er ist in sich selbst vernarrt

infatuation [ɪnˌfætjʊˈeɪʃən] N a *(= state)* Vernarrtheit *f (with* in *+acc)* b *(= object of infatuation)* Angebetete(r) *mf*

infect [ɪnˈfekt] VT a *wound, blood* infizieren; *(lit) person* anstecken, infizieren; *water* verseuchen, verunreinigen; *meat* verderben; **to be ~ed with** *or* **by an illness** sich mit einer Krankheit infiziert *or* angesteckt haben; **his wound became ~ed** seine Wunde entzündete sich; **her cold ~ed all her friends** sie steckte alle ihre Freunde mit ihrer Erkältung an; **this is likely to ~ the rest of the economy** das breitet sich wahrscheinlich auf den Rest der Wirtschaft aus b *(fig: with enthusiasm etc)* anstecken; **for a moment I was ~ed by her fear** für einen Augenblick ließ ich mich von ihrer Angst anstecken

infected [ɪnˈfektɪd] ADJ infiziert; *water, place* verseucht; *meat* verdorben

infection [ɪnˈfekʃən] N a *(= illness)* Infektion *f*, Entzündung *f* b *(= act of infecting)* Infektion *f*; *(of water)* Verseuchung *f*, Verunreinigung *f*

infectious [ɪnˈfekʃəs] ADJ a *(Med) disease* ansteckend, infektiös; **are you still ~?** besteht bei dir noch Ansteckungsgefahr? b *(fig) enthusiasm, laugh* ansteckend; *idea* zündend; *rhythm* mitreißend

infectious hepatitis N epidemische Hepatitis, Hepatitis *f* A

infectiousness [ɪnˈfekʃəsnɪs] N a *(Med)* **the ~ of this disease** die Ansteckungs- *or* Infektionsgefahr bei dieser Krankheit b *(fig)* **the ~ of the rhythm** der zündende Rhythmus; **the ~ of his laughter** sein ansteckendes Lachen; **the ~ of her enthusiasm** ihre mitreißende Begeisterung

infective [ɪnˈfektɪv] ADJ *(Med) agent* infektiös; **~ disease** Infektionskrankheit *f*

infeed [ˈɪnfiːd] N *(mechanism)* Vorschub *m*; *(action)* Zuführung *f*, Aufgabe *f* VT zuführen, aufgeben

infelicitous [ˌɪnfɪˈlɪsɪtəs] ADJ unglücklich; *remark etc* unangebracht, unpassend

infelicity [ˌɪnfɪˈlɪsɪtɪ] N *(form)* **the ~ of the expression** der unglücklich *or* ungeschickt gewählte Ausdruck

infer [ɪnˈfɜːʳ] VT a *(= deduce)* schließen, folgern *(from* aus); **nothing can be ~red from this** daraus kann man nichts schließen *or* folgern b *(= imply)* andeuten, zu verstehen geben

inferable [ɪnˈfɜːrəbl] ADJ ableitbar, zu folgern *pred*, zu schließen *pred*

inference [ˈɪnfərəns] N Schluss(folgerung *f*) *m*; **it has a tiny head and, by ~, a tiny brain** es hat einen winzigen Kopf und demzufolge ein winziges Gehirn; **he said, by ~, that …** implizit sagte er, dass …

inferential [ˌɪnfəˈrenʃəl] ADJ *statistics, thinking* auf Schlussfolgerungen beruhend

inferior [ɪnˈfɪərɪəʳ] ADJ a *(in quality)* minderwertig; *person* unterlegen; *(in rank)* untergeordnet, niedriger; *quality* geringer, minderwertig; *(Jur) court* untergeordnet; **an ~ workman** ein weniger guter Handwerker; **to be ~ to sth** *(in quality)* von minderer *or* geringerer Qualität sein als etw, gegen etw abfallen *or* nicht ankommen; **to be ~ to sb** jdm unterlegen sein; *(in rank)* jdm untergeordnet *or* nachgestellt sein; **he feels ~** er kommt sich *(dat)* unterlegen *or* minderwertig vor
b *(Typ)* **~ letter** tiefstehender Buchstabe
c *(Biol) order, species* niedriger
N **one's ~s** *(in social standing)* Leute *or* Personen *pl* aus einer niedrigeren Schicht; *(in rank)* seine Untergebenen *pl*

inferiority [ɪnˌfɪərɪˈɒrɪtɪ] N *(in quality)* Minderwertigkeit *f*; *(of person)* Unterlegenheit *f (to* gegenüber); *(in rank)* untergeordnete Stellung, niedrigere Stellung, niedrigerer Rang *(to* als)

inferiority complex N Minderwertigkeitskomplex *m*

infernal [ɪnˈfɜːnl] ADJ a *(lit)* Höllen-; **~ fire** Höllenfeuer *nt* b *(fig) cruelty, scheme* teuflisch; *weather* grässlich; *(inf) impudence, nuisance* verteufelt; *noise* höllisch; **this ~ machine** diese Höllenmaschine

infernally [ɪnˈfɜːnəlɪ] ADV *(inf)* teuflisch, verdammt *(inf)*

inferno [ɪnˈfɜːnəʊ] N *(= hell)* Hölle *f*, Inferno *nt*; *(= blazing house etc)* Flammenmeer *nt*; **a blazing ~** ein flammendes Inferno; **it's like an ~ in here** *(fig)* hier ist es wie in einem Brutofen

infertile [ɪnˈfɜːtaɪl] ADJ *soil, womb, person* unfruchtbar; *animal* fortpflanzungsunfähig; *mind* unergiebig, ideenlos

infertility [ˌɪnfɜːˈtɪlɪtɪ] N *(of soil, womb, person)* Unfruchtbarkeit *f*; *(of animal)* Fortpflanzungsunfähigkeit *f*; *(of mind)* Unergiebigkeit *f*, Ideenlosigkeit *f*

infertility clinic N Zentrum *nt* für Sterilitätsbehandlung

infertility treatment N Sterilitätsbehandlung *f*

infest [ɪnˈfest] VT *(rats, lice)* herfallen über *(+acc)*; *(plague also)* befallen; *(fig: unwanted people)* heimsuchen, verseuchen; *(crime, drugs etc)* verseuchen; **to be ~ed with rats** mit Ratten verseucht sein; **to be ~ed** *(with lice etc)* mit Ungeziefer verseucht sein

infestation [ˌɪnfesˈteɪʃən] N Verseuchung *f*; **an ~ of rats** eine Rattenplage

infidel [ˈɪnfɪdəl] N *(Hist, Rel)* Ungläubige(r) *mf*

infidelity [ˌɪnfɪˈdelɪtɪ] N Untreue *f*

in-fighting [ˈɪnfaɪtɪŋ] N *(Boxing)* Nahkampf *m*; *(fig)* interner Machtkampf

infill [ˈɪnfɪl] N *(Build)* Füllmaterial *nt*, Ausfüllung *f*

infiltrate [ˈɪnfɪltreɪt] VT a *(troops)* infiltrieren; *enemy lines* eindringen in *(+acc)*; *(Pol) organization* unterwandern; *spies, informer* einschleusen
b *(liquid)* einsickern in *(+acc)*, durchsickern in *(+acc)*, durchdringen; **to ~ a liquid into a substance** eine Flüssigkeit in eine Substanz einsickern *or* eindringen lassen
VI a *(Mil)* eindringen *(into* in *+acc)*; *(spy, informer)* eindringen, sich einschleusen *(into* in *+acc)*, unterwandern *(into +acc)*; *(fig: ideas)* infiltrieren, eindringen *(into* in *+acc)*
b *(liquid)* **to ~ into a substance** in eine Substanz eindringen *or* einsickern; **to ~ through sth** durch etw durchsickern

infiltration [ˌɪnfɪlˈtreɪʃən] N a *(Mil)* Infiltration *f*; *(Pol)* Unterwanderung *f*; **the ~ of spies** das Einschleusen von Spionen; **by ~ of the enemy's lines** durch Eindringen in die feindlichen Linien, durch Infiltration der feindlichen Linien b *(of liquid)* Eindringen *nt*, Durchsickern *nt*, Einsickern *nt*

infiltrator [ˈɪnfɪlˌtreɪtəʳ] N *(Mil)* Eindringling *m*; *(Pol)* Unterwanderer *m*; **~s** *(Mil)* Sickertruppe *f*

infinite [ˈɪnfɪnɪt] ADJ *(lit)* unendlich; *(fig also) care, trouble, joy, pleasure* grenzenlos; *possibilities* unendlich viele; *choice* unendlich groß, riesig; *knowledge* grenzenlos, unendlich groß; **an ~ amount of time/money** unendlich viel Zeit/Geld; **the organizers, in their ~ wisdom, planned the two events for the same day** die Organisatoren, klug wie sie waren, legten die beiden Veranstaltungen auf den gleichen Tag N **the ~** *(= space)* das Unendliche; *(= God)* der Unendliche

infinitely [ˈɪnfɪnɪtlɪ] ADV unendlich; *(fig also)* grenzenlos; *improved* ungeheuer; *better, worse* unendlich viel

infinitesimal [ˌɪnfɪnɪˈtesɪməl] ADJ unendlich klein, winzig; *(Math)* infinitesimal, unendlich klein

infinitesimal calculus N *(Math)* Infinitesimalrechnung *f*

infinitesimally [ˌɪnfɪnɪˈtesɪməlɪ] ADV *smaller, better, slower* nur ganz geringfügig; *small* zum Verschwinden

infinitive [ɪnˈfɪnɪtɪv] *(Gram)* ADJ Infinitiv-, infinitivisch; **~ form** Infinitivform *f* N Infinitiv *m*, Grundform *f*; **in the ~** im Infinitiv

infinitude [ɪnˈfɪnɪtjuːd] N *(= infinite number)* unbegrenztes Maß *(of* an *+dat)*; *(of facts, possibilities etc)* unendliches Maß *(of* an *+dat)*; *(of space)* unendliche Weite *(of +gen)*

infinity [ɪnˈfɪnɪtɪ] N *(lit)* Unendlichkeit *f*; *(fig also)* Grenzenlosigkeit *f*; *(Math)* das Unendliche; **to ~** (bis) ins Unendliche; **in ~** in der Unendlichkeit/im Unendlichen; **to focus on ~** *(Phot)* (auf) Unendlich einstellen; **an ~ of reasons/details/possibilities** unendlich viele Gründe/Einzelheiten/Möglichkeiten; **I have an ~ of things to do** ich habe unendlich viel zu tun

infirm [ɪnˈfɜːm] ADJ gebrechlich, schwach; **~ of purpose** *(liter)* willensschwach, wenig zielstrebig

infirmary [ɪnˈfɜːmərɪ] N *(= hospital)* Krankenhaus *nt*; *(in school etc)* Krankenzimmer *nt or* -stube *f*; *(in prison, barracks)* (Kranken)revier *nt*, Krankenstation *f*

infirmity [ɪnˈfɜːmɪtɪ] N Gebrechlichkeit *f*; **the infirmities of (old) age** die Altersgebrechen *pl*; **his ~ of purpose** *(liter)* seine Willensschwäche, sein Mangel *m* an Zielstrebigkeit

infix [ɪnˈfɪks] VT *idea* einprägen; *(Ling)* einfügen; **the idea is ~ed in his mind** diese Idee hat sich bei ihm festgesetzt N [ˈɪnfɪks] *(Ling)* Infix *nt*, Einfügung *f*

infixation [ˌɪnfɪkˈseɪʃən] N *(of idea)* Einprägen *nt*, Festsetzen *nt*; *(Ling)* Einfügung *f*

in flagrante delicto [ˌɪnfləˈgræntɪdɪˈlɪktəʊ] ADV in flagranti

inflame [ɪnˈfleɪm] VT **a** *(Med)* entzünden; **her eyes were ~d from crying** ihre Augen waren vom Weinen gerötet; **to become ~d** *(wound, eyes etc)* sich entzünden **b** *person* erzürnen, aufbringen; *feelings* entflammen, entfachen; *situation, public opinion* anheizen; **his speech ~d the people** seine Rede brachte die Menge auf; **they were ~d by the news** die Nachricht brachte sie auf; **~d with passion he ...** von glühender Leidenschaft erfasst, er ...; **he was ~d with rage/jealousy** *etc* er glühte vor Zorn/Eifersucht *etc*

inflammable [ɪnˈflæməbl] ADJ *(lit)* feuergefährlich, (leicht) entzündbar; *fabric* leicht entflammbar; *(fig) temperament* explosiv, leicht reizbar; *situation* brisant, gereizt; **"highly ~"** „Vorsicht Feuergefahr", „feuergefährlich" N feuergefährlicher *or* leicht brennbarer Stoff

inflammation [ˌɪnfləˈmeɪʃən] N **a** *(Med)* Entzündung *f* **b** *(fig, of passion, anger etc)* Aufstacheln *nt*, Aufstachelung *f*

inflammatory [ɪnˈflæmətərɪ] ADJ **a** *rhetoric, statement* aufrührerisch, aufwieglerisch; **~ speech/pamphlet** Hetzrede/-schrift *f* **b** *(Med)* entzündlich; **~ reaction** Entzündungsreaktion *f*

inflatable [ɪnˈfleɪtɪbl] ADJ aufblasbar; **~ dinghy** Schlauchboot *nt*; **~ goods** Aufblasartikel *pl* N *(= boat)* Gummiboot *nt*

inflate [ɪnˈfleɪt] VT **a** *(lit)* aufpumpen; *(by mouth)* aufblasen **b** *(Econ) prices, bill* hochtreiben; **to ~ the currency** die Inflation anheizen, den Geldumlauf steigern; **to ~ the budget** *(for a project etc)* den Etat aufblähen; *(Econ)* inflationäre Haushaltspolitik betreiben **c** *(fig)* steigern, erhöhen; *sb's ego* aufblähen, steigern VI **a** *(lit)* sich mit Luft füllen **b** *(fig: price)* rapide steigen

inflated [ɪnˈfleɪtɪd] ADJ **a** *(lit) (with pump)* aufgepumpt; *(by mouth)* aufgeblasen **b** *(fig) price, salary* überhöht; *pride* übersteigert, übertrieben; *ego* übersteigert; *style, rhetoric* geschwollen, hochtrabend; **to have an ~ opinion of oneself** ein übertriebenes Selbstbewusstsein haben

inflation [ɪnˈfleɪʃən] N **a** *(Econ)* Inflation *f*; **~ rate** Inflationsrate *f*; **to fight ~** die Inflation bekämpfen **b** *(= act of inflating) (with pump)* Aufpumpen *nt*; *(by mouth)* Aufblasen *nt*; *(Econ: of prices)* Steigern *nt*, Hochtreiben *nt*; *(fig)* Steigern *nt*, Erhöhen *nt*; *(of ego)* Aufblähen *nt*

inflationary [ɪnˈfleɪʃənərɪ] ADJ *impact, consequences* inflationär; **~ pressures/spiral/politics** Inflationsdruck *m*/-spirale *f*/-politik *f*

inflationism [ɪnˈfleɪʃənɪzəm] N Inflationspolitik *f*

inflation-proof [ɪnˈfleɪʃənˌpruːf] ADJ inflationssicher, inflationsgeschützt

inflect [ɪnˈflekt] VT **a** *(Gram)* flektieren, beugen **b** *voice* modulieren VI *(Gram)* flektierbar *or* veränderlich sein, gebeugt werden

inflected [ɪnˈflektɪd] ADJ *(Gram) form, ending* flektiert, gebeugt; *language* flektierend

inflection [ɪnˈflekʃən] N = **inflexion**

inflexibility [ɪnˌfleksɪˈbɪlɪtɪ] N *(lit)* Unbiegsamkeit *f*, Starrheit *f*; *(fig)* Unbeugsamkeit *f*, Sturheit *f (pej)*

inflexible [ɪnˈfleksəbl] ADJ *(lit) substance, object* unbiegsam, starr; *(fig) person, attitude, opinion* unbeugsam, inflexibel, stur *(pej)*

inflexion [ɪnˈflekʃən] N **a** *(Gram, of word, language)* Flexion *f*, Beugung *f* **b** *(of voice)* Tonfall *m*

inflexional [ɪnˈflekʃənl] ADJ *(Gram)* Flexions-; **~ ending** Flexionsendung *f*

inflict [ɪnˈflɪkt] VT *punishment, fine* verhängen (*on, upon* gegen), auferlegen (*on or upon sb* jdm); *suffering, damage, pain* zufügen (*on or upon sb* jdm); *wound, defeat* zufügen, beibringen (*on or upon sb* jdm); **to ~ oneself on sb** sich jdm aufdrängen; **the enemy ~ed heavy casualties on us** der Feind fügte uns hohe Verluste zu

infliction [ɪnˈflɪkʃən] N **a** *(= act) (of punishment, fine)* Verhängung *f* (*on, upon* gegen), Auferlegung *f*; *(of suffering, damage, pain)* Zufügen *nt*; *(of wound)* Zufügen *nt*, Beibringen *nt* **b** *(= misfortune)* Plage *f*, Kreuz *nt*

in-flight [ˈɪnflaɪt] ADJ *entertainment, refuelling* während des Fluges; *service* an Bord; **~ magazine** Bordmagazin *nt*

inflorescence [ˌɪnflɔːˈresəns] N Blütenstand *m*

inflow [ˈɪnfləʊ] N **a** *(of water, air) (= action)* Zustrom *m*, Einfließen *nt*, Zufließen *nt*; *(= quantity)* Zuflussmenge *f*; *(= place)* Zufluss *m*; **~ pipe** Zuflussrohr *nt* **b** *(fig) (of foreign currency, goods)* Zustrom *m*; *(of people)* Zustrom *m*, Andrang *m*; *(of ideas etc)* Eindringen *nt*

influence [ˈɪnflʊəns] N Einfluss *m* (*over* auf *+acc*); **to have an ~ on sb/sth** *(person)* Einfluss auf jdn/etw haben; *(fact, weather etc also)* Auswirkungen *pl* auf jdn/etw haben; **the weather had a great ~ on the number of voters** das Wetter beeinflusste die Zahl der Wähler stark; **the book had** *or* **was a great ~ on him** das Buch hat ihn stark beeinflusst; **to have a great deal of ~ with sb** großen Einfluss bei jdm haben; **he was a great ~ in ...** er war ein bedeutender Faktor bei ...; **he's been a bad ~ on you** er war ein schlechter Einfluss für Sie; **to bring ~ to bear on sb, to exert an ~ on sb** Einfluss auf jdn ausüben; **to use one's ~** seinen Einfluss einsetzen; **you have to have ~ to get a job here** Sie müssen schon einigen Einfluss haben, wenn Sie hier eine Stelle haben wollen; **a man of ~** eine einflussreiche Person; **under the ~ of sb/sth** unter jds Einfluss/dem Einfluss einer Sache; **under the ~ of drink/drugs** unter Alkohol-/Drogeneinfluss, unter Alkohol-/Drogeneinwirkung; **under the ~** *(inf)* betrunken; **the changes were due to American ~** die Veränderungen sind auf amerikanische Einflüsse zurückzuführen; **one of my early ~s was Beckett** einer der Schriftsteller, die mich schon früh beeinflusst haben, war Beckett
VT beeinflussen; **to be easily ~d** leicht beeinflussbar *or* zu beeinflussen sein

influential [ˌɪnflʊˈenʃəl] ADJ einflussreich; **these factors were ~ in my decision** diese Faktoren haben meine Entscheidung beeinflusst

influenza [ˌɪnflʊˈenzə] N Grippe *f*

influx [ˈɪnflʌks] N **a** *(of capital, shares, foreign goods)* Zufuhr *f*; *(of people)* Zustrom *m*, Andrang *m*; *(of ideas etc)* Zufluss *m* **b** = **inflow a**

info [ˈɪnfəʊ] N *(inf)* = **information**

infobahn [ˈɪnfəʊbɑːn] N **the ~** die Datenautobahn

infomercial [ˈɪnfəʊmɜːʃəl] N *als Informationssendung getarntes Werbevideo*, Infomercial *nt*

inform [ɪnˈfɔːm] ✪ 12.3, 24.4 VT **a** *person* informieren (*about* über *+acc*), unterrichten; **to ~ sb of sth** jdn von etw unterrichten, jdn über etw informieren; **to ~ sb (that) ...** jdn informieren, dass ...; **I am pleased to ~ you that ...** ich freue mich, Ihnen mitteilen zu können *or* Sie davon in Kenntnis setzen zu können *(form)*, dass ...; **to ~ the police** die Polizei verständigen *or* benachrichtigen *or* informieren; **to keep sb/oneself ~ed** jdn/sich auf dem Laufenden halten (*of* über *+acc*); **to ~ oneself about sth** sich über etw *(acc)* informieren; **until we are better ~ed** bis wir Näheres wissen *or* besser Bescheid wissen *or* genauer informiert sind; **she is better ~ed than most of her colleagues** sie ist besser informiert als die meisten ihrer Kollegen; **why was I not ~ed?** warum wurde mir das nicht mitgeteilt?, warum wurde ich nicht (darüber) informiert?; **I should like to be ~ed just as soon as he arrives** unterrichten Sie mich bitte sofort von seiner Ankunft, informieren Sie mich bitte sofort über seine Ankunft
b *(liter, = permeate)* durchdringen, erfüllen
VI **to ~ against** *or* **on sb** jdn anzeigen *or* denunzieren *(pej)*

informal [ɪnˈfɔːməl] ADJ **a** *(esp Pol: = not official) meeting, talks* nicht formell, nicht förmlich; *visit* inoffiziell, nicht förmlich; *arrangement* inoffiziell **b** *(= simple, without ceremony) meeting, gathering, party, conversation, atmosphere* zwanglos, ungezwungen; *manner, clothes, tone also* leger; *language, speech* ungezwungen, informell; *restaurant* gemütlich; **the ~ use of "du"** die vertraute Anrede „du"; **"dress ~"** „zwanglose Kleidung"; **he is very ~** er ist sehr leger

informality [ˌɪnfɔːˈmælɪtɪ] N **a** *(esp Pol: = unofficial nature) (of meeting, talks)* nicht formeller *or* förmlicher Charakter; *(of visit, arrangement)* inoffizieller Charakter **b** *(= simplicity, lack of ceremony) (of meeting, party, conversation, atmosphere)* Zwanglosigkeit *f*, Ungezwungenheit *f*; *(of manner, tone also)* legere Art; *(of language, speech)* informeller Charakter *or* Ton; *(of restaurant)* Gemütlichkeit *f*

informally [ɪnˈfɔːməlɪ] ADV *(= unofficially)* inoffiziell; *(= casually, without ceremony)* zwanglos, ungezwungen

informant [ɪnˈfɔːmənt] N **a** Informant(in) *m(f)*; **according to my ~ the book is out of print** wie man mir mitteilt *or* berichtet, ist das Buch vergriffen **b** **(police) ~** Polizeispitzel *m*

informatics [ˌɪnfəˈmætɪks] N *sing* Informatik *f*

information [ˌɪnfəˈmeɪʃən] N **a** Auskunft *f*, Informationen *pl*; **a piece of ~** eine Auskunft *or* Information; **for your ~** zu Ihrer Information *or* Kenntnisnahme *(form)*; *(indignantly)* damit Sie es wissen; **his ~ on the subject is most extensive** sein Wissen auf diesem Gebiet ist äußerst umfassend; **to give sb ~ about** *or* **on sb/sth** jdm Auskunft *or* Informationen über jdn/etw geben; **to get ~ about** *or* **on sb/sth** sich über jdn/etw informieren, über jdn/etw Erkundigungen einziehen; **to ask for ~ on** *or* **about sb/sth** um Auskunft *or* Informationen über jdn/etw bitten; **"information"** „Auskunft"; **I have ~ that they will be arriving today** mir liegen Informationen darüber vor, dass sie heute ankommen; **we have no ~ about that** wir wissen darüber nicht Bescheid; **my ~ is that he is unreliable** soweit ich informiert bin, ist er unzuverlässig; **until further ~ is available** bevor wir nichts Näheres wissen; **for further ~ please contact this number ...** Näheres erfahren Sie unter Telefonnummer ...; **what ~ do we have on Kowalsky?** welche Informationen besitzen wir über Kowalsky?; **where did you get your ~?** woher haben Sie diese Kenntnisse *or* Informationen?; **detailed ~** Einzelheiten *pl*
b *(Comput: = information content)* Information *f*; **~ fatigue syndrome** *durch Informationsflut bedingtes Ermüdungssyndrom*

informational [ˌɪnfəˈmeɪʃənl] ADJ informationell; **~ needs** Informationsbedürfnisse *pl*; **~ programme** *(TV)* Informationssendung *f*

information: **information bulletin** N Mitteilungsblatt *nt*; **information bureau** N Auskunft(sbüro *nt*) *f*, Verkehrsbüro *nt*; **information content** N Informationsgehalt *m*; **information desk** N Information *f*, Informationsschalter *m*; **information exchange** N Informationsaustausch *m*; **information highway** N *(Comput)* Datenautobahn *f*; **information officer** N Auskunftsbeamte(r) *m*/-beamtin *f*; **information pack** N Informationsmaterial *nt*; **information processing** N Informationsverarbeitung *f*; **information question** N *(Ling)* Ergänzungsfrage *f*; **information retrieval** N Informations- *or* Datenabruf *m*; **information sciences** PL Informatik *f*; **information scientist** N Informatiker(in) *m(f)*; **information storage** N Datenspeicherung *f*;

information superhighway N Datenautobahn *f*; **information technology** N Informationstechnik *f*; **information theory** N Informationstheorie *f*

informative [ɪnˈfɔːmətɪv] ADJ aufschlussreich, informativ *(geh)*; *book, lecture also* lehrreich; **he's not very ~ about his plans** er ist nicht sehr mitteilsam, was seine Pläne betrifft

informed [ɪnˈfɔːmd] ADJ *(= having information) observer, source* informiert, (gut) unterrichtet; *guess, choice* fundiert; *(= educated)* gebildet

informer [ɪnˈfɔːməʳ] N Informant(in) *m(f)*, Denunziant(in) *m(f) (pej)*; **police ~** Polizeispitzel *m*; **to turn ~** seine Mittäter verraten

infotainment [ˌɪnfəʊˈteɪnmənt] N *(Brit TV)* Infotainment *nt*

infraction [ɪnˈfrækʃən] N **a** *(= infringement)* Verletzung *f*, Verstoß *m* **b** *(Med)* Infraktion *f (spec)*, Knickbruch *m*

infra dig [ˈɪnfrəˈdɪg] ADJ *(inf)* unter meiner/seiner *etc* Würde

infrangible [ɪnˈfrændʒɪbl] ADJ *(form) (= unbreakable)* unzerbrechlich; *(fig: = inviolable)* unverletzlich

infrared [ˈɪnfrəˈred] ADJ infrarot

infrastructure [ˈɪnfrəˌstrʌktʃəʳ] N Infrastruktur *f*

infrequency [ɪnˈfriːkwənsɪ] N Seltenheit *f*

infrequent [ɪnˈfriːkwənt] ADJ selten; **at ~ intervals** in großen Abständen; **her mistakes are so ~** sie macht so selten Fehler

infrequently [ɪnˈfriːkwəntlɪ] ADV selten

infringe [ɪnˈfrɪndʒ] VT verstoßen gegen; *law also* verletzen, übertreten; *copyright also* verletzen; *rights* verletzen, eingreifen in *(+acc)* VI **to ~ (up)on sb's rights** in jds Rechte *(acc)* eingreifen, jds Rechte verletzen

infringement [ɪnˈfrɪndʒmənt] N **a an ~ (of a rule)** ein Regelverstoß *m*; **~ of the law** Gesetzesverletzung *or* -übertretung *f*; **~ of a patent** Patentverletzung *f*; **~ of copyright** Verletzung *f* des Urheberrechts; **the ~ of sb's rights** die Verletzung von jds Rechten, Übergriffe *pl* auf jds Rechte *(acc)* **b** *(of privacy)* Eingriff *m* (*of* in +*acc*)

infuriate [ɪnˈfjʊərɪeɪt] VT wütend *or* rasend machen, zur Raserei bringen; **to be/get ~d** wütend *or* rasend sein/werden

infuriating [ɪnˈfjʊərɪeɪtɪŋ] ADJ (äußerst) ärgerlich; **an ~ habit** eine Unsitte; **an ~ person** ein Mensch, der einen zur Raserei bringen kann *or* der einen rasend *or* wütend machen kann

infuriatingly [ɪnˈfjʊərɪeɪtɪŋlɪ] ADV aufreizend; **she's ~ slow/clumsy** sie ist zum Verzweifeln langsam/so unbeholfen, dass es zum Verzweifeln ist; **~, she couldn't say a word against him** es machte sie rasend, dass sie kein Wort gegen ihn sagen konnte

infuse [ɪnˈfjuːz] VT **a** *courage, enthusiasm etc* einflößen, geben (*into sb* jdm); **~d with excitement** von Aufregung erfüllt **b** *(Cook) tea, herbs* aufbrühen, aufgießen VI ziehen

infuser [ɪnˈfjuːzəʳ] N Tee-Ei *nt*

infusion [ɪnˈfjuːʒən] N **a** *(of hope etc)* Einflößen *nt*; **an ~ of cash/capital** eine Finanzspritze **b** *(Cook)* Aufguss *m*; *(tea-like)* Tee *m*; **an ~ of rosehip tea** Hagebuttentee *m* **c** *(Med)* Infusion *f*

ingenious [ɪnˈdʒiːnɪəs] ADJ genial; *person also* erfinderisch, geschickt, findig; *idea, method also* glänzend, ingeniös *(geh)*; *device, instrument also* raffiniert, geschickt

ingeniously [ɪnˈdʒiːnɪəslɪ] ADV genial, glänzend

ingeniousness [ɪnˈdʒiːnɪəsnɪs] N = **ingenuity**

ingénue [ˌænʒeɪˈnjuː] N naives Mädchen; *(Theat)* Naive *f*

ingenuity [ˌɪndʒɪˈnjuːɪtɪ] N Genialität *f*; *(of person also)* Einfallsreichtum *m*, Findigkeit *f*; *(of idea, method also)* Brillanz *f*; *(of device, instrument also)* Raffiniertheit *f*

ingenuous [ɪnˈdʒenjʊəs] ADJ **a** *(= candid)* offen, aufrichtig, unbefangen **b** *(= naïve)* naiv

ingenuously [ɪnˈdʒenjʊəslɪ] ADV offen, unbefangen; *(= naïvely)* naiv

ingenuousness [ɪnˈdʒenjʊəsnɪs] N **a** *(= candour)* Offenheit *f*, Aufrichtigkeit *f*, Unbefangenheit *f* **b** *(= naïveté)* Naivität *f*

ingest [ɪnˈdʒest] VT *(Biol)* zu sich nehmen, aufnehmen

ingesta [ɪnˈdʒestə] PL *(Biol, Med)* Ingesta *pl (spec)*, aufgenommene Nahrung

ingestion [ɪnˈdʒestʃən] N *(Biol)* Nahrungsaufnahme *f*

inglenook [ˈɪŋgəlnʊk] N Kaminecke *f*

inglorious [ɪnˈglɔːrɪəs] ADJ unrühmlich, unehrenhaft; *defeat* schmählich, ruhmlos

ingloriously [ɪnˈglɔːrɪəslɪ] ADV unrühmlich

ingoing [ˈɪngəʊɪŋ] ADJ *mail* eingehend, einlaufend; **~ tenant** neuer Mieter, neue Mieterin

ingot [ˈɪŋgət] N Barren *m*; **steel ~** Stahlblock *m*

ingrained [ˌɪnˈgreɪnd] ADJ **a** *(fig) habit* fest, eingefleischt; *prejudice* tief verwurzelt *or* eingewurzelt; *belief* fest verankert, unerschütterlich; **to be (deeply) ~** fest verwurzelt sein **b** *dirt* tief eingedrungen, tief sitzend *(attr)*; **the dirt was deeply ~ in the carpet** der Schmutz hatte sich tief im Teppich festgesetzt; **hands ~ with dirt** Hände, bei denen sich der Schmutz in den Poren festgesetzt hat

ingrate [ˈɪngreɪt] N undankbarer Mensch, Undankbare(r) *mf (old, liter)*

ingratiate [ɪnˈgreɪʃɪeɪt] VR **to ~ oneself with sb** sich bei jdm einschmeicheln

ingratiating [ɪnˈgreɪʃɪeɪtɪŋ] ADJ *person, speech, manner* schmeichlerisch, schöntuerisch; *smile* süßlich

ingratiatingly [ɪnˈgreɪʃɪeɪtɪŋlɪ] ADV schmeichlerisch; *smile* süßlich

ingratitude [ɪnˈgrætɪtjuːd] N Undank *m*; **sb's ~** jds Undankbarkeit *f*

ingredient [ɪnˈgriːdɪənt] N Bestandteil *m*, Ingredienz *f (spec)*; *(for recipe)* Zutat *f*; **all the ~s for success** alles, was man zum Erfolg braucht; **the ~s of a man's character** alles, was den Charakter eines Menschen ausmacht

ingress [ˈɪngres] N *(form)* Zutritt *m*, Eintritt *m*; **no right of ~** Zutritt verboten; **to have free ~** Recht auf freien Zugang haben

in-group [ˈɪngruːp] N maßgebliche Leute *pl*, Spitze *f*; *(Sociol)* In-Group *f*

ingrowing [ˈɪngrəʊɪŋ] ADJ *(Med) toenail* eingewachsen

ingrown [ˈɪngrəʊn] ADJ *toenail* eingewachsen; *(= innate)* angeboren; *(= self-contained)* (in sich selbst) zurückgezogen

inguinal [ˈɪŋgwɪnəl] ADJ *(Med)* Leisten-, inguinal *(spec)*; **~ hernia** Leistenbruch *m*

inhabit [ɪnˈhæbɪt] VT bewohnen; *(animals)* leben in *(+dat)*

inhabitable [ɪnˈhæbɪtəbl] ADJ bewohnbar

inhabitant [ɪnˈhæbɪtənt] N *(of house, burrow etc)* Bewohner(in) *m(f)*; *(of island, town also)* Einwohner(in) *m(f)*

inhalation [ˌɪnhəˈleɪʃən] N *(Med)* Inhalation *f*; **smoke ~** Einatmen *nt* von Rauch

inhalator [ˈɪnhəleɪtəʳ] N Inhalationsapparat *m*

inhale [ɪnˈheɪl] VT einatmen; *(Med)* inhalieren VI *(in smoking)* Lungenzüge machen, inhalieren; **do you ~?** rauchen Sie auf Lunge?

inhaler [ɪnˈheɪləʳ] N Inhalationsapparat *m*

inharmonious [ˌɪnhɑːˈməʊnɪəs] ADJ unharmonisch

inhere [ɪnˈhɪəʳ] VI **to ~ in sth** einer Sache *(dat)* innewohnen

inherent [ɪnˈhɪərənt] ADJ innewohnend, eigen, inhärent *(esp Philos)* (*to, in* +*dat*); **the ~ hardness of diamonds** die den Diamanten eigene Härte; **instincts ~ in all animals** allen Tieren inhärente *or* eigene Instinkte

inherently [ɪnˈhɪərəntlɪ] ADV von Natur aus

inherit [ɪnˈherɪt] VT *(lit, fig)* erben; **the problems which we ~ed from the last government** die Probleme, die uns die letzte Regierung hinterlassen *or* vererbt hat VI erben; **to ~ from sb** jdn beerben

inheritable [ɪnˈherɪtəbl] ADJ *(lit, fig)* erblich; *goods* vererbbar

inheritance [ɪnˈherɪtəns] N Erbe *nt (also fig)*, Erbschaft *f*; **it passed to him through** *or* **by ~** er hat es durch eine Erbschaft bekommen; **~ tax** Erbschaftssteuer *f*

inherited [ɪnˈherɪtɪd] ADJ *wealth, property* geerbt, ererbt; *qualities, disease* ererbt

inhibit [ɪnˈhɪbɪt] VT hemmen *(also Psych, Sci)*; *ability, performance* beeinträchtigen; **to ~ sb from doing sth** jdn daran hindern, etw zu tun; **don't let me ~ you** haben Sie meinetwegen keine Hemmungen; **don't let my presence ~ the discussion** lassen Sie sich durch meine Anwesenheit in Ihrer Diskussion nicht stören

inhibited [ɪnˈhɪbɪtɪd] ADJ gehemmt; **to be ~** Hemmungen haben, gehemmt sein

inhibition [ˌɪnhɪˈbɪʃən] N Hemmung *f (also Psych, Sci)*; **he has no ~s about speaking French** er hat keine Hemmungen, Französisch zu sprechen; **to lose one's ~s** seine Hemmungen verlieren; **~ threshold** Hemmschwelle *f*

inhibitory [ɪnˈhɪbɪtərɪ] ADJ *(Psych)* hemmend; *(Physiol also)* behindernd

inhospitable [ˌɪnhɒˈspɪtəbl] ADJ ungastlich; *climate, terrain, region* unwirtlich

inhospitably [ˌɪnhɒˈspɪtəblɪ] ADV ungastlich

inhospitality [ˈɪnˌhɒspɪˈtælɪtɪ] N Ungastlichkeit *f*, mangelnde Gastfreundschaft; *(of climate)* Unwirtlichkeit *f*

in-house [ˈɪnhaʊs] ADJ hausintern; *staff* im Haus; *jobs, work* im Hause zu erledigend *attr or* zu erledigen *pred* [ɪnˈhaʊs] ADV hausintern

inhuman [ɪnˈhjuːmən] ADJ *(lit) monster, shape* nicht menschlich; *(fig) conditions, treatment* unmenschlich

inhumane [ˌɪnhjuːˈmeɪn] ADJ inhuman; *treatment, housing* menschenunwürdig

inhumaneness [ˌɪnhjuːˈmeɪnnɪs] N Inhumanität *f*; *(of treatment, housing)* Menschenunwürdigkeit *f*

inhumanity [ˌɪnhjuːˈmænɪtɪ] N Unmenschlichkeit *f*; **man's ~ to man** die Unmenschlichkeit der Menschen untereinander

inhumation [ˌɪnhjuːˈmeɪʃən] N *(form)* Beisetzung *f (form)*

inhume [ɪnˈhjuːm] VT *(form)* beisetzen *(form)*

inimical [ɪˈnɪmɪkəl] ADJ *(form) (= hostile)* feindselig (*to* gegen); *(= injurious)* abträglich (*to* +*dat*)

inimitable [ɪˈnɪmɪtəbl] ADJ unnachahmlich

iniquitous [ɪˈnɪkwɪtəs] ADJ ungeheuerlich

iniquity [ɪˈnɪkwɪtɪ] N *(no pl: = wickedness)* Ungeheuerlichkeit *f*; *(= sin)* Missetat *f*; *(= crime)* Gräueltat *f* → **den**

initial [ɪˈnɪʃəl] ADJ **a** anfänglich, Anfangs-; **my ~ reaction** meine anfängliche Reaktion; **in the ~ stages** im Anfangsstadium; **according to ~ reports** ersten Berichten zufolge; **~ cost** Startkosten *pl* **b** *(Ling)* anlautend; **~ sound** Anlaut *m* **c** *(Typ)* **~ letter** Anfangsbuchstabe *m*, Initiale *f* N Initiale *f*; *(Typ also)* Anfangsbuchstabe *m*; **to sign a letter with one's ~s** seine Initialen *or (Pol)* Paraphe unter einen Brief setzen; *(Comm)* einen Brief abzeichnen *or* mit seinem Namenszeichen versehen VT *letter, document* mit seinen Initialen unterzeichnen; *(Comm)* abzeichnen; *(Pol)* paraphieren

initialization [ɪˌnɪʃəlaɪˈzeɪʃən] N *(Comput)* Initialisierung *f*

initialize [ɪˈnɪʃəlaɪz] VT *(Comput)* initialisieren

initially [ɪˈnɪʃəlɪ] ADV anfangs, zu *or* am Anfang; *(Ling)* im Anlaut

initial public offering N *(St Ex)* erstes öffentliches Zeichnungsangebot

initiate [ɪˈnɪʃɪeɪt] VT **a** *(= set in motion)* den Anstoß geben zu, initiieren *(geh)*; *negotiations* einleiten; *discussion* eröffnen; *project* in die Wege leiten; *legislation* einbringen; **to ~ proceedings against sb** *(Jur)* gegen jdn einen Prozess anstrengen **b** *(= formally admit) (into club etc)* feierlich aufnehmen; *(in tribal society) adolescents* initiieren **c** *(= instruct: in knowledge, skill)* einweihen; **to ~ sb into sth** jdn in etw *(acc)* einführen **N** *(in club etc)* Neuaufgenommene(r) *mf*; *(in tribal society)* Initiierte(r) *mf*; *(in knowledge)* Eingeweihte(r) *mf*

initiation [ɪˌnɪʃɪ'eɪʃən] N **a** *(of project, fashion etc)* Initiierung *f (geh)*; *(of negotiations)* Einleitung *f*; *(of discussions)* Eröffnung *f* **b** *(into society)* Aufnahme *f*; *(as tribal member)* Initiation *f* **c** *(into branch of knowledge)* Einweihung *f*

initiation ceremony N Aufnahmezeremonie *f*

initiation rite N Initiationsritus *m*

initiative [ɪ'nɪʃətɪv] N Initiative *f*; **to take the ~** die Initiative ergreifen; **on one's own ~** aus eigener Initiative; **to have ~** Initiative haben; **to have the ~** überlegen sein; **to lose the ~** seine Überlegenheit verlieren; **it was an ~ test for me** das hat meine Initiative auf die Probe gestellt

initiator [ɪ'nɪʃieɪtə'] N Initiator(in) *m(f)*

initiatory [ɪ'nɪʃətərɪ] ADJ *(= introductory)* einleitend, einführend

inject [ɪn'dʒekt] VT (ein)spritzen; *drugs, heroin* spritzen; *gas* einblasen; *(fig) comment* einwerfen; *money into economy* pumpen; **to ~ sb with sth** *(Med)* jdm etw spritzen *or* injizieren; **I wanted to ~ some humour into my speech** ich wollte etwas Humor in meine Rede bringen; **they are trying to ~ some life into the economy** sie versuchen, die Wirtschaft neu zu beleben; **he ~ed new life into the team** er brachte neues Leben in das Team

injection [ɪn'dʒekʃən] N *(= act)* Einspritzung *f*; *(of gas)* Einblasen *nt*; *(= substance injected)* Injektion *f*, Spritze *f*; **to give sb an ~** jdm eine Injektion *or* Spritze geben; **to give sth by ~** etw spritzen; **the ~ of more money into the economy** eine größere Finanzspritze für die Wirtschaft; **a £250 million cash ~** eine Finanzspritze von 250 Millionen Pfund; **the team needed an ~ of new life** die Mannschaft brauchte frisches Blut; **~ moulding** Spritzguss *m*; **~ syringe** Injektionsspritze *f*

injector [ɪn'dʒektə'] N Einspritzpumpe *f*

injudicious ADJ, **injudiciously** ADV [ˌɪndʒʊ'dɪʃəs, -lɪ] unklug

injunction [ɪn'dʒʌŋkʃən] N Anordnung *f*; *(Jur)* gerichtliche Verfügung; **to take out a court ~** eine gerichtliche Verfügung erwirken

injure ['ɪndʒə'] VT **a** *(lit)* verletzen; **to ~ one's leg** sich *(dat)* das Bein verletzen, sich *(acc)* am Bein verletzen; **the horse was ~d** das Pferd verletzte sich; **how many were ~d?, how many ~d were there?** wie viele Verletzte gab es?; **the ~d** die Verletzten *pl* **b** *(fig) (= offend) sb, sb's feelings* verletzen, kränken; *(= damage) reputation* schaden *(+dat)*; **his ~d reputation** sein geschädigter Ruf; **the ~d party** *(Jur)* der/die Geschädigte; **~d innocence** gekränkte Unschuld

injurious [ɪn'dʒʊərɪəs] ADJ schädlich; **to be ~ to sb/sth** jdm/einer Sache schaden *or* schädlich sein; **~ to health** gesundheitsschädigend *or* -schädlich

injury ['ɪndʒərɪ] N Verletzung *f (to +gen)*; *(fig also)* Kränkung *f (to +gen)*; **to do sb/oneself an ~** jdn/sich verletzen; **to play ~ time** *(Brit Sport) or* **~ overtime** *(US Sport)* nachspielen, Nachspielzeit haben; **they are into ~ time** *(Brit Sport) or* **~ overtime** *(US Sport)* das ist Nachspielzeit; **~ benefit** *(Brit)* Unfall- *or* Krankengeld *nt*

injury-prone ['ɪndʒərɪˌprəʊn] ADJ verletzungsanfällig

injustice [ɪn'dʒʌstɪs] N *(= unfairness, inequality)* Ungerechtigkeit *f*; *(= violation of sb's rights)* Unrecht *nt no pl*; **to do sb an ~** jdm unrecht tun; **if a real ~ has been done to you ...** wenn Ihnen wirklich Unrecht geschehen ist ...

ink [ɪŋk] **N** Tinte *(also Zool) f*; *(Art)* Tusche *f*; *(Typ)* Druckfarbe *f*; *(for newsprint)* Druckerschwärze *f*; **written in ~** mit Tinte geschrieben; **a sketch in ~** eine Tuschzeichnung **VT** mit Tinte beschmieren; *(Typ)* einfärben

▶ **ink in** VT *sep outline, writing* mit Tinte *or (Art)* Tusche nachziehen; *(= fill in) shape* mit Tinte *or (Art)* Tusche ausmalen *or* ausfüllen

▶ **ink out** VT *sep* mit Tinte übermalen

▶ **ink over** VT *sep* mit Tinte *or (Art)* Tusche nachzeichnen

ink *in cpds* Tinten-; *(Art)* Tusch-; **ink bag** N *(Zool)* Tintenbeutel *m*; **inkblot** N Tintenklecks *m*; **~ test** *(Psych)* Rorschachtest *m*; **ink bottle** N Tintenfass *nt*; **ink drawing** N Tuschzeichnung *f*; **ink eraser** N Tintenradiergummi *m*, Tintenradierer *m (inf)*; **ink-jet (printer)** N Tintenstrahldrucker *m*

inkling ['ɪŋklɪŋ] N *(= vague idea)* dunkle Ahnung; **he didn't have an ~** er hatte nicht die leiseste Ahnung *or* keinen blassen Schimmer *(inf)*; **to give sb an ~** jdm eine andeutungsweise Vorstellung geben; **there was no ~ of the disaster to come** nichts deutete auf die bevorstehende Katastrophe hin

ink: **ink pad** N Stempelkissen *nt*; **inkpot** N Tintenfass *nt*; **inkstain** N Tintenfleck *m*; **inkstained** ADJ tintenbeschmiert; **inkstand** N Tintenfass *nt (mit Halter für Federn etc)*; **inkwell** N Tintenfass *nt (in eine Tischplatte eingelassen)*

inky ['ɪŋkɪ] ADJ *(+er)* **a** *(lit)* tintenbeschmiert, voller Tinte; **~ fingers** Tintenfinger *pl*; **~ newspaper** von Druckerschwärze strotzende Zeitung; **~ smell** Geruch *m* von Druckerschwärze **b** *(fig) darkness, night* tintenschwarz; *blue, black* tintig

inky cap N *(Bot)* Tintling *m*, Tintenpilz *m*

inlaid [ɪn'leɪd] *ptp of* **inlay** ADJ eingelegt *(with* mit); **~ table** Tisch *m* mit Einlegearbeit; **~ work** Einlegearbeit *f*

inland ['ɪnlænd] **ADJ** **a** *waterway* binnenländisch; **~ navigation** Binnenschifffahrt *f*; **~ town** Stadt *f* im Landesinneren **b** *(= domestic) produce* inländisch; **~ mail** Inlandspost *f*; **~ trade** Binnenhandel *m* **ADV** landeinwärts

inland: **inland lake** N Binnensee *m*; **Inland Revenue** N *(Brit)* ≈ Finanzamt *nt*; **inland sea** N Binnenmeer *nt*

inlaw ['ɪnlɔː] N angeheirateter Verwandter, angeheiratete Verwandte; **~s** *(= parents-in-law)* Schwiegereltern *pl*

inlay [ɪn'leɪ] *vb: pret, ptp* **inlaid** **N** *(in table, box)* Einlegearbeit *f*, Intarsien *pl*; *(Dentistry)* Plombe *f*, Füllung *f* **VT** einlegen *(with* mit)

inlet ['ɪnlet] N **a** *(of sea)* Meeresarm *m*; *(of river)* Flussarm *m* **b** *(Tech)* Zuleitung *f*; *(of ventilator)* Öffnung *f*

inlet: **inlet pipe** N Zuleitung(srohr *nt*) *f*; **inlet valve** N Einlassventil *nt*

inliner ['ɪnlaɪnə'] N Inlineskate *m*, Inliner *m*

in-line ['ɪnlaɪn]: **in-line skater** N Inlineskater(in) *m(f)*; **in-line skates** PL Inlineskates *pl*; **in-line skating** N Inlineskating *nt*

in loco parentis [ɪn'ləʊkəʊpə'rentɪs] ADV an Eltern statt

inmate ['ɪnmeɪt] N Insasse *m*, Insassin *f*

inmost ['ɪnməʊst] ADJ = **innermost**

inn [ɪn] N **a** Gasthaus *nt*; *(old) (= hotel)* Herberge *f (old)*; *(= tavern)* Schenke *f*, Schänke *f* **b** *(Jur)* **the Inns of Court** die vier englischen Juristenverbände

innards ['ɪnədz] PL Innereien *pl (also fig)*, Eingeweide *pl*

innate [ɪ'neɪt] ADJ angeboren; **man's ~ desire for happiness** das dem Menschen angeborene Verlangen nach Glück

innately [ɪ'neɪtlɪ] ADV *(= naturally)* von Natur aus

inner ['ɪnə'] **ADJ** **a** innere(r, s); **~ side/door** Innenseite/-tür *f*; **~ court/city** Innenhof *m*/-stadt *f*; **~ sole** Innensohle *f* **b** *(fig) emotions, beauty, voice* innere(r, s); *meaning* verborgen; **his ~ circle of friends** sein engster Freundeskreis; **he wasn't one of the ~ circle** er gehörte nicht zum engeren Kreise; **~ life** Seelenleben *nt*; **~ self** wahres Ich; **the ~ man** *(= soul)* das Innere; **the needs of the ~ man** die inneren Bedürfnisse **N** *(Archery)* Schwarze(s) *nt*

inner-city ['ɪnə'sɪtɪ] ADJ *attr* Innenstadt-; *traffic* innenstädtisch; *housing* in der Innenstadt; *(= of cities generally)* in den Innenstädten; *decay, renewal, problem* der Innenstadt/der Innenstädte; **~ area** Innenstadtbereich *m*; **deprived ~ children** heruntergekommene Stadtkinder

> **INNER CITY**
>
> **Inner city** ist ein ursprünglich amerikanischer Begriff, mit dem vernachlässigte und heruntergekommene Stadtteile beschrieben werden. Eine typische **inner city** ist gekennzeichnet von Armut, Arbeitslosigkeit, unzulänglichen Wohnbedingungen und Spannungen zwischen den Rassen. Der Ausdruck hat sich mittlerweile für jedes heruntergekommene Stadtgebiet etabliert, ganz egal, ob dieses wirklich in der Stadtmitte liegt oder nicht. In den letzten Jahren hat es sowohl in den USA als auch in Großbritannien Versuche gegeben, der Verelendung der **inner cities** Einhalt zu gebieten und die Wohnqualität in diesen Gegenden zu verbessern.

inner: **inner ear** N Innenohr *nt*; **inner harbour** N Innenbecken *nt*; **innermost** ADJ innerste(r, s); **~ in sb** zuinnerst in jdm; **in the ~ recesses of the mind** in den hintersten Winkeln des Gehirns; **his ~ being/heart** sein Innerstes; **in the ~ depths of the forest** im tiefsten Wald; **inner part** N *(Mus)* Mittelstimme *f*; **inner tube** N Schlauch *m*

inning ['ɪnɪŋ] N *(Baseball)* Inning *nt*

innings ['ɪnɪŋz] N *(Cricket)* Innenrunde *f*; **to have one's ~** *(fig inf)* an der Reihe sein; **he has had a good ~** *(fig inf)* er war lange an der Reihe; *(= life)* er hatte ein langes, ausgefülltes Leben

innit ['ɪnɪt] INTERJ *(Brit inf)* **~?** oder? *(inf)*

innkeeper ['ɪnˌkiːpə'] N (Gast)wirt(in) *m(f)*

innocence ['ɪnəsəns] N **a** Unschuld *f*; **to feign ~** vorgeben, unschuldig zu sein, unschuldig tun; **in all ~** in aller Unschuld **b** *(liter, = ignorance)* Unkenntnis *f*

innocent ['ɪnəsənt] **ADJ** **a** unschuldig; *mistake, misrepresentation* unabsichtlich; **she is ~ of the crime** sie ist an dem Verbrechen unschuldig; **a defendant is ~ until proved guilty** ein Angeklagter gilt als unschuldig, bis ihm seine Schuld nachgewiesen wird; **to put on an ~ air** eine Unschuldsmiene aufsetzen; **as ~ as a newborn babe** unschuldig wie ein Lamm; **he is ~ about night life in a big city** er ist die reine Unschuld, was das Nachtleben in einer Großstadt angeht
b *(= innocuous) question* naiv; *remark* arglos; *amusement* harmlos
c **~ of** *(liter) (= ignorant)* nicht vertraut mit; *(= devoid of)* frei von, ohne
N Unschuld *f*; **he's a bit of an ~** er ist eine rechte Unschuld; **the massacre of the Holy Innocents** *(Rel)* der Kindermord zu Bethlehem; **Holy Innocents' Day** das Fest der Unschuldigen Kinder

innocently ['ɪnəsəntlɪ] ADV unschuldig; *(= in all innocence)* in aller Unschuld; **the quarrel began ~ enough** der Streit begann ganz harmlos

innocuous ADJ, **innocuously** ADV [ɪ'nɒkjʊəs, -lɪ] harmlos

innovate ['ɪnəʊveɪt] **VT** neu einführen; **the new techniques which he ~d** die neuen Techniken, die er einführte **VI** Neuerungen einführen

innovation [ˌɪnəʊ'veɪʃən] N Innovation *f*; *(= introduction also)* Neueinführung *f (of +gen)*; *(= thing introduced also)* Neuerung *f*

innovative [ɪnə'veɪtɪv] ADJ innovativ; *idea* originell, neu

innovator ['ɪnəʊveɪtə'] N Neuerer *m*, Neuerin *f*; *(of reform)* Begründer(in) *m(f)*

innuendo [ˌɪnjʊˈendəʊ] N *pl* **-es** versteckte Andeutung; **sexual ~** sexuelle Anspielung

innumerable [ɪˈnjuːmərəbl] ADJ unzählig

innumeracy [ɪˈnjuːmərəsɪ] N Nicht-Rechnen--Können *nt*

innumerate [ɪˈnjuːmərɪt] ADJ **to be ~** nicht rechnen können

innutrition [ˌɪnjuːˈtrɪʃən] N *(spec)* Nahrungsmangel *m*

inoculant [ɪˈnɒkjʊlənt] N *(Med)* Impfstoff *m*

inoculate [ɪˈnɒkjʊleɪt] VT *person* impfen *(against* gegen); **to ~ sb with a virus** jdm einen Virus einimpfen

inoculation [ɪˌnɒkjʊˈleɪʃən] N Impfung *f*; **to give sb an ~ (against smallpox)** jdn (gegen Pocken) impfen

inoculum [ɪˈnɒkjʊləm] N *pl* **inocula** *(Med)* Impfstoff *m*

inodorous [ɪnˈəʊdərəs] ADJ *(geh)* geruchlos

in-off [ˈɪnɒf] N *(inf)* **a** *(Ftbl)* Abprallertor *nt* **b** *(Billiards etc) Kugel, die von einer anderen abprallt und dann in ein Loch geht*

inoffensive [ˌɪnəˈfensɪv] ADJ harmlos

inofficious [ˌɪnəˈfɪʃəs] ADJ *(Jur)* pflichtwidrig; **~ testament** *or* **will** gegen die natürlichen Pflichten des Erblassers verstoßendes Testament

inoperable [ɪnˈɒpərəbl] ADJ *disease, tumour* inoperabel, nicht operierbar; *policy* undurchführbar

inoperative [ɪnˈɒpərətɪv] ADJ **a** *(= ineffective) law, rule* außer Kraft, ungültig **b** *(= not working) (machine, radio)* nicht funktionieren; **to render sth ~** etw außer Betrieb setzen

inopportune [ɪnˈɒpətjuːn] ADJ inopportun; *demand, visit, resignation, moment also* ungelegen; *words* unpassend, nicht angebracht; **to be ~** ungelegen *or* zur Unzeit kommen; **it's very ~ that …** es kommt sehr ungelegen, dass …

inopportunely [ɪnˈɒpətjuːnlɪ] ADV zur Unzeit

inordinate [ɪˈnɔːdɪnɪt] ADJ unmäßig; *number, size, sum of money* übermäßig; *demand, claim, fondness* übertrieben; **to set ~ store by sth** ungeheuer *or* übertrieben viel Wert auf etw *(acc)* legen

inordinately [ɪˈnɔːdɪnɪtlɪ] ADV unmäßig; *large, high, long* übermäßig; **to be ~ fond of sth** etw allzu gern mögen

inorganic [ˌɪnɔːˈgænɪk] ADJ anorganisch; *(fig)* unorganisch

inpatient [ˈɪnpeɪʃnt] N stationär behandelter Patient/behandelte Patientin

inpouring [ˈɪnpɔːrɪŋ] **N** (Her)einströmen *nt* **ADJ** (her)einströmend

input [ˈɪnpʊt] **N** **a** *(into computer)* Eingabe *f*, Input *m or nt*; *(of capital)* Investition *f*; *(of manpower)* (Arbeits)aufwand *m*; *(= power input)* Energiezufuhr *f*; *(of project etc)* Beitrag *m*; **artistic/creative ~** künstlerische/kreative Beiträge *pl*; **their ~ into the project** ihr Beitrag *m* zum Projekt; **~ port** *(Comput)* Eingabeport *m* **b** *(= point of input, input terminal)* Eingang *m* **VT** *(Comput) data, text, information* eingeben

inquest [ˈɪnkwest] N *(Jur: into death)* gerichtliche Untersuchung der Todesursache; *(fig)* Manöverkritik *f*

inquietude [ɪnˈkwaɪətjuːd] N *(liter)* Unruhe *f*

inquire, **enquire** [ɪnˈkwaɪəʳ] **VT** *the time, a name, the way* sich erkundigen nach, fragen nach; **to ~ sth of sb** sich bei jdm nach etw erkundigen; **he ~d what/whether/when** *etc* **…** er erkundigte sich *or* fragte, was/ob/wann *etc* … **VI** sich erkundigen *(about* nach), fragen *(about* nach, wegen); **"inquire within"** „Näheres im Geschäft"

▶ **inquire about** *or* **after** VI *+prep obj person, sb's health* sich erkundigen nach

▶ **inquire for** VI *+prep obj person* fragen nach; *information, details* erfragen

▶ **inquire into** VI *+prep obj* untersuchen

inquirer, **enquirer** [ɪnˈkwaɪərəʳ] N Fragende(r) *mf*

inquiring, **enquiring** [ɪnˈkwaɪərɪŋ] ADJ fragend; *mind* forschend

inquiringly, **enquiringly** [ɪnˈkwaɪərɪŋlɪ] ADV *look* fragend

inquiry [ɪnˈkwaɪərɪ, *(US)* ˈɪnkwɪrɪ], **enquiry** [ɪnˈkwaɪərɪ] N **a** *(= question)* Anfrage *f (about* über *+acc)*; *(for tourist information, direction etc)* Erkundigung *f (about* über *+acc,* nach); **to make inquiries** Erkundigungen einziehen; *(police etc)* Nachforschungen anstellen *(about sb* über jdn, *about sth* nach etw); **all inquiries to …** alle Anfragen an *(+acc)* …; **Inquiries** *(office)* Auskunft *f*; **he is helping the police with their inquiries** *(euph)* er wird von der Polizei vernommen **b** *(= investigation)* Untersuchung *f*; **to hold an ~ into the cause of the accident** eine Untersuchung der Unfallursache durchführen; **court of ~** Untersuchungskommission *f*

inquisition [ˌɪnkwɪˈzɪʃən] N **a** *(Hist Eccl)* **the Inquisition** die Inquisition **b** *(Jur)* Untersuchung *f* **c** *(fig)* Inquisition *f*, Verhör *nt*

inquisitive [ɪnˈkwɪzɪtɪv] ADJ neugierig; *(for knowledge)* wissbegierig; **he's very ~ about my friends** er will alles über meine Freunde wissen

inquisitively [ɪnˈkwɪzɪtɪvlɪ] ADV neugierig

inquisitiveness [ɪnˈkwɪzɪtɪvnɪs] N *(of person)* Neugier *f*; *(for knowledge)* Wissbegier(de) *f*; **the ~ of her look** ihr neugieriger Blick

inquisitor [ɪnˈkwɪzɪtəʳ] N *(Hist Eccl)* Inquisitor *m*; *(fig)* Inquisitor(in) *m(f)*

inquisitorial [ɪnˌkwɪzɪˈtɔːrɪəl] ADJ inquisitorisch; **after an ~ meeting with the headmaster** nachdem ihn der Rektor streng verhört hatte *or* ins Verhör genommen hatte

inquorate [ɪnˈkwɔːreɪt, -rət] ADJ *(Brit)* beschlussunfähig

inroad [ˈɪnrəʊd] N **a** *(Mil)* Einfall *m (into* in *+acc)* **b** *(fig)* **the Japanese are making ~s into the British market** die Japaner dringen in den britischen Markt ein; **these expenses are making great ~s into my bank account** diese Ausgaben greifen mein Bankkonto stark an

inrush [ˈɪnrʌʃ] N Zustrom *m*; *(of water)* Einbruch *m*; **there was a sudden ~ of tourists** die Touristen kamen plötzlich in Strömen

ins **a** *abbr of* **insurance** Vers. **b** *abbr of* **inches**

insalubrious [ˌɪnsəˈluːbrɪəs] ADJ unzuträglich

insane [ɪnˈseɪn] **ADJ** **a** *(lit)* geisteskrank; *(fig inf)* wahnsinnig, irrsinnig; **to drive sb ~** *(lit)* jdn um den Verstand bringen; *(fig inf)* jdn wahnsinnig machen; **to go ~** *(lit)* den Verstand verlieren; *(fig inf)* wahnsinnig werden; **you must be ~!** *(inf)* du bist wohl wahnsinnig!; **that's ~!** *(inf)* das ist Wahnsinn *or* Irrsinn!; **~ jealousy** rasende Eifersucht; **he was judged criminally ~** er wurde als psychisch kranker Straftäter eingeschätzt **b** *(esp US)* **~ asylum/ward** Anstalt *f*/Abteilung *f* für Geisteskranke **PL** **the ~** die Geisteskranken *pl*

insanely [ɪnˈseɪnlɪ] ADV irr; *(fig inf)* verrückt; *jealous* irrsinnig; *laugh* wie ein Geisteskranker/eine Geisteskranke

insanitary [ɪnˈsænɪtərɪ] ADJ unhygienisch

insanity [ɪnˈsænɪtɪ] N Geisteskrankheit *f*, Wahnsinn *m*; *(fig inf)* Irrsinn *m*, Wahnsinn *m*

insatiability [ɪnˌseɪʃəˈbɪlɪtɪ] N Unersättlichkeit *f*; *(of thirst, curiosity, desire)* Unstillbarkeit *f*

insatiable [ɪnˈseɪʃəbl] ADJ unersättlich; *curiosity, desire also* unstillbar; **an ~ hunger/thirst for sth** ein unersättlicher Hunger/unstillbarer Durst nach etw; **he/his mind is ~ for knowledge** er hat einen unersättlichen Wissensdurst

insatiably [ɪnˈseɪʃəblɪ] ADV **he is ~ hungry/curious** er hat einen unersättlichen Hunger/eine unstillbare Neugier

inscribe [ɪnˈskraɪb] VT **a** *(sth on sth* etw in etw *acc) words, symbols etc (= engrave) (on ring, watch etc)* eingravieren; *(on rock, stone, wood)* einmeißeln; *(on tree)* einritzen **b** *book* eine Widmung schreiben in *(+acc)*; **a watch, ~d …** eine Uhr mit der Widmung … **c** **to ~ sth in sb's mind** etw in jds Gedächtnis *(dat)* verankern **d** *(Math)* einbeschreiben *(in a circle etc* einem Kreis etc) **e** *(Fin)* **~d stock** Namensaktien *pl*

inscription [ɪnˈskrɪpʃən] N **a** *(on monument etc)* Inschrift *f*; *(on coin)* Aufschrift *f* **b** *(in book)* Widmung *f*

inscrutability [ɪnˌskruːtəˈbɪlɪtɪ] N Unergründlichkeit *f*

inscrutable [ɪnˈskruːtəbl] ADJ unergründlich *(to* für); **~ face** undurchdringlicher Gesichtsausdruck; **don't pretend to be so ~** tu nicht so geheimnisvoll; **she remained ~ to him** sie blieb für ihn undurchschaubar

insect [ˈɪnsekt] N Insekt *nt*

insect: **insect bite** N Insektenstich *m*; **insect eater** N Insektenfresser *m*; **insect-eating plant** N fleischfressende Pflanze

insecticide [ɪnˈsektɪsaɪd] N Insektengift *nt*, Insektizid *nt (form)*

insectivorous [ˌɪnsekˈtɪvərəs] ADJ insektenfressend

insect: **insect powder** N Insektenpulver *nt*; **insect repellent** N Insektenschutzmittel *nt*; **insect-repellent** [ˈɪnsektrɪˌpelənt] ADJ insektenvertreibend

insecure [ˌɪnsɪˈkjʊəʳ] ADJ **a** *(= uncertain, unsafe)* unsicher; **~ future** ungesicherte Zukunft; **if they feel ~ in their jobs** wenn sie sich in ihrem Arbeitsplatz nicht sicher fühlen **b** *(= loose) load, ladder* ungesichert

insecurely [ˌɪnsɪˈkjʊəlɪ] ADV *fastened* nicht sicher

insecurity [ˌɪnsɪˈkjʊərɪtɪ] N Unsicherheit *f*

inseminate [ɪnˈsemɪneɪt] VT inseminieren *(spec)*, befruchten; *cattle* besamen; *(fig) beliefs* einimpfen

insemination [ɪnˌsemɪˈneɪʃən] N Insemination *f (spec)*, Befruchtung *f*; *(of cattle)* Besamung *f*; *(fig) (of beliefs)* Einimpfung *f*; *(of knowledge)* Vermittlung *f*

insensate [ɪnˈsenseɪt] ADJ *(liter)* **a** *matter, stone* leblos, tot **b** *(fig: = unfeeling)* gefühllos; **she flew into an ~ fury** ein unmäßiger Zorn bemächtigte sich ihrer *(liter)*

insensibility [ɪnˌsensəˈbɪlɪtɪ] N **a** *(bodily)* Unempfindlichkeit *f (to* gegenüber); *(= unconsciousness)* Bewusstlosigkeit *f* **b** *(= lack of feeling)* Gefühllosigkeit *f (to* gegenüber); **~ to art** Unempfindlichkeit *f* für Kunst

insensible [ɪnˈsensəbl] ADJ **a** *(bodily)* unempfindlich *(to* gegen); *(= unconscious)* bewusstlos; **he seems to be ~ to the cold** er scheint kälteunempfindlich zu sein; **his hands became ~ to any feeling** seine Hände verloren jegliches Gefühl **b** *(liter, of beauty, music)* unempfänglich (*of, to* für) **c** *(liter: = unaware)* **~ of** *or* **to sth** einer Sache *(gen)* nicht bewusst **d** *(form: = imperceptible)* unmerklich, nicht wahrnehmbar

insensitive [ɪnˈsensɪtɪv] ADJ **a** *(= unfeeling, uncaring)* gefühllos; *remark* taktlos; *policy, action* rücksichtslos; **to be ~ to** *or* **about sb's problems/fears/feelings** auf jds Probleme/Ängste/Gefühle keine Rücksicht nehmen **b** *(= unappreciative)* unempfänglich; **to be ~ to the beauties of nature** *etc* für Schönheiten der Natur *etc* unempfänglich sein **c** *(physically)* unempfindlich *(to* gegen); **~ to pain/light** schmerz-/lichtunempfindlich **d** *(Econ)* **they are relatively ~ to price** für sie spielt der Preis eine relativ untergeordnete Rolle

insensitivity [ɪnˌsensɪˈtɪvɪtɪ] N **a** *(= unfeeling/uncaring attitude)* Gefühllosigkeit *f (towards* gegenüber); *(of remark)* Taktlosigkeit *f*; *(of policy, action)* Rücksichtslosigkeit *f* **b** *(= unappreciativeness)* Unempfänglichkeit *f (to* für); **his ~ to the reasons behind the demands** seine Verständnislosigkeit *or* sein Unverständnis für die Gründe, die hinter den Forderungen stehen **c** *(physical)* Unempfindlichkeit *f (to* gegen)

inseparability [ɪnˌsepərəˈbɪlɪtɪ] N Untrennbarkeit *f*; *(of friends)* Unzertrennlichkeit *f*

inseparable [ɪnˈsepərəbl] ADJ untrennbar; *friends* unzertrennlich; **these two issues are ~**

diese beiden Fragen sind untrennbar miteinander verbunden

inseparably [ɪnˈsepərəblɪ] ADV untrennbar

insert [ɪnˈsɜːt] VT *(= stick into)* hineinstecken; *(= place in)* hineinlegen; *(= place between)* einfügen; *zip, pocket* einsetzen; *thermometer, suppository* einführen; *coin* einwerfen; *injection needle* einstechen; *text, clause* einfügen; *(Comput) disk* einlegen; *character, space, text* einfügen; **to ~ sth in (-to) sth** *(= stick into)* etw in etw *(acc)* stecken; *(= place in)* etw in etw *(acc)* hineinlegen; *(= place between)* etw in etw *(acc)* einfügen; **to ~ an extra paragraph in(to) a chapter** einen weiteren Absatz in ein Kapitel einfügen; **to ~ an advert in a newspaper** eine Anzeige in die Zeitung setzen, in einer Zeitung inserieren; **he managed to ~ himself between two other students on the crowded benches** es gelang ihm, sich auf den überfüllten Bänken zwischen zwei andere Studenten zu zwängen; **~ mode** *(Comput)* Einfügemodus *m*
N [ˈɪnsɜːt] *(in book)* Einlage *f*; *(= word)* Beifügung *f*, Einfügung *f*; *(in magazine)* Beilage *f*; *(= advertisement)* Inserat *nt*

insertion [ɪnˈsɜːʃən] N **a** *(= sticking into)* Hineinstecken *nt*; *(= placing in)* Hineinlegen *nt*; *(= placing between)* Einfügen *nt*; *(of pocket)* Einsetzen *nt*; *(of thermometer, suppository)* Einführen *nt*; *(of coin)* Einwerfen *nt*; *(of injection needle)* Einstechen *nt*; *(of advert)* Aufgeben *nt*; *(by printer)* Einrücken *nt*; *(of text, clause)* Einfügen *nt*; *(Comput: of disk)* Einlegen *nt* **b** = **insert N c** *(Sew)* Einsatz *m*

insertion point N *(Comput)* Einfügemarke *f*

insert [ˈɪnsɜːt] *(Comput)*: **insert key** N Einfügetaste *f*; **insert mode** N Einfügemodus *m*

in-service [ˈɪn,sɜːvɪs] ADJ *attr* **~ training** (berufsbegleitende) Fortbildung; *(in firm also)* innerbetriebliche Fortbildung; *(course also)* Fortbildungslehrgang *m*

inset *vb: pret, ptp* **inset** VT [ɪnˈset] *map, illustration* einfügen; *(Sew)* einsetzen; **the text is ~ with illustrations** in den Text sind Illustrationen eingefügt [ˈɪnset] N [ˈɪnset] **a** *(= pages)* Einlage *f*, Beilage *f*; *(also* **inset map***)* Nebenkarte *f*; *(on diagram)* Nebenbild *nt* **b** *(Sew)* Einsatz *m*

inshore [ˈɪnˈʃɔːʳ] ADJ Küsten-; **~ fishing/waters** Küstenfischerei *f*/-gewässer *pl* ADV *fish, be* in Küstennähe; *blow, flow* auf die Küste zu; **to be close ~** dicht an der Küste sein; **to go close ~** dicht an die Küste heranfahren

inside [ˈɪnˈsaɪd] N **a** Innere(s) *nt*; *(of pavement)* Innenseite *f*; **the car overtook on the ~** das Auto überholte innen; **it's painted on the ~** es ist innen bemalt; **you'll have to ask someone on the ~** Sie müssen einen Insider *or* Eingeweihten fragen; **to know a company from the ~** interne Kenntnisse über eine Firma haben; **he's seen politics from the ~** er kennt die Politik von innen; **locked from** *or* **on the ~** von innen verschlossen
b the wind blew the umbrella ~ out der Wind hat den Schirm umgestülpt; **her umbrella blew ~ out** ihr Schirm hat sich umgestülpt; **your sweater's ~ out** du hast deinen Pullover links *or* verkehrt herum an; **to turn sth ~ out** etw umdrehen; *(fig) flat etc* etw auf den Kopf stellen; **war turns morality ~ out** im Krieg wird die Moral auf den Kopf gestellt; **to know sth ~ out** etw in- und auswendig kennen; **we know each other ~ out** wir kennen einander in- und auswendig
c *(inf: = stomach: also* **insides***)* Eingeweide *nt*, Innere(s) *nt*; **he felt the excitement grip his ~s** er spürte, wie die Aufregung ihn im Innersten packte
ADJ Innen-, innere(r, s); **it looks like an ~ job** *(crime)* es sieht nach dem Werk von Insidern aus *(inf)*; **~ leg measurement** innere Beinlänge; **~ pocket** Innentasche *f*; **~ seat** Platz *m* an der Wand/am Fenster, Fensterplatz *m*; **~ story** *(Press)* Insidestory *f*; **~ left** Halblinke(r) *mf*; **~ right** Halbrechte(r) *mf*
ADV innen; *(= indoors)* drin(nen); *(direction)* nach innen, herein; **look ~** sehen Sie hinein; *(= search)* sehen Sie innen nach; **come ~!** kommen Sie herein!; **let's go ~** gehen wir hinein; **he played the ball ~** er spielte nach innen ab; **I heard music coming from ~** ich hörte von innen Musik; **there is something/nothing ~** es ist etwas/nichts (innen) drin; **to be ~** *(inf: = in prison)* sitzen *(inf)*
PREP *(esp US: also* **inside of***)* **a** *(place)* innen in *(+dat)*; *(direction)* in *(+acc)* … (hinein); **don't let him come ~ the house** lassen Sie ihn nicht ins Haus (herein); **he was waiting ~ the house** er wartete im Haus; **something ~ me snapped** bei mir hakte etwas aus *(inf)*
b *(time)* innerhalb; **he's well ~ the record time** er liegt noch gut unter der Rekordzeit; **he was 5 seconds ~ the record** er ist 5 Sekunden unter dem Rekord geblieben

inside: **inside forward** N Halbstürmer(in) *m(f)*; **inside information** N Insiderinformationen *pl*, interne Informationen *pl*; **inside knowledge** N Insiderwissen *nt*; **inside lane** N *(Sport)* Innenbahn *f*; *(Aut)* Innenspur *f*

insider [ɪnˈsaɪdəʳ] N Insider(in) *m(f)*, Eingeweihte(r) *mf*

insider dealing, insider trading N *(Fin)* Insiderhandel *m*, Insidergeschäfte *pl*

inside track N Innenbahn *f*

insidious ADJ, **insidiously** ADV [ɪnˈsɪdɪəs, -lɪ] heimtückisch

insight [ˈɪnsaɪt] N **a** *no pl* Verständnis *nt*; **he lacks ~** ihm fehlt das Verständnis; **his ~ into my problems** sein Verständnis für meine Probleme; **~ into human nature** Menschenkenntnis *f* **b** Einblick *m* *(into* in *+acc)*; **to gain (an) ~ into sth** (einen) Einblick in etw gewinnen *or* bekommen; **to give sb (an) ~ into sth** jdm (einen) Einblick in etw *(acc)* geben

insightful [ˈɪnsaɪtfʊl] ADJ *questions, analysis* einsichtsvoll

insignia [ɪnˈsɪgnɪə] PL Insignien *pl*

insignificance [,ɪnsɪgˈnɪfɪkəns] N Bedeutungslosigkeit *f*, Belanglosigkeit *f*; *(of wound, alteration)* Geringfügigkeit *f*; *(of person, appearance)* Unscheinbarkeit *f*

insignificant [,ɪnsɪgˈnɪfɪkənt] ADJ unbedeutend; *sum also, wound, alteration* geringfügig; *little man, person, appearance* unscheinbar; *(= inconsequential) remark* belanglos; **her not ~ talents** ihre nicht unbeträchtlichen Talente; **statistically ~** statistisch vernachlässigbar

insincere [,ɪnsɪnˈsɪəʳ] ADJ unaufrichtig; *person, smile also* falsch

insincerely [,ɪnsɪnˈsɪəlɪ] ADV unaufrichtig; *smile* falsch

insincerity [,ɪnsɪnˈserɪtɪ] N Unaufrichtigkeit *f*; *(of person, smile also)* Falschheit *f*

insinuate [ɪnˈsɪnjʊeɪt] VT **a** *(= hint, suggest)* andeuten *(sth to sb* etw jdm gegenüber*)*; **what are you insinuating?** was wollen Sie damit sagen?; **are you insinuating that I am lying?** willst du damit sagen, dass ich lüge? **b to ~ oneself into sb's favour** *(Brit) or* **favor** *(US)***/the smart set** sich bei jdm/bei der Schickeria einschmeicheln

insinuating [ɪnˈsɪnjʊeɪtɪŋ] ADJ *remark* anzüglich; *article also* voller Anzüglichkeiten; *tone of voice* spitz, bedeutungsvoll

insinuation [ɪn,sɪnjʊˈeɪʃən] N Anspielung *f* *(about* auf *+acc)*; **he objected strongly to any ~ that …** er wehrte sich heftig gegen jede Andeutung, dass …

insipid [ɪnˈsɪpɪd] ADJ fade; *colour* langweilig; *(= vapid) person, novel, lyrics* geistlos

insipidity [,ɪnsɪˈpɪdɪtɪ] N Fadheit *f*; *(= vapidity)* Geistlosigkeit *f*

insist [ɪnˈsɪst] VI **I ~!** ich bestehe darauf!; **if you ~** wenn Sie darauf bestehen; *(= if you like)* wenns unbedingt sein muss; **he ~s on his innocence** *or* **that he is innocent** er behauptet beharrlich, unschuldig zu sein; **to ~ on a point** auf einem Punkt beharren; **to ~ on silence** auf absoluter Ruhe bestehen; **I ~ on the best** ich bestehe auf bester Qualität; **to ~ on doing sth/on sb doing sth** darauf bestehen, etw zu tun/dass jd etw tut; **he will ~ on calling her by the wrong name** er redet sie beharrlich beim falschen Namen an; **if you will ~ on smoking that foul tobacco** wenn Sie schon unbedingt diesen scheußlichen Tabak rauchen müssen
VT **to ~ that …** darauf beharren *or* bestehen, dass …; **he ~s that he is innocent** er behauptet beharrlich, unschuldig zu sein; **"it wasn't me", she ~ed** „ich wars nicht!" sagte sie beharrlich; **but he still ~ed that …** aber er beharrte *or* bestand trotzdem darauf, dass …; **I must ~ that you stop** ich muss darauf bestehen, dass Sie aufhören; **she ~s that she is right** sie besteht darauf, dass sie recht hat

insistence [ɪnˈsɪstəns] N Bestehen *nt* *(on* auf *+dat)*; **the accused's ~ on his innocence** die Unschuldsbeteuerungen des Angeklagten; **in spite of his ~ that he was right** trotz seiner beharrlichen Behauptung, recht zu haben; **I did it at his ~** ich tat es auf sein Drängen, ich tat es, weil er darauf bestand; **I can't understand his ~ on using** *or* **the use of oil** ich kann nicht verstehen, warum er darauf besteht, dass Öl benutzt wird

insistent [ɪnˈsɪstənt] ADJ **a** *person* beharrlich, hartnäckig; *salesman etc* aufdringlich; **I didn't want to but he was ~ (that …)** ich wollte eigentlich nicht, aber er bestand *or* beharrte darauf (, dass …); **he was most ~ about it** er beharrte *or* bestand hartnäckig darauf **b** *(= urgent) demand, tone* nachdrücklich, penetrant *(pej)*; *rhythm* aufdringlich; *ringing* penetrant *(pej)*; *(= constant)* unaufhörlich

insistently [ɪnˈsɪstəntlɪ] ADV mit Nachdruck; **the telephone rang ~** das Telefon klingelte penetrant und unaufhörlich; **this question will be put more and more ~** diese Frage wird immer beharrlicher gestellt werden

in situ [ɪnˈsɪtjuː] ADV in situ *(esp Med, Archeol)*; **this part can be repaired ~** man braucht das Teil nicht auszubauen, um es zu reparieren ADJ **~ investigator** Ermittler(in) *m(f)* vor Ort

insofar [,ɪnsəʊˈfɑːʳ] ADV **~ as** soweit

insole [ˈɪnsəʊl] N Einlegesohle *f*; *(= part of shoe)* Brandsohle *f*

insolence [ˈɪnsələns] N Unverschämtheit *f*, Frechheit *f*; **the ~ of it!** so eine Unverschämtheit *or* Frechheit!

insolent ADJ, **insolently** ADV [ˈɪnsələnt, -lɪ] unverschämt, frech

insolubility [ɪn,sɒljʊˈbɪlɪtɪ] N **a** *(of substance)* Unlöslichkeit *f* **b** *(of problem)* Unlösbarkeit *f*

insoluble [ɪnˈsɒljʊbl] ADJ **a** *substance* unlöslich **b** *problem* unlösbar

insolvency [ɪnˈsɒlvənsɪ] N Zahlungsunfähigkeit *f*, Insolvenz *f* *(geh)*

insolvent [ɪnˈsɒlvənt] ADJ zahlungsunfähig, insolvent *(geh)*

insomnia [ɪnˈsɒmnɪə] N Schlaflosigkeit *f*

insomniac [ɪnˈsɒmnɪæk] N **to be an ~** an Schlaflosigkeit leiden

insomuch [,ɪnsəʊˈmʌtʃ] ADV = **inasmuch**

insouciance [ɪnˈsuːsɪəns] N *(liter)* Unbekümmertheit *f*, Sorglosigkeit *f*

insouciant [ɪnˈsuːsɪənt] ADJ *(liter: = careless)* unbekümmert; **to be ~ about sth** sich nicht um etw kümmern

inspect [ɪnˈspekt] VT **a** *(= examine)* kontrollieren, prüfen; *school, hotel etc* inspizieren; **to ~ sth for sth** etw auf etw *(acc)* (hin) prüfen *or* kontrollieren **b** *(Mil etc: = review)* inspizieren

inspection [ɪnˈspekʃən] N **a** Kontrolle *f*, Prüfung *f*; *(medical)* Untersuchung *f*; *(of school, hotel etc)* Inspektion *f*; **to make an ~ of sth** etw kontrollieren *or* prüfen; *of school etc* etw inspizieren; **on ~** bei näherer Betrachtung *or* Prüfung; **customs ~** Zollkontrolle *f*; **for your ~** zur Prüfung; *(documents also)* zur Einsicht; **~ copy** Ansichtsexemplar *nt*; **~ process** *(Tech etc)* Überprüfungsverfahren *nt or* -prozess *m* **b** *(Mil)* Inspektion *f*

inspector [ɪnˈspektəʳ] N (= *factory inspector, on buses, trains*) Kontrolleur(in) *m(f)*; (*of schools*) Schulrat *m*, Schulrätin *f*; (*of police*) Polizeiinspektor(in) *m(f)*; (*higher*) Kommissar(in) *m(f)*; (*of taxes*) Steuerinspektor(in) *m(f)*; **customs ~** Zollinspektor(in) *m(f)*

inspectorate [ɪnˈspektərɪt] N Inspektion *f*

inspiration [ˌɪnspəˈreɪʃən] N Inspiration *f* (*for* zu *or* für), Eingebung *f* (*for* zu); **he gets his ~ from …** er lässt sich von … inspirieren; **you give me ~** Sie inspirieren mich; **I haven't had any ~ for months** seit Monaten habe ich keine Inspirationen mehr; **to find (one's) ~ in sth** von etw inspiriert werden; **to have a sudden ~** eine plötzliche Inspiration *or* Erleuchtung haben; **you are my ~** du inspirierst mich; **his courage has been an ~ to us all** sein Mut hat uns alle inspiriert

inspirational [ˌɪnspəˈreɪʃənl] ADJ inspirativ

inspire [ɪnˈspaɪəʳ] VT **a** *respect, trust, awe* einflößen (*in sb* jdm); *hope, confidence etc* (er)wecken (*in* in *+dat*); *hate, fear* hervorrufen (*in* bei); **to ~ sb with hope/confidence** jdn mit Hoffnung/Vertrauen erfüllen **b** (= *be inspiration to*) *person* inspirieren; **to ~ sb with an idea** jdn zu einer Idee inspirieren; **I was ~d by his example/courage** sein Vorbild/Mut hat mich inspiriert; **the book was ~d by a real person** die Inspiration zu dem Buch kommt von einer wirklichen Person; **whatever ~d you to change it?** (*iro*) was hat dich bloß dazu inspiriert, es zu ändern?

inspired [ɪnˈspaɪəd] ADJ genial; *work, performance also* voller Inspiration; *author, performer, athlete etc* inspiriert; **in an ~ moment** in einem Augenblick der Inspiration; (*iro*) in einem lichten Moment; **it was an ~ guess/choice** das war genial geraten/gewählt; **the strike was politically ~** der Streik war politisch motiviert; **the divinely ~ word of the Bible** der göttlich geoffenbarte Bibeltext

inspiring [ɪnˈspaɪərɪŋ] ADJ *speech, teacher, leader, speaker, example* inspirierend; **this subject/translation isn't particularly ~** dieses Thema/diese Übersetzung begeistert einen nicht gerade; **she is an ~ teacher** als Lehrerin ist sie eine Inspiration

Inst. *abbr of* **Institute** Inst.

inst. *abbr of* **instant** d. M.

instability [ˌɪnstəˈbɪlɪtɪ] N Instabilität *f*; (*of character also*) Labilität *f*

install [ɪnˈstɔːl] VT installieren (*also Comput*); *telephone also* anschließen; *bathroom, fireplace* einbauen; *person* (in ein Amt) einsetzen *or* einführen; *government* einsetzen; *priest* investieren; **to have electricity ~ed** ans Elektrizitätsnetz angeschlossen werden; **when you've ~ed yourself in your new office** wenn Sie sich in Ihrem neuen Büro installiert *or* eingerichtet haben; **he ~ed himself in the best armchair** (*inf*) er pflanzte sich auf den besten Sessel (*inf*)

installation [ˌɪnstəˈleɪʃən] N **a** (= *action*) Installation *f* (*also Comput*); (*of telephone*) Anschluss *m*; (*of bath, kitchen, engine etc*) Einbau *m*; (*of person in office*) Amtseinsetzung *f or* -einführung *f*; (*of government*) Einsetzung *f*; (*of priest*) Investitur *f*; **~ assistant** (*Comput*) Installationsassistent *m*; **~ program** (*Comput*) Installationsprogramm *nt* **b** (= *machine etc*) Anlage *f*, Einrichtung *f* **c** **military ~** militärische Anlage

installment plan N (*US*) Ratenzahlung *f*; **to buy on the ~** auf Raten kaufen

instalment, (*US*) **installment** [ɪnˈstɔːlmənt] N **a** (*of story, serial*) Fortsetzung *f*; (*Rad, TV*) (Sende)folge *f* **b** (*Fin, Comm*) Rate *f*; **monthly ~** Monatsrate *f*; **to pay in** *or* **by ~s** in Raten *or* ratenweise bezahlen

instalment credit, (*US*) **installment credit** N Teilzahlungs- *or* Abzahlungskredit *m*

instance [ˈɪnstəns] N **a** (= *example*) Beispiel *nt*; (= *case*) Fall *m*; **for ~** zum Beispiel; **as an ~ of** als (ein) Beispiel für; **in many ~s** in vielen Fällen; **there have been many ~s of people refusing to go** es hat viele Fälle gegeben, in denen Leute es abgelehnt haben zu gehen; **in the first ~** zuerst *or* zunächst (einmal); **the appointment will be for two years in the first ~** die Anstellung ist zunächst auf zwei Jahre befristet; **this is a good ~ of the way …** das ist ein gutes Beispiel dafür, wie …
b **at the ~ of** (*form*) auf Ersuchen *or* Betreiben (*+gen*) (*form*), auf Veranlassung von
c (*Jur*) **court of first ~** erste Instanz
VT **a** (= *exemplify*) Beispiele anführen für
b (= *cite*) *cost, example* anführen

instant [ˈɪnstənt] ADJ **a** unmittelbar; *relief, result, reply, success* sofortig *attr*, unmittelbar; **sweets give ~ energy** Süßigkeiten sind sofortige Energielieferanten; **~ photography** Sofortbildfotografie *f*
b (*Cook*) Instant-; **~ milk** Trockenmilch *f*; **~ food** Schnellgerichte *pl*; **~ mashed potatoes** fertiger Kartoffelbrei
c (*Comm*) dieses Monats; **your letter of the 10th inst(ant)** Ihr Schreiben vom 10. dieses Monats
d (*Jur*) **in the ~ case** im vorliegenden Fall
N Augenblick *m*; **this (very) ~** sofort, auf der Stelle; **I'll be ready in an ~** ich bin sofort fertig; **it was all over in an ~** in einem Augenblick *or* im Nu (*inf*) war alles vorbei; **he left the ~ he heard the news** er ging sofort, als er die Nachricht hörte; **at that very ~ …** genau in dem Augenblick …; **the next ~, an ~ later** im nächsten Augenblick; **in the same ~** im gleichen Augenblick

instant access N (*Fin, Comput*) sofortiger Zugriff (*to* auf); **~ account** *Sparkonto ohne Zugriffsbeschränkungen*

instantaneous [ˌɪnstənˈteɪnɪəs] ADJ unmittelbar; **death was ~** der Tod trat sofort *or* unmittelbar ein; **the reaction was almost ~** die Reaktion erfolgte fast sofort

instantaneously [ˌɪnstənˈteɪnɪəslɪ] ADV sofort, unverzüglich

instant camera N Sofortbildkamera *f*

instant coffee N Pulver- *or* Instantkaffee *m*

instanter [ɪnˈstæntəʳ] ADV stante pede, stehenden Fußes (*geh*)

instantly [ˈɪnstəntlɪ] ADV sofort; **the game was ~ forgettable** das Spiel konnte man total vergessen (*inf*)

instant: **instant message** N (*Internet*) Instant Message *f*; **Instant Messenger®** N (*Internet*) Instant Messenger® *m*; **instant replay** N (*TV*) Wiederholung *f*

instead [ɪnˈsted] PREP **~ of** statt (*+gen or* (*inf*) *+dat*), anstelle *or* an Stelle von; **~ of going to school** (an)statt zur Schule zu gehen; **~ of that** statt dessen; **his brother came ~ of him** sein Bruder kam an seiner Stelle *or* statt ihm (*inf*); **he accidentally hit Jim ~ of John** er traf aus Versehen Jim (an)statt John; **this is ~ of a Christmas present** das ist anstelle *or* an Stelle eines Weihnachtgeschenks
ADV stattdessen, dafür; **if he doesn't want to go, I'll go ~** wenn er nicht gehen will, gehe ich (stattdessen); **if he doesn't come here, I shall go there ~** wenn er nicht herkommt, gehe ich stattdessen hin

instep [ˈɪnstep] N **a** (*Anat*) Spann *m*, Rist *m* **b** (*of shoe*) Blatt *nt*

instigate [ˈɪnstɪgeɪt] VT anstiften; *rebellion, strike also* anzetteln; *violence* aufrufen zu; *new idea, reform etc* initiieren

instigation [ˌɪnstɪˈgeɪʃən] N Anstiftung *f*; (*of rebellion, strike also*) Anzettelung *f*, Aufruf *m*; (*of new idea, reform*) Initiierung *f*; **~ of violence** Aufruf *f* zur Gewalt; **at sb's ~** auf jds Betreiben *or* Veranlassung

instigator [ˈɪnstɪgeɪtəʳ] N (*of crime etc*) Anstifter(in) *m(f)*; (*of new idea, reform etc*) Initiator(in) *m(f)*

instil, (*US*) **instill** [ɪnˈstɪl] VT einflößen (*into sb* jdm); *knowledge, attitudes, discipline* beibringen (*into sb* jdm)

instinct [ˈɪnstɪŋkt] N Instinkt *m*; **the sex/survival ~** der Geschlechts-/Überlebenstrieb; **by** *or* **from ~** instinktiv; **to have an ~ for business, to have a good business ~** einen ausgeprägten Geschäftssinn *or* -instinkt haben; **to follow one's ~s** sich auf seinen Instinkt verlassen ADJ (*liter*) **~ with** erfüllt von

instinctive [ɪnˈstɪŋktɪv] ADJ instinktiv; *behaviour also* instinktgesteuert

instinctively [ɪnˈstɪŋktɪvlɪ] ADV instinktiv

institute [ˈɪnstɪtjuːt] VT **a** *new laws, tax, custom, reforms, policy* einführen; (= *found*) *organization etc* einrichten; *search* einleiten; **a newly ~d post** eine neu eingerichtete Stelle **b** (*Jur*) *inquiry* einleiten; *an action* einleiten (*against sb* gegen jdn); *proceedings* anstrengen (*against* gegen); **to ~ divorce proceedings** die Scheidung einreichen N Institut *nt*; (= *home*) Anstalt *f*; **Institute of Technology/Education** technische/pädagogische Hochschule; **educational ~** pädagogische Einrichtung; **women's ~** Frauenverein *m*

institution [ˌɪnstɪˈtjuːʃən] N **a** (*of new laws, customs, reforms*) Einführung *f*; (*of organization*) Einrichtung *f* **b** (*Jur, of inquiry, action*) Einleitung *f*; (*of proceedings*) Anstrengung *f*; **~ of divorce proceedings** Einreichung *f* der Scheidung **c** (= *organization*) Institution *f*, Einrichtung *f* **d** (= *building, home etc*) Anstalt *f* **e** (= *custom*) Institution *f*; **the ~ of marriage** die Institution der Ehe; **he's been here so long he's become an ~** er ist schon so lange hier, dass er zur Institution geworden ist

institutional [ˌɪnstɪˈtjuːʃənl] ADJ **a** (= *of institutions*) *reform, structure, arrangement* institutionell **b** (= *in an institution*) *food, atmosphere* Anstalts-; **~ life/care** Anstaltsleben *nt*/-pflege *f*; **~ care in hospital/an old folk's home** stationäre Versorgung *or* Pflege im Krankenhaus/in einem Altenheim **c** (*US*) **~ advertising** Prestigewerbung *f* **d** (*Fin*) *support, funds* institutionell; **~ buying** Käufe *pl* durch institutionelle Anleger; **~ investors** institutionelle Anleger *pl*

institutionalize [ˌɪnstɪˈtjuːʃənəlaɪz] VT institutionalisieren

institutionalized [ˌɪnstɪˈtjuːʃənəlaɪzd] ADJ **a** *person* in einer Anstalt untergebracht; **to become ~** (*Psych*) sich an das Anstaltsleben gewöhnen **b** (= *organized, established*) *religion, racism, system* institutionalisiert; **homelessness and destitution are becoming ~ here** Obdachlosigkeit und Elend werden hier zur Norm

in-store [ˈɪnstɔːʳ] ADJ *attr* im Laden; **~ surveillance system** geschäftsinternes Überwachungssystem

instruct [ɪnˈstrʌkt] VT **a** (= *teach*) *person* unterrichten; **to ~ sb in the use of a machine** jdn in der Handhabung einer Maschine unterweisen **b** (= *tell, direct*) *person* anweisen; (= *command*) die Anweisung erteilen (*+dat*); (*Brit Jur*) *solicitor* (= *give information to*) unterrichten, instruieren; (= *appoint*) *lawyer* beauftragen; *jury* instruieren, belehren; **I've been ~ed to report to you** ich habe (An)weisung, Ihnen Meldung zu erstatten; **what were you ~ed to do?** welche Instruktionen *or* Anweisungen haben Sie bekommen? **c** (*form*: = *inform*) in Kenntnis setzen

instruction [ɪnˈstrʌkʃən] N **a** (= *teaching*) Unterricht *m*; **course of ~** Lehrgang *m*; **to give sb ~ in fencing** jdm Fechtunterricht erteilen **b** (= *order, command*) Anweisung *f*, Instruktion *f*; (*of jury*) Belehrung *f*, Instruktion *f*; **what were your ~s?** welche Instruktionen *or* Anweisungen hatten Sie?; **on whose ~s did you do that?** auf wessen Anweisung *or* Anordnung haben Sie das getan?; **~s for use** Gebrauchsanweisung *f*, Gebrauchsanleitung *f*; **~ manual** (*Tech*) Bedienungsanleitung *f*

instructive [ɪnˈstrʌktɪv] ADJ instruktiv, aufschlussreich; (= *of educational value*) lehrreich

instructor [ɪnˈstrʌktəʳ] N (*also Sport*) Lehrer *m*; (*US*) Dozent *m*; (*Mil*) Ausbilder *m*

instructress [ɪnˈstrʌktrɪs] N (*also Sport*) Lehrerin *f*; (*US*) Dozentin *f*; (*Mil*) Ausbilderin *f*

instrument [ˈɪnstrʊmənt] N **a** (*Mus, Med, Tech*) Instrument *nt*; (*domestic*) Gerät *nt*; **to fly**

an aircraft on ~s ein Flugzeug nach den (Bord)instrumenten fliegen **b** *(fig: = person)* Werkzeug *nt* **c** *(Jur)* Urkunde *f*, Dokument *nt* **VT** [ˈɪnstrʊˌment] **a** *(Mus)* instrumentieren **b** *(= put into effect)* durchführen, ausführen

instrument *in cpds (Aviat)* Instrumenten-; **~ panel** *or* **board** *(Aviat)* Instrumententafel *f*; *(Aut)* Armaturenbrett *nt*

instrumental [ˌɪnstrʊˈmentl] **ADJ** **a** *role* entscheidend; **she was ~ in my release** sie hat bei meiner Freilassung eine entscheidende Rolle gespielt; **he was ~ in getting her the job** er hat ihr zu dieser Stelle verholfen; **he was ~ in bringing about the downfall of the government** er war maßgeblich am Sturz der Regierung beteiligt **b** *(Mus)* Instrumental-; **~ music/version** Instrumentalmusik *f*/-version *f*; **~ performer** Instrumentalist(in) *m(f)* **N** *(Mus)* Instrumentalstück *nt*

instrumentalist [ˌɪnstrʊˈmentəlɪst] **N** Instrumentalist(in) *m(f)*

instrumentality [ˌɪnstrʊmenˈtælɪtɪ] **N** **through** *or* **by the ~ of sb** durch jds Vermittlung *or* Eingreifen

instrumentation [ˌɪnstrʊmenˈteɪʃən] **N** Instrumentation *f*

insubordinate [ˌɪnsəˈbɔːdənɪt] **ADJ** aufsässig

insubordination [ˈɪnsəˌbɔːdɪˈneɪʃən] **N** Aufsässigkeit *f*; *(Mil)* Gehorsamsverweigerung *f*, Insubordination *f (dated)*

insubstantial [ˌɪnsəbˈstænʃəl] **ADJ** wenig substanziell *or* substantiell; *fear, hopes, accusation, rumour* gegenstandslos; *argument* haltlos; *amount* gering(fügig); *meal, plot, evidence* dürftig

insufferable **ADJ**, **insufferably** **ADV** [ɪnˈsʌfərəbl, -ɪ] unerträglich

insufficiency [ˌɪnsəˈfɪʃənsɪ] **N** *(of supplies)* Knappheit *f*, unzureichende Menge; *(of sb's work)* Unzulänglichkeit *f*

insufficient [ˌɪnsəˈfɪʃənt] **ADJ** nicht genügend; **~ evidence** Mangel *m* an Beweisen; **to take ~ account of sth** etw nicht genug in Betracht ziehen

insufficiently [ˌɪnsəˈfɪʃəntlɪ] **ADV** ungenügend, unzulänglich

insulant [ˈɪnsjələnt] **N** Isolierstoff *m*, Dämmmaterial *nt*; *(for rooms)* Dämmstoff *m*

insular [ˈɪnsjələˈ] **ADJ** **a** *(= narrow-minded)* engstirnig **b** *(= of an island)* Insel-, insular

insularity [ˌɪnsjʊˈlærɪtɪ] **N** *(= narrow-mindedness)* Engstirnigkeit *f*

insulate [ˈɪnsjʊleɪt] **VT** **a** *(lit)* isolieren; **in this anorak you're well ~d against the cold** in diesem Anorak sind Sie gut gegen Kälte geschützt; **to ~ sth from noise** etw schallisolieren; **~d pliers** Isolierzange *f* **b** *(fig: from unpleasantness etc)* abschirmen *(from* gegen)

insulating [ˈɪnsjʊleɪtɪŋ]: **insulating material** **N** Isoliermaterial *nt*; **insulating tape** **N** Isolierband *nt*

insulation [ˌɪnsjʊˈleɪʃən] **N** **a** *(lit)* Isolierung *f*; *(= material)* Isoliermaterial *nt* **b** *(fig)* Geschütztheit *f (from* gegen)

insulator [ˈɪnsjʊleɪtəˈ] **N** *(Elec: = device)* Isolator *m*; *(= material)* Isolierstoff *m*; *(for heat)* Wärmeschutzisolierung *f*

insulin [ˈɪnsjʊlɪn] **N** Insulin *nt*

insult [ɪnˈsʌlt] **VT** beleidigen; *(by words also)* beschimpfen **N** [ˈɪnsʌlt] Beleidigung *f*; *(with words also)* Beschimpfung *f*; **an ~ to the profession** eine Beleidigung für den ganzen Berufsstand; **an ~ to my intelligence** eine Beleidigung meiner Intelligenz; **that's not a salary, it's an ~!** das ist doch kein Gehalt, das ist blanker Hohn *or* das ist eine Beleidigung!; **to add ~ to injury** das Ganze noch schlimmer machen

insulting [ɪnˈsʌltɪŋ] **ADJ** beleidigend; *question* unverschämt; **to use ~ language to sb** jdm gegenüber beleidigende Äußerungen machen, jdn beschimpfen; **he was very ~ to her** er hat sich ihr gegenüber sehr beleidigend geäußert

insultingly [ɪnˈsʌltɪŋlɪ] **ADV** beleidigend; *behave* in beleidigender *or* unverschämter Weise

insuperable [ɪnˈsuːpərəbl] **ADJ** unüberwindlich

insuperably [ɪnˈsuːpərəblɪ] **ADV** **it was ~ difficult** es hat unüberwindliche Schwierigkeiten bereitet; **this could affect its development ~** das könnte seiner Entwicklung einen bleibenden Schaden zufügen

insupportable [ˌɪnsəˈpɔːtəbl] **ADJ** unerträglich

insurable [ɪnˈʃʊərəbl] **ADJ** versicherbar

insurance [ɪnˈʃʊərəns] **N** Versicherung *f*; *(= amount paid out)* Versicherungssumme *f or* -betrag *m*; **the ~ on a building** die Versicherung für ein Gebäude; **to take out ~** eine Versicherung abschließen *(against* gegen)

insurance: **insurance adjuster** **N** *(US)* Schadenssachverständige(r) *mf*; **insurance agent** **N** Versicherungsvertreter(in) *m(f)*; **insurance broker** **N** Versicherungsmakler(in) *m(f)*; **insurance company** **N** Versicherungsgesellschaft *f*; **insurance cover** **N** Versicherungsschutz *m*; **insurance office** **N** Versicherungsanstalt *f*/-büro *nt*; **insurance policy** **N** Versicherungspolice *f*; *(fig)* Sicherheitsvorkehrung *f*; **to take out an ~** eine Versicherung abschließen; *(fig)* Sicherheitsvorkehrungen treffen; **as an ~** *(fig)* für alle Fälle, sicherheitshalber; **as an ~ against sth** *(fig)* als Sicherheitsvorkehrung gegen etw; **insurance premium** **N** Versicherungsprämie *f*; **insurance scheme** **N** Versicherung(smöglichkeit) *f*; **insurance stamp** **N** *(Brit)* Versicherungsmarke *f*

insure [ɪnˈʃʊəˈ] **VT** **a** *car, house* versichern (lassen) *(against* gegen); **he ~d his house contents for £10,000** er schloss eine Hausratsversicherung über £ 10.000 ab; **to ~ one's life** eine Lebensversicherung abschließen; **to ~ oneself against poverty/failure** *etc (fig)* sich gegen Armut/einen Fehlschlag *etc* (ab)sichern **b** = **ensure**

insured [ɪnˈʃʊəd] **ADJ** versichert *(by, with* bei); **~ against fire** feuerversichert **N** **the ~ (party)** der Versicherungsnehmer, die Versicherungsnehmerin, der/die Versicherte

insurer [ɪnˈʃʊərəˈ] **N** Versicherer *m*, Versicherungsgeber *m*

insurgence [ɪnˈsɜːdʒəns], **insurgency** **N** Aufruhr *m*, Aufstand *m*

insurgent [ɪnˈsɜːdʒənt] **ADJ** aufständisch **N** Aufständische(r) *mf*

insurmountable [ˌɪnsəˈmaʊntəbl] **ADJ** unüberwindlich

insurrection [ˌɪnsəˈrekʃən] **N** Aufstand *m*

insurrectionary [ˌɪnsəˈrekʃənərɪ] **ADJ** aufständisch **N** Aufständische(r) *mf*

insurrectionist [ˌɪnsəˈrekʃənɪst] **N** Aufständische(r) *mf*

insusceptible [ˌɪnsəˈseptɪbl] **ADJ** nicht anfällig *(to* für), unempfindlich *(to* gegen); *(fig: = immune)* unempfänglich *(to* für); **~ to pain** schmerzunempfindlich

int. *abbr of* **international** int.

intact [ɪnˈtækt] **ADJ** *(= not damaged)* unversehrt, intakt; *(= whole, in one piece)* intakt; **not one window was left ~** kein einziges Fenster blieb ganz *or* heil; **his confidence remained ~** sein Vertrauen blieb ungebrochen *or* unerschüttert

intake [ˈɪnteɪk] **N** **a** *(= act) (of water, electric current)* Aufnahme *f*; *(of steam)* Ansaugen *nt*; *(= amount) (of water, electricity)* Aufnahme *f*, aufgenommene Menge; *(of steam)* angesaugte *or* einströmende Menge; *(= pipe) (for water)* Zuflussrohr *nt*, Einführungsrohr *nt*; *(for steam)* Einströmungsöffnung *f*, Ansaugöffnung *f*, Einführungsrohr *nt*; **food ~** Nahrungsaufnahme *f*; **(sharp) ~ of breath** (plötzlicher) Atemzug **b** *(Sch, of immigrants)* Aufnahme *f*; *(Mil)* Rekrutierung *f*; **what is your annual ~?** *(Sch)* wie viele neue Schüler nehmen Sie im Jahr auf?; *(Mil)* wie viele Soldaten rekrutieren Sie im Jahr?; **the latest ~ of graduates into our company** die Hochschulabsolventen, die kürzlich in unserer Firma eingestellt worden sind

intake: **intake class** **N** *(Sch)* Anfängerklasse *f*; **intake valve** **N** Einlassventil *nt*; *(= suction valve)* Ansaugventil *nt*

intangible [ɪnˈtændʒəbl] **ADJ** **a** nicht greifbar **b** *fears, longings* unbestimmbar **c** *(Jur, Comm)* **~ property** immaterielle Güter *pl*; **~ capital** immaterielles Kapital

intangible assets **PL** *(Jur, Comm)* immaterielle Werte *pl*

intarsia [ɪnˈtɑːsɪə] **PL** Intarsien *pl*, Einlegearbeiten *pl*

integer [ˈɪntɪdʒəˈ] **N** ganze Zahl

integral [ˈɪntɪgrəl] **ADJ** **a** *part* wesentlich, integral *(geh)*; **to be ~ to sth** ein wesentlicher Bestandteil einer Sache *(gen)* sein; **to play an ~ role in sth** eine wesentliche Rolle bei etw spielen **b** *(= whole)* vollständig, vollkommen **c** *(Math)* Integral- **N** *(Math)* Integral *nt*

integral calculus **N** *(Math)* Integralrechnung *f*

integrate [ˈɪntɪgreɪt] **VT** integrieren; **to ~ sb into** *or* **with sth** jdn in etw *(acc)* integrieren; **to ~ sth into sth** etw in etw *(acc)* integrieren; **to ~ sth with sth** etw auf etw *(acc)* abstimmen; **to ~ a school/college** *(US)* eine Schule/ein College auch für Schwarze *etc* zugänglich machen **VI** *(US: schools etc)* auch für Schwarze *etc* zugänglich werden

integrated [ˈɪntɪgreɪtɪd] **ADJ** integriert; *plan* einheitlich; *piece of work* einheitlich, ein organisches Ganzes bildend; *school, town* ohne Rassentrennung; **an ~ whole** ein integriertes Ganzes; **a fully ~ personality** eine in sich ausgewogene Persönlichkeit

integrated circuit **N** integrierter Schaltkreis

integration [ˌɪntɪˈgreɪʃən] **N** Integration *f (into* in *+acc)*; **(racial) ~** Rassenintegration *f*

integrationist [ˌɪntɪˈgreɪʃənɪst] **N** *(US)* Vertreter(in) *m(f)* der Rassenintegration

integrity [ɪnˈtegrɪtɪ] **N** **a** *(= honesty)* Integrität *f* **b** *(= wholeness)* Einheit *f*

integument [ɪnˈtegjʊmənt] **N** Integument *nt (spec)*

intellect [ˈɪntɪlekt] **N** **a** Intellekt *m*; **a man of keen ~** ein Mensch *m* mit einem scharfen Intellekt; **his powers of ~** seine intellektuellen Fähigkeiten **b** *(= person)* großer Geist

intellectual [ɪntɪˈlektjʊəl] **ADJ** intellektuell; *freedom, climate, property, activity, interests* geistig; **something a little more ~** etwas geistig Anspruchsvolleres **N** Intellektuelle(r) *mf*

intellectualism [ɪntɪˈlektjʊəlɪzəm] **N** Intellektualismus *m*

intellectualize [ɪntɪˈlektjʊəlaɪz] **VT** intellektualisieren **VI** **you always have to ~** du musst immer alles verstandesgemäß angehen, bei dir muss immer alles über den Kopf gehen *(inf)*

intellectually [ɪntɪˈlektjʊəlɪ] **ADV** intellektuell; **~ demanding work** intellektuell anspruchsvolle Arbeit; **he always approaches emotional problems much too ~** er geht an Gefühlsprobleme immer viel zu verstandesmäßig heran

intellectual: **intellectual power** **N** Verstandes- *or* Geisteskraft *f*; **intellectual property rights** **PL** *(Jur)* Urheberrecht *nt*; **intellectual worker** **N** Kopfarbeiter(in) *m(f)*

intelligence [ɪnˈtelɪdʒəns] **N** **a** Intelligenz *f*; **a man of little ~** ein Mensch von geringer Intelligenz; **if he hasn't got the ~ to wear a coat** wenn er nicht gescheit genug ist, einen Mantel anzuziehen **b** *(= news, information)* Informationen *pl*; **according to our latest ~** unseren letzten Meldungen *or* Informationen zufolge **c** *(Mil etc)* Geheim- *or* Nachrichtendienst *m*

intelligence: **intelligence corps** **N** *(Mil)* Geheim- *or* Nachrichtendienst *m*; **intelligence officer** **N** *(Mil)* Nachrichtenoffizier(in) *m(f)*; **intelligence quotient** **N** Intelligenzquotient *m*; **intelligence service** **N** *(Pol)* Geheim- *or* Nachrichtendienst *m*; **intelligence test** **N** Intelligenztest *m*

intelligent [ɪnˈtelɪdʒənt] **ADJ** intelligent; **are there ~ beings on Mars?** gibt es auf dem Mars vernunftbegabte *or* intelligente Lebewesen?

intelligently [ɪn'telɪdʒəntlɪ] ADV intelligent

intelligentsia [ɪn,telɪ'dʒentsɪə] N Intelligenz *f*, Intelligenzija *f*

intelligibility [ɪn,telɪdʒə'bɪlɪtɪ] N Verständlichkeit *f*; *(of handwriting)* Leserlichkeit *f*

intelligible [ɪn'telɪdʒəbl] ADJ zu verstehen *pred*, verständlich *(to sb* für jdn); **in (an) ~ form** in verständlicher Form

intelligibly [ɪn'telɪdʒəblɪ] ADV deutlich

intemperance [ɪn'tempərəns] N *(= lack of moderation)* Maßlosigkeit *f*, Unmäßigkeit *f*; *(= drunkenness)* Trunksucht *f*

intemperate [ɪn'tempərɪt] ADJ **a** *person (= lacking moderation)* unmäßig, maßlos; *(= addicted to drink)* trunksüchtig **b** *climate* extrem; *wind* heftig; *zeal, haste* übermäßig **c** *language, comment* ausfallend, unbeherrscht

intend [ɪn'tend] ✪ 8.1, 8.2, 8.3 VT **a** *(+n)* beabsichtigen, wollen; **I ~ him to go with me, I ~ that he should go with me** ich beabsichtige *or* habe vor, ihn mitzunehmen; *(= insist)* er soll mit mir mitkommen; **I ~ed no harm** es war (von mir) nicht böse gemeint; *(with action)* ich hatte nichts Böses beabsichtigt; **did you ~ that?** hatten Sie das beabsichtigt?, war das Ihre Absicht?; **I didn't ~ it as an insult** das sollte keine Beleidigung sein; **it was ~ed as a compliment** das sollte ein Kompliment sein; **I wondered what he ~ed by that remark** ich fragte mich, was er mit dieser Bemerkung beabsichtigte; **he is ~ed for the diplomatic service** er soll einmal in den diplomatischen Dienst; **this park is ~ed for the general public** dieser Park ist für die Öffentlichkeit gedacht *or* bestimmt; **that remark was ~ed for you** diese Bemerkung war auf Sie gemünzt, mit dieser Bemerkung waren Sie gemeint; **games ~ed for young children** Spiele, die für kleine Kinder gedacht sind; **it was ~ed that he should become an accountant** er sollte eigentlich Buchhalter werden
b *(+vb)* beabsichtigen, fest vorhaben; **he ~s to win** er hat fest vor zu gewinnen; **I ~ to leave next year** ich beabsichtige *or* habe vor, nächstes Jahr zu gehen; **if you don't change your mind I ~ to leave you!** wenn du es dir nicht anders überlegst, verlasse ich dich!; **what do you ~ to do about it?** was beabsichtigen Sie, dagegen zu tun?; **I fully ~ to punish him** ich habe fest vor *or* bin fest entschlossen, ihn zu bestrafen; **this is ~ed to help me** das soll mir helfen; **did you ~ that to happen?** hatten Sie das beabsichtigt?

intendant [ɪn'tendənt] N Intendant(in) *m(f)*

intended [ɪn'tendɪd] ADJ **a** *effect* beabsichtigt, geplant; *victim* ausgeguckt; *target* anvisiert; **what is the ~ meaning of that remark?** was ist mit dieser Bemerkung gemeint? **b** *husband, wife* zukünftig, in spe *pred* N **my ~** *(inf)* mein Zukünftiger *(inf)*, meine Zukünftige *(inf)*

intendment [ɪn'tendmənt] N *(Jur)* wahre Bedeutung; **~ of the law** gesetzgeberische Absicht

intense [ɪn'tens] ADJ **a** *pain, colour, activity* intensiv; *disappointment* bitter, schmerzlich; *pressure, interest, enthusiasm* enorm; *joy, effort* riesig; *heat, cold* ungeheuer; *desire* brennend; *competition, fighting, debate, speculation* heftig; *hatred, jealousy, anger* rasend **b** *person* ernsthaft; *conversation, relationship, feeling, study, life* intensiv; **he suddenly looked very ~** er sah plötzlich ganz ernst aus

intensely [ɪn'tenslɪ] ADV **a** *(= extremely) cold, hot, disappointed, irritated, difficult* äußerst; **~ flavoured** intensiv gewürzt; **an ~ competitive business** eine Branche mit äußerst scharfer Konkurrenz; **I dislike it ~** ich kann es absolut nicht ausstehen **b** *(= with strong emotion, hard) feel, live, stare, work, study* intensiv; **he spoke so ~ that none could doubt his sincerity** er sprach mit einer solchen Intensität, dass niemand an seiner Aufrichtigkeit zweifeln konnte

intenseness [ɪn'tensnɪs] N = **intensity**

intensification [ɪn,tensɪfɪ'keɪʃən] N Intensivierung *f*; *(Phot)* Verstärkung *f*

intensifier [ɪn'tensɪfaɪə'] N *(Gram)* Verstärkungspartikel *f*; **image ~** *(Phys)* Bildverstärker *m*

intensify [ɪn'tensɪfaɪ] VT intensivieren; *meaning, fears* verstärken; *conflict, competition* verschärfen VI zunehmen; *(pain, heat also)* stärker werden; *(fighting also)* sich verschärfen

intension [ɪn'tenʃən] N *(Philos: of a concept)* Intension *f*, Inhalt *m*

intensity [ɪn'tensɪtɪ] N Intensität *f*; *(of feeling, storm also)* Heftigkeit *f*; **~ of a negative** *(Phot)* Dichte *f* eines Negativs

intensive [ɪn'tensɪv] ADJ intensiv, Intensiv-; **to be in ~ care** *(Med)* auf der Intensivstation sein; **~ care unit** Intensivstation *f*; **~ farming** intensive Landwirtschaft; **~ methods** *(Agr)* intensive Bewirtschaftung; **they came under ~ fire** sie kamen unter heftigen Beschuss

intensively [ɪn'tensɪvlɪ] ADV intensiv; **~ reared beef** aus Intensivhaltung stammendes Rindfleisch

intent [ɪn'tent] N Absicht *f*; **with good ~** in guter Absicht; **to all ~s and purposes** im Grunde; **with ~ to** *(esp Jur)* in der Absicht *or* mit dem Vorsatz zu; **to do sth with ~** etw vorsätzlich tun; **letter of ~** (schriftliche) Willenserklärung → **loiter**
ADJ **a** *look* durchdringend, forschend
b to be ~ on achieving sth fest entschlossen sein, etw zu erreichen; **they were ~ on winning** sie wollten unbedingt gewinnen; **she is ~ on a comeback** sie hat die feste Absicht, ein Comeback zu machen; **he was so ~ on catching the bus that he didn't notice the lorry coming** er war so darauf bedacht, den Bus zu erreichen, dass er den Lastwagen nicht kommen sah; **to be ~ on one's work** auf seine Arbeit konzentriert sein

intention [ɪn'tenʃən] ✪ 8.2, 8.3 N **a** Absicht *f*, Intention *f*; **what was your ~ in publishing the article?** mit welcher Absicht haben Sie den Artikel veröffentlicht?; **it is my ~ to punish you severely** ich beabsichtige, Sie streng zu bestrafen; **I have every ~ of doing it** ich habe die feste Absicht, das zu tun; **to have no ~ of doing sth** nicht die Absicht haben, etw zu tun; **I have no** *or* **I haven't the least** *or* **the slightest ~ of staying!** ich habe nicht die geringste Absicht hier zu bleiben, ich denke nicht daran hier zu bleiben; **with good ~s** mit guten Vorsätzen; **with the best of ~s** in der besten Absicht; **with the ~ of ...** in der Absicht zu ..., mit dem Vorsatz zu ...; **his ~s are good, but he seldom carries them out** er hat immer gute Vorsätze *pl*, aber er führt sie selten aus
b ~s *(inf)* (Heirats)absichten *pl*; **his ~s are honourable** er hat ehrliche Absichten

intentional [ɪn'tenʃənl] ADJ absichtlich, vorsätzlich *(esp Jur)*; **it wasn't ~** das war keine Absicht, es war unabsichtlich

intentionally [ɪn'tenʃnəlɪ] ADV absichtlich

intently [ɪn'tentlɪ] ADV *listen, gaze, talk* konzentriert

inter [ɪn'tɜː'] VT *(form)* bestatten

inter- ['ɪntə'-] PREF zwischen-, Zwischen-; *(esp with foreign words)* inter-, Inter-; **interpersonal** zwischenmenschlich; **interdisciplinary** interdisziplinär

interact [,ɪntər'ækt] VI aufeinander wirken; *(Phys)* wechselwirken; *(Psych, Sociol)* interagieren

interaction [,ɪntər'ækʃən] N gegenseitige Einwirkung; *(Phys)* Wechselwirkung *f*; *(Psych, Sociol)* Interaktion *f*

interactive [,ɪntər'æktɪv] ADJ interaktiv; **~ application** *(Comput)* interaktive Anwendung; **~ program** *(Comput)* interaktives Programm; **~ software** *(Comput)* interaktive Software; **~ television** ineraktives Fernsehen

inter alia ['ɪntər'eɪlɪə] ADV unter anderem

interbank ['ɪntə'bæŋk] ADJ *(Fin)* **~ deposits** Bank-bei-Bank-Einlagen *pl*; **~ loan** Bank-an--Bank-Kredit *m*

interbreed ['ɪntə'briːd] VT kreuzen VI *(= inbreed)* sich untereinander vermehren; *(= crossbreed)* sich kreuzen

intercalary [ɪn'tɜːkələrɪ] ADJ Schalt-; **~ day** Schalttag *m*

intercede [,ɪntə'siːd] VI sich einsetzen, sich verwenden *(with* bei, *for, on behalf of* für); *(in argument)* vermitteln

intercellular [,ɪntə'seljʊlə'] ADJ interzellular

intercept [,ɪntə'sept] VT *message, person, plane, pass* abfangen; *(Math)* abschneiden; **they ~ed the enemy** sie schnitten dem Feind den Weg ab

interception [,ɪntə'sepʃən] N *(of message, person, plane etc)* Abfangen *nt*; *(Math)* Abschneiden *nt*; **point of ~** *(Math)* Schnittpunkt *m*

interceptor [,ɪntə'septə'] N *(Aviat)* Abfangjäger *m*

intercession [,ɪntə'seʃən] N Fürsprache *f*; *(in argument)* Vermittlung *f*

interchange ['ɪntə,tʃeɪndʒ] N **a** *(of roads)* Kreuzung *f*; *(of motorways)* (Autobahn)kreuz *nt* **b** *(= exchange)* Austausch *m* VT [,ɪntə'tʃeɪndʒ] **a** *(= switch round)* (miteinander) vertauschen, (aus)tauschen **b** *ideas etc* austauschen *(with* mit)

interchangeable [,ɪntə'tʃeɪndʒəbl] ADJ austauschbar; **the front wheels are ~ with the back ones** Vorder- und Hinterräder sind austauschbar

interchangeably [,ɪntə'tʃeɪndʒəblɪ] ADV austauschbar; **they are used ~** sie können ausgetauscht werden

intercity [,ɪntə'sɪtɪ] ADJ Intercity-; **~ train** Intercityzug *m*

intercollegiate ['ɪntəkə'liːdʒɪɪt] ADJ zwischen Colleges

intercom ['ɪntəkɒm] N (Gegen)sprechanlage *f*; *(in ship, plane)* Bordverständigungsanlage *f*; *(in schools etc)* Lautsprecheranlage *f*

intercommunicate [,ɪntəkə'mjuːnɪkeɪt] VI *(departments, people)* miteinander in Verbindung stehen; *(rooms)* miteinander verbunden sein

intercommunication ['ɪntəkə,mjuːnɪ'keɪʃən] N gegenseitige Verbindung, Verbindung *f* untereinander

intercommunion [,ɪntəkə'mjuːnɪən] N Beziehungen *pl*

interconnect [,ɪntəkə'nekt] VT miteinander verbinden; *loudspeakers, circuits also* zusammenschalten; **~ed problems/events** *etc* zusammenhängende Probleme/Ereignisse *etc*; **are these events ~ed in any way?** besteht irgendein Zusammenhang zwischen diesen Vorfällen?; **to be ~ed by sth** durch etw (miteinander) verbunden sein VI miteinander verbunden sein; *(facts, events)* in Zusammenhang stehen; **to ~ with sth** mit etw verbunden sein/in Zusammenhang stehen; **~ing rooms** miteinander verbundene Zimmer *pl*

interconnection [,ɪntəkə'nekʃən] N Verbindung *f*; *(of circuits etc)* Zusammenschaltung *f*; *(of facts, events etc)* Verbindung *f*, Zusammenhang *m*

intercontinental ['ɪntə,kɒntɪ'nentl] ADJ interkontinental, Interkontinental-; **~ ballistic missile** ballistische Interkontinentalrakete *f*

intercourse ['ɪntəkɔːs] N **a** Verkehr *m*; **commercial ~** Handelsbeziehungen *pl*; **human ~** Verkehr *m* mit Menschen; **social ~** gesellschaftlicher Verkehr **b (sexual) ~** (Geschlechts)verkehr *m*; **anal ~** Analverkehr *m*; **did ~ take place?** hat (Geschlechts)verkehr *or* Beischlaf stattgefunden?

intercross [,ɪntə'krɒs] *(Biol)* VT *animals, plants* kreuzen VI sich kreuzen ['ɪntəkrɒs] N *(crossbreeding)* Kreuzen *nt*; *(hybrid)* Kreuzung

intercultural [,ɪntə'kʌltʃərəl] ADJ interkulturell

intercut [,ɪntə'kʌt] VT **to be ~ with** *(film)* zwischengeschnitten sein mit, mit Zwischenschnitten von ... versehen sein

interdenominational [ˈɪntədɪˌnɒmɪˈneɪʃənl] ADJ interkonfessionell

interdepartmental [ˈɪntəˌdiːpɑːtˈmentl] ADJ *relations, quarrel* zwischen den Abteilungen; *conference, projects* mehrere Abteilungen betreffend; *committee* abteilungsübergreifend

interdependence [ˌɪntədɪˈpendəns] N wechselseitige Abhängigkeit, Interdependenz *f (geh)*

interdependent [ˌɪntədɪˈpendənt] ADJ wechselseitig voneinander abhängig, interdependent *(geh)*

interdict [ˈɪntədɪkt] VT **a** *(Jur)* untersagen, verbieten **b** *(Eccl) person, place* mit dem Interdikt belegen; *priest* suspendieren **c** *(Mil: = intercept) plane, supplies* abfangen N **a** *(Jur)* Verbot *nt* **b** *(Eccl)* Interdikt *nt*

interdiction [ˌɪntəˈdɪkʃən] N *(Jur)* Verbot *nt*, Untersagung *f*; *(Eccl)* Interdikt *nt*

interest [ˈɪntrɪst] ✪ 2.2, 7.5 N **a** Interesse *nt*; **do you have any ~ in chess?** interessieren Sie sich für Schach?, haben Sie Interesse an Schach *(dat)*?; **to take/feel an ~ in sb/sth** sich für jdn/etw interessieren; **after that he took no further ~ in us/it** danach war er nicht mehr an uns *(dat)*/daran interessiert; **to show (an) ~ in sb/sth** Interesse für jdn/etw zeigen; **is it of any ~ to you?** *(= do you want it?)* sind Sie daran interessiert?; **just for ~** nur aus Interesse, nur interessehalber; **he has lost ~** er hat das Interesse verloren; **what are your ~s?** was sind Ihre Interessen(gebiete)?; **his ~s are …** er interessiert sich für …

b *(= importance)* Interesse *nt* *(to* für); **matters of vital ~ to the economy** Dinge *pl* von lebenswichtiger Bedeutung *or* lebenswichtigem Interesse für die Wirtschaft

c *(= advantage, welfare)* Interesse *nt*; **to act in sb's/one's own (best) ~(s)** in jds/im eigenen Interesse handeln; **in the ~(s) of sb** in jds Interesse *(dat)*; **in the ~(s) of sth** im Interesse einer Sache *(gen)*; **the public ~** das öffentliche Wohl; **in the public ~** im öffentlichen Interesse

d *(Fin)* Zinsen *pl*; **~ on an investment** Zinsen aus einer Kapitalanlage; **rate of ~** Zinssatz *m*; **to bear ~ at 4%** 4% Zinsen tragen, mit 4% verzinst sein; **to repay a loan with ~** ein Darlehen mit Zins und Zinseszins zurückzahlen; **to return sb's kindness with ~** *(fig)* jds Freundlichkeit vielfach erwidern; **I'll pay him back with ~** *(fig)* ich werde es ihm mit Zinsen heimzahlen

e *(Comm: = share, stake)* Anteil *m*; *(= interest group)* Kreise *pl*, Interessentengruppe *f*; **shipping/oil ~s** *(= shares)* Reederei-/Ölanteile *pl*; *(= people)* Reedereikreise *pl*/Vertreter *pl* von Ölinteressen; **the landed ~(s)** die Landbesitzer *pl*, die Gutsbesitzer *pl*; **he has a financial ~ in the company** er ist finanziell an der Firma beteiligt; **British trading ~s** britische Handelsinteressen *pl*; **German ~s in Africa** deutsche Interessen *pl* in Afrika; **America has an ~ in helping Russia with its economy** Amerika hat ein Interesse daran, Russland Wirtschaftshilfe zu geben

VT interessieren *(in* für, an *+dat)*; **to ~ sb in doing sth** jdn dafür interessieren, etw zu tun; **can I ~ you in a drink?** kann ich Sie zu etwas Alkoholischem überreden?; **to ~ sb in politics** *etc* jds Interesse an *or* für Politik *etc* wecken, jdn für Politik *etc* interessieren; **to ~ oneself in sb/sth** sich für jdn/etw interessieren

interest: **interest account** N Zinsenkonto *nt*; **interest-bearing** [ˈɪntrɪstˌbeərɪŋ] ADJ *loan* verzinslich; *account, investment* mit Zinsertrag, zinsbringend; **interest coupon** N Zinsabschnitt *m*, Zinsschein *m*

interested [ˈɪntrɪstɪd] ADJ **a** interessiert *(in* an *+dat)*; **I'm not ~** das interessiert mich nicht; **… and I'm not even ~ either** … und es interessiert mich auch gar nicht; **to be ~ in sb/sth** sich für jdn/etw interessieren, an jdm/etw interessiert sein; **would you be ~ in a game of cards?** hätten Sie Interesse, Karten zu spielen?; **I'm going to the cinema, are you ~ (in coming)?** ich gehe ins Kino, haben Sie Interesse daran *or* Lust mitzukommen?; **I'm selling my car, are you ~?** ich verkaufe meinen Wagen, sind Sie interessiert?; **the company is ~ in expanding its sales** die Firma hat Interesse daran *or* ist daran interessiert, ihren Absatz zu vergrößern; **I'd be ~ to know how …** es würde mich ja schon interessieren, wie …; **she was ~ to see what he would do** sie war gespannt, was er wohl tun würde; **I was ~ to hear that** es interessierte mich, das zu hören; **to get sb ~ (in sth)** jdn (für etw) interessieren

b *(= having personal or financial interest)* befangen; *(= involved)* beteiligt; **he is an ~ party** er ist befangen, er ist daran beteiligt

interest: **interest-free** ADJ, ADV zinslos, zinsfrei; **interest group** N Interessengruppe *f*

interesting [ˈɪntrɪstɪŋ] ADJ interessant; **the ~ thing about it is that …** das Interessante daran ist, dass …; **she's in an ~ condition** *(euph)* sie ist in anderen Umständen

interestingly [ˈɪntrɪstɪŋlɪ] ADV auf interessante Weise; **~ enough, I saw him yesterday** interessanterweise habe ich ihn gestern gesehen

interest: **interest instalment**, *(US)* **interest installment** N Zinsrate *f*; **interest rate** N *(Fin)* Zinssatz *m*; **~ policy** Zinspolitik *f*; **interest statement** N Zinsaufstellung *f*

interface [ˈɪntəfeɪs] N **a** Grenzfläche *f*, Grenzschicht *f*; **there's a bigger ~ between these two fields than I thought** diese beiden Gebiete haben mehr Berührungspunkte, als ich gedacht hätte **b** *(Comput)* Schnittstelle *f*, Interface *nt*; **user ~** Benutzeroberfläche *f* VT [ˌɪntəˈfeɪs] koppeln VI [ˌɪntəˈfeɪs] **to ~ with sth** Berührungspunkte mit etw haben

interfacing [ˈɪntəfeɪsɪŋ] N *(Sew)* Einlage *f*

interfere [ˌɪntəˈfɪəˈ] VI **a** *(= meddle) (in argument, sb's affairs)* sich einmischen *(in* in *+acc)*; *(with machinery, sb's property)* sich zu schaffen machen *(with* an *+dat)*; *(euph: sexually)* sich vergehen *(with* an *+dat)*; **don't ~ with the machine** lass die Finger von der Maschine; **who's been interfering with my books?** wer war an meinen Büchern?; **the body has been ~d with** jemand hatte sich an der Leiche zu schaffen gemacht; *(sexually)* die Leiche zeigte Spuren eines Sexualverbrechens

b *(thing, event: = disrupt, obstruct)* **to ~ with sth** etw stören *(also Rad)*; *with work, ability to do sth* etw beeinträchtigen; **to ~ with sb's plans** jds Pläne durchkreuzen

interference [ˌɪntəˈfɪərəns] N **a** *(= meddling)* Einmischung *f*; **I don't want any ~ with my books/papers** ich will nicht, dass jemand an meine Bücher/Papiere geht **b** *(= disruption, Rad, TV)* Störung *f* *(with +gen)*

interfering [ˌɪntəˈfɪərɪŋ] ADJ *person* sich ständig einmischend; **his ~ ways annoy me** es ärgert *or* stört mich, wie er sich immer einmischt; **don't be so ~** misch dich nicht immer ein

interferon [ˌɪntəˈfɪərɒn] N *(Chem)* Interferon *nt*

interfuse [ˌɪntəˈfjuːz] VT *(poet, liter) (= pervade)* durchdringen, durchsetzen; *(= mix)* (ver)mischen VI sich (ver)mischen, sich (miteinander) vermischen

intergalactic [ˌɪntəgəˈlæktɪk] ADJ intergalaktisch

interim [ˈɪntərɪm] N Zwischenzeit *f*, Interim *nt (geh)*; **in the ~** in der Zwischenzeit ADJ vorläufig; **~ agreement/solution** Übergangsabkommen *nt*/-lösung *f*; **~ report** Zwischenbericht *m*; **~ government/president** Interims- *or* Übergangsregierung *f*/-präsident(in) *m(f)*; **~ period** Zwischenzeit *f*; *(= transitional)* Übergangszeit *f*; **~ payment** Interimszahlung *f*

interim dividend N Abschlagsdividende *f*, Zwischendividende *f*

interim financing N Zwischenfinanzierung *f*

interior [ɪnˈtɪərɪəˈ] ADJ **a** *(= inside)* Innen-; **~ wall** Innenwand *f*; **~ space** Innenraum *m*; **~ light** *(Aut)* Innenraumbeleuchtung *f* **b** *(Pol)* **~ minister** Innenminister(in) *m(f)*; **~ ministry** Innenministerium *nt* **c the ~ region(s)** *(of a country)* das Landesinnere N *(of country)* Innere(s) *nt*; *(of house)* Innenausstattung *f*, Interieur *nt (geh)*; *(Phot)* Innenaufnahme *f*; **deep in the ~** tief im Landesinneren; **Department of the Interior** *(US)* Innenministerium *nt*; **the ~ of the house has been newly decorated** das Haus ist innen neu gemacht

interior: **interior angle** N Innenwinkel *m*; **interior decoration** N Innenausstattung *f*; *(= decor also)* Interieur *nt*; **interior decorator** N Innenausstatter(in) *m(f)*; **interior design** N Innenarchitektur *f*; **interior designer** N Innenarchitekt(in) *m(f)*; **interior monologue** N innerer Monolog; **interior-sprung** ADJ Federkern-; **~ mattress** Federkernmatratze *f*

interject [ˌɪntəˈdʒekt] VT *remark, question* einwerfen; **…, he ~ed** …, rief er dazwischen

interjection [ˌɪntəˈdʒekʃən] N *(= exclamation)* Ausruf *m*; *(Ling also)* Interjektion *f*; *(= remark)* Einwurf *m*

interlace [ˌɪntəˈleɪs] VT *threads etc* verflechten; *(in cloth also)* verweben; *cloth (with thread)* durchwirken; *fingers* verschlingen; *(fig) scenes, styles* verflechten VI sich ineinander verflechten; *(twigs)* verschlungen sein

interlacing [ˈɪntəleɪsɪŋ] ADJ verflochten; *branches also* verschlungen N Flechtwerk *nt*

interlanguage [ˈɪntəˌlæŋgwɪdʒ] N Verkehrssprache *f*

interlard [ˌɪntəˈlɑːd] VT **to ~ a speech with facetious comments** witzige Kommentare in eine Rede einflechten; **a speech ~ed with jokes** eine mit Witzen gespickte Rede

interleaf [ˈɪntəliːf] N leeres Zwischenblatt

interleave [ˌɪntəˈliːv] VT mit Zwischenblättern versehen, durchschießen *(spec)*

interlibrary loan [ˈɪntəˌlaɪbrərɪˈləʊn] N Fernleihe *f*; **to have a book on ~** ein Buch über die Fernleihe (ausgeliehen) haben

interline [ˌɪntəˈlaɪn] VT **a** *(Typ) corrections, translation* interlinear einfügen **b** *(Sew)* mit einer Einlage versehen

interlinear [ˌɪntəˈlɪnɪəˈ] ADJ Interlinear-, interlinear; **~ version** Interlinearversion *f*

interlink [ˌɪntəˈlɪŋk] VT ineinanderhängen; *(fig) theories etc* miteinander verknüpfen *or* verbinden VI ineinanderhängen; *(fig: theories etc)* zusammenhängen; **a transport network with bus and rail services ~ing** ein Verkehrsnetz *nt*, in dem Bus und Bahn im Verbund fahren

interlock [ˌɪntəˈlɒk] VT (fest) zusammenstecken, (fest) ineinanderstecken VI ineinandergreifen; *(one piece)* feststecken *or* -sitzen *(with* in *+dat)*; *(chariot wheels etc)* sich verfangen; *(antlers)* sich verhaken, sich verfangen; *(fig: destinies)* verkettet sein

interlocutor [ˌɪntəˈlɒkjʊtəˈ] N Gesprächspartner(in) *m(f)*; *(asking questions)* Fragesteller(in) *m(f)*

interloper [ˈɪntələʊpəˈ] N Eindringling *m*

interlude [ˈɪntəluːd] N Periode *f*; *(Theat) (= interval)* Pause *f*; *(= performance)* Zwischenspiel *nt*; *(Mus)* Interludium *nt*; *(= episode)* Intermezzo *nt*, Episode *f*; **a peaceful ~ in his busy life** eine friedliche Unterbrechung seines geschäftigen Lebens

intermarriage [ˌɪntəˈmærɪdʒ] N *(between groups)* Mischehen *pl*; *(within the group)* Heirat *f* untereinander

intermarry [ˌɪntəˈmærɪ] VI *(= marry within the group)* untereinander heiraten; *(two groups: = marry with each other)* sich durch Heirat vermischen, Mischehen eingehen; **they were not allowed to ~ with another tribe** sie durften keine Mischehen mit einem anderen Stamm eingehen

intermediary [ˌɪntəˈmiːdɪərɪ] N (Ver)mittler(in) *m(f)*, Mittelsperson *f*, Mittelsmann *m* ADJ *(= intermediate)* mittlere(r, s); *(= mediating)* vermittelnd; **~ role** Vermittlerrolle *f*

intermediate [ˌɪntəˈmiːdɪət] ADJ Zwischen-; *French, maths etc* für fortgeschrittene Anfänger; **~ position** Zwischenposition *f*; **~ stage** Zwischenstadium *nt*; **the ~ stations** die dazwischenliegenden Bahnhöfe; **~ step** Zwischenstufe *f*; **an ~ student** ein fortgeschrittener An-

fänger, eine fortgeschrittene Anfängerin; ~ **range ballistic missile** ballistische Mittelstreckenrakete *f*; ~ **goods** (*Econ*: = *semi-finished*) Halbfabrikate *pl*; ~ **treatment** *(Brit) Sozialprogramm für jugendliche Straftäter und sozial gefährdete Jugendliche, das weder Inhaftierung noch Bestrafung beinhaltet*
N fortgeschrittener Anfänger, fortgeschrittene Anfängerin

interment [ɪn'tɜːmənt] N Beerdigung *f*, Bestattung *f*

intermezzo [ˌɪntə'metsəʊ] N Intermezzo *nt*

interminable [ɪn'tɜːmɪnəbl] ADJ endlos; **after what seemed an ~ journey** nach einer Reise, die nicht enden zu wollen schien

interminably [ɪn'tɜːmɪnəblɪ] ADV endlos, ewig

intermingle [ˌɪntə'mɪŋgl] VT vermischen VI sich mischen (*with* unter +*acc*); **people from many countries ~d at the conference** Menschen aus vielen Ländern bekamen bei der Konferenz Kontakt miteinander

intermission [ˌɪntə'mɪʃən] N a Unterbrechung *f*, Pause *f* b (*Theat, Film*) Pause *f*

intermittent [ˌɪntə'mɪtənt] ADJ periodisch auftretend; (*Tech*) intermittierend

intermittent fever N Wechselfieber *nt*

intermittently [ˌɪntə'mɪtəntlɪ] ADV periodisch; (*Tech*) intermittierend; **the patient was only ~ conscious** der Patient war nur zeitweise bei Bewusstsein

intermix [ˌɪntə'mɪks] VT vermischen VI sich vermischen

intern[1] [ɪn'tɜːn] VT *person* internieren; *ship etc* festhalten

intern[2] ['ɪntɜːn] (*US*) N a (= *junior doctor*) Assistenzarzt *m*/-ärztin *f* b (= *trainee*) Praktikant(in) *m(f)* VI das Medizinalpraktikum absolvieren

internal [ɪn'tɜːnl] ADJ (= *inner*) innere(r, s); (*Math*) *angle, diameter* Innen-; (= *within country*) Binnen-, im Inland; (= *within organization*) *policy, debate, investigation, mail, examination* intern; ~ **examiner** (*Univ*) interner Prüfer, interne Prüferin; ~ **flight** Inlandsflug *m*; **Internal Revenue Service** (*US*) Steueramt *nt*, Finanzamt *nt*; ~ **trade** Binnenhandel *m*; ~ **telephone** Haustelefon *nt*; ~ **wall** Innenwand *f*

internal: **internal affairs** PL innere Angelegenheiten *pl*, Inneres *nt*; **internal bleeding** N innere Blutungen *pl*; **internal combustion engine** N Verbrennungsmotor *m*

internalize [ɪn'tɜːnəlaɪz] VT verinnerlichen, internalisieren (*spec*)

internally [ɪn'tɜːnəlɪ] ADV innen, im Inneren; (= *in body*) innerlich; (= *in country*) landesintern; (= *in organization*) intern; **he is bleeding ~** er hat innere Blutungen; **"not to be taken ~"** „nicht zur inneren Anwendung", „nicht zum Einnehmen"

internal: **internal market** N (*Econ*: *in EU etc*) Binnenmarkt *m*; (*in health service etc, within organization*) marktwirtschaftliche Struktur; **internal medicine** N innere Medizin; **internal revenue** N (*Econ*) Staatseinkünfte *pl*

international [ˌɪntə'næʃnəl] ADJ international; ~ **money order** Auslandsanweisung *f*; **International Olympic Committee** Internationales Olympisches Komitee; ~ **relations** internationale Beziehungen *pl* N a (*Sport*) (= *match*) Länderspiel *nt*; (= *player*) Nationalspieler(in) *m(f)* b (*Pol*) **International** Internationale *f*

International: **International Bank for Reconstruction and Development** N Internationale Bank für Wiederaufbau und Entwicklung; **International Court of Justice** N Internationaler Gerichtshof; **International Date Line** N Datumsgrenze *f*

Internationale [ˌɪntəˌnæʃə'nɑːl] N Internationale *f*

internationalism [ˌɪntə'næʃnəlɪzəm] N Internationalismus *m*

internationalist [ˌɪntə'næʃnəlɪst] N Internationalist(in) *m(f)*

internationalize [ˌɪntə'næʃnəlaɪz] VT internationalisieren

International Labour Organization N Internationale Arbeitsorganisation

international law N Völkerrecht *nt*, internationales Recht

international lending N (*Fin*) internationaler Kreditverkehr

internationally [ˌɪntə'næʃnəlɪ] ADV international; *compete* auf internationaler Ebene

International Monetary Fund N (*Econ*) Internationaler Währungsfonds

International Phonetic Alphabet N internationale Lautschrift

International Standards Organization N Internationaler Normenausschuss

interne N, VI = **intern[2]**

internecine [ˌɪntə'niːsaɪn] ADJ a (= *mutually destructive*) für beide Seiten verlustreich; (= *bloody*) mörderisch; ~ **war** gegenseitiger Vernichtungskrieg b (= *internal*) *quarrel, conflict* intern; ~ **strife** innere Zerrissenheit

internee [ˌɪntɜː'niː] N Internierte(r) *mf*

Internet ['ɪntəˌnet] N **the ~** das Internet; **to surf the ~** im Internet surfen

Internet: **Internet access** N Internetanschluss *m* or -zugang *m*; **Internet account** N *auf eine Person bezogener, per Benutzername und Kennwort zugänglicher Internetanschluss*, Internet-Account *m*; **Internet banking** N Internetbanking *nt*; **Internet café** N Internet-Café *nt*; **Internet commerce** N Internethandel *m*, Handel *m* über das Internet; **Internet connection** N Internetanschluss *m* or -verbindung *f*; **Internet-enabled** ADJ *mobile phone, TV etc* internetfähig; **Internet service provider** N Internet-Anbieter *m*; **internet site** N Internetsite *f*

internist [ɪn'tɜːnɪst] N (*US*) Internist(in) *m(f)*

internment [ɪn'tɜːnmənt] N Internierung *f*; ~ **camp** Internierungslager *nt*

internship ['ɪntɜːnʃɪp] N (*US*) a (*Med*) Medizinalpraktikum *nt* b (*as trainee*) Praktikum *nt*

internuncio [ˌɪntə'nʌnsɪəʊ] N Internuntius *m*

interoperability ['ɪntəˌrɒpərə'bɪlɪtɪ] N (*Comput*) Interoperabilität *f*

interparty ['ɪntə'pɑːtɪ] ADJ parteiübergreifend

interpenetrate [ˌɪntə'penɪtreɪt] VT durchdringen VI einander durchdringen

interplanetary [ˌɪntə'plænɪtərɪ] ADJ interplanetar

interplay ['ɪntəpleɪ] N Zusammenspiel *nt*

Interpol ['ɪntəpɒl] N Interpol *f*

interpolate [ɪn'tɜːpəleɪt] VT *remark* einwerfen; *matter into book etc* interpolieren, einfügen; (*Math*) interpolieren

interpolation [ɪnˌtɜːpə'leɪʃən] N (*of remark*) Einwerfen *nt*; (= *remark made*) Einwurf *m*; (*in text*) Interpolation *f*, Einfügung *f*; (*Math*) Interpolation *f*

interpose [ˌɪntə'pəʊz] VT a *object* dazwischenstellen/-legen; **to ~ sth between two things** etw zwischen zwei Dinge stellen/legen; **to be ~d between two things** zwischen zwei Dingen stehen/liegen; **to ~ oneself between two people** sich zwischen zwei Leute stellen b (= *interject*) *remark, question* einwerfen; *objection* vorbringen (*into* in +*dat*) VI (= *intervene*) eingreifen

interpret [ɪn'tɜːprɪt] VT a (= *translate orally*) dolmetschen b (= *explain, understand*) auslegen, interpretieren; *omen, dream* deuten; *world* verstehen; (*Theat, Mus*) interpretieren; **this could be ~ed as meaning** or **to mean that ...** das könnte man so auslegen or interpretieren, dass ...; **how would you ~ what he said?** wie würden Sie seine Worte verstehen or auffassen? VI dolmetschen

interpretation [ɪnˌtɜːprɪ'teɪʃən] N a (= *explanation*) Auslegung *f*, Interpretation *f*; (*of omen, dream*) Deutung *f*; (*of world*) Verständnis *nt*; (*Theat, Mus*) Interpretation *f*; **she put quite a different ~ on the figures** sie legte die Zahlen ganz anders aus, sie interpretierte die Zahlen ganz anders; **the speech can be given several ~s** die Rede kann verschieden ausgelegt or interpretiert werden; **an ~ of a poem** eine Gedichtinterpretation b (*Admin*: = *interpreting*) Dolmetschen *nt*

interpretative [ɪn'tɜːprɪtətɪv] ADJ interpretierend

interpreter [ɪn'tɜːprɪtə'] N a Dolmetscher(in) *m(f)*; (*Theat, Mus*) Interpret(in) *m(f)*; (*of dreams*) Traumdeuter(in) *m(f)* b (*Comput*) Interpreter *m*

interpreting [ɪn'tɜːprɪtɪŋ] N (= *profession*) Dolmetschen *nt*

interpretive [ɪn'tɜːprɪtɪv] ADJ = **interpretative**

interracial [ˌɪntə'reɪʃəl] ADJ (= *between races*) zwischen den or verschiedenen Rassen; (= *multiracial*) gemischtrassig

interregnum [ˌɪntə'regnəm] N *pl* **-s** or **interregna** [ˌɪntə'regnə] Interregnum *nt*

interrelate [ˌɪntərɪ'leɪt] VT *two things* zueinander in Beziehung bringen, eine Beziehung herstellen zwischen (+*dat*); **to ~ one thing with another** eine Sache in Beziehung zu einer anderen bringen; **to be ~d** zueinander in Beziehung stehen, zusammenhängen; **~d factors** zusammenhängende Faktoren *pl* VI zueinander in Beziehung stehen, zusammenhängen; **this influences the way in which we ~ with others** das beeinflusst unsere Beziehungen zu anderen

interrelation [ˌɪntərɪ'leɪʃən] N Beziehung *f* (*between* zwischen +*dat*); (*between factors, events*) Zusammenhang *m* (*between* zwischen +*dat*)

interrogate [ɪn'terəgeɪt] VT verhören; (*father, headmaster etc*) regelrecht verhören

interrogation [ɪnˌterə'geɪʃən] N Verhör *nt*; **to submit to ~** sich verhören lassen; ~ **room** Vernehmungsraum *m* or -zimmer *nt*

interrogative [ˌɪntə'rɒgətɪv] ADJ *look, tone* fragend; (*Gram*) Interrogativ-; ~ **pronoun/clause** Interrogativpronomen *nt*/-satz *m* N (*Gram*) (= *pronoun*) Interrogativpronomen *nt*, Fragefürwort *nt*; (= *mood*) Interrogativ *m*, Frageform *f*; **in the ~** in der Frageform

interrogatively [ˌɪntə'rɒgətɪvlɪ] ADV fragend; (*Gram also*) interrogativ

interrogator [ɪn'terəgeɪtə'] N Vernehmungsbeamte(r) *mf* (*form*); **my/his ~s** die, die mich/ihn verhören

interrogatory [ˌɪntə'rɒgətərɪ] ADJ fragend

interrupt [ˌɪntə'rʌpt] VT (= *break the continuity of*) unterbrechen (*also Elec*); (*in conversation*: *rudely also*) ins Wort fallen (+*dat*); *activity, work also* stören; *traffic flow also* unterbrechen, stören; (= *obstruct*) *view* versperren; ~ **function** (*Comput*) Unterbrechungsfunktion *f* VI (*in conversation*) unterbrechen; (= *interrupt sb's work etc*) stören; **stop ~ing!** fall mir/ihm *etc* nicht dauernd ins Wort! N ['ɪntərʌpt] (*Comput*) Unterbrechungsbefehl *m*, Interrupt *nt*

interrupter [ˌɪntə'rʌptə'] N (*Elec*) Unterbrecher *m*

interruption [ˌɪntə'rʌpʃən] N Unterbrechung *f*; (*of work, activity, traffic flow also*) Störung *f*; (*of view*) Versperrung *f*; **without ~** ohne Unterbrechung, ununterbrochen; **an ~ to her career** eine Unterbrechung ihrer Karriere

intersect [ˌɪntə'sekt] VT durchschneiden; (*Geometry*) schneiden VI sich kreuzen; (*Geometry, in set theory*) sich schneiden; **~ing sets** Schnittmengen *pl*

intersection [ˌɪntə'sekʃən] N (= *crossroads*) Kreuzung *f*; (*Geometry*) Schnittpunkt *m*; **point of ~** Schnittpunkt *m*

intersperse [ˌɪntə'spɜːs] VT (= *scatter*) verteilen; **~d with sth** mit etw dazwischen; **a speech ~d with quotations** eine mit Zitaten gespickte Rede; **periods of sunshine ~d with showers** von Schauern unterbrochener Sonnenschein; **boredom ~d with periods of ...** Langeweile und dazwischen or zwischendurch ...

interstate [ˌɪntəˈsteɪt] ADJ *(US)* zwischen den (US-Bundes)staaten, zwischenstaatlich; **~ highway** (Bundes)autobahn *f*, Interstate Highway *m* N *(US)* (Bundes)autobahn *f*, Interstate (Highway) *m*

interstellar [ˌɪntəˈstelə'] ADJ interstellar

interstice [ɪnˈtɜːstɪs] N Zwischenraum *m*; *(in wall etc also)* Sprung *m*, Riss *m*; *(between panels also)* Fuge *f*

intertextuality [ˈɪntəˈtekstjuːˌælɪtɪ] N *(Liter)* Intertextualität *f*

intertribal [ˌɪntəˈtraɪbl] ADJ zwischen den *or* verschiedenen Stämmen; **~ war** Stammeskrieg *m*

intertwine [ˌɪntəˈtwaɪn] VT verschlingen; *(fig) destinies also* verknüpfen; *stories* verweben VI *(branches, arms etc)* sich ineinander verschlingen; *(threads)* verschlungen sein; *(fig: destinies)* sich verbinden

interurban [ˌɪntəˈɜːbən] ADJ *(US) railroad* städteverbindend

interval [ˈɪntəvəl] N **a** *(in space, time)* Abstand *m*, Intervall *nt (form)*; **at ~s** in Abständen; **at two-weekly ~s** in Abständen von zwei Wochen; **at ~s of two metres** *(Brit) or* **meters** *(US)* in Abständen von zwei Metern; **sunny ~s** *(Met)* Aufheiterungen *pl* **b** *(Sch, Theat etc)* Pause *f* **c** *(Mus)* Intervall *nt*

intervene [ˌɪntəˈviːn] VI *(person)* einschreiten *(in* bei), intervenieren; *(= interrupt)* unterbrechen; *(event, fate)* dazwischenkommen; **if nothing ~s** wenn nichts dazwischenkommt

intervener [ˌɪntəˈviːnə'] N Vermittler(in) *m(f)*; *(Jur)* Nebenintervenient(in) *m(f)*

intervening [ˌɪntəˈviːnɪŋ] ADJ *period of time, space* dazwischenliegend; **in the ~ weeks** in den Wochen dazwischen, in den dazwischenliegenden Wochen; **in the ~ period** in der Zwischenzeit

intervention [ˌɪntəˈvenʃən] N Eingreifen *nt*, Eingriff *m*, Intervention *f*

interventionist [ˌɪntəˈvenʃənɪst] N Interventionist(in) *m(f)* ADJ interventionistisch

intervertebral disc [ˈɪntəˌvɜːtɪbrəlˈdɪsk] N Bandscheibe *f*

interview [ˈɪntəvjuː] ✪ 19.3, 19.5 N **a** *(for job)* Vorstellungsgespräch *nt*; *(with authorities, employer etc)* Gespräch *nt*; *(for grant)* Auswahlgespräch *nt* **b** *(Press, TV etc)* Interview *nt*; **to give an ~** ein Interview *nt* geben **c** *(= formal talk)* Gespräch *nt*, Unterredung *f* VT **a** *job applicant* ein/das Vorstellungsgespräch führen mit; *applicant for grant etc* Fragen stellen *(+dat)*; **he is being ~ed on Monday for the job** er hat am Montag sein Vorstellungsgespräch **b** *(Press, TV etc)* interviewen VI **a** *(for job)* das Vorstellungsgespräch/die Vorstellungsgespräche führen **b** *(Press, TV etc)* interviewen

interviewee [ˌɪntəvjuːˈiː] N *(for job)* Kandidat(in) *m(f)* (für die Stelle); *(Press, TV etc)* Interviewte(r) *mf*

interviewer [ˈɪntəvjuːə'] N *(for job)* Leiter(in) *m(f)* des Vorstellungsgesprächs; *(Press, TV etc)* Interviewer(in) *m(f)*

interwar [ˈɪntəˈwɔː'] ADJ *years, period* zwischen den Weltkriegen; **~ Britain** Großbritannien in der Zeit zwischen den Weltkriegen

interweave [ˌɪntəˈwiːv] VT *(lit, fig)* verweben; *branches, fingers* verschlingen, ineinanderschlingen VI sich verweben; *(branches)* sich ineinanderschlingen

intestate [ɪnˈtestɪt] ADJ *(Jur)* nicht testamentarisch vermacht; **to die ~** ohne Testament sterben

intestinal [ɪnˈtestɪnl] ADJ Darm-, intestinal *(form)*; **~ cancer** Darmkrebs *m*

intestine [ɪnˈtestɪn] N Darm *m*; **small/large ~** Dünn-/Dickdarm *m*

intimacy [ˈɪntɪməsɪ] N Vertrautheit *f*, Intimität *f*; *(euph: = sexual intimacy)* Intimität *f*; **~ took place** *(form euph)* es kam zu Intimitäten

intimate[1] [ˈɪntɪmɪt] ADJ **a** *friend* eng, vertraut, intim; *(sexually)* intim; **we're friends but we are not ~** wir sind befreundet, stehen aber nicht auf so vertraulichem Fuß; **to be on ~ terms with sb** mit jdm auf vertraulichem Fuß stehen; **he was a bit too ~ with my wife** er war ein bisschen zu vertraulich mit meiner Frau; **to be/become ~ with sb** mit jdm vertraut sein/werden; *(sexually)* mit jdm intim sein/werden **b** *(fig)* intim *(geh)*; *feelings, thoughts* geheim, intim; *connection* eng; *knowledge* gründlich; **to have an ~ knowledge of sth** über etw *(acc)* in allen Einzelheiten Bescheid wissen **c** *freshness* im Intimbereich; **~ deodorant** Intimspray *m or nt* N Vertraute(r) *mf*

intimate[2] [ˈɪntɪmeɪt] VT andeuten; **he ~d to them that they should stop** er gab ihnen zu verstehen, dass sie aufhören sollten

intimately [ˈɪntɪmɪtlɪ] ADV *acquainted* bestens; *behave, speak* vertraulich; *related, connected* eng; *know* genau, gründlich; **we know each other but not ~** wir kennen uns, aber nicht besonders gut; **he is ~ involved in local politics** er ist tief in Lokalpolitik verwickelt

intimation [ˌɪntɪˈmeɪʃən] N Andeutung *f*; **he gave no ~ that he was going to resign** er deutete durch nichts an *or* machte keinerlei Andeutungen, dass er zurücktreten würde

intimidate [ɪnˈtɪmɪdeɪt] VT einschüchtern; **they ~d him into not telling the police** sie schüchterten ihn so ein, dass er der Polizei nichts erzählte; **we won't be ~d** wir lassen uns nicht einschüchtern

intimidation [ɪnˌtɪmɪˈdeɪʃən] N Einschüchterung *f*

intimidatory [ɪnˌtɪmɪˈdeɪtərɪ] ADJ *telephone call, behaviour* einschüchternd; **~ tactics** Einschüchterungstaktik *f*

into [ˈɪntʊ] PREP **a** in *(+acc)*; *(= against) crash, drive* gegen; **to translate sth ~ French** etw ins Französische übersetzen; **to change euros ~ pounds** Euro in Pfund umtauschen; **to divide 3 ~ 9** 9 durch 3 teilen *or* dividieren; **3 ~ 9 goes 3** 3 geht dreimal in 9; **to get ~ trouble** in Schwierigkeiten kommen; **to go ~ politics** in die Politik gehen; **they worked far ~ the night** sie arbeiteten bis tief in die Nacht hinein; **he's well ~ his sixties** er ist in den späten Sechzigern; **it turned ~ a nice day** es wurde ein schöner Tag; **I can't get ~ my jeans any more** ich komme nicht mehr in meine Jeans; **research ~ AIDS/cancer** Aids-/Krebsforschung *f* **b** *(inf)* **to be ~ sb/sth** *(= like)* auf jdn/etw *(acc)* stehen *(inf)*; *(= be interested in)* sich für jdn/etw interessieren; **to be ~ sth** *(= use, drugs etc)* etw nehmen; **I'm not really ~ the job yet** ich bin noch nicht ganz drin im Job *(inf)*; **he's ~ local politics in a big way** *(= actively involved)* er ist schwer in der Lokalpolitik aktiv *(inf)*; **she's ~ getting up early** sie ist passionierte Frühaufsteherin; **she's ~ health food** sie steht auf Gesundheitskost *(inf)*; **he's ~ wine** *(= likes)* er ist Weinliebhaber; *(= is expert)* er ist Weinkenner; **he's ~ computers** er ist Computerfan *(inf)*; **well if that's what you're ~ ...** also, wenn das dein Fall ist ...; **I'm not ~ that** darauf stehe ich nicht *(inf)*

intolerable ADJ, **intolerably** ADV [ɪnˈtɒlərəbl, -ɪ] unerträglich

intolerance [ɪnˈtɒlərəns] N **a** Intoleranz *f (of* gegenüber) **b** *(esp Med)* Überempfindlichkeit *f (to, of* gegen)

intolerant [ɪnˈtɒlərənt] ADJ intolerant *(of* gegenüber); *(Med)* überempfindlich *(to, of* gegen)

intolerantly [ɪnˈtɒlərəntlɪ] ADV intolerant; *refuse* intoleranterweise

intonate [ˈɪntəʊneɪt] VT *(Ling)* intonieren

intonation [ˌɪntəʊˈneɪʃən] N Intonation *f*; *(Ling also)* Satzmelodie *f*

intonation pattern N *(Ling)* Intonationsmuster *nt*

intone [ɪnˈtəʊn] VT intonieren

in toto [ɪnˈtəʊtəʊ] ADV im Ganzen, in toto *(geh)*

intoxicant [ɪnˈtɒksɪkənt] N Rauschmittel *nt*

intoxicate [ɪnˈtɒksɪkeɪt] VT *(lit, fig)* berauschen

intoxicated [ɪnˈtɒksɪkeɪtɪd] ADJ betrunken, berauscht *(also fig)*, im Rausch *(also fig)*; **to become ~** sich berauschen *(also fig) (by, with* an *+dat*, von); **~ by drugs** im Drogenrausch; **~ by** *or* **with success** vom Erfolg berauscht

intoxication [ɪnˌtɒksɪˈkeɪʃən] N Rausch *m (also fig)*, (Be)trunkenheit *f*; *(Med: = poisoning)* Vergiftung *f*; **in a state of ~** *(form)* in (be)trunkenem Zustand, im Rausch

intra- [ˌɪntrə-] PREF intra-; **intramuscular** intramuskulär

intractable [ɪnˈtræktəbl] ADJ *metal* unnachgiebig; *nature, problem, illness, pain* hartnäckig; *conflict* unlösbar; *issue* äußerst schwierig

intracutaneous [ˌɪntrəkjuːˈteɪnɪəs] ADJ *(Med)* intrakutan *(spec)*, in der Haut (gelegen); **~ injection** Injektion *f* in die Haut

intramural [ˌɪntrəˈmjʊərəl] ADJ *(esp Univ) course* innerhalb der Universität; *activities* studienspezifisch

intranet [ˈɪntrənet] N *(Comput)* Intranet *nt*

intransigence [ɪnˈtrænsɪdʒəns] N Unnachgiebigkeit *f*

intransigent [ɪnˈtrænsɪdʒənt] ADJ unnachgiebig

intransitive [ɪnˈtrænsɪtɪv] ADJ *verb* intransitiv N Intransitiv *nt*

intraparty [ˈɪntrəˈpɑːtɪ] ADJ parteiintern, innerparteilich

intrastate [ˌɪntrəˈsteɪt] ADJ *(US)* innerhalb des (Bundes)staates

intrauterine device [ˌɪntrəˈjuːtəraɪndɪˌvaɪs] N Intrauterinpessar *nt*

intravenous [ˌɪntrəˈviːnəs] ADJ intravenös; **~ drip** *(Med)* intravenöse Infusion; **~ drug user** Drogenabhängige(r) *mf*, der/die intravenös spritzt

intravenously [ˌɪntrəˈviːnəslɪ] ADV *feed, give, administer* intravenös

in-tray [ˈɪntreɪ] N Ablage *f* für Eingänge

intrepid ADJ, **intrepidly** ADV [ɪnˈtrepɪd, -lɪ] unerschrocken, kühn

intrepidity [ˌɪntrɪˈpɪdɪtɪ] N Unerschrockenheit *f*, Kühnheit *f*

intricacy [ˈɪntrɪkəsɪ] N Kompliziertheit *f*; *(= intricate part: of law, chess etc)* Feinheit *f*; **the intricacies of the job** die Feinheiten der Arbeit

intricate [ˈɪntrɪkɪt] ADJ kompliziert; *(= involved also)* verwickelt

intricately [ˈɪntrɪkɪtlɪ] ADV kompliziert; **these issues are ~ connected** diese Fragen sind auf komplizierte Weise miteinander verknüpft

intrigue [ɪnˈtriːg] VI intrigieren VT *(= arouse interest of)* faszinieren; *(= arouse curiosity of)* neugierig machen; **to be ~d with** *or* **by sth** von etw fasziniert sein; **I would be ~d to know why ...** es würde mich schon interessieren, warum ...; **I'm ~d to hear what she's been saying** ich würde wirklich gerne hören, was sie gesagt hat N [ˈɪntriːg] **a** *(= plot)* Intrige *f*; *(no pl: = plotting)* Intrigen(spiel *nt*) *pl* **b** *(dated: = love affair)* Liaison *f*, Liebschaft *f*

intriguer [ɪnˈtriːgə'] N Intrigant(in) *m(f)*, Ränkeschmied *m*

intriguing [ɪnˈtriːgɪŋ] ADJ faszinierend, interessant N Intrigen(spiel *nt*) *pl*

intriguingly [ɪnˈtriːgɪŋlɪ] ADV auf faszinierende Weise; **her questions were ~ different** ihre Fragen faszinierten durch ihre Andersartigkeit; **most ~, no fingerprints could be found** höchst interessant war die Tatsache, dass man keine Fingerabdrücke finden konnte

intrinsic [ɪnˈtrɪnsɪk] ADJ *merit, value* immanent; *(= essential)* wesenhaft, wesentlich; **~ evidence** *(Jur)* reiner Urkundenbeweis; **is this form ~ to the poem?** ist dies eine dem Gedicht innewohnende Form? *(geh)*; **financial insecurity is ~ to**

capitalism finanzielle Unsicherheit gehört zum Wesen des Kapitalismus

intrinsically [ɪnˈtrɪnsɪkəlɪ] ADV an sich; **these instruments are ~ dangerous** diese Instrumente sind an sich äußerst gefährlich; **~ linked** *or* **connected** untrennbar miteinander verbunden

intro [ˈɪntrəʊ] N *(inf) abbr of* **introduction** Intro *nt (inf)*

introduce [ˌɪntrəˈdjuːs] VT **a** *(= make acquainted) (to person)* vorstellen *(to sb* jdm), bekannt machen *(to* mit); *(butler)* ankündigen; *(to subject)* einführen *(to* in *+acc)*; **have you two been ~d?** hat man Sie bekannt gemacht?; **I don't think we've been ~d** ich glaube nicht, dass wir uns kennen; **to ~ oneself** sich vorstellen; **allow me to** *or* **let me ~ myself** darf ich mich vorstellen?; **he was ~d to drink at an early age** er hat schon früh Bekanntschaft mit dem Alkohol gemacht; **who ~d him to heroin?** durch wen ist er ans Heroin geraten?; **he was ~d to flying by a friend** er ist durch einen Freund zum Fliegen gekommen; **I ~d him to the firm** ich habe ihn in die Firma eingeführt
b *fashion, practice, reform, invention* einführen; *(Parl) bill* einbringen; *mood, competition* bringen *(into* in *+acc)*; *book, subject, era* einleiten; *(= announce) speaker* vorstellen, ankündigen; *programme* ankündigen; **to ~ sth onto the market** etw auf den Markt bringen, etw auf dem Markt einführen
c *(= insert)* einführen *(into* in *+acc)*

introduction [ˌɪntrəˈdʌkʃən] N **a** *(to person)* Vorstellung *f*; **since his ~ to Lord X** seit er Lord X vorgestellt worden ist; **to make** *or* **perform the ~s** die Vorstellung übernehmen; **letter of ~** Einführungsbrief *m or* -schreiben *nt*; **~ agency** Partnervermittlung *f*
b *(= introductory part: to book, music)* Einleitung *f (to* zu)
c *(= elementary course, book)* Einführung *f*; **an ~ to French** eine Einführung ins Französische
d *(= introducing, being introduced) (to subject)* Einführung *f (to* in *+acc)*; *(to habit, hobby)* Bekanntschaft *f (to* mit); *(of fashion, practice, reform etc)* Einführung *f*; *(of bill, competition)* Einbringen *nt*; *(= announcing) (of speaker)* Vorstellung *f*, Ankündigung *f*; *(of programme)* Ankündigung *f*; *(= bringing or carrying in)* Einführung *f (into* in *+dat)*; *(= insertion)* Einführung *f (into* in *+acc)*; **our next guest needs no ~** unser nächster Gast braucht nicht vorgestellt zu werden

introductory [ˌɪntrəˈdʌktərɪ] ADJ *page, paragraph, chapter* einleitend; *words, remarks* einführend; *course, fee, offer* Einführungs-; **~ speech** Einführungsrede *f*; **~ price** Einführungspreis *m*

introit [ˈɪntrɔɪt] N Introitus *m*

introspect [ˌɪntrəʊˈspekt] VI sich selbst beobachten

introspection [ˌɪntrəʊˈspekʃən] N Selbstbeobachtung *f*, Introspektion *f (geh)*

introspective [ˌɪntrəʊˈspektɪv] ADJ *person* selbstbeobachtend, introspektiv *(geh)*; *novel, remarks* introspektiv

introspectiveness [ˌɪntrəʊˈspektɪvnɪs] N *(of novel, remarks)* introspektiver Charakter; *(of person)* Neigung *f* zur Selbstbeobachtung *or* Introspektion *(geh)*

introversion [ˌɪntrəʊˈvɜːʃən] N *(Psych)* Introversion *f*

introvert [ˈɪntrəʊvɜːt] **N** *(Psych)* Introvertierte(r) *mf*; **to be an ~** introvertiert sein **VT** *(Psych)* nach innen wenden; *(Biol)* nach innen stülpen

introverted [ˈɪntrəʊvɜːtɪd] ADJ introvertiert, in sich gekehrt

intrude [ɪnˈtruːd] **VI** stören; **to ~ on sb** jdn stören; **his mother ~d on our relationship** seine Mutter mischte sich in unsere Beziehung ein; **am I intruding?** störe ich?; **to ~ on sb's privacy** jds Privatsphäre verletzen; **my family has been ~d upon by the press** meine Familie ist von der Presse belästigt worden; **to ~ on sb's grief** jdn in seinem Kummer stören; **to ~ on a meeting** eine Besprechung stören; **to ~ into sb's thoughts** jdn in seinen Gedanken stören; **personal feelings cannot be allowed to ~** für persönliche Gefühle ist kein Platz
VT *remark* einwerfen; **to ~ oneself upon sb** sich jdm aufdrängen; **to ~ oneself into sb's affairs** sich in jds Angelegenheiten *(acc)* mischen

intruder [ɪnˈtruːdəʳ] N Eindringling *m*

intrusion [ɪnˈtruːʒən] N **a** Störung *f*; **forgive the ~, I just wanted to ask ...** entschuldigen Sie, wenn ich hier so eindringe, ich wollte nur fragen ...; **the ~ of** *or* **on his privacy** die Verletzung seiner Privatsphäre; **the sudden ~ of the outside world** das plötzliche Eindringen der Außenwelt; **they regarded her presence as an ~** sie betrachteten ihre Anwesenheit als störend **b** *(= forcing: of opinions, advice, one's presence)* Aufdrängen *nt*

intrusive [ɪnˈtruːsɪv] ADJ *person* aufdringlich; *presence* störend; *government, legislation* einmischend; *(Phon)* intrusiv

intubate [ˈɪntjʊbeɪt] VT *(Med)* intubieren

intubation [ˌɪntjʊˈbeɪʃən] N *(Med)* Intubation *f*

intuit [ɪnˈtjʊɪt] VT *(form) thought* intuitiv erahnen

intuition [ˌɪntjuːˈɪʃən] N Intuition *f*; *(of future events etc)* (Vor)ahnung *f (of* von); **to know sth by ~** etw intuitiv wissen

intuitive [ɪnˈtjuːɪtɪv] ADJ intuitiv; *guess, feeling, assessment* instinktiv; **~ powers** Intuition *f*

intuitively [ɪnˈtjuːɪtɪvlɪ] ADV intuitiv; **~ I'd say 50** ich hätte instinktiv 50 gesagt

inundate [ˈɪnʌndeɪt] VT *(lit, fig)* überschwemmen, überfluten; *(with work)* überhäufen; **have you a lot of work on? – I'm ~d** haben Sie viel Arbeit? – ich ersticke darin

inundation [ˌɪnʌnˈdeɪʃən] N *(lit, fig) (with invitations, offers etc)* Überschwemmung *f*; *(with work)* Überhäufung *f*

inure [ɪnˈjʊəʳ] VT gewöhnen *(to* an *+acc)*; *(physically)* abhärten *(to* gegen); *(to danger)* stählen *(to* gegen); **to become ~d to sth** sich an etw *(acc)* gewöhnen; *(physically) to danger* sich gegen etw abhärten/stählen

invade [ɪnˈveɪd] VT *(Mil)* einmarschieren in *(+acc)*; *(fig)* überfallen, heimsuchen; *privacy* eindringen in *(+acc)*, stören; *(Med) cell etc* befallen

invader [ɪnˈveɪdəʳ] N *(Mil)* Invasor *m*; *(fig)* Eindringling *m (of* in *+acc)*; *(of privacy)* Eindringling *(of* in *+acc)*, Störer *m (of +gen)*

invading [ɪnˈveɪdɪŋ] ADJ einmarschierend; *Huns, Vikings etc* einfallend; *virus, organism* eindringend; **~ army/troops** Invasionsarmee *f*/-truppen *pl*

invalid[1] [ˈɪnvəlɪd] **ADJ** **a** krank; *(= disabled)* invalide, körperbehindert **b** *(= for invalids)* Kranken-, Invaliden- **N** Kranke(r) *mf*; *(= disabled person)* Invalide *m*, Invalidin *f*, Körperbehinderte(r) *mf*; **he's been an ~ all his life** er hat sein ganzes Leben lang ein körperliches Leiden gehabt; **to treat sb like an ~** jdn wie einen Invaliden behandeln

▸ **invalid out** VT *sep* dienstunfähig schreiben *or* erklären; **to be invalided out of the army** wegen Dienstunfähigkeit aus der Armee entlassen werden

invalid[2] [ɪnˈvælɪd] ADJ *(esp Jur, Comput)* ungültig; *deduction, argument* nicht schlüssig *or* stichhaltig; *assumption* nicht zulässig; **it makes the argument ~** es entkräftet das Argument; **to declare sth ~** etw für ungültig erklären

invalidate [ɪnˈvælɪdeɪt] VT ungültig machen; *theory, feelings* entkräften

invalidation [ɪnˌvælɪˈdeɪʃən] N *(of document)* Ungültigmachung *f*; *(of theory)* Entkräftung *f*

invalid car N Invaliden(kraft)fahrzeug *nt*

invalid chair N Roll- *or* Krankenstuhl *m*

invalidism [ˈɪnvəlɪdɪzəm] N körperliches Leiden; *(= disability)* Körperbehinderung *f*, Invalidität *f*

invalidity [ɪnvəˈlɪdɪtɪ] N **a** *(esp Jur)* Ungültigkeit *f*; *(of deduction, argument)* mangelnde Schlüssigkeit *or* Stichhaltigkeit; *(of assumption)* Unzulässigkeit *f* **b** *(= disability)* Körperbehinderung *f*, Invalidität *f*

invaluable [ɪnˈvæljʊəbl] ADJ unbezahlbar; *service, role, help, contribution* unschätzbar; *advice, experience, jewel, treasure* von unschätzbarem Wert; **to be ~ (to sb)** (für jdn) von unschätzbarem Wert sein; **to be an ~ source of sth** eine ausgezeichnete Quelle für etw sein

invariable [ɪnˈvɛərɪəbl] **ADJ** *(also Math)* unveränderlich; *reply, characteristic* gleichbleibend; *bad luck* konstant, ständig **N** *(Math)* Konstante *f*

invariably [ɪnˈvɛərɪəblɪ] ADV ständig, unweigerlich; *(= not changing)* unveränderlich; **do you trust his judgement? – ~!** trauen Sie seinem Urteil? – ausnahmslos!

invariant [ɪnˈvɛərɪənt] **ADJ** *(also Math)* unveränderlich **N** *(Math)* Konstante *f*

invasion [ɪnˈveɪʒən] N *(lit, fig)* Invasion *f*; *(of privacy etc)* Eingriff *m (of* in *+acc)*; **the Viking ~** der Einfall der Wikinger; **the German ~ of Poland** der Einmarsch *or* Einfall der Deutschen in Polen

invasive [ɪnˈveɪsɪv] ADJ **a** *(Med)* invasiv **b** *(Mil)* Invasions-; **~ war** Invasionskrieg *m*

invective [ɪnˈvektɪv] N Beschimpfungen *pl (against +gen)*, Schmähungen *pl (geh) (against* gegen), Invektiven *pl (liter)*

inveigh [ɪnˈveɪ] VI **to ~ against sb/sth** *(liter)* jdn/etw schmähen *(liter)*, sich in Schimpfreden gegen jdn/etw ergehen *(geh)*

inveigle [ɪnˈviːgl] VT *(liter)* verleiten *(into* zu); *(= lure)* locken; **to ~ sb into doing sth** jdn dazu verleiten *or* verlocken, etw zu tun

invent [ɪnˈvent] VT erfinden

invention [ɪnˈvenʃən] N **a** Erfindung *f*; **of one's own ~** selbsterfunden **b** *(= inventiveness)* Fantasie *f*

inventive [ɪnˈventɪv] ADJ *(= creative) powers, skills, mind* schöpferisch; *novel, design, menu* einfallsreich; *(= resourceful)* erfinderisch; **~ genius** schöpferisches Genie; **games which encourage a child to be ~** Spiele, die die Fantasie *or* Phantasie des Kindes anregen

inventiveness [ɪnˈventɪvnɪs] N Einfallsreichtum *m*

inventor [ɪnˈventəʳ] N Erfinder(in) *m(f)*

inventory [ˈɪnvəntrɪ] **N** Inventar *nt*, Bestandsaufnahme *f*; **to make** *or* **take an ~ of sth** Inventar von etw *or* den Bestand einer Sache *(gen)* aufnehmen **VT** *(Comm)* inventarisieren

inventory control N Bestandskontrolle *f*

inverse [ˈɪnˈvɜːs] **ADJ** umgekehrt, entgegengesetzt; **in ~ order** in umgekehrter Reihenfolge **N** Gegenteil *nt*

inversion [ɪnˈvɜːʃən] N Umkehrung *f*; *(Mus also, Gram)* Inversion *f*; *(fig: of roles, values)* Verkehrung *f*, Umkehrung *f*

invert [ɪnˈvɜːt] VT umkehren; *object also* auf den Kopf stellen; *order also* umdrehen; *(Gram) subject and object* umstellen; *word order, colours, selection* umkehren; **~ed nipples** Hohlwarzen *pl*

invertebrate [ɪnˈvɜːtɪbrɪt] **N** Wirbellose(r) *m*, Invertebrat *m (spec)* **ADJ** wirbellos

inverted [ɪnˈvɜːtɪd]: **inverted commas** PL *(Brit)* Anführungszeichen *pl*; **his new job, in ~** sein sogenannter neuer Job; **inverted snobbery** N **that's just ~** das ist die umgekehrte Variante von Snobismus

invert sugar [ˈɪnvɜːtˈʃʊgəʳ] N Invertzucker *m*

invest [ɪnˈvest] **VT** **a** *(Fin)* investieren *(in* in *+acc or dat)*, anlegen *(in* in *+dat)*; *(fig)* investieren *(in* in *+acc)* **b** *(form: with rank or authority) president etc* einsetzen, investieren *(old)*; **to ~ sb/sth with sth** jdm/einer Sache etw verleihen; **this number is ~ed with magical qualities** diese Zahl besitzt Zauberkräfte **c** *(Mil: = besiege)* belagern **VI** investieren, Geld anlegen *(in* in *+acc or dat, with* bei); **to ~ in shares** in Aktien investieren, sein Geld in Aktien anlegen; **to ~ in a new car** sich *(dat)* ein neues Auto anschaffen

investigate [ɪnˈvestɪgeɪt] VT untersuchen; *(doing scientific research also)* erforschen; *sb's political beliefs, an insurance claim, business affairs* überprüfen; *complaint* nachgehen *(+dat)*; *motive, reason, cause* erforschen; *crime* untersuchen; **to ~ a case** in einem Fall ermitteln *or* Ermittlungen anstellen VI nachforschen; *(police)* ermitteln, Ermittlungen anstellen

investigation [ɪnˌvestɪˈgeɪʃən] N **a** *(to determine cause)* Untersuchung *f (into +gen)*; *(= official inquiry)* Ermittlung *f*, Untersuchung *f*; **to call for an immediate ~ into sth** die sofortige Untersuchung einer Sache *(gen)* fordern; **to order an ~ into** *or* **of sth** anordnen, dass in einer Sache *(dat)* ermittelt wird; **on ~ it turned out that …** bei näherer Untersuchung stellte (es) sich heraus, dass … **b** *(= looking for sth)* Nachforschung *f*; *(by police)* Ermittlungen *pl*; *(of affairs, applicants, political beliefs etc)* Überprüfung *f*; **to be under ~** überprüft werden; **he is under ~** *(by police)* gegen ihn wird ermittelt; **new methods of criminal ~** neue polizeiliche Ermittlungsmethoden; **(private) ~ agency** Detektei *f*, Detektivbüro *nt* **c** *(= scientific research) (in field)* Forschung *f*; *(of bacteria, object etc)* Erforschung *f (into +gen)*; **recent scientific ~ has shown …** die neuesten wissenschaftlichen Untersuchungen haben gezeigt …

investigative [ɪnˈvestɪgətɪv] ADJ *journalist, series, programme* investigativ; **~ journalism** Enthüllungsjournalismus *m*; **~ mind** Forschergeist *m*; **~ technique/work** Forschungstechnik/-arbeit *f*; **~ report** Untersuchungsbericht *m*; **~ custody** *(Jur)* Untersuchungshaft *f*

investigator [ɪnˈvestɪgeɪtəʳ] N Ermittler(in) *m(f)*; *(= private investigator)* (Privat)detektiv(in) *m(f)*; *(= insurance investigator)* (Schadens)ermittler(in) *m(f)*; *(from government department)* Untersuchungs- *or* Ermittlungsbeamte(r) *m*/-beamtin *f*; **a team of ~s** ein Untersuchungsausschuss *m*, eine Untersuchungskommission

investiture [ɪnˈvestɪtʃəʳ] N *(of president etc)* (feierliche) Einsetzung *f*, Amtseinführung *f*; *(of royalty)* Investitur *f*; *(of honour)* Verleihung *f*; *(= occasion)* Auszeichnungsfeier *f*; **after his ~ with the VC, …** nachdem ihm das Viktoriakreuz verliehen worden war, …

investment [ɪnˈvestmənt] N **a** *(Fin)* Investition *f*; *(= act also)* Anlage *f*; **we need more ~ in industry** in die Industrie muss mehr investiert werden, die Industrie braucht mehr Investitionen; **to make an ~** investieren *(of sth* etw); **foreign ~** Auslandsinvestition(en *pl*) *f*; **return on one's ~s** Anlageertrag *m*; **oil/this company is a good ~** Öl/diese Firma ist eine gute (Kapital)anlage; **a portable TV is a good ~** ein tragbarer Fernseher macht sich bezahlt **b** *(= investiture) (as sth)* (Amts)einsetzung *f*; *(with sth)* Verleihung *f (+gen)* **c** *(Mil: = blockade)* Belagerung *f*

investment: **investment allowance** N Investitionsabschreibung *f*; **investment bonds** PL festverzinsliche Anlagepapiere *pl*; **investment capital** N Anlagekapital *nt*; **investment company** N Investmentgesellschaft *f*; **investment failure** N Fehlinvestition *f*; **investment incentive** N Investitionsanreiz *m*; **investment income** N Kapitalerträge *pl*; **investment management** N Vermögensverwaltung *f*; **investment manager** N Vermögensverwalter(in) *m(f)*, Investmentmanager(in) *m(f)*; **investment trust** N Investmenttrust *m*

investor [ɪnˈvestəʳ] N Kapitalanleger(in) *m(f)*, Investor(in) *m(f)*; **the small ~** die Kleinanleger *pl*

inveterate [ɪnˈvetərɪt] ADJ *dislike, hatred* tief verwurzelt, abgrundtief; *laziness* chronisch; *opposition, prejudice, habit* hartnäckig; *enemies* unversöhnlich; *liar, gambler* unverbesserlich; *collector, traveller* passioniert; **~ smoker/criminal** Gewohnheitsraucher(in) *m(f)*/-verbrecher(in) *m(f)*

invidious [ɪnˈvɪdɪəs] ADJ *remark* gehässig, boshaft; *task, position* unerfreulich, unangenehm; *behaviour, conduct* gemein; *distinctions, comparison, discrimination* ungerecht; **it would be ~ to …** es wäre ungerecht, zu …

invigilate [ɪnˈvɪdʒɪleɪt] *(Brit)* VT *exam* Aufsicht führen bei VI Aufsicht führen

invigilation [ɪnˌvɪdʒɪˈleɪʃən] N *(Brit)* Aufsicht *f*; **to do (the) ~** Aufsicht führen

invigilator [ɪnˈvɪdʒɪleɪtəʳ] N *(Brit)* Aufsicht *f*, Aufsichtführende(r) *mf*, Aufsichtsperson *f*

invigorate [ɪnˈvɪgəreɪt] VT beleben; *(tonic, cure)* kräftigen

invigorating [ɪnˈvɪgəreɪtɪŋ] ADJ *climate* gesund; *sea air, shower* erfrischend, belebend; *tonic, cure* kräftigend, stärkend; *(fig) attitude, frankness* (herz)erfrischend; **he found the American business world very ~** die amerikanische Geschäftswelt stimulierte ihn

invincibility [ɪnˌvɪnsɪˈbɪlɪtɪ] N Unbesiegbarkeit *f*

invincible [ɪnˈvɪnsəbl] ADJ *army etc* unbesiegbar, unschlagbar; *courage, determination* unerschütterlich

invincibly [ɪnˈvɪnsəblɪ] ADV **~ strong** unbesiegbar; **he is ~ placed** er hat eine unschlagbare Position

inviolability [ɪnˌvaɪələˈbɪlɪtɪ] N Unantastbarkeit *f*; *(of frontiers)* Unverletzlichkeit *f*; *(of law, oath)* Heiligkeit *f*

inviolable [ɪnˈvaɪələbl] ADJ unantastbar; *frontiers also* unverletzlich; *law, oath* heilig

inviolate [ɪnˈvaɪəlɪt] ADJ *(form) honour* unbeschadet; *rights* unangetastet

invisibility [ɪnˌvɪzəˈbɪlɪtɪ] N Unsichtbarkeit *f*

invisible [ɪnˈvɪzəbl] ADJ unsichtbar; **to feel ~** sich *(dat)* unsichtbar vorkommen; **~ thread** Nylonfaden *m*; **~ to the naked eye** mit dem bloßen Auge nicht erkennbar N **~s** *(Comm)* unsichtbarer Handel

invisible: **invisible earnings** PL *(Econ)* unsichtbare Einkünfte *pl*; **invisible exports** PL *(Econ)* unsichtbare Exporte *pl*; **invisible ink** N Geheimtinte *f*; **invisible mending** N Kunststopfen *nt*

invisibly [ɪnˈvɪzəblɪ] ADV unsichtbar; **you should have it ~ mended** du solltest es kunststopfen lassen

invitation [ˌɪnvɪˈteɪʃən] ✪ 25.1, 25.2 N Einladung *f*; **by ~ (only)** nur auf Einladung; **at sb's ~** auf jds Aufforderung *(acc)* (hin); **an ~ to burglars** eine Aufforderung zum Diebstahl; **~ card** Einladungskarte *f*

invitational [ˌɪnvɪˈteɪʃənl] ADJ *(Sport) nur für eingeladene Teilnehmer zugänglich*; **~ tournament** Einladungsturnier *nt*

invite [ɪnˈvaɪt] VT **a** *person* einladen; **to ~ sb to do sth** jdn auffordern *or* bitten, etw zu tun; **he ~d me to try for myself** er bot mir an, es doch selbst zu versuchen **b** *(= ask for, attract) suggestions, questions* bitten um; *(behaviour) ridicule, contempt, trouble* auslösen, führen zu; **written in such a way as to ~ further discussion** so geschrieben, dass es zu weiteren Diskussionen auffordert; **it ~s comparison with another theory** der Vergleich mit einer anderen Theorie drängt sich auf; **you're inviting defeat by …** das muss ja zu einer Niederlage führen, wenn du …; **you're inviting ridicule/criticism** du machst dich lächerlich/setzt dich der Kritik aus; **he just seems to ~ trouble** wo er auftaucht, gibt es meistens Unannehmlichkeiten; **it ~s thieves** es lädt geradezu zum Diebstahl ein; **~d lecture** Gastvorlesung *f* [ˈɪnvaɪt] N *(inf)* Einladung *f*

▶ **invite (a)round** VT *sep* (zu sich) einladen

▶ **invite in** VT *sep* hereinbitten, ins Haus bitten; **could I invite you in for (a) coffee?** möchten Sie auf eine Tasse Kaffee hereinkommen?

▶ **invite out** VT *sep* einladen; **I invited her out** ich habe sie gefragt, ob sie mit mir ausgehen möchte; **to invite sb out for a meal** jdn in ein Restaurant einladen

▶ **invite up** VT *sep* heraufbitten

inviting [ɪnˈvaɪtɪŋ] ADJ einladend; *prospect, idea, meal, sea, water* verlockend; *room* heimelig

invitingly [ɪnˈvaɪtɪŋlɪ] ADV einladend; *(= temptingly)* verlockend

in vitro [ɪnˈviːtrəʊ] *(Biol)* ADJ künstlich, In-vitro- *(spec)*; **~ fertilization** künstliche Befruchtung, In-vitro-Fertilisation *f (spec)* ADV *fertilize* künstlich, in vitro *(spec)*

invocation [ˌɪnvəʊˈkeɪʃən] N Beschwörung *f*; *(Eccl)* Invokation *f*; **an ~ to the muses** *(Liter)* eine Anrufung der Musen

invoice [ˈɪnvɔɪs] ✪ 20.7 N *(= bill)* (Waren)rechnung *f*; *(= list)* Lieferschein *m* VT *goods* in Rechnung stellen, berechnen; **to ~ sb for sth** jdm für etw eine Rechnung ausstellen; **has he been ~d for these yet?** hat er dafür schon eine Rechnung bekommen?; **we'll ~ you** wir senden Ihnen die Rechnung

invoice amount N Rechnungsbetrag *m*

invoice clerk N Fakturist(in) *m(f)*

invoicing [ˈɪnvɔɪsɪŋ] N Fakturierung *f*; *(of goods also)* Berechnung *f*, Inrechnungstellung *f*; *(= invoiced sales)* Fakturierungen *pl*

invoke [ɪnˈvəʊk] VT **a** *(= appeal to, call for) God, the law, muse* anrufen; *evil spirits* beschwören; *memories* heraufbeschwören; **to ~ the name of Marx** Marx ins Feld führen; **to ~ God's blessing** Gottes Segen erbitten; **to ~ sb's help** an jds Hilfsbereitschaft *(acc)* appellieren **b** *(= call into operation) treaty etc* sich berufen auf *(+acc)*

involuntarily [ɪnˈvɒləntərɪlɪ] ADV unbeabsichtigt, unabsichtlich; *(= automatically)* unwillkürlich; **he found himself ~ involved** er sah sich unfreiwilligerweise verwickelt

involuntary [ɪnˈvɒləntərɪ] ADJ unbeabsichtigt, ungewollt; *repatriation* unfreiwillig; *shudder, muscle movement etc* unwillkürlich; **I found myself an ~ listener/guest** ich wurde zum unfreiwilligen Zuhörer/Gast; **~ manslaughter** *(Jur)* fahrlässige Tötung

involute [ˈɪnvəluːt] ADJ *(liter: = complex)* verwickelt

involuted [ˌɪnvəˈluːtɪd] ADJ verwickelt, kompliziert

involve [ɪnˈvɒlv] VT **a** *(= entangle)* verwickeln *(sb in sth* jdn in etw *acc)*; *(= include)* beteiligen *(sb in sth* jdn an etw *dat)*; *(= concern)* betreffen; **to ~ sb in a quarrel** jdn in einen Streit verwickeln *or* hineinziehen; **to ~ sb in expense** jdm Kosten verursachen; **the book doesn't ~ the reader** das Buch fesselt *or* packt den Leser nicht; **it wouldn't ~ you at all** du hättest damit gar nichts zu tun; **to be ~d in sth** etwas mit etw zu tun haben; *(= have part in also)* an etw *(dat)* beteiligt sein; *(in sth bad also)* in etw *(acc)* verwickelt sein; **to get ~d in sth** in etw *(acc)* verwickelt werden; *in quarrel, crime etc also* in etw *(acc)* hineingezogen werden; **to ~ oneself in sth** sich in etw *(dat)* engagieren; **to ~ oneself in politics** sich politisch engagieren; **I didn't want to get ~d** ich wollte damit/mit ihm *etc* nichts zu tun haben; **I didn't want to get too ~d** ich wollte mich nicht zu sehr engagieren; **a matter of principle is ~d** es ist eine Frage des Prinzips, es geht ums Prinzip; **the person ~d** die betreffende Person; **we are all ~d in the battle against inflation** der Kampf gegen die Inflation geht uns alle an; **to be/get ~d with sth** etwas mit etw zu tun haben; *(= have part in)* an etw *(dat)* beteiligt sein; *with work etc* mit etw beschäftigt sein; **he got ~d with local politics** er hat sich lokalpolitisch engagiert; **to be ~d with sb** mit jdm zu tun haben; *(sexually)* mit jdm ein Verhältnis haben; **to be romantically ~d (with sb)** eine Liebesbeziehung (zu jdm) haben; **he's very ~d with her** er hat sich bei ihr sehr stark engagiert; **he's ~d with some shady characters** er hat Umgang mit einigen zwielichtigen Gestalten; **to get ~d with sb** mit jdm Kontakt bekommen, sich mit jdm einlassen *(pej)*; **I don't want to get ~d with them** ich will mit ihnen nichts zu tun haben; **he got ~d with a girl** er hat eine Beziehung mit einem Mädchen angefangen

b *(= entail)* mit sich bringen, zur Folge haben; *(= encompass)* umfassen; *(= mean)* bedeuten; **what does the job ~?** worin besteht die Arbeit?; **this problem ~s many separate issues** dieses Problem umfasst viele verschiedene Punkte *or* schließt viele verschiedene Punkte ein; **to ~ considerable expense/a lot of hard work** beträchtliche Kosten/viel Arbeit mit sich bringen *or* zur Folge haben; **such a project ~s considerable planning** zu so einem Projekt gehört eine umfangreiche Planung; **will the post ~ much foreign travel?** ist der Posten mit vielen Auslandsreisen verbunden?; **he doesn't understand what's ~d in this sort of work** er weiß nicht, worum es bei dieser Arbeit geht; **do you realize what's ~d in raising a family?** weißt du denn, was es bedeutet, eine Familie großzuziehen?; **about £1,000 was ~d** es ging dabei um etwa £ 1.000; **the job ~d 50 workmen** für die Arbeit wurden 50 Arbeiter gebraucht; **it would ~ moving to Germany** das würde bedeuten, nach Deutschland umzuziehen; **finding the oil ~d the use of a special drill** um das Öl zu finden, brauchte man einen Spezialbohrer

involved [ɪn'vɒlvd] ADJ kompliziert; *regulations also* verwirrend; *story also* verwickelt; *style* komplex, umständlich *(pej)*; **a long ~ sentence** ein umständlicher Schachtelsatz; **a long ~ explanation** eine lange und komplizierte Erklärung

involvement [ɪn'vɒlvmənt] N *(= being concerned with)* Beteiligung *f* *(in* an *+dat)*; *(in quarrel, crime etc)* Verwicklung *f* *(in* in *+acc)*; *(= commitment)* Engagement *nt*; *(sexually)* Verhältnis *nt*; *(= complexity)* Kompliziertheit *f*, Verworrenheit *f (pej)*; **his ~ with shady characters** sein Umgang *m* mit zwielichtigen Gestalten; **she denied any ~ in** *or* **with drugs** sie leugnete, dass sie etwas mit Drogen zu tun hatte; **the extent of his ~ with her** das Maß, in dem er sich bei ihr engagiert hat; **we don't know the extent of his ~ in the plot/plan** wir wissen nicht, wie weit er an dem Komplott/Plan beteiligt ist; **there is no ~ of the reader in the novel** der Leser fühlt sich von dem Roman nicht angesprochen; **a romantic ~ (with sb)** eine Liebesbeziehung (zu jdm)

invulnerability [ɪn,vʌlnərə'bɪlɪtɪ] N Unverwundbarkeit *f*, Unverletzbarkeit *f*; *(of fortress)* Uneinnehmbarkeit *f*; *(lit, fig: of position)* Unangreifbarkeit *f*

invulnerable [ɪn'vʌlnərəbl] ADJ unverwundbar, unverletzbar; *fortress* uneinnehmbar; *(lit, fig) position* unangreifbar; **~ to attack** unbezwingbar

inward ['ɪnwəd] ADJ **a** *(= inner)* innere(r, s); *smile, life* innerlich; *thoughts* innerste(r, s) **b** *(= incoming) movement* nach innen; *curve* nach innen gehend; *mail* eintreffend; **~ breath** Einatmen *nt*; **~ flow** Zustrom *m* **c** *(Fin)* **~ investment** Investitionen *pl* aus dem Ausland; **~ investor** ausländischer Investor ADV = **inwards**

inward-looking ['ɪnwəd'lʊkɪŋ] ADJ in sich gekehrt, beschaulich

inwardly ['ɪnwədlɪ] ADV innerlich, im Inneren; **to ~ digest sth** etw geistig verarbeiten

inwardness ['ɪnwədnɪs] N Innerlichkeit *f*

inwards ['ɪnwədz] ADV nach innen; **his thoughts turned ~** er versank in Selbstbetrachtung

in-your-face, in-yer-face [,ɪnjə'feɪs] ADJ *(inf) attitude etc* provokativ

I/O *abbr of* **input/output**

IOC *abbr of* **International Olympic Committee** IOK *nt*

iodic [aɪ'ɒdɪk] ADJ *(spec)* jodhaltig, Jod-

iodide ['aɪədaɪd] N Jodid *nt*

iodine ['aɪədiːn] N Jod *nt*

ion ['aɪən] N Ion *nt*

Ionian [aɪ'əʊnɪən] ADJ **~ Sea** Ionisches Meer

Ionic [aɪ'ɒnɪk] ADJ ionisch

ionic [aɪ'ɒnɪk] ADJ Ionen-; **~ bond** Ionenbindung *f*

ionization [,aɪənaɪ'zeɪʃən] N Ionisierung *f*

ionize ['aɪənaɪz] VTI ionisieren

ionosphere [aɪ'ɒnəsfɪə'] N Ionosphäre *f*

iota [aɪ'əʊtə] N Jota *nt*; **not an** *or* **one ~** nicht ein Jota; **not an ~ of truth** kein Funke *m or* Körnchen *nt* Wahrheit; **it won't make an ~ of difference** es wird nicht den geringsten Unterschied machen

IOU [,aɪəʊ'juː] *abbr of* **I owe you** Schuldschein *m*; **to give sb an ~** jdm einen Schuldschein ausschreiben

IPA *abbr of* **International Phonetic Alphabet**

IP address [aɪ'piː-] N *(Comput, Internet)* IP-Adresse *f*

IPO *(St Ex) abbr of* **initial public offering** Erstnotiz *f (einer Aktie)*

ipso facto ['ɪpsəʊ'fæktəʊ] ADV eo ipso

ipso jure ['ɪpsəʊ'dʒʊərɪ] ADV ipso jure, durch das Recht selbst

IP telephony [aɪ'piː-] N *(Comput, Internet)* IP-Telefonie *f*, Internettelefonie *f*

IQ *abbr of* **intelligence quotient** IQ *m*, Intelligenzquotient *m*; **IQ test** Intelligenztest *m*, IQ-Test *m*

IRA *abbr of* **Irish Republican Army** IRA *f*

Iran [ɪ'rɑːn] N (der) Iran

Irangate [ɪ'rɑːngeɪt] N *(Pol)* Iran-Contra-Affäre *f*, Irangate *nt (inf)*

Iranian [ɪ'reɪnɪən] ADJ iranisch N **a** Iraner(in) *m(f)* **b** *(Ling)* Iranisch *nt*

Iraq [ɪ'rɑːk] N (der) Irak

Iraqi [ɪ'rɑːkɪ] ADJ irakisch N Iraker(in) *m(f)*

irascibility [ɪ,ræsɪ'bɪlɪtɪ] N Reizbarkeit *f*, Jähzorn *m*

irascible [ɪ'ræsɪbl] ADJ reizbar, erregbar, jähzornig; *temperament also* jähzornig, heftig, aufbrausend

irascibly [ɪ'ræsɪblɪ] ADV gereizt

irate [aɪ'reɪt] ADJ zornig; *crowd* wütend

irately [aɪ'reɪtlɪ] ADV zornig

ire [aɪə'] N *(liter)* Zorn *m*

Ireland ['aɪələnd] N Irland *nt*; **Northern ~** Nordirland *nt*; **Republic of ~** Republik *f* Irland

iridescence [,ɪrɪ'desəns] N *(liter)* Irisieren *nt*; *(of plumage also, of water)* Schillern *nt*; *(of opals, silk)* Schimmern *nt*

iridescent [,ɪrɪ'desənt] ADJ *(liter)* irisierend; *plumage also, water, bubble* schillernd; *opals, silk* schimmernd

iris ['aɪərɪs] N **a** *(of eye)* Regenbogenhaut *f*, Iris *f* **b** *(Bot)* Iris *f*, Schwertlilie *f*

Irish ['aɪərɪʃ] ADJ **a** irisch; **~ Free State** irischer Freistaat; **~ joke** Irenwitz *m*, ≈ Ostfriesenwitz *m*; **~man** Ire *m*, Irländer *m*; **~ Republican Army** Irisch-Republikanische Armee; **~woman** Irin *f*, Irländerin *f* **b** *(hum inf: = illogical)* unlogisch, blödsinnig N **a** *pl* **the ~** die Iren *pl*, die Irländer *pl* **b** *(Ling)* Irisch *nt*, irisches Gälisch

Irish: Irish coffee N Irish Coffee *m*; **Irish Sea** N Irische See; **Irish setter** N Irischer Setter; **Irish stew** N Irish Stew *nt*

irk [ɜːk] VT verdrießen *(geh)*, ärgern

irksome ['ɜːksəm] ADJ lästig

iron ['aɪən] N **a** Eisen *nt*; **old ~** Alteisen *nt*; **~ tablets** *pl* Eisentabletten *pl*; **a man of ~** ein stahlharter Mann; **a will of ~** ein eiserner Wille; **to rule with a rod of ~** *(Brit)* mit eiserner Rute *or* Hand herrschen; **to pump ~** *(inf)* Krafttraining machen

b *(= electric iron)* Bügeleisen *nt*; **to have other ~s in the fire** *(fig)* noch andere Eisen im Feuer haben; **he has too many ~s in the fire** er macht zu viel auf einmal; **to strike while the ~ is hot** *(Prov)* das Eisen schmieden, solange es heiß ist *(Prov)*

c *(Golf)* Eisen *nt*

d irons PL *(= fetters)* Hand- und Fußschellen *pl*; **to put a man in ~s** jdn in Eisen legen

ADJ **a** *(Chem)* Eisen-; *(= made of iron)* Eisen-, eisern, aus Eisen; **~ bar** Eisenstange *f*; **~ deficiency** Eisenmangel *m*; **~ pyrites** Eisenkies *m*, Pyrit *m*

b *(fig) constitution, hand* eisern; *will* eisern, stählern; *rule* streng, unbarmherzig; **to rule with an ~ hand** mit eiserner Faust regieren; **they soon discovered that here was an ~ fist in a velvet glove** es wurde ihnen bald klar, dass mit ihm *etc* nicht zu spaßen war, obwohl er *etc* so sanft wirkte

VT *clothes* bügeln

VI *(person)* bügeln; *(cloth)* sich bügeln lassen

▶ **iron out** VT *sep (lit, fig)* ausbügeln; *differences also* ausgleichen; *problems, difficulties also* aus dem Weg räumen

iron: Iron Age N Eisenzeit *f*; **Iron Chancellor** N Eiserne(r) Kanzler; **ironclad** ADJ gepanzert N *(obs)* Panzerschiff *nt*; **Iron Curtain** N Eiserne(r) Vorhang; **the ~ countries** die Länder hinter dem Eisernen Vorhang; **Iron Duke** N Wellington *m*; **iron horse** N *(old: = train)* Dampfross *nt (old hum)*

ironic(al) [aɪ'rɒnɪk(əl)] ADJ ironisch; *smile also* spöttisch; *position* paradox; **it's really ~** das ist wirklich witzig *(inf)*; **it's really ~ that now he's got a car he's not allowed to drive** es ist doch paradox *or* wirklich witzig *(inf)*, dass er jetzt, wo er ein Auto hat, nicht fahren darf

ironically [aɪ'rɒnɪkəlɪ] ADV ironisch; **and then, ~ enough, he turned up** komischerweise *or* witzigerweise *(inf)* tauchte er dann auf; **and then, ~, it was he himself who had to do it** und dann hat ausgerechnet er *or* und dann hat paradoxerweise er es tun müssen

ironing ['aɪənɪŋ] N *(= process)* Bügeln *nt*; *(= clothes)* Bügelwäsche *f*; **to do the ~** (die Wäsche) bügeln

ironing board N Bügelbrett *nt*

ironist ['aɪrənɪst] N Ironiker(in) *m(f)*

ironize ['aɪrənaɪz] VTI ironisieren

iron: Iron Lady N *(Brit Pol)* eiserne Lady; **iron lung** N eiserne Lunge; **ironmonger** ['aɪənmʌŋgə'] N *(Brit)* Eisen(waren)händler(in) *m(f)*; **ironmonger's (shop)** N *(Brit)* Eisen- und Haushaltswarenhandlung *f*; **ironmongery** ['aɪən,mʌŋgərɪ] N *(Brit) (= shop)* Eisen- und Haushaltswarenhandlung *f*; *(= goods)* Eisenwaren *pl*; **iron mould**, *(US)* **iron mold** N Rostfleck *m*; **iron ore** N Eisenerz *nt*; **ironware** ['aɪənwɛə'] N Eisenwaren *pl*; *(= household goods)* Haushaltswaren *pl*; **ironwork** N Eisen *nt*; *(on chest, cart etc)* Eisenbeschläge *pl*; **ornamental ~** Eisenverzierungen *pl*; **ironworks** N *sing or pl* Eisenhütte *f*

irony ['aɪrənɪ] N Ironie *f no pl*; **the ~ of the situation** das Ironische an der Situation; **the ~ of it is that …** das Ironische daran ist, dass …, die Ironie liegt darin, dass …; **one of the great ironies of history** eine der ironischsten Fügungen der Geschichte; **life's ironies** die Ironie des Lebens; **by some ~ of fate, he …** durch eine ironische Wendung des Schicksals geschah es, dass er …

irradiate [ɪ'reɪdɪeɪt] VT **a** *(= emit) heat, light rays* ausstrahlen **b** *(liter: = illumine)* erhellen *(liter)* **c** *(= treat by irradiating)* bestrahlen; **~d food** strahlungsbehandelte Lebensmittel *pl*

irradiation [ɪ,reɪdɪ'eɪʃən] N **a** *(= emission)* Ausstrahlung *f* **b** *(Med: treatment; of food)* Bestrahlung *f*; *(of pain)* Ausstrahlung *f*, Irradiation *f (spec)* **c** *(fig, geh: = enlightenment)* Erleuchtung *f (fig)*, Aufklärung *f*

irrational [ɪ'ræʃənl] ADJ **a** *(= illogical, also Math, Psych)* irrational; *fear, belief* unsinnig, irrational; *(= not sensible)* unvernünftig; **he had become quite ~ about it** er hatte eine irrationale Einstellung dazu entwickelt; **if you maintain X, then it is ~ to deny Y** wenn Sie X behaupten, ist es widersinnig *or* unlogisch, Y zu leugnen **b** *(= not having reason) animal* vernunftlos

irrationality [ɪ,ræʃə'nælɪtɪ] N *(= illogicality, Math, Psych)* Irrationalität *f*; *(of fear, belief)* Unsinnigkeit *f*, Irrationalität *f*; *(= lack of good sense)* Unvernünftigkeit *f*

irrationally [ɪ'ræʃnəlɪ] ADV irrational; *(= not sensibly)* unvernünftig; **quite ~, he believed …** er glaubte gegen jede Vernunft *or* völlig unsinnigerweise …; **he's ~ angry with you** er ist grundlos böse auf dich

irreal [ɪ'rɪəl] ADJ *(geh)* irreal, unwirklich

irrebuttable [ˌɪrɪ'bʌtəbl] ADJ *(form)* unwiderlegbar; ~ **presumption** *(Jur)* unwiderlegbare Rechtsvermutung

irreconcilable [ɪˌrekən'saɪləbl] ADJ **a** *enemy, hatred* unversöhnlich **b** *belief, opinion, differences* unvereinbar

irreconcilably [ɪˌrekən'saɪləblɪ] ADV *fight* unversöhnlich; ~ **different** völlig unvereinbar; **to be ~ opposed to sth** absolut gegen etw sein; **they clashed ~** sie konnten ihre Meinungsverschiedenheiten nicht beseitigen

irrecoverable [ˌɪrɪ'kʌvərəbl] ADJ endgültig *or* für immer verloren, unwiederbringlich verloren; *loss* unersetzlich, unersetzbar; *debt* nicht eintreibbar, uneinbringlich; **the company's losses are ~** die Verluste der Firma können nicht mehr wettgemacht werden

irrecoverably [ˌɪrɪ'kʌvrəblɪ] ADV *broken* irreparabel; ~ **lost** für immer verloren

irredeemable [ˌɪrɪ'diːməbl] ADJ **a** *currency, pawned object* nicht einlösbar; *bonds* unkündbar, untilgbar; *annuity, debt* nicht ablösbar **b** *(fig) sinner* (rettungslos) verloren; *loss* unwiederbringlich; *transgression* unverzeihlich

irredeemably [ˌɪrɪ'diːməblɪ] ADV *lost* rettungslos; *confused* hoffnungslos; **he's an ~ wicked man** er ist ein von Grund auf böser *or* ein abgrundtief böser Mensch; **democracy was ~ damaged** die Demokratie hatte irreparablen Schaden genommen

irreducible [ˌɪrɪ'djuːsəbl] ADJ *(Chem, Math)* nicht reduzierbar; **the ~ minimum** das Allermindeste

irrefragable [ɪ'refrəgəbl] ADJ *(form)* unwiderlegbar

irrefutability [ˌɪrɪfjuːtə'bɪlɪtɪ] N Unwiderlegbarkeit *f*

irrefutable [ˌɪrɪ'fjuːtəbl] ADJ unwiderlegbar, unbestreitbar

irrefutably [ˌɪrɪ'fjuːtɪblɪ] ADV unwiderlegbar; *demonstrate also* eindeutig

irregular [ɪ'regjʊlə'] ADJ **a** *(= uneven)* unregelmäßig; *teeth, shape, coastline* ungleichmäßig; *surface* uneben; **at ~ intervals** in unregelmäßigen Abständen; **to be ~ in one's attendance** unregelmäßig erscheinen; **the windows are deliberately ~** die Fenster sind bewusst uneinheitlich; **to keep ~ hours** ein ungeregeltes Leben führen, keine festen Zeiten haben; **he's been a bit ~ recently** *(inf)* er hat in letzter Zeit ziemlich unregelmäßigen Stuhlgang
b *(= not conforming)* unstatthaft; *(= contrary to rules)* unvorschriftsmäßig; *(= contrary to law)* ungesetzlich; *marriage* ungültig; *behaviour* ungebührlich, ungehörig; **well, it's a bit ~, but I'll ...** eigentlich dürfte ich das nicht tun, aber ich ...; **it's a most ~ request, but ...** das ist ein höchst unübliches Ersuchen, aber ...; **this is most ~!** das ist äußerst ungewöhnlich!; **because of ~ procedures, the contract was not valid** wegen einiger Formfehler war der Vertrag ungültig; **she led a somewhat ~ private life** ihr Privatleben war ziemlich turbulent
c *(Gram)* unregelmäßig
d *troops* irregulär
N *(Mil)* Irreguläre(r) *mf*; **the ~s** die irreguläre Truppe

irregularity [ɪˌregjʊ'lærɪtɪ] N **a** *(= unevenness)* Unregelmäßigkeit *f*; *(of teeth, shape, coastline)* Ungleichmäßigkeit *f*; *(of surface)* Unebenheit *f*; *(= lack of uniformity)* Uneinheitlichkeit *f*; *(of sb's life)* Ungeregeltheit *f* **b** *(= failure to conform)* Unstatthaftigkeit *f*; *(= non-observation of rules)* Unvorschriftsmäßigkeit *f*; *(= unlawfulness)* Ungesetzlichkeit *f*; *(of marriage)* unvorschriftsmäßige Durchführung; *(= impropriety: of behaviour)* Ungebührlichkeit *f*, Ungehörigkeit *f*; **a slight ~ in the proceedings** ein kleiner Formfehler **c** *(Gram)* Unregelmäßigkeit *f*

irregularly [ɪ'regjʊləlɪ] ADV **a** *(= unevenly)* unregelmäßig; *shaped* ungleichmäßig; *(= at random intervals) eat, occur, go etc* in unregelmäßigen Abständen **b** *(= inadmissibly)* unstatthaft; *(= against the rules)* unvorschriftsmäßig; *(= against the law)* ungesetzlich; *(= improperly) behave* ungebührlich, ungehörig

irrelevance [ɪ'reləvəns], **irrelevancy** [ɪ'relɪvənsɪ] N Irrelevanz *f no pl*; *(of details also)* Unwesentlichkeit *f*, Nebensächlichkeit *f*; *(of titles, individuals)* Bedeutungslosigkeit *f*; **his speech was full of irrelevancies** vieles in seiner Rede war irrelevant *or* nebensächlich *or* unwesentlich; **it's become something of an ~** es ist ziemlich irrelevant geworden; **she dismissed his opinions as an ~** sie tat seine Ansichten als irrelevant *or* belanglos ab

irrelevant [ɪ'reləvənt] ADJ irrelevant; *details also, information* unwesentlich, nebensächlich; *titles etc* bedeutungslos; **it is ~ whether he agrees or not** es ist irrelevant *or* belanglos, ob er zustimmt; **these issues are ~ to the younger generation** diese Fragen sind für die jüngere Generation irrelevant *or* belanglos; **it's ~ to the subject** das ist für das Thema irrelevant; **his novels are largely ~ to the concerns of today** seine Romane haben wenig Bezug auf die Probleme von heute; **don't be ~** *(in discussion)* bleib bei der Sache; *(in essay writing)* bleiben Sie beim Thema

irrelevantly [ɪ'reləvəntlɪ] ADV belanglos; **..., he said ~** ..., sagte er, obwohl das gar nicht zur Sache gehörte; **he rambled on ~** er schwafelte irrelevantes *or* belangloses Zeug

irreligious [ˌɪrɪ'lɪdʒəs] ADJ unreligiös, irreligiös; *youth* gottlos; *(= lacking respect)* pietätlos

irremediable [ˌɪrɪ'miːdɪəbl] ADJ *character defects, errors* nicht behebbar; *damage* nicht wiedergutzumachen *pred*, nicht wiedergutzumachend *attr*; *situation* nicht mehr zu retten *pred or* rettend *attr*

irremediably [ˌɪrɪ'miːdɪəblɪ] ADV hoffnungslos

irreparable [ɪ'repərəbl] ADJ *damage* irreparabel, nicht wiedergutzumachen *pred*, nicht wiedergutzumachend *attr*; *harm also* bleibend; *loss* unersetzlich; *injury* irreparabel

irreparably [ɪ'repərəblɪ] ADV irreparabel; **his reputation was ~ damaged** sein Ruf war unwiderruflich geschädigt

irreplaceable [ˌɪrɪ'pleɪsəbl] ADJ unersetzlich

irrepressible [ˌɪrɪ'presəbl] ADJ *urge, curiosity, energy, spirit* unbezähmbar; *optimism, sense of humour* unerschütterlich, unverwüstlich; *person* nicht kleinzukriegen; *child* sonnig; *delight* unbändig; **his ~ high spirits** sein sonniges Gemüt; **the ~ Susan** Susan, die sich nicht unterkriegen lässt

irrepressibly [ˌɪrɪ'presəblɪ] ADV *laugh, high-spirited* unbändig; **he was ~ optimistic** sein Optimismus war nicht kleinzukriegen

irreproachable [ˌɪrɪ'prəʊtʃəbl] ADJ *manners* tadellos, einwandfrei; *conduct also* untadelig

irreproachably [ˌɪrɪ'prəʊtʃəblɪ] ADV tadellos

irresistible [ˌɪrɪ'zɪstəbl] ADJ unwiderstehlich (*to* für); **he is ~ to women** er wirkt auf Frauen unwiderstehlich; **he was in ~ form** *(Sport)* er war in unschlagbarer Form; **the truth is ~** *(form)* die Wahrheit kommt immer ans Licht

irresistibly [ˌɪrɪ'zɪstəblɪ] ADV unwiderstehlich; **it's ~ funny** es ist von unwiderstehlicher Komik

irresolute [ɪ'rezəluːt] ADJ unentschlossen, unentschieden

irresolutely [ɪ'rezəluːtlɪ] ADV unentschlossen, unschlüssig

irresoluteness [ɪ'rezəluːtnɪs], **irresolution** [ɪˌrezə'luːʃən] N Unentschiedenheit *f*, Unentschlossenheit *f*

irrespective [ˌɪrɪ'spektɪv] ADJ ~ **of** ungeachtet *(+gen)*, unabhängig von; **candidates should be chosen ~ of sex/race** bei der Auswahl der Kandidaten sollte das Geschlecht/die Rasse keine Rolle spielen; **~ of whether they want to or not** egal *or* gleichgültig, ob sie wollen oder nicht

irresponsibility ['ɪrɪˌspɒnsə'bɪlɪtɪ] N *(of action, behaviour)* Unverantwortlichkeit *f*; *(of person)* Verantwortungslosigkeit *f*

irresponsible [ˌɪrɪ'spɒnsəbl] ADJ *action, behaviour* unverantwortlich; *person* verantwortungslos; **she was ~ to say that** es war unverantwortlich von ihr, das zu sagen

irresponsibly [ˌɪrɪ'spɒnsəblɪ] ADV unverantwortlich; *behave also* verantwortungslos; **he was ~ extravagant with money** es war unverantwortlich, wie verschwenderisch er mit Geld umging

irretrievable [ˌɪrɪ'triːvəbl] ADJ **a** *(= unrecoverable)* nicht mehr wiederzubekommen; *past, happiness etc* unwiederbringlich; *loss* unersetzlich; *debt* nicht eintreibbar; **the erased information is ~** die gelöschte Information kann nicht mehr abgerufen werden **b** *(= irreparable) damage, harm* irreparabel; **~ breakdown of marriage** (unheilbare) Zerrüttung der Ehe

irretrievably [ˌɪrɪ'triːvəblɪ] ADV ~ **lost** für immer verloren; **~ damaged** irreparabel; **her marriage broke down ~** ihre Ehe war (unheilbar) zerrüttet

irreverence [ɪ'revərəns] N *(of behaviour)* Unehrerbietigkeit *f*; *(of remark, attitude)* Respektlosigkeit *f*, Despektierlichkeit *f (geh)*; *(of book, author)* Respektlosigkeit *f*; *(towards religion, the dead)* Pietätlosigkeit *f*

irreverent [ɪ'revərənt] ADJ *behaviour* unehrerbietig; *remark, attitude* respektlos, despektierlich *(geh)*; *book, author* respektlos; *(towards religion, the dead)* pietätlos

irreverently [ɪ'revərəntlɪ] ADV *behave* unehrerbietig; *say, speak, name* respektlos, despektierlich *(geh)*; *write* respektlos; *(towards religion, the dead)* pietätlos

irreversible [ˌɪrɪ'vɜːsəbl] ADJ nicht rückgängig zu machen; *decision, judgement* unwiderruflich; *(Med, Phys, Chem)* irreversibel; *damage* bleibend; *decision* unumstößlich; **to be in ~ decline** sich in einem unaufhaltsamen Abwärtstrend befinden

irreversibly [ˌɪrɪ'vɜːsəblɪ] ADV *change* für immer; **the peace process has been ~ damaged** der Friedensprozess hat einen nicht wiedergutzumachenden Schaden davongetragen

irrevocable ADJ, **irrevocably** ADV [ɪ'revəkəbl, -ɪ] unwiderruflich

irrigate ['ɪrɪgeɪt] VT **a** *land, crop* bewässern **b** *(Med)* spülen

irrigation [ˌɪrɪ'geɪʃən] N **a** *(Agr)* Bewässerung *f*; **~ canal** Bewässerungskanal *m* **b** *(Med)* Spülung *f*, Irrigation *f*; **colonic ~** Darmspülung *f*

irrigator ['ɪrɪgeɪtə'] N **a** *(Agr)* Bewässerungsanlage *f* **b** *(Med)* Spülapparat *m*, Irrigator *m*

irritability [ˌɪrɪtə'bɪlɪtɪ] N Reizbarkeit *f*; *(on occasion)* Gereiztheit *f*

irritable ['ɪrɪtəbl] ADJ *(as characteristic)* reizbar; *(on occasion)* gereizt; **don't be so ~** sei doch nicht so gereizt

irritable bowel syndrome N Reizdarm *m*

irritably ['ɪrɪtəblɪ] ADV gereizt

irritant ['ɪrɪtənt] N *(Med)* Reizerreger *m*; *(= person)* Nervensäge *f (inf)*; *(= noise etc)* Ärgernis *nt*

irritate ['ɪrɪteɪt] VT **a** *(= annoy)* ärgern, aufregen; *(deliberately)* reizen; *(= get on nerves of)* irritieren; **to get ~d** ärgerlich werden; **she's easily ~d** sie ist sehr reizbar *or* schnell verärgert; **I get ~d at** *or* **with him** er reizt *or* ärgert mich, er regt mich auf **b** *(Med)* reizen

irritating ['ɪrɪteɪtɪŋ] ADJ ärgerlich; *cough* lästig; **I find his jokes most ~** seine Witze regen mich wirklich auf; **you really are the most ~ person** du kannst einem wirklich auf die Nerven gehen; **how ~ for you!** wie ärgerlich!; **the ~ thing is that ...** das Ärgerliche ist, dass ...; **she has an ~ habit of snapping her fingers** sie hat die ärgerliche Angewohnheit, mit den Fingern zu schnipsen

irritatingly ['ɪrɪteɪtɪŋlɪ] ADV ärgerlich; **he very ~ changed his mind** ärgerlicherweise hat er seine Meinung geändert

irritation [ˌɪrɪ'teɪʃən] N **a** *(= state)* Ärger *m*, Verärgerung *f*; *(= act)* Ärgern *nt*; *(deliberate)*

Reizen *nt*; *(= thing that irritates)* Ärgernis *nt*, Unannehmlichkeit *f*; **the noise is a source of ~** der Lärm irritiert einen; **to avoid the ~ of a long delay** um eine ärgerliche *or* lästige Verzögerung zu vermeiden **b** *(Med)* Reizung *f*

irrupt [ɪˈrʌpt] VI eindringen, hereinstürzen; *(water also)* hereinbrechen

irruption [ɪˈrʌpʃən] N Eindringen *nt*, Hereinstürzen *nt*; *(of water also)* Hereinbrechen *nt*

IRS *(US) abbr of* **Internal Revenue Service** Finanzamt *nt*

Is *abbr of* **Island(s), Isle(s)**

is [ɪz] *3rd pers sing present of* **be**

ISA [ˈaɪsə] N ABBR *of* **Individual Savings Account** *(Brit Fin) von Zinsabschlagsteuer befreites Sparkonto*

Isaiah [aɪˈzaɪə] N Jesaja *m*

ISBN *abbr of* **International Standard Book Number** ISBN-Nummer *f*

ISDN *abbr of* **Integrated Services Digital Network** ISDN *nt*

-ise [-aɪz] VB *suf* → **-ize**

ish [ɪʃ] ADV *(inf)* ein bisschen; **hungry? – ~** Hunger? – ein bisschen

-ish [-ɪʃ] ADJ *suf (+adj)* -lich; *(+n)* -haft; *(= approximately)* um … herum, circa; **greenish** grünlich; **coldish** ziemlich kalt; **smallish** ziemlich klein; **youngish** ziemlich jung; **boyish** jungenhaft; **fortyish** um vierzig herum, circa vierzig

isinglass [ˈaɪzɪŋglɑːs] N Fischleim *m*

Islam [ˈɪzlɑːm] N *(= religion)* der Islam; *(= Moslems collectively)* die Moslems *pl*

Islamic [ɪzˈlæmɪk] ADJ islamisch

Islamicist [ɪzˈlæmɪsɪst] N Islamist(in) *m(f)*

Islamic radical ADJ radikalislamistisch

Islamist [ˈɪzləmɪst] **N** Islamist(in) *m(f)* **ADJ** islamistisch

islamophobia [ˌɪzlɑːməˈfəʊbɪə] N Islamophobie *f*

island [ˈaɪlənd] N *(lit, fig)* Insel *f*

islander [ˈaɪləndəʳ] N Insulaner(in) *m(f)*, Inselbewohner(in) *m(f)*

island-hopping [ˈaɪləndˌhɒpɪŋ] *(inf)* **N** Inselhüpfen *nt (inf)*; **to go ~** von Insel zu Insel reisen **ADJ ~ holiday** Urlaub *m* mit Inselhüpfen *(inf)*

isle [aɪl] N *(poet)* Eiland *nt (poet)*; **the Isle of Man** die Insel Man

islet [ˈaɪlɪt] N kleines Eiland *(poet)*, Inselchen *nt*

ism [ˈɪzəm] N *(inf)* Ismus *m (inf)*; **Marxism or any other ~** Marxismus oder jeder andere Ismus *(inf)*

isn't [ˈɪznt] *contr of* **is not**

ISO *abbr of* **International Standards Organization**

isobar [ˈaɪsəʊbɑːʳ] N Isobare *f*

isolate [ˈaɪsəʊleɪt] VT **a** *(= separate)* absondern, isolieren; *(Med, Chem)* isolieren; **the causes of crime cannot be ~d from social conditions** man kann die Gründe für kriminelles Verhalten nicht von den gesellschaftlichen Verhältnissen gesondert *or* isoliert betrachten **b** *(= cut off)* abschneiden, isolieren; **to ~ oneself from other people** sich (von anderen) abkapseln; **to ~ oneself from the outside world** sich isolieren, sich von der Außenwelt zurückziehen **c** *(= pinpoint)* herausfinden; *essential factor* herauskristallisieren

isolated [ˈaɪsəʊleɪtɪd] ADJ **a** *(= cut off, marginalized)* abgeschnitten, isoliert; *(= remote)* abgelegen; *existence* zurückgezogen; *(Med)* isoliert; **the islanders feel ~** die Inselbewohner fühlen sich von der Außenwelt abgeschnitten; **she kept her sons ~ from other children** sie hielt ihre Söhne von anderen Kindern fern **b** *(= single)* einzeln; **~ instances** Einzelfälle *pl*

isolating [ˈaɪsəʊleɪtɪŋ] ADJ **~ language** isolierende Sprache

isolation [ˌaɪsəʊˈleɪʃən] N **a** *(= act) (= separation, cutting-off)* Absonderung *f*, Isolierung *f (esp Med, Chem)*; *(= pinpointing)* Herausfinden *nt*; *(of essential factor)* Herauskristallisierung *f* **b** *(= state)* Isoliertheit *f*, Abgeschnittenheit *f*; *(= remoteness)* Abgelegenheit *f*, Abgeschiedenheit *f*; **his ~ from the outside world** seine Abgeschiedenheit von der Außenwelt; **this deliberate and self-imposed social ~** diese absichtliche und selbst auferlegte gesellschaftliche Isolation; **spiritual ~** geistige Isolation; **he felt a sense of ~** er fühlte sich isoliert; **Splendid Isolation** *(Hist)* Splendid Isolation *f*; **he lived in splendid ~ in a bedsitter in the suburbs** *(iro)* er wohnte weitab vom Schuss in einem möblierten Zimmer am Stadtrand *(inf)*; **he was in ~ for three months** er war drei Monate lang isoliert; *(in hospital)* er war drei Monate auf der Isolierstation; **to keep a patient in ~** einen Patienten isolieren; **to live in ~** zurückgezogen leben; **to consider sth in ~** etw gesondert *or* isoliert betrachten; **it doesn't make much sense (when taken) in ~** für sich genommen *or* ohne Zusammenhang ist es ziemlich unverständlich

isolation hospital N Isolierspital *nt*

isolationism [ˌaɪsəʊˈleɪʃənɪzəm] N Isolationismus *m*

isolationist [ˌaɪsəʊˈleɪʃənɪst] **ADJ** isolationistisch **N** Isolationist(in) *m(f)*

isolation ward N Isolierstation *f*

isomer [ˈaɪsəʊməʳ] N *(Chem)* Isomer(e) *nt*

isomeric [ˌaɪsəʊˈmerɪk] ADJ *(Chem)* isomer

isometrics [ˌaɪsəʊˈmetrɪks] N *sing* Isometrie *f*

isomorphic [ˌaɪsəʊˈmɔːfɪk] ADJ *(form)* isomorph

isosceles [aɪˈsɒsɪliːz] ADJ **~ triangle** gleichschenkliges Dreieck

isotherm [ˈaɪsəʊθɜːm] N *(Met)* Isotherme *f*

isotope [ˈaɪsəʊtəʊp] N Isotop *nt*

ISP *(Comput) abbr of* **Internet service provider** Provider *m*

I-spy [ˈaɪˈspaɪ] N *(Brit)* → **spy**

Israel [ˈɪzreɪl] N Israel *nt*

Israeli [ɪzˈreɪlɪ] **ADJ** israelisch **N** Israeli *mf*

Israelite [ˈɪzrɪəlaɪt] N *(Bibl)* Israelit(in) *m(f)*

issei [ˈiːseɪ] N *pl* **issei** *(US) japanischer Einwanderer in den USA*

ISSN *abbr of* **International Standard Serial Number** ISSN *f*

issue [ˈɪʃuː] **VT** **a** *(= give, send out) passport, documents, certificate, driving licence* ausstellen; *tickets, library books* ausgeben; *shares, banknotes* ausgeben, emittieren; *stamps* herausgeben; *coins* ausgeben; *order* erteilen *(to +dat)*; *warning, declaration, statement* abgeben, aussprechen; *proclamation* erlassen; *details* bekannt geben; *ultimatum* stellen; **the issuing authorities** die ausstellende Behörde; **to ~ sb with a visa, to ~ a visa to sb** jdm ein Visum ausstellen; **a warrant for his arrest was ~d** gegen ihn wurde Haftbefehl erlassen; **~d capital** *(Fin)* ausgegebenes Kapital **b** *(= publish) book, newspaper* herausgeben **c** *(= supply) rations, rifles, ammunition* ausgeben; **to ~ sth to sb/sb with sth** etw an jdn ausgeben; **all troops are ~d with …** alle Truppen sind mit … ausgerüstet

VI *(from* aus) *(liquid, gas)* austreten; *(smoke, blood, water)* quellen, austreten; *(sound)* (hervor- *or* heraus)dringen; *(people etc)* (heraus)strömen; **his actions ~ from a desire to help** seine Handlungen entspringen dem Wunsch zu helfen; **the sewage/river ~s into the sea** das Abwasser fließt/der Fluss mündet ins Meer

N **a** *(= question)* Frage *f*; *(= matter)* Angelegenheit *f*; *(problematic)* Problem *nt*; **the main** *or* **key ~ is reducing unemployment** das Wichtigste ist es, die Arbeitslosigkeit zu verringern; **the factual ~s** die Tatsachen *pl*; **to raise an ~** eine Frage aufwerfen; **she raised the ~ of human rights** sie brachte die Frage der Menschenrechte zur Sprache; **the ~ is whether …** es geht darum *or* die Frage ist, ob …; **the whole future of the country is at ~** es geht um die Zukunft des Landes; **what is at ~?** worum geht es?; **this matter/question is not at ~** diese Angelegenheit/Frage steht nicht zur Debatte; **to take ~ with sb over sth** jdm in etw *(dat)* widersprechen; **this has become something of an ~** das ist zu einem Problem geworden; **to make an ~ of sth** etw aufbauschen; **do you want to make an ~ of it?** *(inf)* du willst dich wohl mit mir anlegen?; **to avoid the ~** ausweichen; *(in reply also)* ausweichend antworten

b *(= outcome, result)* Ergebnis *nt*; **that decided the ~** das war entscheidend *or* ausschlaggebend; **to force the ~** eine Entscheidung erzwingen

c *(= giving out, that given out) (of banknotes, shares, coins, stamps etc)* Ausgabe *f*; *(of shares)* Emission *f*, Ausgabe *f*; **place of ~** *(of tickets)* Ausgabestelle *f*; *(of passports)* Ausstellungsort *m*; **date of ~** *(of tickets)* Ausstellungsdatum *nt*; *(of stamps)* Ausgabetag *m*; **~ desk** Ausgabe(-schalter *m*) *f*; **~ price** *(of shares)* Zeichnungs- *or* Emissionspreis *m*

d *(= handing-out)* Ausgabe *f*; *(= supplying, thing supplied)* Lieferung *f*; **the ~ of guns to the troops** die Ausrüstung der Truppen mit Gewehren; **it's part of the clothing ~** es ist Teil der Ausstattung

e *(of book etc)* Herausgabe *f*; *(= book etc)* Ausgabe *f*

f *(of liquid, gas)* Ausströmen *nt*; **~ of pus** Eiterabsonderung *f*; **an ~ of blood from the cut** eine Blutung der Wunde

g *(Jur: = offspring)* Nachkommenschaft *f*

issuer [ˈɪʃuːəʳ] N *(of shares)* Emittent(in) *m(f)*, Ausgeber(in) *m(f)*

issue-related [ˈɪʃuːrɪˈleɪtɪd] ADJ sachbezogen

Istanbul [ˌɪstænˈbuːl] N Istanbul *nt*

isthmus [ˈɪsməs] N Landenge *f*, Isthmus *m*

IT *abbr of* **information technology**

it[1] [ɪt] **PRON** **a** *(when replacing German noun) (subj)* er/sie/es; *(dir obj)* ihn/sie/es; *(indir obj)* ihm/ihr/ihm; **of it** davon; **behind/over/under** *etc* **it** dahinter/darüber/darunter *etc*; **who is it? – it's me** *or (form)* **I** wer ist da? – ich (bins); **who is it? – it's the Browns!** wer ist da? – die Browns!; **once the baby had been fed, it stopped crying** als das Baby gefüttert worden war, hörte es auf zu weinen; **what is it?** was ist es *or* das?; *(= what's the matter?)* was ist los?; **that's not it** *(= not the trouble)* das ist es (gar) nicht; *(= not the point)* darum gehts gar nicht; **the cheek of it!** so eine Frechheit!; **the worst of it is that …** das Schlimmste daran ist, dass …; **I like it here** mir gefällt es hier

b *(indef subject)* es; **it's raining** es regnet; **yes, it is a problem** ja, das ist ein Problem; **it seems simple to me** mir scheint das ganz einfach; **if it hadn't been for her, we would have come** wenn sie nicht gewesen wäre, wären wir gekommen; **it's not that I don't want to go** es ist nicht so, dass ich nicht gehen will; **why is it always me who has to …?** warum muss (ausgerechnet) immer ich …?; **why is it always him who can't …?** warum ist es immer er, der nicht … kann?; **it wasn't me** ICH wars nicht; **it was the Italians who won** es waren die Italiener, die gewannen; **it was ten miles to the station** bis zum Bahnhof waren es zehn Meilen; **I don't think it (is) wise of you …** ich halte es für unklug, wenn du …; **it is said that …** es wird gesagt, dass …, man sagt, dass …

c *(emph)* **it was him** *or* **he** *(form)* **who asked her** ER hat sie gefragt; **it was a cup that he dropped and not …** er hat eine TASSE fallen lassen und nicht …; **it's his appearance I object to** ich habe nur etwas gegen sein Äußeres; **it was for his sake that she lied** nur um seinetwillen hat sie gelogen; **it's the OTHER one I like** ich mag den ANDEREN/das ANDERE *etc*

d *(inf phrases)* **that's it!** *(agreement)* ja, genau!; *(annoyed)* jetzt reichts mir!; **that's it (then)!** *(achievement)* (so,) das wärs!, geschafft!; *(disappointment)* ja, das wars dann wohl; **this is it!** *(before action)* jetzt gehts los! → **at, in, with-it**

N *(inf)* **a** *(in children's games)* **you're it!** du bist!

b **this is really it!** das ist genau das richtige, DAS ist es; **he really thinks he's it** er bildet sich *(dat)* ein, er sei sonst wer

c **my cat's an it** meine Katze ist ein Neutrum **d** *(dated: = sex appeal)* Sexappeal *m*

it² N *(dated sl)* **gin and it** Gin mit italienischem Wermut

ITA *(dated Brit) abbr of* **Independent Television Authority**

ita *abbr of* **initial teaching alphabet** *Lautschrift für den Anfangsunterricht im Lesen*

Italian [ɪ'tæljən] ADJ italienisch N **a** Italiener(in) *m(f)* **b** *(Ling)* Italienisch *nt*

Italianate [ɪ'tæljəneɪt] ADJ nach italienischer Art; **the ~ style of the church** der von der italienischen Schule beeinflusste Stil der Kirche

italic [ɪ'tælɪk] ADJ kursiv; **~ type** Kursivdruck *m*; **~ script** Kurrentschrift *f* N **italics** PL Kursivschrift *f*, Kursive *f*; **in ~s** kursiv (gedruckt)

italicize [ɪ'tælɪsaɪz] VT kursiv schreiben

Italo- [ɪ'tæləʊ-] PREF Italo-, italo-; **~American** italo-amerikanisch

Italy ['ɪtəlɪ] N Italien *nt*

ITC *(Brit) abbr of* **Independent Television Commission**

itch [ɪtʃ] N **a** *(lit)* Jucken *nt*, Juckreiz *m*; **I have an ~** mich juckt es, ich habe einen Juckreiz **b** *(fig inf: = urge)* Lust *f*; **I have the ~ to do sth** es reizt *or* juckt *(inf)* mich, etw zu tun; **the seven-year ~** das verflixte siebte Jahr VI **a** *(lit)* jucken; **my back is ~ing** mein Rücken juckt (mich), mir *or* mich juckt der Rücken; **that rash made me ~ all over** der Ausschlag juckte am ganzen Körper **b** *(fig inf)* **he is ~ing to ...** es reizt *or* juckt *(inf)* ihn, zu ...; **he's ~ing for a fight** er ist auf Streit aus

itching ['ɪtʃɪŋ] ADJ juckend N Jucken *nt*, Juckreiz *m*; **~ powder** Juckpulver *nt*

itchy ['ɪtʃɪ] ADJ *(+er)* **a** *(= itching)* juckend; **my back is ~** mein Rücken juckt; **I've got an ~ leg** mir juckt das Bein; **to become ~** anfangen zu jucken; **I've got ~ feet** *(inf)* ich will hier weg *(inf)*; *(= want to travel also)* mich packt das Fernweh; **he's got ~ fingers** *(inf)* er macht lange Finger *(inf)*; **he's got an ~ (trigger) finger** er hat einen lockeren Finger am Abzug **b** *(= causing itching) cloth* kratzig

it'd ['ɪtəd] *contr of* **it would, it had**

-ite [-aɪt] N *suf (= follower of)* -anhänger(in) *m(f)*; **Blairite** Blair-Anhänger(in) *m(f)*

item ['aɪtəm] ✪ 20.3 N **a** *(in programme, on agenda etc)* Punkt *m*; *(Comm: in account book)* (Rechnungs)posten *m*; *(= article)* Stück *nt*, Ding *nt*, Gegenstand *m*; *(in catalogue etc)* Artikel *m*; *(Brit: in variety show)* Nummer *f*; **~s of furniture/clothing/jewellery** Möbel-/Kleidungs-/ /Schmuckstücke *pl*; **~s of food** Lebensmittel *pl*; **he went through it ~ by ~** er ging die Sache Punkt für Punkt durch; **heating oil is one of the most expensive ~s I have to buy** Heizöl gehört zu den teuersten Dingen, die ich kaufe **b** *(of news)* Bericht *m*; *(short: Rad, TV)* Meldung *f*; **a short news ~** *(in newspaper)* eine Zeitungsnotiz; *(Rad, TV)* eine Kurzmeldung; **the main news ~** die wichtigste Nachricht **c** *(inf)* **Lynn and Craig are an ~** zwischen Lynn und Craig spielt sich was ab *(inf)*

itemization [,aɪtəmaɪ'zeɪʃən] N detaillierte Aufstellung, Einzelaufführung *f*

itemize ['aɪtəmaɪz] VT spezifizieren, einzeln aufführen; **to ~ a bill** die Rechnungsposten einzeln aufführen, die Rechnung spezifizieren

iterate ['ɪtəreɪt] VT *(form)* wiederholen

iteration [ɪtə'reɪʃən] N *(form)* Wiederholung *f*

iterative ['ɪtərətɪv] ADJ *(Gram)* iterativ

itinerant [ɪ'tɪnərənt] ADJ umherziehend, wandernd; *minstrel* fahrend; **an ~ lifestyle** ein Wanderleben *nt*; **~ preacher** Wanderprediger(in) *m(f)*; **~ worker** Saison- *or* Wanderarbeiter(in) *m(f)*; **~ theatre** *(Brit) or* **theater** *(US)* **group** Wandertruppe *f* N *(= worker)* Wanderarbeiter(in) *m(f)*

itinerary [aɪ'tɪnərərɪ] N *(= route)* (Reise)route *f*; *(= map)* Straßenkarte *f*, Wegeverzeichnis *nt*

it'll ['ɪtl] *contr of* **it will, it shall**

ITN *(Brit) abbr of* **Independent Television News** *Nachrichtendienst der Fernsehanstalt ITV*

ITO *abbr of* **International Trade Organization**

its [ɪts] POSS ADJ sein(e)/ihr(e)/sein(e)

it's [ɪts] *contr of* **it is, it has** *as aux*

itself [ɪt'self] PRON **a** *(reflexive)* sich **b** *(emph)* selbst; **and now we come to the text ~** und jetzt kommen wir zum Text selbst; **the frame ~ is worth £1,000** der Rahmen allein *or* schon der Rahmen ist £ 1.000 wert; **she has been kindness ~** sie war die Freundlichkeit in Person; **in ~, the actual amount is not important** der Betrag an sich ist unwichtig; **enthusiasm is not enough in ~** Begeisterung allein genügt nicht **c** **by ~** *(= alone)* allein; *(= automatically)* von selbst, selbsttätig; **seen by ~** einzeln betrachtet; **the bomb went off by ~** die Bombe ging von selbst los

IT specialist N IT-Spezialist(in) *m(f)*

itsy-bitsy ['ɪtsɪ'bɪtsɪ], **itty-bitty** ['ɪtɪ'bɪtɪ] ADJ *(inf: = tiny)* klitzeklein *(inf)*, winzig

ITV *(Brit) abbr of* **Independent Television** *britische Fernsehanstalt*

IUD *abbr of* **intra-uterine device**

IV *(Med) abbr of* **intravenous**

I've [aɪv] *contr of* **I have**

ivied ['aɪvɪd] ADJ efeuumrankt

ivory ['aɪvərɪ] N **a** *(also colour)* Elfenbein *nt*; **the ~ trade** der Elfenbeinhandel **b** *(Art)* Elfenbeinschnitzerei *f* **c** *(inf)* **ivories** *(= piano keys)* Tasten *pl*; *(= billiard balls)* Billardkugeln *pl*; *(= dice)* Würfel *pl*; *(dated: = teeth)* Beißer *pl* *(inf)* ADJ **a** elfenbeinern **b** *(colour)* elfenbeinfarben

Ivory Coast N Elfenbeinküste *f*

ivory tower N *(fig)* Elfenbeinturm *m* ADJ *attr* weltfremd

ivy ['aɪvɪ] N Efeu *m*

Ivy League N *(US)* Eliteuniversitäten *pl* der USA

IVY LEAGUE

Als **Ivy League** bezeichnet man acht Universitäten im Nordosten der Vereinigten Staaten von Amerika, Harvard, Yale, Pennsylvania, Princeton, Columbia, Brown, Dartmouth und Cornell, die neben einem ausgezeichneten akademischen Ruf ein großartiges Renommee haben, das mit dem von Oxford und Cambridge in England verglichen werden kann. **Ivy League** heißen sie deshalb, weil viele der Institutsgemäuer efeubedeckt sind. Der Ausdruck kam erstmals auf, als sich diese Universitäten 1956 zu einer gemeinsamen American Football Liga zusammenschlossen, um den sportlichen Wettkampf unter den Universitäten zu fördern. Studenten dieser ehrwürdigen Universitäten werden „Ivy Leaguer" genannt, eine Bezeichnung, die auch für solche Leute benutzt wird, die Haltung und Moden der Ivy-League-Universitäten annehmen.

-ize [-aɪz] VB *suf* -isieren; **authorize** autorisieren; **rationalize** rationalisieren

J

J, j [dʒeɪ] N J *nt*, j *nt*

jab [dʒæb] VT a *(with stick, elbow etc)* stoßen; *(with knife)* stechen, stoßen; **she ~bed the jellyfish with a stick** sie pik(s)te mit einem Stock in die Qualle (hinein) *(inf)*; **he ~bed his finger at the map** er tippte mit dem Finger auf die Karte; **a sharp ~bing pain** ein scharfer, stechender Schmerz
b *(Brit inf: = give injection to)* eine Spritze geben *(+dat) or* verpassen *(+dat) (inf)*
VI stoßen *(at sb with sth* mit etw nach jdm); *(Boxing)* eine (kurze) Gerade schlagen *(at* auf *+acc)*
N a *(with stick, elbow)* Stoß *m*; *(with needle, knife)* Stich *m*; **he gave the jellyfish a ~ with a stick** er stieß *or* pik(s)te *(inf)* mit einem Stock in die Qualle (hinein); **he got a nasty ~ in the eye when she opened her umbrella** sie stach ihn ins Auge, als sie den Regenschirm öffnete
b *(Brit inf: = injection)* Spritze *f*
c *(Boxing)* (kurze) Gerade

jabber [ˈdʒæbəʳ] VT (daher)plappern *(inf)*; *poem, prayers* herunterrasseln, abhaspeln *(inf)* VI *(also* **jabber away***)* plappern, schwätzen, quasseln *(inf)*; **they sat there ~ing away in Spanish** sie saßen da und quasselten spanisch *(inf)* N Geplapper *nt*, Gequassel *nt (inf)*, Geschnatter *nt*

jabbering [ˈdʒæbərɪŋ] N Geplapper *nt*, Plappern *nt*, Geschnatter *nt*

jabberwocky [ˈdʒæbəˌwɒkɪ] N *(inf: = nonsense)* Nonsens *m*, Kauderwelsch *nt*

jacaranda [ˌdʒækəˈrændə] N Jakaranda(baum) *m*; *(= wood)* Jakarandaholz *nt*, Palisander(holz *nt*) *m*

Jack [dʒæk] N *dim of* **John** Hans *m*; **I'm all right ~** das kann mich überhaupt nicht jucken *(inf)*; **his attitude of I'm all right ~** seine Einstellung „das kann mich überhaupt nicht jucken"

jack [dʒæk] N a Hebevorrichtung *f*; *(Aut)* Wagenheber *m* b *(Cards)* Bube *m* c *(Naut: = flag)* Gösch *f*, Bugflagge *f* → **Union Jack** d *(Bowling)* Zielkugel *f* e *(= bootjack)* Stiefelknecht *m* f *(inf)* **every man ~ (of them)** alle ohne Ausnahme, (alle) geschlossen; **every man ~ of them voted against it** sie stimmten alle geschlossen *or* ohne Ausnahme dagegen

▶ **jack in** VT *sep (Brit inf) university, job etc* stecken *(sl)*, aufgeben; **jack it in!** *(= stop it)* hör auf damit!, stecks *(sl)*

▶ **jack up** VT *sep* a *car* aufbocken b *(inf) prices, wages, interest rates* (in die Höhe) treiben

jackal [ˈdʒækɔːl] N Schakal *m*

jackanapes [ˈdʒækəneɪps] N *pl* - *(old) (= man)* Fant *m (old)*, (eingebildeter) Laffe *(old)*; *(= child)* Racker *m (old)*

jackass [ˈdʒækæs] N *(= donkey)* Eselhengst *m*; *(inf: = person)* Esel *m (inf)*, Blödmann *m (inf)*, Nullchecker(in) *m(f) (inf)*

jackboot [ˈdʒækbuːt] N Schaftstiefel *m*; **to be under the ~ (of)** unter dem Stiefel *(+gen)* stehen

jackdaw [ˈdʒækdɔː] N Dohle *f*

jacket [ˈdʒækɪt] N a *(= garment)* Jacke *f*; *(= man's tailored jacket)* Jackett *nt*; *(= life jacket)* Schwimmweste *f* b *(of book)* Schutzumschlag *m*, Buchhülle *f*; *(US: of record)* Plattenhülle *f* c *(esp US: for papers etc)* Umschlag *m* d **~ potatoes, potatoes (baked) in their ~s** (in der Schale) gebackene Kartoffeln *pl* e *(Tech: of boiler etc)* Mantel *m*, Ummantelung *f*

jack: **Jack Frost** N der Frost, der Reif *(personifiziert)*; **~ has been, ~ has painted the window** es sind Eisblumen am Fenster; **jackhammer** N *(US)* Presslufthammer *m*; **jack-in-office** N Beamtenseele *f*; **jack-in-the-box** N Schachtel- *or* Kastenteufel *m*; **he was up and down like a ~** er sprang immer wieder auf, der reinste Hampelmann

jackknife [ˈdʒæknaɪf] N a (großes) Taschenmesser b *(also* **jackknife dive***)* gehechteter Sprung VI **the lorry ~d** der Lastwagenanhänger hat sich quer gestellt

jack: **jack of all trades** [ˌdʒækəvˈɔːltreɪdz] N Alleskönner *m*; **to be (a) ~ (and master of none)** *(prov)* ein Hansdampf *m* in allen Gassen sein; **jack-o'-lantern** N Kürbislaterne *f*; *(= will-o'-the-wisp)* Irrlicht *nt*; **jack plane** N *(Tech)* Schropp- *or* Doppelhobel *m*; **jack plug** N Bananenstecker *m*; *(for telephone)* Klinkenstecker *m*

jackpot [ˈdʒækpɒt] N Pott *m (inf)*; *(Cards also)* Jackpot *m*; *(in lottery etc)* Hauptgewinn *m*; **the ~ this week stands at £10 million** diese Woche ist der Höchstgewinn zehn Millionen Pfund; **to hit the ~** *(lit)* einen Treffer haben; *(in lottery)* den Hauptgewinn bekommen; *(fig)* das große Los ziehen

jack: **jack rabbit** N Eselhase *m*; **Jack Robinson** [ˌdʒækˈrɒbɪnsən] N **before you could say ~** *(inf)* im Nu, im Handumdrehen; **Jack Russell** [ˌdʒækˈrʌsl] N Jack Russell *m*

jacks [dʒæks] N *sing (= game) Kinderspiel mit kleinem Gummiball und Metallsternchen*

jackstraws [ˈdʒækˌstrɔːz] N *sing* Mikado *nt*

jack: **Jack Tar** N *(Naut inf)* Seebär *m (inf)*; **Jack-the-lad** [ˌdʒækðəˈlæd] N *(Brit inf)* Großmaul *nt (inf)*

Jacob [ˈdʒeɪkəb] N Jakob *m*

Jacobean [ˌdʒækəˈbiːən] ADJ aus der Zeit Jakobs I.

Jacobite [ˈdʒækəbaɪt] N Jakobit(in) *m(f)*

Jacuzzi® [dʒəˈkuːzɪ] N Whirlpool *m*

jade¹ [dʒeɪd] N *(= stone)* Jade *m or f*; *(= colour)* Jadegrün *nt* ADJ Jade-; *(colour)* jadegrün; **a ~ necklace** eine Jadekette, eine Kette aus Jade

jade² N *(old)* a *(= horse)* Schindmähre *f (old)*, Klepper *m (old)* b *(= loose woman)* Weibsbild *nt*, Weibsstück *nt*; *(= pert girl)* freches *or* keckes Weibsbild

jaded [ˈdʒeɪdɪd] ADJ *(physically)* matt, abgespannt; *(permanently)* verbraucht, abgelebt; *(= mentally dulled)* stumpfsinnig, abgestumpft; *(from overindulgence etc)* übersättigt; *appearance* verlebt, verbraucht; *palate* abgestumpft

jade-green ADJ jadegrün

Jag [dʒæg] N *(inf: = car)* Jaguar® *m*

jag [dʒæg] N a *(of rock)* Zacke *f*, Spitze *f*; *(of saw)* Zacke *f* b **to go on a ~** *(inf)* einen draufmachen *(inf)* c *(Scot inf: = injection)* Spritze *f*

jagged [ˈdʒægɪd] ADJ zackig; *edge, hole also* schartig, (aus)gezackt; *teeth* gezackt; *wound, tear* ausgefranst; *coastline, rocks* zerklüftet; *mountains, peaks* spitz

jaguar [ˈdʒægjʊəʳ] N Jaguar *m*

jail [dʒeɪl] N Gefängnis *nt*; **in ~** im Gefängnis; **after two years in ~** nach zwei Jahren Gefängnis, nach zweijähriger Haft; **to go to ~** eingesperrt werden, ins Gefängnis kommen VT einsperren, ins Gefängnis sperren

jail: **jailbait** N *(inf)* **she's ~** die ist noch minderjährig, lass lieber die Finger von ihr *(inf)*; **jailbird** N *(inf)* Knastbruder *m*/-schwester *f (inf)*; **jailbreak** N Ausbruch *m (aus dem Gefängnis)*; **jailbreaker** N Ausbrecher(in) *m(f)*

jailer [ˈdʒeɪləʳ] N Gefängniswärter(in) *m(f)*, Gefängnisaufseher(in) *m(f)*

jail: **jailhouse** N *(US)* Gefängnis *nt*; **jail sentence** N Gefängnisstrafe *f*

jalop(p)y [dʒəˈlɒpɪ] N *(inf)* alte (Klapper)kiste *or* Mühle *(inf)*

jalousie [ˈʒælu(ː)ziː] N Jalousie *f*

jam¹ [dʒæm] N *(Brit)* Marmelade *f*, Konfitüre *f*; **you want ~ on it too, do you?** *(Brit inf)* du kriegst wohl nie genug *or* den Hals voll? *(inf)*; **the company has promised (us) ~ tomorrow** die Firma hat uns auf die Zukunft vertröstet

jam² N a *(= crowd)* Gedränge *nt*, Gewühl *nt*
b *(= traffic jam)* (Verkehrs)stau *m*, Stauung *f*
c *(= blockage: in machine, of logs etc)* Stockung *f*, Stauung *f*
d *(inf: = tight spot)* Klemme *f (inf)*, Patsche *f (inf)*; **to be in a ~** in der Klemme *or* Patsche sitzen *(inf)*; **to get oneself into a ~** ins Gedränge kommen *(inf)*; **to get sb/oneself out of a ~** jdn/sich aus der Patsche ziehen *(inf)*
VT a *(= make stick) window, drawer etc* verklemmen, verkanten; *gun, brakes etc* blockieren; *(= wedge) (to stop rattling etc)* festklemmen; *(between two things)* einklemmen; **to ~ a door open/shut** eine Tür festklemmen(, so dass sie auf/zu bleibt); **be careful not to ~ the lock** pass auf, dass sich das Schloss nicht verklemmt; **they had him ~med up against the wall** sie hatten ihn gegen die Wand gedrängt; **it's ~med** es klemmt; **he got his finger ~med** *or* **he ~med his finger in the door** er hat sich *(dat)* den Finger in der Tür eingeklemmt
b *(= cram, squeeze) (into* in *+acc) things* stopfen, hineinzwängen, quetschen; *people* quetschen, pferchen; **to be ~med together** *(things)* zusammengezwängt sein; *(people)* zusammengedrängt sein; *(in train etc also)* zusammengepfercht sein; **why ~ all the facts into one article?** warum zwängen *or* quetschen *(inf)* Sie alle Fakten in einen Artikel?
c *(= crowd, block) street, town etc* verstopfen, blockieren; *phone lines* blockieren; **spectators ~med the stadium** das Stadion war mit Zuschauern vollgestopft; **a street ~med with cars** eine verstopfte Straße; **the drain was ~med with rubbish** der Abfluss war durch Abfall verstopft; **the passage was ~med with people** Menschen verstopften *or* versperrten den Durchgang; **the switchboard has been ~med all day** sämtliche Leitungen der Telefonzentrale waren den ganzen Tag blockiert
d *(= move suddenly)* **to ~ one's foot on the brake** eine Vollbremsung machen, auf die Bremse steigen *(inf) or* latschen *(inf)*; **he ~med**

his hands into his pockets er steckte die Hände fest in die Taschen → *also* **jam on**
e *(Rad) station, broadcast* stören
VI **a** **the crowd ~med into the bus** die Menschenmenge zwängte sich in den Bus
b *(= become stuck) (brake)* sich verklemmen; *(gun)* Ladehemmung haben; *(door, window etc)* klemmen; **the key ~med in the lock** der Schlüssel blieb im Schloss stecken
c *(Mus)* eine Jamsession machen

▶**jam in** VT *sep* **a** *(= wedge in)* einkeilen; **he was jammed in by the crowd** er war in der Menge eingekeilt **b** *(= press in)* (herein)stopfen in *(+acc)* VI *(= crowd in)* sich hineindrängen

▶**jam on** VT *sep* **a** **to jam on the brakes** eine Vollbremsung machen, voll auf die Bremse latschen *(inf)* **b** **to jam on one's hat** sich *(dat)* den Hut aufstülpen VI *(brakes)* klemmen

▶**jam up** VT *sep* **a** = **jam**[2] **VT a b** *(= block) roads, entrance etc* blockieren, versperren; *drain, pipe* verstopfen, blockieren

Jamaica [dʒəˈmeɪkə] N Jamaika *nt*

Jamaican [dʒəˈmeɪkən] ADJ jamaikanisch N Jamaikaner(in) *m(f)*

Jamaica rum N Jamaikarum *m*

jamb [dʒæm] N *(of door/window)* (Tür-/Fenster)pfosten *m*

jambalaya [ˌdʒʌmbəˈlaɪə] N *aus Louisiana stammendes Gericht aus Reis, Schinken und Meeresfrüchten*

jamboree [ˌdʒæmbəˈriː] N *(Scouts')* Pfadfindertreffen *nt*; *(dated: = party)* Rummel *m (inf)*; **village ~** Dorffest *nt*

James [dʒeɪmz] N Jakob *m*

jam: **jam-full** ADJ *container* vollgestopft, gepfropft voll; *room, bus* überfüllt, knallvoll *(inf)*, proppenvoll *(inf)*; **~ of people** vollgestopft mit Leuten; **jam jar** N *(Brit)* Marmeladenglas *nt*

jammer [ˈdʒæməˈ] N *(Rad)* Störsender *m*

jamming [ˈdʒæmɪŋ] N *(Rad)* Störung *f*; **~ station** Störsender *m*

jammy [ˈdʒæmɪ] ADJ *(+er) (Brit inf: = lucky)* Glücks-; **a ~ shot** ein Glückstreffer *m*; **the ~ bugger won three in a row** der verdammte Glückspilz hat dreimal nacheinander gewonnen *(inf)*

jam: **jam nut** N *(Tech)* Gegenmutter *f*; **jam-packed** ADJ überfüllt, proppenvoll *(inf)*; **~ with tourists** voller Touristen; **jam pot** N Marmeladentöpfchen *nt*; **jam puff** N Blätterteigteilchen *nt* mit Marmelade; **jam roll** N Biskuitrolle *f*; **jam session** N Jamsession *f*; **jam tart** N Marmeladenkuchen *m*, Marmeladentörtchen *nt*

Jan *abbr of* **January** Jan.

Jane [dʒeɪn] N **a** → **plain b** **jane** *(US sl: = woman)* Frau *f*

Jane Doe N *(US Jur) Frau, deren Name nicht bekannt ist*

jangle [ˈdʒæŋgl] VI *(keys, money)* klimpern *(inf)*; *(bells)* bimmeln *(inf)*; *(chains, harness)* klirren, rasseln; **my nerves are jangling** ich bin genervt *(inf)* VT *money* klimpern mit; *bell* bimmeln lassen; *keys, chains* rasseln mit; **it ~d my nerves** das ist mir durch Mark und Bein gegangen N *(of keys, money)* Klimpern *nt*, Geklimper *nt (inf)*; *(of bells)* Bimmeln *nt*; *(of chains, harness)* Klirren *nt*, Rasseln *nt*

jangling [ˈdʒæŋglɪŋ] ADJ *keys, money* klimpernd; *bells* bimmelnd; *chains, harness* klirrend, rasselnd N = **jangle N**

janitor [ˈdʒænɪtəˈ] N Hausmeister(in) *m(f)*; *(of block of flats also)* Hauswart(in) *m(f)*

janitress [ˈdʒænɪtrɪs] N Hausmeisterin *f*

jankers [ˈdʒæŋkəz] PL *(Mil sl: = prison)* Bau *m (Mil sl)*

January [ˈdʒænjʊərɪ] N Januar *m* → *also* **September**

Janus [ˈdʒeɪnəs] N Janus *m*

Jap [dʒæp] N *(pej inf)* Japse *m (pej)*

Japan [dʒəˈpæn] N Japan *nt*

japan [dʒəˈpæn] N schwarzer Lack, Japanlack *m* VT mit Japanlack überziehen

Japanese [ˌdʒæpəˈniːz] ADJ japanisch N **a** Japaner(in) *m(f)* **b** *(Ling)* Japanisch *nt*

jape [dʒeɪp] *(old)* N Spaß *m*, *(Aus also)* Spass *m*, Scherz *m*; *(= trick)* Streich *m* VI spaßen, scherzen

japonica [dʒəˈpɒnɪkə] N Japanische Quitte

jar[1] [dʒɑːˈ] N **a** *(for jam etc)* Glas *nt*; *(without handle)* Topf *m*, Gefäß *nt* **b** *(Brit inf: = drink)* Bierchen *nt (inf)*; **fancy a ~?** kommst du (mit) auf ein Bierchen? *(inf)*

jar[2] N **a** *(= jolt)* Ruck *m*; **he/his neck got quite a ~ in the accident** er/sein Hals hat bei dem Autounfall einen schweren Stoß abbekommen **b** *(fig)* Schock *m*
VI **a** *(= grate: metal etc)* kreischen, quietschen; **to ~ against sth** auf etw *(dat)* quietschen *or* kreischen
b *(= be out of harmony) (note)* schauerlich klingen; *(colours, patterns)* sich beißen *(inf)*, nicht harmonieren *(with* mit); *(ideas, opinions)* sich nicht vertragen, nicht harmonieren *(with* mit)
VT *building etc, brain* erschüttern; *back, knee* sich *(dat)* stauchen; *(= jolt continuously)* durchrütteln; *(fig)* einen Schock versetzen *(+dat)*; **he must have ~red the camera** er muss mit dem Fotoapparat gewackelt haben; **someone ~red my elbow** jemand hat mir an den *or* mich am Ellbogen gestoßen; **the sight of this ~red my memory** dieser Anblick rüttelte alte Erinnerungen wach

▶**jar on** VI *+prep obj* Schauer über den Rücken jagen *(+dat)*; **this noise jars on my nerves** dieser Lärm geht mir auf die Nerven; **her voice jars on my ears** ihre Stimme geht mir durch und durch

jardinière [ˌdʒɑːdɪnɪˈɛəˈ] N Blumenbank *f*

jargon [ˈdʒɑːgən] N Jargon *m (pej)*, Fachsprache *f*

jarring [ˈdʒɑːrɪŋ] ADJ *sound* gellend, kreischend; *colours* sich beißend *attr (inf)*, nicht zusammenpassend *attr*; **to strike a ~ note** einen Misston anschlagen

jasmin(e) [ˈdʒæzmɪn] N Jasmin *m*

Jason [ˈdʒeɪsən] N Jason *m*

jasper [ˈdʒæspəˈ] N Jaspis *m*

jaundice [ˈdʒɔːndɪs] N Gelbsucht *f*

jaundiced [ˈdʒɔːndɪst] ADJ **a** *(lit)* gelbsüchtig **b** *attitude* verbittert, zynisch; **to take a ~ view of sth** in Bezug auf etw *(acc)* zynisch sein; **to regard sth with a ~ eye** eine zynische Einstellung zu etw haben

jaunt [dʒɔːnt] N Trip *m*, Spritztour *f*; **to go for a ~** einen Ausflug *or* eine Spritztour machen; **on his last ~ through Europe** auf seiner letzten Europatour, auf seinem letzten Trip durch Europa

jauntily [ˈdʒɔːntɪlɪ] ADV munter, fröhlich, unbeschwert; *walk also* schwungvoll; **with his hat perched ~ over one ear** den Hut keck aufgesetzt, den Hut keck auf einem Ohr; **she remains ~ confident** sie bewahrt sich ihr unbeschwertes Selbstbewusstsein

jauntiness [ˈdʒɔːntɪnɪs] N Unbeschwertheit *f*, Sorglosigkeit *f*; *(of singing)* Munterkeit *f*, Fröhlichkeit *f*, Heiterkeit *f*; **the ~ of his step** sein schwungvoller *or* munterer Gang

jaunty [ˈdʒɔːntɪ] ADJ *(+er)* munter, fröhlich; *tune also, hat* flott; *steps also* schwungvoll; *attitude* unbeschwert, sorglos; **with a ~ air** unbeschwert; **he wore his hat at a ~ angle** er hatte den Hut keck aufgesetzt

Java [ˈdʒɑːvə] N Java *nt*

Javanese [ˌdʒɑːvəˈniːz] ADJ *(also* **Javan**) javanisch N **a** Javaner(in) *m(f)* **b** *(Ling)* Javanisch *nt*

javelin [ˈdʒævlɪn] N Speer *m*; **in the ~** *(Sport)* beim Speerwerfen; **throwing the ~, ~ throwing** Speerwerfen *nt*; **~ thrower** Speerwerfer(in) *m(f)*

jaw [dʒɔː] N **a** Kiefer *m*, Kinnlade *f*; **the lion opened its ~s** der Löwe riss seinen Rachen auf; **with its prey between its ~s** mit der Beute im Maul; **his ~ dropped** sein Unterkiefer fiel *or* klappte herunter; **his ~ was set (in concentration)** er spannte sein Gesicht (konzentriert) an
b **jaws** PL *(fig: of valley etc)* Mündung *f*, Öffnung *f*; **the horsemen rode into the ~s of death** die Reiter gingen in den sicheren Tod; **snatched from the ~s of death** den Klauen des Todes entrissen
c *(of pincer, vice)* (Klemm)backe *f*
d *(inf) (= chatting)* Gerede *nt*, Geschwätz *nt*; *(= chat)* Schwatz *m*, Schwätzchen *nt*
e *(inf) (= sermonizing)* (Moral)predigen *nt (inf)*; *(= sermon)* Moralpredigt *f (inf)*
VI **a** *(inf: = chat)* quatschen *(inf)*, quasseln *(inf)*
b *(inf: = moralize)* predigen *(inf)*

jaw: **jawbone** N Kieferknochen *m*, Kinnbacke *f*; **jawboning** N *(US Pol inf) Appelle eines Regierungschefs an Wirtschafts- und Gewerkschaftsführer zur Mäßigung bei Preiserhöhungen und Lohnforderungen*; **jawbreaker** N *(inf)* Zungenbrecher *m*

jaw('s)-harp [ˌdʒɔː(z)ˈhɑːp] N *(politically correct form)* Maultrommel *f*, Brummeisen *nt*

jay [dʒeɪ] N Eichelhäher *m*

jay: **jaywalk** VI sich als Fußgänger unachtsam verhalten; **jaywalker** N unachtsamer Fußgänger, unachtsame Fußgängerin; **jaywalking** N Unachtsamkeit *f* (eines Fußgängers) im Straßenverkehr

jazz [dʒæz] N **a** *(Mus)* Jazz *m* **b** *(inf: = talk)* Getön *nt (inf)*, Gewäsch *nt (pej)*; **... and all that ~** ... und all so 'n Zeug *(inf)*, ... und das ganze Drum und Dran *(inf)* *attr* Jazz-; **~ band** Jazzband *f*; **~ music** Jazzmusik *f*, Jazz *m* VI *(dated: = play jazz)* jazzen, Jazz machen

▶**jazz up** VT *sep* aufmöbeln *(inf)*, aufpeppen *(inf)*; **to jazz up the classics** klassische Musik verjazzen

jazz: **jazz ballet** N Jazzballett *nt*; **jazzman** N *pl* **-men** [-men] Jazzer *m*; **jazz rock** N Jazz-Rock *m*

jazzy [ˈdʒæzɪ] ADJ *(+er)* **a** *colour* knallig *(inf)*, auffallend, schreiend *(pej)*; *pattern* wild, stark gemustert, auffallend; *dress, tie* poppig *(inf)*, knallig *(inf)* **b** *music* verjazzt

JC *abbr of* **Jesus Christ** J. Chr.

JCB® [dʒeɪsiːˈbiː] N Erdräummaschine *f*

JCR *(Brit Univ) abbr of* **Junior Common Room** Gemeinschaftsraum *m* für Studenten

jealous [ˈdʒeləs] ADJ **a** *husband, lover, child etc* eifersüchtig; *(= envious: of sb's possessions, success etc)* neidisch, missgünstig; **to be ~ of sb** auf jdn eifersüchtig sein; *(= envious)* jdn beneiden; **I'm not at all ~ of his success** ich bin nicht neidisch auf seinen Erfolg, ich beneide ihn nicht um seinen Erfolg; **in a (fit of) ~ rage** in einem Anfall von rasender Eifersucht
b *(= watchful, careful)* sehr besorgt *(of* um), bedacht *(of* auf *+acc)*; **~ guardian** strenger Wächter *or* Hüter; **to keep a ~ watch over** *or* **a ~ eye on sb** jdn mit Argusaugen bewachen
c *(Bibl)* **a ~ God** ein eifersüchtiger Gott

jealously [ˈdʒeləslɪ] ADV **a** eifersüchtig; *(= enviously)* neidisch; **she's ~ possessive of him** sie stellt eifersüchtige Besitzansprüche an ihn **b** *(= watchfully, carefully) guard* eifersüchtig

jealousy [ˈdʒeləsɪ] N Eifersucht *f (of* auf *+acc)*; *(= envy: of sb's possessions, success etc)* Neid *m*, Missgunst *f*; **their small-minded, petty jealousies** ihre engstirnigen, kleinlichen Eifersüchteleien *pl*

jeans [dʒiːnz] PL Jeans *pl*; **a pair of ~** (ein Paar) Jeans *pl*

Jeep® [dʒiːp] N Jeep® *m*

jeepers (creepers) [ˈdʒiːpəz(ˈkriːpəz)] INTERJ *(US inf)* Mensch *(inf)*

jeer [dʒɪəˈ] N *(= remark)* höhnische Bemerkung; *(= shout, boo)* Buhruf *m*; **~s** Johlen *nt no pl*; *(= laughter)* Hohngelächter *nt* VI höhnische Bemerkungen machen, höhnen *(old, geh)*; *(= shout, boo)* johlen, buhen; *(= laugh)* höhnisch lachen; **to ~ at sb** jdn (laut) verhöhnen; **he's doing his best, don't ~** er versucht sein Bestes, also spotte nicht VT verhöhnen

jeering ['dʒɪərɪŋ] ADJ höhnisch; *(= shouting, booing)* johlend; *(= laughing)* höhnisch lachend N höhnische Bemerkungen *pl*; *(= shouting, booing)* Johlen *nt*, Gejohle *nt*; *(= laughing)* Hohngelächter *nt*

jeeringly ['dʒɪərɪŋlɪ] ADV *laugh, remark, smile* höhnisch

Jehovah [dʒɪ'həʊvə] N Jehova *m*, Jahwe *m*

Jehovah's Witness N Zeuge *m*/Zeugin *f* Jehovas

jejune [dʒɪ'dʒu:n] ADJ *(liter: = dull)* fade, langweilig; *(= naive, simple)* simpel

Jekyll and Hyde ['dʒekələnd'haɪd] N **a ~ (character)** eine Art Jekyll und Hyde

jell [dʒel] VI = **gel**

jellied eels [,dʒelɪd'i:lz] PL Aal *m* in Aspik, Sülzaale *pl*

Jell-O® ['dʒeləʊ] N *(US)* Wackelpeter *m (inf)*

jelly ['dʒelɪ] N **a** Gelee *nt*; *(esp Brit: = dessert)* Götterspeise *f*, Wackelpeter *m (inf)*; *(esp US: = jam)* Marmelade *f*; *(round meat etc)* Aspik *m or nt*, Gallert(e) *m(f)*; **it forms a kind of ~** es bildet eine gelee- *or* gallertartige Masse; **my legs were like ~** ich hatte Pudding in den Beinen *(inf)*; **I** *or* **my legs turned to ~** ich wurde ganz weich in den Knien **b** *(sl: = gelignite)* Dynamit *nt* VT in Aspik einlegen

jelly: **jelly baby** N *(Brit)* ≈ Gummibärchen *nt*; **jellybean** N Geleebonbon *m or nt*; **jellyfish** ['dʒelɪfɪʃ] N Qualle *f*; **jelly jar** N *(US)* = **jam jar**; **jelly roll** N *(US)* Biskuitrolle *f*

jelly shoe N Badeschuh *m or* -sandale *f*

jemmy ['dʒemɪ], *(US)* **jimmy** N Brecheisen *nt*, Stemmeisen *nt*

jenny ['dʒenɪ] N *(= donkey)* Eselin *f*; *(= mule)* weibliches Maultier; *(= spinning jenny)* (frühe) Feinspinnmaschine

jenny wren N Zaunkönigweibchen *nt*; *(in children's stories)* Frau Zaunkönig

jeopardize ['dʒepədaɪz] VT gefährden, in Gefahr bringen

jeopardy ['dʒepədɪ] N Gefahr *f*; **in ~** in Gefahr, gefährdet; **to put sb/sth in ~** jdn/etw gefährden *or* in Gefahr bringen; **to be in ~ of life and limb** in Lebensgefahr schweben *or* sein

jerbil N = **gerbil**

jeremiad [,dʒerɪ'maɪəd] N *(liter)* Jeremiade *f (liter)*, Klagelied *nt*

Jeremiah [,dʒerɪ'maɪə] N Jeremia(s) *m*

Jericho ['dʒerɪkəʊ] N Jericho *nt*

jerk [dʒɜ:k] N **a** Ruck *m*; *(= jump)* Satz *m*; *(= spasm, twitch)* Zuckung *f*, Zucken *nt no pl*; **to give sth a ~** einer Sache *(dat)* einen Ruck geben; *rope, fishing line* an etw *(dat)* ruckartig ziehen; **to give a ~** *(car)* rucken, einen Satz machen; *(= twitch) (person)* zusammenzucken; *(knee etc)* zucken; *(head)* zurückzucken; **the train stopped with a ~** der Zug hielt mit einem Ruck an; **to move in short ~s** sich ruckartig bewegen

b → **physical jerks**

c *(inf: = person)* Dumpfbacke *f (sl)*, Trottel *m (inf)*

VT rucken *or* ruckeln *(inf)* an *(+dat)*; **the impact ~ed his head forward/back** beim Aufprall wurde sein Kopf nach vorn/hinten geschleudert; **she ~ed her thumb toward(s) the car** sie streckte schnell ihren Daumen dem Auto entgegen; **he ~ed the fish out of the water** er zog den Fisch mit einem Ruck aus dem Wasser; **he ~ed his head back to avoid the punch** er riss den Kopf zurück, um dem Schlag auszuweichen; **he ~ed the book away/out of my hand** er riss das Buch weg/mir das Buch aus der Hand; **he ~ed himself free** er riss sich los; **to ~ out one's words** die Worte hervorstoßen

VI *(rope, fishing line)* rucken; *(= move jerkily)* ruckeln *(inf)*; *(body, muscle)* zucken, zusammenzucken; *(head)* zurückzucken; **he ~ed away from me** er sprang mit einem Satz von mir weg; **his head ~ed forward** sein Kopf wurde nach vorne geschleudert; **the car ~ed forward** der Wagen machte einen Satz *or* Ruck nach vorn; **the car ~ed to a stop** das Auto hielt ruckweise an; **to ~ open** aufspringen

▶ **jerk around** VT *sep (inf: = mess around)* an der Nase herumführen *(inf)*

▶ **jerk off** VI *(sl: = masturbate)* sich *(dat)* einen runterholen *(inf)*

jerkily ['dʒɜ:kɪlɪ] ADV ruckartig; *(over cobbles etc)* holpernd, rüttelnd; *speak* holprig

jerkin ['dʒɜ:kɪn] N Jacke *f*; *(Hist)* (Leder)wams *nt*

jerkwater ['dʒɜ:k,wɔ:tə'] ADJ *attr (US inf)* Provinz-; **a ~ town** ein Kaff *nt (inf)*, ein Provinznest *nt (inf)*

jerky ['dʒɜ:kɪ] ADJ *(+er)* **a** ruckartig; *way of speaking* abgehackt; **a ~ ride over cobbles/in an old bus** eine holprige Fahrt über Kopfsteinpflaster/in einem alten Bus **b** *(inf: = foolish)* bekloppt *(inf)*

jeroboam [,dʒerɪ'bəʊəm] N Doppelmagnum(flasche) *f*

Jerome [dʒə'rəʊm] N Hieronymus *m*

Jerry ['dʒerɪ] N *(esp Mil sl) (= German soldier)* deutscher Soldat, Deutsche(r) *m*; *(= the Germans)* die Deutschen *pl*

jerry ['dʒerɪ] N *(dated Brit inf: = chamber pot)* Pott *m (inf)*, Thron *m (inf)*

jerry: **jerry-builder** N schlampiger Bauunternehmer; **jerry-building** N schlampige Bauweise; **jerry-built** ADJ schlampig gebaut; **jerry can** N großer (Blech)kanister

Jersey ['dʒɜ:zɪ] N **a** Jersey *nt* **b** *(= cow)* Jersey(rind) *nt*

jersey ['dʒɜ:zɪ] N Pullover *m*; *(Cycling, Ftbl etc)* Trikot *nt*; *(cloth)* Jersey *m*; **~ wool** Wolljersey *m*

Jerusalem [dʒə'ru:sələm] N Jerusalem *nt*

Jerusalem artichoke N Jerusalem- *or* Erdartischocke *f*, Topinambur *m*

jessamine ['dʒesəmɪn] N Jasmin *m*

jest [dʒest] N *(no pl) (= fun)* Spaß *m*, *(Aus also)* Spass *m*; *(= joke also)* Scherz *m*, Witz *m*; **in ~** im Spaß VI scherzen, spaßen; **you ~, sir!** *(old)* Sie belieben zu scherzen, mein Herr! *(old)*; **to ~ with sb** mit jdm spaßen; **to ~ about sth** über etw *(acc)* Scherze *or* Witze machen

jester ['dʒestə'] N **a** *(Hist)* Narr *m*; **the King's ~** der Hofnarr **b** *(= joker)* Spaßvogel *m*, Witzbold *m (inf)*

jesting ['dʒestɪŋ] ADJ spaßend, scherzhaft N Spaßen *nt*, Scherzen *nt*

jestingly ['dʒestɪŋlɪ] ADV im Spaß, scherzhaft

Jesuit ['dʒezjʊɪt] N Jesuit *m*

Jesuitic(al) [,dʒezjʊ'ɪtɪk(əl)] ADJ jesuitisch

Jesus ['dʒi:zəs] N Jesus *m*; **~ Christ** Jesus Christus INTERJ *(sl)* Mensch *(inf)*; **~ Christ!** Herr Gott, (noch mal)! *(inf)*; *(surprised)* Menschenskind! *(inf)*

jet[1] [dʒet] N **a** *(of water, vapour)* Strahl *m*; **a thin ~ of water** ein dünner Wasserstrahl; **a ~ of gas** (aus einer Düse) austretendes Gas **b** *(= nozzle)* Düse *f* **c** *(= engine)* Düsentriebwerk *nt*; *(also* **jet plane***)* Düsenflugzeug *nt*, Jet *m* VI **a** *(water etc)* schießen **b** *(= go by jet)* mit einem Düsenflugzeug fliegen **c** *(US inf)* abdüsen *(inf)*; **I have to ~** ich muss jetzt weg *attr (Aviat)* Düsen-, Jet-; **~ pilot** Jetpilot(in) *m(f)*

▶ **jet off** VI düsen *(inf)* *(to* nach*)*, jetten *(inf)* *(to* nach*)*; **she's jetting off to Spain next week** nächste Woche düst *or* jettet sie nach Spanien *(inf)*

jet[2] N *(Miner)* Jet(t) *m or nt*, Gagat *m*

jet: **jet airliner** N Jet *m*, Düsenflugzeug *nt*; **jet-black** ADJ kohl(pech)rabenschwarz, pechschwarz; **jet boat** N Jetboot *nt*; **jet engine** N Düsentriebwerk *nt*; **jet-engined** ADJ mit Düsenantrieb; **jet fighter** N Düsenjäger *m*; **jet foil** N Tragflügelboot *nt*; **jet fuel** N Düsentreibstoff *m*; **jet lag** N Jetlag *nt*, Schwierigkeiten *pl* durch den Zeitunterschied; **he's suffering from ~** er hat Jetlag, er ist durch den Zeitunterschied völlig aus dem Rhythmus gekommen; **jetlagged** ADJ **to be ~** an Jetlag leiden; **jetliner** N Jet *m*; **jet plane** N Düsenflugzeug *nt*; **jet-powered**, **jet-propelled** ADJ mit Düsenantrieb; **jet propulsion** N Düsenantrieb *m*

jetsam ['dʒetsəm] N über Bord geworfenes Gut; *(on beach)* Strandgut *nt* → **flotsam**

jet: **jet set** N Jetset *m*; **jet-set** VI **he ~ted off to Rio** er ist im Jet nach Rio gedüst; **jet-setter** N Jetsetter(in) *m(f)*; **he has become a real ~** der ist voll in den Jetset eingestiegen *(inf)*; **jet-setting** ADJ **~ person** Jetsetter(in) *m(f)*; **~ lifestyle** Jetsetleben *nt*; **jet ski** N Wassermotorrad *nt*; **jet-ski** VI Wassermotorrad fahren; **jet stream** N **a** *(= air current)* Jetstream *m* **b** *(of jet engine)* Düsenstrahl *m*

jettison ['dʒetɪsn] VT **a** *(Naut, Aviat)* (als Ballast) abwerfen *or* über Bord werfen **b** *(fig) plan, view, policy* über Bord werfen; *person* abhängen, aufgeben; *unwanted articles* wegwerfen

jetty ['dʒetɪ] N *(= breakwater)* Mole *f*, Hafendamm *m*; *(= landing pier)* Landesteg *m*, Pier *m*, Landungsbrücke *f*

Jew [dʒu:] N **a** Jude *m*, Jüdin *f* **b** *(neg! inf)* Geizkragen *m*, Geizhals *m (inf)*

Jew-baiting ['dʒu:,beɪtɪŋ] N Judenverfolgung *f*, Judenhetze *f*

jewel ['dʒu:əl] N **a** *(= gem)* Edelstein *m*, Juwel *nt (geh)*; *(= piece of jewellery)* Schmuckstück *nt*; **a case full of ~s** ein Koffer voll Juwelen *or* wertvoller Schmuckstücke **b** *(of watch)* Stein *m* **c** *(fig: = person)* Juwel *nt*, Goldstück *nt (inf)*; **this new book is the ~ in her crown** dieses neue Buch ist ihr Meisterwerk

jewel box, **jewel case** N Schmuckkästchen *nt*, Schmuckkasten *m*

jewelled, *(US)* **jeweled** ['dʒu:əld] ADJ mit Juwelen *(geh)* *or* Edelsteinen besetzt; *watch* mit Steinen; *fingers* mit Juwelen geschmückt

jeweller, *(US)* **jeweler** ['dʒu:ələ'] N Juwelier(in) *m(f)*, Schmuckhändler(in) *m(f)*; *(making jewellery)* Goldschmied(in) *m(f)*; **at the ~'s (shop)** beim Juwelier, im Juwelierladen

jewellery, *(US)* **jewelry** ['dʒu:əlrɪ] N Schmuck *m no pl*; **a piece of ~** ein Schmuckstück *nt*

Jewess ['dʒu:ɪs] N Jüdin *f*

Jewish ['dʒu:ɪʃ] ADJ jüdisch

Jewry ['dʒʊərɪ] N die Juden *pl*, das jüdische Volk

jew's-harp [,dʒu:z'hɑ:p] N Maultrommel *f*, Brummeisen *nt*

Jezebel ['dʒezəbel] N *(Bibl)* Isebel *f*; *(fig)* verruchtes Weib

jib [dʒɪb] N **a** *(of crane)* Ausleger *m*, Dreharm *m* **b** *(Naut)* Klüver *m* **c** *(dated inf)* **I don't like the cut of his ~** seine Nase gefällt mir nicht VI *(horse)* scheuen, bocken *(at* vor *+dat)*; **to ~ at sth** *(person)* sich gegen etw sträuben

jib boom N *(Naut)* Klüverbaum *m*

jibe [dʒaɪb] N, VI = **gibe**

jiffy ['dʒɪfɪ], **jiff** [dʒɪf] N *(inf)* Minütchen *nt (inf)*; **I won't be a ~** ich komme sofort *or* gleich; *(= back soon)* ich bin sofort *or* gleich wieder da; **wait a ~!** Augenblick (mal)! *(inf)*; **in a ~** sofort, gleich

Jiffy bag® N *(Brit)* (gepolsterte) Versandtasche; *(smaller)* gefütterter Briefumschlag

jig [dʒɪg] N **a** *(= dance) lebhafter Volkstanz*; **she did a little ~** *(fig)* sie vollführte einen Freudentanz **b** *(Tech)* Spannvorrichtung *f* VI *(= dance)* tanzen; *(fig: also* **jig about***)* herumhüpfen; **to ~ up and down** Sprünge machen, herumspringen VT **to ~ a baby up and down on one's knee** ein Kind auf seinen Knien reiten lassen

jigger ['dʒɪgə'] N **a** *(= sieve)* Schüttelsieb *nt* **b** *(US: = measure) Messbecher für Alkohol: 1½ Unzen* **c** *(= sandflea)* Sandfloh *m*

▶ **jigger up** *(inf)* VT kaputt machen, versauen *(inf)*; *(= tamper with)* herumbasteln an *(+dat)* VI kaputtgehen; *(computer: = crash)* abstürzen

jiggered [ˈdʒɪgəd] ADJ *(inf)* **well, I'll be ~!** da bin ich aber platt *(inf)* or baff *(inf)*; **I'm ~ if I'll do it** den Teufel werde ich tun *(inf)*; **to be ~** *(= tired)* kaputt sein *(inf)*

jiggery-pokery [ˈdʒɪgərɪˈpəʊkərɪ] N *(inf)* Schmu *m (inf)*; **I think there's been some ~ going on here** ich glaube, hier geht es nicht ganz hasenrein zu *(inf)* or hier ist was faul *(inf)*

jiggle [ˈdʒɪgl] VT wackeln mit; *door handle* rütteln an *(+dat)* VI *(also* **jiggle about***)* herumzappeln

jigsaw [ˈdʒɪgsɔː] N **a** *(Tech)* Tischlerbandsäge *f* **b** *(also* **jigsaw puzzle***)* Puzzle(spiel) *nt*

jihad [dʒɪˈhæd] N *(Rel)* Dschihad *m*, Heiliger Krieg

jillion [ˈdʒɪljən] N *(inf)* Unmenge *f*, Unzahl *f*; **~s of …** jede Menge …

jilt [dʒɪlt] VT *lover* den Laufpass geben *(+dat)*; *girl* sitzen lassen; **~ed** verschmäht

Jim [dʒɪm] N *dim of* **James**

Jim Crow [dʒɪmˈkrəʊ] N *(very offensive) (= black person)* Nigger *(very offensive)*, Schwarze(r) *m*; *(= discrimination)* Rassendiskriminierung *f attr law, policy* (gegen Schwarze) diskriminierend; *saloon etc* für Schwarze

jim-dandy [ˈdʒɪmˈdændɪ] ADJ *(US inf)* prima *(inf)*, klasse *(inf)*

jiminy (cricket) [ˈdʒɪmɪnɪ(ˈkrɪkɪt)] INTERJ *(US)* Menschenskind *(inf)*

jimjams [ˈdʒɪmdʒæmz] PL *(Brit inf)* **a** *(inf: = pyjamas)* Pyjama *m* **b** *(sl: = nervousness)* **it gives me the ~** da kriege ich Muffensausen *(inf)* **c** *(sl, = the creeps)* **he gives me the ~** bei dem kriege ich das große Grausen *(inf)*

Jimmy [ˈdʒɪmɪ] N *dim of* **James**

jimmy [ˈdʒɪmɪ] N *(US)* = **jemmy**

jingle [ˈdʒɪŋgl] N **a** *(of keys, bracelets, coins etc)* Geklimper *nt*, Klimpern *nt*; *(of bells)* Bimmeln *nt* **b** *(= catchy verse)* Spruch *m*; *(for remembering)* Merkvers *m*; **(advertising) ~** Jingle *m* VI *(keys, bracelets, coins etc)* klimpern; *(bells)* bimmeln VT *keys, bracelets, coins* klimpern mit; *bells* bimmeln lassen

jingly [ˈdʒɪŋglɪ] ADJ klingelnd, bimmelnd

jingo [ˈdʒɪŋgəʊ] N *pl* **-es** **a** Hurrapatriot(in), Chauvinist(in) *m(f)* **b** *(dated inf)* **by ~!** Tod und Teufel! *(old)*, Teufel, Teufel! *(inf)*

jingoism [ˈdʒɪŋgəʊɪzəm] N Hurrapatriotismus *m*, Chauvinismus *m*

jingoistic [ˌdʒɪŋgəʊˈɪstɪk] ADJ hurrapatriotisch, chauvinistisch

jinks [dʒɪŋks] PL *(inf)* → **high jinks**

jinn [dʒɪn] N Dschinn *m*

jinx [dʒɪŋks] N **there must be** *or* **there's a ~ on it** das ist verhext; **there must be** *or* **there's a ~ on us** wir sind vom Unglück verfolgt; **to put a ~ on sth** etw verhexen

jinxed [dʒɪŋkst] ADJ verhext

jitney [ˈdʒɪtnɪ] N *(US inf)* Fünfcentmünze *f*; *(= bus)* billiger Bus

jitterbug [ˈdʒɪtəbʌg] N **a** *(= dance)* Jitterbug *m* **b** *(inf: = panicky person)* Nervenbündel *nt (inf)* VI Jitterbug tanzen

jitters [ˈdʒɪtəz] PL *(inf)* **the ~** das große Zittern *(inf)* or Bibbern *(inf)*; **his ~** sein Bammel *m (inf)*; **he had (a bad case of) the ~ about the exam** er hatte wegen der Prüfung das große Zittern *(inf)*; **to give sb the ~** jdn ganz rappelig machen *(inf)*

jittery [ˈdʒɪtərɪ] ADJ *(inf)* nervös, rappelig *(inf)*

jiujitsu [dʒuːˈdʒɪtsuː] N Jiu-Jitsu *nt*

jive [dʒaɪv] N **a** *(= dance)* Swing *m* **b** *(US inf: = nonsense)* **don't give me that ~** hör bloß mit dem Quatsch auf *(inf)* VI swingen, Swing tanzen

Joan [dʒəʊn] N Johanna *f*; **~ of Arc** Johanna von Orleans, Jeanne d'Arc

Job [dʒəʊb] N *(Bibl)* Hiob *m*, Job *m*; **the Book of ~** das Buch Hiob; **he has the patience of ~** er hat eine Engelsgeduld

job [dʒɒb] ✪ 19.1, 19.2 N **a** *(= piece of work)* Arbeit *f*; *(Comput)* Job *m*; **I have a ~ to do** ich habe zu tun; **I have several ~s to do** ich habe verschiedene Sachen zu erledigen; **a ~ of work** eine Arbeit, eine Aufgabe; **I have a little ~ for you** ich habe da eine kleine Arbeit *or* Aufgabe für Sie; **it's quite a ~ to paint the house** das ist vielleicht eine Arbeit *or* eine Heidenarbeit *(inf)*, das Haus zu streichen; **the car's in for a paint ~** *(inf)* der Wagen ist zum Lackieren in der Werkstatt; **the plumbers have a lot of ~s on just now** die Klempner haben zurzeit viele Aufträge; **to be paid by the ~** für (die) geleistete Arbeit bezahlt werden, pro Auftrag bezahlt werden; **he's on the ~** *(inf: = at work)* er ist bei *or* an der Arbeit; *(inf: = having sex)* er ist zu Gange *(inf)*; **to make a good/bad ~ of sth** bei etw gute/schlechte Arbeit leisten; **the decorators made a terrible ~ of the kitchen** die Maler haben in der Küche schrecklich gepfuscht; **we could do a far better ~ of running the company** wir könnten die Firma viel besser leiten; **he knows his ~** er versteht sein Handwerk → **odd f**

b *(= employment)* Stelle *f*, Job *m (inf)*; **to look for/get/have a ~** eine Stelle suchen/bekommen/haben; **to lose one's ~** seine Stelle verlieren; **the nice thing about a teaching ~ is …** das Schöne am Lehrberuf *or* an einer Anstellung als Lehrer ist …; **he had a holiday ~** er hatte eine Ferienarbeit *or* einen Ferienjob *(inf)*; **I've got a Saturday ~** ich habe einen Samstagsjob *(inf)*; **500 ~s lost** 500 Arbeitsplätze verloren gegangen; **to bring new ~s to a region** in einer Gegend neue Arbeitsplätze schaffen

c *(= duty)* Aufgabe *f*; **that's not my ~** dafür bin ich nicht zuständig; **it's not my ~ to tell him** es ist nicht meine Aufgabe, ihm das zu sagen; **I'll do my ~ and you do yours** ich mache meine Arbeit, und Sie Ihre; **I had the ~ of breaking the news to her** es fiel mir zu, ihr die Nachricht beizubringen; **he's not doing his ~** er erfüllt seine Aufgabe(n) nicht; **I'm only doing my ~** ich tue nur meine Pflicht; **I'm only doing my ~** ich tue nur meine Pflicht; **drinking a lot of water helps the kidneys do their ~** viel Wasser zu trinken hilft den Nieren bei ihrer Arbeit

d **that's a good ~!** so ein Glück; **what a good ~** *or* **it's a good ~ I brought my cheque book** nur gut, dass ich mein Scheckbuch mitgenommen habe; **to give sb/sth up as a bad ~** jdn/etw aufgeben; **to make the best of a bad ~** das Beste daraus machen; **that should do the ~** das müsste hinhauen *(inf)*; **this is just the ~** das ist goldrichtig *or* genau das Richtige; **a holiday in the sun would be just the ~** Ferien in der Sonne, das wäre jetzt genau das Richtige; **double whisky? – just the ~** einen doppelten Whisky? – prima Idee *(inf)*

e *(= difficulty)* **I had a ~ convincing him** *or* **to convince him** es war gar nicht so einfach, ihn zu überzeugen; **you'll have a ~** das wird gar nicht so einfach sein; **she has a ~ getting up the stairs** es ist gar nicht einfach für sie, die Treppe raufzukommen; **it was quite a ~** das war ganz schön schwer *(inf)* or schwierig

f *(inf: = crime)* Ding *nt (sl)*; **we're going to do a ~ next week** wir drehen nächste Woche ein Ding *(sl)*; **remember that bank ~?** erinnerst du dich an das große Ding in der Bank? *(sl)*

g *(inf: = person, thing)* Ding *nt*; **his new car's a lovely little ~** sein neues Auto ist wirklich große Klasse *(inf)* or eine Wucht *(inf)*; **that blonde's a gorgeous little ~** die Blondine (da) sieht wirklich klasse aus *(inf)*

h *(baby-talk)* **to do a (big/little) ~** ein (großes/kleines) Geschäft machen *(inf)*, Aa/Pipi machen *(baby-talk)*

i *(inf: = operation)* Korrektur *f*; **to have a nose/chin ~ (done)** eine Nasen-/Kinnkorrektur machen lassen

j **to do a ~ on sb** *(inf: = defeat)* jdn in die Pfanne hauen *(inf)*; *(= beat up)* jdn vermöbeln *(inf)*

VI **a** *(= do casual work)* Gelegenheitsarbeiten tun *or* verrichten, jobben *(inf)*; **a graphic designer who ~s for various advertising firms** ein Grafiker, der für verschiedene Werbeagenturen Aufträge *or* Arbeiten ausführt

b *(St Ex)* als Makler tätig sein, Maklergeschäfte betreiben

c *(= profit from public position)* sein Amt (zu privatem Nutzen) missbrauchen

VT *(also* **job out***)* *work* in Auftrag geben, auf Kontrakt *or* auf feste Rechnung vergeben

job advertisement N Stellenanzeige *f*

jobber [ˈdʒɒbəˈ] N **a** *(St Ex)* Makler(in) *m(f)*, Börsenhändler(in) *m(f)* **b** *(= casual worker)* Gelegenheitsarbeiter(in) *m(f)*

jobbery [ˈdʒɒbərɪ] N Schiebung *f*, Amtsmissbrauch *m*

jobbing [ˈdʒɒbɪŋ] ADJ Gelegenheits-; **~ worker/actor** Gelegenheitsarbeiter(in) *m(f)*/-schauspieler *m* N **a** *(= casual work)* Gelegenheitsarbeit *f* **b** *(St Ex)* Börsen- *or* Effektenhandel *m*

jobbing printer N Akzidenzdrucker *m*

job: Jobcentre N *(Brit)* Arbeitsamt *nt*; **job creation** N Arbeitsbeschaffung *f*; **~ scheme** Arbeitsbeschaffungsmaßnahme *f*; **job cuts** PL Arbeitsplatzabbau *m*; **job description** N Tätigkeitsbeschreibung *f*; **job evaluation** N Arbeitsplatzbewertung *f*; **job holder** N Arbeitnehmer(in) *m(f)*; **job hopper** N *(inf) jd, der häufig seine Arbeitsstelle wechselt*; **job-hunter** N Arbeitssuchende(r) *mf*; **job-hunting** N Arbeitssuche *f*, Stellenjagd *f (inf)*; **to be ~** auf Arbeitssuche *or* Stellenjagd *(inf)* sein; **job interview** N Vorstellungsgespräch *nt*, Bewerbungsgespräch *nt*

jobless ADJ arbeitslos, stellungslos N **the ~** *pl* die Arbeitslosen *pl*

jobless rate N Arbeitslosenquote *f*

job: job loss N **there were 1,000 ~es** 1 000 Arbeitsplätze gingen verloren; **job lot** N *(Comm)* (Waren)posten *m*; **job market** N Arbeitsmarkt *m*; **job opportunities** PL Stellenmarkt *m*, Stellenangebote *pl*; **job printer** N Akzidenzdrucker *m*; **job profile** N Stellenbeschreibung *f*, Anforderungsprofil *nt*; **job satisfaction** N Zufriedenheit *f* am Arbeitsplatz; **I've got ~** ich bin mit meiner Arbeit zufrieden

Job's comforter N *jd, der durch seinen Trost die Situation nur verschlimmert*; **you're a real ~** du bist vielleicht ein schöner *or* schwacher Trost

job: job security N Sicherheit *f* des Arbeitsplatzes; **we can offer no ~ guarantees** wir können die Sicherheit des Arbeitsplatzes/der Arbeitsplätze nicht garantieren; **jobseeker** N Arbeitssuchende(r) *mf*; **~'s allowance** *(Brit)* Arbeitslosengeld *nt*; **job sharer** N *jd, der seinen Arbeitsplatz mit anderen teilt*; **job sharing** N Arbeitsplatzteilung *f*, Jobsharing *nt attr scheme* zur Arbeitsplatzteilung

jobsworth [ˈdʒɒbzwɜːθ] N *(inf pej)* Paragrafenreiter(in) *m(f)*

jock [dʒɒk] N *(inf)* **a** *(= disc jockey)* Discjockey *m* **b** *(US pej: = athlete)* Sportfanatiker(in) *m(f)*; **he's a dumb ~** er ist sportlich, aber hirnlos *(inf)*

Jock [dʒɒk] N *(inf)* Schotte *m*, Schottin *f*

jockey [ˈdʒɒkɪ] N Jockey *m*, Jockei *m*, Rennreiter(in) *m(f)* VI **to ~ for position** *(lit)* sich in eine gute Position zu drängeln versuchen, sich gut platzieren wollen; *(fig)* rangeln; **they were all ~ing for office in the new government** sie rangelten alle um ein Amt in der neuen Regierung VT *(= force by crafty manoeuvres)* **to ~ sb into doing sth** jdn dazu bringen, etw zu tun; **he felt he had been ~ed into it** er hatte das Gefühl, dass man ihn da reinbugsiert hatte *(inf)*

jockey shorts PL Jockeyshorts *pl*

jockstrap [ˈdʒɒkstræp] N Suspensorium *nt*

jocose [dʒə'kəʊs] ADJ *(dated)* scherzend, launig *(geh)*

jocosely [dʒə'kəʊslɪ] ADV *(dated)* scherzhaft; *(= as a joke) say* im Scherz

jocular ['dʒɒkjʊlə'] ADJ lustig, spaßig, witzig; **to be in a ~ mood** zu Scherzen *or* Späßen aufgelegt sein

jocularity [ˌdʒɒkjʊ'lærɪtɪ] N Spaßigkeit *f*, Witzigkeit *f*, Scherzhaftigkeit *f*

jocularly ['dʒɒkjʊləlɪ] ADV scherzhaft; *(= as a joke)* im Scherz

jocund ['dʒɒkənd] ADJ heiter, fröhlich, frohsinnig *(geh)*

jodhpurs ['dʒɒdpəz] PL Reithose(n) *f(pl)*

Joe [dʒəʊ] N *dim of* **Joseph** Sepp *(S Ger)*, Jupp *(dial) m*

Joe Bloggs [ˌdʒəʊ'blɒgz], **Joe Public** N *(inf: = ordinary person)* Otto Normalverbraucher *m (inf)*

joey ['dʒəʊɪ] N *(Austral inf)* junges Känguru

jog [dʒɒg] VT stoßen an *(+acc) or* gegen; *person* anstoßen; **he ~ged the child up and down on his knee** er ließ das Kind auf seinen Knien reiten; **he was being ~ged up and down on the horse** das Pferd schüttelte ihn durch; **to ~ sb's memory** jds Gedächtnis *(dat)* nachhelfen *or* auf die Sprünge helfen; **to ~ sb's conscience** jdm Gewissensbisse bereiten
VI trotten, zuckeln *(inf)*; *(Sport)* Dauerlauf machen, joggen; **to ~ up and down** auf und ab hüpfen
N **a** *(= push, nudge)* Stoß *m*, Schubs *m*, Stups *m*; **to give sb's memory a ~** jds Gedächtnis *(dat)* nachhelfen
b *(= run)* trabender Lauf, Trott *m*; *(Sport)* Dauerlauf *m*; **he broke into a ~** er fing an zu traben; **she starts the day with a gentle ~ around the park** für sie fängt der Tag mit einem langsamen Lauf durch den Park an; **to go for a ~** *(Sport)* einen Dauerlauf machen, joggen (gehen); **to set off at a ~** lostraben

▶ **jog about** *(Brit) or* **around** VI hin und her gerüttelt werden VT *sep* durchschütteln, durchrütteln

▶ **jog along** VI **a** *(= go along: person, vehicle)* entlangzuckeln **b** *(fig) (person, worker, industry)* vor sich *(acc)* hin wursteln *(inf)*; *(work)* seinen Gang gehen

jogger ['dʒɒgə'] N **a** *(= person)* Jogger(in) *m(f)*; **~'s nipple** *besonders bei Joggern auftretende Entzündung der Brustwarzen* **b** *(= shoe)* Joggingschuh *m*, Freizeitstiefel *m*

jogging ['dʒɒgɪŋ] N Jogging *nt*, Joggen *nt*

jogging: **jogging pants** PL Jogginghose *f*; **jogging shoes** PL Joggingschuhe *pl*; **jogging suit** N Jogginganzug *m*

joggle ['dʒɒgl] VT schütteln, rütteln N Schütteln *nt*, Rütteln *nt*

jog trot N Trott *m*

John [dʒɒn] N Johannes *m*; **~ the Baptist** Johannes der Täufer

john [dʒɒn] N *(esp US inf) (= toilet)* Klo *nt (inf)*; *(= prostitute's customer)* Freier *m (inf)*

John: **John Barleycorn** [ˌdʒɒn'bɑːlɪkɔːn] N der Gerstensaft; **John Bull** N ein typischer Engländer, John Bull *m*; *(= the English)* die Engländer *pl*; **John Doe** N *(US) (= average man)* Otto Normalverbraucher *m (inf)*; *(Jur) Mann, dessen Name nicht bekannt ist*; **John Hancock** [ˌdʒɒn'hæŋkɒk], **John Henry** [ˌdʒɒn'henrɪ] N *(inf: = signature)* Friedrich Wilhelm *m (inf)*; **to put one's ~ on sth** seinen Friedrich Wilhelm auf etw setzen

Johnny ['dʒɒnɪ] N *dim of* **John** Hänschen *nt*, Hänsel *m (old)*

johnny ['dʒɒnɪ] N *(Brit inf) (= man)* Typ *m (inf)*; *(= condom)* Pariser *m (inf)*

Johnny-come-lately [ˌdʒɒnɪkʌm'leɪtlɪ] N *(inf) (= newcomer)* Neuankömmling *m*; *(= late starter)* Nachzügler(in) *m*

johnson ['dʒɒnsən] N *(US sl: = penis)* Schwanz *m (sl)*

joie de vivre [ˌʒwædə'viːvr] N Lebensfreude *f*, Lebenslust *f*

join [dʒɔɪn] ✪ 25.1 VT **a** *(lit, fig: = connect, unite)* verbinden *(to* mit); **to ~ two things together** zwei Dinge (miteinander) verbinden; *(= attach also)* zwei Dinge zusammenfügen *or* aneinanderfügen; **~ the dots (together)** verbinden Sie die Punkt; **to ~ battle (with the enemy)** den Kampf mit dem Feind aufnehmen; **to ~ hands** *(lit, fig)* sich *(dat) or* einander die Hände reichen; **~ed in marriage** durch das heilige Band der Ehe verbunden *or* vereinigt; **they are ~ed at the hip** *(fig inf)* sie sind völlig unzertrennlich, sie hängen wie Kletten aneinander *(inf)*
b *(= become member of) army* gehen zu; *one's regiment* sich anschließen *(+dat)*, sich begeben zu; *NATO, the EU* beitreten *(+dat)*; *political party, club* beitreten *(+dat)*, Mitglied werden von *or* bei *or* in *(+dat)*, eintreten in *(+acc)*; *religious order* eintreten in *(+acc)*, beitreten *(+dat)*; *university (as student)* anfangen an *(+dat)*; *(as staff) firm* anfangen bei; *group of people, procession* sich anschließen *(+dat)*; **to ~ the queue** sich in die Schlange stellen *or* einreihen; **he has been ordered to ~ his ship at Liverpool** er hat Order bekommen, sich in Liverpool auf seinem Schiff einzufinden *or* zu seinem Schiff zu begeben; **Dr Morris will be ~ing us for a year as guest professor** Dr. Morris wird ein Jahr bei uns Gastprofessor sein
c **he ~ed us in France** er stieß in Frankreich zu uns; **I ~ed him at the station** wir trafen uns am Bahnhof, ich traf mich mit ihm am Bahnhof; **I'll ~ you in five minutes** ich bin in fünf Minuten bei Ihnen; *(= follow you)* ich komme in fünf Minuten nach; **may I ~ you?** kann ich mich Ihnen anschließen?; *(= sit with you)* darf ich Ihnen Gesellschaft leisten?, darf ich mich zu Ihnen setzen?; *(in game, plan etc)* kann ich mitmachen?; **will you ~ us?** machen Sie mit?, sind Sie dabei?; *(= sit with us)* wollen Sie uns nicht Gesellschaft leisten?, wollen Sie sich (nicht) zu uns setzen?; *(= come with us)* kommen Sie mit?; **do ~ us for lunch** wollen Sie nicht mit uns essen?; **will you ~ me in a drink?** trinken Sie ein Glas mit mir?; **Paul ~s me in wishing you ...** Paul schließt sich meinen Wünschen für ... an; **they ~ed us in singing ...** sie sangen mit uns zusammen ...; **Moscow has ~ed Washington in condemning these actions** Moskau hat sich Washington angeschlossen und diese Handlungen verurteilt
d *(river) another river, the sea* einmünden *or* fließen in *(+acc)*; *(road) another road* (ein)münden in *(+acc)*; **his estates ~ ours** seine Ländereien grenzen an unsere (an)
VI **a** *(also* **join together**: *two parts) (= be attached)* (miteinander) verbunden sein; *(= be attachable)* sich (miteinander) verbinden lassen; *(= grow together)* zusammenwachsen; *(= meet, be adjacent)* zusammenstoßen, zusammentreffen; *(estates)* aneinander (an)grenzen; *(rivers)* zusammenfließen, sich vereinigen; *(roads)* sich treffen; **let us all ~ together in the Lord's Prayer** wir wollen alle zusammen das Vaterunser beten; **he ~s with me in wishing you ...** er schließt sich meinen Wünschen für ... an; **to ~ together in doing sth** etw zusammen *or* gemeinsam tun; **Moscow and Washington have ~ed in condemning these actions** Moskau und Washington haben diese Handlungen gemeinsam verurteilt; **they all ~ed together to get her a present** sie taten sich alle zusammen, um ihr ein Geschenk zu kaufen
b *(club member)* beitreten, Mitglied werden
N Naht(stelle) *f*; *(in pipe, knitting)* Verbindungsstelle *f*

▶ **join in** VI *(in activity)* mitmachen *(prep obj* bei); *(in game also)* mitspielen *(prep obj* bei); *(in demonstration also, in protest)* sich anschließen *(prep obj +dat)*; *(in conversation)* sich beteiligen *(prep obj* an *+dat)*; **join in, everybody!** *(in song etc)* alle (mitmachen)!; **everybody joined in the chorus** sie sangen alle zusammen den Refrain, alle fielen in den Refrain ein; **he didn't want to join in the fun** er wollte nicht mitmachen

▶ **join on** VI *(= be attachable)* sich verbinden lassen *(prep obj, -to* mit), sich anfügen lassen (*prep obj, -to* an *+acc)*; *(= be attached)* verbunden sein *(prep obj, -to* mit); *(people: in procession etc)* sich anschließen *(prep obj, -to +dat*, an *+acc)*
VT *sep* verbinden *(prep obj, -to* mit); *(= extend with)* ansetzen *(prep obj, -to* an *+acc)*

▶ **join up** VI **a** *(Brit Mil)* Soldat werden, zum Militär gehen **b** *(= meet: roads etc)* sich treffen, aufeinanderstoßen; *(= join forces)* sich zusammenschließen, sich zusammentun *(inf)* VT *sep* (miteinander) verbinden

joiner ['dʒɔɪnə'] N Tischler(in) *m(f)*, Schreiner(in) *m(f)*

joinery ['dʒɔɪnərɪ] N *(= trade)* Tischlerei *f*, Tischlerhandwerk *nt*; *(= piece of joinery)* Tischlerarbeit *f*

joining fee ['dʒɔɪnɪŋˌfiː] N Aufnahmegebühr *f*

joint [dʒɔɪnt] N **a** *(Anat, tool, in armour etc)* Gelenk *nt*; **ankle ~** Knöchel *m*; **knee ~** Kniegelenk *nt*; **~ pains** Gelenkschmerzen *pl*; **he's a bit stiff in the ~s** *(inf)* er ist ein bisschen steif (in den Knochen); **the times are out of ~** *(fig liter)* die Zeit *or* Welt ist aus den Fugen → **nose**
b *(= join) (in woodwork)* Fuge *f*; *(in pipe etc)* Verbindung(sstelle) *f*; *(welded etc)* Naht(stelle) *f*; *(= junction piece)* Verbindungsstück *nt*
c *(Brit Cook)* Braten *m*; **a ~ of beef** ein Rindsbraten *m*
d *(inf) (= place)* Laden *m (inf)*; *(for gambling)* Spielhölle *f*
e *(inf: of marijuana)* Joint *m (inf)*
VT **a** *(Cook)* (in Stücke) zerlegen *or* zerteilen
b *boards, pipes etc* verbinden
ADJ *attr* gemeinsam; *(in connection with possessions also)* gemeinschaftlich; *(= total, combined) influence, strength* vereint; **he finished ~ second** *or* **in ~ second place** *(Brit)* er belegte gemeinsam mit einem anderen den zweiten Platz; **~ action** gemeinsame Aktion, Gemeinschaftsaktion *f*; **~ committee** gemeinsamer *or* gemischter Ausschuss; **it was a ~ effort** das ist in Gemeinschaftsarbeit entstanden; **it took the ~ efforts of six strong men to move it** es waren die vereinten Anstrengungen *or* Kräfte von sechs starken Männern nötig, um es von der Stelle zu bewegen

joint account N gemeinsames Konto

joint agreement N *Lohnabkommen mehrerer Firmen mit einer Gewerkschaft*

joint capital N Gesellschaftskapital *nt*

JOINT CHIEFS OF STAFF

Joint Chiefs of Staff ist eine Behörde innerhalb des US-Verteidigungsministeriums, deren fünf Mitglieder die wichtigsten militärischen Berater des Präsidenten, des Nationalen Sicherheitsrates und des Verteidigungsministers sind. Diese 1942 eingerichtete Gruppe setzt sich aus einem Vorsitzenden, einem Vizepräsidenten, den Stabschefs der Armee, Luftwaffe und Marine und dem Kommandanten des Marine Corps zusammen. Der wohl bekannteste Vorsitzende aus letzter Zeit ist General Colin Powell, der erste Schwarze auf diesem Posten, der dieses Amt von 1989 bis 1993 innehatte.

joint: **joint custody** N *(Jur)* gemeinsames Sorgerecht *(getrennt lebender Eltern)*; **joint debt** N *(Jur)* gemeinsame Verbindlichkeit

jointed ['dʒɔɪntɪd] ADJ *(= articulated)* mit Gelenken versehen, gegliedert; **a ~ doll** eine Gliederpuppe; **a ~ fishing rod** eine zerlegbare Angel

joint estate N Gemeinschaftsbesitz *m*

joint family N Großfamilie *f*

join-the-dots puzzle [dʒɔɪnðə'dɒts 'pʌzl] N *(esp Brit) Spiel, bei dem man eine Figur zeichnet, indem man einzelne Punkte verbindet*

joint heir N Miterbe *m*, Miterbin *f*; **they were ~s** sie waren gemeinsame Erben

joint life insurance N wechselseitige (Über)lebensversicherung

jointly [ˈdʒɔɪntlɪ] ADV **a** gemeinsam; *decide, work, rule also* zusammen, miteinander; **to be ~ owned by …** im gemeinsamen Besitz von … sein **b** *(Jur)* **to be ~ and severally liable** gesamtschuldnerisch *or* als Gesamtschuldner haften

joint: **joint owner** N Mitbesitzer(in) *m(f)*; **joint ownership** N Miteigentum *nt*, Mitbesitz *m*; **joint partner** N Teilhaber(in) *m(f)*; **joint plaintiff** N Nebenkläger(in) *m(f)*; **~s** gemeinsame Kläger *pl*; **joint production** N *(TV, Film)* Koproduktion *f*; **joint resolution** N *(US Pol)* gemeinsamer Beschluss (beider gesetzgebender Versammlungen); **joint stock** N Aktienkapital *nt*; **joint stock bank** N ≈ Aktienbank *f*; **joint stock company** N ≈ Kapitalgesellschaft *f*

jointure [ˈdʒɔɪntʃəˈ] N *(Jur)* Wittum *nt*

joint venture N Gemeinschaftsunternehmen *nt*, Joint Venture *nt (Comm)*

joist [dʒɔɪst] N Balken *m*; *(of metal, concrete)* Träger *m*

joke [dʒəʊk] **N** Witz *m*; *(= hoax)* Scherz *m*; *(= prank)* Streich *m*; *(inf) (= pathetic person or thing)* Witz *m*; *(= laughing stock)* Gespött *nt*, Gelächter *nt*; **for a ~** zum Spaß, zum *or* aus Jux *(inf)*; **I don't see the ~** ich möchte wissen, was daran so lustig ist *or* sein soll; **he treats the school rules as a big ~** für ihn sind die Schulregeln ein Witz; **he can/can't take a ~** er versteht Spaß/keinen Spaß; **what a ~!** zum Totlachen! *(inf)*, zum Schießen! *(inf)*; **it's no ~** das ist nicht witzig; **the ~ is that …** das Witzige *or* Lustige daran ist, dass …; **it's beyond a ~** *(Brit)* das ist kein Spaß *or* Witz mehr, das ist nicht mehr lustig; **this is getting beyond a ~** *(Brit)* das geht (langsam) zu weit; **the ~ was on me** der Spaß ging auf meine Kosten; **why do you have to turn everything into a ~?** warum müssen Sie über alles Ihre Witze machen?, warum müssen Sie alles ins Lächerliche ziehen?; **I'm not in the mood for ~s** ich bin nicht zu(m) Scherzen aufgelegt; **to play a ~ on sb** jdm einen Streich spielen; **to make a ~ of sth** Witze über etw *(acc)* machen; **to make ~s about sb/sth** sich über jdn/etw lustig machen, über jdn/etw Witze machen *or* reißen *(inf)*
VI Witze machen, scherzen *(geh)* *(about* über *+acc)*; *(= pull sb's leg)* Spaß machen; **I'm not joking** ich meine das ernst; **you must be joking!** das ist ja wohl nicht Ihr Ernst, das soll wohl ein Witz sein; **you're joking!** mach keine Sachen *(inf) or* Witze!; **…, he ~d …**, sagte er scherzhaft

joker [ˈdʒəʊkəˈ] N **a** *(= person)* Witzbold *m*, Spaßvogel *m* **b** *(inf)* Typ *m (inf)*, Kerl *m (inf)* **c** *(Cards)* Joker *m*; **he's/it's the ~ in the pack** *(esp Brit)* er/es ist ein Unsicherheitsfaktor, er/es ist eine unbekannte Größe

jokey ADJ = **joky**

jokily [ˈdʒəʊkɪlɪ] ADV lustig; *say* scherzhaft, im Scherz; *do* im Scherz

joking [ˈdʒəʊkɪŋ] **ADJ** *tone* scherzhaft, spaßend; **in a ~ manner** spaßend; **it's no ~ matter** darüber macht man keine Witze **N** Witze *pl*; **I'm in no mood for ~** ich bin nicht zu Scherzen *or* Späßen aufgelegt; **~ apart** *or* **aside** Spaß *or* Scherz beiseite

jokingly [ˈdʒəʊkɪŋlɪ] ADV im Spaß; *say, call also* scherzhaft

joky [ˈdʒəʊkɪ] ADJ lustig

jollification [ˌdʒɒlɪfɪˈkeɪʃən] N *(hum)* Festivität *f (hum)*; *(= merrymaking: also* **jollifications***)* Festlichkeiten *pl*

jollity [ˈdʒɒlɪtɪ] N Fröhlichkeit *f*, Ausgelassenheit *f*

jolly [ˈdʒɒlɪ] **ADJ** *(+er)* **a** *(esp Brit: = merry)* fröhlich, vergnügt; **everyone had a very ~ time** alle haben sich köstlich amüsiert
b *(inf: = tipsy)* angeheitert *(inf)*
ADV *(dated Brit inf)* ganz schön *(inf)*, vielleicht *(inf)*; *nice, warm, happy, pleased* mächtig *(inf)*; **you are ~ lucky** Sie haben vielleicht Glück *or* ein Mordsglück; **~ good** prima *(inf)*, famos *(dated inf)*; **a ~ good idea** eine tolle Idee; **that's ~ kind of you** das ist furchtbar *or* unheimlich nett von Ihnen; **it's getting ~ late** es wird langsam spät; **he took the news ~ well** er hat die Nachricht wirklich gut verkraftet; **you ~ well will go!** und ob du gehst!; **so you ~ well should be!** das will ich schwer meinen! *(inf)*; **I should ~ well hope/think so!** das will ich auch hoffen/gemeint haben!
VT *(Brit)* **to ~ sb into doing sth** jdn bereden, etw zu tun; **to ~ sb along** jdm aufmunternd zureden; **to ~ sb up** jdn aufmuntern
N **a** *(Brit inf) (= party)* Fete *f (inf)*; *(= trip)* Vergnügungsreise *f*
b *(inf)* **to get one's jollies (from sth)** (von etw) einen Kick bekommen *(sl)*

jolly: **jolly boat** N Beiboot *nt*; **Jolly Roger** N Totenkopfflagge *f*, Piratenflagge *f*

jolt [dʒəʊlt] **VI** *(vehicle)* holpern, rüttelnd fahren; *(= give one jolt)* einen Ruck machen; **to ~ along** rüttelnd entlangfahren; **to ~ to a halt** ruckweise anhalten
VT *(lit) (= shake)* durchschütteln, durchrütteln; *(once)* einen Ruck geben *or* versetzen *(+dat)*; *(fig)* aufrütteln; **she was ~ed awake** sie wurde wachgerüttelt; **she was ~ed back to reality** sie wurde mit einem Ruck wieder in die Wirklichkeit zurückgeholt; **to ~ sb out of his complacency** jdn aus seiner Zufriedenheit aufrütteln *or* reißen; **to ~ sb into doing sth** jdn so aufrütteln, dass er/sie etw tut; **it ~ed him into action** das hat ihn aufgerüttelt
N **a** *(= jerk)* Ruck *m*
b *(fig inf)* Schock *m*; **he realized with a ~ …** mit einem Schlag wurde ihm klar, …; **it gave me a ~** das hat mir einen Schock versetzt

jolting [ˈdʒəʊltɪŋ] N Rütteln *nt*, Schütteln *nt*, Holpern *nt*

jolty [ˈdʒəʊltɪ] ADJ *(+er) cart etc* holp(e)rig, rüttelnd; *road* holp(e)rig, uneben

Jonah [ˈdʒəʊnə] N Jona(s) *m*

jonquil [ˈdʒɒŋkwɪl] N Jonquille *f (Art von Narzisse)*

Jordan [ˈdʒɔːdn] N *(= country)* Jordanien *nt*; *(= river)* Jordan *m*

Joseph [ˈdʒəʊzɪf] N Joseph *m*, Josef *m*

Josephine [ˈdʒəʊzɪfiːn] N Josephine *f*

josh [dʒɒʃ] *(esp US inf)* **VT** aufziehen, veräppeln, verulken *(all inf)* **VI** Spaß machen *(inf)* **N** Neckerei *f*, Hänselei *f*

Joshua [ˈdʒɒʃjʊə] N Josua *m*

joss stick [ˈdʒɒsstɪk] N Räucherstäbchen *nt*

jostle [ˈdʒɒsl] **VI** drängeln; **he ~d against me** er rempelte mich an; **the people jostling round the stalls** die Leute, die sich vor den Buden drängelten; **they are jostling for the top job** sie streiten sich *or* rangeln um den Spitzenjob → **position N a** **VT** anrempeln, schubsen; **they ~d him out of the room** sie drängten *or* schubsten ihn aus dem Zimmer; **he was ~d along with the crowd** die Menge schob ihn mit sich; **to ~ one's way through** sich durchschubsen **N** Gedränge *nt*, Rempelei *f*

jot [dʒɒt] N *(inf, of truth, sense)* Funken *m*, Fünkchen *nt*, Körnchen *nt*; **it won't do a ~ of good** das nützt gar nichts *or* kein bisschen; **this won't affect my decision one ~** das wird meine Entscheidung nicht im Geringsten beeinflussen; **not one ~ or tittle** *(inf)* aber auch nicht das kleinste bisschen *(inf)*, keinen Deut

► **jot down** VT *sep* sich *(dat)* notieren, sich *(dat)* eine Notiz machen von; **to jot down notes** Notizen machen

jotter [ˈdʒɒtəˈ] N *(Brit: = note pad)* Notizblock *m*; *(= notebook)* Notizheft(chen) *nt*

jottings [ˈdʒɒtɪŋz] PL Notizen *pl*

joule [dʒuːl] N *(Phys)* Joule *nt*

journal [ˈdʒɜːnl] N **a** *(= magazine)* Zeitschrift *f*; *(= newspaper)* Zeitung *f* **b** *(= diary)* Tagebuch *nt*; **to keep a ~** Tagebuch führen **c** *(Naut)* Logbuch *nt*, Bordbuch *nt*; *(Comm)* Journal *nt*; *(= daybook)* Tagebuch *nt*; *(Jur)* Gerichtsakten *pl* **d** *(of fax machine)* Sendebericht *m*; *(Mech)* Achszapfen *m*, Achsschenkel *m*

journalese [ˌdʒɜːnəˈliːz] N Zeitungs- *or* Pressejargon *m*

journalism [ˈdʒɜːnəlɪzəm] N Journalismus *m*

journalist [ˈdʒɜːnəlɪst] N Journalist(in) *m(f)*

journalistic [ˌdʒɜːnəˈlɪstɪk] ADJ journalistisch

journalistically [ˌdʒɜːnəˈlɪstɪkəlɪ] ADV im Zeitungsstil

journey [ˈdʒɜːnɪ] **N** Reise *f*; *(by car, train etc also)* Fahrt *f*; **to go on a ~** eine Reise machen, verreisen; **they have gone on a ~** sie sind verreist; **to set out on one's ~** abreisen; **to set out on a ~** eine Reise antreten; **it's a ~ of 50 miles** *or* **a 50-mile ~** es liegt 50 Meilen entfernt; **from X to Y is a ~ of 50 miles/two hours** es sind 50 Meilen/zwei Stunden (Fahrt) von X nach Y; **a two-day ~** eine Zweitagereise; **it's a two-day ~ to get to … from here** man braucht zwei Tage, um von hier nach … zu kommen; **a bus/train ~** eine Bus-/Zugfahrt; **the ~ home** die Heimreise, die Heimfahrt; **he has quite a ~ to get to work** er muss ziemlich weit fahren, um zur Arbeit zu kommen; **to reach one's ~'s end** *(liter)* am Ziel der Reise angelangt sein; **his ~ through life** sein Lebensweg *m*; **a ~ of discovery** eine Entdeckungsreise
VI reisen; **to ~ on** weiterreisen

journeyman [ˈdʒɜːnɪmən] N *pl* **-men** [-mən] Geselle *m*; **~ baker** Bäckergeselle *m*; **~ actor/artist** *etc (of average talent)* durchschnittlicher Schauspieler/Künstler *etc*

joust [dʒaʊst] **VI** im Turnier kämpfen, turnieren *(obs)*; *(fig)* sich rangeln **N** Zweikampf *m* im Turnier

jousting [ˈdʒaʊstɪŋ] N Turnier(kämpfe *pl*) *nt*; *(fig)* Rangeleien *pl*

Jove [dʒəʊv] N Jupiter *m*; **by ~!** *(dated)* Donnerwetter!; **have you/did he** *etc*, **by ~!** tatsächlich!

jovial [ˈdʒəʊvɪəl] ADJ fröhlich, jovial *(esp pej)*; *welcome* freundlich, herzlich; **in (a) ~ mood** gut gelaunt

joviality [ˌdʒəʊvɪˈælɪtɪ] N Fröhlichkeit *f*, Jovialität *f (esp pej)*; *(of welcome)* Herzlichkeit *f*

jovially [ˈdʒəʊvɪəlɪ] ADV fröhlich, jovial; *welcome* freundlich, herzlich

jowl [dʒaʊl] N *(= jaw)* (Unter)kiefer *m*; *(often pl) (= cheek)* Backe *f*; *(= fold of flesh)* Hängebacke *f* → **cheek**

jowly [ˈdʒaʊlɪ] ADJ **to be ~** Hängebacken haben

joy [dʒɔɪ] **N** **a** Freude *f*; **to my great ~** zu meiner großen Freude; **to be full of the ~s of spring** froh und munter sein; **she/the garden is a ~ to behold** sie/der Garten ist eine Augenweide; **it's a ~ to hear him** es ist eine wahre Freude *or* ein Genuss, ihn zu hören; **this car is a ~ to drive** es ist eine Freude, dieses Auto zu fahren; **to wish sb ~** jdm Glück (und Zufriedenheit) wünschen; **I wish you ~ (of it)!** *(iro)* na dann viel Spaß *or* viel Vergnügen!; **one of the ~s of this job is …** eine der erfreulichen Seiten dieses Berufs ist …; **that's the ~ of this system** das ist das Schöne an diesem System → **jump**
b *no pl (Brit inf: = success)* Erfolg *m*; **I didn't get much/any ~** ich hatte nicht viel/keinen Erfolg; **any ~?** hat es geklappt? *(inf)*; **you won't get any ~ out of him** bei ihm werden Sie keinen Erfolg haben

joyful [ˈdʒɔɪfʊl] ADJ freudig, froh

joyfully [ˈdʒɔɪfəlɪ] ADV freudig

joyfulness [ˈdʒɔɪfʊlnɪs] N Fröhlichkeit *f*; *(of person also)* Frohsinn *m*, Heiterkeit *f*

joyless [ˈdʒɔɪlɪs] ADJ freudlos; *person also* griesgrämig

joyous [ˈdʒɔɪəs] ADJ *(liter)* freudig, froh

joyously [ˈdʒɔɪəslɪ] ADV *(liter)* freudig

joy: **joyride** N Spritztour *f (in einem gestohlenen Auto)*; **to take a car for a ~** (ein Auto stehlen und damit) eine Spritztour machen; **joyrider** N *Autodieb, der den Wagen nur für eine Spritztour will*, Joyrider(in) *m(f)*; **joyriding** N Joyriding *nt*; **joystick** N *(Aviat)* Steuerknüppel *m*; *(Comput)* Joystick *m*

JP *(Brit) abbr of* **Justice of the Peace**

jpeg N *(Comput)* JPEG *nt*; ~ **file/format** JPEG-Datei *f*/-Format *nt*

Jr *abbr of* **junior** jr., jun.

JSA *(Brit Admin) abbr of* **job seeker's allowance** ≈ Arbeitslosengeld *nt*

jubilant [ˈdʒuːbɪlənt] ADJ überglücklich; *(= expressing joy)* jubelnd *attr*; *voice* jubelnd *attr*, frohlockend *attr*; *face* strahlend *attr*; *(at sb's failure etc)* triumphierend *attr*; **they gave him a ~ welcome** sie empfingen ihn mit Jubel; **to be ~** überglücklich sein, jubeln, strahlen, triumphieren

jubilation [ˌdʒuːbɪˈleɪʃən] N Jubel *m*; **a cause for ~** ein Grund zum Jubel; **a mood of ~** eine triumphale Stimmung

jubilee [ˈdʒuːbɪliː] N Jubiläum *nt*

Judaea [dʒuːˈdiːə] N Judäa *nt*

Judaeo-Christian, *(US)* **Judeo-Christian** [dʒuːˌdeɪəʊˈkrɪstɪən] ADJ jüdisch-christlich

Judah [ˈdʒuːdə] N Juda *m*

Judaic [dʒuːˈdeɪɪk] ADJ judaisch

Judaism [ˈdʒuːdeɪɪzəm] N Judaismus *m*

Judas [ˈdʒuːdəs] N *(Bibl, fig)* Judas *m*

judas (hole) N Guckloch *nt*

judder [ˈdʒʌdəˈ] *(Brit)* **N** Erschütterung *f*; *(in car etc)* Ruckeln *nt*; **to give a ~** *(car etc)* ruckeln **VI** erzittern; *(car etc)* ruckeln; **the train ~ed to a halt** der Zug kam ruckartig zum Stehen

Judea N = **Judaea**

judge [dʒʌdʒ] ✪ 6.3 **N** **a** *(Jur)* Richter(in) *m(f)*; *(of competition)* Preisrichter(in) *m(f)*; *(Sport)* Punktrichter(in) *m(f)*, Kampfrichter(in) *m(f)*
b *(fig)* Kenner(in) *m(f)*; **he's a good/bad ~ of character** er ist ein guter/schlechter Menschenkenner; **to be a good ~ of wine** ein(e) Weinkenner(in) sein; **I'll be the ~ of that** das müssen Sie mich schon selbst beurteilen lassen
c *(Bibl)* **(the Book of) Judges** (das Buch der) Richter
VT **a** *(Jur) person* die Verhandlung führen über *(+acc)*; *case* verhandeln; *(God)* richten
b *competition* beurteilen, bewerten; *(Sport)* Punktrichter *or* Kampfrichter sein bei
c *(fig: = pass judgement on)* ein Urteil fällen über *(+acc)*; **you shouldn't ~ people by appearances** Sie sollten Menschen nicht nach ihrem Äußeren beurteilen; **don't ~ a book by its cover** *(prov)* man sollte nicht nach dem ersten Eindruck urteilen
d *(= consider, assess, deem)* halten für, erachten für *(geh)*; **this was ~d to be the best way** dies wurde für die beste Methode gehalten *or* erachtet *(geh)*; **you can ~ for yourself which is better** Sie können selbst beurteilen, was besser ist; **you can ~ for yourself how upset I was** Sie können sich *(dat)* denken, wie bestürzt ich war; **I can't ~ whether he was right or wrong** ich kann nicht beurteilen, ob er recht oder unrecht hatte; **I ~d from his manner that he was guilty** ich schloss aus seinem Verhalten, dass er schuldig war; **how would you ~ him?** wie würden Sie ihn beurteilen *or* einschätzen?
e *(= estimate) speed, width, distance etc* einschätzen; **he ~d the moment well** er hat den richtigen Augenblick abgepasst
VI **a** *(Jur)* Richter sein; *(God)* richten; *(at competition)* Preisrichter sein; *(Sport)* Kampfrichter *or* Punktrichter sein
b *(fig) (= pass judgement)* ein Urteil fällen; *(= form an opinion)* (be)urteilen; **who am I to ~?** ich kann mir dazu kein Urteil erlauben; **as** *or* **so far as one can ~** soweit man (es) beurteilen kann; **judging by** *or* **from sth** nach etw zu urteilen; **judging by appearances** dem Aussehen nach; **to ~ by appearances** nach dem Äußeren urteilen; **(you can) ~ for yourself** beurteilen Sie das selbst; **he let me ~ for myself** er überließ es meinem Urteil

judge advocate N *(Mil)* Beisitzer(in) *m(f)* bei einem Kriegsgericht, Kriegsgerichtsrat *m*, Kriegsgerichtsrätin *f*

judg(e)ment [ˈdʒʌdʒmənt] N **a** *(Jur)* (Gerichts)urteil *nt*; *(Eccl)* Gericht *nt*, Richterspruch *m*; *(= divine punishment)* Strafe *f* Gottes; **to await ~** *(Jur)* auf sein *or* das Urteil warten; *(Eccl)* auf das Gericht *or* den Richterspruch (Gottes) warten; **the Day of Judg(e)ment** der Tag des Jüngsten Gerichtes; **to pass** *or* **give ~** *(also fig)* ein Urteil fällen, das Urteil sprechen *(on* über *+acc)*; **to sit in ~ on a case** Richter in einem Fall sein; **to sit in ~ on sb** über jdn zu Gericht sitzen; *(Jur also)* die Verhandlung über jdn führen; **I don't want to sit in ~ on you** ich möchte mich nicht zu Ihrem Richter aufspielen; **it's a ~ from above** das ist die Strafe Gottes; **it's a ~ on him for being so lazy** das ist die Strafe Gottes dafür, dass er so faul ist
b *(= opinion)* Meinung *f*, Ansicht *f*, Urteil *nt*; *(= moral judg(e)ment, value judg(e)ment)* Werturteil *nt*; *(= estimation: of distance, speed etc)* Einschätzung *f*; **to give one's ~ on sth** sein Urteil über etw *(acc)* abgeben, seine Meinung zu etw äußern; **an error of ~** eine falsche Einschätzung, eine Fehleinschätzung; **in my ~** meines Erachtens, meiner Meinung nach; **against one's better ~** gegen (sein) besseres Wissen, wider besseres Wissen
c *(= discernment)* Urteilsvermögen *nt*; **to show ~** ein gutes Urteilsvermögen beweisen *or* zeigen; **it's all a question of ~** das ist Ansichtssache

judg(e)mental [dʒʌdʒˈmentl] ADJ wertend; **don't be so ~** nimm nicht immer gleich Wertungen vor, bewerte nicht immer gleich alles

judg(e)ment: **judg(e)ment call** N *(esp US)* Gewissensentscheidung *f*; **to make a ~** eine Gewissensentscheidung treffen; **Judg(e)ment Day** N Tag *m* des Jüngsten Gerichts; **judg(e)ment seat** N Gottes Richterstuhl *m*

judicable [ˈdʒuːdɪkəbl] ADJ justiziabel; *case* verhandlungsfähig; *person* rechtsfähig

judicature [ˈdʒuːdɪkətʃəˈ] N *(= judges)* Richterstand *m*; *(= judicial system)* Gerichtswesen *nt*, Gerichtsbarkeit *f*

judicial [dʒuːˈdɪʃəl] ADJ **a** *(Jur) inquiry, review* gerichtlich; *power* richterlich; **~ function** Richteramt *nt*; **to take ~ proceedings against sb** ein Gerichtsverfahren *nt* gegen jdn anstrengen *or* einleiten; **~ system** Justizsystem *nt* **b** *(= critical) mind* klar urteilend *attr*, kritisch

judicially [dʒuːˈdɪʃəlɪ] ADV *defeat, approve* gerichtlich; **to apportion blame ~** eine gerichtliche Schuldzuweisung erteilen; **the country is ~ corrupt** das Justizsystem des Landes ist korrupt

judicial murder N Justizmord *m*

judicial separation N Gerichtsbeschluss *m* zur Aufhebung der ehelichen Gemeinschaft

judiciary [dʒuːˈdɪʃɪərɪ] N *(= branch of administration)* Gerichtsbehörden *pl*; *(= legal system)* Gerichtswesen *nt*; *(= judges)* Richterstand *m*

judicious ADJ, **judiciously** ADV [dʒuːˈdɪʃəs, -lɪ] klug, umsichtig

judo [ˈdʒuːdəʊ] N Judo *nt*

Judy [ˈdʒuːdɪ] N *abbr of* **Judith** *(in Punch and Judy)* Gretel *f*

jug[1] [dʒʌg] **N** **a** *(for milk, coffee etc) (with lid)* Kanne *f*; *(without lid)* Krug *m*; *(small)* Kännchen *nt* **b** *(Brit inf: = prison)* Kittchen *nt (inf)*, Knast *m (inf)*; **in ~** hinter schwedischen Gardinen *(inf)*, im Kittchen *(inf) or* Knast *(inf)* **c** **jugs** *(Brit sl: = breasts)* Titten *pl (sl)* **VT** *(Cook)* schmoren

jug[2] N *(of nightingale)* Flöten *nt*

jugged hare [ˈdʒʌgdˈhɛəˈ] N *(Brit Cook)* ≈ Hasenpfeffer *m*

juggernaut [ˈdʒʌgənɔːt] N **a** *(Brit: = lorry)* Schwerlaster *m* **b** *(Rel)* **Juggernaut** Dschagannath *m*, Jagannath *m* **c** *(fig: = destructive force)* verheerende Gewalt; **a media ~** ein Medienkonglomerat *nt*; **the military ~** der Militärapparat; **the ~ of British government** die unaufhaltsame britische Regierungsmaschinerie; **Puritanism, like some huge ~, swept across the country** der Puritanismus rollte mit unaufhaltsamer Gewalt über das Land

juggins [ˈdʒʌgɪnz] N *(Brit inf)* Depp *m (S Ger)*, Trottel *m (inf)*

juggle [ˈdʒʌgl] **VI** jonglieren; **to ~ with the figures** die Zahlen so hindrehen, dass sie passen **VT** *balls* jonglieren (mit); *figures* so hindrehen, dass sie passen; *debts* umverteilen; **many women have to ~ (the demands of) family and career** viele Frauen müssen (die Anforderungen von) Familie und Beruf miteinander vereinbaren; **they ~d the schedules to show the final** die Programmfolge wurde so umgeändert, dass das Endspiel gezeigt werden konnte

juggler [ˈdʒʌgləˈ] N **a** *(lit)* Jongleur(in) *m(f)* **b** *(fig: = trickster)* Schwindler(in) *m(f)*; **~ with words** Wortverdreher(in) *m(f)*

jugglery [ˈdʒʌglərɪ] N = **juggling**

juggling [ˈdʒʌglɪŋ] N **a** *(lit)* Jonglieren *nt* **b** *(fig)* Verdrehen *nt (with* von); **~ with words/figures** Wort-/Zahlenakrobatik *f*; **there has been a bit of ~ here** das ist doch so hingedreht worden, dass es passt, das ist doch nicht ganz hasenrein *(inf)*

juggling act N *(fig)* Balanceakt *m*

jughead [ˈdʒʌghed] N *(US pej sl)* Knallkopf *m (inf)*

Jugoslav [ˈjuːgəʊˌslɑːv] **ADJ** jugoslawisch **N** Jugoslawe *m*, Jugoslawin *f*

Jugoslavia [juːgəʊˈslɑːvɪə] N Jugoslawien *nt*

jugular [ˈdʒʌgjʊləˈ] N **~ (vein)** Drosselvene *f*, Jugularvene *f*; **to go for the ~** *(fig)* zum entscheidenden Schlag ausholen *(fig)*

juice [dʒuːs] N **a** *(of fruit, meat)* Saft *m* **b** *usu pl (of body)* Körpersäfte *pl* **c** *(inf: = electricity, petrol)* Saft *m (inf)*

juice-harp [ˌdʒuːsˈhɑːp] N *(politically correct form)* Maultrommel *f*, Brummeisen *nt*

juice up VT SEP *(US inf)* **a** *car* frisieren *(inf)* **b** *(= spice up) party* aufpeppen *(inf)*; *image, brand* aufmöbeln *(inf)*

juicer [ˈdʒuːsəˈ] N Entsafter *m*

juiciness [ˈdʒuːsɪnɪs] N *(lit)* Saftigkeit *f*; *(fig)* Pikanterie *f*, Schlüpfrigkeit *f*, gewisser Reiz; *(of scandal)* Saftigkeit *f (inf)*

juicy [ˈdʒuːsɪ] ADJ *(+er) fruit* saftig; *(inf) profit* saftig *(inf)*; *squelch* schmatzend, quatschend; *story* pikant, schlüpfrig; *scandal* gepfeffert *(inf)*, saftig *(inf)*; **a big ~ kiss** ein dicker Schmatz *(inf)*; **I've got some really ~ gossip** *(inf)* ich hab die absolute Hammer-Neuigkeit *(inf)*

jujitsu [ˌdʒuːˈdʒɪtsuː] N Jiu-Jitsu *nt*

jujube [ˈdʒuːdʒuːb] N *(Bot)* Jujube *f*; *(= berry also)* Brustbeere *f*

jukebox [ˈdʒuːkbɒks] N Jukebox *f*, Musikbox *f*, Musikautomat *m*; **my favourite song is playing on the ~** die Jukebox spielt mein Lieblingslied

juke joint [ˈdʒuːkdʒɔɪnt] N *(inf)* Bumslokal *nt (inf pej)*

Jul *abbr of* **July**

julep [ˈdʒuːlep] N **a** ≈ Sirup *m*, ≈ Saft *m* **b** → **mint**[2]

Julian [ˈdʒuːlɪən] **N** Julian *m* **ADJ** **~ calendar** julianischer Kalender

Julius Caesar [ˈdʒuːlɪəsˈsiːzəˈ] N Julius Caesar *m*

July [dʒuːˈlaɪ] N Juli *m* → *also* **September**

jumble [ˈdʒʌmbl] **VT** *(also* **jumble up)** **a** *(lit)* durcheinanderwerfen, kunterbunt vermischen; **~d up** durcheinander, kunterbunt vermischt; **a ~d mass of wires** ein Wirrwarr *m* von Kabeln; **to ~ everything up** alles durcheinanderbringen *or* in Unordnung bringen; **his clothes are ~d together on the bed** seine Kleider liegen in einem unordentlichen Haufen auf dem Bett **b** *(fig) facts* durcheinanderbringen; **~d thoughts/memories** verworrene Gedanken/Erinnerungen *pl* **N** **a** *(of objects)* Durcheinander *nt*; *(of ideas, words, memories)* Wirrwarr *m* **b** *no pl (for jumble sale)* gebrauchte Sachen *pl*

jumble sale N *(Brit)* ≈ Flohmarkt *m (von Vereinen veranstalteter Verkauf von gebrauchten Sachen)*; *(for charity)* Wohltätigkeitsbasar *m*

jumbly [ˈdʒʌmblɪ] ADJ wirr, durcheinander

jumbo [ˈdʒʌmbəʊ] N **a** *(inf)* Jumbo *m (inf)* **b** *(= jumbo jet)* Jumbo(jet) *m*

jump [dʒʌmp] **N** **a** *(lit)* Sprung *m*; *(with parachute)* Absprung *m*; *(on race-course)* Hindernis *nt*; **this horse is no good over the ~s** dieses Pferd taugt bei den Hindernissen nichts
b *(fig) (of prices)* (plötzlicher *or* sprunghafter) Anstieg; *(in narrative)* Sprung *m*, abrupter Übergang; **to take a sudden ~** *(prices, temperature)* ruckartig *or* sprunghaft ansteigen (*to* auf *+acc*), in die Höhe schnellen; **a 5% ~ in the number of unemployed people** ein 5%iger Anstieg der Arbeitslosenziffern; **it's a big ~ from medical student to doctor** es ist ein großer Sprung vom Medizinstudenten zum Arzt; **he's always one ~ ahead** er ist immer einen Schritt voraus; **you can take a running ~** *(Brit inf)* das kannst du vergessen
c *(= start)* **to give a ~** zusammenfahren; **my heart gave a ~** mein Herz machte einen Sprung
d *(esp US inf)* **to get a** *or* **the ~ on sb/sth** jdm/etw gegenüber im Vorteil sein; **to give sb a** *or* **the ~ on sb/sth** jdm einen Vorsprung vor jdm/etw verschaffen
VI **a** *(= leap)* springen, einen Satz machen; *(Sport)* springen; *(parachutist)* (ab)springen; **to ~ into a river** in einen Fluss springen; **this horse ~s well** dieses Pferd springt gut *or* nimmt die Hindernisse gut; **to ~ for joy** einen Freudensprung machen; *(heart)* vor Freude hüpfen; **to ~ to one's feet** aufspringen; **to ~ up and down on the spot** auf der Stelle hüpfen; **they ~ed up and down on his stomach** sie hüpften auf seinem Bauch herum; **they're ~ing up and down about it** *(fig)* sie regen sich furchtbar darüber auf; **to ~ to conclusions** vorschnelle Schlüsse ziehen
b *(typewriter)* Buchstaben überspringen *or* auslassen
c *(fig)* springen, unvermittelt übergehen; *(prices, shares)* in die Höhe schnellen, sprunghaft ansteigen; **~ to it!** los schon!, mach schon!; **the film suddenly ~s from the 18th into the 20th century** der Film macht plötzlich einen Sprung vom 18. ins 20. Jahrhundert; **her salary ~ed from £15,000 to £22,000** ihr Gehalt schnellte von £ 15.000 auf £ 22.000; **if you keep ~ing from one thing to another** wenn Sie nie an einer Sache bleiben; **she ~ed from kitchen assistant to chef** sie stieg plötzlich von der Küchenhilfe zur Köchin auf; **let's offer £200 and see which way they ~** *(inf)* machen wir ihnen doch (einfach) ein Angebot von £ 200 und sehen dann, wie sie darauf reagieren
d *(= start)* zusammenfahren, zusammenzucken; **the shout made him ~** er zuckte *or* fuhr bei dem Schrei zusammen; **you made me ~** du hast mich (aber) erschreckt; **his heart ~ed when ...** sein Herz machte einen Satz, als ...
VT **a** *ditch, fence etc* überspringen, hinüberspringen über *(+acc)*; **the horse ~ed a clear round** das Pferd sprang eine fehlerfreie Runde; **he ~ed two metres** er hat zwei Meter übersprungen
b *horse* springen lassen; **he ~ed his horse over the fence** er setzte mit seinem Pferd über den Zaun
c *(= skip)* überspringen, auslassen
d *(pick-up) groove* überspringen; **to ~ the rails** *(train)* entgleisen; **to ~ a man** *(Draughts)* einen überspringen
e *(inf usages)* **to ~ bail** *(Jur)* abhauen *(inf) (während man auf Kaution freigelassen ist)*; **to ~ a claim** einen schon bestehenden Anspruch (auf Land *or* Rechte) übergehen; **to ~ the lights** *or* **a red light** bei Rot rüberfahren *(inf) or* über die Kreuzung fahren; **to ~ the queue** *(Brit)* sich vordrängeln; **to ~ ship** *(Naut, passenger)* das Schiff vorzeitig verlassen; *(sailor)* heimlich abheuern; *(fig: = leave failing organization etc)* das sinkende Schiff verlassen; *(= join rival organization etc)* abspringen (und zur Konkurrenz gehen); **to ~ a train** *(= get on)* auf einen Zug aufspringen; *(= get off)* von einem Zug abspringen; **they ~ed a train to Acapulco** sie fuhren schwarz nach Acapulco; **to ~ sb** jdn überfallen

▶ **jump about** *(Brit) or* **around** VI herumhüpfen *or* -springen

▶ **jump at** VI *+prep obj person (lit)* anspringen; *(fig)* anfahren; *object* zuspringen auf *(+acc)*; *offer* sofort zugreifen bei, sofort ergreifen; *suggestion* sofort aufgreifen; *chance* sofort beim Schopf ergreifen

▶ **jump down** VI herunterhüpfen *or* -springen (*from* von); **to jump down sb's throat** jdn anfahren, jdm dazwischenfahren *(inf)*; **jump down!** spring *or* hüpf (runter)!

▶ **jump in** VI hineinspringen; *(fig)* eingreifen; **jump in!** *(to car)* steig ein!; *(at swimming pool etc)* spring rein!

▶ **jump off** VI **a** *(= leap off)* herunterspringen (*prep obj* von); *(from train, bus)* aussteigen (*prep obj* aus); *(when moving)* abspringen (*prep obj* von); *(from bicycle, horse)* absteigen (*prep obj* von) **b** *(Showjumping)* den Wettbewerb durch ein Stechen entscheiden; **they had to jump off to decide the winner** der Sieger musste durch ein Stechen ermittelt werden

▶ **jump on** **VI** *(lit, onto vehicle)* einsteigen (*prep obj, -to* in *+acc*); *(onto moving train, bus)* aufspringen (*prep obj, -to* auf *+acc*); *(onto bicycle, horse)* aufsteigen (*prep obj, -to* auf *+acc*); **to jump on(to) sb/sth** auf jdn/etw springen; **he jumped on(to) his bicycle** er schwang sich auf sein Fahrrad **VI** *+prep obj (inf) person (= criticize)* anfahren; *(= attack)* überfallen; *suggestion* kritisieren, heruntermachen *(inf)*

▶ **jump out** VI hinausspringen; *(from vehicle)* aussteigen (*of* aus); *(when moving)* abspringen (*of* von); **to jump out of bed** aus dem Bett springen; **to jump out of the window** aus dem Fenster springen, zum Fenster hinausspringen; **the caption jumps out at you** die Überschrift springt einem ins Auge; **to jump out of one's skin** zutiefst erschrocken sein; *(= get angry)* aus der Haut fahren *(inf)*

▶ **jump up** VI hochspringen; *(from sitting or lying position also)* aufspringen; *(onto sth)* hinaufspringen (*onto* auf *+acc*)

jump ball N Schiedsrichterball *m*

jumped-up [ˈdʒʌmptˈʌp] ADJ *(inf)* **this new ~ manageress** dieser kleine Emporkömmling von einer Abteilungsleiterin

jumper [ˈdʒʌmpəʳ] N **a** *(= garment) (Brit)* Pullover *m*; *(US: = dress)* Trägerkleid *nt* **b** *(= person)* Springer(in) *m(f)*; *(= animal)* Springer *m* **c** *(Comput)* Steckbrücke *f*, Jumper *m*

jumper cables N *(US Aut)* = **jump leads**

jumpiness [ˈdʒʌmpɪnɪs] N *(inf)* Nervosität *f*; *(of easily startled person)* Schreckhaftigkeit *f*

jumping jack [ˈdʒʌmpɪŋˈdʒæk] N Hampelmann *m*

jumping-off place [ˌdʒʌmpɪŋˈɒfpleɪs] N *(fig) (for negotiations)* Ausgangsbasis *f*; *(for job)* Sprungbrett *nt*

jump: **jump jet** N Senkrechtstarter *m*; **jump jockey** N *(Brit Horse Racing)* Springreiter(in) *m(f)*; **jump leads** PL *(Brit Aut)* Starthilfekabel *nt*; **jump-off** N *(Showjumping)* Stechen *nt*; **jump pass** N *(Basketball)* Sprungpass *m*; **jump rope** N *(US)* = **skipping rope**; **jump seat** N Notsitz *m*, Klappsitz *m*; **jump shot** N *(Basketball)* Sprungwurf *m*; **jump-start** **N** *(Mot)* Starthilfe *f*; **to give sb a ~** *(lit, fig)* jdm Starthilfe geben **VT** *(Mot)* Starthilfe geben; *(fig: = start)* in Gang setzen *or* bringen, anschieben *(fig)*; **jump suit** N Overall *m*

jumpy [ˈdʒʌmpɪ] ADJ *(+er)* **a** *(inf) person* nervös; *(= easily startled)* schreckhaft; *market* unsicher **b** *motion* ruckartig

Jun *abbr* **a** *of* **June** **b** *of* **junior** jr., jun.

junction [ˈdʒʌŋkʃən] N **a** *(Rail)* Gleisanschluss *m*; *(of roads)* Kreuzung *f*; *(of rivers)* Zusammenfluss *m*; **Clapham Junction** Claphamer Kreuz *nt*; **Hamm is a big railway ~** Hamm ist ein großer Eisenbahnknotenpunkt **b** *(Elec)* Anschlussstelle *f* **c** *(act)* Verbindung *f*

junction box N *(Elec)* Verteilerkasten *m*, Kabelkasten *m*

juncture [ˈdʒʌŋktʃəʳ] N **at this ~** zu diesem Zeitpunkt

June [dʒuːn] N Juni *m* → *also* **September**

jungle [ˈdʒʌŋgl] N Dschungel *m (also fig)*, Urwald *m*; **concrete ~** Betonwüste *f*; **the law of the ~** das Gesetz des Dschungels

jungle: **jungle gym** N *(US)* Klettergerüst *nt*; **jungle juice** N *(hum inf: = alcohol)* Feuerwasser *nt (inf)*

junior [ˈdʒuːnɪəʳ] **ADJ** **a** *(= younger)* jünger; **he is ~ to me** er ist jünger als ich; **Hiram Schwarz, ~** Hiram Schwarz junior; **Smith, ~** *(at school)* Smith II, der kleine Smith; **the ~ miss** die kleine Dame
b *(= subordinate) employee* untergeordnet; *officer* rangniedriger; **to be ~ to sb** unter jdm stehen
c *(Sport)* Junioren-, der Junioren; **~ team** Juniorenmannschaft *f*
N **a** Jüngere(r) *mf*; **he is my ~ by two years, he is two years my ~** er ist zwei Jahre jünger als ich; **where's ~?** wo ist der Junior?
b *(Brit Sch) (at primary school)* Grundschüler(in) *m(f)*; *(at secondary school)* Unterstufenschüler(in) *m(f)*
c *(US Univ) Student(in) im vorletzten Studienjahr*
d *(Sport)* Junior(in) *m(f)*; **the ~s** die Junioren/Juniorinnen *pl*

junior: **junior classes** PL *(Sch)* Unterstufe *f*; **junior clerk** N zweiter Buchhalter; **he's just some ~** er ist bloß ein kleiner Angestellter; **junior college** N *(US Univ) College, an dem man die ersten zwei Jahre eines 4-jährigen Studiums absolviert*; **junior common room** N *(Brit Univ)* Gemeinschaftsraum *m* für Studenten; **junior high (school)** N *(US)* ≈ Mittelschule *f*; **Junior League** N **a** *(Brit Sport)* Amateurliga *f* **b** *(US: for voluntary work) Wohltätigkeitsverband von Frauen, die sich im Sozialbereich engagieren*; **junior management** N untere Führungskräfte *pl*; **junior minister** N Staatssekretär(in) *m(f)*; **junior partner** N jüngerer Teilhaber; *(in coalition)* kleinerer (Koalitions)partner; **junior school** N *(Brit)* Grundschule *f*

juniors' department N *(in department store)* Young-Fashion-Abteilung *f*

juniper [ˈdʒuːnɪpəʳ] N Wacholder *m*; **~ berry** Wacholderbeere *f*

junk[1] [dʒʌŋk] **N** **a** *(= discarded objects)* Trödel *m*, altes Zeug, Gerümpel *nt* **b** *(inf: = trash)* Ramsch *m*, Plunder *m*, Schund *m* **c** *(inf: = drugs)* Stoff *m (inf)* **VT** *(inf: = get rid of) object* wegschmeißen *(inf)*; *idea, attempt* aufgeben

junk[2] N *(boat)* Dschunke *f*

junk: **junk bond** N *(Fin) niedrig eingestuftes Wertpapier mit hohen Ertragschancen bei erhöhtem Risiko*; **junk car** N Schrottauto *nt*; **junk dealer** N Trödler(in) *m(f)*, Altwarenhändler(in) *m(f)*; **junk e-mail** N unerbetene E-Mail mit Werbung

junket [ˈdʒʌŋkɪt] **N** **a** *(Cook)* Dickmilch *f* **b** *(old, hum: = merrymaking)* Gelage *nt*, Fest *nt*, Lustbarkeit *f (old, hum)* **c** *(= trip at public expense)* (Vergnügungs)reise *f* auf Staatskosten **VI** *(old, hum)* ein Gelage abhalten

junketing [ˈdʒʌŋkɪtɪŋ] N **a** *(old, hum, = merrymaking)* Festivitäten *pl (esp hum)*, Lustbarkeit *f (old, hum)* **b** *(= trips at public expense)* (Vergnügungs)reisen *pl* auf Staatskosten

junk: **junk fax** N unerbetenes Fax mit Werbung; **junk food** N Junk food *nt (inf)*, ungesundes Essen; **junk heap** N *(also inf: = car)* Schrotthaufen *m (inf)*; **you'll end up on the ~** du wirst in der Gosse landen

junkie [ˈdʒʌŋkɪ] N *(inf)* Fixer(in) *m(f) (inf)*, Junkie *m (inf)*; **fast food ~** Fan *m* von Fastfood; **computer ~** Computerfreak *m (sl)*

junk: **junk mail** N (Post)wurfsendungen *pl*, Reklame *f*; **junk room** N Rumpelkammer *f*; **junk shop** N Trödelladen *m*; **junk yard** N *(for metal)* Schrottplatz *m*; *(for discarded objects)* Schuttabladeplatz *m*; *(of rag and bone merchant)* Trödellager(platz *m*) *nt*

junta [ˈdʒʌntə] **N** Junta *f*

Jupiter [ˈdʒuːpɪtəˈ] **N** Jupiter *m*

juridical [dʒʊəˈrɪdɪkəl] **ADJ** *(of law)* juristisch; *(of court)* gerichtlich

jurisdiction [ˌdʒʊərɪsˈdɪkʃən] **N** Gerichtsbarkeit *f*; *(= range of authority)* Zuständigkeit(sbereich *m*) *f*; **matters that fall outside the ~ of this court** Fälle, für die dieses Gericht nicht zuständig ist; **this court has no ~ over him** er untersteht diesem Gericht nicht; **that's not within my ~** dafür bin ich nicht zuständig

jurisprudence [ˌdʒʊərɪsˈpruːdəns] **N** Jura *nt*, Rechtswissenschaft *f*, Jurisprudenz *f (old)*

jurist [ˈdʒʊərɪst] **N** Jurist(in) *m(f)*, Rechtswissenschaftler(in) *m(f)*

juror [ˈdʒʊərəˈ] **N** Schöffe *m*, Schöffin *f*; *(for capital crimes)* Geschworene(r) *mf*; *(in competition)* Preisrichter(in) *m(f)*, Jurymitglied *nt*

jury [ˈdʒʊərɪ] **N** **a** *(Jur)* **the ~** die Schöffen *pl*, die Jury; *(for capital crimes)* die Geschworenen *pl*; **they don't have juries there** dort gibt es keine Schöffengerichte *or* keine Jury *or (for capital crimes)* keine Schwurgerichte; **to sit** *or* **be on the ~** Schöffe/Geschworener sein; **Ladies and Gentlemen of the Jury** meine Damen und Herren Schöffen/Geschworenen; **the ~ is (still) out** *(lit)* die Schöffen/Geschworenen beraten noch; *(fig)* es ist noch nichts entschieden; **the ~ is out on whether this is true** es ist noch nicht heraus, ob das stimmt
b *(for examination)* Prüfungsausschuss *m*; *(for exhibition, competition)* Jury *f*, Preisgericht *nt*

jury: **jury box** **N** Schöffenbank *f*; *(for capital crimes)* Geschworenenbank *f*; **juryman** **N** Schöffe *m*; *(for capital crimes)* Geschworene(r) *m*; **jury rig** **N** *(Naut)* Hilfstakelage *f*, Notttakelage *f*; **jury service** **N** Schöffenamt *nt*; *(for capital crimes)* Amt *nt* des Geschworenen; **to do ~** Schöffe/Geschworener sein; **he's never been called for ~** er wurde nie als Schöffe/Geschworener berufen; **jury system** **N** Jurysystem *nt*, Schöffengerichte *pl*; *(for capital crimes)* Schwurgerichte *pl*; **jurywoman** **N** Schöffin *f*; *(for capital crimes)* Geschworene *f*

just[1] [dʒʌst] ✪ 5.4 **ADV** **a** *(immediate past)* gerade, (so)eben; **they have ~ left** sie sind gerade *or* (so)eben gegangen; **she left ~ before I came** sie war, gerade *or* kurz bevor ich kam, weggegangen; **he's ~ been appointed** er ist gerade *or* eben erst ernannt worden; **I met him ~ after lunch** ich habe ihn direkt *or* gleich nach dem Mittagessen getroffen
b *(= at this/that very moment)* gerade; **hurry up, he's ~ going** beeilen Sie sich, er geht gerade; **he's ~ coming** er kommt gerade *or* eben; **I'm ~ coming** ich komme ja schon; **I was ~ going to …** ich wollte gerade …; **~ as I was going** genau in dem Moment *or* gerade, als ich gehen wollte
c *(= barely, almost not)* gerade noch, mit knapper Not; **he (only) ~ escaped being run over** er wäre um ein Haar überfahren worden; **it ~ missed** es hat fast *or* beinahe getroffen; **I've got only ~ enough to live on** mir reicht es gerade so *or* so eben noch zum Leben; **I arrived ~ in time** ich bin gerade (noch) rechtzeitig gekommen
d *(= exactly)* genau, gerade; **it is ~ five o'clock** es ist genau fünf Uhr; **that's ~ like you** das sieht dir ähnlich; **it's ~ on nine o'clock** es ist gerade neun Uhr; **it happened ~ as I expected** es passierte genau so, wie ich es erwartet hatte; **it's ~ because of that that he insists** gerade *or* eben deshalb besteht er darauf; **that's ~ it!** das ists ja gerade *or* eben!; **that's ~ what I was going to say** genau das wollte ich (auch) sagen; **~ what do you mean by that?** was wollen Sie damit sagen?; **~ what does this symbol mean?** was bedeutet dieses Zeichen genau?; **it was ~ there** genau da war es; **~ so!** *(old)* genau, ganz recht; **everything has to be ~ so** es muss alles seine Ordnung haben
e *(= only, simply)* nur, bloß; **I can stay ~ a minute** ich kann nur *or* bloß eine Minute bleiben; **~ you and me** nur wir beide, wir beide allein; **this is ~ to show you how it works** dies soll Ihnen lediglich zeigen, wie es funktioniert; **this is ~ to confirm …** hiermit bestätigen wir, dass …; **he's ~ a boy** er ist doch noch ein Junge; **why don't you want to/like it? – I ~ don't** warum willst du nicht/magst du es nicht? – ich will/mags eben *or* halt *(inf)* nicht; **~ like that** (ganz) einfach so; **I don't know, I ~ don't** ich weiß (es) nicht, beim besten Willen nicht; **you can't ~ assume …** Sie können doch nicht ohne weiteres annehmen …; **it's ~ not good enough** es ist einfach nicht gut genug; **I ~ prefer it this way** ich finds eben *or* einfach besser so
f *(= a small distance: with position)* gleich; **~ round the corner** gleich um die Ecke; **~ above the trees** direkt über den Bäumen; **put it ~ over there** stells mal da drüben hin; **~ here** (genau) hier
g *(= absolutely)* einfach, wirklich; **it was ~ fantastic** es war einfach prima; **it's ~ terrible** das ist ja schrecklich!
h **~ as** genauso, ebenso; **the blue hat is ~ as nice as the red one** der blaue Hut ist genauso hübsch wie der rote; **she didn't understand you – it's ~ as well!** sie hat Sie nicht verstanden – das ist vielleicht auch besser so; **it's ~ as well you stayed at home, you didn't miss anything** es macht nichts, dass Sie zu Hause geblieben sind, Sie haben nichts verpasst; **it's ~ as well you didn't go out** nur gut, dass Sie nicht weggegangen sind; **it would be ~ as well if you came** es wäre doch besser, wenn Sie kämen; **come ~ as you are** kommen Sie so, wie Sie sind; **it's ~ as you please** wie Sie wollen; **~ as I thought!** ich habe es mir doch gedacht!
i **~ about** in etwa, so etwa; **I am ~ about ready** ich bin so gut wie fertig; **it's ~ about here** es ist (so) ungefähr hier; **did he make it in time? – ~ about** hat ers (rechtzeitig) geschafft? – so gerade; **will this do? – ~ about** ist das recht so? – so in etwa; **I am ~ about fed up with it!** *(inf)* so langsam aber sicher hängt es mir zum Hals raus *(inf)*; **that's ~ about the limit!** das ist doch die Höhe!
j **~ now** *(in past)* soeben (erst), gerade erst; **not ~ now** im Moment nicht; **~ now?** jetzt gleich?; **you can go, but not ~ now** Sie können gehen, aber nicht gerade jetzt
k *(other uses)* **~ think** denk bloß; **~ listen** hör mal; **~ try** versuchs doch mal; **~ taste this** probier das mal; *(it's awful)* probier bloß das mal; **~ let me try** lassen Sies mich doch mal versuchen; **~ shut up!** sei bloß still!; **~ wait here a moment** warten Sie hier mal (für) einen Augenblick; **~ a moment** *or* **minute!** Moment mal!; **I can ~ see him as a soldier** ich kann ihn mir gut als Soldat vorstellen; **I can ~ see you getting up so early** *(iro)* du – und so früh aufstehen!; **can I ~ finish this?** kann ich das eben noch fertig machen?; **the possibilities ~ go on for ever** die Möglichkeiten sind ja unerschöpflich; **don't I ~ –!** und ob (ich …); **~ watch it** nimm dich bloß in Acht; **~ you dare** wehe, wenn dus wagst

just[2] **ADJ** *(+er)* **a** *person, decision* gerecht (*to* gegenüber) **b** *punishment, reward* gerecht; *anger* berechtigt; *suspicion* gerechtfertigt, begründet; **a ~ cause** eine gerechte Sache; **I had ~ cause to be alarmed** ich hatte guten Grund, beunruhigt zu sein; **as (it) is only ~** wie es recht und billig ist

justice [ˈdʒʌstɪs] **N** **a** *(Jur)* *(= quality)* Gerechtigkeit *f*; *(system)* Gerichtsbarkeit *f*, Justiz *f*; **British ~** britisches Recht; **is this the famous British ~?** ist das die berühmte britische Gerechtigkeit?; **to bring sb to ~** jdn vor Gericht bringen; **court of ~** Gerichtshof *m*, Gericht *nt*; **to administer ~** Recht sprechen → **poetic justice**
b *(= fairness)* Gerechtigkeit *f*; *(of claims)* Rechtmäßigkeit *f*; **to do him ~** um ihm gegenüber gerecht zu sein, um mal fair zu sein *(inf)*; **this photograph doesn't do her ~** auf diesem Foto ist sie nicht gut getroffen; **she never does herself ~** sie kommt nie richtig zur Geltung; **that's not true, you're not doing yourself ~** das stimmt nicht, Sie unterschätzen sich; **you didn't do yourself ~ in the exams** Sie haben im Examen nicht gezeigt, was Sie können; **they did ~ to the wine** sie wussten den Wein zu würdigen; **and with ~** und (zwar) zu Recht; **there's no ~, is there?** das ist doch nicht gerecht
c *(= judge)* Richter(in) *m(f)*; **Lord Chief Justice** *oberster Richter in Großbritannien*; **Justice of the Peace** Friedensrichter(in) *m(f)*; **Mr Justice Buchanan** Richter Buchanan

justifiable [ˌdʒʌstɪˈfaɪəbl] **ADJ** gerechtfertigt, berechtigt

justifiably [ˌdʒʌstɪˈfaɪəblɪ] **ADV** mit *or* zu Recht, berechtigterweise; **and ~ so** und das mit *or* zu Recht

justification [ˌdʒʌstɪfɪˈkeɪʃən] **N** **a** Rechtfertigung *f* (*of* +*gen*, *for* für); **it can be said in his ~ that …** zu seiner Verteidigung *or* Entschuldigung kann gesagt werden, dass …; **as (a) ~ for his action** zur Rechtfertigung *or* Verteidigung seiner Handlungsweise; **he had no ~ for lying** er hatte keine Rechtfertigung *or* Entschuldigung für seine Lüge **b** *(Typ)* Justieren *nt*; *(Comput)* Randausgleich *m*

justify [ˈdʒʌstɪfaɪ] ✪ 26.1 **VT** **a** *(= show to be right)* rechtfertigen, verteidigen (*sth to sb* etw vor jdm *or* jdm gegenüber); **you don't need to ~ yourself** Sie brauchen sich nicht zu rechtfertigen *or* verteidigen; **don't try to ~ your action** versuchen Sie nicht, Ihre Tat zu entschuldigen *or* zu verteidigen; **am I justified in believing that …?** glaube ich zu Recht, dass …?
b *(= be good reason for)* rechtfertigen, ein Grund sein für; **the future could hardly be said to ~ great optimism** die Zukunft berechtigt wohl kaum zu großem Optimismus; **this does not ~ his being late** das ist kein Grund für sein Zuspätkommen; **he was justified in doing that** es war gerechtfertigt, dass er das tat; **you're not justified in talking to her like that** Sie haben kein Recht, so mit ihr zu reden
c *(Typ)* justieren; *(Comput)* ausrichten; **right/left justified** rechts-/linksbündig

justly [ˈdʒʌstlɪ] **ADV** zu Recht, mit Recht; *treat, try* gerecht; *condemn* gerechterweise

justness [ˈdʒʌstnɪs] **N** *(of cause)* Gerechtigkeit *f*, Billigkeit *f (liter)*; *(of character)* Gerechtigkeit *f*

jut [dʒʌt] **VI** *(also* **jut out***)* hervorstehen, hervorragen, herausragen; *(chin, jaw)* vorspringen; **he saw a gun ~ting (out) from behind the wall** er sah ein Gewehr hinter der Mauer (her)vorragen; **the peninsula ~s out into the sea** die Halbinsel ragt ins Meer hinaus; **to ~ out over the street** über die Straße vorstehen *or* hinausragen **VT** **to ~ one's chin/jaw forward** sein Kinn/seinen Kiefer vorstrecken

jute [dʒuːt] **N** Jute *f*

Jutland [ˈdʒʌtlənd] **N** Jütland *nt*

juvenile [ˈdʒuːvənaɪl] **N** *(Admin)* Jugendliche(r) *mf*; *(= animal)* Jungtier *nt* **ADJ** *(= youthful)* jugendlich; *(= for young people)* für Jugendliche; *(pej)* kindisch, unreif; **~ crime** Jugendkriminalität *f*

juvenile: **juvenile center** **N** *(US)* Heim *nt* für jugendliche Straftäter; **juvenile court** **N** Jugendgericht *nt*; **juvenile delinquency** **N** Jugendkriminalität *f*, Kriminalität *f* bei Jugendlichen; **juvenile delinquent** **N** jugendlicher Straftäter, jugendliche Straftäterin; **juvenile home** **N** *(US)* Heim *nt* für jugendliche Straftäter; **juvenile lead** **N** *(Theat)* Rolle *f* des jugendlichen Hauptdarstellers; *(actor)* jugendlicher Hauptdarsteller; **juvenile offender** **N** *(Jur)* jugendlicher Straftäter, jugendliche Straftäterin

juvenilia [ˌdʒuːvɪˈnɪlɪə] **PL** *(form)* Jugendwerke *pl*

juxtapose [ˈdʒʌkstəˌpəʊz] **VT** nebeneinanderstellen; *ideas also* gegeneinanderhalten; *colours* nebeneinandersetzen

juxtaposition [ˌdʒʌkstəpəˈzɪʃən] **N** *(= act)* Nebeneinanderstellung *f*; **in ~ (with each other)** (direkt) nebeneinander

K

K, k [keɪ] N K *nt*, k *nt*

k N *(Comput)* abbr of **kilobyte** KB

K *abbr (in salaries etc)* -tausend; **15 K** 15.000

Kaffir ['kæfəˈ] N *(also pej)* Kaffer *m*

Kafkaesque [,kæfkə'esk] ADJ kafkaesk

kagoul(e) [kə'gu:l] N = **cagoule**

kagul [kə'gu:l] N = **cagoule**

Kalashnikov [kə'læʃnɪ,kɒf] N Kalaschnikow *f*

kale, kail [keɪl] N Grünkohl *m*

kaleidoscope [kə'laɪdəskəʊp] N Kaleidoskop *nt*; **a ~ of emotion** ein Wechselspiel *nt* der Gefühle

kaleidoscopic [kə,laɪdə'skɒpɪk] ADJ kaleidoskopisch

kamikaze [kæmɪ'kɑ:zɪ] N Kamikaze *nt*; **~ pilot** Kamikazeflieger *m*; **~ mission** Kamikaze-Mission *f*

kangaroo [,kæŋgə'ru:] N Känguru *nt*; **to have ~s in one's top paddock** *(Austral inf)* nicht alle Tassen im Schrank haben *(inf)*

kangaroo court N inoffizielles Gericht, Femegericht *nt*

kaolin ['keɪəlɪn] N Kaolin *m or nt*, Porzellanerde *f*

kapok ['keɪpɒk] N Kapok *m*

Kaposi's sarcoma [kæ'pəʊsɪzsɑ:'kəʊmə] N *(Med)* Kaposisarkom *nt*

kaput [kə'pʊt] ADJ *(inf)* kaputt *(inf)*

karaoke [,kærə'əʊkɪ] N Karaoke *nt*

karaoke machine N Karaoke-Gerät *nt*

karat ['kærət] N = **carat**

karate [kə'rɑ:tɪ] N Karate *nt*

karate chop N Karateschlag *or* -hieb *m*

karma ['kɑ:mə] N Karma *nt*

Karrimat® N **'k[+ae]rlm[+ae]t** Isomatte *f*

kart [kɑ:t] N Gokart *m*

karting ['kɑ:tɪŋ] N Gokartfahren *nt*

Kashmir [kæʃ'mɪəˈ] N Kaschmir *nt*

Kate [keɪt] N *dim of* **Catherine** Kät(h)e *f*

katydid ['keɪtɪdɪd] N Laubheuschrecke *f*

kayak ['kaɪæk] N Kajak *m or nt*

KB *abbr of* **kilobyte**

KBE *(Brit) abbr of* **Knight of the British Empire** *britischer Verdienstorden*

KC *(Brit) abbr of* **King's Counsel**

kc *abbr of* **kilocycle**

kcal ['keɪkæl] *abbr of* **kilocalorie** kcal

KCB *(Brit) abbr of* **Knight Commander of the Bath** *britischer Verdienstorden*

kd rgds *abbr of* **kind regards** MfG

kebab [kə'bæb] N Kebab *m*

kedge [kedʒ] N *(Naut)* Warpauker *m*

kedgeree [,kedʒə'ri:] N *Reisgericht mit Fisch und Eiern*

keel [ki:l] N *(Naut)* Kiel *m*; **to be back on an even ~** *(lit)* sich wieder aufgerichtet haben; **he put the business back on an even ~** er brachte das Geschäft wieder ins Lot *or* wieder auf die Beine *(inf)*; **when things are on a more even ~** wenn sich alles besser eingespielt hat

▶ **keel over** VI *(ship)* kentern; *(fig inf)* umkippen; **she keeled over in a faint** sie klappte zusammen *(inf)*, sie kippte um *(inf)*

keelhaul ['ki:lhɔ:l] VT kielholen

keen¹ [ki:n] ✪ 8.3 ADJ *(+er)* **a** *(= acute, intense) appetite* kräftig; *interest* groß, stark; *pleasure* groß; *anticipation* gespannt; *feeling* stark, tief; *desire, pain* heftig, stark; *mind, intelligence, sense of humour, wit* scharf; *sight, eye, hearing, ear* gut, scharf; *awareness* geschärft; *competition* scharf; **to keep a ~ eye on sth** ein wachsames Auge auf etw *(acc)* haben; **to have a ~ nose for sth** eine gute *or* feine Nase für etw haben; **they have a ~ awareness** *or* **appreciation of the dangers** sie sind sich der Gefahren deutlich bewusst; **he has a ~ sense of history** er hat ein ausgeprägtes Gefühl für Geschichte

b *(= enthusiastic)* begeistert; *football fan, golfer, supporter* leidenschaftlich, begeistert; *(= eager, interested) applicant, learner* stark interessiert; *(= hardworking)* eifrig; **~ to learn** lernbegierig; **~ to know** begierig zu wissen; **try not to seem too ~** versuchen Sie, Ihr Interesse nicht zu sehr zu zeigen; **if he's ~ we can teach him** wenn er wirklich interessiert ist *or* Interesse hat, können wir es ihm beibringen; **he is terribly ~** seine Begeisterung/sein Interesse/sein Eifer kennt kaum Grenzen; **to be ~ on sb** von jdm sehr angetan sein; *(= sexually attracted)* scharf auf jdn sein *(inf)*; *on pop group, actor, author* von jdm begeistert sein; **to be ~ on sth** etw sehr gern mögen; *on classical music, Italian cooking also, football* sehr viel für etw übrighaben; **to be ~ on doing sth** *(= like to do)* etw gern *or* mit Begeisterung tun; **to be ~ to do sth** *(= want to do)* sehr darauf erpicht sein *or* scharf darauf sein *(inf)*, etw zu tun; **to be ~ on mountaineering/dancing** begeisterter *or* leidenschaftlicher Bergsteiger/Tänzer sein, leidenschaftlich gern bergsteigen/tanzen; **he is very ~ on golf/tennis** *etc* er ist ein Golf-/Tennisfan *m etc*; **to become ~ on sb/sth** sich für jdn/etw erwärmen; **I'm not very ~ on him/that idea** ich bin von ihm/dieser Idee nicht gerade begeistert; **he's very ~ on getting the job finished** ihm liegt sehr viel daran, dass die Arbeit fertig wird; **he's not ~ on her coming** er legt keinen (gesteigerten) Wert darauf, dass sie kommt; **he's very ~ that we should go/for us to go** er legt sehr großen Wert darauf *or* ihm ist sehr daran gelegen, dass wir gehen; **they are ~ for revenge** sie sind auf Rache aus

c *(= sharp) blade, wind* scharf; *frost* scharf, klirrend

d *(esp Brit: = competitive) prices* günstig

e *(US inf: = very good)* spitzenmäßig *(inf)*

keen² *(Ir)* **N** Totenklage *f* **VI** die Totenklage halten

keenly ['ki:nlɪ] ADV **a** *(= intensely, acutely) feel* leidenschaftlich, tief, stark; *interested, wish, desire* stark, sehr, leidenschaftlich; *listen* aufmerksam; *observe* scharf; **I am ~ aware that …** ich bin mir deutlich bewusst, dass …; **the match was ~ contested** in dem Spiel wurde hart gekämpft **b** *(= enthusiastically)* mit Begeisterung; **~ awaited** mit Ungeduld erwartet **c** *(esp Brit: = competitively)* **~ priced goods** Waren *pl* zu scharf kalkulierten Preisen

keenness ['ki:nnɪs] N **a** *(of blade, mind, wind, sight)* Schärfe *f* **b** *(= enthusiasm)* Begeisterung *f*; *(of fan, supporter, golfer)* Leidenschaftlichkeit *f*; *(of applicant, learner)* starkes Interesse; *(= hardworking nature)* Eifer *m*; **his ~ to go is suspicious** dass er so unbedingt gehen will, ist verdächtig

keep [ki:p]

vb: pret, ptp **kept**

1 TRANSITIVE VERB	3 NOUN
2 INTRANSITIVE VERB	4 PHRASAL VERBS

When *keep* is part of a set combination, e.g. *keep in mind, keep house, keep goal* etc, look up the noun. For combinations of *keep* with adverbs and prepositions, e.g. *keep in, keep on, keep up* etc, see also the phrasal verbs section.

1 – TRANSITIVE VERB

a [= retain] behalten; **you can keep this book** du kannst dieses Buch behalten; **I can't keep that number in my head** ich kann die Nummer nicht behalten, ich kann mir die Nummer nicht merken; **he wanted to keep the dog for another week** er wollte den Hund noch eine Woche (bei sich) behalten; **to keep a place for sb** einen Platz für jdn frei halten; **to keep one's place in a book** sich *(dat)* die Stelle im Buch markieren; **to keep a note of sth** sich *(dat)* etw notieren; **to keep one's temper** sich beherrschen; **to keep a grip on sth** *(fig)* etw unter Kontrolle halten; **you can keep it!** *(inf)* das kannst du behalten *or* dir an den Hut stecken *(inf)*

b [= maintain in a certain state, place etc] halten; **to keep sb at work** jdn bei der Arbeit halten; **he kept his hands in his pockets** er hat die Hände in der Tasche gelassen; **to keep good health** sich guter Gesundheit erfreuen; **the garden was well kept** der Garten war (gut) gepflegt

♦ **to keep sb/sth doing sth** **to keep sb waiting** jdn warten lassen; **keep her thinking that …** lassen Sie sie in dem Glauben, dass …; **can't you keep him talking?** können Sie ihn nicht in ein Gespräch verwickeln?; **to keep the traffic moving** den Verkehr in Fluss *or* am Fließen halten; **to keep a machine running** eine Maschine laufen lassen; **to keep the conversation going** das Gespräch in Gang halten; **keep it going!** *(Brit)* leg dich ins Zeug! *(inf)*, gib alles! *(inf)*

♦ **to keep sb/sth** + *ADJ* **to keep one's dress clean** sein Kleid nicht schmutzig machen; **to keep sb quiet** zusehen *or* dafür sorgen, dass jd still ist; **that'll keep them quiet for a while** das wird für eine Weile Ruhe schaffen; **just to keep her happy** damit sie zufrieden ist; **to keep sb alive** jdn am Leben halten; **to keep oneself busy** sich selbst beschäftigen; **to keep oneself warm** sich warm halten

c [= have in a certain place, look after] aufbewahren; **where does he keep his money?** wo bewahrt er sein Geld auf?; **where do you keep your spoons?** wo sind die Löffel?

d [= put aside] aufheben; **I've been keeping it for you** ich habe es für Sie aufgehoben; **I'm keep-**

ing the best ones for Christmas die besten hebe ich für Weihnachten auf

e = detain aufhalten, zurückhalten; **I mustn't keep you** ich will Sie nicht aufhalten; **what kept you?** wo waren Sie denn so lang?; **what's keeping him?** wo bleibt er denn?; **to keep sb prisoner** jdn gefangen halten; **to keep sb in prison** jdn in Haft halten; **they kept him in hospital over night** sie haben ihn über Nacht im Krankenhaus behalten; **it kept her in bed for a week** sie musste deswegen eine Woche im Bett bleiben

f = have, look after *shop, hotel, restaurant* haben, unterhalten, führen; *bees, pigs etc* halten; **to keep servants** sich *(dat)* Diener halten; **he keeps an excellent cellar** er hat einen ausgezeichneten Weinkeller

♦ **to keep sb in sth to keep sb in clothes** *(person)* für jds Kleidung sorgen; **I couldn't afford to keep you in drink** ich könnte deine Getränke nicht bezahlen

g = support versorgen, unterhalten; **I earn enough to keep myself** ich verdiene genug für mich (selbst) zum Leben; **I have six children to keep** ich habe sechs Kinder zu unterhalten; **he keeps a mistress** er hält sich *(dat)* eine Geliebte

h = be faithful to, observe *promise* halten; *law, rule* einhalten, befolgen; *treaty* einhalten; *obligations* nachkommen *(+dat)*, erfüllen; *appointment* einhalten; **to keep a vow** einen Schwur halten, ein Gelübde erfüllen; **to keep Lent/the Sabbath** das Fasten/die Sonntagsruhe *or* den Sabbat (ein)halten; **to keep late hours** lange aufbleiben

i = guard, protect (be)hüten; *sheep etc* hüten, aufpassen auf *(+acc)*; **God keep you!** *(old)* Gott befohlen! *(old)* → **keep from VT b**

j accounts, diary etc führen (*of* über *+acc*)

k Comm = *stock* führen, (zu verkaufen) haben

l US = *continue to follow road, path* weitergehen *or* -fahren, folgen *(+dat)*; *direction* einhalten; **to keep one's course** (den) Kurs (ein)halten

m US = *remain in* **to keep one's room** auf seinem Zimmer bleiben; **to keep one's seat** sitzen bleiben

2 – INTRANSITIVE VERB

a = continue in a specified direction **to keep (to the) left/right** sich links/rechts halten; **to keep to the left** *(Aut)* auf der linken Seite bleiben, links fahren; **to keep to the middle of the road** immer in der Mitte der Straße fahren; **keep on this road** bleiben Sie auf dieser Straße; **keep north** gehen/fahren Sie immer Richtung Norden

b = remain in a certain state, position bleiben

♦ **to keep + ADJ to keep fit** fit bleiben, sich in Form halten; **to keep quiet** still sein; **to keep silent** schweigen; **to keep calm** ruhig bleiben, Ruhe bewahren

♦ **to keep doing sth** *(= not stop)* etw weiter tun; *(repeatedly)* etw immer wieder tun; *(constantly)* etw dauernd tun; **to keep walking** weitergehen; **he kept lying to her** er hat sie immer wieder belogen; **if you keep complaining** wenn Sie sich weiter beschweren; **she keeps talking about you all the time** sie redet dauernd von Ihnen; **keep going** machen Sie weiter; **I keep hoping she's still alive** ich hoffe immer noch, dass sie noch lebt; **I keep thinking …** ich denke immer …

c food etc sich halten; **that meat won't keep** dieses Fleisch hält sich nicht *or* bleibt nicht gut

d = be in a certain state of health **how are you keeping?** wie geht es Ihnen so?; **he's not keeping too well** es geht ihm nicht besonders gut; **he's keeping better now** es geht ihm wieder besser

e = wait **that business can keep** das kann warten; **will it keep?** kann das warten?

3 – NOUN

a = livelihood, food Unterhalt *m*; **I got £300 a week and my keep** ich bekam £ 300 pro Woche und freie Kost und Logis; **to earn one's keep** seinen Lebensunterhalt verdienen; **in a poem every word must earn its keep** in einem Gedicht muss jedes Wort seine Daseinsberechtigung haben

b in castle Bergfried *m*; *(as prison)* Burgverlies *nt*

c

♦ **for keeps** *(inf)* für immer; **he's playing for keeps** ihm ists ernst; **it's yours for keeps** das darfst du behalten

4 – PHRASAL VERBS

▶ **keep ahead** VI vorne bleiben; **to keep ahead of one's rivals** seinen Konkurrenten vorausbleiben VT SEP **to keep one step ahead of the others** den anderen einen Schritt voraus sein

▶ **keep at** VI *+prep obj* **a** *(= continue with)* weitermachen mit; **keep at it** machen Sie weiter so **b** *(= nag)* herumnörgeln an *(+dat)*; **keep at him until he says yes** lass ihm so lange keine Ruhe, bis er ja sagt VT *+prep obj* **to keep sb at a task** jdn nicht mit einer Arbeit aufhören lassen; **to keep sb (hard) at it** jdn hart rannehmen *(inf)*, jdn an der Kandare haben; **they kept him at it all day** sie haben ihn den ganzen Tag hart rangenommen *(inf)*

▶ **keep away** VI *(lit)* wegbleiben; *(= not approach)* nicht näher herankommen (*from* an *+acc*); **keep away!** nicht näher kommen!; **keep away from that place** gehen Sie da nicht hin; **he just can't keep away from the pub** es zieht ihn immer wieder in die Wirtschaft; **I just can't keep away** es zieht mich immer wieder hin; **keep away from him** lassen Sie die Finger von ihm; **he just can't keep away from her** er kann einfach nicht von ihr lassen

VT *(always separate) person, children, pet etc* fernhalten (*from* von); **to keep sth away from sth** etw nicht an etw *(acc)* kommen lassen; **keep your hand away from the cutting edge** kommen Sie mit Ihrer Hand nicht an die Schneide; **keep them away from each other** halten Sie sie auseinander; **to keep sb away from school** jdn nicht in die Schule (gehen) lassen; **business kept him away for three months** er war aus geschäftlichen Gründen drei Monate weg; **what's been keeping you away?** wo waren Sie denn so lange?

▶ **keep back** VI zurückbleiben, nicht näher kommen; **keep back!** bleiben Sie, wo Sie sind!, treten Sie zurück!; **please keep back from the edge** bitte gehen Sie nicht zu nahe an den Rand

VT *sep* **a** *(= hold back) person, hair, crowds, enemy* zurückhalten; *water* stauen; *tears* unterdrücken; **to keep sb/sth back from sb** jdn/etw von jdm abhalten

b *(= withhold) money, taxes* einbehalten; *information, facts etc* verschweigen (*from sb* jdm); *(from parent, husband etc)* verheimlichen, verschweigen (*from sb* jdm); **I know you're keeping something back** ich weiß, dass du mir etwas verheimlichst *or* verschweigst; **they are keeping back the names of the victims** die Namen der Opfer werden nicht bekannt gegeben; **keep some cheese back to sprinkle over the top** behalten Sie etwas Käse zum Darüberstreuen zurück

c *(= make late)* aufhalten; *pupil* dabehalten; **I don't want to keep you back** ich möchte Sie nicht aufhalten

d *(= hold up, slow down)* behindern; **being with the slower learners is keeping him back** weil er mit schwächeren Schülern zusammen ist, kommt er nicht so schnell voran

▶ **keep down** VI unten bleiben; **keep down!** duck dich!, bleib unten!

VT *sep* **a** *(lit)* unten lassen; *(= hold down)* unten halten; *head* ducken; *eyes* gesenkt halten; **keep your voices down** reden Sie leise *or* nicht so laut

b *people, revolt* unterdrücken; *dog* bändigen; *rebellious person* im Zaum *or* unter Kontrolle halten; *rabbits, weeds etc* in Grenzen *or* unter Kontrolle halten; **you can't keep a good man down** der Tüchtige lässt sich nicht unterkriegen

c *taxes, rates, prices* niedrig halten; *spending* einschränken; *costs, wages* drücken; **to keep numbers down** die Zahlen gering halten; **to keep one's weight down** nicht zunehmen

d *food, drink* bei sich behalten; **she can't keep anything down** sie kann nichts bei sich behalten

e *(Sch)* wiederholen lassen; **he was kept down** er musste wiederholen

▶ **keep from** VT *+prep obj* **a** *sb* hindern an *(+dat)*; *(from going, doing sth)* abhalten von, hindern an *(+dat)*; **I couldn't keep him from doing it/going there** ich konnte ihn nicht daran hindern *or* davon abhalten, das zu tun/dort hinzugehen; **to keep sb from falling** jdn am Fallen hindern; **to keep oneself from doing sth** sich (davor) hüten, etw zu tun; **shyness keeps him from making new friends** er ist zu schüchtern, um neue Freunde zu gewinnen; **what can we do to keep it from happening again?** was können wir tun, damit es nicht noch einmal passiert?; **the bells keep me from sleeping** die Glocken lassen mich nicht schlafen; **keep them from getting wet** verhindern Sie es, dass sie nass werden; **this will keep the water from freezing** das verhindert, dass das Wasser gefriert; **you shouldn't keep them from their work** Sie sollten sie nicht von der Arbeit abhalten

b *(= protect)* **to keep sb from sth** jdn vor etw *(dat)* bewahren; **to keep sb from harm** jdn vor Schaden *(dat)* bewahren

c *(= withhold)* **to keep sth from sb** jdm etw verschweigen; *piece of news also* jdm etw vorenthalten; **can you keep this from your mother?** können Sie das vor Ihrer Mutter geheim halten *or* verbergen?

VI *+prep obj* **to keep from doing sth** etw nicht tun; *(= avoid doing also)* es vermeiden, etw zu tun; **she bit her lip to keep from crying** sie biss sich *(dat)* auf die Lippe, um nicht zu weinen; **she couldn't keep from laughing** sie musste einfach lachen

▶ **keep in** VT *sep* **a** *schoolboy* nachsitzen lassen; **I've been kept in!** ich musste nachsitzen!; **his parents have kept him in** seine Eltern haben ihn nicht weggelassen *or* gehen lassen **b** *feelings* zügeln **c** *stomach* einziehen VI *(= stay indoors)* drinnen bleiben

▶ **keep in with** VI *+prep obj* sich gut stellen mit; **he's just trying to keep in with her** er will sich nur bei ihr lieb Kind machen

▶ **keep off** VI *(person)* wegbleiben; **if the rain keeps off** wenn es nicht regnet; **"keep off!"** „Betreten verboten!"

VT *sep* **a** *dog, person* fernhalten *(prep obj* von); *one's hands* wegnehmen, weglassen *(prep obj* von); **to keep one's mind off sth** nicht an etw *(acc)* denken; **keep him off me** halten Sie ihn mir vom Leib; **keep your hands off** Hände weg!; **keep the dog off the couch** lassen Sie den Hund nicht aufs Sofa; **to keep sb off drugs** jdn von Drogen fernhalten; **to keep sb off the streets** *(fig)* jdn davon abhalten, auf der Straße zu landen

b *jacket etc* ausbehalten; *hat* abbehalten

VI *+prep obj* vermeiden; **"keep off the grass"** „Betreten des Rasens verboten"; **keep off the whisky** lassen Sie das Whiskytrinken

▶ **keep on** VI **a** *(= continue)* weitermachen, nicht aufhören; **to keep on doing sth** etw weiter tun; *(repeatedly)* etw immer wieder tun; *(incessantly)* etw dauernd tun; **he keeps on swearing** er flucht dauernd; **keep on talking!** reden Sie weiter!; **if you keep on like this** wenn du so weitermachst; **keep on trying** versuchen Sie es weiter; **I keep on telling you** ich sage dir ja immer; **the rain kept on all night** es regnete die ganze Nacht durch; **he kept on crying the whole night** er hat die ganze Nacht unaufhörlich geweint

b *(= keep going)* weitergehen/-fahren; **keep on past the church** fahren Sie immer weiter an der Kirche vorbei; **keep straight on** immer geradeaus

c **to keep on at sb** *(inf)* dauernd an jdm herummeckern *(inf)*; **they kept on at him until he agreed** sie haben ihm so lange keine Ruhe gelassen, bis er zustimmte
d **to keep on about sth** *(inf)* unaufhörlich von etw reden; **there's no need to keep on about it** *(inf)* es ist wirklich nicht nötig, ewig darauf herumzuhacken *(inf)*; **don't keep on so!** *(inf)* hören Sie doch endlich auf damit!
VT *sep* **a** *servant, employee* weiterbeschäftigen, behalten
b *coat etc* anbehalten; *hat* aufbehalten

▶ **keep out** VI *(of room, building)* draußen bleiben; *(of property, land, area)* etw nicht betreten; **keep out of my room!** geh/komm nicht in mein Zimmer; **"keep out"** „Zutritt verboten"; **to keep out of the rain/sun** nicht in den Regen/die Sonne gehen; **to keep out of sight** sich nicht zeigen; *(hiding)* in Deckung bleiben; **to keep out of danger** Gefahr meiden; **to keep out of debt** keine Schulden machen; **that child can't keep out of trouble** das Kind kommt immer in Schwierigkeiten; **to keep out of sb's affairs** sich nicht in jds Angelegenheiten einmischen, sich aus jds Angelegenheiten heraushalten; **you keep out of this!** halten Sie sich da *or* hier raus!
VT *sep* **a** *person* nicht hereinlassen (*of* in *+acc*); *light, cold, rain, enemy etc* abhalten; **this screen keeps the sun out of your eyes** diese Blende schützt Ihre Augen vor Sonne; **how can I keep the rabbits out/out of my garden?** was kann ich tun, dass die Kaninchen nicht hereinkommen/nicht in meinen Garten kommen?
b **to keep sb out of danger/harm's way** jdn vor Gefahr/Gefahren schützen; **I wanted to keep him out of this** ich wollte nicht, dass er da mit hereingezogen wurde; **to keep sb's name out of the papers** jds Namen nicht in der Zeitung erwähnen; **keep him out of my way** halte ihn mir vom Leib; **they kept him out of their plans** sie haben ihn von ihren Plänen ausgeschlossen

▶ **keep to** VI *+prep obj* **a** **to keep to one's promise** sein Versprechen halten, zu seinem Wort stehen; **to keep to one's bed/one's room** im Bett/in seinem Zimmer bleiben; **keep to the main road** bleiben Sie auf der Hauptstraße; **to keep to the schedule/plan** den Zeitplan einhalten, sich an den Zeitplan/Plan halten; **to keep to the speed limit** sich an die Geschwindigkeitsbegrenzung halten; **to keep to the subject/point** bei der Sache *or* beim Thema bleiben; **to keep to the script** sich an den Text halten, am Text bleiben
b **to keep (oneself) to oneself** nicht sehr gesellig sein, ein Einzelgänger sein; **they keep (themselves) to themselves** *(as a group)* sie bleiben unter sich
VT *+prep obj* **to keep sb to his word/promise** jdn beim Wort nehmen; **to keep sth to a minimum** etw auf ein Minimum beschränken; **to keep sth to oneself** etw für sich behalten; **keep it to yourself** behalten Sie das für sich; **keep your hands to yourself!** nehmen Sie Ihre Hände weg!

▶ **keep together** VI *(= stay together)* zusammenbleiben; *(as friends, community etc)* zusammenhalten; *(singers, oarsmen etc)* im Einklang *or* Takt sein VT *sep* zusammen aufbewahren; *(= fix together, unite) things, people* zusammenhalten; *(conductor) orchestra* im Takt halten

▶ **keep under** VT *sep people, race* unterdrücken; *subordinates* streng behandeln, an der Kandare haben; *(= keep under anaesthetic)* unter Narkose halten VI *(under water etc)* unter Wasser bleiben

▶ **keep up** VI **a** *(tent, pole)* stehen bleiben
b *(rain)* (an)dauern; *(weather, hurricane etc)* anhalten; *(prices, output, standard)* gleich hoch bleiben; *(morale, strength, determination)* nicht nachlassen
c **to keep up (with sb/sth)** *(in race, work, with prices)* (mit jdm/etw) Schritt halten, (mit jdm/etw) mithalten können *(inf)*; *(in comprehension)* (jdm/einer Sache) folgen können; **they bought it just to keep up with the Joneses** sie kauften es nur, um den Nachbarn nicht nachzustehen; **to keep up with the times** mit der Zeit gehen; **to keep up with the news** sich auf dem Laufenden halten; **I haven't kept up with my French** ich bin mit meinem Französisch ganz aus der Übung gekommen
d *(= stay in touch)* **to keep up with sb** mit jdm in Kontakt bleiben; **we haven't kept up at all since she went abroad** wir haben nichts mehr voneinander gehört, seit sie im Ausland ist
VT *sep* **a** *pole, tent* aufrecht halten; **the life belt kept him up** der Rettungsring hielt ihn über Wasser; **to keep his trousers up** damit die Hose nicht herunterrutscht
b *(= not stop)* nicht aufhören mit; *study etc* fortsetzen, weitermachen; *quality, prices, output, friendship, tradition, custom* aufrechterhalten; *subscription* beibehalten; *payments etc* weiterbezahlen; *workrate, speed (= maintain)* halten; *(= endure)* durchhalten; **I try to keep up my Spanish** ich versuche, mit meinem Spanisch nicht aus der Übung zu kommen; **to keep up a correspondence** in Briefwechsel bleiben; **to keep one's morale up** den Mut nicht verlieren; **he kept their morale up** er hat ihnen Mut gemacht; **keep it up!** (machen Sie) weiter so!; **he couldn't keep it up** er hat schlappgemacht *(inf)*
c *(= maintain) house* unterhalten; *road* instand *or* in Stand halten
d *(= prevent from going to bed)* am Schlafengehen hindern; **that child kept me up all night** das Kind hat mich die ganze Nacht nicht schlafen lassen; **I was kept up pretty late last night** ich bin gestern Abend ziemlich spät ins Bett gekommen

keeper ['kiːpəʳ] N *(in asylum, zoo)* Wärter(in) *m(f)*, Pfleger(in) *m(f)*, Betreuer(in) *m(f)*; *(of museum)* Kustos *m*, Kustode *m*, Kustodin *f*; *(= guard)* Wächter(in) *m(f)*, Aufseher(in) *m(f)*, Aufpasser(in) *m(f)*; *(Brit inf: = goalkeeper)* Torhüter(in) *m(f)*; **I'm not my brother's ~** ich bin nicht der Hüter meines Bruders

keep fit N Fitnessübungen *pl*

keeping ['kiːpɪŋ] N **a** *(= care)* **to put sth in sb's ~** jdm etw zur Aufbewahrung übergeben → **safe keeping** **b** *(of rule)* Beachten *nt*, Einhalten *nt* **c** **in ~ with** in Übereinstimmung *or* Einklang mit; **her behaviour was out of ~ with the dignity of the occasion** ihr Benehmen entsprach nicht der Feierlichkeit des Anlasses

keepsake ['kiːpseɪk] N Andenken *nt*

keg [keg] N **a** *(= barrel)* kleines Fass, Fässchen *nt* **b** *(also* **keg beer***)* Bier *nt* vom Fass

kegger ['kegəʳ] N *(US inf)* Bierparty *f*

keister ['kiːstəʳ] N *(US inf)* **a** *(= buttocks)* Hintern *m (inf)* **b** *(rare: = case)* Koffer *m*

keks [keks] PL *(Brit inf)* Hose *f*, Buxe *f (N Ger inf)*

kelly-green ['kelɪ'griːn] *(US)* ADJ leuchtend gelbgrün N leuchtendes Gelbgrün

kelp [kelp] N Seetang *m*

kempt ['kempt] ADJ *person, place* gepflegt; *hair* gekämmt

ken [ken] N **that is beyond my ~** das entzieht sich meiner Kenntnis VTI *(Scot)* = **know 1 2**

kennel ['kenl] N **a** Hundehütte *f* **b** **~s** *(= cage)* Hundezwinger *m*; *(for breeding)* Hundezucht *f*; *(boarding)* (Hunde)heim *nt*, Tierheim *nt*; **to put a dog in ~s** einen Hund in Pflege geben

Kenya ['kenjə] N Kenia *nt*

Kenyan ['kenjən] N Kenianer(in) *m(f)* ADJ kenianisch

kepi ['keɪpɪ] N Käppi *nt*

kept [kept] *pret, ptp of* **keep** ADJ **~ woman** Mätresse *f*; **she's a ~ woman** sie lässt sich aushalten

kerb [kɜːb] N *(Brit)* Bordkante *f*, Randstein *m*

kerb: **kerb crawler** N Freier *m* im Autostrich *(inf)*; **kerb crawling** N Autostrich *m*; **kerb crawling area** N Autostrich *m*; **kerb drill** N Verkehrserziehung *f*; **kerb market** N *(St Ex)* Freiverkehr *m*; **kerbside** N Straßenrand *m*; **kerbstone** N Bordstein *m*, Randstein *m*; **kerb weight** N *(of a car)* Leergewicht *nt*

kerchief ['kɜːtʃɪf] N *(old)* Hals- *or* Kopftuch *nt*

kerf [kɜːf] N Kerbe *f*, Einschnitt *m*

kerfuffle [kə'fʌfl] N *(Brit inf) (= noise)* Lärm *m*, Gedöns *nt (inf)*; *(= fight)* Balgerei *f (inf)*; *(= trouble)* Theater *nt (inf)*

kernel ['kɜːnl] N *(lit, fig)* Kern *m*

kerning ['kɜːnɪŋ] N *(Typ, Comput)* Unterschneidung *f*, Kerning *nt*; **automatic pair ~** automatischer Abstand

kerosene ['kerəsiːn] N Kerosin *nt*

kerosene lamp N Petroleum- *or* Paraffinlampe *f*

kestrel ['kestrəl] N Turmfalke *m*

ketch [ketʃ] N Ketsch *f*

ketchup ['ketʃəp] N Ket(s)chup *nt or m*

kettle ['ketl] N Kessel *m*; **I'll put the ~ on** ich stelle mal eben (Kaffee-/Tee)wasser auf; **the ~'s boiling** das Wasser kocht; **this is a different ~ of fish** *(Brit inf)* das ist doch was ganz anderes

kettledrum ['ketldrʌm] N (Kessel)pauke *f*

key [kiː] N **a** Schlüssel *m*
b *(fig: = solution)* Schlüssel *m*; **education is the ~ to success** Bildung ist der Schlüssel zum Erfolg; **the ~ to the mystery** der Schlüssel zum Geheimnis, des Rätsels Lösung; **this was the ~ to the murderer's identity** das gab Aufschluss darüber *or* das gab den Hinweis, wer der Mörder war
c *(= answers)* Lösungen *pl*, Schlüssel *m*; *(Sch)* Schlüssel *m*, Lehrerheft *nt*; *(Math etc)* Lösungsheft *nt*; *(for maps etc)* Zeichenerklärung *f*
d *(of piano, typewriter, Comput)* Taste *f*
e *(Mus)* Tonart *f*; **to sing off ~** falsch singen; **change of ~** Tonartwechsel *m*, Modulation *f*; **in the ~ of C** in C-Dur/c-Moll
f *(Build)* Untergrund *m*
ADJ *attr (= vital)* Schlüssel-, wichtigste(r, s); *witness* wichtigste(r, s); **~ area** Schlüsselbereich *m*; **~ factor** Schlüsselfaktor *m (in sth* bei etw); **education is a ~ issue** Bildung ist eines der entscheidenden Themen; **~ industry** Schlüsselindustrie *f*; **~ man** Schlüsselfigur *f*; **~ point** springender Punkt; **~ position** Schlüsselposition *or* -stellung *f*; **~ question** Schlüsselfrage *f*; **~ role** Schlüsselrolle *f*
VT **a** *speech etc (to or for one's audience)* (auf jdn) abstimmen *or* zuschneiden *(to, for* auf *+acc)*, anpassen *(to, for +dat)*
b *(Comput) (= input) text, data* eingeben; *(= hit) character, F7 etc* drücken
VI *(Comput)* Text/Daten eingeben

▶ **key in** VT *sep (Comput)* eingeben

▶ **key up** VT *sep* **a** **she was (all) keyed up about the interview** sie war wegen des Interviews ganz aufgedreht *(inf)*; **he was all keyed up for the big race** er hatte sich schon ganz auf das große Rennen eingestellt **b** *(Comput)* eingeben

keyboard ['kiːbɔːd] N *(of piano)* Klaviatur *f*, Tastatur *f*; *(of organ)* Manual *nt*; *(of typewriter, Comput)* Tastatur *f*; **~ skills** *(Comput)* Fertigkeiten *pl* in der Texterfassung; **a genius on the ~** *(Mus)* ein Klaviergenie *nt* VTI *(Typ, Comput)* eingeben

keyboarder ['kiːbɔːdəʳ] N *(Typ, Comput)* Texterfasser(in) *m(f)*; **what's she like as a ~?** wie ist sie bei der Texterfassung?

keyboarding [kiːbɔːdɪŋ] N *(Comput)* Texteingabe *f*; **~ skills** Fertigkeiten *pl* in der Texterfassung

keyboard instrument N *(Mus)* Tasteninstrument *nt*

keyboardist ['kiːbɔːdɪst] N *(Mus)* Keyboardspieler(in) *m(f)*, Keyboarder(in) *m(f)*

keyboard: **keyboard operator** N Texterfasser(in) *m(f)*; **keyboard shortcut** N Tastenkombination *f*; **keyboard template** N Tastaturschablone *f*

key: **key card** N Schlüsselkarte *f*; **key case** N Schlüsseletui *nt*; **key chord** N *(Mus)* Grunddreiklang *m*; **key currency** N *(Fin)* Leitwährung *f*

keyhole N Schlüsselloch *nt*

keyhole surgery N minimal invasive Chirurgie, Schlüssellochchirurgie *f*

keying ['kiːɪŋ] N *(Comput)* Texteingabe *f*

key interest rate N *(Fin)* Leitzins *m*

keyless ['kiːlɪs] ADJ ~ **access** Zugang *m* ohne Schlüssel

key: **key money** N Provision *f*, Schlüsselgeld *nt*; **keynote** N *(Mus)* Grundton *m*; *(of a speech)* Leitgedanke *m*, Tenor *m* ADJ ATTR ~ **speech** *(Pol etc)* programmatische Rede; **keynoter** ['kiːnəʊtə'] N *(Pol) jd, der eine programmatische Rede hält*; **keypad** N *(Comput)* Tastenfeld *nt*; **keyring** N Schlüsselring *m*; **key signature** N *(Mus)* Tonartbezeichnung *f*; **keystone** N *(Archit)* Schlussstein *m*; *(fig)* Grundpfeiler *m*; **keystroke** NAnschlag *m*; **keyword** N **a** *(= significant word)* Schlüsselwort *nt*; *(in index)* Stichwort *nt*, Schlagwort *nt* **b** *(= code)* Passwort *nt*, Kennwort *nt*

KFOR troops ['keɪfɔː,truːps] PL *(Mil)* KFOR--Truppen *pl*

KG *(Brit) abbr of* **Knight of the Garter**

kg *abbr of* **kilogramme(s), kilogram(s)** kg

KGB N KGB *m*

khaki ['kɑːkɪ] N Kaki *nt* ADJ kaki(braun *or* -farben)

Khmer Rouge [k'meə'ruːʒ] PL Rote Khmer *pl*

kHz *abbr of* **kilohertz** kHz

kibbutz [kɪ'bʊts] N *pl* **-im** [,kɪbʊt'siːm] Kibbuz *m*

kibitz ['kɪbɪts] VI *(US inf)* **a** *(Cards)* kibitzen *(inf)* **b** *(= chat)* plaudern, quatschen *(inf)*

kibosh ['kaɪbɒʃ] N *(inf)* **to put the ~ on sth** etw vermasseln *(inf)*

kick [kɪk] N **a** *(= act of kicking)* Tritt *m*, Stoß *m*, Kick *m (inf)*; **to take a ~ at sb/sth** nach jdm/etw treten; **to give sth a ~** einer Sache *(dat)* einen Tritt versetzen; **he gave the ball a tremendous ~** er trat mit Wucht gegen den Ball; **a tremendous ~ by Beckenbauer** ein toller Schuss von Beckenbauer; **to get a ~ on the leg** einen Tritt ans Bein bekommen, gegen das *or* ans Bein getreten werden; **what he needs is a good ~ up the backside** *or* **in the pants** *(inf)* er braucht mal einen kräftigen Tritt in den Hintern *(inf)*
b *(inf: = thrill)* **she gets a ~ out of it** es macht ihr einen Riesenspaß *(inf)*; *(physically)* sie verspürt einen Kitzel dabei; **to do sth for ~s** etw zum Spaß *or* Jux *(inf) or* Fez *(inf)* tun; **just for ~s** nur aus Jux und Tollerei *(inf)*; **how do you get your ~s?** was machen Sie zu ihrem Vergnügen?
c *no pl (inf: = power to stimulate)* Feuer *nt*, Pep *m (inf)*; **this drink hasn't much ~ in it** dieses Getränk ist ziemlich zahm *(inf)*; **he has plenty of ~ left in him** er hat immer noch viel Pep *(inf)*
d *(of gun)* Rückstoß *m*
VI *(person)* treten; *(= struggle)* um sich treten; *(baby, while sleeping)* strampeln; *(animal)* austreten, ausschlagen; *(dancer)* das Bein hochwerfen; *(gun)* zurückstoßen *or* -schlagen, Rückstoß haben; *(inf: engine)* stottern *(inf)*; **~ing and screaming** *(fig)* unter großem Protest; **he ~ed into third** *(inf)* er ging in den dritten (Gang)
VT **a** *(person, horse)* sb treten, einen Tritt versetzen *(+dat)*; *door* treten gegen; *football* kicken *(inf)*; *object* einen Tritt versetzen *(+dat)*, mit dem Fuß stoßen; **to ~ sb's backside** jdn in den Hintern treten; **to ~ sb in the head/stomach** jdm gegen den Kopf/in den Bauch treten; **to ~ sb in the teeth** *(fig)* jdn vor den Kopf stoßen *(inf)*; **to ~ a goal** ein Tor schießen; **to ~ one's legs in the air** die Beine in die Luft werfen; **to ~ the bucket** *(inf)* abkratzen *(inf)*, ins Gras beißen *(inf)*; **I could have ~ed myself** *(inf)* ich hätte mich ohrfeigen können, ich hätte mir in den Hintern beißen können *(inf)*
b *(inf: = stop)* **to ~ heroin** vom Heroin runterkommen *(inf)*; **to ~ the habit** es sich *(dat)* abgewöhnen

▶ **kick about** *(Brit) or* **around** VI *(inf)* () person rumhängen *(inf) (prep obj* in *+dat)*; *(thing)* rumliegen *(inf) (prep obj* in *+dat)* VT *sep* **to kick a ball about** *or* **around** (herum)bolzen *(inf)*, den Ball herumkicken *(inf)*; **you shouldn't let them kick you about** *or* **around** Sie sollten sich nicht so herumschubsen lassen; **don't kick that book about** *or* **around** werfen Sie das Buch nicht so herum; **to kick an idea about** *or* **around** *(inf)* eine Idee durchdiskutieren

▶ **kick against** VI *+prep obj* treten gegen

▶ **kick at** VI *+prep obj* treten nach

▶ **kick away** VT *sep* wegstoßen; *(= knock down)* niedertreten

▶ **kick back** VI **a** *(person)* zurücktreten; **if you annoy him he'll kick back** *(fig)* wenn Sie ihn ärgern, gibt er es Ihnen zurück **b** *(gun)* zurückstoßen, einen Rückstoß haben VT *sep blanket* wegstrampeln; *ball* zurückspielen *or* -schießen

▶ **kick down** VT SEP *door* eintreten

▶ **kick in** VT *sep door* eintreten; **to kick sb's teeth in** jdm die Zähne einschlagen VI *(= take effect) (system, fear)* ausgelöst werden; *(drug etc)* wirken

▶ **kick off** VI *(Ftbl)* anstoßen; *(player also)* den Anstoß ausführen; *(fig inf)* losgehen *(inf)*, beginnen; **who's going to kick off?** *(fig inf)* wer fängt an? VT *sep* wegtreten; *shoes* von sich schleudern; **they kicked him off the committee** *(inf)* sie warfen ihn aus dem Ausschuss

▶ **kick out** VI *(horse)* ausschlagen; *(person)* um sich treten; **to kick out at sb** nach jdm treten VT *sep* hinauswerfen (of aus); **he was kicked out of the club** er ist aus dem Verein hinausgeworfen worden *or* geflogen *(inf)*

▶ **kick over** VI *+prep obj* **to kick over the traces** über die Stränge schlagen

▶ **kick up** VT *sep* **a** *dust* aufwirbeln **b** *(fig inf)* **to kick up a row** *or* **a din** Krach machen *(inf)*; **to kick up a fuss** *or* **a stink** Krach schlagen *(inf)*; **to kick up one's heels** *(at a party etc)* einen draufmachen *(inf)*

kick: **kick-ass** ['kɪkæs] ADJ *attr (US inf)* Wahnsinns- *(inf)*, Super- *(inf)*, arschgeil *(sl)*; **kickback** N *(inf) (= reaction)* Auswirkung *f*; *(as bribe)* Provision *f*; *(= perk)* Nebeneinnahme *f*; **kickboxing** N Kickboxen *nt*; **kickdown** N Kick-down *m*

kicker ['kɪkə'] N *Spieler, der Strafstöße etc ausführt*, Strafstoßexperte *m*/-expertin *f*

kick: **kickoff** ['kɪkɒf] N **a** *(Sport)* Anpfiff *m*, Anstoß *m*; **the kick-off is at 3 o'clock** Anpfiff ist um 3 Uhr **b** *(inf: of ceremony etc)* Start *m*, Anfang *m*; **the kick-off is at 3 o'clock** um 3 gehts los *(inf)*; **for a kick-off** *(= to begin with)* erst mal, zunächst; **kickout** N **a** *(Ftbl)* Abschlag *m* **b** *(fig inf: = dismissal)* Rausschmiss *m*; **kick-start(er)** N Kickstarter *m*; **kickturn** N *(Ski)* Kehre *f*

kid [kɪd] N **a** *(= young goat)* Kitz *nt*, Zicklein *nt (liter)*
b *(= leather)* Ziegen- *or* Glacéleder *nt*
c *(inf: = child)* Kind *nt*; **when I was a ~** als ich klein war; **to get the ~s to bed** die Kleinen ins Bett bringen; **it's ~'s stuff** *(= for children)* das ist was für kleine Kinder *(inf)*; *(= easy)* das ist doch ein Kinderspiel; **to be like a ~ in a candy store** *(US)* sich wie ein verwöhntes Kind aufführen
d *(inf) (= man)* Junge *m*, Bursche *m (inf)*; *(= woman)* Kleine *f (inf)*; **listen ~, I didn't mean it** nun hör mir mal gut zu, ich habs doch nicht so gemeint; **listen ~, you keep out of this** hör mal Kleiner, du hältst dich hier raus *(inf)*; **come on ~s!** los Jungs! *(inf)*; **she's some ~** die ist nicht ohne *(inf)*; *(= clever)* die ist ganz schön clever *(inf)*; **he's done it already? some ~!** was, er hat das schon gemacht? tolle Leistung *(inf)*
ADJ *attr* **a** *(inf: = younger)* ~ **brother** kleiner Bruder, Brüderchen *nt*; ~ **sister** kleine Schwester, Schwesterchen *nt*
b *(= of goat leather) boots* aus Glacéleder
VT *(inf)* **to ~ sb (on)** *(= tease)* jdn aufziehen *(inf)*; *(= deceive)* jdm etw vormachen, jdn an der Nase rumführen *(inf)*; **you can't ~ me** mir kannst du doch nichts vormachen; **you're ~ding** *(Brit)*, **you're ~ding me** *(US)* du machst Witze, oder? *(inf)*; **don't ~ yourself!** machen Sie sich doch nichts vor!; **I ~ you not** das ist mein Ernst, ganz ehrlich *(inf)*; **who is she trying to ~?, who is she ~ding?** wem will sie was weismachen?
VI *(inf)* Jux machen *(inf)*; **no ~ding** im Ernst, ehrlich *(inf)*; **you've got to** *or* **you must be ~ding!** das ist doch wohl nicht dein Ernst!

▶ **kid on** VT *sep* = **kid** VT

kidder ['kɪdə'] N *(inf)* Spaßvogel *m*

kiddo ['kɪdəʊ] N *(inf)* = **kid** N **d**

kiddy ['kɪdɪ] N *(inf)* Kleinchen *nt (inf)*, Kindchen *nt (inf)*

kid gloves [kɪd'glʌvz] PL Glacéhandschuhe *pl*; **to handle** *or* **treat sb with ~** *(fig)* jdn mit Samthandschuhen *or* Glacéhandschuhen anfassen

kidnap ['kɪdnæp] VT entführen, kidnappen N Entführung *f*, Kidnapping *nt*

kidnapper ['kɪdnæpə'] N Entführer(in) *m(f)*, Kidnapper(in) *m(f)*

kidnapping ['kɪdnæpɪŋ] N Entführung *f*, Kidnapping *nt*

kidney ['kɪdnɪ] N **a** *(Anat, Cook)* Niere *f* **b** *(fig: = type, temperament)* **of the same ~** vom gleichen Schlag *or* Typ

kidney: **kidney bean** N rote Bohne, Kidneybohne *f*; **kidney dish** N Nierenschale *f*; **kidney failure** N *(Med)* Nierenversagen *nt*; **kidney machine** N künstliche Niere; **kidney-shaped** ADJ nierenförmig; **kidney stone** N *(Med)* Nierenstein *m*

kidology [kɪ'dɒlədʒɪ] N *(inf: = bluffing)* Bluff *m (inf)*

kill [kɪl] VT **a** *(lit)* töten, umbringen; *(by beating)* totschlagen, erschlagen; *(by shooting)* erschießen, totschießen; *(by stabbing)* erstechen, erdolchen; *animals* töten; *(Hunt)* erlegen; *(= slaughter)* schlachten; *(shock)* umbringen; *pain* beseitigen; *weeds* vernichten; **to be ~ed in action** fallen; **to be ~ed in battle/in the war** im Kampf/Krieg fallen; **too many people are ~ed on the roads** zu viele Menschen sterben auf der Straße *or* kommen auf der Straße um; **last year's drought ~ed thousands of animals** bei der letztjährigen Trockenheit kamen Tausende *or* tausende von Tieren um; **her brother was ~ed in a car accident** ihr Bruder ist bei einem Autounfall ums Leben gekommen; **how many were ~ed?** wie viel Todesopfer gab es?; **smoking will ~ you** das Rauchen wird Sie (noch) das Leben kosten; **the frost has ~ed my geraniums** meine Geranien sind erfroren; **she ~ed herself** sie brachte sich um, sie nahm sich *(dat)* das Leben; **he was ~ed with this weapon** dies ist die Mord- *or* Tatwaffe; **please, don't ~ me** bitte, lassen Sie mich leben; **he was ~ed by cancer** er starb an Krebs; **many people were ~ed by the plague** viele Menschen sind der Pest zum Opfer gefallen; **he was ~ed with poison gas** er wurde vergast; **she was ~ed with a knife** sie wurde (mit einem Messer) erstochen; **he was ~ed with an axe** er wurde mit einer Axt erschlagen; **he was ~ed by a stray bullet** er wurde von einer verirrten Kugel getötet; **each man ~s the thing he loves** jeder zerstört das, was er liebt; **I'll ~ him!** *(also fig)* den bring ich um *(inf)*; **the bullet ~ed him** die Kugel traf ihn tödlich, die Kugel tötete ihn
b *(fig) feelings, love etc* töten, zerstören; **to ~ time** die Zeit totschlagen; **we have two hours to ~** wir haben noch zwei Stunden übrig; **to ~ two birds with one stone** *(Prov)* zwei Fliegen mit einer Klappe schlagen *(Prov)*; **these stairs are ~ing me** *(inf)* diese Treppe bringt mich (noch mal) um *(inf)*; **she was ~ing herself (laughing)** *(inf)* sie hat sich totgelacht *or* kaputtgelacht *(inf)*; **this one'll ~ you** *(inf)* da lachst du

dich tot *(inf)*; **a few more weeks won't ~ you** *(inf)* noch ein paar Wochen bringen dich nicht um *(inf)*; **my feet are ~ing me** *(inf)* mir brennen die Füße; **I'll do it (even) if it ~s me** *(inf)* ich mache es, und wenn es mich umbringt *(inf)*; **they're not exactly ~ing themselves** *(inf: = overworking)* sie bringen sich nicht gerade um *(inf)*, sie reißen sich *(dat)* kein Bein aus; **don't ~ yourself** *(iro)* übernehmen Sie sich nicht; **to ~ sb with kindness** es allzu gut mit jdm meinen
c *(= spoil the effect of) taste, performance* verderben, überdecken; *hopes* vernichten, zunichtemachen; **this red ~s the other colours** dieses Rot übertönt *or* erschlägt die anderen Farben
d *(= defeat) parliamentary bill, proposal* zu Fall bringen; *project* zum Scheitern bringen
e *sound* schlucken; **to ~ a ball** eine Bombe schlagen *(inf)*; **~ that light!** *(inf)* Licht aus!
f *(Press etc) paragraph, story* streichen, abwürgen *(inf)*
g *(Tech) engine etc* abschalten, ausschalten; *(Elec) circuit* unterbrechen
h *(inf) bottle* leer machen, auf den Kopf stellen *(inf)*
VI töten; **cigarettes can ~** Zigaretten können tödlich sein *or* tödliche Folgen haben; **she was dressed to ~** sie hatte sich in Schale geworfen *(inf)*
N **a** *(Hunt)* Erlegen *nt*, Abschuss *m*; *(at bullfight)* Todesstoß *m*; **the wolves gathered round for the ~** die Wölfe kreisten die Beute ein, um sie zu erlegen; **the tiger has made a ~** der Tiger hat ein Opfer erlegt *or* geschlagen; **to be in at the ~** *(lit)* beim Abschuss dabei sein; *(fig)* den Schlussakt miterleben; **to move** *or* **close in for the ~** *(lit)* sich an die Beute anschleichen; *(fig)* zum entscheidenden Schlag ausholen
b *(Hunt etc: = animals killed)* Beute *f no pl*

▶**kill off** VT SEP **a** vernichten, töten; *whole race* ausrotten, vernichten; *cows, pigs, elephants* abschlachten; *infection* abtöten; *weeds* vertilgen; *character in TV series* sterben lassen **b** *(fig) hopes* zerstören; *speculation* ein Ende machen *(+dat)*; *jobs* streichen; *company* zugrunde *or* zu Grunde richten

killer [ˈkɪləʳ] **N** *(person)* Mörder(in) *m(f)*, Killer(in) *m(f) (inf)*; **this disease is a ~** diese Krankheit ist tödlich; **it's a ~** *(inf, race, job etc)* das ist der glatte Mord *(inf)* → **lady-killer, weedkiller** **ADJ** *attr (inf: = dangerous)* gefährlich; **a ~ shot** *(Ftbl etc)* ein Bomben- *or* Granatschuss *m (inf)*

killer: **killer bee** N Killerbiene *f*; **killer instinct** N **the ~** *(lit)* der Tötungsinstinkt; **a boxer with the ~** ein Boxer, in dem der Killer wach wird *(inf)*; **a successful businessman needs the ~** ein erfolgreicher Geschäftsmann muss über Leichen gehen können; **killer satellite** N Killersatellit *m*; **killer whale** N Schwertwal *m*, Mordwal *m*

killing [ˈkɪlɪŋ] **N** **a** *(of animals) (Hunt)* Erlegen *nt*; *(at abattoir)* (Ab)schlachten *nt* **b** *(of person)* Töten *nt*, Tötung *f*; **three more ~s in Belfast** drei weitere Morde *or* Todesopfer in Belfast **c** *(fig)* **to make a ~** einen Riesengewinn machen **ADJ** **a** *blow etc* tödlich **b** *(= exhausting) work* mörderisch *(inf)* **c** *(= funny)* urkomisch *(inf)*

killingly [ˈkɪlɪŋlɪ] ADV **~ funny** zum Totlachen *(inf)*

killjoy [ˈkɪldʒɔɪ] N Spielverderber(in) *m(f)*, Miesmacher(in) *m(f)*

kill-time **N** Zeitvertreib *m* **ADJ** als Zeitvertreib, zum Zeitvertreib

kiln [kɪln] N *(for baking, burning)* (Brenn)ofen *m*; *(for minerals)* Röst- *or* Kiesofen *m*; *(for drying bricks etc)* Trockenofen *m*; *(for hops etc)* Darre *f*, Darrofen *m*

kilo [ˈkiːləʊ] N Kilo *nt*

kilobyte [ˈkiːləʊbaɪt] N Kilobyte *nt*

kilocalorie [ˈkɪləʊˌkælərɪ] N Kilokalorie *f*

kilocycle [ˈkɪləʊˌsaɪkl] N Kilohertz *nt*

kilogramme, *(US)* **kilogram** [ˈkɪləʊgræm] N Kilogramm *nt*

kilohertz [ˈkɪləʊhɜːts] N Kilohertz *nt*

kilolitre, *(US)* **kiloliter** [ˈkɪləʊˌliːtəʳ] N Kiloliter *m*

kilometre, *(US)* **kilometer** [kɪˈlɒmɪtəʳ] N Kilometer *m*

kilovolt [ˈkɪləʊˌvəʊlt] N Kilovolt *nt*

kilowatt [ˈkɪləʊwɒt] N Kilowatt *nt*; **~-hour** Kilowattstunde *f*

kilt [kɪlt] N Kilt *m*, Schottenrock *m*

kimono [kɪˈməʊnəʊ] N Kimono *m*

kin [kɪn] **N** Familie *f*, Verwandte *pl*, Verwandtschaft *f*; **has he any ~?** hat er Verwandte *or* Familie? → **kith, next of kin** **ADJ** verwandt *(to* mit)

kind[1] [kaɪnd] N **a** *(= class, variety, nature)* Art *f*; *(of coffee, sugar, paint etc)* Sorte *f*; **they differ in ~** sie sind verschiedenartig; **several ~s of flour** mehrere Mehlsorten; **this ~ of book** diese Art Buch; **all ~s of ...** alle möglichen ...; **what ~ of ...?** was für ein(e) ...?; **what ~ of people does he think we are?** für wen hält er uns denn?; **the only one of its ~** das Einzige seiner Art; **a funny ~ of name** ein komischer Name; **he is not the ~ of man to refuse** er ist nicht der Typ, der Nein *or* nein sagt; **he's not that ~ of person** so ist er nicht; **I'm not that ~ of girl** so eine bin ich nicht; **they're two of a ~** die beiden sind vom gleichen Typ *or* von der gleichen Art; *(people)* sie sind vom gleichen Schlag; **she's one of a ~** sie ist wirklich einzigartig, jemanden wie sie gibt es nur einmal; **I know your ~** deinen Typ kenne ich; **your ~ never do any good** Leute Ihres Schlags *or* Leute wie Sie sind für nichts gut; **this ~ of thing** so etwas; **you know the ~ of thing I mean** Sie wissen, was ich meine; **... of all ~s** alle möglichen ...; **something of the ~** so etwas Ähnliches; **nothing of the ~** nichts dergleichen; **you'll do nothing of the ~** du wirst dich schwer hüten, du wirst das schön bleiben lassen!; **it was beef of a ~** *(pej)* es war Rindfleisch oder so was Ähnliches *(inf)*; **it's not my ~ of holiday** solche Ferien sind nicht mein Fall *(inf) or* nach meinem Geschmack; **she's my ~ of woman** sie ist mein Typ
b **a ~ of ...** eine Art ..., so ein(e) ...; **a ~ of box** so (etwas wie) eine Schachtel, eine Art Schachtel; **in a ~ of way I'm disappointed** *(inf)* ich bin irgendwie enttäuscht; **he was a ~ of worried-looking** *(inf)* er sah irgendwie bedrückt aus; **I ~ of thought that he ...** *(inf) (and he didn't)* ich habe eigentlich gedacht, dass er ...; *(and he did)* ich habe es mir beinahe gedacht, dass er ...; **are you nervous? – ~ of** *(inf)* bist du nervös? – ja, schon *(inf)*
c *(= goods, as opposed to money)* Naturalien *pl*, Ware *f*; **payment in ~** Bezahlung *f* in Naturalien; **I shall pay you back in ~** *(fig)* ich werde es Ihnen in gleicher Münze heimzahlen; **the police responded in ~** die Polizei reagierte, indem sie das Gleiche tat

kind[2] ✪ 4, 21.2 ADJ *(+er)* **a** *(= caring) person* liebenswürdig, nett, freundlich *(to* zu); *voice, smile, face* freundlich; **he's ~ to animals** er ist gut zu Tieren; **the ~est thing to do would be to shoot the wounded animal** das Humanste wäre, das verletzte Tier zu erschießen; **would you be ~ enough to open the door** wären Sie (vielleicht) so nett *or* freundlich *or* lieb, die Tür zu öffnen; **he was so ~ as to show me the way** er war so nett *or* freundlich *or* lieb und zeigte mir den Weg; **it was very ~ of you to help me** es war wirklich nett *or* lieb von Ihnen, mir zu helfen; **you're too ~!** *(also iro)* Sie sind zu liebenswürdig!
b *(= charitable) description, words* freundlich; *(= flattering) description, photograph, lighting* schmeichelhaft; **this dress is ~ to the figure** dieses Kleid schmeichelt der Figur *(dat)*
c *(= gentle)* **to be ~ to your hands/skin** sanft zu den Händen/zur Haut sein; **the years have been ~ to her** die Jahre sind fast spurlos an ihr vorübergegangen

kinda [ˈkaɪndə] ADV *(incorrect)* = **kind of**, → **kind**[1] **b**

kindergarten [ˈkɪndəˌgɑːtn] N Kindergarten *m*

kind-hearted [ˈkaɪndˈhɑːtɪd] ADJ gutherzig, gütig

kind-heartedness [ˈkaɪndˈhɑːtɪdnɪs] N Gutherzigkeit *f*, Güte *f*

kindle [ˈkɪndl] **VT** *fire* entfachen, anzünden, entzünden; *imagination* anregen; *interest* wecken; *enthusiasm* entfachen **VI** *(fire, wood etc)* brennen; *(passions, enthusiasm etc)* entbrennen, aufflammen

kindliness [ˈkaɪndlɪnɪs] N Freundlichkeit *f*, Güte *f*, Liebenswürdigkeit *f*

kindling [ˈkɪndlɪŋ] N *(= wood)* Anzündholz *nt*, Anmachholz *nt*

kindly [ˈkaɪndlɪ] **ADV** **a** *speak, act* freundlich, nett; *treat* liebenswürdig, freundlich; *(= generously) give, donate, offer* großzügig, freundlicherweise; *invite* freundlicherweise; **to look ~ (up)on sb** jdm gewogen sein; **to look ~ (up)on sth** etw positiv betrachten; **to think ~ of sb** nicht schlecht von jdm denken; **they ~ put me up for a night** sie nahmen mich freundlicherweise für eine Nacht auf
b *(with request)* bitte; **~ shut the door** machen Sie doch bitte die Tür zu; **will you ~ do it now** tun Sie das sofort, wenn ich bitten darf; **will you ~ shut up!** halten Sie doch endlich den Mund
c **I don't take ~ to his smoking** sein Rauchen ist mir gar nicht angenehm; **he won't take at all ~ to that** das wird ihm gar nicht gefallen; **I don't take ~ to not being asked** es ärgert mich, wenn ich nicht gefragt werde; **she didn't take ~ to the idea of going abroad** sie konnte sich gar nicht mit dem Gedanken anfreunden, ins Ausland zu gehen; **she didn't take it ~ when I said ...** sie hat es nicht gut aufgenommen, als ich sagte ...
ADJ *(+er) person* lieb, nett, freundlich; *face, eyes, smile* freundlich; *advice* gut gemeint, freundlich; *voice* sanft, gütig; **a ~ soul** ein guter Mensch

kindness [ˈkaɪndnɪs] N **a** *no pl* Freundlichkeit *f (towards* gegenüber), Liebenswürdigkeit *f (towards* gegenüber); *(= goodness of heart)* Güte *f (towards* gegenüber); **thank you very much for all your ~** vielen Dank, dass Sie so freundlich *or* liebenswürdig waren; **to treat sb with ~, to show sb ~** freundlich *or* liebenswürdig zu jdm sein; **out of the ~ of one's heart** aus reiner Nächstenliebe; **would you have the ~ to ...?** hätten Sie die Freundlichkeit *or* Güte, zu ...?
b *(= act of kindness)* Gefälligkeit *f*, Aufmerksamkeit *f*; **to do sb a ~** jdm eine Gefälligkeit erweisen; **it would be a ~ to tell him** man würde ihm einen Gefallen tun, wenn man es ihm sagen würde; **thank you for all your many ~es** vielen Dank für alles, was Sie für mich getan haben

kindred [ˈkɪndrɪd] **N** *no pl (= relatives)* Verwandtschaft *f* **ADJ** *(= related)* verwandt; **~ spirit** Gleichgesinnte(r) *mf*

kinesiology [ˌkiːniːsɪˈɒlədʒɪ] N *(Med)* Kinesiologie *f*

kinetic [kɪˈnetɪk] ADJ kinetisch

kinfolk [ˈkɪnfəʊk] N = **kinsfolk**

king [kɪŋ] N **a** *(lit)* König *m*; **the ~'s highway** *(old, form) eine öffentliche Straße*; **it must have cost a ~'s ransom** das muss eine stolze Summe *or* ein Vermögen gekostet haben; **to live like a ~** leben wie ein Fürst **b** *(fig)* König *m*; **an oil ~** ein Ölkönig *or* -magnat *m* **c** *(Chess, Cards)* König *m*; *(Draughts)* Dame *f*

king: **kingbolt** N *(US)* = **kingpin**; **king crab** N Königskrabbe *f*; **kingcup** N *(= buttercup)* Hahnenfuß *m*, Butterblume *f*; *(= marsh marigold)* Sumpfdotterblume *f*

kingdom [ˈkɪŋdəm] N **a** *(lit)* Königreich *nt* **b** *(Rel)* **~ of heaven** Himmelreich *nt*; **to blow sth to ~ come** *(inf)* etw in die Luft jagen *(inf)*; **you can go on doing that till ~ come** *(inf)* Sie können (so) bis in alle Ewigkeit weitermachen; **he's gone to ~ come** *(inf)* er hat das Zeitliche gesegnet *(hum inf)* **c** *(Zool, Bot)* Reich *nt*; **the animal/plant ~** das Tier-/Pflanzenreich, das Reich der Tiere/Pflanzen

kingfisher ['kɪŋfɪʃəʳ] N Eisvogel *m*

kingfisher-blue [ˌkɪŋfɪʃə'bluː] ADJ eisblau, gletscherblau

kinglet ['kɪŋlɪt] N **a** (*US: Orn*) Goldhähnchen *nt* **b** (*= king*) König *m* eines kleinen oder unbedeutenden Landes

kingly ['kɪŋlɪ] ADJ königlich, majestätisch

king: **kingmaker** N (*lit, fig*) Königsmacher(in) *m(f)*; **kingpin** N (*Tech*) Königsbolzen *m*, Drehzapfen *m*; (*Aut*) Achsschenkelbolzen *m*; (*fig: = person*) Stütze *f*; **he's the ~ of the whole organization** mit ihm steht und fällt die ganze Organisation; **king prawn** N Königskrabbe *f*; **King's Bench** N (*Jur*) *erste Kammer des Obersten Gerichts in Großbritannien*; **King's Counsel** N (*Jur*) Kronanwalt *m*/-anwältin *f* (*Staatsanwalt, der in höheren Strafsachen die Krone vertritt*); **King's English** N englische Hochsprache; **kingship** N Königtum *nt*; **King's highway** N (*Brit*) öffentliche Straße; **king-size(d)** ADJ (*inf*) in Großformat, großformatig; *cigarettes* King-size; *bed* extra groß; **I've got a ~ headache** (*hum*) ich hab vielleicht einen Brummschädel (*inf*) *or* einen dicken Kopf (*inf*); **king's messenger** N (*Diplomacy*) königlicher Gesandter; **King's speech** N Thronrede *f*

kink [kɪŋk] N **a** (*in rope etc*) Knick *m*, Schlaufe *f*; (*in hair*) Welle *f*; **to work out** *or* **iron out the ~s** (*fig*) die Sache geradebiegen (*inf*) **b** (*= mental peculiarity*) Schrulle *f*, Tick *m* (*inf*); (*sexual*) abartige Veranlagung VI (*rope*) Schlaufen bilden, sich verdrehen; (*hair*) sich wellen

kinky ['kɪŋkɪ] ADJ (+*er*) **a** *hair* wellig **b** (*inf*) *person, ideas, mind* verdreht (*inf*), schrullig, spleenig (*inf*); *boots, fashion* verrückt (*inf*); (*sexually*) abartig; *underwear, leather gear* sexy *inv*; **~!** nein, so was! (*inf*), lustig, lustig! (*inf*)

kinsfolk ['kɪnzfəʊk] N Verwandtschaft *f*, Verwandte(n) *pl*

kinship ['kɪnʃɪp] N Verwandtschaft *f*; **to feel ~ with sb** sich jdm verwandt fühlen

kinsman ['kɪnzmən] N *pl* **-men** [-mən] Verwandte(r) *m*

kinswoman ['kɪnzwʊmən] N *pl* **-women** [-wɪmɪn] Verwandte *f*

kiosk ['kiːɒsk] N **a** Kiosk *m*, Verkaufsstand *m*, Bude *f* **b** (*Brit Telec*) (Telefon)zelle *f*

kip [kɪp] (*Brit inf*) N (*= sleep*) Schläfchen *nt*; **I've got to get some ~** ich muss mal 'ne Runde pennen (*inf*); **I need a good ~** ich muss mal (wieder) richtig pennen (*inf*) *or* ratzen (*inf*); **I'm going for a ~** ich geh mal 'ne Runde pennen (*inf*) VI (*also* **kip down**) pennen (*inf*)

kipper ['kɪpəʳ] N Räucherhering *m*, Bückling *m*

kipper tie N breite Krawatte

kir [kɪəʳ] N Kir *m*

Kirghiz ['kɜːgɪz] N Kirgise *m*, Kirgisin *f* ADJ kirgisisch

Kirghizia [kɜː'gɪzɪə] N Kirgisien *nt*

Kirghizstan, Kirgizstan [ˌkɜːgɪz'stɑːn] N Kirgistan *nt*, Kirgisien *nt*

kirk [kɜːk] N (*Scot*) Kirche *f*; **the Kirk** *die Presbyterianische Kirche Schottlands*

kismet ['kɪzmɛt, 'kɪsmɛt] N Kismet *nt*, Schicksal *nt*

kiss [kɪs] N Kuss *m*; **~ of life** Mund-zu-Mund-Beatmung *f*; **that will be the ~ of death for them** das wird ihnen den Todesstoß versetzen VT küssen; (*fig: = touch gently*) sanft berühren; **to ~ sb's cheek** jdn auf die Wange küssen; **to ~ sb's hand** jdm die Hand küssen; *woman's hand* (*in greeting*) jdm einen Handkuss geben; **they ~ed each other** sie gaben sich einen Kuss, sie küssten sich; **to ~ sb back** jds Kuss (*acc*) erwidern, jdn wiederküssen; **to ~ sb good night/goodbye** jdm einen Gutenachtkuss/Abschiedskuss geben; **to ~ sth goodbye** (*fig inf*) sich (*dat*) etw abschminken (*inf*); **come here and I'll ~ it better** komm her, ich werde mal blasen, dann tuts nicht mehr weh VI küssen; (*= kiss each other*) sich küssen; **to ~ and make up** sich mit einem Kuss versöhnen; **to ~ and tell** *Informationen über eine Affäre an die Medien verkaufen*

▶ **kiss away** VT *sep* **she kissed away the child's tears** sie küsste dem Kind die Tränen fort

kissable ['kɪsəbl] ADJ *mouth* zum Küssen einladend *attr*; **a ~ girl** ein Mädchen, das man küssen möchte

KISSAGRAM

Mit einem **kissagram** will man jemanden zum Geburtstag oder zu einem anderen Anlass überraschen. Dabei taucht ein kostümierter Fremder bei der Feier überraschend auf, übermittelt einen lustigen Spruch und küsst dann den glücklich Beschenkten. Mittlerweile haben die **kissagram**-Dienste ihre Angebotspalette auch erweitert, so gibt es zum Beispiel **strippagrams**, bei denen der Überbringer für den Empfänger einen Strip hinlegt.

kiss-and-tell [ˌkɪsən'tel] ADJ **~ story** Enthüllungsstory *f* (*mit Details einer Affäre mit einer prominenten Person*)

kiss curl N Schmachtlocke *f*

kisser ['kɪsəʳ] N **a** **to be a good ~** gut küssen (können) **b** (*inf: = mouth, face*) Fresse *f* (*vulg*), Schnauze *f* (*inf*)

kissing: **kissing disease** ['kɪsɪŋdɪˌziːz] N Kusskrankheit *nt* (*inf*), Pfeiffersches Drüsenfieber; **kissing gate** ['kɪsɪŋˌgeɪt] N Schwinggatter *nt* (*an Weidenzäunen und Hecken, das nur je eine Person durchlässt*)

kiss-off ['kɪsɒf] N (*US inf*) **to give sb the ~** jdn in die Wüste schicken (*inf*); *boyfriend etc* jdm den Laufpass geben (*inf*)

kissogram ['kɪsəgræm] N *Glückwunsch, der von einer Agentur mit einem Kuss überbracht wird*

kissproof ['kɪspruːf] ADJ kussecht

kit [kɪt] N **a** (*= equipment*) (*for fishing, photography etc*) Ausrüstung *f*; (*Mil*) Ausrüstung *f*, Montur *f* (*old*); **~ inspection** (*Mil*) Bekleidungs- *or* Ausrüstungsappell *m* **b** (*Sport: clothes*) Ausrüstung *f*, Zeug *nt* (*inf*), Sachen *pl* (*inf*); **gym ~** Sportzeug *nt*, Sportsachen *pl*; **get your ~ off!** (*inf: = undress*) zieh dich aus! **c** (*= belongings, luggage etc*) Sachen *pl* → **caboodle** **d** (*= set of items*) (*tools*) Werkzeug *nt*; (*in box*) Werkzeugkasten *m*; (*= puncture repair kit*) Flickzeug *nt* **e** (*for self-assembly*) Bastelsatz *m* **f** (*Brit sl: = heroin*) H *nt* (*sl*), Sugar *m* (*sl*)

▶ **kit out** *or* **up** VT *sep* (*Brit*) ausrüsten (*esp Mil*), ausstatten; (*= clothe*) einkleiden; **he arrived kitted out in oilskins** er erschien in Ölzeug

kit: **kitbag** N Seesack *m*; **kit car** N *aus einem Bausatz zusammengebautes Kraftfahrzeug*

kitchen ['kɪtʃɪn] N Küche *f*

kitchenette [ˌkɪtʃɪ'net] N (*= separate room*) kleine Küche; (*= part of one room*) Kochnische *f*

kitchen: **kitchen foil** N Alufolie *f*; **kitchen garden** N Gemüsegarten *m*, Küchengarten *m*; **kitchen knife** N Küchenmesser *nt*; **kitchen-maid** N Küchenmagd *f*; **kitchen range** N Küchenherd *m*; **kitchen roll** N Küchenrolle *f*; **kitchen scales** PL Küchenwaage *f*, Haushaltswaage *f*; **kitchen scissors** PL Küchenschere *f*, Haushaltsschere *f*; **kitchen sink** N Spüle *f*, Ausguss *m*, Spülstein *m*; **I've packed everything but the ~** (*inf*) ich habe den ganzen Hausrat eingepackt; **kitchen-sink drama** N Alltagsdrama *nt*, Wohnküchendrama *nt*; **kitchen timer** N Kurzzeitwecker *m*; **kitchen unit** N Küchenschrank *m*; **kitchenware** N Küchengeräte *pl*

kite [kaɪt] N **a** (*Orn*) Milan *m* **b** (*= toy*) Drachen *m*; **to fly a ~** (*lit*) einen Drachen steigen lassen; (*fig*) einen Versuchsballon steigen lassen; **she's as high as a ~** (*inf*) (*= excited*) sie ist völlig aufgedreht (*inf*); (*= on drugs*) sie ist total high (*inf*) **c** (*Aviat sl*) Vogel *m* (*sl*)

kite flying N Steigenlassen *nt* eines Drachen; (*Econ*) Wechselstreiterei *f*

Kite mark N (*Brit*) *dreieckiges Gütezeichen*

kith [kɪθ] N **~ and kin** Blutsverwandte *pl*; **they came with ~ and kin** sie kamen mit Kind und Kegel

kitsch [kɪtʃ] N Kitsch *m*

kitschy ['kɪtʃɪ] ADJ (+*er*) kitschig

kitten ['kɪtn] N kleine Katze, Kätzchen *nt*; **to have ~s** (*fig inf*) Zustände kriegen (*inf*)

kittenish ['kɪtənɪʃ] ADJ verspielt; (*fig*) *woman* kokett

kittiwake ['kɪtɪweɪk] N Dreizehenmöwe *f*

kitty ['kɪtɪ] N **a** (*= shared money*) (gemeinsame) Kasse; (*Cards etc*) (Spiel)kasse *f*; **we'll have a ~ for the drinks** wir legen für die Getränke zusammen; **there's nothing left in the ~** die Kasse ist leer; **the total prize ~ is now £9 million** in der Gewinnkasse sind jetzt neun Millionen Pfund **b** (*inf: = cat*) Mieze *f*

kiwi ['kiːwiː] N **a** Kiwi *m* **b** (*also* **kiwi fruit**) Kiwi(frucht) *f* **c** (*inf: = New Zealander*) Neuseeländer(in) *m(f)*, Kiwi *m* (*inf*)

KKK *abbr of* **Ku Klux Klan**

Klansman ['klænzmən] N *pl* **-men** [-mən] (*US*) Mitglied *nt* des Ku-Klux-Klan

klaxon ['klæksn] N Horn *nt*, Hupe *f*

Kleenex® ['kliːneks] N Papiertaschentuch *nt*, ≈ Tempo(taschentuch)® *nt*

kleptomania [ˌkleptəʊ'meɪnɪə] N Kleptomanie *f*

kleptomaniac [ˌkleptəʊ'meɪnɪæk] N Kleptomane *m*, Kleptomanin *f* ADJ kleptomanisch

klieg light ['kliːglaɪt] N (*esp US*) *vor allem in Filmstudios verwendete Bogenlampe*

km *abbr of* **kilometre(s)** km

km/h, kmph *abbr of* **kilometres per hour** km/h

knack [næk] N Trick *m*, Kniff *m*; (*= talent*) Talent *nt*, Geschick *nt*; **there's a (special) ~ (to it)** da ist ein (gewisser) Trick *or* Kniff dabei; **there's a (special) ~ to opening it** da ist ein Trick *or* Kniff dabei, wie man das aufbekommt; **to get the ~ of doing sth** (es) herausbekommen, wie man etw macht; **you'll soon get the ~ of it** Sie werden den Dreh bald rausbekommen *or* raushaben; **I never really got the ~ of it** ich habe den Trick nie richtig herausbekommen; **I've lost the ~** ich bekomme *or* kriege (*inf*) das nicht mehr hin *or* fertig; **she's got a ~ of saying the wrong thing** sie hat ein Geschick *or* Talent, immer das Falsche zu sagen

knacker ['nækəʳ] N (*Brit inf, of horses*) Abdecker(in) *m(f)*, Schinder(in) *m(f)*; (*of boats, houses*) Abbruchunternehmer(in) *m(f)*; **to send a horse to the ~'s (yard)** ein Pferd zum Abdecker *or* auf den Schindanger (*old*) bringen

knackered ['nækəd] ADJ (*Brit inf*) (*= exhausted*) geschafft (*inf*); (*= broken*) kaputt (*inf*)

knapsack ['næpsæk] N Proviantbeutel *m*, Tornister *m* (*esp Mil*), Knappsack *m* (*old*)

knave [neɪv] N **a** (*old*) Bube *m* (*old*), Schurke *m* **b** (*Brit Cards*) Bube *m*, Unter *m* (*old*)

knavery ['neɪvərɪ] N (*old*) Bubenstück *nt* (*old*), Büberei *f* (*old*)

knavish ['neɪvɪʃ] ADJ (*Brit old*) bübisch (*old*), schurkisch

knead [niːd] VT *dough* kneten; (*= massage*) *muscles* massieren, durchkneten (*inf*)

knee [niː] N Knie *nt*; **to be on one's ~s** (*lit, fig*) auf den Knien liegen; **on one's ~s, on bended ~(s)** (*liter, hum*) kniefällig; **to go (down) on one's ~s** (*lit*) niederknien, (sich) hinknien; (*fig*) sich auf die Knie werfen; **to go down on one's ~s to sb** (*lit, fig*) sich vor jdm auf die Knie werfen, vor jdm einen Kniefall machen; **to bow** *or* **bend the ~ (to sb)** (vor jdm) die Knie beugen; **to bring sb to his/her** *etc* **~s** (*lit, fig*) jdn in die Knie zwingen; **to bring a country/a government to its ~s** ein Land/eine Regierung in die Knie zwingen; **he sank in up to the** *or* **his ~s** er sank knietief *or* bis zu den Knien ein; **I'll put you over my ~ in a minute** ich lege dich gleich übers Knie
VT mit dem Knie stoßen; **to ~ sb in the groin**

jdm das Knie zwischen die Beine stoßen; **he ~d his opponent in the chest** er hat seinem Gegner mit dem Knie eins gegen den Brustkasten gegeben *(inf)*

knee: **knee bend** N Kniebeuge *f*; **to do a ~** eine Kniebeuge machen; **knee breeches** PL Kniehose *f*, Bundhose *f*; **kneecap** N Kniescheibe *f* VT die Kniescheibe(n) durchschießen *(+dat)*; **knee-deep** ADJ knietief; **the water was ~** das Wasser ging mir *etc* bis zum Knie *or* war knietief; **he was ~ in mud** er steckte knietief im Schlamm; **knee-high** ADJ kniehoch, in Kniehöhe; **knee jerk** N *(Med)* Kniesehnenreflex *m*; **kneejerk reaction** N Kurzschlussreaktion *f*; **knee joint** N *(Med, Tech)* Kniegelenk *nt*

kneel [ni:l] *pret, ptp* **knelt** *or* **kneeled** VI *(before* vor *+dat)* knien; *(also* **kneel down**) niederknien, (sich) hinknien

knee-length ['ni:leŋθ] ADJ *skirt* knielang; *boots* kniehoch; **~ socks** Kniestrümpfe *pl*

kneeler ['ni:ləʳ] N Kniepolster *nt*; *(= stool)* Kniebank *f*

knee: **kneepad** N Knieschützer *m*, Knieleder *nt*; **knee reflex** N Kniesehnenreflex *m*; **knee shot** N *(TV, Film)* Halbtotale *f*; **knee-slapper** N *(inf)* Witz *m* zum Totlachen *(inf)*

knees-up ['ni:zʌp] N *(Brit inf: = dance)* Tanz *m*; *(= party)* Fete *f*, Party *f*

knell [nel] N Geläut *nt*, (Toten)glocke *f*; **to sound the ~** die (Toten)glocke läuten; **to sound the (death) ~ for sb/sth** *(fig)* jdm/etw den Todesstoß geben *or* versetzen

knelt [nelt] *pret, ptp of* **kneel**

Knesset ['knesɪt] N **the ~** die Knesset

knew [nju:] *pret of* **know**

knickerbocker glory [,nɪkəbɒkə'glɔ:rɪ] N *(Brit)* *Eisbecher mit Gelee, Sahne und Obst*

knickerbockers ['nɪkəbɒkəz] PL Knickerbocker *pl*

knickers ['nɪkəz] PL **a** *(Brit)* Schlüpfer *m*; **to get one's ~ in a twist (over sth)** *(inf)* sich *(dat)* (wegen etw) ins Hemd machen *(sl)*; **don't get your ~ in a twist!** *(inf)* dreh nicht gleich durch! *(inf)*; **~ to you!** *(inf: = rubbish)* Quatsch! *(inf)* **b** *(old)* = **knickerbockers**

knick-knack ['nɪknæk] N nette Kleinigkeit, Kinkerlitzchen *nt*; **~s** Krimskrams *m*; *(= figurines)* Nippes *pl*, Nippsachen *pl*

knife [naɪf] N *pl* **knives** Messer *nt*; **~, fork and spoon** Besteck *nt*; **like a (hot) ~ through butter** *(fig)* völlig mühelos; **to be under the ~** *(Med inf)* unterm Messer sein *(inf)*; **to go under the ~** *(Med inf)* unters Messer kommen *(inf)*; **to turn** *or* **twist the ~ (in the wound)** *(fig)* Salz in die Wunde streuen; **to put** *or* **stick the ~ in** *(inf)* böse zuschlagen *(inf)*; **the knives are out for him** *(esp Brit inf)* für ihn wird schon das Messer gewetzt; **before you could say ~** *(inf)* eh man sichs versah, im Nu; **it's war to the ~ between them** sie bekämpfen sich bis aufs Messer; **you could have cut the atmosphere with a ~** die Stimmung war zum Zerreißen gespannt; **he's not the sharpest ~ in the drawer** *(esp US inf)* er ist nicht gerade der Hellste*(inf)*
VT einstechen auf *(+acc)*; *(fatally)* erstechen, erdolchen

knife: **knife blade** N Messerklinge *f*; **knife box** N Besteckkasten *m*; **knife edge** N *(lit)* (Messer)schneide *f*; **to be balanced on a ~** *(fig)* auf Messers Schneide stehen; **knife grinder** N *(= person)* Scherenschleifer(in) *m(f)*; *(= thing)* Schleifrad *nt or* -stein *m*; **knifeman** N *(Brit)* Messerstecher *m*; **knife pleat** N einfache Falte; **knife-point** N **to hold sb at ~** jdn mit einem Messer bedrohen; **to force sb to do sth at ~** jdn mit vorgehaltenem Messer zwingen, etw zu tun

knifer ['naɪfəʳ] N Messerstecher *m*

knife: **kniferest** N Messerbänkchen *nt*; **knife sharpener** N Messerschärfer *m*

knifing ['naɪfɪŋ] N Messerstecherei *f*

knight [naɪt] N *(= title, Hist)* Ritter *m*; *(Chess)* Springer *m*, Pferd(chen) *nt*, Rössel *nt*; **Knight of the Garter** Träger(in) *m(f)* des Hosenbandordens; **~ of the road** *(Brit hum)* Kapitän *m* der Landstraße *(hum)*; **a ~ in shining armour** *(fig)* ein Märchenprinz *m* VT adeln, zum Ritter schlagen

knight: **knight errant** N *pl* **knights errant** fahrender Ritter; **knight errantry** [naɪt'erəntrɪ] N fahrendes Rittertum; *(fig)* Ritterlichkeit *f*

knighthood ['naɪthʊd] N **a** *(= knights collectively)* Ritterschaft *f* **b** *(= rank)* Ritterstand *m*; **to receive a ~** in den Adelsstand erhoben werden; **he's hoping for a ~** er hofft, in den Adelsstand erhoben zu werden

knightly ['naɪtlɪ] ADJ *(+er)* ritterlich

knit [nɪt] *pret, ptp* **knitted** *or* **knit** VT **a** *blanket, scarf etc* stricken; **to ~ sth for sb, to ~ sb sth** jdm etw stricken; **the wool is then ~ted into ...** aus der Wolle wird dann ... gestrickt; **~ three, purl two** drei rechts, zwei links **b to ~ one's brows** die Stirn runzeln VI **a** *(person)* stricken **b** *(bones: also* **knit together, knit up**) verwachsen, zusammenwachsen

▶ **knit together** VT *sep* **a** *stitches* zusammenstricken **b** *(= unite) threads of story* (miteinander) verknüpfen; *people* eng verbinden VI **a** = **knit VI b b** *(= unite)* miteinander verwachsen; **they knit well together** sie harmonieren gut; *(through experience)* sie sind gut aufeinander eingespielt

▶ **knit up** VI **a** *(wool)* sich stricken **b** = **knit VI b** VT *sep jersey* stricken

knitted ['nɪtɪd] ADJ gestrickt; *cardigan, dress etc* Strick-; **~ goods** Strickwaren *or* -sachen *pl*

knitter ['nɪtəʳ] N Stricker(in) *m(f)*

knitting ['nɪtɪŋ] N **a** Stricken *nt*; *(= material being knitted)* Strickzeug *nt*, Strickarbeit *f*; *(= knitted goods)* Gestrickte(s) *nt*, Stricksachen *pl*; **she was doing her ~** sie strickte **b** *(of bones etc)* Verwachsen *nt*, Zusammenwachsen *nt*

knitting: **knitting machine** N Strickmaschine *f*; **knitting needle** N Stricknadel *f*; **knitting wool** N (Strick)wolle *f*, Strickgarn *nt*

knitwear ['nɪtweəʳ] N Strickwaren *pl*, Strick- *or* Wollsachen *pl*

knives [naɪvz] *pl of* **knife**

knob [nɒb] N **a** *(on walking stick)* Knauf *m*; *(on door)* Griff *m*, Knauf *m*; *(on instrument etc)* Knopf *m*; **and the same to you with (brass) ~s on** *(Brit inf)* das beruht auf Gegenseitigkeit **b** *(= swelling)* Beule *f*, Knubbel *m (inf)*; *(on tree)* Knoten *m*, Auswuchs *m* **c** *(= small piece)* Stückchen *nt*; **a ~ of butter** ein Stich *m* Butter **d** *(sl: = penis)* Prügel *m (sl)*, Lanze *f (sl)*

knobbly ['nɒblɪ] ADJ *(+er) wood* knorrig, verwachsen; *surface* uneben, höckrig, knubbelig *(inf)*; **~ knees** Knubbelknie *pl (inf)*

knobby ['nɒbɪ] ADJ *(+er) wood, trunk* knorrig

knock [nɒk] N **a** *(esp Brit) (= blow)* Stoß *m*; *(esp with hand, tool etc)* Schlag *m*; **to get a ~** einen Stoß/Schlag abbekommen; **I got a ~ on the head** *(= was hit)* ich habe einen Schlag auf den Kopf bekommen; *(= hit myself)* ich habe mir den Kopf angeschlagen *or* angestoßen; **he got a ~ from the swing** die Schaukel hat ihn getroffen; **he took a bit of a ~** er hat einiges abbekommen *(inf)*; **the car took a few ~s** mit dem Auto hat es ein paar Mal gebumst *(inf)*; **the furniture has had a few ~s** die Möbel haben ein paar Schrammen abbekommen; **he gave himself a nasty ~** er hat sich böse angeschlagen *or* angestoßen
b *(= noise)* Klopfen *nt no pl*, Pochen *nt no pl (liter)*; *(in engine)* Klopfen *nt no pl*, Klopfgeräusch *nt*; **there was a ~ at the door** es hat (an der Tür) geklopft; **I heard a ~** ich habe es klopfen hören; **I'll give you a ~ at 7 o'clock** *(Brit)* ich klopfe um 7 Uhr (an deine Tür)
c *(esp Brit) (fig: = setback)* (Tief)schlag *m*; **~s** *(inf: = criticism)* Kritik *f*; **to (have to) take a lot of ~s** viele Tiefschläge einstecken (müssen); *(= be criticized)* unter starken Beschuss kommen; **to take a ~** *(self-confidence, pride etc)* erschüttert werden; *(reputation)* geschädigt werden; *(person)* einen Tiefschlag erleben; **the company took a bit of a ~ as a result of the tax changes** die Steuerreform hat der Firma einen Schlag versetzt
VT **a** *(= hit, strike)* stoßen; *(with hand, tool, racket etc)* schlagen; *one's knee, head etc* anschlagen, anstoßen (*on* an *+dat*); *(= nudge, jolt)* stoßen gegen; *(= collide with: car, driver)* rammen; **to ~ one's head/elbow** *etc* sich *(dat)* den Kopf/Ellbogen *etc* anschlagen *or* anstoßen; **he ~ed his foot against the table** er stieß mit dem Fuß gegen den Tisch; **to ~ sb on the head** jdn an *or* auf den Kopf schlagen; **that ~ed his idea on the head** *(Brit inf)* damit konnte er sich die Idee aus dem Kopf schlagen *(inf)*; **I decided to ~ it on the head** *(Brit inf)* ich beschloss, der Sache *(dat)* ein Ende zu machen; **the plan wasn't working so we ~ed it on the head** *(Brit inf)* der Plan klappte nicht, also ließen wir ihn fallen; **to ~ sb to the ground** jdn zu Boden werfen; **to ~ sb unconscious** jdn bewusstlos werden lassen; *(person)* jdn bewusstlos schlagen; **to ~ sb dead** *(fig inf)* jdn umhauen *(inf)*; **go out there and ~ 'em dead** *(inf)* jetzt zeigs denen aber mal! *(inf)*; **he ~ed some holes in the side of the box** er machte ein paar Löcher in die Seite der Kiste; **we ~ed the two rooms into one** wir verbanden die beiden Zimmer indem wir die Verbindungswand abrissen; **to ~ holes in an argument** ein Argument zerpflücken; **to ~ sb/sth out of the way** jdn/etw beiseitestoßen; **he ~ed it as he went past** er ist beim Vorbeigehen dagegengestoßen; *(deliberately)* er hat ihm/ihr *etc* beim Vorbeigehen einen Stoß versetzt *or* gegeben; **she ~ed the glass to the ground** sie stieß gegen das Glas und es fiel zu Boden; **watch you don't ~ your glass off the table** pass auf, dass du dein Glas nicht vom Tisch stößt; **to ~ the nonsense out of sb** jdm den Unsinn austreiben; **to ~ some sense into sb** jdn zur Vernunft bringen; **to ~ sb's confidence** jds Selbstbewusstsein erschüttern; **he was ~ed sideways by it** *(fig inf)* es haute ihn um *(inf)*; **confidence in the legal system has been ~ed sideways** *(inf)* das Vertrauen in das Rechtssystem hat schwer gelitten
b *(inf: = criticize)* (he)runtermachen *(inf)*; **if you haven't tried it, don't ~ it** verurteile es doch nicht, wenn du es noch nie versucht hast
VI **a** *(on door etc)* klopfen, pochen *(liter)*; *(engine etc)* klopfen; **to ~ at** *or* **on the door** an die Tür klopfen, anklopfen; **opportunity was** *or* **came ~ing at his door** ihm bot sich eine Gelegenheit; **he is ~ing on the door of the England team** er wird als Anwärter für die englische Nationalmannschaft gehandelt; **to ~ at** *or* **on the window** gegen das Fenster klopfen; **~ before entering** bitte anklopfen; **he ~ed on the table** er schlug *or* klopfte auf den Tisch
b *(= bump, collide)* stoßen (*into, against* gegen); **he ~ed into** *or* **against the gatepost** er rammte den Türpfosten
c his knees were ~ing (together) ihm zitterten *or* schlotterten *(inf)* die Knie
INTERJ **~ ~!** klopf, klopf

▶ **knock about** *(Brit) or* **around** VI *(inf)* **a** *(person)* herumziehen *(prep obj* in *+dat)*; **to knock around the house** im Haus rumgammeln *(inf)*; **he has knocked about** *or* **around a bit** er ist schon (ganz schön) (he)rumgekommen *(inf)*; **who's he knocking about** *or* **around with these days?** mit wem hängt er denn jetzt so herum? *(inf)*
b *(object)* herumliegen *(prep obj* in *+dat)*; *(boxes etc)* herumstehen
VT *sep* **a** *(= ill-treat)* verprügeln, schlagen; **he was badly knocked about in the accident** er ist bei dem Unfall ziemlich zugerichtet worden; **he knocks her about** *or* **around** er (ver)prügelt sie ständig
b *(= damage)* ramponieren *(inf)*, beschädigen
c to knock a ball about *or* **around** ein paar Bälle schlagen

▶ **knock back** VT *sep (inf)* **a he knocked back his whisky** er kippte sich *(dat)* den Whisky hinter die Binde *(inf)*; **come on, knock it**

back nun trink schon (aus) *(inf)* **b** *(= cost)* **this watch knocked me back £20** ich habe für die Uhr £ 20 hingelegt, die Uhr hat mich £ 20 gekostet; **what did they knock you back for it?** was mussten Sie dafür hinlegen *or* blechen? *(inf)* **c** *(= shock)* schocken, erschüttern **d** *(= reject)* zurückweisen

▶ **knock down** VT *sep* **a** *person, thing* umwerfen, zu Boden werfen; *opponent (by hitting)* niederschlagen; *(car, driver)* anfahren; *(completely)* umfahren; *(fatally)* überfahren; *building* abreißen, niederreißen; *tree* fällen, umhauen; *door* einschlagen; *obstacle, fence* niederreißen; **she was knocked down and killed** sie wurde überfahren; **he knocked him down with one blow** er schlug *or* streckte *(geh)* ihn mit einem Schlag zu Boden
b *price (buyer)* herunterhandeln (*to* auf *+acc*); *(seller)* heruntergehen mit; **I managed to knock him down a pound** ich konnte ein Pfund herunterhandeln; **I knocked him down to £15** ich habe es auf £ 15 heruntergehandelt; **he knocked the price down by £5 for me** er hat mir £ 5 nachgelassen
c *(at auction)* zuschlagen (*to sb* jdm); **to be knocked down at £1** für ein Pfund versteigert werden
d *machine, furniture* zerlegen, auseinandernehmen

▶ **knock in** VT *sep nail* einschlagen

▶ **knock off** VI *(inf)* aufhören, Feierabend *or* Schluss machen *(inf)*; **let's knock off now** Schluss für heute *(inf)*; **to knock off for lunch** Mittag machen
VT *sep* **a** *(lit) vase, cup, person etc* hinunterstoßen; *nose off statue etc* abschlagen; *insect* abschütteln; *high jump bar* reißen; *(off list etc)* streichen; **the branch knocked the rider off (his horse)** der Ast riss den Reiter vom Pferd; **somebody knocked the nose off the statue** jemand hat der Statue *(dat)* die Nase abgeschlagen
b *(inf: = reduce price by)* nachlassen (*for sb* jdm), runtergehen *(inf)*; **he knocked £5 off the bill/price** er hat £ 5 von der Rechnung/vom Preis nachgelassen; **I got something knocked off** ich habe es billiger bekommen
c *(inf: = do quickly) essay, painting* hinhauen *(inf)*; *(with good result)* aus dem Ärmel schütteln *(inf)*
d *(Brit inf: = steal)* klauen *(inf)*
e *(inf: = kill)* umlegen *(inf)*
f *(inf: = stop)* aufhören mit; *smoking, criticizing* stecken *(sl)*; **to knock off work** Feierabend machen; **knock it off!** nun hör schon auf!

▶ **knock on** VI *(Brit inf)* **he's knocking on for fifty** er geht auf die fünfzig zu

▶ **knock out** VT *sep* **a** *tooth* ausschlagen; *nail* herausschlagen (*of* aus); *pipe* ausklopfen; *contents* herausklopfen (*of* aus)
b *(= stun)* bewusstlos werden lassen; *(by hitting)* bewusstlos schlagen, k. o. schlagen; *(Boxing)* k. o. schlagen; *(drink)* umhauen *(inf)*; **he was knocked out** er wurde bewusstlos; *(Boxing)* er wurde k. o. geschlagen; *(by drink)* ihn hats umgehauen *(inf)*; **to knock oneself out** sich so stoßen, dass man bewusstlos wird
c *(from competition)* besiegen (*of* in *+dat*); **to be knocked out** ausscheiden, rausfliegen *(inf)* (*of* aus)
d *(inf: = stun, shock) (good news)* umwerfen, umhauen *(inf)*; *(bad news, sb's death etc)* schocken
e *(inf: = bowl over)* hinreißen *(inf)*, umhauen *(inf)*
f *(inf: = exhaust)* schaffen *(inf)*, kaputtmachen *(inf)*

▶ **knock over** VT *sep* umwerfen, umstoßen; *(car)* anfahren; *(fatally)* überfahren

▶ **knock together** VI **his knees were knocking together** seine Knie zitterten *or* schlotterten *(inf)* VT *sep* **a** *(= make hurriedly) shelter, object* zusammenzimmern; *meal, snack* auf die Beine stellen *(inf)* **b** *(lit)* aneinanderstoßen; **I'd like to knock their heads together** man sollte die beiden zur Räson bringen

▶ **knock up** VI **a** *(Brit Sport)* sich einspielen, ein paar Bälle schlagen
b *(US sl)* bumsen *(inf)*
VT *sep* **a** *(= hit upwards)* hochschlagen
b *(Brit: = wake)* (auf)wecken
c *(= make hurriedly) meal* auf die Beine stellen *(inf)*; *building* hochziehen, hinstellen; *shelter* zusammenzimmern
d *(Brit sl) (= exhaust)* kaputtmachen *(inf)*, schaffen *(inf)*; *(experience, shock)* schaffen *(inf)*
e *(inf: = make pregnant)* ein Kind anhängen *(+dat) (inf)*, ein Kind machen *(+dat) (inf)*; *(US sl: = have sex with)* bumsen mit *(inf)*; **she's knocked up** *(inf)* die hat 'nen dicken Bauch *(sl)*
f *(Cricket)* **to knock up 20 runs** 20 Läufe machen
g *(inf: = do) mileage* fahren; *overtime* machen

knock: **knockabout** ADJ **a** ~ **comedy** *(Theat)* Klamaukstück *nt* **b** ~ **clothes** gammelige Kleidung N *(Naut)* kleiner Einmaster; **knockback** N *(inf: = setback)* Rückschlag *m*; **he wasn't used to getting a ~ from a woman** er war es nicht gewöhnt, von einer Frau zurückgewiesen zu werden *or* einen Korb zu bekommen *(inf)*; **knockdown** ADJ *attr* **a** ~ **price** Schleuderpreis *m*; *(at auction)* Mindestpreis *m* **b** *furniture etc* zerlegbar; ~ **blow** *(Boxing)* Niederschlag *m*; **a ~ drag-out fight** *(US inf) (= fisticuffs)* eine handfeste Schlägerei; *(= argument)* ein handfester Streit; *(= difficult procedure)* ein langwieriger Kampf N *(Boxing)* Niederschlag *m*

knocker ['nɒkəʳ] N **a** *(= door knocker)* (Tür)klopfer *m* **b** *(inf: = breasts)* **(pair of) ~s** Titten *pl (sl)*; **what a pair of ~s!** toller Vorbau *(inf)*, geile Titten *(sl)* **c** *(inf: = critic)* Nörgler(in) *m(f)*

knock-for-knock ['nɒkfə'nɒk] ADJ *(Insur)* ~ **agreement** *Vereinbarung, bei der jede Versicherungsgesellschaft den Schaden des von ihr versicherten Fahrzeugs übernimmt*

knocking ['nɒkɪŋ] N **a** Klopfen *nt*, Pochen *nt (liter)*; *(in engine)* Klopfen *nt* **b** *(inf)* Kritik *f* (*of* an *+dat*); **he has taken a ~** er ist unter Beschuss gekommen

knocking: **knocking copy** N *(in advertising)* Negativwerbung *f*; **knocking-off time** N *(inf)* Feierabend *m*; **knocking-shop** N *(Brit inf)* Puff *m (inf)*

knock: **knock-kneed** [nɒk'ni:d] ADJ x-beinig, X-beinig; **to be ~** X-Beine haben; **knock-me-down** ADJ *(US inf)* überwältigend; **knock-on effect** N *(Brit)* Folgewirkungen *pl* (*on* auf *+acc*)

knockout ['nɒkaʊt] N **a** *(Boxing)* Knockout *m*, K. o. *m*; **he won by a ~** er gewann durch K. o. *or* errang einen K.-o.-Sieg **b** *(inf: = person, thing)* Wucht *f (inf)*; **she looked a ~ in her new dress** sie sah in ihrem neuen Kleid umwerfend aus ATTR **a** *(Boxing, fig)* ~ **blow** K.-o.-Schlag *m*; **to deliver a ~ blow** *or* **punch** einen K.-o.-Schlag landen; ~ **drops** K.-o.-Tropfen *pl*; ~ **mouse** Knockout-Maus *f*, Maus *f* mit Nullmutation **b** ~ **competition** Ausscheidungskampf *m*

knock-up ['nɒkʌp] N *(Brit)* **a** *(Sport)* **to have a ~** ein paar Bälle schlagen **b** **to get knocked up** *(inf: = get pregnant)* sich schwängern lassen

knoll [nəʊl] N Hügel *m*, Kuppe *f*

knot [nɒt] N **a** *(in string, tie, fig)* Knoten *m*; *(in muscle)* Verspannung *f*; **to tie/undo** *or* **untie a ~** einen Knoten machen/aufmachen *or* lösen; **to tie the ~** *(fig)* den Bund fürs Leben schließen; **to tie oneself (up) in ~s** *(fig)* sich immer mehr verwickeln, sich immer tiefer verstricken; **to tie sb (up) in ~s** jdn völlig verwirren; **there was a ~ in his stomach** sein Magen krampfte sich zusammen; **a ~ of muscles** ein Muskelbündel *nt*; **the whole matter is full of legal ~s** die ganze Sache ist rechtlich äußerst verwickelt
b *(Naut: = speed)* Knoten *m*; **to make 20 ~s** 20 Knoten machen → **rate¹ N a**
c *(in wood)* Ast *m*, Verwachsung *f*
d *(= group)* Knäuel *m*; **a ~ of tourists** ein Touristenknäuel *m*
VT einen Knoten machen in *(+acc)*; *(= knot together)* verknoten, verknüpfen; *stomach* verkrampfen; **to ~ sth to sth** etw mit etw verknoten; **to ~ sth around sth** etw um etw knoten; **get ~ted!** *(Brit inf)* du kannst mich mal! *(inf)*, rutsch mir den Buckel runter! *(inf)*; **I told him to get ~ted** *(inf)* ich hab ihm gesagt, er kann mich mal *(inf)* *or* er kann mir den Buckel runterrutschen *(inf)*
VI sich verknoten, Knoten bilden; *(stomach, muscles)* sich verkrampfen; *(forehead)* sich runzeln

▶ **knot together** VT *sep* verknoten

knotgrass ['nɒtgrɑ:s] N *(Bot)* Knöterich *m*

knothole ['nɒthəʊl] N *(in timber)* Astloch *nt*

knotty ['nɒtɪ] ADJ *(+er) wood* astreich, knorrig; *veins, rope* knotig; *problem* verwickelt, verzwickt *(inf)*

knout [naʊt] N Knute *f*

know [nəʊ]

vb: pret **knew**, *ptp* **known**

⊙ 15.1, 15.4, 16.1, 16.4, 26.3

1 TRANSITIVE VERB	4 NOUN
2 INTRANSITIVE VERB	5 PHRASAL VERBS
3 SET STRUCTURES	

1 – TRANSITIVE VERB

a [= have knowledge about] wissen; *answer, facts, dates, details, results etc* kennen, wissen; *French, English etc* können; **he knew her to be guilty** er wusste, dass sie schuldig war; **to know what one is talking about** wissen, wovon man redet; **to know one's own mind** wissen, was man will; **she knows all the answers** sie weiß Bescheid, sie kennt sich aus; *(pej)* sie weiß immer alles besser; **he might even be dead for all I know** vielleicht ist er sogar tot, was weiß ich; **he thinks he knows all the answers** *or* **everything** er meint, er wüsste alles; **that's what I'd like to know (too)** das möchte ich auch wissen; **THAT'S what I'd like to know** das möchte ich wirklich wissen; **that's worth knowing** das ist ja interessant; **that might be worth knowing** es könnte interessant sein, das zu wissen; **before you know where you are** ehe man sichs versieht; **I've been a fool and don't I know it!** *(inf)* ich sehs ja ein, ich war doof *(inf)*, ich war vielleicht doof *(inf)*; **she's angry! – don't I know it!** *(inf)* sie ist wütend! – wem sagst du das! *(inf)*

b [= be acquainted with] *people, places, book, author* kennen; **I know Bavaria well** ich kenne Bayern gut, ich kenne mich gut in Bayern aus; **do you know him to speak to?** kennen Sie ihn näher?; **we all know her as the headmistress/a generous person** wir kennen Sie alle als die Schulleiterin/einen großzügigen Menschen; **if I know John, he'll already be there** wie ich John kenne, ist er schon da; **he didn't want to know me** er wollte nichts mit mir zu tun haben; **know thyself!** erkenne dich selbst! → **name N a**, **sight N b**

c [= recognize] erkennen; **to know sb by his voice/walk** *etc* jdn an der Stimme/am Gang *etc* erkennen; **would you know him again?** würden Sie ihn wiedererkennen?; **he knows a good thing when he sees it** er weiß, was gut ist; **he knows a bargain/good manuscript when he sees one** er weiß, was ein guter Kauf/ein gutes Manuskript ist; **this is the end of the welfare system as we know it** das ist das Ende des uns bekannten Wohlfahrtssystems

d [= be able to distinguish] unterscheiden können; **don't you know your right from your left?** können Sie rechts und links nicht unterscheiden?; **you wouldn't know him from his brother** Sie könnten ihn nicht von seinem Bruder unterscheiden; **do you know the difference between...?** wissen Sie, was der Unterschied zwischen ... ist?; **to know the difference between right and wrong, to know right from**

wrong den Unterschied zwischen Gut und Böse kennen, Gut und Böse unterscheiden können; **he wouldn't know the difference** das merkt er nicht; **he doesn't know one end of a horse/hammer from the other** er hat keine Ahnung von Pferden/keine Ahnung, was ein Hammer ist *(inf)*

e [= experience] erleben; **I've never known it to rain so heavily** so einen starken Regen habe ich noch nie erlebt; **I've never known him (to) smile** ich habe ihn noch nie lächeln sehen, ich habe es noch nie erlebt, dass er lächelt; **have you ever known me (to) tell a lie?** haben Sie mich jemals lügen hören?; **have you ever known such a thing to happen before?** haben Sie je schon so etwas erlebt?, ist Ihnen so etwas schon einmal vorgekommen?

f [Bibl] *(obs: sexually)* erkennen

2 – INTRANSITIVE VERB

wissen; **who knows?** wer weiß?, weiß ichs?; **I know!** ich weiß!, weiß ich (doch)!; *(having a good idea)* ich weiß was!, ich habe eine Idee!; **I don't know** (das) weiß ich nicht; **as far as I know** soviel ich weiß, meines Wissens; **he just didn't want to know** er wollte einfach nicht hören; **afterwards they just didn't want to know** nachher wollten sie einfach nichts mehr davon wissen; **I wouldn't know** *(inf)* weiß ich (doch) nicht *(inf)*; **don't you know?** weißt du das denn nicht?; **how should I know?** wie soll ich das wissen?; **how was I to know?** wie sollte ich das wissen?; **I'm damned if I know** *(inf)* ich habe echt keinen Schimmer *(inf)*; **the channel was rough, as I well know** *or* **as well I know!** die Überfahrt war stürmisch, das kann ich dir sagen

3 – SET STRUCTURES

♦ **to know that ...** wissen, dass ...

Note that while in English *that* can be omitted, in German *dass* must be used to introduce the next sentence.

when I saw the ambulance, I knew (that) something was wrong als ich den Krankenwagen sah, wusste ich, dass etwas nicht stimmte

♦ **to know why...** wissen, warum ...; **he didn't know why** er wusste nicht, warum; **I don't know why you think it's so funny** ich weiß nicht, was du daran so komisch findest

♦ **to know how to know how to do sth** *(in theory)* wissen, wie man etw macht; *(in practice)* etw tun können; **I know how you feel** ich weiß, wie Sie sich fühlen; **I don't know how you can say that!** wie kannst du das nur sagen!; **you don't know how good it is to see you again** Sie wissen gar nicht, wie sehr ich mich freue, Sie wiederzusehen

♦ **to know better I know better than that** ich bin ja nicht ganz dumm; **I know better than to say something like that** ich werde mich hüten, so etwas zu sagen; **he knows better than to eat into the profits** er ist nicht so dumm, den Gewinn anzugreifen; **he/you ought to have known better** das war dumm (von ihm/dir); **he ought to have** *or* **should have known better than to do that** es war dumm von ihm, das zu tun; **you ought to know better at your age** in deinem Alter müsste man das aber (besser) wissen; **they don't know any better** sie kennens nicht anders; **he says he didn't do it, but I know better** er sagt, er war es nicht, aber ich weiß, dass das nicht stimmt

♦ **to know best OK, you know best** o.k., Sie müssens wissen; **mother always knows best** Mutter weiß es am besten

♦ **to get to know to get to know sb** jdn kennenlernen; **to get to know sth** *(methods, techniques, style, pronunciation etc)* etw lernen; *habits, faults, shortcuts etc* etw herausfinden; **to get to know a place** einen Ort kennenlernen

♦ **to let sb know to let sb know sth** *(= not keep back)* jdn etw wissen lassen; *(= tell, inform)* jdm von etw Bescheid sagen *or* geben; **he soon let me know what he thought of it** er hat mich schnell wissen lassen, was er davon hielt; **when can you let me know?** wann können Sie es mich wissen lassen?, wann können Sie mir Bescheid sagen?

♦ **you know... you know, we could/there is ...** weißt du, wir könnten/da ist ...; **he gave it away, you know** er hat es nämlich weggegeben; **it's raining, you know** es regnet; **then there was this man, you know, and ...** und da war dieser Mann, nicht (wahr), und ...; **wear the black dress, you know, the one with the red belt** zieh das schwarze Kleid an, du weißt schon, das mit dem roten Gürtel; **it's long and purple and, you know, sort of crinkly** es ist lang und lila und, na ja, so kraus; **(if you) know what I mean** du weißt schon

♦ **you never know** man kann nie wissen

♦ **I'll have you know it was nothing to do with me, I'll have you know!** es hatte nichts mit mir zu tun, damit du es weißt!

♦ **there's no knowing** *(inf)* das kann keiner sagen, das weiß niemand; **there's no knowing what he'll do** man weiß nie, was er noch tut

♦ **what do you know!** *(inf)* sieh mal einer an!; **what do you know! I've just seen her!** *(inf)* stellen Sie sich vor, ich habe sie eben gesehen

♦ **to be known** → *also* **known**; **to be known (to sb)** (jdm) bekannt sein; **it is (well) known that ...** es ist (allgemein) bekannt, dass ...; **is he/it known here?** ist er/das hier bekannt?, kennt man ihn/das hier?; **to be known for sth** für etw bekannt sein; **he is known to have been here** man weiß, dass er hier war; **he is known as Mr Smith** man kennt ihn als Herrn Smith; **she wishes to be known as Mrs White** sie möchte Frau White genannt werden → *also* **known**

♦ **to make sb/sth known** jdn/etw bekannt machen; **to make it known that ...** bekannt geben, dass ...; **to make oneself known** sich melden (*to sb* bei jdm); *(= introduce oneself)* sich vorstellen (*to sb* jdm); *(= become well-known)* sich *(dat)* einen Namen machen; **to make one's presence known** sich melden (*to* bei)

♦ **to become known** bekannt werden; *(= famous)* berühmt werden

♦ **to let it be known that ...** bekannt geben, dass ...

4 – NOUN

♦ **to be in the know** *inf* eingeweiht sein, im Bild sein *(inf)*, Bescheid wissen *(inf)*; **the people in the know say ...** Leute, die darüber Bescheid wissen, sagen ..., die Fachleute sagen ...

5 – PHRASAL VERBS

▸ **know about** **VI** *+prep obj (= have factual knowledge, experience of) history, maths, politics* sich auskennen in *(+dat)*; *Africa* Bescheid wissen über *(+acc)*; *women, men, cars, horses* sich auskennen mit; *(= be aware of, have been told about)* wissen von; **I know about that** das weiß ich; **I didn't know about that** das wusste ich nicht; **I only knew about it yesterday** ich habe erst gestern davon gehört; **I'd rather not know about it** das möchte ich lieber nicht wissen; **did you know about Maggie?** weißt du über Maggie Bescheid?; **I know about John, but is anyone else absent?** John, das weiß ich, aber fehlt sonst noch jemand?; **to get to know about sb/sth** von jdm/etw hören; **I don't know about that** davon weiß ich nichts; *(= don't agree)* da bin ich aber nicht so sicher; **I don't know about you, but I'm hungry** ich weiß nicht, wie es Ihnen geht, aber ich habe Hunger; **she's very clever, isn't she? – I don't know about clever, but she certainly knows how to use people** sie ist sehr klug, nicht wahr? – klug, na, ich weiß nicht, aber sie weiß Leute auszunutzen

VT *sep +prep obj* **to know a lot/nothing/something about sth** *(= have factual knowledge)* viel/nichts/einiges über etw *(acc)* wissen; *(in history, maths etc)* in etw *(dat)* gut/nicht/ein bisschen Bescheid wissen; *(about cars, horses etc)* viel/nichts/einiges von etw verstehen; *(= be aware of, have been told about)* viel/nichts/einiges von etw wissen; **we don't know anything about him** wir wissen nichts über ihn; **that was the first I knew about it** davon hatte ich nichts gewusst; **not much is known about that** darüber weiß man nicht viel; **I know all about that** da kenne ich mich aus; *(= I'm aware of that)* das weiß ich; *(= I've been told about it)* ich weiß Bescheid; **I know all about you** ich weiß über Sie Bescheid; **that's all you know about it!** *(iro)* das meinst auch nur du!; **I don't know about that!** da bin ich mir nicht so sicher!

▸ **know of** VI *+prep obj café, better method* kennen; *(= have heard of) sb, sb's death* gehört haben von; **I soon got to know of all the facts/all his problems** ich war bald über alle Fakten/all seine Probleme informiert; **I know of him, although I've never met him** ich habe von ihm gehört, aber ich habe ihn noch nie getroffen; **not that I know of** nicht, dass ich wüsste

knowable [ˈnəʊəbl] ADJ den/die/das man wissen kann; **it's not ~** das kann man nicht wissen

know: **know-all** N *(Brit inf)* Alleswisser(in) *m(f)*, Besserwisser(in) *m(f)*; **know-how** N praktische Kenntnis, Know-how *nt*; **he hasn't got the ~ for** *or* **to do the job** er hat nicht die nötige Sachkenntnis für diese Arbeit

knowing [ˈnəʊɪŋ] ADJ *look, smile* wissend; *person* verständnisvoll

knowingly [ˈnəʊɪŋlɪ] ADV **a** *(= consciously)* bewusst, absichtlich, wissentlich **b** *look, smile* wissend

know-it-all [ˈnəʊɪtɔːl] N *(US inf)* = **know-all**

knowledge [ˈnɒlɪdʒ] ✪ 19.2 N **a** *(= understanding, awareness)* Wissen *nt*, Kenntnis *f*; **to have ~ of** Kenntnis haben *or* besitzen von, wissen von; **to have no ~ of** keine Kenntnis haben von, nichts wissen von; **to (the best of) my ~** soviel ich weiß, meines Wissens; **to the best of my ~ and belief** nach bestem Wissen und Gewissen; **not to my ~** nicht, dass ich wüsste; **without his ~** ohne sein Wissen; **without the ~ of her mother** ohne Wissen ihrer Mutter, ohne dass ihre Mutter es weiß; **it has come to my ~ that ...** ich habe erfahren, dass ...; **safe in the ~ that ...** in der Gewissheit, dass ...

b *(= learning, facts learned)* Kenntnisse *pl*, Wissen *nt*; **my ~ of English** meine Englischkenntnisse *pl*; **my ~ of D.H. Lawrence** was ich von D. H. Lawrence kenne; **I have a thorough ~ of this subject** auf diesem Gebiet weiß ich gründlich Bescheid *or* besitze ich umfassende Kenntnisse; **the police have no ~ of him/his activities** die Polizei weiß nichts über ihn/seine Aktivitäten

knowledgeable [ˈnɒlɪdʒəbl] ADJ *person* kenntnisreich, bewandert; *report* gut fundiert; **to be ~** viel wissen (*about* über *+acc*)

knowledgeably [ˈnɒlɪdʒəblɪ] ADV *speak, write* kenntnisreich

known [nəʊn] *ptp of* **know** ADJ bekannt; *expert also* anerkannt; **it is a ~ fact that ...** es ist (allgemein) bekannt, dass ...; **~ quantity** bekannte Größe

knuckle [ˈnʌkl] N (Finger)knöchel *m*; *(of meat)* Hachse *f*, Haxe *f* → **near 2 a, rap**

▸ **knuckle down** VI *(inf)* sich dahinterklemmen *(inf)*, sich dranmachen *(inf)*; **to knuckle down to work** sich hinter die Arbeit klemmen *(inf)*, sich an die Arbeit machen

▸ **knuckle under** VI *(inf)* spuren *(inf)*, sich fügen (*to +dat*); *(to demands)* sich beugen (*to +dat*)

knuckle: **knucklebone** N Knöchelbein *nt*; **knucklebones** PL → **jacks**; **knuckle-duster** N *(esp Brit)* Schlagring *m*; **knucklehead** N *(inf)* Holzkopf *m (inf)*; **knuckle joint** N *(Anat)* Knöchel- *or* Fingergelenk *nt*; *(Tech)* Kardan- *or* Kreuzgelenk *nt*; **knuckle sandwich** N *(Brit inf)* Keile *pl (inf)*, Prügel *pl (inf)*

knurl [nɜːl] **N** Einkerbung *f*, Riffelung *f*; *(Tech)* Rändelrad *nt* **VT** rändeln, kordieren

KO **N** K. o. *m*, K.-o.-Schlag *m* **VT** *(Boxing)* k. o. schlagen; **Jim is totally KO'd** *(inf)* Jim ist total außer Gefecht gesetzt *(inf)* *or* total ausgeknockt *(sl)*

koala [kəʊ'ɑːlə] N *(also* **koala bear**) Koala(bär) *m*

Kolkata [kɒl'kɑːtə] NT Kolkata *nt (new official name for Calcutta)*

kookaburra ['kʊkə,bʌrə] N Rieseneisvogel *m*, Lachender Hans

kooky ['kuːkɪ] ADJ *(+er) (US inf)* komisch *(inf)*, verrückt *(inf)*

kopeck ['kəʊpek] N Kopeke *f*

Koran [kɒ'rɑːn] N Koran *m*

Korea [kə'rɪə] N Korea *nt*

Korean [kə'rɪən] ADJ koreanisch; ~ **war** Koreakrieg *m* N **a** Koreaner(in) *m(f)* **b** *(Ling)* Koreanisch *nt*

kosher ['kəʊʃə'] ADJ **a** koscher **b** *(inf)* in Ordnung; **to make everything ~** alles in Ordnung bringen; **there's something not quite ~ about the deal** an dem Geschäft ist etwas faul *(inf)*

Kosovan ['kɒsɒvən], **Kosovar** ['kɒsɒvɑː'] ADJ kosovarisch; **the ~ Albanians** die Kosovo-Albaner N Kosovare *m*, Kosovarin *f*

Kosovo ['kɒsɒvəʊ] N Kosovo *nt*

kowtow ['kaʊtaʊ] VI einen Kotau machen, dienern; **to ~ to sb** vor jdm dienern *or* katzbuckeln *(inf) or* einen Kotau machen

KP **a** *(US Mil) abbr of* **kitchen police** *(= work)* Küchendienst *m*; *(= soldiers) Soldaten, die Küchendienst haben* **b** *(Med) abbr of* **Kaposi's sarcoma** Kaposisarkom *nt*

kph *abbr of* **kilometres per hour** kph

kraal [krɑːl] N Kral *m*

kraft [krɑːft], **kraft paper** N starkes Packpapier

kraken ['krækən] N Krake *m*

Kraut [kraʊt] N, ADJ *als Schimpfwort gebrauchte Bezeichnung für Deutsche und Deutsches*

Kremlin ['kremlɪn] N **the ~** der Kreml

kremlinologist [,kremlɪ'nɒlədʒɪst] N Kremlforscher(in) *m(f)*

kremlinology [,kremlɪ'nɒlədʒɪ] N Kremlforschung *f*

krona ['krəʊnə] N schwedische Krone

krone ['krəʊnə] N *(Danish)* dänische Krone; *(Norwegian)* norwegische Krone

krypton ['krɪptɒn] N Krypton *nt*

Kt *(Brit) abbr of* **Knight**

kudos ['kjuːdɒs] N Ansehen *nt*, Ehre *f*; **he only did it for the ~** er tat es nur der Ehre wegen

Ku Klux Klan [,kjuːklʌks'klæn] N Ku-Klux-Klan *m*

kumquat ['kʌmkwɒt] N Kumquat *f*, *kleine Orange*

kung fu ['kʌŋ'fuː] N Kung-Fu *nt*; ~ **film** *or* **movie** *(esp US)* Kung-Fu-Film *m*

Kurd [kɜːd] N Kurde *m*, Kurdin *f*

Kurdish ['kɜːdɪʃ] ADJ kurdisch N Kurdisch *nt*

Kuwait [kʊ'weɪt] N Kuwait *nt*

Kuwaiti [kʊ'weɪtɪ] ADJ kuwaitisch N Kuwaiter(in) *m(f)*

kV *abbr of* **kilovolt(s)** kV

kvetch [kvetʃ] *(pej)* N **a** *(= person)* Nörgler(in) *m(f) (pej)* **b** *(= complaint)* Nörgelei *f (pej)* VI nörgeln

kW *abbr of* **kilowatt(s)** kW

kWh, **kwh** *abbr of* **kilowatt hour(s)** kWh

KWIC *(Comput) abbr of* **keyword in context** KWIC

Kyrgyzstan [,kɜːgɪs'tɑːn] N = **Kirghizstan**

L

L, l [el] N L *nt*, l *nt*

L **a** *(Brit Mot) abbr of* **Learner** **b** *abbr of* **large**

l **a** *abbr of* **litre(s)** l. **b** *abbr of* **left** l

LA *abbr of* **Los Angeles**

Lab *(Brit Pol) abbr of* **Labour**

lab [læb] *abbr of* **laboratory**

label ['leɪbl] **N** **a** *(lit)* Etikett *nt*, Label *nt*; *(showing contents, instructions etc)* Aufschrift *f*, Beschriftung *f*; *(on specimen, cage)* Schild *nt*; *(tied on)* Anhänger *m*; *(adhesive)* Aufkleber *m*, Aufklebeetikett *nt*; *(on parcel)* Paketadresse *f*; *(of record company)* Label *nt*, Plattenfirma *f*; **on the Pye ~** unter dem Pye-Label
b *(fig)* Etikett *nt (usu pej)*
VT **a** *(lit)* etikettieren, mit einem Schild/Anhänger/Aufkleber versehen; *(= write on)* beschriften; **the bottle was ~led** *(Brit) or* **~ed** *(US)* **"poison"** die Flasche trug die Aufschrift „Gift"
b *(fig) ideas* bezeichnen; *(pej)* abstempeln; **to ~ sb (as) sth** jdn als etw abstempeln; **he got himself ~led** *(Brit) or* **~ed** *(US)* **as a troublemaker** er brachte sich *(dat)* den Ruf eines Unruhestifters ein

labia ['leɪbɪə] *pl of* **labium**

labial ['leɪbɪəl] **ADJ** *(Anat, Phon)* labial, Lippen-; **~ sound** Labial- *or* Lippenlaut **N** *(Phon)* Labial- *or* Lippenlaut *m*

labiodental [ˌleɪbɪəʊ'dentəl] *(Phon)* **ADJ** labiodental **N** Labiodental *m*

labium ['leɪbɪəm] N *pl* **labia** *(Anat)* Schamlippe *f*, Labium *nt (spec)*

labor *etc (US)* = **labour** *etc*; **labor union** *(US)* Gewerkschaft *f*

> **LABOR DAY**
>
> **Labor Day** ist ein gesetzlicher Feiertag in den USA und Kanada, der jeweils am ersten Montag im September begangen wird. 1894 führte der US-Kongress diesen nationalen Tag der Arbeit zu Ehren der Werktätigen ein, nachdem Arbeiter zwölf Jahre lang einen solchen Tag eingefordert hatten. Heute hat **Labor Day** kaum noch politische Bedeutung, sondern gilt als eine schöne Gelegenheit, zum Abschluss des Sommers und vor Beginn der Schulzeit mit der ganzen Familie noch einmal einen Ausflug oder ein Picknick zu machen - das Verkehrschaos am **Labor Day** ist dementsprechend gefürchtet. Mitunter finden auch noch Paraden und Reden statt.

laboratory [lə'bɒrətərɪ, *(US)* 'læbrəˌtɔːrɪ] N Labor(atorium) *nt*; **~ assistant** Laborant(in) *m(f)*; **~ results** Laborwerte *pl*; **the project was abandoned at the ~ stage** das Projekt wurde im Versuchsstadium abgebrochen

laborious [lə'bɔːrɪəs] ADJ *task, undertaking* mühsam, mühselig; *style* schwerfällig, umständlich

laboriously [lə'bɔːrɪəslɪ] ADV mühsam; *speak* umständlich

labour, *(US)* **labor** ['leɪbə'] **N** **a** *(= work in general)* Arbeit *f*; *(= toil)* Anstrengung *f*, Mühe *f*; **after much ~ the job was at last completed** nach langen Mühen war die Arbeit endlich vollendet
b *(= task)* Aufgabe *f*; **it was a ~ of love** ich/er *etc* tat es aus Liebe zur Sache; **this biography is clearly a ~ of love** diese Biografie ist eindeutig mit viel Liebe zur Sache entstanden; **the ~s of Hercules** die Arbeiten *pl* des Herkules
c *(Jur)* → **hard labour**
d *(= persons)* Arbeiter *pl*, Arbeitskräfte *pl*; **to withdraw one's ~** die Arbeit verweigern
e *(Brit Pol)* **Labour** die Labour Party; **this district is Labour** dies ist ein Labourbezirk
f *(Med)* Wehen *pl*; **to be in ~** in den Wehen liegen, die Wehen haben; **to go into ~** die Wehen bekommen
VT *point, subject* auswalzen, breittreten *(inf)*; **I won't ~ the point** ich will nicht darauf herumreiten
VI **a** *(in fields etc)* arbeiten; *(= work hard)* sich abmühen (*at, with* mit); **they ~ed hard to get the house finished on time** sie gaben sich die größte Mühe, das Haus rechtzeitig fertigzustellen; **to ~ for a cause** sich für eine Sache einsetzen; **to ~ under a misapprehension** sich einer Illusion *(dat)* hingeben; **to ~ under difficulties** mit Schwierigkeiten zu kämpfen haben
b *(= move etc with effort or difficulty)* sich quälen; **the engine is ~ing** der Motor hört sich gequält an; *(in wrong gear)* der Motor läuft untertourig; **to ~ up a hill** sich einen Hügel hinaufquälen, mühsam den Berg hochkriechen; **his breathing became ~ed** er begann, schwer zu atmen

labour camp, *(US)* **labor camp** N Arbeitslager *nt*

Labour Day N der Tag der Arbeit

laboured, *(US)* **labored** ['leɪbəd] ADJ schwerfällig; *breathing* schwer

labourer, *(US)* **laborer** ['leɪbərə'] N (Hilfs)arbeiter(in) *m(f)*; *(= farm labourer)* Landarbeiter(in) *m(f)*; *(= day-labourer)* Tagelöhner(in) *m(f)*

labour exchange N *(dated Brit)* Arbeitsamt *nt*

labour force, *(US)* **labor force** N Arbeiterschaft *f*; *(of company)* Belegschaft *f*

labouring, *(US)* **laboring** ['leɪbərɪŋ] ADJ **~ class** Arbeiterklasse *f*; **~ job** Aushilfsjob *m*

labour-intensive, *(US)* **labor-intensive** [ˌleɪbərɪn'tensɪv] ADJ arbeitsintensiv

labourite ['leɪbəraɪt] N *(pej)* Labour-Anhänger *m*

labour, *(US)* **labor**: **labour market** N Arbeitsmarkt *m*; **labour movement** N Arbeiterbewegung *f*; **labour pains** PL Wehen *pl*

Labour Party N *(Brit)* Labour Party *f*

labour, *(US)* **labor**: **labour relations** PL die Beziehungen *pl* zwischen Unternehmern und Arbeitern *or* Gewerkschaften; **labour-saving** ADJ arbeitssparend; **labour shortage** N Arbeitskräftemangel *m*; **labour supply** N Angebot *nt* an Arbeitskräften; **labour ward** N *(Brit)* Kreißsaal *m*

Labrador ['læbrədɔː'] N Labradorhund *m*

laburnum [lə'bɜːnəm] N Goldregen *m*

labyrinth ['læbɪrɪnθ] N *(lit, fig)* Labyrinth *nt*

labyrinthine [ˌlæbɪ'rɪnθaɪn] ADJ labyrinthisch *(also fig)*, labyrinthähnlich

lace [leɪs] **N** **a** *(= fabric)* Spitze *f*; *(as trimming)* Spitzenborte *f or* -besatz *m*; *(of gold, silver)* Tresse *f*, Litze *f*
b *(of shoe)* (Schuh)band *nt*, Schnürsenkel *m*
VT **a** *corset* schnüren; *(also* **lace up**) *shoe* zubinden; *(fig: also* **lace together**) *fingers* ineinander verschlingen
b **to ~ a drink** einen Schuss Alkohol in ein Getränk geben; **to ~ a drink with drugs/poison** Drogen/Gift in ein Getränk mischen; **~d with brandy** mit einem Schuss Weinbrand; **a ~d drink** ein Getränk mit Schuss; **coffee ~d with cyanide** Kaffee, dem Zyanid beigemischt wurde
c *(fig) speech, conversation* würzen; **her comments were ~d with sarcasm/humour** *(Brit) or* **humor** *(US)* ihre Bemerkungen waren mit Sarkasmus/Humor gewürzt
VI *(shoes etc)* (zu)geschnürt werden

▶ **lace into** VI *+prep obj* **to lace into sb** *(verbally)* jdm eine Standpauke halten, jdn anschnauzen *(inf)*; *(physically)* auf jdn losgehen, jdn verprügeln

▶ **lace up** **VT** *sep* (zu)schnüren **VI** geschnürt werden

lace: **lace-curtain** ADJ der Mittelklasse *or* Mittelschicht; **lace paper** N Papierspitzen *pl*, Spitzenpapier *nt*

lacerate ['læsəreɪt] VT **a** *(lit) hand, skin* verletzen; *clothes* aufreißen; *(by glass etc)* zerschneiden; *(by thorns)* zerkratzen, aufreißen; *(by claws, whip)* zerfetzen; **he ~d his arm** er zog sich *(dat)* tiefe Wunden am Arm zu; **she ~d her wrist with a razor-blade** sie schlitzte sich *(dat)* die Pulsadern mit einer Rasierklinge auf; **her knee was badly ~d** sie hatte tiefe Wunden am Knie **b** *(fig)* zutiefst verletzen

laceration [ˌlæsə'reɪʃən] N Verletzung *f*, Fleischwunde *f*; *(= tear)* Risswunde *f*; *(from blow)* Platzwunde *f*; *(from whip)* Striemen *m*; *(from glass)* Schnittwunde *f*; *(from claws etc)* Kratzwunde *f*

lace-up (shoe) ['leɪsʌp(ʃuː)] N Schnürschuh *m*

lacework ['leɪswɜːk] N *(= fabric)* Spitzenarbeit *f*, Spitzenmuster *nt*; *(of gold and silver)* Filigranmuster *nt*

lachrymose ['lækrɪməʊs] ADJ *(liter) person* weinerlich; *story, film etc* rührselig, ergreifend

lacing ['leɪsɪŋ] N *(of shoe)* Schnürsenkel *pl*, Schuhbänder *pl*; *(of corset)* Schnürung *f*; **uniforms with gold ~** goldbetresste Uniformen *pl*; **tea with a ~ of rum** Tee *m* mit einem Schuss Rum

lack [læk] ✪ 17.1 **N** Mangel *m*; **for** *or* **through ~ of sth** aus Mangel an etw *(dat)*; **they failed for** *or* **through ~ of support** sie scheiterten, weil es ihnen an Unterstützung fehlte *or* mangelte; **though it wasn't for ~ of trying** nicht, dass er sich/ich mich *etc* nicht bemüht hätte; **there was a complete ~ of interest** es bestand überhaupt kein Interesse; **such was their ~ of confidence that ...** sie hatten so wenig Selbstbewusstsein, dass ...; **~ of water/time** Wasser-/ /Zeitmangel *m*; **there is no ~ of money in that family** in dieser Familie fehlt es nicht an Geld; **there was no ~ of applicants** es bestand kein Mangel an Bewerbern, es fehlte nicht an Bewerbern
VT **they ~ the necessary equipment/talent** es fehlt ihnen an der notwendigen Ausrüstung/ am richtigen Talent; **we ~ time** uns fehlt die nötige Zeit
VI **a** **to be ~ing** fehlen; **his sense of humour** *(Brit) or* **humor** *(US)* **is sadly ~ing** mit seinem

Sinn für Humor ist es nicht weit her; **innovation has been sadly ~ing throughout the project** es fehlte leider während des ganzen Projektes an Innovationen
b **he is ~ing in confidence** ihm fehlt es an Selbstvertrauen; **he is completely ~ing in any sort of decency** er besitzt überhaupt keinen Anstand; **I find her ~ing in humour** *(Brit)* or **humor** *(US)* ich vermisse an ihr den Humor; **I find him ~ing in intelligence** ich finde, er ist nicht besonders intelligent
c **he ~ed for nothing** es fehlte ihm an nichts

lackadaisical [ˌlækəˈdeɪzɪkəl] ADJ *(= lacking energy)* lustlos, desinteressiert; *(= careless)* nachlässig, lasch

lackey [ˈlækɪ] N *(lit, fig)* Lakai *m*

lacking [ˈlækɪŋ] ADJ **a** **to be found ~** sich nicht bewähren, der Sache *(dat)* nicht gewachsen sein; **they were not found ~** sie waren der Sache *(dat)* gewachsen **b** *(inf)* geistig minderbemittelt *(inf)*, beschränkt

lacklustre, *(US)* **lackluster** [ˈlækˌlʌstəʳ] ADJ *surface* stumpf, glanzlos; *eyes also* trübe; *style* farblos, langweilig

laconic [ləˈkɒnɪk] ADJ lakonisch; *prose, style* knapp

laconically [ləˈkɒnɪkəlɪ] ADV lakonisch; *write* knapp

lacquer [ˈlækəʳ] **N** Lack *m*; *(= hair lacquer)* Haarspray *nt*; *(= nail lacquer)* Nagellack *m* **VT** lackieren; *hair* sprayen

lacquered [ˈlækəd] ADJ lackiert; *hair* gesprayt; **~ table** Lacktisch *m*

lacrimal gland [ˈlækrɪməlˈglænd] N Tränendrüse *f*

lacrosse [ləˈkrɒs] N Lacrosse *nt*

lactate [ˈlækteɪt] VI Milch absondern, laktieren *(spec)*

lactation [lækˈteɪʃən] N Milchabsonderung *f*, Laktation *f (spec)*; *(= period)* Stillzeit *f*, Laktationsperiode *f (spec)*

lactic acid [ˈlæktɪkˈæsɪd] N Milchsäure *f*

lacto-ovo-vegetarian [ˌlæktəʊˌəʊvəʊˌvedʒɪˈtɛərɪən] N Lacto-ovo-Vegetarier(in) *m(f)*

lactose [ˈlæktəʊs] N Milchzucker *m*, Laktose *f*

lactose-intolerant ADJ **to be ~** eine Laktose-Intoleranz haben

lacuna [ləˈkjuːnə] N *pl* **-e** [ləˈkjuːniː] Lakune *f*

lacy [ˈleɪsɪ] ADJ *(+er)* Spitzen-; *(= like lace)* spitzenartig; **~ underwear** Spitzenunterwäsche

lad [læd] N Junge *m*; *(in stable etc)* Bursche *m*; **young ~** junger Mann; **listen, ~** hör mir mal zu, mein Junge!; **when I was a ~** als ich ein junger Bursche war; **he's only a ~** er ist (doch) noch jung, er ist (doch) noch ein Junge; **a simple country ~** ein einfacher Bauernjunge, ein einfacher Junge vom Land; **all together, ~s, push!** alle Mann anschieben!, alle zusammen, Jungs, anschieben!; **he's a bit of a ~** *(inf)* er ist ein ziemlicher Draufgänger; **he's one of the ~s** *(Brit inf)* er gehört dazu; **he likes a night out with the ~s** *(Brit inf)* er geht gern mal mit seinen Kumpels weg *(inf)*

ladder [ˈlædəʳ] **N** **a** Leiter *f*
b *(fig)* (Stufen)leiter *f*; **to be at the top/bottom of the ~** ganz oben/unten auf der Leiter stehen; **evolutionary ~** Leiter *f* der Evolution; **social ~** Leiter *f* des gesellschaftlichen Erfolges; **to move up the social/career ~** gesellschaftlich/beruflich aufsteigen; **to move up the housing ~** ein anspruchsvolleres Haus kaufen; **it's a first step up the ~** das ist ein Anfang; **a big step up the ~** ein großer Schritt nach vorn → **top**
c *(Brit: in stocking)* Laufmasche *f*
VT *(Brit) stocking* zerreißen; **I've ~ed my tights** ich habe mir eine Laufmasche (in meiner Strumpfhose) geholt
VI *(Brit: stocking)* Laufmaschen bekommen

ladderproof [ˈlædəpruːf] ADJ maschenfest, laufmaschensicher

ladder tournament N *(Sport)* Ranglistenturnier *nt*

laddie [ˈlædɪ] N *(esp Scot inf)* Junge *m*, Bub *m (S Ger, Aus, Sw)*

laddish [ˈlædɪʃ] ADJ *(Brit inf)* machohaft *(inf)*

lade [leɪd] *pret* **laded**, *ptp* **laden** **VT** *ship* beladen; *cargo* verladen **VI** Ladung übernehmen *or* an Bord nehmen

laden [ˈleɪdn] ADJ *(lit, fig)* beladen *(with* mit); **bushes ~ with flowers** blütenschwere Büsche *pl*

la-di-da [ˈlɑːdɪˈdɑː] ADJ ADV *(inf)* affektiert, affig *(inf)*

ladies' fingers [ˈleɪdɪzˌfɪŋgəz] PL Okra *f*

ladies' man [ˈleɪdɪzmæn] N Charmeur *m*, Frauenheld *m*; **he's a bit of a ~** er wirkt auf Frauen

lading [ˈleɪdɪŋ] N *(= act)* Verladen *nt*; *(= cargo)* Ladung *f*

ladle [ˈleɪdl] **N** (Schöpf- *or* Suppen)kelle *f*, Schöpflöffel *m* **VT** schöpfen; **he's ladling money into the business** er steckt *or* pumpt massenhaft Geld in das Geschäft

▶ **ladle out** VT *sep soup etc, money* austeilen

ladleful [ˈleɪdlfʊl] N **one ~** eine Kelle (voll); **each pan holds ten ~s** in jeden Topf passt der Inhalt von zehn Schöpfkellen

lady [ˈleɪdɪ] N **a** Dame *f*; **"Ladies"** *(= lavatory)* „Damen"; **where is the ladies** *or* **the ladies' room?** wo ist die Damentoilette?; **ladies and gentlemen!** sehr geehrte Damen und Herren!, meine Damen und Herren!; **ladies, ...** meine Damen, ...; **~ of the house** Dame *f* des Hauses; **the minister and his ~** der Minister und seine Gattin; **your good ~** *(hum, form)* Ihre Frau Gemahlin *(hum, form)*; **the old ~** *(inf: = mother)* die alte Dame *(inf)*; *(= wife)* meine/deine/seine Alte *(inf)* or Olle *(N Ger inf)*; **a little old ~** eine alte Dame; **young ~** junge Dame; *(scoldingly)* mein Fräulein; **his young ~** seine Freundin; **she's no ~** sie ist keine Dame; **ladies' bicycle** Damen(fahr)rad *nt*
b *(= noble)* Adlige *f*; **Lady** *(as a title)* Lady *f*; **dinner is served, my ~** es ist angerichtet, Mylady *or* gnädige Frau; **to live like a ~** wie eine große Dame leben
c **Our Lady** die Jungfrau Maria, Unsere Liebe Frau; **Church of Our Lady** (Lieb)frauenkirche *f*

lady: **ladybird**, *(US)* **ladybug** N Marienkäfer *m*; **Lady Chapel** N Marienkapelle *f*; **Lady Day** N *(Brit)* Mariä Verkündigung *no art*; **lady doctor** N Ärztin *f*; **ladyfinger** N *(US)* Löffelbiskuit *nt*; **lady friend** N Dame *f*; **lady-in-waiting** N Ehrendame *f*, Hofdame *f*; **lady-killer** N *(inf)* Herzensbrecher *m*; **ladylike** ADJ damenhaft, vornehm; **it's not ~** es ist nicht ladylike, es gehört sich nicht für eine Dame; **ladylove** N *(old)* Geliebte *f*, Feinsliebchen *nt (old)*; **lady mayoress** N *Titel der Frau des Lord Mayor*, Frau *f* (Ober)bürgermeister *(dated)*; **ladyship** N **Her/Your Ladyship** Ihre Ladyschaft; **certainly, Your Ladyship** gewiss, Euer Gnaden; **lady's maid** N (Kammer)zofe *f*

lag[1] [læg] **N** *(= time-lag)* Zeitabstand *m*, Zeitdifferenz *f*; *(= delay)* Verzögerung *f*; **there is too much of a ~** es vergeht zu viel Zeit; **after a ~ of six months** nach sechs Monaten, nachdem sechs Monate vergangen *or* verstrichen waren; **there was a ~ of six months between buying the house and moving in** das Haus konnte erst sechs Monate nach dem Kauf bezogen werden; **the cultural ~ is very apparent** der kulturelle Rückstand ist offensichtlich **VI** *(time)* langsam vergehen, dahinkriechen; *(in pace)* zurückbleiben

▶ **lag behind** VI zurückbleiben; **we lag behind in space exploration** in der Raumforschung liegen wir (weit) zurück *or* hinken wir hinterher *(inf)*; **the government is lagging behind in the polls** die Regierung liegt in den Meinungsumfragen zurück; **why don't you walk beside me instead of always lagging behind?** warum läufst du nicht neben mir, anstatt immer hinterherzutrödeln?; **they are lagging ten points behind** sie liegen zehn Punkte zurück

lag[2] VT *boiler, pipe* umwickeln, isolieren

lag[3] N *(inf: also* **old lag**) (ehemaliger) Knacki *(inf)*

lager [ˈlɑːgəʳ] N helles Bier; **a glass of ~** ein (Glas) Helles

lager lout N *(Brit inf)* betrunkener Rowdy; *(causing damage also)* betrunkener Randalierer

laggard [ˈlægəd] **N** *(= sb who has fallen behind)* Nachzügler(in) *m(f)*; *(= idler)* Trödler(in) *m(f)*; **he is a ~ in love** *(liter, hum)* er ist nicht so stürmisch **ADJ** *student, worker* faul

lagging [ˈlægɪŋ] N Isolierschicht *f*; *(= material)* Isoliermaterial *nt*

lagoon [ləˈguːn] N Lagune *f*

lah-di-dah [ˈlɑːdɪˈdɑː] ADJ ADV *(inf)* = **la-di-da**

laid [leɪd] *pret, ptp of* **lay**[4]

laid-back [ˌleɪdˈbæk] ADJ *(inf)* gelassen, cool *(inf)*

lain [leɪn] *ptp* → **lie**[2]

lair [lɛəʳ] N Lager *nt*; *(= cave)* Höhle *f*; *(= den)* Bau *m*

laird [lɛəd] N *(Scot)* Gutsherr(in) *m(f)*

laissez faire [ˈleɪseɪˈfɛəʳ] N Laisser-faire *nt*; **there's too much ~ here** hier geht es zu leger zu

laissez-faire [ˈleɪseɪˈfɛəʳ] ADJ *(Econ)* Laisser-faire-; *(fig)* leger, lax; **~ economics** Laisser-faire-Wirtschaftspolitik *f*

laity [ˈleɪɪtɪ] N **a** *(= laymen)* Laienstand *m*, Laien *pl* **b** *(= those outside a profession)* Laien *pl*

lake[1] [leɪk] N See *m*

lake[2] N *(colour)* Karm(es)inrot *nt*

lake: **Lake Constance** [ˌleɪkˈkɒnstəns] N der Bodensee; **Lake District** N Lake District *m (Seengebiet im NW Englands)*; **lake dweller** N Pfahlbaubewohner(in) *m(f)*; **lake dwelling** N Pfahlbau *m*; **Lake Poets** PL *Dichter des Lake District: Wordsworth, Coleridge, Southey*; **lakeside** **N** Seeufer *nt* **ATTR** am See

la-la land [ˈlɑːlɑːˌlænd] N *(esp US inf) Bezeichnung für Los Angeles, insbesondere Hollywood*; **to be in ~** *(fig)* ganz weit weg sein

lallygag [ˈlælɪˌgæg] VI *(dated US sl)* = **lollygag**

lam[1] [læm] *(sl)* **VT** vermöbeln *(inf)* **VI** **to ~ into sb** jdn zur Schnecke machen *(inf)*; *(physically)* auf jdn eindreschen *(inf)*

lam[2] N *(US sl)* **he's on the ~** hinter dem sind sie her *(inf)*; **to go on the ~** türmen *(inf)*, die Fliege machen *(sl)*; **he took it on the ~** er türmte *(inf)*, er machte die Fliege *(sl)*

lama [ˈlɑːmə] N *(Rel)* Lama *m*

lamb [læm] **N** **a** *(= young sheep)* Lamm *nt* **b** *(= meat)* Lamm(fleisch) *nt* **c** *(= person)* Engel *m*; **the little ~s** *(children)* die lieben Kleinen; **you poor ~!** du armes Lämmchen!; **she took it like a ~** sie ertrug es geduldig wie ein Lamm; **he followed her like a ~** er folgte ihr wie ein Lamm; **like a ~ to the slaughter** wie das Lamm zur Schlachtbank, wie ein Opferlamm **d** **the Lamb of God** das Lamm Gottes **VI** lammen; **the ~ing season** die Lammungszeit

lambada [læmˈbɑːdə] N *(= dance)* Lambada *m*

lambast [læmˈbæst], **lambaste** [læmˈbeɪst] VT fertigmachen *(inf)*; **to ~ sb for sth** es jdm wegen etw tüchtig geben *(inf)*

lamb: **lamb chop** N Lammkotelett *nt*; **lamblike** ADJ lammfromm, sanft wie ein Lamm; **lambskin** N Lammfell *nt*; **lamb's lettuce** N Feldsalat *m*; **lamb's tail** N *(Bot)* Haselkätzchen *nt*; **lambswool** N Lammwolle *f*

lame [leɪm] **ADJ** *(+er)* **a** lahm; *(as result of stroke etc)* gelähmt; **to be ~ in one leg** auf einem Bein lahm sein; **the animal was ~** das Tier lahmte; **the horse went ~** das Pferd fing an zu lahmen **b** *(fig) excuse* lahm, faul; *argument* schwach, wenig überzeugend; **it's pretty ~** *(US sl)* das ist uncool *(inf)* **VT** lähmen; *horse* lahm machen

lamé [ˈlɑːmeɪ] N Lamé *nt*

lame duck N Niete *f (inf)*; **~ company** unwirtschaftliche Firma

lamella [ləˈmelə] N *pl* **-lae** *or* **-las** Lamelle *f*

lamely ['leɪmlɪ] ADV *argue, say etc* lahm; **to walk ~** hinken; *(horse)* lahmen; **he limped ~ into the room** er humpelte ins Zimmer; **~ he mumbled an excuse** er murmelte eine lahme Entschuldigung vor sich hin

lameness ['leɪmnɪs] N **a** Lähmung *f* *(in, of +gen)*; **his ~** sein Gelähmtsein *nt* **b** *(fig) (of excuse)* Lahmheit *f*; *(of argument)* Schwäche *f*, mangelnde Überzeugungskraft

lament [lə'ment] **N a** Klagen *pl*, (Weh)klage *f*; **in ~** (weh)klagend **b** *(Liter, Mus)* Klagelied *nt*
VT beklagen; *misfortune etc also* bejammern; **to ~ sb** jds Tod beklagen, um jdn trauern; **it is much to be ~ed that …** es ist sehr zu beklagen, dass …; **to ~ the fact that …** die Tatsache bedauern, dass …; **what will become of me now?, he ~ed** was soll nun aus mir werden?, klagte *or* jammerte er
VI (weh)klagen; **to ~ for sb** um jdn trauern; **to ~ over sth** über etw *(acc)* jammern, etw bejammern *or* beklagen; **to ~ over one's lost youth** über seine verlorene Jugend trauern; **she ~ed over his dead body** sie wehklagte über seinem Leichnam

lamentable ['læməntəbl] ADJ beklagenswert; *piece of work* jämmerlich schlecht, erbärmlich

lamentably ['læməntəblɪ] ADV erbärmlich, beklagenswert; **he failed ~** er scheiterte kläglich; **~, this idea is not practicable** bedauerlicherweise lässt sich diese Idee nicht verwirklichen; **she was ~ ignorant of politics** es war traurig *or* zum Weinen, wie wenig sie von Politik wusste; **the level of their commitment is ~ low** es ist jämmerlich, wie wenig sie sich engagieren; **there are ~ few female surgeons** es gibt immer noch beklagenswert wenige Chirurginnen

lamentation [ˌlæmən'teɪʃən] N (Weh)klage *f*; *(= act)* Klagen *nt*, Jammern *nt*; *(= poem, song)* Klagelied *nt*; **he cried out with ~** er brach in lautes Wehklagen aus

laminated ['læmɪneɪtɪd] ADJ geschichtet; *card, book cover* laminiert; **~ glass** Verbundglas *nt*; **~ wood** Sperrholz *nt*; **~ plastic** Resopal® *nt*; **~ working surfaces** Arbeitsflächen aus Resopal®

laminator ['læmɪneɪtəʳ] N Laminiergerät *nt*

lamp [læmp] N Lampe *f*; *(in street)* Laterne *f*; *(Aut, Rail)* Scheinwerfer *m*; *(= rear lamp)* Rücklicht *nt*; *(= torch)* Taschenlampe *f*; *(= sun lamp)* Höhensonne *f*

lamp: **lampblack** N Farbruß *m*; **lamp bracket** N Lampenhalterung *f*; **lamp chimney, lamp glass** N Zylinder *m*; **lamplight** ['læmplaɪt] N Lampenlicht *nt*, Schein *m* der Lampe(n); *(in street)* Licht *nt* der Laterne(n); **by ~** bei Lampenlicht; **in the ~** im Schein der Lampe(n); **lamplighter** N Laternenanzünder *m*

lampoon [læm'puːn] **N** Spott- *or* Schmähschrift *f* **VT** verspotten, verhöhnen

lamppost ['læmppəʊst] N Laternenpfahl *m*

lamprey ['læmprɪ] N Neunauge *nt*, Bricke *f*; *(= sea lamprey)* Lamprete *f*

lamp: **lampshade** ['læmpʃeɪd] N Lampenschirm *m*; **lamp standard** N = **lamppost**

LAN [læn] *(Comput) abbr of* **local area network** LAN *nt*

lance [lɑːns] **N** Lanze *f* **VT** *(Med)* öffnen, aufschneiden

lance corporal N Obergefreite(r) *mf*

lancer ['lɑːnsəʳ] N *(Mil Hist)* Lanzenreiter *m*, Ulan *m*

lancers ['lɑːnsəz] N *sing (= dance)* Lancier *m*, Quadrille *f*

lancet ['lɑːnsɪt] N *(Med)* Lanzette *f*

lancet arch N *(Archit)* Spitzbogen *m*

lancet window N *(Archit)* Spitzbogenfenster *nt*

Lancs [læŋks] *abbr of* **Lancashire**

land [lænd] **N a** *(= not sea)* Land *nt*; **by ~** auf dem Landweg; **by ~ and sea** zu Land und zu Wasser; **as they approached ~** als sie sich dem Land näherten; **to see how the ~ lies** *(lit)* das Gelände erkunden *or* auskundschaften; *(fig)* die Lage sondieren *or* peilen; **the lay** *or* **lie of the ~** *(lit)* die Beschaffenheit des Geländes; **until I've seen the lay** *or* **lie of the ~** *(fig)* bis ich die Lage sondiert habe; **for ~'s sake** *(US, inf)* um Himmels willen → **dry land**
b *(= nation, region: also fig)* Land *nt*; **to be in the ~ of the living** unter den Lebenden sein; **the ~ of opportunity** *(= USA)* das Land der unbegrenzten Möglichkeiten
c *(as property)* Grund und Boden *m*; *(= estates)* Ländereien *pl*; **to own ~** Land besitzen; **she's bought a piece of ~** sie hat ein Stück Land *or (for building)* ein Grundstück gekauft; **get off my ~!** verschwinden Sie von meinem Grundstück *or* von meinem Grund und Boden!
d *(Agr)* Land *nt*; *(= soil)* Boden *m*; **to return to the ~** zur Scholle zurückkehren; **to work on the ~** das Land bebauen; **the drift from the ~** die Landflucht; **to live off the ~** *(= grow own food)* sich vom Lande ernähren, von den Früchten des Landes leben *(liter)*; *(= forage)* sich aus der Natur ernähren
VT a *(Naut) passengers* absetzen, von Bord gehen lassen; *troops* landen; *goods* an Land bringen, löschen; *fish at port* anlanden; *boat* an Land ziehen; **he ~ed the boat on the beach** er zog das Boot an den Strand
b *(Aviat) passengers* absetzen, von Bord gehen lassen; *troops* landen; *goods* abladen; **to ~ a plane** (mit einem Flugzeug) landen; **the helicopter ~ed a doctor on the ship** der Hubschrauber setzte einen Arzt auf dem Schiff ab; **scientists will ~ a space probe on the moon** Wissenschaftler werden eine Raumsonde auf dem Mond landen
c *fish on hook* an Land ziehen
d *(inf: = obtain)* kriegen *(inf)*; *contract* sich *(dat)* verschaffen; *prize* (sich *dat*) holen *(inf)*; *job* an Land ziehen *(inf)*; **she finally ~ed him** sie hat sich *(dat)* ihn schließlich geangelt *(inf)*
e *(Brit inf) blow* landen *(inf)*; **he ~ed him one, he ~ed him a punch on the jaw** er versetzte ihm *or* landete bei ihm einen Kinnhaken
f *(inf: = place)* bringen; **behaviour** *(Brit) or* **behavior** *(US)* **like that will ~ you in trouble/jail** bei einem solchen Betragen wirst du noch mal Ärger bekommen/im Gefängnis landen; **it ~ed me in a mess** dadurch bin ich in einen ganz schönen Schlamassel *(inf)* geraten *or* gekommen; **I've ~ed myself in a real mess** ich bin (ganz schön) in die Klemme geraten *(inf)*; **his attitude ~ed him in trouble** durch seine Einstellung handelte er sich *(dat)* Ärger ein; **buying the house ~ed him in debt** durch den Kauf des Hauses verschuldete er sich; **being overdrawn could ~ you with big bank charges** wenn man sein Konto überzieht, kann einen das hohe Bankgebühren kosten
g *(inf: = lumber)* **to ~ sb with sth** jdm etw aufhalsen *(inf) or* andrehen *(inf)*; **I got ~ed with the job** man hat mir die Arbeit aufgehalst *(inf)*; **I got ~ed with him for two hours** ich hatte ihn zwei Stunden lang auf dem Hals
VI a *(from ship)* an Land gehen
b *(Aviat)* landen; *(bird, insect)* landen, sich setzen; **as it ~ed** *(Aviat)* bei der Landung; **we're coming in to ~** wir setzen zur Landung an
c *(= fall, be placed, strike)* landen; **the bomb ~ed on the building** die Bombe fiel auf das Gebäude; **to ~ on one's feet** *(lit)* auf den Füßen landen; *(fig)* auf die Füße fallen; **to ~ on one's head** auf den Kopf fallen; **he ~ed awkwardly** er ist ungeschickt aufgekommen *or* gelandet *(inf)*

► **land up** VI *(inf)* landen *(inf)*; **you'll land up in trouble** du wirst noch mal Ärger bekommen; **I landed up with nothing** ich hatte schließlich nichts mehr

land agent N Gutsverwalter(in) *m(f)*

land army N Landstreitkräfte *pl*

landau ['lændɔː] N Landauer *m*

land: **land-based** ['lændbeɪst] ADJ *missiles, aircraft* landgestützt; **land breeze** N Landwind *m*; **land defences**, *(US)* **land defenses** PL Landwehr *f*; **land development** N Erschließung *f* von Bauland

landed ['lændɪd] ADJ **the ~ class** die Großgrundbesitzer *pl*; **~ gentry** Landadel *m*; **~ property** Grundbesitz *m*

land: **landfall** N Sichten *nt* von Land; *(= land sighted)* gesichtetes Land; **to make ~** Land sichten; **landfill (site)** N Mülldeponie *f*; **land forces** PL Landstreitkräfte *pl*; **landholder** N *(= land-owner)* Grundbesitzer(in) *m(f)*; *(= tenant)* Pächter(in) *m(f)*

landing ['lændɪŋ] N **a** *(Naut) (of person)* Landung *f*; *(of ship)* Anlegen *nt*, Landung *f*; *(of goods)* Löschen *nt* **b** *(Aviat)* Landung *f* **c** *(on stairs, inside house)* Flur *m*, Gang *m*; *(outside flat door)* Treppenabsatz *m*; *(corridor outside flat doors)* Gang *m*, Etagenabsatz *m*

landing: **landing approach** N *(Aviat)* Landeanflug *m*; **landing card** N Einreisekarte *f*; **landing craft** N Landungsboot *nt*; **landing field** N Landeplatz *m*; **landing gear** N Fahrgestell *nt*; **landing net** N Käscher *m*, Kescher *m*; **landing party** N Landetrupp *m*; **landing place** N *(Naut)* Anlegeplatz *m*; **landing stage** N *(Naut)* Landesteg *m*, Landungsbrücke *f*; **landing strip** N Landebahn *f*; **landing wheels** PL (Lauf)räder *pl*

land: **landlady** N *(of land)* Grundbesitzerin *f*; *(of flat etc)* Vermieterin *f*, Hauswirtin *f*; *(of pub)* Wirtin *f*; **~!** Frau Wirtin!; **land law** N Bodenrecht *nt*; **landless** ADJ landlos; **landline** N *(Telec)* Festnetz *nt*; **landlocked** ADJ von Land eingeschlossen; **a ~ country** ein Land *nt* ohne Zugang zum Meer, ein Binnenstaat *m*; **landlord** N *(of land)* Grundbesitzer *m*; *(of flat etc)* Vermieter *m*, Hauswirt *m*; *(of pub)* Wirt *m*; **~!** Herr Wirt!; **landlubber** ['lændlʌbəʳ] N Landratte *f (inf)*; **landmark** N *(Naut)* Landmarke *f*; *(= boundary mark)* Grenzstein *m*, Grenzpfahl *m*; *(= well-known thing)* Wahrzeichen *nt*; *(fig)* Meilenstein *m*, Markstein *m*; **landmass** N Landmasse *f*; **land mine** N Landmine *f*; **land office** N *(US)* Grundbuchamt *nt*; **to do a land-office business** *(inf)* ein Bombengeschäft machen *(inf)*; **landowner** N Grundbesitzer(in) *m(f)*; **landowning** ADJ *attr* mit Grundbesitz; **the ~ class** die Grundbesitzer *pl*; **land reform** N Boden(rechts)reform *f*; **land register** N *(Brit)* Grundbuch *nt*; **land route** N Landweg *m*; **by the ~** auf dem Landweg; **landscape** ['lændskeɪp] **N a** Landschaft *f*; *(Art also)* **b** *(printing format)* Querformat *nt* **VT** *big area, natural park* landschaftlich gestalten; *garden, grounds* gärtnerisch gestalten, anlegen; **landscape architect** N Landschaftsarchitekt(in) *m(f)*; **landscape gardener** N *(for big areas etc)* Landschaftsgärtner(in) *m(f)*; *(for gardens etc)* Gartengestalter(in) *m(f)*; **landscape gardening** N Landschaftsgärtnerei *or* **-gestaltung** *f*, Gartengestaltung *f*; **landslide** N *(lit, fig)* Erdrutsch *m*; **a ~ victory** ein überwältigender Sieg, ein Erdrutschsieg *m*; **landslip** N Erdrutsch *m*; **land tax** N Grundsteuer *f*; **landward** ADJ *view* zum (Fest)land; **they were sailing in a ~ direction** sie fuhren in Richtung Land *or* **auf das Land zu**; **on the ~ side** auf der Landseite, auf der dem Land zugekehrten Seite; **landward(s)** ADV landwärts; **to landward** in Richtung Land

lane [leɪn] N *(in country) (for walking)* (Feld)weg *m*; *(for driving)* Sträßchen *nt*; *(in town)* Gasse *f*, Weg *m*; *(Sport)* Bahn *f*; *(on road)* Spur *f*; *(= shipping lane)* Schifffahrtsweg *m or* -linie *f*; *(= air lane)* (Flug)route *f*, Luftstraße *f*; **in the left-hand ~** *(Aut)* in *or* auf der linken Spur; **~ markings** *(on road)* Spurmarkierungen *pl*; **three-~** *(motorway etc)* dreispurig; **"get in ~"** „einordnen"

language ['læŋgwɪdʒ] N Sprache *f*; **the English ~** Englisch *nt*, die englische Sprache; **a book on ~** ein Buch über die Sprache; **philosophy of ~** Sprachphilosophie *f*; **the ~ of business/diplomacy** die Sprache der Geschäftswelt/Diplomatie; **the ~ of flowers** die Blumensprache; **to study ~s** Sprachen studieren; **your ~ is appal-**

ling deine Ausdrucksweise ist entsetzlich, du drückst dich entsetzlich aus; **that's no ~ to use to your mother!** so spricht man nicht mit seiner Mutter!; **it's a bloody nuisance! – ~!** verfluchter Mist! – na, so was sagt man doch nicht!; **bad ~** Kraftausdrücke *pl*; **strong ~** Schimpfwörter *pl*, derbe Ausdrücke *pl*; *(= forceful language)* starke Worte *pl*; **he used strong ~, calling them fascist pigs** er beschimpfte sie als Faschistenschweine; **the request/complaint was put in rather strong ~** die Aufforderung/Beschwerde hörte sich ziemlich krass an; **putting it in plain ~ …** *(= simply)* einfach ausgedrückt …; *(= bluntly)* um es ganz direkt *or* ohne Umschweife zu sagen, …; **to talk sb's ~** jds Sprache sprechen; **to talk the same ~ (as sb)** die gleiche Sprache (wie jd) sprechen

language: **language barrier** N Sprachbarriere *f*; **language course** N Sprachkurs(us) *m*; **language lab(oratory)** N Sprachlabor *nt*; **language learning** N Sprachenlernen *nt*; **language-learning** ADJ *facilities, skills* zum Sprachenlernen; **language teacher** N Sprachlehrer(in) *m(f)*

languid ['læŋgwɪd] ADJ träge; *gesture* müde, matt; *manner* lässig, gelangweilt; *walk* lässig, schlendernd; *voice* müde

languidly ['læŋgwɪdlɪ] ADV träge, lässig; **is that all? she said ~** ist das alles?, sagte sie gelangweilt; **the model posed ~ against the sofa** das Modell lehnte sich in einer lässigen Pose gegen das Sofa; **~ she waved to the crowd** mit einer müden *or* matten Geste winkte sie der Menge zu; **the chords build up slowly and ~** die Akkorde bauen sich langsam und schleppend auf

languidness ['læŋgwɪdnɪs] N Trägheit *f*; *(of gesture)* Mattigkeit *f*; *(of manner)* Lässigkeit *f*; **the ~ of her voice** ihre müde Stimme

languish ['læŋgwɪʃ] VI schmachten; *(flowers)* dahinwelken; *(= pine)* sich sehnen *(for* nach); **he ~ed in prison for months** er schmachtete monatelang im Gefängnis; **the panda merely ~ed in its new home** der Panda wurde in seiner neuen Heimat immer apathischer *or* stumpfer; **the child ~ed during his mother's absence** das Kind verzehrte sich nach seiner Mutter *(geh)*; **the products ~ on the shelves** die Waren bleiben in den Regalen liegen; **I ~ without you, he wrote** ich verzehre mich vor Sehnsucht nach dir, schrieb er

languishing ['læŋgwɪʃɪŋ] ADJ schmachtend

languor ['læŋgəʳ] N *(= indolence)* Trägheit *f*, Schläfrigkeit *f*; *(= weakness)* Mattigkeit *f*, Schlappheit *f*; *(emotional)* Stumpfheit *f*, Apathie *f*

languorous ['læŋgərəs] ADJ träge, schläfrig; *heat* schläfrig, wohlig; *feeling* wohlig; *music* schmelzend; *rhythm, metre* gleitend, getragen; *tone, voice* schläfrig; **a ~ beauty** eine schwüle Schönheit

languorously ['læŋgərəslɪ] ADV träge; *speak* mit schläfriger Stimme; **the soft, ~ sentimental mood of the poem** die weiche, schwül-sentimentale Stimmung des Gedichts; **she stretched out ~** sie räkelte *or* rekelte sich verführerisch

langur [l[ae]ŋ'gʊəʳ] N *(Zool)* Langur *m*

lank [læŋk] ADJ *person, body* dürr, hager; *hair* strähnig, kraftlos; *grass* dürr, mager

lanky ['læŋkɪ] ADJ *(+er)* schlaksig N *(inf)* Lange(r) *mf (inf)*

lanolin(e) ['lænəʊlɪn] N Lanolin *nt*

LAN party N *(Comput)* LAN-Party *f*

lantern ['læntən] N *(also Archit)* Laterne *f* → **Chinese lantern**

lantern: **lantern-jawed** ADJ hohlwangig; **lantern slide** N Glasdiapositiv *nt*, Lichtbild *nt*

lanyard ['lænjəd] N *(= cord)* Kordel *f (an der Pfeife oder Messer getragen wird)*; *(Naut)* Taljereep *nt*

Laos [laʊs] N Laos *nt*

Laotian ['laʊʃɪən] ADJ laotisch N Laote *m*, Laotin *f*

lap¹ [læp] N Schoß *m*; **in** *or* **on her ~** auf dem/ihrem Schoß; **his opponent's mistake dropped victory into his ~** durch den Fehler seines Gegners fiel ihm der Sieg in den Schoß; **it's in the ~ of the gods** es liegt im Schoß der Götter; **to live in the ~ of luxury** ein Luxusleben führen

lap² N Überlappung *f* VT *(= overlap)* überlappen VI sich überlappen

lap³ VT *(= wrap)* wickeln

lap⁴ *(Sport)* N *(= round)* Runde *f*; *(fig: = stage)* Etappe *f*, Strecke *f*, Abschnitt *m*; **his time for the first ~** seine Zeit in der ersten Runde; **on the second ~** in der zweiten Runde; **~ of honour** *(esp Brit)* Ehrenrunde *f*; **we're on the last ~ now** *(fig)* wir haben es bald geschafft VT überrunden VI **to ~ at 90 mph** mit einer Geschwindigkeit von 90 Meilen pro Stunde seine Runden drehen; **he's ~ping at 58 seconds** *(athlete)* er läuft die Runde in einer Zeit von 58 Sekunden

lap⁵ N *(= lick)* Schlecken *nt*, Lecken *nt*; *(of waves)* Klatschen *nt*, Schlagen *nt*, Plätschern *nt* VT a *(= lick)* lecken, schlecken b **the waves ~ped the shore** die Wellen rollten *or* plätscherten an das Ufer VI *(waves, water)* plätschern *(against* an *+acc)*, klatschen *(against* gegen); **to ~ over sth** schwappen über etw *(acc)*

▶ **lap up** VT *sep* a *liquid* auflecken, aufschlecken, aufschlabbern *(inf)*; **the children hungrily lapped up their soup** die Kinder löffelten hungrig ihre Suppe b *praise, compliments, sunshine* genießen; **she lapped it up** das ging ihr runter wie Honig *(inf)*; **he lapped up the compliments** die Komplimente gingen ihm wie Honig runter *(inf)*; **the media are lapping up this latest scandal** die Medien haben sich gierig auf diesen neuesten Skandal gestürzt

laparoscopy [ˌlæpə'rɒskəpɪ] N Laparoskopie *f*

laparotomy [ˌlæpə'rɒtəmɪ] N Laparotomie *f*

lap: **lap belt** N Beckengurt *m*; **lap dancer** N *Tänzerin, die über dem Schoß einen Zuschauers einen provokativen Striptease aufführt*; **lap dancing** N *provokativer Striptease, bei dem die Tänzerin über dem Schoß eines Zuschauers tanzt*; **lapdog** N Schoßhund *m*

lapel [lə'pel] N Aufschlag *m*, Revers *nt or m*

lapidary ['læpɪdərɪ] ADJ **~ art** (Edel)steinschneidekunst *f*; **~ inscription** in Stein gehauene Inschrift N Steinschneider(in) *m(f)*

lapis lazuli ['læpɪs'læzjʊlaɪ] N Lapislazuli *m*

Lapland ['læplænd] N Lappland *nt*

Laplander ['læplændəʳ], **Lapp** [læp] N Lappländer(in) *m(f)*, Lappe *m*, Lappin *f*

Lapp [læp] N a = **Laplander** b = **Lappish**

lapping ['læpɪŋ] N *(of water)* Plätschern *nt*, Schlagen *nt*

Lappish ['læpɪʃ] N Lappländisch *nt*, Lappisch *nt*

lap robe N *(US)* Reisedecke *f*

lapse [læps] N a *(= error)* Fehler *m*; *(moral)* Fehltritt *m*, Verfehlung *f*; **~ of judgement** Fehlurteil *nt*; **he had a momentary ~ of concentration** seine Konzentration ließ einen Augenblick nach; **to suffer from ~s of memory** *or* **memory ~s** an Gedächtnisschwäche leiden; **~ of taste** Geschmacksverirrung *f*; **a serious security ~** ein schwerer Verstoß gegen die Sicherheitsvorkehrungen
b *(= decline)* Absinken *nt no pl*, Abgleiten *nt no pl*; **a ~ in confidence** ein Vertrauensschwund *m*; **~ in standards** Niveauabfall *m*; **he noticed her ~ into German** ihm fiel auf, dass sie ins Deutsche verfiel
c *(= expiry)* Ablauf *m*; *(of claim)* Verfall *m*, Erlöschen *nt*; *(= cessation)* Aussterben *nt*, Schwinden *nt*
d *(of time)* Zeitspanne *f*, Zeitraum *m*; **time ~** Zeitspanne *f*, Zeitraum *m*; **after a ~ of 4 months** nach (einem Zeitraum von) 4 Monaten; **there was a ~ in the conversation** es gab eine Gesprächspause
VI a *(= make mistake)* einen Fehler begehen, etwas falsch machen; *(morally)* fehlen *(liter)*, einen Fehltritt begehen, unrecht tun; **to ~ from one's faith** von seinem Glauben abfallen, seinem Glauben abtrünnig werden
b *(= decline)* verfallen *(into* in *+acc)*, abgleiten *(from sth into sth* von etw in etw *acc)*; **to ~ into one's old ways** wieder in seine alten Gewohnheiten verfallen; **he ~d into German/legal jargon** er verfiel ins Deutsche/in den Anwaltsjargon; **he ~d into silence** er versank in Schweigen; **he ~d into a coma** er sank in ein Koma; **he/his work is lapsing** er/seine Arbeit lässt nach, mit ihm/seiner Arbeit geht es bergab
c *(= expire)* ablaufen; *(claims)* verfallen, erlöschen; *(= cease to exist)* aussterben; *(friendship, correspondence)* einschlafen; **after two months have ~d** nach (Ablauf von) zwei Monaten

lapsed [læpst] ADJ *Catholic* abtrünnig, vom Glauben abgefallen; *insurance policy* abgelaufen, verfallen

lap time N *(Sport)* Rundenzeit *f*

laptop ['læptɒp] *(Comput)* N Laptop *m* ATTR Laptop-; **~ PC/computer** Laptop(-PC/Computer) *m*

lapwing ['læpwɪŋ] N Kiebitz *m*

larboard ['lɑːbəd] *(old)* ADJ Backbord-; **~ side** Backbordseite *f* N Backbord *nt*

larcenous ['lɑːsənəs] ADJ diebisch; **~ activities** Diebstähle *pl*

larceny ['lɑːsənɪ] N *(Jur)* Diebstahl *m*

larch [lɑːtʃ] N *(also* **larch tree**) Lärche *f*; *(= wood)* Lärche(nholz *nt*) *f*

lard [lɑːd] N Schweineschmalz *nt* VT *(esp Brit)* mit Schweineschmalz bestreichen; *(with strips of bacon, fig)* spicken

larder ['lɑːdəʳ] N *(esp Brit) (= room)* Speisekammer *f*; *(= cupboard)* Speiseschrank *m*

lardy cake ['lɑːdɪˌkeɪk] N *Schmalzkuchen aus Brotteig mit Rosinen*

large [lɑːdʒ] ADJ *(+er)* a *(= big)* groß; *person* stark, korpulent; *meal* reichlich, groß; *list* lang; **~ print** Großdruck *m*; **"large"** *(on clothing label)* „Large"; **I need a ~r size** ich brauche eine größere Größe; **he's a ~ landowner** er ist ein Großgrundbesitzer *m*; **she looks as ~ as life in that photograph** sie sieht auf dem Foto aus, wie sie leibt und lebt; **there he/it was as ~ as life** da war er/es in voller Lebensgröße
b *(= extensive) interests, power* weitreichend, weit reichend, bedeutend; **his interests were on a ~ scale** er hatte weitreichende *or* breit gestreute Interessen; **taking the ~ view** global betrachtet
ADV groß; **guilt was written ~ all over his face** die Schuld stand ihm deutlich im Gesicht geschrieben
N a **at ~** *(= in general)* im Großen und Ganzen, im Allgemeinen; **people** *or* **the world at ~** die Allgemeinheit; **he wanted to tell his story to the world at ~** er wollte der ganzen Welt seine Geschichte erzählen
b **to be at ~** *(= free)* frei herumlaufen
c **at ~** *(= in detail, at length)* ausführlich, lang und breit
d **strewn at ~** *(= at random)* kreuz und quer verstreut; **scattering accusations at ~** mit Anschuldigungen um sich werfend
e **ambassador at ~** Sonderbotschafter(in) *m(f)*
f *(US inf: = 1000-dollar note)* Riese *m (inf)*; **50 ~** 50 Riesen *pl (inf)*

large-hearted ['lɑːdʒˌhɑːtɪd] ADJ großherzig

largely ['lɑːdʒlɪ] ADV *(= mainly)* zum größten Teil

large-minded ['lɑːdʒˌmaɪndɪd] ADJ aufgeschlossen

largeness ['lɑːdʒnɪs] N a *(= big size)* Größe *f*, Umfang *m*; *(of meal)* Reichlichkeit *f*; *(of list)* Länge *f* b *(= extent: of interests, power)* Bedeutung *f*, Umfang *m* c *(old: = generosity)* Großzügigkeit *f*

large: **large-print** ADJ *book* in Großdruck; **~ edition** Großdruckausgabe *f*; **large-scale** ADJ groß angelegt; *reception, party, changes* in großem Rahmen; **a ~ producer of food** ein Großhersteller *m* von Nahrungsmitteln; **~ production** *(Ind)* Massenproduktion *f*; **~ unrest** Massenaufruhr *m*, Massenunruhen *pl*; **a ~ map** eine (Land)karte in großem Maßstab; **~ integration** *(Comput)* Großintegration *f*; **large screen** N Großbildschirm *m*; **large-sized** ADJ groß

largesse [lɑːˈʒes] N Großzügigkeit *f*, Freigebigkeit *f*; *(= gift)* (großzügige) Gabe

largish [ˈlɑːdʒɪʃ] ADJ ziemlich groß

largo [ˈlɑːgəʊ] N Largo *nt*

lariat [ˈlærɪət] N Lasso *nt or m*

lark¹ [lɑːk] N *(Orn)* Lerche *f*; **to be up with the ~** mit den Hühnern aufstehen; **as happy as a ~** quietschfidel

lark² N *(inf)* **a** *(esp Brit: = joke, fun, frolic)* Jux *m (inf)*, Spaß *m*, *(Aus also)* Spass *m*; **let's go to the party, it'll be a bit of a ~** gehen wir zu der Party, das wird bestimmt lustig; **that's the best ~ we've had for a long time!** so viel Spaß haben wir schon lange nicht mehr gehabt!; **what a ~!** das ist (ja) zum Schreien *or* Schießen!; **to do sth for a ~** etw (nur) zum Spaß *or* aus Jux machen; **to have a ~ with sb** mit jdm zusammen Spaß haben
b *(Brit inf: = business, affair)* **this whole agency ~ is ...** die ganze Geschichte mit der Agentur ist ... *(inf)*; **I wouldn't get involved in that ~** auf so was *or* so 'ne Sache würde ich mich nicht einlassen *(inf)*; **politics and all that ~** Politik und der ganze Kram *(inf)*; **I don't believe in all this horoscopes ~** ich glaube nicht an diesen Blödsinn mit den Horoskopen *(inf)*

▸ **lark about** *or* **around** VI *(Brit inf)* herumblödeln, herumalbern; **to lark about with sth** mit etw herumspielen

larkspur [ˈlɑːkspɜː] N Rittersporn *m*

larrikin [ˈlærɪkɪn] N *(Austral inf)* Rowdy *m*

Larry [ˈlærɪ] N **a** *dim of* **Laurence** *of* **Lawrence** **b** *(dated Brit inf)* **as happy as ~** quietschvergnügt *(inf)*

larva [ˈlɑːvə] N *pl* **-e** [ˈlɑːviː] Larve *f*

larval [ˈlɑːvəl] ADJ Larven-, larvenähnlich; **~ stage** Larvenzustand *m*

laryngeal [ləˈrɪndʒəl] ADJ Kehlkopf-; **~ reflex** Kehlkopfreflex *m*

laryngitis [ˌlærɪnˈdʒaɪtɪs] N Kehlkopfentzündung *f*, Laryngitis *f (spec)*

larynx [ˈlærɪŋks] N Kehlkopf *m*, Larynx *m (spec)*

lasagne, lasagna [ləˈzænjə] N Lasagne *pl*

lascivious [ləˈsɪvɪəs] ADJ lasziv *(geh)*; *movements, person, look, behaviour also* lüstern; *book* schlüpfrig

lasciviously [ləˈsɪvɪəslɪ] ADV lüstern; **the dancer moved ~** die Bewegungen der Tänzerin waren lasziv

lasciviousness [ləˈsɪvɪəsnɪs] N Laszivität *f (geh)*; *(of movement, person, look, behaviour also)* Lüsternheit *f*; *(of book)* Schlüpfrigkeit *f*

laser [ˈleɪzəʳ] N Laser *m*; *(Comput: = printer)* Laserdrucker *m*

laser *in cpds* Laser-; **laser beam** N Laserstrahl *m*; **laser disc** N Laserdisc *f*, Laserdisk *f*; **laser gun** N Laserkanone *f or* -pistole *f*; **laser medicine** N Lasermedizin *f*; **laser printer** N Laserdrucker *m*; **laser show** N Lasershow *f*; **laser surgery** N Laserchirurgie *f*; **laser technology** N Lasertechnik *f*; **laser weapon** N Laserwaffe *f*

lash¹ [læʃ] N *(= eyelash)* Wimper *f*; **she fluttered her ~es at him** sie machte ihm schöne Augen

lash² N **a** *(= whip)* Peitsche *f*; *(= thong)* Schnur *f*
b *(= stroke: as punishment)* (Peitschen)schlag *m*
c *(= lashing, of tail)* Schlagen *nt*; *(of waves, rain)* Peitschen *nt*
d *(fig)* Schärfe *f*; **the ~ of her tongue** ihre scharfe Zunge
VT **a** *(= beat)* peitschen; *(as punishment)* auspeitschen; *(hail, rain, waves)* peitschen gegen; *tail* schlagen mit; **the wind ~ed the sea into a fury** wütend peitschte der Wind die See; **the cow ~ed the flies with its tail** die Kuh schlug mit ihrem Schwanz nach den Fliegen; **to ~ the crowd into a fury** die Menge aufpeitschen
b *(fig: = criticize)* heruntermachen *(inf)*, abkanzeln
c *(= tie)* festbinden (*to* an *+dat*); **to ~ sth together** etw zusammenbinden
VI **to ~ against** peitschen gegen

▸ **lash about** *(Brit) or* **around** VI (wild) um sich schlagen

▸ **lash along** VT *sep* = **lash on**

▸ **lash around** VI = **lash about**

▸ **lash back** VT *sep* festbinden

▸ **lash down** VT *sep (= tie down)* festbinden *or* -zurren VI *(rain etc)* niederprasseln

▸ **lash into** VI *+prep obj* **to lash into sb** *(physically)* auf jdn einschlagen; *(with words)* jdn anfahren *or* anbrüllen *(inf)*

▸ **lash on** *or* **along** VT *sep horse, slaves* mit der Peitsche antreiben

▸ **lash out** VI **a** *(physically)* (wild) um sich schlagen *or* hauen; *(horse)* ausschlagen; **to lash out at sb** auf jdn losgehen; **she lashed out with a knife** sie stieß mit einem Messer; **he lashed out with his fists** er schlug mit den Fäusten zu
b *(in words)* vom Leder ziehen *(inf)*; **to lash out against** *or* **at sb/sth** gegen jdn/etw wettern; **"TUC boss lashes out"** „Gewerkschaftsboss holt zum Schlag aus"
c *(inf: with money)* sich in Unkosten stürzen; **to lash out on sth** sich *(dat)* etw was kosten lassen *(inf)*; **I'm going to lash out on a new car** ich werde mir ein neues Auto leisten; **now we can really lash out** jetzt können wir uns wirklich mal etwas leisten
VT *insep sum of money* springen lassen

▸ **lash up** VT *sep* verschnüren

lashing [ˈlæʃɪŋ] N **a** *(= beating)* Prügel *pl*; *(= punishment)* Auspeitschung *f* **b** *(fig: = criticism)* scharfe Kritik **c** *(= tying)* Verschnürung *f*; *(of prisoner)* Fesseln *pl*; *(Naut)* Tau *nt*, Zurring *m* **d** **lashings** PL *(inf)* eine Unmenge *(inf)*; **~s of money/cream** eine Unmenge *or* massenhaft Geld/Schlagsahne *(inf)*

lass [læs] N (junges) Mädchen, Mädel *nt (dial)*; *(= country lass)* Mädchen *nt* vom Land; *(= sweetheart)* Freundin *f*, Schatz *m*

lassie [ˈlæsɪ] N *(inf: esp Scot, N Engl)* = **lass**

lassitude [ˈlæsɪtjuːd] N Mattigkeit *f*, Trägheit *f*

lasso [læˈsuː] N *pl* **-(e)s** Lasso *m or nt* VT mit dem Lasso einfangen

last¹ [lɑːst] ADJ **a** letzte(r, s); **he was ~ to arrive** er kam als Letzter an; **the ~ person** der Letzte; **the ~ but one, the second ~ (one)** der/die/das Vorletzte; **the third ~ house** das drittletzte Haus; **(the) ~ one there buys the drinks!** der Letzte *or* wer als Letzter ankommt, zahlt die Getränke; **~ Monday, on Monday ~** letzten Montag; **~ year** letztes Jahr, im vorigen Jahr; **during the ~ 20 years, these ~ 20 years** in den letzten 20 Jahren; **~ but not least** nicht zuletzt, last not least
b *(= most unlikely, unsuitable etc)* **that's the ~ thing I worry about** das ist das Letzte, worüber ich mir Sorgen machen würde; **that was the ~ thing I expected** damit hatte ich am wenigsten gerechnet; **that's the ~ thing I wanted to happen** das habe ich am wenigsten gewollt; **he's the ~ person I want to see** er ist der Letzte, den ich sehen möchte; **you're the ~ person to be entrusted with it** du bist der Letzte, dem man das anvertrauen kann
N **a** *(= final one or part, one before)* der/die/das Letzte; **he was the ~ of the visitors to leave** er ging als Letzter der Besucher; **I'm always the ~ to know** ich erfahre immer alles als Letzter; **he withdrew the ~ of his money from the bank** er hob sein letztes Geld von der Bank ab; **each one is better than the ~** eins ist besser als das andere; **this is the ~ of the cake** das ist der Rest des Kuchens; **that's the ~ of the fighting** jetzt hat der Kampf ein Ende; **that was the ~ we saw of him** danach haben wir ihn nicht mehr gesehen; **the ~ we heard of him was ...** das Letzte, was wir von ihm hörten, war ...; **that was the ~ we heard of it/him** seitdem haben wir nichts mehr darüber/von ihm gehört; **I hope this is the ~ we'll hear of it** ich hoffe, damit ist die Sache erledigt; **the ~ I heard, they were getting married** das Letzte, was ich gehört habe, war, dass sie heirateten; **I shall be glad to see the ~ of this/him** ich bin froh, wenn ich das hinter mir habe/wenn ich den los bin *(inf) or* wenn ich den nicht mehr sehe; **we shall never hear the ~ of it** das werden wir noch lange zu hören kriegen; **to look one's ~ on sth** den letzten Blick auf etw *(acc)* werfen; **my ~** *(Comm)* mein letztes Schreiben
b **at ~** endlich; **at long ~** schließlich und endlich; **so you're ready at long ~!** du bist also endlich fertig geworden!; **to the ~** bis zum Schluss
ADV **when did you ~ have a bath** *or* **have a bath ~?** wann hast du das letzte Mal gebadet?; **I ~ heard from him a month ago** vor einem Monat habe ich das letzte Mal von ihm gehört; **he spoke ~** er sprach als Letzter; **the horse came in ~** das Pferd ging als letztes durchs Ziel

last² VT **it will ~ me/a careful user a lifetime** das hält/bei vernünftiger Benutzung hält es ein Leben lang; **the car has ~ed me eight years** das Auto hat acht Jahre (lang) gehalten; **these cigarettes will ~ me a week** diese Zigaretten reichen mir eine Woche; **I didn't think he'd ~ the week** ich hätte nicht gedacht, dass er die Woche durchhält
VI *(= continue)* dauern; *(= remain intact: cloth, flowers, marriage)* halten; **it can't ~** es hält nicht an; **it won't ~** es wird nicht lange anhalten *or* so bleiben; **it's too good to ~** das ist zu schön, um wahr zu sein; **he'll stay as long as the beer ~s** er bleibt, solange Bier da ist; **will this material ~?** ist dieses Material haltbar *or* dauerhaft?; **none of his girlfriends ~s for long** bei ihm hält sich keine Freundin lange; **he won't ~ long in this job** er wird in dieser Stelle nicht alt werden *(inf)*; **the previous boss only ~ed a week** der letzte Chef blieb nur eine Woche

▸ **last out** VT *sep* ausreichen für; *(people)* durchhalten VI *(money, resources)* ausreichen; *(person)* durchhalten

last³ N Leisten *m*; **cobbler, stick to your ~!** Schuster, bleib bei deinem Leisten!

last: **last-chance saloon** N *(Brit inf)* **they are drinking in the ~** es ist ihre letzte Chance; **Last Day** N **the ~** der Jüngste Tag; **last-ditch** [ˈlɑːstdɪtʃ] ADJ allerletzte(r, s); *attempt, proposals, talks etc* in letzter Minute

lasting [ˈlɑːstɪŋ] ADJ *relationship* dauerhaft; *material also* haltbar; *shame etc* anhaltend

Last Judgement N **the ~** das Jüngste *or* Letzte Gericht

lastly [ˈlɑːstlɪ] ADV schließlich, zum Schluss

last: **last-minute** ADJ in letzter Minute; **~ flight** Last-Minute-Flug *m*; **~ deal** Last-Minute-Angebot*n*, Angebot *n* für Kurzentschlossene; **last name** N Nachname *m*, Zuname *m*; **last number recall, last number redial** N *(Telec)* Wahlwiederholung *f*; **last post** N Zapfenstreich *m*; **last rites** PL Letzte Ölung; **Last Supper** N **the ~** das (Letzte) Abendmahl; **last word** N **the ~** *(in fashion)* der letzte Schrei; **to have the ~ (on sth)** das letzte Wort (zu etw) haben; **the ~ on biochemistry/on this subject** das maßgebende Werk über Biochemie/auf diesem Gebiet

Lat *abbr of* **Latin** lat., Lat.

lat *abbr of* **latitude** Br.

latch [lætʃ] N Riegel *m*; **to be on the ~** nicht verschlossen sein, nur eingeklinkt sein; **to leave the door on the ~** die Tür nur einklinken
VT verriegeln

▸ **latch on** VI *(inf)* **a** *(= get hold)* sich festhalten; *(with teeth)* sich festbeißen (*to sth* an etw *dat*); **he latched on to the idea of coming with**

us er hat es sich *(dat)* in den Kopf gesetzt, mitzukommen **b** *(= attach o.s.)* sich anschließen *(to +dat)*; **she latched on to me at the party** sie hängte sich auf der Party an mich *(inf)* **c** *(= understand)* kapieren *(inf)*

latchkey [ˈlætʃkiː] N Hausschlüssel *m*

latchkey child N Schlüsselkind *nt*

late [leɪt] ADJ *(+er)* **a** spät; **to be ~ (for sth)** (zu etw) zu spät kommen; **the train/bus is (five minutes) ~** der Zug/Bus hat (fünf Minuten) Verspätung; **dinner will be ~ tonight** wir essen heute Abend später; *(in hotels)* es wird heute Abend später serviert; **I was ~ in getting up this morning** ich bin heute Morgen zu spät aufgestanden; **he is ~ with his rent** er hat seine Miete noch nicht bezahlt; **he is always ~ with his rent** er bezahlt seine Miete immer zu spät; **my period is ~, I am ~** meine Periode ist noch nicht da; **I don't want to make you ~** ich möchte Sie nicht aufhalten; **you'll make me ~** Ihretwegen werde ich mich verspäten; **that made me ~ for work** dadurch bin ich zu spät zur Arbeit gekommen; **I don't want to make you ~ for work** ich möchte nicht, dass du zu spät zur Arbeit kommst; **that made the coach ~** dadurch hatte der Bus Verspätung; **that made the harvest ~** dadurch verzögerte sich die Ernte; **due to the ~ arrival of …** wegen der verspäteten Ankunft … *(+gen)*; **it's too ~ (in the day) for that** dafür ist es jetzt zu spät; **it's too ~ in the day (for you) to do that** es ist zu spät (für dich), das noch zu tun; **it's not too ~ to change your mind** es ist noch nicht zu spät, um es sich anders zu überlegen; **it's never too ~ to learn** zum Lernen ist es nie zu spät
b **it's ~** es ist spät; **it's getting ~** es ist schon spät; **is it as ~ as that?** ist es schon so spät?
c *hour* spät; *opening hours* lang; **~ train/bus** Spätzug/-bus *m*; **at this ~ hour** zu so später Stunde, so spät; **at a ~ hour** zu später *or* vorgerückter Stunde; **he keeps very ~ hours** er geht sehr spät ins Bett; **they work ~ hours** sie arbeiten bis spät (am Abend); **the night was cold and the hour ~** die Nacht war kalt und es war sehr spät; **they had a ~ dinner yesterday** sie haben gestern spät zu Abend gegessen; **there is no ~ delivery of post on Saturdays** sonnabends gibt es keine zweite Zustellung; **~ night club** Nachtbar *f*; **~ potato/summer/edition/programme** Spätkartoffel *f*/-sommer *m*/-ausgabe *f*/-programm *nt*; **"late opening until 7pm on Fridays"** „freitags verlängerte Öffnungszeiten bis 19 Uhr"; **he's a ~ developer** er ist ein Spätentwickler; **both my babies were ~** meine Kinder sind beide nach dem Termin gekommen; **~ entrants to the examination will be charged £10 extra** für Nachmeldungen zur Prüfung wird eine Gebühr von £ 10 erhoben; **this essay was a ~ entry for the competition** dieser Aufsatz wurde verspätet für den Wettbewerb eingereicht; *(= last-minute)* dieser Aufsatz wurde in letzter Minute eingereicht; **they scored two ~ goals** sie erzielten zwei Tore in den letzten Spielminuten; **it happened in the ~ eighties** es geschah Ende der achtziger Jahre; **a man in his ~ eighties** ein Mann hoch in den Achtzigern, ein Endachtziger; **in the ~ morning** am späten Vormittag; **a ~ 18th-century building** ein Gebäude aus dem späten 18. Jahrhundert; **he came in ~ June** er kam Ende Juni; **Late Stone Age** Jungsteinzeit *f*; **Easter is ~ this year** Ostern liegt *or* ist dieses Jahr spät; **spring is ~ this year** wir haben dieses Jahr einen späten Frühling
d *(= deceased)* verstorben; **the ~ John F. Kennedy** John F. Kennedy
e *(= former)* **the ~ Prime Minister** der frühere *or* vorige Premierminister
f *(= recent)* jüngst; **in the ~ war** im letzten Krieg
g **~ of No 13 White St** ehemals White St Nr. 13; **~ of the Diplomatic Service** ehemals *or* bis vor Kurzem im diplomatischen Dienst tätig
ADV spät; **to come** *or* **arrive ~** *(= after the arranged/scheduled time) (person)* zu spät kommen; *(bus, train)* Verspätung haben; **I'll be home ~ today** ich komme heute spät nach Hause, es wird heute spät; **the train arrived/was running eight minutes ~** der Zug hatte acht Minuten Verspätung; **the baby was born two weeks ~** das Baby kam zwei Wochen nach dem Termin; **we're running ~ today** wir sind heute spät dran; **better ~ than never** lieber *or* besser spät als gar nicht; **to sit** *or* **stay up ~** lange aufbleiben; **don't wait up ~ for me** warte nicht zu lange auf mich; **the chemist is open ~ on Thursdays** die Apotheke hat donnerstags länger geöffnet; **to work ~ at the office** länger im Büro arbeiten; **~ at night** spät abends; **~ last night** spät gestern Abend; **~ in the night** spät in der Nacht; **~ into the night** bis spät in die Nacht; **~ in the afternoon** am späten Nachmittag; **~ last century/in the year** (gegen) Ende des letzten Jahrhunderts/Jahres; **they scored ~ in the second half** gegen Ende der zweiten Halbzeit gelang ihnen ein Treffer; **he took up the piano rather ~ in life** er begann ziemlich spät mit dem Klavierspielen; **Goethe was still active even ~ in life** Goethe war auch im hohen Alter noch aktiv; **we decided rather ~ in the day to come too** wir haben uns ziemlich spät entschlossen, auch zu kommen; **he left it very ~ in the day (to decide)** er hat (mit seiner Entscheidung) bis zum letzten Augenblick gewartet; **of ~** in letzter Zeit; **until as ~ as 1900** noch bis 1900; **it was as ~ as 1900 before child labour** *(Brit) or* **labor** *(US)* **was abolished** erst 1900 wurde die Kinderarbeit abgeschafft

latecomer [ˈleɪtkʌməˈ] N Zuspätkommende(r) *mf*, Nachzügler(in) *m(f) (inf)*; **the product is a ~ to the market** das Produkt ist neu auf dem Markt

lateen sail [ləˈtiːnˈseɪl] N Lateinsegel *nt*

late lamented ADJ kürzlich verstorben *or* verschieden *(geh)*; **my ~ boss** *(iro)* mein heiß geliebter ehemaliger Chef *(iro)*

Late Latin N Spätlatein *nt*

lately [ˈleɪtlɪ] ADV in letzter Zeit; **till ~** bis vor Kurzem

latency [ˈleɪtənsɪ] N Latenz *f*

lateness [ˈleɪtnɪs] N *(= arriving late at work etc)* Zuspätkommen *nt*; *(of train, payments)* Verspätung *f*; *(of meal)* späte Zeit; *(of harvest, seasons)* spätes Eintreten; **the ~ of the hour** die so späte Stunde

late-night [ˈleɪtˌnaɪt] ADJ *period* spät am Abend; **~ movie** Spätfilm *m*; **~ shopping** Einkauf *m* am (späten) Abend, Dämmershopping *nt (inf)*; **~ losses** *(St Ex)* späte Verluste *pl*

latent [ˈleɪtənt] ADJ latent; *strength also* verborgen; *artistic talent, ability also* verborgen, versteckt; *heat also* gebunden; *energy* ungenutzt; **the evil which is ~ in all men** das in jedem Menschen latent vorhandene Böse; **~ period/phase** *(Med, Psych)* Latenzperiode/-phase *f*

later [ˈleɪtəˈ] ADJ später; **at a ~ hour, at a ~ time** später, zu einer späteren Zeit; **this version is ~ than that one** diese Version ist neuer als die andere; **in (his) ~ years** *or* **life** in späteren Jahren, in seinem späteren Leben
ADV später; **Mr Smith, ~ to become Sir John** Mr Smith, der spätere Sir John; **the weather cleared up ~ (on) in the day** das Wetter klärte sich im Laufe des Tages auf; **~ (on) that night/week/day** später in der Nacht/Woche/an dem Tag; **~ (on) in life** später im Leben, in späteren Jahren; **~ (on) in the play** im weiteren Verlauf des Stückes; **I'll tell you ~ (on)** ich erzähle es dir später; **a moment ~** einen Augenblick später, im nächsten Augenblick; **see you ~!** bis nachher, bis später; **I saw him no ~ than yesterday** ich habe ihn (erst) gestern noch gesehen; **come at 7 o'clock and no ~** komm um 7 Uhr und nicht *or* keine Minute später; **not ~ than 1995** spätestens 1995; **they must be handed in no ~ than Monday** sie müssen bis spätestens Montag abgegeben werden

lateral [ˈlætərəl] ADJ seitlich; **~ surface** Seitenfläche *f*; **~ view/window** Seitenansicht *f*/-fenster *nt*

lateral line N *(of fish)* Seitenlinie *f*

laterally [ˈlætərəlɪ] ADV seitlich

lateral thinking N unkonventionelles Denken, Querdenken *nt*

late riser N Langschläfer(in) *m(f)*

latest [ˈleɪtɪst] ADJ **a** *(= most recent) fashion, version* neu(e)ste(r, s); *(= most modern) technology* modernste(r, s); **the ~ news** das Neu(e)ste; **the ~ attempt to rescue them** der jüngste Versuch, sie zu retten; **the ~ thing** *(esp US inf)* der letzte Schrei *(inf)*
b späteste(r, s); **what is the ~ date you can come?** wann kannst du spätestens kommen?; **the ~ possible moment** der letztmögliche *or* allerletzte Augenblick
c *people* letzte(r, s); **the ~ men to resign** die Letzten, die zurückgetreten sind
ADV am spätesten; **he came ~** er kam zuletzt *or* als Letzter
N **a** **he was the ~ to arrive** er kam als Letzter; **the ~ in a series of attacks** der jüngste in einer Reihe von Anschlägen; **what's the ~ (about John)?** was gibts Neues (über John)?; **wait till you hear the ~!** warte, bis du das Neueste gehört hast!; **have you seen John's ~?** *(= girl)* hast du Johns Neu(e)ste schon gesehen?; **have you heard John's ~?** *(= joke)* hast du Johns Neuesten schon gehört?; **it's the ~ in computer games/in technology** es ist das neueste Computerspiel/die neueste Technik
b **at the (very) ~** spätestens

latex [ˈleɪteks] N Latex *m*

lath [læθ] N Latte *f*; **~s** *pl (= structure)* Lattenwerk *nt*

lathe [leɪð] N Drehbank *f*; **~ operator** Dreher(in) *m(f)*

lather [ˈlɑːðəˈ] N (Seifen)schaum *m*; *(= sweat)* Schweiß *m*; **work the soap into a rich ~** die Seife zum Schäumen bringen; **to get** *or* **work oneself up into a ~ (about sth)** *(inf)* sich (über etw *acc*) aufregen, (wegen etw *dat*) durchdrehen *(inf)* VT einschäumen VI schäumen

Latin [ˈlætɪn] ADJ **a** *(= Roman) civilization, world* römisch; *poets, literature* römisch, lateinisch; **~ language** lateinische Sprache; *(= of ancient Latium)* latinische Sprache **b** *(= of Roman origin)* romanisch; *temperament, charm* südländisch **c** *(Rel)* römisch-katholisch N **a** *(= inhabitant of ancient Latium)* Latiner(in) *m(f)*; *(= Roman)* Römer(in) *m(f)*; *(= a member of any Latin race)* Südländer(in) *m(f)*, Romane *m*, Romanin *f* **b** *(Ling)* Latein(isch) *nt*

Latin America N Lateinamerika *nt*

Latin American [ˈlætɪnəˈmerɪkən] ADJ lateinamerikanisch N Lateinamerikaner(in) *m(f)*

latinism [ˈlætɪnɪzəm] N Latinismus *m*

latinist [ˈlætɪnɪst] N Latinist(in) *m(f)*

latinity [ləˈtɪnɪtɪ] N *(rare)* Latinität *f*

latinize [ˈlætɪnaɪz] VT latinisieren

Latin lover N Latin Lover *m*

Latin Quarter N Quartier Latin *nt*

latish [ˈleɪtɪʃ] ADJ ziemlich spät; *applicant, letter* verspätet; *amendment* neuer, später ADV ziemlich spät

latitude [ˈlætɪtjuːd] N Breite *f*; *(fig)* Freiheit *f*, Spielraum *m*

latitudinal [ˌlætɪˈtjuːdɪnl] ADJ Breiten-; **~ lines** Breitengrade *pl*

latrine [ləˈtriːn] N Latrine *f*

latte [ˈlæteɪ] N Caffè latte *m*

latter [ˈlætəˈ] ✪ 26.2 ADJ **a** *(= second of two)* letztere(r, s) **b** *(= at the end)* **the ~ part of the book/story is better** gegen Ende wird das Buch/die Geschichte besser; **the ~ half of the week/year/century** die zweite Hälfte der Woche/des Jahres/des Jahrhunderts; **in the ~ years** in den letzten Jahren; **in his ~ years** in späteren Jahren N **the ~** der/die/das Letztere; *(more than one)* die Letzteren *pl*; **I don't agree with the ~** ich bin mit Letzterem nicht einverstanden; **of these two theories I prefer the ~** von diesen beiden Theorien ziehe ich (die) letztere vor

latter-day ['lætə'deɪ] ADJ modern; **the Latter-day Saints** die Heiligen der Letzten Tage

latterly ['lætəlɪ] ADV *(= recently)* in letzter Zeit; *(= towards end of period)* zuletzt; *(= towards end of life)* in späteren Jahren; **she worked there for 30 years, ~ as manager** sie hat 30 Jahre dort gearbeitet, zuletzt als Geschäftsführerin

lattice ['lætɪs] N Gitter *nt*

latticed ['lætɪst] ADJ vergittert

latticework ['lætɪswɜːk] N Gitterwerk *nt*

Latvia ['lætvɪə] N Lettland *nt*

Latvian ['lætvɪən] ADJ lettisch N a Lette *m*, Lettin *f* b *(Ling)* Lettisch *nt*

laud [lɔːd] VT *(old)* preisen *(geh)*

laudable ['lɔːdəbl] ADJ lobenswert

laudably ['lɔːdəblɪ] ADV lobenswerterweise; **~ unselfish remarks** lobenswert selbstlose Worte *pl*

laudanum ['lɔːdnəm] N Laudanum *nt*

laudatory ['lɔːdətərɪ] ADJ lobend; **a ~ speech** eine Lobrede *or* Laudatio *(geh)*

laugh [lɑːf] N a Lachen *nt*; **no, she said, with a ~** nein, sagte sie lachend; **she let out** *or* **gave a loud ~** sie lachte laut auf; **that woman has a ~ like a hyena** die Frau gackert wie ein Huhn; **what a ~ (she's got)!** die hat vielleicht 'ne Lache! *(inf)*; **to have a good ~ over** *or* **about sth** sich köstlich über etw *(acc)* amüsieren; **to have a good ~ at sb** jdn gründlich auslachen; **you'll have a good ~ about it one day** eines Tages wirst du darüber lachen können; **give us a ~!** *(inf)* bring uns mal zum Lachen!; **it'll give us a ~** *(inf)* das wird lustig; **the ~ was on me** der Witz ging auf meine Kosten; **to have the last ~ (over** *or* **on sb)** es jdm zeigen *(inf)*; **I'll have the last ~** ich werds dir schon noch zeigen *(inf)*; **to get a ~** einen Lacherfolg verbuchen; **to play for ~s** Lacherfolge haben wollen; **he played Hamlet for ~s** er machte aus Hamlet eine komische Figur; **they played "Othello" for ~s** sie machten aus „Othello" eine Komödie
b *(inf: = fun)* **what a ~** (das ist ja) zum Totlachen *or* zum Schreien *(inf)*!; **just for a ~** *or* **for ~s** nur (so) aus Spaß; **it'll be a good ~** es wird bestimmt lustig; **we didn't achieve much, but we had a good ~** wir haben nicht viel geschafft, aber es war trotzdem lustig; **he's a (good) ~** er ist urkomisch *or* zum Schreien *(inf)*; **to be good for a ~** ganz lustig sein; **it was a ~ a minute!** es war zum Schreien! *(inf)*
VI lachen *(about, at, over* über *+acc)*; **to ~ at sb** sich über jdn lustig machen; **to ~ up one's sleeve** sich *(dat)* ins Fäustchen lachen; **she's ~ing up her sleeve at us** sie macht sich heimlich über uns lustig; **it's nothing to ~ about** das ist nicht zum Lachen; **it's all very well for you to ~** du hast gut lachen; **you'll be ~ing on the other side of your face** *(Brit)* *or* **mouth** *(US)* **soon** dir wird das Lachen noch vergehen; **to ~ out loud** laut auflachen; **to ~ in sb's face** jdm ins Gesicht lachen; **he who ~s last ~s longest** *(Prov)* wer zuletzt lacht, lacht am besten *(Prov)*; **you've got to ~** es ist eigentlich zum Lachen; **don't make me ~!** *(iro inf)* dass ich nicht lache! *(inf)*; **if you've got your own house, you're ~ing** *(inf)* wenn man ein eigenes Haus hat, hat man es gut; **he'll be ~ing all the way to the bank** er wird das Geld nur so scheffeln *(inf)* → **drain N a**
VT **to ~ oneself silly** sich tot- *or* kaputtlachen *(inf)*; **he was ~ed out of court** er wurde ausgelacht; **the idea was ~ed out of court** die Idee wurde verlacht; **don't be silly, he ~ed** red keinen Unsinn, sagte er lachend

▶ **laugh away** VT *sep* mit Humor tragen, sich lachend hinwegsetzen über *(+acc)*; **my father laughed away my fears** mein Vater nahm mir mit einem Lachen die Angst VI **he sat there laughing away** er saß da und lachte und lachte

▶ **laugh down** VT *sep* auslachen, mit Gelächter übertönen; **the audience laughed him/his reply down** er/seine Antwort ging im Gelächter des Publikums unter

▶ **laugh off** VT a *always separate* **to laugh one's head off** sich tot- *or* kaputtlachen *(inf)* b *sep (= dismiss)* lachen über *(+acc)*, mit einem Lachen abtun

laughable ['lɑːfəbl] ADJ lachhaft, lächerlich; **if it wasn't so serious, it would be almost ~** wenn es nicht so ernst wäre, könnte man fast darüber lachen

laughably ['lɑːfəblɪ] ADV lächerlich; **we got what was ~ called a double room** wir bekamen ein sogenanntes Doppelzimmer

laughing ['lɑːfɪŋ] ADJ lachend; **it's no ~ matter** das ist nicht zum Lachen, das ist gar nicht komisch N Lachen *nt*; **hysterical ~** hysterisches Gelächter

laughing: **laughing gas** N Lachgas *nt*; **laughing hy(a)ena** N Tüpfel- *or* Fleckenhyäne *f*; **laughing jackass** N Rieseneisvogel *m*

laughingly ['lɑːfɪŋlɪ] ADV *(= with a laugh)* lachend; *(= ridiculously)* lächerlicherweise; **what the government ~ calls its economic policy** das, was die Regierung als Wirtschaftspolitik bezeichnet, obwohl das eigentlich ein Witz ist

laughing stock N Witzfigur *f*; **his visionary ideas made him a ~** mit seinen fantastischen *or* phantastischen Ideen machte er sich lächerlich *or* zum allgemeinen Gespött

laugh lines PL *(US)* Lachfalten *pl*, Lachfältchen *pl*

laughter ['lɑːftəʳ] N Gelächter *nt*; **~ broke out among the audience** das Publikum brach in Gelächter aus; **children's ~** Kinderlachen *nt*; **he shook with silent ~** er schüttelte sich vor Lachen; **at this there was loud ~** das rief lautes Gelächter hervor; **there was a little nervous ~** ein nervöses Lachen war zu hören

laughter lines PL *(Brit)* Lachfalten *pl*, Lachfältchen *pl*

launch [lɔːntʃ] N a *(= vessel)* Barkasse *f*
b *(= launching) (of ship)* Stapellauf *m*; *(of lifeboat)* Aussetzen *nt*; *(of rocket)* Abschuss *m*
c *(= launching) (of company)* Gründung *f*, Eröffnung *f*; *(of new product)* Einführung *f*; *(with party, publicity: of film, play, book)* Lancierung *f*; *(bringing out, of film, play)* Premiere *f*; *(of book)* Herausgabe *f*; *(of shares)* Emission *f*
VT a *new vessel* vom Stapel lassen; *(= christen)* taufen; *lifeboat* zu Wasser lassen, aussetzen; *rocket* abschießen; *plane* katapultieren; **Lady X ~ed the new boat** der Stapellauf fand in Anwesenheit von Lady X statt; **the rocket was ~ed into space** die Rakete wurde in den Weltraum geschossen
b *company, newspaper, initiative* gründen; *new product* einführen, auf den Markt bringen; *(with party, publicity) film, play, book* lancieren; *(= bring out) film* anlaufen lassen; *play* auf die Bühne bringen; *book, series* herausbringen; *plan, investigation* in die Wege leiten; *programme, trend* einführen; *career* starten; *policy* in Angriff nehmen; *shares* emittieren, ausgeben; **to ~ an offensive** *or* **an attack against the enemy** zum Angriff gegen den Feind übergehen; **the attack was ~ed at 15.00 hours** der Angriff fand um 15.00 Uhr statt; **to ~ sb into society** jdn in die Gesellschaft einführen; **this film ~ed him as a comic actor** mit diesem Film machte er sich *(dat)* als Komiker einen Namen; **to ~ sb on his way** jdm einen guten Start geben; **once he is ~ed on this subject ...** wenn er einmal mit diesem Thema angefangen hat *or* bei diesem Thema gelandet ist, ...; **now that he's ~ed himself on the road to success** jetzt, wo er auf Erfolgskurs ist
c *(= hurl)* schleudern; **he ~ed himself into the crowd** er stürzte sich in die Menge

▶ **launch forth** VI = **launch out (a, d)**

▶ **launch into** VI *+prep obj (= question, attack etc vigorously)* angreifen; **the author launches straight into his main theme** der Autor kommt gleich zum Hauptthema; **he launched into a description of his new house** er legte mit einer Beschreibung seines neuen Hauses los *(inf)*

▶ **launch out** VI a *(also* **launch forth***)* **the astronauts launched out into the unknown** die Astronauten starteten ins Unbekannte b *(= diversify)* sich verlegen *(in* auf *+acc)*; **the company launched out in several new directions** die Firma stieg in einige neue Branchen ein c *(inf: = spend a lot)* **to launch out** sich in Unkosten stürzen; **now we can afford to launch out a bit** jetzt können wir es uns leisten, etwas mehr auszugeben *(on* für*)* d *(= start: also* **launch forth***)* anfangen *(into sth* mit etw, etw *acc)*; **to launch out into a new career** eine neue Karriere starten

launcher ['lɔːntʃəʳ] N a *(Mil)* Werfer *m*; *(for rockets)* Abschussvorrichtung *f* b *(Aviat)* Katapult *nt*, Startschleuder *f*

launching ['lɔːntʃɪŋ] N = **launch N b, c**

launching: **launching pad** N Start- *or* Abschussrampe *f*; *(fig)* Sprungbrett *nt*; **launching site** N Abschussbasis *f*

launch: **launch pad** N = **launching pad**; **launch party** N *(for book)* Buchpremiere *f*; *(for film, play)* Premierenfeier *f*; **launch vehicle** N *(Space)* Booster *m*, Startrakete *f*

launder ['lɔːndəʳ] VT waschen und bügeln; *(fig) money* waschen VI waschen und bügeln; **modern fabrics ~ easily** moderne Gewebe lassen sich leicht reinigen *or* sind pflegeleicht

Launderette®, laundrette [,lɔːndə'ret] N *(Brit)* Waschsalon *m*

laundress ['lɔːndrɪs] N Waschfrau *f*, Wäscherin *f*

laundrette [,lɔːn'dret] N *(Brit)* Waschsalon *m*

Laundromat® ['lɔːndrəʊmæt] N *(US)* Waschsalon *m*

laundry ['lɔːndrɪ] N *(= establishment)* Wäscherei *f*; *(= clothes) (dirty)* schmutzige Wäsche; *(washed)* Wäsche *f*; **to do the ~** (Wäsche) waschen

laundry: **laundry bag** N Wäschesack *m*; **laundry basket** N Wäschekorb *m*; **laundry list** N *(fig)* lange Liste *f*; *(of wants)* Wunschzettel *m*; **laundryman** N Wäschemann *m (inf)*

laurel ['lɒrəl] N Lorbeer *m*; **to look to one's ~s** sich behaupten (müssen); **to rest on one's ~s** sich auf seinen Lorbeeren ausruhen; **to win** *or* **gain one's ~s** Lorbeeren ernten

lav [læv] N *(esp Brit inf)* Klo *nt (inf)*

lava ['lɑːvə] N Lava *f*; **~ bed** Lavadecke *f*

lavatory ['lævətrɪ] N Toilette *f*

lavatory: **lavatory attendant** N Toilettenfrau *f*/-mann *m*; **lavatory paper** N Toilettenpapier *nt*; **lavatory seat** N Toilettensitz *m*, Klobrille *f (inf)*

lavender ['lævɪndəʳ] N *(= flower)* Lavendel *m*; *(= colour)* Lavendel *nt* ADJ *(colour)* lavendelfarben; **~ blue eyes** lavendelblaue Augen

lavender: **lavender bag** N Lavendelsäckchen *nt*; **lavender water** N Lavendelwasser *nt*

lavish ['lævɪʃ] ADJ *gifts* großzügig, üppig; *praise, affection* überschwänglich; *banquet* üppig; *party* feudal; *(pej)* verschwenderisch; *expenditure* verschwenderisch; **to be ~ in** *or* **with sth** mit etw verschwenderisch sein *or* umgehen; **he was ~ in his help to others** er half anderen großzügig; **he's ~ in giving money to good causes** für gute Zwecke spendet er großzügig Geld; **you were very ~ with the cream** du hast ja mit der Sahne nicht gespart; **to be ~ with one's money** das Geld mit vollen Händen ausgeben
VT **to ~ sth on sb** jdn mit etw überhäufen; *praise, attention* jdn mit etw überschütten; **she ~ed food and drink on them** sie bewirtete sie fürstlich; **to ~ attention on sth** viel Aufmerksamkeit auf etw *(acc)* richten

lavishly ['lævɪʃlɪ] ADV *give, equipped* großzügig; *praise* überschwänglich; *put paint on, spread* reichlich; *entertain* üppig, reichlich; *illustrated* reich, aufwendig, aufwändig; **they entertain ~** sie geben feudale Feste; **~ furnished** luxuriös *or* aufwendig *or* aufwändig eingerichtet; **to spend (money) ~** das Geld mit vollen Händen ausgeben *(on* für*)*; **he is ~ extravagant in his hospital-**

ity seine Gastfreundschaft kennt keine Grenzen

lavishness [ˈlævɪʃnɪs] N *(of gifts)* Großzügigkeit *f*, Üppigkeit *f*; *(of praise, affection)* Überschwänglichkeit *f*; *(of banquet)* Üppigkeit *f*; *(of person)* Großzügigkeit *f*; *(pej)* Verschwendungssucht *f*; **the ~ of the party** die feudale Party

law [lɔː] N **a** (= *rule, also Jewish, Sci*) Gesetz *nt*; **~ of nature** Naturgesetz *nt*; **it's the ~** das ist Gesetz; **his word is ~** sein Wort ist Gesetz; **to become ~** rechtskräftig werden; **to pass a ~** ein Gesetz verabschieden; **is there a ~ against it?** ist das verboten?; **there is no ~ against asking, is there?** *(inf)* man darf doch wohl noch fragen, oder?; **he is a ~ unto himself** er macht, was er will
b (= *body of laws*) Gesetz *nt no pl*; (= *system*) Recht *nt*; **according to** *or* **in** *or* **by** *or* **under French ~** nach französischem Recht; **by ~** gesetzlich; **by ~ all restaurants must display their prices outside** alle Restaurants sind gesetzlich dazu verpflichtet, ihre Preise draußen auszuhängen; **he is above/outside the ~** er steht über dem Gesetz/außerhalb des Gesetzes; **what is the ~ on drugs?** wie sind die Drogengesetze?; **to keep within the ~** sich im Rahmen des Gesetzes bewegen; **in ~** vor dem Gesetz; **ignorance is no defence** *(Brit)* *or* **defense** *(US)* **in ~** Unwissenheit schützt vor Strafe nicht; **a change in the ~** eine Gesetzesänderung; **the ~ as it relates to property** die gesetzlichen Bestimmungen über das Eigentum; **civil/criminal ~** Zivil-/Strafrecht *nt*
c *(as study)* Jura *no art*, Recht(swissenschaft *f*) *nt*
d *(Sport)* Regel *f*; *(Art)* Gesetz *nt*; **the ~s of harmony** die Harmonielehre; **one of the basic ~s of harmony** eins der grundlegenden Prinzipien der Harmonielehre
e (= *operation of law*) **to practise** *(Brit)* *or* **practice** *(US)* **~** eine Anwaltspraxis haben; **to go to ~** vor Gericht gehen, den Rechtsweg beschreiten; **to take sb to ~** gegen jdn gerichtlich vorgehen, jdn vor Gericht bringen; **to take a case to ~** in einer Sache gerichtlich vorgehen, einen Fall vor Gericht bringen; **to take the ~ into one's own hands** das Recht selbst in die Hand nehmen; **~ and order** Ruhe *or* Recht und Ordnung, Law and Order; **the forces of ~ and order** die Ordnungskräfte *pl*
f the ~ *(inf)* die Polente *(dated inf)*, die Bullen *(sl)*; **I'll get the ~ on you** *(Brit inf)* ich hole die Polizei; **he got the ~ on to me** *(Brit inf)* er hat mir die Polizei auf den Hals gehetzt *(inf)*

law: **law-abiding** ADJ gesetzestreu; **lawbreaker** N Rechtsbrecher(in) *m(f)*; **lawbreaking** ADJ gesetzesübertretend, rechtsbrecherisch N Rechtsbruch *m*, Gesetzesübertretung *f*; **law centre**, *(US)* **law center** N *kostenlose Rechtsberatungsstelle*; **law court** N Gerichtshof *m*, Gericht *nt*; **law enforcement** N **the duty of the police is ~** Aufgabe der Polizei ist es, dem Gesetz Geltung zu verschaffen; **law enforcement authorities** PL Vollstreckungsbehörden *pl*; **law enforcement officer** N Polizeibeamte(r) *m*/-beamtin *f*

lawful [ˈlɔːfʊl] ADJ rechtmäßig; **~ wedded wife** rechtmäßig angetraute Frau; **will you take this man to be your ~ wedded husband?** willst du mit diesem Mann den Bund der Ehe eingehen?

lawfully [ˈlɔːfəlɪ] ADV rechtmäßig; **he is ~ entitled to compensation** er hat einen Rechtsanspruch *or* rechtmäßigen Anspruch auf Entschädigung; **he was careful to carry on his activities ~** er achtete darauf, dass seine Handlungen im Rahmen des Gesetzes blieben

lawfulness [ˈlɔːfʊlnɪs] N Rechtsgültigkeit *f*; (= *permission by law*) Gesetzlichkeit *f*, Gesetzmäßigkeit *f*; (= *recognition by law*) Rechtmäßigkeit *f*, Legitimität *f*

lawgiver [ˈlɔːgɪvəʳ] N Gesetzgeber *m*

lawgiving [ˈlɔːˌgɪvɪŋ] N Gesetzgebung *f* ADJ gesetzgebend; **~ power** gesetzgebende Gewalt

lawless [ˈlɔːlɪs] ADJ *act* gesetzwidrig; *person, society* gesetzlos; *country* ohne Gesetzgebung; *violence* ungezügelt

lawlessness [ˈlɔːlɪsnɪs] N *(of act)* Gesetzwidrigkeit *f*; *(of person, society, country)* Gesetzlosigkeit *f*; **~ among young people** gesetzwidriges Verhalten unter Jugendlichen; **after the coup, the country reverted to ~** nach dem Staatsstreich fiel das Land in einen Zustand der Gesetzlosigkeit zurück

Law Lord N *(Brit)* Lordrichter *m*

lawman [ˈlɔːmən] N *pl* **-men** *(US)* Polizist *m*, Sheriff *m*

lawn¹ [lɔːn] N (= *grass*) Rasen *m no pl*; **the ~s in front of the houses** der Rasen vor den Häusern

lawn² N *(Tex)* Batist *m*, Linon *m*

lawn: **lawn chair** N Liegestuhl *m*; **lawn mower** N Rasenmäher *m*; **lawn party** N *(US)* Gartenfest *nt*, Gartenparty *f*; *(for charity)* Wohltätigkeitsveranstaltung *f* im Freien; **lawn tennis** N Rasentennis *nt*

law office N *(US)* Rechtsanwaltsbüro *nt*, Rechtsanwaltspraxis *f*

lawrencium [lɔˈrensɪəm] N *(Chem)* Lawrencium *nt*

law: **law reports** PL Entscheidungs- *or* Fallsammlung *f*; (= *journal*) Gerichtszeitung *f*; **law school** N *(US)* juristische Fakultät; **law student** N Jurastudent(in) *m(f)*, Student(in) *m(f)* der Rechte *(form)*; **lawsuit** N Prozess *m*, Klage *f*; **he filed a ~ for damages** er strengte eine Schadenersatzklage an; **to bring a ~ against sb** gegen jdn einen Prozess anstrengen

lawyer [ˈlɔːjəʳ] N (Rechts)anwalt *m*, (Rechts)anwältin *f*

LAWYER

In Großbritannien gibt es zwei verschiedene Arten von **lawyers**, Rechtsanwälten: **solicitors** und **barristers** (die in Schottland **advocates** genannt werden). **Solicitors** beschäftigen sich normalerweise mit den allgemeinen Rechtsgeschäften wie An- und Verkauf von Eigentum, Testamenten, Schuldeneintreibung oder Scheidung, und werden von den Klienten direkt angesprochen. Einige dieser Anwälte können nach Fortbildungsmaßnahmen ihre Klienten sowohl in zivil- als auch in strafrechtlichen Angelegenheiten vor Gericht vertreten. **Barristers** beraten in Rechtsfällen, die ihnen meist von den **solicitors**, nicht von den Klienten direkt, vorgelegt werden. Sie haben sich darauf spezialisiert, an den höheren Gerichten zu arbeiten, während die **solicitors** ihre Klienten in den unteren Instanzen vertreten.
In den USA werden die Rechtsanwälte allgemein **attorneys** genannt. Sie können jede Art von Rechtsfall übernehmen und ihre Klienten in allen Instanzen vor Bundes- und Staatsgerichten vertreten. Amerikanische Rechtanwälte bekommen ihr Honorar oft nach dem Prinzip „no win, no fee", dadurch können sich auch ärmere Klienten einen Anwalt nehmen, der nur dann mit einem entsprechend hohen prozentuellen Anteil an der Streitsumme honoriert wird, wenn er den Fall gewinnt. Das hat allerdings dazu geführt, dass die Schadensforderungen weitaus höher liegen als in Europa, und dass gern vor Gericht gezogen wird.

lax [læks] ADJ *(+er)* **a** lax; *discipline* lasch, lax; *morals* locker, lose; **she is rather ~ in her relations with men** sie hat ein recht lockeres Verhältnis zu Männern; **to be ~ about sth** etw vernachlässigen; **he's ~ about washing/imposing discipline** er nimmts mit dem Waschen/der Disziplin nicht so genau; **I've been rather ~ about replying to your letters** ich habe mir mit der Beantwortung Ihrer Briefe reichlich viel Zeit gelassen; **things are very ~ at the school** in der Schule geht es sehr lax *or* undiszipliniert zu **b ~ bowels** dünner Stuhl(gang)

laxative [ˈlæksətɪv] ADJ abführend, laxativ *(spec)* N Abführmittel *nt*, Laxativ(um) *nt (spec)*

laxity [ˈlæksɪtɪ] N (= *lack of vigour, discipline*) Laxheit *f*; (= *carelessness also*) Nachlässigkeit *f*; **his moral ~** seine lockeren *or* laxen moralischen Einstellungen; **sexual ~** lockere Sitten *pl*, sexuelle Freizügigkeit

lay¹ [leɪ] N *(Liter, Mus)* Ballade *f*, Lied *nt*

lay² ADJ Laien-; **~ opinion** die öffentliche Meinung, die Öffentlichkeit; **a ~ opinion** die Meinung eines Laien

lay³ *pret of* **lie²**

lay⁴ *vb: pret, ptp* **laid** N **a** Lage *f* → **land N a**
b *(sl)* **he's an easy ~** er lässt jeden ran *(inf)*; **she's a good ~** sie ist gut im Bett *(inf)*; **that's the best ~ I ever had** das war die beste Nummer, die ich je gemacht habe *(inf)*
VT **a** (= *place, put*) legen *(sth on sth* etw auf etw *acc)*; *wreath* niederlegen; **to ~ (one's) hands on** (= *get hold of*) erwischen, fassen; (= *find*) finden; **to ~ a hand on sb** jdm etwas tun, Hand an jdn legen *(geh)*; **I never laid a hand on him** ich habe ihn überhaupt nicht angefasst, ich habe ihm überhaupt nichts getan; **he took all the money he could ~ his hands on** er nahm alles Geld, das ihm in die Finger kam *(inf)*
b *bricks, foundations, track* legen; *concrete* gießen; *cable, mains, pipes* verlegen; *road* bauen, anlegen; *carpet, lino* (ver)legen
c (= *prepare*) *fire* herrichten; *(esp Brit) table* decken; *mines, ambush* legen; *trap* aufstellen; *plans* schmieden; **to ~ the table for breakfast/lunch** *(esp Brit)* den Frühstücks-/Mittagstisch decken; **to ~ a trap for sb** jdm eine Falle stellen; **even the best-laid plans can go wrong** selbst die ausgeklügeltsten Pläne können schiefgehen
d *(non-material things) burden* auferlegen *(on sb* jdm); **to ~ the blame for sth on sb/sth** jdm/einer Sache die Schuld an etw *(dat)* geben; **to ~ responsibility for sth on sb** jdn für etw verantwortlich machen; **the stress which he ~s on it** der Nachdruck, den er darauf legt
e (= *bring forward*) *complaint* vorbringen *(before* bei); *accusation* erheben; **the police laid a charge of murder against him** die Polizei erstattete gegen ihn Anzeige wegen Mordes; **he laid out his case before them** er trug ihnen seinen Fall vor
f *dust* binden; *ghost* austreiben; *fear* zerstreuen; *doubts* beseitigen; **to ~ waste** verwüsten; **to ~ the ghost of sth** *(fig)* etw endgültig begraben → **low¹**, **open** *etc*
g *eggs (hen)* legen; *(fish, insects)* ablegen
h *bet* abschließen; *money* setzen; **to ~ bets on sth** auf etw *(acc)* wetten; **I ~ you a fiver on it!** ich wette mit dir um 5 Pfund!; **I'll ~ you that ...** ich wette mit dir, dass ...; **I'll ~ you anything ...** ich gehe mit dir jede Wette ein ...
i *(sl)* **to ~ a woman** eine Frau flachlegen *(sl)*; **he just wants to get laid** er will nur bumsen *(inf)*
VI *(hen)* legen

▶ **lay about** VI um sich schlagen VT *sep* losschlagen gegen

▶ **lay aside** *or* **away** VT *sep work etc* weglegen, zur Seite legen; (= *keep in reserve, save*) beiseitelegen, auf die Seite legen; (= *cast away*) ablegen; *doubts* aufgeben; *plans etc* auf Eis legen; **to lay sb away** (= *bury*) jdn zu Grabe tragen

▶ **lay back** VT *sep ears* anlegen; *person* zurücklegen

▶ **lay before** VT *+prep obj* **to lay sth before sb** *(plan)* jdm etw vorlegen; *ideas also* jdm etw unterbreiten; *claim, complaint* etw bei jdm vorbringen

▶ **lay by** VT *sep* beiseitelegen, auf die Seite legen

▶ **lay down** VT *sep* **a** *book, pen etc* hinlegen; **he laid his bag down on the table** er legte seine Tasche auf den Tisch; **she laid herself down to sleep** *(liter)* sie begab sich zur Ruhe

b *(= give up) burden* ablegen; *office* niederlegen; **to lay down one's arms** die Waffen niederlegen; **to lay down one's life** sein Leben geben *or* opfern
c *(= impose, establish) condition* festsetzen *or* -legen; *policy* festsetzen, bestimmen; *rules* aufstellen, festlegen; *price* festsetzen, vorschreiben; **it is laid down that** es wurde festgelegt, dass; **to lay down the law** *(inf)* Vorschriften machen *(to sb* jdm)
d *(= store)* lagern
e *ship* auf Stapel legen
f *deposit* hinterlegen

▶ **lay in** VT *sep food etc* einlagern; *supplies also* anlegen; **they have laid in plenty of water** sie haben (sich *dat*) einen großen Wasservorrat angelegt

▶ **lay into** VI *+prep obj (inf)* **to lay into sb** auf jdn losgehen; *(verbally)* jdn fertigmachen *(inf) or* runterputzen *(inf)*

▶ **lay off** VI *(inf: = stop)* aufhören *(prep obj* mit); **lay off, will you?** hör (mal) auf, ja?; **you'll have to lay off smoking** du wirst das Rauchen aufgeben müssen *(inf)*; **I wish you'd lay off coming here every day** ich wünschte, du würdest nicht mehr jeden Tag hierher kommen; **lay off my little brother, will you!** lass bloß meinen kleinen Bruder in Ruhe! VT *sep workers* Feierschichten machen lassen; *(permanently)* entlassen; **to be laid off** Feierschichten einlegen müssen; *(permanently)* entlassen werden

▶ **lay on** VT *sep* **a** *(= apply) paint* auftragen → **thick**
b *(= prepare, offer) hospitality* bieten *(for sb* jdm); *(= supply) entertainment* sorgen für; *excursion* veranstalten; *extra buses* einsetzen; *water, electricity* anschließen; **if you lay on the drinks I'll get the food** wenn du die Getränke stellst, besorge ich das Essen; **she had laid on a lot of food** sie hatte sehr viel zu essen aufgetischt; **an extra flight was laid on** eine Sondermaschine wurde eingesetzt *or* bereitgestellt
c *(= impose)* **to lay a tax on sth** etw mit einer Steuer belegen, etw besteuern
d *(esp US inf: = tell off)* **he laid it on me** er hat mich zur Sau gemacht *(inf)*

▶ **lay out** VT *sep* **a** *(= spread out)* ausbreiten; **the vast plain laid out before us** die weite Ebene, die sich vor uns ausbreitete
b *(= present)* darlegen; **he laid out his plans for the country** er legte seine Pläne für das Land dar
c *(= prepare) clothes* zurechtlegen; *corpse* (waschen und) aufbahren
d *(= design, arrange)* anlegen, planen; *garden* anlegen, gestalten; *room* aufteilen; *rooms in house* verteilen, anordnen; *office* aufteilen, anordnen; *book* gestalten; *page* umbrechen; *(in magazines)* das Lay-out *(+gen)* machen
e *money (= spend)* ausgeben; *(= invest)* investieren
f *(= knock out)* **to lay sb out** jdn k. o. schlagen; **three whiskies were enough to lay him out** nach drei Whiskys war er erledigt *(inf)*; **he was laid out cold when he fell downstairs** er verlor das Bewusstsein, als er die Treppe hinunterfiel
VR *(dated, = take trouble)* sich bemühen, sich *(dat)* Mühe geben; **to lay oneself out to please** sich Mühe geben zu gefallen

▶ **lay over** VI *(US)* Aufenthalt haben

▶ **lay to** VI *(Naut)* beidrehen

▶ **lay up** VT *sep* **a** *(= store)* lagern; *supply* anlegen; *(= amass, save)* anhäufen, ansammeln; **he's laying up trouble for himself in the future** er wird später noch (viel) Ärger bekommen **b** *(= immobilize) ship* auflegen; *boat* aufbocken; *car* stilllegen, einmotten *(inf)*; **to be laid up (in bed)** auf der Nase *(inf) or* im Bett liegen; **you'd better take it easy or you'll lay yourself up** Sie müssen etwas langsamer treten, sonst liegen Sie nachher flach *or* auf der Nase *(inf)*

lay: **layabout** N *(Brit)* Nichtstuer(in) *m(f)*, Arbeitsscheue(r) *mf*; **layaway** N *(US Comm)* angezahlte und zurückgelegte Ware; **lay brother** N Laienbruder *m*; **lay-by** N *(Brit) (in town)* Parkbucht *f*; *(in country)* Parkplatz *m*; *(big)* Rastplatz *m*

layer [ˈleɪəʳ] N **a** Schicht *f (also Geol)*, Lage *f*; **to arrange the vegetables in ~s** das Gemüse schichten; **we climbed through ~ upon ~ of cloud** wir stiegen durch eine Wolkenschicht nach der anderen auf; **the cake was covered with ~ upon ~ of chocolate** der Kuchen war mit vielen Schokoladenschichten überzogen; **several ~s of clothing** mehrere Kleidungsstücke übereinander; **to put in ~s** *(hairdresser)* die Haare stufen **b** *(Hort)* Ableger *m* **c** *(= hen)* Legehenne *f* VT **a** *(Hort)* absenken **b** *hair* abstufen **c** *vegetables etc* schichten

layer cake N Schichttorte *f*

layette [leɪˈet] N Babyausstattung *f*

lay figure N Gliederpuppe *f*; *(fig)* Marionette *f*

laying [ˈleɪɪŋ] N **~ on of hands** Handauflegen *nt*

lay: **layman** N Laie *m*; **lay-off** N **further ~s were unavoidable** weitere Arbeiter mussten Feierschichten einlegen *or (permanent)* mussten entlassen werden; **he is playing again after a lengthy ~** er spielt wieder nach einer längeren Pause; **layout** N Anordnung *f*, Anlage *f*; *(Typ)* Lay-out *nt*; **the standard ~ of German stations** wie deutsche Bahnhöfe normalerweise angelegt sind; **we have changed the ~ of this office** wir haben dieses Büro anders aufgeteilt; **our house has a different ~** unser Haus hat eine andere Zimmerverteilung *or* ist anders angelegt; **layover** N *(US)* Aufenthalt *m*; **layperson** N Laie *m*; **lay reader** N Hilfsdiakon *m*; **lay sister** N Laienschwester *f*; **laywoman** N Laie *m*

laze [leɪz] N **to have a long ~ in bed** lange faul im Bett (liegen) bleiben VI faulenzen

▶ **laze about** *(Brit) or* **around** VI faulenzen, auf der faulen Haut liegen; **stop lazing about** *or* **around** steh/sitz *etc* nicht so faul herum!

▶ **laze away** VT *sep* verbummeln

lazily [ˈleɪzɪlɪ] ADV faul; *(= languidly, unhurriedly)* träge; *drift, float* gemächlich

laziness [ˈleɪzɪnɪs] N Faulheit *f*; *(= languor)* Trägheit *f*

lazy [ˈleɪzɪ] ADJ *(+er)* **a** *(= not inclined to work)* faul; **to be ~ about doing sth** zu faul sein, etw zu tun; **~ about writing** schreibfaul; **I'm feeling ~ today** ich habe heute einfach keine Lust(, etw zu tun); **he's getting ~ in his old age** *(hum)* er wird auf seine alten Tage faul
b *(= slow-moving)* langsam, träge; *(= lacking activity)* träge; *(= relaxed) lunch, dinner, evening* gemütlich; *smile* träge; **his ~ drawl** seine träge, schleppende Sprache; **~ little streams** träge fließende kleine Bäche *pl*; **the long, ~ days of summer** die langen, trägen Sommertage; **we had a ~ holiday** *(esp Brit) or* **vacation** *(US)* wir haben im Urlaub nur gefaulenzt; **I enjoy a ~ day at home** ich mache mir gerne einen faulen *or* gemütlichen Tag zu Hause
c *(pej: = sloppy) work, writing, style, attitude* schluderig *(inf)*

lazy: **lazybones** [ˈleɪzɪˌbəʊnz] N *sing (inf)* Faulpelz *m*, Faultier *nt*; **lazy eye** N *(Med) zeitweilig schielendes Auge, das weniger belastet wird und daher in der Sehkraft nachlässt*, Amblyopia ex anopsia *f (spec)*; **lazy Susan** N drehbare Tischmenage

lb N *(weight)* ≈ Pfd.

LBO *(Fin) abbr of* **leveraged buyout**

lbw *abbr of* **leg before wicket**

lc *(Typ) abbr of* **lower case**

LCD *abbr of* **liquid crystal display** LCD *nt*; **~ projector** Beamer *m*; **~ screen** LCD-Bildschirm *m*; **~ TV** LCD-TV *nt*, LCD-Fernseher *m*

L-driver [ˈelˌdraɪvəʳ] N *(Brit inf)* Fahrschüler(in) *m(f)*

LEA *(Brit) abbr of* **Local Education Authority**

lea [liː] N *(poet)* Au(e) *f (poet)*, Wiesengrund *m (liter)*

leach [liːtʃ] VT (durch)filtern; *(= extract)* auslaugen

lead¹ [led] N **a** *(= metal)* Blei *nt*; **they pumped him full of ~** *(inf)* sie pumpten ihn mit Blei voll *(inf)* **b** *(in pencil)* Grafit *nt*, Graphit *nt*; *(= single lead)* Mine *f*; **that'll put ~ in your pencil** *(inf)* das wird dir die Glieder stärken *(inf)* **c** *(Naut)* Lot *nt* **d** **leads** PL *(on roof)* Bleiplatten *pl*; *(in window)* Bleifassung *f* VT *(= weight with lead)* mit Blei beschweren

lead² [liːd] ✪ 26.1 *vb: pret, ptp* **led** N **a** *(= front position)* Spitzenposition *f*; *(= leading position, Sport)* Führung *f*, Spitze *f*; *(in league etc)* Tabellenspitze *f*; **to be in the ~** führend sein, in Führung liegen; *(Sport)* in Führung *or* vorn liegen, führen; **to take the ~, to move into the ~** in Führung gehen, die Führung übernehmen; *(in league)* Tabellenführer werden; **this set gives him the ~** mit diesem Satz liegt er in Führung; **this match gives them the ~ in the league** mit diesem Spiel gehen sie in der Liga in Führung; **he took the ~ from the German runner** er übernahm die Führung vor dem deutschen Läufer; **Japan took the ~ from Germany in exports** Japan verdrängte Deutschland auf dem Exportmarkt von der Spitze
b *(= distance, time ahead)* Vorsprung *m*; **to have two minutes' ~ over sb** zwei Minuten Vorsprung vor jdm haben
c *(= example)* Beispiel *nt*; **to give sb a ~** jdm etw vormachen; **to take the ~, to show a ~** mit gutem Beispiel vorangehen
d *(= clue)* Indiz *nt*, Anhaltspunkt *m*; *(in guessing etc)* Hinweis *m*, Tipp *m*; **the police have a ~** die Polizei hat eine Spur; **it gave the police a ~** das brachte die Polizei auf die Spur
e *(Cards)* **it's my ~** ich fange an
f *(Theat) (= part)* Hauptrolle *f*; *(= person)* Hauptdarsteller(in) *m(f)*; **to sing the ~** die Titelpartie *or* die tragende Partie singen
g *(= leash)* Leine *f*; **on a ~** an der Leine
h *(Elec)* Leitung(skabel *nt*) *f*, Kabel *nt*; *(from separate source)* Zuleitung *f (form)*
VT **a** *(= conduct) person, animal* führen; *water* leiten; **to ~ sb in/out** *etc* jdn hinein-/hinaus- *etc* führen; **that road will ~ you back to the station** auf dieser Straße kommen Sie zum Bahnhof zurück; **to ~ the way** *(lit, fig)* vorangehen; *(fig: = be superior)* führend sein; **all this talk is ~ing us nowhere** dieses ganze Gerede bringt uns nicht weiter; **the argument led us round in circles** unsere Argumentation drehte sich im Kreis
b *(= be the leader of, direct)* (an)führen; *expedition, team* leiten; *regiment* führen; *movement, revolution* anführen; *conversation* bestimmen; *orchestra (conductor)* leiten; *(first violin)* führen; **to ~ a government** an der Spitze einer Regierung stehen, Regierungschef sein; **to ~ a party** Parteivorsitzender sein, den Parteivorsitz führen
c *(= be first in)* anführen; **they led us by 30 seconds** sie lagen mit 30 Sekunden vor uns *(dat)*; **Britain ~s the world in textiles** Großbritannien ist auf dem Gebiet der Textilproduktion führend in der Welt
d *card* ausspielen
e *life* führen; **to ~ a life of luxury/deception** ein Luxusleben/betrügerisches Leben führen
f *(= influence)* beeinflussen; **to ~ sb to do sth** jdn dazu bringen, etw zu tun; **to ~ a witness** einen Zeugen/eine Zeugin beeinflussen; **what led him to change his mind?** wie kam er dazu, seine Meinung zu ändern?; **to ~ sb to believe that ...** jdm den Eindruck vermitteln, dass ..., jdn glauben machen, dass ... *(geh)*; **I am led to believe that ...** ich habe Grund zu der Annahme, dass ...; **to ~ sb into error** jdn irreleiten *or* fehlleiten; **to ~ sb into trouble** jdn in Schwierigkeiten bringen; **he is easily led** er lässt sich leicht beeinflussen; *(= deceived)* er lässt sich leicht täuschen *or* sich *(dat)* leicht etwas weismachen; **this led me to the conclusion that ...** daraus schloss ich, dass ...; **I am led to the conclusion that ...** ich komme zu dem Schluss, dass ...; **what ~s you to think that?** woraus schließen Sie das?
g *wire, flex* legen, entlangführen
VI **a** *(= go in front)* vorangehen; *(in race)* in

Führung liegen; **to ~ by 10 metres** einen Vorsprung von 10 Metern haben, mit 10 Metern in Führung liegen; **he easily ~s** er liegt klar in Führung; **he always follows where his brother ~s** er macht alles nach, was sein Bruder macht; **the "Times" led with a story about the financial crisis** die „Times" berichtete auf der ersten Seite ausführlich über die Finanzkrise; **he ~s with his right** *(Boxing)* er ist Rechtsausleger
b (= *be a leader, also in dancing*) führen; **he had shown the ability to ~** er hat gezeigt, dass er Führungsqualitäten besitzt
c *(Cards)* ausspielen (*with sth* etw); **who ~s?** wer spielt aus?, wer fängt an?
d *(street etc)* führen, gehen; **it ~s into that room** es führt zu diesem Raum; **this road ~s nowhere** diese Straße führt nirgendwohin *or* geht nicht weiter
e *(= result in, cause)* führen (*to* zu); **all this talk is ~ing nowhere** dieses ganze Gerede führt zu nichts; **remarks like that could ~ to trouble** solche Bemerkungen können unangenehme Folgen haben; **what will all these strikes ~ to?** wo sollen all diese Streiks hinführen?

▶ **lead along** VT *sep* führen; **he led him along the street** er führte ihn die Straße entlang

▶ **lead aside** VT *sep* auf die Seite nehmen, beiseitenehmen

▶ **lead away** VT *sep* wegführen *or* -bringen; *criminal, prisoner* abführen; **we must not allow this argument to lead us away from the matter in hand** wir dürfen uns durch dieses Argument nicht vom eigentlichen Thema abbringen lassen VI wegführen; **this is leading away from the subject** das führt vom Thema ab

▶ **lead off** VT *sep* abführen; **a policeman led the drunk man off the pitch** ein Polizist führte den Betrunkenen vom Platz VI **a** (= *go off from*) abgehen; **several streets led off the square** mehrere Straßen gingen von dem Platz ab **b** (= *start*) beginnen; **my partner led off with the ten of hearts** mein Partner spielte die Herzzehn aus

▶ **lead on** VI *usu imper* **lead on, sergeant!** führen Sie an, Feldwebel!; **lead on, John!** geh vor, John! VT *sep* (= *deceive*) anführen *(inf)*, hinters Licht führen; (= *tease*) aufziehen, auf den Arm nehmen *(inf)*; **she's just leading him on** sie hält ihn nur zum Narren *or* führt ihn nur an der Nase herum

▶ **lead on to** VI +*prep obj* führen zu

▶ **lead out** VT *sep* hinausführen; **he led his wife out onto the dance floor** er führte seine Frau auf die Tanzfläche VI hinausgehen

▶ **lead up** VT *sep* hinaufführen (*to* auf +*acc*); (= *lead across*) führen (*to* zu); **to lead sb up the garden path** *(fig)* jdm etwas vormachen, jdn an der Nase herumführen
VI **a** (= *come before*) **the events/years that led up to the war** die Ereignisse/Jahre, die dem Krieg voran- *or* vorausgingen
b (= *introduce*) **he was obviously leading up to an important announcement** er schickte sich offensichtlich an, etwas Wichtiges anzukündigen; **his speech was obviously leading up to an important announcement** seine Rede war offensichtlich die Einleitung zu einer wichtigen Ankündigung; **what are you leading up to?** worauf willst du hinaus?; **what's all this leading up to?** was soll das Ganze?

lead [led]: **lead acetate** N Bleiacetat *nt*, Bleiazetat *nt*; **lead content** N Bleigehalt *m*; **lead crystal** N Bleikristall *nt*; **lead-crystal** ['led'krɪstl] ADJ aus Bleikristall; **~ bowl** Bleikristallschale *f*

leaded ['ledɪd] ADJ *petrol* verbleit; **~ glass** Bleiglas *nt*; **~ window** Bleiglasfenster *nt*

leaden ['ledn] ADJ **a** *sky, colour, clouds* bleiern *(geh)*; *heart, limbs, steps* bleischwer; *silence* bedrückend **b** *(pej)* (= *tedious*) *translation, dialogue* schwerfällig; (= *stodgy*) *food* sehr schwer **c** (*old*: = *of lead*) bleiern *(geh)*

leader ['li:də'] N **a** Führer(in) *m(f)*; *(of union, party)* Vorsitzende(r) *mf*, Führer(in) *m(f)*; *(military)* Befehlshaber(in) *m(f)*; *(of gang, rebels)* Anführer(in) *m(f)*; *(of expedition, project)* Leiter(in) *m(f)*; *(Sport) (in league)* Tabellenführer *m*; *(in race)* der/die Erste; *(Mus, of orchestra)* Konzertmeister(in) *m(f)*; *(of choir)* Leiter(in) *m(f)*; *(of brass band)* erster Bläser, erste Bläserin; *(of jazz band, pop group)* Leader(in) *m(f)*; **to be the ~** *(in race, competition)* in Führung liegen; **the ~s** *(in race, competition)* die Spitzengruppe; **~ of the opposition** Oppositionsführer(in) *m(f)*; **the ~s of fashion** die Modemacher *pl*; **the product is a ~/the world ~ in its field** dieses Produkt ist auf diesem Gebiet führend/weltweit führend; **we are still the ~s in biochemical research** wir sind auf dem Gebiet der biochemischen Forschung immer noch führend; **has he the qualities to be a ~ of men?** hat er Führungsqualitäten?
b *(Brit Press)* Leitartikel *m*; **~ writer** Leitartikler(in) *m(f)*
c *(Comput: sign)* Füllzeichen *nt*

> **LEADER OF THE HOUSE**
>
> Leader of the House werden die Führer sowohl des Unterhauses **(Leader of the House of Commons)** als auch des Oberhauses **(Leader of the House of Lords)** genannt. Sie sind hohe Mitglieder der britischen Regierung und verantwortlich für die Gestaltung und Verlesung der wöchentlichen Geschäftsordnung ihres jeweiligen Hauses, wobei sie Rücksprache mit ihren Kollegen aus der Opposition halten.

leaderless ['li:dəlɪs] ADJ führerlos, ohne Führer; *party, union* führungslos

leadership ['li:dəʃɪp] N **a** Führung *f*, Leitung *f*; (= *office*) Vorsitz *m*, Leitung *f*; **under the ~ of** unter (der) Führung von; **a crisis in the ~, a ~ crisis** eine Führungskrise **b** (= *quality*) Führungsqualitäten *pl*; **the country is looking for firm ~** das Land ruft nach einer straffen Führung; **he has ~ potential** er besitzt Führungsqualitäten

lead-free ['ledfri:] ADJ bleifrei; *petrol also* unverbleit N (*also* **lead-free petrol**) unverbleites *or* bleifreies Benzin

lead guitar ['li:d-] N Leadgitarre *f*

lead-in ['li:dɪn] N Einführung *f* (*to* in +*acc*), Einleitung *f* (*to* in +*acc*)

leading[1] ['ledɪŋ] N *(Typ)* Durchschuss *m*

leading[2] ['li:dɪŋ] ADJ **a** (= *first*) vorderste(r, s); *runner, horse, car also* führend; **the ~ car in the procession** das die Kolonne anführende Auto
b (= *most important*) *person, writer, politician, company* führend; **~ product/sportsman** Spitzenprodukt *nt*/-sportler *m*; **~ representative** Spitzenvertreter(in) *m(f)*; **~ part** *or* **role** *(Theat)* Hauptrolle *f*; *(fig)* führende Rolle (*in* bei); **the ~ issue** das Hauptthema, das wichtigste Thema; **we are a ~ company in ...** unsere Firma ist führend auf dem Gebiet ... (+*gen*)

leading ['li:dɪŋ]: **leading article** N Leitartikel *m*; **leading case** N *(Jur)* wichtiger Präzedenzfall; **leading counsel** N *(Brit Jur, for the defence)* Hauptverteidiger(in) *m(f)*; *(for the prosecution)* Kronanwalt *m*/-anwältin *f*; **leading edge** N **a** *(Aviat)* (Flügel)vorderkante *f* **b** **the ~ of technology** die Spitzentechnologie; **to be at** *or* **on the ~ of technology** *(machine etc)* zur Spitzentechnologie gehören; *(country etc)* in der Technologie führend sein; **leading-edge** ADJ *company* führend; **~ technology** Spitzentechnologie *f*; **leading lady** N Hauptdarstellerin *f*; **she was Mel Gibson's ~** sie spielte an der Seite von Mel Gibson die weibliche Hauptrolle; **leading light** N Nummer eins *f*; (= *person also*) großes Licht, Leuchte *f*; **leading man** N Hauptdarsteller *m*; **he was Sharon Stone's ~** er spielte an der Seite von Sharon Stone die männliche Hauptrolle; **leading note** N *(Mus)* Leitton *m*; **leading question** N Suggestivfrage *f*; **leading reins** PL *(for child)* Laufgeschirr *nt*; **leading role** N Hauptrolle *f*

lead [led-]: **lead paint** N Bleifarbe *f*; **lead pencil** N Bleistift *m*; **lead poisoning** N Bleivergiftung *f*; **lead shot** N Schrot *m or nt*

lead ['li:d]: **lead singer** N Leadsänger(in) *m(f)*; **lead story** N Hauptartikel *m*; **lead time** N *(for production)* Produktionszeit *f*; *(for delivery)* Lieferzeit *f*

leaf [li:f] N *pl* **leaves** **a** Blatt *nt*; **to be in ~** grün sein; **to come into ~** grün werden, ausschlagen *(poet)*; **he swept the leaves into a pile** er fegte das Laub auf einen Haufen **b** *(of paper)* Blatt *nt*; **to take a ~ out of** *or* **from sb's book** sich *(dat)* von jdm eine Scheibe abschneiden; **to turn over a new ~** einen neuen Anfang machen; **it's time you turned over a new ~, said the teacher** es wird Zeit, dass du dich änderst, sagte der Lehrer **c** *(of table)* Ausziehplatte *f*; **pull the leaves out** zieh den Tisch aus! **d** *(of metal)* Folie *f*; **gold/silver ~** Blattgold/-silber *nt* VI **to ~ through a book** ein Buch durchblättern

leaf bud N Blattknospe *f*

leafed [li:ft] ADJ belaubt; **four-~** vierblättrig

leaf green N Blattgrün *nt*

leafless ['li:flɪs] ADJ blattlos, kahl

leaflet ['li:flət] N **a** Prospekt *m*; (= *single page*) Handzettel *m*, Reklamezettel *m*; *(with instructions)* Merkblatt *nt*; (= *handout*) Flugblatt *nt*; (= *brochure for information*) Broschüre *f*, Informationsblatt *nt* **b** (= *young leaf*) Blättchen *nt* VT *area* Flugblätter verteilen in (+*dat*); *(Comm)* Werbematerial verteilen in (+*dat*)

leafleting ['li:flətɪŋ] N Flugblattaktionen *pl*; *(Comm)* Verteilen *nt* von Werbematerial; **~ campaign** Flugblattaktion *f*

leaf: **leaf mould**, *(US)* **leaf mold** N (Laub)kompost *m*; **leaf spring** N Blattfeder *f*; **leaf tobacco** N Rohtabak *m*, Blättertabak *m*

leafy ['li:fɪ] ADJ *branch, tree* grün, belaubt; *bower, lane* grün

league[1] [li:g] N *(Measure)* Wegstunde *f*

league[2] N **a** (= *treaty*) Bündnis *nt*, Bund *m*; (= *organization*) Verband *m*, Liga *f*; **League of Nations** Völkerbund *m*; **to enter into a ~** einen Bund schließen; **to be in ~ with sb** mit jdm gemeinsame Sache machen; **to be in ~ with the devil** mit dem Teufel im Bunde sein; **these two boys must be in ~ with each other** diese beiden Jungen stecken sicher unter einer Decke *(inf)*; **to be in ~ against sb** sich gegen jdn verbündet haben
b *(Sport)* Liga *f*; **the club is top of the ~** der Klub ist Tabellen- *or* Ligaführer; **he was not in the same ~** *(fig)* er hatte nicht das gleiche Format; **Peter's car is not in the same ~ as Wendy's** Peters Auto ist eine Nummer kleiner als Wendys; **this is way out of your ~!** das ist einige Nummern zu groß für dich!

league: **league game** N Ligaspiel *nt*; **league leaders** PL Tabellenführer *m*; **league match** N *(Brit)* Ligaspiel *nt*; **league table** N Tabelle *f*

leak [li:k] N **a** (= *hole*) undichte Stelle; *(in container)* Loch *nt*; *(Naut)* Leck *nt*; **to have a ~** undicht sein; *(bucket etc)* laufen, lecken; **my pen has a ~** mein Kugelschreiber läuft aus *or* ist nicht dicht; **there's a ~ in the gas pipe** die Gasleitung ist undicht; **the rain is coming in through a ~ in the roof** es regnet durchs Dach herein
b (= *escape of liquid*) Leck *nt*; **a gas ~** eine undichte Stelle in der Gasleitung; **the tunnel was flooded because of the ~s** der Tunnel wurde vom eindringenden Wasser überflutet; **a faulty joint caused a gas ~** durch die fehlerhafte Verbindung strömte Gas aus
c *(fig)* undichte Stelle; **there was a ~ of information** es sind Informationen durchgesickert; **a security/news ~** eine undichte Stelle; **the news ~ may have been the result of carelessness** die Nachricht kann aufgrund *or* auf Grund einer Unachtsamkeit durchgesickert sein; **a ~ to the press** eine Indiskretion der

Presse gegenüber; **they wanted to break the news gently by a series of ~s to the press** sie wollten die Nachricht langsam an die Presse durchsickern lassen
d *(inf)* **to go for a ~, to have a ~** pissen gehen *(vulg)*
VT **a** *(lit)* durchlassen; *fuel* verlieren; **that tank is ~ing acid** aus diesem Tank läuft Säure aus; **the tanker had ~ed its contents into the river** der Tankerinhalt war in den Fluss gelaufen
b *(fig) information, story, plans* zuspielen *(to sb* jdm); *secret* verraten *(to sb* jdm)
VI **a** *(ship, receptacle, pipe)* lecken; *(roof)* undicht *or* nicht dicht sein; *(pen)* auslaufen, undicht sein
b *(gas)* ausströmen, entweichen; *(liquid)* auslaufen; *(= ooze out)* tropfen *(from* aus); **water is ~ing (in) through the roof** Wasser tropft *or* sickert durch das Dach, es regnet durch (das Dach durch); **to ~ away** auslaufen

▶ **leak out** **VT** *sep news* zuspielen *(to sb* jdm)
VI **a** *(liquid)* auslaufen, durchsickern **b** *(news)* durchsickern

leakage ['liːkɪdʒ] **N** **a** *(= act)* Auslaufen *nt*; *(of body fluids)* Austreten *nt*; **there's a ~ of water into the oil** da läuft *or* tropft Wasser ins Öl; **there's still a slight ~** es ist immer noch etwas undicht; **the ground was polluted by a ~ of chemicals** der Boden war durch auslaufende Chemikalien verunreinigt **b** *(fig)* **~ of information** *(= act)* Durchsickern *nt* von Informationen; **the government was worried by repeated security ~s** die Regierung war besorgt, weil wiederholt Informationen durchgesickert waren

leakproof ['liːkpruːf] **ADJ** dicht, lecksicher *(spec)*; **we'll have to make the department ~** *(fig)* wir müssen undichte Stellen in der Abteilung beseitigen

leaky ['liːkɪ] **ADJ** *(+er)* undicht; *boat also* leck; **the ministry has become rather ~** *(fig inf)* aus dem Ministerium sickert inzwischen einiges durch

lean[1] [liːn] **ADJ** *(+er)* **a** *(= thin)* mager, dünn; *face, person* schmal; *(through lack of food)* hager; *(= fatless) meat* mager; **to grow ~** schlank *or* schmal werden; **to have a ~ build** schlank gebaut sein **b** *(= poor) year, times, harvest* mager; **to go through a ~ patch** eine Durststrecke durchlaufen **c** *(Comm)* schlank; **~er companies** verschlankte Firmen *pl* **N** mageres Fleisch

lean[2] *vb: pret, ptp* **leant** *(esp Brit) or* **leaned** **N** Neigung *f*
VT **a** *(= put in sloping position)* lehnen *(against* gegen, an *+acc)*; **to ~ one's head on sb's shoulder** seinen Kopf an jds Schulter *(acc)* lehnen
b *(= rest)* aufstützen *(on* auf *+dat or acc)*; **to ~ one's elbow on sth** sich mit dem Ellbogen auf etw *(acc)* stützen; **she ~ed her weight on the door** sie lehnte sich mit ihrem Gewicht gegen die Tür
VI **a** *(= be off vertical)* sich neigen *(to* nach); *(trees)* sich biegen; **the box was ~ing dangerously to the side** die Kiste neigte sich gefährlich auf die Seite; **he ~ed across the counter** er beugte sich über den Ladentisch; **a motorcyclist should ~ into the corner** ein Motorradfahrer sollte sich in die Kurve legen
b *(= rest)* sich lehnen; **to ~ against sth** sich gegen etw lehnen; **~ing against the bar** an die Bar gelehnt; **she ~ed on my arm** sie stützte sich auf meinen Arm; **he ~ed on the edge of the table** er stützte sich auf die Tischkante; **to ~ on one's elbow** sich mit dem Ellbogen aufstützen
c *(= tend in opinion etc)* **to ~ toward(s) the left/socialism** nach links/zum Sozialismus tendieren; **to ~ toward(s) sb's opinion** zu jds Ansicht neigen *or* tendieren; **which way does he ~?** in welche Richtung tendiert er?; **he started to ~ away from the party line** er entfernte sich allmählich von der Parteilinie; **at least they're ~ing in the direction of reform** sie neigen immerhin Reformen *(dat)* zu

▶ **lean back** **VI** sich zurücklehnen

▶ **lean forward** **VI** sich vorbeugen

▶ **lean on** **VI** **a** *(= depend on)* **to lean on sb** sich auf jdn verlassen **b** *(inf: = put pressure on)* **to lean on sb** jdn bearbeiten *(inf) or* beknien *(inf)*; **they leaned on him too hard** sie haben ihn zu sehr unter Druck gesetzt *(inf)*

▶ **lean out** **VI** sich hinauslehnen *(of* aus)

▶ **lean over** **VI** **a** *(= be off vertical: object, tree)* sich (vor)neigen **b** *(person)* sich vorbeugen; **they leaned over the side of the bridge** sie beugten sich über das Brückengeländer; **he leaned over her shoulder** er beugte sich über ihre Schulter → **backwards**

lean-burn ['liːnbɜːn] **ADJ** **~ engine** Magermotor *m*

leaning ['liːnɪŋ] **ADJ** schräg, schief; **the Leaning Tower of Pisa** der Schiefe Turm von Pisa **N** Hang *m*, Neigung *f*; **he had a ~ toward(s) the left** er hatte einen Hang nach links; **what are his ~s?** was sind seine Neigungen?; **artistic ~s** künstlerische Neigungen *pl*

leanness ['liːnnɪs] **N** Magerkeit *f*; **the ~ of his face** sein schmales Gesicht; *(through lack of food)* sein hageres Gesicht

lean production **N** *(Comm)* Lean Production *f (spec)*

leant [lent] *(esp Brit) pret, ptp of* **lean[2]**

lean-to ['liːntuː] **N** Anbau *m*; *(= shelter)* Wetterschutz *or* -schirm *m* **ADJ** angebaut

leap [liːp] *vb: pret, ptp* **leapt** *(esp Brit) or* **leaped** **N** Sprung *m*, Satz *m (inf)*; *(fig: in profits, unemployment etc)* sprunghafter Anstieg; **in one ~** mit einem Satz; **to take a ~** einen Satz machen; **a great ~ forward** *(fig)* ein großer Sprung nach vorn; **a ~ into the unknown, a ~ in the dark** *(fig)* ein Sprung ins Ungewisse; **a ~ of imagination is needed** man braucht viel Fantasie *or* Phantasie; **by *or* in ~s and bounds** *(fig)* sprunghaft
VT springen *or* setzen über *(+acc)*; **he ~t the horse across the ditch** er ließ das Pferd über den Graben springen
VI springen; **my heart ~ed (with joy)** mein Herz hüpfte vor Freude *(geh)*, mein Herz machte vor Freude einen Sprung; **to ~ about** herumspringen; **to ~ for joy** vor Freude hüpfen, Freudensprünge machen; **try to ~ over to the other side** versuch mal, auf die andere Seite zu springen; **to ~ to one's feet** aufspringen; **he ~t to her assistance** er sprang ihr zu Hilfe; **the shares ~t by 21p** die Aktien stiegen mit einem Sprung um 21 Pence → *also* **look**

▶ **leap at** **VI** *+prep obj* **to leap at a chance** eine Gelegenheit beim Schopf packen, sofort zugreifen; **to leap at an offer** sich (förmlich) auf ein Angebot stürzen

▶ **leap out** **VI** **a** *(= jump out)* hinausspringen *(of* aus *+dat)*; **he leapt out of the car** er sprang aus dem Auto **b** *(colours)* ins Auge springen, hervorstechen; **the bright colours leap out at you** die hellen Farben springen einem ins Auge

▶ **leap up** **VI** *(person, animals)* aufspringen; *(flames)* hochschlagen; *(prices)* sprunghaft ansteigen, emporschnellen; **he leapt up from behind the wall** er sprang hinter der Mauer hervor; **to leap up into the air** in die Höhe springen

leap day **N** Schalttag *m*

leapfrog ['liːpfrɒg] **N** Bockspringen *nt*; **to play ~** Bockspringen spielen *or* machen *(inf)* **VI** bockspringen; **the children ~ged over one another** die Kinder spielten *or* machten *(inf)* Bocksprünge **VT** **he ~ged him** er machte einen Bocksprung über ihn; **he ~ged his way to the top of the company** er machte in der Firma eine Blitzkarriere

leap of faith **N** Vertrauensvorschuss *m*; **to take *or* make a ~** einen Vertrauensvorschuss gewähren; **it takes a considerable ~ to believe that …** man muss schon eine Menge Vertrauen aufbringen, um zu glauben, dass …

leapt [lept] *(esp Brit) pret, ptp of* **leap**

leap year **N** Schaltjahr *nt*

learn [lɜːn] *pret, ptp* **learnt** *(Brit) or* **learned** **VT** **a** *(= gain knowledge, skill etc)* lernen; *(= memorize) poem etc* auswendig lernen; **where did you ~ that habit?** wo hast du dir das angewöhnt?; **I ~ed (how) to swim** ich habe schwimmen gelernt
b *(= be informed)* erfahren
VI **a** *(= gain knowledge etc)* lernen; **I can't play the piano, but I'm hoping to ~** ich kann nicht Klavier spielen, aber ich hoffe, es zu lernen; **he'll never ~!** er lernt es nie!; **some people never ~!** manche lernens nie!; **to ~ from experience** aus der Erfahrung *or* durch Erfahrung lernen
b *(= find out)* hören, erfahren *(about, of* von)

▶ **learn off** **VT** *sep* lernen

▶ **learn up** **VT** *sep (= learn by study)* lernen, pauken *(inf)*; *(= memorize)* (auswendig) lernen

learned[1] ['lɜːnɪd] **ADJ** gelehrt; *book also, journal* wissenschaftlich; *society also, profession* akademisch; **a ~ man** ein Gelehrter *m*; **my ~ colleague *or* friend** *(Jur)* mein verehrter Herr Kollege, meine verehrte Frau Kollegin

learned[2] [lɜːnd] **PRET, PTP** *of* **learn** **ADJ** *(Psych) behaviour* angelernt; *reaction* antrainiert

learnedly ['lɜːnɪdlɪ] **ADV** gelehrt

learner ['lɜːnəʳ] **N** Anfänger(in) *m(f)*, Lerner(in) *m(f) (esp Ling)*; *(= student)* Lernende(r) *mf*; *(= learner driver)* Fahrschüler(in) *m(f)*; **~s of languages** Sprachschüler *or* -studenten *pl*; **special classes for slow ~s** Sonderklassen *pl* für lernschwache Schüler

learner-centred, *(US)* **learner-centered** ['lɜːnəˌsentəd] **ADJ** auf den Lernenden ausgerichtet

learner driver **N** *(Mot)* Fahrschüler(in) *m(f)*

learning ['lɜːnɪŋ] **N** **a** *(= act)* Lernen *nt*; **difficulties encountered during the ~ of geometry/English** Schwierigkeiten beim Erlernen der Geometrie/beim Englischlernen **b** *(= erudition)* Gelehrsamkeit *f*, Gelehrtheit *f*; **a man of ~** ein Gelehrter *m*; **the ~ contained in these volumes** das in diesen Bänden enthaltene Wissen; **seat of ~** Stätte *f* der Gelehrsamkeit

learning: **learning curve** **N** Lernkurve *f*; **to be on a steep ~** viel dazulernen; **life is a constant ~** man lernt immer noch dazu; **learning disability** **N** Lernbehinderung *f*; **learning-disabled** **ADJ** lernbehindert

learnt [lɜːnt] *(Brit) pret, ptp of* **learn**

lease [liːs] **N** *(of land, farm, business premises etc)* Pacht *f*; *(= contract)* Pachtvertrag *m*; *(of house, flat, office)* Miete *f*; *(= contract)* Mietvertrag *m*; *(of equipment)* Leasing *nt*; *(= contract)* Leasingvertrag *m*; **the ~ was prematurely terminated** die Pacht *or* das Pachtverhältnis/das Mietverhältnis wurde vorzeitig beendet; **to take a ~ on a house** ein Haus mieten; **to take a ~ on business premises** ein Geschäft(sgrundstück) *nt* pachten; **to take a house on a 99-year ~** ein Haus auf 99 Jahre pachten; **you can buy the ~ for a period of 99 years** Sie können einen Pachtvertrag für 99 Jahre abschließen; **we rented the house/farm on a ~** wir haben das Haus gemietet/den Bauernhof gepachtet; **to let sth on a ~** etw verpachten/vermieten; **to be on ~ to …** verpachtet/vermietet sein an *(+acc)* …; **to give sb a new ~ of life** jdm (neuen) Aufschwung geben; **the renovations have given the old farmhouse a new ~ of life** durch die Renovierung ist der alte Bauernhof wieder in Schuss gekommen
VT *(= take)* pachten *(from* von), in Pacht nehmen *(from* bei); *house, flat, office* mieten *(from* von); *equipment* mieten, leasen *(from* von); *(= give: also* **lease out**) verpachten *(to* an *+acc)*, in Pacht geben *(to sb* jdm); *house, flat, office* vermieten *(to* an *+acc)*; *equipment* vermieten, leasen *(to* an *+acc)*

lease: **leaseback** **N** Verkauf und Rückmiete *pl* **ATTR** *arrangement* mit Rückvermietung an den Verkäufer; **leasehold** **N** *(= property)*

Pachtbesitz *m*; *(= land also)* Pachtgrundstück *nt*; *(= building also)* gepachtetes Gebäude; *(= contract, tenure)* Pachtvertrag *m*; **who has the ~ on the property?** wer hat das Land/Gebäude gepachtet?; **we own the house on ~** wir haben das Haus langfristig gepachtet; **~ reform** Mietrechtsreform *f* ADJ gepachtet; **~ property** *(generally)* Pachtbesitz *m*; *(= land)* Pachtgrund *m*, Pachtland *nt*; *(= building)* Pachtobjekt *nt* ADV **to buy a property ~** ein Objekt *nt* mit Pachtvertrag kaufen; **leaseholder** N Pächter(in) *m(f)*

leash [liːʃ] N Leine *f*; **on a ~** an der Leine; **to give sb a longer ~** *(esp US fig)* jdm mehr Freiheit geben → *also* **strain**[1]

leasing [ˈliːsɪŋ] N **a** *(= renting)* Mieten *nt*; *(of land)* Pachten *nt* **b** *(= hiring out)* Vermieten *nt*; *(of land)* Verpachten *nt*; *(of car, computer)* Leasing *nt*

least [liːst] ✪ 26.3 ADJ **a** *(= slightest, smallest)* geringste(r, s)
b *(with uncountable nouns)* wenigste(r, s); **he has the ~ money** er hat am wenigsten Geld
ADV **a** *(+vb)* am wenigsten; **~ of all would I wish to offend him** auf gar keinen Fall möchte ich ihn beleidigen
b *(+adj)* **~ possible expenditure** möglichst geringe Kosten; **the ~ expensive car** das billigste *or* preiswerteste Auto; **the ~ important matter** das Unwichtigste; **of all my worries that's the ~ important** das ist meine geringste Sorge; **the ~ talented player** der am wenigsten talentierte Spieler; **the ~ known** der/die/das Unbekannteste; **the ~ interesting** der/die/das Uninteressanteste; **he's the ~ aggressive of men** er ist nicht im Mindesten *or* mindesten aggressiv; **not the ~ bit drunk** kein bisschen *or* nicht im Geringsten betrunken
N **the ~** der/die/das Geringste *or* wenigste; **that's the ~ of my worries** darüber mache ich mir die wenigsten Sorgen; **I have many worries, and money is the ~ of them** ich habe viele Sorgen, und Geld kümmert mich am wenigsten; **it's the ~ I can do** es ist das wenigste, was ich tun kann; **you gave yourself the ~** du hast dir (selbst) am wenigsten gegeben; **at ~, I think so** ich glaube wenigstens; **at ~ it's not raining** wenigstens *or* zumindest regnet es nicht; **we can at ~ try** wir können es wenigstens versuchen; **there were at ~ eight** es waren mindestens acht da; **we need at ~ three** wir brauchen wenigstens *or* mindestens drei; **we need three at the very ~** allermindestens brauchen wir drei; **there must have been twenty at the very ~** es waren mindestens zwanzig da; **at the very ~ you could apologize** du könntest dich wenigstens *or* zumindest entschuldigen; **all nations love football, not ~ the British** alle Völker lieben Fußball, nicht zuletzt die Briten; **and that's the ~ of it** und das ist noch das wenigste; **not in the ~!** nicht im Geringsten!, ganz und gar nicht!; **he was not in the ~ upset** er war kein bisschen *or* nicht im Geringsten verärgert; **to say the ~** um es milde zu sagen; **the ~ said, the better, ~ said, soonest mended** *(Prov)* je weniger man darüber spricht, desto besser

leastways [ˈliːstweɪz] ADV *(inf)* zumindest, wenigstens

leather [ˈleðəʳ] N Leder *nt*; **~s** *(for motorbike)* Lederzeug *nt* ADJ Leder-, ledern; **~ belt** Ledergürtel *m*; **~ goods** Lederwaren *pl*; **~ jacket** Lederjacke *f*; **~ shoes** Lederschuhe *pl* VT *(inf)* versohlen *(inf)*, ein paar überziehen *(+dat) (inf)*

leatherette [ˌleðəˈret] N Kunstleder *nt*

leathering [ˈleðərɪŋ] N *(Brit inf)* Tracht *f* Prügel

leatherneck [ˈleðənek] N *(US inf)* Ledernacken *m*

leathery [ˈleðərɪ] ADJ *material* lederartig; *skin* ledern; *meat* zäh; **a ~ smell** ein Ledergeruch *m*

leave [liːv] *vb: pret, ptp* **left** N **a** *(= permission)* Erlaubnis *f*; **by your ~** *(form)* mit Ihrer (gütigen) Erlaubnis *(form)*; **to ask sb's ~ to do sth** jdn um Erlaubnis bitten, etw zu tun; **he borrowed my car without so much as a by your ~** er hat sich *(dat)* einfach so mein Auto geliehen
b *(= permission to be absent, Mil)* Urlaub *m*; **to be on ~** auf Urlaub sein, Urlaub haben; **to be on ~ from sth** von etw beurlaubt sein; **I've got ~ to attend the conference** ich habe freibekommen, um an der Konferenz teilzunehmen; **a two-day ~** zwei Tage Urlaub; **~ of absence** Beurlaubung *f*; **to be on ~ of absence** beurlaubt sein
c to take one's ~ sich verabschieden; **to take ~ of sb** sich von jdm verabschieden; **to take ~ of one's senses** den Verstand verlieren
VT **a** *(= depart from, quit) place, person* verlassen; **the train left the station** der Zug fuhr aus dem Bahnhof; **when the plane left Rome** als das Flugzeug von Rom abflog; **when he left Rome** als er von Rom wegging/wegfuhr/abflog *etc*; **would you ~ us, please?** würden Sie uns bitte allein lassen?; **please sir, may I ~ the room?** Herr X, darf ich mal raus?; **to ~ the country** das Land verlassen; *(permanently)* auswandern; **to ~ home** von zu Hause weggehen/wegfahren; *(permanently)* von zu Hause weggehen; **she left her parents' home** sie verließ ihr Elternhaus; **to ~ school** die Schule verlassen; *(prematurely also)* (von der Schule) abgehen; **to ~ the table** vom Tisch aufstehen; **to ~ one's job** seine Stelle aufgeben; **to ~ the road** *(= crash)* von der Straße abkommen; *(= turn off)* von der Straße abbiegen; **to ~ the rails** entgleisen; **the rocket left the ground** die Rakete hob (vom Boden) ab; **I'll ~ you at the station** am Bahnhof trennen wir uns dann; *(in car)* ich setze dich am Bahnhof ab; **he left her for another woman** er verließ sie wegen einer anderen
b *(= allow or cause to remain)* lassen; *bad taste, dirty mark, message, scar, impression* hinterlassen; **I'll ~ my address with you** ich lasse Ihnen meine Adresse da; **I'll ~ the key with the neighbours** *(Brit) or* **neighbors** *(US)* ich hinterlege *or* lasse den Schlüssel bei den Nachbarn; **to ~ one's supper** sein Abendessen stehen lassen; **the postman** *(Brit) or* **mailman** *(US)* **left three letters for you** der Briefträger hat drei Briefe für dich gebracht; **they were left to die** man ließ sie sterben
c *(= leave in a certain condition)* lassen; **who left the window open?** wer hat das Fenster offen gelassen?; **to ~ two pages blank** zwei Seiten frei lassen; **this ~s me free for the afternoon/free to go shopping** dadurch habe ich den Nachmittag frei/Zeit zum Einkaufen; **this new development ~s us with a problem** diese neue Entwicklung stellt uns vor ein Problem; **the death of her uncle left her with no financial worries** nach dem Tod ihres Onkels hatte sie keine finanziellen Probleme mehr; **~ the dog alone** lass den Hund in Ruhe; **~ me alone!** lass mich (in Ruhe)!; **to ~ well alone** die Finger davonlassen *(inf)*; **to ~ sb to do sth** es jdm überlassen, etw zu tun; **I'll ~ you to it** ich lasse Sie jetzt allein weitermachen; **to ~ sb to himself** jdn allein lassen; **to ~ go of sb/sth** jdn/etw loslassen; **let's ~ it at that** lassen wir es dabei (bewenden); **if we ~ it so that he'll contact us** wenn wir dabei verbleiben, dass er sich mit uns in Verbindung setzt; **how did he ~ things at the last meeting?** wobei hat er es beim letzten Treffen belassen?; **to ~ sth to the last minute** mit etw bis zur letzten Minute warten
d *(= forget)* liegen lassen, stehen lassen
e *(after death) person, money* hinterlassen; **he left his wife very badly off** er ließ seine Frau fast mittellos zurück
f to be left *(= remain, be over)* übrig bleiben; **all I have left** alles, was ich noch habe; **I've (got) £6 left** ich habe noch 6 Pfund (übrig); **how many are there left?** wie viele sind noch da *or* übrig?; **3 from 10 ~s 7** 10 minus 3 ist *or* (ist) gleich 7; **what does that ~?** wie viel bleibt übrig?; *(Math)* wie viel gibt *or* ist das?; **there was nothing left for me to do but to sell it** mir blieb nichts anderes übrig, als es zu verkaufen
g *(= entrust)* überlassen *(up to sb* jdm); **~ it to me** lass mich nur machen; **I ~ it to you to judge** es bleibt dir überlassen, zu urteilen; **to ~ sth to chance** etw dem Zufall überlassen
h *(= stop)* **let's ~ this now** lassen wir das jetzt mal
VI *(person)* (weg)gehen; *(in vehicle)* abfahren; *(in plane)* abfliegen; *(train, bus, ship)* abfahren; **we ~ for Sweden tomorrow** wir fahren morgen nach Schweden; **which flight did he ~ on?** welchen Flug hat er genommen?; **his girlfriend has already left** seine Freundin ist schon gegangen

▶ **leave about** *(Brit) or* **around** VT *sep* herumliegen lassen

▶ **leave aside** VT *sep* beiseitelassen; **leaving aside the fact that …** wenn man die Tatsache außer Acht lässt, dass …

▶ **leave behind** VT *sep* **a** *the car, the children* dalassen, zurücklassen; *fingerprints, chaos* hinterlassen; *the past* hinter sich *(dat)* lassen; **we've left all that behind us** das alles liegt hinter uns; **we've left all our worries behind us** *(= settled)* wir sind alle Sorgen los; *(= forgotten)* wir haben all unsere Sorgen vergessen **b** *(= outstrip)* hinter sich *(dat)* lassen; **he left all his fellow students behind** er stellte alle seine Kommilitonen in den Schatten **c** *(= forget)* liegen lassen, stehen lassen

▶ **leave in** VT *sep sentence, scene in play etc* lassen, nicht herausnehmen, drinlassen *(inf)*; **don't leave the dog in all day** lassen Sie den Hund nicht den ganzen Tag im Haus; **how long should the meat be left in?** wie lange muss das Fleisch im Ofen bleiben *or* im Ofen gelassen werden?

▶ **leave off** VT *sep clothes* nicht anziehen; *lid* nicht darauf tun, ablassen *(inf)*; *radio, lights* auslassen; *umlaut* weglassen; **you can leave your coat off** du brauchst deinen Mantel nicht anzuziehen; **don't leave the top off your pen** lass den Füllhalter nicht offen *or* ohne Kappe liegen; **you left her name off the list** Sie haben ihren Namen nicht in die Liste aufgenommen
VI *+prep obj (inf)* aufhören; **we left off work after lunch** wir haben nach dem Mittagessen Feierabend gemacht; **leave off doing that, will you!** hör auf damit, ja?
VI *(inf)* aufhören; **leave off!** lass das!; **he picked up where he left off last year** er machte weiter, wo er letztes Jahr aufgehört hatte

▶ **leave on** VT *sep clothes* anbehalten, anlassen *(inf)*; *lights, fire etc* anlassen; **we left the wallpaper on and painted over it** wir haben die Tapete drangelassen *(inf) or* nicht entfernt und sie überstrichen

▶ **leave out** VT *sep* **a** *(= not bring in)* draußen lassen
b *(= omit)* auslassen; *(= exclude) people* ausschließen *(of* von); **he was instructed to leave out all references to politics** er bekam Anweisung, alle Hinweise auf Politik wegzulassen; **he had been left out in the restructuring** er wurde bei der Neugliederung nicht berücksichtigt; **you leave my wife/politics out of this** lassen Sie meine Frau/die Politik aus dem Spiel; **he got left out of things at school** er wurde in der Schule nie mit einbezogen; **she felt left out** sie fühlte sich ausgeschlossen
c *(= leave available)* dalassen; **I'll leave the books out on my desk** ich lasse die Bücher auf meinem Schreibtisch; **will you leave the tools out ready?** legen Sie bitte das Werkzeug zurecht
d *(= not put away)* nicht wegräumen, liegen lassen

▶ **leave over** VT *sep* **a** *(= leave surplus)* übrig lassen; **to be left over** übrig (geblieben) sein **b** *(= postpone)* verschieben, vertagen

leaven [ˈlevn] N *(also* **leavening)** [-ɪŋ] Treibmittel *nt*; *(= fermenting dough)* Sauerteig *m*; *(fig)* Auflockerung *f*; **even his most serious speeches had a ~ of humour** auch seine ernstesten Reden waren mit Humor gewürzt VT (auf)gehen lassen, treiben; *(fig)* auflockern

leaves [liːvz] *pl of* **leaf**

leave-taking [ˈliːvteɪkɪŋ] N Abschied *m*; *(= act)* Abschiednehmen *nt*

leaving ['li:vɪŋ] N Fortgang *m*, Weggang *m*; **~ was very difficult (for him)** das Weggehen fiel ihm schwer

leaving: **leaving certificate** N *(Brit)* Abgangszeugnis *nt*; **leaving day** N *(Sch)* Schuljahrsabschluss *m*, letzter Schultag; **leaving do** N *(esp Brit inf)* Abschiedsfete *f*, Ausstand *m*; **leaving party** N Abschiedsfeier *or* -party *f*; **leaving present** N Abschiedsgeschenk *nt*

leavings ['li:vɪŋz] PL *(= food)* (Über)reste *pl*; *(= rubbish)* Abfälle *pl*

Lebanese [,lebə'ni:z] ADJ libanesisch N Libanese *m*, Libanesin *f*

Lebanon ['lebənən] N **the ~** der Libanon

lech [letʃ] VI *(esp Brit inf)* **to ~ after sb** *(= chase)* jdm nachstellen; *(in mind)* sich *(dat)* lüsterne Vorstellungen über jdn machen

lecher ['letʃə'] N Lüstling *m*, Wüstling *m*; *(hum)* Lustmolch *m* VI lüstern sein

lecherous ['letʃərəs] ADJ lüstern; *man, behaviour also* geil

lecherously ['letʃərəslɪ] ADV lüstern

lechery ['letʃərɪ] N Lüsternheit *f*, Geilheit *f*; **his reputation for ~** sein Ruf *m* als Wüstling

lectern ['lektɜ:n] N Pult *nt*

lector ['lektə'] N *(Univ: = foreign language assistant)* Lektor(in) *m(f)*

lecture ['lektʃə'] N **a** Vortrag *m*; *(Univ)* Vorlesung *f*; **to give a ~** einen Vortrag/eine Vorlesung halten *(to* für, *on sth* über etw *acc)*; **I asked for a short explanation and got a ~** ich wollte nur eine kurze Erklärung und bekam einen Vortrag zu hören
b *(= scolding)* (Straf)predigt *f*; **to give sb a ~** jdm eine Strafpredigt *or* Standpauke *(inf)* halten *(about* wegen)
VT **a** *(= give a lecture)* **to ~ sb on sth** jdm einen Vortrag/eine Vorlesung über etw *(acc)* halten; **he ~s us in French** wir hören bei ihm (Vorlesungen in) Französisch
b *(= scold)* tadeln, abkanzeln; **to ~ sb** jdm eine Strafpredigt halten *(on* wegen)
VI einen Vortrag halten; *(Univ) (= give lecture)* eine Vorlesung halten; *(= give lecture course)* lesen, Vorlesungen halten *(on* über *+acc)*; **he ~s in English** er ist Dozent für Anglistik; **he ~s on Victorian poetry** er liest über viktorianische Dichtung; **have you ever heard him ~?** hast du schon mal eine Vorlesung bei ihm gehört?; **he ~s at Princeton** er lehrt in Princeton; **he ~s well** seine Vorlesungen sind gut

lecture: **lecture course** N Vorlesungs-/Vortragsreihe *f*; **lecture hall** N Hörsaal *m*; **lecture notes** PL *(professor's)* Manuskript *nt*; *(student's)* Aufzeichnungen *pl*; *(= handout)* Vorlesungsskript *nt*

lecturer ['lektʃərə'] N Dozent(in) *m(f)*; *(= speaker)* Redner(in) *m(f)*; **assistant ~** ≈ Assistent(in) *m(f)*; **senior ~** *Dozent(in) in höherer Position*

lecture room N Hörsaal *m*

lectureship ['lektʃəʃɪp] N Stelle *f* als Dozent, Lehrauftrag *m*

lecture: **lecture theatre**, *(US)* **lecture theater** N Hörsaal *m*; **lecture tour** N Vortragsreise *f*

LED *abbr of* **light-emitting diode**

led [led] *pret, ptp of* **lead²**

LED display N Leuchtanzeige *f*

ledge [ledʒ] N **a** Leiste *f*, Kante *f*; *(along wall)* Leiste *f*; *(of window) (inside)* Fensterbrett *nt*; *(outside)* (Fenster)sims *nt or m*; *(= shelf)* Ablage *f*, Bord *nt*; *(= mountain ledge)* (Fels)vorsprung *m* **b** *(= ridge of rocks)* Riff *nt*

ledger ['ledʒə'] N Hauptbuch *nt*

ledger line N *(Mus)* Hilfslinie *f*

lee [li:] ADJ Lee-; **~ side** Leeseite *f* N **a** *(Naut)* Lee *f* **b** *(= shelter)* Schutz *m*, Windschatten *m*

leech [li:tʃ] N Blutegel *m*; *(fig)* Blutsauger(in) *m(f)*

leek [li:k] N Porree *m*, Lauch *m*

leer [lɪə'] N *(knowing, sexual)* anzügliches Grinsen; *(evil)* heimtückischer Blick VI anzüglich grinsen; einen heimtückischen Blick haben; **he ~ed at the girl** er warf dem Mädchen lüsterne Blicke zu

leery ['lɪərɪ] ADJ *(inf)* misstrauisch; **I'm a bit ~ of him** ich traue ihm nicht so recht

lees [li:z] PL Bodensatz *m*

leeward ['li:wəd] ADJ Lee-; **~ side** Leeseite *f* ADV leewärts; **the ship was anchored ~ of the island** das Schiff ankerte an der Leeseite der Insel N Lee(seite) *f*; **to ~** an der Leeseite; **steer to ~** nach der Leeseite steuern, leewärts steuern

Leeward Islands ['li:wəd,aɪləndz] PL **the ~** die Inseln *pl* über dem Winde *(von den Jungferninseln bis Trinidad)*

leeway ['li:weɪ] N **a** *(Naut)* Abtrift *f*, Leeweg *m* **b** *(fig: = flexibility)* Spielraum *m*; *(in a decision)* Freiheit *f*; *(= time lost)* Zeitverlust *m*; **he has given them too much ~** er hat ihnen zu viel Freiheit *or* Spielraum gelassen; **to make up the ~** den Zeitverlust aufholen; **there's a lot of ~ to make up** es gibt viel nachzuarbeiten, ein großer Rückstand muss aufgeholt werden

left¹ [left] *pret, ptp of* **leave**

left² ADJ *(also Pol)* linke(r, s); **no ~ turn** Linksabbiegen verboten; **he's got two ~ hands** *(inf)* er hat zwei linke Hände *(inf)*; **he's got two ~ feet** *(inf)* er ist sehr ungelenk; **to come out of ~ field** *(esp US)* überraschend kommen
ADV links *(of* von); **turn ~** *(Aut)* links abbiegen; **keep ~** sich links halten, links fahren; **move ~ a little** rücken Sie ein bisschen nach links; **~, right, ~, right** links, rechts, links, rechts; **~ turn!** *(Mil)* links um!
N **a** Linke(r, s); **on the ~** links *(of* von), auf der linken Seite *(of +gen)*; **on** *or* **to sb's ~** links von jdm, zu jds Linken *(form)*; **his wife sat on my ~** seine Frau saß links von mir *or* zu meiner Linken *(form)*; **take the first (on the) ~ after the church** biegen Sie hinter der Kirche die erste (Straße) links ab; **the third/fourth** *etc* **... from the ~** der/die/das dritte/vierte *etc* ... von links; **to keep to the ~** sich links halten; **to drive on the ~** links fahren; **to fall to the ~** nach links fallen
b *(Pol)* Linke *f*; **the parties of the ~** die linken Parteien, die Parteien der Linken; **to be on the ~** links stehen; **to move to the ~** nach links rücken; **he's further to the ~ than I am** er steht weiter links als ich; **to be on the ~ of the party** dem linken Flügel der Partei angehören
c *(Boxing)* Linke *f*

left: **left-aligned** ADJ *(Typ)* linksbündig; **left back** N linker Verteidiger; **left-click** *(Comput)* VI links klicken VT links klicken auf *(+acc)*; **left-footed** [,left'fʊtɪd] *(Ftbl)* ADJ *shot* mit dem linken Fuß; **~ player** Linksfüßer(in) *m(f)*; **he is a ~ player** er ist Linksfüßer, er spielt mit dem linken Fuß ADV **to shoot ~** mit links schießen; **left half** N linker Vorstopper; **left-hand** ADJ **~ drive** Linkssteuerung *f*; **~ side** linke Seite; **he stood on the ~ side of the king** er stand zur Linken des Königs; **~ turn** linke Abzweigung; **take the ~ turn** bieg links ab; **left-handed** ADJ linkshändig; *tool* für Linkshänder; *(fig) compliment* zweifelhaft; **both the children are ~** beide Kinder sind Linkshänder; **a ~ blow** ein linker Treffer ADV *write, bat, bowl etc* mit links; **left-hander** N *(= punch)* Linke *f*; *(= person)* Linkshänder(in) *m(f)*

leftie ['leftɪ] N *(pej)* linker Typ *(pej)*, Rote(r) *mf (pej inf)*

leftish ['leftɪʃ] ADJ linksliberal, links angehaucht *(inf)*; **his views are ~** er ist links angehaucht *(inf)*

leftist ['leftɪst] ADJ linke(r, s), linksgerichtet; **his views are ~** er ist linksgerichtet, er steht links N Linke(r) *mf*

left: **left-luggage locker** N *(Brit)* Gepäckschließfach *nt*; **left-luggage (office)** N *(Brit)* Gepäckaufbewahrung *f*; **is there a ~ in this station?** kann man auf diesem Bahnhof irgendwo sein Gepäck zur Aufbewahrung geben?; **left-of-centre**, *(US)* **left-of-center** ADJ *politician* links von der Mitte stehend; **~ party** Mitte-Links-Partei *f*; **leftover** ADJ übrig geblieben N **a ~s** (Über)reste *pl* **b** *(fig)* **to be a ~ from the past** ein Überbleibsel *nt* aus der Vergangenheit sein; **left property** N Hinterlassenschaft *f*, Nachlass *m*

leftward(s) ['leftwəd(z)] ADJ nach links; **leftward bend** Linkskurve *f*; **a leftward shift** *(Pol)* ein Linksruck *m* ADV *(Pol) move, shift* nach links

left: **left wing** N linker Flügel *(also Sport)*; *(= player)* Linksaußen *m*; **on the ~** *(Pol, Sport)* auf dem linken Flügel; **left-wing** ADJ *(Pol)* linke(r, s); *politician also* linksgerichtet; **~ extremist** Linksextremist(in) *m(f)*; **left-winger** N *(Pol)* Linke(r) *mf*; *(Sport)* Linksaußen *m*

lefty ['leftɪ] *(inf)* N **a** *(Pol)* Linke(r) *mf* **b** *(person)* Linkshänder(in) *m(f)* → **leftie**

leg [leg]¹ N **a** *(also of trousers)* Bein *nt*; **the new-born calf seemed to be all ~s** das neugeborene Kalb schien nur aus Beinen zu bestehen; **to be on one's last ~s** *(= dying)* in den letzten Zügen liegen *(inf)*; *(= exhausted)* auf dem letzten Loch pfeifen *(inf)*; **this carpet is on its last ~s** dieser Teppich hält *or* machts *(inf)* nicht mehr lange; **he hasn't (got) a ~ to stand on** *(fig: = no excuse)* er kann sich nicht herausreden; *(= no proof)* das kann er nicht belegen; **to have ~s** *(esp US inf) (idea, plan)* klappen; *(story)* laufen *(inf)*; **to walk one's ~s off** sich *(dat)* die Füße wund laufen; **to walk sb's ~s off** jdn (ganz schön) scheuchen *(inf)*, jdm davonlaufen; **you've walked my ~s off** du bist mir zu schnell gelaufen; **to run sb's ~s off** *(fig)* jdn herumscheuchen *(inf)*; **he ran the other athletes' ~s off** er rannte den anderen Läufern davon; **I'll take the children to the park and run their ~s off** ich gehe mit den Kindern in den Park, da können sie sich austoben; **to be out ~ before wicket** *(Cricket)* aus sein, weil sein vor dem Mal stehendes Bein von einem Wurf getroffen wurde; **to get one's ~ over** *(Brit inf)* bumsen *(inf)*
b *(as food)* Keule *f*, Hachse *f*; **~ of lamb** Lammkeule *f*
c *(of furniture)* Bein *nt*; *(of bed)* Fuß *m*, Bein *nt*
d *(= stage)* Etappe *f*
VT **to ~ it** *(inf: = go on foot)* laufen, zu Fuß gehen

leg² [ledʒ] N *(sl)* **you're a true ~** du bist ein Held *(inf)*

legacy ['legəsɪ] N *(lit, fig)* Erbschaft *f*, Vermächtnis *nt*; *(fig also)* Erbe *nt*; *(fig pej)* Hinterlassenschaft *f*; **to leave sb a ~ of sth** *(fig)* jdm etw hinterlassen; **our ~ to future generations must not be a polluted world** wir dürfen den zukünftigen Generationen keine verschmutzte Welt hinterlassen; **the tragedy left a ~ of bitterness** die Tragödie hinterließ Bitterkeit

legal ['li:gl] ADJ **a** *(= lawful)* legal, rechtlich zulässig; *(= according to the law) restrictions, obligation, limit* gesetzlich; *(= allowed by law) fare, speed* zulässig; *(= valid before law) will, purchase* rechtsgültig; **to become ~** rechtskräftig werden; **to make sth ~** etw legalisieren; **the ~ age for marriage** das gesetzliche Heiratsalter, die Ehemündigkeit; **it is not ~ to sell drink to children** es ist gesetzlich verboten, Alkohol an Kinder zu verkaufen; **~ limit** *(of blood alcohol when driving)* Promillegrenze *f*; **~ claim** rechtmäßiger Anspruch, Rechtsanspruch *m*; **~ document** *or* **instrument** (rechtskräftige) Urkunde; **~ rights** gesetzlich verankerte Rechte *pl*; **they don't know what their ~ rights are** sie kennen ihre eigenen Rechte nicht; **the ~ custody of the children** das Sorgerecht für die Kinder; **women had no ~ status** Frauen waren nicht rechtsfähig; **he made ~ provision for his ex-wife** er hat die Versorgung seiner geschiedenen Frau rechtlich geregelt
b *(= relating to the law)* Rechts-; *matters, affairs* juristisch, rechtlich; *advice, services, journal, mind* juristisch; *decision* richterlich; *inquiry, investigation* gerichtlich; **from a ~ point of view** aus ju-

ristischer Sicht, rechtlich gesehen; **for ~ reasons** aus rechtlichen Gründen; **what's his ~ position?** wie ist seine rechtliche Stellung?; **~ charges** *or* **fees** *or* **costs** *(solicitor's)* Anwaltskosten *pl*; *(court's)* Gerichtskosten *pl*; **to take ~ advice on** *or* **over** *or* **about sth** in Bezug auf etw *(acc)* juristischen Rat einholen; **to start ~ proceedings against sb** gegen jdn Klage erheben, jdn verklagen; **~ opinion is that ...** die Anwälte sind der Meinung, dass ...; **~ loophole** Gesetzeslücke *f*; **the British ~ system** das britische Rechtssystem; **the ~ profession** der Anwaltsstand, die Anwaltschaft; *(including judges)* die Juristenschaft; **~ representation** Rechtsvertretung *f*; **~ representative** gesetzlicher Vertreter; *(= counsel)* (Rechts)anwalt *m*, (Rechts)anwältin *f*, Verteidiger(in) *m(f)*

legal: **legal action** N Klage *f*; **to take ~ against sb** gegen jdn Klage erheben, jdn verklagen; **legal adviser** N Rechtsberater(in) *m(f)*; **legal aid** N Rechtshilfe *f*; **legal department** N Rechtsabteilung *f*, juristische Abteilung; **legal eagle** N *(hum inf)* Rechtsverdreher(in) *m(f) (hum inf)*; **legal entity** N juristische Person

legalese [ˌliːɡəˈliːz] N *(pej)* Juristensprache *f or* -jargon *m*, Juristendeutsch *nt*

legal fiction N juristische Fiktion

legalistic [ˌliːɡəˈlɪstɪk] ADJ legalistisch

legalistically [ˌliːɡəˈlɪstɪkəlɪ] ADV legalistisch; **to examine the issues ~** die Fragen nach dem Wortlaut des Gesetzes betrachten

legality [liːˈɡælɪtɪ] N Legalität *f*; *(of claim)* Rechtmäßigkeit *f*; *(of tender)* Gesetzlichkeit *f*; *(of restrictions, obligation)* Gesetzmäßigkeit *f*; *(of fare, speed)* Zulässigkeit *f*; *(of contract, will, marriage, purchase, decision, limit)* rechtliche Gültigkeit, Rechtsgültigkeit *f*

legalization [ˌliːɡəlaɪˈzeɪʃən] N Legalisierung *f*

legalize [ˈliːɡəlaɪz] VT legalisieren

legally [ˈliːɡəlɪ] ADV *(= lawfully) transacted, acquire, trade* legal; *married* rechtmäßig; *guaranteed, obliged, set down* gesetzlich; *(= relating to the law) advise* juristisch; *indefensible* rechtlich; **what's the position ~?** wie ist die Lage rechtlich gesehen?; **~, there was no objection** rechtlich *or* juristisch (gesehen) gab es keine Einwände; **~ speaking** vom rechtlichen Standpunkt aus, juristisch gesehen; **it's wrong – ~ or morally?** es ist nicht richtig – aus rechtlicher oder moralischer Sicht?; **~ responsible** vor dem Gesetz verantwortlich; **to be ~ entitled to sth** einen Rechtsanspruch auf etw *(acc)* haben; **~ binding** rechtsverbindlich; **~, he can only stay for 3 months** legal(erweise) kann er nur 3 Monate bleiben; **~ valid** rechtsgültig; **this herbicide can still be ~ sold** dieses Herbizid kann immer noch legal gehandelt werden

legal: **legal offence**, *(US)* **legal offense** N strafbare Handlung; **drug-peddling is a ~** der Handel mit Drogen ist strafbar; **legal practitioner** N Rechtsanwalt *m*, Rechtsanwältin *f*; **legal protection** N Rechtsschutz *m*; **legal separation** N gesetzliche Trennung; **legal successor** N Rechtsnachfolger(in) *m(f)*; **legal tender** N gesetzliches Zahlungsmittel

legate [ˈleɡɪt] N Legat *m*

legatee [ˌleɡəˈtiː] N Vermächtnisnehmer(in) *m(f)*

legation [lɪˈɡeɪʃən] N *(= diplomats)* Gesandtschaft *f*, Vertretung *f*; *(= building)* Gesandtschaftsgebäude *nt*

legend [ˈledʒənd] N **a** Legende *f*; *(fictitious)* Sage *f*; **heroes of Greek ~** griechische Sagenhelden *pl*; **to become a ~ in one's lifetime** schon zu Lebzeiten zur Legende werden **b** *(= inscription, caption)* Legende *f*

legendary [ˈledʒəndərɪ] ADJ **a** legendär; *person* legendär, sagenumwoben; **~ proportions** legendäre Ausmaße *pl*; **to achieve ~ status** zur Legende werden **b** *(= famous)* berühmt

legerdemain [ˌledʒədəˈmeɪn] N Taschenspielerei *f*

-legged [-ˈleɡd, -ˈleɡɪd] ADJ *suf* -beinig; **two-/four-legged** zwei-/vierbeinig; **long-legged** langbeinig; **bare-legged** ohne Strümpfe

leggings [ˈleɡɪŋz] PL (hohe *or* lange) Gamaschen *pl*; *(fireman's, yachtsman's)* Beinlinge *f*; *(= trousers)* Leggings *pl*; *(baby's)* Gamaschenhose *f*

leggy [ˈleɡɪ] ADJ *(+er)* langbeinig; *(= gawky)* staksig

Leghorn [ˈleɡhɔːn] N *(Geog)* Livorno *nt*

legibility [ˌledʒɪˈbɪlɪtɪ] N Lesbarkeit *f*, Leserlichkeit *f*

legible [ˈledʒɪbl] ADJ lesbar; *handwriting also* leserlich

legibly [ˈledʒɪblɪ] ADV lesbar; *write* leserlich

legion [ˈliːdʒən] N **a** Armee *f*; *(= Foreign Legion)* Legion *f* **b** *(Roman)* Legion *f* **c** *(= organization)* **Legion** Legion *f*; **American/British Legion** American/British Legion *f (Verband der Kriegsveteranen)*; **Legion of Honour** Ehrenlegion *f* **d** *(fig: = large number)* Legion *f*; **they are ~** ihre Zahl ist Legion; **his supporters are ~** seine Anhänger sind Legion

> **LEGION**
>
> In Großbritannien ist die **Legion** eine Organisation, die die Veteranen der Streitkräfte und ihre Familien unterstützt und für diese Vereinsheime betreibt. Jeden November ruft die **Legion** mit dem **Poppy Day Appeal** zu Spenden für die Wohlfahrtseinrichtungen der Streitkräfte auf. Die amerikanische **Legion** ist eine ähnliche Einrichtung, die Militärveteranen und ihren Familien finanzielle Unterstützung und Hilfe zur Wiedereingliederung anbietet. Zudem setzt sie sich im Kongress für die Interessen der Veteranen ein und wirbt für eine starke nationale Verteidigung. Für ihre Mitglieder betreibt die **Legion** soziale Einrichtungen auf kommunaler Ebene.

legionary [ˈliːdʒənərɪ] **ADJ** Legions-; **~ cohort** Legionskohorte *f* **N** (*also* **legionnaire**) Legionär *m*

legionnaire [ˌliːdʒəˈneəʳ] N Legionär *m*

legionnaire's disease [ˌliːdʒəˈneəzdɪˌziːz] N Legionärskrankheit *f*

legislate [ˈledʒɪsleɪt] **VI** **a** *(= make laws)* Gesetze/ein Gesetz erlassen; **parliament's job is to ~** die Aufgabe des Parlaments ist die Gesetzgebung **b** *(fig)* **to ~ for sth** etw berücksichtigen; *(= give ruling on)* für etw Regeln aufstellen **VT** **to ~ sth out of existence** etw durch Gesetz aus der Welt schaffen

legislation [ˌledʒɪsˈleɪʃən] N *(= making laws)* Gesetzgebung *f*, Legislatur *f (geh)*; *(= laws)* Gesetze *pl*

legislative [ˈledʒɪslətɪv] ADJ gesetzgebend, legislativ *(geh)*; **~ reforms** Gesetzesreformen *pl*; **~ programme** *(Brit) or* **program** *(US) (of government)* Gesetzgebungsprogramm *nt*

legislator [ˈledʒɪsleɪtəʳ] N Gesetzgeber *m*

legislature [ˈledʒɪsleɪtʃəʳ] N Legislative *f*

legit [lɪˈdʒɪt] ADJ *(inf)* O.K. *(inf)*

legitimacy [lɪˈdʒɪtɪməsɪ] N Rechtmäßigkeit *f*, Legitimität *f*; *(of birth)* Ehelichkeit *f*; *(of conclusion)* Berechtigung *f*; **I don't doubt the ~ of your excuse/reason** ich bezweifle nicht, dass Ihre Entschuldigung/Ihr Grund gerechtfertigt ist

legitimate [lɪˈdʒɪtɪmət] ADJ **a** *(= lawful)* rechtmäßig, legitim; *rights, claim* legitim **b** *(= reasonable)* berechtigt; *excuse* begründet; *reason* zulässig; *target, purpose* legitim; **his use of the company car was not ~** er war nicht berechtigt, den Firmenwagen zu benutzen; **it's perfectly ~ to ask questions** es ist vollkommen in Ordnung, Fragen zu stellen; **it's ~ for them to behave like that** sie dürfen sich so benehmen **c** *(= born in wedlock)* ehelich **d** *(Theat)* **the ~ theatre** das traditionelle Sprechtheater

legitimately [lɪˈdʒɪtɪmətlɪ] ADV *(= lawfully)* legitim; *(= with reason)* berechtigterweise, mit Recht; **he argues, quite ~, that ...** er führt das berechtigte Argument an, dass ...; **it can ~ be expected of people that ...** man kann mit Recht von den Leuten erwarten, dass ...

legitimation [lɪˌdʒɪtɪˈmeɪʃən] N Legitimation *f*; *(= action)* Legitimierung *f*

legitimatize [lɪˈdʒɪtɪmətaɪz], **legitimize** [lɪˈdʒɪtɪmaɪz] VT legitimieren; *children* für ehelich erklären

leg: **legless** ADJ *(= without legs)* ohne Beine; *(Brit inf: = drunk)* sternhagelvoll *(inf)*; **legman** N *(US) kleiner Reporter, der Informationsquellen abklappert (who runs errands)* Laufbursche *m*, Bote *m*; **leg-of-mutton** ADJ *sleeve* keulenförmig; **leg press** N *(in fitness centre)* Beinpresse *f*; **leg-pull** N *(inf)* Scherz *m*, Bluff *m (inf)*; **what he said to us was only a ~** damit wollte er uns nur auf den Arm nehmen; **legroom** N Platz *m* für die Beine, Beinfreiheit *f*; **leg show** N *(inf)* Revue *f*; **leg warmers** PL Stulpen *pl*, Legwarmer *pl*

legume [ˈleɡjuːm] N *(= species)* Hülsenfrüchtler *m*; *(= fruit)* Hülsenfrucht *f*

leguminous [leˈɡjuːmɪnəs] ADJ Hülsenfrucht-, Leguminosen- *(spec)*; **~ plant** Hülsenfrüchtler *m*, Leguminose *f (spec)*

leg: **leg-up** N **to give sb a ~** jdm hochhelfen; **legwarmer** N Legwarmer *m*; **legwork** N Lauferei *f*

Leics *abbr of* **Leicestershire**

leisure [ˈleʒəʳ] N Freizeit *f*; **a gentleman of ~** ein Privatier *m (dated)*; **she decided to give up her job and become a lady of ~** sie entschloss sich, ihren Beruf aufzugeben und in Muße zu leben; **to lead a life of ~** ein Leben in *or* der Muße führen *(geh)*, sich dem (süßen) Nichtstun ergeben; **the problem of what to do with one's ~** das Problem der Freizeitgestaltung; **a park where the public can stroll at ~** ein Park, in dem die Öffentlichkeit in aller Ruhe spazieren gehen kann; **the Prime Minister is seldom at ~** der Premierminister hat selten Zeit für sich *or* hat selten freie Zeit; **do it at your ~** *(= in own time)* tun Sie es, wenn Sie Zeit *or* Ruhe dazu haben; *(= at own speed)* lassen Sie sich *(dat)* Zeit damit; **to have the ~ to do sth** die Zeit *or* Muße haben, etw zu tun

leisure: **leisure activities** PL Hobbys *pl*, Freizeitbeschäftigungen *pl*; **leisure centre** N *(Brit)* Freizeitzentrum *nt*; **leisure clothes** PL Freizeitkleidung *f*

leisured [ˈleʒəd] ADJ **a ~ life** ein Leben *nt* der Muße *(geh)*; **the ~ classes** die feinen Leute

leisure hours PL Freizeit *f*

leisurely [ˈleʒəlɪ] **ADJ** geruhsam; **to go at a ~ pace** *(person)* gemächlich gehen; *(vehicle)* in gemächlichem Tempo fahren; **the train's pace was so ~ that ...** der Zug fuhr so langsam, dass ...; **to have a ~ bath/breakfast** in aller Ruhe baden/frühstücken; **to adopt a more ~ approach** sich mehr Zeit lassen; **to do sth in a ~ way** etw ohne Hast und Eile machen **ADV** *walk, stroll* gemächlich

leisure: **leisure park** N Freizeitpark *m*; **leisure suit** N Jogginganzug *m*; **leisure time** N Freizeit *f*; **leisurewear** N Freizeitbekleidung *f*

leitmotif, leitmotiv [ˈlaɪtməʊˌtiːf] N *(Mus, fig)* Leitmotiv *nt*

lemma [ˈlemə] *pl* **-s** *or* **-ta** [ˈlemətə] N *(Ling)* Lemma *nt*

lemmatization [ˌlemətaɪˈzeɪʃən] N *(Ling)* Lemmatisierung *f*

lemming [ˈlemɪŋ] N Lemming *m*

lemon [ˈlemən] **N** **a** Zitrone *f*; *(= colour)* Zitronengelb *nt*; *(= tree)* Zitrone(nbaum *m*) *f* **b** *(inf: = fool)* Dussel *m (inf)* **c** *(inf: = poor-quality product)* schlechte Ware; **I bought a ~** sie haben mir was angedreht *(inf)* **ADJ** Zitronen-; **~ paint** zitronengelbe Farbe; **~ yellow** Zitronengelb *nt*

lemonade [ˌleməˈneɪd] N Limonade *f*; *(with lemon flavour)* Zitronenlimonade *f*

lemon: **lemon cheese**, **lemon curd** N *zähflüssiger Brotaufstrich mit Zitronengeschmack*; **lemon grass** N *(Bot, Cook)* Zitronengras *nt*; **lemon juice** N Zitronensaft *m*; **lemon law** N *(US) Schutzgesetz für Autokäufer*; **lemon meringue pie** N *mit Baisermasse gedeckter Mürbeteig mit einer Zitronencremefüllung*; **lemon sole** N Rotzunge *f*; **lemon squash** N Zitronensaft *m*; *(in bottle)* Zitronensirup *m*; **lemon squeezer** N Zitronenpresse *f*; **lemon tea** N Zitronentee *m*; **lemon zest** N (geriebene) Zitronenschale

lemony ['lemənɪ] ADJ Zitronen-; **~ flavour** *(Brit) or* **flavor** *(US)* Zitronengeschmack *m*

lemur ['li:məʳ] N Lemur *m*, Maki *m*

lend [lend] *pret, ptp* **lent** VT **a** *(= loan)* leihen *(to sb* jdm); *(banks) money* verleihen *(to* an *+acc)*
b *(fig: = give)* verleihen *(to +dat)*; *name* geben; **I am not going to ~ my name to this** dafür gebe ich meinen (guten) Namen nicht her; **to ~ (one's) support to sb/sth** jdn/etw unterstützen; **to ~ a hand** helfen, mit anfassen
VR **to ~ oneself to sth** sich für etw hergeben; *(= be suitable)* sich für etw eignen; **the programme** *(Brit) or* **program** *(US)* **doesn't really ~ itself to radio** die Sendung ist eigentlich für den Hörfunk ungeeignet; **these problems don't ~ themselves to quick solutions** für diese Probleme gibt es keine schnelle Lösung

▶ **lend out** VT *sep* verleihen; *books also* ausleihen

lender ['lendəʳ] N *(professional)* Geldverleiher(in) *m(f)*; **he paid the £100 back to the ~** er zahlte die £ 100 an den zurück, der sie ihm geliehen hatte

lending ['lendɪŋ] ADJ **~ bank** kreditierende Bank; **~ business** Kreditgeschäft *nt*; **~ country** Gläubigerland *nt*; **~ policy** *(of bank etc)* Kreditpolitik *f*

lending: **lending library** N Leihbücherei *f*; **lending rate** N (Darlehens)zinssatz *m*; **lending rights** PL Verleihrecht *nt*; *(for author)* Anspruch *m* auf Leihbücherei-Tantiemen

lend-lease ['lend'li:s] N **~ agreement** Leih-Pacht-Abkommen *nt*

length [leŋθ] N **a** Länge *f*; **a journey of considerable ~** eine ziemlich lange *or* weite Reise; **to be 4 feet in ~** 4 Fuß lang sein; **what ~ is it?** wie lang ist es?; **what ~ do you want it?** wie lang hätten Sie es gerne?; **of such ~** so lang; **the river, for most of its ~, meanders through meadows** der Fluss schlängelt sich in seinem Verlauf größtenteils durch Wiesen; **the pipe, for most of its ~, ...** fast das ganze Rohr ...; **along the whole ~ of the river/lane** den ganzen Fluss/Weg entlang; **it turns in its own ~** es kann sich um die eigene Achse drehen; **(through) the ~ and breadth of England** in ganz England; *travel* kreuz und quer durch ganz England; **the ~ of skirts** die Rocklänge; **at full ~** in voller Länge
b *(= section, of cloth, rope, pipe)* Stück *nt*; *(of wallpaper)* Bahn *f*; *(of road)* Abschnitt *m*; *(of pool)* Bahn *f*, Länge *f*
c *(of time)* Dauer *f*; *(= great length)* lange Dauer; **at such ~** so lange; **we didn't stay any (great) ~ of time** wir sind nicht lange geblieben; **the ~ of time needed** die Zeit, die man dazu braucht; **in that ~ of time I could have ...** in dieser Zeit hätte ich ...; **for any ~ of time** für längere Zeit; **for what ~ of time?** für wie lange?; **~ of life** *(of people)* Lebenserwartung *f*; *(of animals)* Lebensalter *nt*; *(of machine)* Lebensdauer *f*; **~ of service with a company** Betriebszugehörigkeit *f*; **~ of service with the army** Dienstjahre *pl* bei der Armee; **at ~** *(= finally)* schließlich; *(= for a long time)* lange, ausführlich, lang und breit *(pej)*
d *(Phon, Poet, Sport)* Länge *f*; **to win by half a ~** mit einer halben Länge siegen
e to go to any ~s to do sth vor nichts zurückschrecken, um etw zu tun; **to go to great ~s to do sth** sich *(dat)* sehr viel Mühe geben *or* alles Mögliche versuchen, um etw zu tun; **to go to the ~ of ...** so weit gehen, dass ...

lengthen ['leŋθən] VT verlängern; *clothes, queues* länger machen; **to ~ one's stride** größere Schritte machen VI länger werden

lengthily ['leŋθɪlɪ] ADV ausführlich, langatmig *(pej)*

length mark N *(Phon, Poet)* Längenzeichen *nt*

lengthways ['leŋθweɪz], **lengthwise** ['leŋθwaɪz] ADJ Längen-, Längs-; **~ measurement** Längenmessung *f*; **~ cut** Längsschnitt *m* ADV der Länge nach

lengthy ['leŋθɪ] ADJ *(+er)* sehr lang; *(= dragging on)* langwierig; *speech* ausführlich, langatmig *(pej)*; *meeting, war* lang andauernd; *(= extensive) article, report, statement* sehr umfangreich; *interview, explanation* sehr ausführlich; **a ~ prison sentence** eine lange *or* hohe Gefängnisstrafe; **to have a ~ wait for sth** sehr lange auf etw *(acc)* warten müssen

lenience ['li:nɪəns], **leniency** ['li:nɪənsɪ] N Nachsicht *f* *(towards* gegenüber); *(of judge, attitude, treatment, sentence)* Milde *f*

lenient ['li:nɪənt] ADJ nachsichtig *(towards* gegenüber); *judge, attitude, treatment, sentence* milde; **to be ~ with sb** mit jdm milde umgehen; **to be ~ in one's assessment** milde urteilen

leniently ['li:nɪəntlɪ] ADV nachsichtig; *judge* milde

Leninism ['lenɪnɪzəm] N Leninismus *m*

Leninist ['lenɪnɪst] ADJ leninistisch N Leninist(in) *m(f)*

lenity ['lenɪtɪ] N Nachsicht *f*, Milde *f*

lens [lenz] N *(Anat, Opt, Phot)* Linse *f*; *(in spectacles)* Glas *nt*; *(= camera part containing lens)* Objektiv *nt*; *(= eyeglass)* Klemmlupe *f*; *(for stamps etc)* Vergrößerungsglas *nt*, Lupe *f*

lens: **lens cap** N Schutzkappe *f*; **lens hood** N Sonnenblende *f*, Gegenlichtblende *f*

Lent [lent] N Fastenzeit *f*

lent [lent] *pret, ptp of* **lend**

Lenten ['lentən] ADJ Fasten-; **~ season** Fastenzeit *f*; **~ fast** Fasten *nt* (zur Fastenzeit)

lentil ['lentl] N Linse *f*; **~ soup** Linsensuppe *f*

Leo ['li:əʊ] N *(Astrol)* Löwe *m*; **he's (a) ~** er ist Löwe

leonine ['li:ənaɪn] ADJ Löwen-, löwenartig; **~ courage** *(liter)* Löwenmut *m*; **the ~ bust of Karl Marx** die Büste von Karl Marx mit seiner Löwenmähne

leopard ['lepəd] N Leopard *m*; **a ~ never changes its spots** *(Prov)* die Katze lässt das Mausen nicht *(Prov)*

leotard ['li:ətɑ:d] N Trikot *nt*; *(Gymnastics)* Gymnastikanzug *m*

leper ['lepəʳ] N Leprakranke(r) *mf*, Lepröse(r) *mf (spec)*, Aussätzige(r) *mf (old, fig)*

leper colony N Leprasiedlung *f*, Lepradorf *nt*

lepidoptera [ˌlepɪ'dɒptərə] PL Falter *pl*, Lepidopteren *pl (spec)*

leprechaun ['leprəkɔ:n] N Gnom *m*, Kobold *m*

leprosy ['leprəsɪ] N Lepra *f*, Aussatz *m (old)*

leprous ['leprəs] ADJ leprös, aussätzig *(old)*

lesbian ['lezbɪən] ADJ lesbisch; **~ and gay rights/issues** Rechte *pl*/Probleme *pl* der Lesben und Schwulen; **the ~ and gay community** die Lesben und Schwulen; **~ and gay people** Lesben und Schwule *pl*; **the ~ and gay movement** die Lesben- und Schwulenbewegung N Lesbierin *f*, Lesbe *f (inf)*

lesbianism ['lezbɪənɪzəm] N *(in general)* lesbische Liebe; *(of one person)* Lesbiertum *nt*

lesbo ['lezbəʊ] N *pl* **-bos** *(inf pej)* Lesbe *f (inf)*

lèse-majesté, **lese majesty** ['leɪz'mæʒəsteɪ] N *(= high treason)* Hochverrat *m*; *(= insult to dignity)* (Majestäts)beleidigung *f*

lesion ['li:ʒən] N Verletzung *f*; *(= structural change)* krankhafte Gewebsveränderung; **~s in the brain** Gehirnverletzungen *pl*

Lesotho [lɪ'səʊtəʊ] N Lesotho *nt*

less [les] ✪ 5.1, 5.3, 7.5, 26.3 ADJ, ADV, N weniger; **of ~ importance** von geringerer Bedeutung, weniger bedeutend; **~ noise, please!** nicht so laut, bitte!; **no ~ a person than the bishop** kein Geringerer als der Bischof; **he did it in ~ time** er hat es in kürzerer Zeit *or* schneller getan; **to grow ~** weniger werden; *(= grow at slow rate)* langsamer wachsen; *(= decrease)* abnehmen; **his problem is ~ one of money than of enthusiasm** sein Problem ist weniger das Geld als vielmehr mangelnde Begeisterung; **~ and ~** immer weniger; **she saw him ~ and ~ (often)** sie sah ihn immer seltener; **a sum ~ than £1** eine Summe unter £ 1; **it's nothing ~ than disgraceful/than a disaster** es ist wirklich eine Schande/ein Unglück *nt*; **this is nothing ~ than blackmail** das ist ja direkt Erpressung; **it was little ~ than blackmail** das war schon fast Erpressung, das war so gut wie Erpressung; **he was ~ frightened than angry** er war nicht so sehr ängstlich, sondern eher ärgerlich; **~ beautiful** nicht so schön; **~ quickly** nicht so schnell; **he works ~ than I (do)** er arbeitet weniger als ich; **still** *or* **even ~** noch weniger; **none the ~** trotzdem, nichtsdestoweniger; **I didn't find the film any the ~ interesting** ich fand den Film nicht weniger interessant; **I don't love her any the ~** ich liebe sie nicht weniger; **their apology did not make him any the ~ angry** ihre Entschuldigung konnte seinen Ärger nicht besänftigen; **can't you let me have it for ~?** können Sie es mir nicht etwas billiger lassen?; **I hope you won't think (any the) ~ of me** ich hoffe, du denkst nicht schlecht von mir; **~ of that!** komm mir nicht so!; **x is ~ than/not ~ than 10** *(Math)* x ist kleiner/kleiner (oder) gleich 10
PREP weniger; *(Comm)* abzüglich; **a year ~ 4 days** ein Jahr weniger 4 Tage; **6 ~ 4 is 2** 6 weniger *or* minus 4 ist 2

-less [-lɪs] ADJ *suf* -los; **hopeless** hoffnungslos; **heartless** herzlos; **hatless** ohne Hut; **sunless** ohne Sonne

lessee [le'si:] N Pächter(in) *m(f)*; *(of house, flat)* Mieter(in) *m(f)*; *(of equipment)* Leasingnehmer(in) *m(f)*

lessen ['lesn] VT **a** *(= make less)* verringern; *cost* senken, vermindern; *effect, impact* vermindern, abschwächen; *pain* lindern **b** *(= make seem less important etc)* herabsetzen, herabwürdigen VI nachlassen; *(danger, wind, enthusiasm, difficulty also)* abnehmen; *(value of money)* sich verringern, abnehmen

lessening ['lesnɪŋ] N Nachlassen *nt* *(in sth +gen)*; **~ of value** Wertabnahme *f*; **a ~ in the rate of inflation** ein Rückgang *m or* eine Verringerung der Inflationsrate

lesser ['lesəʳ] ADJ geringer; *(in names)* klein; **to a ~ extent** in geringerem Maße; **a ~ amount** ein kleinerer Betrag; **the ~ weight** das leichtere Gewicht; **~ offence** *(Brit) or* **offense** *(US) (Jur)* Vergehen *nt*, Übertretung *f*; **which is the ~ crime?** welches Verbrechen ist weniger schlimm?; **he is a ~ man than his brother** *(= less good)* er ist kein so guter Mensch wie sein Bruder; *(= less great)* er ist weniger bedeutend als sein Bruder

lesson ['lesn] N **a** *(Sch etc)* Stunde *f*; *(= unit of study)* Lektion *f*; **~s** Unterricht *m*; *(= homework)* (Haus)aufgaben *pl*; **his ~s are boring** sein Unterricht ist *or* seine Stunden sind langweilig; **~s begin at 9** der Unterricht *or* die Schule beginnt um 9; **he's not very good at his ~s** er ist kein besonders guter Schüler; **a French ~** eine Französischstunde; **a driving ~** eine Fahrstunde; **to give** *or* **teach a ~** eine Stunde geben, unterrichten; **we're having a French ~ now** wir haben jetzt Französisch
b *(fig)* Lehre *f*; **to be a ~ to sb** jdm eine Lehre sein; **he has learned his ~** er hat seine Lektion gelernt; **to teach sb a ~** jdm eine Lektion erteilen; **what ~ can we learn from this story?** was können wir von dieser Geschichte lernen?; **it was an important ~ of life for me** das war mir eine wichtige Lehre im Leben
c *(Eccl)* Lesung *f*; **to read the ~** die Lesung halten

lessor [le'sɔː'] N *(form)* Verpächter(in) *m(f)*; *(of flat etc)* Vermieter(in) *m(f)*; *(of equipment)* Leasinggeber(in) *m(f)*

lest [lest] CONJ *(form)* **a** *(= for fear that)* aus Furcht, dass; *(= in order that … not)* damit … nicht; *(= in case)* für den Fall, dass; **I didn't do it ~ somebody should object** ich habe es aus Furcht, dass jemand dagegen sein könnte, nicht getan; **~ we forget** damit wir nicht vergessen **b** *(after fear, be afraid etc)* dass; **I was frightened ~ he should fall** ich hatte Angst, dass er fallen könnte

let[1] [let] N **a** *(Tennis)* Netz(ball *m*) *nt* **b** **without ~ or hindrance** *(Jur)* ungehindert

let[2] N **they are looking for a ~ in this area** sie wollen eine Wohnung/ein Haus in dieser Gegend mieten; **I have this house on a long ~** ich habe dieses Haus für längere Zeit gemietet

let[3] ✪ 9.3, 26.1 *pret, ptp* **let** VT **a** *(= permit)* lassen; **to ~ sb do sth** jdn etw tun lassen; **she ~ me borrow the car** sie lieh mir das Auto, ich durfte ihr Auto nehmen; **we can't ~ that happen** wir dürfen das nicht zulassen; **he wants to but I won't ~ him** er möchte gern, aber ich lasse ihn nicht *or* erlaube es ihm nicht; **the particle wants to escape but the magnetic force won't ~ it** das Teilchen möchte sich frei machen, aber die magnetische Kraft verhindert es; **oh please ~ me** bitte, bitte, lass mich doch (mal)!; **~ me help you** darf ich Ihnen helfen *or* behilflich sein?; **~ me know what you think** sagen Sie mir (Bescheid) *or* lassen Sie mich wissen *(form)*, was Sie davon halten; **to ~ oneself be seen** sich sehen lassen; **to ~ sb be** jdn (in Ruhe) lassen; **to ~ sb/sth go, to ~ go of sb/sth** jdn/etw loslassen; **to ~ sb go** *(= depart)* jdn gehen lassen; **~ me go!** lassen Sie mich los!, loslassen!; **I'm afraid we'll have to ~ you go** *(euph: = dismiss)* wir müssen uns leider von Ihnen trennen; **to ~ oneself go** *(= neglect oneself)* sich gehen lassen; *(= relax)* aus sich herausgehen; **to ~ sth go** *(= neglect)* etw vernachlässigen; **to ~ it go at that** es dabei bewenden lassen; **to ~ sb pass** jdn vorbeilassen; **we'll ~ it pass** *or* **go this once** *(= disregard, error)* wir wollen es mal durchgehen lassen → **drop, fly**[2], **slip**
b *(old: causative)* lassen; **~ the bells be rung** lasset die Glocken ertönen *(liter)*; **~ it be known by all citizens that …** allen Bürgern sei kundgetan, dass … *(old)*; **~ it be known that …** alle sollen wissen, dass …
c **to ~ sb/sth alone** jdn/etw in Ruhe lassen; **we can't improve it any more, we'd better ~ it alone** wir können es nicht mehr verbessern, also lassen wir es lieber so; **please ~ me by/past** bitte, lassen Sie mich vorbei/durch; **to ~ sb/sth through** jdn/etw durchlassen
d **~ alone** *(= much less)* geschweige denn
e **~'s go home** komm, wir gehen nach Hause; **~'s go!** gehen wir!; **~'s get out of here** bloß weg von hier!; **yes, ~'s** oh ja!; **it's late, but yes ~'s** es ist spät, aber na ja, einverstanden; **~'s not** lieber nicht; **don't ~'s** *or* **~'s not fight** wir wollen uns doch nicht streiten; **~'s be happy** lass uns glücklich sein; **~'s be friends** wir wollen Freunde sein; **~'s all be a bit more friendly** seien wir doch alle ein bisschen freundlicher; **~'s look at this in more detail** wir wollen das einmal genauer betrachten; **~ him try (it)!** das soll er nur *or* mal versuchen!; **~ me think** *or* **see, where did I put it?** warte mal *or* Moment mal, wo habe ich das nur hingetan?; **~ their need be never so great** mag ihre Not auch noch so groß sein; **~ there be music** lasst Musik erklingen; **~ there be peace** es soll Friede sein; **~ there be light** es werde Licht; **~ us pray** lasst uns beten; **~ us suppose …** nehmen wir (mal) an, dass … → **equal VI**
f *(esp Brit: = hire out)* vermieten; **"to ~"** „zu vermieten"; **we can't find a house to ~** wir können kein Haus finden, das zu mieten ist
g **to ~ blood** einen Aderlass machen; **they ~ so much of his blood** sie nahmen ihm so viel Blut ab

▸ **let away** VT *sep* **to let sb (get) away with sth** jdm etw durchgehen lassen; **I'll let you (get) away with it just this once** diesmal drücke ich noch ein Auge zu *(inf)*

▸ **let down** VT *sep* **a** *(= lower) rope, person* herunterlassen; *seat* herunterklappen; *hair, window* herunterlassen; **I tried to let him down gently** *(fig)* ich versuchte, ihm das schonend beizubringen; **to let one's guard down** *(lit)* seine Deckung vernachlässigen; *(fig)* sich aus der Reserve locken lassen
b *(= lengthen) dress* länger machen; *hem* auslassen
c *(= deflate)* **to let a tyre** *(Brit)* *or* **tire** *(US)* **down** die Luft aus einem Reifen lassen
d *(= fail to help)* **to let sb down** jdn im Stich lassen *(over* mit); **the weather let us down** das Wetter machte uns einen Strich durch die Rechnung; **to let the side down** die anderen im Stich lassen
e *(= disappoint)* enttäuschen; **to feel let down** enttäuscht sein
f **to let the school/oneself down** die Schule/sich blamieren *or* in Verruf bringen; **you'd be letting yourself down if you only got 5 out of 10** es wäre unter deinem Niveau, nur 5 von 10 Punkten zu bekommen

▸ **let in** VT *sep* **a** *water* durchlassen
b *(= admit) air, cat, visitor* hereinlassen; *(to club etc)* zulassen *(to* zu); **he let himself in (with his key)** er schloss die Tür auf und ging hinein; **he let her/himself into the apartment** er ließ sie/er ging in die Wohnung hinein; **just let yourself in** geh einfach hinein; **I was just letting myself in** ich schloss gerade die Tür auf
c *(= involve in)* **to let sb in for a lot of work** jdm eine Menge Arbeit aufhalsen; **see what you've let me in for now** da hast du mir aber was eingebrockt! *(inf)*; **to let oneself in for sth** sich auf etw *(acc)* einlassen; **I got let in for £50** ich bin £ 50 losgeworden *(inf)*
d *(= allow to know)* **to let sb in on sth, to let sb into sth** jdn in etw *(acc)* einweihen; **she let me in on the secret** sie hat es mir verraten
e *(Sew)* **to let in a panel** eine Bahn einsetzen
VI *(shoes, tent)* Wasser durchlassen, undicht sein

▸ **let off** VT *sep* **a** *(= fire) arrow* abschießen; *gun, shot* abfeuern
b *(= explode) firework, bomb* hochgehen lassen
c *(= emit) vapour* von sich geben; *gases* absondern; *smell* verbreiten; **to let off steam** *(lit)* Dampf ablassen; *(fig also)* sich abreagieren; **to let one off** *(Brit inf: = break wind)* einen (fahren) lassen *(inf)*
VT *always separate* **a** *(= forgive)* **to let sb off** jdm etw durchgehen lassen; **I'll let you off this time** diesmal drücke ich noch ein Auge zu; **OK, I'll let you off, you're quite right** ich will dir mal ausnahmsweise recht geben; **to let sb off sth** jdm etw erlassen; **to let sb off with a warning/fine** jdn mit einer Verwarnung/Geldstrafe davonkommen lassen; **to let sb off lightly** mit jdm glimpflich verfahren; **to be let off lightly** glimpflich davonkommen; **he's been let off** man hat ihn laufen lassen
b *(= allow to go)* gehen lassen; **we were let off early** wir durften früher gehen; **I let the dog off (the leash)** ich machte den Hund (von der Leine) los
c *(from car etc)* herauslassen *(inf)*, aussteigen lassen
VI *(inf: = fart)* einen fahren lassen *(inf)*

▸ **let on** VI **a** *(inf: = tell, give away)* verraten; **don't let on you know** lass dir bloß nicht anmerken, dass du das weißt; **he let on that he had known all the time** er kam damit heraus *(inf)*, dass er es schon die ganze Zeit gewusst hatte; **don't let on about our meeting with John** verrate nichts von unserem Treffen mit John
b *(= pretend)* **to let on that …** vorgeben, dass …

▸ **let out** VT *sep* **a** *(= allow to go out) cat, smell, air* herauslassen; *(from car)* absetzen; **to let oneself out** sich *(dat)* die Tür aufmachen; **I'll let myself out** ich finde alleine hinaus
b *prisoner* entlassen, rauslassen *(inf)*; *(= divulge) news* bekannt geben, bekannt machen; *secret* verraten, ausplaudern *(inf)*; *feelings* freien Lauf lassen *(+dat)*
c *(= emit)* **to let out a long sigh** tief seufzen; **to let out a scream** einen Schrei ausstoßen; **to let out a groan** (auf)stöhnen; **to let one's breath out** ausatmen
d *(= make larger) dress* weiter machen, auslassen; *seam* auslassen
e *fire* ausgehen lassen
f *(= free from responsibility)* **that lets me out (of it)** da komme ich (schon mal) nicht infrage
g *(esp Brit: = rent)* vermieten

▸ **let up** VI **a** *(= cease)* aufhören; **he never lets up about his money** er redet unaufhörlich *or* pausenlos von seinem Geld **b** *(= ease up)* nachlassen **c** **to let up on sb** jdn in Ruhe lassen; **the trainer didn't let up on them until they were perfect** der Trainer hat so lange nicht locker gelassen, bis sie perfekt waren

-let [-lɪt] SUF -lein, -chen; **booklet** Büchlein *nt*; **starlet** Sternchen *nt*

letdown ['letdaʊn] N *(inf: = disappointment)* Enttäuschung *f*

lethal ['liːθəl] ADJ **a** *(= fatal)* tödlich; **a ~-looking knife** ein nach einer tödlichen Waffe aussehendes Messer; **to be ~ to rats/fish** Ratten/Fische töten; **to die/be executed by ~ injection** durch die Todesspritze sterben/hingerichtet werden; **a ~ cocktail of drugs** ein tödlicher Drogencocktail **b** *(fig) (= dangerous) opponent* äußerst gefährlich; *(inf: = strong) drink* tödlich stark *(inf)*; *curry* höllisch scharf *(inf)*; **~ striker** *(Ftbl)* todsicherer Torschütze; **this coffee is pretty ~** *(inf)* dieser Kaffee hats in sich *(inf)*, in diesem Kaffee steht der Löffel *(inf)*

lethargic [lɪ'θɑːdʒɪk] ADJ **a** *appearance, person, atmosphere* träge, lethargisch; *animal* träge; *pace of music* schleppend; *(= uninterested)* lethargisch, teilnahmslos, lustlos; **a ~-looking child** ein teilnahmslos aussehendes Kind; **to feel ~** sich träge fühlen **b** *(Med)* schlafsüchtig, lethargisch **c** *(Comm, St Ex) sales, trading* stagnierend; *market* lustlos

lethargically [lɪ'θɑːdʒɪkəlɪ] ADV träge; *(= without interest)* teilnahmslos, lustlos

lethargy ['leθədʒɪ] N **a** Lethargie *f*, Trägheit *f* **b** *(Med)* Schlafsucht *f*, Lethargie *f*

Letraset® ['letrəˌset] N Letraset® *nt*

let's [lets] *contr of* **let us**

Lett [let] ADJ, N = **Latvian**

letter ['letə'] ✪ 21.1 N **a** *(of alphabet)* Buchstabe *m*; **the ~ of the law** der Buchstabe des Gesetzes; **to the ~** buchstabengetreu, genau; **did he do it? – to the ~** hat er es getan? – ganz nach Vorschrift
b *(= written message)* Brief *m*; *(Comm etc)* Schreiben *nt (form)* *(to* an *+acc)*; **by ~** schriftlich, brieflich; **to write a ~ of complaint/apology** sich schriftlich beschweren/entschuldigen
c *(Liter)* **~s** Literatur *f*; **man of ~s** Belletrist *m*; *(= writer)* Literat *m*
d *(US, = award) als Auszeichnung verliehenes Schulabzeichen*
VT *sign, label* beschriften; **he ~ed the invitations in gold** er ließ die Einladungen in Gold (-buchstaben) drucken

letter: **letter bomb** N Briefbombe *f*; **letter box** N *(Brit)* Briefkasten *m*; **letter card** N Briefkarte *f*; **letter carrier** N *(US)* Briefträger(in) *m(f)*, Postbote *m*/-botin *f*; **letter drop** N Briefeinwurf *m*

lettered ['letəd] ADJ **a** *(rare) person* gelehrt **b** *object* beschriftet; **~ in gold** in Goldschrift

letterhead ['letəhed] N Briefkopf *m*; *(= writing paper)* Geschäfts(brief)papier *nt*

lettering ['letərɪŋ] N Beschriftung *f*

letter: **letter jacket** N *(US: Univ) Jacke, auf die die Initialen des besuchten Colleges gestickt sind*; **letter of credit** N Kreditbrief *m*, Akkreditiv *nt*; **letter opener** N Brieföffner *m*; **letter-perfect** ADJ textsicher, sicher im Text; **to be ~** den Text perfekt beherrschen, den Text bis aufs Wort beherrschen; **letterpress** N Hochdruck *m*; **letter quality** N *(of* *printout)* Korrespondenz- *or* Briefqualität *f*, Schönschrift *f*; **letter-quality** ADJ *script* korrespondenzfähig; *printout* in Korrespondenz- *or* Briefqualität; **~ printer** Schönschriftdrucker *m*; **letter rack** N Briefablage *f*

letters page ['letəz'peɪdʒ] N *(Press)* Leserbriefseite *f*

letters patent ['letəz'peɪtənt] PL Patent(urkunde *f*) *nt*

letting ['letɪŋ] N *(esp Brit)* Vermieten *nt*; **he's in the ~ business** er ist in der Wohnungsbranche

Lettish ['letɪʃ] ADJ, N = **Latvian**

lettuce ['letɪs] N Kopfsalat *m*; *(genus)* Lattich *m*

let-up ['letʌp] N *(inf)* Pause *f*; *(= easing up)* Nachlassen *nt*; **if there is a ~ in the rain** wenn der Regen aufhört/nachlässt

leucocyte, **leukocyte** ['lu:kəʊsaɪt] N *(form)* Leukozyt *m*

leukaemia, *(US)* **leukemia** [lu:'ki:mɪə] N Leukämie *f*

Levant [lɪ'vænt] N Levante *f*

Levantine ['levəntaɪn] **ADJ** levantinisch **N** *(= person)* Levantiner(in) *m(f)*

levee¹ ['leveɪ] N *(Hist) (on awakening)* Lever *nt*; *(at British court)* Nachmittagsempfang *m*

levee² ['levɪ] N Damm *m*, Deich *m*

level ['levl] **ADJ** **a** *(= flat) ground, surface, floor* eben; *spoonful* gestrichen; **try to keep the boat ~** versuchen Sie, das Boot waagerecht zu halten; **the glider maintained a ~ course** das Segelflugzeug behielt die gleiche Flughöhe bei

b *(= at the same height)* auf gleicher Höhe *(with* mit); *(= parallel)* parallel *(with* zu); **the bedroom is ~ with the ground** das Schlafzimmer liegt ebenerdig *or* zu ebener Erde

c *(= equal)* gleichauf; *(fig)* gleich gut; **the two runners are absolutely** *or* **dead ~** die beiden Läufer liegen *or* sind genau auf gleicher Höhe; **Jones was almost ~ with the winner** Jones kam fast auf gleiche Höhe mit dem Sieger; **the two teams are ~ in the league** die beiden Mannschaften haben den gleichen Tabellenstand; **~ race** Kopf-an-Kopf-Rennen *nt*

d *(= steady) tone of voice* ruhig; *(= well-balanced)* ausgeglichen; *judgement* abgewogen, ausgewogen; *head* kühl; **to have/keep a ~ head** einen kühlen Kopf haben/bewahren

e **I'll do my ~ best** *(Brit)* ich werde mein Möglichstes tun

ADV **~ with** in Höhe *(+gen)*; **it should lie ~ with ...** es sollte gleich hoch sein wie ...; **the pipe runs ~ with the ground** das Rohr verläuft zu ebener Erde; *(= parallel)* das Rohr verläuft parallel zum Boden; **they're running absolutely ~** sie laufen auf genau gleicher Höhe; **the value of the shares stayed ~ for some time** der Wert der Aktien blieb für einige Zeit gleich; **to draw ~ with sb** jdn einholen, mit jdm gleichziehen; *(in league etc)* punktgleich mit jdm sein; **the two runners drew ~ on the last lap** in der letzten Runde zogen die beiden Läufer gleich

N **a** *(= instrument)* Wasserwaage *f*

b *(= altitude)* Höhe *f*; **on a ~ (with)** auf gleicher Höhe (mit); **water always finds its own ~** Wasser kehrt immer in die Waagerechte zurück; **at eye ~** in Augenhöhe; **the trees were very tall, almost at roof ~** die Bäume waren sehr hoch, sie reichten fast bis zum Dach; **to be on a ~ with the roof** in Dachhöhe sein

c *(= flat place)* ebene Fläche, ebenes Stück

d *(= storey)* Etage *f*, Stockwerk *nt*; **the house is on four ~s** das Haus hat vier Etagen

e *(= position on scale)* Ebene *f*; *(social, intellectual etc)* Niveau *nt*; **they're on a different ~** sie haben ein unterschiedliches Niveau; **to descend** *or* **come down to that ~** auf ein so tiefes Niveau absinken; **he expects everyone to come down to his ~** er erwartet von jedem, dass er sich auf sein Niveau herabbegibt; **she tried to go beyond her natural ~ of ability** sie versuchte, ihre natürlichen Grenzen zu überschreiten; **to be on a ~ with** auf gleichem Niveau sein wie; **they are on a ~ as far as salaries are concerned** sie bekommen das gleiche Gehalt; **he tried to raise the ~ of the conversation** er versuchte, der Unterhaltung etwas mehr Niveau zu geben; **if profit stays at the same ~** wenn sich der Gewinn auf dem gleichen Stand hält; **the pound has been left to find its own ~** der Pfundkurs wurde freigegeben, um seinen natürlichen Stand zu erreichen; **the rising ~ of inflation** die steigende Inflationsrate; **he maintains his high ~ of excellence** er hält sein äußerst hohes Niveau; **a high ~ of intelligence** ein hoher Intelligenzgrad; **a high ~ of interest** sehr großes Interesse; **a high ~ of support** sehr viel Unterstützung; **a high ~ of civilization** eine hohe Kulturstufe; **the very high ~ of production** das hohe Produktionsniveau; **the higher ~s of academic research** die höheren Stufen der wissenschaftlichen Forschung; **the talks were held at a very high ~** die Gespräche fanden auf hoher Ebene statt; **a low ~ of sales** ein sehr geringer Absatz; **he reduces everything to the commercial ~** er reduziert alles auf eine rein kommerzielle Basis; **on an intellectual ~** auf intellektueller Ebene; **on the moral ~** aus moralischer Sicht; **on a purely personal ~** rein persönlich, auf rein persönlicher Ebene

f *(= amount, degree)* **a high ~ of hydrogen** ein hoher Wasserstoffanteil; **the ~ of alcohol in the blood** der Alkoholspiegel im Blut; **~ of consciousness** Bewusstseinsebene *f*; **cholesterol ~** Cholesterinspiegel *m*; **the ~ of violence** das Ausmaß der Gewalttätigkeit

g **it's on the ~** *(inf: = straightforward, honest) (business)* es ist reell; *(proposition)* es ist ehrlich gemeint; **I guess you're on the ~** du bist wohl schon in Ordnung *(inf)*; **is he on the ~?** meint er es ehrlich?; **to be on the ~ with sb** jdm gegenüber ehrlich *or* aufrichtig sein

VT **a** *ground, site etc* einebnen, planieren; *building* abreißen; *town* dem Erdboden gleichmachen; **to ~ sth to the ground** etw dem Erdboden gleichmachen

b *blow* versetzen, verpassen *(inf) (at sb* jdm); *weapon* richten *(at* auf *+acc)*; *accusation* erheben *(at* gegen); *remark* richten *(at* gegen); *criticism* üben *(at* an *+dat)*; **to ~ a charge against sb** Anklage gegen jdn erheben, jdn anklagen

c *(Sport)* **to ~ the match** den Ausgleich erzielen; **to ~ the score** gleichziehen

VI *(inf)* **to ~ with sb** jdm keinen Quatsch *or* Scheiß erzählen *(inf)*; **I'll ~ with you** ich werd ehrlich mit dir sein

▶ **level down** VT *sep (lit)* einebnen; *(fig)* auf ein tieferes Niveau bringen *or* herabsetzen; *salaries* nach unten angleichen

▶ **level out** **VI** *(also* **level off***)* **a** *(ground)* eben *or* flach werden; *(fig)* sich ausgleichen, sich einpendeln; *(output, growth)* sich stabilisieren **b** *(Aviat, pilot)* das Flugzeug abfangen; *(plane)* sich fangen; *(after rising)* horizontal fliegen **VT** *sep site* planieren, einebnen; *(fig) differences* ausgleichen

▶ **level up** VT *sep (lit)* ausgleichen; *salaries* angleichen; *(fig)* auf ein höheres Niveau bringen; **you sit on the other side of the boat and that'll level it up** du setzt dich auf die andere Seite des Bootes, dann ist das Gleichgewicht (wieder) hergestellt

level: **level crossing** N *(Brit)* (beschrankter) Bahnübergang; **level-headed** ADJ *person* ausgeglichen; *attitude* ausgewogen; *reply, decision* ausgewogen, überlegt

leveller, *(US)* **leveler** ['levlə'] N Gleichmacher *m*; **death is a great ~** der Tod macht alle (Menschen) gleich

levelly ['levəlɪ] ADV *(= calmly)* ruhig; *gaze* gerade

level pegging ['levl'pegɪŋ] ADJ *(Brit)* punktgleich; **with 30 votes each they are ~** mit jeweils 30 Stimmen liegen sie auf gleicher Höhe; **it's ~ as they go round the final bend** sie liegen in der letzten Kurve auf gleicher Höhe

lever ['li:və', *(US)* 'levə'] **N** Hebel *m*; *(= crowbar)* Brechstange *f*; *(fig)* Druckmittel *nt*; **that should give us a ~** *(fig)* das können wir als Druckmittel benutzen **VT** (hoch)stemmen, mit einem Hebel/einer Brechstange (an)heben; **he ~ed the machine-part into place** er hob das Maschinenteil durch Hebelwirkung an seinen Platz; **he ~ed the box open** er stemmte die Kiste auf; **he ~ed himself onto the ledge** er hievte sich auf den Felsvorsprung (hoch); **he seems to have ~ed himself into a position of power** er scheint sich in eine Machtposition manövriert zu haben

▶ **lever out** VT *sep* herausstemmen *or* -brechen; **we'll never lever him out of such a comfortable job** aus diesem bequemen Job werden wir ihn nie herausholen *or* -lotsen können *(inf)*; **he levered himself out of the armchair** er hievte sich aus dem Sessel (hoch)

▶ **lever up** VT *sep* mit einem Hebel/einer Brechstange hochheben, aufstemmen

leverage ['li:vərɪdʒ, *(US)* 'levərɪdʒ] N Hebelkraft *f*; *(fig)* Einfluss *m*; **this spanner can exert considerable ~** dieser Schraubenschlüssel kann eine beträchtliche Hebelwirkung ausüben; **to use sth as ~** *(fig)* etw als Druckmittel benutzen; *(= to one's own advantage)* etw zu seinem Vorteil ausnützen; **this gave us a bit of ~ with the authorities** dadurch konnten wir etwas Druck auf die Behörden ausüben; **his approval gives us a bit of ~ with them** seine Zustimmung verstärkt unsere Position ihnen gegenüber

leveraged ['li:vərɪdʒd] ADJ *(Fin)* fremdfinanziert

leveraged buyout [*(US)* ˌlevərɪdʒd'baɪaʊt] N *(Comm) Aufkauf einer Kapitalgesellschaft durch das eigene Management mithilfe externer Finanzierung*

lever-arch file ['li:vərɑ:tʃ'faɪl] N Leitz-Ordner® *m*

leveret ['levərɪt] N junger Hase, Häschen *nt*

leviathan [lɪ'vaɪəθən] N Leviathan *m*, Meerungeheuer *nt*; *(fig)* Gigant *m*; *(= state)* Leviathan *m*

Levis, **levis**® ['li:vaɪz] PL Levis® *f*, ≈ Jeans *pl*

levitate ['levɪteɪt] **VT** schweben lassen **VI** schweben

levitation [ˌlevɪ'teɪʃən] N Levitation *f*, freies Schweben

Levite ['li:vaɪt] N Levit(e) *m*

levity ['levɪtɪ] N Leichtfertigkeit *f*

levy ['levɪ] **N** *(= act)* (Steuer)einziehung *f or* -eintreibung *f*; *(= tax)* Steuer *f*, Abgaben *pl*; *(Mil)* Aushebung *f*; *(of supplies)* Einziehung *f*, Beschlagnahme *f*; **there were 100 men in the first ~** 100 Männer wurden bei der ersten Aushebung eingezogen; **political ~** *(Brit Pol) zur Unterstützung der Labour Party verwendeter Teil des Gewerkschaftsbeitrags*

VT **a** *(= raise) tax* einziehen, erheben; *charge* erheben; *fine* auferlegen *(on sb* jdm); *sanctions* verhängen; *(Mil) army, troops* ausheben; *supplies* einziehen, beschlagnahmen; **to ~ a tax on beer** Bier mit einer Steuer belegen, Steuern *pl* auf Bier erheben

b *(= wage) war* führen *(against, on* gegen)

lewd [lu:d] ADJ *(+er)* unanständig; *(= lustful)* lüstern; *remark* anzüglich; *joke, song* unanständig, anstößig, anzüglich; *imagination* schmutzig; **don't be ~** werd nicht anzüglich

lewdly ['lu:dlɪ] ADV anzüglich; **he spoke ~ about his amorous adventures** er erzählte lüstern *or* in anzüglicher Weise von seinen amourösen Abenteuern

lewdness ['lu:dnɪs] N *(= being indecent)* Anstößigkeit *f*, Unanständigkeit *f*; *(= being lustful)* Lüsternheit *f*; *(of remark)* Anzüglichkeit *f*; *(of imagination)* Schmutzigkeit *f*

lexical ['leksɪkəl] ADJ lexikalisch

lexicalize ['leksɪkəlaɪz] VT lexikalisieren

lexicographer [ˌleksɪ'kɒgrəfə'] N Lexikograf(in) *m(f)*

lexicographic(al) [ˌleksɪkəʊ'græfɪk(əl)] ADJ lexikografisch

lexicography [ˌleksɪ'kɒgrəfɪ] N Lexikografie *f*

lexicology [ˌleksɪ'kɒlədʒɪ] N Lexikologie *f*

lexicon ['leksɪkən] N Wörterbuch *nt*, Lexikon *nt*; *(in linguistics)* Lexikon *nt*

lexis [ˈleksɪs] N *(Ling)* Lexik *f*

Leyden jar [ˈlaɪdnˈdʒɑːˈ] N Leidener Flasche *f*

l.h.d. *abbr of* **left-hand drive**

liability [ˌlaɪəˈbɪlɪtɪ] N **a** *(= burden)* Belastung *f* **b** *(= being subject to)* **one's ~ for tax** jds Steuerpflicht *f*; **he has a tax ~ of £1,000** er muss £ 1000 Steuern bezahlen; **~ to pay damages** Schadensersatzpflicht *f* **c** *(= proneness)* Anfälligkeit *f* *(to* für); **his ~ to digestive disorders** seine Anfälligkeit für Verdauungsstörungen **d** *(= responsibility)* Haftung *f*; **we accept no ~ for …** wir übernehmen keine Haftung für …; **his ~ for his wife's debts** seine Haftung *or* Haftbarkeit für die Schulden seiner Frau **e** *(Fin)* **liabilities** Verbindlichkeiten *pl*, Verpflichtungen *pl*

liable [ˈlaɪəbl] ADJ **a** *(= subject to)* **to be ~ for** *or* **to sth** einer Sache *(dat)* unterliegen; **to be ~ for tax** *(things)* besteuert werden; *(income, person)* steuerpflichtig sein; **people earning over £X are ~ for surtax** wer mehr als £ X verdient, unterliegt einer Zusatzsteuer *or* ist zusatzsteuerpflichtig; **~ to penalty** strafbar; **to be ~ to prosecution** der Strafverfolgung unterliegen; **you'll make yourself ~ to a heavy fine** Sie können zu einer hohen Geldstrafe verurteilt werden

b *(= prone to)* anfällig; **he's always been ~ to bronchitis** er war schon immer anfällig für Bronchitis; **~ to inflation** inflationsanfällig

c *(= responsible)* **to be ~** haften, haftbar sein; **to be ~ for sth** für etw haftbar sein *or* haften, für etw aufkommen müssen; **he is not legally ~ to pay** er ist nicht gesetzlich verpflichtet zu zahlen

d *(= likely to)* **to be ~ to do sth** *(in future)* wahrscheinlich etw tun (werden); *(habitually)* dazu neigen, etw zu tun; **we are ~ to get shot here** wir können hier leicht beschossen werden; **the pond is ~ to freeze** der Teich friert leicht zu; **is he ~ to come?** ist anzunehmen, dass er kommt?; **he's ~ to tell the police** es wäre ihm zuzutrauen, dass er es der Polizei meldet; **if you don't write it down I'm ~ to forget it** wenn Sie das nicht aufschreiben, kann es durchaus sein, dass ich es vergesse; **the plan is ~ to changes** der Plan wird möglicherweise geändert; **I don't think it's ~ to happen tonight** ich halte es für nicht wahrscheinlich, dass es heute Nacht passiert; **the car is ~ to run out of petrol** *(Brit) or* **gas** *(US)* **any minute** dem Auto kann jede Minute das Benzin ausgehen; **if you tell him that, he's ~ to lose his temper** wenn Sie ihm das sagen, wird er wahrscheinlich wütend

liaise [liːˈeɪz] VI *(= be the contact person)* als Verbindungsperson fungieren; *(= get in contact)* sich in Verbindung setzen *(with* mit); *(= be in contact)* in Verbindung stehen *(with* mit); **social services and health workers ~ closely** das Sozialamt und der Gesundheitsdienst arbeiten eng zusammen

liaison [liːˈeɪzɒn] N **a** *(= coordination)* Verbindung *f*, Zusammenarbeit *f*; *(= person)* Verbindungsmann *m*/-frau *f*, V-Mann *m*/-Frau *f* *(inf)*; *(Mil)* Verbindung *f*; *(person)* Verbindungsoffizier *m* **b** *(= affair)* Liaison *f*

liaison officer N Verbindungsmann *m*/-frau *f*; *(Mil)* Verbindungsoffizier *m*; **the firm's ~** der/die Firmensprecher(in)

liar [ˈlaɪəˈ] N Lügner(in) *m(f)*

Lib *(Brit Pol) abbr of* **Liberal**

lib [lɪb] N *abbr of* **liberation**

libation [laɪˈbeɪʃən] N **a** *(= offering)* Trankopfer *nt* **b** *(inf: = drink)* **we had a few small ~s** wir hatten ein paar getrunken *(inf)*

Lib Dem [ˌlɪbˈdem] *(Brit Pol) abbr of* **Liberal Democrat** **N** Liberaldemokrat(in) *m(f)* **ADJ** liberaldemokratisch; *gain, loss, policy* der Liberaldemokraten

libel [ˈlaɪbəl] **N** (schriftlich geäußerte) Verleumdung *(on +gen)*; **to begin a ~ action against sb** jdn wegen Verleumdung verklagen; **it's a ~ on all of us** das ist eine Verleumdung, die uns alle trifft **VT** verleumden

libellous, *(US)* **libelous** [ˈlaɪbələs] ADJ verleumderisch

liberal [ˈlɪbərəl] **ADJ** **a** *(= generous) offer, supply* großzügig; *helping of food* reichlich; **to be ~ with one's praise/comments** mit Lob/seinen Kommentaren freigebig sein; **to be ~ with one's money** mit seinem Geld großzügig umgehen **b** *(= broad-minded)* liberal **c** *(Pol)* liberal; **the Liberal Party** *(Brit Hist, in Canada)* die Liberale Partei **N** **a** *(Pol)* Liberale(r) *mf* **b** *(= liberal-minded person)* Liberalgesinnte(r) *mf*; **he's a ~ in social matters** er hat eine liberale Einstellung in sozialen Angelegenheiten

liberal: **liberal arts** PL **the ~** *(esp US)* die geisteswissenschaftlichen Fächer; **liberal democracy** N *(Pol)* freiheitliche Demokratie; **Liberal Democrat** *(Brit Pol)* **N** Liberaldemokrat(in) *m(f)* **ADJ** liberaldemokratisch; *gain, loss, policy* der Liberaldemokraten; **the ~ Party** die liberaldemokratische Partei; **liberal education** N Allgemeinbildung *f*

liberalism [ˈlɪbərəlɪzəm] N Liberalität *f*; **Liberalism** *(Pol)* der Liberalismus

liberality [ˌlɪbəˈrælɪtɪ] N **a** *(= generosity)* Großzügigkeit *f* **b** = **liberal-mindedness**

liberalization [ˌlɪbərəlaɪˈzeɪʃən] N Liberalisierung *f*

liberalize [ˈlɪbərəlaɪz] VT liberalisieren

liberally [ˈlɪbərəlɪ] ADV *(= broad-mindedly)* liberal; *(= generously)* großzügig; *(= in large quantities)* reichlich; **he applies the paint very ~** er trägt die Farbe dick *or* reichlich auf

liberal: **liberal-minded** [ˌlɪbərəlˈmaɪndɪd] ADJ *person* liberal (eingestellt); *views, country* liberal; **liberal-mindedness** N *(of person)* liberale Einstellung *or* Gesinnung; *(of views)* Liberalität *f*; **liberal studies** PL *(esp US)* Geisteswissenschaften *pl*

liberate [ˈlɪbəreɪt] VT **a** *(= free) prisoner, country, city* befreien; **to ~ sb from sth** jdn von etw befreien **b** *gas etc* freisetzen

liberated [ˈlɪbəreɪtɪd] ADJ *women, times* emanzipiert

liberation [ˌlɪbəˈreɪʃən] N Befreiung *f*; *(of gases)* Freisetzung *f*

liberator [ˈlɪbəreɪtəˈ] N Befreier(in) *m(f)*

Liberia [laɪˈbɪərɪə] N Liberia *nt*

Liberian [laɪˈbɪərɪən] **ADJ** liberianisch, liberisch **N** Liberianer(in) *m(f)*, Liberier(in) *m(f)*

libertarian [lɪbəˈteərɪən] **ADJ** *(= freedom-loving)* freiheitsliebend; *(= opposed to authority)* antiautoritär, libertär; *policy, politics* liberalistisch; **~ attitude** freiheitliche/antiautoritäre *or* libertäre Gesinnung **N** Verfechter(in) *m(f)* des freien Willens, Liberalist(in) *m(f)* *(esp Pol)*

libertine [ˈlɪbətiːn] N Wüstling *m*, Libertin *m* *(geh)*

liberty [ˈlɪbətɪ] N **a** Freiheit *f*; **individual ~** die Freiheit des Einzelnen; **basic liberties** Grundrechte *pl*; **to set sb at ~** jdn auf freien Fuß setzen; **to be at ~** *(criminal etc)* frei herumlaufen; *(= not busy)* Zeit haben; **to be at ~ to do sth** *(= be permitted)* etw tun dürfen; **I am not at ~ to comment** es ist mir nicht gestattet, darüber zu sprechen; **you are at ~ to go** es steht Ihnen frei zu gehen; **is he at ~ to come?** darf er kommen?

b *(= presumptuous action, behaviour)* **I have taken the ~ of giving your name** ich habe mir erlaubt, Ihren Namen anzugeben; **to take liberties with the truth** es mit der Wahrheit nicht so genau nehmen; **to take liberties with sb** sich jdm gegenüber Freiheiten herausnehmen; **what a ~!** *(inf)* so eine Frechheit!

liberty bodice N Leibchen *nt*

libidinous [lɪˈbɪdɪnəs] ADJ lüstern; *person, behaviour also* triebhaft; *(Psych) urge, effect* libidinös

libido [lɪˈbiːdəʊ] N Libido *f*

Lib-Lab [ˈlɪbˌlæb] ADJ *abbr of* **Liberal-Labour** *(Brit Pol inf)* **~ pact** Pakt *m* zwischen den Liberalen und der Labour Party

LIBOR [ˈliːbɔˈ] N *abbr of* **London Inter-Bank Offer Rate** *bankeninterner Wechselkurs*

Libra [ˈliːbrə] N Waage *f*; **she's (a) ~** sie ist Waage

Libran [ˈliːbrən] N Waage *f*, Waagemensch *m*

librarian [laɪˈbreərɪən] N Bibliothekar(in) *m(f)*

librarianship [laɪˈbreərɪənʃɪp] N **a** *(= subject)* Bibliothekswesen *nt or* -lehre *f* **b** *(= job)* Bibliothekarsstelle *f*

library [ˈlaɪbrərɪ] N **a** *(public)* Bibliothek *f*, Bücherei *f* **b** *(private)* Bibliothek *f* **c** *(= collection of books/records)* (Bücher-/Schallplatten)-sammlung *f* **d** *(= series of books)* Buchreihe *f*, Bibliothek *f*

> **LIBRARY OF CONGRESS**
>
> Die **Library of Congress** in Washington, DC, ist die Nationalbibliothek der Vereinigten Staaten von Amerika. Sie wurde 1800 zunächst als Informationsquelle für die Kongressmitglieder gegründet. Heute ist sie auch für die Vergabe von Urheberrechten zuständig, die in ihrem **Copyright Office** registriert werden müssen. Die Bibliothek erhält von jedem in den USA urheberrechtlich geschützten Buch zwei Exemplare. Sie verfügt über riesige Sammlungen von Büchern und historischen Handschriften, außerdem werden hier Partituren, Landkarten, Filme, Mikrofilme und Tonträger aufbewahrt.

library: **library book** N Leihbuch *nt*; **library card** N Benutzerausweis *m*; **library edition** N Leihbuchausgabe *f*; **library pictures** PL *(TV)* Archivbilder *pl*; **library science** N Bibliothekswissenschaften *pl*; **library ticket** N Leserausweis *m*

librettist [lɪˈbretɪst] N Librettist(in) *m(f)*

libretto [lɪˈbretəʊ] N Libretto *nt*

Libya [ˈlɪbɪə] N Libyen *nt*

Libyan [ˈlɪbɪən] **ADJ** libysch **N** Libyer(in) *m(f)*

lice [laɪs] *pl of* **louse**

licence, *(US)* **license** [ˈlaɪsəns] N **a** *(= permit)* Genehmigung *f*, Erlaubnis *f*; *(by authority)* behördliche Genehmigung, Konzession *f*; *(Comm)* Lizenz *f*; *(= driving licence)* Führerschein *m*; *(= road licence)* Kfz-Steuer *f*; *(= gun licence)* Waffenschein *m*; *(= hunting licence)* Jagdschein *m*; *(= marriage licence)* Eheerlaubnis *f*; *(= radio/television licence)* (Rundfunk-/Fernseh)genehmigung *f*; *(= dog licence)* Hundemarke *f*; **he hasn't paid his (dog) ~** er hat seine Hundesteuer nicht bezahlt; **you have to have a (television) ~** man muss Fernsehgebühren bezahlen; **a ~ to practise medicine** *(Brit)*, **a license to practice medicine** *(US)* die Approbation, die staatliche Zulassung als Arzt; **the restaurant has lost its ~ (to sell drinks)** das Restaurant hat seine Schankerlaubnis *or* Konzession verloren; **we'll get a late ~ for the reception** für den Empfang bekommen wir eine Genehmigung für verlängerte Ausschankzeiten; **a ~ to kill** ein Freibrief *m* zum Töten; **it is just a ~ to print money** *(fig)* es ist ein sehr lukratives Geschäft; **to manufacture sth under ~** etw in Lizenz herstellen; **to give sb ~ to do sth** jdm erlauben, etw zu tun

b *(= freedom)* Freiheit *f*; **translated with considerable ~** sehr frei übersetzt

c *(= excessive freedom)* Zügellosigkeit *f*; **there is too much ~ in sexual matters/the cinema nowadays** in sexuellen Dingen/im Kino geht es heutzutage zu freizügig zu

licence: **licence fee** N *(Brit TV)* ≈ Fernsehgebühr *f*; **licence number**, *(US)* **license number** N *(Aut)* Kraftfahrzeug- *or* Kfz-Kennzeichen *nt*; **licence plate**, *(US)* **license plate** N *(Aut)* Nummernschild *nt*

license [ˈlaɪsəns] **N** *(US)* = **licence** **VT** eine Lizenz/Konzession vergeben an *(+acc)*; **to ~ a pub** einer Gaststätte Schankerlaubnis *or* eine Schankkonzession erteilen; **to be ~d to do sth** die Genehmigung haben, etw zu tun; **he is ~d to practise** *(Brit) or* **practice** *(US)* **medicine** er ist approbierter Arzt, er ist als Arzt zugelassen; **we are not ~d to sell alcohol** wir haben keine

Schankerlaubnis *or* Konzession; **secret agents are ~d to kill** Geheimagenten dürfen Leute umbringen

licensed [ˈlaɪsənst] ADJ **a** *pilot* mit Pilotenschein; *taxi driver* mit Taxischein; *physician* approbiert; **he's a ~ pilot** er hat einen Pilotenschein **b** (= *selling alcohol*) **~ bar/premises** Lokal *nt* mit Schankerlaubnis; **fully ~** mit voller Schankkonzession *or* -erlaubnis; **~ trade** (konzessionierter) Alkoholhandel; **I used to be in the ~ trade** ich war früher Gastwirt; **~ victualler** *Lebensmittelhändler mit einer Konzession für den Verkauf von Alkohol;* **he won't stay at a hotel unless it's ~** er übernachtet nur in Hotels mit Alkoholausschank

licensee [ˌlaɪsənˈsiː] N → **licence** Konzessions-/ /Lizenzinhaber(in) *m(f)*/Inhaber(in) *m(f)* eines Waffenscheins *etc;* (*of bar*) Inhaber(in) *m(f)* einer Schankerlaubnis; **the ~ of our local pub** (*Brit*) *or* **bar** der Wirt unserer Stammkneipe

licenser, licensor [ˈlaɪsənsəʳ] N Lizenzgeber(in) *m(f)*, Konzessionserteiler(in) *m(f)*

licensing [ˈlaɪsənsɪŋ] ADJ **~ agreement** Lizenzabkommen *nt;* **~ hours** Ausschankzeiten *pl;* **~ laws** Schankgesetze *pl,* Gesetz *nt* über den Ausschank und Verkauf alkoholischer Getränke

LICENSING LAWS

In Großbritannien werden alle Gesetze und Verordnungen bezüglich des Verkaufs und Konsums von alkoholischen Getränken unter dem Begriff der **licensing laws** zusammengefasst. Das Mindestalter, ab dem der Konsum von Alkohol in Pubs oder Clubs gestattet ist, liegt bei 18 Jahren. Pubs, Clubs und Restaurants dürfen nur dann Alkohol ausschenken, wenn sie eine Schankerlaubnis, **licence**, besitzen, und auch dann nur zu bestimmten Uhrzeiten. In Lokalen ohne diese Erlaubnis muss man allerdings nicht auf einen guten Schluck Wein oder sein Bier zum Essen verzichten, denn man darf sich seinen eigenen Wein mitbringen (eventuell wird das Öffnen der Flasche in Rechnung gestellt - „corkage charge"). Ein gutes Sortiment verschiedenster Biere und Weine findet sich an fast jeder Ecke in Fachgeschäften, den sogenannten **off-licences**, die so heißen, da der dort verkaufte Alkohol nur privat, außerhalb („off") der lizenzierten Räumlichkeiten konsumiert werden darf.

In den USA bestehen in den einzelnen Bundesstaaten verschiedene Regelungen. Das Mindestalter für den Alkoholkonsum schwankt zwischen 18 und 21 Jahren, einige Staaten haben regelrechte „trockene" Counties, in denen der Konsum und der Verkauf von Alkohol komplett untersagt ist. In einigen Bundesstaaten können alkoholische Getränke nur in den sogenannten **liquor stores** oder auch **package stores** erworben werden. Dafür sind die meisten Restaurants und Clubs im Besitz einer **liquor permit** für den Alkoholausschank.

licensor [ˈlaɪsənsəʳ] N → **licenser**

licentiate [laɪˈsenʃɪɪt] N Lizenziat(in) *m(f)*, Lizentiat(in) *m(f);* (= *degree*) Lizenziat *nt*, Lizentiat *nt*

licentious [laɪˈsenʃəs] ADJ ausschweifend, lasterhaft; *behaviour* unzüchtig; *book* sehr freizügig; *look* lüstern

licentiousness [laɪˈsenʃəsnɪs] N Unmoral *f*, Unzüchtigkeit *f;* (*of book*) Freizügigkeit *f;* (*of look*) Lüsternheit *f*

lichee [ˈlaɪtʃiː] N = **lychee**

lichen [ˈlaɪkən] N Flechte *f*

lichgate, lychgate [ˈlɪtʃgeɪt] N überdachter Kirchhofseingang

licit [ˈlɪsɪt] ADJ erlaubt, gesetzlich

lick [lɪk] N **a** (*with tongue*) Lecken *nt*, Schlecken *nt (dial);* **to give sth a ~** an etw *(dat)* lecken; **the cat gave me/my hand a ~** die Katze leckte mich ab/mir die Hand **b** (= *salt lick*) (Salz)lecke *f;* (*artificial*) Leckstein *m*
c (*inf:* = *small quantity*) **it's time we gave the kitchen a ~ of paint** die Küche könnte auch mal wieder etwas Farbe vertragen *(inf);* **he doesn't do a ~ of work** er tut keinen Schlag
d (*Brit inf:* = *pace*) **the project is coming along at a good ~** das Projekt geht ganz gut voran *(inf);* **to go/drive at a fair old ~** einen ganz schönen Zahn draufhaben *(inf);* **he rushed to the station at full ~** er raste mit Vollgas zum Bahnhof *(inf)*
VT **a** (*with tongue*) lecken; **he ~ed the stamp** er leckte an der Briefmarke; **he ~ed the ice cream** er leckte am Eis; **to ~ one's lips** sich *(dat)* die Lippen lecken; *(fig)* sich *(dat)* die Finger lecken; **the cat ~ed its paws** die Katze leckte sich *(dat)* die Pfoten; **to ~ the bowl out** die Schüssel auslecken; **to ~ one's wounds** *(fig)* seine Wunden lecken; **to ~ sb's boots** *(fig)* vor jdm kriechen *(inf)*, jds Stiefel lecken; **to ~ sb into shape** *(fig)* jdn auf Vordermann bringen *(inf)*
b (*waves*) plätschern an *(+acc);* (*flames*) züngeln an *(+dat)*
c (*inf:* = *beat, defeat*) in die Pfanne hauen *(inf);* **I think we've got it ~ed** ich glaube, wir haben die Sache jetzt im Griff
VI **to ~ at sth** an etw *(dat)* lecken; **flames ~ed around the building** Flammen züngelten an dem Gebäude empor

► **lick off** VT *sep* ablecken; **to lick sth off sth** etw von etw ablecken

► **lick up** VT *sep* auflecken

lickety-split [ˈlɪkɪtɪˈsplɪt] ADV (*US inf*) blitzschnell, mit Volldampf *(inf)*

licking [ˈlɪkɪŋ] N *(inf)* (= *beating*) Tracht *f* Prügel; (= *defeat*) Niederlage *f;* **to give sb a ~** (= *beating*) jdm eine Abreibung geben *(inf);* (= *defeat*) jdn in die Pfanne hauen *(inf)*

licorice [ˈlɪkərɪs] N = **liquorice**

lid [lɪd] N **a** Deckel *m;* **that puts the (tin) ~ on it** *(inf)* das ist doch die Höhe, das schlägt dem Fass den Boden aus; **a documentary that really takes the ~ off Hollywood** ein Dokumentarfilm, der das wahre Gesicht Hollywoods zeigt; **the press took the ~ off the whole plan** die Presse hat den Plan enthüllt *or* aufgedeckt; **to keep a ~ on sth** etw unter Kontrolle halten; *on information* etw geheim halten; **to put the ~ on sth** *(on scandal, affair)* etw vertuschen; **to put the ~ on sb** jdn zum Schweigen bringen **b** (= *eyelid*) Lid *nt*

lidless [ˈlɪdlɪs] ADJ **a** ohne Deckel **b** *eyes* ohne Lider

lido [ˈliːdəʊ] N Freibad *nt*

lie[1] [laɪ] N Lüge *f;* **it's a ~!** das ist eine Lüge!, das ist gelogen!; **to tell a ~** lügen; **I tell a ~, it's actually tomorrow** das stimmt ja gar nicht *or* ich hab mich vertan, es ist morgen; **to give the ~ to sb** jdn der Lüge bezichtigen *or* beschuldigen; **to give the ~ to a claim** die Unwahrheit einer Behauptung *(gen)* zeigen *or* beweisen, eine Behauptung Lügen strafen *(geh)* VI lügen; **to ~ to sb** jdn belügen *or* anlügen; **the camera never ~s** die Kamera lügt nie VT **to ~ one's way out of sth** sich aus etw herauslügen

lie[2] *vb: pret* **lay**, *ptp* **lain** N (= *position*) Lage *f*, Position *f*
VI **a** (*in horizontal or resting position*) liegen; (= *lie down*) sich legen; **he lay where he had fallen** er blieb liegen, wo er hingefallen war; **~ on your back** leg dich auf den Rücken; **obstacles ~ in the way of our success** unser Weg zum Erfolg ist mit Hindernissen verstellt; **the snow didn't ~** der Schnee blieb nicht liegen; **to ~ with sb** (*Bibl, old*) bei jdm liegen (*Bibl, old*)
b (= *be buried*) ruhen; **to ~ at rest** zur letzten Ruhe gebettet sein *(geh)*
c (= *be situated*) liegen; **the runner who is lying third** (*esp Brit*) der Läufer, der auf dem dritten Platz liegt; **Uganda ~s far from the coast** Uganda liegt weit von der Küste ab *or* entfernt; **our road lay along the river** unsere Straße führte am Fluss entlang; **our futures ~ in quite different directions** unsere zukünftigen Wege führen in verschiedene Richtungen; **you are young and your life ~s before you** du bist jung, und das Leben liegt noch vor dir
d (= *be, remain in a certain condition*) liegen; **to ~ asleep** (daliegen und) schlafen; **to ~ helpless** hilflos daliegen; **to ~ dying** im Sterben liegen; **he lay resting on the sofa** er ruhte sich auf dem Sofa aus; **the snow lay deep** es lag tiefer Schnee; **the book lay unopened** das Buch lag ungeöffnet da; **to ~ low** untertauchen, sich nicht mehr sehen lassen; **to ~ heavy on the stomach** schwer im Magen liegen; **to ~ heavy on the conscience** schwer auf dem Gewissen lasten
e (*immaterial things*) liegen; **where does the difficulty ~?** wo liegt die Schwierigkeit?; **it ~s with you to solve the problem** es liegt bei dir, das Problem zu lösen; **his interests ~ in music** seine Interessen liegen auf dem Gebiet der Musik *or* gelten der Musik; **he did everything that lay in his power to help us** er tat alles in seiner Macht Stehende, um uns zu helfen; **that responsibility ~s with your department** dafür ist Ihre Abteilung verantwortlich; **the real solution ~s in education** Bildung ist die wahre Lösung

► **lie about** (*Brit*) *or* **around** VI herumliegen

► **lie back** VI **a** (= *recline*) sich zurücklehnen **b** (*fig:* = *take no action*) es sich gemütlich machen, sich ausruhen; **we can't afford to lie back and relax until the job's finished** wir können uns *(dat)* keine Ruhe gönnen, bis die Arbeit erledigt ist

► **lie behind** VI *+prep obj decision, remarks* stehen hinter *(+dat);* **I don't know what lies behind it** ich weiß nicht, was dahintersteht

► **lie down** VI **a** (*lit*) sich hinlegen; **he lay down on the bed** er legte sich aufs Bett; **lie down!** (*to a dog*) leg dich!, hinlegen! **b** (*fig:* = *accept, submit*) **to lie down under sth** sich *(dat)* etw gefallen *or* bieten lassen; **he won't take that lying down!** das lässt er sich nicht gefallen *or* bieten!; **he didn't take defeat lying down** er nahm die Niederlage nicht tatenlos hin

► **lie in** VI **a** (= *stay in bed*) im Bett bleiben **b** (*old: in childbirth*) im Wochenbett liegen

► **lie off** VI (*Naut:* = *be anchored nearby*) vor Anker liegen; **the ship lay off Aberdeen** das Schiff lag vor Aberdeen vor Anker

► **lie over** VI vertagt *or* zurückgestellt werden

► **lie to** VI (*Naut*) **a** (= *be anchored*) vor Anker liegen, ankern **b** (= *come into a position for anchoring*) beidrehen

► **lie up** VI **a** (= *rest after illness etc*) im Bett bleiben **b** (= *hide*) untertauchen; **the robbers are lying up** die Räuber sind untergetaucht **c** (= *be out of use*) nicht benutzt werden, unbenutzt stehen; (*car*) abgestellt sein

lie-abed [ˈlaɪəbed] N Langschläfer(in) *m(f)*

Liechtenstein [ˈliːxtənʃtaɪn] N Liechtenstein *nt*

Liechtensteiner [ˈliːxtənʃtaɪnəʳ] N Liechtensteiner(in) *m(f)*

lie detector N Lügendetektor *m*

lie-down [ˈlaɪdaʊn] N *(inf)* Schläfchen *nt (inf)*, Nickerchen *nt (inf);* **to have a ~** ein Schläfchen *or* Nickerchen machen *(inf)*

lief [liːf] ADV *(old)* **I would as ~** ich würde ebenso gern; **I would as ~ ... as anything** ich würde nichts lieber tun als ...

liege [liːdʒ] N *(old)* **a** (*also* **liege lord**) Lehnsherr *m;* **my ~** Euer Gnaden **b** (*also* **liege man**) Lehnsmann *m*, Vasall *m*

lie-in [ˈlaɪɪn] N (*Brit inf*) **to have a ~** (sich) ausschlafen

lien [lɪən] N Zurückbehaltungsrecht *nt*, Pfandrecht *nt*

lieu [luː] N (*form*) **money in ~** stattdessen Geld; **in ~ of X** anstelle von X; **in ~ of that** stattdessen; **I work weekends and get time off in ~** (*esp*

Brit) ich arbeite an Wochenenden und kann mir dafür (an anderen Tagen) freinehmen

Lieut. *(Mil) abbr of* **lieutenant** Lt

lieutenancy [lefˈtenənsɪ, *(US)* luːˈtenənsɪ] N Leutnantsrang *m*; **he gained his ~** er ist zum Leutnant befördert worden

lieutenant [lefˈtenənt, *(US)* luːˈtenənt] N a Leutnant *m*; *(Brit)* Oberleutnant *m*; **first ~** *(US)* Oberleutnant *m*; **second ~** Leutnant *m* b *(= governor)* Statthalter(in) *m(f)*, Gouverneur(in) *m(f)*

lieutenant: **lieutenant colonel** N Oberstleutnant *m*; **lieutenant commander** N Korvettenkapitän *m*; **lieutenant general** N *(Brit)* Generalleutnant *m*; **lieutenant governor** N *(US)* Vizegouverneur(in) *m(f)*

life [laɪf] N *pl* **lives** a Leben *nt*; **bird/plant ~** die Vogel-/Pflanzenwelt; **there is not much insect ~ here** hier gibt es nicht viele Insekten; **drawn from ~** lebensnah; **to draw from ~** *(Art)* nach dem Leben zeichnen; **to the ~** lebensecht; **the battle resulted in great loss of ~** bei der Schlacht kamen viele ums Leben; **this is a matter of ~ and death** hier geht es um Leben und Tod; **a ~ and death struggle** ein Kampf auf Leben und Tod; **~ after death** das Leben nach dem Tod; **~ begins at 40** das Leben fängt mit 40 (erst richtig) an; **to be tired of ~** des Lebens überdrüssig sein; **~ goes on** das Leben geht weiter; **to bring sb back to ~** jdn wiederbeleben, jdn ins Leben zurückrufen; **his book brings history to ~** sein Buch lässt die Geschichte lebendig werden; **to come to ~** *(fig)* lebendig werden; **I'm the sort of person who comes to ~ in the evenings** ich bin ein Typ, der erst abends munter wird; **after half an hour the discussion came to ~** nach einer halben Stunde kam Leben in die Diskussion; **to put new ~ into sb** jdm wieder Auftrieb geben; **for dear ~** verzweifelt; **they swam for dear ~** sie schwammen um ihr Leben; **they looked at him in the oxygen tent fighting for dear ~** sie sahen, wie er im Sauerstoffzelt um sein Leben kämpfte; **at my time of ~** in meinem Alter; **marriage should be for ~** eine Ehe sollte fürs Leben geschlossen werden; **he's got a job for ~** er hat eine Stelle auf Lebenszeit; **the murderer was imprisoned for ~** der Mörder wurde zu lebenslänglicher Freiheitsstrafe verurteilt; **he's doing ~ (for murder)** *(inf)* er sitzt lebenslänglich (wegen Mord) *(inf)*; **he got ~** *(inf)* er hat lebenslänglich gekriegt *(inf)*

b *(= individual life)* **how many lives were lost?** wie viele (Menschen) sind ums Leben gekommen?; **the lives of the prisoners** das Leben der Gefangenen; **I've got a new man in my ~** in meinem Leben gibt es einen neuen Mann; **to take sb's ~** jdn umbringen; **to take one's own ~** sich *(dat)* das Leben nehmen; **to save sb's ~** *(lit)* jdm das Leben retten; *(fig)* jdn retten; **I couldn't do it to save my ~** ich kann es beim besten Willen nicht; **the church is my ~** die Kirche ist mein ganzes Leben; **to rule sb's ~** jds Leben bestimmen; **the suspected murderer is on trial for his ~** für den Mordverdächtigen geht es bei dem Prozess um Leben und Tod; **in the next ~** im nächsten Leben; **early in ~, in early ~** in frühen Jahren; **later in ~, in later ~** in späteren Jahren, später im Leben; **she leads a busy ~** bei ihr ist immer etwas los; **she began (her working) ~ as a teacher** sie begann ihr Berufsleben als Lehrerin; **the book started ~ as a screenplay** das Buch war ursprünglich ein Drehbuch; **all his ~** sein ganzes Leben lang; **I've never been to London in my ~** ich war in meinem ganzen Leben noch nicht in London; **to fight for one's ~** um sein Leben kämpfen; **run for your lives!** rennt um euer Leben!; **it gave me the fright of my ~** es hat mich zu Tode erschreckt; **I can't for the ~ of me ...** *(inf)* ich kann beim besten Willen nicht ...; **never in my ~ have I heard such nonsense** ich habe mein Lebtag noch nicht *or* noch nie im Leben so einen Unsinn gehört; **not on your ~!** *(inf)* ich bin doch nicht verrückt! *(inf)*; **would you ever disobey him? – not on your ~!** *(inf)* würdest du je seine Befehle missachten? – nie im Leben!; **get a ~!** *(inf)* sonst hast du keine Probleme? *(inf)*; **to have a ~** etwas vom Leben haben; **to have a ~ of one's own** sein eigenes Leben führen; **it seemed to have a ~ of its own** es scheint seinen eigenen Willen zu haben; **he is a good/bad ~** *(Insur)* er ist ein niedriges/hohes Risiko

c *(= the world, social activity)* **to see ~** die Welt sehen; **there isn't much ~ here in the evenings** hier ist abends nicht viel Leben *or* nicht viel los

d *(= liveliness)* Leben *nt*; **those children are full of ~!** diese Kinder stecken voller Leben *or* sind sehr lebhaft!; **the city centre** *(Brit) or* **center** *(US)* **was full of ~** im Stadtzentrum ging es sehr lebhaft zu; **he's still got so much ~ in him** er ist noch so vital *or* steckt noch voller Leben; **there's ~ in the old girl yet** *(inf)* sie ist noch schwer aktiv *(inf)*; *(of car)* die Kiste bringts noch *(sl)*; **he is the ~ and soul** *(Brit) or* **~** *(US)* **of every party** er bringt Leben in jede Party; **wherever John goes, he wants to be the ~ and soul** *(Brit) or* *(US)* **of the party** John will überall im Mittelpunkt stehen

e *(= way of life)* Leben *nt*; **village ~** das Leben auf dem Dorf; **this is the ~!** ja, ist das ein Leben!; **what a ~!** was für ein Leben!; **such is ~, that's ~** so ist das Leben; **it's a good ~** es ist ein schönes Leben; **the good ~** das süße Leben

f *(= useful or active life)* Lebensdauer *f*; **during the ~ of the present Parliament** während der Legislaturperiode des gegenwärtigen Parlaments; **there's not much ~ left in the battery, the battery's nearing the end of its ~** die Batterie machts nicht mehr lange *(inf)*

g *(= biography)* Biografie *f*; *(of saint, king etc)* Lebensbeschreibung *f*

life: **life annuity** N Leib- *or* Lebensrente *f*; **life assurance** N *(Brit)* Lebensversicherung *f*; **lifebelt** N Rettungsgürtel *m*; **lifeblood** N Blut *nt*; *(fig)* Lebensnerv *m*; **to drain sb's ~** *(fig)* jdn ausbluten lassen; **lifeboat** N *(from shore)* Rettungsboot *nt*; *(from ship also)* Beiboot *nt*; **lifebuoy** N Rettungsring *m*; **life class** N *(Art)* Kurs *m* im Modellzeichnen; **life coach** N Lebensberater(in) *m(f)*; **life cycle** N Lebenszyklus *m*; **life-enhancing** [ˈlaɪfɪnˌhɑːnsɪŋ] ADJ bereichernd; **life expectancy** N Lebenserwartung *f*; **life force** N Lebenskraft *f*; **life-giving** ADJ Leben spendend; **~ aid to poor countries** lebensnotwendige Hilfe für arme Länder; **lifeguard** N a *(on beach)* Rettungsschwimmer(in) *m(f)*; *(in baths)* Bademeister(in) *m(f)* b *(Mil)* Leibwache *f*; **life history** N Lebensgeschichte *f*; *(Biol)* Entwicklungsgeschichte *f*; **the ~ of the salmon** der Lebenskreislauf des Lachses; **life imprisonment** N lebenslängliche Freiheitsstrafe; **life instinct** N *(Psych)* Lebenstrieb *m*; **life insurance** N = **life assurance**; **life interest** N *(Jur)* lebenslänglicher Nießbrauch; **life jacket** N Schwimmweste *f*

lifeless [ˈlaɪflɪs] ADJ a *(= dead, as if dead)* leblos b *(= inanimate)* leblos, tot; *planet* unbelebt, ohne Leben c *(fig: = listless, dull)* lahm *(inf)*, langweilig

lifelessly [ˈlaɪflɪslɪ] ADV leblos; *(fig)* teilnahmslos

lifelessness [ˈlaɪflɪsnɪs] N Leblosigkeit *f*; *(fig)* Teilnahmslosigkeit *f*

life: **lifelike** ADJ lebensecht; *imitation also* naturgetreu; **lifeline** N a Rettungsleine *f*; *(of diver)* Signalleine *f*; *(fig)* Rettungsanker *m*; **the telephone is a ~ for many old people** das Telefon ist für viele alte Leute lebenswichtig; **in doing this they risked severing their financial ~** dadurch haben sie riskiert, dass ihnen der Geldhahn zugedreht wird b *(Palmistry)* Lebenslinie *f*; **lifelong** ADJ lebenslang; **they are ~ friends** sie sind schon ihr Leben lang Freunde; **he's my ~ friend** er war schon immer mein Freund; **we became ~ friends** wir wurden Freunde fürs Leben; **his ~ devotion to the cause** die Sache, in deren Dienst er sein Leben gestellt hat; **her ~ fear of water** ihre angeborene Angst vor Wasser; **life membership** N Mitgliedschaft *f* auf Lebenszeit; **life net** N Sprungtuch *nt*; **life-or-death** ADJ **~ struggle** Kampf *m* auf Leben und Tod; **life peer** N Peer *m* auf Lebenszeit; **life preserver** N a *(Brit)* Totschläger *m* b *(US)* Schwimmweste *f*

lifer [ˈlaɪfəʳ] N *(inf)* Lebenslängliche(r) *mf (inf)*

life: **life raft** N Rettungsfloß *nt*; **life-saver** N a Lebensretter(in) *m(f)*; *(= lifeguard)* Rettungsschwimmer(in) *m(f)* b *(fig)* Retter *m* in der Not; **it was a real ~!** das hat mich gerettet; **life-saving** N Lebensrettung *f*; *(= saving people from drowning)* Rettungsschwimmen *nt* ADJ *techniques, apparatus* zur Lebensrettung; *phone call, drug, operation, treatment* lebensrettend; *drop of whisky* rettend; **~ certificate** Rettungsschwimmabzeichen *nt*; **life science** N *Medizin, Biologie etc*; **life sentence** N lebenslängliche Freiheitsstrafe; **life-size(d)** ADJ in Lebensgröße, lebensgroß; **lifespan** N *(of people)* Lebenserwartung *f*; *(of animals, plants)* Leben(sdauer *f*) *nt*; **life story** N Lebensgeschichte *f*; **lifestyle** N Lebensstil *m*

life support N *(Med)* lebenserhaltende Apparate *pl*; **she's on ~** sie wird künstlich am Leben erhalten

life support machine N Herz-Lungen-Maschine *f*

life support system N Lebenserhaltungssystem *nt*

life: **life table** N Sterblichkeitstabelle *f*; **life-threatening** ADJ lebensbedrohend; **lifetime** N a Lebenszeit *f*; *(of battery, machine, animal)* Lebensdauer *f*; **once in a ~** einmal im Leben; **during** *or* **in my ~** während meines Lebens; **in his ~ there were no buses** zu seiner Zeit gab es keine Busse; **the chance of a ~** eine einmalige Chance, DIE Chance *(inf)*; **a ~'s devotion to charity** ein Leben, das der Wohltätigkeit gewidmet ist; **the work of a ~** ein Lebenswerk *nt* b *(fig)* Ewigkeit *f*; **life vest** N Rettungs- *or* Schwimmweste *f*; **lifework** N Lebenswerk *nt*

lift [lɪft] N a *(= lifting)* Heben *nt*; **the haughty ~ of her head** ihre hochmütige Kopfhaltung; **give me a ~ up** heb mich mal hoch; **give me a ~ with this trunk** hilf mir, den Koffer hochzuheben

b *(Weightlifting)* **that was a good ~** das war eine gute Leistung; **his next ~ is 100 kg** beim nächsten Versuch will er 100 kg heben; **different types of ~** mehrere verschiedene Hebearten *pl*

c *(= emotional uplift)* **to give sb a ~** jdn aufmuntern; *(drug)* jdn aufputschen; *(prospect)* jdm Auftrieb geben

d *(in car etc)* Mitfahrgelegenheit *f*; **to give sb a ~** *(= take along)* jdn mitnehmen; *(as special journey)* jdn fahren; **to get a ~ from sb** von jdm mitgenommen werden/von jdm gefahren werden; **want a ~?** möchten Sie mitkommen?, soll ich dich fahren?; **don't take ~s from strangers** lass dich nicht von Fremden mitnehmen

e *(Brit: = elevator)* Fahrstuhl *m*, Aufzug *m*, Lift *m*; *(for goods)* Aufzug *m*; **he took the ~** er fuhr mit dem Fahrstuhl *etc*

f *(Aviat)* Auftrieb *m*

VT a *(also* **lift up***)* hochheben; *window* hochschieben; *feet, head* heben; *eyes* aufschlagen; *hat* lüften, ziehen; *potatoes etc* ernten; *child etc* hochheben; **to ~ the baby out of his playpen** das Baby aus dem Laufgitter heben; **to ~ one's hand to sb** die Hand gegen jdn erheben; **to ~ the phone** den Hörer abnehmen

b *(fig: also* **lift up***)* heben; *voice* erheben; **to ~ the spirits/mood** die Stimmung heben; **the news ~ed him out of his depression** durch die Nachricht verflog seine Niedergeschlagenheit; **the excellence of his style ~s him far above his contemporaries** sein ausgezeichneter Stil stellt ihn weit über seine Zeitgenossen

c *(= remove) restrictions etc* aufheben; **to ~ the siege of a city** die Belagerung einer Stadt beenden

d *(inf: = steal)* mitgehen lassen *(inf)*, klauen *(inf)*; *(= plagiarize)* abkupfern *(inf)*

e **to have one's face ~ed** sich *(dat)* das Ge-

sicht straffen *or* liften lassen
f *(Brit inf: = arrest)* schnappen *(inf)*
VI **a** *(= be lifted)* sich hochheben lassen; **that chair is too heavy (for you) to ~** dieser Stuhl ist zu schwer zum Hochheben
b *(mist)* sich lichten; *(mood, spirits)* sich heben
c *(rocket, plane)* abheben; **it ~ed slowly into the sky** es stieg langsam zum Himmel auf

▶ **lift down** VT *sep* herunterheben

▶ **lift off** **VT** *sep* abheben **VI** abheben

▶ **lift up** **VT** *sep* = **lift VT a, b; to lift up one's head** *(fig)* den Kopf hoch halten; **I'll never lift up my head again** *(fig)* ich kann niemandem mehr in die Augen blicken **VI** hochgeklappt werden

lift: **lift attendant** N *(Brit)* Fahrstuhlführer(in) *m(f)*; **liftboy** N *(Brit)* Liftboy *m*; **lift cage** N *(Brit)* Fahrstuhl *m*; **liftman** N *(Brit)* = **lift attendant**; **liftoff** N *(Space)* Abheben *nt*, Start *m*; **we have ~** der Start ist erfolgt; **lift-off correction tape** N *(for typewriter)* (Lift-off-)Korrekturband *nt*; **lift operator** N = **lift attendant**; **lift pass** N Skipass *m*; **liftshaft** N *(Brit)* Aufzugsschacht *m*

lig [lɪg] VI *(Brit inf) (at party)* sich selbst einladen, schmarotzen; *(at concert, etc)* ohne Eintrittskarte reingehen *(inf)*

ligament [ˈlɪɡəmənt] N Band *nt*, Ligament *nt*; **he's torn a ~ in his shoulder** er hat einen Bänderriss in der Schulter

ligature [ˈlɪɡətʃəʳ] N *(Med, Mus, Typ)* Ligatur *f*; *(= bandage)* Binde *f*; *(Med: = thread/cord)* Abbindungsschnur *f*/-draht *m*

ligger [ˈlɪɡəʳ] N *(Brit inf) (at party) jd, der sich selbst einlädt*, Schmarotzer(in) *m(f)*; *(at concert etc) jd, der ohne Eintrittskarte hereinkommt*

light¹ [laɪt] *vb: pret, ptp* **lit** *or* **lighted** **N** **a** *(in general)* Licht *nt*; **by the ~ of a candle/the fire** im Schein einer Kerze/des Feuers; **~ and shade** Licht und Schatten; **at first ~** bei Tagesanbruch; **hang the picture in a good ~** häng das Bild ins richtige Licht; **to cast** *or* **throw** *or* **shed ~ on sth** *(lit)* etw beleuchten; *(fig also)* Licht in etw *(acc)* bringen; **the moon cast its silvery ~ on ...** der Mond beleuchtete ... silbern *or* warf sein silbernes Licht auf *(+acc)* ...; **to cast a new** *or* **fresh ~ on sth** neues Licht auf etw *(acc)* werfen; **to be in sb's ~** *(lit)* jdm im Licht stehen; **in the cold ~ of day** *(fig)* bei Licht besehen; **the harsh ~ of reality** die raue Wirklichkeit; **this story shows his character in a bad ~** diese Geschichte wirft ein schlechtes Licht auf seinen Charakter; **to see sb/sth in a different ~** jdn/etw in einem anderen Licht sehen; **it showed him in a different ~** es zeigte ihn in einem anderen Licht; **I don't see things in that ~** ich sehe die Dinge anders *or* in einem anderen Licht; **to see sth in a new ~** etw mit anderen Augen betrachten; **in the ~ of** angesichts *(+gen)*; **the theory, seen in the ~ of recent discoveries** die Theorie im Licht(e) der neuesten Entdeckungen betrachtet; **in the ~ of what you say** in Anbetracht dessen, was Sie sagen; **to bring sth to ~** etw ans Tageslicht bringen; **to come to ~** ans Tageslicht kommen; **to see the ~** *(liter) (= be born)* das Licht der Welt erblicken *(liter)*; *(= be made public)* veröffentlicht werden; **finally I saw the ~** *(inf)* endlich ging mir ein Licht auf *(inf)*; *(morally)* endlich wurden mir die Augen geöffnet; **to see the ~ of day** *(report)* veröffentlicht werden; *(project)* verwirklicht werden; **the ~ dawned** *(fig)* mir ging ein Licht auf *(inf)*; **to go out like a ~** sofort weg sein *(inf)*
b Licht *nt*; *(= lamp)* Lampe *f*; *(= fluorescent light)* Neonröhre *f*; **put out the ~s before you go to bed** mach das Licht aus, bevor du ins Bett gehst; **all the ~s went out during the storm** während des Sturms gingen alle Lichter aus; **(traffic) ~s** Ampel *f*; **the ~s** *(of a car)* die Beleuchtung; **all ships must show a ~ while at sea** alle Schiffe müssen auf See Lichter führen; **~s out** *(Mil)* Zapfenstreich *m*; **~s out for the boys was at 8 pm** um 20 Uhr mussten die Jungen das Licht ausmachen; **~s out!** Licht aus(machen)!; **to hide one's ~ under a bushel** *(prov)* sein Licht unter den Scheffel stellen *(prov)*; **the ~s are on but nobody's (at) home** *(fig inf)* er/sie ist geistig weggetreten *(inf)*
c *(= flame)* **have you (got) a ~?** haben Sie Feuer?; **to put a ~ to sth, to set ~ to sth** etw anzünden
d *(Archit)* (Dach)fenster *nt*; *(= skylight)* Oberlicht *nt*; **leaded ~s** in Blei gefasste Fensterscheiben
e *(in eyes)* Leuchten *nt*; **the ~ went out of her eyes** das Strahlen erlosch in ihren Augen
f *(= standards)* **according to his ~s** nach bestem Wissen und Gewissen
ADJ *(+er)* hell; **a ~ green dress** ein hellgrünes Kleid; **it's getting** *or* **growing ~** es wird hell; **it is ~ now** es ist jetzt hell *or* Tag
VT **a** *(= illuminate)* beleuchten; *lamp, light* anmachen; **a smile lit her face** ein Lächeln erhellte ihr Gesicht; **to ~ the way for sb** jdm leuchten; *(fig)* jdm den Weg weisen; **his pioneering work lit the way for a whole generation of scholars** seine Pionierarbeit war wegweisend für eine ganze Gelehrtengeneration
b *(= ignite)* anzünden; *cigarette* anstecken, anzünden; *fire, candle* anzünden, anmachen; **to ~ a fire under sb** *(esp US fig)* jdm Feuer unter dem Hintern machen *(inf)*
VI *(= begin to burn)* brennen; **this fire won't ~** das Feuer geht nicht an

▶ **light up** **VI** **a** *(= be lit)* aufleuchten; **the shop signs light up after dark** die Leuchtreklamen werden nach Einbruch der Dunkelheit eingeschaltet; **the room suddenly lit up** plötzlich ging das Licht im Zimmer an
b *(face)* sich erhellen; *(eyes)* aufleuchten; **his face lit up with joy** sein Gesicht strahlte vor Freude
c *(= start to smoke)* **the men took out their pipes and lit up** die Männer holten ihre Pfeifen hervor und zündeten sie an
VT *sep* **a** *(= illuminate)* beleuchten; *lights* anmachen; **a smile lit up his face** ein Lächeln erhellte sein Gesicht; **Piccadilly Circus was all lit up** der Piccadilly Circus war hell erleuchtet; **flames lit up the night sky** Flammen erleuchteten den Nachthimmel
b *cigarette etc* anzünden
c *(fig inf)* **to be lit up** angesäuselt sein *(inf)*

light² **ADJ** *(+er)* leicht; *taxes* niedrig; *punishment* milde; **to give sb ~ weight** jdm zu wenig abwiegen; **she has a very ~ touch on the piano** sie hat einen sehr weichen Anschlag; **to be a ~ eater** wenig essen, kein großer Esser sein; **~ comedy** Lustspiel *nt*, Schwank *m*; **~ opera** Operette *f*; **~ reading** Unterhaltungslektüre *f*; **a ~ and cheerful approach to life** eine unbeschwerte, fröhliche Einstellung zum Leben; **with a ~ heart** leichten Herzens; **as ~ as air** *or* **a feather** federleicht; **a bit ~ in the head** *(= crazy)* nicht ganz richtig im Kopf; *(= tipsy)* angeheitert; *(= dizzy)* benommen; **to be ~ on one's feet** sich leichtfüßig bewegen; **to make ~ of one's difficulties** seine Schwierigkeiten auf die leichte Schulter nehmen; **you shouldn't make ~ of her problems** du solltest dich über ihre Probleme nicht lustig machen; **to make ~ work of** spielend fertig werden mit
ADV **to travel ~** mit wenig *or* leichtem Gepäck reisen

light³ VI *pret, ptp* **lighted** *or* **lit** *(liter)* sich niederlassen

▶ **light (up)on** VI *+prep obj (inf)* entdecken, stoßen auf *(+acc)*

light: **light barrier** N Lichtschranke *f*; **light bulb** N Glühlampe *or* -birne *f*; **light-coloured**, *(US)* **light-colored** ADJ *comp* **lighter-colo(u)red**, *superl* **lightest-colo(u)red** hell; **light cream** N *(US)* = **single cream**; **light-emitting diode** N Leuchtdiode *f*

lighten¹ [ˈlaɪtn] **VT** erhellen; *colour, hair* aufhellen; *gloom* aufheitern **VI** hell werden, sich aufhellen; *(mood)* sich heben; *(atmosphere)* sich entspannen; **to thunder and ~** *(Met)* donnern und blitzen

lighten² **VT** *load* leichter machen; **to ~ a ship's cargo** ein Schiff leichtern; **to ~ sb's burden** *or* **load** *(fig)* jds Lage erleichtern; **to ~ sb's workload** jdm etwas Arbeit abnehmen; **the good news ~ed her heart** die gute Nachricht machte ihr das Herz leichter **VI** *(load)* leichter werden; **her heart ~ed** ihr wurde leichter ums Herz

▶ **lighten up** VI *(inf)* die Dinge leichter nehmen; **lighten up!** nimms leicht!

lighter¹ [ˈlaɪtəʳ] N Feuerzeug *nt*

lighter² N *(Naut)* Leichter *m*

lighter fuel N Feuerzeugbenzin *nt*

light: **lightfast** [ˈlaɪtfɑːst] ADJ lichtecht; **light-fingered** [ˌlaɪtˈfɪŋɡəd] ADJ *comp* **lighter-fingered**, *superl* **lightest-fingered** langfingerig; **light fitting, light fixture** N *(= lightbulb holder)* Fassung *f*; *(= bracket)* (Lampen)halterung *f*; **light-footed** ADJ *comp* **lighter-footed**, *superl* **lightest-footed** leichtfüßig; **light-haired** ADJ *comp* **lighter-haired**, *superl* **lightest-haired** hellhaarig; *animals also* mit hellem Fell; **light-handed** ADJ, **light-handedly** ADV geschickt; **light-headed** ADJ *comp* **lighter-headed**, *superl* **lightest-headed** benebelt *(inf)*; *(= dizzy also)* benommen; *(= tipsy also)* angeheitert; *(with fever)* wirr (im Kopf); *(= frivolous)* oberflächlich, leichtfertig; **I felt quite ~ when I heard I'd passed the exam** ich wurde ganz ausgelassen *or* übermütig, als ich hörte, dass ich die Prüfung bestanden hatte; **wine makes me ~** Wein steigt mir in den Kopf; **light-headedness** N benebelter Zustand; *(= dizziness)* Benommenheit *f*; *(= tipsy state)* angeheiterter Zustand; *(with fever)* Verwirrtsein *nt*; *(= frivolity)* Oberflächlichkeit *f*, Leichtfertigkeit *f*; *(= elation)* Ausgelassenheit *f*, Übermut *m*; **light-hearted** ADJ unbeschwert, unbekümmert; *chat* zwanglos; *reply* scherzhaft; *book, film* fröhlich, vergnüglich; *look at life* heiter, unbekümmert; *comedy* leicht; **light-heartedly** ADV unbekümmert, leichten Herzens; *(= jokingly) reply* scherzhaft; **light-heartedness** N Unbeschwertheit *f*, Unbekümmertheit *f*;; *(of chat)* Zwanglosigkeit *f*; *(of reply)* Scherzhaftigkeit *f*; *(of book, film)* Fröhlichkeit, Vergnüglichkeit *f*; *(= amusing nature)* Heiterkeit *f*; **light heavyweight** N Halbschwergewicht *nt*; *(= person)* Halbschwergewichtler(in) *m(f)*; **lighthouse** N Leuchtturm *m*; **lighthouse keeper** N Leuchtturmwärter(in) *m(f)*

lighting [ˈlaɪtɪŋ] N Beleuchtung *f*

lighting-up time [ˌlaɪtɪŋˈʌptaɪm] N *Zeitpunkt, zu dem Straßen- und Fahrzeugbeleuchtung eingeschaltet werden muss*; **when is ~?** wann wird die Beleuchtung angemacht?

lightish [ˈlaɪtɪʃ] ADJ *colour* hell; **a ~ brown** ein helleres Braun

lightless [ˈlaɪtlɪs] ADJ dunkel, lichtlos

light lorry N Kleinlastwagen *m*

lightly [ˈlaɪtlɪ] ADV **a** *touch, rain, eat, wounded, armed, stressed* leicht; *walk, tread* leise; **to sleep ~** einen leichten Schlaf haben; **~ clad (in sth)** leicht (mit etw) bekleidet; **they are ~ taxed** sie haben niedrige Steuern; **to get off ~** glimpflich davonkommen; **to touch ~ on a subject** ein Thema nur berühren *or* streifen
b *(= casually) say* leichthin; **to speak ~ of sb/sth** sich abfällig *or* geringschätzig über jdn/etw äußern; **he spoke ~ of his illness** er nahm seine Krankheit auf die leichte Schulter; **don't take her problems so ~** nimm ihre Probleme etwas ernster; **to treat sth too ~** etw nicht ernst genug nehmen; **she referred ~ to the fact that ...** sie erwähnte leichthin, dass ...; **a responsibility not to be ~ undertaken** eine Verantwortung, die man nicht unüberlegt auf sich nehmen sollte; **it's not a job I'd ~ do again** die Arbeit würde ich so leicht nicht wieder tun

light: **light meter** N Belichtungsmesser *m*; **light-minded** ADJ oberflächlich, leichtfertig

lightness¹ [ˈlaɪtnɪs] N Helligkeit *f*

lightness² N **a** geringes Gewicht, Leichtheit *f*; *(of task, step, movements)* Leichtigkeit *f*; *(of taxes)* Niedrigkeit *f*; *(of punishment)* Milde *f*; *(of soil,* *cake)* Lockerheit *f*; **~ of touch** *(of pianist)* weicher *or* leichter Anschlag; **the ~ of the breeze/music** die leichte Brise/Musik; **a feeling of ~ came over him** ein Gefühl der Erleichterung überkam ihn **b** *(= lack of seriousness)* mangelnder Ernst; **a certain ~ in your attitude toward(s) the authorities** eine gewisse Leichtfertigkeit den Behörden gegenüber

lightning [ˈlaɪtnɪŋ] **N** Blitz *m*; **a flash of ~** ein Blitz *m*; *(doing damage)* ein Blitzschlag *m*; **struck by ~** vom Blitz getroffen; **what causes ~?** wie entstehen Blitze?; **we had some ~ an hour ago** vor einer Stunde hat es geblitzt; **as quick as ~, like (greased) ~** wie der Blitz, wie ein geölter Blitz; **~ never strikes twice in the same place** *(lit, fig)* der Blitz schlägt nie zweimal am gleichen Ort ein **ATTR** blitzschnell, Blitz-; **~ attack** Überraschungs- *or* Blitzangriff *m*; **~ strike** spontaner Streik; **with ~ speed** blitzschnell, mit Blitzesschnelle; **~ visit** Blitzbesuch *m*

lightning conductor, *(US)* **lightning rod** **N** Blitzableiter *m*; **he is a lightning rod for controversy** *(US fig)* er gibt immer Anlass zu Kontroversen

light: **light pen** **N** *(Comput)* Lichtgriffel *m*, Lichtstift *m*; **light pollution** **N** **a** *(in a city)* Lichtüberflutung *f* **b** *(Astrol)* Lichtverschmutzung *f*; **lightproof** **ADJ** lichtundurchlässig; **light railway** **N** Leichteisenbahn *f*; **Docklands Light Railway** *Schnellbahn in den Londoner Docklands*

lights [laɪts] **PL** *(Anat)* Tierlunge *f*

light: **lightship** **N** Feuerschiff *nt*; **light show** **N** Lightshow *f*; **light signal** **N** Leuchtzeichen *nt*, Lichtsignal *nt*; **light-skinned** **ADJ** *comp* **lighter-skinned**, *superl* **lightest-skinned** hellhäutig; **lights out** **N** **~ is at 10 p.m.** um 10 Uhr heißt es „Licht aus"; **light switch** **N** Lichtschalter *m*; **light water reactor** **N** Leichtwasserreaktor *m*; **light wave** **N** (Licht)welle *f*; **lightweight** **ADJ** leicht; *(fig)* schwach; **~ boxer** Leichtgewichtsboxer(in) *m(f)*; **the ~ boxing championship** die Boxmeisterschaft im Leichtgewicht **N** Leichtgewicht *nt*; *(= person)* Leichtgewichtler(in) *m(f)*; *(fig)* Leichtgewicht *nt*; **he is regarded as a ~ in academic circles** er wird in akademischen Kreisen nicht für voll genommen; **light year** **N** Lichtjahr *nt*; **to be ~s ahead of sb** jdm um Lichtjahre voraus sein

ligneous [ˈlɪgnɪəs] **ADJ** hölzern, holzartig

lignite [ˈlɪgnaɪt] **N** Lignit *m*

likable **ADJ** = **likeable**

like[1] [laɪk] ✪ 5.1, 17.2 **ADJ** **a** *(= similar)* ähnlich; **the two boys are very ~** die beiden Jungen sind sich *(dat)* sehr ähnlich
b *(= same)* **of ~ origin** gleicher Herkunft
PREP wie; **to be ~ sb** jdm ähnlich sein; **they are very ~ each other** sie sind sich *(dat)* sehr ähnlich; **to look ~ sb** jdm ähnlich sehen; **who(m) is he ~?** wem sieht er ähnlich?, wem gleicht er?; **what's he ~?** wie ist er?; **he's just bought a new car - what is it ~?** er hat sich gerade ein neues Auto gekauft - wie sieht es aus?; **what's your new coat ~?** wie sieht dein neuer Mantel aus?; **she was ~ a sister to me** sie war wie eine Schwester zu mir; **that's just ~ him!** das sieht ihm ähnlich!, das ist typisch!; **it's not ~ him** es ist nicht seine Art; **I never saw anything ~ it** so (et)was habe ich noch nie gesehen; **that's just ~ a woman!** typisch Frau!; **that's more ~ it!** so ist es schon besser!; **it's on company advice - orders, more ~** *(inf)* es ist auf Anraten der Firma - besser gesagt auf Anordnung; **that hat's nothing ~ as nice as this one** der Hut ist bei Weitem nicht so hübsch wie dieser; **there's nothing ~ a nice cup of tea!** es geht nichts über eine schöne Tasse Tee!; **there's nothing ~ it** das ist einmalig; **is this what you had in mind? – it's something/nothing ~ it** hattest du dir so etwas vorgestellt? – ja, so ähnlich/nein, überhaupt nicht; **that's something ~ a steak!** das ist vielleicht ein Steak!, das nenne ich ein Steak!; **the Americans are ~ that** so sind die Amerikaner; **people ~ that** solche Leute; **a car ~ that** so ein Auto, ein solches Auto; **I found one ~ it** ich habe ein Ähnliches gefunden; **one exactly ~ it** eines, das genau gleich ist; **it will cost something ~ £10** es wird etwa *or* so ungefähr £ 10 kosten; **I was thinking of something ~ a doll** ich habe an so etwas wie eine Puppe gedacht; **that sounds ~ a good idea** das hört sich gut an; **~ a man** wie ein Mann; **~ mad** *(Brit inf)* **~ anything** *(inf)* wie verrückt *(inf) or* wild *(inf)*; **~ that** so; **it wasn't ~ that at all** so wars doch gar nicht; **he thinks ~ us** er denkt wie wir; **A, ~ B, thinks that ...** A wie (auch) B meinen, dass ...
ADV *(inf)* **it's nothing ~** es ist nichts dergleichen; **(as) ~ as not, very ~, ~ enough** höchstwahrscheinlich, sehr wahrscheinlich; **I found this money, ~** *(dial)* ich hab da das Geld gefunden, nich *(sl) or* wa *(dial) or* gell *(S Ger)*
CONJ *(strictly incorrect)* **~ I said** wie ich schon sagte, wie gesagt; **it's just ~ I say** das sage ich ja immer; **~ we used to (do)** wie früher; **do it ~ I do** mach es so wie ich
N *(= equal etc)* **we shall not see his ~ again** einen Mann *or* so etwas *(inf)* wie ihn bekommen wir nicht wieder; **did you ever see the ~?** *(inf)* hast du so was schon gesehen?; **and the ~, and such ~** und dergleichen; **the ~(s) of which** dergleichen; **I've met the ~s of you before** solche wie dich kenne ich schon; **I've no time for the ~s of him** *(inf)* mit solchen Leuten gebe ich mich nicht ab *(inf)*; **~ attracts ~** Gleich und Gleich gesellt sich gern *(prov)*

like[2] ✪ 3.1, 3.3, 7.2, 7.3, 7.4, 8.4, 13, 25.2 **N** *usu pl (= taste)* Geschmack *m*; **she tried to find out his ~s and dislikes** sie wollte herausbekommen, was er mochte und was nicht; **when it comes to food he has far too many ~s and dislikes** beim Essen ist er viel zu wählerisch
VT **a** *person* mögen, gernhaben; **don't you ~ me a little bit?** magst du mich nicht ein kleines bisschen?; **how do you ~ him?** wie gefällt er dir?; **I don't ~ him** ich kann ihn nicht leiden, ich mag ihn nicht; **he is well ~d here** er ist hier sehr beliebt
b *(= find pleasure in)* **I ~ black shoes** ich mag schwarze Schuhe, mir gefallen schwarze Schuhe; **I ~ it** das gefällt mir; **I ~ chocolate** ich mag Schokolade, ich esse gern Schokolade; **I ~ football** *(= playing)* ich spiele gerne Fußball; *(= watching)* ich finde Fußball gut; **I ~ dancing** ich tanze gern; **I ~ this translation** ich finde diese Übersetzung gut; **we ~ it here** es gefällt uns hier; **that's one of the things I ~ about you** das ist eines der Dinge, die ich an dir mag; **how do you ~ your coffee?** wie trinken Sie Ihren Kaffee?; **I ~ wine but wine doesn't ~ me** *(inf)* ich trinke gern Wein, aber er bekommt mir nicht; **how do you ~ Cádiz?** wie gefällt Ihnen Cádiz?; **how would you ~ to go for a walk?** was hältst du von einem Spaziergang?; **how would you ~ a black eye?** du willst dir wohl ein blaues Auge holen!; **your father won't ~ it** deinem Vater wird das nicht gefallen; **well, I ~ that!** *(inf)* das ist ein starkes Stück! *(inf)*; **(well) how do you ~ that?** *(inf)* wie findest du denn das? *(inf)*
c *(= wish, wish for)* **I'd ~ an explanation** ich hätte gerne eine Erklärung; **I should ~ more time** ich würde mir gerne noch etwas Zeit lassen; **they would have ~d to come** sie wären gern gekommen; **I should ~ to know why** ich wüsste (gerne), warum; **I should ~ you to do it** ich möchte, dass du es tust; **I ~ to be obeyed** ich erwarte Gehorsam; **whether he ~s it or not** ob es ihm passt oder nicht, ob er will oder nicht; **I didn't ~ to disturb him** ich wollte ihn nicht stören; **what would you ~?** was hätten *or* möchten Sie gern?, was darf es sein?; **would you ~ a drink?** möchten Sie etwas trinken?; **would you ~ to go to Seville?** würden Sie gern nach Sevilla fahren?; **I would ~ to take this opportunity to welcome Dr Allan** ich möchte diese Gelegenheit ergreifen, um Dr. Allan willkommen zu heißen
VI **he is free to act as he ~s** es steht ihm frei, zu tun, was er will; **as you ~** wie Sie wollen; **if you ~** wenn Sie wollen

-like **ADJ** *suf* -ähnlich, -artig; **cement-like** zementartig *or* -ähnlich

likeable *(Brit)*, **likable** [ˈlaɪkəbl] **ADJ** sympathisch, liebenswert

likeableness *(Brit)*, **likableness** [ˈlaɪkəblnɪs] **N** liebenswertes Wesen; **there's a certain lik(e)ableness about him** er hat etwas Sympathisches *or* Liebenswertes an sich

likelihood [ˈlaɪklɪhʊd] **N** Wahrscheinlichkeit *f*; **in all ~** aller Wahrscheinlichkeit nach; **the ~ is that ...** es ist wahrscheinlich, dass ...; **there is no ~ of that** das ist nicht wahrscheinlich; **there is little/every ~ that ...** es ist kaum/durchaus anzunehmen, dass ...; **is there any ~ of him coming?** besteht die Möglichkeit, dass er kommt?; **what's the ~ of their getting married?** wie wahrscheinlich ist es *or* wie groß ist die Wahrscheinlichkeit, dass die beiden heiraten?; **what's the ~ of you coming out with me tonight?** wie sind die Chancen, dass du heute Abend mit mir ausgehst?

likely [ˈlaɪklɪ] **ADJ** *(+er)* **a** *(= probable)* wahrscheinlich; **he is not ~ to come** es ist unwahrscheinlich, dass er kommt; **they are ~ to accept/refuse** sie werden wahrscheinlich zusagen/ablehnen; **she is hardly ~ to come now** sie wird jetzt kaum kommen; **is it ~ that I would do that?** trauen Sie mir das zu?; **the plan most ~ to succeed** der erfolgversprechendste Plan; **an incident ~ to cause trouble** ein Zwischenfall, der möglicherweise Ärger nach sich zieht; **a ~ explanation** eine mögliche *or* wahrscheinliche Erklärung; *(iro)* wers glaubt, wird selig! *(inf)*; **this is a ~ place for him to stay** es ist gut möglich, dass er sich hier aufhält; **a ~ story** *or* **tale!** *(iro)* das soll mal einer glauben!
b *(inf: = suitable)* geeignet; **a ~ spot for a picnic** ein geeignetes *or* prima *(inf)* Plätzchen für ein Picknick; **he is a ~ person for the job** er kommt für die Stelle infrage *or* in Frage; **~ candidates** aussichtsreiche Kandidaten; **a ~(-looking) lad** ein vielversprechender junger Mann; **a ~-looking target** ein geeignetes Ziel
ADV wahrscheinlich; **as ~ as not** höchstwahrscheinlich; **very ~ they've lost it** höchstwahrscheinlich haben sie es verloren; **they'll ~ be late** *(dial)* sie kommen wahrscheinlich zu spät; **it's more ~ to be early than late** es wird eher früh als spät werden; **not ~!** *(inf iro)* wohl kaum *(inf)*

like-minded [ˈlaɪkˈmaɪndɪd] **ADJ** gleich gesinnt; **~ people** Gleichgesinnte *pl*

liken [ˈlaɪkən] **VT** vergleichen *(to* mit)

like-named [ˈlaɪkˈneɪmd] **ADJ** gleichnamig

likeness [ˈlaɪknɪs] ✪ 5.5 **N** *(= resemblance)* Ähnlichkeit *f*; *(= portrait)* Bild(nis) *nt*; **to have a ~ to sb/one another** jdm/einander ähnlich sehen; **the ghost appeared in the ~ of a monk** der Geist erschien in der Gestalt eines Mönchs; **the god took on the ~ of a bull** der Gott nahm die Form eines Stiers an; **the painting is a good ~ of him** er ist auf dem Gemälde gut getroffen

likewise [ˈlaɪkwaɪz] **ADV** ebenso, gleichermaßen; **he did ~** er machte es ebenso, er tat das Gleiche; **in Italy there is a national dish, ~ in France** in Italien gibt es, ebenso wie in Frankreich, ein Nationalgericht; **my wife is well, the children ~** meiner Frau geht es gut und den Kindern auch; **have a nice weekend – ~** schönes Wochenende! – danke gleichfalls!; **I'm going to the cinema tonight – ~** ich gehe heute Abend ins Kino – ich auch

liking [ˈlaɪkɪŋ] **N** **a** *(for particular person)* Zuneigung *f*; *(for types)* Vorliebe *f*; **to have a ~ for sb** Zuneigung für jdn empfinden, jdn gernhaben; **she took a ~ to him** sie mochte ihn (gut leiden), er war ihr sympathisch **b** *(for thing)* Vorliebe *f*; **to have a ~ for sth** eine Vorliebe für etw haben; **to take a ~ to sth** eine Vorliebe für etw bekommen; **to be to sb's ~** nach jds Geschmack sein; **she asks too many questions for my ~** für meinen Geschmack stellt sie zu viele Fragen

lilac ['laɪlək] **N** **a** *(= plant)* Flieder *m* **b** *(= colour)* (Zart)lila *nt* **ADJ** fliederfarben, (zart)lila

Lilliput ['lɪlɪpət] **N** Liliput *nt*

Lilliputian [ˌlɪlɪ'pju:ʃɪən] **ADJ** winzig, liliputanerhaft **N** Liliputaner(in) *m(f)*

Lilo® ['laɪˌləʊ] **N** *(Brit)* Luftmatratze *f*

lilt [lɪlt] **N** **a** *(of song)* munterer Rhythmus; *(of voice)* singender Tonfall; **she spoke with a Welsh ~** sie sprach mit dem singenden Tonfall der Waliser **b** *(= song)* fröhliches *or* munteres Lied **VT** *song* trällern **VI** **I love the way her voice ~s** ich mag ihren singenden Tonfall; **the tune ~s merrily along** die Melodie plätschert munter dahin

lilting ['lɪltɪŋ] **ADJ** *accent* singend; *ballad, tune, melody* beschwingt, munter

liltingly ['lɪltɪŋlɪ] **ADV** *sing, play* mit beschwingtem Rhythmus

lily ['lɪlɪ] **N** Lilie *f*; *(= water lily)* Seerose *f*; **~ of the valley** Maiglöckchen *nt*

lily: **lily-livered** ['lɪlɪˌlɪvəd] **ADJ** feige; **lily pad** **N** Seerosenblatt *nt*; **lily-white** **ADJ** **a** schnee- *or* blütenweiß; *(fig)* tugendhaft **b** *(US inf: racially) club, suburb* streng weiß

limb [lɪm] **N** **a** *(Anat)* Glied *nt*; **~s** *pl* Glieder *pl*, Gliedmaßen *pl*; **the lower ~s** die unteren Gliedmaßen; **to rest one's tired ~s** seine müden Glieder *or* Knochen *(inf)* ausruhen; **to tear sb ~ from ~** jdn in Stücke reißen; **to risk life and ~** Leib und Leben riskieren *or* aufs Spiel setzen **b** *(of tree)* Ast *m*; **to be out on a ~** *(fig)* exponiert sein; **to go out on a ~** *(fig)* sich exponieren; **John's ideas put him out on a ~** John steht mit seinen Ideen allein auf weiter Flur; **he had left himself out on a ~** er hatte sich in eine prekäre Lage gebracht **c** *(of cross)* Balken *m*; *(of organization etc)* Glied *nt*

-limbed [-lɪmd] **ADJ** *suf* -gliedrig; **short-/long--limbed** kurz-/langgliedrig

limber[1] ['lɪmbə'] **N** *(Mil)* Protze *f*

limber[2] **ADJ** beweglich, gelenkig

▶ **limber up** **VI** Lockerungsübungen machen; *(fig)* sich vorbereiten; **limber up with a few easy exercises** machen Sie sich mit ein paar einfachen Übungen warm

limbless ['lɪmlɪs] **ADJ** *tree* astlos; **a ~ person** *(= with no limbs)* ein Mensch *m* ohne Gliedmaßen

limbo[1] ['lɪmbəʊ] **N** **a** *(Rel)* Vorhölle *f*, Limbus *m (spec)* **b** *(fig)* Übergangs- *or* Zwischenstadium *nt*; **our expansion plans are in ~ because of lack of money** unsere Erweiterungspläne sind wegen Geldmangels in der Schwebe; **I'm in a sort of ~** ich hänge in der Luft *(inf)*

limbo[2] **N** *(= dance)* Limbo *m*

lime[1] [laɪm] **N** **a** *(Geol)* Kalk *m* **b** *(= bird lime)* (Vogel)leim *m* **VT** mit Kalk düngen

lime[2] **N** *(Bot: = linden, also* **lime tree***)* Linde(nbaum *m*) *f*

lime[3] **N** *(Bot: = citrus fruit)* Limone(lle) *f*; *(= tree)* Limonenbaum *m* **ADJ** *(colour)* hellgrün

lime: **lime-green** ['laɪmgri:n] **ADJ** hellgrün; **lime juice** **N** Limonensaft *m*; **limekiln** **N** Kalkofen *m*

limelight ['laɪmlaɪt] **N** Rampenlicht *nt*; **to be in the ~** im Rampenlicht *or* im Licht der Öffentlichkeit stehen; **he never sought the ~** er stand nie gern im Rampenlicht *or* im Licht der Öffentlichkeit

limerick ['lɪmərɪk] **N** Limerick *m*

> **LIMERICK**
>
> Ein **limerick** ist ein kurzes komisches Gedicht in fünf Zeilen, in dem das Reimschema „aabba" verwendet wird. Es handelt normalerweise von einer bestimmten Person, und die Aussage ist oft surreal oder vulgär. **Limericks** beginnen häufig mit „There was a ...". Auf zwei längere Zeilen folgen dann zwei kürzere. Das Ganze endet mit einer Pointe, wobei der letzte Reim nicht unbedingt lupenrein sein muss.

limestone ['laɪmstəʊn] **N** Kalkstein *m*

limewash ['laɪmwɒʃ] **VT** kalken, weißen, tünchen **N** (Kalk)tünche *f*

limey ['laɪmɪ] **N** *(dated US inf)* Engländer(in) *m(f)*

limit ['lɪmɪt] **N** **a** Grenze *f*; *(= limitation)* Beschränkung *f*, Begrenzung *f*; *(= speed limit)* Geschwindigkeitsbegrenzung *f*; *(Comm)* Limit *nt*; **the city ~s** die Stadtgrenzen *pl*; **a 40-mile ~** eine Vierzigmeilengrenze; **the 50 km/h ~** die Geschwindigkeitsbegrenzung von 50 Stundenkilometern; **is there any ~ on the size?** gibt es irgendwelche Größenbeschränkungen?, ist die Größe begrenzt *or* beschränkt?; **to put a ~ on sth, to set a ~ to** *or* **on sth** etw begrenzen, etw beschränken; **that's beyond my financial ~s** das übersteigt meine finanziellen Möglichkeiten; **I am at the ~ of my patience** meine Geduld ist am Ende; **we're constantly working at the ~s of our abilities** unsere Arbeit bringt uns ständig an die Grenzen unserer Leistungsfähigkeit; **there's a ~!** alles hat seine Grenzen!; **there is a ~ to what one person can do** ein Mensch kann nur so viel tun und nicht mehr; **there's a ~ to the time you should spend** Sie sollten nicht allzu viel Zeit darauf verwenden; **there is no ~ to his stupidity** seine Dummheit kennt keine Grenzen; **there's a ~ to the amount of money we can spend** unseren Ausgaben sind Grenzen gesetzt, wir können nicht unbegrenzt Geld ausgeben; **there are ~s!** es gibt (schließlich) Grenzen!; **it is true within ~s** es ist bis zu einem gewissen Grade richtig; **I'll tell you what I can, within ~s** ich sage Ihnen, was ich kann, innerhalb gewisser Grenzen; **without ~s** unbegrenzt, unbeschränkt; **off ~s to military personnel** Zutritt für Militär verboten, für Militär gesperrt; **smoking is off ~s** Rauchen ist nicht erlaubt; **to know no ~s** keine Grenzen kennen; **over the ~** zu viel; *(in time)* zu lange; **you are** *or* **your baggage is over the ~** Ihr Gepäck hat Übergewicht; **you shouldn't drive, you're over the ~** du solltest dich nicht ans Steuer setzen, du hast zu viel getrunken; **he was three times over the ~** er hatte dreimal so viel Promille wie gesetzlich erlaubt; **he had more than the legal ~ (of alcohol) in his blood** er hatte mehr Promille als gesetzlich erlaubt; **top C is my ~** höher als bis zum hohen C komme ich nicht; **I'll offer £400, that's my ~** ich biete £ 400, das ist mein Limit *or* höher kann ich nicht gehen; **50 pages per week is my ~** 50 Seiten pro Woche sind mein Limit **b** *(inf)* **that's (just) the ~!** das ist die Höhe *(inf) or* das Letzte *(inf)*; **that child is the ~!** dieses Kind ist eine Zumutung! *(inf)*; **he's the ~!, isn't he the ~?** das ist 'ne Type! *(inf)* **VT** begrenzen, beschränken; *freedom, spending, possibilities* einschränken; *imagination* hemmen; **to ~ sb/sth to sth** jdn/etw auf etw *(acc)* beschränken; **to ~ oneself to a few remarks** sich auf einige (wenige) Bemerkungen beschränken; **time is the ~ing factor** wir sind zeitlich gebunden; **what are the ~ing factors?** wodurch sind uns *(dat)* Grenzen gesetzt?

limitation [ˌlɪmɪ'teɪʃən] **N** Beschränkung *f*; *(of freedom, spending)* Einschränkung *f*; **damage ~** Schadensbegrenzung *f*; **poor education is a great ~** eine schlechte Schulbildung ist ein großes Handicap; **there is no ~ on exports of coal** es gibt keine Beschränkungen für den Kohleexport; **the ~s of a bilingual dictionary** die beschränkten Möglichkeiten eines zweisprachigen Wörterbuchs; **to have one's/its ~s** seine Grenzen haben

limited ['lɪmɪtɪd] **ADJ** **a** *improvement, number, amount, resources, range* begrenzt, beschränkt; *intelligence, knowledge also* mäßig; *person* beschränkt; **this offer is for a ~ period only** dieses Angebot ist (zeitlich) befristet *or* gilt nur für kurze Zeit; **in a more ~ sense** in engerem Sinn; **this is only true in a ~ sense** *or* **to a ~ extent** dies ist nur in gewissem Maße wahr; **he can only get about/look after himself to a ~ extent** er kann sich nur eingeschränkt bewegen/sich nur teilweise selber versorgen; **they are getting together again to a ~ extent** sie haben sich bis zu einem gewissen Punkt versöhnt **b** *(esp Brit Comm) liability, right, authority* beschränkt; **ABC Travel Limited** ≈ ABC-Reisen GmbH

limited: **limited company** **N** *(esp Brit Comm)* ≈ Gesellschaft *f* mit beschränkter Haftung; **limited edition** **N** limitierte Auflage; *(of car)* limitierte Serie; **limited liability company** **N** *(esp Brit Comm)* = **limited company**; **limited parking zone** **N** Kurzparkzone *f*; **limited partner** **N** *(esp Brit Comm)* Kommanditist(in) *m(f)*; **limited partnership** **N** *(esp Brit Comm)* ≈ Kommanditgesellschaft *f*

limiter ['lɪmɪtə'] **N** **a** *(= limitation)* einschränkender Faktor **b** *(Elec)* (Amplituden)begrenzer *m*

limitless ['lɪmɪtlɪs] **ADJ** grenzenlos

limo ['lɪməʊ] **N** *(inf: = limousine)* Limousine *f*

limousine ['lɪməzi:n] **N** Limousine *f*

limp[1] [lɪmp] **N** Hinken *nt*, Humpeln *nt*; **to walk with a ~** hinken, humpeln; **the accident left him with a ~** seit dem Unfall hinkt er; **he has a bad ~** er hinkt *or* humpelt sehr stark **VI** hinken, humpeln; **the ship managed to ~ into port** das Schiff kam gerade noch *or* mit Müh und Not in den Hafen

limp[2] **ADJ** *(+er)* schlapp, schlaff; *handshake* schlaff; *flowers* welk; *material, cloth* weich; *voice* matt, müde; *(= effeminate)* süßlich; **to hang ~** *(arms, flag)* schlaff herunterhängen; **he's a ~ sort of character** er hat einen schwachen Charakter; **let your body go ~** alle Muskeln entspannen, alles locker lassen

limpet ['lɪmpɪt] **N** Napfschnecke *f*; **to stick to sb like a ~** *(inf)* wie eine Klette an jdm hängen

limpet mine **N** Haftmine *f*

limpid ['lɪmpɪd] **ADJ** klar; *liquid also* durchsichtig; *style* klar

limply ['lɪmplɪ] **ADV** schlapp, schlaff; **~ bound in calfskin** in weiches Kalbsleder gebunden; **..., he said ~** ..., sagte er mit matter Stimme; *(= effeminately)* ..., flötete er *(inf)*

limpness ['lɪmpnɪs] **N** Schlaffheit *f*, Schlappheit *f*; *(of flower)* Welkheit *f*; *(of cloth, material)* Weichheit *f*; *(of voice)* Mattigkeit *f*

limp-wristed ['lɪmp'rɪstɪd] **ADJ** *(inf: = gay)* schwul *(inf)*, warm *(inf)*

limy ['laɪmɪ] **ADJ** *(+er)* kalkhaltig

linage ['laɪnɪdʒ] **N** *(Press)* Zeilenzahl *f*; **advertising ~** Anzeigenzeilenzahl *f*; **~ advertisement** Kleinanzeige *f*

linchpin ['lɪntʃpɪn] **N** Achs(en)nagel *m*, Lünse *f*; *(fig)* Stütze *f*; **accurate timing is the ~ of the entire operation** das ganze Unternehmen steht und fällt mit genauer Zeiteinteilung

linden ['lɪndən] **N** *(also* **linden tree***)* Linde *f*, Lindenbaum *m*

line[1] [laɪn]

✪ 27.3, 27.5, 27.7

1 NOUN	3 PHRASAL VERB
2 TRANSITIVE VERB	

1 – NOUN

a [for washing, fishing] Leine *f*

b [= mark] *on paper, on tennis court etc, on palm* Linie *f*; **drawn in a few bold lines** mit wenigen kühnen Strichen gezeichnet

c [= wrinkle] Falte *f*

d [= boundary] Grenze *f*; **the state line** die Staatsgrenze; **the snow/tree line** die Schnee-/Baumgrenze; **the line** *(= the equator)* die Linie, der Äquator; **the (fine** *or* **thin) line between right and wrong** der (feine) Unterschied zwischen Recht und Unrecht; **to draw a line between** *(fig)* einen Unterschied machen zwischen → *also* **draw**[1]

e [= shape] **the ship's graceful lines** die schnittigen Linien des Schiffes

f [= row] *of people, cars)* (*side by side* Reihe *f*; *(one behind the other)* Schlange *f*; *(of hills)* Kette *f*; *(Sport)* Linie *f*; **in (a) line** in einer Reihe; **in a straight line** geradlinig; **a line of traffic** eine Autoschlange; **a single line of traffic** einspuriger Verkehr

♦ **to be in line** *(buildings etc)* geradlinig sein; **to be in line (with)** *(fig)* in Einklang stehen (mit), übereinstimmen (mit)

♦ **to keep sb/sth in line to keep sb in line** *(fig)* dafür sorgen, dass jd nicht aus der Reihe tanzt; **to keep the party in line** die Einheit der Partei wahren

♦ **into line to bring sb/sth into line (with sth)** *(fig)* jdn/etw auf die gleiche Linie (wie etw) bringen; **it's time these rebels were brought into line** es wird Zeit, dass die Rebellen zurückgepfiffen werden; **to fall** *or* **get into line** *(= abreast)* sich in Reih und Glied aufstellen; *(= behind one another)* sich hintereinander *or* in einer Reihe aufstellen; **the policemen fell into line six abreast** die Polizisten stellten sich in Sechserreihen auf; **he refused to fall into line with the new proposals** er weigerte sich, mit den neuen Vorschlägen konform zu gehen; **it's time these rebels fell into line** es ist Zeit, dass sich diese Rebellen anpassen *or* dass diese Rebellen spuren *(inf)*; **to move into line** sich einreihen; *(fig)* sich anpassen, die gleiche Linie einschlagen

♦ **out of line to be out of line** nicht geradlinig sein; **to be out of line with sth** *(fig)* mit etw nicht übereinstimmen *or* in Einklang stehen; **to step out of line** *(lit)* aus der Reihe treten; *(fig)* aus der Reihe tanzen; **he was stepping out of line telling the director what to do** es war anmaßend von ihm, dem Direktor zu sagen, was er zu tun hätte; **if he steps out of line again** wenn er sich noch einmal etwas zuschulden *or* zu Schulden kommen lässt

g [= queue] *US* Schlange *f*; **to stand in line** Schlange stehen

h [= assembly line] Band *nt*

i [= company] *of aircraft, liners, buses* Gesellschaft *f*, Linie *f*; *(= shipping company)* Reederei *f*

j [indicating succession] **through the male line** durch die männliche Linie; **he was descended from a long line of farmers** er stammte aus einem alten Bauerngeschlecht; **it's the latest in a long line of tragedies** es ist die neueste Tragödie in einer ganzen Serie; **royal line** königliche Familie; **in an unbroken line** in ununterbrochener Folge; **to be next in line** als Nächste(r) an der Reihe sein; **John is next in line for promotion** John ist als Nächster mit der Beförderung an der Reihe; **who is fourth in line to the throne?** wer steht an vierter Stelle der Thronfolge?

k [Rail] *in general* Strecke *f*, Bahnlinie *f*; *(= section of track)* Strecke *f*; **lines** *pl* Gleise *pl*; **to reach the end of the line** *(fig)* am Ende sein

l [Telec] *= cable* Leitung *f*; **the firm has 52 lines** die Firma hat 52 Anschlüsse; **this is a very bad line** die Verbindung ist sehr schlecht; **to be on the line to sb** mit jdm telefonieren; **get off the line!** gehen Sie aus der Leitung!; **hold the line** bleiben Sie am Apparat!; **can you get me a line to Chicago?** können Sie mir eine Verbindung nach Chicago geben?; **an information line** ein Infotelefon *nt*

m [written] Zeile *f*; **lines** *(Brit Sch)* Strafarbeit *f*; **the teacher gave me 200 lines** der Lehrer ließ mich 200 mal … schreiben; **lines** *(Theat)* Text *m*; **to learn one's lines** seinen Text auswendig lernen; **I don't get any good lines in this part** der Text für diese Rolle *or* diese Partie ist sehr dürftig; **he gets all the funny lines** er bekommt immer die lustigen Stellen; **to drop sb a line** jdm ein paar Zeilen *or* Worte schreiben; **to read between the lines** zwischen den Zeilen lesen

n [= direction] **we tried a new line of approach to the problem** wir versuchten, an das Problem anders heranzugehen; **line of argument** Argumentation *f*; **line of attack** *(fig)* Taktik *f*; **what's your line of attack?** wie wollen Sie an die Sache herangehen?; **the police refused to reveal their lines of inquiry** die Polizei weigerte sich zu sagen, in welcher Richtung sie ermittelte; **line of thought** Denkrichtung *f*; **line of vision** Blickrichtung *f*; **I can't see if you stand in my line of vision** ich kann nichts sehen, wenn du mir die Sicht versperrst; **to be on the right lines** *(fig)* auf dem richtigen Weg sein, richtigliegen *(inf)*; **a possible line of development** eine mögliche Entwicklungsrichtung; **the line of least resistance** der Weg des geringsten Widerstandes

♦ **to take + line we must take a firm** *or* **strong line with these people** wir müssen diesen Leuten gegenüber sehr bestimmt auftreten; **the government will take a strong line on inflation** die Regierung wird gegen die Inflation energisch vorgehen; **he took a strong/moderate line in the discussion** er vertrat in der Diskussion einen festen/gemäßigten Standpunkt; **what sort of line do you think I should take when I see him?** wie meinen Sie, soll ich mich verhalten, wenn ich ihn sehe?; **he took the line that …** er vertrat den Standpunkt, dass …; **what line is your thesis going to take?** in welcher Richtung wollen Sie in Ihrer Doktorarbeit argumentieren?

o [Mil] **line of battle** Kampflinie *f*; **to draw up the battle lines** *or* **the lines of battle** *(fig)* (Kampf)stellung beziehen; **enemy lines** feindliche Stellungen *or* Linien *pl*; **lines of communication** Verbindungswege *pl*; **line of retreat** Rückzugslinie *f*; **to keep one's lines of retreat open** sich *(dat)* den Rückzug offenhalten; **the first line of defence** *(Brit) or* **defense** *(US) (fig)* die zuerst gebrauchte Rechtfertigung → **fire**

p [= field] Branche *f*; **what line (of work) is he in?, what's his line (of work)?** was ist er von Beruf?, was macht er beruflich?; **that's not in my line of business** damit habe ich nichts zu tun; **we're in the same line of business** wir sind in der gleichen Berufssparte *or* Branche tätig; **that's not in my line** das liegt mir nicht

q [= course] **it's all in the line of duty** das gehört zu meinen/seinen *etc* Pflichten; **some of the things you do in the line of duty** einige der dienstlichen Pflichten

r [in shop] *= item* Modell *nt*; *(= range)* Kollektion *f*; **we have a new line in spring hats** wir haben eine neue Kollektion Frühjahrshüte; **that line did not sell at all** dieses Modell ließ sich überhaupt nicht verkaufen

s [= talk] *inf* **I've heard that line before** die Platte kenn ich schon *(inf)*; **he has a good line in patter** das ist eine gute Masche, wie er die Leute anquatscht *(inf)*; **to give sb a line about sth** jdm flotte Sprüche über etw *(acc)* erzählen *(inf)*; **chat-up line** *(Brit)* Anmacherspruch *m*

t [= clue, information] **to give sb a line on sth** jdm einen Hinweis auf etw *(acc)* geben; **can you give me a line on it?** können Sie mir darüber etwas sagen?; **the police eventually managed to get a line on him** die Polizei konnte ihm schließlich etwas nachweisen; **once a journalist has got a line on a story …** wenn ein Journalist einer Geschichte erst einmal auf der Spur ist …

u [of cocaine etc] Dosis *f*, Linie *f (sl)*

v [set structures]

♦ **along the line somewhere along the line** *(= at some time)* irgendwann; *(= somewhere)* irgendwo; **all along the line** *(fig)* auf der ganzen Linie

♦ **along the lines of to be along the lines of …** ungefähr so etwas wie … sein; **the essay is written along the lines of the traditional theory** der Aufsatz ist in Richtung der herkömmlichen Lehre verfasst

♦ **along these/the same lines along these lines** ungefähr so; **something along these lines** etwas in dieser Richtung *or* Art; **the story developed along these lines** die Geschichte hat sich so *or* folgendermaßen entwickelt; **I was thinking along the same lines** ich hatte etwas Ähnliches gedacht; **to be on the same lines as** in der gleichen Richtung liegen wie

♦ **to lay it on the line** *(inf)* die Karten auf den Tisch legen *(inf)*; **they laid it on the line to the government, that …** sie erklärten der Regierung klipp und klar, dass … *(inf)*

♦ **to put one's life/job** *etc* **on the line** *(inf)* sein Leben/seine Stelle *etc* riskieren; **to put oneself on the line** sich in die Schusslinie begeben

2 – TRANSITIVE VERB

a [= cross with lines] linieren, liniieren; **worry had lined his face** sein Gesicht war von Sorgen gezeichnet

b [= border] säumen; **an avenue lined with trees** eine von Bäumen gesäumte Straße; **the streets were lined with cheering crowds** eine jubelnde Menge säumte die Straßen; **the crew lined the sides of the ship** die Mannschaft hatte sich auf beiden Seiten des Schiffes aufgestellt; **portraits lined the walls** an den Wänden hing ein Porträt neben dem andern

3 – PHRASAL VERB

► **line up** VI *(= stand in line)* sich aufstellen, antreten; *(= queue)* sich anstellen; **the teams lined up like this** die Mannschaften hatten folgende Aufstellung; **the party lined up behind/against their leader** *(fig)* die Partei stellte sich hinter/gegen ihren Vorsitzenden

VT *sep* **a** *troops, pupils, prisoners* antreten lassen; *boxes, books etc* in einer Reihe *or* nebeneinander aufstellen; **the police lined the gang up with their backs to the wall** die Polizei befahl der Bande, sich mit dem Rücken zur Wand aufzustellen; **they lined the prisoners up along the wall** die Gefangenen mussten sich an der Wand entlang aufstellen

b *(= prepare, arrange) entertainment* sorgen für, auf die Beine stellen *(inf)*; *speakers* bekommen, verpflichten; *support* mobilisieren; **what have you got lined up for me today?** was haben Sie heute für mich geplant?; **I've lined up a meeting with the directors** ich habe ein Treffen mit den Direktoren arrangiert; **I've got a meeting with John lined up for 10 o'clock** um 10 Uhr steht ein Treffen mit John auf dem Programm; **I've got a nice little date lined up for this evening** ich habe für heute Abend eine nette Verabredung arrangiert

---

line[2] VT *clothes* füttern; *pipe* auskleiden, innen beziehen; *floor of attic* auslegen; **~ the box with paper** den Karton mit Papier auskleiden *or* ausschlagen; **to ~ brakes** Bremsbeläge *pl* erneuern (lassen); **the membranes which ~ the stomach** die Schleimhäute, die den Magen auskleiden *or* innen überziehen; **to ~ one's own pockets** *(fig)* sich bereichern, in die eigene Tasche arbeiten *or* wirtschaften *(inf)*

lineage[1] ['lɪnɪɪdʒ] N *(= descent)* Abstammung *f*; *(= descendants)* Geschlecht *nt*

lineage[2] ['laɪnɪdʒ] N = **linage**

lineal ['lɪnɪəl] ADJ *descent* direkt

lineament ['lɪnɪəmənt] N *(form)* Lineament *nt (rare)*; **~s** *pl (of face)* Gesichtszüge *pl*

linear ['lɪnɪə'] ADJ **a** *(Math, Phys)* linear; *motion* linear, geradlinig; **~ foot/metre** Längenfuß *m*/-meter *m or nt* **b** *(form: = sequential) sequence, narrative, thinking* linear; *time* linear fortlaufend; *view* eindimensional

linear: **linear accelerator** N Linearbeschleuniger *m*; **Linear B** N *(Ling)* Linear B *f*; **linear equation** N *(Math)* lineare Gleichung, Gleichung *f* ersten Grades; **linear measure** N Längenmaß *nt*; **linear perspective** N Linearperspektive *f*

line: **line art** N *(Comput, Typ)* Schwarz-Weiß-Grafik *f*, einfarbige Grafik; **linebacker** N *(US Sport)* ≈ Linebacker *m*; **line break** N *(Comput, Typ)* Zeilenumbruch *m*; **line command** N *(Comput)* Zeilenbefehl *m*

lined [laɪnd] ADJ *face etc (of old people)* faltig; *(through worry, tiredness etc)* gezeichnet; *paper* liniert, liniiert; **to become ~ with age** Altersfalten bekommen

line: **line dancing** N Line-Country-Dance *m*; **line drawing** N Zeichnung *f*; **line editor** N

(Comput) Zeileneditor *m*; **line feed** N *(Comput)* Zeilenvorschub *m*; **line judge** N *(Tennis)* Linienrichter(in) *m(f)*; **line manager** N Vorgesetzte(r) *mf*

linen [ˈlɪnɪn] **N** Leinen *nt*; *(= table linen)* Tischwäsche *f*; *(= sheets, garments etc)* Wäsche *f* **ADJ** Leinen-; ~ **blouse** Leinenbluse *f*

linen closet, linen cupboard N Wäscheschrank *m*

line: **line-out** N *(Rugby)* Gasse *f*; **line printer** N *(Comput)* Zeilendrucker *m*; **line print-out** N *(Comput)* Zeilenausdruck *m*

liner [ˈlaɪnəʳ] N *(= ship)* Passagierschiff *nt*, Liniendampfer *m*; *(= plane)* Verkehrsflugzeug *nt*

liner note N *usu pl (US)* Covertext *m*

linesman [ˈlaɪnzmən] N *pl* **-men** [-mən] *(Sport)* Linienrichter *m*; *(Rail)* Streckenwärter *m*; *(Elec, Telec)* Leitungsmann *m*; *(for faults)* Störungssucher *m*

line spacing N Zeilenabstand *m*

lineswoman [ˈlaɪnzwʊmən] N *pl* **-women** [-wɪmɪn] *(Sport)* Linienrichterin *f*

line-up [ˈlaɪnʌp] N *(Sport)* Aufstellung *f*; *(= cast)* Besetzung *f*; *(= alignment)* Gruppierung *f*; *(US: = queue)* Schlange *f*; **she picked the thief out of the ~** sie erkannte den Dieb bei der Gegenüberstellung

line width N Zeilenlänge *f*

ling[1] [lɪŋ] N *(Zool)* Leng(fisch) *m*

ling[2] N *(Bot)* Heidekraut *nt*

linger [ˈlɪŋgəʳ] VI **a** *(also* **linger on)** (zurück)bleiben, verweilen *(liter)*; *(in dying)* zwischen Leben und Tod schweben; *(custom)* fortbestehen, sich halten; *(doubts, suspicions)* zurückbleiben; *(feeling, emotion, pain)* anhalten, bleiben; *(memory)* fortbestehen, bleiben; *(chords)* nachklingen; *(scent)* sich halten; **the party was over, but many of the guests ~ed in the hall** die Party war vorbei, aber viele Gäste standen noch im Flur herum; **it was incredible how Franco ~ed on** es war erstaunlich, wie Franco sich an der Macht festkkrallte
b *(= delay)* sich aufhalten, verweilen *(liter)*; **I mustn't ~ or I'll miss the bus** ich darf mich nicht lange aufhalten, sonst verpasse ich den Bus
c *(= dwell)* **to ~ on a subject** bei einem Thema verweilen *(geh)*; **I let my eyes ~ on the scene** ich ließ meinen Blick auf der Szene ruhen; **to ~ over a meal** sich *(dat)* bei einer Mahlzeit Zeit lassen, sich bei einer Mahlzeit lange aufhalten; **we ~ed over a glass of wine** wir tranken gemächlich ein Glas Wein

lingerie [ˈlænʒəriː] N (Damen)unterwäsche *f*

lingering [ˈlɪŋgərɪŋ] ADJ lang, ausgedehnt; *death* langsam; *illness* langwierig, schleppend; *doubt* zurückbleibend; *look* sehnsüchtig; *chords* lange (nach)klingend; *kiss* innig; **the lovers took a ~ farewell of each other** der Abschied der Liebenden wollte kein Ende nehmen; **I've still got one ~ doubt** es bleibt noch ein Zweifel (zurück); **the customs officer gave him a long ~ look** der Zollbeamte sah ihn lange prüfend an

lingo [ˈlɪŋgəʊ] N *(inf)* Sprache *f*; *(= specialist jargon)* Jargon *m*, Kauderwelsch *nt (inf)*; **I don't speak the ~** ich kann die Sprache (hier/dort) nicht *(inf)*

lingua franca [ˈlɪŋgwəˈfræŋkə] N Verkehrssprache *f*, Lingua franca *f*; *(= official language)* Amtssprache *f*

lingual [ˈlɪŋgwəl] ADJ Zungen-; ~ **sound** Zungenlaut *m*

linguist [ˈlɪŋgwɪst] N **a** *(= speaker of languages)* Sprachkundige(r) *mf*; **he's a good ~** er ist sehr sprachbegabt; **I'm no ~** ich bin nicht sprachbegabt **b** *(= specialist in linguistics)* Linguist(in) *m(f)*, Sprachforscher(in) *m(f)*

linguistic [lɪŋˈgwɪstɪk] ADJ **a** *(= concerning language)* sprachlich; ~ **competence** *or* **ability** Sprachfähigkeit *f*; ~ **knowledge** Sprachkenntnisse *pl* **b** *(= concerning language science)* linguistisch, sprachwissenschaftlich

linguistically [lɪŋˈgwɪstɪkəlɪ] ADV sprachlich, linguistisch; ~ **aware** sprachbewusst; ~ **speaking** vom linguistischen Standpunkt aus (gesehen)

linguistic philosophy N Sprachphilosophie *f*

linguistics [lɪŋˈgwɪstɪks] N *sing* Linguistik *f*, Sprachwissenschaft *f*

liniment [ˈlɪnɪmənt] N Einreibemittel *nt*, Liniment *nt (spec)*

lining [ˈlaɪnɪŋ] N *(of clothes etc)* Futter *nt*; *(= lining material)* Futterstoff *m*; *(of brake)* (Brems)belag *m*; *(of pipe)* Auskleidung *f*; *(of attic floor)* Belag *m*; **the ~ of the stomach** die Magenschleimhaut

link [lɪŋk] **N** **a** *(of chain, fig)* Glied *nt*; *(person)* Verbindungsmann *m*/-frau *f*, Bindeglied *nt*
b *(= connection)* Verbindung *f*; *(Comput)* Link *m*, Verknüpfung *f*; **a new rail ~ for the village** eine neue Zug- *or* Bahnverbindung zum Dorf; **photographs give you a ~ with the past** Fotos verbinden einen mit der Vergangenheit; **cultural ~s** kulturelle Beziehungen *pl*; **this is the first cultural ~ between our two countries** das ist der Anfang der kulturellen Beziehungen zwischen unseren beiden Ländern; **the strong ~s between Britain and Australia** die starken Bindungen *or* engen Beziehungen zwischen Großbritannien und Australien; **are there any ~s between the two phenomena?** besteht zwischen diesen beiden Phänomenen ein Zusammenhang *or* eine Beziehung *or* eine Verbindung?
c *(Measure)* Link *nt*
VT verbinden; *spaceships also* aneinanderkoppeln; **to ~ arms** sich unterhaken *(with* bei); **the police ~ed arms** die Polizisten bildeten einen Kordon; **we are ~ed by telephone to ...** wir sind telefonisch verbunden mit ...; **the two companies are now ~ed** die beiden Firmen haben sich zusammengeschlossen; **do you think these two murders are ~ed?** glauben Sie, dass zwischen den beiden Morden eine Verbindung besteht?; **police are not ~ing him with the crime** die Polizei bringt ihn nicht mit dem Verbrechen in Verbindung; **success in business is closely ~ed with self-confidence** Erfolg im Beruf hängt eng mit Selbstvertrauen zusammen; **his name has been ~ed with several famous women** sein Name ist mit mehreren berühmten Frauen in Verbindung gebracht worden
VI **to ~ (together)** *(parts of story)* sich zusammenfügen lassen; *(parts of machine)* verbunden werden; *(railway lines)* sich vereinigen, zusammenlaufen

▶ **link up** **VI** zusammenkommen; *(people)* sich zusammentun; *(facts)* übereinstimmen, zusammenpassen; *(companies)* sich zusammenschließen; **to link up in space** ein Kopplungsmanöver im Weltraum durchführen; **how does that link up with what Freud says?** wie hängt das mit dem zusammen, was Freud sagt? **VT** *sep* miteinander verbinden; *bits of evidence* miteinander in Verbindung bringen; *spaceships* koppeln

linkage [ˈlɪŋkɪdʒ] N Verbindung *f*; *(Pol)* Junktim *nt*

linkman [ˈlɪŋkmən] N *pl* **-men** [-men] Verbindungsmann *m*; *(Rad, TV)* Moderator *m*

link road N *(Brit)* Verbindungsstraße *f*

links [lɪŋks] PL **a** Dünen *pl* **b** *(= golf course)* Golfplatz *m*

linkup [ˈlɪŋkʌp] N *(Telec, general)* Verbindung *f*; *(of spaceships)* Kopplung(smanöver *nt*) *f*

link verb N *(Ling)* Kopula *f*

linnet [ˈlɪnɪt] N (Blut)hänfling *m*

lino [ˈlaɪnəʊ] N *(esp Brit)* Linoleum *nt*

linocut [ˈlaɪnəʊkʌt] N Linolschnitt *m*

linoleum [lɪˈnəʊlɪəm] N Linoleum *nt*

Linotype® [ˈlaɪnəʊtaɪp] N Linotype® *f*, Zeilensetzmaschine *f*

linseed [ˈlɪnsiːd] N Leinsamen *m*

linseed oil N Leinöl *nt*

lint [lɪnt] N Scharpie *f*, Mull *m*

lintel [ˈlɪntl] N *(Archit)* Sturz *m*

lint-free [ˈlɪntˌfriː] ADJ flusenfrei

lion [ˈlaɪən] N Löwe *m*; **he was one of the literary ~s of his day** er war einer der bedeutendsten *or* größten Schriftsteller seiner Zeit; **to fight** *or* **battle like a ~** kämpfen wie ein Löwe; **to throw sb to the ~s** *(fig)* jdn den Löwen zum Fraß vorwerfen; **the ~'s share** der Löwenanteil

lioness [ˈlaɪənɪs] N Löwin *f*

lionhearted [ˈlaɪənˌhɑːtɪd] ADJ unerschrocken, furchtlos

lionize [ˈlaɪənaɪz] VT **to ~ sb** jdn feiern, jdn zum Helden machen

lip [lɪp] N **a** *(Anat)* Lippe *f*; **he wouldn't open his ~s** er wollte den Mund nicht aufmachen; **to keep a stiff upper ~** Haltung bewahren; **to lick** *or* **smack one's ~s** sich *(dat)* die Lippen lecken; **the question on everyone's ~s** die Frage, die sich *(dat)* jeder stellt **b** *(of jug)* Schnabel *m*; *(of cup, crater)* Rand *m* **c** *(inf: = cheek)* Frechheit(en) *f(pl)*; **to give sb a lot of ~** jdm gegenüber eine (dicke *or* freche) Lippe riskieren *(inf)*; **any more of your ~ and there'll be trouble** wenn du weiterhin so eine (dicke *or* freche) Lippe riskierst, gibts Ärger *(inf)*; **none of your ~!** sei nicht so frech

lip: **lip balm** N = **lip salve**; **lip gloss** N Lipgloss *m*

lipo [ˈlɪpəʊ] N *(inf)* = **liposuction**

liposuction [ˈlɪpəʊˌsʌkʃən] N Fettabsaugung *f*

-lipped [-lɪpt] ADJ *suf* -lippig; **thin-lipped** dünnlippig

lip pencil N Lippencil *m*

lippy [ˈlɪpɪ] N *(Brit inf)* Lippenstift *m*

lip: **lip-read** VT **I could ~ what he said** ich konnte ihm von den Lippen *or* vom Mund ablesen, was er sagte **VI** von den Lippen *or* vom Mund ablesen; **lip-reading** N **deaf people use/learn ~** Taube lesen vom Mund ab/lernen, vom Mund abzulesen; **lip salve** N Lippenfettstift *m*, Lippenpflegestift *m*; **lip service** N **to pay ~ to an idea** ein Lippenbekenntnis zu einer Idee ablegen; **lip-smacking** ADJ *(inf) pleasure* unbändig; *satisfaction, relish* ungemein; **lipstick** N Lippenstift *m*; **lip-sync(h)** [ˈlɪpˌsɪŋk] **VI** *(= talk)* lippensynchron sprechen; *(= sing)* lippensynchron singen **VT** *song* lippensynchron singen; **to ~ sb's words** jdn lippensynchron synchronisieren

liquefaction [ˌlɪkwɪˈfækʃən] N Verflüssigung *f*

liquefy [ˈlɪkwɪfaɪ] **VT** verflüssigen **VI** sich verflüssigen

liqueur [lɪˈkjʊəʳ] N Likör *m*

liquid [ˈlɪkwɪd] **ADJ** **a** flüssig; *(fig) eyes* blank, glänzend; *(fig) notes, song* perlend **b** *(Comm) asset* (frei) verfügbar, flüssig **c** *(Phon)* ~ **consonant** Liquida *f*, Fließlaut *m* **N** **a** Flüssigkeit *f*; **she can only take ~s** sie kann nur Flüssiges zu sich nehmen **b** *(Phon)* Liquida *f*, Fließlaut *m*

liquidate [ˈlɪkwɪdeɪt] VT **a** *(Comm)* liquidieren; *assets* liquidieren, flüssigmachen; *company* auflösen, liquidieren; **to ~ a debt** eine Schuld tilgen **b** *enemy etc* liquidieren

liquidation [ˌlɪkwɪˈdeɪʃən] N **a** *(Comm)* Liquidation *f*, Liquidierung *f*; *(of company)* Auflösung *f*, Liquidation *f*; *(of debts)* Tilgung *f*; **to go into ~** in Liquidation gehen **b** *(of enemy etc)* Liquidierung *f*

liquidator [ˈlɪkwɪdeɪtəʳ] N Liquidator *m*, Abwickler *m*

liquid-crystal [ˈlɪkwɪdˈkrɪstəl] ADJ Flüssigkristall-; ~ **display** Flüssigkristallanzeige *f*

liquidity [lɪˈkwɪdɪtɪ] N Liquidität *f*

liquidize [ˈlɪkwɪdaɪz] VT (im Mixer) pürieren *or* zerkleinern

liquidizer [ˈlɪkwɪdaɪzəʳ] N Mixgerät *nt*

liquid measure N Flüssigkeitsmaß *nt*

liquor [ˈlɪkəʳ] N **a** *(esp US, = whisky, brandy etc)* Spirituosen *pl*; *(= alcohol)* Alkohol *m*; **people who drink hard ~** Leute, die scharfe Sachen trinken, Schnapstrinker *pl*; **a strong ~** ein hochprozentiges Getränk; **the local ~** der am Ort hergestellte Schnaps; **he can't take his ~** er verträgt nichts **b** *(= juice)* Flüssigkeit *f*; **potato ~** Kartoffelwasser *nt*

▶ **liquor up** VT *sep (US inf)* **to get liquored up** sich besaufen *(inf)*; **to be liquored up** besoffen sein *(inf)*

liquorice, licorice ['lɪkərɪs] N *(= plant)* Süßholz *nt*; *(= root)* Süßholzwurzel *f*; *(= flavouring, sweetmeat)* Lakritze *f*

liquor store N *(US)* ≈ Wein- und Spirituosengeschäft *nt*

lira ['lɪərə] N Lira *f*; **500 ~(s)** 500 Lire

L iron ['el,aɪən] N *(Tech)* Winkeleisen *nt*

Lisbon ['lɪzbən] N Lissabon *nt*

lisle [laɪl] N *(also* **lisle thread***)* Florgarn *nt*; **~ stockings** Baumwollstrümpfe *pl*

lisp [lɪsp] **N** Lispeln *nt*; **to speak with a ~, to have a ~** lispeln **VTI** lispeln

lissom(e) ['lɪsəm] ADJ geschmeidig; *person also* gelenkig

list¹ [lɪst] **N** **a** Liste *f*; *(= shopping list)* Einkaufszettel *m*; **it's not on the ~** es steht nicht auf der Liste; **~ of names** Namensliste *f*; *(esp in book)* Namensregister *nt*, Namensverzeichnis *nt*; **~ of prices** Preisliste *f*, Preisverzeichnis *nt*; **~ of applicants** Bewerberliste *f*; **there's a long ~ of people waiting for houses** für Häuser besteht eine lange Warteliste; **it's on my ~ for tomorrow** es steht für morgen auf dem Programm **b** *(= publisher's list)* Programm *nt*; **we'd like to start an educational ~** wir würden gern Lehrbücher in unser Programm aufnehmen
VT aufschreiben, notieren; *single item* in die Liste aufnehmen; *(verbally)* aufzählen; **it is not ~ed** es ist nicht aufgeführt

list² *(Naut)* **N** Schlagseite *f*, Krängung *f (spec)*; **to have a bad ~** schwere Schlagseite haben; **to have a ~ of 20°** sich um 20° auf die Seite neigen; **a ~ to port** Schlagseite nach Backbord **VI** Schlagseite haben, krängen *(spec)*; **to ~ badly** schwere Schlagseite haben

list³ VI *(obs)* lauschen *(old)*

list⁴ VI *(obs, poet)* **the wind bloweth where it ~eth** der Wind bläst, wo er will

listed ['lɪstɪd] ADJ **a** *(Brit) building* unter Denkmalschutz (stehend *attr*); **it's a ~ building** es steht unter Denkmalschutz **b** *(St Ex) company* an der Börse notiert; **~ company** börsennotiertes Unternehmen; **~ option/securities** börsengehandelte Option *f*/Wertpapiere *pl*

listen ['lɪsn] VI **a** *(= hear)* hören *(to sth* etw *acc)*; **to ~ to the radio** Radio hören; **if you ~ hard, you can hear the sea** wenn du genau horchst *or* hinhörst, kannst du das Meer hören; **she ~ed carefully to everything he said** sie hörte ihm genau zu; **to ~ for sth** auf etw *(acc)* horchen; **the boys are ~ing for the bell at the end of the lesson** die Jungen warten auf das Klingeln am Ende der Stunde; **we ~ed for footsteps approaching** wir horchten, ob sich Schritte näherten; **to ~ for sb** horchen *or* hören, ob jd kommt
b *(= heed)* zuhören; **~ to me!** hör mir zu!; **~, I know what we'll do** pass auf, ich weiß, was wir machen; **now ~ here!** nun hör mir mal zu!; **don't ~ to him** hör nicht auf ihn; **if he suggests anything, don't ~** hör nicht darauf, wenn er etwas vorschlägt; **he wouldn't ~** er wollte nicht hören

▶ **listen in** VI (im Radio) hören *(to sth* etw *acc)*; *(= listen secretly)* mithören *(on sth* etw *acc)*; **I'd like to listen in on** *or* **to your discussion** ich möchte mir Ihre Diskussion mit anhören

listener ['lɪsnəʳ] N Zuhörer(in) *m(f)*; *(Rad)* Hörer(in) *m(f)*; **to be a good ~** gut zuhören können

listening ['lɪsnɪŋ] N **he did all the talking, I did all the ~** er redete die ganze Zeit, und ich hörte die ganze Zeit zu; **~ device** Abhörgerät *nt*

listening: listening post N *(Mil, fig)* Horchposten *m*; **listening service** N *(Mil)* Abhördienst *m*

listeria [lɪs'tɪərɪə] N *(Med)* **a** Listeriose *f* **b** **listeria** PL *(= bacteria)* Listerien *pl*

listeriosis [lɪ,stɪərɪ'əʊsɪs] N *(Med)* Listeriose *f*

listing ['lɪstɪŋ] N **a** Auflistung *f*, Verzeichnis *nt* **b** **listings** *(TV, Rad, Film)* Programm *nt*; **~s magazine** Programmzeitschrift *f*

listing paper N *(Comput)* Endlospapier *nt*

listless ['lɪstlɪs] ADJ lustlos; *patient* teilnahmslos

listlessly ['lɪstlɪslɪ] ADV lustlos; **to watch ~** teilnahmslos *or* apathisch zusehen

listlessness ['lɪstlɪsnɪs] N Lustlosigkeit *f*; *(of patient)* Teilnahmslosigkeit *f*, Apathie *f*

list price N Listenpreis *m*

lists [lɪsts] PL *(Hist)* Schranken *pl*; **to enter the ~** *(fig)* in die Schranken treten *(liter)*, zum Kampf antreten; **he entered the ~ after the first ballot** er trat nach dem ersten Wahlgang in den Wahlkampf ein

lit [lɪt] *pret, ptp of* **light¹**

litany ['lɪtənɪ] N Litanei *f*

litchi ['laɪtʃiː] N → **lychee**

lit crit ['lɪt'krɪt] N *(Brit inf) abbr of* **literary criticism**

lite [laɪt] ADJ *(inf: Cook, fig)* Light-, light *pred*; **~ beer** Light-Bier *nt*

liter N *(US)* = **litre**

literacy ['lɪtərəsɪ] N Fähigkeit *f* lesen und schreiben zu können; **many adults have problems with ~** viele Erwachsene haben Probleme mit dem Lesen und Schreiben; **~ campaign** Kampagne *f* gegen das Analphabetentum, Alphabetisierungskampagne *f*; **the ~ rate in this region is only 30%** die Analphabetenquote in dieser Region beträgt 70%; **~ is high here** die Analphabetenquote hier ist niedrig; **~ test** Lese- und Schreibtest *m*

literal ['lɪtərəl] **ADJ** **a** *(esp Typ)* **~ error** Schreib-/Tipp-/Druckfehler *m* **b** *translation, meaning, sense* wörtlich; **in the ~ sense (of the word)** im wörtlichen Sinne **c** *(= real)* **that is the ~ truth** das ist die reine Wahrheit; **it was a ~ disaster** es war im wahrsten Sinne des Wortes eine Katastrophe; **the ~ impossibility of working there** die völlige *or* buchstäbliche Unmöglichkeit, dort zu arbeiten **d** *(= prosaic)* nüchtern, prosaisch; **he has a very ~ mind** *or* **is very ~-minded** er denkt sehr nüchtern, er ist sehr prosaisch **N** Schreib-/Tipp-/Druckfehler *m*

literally ['lɪtərəlɪ] ADV **a** *(= word for word, exactly)* (wort)wörtlich; **to take sb/sth ~** jdn/etw wörtlich nehmen; **to be ~ true** wortwörtlich stimmen **b** *(= really)* buchstäblich, wirklich; **the best meal I've ever had, ~** wirklich das Beste, was ich je gegessen habe; **it was ~ impossible to work there** es war wirklich *or* einfach unmöglich, dort zu arbeiten; **I was ~ shaking with fear** ich zitterte regelrecht vor Angst; **he was quite ~ a giant** er war im wahrsten Sinne des Wortes ein Riese

literariness ['lɪtərərɪnɪs] N literarische Stilebene

literary ['lɪtərərɪ] ADJ literarisch; **he has ~ tastes** er interessiert sich für Literatur; **a ~ man** ein Literaturkenner *m*; *(= author)* ein Literat *or* Autor *m*; **the ~ scene** die Literaturszene

literary: literary agent N Literaturagent(in) *m(f)*; **literary critic** N Literaturkritiker(in) *m(f)*; **literary criticism** N *(as subject)* Literaturwissenschaft *f*; *(= reviews)* Literaturkritik *f*; **literary historian** N Literaturhistoriker(in) *m(f)*; **literary theory** N Literaturtheorie *f*

literate ['lɪtərɪt] ADJ **a** **to be ~** lesen und schreiben können; **they aim to achieve a ~ population in one generation** sie wollen die Bevölkerung in einer Generation alphabetisieren **b** *(= well-educated)* gebildet; **his style is not very ~** er schreibt einen ungeschliffenen Stil

literati [,lɪtə'rɑːtiː] PL Literaten *pl*

literatim [,lɪtə'rɑːtɪm] ADV *(form)* Buchstabe für Buchstabe

literature ['lɪtərɪtʃəʳ] N Literatur *f*; *(inf: = brochures etc)* Informationsmaterial *nt*; *(= specialist literature)* (Fach)literatur *f*

lithe [laɪð] ADJ *(+er)* geschmeidig; *person, body also* gelenkig

lithium ['lɪθɪəm] N Lithium *nt*

litho ['laɪθəʊ] N *(inf)* Litho *nt*

lithograph ['lɪθəʊgrɑːf] **N** Lithografie *f*, Steindruck *m* **VT** lithografieren

lithographer [lɪ'θɒgrəfəʳ] N Lithograf(in) *m(f)*

lithographic [,lɪθəʊ'græfɪk] ADJ lithografisch

lithography [lɪ'θɒgrəfɪ] N Lithografie *f*, Steindruck *m*

lithotripter ['lɪθəʊ,trɪptəʳ] N *(Med)* Lithotripter *m*

Lithuania [,lɪθjʊ'eɪnɪə] N Litauen *nt*

Lithuanian [,lɪθjʊ'eɪnɪən] **ADJ** litauisch **N** **a** Litauer(in) *m(f)* **b** *(Ling)* Litauisch *nt*

litigable ['lɪtɪgəbl] ADJ *(Jur)* streitig, strittig

litigant ['lɪtɪgənt] N prozessführende Partei; **the ~s** die Prozessgegner *pl*, die prozessführenden Parteien

litigate ['lɪtɪgeɪt] VI einen Prozess führen *or* anstrengen

litigation [,lɪtɪ'geɪʃən] N Prozess *m*, Rechtsstreit *m*; **he threatened them with ~** er drohte ihnen mit einem Prozess

litigator ['lɪtɪgeɪtəʳ] N *(Jur)* Prozessanwalt *m*/-anwältin *f*

litigious [lɪ'tɪdʒəs] ADJ prozesssüchtig; **a ~ person** jd, der ständig Prozesse führt, ein Prozesshansel *m (inf)*

litmus ['lɪtməs] N Lackmus *m or nt*

litmus paper N Lackmuspapier *nt*

litmus test N *(lit)* Lackmustest *m*; *(fig)* entscheidender Test

litotes [laɪ'təʊtiːz] N Litotes *f*

litre, *(US)* **liter** ['liːtəʳ] N Liter *m or nt*

litter ['lɪtəʳ] **N** **a** Abfälle *pl*; *(= papers, wrappings)* Papier *nt*; **the park was strewn with ~** der Park war mit Papier und Abfällen übersät; **don't leave** *or* **drop ~** *(on notice)* bitte keinen Abfall zurücklassen; **a ~ of books** ein Haufen *m* Bücher
b *(Zool)* Wurf *m*
c *(= vehicle)* Sänfte *f*; *(Med)* Tragbahre *f*, Trage *f*
d *(= bedding for animals)* Streu *f*, Stroh *nt*; *(for plants)* Stroh *nt*; *(= cat litter)* Katzenstreu *f*
VT **a** **to be ~ed with sth** *(lit, fig)* mit etw übersät sein; **old cans ~ed the countryside** alte Dosen verschandelten die Landschaft; **glass from broken bottles ~ed the streets** Glasscherben lagen überall auf den Straßen herum; **to ~ a room with papers** Papier(e) im Zimmer verstreuen
b *(= give birth to)* werfen
c *plant* abdecken; *animal* Streu geben *(+dat)*
VI **a** *(= have young)* werfen
b *(esp US)* Abfall wegwerfen

litter: litterbag N *(US)* Abfalltüte *f*; **litter basket** N Abfallkorb *m*; **litter bin** N *(Brit)* Abfalleimer *m*; *(hooked on)* Abfallkorb *m*; *(bigger)* Abfalltonne *f*; **litter box** N *(US)* = **litter tray**; **litter bug, litter lout** N *(inf)* Dreckspatz *m (inf)*, Schmutzfink *m (inf)*; **litter tray** N Katzenklo *nt*

little ['lɪtl] **ADJ** klein; **a ~ house** ein Häuschen *nt*, ein kleines Haus; **a funny ~ nose** ein lustiges (kleines) Näschen; **the ~ ones** die Kleinen *pl*; **a nice ~ profit** ein hübscher Gewinn; **the ~ people** *or* **folk** die Elfen; **~ green men** *(inf)* kleine grüne Männchen *pl (inf)*; **he will have his ~ joke** er will auch einmal ein Witzchen machen; **to worry about ~ things** sich *(dat)* über Kleinigkeiten Gedanken machen; **he has a ~ mind** er ist ein Kleingeist; **~ things please ~ minds** so kann man auch mit kleinen Sachen Kindern eine Freude machen; **a ~ while ago** vor Kurzem, vor kurzer Zeit; **it's only a ~ while till I ...** es ist nicht mehr lange, bis ich ...; **in a ~ while** bald

ADV, N a wenig; **of ~ importance/interest** von geringer Bedeutung/geringem Interesse; **he knows ~ Latin and less Greek** er kann (nur) wenig Latein und noch weniger Griechisch; **~ better than** kaum besser als; **~ more than a month ago** vor kaum einem Monat; **~ short of** fast schon, beinahe; **~ did I think that …** ich hätte kaum gedacht, dass …; **~ does he know that …** er hat keine Ahnung, dass …; **they ~ realize what will happen to them** sie sind sich *(dat)* wohl kaum darüber im Klaren, was mit ihnen geschehen wird; **to think ~ of sb/sth** nicht viel von jdm/etw halten; **I walk as ~ as possible** ich laufe so wenig wie möglich; **to spend ~ or nothing** so gut wie (gar) nichts ausgeben; **every ~ helps** Kleinvieh macht auch Mist *(Prov)*; **please donate, every ~ helps** auch die kleinste Spende hilft; **he had ~ to say** er hatte nicht viel zu sagen; **I see very ~ of her nowadays** ich sehe sie in letzter Zeit sehr selten; **there was ~ we could do** wir konnten nicht viel tun; **the ~ of his book that I have read** das wenige *or* bisschen, was ich von seinem Buch gelesen habe; **she did what ~ she could** sie tat das wenige, das sie tun konnte; **~ by ~** nach und nach; **~ by ~, he dragged himself across the room** Stückchen für Stückchen schleppte er sich durch das Zimmer; **to make ~ of sth** etw herunterspielen *or* bagatellisieren; **I could make ~ of this book** ich konnte mit diesem Buch nicht viel anfangen

b **a ~** ein wenig, ein bisschen; **a ~ (bit) hot** etwas *or* ein bisschen heiß; **a ~ (bit) better** etwas *or* ein wenig besser; **with a ~ effort** mit etwas Anstrengung; **I'll give you a ~ advice** ich gebe dir einen kleinen Tipp; **a ~ after five** kurz nach fünf; **we were not a ~ worried** wir waren recht besorgt; **I was not a ~ surprised** ich war einigermaßen überrascht; **we walked on for a ~** wir liefen noch ein bisschen *or* Stück *or* Weilchen weiter; **after a ~** nach einer Weile; **for a ~** für ein Weilchen

little: **little auk** N Krabbentaucher *m*; **Little Englander** [ˈlɪtlˈɪŋgləndəˈ] N *(Brit: = anti-European)* *europafeindlich eingestellter Engländer*; *(Hist)* *Gegner des Imperialismus im 19. Jahrhundert*, Isolationist(in) *m(f)*; **Little League** N *(US Sport)* *Baseball-Liga für Kinder unter 12 Jahren*

littleness [ˈlɪtlnɪs] N Kleinheit *f*, geringe Größe; *(of contribution)* Geringfügigkeit *f*; *(of mind)* Beschränktheit *f*

Little Red Ridinghood [ˌlɪtlredˈraɪdɪŋhʊd] N *(fairy tale)* Rotkäppchen *nt*

little theatre, *(US)* **little theater** N Kleinbühne *f*, Kammerspiele *pl*; *(for experimental theatre)* Experimentierbühne *f*

littoral [ˈlɪtərəl] *(form)* ADJ litoral *(spec)*, Litoral- *(spec)*; *(of lake also)* in Ufernähe; *(of sea also)* in Küstennähe; **~ fauna/flora** Litoralfauna/-flora *f (spec)* N Litorale *nt*; Uferland *nt*; Küstenstrich *m or* -region *f*

liturgical [lɪˈtɜːdʒɪkəl] ADJ liturgisch

liturgy [ˈlɪtədʒɪ] N Liturgie *f*

litz wire [ˈlɪtsˌwaɪəˈ] N *(Elec)* Litze *f*, Litzendraht *m*

livable, **liveable** [ˈlɪvəbl] ADJ *life* erträglich; **the house is ~ (in)** *(inf)* in dem Haus kann man wohnen, in dem Haus lässt es sich wohnen; **arthritis can't be cured, but it can be made ~ (with)** *(inf)* Arthritis ist unheilbar, kann aber erträglich gemacht werden

live[1] [lɪv] VT *life* führen; **to ~ a part** in einer Rolle aufgehen; **he had been living a lie** sein Leben war eine Lüge; **to ~ one's own life** sein eigenes Leben leben; **he ~s and breathes golf** er lebt nur für Golf

VI a *(= be alive, survive)* leben; **there is no man living who can equal him** es gibt niemanden, der es ihm gleichtun könnte; **will he ~, doctor?** wird er (über)leben, Herr Doktor?; **don't worry, you'll ~, it's only a broken ankle** reg dich nicht auf, du stirbst schon nicht, du hast nur einen gebrochenen Knöchel; **long ~ Queen Anne!** lang lebe Königin Anne!; **we ~ and learn** man lernt nie aus; **to ~ and let ~** leben und leben lassen; **to ~ like a king** *or* **lord** fürstlich *or* wie Gott in Frankreich leben; **not many people ~ to be a hundred** nicht viele Menschen werden hundert (Jahre alt); **to ~ to a ripe old age** ein hohes Alter erreichen; **his name will ~ for ever** sein Ruhm wird nie vergehen; **his music will ~ for ever** seine Musik ist unvergänglich; **his spirit still ~s in his work** sein Geist lebt in seinem Werk weiter; **if the spirit of the Renaissance should ever ~ again** wenn der Geist der Renaissance je wieder erwachen sollte; **it was as though the father were living again in the son** es war, als lebte der Vater im Sohn weiter; **to ~ by one's wits** sich (so) durchschlagen; **to ~ by one's pen** von seinen Büchern *or* vom Schreiben leben; **to ~ by crime** von Verbrechen leben; **they ~d in fear of losing their jobs** sie lebten in ständiger Angst, ihre Stelle zu verlieren; **he ~d through two wars** er hat zwei Kriege miterlebt; **to ~ through an experience** eine Erfahrung durchmachen; **the patient was not expected to ~ through the night** man rechnete nicht damit, dass der Patient die Nacht überstehen *or* überleben würde; **people living with HIV and AIDS** Menschen mit HIV und Aids; **I would rather like to ~ to the end of the century** ich möchte die Jahrhundertwende noch miterleben; **to ~ within one's income** nicht über seine Verhältnisse leben; **you'll ~ to regret it** das wirst du noch bereuen; **he ~s for his work/children** er lebt für seine Arbeit/Kinder

b *(= experience real living)* **I want to ~** ich will leben *or* was erleben *(inf)*; **that's existing, not living** das ist doch kein Leben; **you've never skied? you haven't ~d!** du bist noch nie Ski gefahren? du weißt gar nicht, was du versäumt hast!; **you've never ~d until you've discovered Crete** wer Kreta nicht kennt, hat noch nicht gelebt; **before she met him she hadn't ~d** sie begann erst zu leben, als sie ihn kennenlernte

c *(= reside)* wohnen, leben; *(animals)* leben; **he ~s at 19 Marktstraße** er wohnt in der Marktstraße Nr. 19; **he ~s in Gardner St/on the High Street** er wohnt in der Gardner St/auf der *or* in der Hauptstraße; **who ~s in that big house?** wer bewohnt das große Haus?, wer wohnt in dem großen Haus?; **he ~s with his parents** er wohnt bei seinen Eltern; **a house not fit to ~ in** ein unbewohnbares Haus, ein Haus, in dem man nicht wohnen kann; **this house is not fit for a human being to ~ in** dies ist eine menschenunwürdige Behausung

d *(inf: = belong)* **where does this jug ~?** wo gehört der Krug hin?; **the knives ~ in this drawer** die Messer gehören in diese Schublade

e **the other athletes couldn't ~ with him/the pace** die anderen Läufer konnten mit ihm/mit dem Tempo nicht mithalten

▶ **live down** VT *sep scandal, humiliation* hinwegkommen über *(+acc)*, verwinden; *(actively) scandal, mistake* Gras wachsen lassen über *(+acc)*; **he'll never live it down** das wird man ihm nie vergessen

▶ **live in** VI im Haus/im Wohnheim *etc* wohnen, nicht außerhalb wohnen

▶ **live off** VI *+prep obj* a **to live off the land** sich vom Lande ernähren; *(= forage)* sich aus der Natur ernähren; **to live off one's relations** auf Kosten seiner Verwandten leben b = **live on VI** *+prep obj*

▶ **live on** VI *(= continue to live)* weiterleben VI *+prep obj* **to live on eggs** sich von Eiern ernähren, von Eiern leben; **he doesn't earn enough to live on** er verdient nicht genug, um davon zu leben; **to live on hope** (nur noch) von der Hoffnung leben; **to live on one's reputation** von seinem Ruf zehren

▶ **live out** VI außerhalb (des Hauses/des Wohnheims *etc*) wohnen VT *sep life* verbringen; *winter* überleben; **he lived out a life of poverty in the country** er lebte bis an sein Ende in Armut auf dem Land

▶ **live together** VI *(= cohabit)* zusammenleben; *(= share a room, flat etc)* zusammen wohnen

▶ **live up** VT *always separate* **to live it up** *(inf)* die Puppen tanzen lassen *(inf)*; *(extravagantly)* in Saus und Braus leben *(inf)*; **in my young days we really knew how to live it up** in meiner Jugend wussten wir noch, wie man sich so richtig auslebt

▶ **live up to** VI *+prep obj* **the holiday** *(esp Brit)* *or* **vacation** *(US)* **lived up to (my) expectations/the advertiser's claims** der Urlaub hielt, was ich mir davon versprochen hatte/was die Werbung versprochen hatte; **sales have not lived up to expectations** die Verkaufszahlen entsprachen nicht den Erwartungen; **to live up to standards/one's reputation** den Anforderungen/seinem Ruf gerecht werden; **the reality never lives up to the anticipation** die Wirklichkeit kommt nie an die Erwartungen heran; **the holiday didn't live up to our hopes** der Urlaub entsprach nicht dem, was wir uns *(dat)* erhofft hatten; **he's got a lot to live up to** in ihn werden große Erwartungen gesetzt; **if he wants to emulate his father he's got a lot to live up to** er hat sich *(dat)* ein hohes Ziel gesteckt, wenn er seinem Vater nacheifern will; **you should live up to your father's principles** du solltest die Grundsätze deines Vaters anstreben; **I doubt whether he can live up to his brother's success** ich bezweifle, dass er so erfolgreich wie sein Bruder wird

live[2] [laɪv] ADJ a *(= alive)* lebend; *issue, question* aktuell; **a real ~ duke** ein waschechter Herzog; **~ births** Lebendgeburten *pl* b *(= having power or energy) coal* glühend; *match* ungebraucht; *cartridge, shell* scharf; *(Elec)* geladen; **"danger, ~ wires!"** „Vorsicht Hochspannung!"; **she's a real ~ wire** *(fig)* sie ist ein richtiges Energiebündel c *(Rad, TV)* live; **a ~ programme** *(Brit)* *or* **program** *(US)* eine Livesendung; **~ broadcast** *(TV, Rad)* Direktübertragung *f* ADV *(Rad, TV)* live, direkt

liveable [ˈlɪvəbl] ADJ = **livable**

live-cell therapy [ˌlaɪvselˈθerəpɪ] N Frischzellentherapie *f*

lived-in [ˈlɪvdɪn] ADJ *feel* gemütlich, behaglich

live-in [ˈlɪvɪn] ADJ *cook, maid* in Haus wohnend; **her ~ partner** ihr Partner, mit dem sie zusammen wohnt

livelihood [ˈlaɪvlɪhʊd] N Lebensunterhalt *m*; **fishing is their ~** sie verdienen ihren Lebensunterhalt mit Fischfang; **to earn a ~** sich *(dat)* seinen Lebensunterhalt verdienen; **they earned a ~ from farming** sie lebten von der Landwirtschaft

livelock N *(Comput)* *Blockierung der Systemaktivität, wenn zwei Prozesse simultan auf eine Quelle zugreifen*, Livelock *m (spec)*

liveliness [ˈlaɪvlɪnɪs] N Lebhaftigkeit *f*; *(of scene, account, sense of humour, imagination)* Lebendigkeit *f*; *(of tune)* Beschwingtheit *f*; *(of campaign)* Dynamik *f*; *(= rapidity)* Schnelligkeit *f*; *(of mind)* Aufgewecktheit *f*

livelong [ˈlɪvlɒŋ] ADJ **all the ~ day** den lieben langen Tag, den ganzen Tag über; **all the ~ night** die ganze Nacht durch

lively [ˈlaɪvlɪ] ADJ *(+er)* lebhaft; *scene, account, sense of humour* lebendig; *campaign* dynamisch; *pace* flott; *mind* wach, aufgeweckt; *imagination* lebendig, blühend; *tune* schwungvoll; **things are getting ~** es geht hoch her *(inf)*; **at 8 things will start to get ~** um 8 wird es dann lebhafter; **we had a ~ time** es war viel los *(inf)*; **he's having a ~ time of it in his new job** in seiner neuen Stelle kann er sich über Langeweile nicht beklagen; **look ~!** *(= speed up)* mach schnell!, ein bisschen lebhaft, bitte!

liven up [ˈlaɪvənˈʌp] VT *sep* beleben, Leben bringen in *(+acc)* *(inf)* VI in Schwung kommen; *(person)* aufleben

liver[1] [ˈlɪvəˈ] N **clean ~** solider Mensch; **he's a fast ~** er führt ein flottes Leben *(inf)*

liver[2] N *(Anat, Cook)* Leber *f*

liveried [ˈlɪvərɪd] ADJ livriert

liverish ['lɪvərɪʃ] ADJ **a** **to be ~** etwas mit der Leber haben; **I felt a bit ~ after the party** mir ging es nach der Party ziemlich mies *(inf)* **b** *(= bad-tempered)* mürrisch

liver pâté N Leberpastete *f*

Liverpudlian [ˌlɪvə'pʌdlɪən] **N** Liverpooler(in) *m(f)* **ADJ** Liverpooler

liver: **liver salts** PL *salzhaltiges Mittel gegen Magenverstimmung*; **liver sausage** N Leberwurst *f*; **liver spot** N *(Med)* Leberfleck *m*

liverwort ['lɪvəwɜːt] N *(Bot)* Lebermoos *nt*; *(= hepatica)* Leberblümchen *nt*

liverwurst ['lɪvəwɜːst] N *(esp US)* Leberwurst *f*

livery ['lɪvərɪ] N Livree *f*; *(fig liter)* Kleid *nt*

livery: **livery company** N Zunft *f*; **livery stable** N Mietstall *m*

lives [laɪvz] *pl of* **life**

livestock ['laɪvstɒk] N Vieh *nt*; *(= number of animals)* Viehbestand *m*

livestock unit N *(Agr)* Großvieheinheit *f*

liveware ['laɪvwɛəʳ] N *(inf)* Personal *f*, Belegschaft *f*

live wire N *(Elec)* Strom führender Draht; *(fig inf: person)* Energiebündel *nt (inf)*

livid ['lɪvɪd] ADJ **a** *(inf: = furious)* wütend, fuchsteufelswild *(inf)* *(about, at* über *+acc)*; **he was ~ about having to do it himself** er war höchst empört darüber, dass er es selbst machen musste; **to be ~ with rage** eine Stinkwut haben *(inf)*, fuchsteufelswild sein *(inf)*; **he got ~ with us** er hatte eine Stinkwut auf uns *(inf)* **b** *(= dark purple)* dunkelviolett; *(= greyish)* purpurgrau; **~ red** purpurrot; **the sky was a ~ blue** der Himmel war purpurblau

living ['lɪvɪŋ] **ADJ** lebend; *example, faith* lebendig; **the greatest ~ playwright** der bedeutendste noch lebende Dramatiker; **I have no ~ relatives** ich habe keine Verwandten mehr; **a ~ creature** ein Lebewesen *nt*; **not a ~ soul** keine Menschenseele; **(with)in ~ memory** seit Menschengedenken; **he is ~ proof of ...** er ist der lebende Beweis für ...; **her existence was a ~ death** ihr Leben war eine einzige Qual; **~ or dead** tot oder lebendig

N **a** **the living** **PL** die Lebenden *pl*

b *(= way of living)* **the art of ~** Lebenskunst *f*; **he is fond of good ~** er lebt gern gut; **gracious ~** die vornehme Lebensart; **loose ~** lockerer Lebenswandel; **healthy ~** gesundes Leben → **standard N b**

c *(= livelihood)* Lebensunterhalt *m*; **to earn** *or* **make a ~** sich *(dat)* seinen Lebensunterhalt verdienen; **what does he do for a ~?** womit verdient er sich *(dat)* seinen Lebensunterhalt?; **he sells brushes for a ~** er verkauft Bürsten, um sich *(dat)* seinen Lebensunterhalt zu verdienen; **they made a bare ~ out of the soil** sie hatten mit dem Ertrag des Bodens ihr Auskommen; **it is possible to make a very good ~ from modelling** *(Brit)* *or* **modeling** *(US)* von der Arbeit als Model kann man sehr gut leben; **to work for one's ~** arbeiten, um sich *(dat)* seinen Lebensunterhalt zu verdienen; **some of us have to work for a ~** es gibt auch Leute, die arbeiten müssen

d *(Eccl)* Pfründe *f*

living: **living cell** N *(Med)* Frischzelle *f*; **living conditions** PL Wohnverhältnisse *pl*; **living dead** PL Untote *pl*; *(fig)* Scheintote *pl*; **living expenses** PL Spesen *pl*; **living quarters** PL Wohnräume *pl*; *(for soldiers, sailors)* Quartier *nt*; **living room** N Wohnzimmer *nt*; **living space** N *(in house)* Wohnraum *m*; *(for a nation)* Lebensraum *m*; **living wage** N ausreichender Lohn; **£65 a week is not a ~** von £ 65 pro Woche kann man nicht leben; **living will** N Patiententestament *nt*, *testamentartige Erklärung, dass jd im Falle einer tödlichen Erkrankung nicht künstlich am Leben gehalten werden will*

Livy ['lɪvɪ] N Livius *m*

lizard ['lɪzəd] N Eidechse *f*; *(including larger forms also)* Echse *f*

ll *abbr of* **lines** Z

llama ['lɑːmə] N Lama *nt*

LLB *abbr of* **Bachelor of Laws**

LLD *abbr of* **Doctor of Laws** Dr. jur.

LMT *(US) abbr of* **local mean time** Ortszeit *f*

LNG *abbr of* **liquefied natural gas** LNG *nt*, Flüssiggas *nt*

lo [ləʊ] INTERJ *(old)* siehe *(old)*; **lo and behold!** und siehe da

loach [ləʊtʃ] N Schmerle *f*

load [ləʊd] **N** **a** *(= sth carried, burden)* Last *f*; *(= cargo)* Ladung *f*; *(on girder, axle etc, fig)* Belastung *f*, Last *f*; **what sort of ~ was the ship/truck carrying?** was hatte das Schiff/der Lastwagen geladen?; **to put a ~ on sth** etw belasten; **to put too heavy a ~ on sth** etw überlasten; **the maximum ~ for that bridge is 10 tons** die maximale Tragkraft *or* -fähigkeit dieser Brücke beträgt 10 Tonnen; **an arm-load of shopping** ein Arm voll Einkäufe; **a train-~ of passengers** ein Zug voll Reisender; **(work) ~** (Arbeits)pensum *nt*; **he has a heavy teaching ~ this term** er hat in diesem Semester eine hohe Stundenzahl; **he carries a heavy ~ of responsibility** er trägt eine schwere Verantwortung; **I put a ~ in the washing machine** ich habe die Maschine mit Wäsche gefüllt; **that's a ~ off my mind!** da fällt mir ein Stein vom Herzen!; **to take a ~ off sb's mind** jdm eine Last von der Seele nehmen

b *(Elec) (supplied)* Leistung *f*; *(carried)* Spannung *f*

c *(inf usages)* **~s of, a ~ of** massenhaft *(inf)*, jede Menge *(inf)*; **thanks, we have ~s** danke, wir haben jede Menge *(inf)*; **it's a ~ of old rubbish** *(Brit)* das ist alles Blödsinn *(inf)* *or* Quatsch *(inf)*; *(film, book, translation)* das ist alles Mist! *(inf)*; **to take on a ~** (ganz schön) einen heben *(inf)*; **get a ~ of this!** *(= listen)* hör dir das mal an!; *(= look)* guck dir das mal an! *(inf)*

VT **a** *goods* laden; *lorry etc* beladen; **the ship was ~ed with bananas** das Schiff hatte Bananen geladen

b *(= burden, weigh down)* beladen; **the branch was ~ed with pears** der Ast war mit Birnen überladen

c *(fig)* überhäufen; **to ~ sb with honours** *(Brit)* *or* **honors** *(US)* jdn mit Ehrungen überschütten *or* -häufen; **the whole matter is ~ed with problems** die Angelegenheit steckt voller Probleme; **they were ~ed with debt** sie steckten tief in Schulden

d *gun* laden; **to ~ a camera** einen Film (in einen Fotoapparat) einlegen; **is this camera ~ed?** ist ein Film im Apparat?

e *dice* fälschen, präparieren; **to ~ the dice** *(fig)* mit gezinkten Karten spielen; **to ~ the dice against sb** *(fig)* jdn übervorteilen; *(= be a disadvantage)* ein Nachteil *m* für jdn sein; **the dice had been ~ed against him** *(fig)* alles sprach gegen ihn

f *(Comput)* laden

VI **a** *(= load goods, truck)* laden; **"loading and unloading"** „Be- und Entladen"

b *(= load gun)* laden; *(= load camera)* einen Film einlegen; **~!** Gewehr(e) laden!; **how does this gun ~?** wie lädt man dieses Gewehr?; **how does this camera ~?** wie legt man einen Film in diesen Apparat ein?

c *(Comput)* laden

▶ **load down** VT *sep* (schwer) beladen; *(fig)* überladen; **the poor animal was loaded down with luggage** das arme Tier war schwer mit Gepäck beladen; **he is loaded down with guilt** Schuldgefühle lasten schwer auf ihm

▶ **load up** **VI** aufladen **VT** *sep* **a** *lorry* beladen; *goods* aufladen **b** *(Comput)* laden

loadable ['ləʊdəbl] ADJ *(Comput)* ladbar

load: **load-bearing** ['ləʊdˌbɛərɪŋ] ADJ *wall* tragend; **load capacity** N *(Elec)* Belastung(sfähigkeit) *f*; *(of lorry)* maximale Nutzlast; **load center**, *(US)* **load center** N Lastschwerpunkt *m*; **load displacement** N *(Naut)* Ladeverdrängung *f*

loaded ['ləʊdɪd] ADJ beladen; *dice* falsch, präpariert; *camera* mit eingelegtem Film; *gun, software* geladen; **the dice are ~ in their favour** *(Brit) or* **favor** *(US)***/against them** *(fig)* alles spricht für/gegen sie; **a ~ question** eine Fangfrage; **that's a ~ word/term** das ist kein neutrales Wort/kein neutraler Ausdruck; **emotionally ~** *(word, speech)* emotional aufgeladen; **he's ~** *(inf)* *(= rich)* er ist stink- *or* steinreich *(inf)*, er schwimmt im Geld *(inf)*; *(= drunk)* der hat einen in der Krone *(inf)*

loading: **loading bay** ['ləʊdɪŋbeɪ] N Ladeplatz *m*; **loading bridge** ['ləʊdɪŋbrɪdʒ] N Verladebrücke *f*; *(Aviat)* Fluggastbrücke *f*

load: **load line** N Ladelinie *f*; **load space** N *(Aut etc)* Ladefläche *f*; **loadstar** N = **lodestar**; **loadstone** N = **lodestone**

loaf [ləʊf] N *pl* **loaves** Brot *nt*; *(unsliced)* (Brot)laib *m*; *(= meat loaf)* Hackbraten *m*; **a ~ of bread** ein (Laib) Brot; **a small white ~** ein kleines Weißbrot; **half a ~ is better than none** *or* **than no bread** *(Prov)* (wenig ist) besser als gar nichts; **use your ~!** *(inf)* streng deinen Grips an *(inf)*

▶ **loaf about** *(Brit) or* **around** VI *(inf)* faulenzen; **he loafed about** *or* **around the house all day** er hing den ganzen Tag zu Hause herum *(inf)*

loafer ['ləʊfəʳ] N **a** *(inf: = idler)* Faulenzer(in) *m(f)*, Nichtstuer(in) *m(f)* **b** *(esp US: = casual shoe)* Halbschuh *m*, Trotteur *m*

loaf tin, *(US)* **loaf pan** N Kastenform *f*

loam [ləʊm] N Lehmerde *f*

loamy ['ləʊmɪ] ADJ *(+er)* lehmig; **~ soil** Lehmboden *m*

loan [ləʊn] **N** **a** *(= thing lent)* Leihgabe *f*; *(from bank etc)* Darlehen *nt*; *(= public loan)* Anleihe *f*; **my friend let me have the money as a ~** mein Freund hat mir das Geld geliehen; **it's not a gift, it's a ~** es ist nicht geschenkt, sondern nur geliehen; **government ~s** Regierungsdarlehen *nt*; *(= borrowings)* Staatsanleihen *pl*

b **I asked for the ~ of a bicycle** ich bat darum, ein Fahrrad ausleihen zu dürfen; **he gave me the ~ of his bicycle** er hat mir sein Fahrrad geliehen; **conditions governing the ~ of this book** Leihbedingungen *pl* für dieses Buch; **it's on ~** es ist geliehen; *(= out on loan)* es ist verliehen *or* ausgeliehen; **the machinery is on ~ from the American government** die Maschinen sind eine Leihgabe der amerikanischen Regierung; **she's on ~ to us from the CIA** sie ist vom CIA an uns abgestellt worden; **to have sth on ~** etw geliehen haben *(from* von)

VT leihen *(to sb* jdm)

loan: **loan account** N Darlehenskonto *nt*, Kreditkonto *nt*; **loanback facility** N *(Insur)* Beleihungsmöglichkeit *f*; **loan bank** N *(Brit)* Darlehensbank *f*, Kreditanstalt *f*; **loan capital** N Anleihekapital *nt*; **loan collection** N Leihgaben *pl*; **loan shark** N *(inf)* Kredithai *m (inf)*; **loan word** N Lehnwort *nt*

loath, **loth** [ləʊθ] ADJ **to be ~ to do sth** etw ungern tun; **~ as I am to leave** so ungern ich auch gehe; **he was ~ for us to go** er ließ uns ungern gehen; **nothing ~** *(old)* bereitwillig(st)

loathe [ləʊð] VT *thing, person* verabscheuen; *modern art, spinach, jazz etc* nicht ausstehen können; **I ~ the idea** die Vorstellung ist mir zuwider; **I ~ doing it** *(in general)* ich hasse es, das zu tun; *(on particular occasion)* es ist mir zuwider, das zu tun

loathing ['ləʊðɪŋ] N Abscheu *m*

loathly ['ləʊðlɪ] ADJ (sehr) ungern *or* widerwillig

loathsome ['ləʊðsəm] ADJ *thing, person* abscheulich, widerlich; *task* verhasst; *deformity* abstoßend; *wound* Ekel erregend

loathsomeness ['ləʊðsəmnɪs] N Abscheulichkeit *f*, Widerlichkeit *f*; *(of task)* Verhasstheit *f*; *(of deformity)* abstoßender Anblick

loaves [ləʊvz] *pl of* **loaf**

lob [lɒb] **N** *(Tennis)* Lob *m*; *(Ftbl)* Heber *m* **VT** *ball* im Lob spielen, lobben; **he ~bed the gre-**

nade over the wall er warf die Granate im hohen Bogen über die Mauer; **to ~ sth over to sb** jdm etw zuwerfen; **~ it over!** wirf es herüber! VI *(Tennis)* lobben

lobby [ˈlɒbɪ] N *(= entrance hall)* Vor- *or* Eingangshalle *f*; *(of hotel, theatre)* Foyer *nt*; *(= corridor)* Flur *m*, Korridor *m*; *(= anteroom, waiting room)* Vorzimmer *nt*; *(= place in Parliament)* Lobby *f*; *(Pol)* Lobby *f*, Interessengruppe *f or* -verband *m*; **the gun ~** die Waffenlobby
VT **to ~ one's Member of Parliament** auf seinen Abgeordneten Einfluss nehmen; **to ~ a bill through parliament** als Interessengruppe ein Gesetz durchs Parlament bringen
VI auf die Abgeordneten Einfluss nehmen, Lobbyist(in) sein; **they are ~ing for this reform** die Lobbyisten versuchen, diese Reform durchzubringen; **the farmers are ~ing for higher subsidies** die Bauernlobby will höhere Subventionen durchsetzen

lobbying [ˈlɒbɪɪŋ] N Beeinflussung *f* von Abgeordneten (durch Lobbys); **the Prime Minister refused to be influenced by ~** der Premierminister wollte sich nicht von Lobbys *or* Interessenverbänden beeinflussen lassen

lobbyist [ˈlɒbɪɪst] N Lobbyist(in) *m(f)*

lobe [ləʊb] N *(Anat) (of ear)* Ohrläppchen *nt*; *(of lungs, brain)* Lappen *m*, Lobus *m (spec)*; *(of leaf)* Ausbuchtung *f*

lobed [ləʊbd] ADJ gelappt

lobelia [ləʊˈbiːlɪə] N Lobelie *f*

lobotomize [ləʊˈbɒtəmaɪz] VT **to ~ sb** an jdm eine Lobotomie durchführen

lobotomy [ləʊˈbɒtəmɪ] N *(Med)* Lobotomie *f*

lobster [ˈlɒbstəˈ] N Hummer *m*

lobster pot N Hummer(fang)korb *m*

local [ˈləʊkəl] ADJ örtlich; *(= in this area)* hiesig; *(= in that area)* dortig; *anaesthetic* lokal, örtlich; **~ radio** Lokalradio *nt*; **~ radio station** Regionalsender *m*; **~ news** Lokalnachrichten *pl*; **~ newspaper** Lokalzeitung *f*; **~ politician** Kommunalpolitiker(in) *m(f)*; **all the ~ residents** alle Ortsansässigen *pl*; **he's a ~ man** er ist ein Ortsansässiger, er ist von hier *(inf)*; **~ community** Kommune *f*; **~ taxes** Kommunalabgaben *pl*; **~ currency** Landeswährung *f*; **at ~ level** auf lokaler Ebene; **it's only of ~ interest** es ist nur für die Einheimischen interessant; **~ opinion is against the change** die öffentliche Meinung am Ort ist gegen die Änderung; **the latest ~ gossip** der neueste Klatsch (hier/dort); **~ bus** Stadtbus *m*; *(serving the immediate locality)* Nahverkehrsbus *m*; **~ time** Ortszeit *f*; **~ train** Nahverkehrszug *m*; **~ traffic** Ortsverkehr *m*; **~ TV** Lokalfernsehen *nt*; **go into your ~ branch** gehen Sie zu Ihrer Zweigstelle; **vote for your ~ candidate** wählen Sie den Kandidaten Ihres Wahlkreises; **accents with the usual ~ variations** Dialekte mit den üblichen regionalen Unterschieden; **one of our ~ sons** einer der Söhne unserer Gemeinde/Stadt; **we used the ~ shops when we were in Spain** wir haben in den Läden der Einheimischen eingekauft, als wir in Spanien waren; **our village hasn't got a ~ butcher** unser Dorf hat keinen eigenen Schlachter; **there are two ~ grocers** *(esp Brit)* es gibt zwei Lebensmittelhändler am Ort; **the ~ shops aren't very good** die dortigen/hiesigen Geschäfte sind nicht sehr gut; **our ~ doctor back home in Canada** unser Arzt zu Hause in Kanada; **what are their main ~ products there?** was wird dort (in der Gegend) hauptsächlich erzeugt?; **the best ~ wine** der beste Wein der Gegend; **the ~ wine over there will make you sick** von dem dortigen Wein wird es einem schlecht
N **a** *(Brit inf: = pub)* **the ~** *(in village)* der Dorfkrug, die Dorfkneipe *(inf)*; *(in community)* das Stammlokal; **our ~** unsere Stammkneipe *(inf)*, unser Stammlokal *nt*
b *(born in)* Einheimische(r) *mf*; *(living in)* Einwohner(in) *m(f)*
c *(Med inf: = local anaesthetic)* örtliche Betäubung
d *(US) (= branch)* Zweigstelle *f*; *(= train)* Nahverkehrszug *m*

local: **local area network** N *(Comput)* lokales Rechnernetz, LAN *nt*; **local authority** N Kommunalbehörde *f*; **local call** N *(Telec)* Ortsgespräch *nt*; **local colour**, *(US)* **local color** N Lokalkolorit *nt*; **local council** N Gemeindeverwaltung *f*; *(in town)* Stadtverwaltung *f*; *(= councillors)* Gemeinderat *m*; *(in town)* Stadtrat *m*

locale [ləʊˈkɑːl] N Schauplatz *m*

local education authority N örtliche Schulbehörde

local government N Kommunal- *or* Gemeindeverwaltung *f*; **~ expenditure** ≈ der kommunale Haushalt; **~ elections** Kommunalwahlen *pl*; **he is in ~** er ist im Gemeinderat *or (in town)* Stadtrat; **reform of ~** Gemeindereform *f*

locality [ləʊˈkælɪtɪ] N Gegend *f*; **a house in the immediate ~ of shops and schools** ein Haus *nt* in nächster Nähe von Geschäften und Schulen

localize [ˈləʊkəlaɪz] VT **a** *(= detect)* lokalisieren
b this custom, once widespread, has now become very ~d die einst weitverbreitete Sitte ist jetzt auf wenige Orte begrenzt

locally [ˈləʊkəlɪ] ADV am Ort; *(Med)* örtlich; **houses are dear ~** Häuser sind hier teuer; **I prefer to shop ~** ich kaufe lieber im Ort ein; **the shops are situated ~** die Geschäfte befinden sich in der Nähe; **do you live ~?** wohnen Sie am Ort?; **I work in Glasgow but I don't live ~** ich arbeite in Glasgow, wohne aber nicht hier/da; **it is known ~ as Tarzan** es wird von den Einheimischen Tarzan genannt; **was she well-known ~?** war sie in dieser Gegend sehr bekannt?; **it was organized both nationally and ~** es wurde sowohl auf nationaler als auch auf lokaler Ebene organisiert; **if each district is ~ governed** wenn jeder Bezirk regional regiert wird; **the plant grows ~** die Pflanze wächst in dieser Gegend; **~ grown** *or* **produced** in der Region angebaut

lo-carb [ˈləʊkɑːb] ADJ = **low-carb**

locate [ləʊˈkeɪt] VT **a** *(= position)* legen; *headquarters* einrichten; *(including act of building)* bauen, errichten; *sportsground, playground* anlegen; *road* bauen, anlegen; **to be ~d at** *or* **in** sich befinden in *(+dat)*; **the hotel is centrally ~d** das Hotel liegt zentral; **where shall we ~ the new branch?** wohin sollen wir die neue Zweigstelle legen?
b *(= find)* ausfindig machen; *submarine, plane* orten

location [ləʊˈkeɪʃən] N **a** *(= position, site)* Lage *f*; *(of building)* Standort *m*, Lage *f*; *(of road)* Führung *f*; *(of ship)* Position *f*; *(of data file)* Speicherort *m*; **this would be an ideal ~ for the road/airport** das wäre ein ideales Gelände für die Straße/den Flughafen; **they moved the ~ of the rig** sie verlegten die Bohrinsel; **the precise ~ of the accident** der genaue Unfallort; **the doctors haven't determined the precise ~ of the tumour** *(Brit) or* **tumor** *(US)* die Ärzte haben den Tumor noch nicht genau lokalisiert; **that shop is in a good ~** dieses Geschäft hat eine gute Lage
b *(= positioning, siting) (of building, road)* Bau *m*; *(of park)* Anlage *f*; *(of headquarters) (= removal)* Einrichtung *f*; *(= building)* Errichtung *f*; **they discussed the ~ of the proposed road/airport** sie diskutierten, wo die geplante Straße/der geplante Flughafen gebaut werden sollte
c *(= finding)* Auffinden *nt*; *(of tumour)* Lokalisierung *f*; *(of star, ship)* Ortung *f*, Positionsbestimmung *f*; **the ~ of oil in the North Sea** die Entdeckung von Erdöl in der Nordsee
d *(Film)* Drehort *m*; **to be on ~ in Mexico** *(person)* bei Außenaufnahmen in Mexiko sein; **part of the film was shot on ~ in Mexico** ein Teil der Außenaufnahmen für den Film wurde in Mexiko gedreht; **we had a lot of ~ work** wir mussten viele Außenaufnahmen machen

locative [ˈlɒkətɪv] N Lokativ *m*

loc cit [ˈlɒkˈsɪt] *abbr of* **loco citato** l. c., a. a. O.

loch [lɒx] N *(Scot)* See *m*; *(= sea loch)* Meeresarm *m*

loci [ˈlɒkiː] *pl of* **locus**

lock¹ [lɒk] N *(of hair)* Locke *f*; **her wavy ~s** ihr gewelltes Haar

lock² N **a** *(on door, box, gun)* Schloss *nt*; **to put/keep sb under ~ and key** jdn hinter Schloss und Riegel bringen/verwahren; **to put sth under ~ and key** etw wegschließen; **to keep money under ~ and key** Geld unter Verschluss halten; **he offered me the house ~, stock and barrel** er bot mir das Haus mit allem Drum und Dran an *(inf)*; **they destroyed it ~, stock and barrel** sie haben es total zerstört; **to own sth ~, stock and barrel** etw ganz besitzen
b *(= canal lock)* Schleuse *f*
c *(= hold)* Fesselgriff *m*
d *(Aut)* Wendekreis *m*; **the steering wheel was on full ~** das Lenkrad war voll eingeschlagen
VT *door etc* ab- *or* zuschließen; *steering wheel* sperren, arretieren; *wheel* blockieren; *(Comput) file* locken *(spec)*; **to ~ sb in a room** jdn in einem Zimmer einschließen; **the armies were ~ed in combat** die Armeen waren in Kämpfe verwickelt; **they were ~ed in each other's arms** sie hielten sich fest umschlungen; **he ~ed my arm in a firm grip** er umklammerte meinen Arm mit festem Griff; **this bar ~s the wheel in position** diese Stange hält das Rad fest; **the handcuffs were ~ed round his wrists** die Handschellen waren an seinen Handgelenken festgemacht → **stable² N**
VI schließen; *(wheel)* blockieren; **a suitcase that ~s** ein verschließbarer Koffer, ein Koffer, der sich abschließen lässt; **his jaw had ~ed fast** er hatte Mundsperre; **the lion's jaws ~ed round his arm** der Kiefer des Löwen schloss sich fest um seinen Arm

▶ **lock away** VT *sep* wegschließen; *person* einsperren; **he locked the money away in his safe** er schloss das Geld in seinem Safe ein

▶ **lock in** VT *sep* **a** *(= shut in) person, animal* einschließen; **to be locked in** eingesperrt sein
b we're locked into this supplier wir sind an diesen Lieferanten gebunden; **I don't want to get myself locked in** ich will mich nicht zu sehr binden; **to lock in on an idea** sich in eine Idee verbeißen

▶ **lock on** VI *(spaceship etc)* gekoppelt werden (to mit); **the radio automatically locks onto a channel** das Radio hat automatische Feineinstellung; **the missile locks onto its target** das Geschoss richtet sich auf das Ziel VT *sep radio, scanner* einstellen (to auf *+acc*); **with a padlock he locked the extra piece on** er befestigte das zusätzliche Stück mit einem Anhängeschloss

▶ **lock out** VT *sep workers* aussperren; **I've locked myself out** ich habe mich ausgesperrt

▶ **lock together** VI *(rockets)* (miteinander) gekoppelt werden; *(pieces of jigsaw)* sich zusammenstecken lassen VT *sep rockets* (miteinander) koppeln; *currencies* (aneinander) koppeln; *pieces of jigsaw* zusammenstecken; **locked together in a passionate embrace** in einer leidenschaftlichen Umarmung fest umschlungen

▶ **lock up** VT *sep* **a** *thing, house* abschließen; *person* einsperren; **to lock sth up in sth** etw in etw *(dat)* einschließen; **he ought to be locked up!** den müsste man einsperren! **b** *(Comm) capital* fest anlegen VI abschließen

lockable [ˈlɒkəbl] ADJ abschließbar, verschließbar

lockage [ˈlɒkɪdʒ] N **a** *(= canal lock)* Schleusensystem *nt*, Schleusenanlage *f* **b** *(= toll)* Schleusengeld *nt* **c** *(= passage of ship)* (Durch)schleusen *nt*

locker [ˈlɒkəˈ] N Schließfach *nt*; *(Naut, Mil)* Spind *m*

locker room N Umkleideraum *m*

locket [ˈlɒkɪt] N Medaillon *nt*

lock: **lock gate** N Schleusentor *nt*; **lockjaw** N Wundstarrkrampf *m*; **lock keeper** N Schleusenwärter(in) *m(f)*; **locknut** N Gegenmutter *f*; **lockout** N Aussperrung *f*; **locksmith** N Schlosser(in) *m(f)*; **lockstitch** N Steppstich *m*; **lock-up** N **a** *(= shop)* Laden *m*, Geschäft *nt; (= garage)* Garage *f* **b** *(= prison)* Gefängnis *nt*

loco[1] [ˈləʊkəʊ] N *(Rail inf)* Lok *f (inf)*

loco[2] ADJ *(esp US inf)* bekloppt *(inf)*; **he's gone ~** der spinnt *(inf)*

loco citato [ˌlɒkəʊsɪˈtɑːtəʊ] = **loc cit**

locomotion [ˌləʊkəˈməʊʃən] N Fortbewegung *f*; **means of ~** Fortbewegungsmittel *nt*

locomotive [ˌləʊkəˈməʊtɪv] ADJ Fortbewegungs-; **~ power** Fortbewegungsfähigkeit *f* N Lokomotive *f*

locum (tenens) [ˈləʊkəm(ˈtenenz)] N *(Brit)* Vertreter(in) *m(f)*

locus [ˈlɒkəs] N *pl* **loci** geometrischer Ort

locust [ˈləʊkəst] N Heuschrecke *f*

locust tree N Robinie *f*

locution [ləˈkjuːʃən] N Ausdrucksweise *f*; *(= expression)* Ausdruck *m*; **a set ~** eine feste *or* feststehende Redewendung

lode [ləʊd] N Ader *f*

lode: **lodestar** N Leitstern *m*, Polarstern *m*; *(fig) (= person)* Leitbild *nt*; *(= principle)* Leitstern *m*; **lodestone** N Magnetit *m*, Magneteisenstein *m*

lodge [lɒdʒ] N *(in grounds)* Pförtnerhaus *nt*; *(of American Indian)* Wigwam *m*; *(= shooting lodge, skiing lodge etc)* Hütte *f*; *(= porter's lodge)* Pförtnerloge *f*; *(Sch, Univ)* Pedellzimmer *nt*; *(= masonic lodge)* Loge *f*; *(of beaver)* Bau *m*
VT **a** *(Brit) person* unterbringen
b *(with* bei*) complaint* einlegen; *protest* erheben; *claim* geltend machen; *charge, petition, application* einreichen; **to ~ an appeal** Einspruch erheben; *(Jur)* Berufung einlegen
c *(= insert) spear* stoßen; **to be ~d** (fest)stecken
d *jewellery, money* deponieren, hinterlegen
VI **a** *(Brit: = live)* (zur *or* in Untermiete) wohnen *(with sb, at sb's* bei jdm); *(at boarding house)* wohnen *(in* in +*dat)*
b *(object, bullet)* stecken bleiben; **to ~ in sb's mind** jdm in Erinnerung bleiben

lodger [ˈlɒdʒəˈ] N Untermieter(in) *m(f)*; **I was a ~ there once** ich habe dort einmal zur *or* in Untermiete gewohnt; **she takes ~s** sie vermietet (Zimmer), sie nimmt Untermieter auf

lodging [ˈlɒdʒɪŋ] N **a** Unterkunft *f*; **they gave me a night's ~** sie gaben mir Unterkunft *or* ein Zimmer für die Nacht **b** **lodgings** PL ein möbliertes Zimmer, möblierte Zimmer *pl*; **where are your ~s?** wo wohnen Sie?; **we took ~s with Mrs B** wir mieteten uns bei Frau B ein

lodging house N Pension *f*

loess [ˈləʊɪs] N Löss *m*, Löß *m*

loft [lɒft] N **a** Boden *m*, Speicher *m*; *(= hay loft)* Heuboden *m*; **in the ~** auf dem Boden *or* Speicher **b** *(= organ loft, choir loft)* Empore *f*
VT *(Sport)* hochschlagen; **he ~ed the ball over the fence** er schlug den Ball im hohen Bogen über den Zaun

loft conversion N Dachausbau *m*

loftily [ˈlɒftɪlɪ] ADV hoch; *say, speak* stolz, hochmütig; *gaze* hochmütig

loftiness [ˈlɒftɪnɪs] N **a** *(of tree, mountain)* Höhe *f* **b** *(of sentiments)* Erhabenheit *f*; *(of prose)* erlesener *or* gehobener *or* hochtrabender *(pej)* Stil; **the ~ of his ambitions/ideals** seine hochfliegenden Ambitionen/Ideale **c** *(= haughtiness)* Hochmütigkeit *f*

lofty [ˈlɒftɪ] ADJ *(+er)* **a** *(= high)* hoch; **he rose to a ~ position** er stieg in eine gehobene Position auf **b** *(= noble) ideals* hoch(fliegend); *ambitions* hochfliegend; *sentiments* erhaben; *prose, style* erlesen, gehoben, hochtrabend *(pej)* **c** *(= haughty)* stolz, hochmütig N *(inf)* Lange(r) *mf (inf)*

log[1] [lɒg] N Baumstamm *m*; *(= short length of tree trunk)* Block *m*, Klotz *m*; *(for a fire)* Scheit *nt*; **to sleep like a ~** wie ein Stein schlafen

log[2] N **a** *(Naut: = apparatus)* Log *nt* **b** *(= record)* Aufzeichnungen *pl*; *(Naut)* Logbuch *nt*; **to keep a ~ of sth** über etw *(acc)* Buch führen **c** *(Comput)* Protokoll *nt* VT **a** *(= record)* Buch führen über *(+acc)*; *(Naut)* (ins Logbuch) eintragen; *(Comput)* protokollieren; **details are ~ged in the computer** Einzelheiten sind im Computer gespeichert **b** *(= travel)* zurücklegen

▶ **log in** VI *(Comput)* (sich) einloggen

▶ **log off** *(Comput)* VI (sich) ausloggen VT ausloggen, abmelden

▶ **log on** *(Comput)* VI (sich) einloggen VT einloggen, anmelden

▶ **log out** VI *(Comput)* (sich) ausloggen

▶ **log up** VT *sep (Naut)* (ins Logbuch) eintragen; *(= clock up) distance* zurücklegen; *(fig) successes* einheimsen *(inf)*

log[3] *abbr of* **logarithm** log; **~ tables** Logarithmentafel *f*

loganberry [ˈləʊgənbərɪ] N *(= fruit)* Loganbeere *f*; *(= bush)* Loganbeerbusch *m*

logarithm [ˈlɒgərɪθəm] N Logarithmus *m*

logarithmic [ˌlɒgəˈrɪθmɪk] ADJ logarithmisch

logbook [ˈlɒgbʊk] N *(Naut)* Logbuch *nt*; *(Aviat)* Bordbuch *nt*; *(of lorries)* Fahrtenbuch *nt*; *(Aut: = registration book)* Kraftfahrzeug- *or* Kfz-Brief *m*; *(in hospitals, police stations etc)* Dienstbuch *nt*

log cabin N Blockhaus *nt*, Blockhütte *f*

loggerheads [ˈlɒgəhedz] PL **to be at ~ (with sb)** *(esp Brit)* Streit (mit jdm) haben, sich *(dat)* (mit jdm) in den Haaren liegen *(inf)*; **they were constantly at ~ with the authorities** sie standen mit den Behörden dauernd auf Kriegsfuß

loggia [ˈlɒdʒɪə] N Loggia *f*

logging [ˈlɒgɪŋ] N Holzfällen *nt*

logic [ˈlɒdʒɪk] N Logik *f*; **there's no ~ in that** das ist völlig unlogisch

logical [ˈlɒdʒɪkəl] ADJ logisch; *conclusion also* folgerichtig; **he has a ~ mind** er denkt logisch; **they are incapable of ~ thinking** sie können nicht logisch denken; **to take sth to its ~ conclusion** etw bis zur logischen Konsequenz führen

logically [ˈlɒdʒɪkəlɪ] ADV *think, argue* logisch; **~, he may be right** logisch gesehen könnte er recht haben; **it follows ~ from this that ...** daraus lässt sich die logische Schlussfolgerung ziehen, dass ...

logic: **logic analyzer** N *(Comput)* Logikanalysator *m*; **logic bomb** N *(Comput)* Langzeitvirus *m*, Virus-Zeitbombe *f*

logician [lɒˈdʒɪʃən] N Logiker(in) *m(f)*

logic circuit N *(Comput)* logische Schaltung

login [ˈlɒgɪn] N *(Comput)* Einloggen *nt*, Log-in *nt*

logistic [lɒˈdʒɪstɪk] ADJ logistisch

logistically [lɒˈdʒɪstɪkəlɪ] ADV logistisch

logistics [lɒˈdʒɪstɪks] N *sing* Logistik *f*

logo [ˈləʊgəʊ, ˈlɒgəʊ] N Logo *nt*, Emblem *nt*

logoff [ˈlɒgɒf] N *(Comput)* Ausloggen *nt*, Log-off *nt*

logon [ˈlɒgɒn] N *(Comput)* Einloggen *nt*, Log-in *nt*

logout [ˈlɒgaʊt] N *(Comput)* Ausloggen *nt*, Log-out *nt*

logrolling [ˈlɒgrəʊlɪŋ] N *(Pol)* Kuhhandel *m (inf)*; *(Sport) Wettkampf, bei dem zwei Gegner auf einem im Wasser schwimmenden Baumstamm stehen und sich durch Drehen desselben zum Fallen bringen*

loin [lɔɪn] N Lende *f* → **gird up**

loincloth [ˈlɔɪnklɒθ] N Lendenschurz *m*

loiter [ˈlɔɪtəˈ] VI **a** *(= waste time)* trödeln, bummeln **b** *(= hang around suspiciously)* sich herumtreiben, herumlungern; **"no ~ing"** „unberechtigter Aufenthalt verboten"; **to ~ with intent** sich verdächtig machen, sich auffällig verhalten

▶ **loiter about** *(Brit) or* **around** VI herumlungern

loiterer [ˈlɔɪtərəˈ] N Herumtreiber(in) *m(f)*, Herumlungerer *m*; *(= straggler)* Nachzügler(in) *m(f)*, Bummelant(in) *m(f) (inf)*

loll [lɒl] VI **a** sich lümmeln; **he was ~ing in an easy chair** er hing *(inf) or* räkelte sich *or* rekelte sich im Sessel; **to ~ against sth** sich (lässig) gegen *or* an etw *(acc)* lehnen **b** *(= flop) (head)* hängen; *(tongue)* heraushängen

▶ **loll about** *(Brit) or* **around** VI herumlümmeln, herumhängen *(inf)*

▶ **loll back** VI sich zurücklehnen

▶ **loll out** VI heraushängen; **the dog's tongue was lolling out** dem Hund hing die Zunge heraus

lollapalooza [ˌlɒləpəˈluːzəˈ], **lollapaloosa** [ˌlɒləpəˈluːsəˈ] N *(dated US sl: = amazing thing)* Wahnsinnsding *nt (inf)*; *(= large thing)* Riesending *nt (inf)*

lollipop [ˈlɒlɪpɒp] N Lutscher *m*; *(= iced lollipop)* Eis *nt* am Stiel

lollipop lady N *(Brit inf)* ≈ Schülerlotsin *f*

lollipop man N *(Brit inf)* ≈ Schülerlotse *m*

lollop [ˈlɒləp] VI *(also* **lollop along**, *animal)* trotten, zotteln; *(puppy, rabbit)* hoppeln; *(person)* zockeln

lolly [ˈlɒlɪ] N *(esp Brit)* **a** *(inf: = lollipop)* Lutscher *m*; **an ice ~** ein Eis *nt* am Stiel **b** *(inf: = money)* Kohle *f (inf)*

lollygag [ˈlɒlɪgæg], **lallygag** [ˈlælɪˌgæg] VI *(dated US sl)* **a** *(= waste time)* seine Zeit verplempern *(inf)* **b** *(= kiss and cuddle)* schmusen *(inf)*

Lombard [ˈlɒmbɑːd] ADJ lombardisch N Lombarde *m*, Lombardin *f*

Lombardy [ˈlɒmbədɪ] N Lombardei *f*

London [ˈlʌndən] N London *nt* ADJ Londoner

Londoner [ˈlʌndənəˈ] N Londoner(in) *m(f)*

lone [ləʊn] ADJ *(= single)* einzeln; *(= isolated)* einsam; *(= only) survivor, success* einzig; **~ traveller** *(Brit) or* **traveler** *(US)* Alleinreisende(r) *mf*; **he prefers to play a ~ hand** er macht lieber alles im Alleingang; **to be a ~ voice** ein einsamer Rufer sein; **to fight a ~ battle** einen einsamen Kampf führen; **~ mother** alleinerziehende Mutter; **~ father** alleinerziehender Vater; **~ parent** Alleinerziehende(r) *mf*, alleinerziehender Elternteil; **~ parent family** Einelternfamilie *f*, Alleinerziehendenhaushalt *m*

loneliness [ˈləʊnlɪnɪs] N Einsamkeit *f*

lonely [ˈləʊnlɪ] ADJ *(+er)* einsam; **it's ~ at the top** an der Spitze lebt es sich einsam; **~ hearts ad** Kontaktanzeige *f*; **~ hearts column** Kontaktanzeigen *pl*; **~ hearts club** Singletreff *m*, Singleklub *m*

loner [ˈləʊnəˈ] N Einzelgänger(in) *m(f)*

lonesome [ˈləʊnsəm] ADJ *(esp US)* einsam

Lone Star State N *(US)* **the ~** Texas *nt*

lone wolf N *(fig)* Einzelgänger *m*

long[1] *abbr of* **longitude**

long[2] [lɒŋ] ADJ *(+er)* **a** *(in size)* lang; *glass* hoch; *journey* weit; **it is 6 feet ~** es ist 6 Fuß lang; **to be ~ in the leg** lange Beine haben; **to pull a ~ face** ein langes Gesicht machen; **it's a ~ way** das ist weit; **it's a ~ way to Hamburg** nach Hamburg ist es weit; **to have a ~ memory** ein gutes Gedächtnis haben; **to be ~ in the tooth** *(inf)* nicht mehr der/die Jüngste sein; **surely he is a bit ~ in the tooth to be climbing Everest** ist er nicht schon ein bisschen (zu) alt, um den Everest zu besteigen?
b *(in time)* lang; *job* langwierig; **it's a ~ time since I saw her** ich habe sie schon lange nicht mehr gesehen; **will you need it for a ~ time?** brauchen Sie es lange?; **he's been here (for) a ~ time** er ist schon lange hier; **she was abroad for a ~ time** sie war (eine) lange Zeit im Ausland; **well hullo, it's been a ~ time** hallo, schon lange nicht mehr gesehen; **~ time no see** *(inf)* sieht man dich auch mal wieder? *(inf)*; **to take a ~ look at sth** etw lange *or* ausgiebig betrachten; **how ~ is the film?** wie lange dauert der Film?; **a year is 12 months ~** ein Jahr hat 12 Monate; **how ~ are your holidays?** *(Brit)*, **how ~**

is your vacation? *(US)* wie lange haben Sie Urlaub?; **to take the ~ view** etw auf lange Sicht betrachten

c *(Poet, Phon) vowel, syllable* lang

d **a ~ drink** *(mixed)* ein Longdrink *m*; *(= beer)* ein Bier *nt*; **a ~ gin** ein Gin mit Tonic und Eis *etc*; **I'd like something ~ and cool** ich möchte einen kühlen Longdrink

ADV **a** lang(e); **to be ~ in** *or* **about doing sth** lange zu etw brauchen; **don't be ~!** beeil dich!; **don't be too ~ about it** lass dir nicht zu viel Zeit, mach nicht zu lange *(inf)*; **don't be too ~ about phoning me** ruf mich bald (mal) an; **I shan't be ~** *(in finishing)* ich bin gleich fertig; *(in returning)* ich bin gleich wieder da; **two months without you, it's been too ~** zwei Monate ohne dich, das war zu lang(e); **he drank ~ and deep** er nahm einen langen, tiefen Schluck; **all night ~** die ganze Nacht; **~ ago** vor langer Zeit; **not ~ ago** vor Kurzem; **~ before** lange vorher; **~ before now** viel früher; **not ~ before I met you** kurz bevor ich dich kennenlernte; **not ~ before that** kurz davor; **those days are ~ (since) past** diese Tage sind schon lange vorbei; **at the ~est** höchstens; **as ~ as** so lange wie; **we waited as ~ as we could** wir haben gewartet, solange wir konnten; **as ~ as, so ~ as** *(= provided that)* solange → *also* **ago, since**

b *(in comp)* **how much ~er can you stay?** wie lange können Sie noch bleiben?; **I can't wait any ~er** ich kann nicht mehr länger warten; **if that noise goes on any ~er** wenn der Lärm weitergeht; **no ~er** *(= not any more)* nicht mehr; **I'll wait no ~er** ich warte nicht länger; **I'll insist no ~er** ich werde nicht weiter darauf bestehen

c **so ~!** *(inf)* tschüs(s)! *(inf)*, bis später!

N **a** **the ~ and the short of it is that …** kurz gesagt …, der langen Rede kurzer Sinn …; **that's the ~ and the short of it** und damit hat sichs *(inf)*; **before ~** bald; **are you going for ~?** werden Sie länger weg sein?; **I won't stay for ~** ich bleibe nicht lange; **it won't take ~** das dauert nicht lange; **it didn't take ~ before …** es dauerte nicht lange, bis …; **I won't take ~** ich brauche nicht lange (dazu)

b *(Poet)* lange Silbe

long³ VI sich sehnen *(for* nach*)*; *(less passionately)* herbeisehnen, kaum erwarten können *(for sth* etw *acc)*; **he ~ed for his wife to return** er wartete sehnsüchtig auf die Rückkehr seiner Frau; **I'm ~ing for him to resign** ich warte ungeduldig auf seinen Rücktritt; **the children were ~ing for the bell to ring** die Kinder warteten sehnsüchtig auf das Klingeln *or* konnten das Klingeln kaum erwarten; **he is ~ing for me to make a mistake** er möchte zu gern, dass ich einen Fehler mache; **I am ~ing to go abroad** ich brenne darauf, ins Ausland zu gehen; **he ~ed to know what was happening** er hätte zu gerne gewusst, was vorging; **I'm ~ing to see my cat again** ich möchte meine Katze so gern wiedersehen; **I'm ~ing to see that film** ich will den Film unbedingt sehen; **I'm ~ing to hear his reaction** ich bin sehr auf seine Reaktion gespannt; **how I ~ for a cup of tea/a shower** wie ich mich nach einer Tasse Tee/einer Dusche sehne

long: **long-acting** ADJ *(Pharm)* mit Langzeitwirkung; **~ medicine** Depotpräparat *nt*; **longboat** N großes Beiboot; *(of Vikings)* Wikingerboot *nt*; **longbow** N (Lang)bogen *m*; **long-case clock** N Großvateruhr *f*; **long-chain** ADJ *(Chem)* langkettig; **long-distance** ADJ **~ call** Ferngespräch *nt*; **~ lorry driver** *(Brit)* Fernfahrer(in) *m(f)*; **~ flight/race** Langstreckenflug *m*/-rennen *nt*; **~ relationship** Fernbeziehung *f*; **~ runner** Langstreckenläufer(in) *m(f)*; **~ running** Langstreckenlauf *m*; **~ journey/travel** Fernreise *f*/-reisen *pl*; **~ train** Fernverkehrszug *m*; **~ bus** (Fern)reisebus *m*, Überlandbus *m* ADV **to call ~** ein Ferngespräch führen; **long division** N schriftliche Division; **long-drawn-out** ADJ *speech, argument* langatmig; *meeting* ausgedehnt, in die Länge gezogen; *affair, war* sich lange hinziehend; *process* langwierig

longed-for [ˈlɒŋdfɔːˈ] ADJ ersehnt; **the much ~ cup of tea** die heiß ersehnte Tasse Tee

longevity [lɒnˈdʒevɪtɪ] N Langlebigkeit *f*

long: **long-forgotten** ADJ längst vergessen; **long-grain** ADJ **~ rice** Langkornreis *m*; **long-haired** ADJ *person, animal* langhaarig; **~ cow** Kuh *f* mit langhaarigem Fell; **longhand** N Langschrift *f* ADV in Langschrift; **long-haul** ADJ **~ truck driver** Fernfahrer(in) *m(f)*; **long-headed** ADJ *(fig)* klug, weitblickend, weit blickend; **long hill** N *(Ski)* Großschanze *f*; **longhorn** N Longhorn *nt*

longing [ˈlɒŋɪŋ] ADJ *look* sehnsüchtig; *eyes* sehnsuchtsvoll N Sehnsucht *f* *(for* nach*)*; **this sense of ~** diese Sehnsucht; **to have a (great) ~ to do sth** sich (sehr) danach sehnen, etw zu tun

longingly [ˈlɒŋɪŋlɪ] ADV sehnsüchtig

longish [ˈlɒŋɪʃ] ADJ ziemlich lang

longitude [ˈlɒŋgɪtjuːd] N Länge *f*; **lines of ~** Längengrade *pl*

longitudinal [ˌlɒŋgɪˈtjuːdɪnəl] ADJ Längs-; **~ direction** Längsrichtung *f*

longitudinally [ˌlɒŋgɪˈtjuːdɪnəlɪ] ADV der Länge nach

long: **long johns** PL *(inf)* lange Unterhosen *pl*; **long jump** N Weitsprung *m*; **long jumper** N Weitspringer(in) *m(f)*; **long-legged** ADJ langbeinig; **long-life** ADJ *battery etc* mit langer Lebensdauer; **long-life milk** N H-Milch *f*; **long-limbed** ADJ langglied(e)rig; **long-lived** [ˈlɒŋlɪvd] ADJ langlebig; *success* dauerhaft, von Dauer; **~ trees** Bäume, die lange leben; **long-lost** ADJ *person* verloren geglaubt; *ideals, enthusiasm etc* verloren gegangen; **long-playing** ADJ Langspiel-; **~ record** Langspielplatte *f*; **long-range** ADJ *gun* mit hoher Reichweite; *forecast, plan* langfristig; **~ aircraft** Langstreckenflugzeug *nt*; **~ missile** Langstreckenrakete *f*; **~ study** Langzeitstudie *f*; **long-running** ADJ *series* lange laufend; *affair* langjährig; *feud* lange andauernd; **longship** N Wikingerboot *nt*; **longshoreman** N *(US)* Hafenarbeiter *m*; **long shot** N **a** *(Phot)* Fernaufnahme *f* **b** *(inf)* **it's a ~, but it may pay off** es ist gewagt, aber es könnte sich auszahlen; **it was a ~, but it proved to be true** die Vermutung war weit hergeholt, hat sich aber als wahr erwiesen; **that horse is a ~** auf das Pferd zu setzen, ist gewagt; **not by a ~** bei Weitem nicht, noch lange nicht; **long sight** N = **long-sightedness**; **long-sighted** ADJ *(Brit lit, fig)* weitsichtig; **long-sightedness** N *(Brit)* Weitsichtigkeit *f*; *(fig)* Weitsicht *f*; **long-standing** ADJ alt; *friendship* langjährig, alt; *interest, invitation* schon lange bestehend → **standing**; **long-stay** ADJ *(Brit) hospital, patient* Langzeit-; *car park* Dauer-; **long-suffering** ADJ schwer geprüft; **long suit** N *(Cards)* lange Reihe; *(fig)* Trumpf *m*; **long-tailed** ADJ langschwänzig; **long term** N **in the ~** langfristig gesehen; **to plan for the ~** auf lange Sicht planen; **long-term** ADJ *plans, investment, loan, effect, future* langfristig; *relationship* dauerhaft; **~ care insurance** *(US)* ≈ Pflegeversicherung *f*; **~ car park** Langzeitparkplatz *m*; **~ memory** Langzeitgedächtnis *nt*; **the ~ unemployed** die Langzeitarbeitslosen *pl*; **long-time** ADJ **a ~ friend** ein langjähriger *or* alter Freund

longueur [lõːŋˈgɜːˈ] N *(in novel, play etc)* Länge *f*, langweilige Stelle

long: **long vacation** N *(Univ)* (Sommer)semesterferien *pl*; *(Sch)* große Ferien *pl*; **long wave** N Langwelle *f*; **long-wave** ADJ Langwellen-; **~ frequency** Langwellenfrequenz *f*

longways [ˈlɒŋweɪz] ADV der Länge nach, längs

long: **long-winded** ADJ umständlich; *story, speech* langatmig; *affair* langwierig; **long-windedness** N Langatmigkeit *f*

loo [luː] N *(Brit inf)* Klo *nt* *(inf)*; **to go to the ~** aufs Klo gehen *(inf)*; **in the ~** auf dem Klo *(inf)*

loofah [ˈluːfə] N Luffa *f*; *(as sponge)* Luffa(-schwamm) *m*

look [lʊk] ✪ 15.2, 15.3 N **a** *(= glance)* Blick *m*; **she gave me a dirty ~, I got a dirty ~ from her** sie warf mir einen vernichtenden Blick zu; **she gave me a ~ of disbelief** sie sah mich ungläubig an; **he gave me such a ~!** er hat mir (vielleicht) einen Blick zugeworfen!; **we got some very odd ~s** wir wurden komisch angesehen; **to have** *or* **take a ~ at sth** sich *(dat)* etw ansehen; **he had a quick ~ at his watch** er sah kurz auf die Uhr; **can I have a ~?** darf ich mal sehen *or* gucken *(inf)*?; **have a ~ at this!** sieh *or* guck *(inf)* dir das mal an!; **is it in the dictionary? – have a ~ (and see)** steht das im Wörterbuch? – sieh *or* guck *(inf)* mal nach; **let's have a ~** lass mal sehen, zeig mal her; **let's have a ~ at it** lass mal sehen, zeig mal; **let's have a ~ at you** lass dich mal ansehen; **do you want a ~?** willst du mal sehen?; *(at the paper)* willst du mal hineinsehen *or* einen Blick hineinwerfen?; **to take a good ~ at sth** sich *(dat)* etw genau ansehen; **take** *or* **have a good ~** sehen *or* gucken *(inf)* Sie genau hin; **to have a ~ for sth** sich nach etw umsehen; **I can't find it – have another ~** ich finde es nicht – sieh *or* guck *(inf)* noch mal nach; **to have a ~ (a)round** sich umsehen; **shall we have a ~ (a)round the town?** sollen wir uns *(dat)* die Stadt ansehen?

b *(= air, appearance)* Aussehen *nt*; **there was a ~ of despair in his eyes** ein verzweifelter Blick war in seinen Augen; **he put on a serious ~** er machte ein ernstes Gesicht; **he had the ~ of a sailor** er sah wie ein Seeman aus; **I don't like the ~ of him/this wound** er/die Wunde gefällt mir gar nicht; **by the ~ of him** so, wie er aussieht; **judging by the ~ of the sky** wenn man sich *(dat)* den Himmel ansieht, so, wie der Himmel aussieht; **to give sth a new ~** einer Sache *(dat)* ein neues Aussehen verleihen *or* Gesicht geben; **the town has now taken on a new ~** die Stadt hat ein neues Gesicht bekommen

c **looks** PL Aussehen *nt*; **good ~s** gutes Aussehen; **~s aren't everything** auf das Aussehen allein kommt es nicht an; **you can't judge by ~s alone** man kann nicht nur nach dem Aussehen *or* Äußeren urteilen; **she began to lose her ~s** sie verlor allmählich ihr gutes Aussehen

VT **he ~s his age** man sieht ihm sein Alter an; **he's not ~ing himself these days** er sieht in letzter Zeit ganz verändert aus; **he's ~ing his old self again** er ist wieder ganz der Alte; **to ~ one's best** sehr vorteilhaft aussehen; **I want to ~ my best tonight** ich möchte heute Abend besonders gut aussehen; **she ~s best in red** Rot steht ihr am besten; **he ~ed death in the face** er sah dem Tod ins Angesicht *(geh) or* Auge; **~ what you've done!** sieh *or* guck *(inf)* dir mal an, was du da angestellt hast!; **~ what you've done, now she's offended** jetzt hast dus geschafft, nun ist sie beleidigt; **~ what you've made me do** (sieh *or* schau *(dial) or* guck *(inf)* mal,) daran bist du schuld; **can't you ~ what you're doing?** kannst du nicht aufpassen, was du machst?; **~ where you're going!** pass auf, wo du hintrittst!; **just ~ where he's put the car!** sieh *or* schau *(dial) or* guck *(inf)* dir bloß mal an, wo er das Auto abgestellt hat!; **~ who's here!** guck *(inf) or* schau *(dial)* mal *or* sieh doch, wer da ist!

VI **a** *(= see, glance)* gucken *(inf)*, schauen *(liter, dial)*; **to ~ (a)round** sich umsehen; **he ~ed in(to) the chest** er sah *or* schaute *(dial) or* guckte *(inf)* in die Kiste (hinein); **to ~ carefully** genau hinsehen *etc*; **to ~ and see** nachsehen *etc*; **~ here!** hör (mal) zu!; **now ~ here, it wasn't my fault** Moment mal, das war aber nicht meine Schuld; **~, I know you're tired, but …** ich weiß ja, dass du müde bist, aber …; **~, there's a much better solution** da gibt es doch eine wesentlich bessere Lösung; **just ~!** guck mal!; **to ~ the other way** *(fig)* die Augen verschließen; **to ~ over sb's shoulder** jdm über die Schulter sehen; **to ~ over one's shoulder** nach hinten sehen; **~ before you leap** *(Prov)* erst wägen, dann wagen *(Prov)*

b *(= search)* suchen, nachsehen

c *(= seem)* aussehen; **it ~s all right to me** es

scheint mir in Ordnung zu sein; **it ~s suspicious to me** es kommt mir verdächtig vor, es sieht verdächtig aus; **how does it ~ to you?** was meinst du dazu?; **I think the cake is done, how does it ~ to you?** ich glaube, der Kuchen ist fertig, was meinst du?; **the car ~s about 10 years old** das Auto sieht so aus, als ob es 10 Jahre alt wäre; **the trophy ~s well on your mantelpiece** die Trophäe macht sich gut auf deinem Kaminsims
d **to ~ like** aussehen wie; **the picture doesn't ~ like him** das Bild sieht ihm nicht ähnlich; **it ~s like rain, it ~s as if it will rain** es sieht nach Regen aus; **it ~s like cheese to me** (ich finde,) das sieht wie Käse aus; **it ~s as if we'll be late** es sieht (so) aus, als würden wir zu spät kommen; **the festival ~s like being busy** auf dem Festival wird es wahrscheinlich sehr voll (werden)
e *(= face)* gehen nach; **this window ~s (toward(s) the) north** dieses Fenster geht nach Norden; **the village ~s toward(s) the forest** das Dorf liegt dem Wald zugewendet

▶ **look about** VI *(Brit)* sich umsehen *(for sth* nach etw); **to look about one** sich umsehen; **if we look about we might find some more examples** wenn wir suchen, finden wir vielleicht noch ein paar Beispiele

▶ **look after** VI *+prep obj* **a** *(= take care of)* sich kümmern um; **to look after oneself** *(= cook etc)* für sich selbst sorgen, sich selbst versorgen; *(= be capable, strong etc)* auf sich *(acc)* aufpassen; **he's only looking after his own interests** er handelt nur im eigenen Interesse **b** *(temporarily)* sehen nach; *children* aufpassen auf *(+acc)* **c** *(= follow with eyes)* nachsehen *(+dat)*

▶ **look ahead** VI **a** *(lit)* nach vorne sehen *or* gucken *(inf)* **b** *(fig)* vorausschauen; **when we look ahead to the next 30 years/the future of this country** wenn wir die nächsten 30 Jahre/die Zukunft dieses Landes betrachten; **a good manager is one who can look ahead** ein guter Manager muss Weitblick haben

▶ **look around** VI **a** *(generally)* sich umsehen **b** *(in shop etc)* sich umsehen; *(+prep obj)* sich *(dat)* ansehen *or* angucken *(inf)*; **I wanted to look around the exhibition** ich wollte mir die Ausstellung ansehen

▶ **look at** VI *+prep obj* **a** *(= observe) person, object* ansehen, anschauen *(dial)*, angucken *(inf)*; **just look at him!** sieh *etc* dir den mal an!; **look at the time, I'd better go!** so spät ist es schon, ich muss los!; **he looked at his watch** er sah *etc* auf die Uhr; **look at the blackboard** schau(t) an *or* auf die Tafel; **don't look directly at the sun** sehen *etc* Sie nicht direkt in die Sonne; **I can't look at him without feeling …** wenn ich ihn ansehe *etc*, habe ich immer das Gefühl, dass …; **he/it isn't much to look at** *(= not attractive)* er/es sieht nicht besonders (gut) aus; *(= nothing special)* er/es sieht nach nichts aus; **to look at him …** wenn man ihn sieht …
b *(= examine)* sich *(dat)* ansehen *or* -schauen *(dial) or* -gucken *(inf)*; *offer* prüfen; **we'll have to look at the financial aspect** wir müssen die finanzielle Seite betrachten; **has the manuscript been looked at yet?** ist das Manuskript schon durchgesehen worden?
c *(= view)* betrachten, sehen; **they look at life in a different way** sie haben eine andere Einstellung zum Leben, sie sehen das Leben von einer anderen Warte aus
d *(= consider) possibilities* sich *(dat)* überlegen; *suggestions, offer* in Betracht ziehen

▶ **look away** VI **a** *(person)* wegsehen **b** **the house looks away from the sea** das Haus liegt vom Meer abgewendet

▶ **look back** VI sich umsehen; *(fig)* zurückblicken *(on sth, to sth* auf etw *acc)*; **he's never looked back** *(fig inf)* es ist ständig mit ihm bergauf gegangen

▶ **look down** VI hinunter-/heruntersehen *or* -schauen *(dial) or* -gucken *(inf)*; **we looked down the hole** wir sahen *etc* ins Loch hinunter; **look down on the valley below** sieh *etc* ins Tal hinunter

▶ **look down on** VI *+prep obj* herabsehen auf *(+acc)*; **you shouldn't look down on his attempts to help** du solltest ihn nicht belächeln, wenn er versucht zu helfen

▶ **look for** VI *+prep obj* **a** *(= seek)* suchen; **he's looking for trouble** er wird sich *(dat)* Ärger einhandeln; *(actively)* er sucht Streit **b** *(= expect)* erwarten

▶ **look forward to** ✪ 21.2 VI *+prep obj* sich freuen auf *(+acc)*; **I'm so looking forward to seeing you again** ich freue mich so darauf, dich wiederzusehen; **I look forward to hearing from you** ich hoffe, bald von Ihnen zu hören

▶ **look in** VI **a** *(in window etc)* hinein-/hereinsehen *or* -schauen *(dial) or* -gucken *(inf)* **b** *(= visit)* vorbeikommen *(on sb* bei jdm); **would you look in at Smith's and collect my dress?** kannst du bei Smith vorbeigehen und mein Kleid abholen? **c** *(= watch TV)* fernsehen

▶ **look into** VI *+prep obj* **a** **to look into sb's face** jdm ins Gesicht sehen; **to look into the future** in die Zukunft sehen *or* blicken **b** *(= investigate)* untersuchen; *matter, complaint etc* prüfen

▶ **look on** VI **a** *(= watch)* zusehen, zugucken *(inf)* **b** **to look onto** *(window)* (hinaus)gehen auf *(+acc)*; *(building)* liegen an *(+dat)* **c** *+prep obj (also* **look upon**) betrachten, ansehen; **to look on sb as a friend** jdn als Freund betrachten; **I look on him as a good doctor** ich halte ihn für einen guten Arzt; **to look on sb with respect** Achtung *or* Respekt vor jdm haben; **employers look favourably** *(Brit) or* **favorably** *(US)* **on people with experience** Arbeitgeber bevorzugen Leute mit Erfahrung

▶ **look out** VI **a** *(of window etc)* hinaus-/heraussehen *or* -schauen *(dial) or* -gucken *(inf)*; **to look out (of) the window** zum Fenster hinaussehen *etc*, aus dem Fenster sehen *etc* **b** *(building etc)* **to look out on** *or* **over sth** einen Blick auf etw *(acc)* haben **c** *(= take care)* aufpassen; **look out!** pass auf!, Vorsicht! VT *sep* heraussuchen

▶ **look out for** VI *+prep obj* **a** *(= keep watch for)* **we'll look out for you at the station/after the meeting** wir werden auf dem Bahnhof/nach der Versammlung nach dir Ausschau halten; **look out for pickpockets/his left hook** nimm dich vor Taschendieben/seinem linken Haken in Acht, pass auf Taschendiebe/auf seinen linken Haken auf; **the bouncers were told to look out for troublemakers** die Rausschmeißer sollten auf Unruhestifter achten *or* achtgeben; **you must look out for spelling mistakes/snakes** Sie müssen auf Rechtschreibfehler/Schlangen achten
b *(= seek) new job* sich umsehen nach; *new staff, ideas* suchen
c *(= take care of)* sich kümmern um

▶ **look over** VT *sep papers, notes etc* durchsehen; *house* sich *(dat)* ansehen

▶ **look round** VI *(esp Brit)* = **look around**

▶ **look through** VI durchsehen *or* -schauen *(dial) or* -gucken *(inf)* *(prep obj* durch); **he stopped at the window and looked through** er blieb am Fenster stehen und sah *etc* hinein/herein; **he looked through the window** er sah *etc* zum Fenster hinein/herein/hinaus/heraus; **to look straight through sb** durch jdn hindurchgucken VT *sep (= examine)* durchsehen; *(= read)* durchlesen

▶ **look to** VI *+prep obj* **a** *(= rely on)* sich verlassen auf *(+acc)*; **they looked to him to solve the problem** sie verließen sich darauf, dass er das Problem lösen würde; **we look to you for support** wir rechnen auf Ihre *or* mit Ihrer Hilfe; **we look to you to lead the country** wir rechnen damit *or* zählen darauf, dass Sie das Land führen; **there's no point in looking to him for help** es ist sinnlos, von ihm Hilfe zu erwarten; **we look to you for guidance** wir wenden uns an Sie um Rat
b **to look to the future** in die Zukunft sehen *or* blicken
c *(= look after)* sich kümmern um; **look to it that …** sieh zu, dass …

▶ **look up** VI **a** *(lit)* aufsehen *or* -blicken; **don't look up** guck nicht hoch *(inf)* **b** *(= improve)* besser werden; *(shares, prices)* steigen; **things are looking up** es geht bergauf VT *sep* **a** **to look sb up and down** jdn von oben bis unten ansehen *or* mustern **b** *(= visit)* **to look sb up** bei jdm vorbeischauen, jdn besuchen **c** *(= seek) word* nachschlagen; *phone number, address* heraussuchen

▶ **look upon** VI *+prep obj* = **look on c**

▶ **look up to** VI *+prep obj* **to look up to sb** zu jdm aufsehen; **he was always looked up to** andere haben immer zu ihm aufgesehen

look: **lookalike** N Doppelgänger(in) *m(f)*; **a Rupert Murdoch ~** ein Doppelgänger von Rupert Murdoch; **it's not just another ~** es sieht nicht wie all die anderen aus; **look-around** N **to have** *or* **take a ~** sich umsehen

looked-for [ˈlʊktfɔː] ADJ *(= expected)* (lang) ersehnt

looker [ˈlʊkəʳ] N *(inf)* **to be a (good** *or* **real) ~** klasse aussehen *(inf)*

looker-on [ˈlʊkərˈɒn] N Zuschauer(in) *m(f)*, Schaulustige(r) *mf (pej)*

look-in [ˈlʊkɪn] N *(inf)* Chance *f*; **he didn't get a ~** er hatte keine Chance

-looking [-ˈlʊkɪŋ] ADJ *suf* aussehend; **good-looking** gut aussehend; **she/it is not bad-looking** sie/es sieht nicht schlecht aus

looking glass N Spiegel *m*

lookism [ˈlʊkɪzəm] N *Bevorzugung von gut aussehenden Menschen*

look: **lookout** N **a** *(= tower etc) (Mil)* Ausguck *m*; **~ post/station/tower** Beobachtungsposten *m*/-station *f*/-turm *m* **b** *(= person) (Mil)* Wacht- *or* Beobachtungsposten *m*; **the thieves had a ~ on the building opposite** einer der Diebe stand auf dem gegenüberliegenden Gebäude Wache *or* Schmiere *(inf)* **c** **to keep a ~** Ausschau halten; **to be on the ~ for, to keep a ~ for** → **look out for d** *(= prospect)* Aussichten *pl*; **it's a grim ~ for us** es sieht schlecht aus für uns **e** *(inf: = worry)* **that's his ~!** das ist sein Problem!; **look-over** N **to give sth a ~** (sich *dat*) etw flüchtig ansehen, einen flüchtigen Blick auf etw werfen; *(= check)* etw flüchtig (über)prüfen; **look-see** N *(inf)* **to have a ~** nachgucken *(inf) or* -schauen *(dial) or* -sehen; **look-through** N *(inf)* Durchsicht *f*; **would you have a ~?** können Sie sich das mal durchsehen?; **to give sth a quick ~** etw kurz durchsehen

loom¹ [luːm] N Webstuhl *m*

loom² VI *(also* **loom ahead** *or* **up)** *(lit, fig)* sich abzeichnen; *(storm)* heraufziehen; *(disaster)* sich zusammenbrauen; *(danger)* drohen; *(difficulties)* sich auftürmen; *(exams)* bedrohlich näher rücken; **the ship ~ed (up) out of the mist** das Schiff tauchte bedrohlich aus dem Nebel (auf); **the threat of unemployment was ~ing on the horizon** Arbeitslosigkeit zeichnete sich bedrohlich am Horizont ab; **the threat of war ~s ahead** ein Krieg zeichnet sich bedrohlich ab; **the fear of a sudden attack ~ed in his mind** er hatte große Angst vor einem plötzlichen Angriff; **to ~ large** eine große Rolle spielen; **the skyscraper ~s over the city** der Wolkenkratzer ragt über die Stadt

loon¹ [luːn] N *(Orn)* Seetaucher *m*

loon² N *(inf)* Blödmann *m (inf)*

loon pants, loons [luːnz] PL *enge Hüfthose mit Schlag*

loony [ˈluːnɪ] *(inf)* ADJ *(+er)* bekloppt *(inf)* N Verrückte(r) *mf (inf)*, Irre(r) *mf*

loony: **loony bin** N *(inf)* Klapsmühle *f (inf)*; **loony left** *(Brit Pol) (pej inf)* N **the ~** die radikale Linke ADJ ATTR linksradikal

loop [luːp] N **a** *(= curved shape)* Schlaufe *f*; *(of wire)* Schlinge *f*; *(of river, Rail)* Schleife *f*; *(Med)*

Spirale *f*; **to knock** *or* **throw sb for a ~** *(esp US inf)* jdn völlig umhauen *(inf)* **b** *(Aviat)* Looping *m*; **to ~ the ~** einen Looping machen **c** *(Comput)* Schleife *f* **VT** *rope etc* schlingen *(round* um); **to ~ a rope through a ring** ein Seil durch einen Ring ziehen; **she ~ed her arm through his** sie hängte sich bei ihm ein **VI** *(rope etc)* sich schlingen; *(line, road etc)* eine Schleife machen; **the road ~s (a)round the fields** die Straße schlängelt sich um die Felder

▶ **loop back** **VT** *sep* **loop the wire back around the lid** biegen Sie den Draht zurück um den Deckel **VI** **a** *(road)* eine Schleife machen; *(person)* in einem Bogen zurückkehren; **this wire has to loop back** dieser Draht muss zurückgebogen werden **b** *(Comput)* **the program then loops back to ...** die Programmschleife wird dann ab ... nochmals durchlaufen

loop: **loophole** [ˈluːphəʊl] N *(Mil)* Schießscharte *f*; *(fig)* Hintertürchen *nt*; **a ~ in the law** eine Lücke im Gesetz; **loopline** N *(Rail)* Schleife *f*

loopy [ˈluːpɪ] ADJ *(+er)* *(Brit inf)* bekloppt *(inf)*; **to go ~** durchdrehen *(inf)*

loose [luːs] **ADJ** *(+er)* **a** *(= not tight, movable) board, button* lose; *dress, collar* weit; *tooth, bandage, knot, screw, soil, weave* locker; *limbs* beweglich, locker; **he kept his change ~ in his pocket** er hatte sein Kleingeld lose in der Tasche; **a ~ connection** *(Elec)* ein Wackelkontakt *m*; **to come** *or* **work ~** *(screw, handle etc)* sich lockern; *(sole, cover etc)* sich (los)lösen; *(button)* abgehen; **to hang ~** lose herunterhängen; **her hair hung ~** sie trug ihr Haar offen; **to have ~ bowels** Durchfall haben; **just stay** *or* **hang ~** *(inf)* bleib cool *(inf)*; **to sell sth ~** *(= not pre-packed)* etw lose verkaufen

b *(= free)* **to break** *or* **get ~** *(person, animal)* sich losreißen *(from* von); *(ship)* sich (von der Vertäuung) losreißen; *(from group of players etc)* sich trennen, sich lösen; *(= break out)* ausbrechen; *(from commitment, parental home etc)* sich frei machen *(from* von); **to run ~** frei herumlaufen; *(children)* unbeaufsichtigt herumlaufen; **to turn** *or* **let** *or* **set ~** *(animal)* frei herumlaufen lassen; *prisoner* freilassen; *imagination* freien Lauf lassen *(+dat)*; **to let ~ political forces that will be difficult to control** politische Kräfte entfesseln *or* freisetzen, die nur schwer unter Kontrolle zu bringen sind; **I let him ~ on the garden** ich ließ ihn auf den Garten los; **to be at a ~ end** *(fig)* nichts mit sich anzufangen wissen; **to tie up the ~ ends** *(fig)* ein paar offene *or* offenstehende Probleme lösen

c *(= not exact, vague) translation* frei; *account, thinking, planning* ungenau; *connection* lose; **in a ~ sense** im weiteren Sinne; *(= approximately)* grob gesagt

d *(= informal) group, alliance, organization, arrangement* lose, locker

e *(= too free, immoral) conduct* lose; *morals* locker; *person* unmoralisch, lose; **a ~ life** ein lockerer Lebenswandel; **a ~ woman** eine Frau mit lockerem Lebenswandel; **in that bar you get ~ women** in der Bar findest du lose Mädchen; **do you think that's being ~?** meinst du, das ist unmoralisch?; **to have a ~ tongue** nichts für sich behalten können; **~ talk** leichtfertiges Gerede

N *(inf)* **to be on the ~** *(prisoners, dangerous animals)* frei herumlaufen; **he was on the ~ in Paris** er machte Paris unsicher; **the troops were on the ~ in the city** die Truppen wüteten in der Stadt; **oh dear, when these two are on the ~** wehe, wenn sie losgelassen!

VT **a** *(= free)* befreien

b *(= untie)* losmachen

c *(= slacken)* lockern

d *(also* **loose off***) bullet, missile* abfeuern; *arrow* schießen; *gun* feuern; *(fig) tirade, curse* loslassen; **to ~ off a volley** *or* **stream of abuse at sb** eine Schimpfkanonade auf jdn loslassen

loose: **loosebox** N Box *f*; **loose cannon** N **to be a ~** *(= uncontrollable)* unkontrollierbar sein; *(= dangerous)* gemeingefährlich sein; **loose change** N Kleingeld *nt*; **loose chippings** PL *(on roadway)* Rollsplitt *m*; **loose covers** PL Überzüge *pl*; **loose-fitting** ADJ weit; **loose-leaf** N **~ binder** Ringbuch *nt*; **~ book** Loseblattausgabe *f*; **~ pad** Ringbucheinlage *f*; **loose-limbed** ADJ *(= lithe)* gelenkig, beweglich; *(= gangling)* schlaksig; **loose-living** ADJ verkommen, lose

loosely [ˈluːslɪ] ADV **a** lose, locker; *knit, weave* locker; **in hot countries it's better to be ~ dressed in robes** in warmen Ländern trägt man besser weit geschnittene *or* lose hängende Kleider; **his hands dangled ~ from his wrists** er ließ seine Hände locker baumeln; **he held her hand ~ in his** er hielt ihre Hand locker in der seinen

b *(= imprecisely)* **~ speaking** grob gesagt; **~ translated** frei übersetzt; **~ based on Shakespeare** frei nach Shakespeare; **the character is ~ based on X** die Figur ist frei nach X gestaltet; **what is ~ termed socialist realism** das, was man ganz allgemein als sozialistischen Realismus bezeichnet; **I was using the word rather ~** ich habe das Wort ziemlich frei gebraucht; **they are ~ connected** sie hängen lose zusammen

c *(= informally) organized, structured* lose; **a ~ knit group** eine lose Gruppe

d *behave* unmoralisch; **he lives ~** er führt ein loses *or* lockeres Leben

loosen [ˈluːsn] **VT** **a** *(= free)* befreien; *tongue* lösen **b** *(= untie)* losmachen, lösen **c** *(= slacken)* lockern; *belt* lockern, weiter machen; *soil* auflockern; *collar* aufmachen; *reins* locker lassen; **to ~ one's grip on sth** *(lit)* seinen Griff um etw lockern; *(fig) on the party, on power* etw nicht mehr so fest im Griff haben **VI** sich lockern

▶ **loosen up** **VT** *sep muscles* lockern; *soil* auflockern **VI** *(muscles)* locker werden; *(athlete)* sich (auf)lockern; *(= relax)* auftauen

looseness [ˈluːsnɪs] N Lockerheit *f*; *(of clothes)* Weite *f*; *(of thinking)* Ungenauigkeit *f*; *(of translation)* Freiheit *f*; **~ of the bowels** zu rege Darmtätigkeit; **the ~ of her conduct** ihr loses *or* unmoralisches Benehmen; **the ~ of the book's structure** die lockere Struktur des Buches

loot [luːt] **N** Beute *f*; *(dated inf: = money)* Zaster *m (dated sl)* **VTI** plündern

looter [ˈluːtəˊ] N Plünderer *m*

lop [lɒp] VT *(also* **lop off***)* abhacken

lope [ləʊp] VI in großen Sätzen springen; *(hare)* hoppeln; **he ~d along beside her** er lief mit großen Schritten neben ihr her; **to ~ off** davonspringen

lop-eared [ˈlɒpˌɪəd] ADJ mit Hängeohren

lop ears PL Hänge- *or* Schlappohren *(inf) pl*

lopsided [ˈlɒpˈsaɪdɪd] ADJ schief; *(fig)* einseitig

loquacious [ləˈkweɪʃəs] ADJ redselig

loquacity [ləˈkwæsɪtɪ] N Redseligkeit *f*

lord [lɔːd] **N** **a** *(= master, ruler)* Herr *m*; **~ and master** Herr und Meister *m*; *(hum: = husband)* Herr und Gebieter *m*; **tobacco ~s** Tabakkönige *pl*

b *(Brit: = nobleman)* Lord *m*; **the (House of) Lords** das Oberhaus; **my ~** *(to bishop)* Exzellenz; *(to noble, in English contexts)* Mylord; *(to baron)* Herr Baron; *(to earl, viscount)* Euer Erlaucht; *(to judge)* Euer Ehren

c *(Brit: = important official)* **First Lord of the Admiralty** Stabschef *m* der Marine

d *(Rel)* **Lord** Herr *m*; **the Lord (our) God** Gott, der Herr; **(good) Lord!** *(inf)* ach, du lieber Himmel! *(inf)*, (ach,) du meine Güte! *(inf)*; *(annoyed)* mein Gott! *(inf)*; **Lord help him!** *(inf)* (dann) Gnade ihm Gott!; **Lord knows** *(inf)* wer weiß; **Lord knows I've tried often enough** ich habs weiß Gott oft genug versucht

VT **to ~ it** das Zepter schwingen; **to ~ it over sb** jdn herumkommandieren

Lord Chancellor N *(Brit)* Lordsiegelbewahrer *m*, Lordkanzler *m*

Lord Justice N *(Brit) Richter an einem Berufungsgericht*

lordliness [ˈlɔːdlɪnɪs] N Vornehmheit *f*; *(= haughtiness)* Überheblichkeit *f*, Arroganz *f*

lordly [ˈlɔːdlɪ] ADJ *(+er)* **a** *(= magnificent)* vornehm; *house* (hoch)herrschaftlich **b** *(= proud, haughty)* hochmütig, arrogant; *tone of voice* herrisch, gebieterisch

Lord Mayor N *(Brit)* ≈ Oberbürgermeister *m*

Lord's Day [ˈlɔːdzdeɪ] N *(Rel)* **the ~** der Tag des Herrn

Lordship [ˈlɔːdʃɪp] N *(Brit: = title)* Lordschaft *f*; **His/Your ~** Seine/Eure Lordschaft; *(to bishop)* Seine/Eure Exzellenz; *(to judge)* Seine/Euer Ehren *or* Gnaden

Lord's Prayer [ˈlɔːdzˈprɛəˊ] N *(Rel)* **the ~** das Vaterunser

Lord's Supper [ˈlɔːdzˈsʌpəˊ] N *(Rel)* **the ~** das (Heilige) Abendmahl

lore [lɔːˊ] N Überlieferungen *pl*; **in local ~** nach hiesiger Überlieferung; **plant ~** Pflanzenkunde *f*

lorgnette [lɔːˈnjet] N Lorgnette *f*

lorry [ˈlɒrɪ] N *(Brit)* Last(kraft)wagen *m*, Lkw *m*, Laster *m (inf)*; **it fell off the back of a ~** *(hum inf)* ich hab/er hat *etc* das „gefunden" *(hum inf)*

lorry driver N *(Brit)* Last(kraft)wagenfahrer(in) *m(f)*, Lkw-Fahrer(in) *m(f)*

lose [luːz] *pret, ptp* **lost** **VT** **a** *(generally)* verlieren; *pursuer* abschütteln; *one's French* vergessen, verlernen; *prize* nicht bekommen; **to ~ one's job/(driving) licence** *(Brit)* *or* **(driver's) license** *(US)* die Stelle/den Führerschein verlieren; **many men ~ their hair** vielen Männern gehen die Haare aus; **the cat has lost a lot of hair** die Katze hat viel Haar verloren; **they lost 100 planes in one battle** sie haben in einer Schlacht 100 Flugzeuge verloren; **the shares have lost 15% in a month** die Aktien sind in einem Monat um 15% gefallen; **to ~ one's way** *(lit)* sich verirren; *(fig)* die Richtung verlieren; **you will ~ nothing by helping them** es kann dir nicht schaden, wenn du ihnen hilfst; **they have nothing/a lot to ~** sie haben nichts/viel zu verlieren; **that mistake lost him his job/her friendship/the game** dieser Fehler kostete ihn die Stellung/ihre Freundschaft/den Sieg; **she lost her brother in the war** sie hat ihren Bruder im Krieg verloren; **he lost the use of his legs in the accident** seit dem Unfall kann er seine Beine nicht mehr bewegen; **he lost himself in his work** er ging ganz in seiner Arbeit auf; **he likes to ~ himself in his memories** er verliert sich gern in Erinnerungen; **he's lost the desire to live** er hat keinen Lebenswillen mehr; **to ~ no time in doing sth** etw sofort tun; **we lost valuable time just talking** wir haben beim Reden wertvolle Zeit verloren

b **my watch lost three hours** meine Uhr ist drei Stunden nachgegangen

c **you've lost me now with all this abstract argument** bei dieser abstrakten Argumentation komme ich nicht mehr mit

d *(= not catch) opportunity* verpassen; *words* nicht mitbekommen; **to ~ no opportunity to do sth** keine Gelegenheit verpassen, etw zu tun

e *(inf: = go crazy)* **to ~ it** durchdrehen *(inf)*; **he's finally lost it** jetzt ist er völlig durchgedreht *(inf)*

f *(passive usages)* **to be lost** *(things)* verschwunden sein; *(people)* sich verlaufen haben; *(fig)* verloren sein; *(words)* untergehen; **I can't follow the reasoning, I'm lost** ich kann der Argumentation nicht folgen, ich verstehe nichts mehr; **he was soon lost in the crowd** er hatte sich bald in der Menge verloren; **to be lost at sea** auf See geblieben sein; *(ship)* auf See vermisst sein; **the ship was lost with all hands** das Schiff war mit der ganzen Besatzung untergegangen; **all is (not) lost!** (noch ist nicht) alles verloren!; **to get lost** sich verlaufen *or* verirren; *(boxes etc)* verloren gehen; **I got lost after the second chapter** nach dem zweiten Kapitel kam ich nicht mehr mit; **to get lost in the post/move** in der Post/beim Umzug verloren gehen; **get lost!** *(inf)* verschwinde! *(inf)*; **to look lost** (ganz) verloren aussehen; *(fig)* ratlos *or* hilflos aussehen; **you look (as though you're) lost, can I help you?** haben Sie sich verlaufen *or* verirrt, kann ich Ihnen behilflich sein?; **to give sb up for lost** jdn verloren geben; **to give sth up for lost** etw abschreiben; **he was lost to science** er war für die Wissenschaft verloren; **he is lost to all finer feelings** er hat keinen Sinn für höhere Gefühle; **I'm lost without my watch** ohne meine Uhr bin ich verloren *or* aufgeschmissen *(inf)*; **classical music is lost on him** er hat keinen Sinn für klassische Musik; **the joke/remark was lost on her** der Witz/die Bemerkung kam bei ihr nicht an; **the irony was not lost on me** ich verstand die Ironie durchaus; **to be lost for words** sprachlos sein; **to be lost in thought** in Gedanken versunken sein; **to be lost in one's reading/playing** in seine Lektüre/sein Spiel versunken sein; **to be lost to the world** für die Welt verloren sein

VI verlieren; *(watch)* nachgehen; **you can't ~** du kannst nichts verlieren; **the novel ~s a lot in the film** der Roman verliert in der Verfilmung sehr; **you will not ~ by helping him** es kann dir nicht schaden, wenn du ihm hilfst

▶ **lose out** VI *(inf)* schlecht wegkommen *(inf)*, den Kürzeren ziehen (*on* bei); **to lose out to sb/sth** von jdm/etw verdrängt werden

loser ['lu:zəʳ] N Verlierer(in) *m(f)*; **he is a good/bad ~** er ist ein guter/schlechter Verlierer; **he's a born ~** er ist der geborene Verlierer; **what a ~!** *(inf)* was für eine Null! *(inf)*

losing ['lu:zɪŋ] **ADJ** **the ~ team** die unterlegene Mannschaft; **to fight a ~ battle** einen aussichtslosen Kampf führen; **the ~ side/party** die Verliererseite; **to be on the ~ side** verlieren **N** **~s** Verluste *pl*

loss [lɒs] N **a** Verlust *m*; **hair ~** Haarausfall *m*; **weight ~** Gewichtsverlust *m*; **~ of memory, memory ~** Gedächtnisverlust *m*; **progressive ~ of memory** Gedächtnisschwund *m*; **the ~ of the last three games upset the team** die letzten drei Niederlagen brachten die Mannschaft aus der Fassung; **the factory closed with the ~ of 300 jobs** bei der Schließung der Fabrik gingen 300 Stellen verloren; **~ of speed/time** *etc* Geschwindigkeits-/Zeitverlust *m etc*; **~ of picture/sound** *(TV)* Bild-/Tonausfall *m*; **to feel a sense of ~** ein Gefühl *nt* des Verlusts haben; **he felt her ~ very deeply** ihr Tod war ein schwerer Verlust für ihn; **there was a heavy ~ of life** viele kamen ums Leben

b *(= amount, sth lost)* Verlust *m*; **job ~es** Stellenkürzungen *pl*; **how many ~es has the team had so far?** wie viele Spiele hat die Mannschaft bis jetzt verloren?; **the army suffered heavy ~es** die Armee erlitt schwere Verluste; **Conservative ~es in the North** Verluste *pl* der Konservativen im Norden; **his business is running at a ~** er arbeitet mit Verlust; **to sell sth at a ~** etw mit Verlust verkaufen; **it's your ~** es ist deine Sache; **he's no ~** er ist kein (großer) Verlust; **you're a great ~ to the civil service** *(= should have been a civil servant)* an dir ist ein Beamter verloren gegangen; **a dead ~** *(Brit inf)* ein böser Reinfall *(inf)*; *(= person)* ein hoffnungsloser Fall *(inf)*; **total ~** Totalverlust *m*; **to cut one's ~es** *(fig)* Schluss machen, ehe der Schaden (noch) größer wird, Schadensbegrenzung *f* betreiben

c **to be at a ~** nicht mehr weiterwissen; **we are at a ~ with this problem** wir stehen dem Problem ratlos gegenüber; **we are at a ~ for what to do** wir wissen nicht mehr aus noch ein; **to be at a ~ to explain sth** etw nicht erklären können; **we are at a ~ to say why** wir haben keine Ahnung, warum; **to be at a ~ for words** nicht wissen, was man sagen soll; **he's never at a ~ for words/an excuse** er ist nie um Worte/eine Ausrede verlegen

loss: **loss adjuster** N *(Brit Insur)* Schadenssachverständige(r) *mf*; **loss leader** N Lockvogelangebot *nt*; **lossmaker** N *(= company)* mit Verlust arbeitender Betrieb; *(= transaction)* Verlustgeschäft *nt*; *(= product)* Verlustbringer *m*; **loss-making** ADJ **a ~ company** ein Unternehmen, das mit Verlust arbeitet; **loss ratio** N *(= Insur)* Schadensquote *f*

lost [lɒst] *pret, ptp of* **lose** ADJ *attr* verloren; *support* verloren gegangen; *art* ausgestorben; *civilization* untergegangen, versunken; *cause* aussichtslos; *(= missing) person* vermisst; *dog, cat* entlaufen; *(= mislaid) book, glasses etc* verlegt; *(= missed) opportunity* verpasst; **I was groping on the floor for a ~ contact lens** ich tastete auf dem Fußboden nach einer heruntergefallenen Kontaktlinse; **he is mourning his ~ wife** er betrauert den Verlust seiner Frau

lost: **lost-and-found (department)** N *(US)* Fundbüro *nt*; **lost property** N *(Brit)* **a** *(= items)* Fundstücke *pl* **b** = **lost property office**; **lost property office** N *(Brit)* Fundbüro *nt*

lot[1] [lɒt] N **a** *(for deciding)* Los *nt*; **by ~** durch Losentscheid, durch das Los; **to cast** *or* **draw ~s** losen, Lose ziehen; **to draw ~s for sth** etw verlosen; **to draw ~s for a task** eine Aufgabe auslosen; **they drew ~s to see who would begin** sie losten aus, wer anfangen sollte

b *(= destiny)* Los *nt*; **failure was his ~ in life** es war sein Los, immer zu versagen; **it falls to my ~ to tell him** mir fällt die Aufgabe zu, es ihm zu sagen; **to throw in one's ~ with sb** sich mit jdm zusammentun; **to improve one's ~** seine Lage verbessern

c *(= plot)* Parzelle *f*; *(Film)* Filmgelände *nt*; **building ~** Bauplatz *m*; **parking ~** *(US)* Parkplatz *m*; **all over the ~** *(US inf)* *(= everywhere)* überall; *(= in confusion)* völlig durcheinander

d *(= articles of same kind)* Posten *m*; *(at auction)* Los *nt*

e *(esp Brit: = group of things)* **where shall I put this ~?** wo soll ich das hier *or* das Zeug *(inf)* hintun?; **can you carry that ~ by yourself?** kannst du das (alles) alleine tragen?; **divide the books up into three ~s** teile die Bücher in drei Teile *or* Stapel ein; **we moved the furniture in two ~s** wir haben die Möbel in zwei Fuhren befördert; **I'd just finished marking the papers when he gave me another ~** ich war gerade mit dem Korrigieren fertig, da gab er mir einen neuen Packen *or* Stoß *or* noch eine Ladung *(inf)*; **we bought a new ~ of cutlery** wir haben uns (ein) neues Besteck gekauft

f *(esp Brit)* **he/she is a bad ~** *(inf)* er/sie taugt nichts, er/sie ist eine miese Type *(inf)*; **they are a bad ~** *(inf)* das ist ein übles Pack

g *(esp Brit inf: = group)* Haufen *m*; **that ~ in the next office** die Typen vom Büro nebenan *(inf)*; **I'm fed up with you ~** ich hab die Nase voll von euch allen *(inf)* *or* von euch Bande *(inf)*; **are you ~ coming to the pub?** kommt ihr (alle) in die Kneipe?; **us ~ should stick together** wir sollten alle zusammenhalten; **bring your ~ with you** bring die ganze Mannschaft mit

h **the ~** *(inf)* alle; alles; **that's the ~** das ist alles, das wärs *(inf)*; **the whole ~ of them** sie alle; **he's eaten the ~** er hat alles aufgegessen; **big ones, little ones, the ~!** Große, Kleine, alle!

lot[2] **N** **a ~, ~s** viel; **a ~ of money** viel *or* eine Menge Geld; **a ~ of books, ~s of books** viele *or* eine Menge Bücher; **such a ~** so viel; **what a ~!** was für eine Menge!; **what a ~ of time you take to get ready** wie lange du nur brauchst, um dich fertig zu machen; **what a ~ you've got** du hast aber viel; **how much has he got? – ~s** *or* **a ~** wie viel hat er? – jede Menge *(inf)* *or* viel; **quite a ~ of books** ziemlich viele *or* eine ganze Menge Bücher; **such a ~ of books** so viele Bücher; **an awful ~ of things to do** furchtbar viel zu tun; **he made ~s and ~s of mistakes** er hat eine Unmenge Fehler gemacht; **I want ~s and ~s** ich will jede Menge *(inf)*; **we see a ~ of John these days** wir sehen John in letzter Zeit sehr oft; **I'd give a ~ to know ...** ich würde viel drum geben, wenn ich wüsste ...

ADV **a ~, ~s** viel; **things have changed a ~** es hat sich vieles geändert; **I like him a ~** ich mag ihn sehr; **I feel ~s** *or* **a ~ better** es geht mir sehr viel besser; **a ~ you care!** dich interessiert das überhaupt nicht!

loth ADJ = **loath**

Lothario [ləʊ'θɑ:rɪ,əʊ] N *(hum)* Don Juan *m*

lotion ['ləʊʃən] N Lotion *f*; *(esp US: = moisturizer)* Feuchtigkeitscreme *f*

lottery ['lɒtərɪ] N Lotterie *f*; **life is a ~** das Leben ist ein Glücksspiel; **~ ticket** Lotterielos *nt*; *(for Lotto)* Tippschein *inf*, Tippzettel *inf*

lotus ['ləʊtəs] N Lotos *m*

lotus-eater ['ləʊtəs,i:təʳ] N Lotophage *m*, Lotosesser(in) *m(f)*; *(fig)* Müßiggänger(in) *m(f)*

lotus effect N Lotuseffekt *m*

lotus position N Lotossitz *m*

louche [lu:ʃ] ADJ *(= disreputable) person, place* verrufen, berüchtigt

loud [laʊd] **ADJ** *(+er)* **a** laut; *protest, criticism, complaint* lautstark; **he was ~ in his praise of the concert** er lobte das Konzert überschwänglich; **to be ~ in one's condemnation of/opposition to sth** etw lautstark verurteilen/ablehnen **b** *(= obtrusive) behaviour* aufdringlich; *(= garish) colour* grell, schreiend; *tie, clothes* knallbunt **ADV** laut; **~ and clear** laut und deutlich; **to say/read sth out ~** etw laut sagen/lesen; **to laugh/think out ~** laut lachen/denken

loud-hailer [,laʊd'heɪləʳ] N Megafon *nt*, Megaphon *nt*, Flüstertüte *f (inf)*; *(not hand-held)* Lautsprecher *m*

loudly ['laʊdlɪ] ADV **a** laut; *complain, condemn, oppose, criticize* lautstark **b** *(= garishly) clothed* knallbunt; *coloured* grell; **he was ~ dressed in blue** er war in ein grelles Blau gekleidet

loud: **loudmouth** N *(inf)* Großmaul *nt (inf)*; **loudmouthed** ['laʊd,maʊðd] ADJ *(inf)* großmäulig *(inf)*

loudness ['laʊdnɪs] N **a** *(= volume)* Lautstärke *f*; **the ~ of his voice** seine laute Stimme **b** *(= obtrusiveness)* Aufdringlichkeit *f*; *(of colour)* Grellheit *f*; *(of clothes)* Buntheit *f*

loudspeaker [,laʊd'spi:kəʳ] N Lautsprecher *m*; *(of hi-fi also)* Box *f*

lough [lɒx] N *(Ir)* See *m*; *(= sea lough)* Meeresarm *m*

lounge [laʊndʒ] **N** *(in house)* Wohnzimmer *nt*; *(in hotel)* Gesellschaftsraum *m*; *(= lounge bar: on liner etc)* Salon *m*; *(at airport)* Warteraum *m*; **TV ~** Fernsehraum *m* **VI** faulenzen; **to ~ about** *(Brit)* or **around** herumliegen/-sitzen; **to ~ against a wall** sich lässig gegen eine Mauer lehnen; **to ~ back in a chair** sich in einem Stuhl zurücklehnen

lounge: **lounge bar** N Salon *m (vornehmerer Teil einer Gaststätte)*; **lounge chair** N Klubsessel *m*; **lounge lizard** N Salonlöwe *m*

lounger ['laʊndʒəʳ] N **a** Nichtstuer(in) *m(f)*, Faulenzer(in) *m(f)* **b** *(Brit: = reclining chair)* Ruhesessel *m*

lounge: **lounge suit** N Straßenanzug *m*; **lounge suite** N Couch- *or* Polstergarnitur *f*

loupe [lu:p] N *(for jewellers and watchmakers)* Lupe *f*

lour, lower ['laʊəʳ] VI *(person)* ein finsteres Gesicht machen; *(clouds)* sich türmen; **a threatening sky ~ed** der Himmel war bedrohlich dunkel *or* überzogen

louring ['laʊərɪŋ] ADJ finster

louse [laʊs] **N** *pl* **lice** **a** *(Zool)* Laus *f* **b** *(inf)* fieser Kerl *(inf)*; **he behaved like a real ~ to her** er war richtig fies zu ihr *(inf)*, er hat sich richtig fies benommen *(inf)* **VT** *(sl)* **to ~ sth up** etw vermasseln *(inf)*; *friendship* etw kaputt machen *(inf)*

lousy ['laʊzɪ] ADJ **a** verlaust; **he is ~ with money** *(inf)* er ist stinkreich *(inf)*; **this place is ~ with cops** *(inf)* hier wimmelt es nur so von Polizei *(inf)*

b *(inf: = very bad)* mies *(inf)*; *trick etc* fies *(inf)*; **I'm ~ at arithmetic** in Mathe bin ich mies *or* miserabel *(inf)*; **he is ~ at (playing) golf** *or* **a ~ golfer** er spielt miserabel Golf *(inf)*; **you've done a ~ job** du hast saumäßig gearbeitet *(sl)*; **to have ~ luck** saumäßiges Pech haben *(inf)*; **to feel ~** sich mies fühlen *(inf)*; **I feel ~ about**

it mir ist gar nicht wohl bei dem Gedanken daran
c *(inf: = meagre) offer* lausig *(inf)*, mies *(inf)*; **a ~ £3** popelige *or* lausige drei Pfund *(inf)*

lout [laʊt] N Rüpel *m*, Flegel *m*

loutish ['laʊtɪʃ] ADJ rüpelhaft, flegelhaft

louvre, *(US)* **louver** ['lu:və'] N Jalousie *f*; **~ door** Lamellentür *f*

louvred, *(US)* **louvered** ['lu:vəd] ADJ Jalousie-; **~ door** Jalousietür *f*; **~ blinds** Jalousie *f*

lovable ['lʌvəbl] ADJ liebenswert

lovage ['lʌvɪdʒ] N *(Bot)* Liebstöckel *nt or m*

love [lʌv] ✪ 8.4, 21.2, 23.1 **N** **a** *(= affection)* Liebe *f*; **~ is ...** die Liebe ist ...; **the ~ he has for his wife** die Liebe, die er für seine Frau empfindet; **to have a ~ for** *or* **of sb/sth** jdn/etw sehr lieben; **he has a great ~ of soccer/music** er ist ein großer Fußballanhänger/Musikliebhaber; **~ of learning** Freude *f* am Lernen; **~ of adventure** Abenteuerlust *f*; **~ of books** Liebe *f* zu Büchern; **the ~ of God for his creatures** die Liebe Gottes zu seinen Geschöpfen; **~ of (one's) country** Vaterlandsliebe *f*; **for ~** aus Liebe; *(= free)* umsonst; *(= without stakes)* nur zum Vergnügen; **for ~ nor money** nicht für Geld und gute Worte; **for the ~ of** aus Liebe zu; **for the ~ of God!** um Himmels willen!; **he studies history for the ~ of it** er studiert Geschichte aus Liebe zur Sache; **to be in ~ (with sb)** (in jdn) verliebt sein; **to fall in ~ (with sb)** sich (in jdn) verlieben; **there is no ~ lost between them** sie können sich nicht ausstehen; **to make ~** *(sexually)* sich lieben, miteinander schlafen; *(dated) (= flirt)* flirten (*to sb* mit jdm); *(= court)* den Hof machen *(dated)* (*to sb* jdm); **to make ~ to sb** *(sexually)* mit jdm schlafen; **I've never made ~** ich habe noch mit keinem/keiner geschlafen; **make ~ to me** liebe mich; **he's good at making ~** er ist gut in der Liebe; **make ~ not war** Liebe, nicht Krieg
b *(= greetings: in letters etc)* **with all my ~** mit herzlichen Grüßen; **~ from Anna** herzliche Grüße von Anna; **give him my ~** grüß ihn von mir; **to send one's ~ to sb** jdn grüßen lassen; **he sends his ~** er lässt grüßen
c *(= sb/sth causing fondness)* Liebe *f*; **yes, (my) ~** ja, Liebling *or* Schatz; **she's the ~ of my life** sie ist die große Liebe meines Lebens; **sport is the ~ of her life** Sport ist ihre große Liebe; **he sent some roses to his ~** *(dated)* er schickte seiner Liebsten *(dated)* ein paar Rosen; **the child is a little ~** das Kind ist ein kleiner Schatz
d *(inf: form of address)* mein Lieber/meine Liebe; **I'm afraid the bus is full, ~** der Bus ist leider voll
e *(Tennis)* null; **fifteen ~** fünfzehn null
VT lieben; *(= like) thing* gern mögen; **they ~ each other** sie lieben sich; **I ~ tennis** ich mag Tennis sehr gern; *(to play)* ich spiele sehr gern Tennis; **he ~s swimming, he ~s to swim** er schwimmt sehr gern *or* für sein Leben gern; **don't be sad, you know we all ~ you** sei nicht traurig, du weißt doch, dass wir dich alle sehr gernhaben; **I'd ~ to be with you all the time** ich wäre so gerne die ganze Zeit mit dir zusammen; **I'd ~ a cup of tea** ich hätte (liebend) gern(e) eine Tasse Tee; **I'd ~ to come** ich würde sehr *or* liebend gern(e) kommen; **I should ~ to!** sehr *or* liebend gerne!; **we'd all ~ you to come with us** wir würden uns alle sehr freuen, wenn du mitkommen würdest; **I ~ the way she smiles** ich mag es, wie sie lächelt; **I ~ the way he leaves us to do all the work** *(iro)* ist es nicht toll, wie er uns die ganze Arbeit überlässt *(iro)*; **she's going to ~ you for this** *(iro)* das wird sie dir nie vergessen *(iro)*; **she's going to ~ that** *(iro)* na, da wird sie sich aber freuen *(iro)*
VI lieben

love: **love affair** N Liebschaft *f*, Verhältnis *nt*; **the Americans' ~ with firearms** das innige Verhältnis der Amerikaner zu Schusswaffen; **lovebird** N *(Orn)* Unzertrennliche(r) *m*; *(fig inf)* Turteltaube *f*; **lovebite** N Knutschfleck *m* *(inf)*; **love child** N *(dated)* Kind *nt* der Liebe *(dated)*

-loved [-lʌvd] ADJ *suf* -geliebt; **much-loved** viel geliebt; **best-loved** beliebteste(r, s)

love: **love game** N *(Tennis)* Zunullspiel *nt*; **Rosewall lost 3 ~s** Rosewall verlor 3 Spiele zu null; **love handles** PL *(inf)* Rettungsring *m (hum inf)*; **love-hate relationship** N Hassliebe *f*; **they have a ~** zwischen ihnen besteht eine Hassliebe; **loveless** ADJ *life, marriage* ohne Liebe; *home, family, environment* lieblos; **love letter** N Liebesbrief *m*; **love life** N Liebesleben *nt*

loveliness ['lʌvlɪnɪs] N Schönheit *f*; *(of weather, view also)* Herrlichkeit *f*

lovelorn ['lʌvlɔ:n] ADJ *(liter) person* liebeskrank *(liter)*; *song, poem* liebesweh *(liter)*

lovely ['lʌvlɪ] **ADJ** (+er) *(= beautiful)* wunderschön; *baby* niedlich, reizend; *(= delightful)* herrlich, wunderschön; *joke* herrlich; *(= charming, likeable)* liebenswürdig, nett; *personality* einnehmend; *smile* gewinnend; **that dress looks ~ on you** dieses Kleid steht dir sehr gut; **we had a ~ time** es war sehr schön; **it's ~ and warm in this room** es ist schön warm in diesem Zimmer; **all this ~ money** das ganze schöne Geld; **he made a ~ job of it** er hat das wunderbar gemacht; **have a ~ holiday** *(esp Brit) or* **vacation** *(US)!* schöne Ferien!; **it's been ~ to see you** es war schön, dich zu sehen; **how ~ of you to remember!** wie nett *or* lieb, dass Sie daran gedacht haben; **what a ~ thing to say!** wie nett, so was zu sagen!
N *(inf: = person)* Schöne *f*; **yes, my ~** ja, mein schönes Kind

love: **lovemaking** N *(sexual)* Liebe *f*; *(dated: = flirtation)* Flirt *m*; *(dated: = courting)* Liebeswerben *nt (dated)*; **his expert ~** sein gekonntes Liebesspiel; **love match** N Liebesheirat *f*; **love nest** N Liebesnest *nt*; **love philtre** *(old)*, **love potion** N Liebestrank *m*

lover ['lʌvə'] N **a** Liebhaber *m*, Geliebte(r) *m (old, liter)*, Geliebte *f*; **the ~s** die Liebenden *pl*, das Liebespaar; **we were ~s for two years** wir waren zwei Jahre lang zusammen; **Romeo and Juliet were ~s** Romeo und Julia liebten sich; **so she took a ~** da nahm sie sich *(dat)* einen Liebhaber
b **a ~ of books** ein(e) Bücherfreund(in) *m(f)*, ein(e) Liebhaber(in) *m(f)* von Büchern; **a ~ of good food** ein(e) Freund(in) *or* Liebhaber(in) *m(f)* von gutem Essen; **music-~** Musikliebhaber(in) *m(f) or* -freund(in) *m(f)*; **music-lover** Musikliebhaber(in) *m(f) or* -freund(in) *m(f)*; **soccer ~s** Fußballanhänger *or* -begeisterte *pl*

loverboy ['lʌvəbɔɪ] N *(inf)* unser Freund hier *(inf)*; *(= boyfriend)* Freund *m*; **listen, ~** hör mal zu, mein Freund(chen) *(inf)*

love: **love rival** N Nebenbuhler(in) *m(f) (geh)*; **love seat** N Zweiersofa; **love set** N *(Tennis)* Zunullsatz *m*; **lovesick** ADJ liebeskrank; **to be ~** Liebeskummer *m* haben; **love song** N Liebeslied *nt*; **love story** N Liebesgeschichte *f*; **lovestruck** ADJ liebestoll; **love token** N Liebespfand *nt*; **love triangle** N Dreiecksverhältnis *nt*; **love truncheon** N *(Brit hum sl: = penis)* Feuerlöscher *m (sl)*

lovey ['lʌvɪ] N *(Brit inf: address)* Schatz *m (inf)*

lovey-dovey ['lʌvɪ'dʌvɪ] ADJ *(inf)* turtelig, wie die Turteltauben; **to be all ~** völlig vernarrt ineinander sein *(inf)*; **~ couple** (schmusendes) Liebespaar

loving ['lʌvɪŋ] ADJ liebend; *look, disposition, relationship, marriage* liebevoll; **~ kindness** Herzensgüte *f*; *(of God)* Barmherzigkeit *f*; **your ~ son ...** in Liebe Euer Sohn ...; **they are such a ~ couple/family** sie gehen so liebevoll miteinander um

loving cup N Pokal *m*

lovingly ['lʌvɪŋlɪ] ADV liebevoll

low[1] [ləʊ] **ADJ** (+er) **a** niedrig; *form of life, musical key* nieder; *bow, note* tief; *density, intelligence* gering; *food supplies* knapp; *pulse* schwach; *quality* gering; *light* gedämpft, schwach; *(pej)* minderwertig *(pej)*; *(Ling) vowel* offen; *(Math) denominator* klein; **the lamp was ~** die Lampe brannte schwach; **the sun was ~ in the sky** die Sonne stand tief am Himmel; **her dress was ~ at the neck** ihr Kleid hatte einen tiefen Ausschnitt; **~ blow** *or* **punch** Tiefschlag *m*; **that punch was a bit ~** der Schlag war etwas tief; **the river is ~** der Fluss hat *or* führt wenig Wasser; **a ridge of ~ pressure** ein Tiefdruckkeil *m*; **~ density housing** aufgelockerte Bauweise; **activity on the stock exchange is at its ~est** die Börsentätigkeit hat ihren Tiefstand erreicht; **to be ~ in funds** knapp bei Kasse sein *(inf)*
b *(= not loud or shrill)* **to speak in a ~ voice** leise sprechen
c *(= socially inferior, vulgar) birth* nieder, niedrig; *rank, position* untergeordnet, niedrig; *character, company* schlecht; *trick* gemein; **I really felt ~ having to tell him that** ich kam mir richtig gemein vor, dass ich ihm das sagen musste; **how ~ can you get!** wie kann man nur so tief sinken!; **~ cunning** Gerissenheit *f*
d *(= weak in health or spirits) resistance* schwach, gering; *morale* schlecht; **the patient is rather ~ today** der Patient ist heute nicht auf der Höhe; **to be in ~ health** bei schlechter Gesundheit sein; **to be in ~ spirits** in gedrückter Stimmung sein, bedrückt *or* niedergeschlagen sein; **to feel ~** sich nicht wohlfühlen *or* gut fühlen; *(emotionally)* niedergeschlagen sein; **to make sb feel ~** *(events)* jdn mitnehmen, jdm zu schaffen machen; *(people)* jdn mitnehmen *or* bedrücken
ADV *aim* nach unten; *speak, sing* leise; *fly, bow* tief; **they turned the lamps down ~** sie drehten die Lampen herunter; **a dress cut ~ in the back** ein Kleid mit tiefem Rückenausschnitt; **to fall ~** *(morally)* tief sinken; **I would never sink so ~ as to ...** so tief würde ich nie sinken, dass ich ...; **share prices went so ~ that ...** die Aktienkurse fielen so sehr, dass ...; **to buy ~ and sell high** billig kaufen und teuer verkaufen; **to lay sb ~** *(Brit) (punch)* jdn zu Boden strecken; *(disease)* jdn befallen; **he's been laid ~ with the flu** *(Brit)* er liegt mit Grippe im Bett; **to play ~** *(Cards)* um einen niedrigen *or* geringen Einsatz spielen; **to run** *or* **get ~** knapp werden; **we are getting ~ on petrol** *(Brit) or* **gas** *(US)* uns *(dat)* geht das Benzin aus
N **a** *(Met)* Tief *nt*; *(fig also)* Tiefpunkt *m*, Tiefstand *m*; **to reach a new ~** einen neuen Tiefstand erreichen; **this represents a new ~ in advertising** so tief ist die Werbung noch nie zuvor gesunken
b *(Aut: = low gear)* niedriger Gang

low[2] **N** *(of cow)* Muh *nt* **VI** muhen

low: **low-alcohol** ADJ alkoholarm; **lowball** ADJ *(US inf) costs* bewusst zu niedrig veranschlagt; **lowborn** ADJ von niedriger Geburt; **lowboy** N *(US)* niedrige Kommode; **lowbred** ADJ gewöhnlich, ordinär *(pej)*; **lowbrow** **ADJ** (geistig) anspruchslos **N** Anspruchslose(r) *mf*; *(pej: = philistine)* Kulturbanause *m (inf)*; **low-cal** ADJ *(inf)*, **low-calorie** ADJ kalorienarm; **a ~orie diet** eine kalorienarme Diät; **low-carb** ['ləʊkɑ:b] ADJ *(inf)* kohle(n)hydratarm; **~ bread** kohle(n)hydratarmes Brot; **~ lifestyle** kohle(n)hydratarme Lebensweise; **Low Church** N *reformierter, puritanischer Teil der anglikanischen Kirche*; **low comedy** N Schwank *m*, Klamotte *f (pej)*; **low-cost** ADJ preiswert; **~ airline** Billigfluglinie *f*; **Low Countries** PL **the ~** die Niederlande *pl*; **low-cut** ADJ *dress* tief ausgeschnitten; **low-down** ADJ *(esp US inf)* gemein, fies *(inf)*; **lowdown** N *(inf)* Informationen *pl*; **what's the ~ on Kowalski?** was wissen *or* haben *(inf)* wir über Kowalski?; **he gave me the ~ on it** er hat mich darüber aufgeklärt; **to get the ~ on sth** über etw *(acc)* aufgeklärt werden; **low-emission** ADJ *car* schadstoffarm, abgasarm

lower[1] ['ləʊə'] **ADJ** **a** *(in height)* niedriger; *part, half, limb, storey, latitude* untere(r, s); *note* tiefer; *(Geog)* Nieder-; **the Lower Rhine** der Niederrhein; **~ leg/arm** Unterschenkel *m*/-arm *m*; **~ abdomen** Unterleib *m*; **the ~ back** das Kreuz;

~ jaw/lip Unterkiefer *m*/-lippe *f*; **the ~ reaches of the river** der Unterlauf des Flusses; **the ~ parts of the hill** die tiefer gelegenen Teile des Berges; **the ~ of the two holes** das untere der beiden Löcher; **hemlines are ~ this year** die Röcke sind dieses Jahr länger; **the ~ deck** *(of bus)* das untere Deck; *(of ship)* das Unterdeck
b *(in hierarchy) rank, level* niedere(r, s); *(Zool) animals* niedere(r, s); **the ~ classes** *(Sociol)* die unteren Schichten; **a ~ middle-class family** eine Familie aus der unteren Mittelschicht; **the ~ school** die unteren Klassen, die Unter- und Mittelstufe → **lower sixth (form)**
ADV tiefer, leiser; **~ down the mountain** weiter unten am Berg; **~ down the list** weiter unten auf der Liste
VT a *(= let down) boat, injured man, load* herunterlassen; *eyes, gun* senken; *mast* umlegen; *sail, flag* einholen; *bicycle saddle* niedriger machen; **to ~ oneself** sich herunterlassen; **he ~ed himself into an armchair** er ließ sich in einen Sessel nieder; **"lower the lifeboats!"** „Rettungsboote aussetzen!"; **"lower away!"** „holt ein!"
b *(= reduce) pressure, risk* verringern; *price, interest rates, cost, tone, temperature* senken; *morale, resistance* schwächen; *standard* herabsetzen; **~ your voice** sprich leiser; **that is no excuse for ~ing the standards of service** das ist keine Entschuldigung dafür, den Service zu verschlechtern; **to ~ oneself** sich hinunterlassen; *(socially)* sich unter sein Niveau begeben; **to ~ oneself to do sth** sich herablassen, etw zu tun
VI sinken, fallen

lower² ['laʊəʳ] **VI** = **lour**

lower: **Lower Austria N** Niederösterreich *nt*; **lower case N** Kleinbuchstaben *pl*, Gemeine *pl (spec)* **ADJ** klein, gemein *(spec)*; **lower-case ADJ** *pred* **a** Klein-, in Kleinbuchstaben; **~ letter** Kleinbuchstabe *m* **b ADJ** klein, gemein *(spec)*; **Lower Chamber N** Unterhaus *nt*, zweite Kammer; **lower-class ADJ** der Unterschicht; *habit, vocabulary* der unteren *or* niederen Schichten; **~ people** Leute *pl* der Unterschicht *or* unteren Schicht(en); **~ family** Unterschichtfamilie *f*; **a ~ neighbourhood** *(Brit) or* **neighborhood** *(US)* eine sozial schwache Gegend; **lower court N** *(Jur)* untergeordnete Instanz; **Lower Egypt N** Unterägypten *nt*; **lower-income ADJ** *people* gering verdienend *attr*; *household* mit niedrigem Einkommen; **the ~ group** die Gruppe der Geringverdiener; **in the ~ bracket** in der Steuerklasse für Niedrigeinkommen

lowering ['laʊərɪŋ] **ADJ** = **louring**

lower: **Lower Saxony N** Niedersachsen *nt*; **lower sixth (form) N** *(Brit Sch) vorletztes Schuljahr*; **lower world N** Unterwelt *f*, Hölle *f*

low: **low-fat ADJ** *milk, cheese* fettarm, Mager-; **low-flying ADJ** tief fliegend; **~ plane** Tiefflieger *m*; **low frequency N** Niederfrequenz *f*; **Low German N** Platt(deutsch) *nt*; *(Ling)* Niederdeutsch *nt*; **low-grade ADJ** minderwertig; **low-grade petrol N** Benzin *nt* mit niedriger Oktanzahl; **low-heeled ADJ** *shoes* mit flachem *or* niedrigem Absatz; **low-impact ADJ** *aerobics, workout* leicht; **low-income ADJ** einkommensschwach

lowing ['ləʊɪŋ] **N** Muhen *nt*

low: **low-interest ADJ** *credit, loan* zinsgünstig; **low-key ADJ** *approach* gelassen; *handling* besonnen; *production, film's treatment* einfach gehalten, unaufdringlich; *reception* reserviert; *colours* gedämpft; **lowland N** Flachland *nt*; **the Lowlands of Scotland** das schottische Tiefland; **the ~s of Central Europe** die Tiefebenen *pl* Mitteleuropas **ADJ** des Flachlands; *(of Scotland)* des Tieflands; **lowlander N** Flachlandbewohner(in) *m(f)*; **Lowlander N** *(in Scotland)* Bewohner(in) *m(f)* des schottischen Tieflandes; **Low Latin N** nichtklassisches *or* nicht klassisches Latein; **low-level ADJ** *radioactivity* mit niedrigem Strahlungswert; *exposure* schwach; *radiation* niedrig; *attacks, warfare* begrenzt; *(Comput) language* nieder; **~ flying** Tiefflüge *pl*; **lowlife** ['ləʊlaɪf] **N** niederes Milieu; **lowlights** ['ləʊlaɪts] **PL a** *(Hairdressing)* dunkle Strähnchen *pl* **b** *(usu hum)* **one of the season's television ~** ein Tiefpunkt *m* im Fernsehangebot dieser Saison

lowliness ['ləʊlɪnɪs] **N** Bescheidenheit *f*; *(of position, birth also)* Niedrigkeit *f*

low-loader ['ləʊ,ləʊdəʳ] **N** Tieflader *m*

lowly ['ləʊlɪ] **ADJ** *(+er)* bescheiden; *position, birth also* niedrig

low: **low-lying ADJ** tief gelegen; **Low Mass N** (einfache) Messe; **low-minded ADJ** gemein; **low-necked ADJ** tief ausgeschnitten

lowness ['ləʊnɪs] **N a** Niedrigkeit *f*; *(of bow, note)* Tiefe *f*; *(of food, supplies)* Knappheit *f*; *(of light)* Gedämpftheit *f*; *(of sun, shares)* niedriger Stand; *(pej)* Minderwertigkeit *f*; **~ of a river** niedriger Wasserstand eines Flusses **b the ~ of her voice** ihre leise Stimme **c** *(of birth, rank)* Niedrigkeit *f*; *(of taste, manners)* Gewöhnlichkeit *f*; *(of character)* Schlechtheit *f*, Schlechtigkeit *f*; *(of joke)* Geschmacklosigkeit *f*; *(of trick)* Gemeinheit *f* **d** *(of resistance, morale)* Schwäche *f*; **the present ~ of his spirits** seine gegenwärtige Niedergeschlagenheit

low: **low pass N** *(Sport)* Flachpass *m*; **low-pitched ADJ** tief; **low-powered ADJ** *(= requiring little power)* sparsam im Stromverbrauch; **low-pressure ADJ a** *(Tech)* Niederdruck-; **~ system** Niederdrucksystem *nt* **b** *(Met)* Tiefdruck-; **a ~ zone** ein Tiefdruckgebiet *nt*; **low-priced ADJ** günstig; **low-profile ADJ** wenig profiliert; *politician* medienscheu; **a ~ campaign** *(Pol)* eine Kampagne, die in den Medien kaum Beachtung findet; **low-rent ADJ** *housing, flat* mit niedriger Miete; *(fig)* zweitklassig; **low-rise ATTR** niedrig (gebaut); **low-rise jeans PL** Hüftjeans *pl*; **low-scoring ADJ** *game, match* mit wenigen Punkten/Toren; **low season N** Nebensaison *f*; **low-slung ADJ** *chair, sports car* niedrig; **to have ~ hips** kurze Beine haben; **low-spirited ADJ**, **low-spiritedly ADV** niedergeschlagen; **low-start ADJ ~ mortgage** *(Brit) Hypothek, bei der die Rückzahlungen zu Anfang niedrig sind und dann steigen*; **low-tar ADJ** *cigarette* teerarm; **low-tech ADJ** nicht mit Hi-Tech ausgestattet; **it's pretty ~** es ist nicht gerade hi-tech; **low-tension ADJ** *(Elec)* Niederspannungs-; **~ cable** Niederspannungskabel *nt*; **low tide, low water N** Niedrigwasser *nt*; **at ~** bei Niedrigwasser; **low-wage country N** Niedrig- *or* Billiglohnland *nt*; **low-water mark N** Niedrigwassergrenze *f*

loyal ['lɔɪəl] **ADJ** *(+er)* **a** *(= faithful)* treu; **he was very ~ to his friends/country** er hielt (treu) zu seinen Freunden/seinem Land; **he remained ~ to his wife/the king** er blieb seiner Frau/dem König treu; **~ toast** *(Brit)* Toast *m* auf die Königin/den König **b** *(= without emotional involvement)* loyal *(to a party* einer Partei gegenüber); **he's too ~ to say anything against the party/his colleague** er ist zu loyal, um etwas gegen seine Partei/seinen Kollegen zu sagen

loyalist ['lɔɪəlɪst] **N** Loyalist(in) *m(f)*; **the ~s in the army** die regierungstreuen Teile der Armee **ADJ** loyal; *army, troops* regierungstreu

loyally ['lɔɪəlɪ] **ADV a** *(= faithfully) serve* treu **b** *(= without emotional involvement)* loyal; **he ~ refused to give the names** er war zu loyal, um die Namen zu verraten

loyalty ['lɔɪəltɪ] **N a** Treue *f*; **conflicting loyalties** nicht zu vereinbarende Treuepflichten; **torn between ~ to X and ~ to Y** hin- und hergerissen in der Treue zu X und der zu Y **b** *(non-emotional)* Loyalität *f*; **his changing political loyalties** seine wechselnden politischen Bekenntnisse

loyalty card N *(Brit Comm)* Kundenkarte *f*

lozenge ['lɒzɪndʒ] **N a** *(Med)* Pastille *f* **b** *(= shape)* Raute *f*, Rhombus *m*

LP *abbr of* **long player, long-playing record** LP *f*

LPF *abbr of* **light protection factor** *SF*

L-plate ['elpleɪt] **N** *Schild mit der Aufschrift „L" (für Fahrschüler)*

LRAM *(Brit) abbr of* **Licentiate of the Royal Academy of Music**

LRP *(Brit)* **N ABBR** *of* **lead replacement petrol** *Benzin mit integriertem Bleiersatz-Additiv*

LSD *abbr of* **lysergic acid diethylamide** LSD *nt*

lsd N *(old Brit inf: = money)* Geld *nt*, Pinke *f (inf)*

LSE *(Brit) abbr of* **London School of Economics**

Lt *abbr of* **Lieutenant** Lt

LTA *abbr of* **Lawn Tennis Association**

Ltd *abbr of* **Limited** GmbH

lube [lu:b] *(US inf)* **N** Schmieröl *nt*; *(Med)* Gleitmittel *nt* **VT** schmieren, ölen

lubricant ['lu:brɪkənt] **ADJ** Schmier-; **~ oil** Schmieröl *nt* **N** Schmiermittel *nt*; *(Med)* Gleitmittel *nt*

lubricate ['lu:brɪkeɪt] **VT** *(lit, fig)* schmieren, ölen; **~d sheath** Kondom *m* mit Gleitsubstanz; **well-~d** *(hum)* bezecht; **to ~ the wheels of commerce** den Handel reibungslos gestalten

lubricating cream ['lu:brɪkeɪtɪŋ-] **N** Gleitcreme *f*

lubrication [,lu:brɪ'keɪʃən] **N** Schmieren *nt*, Ölen *nt*; *(fig)* reibungslose Gestaltung

lubricator ['lu:brɪkeɪtəʳ] **N** Schmiervorrichtung *f*

lubricity [lu:'brɪsɪtɪ] **N** *(liter: = lewdness)* Schlüpfrigkeit *f*

lucent ['lu:snt] **ADJ** *(liter, poet)* glänzend, strahlend; *(= transparent)* durchsichtig, klar

Lucerne [lu:'sɜ:n] **N** Luzern *nt*; **Lake ~** Vierwaldstätter See *m*

lucid ['lu:sɪd] **ADJ** *(+er)* **a** *(= clear)* klar; *account* klar, präzise; *explanation* einleuchtend, anschaulich **b** *(= sane)* **~ intervals** lichte Augenblicke; **he was ~ for a few minutes** ein paar Minuten lang war er bei klarem Verstand

lucidity [lu:'sɪdɪtɪ] **N** Klarheit *f*; *(of explanation)* Anschaulichkeit *f*

lucidly ['lu:sɪdlɪ] **ADV** klar; *explain* einleuchtend, anschaulich; *write* verständlich

Lucifer ['lu:sɪfəʳ] **N** Luzifer *m*

luck [lʌk] ✪ 23.5 **N** Glück *nt*; **by ~** durch einen glücklichen Zufall; **bad ~** Unglück *nt*, Pech *nt*; **bad** *or* **hard** *or* **tough ~!** so ein Pech!; **bad ~, but it's your own fault** Pech (gehabt), da bist du selbst schuld; **good ~** Glück *nt*; **good ~!** viel Glück!; **good ~ to them!** *(iro)* **and the best of (British) ~!** *(iro)* na dann viel Glück!; **it was his good ~ to be chosen** er hatte das Glück, gewählt zu werden; **here's ~ to you/us!** *(toast)* auf glückliche Zeiten!; **no such ~!** schön wärs! *(inf)*; **just my ~!** Pech (gehabt), wie immer!; **it's just his ~ to miss the train** es musste ihm natürlich wieder passieren, dass er den Zug verpasst hat; **it's the ~ of the draw** man muss es eben nehmen, wies kommt; **with any ~** mit etwas Glück; **any ~?** *(= did it work?)* hats geklappt?; *(= did you find it?)* hast du es gefunden?; **worse ~!** leider, wie schade; **better ~ next time!** vielleicht klappts beim nächsten Mal!; **to be in ~** Glück haben; **to be out of ~** kein Glück haben; **he was a bit down on his ~** er hatte eine Pechsträhne; **tramps and others who are down on their ~** Landstreicher und andere, die kein Glück im Leben haben; **to bring sb good/bad ~** jdm Glück/Unglück bringen; **as ~ would have it** wie es der Zufall wollte; **to have ~ on one's side** das Glück auf seiner Seite haben; **for ~** als Glücksbringer *or* Talisman; **Bernstein kisses his cuff links for ~** Bernstein küsst seine Manschettenknöpfe, damit sie ihm Glück bringen; **to keep sth for ~** etw als Glücksbringer aufheben; **one for ~** und noch eine(n, s); **to try one's ~** sein Glück versuchen

▶ **luck out VI** *(US inf)* Schwein haben *(inf)*

luckily ['lʌkɪlɪ] **ADV** glücklicherweise; **~ for me** zu meinem Glück

luckless ['lʌklɪs] **ADJ** glücklos; *attempt also* erfolglos

lucky ['lʌkɪ] **ADJ** *(+er)* **a** *(= having luck)* Glücks-; **a ~ shot** ein Glückstreffer *m*; **that was a ~ move** der Zug war Glück; **you ~ thing!, ~ you!** du Glückliche(r) *mf*; **who's the ~ man?** wer ist

der Glückliche?; **the ~ winner** der glückliche Gewinner, die glückliche Gewinnerin; **to be ~** Glück haben; **I was ~ enough to meet him** ich hatte das (große) Glück, ihn kennenzulernen; **you are ~ to be alive** du kannst von Glück sagen, dass du noch lebst; **you were ~ to catch him** du hast Glück gehabt, dass du ihn erwischt hast; **to strike (it) ~ (with sb), to get ~ (with sb)** *(inf)* (bei jdm) Glück haben; **he's a ~ man to have a wife like that** mit dieser Frau hat er das große Los gezogen *(inf)*; **you're a ~ man** du bist ein Glückspilz; **you'll be ~ to make it in time** wenn du das noch schaffst, hast du (aber) Glück; **I want another £500 – you'll be ~!** ich will nochmal £ 500 haben – viel Glück!; **I should be so ~!** *(iro)* schön wärs! *(inf)*; **to be ~ at cards/in love** Glück im Spiel/in der Liebe haben; **to be born ~** ein Glücks- *or* Sonntagskind sein; **to be ~ (in) that …** Glück haben, dass …; **we are ~ in having (such) a great teacher** wir haben Glück, dass wir so einen großartigen Lehrer haben; **I am luckier than most: I have a job** ich bin besser dran als die meisten, ich habe (wenigstens) einen Job
b *(= bringing luck) star, day* Glücks-; **~ number** Glückszahl *f*; **~ charm** Glücksbringer *m*, Talisman *m*; **it must be my ~ day** ich habe wohl heute meinen Glückstag; **to be ~** *(charm, number etc)* Glück bringen
c *(= happening fortunately) coincidence* glücklich; **it was ~ I stopped him in time** ein Glück, dass ich ihn rechtzeitig aufgehalten habe, zum Glück habe ich ihn rechtzeitig aufgehalten; **it's ~ for you I remembered the number** dein Glück, dass ich die Nummer noch wusste; **that was very ~ for you** da hast du aber Glück gehabt; **they had a ~ escape from the fire** sie waren dem Feuer glücklich entkommen; **he had a ~ escape in the accident** bei dem Unfall ist er glücklich davongekommen; **that was a ~ escape** da habe ich/hast du *etc* noch mal Glück gehabt

lucky dip N ≈ Glückstopf *m*; **it's something of a ~** *(fig)* es ist Glücksache

lucrative ['lu:krətɪv] ADJ einträglich, lukrativ

lucrativeness ['lu:krətɪvnɪs] N Einträglichkeit *f*

lucre ['lu:kəʳ] N **filthy ~** schnöder Mammon

Lucretius [lu:'kri:ʃəs] N Lukrez *m*

lucubration [ˌlu:kjʊ'breɪʃən] N *(form)* geistige Arbeit

Lucullan [lu:'kʌlən] ADJ *(geh) food* lukullisch

Luddite ['lʌdaɪt] *(Hist, fig)* N Maschinenstürmer *m* ADJ maschinenstürmerisch

ludic ['lʌdɪk] ADJ *(liter)* spielerisch

ludicrous ['lu:dɪkrəs] ADJ grotesk; *sight, words* lächerlich; *idea, suggestion* haarsträubend; *(= low) prices, wages, speed* lächerlich, lachhaft; *(= high) prices, wages, speed* unerhört, haarsträubend; **don't be ~, I can't do it that fast** das ist ja grotesk, so schnell kann ich das nicht (machen); **I've done the most ~ thing!** mir ist etwas Haarsträubendes passiert!

ludicrously ['lu:dɪkrəslɪ] ADV grotesk; *small, little, low* lächerlich; *(= appallingly) high, fast* haarsträubend; **it takes me a ~ long time to …** ich brauche lachhaft lange dazu, zu …; **~ expensive** absurd teuer; **prices are ~ high/low** die Preise sind haarsträubend *or* absurd hoch/lächerlich *or* grotesk niedrig; **the description is ~ inadequate** die Beschreibung ist hoffnungslos unzulänglich

ludicrousness ['lu:dɪkrəsnɪs] N Groteskheit *f*; *(of sight, words, low prices, slow speed)* Lächerlichkeit *f*; *(of high prices, high speed)* Absurdität *f*

ludo ['lu:dəʊ] N ≈ Mensch ärgere dich nicht® *nt*

luff [lʌf] *(Naut)* N Vorliek *nt* VTI (an)luven

lug¹ [lʌg] N **a** *(= earflap)* Klappe *f*; *(Tech)* Haltevorrichtung *f* **b** *(esp Brit inf: = ear)* Ohr *nt*

lug² N = **lugsail**

lug³ VT schleppen; *(towards one)* zerren; **to ~ sth around with one** etw mit sich herumschleppen; **to ~ sth along behind one** etw hinter sich *(dat)* herschleppen

luge [lu:ʒ] N Rodelschlitten *m* VI rodeln

luggage ['lʌgɪdʒ] N Gepäck *nt*

luggage: luggage carrier N Gepäckträger(in) *m(f)*; **luggage compartment** N *(Rail)* Gepäckraum *m*; *(Brit Aut)* Kofferraum *m*; **luggage insurance** N (Reise)gepäckversicherung *f*; **luggage locker** N Gepäckschließfach *nt*; **luggage office** N Gepäckschalter *m*; **luggage rack** N *(Rail etc)* Gepäcknetz *nt or* -ablage *f*; *(Aut)* Gepäckträger *m*; **luggage trolley** N Kofferkuli *m*; **luggage van** N *(Brit Rail)* Gepäckwagen *m*

lugger ['lʌgəʳ] N Logger *m*

lughole ['lʌghəʊl] N *(Brit inf)* Ohr *nt*, Löffel *pl (inf)*

lugsail ['lʌgsl] N Loggersegel *nt*

lugubrious [lu:'gu:brɪəs] ADJ *person, song* schwermütig; *smile, tune* wehmütig; *face, expression* kummervoll

lugubriously [lu:'gu:brɪəslɪ] ADV traurig, kummervoll

lugworm ['lʌgwɜ:m] N Köderwurm *m*

Luke [lu:k] N Lukas *m*

lukewarm ['lu:kwɔ:m] ADJ *(lit, fig)* lauwarm; *applause, support* lauwarm, mäßig; *friendship* lau, oberflächlich; **he's ~ about** *or* **on the idea/about her** er ist von der Idee/von ihr nur mäßig begeistert

lull [lʌl] N Pause *f*; *(Comm)* Flaute *f*; **a ~ in the wind** eine Windstille; **we heard the scream during a ~ in the storm** wir hörten den Schrei, als der Sturm für einen Augenblick nachließ; **a ~ in the conversation/fighting** eine Gesprächs-/ /Gefechtspause; **the ~ before the storm** *(fig)* die Ruhe vor dem Sturm VT *baby* beruhigen; *(fig)* einlullen; *fears etc* zerstreuen, beseitigen; **to ~ a baby to sleep** ein Baby in den Schlaf wiegen; **he ~ed them into a false sense of security** er wiegte sie in trügerische Sicherheit

lullaby ['lʌləbaɪ] N Schlaflied *nt*, Wiegenlied *nt*

lulu ['lu:lu:] N *(inf) (object)* tolles Ding *(inf)*; *(person)* toller Typ *(inf)*; **a ~ of a story** eine tolle Geschichte *(inf)*; **a ~ of a mistake** ein dicker Hund *(inf)*

lumbago [lʌm'beɪgəʊ] N Hexenschuss *m*, Lumbago *f (spec)*

lumbar ['lʌmbəʳ] ADJ Lenden-, lumbal *(spec)*; **the ~ region** die Lendengegend; **~ puncture** Lumbalpunktion *f*

lumber¹ ['lʌmbəʳ] N **a** *(esp US: = timber)* (Bau)holz *nt* **b** *(= junk)* Gerümpel *nt* VT **a** *(also* **lumber up***) space, room* vollstopfen, vollpfropfen **b** *(Brit inf)* **to ~ sb with sth** jdm etw aufhalsen *(inf)*; **he got ~ed with the job** man hat ihm die Arbeit aufgehalst *(inf)*; **I got ~ed with her for the evening** ich hatte sie den ganzen Abend auf dem Hals *(inf)*; **what a job! you've really been ~ed!** was für eine Arbeit! da hat man dir aber was aufgehalst! *(inf)* **c** *(US) hillside, forest* abholzen VI *(US)* Holz fällen, holzen

lumber² VI *(cart)* rumpeln; *(tank)* walzen; *(elephant, person)* trampeln; *(bear)* tapsen; **a big fat man came ~ing into the room** ein dicker, fetter Mann kam ins Zimmer gewalzt; **she went ~ing about the room** sie trampelte im Zimmer herum

lumbering¹ ['lʌmbərɪŋ] ADJ *cart* rumpelnd; *elephant, person* trampelnd; *bear* tapsig; *tank* schwer, klobig; *gait* schwerfällig

lumbering² N *(US)* Holzfällen *nt*, Holzfällerei *f*

lumber: lumberjack ['lʌmbədʒæk] N Holzfäller *m*; **lumberjacket** N Lumberjack *m*; **lumberjack shirt** N bunt kariertes Hemd, Holzfällerhemd *nt*; **lumberman** N *(US)* Holzfäller *m*; **lumbermill** N *(US)* Sägemühle *f or* -werk *nt*; **lumber room** N Rumpelkammer *f*; **lumber trade** N (Bau)holzhandel *m*; **lumberyard** N *(US)* Holzlager *nt*

luminary ['lu:mɪnərɪ] N **a** *(form)* Himmelskörper *m*, Gestirn *nt* **b** *(fig)* Koryphäe *f*, Leuchte *f (inf)*

luminescence [ˌlu:mɪ'nesns] N Lumineszenz *f (spec)*, Leuchten *nt*

luminescent [ˌlu:mɪ'nesnt] ADJ lumineszierend *(spec)*, leuchtend

luminosity [ˌlu:mɪ'nɒsɪtɪ] N *(form)* Helligkeit *f*; *(= emission of light)* Leuchtkraft *f*; *(fig)* Brillanz *f*

luminous ['lu:mɪnəs] ADJ **a** leuchtend; *glow* fluoreszierend; **~ paint/colour** *(Brit) or* **color** *(US)* Leuchtfarbe *f*; **~ dial** Leuchtzifferblatt *nt*; **my watch is ~** meine Uhr leuchtet im Dunkeln **b** *(fig, liter) writings* brillant, luzid *(liter)*

lummox ['lʌməks] N *(US inf)* Trottel *m (inf)*

lummy, lumme ['lʌmɪ] INTERJ *(Brit)* ach, du Schreck!

lump [lʌmp] N **a** Klumpen *m*; *(of sugar)* Stück *nt*
b *(= swelling)* Beule *f*; *(inside the body)* Geschwulst *f*; *(in breast)* Knoten *m*; *(on surface)* Huppel *m (inf)*, kleine Erhebung; **with a ~ in one's throat** *(fig)* mit einem Kloß im Hals, mit zugeschnürter Kehle; **I get a ~ in my throat when I hear that song** wenn ich dieses Lied höre, ist mir die Kehle wie zugeschnürt; **it brings a ~ to my throat** dabei schnürt sich mir die Kehle zu
c *(inf: = person)* Klotz *m*, Trampel *m or nt (inf)*; **a big** *or* **great fat ~ (of a man)** ein Fettkloß *m (inf)*
d **you can't judge them in the ~ like that** du kannst sie doch nicht so pauschal beurteilen *or* nicht alle über einen Kamm scheren; **to pay money in a ~** *(= at once)* auf einmal bezahlen; *(= covering different items)* pauschal bezahlen
VT *(esp Brit inf: = put up with)* **to ~ it** sich damit abfinden; **like it or ~ it you'll have to go to work** *(inf)* du musst zur Arbeit, ob es dir passt oder nicht; **if he doesn't like it he can ~ it** wenns ihm nicht passt, hat er eben Pech gehabt *(inf)*
VI *(sauce, flour)* klumpen

▶ **lump together** VT *sep* **a** *(= put together)* zusammentun; *books* zusammenstellen; *expenses, money* zusammenlegen **b** *(= judge together) persons, topics* in einen Topf werfen, über einen Kamm scheren; **he lumped all the soldiers together as traitors** er urteilte all die Soldaten pauschal als Verräter ab

lumpen ['lʌmpən] ADJ *(= bulky) building etc* klobig; *(inf: = stupid)* blöd *(inf)*

lumpish ['lʌmpɪʃ] ADJ *person* klobig, plump

lump: lump payment N *(at once)* einmalige Bezahlung; *(covering different items)* Pauschalbezahlung *f*; **lump sugar** N Würfelzucker *m*; **lump sum** N Pauschalbetrag *m or* -summe *f*; **to pay sth in a ~** etw pauschal bezahlen

lumpy ['lʌmpɪ] ADJ *(+er) liquid etc, mattress, cushion* klumpig; *figure* pummelig, plump; **to go ~** *(sauce, rice)* klumpen

lunacy ['lu:nəsɪ] N Wahnsinn *m*; **it's sheer ~!** das ist reiner Wahnsinn!; **lunacies** *pl* Verrücktheiten *pl*

lunar ['lu:nəʳ] ADJ Mond-, lunar *(spec)*; **~ landscape** Mondlandschaft *f*

lunar: lunar eclipse N Mondfinsternis *f*; **lunar module** N Mondlandefähre *f or* -fahrzeug *nt*; **lunar orbit** N Mondumlaufbahn *f*

lunatic ['lu:nətɪk] ADJ verrückt, wahnsinnig N Wahnsinnige(r) *mf*, Irre(r) *mf*

lunatic asylum N Irrenanstalt *f*

lunatic fringe N Extremisten *pl*, radikale *or* extremistische Randgruppe

lunch [lʌntʃ] N Mittagessen *nt*; **to have** *or* **take ~** (zu) Mittag essen; **let's do ~** *(inf)* wir sollten uns zum Mittagessen treffen; **to give sb ~** jdn zum Mittagessen einladen; **how long do you get for ~?** wie lange haben Sie Mittagspause?; **when do you have ~ in the office?** wann haben *or* machen Sie im Büro Mittag?; **he's at ~** er ist beim Mittagessen; **to have ~ out** auswärts *or* im Restaurant (zu Mittag) essen; **out to ~** *(inf: = crazy)* weggetreten *(inf)*; **there's no such thing as a free ~** *(fig)* man bekommt im Leben nichts geschenkt

VT zum Mittagessen einladen
VI (zu) Mittag essen; **we ~ed on a salad** zum (Mittag)essen gab es einen Salat

▶ **lunch out** VI auswärts *or* im Restaurant (zu) Mittag essen

lunch: **lunchbox** N **a** Vesperbox *f*, Lunchbox *f* **b** *(Brit hum inf)* Gemächte *nt (old, hum)*; **lunch break** N Mittagspause *f*; **lunch counter** N *(US) (= café)* Imbiss *m*; *(= counter)* Imbisstheke *f*

luncheon [ˈlʌntʃən] N *(form)* Lunch *nt or m*, Mittagessen *nt*

luncheonette [ˌlʌntʃəˈnet] N *(US)* Imbissstube *f*

luncheon: **luncheon meat** N Frühstücksfleisch *nt*; **luncheon voucher** N Essen(s)bon *m or* -marke *f*

lunch: **lunch hour** N Mittagsstunde *f*; *(= lunch break)* Mittagspause *f*; **lunch meeting** N Geschäftsessen *nt (über Mittag)*; **lunch money** N *(US Sch)* Essensgeld *nt*; **lunchpail** N *(US)* = **lunchbox**; **lunchroom** N *(US)* Imbissstube *f*; *(= canteen)* Kantine *f*; **lunchtime** N Mittagspause *f*; **they arrived at ~** sie kamen um die Mittagszeit an, sie kamen gegen Mittag an

lung [lʌŋ] N Lunge *f*; *(= iron lung)* eiserne Lunge; **that baby has plenty of ~ power** das Baby hat eine kräftige Lunge; **he has weak ~s** er hat keine gute Lunge

lung cancer N Lungenkrebs *m*

lunge [lʌndʒ] N Satz *m* nach vorn; *(esp Fencing)* Ausfall *m*; **he made a ~ at his opponent** er stürzte sich auf seinen Gegner; *(Fencing)* er machte einen Ausfall VI (sich) stürzen; *(esp Fencing)* einen Ausfall machen; **to ~ at sb** sich auf jdn stürzen; **the exhausted boxer could only ~ at his opponent** der erschöpfte Boxer schlug nur noch wahllos nach seinem Gegner

▶ **lunge out** VI ausholen; **to lunge out at sb** sich auf jdn stürzen

lunula [ˈluːnjʊlə] N *pl* **-e** Lunula *f (spec)*, Nagelmöndchen *nt*

lupin, *(US)* **lupine** [ˈluːpɪn] N Lupine *f*

lupine [ˈluːpaɪn] ADJ wölfisch

lurch¹ [lɜːtʃ] N **to leave sb in the ~** *(inf)* jdn im Stich lassen, jdn hängen lassen *(inf)*

lurch² N Ruck *m*; *(of boat)* Schlingern *nt*; **with a drunken ~ he started off down the road** betrunken taumelte er die Straße hinunter; **to give a ~** einen Ruck machen; *(boat)* schlingern; **my heart gave a ~** mein Herz stand still; **the party's ~ to the right** der Rechtsruck der Partei; **a ~ into recession** ein Schlittern *nt* in die Rezession
VI **a** einen Ruck machen
b *(= move with lurches)* ruckeln, sich ruckartig bewegen; *(boat)* schlingern; *(person)* taumeln, torkeln; **the train ~ed to a standstill** der Zug kam mit einem Ruck zum Stehen; **he ~ed to his feet** er stand schwankend auf; **to ~ about** hin und her schlingern/taumeln *or* torkeln; **the bus ~ed off down the bumpy track** der Bus ruckelte den holprigen Weg hinunter; **to ~ in/out** *(person)* herein-/hinaustaumeln; **my heart ~ed** mein Herz stand still; **my stomach ~ed** mir drehte sich der Magen um *(inf)*; **to ~ along** dahinruckeln/entlangtorkeln *or* -taumeln; **the economy still manages to ~ along** die Wirtschaft schlittert gerade so eben dahin; **the government ~es from one crisis to the next** die Regierung schlittert von einer Krise in die andere

lure [ljʊəʳ] N *(= bait)* Köder *m*; *(= person, for hawk)* Lockvogel *m*; *(general)* Lockmittel *nt*; *(fig: of city, sea etc)* Verlockungen *pl*; **the ~ of the wild** der lockende Ruf der Wildnis VT anlocken; **to ~ sb away from sth** jdn von etw weg- *or* fortlocken; **to ~ sb/an animal into a trap** jdn/ein Tier in eine Falle locken; **to ~ sb/an animal out** jdn/ein Tier herauslocken

▶ **lure on** VT *sep (inf)* spielen mit

lurgy [ˈlɜːɡɪ] N *(Brit inf)* **to have the ~** *(= flu, cold)* die Schnieferei haben *(inf)*; **to pick up the ~** sich *(dat)* was holen; **to give sb the dreaded ~** jdn anstecken

lurid [ˈljʊərɪd] ADJ **a** *colour, sky* grell; *dress* grellfarben, in grellen Farben; *posters* schreiend; **a ~ sunset of pinks and oranges** ein Sonnenuntergang in grellen Rosa- und Orangetönen; **her taste in clothes is rather ~** sie mag Kleider in ziemlich grellen *or* schreienden Farben; **she was painting her toenails a ~ red** sie lackierte sich die Fußnägel grellrot
b *(fig) language, headline, novel, imagination* reißerisch; *(= bloodthirsty)* blutrünstig; *account, description* reißerisch, sensationslüstern; *(= sordid) detail, crime* widerlich; *photo, image* schaurig; *(= prurient)* anzüglich; **~ tale** Schauergeschichte *f*; **all the love scenes are presented in ~ detail** die Liebesszenen werden in allen widerlichen Einzelheiten dargestellt; **~ details of their quarrels** peinliche Einzelheiten ihrer Streitereien; **he has a ~ imagination** er kann sich *(dat)* die schaurigsten Dinge vorstellen

luridly [ˈljʊərɪdlɪ] ADV **a** *coloured* grell, knallig *(inf)*; **the sky glowed ~** der Himmel leuchtete in grellen Farben; **he sat down on the ~-coloured** *(Brit) or* **~-colored** *(US)* **settee** er setzte sich auf das knallige Sofa *(inf)* **b** *(fig)* reißerisch; *report* reißerisch, sensationslüstern; **~ written/presented** reißerisch aufgemacht; **… his ~ reported private life** … sein Privatleben, über das reißerisch berichtet wird; **Reggie swore briefly and ~** Reggie fluchte kurz und derb

luridness [ˈljʊərɪdnɪs] N **a** *(of colour, sky, dress)* Grellheit *f*; *(of posters)* schreiende Art **b** *(of account)* reißerische *or* sensationslüsterne Aufmachung; *(of details)* grausige Darstellung; **the ~ of his language** seine reißerische Sprache; **the ~ of this tale** diese blutrünstige *or* grausige Geschichte

lurk [lɜːk] VI lauern; **a nasty suspicion ~ed at the back of his mind** er hegte einen fürchterlichen Verdacht; **the fears which still ~ in the unconscious** Ängste, die noch im Unterbewusstsein lauern; **a doubt/the thought still ~ed in his mind** ein Zweifel/der Gedanke plagte ihn noch

▶ **lurk about** *(Brit) or* **around** VI herumschleichen

lurking [ˈlɜːkɪŋ] ADJ heimlich; *doubt also* nagend; *danger* lauernd

luscious [ˈlʌʃəs] ADJ **a** *(= delicious)* köstlich, lecker **b** *(= gorgeous) colour* satt; *girl, boy* zum Anbeißen *(inf)*; *figure (= full)* üppig; *(= pleasing)* fantastisch, phantastisch; *lips* üppig **c** *(= lush) pasture, vegetation* üppig

lusciously [ˈlʌʃəslɪ] ADV köstlich; **~ coated in thick cream** mit einer köstlich dicken Sahneschicht

lusciousness [ˈlʌʃəsnɪs] N Köstlichkeit *f*; *(of fruit also)* Saftigkeit *f*; *(of colour)* Sattheit *f*; *(of girl)* knuspriges *or* appetitliches Aussehen *(inf)*; *(of figure)* Üppigkeit *f*

lush [lʌʃ] ADJ **a** *grass, meadows* saftig, satt; *vegetation* üppig **b** *(inf: = opulent) hotel, house* feudal; *lifestyle* üppig N *(sl)* Säufer(in) *m(f) (inf)*, Rauschkugel *f (inf)*

lushness [ˈlʌʃnɪs] N **a** *(of grass, meadow)* Saftigkeit *f*; *(of vegetation)* Üppigkeit *f* **b** *(inf: = opulence) (of hotel, house)* Feudalität *f*; *(of lifestyle, Mus: of harmonies, sound)* Üppigkeit *f*

lust [lʌst] N *(= inner sensation)* Wollust *f*, Sinneslust *f*; *(= wanting to acquire)* Begierde *f (for* nach); *(= greed)* Gier *f (for* nach); **rape is an act of ~** Vergewaltigungen entspringen triebhafter Gier; **the ~s of the flesh** die fleischlichen (Ge)lüste, die Fleischeslust; **~ for power** Machtgier *f*; **his uncontrollable ~** seine ungezügelte Gier; *(sexual)* seine fleischliche Begierde VI **to ~ after, to ~ for** *(old, hum, sexually)* begehren *(+acc)*; *(greedily)* gieren nach

luster N *(US)* = **lustre**

lusterless ADJ *(US)* = **lustreless**

lustful ADJ, **lustfully** ADV [ˈlʌstfʊl, -fəlɪ] lüstern

lustfulness [ˈlʌstfʊlnɪs] N Lüsternheit *f*, Begierde *f*

lustily [ˈlʌstɪlɪ] ADV kräftig; *work* mit Schwung und Energie; *eat* herzhaft; *sing* aus voller Kehle; *cry, cheer* aus vollem Hals(e)

lustre, *(US)* **luster** [ˈlʌstəʳ] N **a** Schimmer *m*, schimmernder Glanz; *(in eyes)* Glanz *m* **b** *(fig)* Glanz *m*, Ruhm *m*

lustreless [ˈlʌstəlɪs] ADJ glanzlos; *eyes, hair also* stumpf

lustrous [ˈlʌstrəs] ADJ schimmernd, glänzend

lusty [ˈlʌstɪ] ADJ *(+er) person* gesund und munter, voller Leben; *life* urwüchsig; *appetite* herzhaft, kräftig; *cheer, cry* laut, kräftig; *push, kick etc* kräftig, kraftvoll

lute [luːt] N Laute *f*

lutenist [ˈluːtənɪst] N Lautenist(in) *m(f)*, Lautenspieler(in) *m(f)*

lutetium [lʊˈtiːʃɪəm] N *(Chem)* Lutetium *nt*

Luther [ˈluːθəʳ] N Luther *m*

Lutheran [ˈluːθərən] ADJ lutherisch N Lutheraner(in) *m(f)*

Lutheranism [ˈluːθərənɪzəm] N Luthertum *nt*

luvvie, luvvy [ˈlʌvɪ] N *(Brit inf)* **a** *(address)* Schatz *m (inf)* **b** *(= actor)* Akteur(in) *m(f)*

lux *abbr of* **luxury**

luxation [lʌkˈseɪʃən] N *(Med)* Luxation *f (spec)*, Verrenkung *f (eines Gelenks)*

Luxembourg [ˈlʌksəmbɜːɡ] N Luxemburg *nt* ADJ *attr* Luxemburger

Luxembourger [ˈlʌksəmbɜːɡəʳ] N Luxemburger(in) *m(f)*

luxuriance [lʌɡˈzjʊərɪəns] N Üppigkeit *f*; *(of hair also)* Fülle *f*, Pracht *f*

luxuriant [lʌɡˈzjʊərɪənt] ADJ üppig; *flowers, plants* üppig, prächtig; *forest* dicht; *(= thick) beard, hair* üppig, dicht; *(= elaborate) furnishings, style* prunkvoll, prächtig

luxuriantly [lʌɡˈzjʊərɪəntlɪ] ADV üppig; *(= thickly)* dicht

luxuriate [lʌɡˈzjʊərɪeɪt] VI **to ~ in sth** *(people)* sich in etw *(dat)* aalen

luxurious [lʌɡˈzjʊərɪəs] ADJ luxuriös; *food* üppig; **a ~ hotel** ein Luxushotel *nt*; **~ travel** Luxusreisen *pl*; **~ car** Luxusauto *nt*; **he is a man of ~ habits/tastes** er hat einen luxuriösen Lebensstil/einen Hang zum Luxus; **with a ~ sigh** mit einem wohligen Seufzer

luxuriously [lʌɡˈzjʊərɪəslɪ] ADV luxuriös; **to live ~** ein Luxusleben *or* ein Leben im Luxus führen; **he sank back ~ into the cushions** er ließ sich genüsslich in die Kissen sinken

luxury [ˈlʌkʃərɪ] N **a** *(in general)* Luxus *m*; *(of car, house etc)* luxuriöse *or* feudale Ausstattung, Komfort *m*; **to live a life of ~** ein Luxusleben *or* ein Leben im Luxus führen **b** *(= article)* Luxus *m no pl*; **we can't allow ourselves many luxuries** wir können uns *(dat)* nicht viel Luxus leisten; **little luxuries** Luxus *m*; *(to eat)* kleine Genüsse *pl* ADJ *attr* Luxus-; **~ car** Luxusauto *nt*; **~ flat** *(esp Brit) or* **apartment** Luxus- *or* Komfortwohnung *f*; **~ goods** Luxusgüter *pl*; **~ liner** Luxusdampfer *m*; **~ tax** Luxussteuer *f*

LV *(Brit) abbr of* **luncheon voucher**

LW *abbr of* **long wave** LW

lychee [ˈlaɪtʃiː] N Litschi *f*

lychgate N = **lichgate**

Lycra® [ˈlaɪkrə] N Lycra® *nt*

lye [laɪ] N Lauge *f*

lying [ˈlaɪɪŋ] ADJ lügnerisch, verlogen N Lügen *nt*; **that would be ~** das wäre gelogen

lying-in [ˈlaɪɪŋˈɪn] N *(old Med)* Wochenbett *nt (dated)*; **during her ~** im Wochenbett *(dated)*; **~ ward** Wöchnerinnenstation *f (dated)*

lymph [lɪmf] N Lymphe *f*, Gewebsflüssigkeit *f*

lymphatic [lɪmˈfætɪk] ADJ lymphatisch, Lymph-; **~ tissue** Lymphgewebe *nt* N Lymphgefäß *nt*

lymph gland N Lymphdrüse *f*

lymph node N Lymphknoten *m*

lymphocyte [ˈlɪmfəʊˌsaɪt] N Lymphozyt *m*

lymph vessel N Lymphgefäß *nt*

lynch [lɪntʃ] VT lynchen

lynching ['lɪntʃɪŋ] N Lynchen *nt*; **there'll be a ~ soon** er *etc* wird bestimmt gelyncht werden

lynch law N Lynchjustiz *f*

lynx [lɪŋks] N Luchs *m*

lynx-eyed ['lɪŋks,aɪd] ADJ mit Luchsaugen; **the ~ teacher** der Lehrer, der Augen wie ein Luchs hatte

lyre ['laɪə'] N Leier *f*, Lyra *f (geh)*

lyrebird ['laɪəbɜːd] N Leierschwanz *m*

lyric ['lɪrɪk] ADJ lyrisch N *(= poem)* lyrisches Gedicht; *(= genre)* Lyrik *f*; *(= often pl: words of pop song)* Text *m*

lyrical ['lɪrɪkəl] ADJ lyrisch; *(fig: = enthusiastic)* schwärmerisch; **to wax ~ about sth** über etw *(acc)* ins Schwärmen geraten

lyrically ['lɪrɪkəlɪ] ADV **a** lyrisch; *(fig: = enthusiastically)* schwärmerisch; *sing, play, speak* melodisch **b** *(Mus, referring to the text)* textlich; **~, it is full of clichés** der Text ist voller Klischees

lyricism ['lɪrɪsɪzəm] N Lyrik *f*

lyricist ['lɪrɪsɪst] N **a** *(= poet)* Lyriker(in) *m(f)* **b** *(Mus)* Texter(in) *m(f)*

lysergic acid diethylamide [laɪ'sɜːdʒɪk,æsɪd,daɪə'θɪləmaɪd] N Lysergsäurediäthylamid *nt*

Lysol® ['laɪsɒl] N Lysol® *nt*

M, **m** [em] N M *nt*, m *nt*

M *abbr of* **medium**

m a *abbr of* **million(s)** Mill., Mio. b *abbr of* **metre(s)** m c *abbr of* **mile(s)** d *abbr of* **minute(s)** min e *abbr of* **married** verh. f *abbr of* **masculine** m g *abbr of* **female** *(in Internet chat etc)* Girl *nt*

MA *abbr of* **Master of Arts** M. A.

ma [mɑː] N *(inf)* Mama *f (inf)*, Mutti *f (inf)*

ma'am [mæm] N gnä' Frau *f (form)* → *also* **madam a**

mac¹ [mæk] N *(Brit inf)* Regenmantel *m*

mac² N *(esp US inf)* Kumpel *m (inf)*

macabre [məˈkɑːbrə] ADJ makaber

macadam [məˈkædəm] N Schotter *m*, Splitt *m*, Makadam *m or nt*; ~ **road** Schotterstraße *f*

macadamize [məˈkædəmaɪz] VT schottern, makadamisieren *(spec)*

macaque [məˈkɑːk] N *(monkey)* Makak *m*

macaroni [ˌmækəˈrəʊnɪ] N Makkaroni *pl*

macaronic [ˌmækəˈrɒnɪk] ADJ makkaronisch

macaroni cheese N Käsemakkaroni *pl*

macaroon [ˌmækəˈruːn] N Makrone *f*

macaw [məˈkɔː] N Ara *m*

Mace® [meɪs] N *(= gas)* ≈ Tränengas *nt*

mace¹ [meɪs] N *(= weapon)* Streitkolben *m*, Keule *f*; *(mayor's)* Amtsstab *m*

mace² N *(= spice)* Muskatblüte *f*, Mazis *m*

macebearer [ˈmeɪsbɛərəˈ] N Träger(in) *m(f)* des Amtsstabes

Macedonia [ˌmæsɪˈdəʊnɪə] N Makedonien *nt*, Mazedonien *nt*

Macedonian [ˌmæsɪˈdəʊnɪən] N Makedonier(in) *m(f)*, Mazedonier(in) *m(f)* ADJ makedonisch, mazedonisch

macerate [ˈmæsəreɪt] VT aufweichen, einweichen VI aufweichen, weich werden

Mach [mæk] N Mach *nt*; ~ **number** Machzahl *f*; **the jet was approaching ~ 2** das Flugzeug näherte sich (einer Geschwindigkeit von) 2 Mach

machete [məˈtʃeɪtɪ] N Machete *f*, Buschmesser *nt*

Machiavelli [ˌmækɪəˈvelɪ] N Machiavelli *m*

Machiavellian [ˌmækɪəˈvelɪən] ADJ machiavellistisch

machination [ˌmækɪˈneɪʃən] N *usu pl* Machenschaften *pl*

machine [məˈʃiːn] N Maschine *f*, Apparat *m*; *(= vending machine)* Automat *m*; *(= car)* Wagen *m*; *(= cycle, plane)* Maschine *f*; *(fig: = person)* Maschine *f*, Roboter *m*; **by ~** maschinell; **the party ~** *(Pol)* der Parteiapparat; **the political ~** die politischen Drahtzieher *pl*; **the publicity/propaganda ~** die Publicity-/Propagandamaschine *or* -maschinerie; **to be a money-making ~** *(fig)* am laufenden Band Geld machen VT *(Tech)* maschinell herstellen; *(= treat with machine)* maschinell bearbeiten; *(Sew)* mit der Maschine nähen

machine: **machine age** N **the ~** das Maschinenzeitalter; **machine code** N Maschinencode *m*; **machine gun** N Maschinengewehr *nt*; **machine-gun** VT mit dem Maschinengewehr beschießen *or (kill)* erschießen; **machine gunner** N *(Mil)* Maschinengewehrschütze *m*; **machine intelligence** N künstliche Intelligenz; **machine language** N *(Comput)* Maschinensprache *f*; **machine-made** ADJ maschinell hergestellt; **machine operator** N Maschinenarbeiter(in) *m(f)*; *(skilled)* Maschinist(in) *m(f)*; **machine-readable** ADJ ATTR, **machine readable** ADJ PRED *(Comput)* maschinenlesbar; ~ **data** maschinenlesbaren Daten

machinery [məˈʃiːnərɪ] N *(= machines)* Maschinen *pl*, Maschinerie *f*; *(= mechanism)* Mechanismus *m*; *(fig)* Maschinerie *f*; **the ~ of government** der Regierungsapparat

machine: **machine shop** N Maschinensaal *m*; **machine-stitch** VT maschinell *or* mit der Maschine nähen; **machine time** N Betriebszeit *f*; *(= computing time)* Rechenzeit *f*; **the relationship between cost and ~** das Verhältnis der Kosten zur Betriebszeit der Maschine(n); **machine tool** N Werkzeugmaschine *f*; **machine translation** N maschinelle Übersetzung; **machine-washable** ADJ waschmaschinenfest

machinist [məˈʃiːnɪst] N *(Tech: = operator)* Maschinist(in) *m(f)*; *(= constructor, repairer)* Maschinenschlosser(in) *m(f)*; *(Sew)* Näherin *f*

machismo [mæˈkɪzməʊ, mæˈtʃɪzməʊ] N Machismo *m*

macho [ˈmætʃəʊ] ADJ macho *pred*, Macho-; *management* machomäßig; ~ **image** Macho-Image *nt*; **a ~ type** ein Macho-Typ *m*; **a ~ man** ein Macho *m* N Macho *m*

mackerel [ˈmækrəl] N Makrele *f*

mackerel sky N (Himmel *m* mit) Schäfchenwolken

mackintosh [ˈmækɪntɒʃ] N Regenmantel *m*

macramé [məˈkrɑːmɪ] N Makramee *nt*

macro [ˈmækrəʊ] N *(Comput)* Makro *nt*; ~ **virus** Makrovirus *m or nt*

macro- PREF makro-, Makro-; **macrolanguage** Makrosprache *f*

macrobiotic [ˈmækrəʊbaɪˈɒtɪk] ADJ makrobiotisch; ~ **restaurant** *Restaurant, in dem makrobiotische Kost serviert wird*

macrocosm [ˈmækrəʊˌkɒzəm] N Makrokosmos *m*; **the ~ of Italian society** die italienische Gesellschaft als ganzes *or* in ihrer Gesamtheit

macroeconomics [ˈmækrəʊˌiːkəˈnɒmɪks] N *sing or pl* Makroökonomie *f*

macron [ˈmækrɒn] N *(Typ)* Querbalken *m*, Längezeichen *nt*

macroscopic [ˈmækrəʊˈskɒpɪk] ADJ makroskopisch, mit bloßem Auge erkennbar

MAD N *(US Mil) abbr of* **mutual(ly) assured destruction** Gleichgewicht *nt* des nuklearen Zerstörungspotenzials

mad [mæd] ADJ *(+er)* a wahnsinnig; *(= genuinely insane)* geisteskrank; *(inf: = crazy)* verrückt; *(= with rabies) animal* tollwütig; **to go ~** wahnsinnig werden; *(lit: = go insane)* den Verstand verlieren; **to drive sb ~** jdn wahnsinnig machen; *(lit: = drive sb insane)* jdn um den Verstand bringen; **it's enough to drive you ~** es ist zum Verrücktwerden; **he has a ~ look in his eye** er hat einen irren Blick; **he's as ~ as a hatter** *or* **a March hare** *(prov)* er hat einen Dachschaden *(inf)*; **are you raving ~?** bist du total verrückt geworden?; **you must be ~!** du bist wohl wahnsinnig!; **I must have been ~ to believe him** ich war wohl von Sinnen, ihm zu glauben; ~ **dog** tollwütiger Hund; *(fig: = person)* verrückter Typ

b *(inf: = angry)* böse, sauer *(inf)*; **to be ~ at sb** auf jdn böse *or* sauer *(inf)* sein; **to be ~ about** *or* **at sth** über etw *(acc)* wütend *or* sauer *(inf)* sein; **this makes** *or* **drives me ~** das bringt mich auf die Palme *(inf)*; **he makes me so ~** er macht mich so wütend; **don't get ~ at** *or* **with me** sei nicht böse *or* sauer *(inf)* auf mich; **(as) ~ as a hornet** *(US)* fuchsteufelswild *(inf)*

c *(esp Brit: = stupid, rash)* verrückt; **you ~ fool!** du bist ja wahnsinnig *or* verrückt!; **she's ~ doing something like that** sie ist verrückt, so etwas zu tun; **it's a ~ hope** es ist verrückt, darauf zu hoffen; **that was a ~ thing to do** das war Wahnsinn *(inf)*

d *(esp Brit inf: = very keen)* **to be ~ about** *or* **on sth** auf etw *(acc)* verrückt sein; **I'm not exactly ~ about this job** ich bin nicht gerade versessen auf diesen Job; **I'm (just) ~ about you** ich bin (ganz) verrückt nach dir!; **the audience went ~** das Publikum tobte vor Begeisterung; **don't go ~!** *(= don't overdo it)* übertreib es nicht

e *(= wild, frantic)* wahnsinnig *(with* vor *+dat)*; **they ~e a ~ rush** *or* **dash for the door** sie stürzten wie wild zur Tür; **why the ~ rush?** warum diese Hektik?; **the ~ rush toward(s) federalism** die überstürzte Entwicklung zum Föderalismus; **the prisoner ~e a ~ dash for freedom** der Gefangene unternahm einen verzweifelten Ausbruchsversuch; **to be ~ with joy** sich wahnsinnig freuen; **after the news came through the phones went ~** nach der Bekanntgabe der Nachricht standen die Telefone nicht mehr still; **this is bureaucracy gone ~** das ist Bürokratie hoch drei

ADV *(inf)* **to be ~ keen on sb/sth** ganz scharf auf jdn/etw sein *(inf)*; **to be ~ keen to do sth** ganz versessen darauf sein, etw zu tun; **like ~** wie verrückt; **he ran like ~** er rannte wie wild

Madagascan [ˌmædəˈgæskən] ADJ madegassisch N Madegasse *m*, Madegassin *f*

Madagascar [ˌmædəˈgæskəˈ] N Madagaskar *nt*

madam [ˈmædəm] N a gnädige Frau *(old, form)*; **~, would you kindly desist!** würden Sie das bitte unterlassen! *(form)*; **yes, ~** sehr wohl, gnädige Frau *(old, form)*, ja (wohl); **can I help you, ~?** kann ich Ihnen behilflich sein?; **dear ~** *(esp Brit)* sehr geehrte gnädige Frau; **Dear Sir or Madam** *(esp Brit)* Sehr geehrte Damen und Herren b *(Brit inf: = girl)* kleine Prinzessin; **she's a spoiled little ~** sie ist eine verwöhnte kleine Prinzessin c *(of brothel)* Bordellwirtin *f*, Puffmutter *f (inf)*

madcap [ˈmædkæp] ADJ *idea* versponnen; *youth* stürmisch; *tricks* toll; *scheme* hirnverbrannt N impulsiver Mensch

mad cow disease N Rinderwahnsinn *m*

MADD *abbr of* **mothers against drunk driving**

madden [ˈmædn] VT *(= make mad)* verrückt machen; *(= make angry)* ärgern, fuchsen *(inf)*; **it ~s me to think of the opportunity we missed** ich könnte mich schwarzärgern, wenn ich daran denke, was für eine Chance wir vertan haben *(inf)*

maddening ['mædnɪŋ] ADJ unerträglich, zum Verrücktwerden; *delay* unerträglich, lästig; *habit* aufreizend; **the ~ thing is that …** das Verrückte daran ist, dass …; **isn't it ~?** ist das nicht ärgerlich?; **this is ~!** das ist (ja) zum Verrücktwerden!

maddeningly ['mædnɪŋlɪ] ADV unerträglich; **the train ride was ~ slow** es war zum Verrücktwerden, wie langsam der Zug fuhr; **his work is ~ inconsistent** seine Arbeit ist so ungleichmäßig, dass es zum Verrücktwerden ist; **he grinned ~** er grinste, dass es zum Verrücktwerden war

madder ['mædə'] N *(= plant)* Krapp *m*, Färberröte *f*; *(= dye)* Krapprot *nt*, Krappfarbstoff *m*

made [meɪd] *pret, ptp of* **make**

Madeira [mə'dɪərə] N Madeira *nt*; *(= wine)* Madeira *m*

Madeira cake N Sandkuchen *m*

made-to-measure ['meɪdtə'meʒə'] ADJ *(Brit)* maßgeschneidert; *curtains* nach Maß; *furniture etc* spezialangefertigt; **~ suit** Maßanzug *m*; **~ clothes** Maßkonfektion *f*; **~ service** *(Sew)* Maßschneiderei *f*

made up ADJ *(Brit inf: = pleased)* erfreut; **I'm ~ for you** ich freue mich für dich

made-up ['meɪd'ʌp] ADJ **a** *(= invented) story, name, word, character* erfunden **b** *(= wearing make-up) face* geschminkt; **she was over ~ or too heavily ~** sie hatte zu viel Make-up aufgelegt, sie war zu stark geschminkt **c** *(= ready-made)* vorgefertigt; *curtains* fertig genäht; **~ meat products** fertige Fleischprodukte **d** *(= surfaced) road* asphaltiert

madhouse ['mædhaʊs] N *(lit, fig)* Irrenhaus *nt*

madly ['mædlɪ] ADV **a** wie verrückt; **he worked ~ for weeks on end** er arbeitete wochenlang wie besessen *or* verrückt **b** *(inf: = extremely)* wahnsinnig; **to be ~ in love (with sb)** bis über beide Ohren (in jdn) verliebt sein, total (in jdn) verschossen sein *(inf)*; **I'm not ~ keen to go** ich bin nicht wahnsinnig scharf *(inf) or* erpicht darauf (zu gehen)

madman ['mædmən] N *pl* **-men** [-mən] Irre(r) *m*, Verrückte(r) *m*

madness ['mædnɪs] ✪ 2.3 N Wahnsinn *m*; **it's sheer ~!** das ist heller *or* reiner Wahnsinn!; **what ~!** das ist doch Wahnsinn!

Madonna [mə'dɒnə] N Madonna *f*; *(= picture)* Madonnenbild *nt*, Madonna *f*; *(= statue also)* Madonnenfigur *f*

Madrid [mə'drɪd] N Madrid *nt*

madrigal ['mædrɪgəl] N Madrigal *nt*

madwoman ['mædwʊmən] N Verrückte *f*

Maecenas [miː'siːnəs] N Maecenas *m*; *(fig)* Mäzen *m*

maelstrom ['meɪlstrəʊm] N *(lit rare)* Malstrom *m*; *(fig)* Malstrom *m (liter)*, Sog *m*; **he returned to the ~ of public life** er kehrte in den Trubel des öffentlichen Lebens zurück

maestro ['maɪstrəʊ] N Maestro *m*

mae west [,meɪ'west] N *(hum)* Schwimmweste *f*

Mafia ['mæfɪə] N **a** Mafia *f* **b** *(fig)* **the literary/medical mafia** die Literatur-/Medizinmafia

mafioso [,mæfɪ'əʊsəʊ] N *pl* **-sos** *or* **-si** Mafioso *m*

mag [mæg] N *(inf)* Magazin *nt*; *(glossy also)* Illustrierte *f*; **porn ~** Pornoheft *nt*

magalog ['mægəlɒg] N *Bestellkatalog, der wie eine Illustrierte aufgemacht ist*

magazine [,mægə'ziːn] N **a** *(= journal)* Zeitschrift *f*, Magazin *nt* **b** *(in gun)* Magazin *nt* **c** *(Mil: = store)* Magazin *nt (Hist)*, Depot *nt*

magazine rack N Zeitungsständer *m*

mag card ['mægkɑːd] N *(inf)* Magnetkarte *f*

magenta [mə'dʒentə] **N** Fuchsin *nt* **ADJ** tiefrot

maggot ['mægət] N Made *f*

maggoty ['mægətɪ] ADJ madig; **the cheese has gone all ~** der Käse wimmelt von Maden

Magi ['meɪdʒaɪ] PL **the ~** die Heiligen Drei Könige, die drei Weisen aus dem Morgenland

magic ['mædʒɪk] **N** **a** Magie *f*, Zauberei *f*, Zauberkunst *f*; **the witch doctor tried ~ to cure the woman** der Medizinmann versuchte, die Frau durch Magie zu heilen; **he entertained them with a display of ~** er unterhielt sie mit ein paar Zauberkunststücken; **he made the spoon disappear by ~** er zauberte den Löffel weg; **you don't expect the essay to write itself by ~?** glaubst du, dass der Aufsatz sich von alleine schreibt?; **as if by ~** wie durch Zauberei *or* Zauberhand, wie durch ein Wunder; **it worked like ~** *(inf)* es klappte *or* lief wie am Schnürchen *(inf)*

b *(= mysterious charm)* Zauber *m*

ADJ **a** Zauber-; *powers, square* magisch; *moment* zauberhaft; **~ formula** Zauberformel *f*; *(fig)* Patentrezept *nt*; **the ~ word** *(having special effect)* das Stichwort; *(making sth possible)* das Zauberwort; **a pianist with the ~ touch** ein begnadeter Pianist; **he gave it his ~ touch and it worked** er hat es nur angefasst und schon funktionierte es; **he hasn't lost his ~ touch** er hat nichts von seiner Genialität verloren; **"The Magic Flute"** „Die Zauberflöte"

b *(inf: = fantastic)* toll *(inf)*, super *(inf)*

▶ **magic away** VT SEP wegzaubern

▶ **magic up** VT SEP heraufbeschwören

magical ['mædʒɪkəl] ADJ *powers, attraction, light* magisch; *atmosphere* unwirklich; **the effect was ~** das wirkte (wahre) Wunder; *(visually)* die Wirkung war zauberhaft; **~ formula** Zauberformel *f*

magically ['mædʒɪkəlɪ] ADV wunderbar; **~ transformed** auf wunderbare Weise verwandelt; **her headache ~ disappeared** ihre Kopfschmerzen waren auf einmal wie weggeblasen

magic: **magic bullet** N *(inf, Med: for cancer) selektiv wirksames Krebsmedikament, das nur die kranken Zellen zerstört (US fig)* Patentlösung *f*; **magic carpet** N fliegender Teppich; **magic circle** N **a** Zauberkreis *m* **b** *(fig: = cabal)* Clique *f* **c** **Magic Circle** *(= organization)* Gilde *f* der Zauberkünstler; **magic eye** N magisches Auge

magician [mə'dʒɪʃən] N Magier *m*, Zauberer *m*, Zauberin *f*; *(= conjuror)* Zauberkünstler(in) *m(f)*; **I'm not a ~!** ich kann doch nicht hexen!

magic: **magic lantern** N Laterna magica *f*; **magic mushroom** N *(inf)* Magic Mushroom *m*; **magic realism** N *(Liter)* magischer Realismus; **magic spell** N Zauber *m*; *(= words)* Zauberspruch *m*; **the witch cast a ~ on her** die Hexe verzauberte sie; **magic wand** N Zauberstab *m*; **to wave a ~** *(lit, fig)* den Zauberstab schwingen; **there is no ~ to bring about political change** ein politischer Wandel lässt sich nicht herbeizaubern

magisterial [,mædʒɪ'stɪərɪəl] ADJ **a** *(lit) powers, office, robes* eines Friedensrichters **b** *(= imperious)* gebieterisch

magisterially [,mædʒɪs'tɪərɪəlɪ] ADV majestätisch, gebieterisch; **Johnson waves his hand ~** Johnson winkt majestätisch

magistracy ['mædʒɪstrəsɪ] N *(= position)* Amt *nt* des Friedensrichters; *(= judges)* Friedensrichter *pl*

magistrate ['mædʒɪstreɪt] N Friedensrichter(in) *m(f)*, Schiedsmann *m*/-frau *f*

magistrates' court ['mædʒɪstreɪts'kɔːt] N *(Brit)* Friedensgericht *nt*, Schiedsgericht *nt*

maglev ['mæglev] N *(Rail)* Magnet(schwebe)bahn *f*

magma ['mægmə] N *(Geol)* Magma *nt*

magna cum laude ['mægnəkʌm'laʊdeɪ] ADV *(US)* magna cum laude, sehr gut

magnanimity [,mægnə'nɪmɪtɪ] N Großherzigkeit *f*, Großmut *f*; **he acted with great ~** er handelte sehr großherzig

magnanimous [mæg'nænɪməs] ADJ großmütig, großherzig; *(= generous)* großzügig; **to be ~ to sb** sich jdm gegenüber großherzig verhalten; **he was ~ in victory/defeat** er zeigte Großmut im Sieg/in der Niederlage

magnanimously [mæg'nænɪməslɪ] ADV großmütig; *(= generously)* großzügig

magnate ['mægneɪt] N Magnat *m*

magnesia [mæg'niːʃə] N Magnesia *f*

magnesium [mæg'niːzɪəm] N Magnesium *nt*

magnet ['mægnɪt] N *(lit, fig)* Magnet *m*

magnetic [mæg'netɪk] ADJ *(lit)* magnetisch; *(fig) charms* unwiderstehlich; **he has a ~ personality** er hat eine große Ausstrahlung *or* ein sehr anziehendes Wesen; **this perfume has a ~ effect on men** dieses Parfüm übt eine magnetische Wirkung auf Männer aus; **~ attraction** magnetische Anziehungskraft

magnetically [mæg'netɪkəlɪ] ADV *(lit, fig)* magnetisch; **she is ~ attractive/sensual** sie/ihre Sinnlichkeit übt eine magnetische Anziehungskraft aus; **to be ~ drawn to sb/sth** von jdm/etw magnetisch angezogen werden

magnetic: **magnetic card** N Magnetkarte *f*; **magnetic card reader** N Magnetkartenleser *m*; **magnetic compass** N Magnetkompass *m*; **magnetic disk** N *(Comput)* Magnetplatte *f*; **magnetic field** N Magnetfeld *nt*; **magnetic mine** N Magnetmine *f*; **magnetic needle** N Magnetnadel *f*; **magnetic north** N nördlicher Magnetpol; **magnetic pole** N Magnetpol *m*; **magnetic resonance** N *(Med)* Magnetresonanz *f*, Kernspinresonanz *f*; **~ imager** Kernspintomograf *m*; **magnetic resonance imaging** N *(Med)* Kernspintomografie *f*; **magnetic storm** N (erd)magnetischer Sturm; **magnetic strip, magnetic stripe** N Magnetstreifen *m*; **magnetic tape** N Magnetband *nt*

magnetism ['mægnɪtɪzəm] N Magnetismus *m*; *(fig: of person)* Anziehungskraft *f*, Ausstrahlung *f*

magnetize ['mægnɪtaɪz] VT magnetisieren; **the audience was ~d by this incredible performance** das Publikum folgte dieser unglaublichen Darstellung wie gebannt

magneto [mæg'niːtəʊ] N Magnetzünder *m*

magnification [,mægnɪfɪ'keɪʃən] N Vergrößerung *f*; **high/low ~** starke/geringe Vergrößerung; **seen at 300 ~s** in 300facher Vergrößerung, 300fach vergrößert

magnificence [mæg'nɪfɪsəns] N **a** *(= excellence)* Großartigkeit *f*, Größe *f* **b** *(= splendid appearance)* Pracht *f*, Glanz *m* **c** **his Magnificence** Seine Magnifizenz

magnificent [mæg'nɪfɪsənt] ADJ **a** *(= wonderful, excellent)* großartig; *food, meal* hervorragend, ausgezeichnet; **he has done a ~ job** er hat das ganz hervorragend gemacht; **a ~ folly** eine Torheit grandiosen Ausmaßes **b** *(= of splendid appearance)* prachtvoll, prächtig

magnificently [mæg'nɪfɪsəntlɪ] ADV **a** *(= excellently)* großartig; **you did ~** das hast du großartig gemacht; **a ~ rousing finale** ein glanzvolles (und) mitreißendes Finale; **the islands are ~ pure and unspoilt** die Inseln sind herrlich rein und unberührt **b** *(in appearance)* prachtvoll, prächtig

magnifier ['mægnɪfaɪə'] N **a** *(= magnifying glass)* Vergrößerungsglas *nt*, Lupe *f* **b** *(Elec)* Verstärker *m*

magnify ['mægnɪfaɪ] VT **a** *(= make bigger) image* vergrößern; **to ~ sth 7 times** etw 7fach vergrößern **b** *(= exaggerate)* aufbauschen **c** *(obs, liter, = praise) the Lord* lobpreisen *(old, liter)*

magnifying glass ['mægnɪfaɪɪŋ'glɑːs] N Vergrößerungsglas *nt*, Lupe *f*

magniloquence [mæg'nɪləkwəns] N *(liter)* Wortgewalt *f (liter)*

magniloquent [mæg'nɪləkwənt] ADJ *(liter)* wortgewaltig *(liter)*

magnitude ['mægnɪtjuːd] N **a** Ausmaß *nt*, Größe *f*; *(= importance)* Bedeutung *f*; **I didn't appreciate the ~ of the task** ich war mir über den Umfang der Aufgabe nicht im Klaren; **in operations of this ~** bei Vorhaben dieser Größenordnung; **a matter of the first ~** eine Angelegenheit von äußerster Wichtigkeit; **a mistake of the first ~** ein Fehler ersten Ranges; **order of ~** Größenordnung *f* **b** *(Astron)* Größenklasse *f*

magnolia [mæg'nəʊlɪə] N Magnolie *f*; *(also* **magnolia tree**) Magnolienbaum *m*

magnum ['mægnəm] N ≈ Anderthalbliterflasche *f (esp von Sekt)*

magnum opus N Hauptwerk *nt*

magpie ['mægpaɪ] N Elster *f*

Magyar ['mægjɑː'] ADJ madjarisch, magyarisch N Madjar(in) *m(f)*, Magyar(in) *m(f)*

maharajah [,mɑːhə'rɑːdʒə] N Maharadscha *m*

maharani [,mɑːhə'rɑːniː] N Maharani *f*

maharishi [,mɑːhɑː'rɪʃɪ] N Maharischi *m*

mahogany [mə'hɒgənɪ] N Mahagoni *nt*; *(= tree)* Mahagonibaum *m* ADJ Mahagoni-; *(colour)* mahagoni(farben); **~ furniture** Mahagonimöbel *pl*

Mahomet [mə'hɒmɪt] N Mohammed *m*, Mahomet *m (liter)*

Mahometan [mə'hɒmɪtən] *(Hist)* ADJ mohammedanisch *(Hist) (neg!)* N Mohammedaner(in) *m(f) (Hist) (neg!)*

mahout [mə'haʊt] N Mahaut *m*, Elefantenführer *m*

maid [meɪd] N **a** *(= servant)* (Dienst)mädchen *nt*, Hausangestellte *f*; *(in hotel)* Zimmermädchen *nt*; *(= lady's maid)* Zofe *f* **b** *(old, = maiden)* Jungfer *f (obs)*, Maid *f (old, poet)*; *(= young girl)* Mägdelein *nt (poet)*; **the Maid of Orleans** die Jungfrau von Orleans

maidan [maɪ'dɑːn] N *(India)* (Markt)platz *m*, Esplanade *f*

maiden ['meɪdn] N *(liter)* Maid *f (old, poet)*, Mädchen *nt* ADJ *attr* Jungfern-; **~ flight** Jungfernflug *m*; **~ voyage** Jungfernfahrt *f*

maiden: **maiden aunt** N unverheiratete, ältere Tante; **maidenhair** N Frauenhaar *nt*; **maidenhead** N *(Anat)* Jungfernhäutchen *nt*; **she lost her ~** *(liter)* sie hat ihre Unschuld verloren; **maidenhood** N Jungfräulichkeit *f*, Unschuld *f*; *(= time)* Jungmädchenzeit *f*

maidenly ['meɪdnlɪ] ADJ jungfräulich; *(= modest)* mädchenhaft

maiden: **maiden name** N Mädchenname *m*; **maiden over** N *(Cricket)* 6 *Würfe ohne einen Lauf*; **maiden speech** N Jungfernrede *f*

maid: **maid of all work** N *(= person)* Mädchen *nt* für alles; *(= machine)* Allzweckgerät *nt*; **maid of honour**, *(US)* **maid of honor** N Brautjungfer *f*; **maidservant** N Hausangestellte *f*, Hausmädchen *nt*

mail[1] [meɪl] N **a** Post® *f*; **to send sth by ~** etw mit der Post® versenden *or* schicken; **is there any ~ for me?** ist Post für mich da? **b** *(= e-mail)* E-Mail *f* VT aufgeben; *(= put in letter box)* einwerfen; *(= send by mail)* mit der Post® schicken; *(= send by e-mail)* per E-Mail senden, mailen *(inf)*; **to ~ sb** jdm eine E-Mail senden

mail[2] N *(Mil)* Kettenpanzer *m* VT **the ~ed fist of imperialism** die gepanzerte Faust des Imperialismus

mailable ['meɪləbl] ADJ *(esp US)* postversandfähig

mail: **mailbag** N Postsack *m*; **mailboat** N Postdampfer *m*; **mail bomb** N *(US)* Briefbombe *f*; **mailbox** N **a** *(US)* Briefkasten *m* **b** *(Comput)* Mailbox *f*, (elektronischer) Briefkasten; **mailcar** N *(US Rail)* Postwagen *m*; **mail carrier** N *(US)* = **mailman**; **mailcoach** N *(Brit) (Hist)* Postkutsche *f*; *(Rail)* Postwagen *m*; **mail drop** N *(US)* Briefeinwurf *m (form)*, Briefschlitz *m*; **mailer** ['meɪlə'] N *(US)* **a** *(= machine)* Adressiermaschine *f*; *(for stamps)* Frankiermaschine *f* **b** *(= advertisement)* Postwurfsendung *f*; **Mailgram®** N *(US) auf elektronischem Wege an ein Postamt im Bezirk des Empfängers übermittelte Nachricht, die dann als normale Briefsendung zugestellt wird*

mailing ['meɪlɪŋ] N Rundschreiben *nt*

mailing address N *(US)* Postanschrift *f*

mailing list N Adressenliste *f*; *(e-mail)* Mailingliste *f*

mail: **mailman** N *(US)* Briefträger *m*, Postbote *m*; **mail merge** N *(Comput)* Mailmerge *nt*, Serienbrieferstellung*f* (mit automatischer Einfügung von Adressen); **~ program** Dateimischprogramm *nt*; **mail-order** ADJ Versand-; **~ catalogue** *(Brit) or* **catalog** *(US)* Versandhauskatalog *m*; **~ firm, ~ house** Versandhaus *nt*, Versandgeschäft *nt*; **mailroom** N *(esp US)* Poststelle *f*; **mailshot** *(Brit)* N Direktwerbung *f* (per Post®); **to send out a ~** Werbebriefe verschicken VT Werbebriefe verschicken an *(+acc)*; **mail train** N Postzug *m*; **mail van** N *(on roads)* Postauto *nt*; *(Brit Rail)* Postwagen *m*; **mailwoman** N *(US)* Briefträgerin *f*, Postbotin *f*

maim [meɪm] VT *(= mutilate)* verstümmeln; *(= cripple)* zum Krüppel machen; **the wounded and the ~ed** die Verletzten und Versehrten; **he will be ~ed for life** er wird sein Leben lang ein Krüppel bleiben; **he was ~ed in the bomb attack** der Bombenanschlag machte ihn zum Krüppel

main [meɪn] ADJ *attr* Haupt-; **the ~ reason** der Hauptgrund; **the ~ idea in this book** der Haupt- *or* Leitgedanke in diesem Buch; **what is the ~ thing in life?** was ist die Hauptsache im Leben?; **the ~ thing is to ...** die Hauptsache ist, dass ...; **the ~ thing is you're still alive** Hauptsache, du lebst noch

N **a** *(= pipe)* Hauptleitung *f*; **the ~s** *(of town)* das öffentliche Versorgungsnetz; *(for electricity)* das Stromnetz; *(of house)* der Haupthahn; *(for electricity)* der Hauptschalter; **the machine is run directly off the ~s** das Gerät wird direkt ans Stromnetz angeschlossen; **the water/gas/electricity was switched off at the ~s** der Haupthahn/Hauptschalter für Wasser/Gas/Elektrizität wurde abgeschaltet

b *(poet)* **the ~** das offene Meer, die hohe See

c **in the ~** im Großen und Ganzen

d → **might**[2]

main: **mainbrace** N Großbrasse *f*; **to splice the ~** Rum an die Mannschaft ausgeben; **main clause** N *(Gram)* Hauptsatz *m*; **main course** N Hauptgericht *nt*; **main deck** N Hauptdeck *nt*; **main drag** N *(US inf: = main street)* Hauptstraße *f*; **main drain** N Hauptrohr *nt*; *(for sewage)* Hauptkanal *m*; **main establishment** N *(Comm)* Hauptniederlassung *f*; **main force** N rohe Gewalt; **mainframe (computer)** N Großrechner *m*, Mainframe *m*; **mainland** N Festland *nt*; **on the ~ of Europe** auf dem europäischen Festland; **main line** N *(Rail)* Hauptstrecke *f*; **main-line** ADJ **~ train** Schnellzug *m*; **mainline** VI *(sl)* fixen *(inf)*

mainly ['meɪnlɪ] ADV hauptsächlich, in erster Linie; **the meetings are held ~ on Tuesdays** die Besprechungen finden meistens dienstags statt; **the climate is ~ wet** das Klima ist vorwiegend *or* überwiegend feucht

main: **main man** N *(US inf)* **a** *(in film)* Hauptdarsteller *m* **b** *(= best friend)* bester Freund; **mainmast** N Haupt- *or* Großmast *m*; **main memory** N *(Comput)* Hauptspeicher *m*; **main menu** N *(Comput)* Hauptmenü *nt*; **main office** N *(= headquarters)* Zentrale *f*; **main road** N Hauptstraße *f*; **mainsail** N Haupt- *or* Großsegel *nt*; **mainsheet** N *(Naut)* Großschot *f*

mains-operated ['meɪnz,ɒpəreɪtɪd], **mains-powered** ['meɪnz,paʊəd] ADJ für Netzbetrieb, mit Netzanschluss

main: **mainspring** N *(Mech, fig)* Triebfeder *f*; **mainstay** N *(Naut)* Haupt- *or* Großstag *nt*; *(fig)* Stütze *f*

mainstream N **a** Hauptrichtung *f*; **to be in the ~ of sth** der Hauptrichtung einer Sache *(gen)* angehören **b** *(Jazz)* Mainstream *m* ADJ **a** *politician, party, politics* der Mitte; *philosophy, opinion etc* vorherrschend; *schools, education* regulär; **~ society** die Mitte der Gesellschaft; **the ~ press/media** die Hauptvertreter *pl* der Presse/Medien **b** **~ cinema** Mainstreamkino *nt*; **~ jazz** Mainstreamjazz *m* VT *(US Sch)* in die reguläre Schule schicken

maintain [meɪn'teɪn] ✪ 26.2 VT **a** *(= keep up)* aufrechterhalten; *law and order, peace etc* wahren; *speed, attitude* beibehalten; *prices* halten; *life* erhalten; **he wants to ~ his weight at 75 kilos** er möchte sein Gewicht von 75 Kilo beibehalten; **to ~ the status quo** den Status quo (aufrecht)erhalten; **to ~ sth at a constant temperature** etw bei gleichbleibender Temperatur halten

b *(= support) family* unterhalten

c *(= keep in good condition) machine* warten; *roads, building* instand *or* in Stand halten; *car* pflegen; **this old car is too expensive to ~** dieses alte Auto ist im Unterhalt zu teuer; **products which help to ~ healthy skin** Produkte, die die Haut gesund erhalten

d *(= claim)* behaupten; **he still ~ed he was innocent, he still ~ed his innocence** er beteuerte immer noch seine Unschuld

e *(= defend) theory* vertreten; *rights* verteidigen

maintained school [meɪn'teɪndskuːl] N *(Brit)* staatliche Schule

maintenance ['meɪntɪnəns] N **a** *(= keeping up)* Aufrechterhaltung *f*; *(of law and order, peace etc)* Wahrung *f*; *(of speed, attitude)* Beibehaltung *f*; *(of life)* Erhaltung *f* **b** *(Brit) (of family)* Unterhalt *m*; *(= social security)* Unterstützung *f*; **he has to pay ~** er ist unterhaltspflichtig **c** *(= servicing: of machine, car)* Wartung *f*; *(= upkeep) (of road, building etc)* Instandhaltung *f*; *(of gardens)* Pflege *f*; *(= cost)* Unterhalt *m*

maintenance: **maintenance contract** N Wartungsvertrag *m*; **maintenance costs** PL Unterhaltskosten *pl*; **maintenance crew** N Wartungsmannschaft *f*

maintop ['meɪntɒp] N Großmars *m*

maisonette [,meɪzə'net] N *(= small flat)* Appartement *nt*; *(= small house)* Häuschen *nt*

maître d' [,metrə'diː] N *(US: = head waiter)* Oberkellner *m*

maize [meɪz] N Mais *m*

Maj *abbr of* **major**

majestic [mə'dʒestɪk] ADJ majestätisch; *proportions* stattlich; *music* getragen; *(= not slow)* erhaben

majestically [mə'dʒestɪkəlɪ] ADV *move, rise* majestätisch; **~ proportioned buildings** Gebäude von stattlichen Ausmaßen; **the music ends ~** die Musik kommt zu einem erhabenen *or* grandiosen Schluss

majesty ['mædʒɪstɪ] N *(= stateliness)* Majestät *f*; *(of movements etc)* Würde *f*; **the ~ of the mountains** die Majestät *or* Erhabenheit der Bergwelt; **His/Her Majesty** Seine/Ihre Majestät; **Your Majesty** Eure Majestät

Maj Gen *abbr of* **major general**

major ['meɪdʒə'] ADJ **a** Haupt-; *(= of great importance)* bedeutend; *cause, factor* wesentlich; *incident* schwerwiegend, schwer wiegend; *part, role* groß, führend; *(Pol) party* groß, führend; *(= of great extent)* groß; **a ~ road** eine Hauptverkehrsstraße; **a ~ factor in our decision/his defeat** ein wesentlicher Faktor bei unserem Entschluss/seiner Niederlage; **a ~ poet** ein bedeutender Dichter; **Sapporo, the ~ city on Hokkaido** Sapporo, die wichtigste Stadt auf Hokkaido; **matters of ~ interest** Angelegenheiten *pl* von großem *or* größerem Interesse; **of ~ importance** von großer *or* größerer Bedeutung; **a ~ operation** eine größere Operation; **a ~ work of art** ein bedeutendes Kunstwerk

b *(Mus)* Dur-; **~ chord** Durakkord *m*; **~ key** Durtonart *f*; **~ scale** Durtonleiter *f*; **A ~** A-Dur *nt*; **A flat ~** As-Dur *nt*; **G sharp ~** Gis-Dur *nt*; **~ third** große Terz

c **Jenkins Major** Jenkins der Ältere

N **a** *(Mil)* Major(in) *m(f)*

b *(Mus)* Dur *nt*; **in the ~** in Dur

c *(Jur)* **to become a ~** volljährig *or* mündig werden

d *(US: = subject)* Hauptfach *nt*; **he's a psychology ~** Psychologie ist/war sein Hauptfach

VI *(US)* **to ~ in French** Französisch als Hauptfach studieren, das Examen mit Französisch im Hauptfach ablegen

Majorca [məˈjɔːkə] N Mallorca *nt*

Majorcan [məˈjɔːkən] ADJ mallorquinisch N Mallorquiner(in) *m(f)*

major-domo [ˌmeɪdzəˈdəʊməʊ] N Haushofmeister *m*, Majordomus *m*

majorette [ˌmeɪdʒəˈret] N Majorette *f*

major general N Generalmajor(in) *m(f)*

majority [məˈdʒɒrɪtɪ] N **a** Mehrheit *f*; **the ~ of cases** die Mehrheit *or* Mehrzahl der Fälle; **to be in a** *or* **the ~** in der Mehrzahl sein; **to be in a ~ of 3** eine Mehrheit von 3 Stimmen haben; **to have/get a ~** die Mehrheit haben/bekommen; **to have a ~ of 10** eine Mehrheit von 10 Stimmen haben; **what was his ~?** wie groß war seine Mehrheit?; **a two-thirds ~** die Zweidrittelmehrheit; **by a small** *or* **narrow ~** mit knapper Mehrheit **b** *(Jur)* Volljährigkeit *f*, Mündigkeit *f*; **to reach the age of ~** volljährig *or* mündig werden

majority: **majority decision** N Mehrheitsbeschluss *m*; **majority holding** N *(Fin)* Mehrheitsbeteiligung *f*; **majority rule** N Mehrheitsregierung *f*

major: **major league** N (= *US Sport*) oberste Spielklasse; **major-league** ADJ *attr* (= *US Sport*) *football, baseball etc* der obersten Spielklasse; **major premise** N erste Prämisse, Obersatz *m*

make [meɪk]

vb: pret, ptp **made**

1 TRANSITIVE VERB	4 NOUN
2 INTRANSITIVE VERB	5 PHRASAL VERBS
3 REFLEXIVE VERB	

1 – TRANSITIVE VERB

a [= produce, prepare] machen; *bread* backen; *cars* herstellen; *dress* nähen; *coffee* kochen; *peace* stiften; **she made it into a suit** sie machte einen Anzug daraus; **God made the world** Gott erschuf die Welt; **he's as clever as they make 'em** *(inf)* der ist ein ganz gerissener Hund *(inf)*

♦ **made in/of/for/to made in Germany** in Deutschland hergestellt, made in Germany; **it's made of gold** es ist aus Gold; **to show what one is made of** zeigen, was in einem steckt; **the job is made for him** die Arbeit ist wie für ihn geschaffen; **I'm not made for running** ich bin nicht zum Laufen *or* zum Läufer geschaffen; **they're made for each other** sie sind wie geschaffen füreinander; **this car wasn't made to carry eight people** dieses Auto ist nicht dazu gedacht, acht Leute zu transportieren

b [= do, execute] *bow, journey, mistake, attempt, plan, remarks, suggestions etc* machen; *speech* halten; *choice, arrangements* treffen; *decision* fällen, treffen; **to make an application** sich bewerben; **to make a guess** raten; **to make sb a present of sth** jdm etw schenken, jdm etw zum Geschenk machen *(geh)*

c [= cause to be or become] machen

♦ **to make sb/sth + ADJ to make sb happy/angry** *etc* jdn glücklich/wütend *etc* machen; **does that make you happy?** bist du jetzt endlich zufrieden?; **I'll make it easy for you** ich mache es dir leicht *or* es leicht für dich; **to make one's voice heard** mit seiner Stimme durchdringen; **he makes Macbeth very evil** er lässt Macbeth sehr böse erscheinen

♦ **to make sb/sth + NOUN to make sb one's wife** jdn zu seiner Frau machen; **he was made a judge** man ernannte ihn zum Richter; **to make a success of sth, to make sth a success** etw erfolgreich erledigen; **Shearer made it 1-0** Shearer erzielte das 1:0; **they'll never make a soldier of him** *or* **out of him** aus ihm wird nie ein Soldat

♦ **to make a day/night of it we decided to make a day/night of it** wir beschlossen, den ganzen Tag dafür zu nehmen/(die Nacht) durchzumachen

♦ **to make something of oneself/one's life** etwas aus sich/seinem Leben machen

♦ **to make something of it** *(inf)* **do you want to make something of it?** hast du was dagegen? *(inf)*, störts dich etwa? *(inf)*

d [= cause to do or happen] lassen, (dazu) bringen; *(= compel to do)* zwingen

♦ **to make sb do sth** *(= cause to do)* jdn dazu bringen *or* veranlassen *(geh)*, etw zu tun; *(= compel to do)* jdn zwingen, etw zu tun; **to make sb laugh** jdn zum Lachen bringen; **what made you come to this town?** was hat Sie dazu veranlasst, in diese Stadt zu kommen?; **what makes you say that?** warum sagst du das?; **what makes you think you can do it?** was macht Sie glauben, dass Sie es schaffen können?; **it all makes me think that ...** das alles lässt mich denken, dass ...; **how can I make you understand?** wie kann ich es Ihnen verständlich machen?; **that certainly made him think again** das hat ihm bestimmt zu denken gegeben; **what will make you change your mind?** was wird Sie dazu bringen, Ihre Meinung zu ändern?; **what finally made me drop the idea was ...** was mich am Ende dazu veranlasst hat, den Gedanken fallen zu lassen, war ...; **he makes his heroine die** er lässt seine Heldin sterben; **her conduct made him seem polite by comparison** im Vergleich zu ihrem Verhalten machte er einen höflichen Eindruck; **I'll make him suffer for this** dafür soll er mir büßen!; **you can't make me!** mich kann keiner zwingen!; **make me!** *(challenging)* versuch mal, mich zu zwingen!; **I'll make him!** den zwing ich!

♦ **to make sth do sth what makes the engine go?** was treibt den Motor an?, wie wird der Motor angetrieben?; **what made it explode?** was hat die Explosion bewirkt?; **onions make your eyes water** von Zwiebeln tränen einem die Augen; **it makes the room look smaller** es lässt den Raum kleiner wirken; **the chemical makes the plant grow faster** die Chemikalie bewirkt, dass die Pflanze schneller wächst; **that made the cloth shrink** dadurch ging der Stoff ein; **that will make the pain go** das wird den Schmerz vertreiben; **I wish I could make the rain stop** wenn ich nur machen *(inf) or* bewirken könnte, dass der Regen aufhört; **if I could make your problems disappear** wenn ich (nur) Ihre Probleme beseitigen könnte; **you can't make things happen** man kann den Lauf der Dinge nicht erzwingen

♦ **to make do to make do with sth** sich mit etw begnügen; **to make do with less money/on a small income** mit weniger Geld/einem niedrigen Gehalt auskommen

e [= earn] *money* verdienen; *profit, loss, fortune* machen (*on* bei); *reputation* sich *(dat)* verschaffen; **to make a name for oneself** sich *(dat)* einen Namen machen; **how much do you stand to make?** wie viel verdienst du (dabei)?, was bringt dir das ein? *(inf)*

f [= reach, achieve] schaffen, erreichen; *train, plane etc* erwischen *(inf)*, schaffen; *connection* schaffen; *summit, top, shore etc* es schaffen zu; *(ship) 20 knots* machen; **to make land** *(Naut)* anlegen; **to make port** *(Naut)* in den Hafen einlaufen; **we made good time** wir kamen schnell voran; **sorry I couldn't make your party last night** tut mir leid, ich habe es gestern Abend einfach nicht zu deiner Party geschafft; **his first record didn't make the charts** seine erste Platte schaffte es nicht bis in die Hitparade; **we'll never make the airport in time** wir kommen garantiert nicht rechtzeitig zum Flughafen; **he made colonel in one year** er brachte es in einem Jahr zum Obersten; **he made university/the first team** er schaffte es, an die Universität/in die erste Mannschaft zu kommen; **the story made the front page** die Geschichte kam auf die Titelseite

♦ **to make it** *(= succeed)* es schaffen, es zu etwas bringen; **he just made it** er hat es gerade noch geschafft; **we've made it!** wir haben es geschafft!; **he'll never make it through the winter** *(= survive)* er wird den Winter nie überstehen

♦ **to make it (with sb)** *(inf: = have sex)* mit jdm schlafen; **they were making it all night** sie liebten sich die ganze Nacht

♦ **to make good to make good as a writer** es als Schriftsteller(in) schaffen *or* zu etwas bringen; **he is a poor boy made good** er ist ein armer Junge, der es zu etwas gebracht hat

g [= cause to succeed] berühmt machen, zum Erfolg verhelfen *(+dat)*; **this film made her** mit diesem Film schaffte sie es *or* schaffte sie den Durchbruch; **his performance makes the play** das Stück lebt von seiner schauspielerischen Leistung; **you'll be made for life** Sie werden ausgesorgt haben; **he's got it made** *(inf)* er hat ausgesorgt; **he's a made man** er ist ein gemachter Mann; **but what really made the evening was ...** die eigentliche Krönung des Abends war ...

♦ **to make sb's day that makes my day!** das freut mich unheimlich!; *(iro)* das hat mir gerade noch gefehlt!; **seeing the Queen made her day** sie war selig, als sie die Königin gesehen hatte; **you've made my day** ich könnte dir um den Hals fallen! *(inf)*

♦ **to make or break sth/sb the weather will make or break the parade** der Festzug steht und fällt mit dem Wetter; **he can make or break you** er hat dein Schicksal in der Hand

h [= be, constitute] sein, machen, (ab)geben; **he made a good father** er gab einen guten Vater ab; **he'll never make a soldier/an actor** aus dem wird nie ein Soldat/Schauspieler; **you'd make someone a good wife** Sie würden eine gute Ehefrau abgeben; **she made him a good wife** sie war ihm eine gute Frau; **he'd make a fantastic Hamlet/a good teacher** er wäre ein fantastischer *or* phantastischer Hamlet/ein guter Lehrer, er gäbe einen fantastischen *or* phantastischen Hamlet/einen guten Lehrer ab; **they make a good/an odd couple** sie sind ein gutes/ungleiches Paar; **it makes good television/publicity** es ist sehr fernsehwirksam/werbewirksam; **it made a very strange sight** es war ein sehr merkwürdiger Anblick; **to make a fourth at bridge** den vierten Mann beim Bridge machen

i [= equal] sein, (er)geben; **2 plus 2 makes 4** 2 und 2 ist 4; **1760 yards make 1 mile** 1760 Yards sind eine Meile; **that makes £55 you owe me** Sie schulden mir damit (nun) £ 55; **how much does that make altogether?** was macht das insgesamt?

j [= reckon] *distance, total* schätzen auf *(+acc)*; **I make the total 107** ich komme auf 107

♦ **to make it + time, date, figure what time do you make it?** wie spät hast du es?, wie spät ist es bei dir?; **I make it 3.15** ich habe 3.15 Uhr, auf meiner Uhr ist es 3.15 Uhr; **I make it 3 miles** ich schätze 3 Meilen; **how many do you make it?** wie viele sind es nach deiner Zählung?; **shall we make it 7 o'clock?** *(= agree)* sagen wir 7 Uhr?; **let's make it Monday** sagen wir Montag

k [Cards] *(= fulfil contract)* erfüllen; *(= win) trick* machen; *(= shuffle) pack* mischen → **bid**

l [Elec] *circuit* schließen; *contact* herstellen

m [Naut] *(= signal)* senden, funken; **make (the following message) to HMS Victor** machen Sie die folgende Meldung an HMS Victor

n [US] *(= recognize)* erkennen

2 – INTRANSITIVE VERB

a [= go] **to make toward(s) a place** auf einen Ort zuhalten; *(ship)* Kurs auf einen Ort nehmen; **to make after sb** jdm nachsetzen → **make for**

b [= profit] **to make on a deal** bei einem Geschäft verdienen

c [= act]

♦ **to make as if to do sth** Anstalten machen, etw zu tun; *(as deception)* so tun, als wolle man etw tun

♦ **to make to...** *(= try)* **I made to speak** ich setzte zur Rede an

♦ **to make like…** *(inf)* so tun, als ob…; **he made like he was dying** er tat so, als ob er am Sterben wäre, er markierte *(inf)* or spielte den Sterbenden; **he's started making like a big-shot** er hat angefangen, den starken Mann zu spielen or zu markieren *(inf)*

3 – REFLEXIVE VERB

♦ **to make oneself** + *ADJ or NOUN (= cause oneself to be)* **to make oneself useful** sich nützlich machen; **to make oneself comfortable** es sich *(dat)* bequem machen; **make yourself small** mach dich klein; **to make oneself conspicuous** auffallen; **you'll make yourself ill!** du machst dich damit krank!; **to make oneself heard** sich *(dat)* Gehör verschaffen; **to make oneself understood** sich verständlich machen; **he made himself Emperor for life** er krönte or machte sich selbst zum Kaiser auf Lebenszeit

♦ **to make oneself sth** *(= to make sth for oneself)* sich *(dat)* etw machen; **he made himself a cup of tea/a sandwich** er machte sich *(dat)* eine Tasse Tee/ein Butterbrot; **she made herself a lot of money on the deal** sie hat bei dem Geschäft eine Menge Geld verdient

♦ **to make oneself do sth** *(= force oneself)* sich dazu zwingen, etw zu tun; **I made myself apologize to him** ich zwang mich dazu, mich bei ihm zu entschuldigen; **he's just made himself look ridiculous** er hat sich nur lächerlich gemacht

4 – NOUN

a [= brand] Marke *f*, Fabrikat *nt*; **what make of car do you have?** welche (Auto)marke fahren Sie?; **it's a good make** das ist eine gute Marke; **these are my own make** die sind selbst gemacht, die sind Eigenfabrikat *(hum)*

b

♦ **on the make** *(pej inf, for profit)* profitgierig *(inf)*, auf Profit aus; *(= ambitious)* karrieresüchtig *(inf)*, auf Karriere aus; *(sexually)* sexhungrig *(inf)*, auf sexuelle Abenteuer aus

5 – PHRASAL VERBS

▶ **make away** VI = **make off**

▶ **make away with** VI *+prep obj* **to make away with sb** jdn beseitigen or umbringen; **to make away with oneself** sich umbringen

▶ **make for** VI *+prep obj* **a** *(= head for)* zuhalten auf *(+acc)*; *(crowd)* zuströmen *(+dat,* auf *+acc)*; *(= attack)* losgehen auf *(+acc)*; *(vehicle)* losfahren auf *(+acc)*; **where are you making for?** wo willst du hin?; **we are making for London** wir wollen nach London; *(by vehicle)* wir fahren or wollen Richtung London; *(by ship)* wir halten Kurs auf London
b *(= promote) happy marriage, successful parties* den Grund legen für; **such tactics don't make for good industrial relations** solche Praktiken wirken sich nicht gerade günstig auf das Arbeitsklima aus; **the trade figures make for optimism** die Handelsziffern geben Anlass zum Optimismus

▶ **make of** VI *+prep obj* halten von; **I didn't make much of it** ich konnte nicht viel dabei finden; **well, what do you make of that?** nun, was halten Sie davon?, was sagen Sie dazu?; **don't make too much of it** überbewerten Sie es nicht

▶ **make off** VI sich davonmachen *(with sth* mit etw)

▶ **make out** VT *sep* **a** *(= write out) cheque, receipt* ausstellen *(to* auf *+acc)*; *list, bill* aufstellen, zusammenstellen; *(= fill out) form* ausfüllen; **to make out a case for sth** für etw argumentieren
b *(= see, discern)* ausmachen; *(= decipher)* entziffern; *(= understand)* verstehen; *person, actions* schlau werden aus; **I can't make out what he wants** ich komme nicht dahinter, was er will; **how do you make that out?** wie kommst du darauf?
c *(= claim)* behaupten
d *(= imply)* **to make out that …** es so hinstellen, als ob …; **he made out that he was hurt** er tat, als sei er verletzt; **to make sb out to be clever/a genius** jdn als klug/Genie hinstellen; **she's not as rich as he makes out** sie ist nicht so reich, wie er es hinstellt; **he tried to make out it was my fault** er versuchte, es so hinzustellen, als wäre ich daran schuld; **Jesus is made out to be a Communist** Jesus wird zum Kommunisten gemacht
VI **a** *(inf) (= get on)* zurechtkommen; *(with people)* auskommen; *(= succeed)* es schaffen; **he didn't make out with her** er ist bei ihr nicht gelandet *(inf)*
b *(US inf: = pet)* knutschen *(inf)*, fummeln *(inf)*

▶ **make over** VT *sep* **a** *(= assign)* überschreiben *(to sb* jdm); *(= bequeath) property, money* vermachen *(to sb* jdm) **b** *(= convert)* umändern, umarbeiten; *house* umbauen; **the gardens have been made over into a parking lot** man hat die Anlagen in einen Parkplatz umgewandelt

▶ **make up** VT *sep* **a** *(= constitute)* bilden; **to be made up of** bestehen aus, sich zusammensetzen aus
b *(= put together) food, medicine, bed* zurechtmachen; *parcel* packen; *list, accounts* zusammenstellen, aufstellen; *team* zusammenstellen; *(Typ) page* umbrechen; *(= design) layout* aufmachen; **to make material up into sth** Material zu etw verarbeiten; **they made the daffodils up into bunches** sie banden die Osterglocken zu Sträußen
c *quarrel* beilegen, begraben; **to make it up (with sb)** sich (mit jdm) wieder vertragen, sich (mit jdm) aussöhnen; **come on, let's make it up** komm, wir wollen uns wieder vertragen
d *face, eyes* schminken; **to make sb/oneself up** jdn/sich schminken; **the way she's made up** wie sie geschminkt ist
e **to make up one's mind (to do sth)** sich (dazu) entschließen(, etw zu tun); **make up your mind!** entschließ dich!; **my mind is quite made up** mein Entschluss steht fest; **once his mind is made up, that's it** wenn er einmal einen Entschluss gefasst hat, bleibt es dabei; **I can't make up your mind for you** ich kann das nicht für dich entscheiden; **to make up one's mind about sb/sth** sich *(dat)* eine Meinung über jdn/etw bilden; **I can't make up my mind about him** ich weiß nicht, was ich von ihm halten soll
f *(= invent)* erfinden, sich *(dat)* ausdenken; **you're making that up!** jetzt schwindelst du aber! *(inf)*; **he makes it up as he goes along** *(storyteller)* er macht das aus dem Stegreif; *(child playing)* er macht das, wie es ihm gerade einfällt; *(making excuses, telling lies)* er saugt sich *(dat)* das nur so aus den Fingern; **it was all made up** das war alles nur erfunden
g *(= complete) crew* vollständig or komplett *(inf)* machen; **I'll make up the other £20** ich komme für die restlichen £ 20 auf; **he made the gift up to £50** er rundete das Geschenk auf £ 50 auf; **add water to make it up to one pint** mit Wasser auf 0,57 Liter auffüllen; **he made up the four at bridge** er war der vierte Mann zum or beim Bridge
h *(= compensate for) loss* ausgleichen; *time* einholen, aufholen; *sleep* nachholen; **to make it up to sb (for sth)** *(= compensate)* jdn (für etw) entschädigen; *(emotionally, return favour etc)* jdm etw wiedergutmachen
i *fire* (wieder) anschüren or anfachen
VI **a** *(after quarrelling)* sich versöhnen, sich wieder vertragen; **let's kiss and make up** komm, gib mir einen Kuss und wir vertragen uns wieder
b *(material)* **this material will make up into a nice coat** dieser Stoff wird sich als Mantel gut machen
c *(= catch up)* aufholen; **to make up on sb** jdn einholen, an jdn herankommen; **you've a lot of making up to do** du hast viel nachzuholen or aufzuarbeiten

▶ **make up for** VI *+prep obj* **to make up for sth** etw ausgleichen; **to make up for lost time** verlorene Zeit aufholen; **to make up for the loss of sb/lack of sth** jdn/etw ersetzen; **that still doesn't make up for the fact that you were very rude** das macht noch lange nicht ungeschehen, dass du sehr unhöflich warst

▶ **make up to** VI *+prep obj (inf)* sich heranmachen an *(+acc)*

▶ **make with** VI *+prep obj (US inf)* **he started making with his trumpet** er legte mit seiner Trompete los *(inf)*; **OK, let's make with the paint brushes** na dann, schnappen wir uns die Pinsel *(inf)*; **just make with the scissors** mach schon los mit der Schere *(inf)*

makebelieve [ˈmeɪkbɪliːv] VT sich *(dat)* vorstellen

make-believe [ˈmeɪkbɪliːv] ADJ *attr* Fantasie-, Phantasie-, imaginär; **a ~ world** eine Fantasie- or Phantasie- or Scheinwelt N Fantasie *f*, Phantasie *f*; **a world of ~** eine Fantasie- or Phantasie- or Scheinwelt; **don't be afraid, it's only ~** hab keine Angst, das ist doch nur eine Geschichte

make-or-break [ˈmeɪkɔːˈbreɪk] ADJ *attr (inf)* kritisch, entscheidend

makeover [ˈmeɪkəʊvəʳ] N *(= beauty treatment)* Schönheitskur *f*; *(of car, building)* Verschönerung *f*; **to give sb a complete ~** *(= give new clothes, hairstyle etc)* jdm einen neuen Look verpassen *(inf)*

maker [ˈmeɪkəʳ] N *(= manufacturer)* Hersteller(in) *m(f)*; **our Maker** unser Schöpfer *m*; **to go to meet one's Maker** zum Herrn eingehen *(geh)*

-maker [ˈmeɪkəʳ] N *suf (hat-maker, clockmaker)* -macher(in) *m(f)*

make-ready [ˈmeɪkredɪ] N *(Typ)* Zurichtung *f*

make-ready time N *(Ind)* Vorbereitungszeit *f*

makeshift [ˈmeɪkʃɪft] ADJ improvisiert; *office* provisorisch; *weapon, tool, repairs* behelfsmäßig; **~ accommodation** Notunterkunft *f*; **~ hospital** Notkrankenhaus *nt* N Übergangslösung *f*, Notbehelf *m* → **shift N d**

make-up [ˈmeɪkʌp] N **a** Make-up *nt*; *(Theat)* Maske *f*, Schminke *f*; **the star does his own ~** der Star schminkt sich selbst or macht seine Maske selbst; **she spends hours on her ~** sie braucht Stunden zum Schminken **b** *(= composition: of team, party etc)* Zusammenstellung *f*; *(= character)* Veranlagung *f*; **psychological ~** Psyche *f*; **loyalty is part of his ~** er ist loyal veranlagt; **it's part of their national ~** das gehört zu ihrem Nationalcharakter **c** *(Typ)* Umbruch *m*; *(= layout)* Aufmachung *f*

make-up: **make-up artist** N Maskenbildner(in) *m(f)*; **make-up bag** N Kosmetiktasche *f*; **make-up brush** N Make-up-Pinsel *m*; **make-up girl** N Maskenbildnerin *f*; **make-up kit** N Schminkset *nt*; **make-up man** N Maskenbildner *m*; **make-up mirror** N Schminkspiegel *m*; **make-up woman** N Maskenbildnerin *f*

makeweight [ˈmeɪkweɪt] N **a** *(lit)* **he added a few more as ~s** er gab noch ein paar dazu, um das Gewicht vollzumachen **b** *(fig)* Lückenbüßer *m*; *(= person)* Lückenbüßer(in) *m(f)*; **to use sth as a ~** etw in die Waagschale werfen

making [ˈmeɪkɪŋ] N **a** *(= production)* Herstellung *f*; *(of food)* Zubereitung *f*; **in the ~** im Werden, im Entstehen; **the film was three months in the ~** der Film wurde in drei Monaten gedreht; **here you can see history in the ~** hier hat man den Finger am Puls der Geschichte *(liter)*; **a star/dictator in the ~** ein werdender Star/Diktator; **it's a civil war/a disaster in the ~** es bahnt sich ein Bürgerkrieg/eine Katastrophe an; **the mistake was not of my ~** der Fehler war nicht mein Werk; **many of her problems are of her own ~** an vielen ihrer Probleme ist sie selbst schuld; **it was the ~ of him** das hat ihn zum Mann gemacht; *(= made him successful)* das hat ihn zu dem gemacht, was er (heute) ist
b **makings** PL Voraussetzungen *pl* (of zu); **he has the ~s of an actor/a general** *etc* er hat das Zeug zu einem Schauspieler/General *etc*; **the situation has all the ~s of a strike** die Situation bietet alle Voraussetzungen für einen Streik

maladjusted [ˌmælə'dʒʌstɪd] ADJ *(Psych, Sociol)* verhaltensgestört; **psychologically ~** verhaltensgestört; **emotionally ~** emotional gestört; **~ youths** fehlangepasste *or* nicht angepasste Jugendliche *pl*

maladjustment [ˌmælə'dʒʌstmənt] N *(Psych, Sociol)* Verhaltensstörung *f*

maladministration ['mæləd,mɪnɪs'treɪʃən] N schlechte Verwaltung

maladroit ADJ, **maladroitly** ADV [ˌmælə'drɔɪt, -lɪ] ungeschickt

maladroitness [ˌmælə'drɔɪtnɪs] N Ungeschicklichkeit *f*

malady ['mælədɪ] N Leiden *nt*, Krankheit *f*; **social ~** gesellschaftliches Übel

malaise [mæ'leɪz] N Unwohlsein *nt*; *(fig)* Unbehagen *nt*; **I have a vague feeling of ~ about the future** mich überkommt ein leises Unbehagen, wenn ich an die Zukunft denke

malapropism ['mæləprɒpɪzəm] N Malapropismus *m*

malaria [mə'lɛərɪə] N Malaria *f*

malarial [mə'lɛərɪəl] ADJ Malaria-

malarkey [mə'lɑːkɪ] N *(inf)* *(= messing about)* Blödelei *f (inf)*; *(= nonsense)* Hokuspokus *m (sl)*; *(= goings-on)* Gedöns *nt (inf)*

Malawi [mə'lɑːwɪ] N Malawi *nt*

Malay [mə'leɪ] ADJ malaiisch; **the ~ Archipelago** der Malaiische Archipel; **the ~ Peninsula** die Malaiische Halbinsel, die Halbinsel Malakka N **a** Malaie *m*, Malaiin *f* **b** *(Ling)* Malaiisch *nt*

Malaya [mə'leɪə] N Malaya *nt*

Malayan [mə'leɪən] ADJ malaiisch N Malaie *m*, Malaiin *f*

Malaysia [mə'leɪzɪə] N Malaysia *nt*

Malaysian [mə'leɪzɪən] ADJ malaysisch N Malaysier(in) *m(f)*

malcontent ['mælkən,tent] ADJ unzufrieden N Unzufriedene(r) *mf*

Maldive Islands ['mɔːldaɪv'aɪləndz], **Maldives** ['mɔːldaɪvz] PL Malediven *pl*

male [meɪl] ADJ **a** männlich; **~ child** Junge *m*; **a ~ doctor** ein Arzt *m*; **~ nurse** Krankenpfleger *m*; **~ prostitute** Strichjunge *m (inf)*; **~ sparrow/crocodile** Spatzen-/Krokodilmännchen *nt*; **~ violence** männliche Gewalt

b *choir, voice* Männer-; **an all-~ club** ein reiner Männerverein; **that's a typical ~ attitude** das ist typisch männlich

c *(= manly)* männlich; **~ bonding** Verbundenheit *f* unter Männern

d *(Mech)* **~ screw** Schraube *f*; **~ thread** Außengewinde *nt*; **~ plug** *(Elec)* Stecker *m*; **~ connector** Stiftstecker *m*

N *(= animal)* Männchen *nt*; *(inf: = man)* Mann *m*, männliches Wesen; **the ~ of the species** das männliche Tier, das Männchen; **that's typical of a ~** *(inf)* das ist typisch Mann *(inf)*

male: **male chauvinism** N Chauvinismus *m*; **male chauvinist** N Chauvi *m (inf)*; **~ attitude** chauvihafte Haltung *(inf)*; **~ remark** chauvihafte Bemerkung *(inf)*; **male chauvinist pig** N *(pej inf)* Chauvi *m (inf)*, Chauvinistenschwein *nt (pej)*

malediction [ˌmælɪ'dɪkʃən] N Fluch *m*, Verwünschung *f*

male-dominated [meɪl'dɒmɪneɪtɪd] ADJ von Männern beherrscht; **~ society** Männergesellschaft *f*

malefactor ['mælɪfæktə'] N Übeltäter(in) *m(f)*, Missetäter(in) *m(f)*

male menopause N *(hum)* Wechseljahre *pl* (des Mannes)

maleness ['meɪlnɪs] N Männlichkeit *f*

malevolence [mə'levələns] N Boshaftigkeit *f*; *(of action)* Böswilligkeit *f*; **to feel ~ toward(s) sb** einen Groll gegen jdn hegen

malevolent [mə'levələnt] ADJ boshaft; *gods* übelwollend; *action* böswillig; *power, force* böse; *fate* grausam; *presence* unheilvoll

malfeasance [mæl'fiːzəns] N *(Jur)* strafbare Handlung, (Amts)vergehen *nt*

malformation [ˌmælfɔː'meɪʃən] N Missbildung *f*

malformed [mæl'fɔːmd] ADJ missgebildet; *characters* verzerrt

malfunction [ˌmæl'fʌŋkʃən] N *(of liver etc)* Funktionsstörung *f*; *(of machine)* Defekt *m*; **a ~ of the carburettor** ein Defekt *m* im Vergaser, ein defekter Vergaser VI *(liver etc)* nicht richtig arbeiten; *(machine etc)* defekt sein, nicht richtig funktionieren; *(system)* versagen, nicht richtig funktionieren; **the ~ing part** das defekte Teil

malice ['mælɪs] N **a** Bosheit *f*, Bösartigkeit *f*; *(of action)* Böswilligkeit *f*; **a look of ~** ein boshafter Blick; **out of ~** aus Bosheit; **to bear sb ~** einen Groll gegen jdn hegen; **I bear him no ~** ich bin ihm nicht böse **b** *(Jur)* **with ~ aforethought** in böswilliger Absicht, vorsätzlich

malicious [mə'lɪʃəs] ADJ **a** *person, words* boshaft; *behaviour* bösartig, böswillig; *letter, phone call* bedrohend; *crime* gemein, arglistig; *action* böswillig **b** *(Jur) damage* mutwillig, böswillig; **with ~ intent** in böswilliger Absicht

malicious falsehood N *(Jur)* böswillige Verleumdung

maliciously [mə'lɪʃəslɪ] ADV *act* böswillig; *say, smile* boshaft

malicious: **malicious slander** N *(Jur)* böswillige Verleumdung; **malicious wounding** N *(Jur)* vorsätzliche Körperverletzung

malign [mə'laɪn] ADJ *(liter) person* boshaft; *force, intent* böse; *influence, effect* unheilvoll → *also* **malignant** VT verleumden; *(= run down)* schlechtmachen; **without wishing in any way to ~ her ...** ich will ihr ja nichts (Schlechtes) nachsagen, aber ...

malignancy [mə'lɪgnənsɪ] N Bösartigkeit *f*; *(Med)* Malignität *f (spec)*, Bösartigkeit *f*; *(fig: = evil thing)* Übel *nt*

malignant [mə'lɪgnənt] ADJ bösartig; *(Med also)* maligne *(spec)*; *effect* negativ; **he took a ~ delight in our misfortunes** unser Unglück bereitete ihm ein hämisches Vergnügen; **a ~ growth** *(Med, fig)* ein bösartiges Geschwür; **~ melanoma** *(Med)* malignes Melanom

malignantly [mə'lɪgnəntlɪ] ADV *look, say* boshaft; **his eyes looked ~ at me** seine Augen schauten mich mit boshaftem Blick an

malignity [mə'lɪgnɪtɪ] N Bösartigkeit *f*; *(Med also)* Malignität *f (spec)*

malinger [mə'lɪŋgə'] VI simulieren, krank spielen

malingerer [mə'lɪŋgərə'] N Simulant(in) *m(f)*

mall [mɔːl, mæl] N *(US: also* **shopping mall***)* Einkaufszentrum *nt*

mallard ['mælɑːd] N Stockente *f*

malleability [ˌmælɪə'bɪlɪtɪ] N Formbarkeit *f*; *(of clay, wax also)* Geschmeidigkeit *f*

malleable ['mælɪəbl] ADJ formbar *(also fig)*, weich; *(of clay, wax also)* geschmeidig

mallet ['mælɪt] N Holzhammer *m*; *(Croquet)* (Krocket)hammer *m*; *(Polo)* (Polo)schläger *m*

mallow ['mæləʊ] N Malve *f*

mallrats ['mɔːlræts] PL *(US sl)* *Jugendliche, die sich zum Zeitvertreib ständig in Einkaufszentren aufhalten*

malmsey ['mɑːmzɪ] N Malvasier(wein) *m*

malnourished [ˌmæl'nʌrɪʃt] ADJ *(form) person* unterernährt; **severely ~** stark unterernährt

malnutrition [ˌmælnjʊ'trɪʃən] N Unterernährung *f*

malodorous [mæl'əʊdərəs] ADJ *(form)* übel riechend

malpractice [ˌmæl'præktɪs] N Berufsvergehen *nt*, Verstoß *m* gegen das Berufsethos, Amtsvergehen *nt (eines Beamten)*

malpractice suit N *(US: Jur, Med)* *Strafverfolgung wegen Verletzung der Berufspflichten*; **to bring a ~ against a surgeon** einen Chirurg wegen eines Kunstfehlers vor Gericht bringen

malt [mɔːlt] N Malz *nt* VT *barley* malzen, mälzen; *drink etc* mit Malz versetzen *or* mischen; **~ed barley** gemälzte Gerste

Malta ['mɔːltə] N Malta *nt*

malted milk ['mɔːltɪd'mɪlk] N Malzmilch *f*

Maltese [ˌmɔːl'tiːz] ADJ maltesisch N **a** Malteser(in) *m(f)* **b** *(Ling)* Maltesisch *nt*

Maltese cross N Malteserkreuz *nt*

malt: **malt extract** N Malzextrakt *m*; **malt liquor** N *aus Malz gebrautes alkoholisches Getränk* *(US: = beer)* Starkbier *nt*; **malt loaf** N ≈ Rosinenbrot *nt*

maltreat [ˌmæl'triːt] VT schlecht behandeln; *(using violence)* misshandeln

maltreatment [ˌmæl'triːtmənt] N schlechte Behandlung; *(violent)* Misshandlung *f*

malt whisky N Malt Whisky *m*

malware ['mælwɛə'] N *(Comput)* Schadsoftware *f*

mamba ['mæmbə] N Mamba *f*

mambo ['mæmbəʊ] N Mambo *m*

mam(m)a [mə'mɑː] N *(inf)* Mama *f (inf)*

mammal ['mæməl] N Säugetier *nt*, Säuger *m*

mammalian [mæ'meɪlɪən] ADJ der Säugetiere

mammary ['mæmərɪ] ADJ Brust-; **~ gland** Brustdrüse *f*

mammogram ['mæməgræm] N *(Med)* Mammogramm *nt*

mammography [mæ'mɒgrəfɪ] N Mammografie *f*

mammon ['mæmən] N Mammon *m*, Reichtum *m*; **Mammon** der Mammon

mammoth ['mæməθ] N Mammut *nt* ADJ Mammut-; *cost, enterprise* kolossal; *change* gewaltig; *proportions* riesig; **a ~ task** eine Mammutaufgabe, eine kolossale Aufgabe

mammy ['mæmɪ] N *(inf)* Mami *f (inf)*; *(dated US)* (schwarze) Kinderfrau, schwarze Mami *(inf)*

man [mæn] N *pl* **men** **a** *(= adult male)* Mann *m*; **be a ~!** sei ein Mann!; **to make a ~ out of sb** einen Mann aus jdm machen; **this incident made a ~ out of him** dieses Ereignis hat ihn zum Mann gemacht; **we'll never make a ~ out of him** aus ihm wird nie ein Mann; **he's only half a ~** er ist kein richtiger Mann; **I'm only half a ~ without you** ohne dich bin ich nur ein halber Mensch; **he took it like a ~** er hat es wie ein Mann *or* mannhaft ertragen; **that's just like a ~** das ist typisch Mann *(inf)*; **her ~** *(inf)* ihr Mann; **~ and boy** von Kindheit/Jugend an; **they are ~ and wife** sie sind Mann und Frau; **the ~ in the street** der Mann auf der Straße, der kleine Mann; **the ~ on the Clapham omnibus** *(Brit)* der Mann auf der Straße; **~ of God** Mann *m* Gottes; **~ of letters** *(= writer)* Schriftsteller *m*, Literat *m*; *(= scholar)* Gelehrter *m*; **~ of property** vermögender Mann; **you're a ~ about town, you know where ...** *(Brit)* du kennst dich aus, du weißt, wo ...; **he used to be something of a ~ about town** *(Brit)* er hatte früher ein reges gesellschaftliches Leben; **a suit for the ~ about town** *(Brit)* ein Anzug für den feinen Herrn; **a ~ of the world** ein Mann *m* von Welt; **as one ~ to another** von Mann zu Mann; **well done, that ~!** gut gemacht, alter Junge! *(inf)*; **to be ~ enough (to do sth)** Manns genug sein(, etw zu tun); **~'s bicycle/jacket** Herrenfahrrad *nt*/-jacke *f*; **old ~** *(dated)* alter Junge *(dated) or* Knabe *(dated)* → **good**

b *(= human race: also* **Man***)* der Mensch, die Menschen; **that's no use** *or* **good to ~ or beast** das nützt niemandem etwas

c *(= person)* man; **no ~** keiner, niemand; **any ~** jeder; **any ~ who believes that ...** wer das glaubt, ...; **sometimes a ~ needs a change** *(inf)* manchmal braucht man einfach etwas Abwechslung; **that ~ Jones** dieser *or* der Jones; **our ~ in Beirut** unser Mann in Beirut; **the strong ~ of the government** der starke Mann (in) der Regierung; **as one ~** geschlossen, wie ein Mann; **they are communists to a ~** sie sind allesamt Kommunisten

d *(= type)* **the right/wrong ~** der Richtige/Falsche; **you've come to the right ~** da sind *or* liegen *(inf)* Sie bei mir richtig; **then I am your ~** dann bin ich genau der Richtige (für Sie); **he's not the ~ for the job** er ist nicht der Richtige für diese Aufgabe; **he's not the ~ to make a mistake like that** so etwas würde ihm bestimmt nicht passieren; **he's not a ~ to …** er ist nicht der Typ, der …; **he's not a ~ to meddle with** mit ihm ist nicht gut Kirschen essen; **he is a Cambridge ~** er hat in Cambridge studiert; **family ~** Familienvater *m*; **he's a family ~** *(= home-loving)* er ist sehr häuslich; **it's got to be a local ~** es muss jemand von hier *or* aus dieser Gegend sein; **I'm not a drinking ~** ich bin kein großer Trinker; **I'm a whisky ~ myself** ich bin mehr für Whisky; **he's a leg/tit ~** *(inf)* er steht bei Frauen vor allem auf Beine/Titten *(inf)*; **I'm not a football ~** ich mache mir nicht viel aus Fußball; **he's a ~'s ~** er bevorzugt Männergesellschaft

e *(inf: interj)* Mensch *(inf)*, Mann *(inf)*; **you can't do that, ~** Mensch *or* Mann, das kannst du doch nicht machen! *(inf)*; **fantastic, ~!** klasse, Mann! *(inf)*; **see you, ~!** bis später; **are you coming with us, ~?** du, kommst du noch mit?

f *(= employee, soldier etc)* Mann *m*; *(= servant)* Bedienstete(r) *m*; **she has a ~ to do the garden** sie hat jemanden, der den Garten macht; **officers and men** Offiziere und Mannschaften; **follow me, men!** mir nach, Leute!

g *(Chess)* Figur *f*; *(in draughts)* Stein *m*

h **the Man** *(US inf: = boss)* der Boss *(inf)*, der Alte *(inf)*; *(= police)* die Bullen *pl (sl)*; *(= white man)* die Weißen *pl*

VT *ship* bemannen; *fortress, barricades, checkpoint* besetzen; *power station, pump, gun, telephone etc* bedienen; *pickets* bewachen; **the ship is ~ned by a crew of 30** das Schiff hat 30 Mann Besatzung; **a fully ~ned ship** ein voll bemanntes Schiff; **he left 10 soldiers behind to ~ the fortress** er ließ 10 Soldaten als Besatzung für die Festung zurück; **~ the guns/pumps!** an die Geschütze/Pumpen!; **the captain gave the signal to ~ the guns** der Kapitän gab das Zeichen zur Besetzung der Geschütze

manacle ['mænəkl] **N** *usu pl* Handfesseln *pl*, Ketten *pl* **VT** *person* in Ketten legen; *hands* (mit Ketten) fesseln; **they were ~d together** sie waren aneinandergekettet; **he was ~d to the wall** er war an die Wand gekettet

manage ['mænɪdʒ] **VT** **a** *company, organization, economy* leiten; *property* verwalten; *affairs* in Ordnung halten, regeln; *time, money, resources* einteilen; *football team, pop group* managen; **he ~d the election** er war Wahlleiter; **the election was ~d** *(pej)* die Wahl war manipuliert

b *(= handle, control) person, child, animal* zurechtkommen mit, fertig werden mit; *car, ship* zurechtkommen mit, handhaben; **the car is too big for her to ~** sie kommt mit dem großen Auto nicht zurecht; **she can't ~ children** sie kann nicht mit Kindern umgehen; **I can ~ him** mit dem werde ich schon fertig

c *task* bewältigen, zurechtkommen mit; *another portion* bewältigen, schaffen; **£50/two hours is the most I can ~** ich kann mir höchstens £ 50 leisten/zwei Stunden erlauben; **I'll ~ it** das werde ich schon schaffen; **he ~d it very well** er hat das sehr gut gemacht; **you'll ~ it next time** nächstes Mal schaffst dus; **I'll do that as soon as I can ~ it** ich mache das, sobald ich kann *or* sobald ich es schaffe; **he should take some exercise as soon as he can ~ it** er sollte sich so bald wie möglich Bewegung verschaffen; **can you ~ the cases?** kannst du die Koffer (allein) tragen?; **thanks, I can ~ them** danke, das geht schon; **she can't ~ the stairs** sie schafft die Treppe nicht; **can you ~ two more in the car?** kriegst du noch zwei Leute in dein Auto? *(inf)*; **can you ~ 8 o'clock?** 8 Uhr, ginge *or* geht das?; **could you ~ (to be ready by) 8 o'clock?** kannst du um 8 Uhr fertig sein?; **can you ~ another cup?** darfs noch eine Tasse sein?; **could you ~ another whisky?** schaffst du noch einen Whisky?; **I think I could ~ another piece of cake** ich glaube, ich könnte noch ein Stück Kuchen vertragen; **I couldn't ~ another thing** ich könnte keinen Bissen mehr runterbringen; **she ~d a weak smile** sie brachte ein schwaches Lächeln über sich *(acc)*; **he ~d a few words about his visit** er verlor nur ein paar Worte über seinen Besuch

d **to ~ to do sth** es schaffen, etw zu tun; **we have ~d to reduce our costs** es ist uns gelungen, die Kosten zu senken; **do you think you'll ~ to do it?** meinen Sie, Sie können *or* schaffen das?; **I hope you'll ~ to come** ich hoffe, Sie können kommen; **how did you ~ to get a salary increase?** wie hast du es geschafft *or* angestellt, eine Gehaltserhöhung zu bekommen?; **he ~d to control himself** es gelang ihm, sich zu beherrschen; **he ~d not to get his feet wet** es ist ihm gelungen, keine nassen Füße zu bekommen; **how did you ~ to miss that?** wie konnte Ihnen das nur entgehen?; **how could you possibly ~ to do that?** wie hast du denn das fertiggebracht?; **how could anybody possibly ~ to be so stupid?** wie kann ein Mensch nur so dumm sein?; **could you possibly ~ to close the door?** *(iro)* wäre es vielleicht möglich, die Tür zuzumachen?

VI zurechtkommen, es schaffen; **can you ~?** geht es?; **thanks, I can ~** danke, es geht schon *or* ich komme schon zurecht; **I thought I could cope with things, but I can't ~** ich dachte, ich käme zurecht, aber ich schaffe es nicht *or* ich bringe es nicht fertig; **she ~s well enough** sie kommt ganz gut zurecht; **how do you ~?** wie schaffen *or* machen Sie das bloß?; **to ~ without sth** ohne etw auskommen, sich *(dat)* ohne etw behelfen; **we'll just have to ~ without** dann müssen wir uns *(dat)* eben so behelfen, dann müssen wir eben so auskommen; **to ~ without sb** ohne jdn auskommen *or* zurechtkommen; **I can ~ by myself** ich komme (schon) allein zurecht; **how do you ~ on £20 a week?** wie kommen Sie mit £ 20 pro Woche aus?

manageable ['mænɪdʒəbl] **ADJ** *child* folgsam, fügsam; *horse* fügsam; *amount, job, task* zu bewältigen; *hair* leicht frisierbar, geschmeidig; *number, proportions* überschaubar; *car* leicht zu handhaben; **since the treatment he's been less violent, more ~** seit der Behandlung ist er nicht mehr so gewalttätig, man kann besser mit ihm umgehen *or* zurechtkommen; **the children are no longer ~ for her** sie wird mit den Kindern nicht mehr fertig; **is that ~ for you?** schaffen Sie das?; **the situation is ~** die Situation lässt sich in den Griff bekommen; **this company is just not ~** es ist unmöglich, dieses Unternehmen (erfolgreich) zu leiten; **to keep sth to a ~ level** etw im überschaubaren Rahmen halten; **you should try and keep the book within ~ limits** Sie sollten versuchen, das Buch in überschaubaren Grenzen zu halten; **pieces of a more ~ size** Stücke, die leichter zu handhaben sind, Stücke *pl* in handlicher Größe; **a job of ~ size** eine überschaubare Aufgabe; **the staircase isn't ~ for an old lady** die Treppe ist für eine alte Dame zu beschwerlich

managed: **managed economy** **N** Planwirtschaft *f*; **managed fund** ['mænɪdʒd'fʌnd] **N** Investmentfonds *m (mit gelegentlicher Umschichtung des Aktienbestandes)*

management ['mænɪdʒmənt] **N** **a** *(= act) (of company)* Leitung *f*, Führung *f*, Management *nt*; *(of non-commercial organization)* Leitung *f*; *(of estate, assets, money)* Verwaltung *f*; *(of affairs)* Regelung *f*; **crisis/time/people ~** Krisen-/Zeit-/ /Personalmanagement *nt*; **~ by objectives** Führen *nt* durch Zielvereinbarung **b** *(= persons)* Unternehmensleitung *f*; *(of single unit or smaller factory)* Betriebsleitung *f*; *(non-commercial)* Leitung *f*; *(Theat)* Intendanz *f*; **"under new ~"** „neuer Inhaber"; *(shop)* „neu eröffnet"; *(pub)* „unter neuer Bewirtschaftung"

management: **management accounting** **N** Kosten- und Leistungsrechnung *f*; **management accounts** **PL** Geschäftsbilanz *pl*; **management buyout** **N** *Aufkauf eines Unternehmens durch Mitglieder der Geschäftsleitung*, Management-Buy-out *nt*; **management consultancy** **N** Unternehmensberatung *f*; **management consultant** **N** Unternehmensberater(in) *m(f)*; **management course** **N** Managerkurs *m*; **management fee** **N** Verwaltungsgebühr *f*; **management skills** **PL** Führungsqualitäten *pl*; **management studies** **N** Betriebswirtschaft *f*; **management style** **N** Führungsstil *m*; **management team** **N** Führungsriege *f*

manager ['mænɪdʒəʳ] **N** *(Comm etc)* Geschäftsführer(in) *m(f)*, Manager(in) *m(f)*; *(of restaurant)* Geschäftsführer(in) *m(f)*; *(of smaller firm or factory)* Betriebsleiter(in) *m(f)*; *(of bank, chain store)* Filialleiter(in) *m(f)*; *(of department)* Abteilungsleiter(in) *m(f)*; *(of estate etc)* Verwalter(in) *m(f)*; *(Theat)* Intendant(in) *m(f)*; *(of hotel)* Direktor(in) *m(f)*; *(of pop group, boxer etc)* Manager(in) *m(f)*; *(of team)* Trainer(in) *m(f)*; **sales ~** Verkaufsleiter(in) *m(f)*; **publicity ~** Werbeleiter(in) *m(f)*; **business ~** *(for theatre)* Verwaltungsdirektor(in) *m(f)*; *(of pop star etc)* Manager(in) *m(f)*

manageress [ˌmænɪdʒə'res] **N** *(Comm etc)* Geschäftsführerin *f*, Managerin *f*; *(of restaurant)* Geschäftsführerin *f*; *(of chain store)* Filialleiterin *f*; *(of hotel)* Direktorin *f*

managerial [ˌmænə'dʒɪərɪəl] **ADJ** geschäftlich; *(= executive)* Management-; *post, staff* leitend; **the ~ team** das Management(team); **at ~ level** auf der Führungsebene; **he has no ~ skills** er ist für leitende Funktionen ungeeignet; **proven ~ skills** nachgewiesene Führungs- *or* Leitungsfähigkeit *f*; **~ career** Karriere *f* als Manager; *(Ftbl)* Trainerkarriere *f*; **~ responsibilities** Führungs- *or* Leitungsaufgaben *pl*; **~ style** Führungsstil *m*; **~ class** Führungsklasse *f*

managing board ['mmænɪdʒɪŋˌbɔːd] **N** Direktorium *nt*, geschäftsführender Vorstand

managing director ['mænɪdʒɪŋdɪ'rektəʳ] **N** Geschäftsführer(in) *m(f)*

managing partner **N** geschäftsführende(r) Gesellschafter(in) *m(f) or* Teilhaber(in) *m(f)*

man-at-arms [ˌmænət'ɑːmz] **N** *pl* **men-at-arms** [ˌmenət'ɑːmz] Soldat *m*, Krieger *m (old)*

manatee [ˌmænə'tiː] **N** (Rundschwanz)seekuh *f*

Manchuria [mæn'tʃʊərɪə] **N** die Mandschurei

Manchurian [mæn'tʃʊərɪən] **ADJ** mandschurisch **N** **a** Mandschu *m* **b** *(Ling)* Mandschu *nt*

Mancunian [mæŋ'kjuːnɪən] **N** Bewohner(in) *m(f)* Manchesters; **he's a ~** er kommt *or* ist aus Manchester **ADJ** aus Manchester

mandarin ['mændərɪn] **N** **a** *(= Chinese official)* Mandarin *m*; *(= official)* hoher Funktionär, Bonze *m (pej)* **b** *(Ling)* **Mandarin** Hochchinesisch *nt* **c** *(= fruit)* Mandarine *f*

mandate ['mændeɪt] **N** Auftrag *m*; *(Pol)* Mandat *nt*; *(= territory)* Mandat(sgebiet) *nt*; **to give sb a ~ to do sth** jdm den Auftrag geben *or* jdn damit beauftragen, etw zu tun; **we have a clear ~ from the country to …** wir haben den eindeutigen Wählerauftrag, zu … **VT** **to ~ a territory to sb** ein Gebiet jds Verwaltung *(dat)* unterstellen, ein Gebiet als Mandat an jdn vergeben

mandated ['mændeɪtɪd] **ADJ** **~ territory** Mandatsgebiet *nt*

mandatory ['mændətərɪ] **ADJ** **a** obligatorisch, erforderlich; **~ retirement age** vorgeschriebenes Rentenalter; **the ~ nature of this ruling** der Zwangscharakter dieser Regelung; **union membership is ~** Mitgliedschaft in der Gewerkschaft ist Pflicht; **it is ~ for him to do this** er ist dazu verpflichtet, das zu tun

b *(Jur) sentence, ban, fine* vorgeschrieben; **murder carries a ~ death sentence** bei Mord ist die Todesstrafe vorgeschrieben; **Singapore has a ~ death penalty for drug offences** *(Brit) or* **offenses** *(US)* auf Drogendelikte steht in Singapur die Todesstrafe

c *(Pol)* **~ state** *(= having a mandate)* Mandatarstaat *m*; *(= being a mandate)* Mandat *nt*; **Mandatory Palestine** das Mandat(sgebiet) Palästina; **to be a ~ power** Mandatarstaat *or* Mandatsherr sein; **to have ~ powers** über Vollmachten verfügen

man-day ['mæn'deɪ] **N** Manntag *m*

Mandelbrot set ['mændlbrɒt,set] N *(Math)* Mandelbrotmenge *f*

mandible ['mændɪbl] N *(of vertebrates)* Unterkiefer(knochen) *m*, Mandibel *f (spec)*; **~s** *(of insects)* Mundwerkzeuge *pl*, Mundgliedmaßen *pl*, Mandibel *f (spec)*; *(of birds)* Schnabel *m*

mandolin(e) ['mændəlɪn] N Mandoline *f*

mandrake ['mændreɪk] N Mandragore *f*; **~ root** Alraune *f*

mandrill ['mændrɪl] N Mandrill *m*

mane [meɪn] N *(lit, fig)* Mähne *f*

man-eater ['mæn,iːtəʳ] N Menschenfresser *m*; *(= shark)* Menschenhai *m*; *(inf: = woman)* männermordendes Weib *(inf)*

man-eating ['mæn,iːtɪŋ] ADJ menschenfressend; **~ shark** Menschenhai *m*

maneuver N, VTI *(US)* = **manoeuvre**

man Friday N *(= male helper)* rechte Hand *(fig)*, Mädchen *nt* für alles *(inf iro)*

manful ADJ, **manfully** ADV ['mænfʊl, -fəlɪ] mannhaft *(geh)*, mutig, beherzt

manga ['mæŋgə] N Manga *m*, *japanischer Comic*

manganese [,mæŋgə'niːz] N Mangan *nt*

mange [meɪndʒ] N Räude *f*; *(of man)* Krätze *f*

mangel(wurzel) ['mæŋgl(,wɜːzl)] N Runkel- *or* Futterrübe *f*

manger ['meɪndʒəʳ] N Krippe *f*

mangetout ['mɑ̃ːʒ'tuː] N *(Brit: also* **mangetout pea***)* Zuckererbse *f*

mangle¹ ['mæŋgl] **N** Mangel *f* **VT** *clothes* mangeln

mangle² VT *(also* **mangle up***)* (übel) zurichten

mangler ['mæŋgləʳ] N Hackmaschine *f*, Fleischwolf *m*; *(fig: person)* Verstümmler(in) *m(f)*

mango ['mæŋgəʊ] N *(= fruit)* Mango *f*; *(= tree)* Mangobaum *m*

mangold(wurzel) ['mæŋgəld(,wɜːzl)] N = **mangel(wurzel)**

mangrove ['mæŋgrəʊv] N Mangrove(n)baum *m*; **~ swamp** Mangrove *f*

mangy ['meɪndʒɪ] ADJ *(+er) dog* räudig; *carpet* schäbig; *hotel* schäbig, heruntergekommen

manhandle ['mænhændl] VT **a** *person* grob *or* unsanft behandeln; **he was ~d into the back of the van** er wurde recht unsanft *or* gewaltsam in den Laderaum des Wagens verfrachtet **b** *piano etc* hieven

manhole ['mænhəʊl] N Kanal- *or* Straßenschacht *m*; *(in boiler etc)* Mannloch *nt*, Einsteigöffnung *f*

manhood ['mænhʊd] N **a** *(= state)* Mannesalter *nt* **b** *(= manliness)* Männlichkeit *f* **c** *(= men)* Männer *pl*; **a fine example of American ~** ein gutes Beispiel für den amerikanischen Mann **d** *(euph: = penis)* Männlichkeit *f (inf)*

man: **man-hour** N Arbeitsstunde *f*; **manhunt** N Fahndung *f*; *(hum, of woman)* Männerfang *m*

mania ['meɪnɪə] N **a** *(= madness)* Manie *f*; **persecution ~** Verfolgungswahn *m* **b** *(inf: = enthusiasm)* Manie *f*, Tick *m (inf)*, Fimmel *m (inf)*; **this ~ for nationalization** diese Verstaatlichungsmanie; **Gazza ~** Gazza-Manie *f*, Gazza-Rummel *m*; **this current ~ for the 1920's** die derzeitige Manie für die 20er Jahre; **he has a ~ for collecting old matchboxes** er hat den Tick *or* Fimmel, alte Streichholzschachteln zu sammeln *(inf)*; **he has a ~ for collecting things** er hat einen Sammeltick *(inf) or* -fimmel *(inf)*; **~ for cleanliness** Sauberkeitstick *m (inf)*, Reinlichkeitsfimmel *m (inf)*; **tennis has become a ~ with him** Tennis ist bei ihm zur Manie geworden

maniac ['meɪnɪæk] **ADJ** wahnsinnig **N a** Wahnsinnige(r) *mf*, Irre(r) *mf* **b** *(fig)* **these sports ~s** diese Sportfanatiker *pl*; **you ~** du bist ja wahnsinnig!

maniacal [mə'naɪəkəl] ADJ wahnsinnig

maniacally [mə'naɪəkəlɪ] ADV *grin, laugh* wie ein Irrer/eine Irre; **they were laughing ~** sie lachten wie die Irren

manic ['mænɪk] ADJ **a** *(= frenzied) activity, excitement* fieberhaft; *energy, person* rasend **b** *(= insane) grin, laughter, sense of humour* wahnsinnig, irre; *jealousy* rasend **c** *(Psych) state, depression* manisch

manic-depressive ['mænɪkdɪ'presɪv] **ADJ** manisch-depressiv **N** Manisch-Depressive(r) *mf*; **he is a ~** er ist manisch-depressiv

manicure ['mænɪ,kjʊəʳ] **N** Maniküre *f*; **to have a ~** sich *(dat)* (die Hände) maniküren lassen; **to give sb a ~** jdm die Hände maniküren, jdn maniküren **VT** maniküren

manicured ['mænɪkjʊəd] ADJ *nails, hands* manikürt; *lawn, garden* gepflegt; **his well-~ hands** seine gepflegten Hände, seine sorgfältig manikürten Hände

manicure set N Nagelnecessaire *nt*, Nagel- *or* Maniküreetui *nt*

manicurist ['mænɪ,kjʊərɪst] N Handpflegerin *f*

manifest ['mænɪfest] **ADJ** offenkundig, offenbar; *(= definite)* eindeutig; **I think it's ~ that ...** es liegt doch wohl auf der Hand, dass ...; **to make sth ~** etw klarmachen *or* deutlich machen; **he made it ~ that ...** er machte klar *or* deutlich, dass ... **N** *(Naut)* Manifest *nt* **VT** zeigen, bekunden **VR** sich zeigen; *(Sci, Psych etc)* sich manifestieren; *(ghost)* erscheinen; *(guilt etc)* sich offenbaren, offenbar werden

> **MANIFEST DESTINY**
>
> **Manifest Destiny** war eine gängige Auffassung im Amerika des 19. Jahrhunderts, gemäß der es göttlicher Wille sei, dass die Vereinigten Staaten die Pflicht und die Bestimmung hätten, ihr Territorium und ihren Einfluss auf dem nordamerikanischen Kontinent auszubreiten. Mit diesem Konzept wurde die Siedlerbewegung nach Westen und in Richtung Mexiko gerechtfertigt und ebenso der spanisch-amerikanische Krieg 1898, durch den Puerto Rico und die Philippinen dazugewonnen wurden. Auch wenn das **Manifest Destiny** in der heutigen Zeit nicht mehr angeführt wird, ist es doch immer noch eine unterschwellige Grundeinstellung vieler Amerikaner, wenn es um die Vorrangstellung ihres Landes in der Neuen Welt und rund um den Pazifischen Ozean geht und wird als Legitimation für interventionistische Politik bemüht.

manifestation [,mænɪfe'steɪʃən] N *(= act of showing)* Ausdruck *m*, Manifestierung *f*, Bekundung *f*; *(= sign)* Anzeichen *nt*, Manifestation *f*; *(of spirit)* Erscheinung *f*

manifestly ['mænɪfestlɪ] ADV eindeutig, offensichtlich; **it's so ~ obvious** es ist so völlig offensichtlich; **the policy ~ failed to work** die Politik funktionierte offenkundig nicht

manifesto [,mænɪ'festəʊ] N *pl* **-(e)s** Manifest *nt*

manifold ['mænɪfəʊld] **ADJ** mannigfaltig *(geh)*, vielfältig; **~ uses** vielseitige Anwendung; **there are ~ problems/dangers** es gibt vielfache Probleme/Gefahren **N** *(Aut) (= inlet manifold)* Ansaugrohr *nt*; *(= exhaust manifold)* Auspuffrohr *nt*

manikin ['mænɪkɪn] N *(= dwarf)* Männchen *nt*, Knirps *m*; *(Art)* Modell *nt*, Gliederpuppe *f*

manila, **manilla** [mə'nɪlə] N **a** *(= manila paper)* Hartpapier *nt*; **~ envelopes** braune Umschläge **b** *(= manila hemp)* Manilahanf *m*

manioc ['mænɪɒk] N Maniok *m*

manipulate [mə'nɪpjʊleɪt] VT **a** *public opinion, person, prices, data, media* manipulieren; *accounts, figures* manipulieren, frisieren *(inf)*; **to ~ sb into doing sth** jdn so manipulieren, dass er/sie etw tut **b** *machine etc* handhaben, bedienen; *bones* einrenken; *(after fracture)* zurechtrücken

manipulation [mə,nɪpjʊ'leɪʃən] N Manipulation *f*

manipulative [mə'nɪpjʊlətɪv] ADJ **a** *(pej) behaviour, skill* manipulativ; *film, article, speech* manipulierend; **~ person** Manipulant(in) *m(f)*; **he was very ~** er konnte andere sehr gut manipulieren **b** *(Med)* **~ therapy** Manipulationstherapie *f*; **~ technique** Manipulationstechnik *f*; **~ treatment** Manipulation *f*; **~ operation** manipulativer Eingriff

manipulator [mə'nɪpjʊleɪtəʳ] N Manipulator(in) *m(f)*, Manipulant(in) *m(f)*; **he's a skilled ~ of public opinion** er versteht es, die öffentliche Meinung geschickt zu manipulieren

mankind [mæn'kaɪnd] N die Menschheit

manky ['mæŋkɪ] ADJ *(Brit inf)* dreckig *(inf)*

manlike ['mænlaɪk] ADJ menschlich; *(= like a male)* männlich; *robot* menschenähnlich

manliness ['mænlɪnɪs] N Männlichkeit *f*

manly ['mænlɪ] ADJ *(+er)* männlich; **to behave in a ~ fashion** sich als Mann erweisen

man-made ['mæn'meɪd] ADJ **a** *(= artificial)* künstlich; **~ fibres** *(Brit) or* **fibers** *(US)* Kunstfasern *pl*, synthetische Fasern *pl*; **~ leather/silk** Kunstleder *nt*/-seide *f* **b** *(= caused by man) disaster, pollution* vom Menschen verursacht; *world, environment, laws* vom Menschen geschaffen

man-mark ['mænmɑːk] VT *(Sport) player, opponent* in Manndeckung nehmen

man-marker ['mæn,mɑːkəʳ] N *(Sport Ftbl)* Manndecker(in) *m(f)*

man-marking ['mæn,mɑːkɪŋ] N *(Sport Ftbl)* Manndeckung *f*

manna ['mænə] N Manna *nt*

manned [mænd] ADJ *satellite etc* bemannt

mannequin ['mænɪkɪn] N *(Fashion)* Mannequin *nt*; *(Art)* Modell *nt*; *(= dummy)* Gliederpuppe *f*

manner ['mænəʳ] N **a** *(= mode)* Art *f*, (Art und) Weise *f*; **in** *or* **after this ~** auf diese Art und Weise; **in** *or* **after the ~ of Petrarch** im Stile Petrarcas; **in the Spanish ~** im spanischen Stil; **in like ~** *(form)* auf die gleiche Weise, ebenso; **in such a ~ that ...** so ..., dass ...; **a painter in the grand ~** ein Maler der alten Schule; **a ball in the grand ~** ein Ball alten Stils *or* im alten Stil; **in a ~ of speaking** sozusagen, gewissermaßen; **in a ~ of speaking, the job's finished** die Arbeit ist sozusagen *or* gewissermaßen fertig; **it's just a ~ of speaking** *(of idiom)* das ist nur so eine Redensart; **I didn't mean to insult him, it was just a ~ of speaking** das sollte keine Beleidigung sein, ich habe das nur so gesagt; **as to the ~ born** als sei er/sie dafür geschaffen; **a horseman as to the ~ born** ein geborener Reiter

b *(= behaviour etc)* Art *f*; **he has a very kind ~** er hat ein sehr freundliches Wesen; **his ~ to his parents** sein Verhalten gegenüber seinen Eltern; **I don't like his ~** ich mag seine Art nicht; **there's something odd about his ~** er benimmt sich irgendwie komisch

c manners PL *(good, bad etc)* Manieren *pl*, Benehmen *nt*, Umgangsformen *pl*; **road ~s** Verhalten *nt* im Straßenverkehr; **he hasn't got any road ~s** er ist ein sehr unhöflicher *or* rücksichtsloser Fahrer; **that's bad ~s** das *or* so etwas gehört sich nicht, das ist unanständig; **~s!** benimm dich!; **it's bad ~s to ...** es gehört sich nicht *or* es ist unanständig, zu ...; **to have bad ~s** schlechte Manieren haben; **he has no ~s** er hat keine Manieren, er kann sich nicht benehmen; **have you forgotten your ~s?** wo hast du denn deine Manieren gelassen?; **now, don't forget your ~s!** du weißt doch, was sich gehört!; **to teach sb some ~s** jdm Manieren beibringen **d manners** PL *(of society)* Sitten (und Gebräuche) *pl*; **a novel of ~s** ein Sittenroman *m*; **a comedy of ~s** eine Sittenkomödie

e *(= class, type)* Art *f*; **all ~ of birds** die verschiedensten Arten von Vögeln; **we saw all ~ of interesting things** wir sahen allerlei Interessantes *or* so manches Interessante; **I've got all ~ of things to do yet** ich habe noch allerlei *or* tausenderlei zu tun; **by no ~ of means** keineswegs, in keinster Weise *(inf)*; **what ~ of man is he?** *(liter)* was ist er für ein Mensch?

mannered ['mænəd] ADJ **a** *(= affected, fussy) style, work of art, gestures* manieriert; *friendliness,* *subservience etc* betont, prononciert *(geh)* **b** *(with adv)* **to be well-/ill-/impeccably ~** gute/schlechte/tadellose Manieren haben; **a well-/ill-/impeccably ~ man** ein Mann mit guten/schlechten/tadellosen Manieren

mannerism ['mænərɪzəm] N **a** *(in behaviour, speech)* Angewohnheit *f*, Eigenheit *f* **b** *(of style)* Manieriertheit *f*; **his ~s** seine Manierismen

mannerliness ['mænəlɪnɪs] N Wohlerzogenheit *f*

mannerly ['mænəlɪ] ADJ wohlerzogen

mannish ['mænɪʃ] ADJ *woman, clothes* männlich wirkend

mannishly ['mænɪʃlɪ] ADV *dress* maskulin; *walk, behave* wie Männer/ein Mann

manoeuvrability, *(US)* **maneuverability** [mə,nu:vrə'bɪlɪtɪ] N Manövrierfähigkeit *f*, Wendigkeit *f*

manoeuvrable, *(US)* **maneuverable** [mə'nu:vrəbl] ADJ manövrierfähig, wendig; **easily ~** leicht zu manövrieren

manoeuvre, *(US)* **maneuver** [mə'nu:və'] **N** **a** *(Mil)* Feldzug *m*; **in a well-planned ~** durch einen geschickt geplanten Feldzug

b **manoeuvres** PL *(Mil)* Manöver *nt or pl*, Truppenübung *f*; **the troops were out on ~s** die Truppen befanden sich im Manöver

c *(= clever plan)* Manöver *nt*, Winkelzug *m*, Schachzug *m*; **rather an obvious ~** ein ziemlich auffälliges Manöver

VT manövrieren; **he ~d his troops out onto the plain** er dirigierte *or* führte seine Truppen hinaus auf die Ebene; **to ~ a gun into position** ein Geschütz in Stellung bringen; **to ~ sb into doing sth** jdn dazu bringen, etw zu tun; **he ~d his brother into a top job** er manövrierte *or* lancierte seinen Bruder in eine Spitzenposition

VI manövrieren; *(Mil)* (ein) Manöver durchführen; **to ~ for position** *(lit, fig)* sich in eine günstige Position manövrieren; **room to ~** Spielraum *m*, Manövrierfähigkeit *f*

man-of-war [,mænəv'wɔ:'] N *pl* **men-of-war** [,menəv'wɔ:'] *(old)* → **Portuguese man-of-war**

manometer [mə'nɒmɪtə'] N *(Tech)* Manometer *nt*

manor ['mænə'] N Gutshof *m*, (Land)gut *nt*; **lord/lady of the ~** Gutsherr *m*/-herrin *f*

manor house N Herrenhaus *nt*

manpower ['mæn,paʊə'] N Leistungspotenzial *nt or* -potential *nt*; *(Mil)* Stärke *f*; **we haven't got the ~** wir haben dazu nicht genügend Personal *or* Arbeitskräfte *pl*; **Manpower Services Commission** *(Brit) Behörde für Arbeitsbeschaffung, Arbeitsvermittlung und Berufsausbildung*

manqué ['mɒŋkeɪ] ADJ *pred (= failed)* gescheitert; *(= unrecognized)* verkannt; **he's a novelist ~** *(= unfulfilled)* an ihm ist ein Schriftsteller verloren gegangen

mansard ['mænsɑ:d] N, **mansard roof** N Mansardendach *nt*

manse [mæns] N Pfarrhaus *nt*

manservant ['mænsɜ:vənt] N *pl* **menservants** ['mensɜ:vənts] Diener *m*

mansion ['mænʃən] N Villa *f*; *(of ancient family)* Herrenhaus *nt*

man: **man-sized** ADJ Riesen-; **~ portion/steak** Riesenportion *f*/-steak *nt*; **manslaughter** N Totschlag *m*

manta (ray) ['mæntə(reɪ)] N Teufelsrochen *m*, Manta *m*

mantelpiece ['mæntlpi:s] N *(above fireplace)* Kaminsims *nt or m*; *(around fireplace)* Kaminverkleidung *or* -einfassung *f*

mantelshelf ['mæntlʃelf] N *pl* **-shelves** [-ʃelvz] = **mantelpiece**

mantilla [mæn'tɪlə] N Mantille *f*, Mantilla *f*

mantis ['mæntɪs] N = **praying mantis**

mantle ['mæntl] **N** **a** Umhang *m*; *(fig)* Deckmantel *m*; **a ~ of snow** eine Schneedecke **b** *(= gas mantle)* Glühstrumpf *m* **VT** *(liter)* bedecken

man: **man-to-man** [,mæntə'mæn] ADJ, ADV **a** *(= frank)* von Mann zu Mann; **a ~ talk** ein Gespräch *nt* von Mann zu Mann **b** *(Sport)* **~ marking** Manndeckung *f*; **~ marker** Manndecker *m*; **man-trained** ['mæntreɪnd] ADJ *dog* auf den Mann dressiert; **mantrap** N Fußangel *f*

manual ['mænjʊəl] **ADJ** manuell; *labour* körperlich; **~ work** manuelle Arbeit, Handarbeit *f*; **~ labourer** *(Brit) or* **laborer** *(US)* Schwerarbeiter(in) *m(f)*; **~ worker** Handarbeiter(in) *m(f)*; **~ skill** Handwerk *nt*; **he was trained in several ~ skills** er hatte verschiedene Handwerksberufe *pl* erlernt; **~ gear change** *(Brit) or* **shift** *(US)* Schaltung *f* von Hand; **~ control** Handsteuerung *f*; **~ operation** Handbetrieb *m*

N **a** *(= book)* Handbuch *nt*; *(Comput)* Benutzerhandbuch *nt*

b *(Mus)* Manual *nt*

c *(= manual operation)* Handbetrieb *m*, manueller Betrieb; **to run on ~** im Handbetrieb laufen; **to put a machine on ~** eine Maschine auf Handbetrieb stellen

manual gearbox ['mænjʊəl'gɪəbɒks] N *(Brit)* Schaltgetriebe *nt*

manually ['mænjʊəlɪ] ADV von Hand, manuell; **~ operated** handbetrieben; **~ controlled** handgesteuert

manual strangulation N Erwürgen *nt* mit bloßen Händen

manual transmission N Schaltgetriebe *nt*

manufacture [,mænjʊ'fæktʃə'] **N** *(= act)* Herstellung *f*; *(pl: = products)* Waren *pl*, Erzeugnisse *pl*; **articles of foreign ~** ausländische Erzeugnisse *pl* **VT** **a** *(lit)* herstellen; **~d goods** Fertigware *f*, Fertigerzeugnisse *pl* **b** *(fig) excuse* erfinden **VI** **we started manufacturing …** wir begannen mit der Herstellung …

manufacturer [,mænjʊ'fæktʃərə'] N *(= person)* Hersteller(in) *m(f)*; *(= company)* Hersteller *m*; **this country/firm has always been a big ~ of …** dieses Land/Unternehmen hat schon immer eine bedeutende Rolle bei der Herstellung von … gespielt; **~'s recommended price** unverbindliche Preisempfehlung (des Herstellers)

manufacturing [,mænjʊ'fæktʃərɪŋ] **ADJ** Herstellungs-, Produktions-; *industry* verarbeitend; **~ techniques/costs/process** Herstellungs- *or* Produktionstechniken *pl*/-kosten *pl*/-verfahren *nt*; **~ company** Herstellerfirma *f*; **~ town/city** Industriestadt *f*; **~ output** Produktionsmenge *f*; **the ~ sector** das verarbeitende Gewerbe **N** Erzeugung *f*, Herstellung *f*

manure [mə'njʊə'] **N** Dung *m*, Mist *m*; *(esp artificial)* Dünger *m*; **liquid ~** Jauche *f*; **artificial ~** Kunstdünger *m* **VT** *field* düngen

manuscript ['mænjʊskrɪpt] N Manuskript *nt*; *(ancient also)* Handschrift *f*; **the novel is still in ~** der Roman ist noch in Manuskriptform; **I read it first in ~ form** ich habe es zuerst als Manuskript gelesen

Manx [mæŋks] **ADJ** der Insel Man **N** *(Ling)* Manx *nt*

Manx: **Manx cat** N Manx-Katze *f (stummelschwänzige Katze)*; **Manxman** ['mæŋksmən] N *pl* **-men** [-mən] Bewohner *m* der Insel Man; **Manxwoman** ['mæŋkswʊmən] N *pl* **-women** [-wɪmɪn] Bewohnerin *f* der Insel Man

many ['menɪ] **ADJ, PRON** viele; **~ people** viele (Menschen *or* Leute); **she has ~** sie hat viele (davon); **he hasn't got ~** er hat nicht viele (davon); **there were as ~ as 20** es waren sogar 20 da; **fifty went to France and as ~ to Germany** fünfzig gingen nach Frankreich und ebenso viele nach Deutschland; **as ~ again** noch einmal so viele; **they are just so ~ cowards** das sind lauter Feiglinge; **there's one too ~** einer ist zu viel; **he's had one too ~** *(inf)* er hat einen zu viel *or* einen über den Durst getrunken *(inf)*; **they were too ~ for us** sie waren zu viele *or* zu zahlreich für uns; **he made one mistake too ~** er hat einen Fehler zu viel gemacht; **a good/great ~ houses** eine (ganze) Reihe *or* Anzahl Häuser; **~ a good soldier** so mancher gute Soldat; **~ a time** so manches Mal; **she waited ~ a long year** *(liter)* sie wartete gar manches lange Jahr *(liter)*; **~'s the time I've heard that old story** ich habe diese alte Geschichte so manches Mal gehört

N **the ~** die (große) Masse

many: **many-coloured**, *(US)* **many-colored** ADJ bunt, vielfarbig; **many-sided** ADJ vielseitig; *figure also* vieleckig; **it's a ~ problem** das Problem hat sehr viele verschiedene Aspekte

Maoist ['maʊɪst] N Maoist(in) *m(f)*

Maori ['maʊrɪ] **ADJ** Maori-; **~ chief** Maorihäuptling *m* **N** **a** Maori *mf* **b** *(Ling)* Maori *nt*

map [mæp] **N** (Land)karte *f*; *(of streets, town)* Stadtplan *m*; *(showing specific item)* Karte *f*; **a ~ of the stars/rivers** eine Stern-/Flusskarte; **is it on the ~?** ist das auf der Karte (eingezeichnet)?; **this will put Cheam on the ~** *(fig)* das wird Cheam zu einem Namen verhelfen; **it's right off the ~** *(fig)* das liegt (ja) am Ende der Welt *or* hinter dem Mond *(inf)*; **entire cities were wiped off the ~** ganze Städte wurden ausradiert

VT **a** *(= measure)* vermessen; *(= make a map of)* eine Karte anfertigen von; **the history of her suffering was ~ped on her face** ihr Gesicht war von Leid gezeichnet

b *(Math, Comput: = assign)* zuordnen

▶ **map out** VT *sep* **a** *(lit)* = **map VT b** *(fig: = plan)* entwerfen; **the essay is well mapped out** der Aufsatz ist gut angelegt; **the conference schedule was all mapped out in advance** der Zeitplan für die Konferenz war schon im Voraus genau festgelegt; **he has mapped out what he will do** er hat bereits geplant, was er tun wird

maple ['meɪpl] N *(= wood, tree)* Ahorn *m*

maple: **maple leaf** N Ahornblatt *nt*; **maple sugar** N Ahornzucker *m*; **maple syrup** N Ahornsirup *m*

map: **mapmaker** N Kartograf(in) *m(f)*; **mapmaking** N Kartografie *f*

mapping ['mæpɪŋ] N *(Comput)* Abbildung *f*, Mapping *nt*; *(Math, Comput)* Zuordnung *f*

map: **mapreader** N Kartenleser(in) *m(f)*; **map-reading** N Kartenlesen *nt*

maquis [mæ'ki:] N **a** **the Maquis** der Maquis *(französische Widerstandsbewegung im Zweiten Weltkrieg)* **b** *(Bot)* Macchia *f*

Mar *abbr of* **March** Mrz

mar [mɑ:'] VT verderben; *happiness* trüben; *beauty* mindern; **not a cloud to ~ the sky** kein Wölkchen trübte den Himmel; **his essay was ~red by careless mistakes** durch seine Flüchtigkeitsfehler verdarb er (sich) den ganzen Aufsatz

marabou ['mærəbu:] N Marabu *m*

maracas [mə'rækəz] PL Rassel *f*, Maracá *f*

maraschino [,mærə'ski:nəʊ] N *(= drink)* Maraschino *m*; *(= maraschino cherry)* Maraschinokirsche *f*

marathon ['mærəθən] **N** **a** *(lit)* Marathon(-lauf) *m*; **~ runner** Marathonläufer(in) *m(f)* **b** *(fig)* Marathon *nt*; **this film is a real ~** das ist wirklich ein Marathonfilm **ADJ** Marathon-; *negotiations* endlos (lang); **~ speech/film** Marathonrede *f*/-film *m*

maraud [mə'rɔ:d] **VI** plündern; **they went ~ing about the countryside** sie zogen plündernd durch die Lande **VT** plündern

marauder [mə'rɔ:də'] N Plünderer *m*, Plünderin *f*; *(= animal)* Räuber *m*

marauding [mə'rɔ:dɪŋ] ADJ plündernd; **the deer fled from the ~ wolf** das Reh floh vor dem Beute suchenden Wolf

marble ['mɑ:bl] **N** **a** Marmor *m* **b** *(= work in marble)* Marmorplastik *f* **c** *(= glass ball)* Murmel *f*, Klicker *m (inf)*; **he's lost his ~s** *(inf)* er hat nicht mehr alle Tassen im Schrank *(inf)*; **to pick up one's ~s and go home** *(US)* die Koffer packen und nach Hause gehen **ADJ** Marmor-; **~ pillar/staircase** Marmorsäule *f*/-treppe *f*

marble cake N Marmorkuchen *m*

marbled ['mɑ:bld] ADJ *surface, paper, wall, soap, colour* marmoriert; **~ effect/finish** Marmoreffekt *m*; **meat ~ with fat** durchwachsenes Fleisch

March [mɑ:tʃ] N März *m* → *also* **September**

march[1] [mɑ:tʃ] **N** **a** *(Mil, Mus)* Marsch *m*; *(= demonstration)* Demonstration *f*; *(fig: = long walk)* Weg *m*; **to move at a good stiff ~** mit strammen Schritten *or* stramm marschieren; **we had been five days on the ~** wir waren fünf Tage lang marschiert; **it's two days' ~** es ist ein Zwei-Tage-Marsch; **he went for a good ~ across the moors** er ist durchs Moorland marschiert
b *(of time, history, events)* Lauf *m*
c **to steal a ~ on sb** jdm zuvorkommen
VT *soldiers* marschieren lassen; *distance* marschieren; **to ~ sb off** jdn abführen
VI marschieren; **forward ~!** vorwärts(, marsch)!; **quick ~!** im Laufschritt, marsch!; **to ~ in** einmarschieren; **she just ~ed into the room** sie marschierte einfach (ins Zimmer) hinein; **time ~es on** die Zeit bleibt nicht stehen; **to ~ out** abmarschieren, ausrücken; **to ~ past sb** an jdm vorbeimarschieren; **she ~ed straight up to him** sie marschierte schnurstracks auf ihn zu

march[2] N *(Hist)* Grenzmark *f*; **the Welsh ~es** das Grenzland zwischen England und Wales

marcher ['mɑ:tʃə] N *(in demo)* Demonstrant(in) *m(f)*

marching ['mɑ:tʃɪŋ]: **marching orders** PL *(Brit) (Mil)* Marschbefehl *m*; *(inf)* Entlassung *f*; **the new manager got his ~** der neue Manager ist gegangen worden *(inf)*; **she gave him his ~** sie hat ihm den Laufpass gegeben; **marching song** N Marschlied *nt*

marchioness ['mɑ:ʃənɪs] N Marquise *f*

march past N Vorbeimarsch *m*, Aufmarsch *m*, Defilee *nt*

Mardi Gras ['mɑ:dɪ'grɑ:] N Karneval *m*

mare [mɛə'] N *(= horse)* Stute *f*; *(= donkey)* Eselin *f*

mare's-nest ['mɛəznest] N Windei *nt*, Reinfall *m*

Margaret ['mɑ:gərɪt] N Margarete *f*

margarine [,mɑ:dʒə'ri:n], **marge** [mɑ:dʒ] *(inf)* N Margarine *f*

margarita [,mɑ:gə'ri:tə] N, **marguerita** [,mɑ:gə'ri:tə] N Margarita *m (Tequila mit Zitronensaft)*

margin ['mɑ:dʒɪn] N **a** *(on page)* Rand *m*; **a note (written) in the ~** eine Randbemerkung, eine Bemerkung am Rand **b** *(= extra amount)* Spielraum *m*; **~ of error** Fehlerspielraum *m*; **to allow for a ~ of error** etwaige Fehler mit einkalkulieren; **he left a safety ~ of one hour** sicherheitshalber kalkulierte er einen Spielraum von einer Stunde ein; **by a narrow ~** knapp; **it's within the safety ~** das ist noch sicher **c** *(Comm: also* **profit margin***)* Gewinnspanne *f*, Verdienstspanne *f* **d** *(liter, = edge)* Rand *m*, Saum *m (liter)*; **the grassy ~ of the lake** das grüne Seeufer

marginal ['mɑ:dʒɪnl] ADJ **a** *(= slight) improvement, difference* geringfügig, unwesentlich; *issue* nebensächlich; **to be of ~ importance** nebensächlich sein; **~ figure** Randfigur *f* **b** *(Sociol) people, groups* randständig **c** *(= borderline) (Brit Parl) constituency, seat* mit knapper Mehrheit; **this is a ~ constituency for the Tories** die Tories haben in diesem Wahlkreis nur eine knappe Mehrheit; **~ case** Grenzfall *m* **d** *(= barely profitable) business* kaum rentabel; *land* ertragsarm; **~ cost** Grenzkosten *pl* **e** **~ note** Randbemerkung *f*

> **MARGINAL SEAT**
>
> In Großbritannien spricht man dann von einem **marginal seat** oder einer **marginal constituency**, wenn eine bestimmte politische Partei nur mit einer knappen Mehrheit die Macht in einem Wahlbezirk behaupten kann. Bei einer Neuwahl bestehen dann gute Chancen, dass dieser Sitz von einer Oppositionspartei erobert wird. Wenn es für einen **marginal seat** zu einer **by-election**, einer Nachwahl aufgrund des Todes oder des Rücktritts eines Parlamentsmitgliedes kommt, wird das Wahlergebnis häufig von den Medien genauestens analysiert, um eventuelle Rückschlüsse auf die landesweite Beliebtheit der Regierung zu ziehen. Wenn ein Sitz von einer Partei stets mit großer Mehrheit gewonnen wird, spricht man von einem **safe seat.**

marginalization [,mɑ:dʒɪnəlaɪ'zeɪʃən] N Marginalisierung *f (geh)*

marginalize ['mɑ:dʒɪnəlaɪz] VT marginalisieren *(geh)*

marginally ['mɑ:dʒɪnəlɪ] ADV geringfügig; *higher, lower, faster etc* etwas; **is that better? – ~** ist das besser? – etwas *or* ein wenig; **he failed, but only just ~** es gelang ihm nicht, aber nur ganz knapp; **it's only ~ useful** es hat nur sehr begrenzte Anwendungsmöglichkeiten

margin: **margin release** N Randlöser *m*; **margin stop** N Randsteller *m*

marguerite [,mɑ:gə'ri:t] N Margerite *f*

marigold ['mærɪgəʊld] N *(= African or French marigold)* Tagetes *f*, Studentenblume *f*; *(= common or pot marigold)* Ringelblume *f*

marihuana, **marijuana** [,mærɪ'hwɑ:nə] N Marihuana *nt*

marimba [mə'rɪmbə] N Marimba *f*

marina [mə'ri:nə] N Yacht- *or* Jachthafen *m*

marinade [,mærɪ'neɪd] N Marinade *f*

marinate ['mærɪneɪt] VT marinieren

marine [mə'ri:n] **ADJ** Meeres-, See-; **~ life** Meeresfauna und -flora *f*; **~ animal** Meerestier *nt*; **~ bird** Seevogel *m*; **~ plant** Meerespflanze *f*; **~ pollution** Meeresverschmutzung *f*; **~ environment** Meeresumwelt *f* **N** **a** *(= fleet)* Marine *f* **b** *(= person)* Marineinfanterist(in) *m(f)*; **the ~s** die Marineinfanterie *pl*, die Marinetruppen *pl*; **tell that to the ~s!** *(Brit inf)* das kannst du mir nicht weismachen, das kannst du deiner Großmutter erzählen! *(inf)*

marine: **marine biologist** N Meeresbiologe *m*, Meeresbiologin *f*; **marine biology** N Meeresbiologie *f*; **marine dumping** N Verklappung *f*; **marine engineer** N Marineingenieur(in) *m(f)*; **marine insurance** N Seeversicherung *f*

mariner ['mærɪnə'] N Seefahrer *m*, Seemann *m*

marine science N Meereskunde *f*

marine underwriter N *(Insur)* Seeversicherer *m*

marionette [,mærɪə'net] N Marionette *f*

marital ['mærɪtl] ADJ ehelich

marital: **marital bed** N Ehebett *nt*; **marital bliss** N Eheglück *nt*; **they lived together in ~** sie genossen ein glückliches Eheleben; **marital rape** N Vergewaltigung *f* in der Ehe; **marital status** N Familienstand *m*; **marital vows** PL Ehegelübde *nt*

maritime ['mærɪtaɪm] ADJ See-; **~ warfare** Seekrieg *m*; **~ regions** Küstenregionen *pl*; **~ museum** *(for seafaring)* Schifffahrtsmuseum *nt*; *(for marine science)* Meereskundemuseum *nt*

maritime: **maritime law** N Seerecht *nt*; **maritime nation** N Seefahrernation *f*; **maritime power** N Seemacht *f*; **Maritime Provinces** PL *(Canada)* **the ~** die (kanadischen) Ostprovinzen

marjoram ['mɑ:dʒərəm] N Majoran *m*

Mark [mɑ:k] N Markus *m*; **~ Antony** Mark Anton

mark[1] [mɑ:k] N *(Hist Fin)* Mark *f*

mark[2] **N** **a** *(= stain, spot etc)* Fleck *m*; *(= scratch)* Kratzer *m*, Schramme *f*; **to make a ~ on sth** einen Fleck/Kratzer auf etw *(acc)* machen; **dirty ~s** Schmutzflecken *pl*; **with not a ~ on it** in makellosem Zustand; **will the operation leave a ~?** wird die Operation Spuren *or* Narben hinterlassen?; **the ~s of violence** die Spuren der Gewalt; **he left the ring without a ~ on him/his body** er verließ den Ring, ohne auch nur eine Schramme abbekommen zu haben; **the corpse didn't have a ~ on it** die Leiche wies keine Verletzungen auf
b *(= marking) (on animal)* Fleck *m*; *(on person)* Mal *nt*; *(on plane, football pitch etc)* Markierung *f*; *(= sign: on monument etc)* Zeichen *nt*
c *(in exam)* Note *f*; **high** *or* **good ~s** gute Noten *pl*; **the ~s are out of 100** insgesamt kann man 100 Punkte erreichen; **you get no ~s at all for your cooking** *(fig)* in puncto Kochen bist du ja nicht gerade eine Eins *(inf)*; **there are no ~s for guessing** *(fig)* das ist ja wohl nicht schwer zu erraten; **he gets full ~s for punctuality** *(fig)* in Pünktlichkeit verdient er eine Eins
d *(= sign, indication)* Zeichen *nt*; **he had the ~s of old age** er war vom Alter gezeichnet; **it bears the ~s of genius** das trägt geniale Züge; **it's the ~ of a gentleman** daran erkennt man den Gentleman
e *(instead of signature)* **to make one's ~** drei Kreuze (als Unterschrift) machen
f *(= level)* **expenses have reached the £100 ~** die Ausgaben haben die 100-Pfund-Grenze erreicht; **the temperature reached the 35° ~** die Temperatur stieg bis auf 35° an
g **Cooper Mark II** Cooper, II; **the new secretary, a sort of Miss Jones ~ 2** die neue Sekretärin, eine zweite Ausführung von Fräulein Jones
h *(phrases)* **to be quick off the ~** *(Sport)* einen guten Start haben; *(fig)* blitzschnell handeln *or* reagieren; **you were quick off the ~** *(fig)* du warst aber fix!; **he was quickest off the ~** er war der Schnellste; **to be slow off the ~** *(Sport)* einen schlechten Start haben; *(fig)* nicht schnell genug schalten *or* reagieren; *(as characteristic)* eine lange Leitung haben *(inf)*; **to be up to the ~** den Anforderungen entsprechen; **his work is not up to the ~** seine Arbeit ist unter dem Strich; **I'm not feeling quite up to the ~** ich bin *or* fühle mich nicht ganz auf dem Posten; **to leave one's ~ (on sth)** seine Spuren (an etw *dat*) hinterlassen; **to make one's ~** sich *(dat)* einen Namen machen; **on your ~s!** auf die Plätze!; **to be wide of the ~** *(shooting)* danebentreffen, danebenschießen; *(fig: in guessing, calculating)* danebentippen, sich verhauen *(inf)*; **your calculations were wide of the ~** mit deiner Kalkulation hast du dich ganz schön verhauen *(inf)*; **to hit the ~** *(lit, fig)* ins Schwarze treffen
i *(Rugby)* Freifang *m*; **"mark!"** „Marke!"
VT **a** *(adversely)* beschädigen; *(= stain)* schmutzig machen, Flecken machen auf *(+acc)*; *(= scratch)* zerkratzen; **the other boxer was not ~ed at all** der andere Boxer hatte nicht eine Schramme abbekommen *or* überhaupt nichts abbekommen; **her face was ~ed for life** sie hat bleibende Narben im Gesicht zurückbehalten; **the experience ~ed him for life** das Erlebnis hat ihn für sein Leben gezeichnet
b *(for recognition, identity)* markieren, bezeichnen; *(= label)* beschriften; *(= price)* auszeichnen; *playing cards* zinken; **~ed with the name and age of the exhibitor** mit Namen und Alter des Ausstellers versehen; **the bottle was ~ed "poison"** die Flasche trug die Aufschrift „Gift"; **the chair is ~ed at £2** der Stuhl ist mit £ 2 ausgezeichnet; **the picture isn't ~ed** das Bild ist ohne Angaben; **the cage isn't ~ed** der Käfig hat keine Aufschrift; **~ where you have stopped in your reading** mach dir ein Zeichen, bis wohin du gelesen hast; **to ~ sth with an asterisk** etw mit einem Sternchen versehen; **X ~s the spot** X markiert *or* bezeichnet die Stelle; **the teacher ~ed him absent** der Lehrer trug ihn als fehlend ein; **it's not ~ed on the map** es ist nicht auf der Karte eingezeichnet; **it's ~ed with a blue dot** es ist mit einem blauen Punkt gekennzeichnet; **he ~ed his own books with a secret sign** er kennzeichnete seine eigenen Bücher mit einem Geheimzeichen
c *(= characterize)* kennzeichnen; **a decade ~ed by violence** ein Jahrzehnt, das im Zeichen

der Gewalt stand; **the new bill ~s a change of policy** das neue Gesetz deutet auf einen politischen Kurswechsel hin; **it ~ed the end of an era** damit ging eine Ära zu Ende; **it ~s him as a future star** daran zeigt sich, dass er eine große Karriere vor sich *(dat)* hat; **a month ~ed by inactivity** ein Monat, der sich durch Untätigkeit auszeichnete

d *(usu pass)* zeichnen; **~ed with grief** von Schmerz gezeichnet; **a beautifully ~ed bird** ein schön gezeichneter Vogel

e *exam, paper* korrigieren (und benoten); **to ~ a paper A** eine Arbeit mit (einer) Eins benoten; **to ~ a candidate** einem Kandidaten eine Note geben; **the candidate was ~ed …** der Kandidate erhielt die Note …; **we ~ed him A** wir haben ihm eine Eins gegeben; **to ~ sth wrong** etw anstreichen

f *(= heed)* hören auf *(+acc)*; **~ my words** eins kann ich dir sagen; *(threatening, warning also)* lassen Sie sich das gesagt sein!; **~ you, he may have been right** er könnte gar nicht so unrecht gehabt haben; **~ you, I didn't believe him** ich habe ihm natürlich nicht geglaubt

g *(old, = notice)* bemerken; **did you ~ where it fell?** hast du dir gemerkt, wo es hingefallen ist?

h *(Sport) player, opponent* decken

i **to ~ time** *(Mil, fig)* auf der Stelle treten

VI **a** *(= get dirty)* schmutzen, schmutzig werden; *(= scratch)* Kratzer bekommen

b **her skin ~s easily** sie bekommt leicht blaue Flecken

c *(Sport)* decken

▶ **mark down** VT *sep* **a** *(= note down)* (sich *dat*) notieren **b** *prices* herab- *or* heruntersetzen

▶ **mark off** VT *sep* kennzeichnen; *boundary* markieren; *football pitch etc* abgrenzen; *danger area etc* absperren; **these characteristics mark him off from the others** durch diese Eigenschaften unterscheidet er sich von den anderen

▶ **mark out** VT *sep* **a** *tennis court etc* abstecken **b** *(= note)* bestimmen *(for* für); **he's been marked out for promotion** er ist zur Beförderung vorgesehen; **the area has been marked out for special government grants** für das Gebiet sind besondere staatliche Zuschüsse vorgesehen **c** *(= identify)* **his speeches have marked him out as a communist** aus seinen Reden kann man schließen, dass er Kommunist ist; **what marks this example out as being different?** worin unterscheidet sich dieses Beispiel?

▶ **mark up** VT *sep* **a** *(= write up)* notieren *(on* auf *+dat)*; *(Typ)* auszeichnen **b** *price* heraufsetzen, erhöhen

markdown [ˈmɑːkdaʊn] N *(Comm)* Preissenkung *f (of um)*; **~ price** herabgesetzter Preis

marked [mɑːkt] ADJ **a** *contrast* merklich, deutlich; *accent* stark, deutlich; *improvement* spürbar, merklich; **in ~ contrast (to sb/sth)** in scharfem Gegensatz (zu jdm/etw); **it is becoming more ~** es wird immer deutlicher, es tritt immer deutlicher zutage *or* zu Tage **b** **he's a ~ man** er steht auf der schwarzen Liste **c** *(= signposted) path, trail* ausgezeichnet

markedly [ˈmɑːkɪdlɪ] ADV *improve, increase, differ, change* merklich; *quicker, slower, more, less* wesentlich; **it is ~ better** es ist wesentlich *or* bedeutend besser; **not ~ so** nicht, dass es auffallen würde; **they are not ~ different** es besteht kein wesentlicher *or* großer Unterschied zwischen ihnen

marker [ˈmɑːkəˈ] N **a** Marke *f*; *(to turn at)* Wendemarke *f*, Wendepunkt *m*; *(on road)* Schild *nt*, Wegweiser *m*; *(in book)* Lesezeichen *nt* **b** *(= indication)* **a ~ for sth** eine Kennzeichnung für etw **c** *(for exams)* Korrektor(in) *m(f)*; *(= scorekeeper in games)* Punktezähler(in) *m(f)*; **will you be the ~?** schreibst du (die Punkte) auf? **d** *(Ftbl)* Beschatter(in) *m(f)* **e** *(= pen)* Markierstift *m*, Marker *m*

market [ˈmɑːkɪt] **N** **a** Markt *m*; **when is the next ~?** wann ist wieder Markt(tag)?; **he took his sheep to ~** er brachte seine Schafe zum Markt; **at the ~** auf dem Markt; **to go to ~** auf den Markt gehen

b *(= trade)* Markt *m*; **world ~** Weltmarkt *m*; **open ~** offener Markt; **to be in the ~ for sth** an etw *(dat)* interessiert sein; **to be on the ~** auf dem Markt sein; **to come on(to) the ~** auf den Markt kommen; **to put on the ~** auf den Markt bringen; *house* zum Verkauf anbieten

c *(= demand)* (Absatz)markt *m*; *(= area)* Absatzgebiet *nt or* -markt *m*; **to create a ~** Nachfrage erzeugen; **to find a ready ~** guten Absatz finden

d *(= stock market)* Börse *f*; **to play the ~** (an der Börse) spekulieren

VT vertreiben; **to ~ a (new) product** ein (neues) Produkt auf den Markt bringen; **it's a nice idea, but we can't ~ it** das ist eine gute Idee, sie lässt sich nur nicht verkaufen *or* vermarkten; **the reason it didn't sell was simply that it wasn't properly ~ed** es fand wegen unzureichenden Marketings keinen Absatz

VI sich verkaufen, Absatz finden, gehen *(inf)*

marketability [ˌmɑːkɪtəˈbɪlɪtɪ] N Marktfähigkeit *f*

marketable [ˈmɑːkɪtəbl] ADJ absetzbar, marktfähig; *(fig) actor, sportsperson* vermarktbar

market: **market analysis** N Marktanalyse *f*; **market behaviour** N Marktverhalten *nt*; **market cleansing** N *(Econ)* Marktbereinigung *f*; **market condition** N *usu pl* Marktlage *f*, Konjunktur *f*; **market day** N Markttag *m*; **market dealings** PL *(Brit St Ex)* Börsenhandel *m*; **market dominance** N *(Econ)* Marktbeherrschung *f*; **market-driven**, **market-led** ADJ *product, decision, change, company* marktbestimmt, marktgesteuert; **market economy** N Marktwirtschaft *f*; **market expert** N Marktexperte *m*, Marktexpertin *f*; **market forces** PL Marktkräfte *pl*; **market garden** N Gemüseanbaubetrieb *m*, Gärtnerei *f*; **market gardener** N Gärtner(in) *m(f)*; **market gardening** N (gewerbsmäßiger) Anbau von Gemüse

marketing [ˈmɑːkɪtɪŋ] N Marketing *nt*

marketing manager N Marketingmanager(in) *m(f)*

market: **market leader** N Marktführer *m*; **market niche** N Marktnische *f*; **marketplace** N **a** Marktplatz *m*; **on the ~** auf dem Marktplatz **b** *(= world of trade)* Markt *m*; **in the ~** auf dem Markt; **market price** N Marktpreis *m*; **market research** N Marktforschung *f*; **market researcher** N Marktforscher(in) *m(f)*; **market sector** N *(Econ)* Marktsegment *nt or* -sektor *m*; **market share** N Marktanteil *m*; **market square** N Marktplatz *m*; **market stall** N Marktbude *f*; **market survey** N Marktuntersuchung *f*; **market swing** N *(US)* Konjunkturumschwung *m*; **market town** N Marktstädtchen *nt*; **market trader** N *(Brit)* Markthändler(in) *m(f)*; **market trends** PL Markttendenzen *pl*; **market value** N Marktwert *m*

marking [ˈmɑːkɪŋ] N **a** Markierung *f*; *(on animal)* Zeichnung *f* **b** *(of exams) (= correcting)* Korrektur *f*; *(= grading)* Benotung *f* **c** *(Sport)* Decken *nt*, Deckung *f*

marking ink N Wäschetinte *f*

marksman [ˈmɑːksmən] N *pl* **-men** [-mən] Schütze *m*; *(police etc)* Scharfschütze *m*

marksmanship [ˈmɑːksmənʃɪp] N Treffsicherheit *f*

markswoman [ˈmɑːksˌwʊmən] N *pl* **-women** [-ˌwɪmɪn] Schützin *f*; *(police etc)* Scharfschützin *f*

mark-up [ˈmɑːkʌp] N **a** Handelsspanne *f*; *(= amount added)* Preiserhöhung *f or* -aufschlag *m*; **~ price** Verkaufspreis *m* **b** *(Typ)* Auszeichnung *f*

marl [mɑːl] N Mergel *m*

marlin [ˈmɑːlɪn] N Fächerfisch *m*, Marlin *m*

marlinspike [ˈmɑːlɪnspaɪk] N Marlspieker *m*, Splisseisen *nt*

marmalade [ˈmɑːməleɪd] N Marmelade *f* aus Zitrusfrüchten; **(orange) ~** Orangenmarmelade *f*

marmoreal [mɑːˈmɔːrɪəl] ADJ marmorn, aus Marmor; *(= resembling marble)* marmorartig

marmoset [ˈmɑːməʊzet] N Krallenaffe *m*, Pinseläffchen *nt*

marmot [ˈmɑːmət] N Murmeltier *nt*

maroon[1] [məˈruːn] **ADJ** kastanienbraun, rötlich braun **N** *(= colour)* Kastanienbraun *nt*

maroon[2] VT aussetzen; **~ed** von der Außenwelt abgeschnitten; **~ed by floods** vom Hochwasser eingeschlossen

marque [mɑːk] N *(= brand)* Marke *f*

marquee [mɑːˈkiː] N **a** Festzelt *nt* **b** *(US: of theatre etc)* Vordach *nt*, Canopy *nt*; **his name's on all the ~s** sein Name ist auf allen Anzeigetafeln zu sehen

marquess [ˈmɑːkwɪs] N Marquis *m*

marquetry [ˈmɑːkɪtrɪ] N Marketerie *f*, Einlegearbeit *f*

marquis [ˈmɑːkwɪs] N = **marquess**

marram grass [ˈmærəmˌgrɑːs] N Strandhafer *m*, Dünengras *nt*

marriage [ˈmærɪdʒ] ✪ 24.3 N **a** *(state)* die Ehe; *(= wedding)* Hochzeit *f*, Heirat *f*; *(= marriage ceremony)* Trauung *f*; **~ of convenience** Vernunftehe *f*; **relations by ~** angeheiratete Verwandte; **to be related by ~** *(in-laws)* miteinander verschwägert sein; *(others)* miteinander verwandt sein; **to give sb in ~ to sb** jdn jdm zur Frau geben; **to give sb in ~** jdn verheiraten; **an offer of ~** ein Heiratsantrag *m* **b** *(fig)* Verbindung *f*; **a ~ of two minds** eine geistige Ehe

marriageable [ˈmærɪdʒəbl] ADJ heiratsfähig; **of ~ age** im heiratsfähigen Alter

marriage: **marriage bed** N Ehebett *nt*; **marriage broker** N Heiratsvermittler(in) *m(f)*; *(Jur)* Ehemakler(in) *m(f)*; **marriage bureau** N Heiratsinstitut *nt*; **marriage ceremony** N Trauzeremonie *f*; **marriage certificate** N Heiratsurkunde *f*; **marriage contract** N *(Jur)* Ehevertrag *m*; **marriage counselling**, *(US)* **marriage counseling** N Eheberatung *f*; **marriage counsellor**, *(US)* **marriage counselor** N Eheberater(in) *m(f)*; **marriage guidance** N Eheberatung *f*; **marriage guidance centre**, **marriage guidance center** *(US)* N Eheberatungsstelle *f*; **marriage guidance counsellor**, **marriage guidance counselor** *(US)* N Eheberater(in) *m(f)*; **marriage licence**, *(US)* **marriage license** N Eheerlaubnis *f*; **marriage lines** PL Trauschein *m*; **marriage plans** PL Hochzeitspläne *pl*; **marriage portion** N *(old)* Mitgift *f*; **marriage problems** PL Eheprobleme *pl*; **marriage proposal** N Heiratsantrag *m*; **marriage settlement** N Ehevertrag *m*; **marriage vow** N Ehegelübde *nt*

married [ˈmærɪd] ADJ *man, woman* verheiratet *(to sb* mit jdm); **just** *or* **newly ~** frisch vermählt; **~ couple** Ehepaar *nt*; **~ life** das Eheleben; **he/she is a ~ man/woman** er/sie ist verheiratet

married: **married name** N Ehename *m*; **married quarters** PL Unterkünfte *pl* für Eheleute

marrow [ˈmærəʊ] N **a** *(Anat)* (Knochen)mark *nt*; **he's a Scot to the ~** er ist durch und durch Schotte; **to be frozen to the ~** völlig durchgefroren sein **b** *(fig: of statement etc)* Kern *m*, Wesentliche(s) *nt* **c** *(Brit Bot: also* **vegetable marrow**) Gartenkürbis *m*

marrowbone [ˈmærəʊbəʊn] N Markknochen *m*

marrowfat [ˈmærəʊfæt] N, **marrowfat pea** N Markerbse *f*

marry [ˈmærɪ] ✪ 24.3 **VT** **a** *(= get married to)* heiraten; **to ~ money** reich heiraten; **will you ~ me?** willst du mich heiraten?

b *(priest)* trauen

c *(father)* verheiraten; **he married all his daughters into very rich families** er hat zugesehen, dass alle seine Töchter in reiche Familien einheirateten

VI **a** *(also* **get married**) heiraten, sich verheiraten; *(couple)* heiraten, sich vermählen

(geh); **to ~ into a rich family** in eine reiche Familie einheiraten; **to ~ into money** reich heiraten; **he married into a small fortune** durch die Heirat ist er an ein kleines Vermögen gekommen; **he's not the ~ing kind** er ist nicht der Typ, der heiratet; **~ in haste, repent at leisure** *(prov)* Heiraten in Eile bereut man in Weile *(prov)*
b *(fig: two pieces of wood etc)* ineinanderpassen

▶ **marry off** VT *sep* an den Mann/die Frau bringen *(inf)*; *girl also* unter die Haube bringen *(inf)*; **he has married off his daughter to a rich young lawyer** er hat dafür gesorgt, dass seine Tochter einen reichen jungen Anwalt heiratet

Mars [mɑːz] N Mars *m*

Marseillaise [ˌmɑːsəˈleɪz] N **the ~** die Marseillaise

Marseilles [mɑːˈseɪlz] N Marseille *nt*

marsh [mɑːʃ] N Sumpf *m*

marshal [ˈmɑːʃəl] **N** *(Mil, of royal household)* Marschall *m*; *(at sports meeting etc)* Platzwärter(in) *m(f)*; *(at demo etc)* Ordner(in) *m(f)*; *(US)* Bezirkspolizeichef(in) *m(f)* **VT** *facts, arguments* ordnen; *soldiers* antreten lassen; *(= lead)* geleiten, führen

marshalling yard, *(US)* **marshaling yard** [ˈmɑːʃəlɪŋˈjɑːd] N Rangier- *or* Verschiebebahnhof *m*

marsh: **marsh gas** N Methangas *nt*, Sumpf- *or* Grubengas *nt*; **marshland** N Marschland *nt*; **marshmallow** N *(= sweet)* Marshmallow *nt*; *(Bot)* Eibisch *m*; **marsh marigold** N Sumpfdotterblume *f*

marshy [ˈmɑːʃɪ] ADJ *(+er)* sumpfig; **a ~ district** ein Sumpfgebiet *nt*

marsupial [mɑːˈsuːpɪəl] **ADJ** **~ animal** Beuteltier *nt* **N** Beuteltier *nt*

mart [mɑːt] N *(old)* Markt *m*

marten [ˈmɑːtɪn] N Marder *m*

martial [ˈmɑːʃəl] ADJ *music* kriegerisch; *bearing* stramm, soldatisch

martial art N **the ~s** die Kampfkunst; **the ~ of judo** der Kampfsport Judo

martial law N Kriegsrecht *nt*; **the state was put under ~** über den Staat wurde (das) Kriegsrecht verhängt

Martian [ˈmɑːʃɪən] **ADJ** *atmosphere, exploration* des Mars; *invaders* vom Mars **N** Marsbewohner(in) *m(f)*, Marsmensch *m*

martin [ˈmɑːtɪn] N Schwalbe *f*

martinet [ˌmɑːtɪˈnet] N (strenger) Zuchtmeister; **he's a real ~** er führt ein strenges Regiment

martingale [ˈmɑːtɪngeɪl] N *(Horseriding)* Martingal *nt*

martini [mɑːˈtiːnɪ] N Martini *m*

Martinique [ˌmɑːtɪˈniːk] N Martinique *nt*

Martinmas [ˈmɑːtɪnməs] N Martinstag *m*, Martini *nt*

martyr [ˈmɑːtəʳ] **N** Märtyrer(in) *m(f)*; **he was a ~ to the cause of civil rights** er wurde zum Märtyrer für die Sache der Bürgerrechtsbewegung; **to be a ~ to arthritis** entsetzlich unter Arthritis zu leiden haben; **there's no need to make a ~ of yourself** *(inf)* du brauchst hier nicht den Märtyrer zu spielen *(inf)* **VT** martern, (zu Tode) quälen; **thousands of Christians were ~ed** tausende *or* Tausende von Christen starben den Märtyrertod

martyrdom [ˈmɑːtədəm] N *(= suffering)* Martyrium *nt*; *(= death)* Märtyrertod *m*

marvel [ˈmɑːvəl] **N** Wunder *nt*; **the ~s of modern science** die Wunder der modernen Wissenschaft; **this medicine is a ~** diese Medizin wirkt Wunder; **if he ever gets there it will be a ~** *(inf)* wenn er jemals dort ankommt, ist das ein Wunder; **it's a ~ to me that he escaped unhurt** es kommt mir wie ein Wunder vor, dass er ohne Verletzungen davonkam; **it's a ~ to me how he does it** *(inf)* es ist mir einfach unerklärlich *or* schleierhaft, wie er das macht; **her desk is a ~ of tidiness** ihr Schreibtisch ist ein Muster an Ordnung; **you're a ~!** *(inf)* du bist ein Engel!; *(= clever)* du bist ein Genie!
VI staunen *(at* über *+acc)*; **to ~ at a sight** einen Anblick bestaunen; **they ~led** *(Brit) or* **~ed** *(US)* **at her beauty** *(liter)* sie bewunderten ihre Schönheit

marvellous, *(US)* **marvelous** [ˈmɑːvələs] ADJ wunderbar, fantastisch, phantastisch, fabelhaft; **isn't it ~?** ist das nicht herrlich?; *(iro)* gut, nicht! *(iro)*; **they've done a ~ job** das haben sie hervorragend gemacht

marvellously, *(US)* **marvelously** [ˈmɑːvələslɪ] ADV *(with adj)* herrlich; *(with vb)* großartig, fabelhaft

marvy [ˈmɑːvɪ] ADJ *(+er)* *(US sl)* prima, klasse *(inf)*

Marxian [ˈmɑːksɪən] ADJ Marxisch

Marxism [ˈmɑːksɪzəm] N der Marxismus

Marxist [ˈmɑːksɪst] **ADJ** marxistisch **N** Marxist(in) *m(f)*

Mary [ˈmɛərɪ] N Maria *f*

marzipan [ˌmɑːzɪˈpæn] N Marzipan *nt or m*

mascara [mæˈskɑːrə] **N** Wimperntusche *f*, Maskara *f* **VT** tuschen

mascaraed [mæsˈkɑːrəd] ADJ getuscht

mascot [ˈmæskət] N Maskottchen *nt*

masculine [ˈmæskjʊlɪn] **ADJ** männlich; *woman, room, decor* maskulin; *(Gram)* maskulin, männlich **N** *(Gram)* Maskulinum *nt*

masculinist [ˈmæskjʊlɪnɪst] ADJ maskulinistisch

masculinity [ˌmæskjʊˈlɪnɪtɪ] N Männlichkeit *f*

MASH N *(US) abbr of* **Mobile Army Surgical Hospital** mobiles Lazarett

mash [mæʃ] **N** Brei *m*; *(for animals)* Futterbrei *m*, Schlempe *f*; *(= potatoes)* Püree *nt*; *(in brewing)* Maische *f* **VT** zerstampfen

mashed [mæʃt] ADJ **~ potatoes** Kartoffelbrei *m or* -püree *nt*

masher [ˈmæʃəʳ] N Stampfer *m*; *(for potatoes)* Kartoffelstampfer *m*

mashy [ˈmæʃɪ] ADJ *(+er)* *(= pulpy)* breiig

mask [mɑːsk] **N** *(lit, fig, Comput)* Maske *f*; **the ~ slipped** *(fig)* er/sie *etc* ließ die Maske fallen; **surgeon's ~** Mundschutz *m* **VT** maskieren; *(clouds, trees etc)* verdecken; *feelings* verbergen; *intentions* maskieren

masked [mɑːskt] ADJ maskiert

masked ball N Maskenball *m*

masking tape N *(= adhesive tape)* Kreppband *m*

masochism [ˈmæsəʊkɪzəm] N Masochismus *m*

masochist [ˈmæsəʊkɪst] N Masochist(in) *m(f)*

masochistic [ˌmæsəʊˈkɪstɪk] ADJ masochistisch

masochistically [ˌmæsəʊˈkɪstɪkəlɪ] ADV masochistisch

mason [ˈmeɪsn] N **a** *(= builder)* Steinmetz(in) *m(f)*; *(in quarry)* Steinhauer(in) *m(f)* → **monumental mason** **b** *(= freemason)* Freimaurer *m*

MASON-DIXON LINE

Die **Mason-Dixon line** ist die symbolische Linie, die den Norden der Vereinigten Staaten von Amerika vom Süden abtrennt. Die 233 Meilen lange Linie wurde im 18. Jahrhundert zunächst festgelegt, um den Grenzstreitigkeiten zwischen Maryland und Pennsylvania ein Ende zu setzen, danach wurde sie auf die Grenzlinie zwischen Pennsylvannia und Virginia ausgedehnt. Bis zum Ende des Bürgerkriegs trennte diese Grenze die Sklavenstaaten von den freien Staaten. Heute wird die **Mason-Dixon line** immer noch herangezogen, um einen Südstaatler und den Süden im Allgemeinen zu definieren: „Sie wurde auf einer Farm geboren, die zu ihrem größten Bedauern ein paar Meilen nördlich der Mason-Dixon-Linie lag." Country-Sänger träumen in ihren Liedern häufig von „crossing that Mason-Dixon line", der Heimkehr in den Süden.

masonic [məˈsɒnɪk] ADJ Freimaurer-; *handshake* unter Freimaurern; **~ lodge/order** Freimaurerloge *f*/-orden *m*

masonry [ˈmeɪsnrɪ] N **a** *(= stonework)* Mauerwerk *nt* **b** *(= free masonry)* Freimaurerei *f*, Freimaurertum *nt*

masque [mɑːsk] N Maskenspiel *nt*

masquerade [ˌmæskəˈreɪd] **N** Maskerade *f*; **that's just a ~, she's not really like that at all** *(fig)* das ist alles nur Theater, in Wirklichkeit ist sie gar nicht so **VI** **to ~ as ...** sich verkleiden als ...; *(fig)* sich ausgeben als ..., vorgeben, ... zu sein; **this cheap trash masquerading as literature** dieser Schund, der als Literatur ausgegeben wird

mass¹ [mæs] N *(Eccl)* Messe *f*; **High Mass** Hochamt *nt*; **to go to ~** zur Messe gehen; **to hear ~** die Messe feiern; **to say ~** die Messe lesen

mass² **N** **a** *(general, Phys)* Masse *f*; *(of people)* Menge *f*; **a ~ of snow** eine Schneemasse; **a ~ of rubble** ein Schutthaufen *m*; **the ~ of rubble** der Haufen Schutt; **a ~ of cold air** eine kalte Luftmasse; **a ~ of red hair** ein Wust *m* roter Haare; **a ~ of flames** ein einziges Flammenmeer; **this confused ~ of thoughts** dieser wirre Gedankenwust; **the essay is one great ~ of spelling mistakes** der Aufsatz wimmelt nur so von Schreibfehlern; **he's a ~ of bruises** er ist voller blauer Flecken; **the garden is a ~ of yellow/colour** *(Brit) or* **color** *(US)* der Garten ist ein Meer *nt* von Gelb/ein Farbenmeer *nt*; **the ~es** die Masse(n *pl*); **the great ~ of the population** die (breite) Masse der Bevölkerung; **the nation in the ~** die breite(n) Volksmasse(n); **people, in the ~, prefer ...** die breite Masse (der Menschen) zieht es vor, ...
b *(= bulk)* **the great ~ of the mountains** das riesige Bergmassiv; **the huge ~ of the ship loomed up out of the night** die riesige Form des Schiffes tauchte aus der Nacht auf
c **masses** **PL** *(inf)* massenhaft, eine Masse *(inf)*; **he has ~es of money/time** er hat massenhaft *or* massig *(inf) or* eine Masse *(inf)* Geld/Zeit; **the factory is producing ~es of cars** die Fabrik produziert Unmengen von Autos; **I've got ~es (of things) to do** ich habe noch massig *(inf)* zu tun
VT *troops* massieren, zusammenziehen
VI *(Mil)* sich massieren; *(Red Indians etc)* sich versammeln; *(clouds)* sich (zusammen)ballen; **they're ~ing for an attack** sie sammeln sich zum Angriff

massacre [ˈmæsəkəʳ] **N** Massaker *nt* **VT** niedermetzeln, massakrieren; **last Saturday they ~d us 6-0** *(inf)* letzten Samstag haben sie uns mit 6:0 fertiggemacht *(inf)*

massage [ˈmæsɑːʒ] **N** Massage *f* **VT** massieren

massage parlour, *(US)* **massage parlor** N Massagesalon *m*

mass: **mass culture** N Massenkultur *f*; **mass destruction** N Massenvernichtung *f*; **weapons of ~** Massenvernichtungswaffen *pl*

massed [mæst] ADJ *troops, tanks* zusammengezogen; *people, plants* dicht gedrängt; **~ ranks** dicht gedrängte Reihen; **~ sprint** *(Cycling)* Massensprint *m*; **the ~ bands of the Royal Navy** die vereinigten Militärkapellen der königlichen Marine; **sung by ~ choirs** von den Stimmen mehrerer Chöre gesungen; **the ~ weight of medical opinion** das ganze Gewicht der ärztlichen Meinung

mass education N Massenerziehung *f*

masseur [mæˈsɜːʳ] N Masseur *m*

masseuse [mæˈsɜːz] N Masseuse *f*

mass: **mass funeral** N Massenbegräbnis *nt*; **mass grave** N Massengrab *nt*; **mass hysteria** N Massenhysterie *f*

massif [mæˈsiːf] N *(Geog)* (Gebirgs)massiv *nt*

massive [ˈmæsɪv] ADJ *(= huge)* riesig, enorm; *task* gewaltig; *attack, pressure, support, heart attack, stroke* massiv; *(= bulky, weighty) structure, wall* massiv, wuchtig; *forehead* breit, wuchtig; *boxer* wuchtig, massig; **he weighs in at a ~ 17 stone** er wiegt beachtliche 108 Kilo; **~ furniture** Massivholzmöbel *pl*; **on a ~ scale** in riesigem Umfang; **the ship was designed on a ~ scale** das Schiff hatte riesenhafte Ausmaße; **the symphony is conceived on a ~ scale** die Sinfonie *or* Symphonie ist grandios konzipiert; **space research is financed on a ~ scale** Raumforschung wird mit riesigen Summen finanziert

massively ['mæsɪvlɪ] ADV *(= hugely) popular, expensive, increase* enorm; *(= bulkily) made* massiv; **a ~ built man** ein Schrank *m* von einem Mann; **~ in debt** enorm verschuldet; **to invest/borrow ~** riesige Summen investieren/aufnehmen

massiveness ['mæsɪvnɪs] N *(of expanse of land, plane, ship, hotel etc)* riesige *or* gewaltige Ausmaße *pl*; *(of fortune, expenditure, orchestra)* enorme Größe; *(of structure, wall)* Wuchtigkeit *f*, Massivität *f*; *(of boxer, forehead)* Wuchtigkeit *f*; **the ~ of the task** die gewaltige Aufgabe

mass: **mass killing** N Massenmord *m*; **mass market** N Massenmarkt *m*; **mass-market** ADJ **~ paperbacks** Taschenbücher *pl* für den Massenmarkt; **mass marketing** N massenweise Vermarktung; **mass media** PL Massenmedien *pl*; **mass meeting** N Massenveranstaltung *f*; *(in company)* Betriebsversammlung *f*; *(of trade union)* Vollversammlung *f*; *(Pol)* Massenkundgebung *f*; **mass murderer** N Massenmörder(in) *m(f)*; **mass murders** PL Massenmord *m*; **mass number** N *(Phys)* Massenzahl *f*; **mass-produce** VT in Massenproduktion herstellen; *cars, engines etc* serienweise herstellen; **mass-produced** ADJ **~ items** Massenartikel *pl*; **it looks as though it was ~** das sieht sehr nach Massenware aus; **mass production** N Massenproduktion *f*; **mass protests** PL Massenproteste *pl*; **mass psychology** N Massenpsychologie *f*; **mass rally** N Massenkundgebung *f*; **mass storage (device)** N *(Comput)* Massenspeicher *m*; **mass survey** N *(Med)* Reihenuntersuchung *f*; **mass tourism** N Massentourismus *m*; **mass unemployment** N Massenarbeitslosigkeit *f*

mast¹ [mɑːst] N *(Naut)* Mast(baum) *m*; *(Rad etc)* Sendeturm *m*; **10 years before the ~** 10 Jahre auf See

mast² N *(Bot)* Mast *f*

mastectomy [mæ'stektəmɪ] N Brustamputation *f*

-masted [-mɑːstɪd] ADJ *suf* -mastig; **two-masted** zweimastig; **a three-masted vessel** ein Dreimaster *m*

master ['mɑːstə'] **N** **a** *(of the house, dog, servants)* Herr *m*; **Master** *(= Christ)* der Herr; *(in address)* Meister; **to be ~ in one's own house** *(also fig)* Herr im Hause sein; **to be one's own ~** sein eigener Herr sein

b *(Naut)* Kapitän *m*; **~'s certificate** Kapitänspatent *nt*

c *(= musician, painter etc)* Meister(in) *m(f)*

d *(= teacher)* Lehrer *m*; *(of apprentice)* Meister *m*

e **to be ~ of sth** etw beherrschen; **to be ~ of the situation** Herr *m* der Lage sein; **to be the ~ of one's fate** sein Schicksal in der Hand haben → **grand master, past master**

f *(= boy's title)* Master *m*, Meister *m (old)*

g *(of college)* Leiter *m*, Rektor *m*

h *(= master copy)* Original *nt*

i *(Univ: = Master of Art etc)* **to do a ~'s** seinen Magister machen *(in* in *+dat)*; **~'s degree** Magister(grad) *m*

VT meistern; *one's emotions* unter Kontrolle bringen; *technique, method* beherrschen; **to ~ the violin** das Geigenspiel beherrschen; **to ~ one's temper** sich beherrschen, sein Temperament zügeln

master *in cpds (with trades)* -meister(in) *m(f)*; **master-at-arms** N Bootsmann *m* mit Polizeibefugnis; **master baker** N Bäckermeister(in) *m(f)*; **master bedroom** N großes Schlafzimmer; **master builder** N Baumeister *m*; **master card** N *(fig)* Trumpf *m*; **to play one's ~** seinen Trumpf ausspielen; **master chef** N Meisterkoch *m*/-köchin *f*; **master copy** N Original *nt*; **master craftsman** N Handwerksmeister *m*; **master criminal** N Meister(in) *m(f)* des Verbrechens; **master data** PL *usu with sing* Stammdaten *pl*; **master disk** N Hauptplatte *f*; **master file** N *(Comput)* Stammdatei *f*

masterful ['mɑːstəfʊl] ADJ meisterhaft; *ball control* gekonnt; *(= dominating) personality* gebieterisch; **he's got a ~, yet polite attitude** er hat eine bestimmte, aber trotzdem höfliche Art; **he said in a ~ tone** sagte er in bestimmtem Ton; **we were amazed at his ~ control of the meeting** wir staunten darüber, wie überlegen *or* souverän er die Sitzung in der Hand hatte

masterfully ['mɑːstəfəlɪ] ADV meisterhaft; *control* überlegen, souverän; *play, kick etc* gekonnt

master key N Haupt- *or* Generalschlüssel *m*

masterly ['mɑːstəlɪ] ADJ meisterhaft, gekonnt; **in a ~ fashion** meisterhaft, gekonnt; **..., he said with ~ understatement** ..., sagte er, meisterhaft untertreibend

master: **master magician** N Zaubermeister(in) *m(f)*; **master mariner** N Kapitän *m*; **master mason** N Steinmetzmeister *m*; **mastermind** **N** (führender) Kopf; **who's the ~ who planned all these operations?** wer ist der Kopf, der hinter der Planung dieser Unternehmungen steckte? **VT** **who ~ed the robbery?** wer steckt hinter dem Raubüberfall?; **Master of Arts/Science** N ≈ Magister *m* (der philosophischen/naturwissenschaftlichen Fakultät); **master of ceremonies** N *(at function)* Zeremonienmeister(in) *m(f)*; *(on stage)* Conférencier *m*; *(on TV)* Showmaster(in) *m(f)*; **master of (fox)hounds** N Master *m*; **masterpiece** N Meisterwerk *nt*; **master plan** N *(overall)* Gesamtplan *m*; *(masterly)* Meisterplan *m*; **master race** N Herrenvolk *nt*; **master sergeant** N *(US)* Oberfeldwebel *m*; **master spy** N Meisterspion(in) *m(f)*; **masterstroke** N Meister- *or* Glanzstück *nt*; **master switch** N Hauptschalter *m*; **master tape** N Originalband *nt*; *(Comput)* Stammband *nt*; **master thief** N Meisterdieb(in) *m(f)*; **masterwork** N Meisterwerk *nt*

mastery ['mɑːstərɪ] N *(= control: of language, technique, instrument etc)* Beherrschung *f*; *(= skill)* Können *nt*; *(over competitors etc)* Oberhand *f*; **~ of the seas** Herrschaft *f* über die Meere; **the painter's ~ of form** des Malers meisterhafter Gebrauch von Form; **to gain the ~ of sth** etw beherrschen

masthead ['mɑːsthed] N **a** *(Naut)* Mars *m*, Mastkorb *m* **b** *(Press: in newspaper, magazine)* Impressum *nt*

mastic ['mæstɪk] N *(Build)* Mastix *m*

masticate ['mæstɪkeɪt] VTI kauen; *(for young)* vorkauen

mastication [,mæstɪ'keɪʃən] N Kauen *nt*; *(for young)* Vorkauen *nt*

mastiff ['mæstɪf] N Dogge *f*

mastitis [mæ'staɪtɪs] N Brust(drüsen)entzündung *f*, Mastitis *f*

mastodon ['mæstədɒn] N Mastodon *nt*

mastoid ['mæstɔɪd] **ADJ** warzenförmig, mastoid *(spec)* **N** Warzenfortsatz *m*, Mastoid *nt (spec)*

masturbate ['mæstəbeɪt] VI masturbieren, onanieren

masturbation [,mæstə'beɪʃən] N Masturbation *f*, Onanie *f*

masturbatory [,mæstə'beɪtərɪ] ADJ masturbatorisch

mat¹ [mæt] **N** Matte *f*; *(= door mat)* Fußmatte *f*; *(on table)* Untersetzer *m*; *(of cloth)* Deckchen *nt*; *(of hair)* Gewirr *nt*; **to go to the ~ for sb** *(US)* sich für jdn auf einen Streit einlassen; **to go to the ~ to do sth** *(US)* einen Streit riskieren, um etw zu tun **VT** **the sea-water had ~ted his hair** durch das Salzwasser waren seine Haare verfilzt geworden **VI** verfilzen

mat² ADJ = **matt**

matador ['mætədɔː'] N Matador *m*

match¹ [mætʃ] N Streichholz *nt*, Zündholz *nt*

match² ✪ 5.3 **N** **a** *(= sb/sth similar, suitable etc)* **to be** *or* **make a good ~** gut zusammenpassen; **the skirt is a good ~ for the sweater** der Rock passt gut zum Pullover; **I want a ~ for this yellow paint** ich möchte Farbe in diesem Gelbton; **this chair is a ~ for that one** dieser Stuhl ist das Gegenstück zu dem

b **to be a/no ~ for sb** *(= be able to compete with)* sich mit jdm messen/nicht messen können; *(= be able to handle)* jdm gewachsen/nicht gewachsen sein; **he's a ~ for anybody** er kann es mit jedem aufnehmen; **A was more than a ~ for B** A war B weit überlegen; **to meet one's ~** seinen Meister finden

c *(= marriage)* Heirat *f*; **who thought up this ~?** wer hat die beiden zusammengebracht?; **she made a good ~** sie hat eine gute Partie gemacht; **he's a good ~** er ist eine gute Partie

d *(Sport) (general)* Wettkampf *m*; *(= team game)* Spiel *nt*; *(Tennis)* Match *nt*, Partie *f*; *(Boxing, Fencing)* Kampf *m*; *(= quiz)* Wettkampf *m*, Wettbewerb *m*; **athletics ~** Leichtathletikkampf *m*; **I'll give you a ~** ich werde einmal gegen Sie spielen; **we must have another ~ some time** wir müssen wieder einmal gegeneinander spielen; **that's ~** *(Tennis)* Match!, damit ist das Match entschieden

VT **a** *(= pair off)* (einander) anpassen; **~ each diagram with its counterpart** ordnen Sie die Schaubilder einander zu

b *(= equal)* gleichkommen *(+dat) (in* an *+dat)*; **A doesn't quite ~ B in originality** A kann es an Originalität nicht mit B aufnehmen; **nobody can ~ him in argument** niemand kann so gut argumentieren wie er; **a quality that has never been ~ed since** eine Qualität, die bislang unerreicht ist *or* noch ihresgleichen sucht *(geh)*; **no knight could ~ him in battle** kein Ritter konnte sich mit ihm messen; **I can't ~ him in chess** im Schach kann ich es mit ihm nicht aufnehmen; **that sort of easy self-confidence which is not ~ed by any great degree of intelligence** jene Selbstsicherheit, die nicht mit der entsprechenden Intelligenz gepaart ist; **~ that if you can!** das soll erst mal einer nachmachen, das macht so leicht keiner nach!; **three kings! ~ that!** drei Könige! kannst du da noch mithalten?; **this climate/whisky can't be ~ed anywhere in the world** so ein Klima/so einen Whisky gibt es nicht noch einmal

c *(= correspond to)* entsprechen *(+dat)*; **the results did not ~ our hopes** die Ergebnisse entsprachen nicht unseren Hoffnungen; **~ case** *(Comput)* Groß-/Kleinschreibung beachten; **~ing words** Wortentsprechungen *pl*

d *(clothes, colours)* passen zu; **she ~ed the carpet with a nice rug** sie fand einen hübschen, zum Teppich passenden Läufer; **can you ~ this fabric?** haben Sie etwas, das zu diesem Stoff passt?; **to ~ textures and fabrics so that ...** Strukturen und Stoffe so aufeinander abstimmen, dass ...; **his face ~ed the red of his sweater** sein Gesicht war so rot wie sein Pullover

e *(= pit)* **he decided to ~ his team against** *or* **with the champions** er beschloss, seine Mannschaft gegen die Meister antreten zu lassen; **to be ~ed against sb** gegen jdn antreten; **to ~ one's wits against sb** sich geistig mit jdm messen; **to ~ one's strength against sb** seine Kräfte mit jdm messen

VI zusammenpassen; **it doesn't ~** das passt nicht (zusammen); **with a skirt to ~** mit (dazu) passendem Rock

▶ **match up** **VI** **a** *(= correspond)* zusammenpassen **b** *(= be equal)* **he matched up to the situation** er war der Situation gewachsen **VT** *sep colours* aufeinander abstimmen; **I matched the lampshade up with the wallpaper** ich fand den passenden Lampenschirm zu der Tapete

match: **matchbook** N *(esp US)* Streichholzheftchen *nt*; **matchbox** N Streichholzschachtel *f*; **match day** N *(Brit Sport)* Spieltag *m*

matched [mætʃt] ADJ *pair, set* zusammenpassend; **they're well ~** *(couple)* die beiden passen gut zusammen; *(colours)* sie sind gut aufeinander abgestimmt; **the two boxers were well ~** die beiden Boxer waren einander ebenbürtig; **the**

teams are closely *or* **evenly ~** die Mannschaften sind gleichwertig

match-fit ['mætʃfɪt] ADJ (*Brit Sport*) in guter Spielform

match-fitness [,mætʃ'fɪtnɪs] N (*Brit Sport*) **to regain ~** wieder in gute Spielform kommen

matching ['mætʃɪŋ] ADJ (dazu) passend; **they form a ~ pair** sie passen *or* gehören zusammen; **a ~ set of wine glasses** ein Satz *m* Weingläser

matching: **matching funds** PL *Geldmittel, die von der Regierung oder einem Unternehmen zur Verfügung gestellt werden, um von privater Seite aufgebrachte Spenden etc zu verdoppeln*; **matching test** N Vergleichsprobe *f*

matchless ['mætʃlɪs] ADJ einzigartig, unvergleichlich

match: **matchlock** N Luntenschloss *nt*; **matchmaker** N Ehestifter(in) *m(f)*, Kuppler(in) *m(f)* *(pej)*; **matchmaking** N **she loves ~** sie verkuppelt die Leute gern *(inf)*; **match penalty** N *(Ice hockey)* Matchstrafe *f*; **match point** N *(Tennis)* Matchball *m*; **matchstick** N Streichholz *nt*; **matchwood** N *Holz zur Herstellung von Streichhölzern* **reduced to ~** *(fig)* zu Kleinholz gemacht *(inf)*

mate[1] [meɪt] (*Chess*) N Matt *nt* VT matt setzen VI **white ~s in two** Weiß setzt den Gegner in zwei Zügen matt

mate[2] N **a** *(= fellow worker)* Arbeitskollege *m*/-kollegin *f*, Kumpel *m*
b *(= helper)* Gehilfe *m*, Gehilfin *f*
c *(Naut)* Maat *m*
d *(of animal) (male)* Männchen *nt*; *(female)* Weibchen *nt*; **his ~** das Weibchen
e *(inf: = friend)* Freund(in) *m(f)*, Kamerad(in) *m(f)*; **listen, ~** hör mal, Freundchen! *(inf)*; **got a light, ~?** hast du Feuer, Kumpel? *(inf)*
f *(hum inf) (= husband)* Mann *m*; *(= wife)* Frau *f*; *(of animal, male)* Partner *m*; *(female)* Partnerin *f*
g *(of pair)* **here's one sock, where's its ~?** hier ist eine Socke, wo ist die andere *or* zweite?
VT *animals* paaren; *female animal* decken lassen; *(fig hum)* verkuppeln; **they ~d their mare with our stallion** sie haben ihre Stute von unserem Hengst decken lassen
VI *(Zool)* sich paaren

mater ['meɪtəʳ] N (*Brit inf*) Mama *f*

material [mə'tɪərɪəl] ADJ **a** *(= of matter, things)* materiell; **~ damage** Sachschaden *m*
b *(= physical) needs, comforts* materiell
c *(esp Jur: = important) evidence, witness* wesentlich; *difference* grundlegend, wesentlich; *fact, information* relevant; **that's not ~** das ist nicht relevant
N **a** Material *nt*; *(for report, novel etc)* Stoff *m*; **he's good editorial ~** er hat das Zeug zum Redakteur; **this group would be good ~ for our show** diese Band wäre für unsere Show ganz brauchbar
b materials PL Material *nt*; **building ~s** Baustoffe *pl*, Baumaterial *nt*; **raw ~s** Rohstoffe *pl*; **writing ~s** Schreibzeug *nt*
c *(= cloth)* Stoff *m*, Material *nt*

materialism [mə'tɪərɪəlɪzəm] N der Materialismus

materialist [mə'tɪərɪəlɪst] N Materialist(in) *m(f)*

materialistic ADJ, **materialistically** ADV [mə,tɪərɪə'lɪstɪk, -əlɪ] materialistisch

materialization [mə,tɪərɪəlaɪ'zeɪʃən] N Verkörperung *f*; *(of ghosts)* Materialisation *f*

materialize [mə'tɪərɪəlaɪz] VI **a** *(idea, plan)* sich verwirklichen; *(promises, hopes etc)* wahr werden; **this idea will never ~** aus dieser Idee wird nie etwas; **the meeting never ~d** das Treffen kam nie zustande *or* zu Stande; **if this deal ever ~s** wenn aus diesem Geschäft je etwas wird, wenn dieses Geschäft je zustande *or* zu Stande kommt; **the money he'd promised me never ~d** von dem Geld, das er mir versprochen hatte, habe ich nie etwas gesehen **b** *(ghost)* erscheinen; *(indistinct object)* auftauchen

materially [mə'tɪərɪəlɪ] ADV grundlegend, wesentlich; **they are not ~ different** sie unterscheiden sich nicht wesentlich

matériel [mə,tɪərɪ'el] N *(US)* Ausrüstung *f*

maternal [mə'tɜːnl] ADJ mütterlich; **~ grandfather** Großvater mütterlicherseits; **~ affection** *or* **love** Mutterliebe *f*; **~ instincts** Mutterinstinkte *pl*, mütterliche Instinkte *pl*; **to be ~ to sb** sich jdm gegenüber mütterlich *or* wie eine Mutter verhalten; **~ health care** medizinische Betreuung für Mütter; **~ death rate** Müttersterblichkeit *f*

maternal deprivation N *(Psych)* Verlust *m* der Mutter

maternity [mə'tɜːnɪtɪ] N Mutterschaft *f*; **the idea of ~ never appealed to her** sie konnte sich nicht mit dem Gedanken befreunden, Mutter zu werden

maternity: **maternity allowance**, **maternity benefit** N *(Brit)* Mutterschaftshilfe *f*, Mutterschaftsgeld *nt*; **maternity dress** N Umstandskleid *nt*; **maternity home**, **maternity hospital** N Entbindungsheim *nt*; **maternity leave** N Mutterschaftsurlaub *m*; **maternity pay** N *(Brit)* Mutterschaftsgeld *nt (als Lohnfortzahlung)*; **maternity unit** N Entbindungsstation *f*; **maternity ward** N Entbindungsstation *f*

matey ['meɪtɪ] (*Brit inf*) ADJ (+er) *person* freundlich, kollegial; *(pej)* vertraulich; *atmosphere* freundschaftlich, kollegial; *gathering* vertraulich; **careful what you say, he's ~ with the director** sei vorsichtig mit dem, was du sagst, er steht mit dem Direktor auf Du und Du; **he was getting just a bit too ~ with my wife** er wurde ein wenig zu vertraulich mit meiner Frau N Kumpel *m*; *(warningly)* Freundchen *nt (inf)*

math [mæθ] N *(US inf)* Mathe *f (inf)*

mathematical [,mæθə'mætɪkəl] ADJ mathematisch

mathematically [,mæθə'mætɪkəlɪ] ADV mathematisch; *possible, impossible, complicated* rechnerisch; **~ speaking** *(= numerically speaking)* rein zahlenmäßig

mathematician [,mæθəmə'tɪʃən] N Mathematiker(in) *m(f)*

mathematics [,mæθə'mætɪks] N **a** *sing* Mathematik *f* **b** *pl* **the ~ of this are complicated** das ist mathematisch kompliziert

maths [mæθs] N *sing* (*Brit inf*) Mathe *f (inf)*

matinée ['mætɪneɪ] N Matinee *f*; *(in the afternoon)* Frühvorstellung *f*; **~ coat**, **~ jacket** *(for baby)* Ausfahrjäckchen *nt*

mating ['meɪtɪŋ] N Paarung *f*

mating: **mating call** N Lockruf *m*; *(of birds also)* Balzlaut *m*; *(of deer also)* Brunstschrei *m*; **mating dance** N Paarungstanz *m*; **mating season** N Paarungszeit *f*

matins ['mætɪnz] N *sing (Catholic)* Matutin *f*, Morgenlob *nt*; *(Anglican)* Morgenandacht *f*

matriarch ['meɪtrɪɑːk] N Matriarchin *f*

matriarchal [,meɪtrɪ'ɑːkl] ADJ matriarchalisch

matriarchy ['meɪtrɪɑːkɪ] N Matriarchat *nt*

matric [mə'trɪk] N *(inf)* = **matriculation**

matrices ['meɪtrɪsiːz] *pl of* **matrix**

matricide ['meɪtrɪsaɪd] N *(= act)* Muttermord *m*; *(= person)* Muttermörder(in) *m(f)*

matriculate [mə'trɪkjʊleɪt] VI sich immatrikulieren VT immatrikulieren

matriculation [mə,trɪkjʊ'leɪʃən] N Immatrikulation *f*; *(= ceremony)* Immatrikulationsfeier *f*

matrimonial [,mætrɪ'məʊnɪəl] ADJ ehelich

matrimonial: **matrimonial bed** N Ehebett *nt*; **matrimonial law** N Eherecht *nt*; **matrimonial vow** N Ehegelübde *nt*

matrimony ['mætrɪmənɪ] N *(form)* Ehe *f*; **to enter into holy ~** in den heiligen Stand der Ehe treten

matrix ['meɪtrɪks] N *pl* **matrices** *or* **-es** **a** *(= mould)* Matrize *f*, Mater *f* **b** *(Geol, Math)* Matrix *f*

matrix printer N Matrixdrucker *m*

matron ['meɪtrən] N **a** *(in hospital)* Oberin *f*, Oberschwester *f*; *(in school)* Schwester *f* **b** *(= married woman)* Matrone *f*

matronly ['meɪtrənlɪ] ADJ matronenhaft

matron of honour ['meɪtrənəv'ɒnəʳ] N *pl* **matrons of honour** *verheiratete Frau, die als Brautjungfer fungiert*

matt [mæt] ADJ matt, mattiert; **a paint with a ~ finish** ein Mattlack *m*

matted ['mætɪd] ADJ verfilzt; **hair ~ with blood/mud** mit Blut/Schlamm verkrustetes Haar

matter ['mætəʳ] N **a** *(= substance, not mind)* die Materie; **organic/inorganic ~** organische/anorganische Stoffe *pl*
b *(particular kind)* Stoff *m*; **advertising ~** Reklame *f*, Werbung *f*; **printed ~** Büchersendung *f*; **colouring ~** Farbstoff(e) *m(pl)*; **vegetable ~** pflanzliche Stoffe *pl*
c *(Med, = pus)* Eiter *m*
d *(Typ) (= copy)* Manuskript *nt*; *(= type set up)* Satz *m*
e *(= content)* Inhalt *m*; **the main ~ of his speech was …** (der) Hauptgegenstand seiner Rede war …
f *(= question, affair)* Sache *f*, Angelegenheit *f*; *(= topic)* Thema *nt*, Stoff *m*; **can I talk to you on a ~ of great urgency?** kann ich Sie in einer äußerst dringenden Angelegenheit sprechen?; **this is a ~ I know little about** darüber weiß ich wenig; **in the ~ of …** was … *(+acc)* anbelangt, hinsichtlich … *(+gen)*; **in the ~ of clothes** *etc* in puncto Kleidung *etc*; **there's the ~ of my expenses** da ist (noch) die Sache *or* Frage mit meinen Ausgaben; **it's no great ~** das macht nichts, das ist nicht so wichtig; **that's quite another ~** das ist etwas (ganz) anderes; **that's another ~ altogether, that's a very different ~** das ist etwas völlig anderes; **it will be no easy ~ (to) …** es wird nicht einfach sein, zu …; **it's a serious ~** das ist eine ernste Angelegenheit, die Sache ist ernst; **the ~ is closed** die Sache *or* der Fall ist erledigt
g matters PL Angelegenheiten *pl*; **business ~s** geschäftliche Angelegenheiten *or* Dinge *pl*, Geschäftliche(s) *nt*; **as ~s stand** wie die Dinge liegen; **to make ~s worse** zu allem Unglück (noch)
h for that ~ eigentlich; **I haven't seen him for weeks, nor for that ~ has anybody else** ich habe ihn seit Wochen schon nicht mehr gesehen, und eigentlich hat ihn sonst auch niemand gesehen; **he wants to complain about it and for that ~, so do I** er will sich darüber beschweren und ich eigentlich auch
i a ~ of eine Frage *(+gen)*, eine Sache von; **it's a ~ of form/time** das ist eine Formsache/Zeitfrage *or* Frage der Zeit; **it's a ~ of taste/opinion** das ist Geschmacks-/Ansichtssache; **it's a ~ of adjusting this part exactly** es geht darum, dieses Teil genau einzustellen; **it will be a ~ of a few weeks** es wird ein paar Wochen dauern; **it's a ~ of 10 miles from …** es sind 10 Meilen von …; **it's a ~ of a couple of hours** das ist eine Sache von ein paar Stunden; **if it's just a ~ of another 10 minutes, then I'll wait** wenn es sich nur noch um 10 Minuten handelt, dann warte ich solange; **in a ~ of minutes** innerhalb von Minuten; **it's a ~ of great concern to us** die Sache ist für uns von großer Bedeutung; **it's not just a ~ of increasing the money supply** es ist nicht damit getan, die Geldzufuhr zu erhöhen; **it's just a ~ of trying harder** man muss sich ganz einfach etwas mehr anstrengen; **as a ~ of course** selbstverständlich; **it's a ~ of course with us** für uns ist das eine Selbstverständlichkeit; **you should always take your passport with you as a ~ of course** es sollte für Sie eine Selbstverständlichkeit sein, stets Ihren Pass bei sich zu haben; **earthquakes happen as a ~ of course in that part of the world** Erdbeben sind in der Gegend an der Tagesordnung
j no ~! macht nichts; **I've decided to leave tomorrow, no ~ what** ich gehe morgen, egal

was passiert; **no ~ how/what/when/where** *etc* **...** egal, wie/was/wann/wo *etc* ...; **no ~ how you do it** wie du es auch machst, egal, wie du es machst; **no ~ how hot it was** auch *or* selbst bei der größten Hitze; **no ~ how hard he tried** so sehr er sich auch anstrengte

k **sth is the ~ with sb/sth** etw ist mit jdm/etw los; *(ill)* etw fehlt jdm; **what's the ~?** was ist (denn) los?, was ist (denn)?; **what's the ~ with you this morning? – nothing's the ~** was hast du denn heute Morgen? – gar nichts; **what's the ~ with having a little fun?** was ist denn schon dabei, wenn man ein bisschen Spaß hat?; **something's the ~ with the lights** mit dem Licht ist irgendetwas nicht in Ordnung; **as if nothing was the ~** als ob nichts (los) wäre

VI **it doesn't ~** (es *or* das) macht nichts, ist schon gut; **what does it ~?** was macht das schon?; **I forgot it, does it ~? – yes, it does ~** ich habs vergessen, ist das schlimm? – ja, das ist schlimm; **does it ~ to you if I go?** macht es dir etwas aus, wenn ich gehe?; **doesn't it ~ to you at all if I leave you?** macht es dir denn gar nichts aus, wenn ich dich verlasse?; **why should it ~ to me?** warum sollte mir das etwas ausmachen?; **why should it ~ to me if people are starving?** was geht es mich an, wenn Menschen verhungern?; **it doesn't ~ to me what you do** es ist mir (ganz) egal, was du machst; **some things ~ more than others** es ist aber nicht alles gleich wichtig; **the things which ~ in life** was im Leben wichtig ist *or* zählt; **poverty ~s** Armut geht jeden etwas an

matter-of-course [ˌmætərəvˈkɔːs] ADJ *attr* selbstverständlich, natürlich

matter-of-fact [ˌmætərəvˈfækt] ADJ *attr* sachlich, nüchtern; **he was very ~ about it** er blieb sehr sachlich *or* nüchtern

matter-of-factly [ˌmætərəvˈfæktlɪ] ADV *say, answer* nüchtern, sachlich; *explain* sachlich; **I hated her, he said ~** ich habe sie gehasst, sagte er nüchtern

Matthew [ˈmæθjuː] N Matthias *m*; *(Bibl)* Matthäus *m*

matting [ˈmætɪŋ] N Matten *pl*; *(= material)* Mattenmaterial *nt*

mattock [ˈmætək] N Breithacke *f*

mattress [ˈmætrɪs] N Matratze *f*

maturate [məˈtjʊəreɪt] VI **a** *(lit, fig)* reifen **b** *(Med, abscess etc)* reifen, zum Reifen kommen

maturation [ˌmætjʊˈreɪʃən] N Reifeprozess *m*, Reifung *f*

mature [məˈtjʊəˈ] **ADJ** *(+er)* **a** *person, mind* reif; *child* verständig, vernünftig; *(euph: = middle-aged)* gereift; **~ skin** reifere Haut; **his mind is very ~** geistig ist er schon sehr reif; **of ~ years, in his/her ~ years** im reiferen *or* vorgerückten Alter

b *wine* ausgereift; *sherry, port, cheese* reif; *fruit* reif, ausgereift; *plant* ausgewachsen; *plans* ausgereift; **after ~ deliberation** nach reiflicher Überlegung; **his ~r poems** seine reiferen Gedichte

c *(Comm) bill, debt* fällig

VI **a** *(person)* heranreifen *(geh)*, reifer werden; *(animal)* auswachsen; **his character ~d during the war years** der Krieg ließ ihn reifer werden *or* machte ihn reifer

b *(wine, cheese)* reifen, reif werden

c *(Comm)* fällig werden

VT **a** *person* reifer machen

b *wine, cheese* reifen lassen

maturely [məˈtjʊəlɪ] ADV *behave* verständig, vernünftig; **a more ~ conceived novel** ein ausgereifterer Roman

mature student N Spätstudierende(r) *mf*

maturity [məˈtjʊərɪtɪ] N **a** Reife *f*; **to reach ~** *(person)* erwachsen werden; *(legally)* volljährig werden; *(animal)* ausgewachsen sein; **poems of his ~** Gedichte *pl* seiner reiferen Jahre; **he's somewhat lacking in ~** ihm fehlt die nötige Reife **b** *(Comm)* Fälligkeit *f*; *(= date)* Fälligkeitsdatum *nt*

maty [ˈmeɪtɪ] ADJ, N *(Brit inf)* = **matey**

matzo [ˈmɒtsə] N Matze *f*, Matzen *m*

maudlin [ˈmɔːdlɪn] ADJ *story, play, sentimentality* rührselig; *person* sentimental, gefühlsselig; **don't get ~ about it** werden Sie deswegen nicht gleich sentimental

maul [mɔːl] VT übel zurichten; *(fig) writer, play etc* verreißen

mauling [ˈmɔːlɪŋ] N **to get a ~** *(player, team)* vernichtend geschlagen werden; *(author, book)* von der Kritik verrissen werden

Maundy money [ˈmɔːndɪˌmʌnɪ] N *speziell geprägte Münzen, die am Gründonnerstag vom britischen Monarchen als Almosen verteilt werden*

Maundy Thursday N Gründonnerstag *m*

Mauritius [məˈrɪʃəs] N Mauritius *nt*

mausoleum [ˌmɔːsəˈlɪəm] N Mausoleum *nt*

mauve [məʊv] **ADJ** mauve, malvenfarben **N** Mauvein *nt*

maverick [ˈmævərɪk] N **a** *(US Agr)* herrenloses Kalb/Rind *nt* ohne Brandzeichen **b** *(= dissenter)* Abtrünnige(r) *mf* **c** *(= independent person)* Alleingänger(in) *m(f)*, Einzelgänger(in) *m(f)*

maw [mɔː] N **a** *(Anat)* Magen *m*; *(of cow)* (Lab)-magen *m*; *(of bird)* Hals *m* **b** *(liter)* Maul *nt*; *(fig)* Rachen *m*, Schlund *m*

mawkish [ˈmɔːkɪʃ] ADJ rührselig, sentimental

mawkishness [ˈmɔːkɪʃnɪs] N Rührseligkeit *f*, Sentimentalität *f*

max **N** *abbr of* **maximum** max.; **to the ~** *(inf, run up debts, fill up tank)* bis zum Maximum; *enjoy life, live* in vollen Zügen; **to go to the ~** *(in partying)* die Sau rauslassen *(inf)*; **stressed to the ~** total gestresst *(inf)* **VT** **to ~ out sth, to ~ sth out** *(US inf)* etw ausschöpfen; **to ~ out one's credit card** seinen Kredit (auf der Kreditkarte) voll ausschöpfen

maxi [ˈmæksɪ] N *(Tex)* Maxirock *m*/-kleid *nt*/-mantel *m*

maxim [ˈmæksɪm] N Maxime *f*

maximal [ˈmæksɪməl] ADJ maximal

maximization [ˌmæksɪmaɪˈzeɪʃən] N Maximierung *f*

maximize [ˈmæksɪmaɪz] VT maximieren; *(Comput) window* maximieren, in maximaler Standardgröße darstellen

maximum [ˈmæksɪməm] **ADJ** *attr* Höchst-; *size, height, costs, length* maximal; **~ amount** *(= money)* Höchstbetrag *m*; **~ penalty/sentence** Höchststrafe *f*; **~ fine** maximale Geldstrafe; **~ credible accident** größter anzunehmender Unfall, GAU *m*; **for ~ effect** um die größte Wirkung zu erzielen; **they capitalized on our mistakes to ~ effect** sie haben unsere Fehler maximal ausgenutzt; **he scored ~ points** er hat die höchste Punktzahl erreicht; **a ~ speed of ...** eine Höchstgeschwindigkeit von ...; **we are producing at ~ speed** wir produzieren mit maximaler Geschwindigkeit; **five is the ~ number allowed in a taxi** maximal *or* höchstens fünf Leute dürfen in ein Taxi; **~ security wing/prison** Hochsicherheitstrakt *m*/-gefängnis *nt*

N *pl* **-s** *or* **maxima** [ˈmæksɪmə] Maximum *nt*; **up to a ~ of £8** bis zu maximal *or* höchstens £ 8; **temperatures reached a ~ of 34°** die Höchsttemperatur betrug 34°; **is that the ~ you can offer?** ist das Ihr höchstes Angebot?; **£20 at the ~** maximal 20 Pfund; **my salary is now at its ~** ich bin jetzt in der höchsten *or* obersten Gehaltsstufe; **to exploit sth to the ~** etw maximal ausnutzen

ADV *(= at the most)* maximal; **drink two cups of coffee a day ~** trinken Sie maximal zwei Tassen Kaffee pro Tag

maxiskirt [ˈmæksɪˌskɜːt] N Maxirock *m*

May [meɪ] **N** Mai *m* **VI** **to go maying** den Mai feiern

may [meɪ] ✪ 3.3, 9.1, 15.2, 26.3 VI *pret* **might** → *also* **might**[1] **a** *(possibility: also* **might***)* können; **it ~ rain** es könnte regnen, vielleicht regnet es; **it ~ be that ...** vielleicht..., es könnte sein, dass ...; **although it ~ have been useful** obwohl es hätte nützlich sein können; **he ~ not be hungry** vielleicht hat er keinen Hunger; **I ~ have said so** es kann *or* könnte sein, dass ich das gesagt habe; **you ~ be right** Sie könnten recht haben; **there ~ not be a next time** vielleicht gibts gar kein nächstes Mal; **they ~ be brothers for all I know** es kann *or* könnte sein, dass sie Brüder sind; **yes, I ~** ja, das ist möglich *or* das kann sein; **I ~ just do that** vielleicht tue ich das wirklich; **that's as ~ be** *(not might)* das mag ja sein(, aber ...); **one ~ well wonder why ...** die Frage wäre wohl berechtigt, warum ...; **you ~ well ask** das kann man wohl fragen

b *(permission)* dürfen; **~ I go now?** darf ich jetzt gehen?; **yes, you ~** ja, Sie dürfen

c **I hope he ~ succeed** ich hoffe, dass es ihm gelingt; **I had hoped he might succeed this time** ich hatte gehofft, es würde ihm diesmal gelingen; **such a policy as ~ or might bring peace** eine Politik, die zum Frieden führen könnte; **we ~ or might as well go** ich glaube, wir können (ruhig) gehen; **you ~ or might as well go now** du kannst jetzt ruhig gehen; **if they don't have it we ~ or might as well go to another firm** wenn sie es nicht haben, gehen wir am besten zu einer anderen Firma; **if they won't help we ~ or might just as well give up** wenn sie uns nicht helfen, können wir (ja) gleich aufgeben

d *(in wishes)* **~ you be successful!** (ich wünsche Ihnen) viel Erfolg!; **~ your days be full of joy** mögen Ihnen glückliche Tage beschieden sein; **~ you be very happy together** ich wünsche euch, dass ihr sehr glücklich miteinander werdet; **~ the Lord have mercy on your soul** der Herr sei deiner Seele gnädig; **~ you be forgiven** *(inf)* so was tut man doch nicht!; **~ I be struck dead if I lie!** ich will auf der Stelle tot umfallen, wenn das nicht stimmt

e *(in questions)* **who ~ or might you be?** und wer sind Sie?, wer sind Sie denn?

Maya [ˈmeɪjə] N **a** Maya *mf* **b** *(Ling)* Maya *nt*, Mayasprache *f*

Mayan [ˈmeɪjən] **ADJ** Maya-; **~ ruins** Mayaruinen *pl* **N** **a** Maya *mf* **b** *(Ling)* Maya(sprache *f*) *nt*

maybe [ˈmeɪbiː] ✪ 2.2, 4 ADV vielleicht, kann sein(, dass ...); **that's as ~** kann schon sein; **~, ~ not** vielleicht, vielleicht auch nicht

May: **May beetle, May bug** N *(Zool)* Maikäfer *m*; **May Day** N der 1. Mai, der Maifeiertag; **Mayday** N *(= distress call)* Maydaysignal *nt*, SOS-Ruf *m*; *(said)* Mayday

mayest [ˈmeɪəst] *(obs)*, **mayst** *(obs) 2nd pers sing of* **may**

mayfly [ˈmeɪflaɪ] N Eintagsfliege *f*

mayhem [ˈmeɪhem] N **a** *(US Jur)* (schwere) Körperverletzung **b** *(= havoc)* Chaos *nt*

mayn't [meɪnt] *contr of* **may not**

mayo [ˈmeɪəʊ] N *(US inf)* Mayonnaise *f*, Majonäse *f*, Mayo *f (inf)*

mayonnaise [ˌmeɪəˈneɪz] N Mayonnaise *f*, Majonäse *f*

mayor [mɛəˈ] N Bürgermeister(in) *m(f)*

mayoral [ˈmɛərəl] ADJ des Bürgermeisters

mayoralty [ˈmɛərəltɪ] N *(= office)* Bürgermeisteramt *nt*, Amt *nt* des Bürgermeisters; **during his ~ ...** als er Bürgermeister war ..., während seiner Zeit als Bürgermeister ...

mayoress [ˈmɛəres] N Frau *f* Bürgermeister; *(= lady mayor)* Bürgermeisterin *f*

may: **maypole** N Maibaum *m*; **May queen** N Maikönigin *f*

mayst [meɪst] *(obs)* = **mayest**

maze [meɪz] N Irrgarten *m*; *(= puzzle)* Labyrinth *nt*; *(fig)* Wirrwarr *m*, Gewirr *nt*; **the ~ of streets** das Gewirr der Straßen

mazurka [məˈzɜːkə] N Mazurka *f*

MB[1] *abbr of* **Bachelor of Medicine**

MB[2] *abbr of* **megabyte**

MBA *abbr of* **Master of Business Administration**; **he's doing an ~** er studiert Betriebswirtschaft; **he has an ~** er ist Betriebswirt

MBE *abbr of* **Member of the Order of the British Empire** *britischer Verdienstorden*

MBO N **a** *(Fin) abbr of* **management buyout** **b** *abbr of* **management by objectives**

MC **a** *abbr of* **Master of Ceremonies** **b** *abbr of* **Military Cross**

MCA *abbr of* **maximum credible accident**

MCAT N *(US Univ) abbr of* **Medical College Admissions Test**

MCC *abbr of* **Marylebone Cricket Club**

McCoy [mə'kɔɪ] N → **real**

m-commerce N *(Comm)* M-Commerce *m*, mobiler Handel

MCP *(Brit inf) abbr of* **male chauvinist pig**

MD **a** *abbr of* **Doctor of Medicine** Dr. med. **b** *abbr of* **managing director** **c** *abbr of* **Minidisc** MD *f*; **MD-player** MD-Spieler *m*

m.d. *abbr of* **mentally deficient**

me [mi:] PRON **a** *(dir obj, with prep +acc)* mich; *(indir obj, with prep +dat)* mir; **with my books about me** mit meinen Büchern um mich herum; **he's older than me** er ist älter als ich **b** *(emph)* ich; **who, me?** wer, ich?; **it's me** ich bins

ME **a** *abbr of* **Middle English** **b** *(US) abbr of* **medical examination**

mead[1] [mi:d] N *(= drink)* Met *m*

mead[2] N *(old, poet)* Aue *f*

meadow ['medəʊ] N Wiese *f*, Weide *f*; **in the ~** auf der Wiese *or* Weide

meadow: **meadowland** ['medəʊlænd] N Weideland *nt*; **meadowlark** N Wiesenstärling *m*; **meadowsweet** N Mädesüß *nt*

meagre, *(US)* **meager** ['mi:gəʳ] ADJ **a** spärlich; *amount, crowd* kläglich; *meal* dürftig, kärglich; **to eke out a ~ existence** ein kümmerliches Dasein fristen; **he earns a ~ £500 a month** er verdient magere *or* mickrige *(inf)* £ 500 im Monat **b** *(liter. = lean)* hager

meagrely, *(US)* **meagerly** ['mi:gəlɪ] ADV spärlich; *live* kärglich

meagreness, *(US)* **meagerness** ['mi:gənɪs] N Spärlichkeit *f*; *(of amount, crowd)* Kläglichkeit *f*; *(of meal)* Dürftigkeit *f*, Kärglichkeit *f*

meal[1] [mi:l] N Schrot(mehl *nt*) *m*; **meat and bone ~** Tiermehl *nt*

meal[2] N **a** Mahlzeit *f*; *(= food)* Essen *nt*; **come round for a ~** komm zum Essen (zu uns); **to go for a ~** essen gehen; **to have a (good) ~** (gut) essen; **hot ~s** warme Mahlzeiten *pl*, warmes Essen; **I haven't had a ~ for two days** ich habe seit zwei Tagen nichts Richtiges mehr gegessen; **to make a ~ of sth** *(inf)* etw auf sehr umständliche Art machen; **don't make a ~ of it** *(inf)* nun übertreibs mal nicht *(inf)* **b** *(= set meal)* Menü *nt*

mealie meal ['mi:lɪmi:l] N Maismehl *nt*

meal: **meals on wheels** N Essen *nt* auf Rädern; **meal ticket** N **a** *(US: lit)* Essensbon *m* *or* -marke *f* **b** *(fig)* **that letter of introduction was his ~ for the next few months** dank des Empfehlungsschreibens konnte er sich die nächsten paar Monate über Wasser halten; **a boyfriend is just a ~ to a lot of girls** viele Mädchen haben nur einen Freund, um sich von ihm aushalten zu lassen; **mealtime** N Essenszeit *f*; **you shouldn't smoke at ~s** Sie sollten während des Essens nicht rauchen

mealworm ['mi:lwɜ:m] N Mehlwurm *m*

mealy ['mi:lɪ] ADJ mehlig

mealy-mouthed ['mi:lɪ'maʊðd] ADJ unaufrichtig; *politician* schönfärberisch; **let's not be ~ about it** wir wollen doch mal nicht so um den heißen Brei herumreden

mean[1] [mi:n] ADJ *(+er)* **a** *(esp Brit: = miserly)* geizig, knauserig; **don't be ~!** sei doch nicht so geizig *or* knauserig!; **you ~ thing!** du Geizhals *or* Geizkragen!

b *(= unkind, spiteful)* gemein; **don't be ~!** sei nicht so gemein *or* fies! *(inf)*; **you ~ thing!** du gemeines *or* fieses Stück! *(inf)*, du Miststück! *(inf)*; **it made me feel ~** ich kam mir richtig schäbig *or* gemein vor

c *(= base, inferior) birth, motives* niedrig; **the ~est citizen** der Geringste unter den Bürgern *(old)*

d *(= shabby, unimpressive) shack, house* schäbig, armselig

e *(= vicious)* bösartig; *look* gehässig, hinterhältig; *criminal* niederträchtig, abscheulich

f **he is no ~ player** er ist ein beachtlicher Spieler; **he plays a ~ game of poker** er ist ein ausgefuchster Pokerspieler *(inf)*; **that's no ~ feat** diese Aufgabe ist nicht zu unterschätzen *or* nicht von Pappe *(inf)*; **a sportsman/politician of no ~ ability** ein sehr fähiger Sportler/Politiker

mean[2] **N** *(= middle term)* Durchschnitt *m*; *(Math)* Durchschnitt *m*, Mittelwert *m*, Mittel *nt*; **the golden** *or* **happy ~** die goldene Mitte **ADJ** mittlere(r, s); **~ sea level** Normalnull *nt*

mean[3] ✪ 6.3, 8.2, 16.1, 26.3 *pret, ptp* **meant** VT **a** *(= signify)* bedeuten; *(person: = refer to, have in mind)* meinen; **what do you ~ by that?** was willst du damit sagen?; **the name ~s nothing to me** der Name sagt mir nichts; **it ~s starting all over again** das bedeutet *or* das heißt, dass wir wieder ganz von vorne anfangen müssen; **this will ~ great changes** dies wird bedeutende Veränderungen zur Folge haben; **a pound ~s a lot to her** für sie ist ein Pfund eine Menge Geld; **your friendship/he ~s a lot to me** deine Freundschaft/er bedeutet mir viel; **you ~ everything to me** du bist alles für mich

b *(= intend)* beabsichtigen; **to ~ to do sth** etw tun wollen; *(= do on purpose)* etw absichtlich tun; **to be ~t for sb/sth** für jdn/etw bestimmt sein; **to ~ sb to do sth** wollen, dass jd etw tut; **sth is ~t to be sth** etw soll etw sein; **what do you ~ to do?** was wirst du tun?, was hast du vor?; **I only ~t to help** ich wollte nur helfen; **of course it hurt, I ~t it to** *or* **it was ~t to** natürlich tat das weh, das war Absicht; **without ~ing to sound rude** ich möchte nicht unverschämt klingen(, aber …); **I ~t it as a joke** das sollte ein Witz sein; **I ~t you to have it** das solltest du haben; **I was ~t to do that** ich hätte das tun sollen; **you are ~t to be on time** du solltest pünktlich sein; **he wasn't ~t to be a leader** er war nicht zum Führer bestimmt; **I thought it was ~t to be hot in the south** ich dachte immer, dass es im Süden so heiß sei; **I ~ to be obeyed** ich verlange, dass man mir gehorcht; **I ~ to have it** ich bin fest entschlossen, es zu bekommen; **this pad is ~t for drawing** dieser Block ist zum Zeichnen gedacht *or* da *(inf)*; **if he ~s to be awkward …** wenn er vorhat, Schwierigkeiten zu machen …; **this present was ~t for you** dieses Geschenk sollte für dich sein *or* war für dich gedacht → **business**

c *(= be serious about)* ernst meinen; **I ~ it!** das ist mein Ernst!, ich meine das ernst!; **do you ~ to say you're not coming?** willst du damit sagen *or* soll das heißen, dass du nicht kommst?; **I ~ what I say** ich sage das im Ernst; **do you really ~ it this time?** ist es dir diesmal ernst *or* Ernst damit?

d **he ~s well/no harm** er meint es gut/nicht böse; **to ~ well by sb** es gut mit jdm meinen; **to ~ sb no harm** es gut mit jdm meinen, jdm nichts Böses wollen; *(physically)* jdm nichts tun; *(in past tense)* jdm nichts tun wollen; **I ~t no harm by what I said** was ich da gesagt habe, war nicht böse gemeint

meander [mɪ'ændəʳ] VI *(river)* sich (dahin)schlängeln, mäandern; *(person)* wirr sein; *(= go off subject)* (vom Thema) abschweifen; *(walking)* schlendern

meanderings [mɪ'ændərɪŋz] PL *(of river)* Windungen *pl*, Mäander *m*; *(= talk)* Gefasel *nt*; *(off subject)* Abschweifungen *pl*, Exkurse *pl*; **the ~ of his mind** seine verworrenen Gedankengänge

meanie ['mi:nɪ] N *(esp Brit inf: = miserly person)* Geizhals *or* -kragen *m*; *(= nasty person)* Miststück *nt (inf)*

meaning ['mi:nɪŋ] **ADJ** *look etc* vielsagend, bedeutsam **N** Bedeutung *f*; *(= sense: of words, poem etc also)* Sinn *m*; **a look full of ~** ein bedeutungsvoller *or* bedeutsamer Blick; **what's the ~ of (the word) "hick"?** was soll das Wort „hick" heißen *or* bedeuten?; **to mistake sb's ~** jdn missverstehen; **do you get my ~?** haben Sie mich (richtig) verstanden?; **you don't know the ~ of love/hunger** du weißt ja gar nicht, was Liebe/Hunger ist *or* bedeutet; **what's the ~ of this?** was hat denn das zu bedeuten?, was soll denn das (heißen)?

meaningful ['mi:nɪŋfʊl] ADJ **a** *(= having meaning) word, statement, symbol* mit Bedeutung; *(Ling) unit* bedeutungstragend; *poem, film* bedeutungsvoll; *(= expressive) look, glance* bedeutungsvoll; **to be ~** eine Bedeutung haben **b** *(= comprehensible) advice, information, question, answer, results* sinnvoll; **the statistics only become ~ when …** die Zahlen ergeben nur dann einen Sinn, wenn … **c** *(= purposeful) job, negotiations* sinnvoll; *relationship* tiefer gehend

meaningfully ['mi:nɪŋfəlɪ] ADV **a** *(= pointedly) look* bedeutungsvoll; *say, add* vielsagend **b** *(= comprehensibly) explain, answer* sinnvoll **c** *(= purposefully) spend one's time, participate, negotiate* sinnvoll

meaningless ['mi:nɪŋlɪs] ADJ **a** *(semantically) word, symbol etc* ohne Bedeutung, bedeutungslos **b** sinnlos; **my life is ~** mein Leben hat keinen Sinn

meanly ['mi:nlɪ] ADV **a** *(esp Brit: = ungenerously)* geizig, knauserig **b** *(= unkindly) behave, treat* gemein; **~, he took her last cigarette** er war so gemein, ihre letzte Zigarette zu nehmen

meanness ['mi:nnɪs] N **a** *(esp Brit: = miserliness)* Geiz *m*, Knauserigkeit *f* **b** *(= unkindness, spite)* Gemeinheit *f* **c** *(= baseness: of birth, motives)* Niedrigkeit *f* **d** *(= shabbiness)* Schäbigkeit *f*, Armseligkeit *f* **e** *(= viciousness)* Bösartigkeit *f*; *(of look)* Gehässigkeit *f*, Hinterhältigkeit *f*; *(of criminal)* Niedertracht *f*

means [mi:nz] ✪ 17.1 N **a** *sing (= method)* Möglichkeit *f*; *(= instrument)* Mittel *nt*; **a ~ of transport** ein Beförderungsmittel *nt*; **a ~ of escape** eine Fluchtmöglichkeit; **a ~ to an end** ein Mittel *nt* zum Zweck; **I have/there is no ~ of doing it** es ist mir/es ist unmöglich, das zu tun; **is there any ~ of doing it?** ist es irgendwie möglich, das zu tun?; **there must be a ~ of doing it** es muss doch irgendwie *or* auf irgendeine Art zu machen sein; **we've no ~ of knowing** wir können nicht wissen; **he was the ~ of sending it** man ließ es durch ihn überbringen; **they used him as the ~ of getting the heroin across the border** sie benutzten ihn, um das Heroin über die Grenze zu bringen; **all known ~ have been tried** man hat alles Mögliche versucht; **by ~ of sth** durch etw, mittels einer Sache *(gen) (form)*; **by ~ of doing sth** dadurch, dass man etw tut; **by this ~** dadurch, auf diese Weise; **by some ~ or other** auf irgendeine Art und Weise, irgendwie

b *sing* **by all ~!** (aber) selbstverständlich *or* natürlich!; **by all ~ take one** nehmen Sie sich ruhig (eins); **by no ~, not by any ~** keineswegs, durchaus nicht; *(= under no circumstances)* auf keinen Fall

c *pl (= wherewithal)* Mittel *pl*; *(= financial means)* Gelder *pl*, Mittel *pl*; **a man of ~** ein vermögender Mann; **private ~** private Mittel *pl*; **that is within/beyond my ~** das kann ich mir leisten/nicht leisten; **to live beyond one's ~** über seine Verhältnisse leben; **to live within one's ~** seinen Verhältnissen entsprechend leben

mean-spirited [mi:n'spɪrɪtɪd] ADJ geizig, knauserig

means test N Einkommens- *or* Vermögensveranlagung *f*

meant [ment] *pret, ptp of* **mean**[3]

meantime ['mi:ntaɪm] **ADV** inzwischen **N** **for the ~** vorerst, im Augenblick, einstweilen; **in the ~** in der Zwischenzeit, inzwischen

meanwhile ['mi:nwaɪl] ADV **a** *(= in the meantime)* inzwischen **b** *(= in contrast)* währenddessen; **every packet carries a warning, ~ many continue to smoke** auf jeder Packung steht eine Warnung, trotzdem rauchen viele auch weiterhin

measles ['mi:zlz] N *sing* Masern *pl*

measly ['mi:zlɪ] ADJ *(+er) (inf)* mick(e)rig *(inf)*, poplig *(inf)*

measurable ['meʒərəbl] ADJ messbar; *(= perceptible)* erkennbar

measurably ['meʒərəblɪ] ADV messbar; *(= perceptibly)* deutlich

measure ['meʒəʳ] **N** **a** *(= unit of measurement)* Maß(einheit *f*) *nt*; **a ~ of length** ein Längenmaß *nt*; **to have sth made to ~** etw nach Maß anfertigen lassen; **the furniture has been made to ~** die Möbel sind Maßarbeit; **beyond ~** grenzenlos; **her joy was beyond** *or* **knew no ~** ihre Freude kannte keine Grenzen → **weight**
b *(= object for measuring)* Maß *nt*; *(graduated for length)* Maßstab *m*; *(graduated for volume)* Messbecher *m*
c *(= amount measured)* Menge *f*; **a small ~ of flour** ein wenig Mehl; **wine is sold in ~s of 1/4 litre** *(Brit)* *or* **liter** *(US)* Wein wird in Vierteln ausgeschenkt; **to give sb full/short ~** *(barman)* richtig/zu wenig ausschenken; *(grocer)* richtig/zu wenig abwiegen; **in full ~** in höchstem Maße; **for good ~** zur Sicherheit, sicherheitshalber; **... and another one for good ~** ... und noch eines obendrein
d *(fig: = yardstick)* Maßstab *m (of* für); **can we regard this exam as a ~ of intelligence?** kann diese Prüfung als Intelligenzmaßstab gelten?; **MacLeod's approval is the ~ of a good whisky** MacLeods Urteil in Bezug auf Whisky ist (für mich) maßgebend *or* ausschlaggebend; **please consider this as a ~ of my esteem for ...** bitte betrachten Sie dies als Ausdruck meiner Anerkennung für ...; **it gave us some ~ of the difficulty** es gab uns einen Begriff von der Schwierigkeit; **it's a ~ of his skill as a writer that ...** seine schriftstellerischen Fähigkeiten lassen sich daran beurteilen, dass ...; **words cannot always give the ~ of one's feelings** Worte können Gefühle nicht immer angemessen ausdrücken
e *(= extent)* **in some ~** in gewisser Hinsicht *or* Beziehung; **some ~ of** ein gewisses Maß an; **to a large ~, in large ~** in hohem Maße; **to get the ~ of sb/sth** jdn/etw (richtig) einschätzen
f *(= step)* Maßnahme *f*; **to take ~s to do sth** Maßnahmen ergreifen, um etw zu tun
g *(Poet)* Versmaß *nt*
h *(US Mus)* Takt *m*
i *(old, = dance)* Tanz *m*; **to tread a ~ with sb** mit jdm ein Tänzchen wagen
VT messen; *length also* abmessen; *room also* ausmessen; *(= take sb's measurements)* Maß nehmen bei; *(fig)* beurteilen, abschätzen; *words* abwägen; **a ~d mile** genau eine Meile; **to ~ one's length** *(fig)* der Länge nach hinfallen
VI messen; **what does it ~?** wie viel misst es?, wie groß ist es?

▶ **measure off** VT *sep area, length of cloth* abmessen

▶ **measure out** VT *sep* abmessen; *weights also* abwiegen

▶ **measure up** **VT** *sep* **a** *(= take measurements of) wood, room etc* abmessen; *person for suit etc* Maß nehmen bei **b** *(fig: = assess) situation* abschätzen; *person* einschätzen **VI** **a** *(= be good enough, compare well)* **he didn't measure up** er hat enttäuscht; **to measure up to sth** an etw *(acc)* herankommen; **visually he measured up (to the description)** vom Aussehen her passte er (auf die Beschreibung); **it's a hard job, but he should measure up** das ist eine schwierige Aufgabe, aber er sollte ihr gewachsen sein **b** *(= take measurements)* Maß nehmen, messen

measured ['meʒəd] ADJ *tread* gemessen *(liter)*; *tone* bedacht, bedächtig; *words* wohlüberlegt, durchdacht; *approach, response* maßvoll; **he walked with ~ steps** er ging gemessenen Schrittes *(liter)*; **at a ~ pace** in gemäßigtem Tempo; **he is becoming calmer and more ~** er wird ruhiger und bedächtiger

measureless ['meʒəlɪs] ADJ unermesslich

measurement ['meʒəmənt] N **a** *(= act)* Messung *f*; **the metric system of ~** das metrische Maßsystem **b** *(= measure)* Maß *nt*; *(= figure)* Messwert *m*; *(fig)* Maßstab *m*; **to take sb's ~s** an jdm *or* bei jdm Maß nehmen

measuring ['meʒərɪŋ] N Messen *nt*; **to take ~s of sth** etw messen

measuring ['meʒərɪŋ] *in cpds* Mess-; **measuring device** N Messgerät *nt*; **measuring equipment** N Messvorrichtungen *pl*; **measuring instrument** N Messinstrument *nt*; **measuring jug** N Messbecher *m*; **measuring range** N *(Phys)* Messbereich *m*; **measuring tape** N Bandmaß *nt*, Metermaß *nt*

meat [mi:t] N **a** Fleisch *nt*; **cold ~** kalter Braten; *(= sausage)* Wurst *f*; **assorted cold ~s** Aufschnitt *m* **b** *(old: = food)* Essen *nt*, Speise *f* *(liter)*; **food and drink** Speise und Trank; **one man's ~ is another man's poison** *(Prov)* des einen Freud, des andern Leid *(Prov)* **c** *(fig: of argument, book)* Substanz *f*; **a book with some ~ in it** ein aussagestarkes Buch

meat *in cpds* Fleisch-; **meatball** N Fleischkloß *m*; **meat-chopper** N **a** *(= knife)* Hackmesser *nt* **b** *(= mincer)* Fleischhackmaschine *f*, Fleischwolf *m*; **meat-grinder** N *(US)* Fleischwolf *m*; **meathead** N *(US inf)* Dummkopf *m*; **meat loaf** N ≈ Fleischkäse *m*; **meat market** N **a** *(for animals)* Viehmarkt *m* **b** *(pej inf) (for people)* Aufreißschuppen *m (inf)*; *(= beauty contest etc)* Fleischbeschau *f (inf)*; **meat meal** N Fleischmehl *nt*; **meatpacker** N *(US Comm)* Arbeiter(in) *m(f)* in der Fleischverarbeitung; **meatpacking** N *(US Comm)* Fleischverarbeitung *f*; *(= industry)* Fleischverarbeitungsindustrie *f*; **meat products** PL Fleisch- und Wurstwaren *pl*; **meat safe** N Fliegenschrank *m*

meaty ['mi:tɪ] ADJ *(+er)* **a** *soup, sauce, meal, dish* mit viel Fleisch; **~ chunks** Fleischbrocken *pl*; **~ texture** Fleischstruktur *f*; **this is a ~ fish** dieser Fisch hat Fleischcharakter **b** *(= fleshy) arms, hands* fleischig **c** *(fig) book* aussagestark, gehaltvoll; *role, part* anspruchsvoll

Mecca ['mekə] N *(lit, fig)* Mekka *nt*

mechanic [mɪ'kænɪk] N Mechaniker(in) *m(f)*

mechanical [mɪ'kænɪkəl] ADJ *(lit, fig)* mechanisch; *toy* technisch; **a ~ device** ein Mechanismus *m*

mechanical: **mechanical digger** N Bagger *m*; *(also* **mechanical shovel**) Löffelbagger *m*; **mechanical engineer** N Maschinenbauer(in) *or* -bauingenieur(in) *m(f)*; **mechanical engineering** N Maschinenbau *m*

mechanically [mɪ'kænɪkəlɪ] ADV *(lit, fig)* mechanisch; **~-minded** technisch begabt; **~ recovered meat** Separatorenfleisch *nt*

mechanical shovel N Löffelbagger *m*

mechanician [ˌmekə'nɪʃən] N → **mechanic**

mechanics [mɪ'kænɪks] N **a** *sing (= subject) (= engineering)* Maschinenbau *m*; *(Phys)* Mechanik *f*; **home ~ for the car-owner** kleine Maschinenkunde für den Autobesitzer **b** *pl (= technical aspects)* Mechanik *f*, Mechanismus *m*; *(fig: of writing etc)* Technik *f*; **there is something wrong with the ~ of the car** das Auto ist mechanisch nicht in Ordnung; **I don't understand the ~ of parliamentary procedure** ich verstehe den Mechanismus parlamentarischer Abläufe nicht

mechanism ['mekənɪzəm] N Mechanismus *m*

mechanistic ADJ, **mechanistically** ADV [ˌmekə'nɪstɪk, -əlɪ] mechanistisch

mechanization [ˌmekənaɪ'zeɪʃən] N Mechanisierung *f*

mechanize ['mekənaɪz] VT mechanisieren

mechanized ['mekənaɪzd] ADJ mechanisiert; **highly ~ production** stark automatisierte Produktion

med *abbr of* **medium**

medal ['medl] N Medaille *f*; *(= decoration)* Orden *m*

medalist N *(US)* = **medallist**

medallion [mɪ'dæljən] N Medaillon *nt*; *(= medal)* Medaille *f*

medallist, *(US)* **medalist** ['medəlɪst] N Medaillengewinner(in) *m(f)*

meddle ['medl] VI *(= interfere)* sich einmischen *(in* in *+acc)*; *(= tamper)* sich zu schaffen machen, herumfummeln *(inf)* *(with* an *+dat)*; **to ~ with sb** sich mit jdm einlassen; **he's not a man to ~ with** mit ihm ist nicht gut Kirschen essen; **he's always meddling** er mischt sich in alles ein

meddler ['medləʳ] N **he's a terrible ~** er muss sich immer in alles einmischen

meddlesome ['medlsəm] ADJ, **meddling** ['medlɪŋ] ADJ *attr* **she's a ~ old busybody** sie mischt sich dauernd in alles ein

media ['mi:dɪə] N *pl of* **medium** Medien *pl*; **he works in the ~** er ist im Mediensektor tätig *or* beschäftigt; **~ coverage** Berichterstattung *f* in den Medien; **to get too much ~ coverage** zu viel Publicity bekommen; **~ bashing** *(inf)* Medienschelte *f*

media competence N Medienkompetenz *f*

mediaeval ADJ = **medieval**

mediaevalist N = **medievalist**

media: **media environment** N *(fig)* Medienlandschaft *f*; **media event** N Medienereignis *nt*

mediagenic [ˌmi:dɪə'dʒi:nɪc] ADJ *(esp US) event, story, politician etc* medienwirksam

medial ['mi:dɪəl] ADJ *(= in the middle)* mittlere(r, s); **in (word) ~ position** *(Ling)* im Inlaut

media landscape N *(fig)* Medienlandschaft *f*

media mogul N Medienmogul *m*

median ['mi:dɪən] **ADJ** mittlere(r, s) **N** *(Math)* Zentralwert *m*

median strip N *(US)* Mittelstreifen *m*

media: **mediaperson** N *pl* **mediapeople** *(well-known)* Medienstar *m*; **media player** N *(Comput: program)* Medienwiedergabe *f*; **media resonance** N Medienresonanz *f*; **media studies** PL Medienwissenschaft *f*

mediate[1] ['mi:dɪət] ADJ *(rare)* mittelbar

mediate[2] ['mi:dɪeɪt] **VI** vermitteln **VT** *settlement* aushandeln, herbeiführen

mediation [ˌmi:dɪ'eɪʃən] N Vermittlung *f*

mediator ['mi:dɪeɪtəʳ] N Vermittler(in) *m(f)*, Mittelsmann *m*, Mittelsperson *f*

mediatorship ['mi:dɪeɪtəʃɪp] N **a** *(= role of mediator)* Vermittleramt *nt*, Vermittlerrolle *f* **b** *(= help, arrangement)* Vermittlung *f*

mediatory ['mi:dɪətərɪ] ADJ vermittelnd, des Vermittlers; **in a ~ capacity** als Vermittler

medic ['medɪk] N *(inf)* Mediziner(in) *m(f) (inf)*

Medicaid ['medɪˌkeɪd] N *(US) staatliche Krankenversicherung und Gesundheitsfürsorge für Einkommensschwache unter 65 in den USA* → *also* **Medicare**

MEDICAID, MEDICARE

Medicaid ist ein gemeinsames Programm der US-Bundesregierung und der Bundesstaaten, mit dem die stationäre Krankenhausbehandlung und medizinische Versorgung für all diejenigen Personen unter 65 Jahren finanziert wird, die an oder unterhalb der offiziellen staatlichen Armutsgrenze leben. Die Berechtigungskriterien wie auch die Leistungspalette variieren von Staat zu Staat und können auch Kosten beinhalten, die nicht von **Medicare** getragen werden.
Medicare ist das staatlich finanzierte US-Krankenversicherungsprogramm, das speziell die Kosten für Krankenhausbehandlung und medizinische Versorgung für über 65-jährige, Nierenpatienten und einige Behinderte übernimmt. Die Mitglieder zahlen einen monatlichen Beitrag. Die Behandlung erfolgt durch bestimmte Krankenhäuser und Ärzte, die am Programm teilnehmen. Parallel dazu gibt es ein Privatversicherungsprogramm, **Medigap**, das als Zusatzversicherung zu **Medicare** fungiert.
Alle, die nicht durch **Medicare** oder **Medicaid** abgedeckt sind, müssen ihre medizinische Versorgung durch private Krankenversicherungen absichern.

medical ['medɪkəl] ADJ *(= related to science) research, study, journal, faculty, training* medizinisch; *(in military contexts)* Sanitäts-; *(= relating to doctors) test, examination, treatment, attention, advice, expertise, care, staff* ärztlich; ~ **advances** Fortschritte *pl* in der Medizin; **the ~ profession** die Ärzteschaft; **the ~ world** die Welt der Medizin; *(= doctors)* die Ärzteschaft; **I'm not a ~ man** ich bin kein Arzt; ~ **condition** *or* **disorder** Erkrankung *f*; ~ **opinion** ärztliches Gutachten
N (ärztliche) Untersuchung; **have you had your ~?** bist du zur Untersuchung gewesen?, hast du dich untersuchen lassen?

medical: **medical assistant** N medizinischer Assistent, medizinische Assistentin; *(US)* ≈ Arzthelfer(in) *m(f)*; **medical authority** N Gesundheitsbehörde *f*; **medical card** N *(Brit)* Krankenversicherungsausweis *m*; **medical centre**, *(US)* **medical center** N *(Brit)* Ärztehaus *nt*; *(US)* Krankenhaus *nt*, Klinik *f*; **medical certificate** N ärztliches Attest; **Medical College Admissions Test** N *(US Univ)* Zulassungsprüfung *f* zum Medizinstudium; **medical corps** N *(Mil)* Sanitätstruppe *f*; **medical doctor** N Arzt *m*, Ärztin *f*; **medical examiner** N *(US Jur)* Gerichtsmediziner(in) *m(f)*; **medical history** N **a** *(= medical background)* **her ~** ihre Krankengeschichte **b** *(= history of medicine)* die Geschichte der Medizin; **that made ~** das hat in der Medizin Geschichte gemacht; **medical insurance** N Krankenversicherung *f*; **medical jurisprudence** N Gerichtsmedizin *f*

medically ['medɪkəlɪ] ADV medizinisch; *examine* ärztlich; **to be ~ qualified/trained** eine medizinische Ausbildung absolviert/gemacht haben

medical: **medical officer** N *(Mil)* Stabsarzt *m*; *(= official)* Amtsarzt *m*; **medical practice** N *(= business)* Arztpraxis *f*; *(= procedure)* medizinisches Verfahren; **in western ~** in der westlichen Medizin; **medical practitioner** N Arzt *m*, Ärztin *f*; **medical profession** N **a** *(= doctor's job)* Arztberuf *m* **b** *(= doctors as a whole)* Ärzteschaft *f no pl*; **medical record** N *(= medical background)* Krankengeschichte *f*; **~s** *(= detailed notes)* Krankenblatt *nt*; **Medical Register** N *(Brit)* Ärzteregister *nt*; **to strike sb off the ~** jdm die Approbation entziehen; **Medical Research Council** N *(Brit) Organisation zur Förderung der medizinischen Forschung*; **medical school** N ≈ medizinische Hochschule; **medical science** N die ärztliche Wissenschaft; **medical student** N Medizinstudent(in) *m(f)*; **medical unit** N *(Mil)* Sanitätsbataillon *nt*; **medical ward** N Innere Abteilung

medicament [me'dɪkəmənt] N Medikament *nt*, Mittel *nt*

Medicare ['medɪˌkeəʳ] N *(US) staatliche Krankenversicherung und Gesundheitsfürsorge für ältere Bürger in den USA* → *also* **Medicaid**

medicate ['medɪkeɪt] VT (medizinisch) behandeln

medicated ['medɪkeɪtɪd] ADJ medizinisch

medication [ˌmedɪ'keɪʃən] N *(act)* (medizinische) Behandlung; *(= drugs etc)* Verordnung *f*, Medikamente *pl*

medicinal [me'dɪsɪnl] ADJ Heil-, heilend; **for ~ purposes** zu medizinischen Zwecken; **I need a whisky - for ~ purposes** *(hum)* ich brauche einen Whisky, aus medizinischen Gründen; **the ~ properties of various herbs** die Heilkraft verschiedener Kräuter

medicinally [me'dɪsɪnəlɪ] ADV *use, take* zu Heilzwecken, zu medizinischen Zwecken; *valuable* medizinisch; **~, it aids digestion** medizinisch gesehen fördert es die Verdauung

medicine ['medsɪn, 'medɪsɪn] N **a** Arznei *f*, Medizin *f (inf)*; *(= one particular preparation)* Medikament *nt*; **to take one's ~** *(lit)* seine Arznei einnehmen; *(fig)* die bittere Pille schlucken, in den sauren Apfel beißen; **to give sb a taste of his own ~** *(fig)* es jdm mit gleicher Münze heimzahlen *or* zurückzahlen; **now we'll see how you like a taste of your own ~** jetzt werden wir sehen, wie es dir schmeckt, wenn dir das passiert **b** *(= science)* Medizin *f*; **to practise** *(Brit) or* **practice** *(US)* ~ den Arztberuf ausüben

medicine: **medicine ball** N Medizinball *m*; **medicine chest** N Hausapotheke *f*, Arzneischränkchen *nt*; **medicine man** N Medizinmann *m*; **medicine show** N *(US Hist) Schau eines reisenden Wunderdoktors*

medico ['medɪkəʊ] N *(dated inf)* Medikus *m (dated, hum)*

medieval [ˌmedɪ'iːvəl] ADJ *(lit, fig)* mittelalterlich; **in ~ times** im Mittelalter; **it's positively ~** *(practice, attitude)* es ist wie im Mittelalter

medieval history N die Geschichte des Mittelalters

medievalist [ˌmedɪ'iːvəlɪst] N Mediävist(in) *m(f)*

Medigap ['medɪgæp] N *(US)* Zusatzkrankenversicherung *f*

mediocre [ˌmiːdɪ'əʊkəʳ] ADJ mittelmäßig

mediocrity [ˌmiːdɪ'ɒkrɪtɪ] N **a** *(= quality)* Mittelmäßigkeit *f* **b** *(= person)* kleines Licht

meditate ['medɪteɪt] VT **to ~ revenge** auf Rache sinnen *(liter)* VI nachdenken *(upon, on* über *+acc)*; *(Rel, Philos)* meditieren

meditation [ˌmedɪ'teɪʃən] N Nachdenken *nt*; *(Rel, Philos)* Meditation *f*; **"A Meditation on Life"** „Betrachtungen über das Leben"

meditative ['medɪtətɪv] ADJ nachdenklich; *(Rel, Philos)* Meditations-; **~ techniques** Meditationstechniken *pl*

meditatively ['medɪtətɪvlɪ] ADV nachdenklich; *sit, look* meditierend

Mediterranean [ˌmedɪtə'reɪnɪən] N Mittelmeer *nt*; **in the ~** *(= in sea)* im Mittelmeer; *(= in region)* am Mittelmeer, im Mittelmeerraum ADJ Mittelmeer-; *scenery, character, person* südländisch; **~ climate/nations** Mittelmeerklima *nt*/-länder *pl*; **~ island** Mittelmeerinsel *f*; **~ fruit** Südfrüchte *pl*; **~ types** Südländer *pl*; **~ cruise** Kreuzfahrt *f* im Mittelmeer; **~ holiday** *(Brit) or* **vacation** *(US)* Urlaub *m* im Mittelmeerraum

Mediterranean Sea N **the ~** das Mittelmeer

medium ['miːdɪəm] ADJ *quality, size, height, length etc* mittlere(r, s); *steak* halb durch, medium; *(= medium-sized)* mittelgroß; **~ brown** mittelbraun; **of ~ height/build/size** mittelgroß; **of ~ difficulty** mittelschwer; **cook over a ~ heat** bei mittlerer Hitze kochen; **in/over the ~ term** mittelfristig
N *pl* **media** *or* **-s** **a** *(= means)* Mittel *nt*; *(TV, Rad, Press)* Medium *nt*; *(Art, Liter)* Ausdrucksmittel *nt*; **~ of exchange** Tauschmittel *nt*; **through the ~ of the press** durch die Presse; **advertising ~** Werbeträger *m*
b *(= surrounding substance) (Phys)* Medium *nt*; *(= environment)* Umgebung *f*; *(air, water etc)* Element *nt*
c *(= midpoint)* Mitte *f*; **happy ~** goldener Mittelweg; **to strike a happy ~** den goldenen Mittelweg finden
d *(= spiritualist)* Medium *nt*

medium *in cpds* mittel-; **medium-dry** ADJ *wine, sherry* halbtrocken; **medium-priced** ADJ **a ~ hotel/whisky** ein Hotel *nt*/ein Whisky *m* mittlerer Preislage; **in the ~ range** in der mittleren Preislage; **medium-range** ADJ Mittelstrecken-; **~ aircraft/missile** Mittelstreckenflugzeug *nt*/-rakete *f*; **medium-rare** ADJ rosa, englisch; **mediumship** N Tätigkeit *f* als Medium; **medium-size**, **medium-sized** ADJ mittelgroß; **medium-sweet** ADJ *wine* fruchtig; *sherry, cider* halbsüß; **medium-term** ADJ mittelfristig; **medium wave** N Mittelwelle *f*; **medium-wave** ADJ **~ transmission** Mittelwellenübertragung *f*; **~ transmitter** Mittelwellensender *m*

medley ['medlɪ] N Gemisch *nt*; *(Mus)* Potpourri *nt*, Medley *nt*

medley relay N *Staffellauf, bei dem die einzelnen Teilnehmer über verschieden lange Strecken laufen, z. B. Schwedenstaffel, olympische Staffel (Swimming)* Lagenstaffel *f*

med school ['medskuːl] *(esp US) abbr of* **medical school**

medulla [me'dʌlə] N Mark *nt*; *(of spine)* Rückenmark *nt*; *(= renal medulla)* Nierenmark *nt*

meek [miːk] ADJ *(+er)* sanft(mütig), lammfromm *(inf)*; *(pej)* duckmäuserisch; *(= uncomplaining)* duldsam, geduldig; *voice* schüchtern; *acceptance* widerstandslos; **as ~ as a lamb** sanft wie ein Lamm; **don't be so ~ and mild** lass dir doch nicht (immer) alles gefallen! N *(Bibl)* **the ~** *pl* die Sanftmütigen *pl*

meekly ['miːklɪ] ADV sanft, lammfromm *(inf)*; *(pej)* duckmäuserisch; *agree* widerspruchslos; *submit, accept* widerstandslos; *listen, sit, stand* geduldig

meekness ['miːknɪs] N Sanftmut *f*; *(pej)* Duckmäuserei *f*; *(= tolerance)* Duldsamkeit *f*

meerschaum ['mɪəʃəm] N Meerschaum *m*; *(= pipe)* Meerschaumpfeife *f*

meet[1] [miːt] ADJ *(obs)* geziemend *(liter)*; **it is ~ that ...** es ist billig *or* (ge)ziemt sich *(liter, old)*, dass ...; **to be ~ for** sich (ge)ziemen für *(liter, old)*

meet[2] [miːt] *vb: pret, ptp* **met** VT **a** *(= encounter) person* treffen, begegnen *(+dat)*; *(by arrangement)* treffen, sich treffen mit; *difficulty* stoßen auf *(+acc)*; *(Sport)* treffen auf *(+acc)*; **I'll ~ you outside** ich treffe euch draußen; **he met his guests at the door** er empfing seine Gäste an der Tür; **he met him in a duel** er duellierte sich mit ihm; **he met his death in 1800** im Jahre 1800 fand er den Tod; **to ~ death calmly** dem Tod gefasst entgegentreten; **to arrange to ~ sb** sich mit jdm verabreden; **to ~ a challenge** sich einer Herausforderung *(dat)* stellen; **the last time the two teams met there was a riot** bei der letzten Begegnung zwischen beiden Teams kam es zu heftigen Auseinandersetzungen; **his eyes** *or* **gaze met mine** unsere Blicke trafen sich; **she refused to ~ his eyes** *or* **gaze** sie wich seinem Blick aus; **I could not ~ his eyes** ich konnte ihm nicht in die Augen sehen; **there's more to it than ~s the eye** da steckt mehr dahinter, als man auf den ersten Blick meint
b *(= get to know)* kennenlernen; *(= be introduced to)* bekannt gemacht werden mit; **you don't know him? come and ~ him** du kennst ihn nicht? komm, ich mache dich mit ihm bekannt; **pleased to ~ you!** guten Tag/Abend, sehr angenehm! *(form)*
c *(= await arrival, collect)* abholen *(at* an *+dat*, von); *(= connect with) train, boat etc* Anschluss haben an *(+acc)*; **I'll ~ your train** ich hole dich vom Zug ab; **the car will ~ the train** der Wagen wartet am Bahnhof *or* steht am Bahnhof bereit
d *(= join, run into)* treffen *or* stoßen auf *(+acc)*; *(= converge with)* sich vereinigen mit; *(river)* münden *or* fließen in *(+acc)*; *(= intersect)* schneiden; *(= touch)* berühren; **where East ~s West** *(fig)* wo Ost und West sich treffen
e *expectations, target, obligations, deadline* erfüllen; *requirement, demand, wish* entsprechen *(+dat)*, gerecht werden *(+dat)*; *deficit, expenses, needs* decken; *debt* bezahlen, begleichen; *charge, objection, criticism* begegnen *(+dat)*
VI **a** *(= encounter) (people)* sich begegnen; *(by arrangement)* sich treffen; *(society, committee etc)* zusammenkommen, tagen; *(Sport)* aufeinandertreffen; *(in duel)* sich duellieren; **keep it until we ~ again** behalten Sie es, bis wir uns mal wiedersehen; **until we ~ again!** bis zum nächsten Mal!; **to ~ halfway** einen Kompromiss schließen
b *(= become acquainted)* sich kennenlernen; *(= be introduced)* bekannt gemacht werden; **we've met before** wir kennen uns bereits; **haven't we met before somewhere?** sind wir uns nicht schon mal begegnet?, kennen wir uns nicht irgendwoher?
c *(= join)* sich treffen, aufeinanderstoßen; *(= converge)* sich vereinigen; *(rivers)* ineinanderfließen; *(= intersect)* sich schneiden; *(= touch)* sich berühren; *(fig: = come together)* sich treffen; **our**

eyes met unsere Blicke trafen sich; **the skirt wouldn't ~ round her waist** der Rock ging an der Taille nicht zu
N *(Brit Hunt)* Jagd(veranstaltung) *f*; *(US) (Athletics)* Sportfest *nt*; *(Swimming)* Schwimmfest *nt*

▶ **meet up** VI sich treffen

▶ **meet with** VI *+prep obj* **a** *(= encounter, experience) hostility, opposition, problems* stoßen auf *(+acc)*; *success, accident* haben; *disaster, loss, shock* erleiden; *setback* erleben; *approval, encouragement, an untimely death* finden; **to meet with derision** verspottet werden; **to meet with kindness/a warm welcome** freundlich behandelt/herzlich empfangen werden; **I was met with a blank stare** sie/er *etc* starrte mich unwissend an **b** *person* treffen; *(esp US: = have a meeting with)* (zu einer Unterredung) zusammenkommen mit

meeting ['mi:tɪŋ] N **a** Begegnung *f*, Zusammentreffen *nt*; *(arranged)* Treffen *nt*; *(= business meeting)* Besprechung *f*, Konferenz *f*; **the minister had a ~ with the ambassador** der Minister traf zu Gesprächen mit dem Botschafter zusammen
b *(of committee, board of directors, council)* Sitzung *f*; *(of members, employees, citizens)* Versammlung *f*, Meeting *nt*; **at the last ~** bei der letzten Sitzung; **the committee has three ~s a year** der Ausschuss tagt dreimal im Jahr; **Mr Jones is at/in a ~** Herr Jones ist (gerade) in einer Sitzung; **~ of creditors** Gläubigerversammlung *f*
c *(Sport)* Veranstaltung *f*; *(between teams, opponents)* Begegnung *f*, Treffen *nt*
d *(of rivers)* Zusammenfluss *m*; **at the ~ of the X and the Y** wo X und Y zusammenfließen

meeting: **meeting house** N Gemeindehaus *nt* (der Quäker); **meeting place** N Treffpunkt *m*; **meeting point** N Treffpunkt *m*; *(of rivers)* Zusammenfluss *m*; *(of lines)* Berührungspunkt *m*; **at the ~ of the two roads** wo die beiden Straßen zusammentreffen; **at the ~ of the two cultures** wo sich die beiden Kulturen treffen; **meeting room** N Sitzungssaal *m*

meg [meg] N *(Comput inf)* Mega(byte) *nt*

mega ['megə] *(inf)* **ADJ** klasse *(inf)*, mega *(sl)*, geil *(sl)*; **they are ~ rich** sie sind stinkreich *(inf)* **ADV** wahnsinnig *(inf)*

mega- ['megə-] **PREF** Mega-; **megabucks** PL *(inf)* **he's making ~** er verdient ein Schweinegeld *(inf)*, er macht einen Haufen Kohle *(inf)*

megabyte ['megə͵baɪt] N *(Comput)* Megabyte *nt*; **a 40-~ memory** ein 40-Megabyte-Speicher *m*

megalith ['megəlɪθ] N Megalith *m*

megalithic [͵megə'lɪθɪk] ADJ megalithisch

megalomania [͵megələʊ'meɪnɪə] N Größenwahn *m*, Megalomanie *f* *(spec)*

megalomaniac [͵megələʊ'meɪnɪæk] **N** Größenwahnsinnige(r) *mf*; **he's a ~** er leidet an Größenwahn, er ist größenwahnsinnig **ADJ** *person, ambition* größenwahnsinnig; *(Psych) delusions* megaloman(isch); **~ frenzy** Anfall *m* von Megalomanie *or* Größenwahn

mega: **megaphone** N Megafon *nt*, Megaphon *nt*; **megastar** N Megastar *m*; **megastore** N Großmarkt *m*; **megaton** N *(Phys)* Megatonne *f*; **megavolt** N Megavolt *nt*; **megawatt** N Megawatt *nt*

meiosis [maɪ'əʊsɪs] N *pl* **-ses** [-si:z] *(Biol)* Meiose *f*

melamine ['meləmi:n] N Melamin *nt*

melancholia [͵melən'kəʊlɪə] N Schwermut *f*, Melancholie *f*

melancholic [͵melən'kɒlɪk] **ADJ** melancholisch, schwermütig **N** *(liter)* Melancholiker(in) *m(f)*

melancholy ['melənkəlɪ] **ADJ** melancholisch, schwermütig; *duty, sight, truth etc* traurig; *place* trist **N** Melancholie *f*, Schwermut *f*

melange, mélange [meɪ'lɑ:nʒ] N Mischung *f*

melanoma [͵melə'nəʊmə] N *(Med)* Melanom *nt*

Melba toast ['melbə'təʊst] N dünner, harter Toast

meld [meld] **VT** vermischen, verschmelzen; **to ~ sth into sth** etw zu etw kombinieren **VI** sich vermischen, ineinander verschmelzen **N** Mischprodukt *nt*, Kombination *f*

mêlée ['meleɪ] N *(= confused struggle)* Gedränge *nt*, Gewühl *nt*; *(= fighting)* Handgemenge *nt*

mellifluous [me'lɪflʊəs] ADJ wohltönend, wohlklingend

mellifluously [me'lɪflʊəslɪ] ADV klangvoll; **..., he said ~** ..., sagte er mit wohltönender *or* klangvoller Stimme

Mellotron® ['melətrɒn] N Mellotron® *nt*

mellow ['meləʊ] **ADJ** *(+er)* **a** *fruit* ausgereift, saftig; *wine* ausgereift; *brandy, whisky, flavour* mild; *colour, light, stone, brick* warm; *sound* voll, rund; *(= soft)* weich; *voice* weich, sanft; **a ~ instrument** ein Instrument mit einem vollen, weichen Klang
b *person (= relaxed)* abgeklärt, gesetzt; *(= affable)* umgänglich; *(= in a good mood)* gut gelaunt; *(fig: = slightly drunk)* angeheitert; **in the ~ later years** im gesetzteren Alter; **in a ~ mood** guter Laune, stillvergnügt
VT reifen, heranreifen lassen; *(= relax)* heiter stimmen; *sounds, colours* dämpfen, abschwächen; *taste* mildern; **the rum began to ~ her** der Rum versetzte sie allmählich in freundlichere Stimmung
VI *(wine, fruit)* reif werden, (heran)reifen; *(colours, sounds)* weicher werden; *(person) (= become more relaxed)* abgeklärter *or* gesetzter werden; *(= become more affable)* umgänglicher werden

mellowness ['meləʊnɪs] N **a** *(of fruit)* Ausgereiftheit *f*, Saftigkeit *f*; *(of wine)* Ausgereiftheit *f*; *(of brandy, whisky, flavour)* Milde *f*; *(of colour, light, stone, brick)* Wärme *f*; *(= softness)* Weichheit *f*; *(= mellow sound)* weicher *or* sanfter Klang **b** *(of person) (= relaxed attitude)* Abgeklärtheit *f*, Gesetztheit *f*; *(= affability)* Umgänglichkeit *f*; *(= good mood)* gute Laune; *(= slight tipsiness)* angeheiterte Stimmung

melodic ADJ, **melodically** ADV [mɪ'lɒdɪk, -əlɪ] melodisch

melodious [mɪ'ləʊdɪəs] ADJ melodiös, melodisch, wohlklingend; **a ~ tune** eine harmonische Melodie

melodiously [mɪ'ləʊdɪəslɪ] ADV melodiös, melodisch

melodiousness [mə'ləʊdɪəsnɪs] N Wohlklang *m*, Melodik *f*

melodrama ['meləʊ͵drɑ:mə] N Melodrama *nt*

melodramatic ADJ, **melodramatically** ADV [͵meləʊdrə'mætɪk, -əlɪ] melodramatisch

melody ['melədɪ] N Melodie *f*; *(fig: of poetry etc)* Melodik *f*

melon ['melən] N Melone *f*

melt [melt] **VT** **a** *(lit)* schmelzen; *snow* schmelzen, zum Schmelzen bringen; *butter* zergehen lassen, zerlassen; *sugar, grease* auflösen **b** *(fig) heart etc* erweichen; **her tears ~ed my heart** der Anblick ihrer Tränen erweichte mein Herz **VI** **a** schmelzen; *(sugar, grease)* sich (auf)lösen; **it just ~s in the mouth** es zergeht einem nur so auf der Zunge **b** *(fig) (person)* dahinschmelzen; *(anger)* verfliegen; **... and then his heart ~ed** ... und dann ließ er sich erweichen

▶ **melt away** VI **a** *(lit)* (weg)schmelzen **b** *(fig)* sich auflösen; *(crowd)* dahinschmelzen; *(anger, anxiety)* verfliegen; *(suspicion, money)* zerrinnen

▶ **melt down** **VT** *sep* einschmelzen **VI** *(reactor core)* schmelzen

meltdown ['meltdaʊn] N Kernschmelze *f*; *(fig) (of market, industry)* Crash *m*; *(of company)* Zusammenbruch *m*

melting ['meltɪŋ]: **melting point** N Schmelzpunkt *m*; **what is the ~ of iron?** welchen Schmelzpunkt hat Eisen?; **melting pot** N *(lit, fig)* Schmelztiegel *m*; **to be in the ~** in der Schwebe sein

member ['membə'] N **a** Mitglied *nt*; *(of tribe, species)* Angehörige(r) *mf*; **"members only"** „nur für Mitglieder"; **~ of the family** Familienmitglied *nt*; **if any ~ of the audience ...** falls einer der Zuschauer/Zuhörer ...; **you have to be a ~** Sie müssen Mitglied sein; **the ~ countries/states** die Mitgliedsstaaten *pl*
b *(Parl)* Abgeordnete(r) *mf*; **~ of parliament** Parlamentsmitglied *nt*; *(in GB)* Abgeordnete(r) *mf* des Unterhauses; *(Ger)* Bundestagsabgeordnete(r) *mf*; **~ of the European Parliament** Europaabgeordnete(r) *mf*; **the ~ for Woodford** der/die Abgeordnete für den Wahlkreis Woodford
c *(Math, Logic)* Glied *nt*

membership ['membəʃɪp] N Mitgliedschaft *f* *(of in +dat)*; *(= number of members)* Mitgliederzahl *f*; **when I applied for ~ of the club** als ich mich um die Klubmitgliedschaft bewarb

membership: **membership card** N Mitgliedsausweis *m*; **membership fee** N Mitgliedsbeitrag *m*; **membership list** N Mitgliederkartei *f*

member state N *(of EU etc)* Mitglied(s)staat *m*

membrane ['membreɪn] N Membran(e) *f*

membranous [mem'breɪnəs] ADJ membranartig

memento [mə'mentəʊ] N *pl* **-(e)s** Andenken *nt* *(of an +acc)*

memo ['meməʊ] N *abbr of* **memorandum** Mitteilung *f*, Notiz *f*, Memo *nt*

memoir ['memwɑ:'] N **a** Kurzbiografie *f* **b memoirs** PL Memoiren *pl*

memo pad N Notizblock *m*

memorable ['memərəbl] ADJ unvergesslich; *(= important)* denkwürdig; **on one ~ occasion he/she ...** unvergesslich bleibt, wie er/sie einmal ...; **the play was not at all ~** das Stück kann man vergessen

memorably ['memərəblɪ] ADV bemerkenswert; **she sang ~** ihr Gesang war unvergesslich

memorandum [͵memə'rændəm] N *pl* **memoranda** [͵memə'rændə] **a** *(in business)* Mitteilung *f*; *(= personal reminder)* Notiz *f*, Vermerk *m* **b** *(Pol)* Memorandum *nt*

memorial [mɪ'mɔ:rɪəl] **ADJ** Gedenk-; **~ plaque** Gedenktafel *f* **N** Denkmal *nt* *(to* für)

memorial: **Memorial Day** N *(US)* ≈ Volkstrauertag *m*; **memorial park** N *(US: = cemetery)* Friedhof *m*; **memorial service** N Gedenkgottesdienst *m*

memorize ['meməraɪz] VT sich *(dat)* einprägen

memory ['memərɪ] N **a** Gedächtnis *nt*; *(= faculty)* Erinnerungsvermögen *nt*; **from ~** aus dem Kopf; **to lose one's ~** sein Gedächtnis verlieren; **to commit sth to ~** sich *(dat)* etw einprägen; *poem* etw auswendig lernen; **to have a long ~** ein langes Gedächtnis haben; **I have a bad ~ for faces/names** ich habe ein schlechtes Personengedächtnis/Namensgedächtnis; **if my ~ serves me right** wenn ich mich recht entsinne → **living**
b *(= thing remembered)* Erinnerung *f* *(of* an *+acc)*; **I have no ~ of it** ich kann mich nicht daran erinnern; **he had happy memories of his father** er verband angenehme Erinnerungen mit seinem Vater
c *(Comput)* (Arbeits-, Haupt)speicher *m*
d to honour *(Brit) or* **honor** *(US)* **sb's ~** jds Andenken *nt* ehren; **in ~ of** zur Erinnerung *or* zum Gedenken *(form)* an *(+acc)*

memory: **memory access** N *(Comput)* Speicherzugriff *f*; **memory address** N *(Comput)* Speicheradresse *f*; **memory bank** N *(Comput)* Datenbank *f*; **memory capacity** N *(Comput)* Speicherkapazität *f*; **memory card** N *(Comput)* Speicherkarte *f*; **memory chip** N *(Comput)* Speicherchip *m*; **memory expansion** N *(Comput)* Speichererweiterung *f*; **memory expansion card** N *(Comput)* Speichererweiterungskarte *f*; **memory function** N *(Comput)* Speicherfunktion *f*; **memory lane** N **to take a trip** *or* **to walk down ~** in Erinnerungen schwelgen; **memory management** N *(Comput)* Speicherverwaltung *f*; **memory module** N *(Comput)* Speichermodul *nt*; **memory protection** N *(= Comput)* Speicherschutz *m*; **memory range** N *(Comput)* Speicherbereich *m*; **memo-**

ry-resident ADJ *(Comput)* speicherresident; **memory stick** N *(Comput)* Speicherkarte *f*, Memory Stick *m*

men [men] *pl of* **man**

menace [ˈmenɪs] **N** **a** Bedrohung *f* *(to +gen)*; *(issued by a person)* Drohung *f*; *(= imminent danger)* drohende Gefahr; **to demand money with ~s** unter Androhung von Gewalt Geld fordern **b** *(inf: = nuisance)* (Land)plage *f*; **she's a ~ on the roads** sie gefährdet den ganzen Verkehr **VT** bedrohen

menacing [ˈmenɪsɪŋ] ADJ drohend; *threat* gefährlich; **to look ~** bedrohlich aussehen

menacingly [ˈmenɪsɪŋlɪ] ADV drohend; **..., he said ~** ..., sagte er mit drohender Stimme

ménage [meˈnɑːʒ] N Haushalt *m*; **~ à trois** Dreiecksverhältnis *nt*

menagerie [mɪˈnædʒərɪ] N Menagerie *f*

mend [mend] **N** *(in shoe)* reparierte Stelle; *(in piece of metal, cloth etc also)* Flickstelle *f*; *(in roof, fence etc also)* ausgebesserte Stelle; **the ~ is almost invisible** man sieht kaum, dass es repariert/geflickt/ausgebessert worden ist; **to be on the ~** *(fig, lit: person)* sich (langsam) erholen, sich auf dem Wege der Besserung befinden *(form)*; **the fracture is on the ~** der Bruch heilt schon wieder *or* ist am Verheilen *(inf)*
VT **a** *(= repair)* reparieren; *roof, fence* ausbessern, reparieren; *hole, clothes* flicken; **my shoes need ~ing** ich muss meine Schuhe reparieren *or* machen *(inf)* lassen
b *(= improve)* **to ~ relations with sb** die Beziehungen zu jdm verbessern; **to ~ one's ways** sich bessern; **you'd better ~ your ways** das muss aber anders werden mit dir!; **to ~ matters** eine Angelegenheit bereinigen; **that won't ~ matters** das macht die Sache auch nicht besser; **to ~ fences** *(fig)* Unstimmigkeiten ausbügeln; **to ~ one's marriage** seine Ehe kitten
VI *(bone)* (ver)heilen; **make do and ~** *(prov)* aus Alt mach Neu *(prov)*

mendacious [menˈdeɪʃəs] ADJ lügnerisch, verlogen

mendaciously [menˈdeɪʃəslɪ] ADV unwahrheitsgemäß

mendacity [menˈdæsɪtɪ] N Verlogenheit *f*

Mendelian [menˈdiːlɪən] ADJ mendelsch

mendicant [ˈmendɪkənt] **ADJ** bettelnd; **~ monk** Bettelmönch *m*; **~ order** Bettelorden *nt* **N** *(= beggar)* Bettler(in) *m(f)*; *(= monk)* Bettelmönch *m*

mending [ˈmendɪŋ] N *(= articles to be mended)* Flickarbeit *f*

menfolk [ˈmenfəʊk] PL Männer *pl*, Mannsvolk *nt (old)*

menhir [ˈmenhɪəˈ] N *(Archeol)* Menhir *m*

menial [ˈmiːnɪəl] **ADJ** niedrig, untergeordnet; **she regards no task as too ~ for her** sie betrachtet keine Arbeit für unter ihrer Würde; **the ~ staff** die (unteren) Dienstboten, das Gesinde **N** *(pej)* Dienstbote *m*/-botin *f*

meningitis [ˌmenɪnˈdʒaɪtɪs] N Hirnhautentzündung *f*, Meningitis *f*

meniscus [mɪˈnɪskəs] N *pl* **menisci** [mɪˈnɪsaɪ] Meniskus *m*

menopause [ˈmenəʊpɔːz] N Wechseljahre *pl*, Menopause *f (spec)*

menorrhagia [ˌmenɔːˈreɪdʒɪə] N *(Med)* überhöhte Menstruationsblutung

Mensa [ˈmensə] N Mensa *no art*

men's department [ˈmenzdɪˌpɑːtmənt] N *(in department store)* Herrenabteilung *f*

menses [ˈmensiːz] PL *(rare)* Menses *pl (dated)*

men's room [ˈmenzruːm] N *(esp US)* Herrentoilette *f*

menstrual [ˈmenstrʊəl] ADJ Menstruations-, menstrual *(spec)*; **~ bleeding** Monatsblutung *f*; **~ cramps** Menstruationskrämpfe *pl*

menstrual: **menstrual cycle** N Menstruationszyklus *m*; **menstrual period** N Menstruation *f*

menstruate [ˈmenstrʊeɪt] VI menstruieren *(spec)*, die Menstruation haben

menstruation [ˌmenstrʊˈeɪʃən] N die Menstruation *or* Periode

menswear [ˈmenzwɛəˈ] N Herrenbekleidung *f*

mental [ˈmentl] ADJ **a** geistig; *strain* psychisch; *cruelty* seelisch; **to make a ~ note of sth** sich *(dat)* etw merken; **~ process** geistiger *or* gedanklicher Prozess, Denkvorgang *m*; **the causes are ~ not physical** die Ursachen sind eher psychischer als physischer Natur; **he still shows great ~ agility** er ist geistig noch immer sehr rege **b** *(inf: = mad)* übergeschnappt *(inf)*; **to go ~** verrückt werden, durchdrehen *(inf)*; *(= get furious)* ausrasten *(inf)*

mental: **mental age** N **he has a ~ of ten** er ist auf dem geistigen Entwicklungsstand eines Zehnjährigen; **mental arithmetic** N Kopfrechnen *nt*; **mental block** N Bewusstseinsstörung *f*; **to have a ~** eine Bewusstseinsstörung haben, geistig weggetreten sein *(inf)*; *(due to alcohol)* einen Filmriss haben *(inf)*; **to have a ~** *(in exam)* ein Brett vor dem Kopf haben *(inf)*; **mental breakdown** N Nervenzusammenbruch *m*; **mental deficiency** N Geistesschwäche *f*, Geistesstörung *f*; **mental health** N Geisteszustand *m*; **mental home** N (Nerven)heilanstalt *f*; **mental hospital** N psychiatrische Klinik, Nervenklinik *f*; **mental illness** N Geisteskrankheit *f*; **mental institution** N (Nerven)heilanstalt *f*

mentality [menˈtælɪtɪ] N Mentalität *f*; **how can we change this class ~?** wie können wir dieses Klassendenken ändern?

mentally [ˈmentəlɪ] ADV **a** geistig; **~ handicapped** geistig behindert; **~ deficient** geistesschwach; **he is ~ ill** er ist geisteskrank **b** *(= in one's head)* im Kopf

mental patient N Geisteskranke(r) *mf*

mental reservation N (stille) Bedenken *pl*, Vorbehalte *pl*

menthol [ˈmenθɒl] N Menthol *nt*; **~ cigarettes** Mentholzigaretten *pl*

mentholated [ˈmenθəleɪtɪd] ADJ mit Menthol

mention [ˈmenʃən] ✪ 19.4, 26.2, 26.3 **N** Erwähnung *f*; **to get** *or* **receive a ~** erwähnt werden; **he received a ~ for bravery** er erhielt eine Auszeichnung *or* Belobigung für seine Tapferkeit; **to give sb/sth a ~** jdn/etw erwähnen; **there is a/no ~ of it** es wird erwähnt/nicht erwähnt; **I can't find any ~ of his name** ich kann seinen Namen nirgendwo finden; **his contribution deserves special ~** sein Beitrag verdient es, besonders hervorgehoben zu werden; **~ should also be made of ...** ... sollte Erwähnung finden *(form)*; **it's hardly worth a ~** es ist kaum erwähnenswert, es lohnt sich kaum, das zu erwähnen; **at the ~ of his name/the police ...** als sein Name/das Wort Polizei fiel *or* erwähnt wurde ...
VT erwähnen *(to sb* jdm gegenüber*)*; **he was ~ed in several dispatches** er wurde mehrfach lobend erwähnt; **not to ~ ...** nicht zu vergessen ..., geschweige denn ...; **France and Spain, not to ~ Holland** Frankreich und Spanien, von Holland ganz zu schweigen *or* ganz abgesehen von Holland; **too numerous to ~** zu zahlreich, um sie einzeln erwähnen zu können; **don't ~ it!** (das ist doch) nicht der Rede wert!, (bitte,) gern geschehen!; **if I may ~ it** wenn ich das einmal sagen darf; **it hardly needs ~ing that we're very grateful** es versteht sich wohl von selbst, dass wir sehr dankbar sind; **to ~ sb in one's will** jdn in seinem Testament berücksichtigen; **~ me to your parents!** empfehlen Sie mich Ihren Eltern! *(form)*, viele Grüße an Ihre Eltern!

mentor [ˈmentɔːˈ] N Mentor(in) *m(f)*

menu [ˈmenjuː] N **a** *(= bill of fare)* Speisekarte *f*; *(= dishes served)* Menü *nt*; **may we see the ~?** können *or* würden Sie uns bitte die Karte bringen?, können wir bitte die Karte sehen?; **what's on the ~?** was steht heute auf dem Speisezettel?, was gibt es heute (zu essen)?; **they have a very good ~ there** man kann dort ausgezeichnet essen; **the typical British ~ consists of ...** ein typisches britisches Essen besteht aus ... **b** *(Comput)* Menü *nt*

menu *(Comput)*: **menu bar** N Menüleiste *f*; **menu-driven** ADJ menügesteuert; **menu item** N Menüeintrag *or* -befehl *m*; **menu line** N Menüzeile *f*; **menu option** N Menüoption *f*; **menu point** N Menübefehl *m*

meow N, VI = **miaow**

MEP *abbr of* **Member of the European Parliament** Mitglied *nt* des Europäischen Parlaments

mercantile [ˈmɜːkəntaɪl] ADJ Handels-; *nation also* Handel treibend; **the ~ marine** die Handelsmarine

mercantilism [ˈmɜːkəntɪlɪzəm] N Merkantilismus *m*

mercenary [ˈmɜːsɪnərɪ] **ADJ** **a** *person* geldgierig; **his motives were purely ~** er tat es nur des Geldes wegen; **don't be so ~** sei doch nicht so hinter dem Geld her *(inf)* **b** *(Mil)* Söldner-; **~ army** Söldnerarmee *f* **N** Söldner(in) *m(f)*

mercerized [ˈmɜːsəraɪzd] ADJ *thread* merzerisiert

merchandise [ˈmɜːtʃəndaɪz] N (Handels)ware *f*; **"please do not handle the ~"** „das Berühren der Ware(n) ist verboten"

merchandiser [ˈmɜːtʃəndaɪzəˈ] N Verkaufsförderungsexperte *m*/-expertin *f*

merchandising [ˈmɜːtʃəndaɪzɪŋ] N Verkaufsförderung *f*

merchant [ˈmɜːtʃənt] N **a** Kaufmann *m*/-frau *f*; **corn/fruit/diamond ~** Getreide-/Obst-/Diamantenhändler(in) *m(f)* **b** *(Brit inf)* Typ *m (sl)*; **he's a real speed ~** der ist ein Raser *(inf)*, der fährt wie die gesengte Sau *(inf)*; **he is a rip-off ~** er zockt seine Kunden ganz schön ab *(inf)*

merchant *in cpds* Handels-; **merchant bank** N *(Brit)* Handelsbank *f*; **merchant banker** N *(Brit)* Handelsbankier *m*; **merchant fleet** N Handelsflotte *f*; **merchantman** N Handelsschiff *nt*; **merchant marine** N *(US)* Handelsmarine *f*; **merchant navy** N *(Brit)* Handelsmarine *f*; **merchant prince** N reicher Kaufmann, Handelsboss *m (inf)*; **merchant seaman** N Matrose *m* in der Handelsmarine; **merchant ship** N Handelsschiff *nt*

merciful [ˈmɜːsɪfʊl] ADJ gnädig *(to sb* jdm gegenüber*)*; **o ~ Lord** gütiger Gott; **O Lord be ~!** Gott, sei uns *(dat)* gnädig!; **I begged him to be ~** ich bat ihn um Gnade; **his death was a ~ release from pain** sein Tod war für ihn eine Erlösung; **~ heavens!** *(dated)* gütiger Himmel! *(dated)*

mercifully [ˈmɜːsɪfəlɪ] ADV *act* barmherzig; *treat sb* gnädig; *(= fortunately)* glücklicherweise; **his suffering was ~ short** es war eine Gnade, dass er nicht lange leiden musste; **the country is ~ free from ethnic tensions** das Land ist glücklicherweise frei von ethnischen Spannungen

merciless [ˈmɜːsɪlɪs] ADJ unbarmherzig, erbarmungslos; *destruction* schonungslos; *(= unrelenting) treatment, scrutiny, competition, glare, sun* gnadenlos

mercilessly [ˈmɜːsɪlɪslɪ] ADV erbarmungslos; *glare* gnadenlos

mercurial [mɜːˈkjʊərɪəl] ADJ **a** *(Chem: = containing mercury)* quecksilberhaltig **b** *(fig)* *(= volatile)* sprunghaft, wechselhaft; *(= lively)* quicklebendig

Mercury [ˈmɜːkjʊrɪ] N Merkur *m*

mercury [ˈmɜːkjʊrɪ] N Quecksilber *nt*

mercy [ˈmɜːsɪ] N **a** *no pl (= feeling of compassion)* Erbarmen *nt*; *(= action, forbearance from punishment)* Gnade *f*; *(= God's mercy)* Barmherzigkeit *f*; **to beg for ~** um Gnade bitten *or* flehen; **to have ~/no ~ on sb** mit jdm Erbarmen/kein Erbarmen haben; **have ~!** Gnade!, Erbarmen!; **Lord have ~ upon us** Herr, erbarme dich unser; **to show sb ~/no ~** Erbarmen/kein Erbarmen mit jdm haben; **to throw oneself on sb's ~** sich jdm auf Gnade und Ungnade ausliefern; **to be**

at the ~ of sb jdm (auf Gedeih und Verderb) ausgeliefert sein; **to be at the ~ of sth** einer Sache *(dat)* ausgeliefert sein; **we're at your ~** wir sind in Ihrer Gewalt *or* Hand; **at the ~ of the elements** dem Spiel der Elemente preisgegeben; **a mission of ~** eine Hilfsaktion
b *(inf: = blessing)* Segen *m*, Glück *nt*; **it's a ~ nobody was hurt** man kann von Glück sagen, dass niemand verletzt wurde; **we must be thankful for small mercies** man muss schon mit wenigem zufrieden *or* für weniges dankbar sein

mercy: **mercy killing** N Euthanasie *f*, Töten *nt* aus Mitleid; **mercy seat** N Gnadenthron *or* -stuhl *m*

mere[1] [mɪəʳ] N *(poet)* See *m*

mere[2] ADJ **a** bloß; *formality also, nonsense* rein; **a ~ mortal** ein gewöhnlicher Sterblicher, eine gewöhnliche Sterbliche; **he's a ~ clerk** er ist bloß ein kleiner Angestellter; **a ~ 3%/two hours** bloß *or* lediglich 3%/zwei Stunden; **a ~ nothing** eine (bloße) Lappalie; **but she's a ~ child** aber sie ist doch noch ein Kind!; **the ~ thought of food made me hungry** schon *or* allein beim Gedanken an Essen bekam ich Hunger; **the ~ sight of him makes me shiver** sein bloßer Anblick lässt es mir kalt über den Rücken laufen; **the ~ fact that we have won is enough** allein die Tatsache, dass wir gewonnen haben, genügt
b the ~st ... *(= slightest)* der/die/das kleinste ...; *suspicion, sign* der/die/das geringste ...; **the ~st hint of any corruption** das geringste Zeichen von Korruption; **they giggle at the ~st mention of sex** sie kichern jedes Mal, wenn Sex auch nur erwähnt wird

merely ['mɪəlɪ] ADV lediglich, bloß; **it's not ~ broken, it's ruined** es ist nicht bloß kaputt, es ist völlig ruiniert

meretricious [,merɪ'trɪʃəs] ADJ trivial; *(= kitschy)* kitschig

merge [mɜːdʒ] **VI a** *(= come together)* zusammenkommen; *(colours)* ineinander übergehen; *(roads)* zusammenlaufen *or* -führen; *(US Aut)* sich einordnen; **to ~ with sth** mit etw verschmelzen, sich mit etw vereinen; *(colour)* in etw *(acc)* übergehen; *(road)* in etw *(acc)* einmünden; **to ~ (in) with/into the crowd** in der Menge untergehen/untertauchen; **to ~ into sth** in etw *(acc)* übergehen; **the bird ~d in with its background of leaves** der Vogel verschmolz mit dem Laubwerk im Hintergrund; **"motorways ~"** „Autobahneinmündung"; **to ~ to the left** *(US Aut)* sich links einordnen
b *(Comm)* fusionieren, sich zusammenschließen
VT a *(= bring together)* miteinander vereinen *or* verbinden *or* verschmelzen; *colours* (miteinander) verschmelzen, ineinander übergehen lassen; *metals* legieren; *(Comput) files* zusammenführen; **to ~ sth with sth** etw mit etw vereinen *or* verbinden *or* verschmelzen; etw in etw *(acc)* übergehen lassen
b *(Comm)* zusammenschließen, fusionieren; **they were ~d into one company** sie wurden zu einer Firma zusammengeschlossen; **they were ~d with ...** sie haben mit ... fusioniert

merger ['mɜːdʒəʳ] N *(Comm)* Fusion *f*

merging lane ['mɜːdʒɪŋ,leɪn] N *(US)* Spur *f* zum Einordnen, Abbiegespur *f*

meridian [mə'rɪdɪən] N *(Astron, Geog)* Meridian *m*; *(fig)* Höhepunkt *m*, Gipfel *m*

meridian system N *(Med)* Meridiansystem *nt*

meridian therapy N *(Med)* Meridiantherapie *f*

meringue [mə'ræŋ] N Meringe *f*, Baiser *nt*

merino [mə'riːnəʊ] N **a** *(= sheep)* Merino *m*, Merinoschaf *nt* **b** *(= wool)* Merinowolle *f*

merit ['merɪt] **N a** *(= achievement)* Leistung *f*, Verdienst *nt*; *(= advantage)* Vorzug *m*; **to look** *or* **inquire into the ~s of sth** etw auf seine Vorteile *or* Vorzüge untersuchen; **a work of great literary ~** ein Werk von großem literarischem Wert; **what are the particular ~s of Greek drama?** wodurch zeichnet sich das griechische Drama besonders aus?; **she was elected on ~ alone** sie gewann die Wahl aufgrund *or* auf Grund persönlicher Fähigkeiten; **judged on one's own ~s** ausschließlich nach Leistung(en) *or* Verdiensten beurteilt; **judged on its own ~s** für sich selbst beurteilt; **to judge a case on its ~s** einen Fall für sich selbst *or* gesondert behandeln; **I don't see any ~ in being rich** ich betrachte Reichtum als kein besonderes Verdienst; **he sees little ~ in paying for research** er sieht nicht viel Sinn darin, für Forschungsvorhaben zu bezahlen; **there's no particular ~ in coming early** es ist keine besondere Leistung *or* kein besonderes Verdienst, früh zu kommen; **to pass an exam with ~** ein Examen mit Auszeichnung bestehen; **certificate of ~** *(Sch, Univ) Urkunde für besonders gute Leistungen an Schule oder Universität*
VT verdienen; **it ~s your consideration** das ist es wert, dass Sie sich damit beschäftigen

meritocracy [,merɪ'tɒkrəsɪ] N Leistungsgesellschaft *f*, Meritokratie *f (geh)*

meritocratic [,merɪtə'krætɪk] ADJ leistungsorientiert

meritorious ADJ, **meritoriously** ADV [,merɪ'tɔːrɪəs, -lɪ] lobenswert

Merlin ['mɜːlɪn] N *(Myth)* Merlin *m (Zauberer in der keltischen Sage)*

mermaid ['mɜːmeɪd] N Nixe *f*, See- *or* Meerjungfrau *f*

merman ['mɜːmæn] N *pl* **-men** [-men] Nix *m*, Wassergeist *m*

merrily ['merɪlɪ] ADV **a** *(= happily)* vergnügt; *(fig) boil* munter; **to burn ~** *(fire in grate)* munter vor sich hin brennen **b** *(= blithely) continue, say* munter

merriment ['merɪmənt] N Heiterkeit *f*, Fröhlichkeit *f*; *(= laughter)* Gelächter *nt*; **at this there was much ~** das erregte allgemeine Heiterkeit, das rief großes Gelächter hervor

merry ['merɪ] ✪ 23.2 ADJ *(+er)* **a** *(= cheerful)* fröhlich, vergnügt, lustig; *song, tune* fröhlich; **to make ~** lustig und vergnügt sein; **Merry Christmas!** fröhliche *or* frohe Weihnachten!; **a Merry Christmas to all our readers** allen unseren Lesern ein frohes Weihnachtsfest; **Merry England** das gute alte England
b *(fig)* **to lead sb a ~ dance** jdn ganz schön an der Nase herumführen; **to play ~ hell with sth** *(inf)* etw total durcheinanderbringen; **to give sb ~ hell** *(inf)* jdm einheizen *(inf)*; **to go one's ~ way** seiner Wege gehen
c *(Brit inf: = tipsy)* beschwipst, angeheitert *(inf)*; **to get ~** sich *(dat)* einen anpicheln *(inf)*

merry: **merry-go-round** ['merɪgəʊraʊnd] N Karussell *nt*; **merrymaker** N Festgast *m*, Feiernde(r) *mf*; **merrymaking** N Feiern *nt*, Belustigung *f*, Lustbarkeit *f (liter)*; **after the ~ had finished** nach Beendigung des Festes *or* der Lustbarkeiten *(liter)*

mesa ['meɪsə] N Tafelberg *m*

mescalin(e) ['meskəlɪn] N Meskalin *nt*

mesh [meʃ] **N a** *(= hole)* Masche *f*; *(= size of hole)* Maschenweite *f*; **caught in the fine ~ of the net** in den feinen Maschen des Netzes gefangen; **fine ~ stockings** feinmaschige Strümpfe *pl*; **the big ~ of this material makes it ideal** die Grobmaschigkeit dieses Materials ist ideal; **a 5mm ~ screen** ein 5 mm Maschendraht; **the ~ is big enough to see through** es ist großmaschig genug, um durchzusehen
b *(material) (= wire mesh)* Maschendraht *m*; *(= network of wires)* Drahtgeflecht *nt*; *(Tex)* Gittergewebe *nt*
c *(Mech)* **out of ~** nicht im Eingriff; **in ~** im Eingriff; **the tight ~ of the cogwheels** die enge Verzahnung der Räder
d *(fig)* **to catch** *or* **entangle sb in one's ~es** jdn umgarnen, jdn in sein Netz locken; **to be caught in sb's ~es** jdm ins Netz gegangen sein; **a ~ of lies** ein Lügengespinst *nt*
VI a *(Mech)* eingreifen *(with* in *+acc)*; **the gears ~ (together)** die Zahnräder greifen ineinander
b *(fig: views, approach)* sich vereinen lassen; **he tried to make the departments ~ (together)** er versuchte, die einzelnen Abteilungen miteinander zu koordinieren
VT = **enmesh**

mesh stocking N Netzstrumpf *m*

meshugge [mɪ'ʃʊgə] ADJ *(US sl)* meschugge *(inf)*

mesmeric [mez'merɪk] ADJ hypnotisch; *movement* hypnotisierend

mesmerism ['mezmərɪzəm] N hypnotische Wirkung; *(old)* Mesmerismus *m*

mesmerize ['mezməraɪz] VT hypnotisieren; *(fig)* faszinieren, fesseln; **the audience sat ~d** die Zuschauer saßen wie gebannt

mesmerizing ['mezməraɪzɪŋ] ADJ *effect* hypnotisch; *rhythm, presence, experience* hypnotisierend; *smile, voice* faszinierend

meson ['miːzɒn] N *(Phys)* Meson *nt*

Mesopotamia [,mesəpə'teɪmɪə] N Mesopotamien *nt*

mess[1] [mes] **N a** Durcheinander *nt*; *(dirty)* Schweinerei *f*; **to be (in) a ~** unordentlich sein, in einem fürchterlichen Zustand sein; *(= disorganized)* ein einziges Durcheinander sein; *(fig: one's life, marriage, career etc)* verkorkst sein *(inf)*; **to be a ~** *(piece of work)* eine Schweinerei sein *(inf)*; *(= disorganized)* ein einziges *or* heilloses Durcheinander sein; *(person) (in appearance)* unordentlich aussehen; *(psychologically)* verkorkst sein *(inf)*; **to look a ~** *(person)* unmöglich aussehen; *(= untidy also)* schlampig *or* unordentlich aussehen; *(= dirty also)* völlig verdreckt sein; *(room, piece of work)* unordentlich *or* schlimm aussehen; **to make a ~** *(= be untidy)* Unordnung machen; *(= be dirty)* eine Schweinerei machen *(inf)*; **to make a ~ of sth** *(= make untidy)* etw in Unordnung bringen, etw durcheinanderbringen; *(= make dirty)* etw verdrecken; *(= bungle, botch)* etw verpfuschen, bei etw Mist bauen *(inf)*; *of one's life* etw verkorksen *(inf) or* verpfuschen; **I made a ~ of sewing it on** ich habe beim Annähen Mist gebaut *(inf)*; **you've really made a ~ of things** du hast alles total vermasselt *(inf)*; **a fine ~ you've made of that** da hast du was Schönes angerichtet; **what a ~!** wie sieht das denn aus!, das sieht ja vielleicht aus!; *(fig)* ein schöner Schlamassel! *(inf)*; **I'm not tidying up your ~** ich räume nicht für dich auf; **a ~ of beer cans/pots and pans** ein Haufen Bierdosen/Töpfe und Pfannen
b *(= awkward predicament)* Schwierigkeiten *pl*, Schlamassel *m (inf)*; **cheating got him into a ~** durch seine Mogelei ist er in ziemliche Schwierigkeiten geraten; **he got into a ~ with the police** er hat Ärger mit der Polizei bekommen
c *(euph: = excreta)* Dreck *m*; **the cat/baby has made a ~ on the carpet** die Katze/das Baby hat auf den Teppich gemacht
VI = **mess about VI c, d**

▶ **mess about** *(Brit) or* **around** *(inf)* **VT** *sep (= fiddle, tinker with)* herumpfuschen an *(+dat) (inf)*; *person* an der Nase herumführen *(inf)*; *(boss, person in authority)* herumschikanieren; *(by delaying decision)* hinhalten
VI a *(= play the fool)* herumalbern *or* -blödeln *(inf)*
b *(= do nothing in particular)* herumgammeln *(inf)*; **he enjoys messing about** *or* **around on the river** *(in boat)* er gondelt gern (im Boot) auf dem Fluss herum
c *(= tinker, fiddle)* herumfummeln *(inf) or* -spielen *(with* an *+dat)*; *(as hobby etc)* herumbasteln *(with* an *+dat) (inf)*; **that'll teach you to mess about** *or* **around with explosives** das soll dir eine Lehre sein, nicht mit Sprengkörpern herumzuspielen; **I don't like film directors messing about** *or* **around with my scripts** ich kann es nicht haben, wenn Regisseure an meinen Drehbüchern herumändern
d to mess around with sb *(= associate with)* sich mit jdm einlassen *or* abgeben; *(= not take seriously)* jdn zum Narren haben; **he was messing about** *or* **around with my wife** *(= having affair)* er trieb es mit meiner Frau

▶**mess up** VT *sep* durcheinanderbringen; *(= make dirty)* verdrecken; *(= botch, bungle)* verpfuschen, verhunzen *(inf)*; *marriage* kaputt machen *(inf)*, ruinieren; *life, person* verkorksen *(inf)*; *person (as regards looks)* übel zurichten; **missing the connection messed up the whole journey** dadurch, dass wir den Anschluss verpassten, lief die ganze Reise schief; **her visit really messed me up** *(inf)* ihr Besuch hat mir wirklich alles vermasselt *(inf)*; **that's really messed things up** das hat wirklich alles verdorben *or* vermasselt *(inf)*

mess[2] *(Mil)* **N** Kasino *nt*, *(Aus also)* Casino *nt*; *(on ships)* Messe *f*; *(= food)* Essen *nt* **VI** essen, das Essen einnehmen

message ['mesɪdʒ] ✪ 27.6 N **a** Mitteilung *f*, Nachricht *f*, Botschaft *f (old, form)*; *(Comput)* Meldung *f*; *(= radio message)* Funkspruch *m or* -meldung *f*; *(= report, police message)* Meldung *f*; **to take a ~ to sb** jdm eine Nachricht überbringen; **to give sb a ~** *(verbal)* jdm etwas ausrichten; *(written)* jdm eine Nachricht geben; **would you give John a ~ (for me)?** könnten Sie John etwas (von mir) ausrichten?; **have you given him my ~ yet?** hast du es ihm schon ausgerichtet?; **to send a ~ to sb, to send sb a ~** jdn benachrichtigen; **to leave a ~ for sb** *(written)* jdm eine Nachricht hinterlassen; *(verbal)* jdm etwas ausrichten lassen; **can I take a ~ (for him)?** *(on telephone)* kann ich (ihm) etwas ausrichten?; **the Queen's ~** die (Fernseh)ansprache der Königin
b *(= moral)* Botschaft *f*; **the ~ of the play is ...** die Aussage des Stückes ist ..., das Stück will Folgendes sagen ...; **a pop song with a ~** ein Schlagertext, der einem etwas zu sagen hat; **to get the** *or* **one's ~ across to sb** es jdm verständlich machen
c *(fig inf)* **to get the ~** kapieren *(inf)*; **I got the ~** ich habe schon verstanden *or* kapiert *(inf)*
d *(Scot: = errand)* Einkauf *m*; **to do** *or* **get one's ~s** einkaufen

message board N *(Internet)* Forum *nt*

message switching ['mesɪdʒ,swɪtʃɪŋ] N *(Comput)* Speichervermittlung *f*

messaging ['mesɪdʒɪŋ] N Datentransfer *m*

mess deck N Speisedeck *nt*

messenger ['mesɪndʒə'] N **a** Bote *m (old, form)*, Botin *f (old, form)*, Überbringer(in) *m(f)*, (einer Nachricht); *(Mil)* Kurier(in) *m(f)*; **bank ~** Bankbote *m*/-botin *f*; **don't shoot the ~** *(fig)* lassen Sie Ihren Zorn an dem Verantwortlichen aus **b** *(Med, Biol)* Botenstoff *m*

messenger boy N Botenjunge *m*, Laufbursche *m*

mess hall N Kasino *nt*, *(Aus also)* Casino *nt*

Messiah [mɪ'saɪə] N Messias *m*

messianic [,mesɪ'ænɪk] ADJ messianisch

messily ['mesɪlɪ] ADV unordentlich; **they divorced ~** ihre Scheidung war eine unerfreuliche Angelegenheit

mess: **mess jacket** N Affenjäckchen *nt (inf)*; **mess kit** N **a** *(Brit) Uniform für gesellschaftliche Anlässe* **b** *(US)* Essgeschirr *nt*; **messmate** N **they were ~s** sie waren Kameraden bei der Armee

Messrs ['mesəz] PL *of* **Mr** *abbr of* **Messieurs**; **to ~ ...** an die Herren ...

mess tin N Ess- *or* Kochgeschirr *nt*

mess-up ['mesʌp] N Kuddelmuddel *nt (inf)*; **it's a complete ~** da ist alles schiefgelaufen *(inf)*

messy ['mesɪ] ADJ (+er) **a** *(= dirty)* dreckig, schmutzig; *(= untidy)* unordentlich; **~ writing** fürchterliche Klaue *(inf)*; **he's a ~ eater** er kann nicht ordentlich essen, er isst wie ein Schwein **b** *(fig) situation* verfahren; *(= confused)* durcheinander; *(= unpleasant)* unschön; *process, relationship* schwierig; *dispute* unschön; **their divorce was a ~ business, they had a ~ divorce** ihre Scheidung war eine unerfreuliche Angelegenheit

Met [met] N *(inf)* **a** *(US) abbr of* **Metropolitan Opera Company** Metropolitan (Oper) *f* **b** *(US) abbr of* **Metropolitan Museum of Art** *Kunstmuseum in New York* **c** *(Brit) abbr of* **Metropolitan Police**

met[1] [met] *pret, ptp of* **meet**[2]

met[2] *abbr of* **meteorological**

meta- ['metə-] PREF meta-, Meta-

metabolic [,metə'bɒlɪk] ADJ Stoffwechsel-, metabolisch

metabolic disorder N Stoffwechselkrankheit *f*

metabolic rate N Stoffwechselrate *f*

metabolism [me'tæbəlɪzəm] N Stoffwechsel *m*, Metabolismus *m*

metacarpal [,metə'kɑːpl] N Mittelhandknochen *m*

metal ['metl] **N** **a** Metall *nt*; *(Brit: on road)* Schotter *m* **b metals** **PL** *(Rail)* Schienen *pl* **c** *(Mus: = heavy metal)* Heavy Metal *nt* **VT** *(Brit) road* beschottern; **~led road** Asphaltstraße *f (mit Schotterunterbau)*

metalanguage ['metəlæŋgwɪdʒ] N Metasprache *f*

metal: **metal-arc welding** N *(Tech)* Metalllichtbogenschweißen *nt*; **metal detector** N Metallsuchgerät *nt*

metalled, *(US)* **metaled** ['metld] ADJ *road* Schotter-

metallic [mɪ'tælɪk] ADJ metallisch; **~ finish/paint** Metalliclackierung *f*/-lack *m*; **~ blue/green** blau-/grünmetallic; **a ~ blue car** ein Auto *nt* in Blaumetallic

metallurgic(al) [,metə'lɜːdʒɪk(əl)] ADJ metallurgisch

metallurgist [me'tælədʒɪst] N Metallurg(e) *m*, Metallurgin *f*

metallurgy [me'tælədʒɪ] N Hüttenkunde *f*, Metallurgie *f*

metal *in cpds* Metall-; **metal plating** N Metallschicht *f*; *(= act)* Plattierung *f*; **metal polish** N Metallpolitur *f*; **metal processing** N Metallverarbeitung *f*; **metalwork** N Metall *nt*; **we did ~ at school** wir haben in der Schule Metallarbeiten gemacht; **metalworker** N Metallarbeiter(in) *m(f)*; **metalworking** N Metallbearbeitung *f*

metamorphose [,metə'mɔːfəʊz] **VT** verwandeln; *(Sci)* umwandeln **VI** sich verwandeln; *(Sci)* sich umwandeln

metamorphosis [,metə'mɔːfəsɪs] N *pl* **metamorphoses** [,metə'mɔːfəsiːz] Metamorphose *f*; *(fig)* Verwandlung *f*

metaphor ['metəfə'] N Metapher *f*; **to mix one's ~s** unterschiedliche Metaphern zusammen verwenden

metaphorical [,metə'fɒrɪkəl] ADJ metaphorisch

metaphorically [,metə'fɒrɪkəlɪ] ADV metaphorisch; **~ speaking** metaphorisch ausgedrückt, bildlich gesprochen

metaphysical ADJ, **metaphysically** ADV [,metə'fɪzɪkəl, -ɪ] metaphysisch

metaphysician [,metəfɪ'zɪʃn] N Metaphysiker(in) *m(f)*

metaphysics [,metə'fɪzɪks] N *sing* Metaphysik *f*

metastasis [mɪ'tæstəsɪs] N *pl* **metastases** [mɪ'tæstəsiːz] Metastasenbildung *f*, Metastasierung *f*

metatarsal [,metə'tɑːsl] ADJ Mittelfuß-, metatarsal *(spec)*; **~ bone** Mittelfußknochen *m*

metathesis [me'tæθəsɪs] N *pl* **metatheses** [me'tæθəsiːz] Metathese *f*, Metathesis *f*

metazoan [metə'zəʊən] **N** Metazoon *nt (spec)*, Vielzeller *m* **ADJ** vielzellig, metazoisch *(spec)*

mete [miːt] VT **to ~ out** zuteilwerden lassen *(to sb* jdm); *praise* austeilen; *rewards* verteilen; **to ~ out punishment to sb** jdn bestrafen; **the function of the courts is to ~ out justice** es ist Aufgabe der Gerichte zu richten; **justice was ~d out to them** es wurde über sie gerichtet

metempsychosis [,metəmsaɪ'kəʊsɪs] N *pl* **metempsychoses** [,metəmsaɪ'kəʊsiːz] Metempsychose *f*

meteor ['miːtɪə'] N Meteor *m*

meteoric [,miːtɪ'ɒrɪk] ADJ meteorisch; *(fig)* kometenhaft

meteorite ['miːtɪəraɪt] N Meteorit *m*

meteoroid ['miːtɪərɔɪd] N Sternschnuppe *f*

meteorological [,miːtɪərə'lɒdʒɪkəl] ADJ Wetter-, meteorologisch; **~ station** Wetterstation *f*

Meteorological Office N **the ~** *(Brit)* das Wetteramt

meteorologist [,miːtɪə'rɒlədʒɪst] N Meteorologe *m*, Meteorologin *f*

meteorology [,miːtɪə'rɒlədʒɪ] N Meteorologie *f*, Wetterkunde *f*

meteor shower N Meteoritenschauer *m*

meter[1] ['miːtə'] **N** Zähler *m*; *(= gas meter also)* Gasuhr *f*; *(= water meter)* Wasseruhr *f*; *(= parking meter)* Parkuhr *f*; *(= exposure or light meter)* Belichtungsmesser *m*; *(= coin meter)* Münzzähler *m*; **the ~ has run out** *(parking meter)* die Parkuhr ist abgelaufen; *(coin meter)* es ist kein Geld mehr im Zähler; **to turn the water/gas off at the ~** das Wasser/Gas am Hauptschalter abstellen; **to turn the electricity off at the ~** den Strom am Hauptschalter abschalten **VT** messen

meter[2] N *(US)* = **metre**

meter maid N *(inf)* Politesse *f*

methadone ['meθədəʊn] N *(Pharm)* Methadon *nt*

methamphetamine [,meθæm'fetəmiːn] N Metamphetamin *nt*

methane ['miːθeɪn] N Methan *nt*

methanol ['meθənɒl] N Methanol *nt*

methinks [mɪ'θɪŋks] *pret* **methought** [mɪ'θɔːt] VI *impers (obs)* mich deucht *(obs)*, mir *or* mich dünkt *(old)*

method ['meθəd] N Methode *f*; *(= process)* Verfahren *nt*; *(Cook)* Zubereitung *f*; *(in experiment)* Vorgehens- *or* Verfahrensweise *f*; **~ of payment/application** Zahlungs-/Anwendungsweise *f*; **there's ~ in his madness** sein Wahnsinn hat Methode

method acting N *(Theat) Schauspielen nach dem System Stanislawski*

methodical ADJ, **methodically** ADV [mɪ'θɒdɪkəl, -ɪ] methodisch

Methodism ['meθədɪzəm] N Methodismus *m*

Methodist ['meθədɪst] **ADJ** methodistisch **N** Methodist(in) *m(f)*

methodology [,meθə'dɒlədʒɪ] N Methodik *f*, Methodologie *f*

methought [mɪ'θɔːt] PRET *of* **methinks**

meths [meθs] N *sing abbr of* **methylated spirits** Spiritus *m*; **~ drinker** ≈ Fuseltrinker(in) *m(f)*

Methuselah [mə'θuːzələ] N Methusalem *m*; **as old as ~** so alt wie Methusalem

methyl alcohol ['miːθaɪl'ælkəhɒl] N Methylalkohol *m*

methylated spirits ['meθɪleɪtɪd'spɪrɪts] N *sing* Äthylalkohol *m*, (Brenn)spiritus *m*

meticulous [mɪ'tɪkjʊləs] ADJ sorgfältig, genau, exakt; *(= fastidious)* peinlich genau; **to be ~ about sth** es mit etw sehr genau nehmen; **with ~ attention to detail** mit besonderer Sorgfalt für das Detail

meticulously [mɪ'tɪkjʊləslɪ] ADV sorgfältig; *(= fastidiously)* peinlich genau; **~ clean** peinlich sauber

métier ['meɪtɪeɪ] N Metier *nt*

me time, me-time N Ichzeit *m*, Zeit *f* für sich selbst

met office ['met,ɒfɪs] N *(Brit)* Wetteramt *nt*

metonymy [mə'tɒnɪmɪ] N Metonymie *f*

me-too product N *(Comm)* Me-too-Produkt *nt*, Nachahmerprodukt *nt*

metre, *(US)* **meter** ['miːtə'] N **a** *(Measure)* Meter *m or nt* **b** *(Poet)* Metrum *nt*

metric ['metrɪk] ADJ metrisch; **the ~ system** das metrische Maßsystem; **to go ~** auf das metrische Maßsystem umstellen

metrical ['metrɪkəl] ADJ *(Poet)* metrisch

metrication [ˌmetrɪ'keɪʃən] N Umstellung *f* auf das metrische Maßsystem

metric ton N Metertonne *f*

metronome ['metrənəʊm] N Metronom *nt*

metronomic [ˌmetrə'nɒmɪk] ADJ metronomartig; **variety is the charm of tennis, which could otherwise become a ~ bore** der Reiz von Tennis liegt in der Abwechslung, sonst könnte es leicht so eintönig wie ein Metronom werden

metropolis [mɪ'trɒpəlɪs] N Metropole *f*, Weltstadt *f*; *(= capital)* Hauptstadt *f*

metropolitan [ˌmetrə'pɒlɪtən] ADJ **a** weltstädtisch; *(of a capital)* hauptstädtisch; **~ diocese** Erzdiözese *f*; **~ bishop** Diözesanbischof *m*; **a ~ city** eine Weltstadt; **~ district/area** Stadtgebiet *nt* **b** *(= mainland)* **~ France** das französische Mutterland N **a** Weltbürger(in) *m(f)*; *(= citizen)* Großstädter(in) *m(f)*, Hauptstädter(in) *m(f)* **b** *(Eccl)* Metropolit *m*

Metropolitan Police N Londoner/New Yorker Polizei

mettle ['metl] N *(= spirit)* Courage *f*, Stehvermögen *nt*; *(of horse)* Zähigkeit *f*; *(= temperament)* Feuer *nt*; **a man of ~** ein Mann von echtem Schrot und Korn; **to show one's ~** zeigen, was in einem steckt; **to test sb's ~, to be a test of sb's ~** *(thing)* zeigen, was in jdm steckt; *(person)* herausfinden, was in jdm steckt; **to be on one's ~** auf dem Posten sein; **to put sb on his ~** jdn fordern

mettlesome ['metlsəm] ADJ *person* couragiert, schneidig; *horse* feurig

mew [mjuː] N Miau(en) *nt* VI miauen

mewl [mjuːl] VI *(cat)* maunzen, mauzen; *(baby)* wimmern

mews [mjuːz] N *sing or pl (= houses) Siedlung ehemaliger zu modischen Wohnungen umgebauter Kutscherhäuschen* *(= street)* Gasse *f*; *(old, = stables)* Stall *m*, Stallungen *pl*; **a ~ cottage** ein ehemaliges Kutscherhäuschen

Mexican ['meksɪkən] ADJ mexikanisch N Mexikaner(in) *m(f)*

Mexican wave N La-Ola-Welle *f*

Mexico ['meksɪkəʊ] N Mexiko *nt*

Mexico City N Mexiko City *nt*

mezzanine ['mezəniːn] N Mezzanin *nt*

mezzo-soprano [ˌmetsəʊsə'prɑːnəʊ] N *(= voice)* Mezzosopran *m*; *(= singer)* Mezzosopranistin *f*

mezzotint ['metsəʊˌtɪnt] N Mezzotint *nt*

mfd *abbr of* **manufactured** hergest.

MG *abbr of* **machine gun** MG *nt*

mg *abbr of* **milligram(s), milligramme(s)** mg

MHz *abbr of* **megahertz** MHz

mi. *abbr of* **mile(s)**

MI *abbr of* **machine intelligence**

MI5 *(Brit) abbr of* **Military Intelligence, section 5** MI5 *m*, *Spionageabwehrdienst der britischen Regierung*

MI6 *(Brit) abbr of* **Military Intelligence, section 6** MI6 *m*, *britischer Auslandsgeheimdienst*

miaow [miː'aʊ] *(Brit)* N Miau(en) *nt* VI miauen

miasma [mɪ'æzmə] N *pl* **miasmata** *or* **miasmas** [mɪ'æzmətə, mɪ'æzməz] Miasma *nt*

mica ['maɪkə] N Muskovit *m*

mice [maɪs] *pl of* **mouse**

Michaelmas ['mɪklməs] N Michaeli(s) *nt*

Michaelmas daisy N Herbstaster *f*

Michaelmas Day N Michaelis(tag *m*) *nt*

mickey ['mɪkɪ] N *(Brit inf)* **to take the ~ out of sb** jdn auf den Arm *or* auf die Schippe nehmen *(inf)*, jdn veräppeln *(inf)*; **are you taking the ~?** du willst mich/ihn *etc* wohl veräppeln *etc* *(inf)*

Mickey D's [ˌmɪkɪ'diːz] N *(US inf: = McDonald's)* Mäc *m (inf)*

Mickey Finn ['mɪkɪ'fɪn] N *(Brit inf)* Betäubungsmittel *nt*; *(= drink)* präparierter Drink; **they slipped him a ~** sie haben ihm was in den Drink getan *(inf)*

Mickey Mouse N Mickymaus *f* ADJ *attr (inf) company etc* lachhaft; **~ ears** Mickymaus-Ohren *pl*; **~ money** Spielgeld *nt*

micro ['maɪkrəʊ] N *(Comput)* Mikro(computer) *m*

micro- PREF mikro-, Mikro-

microbe ['maɪkrəʊb] N Mikrobe *f*

micro: microbiology N Mikrobiologie *f*; **microblog** N *(Internet)* Microblog *m or nt*; **microchannel architecture** N *(Comput)* Microchannel-Architektur *f*; **microchip** N Mikrochip *nt*; **microcircuit** N Mikroschaltung *f*; **microcircuitry** N Mikroschaltung *f*; **microclimate** N Mikroklima *nt*; **microcomputer** N Mikrorechner *m*, Mikrocomputer *m*; **microcosm** N Mikrokosmos *m*; **microdiskette** N Mikrofloppy *f*, Mikrodiskette *f*; **microdot** N Mikrobild *nt*; **microeconomics** N *sing* Mikroökonomie *f*; **microelectronics** N *sing* Mikroelektronik *f*; **micro fibre**, *(US)* **micro fiber** N *(Tex)* Mikrofaser *f*; **microfiche** N Mikrofiche *m or nt*, Mikrokarte *f*; **microfilm** N Mikrofilm *m* VT auf Mikrofilm aufnehmen; **microgravity** N *(Phys)* Mikrogravitation *f*; **microlight** N Ultraleichtflugzeug *nt*; **micrological** ADJ, **micrologically** ADV pedantisch, kleinlich; **micromesh** ADJ *stockings* feinmaschig; **micrometer** [maɪ'krÁmIt@'] N *(= gauge)* Mikrometerschraube *f*, Messschraube *f*; **micrometre**, *(US)* **micrometer** N Mikrometer *m or nt*

micron ['maɪkrɒn] N Mikron *nt*, Mikrometer *m or nt*

micro: microorganism N Mikroorganismus *m*; **microphone** N Mikrofon *nt*, Mikrophon *nt*; **microprocessor** N Mikroprozessor *m*; **microscope** N Mikroskop *nt*

microscopic [ˌmaɪkrə'skɒpɪk] ADJ *(in size)* mikroskopisch (klein); **~ creature** mikroskopisch kleines Lebewesen; **~ details** feinste Details; **in ~ detail** bis ins kleinste Detail

microscopically [ˌmaɪkrə'skɒpɪkəlɪ] ADV mikroskopisch

micro: microsecond N Mikrosekunde *f*; **microspacing** N *(Comput)* Feinausgleich *m*; **microstructural** ADJ mikrostrukturell; **microsurgery** N Mikrochirurgie *f*; **microsurgical** ADJ mikrochirurgisch; **microtransmitter** N Mikrosender *m*

microwave ['maɪkrəʊˌweɪv] N Mikrowelle *f*

microwavable, microwaveable ['maɪkrəʊˌweɪvəbl] ADJ *food* mikrowellen(herd)geeignet, -tauglich

microwave oven N Mikrowellenherd *m*

microwave-safe ADJ mikrowellenbeständig *or* -sicher

micturate ['mɪktjʊreɪt] VI *(Med: = urinate)* urinieren, harnen *(form)*

micturition [ˌmɪktjʊ'rɪʃən] N *(Med: = urinating)* Urinieren *nt*, Miktion *f (spec)*

mid [mɪd] PREP *(poet)* = **amid(st)** ADJ **in ~ January/June** Mitte Januar/Juni; **in the ~ 1950s** Mitte der fünfziger Jahre; **in the ~ 20th century** Mitte des 20. Jahrhunderts; **temperatures in the ~ eighties** Temperaturen um 85° Fahrenheit; **to be in one's ~ forties** Mitte vierzig *or* Mittvierzige(r) *mf* sein; **in ~ morning/afternoon** am Vormittag/Nachmittag; **a ~-morning/-afternoon break** eine Frühstücks-/Nachmittagspause; **a ~-morning snack** ein zweites Frühstück; **a ~-afternoon snack** ein Imbiss *m* am Nachmittag; **in ~ channel** in der Mitte des Kanals; **in ~ ocean** mitten auf dem Meer; **in ~ air** in der Luft; **in ~ flight** während des Flugs

mid-air [ˌmɪd'eə'] ADJ **~ collision** Zusammenstoß *m* in der Luft

Midas ['maɪdəs] N Midas *m*; **the ~ touch** eine glückliche Hand, Glück *nt*; **he has the ~ touch** er macht aus Dreck Geld *(inf)*

mid-Atlantic [ˌmɪdət'læntɪk] ADJ *accent etc* angloamerikanisch

midday ['mɪd'deɪ] N Mittag *m*; **at ~** mittags, gegen Mittag, um die Mittagszeit ADJ *attr* mittäglich; **~ meal** Mittagessen *nt*; **~ sun/heat** Mittagssonne/-hitze *f*

midden ['mɪdn] N *(Archeol)* Muschelhaufen *m*; *(dial) (= dustbin)* Mülleimer *m*; *(= rubbish dump)* Müll *m*

middle ['mɪdl] N Mitte *f*; *(= central section: of book, film etc)* Mittelteil *m*, mittlerer Teil; *(= inside: of fruit, nut etc)* Innere(s) *nt*; *(= stomach)* Bauch *m*, Leib *m*; *(= waist)* Taille *f*; **in the ~ of the table** mitten auf dem Tisch; *(= in exact centre)* in der Mitte des Tisches; **he passed the ball to the ~ of the field** er spielte den Ball zur (Feld)mitte; **in the ~ of the night** mitten in der Nacht; **in the ~ of the day** mitten am Tag; *(= around midday)* gegen Mittag; **to live in the ~ of nowhere** am Ende der Welt wohnen; **in the ~ of summer** mitten im Sommer; *(= height of summer season)* im Hochsommer; **in** *or* **about the ~ of May** Mitte Mai; **in the ~ of the century** um die Jahrhundertmitte, Mitte des Jahrhunderts; **we were in the ~ of lunch** wir waren mitten beim Essen; **in the ~ of my back** im Kreuz; **to be in the ~ of doing sth** mitten dabei sein, etw zu tun; **I'm in the ~ of reading it** ich bin mittendrin; **down the ~** in der Mitte; **he parts his hair down the ~** er hat einen Mittelscheitel ADJ mittlere(r, s); **the ~ house** das mittlere Haus, das Haus in der Mitte; **to be in one's ~ twenties/thirties** Mitte zwanzig/dreißig sein; **I'm the ~ child of three** ich bin das mittlere der drei Kinder

middle *in cpds* Mittel-, mittel-; **middle age** N mittleres Lebensalter; **middle-aged** ADJ in den mittleren Jahren, mittleren Alters; *feeling, appearance* alt; *attitudes* spießig *(pej)*, altmodisch; **Middle Ages** PL Mittelalter *nt*; **Middle America** N **a** *(Geog)* Mittelamerika *nt* **b** *(= class)* die amerikanische Mittelschicht; **middlebrow** ADJ für den (geistigen) Normalverbraucher; **~ tastes** Durchschnittsgeschmack *m* N (geistiger) Normalverbraucher; **middle C** N (eingestrichenes) C; **middle-class** ADJ bürgerlich, spießig *(pej)*; *(Sociol)* mittelständisch; **he's so typically ~** er ist ein typischer Vertreter der Mittelklasse, er ist ein richtiger Spießer *(pej)*; **middle class(es)** N(PL) Mittelstand *m or* -schicht *f*; **middle distance** N mittlere Entfernung; *(Sport)* Mittelstrecke *f*; *(Art)* Mittelgrund *m*; **middle-distance runner** N Mittelstreckenläufer(in) *m(f)*; **middle-distance running** N Mittelstreckenlauf *m*; **~ is ...** der Mittelstreckenlauf ist ...; **middle ear** N Mittelohr *nt*; **Middle East** N Naher Osten; *(from Iran and Iraq to India)* Mittlerer Osten; **Middle England** N *(fig: = middle classes)* die englische Mittelschicht; **Middle English** N Mittelenglisch *nt*; **middle finger** N Mittelfinger *m*; **Middle High German** N Mittelhochdeutsch *nt*; **middle-income** ADJ *family* mit mittlerem Einkommen; **~ earner** Mittelverdiener(in) *m(f)*; **Middle Low German** N Mittelniederdeutsch *nt*; **middleman** N Mittelsmann *m*, Mittelsperson *f*; *(Comm)* Zwischenhändler *m*; **middle management** N mittleres Management; **middle manager** N mittlerer Manager, mittlere Managerin, mittlere Führungskraft; **middle name** N zweiter (Vor)name; **modesty is my ~** *(fig)* ich bin die Bescheidenheit in Person; **middle-of-the-road** ADJ **a** *(= moderate)* gemäßigt; *policy, politician* der gemäßigten Mitte **b** *(= conventional) style, person* konventionell; *music* anspruchslos, für den Normalverbraucher; **middle-of-the-roader** N Vertreter(in) *m(f)* der gemäßigten Mitte; **middle-ranking** ADJ mittlere(r, s); **~ army officers** Armeeoffiziere *pl* mittleren Ranges; **middle school** N *(Brit) Schule für 9-12-jährige*; **middle watch** N Mittelwache *f*; **middleweight** *(Sport)* N Mittelgewicht *nt*; *(= person also)* Mittelgewichtler(in) *m(f)* ADJ Mittelgewichts-; **~ champion** Mittelgewichtsmeister(in) *m(f)*, Meister(in) *m(f)* im Mittelgewicht

middling [ˈmɪdlɪŋ] ADJ mittelmäßig; *(of size)* mittlere(r, s); **how are you? – ~** wie geht es dir? – mittelprächtig *(inf)* *or* einigermaßen; **what was the weather like? – ~** wie war das Wetter? – durchwachsen *or* so lala *(inf)* ADV *(inf: = fairly)* **~ rich** ziemlich reich

Middx *abbr of* **Middlesex**

Mideast [mɪdˈiːst] *(US)* N **the ~** der Nahe Osten; *(from Iran and Iraq to India)* der Mittlere Osten ADJ Nahost-; *(from Iran and Iraq to India)* des Mittleren Ostens; **a ~ peace conference** eine Nahost-Friedenskonferenz/eine Friedenskonferenz des Mittleren Ostens

midfield [ˌmɪdˈfiːld] N Mittelfeld *nt* ADJ Mittelfeld-; **~ player/position** Mittelfeldspieler(in) *m(f)*/-position *f*

midfielder [mɪdˈfiːldəʳ] N *(Ftbl)* Mittelfeldspieler(in) *m(f)*

midge [mɪdʒ] N *(Brit)* Mücke *f*

midget [ˈmɪdʒɪt] N kleiner Mensch, Liliputaner(in) *m(f)*; *(= child)* Knirps *m* ADJ winzig; **~ submarine** Kleinst-U-Boot *nt*

MIDI [ˈmɪdɪ] *abbr of* **musical instrument digital interface** N Midi-System *nt or* -Anlage *f* ADJ Midi-

midi (system) [ˈmɪdɪ(ˌsɪstəm)] N Midi-System *nt or* -Anlage *f*

mid: **midland** ADJ *attr* im Landesinneren (gelegen) N Landesinnere(s) *nt* → **Midlands**; **Midlands** PL **the ~** die Midlands; **midlife crisis** N Midlifecrisis *f*, Midlife-Crisis *f*, Krise *f* in der Mitte des Lebens; **he's having his ~** er befindet sich in der Midlifecrisis *or* Midlife-Crisis; **midnight** N Mitternacht *f*; **at ~** um Mitternacht ADJ *attr* mitternächtlich, Mitternachts-; **~ mass** Mitternachtsmesse *f*; **the ~ hour** die Mitternachtsstunde, Mitternacht *f*; **the ~ sun** die Mitternachtssonne; **midnight-blue** ADJ nachtblau; **midpoint** N mittlerer Punkt; *(Geometry)* Mittelpunkt *m*; **to pass ~** die Hälfte hinter sich *(dat)* haben; **mid-price** ADJ im mittleren Preisbereich N mittlerer Preisbereich, Mittelpreislage *f*; **at ~** im mittleren Preisbereich; **mid-range** ADJ *hotel, computer* der Mittelklasse *pred*, im mittleren Bereich; **a ~ car** ein Mittelklassewagen *m*

midriff [ˈmɪdrɪf] N Taille *f*; **a punch to the ~** ein Schlag in die Magengegend *or* -grube

mid: **midshipman** N Fähnrich *m* zur See; **midships** ADV mittschiffs; **mid-sized** ADJ mittelgroß; *company* mittelständisch

midst [mɪdst] N Mitte *f*; **in the ~ of** mitten in; **we are in the ~ of an economic crisis** wir stecken mitten in einer Wirtschaftskrise; **and in the ~ of our troubles Grandpa died** und zu allem Unglück starb noch Großvater; **in our ~** unter uns, in unserer Mitte *(geh)*; **in the ~ of life (we are in death)** *(Bibl)* mitten im Leben sind wir vom Tod umgeben PREP *(old poet)* = **amid(st)**

mid: **midstream** N **in ~** *(lit)* in der Mitte des Flusses; *(fig)* auf halber Strecke, mittendrin; **midsummer** N Hochsommer *m* ADJ *days, nights, festival* im Hochsommer; **"A Midsummer Night's Dream"** „Ein Sommernachtstraum"; **midsummer madness** N Sommerkoller *m* *(inf)*; **that was ~** das war eine Schnapsidee *(inf)*; **Midsummer's Day** N Sommersonnenwende *f*, Johannistag *m*; **midterm** N **in ~** *(three-term year)* mitten im Trimester; *(two-term year)* mitten im Schulhalbjahr *or (Univ)* Semester; **by ~** bis zur Trimesterhälfte/bis zur Mitte des Schulhalbjahres/Semesters; **it was ~ before ...** das halbe Trimester/Schulhalbjahr/Semester war schon vorbei, bevor ... ADJ **~ elections** *(Pol)* Zwischenwahlen *pl*; **~ examinations** *Prüfungen in der Mitte eines Trimesters/Schulhalbjahres/Semesters*; **midtown** *(US)* N Stadtzentrum *nt* ADJ im Stadtzentrum; **the ~ bus** der Bus ins Stadtzentrum; **a ~ Manhattan hotel** ein Hotel im Zentrum von Manhattan

midway ADV auf halbem Weg; **Düsseldorf is ~ between Krefeld and Cologne** Düsseldorf liegt auf halber Strecke zwischen Krefeld und Köln; **~ through sth** mitten in etw *(dat)*; **we are now ~** die Hälfte haben wir hinter uns *(dat)* ADJ **X is the ~ point between A and B** X liegt auf halbem Wege zwischen A und B; **we've now reached the ~ point** *or* **stage in the project** das Projekt ist jetzt zur Hälfte fertig N *(US: at fair)* *Mittelweg eines Jahrmarkts, an dem sich die Hauptattraktionen befinden*

mid: **midweek** ADV mitten in der Woche; **by ~** Mitte der Woche ADJ *attr* Mitte der Woche; **he booked a ~ flight** er buchte einen Flug für Mitte der Woche; **Midwest** N Mittelwesten *m*; **Midwestern** ADJ mittelwestlich; *songs, dialect etc also* des Mittelwestens; **Midwesterner** N *(US)* Bewohner(in) *m(f)* des Mittelwestens

midwife [ˈmɪdwaɪf] N *pl* **-wives** Hebamme *f*

midwifery [ˌmɪdˈwɪfərɪ] N Geburtshilfe *f*

midwife toad N *(Zool)* Geburtshelferkröte *f*

midwinter [ˌmɪdˈwɪntəʳ] N Mitte *f* des Winters, Wintermitte *f* ADJ um die Mitte des Winters, mittwinterlich

midwives [ˈmɪdwaɪvz] *pl of* **midwife**

mien [miːn] N *(liter)* Miene *f*

miff [mɪf] VT *(inf)* **to be ~ed at** *or* **about sth** *(= annoyed)* über etw *(acc)* verärgert sein; *(= offended)* sich wegen etw auf den Schlips getreten fühlen *(inf)*; **to get ~ed at sth** sich über etw *(acc)* erhitzen

miffy [ˈmɪfɪ] ADJ *(+er)* *(inf: = easily annoyed)* leicht beleidigt, mimosenhaft; *plant* empfindlich

might[1] [maɪt] ✪ 15.2, 15.3 *pret of* **may**; **they ~ be brothers, they look so alike** sie könnten Brüder sein, sie sehen sich so ähnlich; **as you ~ expect** wie zu erwarten war; **... I ~ add ...** möchte ich hinzufügen; **how old ~ he be?** wie alt er wohl ist?; **~ I smoke?** dürfte ich wohl rauchen?; **you ~ try Smith's** Sie könnten es ja mal bei Smiths versuchen; **he ~ at least have apologized** er hätte sich wenigstens entschuldigen können; **I ~ have known** das hätte ich mir denken können; **she was thinking of what ~ have been** sie dachte an das, was hätte sein können

might[2] N Macht *f*; **with all one's ~** mit aller Kraft; **superior ~** Übermacht *f*, Überlegenheit *f*; **~ is right** *(Prov)* Macht geht vor Recht *(Prov)*

mightily [ˈmaɪtɪlɪ] ADV **a** mit aller Macht; *(fig: = majestically, imposingly)* gewaltig **b** *(inf: = extremely)* mächtig *(inf)*; **a ~ improved team** eine stark verbesserte Mannschaft; **~ impressive** höchst beeindruckend; **I was ~ impressed/relieved** ich war überaus beeindruckt/erleichtert

mightiness [ˈmaɪtɪnɪs] N Macht *f*; *(of wave, shout, scream)* Gewalt *f*; *(of warrior, noise, cheer)* Stärke *f*; *(of ship, tree etc)* gewaltige Ausmaße *pl*

mightn't [ˈmaɪtnt] *contr of* **might not**

mighty [ˈmaɪtɪ] ADJ **a** *(= wielding power) person, force, army* mächtig; **the ~** die Mächtigen *pl*; **how are the ~ fallen** wie sind die Helden gefallen *(Bibl)*, Hochmut kommt vor dem Fall *(Prov)*; **a ~ warrior** ein großer Krieger **b** *(= massive) building, noise, load, crowd, ship* gewaltig; *river, tree, wave, effect, blow* mächtig, gewaltig; *cheer* lautstark ADV *(esp US inf)* mächtig *(inf)*

mignonette [ˌmɪnjəˈnet] N Reseda *f*, Resede *f*

migraine [ˈmiːgreɪn] N Migräne *f*

migrant [ˈmaɪgrənt] ADJ **~ bird** Zugvogel *m*; **~ butterfly** Wanderfalter *m*; **~ worker** Wanderarbeiter(in) *m(f)*; *(esp in EC)* Migrant(in) *m(f)*, Gastarbeiter(in) *m(f)* *(neg!)*; **~ labour** *(Brit) or* **labor** *(US)* Wanderarbeiter *pl*; *(esp in EC)* Gastarbeiter *pl* *(neg!)*; **~ family** Migrantenfamilie *f*; **~ child** Migrantenkind *nt* N **a** *(= bird)* Zugvogel *m* **b** *(= worker)* Wanderarbeiter(in) *m(f)*; *(esp in EC)* Migrant(in) *m(f)*, Gastarbeiter(in) *m(f)* *(neg!)*

migrate [maɪˈgreɪt] VI *(animals, workers)* (ab)wandern; *(birds)* nach Süden ziehen; *(fig: townsfolk etc)* ziehen; **do these birds ~?** sind das Zugvögel?

migration [maɪˈgreɪʃən] N **a** Wanderung *f*; *(of birds)* (Vogel)zug *m*; *(fig: of people)* Abwanderung *f*, Migration *f*; *(seasonal)* Zug *m*; *(Comput) (of software infrastructute etc)* Migration *f* **b** *(= number)* Schwarm *m*

migratory [maɪˈgreɪtərɪ] ADJ Wander-; *population* wandernd; **~ habits** Wanderungsgewohnheiten *pl*; **~ life** Wanderleben *nt*; **~ instinct** Wandertrieb *m*; **~ worker** Wanderarbeiter(in) *m(f)*; **~ labour** *(Brit) or* **labor** *(US)* Wanderarbeiter *pl*; **~ birds** Zugvögel *pl*; **~ creatures** *or* **animals** Tiere, die auf Wanderung gehen, wandernde Tiere; **~ fish** Wanderfisch *m*; **sea turtles are ~** Meeresschildkröten sind wandernde Tiere

Mike [maɪk] N **a** *dim of* **Michael b for the love of ~!** *(inf)* um Himmels willen *(inf)*

mike [maɪk] N *(inf)* Mikro *nt (inf)*, Mikrofon *nt*, Mikrophon *nt*

milady [mɪˈleɪdɪ] N Mylady *f*, gnädige Frau

milage N = **mileage**

Milan [mɪˈlæn] N Mailand *nt*

mild [maɪld] ADJ *(+er)* **a** *(= gentle) climate, weather, soap, punishment, spring day* mild; *breeze, criticism, rebuke* leicht, sanft; *medicine* leicht; *person, character, eyes* sanft **b** *(in flavour) taste, cigar, cheese, whisky* mild; *cigarettes* mild, leicht; **this cheese has a very ~ taste** der Käse ist sehr mild (im Geschmack); **~ ale** leichtes dunkles Bier **c** *(= slight) illness* leicht; **a ~ form/case of meningitis** eine leichte Gehirnhautentzündung N *(Brit: = beer)* leichtes dunkles Bier

mildew [ˈmɪldjuː] N Schimmel *m*; *(on plants)* Mehltau *m* VI verschimmeln, Schimmel ansetzen; *(plants)* von Mehltau befallen sein

mildewy [ˈmɪldjuːɪ] ADJ schimmelig, verschimmelt; *plants* von Mehltau befallen

mildly [ˈmaɪldlɪ] ADV leicht; *say, ask* sanft; *scold, rebuke, protest, curse, reply* milde; **to put it ~** gelinde gesagt; **... and that's putting it ~** ... und das ist noch milde ausgedrückt; **they seemed ~ interested** sie machten einen leicht interessierten Eindruck; **to be ~ critical of sth** etw milde kritisieren

mildness [ˈmaɪldnɪs] N **a** *(= gentleness) (of climate, weather, day, soap, punishment)* Milde *f*; *(of breeze, criticism, rebuke)* Sanftheit *f*; *(of medicine)* Leichtheit *f*; *(of person, character)* Sanftmütigkeit *f* **b** *(in flavour)* Milde *f*; *(of cigarettes)* Milde *f*, Leichtheit *f* **c** *(= slightness: of illness)* leichte Form

mile [maɪl] N Meile *f*; **how many ~s per gallon does your car do?** wie viel verbraucht Ihr Auto?; **a fifty-~ journey** eine Fahrt von fünfzig Meilen; **it's 12 ~s to Manchester** bis Manchester sind es 12 Meilen; **~s (and ~s)** *(inf)* meilenweit; **~ upon ~ of sandy beaches** meilenweite Sandstrände *pl*; **to go the extra ~** *(fig)* besondere Anstrengungen unternehmen; **the President is willing to go the extra ~ for peace** der Präsident ist bereit, für den Frieden Zugeständnisse zu machen; **they live ~s away** sie wohnen meilenweit weg; **sorry, I was ~s away** *(inf)* tut mir leid, ich war mit meinen Gedanken ganz woanders *(inf)*; **you can tell it a ~ off, it stands** *or* **sticks out a ~** das sieht ja ein Blinder (mit Krückstock) *(inf)*; **it smelled for ~s around** das roch 10 Kilometer gegen den Wind *(inf)*; **you were ~s off the target** du hast meilenweit danebengetroffen; **he's ~s better at tennis than she is** er spielt hundertmal besser Tennis als sie *(inf)*; **not a million ~s from here** *(fig)* in nächster Nähe, gar nicht weit weg; **if she invited me for dinner, I'd run a ~** *(fig inf)* wenn sie mich zum Abendessen einladen würde, würde mich das kalte Grausen packen *(inf)*; **to talk a ~ a minute** *(US inf)* das Blaue vom Himmel (herunter)reden *(inf)*

mileage [ˈmaɪlɪdʒ] N Meilen *pl*; *(on odometer)* Meilenstand *m*, Meilenzahl *f*; **what ~ did you do yesterday?** wie viele Meilen seid ihr gestern gefahren?; **~ per gallon** Benzinverbrauch *m*; **you get a much better ~ (per gallon) from this car if ...** dieser Wagen ist viel sparsamer im Verbrauch, wenn ...; **unlimited ~** *(for hired car)* unbegrenzte Kilometerzahl; **~ allowance** ≈ Kilometerpauschale *f*; **we got a lot of ~ out of it** *(fig inf)* das war uns *(dat)* sehr dienlich; **it's still**

got a lot of ~ left in it *(fig inf)* da steckt noch einiges drin *(inf)*; **he decided there was no ~ in provoking a row with his boss** er entschied, dass es nichts bringen würde, mit dem Chef einen Streit anzufangen *(inf)*

mileometer [maɪˈlɒmɪtəʳ] N *(Brit)* ≈ Kilometerzähler *m*

milepost [ˈmaɪlpəʊst] N Meilenanzeiger *m or* -pfosten *m*

miler [ˈmaɪləʳ] N 1500-Meter-Läufer(in) *m(f)*

milestone [ˈmaɪlstəʊn] N *(lit, fig)* Meilenstein *m*

milieu [ˈmiːljɜː] N Milieu *nt*

militant [ˈmɪlɪtənt] **ADJ** militant; **to be in (a) ~ mood** in militanter Stimmung sein **N** militantes Element; **the ~s among the students** die militanten Studenten

militantly [ˈmɪlɪtəntlɪ] ADV *(= fiercely)* militant; **the army is ~ nationalist** die Armee ist militant-nationalistisch

Militant Tendency N *(Brit Pol) trotzkistische Splittergruppe innerhalb der Labour Party*

militarily [ˈmɪlɪtrɪlɪ] ADV *intervene, respond* militärisch; *(= from a military point of view)* militärisch (gesehen), auf militärischem Gebiet; **to get involved ~** in Militäraktionen *(acc)* verwickelt werden

militarism [ˈmɪlɪtərɪzəm] N Militarismus *m*

militarist [ˈmɪlɪtərɪst] **ADJ** militaristisch **N** Militarist(in) *m(f)*

militaristic [ˌmɪlɪtəˈrɪstɪk] ADJ militaristisch

militarize [ˈmɪlɪtəraɪz] VT militarisieren; **fully ~d** hoch militarisiert

military [ˈmɪlɪtərɪ] **ADJ** militärisch; **~ government** Militärregierung *f*; **~ personnel** Militär- *or* Armeeangehörige *pl*; **to do sth with ~ precision** etw mit militärischer Präzision tun; **the top ~ men** die führenden Militärs **N** **the ~** das Militär

military: **military academy** N Militärakademie *f*; **military band** N Militärkapelle *f*; **military base** N Militär- *or* Armeestützpunkt *m*; **military-industrial complex** N **the ~** *(US)* der militärisch-industrielle Komplex; **military police** N Militärpolizei *f*; **military policeman** N Militärpolizist *m*; **military policewoman** N Militärpolizistin *f*; **military school** N Militärschule *f*; **military service** N Militärdienst *m*, Wehrdienst *m*; **to do one's ~** seinen Wehr- *or* Militärdienst ableisten *or* machen *(inf)*; **he's doing his ~** er ist gerade beim Militär; **military spending** N Militärausgaben *pl*

militate [ˈmɪlɪteɪt] VI **to ~ against/in favour** *(Brit) or* **favor** *(US)* **of sth** für/gegen etw sprechen

militia [mɪˈlɪʃə] N Miliz *f*, Bürgerwehr *f*

militiaman [mɪˈlɪʃəmən] N *pl* **-men** [-mən] Milizsoldat *m*

milk [mɪlk] **N** Milch *f*; **the land of** *or* **flowing with ~ and honey** das Land, wo Milch und Honig fließt; **the ~ of human kindness** die Milch der frommen Denk(ungs)art *(liter)*; **she was not exactly flowing over with the ~ of human kindness** sie strömte nicht gerade über vor Freundlichkeit; **it's** *or* **there's no use crying over spilled ~** *(prov)* was passiert ist, ist passiert **VT** *(lit, fig)* melken; **the little old lady was ~ed dry by some heartless swindler** die alte Frau wurde von einem gewissenlosen Betrüger nach Strich und Faden ausgenommen *(inf)* **VI** Milch geben, milchen *(dial)*

milk *in cpds* Milch-; **milk-and-water** ADJ *(fig)* seicht, verwässert; **he dismissed the report as milk and water** er tat den Bericht als nichtssagend ab; **milk bar** N Milchbar *f*; **milk carton** N Milchtüte *f*, Milchkarton *m*; **milk chocolate** N Vollmilchschokolade *f*; **milk churn** N Milchkanne *f*; **milk float** N Milchauto *nt*

milkiness [ˈmɪlkɪnɪs] N Milchigkeit *f*

milking [ˈmɪlkɪŋ] N Melken *nt*

milking machine N Melkmaschine *f*

milking stool N Melkschemel *m*

milk: **milkmaid** N Milchmädchen *nt*; **milkman** N Milchmann *m*; **milk of magnesia** N Magnesiamilch *f*; **milk powder** N Milchpulver *nt*; **milk product** N Milchprodukt *nt*; **milk pudding** N *(Brit)* Milchspeise *f*; **milk round** N *(Brit)* **a** *(of milkman)* Milchrunde *f* **b** *(Univ) regelmäßige Besuche von Personalvertretern großer Firmen an Universitäten, um mögliche Mitarbeiter zu rekrutieren*; **milk run** N *(Aviat inf)* Routineflug *m*; **milkshake** N Milchmixgetränk *nt*, Milchshake *m*; **milksop** N Milchbart *m*, Milchgesicht *nt*; **milk stout** N *(Brit)* ≈ Malzbier *nt*; **milk tooth** N Milchzahn *m*; **milkweed** N *(US)* Schwalbenwurzgewächs *nt*; **milk-white** ADJ milchig-weiß, milchweiß

milky [ˈmɪlkɪ] ADJ *(+er)* milchig; **~ green/blue/white** milchig grün/blau/weiß; **~ drink** Milchgetränk *nt*; **~ coffee** Milchkaffee *m*; **rich ~ chocolate** sahnige Vollmilchschokolade

Milky Way [ˌmɪlkɪˈweɪ] N Milchstraße *f*

mill [mɪl] **N** **a** *(= building)* Mühle *f* **b** *(= machine)* Mühle *f*; **the poor man really went through the ~** *(inf)* der Arme hat wirklich viel durchmachen müssen; *(= was questioned hard)* der Arme wurde wirklich durch die Mangel gedreht *(inf)*; **in training you're really put through the ~** *(inf)* im Training wird man ganz schön hart rangenommen *(inf)* **c** *(= paper, steel mill etc)* Fabrik *f*; *(= cotton mill, for thread)* Spinnerei *f*; *(for cloth)* Weberei *f* **VT** *flour, coffee etc* mahlen; *metal, paper* walzen; *(with milling machine) metal* fräsen; *coin* rändeln

▶ **mill about** *(Brit) or* **around** VI umherlaufen; **people were milling about** *or* **around the office** es herrschte ein Kommen und Gehen im Büro; **the crowds milling about** *or* **around the stalls in the marketplace** die Menschenmenge, die sich zwischen den Marktständen einherschob

millboard [ˈmɪlbɔːd] N *(= pasteboard)* starke Pappe, Pappdeckel *m*

milled [mɪld] ADJ *grain* gemahlen; *coin, edge* gerändelt; **freshly-~ pepper** frisch gemahlener Pfeffer

millenarian [ˌmɪləˈneərɪən] ADJ *(Rel)* millenaristisch, chiliastisch

millennial [mɪˈlenɪəl] ADJ Jahrtausend-, Millennium(s)-

millennium [mɪˈlenɪəm] N *pl* **-s** *or* **millennia** [mɪˈlenɪə] *(= 1,000 years)* Jahrtausend *nt*, Millennium *nt*; *(= state of perfection)* Tausendjähriges Reich, Millennium *nt*

millennium: **millennium bug** N *(Comput inf)* Jahrtausendfehler *m or* -problem *nt*; **Millennium Fund** N *(Brit) Fonds für die Finanzierung von Projekten zur Feier der Jahrtausendwende*

millepede [ˈmɪlɪpiːd] N = **millipede**

miller [ˈmɪləʳ] N Müller(in) *m(f)*

millet [ˈmɪlɪt] N Hirse *f*

milli- [ˈmɪlɪ-] PREF Milli-; **millisecond** Millisekunde *f*

milliard [ˈmɪlɪɑːd] N *(Brit)* Milliarde *f*

milli: **millibar** N Millibar *nt*; **milligram(me)** N Milligramm *nt*; **millilitre**, *(US)* **milliliter** N Milliliter *m or nt*; **millimetre**, *(US)* **millimeter** N Millimeter *m or nt*

milliner [ˈmɪlɪnəʳ] N Hutmacher *m*, Hut- *or* Putzmacherin *f*, Modistin *f*; **at the ~'s (shop)** im Hutgeschäft *or* -laden

millinery [ˈmɪlɪnərɪ] N *(= trade)* Hut- *or* Putzmacherhandwerk *nt*; *(= articles)* Hüte *pl*

milling machine [ˈmɪlɪŋməʃiːn] N *(for coins)* Rändel(eisen) *nt*; *(for metal)* Fräse *f*, Fräsmaschine *f*

million [ˈmɪljən] N Million *f*; **4 ~ people** 4 Millionen Menschen; **for ~s and ~s of years** für millionen und abermillionen *or* Millionen und Abermillionen von Jahren; **the starving ~s** die Millionen, die Hunger leiden; **she's one in a ~** *(inf)* so jemanden wie sie findet man sobald nicht wieder, sie ist einsame Klasse *(inf)*; **it will sell a ~** *(inf)* das wird ein Millionenerfolg; **I've done it ~s of times** *(inf)* das habe ich schon tausendmal gemacht; **to feel (like) a ~ dollars** *(inf)* sich pudelwohl fühlen; **to look (like) a ~ dollars** *(inf)* umwerfend aussehen *(inf)*

millionaire [ˌmɪljəˈneəʳ] N Millionär *m*

millionairess [ˌmɪljəˈneəres] N Millionärin *f*

millionfold [ˈmɪljənfəʊld] *(liter)* **ADJ** millionenfach **ADV** **a ~** millionenfach, millionenfältig

millionth [ˈmɪljənθ] **ADJ** *(= fraction)* millionstel; *(in series)* millionste(r, s) **N** Millionstel *nt*

millipede [ˈmɪlɪpiːd] N Tausendfüß(l)er *m*

mill: **millpond** N Mühlteich *m*; **millrace** N Mühlbach *or* -graben *m*; **millstone** N Mühlstein *m*, Mahlstein *m*; **she's/it's a ~ around his neck** sie/das ist für ihn ein Klotz am Bein; **millstream** N Mühlbach *m*; **millwheel** N Mühlrad *nt*

milord [mɪˈlɔːd] N *(= person)* Mylord *m*, Lord *m*; *(as address)* Mylord *m*; **like some English ~** wie ein englischer Lord

milt [mɪlt] N *(Fishing)* Milch *f*

mime [maɪm] **N** *(= acting)* Pantomime *f*; *(= actor)* Pantomime *m*, Pantomimin *f*; *(= ancient play, actor)* Mimus *m*; **the art of ~** die Pantomimik, die Kunst der Pantomime; **to do a ~** eine Pantomime darstellen **VT** pantomimisch darstellen **VI** Pantomimen spielen

mime artist N Pantomime *m*, Pantomimin *f*

mimeograph [ˈmɪmɪəgrɑːf] **N** Vervielfältigungsapparat *m* **VT** vervielfältigen, abziehen *(inf)*

mimic [ˈmɪmɪk] **N** Imitator(in) *m(f)*; **he's a very good ~** er kann sehr gut Geräusche/andere Leute nachahmen *or* -machen **VT** nachahmen *or* -machen; *(= ridicule)* nachäffen

mimicry [ˈmɪmɪkrɪ] N Nachahmung *f*; *(Biol)* Mimikry *f*; **protective ~** Schutzfärbung *f*, Tarnfarbe *f*; **his talent for ~** sein Talent dafür, andere nachzuahmen

mimosa [mɪˈməʊzə] N **a** *(Bot)* Mimose *f* **b** *(US: = drink)* Sekt *m* mit Orangensaft

Min **a** *abbr of* **Minister** Min. **b** *abbr of* **Ministry** Min.

min **a** *abbr of* **minute(s)** min **b** *abbr of* **minimum** min.

minaret [ˌmɪnəˈret] N Minarett *nt*

mince [mɪns] **N** *(esp Brit)* Hackfleisch *nt*, Gehackte(s) *nt* **VT** *(esp Brit) meat* hacken, durch den Fleischwolf drehen; **he doesn't ~ his words** er nimmt kein Blatt vor den Mund; **he didn't ~ matters** er sagte es mal ganz deutlich *or* brutal *(inf)* **VI** *(Brit) (= walk)* tänzeln, trippeln, scharwenzeln; *(= behave/speak)* sich geziert benehmen/ausdrücken

minced [mɪnst] ADJ **a** *meat* klein gehackt; *onion* klein geschnitten **b** *(Brit inf: = drunk)* hackedicht *(inf)*

mince: **mincemeat** N *süße Gebäckfüllung aus Dörrobst und Sirup*; **to make ~ of sb** *(inf) (physically)* Hackfleisch aus jdm machen *(inf)*; *(verbally)* jdn zur Schnecke machen *(inf)*; **to make ~ of sth** *(inf)* keinen guten Faden an etw *(dat)* lassen; **mince pie** N *mit Mincemeat gefülltes Gebäck*

mincer [ˈmɪnsəʳ] N *(esp Brit)* Fleischwolf *m*

mincing [ˈmɪnsɪŋ] ADJ *(Brit)* geziert; *steps* tänzelnd, trippelnd

mincingly [ˈmɪnsɪŋlɪ] ADV *(Brit)* gekünstelt; **he walked ~ away from her** er entfernte sich tänzelnd von ihr

mincing machine N *(esp Brit)* Fleischwolf *m*

mind [maɪnd]
✪ 4, 9.1

1 NOUN	3 INTRANSITIVE VERB
2 TRANSITIVE VERB	4 PHRASAL VERB

1 – NOUN

a [= intellect] Geist *m (also Philos)*, Verstand *m*; **things of the mind** Geistiges *nt*; **the conscious and unconscious mind** das Bewusste und das Unbewusste; **to have a good mind** ein heller Kopf sein; **one of the finest minds of our times** einer der großen Geister unserer Zeit; **it's all in the mind** das ist alles Einbildung; **in one's mind's eye** vor seinem geistigen Auge, im Geiste; **to blow sb's mind** *(inf)* jdn umwerfen *(inf)*; *(drugs)* jdn high machen *(inf)* → **boggle, great, improve**

♦ **mind over matter** **it's a question of mind over matter** es ist eine Willenssache *or* -frage; **a triumph of mind over matter** ein Triumph des Geistes *or* Willens über den Körper

b [= way of thinking] Denkweise *f*; *(= type of mind)* Geist *m*, Kopf *m*; **to the child's/Victorian mind** in der Denkweise des Kindes/der viktorianischen Zeit; **he has that kind of mind** er ist so veranlagt; **to have a literary/logical** *etc* **mind** literarisch/logisch *etc* veranlagt sein; **he has the mind of a five-year old** er verhält sich wie ein Fünfjähriger; **in the public mind prostitution is immoral** nach dem Empfinden der Öffentlichkeit ist Prostitution unmoralisch; **state** *or* **frame of mind** (seelische) Verfassung, (Geistes)zustand *m*

c [= thoughts] Gedanken *pl*; **to be clear in one's mind about sth** sich *(dat)* über etw im Klaren sein; **to put** *or* **set one's mind to sth** *(= try to do sth)* sich anstrengen, etw zu tun; *(= think about sth)* sich auf etw *(acc)* konzentrieren; **if you put** *or* **set your mind to it** wenn du dich anstrengst; **he had something on his mind** ihn beschäftigte etwas; **I've a lot on my mind** ich muss mich um (so) viele Dinge kümmern; **you are always on my mind** ich denke ständig an dich; **keep your mind on the job** bleib mit den Gedanken *or* dem Kopf bei der Arbeit; **she couldn't get** *or* **put the song/him out of her mind** das Lied/er ging ihr nicht aus dem Kopf; **you can put that idea out of your mind!** den Gedanken kannst du dir aus dem Kopf schlagen!; **to take sb's mind off things** jdn auf andere Gedanken bringen; **to take sb's mind off sth** jdn etw vergessen lassen; **my mind isn't on my work** ich kann mich nicht auf meine Arbeit konzentrieren; **don't let your mind dwell on the problem** grüble nicht über dieses Problem nach; **he can't keep his mind off sex** er denkt nur an Sex *or* an nichts anderes als Sex; **the idea never entered my mind** daran hatte ich überhaupt nicht gedacht; **it's been going through my mind** es ging mir im Kopf herum; **nothing was further from my mind** nichts lag mir ferner; **his mind is set on that** er hat sich *(dat)* das in den Kopf gesetzt; **he guessed what was in my mind** er erriet meine Gedanken; **in my mind's eye** vor meinem inneren Auge → **cross**[1]

d [= memory] Gedächtnis *nt*; **it went right out of my mind** daran habe ich überhaupt nicht mehr gedacht; **that quite put it out of my mind** dadurch habe ich es vergessen; **to bring** *or* **call sth to mind** etw in Erinnerung rufen, an etw *(acc)* erinnern → **sight, slip**

e [= inclination] Lust *f*; *(= intention)* Sinn *m*, Absicht *f*; **I've half a mind/a good mind to ...** ich hätte Lust/große *or* gute Lust, zu ...; **to be of a mind to do sth** geneigt sein, etw zu tun *(geh)* → **read**[1]

f [= opinion] Meinung *f*, Ansicht *f*; **to change one's mind** seine Meinung ändern (*about* über *+acc*), es sich *(dat)* anders überlegen; **to be in two minds about sth** sich *(dat)* über etw *(acc)* nicht im Klaren sein; **to be of one** *or* **of the same mind** eines Sinnes *(geh)* *or* gleicher Meinung sein; **I'm of the same mind as you** ich denke wie du, ich bin deiner Meinung; **with one mind** wie ein Mann; **to my mind he's wrong** meiner Ansicht nach *or* nach meiner Meinung irrt er sich; **to have a mind of one's own** (*person, = think for oneself*) eine eigene Meinung haben; *(= not conform)* seinen eigenen Kopf haben; *(hum, machine etc)* seine Mucken haben *(inf)* → **close**[2], **know, make up, open, piece, speak**

g [= sanity] Verstand *m*, Sinne *pl*; **his mind was wandering** *(out of boredom etc)* seine Gedanken wanderten umher; **to lose one's mind** verrückt werden, den Verstand verlieren; **nobody in his right mind** kein normaler Mensch; **while the balance of his mind was disturbed** *(Jur)* wegen Verlusts des seelischen Gleichgewichts

h [set structures]

♦ **in mind** **to bear** *or* **keep sth in mind** etw nicht vergessen; *facts also, application* etw im Auge behalten; **to bear** *or* **keep sb in mind** an jdn denken; *applicant also* jdn im Auge behalten; **with this in mind...** mit diesem Gedanken im Hinterkopf...; **to have sb/sth in mind** an jdn/etw denken; **to have in mind to do sth** vorhaben *or* im Sinn haben, etw zu tun; **to have it in mind to do sth** beabsichtigen *or* sich *(dat)* vorgenommen haben, etw zu tun; **it puts me in mind of sb/sth** es weckt in mir Erinnerungen an jdn/etw

♦ **out of one's mind** **to go out of one's mind** verrückt werden, den Verstand verlieren; **to be out of one's mind** verrückt sein; **to go out of one's mind with worry/grief** vor Sorge/Trauer den Verstand verlieren; **to drive sb out of his mind** jdn um den Verstand bringen, jdn wahnsinnig machen; **I'm bored out of my mind** ich langweile mich zu Tode

2 – TRANSITIVE VERB

a [= look after] aufpassen auf *(+acc)*; *sb's chair, seat* frei halten; **I'm minding the shop** *(fig)* ich sehe nach dem Rechten

b [= be careful of] aufpassen auf *(+acc)*; *(= pay attention to)* achten auf *(+acc)*; *(= act in accordance with)* beachten; **mind what you're doing!** pass (doch) auf!; **mind what you're doing with that car** pass mit dem Auto auf; **mind what I say!** lass dir das gesagt sein; *(= do as I tell you)* hör auf das, was ich dir sage; **mind how you go** passen Sie auf, wo Sie hintreten; **mind your language!** drück dich anständig aus!; **mind the step!** *(Brit)* Vorsicht Stufe!; **mind your head!** *(Brit)* Kopf einziehen *(inf)*, Vorsicht, niedrige Tür/Decke *etc*; **mind your feet!** *(Brit)* *(when sitting)* zieh die Füße ein!; *(when moving)* pass auf, wo du hintrittst!; **mind your own business** kümmern Sie sich um Ihre eigenen Angelegenheiten

c [= care about] sich kümmern um; *(= object to)* etwas haben gegen; **she minds/doesn't mind it** es macht ihr etwas/nichts aus; *(= is/is not bothered, annoyed by)* es stört sie/stört sie nicht; *(= is not/is indifferent to)* es ist ihr nicht egal/ist ihr egal; **I don't mind the cold** die Kälte macht mir nichts aus; **I don't mind what he does** es ist mir egal, was er macht; **I don't mind four but six is too many** ich habe nichts gegen vier, aber sechs sind zu viel; **do you mind coming with me?** würde es dir etwas ausmachen mitzukommen?; **would you mind opening the door?** wären Sie so freundlich, die Tür aufzumachen?; **do you mind my smoking?** macht es Ihnen etwas aus *or* stört es Sie *or* haben Sie etwas dagegen, wenn ich rauche?; **I don't mind telling you, I was shocked** ich war schockiert, das kannst du mir glauben; **I hope you don't mind my asking you/sitting here** ich hoffe, Sie haben nichts dagegen, wenn ich Sie frage/dass ich hier sitze; **don't mind me** lass dich (durch mich) nicht stören; *(iro)* nimm auf mich keine Rücksicht; **I wouldn't mind a cup of tea** ich hätte nichts gegen eine Tasse Tee

♦ **never mind** + *sb/sth* **never mind the expense** (es ist) egal, was es kostet; **never mind that now** das ist jetzt nicht wichtig, lass das doch jetzt; **never mind your back, I'm worried about ...** dein Rücken ist mir doch egal, ich mache mir Sorgen um ...; **never mind him** kümmere dich nicht um ihn

3 – INTRANSITIVE VERB

a [= care, worry] sich kümmern, sich *(dat)* etwas daraus machen; *(= object)* etwas dagegen haben; **he doesn't seem to mind about anything** ihn scheint nichts zu kümmern; **I wish he minded a little** ich wünschte, es würde ihm etwas ausmachen *or* ihn ein bisschen kümmern; **nobody seemed to mind** es schien keinem etwas auszumachen, niemand schien etwas dagegen zu haben; **I'd prefer to stand, if you don't mind** ich würde lieber stehen, wenn es Ihnen recht ist; **do you mind?** macht es Ihnen etwas aus?; **do you mind!** *(iro)* na hör mal!, ich möchte doch sehr bitten!; **do you mind if I open** *or* **would you mind if I opened the window?** macht es Ihnen etwas aus, wenn ich das Fenster öffne?; **I don't mind if I do** ich hätte nichts dagegen

♦ **never mind** macht nichts, ist doch egal; *(in exasperation)* ist ja auch egal, schon gut; **never mind, you'll find another** mach dir nichts draus, du findest bestimmt einen anderen; **oh, never mind, I'll do it myself** ach, lass (es) *or* schon gut, ich mache es selbst; **never mind about that now!** lass das doch jetzt!, das ist doch jetzt nicht wichtig; **never mind about what you said to him, what did he say to you?** es ist doch egal *or* unwichtig, was du zu ihm gesagt hast, was hat er zu dir gesagt?; **never mind about that mistake** mach dir nichts aus dem Fehler; **never mind about your shoes** *(in exasperation)* deine Schuhe sind mir doch egal; **I'm not going to finish school, never mind go to university** ich werde die Schule nicht beenden und schon gar nicht zur Universität gehen

♦ **never you mind!** kümmere du dich mal nicht darum; *(= none of your business)* das geht dich überhaupt nichts an!

b [= be sure] aufpassen; **mind and see if ...** sieh zu, ob ...; **mind you get that done** sieh zu, dass du das fertig bekommst; **I'm not saying I'll do it, mind** ich will damit aber nicht sagen, dass ich es tue; **he's not a bad lad, mind, just ...** er ist eigentlich kein schlechter Junge, nur ...; **he didn't do it, mind** er hat es (ja) nicht getan

♦ **mind you** allerdings; **mind you, I'd rather not go** ich würde eigentlich *or* allerdings lieber nicht gehen; **it was raining at the time, mind you** allerdings hat es da geregnet; **mind you, he did try/ask** er hat es immerhin versucht/hat immerhin gefragt; **he's quite good, mind you** er ist eigentlich ganz gut

4 – PHRASAL VERB

▶ **mind out** VI *(Brit)* aufpassen (*for* auf *+acc*); **mind out!** pass (doch) auf!

---

mind: **mind-bending** ADJ *(inf)* Wahnsinns- *(inf)*; *drug, substances* bewusstseinsverändernd; **mind-blowing** ADJ *(inf)* Wahnsinns- *(inf)*; *simplicity* atemberaubend; **mind-boggling** ADJ *(inf)* irrsinnig *(inf)*, verrückt *(inf)*; **it's ~ that ...** es ist kaum zu fassen, dass ...; **~ statistics** schwindelerregende Statistiken

minded [ˈmaɪndɪd] ADJ gesonnen *(geh)*, gewillt; **if you are so ~** wenn Ihnen der Sinn danach steht *(geh)*

-minded ADJ *suf* **romantically-minded** romantisch veranlagt; **nasty-minded** übel gesinnt; **she's very politically-minded** sie interessiert sich sehr für Politik; **I'm not really opera-minded** ich mache mir nichts aus Opern

minder [ˈmaɪndəʳ] N *(inf)* Aufpasser(in) *m(f)*

mind-expanding [ˈmaɪndɪksˌpændɪŋ] ADJ bewusstseinserweiternd

mindful [ˈmaɪndfʊl] ADJ **to be ~ of sth** etw berücksichtigen *or* bedenken; **ever ~ of the risks, she ...** weil sie sich *(dat)* der Risiken bewusst war, ... sie ...; **ever ~ of her words** immer an ihre Worte denkend

mindfulness [ˈmaɪndfʊlnɪs] N Achtsamkeit *f*, Aufmerksamkeit *f*

mind: **mind game** N psychologisches Spiel; **to play ~s with sb** jdn verunsichern; **mindless** ADJ **a** *(= senseless) destruction, crime, violence* sinnlos; *(= unchallenging) work, entertainment, routine* stumpfsinnig; *occupation* geistlos; *(= stupid)* hirnlos, ohne Verstand; **~ idiot** hirnloser Idiot; **~ thug** hirnloser Schlägertyp **b** **to be ~ of sth** nicht an etw *(acc)* denken; **mindlessly** ADV *(= tediously)* stumpfsinnig; *(= stupidly)* hirnlos; **mind-reader** N Gedankenleser(in) *m(f)*; **I'm not a ~** ich bin doch kein Gedankenleser;

mindset N Mentalität *f*, Denkweise *f*, Geisteshaltung *f*

mine[1] [maɪn] POSS PRON meine(r, s); **this car is ~** das ist MEIN Auto, dieses Auto gehört mir; **is this ~?** gehört das mir?, ist das meine(r, s)?; **his friends and ~** seine und meine Freunde; **a friend of ~** ein Freund von mir; **will you be ~?** *(old)* willst du die Meine werden? *(old)*; **~ is a rather different job** meine Arbeit ist ziemlich anders; **no advice of ~ could ...** keiner meiner Ratschläge konnte ...; **a favourite** *(Brit)* or **favorite** *(US)* **expression of ~** einer meiner Lieblingsausdrücke ADJ *(obs)* mein(e)

mine[2] N **a** *(Min)* Bergwerk *nt*; *(= gold mine, silver mine)* Bergwerk *nt*, Mine *f*; *(= coal mine)* Zeche *f*, Bergwerk *nt*; **to work down the ~s** unter Tage arbeiten
b *(Mil, Naut etc)* Mine *f*; **to lay ~s** Minen legen
c *(fig)* **the book is a ~ of information** das Buch ist eine wahre Fundgrube; **he is a ~ of information** er ist ein wandelndes Lexikon *(inf)*; **he's a ~ of information about history** er besitzt ein schier unerschöpfliches Geschichtswissen
VT **a** *coal, metal* fördern, abbauen; *area* Bergbau betreiben *or* Bodenschätze abbauen in *(+dat)*
b *(Mil, Naut) channel, road* verminen; *(= blow up)* (mit einer Mine) sprengen
VI Bergbau betreiben; **to ~ for sth** nach etw graben; **they ~d deep down into the mountain** sie trieben einen Stollen bis tief in den Berg hinein

mine: **mine detector** N Minensuchgerät *nt*; **mine disaster** N Grubenunglück *nt*; **minefield** N Minenfeld *nt*; **to enter a (political) ~** sich auf (politisch) gefährliches Terrain begeben; **it's an absolute ~!** das ist Sprengstoff!; **mine gas** N Grubengas *nt*, schlagende Wetter *pl*; **minehunter** N Minensuchboot *nt*; **minelayer** N Minenleger *m*

miner [ˈmaɪnəʳ] N Bergarbeiter(in) *m(f)*, Bergmann *m*

mineral [ˈmɪnərəl] N Mineral *nt* ADJ mineralisch; **~ deposits** Mineralbestände *pl*; **~ exploration** Mineraliensuche *f*

mineralogical [ˌmɪnərəˈlɒdʒɪkəl] ADJ mineralogisch

mineralogist [ˌmɪnəˈrælədʒɪst] N Mineraloge *m*, Mineralogin *f*

mineralogy [ˌmɪnəˈrælədʒɪ] N Mineralogie *f*

mineral: **mineral oil** N Mineralöl *nt*; **mineral spring** N Mineralquelle *f*, Heilbrunnen *m*; **mineral water** N Mineralwasser *nt*

miner's lamp [ˈmaɪnəzlæmp] N Grubenlampe *f*

mineshaft [ˈmaɪnʃɑːft] N Schacht *m*

minestrone [ˌmɪnɪˈstrəʊnɪ] N Minestrone *f*, Gemüsesuppe *f*

mine: **minesweeper** N Minenräumboot *nt* or -suchboot *nt* or -sucher *m*; **mine workings** PL Stollen *pl*

Ming [mɪŋ] ADJ Ming-; **~ Dynasty** Ming-Dynastie *f*; **~ vase** Mingvase *f*

minger [ˈmɪndʒəʳ] N *(Brit sl) jd, der eklig aussieht*

minging [ˈmɪndʒɪŋ] ADJ *(Brit sl: = disgusting)* eklig, asslig *(sl)*

mingle [ˈmɪŋgl] VI sich vermischen; *(people, groups)* sich untereinander vermischen; **he ~d with people of all classes** er hatte Umgang mit Menschen aller gesellschaftlichen Schichten; **to ~ with the crowd** sich unters Volk mischen; **she ~d for a while, then sat down with her husband** *(at party)* sie mischte sich eine Zeit lang unter die Gäste und setzte sich dann mit ihrem Mann hin VT mischen *(with* mit); *(liter) waters* vermischen; **love ~d with hate** mit Hass vermischte *or* gemischte Liebe

mingy [ˈmɪndʒɪ] ADJ *(+er)* *(Brit inf)* knickerig *(inf)*; *amount* lumpig *(inf)*, mickerig *(inf)*

mini- [ˈmɪnɪ-] PREF Mini-

miniature [ˈmɪnɪtʃəʳ] N Miniatur- *or* Kleinausgabe *f*; *(Art)* Miniatur *f*; *(= bottle)* Miniflasche *f*; **in ~** en miniature, im kleinen ADJ *attr* Miniatur-; **~ world** Miniaturmodell *nt*

miniature: **miniature camera** N Kleinbildkamera *f*; **miniature golf** N Mini- *or* Kleingolf *nt*; **~ course** Minigolfplatz *m*; **miniature poodle** N Zwergpudel *m*; **miniature railway** N Liliputbahn *f*; **miniature submarine** N Kleinst-U-Boot *nt*

miniaturist [ˈmɪnɪtʃərɪst] N Miniaturmaler(in) *m(f)*

miniaturize [ˈmɪnɪtʃəraɪz] VT verkleinern

mini: **minibar** N Minibar *f*; **minibreak** N Kurzurlaub *m*; **minibudget** N *Etat, der nur Teilbereiche bzw. nur einen Teil des Rechnungsjahres abdeckt*, Zwischenetat *m*; **minibus** N Kleinbus *m*; **minicab** N Minicar *m*, Kleintaxi *nt*; **minicassette** N Minikassette *f*; **minicomputer** N Minicomputer *m*, Kleinrechner *m*; **Minidisc**® [ˈmɪnɪdɪsk] N *(Mus)* Minidisc *f*; **~ player** Minidisc-Spieler *m*; **minidress** N Minikleid *nt*

minim [ˈmɪnɪm] N *(Brit Mus)* halbe Note

minimal [ˈmɪnɪml] ADJ minimal; **at ~ cost** zu minimalen Kosten; **with ~ effort** mit minimalem Aufwand

minimal artist N *(Art)* Minimalist(in) *m(f)*

minimalism [ˈmɪnɪməlɪzəm] N Minimalismus *m*

minimalist [ˈmɪnɪməlɪst] ADJ minimalistisch

minimally [ˈmɪnɪmlɪ] ADV *(= marginally)* minimal; **this album sold ~ in the UK** dieses Album verkaufte sich in Großbritannien nur minimal; **~ invasive surgery** *(Med)* minimal invasive Chirurgie

minimize [ˈmɪnɪmaɪz] VT **a** *(= reduce) expenditure, time lost etc* auf ein Minimum reduzieren, minimieren *(form)*; *(Comput) window* minimieren, verkleinern **b** *(= belittle, underestimate)* schlechtmachen, herabsetzen

minimum [ˈmɪnɪməm] N Minimum *nt*; **the temperature fell to a ~ of 5 degrees** die Temperatur fiel auf Tiefstwerte von 5 Grad; **with a ~ of inconvenience** mit einem Minimum an Unannehmlichkeiten; **what is the ~ you will accept?** was ist für Sie das Minimum *or* der Mindestbetrag?; **a ~ of 2 hours/£50/10 people** mindestens 2 Stunden/£ 50/10 Leute; **to keep sth to a** *or* **the ~** etw auf ein Minimum beschränken; **to reduce sth to a ~** etw auf ein Minimum *or* Mindestmaß reduzieren; **at a** *or* **the ~** *(= at least)* mindestens
ADJ *attr* Mindest-; **~ age** Mindestalter *nt*; **~ charge** Mindestgebühr *f*; **to achieve maximum possible profits from ~ possible expenditure** möglichst hohe Gewinne mit möglichst geringen Ausgaben erzielen; **the ~ expenditure will be ...** das wird mindestens ... kosten; **~ temperature** Tiefsttemperatur *f*; **a ~ level of discontent** ein Mindestmaß *nt* an Unzufriedenheit; **the ~ level of aluminium in the body** die Mindestmenge von Aluminium im Körper

minimum lending rate N *(Brit Fin)* Diskontsatz *m*

minimum wage N Mindestlohn *m*

mining [ˈmaɪnɪŋ] N **a** *(Min)* Bergbau *m*; *(= work at the face)* Arbeit *f* im Bergwerk **b** *(Mil)* *(of area)* Verminen *nt*; *(of ship)* Befestigung *f* einer Mine *(of* an *+dat)*; *(= blowing-up)* Sprengung *f* (mit einer Mine)

mining: **mining area** N Bergbaugebiet *nt*, Revier *nt*; **mining disaster** N Grubenunglück *nt*; **mining engineer** N Berg(bau)ingenieur(in) *m(f)*; **mining industry** N Bergbau *m*; **mining town** N Bergarbeiterstadt *f*

minion [ˈmɪnɪən] N *(old)* Günstling *m*; *(fig)* Trabant *m*; **she delegated the job to one of her ~s** sie beauftragte einen/eine ihrer Untergebenen, die Sache zu erledigen

mini: **minipill** N Minipille *f*; **miniquake** N *(esp US)* kleines Erdbeben, Erdstoß *m*; **miniski** N Kurzski *m*; **miniskirt** N Minirock *m*; **ministate** N Zwergstaat *m*

minister [ˈmɪnɪstəʳ] N **a** *(Pol)* Minister(in) *m(f)* **b** *(Eccl)* Pfarrer(in) *m(f)*, Pastor(in) *m(f)*; **good morning, ~** guten Morgen, Herr Pfarrer *or* Herr Pastor VI **to ~ to sb** sich um jdn kümmern; **to ~ to sb's needs/wants** jds Bedürfnisse/Wünsche *(acc)* befriedigen; **a ~ing angel** *(liter)* ein barmherziger Engel

ministerial [ˌmɪnɪˈstɪərɪəl] ADJ *(Pol)* ministeriell, Minister-; *source* ministeriell; **~ post** Ministerposten *m*; **his ~ duties** seine Pflichten als Minister; **at ~ level** auf Ministerebene; **those of ~ rank** diejenigen, die im Rang eines Ministers stehen *(form)* or die einen Ministerposten innehaben

ministration [ˌmɪnɪˈstreɪʃən] N *usu pl* Pflege *f*, Fürsorge *f*

ministry [ˈmɪnɪstrɪ] N **a** *(Pol)* Ministerium *nt*; **~ of education/agriculture** Bildungs-/Landwirtschaftsministerium *nt*; **during his ~** in *or* während seiner Amtszeit (als Minister); **during the ~ of X** als X Minister war **b** *(Eccl)* geistliches Amt; **to join** *or* **enter** *or* **go into the ~** Pfarrer(in) *or* Geistliche(r) werden; **to train for the ~** Theologie studieren, um Geistlicher zu werden **c** *(= ministering)* Sendungsbewusstsein *nt*; **Christ's ~ here on earth** das Wirken Christi auf Erden

minivan [ˈmɪnɪvæn] N Minivan *m*

miniver [ˈmɪnɪvəʳ] N Hermelin *m*

mink [mɪŋk] N Nerz *m*; **~ coat** Nerzmantel *m*

minnow [ˈmɪnəʊ] N Elritze *f*

Minoan [mɪˈnəʊən] ADJ minoisch

minor [ˈmaɪnəʳ] ADJ **a** *(= of lesser extent)* kleiner; *(= of lesser importance)* unbedeutend, unwichtig; *offence, illness, operation, injuries* leicht; *surgery* klein; *interest, importance* geringer; *poet, position* unbedeutend; *prophet, planet* klein; **~ road** Nebenstraße *f*; **a ~ role** eine Nebenrolle, eine kleinere Rolle; **he only played a ~ role in the company** er spielte in der Firma nur eine untergeordnete Rolle; **I have one or two ~ criticisms of the hotel** ich habe an dem Hotel nur ein paar Kleinigkeiten auszusetzen
b *(Mus)* Moll-; **~ key** Molltonart *f*; **~ scale** Molltonleiter *f*; **G/E flat/C sharp ~** g-/es-/cis-Moll *nt*; **~ third** kleine Terz; **the novel ends in a ~ key** *or* **on a ~ note** der Roman endet mit einer traurigen Note
c *(Brit Sch inf)* **Smith ~** Smith der Jüngere
N **a** *(Mus)* **the ~** Moll *nt*; **the music shifts to the ~** die Musik wechselt nach Moll über *or* geht in die Molltonart über
b *(Jur)* Minderjährige(r) *mf*
c *(US Univ)* Nebenfach *nt*
VI *(US Univ)* im Nebenfach studieren *(in +acc)*

Minorca [mɪˈnɔːkə] N Menorca *nt*

Minorcan [mɪˈnɔːkən] ADJ menorkinisch N Menorkiner(in) *m(f)*

minority [maɪˈnɒrɪtɪ] N **a** Minderheit *f*, Minorität *f*; **to be in a** *or* **the ~** in der Minderheit sein; **the reforms will affect only a small ~ of the population** die Reformen werden sich nur auf eine kleine Minderheit in der Bevölkerung auswirken; **you are in a ~ of one** Sie stehen allein da
b *(Jur)* Minderjährigkeit *f*
ADJ *attr* **a** Minderheits-; **~ group** Minderheit *f*, Minorität *f*; **~ community** Minderheit *f*; **(ethnic) ~ students** Studenten *pl*, die einer (ethnischen) Minderheit angehören; **~ opinion** Minderheitsmeinung *f*; **a ~ view** die Ansicht einer Minderheit; **~ rights** *(Pol)* Minderheitenrechte *pl*; **~ programme** *(Brit)* or **program** *(US)* *(Rad/TV)* Programm, das nur einen kleinen Hörerkreis/Zuschauerkreis anspricht
b *(US Pol: = opposition)* **House/Senate Minority Leader** Oppositionsführer(in) *m(f)* *(im Repräsentantenhaus/Senat)*

minority: **minority government** N Minderheitsregierung *f*; **minority holding**, **minority interest** N *(Fin)* Minderheitsbeteiligung *f*; **minority shareholder** N *(Fin)* Kleinaktionär(in) *m(f)*

minor league ADJ *person* zweitklassig; *subject* zweitrangig; ~ **baseball** *(US)* Baseball *m or nt* in den unteren Ligen

minor premise N Untersatz *m*

Minotaur ['maɪnətɔː'] N Minotaur(us) *m*

minster ['mɪnstə'] N Münster *nt*

minstrel ['mɪnstrəl] N *(medieval)* Spielmann *m*; *(wandering)* (fahrender) Sänger; *(= ballad-singer)* Bänkelsänger *m*; *(= singer of love songs)* Minnesänger *m*; *(esp US: modern) weißer, als Schwarzer zurechtgemachter Sänger und Komiker*

mint[1] [mɪnt] **N** Münzanstalt *f*, Munzstätte *f*, Münze *f*; **(Royal) Mint** (Königlich-)Britische Münzanstalt; **to be worth a ~** *(inf)* Gold wert sein, unbezahlbar sein; **he is making a ~ (of money)** *(inf)* er verdient ein Heidengeld *(inf)*; **his father made a ~** *(inf)* sein Vater hat einen Haufen Geld gemacht *(inf)* **ADJ** *stamp* postfrisch, ungestempelt; **in ~ condition** in tadellosem Zustand **VT** *coin, phrase* prägen

mint[2] N *(Bot)* Minze *f*; *(= sweet)* Pfefferminz *nt*

-minted [-'mɪntɪd] ADJ *suf* **newly-/freshly-minted** nagelneu *(inf)*; **a freshly-minted medical doctor** ein frischgebackener Arzt

mint: **mint julep** N *Whisky mit Eis und frischer Minze*; **mint sauce** N Minzsoße *f*; **mint tea** N Pfefferminztee *m*

minuet [ˌmɪnjʊ'et] N Menuett *nt*

minus ['maɪnəs] **PREP** **a** minus, weniger; **£100 ~ taxes** £ 100 abzüglich (der) Steuern **b** *(= without, deprived of)* ohne; **he returned from the war ~ an arm** er kam mit einem Arm weniger aus dem Krieg zurück **ADJ** Minus-; *quantity, value* negativ; **~ point** Minuspunkt *m*; **~ temperatures** Minustemperaturen *pl*, Temperaturen *pl* unter null; **~ three degrees centigrade** drei Grad minus; **an A ~** *(in grading)* eine Eins minus **N** **a** *(= sign)* Minus(zeichen) *nt*; **two ~es make a plus** minus mal minus gibt plus; **if the result is a ~ ...** wenn das Ergebnis negativ ist *or* eine negative Größe ist ... **b** *(= disadvantage)* Minus *nt*

minuscule ['mɪnɪskjuːl] ADJ winzig

minus sign N Minuszeichen *nt*

minute[1] ['mɪnɪt] **N** **a** *(of time, degree)* Minute *f*; **it's 23 ~s past 3** es ist 3 Uhr und 23 Minuten; **in a ~** gleich, sofort; **this (very) ~!** auf der Stelle!; **at this very ~** gerade jetzt *or* in diesem Augenblick; **I shan't be a ~** es dauert nicht lang; **just a ~!** einen Moment bitte!; **any ~ (now)** jeden Augenblick; **tell me the ~ he comes** sag mir sofort Bescheid, wenn er kommt; **let me know the ~ it stops** sagen Sie mir Bescheid, sobald es aufhört; **we timed it to the ~** wir haben die Zeit auf die Minute genau genommen; **have you got a ~?** hast du mal eine Minute *or* einen Augenblick Zeit?; **it won't take a ~/5 ~s** es dauert keine Minute/keine 5 Minuten; **I enjoyed every ~ of it** ich habe es von Anfang bis Ende genossen; **I don't believe for a** *or* **one ~ that ...** ich glaube nicht einen Augenblick, dass...; **at the last ~** in letzter Minute

b *(= official note)* Notiz *f*; **~s** Protokoll *nt*; **to take the ~s** das Protokoll führen

VT *meeting* protokollieren; *remark, fact* zu Protokoll nehmen

minute[2] [maɪ'njuːt] ADJ *(= small)* winzig; *resemblance* ganz entfernt; *(= detailed, exact)* minutiös; *detail* kleinste(r, s)

minute ['mɪnɪt]: **minute book** N Protokollbuch *nt*; **minute hand** N Minutenzeiger *m*

minutely [maɪ'njuːtlɪ] ADV *(= by a small amount)* ganz geringfügig; *(= in detail)* genauestens; **anything ~ resembling a fish** alles, was auch nur annähernd nach Fisch aussieht; **a ~ detailed account** eine sehr detaillierte Schilderung; **a ~ folded piece of paper** ein klitzeklein gefaltetes Stück Papier

Minuteman ['mɪnɪtmæn] N *pl* **-men** [-men] *(US) Freiwilliger im Unabhängigkeitskrieg, der auf Abruf bereitstand*

minuteness [maɪ'njuːtnɪs] N *(= small size)* Winzigkeit *f*; *(of account, description)* Ausführlichkeit *f*; *(of detail)* Genauigkeit *f*

minute steak ['mɪnɪt-] N Minutensteak *nt*

minutiae [mɪ'njuːʃiː] PL genaue Einzelheiten *pl*; **the ~ of daily life** die tägliche Kleinarbeit

minx [mɪŋks] N Biest *nt (inf)*

miracle ['mɪrəkəl] N Wunder *nt*; **to work** *or* **perform ~s** *(lit)* Wunder tun *or* wirken *or* vollbringen; **I can't work ~s** ich kann nicht hexen *or* zaubern; **by a ~** *(fig)* **by some ~** *(fig)* wie durch ein Wunder; **it will be a ~ if ...** das wäre ein Wunder, wenn ...; **it's a ~ he ...** es ist ein Wunder, dass er ...; **her recovery/his victory was a ~** es war ein Wunder, dass sie wieder gesund geworden ist/dass er gewonnen hat; **it'll take a ~ for us** *or* **we'll need a ~ to be finished on time** da müsste schon ein Wunder geschehen, wenn wir noch rechtzeitig fertig werden sollen

miracle: **miracle drug** N Wunderdroge *f*; **miracle play** N Mirakelspiel *nt*, geistliches Drama; **miracle worker** N Wundertäter *m*; **I'm not a ~, you know** *(inf)* ich kann doch keine Wunder vollbringen

miraculous [mɪ'rækjʊləs] ADJ **a** *escape, recovery* wundersam; **~ powers** Wunderkräfte *pl*; **that is nothing/little short of ~** das grenzt an ein Wunder **b** *(= unbelievable, wonderful)* wunderbar; *achievement, improvement, transformation* erstaunlich; **there was a ~ change in her appearance** es war kaum zu fassen, wie sie sich verändert hatte

miraculously [mɪ'rækjʊləslɪ] ADV **a** *escape* auf wundersame Weise; **~ intact/unharmed** wie durch ein Wunder unbeschädigt; **~ the baby was unhurt** es war wie ein Wunder, dass das Baby unverletzt blieb **b** *(= unbelievably, wonderfully)* wunderbar; **she was somehow ~ changed** es war nicht zu fassen, wie verändert sie war

mirage ['mɪrɑːʒ] N Fata Morgana *f*, Luftspiegelung *f*; *(fig)* Trugbild *nt*, Illusion *f*

MIRAS ['maɪræs] N *(Brit Fin) abbr of* **mortgage interest relief at source** *Steuervergünstigung bei der Zahlung von Hypothekenzinsen*

mire ['maɪə'] N Morast *m (also fig)*, Schlamm *m*; **the football pitch was an absolute ~** der Fußballplatz war ein einziges Schlammfeld; **to drag sb/sth through the ~** *(fig)* jdn/etw in den Schmutz ziehen

mired ['maɪəd] ADJ *(esp liter* **a** *(= dirtied)* **~ in mud** *(vehicle)* im Schlamm versunken; *road* schlammbedeckt **b** *: = involved)* **~ in debt** tief verschuldet; **~ in scandal** von Skandalen umwittert *or* verfolgt

mirror ['mɪrə'] **N** Spiegel *m*; **a ~ of 19th century life** ein Spiegelbild *nt* des Lebens im 19. Jahrhundert; **to hold a ~ up to sth** etw widerspiegeln **VT** widerspiegeln, spiegeln; **the trees ~ed in the lake** die Bäume, die sich im See (wider)-spiegelten

mirror: **mirror image** N Spiegelbild *nt*; **mirror site** N *(Comput)* Mirrorsite *f*; **mirror writing** N Spiegelschrift *f*

mirth [mɜːθ] N Freude *f*, Frohsinn *m*; *(= laughter)* Heiterkeit *f*; **shrieks of ~ coming from the classroom** frohes *or* fröhliches Lachen, das aus dem Klassenzimmer drang

mirthful ['mɜːθfʊl] ADJ froh, heiter, fröhlich

mirthless ['mɜːθlɪs] ADJ freudlos; *laughter* unfroh, beklemmt

mirthlessly [mɜːθlɪslɪ] ADV *(liter) smile* betrübt; *laugh* unfroh, beklemmt

miry ['maɪərɪ] ADJ morastig, schlammig

misadventure [ˌmɪsəd'ventʃə'] N Missgeschick *nt*; **death by ~** Tod *m* durch Unfall

misalliance [ˌmɪsə'laɪəns] N Mesalliance *f*

misanthrope ['mɪzənθrəʊp] N = **misanthropist**

misanthropic [ˌmɪzən'θrɒpɪk] ADJ misanthropisch, menschenfeindlich

misanthropist [mɪ'zænθrəpɪst] N Misanthrop(in) *m(f)*, Menschenfeind(in) *m(f)*

misanthropy [mɪ'zænθrəpɪ] N Misanthropie *f*, Menschenfeindlichkeit *f*

misapply ['mɪsə'plaɪ] VT falsch anwenden; *funds* falsch verwenden; *one's energy* verschwenden

misapprehend ['mɪsˌæprɪ'hend] VT missverstehen

misapprehension ['mɪsˌæprɪ'henʃən] N Missverständnis *nt*; **I think you are under a ~** ich glaube, bei Ihnen liegt (da) ein Missverständnis vor; **he was under the ~ that ...** er hatte fälschlicherweise *or* irrtümlicherweise angenommen, dass ...

misappropriate ['mɪsə'prəʊprɪeɪt] VT entwenden; *money* veruntreuen

misappropriation ['mɪsəˌprəʊprɪ'eɪʃən] N Entwendung *f*; *(of money)* Veruntreuung *f*

misbegotten ['mɪsbɪ'gɒtn] ADJ *(liter: = illegitimate)* unehelich; *(fig: = ill-conceived)* schlecht konzipiert

misbehave ['mɪsbɪ'heɪv] VI sich schlecht *or* unanständig benehmen; *(child also)* ungezogen sein; **I saw him misbehaving with my wife** ich habe ihn in einer unmissverständlichen *or* eindeutigen Situation mit meiner Frau gesehen

misbehaviour, *(US)* **misbehavior** ['mɪsbɪ'heɪvjə'] N schlechtes Benehmen; *(of child also)* Ungezogenheit *f*; **sexual ~** sexuelles Fehlverhalten

misbelief ['mɪsbɪ'liːf] N irrige Annahme; *(Rel)* Irrglaube *m*

misc. *abbr of* **miscellaneous**

miscalculate ['mɪs'kælkjʊleɪt] **VT** falsch berechnen; *(= misjudge)* falsch einschätzen **VI** sich verrechnen; *(= estimate wrongly)* sich verkalkulieren; *(= misjudge)* sich verschätzen

miscalculation ['mɪsˌkælkjʊ'leɪʃən] N Rechenfehler *m*; *(= wrong estimation)* Fehlkalkulation *f*; *(= misjudgement)* Fehleinschätzung *f*; **to make a ~ in sth** bei etw einen Rechenfehler machen/etw falsch kalkulieren/etw falsch einschätzen

miscall ['mɪs'kɔːl] VT *(Sport) shot* falsch bewerten *or* aufrufen

miscarriage ['mɪsˌkærɪdʒ] N **a** *(Med)* Fehlgeburt *f* **b** **~ of justice** Justizirrtum *m* **c** *(form, of letter)* Fehlleitung *f*

miscarry [ˌmɪs'kærɪ] VI **a** *(Med)* eine Fehlgeburt haben **b** *(= fail: plans)* fehllaufen, fehlschlagen **c** *(form, letter, goods)* fehlgeleitet werden

miscast ['mɪs'kɑːst] *pret, ptp* **miscast** VT *play* falsch *or* schlecht besetzen, fehlbesetzen; **the actor was clearly ~ in this role** mit diesem Schauspieler war die Rolle eindeutig fehlbesetzt

miscegenation [ˌmɪsɪdʒɪ'neɪʃən] N Rassenmischung *f*

miscellanea [ˌmɪsə'leɪnɪə] PL Verschiedenes *nt*; *(of literary compositions, objects)* (bunte) Sammlung

miscellaneous [ˌmɪsɪ'leɪnɪəs] ADJ verschieden; *poems* vermischt, verschiedenerlei; *collection, crowd* bunt; **~ expenses/costs/income** sonstige Aufwendungen/Kosten/Erträge; **~ items** verschiedene Artikel; *(= news items)* Verschiedenes; **a ~ collection of junk** bunt gemischtes altes Zeug; **"miscellaneous"** *(on agenda, list)* „Sonstiges"; **a ~ section** Vermischtes

miscellaneously [ˌmɪsɪ'leɪnɪəslɪ] ADV verschieden; *grouped, collected* bunt, wahllos

miscellany [mɪ'selənɪ] N *(= collection)* (bunte) Sammlung, (buntes) Gemisch; *(= variety)* Vielfalt *f*; *(of writings)* vermischte Schriften *pl*; *(of poems, articles)* Sammelband *m*, Auswahl *f*

mischance [ˌmɪs'tʃɑːns] N unglücklicher Zufall; **by some ~** durch einen unglücklichen Zufall

mischief ['mɪstʃɪf] N **a** *(= roguery)* Schalk *m*, Verschmitztheit *f*; *(= naughty, foolish behaviour)* Unsinn *m*, Unfug *m*; **she's full of ~** sie hat nur Unfug im Kopf; **he's up to ~** er führt etwas im Schilde; **he's always getting into ~** er stellt dauernd etwas an; **to keep sb out of ~** aufpassen, dass jd keine Dummheiten macht; **to keep out of ~** keinen Unfug machen; **that'll keep you**

out of ~ dann kannst du wenigstens nichts anstellen, dann kommst du wenigstens auf keine dummen Gedanken **b** *(= trouble)* **to cause** *or* **make ~** Unfrieden stiften; **to make ~ for sb** jdm Unannehmlichkeiten bereiten, jdn in Schwierigkeiten bringen **c** *(= damage, physical injury)* Schaden *m*; **to do sb/oneself a ~** jdm/sich Schaden zufügen; *(physically)* jdm/sich etwas (an)tun; **to do ~ to sth** Schaden bei etw anrichten **d** *(= person)* Schlawiner *m*; *(= child, puppy)* Racker *m*

mischief-maker [ˈmɪstʃɪfˌmeɪkəʳ] N Unruhestifter(in) *m(f)*

mischievous [ˈmɪstʃɪvəs] ADJ **a** *(= roguish, playful) expression, smile* schelmisch, verschmitzt, spitzbübisch; **a ~ person** ein Schlawiner *m*; **a ~ child** ein Schlingel *or* Racker *m*; **her son is really ~** ihr Sohn ist ein Schlingel *or* hat nur Unfug im Sinn; **what ~ pranks are you up to now?** welche üblen Streiche heckst du jetzt aus?; **a ~ elf** eine Elfe, die Schabernack treibt **b** *(= malicious, troublemaking) rumour, suggestion* bösartig; *person* boshaft; *strike* schädlich; *(= physically disabling) blow* verletzend

mischievously [ˈmɪstʃɪvəslɪ] ADV **a** *(= roguishly) smile, say* schelmisch, verschmitzt, spitzbübisch; **to behave ~** Unfug anstellen, Schabernack treiben **b** *(= maliciously)* bösartig, boshaft

mischievousness [ˈmɪstʃɪvəsnɪs] N *(= roguery)* Verschmitztheit *f*

miscible [ˈmɪsɪbl] ADJ *(form)* mischbar

misconceive [ˈmɪskənˈsiːv] VT *(= understand wrongly)* verkennen, eine falsche Vorstellung haben von; *(= base on false assumption)* von einer falschen Voraussetzung ausgehen bei

misconceived [ˈmɪskənˈsiːvd] ADJ *(= mistaken) policy* verfehlt; *idea* irrig, falsch; *approach, action* falsch; **such fears are ~** solche Befürchtungen sind unbegründet

misconception [ˈmɪskənˈsepʃən] N fälschliche *or* irrtümliche Annahme; *(no pl: = misunderstanding)* Verkennung *f*

misconduct [ˌmɪsˈkɒndʌkt] **N** **a** *(= improper behaviour)* schlechtes Benehmen; *(professional)* Berufsvergehen *nt*, Verfehlung *f* im Amt; *(sexual)* Fehltritt *m*; **gross ~** grobes Fehlverhalten **b** *(= mismanagement)* schlechte Verwaltung **VT** [ˌmɪskənˈdʌkt] schlecht verwalten **VR** [ˌmɪskənˈdʌkt] **to ~ oneself** sich schlecht benehmen; *(professionally)* sich falsch verhalten

misconstruction [ˈmɪskənˈstrʌkʃən] N falsche Auslegung, Fehlinterpretation *f*, Missdeutung *f*

misconstrue [ˈmɪskənˈstruː] VT missverstehen, missdeuten, falsch auslegen; **you have ~d my meaning** Sie haben mich falsch verstanden; **to ~ sth as sth** etw irrtümlicherweise für etw halten

miscount [ˈmɪsˈkaʊnt] **N** **there was a ~** da hat sich jemand verzählt **VT** falsch (aus)zählen **VI** sich verzählen

miscreant [ˈmɪskrɪənt] N *(old)* Bösewicht *m (old)*, Schurke *m*

misdate [ˌmɪsˈdeɪt] VT *letter* falsch datieren

misdeal [ˈmɪsˈdiːl] *pret, ptp* **misdealt** [ˈmɪsˈdelt] **VT** *cards* falsch (aus)geben **VI** sich vergeben, falsch geben

misdeed [ˈmɪsˈdiːd] N Missetat *f (old)*

misdemeanour, *(US)* **misdemeanor** [ˌmɪsdɪˈmiːnəʳ] N schlechtes Betragen *or* Benehmen; *(Jur)* Vergehen *nt*, Übertretung *f*; **she was guilty of a slight ~ at the party** sie benahm sich auf der Party leicht daneben

misdiagnose [ˈmɪsdaɪəgnəʊz] VT **a** *(Med) illness* falsch diagnostizieren; *patient* eine falsche Diagnose stellen *(+dat)* **b** *(= analyse wrongly) problem, situation* falsch diagnostizieren *or* einschätzen

misdiagnosis [ˌmɪsdaɪəgˈnəʊsɪs] N *pl* **misdiagnoses** [ˌmɪsdaɪəgˈnəʊsiːz] **a** *(Med: of illness)* Fehldiagnose *f*, falsche Diagnose *f* **b** *(= wrong analysis: of problem, situation)* Fehleinschätzung *f*

misdial [ˈmɪsˈdaɪəl] VTI *(Telec)* **to ~ (the number)** sich verwählen

misdirect [ˈmɪsdɪˈrekt] VT **a** *letter (= send to wrong address)* fehlleiten; *(= address wrongly)* falsch adressieren; *energies* falsch einsetzen, vergeuden; *pass, volley* falsch platzieren; *person (= send astray)* in die falsche Richtung schicken; *(= misinform)* falsch informieren, eine falsche Auskunft geben *(+dat)*; *(Jur) jury* falsch belehren **b** *campaign, operation* schlecht durchführen

misdirected [ˈmɪsdɪˈrektɪd] ADJ **a** *(lit) mail* fehlgeleitet; *(= wrongly addressed)* falsch adressiert; *shot, pass* unplatziert; **the shot was ~** der Schuss verfehlte sein Ziel **b** *(fig) (= misapplied) energy, effort* vergeudet; *spending, feeling* fehlgeleitet; *(= misconceived) policy, campaign* verfehlt

misdirection [ˈmɪsdɪˈrekʃən] N **a** *(of letter) (= sending to wrong address)* Fehlleiten *nt*; *(= addressing wrongly)* falsche Adressierung; *(of energies)* falscher Einsatz, Vergeudung *f*; *(of person) (= sending astray)* falsche Richtungsweisung; *(= misinforming)* falsche Information, falsche Unterrichtung **b** *(of campaign, operation)* schlechte Durchführung

mise en scène [ˌmiːzɑ̃nˈseɪn] N *(Theat, fig)* Kulisse *f*

miser [ˈmaɪzəʳ] N Geizhals *m*, Geizkragen *m*

miserable [ˈmɪzərəbl] ADJ **a** *(= unhappy) person* unglücklich, trostlos; *colour* trist; *(= ill-tempered)* griesgrämig; **I feel ~ today** ich fühle mich heute elend *or (ill)* miserabel; **~ with hunger/cold** elend vor Hunger/Kälte; **a ~ old hag** eine missmutige alte Hexe; **to make sb ~** jdm Kummer machen *or* bereiten, jdn unglücklich machen; **to make life ~ for sb, to make sb's life ~** jdm das Leben zur Qual machen **b** *(= wretched, causing distress) headache, cold, weather* grässlich, fürchterlich; *life, existence, hovel, spectacle* erbärmlich, elend, jämmerlich; *place* öde, trostlos; **he died a ~ death** er ist elend *or* jämmerlich zugrunde *or* zu Grunde gegangen **c** *(= contemptible)* miserabel, jämmerlich, erbärmlich; *person* gemein, erbärmlich; *treatment, behaviour* gemein; *sum, failure* kläglich, jämmerlich; **a ~ £3** mickrige 3 Pfund *(inf)*; **you ~ little wretch!** du mieses kleines Biest!, du Miststück! *(inf)*; **to be a ~ failure** kläglich versagen

miserably [ˈmɪzərəblɪ] ADV **a** *(= unhappily)* unglücklich; *say also* kläglich **b** *(= wretchedly, distressingly) hurt, ache, rain* grässlich, fürchterlich; *live, die* elend, jämmerlich; *poor* erbärmlich; **~ unhappy** todunglücklich *(inf)*; **it was ~ cold** es war erbärmlich kalt **c** *(= contemptibly) pay, feed, play* miserabel; *fail* kläglich, jämmerlich; *treat, behave* gemein; **the wages were ~ low** die Löhne waren miserabel

misericord [ˈmɪzərɪkɔːd] N Miserikordie *f*

miserliness [ˈmaɪzəlɪnɪs] N Geiz *m*

miserly [ˈmaɪzəlɪ] ADJ geizig; *hoarding* kleinlich; *offer* knauserig; **a ~ £8** miese *or* mickrige £ 8 *(inf)*; **to be ~ with sth** mit etw geizen

misery [ˈmɪzərɪ] N **a** *(= sadness)* Kummer *m*, Trauer *f*; **she looked the picture of ~** sie war ein Bild des Jammers **b** *(= suffering)* Qualen *pl*; *(= wretchedness)* Elend *nt*; **the ~ caused by war** das Elend des Krieges; **a life of ~** ein erbärmliches *or* jämmerliches *or* elendes Leben; **to make sb's life a ~** jdm das Leben zur Qual *or* zur Hölle machen; **to put an animal out of its ~** ein Tier von seinen Qualen erlösen; **to put sb out of his ~** *(fig)* jdn nicht länger auf die Folter spannen **c** *(Brit inf: = person)* Miesepeter *m (inf)*

misery-guts [ˈmɪzərɪgʌts] N *(Brit inf)* Miesmacher(in) *m(f) (inf)*

misfire [ˈmɪsˈfaɪəʳ] VI *(engine)* fehlzünden, eine Fehlzündung haben; *(plan)* fehlschlagen; *(joke, trick)* danebengehen

misfit [ˈmɪsfɪt] N *(= person)* Außenseiter(in) *m(f)*; *(= social misfit also)* Nichtangepasste(r) *mf*; **society's ~s** die Außenseiter der Gesellschaft; **he's a real ~** er ist ein sehr schwieriger Fall; **he's always been a ~ here** er hat nie richtig hierher gepasst, er hat sich hier nie angepasst; **I felt (like) a ~** ich fühlte mich fehl am Platze

misfortune [mɪsˈfɔːtʃuːn] N *(= ill fortune, affliction)* (schweres) Schicksal *or* Los *nt*; *(= bad luck)* Pech *nt no pl*; *(= unlucky incident)* Missgeschick *nt*; **companion in ~** Leidensgenosse *m*/-genossin *f*; **it was my ~** *or* **I had the ~ to ...** ich hatte das Pech, zu ...; **a victim of ~** ein Unglücksrabe *or* Pechvogel *m*; **~ seldom comes alone** ein Unglück kommt selten allein *(prov)*; **financial ~s** finanzielle Fehlschläge *pl*

misgiving [mɪsˈgɪvɪŋ] ✪ 26.3 N Bedenken *pl*; **I had (certain) ~s about the scheme** bei dem Vorhaben war mir nicht ganz wohl; **I had (certain) ~s about lending him the money** bei dem Gedanken, ihm das Geld zu leihen, war mir nicht ganz wohl

misgovern [ˈmɪsˈgʌvən] VT schlecht regieren, schlecht verwalten

misgovernment [ˈmɪsˈgʌvənmənt] N Misswirtschaft *f (of* in *+dat)*

misguided [ˈmɪsˈgaɪdɪd] ADJ töricht; *decision also, opinions* irrig; *(= misplaced) kindness, enthusiasm, solicitude* unangebracht, fehl am Platz; **to be ~ in sth** mit etw falschliegen; **I think it was ~ of you** *or* **you were ~ to accept his proposal** meiner Ansicht nach waren Sie schlecht beraten, seinen Vorschlag anzunehmen

misguidedly [ˈmɪsˈgaɪdɪdlɪ] ADV töricht; *believe* irrigerweise

mishandle [ˈmɪsˈhændl] VT *case* falsch *or* schlecht handhaben

mishap [ˈmɪshæp] N Missgeschick *nt*; **without (further) ~** ohne (weitere) Zwischenfälle; **he's had a slight ~** ihm ist ein kleines Missgeschick *or* Malheur passiert

mishear [ˈmɪsˈhɪəʳ] *pret, ptp* **misheard** [ˈmɪsˈhɜːd] **VT** falsch hören **VI** sich verhören

mishmash [ˈmɪʃmæʃ] N Mischmasch *m*

misinform [ˈmɪsɪnˈfɔːm] VT falsch informieren *or* unterrichten; **you've been ~ed** man hat Sie *or* Sie sind falsch informiert; **does the press ~ the public?** verbreitet die Presse falsche Informationen?

misinformation [ˈmɪsɪnfəˈmeɪʃən] N Fehlinformation *f*, Fehlinformationen *pl*

misinterpret [ˈmɪsɪnˈtɜːprɪt] VT falsch auslegen *or* deuten; *play, novel* fehlinterpretieren, falsch auslegen; *(interpreter)* falsch wiedergeben; **it could easily be ~ed as implying ingratitude** es könnte leicht als Undankbarkeit ausgelegt werden; **he ~ed her silence as agreement** er deutete ihr Schweigen fälschlich als Zustimmung

misinterpretation [ˈmɪsɪnˌtɜːprɪˈteɪʃən] N Fehldeutung *f*, falsche Auslegung; *(of play, novel)* Fehlinterpretation *f*, falsche Auslegung; *(by interpreter)* falsche Wiedergabe

misjudge [ˈmɪsˈdʒʌdʒ] VT falsch einschätzen, sich verschätzen in *(+dat)*; *person also* falsch beurteilen

misjudgement [ˌmɪsˈdʒʌdʒmənt] N Fehleinschätzung *f*; *(of person also)* falsche Beurteilung

miskick [ˌmɪsˈkɪk] **VT** **to ~ the ball** den Ball nicht richtig treffen **N** Fehlschuss *m*

mislay [ˌmɪsˈleɪ] *pret, ptp* **mislaid** [ˌmɪsˈleɪd] VT verlegen

mislead [ˌmɪsˈliːd] *pret, ptp* **misled** VT **a** *(= give wrong idea)* irreführen; **you have been misled** Sie irren *or* täuschen sich, Sie befinden sich im Irrtum *(form)*; **don't be misled by appearances** lassen Sie sich nicht durch Äußerlichkeiten täuschen; **the ad misled me into thinking that ...** die Anzeige ließ mich irrtümlicherweise annehmen, dass ... **b** *(= lead into bad ways)* verleiten *(into* zu) **c** *(in guiding)* in die Irre *or* in die falsche Richtung führen

misleading [ˌmɪsˈliːdɪŋ] ADJ irreführend; **the ~ simplicity of his style** die täuschende Einfachheit seines Stils

misleadingly [ˌmɪsˈliːdɪŋlɪ] ADV *tell, say etc* irreführenderweise; *presented* irreführend; *(= deceptively)* trügerisch; **the film has a ~ violent trailer** die brutale Vorankündigung für diesen Film war irreführend; **they looked ~ angelic** sie machten einen trügerisch engelhaften Eindruck

misled [ˌmɪsˈled] *pret, ptp of* **mislead**

mismanage [ˈmɪsˈmænɪdʒ] VT *company, finances* schlecht verwalten; *affair, deal* schlecht abwickeln *or* handhaben

mismanagement [ˈmɪsˈmænɪdʒmənt] N Misswirtschaft *f*

mismatch [mɪsˈmætʃ] **N** **to be a ~** nicht zusammenpassen **VI** nicht zusammenpassen

misname [ˈmɪsˈneɪm] VT unzutreffend benennen

misnomer [ˈmɪsˈnəʊməʳ] N unzutreffende Bezeichnung

misogamist [mɪˈsɒɡəmɪst] N Misogam *m*

misogamy [mɪˈsɒɡəmɪ] N Misogamie *f*

misogynist [mɪˈsɒdʒɪnɪst] N Frauenfeind *m*, Misogyn *m (geh)*

misogynistic [mɪˌsɒdʒɪˈnɪstɪk] ADJ frauenfeindlich, misogyn *(geh)*

misogyny [mɪˈsɒdʒɪnɪ] N Frauenfeindlichkeit *f*, Misogynie *f (geh)*

misplace [ˈmɪsˈpleɪs] VT **a** *document, file etc* falsch einordnen; *(= mislay)* verlegen **b** **to be ~d** *(confidence, trust, affection)* fehl am Platz sein, unangebracht sein; **her ~d trust** ihr törichtes Vertrauen

misplay [ˌmɪsˈpleɪ] VT verschießen

misprint [ˈmɪsprɪnt] **N** Druckfehler *m* **VT** [ˌmɪsˈprɪnt] verdrucken

mispronounce [ˈmɪsprəˈnaʊns] VT falsch aussprechen

mispronunciation [ˈmɪsprəˌnʌnsɪˈeɪʃən] N falsche *or* fehlerhafte Aussprache

misquotation [ˈmɪskwəʊˈteɪʃən] N falsches Zitat; **his constant ~ of Shakespeare** dass er Shakespeare ständig falsch zitiert

misquote [ˈmɪsˈkwəʊt] VT falsch zitieren; **he was ~d as having said …** man unterstellte ihm, gesagt zu haben …

misread [ˈmɪsˈriːd] *pret, ptp* **misread** [ˈmɪsˈred] VT falsch *or* nicht richtig lesen; *(= misinterpret)* falsch verstehen

misrepresent [ˈmɪsˌreprɪˈzent] VT falsch darstellen; *facts also* verdrehen; *ideas* verfälschen; **he was ~ed in the papers** seine Worte *etc* wurden von der Presse verfälscht *or* entstellt wiedergegeben; **he was ~ed as being for the strike** er wurde zu Unrecht als Befürworter des Streiks hingestellt

misrepresentation [ˈmɪsˌreprɪzenˈteɪʃən] N falsche Darstellung; *(of facts also)* Verdrehung *f*; *(of theory)* Verfälschung *f*; **to be accused of ~** der Verdrehung *(gen)* von Tatsachen beschuldigt werden

misrule [ˈmɪsˈruːl] **N** schlechte Regierung; *(by government also)* Misswirtschaft *f* **VT** schlecht regieren

miss[1] [mɪs] **N** **a** *(= shot)* Fehltreffer *m or* -schuss *m*; *(= failure)* Misserfolg *m*, Pleite *f (inf)*, Reinfall *m (inf)*; **his first shot was a ~** sein erster Schuss ging daneben; **it was a near ~** das war eine knappe Sache; *(shot)* das war knapp daneben; **we had a near ~ with that car** wir wären fast mit diesem Auto zusammengestoßen; **the sales department voted it a ~** in der Verkaufsabteilung räumte man dem keine Chance ein; **a ~ is as good as a mile** *(prov)* knapp vorbei ist auch daneben

b **to give sth a ~** *(inf)* sich *(dat)* etw schenken

VT **a** *(= fail to hit, catch, reach, find, attend etc: by accident)* verpassen; *chance, appointment, bus, concert* verpassen, versäumen; *(= deliberately not attend)* nicht gehen zu *or* in *(+acc)*; *(= not hit, find) target, ball, way, step, vocation, place, house* verfehlen; *(shot, ball)* verfehlen, vorbeigehen an *(+dat)*; **to ~ breakfast** nicht frühstücken; *(= be too late for)* das Frühstück verpassen; **they ~ed each other in the crowd** sie verpassten *or* verfehlten sich in der Menge; **to ~ the boat** *or* **bus** *(fig)* den Anschluss verpassen; **he ~ed school for a week** er hat eine Woche lang die Schule versäumt; **~ a turn** einmal aussetzen; **have I ~ed my turn?** bin ich übergangen worden?; **if you ~ a pill** wenn Sie vergessen, eine Pille zu nehmen

b *(= fail to experience)* verpassen; *(deliberately)* sich *(dat)* entgehen lassen; *(= fail to hear or perceive)* nicht mitbekommen, verpassen; *(deliberately)* überhören/-sehen; **I ~ed that** das ist mir entgangen; **he doesn't ~ much** *(inf)* ihm entgeht so schnell nichts; **you haven't ~ed much!** da hast du nicht viel verpasst *or* versäumt!; **I wouldn't have ~ed it for anything** das hätte ich mir nicht entgehen lassen wollen

c *(= fail to achieve) prize* nicht bekommen *or* schaffen *(inf)*; **he narrowly ~ed being first/becoming president** er wäre beinahe auf den ersten Platz gekommen/Präsident geworden

d *(= avoid) obstacle* (noch) ausweichen können *(+dat)*; *(= escape)* entgehen *(+dat)*; **to ~ doing sth** etw fast *or* um ein Haar tun; **the car just ~ed the tree** das Auto wäre um ein Haar gegen den Baum gefahren; **we narrowly ~ed having an accident** wir hätten um ein Haar einen Unfall gehabt

e *(= leave out)* auslassen; *(= overlook, fail to deal with)* übersehen; **my heart ~ed a beat** mir stockte das Herz

f *(= notice or regret absence of)* vermissen; **I ~ him/my old car** er/mein altes Auto fehlt mir; **he won't be ~ed** keiner wird ihn vermissen; **he'll never ~ it** er wird es nie merken(, dass es ihm fehlt)

VI **a** *(= not hit)* nicht treffen; *(punching)* danebenschlagen; *(shooting)* danebenschießen; *(= not catch)* danebengreifen; *(= not be present, not attend)* fehlen; *(ball, shot, punch)* danebengehen

b *(inf: = fail)* **you can't ~** da kann nichts schiefgehen; **he never ~es** er schafft es immer

▶ **miss out** **VT** *sep* auslassen; *(= accidentally not see)* übersehen; *last line or paragraph etc* weglassen; **my name was missed out from the list** mein Name fehlte auf der Liste **VI** *(inf)* zu kurz kommen; **to miss out on sth** etw verpassen; *(= get less)* bei etw zu kurz kommen; **he's been missing out on life** er ist im Leben zu kurz gekommen

miss[2] N **a** **Miss** Fräulein *nt*, Frl. *abbr*; **Miss Germany 1998** (die) Miss Germany von 1998 **b** *(= girl)* **a proper little ~** ein richtiges kleines Fräulein; **look here, you cheeky little ~!** hör mal, mein (kleines) Fräulein! **c** *(= term of address) (to waitress etc)* Bedienung, Fräulein *(dated)*; *(to teacher)* Frau X

missal [ˈmɪsəl] N Messbuch *nt*, Missale *nt*

misshapen [ˈmɪsˈʃeɪpən] ADJ missgebildet; *plant, tree also* verwachsen; *vegetables* unförmig, missraten

missile [ˈmɪsaɪl] N **a** *(= stone, javelin etc)* (Wurf)geschoss *nt* **b** *(= rocket)* Rakete *f*, Flugkörper *m (form)*

missile: **missile base** N Raketenbasis *f*; **missile defence system** *(Brit)*, **missile defense system** *(US)* N Raketenabwehrsystem *nt*; **missile launcher** N Abschuss- *or* Startrampe *f*; *(= vehicle)* Raketenwerfer *m*; **missile site** N Raketenbasis *f*

missilry [ˈmɪsɪlrɪ] N *(= science)* Raketentechnik *f*; *(= missiles)* Raketen(waffen) *pl*

missing [ˈmɪsɪŋ] ADJ *(= not able to be found) person, soldier, aircraft, boat* vermisst; *object* verschwunden; *(= not there)* fehlend; **to be ~/have gone ~** fehlen; *(person, aircraft, boat etc)* vermisst werden; **to go ~** *(person, aircraft, boat etc)* vermisst werden; *(object)* verloren gehen; **the coat has two buttons ~, two buttons are ~ from the coat** an dem Mantel fehlen zwei Knöpfe; **my name is ~ from the list** mein Name fehlt auf der Liste; **he has a tooth ~** er hat eine Zahnlücke; **we are £50 ~** uns *(dat)* fehlen £ 50; **the ~ clue to his identity** der Schlüssel zu seiner Identität; **~ in action** vermisst; *(Biol)* Missing link *nt*, Übergangs- *or* Zwischenform *f*

missing link N fehlendes Glied

missing person N Vermisste(r) *mf*; **~s bureau/file** Vermisstenbüro *nt*/-liste *f*

mission [ˈmɪʃən] N **a** *(= business, task)* Auftrag *m*; *(= calling)* Aufgabe *f*, Berufung *f*; *(Mil)* Befehl *m*; *(= operation)* Einsatz *m*; **what is their ~?** welchen Auftrag haben sie?, wie lauten ihre Befehle?; **our ~ is to …** wir sind damit beauftragt, zu …; **the soldiers' ~ was to …** die Soldaten hatten den Befehl erhalten, zu …; **to send sb on a secret ~** jdn mit einer geheimen Mission beauftragen; **he's on a secret ~** er ist in geheimer Mission unterwegs; **sense of ~** Sendungsbewusstsein *nt*; **~ accomplished** *(Mil, fig)* Befehl ausgeführt; *(without military overtones)* Auftrag ausgeführt

b *(= journey)* Mission *f*; **~ of inquiry** Erkundungsreise *f*; **Henry Kissinger's ~ to the Middle East** Kissingers Nahostmission

c *(= people on mission)* Gesandtschaft *f*, Delegation *f*; *(Pol)* Mission *f*; **trade ~** Handelsreise *f*

d *(Rel)* Mission *f*; **~ hut** Mission(sstation) *f*

missionary [ˈmɪʃənrɪ] **N** Missionar(in) *m(f)* **ADJ** missionarisch

missionary position N *(fig inf)* Missionarsstellung *f*

mission: **mission control** N *(Space)* Kontrollzentrum *nt*, Flugleitung *f*; **mission controller** N *(Space)* Flugleiter(in) *m(f)*; **mission statement** N *(of company)* (Kurzdarstellung der) Firmenphilosophie *f*

missis [ˈmɪsɪz] N *(Brit inf: = wife)* bessere Hälfte *(hum inf)*, Alte *f (pej inf)*, Olle *f (inf)*; *(= mistress of household)* Frau *f* des Hauses; **yes, ~** ja (-wohl)

Mississippi [mɪsɪˈsɪpɪ] N Mississippi *m*

missive [ˈmɪsɪv] N *(form, old)* Schreiben *nt (form)*

Missouri [mɪˈzʊːrɪ] N *(= state)* Missouri *nt*

misspell [ˈmɪsˈspel] *pret, ptp* **misspelled** *or* **misspelt** VT falsch schreiben

misspelling [ˈmɪsˈspelɪŋ] N *(= act)* falsches Schreiben; *(= spelling mistake)* Rechtschreibfehler *m*

misspelt [ˈmɪsˈspelt] *pret, ptp of* **misspell**

misspent [ˌmɪsˈspent] ADJ vergeudet, verschwendet; **I regret my ~ youth** ich bedaure es, in meiner Jugend so ein liederliches Leben geführt zu haben; *(= wasted youth)* ich bedaure es, meine Jugend so vergeudet *or* vertan zu haben

misstate [ˈmɪsˈsteɪt] VT falsch darlegen *or* darstellen

misstatement [ˈmɪsˈsteɪtmənt] N falsche Darstellung

missus [ˈmɪsɪz] N *(inf)* = **missis**

missy [ˈmɪsɪ] N *(inf)* Fräuleinchen *nt (inf)*, kleines Fräulein

mist [mɪst] **N** **a** Nebel *m*; *(in liquid)* Trübung *f*; *(= haze)* Dunst *m*; *(on glass etc)* Beschlag *m* **b** *(fig)* **through a ~ of tears** durch einen Tränenschleier; **it is lost in the ~s of time** das liegt im Dunkel der Vergangenheit; **the ~s of confusion surrounding the affair** das undurchsichtige Dunkel, in das die Angelegenheit gehüllt ist **VI** **a** *(window etc)* beschlagen **b** *(fig: eyes)* sich verschleiern *(geh)*

▶ **mist over** **VI** *(= become cloudy)* sich trüben; *(glass, mirror: also* **mist up***)* (sich) beschlagen; **her eyes misted over with tears** Tränen verschleierten ihren Blick *(liter)* **VT** *sep* **the condensation is misting over the windows** durch den Dampf beschlagen die Fensterscheiben

mistakable [mɪˈsteɪkəbl] ADJ **the twins are easily ~** man kann die Zwillinge leicht miteinander verwechseln

mistake [mɪˈsteɪk] **N** Fehler *m*; **to make a ~** *(in writing, calculating etc)* einen Fehler machen; *(= be mistaken)* sich irren; **you're making a big ~ in marrying him** Sie machen *or* begehen *(form)* einen schweren Fehler, wenn Sie ihn heiraten; **to make the ~ of asking too much** den Fehler

machen *or* begehen *(form)*, zu viel zu verlangen; **my biggest ~ was to …** mein größter Fehler war, zu …; **what a ~ (to make)!** wie kann man nur (so einen Fehler machen)!; **by ~** aus Versehen, versehentlich; **she was shot in ~ for her sister** sie wurde irrtümlicherweise anstelle ihrer Schwester erschossen; **there must be some ~** da muss ein Fehler *or* Irrtum vorliegen; **the ~ is mine** der Fehler liegt bei mir; **there's no ~ about it, …** (es besteht) kein Zweifel, …; **let there be no ~ (about it)** ein(e)s steht fest: …; **make no ~, I mean what I say** damit wir uns nicht falsch verstehen: mir ist es ernst *or* Ernst; **it's freezing and no ~!** *(inf)* (ich kann dir sagen,) das ist vielleicht eine Kälte! *(inf)*
VT *pret* **mistook**, *ptp* **mistaken** **a** *words, meaning, remarks etc* falsch auffassen *or* verstehen; *seriousness, cause* verkennen, nicht erkennen; *house, road, time of train* sich irren *or* vertun *(inf)* in *(+dat)*; **to ~ sb's meaning** jdn falsch verstehen; **I mistook you** *or* **what you meant** ich habe Sie falsch *or* nicht richtig verstanden; **to ~ sb's identity** jdn verwechseln; **there's no mistaking the urgency of the situation** die Dringlichkeit der Situation steht außer Frage; **there's no mistaking her writing** ihre Schrift ist unverkennbar; **there's no mistaking what he meant** er hat sich unmissverständlich ausgedrückt; **there was no mistaking his anger** er war eindeutig wütend
b **to ~ A for B** A mit B verwechseln, A für B halten; **it cannot possibly be ~n for anything else** das ist doch unverkennbar!, das kann man doch gar nicht verwechseln!
c **to be ~n** sich irren; **to be ~n about sth/sb** sich in etw/jdm irren; **to be ~n in thinking that …** fälschlicherweise annehmen, dass …; **you are badly ~n there** da irren Sie sich aber gewaltig!; **if I am not ~n …, unless I am (very much) ~n …** wenn mich nicht alles täuscht …, wenn ich mich nicht irre …

mistaken [mɪˈsteɪkən] ✪ 12.1 **ADJ** *(= wrong) idea* falsch; *(= misplaced) loyalty, kindness* unangebracht, fehl am Platz; *affection, trust* töricht; **in the ~ belief that …** in der falschen *or* irrigen Annahme, dass …; **to be under** *or* **have the ~ impression that …** fälschlicherweise vermuten, dass …; **a case of ~ identity** eine Verwechslung

mistakenly [mɪˈsteɪkənlɪ] **ADV** fälschlicherweise, irrtümlicherweise; *(= by accident)* versehentlich

mister [ˈmɪstəʳ] **N** **a** *(abbr* **Mr***)* Herr *m*; *(on envelope)* Herrn; *(with politicians' names etc) not translated* **b** *(inf: = sir) not translated*; **please, ~, can you tell me …?** können Sie mir bitte sagen …?; **now listen here, ~** hören Sie mal her

mistime [ˈmɪsˈtaɪm] **VT** **a** *act* einen ungünstigen Zeitpunkt wählen für; **a badly ~d political announcement** eine politische Erklärung, die zu einem denkbar ungünstigen Zeitpunkt kommt; **he ~d his entrance** *(actor)* er trat zum falschen Zeitpunkt auf **b** *race* falsch stoppen

mistle thrush [ˈmɪsl̩θrʌʃ] **N** Misteldrossel *f*

mistletoe [ˈmɪsltəʊ] **N** Mistel *f*; *(= sprig)* Mistelzweig *m*

mistook [mɪˈstʊk] *pret of* **mistake**

mistral [mɪˈstrɑːl] **N** Mistral *m*

mistranslate [ˈmɪstrænzˈleɪt] **VT** falsch übersetzen

mistranslation [ˈmɪstrænzˈleɪʃən] **N** *(= act)* falsche Übersetzung; *(= error also)* Übersetzungsfehler *m*

mistreat [ˌmɪsˈtriːt] **VT** schlecht behandeln; *(violently)* misshandeln

mistreatment [ˌmɪsˈtriːtmənt] **N** schlechte Behandlung; *(violent)* Misshandlung *f*

mistress [ˈmɪstrɪs] **N** **a** *(of house, horse, dog)* Herrin *f*; **she is now ~ of the situation** sie ist jetzt Herr der Lage **b** *(= lover)* Geliebte *f*, Mätresse *f (old)* **c** *(= teacher)* Lehrerin *f* **d** *(old, = Mrs)* Frau *f*

mistrial [ˌmɪsˈtraɪəl] **N** **it was declared a ~** das Urteil wurde wegen Verfahrensmängeln aufgehoben

mistrust [ˈmɪsˈtrʌst] **N** Misstrauen *nt* (*of* gegenüber) **VT** misstrauen *(+dat)*

mistrustful [ˌmɪsˈtrʌstfʊl] **ADJ** misstrauisch; **to be ~ of sb/sth** jdm/einer Sache misstrauen

misty [ˈmɪstɪ] **ADJ** *(+er)* **a** *day, morning* neblig; *(= hazy)* dunstig; *mountain peaks* in Nebel gehüllt; *colour* gedeckt; *(= fine) rain* fein; **~ weather** Nebelwetter *nt*, Nebel *m*; **a ~ view of the valley** ein Blick auf das (nebel)verhangene *or* dunstige Tal; **a ~ drizzle** ein feiner Regenschleier **b** *(fig: = blurred) form, figure, memory* verschwommen; **her eyes grew ~, a ~ look came into her eyes** ihr Blick verschleierte sich; **~-eyed, with ~ eyes** mit verschleiertem Blick **c** *glasses (= misted up)* beschlagen; *(= opaque)* milchig; *liquid* trübe; **the window is getting ~** das Fenster beschlägt

misunderstand [ˈmɪsʌndəˈstænd] *pret, ptp* **misunderstood** **VT** falsch verstehen, missverstehen; **don't ~ me …** verstehen Sie mich nicht falsch … **VI** **I think you've misunderstood** ich glaube, Sie haben das missverstanden *or* falsch verstanden

misunderstanding [ˈmɪsʌndəˈstændɪŋ] **N** **a** Missverständnis *nt*; **there must be some ~** da muss ein Missverständnis vorliegen; **so that no ~ is possible** um Missverständnissen vorzubeugen; **let there be no ~ (about it) …** damit keine Missverständnisse entstehen: …, damit wir uns nicht missverstehen: … **b** *(= disagreement)* Meinungsverschiedenheit *f*

misunderstood [ˈmɪsʌndəˈstʊd] *ptp of* **misunderstand** **ADJ** unverstanden; *artist, playwright* verkannt

misuse [ˈmɪsˈjuːs] **N** Missbrauch *m*; *(of words)* falscher Gebrauch; *(of funds)* Zweckentfremdung *f*; **~ of power/authority** Macht-/Amtsmissbrauch *m* [ˈmɪsˈjuːz] **VT** missbrauchen; *words* falsch gebrauchen; *funds* zweckentfremden

misword [ˈmɪsˈwɜːd] **VT** *contract etc* falsch formulieren

MIT *(US) abbr of* **Massachusetts Institute of Technology**

mite¹ [maɪt] **N** *(Zool)* Milbe *f*

mite² **N** **a** *(Hist, = coin)* Scherf *m*, Heller *m*; **to contribute one's ~ to sth** sein Scherflein zu etw beitragen **b** *(= small amount)* bisschen *nt*; **well, just a ~ then** na gut, ein (ganz) kleines bisschen **c** *(Brit = child)* Würmchen *nt (inf)*; **poor little ~!** armes Wurm! *(inf)* **ADV** *(inf)* **a ~ surprised/disappointed** etwas *or* ein bisschen überrascht/enttäuscht; **could you wait a ~ longer?** können Sie noch ein Momentchen warten? *(inf)*

miter **N** *(US)* = **mitre**

mitigate [ˈmɪtɪgeɪt] **VT** *pain* lindern; *punishment* mildern; **mitigating circumstances/factors** mildernde Umstände *pl*

mitigation [ˌmɪtɪˈgeɪʃən] **N** *(of pain)* Linderung *f*; *(of punishment)* Milderung *f*; **to say something in ~** etwas zu jds/seiner Verteidigung anführen; **have you anything to say in ~ of sentence?** haben Sie zu dem Urteil noch irgendetwas Entlastendes vorzubringen?

mitre, *(US)* **miter** [ˈmaɪtəʳ] **N** **a** *(Eccl)* Mitra *f* **b** *(Tech: also* **mitre joint***)* Gehrung *f*, Gehrfuge *f* **VT** *(Tech)* gehren

mitt [mɪt] **N** **a** = **mitten** **b** *(= baseball glove)* Baseballhandschuh *m* **c** *(inf: = hand)* Pfote *f (inf)*

mitten [ˈmɪtn] **N** **a** Fausthandschuh *m*, Fäustling *m*; *(with bare fingers)* Handschuh *m* ohne Finger *or* mit halben Fingern **b** **mittens** **PL** *(Boxing)* Boxhandschuhe *pl*

mix [mɪks] **N** Mischung *f*; **a real ~ of people** eine bunte Mischung von Menschen; **a good social ~ at the gala performance** ein gut gemischtes Publikum auf der Galavorstellung; **a broad racial ~** ein breites Spektrum verschiedener Rassen; **product ~** Produktspanne *f*; **cement ~** Zementmischung *f*; **a wool ~ pullover** ein Pullover *m* aus verschiedenen Fasern
VT **a** *(= combine)* (ver)mischen; *drinks (= prepare)* mischen, mixen; *(Cook) ingredients* verrühren; *dough* zubereiten; *salad* untermengen, wenden; **you shouldn't ~ your drinks** man sollte nicht mehrere Sachen durcheinandertrinken; **to ~ sth into sth** etw unter etw *(acc)* mengen *or* mischen; **I never ~ business with** *or* **and pleasure** ich vermische nie Geschäftliches und Privates
b *(= confuse)* durcheinanderbringen; **to ~ sb/sth with sb/sth** jdn/etw mit jdm/etw verwechseln
c **to ~ it** *(dated inf)* sich prügeln, sich kloppen *(inf)*; **the gangs were really ~ing it** die Banden haben sich eine ganz schöne Schlägerei geliefert *(inf)*
VI **a** *(= combine)* sich mischen lassen; *(chemical substances, races)* sich vermischen
b *(= go together)* zusammenpassen; **business and pleasure don't ~** Arbeit und Vergnügen lassen sich nicht verbinden
c *(people) (= get on)* miteinander auskommen; *(= mingle)* sich vermischen; *(= associate)* miteinander verkehren; **to ~ with sb** mit jdm auskommen, sich unter jdn mischen, mit jdm verkehren; **he finds it hard to ~** er ist nicht sehr gesellig *or* kontaktfreudig; **to ~ well** kontaktfreudig *or* gesellig sein; **he ~es in high society** er verkehrt in den besseren Kreisen

▶ **mix in** **VT** *sep egg, water* unterrühren

▶ **mix up** **VT** *sep* **a** *(= combine)* vermischen; *ingredients* verrühren; *(= prepare) medicine* mischen **b** *(= get in a muddle)* durcheinanderbringen; *(= confuse with sb/sth else)* verwechseln **c** *(= involve)* **to mix sb up in sth** jdn in etw *(acc)* hineinziehen; *in crime etc also* jdn in etw *(acc)* verwickeln; **to be mixed up in sth** in etw *(acc)* verwickelt sein; **he's got himself mixed up with the police** er hat Scherereien mit der Polizei bekommen; **he's got himself mixed up with that gang** er hat sich mit dieser Bande eingelassen **d** **to mix it up** *(US inf)* sich prügeln *(with* mit); *(non-physically)* sich anlegen *(with* mit)

mixed [mɪkst] **ADJ** **a** *(= assorted)* gemischt; **~ nuts/biscuits** Nuss-/Keksmischung *f* **b** *(= of both sexes) choir, bathing, school* gemischt; **in ~ company** in gemischter Gesellschaft **c** *(= varied)* gemischt; *(= both good and bad)* unterschiedlich; **of ~ race** *or* **parentage** gemischtrassig; **a class of ~ ability** eine Klasse mit Schülern unterschiedlicher Leistungsstärke; **a ~ set of people** eine bunt zusammengewürfelte Gruppe; **I have ~ feelings about him** ich habe ihm gegenüber zwiespältige Gefühle; **to have ~ feelings about sth** etw mit gemischten Gefühlen betrachten; **with ~ results** mit wechselndem *or* geteiltem Erfolg

mixed: **mixed-ability** **ADJ** *group, class* mit unterschiedlicher Leistungsstärke; **~ teaching** *gemeinsamer Unterricht für Schüler mit unterschiedlicher Leistungsstärke*; **mixed bag** **N** bunte Mischung; **the students are a bit of a ~** die Studenten sind eine ziemlich bunt gemischte Truppe *(inf)*; **a very ~ of activities** eine bunte Mischung unterschiedlichster Aktivitäten; **mixed blessing** **N** **it's a ~** das ist ein zweischneidiges Schwert; **children are a ~** Kinder sind kein reines Vergnügen; **mixed bunch** **N** *(lit)* bunt gemischter Blumenstrauß; *(fig: = people)* eine bunt gemischte Truppe *(inf)*; **a ~ of products** ein bunt gemischtes Angebot; **mixed cloth** **N** meliertes Tuch; **mixed doubles** **PL** *(Sport)* gemischtes Doppel; **mixed drink** **N** Mixgetränk *nt*; **mixed economy** **N** gemischte Wirtschaftsform; **mixed farming** **N** Ackerbau und Viehzucht *(+pl vb)*; **mixed grill** **N** Grillteller *m*; **mixed marriage** **N** Mischehe *f*; **mixed-media** **ADJ** *work* mittelmedial; **mixed metaphor** **N** gemischte Metapher, Bildervermengung *f*; **mixed pickles** **PL** Mixed Pickles *pl*, Mixedpickles *pl*; **mixed-race** **ADJ** *children* gemischtrassig; **mixed**

school N Koedukationsschule *f*; **mixed-up** ADJ ATTR, **mixed up** ADJ PRED durcheinander *pred*; *(= muddled) person also, ideas* konfus; **she's just a crazy ~ kid** *(inf)* sie ist total verdreht; **I'm all mixed up** ich bin völlig durcheinander; **he got all mixed up** er hat alles durcheinandergebracht; **I got mixed up about the times** ich habe die Zeiten verwechselt

mixer ['mɪksəʳ] N **a** *(= food mixer)* Mixer *m*, Mixgerät *nt*; *(= cement mixer)* Mischmaschine *f* **b** *(for drink) Cola, Ginger Ale, Tonic etc zum Auffüllen von alkoholischen Mixgetränken* **c** *(Rad) (= person)* Toningenieur(in) *m(f)*, Mixer(in) *m(f)*; *(= thing)* Mischpult *nt* **d** *(= sociable person)* **to be a good ~** kontaktfreudig sein; **David's not much of a ~** David ist ziemlich kontaktarm *or* verschlossen **e** *(US inf)* Party *f* zum Kennenlernen; *(for new students)* Erstsemesterfete *f*

mixer tap N *(Brit)* Mischbatterie *f*

mixture ['mɪkstʃəʳ] N Mischung *f*; *(Med)* Mixtur *f*; *(Cook)* Gemisch *nt*; *(= cake mixture, dough)* Teig *m*; **~ of teas** Teemischung *f*; **~ of gases** Gasgemisch *nt*; **they spoke to each other in a ~ of French and English** sie haben miteinander eine Mischung aus Französisch und Englisch gesprochen; **I've had quite a ~ of drinks tonight** ich habe heute Abend ziemlich viel durcheinandergetrunken; **a ~ of comedy and tragedy** eine Mischung aus Komödie und Tragödie; **fold the eggs into the cheese ~** heben Sie die Eier ins Käsegemisch *or* in die Käsemischung unter

mix-up ['mɪksʌp] N Durcheinander *nt*; **there seemed to be some ~ about which train ...** es schien völlig unklar, welchen Zug ...; **there must have been a ~** da muss irgendetwas schiefgelaufen sein *(inf)*

MLA *(Brit Pol) abbr of* **Member of the Legislative Assembly** Mitglied *nt* der legislativen Versammlung Nordirlands

MLR *(Brit) abbr of* **minimum lending rate**

M'lud [mə'lʌd] *(Brit Jur) abbr of* **My Lord** Euer Ehren

mm *abbr of* **millimetre(s)** mm

MMR *(Med) abbr of* **measles, mumps, rubella**

MMS *(Telec) abbr of* **Multimedia Messaging Service** MMS *m*

mnemonic [nɪ'mɒnɪk] ADJ **a** Gedächtnis-; **~ trick** *or* **device** Gedächtnisstütze *f*; **~ rhyme** Eselsbrücke *f (inf)* **b** *(Comput)* mnemotechnisch N Gedächtnisstütze *or* -hilfe *f*, Eselsbrücke *f (inf)*

MO **a** *abbr of* **money order** **b** *abbr of* **medical officer** **c** *abbr of* **modus operandi**

mo [məʊ] N *(inf) abbr of* **moment**

moan [məʊn] N **a** *(= groan)* Stöhnen *nt*; *(of wind)* Seufzen *nt*, Raunen *nt (geh)*; *(of trees etc)* Raunen *nt (geh)* **b** *(= grumble)* Gejammer *nt no pl (inf)*; **to have a ~ about sth** über etw *(acc)* jammern *or* schimpfen VI **a** *(= groan)* stöhnen; *(wind, trees)* raunen *(geh)* **b** *(= grumble)* jammern, schimpfen *(about* über *+acc)*; **~, ~, ~, that's all she does** sie ist ständig am Maulen *(inf)* VT **..., he ~ed ...** stöhnte er; **he ~ed a sigh of relief** er stöhnte erleichtert auf

moaner ['məʊnəʳ] N *(inf)* Miesepeter *m (inf)*, Mäkelliese *f (inf)*

moaning ['məʊnɪŋ] N **a** Stöhnen *nt*; *(of wind)* Seufzen *nt*; *(of trees etc)* Raunen *nt (geh)* **b** *(= grumbling)* Gestöhn(e) *nt*

moat [məʊt] N Wassergraben *m*; *(of castle also)* Burggraben *m*

moated ['məʊtɪd] ADJ von einem Wassergraben umgeben

mob [mɒb] N **a** *(= crowd)* Horde *f*, Schar *f*; *(riotous, violent)* Mob *m no pl*; **an undisciplined ~** ein undisziplinierter Haufen; **a ~ gathered to burn the houses** der Mob *or* Pöbel lief zusammen, um die Häuser zu verbrennen; **the crowd became a ~** das Volk wurde zur wütenden Menge; **they went in a ~ to the town hall** sie stürmten zum Rathaus **b** *(inf) (= criminal gang)* Bande *f*; *(fig: = clique)* Haufen *m*, Bande *f*; **which ~ were you in?** *(Mil)* bei welchem Haufen warst du denn? *(inf)*; **the Mob** *(= the Mafia)* die Maf(f)ia **c** **the ~** *(pej: = the masses)* die Masse(n *pl*) VT herfallen über *(+acc)*, sich stürzen auf *(+acc)*; *actor, pop star also* belagern; **the prisoner was ~bed** die Menge fiel über den Gefangenen her

mobcap ['mɒbkæp] N *(Hist)* (Spitzen)haube *f*

mobile ['məʊbaɪl] ADJ **a** *person* beweglich, mobil; *(= having means of transport)* beweglich, motorisiert; *(Sociol)* mobil; **the patient is ~ already** der Patient kann schon aufstehen **b** *X-ray unit etc* fahrbar; *missile launcher, laboratory* mobil **c** *mind* wendig, beweglich; *face, expression, features* lebhaft, beweglich N **a** *(= mobile phone)* Handy *nt* **b** *(= decoration)* Mobile *nt*

mobile: **mobile canteen** N Kantine *f* auf Rädern, mobile Küche; *(Mil)* Feldküche *f*; **mobile home** N Wohnwagen *m*; **mobile library** N Fahrbücherei *f*; **mobile phone** N Mobiltelefon *nt*, Handy *nt*; **mobile radio** N Mobilfunk *m*; *(= device)* Funkgerät *nt*; **mobile shop** N *(Brit)* Verkaufswagen *m*; **mobile walkway** N *(US)* Rollsteg *m*

mobility [məʊ'bɪlɪtɪ] N *(of person)* Beweglichkeit *f*; *(of mind also)* Wendigkeit *f*; *(of features, face etc also)* Lebhaftigkeit *f*; *(of work force, Sociol)* Mobilität *f*; **a car gives you ~** ein Auto macht Sie beweglicher

mobilization [ˌməʊbɪlaɪ'zeɪʃən] N Mobilisierung *f*; *(Mil also)* Mobilmachung *f*

mobilize ['məʊbɪlaɪz] VT mobilisieren; *(Mil also)* mobil machen VI mobil machen

mob rule N Herrschaft *f* des Pöbels

mobster ['mɒbstəʳ] N *(esp US)* Gangster(in) *m(f)*, Bandit(in) *m(f)*

mob violence N Massenausschreitungen *pl*

moccasin ['mɒkəsɪn] N Mokassin *m*

mocha ['mɒkə] N Mokka *m*

mock [mɒk] N **a** **to make a ~ of sth** etw ad absurdum führen; *(= put an end to)* etw vereiteln *or* zunichtemachen **b** **mocks** *(Brit Sch inf)* Probeprüfungen *pl* ADJ *attr emotions* gespielt; *crash, examination* simuliert; *execution, trial* gestellt; **~ leather/fur** Kunstleder *nt*/-pelz *m*; **the house is ~ Tudor** das Haus ist nachgemachtes Tudor; **~ attack/fight** Scheinangriff/-kampf *m* VT **a** *(= ridicule)* sich lustig machen über *(+acc)*, verspotten **b** *(= mimic)* nachmachen, nachäffen **c** *(= defy)* trotzen *(+dat)*; *law* sich hinwegsetzen über *(+acc)*; *(= set at nought) plans, efforts* vereiteln, zunichtemachen VI **to ~ at sb/sth** sich über jdn/etw lustig machen; **don't ~** mokier dich nicht!, spotte nicht! *(geh)*

mocker ['mɒkəʳ] N **a** Spötter(in) *m(f)*, spöttischer Mensch **b** **to put the ~s on sth** *(Brit inf)* etw vermasseln *(inf)*

mockery ['mɒkərɪ] N **a** *(= derision)* Spott *m* **b** *(= object of ridicule)* Gespött *nt*; **they made a ~ of him** sie machten ihn zum Gespött der Leute; **to make a ~ of sth** etw lächerlich machen; *(= prove its futility)* etw ad absurdum führen; **inflation will make a ~ of our budget** durch die Inflation wird unser Haushaltsplan zur Farce **c** **this is a ~ of justice** das spricht jeglicher Gerechtigkeit Hohn; **it was a ~ of a trial** der Prozess war eine einzige Farce; **what a ~ (this is)!** das ist doch glatter Hohn *or* der reinste Hohn!

mock: **mock-heroic** ADJ *(Liter)* heroisch-komisch; **~ poem** komisches Epos; **mock-heroics** PL *(Liter)* heroisch-komische Passage(n) *f(pl)*

mocking ['mɒkɪŋ] ADJ spöttisch N Spott *m*

mockingbird ['mɒkɪŋˌbɜːd] N Spottdrossel *f*

mockingly ['mɒkɪŋlɪ] ADV spöttisch, voller Spott; **she ~ repeated his words** sie äffte seine Worte nach

mock: **mock moon** N *(Astron)* Nebenmond *m*; **mock orange** N Falscher Jasmin, Pfeifenstrauch *m*; **mock trial** N *(Jur)* Scheinprozess *m*; **mock turtle soup** N Mockturtlesuppe *f*; **mock-up** ['mɒkʌp] N Modell *nt* in Originalgröße

MOD *(Brit) abbr of* **Ministry of Defence**

mod [mɒd] ADJ *(dated sl)* modern, poppig *(inf)* N *(dated sl) modisch gekleideter Halbstarker in den 60er Jahren*

modal ['məʊdl] ADJ modal; **~ verb** Modalverb *nt*

modality [məʊ'dælɪtɪ] N Modalität *f*

mod cons ['mɒd'kɒnz] *(Brit inf) pl abbr of* **modern conveniences** mod. Komf., (moderner) Komfort

mode [məʊd] N **a** *(Gram)* Modus *m*; *(Mus)* Tonart *f*; *(Philos)* Modalität *f* **b** *(= way)* Art *f* (und Weise); *(= form)* Form *f*; **~ of transport** Transportmittel *nt*; **~ of life** Lebensweise *f*; *(Biol)* Lebensform *f*; **~ of address** Anrede *f* **c** *(Fashion)* Mode *f*; **to be the ~** in Mode sein **d** *(Comput)* Modus *m*

model ['mɒdl] N **a** Modell *nt*; **to make sth on the ~ of sth** etw *(acc)* einer Sache *(dat)* nachbilden; **it is built on the ~ of the Doge's Palace** es ist eine Nachbildung des Dogenpalastes; **our democracy is based on the ~ of Greece** unsere Demokratie ist nach dem Vorbild Griechenlands aufgebaut **b** *(= perfect example)* Muster *nt (of* an *+dat)*; **this book is a ~ of objectivity** dieses Buch ist ein Muster an Objektivität; **to hold sb up as a ~** jdn als Vorbild hinstellen **c** *(artist's, photographer's)* Modell *nt*; *(= fashion model)* Mannequin *nt*; *(= male model)* Dressman *m* **d** *(of car, dress, machine etc)* Modell *nt* ADJ **a** Modell-; **~ railway** *(Brit) or* **railroad** *(US)* Modelleisenbahn *f*; **~ house** Puppenhaus *nt* **b** *(= perfect)* vorbildlich, mustergültig; **~ pupil** Musterschüler(in) *m(f)* VT **a** **to ~ X on Y** Y als Vorlage *or* Muster für X benutzen; **X is ~led** *(Brit) or* **~ed** *(US)* **on Y** Y dient als Vorlage *or* Muster für X; **this building is ~led** *(Brit) or* **~ed** *(US)* **on the Parthenon** dieses Gebäude ist dem Parthenon nachgebildet; **the system was ~led** *(Brit) or* **~ed** *(US)* **on the American one** das System war nach amerikanischem Muster aufgebaut; **this poem is ~led** *(Brit) or* **~ed** *(US)* **on Shakespeare's sonnets** dieses Gedicht ist Shakespeares Sonetten nachempfunden; **it's not ~led** *(Brit) or* **~ed** *(US)* **on anything** es ist frei entstanden, dafür gibt es keine Vorlage; **to ~ oneself/one's life on sb** sich *(dat)* jdn zum Vorbild nehmen **b** *(= make a model)* modellieren, formen; **her finely ~led** *(Brit) or* **~ed features** *(US, fig)* ihre fein geschnittenen Gesichtszüge **c** *dress etc* vorführen VI **a** *(= make models)* modellieren **b** *(Art, Phot)* als Modell arbeiten *or* beschäftigt sein; *(Fashion)* als Mannequin/Dressman arbeiten; **to ~ for sb** *(Art, Phot)* jdm Modell stehen; *(Fashion)* jds Kreationen vorführen

modelling, *(US)* **modeling** ['mɒdlɪŋ] N **a** *(of statue etc)* Modellieren *nt*; *(fig: of features)* Schnitt *m* **b** **to do some ~** *(Phot, Art)* als Modell arbeiten; *(Fashion)* als Mannequin/Dressman arbeiten

modem ['məʊdem] N Modem *nt*

modem card N Modemkarte *f*

moderate ['mɒdərɪt] ADJ gemäßigt *(also Pol)*; *appetite, enjoyment, lifestyle, speed, increase* mäßig; *gain, improvement* leicht; *demands, price* vernünftig, angemessen; *drinker, eater* maßvoll; *income, success* (mittel)mäßig, bescheiden; *punishment, winter* mild; **a ~ amount** einigermaßen viel; **~-sized, of ~ size** mittelgroß; **over a ~ heat** bei mittlerer Hitze; **in a ~ oven** im Backofen bei mittlerer Hitze; **~ drinking** Alkoholgenuss *m* in Maßen N *(Pol)* Gemäßigte(r) *mf* ['mɒdəreɪt] VT **a** *(= attenuate) demands, position, behaviour* mäßigen; **the climate is ~d by the Gulf Stream**

das Klima wird durch den Golfstrom gemäßigter; **to have a moderating influence on sb** mäßigend auf jdn wirken
b *meeting, discussion* den Vorsitz führen bei; *(TV, Rad)* moderieren ['mɒdəreɪt]
VI a nachlassen, sich mäßigen; *(wind etc)* nachlassen, sich abschwächen; *(demands)* gemäßigter werden
b *(in meeting, discussion)* den Vorsitz führen; *(TV, Rad)* moderieren

moderately ['mɒdərɪtlɪ] ADV a *(with adj/adv)* einigermaßen; *increase, decline* mäßig; **a ~ priced suit** ein nicht allzu *or* übermäßig teurer Anzug; **the house was ~ large** das Haus war mäßig groß b *(= in moderation) drink, eat, exercise* in Maßen; *act* maßvoll

moderation [,mɒdə'reɪʃən] N Mäßigung *f*; **in ~** mit Maß(en)

moderator ['mɒdəreɪtə'] N *(Eccl)* Synodalpräsident *m*

modern ['mɒdən] ADJ modern *(also Art, Liter)*; *times, world also* heutig; *history* neuere und neueste; **Modern Greek** *etc* Neugriechisch *nt etc* N Anhänger(in) *m(f)* der Moderne

modern-day [,mɒdən'deɪ] ADJ modern; **~ America** das heutige Amerika

modernism ['mɒdənɪzəm] N Modernismus *m*

modernist ['mɒdənɪst] ADJ modernistisch N Modernist(in) *m(f)*

modernistic [,mɒdə'nɪstɪk] ADJ modernistisch

modernity [mɒ'dɜːnɪtɪ] N Modernität *f*

modernization [,mɒdənaɪ'zeɪʃən] N Modernisierung *f*

modernize ['mɒdənaɪz] VT modernisieren

modern languages PL neuere Sprachen *pl*, moderne Fremdsprachen *pl*; *(Univ)* Neuphilologie *f*

modernly ['mɒdənlɪ] ADV *(= fashionably)* modern; **more ~ known as ...** in neuerer Zeit als ... bekannt

modernness ['mɒdənnɪs] N = **modernity**

modern studies PL Gegenwartskunde *f* und Kulturwissenschaft *f*

modest ['mɒdɪst] ADJ a *(= not boastful, humble)* bescheiden; **to be ~ about one's successes** nicht mit seinen Erfolgen prahlen b *(= moderate)* bescheiden; *requirements also* gering; *price* mäßig; **a man of ~ means** ein Mann mit bescheidenen Mitteln; **on a ~ scale** in bescheidenem Rahmen; **a ~ crowd turned out for the occasion** die Veranstaltung war (nur) mäßig besucht c *(= chaste, proper)* schamhaft; *(in one's behaviour)* anständig, sittsam *(geh)*, züchtig *(old)*; **to be ~ in one's dress** sich anständig kleiden

modestly ['mɒdɪstlɪ] ADV a *(= unassumingly, moderately)* bescheiden; **~ successful** in bescheidenem Maße erfolgreich; **~ priced goods** Waren zu gemäßigten Preisen; **he still gambled ~** er spielte immer noch in Maßen b *(= chastely, properly)* schamhaft; *behave* anständig, züchtig *(old)*; *dress* anständig

modesty ['mɒdɪstɪ] N a *(= humbleness)* Bescheidenheit *f*; **in all ~** bei aller Bescheidenheit; **the ~ of the man!** *(iro)* der ist ja überhaupt nicht von sich eingenommen! *(iro inf)* b *(= moderation)* Bescheidenheit *f*, Genügsamkeit *f*; *(of price)* Mäßigkeit *f* c *(= chasteness)* Schamgefühl *nt*; *(in behaviour)* Anstand *m*, Sittsamkeit *f (geh)*, Züchtigkeit *f (old)*; *(in dress)* Unauffälligkeit *f*, Dezentheit *f*

modicum ['mɒdɪkəm] N **a ~ (of)** ein wenig, ein bisschen; **with a ~ of luck** mit ein wenig *or* mit einem Quäntchen Glück; **a ~ of hope/intelligence** ein Funke *m* (von) Hoffnung/Intelligenz; **a ~ of truth** ein Körnchen *nt* Wahrheit

modifiable ['mɒdɪfaɪəbl] ADJ modifizierbar

modification [,mɒdɪfɪ'keɪʃən] N (Ver)änderung *f*; *(of design)* Abänderung *f*; *(of terms, contract, wording)* Modifizierung *f*, Modifikation *f*; **to make ~s to sth** (Ver)änderungen an etw *(dat)* vornehmen; etw abändern; etw modifizieren; **the suggested ~s to his design** die Änderungsvorschläge *pl* zu seinem Entwurf

modifier ['mɒdɪfaɪə'] N *(Gram)* Bestimmungswort *nt*, nähere Bestimmung

modify ['mɒdɪfaɪ] VT a *(= change)* (ver)ändern; *design* abändern; *terms, contract, wording* modifizieren; *(Comput)* ändern b *(= moderate)* mäßigen c *(Gram)* näher bestimmen

modish ['məʊdɪʃ] ADJ *(= fashionable)* modisch; *(= stylish)* schick; **it is very ~** es ist große Mode

modishly ['məʊdɪʃlɪ] ADV *(= fashionably)* modisch; *(= stylishly)* schick; **he ~ professed his solidarity with the working classes** er folgte dem herrschenden Trend und bekannte sich mit der Arbeiterklasse solidarisch

modiste [məʊ'diːst] N Modistin *f*

modular ['mɒdjʊlə'] ADJ aus Elementen zusammengesetzt; *(Comput)* modular; *(esp Brit Sch, Univ) course, degree etc* modular aufgebaut; **the ~ design of their furniture** ihre als Bauelemente konzipierten Möbel

modulate ['mɒdjʊleɪt] *(Mus, Rad)* VI modulieren; **the key ~d from major to minor** die Tonart wechselte von Dur nach Moll VT modulieren

modulated ['mɒdjʊleɪtɪd] ADJ **(beautifully) ~** *(voice)* (harmonisch) ausgewogen

modulation [,mɒdjʊ'leɪʃən] N *(Mus, Rad)* Modulation *f*

module ['mɒdjuːl] N (Bau)element *nt*; *(in education)* Kurs *m*; *(Comput)* Modul *nt*; *(Space)* Raumkapsel *f*

modus operandi ['məʊdəs,ɒpə'rændɪ] N Modus Operandi *m*

modus vivendi ['məʊdəs,vɪ'vendɪ] N Modus Vivendi *m*; *(= way of life)* Lebensstil *m*, Lebensweise *f*

moggy ['mɒgɪ] N *(Brit inf)* Mieze *f (inf)*

mogul¹ ['məʊgəl] N a *(lit, fig)* Mogul *m* b *(Hist)* **Mogul emperor** Mogulkaiser *m*; **Mogul empire** Mogulreich *nt*; **Mogul invasion** Invasion *f* durch die Moguln; **Mogul city** mogulische Stadt

mogul² N *(Ski)* Buckel *m*

MOH *abbr of* **Medical Officer of Health**

mohair ['məʊhɛə'] N Mohair *m*, Mohär *m*

Mohammed [məʊ'hæmed] N Mohammed *m*

Mohammedan [məʊ'hæmɪdən] *(Hist) (neg!)* ADJ mohammedanisch *(Hist) (neg!)* N Mohammedaner(in) *m(f) (Hist) (neg!)*

Mohammedanism [mə'hæmədənɪzəm] N *(Hist) (neg!)* Islam *m*

Mohican [məʊ'hiːkən] N a Mohikaner(in) *m(f)* b **mohican** *(Brit: = haircut)* Irokesenschnitt *m*

mohican [məʊ'hiːkən] N *(Brit: = haircut)* Irokesenschnitt *m*

moiety ['mɔɪɪtɪ] N *(Jur: = half)* Hälfte *f*; *(liter) (= small amount)* Hauch *m (geh)* (of an *+dat*); *(= small share)* Bruchteil *m*

moist [mɔɪst] ADJ *(+er)* feucht *(from, with* vor *+dat)*; **~ with tears** feucht von Tränen, tränenfeucht; **~ with dew** taufeucht

moisten ['mɔɪsn] VT anfeuchten; **to ~ sth with sth** etw mit etw befeuchten VI feucht werden

moistness ['mɔɪstnɪs] N Feuchtigkeit *f*

moisture ['mɔɪstʃə'] N Feuchtigkeit *f*; **drops of ~** *(= water)* Wassertropfen *pl*; *(= sweat)* Schweißtropfen *pl*

moisturize ['mɔɪstʃəraɪz] VT *skin* mit einer Feuchtigkeitscreme behandeln; *(cosmetic)* geschmeidig machen, Feuchtigkeit verleihen *(+dat)*; *air* befeuchten; **moisturizing gloves/socks** *Handschuhe/Socken mit integrierter cremehaltiger Schicht*

moisturizer ['mɔɪstʃəraɪzə'], **moisturizing cream** ['mɔɪstʃəraɪzɪŋ'kriːm] N Feuchtigkeitscreme *f*

molar (tooth) ['məʊlə'(,tuːθ)] N Backenzahn *m*

molasses [məʊ'læsɪz] N Melasse *f*; **to be as slow as ~ (in winter)** *(US inf)* eine (fürchterliche) Transuse sein *(inf)*

mold *etc (US)* = **mould** *etc*

Moldavia [mɒl'deɪvɪə] N = **Moldova**

Moldavian [mɒl'deɪvɪən] N, ADJ = **Moldovan**

Moldova [mɒl'dəʊvə] N Moldawien *nt*

Moldovan [mɒl'dəʊvən] N *(Ling)* Moldawisch ADJ moldawisch; **he is ~** er ist Moldawier

mole¹ [məʊl] N *(Anat)* Pigmentmal *nt (form)*, Leberfleck *m*

mole² N *(Zool)* Maulwurf *m*; *(inf: = secret agent)* Spion(in) *m(f)*

mole³ N *(Naut)* Mole *f*

molecular [məʊ'lekjʊlə'] ADJ molekular, Molekular-

molecular biology N Molekularbiologie *f*

molecule ['mɒlɪkjuːl] N Molekül *nt*

mole: **molehill** N Maulwurfshaufen *or* -hügel *m*; **moleskin** N *(= fur)* Maulwurfsfell *nt*; *(= coat/jacket etc)* Mantel/Jacke *etc* aus Maulwurfsfell; *(= fabric)* Moleskin *m or nt*

molest [məʊ'lest] VT belästigen

molestation [,məʊles'teɪʃən] N Belästigung *f*

moll [mɒl] N *(inf)* Gangsterbraut *f (inf)*

mollify ['mɒlɪfaɪ] VT besänftigen, beschwichtigen; **he was somewhat mollified by this** daraufhin beruhigte er sich etwas

mollusc ['mɒləsk] N Molluske *f (spec)*, Weichtier *nt*

mollycoddle ['mɒlɪ,kɒdl] VT verhätscheln, verpäppeln, verzärteln N Weichling *m*

Moloch ['məʊlɒk] N Moloch *m*

Molotov cocktail ['mɒlətɒf'kɒkteɪl] N Molotowcocktail *m*

molt N, VTI *(US)* = **moult**

molten ['məʊltən] ADJ geschmolzen; *glass, lava* flüssig

Molucca [məʊ'lʌkə] N **the ~ Islands, the ~s** die Molukken *pl*

mom [mɒm] N *(US inf)* = **mum²**

mom-and-pop store ['mɒmən'pɒp,stɔː'] N *(US inf)* Tante-Emma-Laden *m (inf)*

moment ['məʊmənt] N a Augenblick *m*, Moment *m*; **there were one or two ~s when I thought ...** ein paar Mal dachte ich ...; **from ~ to ~** zusehends, von Minute zu Minute; **any ~ now, (at) any ~** jeden Augenblick; **at any ~** *(= any time)* jederzeit; **at the ~** im Augenblick, momentan; **at the ~ when ...** zu dem Zeitpunkt, als ...; **not at the** *or* **this ~** im Augenblick *or* zurzeit nicht; **at the ~ of impact** beim Aufprall, im Augenblick des Aufpralls; **at the last ~** im letzten Augenblick; **at this (particular) ~ in time** momentan, augenblicklich; **for the ~** im Augenblick, vorläufig; **for a ~** (für) einen Moment; **for one ~ it seemed to have stopped** einen Augenblick lang schien es aufgehört zu haben; **not for a** *or* **one ~ ...** nie(mals) ...; **I didn't hesitate for a ~** ich habe keinen Augenblick gezögert; **in a ~** gleich; **in a ~ of madness** in einem Anflug von geistiger Umnachtung; **it was all over in a ~** *or* **in a few ~s** das ganze dauerte nur wenige Augenblicke; **to leave things until the last ~** alles erst im letzten Moment erledigen *or* machen *(inf)*; **half a ~!, one ~!** einen Moment!; **just a ~!, wait a ~!** Moment mal!; **I shan't be a ~** ich bin gleich wieder da; *(= nearly ready)* ich bin gleich so weit; **do it this very ~!** tu das auf der Stelle!; **I have just this ~ heard about it** ich habe es eben *or* gerade erst erfahren; **we haven't a ~ to lose** wir haben keine Minute zu verlieren; **not a ~ too soon** keine Minute zu früh, in letzter Minute; **not a ~'s peace** *or* **rest** keine ruhige Minute; **one ~ she was laughing, the next she was crying** zuerst lachte sie, einen Moment später weinte sie; **the ~ it happened** (in dem Augenblick,) als es passierte; **the ~ I saw him I knew ...** als ich ihn sah, wusste ich sofort ...; **the ~ he arrives there's trouble** sobald er auftaucht, gibt es Ärger; **tell me the ~ he comes** sagen Sie mir sofort Bescheid, wenn er kommt; **the ~ of truth** die Stunde der Wahrheit; **he is the man of the ~** er ist der Mann des Tages; **the film has its ~s** streckenweise hat der Film was *(inf)* **b** *(Phys)* Moment *nt*; **~ of acceleration/inertia** Beschleunigungs-/Trägheitsmoment *nt* **c** *(= importance)* Bedeutung *f*; **of little ~** bedeutungslos, unwichtig

momentarily ['məʊməntərɪlɪ] ADV **a** (für) einen Augenblick *or* Moment; **she shivered ~** sie zitterte einen Moment lang **b** *(US) (= very soon)* jeden Augenblick *or* Moment; *(= from moment to moment)* zusehends

momentary ['məʊməntərɪ] ADJ kurz; *glimpse also* flüchtig; *lapse of memory/concentration* momentan, vorübergehend; **a ~ feeling of nausea** eine momentane Übelkeit; **there was a ~ silence** einen Augenblick lang herrschte Stille

momentous [məʊ'mentəs] ADJ *(= memorable, important)* bedeutsam, bedeutungsvoll; *(= of great consequence)* von großer Tragweite; **of ~ significance** von entscheidender Bedeutung

momentousness [məʊ'mentəsnɪs] N Bedeutsamkeit *f*; *(of decision)* Tragweite *f*

momentum [məʊ'mentəm] N *(of moving object)* Schwung *m*; *(at moment of impact)* Wucht *f*; *(Phys)* Impuls *m*; *(fig)* Schwung *m*; **the rock's ~ carried it through the wall** der Felsbrocken hatte eine solche Wucht, dass er die Mauer durchschlug; **he let the car go under its own ~** er ließ das Auto von allein weiterrollen; **to gather** *or* **gain ~** *(lit)* sich beschleunigen, in Fahrt kommen *(inf)*; *(fig, idea, movement, plan)* in Gang kommen; **the campaign is now gathering** *or* **gaining ~** die Kampagne kommt nun in Gang *or* in Schwung; **to keep going under its own ~** *(lit)* sich aus eigener Kraft weiterbewegen; *(fig)* eine Eigendynamik entwickelt haben; **to lose ~** *(lit, fig)* Schwung verlieren

momma ['mɒmə] N *(US)* = **mummy**

momma's boy ['mɒməz,bɔɪ] N *(US inf)* Muttersöhnchen *nt (inf)*

Mon *abbr of* **Monday** Mo

Monaco ['mɒnəkəʊ] N Monaco *nt*

monad ['mɒnæd] N **a** *(Philos)* Monade *f* **b** *(Biol: dated)* Einzeller *m* **c** *(Chem)* einwertiges Element *or* Atom *or* Radikal

monarch ['mɒnək] N Monarch(in) *m(f)*, Herrscher(in) *m(f)*; *(fig)* König *m*; **absolute ~** Alleinherrscher(in) *m(f)*

monarchic(al) [mɒ'nɑːkɪk(əl)] ADJ monarchisch; *(= favouring monarchy)* monarchistisch

monarchism ['mɒnəkɪzəm] N *(= system)* Monarchie *f*; *(= advocacy of monarchy)* Monarchismus *m*

monarchist ['mɒnəkɪst] **ADJ** monarchistisch **N** Monarchist(in) *m(f)*, Anhänger(in) *m(f)* der Monarchie

monarchy ['mɒnəkɪ] N Monarchie *f*

monastery ['mɒnəstərɪ] N (Mönchs)kloster *nt*

monastic [mə'næstɪk] ADJ mönchisch, klösterlich; **~ life** Klosterleben *nt*; **~ building** Klostergebäude *nt*; **~ order** Mönchsorden *m*; **~ vows** Ordensgelübde *nt*; **he leads a ~ existence** *(fig)* er lebt wie ein Mönch

monasticism [mə'næstɪsɪzəm] N Mönch(s)tum *nt*

Monday ['mʌndɪ] N Montag *m* → *also* **Tuesday**

Monegasque [mɒnə'gæsk] **N** Monegasse *m*, Monegassin *f* **ADJ** monegassisch

monetarism ['mʌnɪtərɪzəm] N Monetarismus *m*

monetarist ['mʌnɪtərɪst] **N** Monetarist(in) *m(f)* **ADJ** monetaristisch

monetary ['mʌnɪtərɪ] ADJ **a** *(= pertaining to finance or currency)* währungspolitisch, Währungs-; **~ area** Währungsgebiet *nt*; **~ policy** Geld- *or* Währungspolitik *f*; **~ reform** Währungsreform *f*; **~ reserves** Geldreserven *pl*; **~ stability** Geldwertstabilität *f*; **~ system** Währungssystem *nt*; **~ targeting** Geldmengenpolitik *f*; **~ union** Währungsunion *f* **b** *(= pecuniary) considerations etc* geldlich

monetary unit N Geld- *or* Währungseinheit *f*

money ['mʌnɪ] N Geld *nt*; *(= medium of exchange)* Zahlungsmittel *nt*; **monies** Zahlungsmittel *pl*; **they use these stones as ~** sie benutzen diese Steine als Zahlungsmittel, sie benutzen diese Steine anstelle *or* an Stelle von Geld; **to make ~** *(person)* (viel) Geld verdienen; *(business)* etwas einbringen, sich rentieren; **to lose ~** *(person)* Geld verlieren; *(business)* Verluste machen *or* haben; **he spends ~ like water** er wirft mit dem Geld nur so um sich; **there's ~ in it** das ist sehr lukrativ; **if you help me, there's ~ in it for you** wenn du mir hilfst, springt für dich auch etwas dabei heraus *(inf)*; **it's a bargain for the ~** das ist eine günstige Anschaffung; **what can you expect for the ~?** was kann man bei dem Preis schon verlangen?; **that's the one for my ~!** ich tippe auf ihn/sie *etc*; **the smart ~'s on him** er hat die besten Chancen; **it's ~ for jam** *or* **old rope** *(Brit inf)* da wird einem das Geld ja nachgeworfen *(inf)*; **to be in the ~** *(inf)* Geld wie Heu haben; **what's the ~ like in this job?** wie wird der Job bezahlt?; **to earn good ~** gut verdienen; **to get one's ~'s worth** etwas für sein Geld bekommen; **I've really had my ~'s worth** *or* **my ~ out of that car** der Wagen hat sich wirklich bezahlt gemacht *or* war wirklich sein Geld wert; **do you think I'm made of ~?** *(inf)* ich bin doch kein Krösus!; **to throw ~ at sth** viel Geld in etw *(acc)* stecken; **to throw ~ at a problem** ein Problem dadurch zu lösen versuchen, dass man viel Geld dafür ausgibt; **to throw ~ at a solution** eine Lösung finden, indem man viel Geld dafür ausgibt; **that's throwing good ~ after bad** das ist rausgeschmissenes Geld *(inf)*, das ist gutes Geld dem schlechten nachgeworfen; **your ~ or your life!** Geld oder Leben!; **to put one's ~ where one's mouth is** *(inf)* (nicht nur reden, sondern) Taten sprechen lassen; **~ talks** *(inf)* mit Geld geht alles; **~ isn't everything** *(prov)* Geld (allein) macht nicht glücklich *(prov)*; **his analysis was right on the ~** *(US)* seine Analyse stimmte haargenau

money: **money bag** N Geldsack *m*; **moneybags** N *sing (inf)* Geldsack *m*; **money belt** N ≈ Gürteltasche *f (mit Geldfächern)*; **moneybox** N Sparbüchse *f*; **moneychanger** N *(= person)* (Geld)wechsler(in) *m(f)*

moneyed ['mʌnɪd] ADJ begütert

money: **money-grubber** N *(Brit inf)* Raffke *m (inf)*; **money-grubbing** *(Brit inf)* **ADJ** geld- *or* raffgierig **N** Geld- *or* Raffgier *f*; **money laundering** N Geldwäsche *f*; **money laundry** N Geldwaschanlage *f*; **moneylender** N Geldverleiher(in) *m(f)*; **moneylending** N Geldverleih *m*; **money machine** N *(US)* Geldautomat *m*; **moneymaker** N *(= idea)* einträgliche Sache; *(= product)* Verkaufserfolg *m*; *(= company)* gewinnbringendes *or* Gewinn bringendes Unternehmen, gut gehendes Unternehmen; **moneymaking** **ADJ** *idea, plan* gewinnbringend, Gewinn bringend, einträglich **N** Geldverdienen *nt*; **money market** N Geldmarkt *m*; **money matters** PL Geldangelegenheiten *or* -dinge *pl*; **money order** N Zahlungsanweisung *f*; **money prize** N Geldpreis *m*; **money spider** N *kleine Spinne*; **money-spinner** N *(inf)* Verkaufsschlager *m (inf) or* -hit *m (inf)*; **money-spinning** ADJ *(Brit inf)* **a ~ idea** eine Idee, mit der sich viel Geld machen lässt; **money supply** N Geldvolumen *nt*

mongol ['mɒŋgəl] **ADJ** **a** *(pej)* mongolisch **b** *(Med)* ~ mongoloid **N** **a** **Mongol** = **Mongolian** **b** *(Med)* **he's a ~** er ist mongoloid

Mongolia [mɒŋ'gəʊlɪə] N Mongolei *f*

Mongolian [mɒŋ'gəʊlɪən] N **a** Mongole *m*, Mongolin *f* **b** *(= language)* Mongolisch *nt*

mongolism ['mɒŋgəlɪzəm] N *(Med) (neg!)* Downsyndrom *nt*, Mongolismus *m (neg!)*

mongoloid ['mɒŋgəlɔɪd] ADJ **a** *(neg!)* mit Downsyndrom, mongolid *(neg!)* **b** *(Med)* ~ mongoloid

mongoose ['mɒŋguːs] N *pl* **-s** Mungo *m*

mongrel ['mʌŋgrəl] **ADJ** **~ race** Mischrasse *f* **N** *(= mongrel dog)* Promenadenmischung *f*; *(pej)* Köter *m*; *(pej: = person)* Mischling *m*

moni(c)ker ['mɒnɪkə'] N *(Brit inf: = signature)* Name *m*, (Friedrich) Wilhelm *m (inf)*

monition [mə'nɪʃən] N **a** *(form: = reprimand)* (Er)mahnung *f* **b** *(= warning)* Warnung *f* **c** *(Jur)* Vorladung *f*

monitor ['mɒnɪtə'] **N** **a** *(Sch)* Schüler(in) *m(f)* mit besonderen Pflichten; **stationery/book ~** Schreibwaren-/Bücherwart(in) *m(f)* **b** *(TV, Tech: = screen)* Monitor *m* **c** *(= observer)* Überwacher(in) *m(f)*; *(of telephone conversations)* Abhörer(in) *m(f)*; *(Rad)* Mitarbeiter(in) *m(f)* am Monitordienst **d** *(also* **monitor lizard**) Waran *m*, Waranechse *f* **VT** **a** *foreign station, telephone conversation* abhören; *TV programme* mithören **b** *(= control, check)* überwachen; *personal expenditure etc* kontrollieren

monitoring ['mɒnɪtərɪŋ] **N** **a** *(of foreign station, telephone conversation)* Abhören *nt*; *(of TV programme)* Mithören *nt* **b** *(= controlling, checking)* Überwachung *f*; *(of personal expenditure etc)* Kontrolle *f* **ADJ** *attr* Überwachungs-, Kontroll-; **~ body** Kontrollorgan *nt*; **~ function** Überwachungs- *or* Kontrollfunktion *f*

monk [mʌŋk] N Mönch *m*

monkey ['mʌŋkɪ] **N** Affe *m*; *(fig: = child)* Strolch *m*, Schlingel *m*; **to make a ~ out of sb** *(inf)* jdn verhohnepipeln *(inf)*; **well, I'll be a ~'s uncle** *(inf)* (ich glaub,) mich laust der Affe *(inf)*; **to have a ~ on one's back** *(US inf)* an der Nadel hängen *(inf)*; **I don't give a ~'s (about it)** *(Brit inf)* das ist mir scheißegal *(inf) or* schnurzpiepe *(hum inf)*; **as clever as a cartload** *or* **barrel (load) of ~s** *(Brit inf)* ganz schön clever *(inf)* **VI** **to ~ around** *(inf)* herumalbern; **to ~ around with sth** an etw *(dat)* herumspielen *or* -fummeln *(inf)*

monkey: **monkey bars** PL Klettergerüst *nt*; **monkey business** N *(inf)* **no ~!** mach(t) mir keine Sachen! *(inf)*; **there's too much ~** da ist zu viel faul *(inf)*; **what ~ have you been getting up to?** was hast du jetzt schon wieder angestellt?; **monkey engine** N *(Tech: = pile-driver)* Pfahlramme *f*; **monkey jacket** N Affenjäckchen *nt (inf)*; **monkey nut** N Erdnuss *f*; **monkey puzzle (tree)** N Andentanne *f*, Araukarie *f (spec)*; **monkeyshines** ['mʌŋkɪʃaɪnz] PL *(US inf)* Streiche *pl*; **monkey suit** N *(inf: = tails)* Frack *m*; **he was all done up in his ~** er hatte sich in volle Montur *or* in Schale geworfen *(inf)*; **monkey tricks** PL Unfug *m*, dumme Streiche *pl*; **no ~!** mach(t) mir keinen Unfug!; **I bet he's been getting up to some ~ again!** der hat doch sicher wieder irgendwas ausgeheckt *(inf)*; **monkey wrench** N verstellbarer Schraubenschlüssel, Engländer *m*; **to throw a ~ into the works** *(US inf)* jdm einen Knüppel zwischen die Beine werfen *(inf)*

monkfish ['mʌŋkfɪʃ] N Seeteufel *m*

monkish ['mʌŋkɪʃ] ADJ mönchisch; *(fig pej)* pastorenhaft; **he leads a ~ life** er führt ein Leben wie ein Mönch

monk seal N *(Zool)* Mönchsrobbe *f*

mono ['mɒnəʊ] **N** Mono *nt* **ADJ** Mono-, mono-; *record also* in Mono *pred*; **~ recording** Monoaufnahme *f*

mono- PREF Mono-, mono-

monochrome ['mɒnəkrəʊm] **ADJ** monochrom, einfarbig; *(Comput)* monochrom; **~ screen** Monochrombildschirm *m*; **~ television** Schwarz-Weiß-Fernsehen *nt* **N** *(Art)* monochrome Malerei, in einer Farbe gehaltene Malerei; *(TV)* Schwarzweiß *nt*

monocle ['mɒnəkəl] N Monokel *nt*

monocled ['mɒnəkld] ADJ Monokel tragend

monocoque ['mɒnəkɒk] N **a** *(Aviat)* Schalenrumpf *m*; **~ construction** Schalenbau *m*, Schalenbauweise *f* **b** *(Aut, of racing car)* Monocoque *nt*

monogamous [mɒ'nɒgəməs] ADJ monogam

monogamy [mɒ'nɒgəmɪ] N Monogamie *f*

monogram ['mɒnəgræm] N Monogramm *nt*

monogrammed ['mɒnəgræmd] ADJ mit Monogramm

monograph ['mɒnəgrɑːf] N Monografie *f*

monokini [,mɒnə'kiːniː] N Monokini *m*

monolingual [,mɒnə'lɪŋgwəl] ADJ einsprachig

monolith ['mɒnəʊlɪθ] N Monolith *m*

monolithic [,mɒnəʊ'lɪθɪk] ADJ *(lit)* monolithisch; *(fig)* gigantisch, riesig

monologize [mə'nɒlədʒaɪz] VI *(geh)* monologisieren; *(to oneself)* ein Selbstgespräch führen

monologue, *(US)* **monolog** ['mɒnəlɒg] N Monolog *m*

mono: **monomania** N Monomanie *f*; **monoplane** N Eindecker *m*

monopolist [mə'nɒpəlɪst] N Monopolist(in) *m(f)*

monopolistic [mə'nɒpəlɪstɪk] ADJ monopolistisch

monopolization [mə,nɒpəlaɪ'zeɪʃən] N *(lit)* Monopolisierung *f*; *(fig) (of bathroom, best seat etc)* Beschlagnahme *f*; *(of person, sb's time etc)* völlige Inanspruchnahme; *(of conversation etc)* Beherrschung *f*

monopolize [mə'nɒpəlaɪz] VT *(lit) market* monopolisieren, beherrschen; *(fig) person, place, sb's time etc* mit Beschlag belegen, in Beschlag nehmen; *conversation, discussion* beherrschen, an sich *(acc)* reißen; **to ~ the supply of ...** eine Monopolstellung für die Lieferung von ... haben; **she wants to ~ his attention** sie möchte seine Aufmerksamkeit ganz für sich haben

Monopoly® [mə'nɒpəlɪ] N *(= game)* Monopoly® *nt*; **~ money** *(inf: = large amount)* Wahnsinnssummen *pl (inf)*; *(pej: = foreign currency)* ausländisches Geld, Spielgeld *nt (pej)*

monopoly [mə'nɒpəlɪ] N **a** *(lit)* Monopol *nt*; **~ position** Monopolstellung *f*; **coal is a government ~** der Staat hat das Kohlenmonopol *or* das Monopol für Kohle; **Monopolies and Mergers Commission** *(Brit) britisches Kartellamt* **b** *(fig)* **to have the** *or* **a ~ on** *or* **of sth** etw für sich gepachtet haben *(inf)*; **you haven't got a ~ on me** ich bin doch nicht dein Eigentum

monorail ['mɒnəreɪl] N Einschienenbahn *f*

monosodium glutamate [mɒnəʊ'səʊdɪəm'gluːtəmeɪt] N Monosodiumglutamat *nt*

mono: **monosyllabic** ADJ *(lit)* einsilbig, monosyllabisch *(Ling)*; *(fig) person* einsilbig; **his English was fairly ~** sein Englisch beschränkte sich größtenteils auf einsilbige Wörter; **monosyllable** N einsilbiges Wort, Einsilber *m*; **to speak/answer in ~s** einsilbig sein/antworten, einsilbige Antworten geben; **monotheism** N Monotheismus *m*; **monotheistic** ADJ monotheistisch

monotone ['mɒnətəʊn] N monotoner Klang; *(= voice)* monotone Stimme

monotonous [mə'nɒtənəs] ADJ *(lit, fig)* eintönig, monoton; **with ~ regularity** regelmäßig; **it's getting ~** es wird allmählich langweilig

monotonously [mə'nɒtənəslɪ] ADV monoton; **the days were ~ alike** die Tage waren eintönig in ihrer Ähnlichkeit

monotony [mə'nɒtənɪ] N *(lit, fig)* Eintönigkeit *f*, Monotonie *f*; **the sheer ~ of it!** dieses ewige Einerlei!; *(of work etc also)* dieser Stumpfsinn!

Monotype® ['mɒnəʊtaɪp] N Monotype-Verfahren® *nt*; **monotype machine** Monotype® *f*

monoxide [mɒ'nɒksaɪd] N Monoxid *nt*

Monsignor [mɒn'siːnjə'] N Monsignore *m*

monsoon [mɒn'suːn] N Monsun *m*; **the ~ rains** der Monsunregen; **the ~s, the ~ season** die Monsunzeit

monster ['mɒnstə'] N **a** *(= big animal, thing)* Ungetüm *nt*, Monstrum *nt*; *(= animal)* Ungeheuer *nt*, Ungetüm *nt*; **a real ~ of a fish** ein wahres Monstrum *or* Ungeheuer von (einem) Fisch; **a ~ of a book** ein richtiger Schinken *(inf)*, ein Mammutwerk *nt*; **a ~ of greed** ein (hab)gieriges Monster **b** *(= abnormal animal)* Ungeheuer *nt*, Monster *nt*, Monstrum *nt*; *(= legendary animal)* (groteskes) Fabelwesen **c** *(= cruel person)* Unmensch *m*, Ungeheuer *nt* ATTR **a** *(= enormous)* riesenhaft; **~ film** Monster- *or* Mammutfilm *m* **b** *(= to do with monsters)* Monster-; **~ hunt** Monsterjagd *f*

monstrance ['mɒnstrəns] N *(Eccl)* Monstranz *f*

monstrosity [mɒn'strɒsɪtɪ] N *(= quality)* Ungeheuerlichkeit *f*, Monstrosität *f*; *(= thing)* Monstrosität *f*; *(= cruel deed)* Gräueltat *f*; **it's a ~ that ...** es ist unmenschlich *or* schändlich, dass ...

monstrous ['mɒnstrəs] ADJ **a** *(= huge)* ungeheuer (groß), riesig **b** *(= shocking, horrible)* abscheulich; *crime, thought, colour* grässlich, abscheulich; *suggestion* ungeheuerlich; **it's ~ that ...** es ist einfach ungeheuerlich *or* schändlich, dass ...

monstrously ['mɒnstrəslɪ] ADV schrecklich, fürchterlich

mons veneris ['mɒnz'venərɪs] N *pl* **montes veneris** ['mɒntiːz'venərɪs] Venusberg *m*

montage [mɒn'tɑːʒ] N Montage *f*

Montenegran [,mɒntɪ'niːgrən] N, ADJ = **Montenegrin**

Montenegrin [,mɒntɪ'niːgrɪn] ADJ montenegrisch; **he is ~** er ist Montenegriner N Montenegriner(in) *m(f)*

Montenegro [,mɒntɪ'niːgrəʊ] N Montenegro *nt*

month [mʌnθ] N Monat *m*; **in the ~ of October** im Oktober; **six ~s** ein halbes Jahr, sechs Monate; **in** *or* **for ~s** seit Langem; **it went on for ~s** es hat sich monatelang hingezogen; **in the early ~s of the war** in den ersten Kriegsmonaten; **one ~'s salary** ein Monatsgehalt; **paid by the ~** monatlich bezahlt

monthly ['mʌnθlɪ] ADJ monatlich; **~ magazine** Monats(zeit)schrift *f*; **~ cycle** Monatszyklus *m*; **~ salary** Monatsgehalt *nt*; **~ ticket/payment** Monatskarte/-rate *f*; **they have ~ meetings** sie treffen sich einmal im Monat; **to pay on a ~ basis** monatlich zahlen ADV monatlich; **twice ~** zweimal im *or* pro Monat N Monats(zeit)schrift *f*

monty, monte ['mɒntɪ] N *(inf)* **the full ~** absolut alles; **to go the full ~** *(= strip)* alle Hüllen fallen lassen *(hum)*; *(= go the whole hog)* aufs Ganze gehen

monument ['mɒnjʊmənt] N Denkmal *nt*; *(big also)* Monument *nt*; *(small, on grave etc)* Gedenkstein *m*; *(fig)* Zeugnis *nt (to +gen)*; **his great trilogy survives as a ~ to his talent** seine große Trilogie legt Zeugnis von seinem Talent ab

monumental [,mɒnjʊ'mentl] ADJ **a** *(= very great)* enorm, monumental *(geh)*; *proportions, achievement* gewaltig; *ignorance, stupidity, error* kolossal, ungeheuerlich; **on a ~ scale, of ~ proportions** *(disaster, crisis)* von riesigem Ausmaß; *building, work of art* monumental **b ~ inscription** Grabinschrift *f*; **~ sculptures** Steinfiguren *pl*

monumentally [,mɒnjʊ'mentəlɪ] ADV *(inf: = immensely) stupid, incompetent, ugly* ungeheuerlich; *drink* übermäßig; *fail* katastrophal

monumental mason N Steinmetz(in) *m(f)*, Steinbildhauer(in) *m(f)*

moo [muː] N **a** Muhen *nt*; **the cow gave a ~** die Kuh muhte *or* machte „muh" *(inf)* **b** *(inf: = woman)* Kuh *f (inf)* VI muhen, „muh" machen *(inf)*

mooch [muːtʃ] *(inf)* VI tigern *(inf)*; **I spent all day just ~ing about** *(Brit)* *or* **around the house** ich habe den ganzen Tag zu Hause herumgegammelt *(inf)* VT *(US inf)* abstauben *(inf)*

moo-cow ['muːkaʊ] N *(baby-talk)* Muhkuh *f (baby-talk)*

mood[1] [muːd] N **a** *(of party, town etc)* Stimmung *f*; *(of one person)* Laune *f*, Stimmung *f*; **he was in a good/bad/foul ~** er hatte gute/schlechte/eine fürchterliche Laune, er war gut/schlecht/fürchterlich gelaunt; **to be in a cheerful ~** gut aufgelegt sein; **to be in a festive/forgiving ~** feierlich/versöhnlich gestimmt sein; **to be in a generous ~** in Geberlaune sein; **in one of his crazy** *or* **mad ~s** aus einer plötzlichen Laune heraus, in einer seiner Anwandlungen; **I'm in no ~ for laughing** mir ist nicht nach *or* zum Lachen zumute *or* zu Mute; **to be in the ~ for sth** zu etw aufgelegt sein; **to be in the ~ to do sth** dazu aufgelegt sein, etw zu tun; **to be in no ~ to do sth** nicht in der Stimmung sein, etw zu tun; **I'm not in the ~ for work** *or* **to work** ich habe keine Lust zum Arbeiten; **I'm not in the ~ for this type of music** ich bin nicht in der Stimmung für diese Musik; **I'm not in the ~** ich bin nicht dazu aufgelegt; *(to do sth also)* ich habe keine Lust; *(for music etc also)* ich bin nicht in der richtigen Stimmung; **~ music** stimmungsvolle Musik **b** *(= bad mood)* schlechte Laune; **he's in one of his ~s** er hat mal wieder eine seiner Launen; **he's in a ~** er hat schlechte Laune; **he has ~s** er ist sehr launisch

mood[2] N *(Gram)* Modus *m*; **indicative ~** Indikativ *m*; **imperative ~** Imperativ *m*; **subjunctive ~** Konjunktiv *m*

moodily ['muːdɪlɪ] ADV launisch, launenhaft; *(= in a bad mood)* schlecht gelaunt, übellaunig

moodiness ['muːdɪnɪs] N Launenhaftigkeit *f*; *(= bad mood)* schlechte Laune; *(of look, answer)* Verdrossenheit *f*; **his ~** sein launisches Wesen

mood swing N Stimmungsschwankung *f*

moody ['muːdɪ] ADJ *(+er)* launisch, launenhaft; *(= bad-tempered)* schlecht gelaunt; *look, answer* verdrossen, übellaunig; *picture, film, piece of music* stimmungsvoll

moola(h) ['muːlɑː] N *(dated US inf: = money)* Kohle *f (inf)*

moon [muːn] N Mond *m*; **is there a ~ tonight?** scheint heute der Mond?; **when the ~ is full** bei Vollmond; **the man in the ~** der Mann im Mond; **you're asking for the ~!** du verlangst Unmögliches!; **to promise sb the ~** jdm das Blaue vom Himmel versprechen; **to be over the ~** *(inf)* überglücklich sein VI **a** *(= mope)* (vor sich *acc* hin) träumen **b** *(inf, with backside)* seinen nackten Hintern herausstrecken

▶ **moon about** *(Brit) or* **around** VI (vor sich *acc* hin) träumen; **to moon about** *or* **around (in) the house** zu Hause hocken

▶ **moon away** VT *sep time* verträumen

moon *in cpds* Mond-; **moonbeam** N Mondstrahl *m*; **moon blindness** N **a** *(Vet)* Mondblindheit *f* **b** *(Med)* Nachtblindheit *f*; **moonboots** PL Moonboots *pl*; **moonbuggy** N Mondauto *or* -fahrzeug *nt*; **mooncalf** N *(dated)* Schwachsinnige(r) *mf*; *(inf)* Mondkalb *nt*; **moon-faced** ['muːn,feɪst] ADJ mit einem Mondgesicht, mondgesichtig

Moonie ['muːnɪ] N *(inf)* Anhänger(in) *m(f)* der Mun-Sekte, Moonie *m (inf)*

moon: **moon landing** N Mondlandung *f*; **moonless** ADJ *night* mondlos; **moonlight** N Mondlicht *nt or* -schein *m*; **it was ~** der Mond schien; **a ~ walk** ein Mondscheinspaziergang *m* → **flit** VI *(inf)* schwarzarbeiten; **moonlighter** N *(inf)* Schwarzarbeiter(in) *m(f)*; **moonlighting** N *(inf)* Schwarzarbeit *f*; **moonlit** ADJ *object* mondbeschienen; *night, landscape, lawn* mondhell; **moonscape** ['muːnskeɪp] N Mondlandschaft *f*; **moonshine** N **a** *(= moonlight)* Mondschein *m* **b** *(inf: = nonsense)* Unsinn *m* **c** *(inf: = illegal whisky) illegal gebrannter Whisky*; **moonshiner** N *(inf)* Schwarzbrenner(in) *m(f)*; **moonshot** N Mondflug *m*; **moonstone** N Mondstein *m*; **moonstruck** ADJ *(= mad)* mondsüchtig; *(fig)* vernarrt

moony ['muːnɪ] ADJ *(+er) (inf: = dreamy)* verträumt

Moor [mʊə'] N Maure *m*; *(old, = black man)* Mohr *m*

moor[1] [mʊə'] N (Hoch)moor *nt*; *(Brit: for game)* Moorjagd *f*; **a walk on the ~s** ein Spaziergang *m* übers Moor

moor[2] VT festmachen, vertäuen; *(at permanent moorings)* muren VI festmachen, anlegen

moorage ['mʊərɪdʒ] N *(= place)* Anlegeplatz *m*; *(= charge)* Anlegegebühren *pl*

moorhen ['mʊərhen] N Teichhuhn *nt*

mooring ['mʊərɪŋ] N *(= act of mooring)* Anlegen *nt*; *(= place)* Anlegeplatz *m*; **~s** *(= ropes, fixtures)* Verankerung *f*; **to lose one's ~s** *(fig)* den Halt verlieren

mooring buoy N Muringsboje *f*

Moorish ['mʊərɪʃ] ADJ maurisch; *invasion* der Mauren

moorland ['mʊərlənd] N Moor- *or* Heideland *nt*

moose [mu:s] N *pl* - Elch *m*

moot [mu:t] ADJ **a ~ point** *or* **question** eine fragliche Sache; **it's a ~ point** *or* **question whether …** es ist noch fraglich *or* die Frage *(inf)*, ob … VT aufwerfen; *suggestion* vorbringen; **it has been ~ed that …** es wurde zur Debatte gestellt, dass …

mop [mɒp] N *(= floor mop)* (Nass)mop *m*; *(= dish mop)* Spülbürste *f*; *(= sponge mop)* Schwammmopp *m*; *(inf: = hair)* Mähne *f*, Zotteln *pl (inf)*; **her ~ of hair** ihre Mähne; **her ~ of curls** ihr Wuschelkopf *m* VT *floor, kitchen* wischen; **to ~ one's face/brow** sich *(dat)* den Schweiß vom Gesicht/von der Stirn wischen; **to ~ one's eyes** sich *(dat)* die Tränen abwischen

▶ **mop down** VT *sep walls* abwischen; *floor* wischen

▶ **mop up** VT *sep* **a** *water etc* aufwischen; **she mopped up the sauce with a piece of bread** sie tunkte die Soße mit einem Stück Brot auf **b** *(Mil)* säubern *(inf)*; **mopping-up operations** Säuberungsaktion *f*; *(hum)* Aufräumungsarbeiten *pl* VI (auf)wischen

mopboard ['mɒpbɔ:d] N *(US)* Scheuerleiste *f*

mope [məʊp] VI Trübsal blasen *(inf)*

▶ **mope about** *(Brit) or* **around** VI mit einer Jammermiene herumlaufen; **to mope about** *or* **around the house** zu Hause hocken und Trübsal blasen *(inf)*

moped ['məʊped] N Moped *nt*; *(very small)* Mofa *nt*

mopes [məʊps] PL *(inf)* **to have a case of the ~** seinen *or* den Moralischen haben *(inf)*

mopy ['məʊpɪ] ADJ *(+er) (inf)* trübselig; **I'm feeling a bit ~ today** ich bin heute etwas in Tiefstimmung *(inf)*

MOR *(Mus) abbr of* **middle-of-the-road** für den Massenmarkt

moraine [mɒ'reɪn] N Moräne *f*

moral ['mɒrəl] ADJ **a** moralisch, sittlich; *support, victory, obligation, principles* moralisch; **~ values** sittliche Werte *pl*, Moralvorstellungen *pl*; **~ code** *(of individual)* Auffassung *f* von Moral; *(of society)* Sitten- *or* Moralkodex *m*; **a ~ imperative** ein Gebot *nt* der Moral; **~ standards** Moral *f*; **~ sense** Gefühl *nt* für Gut und Böse, moralisches Bewusstsein; **~ support** moralische Unterstützung; **to give sb ~ support** jdn moralisch unterstützen; **~ courage** Charakter *m*; **~ lecture** Moralpredigt *f*

b *(= virtuous)* integer, moralisch einwandfrei; *(sexually)* tugendhaft; *(= moralizing) story, book* moralisch

c it's a ~ certainty that … es ist mit Sicherheit anzunehmen, dass …; **to have a ~ right to sth** jedes Recht auf etw *(acc)* haben

N **a** *(= lesson)* Moral *f*; **to draw a ~ from sth** eine Lehre aus etw ziehen

b morals PL *(= principles)* Moral *f*; **his ~s are different from mine** er hat ganz andere Moralvorstellungen als ich; **to have loose ~s** eine recht lockere Moral haben

morale [mɒ'rɑ:l] N Moral *f*; **to boost sb's ~** jdm (moralischen) Auftrieb geben; **to destroy sb's ~** jdn entmutigen; **to be a ~ booster for sb** jdm (moralischen) Auftrieb geben

moralist ['mɒrəlɪst] N *(Philos, fig)* Moralist(in) *m(f)*

moralistic [,mɒrə'lɪstɪk] ADJ moralisierend; *(Philos)* moralistisch

morality [mə'rælɪtɪ] N Moralität *f*; *(= moral system)* Moral *f*, Ethik *f*

morality play N Moralität *f*

moralize ['mɒrəlaɪz] VI moralisieren; **to ~ about sb/sth** sich über jdn/etw moralisch entrüsten; **stop your moralizing!** hör mit deinen Moralpredigten auf!

moralizer ['mɒrəlaɪzəʳ] N Moralprediger(in) *m(f)*, Moralapostel *m (inf)*

morally ['mɒrəlɪ] ADV **a** *(= ethically)* moralisch; **I am ~ certain that …** ich bin moralisch überzeugt, dass … **b** *(= virtuously)* integer, moralisch einwandfrei; *(sexually)* tugendhaft

moral: **Moral Majority** N *(US Pol)* moralische Mehrheit; **moral philosopher** N Moralphilosoph(in) *m(f)*; **moral philosophy** N Moralphilosophie *f*; **Moral Rearmament** N moralische Aufrüstung

morass [mə'ræs] N Morast *m*, Sumpf *m (also fig)*; **to be sucked into the ~ (of vice)** sich immer tiefer (im Laster) verstricken; **a ~ of problems** ein Wust *m* von Problemen; **a ~ of emotions** ein Wirrwarr *m* der Gefühle

moratorium [,mɒrə'tɔ:rɪəm] N Stopp *m*; *(Mil)* Stillhalteabkommen *nt*; *(on treaty etc)* Moratorium *nt*; *(Fin)* Zahlungsaufschub *m*; **a ~ on nuclear armament** ein Atomwaffenstopp *m*; **to declare a ~ on sth** etw (vorläufig) mit einem Stopp belegen; in der Frage einer Sache *(gen)* ein Moratorium beschließen; **there's been a ~ on new transplant techniques** neue Transplantationstechniken wurden vorläufig gestoppt

Moravia [mə'reɪvɪə] N Mähren *nt*

morbid ['mɔ:bɪd] ADJ **a** *idea, thought, jealousy, curiosity etc* krankhaft; *interest, attitude* unnatürlich, krankhaft; *sense of humour, talk etc* makaber; *(= gloomy) outlook, thoughts* düster; *person* trübsinnig; *(= pessimistic)* schwarzseherisch; *poet, novel, music etc* morbid; **that's ~!, that's a ~ thought** *or* **idea!** das ist ja makaber; **don't be so ~!** sieh doch nicht alles so schwarz!; **he's such a ~ little boy** er hat einen Hang zum Makabren **b** *(Med)* morbid; *growth* krankhaft

morbid anatomy N *(Med)* Pathologie *f*

morbidity [mɔ:'bɪdɪtɪ] N **a** *(of idea, thought, jealousy, curiosity etc)* Krankhaftigkeit *f*; *(of interest, attitude)* Unnatürlichkeit *f*; *(of sense of humour, talk)* Düsterkeit *f*; *(of novel, music)* Morbidität *f*; *(of person)* Trübsinn *m*; *(of poet etc)* Hang *m* zu düsteren Gedanken, Morbidität *f*; *(= gloominess)* Morbidität *f* **b** *(Med)* Morbidität *f*; *(of growth)* Krankhaftigkeit *f*

morbidly ['mɔ:bɪdlɪ] ADV **to think ~** krankhafte *or* düstere *or* morbide *(geh)* Gedanken haben; **he is ~ interested in bad crashes** er hat ein krankhaftes Interesse an schweren Unfällen; **staring ~ out of the window** trübsinnig *or* düster aus dem Fenster schauend; **maybe I'll be dead then, he said ~** vielleicht bin ich dann schon tot, sagte er düster

mordacious [mɔ:'deɪʃəs] ADJ = **mordant**

mordacity [mɔ:'dæsɪtɪ], **mordancy** ['mɔ:dənsɪ] N beißender Humor; **the ~ of his wit** sein beißender Humor

mordant ['mɔ:dənt] ADJ beißend, ätzend

more [mɔ:ʳ] ✪ 7.3, 12.2 N, PRON **a** *(= greater amount)* mehr; *(= a further or additional amount)* noch mehr; *(of countable things)* noch mehr *or* welche; **~ and ~** immer mehr; **I want a lot ~** ich will viel mehr; *(in addition)* ich will noch viel mehr; **three ~** noch drei; **a few ~** noch ein paar; **a little ~** etwas mehr; *(in addition)* noch etwas mehr; **many/much ~** viel mehr; **not many/much ~** nicht mehr viele/viel; **no ~** nichts mehr; *(countable)* keine mehr; **some ~** noch etwas; *(countable)* noch welche; **any ~?** noch mehr *or* etwas?; *(countable)* noch mehr *or* welche?; **there isn't/aren't any ~** mehr gibt es nicht; *(here, at the moment, left over)* es ist nichts/es sind keine mehr da; **is/are there any ~?** gibt es noch mehr?; *(left over)* ist noch etwas/sind noch welche da?; **even ~** noch mehr; **I shall have ~ to say about this** dazu habe ich noch etwas zu sagen; **let's say no ~ about it** reden wir nicht mehr darüber; **we shall hear/see ~ of you** wir werden öfter von dir hören/dich öfter sehen; **there's ~ to come** da kommt noch etwas, das ist noch nicht alles; **what ~ do you want?** was willst du denn noch?; **what ~ could one want?** mehr kann man sich doch nicht wünschen; **there's ~ to it** da steckt (noch) mehr dahinter; **there's ~ to bringing up children than just …** zum Kindererziehen gehört mehr als nur …; **and what's ~, he …** und außerdem *or* obendrein hat er … (noch) …; **they are ~ than we are** sie sind in der Mehrzahl; **there's ~ where that came from** davon gibts noch mehr

b (all) the ~ umso mehr; **the ~ you give him, the ~ he wants** je mehr du ihm gibst, desto mehr verlangt er; **it makes me (all) the ~ ashamed** das beschämt mich umso mehr; **the ~ the merrier** je mehr, desto besser *or* umso besser

ADJ mehr; *(in addition)* noch mehr; **two/five ~ bottles** noch zwei/fünf Flaschen; **one ~ day, one day ~** noch ein Tag; **~ and ~ money/friends** immer mehr Geld/Freunde; **a lot/a little ~ money** viel/etwas mehr Geld; *(in addition)* noch viel/noch etwas mehr Geld; **a few ~ friends/weeks** noch ein paar Freunde/Wochen; **you won't have many ~ friends/much ~ money left** du hast nicht mehr viele Freunde/nicht mehr viel Geld übrig; **no ~ money/friends** kein Geld/keine Freunde mehr; **no ~ singing/squabbling!** Schluss mit der Singerei/mit dem Zanken!; **do you want some ~ tea/books?** möchten Sie noch etwas Tee/noch ein paar Bücher?; **is there any ~ wine in the bottle?** ist noch (etwas) Wein in der Flasche?; **there isn't any ~ wine** es ist kein Wein mehr da; **there aren't any ~ books** mehr Bücher gibt es nicht; *(here, at the moment)* es sind keine Bücher mehr da; **(the) ~ fool you!** du bist ja vielleicht ein Dummkopf!; **(the) ~ fool you for giving him the money** dass du auch so dumm bist und ihm das Geld gibst

ADV **a** mehr; **~ and ~** immer mehr; **it will weigh/grow a bit ~** es wird etwas mehr wiegen/noch etwas wachsen; **will it weigh/grow any ~?** wird es mehr wiegen/noch wachsen?; **it'll grow ~ if you …** es wächst besser, wenn du …; **to like/want sth ~** etw lieber mögen/wollen; **~ than** mehr als; **£5/2 hours ~ than I thought** £ 5 mehr/2 Stunden länger, als ich dachte; **it will ~ than meet the demand** das wird die Nachfrage mehr als genügend befriedigen; **he's ~ lazy than stupid** er ist eher faul als dumm; **no ~ than, not ~ than** nicht mehr als; **no ~ a duchess than I am** genauso wenig eine Herzogin wie ich (eine bin); **nothing ~ than a wild guess** eine reine Vermutung; **he's ~ like a brother to me** er ist eher wie ein Bruder (für mich); **no ~ do I** ich auch nicht; **he has resigned – that's no ~ than I expected** er hat gekündigt – das habe ich ja erwartet

b *(= again)* **once ~** noch einmal, noch mal *(inf)*; **never ~** nie mehr *or* wieder

c *(= longer)* mehr; **no ~, not any ~** nicht mehr; **to be no ~** *(person)* nicht mehr sein *or* leben; *(thing)* nicht mehr existieren; **if he comes here any ~ …** wenn er noch weiter *or* länger hierher kommt …

d *(to form comp of adj, adv)* -er *(than* als); **~ beautiful** schöner; **~ and ~ beautiful** immer schöner; **~ seriously** ernster; **no ~ stupid than I am** (auch) nicht dümmer als ich

e ~ or less mehr oder weniger; **neither ~ nor less, no ~, no less** nicht mehr und nicht weniger

moreish ['mɔ:rɪʃ] ADJ *(Brit inf)* **these biscuits are very ~** diese Plätzchen schmecken nach mehr *(inf)*

morello [mɒ'reləʊ] N Sauerkirsche *f*, Morelle *f*

moreover [mɔ:'rəʊvəʳ] ✪ 26.1 ADV überdies, zudem, außerdem

mores ['mɔ:reɪz] PL Sittenkodex *m*

morganatic [,mɔ:gə'nætɪk] ADJ morganatisch

morgue [mɔːg] N **a** *(= mortuary)* Leichenschauhaus *nt*; **to be like a ~** wie ausgestorben sein **b** *(Press)* Archiv *nt*

MORI ['mɔːrɪ] *(Brit) abbr of* **Market and Opinion Research Institute** *britisches Meinungsforschungsinstitut*; **~ poll** Meinungsumfrage *f*

moribund ['mɒrɪbʌnd] ADJ *person* todgeweiht *(geh)*, moribund *(spec)*; *species* im Aussterben begriffen; *(fig) plan, policy* zum Scheitern verurteilt; *customs, way of life* zum Aussterben verurteilt; **the empire was in a ~ state** das Weltreich stand vor dem Untergang *or* ging seinem Untergang entgegen

Mormon ['mɔːmən] ADJ mormonisch, Mormonen-; *doctrine* der Mormonen; **~ church** Mormonenkirche *f* N Mormone *m*, Mormonin *f*

Mormonism ['mɔːmənɪzəm] N Mormonentum *nt*

morn [mɔːn] N *(poet)* Morgen *m*

mornay ['mɔːneɪ] ADJ **~ sauce** Mornay- *or* Käsesoße *f*; **cauliflower/eggs ~** Blumenkohl/hart gekochte Eier in Käsesoße

morning ['mɔːnɪŋ] N Morgen *m*; *(as opposed to afternoon also)* Vormittag *m*; *(fig) (of life)* Frühling *m (liter)*; *(of an era)* Anfänge *pl*, Beginn *m*; **~ dawned** es dämmerte; **in the ~** morgens, am Morgen, vormittags, am Vormittag; *(= tomorrow)* morgen früh; **early in the ~** früh(morgens), in der Frühe, am frühen Morgen; *(= tomorrow)* morgen früh; **very early in the ~** in aller Frühe, ganz früh (am Morgen); *(= tomorrow)* morgen ganz früh; **late (on) in the ~** am späten Vormittag, gegen Mittag; **(at) 7 in the ~** (um) 7 Uhr morgens *or* früh; *(= tomorrow)* morgen (früh) um 7; **I didn't get back until 2 in the ~** ich bin erst um 2 Uhr früh nach Hause gekommen; **this/yesterday ~** heute/gestern Morgen, heute/gestern Vormittag; **tomorrow ~** morgen früh, morgen Vormittag; **on the ~ of November 28th** am Morgen des 28. November, am 28. November morgens; **it was the ~ after** es war am nächsten *or* anderen Tag *or* Morgen; **the ~ after the night before, the ~-after feeling** der Katzenjammer *or* die Katerstimmung am nächsten Morgen; **~, noon and night** morgens, mittags und nachts, Tag und Nacht

ATTR am Morgen; *(= regularly in the morning)* morgendlich; **~ flight** Vormittagsflug *m*; **~ train** Frühzug *m*; **what time is ~ coffee?** *(at work)* wann ist morgens die Kaffeepause?; *(in café)* ab wann wird vormittags Kaffee serviert?

morning: **morning-after pill** N die Pille danach; **morning coat** N Cut(away) *m*; **morning dress** N *no pl* Cut(away) *m*; *(dark)* Stresemann *m*; **morning-glory** N *(Bot)* Winde *f*; **morning gown** N Hauskleid *nt*; **morning market** N *(Comm)* Vormittagsmarkt *m*; **Morning Prayer** N Morgenandacht *f*, Frühgottesdienst *m*; **morning room** N Frühstückszimmer *nt*; **morning sickness** N (Schwangerschafts)übelkeit *f*; **morning star** N Morgenstern *m*; **morning suit** N Cut(away) *m*; *(dark)* Stresemann *m*

Moroccan [mə'rɒkən] ADJ marokkanisch N Marokkaner(in) *m(f)*

Morocco [mə'rɒkəʊ] N Marokko *nt*

morocco [mə'rɒkəʊ] N *(also* **morocco leather***)* Maroquin *nt*

moron ['mɔːrɒn] N *(Med)* Geistesschwache(r) *mf*, Debile(r) *mf (spec)*; *(inf)* Trottel *m (inf)*, Schwachkopf *m (inf)*; **you're such a ~!** *(inf)* du bist echt grenzdebil! *(inf)*

moronic [mə'rɒnɪk] ADJ *(Med)* geistesschwach, debil *(spec)*; *(inf)* idiotisch *(inf)*

morose ADJ, **morosely** ADV [mə'rəʊs, -lɪ] verdrießlich, missmutig

moroseness [mə'rəʊsnɪs] N Verdrießlichkeit *f*, Missmut *m*

morpheme ['mɔːfiːm] N Morphem *nt*

morphia N = **morphine**

morphine ['mɔːfiːn] N Morphium *nt*, Morphin *nt (spec)*

morphing ['mɔːfɪŋ] N Morphing *nt*

morphological [ˌmɔːfə'lɒdʒɪkəl] ADJ morphologisch

morphology [mɔː'fɒlədʒɪ] N Morphologie *f*

morris dance ['mɒrɪs'dɑːns] N Moriskentanz *m, alter englischer Volkstanz*

morrow ['mɒrəʊ] N *(old)* **the ~** der kommende *or* folgende Tag; **on the ~** tags darauf; **good ~!** guten Morgen!

morse [mɔːs] N *(also* **Morse code***)* Morsezeichen *pl*, Morseschrift *f*; **do you know ~** *or* **(the) Morse code?** können Sie morsen?

morse alphabet N Morsealphabet *nt*

morsel ['mɔːsl] N *(of food)* Bissen *m*, Happen *m*; *(fig)* bisschen *nt*; *(of information)* Brocken *m*; **not a ~ of food** kein Bissen zu essen; **a ~ of comfort** ein kleiner Trost

mortal ['mɔːtl] ADJ **a** *(= liable to die)* sterblich; *(= causing death) injury, combat* tödlich; **to deal (sb/sth) a ~ blow** (jdm/einer Sache) einen tödlichen Schlag versetzen; **to be locked in ~ combat** auf Leben und Tod miteinander kämpfen

b *(= extreme)* tödlich, Todes-; *(inf) hurry, embarrassment* irrsinnig *(inf)*; **~ fear** Todesangst *f*; **~ agony** Todesqualen *pl*; **to live in ~ fear** *or* **dread that ...** eine Todesangst haben, dass ...; **~ enemy** Todfeind(in) *m(f)*

c *(inf, = conceivable)* **no ~ use** überhaupt kein Nutzen

d *(inf, = tedious) hours, boredom* tödlich *(inf)*

N Sterbliche(r) *mf*; **ordinary ~** *(inf)* Normalsterbliche(r) *mf (inf)*; **a mere ~** ein bloßer Sterblicher

mortality [mɔː'tælɪtɪ] N **a** *(= mortal state)* Sterblichkeit *f* **b** *(= number of deaths)* Todesfälle *pl*; *(= rate)* Sterblichkeit(sziffer) *f*, Mortalität *f (form)*; **~ rate, rate of ~** Sterbeziffer *f*, Sterblichkeitsziffer *f*, Mortalität *f (form)*

mortally ['mɔːtəlɪ] ADV **a** *(= fatally)* tödlich; **~ ill** todkrank **b** *(fig: = extremely) shocked etc* zu Tode; *wounded* zutiefst; *offended* tödlich; **I was ~ afraid** ich habe Todesängste ausgestanden; **she is ~ embarrassed** es ist ihr höchst peinlich

mortal sin N Todsünde *f*

mortar[1] ['mɔːtə'] N **a** *(= bowl)* Mörser *m* **b** *(= cannon)* Minenwerfer *m*

mortar[2] N *(= cement)* Mörtel *m* VT mörteln

mortarboard ['mɔːtəˌbɔːd] N **a** *(Univ)* Doktorhut *m* **b** *(Build)* Mörtelbrett *nt*

mortgage ['mɔːgɪdʒ] N Hypothek *f* (*on* auf *+acc/dat*); **a ~ for £50,000/for that amount** eine Hypothek über *or* von £ 50.000/über diesen Betrag VT *house, land* hypothekarisch belasten; **to ~ one's future** *(fig)* sich *(dat)* die *or* seine Zukunft verbauen

mortgage: **mortgage bond** N (Hypotheken)pfandbrief *m*; **mortgage deed** N *(Jur)* **a** Pfandbrief *m* **b** Hypothekenbrief *m*

mortgagee [ˌmɔːgə'dʒiː] N Hypothekar *m*

mortgage rate N Hypothekenzinssatz *m*

mortgage relief N *Steuervergünstigung bei der Zahlung von Hypothekenzinsen*

mortgagor [ˌmɔːgə'dʒɔː'] N Hypothekenschuldner(in) *m(f)*

mortice ['mɔːtɪs] N, VT = **mortise**

mortician [mɔː'tɪʃən] N *(US)* Bestattungsunternehmer(in) *m(f)*

mortification [ˌmɔːtɪfɪ'keɪʃən] N **a** Beschämung *f*; *(= embarrassment)* äußerste Verlegenheit; *(= humiliation)* Demütigung *f*; **much to his ~, she ...** er empfand es als sehr beschämend, dass sie ...; *(embarrassment)* es war ihm äußerst peinlich, dass sie ...; *(humiliation)* er empfand es als eine Schmach, dass sie ...; **I discovered to my ~ that I had made a mistake** ich stellte zu meiner größten Verlegenheit fest, dass ich einen Fehler gemacht hatte; **because of her ~ at what had happened** weil ihr das, was geschehen war, so überaus peinlich war; **he felt great ~ at being rejected** er empfand es als eine Schmach *or* Schande, dass er nicht angenommen wurde

b *(Rel)* Kasteiung *f*

c *(Med)* Brand *m*

mortify ['mɔːtɪfaɪ] VT *usu pass* **a** *(= shame)* beschämen; *(= embarrass)* äußerst peinlich sein *(+dat)*; **he was mortified** er empfand das als beschämend; *(= embarrassed)* es war ihm äußerst peinlich; **embarrassed? I was mortified!** peinlich? ich wäre am liebsten im Boden versunken!; **a mortified look** ein äußerst betretener Gesichtsausdruck **b** *(Rel)* kasteien **c** *(Med)* absterben lassen; **to be mortified** abgestorben sein VI *(Med)* absterben

mortifying ADJ, **mortifyingly** ADV ['mɔːtɪfaɪɪŋ, -lɪ] beschämend; *(= embarrassing)* peinlich

mortise ['mɔːtɪs] N Zapfenloch *nt* VT verzapfen (*into* mit)

mortise and tenon joint N Zapfenverbindung *f*

mortise lock N (Ein)steckschloss *nt*

mortuary ['mɔːtjʊərɪ] N Leichenhalle *f*

Mosaic [məʊ'zeɪɪk] ADJ mosaisch

mosaic [məʊ'zeɪɪk] N Mosaik *nt* ATTR Mosaik-; **~ floor** Mosaikboden *m*

Moscow ['mɒskəʊ] N Moskau *nt*

Moselle [məʊ'zel] N Mosel *f*; *(also* **Moselle wine***)* Mosel(wein) *m*

Moses ['məʊzɪz] N Mose(s) *m*

Moses basket N Körbchen *nt*

Moslem ['mɒzlem] ADJ, N = **Muslim**

mosque [mɒsk] N Moschee *f*

mosquito [mɒ'skiːtəʊ] N *pl* **-es** Stechmücke *f*; *(in tropics)* Moskito *m*

mosquito net N Moskitonetz *nt*

moss [mɒs] N Moos *nt*

Mossad ['mɒsæd] N Mossad *m (israelischer Geheimdienst)*

mossy ['mɒsɪ] ADJ *(+er)* *(= moss-covered)* moosbedeckt, bemoost; *lawn* vermoost; *(= mosslike)* moosig, moosartig

most [məʊst] ADJ *superl* **a** meiste(r, s); *(= greatest) satisfaction, pleasure etc* größte(r, s); *(= highest) speed etc* höchste(r, s); **who has (the) ~ money?** wer hat am meisten *or* das meiste Geld?; **that gave me (the) ~ pleasure** das hat mir am meisten Freude *or* die größte Freude gemacht; **for the ~ part** größtenteils, zum größten Teil; *(= by and large)* im Großen und Ganzen

b *(= the majority of)* die meisten; **~ men/people** die meisten (Menschen/Leute); **he's better than ~ people** er ist besser als die meisten anderen

N, PRON *(uncountable)* das meiste; *(countable)* die meisten; **~ of it** das meiste; **~ of them** die meisten (von ihnen); **~ of the money** das meiste Geld; **~ of his friends** die meisten seiner Freunde; **~ of the winter/day** fast den ganzen Winter/Tag über; **~ of the time** die meiste Zeit, fast die ganze Zeit; *(= usually)* meist(ens); **at (the) ~** höchstens; **at (the) very ~** allerhöchstens; **to make the ~ of sth** *(= make good use of)* etw voll ausnützen; *(= enjoy)* etw in vollen Zügen genießen; **to make the ~ of a story** so viel wie möglich aus einer Geschichte machen; **to make the ~ of one's looks** *or* **of oneself** das Beste aus sich machen; **the hostess with the ~est** *(inf)* die Supergastgeberin *(inf)*; **it's the ~!** *(dated sl)* das ist dufte! *(dated sl)*

ADV **a** *superl (+vbs)* am meisten; *(+adj)* -ste(r, s); *(+adv)* am -sten; **the ~ beautiful/difficult** *etc* **...** der/die/das schönste/schwierigste *etc* ...; **who did it ~ easily?** wem ist es am leichtesten gefallen?; **what ~ displeased him ..., what displeased him ~ ...** was ihm am meisten missfiel ...; **~ of all** am allermeisten; **~ of all because ...** vor allem, weil ...

b *(= very)* äußerst, überaus; **~ likely** höchstwahrscheinlich; **he added ~ unnecessarily ...** er sagte noch völlig unnötigerweise ...; **he had told you ~ explicitly** er hat Ihnen doch ganz eindeutig gesagt ...

c *(old, dial, = almost)* fast, so ziemlich *(inf)*, schier *(old, S Ger)*

most-favoured-nation clause, *(US)* **most-favored-nation clause** [ˌməʊstˈfeɪvədˈneɪʃnˌklɔːz] N *(Pol)* Meistbegünstigungsklausel *f*

mostly [ˈməʊstlɪ] ADV *(= principally)* hauptsächlich; *(= most of the time)* meistens; *(= by and large)* zum größten Teil; **they are ~ women/over fifty** die meisten sind Frauen/über fünfzig; **~ because …** hauptsächlich, weil …

MOT [ˌeməʊˈtiː] *(Brit)* **N** **a** *abbr of* **Ministry of Transport** **b** **~ (test)** ≈ TÜV *m*; **it failed its ~** ≈ es ist nicht durch den TÜV gekommen; **~ certificate** ≈ TÜV-Plakette *f* **VT** **to get one's car ~'d** ≈ sein Auto zum TÜV bringen; **I got my car ~'d** *(successfully)* ≈ mein Auto hat den TÜV bestanden; **the car is ~'d till June** ≈ das Auto hat noch TÜV bis Juni

mote [məʊt] N *(old)* Staubkorn *nt*, Stäubchen *nt*; **to see the ~ in one's neighbour's eye (and not the beam in one's own)** den Splitter im Auge des anderen (und nicht den Balken im eigenen Auge) sehen

motel [məʊˈtel] N Motel *nt*

motet [məʊˈtet] N Motette *f*

moth [mɒθ] N Nachtfalter *m*; *(wool-eating)* Motte *f*; **to be attracted like a ~ to a flame** wie die Motten vom Licht angezogen werden

moth: **mothball** **N** Mottenkugel *f*; **to put in ~s** *(lit, fig)* einmotten; *ship* stilllegen, außer Dienst stellen **VT** *plan, equipment etc* einmotten; *factory* stillegen; **moth-eaten** ADJ *(lit)* mottenzerfressen; *(fig)* ausgedient, vermottet *(inf)*

mother [ˈmʌðəˈ] **N** **a** Mutter *f*; *(= animal)* Muttertier *nt*, Mutter *f*; *(= address to elderly lady)* Mütterchen; **Mother of God** Muttergottes *f*, Mutter *f* Gottes;; **a ~'s love** Mutterliebe *f*; **she's a ~ of three** sie hat drei Kinder; **she's her ~'s daughter** sie ist wie ihre Mutter; **I had the ~ and father of a headache** *(inf)* ich hatte vielleicht Kopfschmerzen!; **the ~ of all battles/confrontations/traffic jams** die Mutter aller Kriege/Auseinandersetzungen/Staus; **shall I be ~?** *(inf) (= pour tea)* soll ich eingießen?; *(= serve food)* soll ich austeilen?
b *(US sl)* Arschloch *nt (vulg)*, Saftsack *m (inf)*; **a real ~ of a day** ein Scheißtag *m (inf)*
ATTR Mutter-; **~ plant** Mutterpflanze *f*; **~ bird** Vogelmutter *f*; **~ hen** Glucke *f*
VT *(= care for) young* auf- *or* großziehen; *(= give birth to)* zur Welt bringen; *(= cosset)* bemuttern

mother: **motherboard** N *(Comput)* Mutterplatine *f*, Hauptplatine *f*; **mother country** N *(= native country)* Vaterland *nt*, Heimat *f*; *(= head of empire)* Mutterland *nt*; **mothercraft** N Kinderpflege *f*; **mother earth** N Mutter *f* Erde; **mother figure** N Mutterfigur *f*; **motherfucker** N *(US vulg)* Arschloch *nt (vulg)*, Arschficker *m (vulg)*; **motherfucking** ADJ *(US vulg)* Scheiß- *(sl)*; **motherhood** N Mutterschaft *f*

Mothering Sunday [ˈmʌðərɪŋˈsʌndɪ] N ≈ Muttertag *m*

mother: **mother-in-law** N *pl* **mothers-in-law** Schwiegermutter *f*; **motherland** N *(= native country)* Vaterland *nt*, Heimat *f*; *(= ancestral country)* Land *nt* der Väter *or* Vorfahren; **motherless** ADJ mutterlos; **he was left ~ at the age of 2** er verlor mit 2 Jahren seine Mutter; **mother lode** N *(Min)* Hauptader *f*; **mother love** N Mutterliebe *f*

motherly [ˈmʌðəlɪ] ADJ mütterlich

mother-naked ADJ *pred* [ˌmʌðəˈneɪkɪd] splitternackt *(inf)*

mother nature N Mutter *f* Natur

mother-of-pearl [ˌmʌðərəvˈpɜːl] **N** Perlmutt *nt*, Perlmutter *f* **ADJ** Perlmutt-; **~ button** Perlmuttknopf *m*

Mother's Day N Muttertag *m*

mother's help N Haus(halts)hilfe *f*

mother: **mother ship** N Mutterschiff *nt*; **mother superior** N Mutter Oberin *f*; **mother tie** N *(Psych)* Mutterbindung *f*; **mother-to-be** N *pl* **mothers-to-be** werdende Mutter; **mother tongue** N Muttersprache *f*; **mother wit** N Mutterwitz *m*

moth: **mothhole** N Mottenloch *nt*; **mothproof** **ADJ** mottenfest **VT** mottenfest machen

motif [məʊˈtiːf] N *(Art, Mus)* Motiv *nt*; *(Sew)* Muster *nt*

motion [ˈməʊʃən] **N** **a** *no pl (= movement)* Bewegung *f*; **to be in ~** sich bewegen; *(engine, machine etc)* laufen; *(train, bus etc)* fahren; **to set** *or* **put sth in ~** etw in Gang bringen *or* setzen; **to set the wheels in ~ (to do sth)** die Dinge ins Rollen bringen(, um etw zu tun)
b *(= gesture)* Bewegung *f*; **to go through the ~s of doing sth** *(because protocol, etiquette etc demands it)* etw pro forma *or* der Form halber tun; *(= pretend)* so tun, als ob man etw täte, den Anschein erwecken, etw zu tun; *(= do mechanically)* etw völlig mechanisch tun
c *(= proposal)* Antrag *m*; **to propose** *or* **make** *(US)* **a ~** einen Antrag stellen
d *(in debate)* Thema *nt*
e *(Brit: = bowel motion)* Stuhlgang *m*; *(= faeces)* Stuhl *m*; **to have a ~** Stuhlgang haben
VT **to ~ sb to do sth** jdm bedeuten, etw zu tun *(geh)*, jdm ein Zeichen geben, dass er etw tun solle; **he ~ed me to a chair** er wies mir einen Stuhl an; **he ~ed me in** er winkte mich herein; **she ~ed me away** sie gab mir ein Zeichen, wegzugehen
VI **to ~ to sb to do sth** jdm bedeuten, etw zu tun *(geh)*, jdm ein Zeichen geben, dass er etw tun solle

motion: **motionless** ADJ unbeweglich, reg(ungs)los; **to stand ~** bewegungslos dastehen; **motion picture** N *(esp US)* Film *m*; **motion sensor** N Bewegungsmelder *m*; **motion sickness** N *(Med)* Kinetose *f (spec)*, Seekrankheit *f*; *(in the air)* Luftkrankheit *f*; *(in car)* Autokrankheit *f*; **motion study** N *(Econ)* Bewegungsstudie *f*

motivate [ˈməʊtɪveɪt] VT motivieren

motivated [ˈməʊtɪveɪtɪd] ADJ motiviert; **highly ~** hoch motiviert; **to keep sb ~** jds Motivation erhalten; **he's just not ~ enough** es fehlt ihm einfach die nötige Motivation

motivation [ˌməʊtɪˈveɪʃən] N Motivation *f*

motivational [ˌməʊtɪˈveɪʃənəl] ADJ motivationsfördernd

motive [ˈməʊtɪv] **N** **a** *(= incentive, reason)* Motiv *nt*, Beweggrund *m*; *(for crime)* (Tat)motiv *nt*; **the profit ~** Gewinnstreben *nt*; **with the purest of ~s** mit den besten Absichten **b** = **motif** **ADJ** **~ power/force** Antriebs- *or* Triebkraft *f*

motiveless [ˈməʊtɪvlɪs] ADJ grundlos, ohne Motiv, unmotiviert

mot juste [ˈməʊˈʒuːst] N passender *or* treffender Ausdruck

motley [ˈmɒtlɪ] **ADJ** kunterbunt; *(= varied also)* bunt (gemischt); *(= multicoloured also)* bunt (gescheckt) **N** Narrenkostüm *or* -kleid *nt*; **on with the ~!** lache, Bajazzo!

motocross [ˈməʊtəkrɒs] N Motocross *nt*

motor [ˈməʊtəˈ] **N** **a** Motor *m* **b** *(Brit inf: = car)* Auto *nt* **VI** *(dated)* (mit dem Auto) fahren **ATTR** **a** *(Physiol)* motorisch **b** *(= motor-driven)* Motor-; **~ yacht** Motorjacht *f* **c** *(= relating to motor vehicles)* Kraftfahrzeug-, Kfz-; **~ manufacturer** Kraftfahrzeughersteller *m*; *(esp making cars)* Automobilhersteller *m*; **the ~ trade** die Kraftfahrzeugbranche, die Kfz-Branche

motor: **motor-assisted** ADJ mit Hilfsmotor; **motorbike** [ˈməʊtəbaɪk] N Motorrad *nt*; **motorboat** [ˈməʊtəbəʊt] N Motorboot *nt*

motorcade [ˈməʊtəkeɪd] N Fahrzeug- *or* Wagenkolonne *f*

motor: **motorcar** N *(dated, form)* Automobil *nt (dated)*, Auto *nt*; **motor caravan** N *(Brit)* Wohnmobil *nt*; **motorcoach** N *(dated)* Autobus *m*; **motorcycle** N Motorrad *nt*, Kraftrad *nt (form)*; **~ combination** Motorrad *nt* mit Beiwagen; **motorcycling** N Motorradfahren *nt*; *(Sport)* Motorradsport *m*; **motorcyclist** N Motorradfahrer(in) *m(f)*; **motor-driven** ADJ mit Motorantrieb

-motored [-ˈməʊtəd] ADJ *suf* -motorig; **tri-motored** dreimotorig

motor home N Wohnmobil *nt*

motor industry N Kraftfahrzeugindustrie *f*; *(esp making cars)* Automobilindustrie *f*

motoring [ˈməʊtərɪŋ] *(esp Brit)* **ADJ** *attr* Auto-; **~ accident** Autounfall *m*; **~ offence** Verkehrsdelikt *nt*; **the ~ public** die Autofahrer *pl* **N** Autofahren *nt*; **school of ~** Fahrschule *f*

motor inn N *(US)* = **motor lodge**

motor insurance N Kraftfahrzeugversicherung *f*, Kfz-Versicherung *f*

motorist [ˈməʊtərɪst] N Autofahrer(in) *m(f)*

motorization [ˌməʊtəraɪˈzeɪʃən] N Motorisierung *f*

motorize [ˈməʊtəraɪz] VT motorisieren; **to be ~d** motorisiert sein; *(private person also)* ein Auto haben

motor: **motor lodge**, **motor inn** N *(US)* Motel *nt*; **motorman** N *(of train)* Zugführer(in) *m(f)*; *(of tram)* Straßenbahnfahrer(in) *m(f)*; **motor mechanic** N Kraftfahrzeugmechaniker(in) *m(f)*, Kfz-Mechaniker(in) *m(f)*; **motor nerve** N motorischer Nerv; **motor neuron disease** N *(Med)* amyotrophe Lateralsklerose; **motor oil** Motorenöl *nt*, Motoröl *nt*; **motor race** N (Auto)rennen *nt*; **motor racing** N Rennsport *m*; **he did a lot of ~** er hat an vielen Autorennen teilgenommen; **motor road** N Fahrstraße *f*; **motor scooter** N *(form)* Motorroller *m*; **motor show** N Automobilausstellung *f*; **motor sport** N Motorsport *m*; *(with cars also)* Automobilsport *m*; **motor torpedo boat** N Torpedoboot *nt*; **motor truck** N *(dated US)* Lastwagen *m*; **motor vehicle** N *(form)* Kraftfahrzeug *nt*; **motor vessel** N Motorschiff *nt*; **motorway** N *(Brit)* Autobahn *f*; **~ driving** das Fahren auf der Autobahn, das Autobahnfahren; **~ junction** Autobahndreieck *nt*; **~ madness** Geschwindigkeitsrausch *m*

mottled [ˈmɒtld] ADJ gesprenkelt; *complexion* fleckig; **~ brown and white** braun und weiß gesprenkelt

motto [ˈmɒtəʊ] N *pl* **-es** Motto *nt*, Wahlspruch *m*; *(personal also)* Devise *f*; *(Her also)* Sinnspruch *m*; *(in cracker, on calendar)* Spruch *m*; **the school ~** das Motto der Schule

mould[1], *(US)* **mold** [məʊld] **N** **a** *(= hollow form)* (Guss)form *f*; *(Typ also)* Mater *f*; *(= shape, Cook)* Form *f*
b *(= jelly, blancmange)* Pudding *m*, Wackelpeter *m (inf)*
c *(fig: = character, style)* **to be cast in** *or* **from the same/a different ~** *(people)* vom gleichen/von einem anderen Schlag sein, aus dem gleichen/einem anderen Holz geschnitzt sein; *(novel characters)* nach demselben/einem anderen Muster geschaffen sein; **the two painters/novelists** *etc* **are cast in** *or* **from the same/a different ~** die beiden Maler/Schriftsteller *etc* verbindet viel/wenig miteinander; **to break the ~** *(fig)* mit der Tradition brechen; **they broke the ~ when they made him** er hat nicht seinesgleichen; **to fit sb/sth into a ~** jdn/etw in ein Schema zwängen
VT **a** *(lit) (= fashion)* formen (*into* zu); *(= cast)* gießen
b *(fig) character, person* formen; **to ~ sb into sth** etw aus jdm machen
VR **to ~ oneself on sb** sich *(dat)* jdn zum Vorbild nehmen; **to ~ oneself on an ideal** sich an einem Ideal orientieren

mould[2], *(US)* **mold** N *(= fungus)* Schimmel *m*

mould[3], *(US)* **mold** N *(= soil)* Humus(boden) *m*, Humuserde *f*

moulder[1], *(US)* **molder** [ˈməʊldəˈ] N *(Tech: = person)* Former(in) *m(f)*, (Form)gießer(in) *m(f)*

moulder[2], *(US)* **molder** VI *(lit)* vermodern; *(leaves also)* verrotten; *(food)* verderben; *(carcass)* verwesen; *(fig) (mental faculties, building)* zerfallen; *(equipment)* vermodern, vergammeln *(inf)*; *(person)* verkümmern

mouldiness, *(US)* **moldiness** [ˈməʊldɪnɪs] N Schimmel *m (of* auf *+dat)*, Schimmligkeit *f*

moulding, *(US)* **molding** [ˈməʊldɪŋ] N **a** *(= act)* Formen *nt*; *(of metals)* Gießen *nt* **b** *(= cast)* Abdruck *m*; *(of metal)* (Ab)guss *m*; *(= ceiling moulding)* Deckenfries *m or* -stuck *m* **c** *(fig)* Formen *nt*

mouldy, *(US)* **moldy** [ˈməʊldɪ] ADJ *(+er)* **a** *(= covered with mould)* verschimmelt, schimmelig; *(= musty)* mod(e)rig; **to go ~** *(food)* verschimmeln **b** *(dated inf) (= pathetic, contemptible)* miserabel *(inf)*; *(= mean) person* schäbig; *amount* lumpig *(inf)*

moult, *(US)* **molt** [məʊlt] N *(of birds)* Mauser *f (also Comput)*; *(of mammals)* Haarwechsel *m*; *(of snakes)* Häutung *f* VT *hairs* verlieren; *feathers, skin* abstreifen VI *(bird)* sich mausern; *(mammals)* sich haaren; *(snake)* sich häuten

mound [maʊnd] N **a** *(= hill, burial mound)* Hügel *m*; *(= earthwork)* Wall *m*; *(Baseball)* Wurfmal *nt* **b** *(= pile)* Haufen *m*; *(of books, letters)* Stoß *m*, Stapel *m*

mount[1] [maʊnt] N **a** *(poet: = mountain, hill)* Berg *m* **b** *(in names)* **Mount Etna/Kilimanjaro** *etc* der Ätna/Kilimandscharo *etc*; **Mount Everest** Mount Everest *m*; **on Mount Sinai** auf dem Berg(e) Sinai

mount[2] N **a** *(= horse etc)* Reittier *nt*, Ross *nt (old, liter)*
b *(= support, base) (of machine)* Sockel *m*, Untersatz *m*; *(of jewel)* Fassung *f*; *(of photo, picture)* Passepartout *nt*; *(= backing)* Unterlage *f*, Rücken *m*; *(= stamp mount)* Falz *m*
VT **a** *(= climb onto)* besteigen, steigen auf *(+acc)*
b *(= place in/on mount)* montieren; *picture, photo* aufziehen; *colour slide* rahmen; *microscope slide, specimen, animal* präparieren; *jewel* (ein)fassen; *stamp* aufkleben
c *(= organize) play* inszenieren; *attack, expedition, exhibition* organisieren, vorbereiten; *army* aufstellen
d **to ~ a guard** eine Wache aufstellen *(on, over* vor *+dat)*; **to ~ guard** Wache stehen *or* halten *(on, over* vor *+dat)*
e *(= mate with)* bespringen; *(inf: person)* besteigen
f *(= provide with horse)* mit Pferden/einem Pferd versorgen
g *(Comput) data system, disk drive etc* mounten, verfügbar machen
VI **a** *(= get on)* aufsteigen; *(on horse)* aufsitzen, aufsteigen
b *(also* **mount up***)* wachsen, zunehmen; *(evidence)* sich häufen; **the death toll has ~ed to 800** die Todesziffer ist auf 800 gestiegen; **pressure is ~ing on him to resign** er sieht sich wachsendem Druck ausgesetzt, zurückzutreten

mountain [ˈmaʊntɪn] N *(lit, fig)* Berg *m*; **in the ~s** im Gebirge, in den Bergen; **to make a ~ out of a molehill** aus einer Mücke einen Elefant(en) machen *(inf)*; **we have a ~ to climb** *(esp Brit fig)* wir haben eine riesige Aufgabe vor uns; **faith can move ~s** der Glaube kann Berge versetzen; **if Mohammed won't go to the ~, the ~ must go to Mohammed** *(prov)* wenn der Berg nicht zum Propheten kommen will, muss der Prophet zum Berge gehen *(prov)*

mountain *in cpds* Berg-; *(alpine, Himalayan etc)* Gebirgs-; **~ road** Berg-/Gebirgsstraße *f*; **~ air** Bergluft *f*; **mountain ash** N Eberesche *f*; **mountain bike** N Mountainbike *nt*; **mountain biker** N Mountainbiker(in) *m(f)*; **mountain chain** N Berg- *or* Gebirgskette *f*, Gebirgszug *m*; **mountain climber** N Bergsteiger(in) *m(f)*; **mountain dew** N *(inf) illegal gebrannter Whisky*

mountaineer [ˌmaʊntɪˈnɪəʳ] N Bergsteiger(in) *m(f)* VI bergsteigen

mountaineering [ˌmaʊntɪˈnɪərɪŋ] N Bergsteigen *nt* ATTR Bergsteiger-; **~ expedition** Bergpartie *f*; **~ school** Bergsteigerschule *f*; **~ skill** bergsteigerisches Können; **learn ~ skills with …** erlernen Sie das Bergsteigen mit …; **in ~ circles** unter Bergsteigern

mountain goat N Bergziege *f*

mountain lion N Puma *m*, Silberlöwe *m*

mountainous [ˈmaʊntɪnəs] ADJ bergig, gebirgig; *(fig: = huge)* riesig; *waves* meterhoch; **~ seas** stürmische See (mit meterhohen Wellen)

mountain: **mountain pass** N Gebirgspass *m*; **mountain people** PL Berg- *or* Gebirgsbewohner *pl*; **mountain range** N Gebirgszug *m or* -kette *f*; **mountain rescue** N Bergrettungsaktion *f*; **~ team** Bergrettungsteam *nt or* -mannschaft *f*

mountains classification N *(Cycling)* Bergwertung *f*

mountain: **mountain sheep** N Dickhornschaf *nt*; **mountain sickness** N Höhen- *or* Bergkrankheit *f*; **mountainside** N (Berg)hang *m*; **mountain slide** N Bergrutsch *m*; **mountaintop** N Berggipfel *m* ADJ *attr* Gipfel-

mountebank [ˈmaʊntɪbæŋk] N Quacksalber *m*, Scharlatan *m*

mounted [ˈmaʊntɪd] ADJ *(= on horseback)* beritten; *(Mil, = with motor vehicles)* motorisiert

Mountie [ˈmaʊntɪ] N *(inf) berittener kanadischer Polizist*

mounting [ˈmaʊntɪŋ] ADJ *(= increasing)* wachsend, zunehmend; **there is ~ evidence that …** es häufen sich die Beweise dafür, dass … N **a** *(of horse)* Besteigen *nt* **b** *(of picture, photo)* Aufziehen *nt*; *(of jewel)* (Ein)fassen *nt* **c** *(= frame etc)* = **mount**[2] **N b**

mourn [mɔːn] VT *person* trauern um, betrauern; *sb's death* beklagen, betrauern; *(with wailing)* beklagen; *(fig)* nachtrauern *(+dat)*; **who is she ~ing?** um wen trauert sie?; *(= wear mourning for)* warum trägt sie Trauer?; **he is still ~ing the break-up of his relationship** er trauert noch immer über das Ende seiner Beziehung; **what is to become of us?, she ~ed** was soll aus uns werden?, klagte sie VI trauern; *(= wear mourning)* Trauer tragen, in Trauer gehen; **to ~ for** *or* **over sb** um jdn trauern, jds Tod *(acc)* betrauern; **to ~ for** *or* **over sth** einer Sache *(dat)* nachtrauern

mourner [ˈmɔːnəʳ] N Trauernde(r) *mf*; *(= non-relative at funeral)* Trauergast *m*

mournful [ˈmɔːnfʊl] ADJ *(= sad) person, occasion, atmosphere, look* traurig, trauervoll; *person (as character trait), voice* weinerlich; *sigh, appearance* kläglich, jämmerlich; *sound, cry* klagend

mournfully [ˈmɔːnfəlɪ] ADV *(= sadly)* traurig, trauervoll; *wail, cry* klagend

mournfulness [ˈmɔːnfʊlnɪs] N Traurigkeit *f*; *(of voice)* Weinerlichkeit *f*; *(of sigh, appearance)* Jämmerlichkeit *f*

mourning [ˈmɔːnɪŋ] N *(= act)* Trauer *f*, Trauern *nt (of* um*)*; *(with wailing)* Wehklage *f*; *(= period etc)* Trauerzeit *f*; *(= dress)* Trauer(kleidung) *f*; **to be in ~ for sb** um jdn trauern; *(= wear mourning)* Trauer tragen; **to come out of ~** die Trauer ablegen; **to go into ~** trauern; *(= wear mourning)* Trauer anlegen; **next Tuesday has been declared a day of national ~** für den kommenden Dienstag wurde Staatstrauer angeordnet

mouse [maʊs] N *pl* **mice** **a** Maus *f (also Comput)* **b** *(inf: = person) (shy)* schüchternes Mäuschen; *(nondescript)* graue Maus VI Mäuse fangen, mausen; **to go mousing** auf Mäusejagd gehen

mouse *in cpds* Mause-; *(Comput)* Maus-; **mouse button** N *(Comput)* Maustaste *f*; **mouse click** N *(Comput)* Mausklick *m*; **mouse-coloured** ADJ mausgrau; **mouse control** N *(Comput)* Maussteuerung *f*; **mouse-controlled**, **mouse-driven** ADJ *(Comput)* mausgesteuert; **mousehole** N Mauseloch *nt*; **mouse mat**, **mouse pad** N *(Comput)* Mausmatte *f*; **mouse pointer** N *(Comput)* Mauszeiger *m*; **mouse potato** N *(hum: = computer freak)* Computerjunkie *m (inf)*, Mouse-Potato *f (inf)*

mouser [ˈmaʊsəʳ] N Mäusefänger(in) *m(f)*, Mäusejäger(in) *m(f)*

mousetrap [ˈmaʊstræp] N Mausefalle *f*

mouse wheel N *(Comput)* Mausrad *nt*

mousey ADJ = **mousy**

moussaka [mʊˈsɑːkə] N Moussaka *f*

mousse [muːs] N **a** Creme(speise) *f* **b** *(also* **styling mousse***)* Schaumfestiger *m*

moustache, *(US)* **mustache** [məˈstɑːʃ] N Schnurrbart *m*

mousy, **mousey** [ˈmaʊsɪ] ADJ *(+er) (= timid, shy)* schüchtern; *(= nondescript)* farblos, unscheinbar; *colour, hair* mausgrau

mouth [maʊθ] N *(of person)* Mund *m*; *(of animal)* Maul *nt*; *(of bird)* Rachen *m*; *(of bottle, cave, vice etc)* Öffnung *f*; *(of river)* Mündung *f*; *(of harbour)* Einfahrt *f*; **to be down in the ~** *(inf)* deprimiert *or* niedergeschlagen sein; **to keep one's (big) ~ shut (about sth)** *(inf)* (über etw *acc*) den Mund *or* die Klappe *(inf)* halten; **me and my big ~!** *(inf)* ich konnte wieder nicht den Mund *or* die Klappe *(inf)* halten; **he's all ~ and (no) trousers** *(Brit inf)* große Klappe, nichts dahinter *(inf)*; **to have a foul ~** ein grobes *or* ungewaschenes Maul haben *(inf)*; **watch your ~!** pass auf, was du sagst; **to speak** *or* **talk out of both sides of one's ~** *(US)* mit doppelter *or* gespaltener Zunge sprechen; **he has three ~s to feed** er hat drei Mäuler zu ernähren *or* stopfen *(inf)* → **word** [maʊð]
VT *(= say affectedly)* (über)deutlich artikulieren; *(= articulate soundlessly)* mit Lippensprache sagen

mouthful [ˈmaʊθfʊl] N *(of drink)* Schluck *m*; *(of food)* Bissen *m*, Happen *m (inf)*; *(fig) (= difficult word)* Zungenbrecher *m*; *(= long word)* Bandwurm *m*; **the diver gulped in great ~s of air** der Taucher machte ein paar tiefe Atemzüge; **I got a ~ of salt water** ich habe einen ganzen Schwall Salzwasser geschluckt; **you said a ~** *(US inf)* das kann man wohl sagen

mouth *in cpds* Mund-; **mouth guard** N Mundschutz *m*; **mouth organ** N Mundharmonika *f*; **mouthpiece** N Mundstück *nt*; *(of telephone)* Sprechmuschel *f*; *(fig: = spokesman, publication)* Sprachrohr *nt*; **mouth-to-mouth** ADJ **~ resuscitation** Mund-zu-Mund-Beatmung *f*; **mouthwash** N Mundwasser *nt*; **mouthwatering** ADJ lecker; *(fig) prospect, car etc* verlockend; **that smells/looks really ~** da läuft einem ja das Wasser im Mund(e) zusammen!; **a ~ sum** ein hübsches Sümmchen *(inf)*; **to look ~** *(boy, girl)* appetitlich aussehen; **mouthwateringly** ADV appetitlich

mouthy [ˈmaʊθɪ] ADJ *(inf)* **to be ~** eine große Klappe haben *(inf)*

movability [ˌmuːvəˈbɪlɪtɪ] N Beweglichkeit *f*; *(= transportability)* Transportfähigkeit *f*

movable [ˈmuːvəbl] ADJ beweglich *(auch Jur, Eccl)*; *(= transportable)* transportierbar, transportfähig; **not easily ~** schwer zu bewegen/transportieren N **a** *(= portable object)* bewegliches Gut; **~s** *pl* Mobiliar *nt*, Mobilien *pl* **b** *usu pl (Jur)* bewegliches Vermögen, Mobiliarvermögen *nt*

move [muːv]

1 TRANSITIVE VERB	3 NOUN
2 INTRANSITIVE VERB	4 PHRASAL VERBS

1 – TRANSITIVE VERB

a = make sth move bewegen; *wheel, windmill etc* (an)treiben; *(= shift) objects, furniture* woanders hinstellen; *(= move away)* wegstellen; *(= shift about)* umstellen, umräumen; *chest, chair* rücken; *(Comput) window, file* verschieben; *vehicle (driver)* wegfahren; *engine* von der Stelle bewegen; *(= transport)* befördern; *(= remove) soil, dirt, rubble* wegschaffen; *obstacle* aus dem Weg räumen; *rock* von der Stelle bewegen; *chess piece etc* ziehen mit, einen Zug machen mit; **to move sth to a different place** etw an einen anderen Platz stellen; **to move sth to the recycle bin** *(Comput)* etw in den Papierkorb verschieben; **to be unable to move sth** *(= lift)* etw nicht von der Stelle *or* vom Fleck *(inf)* bringen; *screw, nail* etw nicht losbekommen; **I can't**

move this lid/handle der Deckel/Griff lässt sich nicht bewegen; **you'll have to move these books/your car (out of the way)** Sie müssen diese Bücher wegräumen/Ihr Auto wegfahren; **don't move anything, said the detective** verändern Sie nichts *or* lassen Sie alles so, wie es ist, sagte der Detektiv; **you must have moved the camera** da haben Sie wahrscheinlich gewackelt; **recent events have moved the share index upwards/downwards** infolge der jüngsten Ereignisse ist der Aktienindex gestiegen/gefallen

b [parts of body] bewegen; *(= take away) arm* wegnehmen; *one's foot, hand* wegziehen; **could you move your head a little to the side?** können Sie vielleicht Ihren Kopf ein wenig zur Seite drehen?; **he moved his face a little closer** er ging mit dem Gesicht etwas näher heran; **move your feet off the table!** nimm deine Füße vom Tisch!; **move yourself, can't you?** *(= make room)* können Sie nicht mal etwas Platz machen?

c [people: enemy, demonstrators] vertreiben; *patient* bewegen; *(= transport)* transportieren; *(= transfer)* verlegen; *refugees* transportieren; *(out of area)* evakuieren; *employee (to different department)* versetzen; *pupil (by authorities)* versetzen; **move those people** schicken Sie die Leute da weg; **to move sb to a hospital** jdn ins Krankenhaus einliefern; **to move soldiers into a city** Soldaten in eine Stadt versetzen; **I'm going to move you to sales manager** ich werde Sie jetzt als Verkaufsleiter einsetzen; **his parents moved him to another school** seine Eltern haben ihn in eine andere Schule getan *or* gegeben

d [= change location of] *offices, troops, production* verlegen; *(Comput) text block* verschieben; **the removal men are moving us on Friday** die Spediteure machen am Freitag unseren Umzug; **we've been moved to a new office** wir mussten in ein anderes Büro umziehen

♦ **to move house** *(Brit)* umziehen

♦ **to move office** (in ein anderes Büro) umziehen

e [= change timing of] *event, date* verlegen; *(= put back)* verschieben; **they've moved the meeting to 3 o'clock on Tuesday** sie haben die Sitzung auf Dienstag 15 Uhr verlegt/verschoben

f [= cause emotion in] rühren, bewegen; *(= upset)* erschüttern, ergreifen; **to be moved** gerührt/erschüttert sein; **I'm not easily moved, but ...** ich bin ja sonst nicht so schnell gerührt/leicht zu erschüttern, aber ...; **his speech really moved them** sie waren von seiner Rede tief bewegt; **to move sb from an opinion** *etc (= sway)* jdn von einer Meinung *etc* abbringen; **I shall not be moved** ich bleibe hart *or* dabei

♦ **to move sb to... to move sb to tears** jdn zu Tränen rühren; **to move sb to anger/pity** jds Zorn/Mitleid erregen; **to move sb to action** jdn veranlassen, etw zu unternehmen

♦ **to move sb to do sth** jdn veranlassen *or* bewegen *(geh) or* dazu bringen, etw zu tun

g [= propose] *form* beantragen; **she moved an amendment to the motion** sie stellte einen Abänderungsantrag; **I move that we adjourn** ich beantrage eine Vertagung

h [Med] **to move the** *or* **one's bowels** Stuhlgang haben; **this mixture will help to move the bowels** dieses Mittel regt die Verdauung an *or* ist verdauungsfördernd

i [Comm] *(= sell)* absetzen

2 – INTRANSITIVE VERB

a sich bewegen; **the wheel/vehicle began to move** das Rad/Fahrzeug setzte sich in Bewegung; **she moves gracefully/like a cat** ihre Bewegungen sind anmutig/katzenhaft; **nothing/nobody moved** nichts/niemand rührte sich; **don't move!** still halten!; **don't move or I'll shoot!** keine Bewegung, oder ich schieße!

b [= not be stationary] *vehicle, ship* fahren; *(traffic)* vorankommen; **to keep moving** nicht stehen bleiben; **to keep sb/sth moving** jdn/etw in Gang halten; **keep those people moving!** sorgen Sie dafür, dass die Leute weitergehen!

c [= move house] umziehen; **we moved to London/to a bigger house** wir sind nach London/in ein größeres Haus umgezogen; **they moved to Germany** sie sind nach Deutschland gezogen; **they moved from London** sie sind von London weggezogen

d [= change place] gehen; *(in vehicle)* fahren; **he has moved to room 52** er ist jetzt in Zimmer 52; **she has moved to another department/a different company** sie hat die Abteilung/Firma gewechselt; **he used to sit here, has he moved?** das war doch sein Platz, sitzt er nicht mehr da?; **he has moved to Brown's** er ist zu Brown gegangen *or* gewechselt; **have the troops moved?** sind die Truppen abgezogen?; **the troops moved to another base** die Truppen zogen zu einem anderen Stützpunkt weiter; **move!** weitergehen!; *(= go away)* verschwinden Sie!; **don't move** gehen Sie nicht weg; **I won't move from here** ich rühre mich nicht von der Stelle; **it's time we were moving** *or* **we moved** es wird Zeit, dass wir gehen

e [= change, progress] **to move (away) from sth** sich von etw entfernen; **to move (closer) to (-wards) sth** sich einer Sache *(dat)* nähern; **which way are events moving?** in welche Richtung entwickeln sich die Dinge?; **things are moving at last** endlich kommen die Dinge in Gang, endlich geschieht etwas; **technology moves at an ever faster rate** die Technik macht immer raschere Fortschritte; **to move with the times** mit der Zeit gehen; **let's move to another subject** wechseln wir das Thema

f [= go fast] *inf* einen Zahn *or* ein Tempo draufhaben *(inf)*; *(= hurry up)* zumachen *(inf)*, einen Zahn zulegen *(inf)*; **he can really move** der ist unheimlich schnell *(inf)*; **150? that's moving!** 150? das ist aber ein ganz schönes Tempo! *(inf)*

g [= be part of] **to move in high society/in royal circles** *etc* in der feinen Gesellschaft/in königlichen Kreisen *etc* verkehren

h [in games] *= make a move* einen Zug machen, ziehen; *(= have one's turn)* am Zug sein, ziehen

i [= act] *fig* etwas unternehmen, Maßnahmen ergreifen; **they must move first** sie müssen den ersten Schritt tun; **we'll have to move quickly (in order to avoid this)** wir müssen schnell handeln(, um dies zu vermeiden); **the government won't move until ...** die Regierung wird nichts unternehmen, bis ...

j [= propose, request] *form* **to move for sth** etw beantragen

k [Comm] *(= sell)* sich absetzen lassen, gehen *(inf)*

3 – NOUN

a [in game] Zug *m*; *(fig) (= step, action)* Schritt *m*; *(= measure taken)* Maßnahme *f*; **it's my move** *(lit, fig)* ich bin am Zug, ich bin dran *(inf)*; **that was a bad/good/clever move** *(lit, fig)* das war ein schlechter/guter/raffinierter Zug

♦ **to make a move** *(lit, fig)* einen Zug machen

♦ **to make the first move** *(fig)* den ersten Zug machen, den ersten Schritt tun

b [= movement] Bewegung *f*; **to watch sb's every move** jdn nicht aus den Augen lassen

♦ **to make a move** *(= go, leave)* **nobody had made a move (toward(s) going)** keiner hatte Anstalten gemacht zu gehen; **it's time we made a move** es wird Zeit, dass wir gehen *or* dass wir uns auf den Weg machen

♦ **to make a move to do sth** *(fig)* Anstalten machen, etw zu tun

♦ **to be on the move** *(things, people)* in Bewegung sein; *(fig: developments)* im Fluss sein; *(person: in different places)* unterwegs *or* auf Achse *(inf)* sein; *(vehicle)* fahren; *(country, institutions etc)* sich im Umbruch befinden

♦ **to get a move on (with sth)** *(inf: = hurry up)* sich beeilen (mit etw); *(= make quick progress)* (mit etw) vorankommen; **get a move on!** nun mach schon! *(inf)*, mach mal zu! *(inf)*

c [= change] *of house etc* Umzug *m*; *(to different job)* Stellenwechsel *m*; *(to different department)* Wechsel *m*; *(to different system etc)* Übergang *m*

4 – PHRASAL VERBS

► **move about** *(Brit)* **VT** *sep (= place in different positions)* umarrangieren; *furniture, ornaments etc* umstellen, umräumen; *parts of body* (hin und her) bewegen; *(= fiddle with)* herumspielen mit; *employee* versetzen; *(= make travel)* umher- *or* herumschicken; **the families of servicemen get moved about a lot** die Familien von Militärpersonal müssen oft umziehen **VI** sich (hin und her) bewegen; *(= fidget)* herumzappeln; *(= travel)* unterwegs sein; *(= move house)* umziehen; **I can hear him moving about** ich höre ihn herumlaufen; **the car/stick will help her to move about** mit dem Auto/Stock ist sie beweglicher

► **move along** **VT** *sep* weiterrücken; *car* vorfahren; *bystanders etc* zum Weitergehen veranlassen; **they are trying to move things along** sie versuchen, die Dinge voranzutreiben **VI** *(along seat etc)* auf- *or* durchrücken; *(along pavement, bus etc)* weitergehen; *(cars)* weiterfahren

► **move around** VTI *sep* = **move about**

► **move aside** **VT** *sep* zur Seite rücken *or* schieben, beiseiterücken *or* -schieben; *person* beiseitedrängen **VI** zur Seite gehen, Platz machen

► **move away** **VT** *sep* wegräumen; *car* wegfahren; *person* wegschicken; *(to different town, job etc)* versetzen; *troops* abziehen; *(pupil)* wegsetzen; **to move sb away from sb/sth** jdn von jdm/etw entfernen **VI** **a** *(= move aside)* aus dem Weg gehen, weggehen; *(= leave, people)* weggehen; *(vehicle)* losfahren; *(= move house)* fort- *or* wegziehen *(from* aus, von); *(firm)* wegziehen *(from* von, aus), verziehen; *(person, from department)* verlassen *(from +acc)*; *(from job)* wechseln *(from +acc)* **b** *(fig)* sich entfernen *(from* von); **the country is moving away from communism** das Land entfernt sich vom Kommunismus

► **move back** **VT** *sep* **a** *(to former place)* zurückstellen; *people* zurückbringen; *(into old house, town)* wieder unterbringen *(into* in *+dat)*; *(to job)* zurückversetzen; *soldiers* zurückbeordern; **they'll move you back when the danger is past** Sie werden zurückgeschickt, wenn die Gefahr vorbei ist

b *(to the rear) things* zurückschieben *or* -rücken; *car* zurückfahren; *chess piece* zurückziehen, zurückgehen mit; *people* zurückdrängen; *troops* zurückziehen

VI **a** *(to former place)* zurückkommen; *(into one's house)* wieder einziehen *(into* in *+acc)*; *(into old job)* zurückgehen *(to* zu); *(fig, to theory, ideology)* zurückkehren *(to* zu)

b *(to the rear)* zurückweichen; *(troops)* sich zurückziehen; *(car)* zurückfahren; **move back, please!** bitte zurücktreten!

► **move down** **VT** *sep (downwards)* (weiter) nach unten stellen; *(along)* (weiter) nach hinten stellen; *pupil* zurückstufen; *(Sport)* absteigen lassen; **move that item further down the list** führen Sie diesen Punkt weiter unten auf der Liste auf; **he moved the cows/soldiers down to the plains** er trieb die Kühe/beorderte die Soldaten ins Flachland hinunter

VI *(downwards)* nach unten rücken *or* rutschen; *(along)* weiterrücken *or* -rutschen; *(in bus etc)* nach hinten aufrücken; *(pupil)* zurückgestuft werden; *(team etc)* absteigen, zurückfallen *(to* auf *+acc)*; **move (right) down the bus, please!** rücken Sie bitte (ans hintere Ende des Busses) auf!; **he had to move down a year** *(pupil)* er musste eine Klasse zurück; **when the nomads/cows moved down to the plains** als die Nomaden/Kühe ins Flachland herunterkamen

► **move forward** **VT** *sep* **a** *person* vorgehen lassen; *chair, table etc* vorziehen, vorrücken; *chess piece* vorziehen, vorgehen mit; *car* vorfahren; *troops* vorrücken lassen **b** *(fig: = advance) event, date* vorverlegen; **to move the clock forward** die Uhr vorstellen **VI** *(person)* vorrücken; *(crowd)* sich vorwärts bewegen; *(car)* vorwärts fahren; *(troops)* vorrücken; **the clocks move forward tomorrow** morgen werden die Uhren vorgestellt

▶ **move in** VT *sep* **a** *police, troops, extra staff* einsetzen (*-to* in *+dat*); (*= march/drive in*) einrücken lassen (*-to* in *+acc*); (*= take inside*) *luggage etc* hineinstellen (*-to* in *+acc*); *car* hineinfahren (*-to* in *+acc*)
b **the council hasn't moved us in(to the house) yet** die Stadt hat uns noch nicht im Haus untergebracht; **when will the removal firm** (*Brit*) *or* **moving company** (*US*) **move our things in?** wann macht die Spedition unseren Umzug?
VI **a** (*into accommodation*) einziehen (*-to* in *+acc*); **to move in together** zusammenziehen
b (*= come closer*) sich nähern (*on dat*), näher herankommen (*on* an *+acc*); (*camera*) näher herangehen (*on* an *+acc*); (*police, troops*) anrücken; (*= start operations*) (*workers*) (an)kommen, anfangen; (*hooligans, firms*) auf den Plan treten; **to move in on sb** (*police, troops*) gegen jdn vorrücken; **the big concerns moved in on the market** die großen Konzerne etablierten sich auf dem Markt; **the troops moved into the town** die Truppen rückten in die Stadt ein

▶ **move off** VT *sep people* wegschicken; **move her off!** (*inf: car, train etc*) fahr los! VI **a** (*= go away*) (*people*) weggehen; (*troops*) abziehen
b (*= start moving*) sich in Bewegung setzen

▶ **move on** VT *sep* **the policeman moved them on** der Polizist forderte sie auf weiterzugehen/weiterzufahren; **he moved the discussion on to the next point** er leitete die Diskussion zum nächsten Punkt über
VI (*people*) weitergehen; (*vehicles*) weiterfahren; **it's about time I was moving on** (*fig, to new job etc*) es wird Zeit, dass ich (mal) etwas anderes mache; **to move on to higher things** sich Höherem zuwenden; **to move on to a more responsible job** zu einem verantwortungsvolleren Posten aufsteigen; **they moved on to discuss the future of the company** als Nächstes besprachen sie die Zukunft der Firma; **let's move on to the next point** gehen wir zum nächsten Punkt über; **time is moving on** die Zeit vergeht

▶ **move out** VT *sep* **a** *car* herausfahren (*of* aus); **we had to move the furniture out** wir mussten die Möbel hinausräumen *or* -stellen; **move the table out of the corner** stellen *or* rücken Sie den Tisch von der Ecke weg; **she moved it out from under the bed** sie zog es unter dem Bett (her)vor
b (*= withdraw*) *troops* abziehen; **they are being moved out (of their house)** sie müssen (aus ihrem Haus) ausziehen; **they were moved out for non-payment of rent** wegen Nichtzahlung der Miete wurden sie gezwungen, ihre Wohnung zu räumen; **they moved everybody out of the danger zone** alle mussten die Gefahrenzone verlassen *or* räumen; **the removal men are moving us out tomorrow** die Spediteure machen morgen unseren Umzug
VI **a** (*= leave accommodation*) ausziehen; (*= withdraw: troops*) abziehen; **to move out of an area** ein Gebiet räumen
b (*= leave: train etc*) abfahren

▶ **move over** VT *sep* herüberschieben; **move your bottom over** (*inf*) rück *or* rutsch mal ein Stück zur Seite (*inf*); **he moved the car over to the side** er fuhr an die Seite heran
VI zur Seite rücken *or* rutschen; **move over, we all want to sit down** rück *or* rutsch mal ein Stück, wir wollen uns auch hinsetzen (*inf*); **move over to your side of the bed** leg dich in deine Hälfte des Betts; **he moved over to his own side of the bed** er rückte herüber in seine Betthälfte; **to move over to a new system** ein neues System einführen; **if he can't do the job he should move over and let someone else do it** wenn er die Arbeit nicht machen kann, sollte er einen anderen ranlassen (*inf*)

▶ **move up** VT *sep* **a** (*= change to higher position*) (weiter) nach oben stellen; (*= promote*) befördern; *pupil* versetzen; (*Sport*) aufsteigen lassen; **move that up to the top of the list** stellen Sie das ganz oben an die Liste, führen Sie das ganz oben auf; **they moved him up two places** sie haben ihn zwei Plätze vorgerückt; **they moved the cows up to the pastures** sie trieben die Kühe auf die Alm (hinauf); **the general moved his men up onto the hill** der General beorderte seine Leute auf den Hügel hinauf; **to move sb up the line** jdn weiter vorn platzieren
b *troops etc* (*into battle area*) aufmarschieren lassen; (*to front line*) vorrücken lassen; *guns, artillery* auffahren
VI **a** (*fig*) aufsteigen; (*shares, rates etc*) steigen; (*= be promoted*) befördert werden; (*Sch*) versetzt werden; **the nomads moved up to the hills for the summer** die Nomaden zogen den Sommer über in die Berge hinauf; **to move up in the world** die gesellschaftliche Leiter hinaufklettern
b (*= move along*) auf- *or* weiterrücken; **move up the bus!** rücken Sie auf *or* weiter!

moveable ADJ, N = **movable**

movement ['mu:vmənt] N **a** (*= motion*) Bewegung *f*; (*of troops etc*) Truppenbewegung *f*; (*fig*) (*= trend*) Trend *m* (*towards* zu); (*of events*) Entwicklung *f*; (*of prices/rates*) Preis-/Kursbewegung *f*; **a slight downward/upward ~** eine leichte Abwärts-/Aufwärtsbewegung; **the ~ of traffic** der Verkehrsfluss; **~ (of the bowels)** (*Med*) Stuhlgang *m*; **there was a ~ toward(s) the door** alles drängte zur Tür; **a marked ~ to the right** ein merklicher *or* deutlicher Rechtsruck; **the flowing ~ of the piece** (*Mus*) der fließende Rhythmus des Stückes; **the free ~ of capital and goods** der freie Kapital- und Warenverkehr
b (*= political, artistic etc movement*) Bewegung *f*
c (*= transport: of goods etc*) Beförderung *f*
d (*Mus*) Satz *m*
e (*= mechanism*) Antrieb(smechanismus) *m*, Getriebe *nt*; (*of clock*) Uhrwerk *nt*

mover ['mu:və'] N **a** (*of proposition*) Antragsteller(in) *m(f)* **b** (*= remover*) Möbelpacker(in) *m(f)* **c** (*= walker, dancer etc*) **he is a good/poor** *etc* **~** seine Bewegungen sind schön/plump *etc*
d **the ~s and shakers** (*inf*) die Leute *pl* mit Einfluss; **to be a fast ~** (*inf*) von der schnellen Truppe sein (*inf*)

movie ['mu:vɪ] N (*esp US*) Film *m*; **(the) ~s** der Film; **to go to the ~s** ins Kino gehen

> **MOVIE RATING, FILM RATING**
>
> Es ist Aufgabe des „British Board of Film Classification", die in Großbritannien erscheinenden Filme und Videos einzustufen. Jeder Film erhält danach eine Klassifizierung: **U (Universal)** - für jedes Alter geeignet; **PG (Parental Guidance)** - einige Szenen könnten für jüngere Kinder ungeeignet sein; **12A** - Kinder unter 12 müssen von einem Erwachsenen begleitet werden; „12", „15" oder „18" - das ist das jeweilige Mindestalter der Zuschauer; „Restricted 18" - darf nur in bestimmten Lokalitäten, z. B. Kinoklubs, gezeigt werden.
> In den USA erfüllt die „Motion Picture Association of America" eine ähnliche Aufgabe. Hier werden folgende Klassifizierungen vergeben: **G (General)** - für jedes Alter geeignet; **PG (Parental Guidance)** - einige Szenen könnten für jüngere Kinder ungeeignet sein; „PG13" - einige Szenen könnten für Kinder unter 13 nicht geeignet sein; „R" **(Restricted)** - jeder unter 17 muss von einem Elternteil oder einer erwachsenen Aufsichtsperson begleitet werden; „NC-17" oder „X" - keine Jugendlichen unter 17.

movie (*esp US*) *in cpds* Film-; **movie camera** N Filmkamera *f*; **moviegoer** N Kinogänger(in) *m(f)*; **movie house** N Kino *nt*, Filmtheater *nt*; **movie star** N Filmstar *m*; **movie theater** N Kino *nt*

moving ['mu:vɪŋ] ADJ **a** (*= that moves*) beweglich **b** (*= causing emotion*) ergreifend; *tribute* rührend **c** (*Tech: = motive*) Antriebs-; **~ power** Antriebskraft *f*; **the ~ spirit** *or* **force** (*fig*) die treibende Kraft (*behind sth* hinter etw *dat*) **d** (*= of removal*) **~ costs/expenses** Umzugskosten *pl*

moving company N (*US*) Umzugsunternehmen *nt*

movingly ['mu:vɪŋlɪ] ADV ergreifend

moving: **moving pavement** N (*esp Brit*) Rollband *nt*; **moving sidewalk** N (*US*) Rollband *nt*; **moving staircase** N, **moving stairs** PL Rolltreppe *f*; **moving van** N (*US*) Möbelwagen *m*

mow[1] [məʊ] *pret* **mowed**, *ptp* **mown** *or* **mowed** VTI mähen

▶ **mow down** VT *sep* abmähen; (*fig: = slaughter*) niedermähen

mow[2] N (*US*) Heuhaufen *m*; (*= storing place*) Heuboden *m*

mower ['məʊə'] N (*= person*) Mäher *m*, Schnitter *m* (*old*); (*= machine: on farm*) Mähmaschine *f*; (*= lawnmower*) Rasenmäher *m*

mowing ['məʊɪŋ] N Mähen *nt*; **~ machine** Mähmaschine *f*

mown [məʊn] *ptp of* **mow**

moxie ['mɒksɪ] N (*US sl*) (*= verve, determination*) Power *f* (*inf*); (*= courage*) Mumm *f* (*inf*); (*= skill, know-how*) Fachwissen *nt*, Sachkenntnis *f*; **he's got the ~** er ist ein Powertyp (*inf*)

Mozambique [,məʊzəm'bi:k] N Mosambik *nt*, Moçambique *nt*

MP **a** *abbr of* **Member of Parliament** **b** *abbr of* **Military Police** **c** *abbr of* **Metropolitan Police**

MP3 N MP3; **~ player** MP3-Player *m*

mpg *abbr of* **miles per gallon**

mph *abbr of* **miles per hour**

MPhil *abbr of* **Master of Philosophy**

MPV *abbr of* **multipurpose vehicle**

Mr ['mɪstə'] *abbr of* **Mister** Herr *m*

MRC N (*Brit*) *abbr of* **Medical Research Council** *Organisation zur Förderung der medizinischen Forschung*

MRI *abbr of* **magnetic resonance imaging**

MRM *abbr of* **mechanically recovered meat**

MRP *abbr of* **manufacturer's recommended price**

Mrs ['mɪsɪz] *abbr of* **Mistress** Frau *f*

MRSA *abbr of* **methicillin-resistant Staphylococcus aureus** MRSA *m* (*Keim, gegen den die üblichen Antibiotika unwirksam sind*)

Mrs Mop ['mɪsɪz'mɒp] N (*dated Brit inf*) Putzfrau *f*

MS N *abbr of* **multiple sclerosis**

Ms [mɪz] N Frau *f* (*auch für Unverheiratete*)

> **Ms**
>
> **Ms** ist die schriftliche Anredeform für Frauen, mit der man die traditionelle Unterscheidung nach verheiratetem **(Mrs)** und unverheiratetem **(Miss)** Familienstand vermeidet. Es handelt sich dabei um die formale weibliche Entsprechung der männlichen Anrede **Mr.** Zunächst wurde **Ms** von vielen belächelt, doch heutzutage ist diese Anredeform weitverbreitet.

ms *abbr of* **manuscript** Ms, Mskr.

MSC (*Brit*) *abbr of* **Manpower Services Commission**

MSc *abbr of* **Master of Science**

MSF N (*Brit*) *abbr of* **Manufacturing, Science, Finance** *britische Angestelltengewerkschaft*

Msg *abbr of* **Monsignor** Msgr., Mgr.

MSP (*Brit Pol*) *abbr of* **Member of the Scottish Parliament** Mitglied *nt* des schottischen Parlaments

MSS, **mss** *abbr of* **manuscripts**

MT *abbr of* **machine translation**

Mt *abbr of* **Mount**

much [mʌtʃ] ADJ, N **a** viel *inv*; **how ~** wie viel *inv*; **not ~** nicht viel; **that ~** so viel; **but that ~ I do know** aber DAS weiß ich; **~ of this is true** viel *or* vieles daran ist wahr; **we don't see ~ of**

each other wir sehen uns nicht oft *or* nur selten; **he's/it's not up to ~** *(inf)* er/es ist nicht gerade berühmt *(inf)*; **I'm not ~ of a musician/cook/player** ich bin nicht sehr musikalisch/keine große Köchin/kein (besonders) guter Spieler; **not ~ of a choice** keine große Auswahl; **that wasn't ~ of a dinner/party** das Essen/die Party war nicht gerade besonders; **I find that a bit (too) ~ after all I've done for him** nach allem was ich für ihn getan habe, finde ich das ein ziemlich starkes Stück *(inf)*

b **too ~** *(in quantity, money etc, inf: = more than one can take)* zu viel *inv*; *(with emphatic too)* zu viel; *(inf) (= marvellous, hilarious)* Spitze *(sl)*; *(= ridiculous)* das Letzte *(inf)*; **to be too ~ for sb** *(in quantity)* zu viel für jdn sein; *(= too expensive)* jdm zu viel *or* zu teuer sein; **that insult was too ~ for me** die Beleidigung ging mir zu weit; **the sight of her face was too ~ for me** *(inf, = outrageous)* ihr Gesicht war zum Schreien *(inf)*; **he's just too ~** *(inf: = hilarious)* er ist zum Schießen *(inf)*; **these children are/this job is too ~ for me** ich bin den Kindern/der Arbeit nicht gewachsen; **he'd be too ~ for anybody** er wäre für jeden eine Zumutung; **he doesn't do too ~** er tut nicht übermäßig viel; **far too ~, too ~ by half** viel zu viel

c **(just) as ~** ebenso viel *inv*, genauso viel *inv*; **about/not as ~** ungefähr/nicht so viel; **three times as ~** dreimal so viel; **as ~ as you want/can** *etc* so viel du willst/kannst *etc*; **as ~ as possible** so viel wie möglich; **he spends as ~ as he earns** er gibt (genau)so viel aus, wie er verdient; **they hope to raise as ~ as £2m** sie hoffen, nicht weniger als zwei Millionen Pfund aufzubringen; **as ~ again** noch einmal so viel; **I feared/thought** *etc* **as ~** (genau) das habe ich befürchtet/mir gedacht *etc*; **it's as ~ as I can do to stand up** es fällt mir schwer genug aufzustehen; **as ~ as to say ...** was so viel heißt *or* bedeutet wie ...

d **so ~** so viel *inv*; *(emph so, with following that)* so viel; **it's not so ~ a problem of modernization as ...** es ist nicht so sehr ein Problem der Modernisierung, als ...; **you know so ~** du weißt so viel → *also* **so**

e **to make ~ of sb/sth** viel Wind um jdn/etw machen; **Glasgow makes ~ of its large number of parks** Glasgow rühmt sich seiner vielen Parks; **I couldn't make ~ of that chapter** mit dem Kapitel konnte ich nicht viel anfangen *(inf)*

ADV **a** *(with adj, adv)* viel; *(with vb)* sehr; *(with vb of physical action) drive, sleep, think, talk, laugh etc* viel; *come, visit, go out etc* oft, viel *(inf)*; **a ~-admired/-married woman** eine viel bewunderte/oft verheiratete Frau; **he was ~ dismayed/embarrassed** *etc* er war sehr bestürzt/verlegen *etc*; **so ~** so viel; so sehr; **too ~** zu viel, zu sehr; **I like it very/so ~** es gefällt mir sehr gut/so gut *or* so sehr; **I don't like him/it too ~** ich kann ihn/es nicht besonders leiden; **thank you very ~** vielen Dank; **thank you (ever) so ~** vielen herzlichen Dank; **I don't ~ care** *or* **care ~** es ist mir ziemlich egal; **however ~ he tries** sosehr *or* wie sehr er sich auch bemüht; **~ to my astonishment** sehr zu meinem Erstaunen; **~ as I should like to** so gern ich möchte; **~ as I like him** sosehr ich ihn mag; **there wasn't enough water to drink, ~ less wash in** es gab nicht genug Wasser zu trinken, ganz zu schweigen, um sich damit zu waschen → *also* **so**

b *(= by far)* weitaus, bei Weitem; **~ the biggest** weitaus *or* bei Weitem der/die/das größte; **I would ~ prefer to** *or* **~ rather stay** ich würde viel lieber bleiben

c *(= almost)* beinahe; **they are ~ of an age** *or* **~ the same age** sie sind fast *or* beinahe gleichaltrig; **they're (fairly) ~ the same size** sie sind beinahe *or* so ziemlich gleich groß; **they are produced in ~ the same way** sie werden auf sehr ähnliche Art hergestellt

muchness ['mʌtʃnɪs] N *(Brit inf)* **they're much of a ~** *(things)* das ist eins wie das andere; *(people)* sie sind einer wie der andere

mucilaginous [ˌmju:sɪ'lædʒɪnəs] ADJ klebrig

muck [mʌk] N **a** *(= dirt)* Dreck *m*; *(euph: = cat's/dog's muck)* Kot *m*; *(= manure)* Dung *m*, Mist *m*; *(= liquid manure)* Jauche *f*; **where there's ~, there's brass** *or* **money** *(Prov)* Dreck und Geld liegen nahe beisammen *(prov)* **b** *(fig) (= rubbish)* Mist *m*; *(= obscenities)* Schund *m*; *(= food etc)* Zeug *nt (inf)*; **Lord Muck** *(Brit hum inf)* Graf Rotz *(inf)*; **Lady Muck** *(Brit hum inf)* die feine Dame

▶ **muck about** *or* **around** *(Brit inf)* VT *sep* **a** **to muck sb about** mit jdm machen, was man will, jdn verarschen *(inf)*; *(by not committing oneself)* jdn hinhalten; **the travel agents really mucked us about** das war ein ewiges Hin und Her mit dem Reisebüro *(inf)*; **stop mucking me about!** sag mir endlich, woran ich bin *or* was los ist!

b *(= fiddle around with, spoil)* herumpfuschen an *(+dat) (inf)*; **to muck things about** alles durcheinanderbringen

VI **a** *(= lark about)* herumalbern *or* -blödeln *(inf)*; *(= do nothing in particular)* herumgammeln *(inf)*; **to muck about** *or* **around in boats** sich mit Booten beschäftigen; **to muck around (at) doing sth** Zeit damit vertrödeln, etw zu tun *(inf)*

b *(= tinker with)* herumfummeln *(with* an *+dat)*

c **to muck about** *or* **around with sb** jdn an der Nase herumführen *(inf)*

▶ **muck in** VI *(Brit inf)* mit anpacken *(inf)*

▶ **muck out** *(Brit)* VT *sep* (aus)misten VI ausmisten

▶ **muck up** VT *sep (Brit inf)* **a** *(= dirty)* dreckig machen *(inf)*; **you've really mucked up this place** ihr habt hier ja eine (ganz) schöne Schweinerei angerichtet! **b** *(= spoil)* vermasseln *(inf)*; *person (emotionally)* verkorksen *(inf)*; **that's really mucked me/my plans up** das hat mir alles/meine Pläne vermasselt *(inf)*

mucker ['mʌkə'] N **a** *(Brit inf)* Kumpel *m (inf)* **b** *(US inf)* ungehobelter Kerl, Bauer *m (inf)* **c** *(Min: = person who removes muck)* Lader *m*

muckiness ['mʌkɪnɪs] N Schmutzigkeit *f*

muck: **muckrake** VI *(fig inf)* im Schmutz wühlen; **muckraker** N *(fig inf)* Sensationshai *m (inf)*; **muckraking** N *(fig inf)* Sensationsmache(rei) *f (inf)* ADJ *(fig inf) person* sensationslüstern; **a ~ newspaper** ein Skandalblatt *nt*; **muck-spread** VI Mist streuen; **muck-spreading** N Miststreuen *nt*; **muck-up** N *(Brit inf)* Durcheinander *nt*; *(= fiasco)* Katastrophe *f*; **there's been a ~ with the invitations** bei den Einladungen hat jemand/habe ich *etc* Mist gemacht *(inf)*

mucky ['mʌkɪ] ADJ *(+er)* dreckig *(inf)*, schmutzig; *soil etc* matschig; **to get oneself/sth all ~** sich/etw ganz dreckig *(inf)* *or* schmutzig machen; **you ~ thing** *or* **pup!** *(Brit inf)* du Ferkel! *(inf)*; **keep your ~ paws off!** *(hum inf)* nimm deine dreckigen Pfoten weg! *(inf)*

mucous ['mju:kəs] ADJ schleimig, Schleim-; **~ secretion** Schleimabsonderung *f*

mucous membrane N Schleimhaut *f*

mucoviscidosis [ˌmju:kəʊvɪsɪ'dəʊsɪs] N *(Med)* Mukoviszidose *f*

mucus ['mju:kəs] N Schleim *m*

mud [mʌd] N **a** Schlamm *m*; *(on roads etc)* Matsch *m*; **(here's) ~ in your eye!** *(dated)* zum Wohl!, prösterchen! *(hum)*

b *(fig)* **his name is ~** *(inf)* er ist unten durch *(inf)*; **to drag sb/sb's name** *or* **reputation through the ~** jdn/jds guten Namen in den Schmutz zerren *or* ziehen; **to throw** *or* **sling ~** im Schmutz *or* Dreck *(inf)* wühlen; **to throw** *or* **sling ~ at sb** jdn mit Schmutz bewerfen; **to throw** *or* **sling ~ at sth** etw in den Dreck *(inf)* *or* Schmutz ziehen; **some of the ~ has stuck/is bound to stick** etwas ist hängen geblieben/bleibt immer hängen; **~ sticks** etwas bleibt immer hängen

mud: **mud bath** N Schlammbad *nt*; *(Med)* Moorbad *nt*; **mud-coloured** ADJ schmutzig grau

muddle ['mʌdl] N Durcheinander *nt*; **to get in(to) a ~** *(things)* durcheinandergeraten; *(person)* konfus werden; **to get oneself in(to) a ~ over sth** mit etw nicht klarkommen *(inf)*; **how did things get into such a ~?** wie ist denn dieses Durcheinander entstanden?; **to be in a ~** völlig durcheinander sein; **this room is (in) a real ~** in diesem Zimmer herrscht ein einziges Durcheinander; **her office was a ~ of files and papers** in ihrem Büro lagen Akten und Papiere wild durcheinander; **to make a ~ of sth** etw völlig durcheinanderbringen

VT durcheinanderbringen; *two things or people also* verwechseln; *(= make confused) person* verwirren, durcheinanderbringen; **you're only muddling the issue** du machst die Sache nur verworrener

▶ **muddle along** *or* **on** VI vor sich *(acc)* hinwursteln *(inf)*

▶ **muddle through** VI durchkommen, sich (irgendwie) durchwursteln *(inf)* *or* durchschlagen

▶ **muddle up** VT *sep* = **muddle VT**

muddled ['mʌdld] ADJ konfus; *person also* durcheinander *pred*; *thoughts, ideas also* verworren, wirr; **to get ~ (up)** *(things)* durcheinandergeraten; *(person)* konfus werden; **to be ~ about sth** verwirrt über etw *(acc)* sein; **set out in a ~ way** ziemlich konfus angelegt; **he has a rather ~ way of doing things** er macht alles ziemlich kompliziert; **in a ~ way it does make sense** es ist zwar verworren, ergibt aber doch einen Sinn

muddleheaded ['mʌdlˌhedɪd] ADJ *person* zerstreut; *ideas* konfus, verworren

muddler ['mʌdlə'] N *(= person)* Tölpel *m*, Dussel *m (inf)*

muddy ['mʌdɪ] ADJ *(+er)* **a** *floor, shoes, hands etc* schmutzig, schlammbeschmiert; *road, ground etc* schlammig, matschig; *liquid* schlammig, trübe; **to get sb/oneself/sth ~** jdn/sich/etw schmutzig machen *or* mit Schlamm beschmieren; **I'm all ~** ich bin ganz voll Schlamm **b** *(fig) complexion* gräulich schimmernd; *style* verworren VT schmutzig machen, mit Schlamm beschmieren; *water, river* verschlammen; *(fig: = confuse) situation, issue* verwirren, in Verwirrung bringen; **his explanation only helped to ~ the waters** durch seine Erklärung ist die Sache nur noch verworrener geworden

mud: **mudflap** N *(Aut etc)* Schmutzfänger *m*; **mud flat** N Watt(enmeer) *nt no pl*; **mudguard** N *(Brit) (on cycles)* Schutzblech *nt*; *(on cars)* Kotflügel *m*; **mud hut** N Lehmhütte *f*; **mudpack** N Schlammpackung *f*; **mud pie** N Kuchen *m (aus Sand, Erde etc)*; **mudslinger** N Dreckschleuder *f (inf)*; **mudslinging** N Schlechtmacherei *f*; **all that ~ before every election** diese gegenseitige Verunglimpfung vor jeder Wahl; **we've had enough ~** es ist genug im Schmutz *or* Dreck *(inf)* gewühlt worden ADJ **a ~ election campaign** ein Wahlkampf, der darin besteht, sich gegenseitig mit Schmutz zu bewerfen; **the election turned into a ~ match** die Wahlen arteten zur reinsten Schlammschlacht aus; **mud wrestling** N Schlammringen *nt*

muesli ['mju:zlɪ] N Müsli *nt*, Müesli *nt (Sw)*

muezzin [mu:'ezɪn] N Muezzin *m*

muff[1] [mʌf] N Muff *m*

muff[2] *(inf)* N **to make a ~ of = to muff** VT vermasseln *(inf)*, verpatzen *(inf)*; *exam also* verhauen *(inf)*; *question* danebenhauen *or* sich verhauen bei *(inf)*; *kick, shot, ball* danebensetzen *(inf)*; *lines, text, passage* verpatzen *(inf)*; **to ~ a catch** danebengreifen *(inf)*, schlecht fangen

muffin ['mʌfɪn] N **a** Muffin *m, kleiner, in Förmchen gebackener Kuchen* **b** *(Brit) weiches, flaches Milchbrötchen, meist warm gegessen*

muffle ['mʌfl] VT **a** *(= wrap warmly: also* **muffle up***) person* einmummen **b** *(= deaden) sound, shot etc* dämpfen; *noise* abschwächen; *shouts* ersticken; *bells, oars, drum* umwickeln

muffled [ˈmʌfld] ADJ *sound, voice etc* gedämpft; *shouts* erstickt; *drum, bells, oars* umwickelt; **a ~ conversation** eine Unterhaltung in gedämpftem Ton

muffler [ˈmʌflәʳ] N **a** *(= scarf)* (dicker) Schal **b** *(Tech)* Schalldämpfer *m*; *(US Aut)* Auspuff(-topf) *m*

mufti [ˈmʌftɪ] N *(= clothing)* Zivil(kleidung *f*) *nt*; **in ~** in Zivil

mug [mʌg] **N a** *(= cup)* Becher *m*; *(for beer)* Krug *m* **b** *(esp Brit inf: = dupe)* Trottel *m (inf)*; **have you found some ~ to do it?** hast du einen Dummen dafür gefunden? *(inf)*; **I was left looking a real ~** ich stand dann blöd da *(inf)*; **don't be such a ~** sei doch nicht so blöd *(inf)*; **to take sb for a ~** jdn für blöd halten *(inf)*; **that's a ~'s game** das ist doch schwachsinnig **c** *(inf: = face)* Visage *f (inf)* **VT a** *(= attack and rob)* überfallen **b** *(US sl: = photograph)* fotografieren

▶ **mug up** VT *sep* **a** *(Brit inf: also* **mug up on***)* **to mug sth/one's French up, to mug up on sth/one's French** etw/Französisch pauken *(inf)* **b to mug it up** *(US)* zu dick auftragen

mugger [ˈmʌgәʳ] N Straßenräuber(in) *m(f)*

mugging [ˈmʌgɪŋ] N Straßenraub *m no pl*; **a lot of ~s** viele Überfälle auf offener Straße

muggins [ˈmʌgɪnz] N *sing (Brit inf)* Blödmann *m (inf)*; **while ~ does all the work** und ich bin mal wieder der/die Dumme und kann die ganze Arbeit allein machen *(inf)*; **and ~ here forgot …** und ich Blödmann vergesse *(inf)* …, und der Blödmann hier vergisst *(inf)*

muggy [ˈmʌgɪ] ADJ *(+er)* schwül; *heat* drückend

mug shot N *(inf)* Verbrecherfoto *nt (inf)*

mugwump [ˈmʌgwʌmp] N *(US Pol)* Unabhängige(r) *mf*

Muhammad [muːˈhʌmʌd] N Mohammed *m*

Mujaheddin [ˌmuːdʒәheˈdiːn] N Mudschahed-din *m*

mulatto [mjuːˈlætәʊ] **ADJ** Mulatten-; *features* eines Mulatten/einer Mulattin; **~ child** Mulattenkind *nt* **N** *pl* **-es** Mulatte *m*, Mulattin *f*

mulberry [ˈmʌlbәrɪ] N *(= fruit)* Maulbeere *f*; *(= tree)* Maulbeerbaum *m*; *(= colour)* Aubergine *nt*, dunkles Violett

mulch [mʌltʃ] *(Hort)* **N** Krümelschicht *f*, Mulch *m (spec)* **VT** mulchen *(spec)*, abdecken

mulct [mʌlkt] VT **a** *(= fine)* mit einer Geldstrafe belegen *(form)* **b** *(= defraud)* **to ~ sb of sth** jdm etw abschwindeln

mule[1] [mjuːl] N **a** *(of donkey and mare)* Maultier *nt*; *(of stallion and donkey)* Maulesel *m* **b** *(inf: = person)* Maulesel *m*; **(as) stubborn as a ~** (so) störrisch wie ein Maulesel **c** *(Tech)* Selfaktor *m* **d** *(inf: = drugs courier)* Drogenkurier(in) *m(f)*

mule[2] N *(= slipper)* Schlappen *m (dial)*, Pantoffel *m*

mule skinner N *(US inf)* Maultiertreiber *m*

muleteer [ˌmjuːlɪˈtɪәʳ] N Maultiertreiber(in) *m(f)*

mule track N Saumpfad *m*

mulish [ˈmjuːlɪʃ] ADJ störrisch, stur

mulishly [ˈmjuːlɪʃlɪ] ADV stur, starrsinnig

mulishness [ˈmjuːlɪʃnɪs] N Starrsinn *m*, Sturheit *f*

mull [mʌl] VT *mit Zucker und Gewürzen ansetzen und erhitzen* **to ~ wine** Glühwein zubereiten

▶ **mull over** VT *sep* sich *(dat)* durch den Kopf gehen lassen

mullah [ˈmʌlә] N Mullah *m*

mulled wine [mʌld-] N Glühwein *m*

mullet [ˈmʌlɪt] N Meeräsche *f*

mulligatawny [ˌmʌlɪgәˈtɔːnɪ] N Currysuppe *f*

mullion [ˈmʌlɪәn] N **a** Längs- *or* Zwischenpfosten *m* **b mullions** PL *(in Gothic Archit)* Stabwerk *nt*

mullioned [ˈmʌlɪәnd] ADJ *window* längs unterteilt

multi [ˈmʌltɪ] N *(inf: = company)* Multi *m (inf)*

multi- PREF mehr-, Mehr-; *(with Latin stem in German)* Multi-, multi-; **multisyllabic** mehrsilbig; **multidisciplinary** multidisziplinär

multi: **multiaccess** ADJ *(Comput)* Mehrplatz-; **~ system** Mehrplatzsystem *nt*; **multiband** ADJ *(Telec)* Mehrband-; **~ radio** Mehrbandfunk *m*; **multicellular** ADJ viel- *or* mehrzellig; **multichannel** ADJ *(TV)* mehrkanalig, Mehrkanal-; **~ broadcasting** Mehrkanalfernsehen *nt*; **multicoloured**, *(US)* **multicolored** ADJ mehrfarbig; *material also, lights, decorations* bunt; *bird* bunt gefiedert; *fish* bunt schillernd; **multicultural** ADJ multikulturell; **multifaceted** ADJ vielseitig

multifarious [ˌmʌltɪˈfɛәrɪәs] ADJ vielfältig, mannigfaltig

multi: **multifocals** [ˈmʌltɪˌfәʊkәlz] PL Gleitsichtgläser *pl*; *(= spectacles)* Gleitsichtbrille *f*; **multifold** ADJ vielfältig; **multiform** ADJ vielgestaltig; **multifunctional** ADJ multifunktional; *(Comput)* Multifunktions-; **~ keyboard** Multifunktionstastatur *f*; **multigrade** ADJ **~ oil** Mehrbereichsöl *nt*; **multigym** N Multifunktionstrainer *m*; **multihull** N *(Naut)* Mehrkörperschiff *nt*; **multilateral** ADJ *(Pol)* multilateral; *(Math)* mehrseitig; **multilateralist** *(Pol)* **ADJ** *campaigner* für die multilaterale atomare Abrüstung **N** Befürworter(in) *m(f)* der multilateralen atomaren Abrüstung; **multilevel** ADJ *shopping centre etc* mehrstöckig; *(fig) marketing etc* mehrschichtig; **multilingual** ADJ mehrsprachig; **multimedia** ADJ multimedial; *(Comput etc)* Multimedia-; **~ presentation** Multimediapräsentation *f*; **multimillionaire** N Multimillionär(in) *m(f)*; **multinational N** multinationaler Konzern, Multi *m (inf)* **ADJ** multinational; *aid, effort* international; **~ state** Vielvölkerstaat *m*; **multipack** N Multipack *nt or m*; **multipage** ADJ *attr document* mehrseitig; **multiparty** ADJ *(Pol)* Mehrparteien-; **~ system** Mehrparteiensystem *nt*; **multiplane** N *(Aviat)* Mehrdecker *m*, Vieldecker *m*

multiple [ˈmʌltɪpl] **ADJ a** *(with sing n: = of several parts)* mehrfach; **~ collision** *or* **crash** Massenkarambolage *f* **b** *(with pl n: = many)* mehrere; **he died of ~ injuries** er erlag seinen zahlreichen Verletzungen **N a** *(Math)* Vielfache(s) *nt*; **eggs are usually sold in ~s of six** Eier werden gewöhnlich in Einheiten zu je sechs verkauft **b** *(Brit: = store)* Ladenkette *f*

multiple: **multiple birth** N Mehrlingsgeburt *f*; **multiple choice** N Multiple Choice *nt*; **multiple-column** ADJ *attr text, document* mehrspaltig *nt*; **multiple cropping** N mehrfache Bebauung; **multiple-entry visa** N *für wiederholte Einreisen gültiges Visum*; **multiple personality** N *(Psych)* alternierende Persönlichkeit; **~ disorder** Persönlichkeitsspaltung *f*; **multiple sclerosis** N multiple Sklerose; **multiple star** N *(Astron)* Sternhaufen *m*; **multiple store** N Ladenkette *f*; **multiple unit** N *(= train)* Triebwagen *m*; **multiple voting** N mehrfache Stimmabgabe

multiplex [ˈmʌltɪpleks] **N** *(= cinema)* Multiplexkino *nt* **ADJ** *(Tech)* Mehrfach-, Vielfach- **VI** *(Telec)* gleichzeitig senden

multiplexer, multiplexor [ˈmʌltɪpleksәʳ] N *(Telec)* Multiplexer *m*

multiplicand [ˌmʌltɪplɪˈkænd] N Multiplikand *m*

multiplication [ˌmʌltɪplɪˈkeɪʃәn] N **a** *(Math)* Multiplikation *f* **b** *(fig)* Vervielfachung *f*, Vermehrung *f*

multiplication: **multiplication sign** N *(Math)* Multiplikationszeichen *nt*; **multiplication table** N *(Math)* Multiplikationstabelle *f*; **he knows all his ~s** er kann das Einmaleins

multiplicity [ˌmʌltɪˈplɪsɪtɪ] N Vielzahl *f*, Fülle *f*; **for a ~ of reasons** aus vielerlei Gründen

multiplier [ˈmʌltɪplaɪәʳ] N *(Math)* Multiplikator *m*

multiply [ˈmʌltɪplaɪ] **VT a** *(Math)* multiplizieren, malnehmen; **to ~ 8 by 7** 8 mit 7 multiplizieren *or* malnehmen; **4 multiplied by 6 is 24** 4 mal 6 ist 24 **b** *(fig)* vervielfachen, vermehren **VI a** *(Math) (person)* multiplizieren; *(numbers)* sich multiplizieren lassen **b** *(fig)* zunehmen, sich vermehren *or* vervielfachen **c** *(= breed)* sich vermehren

multi: **multipurpose** ADJ Mehrzweck-; **~ gadget** Mehrzweckgerät *nt*; **~ cleaner** Allzweckreiniger *m*; **multipurpose vehicle** N Mehrzweckfahrzeug *nt*; **multiracial** ADJ gemischtrassig; **~ policy** Politik *f* der Rassenintegration; **~ school** Schule *f* ohne Rassentrennung; **multistage** ADJ Mehrstufen-; **~ rocket** Mehrstufenrakete *f*; **multistorey**, *(US)* **multistory** ADJ mehrstöckig; **~ flats** *(Brit)*, **multistory apartments** *(US)* (Wohn)hochhäuser *pl*; **~ building** Hochhaus *nt*; **~ car park** *(Brit)* Park(hoch)haus *nt*; **multistrike** ADJ *(Mil)* **~ capability** Fähigkeit *f* zum Angriff auf mehrere Ziele; **multitasking** N *(Comput)* Multitasking *nt*; **multitrack** ADJ mehrspurig; **~ recording** Mehrspuraufzeichnung *f*

multitude [ˈmʌltɪtjuːd] N Menge *f*; **a ~ of** eine Vielzahl von, eine Menge; *(of people also)* eine Schar (von); **for a ~ of reasons** aus vielerlei Gründen; **they came in their ~s** sie kamen scharenweise

multitudinous [ˌmʌltɪˈtjuːdɪnәs] ADJ zahlreich

multi-user [ˈmʌltɪˈjuːzәʳ] ADJ *(Comput)* Mehrplatz-, Mehrbenutzer-; **~ system** Mehrplatz- *or* Mehrbenutzersystem *nt*

mum[1] [mʌm] N, ADJ *(inf)* **~'s the word!** nichts verraten! *(inf)*; **to keep** *or* **stay ~** den Mund halten *(about* über *+acc) (inf)*

mum[2] N *(Brit inf) (= mother)* Mutter *f*; *(as address)* Mutti *f (inf)*

mum[3] N *(US inf: = chrysanthemum)* Chrysantheme *f*

Mumbai [ˈmʊmbaɪ] NT Mumbai *nt (new official name for Bombay)*

mumble [ˈmʌmbl] **N** Gemurmel *nt*, Murmeln *nt* **VT** murmeln; **he ~d the words** er nuschelte **VI** vor sich hin murmeln; *(= speak indistinctly)* nuscheln; **don't ~ (into your beard)** murm(e)le doch nicht so in deinen Bart

mumbler [ˈmʌmblәʳ] N **he's a real ~** er nuschelt so

mumblingly [ˈmʌmblɪŋlɪ] ADV undeutlich

mumbo jumbo [ˈmʌmbәʊˈdʒʌmbәʊ] N *(= empty ritual, superstition)* Hokuspokus *m*; *(= gibberish)* Kauderwelsch *nt*; *(= idol)* Abgott *m*

mummer [ˈmʌmәʳ] N *(old)* Mime *m (old)*

mummery [ˈmʌmәrɪ] N *(old)* Pantomimenspiel *nt*; *(fig)* Mummenschanz *m*

mummification [ˌmʌmɪfɪˈkeɪʃәn] N Mumifizierung *f*

mummify [ˈmʌmɪfaɪ] VTI mumifizieren

mummy[1] [ˈmʌmɪ] N *(= corpse)* Mumie *f*

mummy[2] N *(Brit inf: = mother)* Mami *f (inf)*, Mama *f (inf)*

mummy's boy [ˈmʌmɪzˌbɔɪ] N *(Brit inf)* Muttersöhnchen *nt (inf)*

mumps [mʌmps] N *sing* Mumps *m or f (inf) no art*

mumsy [ˈmʌmzɪ] ADJ *(inf)* mütterlich

munch [mʌntʃ] VTI mampfen *(inf)*

▶ **munch away** VI vor sich hin mampfen *(inf)*; **he was munching away on** *or* **at an apple** er mampfte einen Apfel *or* an einem Apfel

munchies [ˈmʌnʃɪz] PL *(US inf)* Knabberei *f (inf)*

mundane [ˌmʌnˈdeɪn] **ADJ** *(= worldly)* weltlich, profan; *(fig: = everyday)* alltäglich; *(pej) (= humdrum)* banal; *(= boring)* langweilig **N the ~** das Alltägliche

mundanely [ˌmʌnˈdeɪnlɪ] ADV weltlich; *(= in a down-to-earth way) remark, describe* nüchtern; **~ obvious** allzu offensichtlich

mundaneness [ˌmʌnˈdeɪnnɪs] N *(= worldliness)* Weltlichkeit *f*; *(= everyday nature)* Alltäglichkeit *f*; *(= humdrum nature)* Banalität *f*; *(= tediousness)* Langweiligkeit *f*

Munich ['mju:nɪk] N München *nt* ADJ *attr* Münchner

municipal [mju:'nɪsɪpəl] ADJ städtisch; **~ council** Stadt- *or* Gemeinderat *m*; **~ elections** Stadtrats- *or* Gemeinderatswahl *f*

municipality [mju:,nɪsɪ'pælɪtɪ] N (*= place*) Ort *m*, Gemeinde *f*; (*= council*) Stadt *f*, Gemeinde *f*

municipalization [,mju:nɪsɪpəlaɪ'zeɪʃən] N Übernahme *f* durch die Stadt *or* durch die Gemeinde

municipalize [,mju:'nɪsɪpəlaɪz] VT *bus service, baths etc* unter städtische Verwaltung *or* Gemeindeverwaltung bringen

municipally [mju:'nɪsɪpəlɪ] ADV von der Stadt *or* Gemeinde; **~ owned** im Besitz der Stadt *or* Gemeinde

municipal rates PL (*Brit*), **municipal taxes** PL (*US*) Gemeindesteuern *pl*, Gemeindeabgaben *pl*

munificence [mju:'nɪfɪsns] N (*form*) Großzügigkeit *f*, Generosität *f* (*geh*)

munificent [mju:'nɪfɪsnt] ADJ (*form*) großzügig; *person also* generös (*geh*)

munificently [mju:'nɪfɪsntlɪ] ADV (*form*) großzügig, generös (*geh*); **~ donated by ...** großzügigerweise gespendet von ...

muniments ['mju:nɪmənts] PL (*Jur, form*) Urkunde *f*

munition [mju:'nɪʃən] N *usu pl* Kriegsmaterial *nt no pl*, Waffen *pl* und Munition *f*

munitions dump [mju:'nɪʃənz'dʌmp] N (Waffen- und) Munitionslager *or* -depot *nt*

mural ['mjʊərəl] N Wandgemälde *nt* ADJ Wand-; **~ painting** Wandmalerei *f*

murder ['mɜːdəʳ] N **a** (*lit*) Mord *m*; **the ~ of John F. Kennedy** der Mord an John F. Kennedy, die Ermordung John F. Kennedys; **to stand accused of ~** unter Mordverdacht stehen
b (*fig inf*) **it was/it's ~** es war/ist mörderisch; **it'll be ~** es wird schrecklich werden; (*= exhausting also*) das ist glatter Mord (*inf*); **to scream blue** (*Brit*) *or* **bloody ~** Zeter und Mordio schreien, ein Mordsspektakel *or* -theater machen (*inf*); **to get away with ~** sich (*dat*) alles erlauben können
VT **a** (*lit*) ermorden, umbringen (*inf*); (*= slaughter*) morden; (*fig inf*) *opponents* haushoch schlagen
b (*inf: = ruin*) *music, play etc* verhunzen (*inf*)

murderer ['mɜːdərəʳ] N Mörder(in) *m(f)*

murderess ['mɜːdərɪs] N Mörderin *f*

murderous ['mɜːdərəs] ADJ **a** *villain, soldiers etc* mordgierig, blutrünstig; *weapon* mörderisch; **~ attack** Mordanschlag *m*; **~ intent** Mordabsicht *f*; **a ~ type** ein brutaler Typ; **there was a ~ look about him** er hatte etwas Brutales an sich; **he gave me a ~ look** er erdolchte mich mit Blicken; **once he had started on this ~ course** als er erst einmal den Weg der Gewalt eingeschlagen hatte **b** (*inf: = hellish*) *heat, conditions, traffic* mörderisch (*inf*)

murderously ['mɜːdərəslɪ] ADV mordgierig, blutdürstig; (*fig*) mörderisch; **a ~ cunning trap** eine teuflische Falle

murder: **murder trial** N Mordprozess *m*; **murder victim** N Mordopfer *nt*; **murder weapon** N Mordwaffe *f*

murk [mɜːk] N Düsternis *f*; (*in water*) trübes Wasser

murkily ['mɜːkɪlɪ] ADV trübe; **the wreck could be seen ~ through the muddy water** das Wrack zeichnete sich undeutlich im schlammigen Wasser ab

murkiness ['mɜːkɪnɪs] N **a** (*= gloominess*) Trübheit *f*; (*of room, street, sky*) Düsterheit *f*; (*of night*) Finsternis *f*, Dunkelheit *f* **b** (*= shady nature*) (*of character, deed*) Finsterkeit *f*; (*of past*) Dunkel *nt*

murky ['mɜːkɪ] ADJ (+*er*) **a** (*= gloomy*) trüb; *room, street* düster, dunkel; *night* finster; *sky* verhangen, düster; *water* trüb, schmutzig; *fog* dicht; *outline* unscharf, unklar; **~ brown/green** trüb-braun/-grün; **it's really ~ outside** draußen ist es so düster **b** (*= shady*) *character, deed* finster; *past* dunkel; **the ~ waters of politics** der Sumpf der Politik; **that's a pretty ~ area** das ist eine ziemlich undurchsichtige Sache

murmur ['mɜːməʳ] N (*= soft speech*) Murmeln *nt*, Raunen *nt* (*liter*); (*of discontent*) Murren *nt*; (*of water, wind, leaves, traffic*) Rauschen *nt*; **there was a ~ of approval/discontent** ein beifälliges/unzufriedenes Murmeln erhob sich; **a soft ~ of voices** gedämpftes Stimmengemurmel; **..., she said in a ~** ..., murmelte sie; **not a ~** kein Laut; **without a ~** ohne zu murren VT murmeln; (*with discontent*) murren VI murmeln; (*with discontent*) murren (*about, against* über +*acc*); (*fig*) rauschen

murmuring ['mɜːmərɪŋ] N Murmeln *nt no pl*; (*of water, wind, leaves*) Rauschen *nt no pl*; **~s (of discontent)** Unmutsäußerungen *pl* (*from* +*gen*); **do I hear ~? asked the chairman** irgendwelche Unstimmigkeiten? fragte der Vorsitzende

Murphy's Law ['mɜːfɪz,lɔː] N (*hum inf*) Murphys Gesetz *nt*, *„Gesetz", demzufolge eine Sache, die schiefgehen kann, auch bestimmt schiefgehen wird*

muscadel(le) [,mʌskə'del] N (*= wine*) Muskateller *m*

muscat ['mʌskət] N (*= grape*) Muskatellertraube *f*

muscatel [,mʌskə'tel] N (*= wine*) Muskateller *m*

muscle ['mʌsl] N Muskel *m*; (*fig: = power*) Macht *f*; **he's all ~** er besteht nur aus Muskeln, er ist sehr muskulös (gebaut); **to have financial ~** finanzstark *or* -kräftig sein; **he never moved a ~** er rührte sich nicht

▶ **muscle in** VI (*inf*) mitmischen (*inf*) (*on* bei); **to muscle in on sb's territory** jdm dazwischenfunken (*inf*)

muscle: **muscle-bound** ADJ (*inf: = muscular*) muskelbepackt (*inf*); **to be ~** ein Muskelpaket *m* sein (*inf*); **muscle building** N Muskelaufbau *m*; **muscle cramp** N Muskelkrampf *m*; **muscleman** N Muskelmann *m*, Muskelprotz *m* (*pej*); **muscle power** N Muskelkraft *f*

muscl(e)y ['mʌsəlɪ] ADJ (*inf*) muskulös, muskelbepackt (*inf*)

Muscovite ['mʌskəvaɪt] ADJ Moskauer; (*Hist*) moskowitisch N Moskauer(in) *m(f)*; (*Hist*) Moskowiter(in) *m(f)*

Muscovy ['mʌskəvɪ] N (*Hist*) Moskauer Staat *m*

Muscovy duck N (*Zool*) Moschusente *f*

muscular ['mʌskjʊləʳ] ADJ **a** (*= relating to muscles*) Muskel-, muskulär (*form*); **~ cramp** *or* **spasm** Muskelkrampf *m*; **~ control** Muskelbeherrschung *f*; **~ pains** Muskelschmerzen *pl* **b** (*= having strong muscles*) muskulös; **to be of ~ build** muskulös gebaut sein

muscular atrophy N Muskelatrophie *f*, Muskelschwund *m*

muscular dystrophy N Muskeldystrophie *f*, Muskelschwund *m*

musculature ['mʌskjʊlətʃəʳ] N Muskulatur *f*

Muse [mju:z] N (*Myth*) Muse *f*

muse [mju:z] VI nachgrübeln, nachsinnen (*liter*) (*about, on* über +*acc*) VT grüblerisch *or* sinnierend (*liter*) sagen N Muse *f*

museum [mju:'zɪəm] N Museum *nt*

museum piece N (*lit, hum*) Museumsstück *nt*

mush[1] [mʌʃ] N **a** Brei *m*; (*of fruit also*) Mus *nt* **b** (*inf*) Schmalz *m*; **he always sings such ~** er singt immer solche Schnulzen

mush[2] [mʊʃ] N (*Brit inf*) **a** (*= face*) Visage *f* (*inf*) **b** (*= person*) **hey, ~!** he, du da!

mushroom ['mʌʃrʊm] N (essbarer) Pilz; (*= button mushroom*) Champignon *m*; (*= atomic mushroom*) Pilz *m*; **a great ~ of smoke** ein großer Rauchpilz; **to spring up** *or* **sprout like ~s** wie die Pilze aus dem Boden schießen
ATTR **a** (*made of mushrooms*) Pilz-, Champignon-; **~ soup** Pilz- *or* Champignonsuppe *f*; **~ farm** Pilzzuchtbetrieb *m*; **~-picker** Pilzsammler(in) *m(f)*
b (*= mushroom-shaped*) pilzförmig
c (*= rapid and ephemeral*) *growth* sprunghaft
VI **a** **to go ~ing** in die Pilze gehen, Pilze sammeln (gehen)
b (*= grow rapidly*) wie die Pilze aus dem Boden schießen; **unemployment has ~ed** die Arbeitslosigkeit ist explosionsartig angestiegen; **to ~ into sth** sich rasch zu etw entwickeln

mushroom cloud N Atompilz *m*

mushroom town N Stadt, die aus dem Boden geschossen ist

mushy ['mʌʃɪ] ADJ (+*er*) **a** matschig; *liquid, consistency* breiig; (*= puréed*) *food, vegetables* püriert; **~ snow** Schneematsch *m*; **to go ~** zu Brei werden; (*= go off: fruit*) matschig werden **b** (*inf: = maudlin*) schmalzig

mushy peas PL Erbsenmus *nt*

music ['mju:zɪk] N Musik *f*; (*of voice*) Musikalität *f*; (*= written score*) Noten *pl*; **I can't read ~** ich kann keine Noten lesen; **do you use ~?** spielen/singen Sie nach Noten?; **to set** *or* **put sth to ~** etw vertonen; **it was (like) ~ to my ears** das war Musik für mich *or* in meinen Ohren; **to face the ~** (*fig*) dafür gradestehen

musical ['mju:zɪkəl] ADJ **a** (*of music*) musikalisch; **~ note** Note *f*; **~ evening** musikalischer Abend, Musikabend *m* **b** (*= tuneful*) melodisch **c** (*= musically-minded*) musikalisch N Musical *nt*

musical: **musical box** N Spieluhr *f or* -dose *f*; **musical chairs** N *sing* Reise *f* nach Jerusalem; **political ~** ein politisches Stühlerücken; **Labour and Tories play ~ in local government** Labour und die Konservativen wechseln sich in der Kommunalverwaltung ab; **musical director** N (*esp US*) (*of orchestra*) Chefdirigent(in) *m(f)*; (*of show*) musikalischer Leiter, musikalische Leiterin; **musical instrument** N Musikinstrument *nt*

musicality [,mju:zɪ'kælɪtɪ] N Musikalität *f*

musically ['mju:zɪkəlɪ] ADV **a** musikalisch; **I'm ~ trained** ich habe eine musikalische Ausbildung **b** (*= tunefully*) melodisch

musical score N (*written*) Partitur *f*; (*for film etc*) Musik *f*

music *in cpds* Musik-; **music box** N Spieldose *f or* -uhr *f*; **music centre** N Kompaktanlage *f*, Musikcenter *nt*; **music drama** N Musikdrama *nt*; **music hall** N Varieté *nt*, Varietee *nt*

musician [mju:'zɪʃən] N Musiker(in) *m(f)*

musicianship [mju:'zɪʃənʃɪp] N musikalisches Können

music lover N Musikliebhaber(in) *m(f)*

musicological [,mju:zɪkə'lɒdʒɪkəl] ADJ musikwissenschaftlich

musicologist [,mju:zɪ'kɒlədʒɪst] N Musikwissenschaftler(in) *m(f)*

musicology [,mju:zɪ'kɒlədʒɪ] N Musikwissenschaft *f*

music: **music paper** N Notenpapier *nt*; **music shop** N Musikalienhandlung *f*; **music stand** N Notenständer *m*; **music stool** N Klavierstuhl *m or* -hocker *m*; **music video** N Musikvideo *nt*

musing ['mju:zɪŋ] ADJ grüblerisch, nachdenklich, sinnierend (*liter*); *philosopher, book, article* gedankenvoll N Überlegungen *pl* (*on* zu)

musk [mʌsk] N **a** (*= secretion, smell*) Moschus *m* **b** (*Bot*) Moschuskraut *nt*

musk: **musk deer** N Moschustier *nt*, Moschushirsch *m*; **musk duck** N Moschusente *f*

musket ['mʌskɪt] N Muskete *f*

musketeer [,mʌskɪ'tɪəʳ] N Musketier *m*

musketry ['mʌskɪtrɪ] N (*= muskets*) Musketen *pl*; (*= troops*) Musketiere *pl*

musk: **muskmelon** N Zucker- *or* Gartenmelone *f*; **musk ox** N Moschusochse *m*; **muskrat** N Bisamratte *f*; **musk rose** N Moschusrose *f*

musky ['mʌskɪ] ADJ (+*er*) moschusartig *or* -ähnlich; **~ smell** *or* **scent** Moschusduft *m*

Muslim ['mʊzlɪm] ADJ mohammedanisch N Muslim(in) *m(f)*, Moslem(in) *m(f)*; *(= woman also)* Muslime *f*, Moslime *f*

muslin ['mʌzlɪn] N Musselin *m* ADJ aus Musselin

musquash ['mʌskwɒʃ] N Bisamratte *f*

muss [mʌs] *(US inf)* N Durcheinander *nt*; **to be in a ~** durcheinander *(inf)* or unordentlich sein VT *(also* **muss up***)* in Unordnung bringen; *hair, room also* durcheinanderbringen *(inf)*; **to get ~ed (up)** in Unordnung geraten

mussel ['mʌsl] N (Mies)muschel *f*; **~ bed** Muschelbank *f*

Mussulman ['mʌslmən] N *pl* **-mans** *(old)* Muselman(in) *m(f)*

mussy ['mʌsɪ] ADJ *(+er)* *(US inf)* unordentlich, durcheinander *pred (inf)*

must[1] [mʌst] ✪ 4, 9.5, 10.1, 15.1, 15.2 VB AUX *present tense only* **a** müssen; **you ~ (go and) see this church** Sie müssen sich *(dat)* diese Kirche unbedingt ansehen; **do it if you ~** tu, was du nicht lassen kannst; **if you ~ know** wenn du es unbedingt wissen willst; **~ you/I etc?** *(= really?)* ja (wirklich)?; *(= do you/I have to?)* muss das sein?; **we ~ away** *(old)* wir müssen fort

b *(in neg sentences)* dürfen; **I ~n't forget that** ich darf das nicht vergessen

c *(= be certain to)* **he ~ be there by now** er ist wohl inzwischen da; *(= is bound to)* er ist inzwischen bestimmt da, er muss (wohl) inzwischen da sein; **he (surely) ~ be there by now** er MUSS doch inzwischen da sein; **I ~ have lost it** ich habe es wohl verloren, ich muss es wohl verloren haben; *(with stress on must)* ich muss es verloren haben; **you ~ have heard of him** Sie haben bestimmt schon von ihm gehört; *(with stress on must)* Sie müssen doch schon von ihm gehört haben; **there ~ have been five of them** es müssen fünf gewesen sein; *(about five)* es waren wohl etwa fünf; *(at least five)* es waren bestimmt fünf; **he ~ be older than that** er muss älter sein; **there ~ be a reason for it** es gibt bestimmt eine Erklärung dafür; *(with stress on must)* es muss doch eine Erklärung dafür geben; **it ~ be about 3 o'clock** es wird wohl (so) etwa 3 Uhr sein, es muss so gegen 3 Uhr sein; **I ~ have been dreaming** da habe ich wohl geträumt; **I ~ have been mad** ich muss (wohl) wahnsinnig gewesen sein; **you ~ be crazy!** du bist ja *or* wohl wahnsinnig!

d *(showing annoyance)* müssen; **he ~ come just now** natürlich muss er gerade jetzt kommen

N *(inf)* Muss *nt*; **a sense of humour** *(Brit) or* **humor** *(US)***/an umbrella is a ~** man braucht unbedingt Humor/einen Schirm, Humor/ein Schirm ist unerlässlich; **tighter security is a ~** bessere Sicherheitskontrollen sind unerlässlich; **this novel/film is a ~ for everyone** diesen Roman/diesen Film muss man einfach *or* unbedingt gelesen/gesehen haben

must[2] N *(= mustiness)* Muffigkeit *f*

must[3] N *(Winemaking)* Most *m*

must- [mʌst] PREF *(inf)* **a ~see movie** ein Film, den man gesehen haben muss; **a ~read** ein Buch, das man gelesen haben muss; **it's a ~visit** dort muss man gewesen sein

mustache N *(US)* = **moustache**

mustachio [mʌ'stæʃɪəʊ] N *pl* **-s** Schnauzbart *m*

mustachioed [mʌ'stæʃɪəʊd] ADJ *(esp Brit)* schnauzbärtig

mustang ['mʌstæŋ] N Mustang *m*

mustard ['mʌstəd] N Senf *m*; *(= colour)* Senfgelb *nt*; **to be as keen as ~** Feuer und Flamme sein; **to cut the ~** *(inf)* es bringen *(sl)* ATTR Senf-; *(= yellow)* senffarben; **~ sauce** Senfsoße *f*

mustard *in cpds* Senf-; **mustard gas** N Senfgas *nt*; **mustard plaster** N Senfpackung *f*; **mustard powder** N Senfmehl *nt*; **mustard seeds** PL Senfkörner *pl*; **mustard yellow** N Senfgelb *nt*; **mustard-yellow** ADJ senfgelb

muster ['mʌstə'] N *(esp Mil: = assembly)* Appell *m*; *(= cattle muster)* Zusammentreiben *nt* der Herde; **to pass ~** *(fig)* den Anforderungen genügen; **~ station** *(on ship)* Sammelplatz *m* VT **a** *(= summon)* versammeln, zusammenrufen; *(esp Mil)* antreten lassen; *cattle* zusammentreiben; **the men were ~ed at 14.00** die Leute mussten um 14.00 Uhr zum Appell antreten **b** *(= manage to raise: also* **muster up***)* zusammenbekommen, aufbringen; *(fig) intelligence* aufbieten; *strength, courage* aufbringen; *all one's strength, courage* zusammennehmen VI sich versammeln; *(esp Mil)* (zum Appell) antreten

▸ **muster in** VT *sep (US) troops, recruits* einziehen

▸ **muster out** VT *sep (US) troops* entlassen

mustiness ['mʌstɪnɪs] N Modergeruch *m*

mustn't ['mʌsnt] *contr of* **must not**

must-read ADJ *(esp US)* **a must-read book** ein Buch, das man unbedingt gelesen haben muss

musty ['mʌstɪ] ADJ *(+er)* moderig; *air* muffig

mutability [,mju:tə'bɪlɪtɪ] N Wandlungsfähigkeit *f*, Mutabilität *f (spec)*

mutable ['mju:təbl] ADJ variabel, veränderlich; *(Biol)* mutabel

mutagen ['mju:tədʒən] N *(Biol)* Mutagen *nt*

mutant ['mju:tənt] N Mutante *f (spec)*, Mutation *f* ADJ mutierend

mutate [mju:'teɪt] VI sich verändern; *(Biol)* mutieren *(to* zu); *(Ling)* sich verwandeln *(to* in *+acc)*; **to ~ into sth** *(fig)* sich in etw *(acc)* verwandeln VT wandeln; *(Biol)* zu einer Mutation führen bei

mutation [mju:'teɪʃən] N *(= process)* Veränderung *f*; *(= result)* Variante *f*; *(Biol)* Mutation *f*; *(Ling)* Wandel *m (to* zu)

mute [mju:t] ADJ stumm *(also Ling)*; *amazement, rage* sprachlos; **~** *(Comput: command)* Ton aus; **to be ~ about sth** über etw *(acc)* schweigen; **to sit ~** schweigend dasitzen; **he was ~ with rage** er brachte vor Wut kein Wort heraus N **a** *(= dumb person)* Stumme(r) *mf* **b** *(= hired mourner)* Totenkläger *m*; *(= woman)* Klageweib *nt* **c** *(Mus)* Dämpfer *m* VT dämpfen

muted ['mju:tɪd] ADJ gedämpft; *(fig) criticism etc* leise, leicht

mute swan N Höckerschwan *m*

mutilate ['mju:tɪleɪt] VT *person, animal, story, play* verstümmeln; *painting, building etc* verschandeln *(inf)*

mutilation [,mju:tɪ'leɪʃən] N Verstümmelung *f*; *(of painting, building etc)* Verschandelung *f (inf)*

mutineer [,mju:tɪ'nɪə'] N Meuterer *m*, Meuterin *f*

mutinous ['mju:tɪnəs] ADJ *(Naut)* meuterisch, aufrührerisch; *(fig)* rebellisch

mutiny ['mju:tɪnɪ] *(Naut, fig)* N Meuterei *f* VI meutern

mutism ['mju:tɪzəm] N *(Psych)* Mutismus *m*

mutt [mʌt] N *(pej inf)* *(= dog)* Köter *m*; *(= idiot)* Dussel *m (inf)*

mutter ['mʌtə'] N Murmeln *nt*, Gemurmel *nt*; *(of discontent)* Murren *nt*; **a ~ of voices** ein Stimmengemurmel *nt*; **a ~ of discontent** ein unzufriedenes Murren VT murmeln, brummeln; **they ~ed their discontent** sie murrten unzufrieden; **are you ~ing threats at me?** höre ich Sie Drohungen (gegen mich) brummeln? VI murmeln; *(with discontent)* murren

muttering ['mʌtərɪŋ] N *(= act)* Gemurmel *nt*; *(with discontent)* Murren *nt*; *(= remark)* Gemurmel *nt no pl*, Meckerei *f (inf)*

mutton ['mʌtn] N Hammel(fleisch *nt*) *m*; **as dead as ~** mausetot *(inf)*; **she's ~ dressed (up) as lamb** *(inf)* sie macht auf jung *(inf)*

mutton: **muttonchops** PL *(= whiskers)* Koteletten *pl*; **muttonhead** N *(fig inf)* Schafskopf *m (inf)*

mutual ['mju:tjʊəl] ADJ *(= reciprocal) trust, respect, affection etc* gegenseitig; *(= bilateral) troop withdrawals, efforts, détente, satisfaction* beiderseitig; *(= shared, in common) interest, friends, dislikes etc* gemeinsam; **the divorce was by ~ consent** sie haben sich im gegenseitigen Einvernehmen scheiden lassen; **it would be for our ~ benefit** es wäre für uns beide von Vorteil *or* zu unser beider Nutzen *(form)*; **the feeling is ~** das beruht (ganz) auf Gegenseitigkeit; **I hate you! – the feeling is ~** ich hasse dich! – ganz meinerseits *(inf)*

mutual: **mutual fund** N *(US Fin)* Mutual Fund *m*, offener Investmentfonds; **mutual insurance** N Versicherung *f* auf Gegenseitigkeit

mutuality [,mju:tjʊ'ælɪtɪ] N Gegenseitigkeit *f*

mutually ['mju:tjʊəlɪ] ADV beide; *(= reciprocally) distrust* gegenseitig; *satisfactory, beneficial* für beide Seiten; *agreed, rejected* von beiden Seiten; **at a ~ convenient time** zu einem für beide Seiten annehmbaren Zeitpunkt; **~ contradictory** einander widersprechend; **a gentleman ~ known to us** ein Herr, den wir beide kennen; **~ assured destruction** *(Mil)* beiderseitige Bereitschaft zum nuklearen Gegenschlag

Muzak® ['mju:zæk] N funktionelle Musik, Berieselungsmusik *f (inf)*

muzziness ['mʌzɪnɪs] N *(= dizziness, dazed state)* Benommenheit *f*; *(= blurred state)* Verschwommenheit *f*; *(of noise)* Verzerrtheit *f*

muzzle ['mʌzl] N **a** *(= snout, mouth)* Maul *nt* **b** *(for dog etc)* Maulkorb *m* **c** *(of gun)* Mündung *f*; *(= barrel)* Lauf *m* VT *animal* einen Maulkorb um- *or* anlegen *(+dat)*; *(fig) critics, the press* mundtot machen; *criticism, protest* ersticken

muzzle: **muzzle-loader** N Vorderlader *m*; **muzzle-loading** ['mʌzl,ləʊdɪŋ] ADJ *gun* mit Vorderladung; **muzzle velocity** N Mündungs- *or* Auffangsgeschwindigkeit *f*

muzzy ['mʌzɪ] ADJ *(+er)* *(= dizzy, dazed)* benommen, benebelt; *(= blurred) view, memory etc* verschwommen; *noise* verzerrt

MVP N *(US Sport) abbr of* **most valuable player** bester Spieler, beste Spielerin

MW *abbr of* **medium wave** MW

my [maɪ] POSS ADJ mein; **I've hurt my leg/arm** ich habe mir das Bein/den Arm verletzt; **my father and mother** mein Vater und meine Mutter; **of course, my darling** natürlich, Liebling; **in my country** bei uns, in meinem Land *(form)*; **my God!** mein Gott!; **my goodness!** (du) meine Güte! INTERJ *(surprise)* (du) meine Güte, du liebe Zeit; *(delight)* ach, oh; **my, my, hasn't she grown!** nein so was, die ist vielleicht groß geworden

Myanmar ['maɪænma:'] N Myanmar *nt*

mycosis [maɪ'kəʊsɪs] N *(Med)* Mykose *nt (spec)*, Pilzkrankheit *f*

myna(h) bird ['maɪnə,bɜ:d] N Hirtenstar *m*

myocardial infarction ['maɪəʊ,ka:dɪəlɪn'fa:kʃən] N *(Med)* Myokardinfarkt *m*

myopia [maɪ'əʊpɪə] N Kurzsichtigkeit *f*, Myopie *f (spec)*

myopic [maɪ'ɒpɪk] ADJ kurzsichtig

myriad ['mɪrɪəd] N Myriade *f*; **a ~ of** Myriaden von ADJ *(= innumerable)* unzählige

myrrh [mɜ:'] N Myrr(h)e *f*

myrtle ['mɜ:tl] N Myrte *f*

myrtle-green ['mɜ:tl'gri:n] ADJ moosgrün

myself [maɪ'self] PERS PRON **a** *(dir obj, with prep +acc)* mich; *(indir obj, with prep +dat)* mir; **I said to ~** ich sagte mir; **singing to ~** vor mich hin singend; **I wanted to see (it) for ~** ich wollte es selbst *or* selber sehen; **I tried it out on ~** ich habe es an mir selbst *or* selber ausprobiert; **I addressed the letter to ~** ich habe den Brief an mich selbst adressiert

b *(emph)* (ich) selbst; **my wife and ~** meine Frau und ich; **I did it ~** ich habe es selbst gemacht; **I thought so ~** das habe ich auch gedacht; **… if I say so** *or* **it ~** … auch wenn ich es selbst sage; **(all) by ~** (ganz) allein(e); **I ~ believe that …, ~, I believe that …** ich persönlich *or* ich selbst bin der Ansicht, dass …; **~, I doubt it** ich persönlich *or* ich für meinen Teil bezweifle das

c *(= one's normal self)* **I'm not (feeling) ~ today** mit mir ist heute etwas nicht in Ordnung; *(healthwise also)* ich bin heute nicht ganz auf der Höhe; **I just tried to be ~** ich versuchte, mich ganz natürlich zu benehmen

mysterious [mɪˈstɪərɪəs] ADJ *(= puzzling)* rätselhaft, mysteriös; *(= secretive)* geheimnisvoll; *atmosphere, stranger* geheimnisvoll; **she is being quite ~ about it/him** sie macht ein großes Geheimnis daraus/um ihn; **why are you being so ~?** warum tust du so geheimnisvoll?; **for some ~ reason** aus unerfindlichen Gründen; **the Lord moves in ~ ways** die Wege des Herrn sind unergründlich

mysteriously [mɪˈstɪərɪəslɪ] ADV *vague, unwilling, pleased* sonderbar; *(= puzzlingly) vanish, change, die* auf rätselhafte *or* geheimnisvolle *or* mysteriöse Weise; *disappointed, missing* unerklärlicherweise; *(= secretively)* geheimnisvoll

mystery [ˈmɪstərɪ] N *(= puzzle)* Rätsel *nt*; *(= secret)* Geheimnis *nt*; **to be shrouded** *or* **surrounded in ~** von einem Geheimnis umwittert *or* umgeben sein; **there's no ~ about it** da ist überhaupt nichts Geheimnisvolles dabei; **it's a ~ to me** das ist mir schleierhaft *or* ein Rätsel; **don't make a great ~ of it!** mach doch kein so großes Geheimnis daraus!; **why all the ~?** was soll denn die Geheimnistuerei?

mystery: **mystery caller** N Testanrufer(in) *m(f)*; **mystery calling** N Testanruf *m*; **mystery model** N *(Aut)* Erlkönig *m (fig)*; **mystery monger** [ˈmɪstərɪˌmʌŋgəʳ] N Geheimniskrämer(in) *m(f)*; **mystery novel** N = **mystery story**; **mystery play** N Mysterienspiel *nt*; **mystery shopper** N Testkäufer(in) *m(f)*; **mystery shopping** N Testkauf *m*; **mystery story** N Kriminalgeschichte *f*, Krimi *m (inf)*; **mystery tour** N Fahrt *f* ins Blaue; **a ~ of the Black Forest** eine Entdeckungsreise durch den Schwarzwald; **mystery visitor** N Testbesucher(in) *m(f)*; **mystery writer** N Kriminalschriftsteller(in) *m(f)*

mystic [ˈmɪstɪk] **ADJ** mystisch; *writing, words, beauty also* geheimnisvoll **N** Mystiker(in) *m(f)*

mystical [ˈmɪstɪkəl] ADJ mystisch

mysticism [ˈmɪstɪsɪzəm] N Mystizismus *m*; *(of poetry etc)* Mystik *f*, Mystische(s) *nt*

mystification [ˌmɪstɪfɪˈkeɪʃən] N *(= bafflement)* Verwunderung *f*, Verblüffung *f*; *(= act of bewildering)* Verwirrung *f*

mystified [ˈmɪstɪfaɪd] ADJ *person, look, frown* verblüfft; **she was ~ about it** es verblüffte sie, es war ihr rätselhaft *or* ein Rätsel; **I am ~ as to how this could happen** es ist mir ein Rätsel, wie das passieren konnte

mystify [ˈmɪstɪfaɪ] VT vor ein Rätsel stellen; **his explanation mystified us all** seine Erklärung blieb uns allen ein Rätsel; **the conjurer's tricks mystified the audience** die Kunststücke des Zauberers verblüfften das Publikum

mystifying [ˈmɪstɪfaɪɪŋ] ADJ unerklärlich, rätselhaft

mystique [mɪˈstiːk] N geheimnisvoller Nimbus; **modern women have little ~, there is little ~ about modern women** die moderne Frau hat wenig Geheimnisvolles an sich

myth [mɪθ] N Mythos *m*; *(fig)* Märchen *nt*; **it's a ~** *(fig)* das ist doch ein Gerücht *or* Märchen

mythic [ˈmɪθɪk] ADJ = **mythical a, b**

mythical [ˈmɪθɪkəl] ADJ **a** *(of myth)* mythisch; **the ~ figure/character of Arthur** die mythische Artusfigur, die Sagengestalt des Artus **b** *(= fantastic) proportions, status, figure* legendär; **their rivalry has taken on ~ proportions** ihre Rivalität ist zur Legende geworden **c** *(= unreal) figure, world* fantastisch, phantastisch; *(= invented)* erfunden

mythological [ˌmɪθəˈlɒdʒɪkəl] ADJ mythologisch

mythology [mɪˈθɒlədʒɪ] N Mythologie *f*

myxomatosis [ˌmɪksəʊməˈtəʊsɪs] N Myxomatose *f*

N

N, n [en] N N *nt*, n *nt*

N *abbr of* **north** N

n **a** *(Math)* n **b** **'n** *(inf)* = **and** **c** *(inf: = many)* x *(inf)*; **n times** x-mal *(inf)*

n **a** *abbr of* **noun** Subst. **b** *abbr of* **neuter** nt

n/a *abbr of* **not applicable** entf.

NAACP *(US) abbr of* **National Association for the Advancement of Colored People** *Vereinigung zur Förderung Farbiger*

Naafi ['næfɪ] *abbr of* **Navy, Army and Air Force Institutes** *(= shop) Laden der britischen Armee (= canteen) Kantine der britischen Armee*

nab [næb] VT *(inf)* **a** *(= catch)* erwischen; *(police)* schnappen *(inf)*, erwischen *(inf)*; **the police ~bed him when he …** die Polizei hat ihn dabei erwischt, wie er … *(inf)* **b** *(= take for oneself)* sich *(dat)* grapschen *(inf)*; **somebody had ~bed my seat** mir hatte jemand den Platz geklaut *(inf)*

nabob ['neɪbɒb] N Nabob *m*; *(fig also)* Krösus *m*

nacelle [næ'sel] N **a** *(on aeroplane)* (Flugzeug)-rumpf *m* **b** *(= gondola) (on airship)* (Luftschiff) gondel *f*; *(on balloon)* (Ballon)korb *m*

nacre ['neɪkəʳ] N Perlmutter *f or nt*, Perlmutt *nt*

nacreous ['neɪkriːəs] ADJ perlmutterartig, Perlmutt(er)-

nadir ['neɪdɪəʳ] N **a** *(Astron)* Nadir *m*, Fußpunkt *m* **b** *(fig)* Tiefstpunkt *m*; **the ~ of despair** tiefste Verzweiflung

naff [næf] ADJ *(Brit inf)* **a** *(= stupid) idea, thing to do, suggestion* blöd *(inf)* **b** *(= not much use) management, company* lahm *(inf)*; *computer, gadget etc* nutzlos; **this new monitor's a bit ~** dieser neue Monitor bringts nicht *(inf) or* ist nicht das Wahre *(inf)* **c** *(= not perceived as good style) colour, jacket, tie, design, book cover, car* ordinär; **it looks a bit ~, doesn't it?** es sieht nicht gerade schick aus, oder?

▶ **naff off** VI *(Brit inf)* verschwinden *(inf)*; **naff off!** *(= go away)* hau ab! *(inf)*; *(expressing refusal)* du spinnst wohl!

naffing ['næfɪŋ] ADJ *(Brit inf)* verdammt *(inf)*

NAFTA ['næftə] N *abbr of* **North American Free Trade Agreement** NAFTA *f*

nag¹ [næg] VT *(= find fault with)* herumnörgeln an *(+dat)*; *(= pester)* keine Ruhe lassen *(+dat)* (for wegen); **she's forever ~ging me** sie nörgelt immerzu an mir herum, sie hat dauernd etwas an mir auszusetzen; **don't ~ me** nun lass mich doch in Ruhe!; **to ~ sb about sth** jdm wegen etw keine Ruhe lassen; **to ~ sb to do sth** jdm schwer zusetzen *or* die Hölle heißmachen, damit er etw tut; **she kept on ~ging him until he did it** sie hat ihm solange zugesetzt *or* keine Ruhe gelassen, bis er es machte; **one thing that's been ~ging me for some time is …** was mich schon seit einiger Zeit plagt *or* nicht in Ruhe lässt, ist …

VI *(= find fault)* herumnörgeln, meckern *(inf)*; *(= be insistent)* keine Ruhe geben; **to ~ at sb** an jdm herumnörgeln, jdm keine Ruhe lassen; **stop ~ging** hör auf zu meckern *(inf)*

N *(= fault-finder)* Nörgler(in) *m(f)*; *(= woman also)* Meckerliese *f (inf)*, Meckerziege *f (inf)*; *(= man also)* Meckerfritze *m (inf)*; *(pestering)* Quälgeist *m*; **don't be a ~** nun meckre nicht immer *(inf)*

nag² N *(= old horse)* Klepper *m*, Mähre *f*; *(inf: = horse)* Gaul *m*

nagger ['nægəʳ] N = **nag¹ N**

nagging ['nægɪŋ] ADJ **a** *wife, voice* meckernd *(inf)*, nörglerisch; *(= pestering)* ewig drängend **b** *pain* dumpf; *worry, doubt* quälend; *question* brennend; *fear* drückend N *(= fault-finding)* Meckern *nt (inf)*, Nörgelei *f*; *(= pestering)* ewiges Drängen

nah [nɑː] INTERJ *(Brit inf)* nein, nee *(inf)*

NAHT *(Brit) abbr of* **National Association of Head Teachers**

naiad ['naɪæd] N Najade *f*, Wassernymphe *f*

NAICS *abbr of* **North American Industry Classification System** ≈ DIN®

nail [neɪl] N **a** *(Anat)* Nagel *m* **b** *(Tech)* Nagel *m*; **as hard as ~s** knallhart *(inf)*, (unheimlich) hart; *(physically)* zäh wie Leder; **on the ~** *(Brit fig inf)* auf der Stelle, sofort; **cash on the ~** *(Brit inf)* Bargeld *nt*; **to hit the ~ (right) on the head** *(fig)* den Nagel auf den Kopf treffen; **to drive a ~ into sb's coffin** *(fig)* **to be a ~ in sb's coffin** *(fig)* ein Nagel zu jds Sarg sein

VT **a** *(= fix with nails, put nails into)* nageln; **to ~ sth to the floor/door/wall** etw an den Boden/an die Tür/Wand nageln, etw auf dem Boden/an der Tür/Wand festnageln; **~ this on here** nageln Sie das hier an *or* fest; **he ~ed his opponent to the canvas** er pinnte seinen Gegner auf die Matte *(inf)*

b *(fig) person* festnageln; **fear ~ed him to the spot** er war vor Furcht wie auf der Stelle festgenagelt; **they ~ed the deal** sie haben den Handel unter Dach und Fach gebracht; **to ~ a lie** eine Lüge entlarven *or* entblößen

c *(inf)* **to ~ sb** sich *(dat)* jdn schnappen *(inf)*; *(= charge)* jdn drankriegen *(inf)*

▶ **nail down** VT *sep* **a** *(lit) box* zunageln; *carpet, lid* festnageln **b** *(fig) person* festnageln (to auf *+acc*); **I nailed him down to coming at 6 o'clock** ich nagelte ihn auf 6 Uhr fest

▶ **nail up** VT *sep picture etc* annageln; *door, window* vernageln; *box* zunageln

nail *in cpds* Nagel-; **nailbiter** N **a** Nägelkauer(in) *m(f)* **b** *(inf: = Film)* spannender Film; *(= book)* spannendes Buch; **nail-biting** N Nägelkauen *nt* ADJ *(inf) suspense* atemlos; *match* spannungsgeladen; **it's a ~ time for them** sie machen eine spannungsreiche Zeit durch; **nailbrush** N Nagelbürste *f*; **nail clippers** PL Nagelzwicker *m*; **nailfile** N Nagelfeile *f*; **nail hardener** N Nagelhärter *m*; **nail polish** N Nagellack *m*; **nail polish remover** N Nagellackentferner *m*; **nail scissors** PL Nagelschere *f*; **nail varnish** N *(Brit)* Nagellack *m*; **nail varnish remover** N Nagellackentferner *m*

naïve [naɪ'iːv] ADJ *(+er)* naiv *(also Art)*; *person, remark also* einfältig

naïvely [naɪ'iːvlɪ] ADV naiv; **he ~ believed me** er war so naiv, mir zu glauben, in seiner Einfalt glaubte er mir; **I ~ thought that …** naiverweise dachte ich, dass …

naïveté [naɪ'iːvteɪ], **naïvety** [naɪ'iːvɪtɪ] N Naivität *f*; *(of person also)* Einfalt *f*

naked ['neɪkɪd] ADJ **a** *person* nackt, unbekleidet, bloß *(liter)*; *animal (= without fur)* ohne Fell; *bird (= without feathers)* federlos; *branch* nackt, kahl; *countryside* kahl; *sword* bloß, blank, nackt; *flame, light* ungeschützt; *wire* blank; **to go ~** nackt gehen; **~ to the waist** mit freiem *or* nacktem Oberkörper; **I feel ~ without my wristwatch/make-up** ich fühle mich ohne meine Armbanduhr/ohne Make-up ganz nackt; **(as) ~ as nature intended** *(hum, man)* im Adamskostüm *(hum)*; *woman* im Evaskostüm *(hum)*; **(as) ~ as the day (that) he was born** splitterfasernackt *(hum)*; **the ~ eye** das bloße Auge; **visible/invisible to the ~ eye** mit bloßem Auge erkennbar/nicht erkennbar; **a room with one ~ bulb** ein Zimmer, in dem nur eine Glühbirne hing

b *(= defenceless)* schutzlos; **the President/army was left ~** der Präsident/das Heer stand schutzlos da

c *(= pure) truth, facts, aggression* nackt; *hatred, misery, anxiety* blank, nackt

nakedly ['neɪkɪdlɪ] ADV **a** *(= unashamedly)* offen; **the new government is far more ~ military than the old** die neue Regierung zeigt ihren militärischen Charakter viel offener als die alte **b** *(= utterly) alone* vollkommen **c** *(= without clothes)* nackt; **a mass of bodies, writhing ~** eine Masse nackter, sich wälzender Körper

nakedness ['neɪkɪdnɪs] N Nacktheit *f*, Blöße *f (liter)*

NALGO ['nælgəʊ] *(Brit) abbr of* **National and Local Government Officers' Association** *Gewerkschaft der staatlichen und kommunalen Verwaltungsangestellten*

Nam [næm] N *(US) abbr of* **Vietnam**

namby-pamby ['næmbɪ'pæmbɪ] *(esp Brit inf)* N Mutterkind *nt*; *(= boy also)* Muttersöhnchen *nt* ADJ *person* verweichlicht, verzärtelt *(inf)*; *(= indecisive)* unentschlossen

name [neɪm] N **a** Name *m*; **what's your ~?** wie heißen Sie?, wie ist Ihr Name? *(form)*; **my ~ is …** ich heiße …, mein Name ist … *(form)*; **what's the ~ of this street?** wie heißt diese Straße?; **this man, Smith by ~** dieser Mann namens Smith; **a man (going) by the ~ of Gunn** ein Mann namens *or* mit Namen Gunn; **I know him only by ~** ich kenne ihn nur dem Namen nach; **he knows all his customers by ~** er kennt alle seine Kunden bei Namen; **to refer to sb/sth by ~** jdn/etw namentlich *or* mit Namen nennen; **in ~ alone** *or* **only** nur dem Namen nach; **a marriage in ~ only** eine nur auf dem Papier bestehende Ehe; **I won't mention any ~s** ich möchte keine Namen nennen; **he writes under the ~ of X** er schreibt unter dem Namen X; **fill in your ~(s) and address(es)** Namen und Adresse eintragen; **they married to give the child a ~** sie haben geheiratet, damit das Kind einen Namen hatte; **what ~ shall I say?** wie ist Ihr Name, bitte?; *(on telephone)* wer ist am Apparat?; *(before showing sb in)* wen darf ich melden?; **to have one's ~ taken** *(Ftbl, Police etc)* aufgeschrieben werden; **in the ~ of** im Namen *(+gen)*; **stop in the ~ of the law** halt, im Namen des Gesetzes; **in the ~ of goodness/God** um Himmels/Gottes willen; **what in God's ~ …** was in Gottes Namen …; **all the big ~s were there** alle großen Namen waren da; **I'll put my/your ~ down** *(on list, in register etc)* ich trage mich/dich ein; *(for school, class, excursion, compe-*

tition etc) ich melde mich/dich an *(for* zu, *for a school* in einer Schule); *(for tickets, goods etc)* ich lasse mich/dich vormerken; *(on waiting list)* ich lasse mich *or* meinen Namen/dich *or* deinen Namen auf die Warteliste setzen; **I'll put your ~ down, Sir/Madam** ich werde Sie vormerken; **to call sb ~s** jdn beschimpfen; **you can call me all the ~s you like …** du kannst mich nennen, was du willst …; **not to have a penny/cent to one's ~** völlig pleite sein *(inf)*, keinen roten Heller haben *(dated)*; **what's in a ~?** was ist *or* bedeutet schon ein Name?, Name ist Schall und Rauch *(Prov)*; **in all but ~** praktisch; **that's the ~ of the game** *(inf)* darum geht es; **for these people survival is the ~ of the game** diesen Leuten geht es ums Überleben; **I'll do it or my ~'s not Bob Brown** ich mache das, so wahr ich Bob Brown heiße

b *(= reputation)* Name *m*, Ruf *m*; **to have a good/bad ~** einen guten/schlechten Ruf *or* Namen haben; **to get a bad ~** in Verruf kommen; **to give sb a bad ~** jdn in Verruf bringen; **to protect one's good ~** seinen Ruf *or* guten Namen wahren; **to make one's ~ as, to make a ~ for oneself as** sich *(dat)* einen Namen machen als; **to make one's ~** berühmt werden; **this book made his ~** mit diesem Buch machte er sich einen Namen; **to have a ~ for sth** für etw bekannt sein

c *(= important person)* Persönlichkeit *f*

d *(Brit: = Lloyd's investor)* Lloyd's-Gesellschafter(in) *m(f)*

VT a *(= call by a name, give a name to) person* nennen; *plant, new star etc* benennen, einen Namen geben *(+dat)*; *ship* taufen, einen Namen geben *(+dat)*; **I ~ this child/ship X** ich taufe dieses Kind/Schiff auf den Namen X; **a person ~d Smith** jemand namens *or* mit Namen Smith; **the child is ~d Peter** das Kind hat den *or* hört auf den Namen Peter; **to ~ a child after** *or (US)* **for sb** ein Kind nach jdm nennen; **to ~ sb as a witness** jdn als Zeugen/Zeugin nennen; **he was ~d as the thief/culprit/victim** er wurde als der Dieb/der Schuldige/das Opfer genannt *or* bezeichnet; **they refused to ~ the victim** sie hielten den Namen des Opfers geheim; **to ~ ~s** Namen nennen

b *(= appoint, nominate)* ernennen; **to ~ sb mayor/as leader** jdn zum Bürgermeister/Führer ernennen; **to ~ sb for the post of mayor** jdn für das Amt des Bürgermeisters vorschlagen; **he has been ~d as Nobel Prize winner** ihm wurde der Nobelpreis verliehen; **they ~d her as the winner of the award** sie haben ihr den Preis verliehen; **to ~ sb as one's heir** jdn zu seinem Erben bestimmen

c *(= describe, designate)* **to ~ sb (as) sth** jdn als etw bezeichnen

d *(= specify, list)* nennen; **~ the main plays by Shakespeare** nenne mir die wichtigsten Dramen Shakespeares; **~ your price** nennen Sie Ihren Preis; **to ~ the day** *(inf)* den Hochzeitstag festsetzen; **~ the date and I'll be there** bestimmen Sie den Tag, und ich werde da sein; **you ~ it, they have it/he's done it** es gibt nichts, was sie nicht haben/was er noch nicht gemacht hat

name-calling [ˈneɪmˌkɔːlɪŋ] N Beschimpfung(en) *f(pl)*, Schimpferei(en) *f(pl)*

-named [-neɪmd] ADJ *suf* genannt; **the first-/last--named** der Erst-/Letztgenannte, der zuerst/zuletzt Genannte

name: name day N Namenstag *m*; **name--drop** VI *(inf)* berühmte Bekannte in die Unterhaltung einfließen lassen; **she's always ~ping** sie muss dauernd erwähnen, wen sie alles kennt; **name-dropper** N *(inf)* **he's a terrible ~** er muss dauernd erwähnen, wen er alles kennt; **name-dropping** N *(inf)* Angeberei *f* mit berühmten Bekannten; **his constant ~ is most tedious** es ist nicht auszuhalten, wie er ständig mit berühmten Namen um sich wirft; **nameless** ADJ **a** *(= unknown) person* unbekannt **b** *(= undesignated)* namenlos; *grave* anonym; **a person who shall be/remain ~** jemand, der nicht genannt werden soll/der ungenannt bleiben soll **c** *(= undefined) sensation, emotion* unbeschreiblich; *longing, terror, suffering also* namenlos **d** *(= shocking) vice, crime* unaussprechlich

namely [ˈneɪmlɪ] ADV nämlich

name: namepart N Titelrolle *f*; **nameplate** N Namensschild *nt*; *(on door also)* Türschild *nt*; *(on business premises)* Firmenschild *nt*; **namesake** N Namensvetter(in) *m(f)*; **name tag** N *(= badge)* Namensschild *nt*; **nametape** N Wäschezeichen *nt*

Namibia [næˈmɪbɪə] N Namibia *nt*

Namibian [næˈmɪbɪən] ADJ namibisch

naming [ˈneɪmɪŋ] N Namen(s)gebung *f*

nan(a) [ˈnæn(ə)] N Oma *f (inf)*

nana [ˈnɑːnə] N *(inf)* Trottel *m (inf)*

nan bread [ˈnɑːnˈbred] N *warm serviertes, fladenförmiges Weißbrot als Beilage zu indischen Fleisch- und Gemüsegerichten*

nancy [ˈnænsɪ] N, **nancy-boy** N *(dated esp Brit inf)* **a** *(= homosexual)* Schwule(r) *m* **b** *(= softy)* Weichling *m (pej)*

nankeen [nænˈkiːn] N, *no pl (= cloth)* Nanking(-stoff) *m*

nanny [ˈnænɪ] N **a** Kindermädchen *nt* **b** *(inf: also* **nana**) Oma *f*, Omi *f (inf)* **c** *(also* **nanny goat**) Geiß *f*, Ziege *f*

nannying [ˈnænɪɪŋ] N **a** *(= job)* Arbeit *f* als Kindermädchen **b** *(pej: = mollycoddling)* Bemutterung *f* ADJ *(pej)* bemutternd; **stupid, ~ legislation** dumme Gesetze, die die Bürger bevormunden wollen

nanny state N *(esp Brit pej)* Bevormundungsstaat *m*; *(all-providing)* Versorgerstaat *m*

nanosecond [ˈnænəʊˌsekənd] N Nanosekunde *f*

nanotechnology [ˌnænəʊtekˈnɒlədʒɪ] N Nanotechnologie *f*

nap[1] [næp] **N** Schläfchen *nt*, Nickerchen *nt*; **afternoon ~** Nachmittagsschläfchen *nt*; **to have** *or* **take a ~** ein Schläfchen *or* ein Nickerchen machen; **he always has** *or* **takes a 20 minute ~ after lunch** nach dem Mittagessen legt er sich immer 20 Minuten aufs Ohr *or* hin **VI** **to catch sb ~ping** *(fig)* jdn überrumpeln

nap[2] N *(Tex)* Flor *m*; *(Sew)* Strich *m*

nap[3] *(Racing)* **VT** *winner, horse* setzen auf *(+acc)* **N** Tip *m*; **to select a ~** auf ein bestimmtes Pferd setzen

napalm [ˈneɪpɑːm] **N** Napalm® *nt* **VT** mit Napalm bewerfen

napalm: napalm bomb N Napalmbombe *f*; **napalm bombing** N Abwurf *m* von Napalmbomben

nape [neɪp] N **~ of the/one's neck** Nacken *m*, Genick *nt*

naphtha [ˈnæfθə] N Naphtha *nt or f*

naphthalene [ˈnæfθəliːn] N Naphthalin *nt*

napkin [ˈnæpkɪn] N **a** *(= table napkin)* Serviette *f*, Mundtuch *nt (old)* **b** *(for baby)* Windel *f*; *(US: = sanitary napkin)* (Damen)binde *f*

napkin ring N Serviettenring *m*

Naples [ˈneɪplz] N Neapel *nt*

Napoleon [nəˈpəʊlɪən] N Napoleon *m*

Napoleonic [nəˌpəʊlɪˈɒnɪk] ADJ napoleonisch

nappa [ˈnæpəˈ] N Nappa(leder) *nt*

napper [ˈnæpəˈ] N *(Brit inf: = a person's head)* Birne *f (inf)*

nappy [ˈnæpɪ] N *(Brit)* Windel *f*

nappy rash N Wundsein *nt*, Windeldermatitis *f (spec)*; **little Jonathan's got ~** der kleine Jonathan ist wund

narc [nɑːk] N *(US sl)* Rauschgiftfahnder(in) *m(f)*

narcissi [nɑːˈsɪsaɪ] *pl of* **narcissus**

narcissism [nɑːˈsɪsɪzəm] N Narzissmus *m*

narcissistic [ˌnɑːsɪˈsɪstɪk] ADJ narzisstisch

narcissus [nɑːˈsɪsəs] N **a** *pl* **narcissi** *(Bot)* Narzisse *f* **b** *(Myth)* **Narcissus** Narziss *m*

narcosis [nɑːˈkəʊsɪs] N Narkose *f*

narco-terrorism [ˌnɑːkəʊˈterəˌrɪzəm] N Narkoterrorismus *m*

narcotic [nɑːˈkɒtɪk] **ADJ a ~ substance/drug** Rauschgift *nt* **b** *(Med)* narkotisch **N a** Rauschgift *nt*; **~s** Rauschgift *nt*; *(= illegal drugs also)* Drogen *pl*; **~s industry** Drogenindustrie *f*; **the ~s squad** das Rauschgiftdezernat; **~s offence** Drogendelikt *nt*; **to be on a ~s charge** wegen eines Drogendelikts angeklagt sein **b** *(Med)* Narkotikum *nt*

narcotics [nɑːˈkɒtɪks]: **narcotics agent** N Rauschgiftfahnder(in) *m(f)*; **narcotics crime** N Drogenkriminalität *f*; **narcotics trade, narcotics traffic** N Drogenhandel *m*; **narcotics trafficker** N Drogendealer(in) *m(f) (inf)*

nark [nɑːk] *(Brit)* **VT** *(inf)* ärgern; **to get ~ed** wütend werden; **to feel ~ed** sich ärgern **N** *(inf)* Spitzel *m*

narky [ˈnɑːkɪ] ADJ *(+er) (Brit inf)* gereizt

narrate [nəˈreɪt] VT erzählen; *events, journey etc* schildern

narration [nəˈreɪʃən] N Erzählung *f*; *(of events, journey)* Schilderung *f*

narrative [ˈnærətɪv] **N a** *(= story)* Erzählung *f*; *(= account)* Schilderung *f*; *(= text)* Text *m* **b** *(= act of narrating)* Erzählen *nt*; *(of events, journey)* Schilderung *f*; **he has a gift for ~** er ist ein talentierter Erzähler **ADJ** erzählend; *ability etc* erzählerisch; **~ poem** Ballade *f*; *(modern)* Erzählgedicht *nt*; **~ structure** Erzählstruktur *f*

narrator [nəˈreɪtəˈ] N Erzähler(in) *m(f)*; **first-person ~** Icherzähler(in) *m(f)*; **third-person ~** Erzähler(in) *m(f)*

narrow [ˈnærəʊ] **ADJ** *(+er)* **a** eng; *road, path, passage, valley* eng, schmal; *shoulders, hips* schmal; **to become ~** eng werden; *(road etc)* sich verengen

b *(fig) person, attitudes, ideas, views* engstirnig, beschränkt; *sense, meaning, interpretation* eng; *existence* beschränkt; *band, margin* schmal, eng; *range* eng, begrenzt; *majority, victory, defeat, lead* knapp; *scrutiny* peinlich genau; **to have a ~ mind** engstirnig sein; **to have a ~ escape** mit knapper Not davonkommen, gerade noch einmal davonkommen; **that was a ~ escape** *(inf)* das war knapp, das wäre beinahe ins Auge gegangen *(inf)*

c *(Ling) vowel* geschlossen

N narrows PL enge Stelle

VT *road etc* enger machen, verengen; *(= reduce) gap* verkleinern; **to ~ the field** *(fig)* die Auswahl reduzieren *(to* auf *+acc)*; **they decided to ~ the focus of their investigation** sie beschlossen, ihre Untersuchung einzuengen; **with ~ed eyes** mit zusammengekniffenen Augen

VI enger werden, sich verengen; *(difference, majority)* geringer werden, sich verringern; **the field ~ed to two candidates** die Auswahl war auf zwei Kandidaten zusammengeschrumpft

► **narrow down VI** *(to* auf *+acc)* sich beschränken; *(= be concentrated)* sich konzentrieren; **the choice narrows down to this** die Auswahl reduziert sich hierauf **VT** *sep (to* auf *+acc) (= limit)* beschränken, einschränken; *possibilities etc* beschränken; *(= concentrate)* konzentrieren; **that narrows it down a bit** dadurch wird die Auswahl kleiner

narrow: narrow boat N *(esp Brit)* (langes, schmales) Kanalboot; **narrowcast** VI *(TV, Rad)* zielgruppenorientierte Programme ausstrahlen; **narrowcasting** N *(TV, Rad)* Spartenfernsehen *nt*/-radio *nt*; **narrow-gauge** ADJ schmalspurig; **~ railway** Schmalspurbahn *f*

narrowly [ˈnærəʊlɪ] ADV **a** *(= by a small margin) defeat, fail, avoid* knapp; *escape* mit knapper Not; **he ~ escaped being knocked down** er wäre um ein Haar *or* beinahe überfahren worden; **you ~ missed (seeing) him** du hast ihn gerade verpasst **b** *interpret, define, focus* eng; *examine* peinlich genau; *watch* genau, scharf; **to be ~ based** eine schmale Basis haben; **to focus too ~ on sth** sich zu sehr auf etw *(acc)* beschränken; **she looks at things/life much too ~** sie sieht die Dinge/das Leben viel zu eng

narrow: **narrow-minded** ADJ, **narrow-mindedly** ADV engstirnig; **narrow-mindedness** N Engstirnigkeit *f*; **narrowness** N Enge *f*; **narrow-shouldered** ADJ schmalschult(e)rig

narwhal ['nɑːwəl] N Narwal *m*

nary ['nɛərɪ] ADJ *(old)* **with ~ a word** ohne ein Wort zu sagen

NASA ['næsə] *abbr of* **National Aeronautics and Space Administration** NASA *f*

nasal ['neɪzəl] **ADJ** **a** *(Anat, Med)* Nasen-; **~ cavities** Nasenhöhle *f*; **~ membrane** Nasenschleimhaut *f*; **~ congestion** Nasenverstopfung *f*; **~ discharge** Ausfluss *m* aus der Nase **b** *(Ling)* nasal; *accent, voice, intonation* näselnd; **to speak in a ~ voice** durch die Nase sprechen, näseln; **~ sound** Nasallaut *m* **N** *(Ling)* Nasal (-laut) *m*

nasalization [,neɪzəlaɪ'zeɪʃən] N Nasalierung *f*

nasalize ['neɪzəlaɪz] VT nasalieren

nasally ['neɪzəlɪ] ADV *pronounce* nasal; *speak* durch die Nase, näselnd

nasal: **nasal passage** N Nasengang *m*; **nasal spray** N Nasenspray *nt*; **nasal strip** N *(esp Sport)* Nasenpflaster *nt*

nascent ['næsnt] ADJ **a** *(liter) republic, world, culture* werdend, im Entstehen begriffen; *doubt, hope, pride* aufkommend **b** *(Chem)* naszierend

nastily ['nɑːstɪlɪ] ADV **a** *(= unpleasantly)* scheußlich; *speak, say, laugh* gehässig, gemein; *behave* gemein, scheußlich; **to speak ~ to sb** zu jdm gehässig sein, jdn angiften *(inf)* **b** *(= awkwardly, dangerously) fall, cut oneself* böse, schlimm; *skid, veer* gefährlich

nastiness ['nɑːstɪnɪs] N *no pl* **a** *(= unpleasantness)* Scheußlichkeit *f*; *(of medicine)* Ekelhaftigkeit *f*; *(of weather)* Abscheulichkeit *f*; *(= seriousness: of break, wound)* schlimme Art; *(= objectionableness: of crime, behaviour, language)* Abscheulichkeit *f*; *(= dirtiness)* Schmutzigkeit *f*; *(= dangerousness)* Gefährlichkeit *f*
b *(= malice) (of behaviour etc)* Gemeinheit *f*; *(of person)* Bosheit *f*, Gemeinheit *f*; *(of remarks etc)* Gehässigkeit *f*, Gemeinheit *f*; *(= behaviour)* gemeines *or* scheußliches Benehmen (*to* gegenüber); *(= remarks)* Gehässigkeit(en *pl*) *f* (*to(-wards)* gegenüber)
c *(= offensiveness)* Anstößigkeit *f*; *(of film, book also)* Ekelhaftigkeit *f*; **the ~ of his mind** seine üble/schmutzige Fantasie *or* Phantasie

nasturtium [nəs'tɜːʃəm] N (Kapuziner)kresse *f*, Kapuziner *m*

nasty ['nɑːstɪ] **ADJ** (+er) **a** *(= unpleasant)* scheußlich; *smell, taste* scheußlich, widerlich; *medicine* ekelhaft, widerlich; *weather, habit* abscheulich, scheußlich; *surprise* böse, unangenehm; *(= serious) break, cough, wound, fall* böse, schlimm; *situation, problem, accident* schlimm; *moment* böse; *(= objectionable) crime, behaviour, language, word, names* abscheulich; *(= dirty)* schmutzig; *(= dangerous) virus, disease* böse, gefährlich; *corner, bend, fog* böse, übel, gefährlich; **that's a ~-looking sky/cut** der Himmel/der Schnitt sieht böse aus; **she had a ~ fall** sie ist böse *or* schlimm gefallen; **history has a ~ habit of repeating itself** die Geschichte hat die unangenehme Gewohnheit, sich zu wiederholen; **he had a ~ time of it** es ging ihm sehr schlecht *or* ganz übel; **he has a ~ look in his eyes** sein Blick verheißt nichts Gutes; **don't touch that, that's ~** pfui, fass das nicht an; **they pulled all his teeth out – ~!** sie haben ihm alle Zähne gezogen – wie scheußlich *or* unangenehm!; **a ~ surprise** *or* **shock** eine böse *or* unangenehme Überraschung; **to turn ~** *(situation, person)* unangenehm werden; *(animal)* wild werden; *(weather)* schlecht werden, umschlagen; **events took a ~ turn** die Dinge nahmen eine Wendung zum Schlechten
b *(= malicious) person, behaviour* gemein, gehässig, garstig *(dated)*, fies *(inf)* (*to sb* jdm gegenüber); *trick* gemein, übel; *remark, word* gemein; *rumour* gehässig, übel; **he has a ~ temper** mit ihm ist nicht gut Kirschen essen; **don't say that, that's ~** pfui, so was sagt man doch nicht; **to be ~ about sb** gemein über jdn reden; **that was a ~ thing to say/do** das war gemein *or* fies *(inf)*; **you ~ little boy (you)!** du böser Junge; **a ~ little man** ein Giftzwerg *m (inf)*; **what a ~ man** was für ein ekelhafter Mensch; **he's a ~ bit** *or* **piece of work** *(inf)* er ist ein übler Kunde *(inf) or* Typ *(inf)*
c *(= offensive)* anstößig; **to have a ~ mind** eine üble Fantasie *or* Phantasie haben; *(= obsessed with sex)* eine schmutzige Fantasie *or* Phantasie haben
N **nasties** *pl* (*inf*: *= nasty things*) ekelhafte Sachen *pl* → *also* **video nasty**

Nat *abbr of* **national**

Natal [nə'tæl] N Natal *nt*

natal ['neɪtl] ADJ Geburts- → **antenatal, postnatal** *etc*

natality [nə'tælɪtɪ] N *(esp US)* Geburtenziffer *f*

natch [nætʃ] INTERJ *(inf)* natürlich!, klar!, logo! *(inf)*

NATFHE *(Brit) abbr of* **National Association of Teachers in Further and Higher Education**

nation ['neɪʃən] N Volk *nt*; *(= people of one country)* Nation *f*; **people of all ~s** Menschen aller Nationen; **the voice of the ~** die Stimme des Volkes; **in the service of the ~** im Dienste des Volkes; **to address the ~** zum Volk sprechen; **the whole ~ watched him do it** das ganze Land sah ihm dabei zu; **the Sioux ~** die Siouxindianer *pl*, das Volk der Sioux(indianer)

national ['næʃənəl] **ADJ** national; *problem, affairs also* das (ganze) Land betreffend, des Landes, des Staates; *election* national, landesweit; *strike, scandal* landesweit; *(= not local) agreement, radio station, press etc* überregional; **the ~ average** der Landesdurchschnitt; **~ character** Nationalcharakter *m*; **~ colours** *(Brit) or* **colors** *(US)* Landesfarben *pl*; **~ defence** *(Brit) or* **defense** *(US)* Landesverteidigung *f*; **~ economy** Volkswirtschaft *f*; **~ language** Landessprache *f*; **~ monument** nationales Denkmal, Nationaldenkmal *nt*; **~ news** Inlandsnachrichten *pl*; **~ status** Landeszugehörigkeit *f*; **~ strip** *(Brit) or* **jersey** *(US)*) (*(Sport)* Nationaltrikot *nt*; **~ team** Nationalmannschaft *f*
N **a** *(= person)* Staatsbürger(in) *m(f)*; **foreign ~** Ausländer(in) *m(f)*; **Commonwealth ~s** Angehörige *pl* des Commonwealth
b (*inf*: *= newspaper*) überregionale Zeitung
c *(Sport)* = **Grand National**

national: **national anthem** N Nationalhymne *f*; **national assistance** N Sozialhilfe *f*; **national bank** N National- *or* Staatsbank *f*; **national costume**, **national dress** N National- *or* Landestracht *f*

national currency N Landeswährung *f*

NATIONAL CURRICULUM

Der **National Curriculum** ist der zentrale Lehrplan für die Pflichtfächer an allen englischen und walisischen Schulen. Die Fächer sind dabei Englisch, Mathematik, Naturwissenschaften, Technik, Geschichte, Erdkunde, Musik, Kunst, Sport und eine Fremdsprache (und in Wales noch zusätzlich Walisisch). In Englisch, Mathematik und Naturwissenschaften gibt es landesweite Prüfungen zu bestimmten Abschnitten der Grund- und weiterführenden Ausbildung. Religionsunterricht müssen alle Grund- und weiterführenden Schulen anbieten, die weiterführenden darüber hinaus Sexualkunde, wobei den Eltern das Recht eingeräumt wird, ihre Kinder von diesem Unterricht befreien zu lassen. In Nordirland gibt es ein überwiegend identisches System, während in Schottland der Lehrplan in den Verantwortungsbereich der lokalen Schulbehörden und der jeweiligen Schulen fällt.

national: **national debt** N Staatsverschuldung *f*; **national dish** N Nationalgericht *nt*; **national flag** N National- *or* Landesflagge *f*; **National Front** N *(Brit) rechtsradikale Partei*; **national government** N nationale Regierung; *(in Germany)* Bundesregierung *f*; *(= coalition government)* ≈ Große Koalition; **National Guard** N *(esp US)* Nationalgarde *f*; **National Guardsman** N *(US)* Mitglied *nt* der Nationalgarde; **National Health** ADJ *attr* ≈ Kassen-; **~ patient** ≈ Kassenpatient(in) *m(f)*; **National Health (Service)** N *(Brit)* staatlicher Gesundheitsdienst; **I got it on the ~** ≈ das hat die Krankenkasse bezahlt; **national holiday** N gesetzlicher *or* staatlicher Feiertag; **National Hunt racing** N *(Brit Horseracing)* Hindernisrennen *nt*; **national income** N Volkseinkommen *nt*; **national insurance** N *(Brit)* Sozialversicherung *f*; **~ contributions** Sozialversicherungsbeiträge *pl*; **~ benefits** Arbeitslosen- und Krankengeld *nt*

NATIONAL INSURANCE

National Insurance ist das System der staatlichen Sozialversicherung in Großbritannien, in das alle Arbeiter und Angestellten, deren Arbeitgeber sowie Selbstständige einzahlen müssen. Ein Teil dieses Geldes wird für die Finanzierung des Gesundheitsdienstes (NHS) verwendet, doch der Großteil des Geldes fließt in die staatlichen Unterhaltsleistungen wie Rente, Arbeitslosengeld, Witwenrente, Invalidenrente und Schwangerschaftsbeihilfe. Nur wer lang genug in die **National Insurance** eingezahlt hat, ist berechtigt, im Bedarfsfall diese beitragspflichtigen Zuschüsse zu beziehen → NHS

nationalism ['næʃnəlɪzəm] N Nationalismus *m*; **feeling of ~** Nationalgefühl *nt*

nationalist ['næʃnəlɪst] **ADJ** nationalistisch **N** Nationalist(in) *m(f)*

nationalistic [,næʃnə'lɪstɪk] ADJ nationalistisch

nationality [,næʃə'nælɪtɪ] N Staatsangehörigkeit *f*, Nationalität *f*; **what ~ is he?** welche Staatsangehörigkeit hat er?; **she is of German ~** sie hat die deutsche Staatsangehörigkeit; **the many nationalities present** die Menschen verschiedener Nationalitäten, die anwesend sind

nationalization [,næʃnəlaɪ'zeɪʃən] N Verstaatlichung *f*

nationalize ['næʃnəlaɪz] VT *industries etc* verstaatlichen

national: **National League** N *(US Sport) eine der beiden bedeutendsten US-Baseballligen*; **National Lottery** N *(Brit)* ≈ Lotto *nt*

nationally ['næʃnəlɪ] ADV *(= as a nation)* als Nation; *(= nationwide)* im ganzen Land, landesweit; *recognized* landesweit; **~ televised** landesweit im Fernsehen übertragen

national: **national park** N Nationalpark *m*; **National Rifle Association** N *(US) amerikanische Organisation, die das Recht der Bürger auf freien Kauf und Besitz von Waffen verteidigt*; **National Savings** PL *(Brit)* ≈ Postsparkasse *f*; **national savings certificate** N *(Brit) festverzinsliches öffentliches Sparpapier*; **national security** N Staatssicherheit *f*; **National Security Council** N *(US)* Nationaler Sicherheitsrat; **national service** N Wehrdienst *m*; **National Socialism** N der Nationalsozialismus; **National Socialist** **N** Nationalsozialist(in) *m(f)* **ADJ** nationalsozialistisch; **National Trust** N *(Brit)* National Trust *m*, *Natur- und Denkmalschutzverein in Großbritannien*; **~ property** *(= building)* Gebäude *nt* im Besitz des National Trust; *(= estate)* Gelände *nt* im Besitz des National Trust

nationhood ['neɪʃənhʊd] N nationale Einheit *or* Geschlossenheit

nationwide ['neɪʃən,waɪd] ADJ, ADV landesweit; *(in Germany also)* bundesweit; **the speech was broadcast ~** die Rede wurde landesweit *or (in Germany also)* bundesweit übertragen; **the film opens ~ on Friday** der Film läuft am Freitag landesweit *or* im ganzen Land *or (in Ger-*

many also) bundesweit an; **we have 300 branches ~** wir haben 300 Niederlassungen im ganzen Land

native ['neɪtɪv] ADJ **a** *product, costume, customs, habits, plants* einheimisch; *(= associated with natives)* der Eingeborenen; *population* eingeboren; **~ country** Heimatland *nt*; **~ town/city** Heimatstadt *f*; **~ language** *or* **tongue** Muttersprache *f*; **the ~ inhabitants** *or* **people** die Einheimischen *pl*; *(in colonial context)* die Eingeborenen *pl*; *(= original inhabitants)* die Ureinwohner *pl*; **~ tribe** Eingeborenenstamm *m*; **the ~ habitat of the tiger** die Heimat *or* der natürliche Lebensraum des Tigers; **my ~ Germany** mein Heimatland *nt or* meine Heimat Deutschland; **his ~ Berlin** seine Heimatstadt *or* Vaterstadt Berlin; **a ~ German** ein gebürtiger Deutscher, eine gebürtige Deutsche; **California's most famous ~ son** der berühmteste Sohn Kaliforniens; **an animal/tree ~ to India** ein in Indien beheimatetes Tier/beheimateter Baum; **to go ~** wie die Eingeborenen leben
b *(= inborn) wit, quality* angeboren
c *metal* gediegen
N **a** *(= person)* Einheimische(r) *mf*; *(in colonial contexts)* Eingeborene(r) *mf*; *(= original inhabitant)* Ureinwohner(in) *m(f)*; **a ~ of Britain/Germany** ein gebürtiger Brite/Deutscher, eine gebürtige Britin/Deutsche
b to be a ~ of ... *(plant, animal)* in ... beheimatet sein

Native American ADJ indianisch N Indianer(in) *m(f)*

> **NATIVE AMERICAN**
> **Native American** ist der heutzutage gängige Begriff für die Urbevölkerung Amerikas, mit dem man diese von den Menschen europäischer, afrikanischer oder asiatischer Abstammung unterscheidet. Daneben kann man noch **American Indian** verwenden, doch **Red Indian** oder gar **Redskin** sollte man vermeiden, da dies als herablassend oder beleidigend empfunden wird. Es ist auch üblich, direkt den Namen des jeweiligen Volkes oder Stammes zu verwenden, wie zum Beispiel „Iroquois", „Navaho" oder „Mohawk", da sich diese durch ihre verschiedenen Kulturen und Sprachen unterscheiden → BUREAU OF INDIAN AFFAIRS

native: **native-born** ADJ *attr* gebürtig; **native country** N Heimatland *nt*, Vaterland *nt*; **native land** N Vaterland *nt*; **native speaker** N Muttersprachler(in) *m(f)*; **I'm not a ~ of English** Englisch ist nicht meine Muttersprache; **he speaks English like a ~** er spricht Englisch, als wäre es seine Muttersprache

nativity [nə'tɪvɪtɪ] N Geburt *f*; **the Nativity** Christi Geburt *f*; *(= picture)* die Geburt Christi; **~ play** Krippenspiel *nt*

NATO ['neɪtəʊ] *abbr of* **North Atlantic Treaty Organization** NATO *f*

natter ['nætə'] *(Brit inf)* VI *(= gossip)* schwatzen *(inf)*; *(= chatter also)* quasseln *(inf)*; **to ~ away in German** deutsch quasseln *(inf)*; **to ~ on about sth** über etw *(acc)* quasseln *(inf)* N Schwatz *m (inf)*; **to have a ~** einen Schwatz halten *(inf)*

natty ['nætɪ] ADJ *(+er) (inf)* **a** *(= neat) dress* schick, schmuck *(dated)*; *person* schick, adrett; **he's a ~ dresser** er zieht sich immer elegant *or* schmuck *(dated)* an **b** *(= handy) tool, gadget* handlich

natural ['nætʃrəl] ADJ **a** natürlich, Natur-; *rights* naturgegeben; *(= understandable) mistake* verständlich; **~ phenomenon** Naturphänomen *nt*; **it is (only) ~ for you/him to think ...** es ist nur natürlich, dass Sie denken/er denkt ...; **~ resources** Naturschätze *pl*; **the ~ world** die Natur; **in its ~ state** im Naturzustand; **to die a ~ death** *or* **of ~ causes** eines natürlichen Todes sterben; **death from ~ causes** *(Jur)* Tod durch natürliche Ursachen; **to be imprisoned for the rest of one's ~ life** *(Jur)* eine lebenslängliche Gefängnisstrafe verbüßen; **a ~ son of Utah** in Utah geboren
b *(= chemical-free) food, hair colour* natürlich; **~ cosmetics** Naturkosmetik *f*; **~ remedy** Naturheilmittel *nt*; **she is a ~ blonde** sie ist von Natur aus blond, blond ist ihre natürliche Haarfarbe
c *(= inborn) gift, ability, quality* angeboren; **to have a ~ talent for sth** eine natürliche Begabung für etw haben; **he is a ~ artist/comedian** er ist der geborene Künstler/Komiker; **it is ~ for birds to fly** Vögel können von Natur aus fliegen; **sth comes ~ to sb** etw fällt jdm leicht
d *(= unaffected) manner* natürlich, ungekünstelt; *person, charm* natürlich; **there was something not quite ~ about her way of speaking** ihre Sprechweise hatte etwas Gekünsteltes
e *(Math) number* natürlich
f *parents* leiblich; *(old) child* natürlich
N **a** *(Mus) (= symbol)* Auflösungszeichen *nt*; *(= note)* Note *f* ohne Vorzeichen; *(= note with a natural symbol)* Note *f* mit Auflösungszeichen; **B ~** H, h; **D ~** D, d; **you played F sharp instead of F ~** Sie haben fis statt f gespielt → *also* **major, minor**
b *(inf: = person)* Naturtalent *nt*; **he's a ~ for this part** diese Rolle ist ihm wie auf den Leib geschrieben
c *(inf: = life)* Leben *nt*; **I've never heard the like in all my ~** ich habe so was mein Lebtag noch nicht gehört *(inf)*
d *(old: = idiot)* Einfaltspinsel *m*

natural: **natural-born** ADJ *attr* geboren, von Natur aus begabt; **she'a a ~ teacher** sie ist die geborene Lehrerin; **natural childbirth** N natürliche Geburt; *(= method)* die schmerzlose Geburt; **natural disaster** N Naturkatastrophe *f*; **natural food** N naturbelassene Lebensmittel *pl*; **natural forces** PL Naturgewalten *pl*; **natural gas** N Erdgas *nt*; **natural history** N Naturkunde *f*; *(concerning evolution)* Naturgeschichte *f*

naturalism ['nætʃrəlɪzəm] N Naturalismus *m*

naturalist ['nætʃrəlɪst] N **a** Naturforscher(in) *m(f)* **b** *(Art, Liter)* Naturalist(in) *m(f)*

naturalistic [ˌnætʃrə'lɪstɪk] ADJ *(Art, Liter)* naturalistisch

naturalization [ˌnætʃrəlaɪ'zeɪʃən] N Naturalisierung *f*, Einbürgerung *f*; **~ papers** Einbürgerungsurkunde *f*

naturalize ['nætʃrəlaɪz] VT **a** *person* einbürgern, naturalisieren; **to become ~d** eingebürgert werden **b** *animal, plants* heimisch machen; *word* einbürgern; **to become ~d** heimisch werden/sich einbürgern

natural: **natural justice** N Naturrecht *nt*; **natural landscape** N Naturlandschaft *f*; **natural laws** PL Naturgesetze *pl*

naturally ['nætʃrəlɪ] ADV **a** *(= of course)* natürlich; *(= understandably)* verständlicherweise **b** *(= unaffectedly) behave, speak* natürlich, ungekünstelt **c** *(= by nature)* von Natur aus; **he is ~ artistic/lazy** er ist künstlerisch veranlagt/von Natur aus faul **d** *(= not taught)* natürlich, instinktiv; **to do what comes ~** seiner Natur *or* seinem Trieb folgen; **it comes ~ to him** das fällt ihm leicht; **concern for the elderly comes ~ to him** die Sorge um ältere Menschen ist für ihn selbstverständlich

naturalness ['nætʃrəlnɪs] N Natürlichkeit *f*

natural: **natural philosopher** N Naturphilosoph(in) *m(f)*; **natural philosophy** N Naturwissenschaft *f*, Naturlehre *f (old)*; **natural science** N Naturwissenschaft *f*; **the ~s** die Naturwissenschaften *pl*; **natural selection** N natürliche Auslese; **natural sign** N *(Mus)* Auflösungszeichen *nt*; **natural wastage** N natürliche Personalreduzierung; **to make job cuts through ~** Personal durch natürliche Fluktuation abbauen; **natural wonder** N Naturwunder *nt*

nature ['neɪtʃə'] N **a** Natur *f*; **Nature** die Natur; **laws of ~** Naturgesetze *pl*; **against ~** gegen die Natur; **in a state of ~** *(= uncivilized, inf: = naked)* im Naturzustand; **to return to ~** *(person)* zur Natur zurückkehren; *(garden)* in den Naturzustand zurückkehren; **to get back to ~** zur Natur zurückkehren; **to paint from ~** nach der Natur malen; **~ calls** *(euph)* ich muss mal *(inf)*
b *(of person)* Wesen(sart *f*) *nt*, Natur *f*; **it is not in my ~ to say things like that** es entspricht nicht meiner Art *or* meinem Wesen, so etwas zu sagen; **it is in the ~ of young people to want to travel** es liegt im Wesen junger Menschen, reisen zu wollen; **cautious by ~** von Natur aus vorsichtig
c *(of object, material)* Beschaffenheit *f*; **it's in the ~ of things** das liegt in der Natur der Sache; **the ~ of the case is such ...** der Fall liegt so ...; **that's the ~ of the beast** *(fig)* das ist die Natur dieser Sache; **cash is, by its (very) ~, easy to steal** Geld ist aufgrund seiner Beschaffenheit leicht zu stehlen
d *(= type, sort)* Art *f*; **things of this ~** derartiges; **something in the ~ of an apology** so etwas wie eine Entschuldigung; **... or something of that ~** ... oder etwas in der Art

nature: **nature conservancy** N Naturschutz *m*; **nature cure** N Naturheilverfahren *nt*

-natured [-'neɪtʃəd] ADJ *suf things, animals* -artig; *person* mit einem ... Wesen; **good-natured** *(person)* gutmütig; *animal, thing* gutartig; **ill-natured** bösartig

nature: **nature lover** N Naturfreund(in) *m(f)*; **nature poet** N Naturdichter(in) *m(f)*; **nature reserve** N Naturschutzgebiet *nt*; **nature study** N Naturkunde *f*; **nature trail** N Naturlehrpfad *m*; **nature worship** N Naturreligion *f*

naturism ['neɪtʃərɪzəm] N Freikörperkultur *f*, FKK *no art*

naturist ['neɪtʃərɪst] N Anhänger(in) *m(f)* der Freikörperkultur, FKK-Anhänger(in) *m(f)* ADJ FKK-; **~ beach** FKK-Strand *m*

naught [nɔːt] N *(old, form)* = **nought b**

naughtily ['nɔːtɪlɪ] ADV frech, dreist; *(esp of child) say, remark* ungezogen, frech; *behave* unartig, ungezogen; **I very ~ opened your letter** ich war so frech und habe deinen Brief aufgemacht; **but he very ~ did it all the same** aber frecherweise hat er es trotzdem getan

naughtiness ['nɔːtɪnɪs] N **a** Frechheit *f*, Dreistigkeit *f*; *(of child)* Unartigkeit *f*, Ungezogenheit *f*; *(of dog)* Unartigkeit *f*; *(= disobedience)* Ungehorsam *m* **b** *(= shocking nature: of joke, word, story)* Unanständigkeit *f*

naughty ['nɔːtɪ] ADJ *(+er)* **a** frech, dreist; *child* unartig, ungezogen; *dog* unartig; *(= disobedient)* ungehorsam; **you ~ boy/dog!** du böser *or* unartiger Junge/Hund!; **it was ~ of him to break it** das war aber gar nicht lieb von ihm, dass er das kaputt gemacht hat; **I was ~ and ate a whole bar of chocolate** ich habe schwer gesündigt und eine ganze Tafel Schokolade gegessen; **~, ~!** aber, aber!; **how ~ of me/him!** das war ja gar nicht lieb!; **the kitten's been ~ on the carpet** *(inf)* das Kätzchen hat auf den Teppich gemacht
b *(= fattening: of food)* **(it's) ~ but nice** es ist ungesund, dafür aber lecker
c *(= shocking) joke, word, story* unanständig; **~!** nein, wie unanständig!; **the ~ nineties** die frechen neunziger Jahre *or* Neunzigerjahre; **the ~ bits** *(hum: = genitals)* die Genitalien *pl*

nausea ['nɔːsɪə] N *(Med)* Übelkeit *f*; *(fig)* Ekel *m*; **a feeling of ~** Übelkeit *f*; *(fig)* ein Gefühl *nt* des Ekels; **the very thought fills me with ~** bei dem Gedanken allein wird mir schon übel

nauseate ['nɔːsɪeɪt] VT **to ~ sb** *(Med)* (bei) jdm Übelkeit verursachen, in jdm Übelkeit erregen; *(fig)* jdn anwidern

nauseating ['nɔːsɪeɪtɪŋ] ADJ *sight, smell, violence, food* ekelerregend; *film, book, style* grässlich; *hypocrisy* widerlich; *person* ekelhaft, widerlich

nauseatingly ['nɔːsɪeɪtɪŋlɪ] ADV widerlich

nauseous ['nɔːsɪəs] ADJ **a** *(Med)* **that made me (feel) ~** dabei wurde mir übel **b** *(fig)* widerlich

nautical [ˈnɔːtɪkəl] ADJ nautisch; *prowess, superiority* zur See, seefahrerisch; *distance* zur See; *stories* von der Seefahrt; *language, tradition, appearance* seemännisch; ~ **chart** Seekarte *f*; **a ~ nation** eine Seefahrernation; **he is interested in ~ matters, he's a very ~ person** er interessiert sich für die Seefahrt; **the music/play has a ~ flavour** die Musik/das Stück beschwört die See herauf

nautically [ˈnɔːtɪkəlɪ] ADV *superior* in Bezug auf die Seefahrt

nautical mile N Seemeile *f*

nautilus [ˈnɔːtɪləs] N Nautilus *m*, Schiffsboot *nt*

naval [ˈneɪvəl] ADJ der Marine; **his interests are ~ not military** er interessiert sich für die Marine und nicht für das Heer

naval: **naval academy** N Marineakademie *f*; **naval architect** N Schiffsbauingenieur(in) *m(f)*; **naval architecture** N Schiffsbau *m*; **naval aviation** N Seeflugwesen *nt*; **naval base** N Flottenbasis *f or* -stützpunkt *m*; **naval battle** N Seeschlacht *f*; **naval blockade** N Seeblockade *f*; **naval college** N Marineschule *f*; **naval forces** PL Seestreitkräfte *pl*; **naval officer** N Marineoffizier(in) *m(f)*; **naval port** N Kriegshafen *m*, Flottenstützpunkt *m*; **naval power** N Seemacht *f*; **naval warfare** N Seekrieg *m*

nave [neɪv] N **a** *(of church)* Haupt- *or* Mittel- *or* Längsschiff *nt* **b** *(of wheel)* (Rad)nabe *f*

navel [ˈneɪvəl] N **a** *(Anat)* Nabel *m* **b** *(also* **navel orange***)* Navelorange *f*

navel-gazing [ˈneɪvəlˌgeɪzɪŋ] N *(pej)* Nabelschau *f*

navel-piercing N *(Fashion)* Nabelpiercing *nt*

navigable [ˈnævɪgəbl] ADJ **a** schiffbar; **in a ~ condition** *(ship)* seetüchtig **b** *balloon, airship* lenkbar

navigate [ˈnævɪgeɪt] VI *(in plane, ship)* navigieren; *(in car)* den Fahrer dirigieren; *(in rally)* der Beifahrer sein; **who was navigating?** *(in plane, ship)* wer war für die Navigation zuständig?; *(in car)* wer war der Beifahrer?; **I don't know the route, you'll have to ~** ich kenne die Strecke nicht, du musst mir sagen, wie ich fahren muss *or* du musst mich dirigieren

VT **a** *aircraft, ship, spaceship* navigieren; **to ~ sth through sth** etw durch etw (hindurch)navigieren; *(fig)* etw durch etw hindurchschleusen; **he ~d his way through the crowd** er bahnte sich *(dat)* einen Weg durch die Menge **b** *(= journey through)* durchfahren; *(plane, pilot)* durchfliegen; *ocean* durchqueren; *river* befahren

navigation [ˌnævɪˈgeɪʃən] N **a** *(= act of navigating)* Navigation *f* **b** *(= shipping)* Schiffsverkehr *m* **c** *(= skill: in ship, plane)* Navigation *f*; **how's your ~?** *(in car)* bist du als Beifahrer gut zu gebrauchen?; **his ~ was lousy, we got lost** *(in car)* er hat mich so schlecht dirigiert, dass wir uns verirrt haben

navigation: **navigation channel** N *(Naut)* Fahrwasser *nt*; **navigation law** N Schifffahrtsregelung *f*; **navigation light** N Positionslicht *nt or* -lampe *f*; **navigation system** N *(Tech, Aut)* Navigationssystem *nt*

navigator [ˈnævɪgeɪtəˈ] N *(Naut)* Navigationsoffizier(in) *m(f)*; *(Aviat)* Navigator(in) *m(f)*; *(Mot)* Beifahrer(in) *m(f)*

navvy [ˈnævɪ] N *(Brit)* Bauarbeiter(in) *m(f)*; *(on road also)* Straßenarbeiter(in) *m(f)*

navy [ˈneɪvɪ] N **a** (Kriegs)marine *f*; **to serve in the ~** in der Marine dienen **b** *(also* **navy blue***)* Marineblau *nt* ADJ **a** *attr* Marine-; **~ ship** Marineschiff *nt* **b** *(also* **navy-blue***)* marineblau

navy bean N *(US)* weiße Bohne

Navy Department N *(US)* Marineministerium *nt*

nawab [nəˈwɒb] N = **nabob**

nay [neɪ] ADV **a** *(obs, dial)* nein **b** *(liter)* **surprised, ~ astonished** überrascht, nein vielmehr verblüfft N Nein *nt*, Neinstimme *f* → **yea**

Nazarene [ˈnæzəriːn] N Nazaräer(in) *m(f)*

Nazi [ˈnɑːtsɪ] N Nazi *m*; *(fig pej)* Faschist(in) *m(f)* ADJ Nazi-; **~ criminal** Naziverbrecher(in) *m(f)*

Nazism [ˈnɑːtsɪzəm] N Nazismus *m*

NB *abbr of* **nota bene** NB

NCB *(Brit old) abbr of* **National Coal Board** *Verband der britischen Kohleindustrie*

NCO *abbr of* **noncommissioned officer** Uffz. *m*

NDE *abbr of* **near-death experience** NTE *f*

NE *abbr of* **north-east** NO

Neanderthal [nɪˈændətɑːl] ADJ **a** *(Hist)* Neandertaler *attr* **b** *(inf) (= brutish) person* massig; *appearance, grunt, conversation* roh; *(= reactionary) person, attitude, view* rückständig; *system, method* vorsintflutlich N **a** *(Hist)* Neandertaler *m* **b** *(inf) (= brute)* Schlägertyp *m (inf)*; *(= reactionary)* Neandertaler(in) *m(f) (inf)*

Neanderthal man N der Neandertaler

neap [niːp] N *(also* **neap-tide***)* Nippflut *f*, Nippzeit *f*, Nipptide *f (N Ger)*

Neapolitan [nɪəˈpɒlɪtən] ADJ neapolitanisch; **~ ice cream** Fürst-Pückler-Eis *nt* N Neapolitaner(in) *m(f)*

near [nɪəˈ] *(+er)*

1 ADVERB	4 TRANSITIVE VERB
2 PREPOSITION	5 INTRANSITIVE VERB
3 ADJECTIVE	

1 – ADVERB

a [= close in space or time] nahe; **he lives quite near** er wohnt ganz in der Nähe; **don't sit/stand so near** setzen Sie sich/stehen Sie nicht so nahe (daran); **you live nearer/nearest** du wohnst näher/am nächsten; **to move/come nearer** näher kommen; **could you move nearer together?** könnten Sie näher *or* enger zusammenrücken?; **that was the nearest I ever got to seeing him** da hätte ich ihn fast gesehen; **this is the nearest I can get to solving the problem** besser kann ich das Problem nicht lösen; **that's the nearest I ever got to being fired** da hätte nicht viel gefehlt und ich wäre rausgeworfen worden; **the nearer it gets to the election, the more they look like losing** je näher die Wahl kommt *or* rückt, desto mehr sieht es danach aus, dass sie verlieren werden

♦ **to be near at hand** zur Hand sein; *(shops)* in der Nähe sein; *(help)* ganz nahe sein; *(event)* unmittelbar bevorstehen → **draw**

b [= closely, accurately] genau; **as near as I can tell** soweit ich es beurteilen kann; **the same size as near as dammit** *(inf)* fast genau die gleiche Größe

♦ **near enough (that's) near enough** so gehts ungefähr, das haut so ungefähr hin *(inf)*; **... no, but near enough** ... nein, aber es ist nicht weit davon entfernt; **there were near enough 60 people at the party** es waren knapp 60 Leute auf der Party

♦ **as near as makes no difference they're the same length or as near as makes no difference** sie sind so gut wie gleich lang; **it's as near stopped as makes no difference** es hat so gut wie aufgehört

c [= almost] fast, beinahe; *impossible* nahezu, fast; *dead* nahezu; **he very near succeeded** fast *or* beinahe wäre es ihm gelungen

d [in negative statements] **it's nowhere near enough** das ist bei Weitem nicht genug; **it's nowhere near right** das ist weit gefehlt; **we're not any nearer (to) solving the problem** wir sind der Lösung des Problems kein bisschen näher gekommen; **we're nowhere** *or* **not anywhere near finishing the book** wir haben das Buch noch lange nicht fertig; **nowhere near as much** lange *or* bei Weitem nicht so viel; **you are nowhere** *or* **not anywhere near the truth** das ist weit gefehlt, du bist weit von der Wahrheit entfernt; **he is nowhere** *or* **not anywhere near as clever as you** er ist lange *or* bei Weitem nicht so klug wie du

2 – PREPOSITION

(also ADV: **near to***)*

a [= close to] *position* nahe an *(+dat)*, nahe *(+dat)*; *(with motion)* nahe an *(+acc)*; *(= in the vicinity of)* in der Nähe von *or +gen*; *(with motion)* in die Nähe von *or +gen*; **to get near (to) the church** in die Nähe der Kirche kommen; **he lives near (to) the border** er wohnt in der Nähe der Grenze *or* nahe der Grenze; **the hotel is very near (to) the station** das Hotel liegt ganz in der Nähe des Bahnhofs; **move the chair near/nearer (to) the table** rücken Sie den Stuhl an den/näher an den Tisch; **to get near/nearer (to) sb/sth** nahe/näher an jdn/etw herankommen; **to stand near/nearer (to) the table** nahe/näher am Tisch stehen; **he won't go near anything illegal** mit Ungesetzlichem will er nichts zu tun haben; **when we got near (to) the house** als wir an das Haus herankamen *or* in die Nähe des Hauses kamen; **when we are nearer home** wenn wir nicht mehr so weit von zu Hause weg sind; **keep near me** bleib in meiner Nähe; **near here/there** hier/dort in der Nähe; **don't come near me** komm mir nicht zu nahe; **near (to) where I had seen him** nahe der Stelle, wo ich ihn gesehen hatte; **to be nearest to sth** einer Sache *(dat)* am nächsten sein; **take the chair nearest (to) you/the table** nehmen Sie den Stuhl direkt neben Ihnen/dem Tisch; **that's nearer it** das trifft schon eher zu; **the adaptation is very near (to) the original** die Bearbeitung hält sich eng ans Original; **to be near (to) sb's heart** *or* **sb** jdm am Herzen liegen; **to be near (to) the knuckle** *or* **bone** *(joke)* gewagt sein; *(remark)* hart an der Grenze sein

b [= close in time] *with time stipulated* gegen; **near (to) death** dem Tode nahe; **she is near her time** es ist bald so weit (bei ihr); **near (to) the appointed time** um die ausgemachte Zeit herum; **phone again nearer (to) Christmas** rufen Sie vor Weihnachten noch einmal an; **come back nearer (to) 3 o'clock** kommen Sie gegen 3 Uhr wieder; **on the Wednesday nearest Easter** am Mittwoch (direkt) vor Ostern; **to be nearer/nearest (to) sth** einer Sache *(dat)* zeitlich näher liegen/am nächsten liegen; **near (to) the end of my stay/the play/the book** gegen Ende meines Aufenthalts/des Stücks/des Buchs; **I'm near (to) the end of the book** ich habe das Buch fast zu Ende gelesen; **she's near (to) the end of her stay** ihr Aufenthalt ist fast zu Ende *or* vorbei; **her birthday is near (to) mine** ihr und mein Geburtstag liegen nahe beieinander; **the sun was near (to) setting** die Sonne war am Untergehen; **it is drawing near (to) Christmas** es geht auf Weihnachten zu; **as it drew near/nearer (to) his departure** als seine Abreise heranrückte/näher heranrückte

c [= on the point of] **to be near (to) doing sth** nahe daran sein, etw zu tun; **to be near (to) tears/despair** *etc* den Tränen/der Verzweiflung *etc* nahe sein; **she was near (to) laughing out loud** sie hätte beinahe laut gelacht; **the project is near/nearer (to) completion** das Projekt steht vor seinem Abschluss/ist dem Abschluss näher gekommen; **he came near to ruining his chances** er hätte sich seine Chancen beinahe verdorben, es hätte nicht viel gefehlt, und er hätte sich seine Chancen verdorben; **we were near to being drowned** wir waren dem Ertrinken nahe, wir wären beinahe ertrunken

d [= similar to] ähnlich *(+dat)*; **German is nearer (to) Dutch than English is** Deutsch ist dem Holländischen ähnlicher als Englisch; **it's the same thing or near it** es ist so ziemlich das Gleiche; **nobody comes anywhere near him at swimming** *(inf)* im Schwimmen kann es niemand mit ihm aufnehmen *(inf)*

3 – ADJECTIVE

a [= close in space or time] nahe; **to be near** *(person, object)* in der Nähe sein; *(danger, end, help)* nahe sein; *(event, departure, festival)* bevorstehen; **to be very near** ganz in der Nähe sein; *(in time)* nahe *or* unmittelbar bevorstehen; *(danger etc)* ganz nahe sein; **to be nearer/nearest** näher/am nächsten sein; *(event etc)* zeitlich näher/am nächsten liegen; **it looks very near** es sieht so aus, als ob es ganz nah wäre; **our nearest neighbours are 5 miles away** unsere nächsten Nachbarn sind 5 Meilen entfernt; **these glasses make things look nearer** diese Brille lässt alles näher erscheinen; **his answer was nearer than mine/nearest** seine Antwort traf eher zu als meine/traf die Sachlage am ehesten; **when death is so near** wenn man dem Tod nahe ist; **these events are still very near** diese Ereignisse liegen noch nicht lange zurück; **the hour is near (when …)** *(old)* die Stunde ist nahe(, da …) *(old)*; **her hour was near** *(old)* ihre Stunde war nahe *(old)*

b [fig] *escape* knapp; **a near disaster/accident** beinahe *or* fast ein Unglück *nt*/ein Unfall *m*; **his nearest rival** sein schärfster Rivale, seine schärfste Rivalin; **our nearest competition** unsere stärkste Konkurrenz; **to be in a state of near collapse/hysteria** am Rande eines Zusammenbruchs/der Hysterie sein; **round up the figure to the nearest pound** runden Sie die Zahl auf das nächste Pfund auf; **£50 or nearest offer** *(Comm)* Verhandlungsbasis £ 50; **we'll sell it for £50, or nearest offer** wir verkaufen es für £ 50 oder das nächstbeste Angebot; **the nearest in line to the throne** der unmittelbare Thronfolger; **this is the nearest equivalent** das kommt dem am Nächsten; **this is the nearest translation you'll get** besser kann man es kaum übersetzen, diese Übersetzung trifft es noch am ehesten; **that's the nearest thing you'll get to a compliment/an answer** ein besseres Kompliment/eine bessere Antwort kannst du kaum erwarten

c [= closely related, intimate] *relation* nah; *friend* nah, vertraut; **my nearest and dearest** meine Lieben *pl*; **a near and dear friend** ein lieber und teurer Freund

4 – TRANSITIVE VERB

sich nähern *(+dat)*; **he was nearing his end** sein Leben neigte sich dem Ende zu; **to be nearing sth** *(fig)* auf etw *(acc)* zugehen; **she was nearing fifty** sie ging auf die Fünfzig zu; **to near completion** kurz vor dem Abschluss stehen

5 – INTRANSITIVE VERB

(time, event) näher rücken; **the time is nearing when …** die Zeit rückt näher, da …

near beer N alkoholarmes *or* -freies Bier

near beginner N Anfänger(in) *m(f)* mit Vorkenntnissen

nearby [nɪə'baɪ] ADV *(also* **near by**) in der Nähe ADJ nahe gelegen

near: **near-death experience** N Nahtoderfahrung *f*; **Near East** N Naher Osten; **in the ~** im Nahen Osten; **near letter-quality** N Schönschrift *f*, Korrespondenz- *or* Briefqualität *f*

nearly ['nɪəlɪ] ADV **a** *(= almost)* beinahe, fast; **I ~ laughed** ich hätte fast *or* beinahe gelacht; **she was ~ crying** *or* **in tears** sie war den Tränen nahe; **we are ~ there** *(at a place)* wir sind fast da; *(with a job)* wir sind fast so weit; **he very ~ drowned** er wäre um ein Haar ertrunken **b not ~** bei Weitem nicht, nicht annähernd; **not ~ enough** bei Weitem nicht genug

nearly-new [ˌnɪəlɪ'njuː] ADJ *clothes* fast neu; **~ shop** Second-Hand-Laden *m (der besonders gute Qualität anbietet)*

near miss N *(Aviat)* Beinahezusammenstoß *m* → *also* **miss¹ N a**

nearness ['nɪənɪs] N Nähe *f*

near: **nearside** ADJ auf der Beifahrerseite; *(when driving on the left also)* linke(r, s); *(when driving on the right also)* rechte(r, s) N Beifahrerseite *f*; **near-sighted** ADJ kurzsichtig; **near-sightedness** N Kurzsichtigkeit *f*; **near thing** N **that was a ~** das war knapp

neat [niːt] ADJ *(+er)* **a** *(= tidy) person, house, hairstyle* ordentlich; *worker, work, handwriting, sewing* sauber, ordentlich; *hair, appearance* gepflegt; **he likes everything ~ and tidy** er will alles hübsch ordentlich haben; **to make a ~ job of sth** etw tadellos machen; **he made a very ~ job of repairing the window** er hat das Fenster tadellos repariert → **pin**

b *(= precise) fit, category* genau; *division* sauber; *summary* prägnant; *explanation* prägnant formuliert; **it's a ~ fit in the corner** es passt genau in die Ecke

c *(= pleasing)* nett; *clothes* nett, adrett; *person, figure* hübsch, nett; *ankles* schlank; **she has a ~ figure** sie hat ein nettes Figürchen; **~ little suit** schmucker *or* netter Anzug

d *(= skilful) gadget, speech* gelungen; *style* gewandt; *solution* sauber, elegant; *plan* elegant; *trick* schlau; **that's very ~** das ist sehr schlau

e *(esp Brit: = undiluted) spirits* pur; *wines* unverdünnt; **to drink one's whisky ~** Whisky pur trinken

f *(US inf: = excellent)* prima *(inf)*, klasse *inv (inf)*; **a ~ guy** ein großartiger *or* toller Typ *(inf)*

neaten ['niːtn] VT *(also* **neaten up**) in Ordnung bringen; *phrasing* glätten

'neath [niːθ] PREP *(poet)* unter *(+dat)*, unterhalb *(+gen)*; *(with motion)* unter *(+acc)*

neatly ['niːtlɪ] ADV **a** *(= tidily)* ordentlich; *write, work, sew* ordentlich, sauber **b** *(= pleasingly)* nett, adrett, hübsch; **a ~ turned ankle** eine hübsche schlanke Fessel **c** *(= skilfully)* gewandt; *solve* sauber, elegant; **that was ~ done** das hast du/hat er *etc* schlau gemacht; **~ put** prägnant formuliert; **~ turned phrases** prägnant formulierte Sätze *pl*

neatness ['niːtnɪs] N **a** *(= tidiness)* Ordentlichkeit *f*; *(of work, writing, sewing)* Ordentlichkeit *f*, Sauberkeit *f* **b** *(= precision) (of category)* Genauigkeit *f*; *(of division)* Sauberkeit *f*; *(of summary, explanation)* Prägnanz *f* **c** *(= pleasing nature)* Nettheit *f*; *(of clothes)* nettes Aussehen, Adrettheit *f*; *(of person, figure)* hübsches Aussehen; *(of ankles)* Schlankheit *f* **d** *(= successfulness)* Gelungenheit *f*; *(= skilfulness) (of speech, style)* Gewandtheit *f*; *(of solution)* Sauberkeit *f*, Eleganz *f*; *(of trick)* Schlauheit *f*

nebbish ['nebɪʃ] N *(sl)* Schlappschwanz *m (inf)*

nebula ['nebjʊlə] N *pl* **-e** ['nebjʊliː] **a** *(Astron)* Nebel *m*, Nebelfleck *m* **b** *(Med)* Trübung *f*

nebulous ['nebjʊləs] ADJ **a** *(Astron)* nebelartig **b** *(fig)* unklar, verworren, nebulös

necessarily ['nesɪsərɪlɪ] ✪ 16.1 ADV notwendigerweise *(also Logic)*, unbedingt; **not ~** nicht unbedingt; **if that is true, then it is not ~ the case that …** wenn das stimmt, muß es nicht unbedingt sein, dass …

necessary ['nesɪsərɪ] ADJ **a** notwendig, nötig, erforderlich *(to, for* für); **it is ~ to …** man muss …; **is it really ~ for me to come too?** muss ich denn wirklich auch kommen?; **it's not ~ for you to come** Sie brauchen nicht zu kommen; **it is ~ for him to be there** es ist nötig *or* notwendig, dass er da ist, er muss da sein; **all the ~ qualifications** alle erforderlichen Qualifikationen; **~ condition** Voraussetzung *f*; *(Logic)* notwendige Voraussetzung; **to be/become ~ to sb** jdm unentbehrlich sein/werden; **to make it ~ for sb to do sth** es erforderlich machen, dass jd etw tut; **if/when ~** wenn nötig, nötigenfalls; **where ~** wo nötig; **you were rude to him, was that ~?** du warst grob zu ihm, war das denn notwendig *or* nötig?; **that won't be ~** das wird nicht nötig sein; **to make the ~ arrangements** die erforderlichen *or* notwendigen Maßnahmen treffen; **to do everything ~, to do whatever is ~** alles Nötige tun; **to do no more than is (strictly) ~** nicht mehr tun, als unbedingt notwendig *or* nötig ist; **good food is ~ to health** gutes Essen ist für die Gesundheit notwendig

b *(= unavoidable) conclusion, change, result* unausweichlich; **we drew the ~ conclusions** wir haben die entsprechenden Schlüsse daraus gezogen; **a ~ evil** ein notwendiges Übel

N **a** *(inf: = what is needed)* **the ~** das Notwendige; **will you do the ~?** wirst du das Notwendige *or* Nötige erledigen?

b *(inf: = money)* **the ~** das nötige Kleingeld

c *usu pl* **the ~** *or* **necessaries** das Notwendige

necessitate [nɪ'sesɪteɪt] VT notwendig *or* erforderlich machen, erfordern *(form)*; **the heat ~d our staying indoors** die Hitze zwang uns, im Haus zu bleiben

necessitous [nɪ'sesɪtəs] ADJ *(old, form)* dürftig, armselig

necessity [nɪ'sesɪtɪ] N **a** *no pl* Notwendigkeit *f*; **from** *or* **out of ~** aus Not; **of ~** notgedrungen, notwendigerweise; **to be born of ~** aus Notwendigkeit (heraus) geschehen; **he did not realize the ~ for a quick decision** er hat nicht erkannt, wie wichtig *or* notwendig eine schnelle Entscheidung war; **it is a case of absolute ~** es ist unbedingt notwendig; **there is no ~ for you to do that** es besteht nicht die geringste Notwendigkeit, dass Sie das tun; **~ is the mother of invention** *(Prov)* Not macht erfinderisch *(Prov)*

b *no pl (= poverty)* Not *f*, Armut *f*; **to live in ~** Not leiden, in Armut leben

c *(= necessary thing)* Notwendigkeit *f*; **the bare necessities (of life)** das Notwendigste (zum Leben)

neck [nek] N **a** Hals *m*; **to break one's ~** sich *(dat)* das Genick *or* den Hals brechen; **but don't break your ~** *(inf)* bring dich nicht um *(inf)*; **to risk one's ~** Kopf und Kragen riskieren; **to save one's ~** seinen Hals aus der Schlinge ziehen; **a stiff ~** ein steifer Hals *or* Nacken; **to win by a ~** um eine Kopflänge gewinnen; **to have sb round one's ~** *(fig inf)* jdn auf dem *or* am Halse haben; **to be up to one's ~ in work** bis über den Hals *or* über die Ohren in der Arbeit stecken; **he's in it up to his ~** *(inf)* er steckt bis über den Hals drin; **to get it in the ~** *(inf)* eins aufs Dach bekommen *(inf)*; **to stick one's ~ out** seinen Kopf riskieren; **in this ~ of the woods** *(inf)* in diesen Breiten; **she's from your ~ of the woods** *(inf)* sie kommt aus der g[illegible]hen Ecke wie du *(inf)* → *also* **breathe VI**

b *(Cook)* **~ of lamb** Halsstück *nt* vom Lamm

c *(of bottle, vase, violin, bone)* Hals *m*; *(of land)* Landenge *f*

d *(of dress etc)* Ausschnitt *m*; **it has a high ~** es ist hochgeschlossen

e *(also* **neck measurement**) Halsweite *f*

VI *(inf)* knutschen *(inf)*, schmusen *(inf)*

neck: **neck and neck** *(lit, fig)* ADJ *attr* Kopf-an-Kopf-; **a ~ race** ein Kopf-an-Kopf-Rennen *nt* ADV Kopf an Kopf; **neckband** N Besatz *m*; *(of shirt)* Kragensteg *m*; *(of pullover)* Halsbündchen *nt*; **neckcloth** N *(obs)* Halstuch *nt*

neckerchief ['nekətʃiːf] N Halstuch *nt*

necklace ['neklɪs] N (Hals)kette *f*

necklet ['neklɪt] N Kettchen *nt*

neck: **neckline** N Ausschnitt *m*; **a dress with a low ~** ein tief ausgeschnittenes Kleid; **necktie** N *(esp US)* Krawatte *f*, Binder *m*, Schlips *m*

necrology [ne'krɒlədʒɪ] N *(form)* Totenverzeichnis *nt*, Nekrologium *nt*; *(= obituary)* Nachruf *m*, Nekrolog *m*

necromancer ['nekrəʊmænsəʳ] N Toten- *or* Geisterbeschwörer(in) *m(f)*, Nekromant(in) *m(f)*

necromancy ['nekrəʊmænsɪ] N Toten- *or* Geisterbeschwörung *f*, Nekromantie *f*

necrophilia [ˌnekrəʊ'fɪlɪə] N Leichenschändung *f*, Nekrophilie *f*

necrophiliac [ˌnekrəʊ'fɪlɪæk] ADJ nekrophil N Leichenschänder *m*, Nekrophile(r) *m*

necropolis [ne'krɒpəlɪs] N Totenstadt *f*, Nekropole *f*, Nekropolis *f*

necrotising fasciitis ['nekrəʊtaɪzɪŋfæʃɪ'aɪtɪs] N *(Med)* nekrotisierende Fasciitis

nectar ['nektəʳ] N *(lit, fig)* Nektar *m*

nectarine ['nektərɪn] N *(= fruit)* Nektarine *f*; *(= tree)* Nektarine(nbaum *m*) *f*

ned [ned] N *(inf)* Rowdy *m*; *(= criminal type)* Halunke *m*

NEDC *(Brit) abbr of* **National Economic Development Council** *Rat für Wirtschaftsentwicklung*

née [neɪ] ADJ **Mrs Smith, ~ Jones** Frau Smith, geborene Jones

need [ni:d] ✪ 1.1, 9.4, 10.2 **N** **a** *no pl (= necessity)* Notwendigkeit *f (for +gen)*; **if ~ be** nötigenfalls, wenn nötig; **in case of ~** notfalls, im Notfall; **(there is) no ~ for sth** etw ist nicht nötig; **(there is) no ~ to do sth** etw braucht nicht *or* muss nicht unbedingt getan werden; **there is no ~ for sb to do sth** jd braucht etw nicht zu tun; **there is no ~ for tears** du brauchst nicht zu weinen; **there was no ~ to send it immediately** es war nicht nötig, es sofort zu schicken; **there's no ~ to get angry** du brauchst nicht gleich wütend zu werden; **to be (badly) in ~ of sth** *(person)* etw (dringend) brauchen; **those most in ~ of help** diejenigen, die Hilfe am nötigsten brauchen; **to be in ~ of repair** reparaturbedürftig sein; **to be in ~ of an overhaul** (dringend) überholt werden müssen; **this window is in ~ of a coat of paint** dieses Fenster könnte ein wenig Farbe gut gebrauchen; **to have no ~ of sth** etw nicht brauchen; **to have no ~ to do sth** etw nicht zu tun brauchen
b *no pl (= misfortune)* Not *f*; **in time(s) of ~** in schwierigen Zeiten, in Zeiten der Not; **do not fail me in my hour of ~** *(usu iro)* verlass mich nicht in der Stunde der Not
c *no pl (= poverty)* Not *f*; **to be in great ~** große Not leiden; **those in ~** die Notleidenden *pl*, die Not Leidenden *pl*
d *(= requirement)* Bedürfnis *nt*; **the body's ~ for oxygen** das Sauerstoffbedürfnis des Körpers; **my ~s are few** ich stelle nur geringe Ansprüche; **a list of all your ~s** eine Aufstellung all dessen, was Sie brauchen; **your ~ is greater than mine** Sie haben es nötiger als ich; **there is a great ~ for ...** es besteht ein großer Bedarf an *(+dat)* ...; **investment is one of the firm's greatest ~s** die Firma braucht dringend Investitionen
VT **a** *(= require)* brauchen; **he ~ed no second invitation** man musste ihn nicht zweimal bitten; **to ~ no introduction** keine spezielle Einführung brauchen; **much ~ed** dringend notwendig; **what I ~ is a good drink** ich brauche etwas zu trinken; **just what I ~ed** genau das Richtige; **that's/you're all I ~ed** *(iro)* das hat/du hast mir gerade noch gefehlt; **this incident ~s some explanation** dieser Vorfall bedarf einer Erklärung *(gen)*; **it ~s a service/a coat of paint/careful consideration** es muss gewartet/gestrichen/gründlich überlegt werden; **is a visa ~ed to enter the USA?** braucht man für die Einreise in die USA ein Visum?; **it ~ed a revolution to change that** es bedurfte einer Revolution, um das zu ändern; **it ~ed an accident to make him drive carefully** er musste erst einen Unfall haben, bevor er vernünftig fuhr
b *(in verbal constructions)* **sth ~s doing** *or* **to be done** etw muss gemacht werden; **he ~s watching/cheering up** man muss ihn beobachten/aufheitern, er muss beobachtet/aufgeheitert werden; **to ~ to do sth** *(= have to)* etw tun müssen; **not to ~ to do sth** etw nicht zu tun brauchen; **he doesn't ~ to be told** man braucht es ihm nicht zu sagen; **you shouldn't ~ to be told** das müsste man dir nicht erst sagen müssen; **it doesn't ~ me to tell you that** das brauche ich dir ja wohl nicht zu sagen; **she ~s to have everything explained to her** man muss ihr alles erklären
VB AUX **a** *(indicating obligation: in positive contexts)* müssen; **~ he go?** muss er gehen?; **~ I say more?** mehr brauche ich ja wohl nicht zu sagen; **I ~ hardly say that ...** ich brauche wohl kaum zu erwähnen, dass ...; **no-one ~ go** *or* **~s to go home yet** es braucht noch keiner nach Hause zu gehen; **you only ~ed (to) ask** du hättest nur (zu) fragen brauchen; **one ~ only look** ein Blick genügt
b *(indicating obligation: in negative contexts)* brauchen; **you ~n't wait** du brauchst nicht (zu) warten; **we ~n't have come/gone** wir hätten gar nicht kommen/gehen brauchen; **I/you ~n't have bothered** das war nicht nötig
c *(indicating logical necessity)* **~ that be true?** ist das notwendigerweise wahr?; **that ~n't be the case** das muss nicht unbedingt der Fall sein; **it ~ not follow that ...** daraus folgt nicht unbedingt, dass ...

needful ['ni:dfʊl] **ADJ** *(old)* notwendig, nötig *(for, to* für, zu) **N** *(inf: = what is necessary)* **to do the ~** das Nötige tun

neediness ['ni:dɪnɪs] N Armut *f*, Bedürftigkeit *f*

needle ['ni:dl] **N** *(all senses)* Nadel *f*; **it's like looking for a ~ in a haystack** es ist, als ob man eine Stecknadel im Heuhaufen suchte; **to give sb the ~** *(inf)* jdn reizen **VT** **a** *(inf: = goad)* ärgern, piesacken *(inf)*; **what's needling him?** was ist ihm über die Leber gelaufen? *(inf)* **b** *(US inf)* **to ~ a drink** einen Schuss Alkohol in ein Getränk geben

needle: **needle-book** N Nadelheft *nt*; **needle-case** N Nadeletui *nt*; **needlecord** N *(Tex)* Feincord *m*; **needlecraft** N handarbeitliches Geschick; **needle exchange** N *(= centre)* ≈ Fixerstube *f*; *(= drugs treatment programme)* Spritzentausch *m*; **needle match** N spannendes Spiel; **needle-sharp** ADJ *(inf)* clever *(inf)*, schwer auf Zack *(inf)*

needless ['ni:dlɪs] ADJ unnötig; *remark etc also* überflüssig; *death, killing, pain, destruction* sinnlos; **~ to say, he didn't come** er kam natürlich nicht

needlessly ['ni:dlɪslɪ] ADV unnötig(erweise), überflüssig(erweise); *destroy, kill* sinnlos; **he was quite ~ rude** er war ganz unnötig grob; **you are worrying quite ~** Ihre Sorgen sind vollkommen unbegründet

needlessness ['ni:dlɪsnɪs] N Unnötigkeit *f*

needle: **needlewoman** N Näherin *f*; **needlework** N Handarbeit *f*; **a piece of ~** eine Handarbeit

needs [ni:dz] ADV *(obs)* **I must ~ away/obey** ich muss fort/notwendigerweise gehorchen; **~ must if the devil drives** *(prov)* nolens volens

need-to-know [,ni:dtə'nəʊ] N **on a ~ basis** nur bei tatsächlichem Informationsbedarf, nach dem „need to know"-Prinzip

needy ['ni:dɪ] **ADJ** (+er) ärmlich, bedürftig **N** **the ~** die Bedürftigen *pl*

ne'er [nɛəʳ] ADV *(old, poet: = never)* nie, niemals

ne'er-do-well ['nɛədu:,wel] *(dated)* **N** Tunichtgut *m*, Taugenichts *m (dated)* **ADJ** nichtsnutzig

ne'ertheless [,nɛəðə'les] ADV *(old, poet)* nichtsdestoweniger

nefarious [nɪ'fɛərɪəs] ADJ *(form)* schändlich, ruchlos *(liter)*; **~ deed** Freveltat *f (liter)*, ruchlose Tat

negate [nɪ'geɪt] VT *(= nullify)* zunichtemachen; *(= deny)* verneinen *(also Gram)*, negieren *(geh)*

negation [nɪ'geɪʃən] N Verneinung *f*; *(of statement, negative form also)* Negation *f*

negative ['negətɪv] **ADJ** negativ; *answer* verneinend; *(Gram) form* verneint; **~ ion** Anion *nt*; **~ cash flow** *(Fin)* Überhang *m* der Zahlungsausgänge; **~ campaigning** *(Pol) negativer Wahlkampf*; **~ vote** Gegenstimme *f*; **I got a ~ reply to my request** ich habe auf meinen Antrag einen abschlägigen Bescheid bekommen
N **a** *(also Gram)* Verneinung *f*; **to answer in the ~** eine verneinende Antwort geben; *(= say no)* mit Nein antworten; *(= refuse)* einen abschlägigen Bescheid geben; **his answer was a curt ~** er antwortete mit einem knappen Nein; **put this sentence into the ~** verneinen Sie diesen Satz; **how do you express this statement in the ~?** wie drückt man diesen Satz verneint *or* in der Verneinungsform aus?
b *(Gram: = word)* Verneinungswort *nt*, Negation *f*; *(Math)* negative Zahl; **two ~s make a positive** *(Math)* zweimal minus gibt plus
c *(Phot)* Negativ *nt*
d *(Elec)* negativer Pol
INTERJ nein
VT *amendment, plan* ablehnen; *statement* negieren

negative equity N *(Fin) Differenz zwischen dem gefallenen Wert einer Immobilie und der auf ihr lastenden höheren Hypothekenschuld*

negative feedback N *(Elec)* negative Rückkopplung, Gegenkopplung *f*; *(= criticism)* negatives Feedback, negative Reaktion; **to give sb ~ (about sb/sth)** jdm eine negative Rückmeldung (zu jdm/etw) geben; **to get ~ (about sb/sth)** eine negative Rückmeldung (zu jdm/etw) erhalten

negatively ['negətɪvlɪ] ADV negativ; *(= in the negative)* verneinend; **to respond ~** ablehnend *or* negativ reagieren

negative sign N *(Math)* Minuszeichen *nt*, negatives Vorzeichen

negativity [negə'tɪvɪtɪ] N negative Einstellung

neglect [nɪ'glekt] **VT** vernachlässigen; *promise* nicht einhalten; *advice* nicht befolgen; *opportunity* versäumen; **to ~ to do sth** es versäumen *or* unterlassen, etw zu tun **N** Vernachlässigung *f*; *(of promise)* Nichteinhalten *nt*; *(of opportunity)* Versäumen *nt*; *(of advice)* Nichtbefolgung *f*; *(= negligence)* Nachlässigkeit *f*; **~ of one's duties** Pflichtvergessenheit *f*, Pflichtversäumnis *nt*; **to be in a state of ~** verwahrlost sein, völlig vernachlässigt sein; **the garden suffered through (our) ~** der Garten hat darunter gelitten, dass wir ihn vernachlässigt haben

neglected [nɪ'glektɪd] ADJ vernachlässigt; *area, garden etc also* verwahrlost; **to feel ~** sich vernachlässigt fühlen

neglectful [nɪ'glektfʊl] ADJ nachlässig; *father, government etc* pflichtvergessen; **to be ~ of sb/sth** sich nicht um jdn/etw kümmern, jdn/etw vernachlässigen

neglectfully [nɪ'glektfəlɪ] ADV nachlässig

négligé(e) ['neglɪʒeɪ] N Negligee *nt*, Negligé *nt*

negligence ['neglɪdʒəns] N *(= carelessness)* Nachlässigkeit *f*; *(causing danger, Jur)* Fahrlässigkeit *f*

negligent ['neglɪdʒənt] ADJ **a** nachlässig; *(causing danger, damage)* fahrlässig; **to be ~ of sb/sth** jdn/etw vernachlässigen; **to be ~ of one's duties** pflichtvergessen sein; **both drivers were ~** beide Fahrer haben sich fahrlässig verhalten **b** *(= off-hand)* lässig

negligently ['neglɪdʒəntlɪ] ADV **a** nachlässig; *(= causing danger, damage)* fahrlässig; **he very ~ forgot** in seiner Nachlässigkeit *or* nachlässigerweise vergaß er es **b** *(= in an offhand manner)* lässig

negligible ['neglɪdʒəbl] ADJ unwesentlich, unbedeutend; *quantity, amount, sum also* geringfügig, unerheblich; **the opposition in this race is ~** in diesem Rennen gibt es keinen ernst zu nehmenden Gegner

negotiable [nɪ'gəʊʃɪəbl] ADJ **a** *(Comm) (= can be sold)* verkäuflich, veräußerlich; *(= can be transferred)* übertragbar; **not ~** nicht verkäuflich/übertragbar **b** **these terms are ~** über diese Bedingungen kann verhandelt werden **c** *road* befahrbar; *river, mountain, pass* passierbar; *obstacle, difficulty* überwindbar

negotiate [nɪ'gəʊʃɪeɪt] **VT** **a** *(= discuss)* verhandeln über *(+acc)*; *(= bring about)* aushandeln **b** *bend in road* nehmen; *(horse) fence* nehmen; *river, mountain, rapids* passieren; *obstacle, difficulty* überwinden **c** *(Comm) shares* handeln mit; *sale* tätigen *(form)* **VI** verhandeln *(for* über *+acc)*

negotiating table [nɪ'gəʊʃɪeɪtɪŋ,teɪbl] N Verhandlungstisch *m*

negotiation [nɪ,gəʊʃɪ'eɪʃən] N **a** *(= discussion)* Verhandlung *f*; *(= bringing about)* Aushandlung *f*; **the matter is still under ~** über diese Sache wird noch verhandelt; **the price is a matter for ~** über den Preis kann verhandelt werden; **by ~** auf dem Verhandlungsweg; **~ skills** Verhandlungsgeschick *nt* **b** *usu pl (= talks)* Verhandlung *f*; **to begin ~s with sb** Verhandlungen *pl* mit jdm aufnehmen; **to be in ~(s) with sb** mit jdm in Verhandlungen stehen **c** *(of river, moun-*

tain, rapids) Passage *f*, Passieren *nt*; *(of obstacle, difficulty)* Überwindung *f*

negotiator [nɪˈgəʊʃieɪtəˈ] N Unterhändler(in) *m(f)*

Negress [ˈniːgres] N *(neg!)* Schwarze *f*, Negerin *f (neg!)*

Negro [ˈniːgrəʊ] *(neg!)* ADJ Neger- *(neg!)*; **~ slave** Negersklave *m*/-sklavin *f* N Schwarze(r) *m*, Neger *m (neg!)*

Negroid [ˈniːgrɔɪd] ADJ negroid

neigh [neɪ] VI wiehern N Wiehern *nt*

neighbour, *(US)* **neighbor** [ˈneɪbəˈ] N **a** Nachbar(in) *m(f)*; *(at table)* Tischnachbar(in) *m(f)* → **next-door b** *(Bibl)* Nächste(r) *mf* VT *(= adjoin) country, river* angrenzen an *(+acc)* VI **a to ~ on** *(= adjoin)* (an)grenzen an *(+acc)*; *(= approach)* grenzen an *(+acc)* **b** *(US inf)* **to neighbor with sb** gutnachbarliche Beziehungen *pl* zu jdm haben

neighbourhood, *(US)* **neighborhood** [ˈneɪbəhʊd] N *(= district)* Gegend *f*, Viertel *nt*; *(= people)* Nachbarschaft *f*; **get to know your ~** lernen Sie Ihre nähere Umgebung *or (people also)* Ihre Nachbarschaft kennen; **all the children from the ~** all die Kinder aus der Nachbarschaft *or* der Gegend; **she is very popular in this ~** sie ist bei allen Nachbarn *or* in der ganzen Nachbarschaft sehr beliebt; **your friendly ~ policeman** der freundliche Polizist in Ihrer Nachbarschaft; **in the ~ of sth** in der Nähe von etw; *(fig: = approximately)* um etw herum

neighbourhood watch N *(Brit) Vereinigung von Bürgern, die durch Straßenwachen etc in ihrem Bezirk die Polizei bei der Verbrechensbekämpfung unterstützen*

neighbouring, *(US)* **neighboring** [ˈneɪbərɪŋ] ADJ benachbart, angrenzend; **~ village/house** Nachbardorf/-haus *nt*; **~ country** Nachbarland *nt*; **in ~ Latvia** im benachbarten Lettland

neighbourly, *(US)* **neighborly** [ˈneɪbəlɪ] ADJ *person* nachbarlich; *action, relations* gutnachbarlich; **they are ~ people** sie sind gute Nachbarn

neighing [ˈneɪɪŋ] N Wiehern *nt*

neither [ˈnaɪðəˈ] ADV **~ ... nor** weder ... noch; **he ~ knows nor cares** er weiß es nicht und will es auch nicht wissen
CONJ auch nicht; **if you don't go, ~ shall I** wenn du nicht gehst, gehe ich auch nicht; **I'm not going – ~ am I** ich gehe nicht – ich auch nicht; **he didn't do it (and) ~ did his sister** weder er noch seine Schwester haben es getan; **I can't go, ~ do I want to** ich kann und will auch nicht gehen
ADJ keine(r, s) (der beiden); **~ one of them** keiner von beiden; **in ~ case** in keinem Fall, weder in dem einen noch in dem anderen Fall
PRON keine(r, s); **~ of them** keiner von beiden; **which will you take? – ~** welches nehmen Sie? – keines (von beiden)

nelly [ˈnelɪ] N **not on your ~** *(Brit hum inf)* nie im Leben

nelson [ˈnelsən] N *(Wrestling)* Nelson *m*

nem con [ˌnemˈkɒn] ADV ohne Gegenstimme

nemesis [ˈnemɪsɪs] N Nemesis *f (liter)*, die gerechte Strafe

neo- [ˈniːəʊ-] PREF neo-, Neo-; **neoclassical** ADJ klassizistisch; **neoclassicism** N Klassizismus *m*; **neocolonial** ADJ neokolonialistisch; **neocolonialism** N Neokolonialismus *m*

neodymium [ˌniːəʊˈdɪmɪəm] N *(Chem)* Neodym *nt*

neo: **neofascism** N Neofaschismus *m*; **neofascist** ADJ neofaschistisch N Neofaschist(in) *m(f)*

neolithic [ˌniːəʊˈlɪθɪk] ADJ jungsteinzeitlich, neolithisch

neologism [nɪˈɒlədʒɪzəm] N *(Ling)* (Wort)neubildung *f*, Neologismus *m*

neologize [nɪˈɒlədʒaɪz] VI *(Ling)* neue Wörter bilden *or* benutzen

neon [ˈniːɒn] N *(Chem)* Neon *nt* ADJ *attr* Neon-; **~ tube** Neonröhre *f*

neo-Nazi [ˌniːəʊˈnɑːtsɪ] N Neonazi *m* ADJ neonazistisch

neon light N Neonlicht *nt*

neon sign N *(= name)* Neon- *or* Leuchtschild *nt*; *(= advertisement)* Neon- *or* Leuchtreklame *f no pl*

neophyte [ˈniːəʊfaɪt] N Neubekehrte(r) *mf*, Neophyt(in) *m(f) (spec)*; *(in RC church)* neu geweihter Priester

Neo: **Neo-Platonic** [ˌniːəʊpləˈtɒnɪk] ADJ neuplatonisch; **Neo-Platonism** N Neuplatonismus *m*; **Neo-Platonist** N Neuplatoniker(in) *m(f)*

Nepal [nɪˈpɔːl] N Nepal *nt*

Nepalese [ˌnepəˈliːz], **Nepali** [nɪˈpɔːlɪ] ADJ nepalesisch, nepalisch N **a** Nepalese *m*, Nepalesin *f* **b** *(Ling)* Nepalesisch *nt*

nephew [ˈnevjuː, ˈnefjuː] N Neffe *m*

nephritis [neˈfraɪtɪs] N Nierenentzündung *f*, Nephritis *f (spec)*

nepotism [ˈnepətɪzəm] N Vetternwirtschaft *f*, Nepotismus *m*

Neptune [ˈneptjuːn] N *(Astron, Myth)* Neptun *m*

neptunium [nepˈtjuːnɪəm] N *(Chem)* Neptunium *nt*

nerd [nɜːd] N *(inf)* Dumpfbacke *f (sl)*; **computer ~** Computerfreak *m (inf)*

nerdy [ˈnɜːdɪ] ADJ *(inf)* **a** *person* freakig *(inf)*, *intelligent aber nicht gesellschaftsfähig* **b** *thing* beknackt *(sl)*; *(= cool)* geil *(sl)*

nereid [ˈnɪərɪɪd] N *(Myth)* Nereide *f*, Meerjungfrau *f*

nerve [nɜːv] N **a** *(Anat)* Nerv *m*; **to suffer from ~s** nervös sein; **to have an attack of ~s** in Panik geraten, durchdrehen *(inf)*; *(before exam also)* Prüfungsangst haben; **to be in a terrible state of ~s** mit den Nerven völlig fertig *or* herunter sein; **it's only ~s** du bist/er ist *etc* nur nervös; **to be all ~s** ein Nervenbündel sein; **his ~s are bad** er hat schlechte Nerven; **to get on sb's ~s** *(inf)* jdm auf die Nerven gehen *or* fallen; **he doesn't know what ~s are** er hat die Ruhe weg *(inf)*; **to live on one's ~s** nervlich angespannt sein, völlig überreizt sein; **to have ~s of steel** Nerven wie Drahtseile haben; **his speech touched** *or* **struck a (raw) ~** seine Rede berührte einen wunden Punkt
b *no pl (= courage)* Mut *m*; **to lose/hold** *or* **keep one's ~** die Nerven verlieren/nicht verlieren; **to regain one's ~**, **to get one's ~ back** seine Angst überwinden; **his ~ failed him** ihn verließ der Mut, er bekam Angst; **to have the ~ to do sth** sich trauen, etw zu tun; **a test of ~** eine Nervenprobe
c *no pl (inf: = impudence)* Frechheit *f*, Unverschämtheit *f*; **to have the ~ to do sth** die Frechheit besitzen, etw zu tun; **he's got a ~!** der hat Nerven! *(inf)*; **what a ~!, the ~ of it!** so eine Frechheit!
d *(Bot)* Ader *f*, Nerv *m*
VR **to ~ oneself for sth/to do sth** sich seelisch und moralisch auf etw *(acc)* vorbereiten/darauf vorbereiten, etw zu tun; **I can't ~ myself to do it** ich bringe einfach den Mut nicht auf, das zu tun
VT **to ~ sb for sth** jdm den Mut geben, etw zu tun

nerve *in cpds* Nerven-; **nerve cell** N Nervenzelle *f*; **nerve centre**, *(US)* **nerve center** N *(Anat)* Nervenzentrum *nt*; *(fig also)* Schaltstelle *or* -zentrale *f*; **nerve ending** N Nervende *nt*; **nerve gas** N Nervengas *nt*

nerveless [ˈnɜːvlɪs] ADJ **a** *(= without nerves)* ohne Nerven; *plant* ohne Adern *or* Nerven **b** *(= confident) person* gelassen, seelenruhig

nerve-racking, **nerve-wracking** [ˈnɜːvrækɪŋ] ADJ nervenaufreibend

nervous [ˈnɜːvəs] ADJ **a** *(Anat)* Nerven-; *(= related to the nerves) problem, disorder* nervös (bedingt); *exhaustion, reflex* nervös; **~ tension** Nervenanspannung *f*
b *(= apprehensive, timid)* ängstlich; *(= on edge)* nervös; **to be** *or* **feel ~** *(= be afraid)* Angst haben; *(= be worried)* sich *(dat)* Sorgen machen; *(= be on edge)* nervös sein; **you make me (feel) ~** du machst mich (noch) ganz nervös; **I am ~ about the exam/him** mir ist bange vor dem Examen/um ihn; **I was rather ~ about giving him the job** mir war nicht wohl bei dem Gedanken, ihm die Stelle zu geben; **I am rather ~ about diving** ich habe eine ziemliche Angst vor dem Tauchen; **to be in a ~ state** nervös sein

nervous *in cpds* Nerven-; **nervous breakdown** N Nervenzusammenbruch *m*; **nervous disease** N Nervenkrankheit *f*; **nervous energy** N Vitalität *f*; **after the exam I still had a lot of ~** nach dem Examen war ich noch ganz aufgedreht

nervously [ˈnɜːvəslɪ] ADV *(= apprehensively)* ängstlich; *(= on edge)* nervös

nervous Nellie [-ˈnelɪ] N *(US inf)* Flattermann *m (inf)*

nervousness [ˈnɜːvəsnɪs] N Ängstlichkeit *f*; *(= edgy state)* Nervosität *f*; **his ~ about flying** seine Angst vor dem Fliegen

nervous: **nervous strain** N Nervenanspannung *f*; **nervous system** N Nervensystem *nt*; **nervous tension** N Nervenanspannung *f*; **nervous wreck** N *(inf)* **to be/look a ~** mit den Nerven völlig am Ende *or* fertig sein

nervy [ˈnɜːvɪ] ADJ *(+er)* **a** *(Brit: = tense)* nervös **b** *(dated US inf: = cheeky)* frech, unverschämt

nescient [ˈnesɪənt] ADJ *(geh)* unwissend

nest [nest] N **a** *(of birds, bees, ants)* Nest *nt*; **to leave** *or* **fly the ~** *(lit, fig)* das Nest verlassen **b** *(of boxes etc)* Satz *m*; **a ~ of tables** ein Satz *m* Tische *or* von Tischen **c** *(fig: = den)* Schlupfwinkel *m*; **a ~ of spies/criminals** ein Agenten-/ /Verbrechernest *nt*; **a ~ of machine guns** eine Maschinengewehrstellung VI **a** *(bird)* nisten **b to go ~ing** Nester ausheben *or* ausnehmen

nest box N Nistkasten *m*

nested [ˈnestɪd] ADJ *(Comput) menu* verschachtelt

nest egg N *(lit)* Nestei *nt*; *(fig)* Notgroschen *m*; **to have a nice little ~** *(fig)* sich *(dat)* einen Notgroschen zurückgelegt haben

nesting [ˈnestɪŋ]: **nesting box** N Nistkasten *m*; **nesting instinct** N *(lit, fig)* Nistinstinkt *m* or -trieb *m*

nestle [ˈnesl] VI **to ~ down in bed** sich ins Bett kuscheln; **to ~ up to sb** sich an jdn schmiegen *or* kuscheln; **to ~ against sb** sich an jdn anschmiegen; **the village nestling in the hills** das Dorf, das zwischen den Bergen eingebettet liegt; **a house nestling** *or* **~d among the trees** ein von Bäumen eingerahmtes Haus

nestling [ˈneslɪŋ] N Nestling *m*

Net [net] N *(inf)* **the ~** *(Comput)* das Internet

net[1] [net] N **a** *(lit, fig)* Netz *nt*; **to make ~s** Netze knüpfen; **to be caught in the ~** *(fig)* in die Falle gehen; **to be caught in the police ~** *(fig)* der Polizei ins Netz *or* Garn gehen; **he felt the ~ closing round him** *(fig)* er fühlte, wie sich die Schlinge immer enger zog; **to cast one's ~ wider** die Auswahl erweitern; **to slip through the ~** *(criminal)* durch die Maschen schlüpfen
b *(Sport)* Netz *nt*; **to come up to the ~** ans Netz gehen; **the ball's in the ~** der Ball ist im Tor *or* Netz; **the ~s** *(Cricket) von Netzen umspannter Übungsplatz*
c *(Tex)* Netzgewebe *nt*; *(for curtains, clothes etc)* Tüll *m*
VT **a** *fish, game, butterfly* mit dem Netz fangen; *(fig) criminal* fangen; **the police have ~ted the criminals** die Verbrecher sind der Polizei ins Netz gegangen
b *(Sport) ball* ins Netz schlagen; **to ~ a goal** ein Tor schießen *or* erzielen

net[2] ADJ **a** *price, income, weight* netto, Netto-; **~ disposable income** verfügbares Nettoeinkommen; **it costs £15 ~** es kostet £ 15 netto **b** *(fig)* End-, letztendlich; **~ result** Endergebnis *nt*; **~ effect** Endeffekt *m* VT netto einnehmen; *(in wages, salary)* netto verdienen; *(show, deal* *etc)* einbringen; **I ~ted a salary of £850 a month** ich bezog ein Gehalt von £ 850 netto im Monat, ich hatte ein monatliches Nettogehalt von £ 850

net: **net assets** PL Nettovermögen *nt*; **net bag** N (Einkaufs)netz *nt*; **net balance** N *(Econ)* Nettosaldo *m*, Reinüberschuss *m*; **netball** N *(Brit)* Korbball *m*; **net card** N *(Comput)* Netzwerkkkarte *f*; **net cord** N *(Tennis)* Netzkante *f*; **net curtain** N *(Brit)* Tüllgardine *f*, Store *m*

nether ['neðəʳ] ADJ *(liter)* untere(r, s); **~ regions** Unterwelt *f*; *(hum inf)* untere Regionen *pl (hum inf)*

Netherlander ['neðə,lændəʳ] N Niederländer(in) *m(f)*

Netherlands ['neðələndz] PL **the ~** die Niederlande *pl*

nethermost ['neðəməʊst] ADJ *(liter)* unterste(r, s)

netherworld ['neðəwɜ:ld] N *(liter)* Unterwelt *f*

netiquette ['netɪket] N *(Comput)* Netiquette *f*, Net(t)ikette *f*

netizen ['netɪzn] N *(Comput)* Netizen *m*, Dauersurfer(in) *m(f)*

net: **net play** N *(Tennis)* Spiel *nt* am Netz; **net profit** N Reingewinn *m*, Nettoertrag *m*; **netspeak** ['netspi:k] N *(Comput inf)* Internetjargon *m*; **net stocking** N Netzstrumpf *m*; **Net surfer** N Internetsurfer(in) *m(f)*

nett ADJ = **net²**

netting ['netɪŋ] N Netz *nt*; *(= wire netting)* Maschendraht *m*; *(= fabric)* Netzgewebe *nt*; *(for curtains etc)* Tüll *m*

nettle ['netl] **N** *(Bot)* Nessel *f*; **to grasp the ~** *(fig)* in den sauren Apfel beißen **VT** *(fig inf) person* ärgern, wurmen *(inf)*, fuchsen *(inf)*

nettle: **nettle rash** N Nesselausschlag *m*; **nettle sting** N Brennnesselstich *m*; **her legs were covered in ~s** ihre Beine waren von den Brennnesseln völlig zerstochen

network ['netwɜ:k] **N** **a** *(lit, fig)* Netz *nt* **b** *(Rad, TV)* Sendenetz *nt*; *(Elec, Comput)* Netzwerk *nt*; **~ card/driver/server** *(Comput)* Netzwerkkarte *f*/-treiber *m*/-server *m* **VT** *(inf) programme* im ganzen Netzbereich ausstrahlen **VI** *(= make contacts)* Kontakte knüpfen

network access N *(Comput)* Netzzugang *m*

network drive N *(Comput)* Netzlaufwerk *nt*

networking ['netwɜ:kɪŋ] N **a** *(Comput)* Vernetzung *f*; *(= operating a network)* Netzwerkbetrieb *m* **b** *(= making contacts)* Knüpfen *nt* von Kontakten; Networking *nt*

network operator N *(Comput)* Netzbetreiber *m*

neural ['njʊərəl] ADJ Nerven-; **~ cell** Nervenzelle *f*

neuralgia [njʊə'rældʒə] N Neuralgie *f*, Nervenschmerzen *pl*

neural network N *(Anat)* Nervennetzwerk *nt*; *(Comput)* neurales Netz

neurasthenia [,njʊərəs'θi:nɪə] N Neurasthenie *f*, Nervenschwäche *f*

neurasthenic [,njʊərəs'θenɪk] **N** Neurastheniker(in) *m(f)* **ADJ** neurasthenisch

neuritis [njʊə'raɪtɪs] N Neuritis *f*, Nervenentzündung *f*

neuro- ['njʊərəʊ-] *in cpds* Neuro-, neuro-; **neurobiology** N Neurobiologie *f*; **neurochemistry** N Neurochemie *f*; **neurolinguistic programming** N neurolinguistisches Programmieren

neurological [,njʊərə'lɒdʒɪkəl] ADJ neurologisch

neurologist [njʊə'rɒlədʒɪst] N Neurologe *m*, Neurologin *f*, Nervenarzt *m*/-ärztin *f*

neurology [njʊə'rɒlədʒɪ] N Neurologie *f*

neuron ['njʊərɒn], **neurone** ['njʊərəʊn] N *(Biol)* Neuron *nt*

neuropath ['njʊərəpæθ] N Nervenkranke(r) *mf*

neuropathic [njʊərəʊ'pæθɪk] ADJ neuropathisch

neuropathology [,njʊərəʊpə'θɒlədʒɪ] N Neuropathologie *f*, Lehre *f* von den Nervenkrankheiten

neurosis [njʊə'rəʊsɪs] N *pl* **neuroses** [njʊə'rəʊsi:z] Neurose *f*

neurosurgeon ['njʊərəʊ,sɜ:dʒən] N Neurochirurg(in) *m(f)*

neurosurgery ['njʊərəʊ,sɜ:dʒərɪ] N Neurochirurgie *f*

neurosurgical [,njʊərəʊ'sɜ:dʒɪkəl] ADJ neurochirurgisch

neurotic [njʊə'rɒtɪk] **ADJ** neurotisch; **to be ~ about sth** in Bezug auf etw *(acc)* neurotisch sein; **he's getting rather ~ about this problem** das Problem ist bei ihm schon zur Neurose geworden **N** Neurotiker(in) *m(f)*

neurotically [njʊə'rɒtɪkəlɪ] ADV neurotisch

neurotoxin [,njʊərəʊ'tɒksɪn] N *(Pharm)* Neurotoxin *nt (spec)*, Nervengift *nt*

neuter ['nju:təʳ] **ADJ** **a** *(Gram)* sächlich; **this word is ~** dieses Wort ist sächlich *or* ein Neutrum **b** *animal, person* geschlechtslos; *(= castrated)* kastriert; *plant* ungeschlechtlich **N** **a** *(Gram)* Neutrum *nt*; *(= noun)* Neutrum *nt*, sächliches Substantiv; **in the ~** in der sächlichen Form, im Neutrum **b** *(= animal)* geschlechtsloses Wesen; *(castrated)* kastriertes Tier; *(= plant)* ungeschlechtliche Pflanze **VT** *cat, dog* kastrieren; *female, male* sterilisieren; *(esp Brit fig: = render ineffective)* kastrieren

neutral ['nju:trəl] **ADJ** neutral; *(= colourless) shoe cream* farblos; **you have a very ~ English accent** an Ihrem Akzent erkennt man nicht, woher in England Sie stammen **N** **a** *(= person)* Neutrale(r) *mf*; *(= country)* neutrales Land **b** *(Aut)* Leerlauf *m*; **to be in ~** im Leerlauf sein; **to put the car/gear in ~** den Gang herausnehmen

neutralism ['nju:trəlɪzəm] N Neutralismus *m*

neutrality [nju:'trælɪtɪ] N Neutralität *f*

neutralization [,nju:trəlaɪ'zeɪʃən] N Neutralisation *f*; *(fig)* Aufhebung *f*

neutralize ['nju:trəlaɪz] VT neutralisieren *(also Chem)*; *(fig)* aufheben; *the force of an argument* die Spitze nehmen *(+dat)*; **neutralizing agent** neutralisierender Wirkstoff

neutrino [nju:'traɪnəʊ] N Neutrino *nt*

neutron ['nju:trɒn] N Neutron *nt*

neutron: **neutron bomb** N Neutronenbombe *f*; **neutron star** N Neutronenstern *m*

never ['nevəʳ] ✪ 6.3, 18.3 ADV **a** *(= not ever)* nie, niemals *(geh)*; **I ~ eat it** das esse ich nie; **I have ~ seen him** ich habe ihn (noch) nie gesehen; **~ again** nie wieder; **~ do that again** mach das bloß nie wieder *or* nicht noch einmal; **~ say ~** sag niemals nie; **I'll ~ try that again** das werde ich nie wieder *or* nicht noch einmal versuchen; **~ again will I see my own country** ich werde meine Heimat nie wiedersehen; **~ before** noch nie; **I had ~ seen him before today** ich hatte ihn (vor heute) noch nie gesehen; **~ before have men climbed this peak** nie zuvor haben Menschen diesen Gipfel erklommen; **~ before had there been such a disaster** eine solche Katastrophe hatte es noch nie (zuvor) gegeben; **~ even** nicht einmal; **~ ever** absolut *or* garantiert nie; **I have ~ ever been so insulted** ich bin noch nie so beleidigt worden; **I have ~ yet been able to find ...** ich habe ... bisher noch nicht finden können; **I ~ heard such a thing!** so etwas ist mir noch nie zu Ohren gekommen!

b *(emph: = not)* **that will ~ do!** das geht ganz und gar nicht!; **I ~ slept a wink** *(inf)* ich habe kein Auge zugetan; **he ~ so much as smiled** er hat nicht einmal gelächelt; **he said ~ a word** er hat kein einziges Wort gesagt; **you've ~ left it behind!** *(inf)* du hast es doch wohl nicht etwa liegen lassen! *(inf)*; **you've ~ done that!** hast du das wirklich gemacht?; **would you do it again? – ~!** würdest du das noch einmal machen? – bestimmt nicht; **Spurs were beaten – ~!** *(inf)* Spurs ist geschlagen worden – das ist doch nicht möglich! *or* nein! *or* nein wirklich? *(iro)*; **well I ~ (did)!** *(inf)* nein, so was!; **~ fear** keine Angst

never: **never-ending** ADJ endlos, unaufhörlich; *discussions, negotiations also* nicht enden wollend *attr*; **it seemed ~** es schien kein Ende nehmen zu wollen; **a ~ job** eine Arbeit ohne Ende; **never-failing** ADJ *method etc* unfehlbar; *source, spring etc* unversieglich; **nevermore** ADV *(liter)* nimmermehr *(liter)*, niemals wieder; **he departed ~ to return** er ging und kehrte niemals wieder *(liter)*; **never-never** N *(Brit inf)* **on the ~** auf Pump *(inf)*; **never-never land** N Wunsch- *or* Traumwelt *f*

nevertheless [,nevəðə'les] ✪ 26.2 ADV trotzdem, dennoch, nichtsdestoweniger *(geh)*

never-to-be-forgotten ['nevətəbi:fə'gɒtn] ADJ *attr* unvergesslich

new [nju:] ADJ *(+er)* **a** neu; **the ~ people at number five** die Neuen in Nummer fünf; **that's nothing ~** das ist nichts Neues; **that's something ~** das ist wirklich ganz was Neues!; **what's ~?** *(inf)* was gibts Neues? *(inf)*; **to make sth (look) like ~** etw wie neu machen; **as ~** wie neu; **this system is ~ to me** dieses System ist mir neu; **he is a ~ man** *(fig)* er ist ein neuer Mensch; **that's a ~ one on me** *(inf)* das ist mir ja ganz neu; *(joke)* den kenne ich noch nicht; **a ~ kind of engine** ein neuartiger Motor

b *(= fresh) potatoes* neu; *wine* neu, jung; *bread* frisch; **~ snow** Neuschnee *m*

c *(= modern, novel)* modern; *fashion, style* neu; **the ~ woman** die moderne Frau; **the ~ diplomacy** die neue Diplomatie; **the New Look** *(Fashion)* der New Look

d *(= lately arrived, inexperienced) person, pupil, recruit* neu; **the ~ boys/girls** die Neuen *pl*, die neuen Schüler *pl*; **~ mother** junge Mutter; **the ~ rich** die Neureichen *pl*; **I'm quite ~ to this job/to the company** ich bin neu in dieser Stelle/Firma; **to be ~ to business** ein Neuling *m* im Geschäftsleben sein; **are you ~ here?** sind Sie neu hier?; **I am ~ to this place** ich bin erst seit Kurzem hier; **she's ~ to the game** *(Sport)* sie ist erst seit Kurzem bei diesem Sport dabei; *(fig)* sie ist neu auf diesem Gebiet

New Ager N *(inf)* Newagejünger(in) *m(f)*, New-Age-Jünger(in) *m(f)*

New Age Traveller N *(Brit)* Aussteiger(in) *m(f)*

newbie ['nju:bɪ] N *(inf: = newcomer)* Neuling *m*, Neue(r) *mf (inf)*

new: **new blood** N *(fig)* frisches Blut; **newborn** ADJ neugeboren; **the ~ babies** die Neugeborenen; **~ screening** *(Med)* Neugeborenenscreening *nt*; **new broom** N *(fig)* neuer Besen; **newcomer** N *(who has just arrived)* Neuankömmling *m*; *(in job, subject etc)* Neuling *m (to in +dat)*; *(in business)* Neueinsteiger(in) *m(f)*; **they are ~s to this town** sie sind neu in dieser Stadt, sie sind Zuzügler; **for the ~s I will recap** für diejenigen, die neu dazugekommen sind, fasse ich kurz zusammen; **New Delhi** [,nju:'delɪ] N Neu-Delhi *nt*

newel ['nju:əl] N *(of spiral staircase)* Spindel *f*; *(supporting banister)* Pfosten *m*

new: **New England** N Neuengland *nt*; **New Englander** N Neuengländer(in) *m(f)*; **new face** N neues Gesicht, Neuling *m*; **newfangled** ADJ neumodisch; **new-fashioned** ADJ modisch, modern; **new-found** ADJ *friend, happiness* neu(gefunden); *confidence* neugeschöpft

Newfoundland ['nju:fəndlənd] **N** Neufundland *nt* **ADJ** *attr* neufundländisch; **~ dog** Neufundländer *m*

Newfoundlander [,nju:fənd'ləndəʳ] N Neufundländer(in) *m(f)*

New Guinea N Neuguinea *nt*

newish ['nju:ɪʃ] ADJ ziemlich neu

new: **New Lad** N *(Brit inf)* Macho *m* neuen Stils; **new-laid** ADJ frisch; **new-look** ADJ *(inf)* neu

newly ['nju:lɪ] ADV frisch; **a ~ dug trench** ein frisch gezogener Graben; **a ~ dug grave** ein frisches Grab; ~ **made** ganz neu; *bread, cake etc* frisch gebacken; *road, gardens etc* neu angelegt; ~ **arrived** neu angekommen; ~ **awakened** neu erwacht; ~ **formed/found** neu geschaffen/gefunden; ~ **married** frisch vermählt; **a ~ industrialized** *or* **industrializing country** ein industrielles Schwellenland

newlyweds ['nju:lɪwedz] PL *(inf)* Neu- *or* Frischvermählte *pl*

new: **New Mexico** N New Mexico *nt*; **new moon** N Neumond *m*; **there's a ~ tonight** heute Nacht ist Neumond; **new-mown** ADJ frisch gemäht

newness ['nju:nɪs] N Neuheit *f*; *(of bread, cheese etc)* Frische *f*; **his ~ to this job/the trade/this town** die Tatsache, dass er neu in dieser Arbeit ist/dass er Neuling ist/dass er erst seit Kurzem in dieser Stadt ist

New Orleans [,nju:ɔ:'li:nz] N New Orleans *nt*

news [nju:z] N *no pl* **a** *(= report, information)* Nachricht *f*; *(= recent development)* Neuigkeit(en) *f(pl)*; **a piece of ~** eine Neuigkeit; **I have ~/no ~ of him** ich habe von ihm gehört/nicht von ihm gehört, ich weiß Neues/nichts Neues von ihm; **there is no ~** es gibt nichts Neues zu berichten; **have you heard the ~?** haben Sie schon (das Neueste) gehört?; **have you heard the ~ about Fred?** haben Sie schon das Neueste über Fred gehört?; **tell us your ~** erzähl uns die Neuigkeiten *or* das Neueste; **let us have** *or* **send us some ~ of yourself** lassen Sie mal von sich hören; **what's your ~?** was gibts Neues?; **is there any ~?** gibt es etwas Neues?; **I have ~ for you** *(iro)* ich habe eine Überraschung für dich; **bad/sad/good ~** schlimme *or* schlechte/traurige/gute Nachricht(en); **that is good ~** das ist erfreulich zu hören, das sind ja gute Nachrichten; **that's bad ~ for English football** das ist ein schwerer Schlag für den englischen Fußball; **when the ~ of his death/the ~ broke** als sein Tod/es bekannt wurde; **who will break the ~ to him?** wer wird es ihm sagen *or* beibringen?; **that is ~ (to me)!** das ist (mir) ganz neu!; **that isn't exactly ~** das ist nichts Neues; **it will be ~ to him that ...** er wird staunen, dass ...; **~ travels fast** wie sich doch alles herumspricht; **bad ~ travels fast** schlechte Nachrichten verbreiten sich schnell; **as far as I'm concerned, he's bad ~** *(inf)* für mich bedeutet er (nichts als) Ärger; **no ~ is good ~** keine Nachricht ist gute Nachricht

b *(Press, Film, Rad, TV)* Nachrichten *pl*; **~ in brief** Kurznachrichten *pl*; **financial ~** Wirtschaftsbericht *m*; **sports ~** Sportnachrichten *pl*; **here is the ~** Sie hören nun Nachrichten; **it was on the ~** das kam in den Nachrichten; **to be in the ~** von sich reden machen; **to make ~** Schlagzeilen machen; **that's not ~** damit kann man keine Schlagzeilen machen

news: **news agency** N Nachrichtenagentur *f*, Nachrichtendienst *m*; **newsagent** N *(Brit)* Zeitungshändler(in) *m(f)*; **newsboy** N *(US)* Zeitungsjunge *m*; **news bulletin** N Bulletin *nt*; **newscast** N Nachrichtensendung *f*; **newscaster** N Nachrichtensprecher(in) *m(f)*; **news cinema** N Aktualitätenkino *nt*; **newscopy** N *(Press, TV)* Bericht *m*; **newsdealer** N *(US)* Zeitungshändler(in) *m(f)*; **news desk** N Nachrichtenredaktion *f*; **news editor** N Nachrichtenredakteur(in) *m(f)*; **newsflash** N Kurzmeldung *f*; **news gathering** N *no pl* Sammeln *nt* von Informationen; **newsgirl** N *(US)* Reporterin *f*; **newsgroup** N *(Internet)* Newsgroup *f*; **news hawk** N *(inf)* Zeitungsmann *m*/-frau *f* *(inf)*, Reporter(in) *m(f)*; **news headlines** PL Kurznachrichten *pl*; *(= recap)* Nachrichten *pl* in Kürze; **news hound** N = **news hawk**; **news item** N Neuigkeit *f*, Nachricht *f*; **the three main ~s today** die drei Hauptpunkte der Nachrichten; **a short ~** *(in paper)* eine Pressenotiz, eine Zeitungsnotiz; **newsletter** N Rundschreiben *nt*, Mitteilungsblatt *nt*; **newsmaker** N *jd, der/etw, das Schlagzeilen macht*; **newsman** N *(esp US)* **a** *(= journalist)* Reporter *m*; *(= newsreader)* Nachrichtensprecher *n*; *(= anchor)* Moderator *m* **b** *(= paper man)* Zeitungsausträger *m*; *(selling newspapers)* Zeitungsverkäufer *m*; **newsmonger** N Klatschmaul *nt*; *(in paper)* Klatschspaltenschreiber(in) *m(f)*

New South Wales N Neusüdwales *nt*

newspaper ['nju:z,peɪpəʳ] N Zeitung *f*; **daily/weekly ~** Tages-/Wochenzeitung *f*; **he works on a ~** er ist bei einer Zeitung beschäftigt

newspaper: **newspaper article** N Zeitungsartikel *m*; **newspaper boy** N Zeitungsjunge *m*; **newspaper cutting** N Zeitungsausschnitt *m*; **newspaperman** N Zeitungsverkäufer *m*, Zeitungsmann *m* *(inf)*; *(= journalist)* Journalist *m*; **newspaper office** N Redaktion *f*; **newspaper report** N Zeitungsbericht *m*; **newspaperwoman** N Zeitungsverkäuferin *f*, Zeitungsfrau *f* *(inf)*; *(= journalist)* Journalistin *f*

news: **newsprint** N Zeitungspapier *nt*; **newsreader** N Nachrichtensprecher(in) *m(f)*; **newsreel** N Wochenschau *f*; **news release** N *(esp US)* = **press release**; **newsroom** N *(of newspaper)* Nachrichtenredaktion *f*; *(TV, Rad also)* Nachrichtenstudio *nt or* -zentrale *f*; **news satellite** N Nachrichtensatellit *m*; **news sheet** N Informationsblatt *nt*; **newsstand** N Zeitungsstand *m*; **news story** N Bericht *m*; **news theatre** N Aktualitätenkino *nt*

new-style ['nju:staɪl] ADJ im neuen Stil; **~ calendar** Kalender *m* nach neuer Zeitrechnung

news vendor N Zeitungsverkäufer(in) *m(f)*

newswoman N *(esp US)* **a** *(= journalist)* Reporterin *f*; *(= newsreader)* Nachrichtensprecherin *f*; *(= anchor)* Moderatorin *f* **b** *(= paper woman)* Zeitungsausträgerin *f*; *(selling newspapers)* Zeitungsverkäuferin *f*

newsworthiness N Neuigkeitswert *m*, Interessantheit *f* für die Medien

newsworthy ADJ berichtenswert, schlagzeilenträchtig; **to be ~** Neuigkeitswert haben

newsy ['nju:zɪ] ADJ *(+er)* *(inf)* voller Neuigkeiten

newt [nju:t] N Wassermolch *m*; **as pissed as a ~** *(Brit inf)* voll wie eine Strandhaubitze *(inf)*, stockbesoffen *(inf)*

new: **New Testament** N **the ~** das Neue Testament ADJ *attr* neutestamentlich, des Neuen Testaments; **new town** N neue Stadt, ≈ Retortenstadt *f* *(pej)*; **new wave** N *(in films)* neue Welle ADJ *attr* der neuen Welle; **new wool** N Schurwolle *f*; **pure ~** reine Schurwolle; **New World** N **the ~** die Neue Welt

New Year ✪ 23.2 N neues Jahr; *(= New Year's Day)* Neujahr *nt*; **to bring in** *or* **see in the ~** das neue Jahr begrüßen; **Happy ~!** (ein) glückliches *or* gutes neues Jahr!; **over/at ~** über/an Neujahr; **she's expecting a baby in the ~** sie erwartet im neuen Jahr ihr Baby; **~ resolution** (guter) Vorsatz für das neue Jahr

New Year's ['nju:jɪəz] N *(US inf)* = **New Year's Day, New Year's Eve**

New Year's Day N Neujahr *nt*, Neujahrstag *m*

New Year's Eve N Sylvester *nt*

New: **New York** N New York *nt* ADJ *attr* New Yorker; **New Yorker** N New Yorker(in) *m(f)*; **New Zealand** N Neuseeland *nt* ADJ *attr* Neuseeländer *attr*, neuseeländisch; **New Zealander** N Neuseeländer(in) *m(f)*

next [nekst] ADJ **a** *(in place)* nächste(r, s); ~ *(Comput: command)* weiter

b *(in time)* nächste(r, s); **come back ~ week/Tuesday** kommen Sie nächste Woche/nächsten Dienstag wieder; **he came back the ~ day/week** er kam am nächsten Tag/in der nächsten Woche wieder; **(the) ~ time I see him** wenn ich ihn das nächste Mal sehe; **(the) ~ moment he was gone** im nächsten Moment war er weg; **from one moment to the ~** von einem Moment zum anderen; **this time ~ week** nächste Woche um diese Zeit; **the year after ~** übernächstes Jahr; **the week after ~** übernächste Woche; **the ~ day but one** der übernächste Tag

c *(order)* nächste(r, s); **who's ~?** wer ist der Nächste?; **you're ~** Sie sind dran *(inf)* *or* an der Reihe; **~ please!** der Nächste bitte!; **I come ~ after you** ich bin nach Ihnen an der Reihe *or* dran *(inf)*; **I knew I was the ~ person to speak** ich wusste, dass ich als Nächster sprechen sollte; **I'll ask the very ~ person (I see)** ich frage den Nächsten(, den ich sehe); **my name is ~ on the list** mein Name kommt als nächster auf der Liste; **the ~ but one** der/die/das Übernächste; **the ~ thing to do is (to) polish it** als Nächstes poliert man (es); **the ~ thing I knew I ...** bevor ich wusste, wie mir geschah, ... ich ...; *(after fainting etc)* das Nächste, woran ich mich erinnern kann, war, dass ich ...; **the ~ size up/down** die nächstkleinere/nächstgrößere Größe

ADV **a** *(= the next time)* das nächste Mal; *(= afterwards)* danach; **what shall we do ~?** und was sollen wir als Nächstes machen?; **when shall we meet ~?** wann treffen wir uns wieder *or* das nächste Mal?; **a new dress! what ~?** ein neues Kleid? sonst noch was?; **whatever ~?** *(in surprise)* Sachen gibts! *(inf)*; *(despairingly)* wo soll das nur hinführen?

b **~ to sb/sth** neben jdm/etw; *(with motion)* neben jdn/etw; **the ~ to last row** die vorletzte Reihe; **he was ~ to last** er war der Vorletzte; **the ~ to bottom shelf** das vorletzte Brett, das zweitunterste Brett; **~ to the skin** (direkt) auf der Haut; **~ to nothing/nobody** so gut wie nichts/niemand; **~ to impossible** nahezu unmöglich; **I kept it ~ to my heart** *(most important thing)* es lag mir am meisten am Herzen; *(dearest thing)* es war mir das Liebste; **~ to useless** praktisch wertlos

c **the ~ best** der/die/das Nächstbeste; **this is the ~ best thing** das ist das Nächstbeste; **the ~ tallest/oldest boy** *(= second in order)* der zweitgrößte/zweitälteste Junge; **she is my ~ best friend** sie ist meine zweitbeste Freundin

N Nächste(r) *mf*; *(= child)* Nächste(s) *nt*

PREP *(old)* neben *(+dat)*

next door ['neks'dɔ:ʳ] ADV nebenan; **let's go ~** gehen wir nach nebenan; **they live ~ to us** sie wohnen (direkt) neben uns *or* (gleich) nebenan; **he has the room ~ to me** er hat das Zimmer neben mir; **we live ~ to each other** wir wohnen Tür an Tür; **the boy ~** der Junge von nebenan; **it's ~ to madness** das grenzt an Wahnsinn

next-door ['neks'dɔ:ʳ] ADJ **the ~ neighbour** *(Brit)* *or* **neighbor** *(US)* der direkte Nachbar; **we are ~ neighbours** *(Brit)* *or* **neighbors** *(US)* wir wohnen Tür an Tür; **the ~ house** das Nebenhaus; **the ~ room** das Zimmer nebenan, das Nebenzimmer

next friend N *(Jur)* Prozesspfleger(in) *m(f)* *(eines Minderjährigen)*

next of kin N *pl* - nächster Verwandter, nächste Verwandte, nächste Verwandte *pl*

nexus ['neksəs] N Verknüpfung *f*, Verkettung *f*

NF *(Brit) abbr of* **National Front**

NFL *(US) abbr of* **National Football League** *amerikanische Fußball-Nationalliga*

NFU *(Brit) abbr of* **National Farmers' Union** *Bauerngewerkschaft*

NG *(US) abbr of* **National Guard**

NGO *abbr of* **non-governmental organization**

NHS *(Brit) abbr of* **National Health Service**; **~ abortion** ≈ Abtreibung *f* auf Krankenschein

> **NHS**
>
> Der **National Health Service** oder auch **NHS** ist das Gesundheitswesen, das seit 1948 allen Einwohnern Großbritanniens eine kostenlose medizinische Versorgung garantiert. Der **NHS** wird überwiegend aus Steuergeldern finanziert. Dazu kommen noch andere Quellen wie die Beiträge zur **National Insurance**, die von Arbeitgebern wie Arbeitnehmern gezahlt werden, oder die Gebühren für Rezepte oder Zahnbehandlung.
> Verschiedene Regierungen haben einige umstrittene Änderungen am System des **NHS** durchgeführt, doch immer mehr Menschen äußern ihre Unzufriedenheit über den **NHS**, weil man zur Behandlung durch einen Spezi-

alisten zunächst eine Überweisung vom Hausarzt, dem **GP** braucht, oder weil z. B. Patienten, die eine Operation benötigen, recht lange Wartezeiten in Kauf nehmen müssen → NATIONAL INSURANCE

niacin ['naɪəsɪn] N Nikotinsäure *f*, Niacin *nt* *(spec)*

Niagara [naɪ'ægrə] N Niagara *m*; **~ Falls** die Niagarafälle *pl*

nib [nɪb] N Feder *f*; *(= point of nib)* (Feder)spitze *f*

nibble ['nɪbl] VT knabbern; *(= pick at) food* nur anessen, herumnagen an *(+dat)* *(inf)* VI *(at* an *+dat)* knabbern; *(= pick at)* herumnagen; *(fig)* sich interessiert zeigen; **to ~ at the bait** *(fig)* sich interessiert zeigen N **I think I've got a ~** ich glaube, bei mir beißt einer an; **I feel like a ~** *(inf)* ich habe Appetit auf etwas, ich brauche etwas zwischen die Zähne *(hum inf)*; **~s** *(Brit: = snacks)* Knabbereien *pl*

niblick ['nɪblɪk] N *(Golf)* Niblick *m*

nibs [nɪbz] N *(hum inf)* **his ~** der hohe Herr *(hum)*, Seine Herrlichkeit *(hum inf)*

NIC N **a** *(Brit) abbr of* **national insurance contribution** Sozialversicherungsbeitrag *m* **b** *abbr of* **newly industrialized** *or* **industrializing country** industrielles Schwellenland

Nicaragua [ˌnɪkə'rægjʊə] N Nicaragua *nt*

Nicaraguan [ˌnɪkə'rægjʊən] ADJ nicaraguanisch N Nicaraguaner(in) *m(f)*

nice [naɪs] ADJ *(+er)* **a** nett; *person, ways, voice* nett, sympathisch; *(= nice-looking) girl, dress, looks etc* nett, hübsch; *weather* schön, gut; *taste, smell, meal, whisky* gut; *warmth, feeling, car* schön; *food* gut, lecker; *(= skilful) workmanship, work* gut, schön, fein; **be ~ to him** sei nett zu ihm; **that's not ~!** das ist aber nicht nett; **be a ~ girl and ...** sei lieb und ...; **he always tries to be Mr Nice Guy** er will sich immer bei allen beliebt machen; **no more Mr Nice Guy** jetzt werden andere Saiten aufgezogen; **to have a ~ time** sich gut amüsieren; **have a ~ day!** *(esp US)* schönen Tag noch!; **that was the ~ thing about Venice** das war das Schöne an Venedig; **it's (so) ~ to meet you at last/to see you again** es freut mich (sehr), Sie endlich (persönlich) kennenzulernen/Sie wieder zu treffen; **it's been ~ meeting you** ich habe mich gefreut, Sie kennenzulernen; **I had a ~ rest** ich habe mich gut *or* schön ausgeruht; **it's ~ to be needed** es ist schön, gebraucht zu werden; **how ~ of you to ...** wie nett *or* lieb von Ihnen, zu ...; **~ one!** toll! *(inf)*, sauber! *(inf)*; **he has a ~ taste in ties** er hat einen guten Geschmack, was Krawatten angeht
b *(intensifier)* schön; **a ~ long bath** ein schönes, langes Bad; **~ and warm/near/quickly** schön warm/nahe/schnell; **~ and easy** ganz leicht; **take it ~ and easy** überanstrengen Sie sich nicht; **~ and easy does it** immer schön sachte
c *(= respectable)* nett; *district* fein; *words* schön; *(= refined) manners* gut, fein; **not a ~ word/district/book** gar kein schönes Wort/Viertel/Buch
d *(iro)* nett, schön, sauber *(all iro)*; **here's a ~ state of affairs!** das sind ja schöne *or* nette Zustände!; **you're in a ~ mess** du sitzt schön im Schlamassel *(inf)*; **that's a ~ way to talk to your mother** das ist ja eine schöne Art, mit deiner Mutter zu sprechen, wie sprichst du denn mit deiner Mutter?
e *(= subtle) distinction, shade of meaning* fein, genau; **overly ~ distinctions** überfeine *or* subtile Unterscheidungen; **that was a ~ point** das war eine gute Bemerkung; **one or two ~ points** ein paar brauchbare *or* gute Gedanken
f *(= hard to please) person* anspruchsvoll; **to be ~ about one's food** in Bezug aufs Essen wählerisch sein

nice-looking ['naɪs'lʊkɪŋ] ADJ schön; *woman also, man* gut aussehend; *face, dress etc* nett; *hotel, village* hübsch; **to be ~** gut aussehen

nicely ['naɪslɪ] ADV **a** *(= pleasantly)* nett; *(= well) go, speak, behave, placed* gut; **to go ~** wie geschmiert laufen *(inf)*; **to be coming along ~** sich gut machen *or* entwickeln; **she thanked me ~** sie hat sich nett bei mir bedankt; **to ask ~** höflich fragen; **eat up/say thank you ~!** iss mal schön auf/sag mal schön danke!; **that will do ~** das reicht vollauf; **how's it going? – ~, thank you** wie geht es so? – danke, ganz gut; **he's doing very ~ for himself** er ist sehr gut gestellt; *(= making money)* er scheffelt Geld *(inf)*; **a ~ situated home** ein hübsch gelegenes Haus; **to be ~ spoken** sich gepflegt ausdrücken; **he's such a ~ spoken young man** es ist eine Freude, diesem jungen Mann zuzuhören; **~ done** gut gemacht, prima *(inf)*; **when the engine's ~ warmed up** wenn der Motor schön warm gelaufen ist
b *(= carefully) distinguish* genau, fein

niceness ['naɪsnɪs] N **a** *(= pleasantness: of person, behaviour)* Nettigkeit *f*; *(= nice appearance)* nettes *or* hübsches Aussehen; *(= skilfulness)* Qualität *f*, Feinheit *f* **b** *(= subtlety)* Feinheit *f*, Genauigkeit *f* **c** *(= fastidiousness)* anspruchsvolle Art, Pingeligkeit *f* *(inf)*, Heikelkeit *f* *(dial)*

nicety ['naɪsɪtɪ] N **a** *(= subtlety)* Feinheit *f*; *(of judgement)* Schärfe *f*; *(= precision)* (peinliche) Genauigkeit; **to a ~** äußerst *or* sehr genau **b** **niceties** PL Feinheiten *pl*, Details *pl*

niche [niːʃ] N *(Archit)* Nische *f*; *(fig)* Plätzchen *nt*; **to carve a ~ for oneself** eine Nische für sich finden; **~ market** *(Comm)* Nischenmarkt *m*

Nicholas ['nɪkələs] N Nikolaus *m*

nick¹ [nɪk] N **a** Kerbe *f*; **I got a little ~ on my chin** ich habe mich leicht am Kinn geschnitten **b** **in the ~ of time** gerade noch (rechtzeitig) **c** *(Brit inf: = condition)* **in good/bad ~** gut/nicht gut in Schuss *(inf)* VT **a** *wood, stick* einkerben; **to ~ oneself** *(inf)* sich schneiden; **to ~ one's chin** *(inf)* sich am Kinn schneiden **b** *(bullet) person, wall, arm* streifen

nick² *(Brit)* VT *(inf)* **a** *(= arrest)* einsperren *(inf)*, einlochen *(inf)*; *(= catch)* schnappen *(inf)*; **he got ~ed** den haben sie sich *(dat)* gegriffen *(sl)* *or* geschnappt *(inf)*; **you're ~ed!** Sie sind verhaftet! **b** *(= steal)* klauen *(inf)*, mitgehen lassen *(inf)* N *(inf)* *(= prison)* Kittchen *nt* *(inf)*, Knast *m* *(inf)*; *(= police station)* Wache *f*, Revier *nt*

nick³ VT *(US sl)* **to ~ sb for sth** jdm etw abknöpfen *(inf)*

Nick [nɪk] N *abbr of* **Nicholas**; **Old ~** *(inf)* der Böse, der Leibhaftige *(old)*

nickel ['nɪkl] N **a** *(= metal)* Nickel *nt* **b** *(US)* Nickel *m*, Fünfcentstück *nt*

nickel-and-dime ['nɪklən'daɪm] *(US inf)* ADJ billig; *criminal etc* klein VT **to ~ sb** jdm sehr kleine (Geld)beträge abknöpfen *(inf)*

nickelodeon [ˌnɪkəl'əʊdɪən] N *(dated US)* **a** (Film)theater *nt* *(mit Eintrittspreisen von 5 Cent)* **b** *(= juke-box)* Musikbox *f*

nickel-plated ['nɪklˌpleɪtɪd] ADJ vernickelt

nicker ['nɪkə'] N *pl* - *(Brit inf: = pound)* **50 ~** 50 Eier *(sl)*

nickel silver N Neusilber *nt*

nickname ['nɪkneɪm] N Spitzname *m* VT *person* betiteln, taufen *(inf)*; **they ~d him Baldy** sie gaben ihm den Spitznamen Glatzköpfchen; **Chicago is ~d the Windy City** Chicago hat den Spitznamen Windy City

nicotine ['nɪkətiːn] N Nikotin *nt*

nicotine: **nicotine patch** N Nikotinpflaster *nt*; **nicotine poisoning** N Nikotinvergiftung *f*; **nicotine-stained** ADJ gelb von Nikotin; *fingers also* nikotingelb

niece [niːs] N Nichte *f*

Nielsen rating ['niːlsənˌreɪtɪŋ] N *(US)* Zuschauerquote *f*

niff [nɪf] N *(Brit inf)* Mief *m* *(inf)*

niffy ['nɪfɪ] ADJ *(+er)* *(Brit inf)* muffig *(inf)*

nifty ['nɪftɪ] ADJ *(+er)* *(inf)* *(= smart)* flott *(inf)*; *gadget, tool* schlau *(inf)*; *(= quick) person* flott *(inf)*, fix *(inf)*; **~ footwork** *(fig)* flotte Fußarbeit; **a ~ piece of work** gute Arbeit; **he's pretty ~ with a gun** er hat ein lockeres Händchen mit dem Schießeisen *(inf)*; **you'd better be ~ about it!** und ein bisschen dalli *(inf)*; **a ~ little car** ein netter kleiner Flitzer *(inf)*

Niger ['naɪdʒə'] N Niger *m*

Nigeria [naɪ'dʒɪərɪə] N Nigeria *nt*

Nigerian [naɪ'dʒɪərɪən] ADJ nigerianisch N Nigerianer(in) *m(f)*

niggard ['nɪgəd] N *(= miser)* Geizhals *m* *(pej)*

niggardliness ['nɪgədlɪnɪs] N *(of person)* Knaus(e)rigkeit *f*; *(of amount, portion also)* Armseligkeit *f*, Kümmerlichkeit *f*

niggardly ['nɪgədlɪ] ADJ *person* knaus(e)rig; *amount, portion also* armselig, kümmerlich

nigger ['nɪgə'] N *(very offensive)* Nigger *m* *(very offensive)*; **so you're the ~ in the woodpile** *(Brit inf)* Sie sind es also, der querschießt; **there's a ~ in the woodpile** *(Brit inf)* irgendjemand schießt quer *(inf)*; *(= snag)* da ist ein Haken dran *(inf)*

niggle ['nɪgl] VI *(= complain)* (herum)kritteln *(inf)*, herumkritisieren *(about* an *+dat)* VT *(= worry)* plagen, quälen, zu schaffen machen *(+dat)*

niggling ['nɪglɪŋ] ADJ *person* kritt(e)lig *(inf)*, überkritisch; *question, doubt, pain* bohrend, quälend; *injury* lästig; *detail* pingelig *(inf)*; *feeling* ungut N Kritteln *nt*, Meckern *nt* *(inf)*

nigh [naɪ] ADJ *(old, liter)* nahe; **the end (of the world) is ~** das Ende der Welt ist nah ADV **a** *(old, liter)* **to draw ~** sich nahen *(old, geh)* *(to +dat)* **b** **~ on** nahezu *(geh)*; **well ~ impossible** nahezu unmöglich PREP *(old, liter)* nahe *(+dat)*

night [naɪt] N **a** Nacht *f*; *(= evening)* Abend *m*; **~ is falling** die Nacht bricht herein; **I saw him last ~** ich habe ihn gestern Abend gesehen; **I'll see him tomorrow ~** ich treffe ihn morgen Abend; **I stayed with them last ~** ich habe heute *or* letzte Nacht bei ihnen übernachtet; **to stay four ~s with sb** vier Nächte lang bei jdm bleiben; **I'll stay with them tomorrow ~** ich übernachte morgen Nacht bei ihnen; **to look for somewhere to stay the ~** eine Übernachtungsmöglichkeit suchen; **on Friday ~** Freitagabend/-nacht; **on the ~ of (Saturday) the 11th** am (Samstag dem) 11. nachts; **11 o'clock at ~** 11 Uhr nachts; **6 o'clock at ~** 6 Uhr abends; **she works at ~** sie arbeitet nachts; **to travel by ~** nachts reisen; **to see Paris by ~** Paris bei Nacht sehen; **far into the ~** bis spät in die Nacht, bis in die späte Nacht; **in/during the ~** in/während der Nacht; **the ~ before they were ...** am Abend/die Nacht zuvor waren sie ...; **the ~ before last they were ...** vorgestern Abend/vorletzte Nacht waren sie ...; **to spend the ~ at a hotel** in einem Hotel übernachten; **to have a good/bad ~** *or* **~'s sleep** gut/schlecht schlafen; *(patient also)* eine gute/schlechte Nacht haben; **I need a good ~'s sleep** ich muss mal wieder ordentlich schlafen; **~~!** *(inf)* gut Nacht! *(inf)*; **~ after ~** jede Nacht, Nacht um Nacht *(geh)*; **all ~ (long)** die ganze Nacht; **~ and day** *(lit, fig)* Tag und Nacht; **to have a ~ out** (abends) ausgehen; **a ~ out with the lads** *(Brit) or* **boys** ein Abend mit den Kumpeln; **to make a ~ of it** durchmachen *(inf)*; **to have a late/an early ~** spät/früh ins Bett kommen, spät/früh schlafen gehen; **too many late ~s!** zu wenig Schlaf!; **after your early ~** nachdem du so früh schlafen gegangen bist; **to work ~s** nachts arbeiten; **to be on ~s** Nachtdienst haben; *(shift worker)* Nachtschicht haben; **the dark ~ of the soul** *(fig)* die dunkle Nacht der Seele
b *(Theat)* Abend *m*; **the last three ~s of ...** die letzten drei Abende von ...; **a Mozart ~** ein Mozartabend *m* → **first night**
ADV **~s** *(esp US)* nachts

night *in cpds* Nacht-; **night bird** N Nachtvogel *m*; *(fig)* Nachteule *f* *(inf)*, Nachtschwärmer(in) *m(f)*; **night blindness** N Nachtblindheit *f*; **nightcap** N **a** *(= garment)* Nachtmütze *f*; *(for woman)* Nachthaube *f* **b** *(= drink)* Schlaftrunk *m* *(inf)*; **nightclothes** PL Nachtzeug *nt*, Nachtwäsche *f* *(esp Comm)*; **nightclub** N Nachtlokal *nt* *or* -klub *m*; **night cream** N

Nachtcreme *f*; **night depository** N Nachttresor *m*; **nightdress** N Nachthemd *nt*; **night duty** N Nachtdienst *m*; **to be on ~** Nachtdienst haben; **night editor** N Nachtredakteur(in) *m(f)*; **nightfall** N Einbruch *m* der Dunkelheit; **at ~** bei Einbruch der Dunkelheit; **night fighter** N Nachtjäger *m*; **night flight** N Nachtflug *m*; **nightgown** N Nachthemd *nt*; **nighthawk** N *(US) (lit)* Amerikanischer Ziegenmelker; *(fig)* Nachtschwärmer(in) *m(f)*

nightie ['naɪtɪ] N *(inf)* Nachthemd *nt*

nightingale ['naɪtɪŋgeɪl] N Nachtigall *f*

night: **nightjar** N Ziegenmelker *m*, Nachtschwalbe *f*; **night leave** N *(Mil)* Urlaub *m* bis zum Wecken; **night letter** N *(US) (zu billigem Tarif gesandtes)* Nachttelegramm *nt*; **nightlife** N Nachtleben *nt*; **night-light** N **a** *(for child etc)* Nachtlicht *nt* **b** *(for teapot etc)* Teelicht *nt*; **nightlong** ADJ sich über die ganze Nacht hinziehend; *(= lasting several nights)* nächtelang; **after their ~ vigil** nachdem sie die ganze Nacht gewacht hatten

nightly ['naɪtlɪ] ADJ *(= every night)* (all)nächtlich; *(= every evening)* (all)abendlich; **~ performances** *(Theat)* allabendliche Vorstellung; **the ~ television news** die Abendnachrichten im Fernsehen ADV *(= every night)* jede Nacht; *(= every evening)* jeden Abend; **performances ~** jeden Abend Vorstellung; **three performances ~** jeden Abend drei Vorstellungen; **twice ~** zweimal pro Abend

nightmare ['naɪtmɛəʳ] N *(lit, fig)* Albtraum *m*, Alptraum *m*; **to suffer from ~s** Albträume haben *(over, about* wegen); **that was a ~ of a journey** die Reise war ein Albtraum; **~ scenario** eine Albtraum- *or* Schreckensvision

nightmarish ['naɪtmɛərɪʃ] ADJ grauenhaft, albtraumhaft, alptraumhaft

night: **night nurse** N Nachtschwester *f*; *(= man)* Nachtpfleger *m*; **night owl** N *(inf)* Nachteule *f (inf)*; **night porter** N Nachtportier *m*; **night safe** N Nachtsafe *m*; **night school** N Abendschule *f*

nightshade ['naɪtʃeɪd] N Nachtschatten *m* → **deadly nightshade**

night: **night shelter** N Nachtquartier *nt*; **night shift** N Nachtschicht *f*; **to be** *or* **work on ~** Nachtschicht haben *or* arbeiten; **nightshirt** N (Herren)nachthemd *nt*; **night sky** N nächtlicher Himmel; **nightspot** N Nachtlokal *nt*; **night stand** N *(US)* Nachttisch *m*; **night stick** N *(US)* Schlagstock *m*; **night-storage heater** N Nachtspeicherofen *m*; **night table** N *(US)* Nachttisch *m*; **night-time** N Nacht *f*; **at ~** nachts; **in the ~** während der Nacht, nachts ADJ *attr* nächtlich; **~ temperature** Nachttemperatur *f*; **night vision** N Nachtsichtigkeit *f*; **night-vision** ADJ Nachtsicht-; **night vision aid, night vision scope** N Nachtsichtgerät *nt*; **night watch** N Nachtwache *f*; **night watchman** N Nachtwächter(in) *m(f)*; **nightwear** N Nachtzeug *nt*, Nachtwäsche *f (esp Comm)*

nihilism ['naɪɪlɪzəm] N Nihilismus *m*

nihilist ['naɪɪlɪst] N Nihilist(in) *m(f)*

nihilistic [,naɪɪ'lɪstɪk] ADJ nihilistisch

Nikkei average [nɪ,keɪ'ævərɪdʒ], **Nikkei index** [nɪ,keɪ'ɪndeks] N Nikkei-(Durchschnitts)index *m*

nil [nɪl] N *(= zero)* null *(also Sport)*; *(= nothing)* nichts; **the score was one-~** es stand eins zu null; **the response** *etc* **was ~** die Reaktion *etc* war gleich null → *also* **zero**

Nile [naɪl] N Nil *m*

nimble ['nɪmbl] ADJ *(+er) (= quick) fingers, feet* flink; *person also* behände *(geh)*; *(= agile)* gelenkig, wendig, beweglich; *car* wendig; *(= skilful)* geschickt; *mind* beweglich; **to be very ~ at operating sth** sehr geschickt im Umgang mit etw sein; **as ~ as a goat** leichtfüßig (wie eine Gämse); **she is still ~** sie ist noch sehr rüstig

nimble: **nimble-fingered** ADJ fingerfertig; **nimble-footed** ADJ leichtfüßig

nimbleness ['nɪmblnɪs] N *(of fingers, feet)* Flinkheit *f*; *(of person)* Flinkheit *f*, Behändigkeit *f (geh)*; *(= agility)* Gelenkigkeit *f*, Wendigkeit *f*, Beweglichkeit *f*; *(= skilfulness)* Geschicklichkeit *f*, Geschick *nt*; *(of mind)* Beweglichkeit *f*

nimble-witted ['nɪmbl,wɪtɪd] ADJ schlagfertig

nimbly ['nɪmblɪ] ADV *work, respond* flink; *dance* leicht(füßig); *jump, climb, step* gelenkig, behände *(geh)*; **her fingers moved ~** ihre Finger bewegten sich leicht und flink

nimbus ['nɪmbəs] N **a** *(Liter. = halo)* Nimbus *m (geh)*, Heiligenschein *m* **b** *(Met)* → **cumulonimbus**

nimby, Nimby ['nɪmbɪ] *abbr of* **not in my back yard** *jd, der Unangenehmes aber Notwendiges nicht in seiner Nachbarschaft haben will, sondern möglichst weit weg* ADJ ablehnend; **~ attitude** Ohne-Mich-Haltung *f*

nincompoop ['nɪŋkəmpu:p] N *(inf)* Trottel *m (inf)*, Simpel *m (inf)*

nine [naɪn] ADJ neun; **~ times out of ten** in neun Zehntel der Fälle, so gut wie immer; **to have ~ lives** ein zähes Leben haben; **a ~ days' wonder** eine Eintagsfliege *(inf)* N Neun *f*; **dressed (up) to the ~s** in Schale *(inf)* → *also* **six**

ninepin alley [,naɪnpɪn'ælɪ] N Kegelbahn *f*

ninepins ['naɪnpɪnz] N *(= game)* Kegeln *nt*; **to go down like ~** *(fig)* wie die Fliegen umfallen *(inf)*

nineteen ['naɪn'ti:n] ADJ neunzehn N Neunzehn *f*; **she talks ~ to the dozen** *(Brit inf)* sie redet wie ein Wasserfall *(inf)*; **they were talking ~ to the dozen** *(Brit inf)* sie redeten, was das Zeug hielt *(inf)*; **19-inch monitor** *(Comput)* 19-Zoll-Monitor *m*, 19-Zöller *m (inf)*

nineteenth ['naɪn'ti:nθ] ADJ *(in series)* neunzehnte(r, s); *(as fraction)* neunzehntel; **the ~ (hole)** *(Golf inf)* das neunzehnte Loch *(Bar im Klubhaus)* N Neunzehnte(r, s); *(= fraction)* Neunzehntel *nt* → *also* **sixteenth**

ninetieth ['naɪntɪɪθ] ADJ *(in series)* neunzigste(r, s); *(as fraction)* neunzigstel N Neunzigste(r, s); *(= fraction)* Neunzigstel *nt*

nine-to-five [,naɪntə'faɪv] ADJ Büro-; **~ job/worker** Bürojob *m*/-angestellte(r) *mf*; **~ mentality** Angestelltenmentalität *f*

nine-to-fiver [,naɪntə'faɪvəʳ] N *(US inf)* Büroangestellte(r) *mf*, Bürohengst *m (pej inf)*

ninety ['naɪntɪ] ADJ neunzig N Neunzig *f* → *also* **sixty**

ninny ['nɪnɪ] N *(inf)* Dussel *m (inf)*

ninth [naɪnθ] ADJ *(in series)* neunte(r, s); *(as fraction)* neuntel N Neunte(r, s); *(= fraction)* Neuntel *nt*; *(Mus)* None *f* → *also* **sixth**

niobium [naɪ'əʊbɪəm] N *(Chem)* Niob *nt*

Nip [nɪp] N *(pej)* Japs *m (pej inf)*

nip¹ [nɪp] N **a** *(= pinch)* Kniff *m*; *(= bite: from animal etc)* Biss *m*; **to give sb a ~ on the leg** jdn ins Bein zwicken *or* kneifen; *(dog)* jdn leicht ins Bein beißen; **the dog gave him a ~** der Hund hat kurz zugeschnappt → **nip and tuck**

b there's a ~ in the air today es ist ganz schön frisch heute

VT **a** *(= bite)* zwicken; *(= pinch)* kneifen; **the dog ~ped his ankle** der Hund hat ihn am Knöchel gezwickt

b *(Hort) bud, shoot* abknipsen; **to ~ sth in the bud** *(fig)* etw im Keim ersticken

c *(cold, frost etc) plants* angreifen; **the cold air ~ped our faces** die Kälte schnitt uns ins Gesicht; **the plants had been ~ped by the frost** die Pflanzen hatten Frost abbekommen

VI *(Brit inf)* sausen *(inf)*, flitzen *(inf)*; **to ~ up (-stairs)/down(stairs)** hoch-/runtersausen *(inf)* *or* -flitzen *(inf)*; **I'll just ~ down to the shops** ich gehe mal kurz einkaufen *(inf)*; **I'll just ~ round to his place** ich gehe mal kurz bei ihm vorbei *(inf)*; **I'll ~ on ahead** ich gehe schon mal voraus *(inf)*

▶ **nip along** VI *(Brit inf)* entlangsausen *(inf) or* -flitzen *(inf)*; **nip along to Joan's house** lauf *or* saus mal schnell zu Joan rüber *(inf)*

▶ **nip in** VI *(Brit inf)* hereinsausen *(inf)*; *(= call in)* auf einen Sprung vorbeikommen; **I've just nipped in for a chat** ich bin nur auf ein Schwätzchen vorbeigekommen *(inf)*; **he just nipped into the pub for a drink** er ging auf einen Sprung *or* nur mal kurz in die Kneipe *(inf)*; **to nip in and out of the traffic** sich durch den Verkehr schlängeln

▶ **nip off** VI *(Brit inf)* davonsausen *(inf)* VT *sep twig* abknicken; *(with clippers etc)* abzwicken; **he nipped off the end of his finger** er hat sich *(dat)* die Fingerspitze gekappt

▶ **nip out** VI *(Brit inf)* heraussausen *(inf)*; *(out of house etc)* kurz weggehen *(inf)*

nip² N *(inf: = drink)* Schlückchen *nt*

nip and tuck ['nɪpənd'tʌk] N *(inf)* **a** *(= cosmetic surgery)* Schönheitsoperation *f* **b** *(esp US)* **it was ~** das war eine knappe Sache; **to be ~** *(in race etc)* Kopf an Kopf liegen; **it was ~ as they came up to the finishing line** sie lagen vor dem Ziel praktisch auf gleicher Höhe

nip-and-tuck ['nɪpənd'tʌk] ADJ *attr (inf)* **a ~ race** ein Kopf-an-Kopf-Rennen

nipper ['nɪpəʳ] N **a** *(Zool)* Schere *f*, Zange *f* **b** *(Brit inf: = child)* Steppke *m (inf)*

nipple ['nɪpl] N **a** *(Anat)* Brustwarze *f*, Nippel *m (inf)*; *(US: on baby's bottle)* Sauger *m*, Schnuller *m (inf)* **b** *(Tech)* Nippel *m*

nippy ['nɪpɪ] ADJ *(+er)* **a** *(Brit inf)* flink, flott; *car, motor* spritzig; **to be ~** sich beeilen **b** *(= sharp, cold) weather* frisch; *wind* frisch, beißend

Nirvana [nɪə'vɑ:nə] N Nirwana *nt*

nisi ['naɪsaɪ] CONJ → **decree**

Nissen hut ['nɪsn,hʌt] N *(Brit)* Nissenhütte *f*

nit [nɪt] N **a** *(Zool)* Nisse *f* **b** *(Brit inf)* Dummkopf *m*, Schwachkopf *m (inf)*

niter N *(US)* = **nitre**

nit-pick ['nɪtpɪk] VI *(inf)* kleinlich *or* pingelig *(inf)* sein

nit-picker ['nɪtpɪkəʳ] N *(inf)* Kleinigkeitskrämer(in) *m(f) (inf)*

nit-picking ['nɪtpɪkɪŋ] ADJ *(inf)* kleinlich, pingelig *(inf)*

nitrate ['naɪtreɪt] N Nitrat *nt*

nitration [naɪ'treɪʃən] N Nitrierung *f*

nitre, *(US)* **niter** ['naɪtəʳ] N Salpeter *m or nt*

nitric ['naɪtrɪk] *in cpds (= of nitrogen)* Stickstoff-; *(= of nitre)* Salpeter-; **nitric acid** N Salpetersäure *f*; **nitric oxide** N Stick(stoffmon)oxid *nt*

nitro ['naɪtrəʊ] *(inf) abbr of* **nitroglycerin(e)** Nitroglyzerin *nt*

nitro- PREF Nitro-; **~phosphates** Nitrophosphate *pl*

nitrogen ['naɪtrədʒən] N Stickstoff *m*

nitrogen *in cpds* Stickstoff-; **~ compound** Stickstoffverbindung *f*

nitrogen dioxide N Stickstoffdioxid *nt*

nitroglycerin(e) ['naɪtrəʊ'glɪsəri:n] N Nitroglyzerin *nt*

nitrous ['naɪtrəs]: **nitrous acid** N salpetrige Säure; **nitrous oxide** N Distickstoffmonoxid *nt*, Lachgas *nt*

nitty-gritty ['nɪtɪ'grɪtɪ] N *(inf)* **to get down to the ~** zur Sache kommen; **the ~ of everyday life/of politics** die wahre Realität des alltäglichen Lebens/der Politik

nitwit ['nɪtwɪt] N *(inf)* Dummkopf *m*, Schwachkopf *m (inf)*

nix [nɪks] N *(inf)* nix *(inf)* VT *(US inf) proposal* über den Haufen werfen *(inf)*

NLP *abbr of* **neurolinguistic programming** NLP *nt*

NLQ *abbr of* **near letter-quality** NLQ; **in ~ mode** im NLQ-Druckmodus

NNE *abbr of* **north-northeast** NNO

NNW *abbr of* **north-northwest** NNW

No, no a *abbr of* **north** N b *abbr of* **number** Nr.

no [nəʊ] ADV a *(negative)* nein; **oh no!** o nein!; **to answer no** *(to question)* mit Nein antworten, verneinen; *(to request)* Nein *or* nein sagen; **she can't say no** sie kann nicht Nein *or* nein sagen; **the answer is no** da muss ich Nein *or* nein sagen; *(as emphatic reply also)* nein (und noch mal nein)
b *(= not)* nicht; **whether he comes or no** ob er kommt oder nicht; **hungry or no, you'll eat it** ob du Hunger hast oder nicht, das wird gegessen *(inf)*
c *(with comp)* nicht; **I can bear it no longer** ich kann es nicht länger ertragen; **I have no more money** ich habe kein Geld mehr; **he has no more than anyone else** er hat auch nicht mehr als jeder andere; **I'm no less tired than you are** ich bin auch nicht weniger müde als du; **he returned to England in an aircraft carrier no less** er kehrte auf nichts Geringerem als einem Flugzeugträger nach England zurück; **no later than Monday** spätestens Montag; **no longer ago than last week** erst letzte Woche
ADJ a *(= not any: also with numerals and "other")* kein; **a person of no intelligence** ein Mensch ohne jede Intelligenz; **he has no integrity** er ist ein unredlicher Mensch; **no one person could do it** keiner könnte das allein tun; **no two men could be less alike** zwei verschiedenere Menschen könnte es nicht geben; **no other man** kein anderer; **it's of no interest/importance** das ist belanglos/unwichtig; **it's no use** *or* **no good** das hat keinen Zweck
b *(forbidding)* **no parking/smoking** Parken/Rauchen verboten; **no surrender!** wir kapitulieren nicht!
c *(with gerund)* **there's no saying** *or* **telling what he'll do next** man kann nie wissen, was er als Nächstes tun wird; **there's no denying it** es lässt sich nicht leugnen; **there's no pleasing him** ihm kann man es auch nie recht machen
d *(emph)* **he's no genius** er ist nicht gerade ein Genie; **she's no beauty** sie ist nicht gerade eine Schönheit; **president or no president** Präsident oder nicht; **this is no place for children** das ist hier nichts für Kinder; **I'm no expert, but ...** ich bin ja kein Fachmann, aber ...; **in no time** im Nu; **it's no small matter** das ist keine Kleinigkeit; **at no little expense** zu großen Kosten; **theirs is no easy task** sie haben keine leichte Aufgabe; **there is no such thing** so etwas gibt es nicht; **it was/we did no such thing** bestimmt nicht, nichts dergleichen; **I'll do no such thing** ich werde mich hüten
N *pl* **-es** Nein *nt*; *(= no vote)* Neinstimme *f*; **I won't take no for an answer** ich bestehe darauf, ich lasse nicht locker; **he's the type who won't take no for an answer** er lässt sich nicht mit einem Nein abspeisen; **the noes have it** die Mehrheit ist dagegen

no-account ['nəʊə,kaʊnt] *(US inf)* ADJ *(= no use)* nutzlos; *(= up to no good)* nichtsnutzig N *(no use)* Niete *f (inf)*; *(up to no good)* Nichtsnutz *m*

Noah ['nəʊə] N Noah *m*

Noah's ark ['nəʊəz'ɑːk] N *(Bibl)* die Arche Noah

nob[1] [nɒb] N *(inf)* einer der besseren Leute *(inf)*; **all the ~s** all die besseren Leute *(inf)*, alles, was Rang und Namen hat

nob[2] N *(inf: = head)* Rübe *f (inf)*

no-ball ['nəʊ'bɔːl] N *(Cricket) wegen Übertreten ungültiger Ball*

nobble ['nɒbl] VT *(Brit inf)* a *horse, dog* lahm legen *(inf)* b *(= catch)* sich *(dat)* schnappen *(inf)* c *(= obtain dishonestly) votes etc* sich *(dat)* kaufen; *money* einsacken *(inf)* d *jury, witness* bestechen e *(= thwart) plan* durchkreuzen

Nobel ['nəʊbel] N **~ prize** Nobelpreis *m*; **~ peace prize** Friedensnobelpreis *m*; **~ prize winner** Nobelpreisträger(in) *m(f)*; **alternative ~ prize** alternativer Nobelpreis

nobelium [nəʊ'biːlɪəm] N Nobelium *nt*

nobility [nəʊ'bɪlɪtɪ] N *no pl* a *(= people)* (Hoch)adel *m*; **she is one of the ~** sie ist eine Adlige b *(= quality)* Adel *m*, Edle(s) *nt*; **~ of mind/thought** geistiger Adel; **~ of sentiment** edles Gefühl

noble ['nəʊbl] ADJ *(+er)* a *(= aristocratic) person, rank* adlig; **to be of ~ birth** adlig sein, von edler *or* adliger Geburt sein
b *(= fine, distinguished) person, deed, thought etc* edel, nobel; *appearance* vornehm; *monument* stattlich, prächtig; *stag also* kapital; *(= brave) resistance* heldenhaft, wacker; **the ~ art of self-defence** die edle Kunst der Selbstverteidigung; **that was a ~ attempt** das war ein heldenhafter Versuch; **the ~ savage** *(Liter)* der edle Wilde
c *(inf: = selfless)* edel, großmütig, edelmütig; **how ~ of you!** *(iro)* zu gütig
d *metal* edel
N Adlige(r) *mf*, Edelmann *m (Hist)*; **the ~s** die Adligen *or* Edelleute *(Hist)*

noble: **noble gas** N Edelgas *nt*; **nobleman** N Adlige(r) *m*, Edelmann *m (Hist)*; **noble-minded** ADJ edel gesinnt, vornehm

nobleness ['nəʊblnɪs] N a *(of person)* Adligkeit *f*; *(of birth, rank)* Vornehmheit *f* b *(of deed, thought etc)* Vornehmheit *f*; *(of person)* edle *or* noble Gesinnung; *(= braveness)* Heldenhaftigkeit *f* c *(= impressiveness)* Stattlichkeit *f* d *(inf: = selflessness)* Großmütigkeit *f*; *(of person)* Großmut *m*, Edelmut *m*

noblesse [nəʊ'bles] N Noblesse *f*; **~ oblige** Adel verpflichtet, noblesse oblige

noblewoman ['nəʊblwʊmən] N *pl* **-women** [-wɪmɪn] Adlige *f*; *(married also)* Edelfrau *f (Hist)*; *(unmarried also)* Edelfräulein *nt (Hist)*

nobly ['nəʊblɪ] ADV a *(= aristocratically)* vornehm; **~ born** von edler Geburt b *(= finely)* edel, vornehm; *(= bravely)* wacker, heldenhaft; **you've done ~** du hast dich wacker geschlagen *(inf)* c *(= impressively) proportioned* prächtig, prachtvoll d *(inf: = selflessly)* großmütig; **he ~ gave up his weekend** großmütigerweise opferte er sein Wochenende

nobody ['nəʊbədɪ] PRON niemand, keiner; **who saw him? – ~** wer hat ihn gesehen? – niemand; **~ knows better than I** niemand *or* keiner weiß besser als ich; **there was ~ else** da war niemand anderes *or* sonst niemand; **~ else could have done it** es kann niemand anders *or* kein anderer gewesen sein; **~ else but you can do it** nur du kannst das, außer dir kann das niemand; **~ else offered to give them money** sonst hat sich keiner *or* niemand angeboten, ihnen Geld zu geben; **like ~'s business** wie nichts; **he's ~'s fool** er ist nicht auf den Kopf gefallen
N Niemand *m no pl*, Nichts *nt no pl*; **he's a mere ~** er ist überhaupt nichts, er ist doch ein Niemand *or* Nichts; **to marry a ~** jdn heiraten, der nichts ist und nichts hat; **they are nobodies** sie sind doch niemand; **I worked with him when he was (a) ~** ich habe mit ihm gearbeitet, als er noch ein Niemand war

no-brainer [nəʊ'breɪnə'] N *(esp US inf)* Kinderspiel *m*, leichte Entscheidung; **it's a ~** da muss man nicht lange überlegen, das versteht sich von selbst

no-claim(s) bonus ['nəʊ,kleɪm(z)'bəʊnəs] N Schadenfreiheitsrabatt *m*

nocturnal [nɒk'tɜːnl] ADJ nächtlich; *sound also* der Nacht; **~ animal/bird** Nachttier *nt*/-vogel *m*; **~ flowers** Nachtblüher *pl*

nocturne ['nɒktɜːn] N *(Mus)* Nocturne *f*

nod [nɒd] N a Nicken *nt*; **he gave a quick ~** er nickte kurz; **to give sb a ~** jdm zunicken; **to give sb the ~** *(fig)* jdm grünes Licht geben; **to answer with a ~** (zustimmend) nicken; **to give sb a ~ and a wink** *(fig)* jdm im Stillen zustimmen; **a ~ is as good as a wink (to a blind man)** *(inf)* schon verstanden, das wird er schon verstehen; **to go through on the ~** *(inf)* ohne Einwände angenommen werden
b *(inf: = sleep)* **the land of Nod** das Land der Träume
VI a *(person, flowers)* nicken; *(plumes)* wippen; **to ~ to sb** jdm zunicken; **to ~ toward(s) sth** mit dem Kopf auf etw zeigen; **to ~ in agreement** zustimmend nicken; **he ~ded to me to leave** er gab mir durch ein Nicken zu verstehen, dass ich gehen sollte
b *(= doze)* ein Nickerchen machen *(inf)*; **she was ~ding over a book** sie war über einem Buch eingenickt *(inf)*
c **even Homer ~s** Irren *or* irren ist menschlich *(Prov)*
VT a **to ~ one's head** mit dem Kopf nicken; **to ~ one's agreement/approval** zustimmend nicken; **to ~ a greeting/welcome to sb** jdm zum Gruß/zur Begrüßung zunicken
b *(Sport) ball* köpfen

▶ **nod in** VT SEP *goal, ball* einköpfen

▶ **nod off** VI einnicken *(inf)*

nodal ['nəʊdl] ADJ knotenartig; **~ point** *(fig)* Knotenpunkt *m*

nodding ['nɒdɪŋ] ADJ **to have a ~ acquaintance with sb** jdn flüchtig kennen

noddle ['nɒdl] N *(Brit inf: = head)* Dez *m (inf)*, Schädel *m (inf)*

node [nəʊd] N Knoten *m*

nodular ['nɒdjʊlə'] ADJ knötchenartig

nodule ['nɒdjuːl] N *(Med, Bot)* Knötchen *nt*; *(Geol)* Klümpchen *nt*

no-fault ['nəʊ,fɔːlt] *(US)* ADJ a *divorce* in gegenseitigem Einvernehmen b *(Insur) coverage* mit garantierter Entschädigungssumme N *(also* **no-fault insurance**) *Kraftfahrzeugversicherung mit garantierter Auszahlung einer Entschädigungssumme ohne vorherige Klärung der Unfallschuld*

no-fly zone ['nəʊ,flaɪ'zəʊn] N *(Mil)* Flugverbotszone *f*

no-frills ['nəʊ'frɪlz] ADJ *attr package, deal etc* ohne (alle) Extras; *style, decor etc* (schlicht und) einfach; **~ airline** Billigflieger *m*

noggin ['nɒgɪn] N a *(inf: = head)* Birne *f (inf)* b *(Measure)* Becher *m (ca. 0,15 Liter)*; **let's have a ~** *(inf)* wie wärs mit 'nem Gläschen? *(inf)*

no-go area ['nəʊ,gəʊ'ɛərɪə] N Sperrgebiet *nt*; **this street is a ~** diese Straße sollte man meiden

no: **no-good** ADJ *person* nichtsnutzig N *(= person)* Nichtsnutz *m*; **no-growth** ADJ *attr* nicht wachstumsorientiert; *(= preventing growth)* wachstumshemmend; **we have a ~ economy** unsere Wirtschaft zeigt kein Wachstum; **no-holds-barred** ADJ *contest, attack* kompromisslos; **no-hoper** N *(inf)* völlige Niete *(inf)*, Nulpe *f (dial inf)*; **nohow** ADV *(incorrect, hum)* **not never not ~** nie und nimmer

noise [nɔɪz] N Geräusch *nt*; *(= loud, irritating sound)* Lärm *m*, Krach *m*; *(Elec: = interference)* Rauschen *nt*; **what was that ~?** was war das für ein Geräusch?; **a hammering ~** ein hämmerndes Geräusch; **the ~ of (the) jet planes** der Düsenlärm; **the ~ of the traffic** der Straßenlärm; **the ~ of the bells** der Lärm der Glocken; **the ~ of horses coming up the street** Pferdegetrappel die Straße herauf; **~s in the ears** *(Med)* Ohrensausen *nt*; **the rain made a ~ on the roof** der Regen prasselte aufs Dach; **it made a lot of ~** es war sehr laut, es hat viel Krach gemacht; **don't make a ~!** sei leise!; **stop making such a (lot of) ~** hör auf, solchen Lärm *or* Krach zu machen; **she made ~s about leaving early** sie ließ immer wieder fallen, dass sie früh gehen wollte *(inf)*; **he's always making ~s about resigning** er redet dauernd davon, dass er zurücktreten will; **to make reassuring/placatory ~s** beruhigende/besänftigende Geräusche machen; **she made (all) the right ~s** sie reagierte richtig; **to make a lot of ~ about sth** *(inf)* viel Geschrei um etw machen; **to make a ~ in the world** Aufsehen erregen, von sich reden machen; **a big ~** *(fig inf)* ein großes Tier *(inf)*; **~ abatement/prevention** Lärmbekämpfung *f*
VT **to ~ sth abroad** *or* **about** *(old, hum)* etw verbreiten; **it was ~d about that ...** es ging das Gerücht (um), dass ...

noise: **noise abatement** N Lärmbekämpfung *f*; *(Tech)* Schallschutz *m*; **~ zone** Lärmschutzzone *f*; **noise barrier** N Lärmschutzwall *m*; *(= fence)* Lärmschutzzaun *m*; **noise control** N Lärmbekämpfung *f*; *(Tech)* Schallschutz *m*; **noiseless** ['nɔɪzlɪs] ADJ geräuschlos; *tread, step also* lautlos; **noiselessly** ['nɔɪzlɪslɪ] ADV geräuschlos; *move also* lautlos; **noise level** N Geräuschpegel *m*; **noise nuisance, noise pollution** N Lärmbelästigung *f*

noisily ['nɔɪzɪlɪ] ADV laut; *protest, welcome, debate* lautstark

noisiness ['nɔɪzɪnɪs] N Lärm *m*; *(of person)* laute Art; *(of children)* Krachmacherei *f (inf)*; *(of protest, welcome, debate)* Lautstärke *f*; **the ~ of these pupils/this car** der Lärm *or* Krach, den diese Schüler machen/dieses Auto macht

noisome ['nɔɪsəm] ADJ **a** *smell* widerlich, eklig **b** *(= noxious)* giftig, (gesundheits)schädlich

noise protection N Lärmschutz *m*

noisy ['nɔɪzɪ] ADJ *(+er)* laut; *traffic, child also* lärmend; *machine, behaviour, work also* geräuschvoll; *protest, welcome, debate* lautstark; **don't be so ~** sei nicht so laut, mach nicht so viel Lärm; **this is a ~ house** in dem Haus ist es laut

no-jump ['nəʊdʒʌmp] N *(Sport)* Fehlsprung *m*, ungültiger Versuch *(beim Springen)*

nomad ['nəʊmæd] N Nomade *m*, Nomadin *f*

nomadic [nəʊ'mædɪk] ADJ nomadisch, Nomaden-; **~ tribe** Nomadenstamm *m*; **~ lifestyle** Nomadenleben *nt*

no-man's-land ['nəʊmænzlænd] N *(lit, fig)* Niemandsland *nt*

nom de plume ['nɒmdə'plu:m] N Pseudonym *nt*

nomenclature [nəʊ'menklətʃə'] N Nomenklatur *f*

nomenklatura [ˌnəʊmenklə'tʊərə] N **the ~** *(Pol)* die Nomenklatura

nominal ['nɒmɪnl] ADJ **a** *(= in name)* nominell; **~ shares** Stamm- *or* Gründungsaktien *pl* **b** *(= small) salary, fee, amount, rent* nominell, symbolisch **c** *(Gram)* Nominal-; **~ clause** Nominalphrase *f*

nominal interest N *(Fin)* Nominalzins *m*, Nominalzinsfuß *m*

nominalism ['nɒmɪnəlɪzəm] N *(Philos)* Nominalismus *m*

nominalize ['nɒmɪnəlaɪz] VT *(Gram)* nominalisieren; *word also* substantivieren

nominally ['nɒmɪnəlɪ] ADV nominell; **it's ~ worth £500** auf dem Papier ist es £ 500 wert

nominal value N *(of shares, voucher, banknote etc)* Nennwert *m*

nominate ['nɒmɪneɪt] VT **a** *(= appoint)* ernennen; **he was ~d chairman** er wurde zum Vorsitzenden ernannt **b** *(= propose)* nominieren, aufstellen; **he was ~d for the presidency** er wurde als Präsidentschaftskandidat aufgestellt; **to ~ sb/sth for an award** jdn/etw für eine Auszeichnung nominieren

nomination [ˌnɒmɪ'neɪʃən] N **a** *(= appointment)* Ernennung *f* **b** *(= proposal)* Nominierung *f*, Kandidatenvorschlag *m*

nominative ['nɒmɪnətɪv] *(Gram)* N Nominativ *m*, Werfall *m* ADJ **(the) ~ case** der Nominativ, der Werfall

nominee [ˌnɒmɪ'ni:] N Kandidat(in) *m(f)*

non- [nɒn-] PREF nicht-; **non-absorbent** ADJ nicht absorbierend; **nonacceptance** N *(Comm, Fin)* Nichtannahme *f*, Annahmeverweigerung *f*; **non-achiever** N Leistungsschwache(r) *mf*; **non-adjustable** ADJ nicht verstellbar, unverstellbar; **non-affiliated** ADJ *(to an +acc) business, industry* nichtangeschlossen *attr*, nicht angeschlossen *pred*

nonagenarian [ˌnɒnədʒɪ'neərɪən] N Neunziger(in) *m(f)* ADJ in den Neunzigern

nonaggression [nɒnə'greʃən] N Nichtangriff *m*; **~ treaty** *or* **pact** Nichtangriffspakt *m*

nonagon ['nɒnəgɒn] N Neuneck *nt*, Nonagon *nt*

non-: **nonalcoholic** ADJ nichtalkoholisch, nicht alkoholisch, alkoholfrei; **nonaligned** ADJ *(Pol)* blockfrei, bündnisfrei; **nonalignment** N *(Pol)* Blockfreiheit *f*, Bündnisfreiheit *f*; **~ policy** Neutralitätspolitik *f*; **no-name** ADJ *attr* No-Name; *person* unauffällig, nullachtfünfzehn *(inf)*; *(unimportant)* unbedeutend; **~ product** Billigprodukt *nt*; **nonappearance** N Nichterscheinen *nt*; **nonarrival** N Ausbleiben *nt*; *(of train, plane, letter also)* Nichteintreffen *nt*; **nonattendance** N Nichtteilnahme *f (at an +dat)*; **nonavailability** N Unerhältlichkeit *f*; *(of person)* Unabkömmlichkeit *f*; **nonavailable** ADJ nicht erhältlich; *person* unabkömmlich; **nonbelligerent** N Kriegsunbeteiligte(r) *mf*; **to be a ~** nicht am Krieg teilnehmen ADJ nicht Krieg führend, kriegsunbeteiligt; **nonbook** N *(pej)* rein kommerzielles Buch ADJ *(= relating to media other than books)* Non-Book-; **~ item** Non-Book-Artikel *m*; **~ media** andere Medien als Bücher; **non-breakable** ADJ unzerbrechlich, nicht zerbrechlich; **non-breaking** ADJ *(Comput)* geschützt; **~ hyphen** geschützter Trennstrich; **~ space** geschütztes Leerzeichen; **non-cash** ADJ *(Fin) payment* bargeldlos; **~ assets** Sachwerte *pl*; **~ benefits** geldwerte Vorteile *pl*

nonce word ['nɒnswɜ:d] N Ad-hoc-Bildung *f*

nonchalance ['nɒnʃələns] N Lässigkeit *f*, Nonchalance *f*

nonchalant ADJ, **nonchalantly** ADV ['nɒnʃələnt, -lɪ] lässig, nonchalant

non: **non-Christian** N Nichtchrist(in) *m(f)* ADJ nichtchristlich, nicht christlich; **non-collegiate** ADJ *university* nicht aus Colleges bestehend; **non-com** N *(Mil inf)* Uffz *m (sl)*; **noncombatant** N Nichtkämpfer(in) *m(f)*, Nonkombattant(in) *m(f) (spec)* ADJ nicht am Kampf beteiligt; **noncombustible** ADJ nicht brennbar N nicht brennbarer Stoff; **noncommissioned** ADJ *(Mil)* **~ officer** Unteroffizier(in) *m(f)*; **noncommittal** ADJ zurückhaltend; *answer also* unverbindlich; **to be ~ about whether ...** sich nicht festlegen, ob ...; **he's so ~** er legt sich nie fest; **noncommittally** ADV *answer, say* unverbindlich; **non-communicant** N *(Eccl)* Nichtkommunikant(in) *m(f)*; **non-completion** N Nichtbeendung *f*; *(of work also, contract)* Nichtabschluss *m*; **noncompliance** N *(with regulations etc)* Nichteinhaltung *f*, Nichterfüllung *f (with +gen)*; *(with wishes, orders)* Zuwiderhandlung *f*, Zuwiderhandeln *nt (with* gegen)

non compos mentis ['nɒnˌkɒmpəs'mentɪs] ADJ nicht zurechnungsfähig, unzurechnungsfähig; **to be ~** *(inf)* nicht ganz da sein *(inf)*

non: **nonconformism** N Nonkonformismus *m*; **his social ~** seine mangelnde Anpassung an die Gesellschaft; **the ~ of his views** seine nonkonformistischen Ansichten; **nonconformist** N Nonkonformist(in) *m(f)* ADJ nonkonformistisch; **nonconformity** N *(with rules)* Nichteinhaltung *f (with +gen)*, Nichtkonformgehen *nt (form) (with* mit); **noncontributory** ADJ *benefits, insurance, pension scheme* ohne Eigenbeteiligung; *member* beitragsfrei; **noncontroversial** ADJ für alle annehmbar, nicht kontrovers; **to be ~** keinen Anlass zu Kontroversen bieten; **nonconvertible** ADJ *(Fin)* nicht konvertierbar; **noncooperation** N unkooperative Haltung; **noncooperative** ADJ unkooperativ; **non-crease** ADJ *shirt etc* knitterfrei, knitterfest; **non-deciduous** ADJ *(Bot) tree* immergrün; *leaves* nicht abfallend; **non-delivery** N Nichtlieferung *f*; **nondenominational** ADJ konfessionslos; **non-departure** N *(of train, flight)* Ausfall *m*

nondescript ['nɒndɪskrɪpt] ADJ *taste, colour* unbestimmbar; *person, appearance* unauffällig, unscheinbar *(pej)*

non: **nondetachable** ADJ *handle, hood etc* nicht abnehmbar, fest angebracht; *lining* nicht ausknöpfbar; *(without zip)* nicht ausreißbar; **nondiscrimination** N Nichtdiskriminierung *f (against, towards +gen)*; **~ principle** Diskriminierungsverbot *nt*; **nondiscriminatory** ADJ nicht diskriminierend; **nondrinker** N Nichttrinker(in) *m(f)*; **she is a ~** sie trinkt keinen Alkohol; **nondriver** N Nichtfahrer(in) *m(f)*; **~s are ...** wer selbst nicht (Auto) fährt, ist ...; **non-dutiable** ADJ unverzollbar

none [nʌn] PRON keine(r, s), keine; *(on form)* keine; **~ of the boys/the chairs/them** keiner der Jungen/Stühle/von ihnen; **~ of the girls** keines der Mädchen; **~ of this/the cake** nichts davon/von dem Kuchen; **~ of this is any good** das ist alles nicht gut; **~ of this money is mine** von dem Geld gehört mir nichts; **do you have any bread/apples? – ~ (at all)** haben Sie Brot/Äpfel? – nein, gar keines/keine; **there is ~ left** es ist nichts übrig; **money have I ~** *(liter)* Geld hab ich keines; **~ but he** nur er; **their guest was ~ other than ...** ihr Gast war kein anderer als ...; **there is ~ better than him at climbing** niemand kann besser klettern als er; **but ~ of your silly jokes** aber lass bitte deine dummen Witze; **I want ~ of your excuses** und ich will keine Entschuldigungen hören; **(we'll have) ~ of that!** jetzt reichts aber!; **I want ~ of this/this nonsense** ich will davon/von diesem Unsinn nichts hören; **I'll have ~ of your rudeness** *(inf)* ich dulde diese Unhöflichkeit nicht; **he would have ~ of it** er wollte davon nichts wissen

ADV **to be ~ the wiser** um nichts schlauer sein; **she looks ~ the worse for her ordeal** trotz allem, was sie durchzustehen hatte, sieht sie gut aus; **it's ~ too warm** es ist nicht *or* keineswegs zu warm; **he was ~ too happy about it** er war darüber gar nicht erfreut; **~ too sure/easy** durchaus nicht sicher/einfach

nonentity [nɒ'nentɪtɪ] N *(= person)* Nullität *f*, unbedeutende Figur

nonessential [nɒnɪ'senʃəl] ADJ unnötig; *workers* nicht unbedingt nötig; *services* nicht lebenswichtig N **nonessentials** PL nicht (lebens)notwendige Dinge *pl*

nonetheless [ˌnʌnðə'les] ✪ 26.3 ADV nichtsdestoweniger, trotzdem

non: **nonevent** N *(inf)* Reinfall *m (inf)*, Pleite *f (inf)*, Schlag *m* ins Wasser *(inf)*; **nonexecutive** ADJ **in a ~ capacity** ohne Entscheidungsbefugnis; **~ director** ≈ Aufsichtsratsmitglied *nt (ohne Entscheidungsbefugnis)*; **nonexistence** N Nichtvorhandensein *nt*; *(Philos)* Nichtexistenz *f*; **nonexistent** ADJ nicht vorhanden; *(Philos)* nicht existent; **discipline is practically ~ here** hier herrscht praktisch keine Disziplin; **non-fat** ADJ *diet* fettlos; *food* fettarm; **non-fat creamer** N milchfreier Kaffeeweißer; **non-fat milk** N Milchersatz *m (auf pflanzlicher Basis)*; **nonfattening** ADJ nicht dick machend *attr*; **fruit is ~** Obst macht nicht dick; **nonferrous** ADJ nicht eisenhaltig; **nonfiction** N Sachbücher *pl* ADJ **~ book/publication** Sachbuch *nt*; **~ department** Sachbuchabteilung *f*; **nonfinite** ADJ *(Gram)* infinit; **nonflammable** ADJ nichtentzündbar, nicht entzündbar; **non-flowering** ADJ nichtblühend, nicht blühend; **non-governmental** ADJ **~ organization** regierungsunabhängige Organisation; **nonhereditary** ADJ nichtvererbbar, nicht vererbbar; *disease also* nichtvererblich, nicht vererblich; **non-impact printer** N Non-Impact-Drucker *m*, anschlagfreier Drucker; **non-infectious** ADJ nichtansteckend, nicht ansteckend, nicht infektiös *(form)*; **non-inflammable** ADJ nicht feuergefährlich; **non-interest-bearing** ADJ zinslos, unverzinslich; **noninterference** N Nichteinmischung *f (in* in *+acc)*; **nonintervention** N *(Pol etc)* Nichteinmischung *f*, Nichteingreifen *nt (in* in *+acc)*; **noninterventionist** ADJ *policy* der Nichteinmischung; **noniron** ADJ bügelfrei; **non-league** ADJ *(Brit Sport)* außerhalb der Spitzenligen, Amateur-; **~ football** Amateurfußball *m*; **non-medical practitioner** N Heilpraktiker(in) *m(f)*; **nonmember** N Nichtmitglied *nt*; *(of society also)* Nichtangehörige(r) *mf*; **open to ~s** Gäste willkommen; **non-migratory** ADJ **~ bird** Standvogel *m*, Nichtzieher *m (spec)*; **non-milk** ADJ **~ fat(s)** nichttierische *or* nicht tierische Fette *pl*; **non-negotiable** ADJ *ticket* nicht übertragbar; **the price is ~** über den Preis lässt sich nicht verhandeln; **non-nuclear** ADJ *weapons, forces, en-*

ergy nicht nuklear; *world* atomwaffenfrei; **~ state** Nichtnuklearstaat *m*

no-no ['nəʊnəʊ] N *(inf)* **to be a ~** verboten *or* tabu sein; **that's/she's a ~!** das/sie kommt nicht infrage *or* in Frage! *(inf)*; **that's a ~!** *(= you mustn't do it)* das gibts nicht!

non: **non-obligatory** ADJ freiwillig, nicht Pflicht *pred*, freigestellt *pred*; **non-observance** N Nicht(be)achtung *f*

no-nonsense ['nəʊ,nɒnsəns] ADJ (kühl und) sachlich, nüchtern

non: **non-paid** ADJ *service etc* unbezahlt; **nonpareil** [nɒnpə'reɪ] ADJ *(liter)* unerreicht N *(liter)* *(= thing)* Nonplusultra *nt*; *(= person)* unerreichter Meister; **nonpartisan** ADJ unparteiisch; **nonpayment** N Nichtzahlung *f*, Zahlungsverweigerung *f*; **nonperishable** ADJ dauerhaft, haltbar; **non-person** N Unperson *f*

nonplus ['nɒn'plʌs] VT verblüffen; **completely ~sed** völlig verdutzt *or* verblüfft

non: **nonpoisonous** ADJ nicht giftig, ungiftig; **nonpolitical** ADJ nichtpolitisch, nicht politisch; **nonpolluting** ADJ umweltschonend; **nonporous** ADJ nichtporös, nicht porös; **nonprinting** ADJ nicht druckend; **~ character** nicht druckendes Zeichen; **nonproductive** ADJ **~ industries** Dienstleistungssektor *m*; **~ worker** Angestellte(r) *mf* im Dienstleistungssektor; **non-profit-making**, *(US)* **nonprofit** ADJ keinen Gewinn anstrebend *attr*; *charity etc also* gemeinnützig; **on a ~ basis** auf gemeinnütziger Basis; **nonproliferation** N Nichtverbreitung *f* von Atomwaffen; **~ treaty** Atomsperrvertrag *m*; **nonpublication** N Nichterscheinen *nt*; **nonradioactive** ADJ *substance* nicht radioaktiv, strahlenfrei; **nonreader** N Analphabet(in) *m(f)*; **there are still five ~s in this class** in dieser Klasse können fünf Schüler noch nicht lesen; **nonrecognition** N Nichtanerkennung *f*; **non-refillable** ADJ Wegwerf-, Einweg-; **~ bottle** Wegwerf- *or* Einwegflasche *f*; **nonresident** ADJ nicht ansässig; *(in hotel)* nicht im Hause wohnend N Nicht(orts)ansässige(r) *mf*; *(in hotel)* nicht im Haus wohnender Gast; **open to ~s** auch für Nichthotelgäste; **nonreturnable** ADJ **~ bottle** Einwegflasche *f*; **~ deposit** Anzahlung *f*; **non-run** ADJ *(esp US) stockings* maschenfest, laufmaschensicher; **non-scene** ADJ *(inf) gay* der nicht zur Szene gehört; **nonscheduled** ADJ *flight, train* außerplanmäßig; **nonsectarian** ADJ nichtkonfessionell, nicht konfessionell; *assembly* nicht konfessionsgebunden

nonsense ['nɒnsəns] N *no pl (also as interjection)* Unsinn *m*, Quatsch *m (inf)*, Nonsens *m (geh)*; *(verbal also)* dummes Zeug; *(= silly behaviour)* Dummheiten *pl*; **a piece of ~** ein Quatsch *m (inf) or* Unsinn *m*; **that's a lot of ~!** das ist (ja) alles dummes Zeug!; **I've had enough of this ~** jetzt reichts mir aber; **to make (a) ~ of sth** etw ad absurdum führen, etw sinnlos machen; **what's all this ~ about a cut in salary/about them not wanting to go?** was soll all das Gerede von einer Gehaltskürzung/all das Gerede, dass sie nicht mitgehen wollen?; **no more of your ~!** Schluss mit dem Unsinn!; **and no ~** und keine Dummheiten; **I will stand** *or* **have no ~ from you** ich werde keinen Unsinn *or* keine Dummheiten dulden; **he will stand no ~ from anybody** er lässt nicht mit sich spaßen; **he won't stand any ~ over that** was das betrifft, verträgt er keinen Spaß; **a man with no ~ about him** ein nüchterner *or* kühler und sachlicher Mensch → **stuff N a**

nonsense verse N Nonsensvers *m*, Unsinnsvers *m*; *(= genre)* Nonsensverse *pl*, Unsinnsverse *pl*

nonsensical [nɒn'sensɪkəl] ADJ *idea, action* unsinnig

nonsensically [nɒn'sensɪkəlɪ] ADV *argue etc* unsinnigerweise

non sequitur [,nɒn'sekwɪtə'] N unlogische (Schluss)folgerung

non: **nonshrink** ADJ nicht einlaufend; **to be ~** nicht einlaufen; **nonskid** ADJ rutschsicher; **nonslip** ADJ rutschfest; **nonsmoker** N **a** *(= person)* Nichtraucher(in) *m(f)* **b** *(Rail)* Nichtraucherabteil *nt*; **nonsmoking** ADJ Nichtraucher-; **~ area** *or* **section** Nichtraucherbereich *m*; **we have a ~ policy** bei uns herrscht Rauchverbot, bei uns darf nicht geraucht werden; **nonspecific** ADJ **a** *(Med)* unspezifisch **b** *(= imprecise)* allgemein; **nonstandard** ADJ nicht der Norm entsprechend; *(= not usually supplied) fittings* nicht üblich; **~ size** Sondergröße *f*; **nonstarter** N **a** *(in race) (= person)* Nichtstartende(r) *mf*; *(= horse)* nicht startendes Pferd; **there were two ~s** zwei traten nicht an **b** *(fig) (= idea)* Blindgänger *m*; *(= person)* Blindgänger(in) *m(f)*; **nonstick** ADJ *pan, surface* kunststoffbeschichtet, Teflon-®; **nonstop** ADJ *train* durchgehend; *journey, performances* ohne Unterbrechung; *music* dauernd; **~ flight** Nonstop-Flug *m*, Nonstopflug *m* ADV *talk, work* ununterbrochen; *fly* nonstop; *travel* ohne Unterbrechung, nonstop; **non-survival** N Aussterben *nt*; **nonswimmer** N Nichtschwimmer(in) *m(f)*; **nontaxable** ADJ nicht steuerpflichtig; **nontechnical** ADJ *language etc* für den Laien verständlich; *subject* nichttechnisch, nicht technisch; **~ people** technische Laien *pl*; **nontoxic** ADJ ungiftig; **non-U** ADJ *(Brit) charakteristisch für die Gewohnheiten, Sprechweise etc des Kleinbürgertums*, nicht vornehm; **nonunion** ADJ *worker, labour* nicht organisiert; **nonverbal** ADJ *communication* nichtverbal, nicht verbal, wortlos, ohne Worte; **nonviolence** N Gewaltlosigkeit *f*; **nonviolent** ADJ gewaltlos; *crime, offender* nicht gewalttätig; **nonvocational** ADJ *subject, course* nicht berufsorientiert; **nonvolatile** ADJ *(Chem, Comput)* nicht flüchtig; **nonvoter** N Nichtwähler(in) *m(f)*; **nonvoting** ADJ **~ shares** stimmrechtslose Aktien *pl*; **non-White** N Farbige(r) *mf* ADJ farbig

noodle ['nu:dl] N **a** *(Cook)* Nudel *f* **b** *(dated inf, = fool)* Dummerjan *m (dated inf)* **c** *(US inf: = head)* Birne *f (inf)*; **use your ~** streng deinen Grips an *(inf)*

nook [nʊk] N *(= corner)* Ecke *f*, Winkel *m*; *(= remote spot)* Winkel *m*; **a shady ~** ein schattiges Fleckchen; **a cosy ~** ein gemütliches Eckchen; **in every ~ and cranny** in jedem Winkel

nooky, **nookie** ['nʊkɪ] N *(inf: = sex)* Nümmerchen *nt (inf)*; **to have a bit of ~** (ein bisschen) bumsen *(inf)*

noon [nu:n] N Mittag *m*; **at ~** um 12 Uhr mittags ADJ 12-Uhr-; *deadline* bis 12 Uhr; **~ flight** 12-Uhr-Flug *m*

noonday ['nu:ndeɪ] ADJ *attr* Mittags-, mittäglich; **~ sun** Mittagssonne *f*

no-one, **no one** ['nəʊwʌn] PRON = **nobody** PRON

noon: **noontide** N *(liter)* = **noontime**; **noontime** *(esp US)* N Mittagszeit *f*, Mittagsstunde *f (geh)*; **at ~** um die Mittagsstunde *(geh)* ADJ *meal, sun, light, class, service, crowd* zur Mittagszeit

noose [nu:s] N Schlinge *f*; **to put one's head in the ~** *(prov)* den Kopf in die Schlinge stecken

no-passing zone N *(US: Mot)* Überholverbotszone *f*

nope [nəʊp] ADV *(inf)* ne(e) *(dial)*, nein

no place ADV *(esp US inf)* = **nowhere**

nor [nɔ:'] CONJ **a** noch; **neither ... ~** weder ... noch **b** *(= and not)* und ... auch nicht; **I shan't go, ~ will you** ich gehe nicht, und du auch nicht; **~ do/have/am I** ich auch nicht; **~ was this all** und das war noch nicht alles

Nordic ['nɔ:dɪk] ADJ nordisch; **~ walking** *(Sport)* Nordic Walking *nt*

nor'east [nɔ:'ri:st] *(Naut)* = **northeast**

norm [nɔ:m] N Norm *f*; **our ~ is ...** unsere Norm liegt bei ...

normal ['nɔ:məl] ADJ **a** normal; *(= customary)* üblich; **it's a perfectly** *or* **quite a ~ thing** das ist völlig normal; **it's perfectly ~ for you to feel that way** es ist vollkommen normal, dass Sie so empfinden; **it's ~ practice** das ist so üblich; **~ temperature/consumption/output** Normaltemperatur *f*/-verbrauch *m*/-leistung *f*; **~ view** *(Comput)* Normalansicht *f*; **he is not his ~ self today** er ist heute so anders; **a higher than ~ risk of infection** ein Infektionsrisiko, das über dem Normalen liegt
b *(Math)* senkrecht
c *(Chem)* **~ solution** Normallösung *f*
N *no pl (of temperature)* Normalwert *m*, Durchschnitt *m*; *(Math)* Senkrechte *f*; *(to tangent)* Normale *f*; **temperatures below ~** Temperaturen unter dem Durchschnitt; **her temperature is below/above ~** sie hat Untertemperatur/erhöhte Temperatur; **when things/we are back to** *or* **return to ~** wenn sich alles wieder normalisiert hat; **just carry on as ~** machen Sie einfach normal weiter; **life went on as ~** das Leben ging normal weiter

normalcy ['nɔ:məlsɪ] N = **normality**

normal hill N *(ski jumping)* Normalschanze *f*

normality [nɔ:'mælɪtɪ] N Normalität *f*; **the return to ~ after war** die Normalisierung (des Lebens) *or* die Wiederaufnahme eines normalen Lebens nach dem Krieg; **to return to ~** sich wieder normalisieren; **despite his apparent ~** obwohl er ganz normal zu sein scheint

normalization [,nɔ:məlaɪ'zeɪʃən] N Normalisierung *f*

normalize ['nɔ:məlaɪz] VT normalisieren; *relations* wiederherstellen; **to be ~d** sich normalisiert haben

normally ['nɔ:məlɪ] ADV *(= usually)* normalerweise, gewöhnlich; *(= in normal way)* normal

normal school N *(US, old)* pädagogische Hochschule

Norman ['nɔ:mən] ADJ normannisch; **the ~ Conquest** der normannische Eroberungszug N Normanne *m*, Normannin *f*

Normandy ['nɔ:məndɪ] N Normandie *f*

normative ['nɔ:mətɪv] ADJ normativ

nor'-nor'east [,nɔ:nɔ:'ri:st] *(Naut)* = **north-northeast**

nor'-nor'west [,nɔ:nɔ:'west] *(Naut)* = **north-northwest**

Norse [nɔ:s] ADJ *mythology* altnordisch N *(Ling)* **Old ~** Altnordisch *nt*

Norse: **Norseman** N *(Hist)* Normanne *m*, Wikinger *m*; **Norsewoman** N *(Hist)* Normannin *f*, Wikingerin *f*

north [nɔ:θ] N **a** Norden *m*; **in/from the ~** im/aus dem Norden; **to live in the ~** im Norden leben; **to the ~ of** nördlich von, im Norden von; **to veer/go to the ~** in nördliche Richtung *or* nach Norden drehen/gehen; **the wind is in the ~** es ist Nordwind; **to face (the) ~** nach Norden liegen; **the North (of Scotland/England)** Nordschottland/-england *nt*
b *(US Hist)* **the North** der Norden, die Nordstaaten *pl*
ADJ *attr* Nord-; **North German** norddeutsch
ADV *(= towards North)* nach Norden, gen Norden *(liter)*, nordwärts *(liter, Naut)*; *(Met)* in nördliche Richtung; **~ of** nördlich *or* im Norden von; **~ of one million** *(US fig)* über eine Million

north *in cpds* Nord-; **North Africa** N Nordafrika *nt*; **North African** ADJ nordafrikanisch N Nordafrikaner(in) *m(f)*; **North America** N Nordamerika *nt*; **North American** ADJ nordamerikanisch N Nordamerikaner(in) *m(f)*

Northants [nɔ:'θænts] *abbr of* **Northamptonshire**

north: **North Atlantic** N Nordatlantik *m*; **northbound** ADJ *carriageway* nach Norden (führend); *traffic* in Richtung Norden; **north country** N **the ~** Nordengland *nt*; **north-country** ADJ nordenglisch; **North Dakota** ['nɔ:θ,də'kəʊtə] N Norddakota *nt*; **northeast** N Nordosten *m*, Nordost *m (esp Naut)*; **in the ~** im Nordosten; **from the ~** von Nordost ADJ Nordost-, nordöstlich; **~ England** Nordostengland *nt* ADV nach Nordosten; **~ of** nordöstlich von; **northeasterly** ADJ nordöstlich N *(= wind)* Nordostwind *m*; **northeastern** ADJ *provinces* nordöstlich, im Nordosten; **northeastwards** ADV nordostwärts, nach Nordost(en)

northerly [ˈnɔːðəlɪ] ADJ *wind, direction, latitude* nördlich ADV nach Norden, nordwärts *(liter, Naut)* N Nordwind *m*

northern [ˈnɔːðən] ADJ *hemisphere, counties* nördlich; **~ Germany/Italy** Norddeutschland/-italien *nt*; **Northern Irish** nordirisch; **with a ~ outlook** mit Blick nach Norden

Northern Alliance N *(Pol: in Afghanistan)* Nordallianz *f*

northerner [ˈnɔːðənəˈ] N **a** Bewohner(in) *m(f)* des Nordens, Nordengländer(in) *m(f)*/-deutsche(r) *mf etc*; **he is a ~** er kommt aus dem Norden (des Landes) **b** *(US)* Nordstaatler(in) *m(f)*

Northern Ireland N Nordirland *nt*

northern lights PL **the ~** das Nordlicht

northernmost [ˈnɔːðənməʊst] ADJ *area* nördlichste(r, s)

northing [ˈnɔːðɪŋ] N **a** *(Astron)* nördliche Deklination *(eines Planeten)* **b** *(= Naut)* Weg *m* *or* Distanz *f* nach Norden

north: **North Korea** N Nordkorea *nt*; **North Korean** ADJ nordkoreanisch N Nordkoreaner(in) *m(f)*; **north-northeast** N Nordnordosten *m*, Nordnordost *m (esp Naut)* ADJ nordnordöstlich ADV nach Nordnordost(en); **~ of** nordnordöstlich von; **north-northwest** N Nordnordwesten *m*, Nordnordwest *m (esp Naut)* ADJ nordnordwestlich ADV nach Nordnordwest(en); **~ of** nordnordwestlich von; **North Pole** N Nordpol *m*; **North Sea** N Nordsee *f* ADJ Nordsee-; **~ gas/oil** Nordseegas *nt*/-öl *nt*; **North-South divide** N Nord-Süd-Gefälle *nt*

> **NORTH/SOUTH DIVIDE**
>
> **North/South divide** bezeichnet eine Art umgekehrtes Nord-Süd-Gefälle in Großbritannien, das in wirtschaftlicher wie sozialer Hinsicht zwischen dem Norden und dem Süden Großbritanniens herrscht. Im Allgemeinen heißt es, dass die Menschen im Süden Englands wohlhabender sind, die besseren Arbeitsperspektiven haben und einen gesünderen Lebensstil praktizieren. Außerdem glaubt man, dass der Süden, besonders die Gegend rund um London, von der Regierung bevorzugt behandelt wird. Viele traditionelle Industriezweige im Norden sind verschwunden, und die Regierung wird häufig beschuldigt, nicht energisch genug einzugreifen, um Wirtschaft und Infrastruktur der betroffenen Gebiete wieder zu beleben.

North Star N Nordstern *m*

Northumb *(Brit) abbr of* **Northumberland**

north: **North Vietnam** N Nordvietnam *nt*; **North Vietnamese** ADJ nordvietnamesisch N Nordvietnamese *m*/-vietnamesin *f*; **northward** ADJ nördlich; **in a ~ direction** nach Norden, (in) Richtung Norden ADV *(also* **northwards***)* nach Norden, nordwärts; **northwardly** ADJ ADV = **northward**; **northwest** N Nordwesten *m*, Nordwest *m (esp Naut)* ADJ Nordwest-, nordwestlich; **~ England** Nordwestengland *nt*; **the Northwest Passage** die Nordwestpassage ADV nach Nordwest(en); **~ of** nordwestlich von; **northwesterly** ADJ nordwestlich N Nordwestwind *m*

Norway [ˈnɔːweɪ] N Norwegen *nt*

Norwegian [nɔːˈwiːdʒən] ADJ norwegisch N **a** Norweger(in) *m(f)* **b** *(Ling)* Norwegisch *nt*

nor'west [nɔːˈwest] *(Naut)* = **northwest**

Nos., **nos.** *abbr of* **numbers** Nrn.

nose [nəʊz] N **a** Nase *f*; **to hold one's ~** sich *(dat)* die Nase zuhalten; **to speak through one's ~** durch die Nase sprechen; **the tip of one's ~** die Nasenspitze; **my ~ is bleeding** ich habe Nasenbluten; **follow your ~** immer der Nase nach; **she always has her ~ in a book** sie hat dauernd den Kopf in einem Buch (vergraben); **to do sth under sb's (very) ~** etw vor jds Augen tun; **it was right under his ~ all the time** er hatte es die ganze Zeit direkt vor der Nase; **I just followed my ~** ich bin immer der Nase nach gegangen; **she leads him by the ~** er tanzt ganz nach ihrer Pfeife *(inf)*; **don't let him lead you by the ~** lass dich von ihm nicht unterbuttern!; **he can't see beyond** *or* **further than the end of his ~** er kann nicht weiter sehen, als sein eigener Schatten reicht; **to get up sb's ~** *(fig inf)* jdm auf den Geist *or* auf die Nerven gehen *(inf)*; **to poke** *or* **stick one's ~ into sth** *(fig)* seine Nase in etw *(acc)* stecken; **you keep your ~ out of this** *(inf)* halt du dich da raus *(inf)*; **to cut off one's ~ to spite one's face** *(prov)* sich ins eigene Fleisch schneiden; **to look down one's ~ at sb/sth** auf jdn/etw herabblicken; **with one's ~ in the air** mit hocherhobenem Kopf, hochnäsig; **to pay through the ~** *(inf)* viel blechen *(inf)*, sich dumm und dämlich zahlen *(inf)*; **to win by a ~** *(horse)* um eine Nasenlänge gewinnen; **to put sb's ~ out of joint** jdn vor den Kopf stoßen; **his ~ is out of joint over this** er fühlt sich dadurch vor den Kopf gestoßen; **to keep one's ~ clean** *(inf)* sauber bleiben *(inf)*, eine saubere Weste behalten *(inf)*; **to pay on the ~** sofort bezahlen

b *(= sense of smell)* Nase *f*; *(fig)* Riecher *m* *(inf)*, Nase *f*; **to have a ~ for sth** *(fig)* eine Nase *or* einen Riecher *(inf)* für etw haben

c *(of wines)* Blume *f*

d *(of plane)* Nase *f*; *(of car)* Schnauze *f*; *(of boat)* Bug *m*; *(of torpedo)* Kopf *m*; **~ to tail** *(cars)* Stoßstange an Stoßstange

VT **the car/ship ~d its way through the fog** das Auto/Schiff tastete sich durch den Nebel; **the car ~d its way into the stream of traffic** das Auto schob sich in den fließenden Verkehr vor; **I ~d the car toward(s) the gate** ich manövrierte das Auto langsam zum Tor

VI **a boat ~d through the mist** ein Boot tastete sich durch den Nebel; **the car ~d forward** das Auto schob sich langsam vor; **to ~ into sb's affairs** *(fig)* seine Nase in jds Angelegenheiten *(acc)* stecken *(inf)*

▶ **nose about** *(Brit) or* **around** VI herumschnüffeln *(inf)*; *(person also)* herumspionieren *(inf)*

▶ **nose out** VT *sep (Brit inf)* aufspüren; *secret, scandal* ausspionieren *(inf)*, ausschnüffeln *(inf)* VI *(car)* sich vorschieben

nose: **nosebag** N Futtersack *m*; **noseband** N Nasenriemen *m*; **nosebleed** N Nasenbluten *nt*; **to have a ~** Nasenbluten haben; **nose cone** N *(Aviat)* Raketenspitze *f*; **nosedive** N *(Aviat)* Sturzflug *m*; **to go into a ~** zum Sturzflug ansetzen; **the car/he took a ~ into the sea** das Auto stürzte vornüber/er stürzte kopfüber ins Meer; **the company's profits took a ~** mit der Firma ging es rapide bergab; **his career took a ~** seine Karriere nahm einen scharfen Knick nach unten; **his reputation took a ~** sein Ruf nahm starken Schaden VI *(plane)* im Sturzflug herabgehen; *(fig: career, reputation)* den Bach runtergehen *(inf)*; **to ~ off sth** vornüber von etw stürzen; *(person)* kopfüber von etw stürzen; **nosedrops** PL Nasentropfen *pl*; **nose flute** N Nasenflöte *f*; **nosegay** N (Biedermeier)sträußchen *nt*; **nose job** N *(inf)* Nasenkorrektur *f*; **to have a ~** sich einer Nasenkorrektur unterziehen; **nose-picking** N Nasenbohren *nt*; **nose plaster** N *(esp Sport)* Nasenpflaster *nt*; **nose ring** N Nasenring *m*; **nosewheel** N Bugrad *nt*

nosey ADJ = **nosy**

nosey parker [ˌnəʊzɪˈpɑːkəˈ] N *(Brit inf)* Schnüffler(in) *m(f)* *(inf)*; **I don't like ~s** ich mag Leute nicht, die ihre Nase in alles stecken *(inf)*; **~!** sei doch nicht so neugierig!

nosh [nɒʃ] *(Brit sl)* N *(= food)* Futter *nt (inf)*; *(= meal)* Schmaus *m*; **to have some ~** was essen *or* futtern *(inf)* VI futtern *(inf)*

no-show [ˈnəʊʃəʊ] N *(Aviat)* No-Show *m*, fehlender Flugpassagier

nosh-up [ˈnɒʃʌp] N *(Brit inf)* Schmaus *m*, Fressgelage *nt (inf)*

no-smoking ADJ *attr* Nichtraucher-

nostalgia [nɒˈstældʒɪə] N Nostalgie *f (for* nach); **to feel ~ for sth** sich nach etw zurücksehnen

nostalgic [nɒˈstældʒɪk] ADJ nostalgisch; *(= wistful)* wehmütig; **to feel/be ~ for** *or* **about sth** sich nach etw zurücksehnen

nostalgically [nɒˈstældʒɪklɪ] ADV nostalgisch; *(= wistfully)* wehmütig; **they look back ~ to the war** sie blicken mit Nostalgie auf den Krieg zurück

no-strike [ˈnəʊstraɪk] ADJ *attr* **~ deal/agreement** Streikverzichtabkommen *nt*

nostril [ˈnɒstrəl] N Nasenloch *nt*; *(of horse, zebra etc)* Nüster *f*

nostrum [ˈnɒstrəm] N *(old lit, fig)* Patentrezept *nt*

nosy [ˈnəʊzɪ] ADJ *(+er) (inf)* neugierig

not [nɒt] ADV **a** nicht; **he told me ~ to come/~ to do that** er sagte, ich solle nicht kommen/ich solle das nicht tun; **do ~** *or* **don't come** kommen Sie nicht; **that's how ~ to do it** so sollte man es nicht machen; **he was wrong in ~ making a protest** es war falsch von ihm, nicht zu protestieren; **~ wanting to be heard, he …** da er nicht gehört werden wollte, … er …; **~ I!** ich nicht!; **fear ~!** *(old)* fürchte dich nicht!

b *(emphatic)* nicht; **~ a sound/word** *etc* kein Ton/Wort *etc*, nicht EIN Ton/Wort *etc*; **~ a bit** kein bisschen; **~ a sign of …** keine Spur von …; **~ one of them** kein Einziger, nicht einer; **~ a thing** überhaupt nichts; **they were here ~ ten minutes ago** vor nicht einmal zehn Minuten waren sie noch hier; **~ any more** nicht mehr; **~ yet** noch nicht; **~ even** nicht einmal; **~ so** *(as reply)* nein; **say ~ so** *(old)* sag, dass es nicht wahr ist

c *(in tag or rhetorical questions)* **it's hot, isn't it?** *or (form)* **is it ~?** es ist heiß, nicht wahr *or* nicht? *(inf)*; **isn't it hot?** (es ist) heiß, nicht wahr?, ist das vielleicht heiß!; **isn't he naughty!** ist er nicht frech?, (er ist) ganz schön frech, nicht! *(inf)*; **you are coming, aren't you** *or* **are you ~?** Sie kommen doch, oder?; **you have got it, haven't you?** Sie haben es doch, oder?, Sie haben es, nicht wahr?; **you like it, don't you?** *or (form)* **do you ~?** das gefällt dir, nicht (wahr)?; **you are ~ angry, are you?** Sie sind nicht böse, oder?; **you are ~ angry – or are you?** Sie sind doch nicht etwa böse?

d *(as substitute for clause)* nicht; **is he coming? – I hope/I believe ~** kommt er? – ich hoffe/glaube nicht; **it would seem** *or* **appear ~** anscheinend nicht; **he's decided ~ to do it – I should think/hope ~** er hat sich entschlossen, es nicht zu tun – das möchte ich auch meinen/hoffen

e *(elliptically)* **are you cold? – ~ at all** ist dir kalt? – überhaupt *or* gar nicht; **thank you very much – ~ at all** vielen Dank – keine Ursache *or* gern geschehen; **~ in the least** überhaupt *or* gar nicht, nicht im Geringsten; **~ that I care** nicht, dass es mir etwas ausmacht(e); **~ that I know of** nicht, dass ich wüsste; **it's ~ that I don't believe him** ich glaube ihm ja, es ist ja nicht so, dass ich ihm nicht glaube

notability [ˌnəʊtəˈbɪlɪtɪ] N **a** *(= person)* bedeutende Persönlichkeit; **the notabilities of the town** die Honoratioren *pl* der Stadt **b** *(= eminence)* Berühmtheit *f*, Bedeutung *f*

notable [ˈnəʊtəbl] ADJ *(= eminent) person* bedeutend; *(= worthy of note) success, fact, event also* bemerkenswert, beachtenswert *(for* wegen); *(= big) difference, improvement* beträchtlich, beachtlich; *(= conspicuous)* auffallend; **with a few ~ exceptions** bis auf einige rühmliche Ausnahmen; **he was ~ by his absence** er glänzte durch Abwesenheit N = **notability a**

notably ['nəʊtəblɪ] ADV **a** (= *strikingly*) auffallend; *improved, different* beträchtlich; **to be ~ absent** durch Abwesenheit glänzen; **they were ~ unimpressed** sie zeigten sich bemerkenswert unbeeindruckt **b** (= *in particular*) hauptsächlich, insbesondere; **most ~** vor allem

notarial [nəʊ'tɛərɪəl] ADJ *seal, deed, style* notariell; *fees* Notar-

notarize ['nəʊtəraɪz] VT notariell beglaubigen

notary (public) ['nəʊtərɪ('pʌblɪk)] N Notar(in) *m(f)*; **attested by (a) ~** notariell beglaubigt

notate [nəʊ'teɪt] VT (*Mus*) in Notenschrift schreiben

notation [nəʊ'teɪʃən] N **a** (= *system*) Zeichensystem *nt*, Notation *f* (*spec*); (= *symbols*) Zeichen *pl*; (*Mus*) Notenschrift *f*, Notation *f*; (*Math, Comput*) Notation *f* **b** (= *note*) Notiz *f*, Anmerkung *f*

notch [nɒtʃ] **N** Kerbe *f*; (*of handbrake, for adjustment etc*) Raste *f*; (*in belt*) Loch *nt*; (= *point, degree*) Grad *m*, Stufe *f*; **to cut a ~ in sth** eine Kerbe in etw (*acc*) machen; **our team is a ~ above theirs** unsere Mannschaft ist eine Klasse besser als ihre; **several ~es better** um einiges besser → **top-notch** **VT** einkerben, einschneiden; (*esp Sport*) *win, success* verzeichnen können

▶ **notch up** VT *sep score, points* erzielen, einheimsen (*inf*); *record* erringen, verzeichnen; *success* verzeichnen können

note [nəʊt] ✪ 20.7, 26.3 **N** **a** Notiz *f*, Anmerkung *f*; (= *notice, comment*) Hinweis *m* (*also Comput*); (= *footnote*) Anmerkung *f*, Fußnote *f*; (*official: in file etc*) Vermerk *m*; (= *diplomatic note*) Note *f*; (= *informal letter*) Briefchen *nt*, paar Zeilen *pl*; **~s** (= *summary*) Aufzeichnungen *pl*; (= *plan, draft*) Konzept *nt*; **a few rough ~s** ein paar Stichworte *pl*; **lecture ~s** (*professor's*) Manuskript *nt*; (*student's*) Aufzeichnungen *pl*; (= *handout*) Vorlesungsskript *nt*; **to speak without ~s** frei sprechen, ohne Vorlage sprechen; **to speak from ~s** (von einer Vorlage) ablesen; **"Author's Note"** „Anmerkung des Verfassers"; **exchange of ~s** (*Pol*) Notenaustausch *m*; **to send/leave sb a ~** jdm ein paar Zeilen schicken; **to write a hasty ~** schnell ein paar Zeilen schreiben; **to take** *or* **make ~s** Notizen machen; (*in lecture also, in interrogation*) mitschreiben; **to make ~s on a case** (sich *dat*) Notizen zu einem Fall machen; **to take** *or* **make a ~ of sth** sich (*dat*) etw notieren
b *no pl* (= *notice*) **to take ~ of sth** von etw Notiz nehmen, etw zur Kenntnis nehmen; (= *heed*) einer Sache (*dat*) Beachtung schenken; **take no ~ of what he says** nehmen Sie keine Notiz von dem, was er sagt, achten Sie nicht darauf, was er sagt; **take ~ of what I tell you** hören Sie auf das, was ich zu sagen habe; **worthy of ~** beachtenswert, erwähnenswert
c *no pl* (= *importance*) **a man of ~** ein bedeutender Mann; **nothing of ~** nichts Beachtens- *or* Erwähnenswertes
d (*Mus*) (= *sign*) Note *f*; (= *sound: on piano etc*) Ton *m*; (= *song of bird etc*) Lied *nt*, Gesang *m*; **to give the ~** den Ton angeben; **to play/sing the right/wrong ~** richtig/falsch spielen/singen; **to strike the right ~** (*fig*) den richtigen Ton treffen; **it struck a wrong** *or* **false ~** (*fig*) da hat er *etc* sich im Ton vergriffen; (= *wasn't genuine*) es klang nicht echt
e (= *quality, tone*) Ton *m*, Klang *m*; **on a personal ~** persönlich gesprochen; **on a more optimistic/positive ~** aus optimistischer/positiver Sicht; **his voice took on a ~ of desperation** aus seiner Stimme klang Verzweiflung, seine Stimme hatte einen verzweifelten Klang; **a ~ of nostalgia** eine nostalgische Note; **to sound** *or* **strike a ~ of warning** warnen; **to sound a ~ of caution** zur Vorsicht mahnen; **there was a ~ of warning in his voice** seine Stimme hatte einen warnenden Unterton
f (*Brit Fin*) Note *f*, Schein *m*; **a £5 ~, a five-pound ~** eine Fünfpfundnote, ein Fünfpfundschein *m*
VT **a** (= *notice*) bemerken; (= *take note of*) zur Kenntnis nehmen; (= *pay attention to*) beachten
b = **note down**

▶ **note down** VT *sep* notieren, aufschreiben; (*as reminder*) sich (*dat*) notieren *or* aufschreiben

note: **notebook** ['nəʊtbʊk] N Notizbuch *or* -heft *nt*; **~ (computer)** Notebook *nt*, Notebookcomputer *m*; **notecase** N Brieftasche *f*

noted ['nəʊtɪd] ADJ bekannt, berühmt (*for* für, wegen)

notelet ['nəʊtlɪt] N Briefkarte *f*

note: **notepad** N **a** Notizblock *m* **b** (*Comput*) Notepad *nt*; **notepaper** N Briefpapier *nt*; **note row** ['nəʊtrəʊ] N (*twelve-tone music*) Reihe *f*

noteworthy ['nəʊtwɜːðɪ] ADJ beachtenswert, erwähnenswert

nothing ['nʌθɪŋ] **N, PRON, ADV** **a** nichts; **~ pleases him** nichts gefällt ihm, ihm gefällt nichts; **~ could be easier** nichts wäre einfacher; **it was reduced to ~** es blieb nichts davon übrig; **she is five foot ~** (*inf*) sie ist genau fünf Fuß; **it was all or ~** es ging um alles oder nichts
b (*with vb*) nichts; **she is** *or* **means ~ to him** sie bedeutet ihm nichts; **£500 is ~ to her** £ 500 sind für sie gar nichts; **she is ~ (compared) to her sister** sie ist nichts im Vergleich zu ihrer Schwester; **that's ~ to what is to come** das ist noch gar nichts im Vergleich zu dem, was noch kommen wird; **it came to ~** da ist nichts draus geworden; **I can make ~ of it** das sagt mir nichts, ich werde daraus nicht schlau; **he thinks ~ of doing that** er findet nichts dabei(, das zu tun); **think ~ of it** keine Ursache!; **will you come? – ~ doing!** (*inf*) kommst du? – ausgeschlossen! *or* kein Gedanke (*inf*); **there was ~ doing at the club** (*inf*) im Klub war nichts los; **I tried, but there's ~ doing** (*inf*) ich habs versucht, aber keine Chance (*inf*) *or* aber da ist nichts zu machen
c (*with prep*) **all his fame stood** *or* **counted for ~** (*liter*) sein Ruhm galt nichts; **for ~** (= *free, in vain*) umsonst; **it's not for ~ that he's called X** er heißt nicht umsonst *or* ohne Grund X; **there's ~ (else) for it but to leave** da bleibt einem nichts übrig als zu gehen; **there's ~ (else) for it, we'll have to ...** da hilft alles nichts, wir müssen ...; **there was ~ in it for me** das hat sich für mich nicht gelohnt, ich hatte nichts davon; (*financially also*) dabei sprang nichts für mich heraus (*inf*); **there's ~ in the rumour** (*Brit*) *or* **rumor** (*US*) das Gerücht ist völlig unfundiert *or* aus der Luft gegriffen, an dem Gerücht ist nichts (Wahres); **that is ~ to you** für dich ist das doch gar nichts; (= *isn't important*) das kümmert *or* berührt dich nicht, das ist dir egal; **there's ~ to it** (*inf*) das ist kinderleicht (*inf*)
d (*with adj, adv*) **~ but** nur; **he does ~ but eat** er isst nur *or* ständig, er tut nichts anderes als essen; **~ else** sonst nichts; **~ more** sonst nichts; **I'd like ~ more than that** ich möchte nichts lieber als das; **I'd like ~ more than to go to Canada** ich würde (nur) zu gern nach Kanada gehen; **~ much** nicht viel; **~ less than** nur; **~ if not polite** äußerst *or* überaus höflich; **~ new** nichts Neues; **it was ~ like as big as we thought** es war lange nicht so groß, wie wir dachten
e **in ~ flat** (*US inf*) in null Komma nichts (*inf*); **you don't know from ~** (*US inf*) du hast (überhaupt) keine Ahnung (*inf*); **he has ~ on her** (*inf*) er kann ihr nicht das Wasser reichen (*inf*)
N **a** (*Math*) Null *f*
b (= *thing, person of no value*) Nichts *nt*; **it's a mere ~ compared to what he spent last year** im Vergleich zu dem, was er letztes Jahr ausgegeben hat, ist das gar nichts; **it was a mere ~** das war doch nicht der Rede wert, das war doch nur eine winzige Kleinigkeit; **thank you – it was ~** danke – das war doch selbstverständlich; **don't apologize, it's ~** entschuldige dich nicht, es ist nicht der Rede wert; **what's wrong with you? – (it's) ~** was ist mit dir los? – nichts; **to whisper sweet ~s to sb** jdm Zärtlichkeiten ins Ohr flüstern

nothingness ['nʌθɪŋnɪs] N Nichts *nt*

no through road N **it's a ~** es ist keine Durchfahrt

no-throw ['nəʊ'θrəʊ] N Fehlwurf *m*

notice ['nəʊtɪs] **N** **a** (= *warning, communication*) Bescheid *m*, Benachrichtigung *f*; (= *written notification*) Mitteilung *f*; (*of forthcoming event, film etc*) Ankündigung *f*; **~ to pay** (*Comm*) Zahlungsaufforderung *f*; **final ~** letzte Aufforderung; **we need three weeks' ~** wir müssen drei Wochen vorher Bescheid wissen; **to give ~ of sth** von etw Bescheid geben; *of film, change etc* etw ankündigen; *of arrival etc* etw melden; **to give sb one week's ~ of sth** jdn eine Woche vorher von etw benachrichtigen, jdm eine Woche vorher über etw (*acc*) Bescheid geben; **to give sb ~ of sth** jdn von etw benachrichtigen, jdm etw mitteilen; **to give ~ of appeal** (*Jur*) Berufung einlegen; **we must give advance ~ of the meeting** wir müssen das Treffen ankündigen; **to give official ~ that ...** öffentlich bekannt geben, dass ...; (*referring to future event*) öffentlich ankündigen, dass ...; **without ~** ohne Ankündigung; (*of arrival also*) unangemeldet; **~ is hereby given that ...** hiermit wird bekannt gegeben, dass ...; **he didn't give us much ~, he gave us rather short ~** er hat uns nicht viel Zeit gelassen *or* gegeben; **to have ~ of sth** von etw Kenntnis haben; **I must have ~** *or* **you must give me some ~ of what you intend to do** ich muss Bescheid wissen *or* Kenntnis davon haben (*form*), was Sie vorhaben; **to serve ~ on sb** (*Jur, to appear in court*) jdn vorladen; **at short ~** kurzfristig; **at a moment's ~** jederzeit, sofort; **at three days' ~** binnen drei Tagen, innerhalb von drei Tagen; **until further ~** bis auf Weiteres
b (= *public announcement*) (*on notice board etc*) Bekanntmachung *f*, Anschlag *m*; (= *poster*) Plakat *nt*; (= *sign*) Schild *nt*; (*in newspaper*) Mitteilung *f*, Bekanntmachung *f*; (*short*) Notiz *f*; (*of birth, wedding, vacancy etc*) Anzeige *f*; **the ~ says ...** da steht ...; **to post a ~** einen Anschlag machen, ein Plakat *nt* aufhängen; **public ~** öffentliche Bekanntmachung; **birth/marriage/death ~** Geburts-/Heirats-/Todesanzeige *f*; **I saw a ~ in the paper about the concert** ich habe das Konzert in der Zeitung angekündigt gesehen
c (*prior to end of employment, residence etc*) Kündigung *f*; **~ to quit** (*Brit*) *or* **to vacate** (*US*) Kündigung *f*; **to give sb ~** (*employer, landlord*) jdm kündigen; (*lodger, employee also*) bei jdm kündigen; **to give** *or* **hand** *or* **turn** (*US*) **in one's ~** kündigen; **I am under ~ of redundancy, I got my ~** mir ist gekündigt worden; **a month's ~** eine einmonatige Kündigungsfrist; **I have to give (my landlady) a week's ~** ich habe eine einwöchige Kündigungsfrist; **she gave me** *or* **I was given a month's ~** mir wurde zum nächsten Monat gekündigt
d (= *review*) Kritik *f*, Rezension *f*
e (= *attention*) **to take ~ of sth** von etw Notiz nehmen; (= *heed*) etw beachten, einer Sache (*dat*) Beachtung schenken; **I'm afraid I wasn't taking much ~ of what they were doing** ich muss gestehen, ich habe nicht aufgepasst, was sie machten; **to take no ~ of sb/sth** jdn/etw ignorieren, von jdm/etw keine Notiz nehmen, jdm/etw keine Beachtung schenken; **take no ~!** kümmern Sie sich nicht darum!; **a lot of ~ he takes of me!** als ob er mich beachten würde!; **to attract ~** Aufmerksamkeit erregen; **that has escaped his ~** das hat er nicht bemerkt; **it might not have escaped your ~ that ...** Sie haben vielleicht bemerkt, dass ...; **to bring sth to sb's ~** jdn auf etw (*acc*) aufmerksam machen; (*in letter etc*) jdn von etw in Kenntnis setzen; **it came to his ~ that ...** er erfuhr, dass ..., es ist ihm zu Ohren gekommen, dass ...
VT bemerken; (= *feel, hear, touch also*) wahrnehmen; (= *realize also*) merken; (= *recognize, acknowledge existence of*) zur Kenntnis nehmen; *difference* feststellen; **~ the beautiful details** achten Sie auf die schönen Einzelheiten; **without my noticing it** ohne dass ich etwas ge-

merkt *or* bemerkt habe, von mir unbemerkt; **did anybody ~ him leave?** hat jemand sein Gehen bemerkt?; **I ~d her hesitating** ich bemerkte *or* merkte, dass sie zögerte; **did he wave? – I never ~d** hat er gewinkt? – ich habe es nicht bemerkt *or* gesehen; **I ~ you have a new dress** ich stelle fest, du hast ein neues Kleid, wie ich sehe, hast du ein neues Kleid; **to get oneself ~d** Aufmerksamkeit erregen, auf sich *(acc)* aufmerksam machen; *(negatively)* auffallen

noticeable [ˈnəʊtɪsəbl] ADJ erkennbar, wahrnehmbar; *(= visible)* sichtbar; *(= obvious, considerable)* deutlich; *relief, pleasure, disgust etc* sichtlich, merklich; **the stain is very ~** der Fleck fällt ziemlich auf; **his incompetence was very ~** seine Unfähigkeit trat klar zum Vorschein *or* zeigte sich deutlich; **the change was ~** man konnte eine Veränderung feststellen; **it is hardly ~, it isn't really ~** man merkt es kaum; *(= visible also)* man sieht es kaum; **it is ~ that …** man merkt, dass …; **she was ~ by her absence/because of her large hat** sie fiel durch ihre Abwesenheit/ihren großen Hut auf

noticeably [ˈnəʊtɪsəblɪ] ADV deutlich, merklich; *relieved, pleased, annoyed etc* sichtlich; **he was ~ lacking in confidence** es war deutlich, dass ihm das Selbstvertrauen fehlte

notice board [ˈnəʊtɪsbɔːd] N *(esp Brit)* Anschlagbrett *nt*; *(in school etc also)* Schwarzes Brett; *(= sign)* Schild *nt*, Tafel *f*

notifiable [ˈnəʊtɪfaɪəbl] ADJ meldepflichtig

notification [ˌnəʊtɪfɪˈkeɪʃən] N Benachrichtigung *f*, Mitteilung *f*; *(of disease, crime, loss, damage etc)* Meldung *f*; *(= written notification: of birth etc)* Anzeige *f*; **to send ~ of sth to sb** jdm etw schriftlich mitteilen

notify [ˈnəʊtɪfaɪ] VT *person, candidate* benachrichtigen, unterrichten *(form)*; *change of address, loss, disease etc* melden; **to ~ sb of sth** jdn von etw benachrichtigen, jdm etw mitteilen; *authorities, insurance company* jdm etw melden; **to be notified of sth** über etw *(acc)* informiert werden, von etw benachrichtigt *or* unterrichtet *(form)* werden

notion [ˈnəʊʃən] N **a** *(= idea, thought)* Idee *f*; *(= conception)* Vorstellung *f*, Idee *f*; *(= vague knowledge)* Ahnung *f*; *(= opinion)* Meinung *f*, Ansicht *f*; **I haven't the foggiest** *(inf)* *or* **slightest ~ (of what he means)** ich habe keine Ahnung *or* nicht die leiseste Ahnung(, was er meint); **I have no ~ of time** ich habe überhaupt kein Zeitgefühl; **to give sb ~s** jdn auf Gedanken *or* Ideen bringen; **that gave me the ~ of inviting her** das brachte mich auf die Idee *or* den Gedanken, sie einzuladen; **where did you get the ~** *or* **what gave you the ~ that I …?** wie kommst du denn auf die Idee, dass ich …?; **he got the ~ (into his head) that she wouldn't help him** irgendwie hat er sich *(dat)* eingebildet, sie würde ihm nicht helfen; **I have a ~ that …** ich habe den Verdacht, dass …
b *(= whim)* Idee *f*; **to have a ~ to do sth** Lust haben, etw zu tun; **if he gets a ~ to do something, nothing can stop him** wenn er sich *(dat)* etwas in den Kopf gesetzt hat, kann ihn keiner davon abhalten; **she has some strange ~s** sie kommt manchmal auf seltsame Ideen *or* Gedanken; **I hit (up)on** *or* **suddenly had the ~ of going to see her** mir kam plötzlich die Idee, sie zu besuchen
c notions PL *(esp US inf)* Kurzwaren *pl*

notional [ˈnəʊʃənl] ADJ **a** *(= hypothetical)* fiktiv, angenommen; *(= nominal) payment* nominell, symbolisch **b** *(esp US)* versponnen, verträumt **c** *(Philos)* spekulativ

notionally [ˈnəʊʃənəlɪ] ADV nominell

notoriety [ˌnəʊtəˈraɪətɪ] N traurige Berühmtheit

notorious [nəʊˈtɔːrɪəs] ADJ *person, fact* berüchtigt; *place also* verrufen, verschrieen; *(= well-known) gambler, criminal, liar* notorisch; **a ~ woman** eine Frau von schlechtem Ruf; **to be ~ for/as sth** für/als etw berüchtigt sein; **it is a ~ fact that …** es ist leider nur allzu bekannt, dass …

notoriously [nəʊˈtɔːrɪəslɪ] ADV notorisch; *(= as is well known)* bekanntlich; **it is ~ difficult to treat** es lässt sich bekanntlich nur sehr schwer behandeln; **to be ~ unreliable/inefficient/violent** *etc* für seine Unzuverlässigkeit/Untüchtigkeit/Gewalttätigkeit *etc* berüchtigt *or* bekannt sein; **a ~ violent man** ein für seine Gewalttätigkeit bekannter Mann

no-trump [ˈnəʊˈtrʌmp] *(Cards)* ADJ Sans-Atout-; **~ contract** Sans-Atout-Kontrakt *m* N *(also* **no-trumps***)* Sans-Atout *nt*

Notts [nɒts] *abbr of* **Nottinghamshire**

notwithstanding [ˌnɒtwɪθˈstændɪŋ] *(form)* PREP ungeachtet *(+gen) (form)*, trotz *(+gen)* ADV dennoch, trotzdem, nichtsdestotrotz *(form)* CONJ **~ that …** obwohl *or* obgleich …

nougat [ˈnuːgɑː] N Nougat *m*, Nugat *m*

nought [nɔːt] N **a** *(= number)* Null *f*; **~s and crosses** *(Brit)* Tic Tac Toe *nt*, *Kinderspiel mit Nullen und Kreuzen* → *also* **zero b** *(liter. = nothing)* Nichts *nt*; **to come to ~** sich zerschlagen; **to bring to ~** zunichtemachen

noughties [ˈnɔːtɪz] PL *(inf) das erste Jahrzehnt des dritten Jahrtausends*, Nullerjahre *pl (rare)*, Nulliger *pl (rare)*

noun [naʊn] N Substantiv(um) *nt*, Hauptwort *nt*; **abstract ~** Abstraktum *nt*; **collective ~** Sammelbegriff *m*; **common ~** Gattungsname *or* -begriff *m*; **proper ~** Name *m*; **~ group** *or* **phrase** Nominalphrase *f*

nourish [ˈnʌrɪʃ] VT **a** *(lit)* nähren; *person* ernähren; *leather* pflegen; **a good diet ~ed her back to health** gute Ernährung brachte sie wieder zu Kräften **b** *(fig) hopes etc* nähren, hegen; **literature to ~ their minds** Literatur als geistige Nahrung VI nahrhaft sein

nourishing [ˈnʌrɪʃɪŋ] ADJ *food, diet, drink* nahrhaft

nourishing cream N Nährcreme *f*

nourishment [ˈnʌrɪʃmənt] N *(= food)* Nahrung *f*; **to take ~** Nahrung *f* zu sich *(dat)* nehmen; **you need some real ~** du brauchst gutes Essen

nous [naʊs] N *(Brit inf)* Grips *m (inf)*

nouveau riche [ˌnuːvəʊˈriːʃ] N *pl* **-x -s** [ˌnuːvəʊˈriːʃ] Neureiche(r) *mf* ADJ typisch neureich

nouvelle cuisine [ˌnuːvelkwɪˈziːn] N Nouvelle cuisine *f*

Nov *abbr of* **November** Nov

nova [ˈnəʊvə] N *pl* **-s** *or* **-e** [ˈnəʊviː] Nova *f*

Nova Scotia [ˈnəʊvəˈskəʊʃə] N Neuschottland *nt*

Nova Scotian [ˈnəʊvəˈskəʊʃən] ADJ neuschottisch N Neuschotte *m*, Neuschottin *f*

novel¹ [ˈnɒvəl] N Roman *m*

novel² ADJ neu(artig)

novelette [ˌnɒvəˈlet] N *(pej)* Romänchen *nt*, Kitschroman *m*

novelettish [ˌnɒvəˈletɪʃ] ADJ *(pej) situation* rührselig, kitschig

novelist [ˈnɒvəlɪst] N Romanschriftsteller(in) *m(f)*, Romancier *m*

novelistic [nɒvəˈlɪstɪk] ADJ romanhaft

novella [nəˈvelə] N Novelle *f*

novelty [ˈnɒvəltɪ] N **a** *(= newness)* Neuheit *f*; **once the ~ has worn off** wenn der Reiz des Neuen *or* der Neuheit vorbei ist **b** *(= innovation)* Neuheit *f*, Novum *nt*; **it was quite a ~** das war etwas ganz Neues, das war ein Novum **c** *(Comm: = trinket)* Krimskrams *m*

November [nəʊˈvembəʳ] N November *m* → *also* **September**

novena [nəʊˈviːnə] N Novene *f*

novice [ˈnɒvɪs] N *(Eccl)* Novize *m*, Novizin *f*;; *(= racehorse) Pferd, das noch nicht eine bestimmte Anzahl von Rennen gewonnen hat*; *(fig)* Neuling *m*, Anfänger(in) *m(f)* *(at* bei, in *+dat)*

noviciate, novitiate [nəʊˈvɪʃɪɪt] N *(Eccl)* **a** *(= state)* Noviziat *nt* **b** *(= place)* Novizenhaus *nt*

Novocaine® [ˈnəʊvəʊkeɪn] N Novokain *nt*, Novocain® *nt*

now [naʊ] ✪ 26.1 ADV **a** jetzt, nun; *(= immediately)* jetzt, sofort, gleich; *(= at this very moment)* gerade, (so)eben; *(= nowadays)* heute, heutzutage; **she ~ realized why …** nun *or* da erkannte sie, warum …; **just ~** gerade; *(= immediately)* gleich, sofort; **~ is the time to do it** jetzt ist der richtige Moment dafür; **I'll do it just** *or* **right ~** ich mache es jetzt gleich *or* sofort; **do it (right) ~** mach es jetzt (sofort); **it's ~ or never** jetzt oder nie; **even ~ it's not right** es ist immer noch nicht richtig; **~ for it** los!; **~ for a look at the weather forecast** und nun zum Wetterbericht; **what is it ~?** was ist denn jetzt *or* nun schon wieder?; **by ~** *(present, past)* inzwischen, mittlerweile; **they have/had never met before ~** sie haben sich bis jetzt/sie hatten sich bis dahin noch nie getroffen; **before ~ it was thought …** früher dachte man, dass …; **we'd have heard before ~** das hätten wir (inzwischen) schon gehört; **I've been there before ~** ich war schon (früher) da; **for ~** (jetzt) erst einmal, im Moment, vorläufig; **even ~** auch *or* selbst jetzt noch; **any day/moment ~** jetzt jeden Tag/Moment; **from ~ on(wards)** von nun an; **between ~ and the end of the week** bis zum Ende der Woche; **in three days from ~** (heute) in drei Tagen; **from ~ until then** bis dahin; **up to ~, till ~, until ~** bis jetzt
b *(alternation)* **~ … ~** bald … bald; **(every) ~ and then, ~ and again** ab und zu, von Zeit zu Zeit, gelegentlich
CONJ **a ~ (that) you've seen him** jetzt, wo Sie ihn gesehen haben, nun, da Sie ihn gesehen haben *(geh)*
b *(in explanation etc)* nun
INTERJ also; **~, ~!** na, na!; **well ~** also; **~ then** also (jetzt); **stop that ~!** Schluss jetzt!; **come ~, don't exaggerate** nun übertreib mal nicht; **~, why didn't I think of that?** warum habe ich bloß nicht daran gedacht?

nowadays [ˈnaʊədeɪz] ✪ 26.1 ADV heute, heutzutage

no way [ˈnəʊˈweɪ] ADV → **way 1 g**

nowhere [ˈnəʊwɛəʳ] ADV nirgendwo, nirgends; *(with verbs of motion)* nirgendwohin; **~ special** irgendwo; *(with motion)* irgendwohin; **~ is** *or* **there is ~ more romantic than Paris** nirgends ist es romantischer als in Paris; **there's ~ I'd rather be** nirgends wäre ich lieber; **it's ~ you know** du kennst den Ort nicht; **it's ~ you'll ever find it** es ist an einem Platz, wo du es bestimmt nicht findest; **they have ~ (else) to go** sie können (sonst) nirgends unterkommen; *(fig: = have no escape)* es gibt für sie (sonst) keinen Ausweg; **there was ~ to hide** man konnte sich nirgends verstecken; **there was ~ to hide from the wind** es gab keinen Schutz vor dem Wind; **to have ~ to live** kein Zuhause *or* keine Bleibe haben; **to appear from** *or* **out of ~** ganz plötzlich *or* aus heiterem Himmel auftauchen; **to come ~** *(Sport)* unter „ferner liefen" kommen *or* enden; **to come from ~ and win** *(Sport)* überraschend siegen; **we're getting ~ (fast)** wir machen keine Fortschritte, wir kommen nicht weiter; **rudeness will get you ~** Grobheit bringt dir gar nichts ein, mit Grobheit bringst du es auch nicht weiter; **a pound goes ~ these days** mit einem Pfund kommt man heute nicht mehr weit → **near 1 d**

no-win situation [ˌnəʊwɪnsɪtjʊˈeɪʃən] N verzwickte Situation *(in der man so oder so nicht gewinnen kann)*; **it's a ~** wie mans macht ists falsch

nowt [naʊt] N, PRON, ADV *(Brit, dial)* nix *(inf)*, nischt *(dial, inf)*

noxious [ˈnɒkʃəs] ADJ **a** *(= harmful)* schädlich; *(= toxic) fumes, gas, substance* giftig **b** *(= repugnant) smell, habit* übel; *attitude* widerlich

nozzle [ˈnɒzl] N Düse *f*; *(of syringe)* Kanüle *f*

nr *abbr of* **near** b., bei

NRA *(US) abbr of* **National Rifle Association** *amerikanische Organisation, die das Recht der Bürger auf freien Kauf und Besitz von Waffen verteidigt*

NS *abbr of* **Nova Scotia**

n/s N *abbr of* **nonsmoker** Nichtraucher(in) *m* ADJ *abbr of* **nonsmoking** Nichtraucher-

NSB *(Brit) abbr of* **National Savings Bank** ≈ Postsparkasse *f*

NSPCC *(Brit) abbr of* **National Society for the Prevention of Cruelty to Children** ≈ Kinderschutzbund *m*

NSU *(Med) abbr of* **nonspecific urethritis** unspezifische Urethritis, unspezifische Harnröhrenentzündung

NSW *abbr of* **New South Wales**

NT a *abbr of* **New Testament** N. T. *nt* b *abbr of* **Northern Territory**

nth [enθ] ADJ **the ~ power** *or* **degree** die n-te Potenz; **for the ~ time** zum x-ten Mal *(inf)*

nt. wt. *abbr of* **net weight**

nuance [ˈnjuːɑːns] N Nuance *f*; *(of colour also)* Schattierung *f*; **~s of colour** *(Brit) or* **color** *(US)* Farbnuancen *pl*

nub [nʌb] N a *(= piece)* Stückchen *nt*, Klümpchen *nt* b *(fig)* **the ~ of the matter** der springende Punkt, der Kernpunkt

Nubia [ˈnjuːbɪə] N Nubien *nt*

Nubian [ˈnjuːbɪən] ADJ nubisch N Nubier(in) *m(f)*

nubile [ˈnjuːbaɪl] ADJ *girl* heiratsfähig; *(= attractive)* gut entwickelt

nuclear [ˈnjuːklɪəʳ] ADJ Atom-; *fuel* nuklear, atomar; **to go ~** *(country, = develop nuclear weapons)* Atomwaffen entwickeln; *(= use nuclear energy)* zur Atomenergie übergehen

nuclear: **nuclear attack** N Atomangriff *m*; **nuclear deterrent** N nukleares Abschreckungsmittel; **nuclear disarmament** N nukleare *or* atomare Abrüstung; **nuclear division** N Kernteilung *f*; **nuclear energy** N = **nuclear power**; **nuclear family** N Klein- *or* Kernfamilie *f*; **nuclear fission** N Kernspaltung *f*; **nuclear-free** ADJ atomwaffenfrei; **nuclear fuel rod** N Kernbrennstab *m*; **nuclear holocaust** N Atominferno *nt*; **nuclear magnetic resonance** N kernmagnetische Resonanz; **nuclear medicine** N Nuklearmedizin *f*; **nuclear missile** N Atomrakete *f*; **Nuclear Non-Proliferation Treaty** N Atomwaffensperrvertrag *m*; **nuclear physicist** N Kernphysiker(in) *m(f)*; **nuclear physics** N Kernphysik *f*; **nuclear pile** N Atommeiler *m*; **nuclear plant** N Atomanlage *f*; **nuclear power** N Atomkraft *f*, Kernenergie *f*; **nuclear-powered** ADJ atomgetrieben; **nuclear power plant**, **nuclear power station** N Kern- *or* Atomkraftwerk *nt*; **nuclear reaction** N Kernreaktion *f*; **nuclear reactor** N Kern- *or* Atomreaktor *m*; **nuclear reprocessing plant** N nukleare Wiederaufbereitungsanlage; **nuclear scientist** N Nuklearwissenschaftler(in) *m(f)*; **nuclear submarine** N Atom-U-Boot *nt*; **nuclear test** N Atom(waffen)test *m*; **nuclear umbrella** N Atom- *or* Nuklearschirm *m*; **nuclear war** N Atomkrieg *m*; **nuclear warfare** N Atomkrieg *m*; **nuclear warhead** N Atomsprengkopf *m*; **nuclear waste** N Atommüll *m*; **nuclear weapon** N Atomwaffe *f*; **nuclear winter** N nuklearer Winter

nuclei [ˈnjuːklɪaɪ] PL *of* **nucleus**

nucleic acid [njuːˈkleɪɪkˈæsɪd] N Nukleinsäure *f*

nucleus [ˈnjuːklɪəs] N *pl* **nuclei** *(Phys, Astron, fig)* Kern *m*; *(Biol, of cell also)* Nukleus *m*; **atomic ~** Atomkern *m*

nude [njuːd] ADJ nackt; *(Art)* Akt-; **~ photograph** Aktfoto *nt*; **~ study** *(Art)* Akt *m*, Aktstudie *f*; **~ figure/portrait** Akt *m*; **~ scene** *(Film)* Nacktszene *f* N *(= person)* Nackte(r) *mf*; *(Art)* *(= painting, sculpture etc)* Akt *m*; *(= model)* Aktmodell *nt*; **to paint from the ~** einen Akt malen; **in the ~** nackt

nudge [nʌdʒ] VT stupsen, anstoßen; **she ~d him forward** sie schubste ihn vorwärts; **to ~ sb into doing sth** jdm den Austoß dazu geben, etw zu tun; **to ~ sb's memory** *(fig)* jds Gedächtnis *(dat)* (ein wenig) nachhelfen; **the temperature was nudging 35°C** die Temperatur erreichte fast 35°C; **she's nudging 40** sie geht stramm auf die 40 zu N Stups *m*, kleiner Stoß; **to give sb a ~** jdm einen Stups geben, jdn stupsen; **a ~ and a wink** ein Augenzwinkern *nt*; **~-nudge, wink-wink** *(inf)* na, du weißt schon

nudie [ˈnjuːdɪ] ADJ *(inf)* **~ picture** Nacktfoto *nt*; **~ magazine** Pornomagazin *nt*

nudism [ˈnjuːdɪzəm] N Freikörperkultur *f*, Nudismus *m*

nudist [ˈnjuːdɪst] N Anhänger(in) *m(f)* der Freikörperkultur, FKK-Anhänger(in) *m(f)*, Nudist(in) *m(f)*

nudist: **nudist beach** N FKK-Strand *m*, Nacktbadestrand *m*; **nudist camp** N FKK-Platz *m*, Nudistenplatz *m*; **nudist colony** N FKK-Kolonie *f*, Nudistenkolonie *f*

nudity [ˈnjuːdɪtɪ] N Nacktheit *f*; **there's a lot of ~ in this film** in diesem Film gibt es viele Nacktszenen

nugatory [ˈnjuːgətərɪ] ADJ *(liter)* belanglos, nichtig *(geh)*

nugget [ˈnʌgɪt] N *(of gold etc)* Klumpen *m*; *(fig: of information, knowledge)* Brocken *m*, Bröckchen *nt*

nuisance [ˈnjuːsns] N a *(= person)* Plage *f*; *(esp pestering)* Nervensäge *f*; *(esp child)* Quälgeist *m*; **he can be a ~** er kann einen aufregen, er kann einem auf die Nerven *or* den Geist *(inf)* gehen; **sorry to be a ~** entschuldigen Sie, wenn ich störe; **to make a ~ of oneself** lästig werden; **to have (some** *or* **a certain) ~ value** als Störfaktor wirken; *(esp Pol)* für einige Umtriebe sorgen *(inf)*
b *(= thing, event)* **to be a ~** lästig sein; *(annoying)* ärgerlich sein; **what a ~, having to do it again** wie ärgerlich *or* lästig, das noch einmal machen zu müssen; **to become a ~** lästig werden; **this wind is a ~** dieser Wind ist eine Plage
c *(Jur)* **public ~** öffentliches Ärgernis; **to cause a (public) ~** (öffentliches) Ärgernis erregen

nuisance: **nuisance call** N *(Telec)* Schockanruf *m*; **~s** *pl* Telefonterror *m (inf)*; **nuisance caller** N *(Telec)* Schockanrufer(in) *m(f)*

NUJ *(Brit) abbr of* **National Union of Journalists** *Journalistengewerkschaft*

nuke [njuːk] *(sl)* N a *(US: = power plant)* Kern- *or* Atomkraftwerk *nt* b *(= bomb)* Atombombe *f* VT *(= attack)* mit Atomwaffen angreifen; *(= destroy)* atomar vernichten

null [nʌl] ADJ *(Jur) act, decree* (null und) nichtig, ungültig; **to render sth ~ and void** etw null und nichtig machen

nullification [ˌnʌlɪfɪˈkeɪʃən] N a Annullierung *f*, Aufhebung *f* b *(US)* unterlassene Amts- *or* Rechtshilfe

nullify [ˈnʌlɪfaɪ] VT annullieren, für (null und) nichtig erklären

nullity [ˈnʌlɪtɪ] N *(Jur)* Ungültigkeit *f*, Nichtigkeit *f*

NUM *(Brit) abbr of* **National Union of Mineworkers** *Bergarbeitergewerkschaft*

numb [nʌm] ADJ *(+er)* taub, empfindungslos, gefühllos; *feeling* taub; *(emotionally)* benommen, wie betäubt; **hands ~ with cold** Hände, die vor Kälte taub *or* gefühllos sind; **~ with grief** starr *or* wie betäubt vor Schmerz; **~ with disbelief** starr vor Ungläubigkeit VT *(cold)* taub *or* gefühllos machen; *(injection, fig)* betäuben; **~ed with fear/grief** starr vor Furcht/Schmerz

number [ˈnʌmbəʳ] ✪ 27.1, 27.3, 27.4, 27.7 N
a *(Math)* Zahl *f*; *(= numeral)* Ziffer *f*; **the ~ of votes cast** die abgegebenen Stimmen
b *(= quantity, amount)* Anzahl *f*; **a ~ of problems/applicants** eine (ganze) Anzahl von Problemen/Bewerbern; **large ~s of people/books** (sehr) viele Leute/Bücher; **on a ~ of occasions** des Öfteren; **boys and girls in equal ~s** ebenso viele Jungen wie Mädchen, Jungen und Mädchen zu gleicher Zahl *(geh)*; **in a small ~ of cases** in wenigen Fällen; **ten in ~** zehn an der Zahl; **they were few in ~** es waren nur wenige; **to be found in large ~s** zahlreich vorhanden sein, häufig zu finden sein; **in small/large ~s** in kleinen/großen Mengen; **many in ~** zahlreich; **a fair ~ of times** ziemlich oft; **times without ~** unzählige Male *pl*; **any ~ can play** beliebig viele Spieler können teilnehmen; **any ~ of cards** *etc (when choosing)* beliebig viele Karten *etc*; *(= many)* sehr viele Karten *etc*; **I've told you any ~ of times** ich habe es dir zigmal *or* x-mal gesagt *(inf)*; **to win by force of ~s** aufgrund *or* auf Grund zahlenmäßiger Überlegenheit gewinnen; **they have the advantage of ~s** sie sind zahlenmäßig überlegen; **they were defeated by superior ~s** sie wurden von einer zahlenmäßigen Übermacht geschlagen
c *(of house, room, phone)* Nummer *f*; *(of page)* Seitenzahl *f*; *(of car)* (Auto)nummer *f*; *(Mil, of soldier etc)* Kennnummer *f*; **at ~ 4** (in) Nummer 4; **Number Ten (Downing Street)** Nummer zehn (Downing Street); **the ~ 47 bus** die Buslinie 47, der 47er *(inf)*; **I've got the wrong ~** ich habe mich verwählt; **it was a wrong ~** ich/er *etc* war falsch verbunden; **~ to dial** Rufnummer *f*; **the ~ one pop star/tennis player** *(inf)* der Popstar/Tennisspieler Nummer eins *(inf)*; **the single went straight to** *or* **straight in at ~ one** die Single stieg gleich auf Nummer eins ein; **he has never had a ~ one** *(inf)* er hat nie einen Nummer-Eins-Hit gehabt; **to take care of** *or* **look after ~ one** *(inf)* (vor allem) an sich *(acc)* selbst denken; **he's my ~ two** *(inf)* er ist mein Vize *(inf) or* Stellvertreter *m*; **I'm (the) ~ two in the department** ich bin die Nummer zwei in der Abteilung; **his ~'s up** *(inf)* er ist dran *(inf)*; **to do a ~ one/two** *(baby-talk)* klein/groß machen *(baby-talk)*; **I have to go ~ two** *(baby-talk)* ich muss mal groß *(baby-talk)*; **to get sb's ~** *(inf)* jdn einschätzen *or* einordnen *or* durchschauen; **to do sth by (the** *US***) ~s** etw nach Schema F *(esp pej) or* rein mechanisch erledigen
d *(= song, act etc)* Nummer *f*; *(= issue of magazine etc)* Ausgabe *f*, Nummer *f*, Heft *nt*; *(= dress)* Kreation *f*; **the June ~** das Juniheft, die Juniausgabe *or* -nummer
e *(Gram)* Numerus *m*
f *(Eccl)* **The Book of Numbers** das Vierte Buch Mose, Numeri *pl*
g *(= company)* **one of their/our ~** eine(r) aus ihren/unseren Reihen
h **numbers** PL *(= arithmetic)* Rechnen *nt*
VT a *(= give a number to)* nummerieren; **~ed account** Nummernkonto *nt*
b *(= include)* zählen *(among* zu)
c *(= amount to)* zählen; **the group ~ed 50** es waren 50 (Leute in der Gruppe); **the library ~s 30,000 volumes** die Bibliothek hat 30.000 Bände
d *(= count)* zählen; **to be ~ed** *(= limited)* begrenzt sein; **his days are ~ed** seine Tage sind gezählt
VI *(Brit Mil etc: also* **number off***)* abzählen

number: **number block** N *(Comput)* Nummernblock *m*; **number cruncher** [ˈnʌmbəˈkrʌntʃəʳ] N *(Comput)* Numbercruncher *m*, Number Cruncher *m*, Supercomputer *m*; *(= person)* Zahlenzauberer *m*, Zahlenzauberin *f*; **number crunching** [ˈnʌmbəˈkrʌntʃɪŋ] N *(Comput)* Numbercrunching *nt*, Number Crunching *nt*, *das Ausführen umfangreicher und komplexer numerischer Berechnungen*

numbering [ˈnʌmbərɪŋ] N *(of houses etc)* Nummerierung *f*; **~ system** Nummeriersystem *nt*

numbering machine N Nummernstempel *m*

number: **numberless** ADJ zahllos, unzählig; **number pad** N *(Comput)* Ziffernblock *m*; **numberplate** N *(Brit)* Nummernschild *nt*, Kennzeichen *nt*; **number pool** N *(US)* ≈ Zahlenlotto *nt*

numbers game N Zahlenspiel *nt*; **to play the ~** Zahlenspielerei betreiben

number sign N *(Typ)* Nummernzeichen *nt*

numbers lock N *(Comput)* Zahlenverriegelung *f*

number theory N *(Math)* Zahlentheorie *f*

numbly [ˈnʌmlɪ] ADV benommen, wie betäubt

numbness ['nʌmnɪs] N *(of limbs etc)* Taubheit *f*, Starre *f*; *(fig: of mind, senses)* Benommenheit *f*, Betäubung *f*

numbnuts ['nʌmnʌts] N *(US inf)* taube Nuss *(inf)*, (Ober)trottel *m (inf)*

numbskull ['nʌmskʌl] N *(inf)* Holzkopf *m (inf)*

numeracy ['nju:mərəsɪ] N Rechnen *nt*; **his ~** seine rechnerischen Fähigkeiten

numeral ['nju:mərəl] N Ziffer *f*

numerate ['nju:mərɪt] ADJ rechenkundig; **to be (very) ~** (gut) rechnen können

numeration [ˌnju:mə'reɪʃən] N Nummerierung *f*

numerator ['nju:məreɪtə'] N *(Math)* Zähler *m*, Dividend *m*

numeric [nju:'merɪk] ADJ **~ (key)pad** Zehnertastatur *f*, numerisches Tastenfeld

numerical [nju:'merɪkəl] ADJ *equation, order, data* numerisch; *superiority* zahlenmäßig; **~ symbols** Zahlensymbole *pl*; **~ value** Zahlenwert *m*

numerically [nju:'merɪkəlɪ] ADV zahlenmäßig; **the reports are ~ incorrect** die Zahlenangaben in den Berichten stimmen nicht

numerous ['nju:mərəs] ADJ zahlreich; *family* kinderreich; **on ~ occasions** bei vielen Gelegenheiten; **it happened ~ times** es geschah sehr oft

numismatic [ˌnju:mɪz'mætɪk] ADJ numismatisch

numismatics [ˌnju:mɪz'mætɪks] N *sing* Münzkunde *f*, Numismatik *f*

numismatist [nju:'mɪzmətɪst] N Numismatiker(in) *m(f)*

numpty ['nʌmptɪ] N *(Brit inf)* (Ober)trottel *m (inf)*

numskull ['nʌmskʌl] N *(inf)* Holzkopf *m (inf)*

nun [nʌn] N Nonne *f*

nunciature ['nʌnʃɪətjʊə'] N Nuntiatur *f*

nuncio ['nʌnʃɪəʊ] N *(= Papal nuncio)* Nuntius *m*

nunnery ['nʌnərɪ] N *(old)* (Nonnen)kloster *nt*

NUPE ['nju:pɪ] *(Brit) abbr of* **National Union of Public Employees** *Gewerkschaft der Angestellten im öffentlichen Dienst*

nuptial ['nʌpʃəl] ADJ *bliss* ehelich; **~ celebrations** Hochzeitsfeier *f*; **~ vows** Ehegelöbnis *nt or* -gelübde *nt*; **the ~ day** *(hum)* der Hochzeitstag N **nuptials** PL *(hum, liter)* **the ~s** die Hochzeit *f*

NUR *(Brit old) abbr of* **National Union of Railwaymen** *Eisenbahnergewerkschaft*

nurd N *(US sl)* = **nerd**

Nuremberg ['njʊərəm,bɜ:g] N Nürnberg *nt*

nurse [nɜ:s] N Schwester *f*; *(as professional title)* Krankenschwester *f*; *(= nanny)* Kindermädchen *nt*, Kinderfrau *f*; *(= wet nurse)* Amme *f*; **male ~** Krankenpfleger *m*

VT a *sb* pflegen; *plant also* hegen; *(fig) plan* hegen; *hope, wrath etc* hegen, nähren *(geh)*; *fire* bewachen; *(= treat carefully)* schonen; *business* sorgsam verwalten; **to ~ sb back to health** jdn gesund pflegen; **to ~ sb through an illness** jdn während einer Krankheit pflegen; **to ~ a cold** an einer Erkältung herumlaborieren *(inf)*; **he stood there nursing his bruised arm** er stand da und hielt seinen verletzten Arm; **to ~ a grudge (against sb)** (gegen jdn) einen Groll hegen; **to ~ the economy** die Wirtschaft hegen und pflegen

b *(= suckle) child* stillen; *(= cradle)* (in den Armen) wiegen

VI *(baby)* gestillt werden

nurseling ['nɜ:slɪŋ] N = **nursling**

nursemaid ['nɜ:smeɪd] N *(= nanny, hum: = servant)* Kindermädchen *nt*

nursery ['nɜ:sərɪ] N a *(= room)* Kinderzimmer *nt*; *(in hospital)* Säuglingssaal *m* b *(= institution)* Kindergarten *m*; *(all-day)* Kindertagesstätte *f*, Hort *m* c *(Agr, Hort) (for plants)* Gärtnerei *f*; *(for trees)* Baumschule *f*; *(fig)* Zuchtstätte *f*

nursery: **nurseryman** N Gärtner *m*; **nursery nurse** N Kindermädchen *nt*, Kinderfrau *f*; *(in day nursery)* Kindergärtnerin *f*, Kinderpflegerin *f*; **nursery rhyme** N Kinderreim *m*; **nursery school** N Kindergarten *m*; **nursery school teacher** N Kindergärtner(in) *m(f)*; **nursery slope** N *(Ski)* Idiotenhügel *m (hum)*, Anfängerhügel *m*

nurse's aid [ˌnɜ:sɪz'eɪd] N Schwesternhelferin *f*; *(male)* Hilfspfleger *m*

nursing ['nɜ:sɪŋ] N a *(= care of invalids)* Pflege *f*, Pflegen *nt* b *(= profession)* Krankenpflege *f*; **she's going in for ~** sie will in der Krankenpflege arbeiten c *(= feeding)* Stillen *nt* ADJ *attr* Pflege-; *abilities* pflegerisch; **~ staff** Pflegepersonal *nt*; **the ~ profession** die Krankenpflege; *(= nurses collectively)* die pflegerischen Berufe, die Pflegeberufe *pl*

nursing: **nursing auxiliary** N Schwesternhelferin *f*; **nursing bottle** N *(US)* Flasche *f*, Fläschchen *nt*; **nursing bra** N Still-BH *m*; **nursing care** N Pflege *f*; **nursing fees** PL Pflegekosten *pl*; **nursing home** N Privatklinik *f*; *(Brit: = maternity hospital)* Entbindungsklinik *f*; *(= convalescent home)* Pflegeheim *nt*; **nursing mother** N stillende Mutter; **nursing officer** N *(Brit)* Oberpfleger *m*, Oberschwester *f*; **nursing sister** N Oberschwester *f*

nursling ['nɜ:slɪŋ] N Pflegling *m*

nurture ['nɜ:tʃə'] N *(= nourishing)* Hegen *nt*; *(= upbringing)* Erziehung *f*, Bildung *f* VT a *sb's talent* entwickeln; *idea, ambitions* hegen; **to ~ sb on sth** *(lit, fig)* jdn mit etw aufziehen b *(fig: = train)* hegen und pflegen

NUS *(Brit)* a *abbr of* **National Union of Students** *Studentengewerkschaft* b *abbr of* **National Union of Seamen** *Seeleutegewerkschaft*

NUT *(Brit) abbr of* **National Union of Teachers**

nut [nʌt] N a *(Bot)* Nuss *f*; *(of coal)* kleines Stück; **a packet of ~s and raisins** eine Tüte Studentenfutter; **a hard** *or* **tough ~ to crack** *(fig)* eine harte Nuss

b *(inf: = head)* Nuss *f (inf)*, Birne *f (inf)*; **use your ~!** streng deinen Grips an! *(inf)*; **to be off one's ~** nicht ganz bei Trost sein *(inf)*, spinnen *(inf)*; **to go off one's ~** durchdrehen *(inf)*; **to do one's ~** *(Brit inf)* durchdrehen *(inf)* → *also* **nuts**

c *(inf: = person)* Spinner(in) *m(f) (inf)*; **he's a tough ~** *(inf)* er ist ein harter *or* zäher Brocken *(inf)*

d *(inf: = enthusiast)* Fan *m*, Freak *m (inf)*; **computer ~** Computerfreak *m (inf)*; **to be a car/football ~** autonärrisch/fußballverrückt sein *(inf)*

e *(Mech)* (Schrauben)mutter *f*; **the ~s and bolts of a theory** die Grundbestandteile einer Theorie

f **nuts** PL *(sl: = testicles)* Eier *pl (sl)*

nut: **nutbrown** ADJ nussbraun; **nutcase** N *(inf)* Spinner(in) *m(f) (inf)*; **nutcracker** N, **nutcrackers** PL Nussknacker *m*; **nuthatch** N Kleiber *m*; **nuthouse** N *(inf, lit, fig)* Irrenhaus *nt (inf)*; *(lit also)* Klapsmühle *f (inf)*; **nutmeg** N a *(= spice)* Muskat(nuss *f*) *m*; *(also* **nutmeg tree***)* Muskatnussbaum *m* b *(Ftbl inf: = play of ball through opponent's legs)* Tunneln *nt*; **~!** super *(inf) or* endgeil *(sl)* getunnelt VT *(Ftbl inf)* tunneln; **to ~ the goalie** dem Torwart durch die Hosenträger spielen *(inf)*

NutraSweet® ['nju:trəswi:t] N *ein Süßstoff*

nutrient ['nju:trɪənt] ADJ *substance* nahrhaft; **~ cream/solution** Nährcreme *f*/-lösung *f* N Nährstoff *m*

nutriment ['nju:trɪmənt] N *(form)* Nahrung *f*

nutrition [nju:'trɪʃən] N *(= diet, science)* Ernährung *f*

nutritional [nju:'trɪʃənl] ADJ Nähr-; **~ value** Nährkraft *f*, Nährwert *m*; **~ content** Nähr(stoff)gehalt *m*; **~ information** Nährwertangaben *pl*; **~ supplements** Nahrungsergänzungsmittel *pl*

nutritionist [nju:'trɪʃənɪst] N Ernährungswissenschaftler(in) *m(f)*; *(= nutritional adviser)* Ernährungsberater(in) *m(f)*

nutritious [nju:'trɪʃəs] ADJ nahrhaft

nutritiousness [nju:'trɪʃəsnɪs] N Nahrhaftigkeit *f*

nutritive ['nju:trɪtɪv] ADJ nahrhaft

nuts [nʌts] ADJ *pred (inf)* **to be ~** spinnen *(inf)*; **to go ~** durchdrehen *(inf)*, anfangen zu spinnen *(inf)*; **to be ~ about sb/sth** ganz verrückt nach jdm/auf etw *(acc)* sein *(inf)*; **~!** *(dated US)* Quatsch! *(inf)*; *(in annoyance)* Mist *(inf)*!; **~ to him!** *(dated US)* er kann mich mal (gern haben)! *(inf)*

nutshell ['nʌtʃel] N Nussschale *f*; **in a ~** *(fig)* kurz gesagt, mit einem Wort; **to put the matter in a ~** *(fig)* um es (ganz) kurz *or* kurz und bündig zu sagen

nutter ['nʌtə'] N *(Brit inf)* Spinner(in) *m(f) (inf)*; *(dangerous)* Verrückte(r) *mf*; **he's a ~** er hat einen Stich *(inf) or* Vogel *(inf)*

nutty ['nʌtɪ] ADJ *(+er)* a *(= like nuts)* nussartig; *(= with nuts)* mit Nüssen; *aroma* nussig; **~ flavour** Nussgeschmack *m* b *(inf: = crazy)* bekloppt *(inf)*; **to be ~ about sb/sth** ganz verrückt nach jdm/auf etw *(acc)* sein *(inf)*

nuzzle ['nʌzl] VT *(pig)* aufwühlen; *(dog)* beschnüffeln, beschnuppern VI **to ~ (up) against sb, to ~ up to sb** *(person, animal)* sich an jdn schmiegen *or* drücken

> **NVQ**
>
> **National Vocational Qualifications** oder **NVQs** sind berufsbezogene Qualifizierungen, die überwiegend für Menschen gedacht sind, die bereits im Berufsleben stehen, auch wenn einige Schulen diesen Abschluss zusätzlich zu oder anstelle der Hochschulzugangsqualifikationen wie GSCE oder A levels anbieten. Die Beurteilung erfolgt aufgrund der Leistungen im praktischen und theoretischen Unterricht sowie mündlichen und schriftlichen Prüfungen. Das System gilt in England, Wales und Nordirland, wobei es in Schottland ein ähnliches System, die **Scottish Vocational Qualifications** (oder auch „SVQs") gibt. → A LEVELS, GCSE

NW *abbr of* **north-west** NW

NY *abbr of* **New York**

Nyasaland [naɪ'æsəlænd] N Njassaland *nt*

NYC *abbr of* **New York City**

nylon ['naɪlɒn] N a *(Tex)* Nylon® *nt* b **nylons** PL Nylonstrümpfe *pl* ADJ Nylon-; **~ shirt** Nylonhemd *nt*; **~ material** Nylon *nt*

nymph [nɪmf] N a *(Myth)* Nymphe *f* b *(Zool)* Nymphe *f*

nymphet [nɪm'fet] N Nymphchen *nt*

nympho ['nɪmfəʊ] N *(inf)* Nymphomanin *f*

nymphomania [ˌnɪmfəʊ'meɪnɪə] N Nymphomanie *f*

nymphomaniac [ˌnɪmfəʊ'meɪnɪæk] N Nymphomanin *f*

NYPD *(US) abbr of* **New York Police Department**

NYSE *(US) abbr of* **New York Stock Exchange**

NZ *abbr of* **New Zealand**

O

O INTERJ **a** *(Poet)* o; **O my people** o du mein Volk! **b** *(expressing feeling)* oh, ach; **O how wrong he was** wie hatte er sich da (doch) geirrt; **O for a bit of fresh air!** ach, wenn es doch nur ein bisschen frische Luft gäbe!; **O to be in France** (ach,) wäre ich nur in Frankreich! → *also* **oh**

O, o [əʊ] N **a** O *nt*, o *nt* **b** [*(Brit)* əʊ] [*(US)* 'zɪərəʊ] *(Telec)* Null *f*

o' [ə] PREP *abbr of* **of**

oaf [əʊf] N *pl* **-s** *or* **oaves** Flegel *m*, Lümmel *m*; **you clumsy ~!** du altes Trampel! *(inf)*

oafish ['əʊfɪʃ] ADJ flegelhaft, lümmelhaft; *(= clumsy)* tölpelhaft

oak [əʊk] N Eiche *f*; *(= wood also)* Eichenholz *nt*; **he has a heart of ~** er hat ein unerschütterliches Gemüt; **dark ~** *(= colour)* (in) dunkel Eiche; **great ~s from little acorns grow** *(prov)* aus kleinen Dingen entwickeln sich oft erstaunliche Sachen

oak *in cpds* Eichen-; **~ tree** Eichenbaum *m*

oak apple N Gallapfel *m*

oaken ['əʊkən] ADJ *(liter)* Eichen-, eichen; **~ door** Eichentür *f*

oakum ['əʊkəm] N Werg *nt*

OAP *(Brit) abbr of* **old-age pensioner**

OAPEC [əʊ'eɪpek] *abbr of* **Organization of Arab Petroleum Exporting Countries**

oar [ɔː'] N **a** Ruder *nt*, Riemen *m (spec)*; **to pull at the ~s** sich in die Riemen legen; **he always has to put** *or* **stick his ~ in** *(fig inf)* er muss (aber auch) immer mitmischen *(inf)*; **to rest on one's ~s** *(fig)* langsamer treten *(inf)* **b** *(= person)* Ruderer *m*, Ruderin *f*

-oared [-ɔːd] ADJ *suf* mit … Rudern; **four-oared boat** Boot *nt* mit vier Rudern

oarlock ['ɔːlɒk] N *(US)* (Ruder)dolle *f*

oarsman ['ɔːzmən] N Ruderer *m*

oarsmanship ['ɔːzmənʃɪp] N Rudertechnik *or* -kunst *f*

OAS *abbr of* **Organization of American States** OAS *f*

oasis [əʊ'eɪsɪs] N *pl* **oases** [əʊ'eɪsiːz] *(lit, fig)* Oase *f*

oast [əʊst] N Darre *f*, Trockenboden *m*

oast house N Trockenschuppen *m or* -haus *nt*

oat [əʊt] N *usu pl* Hafer *m*; **~s** *pl (Cook)* Haferflocken *pl*; **to sow one's wild ~s** *(fig)* sich *(dat)* die Hörner abstoßen; **he's feeling his ~s** ihn sticht der Hafer; **to be off one's ~s** *(hum inf)* keinen Appetit haben; **he hasn't had his ~s for some time** *(hum inf)* der hat schon lange keine mehr vernascht *(hum sl)*

oatcake ['əʊtkeɪk] N Haferkeks *m*

oaten ['əʊtn] ADJ *attr* **a** *(of oat straw)* aus Haferstroh **b** *(of oatmeal)* Hafer(mehl)-, aus Hafermehl

oath [əʊθ] N **a** Schwur *m*; *(Jur)* Eid *m*; **to take** *or* **make** *or* **swear an ~** schwören; *(Jur)* einen Eid ablegen *or* leisten; **he took an ~ of loyalty to the government** er schwor der Regierung Loyalität; **to declare under ~** *or* **on ~** *(Jur)* unter Eid aussagen; **to be under ~** *(Jur)* unter Eid stehen; **to break one's ~** seinen Schwur brechen; **to put sb on ~** *(Jur)* jdn vereidigen; **to take the ~** *(Jur)* vereidigt werden; **he refused to take the ~** *(Jur)* er verweigerte den Eid; **on my ~!** *(obs)* bei meiner Seele! *(obs)* **b** *(= curse, profanity)* Fluch *m*

oatmeal ['əʊtmiːl] N *no pl* Haferschrot *m*, Hafermehl *nt* ADJ **a** *biscuits, bread* aus Hafermehl **b** *colour, dress* hellbeige

OAU *abbr of* **Organization of African Unity** OAU *f*

oaves [əʊvz] PL *of* **oaf**

OB *(Brit) abbr of* **outside broadcast** Außenreportage *f*

ob *abbr of* **obiit** gest.

obbligato N, ADJ = **obligato**

obduracy ['ɒbdjʊrəsɪ] N *(= stubbornness)* Hartnäckigkeit *f*; *(of sinner)* Verstocktheit *f*, Halsstarrigkeit *f*; *(= hardheartedness)* Unnachgiebigkeit *f*

obdurate ['ɒbdjʊrɪt] ADJ *(= stubborn)* hartnäckig; *sinner* verstockt, halsstarrig; *(= hard-hearted)* unnachgiebig, unerbittlich

obdurately ['ɒbdjʊrɪtlɪ] ADV *(= stubbornly)* hartnäckig; *(= hardheartedly)* unerbittlich; **she remained ~ silent** sie verharrte verbissen in Schweigen

OBE *abbr of* **Officer of the Order of the British Empire** *britischer Verdienstorden*

obedience [ə'biːdɪəns] N *no pl* Gehorsam *m*; **in ~ to the law** dem Gesetz entsprechend; **in ~ to your wishes** *(form)* Ihren Wünschen gemäß; **to teach sb ~** jdn gehorchen lehren

obedient [ə'biːdɪənt] ADJ gehorsam; *child, dog also* folgsam; **to be ~** gehorchen *(to +dat)*; *(child, dog also)* folgen *(to +dat)*; *(steering, controls, car also)* reagieren, ansprechen *(to* auf *+acc)*; **your ~ servant** *(old, in letters)* Ihr ergebenster Diener, Ihre ergebenste Dienerin *(old)*

obediently [ə'biːdɪəntlɪ] ADV gehorsam; **the car responded ~** das Auto reagierte prompt

obeisance [əʊ'beɪsəns] N **a** *(form: = homage, respect)* Ehrerbietung *f*, Reverenz *f (geh)*, Huldigung *f (liter)*; **to make** *or* **pay ~ (to sb)** (jdm) seine Huldigung darbringen, (jdm) huldigen **b** *(obs, = deep bow)* Verbeugung *f*, Verneigung *f*

obelisk ['ɒbɪlɪsk] N **a** *(Archit)* Obelisk *m* **b** *(Typ)* Kreuz *nt*

obese [əʊ'biːs] ADJ fettleibig *(form, Med)*, feist *(pej)*

obeseness [əʊ'biːsnɪs], **obesity** [əʊ'biːsɪtɪ] N Fettleibigkeit *f (form, Med)*, Feistheit *f (pej)*

obey [ə'beɪ] VT gehorchen *(+dat)*; *conscience also* folgen *(+dat)*; *(child, dog also)* folgen *(+dat)*; *law, rules* sich halten an *(+acc)*, befolgen; *order* befolgen; *(Jur) summons* nachkommen *(+dat)*, Folge leisten *(+dat)*; *(machine, vehicle) controls* reagieren *or* ansprechen auf *(+acc)*; *driver* gehorchen *(+dat)*; **to ~ sb implicitly** jdm absoluten Gehorsam leisten; **I expect to be ~ed** ich erwarte, dass man meine Anordnungen befolgt VI gehorchen; *(child, dog also)* folgen; *(machine, vehicle also)* reagieren; **the troops refused to ~** die Truppen verweigerten den Gehorsam

obfuscate ['ɒbfəskeɪt] VT *(liter) mind* verwirren, trüben; *issue* unklar *or* verworren machen, vernebeln

obituarist [ə'bɪtjʊərɪst] N Nachrufverfasser(in) *m(f)*

obituary [ə'bɪtjʊərɪ] N Nachruf *m*; **~ notice** Todesanzeige *f*; **I saw his ~ notice today** ich habe seinen Namen heute im Sterberegister gelesen; **~ column** Sterberegister *nt*

object¹ ['ɒbdʒɪkt] N **a** *(= thing)* Gegenstand *m*, Ding *nt*; *(Philos, abstract etc)* Objekt *nt*, Ding *nt*; **he treats her like an ~** er behandelt sie wie ein Ding *or* Objekt; **she became an ~ of pity** mit ihr musste man Mitleid haben; **he was an ~ of scorn** er war die Zielscheibe der Verachtung; **the cat is the sole ~ of her love** ihre ganze Liebe gilt ihrer Katze
b *(= aim)* Ziel *nt*, Absicht *f*, Zweck *m*; **with this ~ in view** *or* **in mind** mit diesem Ziel vor Augen; **with the sole ~ (of doing)** mit dem einzigen Ziel *or* nur in der Absicht(, zu …); **he has no ~ in life** er hat kein Ziel im Leben *or* kein Lebensziel; **what's the ~ (of staying here)?** wozu *or* zu welchem Zweck (bleiben wir hier)?; **the ~ of the exercise** der Zweck *or (fig also)* Sinn der Übung; **that defeats the ~** das macht es sinnlos, das verfehlt seinen Sinn *or* Zweck; **he made it his ~ to …** er setzte es sich *(dat)* zum Ziel, zu …
c *(= obstacle)* Hinderungsgrund *m*; **money/distance is no ~** Geld/Entfernung spielt keine Rolle, Geld/Entfernung (ist) nebensächlich
d *(Gram)* Objekt *nt*; **direct/indirect ~** direktes/indirektes Objekt, Akkusativ-/Dativobjekt *nt*
e *(inf, = odd thing)* Ding *nt*, Dings *nt (inf)*; *(= odd person)* Subjekt *nt*, Vogel *m (inf)*

object² [əb'dʒekt] ✪ 9.2, 12.1, 26.3 VI dagegen sein; *(= make objection, protest)* protestieren; *(= be against: in discussion etc)* Einwände haben *(to* gegen); *(= raise objection)* Einwände erheben; *(= disapprove)* Anstoß nehmen *(to* an *+dat)*, sich stören *(to* an *+dat)*; **to ~ to sth** *(= disapprove)* etw ablehnen *or* missbilligen; **I don't ~ to that** ich habe nichts dagegen (einzuwenden); **if you don't ~** wenn es (Ihnen) recht ist, wenn Sie nichts dagegen haben; **do you ~ to my smoking?** stört es (Sie), wenn ich rauche?, haben Sie etwas dagegen, wenn ich rauche?; **he ~s to my drinking** er nimmt daran Anstoß *or* er hat etwas dagegen, dass ich trinke; **I ~ to your tone** ich verbitte mir diesen Ton; **I ~ to people smoking in my living room** ich verbitte mir, dass in meinem Wohnzimmer geraucht wird; **I ~ most strongly to his smoking** ich missbillige es aufs Äußerste, dass er raucht; **I ~ most strongly to his argument** ich lehne seine Argumentation energisch ab; **I ~ to him bossing me around** ich wehre mich dagegen, dass er mich (so) herumkommandiert; **I ~ to orange curtains with green wallpaper** Vorhänge in Orange mit grünen Tapeten, da protestiere ich!; **she ~s to all that noise** sie stört sich an dem vielen Lärm; **he doesn't ~ to the odd drink** er hat nichts gegen ein Gläschen ab und zu (einzuwenden); **I ~!** ich protestiere!, ich erhebe Einspruch *(form)*; **to ~ to a witness** *(Jur)* einen Zeugen ablehnen
VT einwenden

object: **object clause** ['ɒbdʒɪkt,klɔːz] N Objektsatz *m*; **object deletion** N *(Gram)* Unterdrückung *f* des Objekts

objection [əbˈdʒekʃən] N **a** *(= reason against)* Einwand *m* (*to* gegen); **to make** *or* **raise an ~ (to sth)** einen Einwand (gegen etw) machen *or* erheben *(geh)*; **I have no ~ to his going away** ich habe nichts dagegen (einzuwenden), dass er weggeht; **are there any ~s?** irgendwelche Einwände?; **I see no ~ to it** ich sehe nichts, was dagegen spricht; **what are your ~s to it/him?** was haben Sie dagegen/gegen ihn (einzuwenden)?, welche Einwände haben Sie dagegen/gegen ihn?; **~!** *(Jur)* Einspruch!
b *(= dislike)* Abneigung *f*; *(= disapproval)* Einspruch *m*, Widerspruch *m*; **I have no ~ to him** *(as a person)* ich habe nichts gegen ihn

objectionable [əbˈdʒekʃənəbl] ADJ störend; *conduct* anstößig, nicht einwandfrei; *remark, language* anstößig, unanständig; *smell* unangenehm, übel; **he's a most ~ person** er ist unausstehlich *or* ekelhaft; **he became ~** er wurde unangenehm; **I find this (really) ~** ich habe starke Einwände dagegen; *(= offensive)* ich finde das anstößig; **this attitude was ~ to them** sie fanden diese Einstellung anstößig

objectionably [əbˈdʒekʃənəblɪ] ADV unangenehm

objective [əbˈdʒektɪv] ADJ **a** *(= impartial) person, article* objektiv, sachlich; **to take an ~ look at sth** etw objektiv betrachten **b** *(= real)* objektiv; **~ fact** Tatsache *f* N **a** *(= aim)* Ziel *nt*; *(esp Comm)* Zielvorstellung *f*; *(Mil)* Angriffsziel *nt*; **in establishing our ~s** bei unserer Zielsetzung **b** *(Opt, Phot)* Objektiv *nt*

objectively [əbˈdʒektɪvlɪ] ADV **a** *(= unemotionally)* objektiv, sachlich **b** *(= in real life etc)* tatsächlich, wirklich

objectivism [əbˈdʒektɪvɪzəm] N Objektivismus *m*

objectivity [ˌɒbdʒekˈtɪvɪtɪ] N Objektivität *f*

object lesson [ˈɒbdʒɪktˌlesn] N **a** *(fig)* Paradebeispiel *nt*, Musterbeispiel *nt* (*in, on* für, +*gen*) **b** *(Sch)* Anschauungsunterricht *m*

objector [əbˈdʒektəʳ] N Gegner(in) *m(f)* (*to* +*gen*)

objet d'art [ˈɒbʒeɪˈdɑː] N Kunstgegenstand *m*

objurgate [ˈɒbdʒɜːgeɪt] VT *(form)* rügen *(geh)*, tadeln

objurgation [ˌɒbdʒɜːˈgeɪʃən] N *(form)* Tadel *m*, Rüge *f*

oblate[1] [ˈɒbleɪt] ADJ *(Math)* abgeplattet

oblate[2] N *(Eccl)* Oblate *m*

oblation [əʊˈbleɪʃən] N *(Eccl)* Opfergabe *f*, Opfer *nt*

obligate [ˈɒblɪgeɪt] VT *(form)* verpflichten (*sb to do sth* jdn, etw zu tun)

obligated [ˈɒblɪgeɪtɪd] ADJ *(form)* verpflichtet; **to be ~ to sb** in jds Schuld sein *or* stehen; **to feel ~ to do sth** sich verpflichtet fühlen, etw zu tun

obligation [ˌɒblɪˈgeɪʃən] N Verpflichtung *f*, Pflicht *f*; **to be under an ~ to do sth** verpflichtet sein *or* die Pflicht haben, etw zu tun; **to be under no ~ to do sth** nicht verpflichtet sein, etw zu tun; **to be under** *or* **have an ~ to sb** jdm verpflichtet sein; **you have placed us all under a great ~** wir sind Ihnen alle sehr verpflichtet; **without ~** *(Comm)* unverbindlich, ohne Obligo *(form)*; **with no ~ to buy** ohne Kaufzwang

obligato [ˌɒblɪˈgɑːtəʊ] N *(= part)* Obligato *nt* ADJ obligato

obligatory [ɒˈblɪgətərɪ] ADJ obligatorisch; *rule* verbindlich; **~ subject** Pflichtfach *nt*; **biology is ~** Biologie ist Pflicht; **attendance is ~** Anwesenheit ist vorgeschrieben; **it's ~ to pay tax** jeder ist steuerpflichtig; **to make it ~ to do sth/for sb to do sth** vorschreiben, dass etw getan wird/dass jd etw tut; **identity cards were made ~** Personalausweise wurden Vorschrift; **with the ~ piper** mit dem obligaten Dudelsackpfeifer

oblige [əˈblaɪdʒ] ✪ 4 VT **a** *(= compel)* zwingen; *(because of duty)* verpflichten (*sb to do sth* jdn, etw zu tun); *(Jur)* vorschreiben (*sb to do sth* jdm, etw zu tun); **to feel ~d to do sth** sich verpflichtet fühlen, etw zu tun; **I was ~d to go** ich sah mich gezwungen zu gehen; **you are not ~d to do it** Sie sind nicht dazu verpflichtet; **you are not ~d to answer this question** Sie brauchen diese Frage nicht zu beantworten
b *(= do a favour to)* einen Gefallen tun (+*dat*), gefällig sein (+*dat*); **could you ~ me with a light?** wären Sie so gut, mir Feuer zu geben?; **please ~ me by opening a window** würden Sie mir bitte den Gefallen tun und ein Fenster öffnen?; **he ~d us with a song** er gab uns ein Lied zum Besten; **would you ~ me by not interrupting, I would be ~d if you wouldn't interrupt** hätten Sie die Güte, mich nicht zu unterbrechen; **anything to ~ a friend** was tut man nicht alles für einen Freund!
c much ~d! herzlichen Dank!; **I am much ~d to you for this!** ich bin Ihnen dafür sehr verbunden *or* dankbar
VI **she is always ready to ~** sie ist immer sehr gefällig *or* hilfsbereit; *(hum)* sie ist niemals abgeneigt; **they called for a song, but no-one ~d** sie verlangten nach einem Lied, aber niemand kam der Aufforderung nach; **we asked him the way and he ~d with directions** wir fragten ihn nach dem Weg, und er gab bereitwillig Auskunft; **anything to ~** stets zu Diensten!; **a prompt reply would ~** *(Comm)* wir bitten um baldige Antwort

obliging [əˈblaɪdʒɪŋ] ADJ entgegenkommend, gefällig; *personality* zuvorkommend

obligingly [əˈblaɪdʒɪŋlɪ] ADV entgegenkommenderweise, freundlicherweise, liebenswürdigerweise

obligingness [əˈblaɪdʒɪŋnɪs] N Gefälligkeit *f*, Zuvorkommenheit *f*

oblique [əˈbliːk] ADJ **a** *line* schief, schräg, geneigt; *angle* schief; *(Gram) case* abhängig; **~ stroke** Schrägstrich *m* **b** *(fig) look* schief, schräg; *course* schräg; *method, style, reply* indirekt; *hint, reference* indirekt, versteckt; *warning* versteckt; *criticism* verdeckt; **an ~ approach to the problem** eine indirekte Art, an das Problem heranzugehen; **he achieved his goal by rather ~ means** er erreichte sein Ziel auf Umwegen *or (dishonestly)* auf krummen Wegen N Schrägstrich *m*; **and ~ or** und Strich oder

obliquely [əˈbliːklɪ] ADV **a** schräg **b** *(fig)* indirekt

obliqueness [əˈbliːknɪs] N **a** Schiefe *f*, Schräge *f*, Neigung *f* **b** *(fig: of means)* Indirektheit *f*

obliterate [əˈblɪtəreɪt] VT *(= erase, abolish)* auslöschen; *past, memory also* tilgen *(geh)*; *city also* vernichten; *(inf) opposite team etc* vernichten; *(= hide from sight) sun, view* verdecken; **the coffee stain has ~d most of the text** der Kaffeefleck hat den Text fast ganz unkenntlich gemacht; **by the 19th century this disease had been completely ~d** im 19. Jahrhundert war dann diese Krankheit völlig ausgerottet

obliteration [əˌblɪtəˈreɪʃən] N Auslöschen *nt*; *(inf: of opponent)* Vernichtung *f*; *(= hiding)* Verdecken *nt*

oblivion [əˈblɪvɪən] N **a** Vergessenheit *f*, Vergessen *nt*; **to sink** *or* **fall into ~** in Vergessenheit geraten, der Vergessenheit anheimfallen *(geh)*; **to rescue sb/sth from ~** jdn/etw wieder ins Bewusstsein *or* ans Tageslicht bringen; **he drank himself into ~** er trank bis zur Bewusstlosigkeit; **to be bombed/blasted into ~** *(town etc)* dem Erdboden gleichgemacht werden **b** *(= unawareness)* = **obliviousness**

oblivious [əˈblɪvɪəs] ADJ **to be ~ of** *or* **to sth** sich *(dat)* etw nicht bewusst machen, sich *(dat)* einer Sache *(gen)* nicht bewusst sein; **he was quite ~ of his surroundings** er nahm seine Umgebung gar nicht wahr; **they are ~ to the beauty of their surroundings** sie haben für die Schönheit ihrer Umgebung keinen Sinn; **he was totally ~ of what was going on in his marriage** er (be)merkte gar nicht, was in seiner Ehe vor sich ging; **~ of the world** weltvergessen

obliviously [əˈblɪvɪəslɪ] ADV **to carry on ~** einfach (unbeirrt) weitermachen

obliviousness [əˈblɪvɪəsnɪs] N **because of his ~ to the danger he was in** weil er sich *(dat)* nicht der Gefahr bewusst war, in der er schwebte; **a state of blissful ~ to the world** ein Zustand *m* seliger Weltvergessenheit

oblong [ˈɒblɒŋ] ADJ rechteckig N Rechteck *nt*

obloquy [ˈɒbləkwɪ] N *(liter)* **a** *(= blame, abuse)* Schmähung *f (liter)*, Beschimpfung *f* **b** *(= disgrace)* Schande *f*, Schmach *f*

obnoxious [ɒbˈnɒkʃəs] ADJ widerlich, widerwärtig; *person also, behaviour* unausstehlich; **an ~ person** ein Ekel *nt (inf)*; **don't be so ~ to her** sei nicht so gemein *or* fies *(inf)* zu ihr

obnoxiously [ɒbˈnɒkʃəslɪ] ADV widerlich; *behave* unausstehlich

obnoxiousness [ɒbˈnɒkʃəsnɪs] N Widerlichkeit *f*, Widerwärtigkeit *f*; *(of person also, behaviour)* Unausstehlichkeit *f*

o.b.o. *abbr of* **or best offer** ≈ VB, Verhandlungsbasis *f* → **offer**

oboe [ˈəʊbəʊ] N Oboe *f*

oboist [ˈəʊbəʊɪst] N Oboist(in) *m(f)*

obscene [əbˈsiːn] ADJ obszön; *word, picture, book also* unzüchtig; *language, joke also* zotig; *gesture, posture, thought also* schamlos, unzüchtig; *(non-sexually: = repulsive)* ekelerregend; *prices, demands* unverschämt; **~ publication** Veröffentlichung *f* mit pornografischem Inhalt; **Obscene Publications Act** *(Brit) Gesetz über die Veröffentlichung pornografischen Materials*; **this colour scheme is positively ~** diese Farbzusammenstellung widert einen an *or* ist widerlich

obscenely [əbˈsiːnlɪ] ADV obszön; *(= repulsively)* ekelerregend; **she earns ~ large amounts of money** sie verdient unverschämt viel Geld

obscenity [əbˈsenɪtɪ] N Obszönität *f*; **he used an ~** er benutzte *or* gebrauchte einen ordinären Ausdruck

obscurantism [ˌɒbskjʊəˈræntɪzəm] N Obskurantismus *m*, Aufklärungsfeindlichkeit *f*

obscurantist [ˌɒbskjʊəˈræntɪst] N Gegner(in) *m(f)* der Aufklärung

obscuration [ˌəbskjʊəˈreɪʃən] N Verdunkelung *f*

obscure [əbˈskjʊəʳ] ADJ (+*er*) **a** *(= hard to understand)* dunkel; *style* unklar, undurchsichtig; *argument* verworren; *language, word, book, poet* schwer verständlich
b *(= indistinct) feeling, memory* dunkel, undeutlich, unklar; **for some ~ reason** aus einem unerfindlichen Grund
c *(= unknown, little known)* obskur; *poet, village* unbekannt; *(= humble) beginnings* unbedeutend; *life* wenig beachtenswert; **of ~ birth** von unbekannter Herkunft; **he holds some ~ post in the Civil Service** er hat so ein obskures Pöstchen im Staatsdienst
d *(rare, = dark)* düster, finster
VT **a** *(= hide) sun, view* verdecken; **the tree ~d the bay from our view** der Baum nahm uns *(dat)* die Sicht auf die Bucht
b *(= confuse)* verworren *or* unklar machen; *mind* verwirren; *truth, facts, issues* verschleiern

obscurely [əbˈskjʊəlɪ] ADV **a** *written, presented, argued, remember* undeutlich, unklar **b a movement which began ~ in the depths of Russia** eine Bewegung mit obskuren Anfängen im tiefsten Russland **c** *lit* schwach

obscurity [əbˈskjʊərɪtɪ] N **a** *no pl (of a wood, night)* Dunkelheit *f*, Finsternis *f*, Dunkel *nt* **b** *(of style, ideas, argument)* Unklarheit *f*, Unverständlichkeit *f*, Verworrenheit *f*; **to lapse into ~** verworren *or* unklar werden; **he threw some light on the obscurities of the text** er erhellte einige der unklaren Textstellen **c** *no pl (of birth, origins)* Dunkel *nt*; **to live in ~** zurückgezogen leben; **to rise from ~** aus dem Nichts auftauchen; **in spite of the ~ of his origins** trotz seiner unbekannten Herkunft; **to sink into ~** in Vergessenheit geraten

obsequies [ˈɒbsɪkwɪz] PL *(form)* Beerdigungsfeier *f*, Leichenbegängnis *nt (liter)*

obsequious [əbˈsiːkwɪəs] ADJ unterwürfig, servil *(geh)* (*to(wards)* gegen, gegenüber)

obsequiously [əb'siːkwɪəslɪ] ADV unterwürfig

obsequiousness [əb'siːkwɪəsnɪs] N Unterwürfigkeit *f*, Servilität *f (geh)*

observable [əb'zɜːvəbl] ADJ sichtbar, erkennbar; *universe* sichtbar; **as is ~ in rabbits** wie bei Kaninchen zu beobachten ist *or* beobachtet wird; **a welcome improvement has recently become ~** in letzter Zeit zeichnet sich eine willkommene Verbesserung ab; **there has been no ~ change in his condition today** es wurde heute keine Veränderung seines Befindens beobachtet

observably [əb'zɜːvəblɪ] ADV *(= visibly)* sichtlich

observance [əb'zɜːvəns] N **a** *(of law)* Befolgung *f*, Beachtung *f*, Beachten *nt* **b** *(Eccl) (= keeping: of rites etc)* Einhalten *nt*, Einhaltung *f*, Beachten *nt*; *(= celebration)* Kirchenfest *nt*; *(in a convent etc)* (Ordens)regel *f*, Observanz *f*; **~ of the Sabbath** Einhaltung *f* des Sabbats *or (non--Jewish)* des Sonntagsgebots; **religious ~s** religiöse *or (Christian also)* kirchliche Feste

observant [əb'zɜːvənt] ADJ **a** *(= watchful) person* aufmerksam, wach(sam), achtsam; **that's very ~ of you** das hast du aber gut bemerkt; **if you'd been a little more ~** wenn du etwas besser aufgepasst hättest **b** *(= strict in obeying rules)* **you should be a little more ~ of the law** Sie sollten sich etwas mehr an das Gesetz halten

observantly [əb'zɜːvəntlɪ] ADV aufmerksam; **... which he very ~ spotted** ..., wie er sehr gut bemerkt hat

observation [ˌɒbzə'veɪʃən] N **a** Beobachtung *f*; **to keep sb/sth under ~** jdn/etw unter Beobachtung halten; *(by police)* jdn/etw überwachen *or* observieren *(form)*; **~ of nature** Naturbeobachtung *f*; **to take an ~** *(Naut)* das Besteck nehmen; **powers of ~** Beobachtungsgabe *f*; **he's in hospital for ~** er ist zur Beobachtung im Krankenhaus; **to escape sb's ~** (von jdm) unbemerkt bleiben, jdm entgehen **b** *(of rules, Sabbath)* Einhalten *nt* **c** *(= remark)* Bemerkung *f*, Äußerung *f*; **~s on Kant** Betrachtungen über *or* zu Kant; **his ~s on the experiment** seine Versuchserläuterungen

observational [ˌɒbzə'veɪʃənəl] ADJ empirisch, aufgrund *or* auf Grund von Beobachtungen gewonnen; **~ skills** *or* **faculties** Beobachtungsgabe *f*; **~ study** Beobachtungsstudie *f*

observation: **observation car** N *(Rail)* Aussichtswagen *m*, Panoramawagen *m*; **observation deck** N Aussichtsdeck *nt*; **observation lounge** N Aussichtsrestaurant *nt*; **observation post** N Beobachtungsposten *m*; **observation tower** N Aussichtsturm *m*; **observation ward** N Beobachtungsstation *f*

observatory [əb'zɜːvətrɪ] N Observatorium *nt*, Sternwarte *f*; *(Met)* Observatorium *nt*, Wetterwarte *f*

observe [əb'zɜːv] ✪ 26.2 VT **a** *(= see, notice)* beobachten, bemerken; *difference, change* beobachten, wahrnehmen; **did you actually ~ him do it?** haben Sie ihn wirklich dabei beobachtet?; **the thief was ~d to ...** der Dieb wurde dabei beobachtet, wie er ...
b *(= watch carefully, study)* beobachten; *(by police)* überwachen
c *(= remark)* bemerken, feststellen, äußern
d *(= obey)* achten auf *(+acc)*; *rule, custom, ceasefire, Sabbath* einhalten; *anniversary etc* begehen, feiern; **to ~ a minute's silence** *or* **a moment's silence** *(US)* eine Schweigeminute einlegen; **failure to ~ the law** ein Verstoß *m* gegen das Gesetz
VI **a** *(= watch)* zusehen; *(= act as an observer)* beobachten
b *(= remark)* bemerken, feststellen *(on* zu, über *+acc)*; **you were about to ~ ...?** Sie wollten gerade sagen ...?

observer [əb'zɜːvə'] N *(= watcher)* Zuschauer(in) *m(f)*; *(Mil, Aviat, Pol)* Beobachter(in) *m(f)*

obsess [əb'ses] VT **to be ~ed by** *or* **with sb/sth** von jdm/etw besessen sein; **to be ~ed about sth** von etw besessen sein; **to be ~ed about doing sth** davon besessen sein, etw zu tun; **sth ~es sb** jd ist von etw besessen; **his one ~ing thought** der ihn ständig verfolgende Gedanke; **don't become ~ed by it** lass das nicht zum Zwang *or* zur Manie werden

obsession [əb'seʃən] N **a** *(= fixed idea)* fixe Idee, Manie *f*; *(= fear etc)* Zwangsvorstellung *f*, Obsession *f (spec)*; **she has an ~ with her cat** die Katze ist ihre ganze Leidenschaft; **it's an ~ with him** das ist eine fixe Idee von ihm; *(hobby etc)* er ist davon besessen; **watching TV is an ~ with him** Fernsehen ist bei ihm zur Sucht geworden **b** *(= state)* Besessenheit *f (with* von), Monomanie *f*; **this ~ with order/quality** dieser Ordnungs-/Qualitätswahn *m*; **an unnatural ~ with detail** eine (ganz) unnatürliche Detailbesessenheit; **because of his ~ with her** weil er ihr gänzlich verfallen ist

obsessional [əb'seʃənl] ADJ *(Psych) behaviour, personality* zwanghaft; *love, hatred, jealousy* obsessiv

obsessionally [əb'seʃənlɪ] ADV *(Psych) (+adj)* zwanghaft, obsessiv; *jealous* zwanghaft; *(+vb)* wie besessen, fanatisch

obsessive [əb'sesɪv] ADJ zwanghaft, obsessiv *(spec)*; **to be ~ about sth** von etw besessen sein; **to be ~ about tidiness** eine übertriebene Ordnungsliebe haben; **to be ~ about cleanliness** einen Sauberkeitsfimmel haben *(inf)*; **she's ~ about organic food** Biokost ist bei ihr zur Manie geworden; **to have an ~ need to do sth** den Zwang verspüren, etw tun zu müssen; **to become ~** zum Zwang *or* zur Manie werden; **an ~ thought/memory** ein Gedanke, der/eine Erinnerung, die einen nicht loslässt; **an ~ desire for wealth** eine Sucht nach Reichtum; **he is an ~ reader** er liest wie besessen, er hat die Lesewut *(inf)*
N Zwangsneurotiker(in) *m(f)*

obsessive-compulsive disorder [əb'sesɪvkəm'pʌlsɪvdɪs'ɔːdə'] N *(Psych)* zwanghafte Verhaltensstörung

obsessively [əb'sesɪvlɪ] ADV wie besessen; **to be ~ concerned about sb/sth** von der Sorge um jdn/etw besessen sein; **she is ~ preoccupied with cleanliness** sie huldigt einem Sauberkeitswahn; **he is ~ devoted to her** er ist ihr bedingungslos ergeben; *(lover)* er liebt sie wie besessen

obsessive neurosis N *(Psych)* Zwangsneurose *f*

obsolescence [ˌɒbsə'lesns] N Veralten *nt* → **planned obsolescence**

obsolescent [ˌɒbsə'lesnt] ADJ allmählich außer Gebrauch kommend; **to be ~** anfangen zu veralten; *(machine, process etc)* technisch (fast) überholt sein

obsolete ['ɒbsəliːt] ADJ veraltet, überholt, obsolet *(geh)*; **to become ~** veralten

obstacle ['ɒbstəkl] N *(lit, fig)* Hindernis *nt*; **to be an ~ to sb/sth** jdm/einer Sache im Weg(e) stehen, jdn/etw (be)hindern; **if they put any ~ in the way of our plans** wenn man uns Steine in den Weg legt *or* unsere Pläne behindert; **that's no ~ to our doing it** das wird uns nicht daran hindern; **all the ~s to progress/peace** *etc* alles, was den Fortschritt/Frieden *etc* behindert

obstacle course N Hindernisstrecke *f*; **getting from the desk to the door is a real ~** der Weg vom Schreibtisch zur Tür ist mit Hindernissen übersät

obstacle race N *(Sport, fig)* Hindernisrennen *nt*

obstetric(al) [ɒb'stetrɪk(əl)] ADJ *(Med) techniques etc* bei der Geburtshilfe; **obstetric care** Geburtshilfe *f*; **obstetric problems** Probleme *pl* bei der Entbindung; **obstetric specialist** Geburtshelfer(in) *m(f)*

obstetric clinic N Entbindungsheim *nt*, Geburtsklinik *f*

obstetrician [ˌɒbstə'trɪʃən] N Geburtshelfer(in) *m(f)*

obstetrics [ɒb'stetrɪks] N *sing* Geburtshilfe *f*, Obstetrik *f (spec)*; *(= ward)* Wöchnerinnenstation *f*

obstetric ward N Entbindungsstation *f*

obstinacy ['ɒbstɪnəsɪ] N **a** *(of person)* Hartnäckigkeit *f*, Starrsinn *m*; **his ~ in doing sth** die Hartnäckigkeit, mit der er etw tut **b** *(of illness, resistance)* Hartnäckigkeit *f*

obstinate ['ɒbstɪnɪt] ADJ **a** *person* hartnäckig, starrsinnig; *stain, weeds* hartnäckig; *nail etc* widerspenstig; **to remain ~** stur bleiben; **to have an ~ streak** zur Sturheit neigen; **he was ~ in insisting that ...** er bestand stur *or* hartnäckig darauf, dass ... **b** *resistance, illness* hartnäckig

obstinately ['ɒbstɪnɪtlɪ] ADV hartnäckig, stur; **unemployment figures remain ~ high** die Arbeitslosenzahlen verharren auf unverändert hohem Niveau

obstreperous [əb'strepərəs] ADJ aufmüpfig *(inf)*; *child* aufsässig; **the drunk became ~** der Betrunkene fing an zu randalieren; **it's not a real complaint, he's just being ~** es ist keine echte Beschwerde, er will nur Schwierigkeiten machen

obstreperously [əb'strepərəslɪ] ADV aufmüpfig *(inf)*; *(referring to child)* aufsässig

obstreperousness [əb'strepərəsnɪs] N Aufmüpfigkeit *f (inf)*; *(of child)* Aufsässigkeit *f*

obstruct [əb'strʌkt] VT **a** *(= block)* blockieren; *passage, road* versperren, blockieren; *view* versperren; *(Med) artery, pipe* blockieren, verstopfen; **you're ~ing my view** Sie nehmen *or* versperren mir die Sicht **b** *(= hinder)* (be)hindern; *navigation* behindern; *traffic, progress* behindern, aufhalten; *(Sport)* behindern; *(in possession of ball)* sperren; **to ~ a bill** *(Parl)* einen Gesetzentwurf blockieren; **to ~ (the course of) justice** die Rechtsfindung behindern; **to ~ the police** die Arbeit der Polizei behindern VI *(= be obstructionist)* obstruieren, Obstruktion treiben; *(Sport)* sperren

obstruction [əb'strʌkʃən] N **a** *(= blocking)* Blockierung *f*; *(of view)* Versperren *nt*; *(of artery, pipe also)* Verstopfung *f*; *(of road)* Sperrung *f* **b** *(= hindering)* Behinderung *f*; *(Sport)* Sperren *nt*; **to cause an ~** den Verkehr behindern **c** *(= obstacle)* Hindernis *nt*, Hemmnis *nt (esp fig)*; **there is an ~ in the pipe** das Rohr ist blockiert *or* verstopft; **all ~s to progress** alles, was den Fortschritt aufhält *or* hemmt **d** *(Pol)* Obstruktion *f*, Behinderung *f*

obstructionism [əb'strʌkʃənɪzəm] N Obstruktionspolitik *f*

obstructionist [əb'strʌkʃənɪst] N Obstruktionspolitiker(in) *m(f)*

obstructive [əb'strʌktɪv] ADJ obstruktiv *(esp Pol)*, behindernd; **to be ~** *(person)* Schwierigkeiten machen, sich querstellen *(inf)*; **to be ~ to progress** dem Fortschritt hinderlich sein

obtain [əb'teɪn] VT erhalten, bekommen; *result, votes also* erzielen; *knowledge* erwerben; **to ~ sth through hard work** etw durch harte Arbeit erreichen; *possession* sich *(dat)* etw mühsam erarbeiten; **to ~ a divorce** die Scheidung ausgesprochen bekommen; **to ~ an injunction** eine einstweilige Verfügung erteilt bekommen; **to ~ sth for sb** jdm etw beschaffen *or* verschaffen; **they ~ed the release of the hostages** sie erreichten die Freilassung der Geiseln VI *(form)* gelten; *(rules also)* in Kraft sein; *(customs)* bestehen, herrschen

obtainable [əb'teɪnəbl] ADJ erhältlich

obtrude [əb'truːd] VT **a** **to ~ oneself** sich anderen aufdrängen **b** *(= push out)* hervorstrecken, hervorschieben VI **a** *(= intrude)* sich aufdrängen **b** *(= protrude)* (her)vorstehen; *(fig)* hervortreten

obtrusion [əb'truːʒən] N **a** Aufdrängen *nt*; **because of this ~ of himself/his ideas upon others** weil er sich/seine Ideen anderen aufdrängen will **b** *(= pushing out)* Hervorstrecken *nt* **c** *(= sticking out)* Herausragen *nt*

obtrusive [əb'tru:sɪv] ADJ *person, music* aufdringlich; *smell also* penetrant; *building, furniture* zu auffällig

obtrusively [əb'tru:sɪvlɪ] ADV (zu) auffällig; *smell* penetrant

obtrusiveness [əb'tru:sɪvnɪs] N *(of person)* Aufdringlichkeit *f*; *(of smell also)* Penetranz *f*; *(of appearance, dress, building)* Auffälligkeit *f*

obtuse [əb'tju:s] ADJ **a** *(Geometry)* stumpf **b** *person* begriffsstutzig, beschränkt; **are you just being ~?** tust du nur so beschränkt?

obtuseness [əb'tju:snɪs] N Begriffsstutzigkeit *f*, Beschränktheit *f*

OB van [,əubi:'væn], **outside broadcast van** N *(Rad, TV)* Übertragungswagen *m*

obverse ['ɒbvɜ:s] ADJ **~ side** Vorderseite *f* N **a** *(of coin)* Vorderseite *f*, Avers *m (spec)* **b** *(of statement, truth)* andere Seite, Kehrseite *f*

obviate ['ɒbvɪeɪt] VT vermeiden, umgehen; *need* vorbeugen *(+dat)*

obvious ['ɒbvɪəs] ADJ offensichtlich, deutlich; *(visually also)* augenfällig; *(= not subtle)* plump; *proof* klar, eindeutig; *difference, fact* eindeutig, offensichtlich, offenkundig; *statement* naheliegend, selbstverständlich; *reason* (leicht) ersichtlich; *dislike, reluctance, surprise* sichtlich; **an ~ truth** eine offenkundige Tatsache; **because of the ~ truth of what he maintains** da es so eindeutig *or* offensichtlich wahr ist, was er sagt; **that's the ~ translation/solution** das ist die am nächsten liegende *or* nächstliegende Übersetzung/Lösung; **for ~ reasons** aus naheliegenden Gründen; **he was the ~ choice** es lag nahe, ihn zu wählen; **it was ~ he didn't want to come** er wollte offensichtlich nicht kommen; **it's quite ~ he doesn't understand** man merkt doch (sofort) *or* es ist doch klar, dass er nicht versteht; **to make sth a little more ~** etw etwas deutlicher *or* eindeutiger machen; **there's no need to make it so ~** man braucht das (doch) nicht so deutlich werden zu lassen; **do I have to make it even more ~?** muss ich denn noch deutlicher werden?; **we must not be too ~ about it** wir dürfen es nicht zu auffällig machen; **I would have thought that was perfectly ~** das liegt doch auf der Hand; *(= noticeable)* das springt doch ins Auge; **that should be ~ to you** das sollte für Sie offensichtlich sein; **with the ~ exception of ...** natürlich mit Ausnahme von ...; **subtle? he's the most ~ person I know** raffiniert? ich kenne niemanden, der einfacher zu durchschauen wäre!; **even if I am stating the ~** selbst wenn ich hier etwas längst Bekanntes sage; **he has a gift for stating the ~** der merkt aber auch alles! *(inf)*; **don't just state the ~, try to be original** sagen Sie nicht, was sich von selbst versteht, sondern bemühen Sie sich um Originalität; **what's the ~ thing to do?** was ist das Naheliegendste?, was bietet sich am ehesten an?

obviously ['ɒbvɪəslɪ] ADV offensichtlich, offenbar; *(= noticeably)* (offen)sichtlich; **he's ~ French** er ist eindeutig ein Franzose; **she is not ~ drunk** es ist nicht offensichtlich, dass sie betrunken ist; **~!** natürlich!, selbstverständlich!; **is he there? – well, ~ not** ist er da? – offensichtlich nicht; **~ he's not going to like it** das wird ihm natürlich nicht gefallen; **he's ~ not going to get the job** er bekommt die Stelle nicht, das ist ja klar *(inf)*

obviousness ['ɒbvɪəsnɪs] N Offensichtlichkeit *f*, Deutlichkeit *f*; **amused by the ~ of his reply** belustigt über die Eindeutigkeit *or* Plumpheit seiner Antwort

OC N *abbr of* **Officer Commanding** *(Mil)* Oberbefehlshaber(in) *m(f)*; **who's OC paper supply in the office?** *(inf)* wer ist hier im Büro der Papierhengst? *(inf)*

ocarina [,ɒkə'ri:nə] N Okarina *f*

Occam's razor ['ɒkəmz'reɪzəʳ] N **to apply ~ to sth** etw komprimieren, etw auf das Wesentliche beschränken

occasion [ə'keɪʒən] N **a** *(= point in time)* Gelegenheit *f*, Anlass *m*; **on that ~** damals, bei *or* zu jener Gelegenheit *or* jenem Anlass *(geh)*; **on another ~** ein anderes Mal, bei einer anderen Gelegenheit *etc*; **on several ~s** mehrmals, bei *or* zu mehreren Gelegenheiten *etc*; **(on) the first ~** beim ersten Mal, das erste Mal; **on ~** gelegentlich; *(= if need be)* wenn nötig; **it does not befit the ~** es ist unpassend für diesen *or* zu diesem Anlass; **to rise to the ~** sich der Lage gewachsen zeigen

b *(= special time)* Ereignis *nt*; **~s of state** Staatsanlässe *pl*; **on the ~ of his birthday** anlässlich *or* aus Anlass seines Geburtstages *(geh)*; **one's 21st birthday should be something of an ~** ein 21. Geburtstag sollte schon ein besonderes Ereignis sein

c *(= opportunity)* Gelegenheit *f*, Möglichkeit *f*; **I never had the ~ to congratulate him** es bot sich mir keine Gelegenheit *or* ich hatte nicht die Möglichkeit, ihm zu gratulieren; **I would like to take this ~ to ...** *(form)* ich möchte diese Gelegenheit ergreifen, um ...

d *(= reason)* Grund *m*, Anlass *m*, Veranlassung *f*; **should the ~ arise** sollte es nötig sein *or* werden; **to give ~ to sth** *(form)* zu etw Anlass geben; **if you have ~ to ...** sollten Sie Veranlassung haben, zu ...; **not an ~ for merriment** kein Grund zur Freude

VT *(form)* verursachen, Anlass geben zu, zeitigen *(geh)*; **to ~ sb to do sth** jdn dazu veranlassen, etw zu tun

occasional [ə'keɪʒənl] ADJ **a** *visit, visitor, meeting, outburst, lapse* gelegentlich; **he likes an** *or* **the ~ cigar** er raucht hin und wieder ganz gerne *or* gelegentlich ganz gern eine Zigarre; **she made ~ visits to England** sie fuhr ab und zu nach England **b** *(= designed for special event)* Gelegenheits-; **~ poem** Gelegenheitsgedicht *nt*

occasionally [ə'keɪʒənəlɪ] ADV gelegentlich, hin und wieder, zuweilen *(geh)*; **very ~** sehr selten, nicht sehr oft

occasional table N kleiner Wohnzimmertisch

occident ['ɒksɪdənt] N *(liter)* Abendland *nt*, Okzident *m (geh)*; **the Occident** *(Pol)* der Westen

occidental [,ɒksɪ'dentəl] ADJ *(liter)* abendländisch N *(rare)* Abendländer(in) *m(f)*

occipital [ɒk'sɪpɪtəl] ADJ *(spec)* des Hinterkopfs

occiput ['ɒksɪpʌt] N *(spec)* Hinterkopf *m*

occlude [ɒ'klu:d] *(spec)* VT *(Anat, Med) pores, artery* verschließen, verstopfen, okkludieren *(spec)*; *(Chem) gas* adsorbieren VI *(Dentistry)* eine normale Bissstellung haben

occluded front [ɒ'klu:dɪd'frʌnt] N *(Met)* Okklusion *f*

occlusion [ɒ'klu:ʒən] N *(spec)* *(Med: of artery)* Verschluss *m*, Okklusion *f (spec)*; *(Dentistry)* Biss *m*, normale Bissstellung; *(Phon)* Verschluss *m*; *(Chem)* Adsorption *f*; *(Met)* Okklusion *f*

occult [ɒ'kʌlt] ADJ okkult; *(= of occultism)* okkultistisch; *(= secret)* geheimnisvoll N Okkulte(s) *nt*

occultism ['ɒkəltɪzəm] N Okkultismus *m*

occultist [ɒ'kʌltɪst] N Okkultist(in) *m(f)*

occupancy ['ɒkjʊpənsɪ] N Bewohnen *nt*; *(= period)* Wohndauer *f*; **a change of ~** ein Besitzerwechsel *m*; *(of rented property)* ein Mieterwechsel *m*; **multiple ~** Mehrfachbelegung *f* von Wohnraum; **levels of hotel ~** Übernachtungsziffern *pl*

occupant ['ɒkjʊpənt] N *(of house)* Bewohner(in) *m(f)*; *(of post)* Inhaber(in) *m(f)*; *(of car)* Insasse *m*, Insassin *f*

occupation [,ɒkjʊ'peɪʃən] N **a** *(= employment)* Beruf *m*, Tätigkeit *f*; **what is his ~?** was ist er von Beruf?, welche Tätigkeit übt er aus?; **he is a teacher by ~** er ist Lehrer von Beruf **b** *(= pastime)* Beschäftigung *f*, Betätigung *f*, Tätigkeit *f* **c** *(Mil)* Okkupation *f*; *(= act)* Besetzung *f* *(of* von), Okkupation *f* *(of* von); **army of ~** Besatzungsarmee *f* **d** *(of house etc)* Besetzung *f*; **to be in ~ of a house** ein Haus bewohnen; **ready for ~** bezugsfertig, schlüsselfertig; **we found them already in ~** wir sahen, dass sie schon eingezogen waren ADJ Besatzungs-, Okkupations-; **~ troops** Besatzungs- *or* Okkupationstruppen *pl*

occupational [,ɒkjʊ'peɪʃənl] ADJ Berufs-, beruflich; **~ accident** Berufsunfall *m*; **~ disease** Berufskrankheit *f*; **~ group** Berufsgruppe *f*; **~ hazard** *or* **risk** Berufsrisiko *nt*

occupationally [,ɒkjʊ'peɪʃənəlɪ] ADV beruflich; **equality for women politically and ~** die Gleichberechtigung der Frau in Politik und Beruf

occupational: **occupational pension (scheme)** N betriebliche Altersversorgung; **Occupational Safety and Health Administration** N *(US)* Arbeitsschutzbehörde *f*; **occupational therapist** N Beschäftigungstherapeut(in) *m(f)*; **occupational therapy** N Beschäftigungstherapie *f*

occupied ['ɒkjʊpaɪd] ADJ **a** *house, room* belegt; **a room ~ by four people** ein von vier Personen bewohntes Zimmer; **is this seat ~?** ist dieser Platz belegt? **b** *(Mil etc) country, territory* besetzt **c** *(= busy)* beschäftigt; **to be ~ with sth** mit etw beschäftigt sein; **to keep sb ~** jdn beschäftigen; **that'll keep him ~** dann hat er was zu tun, dann ist er beschäftigt; **he kept his mind ~** er beschäftigte sich geistig

occupier ['ɒkjʊpaɪəʳ] N *(of house, land)* Bewohner(in) *m(f)*; *(of post)* Inhaber(in) *m(f)*

occupy ['ɒkjʊpaɪ] VT **a** *house* bewohnen; *seat, room* belegen, besetzen; *hotel room* belegen; **you ~ a special place in my heart** du hast einen besonderen Platz in meinem Herzen (inne)

b *(Mil etc)* besetzen; *country* okkupieren, besetzen

c *post, position* innehaben, bekleiden *(geh)*

d *(= take up)* beanspruchen; *space* einnehmen; *time* in Anspruch nehmen, beanspruchen; *(= help pass)* ausfüllen; **can't you find some better way of ~ing your time?** kannst du mit deiner Zeit nicht etwas Besseres anfangen?

e *(= busy)* beschäftigen; **to ~ oneself** sich beschäftigen; **a thought which has been ~ing my mind** ein Gedanke, der mich beschäftigt

occur [ə'kɜ:ʳ] VI **a** *(= take place) (event)* geschehen, sich ereignen, vorkommen; *(difficulty)* sich ergeben; *(change)* stattfinden; **that doesn't ~ very often** das kommt nicht oft vor, das gibt es nicht oft; **don't let it ~ again** lassen Sie das nicht wieder vorkommen, dass das nicht wieder passiert!; **should a fault ~** sollte ein Fehler auftreten; **if the opportunity ~s** wenn sich die Gelegenheit bietet *or* ergibt

b *(= be found: disease)* vorkommen

c *(= come to mind)* einfallen, in den Sinn kommen *(geh)* *(to sb* jdm); **if it ~s to you that he is wrong** falls es Ihnen so vorkommt, als habe er sich geirrt; **it ~s to me that ...** ich habe den Eindruck, dass ...; **the idea just ~red to me** es ist mir gerade eingefallen; **it never ~red to me** darauf bin ich noch nie gekommen; **it didn't even ~ to him to ask** er kam erst gar nicht auf den Gedanken, zu fragen; **did it ever ~ to you to apologize?** hast du eigentlich je daran gedacht, dich zu entschuldigen?

occurrence [ə'kʌrəns] N **a** *(= event)* Ereignis *nt*, Begebenheit *f* **b** *(= presence, taking place)* Auftreten *nt*; *(of minerals)* Vorkommen *nt*; **further ~s of this nature must be avoided** weitere Vorkommnisse dieser Art müssen vermieden werden

ocean ['əʊʃən] N **a** Ozean *m*, Meer *nt* **b an ~ of flowers** ein Blumenmeer *nt*; **~s of** *(inf)* jede Menge *(inf)*, massenhaft

ocean: **ocean bed** N Meeresboden *m or* -grund *m*; **ocean chart** N Seekarte *f*; **ocean climate** N Meeresklima *nt*, maritimes Klima; **ocean-going** ADJ hochseetauglich; **~ tug** Hochseeschlepper *m*

Oceania [,əʊʃɪ'eɪnɪə] N Ozeanien *nt*

Oceanian [,əʊʃɪ'eɪnɪən] ADJ ozeanisch N Ozeanier(in) *m(f)*

oceanic [,əʊʃɪ'ænɪk] ADJ **a** Meeres-; **~ plant** Meerespflanze *f* **b** *(fig)* riesenhaft

ocean liner N Ozeandampfer *m*

oceanographer [ˌəʊʃəˈnɒgrəfəʳ] N Ozeanograf(in) *m(f)*, Meereskundler(in) *m(f)*

oceanography [ˌəʊʃəˈnɒgrəfɪ] N Ozeanografie *f*, Meereskunde *f*

ocean: **Ocean State** N **the ~** *(US)* Rhode Island *nt*; **ocean voyage** N Schiffsreise *f*, Seereise *f*

ocelot [ˈɒsɪlɒt] N Ozelot *m*

och [ɒx] INTERJ *(Scot)* ach was, ach wo; **~ aye** ach ja

ochre, *(US)* **ocher** [ˈəʊkəʳ] **N** Ocker *m or nt*; **red ~** roter *or* rotes Ocker; **yellow ~** *(= substance)* Ocker *m or nt*; *(= colour)* Ocker *m or nt*, Ockergelb *nt* **ADJ** ockerfarben

o'clock [əˈklɒk] ADV **a** **at 5 ~** um 5 Uhr; **it is 5 ~ in the morning/evening** es ist 5 Uhr morgens/abends; **what ~ is it?** *(obs)* was ist die Uhr?; **the 9 ~ news** die 9-Uhr-Nachrichten; **the 9 ~ train** der 9-Uhr-Zug **b** **aircraft approaching at 5 ~** Flugzeug aus Südsüdost

OCR *abbr of* **optical character reader, optical character recognition ~ font** OCR-Schrift *f*

Oct *abbr of* **October** Okt.

octagon [ˈɒktəgən] N Achteck *nt*, Oktogon *nt*, Oktagon *nt*

octagonal [ɒkˈtægənl] ADJ achteckig, oktogonal

octahedron [ˌɒktəˈhiːdrən] N Oktaeder *m*, Achtflächner *m*

octane [ˈɒkteɪn] N Oktan *nt*; **high-~ fuel** Benzin *nt* mit hoher Oktanzahl

octane number, **octane rating** N Oktanzahl *f*

octangle [ˈɒktæŋgl] N *(Math)* Achteck *nt*

octave [ˈɒktɪv] N **a** *(Mus)* Oktave *f* **b** *(of sonnet)* Oktett *nt*

octavo [ɒkˈteɪvəʊ] N Oktav(format) *nt*; *(also* **octavo volume**) Oktavband *m*

octet [ɒkˈtet] N *(Mus, Poet)* Oktett *nt*

October [ɒkˈtəʊbəʳ] N Oktober *m*; **the ~ Revolution** die Oktoberrevolution → *also* **September**

octogenarian [ˌɒktəʊdʒɪˈnɛərɪən] **N** Achtziger(in) *m(f)*, Achtzigjährige(r) *mf* **ADJ** achtzigjährig

octopus [ˈɒktəpəs] N Tintenfisch *m*, Krake *f*

ocular [ˈɒkjʊləʳ] ADJ *(form)* okular *(spec)*

oculist [ˈɒkjʊlɪst] N Augenspezialist(in) *m(f)*

OD *(inf)* **N** Überdosis *f* **VI** eine Überdosis nehmen; **to OD on heroin** sich *(dat)* den goldenen Schuss setzen *(inf)*

odalisque [ˈəʊdəlɪsk] N Odaliske *f*

odd [ɒd] **ADJ** (+er) **a** *(= peculiar)* merkwürdig, seltsam, sonderbar; *person, thing, idea* eigenartig, seltsam; **how ~ that we should meet him** (wie) eigenartig *or* seltsam, dass wir ihn trafen; **it is an ~ thing to do** es ist seltsam, so etwas zu tun; **the ~ thing about it is that ...** das Merkwürdige *etc* daran ist, dass ...; **there was something ~ about it** daran stimmte irgendetwas nicht; **it seemed ~ to me** es kam mir komisch vor; **he's got some ~ ways** er hat eine schrullige *or* verschrobene Art

b *number* ungerade

c *(= one of a pair or a set) shoe, glove* einzeln; **he/she is (the) ~ man** *or* **one out** er/sie ist übrig *or* überzählig *or* das fünfte Rad am Wagen; *(in character)* er/sie steht (immer) abseits, er/sie ist ein Außenseiter/eine Außenseiterin; **in each group underline the word/picture which is the ~ man** *or* **one out** unterstreichen Sie in jeder Gruppe das nicht dazugehörige Wort/Bild

d *(= slightly over)* **600-~ euros** gut 600 Euro

e *(= surplus, extra)* übrig, restlich, überzählig; **the ~ one left over** der/die/das Überzählige; **have you got an ~ piece of paper?** haben Sie ein Blatt Papier übrig?

f *(= not regular or specific) moments, times* zeitweilig; *(Comm) size* ausgefallen; **any ~ piece of wood** irgendein Stück(chen) Holz; **at ~ moments** *or* **times** ab und zu; **at ~ moments during the day** zwischendurch; **he likes the ~ drink** er trinkt gerne mal einen; **~ job** (gelegentlich) anfallende Arbeit; **he does all the ~ jobs** er macht alles, was an Arbeit anfällt

ADV *(inf)* **he was acting a bit ~** er benahm sich etwas komisch

oddball [ˈɒdbɔːl] *(inf)* **N** Spinner(in) *m(f)*; *(more harmless)* komischer Kauz; *(less harmless: = weirdo)* Verrückte(r) *mf* **ADJ** *ideas, friends* komisch

odd bod [ˈɒdbɒd] N *(Brit inf)* komischer Kauz

oddity [ˈɒdɪtɪ] N **a** *(= strangeness) (of person)* Wunderlichkeit *f*, Absonderlichkeit *f*, Eigenartigkeit *f*; *(= strangeness: of thing)* Ausgefallenheit *f* **b** *(= odd person)* komischer Kauz *or* Vogel; *(who doesn't fit)* Kuriosität *f*; *(= odd thing)* Kuriosität *f*

odd-jobman [ˌɒdˈdʒɒbmæn] Mädchen *nt* für alles

oddly [ˈɒdlɪ] ADV *speak, behave* eigenartig, sonderbar, merkwürdig; **an ~ shaped room** ein Raum, der eine seltsame Form hat; **I find her ~ attractive** ich finde sie auf (eine) seltsame Art anziehend; **they are ~ similar** sie sind sich seltsam *or* merkwürdig ähnlich; **the street was ~ familiar** die Straße kam mir merkwürdig bekannt vor; **~ enough she was at home** merkwürdigerweise *or* seltsamerweise war sie zu Hause; **~ enough you are right** Sie werden überrascht sein, aber das stimmt

oddment [ˈɒdmənt] N *usu pl* Restposten *m*; *(of cloth also)* Rest *m*; *(= single piece also)* Einzelstück *nt*

oddness [ˈɒdnɪs] N Merkwürdigkeit *f*, Seltsamkeit *f*

odds [ɒdz] PL **a** *(Betting)* Odds *pl*; *(of bookmaker)* Kurse *pl*, Odds *pl*; **the ~ are 6 to 1** die Chancen stehen 6 zu 1 *(written: 6:1)*; **long/short ~** geringe/hohe Gewinnchancen *pl*; **he won at long ~** er hat mit einer hohen Gewinnquote gewonnen; **fixed ~** feste Kurse *pl*; **to lay** *or* **give ~ of 2 to 1 (against sb)** den Kurs mit 2 zu 1 *(written: 2:1)* (gegen jdn) angeben; **I'll lay ~ (of 3 to 1) that ...** *(fig)* ich wette (3 gegen 1), dass ...

b *(= chances for or against)* Chance(n) *f(pl)*; **the ~ were against us** alles sprach gegen uns; **in spite of the tremendous ~ against him ...** obwohl alles so völlig gegen ihn sprach *or* war ...; **the ~ were in our favour** *(Brit) or* **favor** *(US)* alles sprach für uns; **against all the ~ he won** wider Erwarten *or* entgegen allen Erwartungen gewann er; **what are the ~ on/against ...?** wie sind *or* stehen die Chancen, dass .../dass ... nicht?; **to fight against heavy/overwhelming ~** *(Mil)* gegen eine große/überwältigende gegnerische Übermacht ankämpfen; **to struggle against impossible ~** so gut wie keine Aussicht auf Erfolg haben; **the ~ are that he will come** es sieht ganz so aus, als ob er käme *or* kommen würde; **to lengthen/shorten the ~** die Chancen erhöhen/verringern

c *(inf)* **to pay over the ~** zu viel bezahlen; **foreign buyers who are prepared to pay over the ~** Ausländer, die gewillt sind, überhöhte Preise zu bezahlen

d *(= difference)* **what's the ~?** was macht das schon (aus)?; **it makes no ~** es spielt keine Rolle; **it makes no ~ to me** es ist mir (völlig) einerlei; **does it really make any ~ if I don't come?** macht es etwas aus, wenn ich nicht komme?

e *(= variance)* **to be at ~ with sb over sth** mit jdm in etw *(dat)* nicht übereinstimmen; **we are at ~ as to the best solution** wir gehen nicht darin einig, wie das am besten gelöst werden soll; **to be at ~ with oneself** mit sich selbst nicht klarkommen

odds and ends PL Krimskrams *m*, Kram *m*; *(of food)* Reste *pl*; *(of cloth)* Reste *pl*, Flicken *pl*; **bring all your ~** bringen Sie Ihren ganzen Kram *or* Ihre Siebensachen *(inf)*

odds and sods PL *(Brit hum inf)* Kleinkram *m*; **I've got a few ~ to tidy up** ich muss hier und da noch ein paar Sachen in Ordnung bringen; **a few ~** *(= people)* ein paar Leute

odds-on [ˈɒdzɒn] **ADJ** **the ~ favourite** *(Brit) or* **favorite** *(US)* der klare Favorit; **she's ~ favourite** *(Brit) or* **favorite** *(US)* **for the job** sie hat die größten Aussichten, die Stelle zu bekommen; **he has an ~ chance (of winning)** er hat die besten (Gewinn)chancen **ADV** **it's ~ that he'll come** es ist so gut wie sicher, dass er kommt

ode [əʊd] N Ode *f* *(to, on* an *+acc)*

odious [ˈəʊdɪəs] ADJ *person* abstoßend, ekelhaft; *action* abscheulich, verabscheuenswürdig; **an ~ person** ein Ekel *nt*; **what an ~ thing to say** wie abscheulich, so etwas zu sagen; **to make ~ comparisons** hässliche Vergleiche machen

odium [ˈəʊdɪəm] N *(= being hated)* Hass *m*; *(= repugnance)* Abscheu *m*

odometer [ɒˈdɒmɪtəʳ] N Kilometerzähler *m*

odontologist [ˌɒdɒnˈtɒlədʒɪst] N Odontologe *m*, Odontologin *f*, Facharzt *m*/-ärztin *f* für Zahnheilkunde

odontology [ˌɒdɒnˈtɒlədʒɪ] N Odontologie *f*, Zahnheilkunde *f*

odor *etc (US)* = **odour** *etc*

odoriferous [ˌəʊdəˈrɪfərəs] ADJ *(form)* wohlriechend, duftend

odorous [ˈəʊdərəs] ADJ *(esp poet)* duftend, wohlriechend

odour, *(US)* **odor** [ˈəʊdəʳ] N **a** *(lit, fig)* Geruch *m*; *(= sweet smell)* Duft *m*, Wohlgeruch *m*; *(= bad smell)* Gestank *m* **b** **to be in good/bad ~ with sb** gut/schlecht bei jdm angeschrieben sein

odour-free, *(US)* **odor-free** [ˈəʊdəfriː] ADJ geruchsfrei

odourless, *(US)* **odorless** [ˈəʊdəlɪs] ADJ geruchlos

Odyssey [ˈɒdɪsɪ] N *(Myth, fig)* Odyssee *f*

OE *abbr of* **Old English**

OECD *abbr of* **Organization for Economic Cooperation and Development** OECD *f*

oecumenical [ˌiːkjuːˈmenɪkəl] ADJ = **ecumenical**

oedema, *(US)* **edema** [ɪˈdiːmə] N Ödem *nt*

Oedipus [ˈiːdɪpəs] N Ödipus *m*

Oedipus complex [ˈiːdɪpəsˈkɒmpleks] N Ödipuskomplex *m*

OEIC [ɔɪk] N ABBR *of* **open-ended investment company** *(Brit Fin)* Investmentgesellschaft *f (mit eingeschränkten Befugnissen)*

o'er [ˈəʊəʳ] PREP, ADV *(poet) contr of* **over**

oesophagus, *(US)* **esophagus** [iːˈsɒfəgəs] N Speiseröhre *f*

oestrogen [ˈiːstrəʊdʒən] N *(Brit) (Med, Pharm)* Östrogen *nt*

of [ɒv, əv] PREP **a** *(indicating possession or relation)* von *(+dat)*, *use of gen*; **the wife of the doctor** die Frau des Arztes, die Frau vom Arzt; **a friend of ours** ein Freund/eine Freundin von uns; **a painting of the Queen** ein Gemälde *nt* der *or* von der Königin; **a painting of the Queen's** *(= belonging to her)* ein Gemälde (im Besitz) der Königin; *(= painted by her)* ein Gemälde (von) der Königin; **of it** davon; **the first of May** der Erste Mai; **the first of the month** der Erste (des Monats), der Monatserste; **that damn dog of theirs** *(inf)* ihr verdammter Hund *(inf)*; **it is very kind of you** es ist sehr freundlich von Ihnen; **it was nasty of him to say that** es war gemein von ihm, das zu sagen

b *(indicating separation in space or time)* **south of Paris** südlich von Paris; **within a month of his death** einen Monat nach seinem Tod; **a quarter of six** *(US)* Viertel vor sechs

c *(indicating cause)* **he died of poison/cancer** er starb an Gift/Krebs; **he died of hunger** er verhungerte, er starb hungers *(geh)*; **it did not happen of itself** *(liter)* das ist nicht von selbst *or* von allein geschehen; **it tastes of garlic** es schmeckt nach Knoblauch; **she is proud of him** sie ist stolz auf ihn; **I am ashamed of it** ich schäme mich dafür

d *(indicating deprivation, riddance)* **he was cured of the illness** er wurde von der Krankheit geheilt; **trees bare of leaves** Bäume ohne Blätter;

free of charge kostenlos
e *(indicating material)* aus; **dress made of wool** Wollkleid *nt*, Kleid *nt* aus Wolle
f *(indicating quality, identity etc)* **house of ten rooms** Haus *nt* mit zehn Zimmern; **man of courage** mutiger Mensch, Mensch *m* mit Mut; **girl of ten** zehnjähriges Mädchen, Mädchen *nt* von zehn Jahren; **a matter of no importance** eine Sache ohne Bedeutung; **the city of Paris** die Stadt Paris; **person of swarthy complexion** dunkelhäutige Person; **a town of narrow streets** eine Stadt mit engen Straßen; **where is that rascal of a boy?** wo ist dieser verflixte Bengel?; **that idiot of a waiter** dieser Idiot von Kellner
g *(objective genitive)* **fear of God** Gottesfurcht *f*; **his love of his father** die Liebe zu seinem Vater; **he is a leader of men** er hat die Fähigkeit, Menschen zu führen; **great eaters of fruit** große Obstesser *pl*; **writer of legal articles** Verfasser von juristischen Artikeln; **love of money** Liebe zum Geld
h *(subjective genitive)* **love of God for man** Liebe Gottes zu den Menschen; **affection of a mother** Mutterliebe *f*
i *(partitive genitive)* **the whole of the house** das ganze Haus; **half of the house** das halbe Haus; **how many of them do you want?** wie viele möchten Sie (davon)?; **many of them came** viele (von ihnen) kamen; **there were six of us** wir waren zu sechst, wir waren sechs; **he is not one of us** er gehört nicht zu uns; **one of the best** einer der Besten; **he asked the six of us to lunch** er lud uns sechs zum Mittagessen ein; **of the ten only one was absent** von den zehn fehlte nur einer; **today of all days** ausgerechnet heute; **you of all people ought to know** gerade Sie sollten das wissen; **they are the best of friends** sie sind die besten Freunde; **the best of teachers** der (aller)beste Lehrer; **the bravest of the brave** der Mutigste der Mutigen; **he drank of the wine** *(liter)* er trank von dem Weine *(liter)*
j *(= concerning)* **what do you think of him?** was halten Sie von ihm?; **what has become of him?** was ist aus ihm geworden?; **he warned us of the danger** er warnte uns vor der Gefahr; **doctor of medicine** Doktor der Medizin; **what of it?** ja und?
k *(obs, liter, = by)* **forsaken of men** von allen verlassen; **beloved of all** von allen geliebt
l *(in temporal phrases)* **he's become very quiet of late** er ist letztlich *or* seit Neuestem so ruhig geworden; **they go out of an evening** *(inf)* sie gehen abends (schon mal) aus *(inf)*; **he died of a Saturday morning** *(dial)* er starb an einem Samstagmorgen

off [ɒf] ADV **a** *(distance)* **the house is 5 km ~** das Haus ist 5 km entfernt; **some way ~ (from here)** in einiger Entfernung (von hier); **it's a long way ~** das ist weit weg; *(time)* das liegt in weiter Ferne; **August isn't/the exams aren't very far ~** es ist nicht mehr lang bis August/bis zu den Prüfungen; **Christmas is only a week ~** es ist nur noch eine Woche bis Weihnachten; **noises ~** *(Theat)* Geräusche *pl* hinter den Kulissen
b *(departure)* **to be/go ~** gehen; **he's ~ to school** er ist zur Schule gegangen; **(be) ~ with you!** fort mit dir!, mach, dass du wegkommst!; **~ with him!** fort *or* weg mit ihm!; **I must be ~** ich muss (jetzt) gehen *or* weg *(inf)*; **it's time I was ~** es wird *or* ist (höchste) Zeit, dass ich gehe; **where are you ~ to?** wohin gehen Sie denn?, wohin gehts denn? *(inf)*; **~ we go!** los!, auf los gehts los!, na denn man los! *(inf)*; **he's ~ playing tennis every evening** er geht jeden Abend Tennis spielen; **they're ~** *(Sport)* sie sind vom Start; **she's ~ again** *(inf: = complaining etc)* sie legt schon wieder los *(inf)*
c *(removal)* **he had his coat ~** er hatte den Mantel aus; **he helped me ~ with my coat** er half mir aus dem Mantel; **with his shirt ~** ohne Hemd; **~ with those wet clothes!** raus aus den nassen Kleidern!; **the handle has come ~** der Griff ist abgegangen; **there are two buttons ~** es fehlen zwei Knöpfe, da sind zwei Knöpfe ab *(inf)*; **~ with his head!** herunter mit seinem Kopf!, Kopf ab!; **he had the back of the TV ~** er hatte die Rückwand des Fernsehers abgenommen; **the lid is ~** der Deckel ist nicht drauf
d *(= discount)* **3% ~** *(Comm)* 3% Nachlass *or* Abzug; **3% ~ for cash** *(Comm)* 3% Skonto, bei Barzahlung 3%; **to give sb £5/something ~** jdm £ 5 Ermäßigung/eine Ermäßigung geben; **he let me have £5 ~** er gab es mir (um) £ 5 billiger
e *(= not at work)* **to have time ~ to do sth** (Zeit) freibekommen haben, um etw zu tun; **I've got a day ~** ich habe einen Tag frei(bekommen); **she's nearly always ~ on Tuesdays** dienstags hat sie fast immer frei; **to be ~ sick** wegen Krankheit fehlen
f *(in phrases)* **~ and on, on and ~** ab und zu, ab und an; **it rained ~ and on** es regnete mit Unterbrechungen; **right** *or* **straight ~** gleich
ADJ **a** *attr (= substandard) year, day etc* schlecht; **I'm having an ~ day today** ich bin heute nicht in Form
b *pred (Brit: = not fresh)* verdorben, schlecht; *milk* schlecht, sauer; *butter* ranzig; **to go ~** schlecht werden
c *pred (= cancelled) match, party, talks* abgesagt; *(= not available: in restaurant) chops, fish* aus; **I'm afraid veal is ~ today** Kalbfleisch gibt es heute leider nicht; **the bet/agreement is ~** die Wette/Abmachung gilt nicht (mehr); **their engagement is ~** ihre Verlobung ist gelöst; **the play is ~** *(= cancelled)* das Stück wurde abgesagt; *(= no longer running)* das Stück wurde abgesetzt
d *TV, light, machine* aus(geschaltet); *tap* zu(gedreht); **the gas/electricity was ~** das Gas/der Strom war abgeschaltet; **the brake was ~** die Bremse war gelöst
e **they are badly/well** *or* **comfortably ~** sie sind nicht gut/(ganz) gut gestellt, sie stehen sich schlecht/(ganz) gut; **I am badly ~ for money/time** mit Geld/Zeit sieht es bei mir nicht gut aus; **how are we ~ for time?** wie sieht es mit der Zeit aus?, wie viel Zeit haben wir noch?; **he is better/worse ~ staying in England** er steht sich in England besser/schlechter
f *pred (= wide of the truth etc)* **you're ~ there** da irrst du gewaltig, da vertust du dich; **he was quite a bit ~ in his calculations** er hatte sich in seinen Berechnungen ziemlich *or* schwer *(inf)* vertan
g *pred (inf)* **that's a bit ~!** das ist ein dicker Hund! *(inf)*; **it's a bit ~ not letting me know** das ist ja nicht die feine Art, mir nicht Bescheid zu sagen; **his behaviour** *(Brit) or* **behavior** *(US)* **was a bit ~** er hat sich ziemlich danebenbenommen; **she's been a bit ~ with me all week** sie hat sich die ganze Woche mir gegenüber etwas komisch verhalten; *(= has been angry)* sie war die ganze Woche über etwas sauer auf mich *(inf)*
PREP **a** *(indicating motion, removal etc)* von *(+dat)*; **he jumped ~ the roof** er sprang vom Dach; **once you are ~ the premises** sobald Sie vom Gelände (herunter) sind; **I got it ~ my friend** *(inf)* ich habs von meinem Freund (gekriegt) *(inf)*; **he borrowed money ~ his father** *(inf)* er lieh sich *(dat)* von seinem Vater Geld; **they dined ~ chicken** sie aßen Hühnchen; **we live ~ cheese on toast** wir leben von Käse und Toastbrot; **I'll take something ~ the price for you** ich lasse Ihnen vom *or* im Preis etwas nach; **he got £2 ~ the shirt** er bekam das Hemd £ 2 billiger; **the lid had been left ~ the tin** jemand hatte den Deckel nicht wieder auf die Büchse getan; **the coat has two buttons ~ it** am Mantel fehlen zwei Knöpfe; **which coat is that button ~?** von welchem Mantel ist dieser Knopf?
b *(= distant from)* ab(gelegen) von *(+dat)*; *(= in a side street from)* in einer Nebenstraße von *(+dat)*; *(Naut)* vor *(+dat)*; **the house was just ~ the main road** das Haus lag in unmittelbarer Nähe der Hauptstraße; **one mile ~ the main road** eine Meile von der Hauptstraße weg *or* entfernt; **height ~ the ground** Höhe vom Boden (weg); **just ~ Piccadilly** in der Nähe von Piccadilly, gleich bei Piccadilly; **a road ~ Bank Street** eine Querstraße zur Bank Street
c **~ the map** nicht auf der Karte; **I just want it ~ my hands** ich möchte das nur loswerden → **duty, food** *etc*
d **I'm ~ sausages/beer/him** *(= don't like at the moment)* Wurst/Bier/er kann mich zurzeit nicht reizen

off: off air ADV *(TV, Rad)* nicht auf Sendung; **to go ~** *(broadcast)* enden; *(for good: station)* den Sendebetrieb einstellen; **off-air** ADJ *(TV, Rad) argument, discussion* bei abgeschaltetem Mikrofon; **a special ~ advice line** ein besonderes Sorgentelefon, dessen Gespräche nicht gesendet werden

offal [ˈɒfəl] N *no pl* Innereien *pl*; *(fig)* Abfall *m*, Ausschuss *m*

off: off-balance ADJ nicht im Gleichgewicht *pred*; **he was in an ~ position** er war aus dem Gleichgewicht gekommen → *also* **balance**; **off-beam** ADJ *(inf)* **to be ~** *(person, statement)* danebenliegen *(inf)*; **offbeat** ADJ **a** *(= unusual)* unkonventionell, ausgefallen, ungewöhnlich **b** *jazz* synkopiert N unbetonte Taktzeit;; **off-Broadway** ADJ *in New York außerhalb des Broadway aufgeführt/gelegen*, Off-Broadway-; **~ musical** Off-Broadway-Musical *nt* ADV *in New York außerhalb des Broadway*, off-Broadway

OFF-BROADWAY

Off-Broadway heißen in New York diejenigen Theaterproduktionen, die nicht in den berühmten Broadway-Häusern gespielt werden. Der Ausdruck wurde in den Fünfzigerjahren geprägt, als Dramatiker wie Tennessee Williams und Edward Albee kreative Low-Budget-Produktionen zur Aufführung brachten. Off-Broadway-Theater sind normalerweise kleiner und die Eintrittskarten kosten weniger als bei den berühmteren Häusern, wobei neben professionellen Truppen auch Laiengruppen Aufführungen anbieten.
Heute werden insbesondere avantgardistische Theater als **„off-off-Broadway"** bezeichnet.

off: off-campus ADJ *(Univ) activities* außerhalb der Universität; *area* außerhalb des Universitätsgeländes; **several colleges hold classes at ~ sites** mehrere Institute halten außerhalb des Universitätsgeländes Lehrveranstaltungen ab ADV außerhalb des Universitätsgeländes; **off-centre,** *(US)* **off-center** ADJ *(lit)* nicht in der Mitte; *construction* asymmetrisch; **his translation/explanation was a bit ~** seine Übersetzung/Erklärung war schief *or* ging an der Sache vorbei ADV *(= askew)* schief; **the tablecloth was hanging ~** die Tischdecke hing an einer Seite zu weit herunter; **off chance** N **I just did it on the ~** ich habe es auf gut Glück getan; **to do sth on the ~ that …** etw auf den Verdacht hin *or* in der unbestimmten Hoffnung tun, dass …; **he bought it on the ~ that it would come in useful** er kaufte es, weil es vielleicht irgendwann mal nützlich sein könnte; **I came on the ~ of seeing her** ich kam in der Hoffnung, sie vielleicht zu sehen; **off-colour,** *(US)* **off-color** ADJ *(esp Brit)* **a** *(= unwell)* unwohl; **to feel/be ~** sich nicht wohlfühlen, sich danebenfühlen *(inf)* **b** *(= indecent)* schlüpfrig, gewagt; **off-duty** ADJ *attr soldier, nurse, policeman* außer Dienst; *hours* dienstfrei; **there was nothing to do in their ~ hours** wenn sie außer Dienst waren, gab es für sie nichts zu tun

offence, *(US)* **offense** [əˈfens] N **a** *(Jur) (= crime)* Straftat *f*, Delikt *nt*; *(minor)* Vergehen *nt*; **to commit an ~** sich strafbar machen; **it is an ~ to …** … ist bei Strafe verboten; **first ~** erste Straftat, erstes Vergehen; **second ~** Rückfall *m*; **an ~ against …** ein Verstoß *m* gegen …
b *(fig)* **an ~ against good taste** eine Beleidigung des guten Geschmacks; **an ~ against common decency** eine Erregung öffentlichen Ärger-

nisses
c *no pl (to sb's feelings)* Kränkung *f*, Beleidigung *f*; *(to sense of decency, morality etc)* Anstoß *m*; **to cause** *or* **give ~ to sb** jdn kränken *or* beleidigen; **without giving ~** ohne kränkend zu sein; **to take ~ at sth** wegen etw gekränkt *or* beleidigt sein; **she is quick to take ~** sie ist leicht gekränkt *or* beleidigt; **I meant no ~** ich habe es nicht böse gemeint; **no ~ to the Germans, of course!** damit will/wollte ich natürlich nichts gegen die Deutschen gesagt haben; **no ~ (meant)** nichts für ungut; **no ~ (taken)** ich nehme dir das nicht übel
d *(Eccl, = sin)* Sünde *f*
e [ɒ'fens] *(= attack, US: = attacking part of team)* Angriff *m*; **~ is the best defence** *(Brit)* **offense is the best defense** *(US)* Angriff ist die beste Verteidigung

offend [ə'fend] **VT** **a** *(= hurt feelings of)* kränken; *(= be disagreeable to)* Anstoß erregen bei; **this novel would ~ a lot of people** dieser Roman würde bei vielen Leuten Anstoß erregen
b *ear, eye* beleidigen; *reason* verstoßen gegen; *sense of justice* gehen gegen, verletzen **VI** **a** *(= give offence)* beleidigend sein **b** *(= do wrong)* (ein) Unrecht tun, unrecht tun

▶ **offend against** **VI** *+prep obj taste, common sense* verstoßen gegen; *God* sündigen gegen

offended [ə'fendɪd] **ADJ** beleidigt, gekränkt; **don't be ~** seien Sie (doch) nicht beleidigt, nehmen Sie mir *etc* das nicht übel; **to be ~ by sth** sich von etw verletzt fühlen; **to look ~** eine beleidigte Miene machen

offender [ə'fendə'] **N** *(= law-breaker)* (Straf)täter(in) *m(f)*; *(against traffic laws)* Verkehrssünder(in) *m(f)*; **sex ~** Sexualstraftäter(in) *m(f)*; **who left that here? – I'm afraid I was the ~** wer hat das da liegen lassen? – ich war der Übeltäter; **they are the worst ~s when it comes to ...** wenn es um ... geht, sind sie die schlimmsten → **first offender, young offender**

offending [ə'fendɪŋ] **ADJ** **a** *(= giving offence) remark* kränkend, beleidigend **b** *(= law-breaking) person* zuwiderhandelnd; *behaviour* kriminell; **the ~ party** *(Jur)* die schuldige Partei; *(fig)* der/die Schuldige **c** *(= causing problem)* störend; *(= faulty) wire, part* defekt; **the ~ object** der Stein des Anstoßes

offense **N** *(US)* = **offence**

offensive [ə'fensɪv] **ADJ** **a** *(Jur)* Angriffs-; *(Mil)* Offensiv-; *action* offensiv; **~ play** *(Sport)* Offensivspiel *nt*; **~ player** Offensivspieler(in) *m(f)*
b *(= unpleasant) smell, sight* übel, abstoßend, widerlich; *language, film, book* anstößig, Anstoß erregend; *(= insulting, abusive) remark, gesture, behaviour* beleidigend, unverschämt; **his language was ~ to his parents** seine Ausdrucksweise erregte Anstoß bei seinen Eltern; **to find sb/sth ~** jdn/etw abstoßend finden; *behaviour, language* Anstoß an etw *(dat)* nehmen; **he was ~ to her** er beleidigte sie; **I don't mean to be ~** ich möchte nicht beleidigend wirken; **there's no need to get ~** kein Grund, ausfällig *or* ausfallend zu werden
N *(Mil, Sport)* Angriff *m*, Offensive *f*; **to take the ~** in die Offensive gehen; **to go over** *or* **on to the ~** zum Angriff übergehen; **on the ~** in der Offensive; **to mount an ~ (against sb/sth)** eine Offensive (gegen jdn/etw) starten

offensive capability **N** *(Mil)* Angriffsfähigkeit *f*

offensively [ə'fensɪvlɪ] **ADV** **a** *(= unpleasantly)* übel, widerlich; *(in moral sense)* anstößig; *(= abusively)* beleidigend, unverschämt; *(= obscenely)* unflätig **b** *(Mil, Sport)* offensiv

offensiveness [ə'fensɪvnɪs] **N** *(of smell, sight)* Widerlichkeit *f*; *(of language, film, book)* Anstößigkeit *f*; *(of remark, gesture, behaviour)* Unverschämtheit *f*

offensive operation **N** *(Mil)* Angriffsaktion *f*

offensive weapon **N** Angriffswaffe *f*, Offensivwaffe *f*

Offer ['ɒfə] **N** *(Brit) abbr of* **Office of Electricity Regulation** *Regulierungsbehörde für die Stromindustrie*

offer ['ɒfə'] ✪ 3.1, 18.1, 19.5, 20.2, 26.1 **N** Angebot *nt*; *(also* **offer of marriage***)* (Heirats)antrag *m*; **the ~'s there** das Angebot gilt *or* steht; **did you have many ~s of help?** haben Ihnen viele Leute ihre Hilfe angeboten?; **any ~s?** ist jemand interessiert?; **to make sb an ~ of sth** jdm etw anbieten; **he made me an ~ (of £50)** er machte mir ein Angebot (von £ 50); **an ~ I couldn't refuse** ein Angebot, zu dem ich nicht Nein *or* nein sagen konnte; **~s over £75,000** Angebote nicht unter £ 75.000; **on ~** *(Comm) (= on special offer)* im Angebot; *(= for sale)* verkäuflich → **near 3 b**
VT **a** *help, money, job, food, friendship etc* anbieten; *reward, prize* aussetzen; **to ~ to do sth** anbieten, etw zu tun; *(= offer one's services)* sich bereit erklären, etw zu tun; **he ~ed to give me £5 for it** er bot mir dafür £ 5 an; **he ~ed to help** er bot seine Hilfe an; **to ~ one's services** sich anbieten; **he was ~ed the job** ihm wurde die Stelle angeboten; **did he ~ to?** hat er sich angeboten?; **he's got nothing to ~** er hat nichts zu bieten
b *advice* anbieten; *plan, suggestion* unterbreiten; *remark* beisteuern; *excuse* vorbringen; *consolation* spenden; *condolences* aussprechen; **to ~ an opinion** sich (dazu) äußern; **to ~ one's resignation** seinen Rücktritt anbieten
c *(= present in worship or sacrifice) prayers, homage, sacrifice* darbringen; *one's life* opfern; **nuns ~ their lives to God** Nonnen stellen ihr Leben in den Dienst Gottes
d *(= put up, attempt to inflict) resistance* bieten; **to ~ violence** gewalttätig werden (*to* gegen) → **battle**
e *(= afford, make available) sleeping accommodation etc* bieten; **the bay ~ed a fine view** von der Bucht bot sich eine schöne Aussicht
f *subject (for exam)* machen
VI **whenever the opportunity ~s** wann immer sich die Gelegenheit bietet *or* ergibt; **did he ~?** hat er es angeboten?

▶ **offer up** **VT** *sep prayers, sacrifice* darbringen (*to sb* jdm); **to offer up one's life** sein Leben opfern; **to offer oneself up to a life of public service** sein Leben in den Dienst der Öffentlichkeit stellen

offering ['ɒfərɪŋ] **N** Gabe *f*; *(Rel) (= collection)* Opfergabe *f*; *(= sacrifice)* Opfer *nt*; *(iro: = essay, play etc)* Vorstellung *f*

offer price **N** Angebotspreis *m*

offertory ['ɒfətərɪ] **N** *(Eccl) (= part of service)* Opferung *f*, Offertorium *nt*; *(= collection)* Kollekte *f*, Geldsammlung *f*; **~ hymn** Lied *nt* während der Opferung

offertory box **N** *(Eccl)* Opferstock *m*

offhand [ˌɒf'hænd] **ADJ** *(also* **off-handed***: = casual) remark, manner* lässig; **to be ~ with sb** sich jdm gegenüber lässig benehmen; **to be ~ about sth** etw leichthin abtun **ADV** so ohne Weiteres, aus dem Stand *(inf)*; **I couldn't tell you ~** das könnte ich Ihnen auf Anhieb *or* so ohne Weiteres nicht sagen

offhandedly [ˌɒf'hændɪdlɪ] **ADV** lässig, leichthin

offhandedness [ˌɒf'hændɪdnɪs] **N** Lässigkeit *f*

office ['ɒfɪs] **N** **a** Büro *nt*; *(of lawyer)* Kanzlei *f*; *(= part of organization)* Abteilung *f*; *(= branch)* Geschäftsstelle *f*; **at the ~** im Büro; **local government ~s** Gemeindeverwaltung *f*
b *(= public position)* Amt *nt*; **to take ~** sein *or* das Amt antreten; *(political party)* die Regierung übernehmen, an die Regierung kommen; **to be in** *or* **hold ~** im Amt sein; *(party)* an der Regierung sein; **to be out of ~** nicht mehr an der Regierung sein; *(person)* nicht im Amt sein; **to be barred** *or* **disqualified from (holding) public ~** von allen öffentlichen Ämtern ausgeschlossen sein
c *(= duty)* Aufgabe *f*, Pflicht *f*
d *usu pl (= attention, help)* **through his good ~s** durch seine guten Dienste; **through the ~s of** ... durch Vermittlung von ...
e *(Eccl)* Gottesdienst *m*; **~ for the dead** Totenamt *nt*; *(RC)* Totenmesse *f*
f *(Brit)* **"usual ~s"** „übliche Nebenräume“

office: **office automation** **N** Büroautomation *f*; **office bearer** **N** Amtsträger(in) *m(f)*, Amtsinhaber(in) *m(f)*; **office block** **N** Bürohaus *or* -gebäude *nt*; **office boy** **N** Laufjunge *m*; **office clerk** **N** Büroangestellte(r) *mf*; **office furniture** **N** Büromöbel *pl*; **office holder** **N** Amtsinhaber(in) *m(f)*; **office hours** **PL** Arbeitsstunden *pl*, Dienstzeit *f*; *(on sign)* Geschäfts- *or* Öffnungszeiten *pl*; **to work ~** normale Arbeitszeiten haben; **office hunter** **N** Postenjäger(in) *m(f)*; **office job** **N** Stelle *f* im Büro; **office junior** **N** Bürogehilfe *m*/-gehilfin *f*; **office manager(ess)** **N** Büroleiter(in) *m(f)*; **Office of Fair Trading** **N** *(Brit)* Behörde *f* gegen unlauteren Wettbewerb; **Office of Management and Budget** **N** *(US) US-Behörde für die Verwaltung der Ministerien und der Vorbereitung des Haushalts*; **office party** **N** Büroparty *f*

officer ['ɒfɪsə'] **N** **a** *(Mil, Naut, Aviat)* Offizier(in) *m(f)*; **~ of the day** diensthabender Offizier, Offizier *m* vom Dienst; **Officers' Training Corps** *(Brit) Verband zur Offiziersausbildung*
b *(= official)* Beamte(r) *m*, Beamtin *f*; *(= police officer)* Polizeibeamte(r) *m*/-beamtin *f*, Polizist(in) *m(f)*; *(of club, society)* Vorstandsmitglied *nt*, Funktionär(in) *m(f)*; **medical ~** Amtsarzt *m*/-ärztin *f*; *(Mil)* Stabsarzt *m*/-ärztin *f*

officers' mess ['ɒfɪsəz'mes] **N** Offizierskasino *nt*

office: **office seeker** **N** *(esp US)* **a** *(= job seeker)* Stellensuchende(r) *mf* **b** *(= office hunter)* Postenjäger(in) *m(f)*; **office supplies** **PL** Büroartikel *pl*, Bürobedarf *m*; **office worker** **N** Büroangestellte(r) *mf*

official [ə'fɪʃəl] **ADJ** offiziell; *report, duties, meeting, visit also* amtlich; *(= formal) ceremony, style* förmlich, formell; *(= authorized) biography* autorisiert; **~ language** Amtssprache *f*; **~ religion** Staatsreligion *f*; **~ statement** amtliche Verlautbarung; **is that ~?** ist das amtlich?; *(= publicly announced)* ist das offiziell?; **~ residence** *(of mayor, governor)* Amtssitz *m*; **~ strike** offizieller Streik, gewerkschaftlich genehmigter Streik; **acting in one's ~ capacity** in Ausübung seiner Amtsgewalt; **~ uniform** Dienstuniform *f*
N *(= railway official, post office official etc)* Beamte(r) *m*, Beamtin *f*; *(of club, at race-meeting)* Funktionär(in) *m(f)*; **government ~** Regierungsbeamte(r) *m*/-beamtin *f*; **trade union ~** *(Brit)* Gewerkschaftsfunktionär(in) *m(f)*

officialdom [ə'fɪʃəldəm] **N** *(pej)* Bürokratie *f*, Beamtentum *nt*

officialese [əˌfɪʃə'liːz] **N** Behördensprache *f*, Beamtenchinesisch *nt (pej)*

officially [ə'fɪʃəlɪ] **ADV** offiziell; **~ approved** offiziell anerkannt

official: **Official Receiver** **N** Konkursverwalter(in) *m(f)*; **official seal** **N** Dienstsiegel *nt*, Amtssiegel *nt*; **official secret** **N** Dienstgeheimnis *nt*, Amtsgeheimnis *nt*; **Official Secrets Act** *(Brit)* Gesetz *nt* zur amtlichen Schweigepflicht

officiate [ə'fɪʃɪeɪt] **VT** amtieren, fungieren (*at* bei); **to ~ as president** als Präsident fungieren, das Amt des Präsidenten ausüben; **to ~ at a wedding** eine Trauung vornehmen

officious [ə'fɪʃəs] **ADJ** (dienst)beflissen, übereifrig; **to be ~** sich vor (Dienst)eifer überschlagen

officiousness [ə'fɪʃəsnɪs] **N** (Dienst)beflissenheit *f*, Übereifer *m*

offing ['ɒfɪŋ] **N** **in the ~** in Sicht; **there's a pay rise** *(Brit)* *or* **raise** *(US)* **in the ~ for us** uns steht eine Gehaltserhöhung bevor, wir haben Aussicht auf eine Gehaltserhöhung

offish **ADJ**, **offishly** **ADV** ['ɒfɪʃ, -lɪ] *(inf)* reserviert, unnahbar, kühl *(fig)*, steif *(fig)*

off: **off-key** **ADJ** *attr*, **off key** **ADJ** *pred (Mus)* falsch; **off-licence** **N** *(Brit)* **a** *(= shop)* Wein- und Spirituosenhandlung *f* **b** *(= permit)* Lizenz *f* zum Alkoholvertrieb *or* -verkauf, Alkohollizenz *f*; **off-limits** ADJ *attr*, **off limits** ADJ *pred* **a** *(= out of bounds) place* gesperrt; **this area is off limits** das Betreten dieses Gebiets ist verboten; **this room is off limits to** *or* **for the kids** die Kinder dürfen diesen Raum nicht betreten → *also* **limit N a b** *(fig: = forbidden) activity* verboten; **chocolates are off limits** Pralinen sind nicht erlaubt; **all drugs should be declared off limits for teenagers** alle Drogen sollten für Teenager verboten sein; **off line** *(Comput)* ADJ *pred* offline ADV off line; **to go ~** auf Offlinebetrieb schalten; **to put a printer ~** einen Drucker auf Offlinebetrieb schalten; **off-line** ADJ *attr (Comput)* Offline-; **~ mode** Offlinebetrieb *m*; **off-load** VT *goods* ausladen, entladen; *passengers* aussteigen lassen; **off-peak** ADJ **~ central heating** Nacht(strom)speicherheizung *f*; **~ electricity** Strom *m* außerhalb der Hauptabnahmezeit, Nachtstrom *m*; **~ charges** verbilligter Tarif; *(Elec)* ≈ Nachttarif *m*; **at ~ times, during ~ hours** außerhalb der Stoßzeiten; *(Telec)* außerhalb der Spitzenzeiten; **~ service** *(Rail)* Zugverkehr *m* außerhalb der Hauptverkehrszeit; **~ trains** Züge *pl* außerhalb der Hauptverkehrszeit; **~ ticket** verbilligte Fahrkarte/Flugkarte außerhalb der Stoßzeit; **off-piste** ADJ, ADV abseits der Piste; **offprint** N Sonderabdruck *m*; **off-putting** ADJ *(esp Brit) smell, behaviour* abstoßend; *sight also, meal* wenig einladend; *thought, idea, story* wenig ermutigend; *(= daunting)* entmutigend; *interviewer* wenig entgegenkommend; *job* unsympathisch; **it can be rather ~ to see how sausages are made** es kann einem den Appetit verderben *or* die Lust am Essen nehmen, wenn man sieht, wie Wurst gemacht wird; **off-road** ADJ *driving, racing* im Gelände; *car* geländegängig; **~ vehicle** Geländefahrzeug *nt*; **off-roader** N Geländefahrzeug *nt*; **off-sales** N *(Brit)* **a** *pl* Verkauf *m* aus dem Haus **b** *sing* = **off-licence a**; **off-screen** ADJ, ADV *(Film, TV: = in real life)* im wirklichen Leben; **off season** N *(in tourism)* Nebensaison *f*; **in the ~** außerhalb der Saison; **off-season** ADJ *travel, prices* außerhalb der Saison

offset [ˈɒfset] *pret, ptp* **offset** VT **a** *(financially, statistically etc)* ausgleichen; *(= make up for)* wettmachen, aufwiegen **b** [ɒfˈset] *(= place non-centrally)* versetzen N **a** *(Typ)* **~ (lithography/printing)** Offsetdruck *m* **b** *(Hort)* Ableger *m* **c** *(fig: = counterbalancing factor)* Ausgleich *m*; **as an ~** zum Ausgleich, als Ausgleich (*to* für)

off: **offshoot** N **a** *(of plant)* Ausläufer *m*, Ableger *m*; *(of tree)* Schössling *m*, Spross *m* **b** *(fig) (of family)* Nebenlinie *f*; *(of organization)* Nebenzweig *m*; *(of discussion, action etc)* Randergebnis *nt*; **offshore** ADJ **a** *island* küstennah; *wind* ablandig; *oilfield, installations etc* im Meer; **~ drilling rig** Bohrinsel *f*; **the ~ industry/business** *(= oil)* die Offshoreindustrie **b** *(Fin: = abroad) investment, funds* im Ausland ADV **a** *drill, explore* im Meer; *work, live* auf einer Bohrinsel; **20 miles ~** 20 Meilen vor der Küste; **the wind blew ~** der Wind kam vom Land; **the ship anchored ~** das Schiff ankerte vor der Küste; **a gentle current carried him ~** eine leichte Strömung trug ihn aufs Meer hinaus; **50% of our oil comes from ~** 50% unseres Erdöls kommt *or* stammt aus dem Meer **b** *(Fin: = abroad)* im Ausland; **to move one's operation ~** sein Unternehmen ins Ausland verlegen

offshore: **offshore banking** N *(Fin)* Offshorebankgeschäfte *pl*; **offshore company** N *(Fin)* Offshorefirma *f*; **offshore fishery** N Küstenfischerei *f*; **offshore well** N Offshorebohrloch *nt*; **offshore worker** N Offshorearbeiter(in) *m(f)*

offside [ˌɒfˈsaɪd] ADJ **a** *(Sport)* im Abseits; **to be ~** *(player)* im Abseits sein *or* stehen; *(goal)* ein Abseitstreffer *m* sein; **in an ~ position** in einer Abseitsposition, im Abseits; **~ rule** Abseitsregel *f*; **~ trap** Abseitsfalle *f* **b** *(Aut)* auf der Fahrerseite; *(when driving on the left also)* rechte(r, s); *(when driving on the right also)* linke(r, s) N *(Aut)* Fahrerseite *f* ADV *(Sport)* abseits, im Abseits

off site ADV außerhalb des Geländes

off-site [ˌɒfˈsaɪt] ADJ außerhalb des Geländes befindlich

offspring [ˈɒfsprɪŋ] N **a** *sing* Sprössling *m*, Kind *nt*, Abkömmling *m*; *(of animal)* Junge(s) *nt* **b** *pl (form, hum, of people)* Nachwuchs *m (hum)*, Nachkommen *pl*; *(of animals)* Junge *pl*; **how are your ~?** *(hum)* wie gehts dem Nachwuchs? *(hum)*

offstage [ˌɒfˈsteɪdʒ] ADJ hinter den Kulissen; *voice, music etc* aus den Kulissen; **his ~ life** sein Leben abseits der Bühne ADV *go, walk* von der Bühne; *stand* hinter den Kulissen; **she was booed ~** sie wurde von der Bühne gebuht

off: **off-street parking** N *(provided with flat/house, = single place)* Stellplatz *m*; *(= spaces)* Stellplätze *pl*; **there isn't much ~ in this area** in dieser Gegend gibt es wenige Parkhäuser und Parkplätze; **off-the-cuff** ADJ *remark, speech* aus dem Stegreif; **off-the-job training** N außerbetriebliche Weiterbildung; **off-the-peg** ADJ *attr*, **off the peg** ADJ *pred (Brit)*, **off-the-rack** ADJ *attr*, **off the rack** ADJ *pred (US) dress, suit* von der Stange; **~ clothes** Konfektionskleidung *f*; **off-the-record** ADJ *attr*, **off the record** ADJ *pred remark, statement* inoffiziell; *(= confidential)* vertraulich; **off-the-shelf** ADJ *attr* **a** *(= take-away, cash-and-carry) goods, merchandise* Mitnahme-, zum Mitnehmen **b** *solution, computer, software etc* Standard-; **off-the-shoulder** ADJ *dress* schulterfrei; **off-the-wall** ADJ *attr*, **off the wall** ADJ *pred (inf: = zany)* irre *(inf)*, verrückt; **off-white** ADJ gebrochen weiß N gebrochenes Weiß

Ofgas [ˈɒfgæs] N *(Brit) abbr of* **Office of Gas Supply** *Regulierungsbehörde für die Gasindustrie*

Ofgem [ˈɒfdʒem] N *(Brit) abbr of* **Office of Gas and Electricity Markets** *Regulierungsbehörde für die Stromindustrie*

Oflot [ˈɒflɒt] N *(Brit) abbr of* **Office of the National Lottery** *Regulierungsbehörde für die britische Staatslotterie*

OFT *(Brit) abbr of* **Office of Fair Trading**

oft [ɒft] ADV *(liter)* oft; **an ~-told story** eine gar oft erzählte Geschichte *(liter)*

Oftel [ˈɒftel] N *(Brit) abbr of* **Office of Telecommunications** *Regulierungsbehörde für die Telekommunikationsindustrie*

often [ˈɒfən] ✪ 26.1 ADV oft, häufig; **he went there ~, he ~ went there** er ging oft *or* häufig da hin; **you have been there as ~ as I have** Sie sind schon (eben)so oft wie ich dort gewesen; **do you go there as ~ as twice a week?** gehen Sie tatsächlich zweimal in der Woche dahin?; **not as ~ as twice a week** weniger als zweimal in der Woche; **as ~ as I ask you ...** jedes Mal wenn ich Sie frage ...; **more ~ than not, as ~ as not** meistens; **every so ~** öfters, von Zeit zu Zeit; **he did it once too ~** er hat es einmal zu oft *or* zu viel getan; **how ~?** wie oft?; **it is not ~ that ...** es kommt selten vor, dass ..., es geschieht nicht oft, dass ...; **oft(en) times** *(obs)* oftmals, gar viele Male *(old)*

Ofwat [ˈɒfwɒt] N *(Brit) abbr of* **Office of Water Services** *Regulierungsbehörde für die Wasserindustrie*

ogle [ˈəʊgl] VT kein Auge lassen *or* wenden von, begaffen *(pej)*; *(flirtatiously)* liebäugeln mit, schöne Augen machen *(+dat)*; *legs, girls* schielen nach, beäuge(l)n *(esp hum)*, beaugapfeln *(hum)*

O grade [ˈəʊgreɪd] N *(Scot formerly)* = **O level**

ogre [ˈəʊgəˈ] N *(Myth)* Menschen fressender Riese; *(fig)* Ungeheuer *nt*, Unmensch *m*

ogress [ˈəʊgrɪs] N *(Myth)* menschenfressende Riesin; *(fig)* Ungeheuer *nt*, Unmensch *m*

oh [əʊ] INTERJ ach; *(admiring, surprised, disappointed)* oh; *(questioning, disinterested, in confirmation)* tatsächlich, wahrhaftig; **oh good!** prima! *(inf)*; **oh well** na ja!; **oh bother!** *(dated Brit)* Mist! *(inf)*; **oh damn!** *(inf)* verdammt! *(inf)*; **oh dear!** o je!; **oh yes?** *(interested)* ach ja?; *(disbelieving)* so, so; **oh yes, that's right** ach ja, das stimmt; **oh yes, of course there'll be room** o ja, klar haben wir Platz; **oh my God!** o Gott!, ach du lieber Gott!

ohm [əʊm] N Ohm *nt*

OHMS *abbr of* **On His/Her Majesty's Service** *Aufdruck auf amtlichen Postsendungen*

Ohm's law [ˈəʊmzˈlɔː] N ohmsches Gesetz

OHP *abbr of* **overhead projector**

oi(c)k [ɔɪk] N *(Brit pej sl)* Prolo *m (sl)*

oil [ɔɪl] N **a** Öl *nt*; **to pour ~ on troubled waters** die Wogen glätten, Öl auf die Wogen gießen **b** *(= petroleum)* (Erd)öl *nt*; **to strike ~** *(lit)* auf Öl stoßen; *(fig)* einen guten Fund machen; *(= get rich)* das große Los ziehen **c** *(Art: = painting)* Ölgemälde *nt*; **to paint in ~s** in Öl malen; **a painting in ~s** ein Ölgemälde *nt* **d** *(inf, = flattery)* Schmeicheleien *pl* VT ölen, schmieren; *table, furniture* einölen; **to ~ sb's tongue** *(fig)* jdm die Zunge ölen *or* schmieren; **to ~ the wheels** *(fig)* die Dinge erleichtern

oil *in cpds* Öl-; **oil baron** N Ölmagnat *m*; **oil-based** ADJ auf Ölbasis; **~ paint** Ölfarbe *f*; **oil-bearing** ADJ **a** *materials* ölhaltig **b** *(Geol) layer etc* Öl führend; **oil-burning** ADJ Öl-; **~ lamp/stove** Öllampe *f*/-ofen *m*; **oilcake** N Ölkuchen *m*; **oilcan** N Ölkanne *f*; *(for lubricating also)* Ölkännchen *nt*; **oil change** N Ölwechsel *m*; **to do an ~** einen Ölwechsel machen *or* vornehmen; **I took the car in for an ~** ich habe den Wagen zum Ölwechsel(n) gebracht; **oilcloth** N Wachstuch *nt*; **oil colours**, *(US)* **oil colors** PL Ölfarben *pl*; **oil company** N Ölkonzern *m*; **oil drum** N Ölfass *nt*

oiled [ɔɪld] ADJ **a ~ silk** Ölhaut *f* **b he's well-~** *(inf: = drunk)* der ist ganz schön voll *(inf)*, der hat ganz schön getankt *(inf)*

oil: **oil-exporting** ADJ Öl exportierend; **oilfield** N Ölfeld *nt*; **oil-fired** ADJ Öl-, mit Öl befeuert; **~ power station** Ölkraftwerk *nt*; **oil gauge**, *(US)* **oil gage** N Ölstandsanzeiger *m*, Ölstandsmesser *m*; **oil industry** N Ölindustrie *f*

oiliness [ˈɔɪlɪnɪs] N **a** ölige Beschaffenheit; *(of food)* Fettigkeit *f* **b** *(fig: of person)* aalglattes Wesen

oil: **oil lamp** N Öllampe *f*; **oil level** N Ölstand *m*; **oilman** N Ölindustrielle(r) *mf*; *(= trader)* Ölhändler(in) *m(f)*; **oil paint** N Ölfarbe *f*; **oil painting** N *(= picture)* Ölgemälde *nt*; *(= art)* Ölmalerei *f*; **she's no ~** *(inf)* sie ist nicht gerade eine Schönheit; **oilpan** N Ölwanne *f*; **oil platform** N Bohrinsel *f*, Bohrplattform *f*; **oil pollution** N Ölverschmutzung *f*; **oil-producing** ADJ ölproduzierend; **oil refinery** N (Erd)ölraffinerie *f*; **oil-rich** ADJ ölreich; **oil rig** N (Öl)bohrinsel *f*; **oil sheik** N Ölscheich *m*; **oilskin** N **a** *(= cloth)* Öltuch *nt* **b oilskins** PL *(= clothing)* Ölzeug *nt*; **oil slick** N Ölteppich *m*; **oil spill** N Ölkatastrophe *f*; **oilstone** N geölter Wetzstein; **oil stove** N Ölofen *m*; **oil tanker** N *(= ship)* (Öl)tanker *m*, Tankschiff *nt*; *(= lorry)* Tankwagen *m*; **oil terminal** N Ölhafen *m*; **oil well** N Ölquelle *f*

oily [ˈɔɪlɪ] ADJ (+er) **a** ölig; *hair, skin, food* fettig; *clothes, fingers* voller Öl; **~ fish** Fisch *m* mit hohem Ölgehalt **b** *(fig)* aalglatt, schleimig, ölig

oink [ɔɪŋk] INTERJ *(pig)* grunz

ointment [ˈɔɪntmənt] N Salbe *f*

OK, okay [ˈəʊˈkeɪ] *(inf)* INTERJ okay *(inf)*; *(= agreed also)* einverstanden, in Ordnung; **OK, OK!** ist ja gut! *(inf)*, okay, okay! *(inf)*; **I'll come too, OK?** ich komme auch, okay *(inf)* *or* einverstanden?; **OK, that's enough of that** *(call for attention)* nun mal Schluss damit!; **OK, let's go!** also, gehen wir!

ADJ in Ordnung, okay *(inf)*; **that's OK with** *or* **by me** *(= that's convenient)* das ist mir recht, mir ists recht; *(= I don't mind that)* von mir aus, mir solls recht sein; **is it OK (with you) if ...?** macht es (dir) etwas aus, wenn ...?; **how's your mother? – she's OK** wie gehts deiner Mutter? – gut *or (not too well)* so einigermaßen *(inf)*; **I feel OK** es geht mir einigermaßen *(inf)*; **she looks OK** sie sieht einigermaßen aus *(inf)*; **to be OK (for time/money** *etc*) (noch) genug (Zeit/Geld *etc*) haben; **is your car OK?** ist Ihr Auto in Ordnung?; **is that OK?** geht das?, ist das okay? *(inf)*; **what do you think of him? – he's OK** was halten Sie von ihm? – der ist in Ordnung *(inf)*; **he's an OK guy** *(esp US)* er ist ein prima Kerl *(inf)*

ADV **a** *(= well)* gut; *(= not too badly)* einigermaßen (gut); *(= for sure)* schon; **to do OK** ganz gut zurechtkommen; *(Sch, in subject)* nicht schlecht sein; **they must be doing OK** *(= be affluent)* es muss ihnen ganz gut gehen; **can you mend it OK?** kannst du das reparieren?; **can you manage it OK?** kommst du damit klar?; **he'll come OK** der kommt schon

b *(inf: = admittedly)* **OK it's difficult but …** zugegeben, es ist schwer, aber …; **OK, so he's not a real count** na gut, er ist also kein richtiger Graf

VT *order, plan, suggestion* gutheißen, billigen; *document, proposed expenses* genehmigen; **you have to get the boss to OK it, you have to OK it with the boss** das muss der Chef bewilligen

N Zustimmung *f*; **to give (sb/sth) the OK** (jdm/zu etw) seine Zustimmung geben; **if the boss gives his OK** wenn der Chef das bewilligt; **I can start work as soon as I get the OK** ich kann mit der Arbeit anfangen, sobald ich grünes Licht bekomme

okapi [əʊˈkɑːpɪ] N *pl* **-s** *or* **-** Okapi *nt*

okey-doke [ˈəʊkɪˈdəʊk], **okey-dokey** [ˈəʊkɪˈdəʊkɪ] INTERJ *(inf)* okay *(inf)*

Okla *abbr of* **Oklahoma**

okra [ˈɒkrə] N Okra *f*

ol' [əʊl] ADJ *(esp US inf)* = **old**

old [əʊld] ADJ (+er) **a** alt; **~ people** *or* **folk(s)** alte Leute, die Alten *pl*; **if I live to be that ~** wenn ich (je) so alt werde; **~ Mr Smith, ~ man Smith** *(esp US)* der alte (Herr) Smith; **he/the building is 40 years ~** er/das Gebäude ist 40 Jahre alt; **at ten months ~** im Alter von zehn Monaten; **two-year-~** Zweijährige(r) *mf*; **the ~ part of Ulm** die Ulmer Altstadt; **the ~ (part of) town** die Altstadt; **in the ~ days** früher; **the good/bad ~ days** die gute/schlechte alte Zeit; **my ~ school** *(= former)* meine alte *or* ehemalige Schule

b *(inf, as intensifier)* **she dresses any ~ how** die ist vielleicht immer angezogen *(inf)*; **any ~ thing** irgendwas, irgendein Dings *(inf)*; **any ~ bottle/blouse** *etc* irgendeine Flasche/Bluse *etc* *(inf)*; **~ Mike** der Michael *(inf)*; **good ~ Tim** *(inf)* der gute alte Tim; **always the same ~ excuse** immer wieder dieselbe Ausrede; **we had a great ~ time** wir haben uns prächtig amüsiert; **funny ~ guy** komischer Typ *(inf)*

N **a** *pl (= old people)* **the ~** die Alten; **it caters for young and ~** es hat Angebote für Jung und Alt

b in days of ~ *(= former times)* in alten *or* früheren Zeiten; **I know him of ~** ich kenne ihn von früher; **as of ~** wie in alten Zeiten

old: **old age** N das Alter; **to reach ~** ein hohes Alter erreichen; **in one's ~** im Alter, auf seine alten Tage *(also hum)*; **old-age pension** N (Alters)rente *f*; **old-age pensioner** N Rentner(in) *m(f)*; **Old Bill** PL *(Brit inf)* **the ~** die Bullen *pl (sl)*, die Bullerei *(sl)*; **old boy** N **a** *(Brit Sch)* ehemaliger Schüler, Ehemalige(r) *m*; **the old-boy network** Beziehungen *pl* (von der Schule her) **b** *(inf: = old man)* **the ~ next door** der Alte von nebenan **c** *(dated inf, as address)* alter Junge *(inf)*; **old country** N Mutterland *nt*, alte Heimat; **Old Dominion** N *(US: = Virginia)* Virginia *nt*

olde [ˈəʊldɪ] ADJ *(archaic)* alt, aus alter Zeit

olden [ˈəʊldən] ADJ *(liter)* alt; **in ~ times** *or* **days** früher, vordem *(liter)*, in alten Zeiten; **city of ~ times** Stadt vergangener Zeiten

old: **Old English** N Altenglisch *nt* ADJ altenglisch; **Old English sheepdog** N Bobtail *m*; **old-established** ADJ *family, firm* alteingesessen; *custom* seit Langem bestehend, alt

olde-worlde [ˈəʊldɪˈwɜːldɪ] ADJ altertümlich; *(pej)* auf alt getrimmt *(inf) or* gemacht

old: **old-fashioned** [ˈəʊldˈfæʃnd] ADJ altmodisch; **a good ~ love story** eine Liebesgeschichte wie sie sein sollte; **to give sb an ~ look** jdn missbilligend ansehen N *(US: = cocktail) Cocktail aus Whiskey, Bitterlikör, Zucker und Früchten*; **old flame** N alte Liebe; **old folk's home** N *(inf)* Altenheim *nt*; **Old French** N *(Ling)* Altfranzösisch *nt*; **old girl** N **a** *(inf: = old woman)* Alte *f*, alte Dame; *(= animal)* altes Mädchen; **my ~** *(dated: = wife)* meine Alte **b** *(Brit Sch)* Ehemalige *f*, ehemalige Schülerin; **Old Glory** N *(US: = flag)* das Sternenbanner; **old gold** N Altgold *nt*; **old guard** N *(fig)* alte Garde; **old hand** N alter Hase *(at sth* in etw *dat)*; **Old Harry** [ˈəʊldˈhærɪ] N *(= Devil)* der Leibhaftige; **to play ~ with sth** etw vollständig durcheinanderbringen; **old hat** N *(fig)* alter Hut *(fig)*; **that's ~** das ist ein alter Hut, das ist uninteressant; **Old High German** N *(Ling)* Althochdeutsch *nt*

oldie [ˈəʊldɪ] N *(inf) (= joke)* alter Witz; *(= song)* Oldie *m*; *(= record)* alte Platte, Oldie *m*; **the ~s** *(= people)* die Alten *pl*, die Oldies *pl (inf)*; **that's a real ~** *(joke)* der hat so einen Bart *(inf)*

oldish [ˈəʊldɪʃ] ADJ ältlich

old: **old lady** N *(inf)* **my ~** *(= wife)* meine Alte *(inf)*; *(= mother also)* meine alte Dame *(inf)*; **old lag** N *(sl)* Knastbruder *m (inf)*; **old-line** ADJ *(= following tradition)* der alten Schule; *(= long-established)* alteingesessen; **old maid** N alte Jungfer; **old-maidish** ADJ altjüngferlich, altbacken; **old man** N *(inf)* **my ~** *(= husband)* mein Alter *(inf)*; *(= father also)* mein alter Herr *(inf)*; **the ~** *(= boss etc)* der Alte; **old master** N alter Meister; **Old Nick** N *(hum: = the devil)* der Leibhaftige; **old people's home** N Altenheim *nt*; **old rose** ADJ altrosa N Altrosa *nt*; **old salt** N (alter) Seebär; **old school** N *(fig)* alte Schule; **old school tie** N *(lit)* Schulschlips *m*; *(fig) Gehabe, das von Ehemaligen einer Public School erwartet wird*; **old soldier** N alter Soldat; *(fig: = old hand)* alter Hase; **Old South** N *Südstaaten der USA vor dem amerikanischen Bürgerkrieg*; **old stager** N *(inf)* alter Hase *(inf)*

oldster [ˈəʊldstəʳ] N *(US inf)* älterer Mann; **some of us ~s** einige von uns Alten

old: **old-style** ADJ im alten Stil; *furniture, car etc* altertümlich; **~ calendar** Kalender *m* alten Stils *or* nach alter Zeitrechnung; **Old Testament** *(Bibl)* N Altes Testament ADJ *prophet* alttestamentarisch; **old-timer** N Veteran(in) *m(f)*; **old wives' tale** N Ammenmärchen *nt*; **old woman** N **a** = **old lady b he's an ~** er ist wie ein altes Weib; **old-womanish** ADJ tuntig *(inf)*; **Old World** N **the ~** die Alte Welt; **old-world** ADJ **a** *(= quaint) politeness, manners* altväterlich; *cottage, atmosphere* altehrwürdig, heimelig **b** *(esp US: = European etc)* zur Alten Welt gehörend

OLE *(Comput) abbr of* **object linking and embedding** OLE *nt*

oleaginous [ˌəʊlɪˈædʒɪnəs] ADJ *(form) consistency* ölig; *(= containing oil)* ölhaltig; *(fig) person* ölig

oleander [ˌəʊlɪˈændəʳ] N Oleander *m*

oleomargarine [ˈəʊlɪəʊˌmɑːdʒəˈriːn] N *(esp US)* Margarine *f*

O level [ˈəʊlevl] N *(Brit formerly)* Abschluss *m* der Sekundarstufe 1, ≈ mittlere Reife; **to do one's ~s** ≈ die mittlere Reife machen; **to have an ~ in English** ≈ bis zur mittleren Reife Englisch gelernt haben; **he failed his English ~** er fiel durch die O-Level-Prüfung in Englisch; **3 ~s** ≈ die mittlere Reife in 3 Fächern

olfactory [ɒlˈfæktərɪ] ADJ Geruchs-, olfaktorisch *(spec)*

olfactory nerve N Geruchsnerv *m*

oligarchic(al) [ˌɒlɪˈgɑːkɪk(əl)] ADJ oligarchisch

oligarchy [ˈɒlɪgɑːkɪ] N Oligarchie *f*

olive [ˈɒlɪv] N **a** Olive *f*; *(also* **olive tree***)* Olivenbaum *m*; *(also* **olive wood***)* Olive(nholz *nt*) *f* **b** *(= colour)* Olive *nt* ADJ *(also* **olive-coloured***)* olivgrün; *complexion* dunkel

olive: **olive branch** N *(lit, fig)* Ölzweig *m*; **to hold out** *or* **offer the ~ to sb** *(fig)* jdm seinen Willen zum Frieden bekunden; **olive green** N Olivgrün *nt*; **olive-green** ADJ *cloth* olivgrün; **olive grove** N Olivenhain *m*; **olive oil** N Olivenöl *nt*

Olympiad [əʊˈlɪmpɪæd] N Olympiade *f*

Olympian [əʊˈlɪmpɪən] ADJ olympisch N **the ~s** die Olympier *pl*

Olympic [əʊˈlɪmpɪk] ADJ olympisch; **~ medallist** *(Brit) or* **medalist** *(US)* Olympiamedaillengewinner(in) *m(f)* N **Olympics** PL **the ~s** die Olympiade, die Olympischen Spiele

Olympic: **Olympic champion** N Olympiasieger(in) *m(f)*; **Olympic flame** N olympisches Feuer; **Olympic Games** PL **the ~** die Olympiade, die Olympischen Spiele; **Olympic stadium** N Olympiastadion *nt*; **Olympic torch** N olympisches Feuer

Olympus [əʊˈlɪmpəs] N *(also* **Mount Olympus***)* der Olymp

OM *abbr of* **Order of Merit**

Oman [əʊˈmɑːn] N Oman *nt*

Omani [əʊˈmɑːnɪ] ADJ omanisch N Omaner(in) *m(f)*

omasum [əʊˈmɑːsəm] N Blättermagen *m*

OMB *(US) abbr of* **Office of Management and Budget**

ombudsman [ˈɒmbʊdzmən] N *pl* **-men** [-mən] Ombudsmann *m*

ombudswoman [ˌɒmbʊdzwʊmən] N *pl* **-women** [-wɪmɪn] Ombudsfrau *f*

omega [ˈəʊmɪgə] N Omega *nt*

omelette, *(US)* **omelet** [ˈɒmlɪt] N Omelett(e) *nt*; **you can't make an ~ without breaking eggs** *(Prov)* wo gehobelt wird, da fallen Späne *(Prov)*

omen [ˈəʊmen] N Omen *nt*, Zeichen *nt*; **it is an ~ of greatness** das bedeutet Erfolg; **a bird of ill ~** ein Unglücksvogel *m*

ominous [ˈɒmɪnəs] ADJ bedrohlich, ominös; *event, appearance also* drohend; *look, voice also* Unheil verkündend, unheilschwanger; *sign also* verhängnisvoll; *sky* bedrohlich; **that's ~** das lässt nichts Gutes ahnen; **that sounds/looks ~** *(fig)* das verspricht nichts Gutes

ominously [ˈɒmɪnəslɪ] ADV bedrohlich, ominös; *say* in einem Unheil verkündenden Ton; **it sounds ~ like a declaration of war** es klingt ominös nach einer Kriegserklärung; **more ~, the government is talking of reprisals** schlimmer noch, die Regierung spricht von Vergeltungsmaßnahmen

omission [əʊˈmɪʃən] N *(= omitting: of word, detail etc)* Auslassen *nt*; *(= word, thing etc left out)* Auslassung *f*; *(= failure to do sth)* Unterlassung *f*; **with the ~ of …** unter Auslassung *(+gen)* …; **sin of ~** *(Eccl, fig)* Unterlassungssünde *f*

omit [əʊˈmɪt] VT **a** *(= leave out)* auslassen; **please ~ any reference to me** bitte erwähnen Sie mich nicht, bitte unterlassen Sie jeden Hinweis auf mich **b** *(= fail) (to do sth* etw zu tun) unterlassen; *(accidentally)* versäumen

omnibus [ˈɒmnɪbəs] N **a** *(form: = bus)* Omnibus *m*, Autobus *m* **b** *(also* **omnibus edition***: = book)* Sammelausgabe *f*, Sammelband *m*; *(TV)* Fernseh- *oder* Radioprogramm, *das zwei oder mehrere Folgen einer Serie als eine Sendung zeigt* ADJ *(esp US)* allgemein, umfassend; **~ bill** *(Parl)* Sammelgesetz *nt*

omnibus edition N → **omnibus N b**

omnidirectional [ˌɒmnɪdɪˈrekʃənl] ADJ Rundstrahl-; **~ antenna** Rundstrahlantenne *f*

omnipotence [ɒmˈnɪpətəns] N *no pl* Allmacht *f*, Omnipotenz *f*

omnipotent [ɒmˈnɪpətənt] ADJ allmächtig, omnipotent N **The Omnipotent** der Allmächtige

omnipresence [ˈɒmnɪˈprezəns] N Allgegenwart *f*

omnipresent [ˈɒmnɪˈprezənt] ADJ allgegenwärtig

omniscience [ɒmˈnɪsɪəns] N Allwissenheit *f*

omniscient [ɒmˈnɪsɪənt] ADJ allwissend

omnivore [ˈɒmnɪˌvɔː] N Allesfresser *m*, Omnivore *m (spec)*

omnivorous [ɒmˈnɪvərəs] ADJ *(lit)* alles fressend, omnivor *(spec)*; **an ~ reader** ein Vielfraß *m*, was Bücher angeht

on [ɒn]

1 PREPOSITION	3 ADJECTIVE
2 ADVERB	

1 – PREPOSITION

When *on* is the second element in a phrasal verb, eg *live on, lecture on*, look up the verb. When it is part of a set combination, eg *on the right, on request, on occasion*, look up the other word.

a indicating place, position auf *(+dat)*; *(with vb of motion)* auf *(+acc)*; *(on vertical surface, part of body)* an *(+dat)*; *(with vb of motion)* an *(+acc)*; **the book is on the table** das Buch ist auf dem Tisch; **he put the book on the table** er legte das Buch auf den Tisch; **it was on the blackboard** es stand an der Tafel; **he hung it on the wall/nail** er hängte es an die Wand/den Nagel; **a house on the coast/main road** ein Haus am Meer/an der Hauptstraße; **on the bank of the river** am Flussufer; **with a smile on her face** mit einem Lächeln auf den Lippen; **a ring on his finger** ein Ring am Finger; **her name is on the list** ihr Name ist auf der Liste; **he hit his head on the table/on the ground** er hat sich *(dat)* den Kopf am Tisch/auf dem *or* am Boden angeschlagen; **they came on(to) the stage** sie kamen auf die Bühne; **they advanced on the fort** sie rückten zum Fort vor; **on TV/the radio** im Fernsehen/Radio; **on video** auf Video; **held on computer** auf Computer *(dat)* gespeichert; **who's on his show tonight?** wer ist heute in seiner Show?; **I have no money on me** ich habe kein Geld bei mir; **we had something to eat on the train** wir haben im Zug etwas gegessen → *also* **onto**

b = by means of, using **we went on the train/bus** wir fuhren mit dem Zug/Bus; **on a bicycle** mit dem (Fahr)rad; **on foot/horseback** zu Fuß/Pferd; **the heating runs on oil** die Heizung wird mit Öl betrieben; **to count sth on one's fingers** etw an den Fingern abzählen

c = about, concerning über *(+acc)*; **a book on German grammar** ein Buch über deutsche Grammatik; **we read Stalin on Marx** wir lasen Stalins Ausführungen zu Marx; **have you heard him on the subject?** haben Sie ihn zu diesem Thema gehört?; **he has nothing on me** *(= no damaging information etc)* er hat nichts gegen mich in der Hand, er kann mir nichts anhaben

d in expressions of time an *(+dat)*; **on Sunday** (am) Sonntag; **on Sundays** sonntags; **on December the first** am ersten Dezember; **stars visible on clear nights** Sterne, die in klaren Nächten sichtbar sind; **on or about the twentieth** um den Zwanzigsten herum; **on and after the twentieth** am Zwanzigsten und danach

e = earning, getting **I'm on £18,000 a year** ich bekomme £ 18.000 im Jahr; **how much are you on?** wie viel verdienst *or* bekommst du?; **he retired on a good pension** er trat mit einer guten Rente in den Ruhestand

f = at the time of bei *(+dat)*; **on my arrival** bei meiner Ankunft; **on examination** bei der Untersuchung; **on hearing this he left** als er das hörte, ging er

g = as a result of auf ... *(acc)* hin; **on receiving my letter** auf meinen Brief hin

h indicating membership in *(+dat)*; **he is on the committee/the board** er gehört dem Ausschuss/Vorstand an, er sitzt im Ausschuss/Vorstand; **he is on the "Evening News"** er ist bei der „Evening News"; **he is on the teaching staff** er gehört zum Lehrpersonal

i = doing **to be on a course** *(Sch, Univ)* an einem Kurs teilnehmen; **I am working on a new project** ich arbeite gerade an einem neuen Projekt; **he was away on business** er war geschäftlich unterwegs; **I am on overtime** ich mache Überstunden; **we're on the past tense** *(Sch)* wir sind bei der Vergangenheit; **we were on page 72** wir waren auf Seite 72

j = at the expense of **this round is on me** diese Runde geht auf meine Kosten; **have it on me** das spendiere ich (dir), ich gebe (dir) das aus → **house**

k = compared with im Vergleich zu; **prices are up on last year('s)** im Vergleich zum letzten Jahr sind die Preise gestiegen; **he has nothing on me** *(= not as good as)* er kann mir nicht das Wasser reichen

l = taking **to be on drugs/the pill** Drogen/die Pille nehmen; **what is he on?** *(inf)* er tickt wohl nicht ganz richtig! *(inf)*

m indicating repetition **he made mistake on mistake** er machte einen Fehler nach dem anderen

n musical instrument **he played (it) on the violin/trumpet** er spielte (es) auf der Geige/Trompete; **on drums/piano** am Schlagzeug/Klavier; **Roland Kirk on tenor sax** Roland Kirk, Tenorsaxofon

o = according to nach *(+dat)*; **on your theory** Ihrer Theorie nach *or* zufolge, nach Ihrer Theorie

2 – ADVERB

a = in place, covering **he screwed the lid on** er schraubte den Deckel drauf; **she had nothing on** sie hatte nichts an; **what did he have on?** was hatte er an?; **he had his hat on crooked** er hatte den Hut schief auf; **he put his hat on** er setzte seinen Hut auf; **he put his coat on** er zog seinen Mantel an

b indicating position **put it this way on** stellen/legen Sie es so herum (darauf); **sideways on** längs

c indicating forward movement **move on!** gehen Sie weiter!, weitergehen!; **on! on!** weiter! weiter!; **to pass a message on** eine Nachricht weitergeben

d indicating time **from now on** von jetzt an; **from that day on** von diesem Tag an; **later on** später; **it was well on in the night** es war zu vorgerückter Stunde, es war spät in der Nacht; **it was well on into September** es war spät im September; **early on in her career** schon früh in ihrer Karriere

e indicating continuation **to keep on talking** immer weiterreden, in einem fort reden; **they walked on in silence** sie gingen schweigend weiter; **go on with your work** machen Sie Ihre Arbeit weiter

f set structures

♦ **on and on they talked on and on** sie redeten und redeten, sie redeten unentwegt; **the noise went on and on** der Lärm hörte überhaupt nicht auf; **she went on and on** sie hörte gar nicht mehr auf

♦ **to be on at sb** *(inf)* **he's always on at me** er hackt dauernd auf mir herum, er meckert dauernd an mir herum *(inf)*; **he's always on at me to get my hair cut** er liegt mir dauernd in den Ohren, dass ich mir die Haare schneiden lassen soll; **he's been on at me about that several times** er ist mir ein paar Mal damit gekommen *(inf)*

♦ **to be on about sth** *(inf)* **she's always on about her experiences in Italy** sie kommt dauernd mit ihren Italienerfahrungen *(inf)*; **what's he on about?** wovon redet er nun schon wieder?; **he knows what he's on about** er weiß, wovon er redet

3 – ADJECTIVE

a = switched on, functioning *lights, TV, radio* an; *brake* angezogen; *electricity, gas* an(gestellt); **to leave the engine on** den Motor laufen lassen; **the "on" switch** der Einschalter; **in the "on" position** auf „ein" gestellt; **it wasn't one of his on days** *(inf)* er war nicht gerade in Form

b = in place *lid, cover* drauf; **his hat/tie was on crookedly** sein Hut saß/sein Schlips hing schief; **his hat/coat was already on** er hatte den Hut schon auf/den Mantel schon an

c = taking place **there's a tennis match on at the moment** ein Tennismatch ist gerade im Gang; **there's a tennis match on tomorrow** morgen findet ein Tennismatch statt; **I have nothing on tonight** ich habe heute Abend nichts vor; **what's on in London?** was ist los in London?; **there's never anything on in this town** in dieser Stadt ist nie was los; **the search is on for a new managing director** jetzt wird nach einem neuen Geschäftsführer gesucht

d = being performed, performing **to be on** *(in theatre, cinema)* gegeben *or* gezeigt werden; *(on TV, radio)* gesendet *or* gezeigt werden; **is that programme** *(Brit) or* **program** *(US)* **still on?** läuft das Programm noch?; **the play is still on** *(= still running)* das Stück wird immer noch gegeben *or* gespielt; **what's on tonight?** was ist *or* steht heute Abend auf dem Programm?; **who's on tonight?** *(Theat, Film)* wer spielt heute Abend?, wer tritt heute Abend auf?; *(TV)* wer kommt heute Abend (im Fernsehen)?; **you're on now** *(Theat, Rad, TV)* Ihr Auftritt!, Sie sind (jetzt) dran *(inf)*; **tell me when the English team is on** sagen Sie mir, wenn die englische Mannschaft dran ist *or* drankommt

e indicating agreement, acceptability **to be on** *(bet, agreement)* gelten; **you're on!** abgemacht!; **are you on?** *(inf, = are you with us)* bist du mit von der Partie? *(inf)*, machst du mit?; **are you on for dinner tonight?** sehen wir uns zum Abendessen?; **you're/he's not on** *(Brit inf)* das ist nicht drin *(inf)*; **it's just not on** *(Brit inf: = not acceptable)* das ist einfach nicht drin *(inf)*, das gibt es einfach nicht; **his behaviour was really not on** *(Brit inf)* sein Benehmen war unmöglich

onanism [ˈəʊnənɪzəm] N *(form)* Coitus interruptus *m*; *(= masturbation)* Onanie *f*, Masturbation *f*

on-camera ADJ, ADV *(Film, TV)* vor der Kamera

once [wʌns] ADV **a** *(= on one occasion)* einmal; **~ a week/month/year** einmal in der Woche/im Monat/im Jahr, einmal pro Woche/Monat/Jahr; **~ only** nur einmal; **this has happened only ~ before** das ist nur einmal zuvor passiert; **he tried this ~ before** er hat das schon einmal probiert; **~ again** *or* **more** noch einmal; **~ again we find that ...** wir stellen wiederum *or* erneut fest, dass ...; **~ or twice** *(lit)* ein- oder zweimal; *(fig)* nur ein paar Mal; **~ and for all** ein für alle Mal; **(every) ~ in a while, ~ in a way** ab und zu mal; **you can come (just) this ~** dieses eine Mal können Sie kommen; **for ~** ausnahmsweise einmal; **I never ~ wondered where you were** ich habe mich kein einziges Mal gefragt, wo Sie wohl waren; **she walked away, without ~ looking back** sie ging davon, ohne auch nur ein einziges Mal zurückzublicken; **if ~ you begin to hesitate** wenn Sie erst einmal anfangen zu zögern; **~ a smoker, always a smoker** einmal Raucher, immer Raucher; **~ is enough** einmal reicht

b *(= in past)* einmal; **he was ~ famous** er war früher einmal berühmt; **~ upon a time there was ...** es war einmal ...

c at ~ *(= immediately)* sofort, auf der Stelle; *(= at the same time)* auf einmal, gleichzeitig; **all at ~** auf einmal; *(= suddenly)* ganz plötzlich; **they came all at ~** sie kamen alle zur gleichen Zeit; **don't spend it all at ~** gib es nicht alles auf einmal aus

CONJ wenn; *(with past tense)* als; **~ you understand, it's easy** wenn Sie es einmal verstehen, ist es einfach; **~ the sun had set, it turned cold** als die Sonne erst einmal untergegangen war, wurde es kalt; **~ learned, it isn't easily forgotten** wenn man das erst einmal gelernt hat, vergisst man es nicht so leicht wieder

once-in-a-lifetime ADJ *attr chance etc* einmalig

once-over ['wʌnsəʊvəʳ] N (*inf*: = *quick look*) flüchtige Überprüfung, kurze Untersuchung; **to give sb/sth the** *or* **a ~** (= *appraisal*) jdn/etw mal begucken (*inf*) *or* kurz überprüfen *or* inspizieren; (= *clean*) mal kurz über etw (*acc*) gehen (*inf*); **to give sb the** *or* **a ~** (= *beat up*) jdn in die Mache nehmen (*inf*)

oncologist [ɒŋ'kɒlədʒɪst] N Onkologe *m*, Onkologin *f*

oncology [ɒŋ'kɒlədʒɪ] N Onkologie *f*

oncoming ['ɒnkʌmɪŋ] ADJ **a** (= *approaching*) *car, traffic* entgegenkommend; *troops, forces* heranrückend; *danger* nahend, drohend; **the ~ traffic** der Gegenverkehr **b** (= *imminent*) *winter, night* (her)einbrechend **N** (*of winter etc*) Nahen *nt*, Kommen *nt*

oncomouse ['ɒŋkəʊmaʊs] N (*Med*) *Maus mit eingepflanztem Krebsgen*, Onkomaus *f*, Krebsmaus *f*; **~ patent** Krebsmauspatent *nt*

OND (*Brit*) *abbr of* **Ordinary National Diploma**

one [wʌn] ADJ **a** (= *number*) ein/eine/ein; (*counting*) eins; **~ man in a thousand** einer von tausend; **there was ~ person too many** da war einer zu viel; **~ girl was pretty, the other was ugly** das eine Mädchen war hübsch, das andere hässlich; **she was in ~ room, he was in the other** sie war im einen Zimmer, er im anderen; **the baby is ~ (year old)** das Kind ist ein Jahr (alt); **it is ~ (o'clock)** es ist eins, es ist ein Uhr; **~ hundred pounds** hundert Pfund; (*on cheque etc*) einhundert Pfund; **that's ~ way of doing it** so kann mans (natürlich) auch machen
b (*indefinite*) **~ morning/day** *etc* **he realized …** eines Morgens/Tages *etc* bemerkte er …; **~ morning next week** nächste Woche einmal morgens; **~ day next week** nächste Woche einmal; **~ day soon** bald einmal; **~ sunny summer's day** an einem sonnigen Sommertag
c (= *a certain*) **~ Mr Smith** ein gewisser Herr Smith
d (= *sole, only*) **he is the ~ man to tell you** er ist der Einzige, der es Ihnen sagen kann; **no ~ man could do it** niemand konnte es allein tun; **my ~ (and only) hope** meine einzige Hoffnung; **the ~ and only Brigitte Bardot** die unvergleichliche Brigitte Bardot
e (= *same*) **they all came in the ~ car** sie kamen alle in dem einen Auto; **they are ~ and the same person** das ist ein und dieselbe Person; **it is ~ and the same thing** das ist ein und dasselbe; **it's all ~ to me** das ist mir alles einerlei
f (= *united*) **God is ~** Gott ist unteilbar; **are they ~ with us?** sind sie mit uns eins?; **we are ~ on the subject** wir sind uns über dieses Thema einig; **they were ~ in wanting that** sie waren sich darin einig, dass sie das wollten; **the crowd rose as ~** die Menge erhob sich geschlossen
PRON **a** eine(r, s); **the ~ who …** der(jenige), der …/die(jenige), die …/das(jenige), das …; **he/that was the ~** er/das wars; **do you have ~?** haben Sie einen/eine/ein(e)s?; **the red/big** *etc* **~** der/die/das Rote/Große *etc*; **he has some very fine ~s** er hat sehr Schöne; **my ~** (*inf*) meiner/meine/mein(e)s; **his ~** (*inf*) seiner/seine/sein(e)s; **not (a single) ~ of them, never ~ of them** nicht eine(r, s) von ihnen, kein Einziger/keine Einzige/kein Einziges; **no ~ of these people** keiner dieser Leute; **any ~** irgendeine(r, s); **every ~** jede(r, s); **this ~** diese(r, s); **that ~** der/die/das, jene(r, s) (*geh*); **which ~?** welche(r, s)?; **the little ~s** (= *children*) die Kleinen *pl*; (= *animals*) die Jungen *pl*; **that's a good ~** (*inf*) der (Witz) ist gut; (*iro, excuse etc*) (das ist ein) guter Witz; **let's have a quick ~ after work** (*inf*) lasst uns nach der Arbeit noch kurz einen trinken gehen; **I'm not ~ to go out often** ich bin nicht der Typ, der oft ausgeht; **I'm not usually ~ to go out on a week night, but today …** ich gehe sonst eigentlich nicht an Wochentagen aus, aber heute …; **I am not much of a ~ for cakes** (*inf*) ich bin kein großer Freund von Kuchen (*inf*), Kuchen ist eigentlich nicht mein Fall (*inf*); **she was never ~ to cry** Weinen war noch nie ihre Art; (*but she did*) sonst weinte sie nie; **he's never ~ to say no** er sagt nie Nein *or* nein; **what a ~ he is for the girls!** der ist vielleicht ein Schwerenöter! (*inf*); **he's a great ~ for discipline/turning up late** der ist ganz groß, wenns um Disziplin/ums Zuspätkommen geht; **ooh, you are a ~!** (*inf*) oh, Sie sind mir vielleicht eine(r)! (*inf*); **she is a teacher, and he/her sister wants to be ~ too** sie ist Lehrerin, und er möchte auch gern Lehrer werden/ihre Schwester möchte auch gern eine werden; **I, for ~, think otherwise** ich, zum Beispiel, denke anders; **they came ~ and all** sie kamen alle (ohne Ausnahme); **~ by ~** einzeln; **~ after the other** eine(r, s) nach dem/der/dem anderen; **take ~ or the other** nehmen Sie das eine oder das andere/den einen oder den anderen/die eine oder die andere; **you can't have ~ without the other** Sie können das eine nicht ohne das andere haben; **~ or other of them will do it** der/die eine oder andere wird es tun; **he's not ~ of our group** er gehört nicht zu unserer Gruppe; **he is ~ of us** er ist einer von uns; **~ who knows the country** jemand, der das Land kennt; **in the manner of ~ who …** in der Art von jemandem, der …; **like ~ demented/possessed** wie verrückt/besessen
b (*impers*) (*nom*) man; (*acc*) einen; (*dat*) einem; **~ must learn to keep quiet** man muss lernen, still zu sein; **to hurt ~'s foot** sich (*dat*) den Fuß verletzen; **to wash ~'s face/hair** sich (*dat*) das Gesicht/die Haare waschen; **~ likes to see ~'s** *or* **his** (*US*) **friends happy** man sieht seine Freunde gern glücklich
N (= *written figure*) Eins *f*; **Chapter ~** Kapitel eins; **in ~s and twos** in kleinen Gruppen; **they became ~** sie wurden eins; **they were made ~** sie wurden vereint; **to be at ~ (with sb)** sich (*dat*) (mit jdm) einig sein; **he was at ~ with the world** er war mit der Welt im Einklang; **he is not at ~ with himself** er ist mit sich selbst nicht im Reinen; **it was a bedroom and sitting room (all) in ~** es war Schlaf- und Wohnzimmer in einem; **T-shirt and shorts all in ~** T-shirt und Shorts in einem Stück; **I landed him ~** (*inf*) dem habe ich eine(n) *or* eins verpasst (*inf*); **to be ~ up on sb** (*inf*) (= *know more*) jdm eins voraus sein; (= *have more*) jdm etwas voraushaben; **Rangers were ~ up after the first half** Rangers hatten nach der ersten Halbzeit ein Tor Vorsprung

one-acter ['wʌnˌæktəʳ], **one-act play** ['wʌnækt'pleɪ] N Einakter *m*

one another = **each other**, → **each PRON b**

one: **one-armed** ADJ einarmig; **one-armed bandit** N (*inf*) einarmiger Bandit; **one-day** ADJ *seminar, course* eintägig; **one-dimensional** ADJ (*Math*) eindimensional; (*fig*) *character* eindimensional; *story* eindimensional, einfallslos; **one-eyed** ADJ einäugig; **one-handed** ADJ *person* einhändig ADV mit einer Hand; **one-horse** ADJ **a** *vehicle* einspännig; **to be a ~ race** (*fig*) einen sicheren Sieger haben **b** (*inf*: = *inferior*) **~ town** Kuhdorf *nt* (*inf*); **one-legged** ADJ *person* einbeinig; **one-line** ADJ *message etc* einzeilig; **one-liner** N (*inf*) witzige Bemerkung; **one-man** ADJ Einmann-; **~ canoe** Einerkanu *nt*; **~ job** Arbeit *f* für einen Einzelnen; **she's a ~ woman** ihr liegt nur an einem Mann etwas; **one-man band** N Einmannkapelle *f*; (*fig inf*) Einmannbetrieb *m*; **one-man show** N (*Art*) Ausstellung *f* eines (einzigen) Künstlers; (*Theat etc*) Einmannshow *f*

oneness ['wʌnnɪs] N Einheit *f*; (*of personality, thought*) Geschlossenheit *f*; (= *concord: with nature, fellow men*) Einklang *m*

one: **one-night stand** N (*fig*) One-Night-Stand *m*; (= *sex also*) Sex *m* für eine Nacht; **he's just after a ~** er sucht nur eine für eine Nacht; **one-off** (*Brit inf*) ADJ einmalig N **a ~** etwas Einmaliges; **that mistake** *etc* **was just a ~** dieser Fehler *etc* war eine Ausnahme; **one-one**, **one-on-one** ADJ (*US*) = **one-to-one**; **one-parent family** N Einelternteilfamilie *f*; **one-party** ADJ (*Pol*) Einparteien-; **~ state/system** Einparteienstaat *m*/-system *nt*; **one-person household** N Single-Haushalt *m*; **one-piece** ADJ einteilig N (= *bathing costume*) (einteiliger) Badeanzug, Einteiler *m*; **one-room** ATTR, **one-roomed** ADJ Einzimmer-; **~ flat** (*Brit*) *or* **apartment** Einzimmerwohnung *f*

onerous ['ɒnərəs] ADJ *responsibility* schwer(wiegend); *task, duty* beschwerlich, schwer

oneself [wʌn'self] PRON **a** (*dir and indir, with prep*) sich; (= *oneself personally*) sich selbst *or* selber **b** (*emph*) (sich) selbst → *also* **myself**

one: **one-shot** ADJ, N (*US*) = **one-off**; **one-sided** ADJ einseitig; *judgement, account also* parteiisch; **one-time** ADJ ehemalig; **one-to-one** ADJ **a** (= *between two people*) *conversation, meeting* unter vier Augen; **~ teaching** *or* **tuition** Einzelunterricht *m*; **~ therapy** Einzeltherapie *f*; **~ relationship** Zweierbeziehung *f* **b** (= *corresponding exactly*) *correspondence, correlation* sich Punkt für Punkt entsprechend, eins zu eins; **a ~ exchange rate** ein Wechselkurs *m* im Verhältnis eins zu eins ADV **a** (= *person to person*) *talk, discuss* unter vier Augen; **they fought ~** sie kämpften einzeln gegeneinander **b** (= *in exact correspondence*) im Verhältnis eins-zu-eins N (= *conversation*) Gespräch *nt* unter vier Augen; **to have a ~ with sb** ein Gespräch *nt* unter vier Augen mit jdm führen; **one-track** ADJ **he's got a ~ mind** der hat immer nur das eine im Sinn *or* Kopf; **one-two** N **a** (*Boxing*) Rechts-links-Kombination *f*; **to give sb the old ~** jdm eine klassische Rechts-links-Kombination verpassen **b** (*Ftbl*) Doppelpass *m* **c** (*in race*) *erster und zweiter Platz für Teamkollegen*; **one-upmanship** [ˌwʌn'ʌpmənʃɪp] N **that's just a form of ~** damit will er *etc* den anderen nur um eine Nasenlänge voraus sein; **the game of ~** (*hum*) die Kunst, allen anderen um einen Schritt *or* eine Nasenlänge voraus zu sein; **one-way** ADJ **a** (= *in one direction*) *traffic etc* in einer Richtung; **~ street** Einbahnstraße *f*; **~ system** System *nt* von Einbahnstraßen; **~ ticket** (*US Rail*) einfache Fahrkarte; **~ trip** einfache Fahrt **b** (= *one-sided*) *relationship, deal* einseitig; *process* einseitig, eingleisig **c** *mirror, glass* von einer Seite durchsichtig; **one-woman** ADJ Einfrau-; **~ show** Einfraushow *f*

ongoing ['ɒngəʊɪŋ] ADJ (= *in progress*) *research, project* im Gang befindlich, laufend; (= *long-term, continuing*) *development, relationship* andauernd; **~ crisis** Dauerkrise *f*; **this is an ~ situation** diese Situation ist von Dauer

onion ['ʌnjən] N Zwiebel *f*; **he knows his ~s** (*Brit inf*) er kennt seinen Kram (*inf*)

onion: **onion dome** N Zwiebelturm *m*; **onion ring** N (*Cook*) Zwiebelring *m*; **onion-shaped** ADJ zwiebelförmig; **onionskin** N Zwiebelschale *f*; (= *paper*) Florpost *f*; **onion soup** N Zwiebelsuppe *f*

on line [ɒn'laɪn] (*Comput*) ADJ *pred* online ADV online, on line; **to go ~** auf Onlinebetrieb schalten; **to put a printer ~** einen Drucker auf Onlinebetrieb schalten; **to be ~ to sb/sth** mit jdm/etw verbunden sein

on-line ['ɒnlaɪn] ADJ *attr* (*Comput*) Online-; **~ database** Onlinedatenbank *f*; **~ dating** Kennenlernen *nt* übers Internet; **~ help** Online-Hilfe *f*; **~ mode** Onlinebetrieb *m*; **~ service provider** (*Internet*) Onlinedienst *m*; **~ shopping** Einkaufen *nt* übers Internet ADV **a** (*Comput*) online; **to go ~** (*user*) online gehen; (*computer also*)*auf Onlinebetrieb gehen* **to order ~** online bestellen **b** (*Ind*) **to go ~** (*factory etc*) in Betrieb gehen, den Betrieb aufnehmen

onlooker ['ɒnlʊkəʳ] N Zuschauer(in) *m(f)*

only ['əʊnlɪ] ADJ *attr* einzige(r, s); **he's an/my ~ child** er ist ein Einzelkind *nt*/mein einziges Kind; **the ~ one** *or* **person** der/die Einzige; **the ~ ones** *or* **people** die Einzigen; **he was the ~ one to leave** *or* **who left** er ist als Einziger gegangen; **the ~ thing** das Einzige; **the ~ thing I could suggest would be to invite him too** ich könnte höchstens vorschlagen, dass wir *etc* ihn auch einladen; **that's the ~ thing for it/the**

~ thing to do das ist die einzige Möglichkeit; **the ~ thing I have against it is that …** ich habe nur eins dagegen einzuwenden, nämlich, dass …; **the ~ thing** *or* **problem is …** nur …; **the ~ thing is (that) it's too late** es ist bloß *or* nur schon zu spät; **my ~ wish/regret** das einzige, was ich mir wünsche/was ich bedaure; **the ~ real problem** das einzig wirkliche Problem; **her ~ answer was a grin** *or* **to grin** ihre Antwort bestand nur aus einem Grinsen → **one ADJ d**
ADV **a** nur; **it's ~ five o'clock** es ist erst fünf Uhr; **~ yesterday/last week** erst gestern/letzte Woche; **she's ~ young** sie ist noch jung; **I ~ hope he gets here in time** ich hoffe nur, dass es noch rechtzeitig hier eintrifft; **I ~ wanted to be with you** ich wollte nur mit dir zusammen sein; **you ~ have to ask** Sie brauchen nur zu fragen; **I wanted ~ to be with you** *(esp liter)* ich wollte weiter nichts, als mit dir zusammen zu sein; **"members ~"** „(Zutritt) nur für Mitglieder"; **~ think of it!** stellen Sie sich das nur (mal) vor!; **~ to think of it made him ill** der bloße Gedanke *or* schon der Gedanke daran machte ihn krank
b *(in constructions)* **~ too true/easy** *etc* nur (all)zu wahr/leicht *etc*; **I'd be ~ too pleased to help** ich würde nur zu gerne helfen; **if ~ that hadn't happened** wenn das bloß *or* nur nicht passiert wäre; **we ~ just caught the train** wir haben den Zug gerade noch gekriegt; **he has ~ just arrived** er ist gerade erst angekommen; **I've ~ just got enough** ich habe gerade genug; **not ~ … but also …** nicht nur …, sondern auch …
CONJ bloß, nur; **I would do it myself, ~ I haven't time** ich würde es selbst machen, ich habe bloß *or* nur keine Zeit; **she looks like me, ~ taller** sie sieht aus wie ich, nur dass sie etwas größer ist

ono, o.n.o. *abbr of* **or near(est) offer**

on-off switch ['ɒn'ɒfswɪtʃ] **N** Ein- und Ausschalter *m*

onomatopoeia [ˌɒnəʊmætəʊ'piːə] **N** Lautmalerei *f*, Onomatopöie *f (spec)*

onomatopoeic [ˌɒnəˌmætəʊ'piːɪk], **onomatopoetic** [ˌɒnəˌmætəpəʊ'etɪk] **ADJ** lautmalend, onomatopoetisch *(spec)*

onrush ['ɒnrʌʃ] **N** *(of people)* Ansturm *m*; *(of water)* Schwall *m*

onrushing ['ɒnˌrʌʃɪŋ] **ADJ** *vehicle* heranbrausend; *tide, water* hereinbrechend

on-screen ['ɒnskriːn] **ADJ** **a** *(Comput)* auf dem Bildschirm; **read the ~ text** lesen Sie den Text auf dem Bildschirm; **~ display** Bildschirmanzeige *f* **b** *romance, kiss etc (TV)* Bildschirm-; *(Film)* Film-; **an ~ adventure** ein Bildschirm-/ /Filmabenteuer *nt* [ˌɒn'skriːn] **ADV** *(Film)* auf der Leinwand; *(TV, Comput)* auf dem Bildschirm

onset ['ɒnset] **N** Beginn *m*; *(of cold weather also)* Einbruch *m*; *(of illness)* Ausbruch *m*; **the sudden ~ of winter** der plötzliche Wintereinbruch; **the ~ of this illness is quite gradual** diese Krankheit kommt nur allmählich zum Ausbruch; **with the ~ of old age he …** als er alt zu werden begann …

onshore ['ɒnʃɔː'] **ADJ** an Land; *oilfield, job* auf dem Festland; **~ wind** Seewind *m* [ɒn'ʃɔː'] **ADV** *(also* **on shore***)* an Land; *(= on the mainland)* auf dem Festland; *blow* landwärts, küstenwärts

onside [ɒn'saɪd] **ADV** nicht im Abseits; **to stay ~** nicht ins Abseits laufen

on-site [ɒn'saɪt] **ADJ** *supervision, maintenance, personnel etc* vor Ort

onslaught ['ɒnslɔːt] **N** *(Mil)* (heftiger) Angriff (*on* auf *+acc*); *(fig also)* Attacke *f* (*on* auf *+acc*); **to make an ~ on sb/sth** *(fig) (verbally)* jdn/etw angreifen *or* attackieren; *(on work)* einer Sache *(dat)* zu Leibe rücken; **the constant ~ of advertisements on TV** das ständige Bombardement der Fernsehzuschauer mit Werbung

on-street parking [ˌɒnstriːt'pɑːkɪŋ] **N** Parken *nt* auf der Straße

Ont *abbr of* **Ontario**

on-the-job training [ˈɒnðəˌdʒɒb'treɪnɪŋ] **N** Ausbildung *f* am Arbeitsplatz, innerbetriebliche Ausbildung

on-the-spot [ˌɒnðə'spɒt] **ADJ** *fine* an Ort und Stelle verhängt; *decision, diagnosis, investigation, assessment* an Ort und Stelle; *reporting, coverage* vom Ort des Geschehens → *also* **spot**

onto ['ɒntʊ] **PREP** **a** *(= upon, on top of)* auf *(+acc)*; *(on sth vertical)* an *(+acc)*; **to clip sth ~ sth** etw an etw *(acc)* anklemmen; **to get ~ the committee** in den Ausschuss kommen
b *(in verbal expressions, see also vb +on)* **to get/come ~ a subject** auf ein Thema zu sprechen kommen; **to come ~ the market** auf den Markt kommen; **are you ~ the next chapter already?** sind Sie schon beim nächsten Kapitel?; **when will you get ~ the next chapter?** wann kommen Sie zum nächsten Kapitel?; **the windows look ~ the lake** die Fenster gehen zur Seeseite hinaus; **to be ~** *or* **on to sb** *(= find sb out)* jdm auf die Schliche gekommen sein *(inf)*; *(police)* jdm auf der Spur sein; **I think we're ~ something** ich glaube, hier sind wir auf etwas gestoßen

ontogeny [ɒn'tɒdʒənɪ] **N** Ontogenese *f*

ontological [ˌɒntə'lɒdʒɪkəl] **ADJ** ontologisch

ontology [ɒn'tɒlədʒɪ] **N** Ontologie *f*

onus ['əʊnəs] **N** *no pl* Pflicht *f*; *(= burden)* Last *f*, Bürde *f (geh)*; **to shift the ~ for sth onto sb** jdm die Verantwortung für etw zuschieben; **the ~ to do it is on him** *or* **lies with him** es liegt an ihm, das zu tun; **the ~ of proof lies with the prosecution** die Anklage trägt die Beweislast

onward ['ɒnwəd] **ADJ** **a** *(lit)* **~ flight** Anschlussflug *m*; **~ journey** Weiterreise *f*; **~ movement** Weiterbewegung *f*; *(on journey)* Weiterreise *f*; *(of goods)* Weitertransport *m* **b** *(fig)* **~ progress** weitere Fortschritte *pl*; **the ~ march of time/progress** das Fortschreiten der Zeit/der Vormarsch des Fortschritts **ADV** *(also* **onwards***)* voran, vorwärts; *march* weiter; **from today/this time ~** von heute/der Zeit an **INTERJ** *(also* **onwards***)* voran, vorwärts

onyx ['ɒnɪks] **N** Onyx *m* **ADJ** Onyx-; **~ jewellery** *(Brit) or* **jewelry** *(US)* Onyxschmuck *m*

oodles ['uːdlz] **PL** *(inf)* jede Menge *(inf)*; **~ and ~** Unmengen *pl (inf)*; **~ (and ~) of money** Geld wie Heu *(inf)*; **~ (and ~) of time** massenhaft Zeit *(inf)*

ooh [uː] **INTERJ** oh **VI** **there was a lot of ~ing and ahing** es gab viele Ohs und Ahs

oompah music ['uːmpɑːˌmjuːzɪk] **N** *(inf)* Blechblasmusik *f*

oomph [ʊmf] **N** *(inf)* **a** *(= energy)* Pep *m (inf)*, Schwung *m* **b** *(= sex appeal)* Sex *m (inf)*; **to have ~** sexy sein *(inf)*

oops [uːps, ʊps] **INTERJ** *(inf)* hoppla!

ooze [uːz] **N** **a** *(of mud, glue, resin)* Quellen *nt*; *(of water, blood)* Sickern *nt*, Triefen *nt*
b *(= mud)* Schlamm *m*
VI **a** *(lit)* triefen; *(water, blood)* sickern, triefen; *(wound)* nässen; *(resin, mud, glue)* (heraus)quellen
b *(fig)* **to ~ with charm/kindness** Liebenswürdigkeit/Güte verströmen; **the house ~s with wealth** *or* **money/culture** das Haus verströmt eine Atmosphäre von Reichtum/Kultur; **he stood there, charm oozing out of** *or* **from every pore** er stand da, förmlich triefend vor Liebenswürdigkeit
VT **a** (aus)schwitzen, absondern; *blood* triefen von; **my shoes were oozing water** das Wasser quoll mir aus den Schuhen
b *(fig) charm* triefen von *(pej)*, verströmen; *confidence, sex appeal* strotzen von; *insincerity* stinken vor *(+dat) (inf)*

► **ooze away** **VI** wegsickern; *(into ground)* versickern; *(fig: courage, pride, affection etc)* schwinden

► **ooze out** **VI** herausquellen; *(water, blood etc)* heraussickern

op[1] [ɒp] *abbr of* **opus** op

op[2] **N** *(inf)* = **operation**

OPAC *abbr of* **on-line public access catalogue** elektronischer Bibliothekskatalog

opacity [əʊ'pæsɪtɪ] **N** **a** Undurchsichtigkeit *f*, Lichtundurchlässigkeit *f*; *(of paint)* Deckkraft *f* **b** *(fig: of essay, meaning etc)* Undurchsichtigkeit *f*

opal ['əʊpəl] **N** *(= stone)* Opal *m*; *(= colour)* beigegraue Farbe **ADJ** Opal-, opal-; *(colour)* opalen *(liter)*, beigegrau schimmernd; **~ blue** opalblau; **~ ring** Opalring *m*

opalescence [ˌəʊpə'lesns] **N** Schimmern *nt*, Opaleszenz *f*

opalescent [ˌəʊpə'lesnt] **ADJ** schimmernd, opaleszierend

opal glass **N** Opalglas *nt*

opaline ['əʊpəliːn] **ADJ** opalen *(liter)*

opaque [əʊ'peɪk] **ADJ** **a** opak; *liquid* trüb; *paper, glass, window* undurchsichtig; *tights, stockings* blickdicht **b** *(fig) essay, prose, text* undurchsichtig, unklar

op art ['ɒp'ɑːt] **N** Op-Art *f*

op cit [ɒp'sɪt] *abbr of* **opere citato** op. cit.

OPEC ['əʊpek] *abbr of* **Organization of Petroleum Exporting Countries** OPEC *f*; **~ country** OPEC-Land *nt*

open ['əʊpən] **ADJ** **a** *door, bottle, book, eye, flower etc* offen, auf *pred*, geöffnet; *circuit* offen; *lines of communication* frei; *wound etc* offen; **to keep/hold the door ~** die Tür offen lassen *or* auflassen/offen halten *or* aufhalten; **to fling** *or* **throw the door ~** die Tür aufstoßen; **I can't keep my eyes ~** ich kann die Augen nicht offen halten *or* aufhalten; **the window flew ~** das Fenster flog auf; **the thugs split his head ~** die Schläger brachten ihm eine klaffende Wunde am Kopf bei; **his defeat blew the competition wide ~** durch seine Niederlage war der Ausgang des Wettbewerbs weit offen; **he threatened to blow the operation wide ~** *(= reveal sth secret)* er drohte damit, die Aktion offenzulegen; **a shirt ~ at the neck** ein am Hals offenes Hemd
b *(= open for business: shop, bank etc)* geöffnet; **the baker/baker's shop is ~** der Bäcker hat/der Bäckerladen ist *or* hat geöffnet *or* hat auf *(inf)*
c *(= not enclosed)* offen; *country, ground* offen, frei; *view* frei; *carriage, car* offen, ohne Verdeck; **in the ~ air** im Freien; **on ~ ground** auf offenem *or* freiem Gelände; *(= waste ground)* auf unbebautem Gelände
d *(= not blocked) Ling* offen; *road, canal, pores* offen, frei (*to* für), geöffnet; *rail track, river* frei (*to* für); *(Mus) string* leer; *pipe* offen; **~ note** Grundton *m*; **have you had your bowels ~ today?** *(Med form)* haben Sie heute Stuhlgang gehabt?; **~ to traffic/shipping** für den Verkehr/die Schifffahrt freigegeben; **"road ~ to traffic"** „Durchfahrt frei"
e *(= officially in use) building* eingeweiht; *road, bridge* (offiziell) freigegeben; *exhibition* eröffnet; **to declare sth ~** etw einweihen/freigeben/für eröffnet erklären
f *(= not restricted, accessible) letter, scholarship* offen; *market, competition* offen, frei; *(= public) meeting, trial* öffentlich; **to be ~ to sb** *(competition, membership, possibility)* jdm offenstehen; *(admission)* jdm freistehen; *(place)* für jdn geöffnet sein; *(park)* jdm zur Verfügung stehen; **my house is always ~ to you** mein Haus steht dir immer offen; **the director's door is always ~** die Tür des Direktors ist immer offen; **in ~ court** *(Jur)* in öffentlicher Verhandlung; **~ to the public** der Öffentlichkeit zugänglich; **park ~ to the public** öffentlicher Park; **~ forum** öffentliches Forum; **she gave us an ~ invitation to visit** sie lud uns ein, jederzeit bei ihr vorbeizukommen; **an unlocked window is an ~ invitation to a thief** ein unverschlossenes Fenster lädt geradezu zum Diebstahl ein
g **to be ~ to advice/suggestions/ideas** Ratschlägen/Vorschlägen/Ideen zugänglich sein *or* gegenüber offen sein; **I'm ~ to persuasion** ich lasse mich gern überreden; **I'm ~ to offers** ich lasse gern mit mir handeln *or* reden; **~ to**

bribes Bestechungen zugänglich
h (= not filled) *evening, time* frei; *job, post* frei, offen
i (= not concealed) *campaign, secret, resistance* offen; *hostility* offen, unverhüllt
j (= not decided or settled) *question* offen, ungeklärt, ungelöst; **they left the matter ~** sie ließen die Angelegenheit offen *or* ungeklärt; **to keep one's options ~** es offenlassen; **to keep an ~ mind** alles offenlassen; (judge, jury) unvoreingenommen sein; **to have an ~ mind on sth** einer Sache (*dat*) aufgeschlossen gegenüberstehen; **keep your mind ~ to new suggestions** verschließen Sie sich neuen Vorschlägen nicht; **to be ~ to debate** zur Debatte stehen
k (= exposed, not protected) (Mil) *town* offen; *coast* ungeschützt; **a position ~ to attack** eine exponierte *or* leicht angreifbare Position; **~ to the elements** Wind und Wetter ausgesetzt; **to be ~ to criticism/attack** der Kritik/Angriffen ausgesetzt sein; **to lay oneself ~ to criticism/attack** sich der Kritik/Angriffen aussetzen; **he left himself wide ~ to criticism** er setzte sich breiter Kritik aus; **a theory ~ to criticism** eine anfechtbare Theorie; **to be ~ to abuse** sich leicht missbrauchen lassen; **to be ~ to doubt** anzweifelbar sein
l *weave* locker; *fabric, pattern* durchbrochen
m (= frank) *character, face, person* offen, aufrichtig; **he was ~ with us** er war ganz offen mit uns
N **in the ~** (= outside) im Freien; (= on open ground) auf freiem Feld; **it's all out in the ~ now** nun ist alles heraus (*inf*), nun ist es alles zur Sprache gekommen; **to bring sth out into the ~** mit etw nicht länger hinterm Berg halten; **to come out into the ~** (fig, person) Farbe bekennen, sich erklären; (affair) herauskommen; **he eventually came out into the ~ about what he meant to do** er rückte endlich mit der Sprache heraus (*inf*), was er tun wollte; **to force sb out into the ~** jdn zwingen, sich zu stellen; (fig) jdn zwingen, Farbe zu bekennen; **to force sth out into the ~** (fig) etw zur Sprache bringen
VT **a** *door, mouth, bottle, letter etc* öffnen, aufmachen (*inf*); *book* aufschlagen, öffnen; *newspaper* aufschlagen; *throttle, circuit* öffnen; **he didn't ~ his mouth once** er hat kein einziges Mal den Mund aufgemacht (*inf*); **to ~ ranks** (Mil) weg- *or* abtreten
b (officially) *exhibition* eröffnen; *building* einweihen; *motorway* (für den Verkehr) freigeben
c *region* erschließen; **they ~ed a road through the mountains** durch die Berge wurde eine Straße gebaut
d (= reveal, unfold) öffnen; **to ~ one's heart to sb** sich jdm eröffnen (*geh*), jdm sein Herz aufschließen (*geh*); **to ~ sb's mind** jds Horizont erweitern; **~ your mind to new possibilities** öffnen Sie sich (*dat*) den Blick für neue Möglichkeiten; **it had ~ed new horizons for him** dadurch erschlossen sich ihm neue Horizonte
e (= start) *case, trial, account* eröffnen; *debate, conversation etc* beginnen
f (= set up) *shop* eröffnen, aufmachen (*inf*); *school* einrichten
g (Med) *pores* öffnen; **to ~ the bowels** (person) Stuhlgang haben; (medicine) abführen
h to ~ fire (Mil) das Feuer eröffnen (*on* auf *+acc*)
VI **a** aufgehen; (eyes) sich öffnen; (door, flower, book, wound, pores, window) sich öffnen, aufgehen; **I couldn't get the box/bottle to ~** ich habe die Schachtel/Flasche nicht aufbekommen; **it won't ~** es geht nicht auf
b (shop, museum) öffnen, aufmachen
c (= afford access: door) führen (*into* in *+acc*); **the two rooms ~ into one another** diese zwei Zimmer sind durch eine Tür verbunden → *also* **open on to**
d (= start) beginnen (*with* mit); (Cards, Chess) eröffnen; **the play ~s next week** das Stück wird ab nächster Woche gegeben; **when the play ~ed in Hull** bei der ersten Vorstellung in Hull

▶ **open on to** VI *+prep obj* (window) gehen auf (*+acc*); (door also) führen auf (*+acc*)

▶ **open out** VI **a** (= become wider) (river, street) sich verbreitern (*into* zu); (view) sich weiten, sich öffnen **b** (flower) sich öffnen, aufgehen **c** (map) sich ausfalten lassen **d** (fig: person) aus sich herausgehen; (business) sich ausdehnen (*into* auf *+acc*); (new horizons) sich auftun
VT sep **a** (= unfold) *map, newspaper etc* auseinanderfalten, aufmachen (*inf*) **b** (= make wider) *hole* erweitern, vergrößern **c** (fig) (= make expansive) *person* aus der Reserve locken; (= develop) *business* ausdehnen, erweitern

▶ **open up** VI **a** (flower) sich öffnen, aufgehen; (fig) (prospects) sich eröffnen, sich ergeben, sich erschließen; (field, new horizons) sich auftun, sich erschließen
b (= become expansive) gesprächiger werden; **to open up to sb** sich jdm gegenüber öffnen; **to get sb to open up** jdn zum Reden bringen; **to open up about sth** über etw (*acc*) sprechen *or* reden
c (inf: = accelerate) aufdrehen (*inf*)
d (= unlock doors: of house, shop etc) aufschließen, aufmachen; **open up!** aufmachen!
e (= start up: new shop) aufmachen
f (= start firing: guns, enemy) das Feuer eröffnen
g (Sport: game) sich auflockern
VT sep **a** (= make accessible) *territory, mine, prospects* erschließen; *new horizons etc* auftun, erschließen; (= unblock) *disused tunnel etc* frei machen; **to open up a country to trade** ein Land für den Handel erschließen; **to open oneself up to sth** sich für etw öffnen
b (= cut, make) *passage* bauen; *gap* schaffen; *hole* machen; (= make wider) *hole* größer *or* weiter machen, vergrößern
c (= unlock) *house, shop, car etc* aufschließen, aufmachen
d (= start) *business* eröffnen; *shop also* aufmachen; *debate* eröffnen
e (Sport) *game* auflockern; **to open up a lead** eine Führung herausarbeiten

open: **open-access library** N (Brit) Freihandbibliothek *f*; **open-air** ADJ im Freien; **open-air concert** N Freilichtkonzert *nt*; **open-air performance** N Freilichtaufführung *f*, Open-Air-Aufführung *f*; **open-air swimming pool** N Freibad *nt*; **open-air theatre**, (US) **open-air theater** N Freilichtbühne *f*, Freilichttheater *nt*; **open-and-shut** ADJ simpel; **it's an ~ case** es ist ein glasklarer Fall; **open-cast** ADJ *coal mine* über Tage *pred*; **~ mining** Tagebau *m*; **open cheque** N (Brit) Barscheck *m*; **open-cut** ADJ (US) = **open-cast**; **open day** N (Brit) Tag *m* der offenen Tür; **open-door** ADJ **~ policy** Politik *f* der Offenheit *or* der offenen Tür; **open-ended** ADJ **a** (lit) *box, tube, barrel* (an einer Seite) offen **b** (fig) *contract* offen, zeitlich nicht begrenzt; *offer, commitment* unbegrenzt; *discussion* alles offenlassend *attr*; *subject, category* endlos, uferlos; **this question/subject is ~** über diese Frage/dieses Thema kann man endlos weiterdiskutieren; **open enrollment** N (US Univ) *Einschreibung ohne Zulassungsvoraussetzungen*

opener ['əʊpnəʳ] N **a** Öffner *m* **b for ~s** (*inf*) für den Anfang

open: **open-eyed** ADJ mit weit offenen Augen; **open-face sandwich** N (US) belegtes Brot; **open government** N transparente Politik; **open-handed** ADJ freigebig, großzügig; **open-handedness** N Freigebigkeit *f*, Großzügigkeit *f*; **open-hearted** ADJ offen, offenherzig; **open-hearth** ADJ (Tech) **~ furnace** Herdofen *m*; **~ process** Siemens-Martin-Verfahren *nt*; **open-heart surgery** N Eingriff *m* am offenen Herzen; **open house** N **it's ~ there** das ist ein gastfreundliches Haus, das ist ein Haus der offenen Tür; **to keep ~** ein offenes Haus führen; **open housing** N (US) *Wohnraumvergabe ohne (Rassen)diskriminierung*

opening ['əʊpnɪŋ] N **a** Öffnung *f*; (in hedge, branches, clouds, wall etc also) Loch *nt*; (= cleft) Spalt *m*; (in traffic stream) Lücke *f*; (= forest clearing) Lichtung *f*; (fig: in conversation) Anknüpfungspunkt *m*
b (= beginning, initial stages) Anfang *m*; (Chess, Cards) Eröffnung *f*
c (= official opening) (of exhibition, stores) Eröffnung *f*; (of building) Einweihung *f*, Eröffnung *f*; (of motorway) Freigabe *f* (für den Verkehr); **Opening of Parliament** Parlamentseröffnung *f*
d (= action) (of door, mouth, bottle, letter, pub, shop etc) Öffnen *nt*; (of flower) Aufgehen *nt*; (of account) Eröffnung *f*; (= setting up: of shop, school etc) Eröffnen *nt*, Aufmachen *nt*; **hours of ~** Öffnungszeiten *pl*
e (= opportunity) Möglichkeit *f*, Chance *f*; (= job vacancy) (freie) Stelle; **he gave his adversary an ~** er bot seinem Gegner eine Blöße; **leave an ~ for negotiations** lassen Sie die Möglichkeit für Verhandlungen offen
ATTR (= initial, first) erste(r, s); *remarks* einführend; **~ speech** Eröffnungsrede *f*; **~ move** erster Zug; (Chess also) Eröffnungszug *m*

opening: **opening ceremony** N Eröffnungsfeierlichkeiten *pl*; **opening hours** PL Öffnungszeiten *pl*; **opening night** N Eröffnungsvorstellung *f* (am Abend); **opening price** N (St Ex) Eröffnungs- *or* Anfangskurs *m*; **opening stock market** N (St Ex) Börsenbeginn *m*; **opening time** N Öffnungszeit *f*; **what are the bank's ~s?** wann hat die Bank geöffnet?; **when is ~ on Sundays?** wann machen am Sonntag die Lokale auf?

openly ['əʊpənlɪ] ADV (= without concealment) offen; *speak also* freiheraus; (= publicly) öffentlich; **to be ~ critical of sb/sth** jdn/etw offen kritisieren; **he was ~ gay** er machte keinen Hehl aus seiner Homosexualität

open: **open-minded** ADJ aufgeschlossen; **open-mindedness** N Aufgeschlossenheit *f*; **open-mouthed** [,əʊpn'maʊðd] ADJ (in surprise or stupidity) mit offenem Mund, baff *pred* (*inf*); **she stood in ~ amazement** sie sperrte vor Staunen den Mund auf; **open-necked** ADJ *shirt* mit offenem Kragen

openness ['əʊpnnɪs] N **a** (= frankness) Offenheit *f*, Aufrichtigkeit *f*; (= publicness) Öffentlichkeit *f*, Offenheit *f* **b** (fig: of mind) Aufgeschlossenheit *f* (*to* für) **c** (of countryside, coast) Offenheit *f* **d** (= looseness: of weave) Lockerheit *f*

open: **open-plan** ADJ *flat etc* offen angelegt; **~ office** Großraumbüro *nt*; **open prison** N offenes Gefängnis; **open sandwich** N (Brit) belegtes Brot; **open season** N (Hunt) Jagdzeit *f*; **open-shelf library** N (US) Freihandbibliothek *f*; **open shop** N Open Shop *m*; **we have an ~** wir haben keinen Gewerkschaftszwang; **open-stack library** N (US) Freihandbibliothek *f*; **open-top(ped)** ADJ *bus* mit offenem Oberdeck; *car* mit offenem Verdeck; **Open University** N (Brit) Fernuniversität *f*; **to do an ~ course** ein Fernstudium machen *or* absolvieren

OPEN UNIVERSITY

Die **Open University** ist eine britische Fernuniversität, die 1969 gegründet wurde. Für die Kurse, die mit einem ersten akademischen Grad abschließen, werden keine formellen Aufnahmeanforderungen gestellt. Der Unterricht erfolgt über Radio- und Fernsehprogramme, die von der BBC ausgestrahlt werden. Schriftliche Arbeiten werden per Post verschickt. Zusätzlich müssen bestimmte Kurse, häufig im Sommer, in einer Art Internat besucht werden.

open verdict N **to record an ~** keine Erklärung zur Todesursache abgeben

openwork ['əʊpənwɜːk] N (Sew) Durchbrucharbeit *f*; (Archit) Durchbruchmauerwerk *nt* ADJ durchbrochen

opera [ˈɒpərə] N Oper *f*; **to go to the ~** in die Oper gehen

operable [ˈɒpərəbl] ADJ **a** *(Med)* operierbar, operabel **b** *(= practicable)* durchführbar, praktikabel

opera *in cpds* Opern-; **opera company** N Opernensemble *nt*; **opera glasses** PL Opernglas *nt*; **opera hat** N Chapeau claque *m*; **opera house** N Opernhaus *nt*

operand [ˈɒpəˌrænd] N *(Math, Comput)* Operand *m*

opera singer N Opernsänger(in) *m(f)*

operate [ˈɒpəreɪt] **VI** **a** *(machine, mechanism)* funktionieren; *(= be powered)* betrieben werden *(by, on* mit); *(= be in operation)* laufen, in Betrieb sein; *(fig: worker)* arbeiten; **how does it ~?** wie funktioniert es?; **to ~ at maximum capacity** *(lit, fig)* Höchstleistung bringen
b *(theory, plan, law)* sich auswirken; *(causes, factors)* hinwirken *(on, for* auf *+acc)*; *(organization, system)* arbeiten; *(medicine)* wirken; **I don't understand how his mind ~s** ich verstehe seine Gedankengänge nicht; **to ~ against sb/sth** gegen jdn/etw wirken; **to ~ in favour of sb/sth** zugunsten *or* zu Gunsten von jdm/etw wirken
c *(= carry on one's business)* operieren; *(company)* operieren, Geschäfte tätigen; *(airport, station)* in Betrieb sein; *(buses, planes)* verkehren; **I don't like the way he ~s** ich mag seine Methoden nicht; **that firm ~s by defrauding its customers** es gehört zu den (Geschäfts)methoden der Firma, die Kunden zu betrügen
d *(Mil)* operieren
e *(Med)* operieren *(on sb/sth* jdn/etw); **to be ~d on** operiert werden; **he ~d on him for appendicitis/a cataract** er operierte ihn am Blinddarm/auf grauen Star
VT **a** *(person) machine, switchboard etc* bedienen; *(= set in operation)* in Betrieb setzen; *brakes etc* betätigen; *(lever, button etc)* betätigen; *(electricity, batteries etc)* betreiben
b *(= manage) business* betreiben, führen
c *(= put into practice) system, law* anwenden, arbeiten nach; *policy also* betreiben
d *(airline etc) route* bedienen; *bus etc service* unterhalten; *holiday, tours* veranstalten

operatic [ˌɒpəˈrætɪk] ADJ Opern-; **~ aria/singer** Opernarie *f*/-sänger(in) *m(f)*

operatics [ˌɒpəˈrætɪks] N *sing* **(amateur) ~** Amateuropern *pl*

operating [ˈɒpəreɪtɪŋ] ADJ *attr* **a** *(Tech, Comm)* Betriebs-; **~ pressure** Betriebsdruck *m*; **~ profit** Betriebsgewinn *m*; **~ statement** *(US)* Gewinn- und Verlustrechnung *f* **b** *(Med)* Operations-

operating: **operating licence**, *(US)* **operating license** N Betriebserlaubnis *f*; **operating manual** N Betriebsanleitung *f*, Bedienungsanleitung *f*; **operating room** N *(US Med)* Operationssaal *m*, OP *m*; **operating system** N *(Comput)* Betriebssystem *nt*; **operating table** N *(Med)* Operationstisch *m*; **operating theatre** N *(Brit Med)* Operationssaal *m*, OP *m*

operation [ˌɒpəˈreɪʃən] N **a** *(= act of operating as in vi) (of machine, mechanism, system)* Funktionieren *nt*; *(of plan)* Durchführung *f*; *(of theory)* Anwendung *f*; *(= method of functioning) (of machine, organization)* Arbeitsweise *f*; *(of system, organ)* Funktionsweise *f*; *(of law)* Wirkungsweise *f*; **to be in ~** *(machine)* in Betrieb sein; *(law)* in Kraft sein; *(plan)* durchgeführt werden; **to be out of ~** außer Betrieb sein; *(fig: person)* nicht einsatzfähig sein; **to come into ~** *(machine)* in Gang kommen; *(law)* in Kraft treten; *(plan)* zur Anwendung gelangen; **to bring** *or* **put a law into ~** ein Gesetz in Kraft setzen
b *(= act of operating as in vt) (of machine etc)* Bedienung *f*, Handhabung *f*; *(of small mechanism)* Betätigung *f*; *(of business)* Betreiben *nt*, Führen *nt*; *(of system, policy)* Anwendung *f*; *(of plan, law)* Durchführung *f*; *(of route)* Bedienung *f*; *(of bus service etc)* Unterhaltung *f*; *(of tours)* Veranstaltung *f*
c *(Med)* Operation *f (on* an *+dat)*; **to have an ~** operiert werden; **to have a serious/heart ~** sich einer schweren Operation/einer Herzoperation unterziehen; **to have an ~ for a hernia** wegen eines Bruchs operiert werden
d *(= enterprise)* Unternehmen *nt*, Unternehmung *f*, Operation *f*; *(= task, stage in undertaking)* Arbeitsgang *m*; *(Math)* Rechenvorgang *m*, Operation *f*; **(business) ~s** Geschäfte *pl*; **to cease/resume ~s** den Geschäftsverkehr einstellen/wieder aufnehmen
e *(esp Mil: = campaign)* Operation *f*, Einsatz *m*, Unternehmen *nt*; *(in police force etc)* Einsatz *m*; **Operation Cynthia** Operation Cynthia

operational [ˌɒpəˈreɪʃənl] ADJ **a** *(= ready for use or action) machine, vehicle* betriebsbereit *or* -fähig; *army unit, aeroplane, tank etc* einsatzbereit *or* -fähig; *(fig) worker etc* einsatzbereit *or* -fähig; *(= in use or action) machine, vehicle etc* in Betrieb, in *or* im Gebrauch; *airport* in Betrieb; *army unit etc* im Einsatz
b *(= relating to operation, Tech, Comm)* Betriebs-; *(Mil)* Einsatz-; *problems, duties* operativ; **~ costs** Betriebskosten *pl*; **for ~ reasons** aus operativen Gründen; **~ research** betriebliche Verfahrens- *or* Planungsforschung, Operations Research *f*; **~ staff** *(for machinery)* Bedienungspersonal *nt*; *(in military, police action)* Einsatzkräfte *pl*; **~ range** *(of radar etc)* Einflussbereich *m*; *(of aircraft)* Flugbereich *m*; **~ plan** *(Mil)* Einsatzplan *m*; **~ flight** *(Mil)* Einsatzflug *m*; **~ base** *(Mil)* Operationsbasis *f*; **these submarines have never seen ~ service** diese U-Boote sind nie eingesetzt worden *or* kamen nie zum Einsatz

operations [ˌɒpəˈreɪʃənz]: **operations research** N *(Econ)* betriebliche Verfahrens- *or* Planungsforschung, Operations Research *f*; **operations room** N *(Mil, Police)* Hauptquartier *nt*

operative [ˈɒpərətɪv] **ADJ** **a** *(= producing an effect) measure, laws* wirksam; *clause* maßgeblich, entscheidend; *(= in effect) law* rechtsgültig, geltend; *plan, system, service* operativ; **"if" being the ~ word** wobei „wenn" das entscheidende Wort ist; **to become ~** *(law)* in Kraft treten; *(system etc)* verbindlich eingeführt werden **b** *(Med) treatment* operativ; **~ report** Operationsbericht *m*; **~ risk** Operationsrisiko *nt* **N** *(of machinery)* Maschinenarbeiter(in) *m(f)*; *(= detective)* Detektiv(in) *m(f)*; *(= spy)* Agent(in) *m(f)*; *(US Pol: = campaign worker)* Parteiarbeiter(in) *m(f)*

operator [ˈɒpəreɪtəˈ] N **a** *(Telec)* ≈ Vermittlung *f*; **a call through the ~** ein handvermitteltes Gespräch **b** *(of machinery)* (Maschinen)arbeiter(in) *m(f)*; *(of vehicle, lift)* Führer(in) *m(f)*; *(of electrical equipment)* Bediener(in) *m(f)*; *(of computer etc)* Operator(in) *m(f)*; **lathe** *etc* **~** Arbeiter(in) *m(f)* an der Drehbank *etc* **c** *(= private company)* Unternehmen *nt*; *(= company owner)* Unternehmer(in) *m(f)*; *(Fin)* (Börsen)makler(in) *m(f)*; *(= tour operator)* Veranstalter(in) *m(f)* **d** *(inf)* raffinierter Typ *m (inf)*; *(= criminal)* Gauner(in) *m(f)*; **to be a smooth/clever ~** raffiniert vorgehen

operetta [ˌɒpəˈretə] N Operette *f*

ophthalmic [ɒfˈθælmɪk] ADJ Augen-

ophthalmic optician N Optiker(in) *m(f)*; *(prescribing)* Augenarzt *m*, Augenärztin *f*; *(dispensing)* Optiker(in) *m(f)*

ophthalmic surgeon N Augenchirurg(in) *m(f)*

ophthalmologist [ˌɒfθælˈmɒlədʒɪst] N Ophthalmologe *m*, Ophthalmologin *f*

ophthalmology [ˌɒfθælˈmɒlədʒɪ] N Augenheilkunde *f*, Ophthalmologie *f (spec)*

ophthalmoscope [ɒfˈθælməskəʊp] N Augenspiegel *m*

opiate [ˈəʊpɪɪt] **N** Opiat *nt*; *(fig)* Beruhigungsmittel *nt* **ADJ** opiumhaltig

opine [əʊˈpaɪn] VT *(liter)* dafürhalten *(geh)*, meinen

opinion [əˈpɪnjən] ✪ 1.1, 2.1, 6.1, 6.2, 6.3, 11.1, 13, 26.2 N **a** *(= belief, view)* Meinung *f (about, on* zu), Ansicht *f (about, on* zu); *(political, religious)* Anschauung *f*; **in my ~** meiner Meinung *or* Ansicht nach, meines Erachtens; **in the ~ of the experts** nach Ansicht der Experten; **to be of the ~ that ...** der Meinung *or* Ansicht sein, dass ...; **to express** *or* **put forward an ~** seine Meinung äußern *or* vorbringen; **to ask sb's ~** jdn nach seiner Meinung fragen; **it is a matter of ~** das ist Ansichtssache; **I have no ~ about it** *or* **on the matter** dazu habe ich keine Meinung
b *no pl (= estimation)* Meinung *f*; **to have a good** *or* **high/low** *or* **poor ~ of sb/sth** eine gute *or* hohe/keine gute *or* eine schlechte Meinung von jdm/etw haben; **to form an ~ of sb/sth** sich *(dat)* eine Meinung über jdn/etw bilden
c *(= professional advice)* Gutachten *nt*; *(esp Med)* Befund *m*; **it is the ~ of the court that ...** das Gericht ist zu der Auffassung *or* Ansicht gekommen, dass ...; **to seek** *or* **get a second ~** *(esp Med)* ein zweites Gutachten *or* einen zweiten Befund einholen

opinionated [əˈpɪnjəneɪtɪd] ADJ selbstherrlich, rechthaberisch

opinion poll N Meinungsumfrage *f*

opinion pollster N Meinungsforscher(in) *m(f)*

opium [ˈəʊpɪəm] N *(lit, fig)* Opium *nt*; **the ~ of the masses** Opium *nt* für das Volk

opium *in cpds* Opium-; **opium den** N Opiumhöhle *f*; **opium fiend** N Opiumsüchtige(r) *mf*; **opium poppy** N Schlafmohn *m*

opossum [əˈpɒsəm] N Opossum *nt*

opp. *abbr of* **opposite** **a** *(= reverse)* Gegent. **b** *(= opposite from)* ggb.

opponent [əˈpəʊnənt] ✪ 14 N Gegner(in) *m(f)*; *(in debate, battle of wits etc also)* Opponent *m*

opportune [ˈɒpətjuːn] ADJ *time* gelegen, günstig; *remark* an passender Stelle; *action, event* rechtzeitig, opportun *(geh)*; **at an ~ moment** zu einem günstigen Zeitpunkt

opportunely [ˈɒpətjuːnlɪ] ADV gelegen, günstig, opportun *(geh)*; *remark* an passender Stelle

opportunism [ˌɒpəˈtjuːnɪzəm] N Opportunismus *m*

opportunist [ˌɒpəˈtjuːnɪst] **N** Opportunist(in) *m(f)* **ADJ** opportunistisch; **~ goal** Gelegenheitstor *nt*; **~ thief** Gelegenheitsdieb(in) *m(f)*

opportunity [ˌɒpəˈtjuːnɪtɪ] N **a** Gelegenheit *f*; **at the first** *or* **earliest ~** bei der erstbesten Gelegenheit; **I have little/no ~ for listening** *or* **to listen to music** ich habe wenig/nie Gelegenheit, Musik zu hören; **to take/seize the ~ to do sth** *or* **of doing sth** die Gelegenheit nutzen/ergreifen, etw zu tun; **as soon as I get the ~** sobald sich die Gelegenheit ergibt; **~ makes the thief** *(Prov)* Gelegenheit macht Diebe *(Prov)* **b** *(= chance to better oneself)* Chance *f*, Möglichkeit *f*; **opportunities for promotion** Aufstiegsmöglichkeiten *or* -chancen *pl*; **equality of ~** Chancengleichheit *f*

oppose [əˈpəʊz] VT **a** *(= be against)* ablehnen; *(= fight against)* sich entgegenstellen *or* entgegensetzen *(+dat)*, opponieren gegen *(form)*; *leadership, orders, plans, decisions, sb's wishes* sich widersetzen *(+dat)*; *government* sich stellen gegen; **if you think he is the best I won't ~ you** wenn Sie meinen, dass er der Beste ist, werde ich mich nicht dagegen stellen; **he ~s our coming** er ist absolut dagegen, dass wir kommen; **the President ~s sending the refugees back** der Präsident lehnt eine Rückführung der Flüchtlinge ab
b *(= stand in opposition: candidate)* kandidieren gegen
c *(form) (against, to +dat) (= set up in opposition)* entgegensetzen, entgegenstellen; *(= contrast)* gegenüberstellen

opposed [əˈpəʊzd] ✪ 12.1, 14 ADJ **a** *pred (= hostile)* dagegen; **to be ~ to sb/sth** gegen jdn/etw sein; **I am ~ to your going away** ich bin dagegen, dass Sie gehen **b** *(= opposite, contrasted)* entgegengesetzt, gegensätzlich; *aims, views, attitudes* gegensätzlich; **~ to all reason** entgegen aller Vernunft **c** **as ~ to** im Gegensatz zu

opposing [əˈpəʊzɪŋ] ADJ *team* gegnerisch; *army* feindlich; *characters* entgegengesetzt, gegensätzlich; *views* gegensätzlich; *minority* opponierend; **to be on ~ sides** auf entgegengesetzten Seiten stehen

opposing counsel N *(Jur)* Anwalt *m*/Anwältin *f* der Gegenpartei

opposing party N *(Jur)* Gegenpartei *f*

opposite [ˈɒpəzɪt] ADJ a *(in place)* entgegengesetzt; *(= facing)* gegenüberliegend *attr*, gegenüber *pred*; **to be ~** gegenüberliegen/-stehen/-sitzen *etc*; **on the ~ page** auf der Seite gegenüber, auf der gegenüberliegenden *or* anderen Seite
b *(= contrary)* entgegengesetzt (*to, from +dat*, zu); **in the ~ direction** in entgegengesetzter Richtung; **the ~ sex** das andere Geschlecht; **~ poles** *(Geog)* entgegengesetzte Pole *pl*; *(Elec also)* Gegenpole *pl*; *(fig)* zwei Extreme; **they've got quite ~ characters** sie sind ganz gegensätzliche Charaktere; **it had the ~ effect** es bewirkte das genaue Gegenteil
N Gegenteil *nt*; *(= contrast: of pair)* Gegensatz *m*; **black and white are ~s** Schwarz und Weiß sind Gegensätze; **quite the ~!** ganz im Gegenteil!; **she's quite the ~ of her husband** sie ist genau das Gegenteil von ihrem Mann
ADV gegenüber, auf der anderen *or* gegenüberliegenden Seite; **they sat ~** sie saßen uns/ihnen/sich *etc* gegenüber
PREP gegenüber *(+dat)*; **~ one another** sich gegenüber; **they live ~ us** sie wohnen uns gegenüber, sie wohnen gegenüber von uns; **to play ~ sb** *(Theat)* jds Gegenspieler(in) sein, die Gegenrolle zu jdm spielen

opposite number N Pendant *nt*

opposition [ˌɒpəˈzɪʃən] N a *(= resistance)* Widerstand *m*, Opposition *f*; *(= people resisting)* Opposition *f*; **to offer ~ to sb/sth** jdm/einer Sache Widerstand entgegensetzen; **to act in ~ to sth** einer Sache *(dat)* zuwiderhandeln; **to start up a business in ~ to sb** ein Konkurrenzunternehmen zu jdm aufmachen; **without ~** widerstandslos
b *(= contrast)* Gegensatz *m*; **to be in ~ to sb** anderer Meinung als jd sein; **to be in ~ to sth** im Gegensatz zu etw stehen; **he found himself in ~ to the general opinion** er sah sich im Widerspruch zur allgemeinen Meinung
c *(Astron)* Opposition *f*, Gegenschein *m*; **planet in ~** Planet *m* in Opposition *or* im Gegenschein
d *(esp Brit Parl)* **Opposition** Opposition *f*; **the Opposition, Her Majesty's Opposition** die Opposition; **leader of the Opposition** Oppositionsführer(in) *m(f)*
e *(Sport)* Gegner *pl*

Opposition benches PL *(esp Brit Parl)* Oppositionsbank *f*

oppositionist [ˌɒpəˈzɪʃənɪst] N *(Pol)* Oppositionelle(r) *mf*

opposition parties PL *(Pol)* Oppositionsparteien *pl*

oppress [əˈpres] VT a *(= tyrannize)* unterdrücken b *(= weigh down)* bedrücken, lasten auf *(+dat)*; *(heat)* lasten auf *(+dat)*; **the climate ~es me** das Klima macht mir schwer zu schaffen; **I feel ~ed by the heat** die Hitze lastet schwer auf mir

oppression [əˈpreʃən] N a *(= tyranny)* Unterdrückung *f* b *(fig: = depression)* Bedrängnis *f*, Bedrücktheit *f*; *(due to heat, climate)* bedrückende Atmosphäre; **the ~ of his spirits** seine Bedrängtheit

oppressive [əˈpresɪv] ADJ a *(= tyrannical) regime, laws* repressiv; *taxes* (er)drückend b *(fig)* drückend; *thought, mood* bedrückend; *heat* drückend, schwül

oppressively [əˈpresɪvlɪ] ADV a *rule* repressiv; **to tax ~** drückende Steuern *pl* erheben b *(fig) hot* drückend; **~ drab and grey** bedrückend grau in grau

oppressiveness [əˈpresɪvnɪs] N a Unterdrückung *f* (*of* durch); *(of taxes)* (er)drückende Last b *(fig)* bedrückende Atmosphäre; *(of thought)* schwere Last; *(of heat, climate)* Schwüle *f*

oppressor [əˈpresəʳ] N Unterdrücker(in) *m(f)*

opprobrious [əˈprəʊbrɪəs] ADJ *invective, remark* verächtlich, schmähend; *conduct* schändlich, schandhaft, schimpflich

opprobrium [əˈprəʊbrɪəm] N *(= disgrace)* Schande *f*, Schmach *f*; *(= scorn, reproach)* Schmähung *f*; **a term of ~** ein Schmähwort *nt*

opt [ɒpt] VI **to ~ for sth** sich für etw entscheiden; **to ~ to do sth** sich entscheiden, etw zu tun; **to ~ to join the single currency** seine Option wahrnehmen, der Währungsunion beizutreten

▶ **opt in** VI *(= join)* beitreten *(+dat)*; *(= participate)* mitmachen

▶ **opt out** VI sich anders entscheiden; *(of awkward situation also)* abspringen (*of* bei); *(of responsibility, invitation)* ablehnen (*of +acc*); *(= give up membership) (also Rad, TV)* austreten (*of* aus); *(of insurance scheme)* kündigen (*of +acc*); *(Brit: school, hospital)* aus der Kontrolle der Kommunalverwaltung austreten; **he opted out of going to the party** er entschied sich, doch nicht zur Party zu gehen

optative [ˈɒptətɪv] N Optativ *m*, Wunschform *f* ADJ optativ

optic [ˈɒptɪk] ADJ optisch

optical [ˈɒptɪkəl] ADJ optisch

optical: **optical character reader** N *(Comput)* optischer Klarschriftleser; **optical character recognition** N *(Comput)* optische Zeichenerkennung; **optical disk** N optische Platte; **optical fibre**, *(US)* **optical fiber** N *(= material)* Glasfaser *f*; *(= cable)* Glasfaserkabel *nt*; **optical illusion** N optische Täuschung; **optical scanner** N optischer Scanner

optician [ɒpˈtɪʃən] N Augenarzt *m*, Augenärztin *f*, Optiker(in) *m(f)*

optic nerve N Sehnerv *m*

optics [ˈɒptɪks] N *sing* Optik *f*

optima [ˈɒptɪmə] *pl of* **optimum**

optimal [ˈɒptɪml] ADJ optimal

optimism [ˈɒptɪmɪzəm] N Optimismus *m*

optimist [ˈɒptɪmɪst] N Optimist(in) *m(f)*

optimistic [ˌɒptɪˈmɪstɪk] ADJ optimistisch; **to be ~ about sth** in Bezug auf etw *(acc)* optimistisch sein; **I'm not very ~ about it** da bin ich nicht sehr optimistisch; **the talks ended on an ~ note** die Gespräche endeten optimistisch

optimistically [ˌɒptɪˈmɪstɪkəlɪ] ADV optimistisch

optimize [ˈɒptɪmaɪz] VT optimieren

optimum [ˈɒptɪməm] ADJ optimal; *results, conditions also* bestmöglich; **for ~ health** für beste Gesundheit N *pl* **optima** *or* **-s** Optimum *nt*; **at an ~** optimal

option [ˈɒpʃən] N a *(= choice)* Wahl *f no pl*; *(= possible course of action)* Möglichkeit *f*; **you have the ~ of leaving or staying** Sie haben die Wahl, ob Sie gehen oder bleiben wollen; **to give sb the ~ of doing sth** jdm die Wahl lassen, etw zu tun; **I have little/no ~** mir bleibt kaum eine/keine andere Wahl; **he had no ~ but to come** ihm blieb nichts anderes übrig, als zu kommen; **you have only two ~s (open to you)** es stehen Ihnen nur zwei Möglichkeiten zur Wahl; **that leaves us no ~** das lässt uns keine andere Wahl; **to keep** *or* **leave one's ~s open** sich *(dat)* alle Möglichkeiten offenlassen; **imprisonment without the ~ of a fine** *(Jur)* Gefängnisstrafe *f* ohne Zulassung einer ersatzweisen Geldstrafe; **the military ~** die militärische Lösung
b *(Comm)* Option *f* (*on* auf *+acc*); *(on house, goods etc)* Vorkaufsrecht *nt* (*on* an *+dat*); *(on shares)* Bezugsrecht *nt* (*on* für); **with an ~ to buy** mit einer Kaufoption *or (on shares)* Bezugsoption; *(= on approval)* zur Ansicht; **to have a 20-day ~** eine Option mit einer Frist von 20 Tagen haben
c *(Univ, Sch)* Wahlfach *nt*

optional [ˈɒpʃənl] ADJ *(= not compulsory)* freiwillig; *(= not basic) trim, mirror etc* auf Wunsch erhältlich; **"evening dress ~"** „Abendkleidung nicht Vorschrift"; **"fancy dress ~"** „kein Kostümzwang"; **~ extras** Extras *pl*; **the cigar lighter is an ~ extra** der Zigarettenanzünder wird auf Wunsch eingebaut; **~ subject** *(Sch, Univ)* Wahlfach *nt*

optometrist [ɒpˈtɒmətrɪst] N *(US: = optician)* Optiker(in) *m(f)*

optometry [ɒpˈtɒmətrɪ] N Optometrie *f*

opt-out [ˈɒptaʊt] ADJ *attr* a *(Brit) school, hospital* aus der Kontrolle der Kommunalverwaltung ausgetreten b **~ clause** Rücktrittsklausel *f* N a *(Brit: by school, hospital)* Austritt *m* aus der Kontrolle der Kommunalverwaltung b *(from agreement, treaty)* Rücktritt *m*

opulence [ˈɒpjʊləns] N *no pl* Reichtum *m*; *(of person's appearance also)* Wohlhabenheit *f*; *(of clothes, building, room)* Prunk *m*, Stattlichkeit *f*; *(of car, chairs, carpet)* Feudalität *f*; *(of décor, lifestyle, vegetation)* Üppigkeit *f*; *(of figure)* Üppigkeit *f*, Fülligkeit *f*; **to live in ~** im Überfluss leben

opulent [ˈɒpjʊlənt] ADJ reich; *appearance (of person) also* wohlhabend; *clothes, building, room* prunkvoll, stattlich; *car, chairs, carpets* feudal; *décor, lifestyle, vegetation* üppig; *figure* üppig, füllig; *feel, look, film, production* opulent

opus [ˈəʊpəs] N *pl* **opera** [ˈɒpərə] *(Mus)* Opus *nt*

OR a *(Sport) abbr of* **Olympic record** b *(Med) abbr of* **operating room** OP *m*

or[1] [ɔːʳ] N *(Her)* Gold *nt*

or[2] ✪ 26.2 CONJ a oder; *(with neg)* noch; **he could not read or write** er konnte weder lesen noch schreiben; **without food or water** ohne Nahrung oder Wasser; **in a day/month or two** in ein bis *or* oder zwei Tagen/Monaten; **I'm coming, ready or not** ich komme!; **we're going outside, rain or no rain** wir gehen nach draußen, ob es nun regnet oder nicht
b *(= that is)* (oder) auch; **the Lacedaemonians, or Spartans** die Lazedämonier, (oder) auch Spartaner; **Rhodesia, or rather, Zimbabwe** Rhodesien, beziehungsweise Simbabwe
c *(= otherwise)* sonst; **you'd better go or (else) you'll be late** gehen Sie jetzt besser, sonst kommen Sie zu spät; **you'd better do it or else!** tu das lieber, sonst …!

oracle [ˈɒrəkl] N a Orakel *nt*; *(= person)* Seher(in) *m(f)*; *(fig)* Alleswisser(in) *m(f)* b **Oracle®** *britisches Videotext-System*

oracular [ɒˈrækjʊləʳ] ADJ *inscriptions, utterances, tone* orakelhaft; *powers* seherisch; *(fig)* weise; **~ shrine** Orakelstätte *f*

oral [ˈɔːrəl] ADJ a *consonant, phase, contraceptive* oral; *vaccine* oral verabreicht; *medicine* zum Einnehmen b *(= verbal) communication, agreement, examination, tradition etc* mündlich; **to give ~ evidence to a committee** vor einer Kommission aussagen; **to improve one's ~ skills in a language** eine Sprache besser sprechen lernen N Mündliche(s) *nt*

oral: **oral cavity** N Mundhöhle *f*; **oral history** N Oral History *f*, mündliche Geschichtsdokumentation; **oral hygiene** N Mundhygiene *f*; **oral intercourse** N Oralverkehr *m*

orally [ˈɔːrəlɪ] ADV a oral; **to take a medicine ~** eine Medizin oral einnehmen b *(= verbally)* mündlich

oral: **oral sex** N Oralverkehr *m*; **oral surgeon** N Kieferchirurg(in) *m(f)*; **oral surgery** N Kieferchirurgie *f*; **oral vaccination** N Schluckimpfung *f*

orange [ˈɒrɪndʒ] N a *(= fruit)* Orange *f*, Apfelsine *f*; *(= tree)* Orangen- *or* Apfelsinenbaum *m*; *(= drink)* Orangensaft *m* b *(= colour)* Orange *nt* ADJ a Orangen-; **~ flavour** *(Brit) or* **flavor** *(US)* Orangengeschmack *m* b *(colour)* orange *inv*, orange(n)farben *or* -farbig; **bright ~** grellorange

orangeade [ˈɒrɪndʒˈeɪd] N Orangeade *f*, Orangenlimonade *f*

orange: **orange blossom** N Orangenblüte *f* *(wird von Bräuten zur Hochzeit getragen)*; **orange box** N Obst- *or* Apfelsinenkiste *f*; **orange-coloured**, *(US)* **orange-colored** ADJ orange(n)farben *or* -farbig; **Orange Day** N *Jahrestag der Schlacht an der Boyne (1690) am 12. Juli (Festtag der Protestanten in Nordirland)*; **orange flower water** N Orangenblütenwasser *nt*; **Orange Free State** N Oranjefreistaat *m*; **orange grove** N Orangenhain *m*; **orange juice** N Orangensaft *m*, O-Saft *m (inf)*; **Orangeman** N Mitglied *nt* des Oranierordens; **Orangeman's Day** N = **Orange Day**; **Orange March** N Demonstration *f* des Oranienordens; **orange marmalade** N Orangenmarmelade *f*; **Orange Order** N Oranienorden *m (protestantische Vereinigung, die den Namen Wilhelms von Oranien trägt)*; **orange peel** N Orangen- *or* Apfelsinenschale *f*

orangery ['ɒrɪndʒərɪ] N Orangerie *f*

orange: **orange squash** N *(Brit)* Orangenkonzentrat *nt*; *(diluted)* Orangengetränk *nt*; **orange stick** N Manikürstäbchen *nt*; **orange zest** N geriebene Orangenschale

orang-outang, **orang-utan** [ɔːˌræŋuːˈtæŋ, -n] N Orang-Utan *m*

orate [ɒ'reɪt] VI Reden/eine Rede halten *(to* vor *+dat)*

oration [ɒ'reɪʃən] N Ansprache *f*; **funeral ~** Grabrede *f*

orator ['ɒrətə'] N Redner(in) *m(f)*, Orator *m (rare, Hist)*

oratorical [ˌɒrə'tɒrɪkəl] ADJ oratorisch

oratorio [ˌɒrə'tɔːrɪəʊ] N *(Mus)* Oratorium *nt*

oratory[1] ['ɒrətərɪ] N *(= art of making speeches)* Redekunst *f*

oratory[2] N *(Eccl)* Oratorium *nt*

orb [ɔːb] N **a** *(poet)* Ball *m*; *(= star)* Gestirn *nt (geh)*; *(= eye)* Auge *nt* **b** *(of sovereignty)* Reichsapfel *m*

orbit ['ɔːbɪt] **N a** *(Astron, Space) (= path)* Umlaufbahn *f*, Kreisbahn *f*, Orbit *m*; *(= single circuit)* Umkreisung *f*, Umlauf *m*; **to be in ~ ((a)round the earth)** in der (Erd)umlaufbahn sein; **to go into ~ ((a)round the sun)** in die (Sonnen)umlaufbahn eintreten; **to put a satellite into ~** einen Satelliten in die Umlaufbahn schießen **b** *(fig)* Kreis *m*; *(= sphere of influence)* (Macht)bereich *m*, Einflusssphäre *f* **VT** umkreisen **VI** kreisen

orbital ['ɔːbɪtl] **ADJ** orbital; *flight* im Orbit; **~ motion** Kreisbewegung *f* **N** *(also* **orbital motorway)** Ringautobahn *f*

orbiter ['ɔːbɪtə'] N *(Space)* Orbiter *m*, Raumflugkörper *m*

orchard ['ɔːtʃəd] N Obstgarten *m*; *(commercial)* Obstplantage *f*; **apple/cherry ~** Obstgarten *m* mit Apfel-/Kirschbäumen; *(commercial)* Apfel-/ /Kirschplantage *f*

orchestra ['ɔːkɪstrə] N Orchester *nt*

orchestral [ɔː'kestrəl] ADJ Orchester-, orchestral; **~ music** Orchestermusik *f*; **~ musician** *or* **player** Orchestermusiker(in) *m(f)*; **~ work** Orchesterwerk *nt*

orchestrally [ɔː'kestrəlɪ] ADV orchestral

orchestra: **orchestra pit** N Orchestergraben *m*; **orchestra stalls** PL Orchestersitze *pl*; **a seat in the ~** ein Orchestersitz *m*

orchestrate ['ɔːkɪstreɪt] VT orchestrieren

orchestrated ['ɔːkɪstreɪtɪd] ADJ *(fig) attempt, campaign* gezielt; **a carefully ~ protest** eine sorgfältig organisierte Protestaktion

orchestration [ˌɔːkɪs'treɪʃən] N Orchestrierung *f*, Orchesterbearbeitung *f*

orchid ['ɔːkɪd] N Orchidee *f*

ordain [ɔː'deɪn] VT **a** *sb* ordinieren; *(Eccl) a priest* weihen; **to be ~ed priest/to the ministry** ordiniert werden; *(Catholic also)* zum Priester geweiht werden **b** *(= destine: God, fate)* wollen, bestimmen; **God has ~ed that man should die** Gott hat es gewollt *or* hat bestimmt, dass der Mensch sterbe; **fate ~ed that he should die, it was ~ed that he should die** das Schicksal hat es so gefügt *or* es war ihm vom Schicksal bestimmt, dass er sterben sollte **c** *(= decree) (law)* bestimmen; *(ruler)* verfügen

ordeal [ɔː'diːl] N **a** Tortur *f*; *(stronger, long-lasting)* Martyrium *nt*; *(= torment, emotional ordeal)* Qual *f* **b** *(Hist: = trial)* Gottesurteil *nt*; **~ by fire/water** Feuer-/Wasserprobe *f*

order ['ɔːdə'] ✪ 20.3, 20.4 **N a** *(= sequence)* (Reihen)folge *f*, (An)ordnung *f*; **word ~** Wortstellung *f*, Wortfolge *f*; **are they in ~/in the right ~?** sind sie geordnet/in der richtigen Reihenfolge?; **in ~ of preference/merit** in der bevorzugten/in der ihren Auszeichnungen entsprechenden Reihenfolge; **to put sth in (the right) ~** etw ordnen; **to be in the wrong ~** *or* **out of ~** durcheinander sein; *(one item)* nicht am richtigen Platz sein; **to get out of ~** durcheinandergeraten; *(one item)* an eine falsche Stelle kommen → **cast N d**

b *(= system)* Ordnung *f*; **there's no ~ in his work** seiner Arbeit fehlt die Systematik; **he has no sense of ~** er hat kein Gefühl für Systematik *or* Methode; **the ~ of the world** die Weltordnung; **it is in the ~ of things** es liegt in der Natur der Dinge; **a new social/political ~** eine neue soziale/politische Ordnung

c *(= tidy or satisfactory state)* Ordnung *f*; **his passport was in ~** sein Pass war in Ordnung; **to put** *or* **set one's life/affairs in ~** Ordnung in sein Leben/seine Angelegenheiten bringen

d *(= discipline) (in society)* Ordnung *f*; *(in school, team)* Disziplin *f*, Ordnung *f*; **to keep ~** die Ordnung wahren, die Disziplin aufrechterhalten; **to keep the children in ~** die Kinder unter Kontrolle halten; **~ in court** *(Brit) or* **the courtroom** *(US)*! Ruhe im Gerichtssaal!; **~, ~!** Ruhe!

e *(= working condition)* Zustand *m*; **to be in good ~** in gutem Zustand sein; *(= work well)* in Ordnung sein; **to be out of/in ~** *(car, radio, telephone)* nicht funktionieren/funktionieren; *(machine, lift also)* außer/in Betrieb sein; **"out of ~"** „außer Betrieb" → **working ADJ c**

f *(= command)* Befehl *m*, Order *f (old, hum)*; **by ~ of the court** laut gerichtlicher Anweisung; **~s are ~s** Befehl ist Befehl; **"no parking/smoking by ~"** „Parken/Rauchen verboten!"; **"no parking - by ~ of the Town Council"** „Parken verboten - die Stadtverwaltung"; **by ~ of the minister** auf Anordnung des Ministers; **I don't take ~s from anyone** ich lasse mir von niemandem befehlen; **to be under ~s to do sth** Instruktionen haben, etw zu tun; **until further ~s** bis auf weiteren Befehl

g *(in restaurant etc, Comm)* Bestellung *f*; *(= contract to manufacture or supply)* Auftrag *m*; **to place an ~ with sb** eine Bestellung bei jdm aufgeben *or* machen/jdm einen Auftrag geben; **to put sth on ~** etw in Bestellung/Auftrag geben; **to be on ~** bestellt sein; **two ~s of French fries** *(esp US)* zwei Portionen Pommes frites; **made to ~** auf Bestellung (gemacht *or* hergestellt)

h *(Fin)* **cheque** *(Brit) or* **check** *(US)* **to ~** Orderscheck *m*, Namensscheck *m*; **pay to the ~ of** zahlbar an *(+acc)*; **pay X or Order** (zahlbar) an X oder dessen Order

i **in ~ to do sth** um etw zu tun; **in ~ that** damit

j *(= correct procedure at meeting, Parl etc)* **a point of ~** eine Verfahrensfrage; **to be out of ~** gegen die Verfahrensordnung verstoßen; *(Jur: evidence)* unzulässig sein; *(fig)* aus dem Rahmen fallen; **to call sb to ~** jdn ermahnen, sich an die Verfahrensordnung zu halten; **to call the meeting/delegates to ~** die Versammlung/die Delegierten zur Ordnung rufen; **an explanation/a drink would seem to be in ~** eine Erklärung/ein Drink wäre angebracht; **congratulations are in ~** Glückwünsche sind angebracht; **is it in ~ for me to go to Paris?** ist es in Ordnung, wenn ich nach Paris fahre?; **his demand is quite in ~** seine Forderung ist völlig berechtigt; **what's the ~ of the day?** was steht auf dem Programm *(also fig) or* auf der Tagesordnung?; *(Mil)* wie lautet der Tagesbefehl?

k *(Archit)* Säulenordnung *f*; *(fig: = class, degree)* Art *f*; **intelligence of a high** *or* **the first ~** hochgradige Intelligenz; **the present crisis is of a different ~** die gegenwärtige Krise ist andersgeartet; **something in the ~ of ten per cent** in der Größenordnung von zehn Prozent; **something in the ~ of one in ten applicants** etwa einer von zehn Bewerbern

l *(Mil: = formation)* Ordnung *f*

m *(social)* Schicht *f*; **the higher/lower ~s** die oberen/unteren Schichten; **the ~ of baronets** der Freiherrnstand

n *(Eccl: of monks etc)* Orden *m*; **Benedictine ~** Benediktinerorden *m*

o **orders PL (holy) ~s** *(Eccl)* Weihe(n) *f(pl)*; *(of priesthood)* Priesterweihe *f*; **to take (holy) ~s** die Weihen empfangen; **he is in (holy) ~s** er gehört dem geistlichen Stand an

p *(= honour, society of knights)* Orden *m*; **Order of Merit** *(Brit)* Verdienstorden *m* → **garter**

VT a *(= command, decree) sth* befehlen, anordnen; *(= prescribe: doctor)* verordnen *(for sb* jdm); **to ~ sb to do sth** jdn etw tun heißen *(geh)*, jdm befehlen *or (doctor)* verordnen, etw zu tun; *(esp Mil)* jdn dazu beordern, etw zu tun; **to ~ sb's arrest** jds Verhaftung anordnen; **he was ~ed to be quiet** man befahl ihm, still zu sein; *(in public)* er wurde zur Ruhe gerufen; **the army was ~ed to retreat** dem Heer wurde der Rückzug befohlen; **he ~ed his gun to be brought (to him)** er ließ sich *(dat)* sein Gewehr bringen; **to ~ sb out/home** jdn heraus-/heimbeordern *(form, hum) or* -rufen; *(= send out etc)* jdn hinaus-/heimbeordern *(form, hum) or* -schicken

b *(= direct, arrange) one's affairs, life* ordnen; **to ~ arms** *(Mil)* das Gewehr abnehmen

c *(Comm etc) goods, dinner, taxi* bestellen; *(to be manufactured) ship, suit, machinery etc* in Auftrag geben *(from sb* bei jdm)

VI bestellen

▶ **order about** *(Brit) or* **around** VT *sep* herumkommandieren

▶ **order in** VT *(esp US) food* (bei einem Heimservice) bestellen

order: **order book** N *(Comm)* Auftragsbuch *nt*; **the ~s are full** die Auftragsbücher sind voll; **order cheque** N Orderscheck *m*, Namensscheck *m*; **order form** N Bestellformular *nt*, Bestellschein *m*

orderliness ['ɔːdəlɪnɪs] N **a** Ordentlichkeit *f*; **the ~ of his life** sein geregeltes Leben **b** *(of group, demonstration)* Friedlichkeit *f*, Gesittetheit *f*

orderly ['ɔːdəlɪ] **ADJ a** *(= tidy, methodical)* ordentlich, geordnet; *life* geordnet, geregelt; *person, mind* ordentlich, methodisch; **in an ~ fashion** *or* **manner** geordnet **b** *group, demonstration* ruhig, friedlich, gesittet **N a** *(Mil, attached to officer)* Bursche *m (dated)* **b** **(medical) ~** Pfleger(in) *m(f)*; *(Mil)* Sanitäter(in) *m(f)*

orderly: **orderly officer** N diensthabender Offizier, diensthabende Offizierin, Offizier(in) *m(f)* vom Dienst; **orderly room** N Schreibstube *f*

order paper N *(esp Parl)* Tagesordnung *f*

ordinal ['ɔːdɪnl] *(Math)* **ADJ** Ordnungs-, Ordinal- **N** Ordnungs- *or* Ordinalzahl *f*, Ordinale *f (spec)*

ordinal number N *(Math)* Ordnungszahl *f*, Ordinalzahl *f*

ordinance ['ɔːdɪnəns] N **a** *(= order) (of government)* Verordnung *f*; *(Jur)* Anordnung *f*; *(of fate)* Fügung *f (geh)* **b** *(Eccl) (= sacrament)* Sakrament *nt*; *(= rite)* Ritus *m*

ordinand ['ɔːdɪˌnænd] N Priesteramtskandidat(in) *m(f)*

ordinarily ['ɔːdnrɪlɪ] ADV normalerweise, gewöhnlich; *(+adj)* normal, wie gewöhnlich; **more than ~ stupid/intelligent** außergewöhnlich dumm/intelligent

ordinary ['ɔːdnrɪ] **ADJ a** *(= usual)* gewöhnlich, normal; **to do sth in the ~ way** etw auf die normale *or* gewöhnliche Art und Weise tun; **in the**

~ **way I would ...** normalerweise *or* gewöhnlich würde ich ...; ~ **use** normaler Gebrauch; **my ~ doctor** der Arzt, zu dem ich normalerweise gehe
b *(= average)* normal, durchschnittlich; *(= nothing special, commonplace)* gewöhnlich, alltäglich; **the ~ Englishman** der normale Engländer; **a very ~ kind of person** ein ganz gewöhnlicher Mensch; **this is no ~ car** dies ist kein gewöhnliches Auto
N a out of the ~ außergewöhnlich, außerordentlich; **nothing/something out of the ~** nichts/etwas Außergewöhnliches *or* Ungewöhnliches; **to be a cut above the ~** besser als der Durchschnitt sein; **intelligence above the ~** überdurchschnittliche *or* außergewöhnliche Intelligenz
b *(form)* **physician/painter in ~ to the king** königlicher Leibarzt/Hofmaler
c *(Eccl)* **the ~ of the mass** Ordo *m* Missae

ordinary: **Ordinary grade** N *(Brit)* = **O grade**; **Ordinary level** N *(Brit)* = **O level**; **Ordinary National Certificate** N *(Brit) Qualifikationsnachweis von einer Fachschule*; **Ordinary National Diploma** N *(Brit) Diplom einer technischen Fachschule*; **ordinary seaman** N Maat *m*; **ordinary share** N *(Fin)* Stammaktie *f*

ordination [ˌɔːdɪˈneɪʃən] N Ordination *f*

ordnance [ˈɔːdnəns] *(Mil)* N **a** *(= artillery)* (Wehr)material *nt* **b** *(= supply)* Material *nt*, Versorgung *f*; *(= corps)* Technische Truppe; *(in times of war)* Nachschub *m*

ordnance: **ordnance factory** N Munitionsfabrik *f*; **ordnance map** N **a** *(Brit)* → **Ordnance Survey map b** *(US Mil)* Generalstabskarte *f*; **Ordnance Survey** N *(Brit)* ≈ Landesvermessungsamt *nt*; **Ordnance Survey map** N *(Brit)* amtliche topografische Karte *(form)*, Messtischblatt *nt*

ordure [ˈɔːdjʊəʳ] N *(liter)* *(= excrement)* Kot *m*; *(= rubbish)* Unrat *m*, Unflat *m (geh)*; *(liter fig)* Schmutz *m no pl*

ore [ɔːʳ] N Erz *nt*

ore-bearing ADJ *(Geol) layer etc* Erz führend, erzhaltig

Ore(g) *abbr of* **Oregon**

oregano [ˌɒrɪˈgɑːnəʊ] N Origano *m*, Oregano *m*

organ [ˈɔːgən] N **a** *(Anat)* Organ *nt*; *(= penis)* Geschlecht *nt*; ~ **of speech** Sprechorgan *nt* **b** *(Mus)* Orgel *f*; **to be at the ~** die Orgel spielen **c** *(= mouthpiece of opinion)* Sprachrohr *nt*; *(= newspaper)* Organ *nt* **d** *(= means of action)* Organ *nt*

organ bank N *(Med)* Organbank *f*

organdie, *(US)* **organdy** [ˈɔːgəndɪ] N Organdy *m*

organ: **organ donor** N Organspender(in) *m(f)*; **organ donor card** N Organspenderausweis *m*; **organ-grinder** N Drehorgelspieler(in) *m(f)*; *(= man also)* Leierkastenmann *m*; **I want to talk to the ~, not the monkey** *(inf)* ich will den sprechen, der das Sagen hat

organic [ɔːˈgænɪk] ADJ **a** *(Sci, Med)* organisch **b** *vegetables, farming* biodynamisch; ~ **wine/flour** Wein *m*/Mehl *nt* aus biologisch kontrolliertem Anbau; ~ **beer** *Bier aus Zutaten, die aus biologisch kontrolliertem Anbau stammen*; ~ **meat** Fleisch *nt* aus biologisch kontrollierter Zucht; ~ **methods** *(Agr)* naturnahe Bewirtschaftung **c** *(fig) whole, unity* organisch; *part of whole* substanziell, substantiell; *fault* immanent

organically [ɔːˈgænɪkəlɪ] ADV **a** *(Sci, Med)* organisch **b** *farm, grow* biodynamisch **c** *(fig) integrated, connected etc* organisch

organic: **organic chemistry** N organische Chemie; **organic farm** N Bio-Landwirtschaftsbetrieb *m*; **organic farmer** N Bio-Bauer *m*, Bio-Bäuerin *f*; **organic waste** N organische Abfallprodukte *pl*, Biomüll *m*

organism [ˈɔːgənɪzəm] N *(Biol, fig)* Organismus *m*

organist [ˈɔːgənɪst] N Organist(in) *m(f)*

organization [ˌɔːgənaɪˈzeɪʃən] N **a** *(= act)* Organisation *f (also Pol)*; *(of time)* Einteilung *f* **b** *(= arrangement)* Ordnung *f*; *(of facts, work)* Organisation *f*; *(of time)* Einteilung *f*; *(of essay)* Aufbau *m*; *(of sb's life)* Planung *f* **c** *(= institution)* Organisation *f*; *(Comm)* Unternehmen *nt*

organizational [ˌɔːgənaɪˈzeɪʃənəl] ADJ organisatorisch; **at an ~ level** im strukturellem Bereich

organization: **organization chart** N Organisationsplan *m*; **Organization for Economic Cooperation and Development** N Organisation *f* für wirtschaftliche Zusammenarbeit und Entwicklung; **Organization of African Unity** N Organisation *f* für Afrikanische Einheit; **Organization of American States** N Organisation *f* Amerikanischer Staaten; **Organization of Arab Petroleum Exporting Countries** N Organisation *f* der arabischen Erdöl exportierenden Länder; **Organization of Petroleum Exporting Countries** N Organisation *f* der Erdöl exportierenden Länder

organize [ˈɔːgənaɪz] VT **a** *(= give structure to, systematize)* ordnen; *facts* organisieren, ordnen; *time* einteilen; *work* organisieren, einteilen; *essay* aufbauen; *one's/sb's life* planen; *one's thoughts* ordnen; **to get (oneself) ~d** *(= get ready)* alles vorbereiten; *(to go out)* sich fertig machen; *(for term, holiday etc)* sich vorbereiten; *(= sort things out)* seine Sachen in Ordnung bringen; *(= sort out one's life)* ein geregeltes Leben anfangen; **I'll have to get better ~d** ich muss das alles besser organisieren; **I'll come as soon as I've got (myself) ~d** ich komme, sobald ich so weit bin; **I've only just taken over the business, but as soon as I've got ~d I'll contact you** ich habe das Geschäft gerade erst übernommen, aber sobald alles (richtig) läuft, melde ich mich bei Ihnen; **it took us quite a while to get ~d in our new house** wir haben eine ganze Zeit gebraucht, uns in unserem neuen Haus (richtig) einzurichten
b *(= arrange) party, meeting etc* organisieren; *food, music for party etc* sorgen für; *sports event* organisieren, ausrichten; *(into teams, groups)* einteilen; **to ~ things so that ...** es so einrichten, dass ...; **they ~d (it) for me to go to London** sie haben meine Londonreise arrangiert; **organizing committee** Organisationskomitee *nt*
c *(Pol: = unionize)* organisieren
VI *(Pol)* sich organisieren

organized [ˈɔːgənaɪzd] ADJ **a** *(Sci)* organisch **b** *(= structured, systematized)* organisiert; *life* geregelt; **he isn't very ~** bei ihm geht alles drunter und drüber *(inf)*; **you have to be ~** du musst planvoll *or* systematisch *or* mit System vorgehen; **as far as his work/social life is concerned, he's well ~** was seine Arbeit/sein gesellschaftliches Leben angeht, so läuft bei ihm alles sehr geregelt ab; **he's well ~** *(in new flat etc)* er ist bestens eingerichtet; *(= well-prepared)* er ist gut vorbereitet **c** *(Pol: = unionized)* organisiert

organized crime N organisiertes Verbrechen

organized labour, *(US)* **organized labor** N organisierte Arbeitnehmerschaft

organizer [ˈɔːgənaɪzəʳ] N **a** Organisator(in) *m(f)*, Veranstalter(in) *m(f)*; *(of sports event)* Ausrichter(in) *m(f)* **b** = **personal organizer**

organ loft N Orgelempore *f*, Orgelbühne *f*

organophosphate [ɔːˌgənəʊˈfɒsfeɪt] N Organophosphat *nt*

organ: **organ pipe** N *(Mus)* Orgelpfeife *f*; **organ stop** N *(Mus)* Orgelregister *nt*, -zug *m*; **organ transplant** N **a** *(= operation)* Organtransplantation *f* **b** *(= organ)* Organtransplantat *nt*

organza [ɔːˈgænzə] N Organza *m*

orgasm [ˈɔːgæzəm] **N** *(lit, fig)* Orgasmus *m*; **to go into ~s** *(fig inf)* einen Orgasmus nach dem anderen kriegen *(inf)*; **to be having ~s** *(fig inf)* ganz aus dem Häuschen sein *(inf)* **VI** einen Orgasmus haben

orgasmic [ɔːˈgæzmɪk] ADJ orgasmisch

orgiastic [ˌɔːdʒɪˈæstɪk] ADJ orgiastisch

orgy [ˈɔːdʒɪ] N *(lit, fig)* Orgie *f*; **drunken ~** Sauforgie *f*; **an ~ of killing** eine Blutorgie; **~ of spending** Kauforgie *f*; **an ~ of colour** *(Brit) or* **color** *(US)* eine orgiastische Farbenpracht

oriel (window) [ˈɔːrɪəl(ˈwɪndəʊ)] N Erker(fenster *nt*) *m*

orient [ˈɔːrɪənt] **N** *(also* **Orient***)* Orient *m*; *(poet also)* Morgenland *nt* **ADJ** *(poet) sun, moon* aufgehend **VT** = **orientate**

oriental [ˌɔːrɪˈentl] **ADJ** orientalisch; *languages also* östlich; *(Univ)* orientalistisch; ~ **rug** Orientteppich *m*; ~ **studies** *pl* Orientalistik *f* **N** *(= person)* **Oriental** Orientale *m*, Orientalin *f*

orientalist [ˌɔːrɪˈentəlɪst] N Orientalist(in) *m(f)*

orientate [ˈɔːrɪənteɪt] **VR** *(lit)* sich orientieren *(by* an *+dat, by the map* nach der Karte); *(fig also)* sich zurechtfinden **VT** ausrichten *(towards* auf *+acc)*; *new employees etc* einführen; *thinking* orientieren *(towards* an *+dat)*; **money-~d** materiell ausgerichtet; **family-~d** familienorientiert

orientation [ˌɔːrɪənˈteɪʃən] N **a** *(= getting one's bearing)* Orientierung *f*; *(fig)* Ausrichtung *f*, Orientierung *f* **b** *(= position, direction)* *(lit: of boat, spaceship etc)* Kurs *m*; *(fig)* Orientierung *f*; *(= attitude)* Einstellung *f (towards* zu); *(Comput: for printing)* Ausrichtung *f*; *(= leaning)* Ausrichtung *f (towards* auf *+acc)*; **sexual ~** sexuelle Orientierung

-oriented [ˈɔːrɪəntɪd] ADJ *suf* -orientiert; **market-oriented** marktorientiert

orienteering [ˌɔːrɪənˈtɪərɪŋ] N Orientierungslauf *m*

orifice [ˈɒrɪfɪs] N Öffnung *f*

origami [ˌɒrɪˈgɑːmɪ] N Origami *nt*

origin [ˈɒrɪdʒɪn] N **a** Ursprung *m*, Herkunft *f*; *(of person, family)* Herkunft *f*, Abstammung *f*; *(of world)* Entstehung *f*; *(of river)* Ursprung *m (geh)*; **to have its ~ in sth** auf etw *(acc)* zurückgehen; *(river)* in etw *(dat)* entspringen; **his family had its ~ in France** seine Familie ist französischer Herkunft; **country of ~** Herkunftsland *nt*; **nobody knew the ~ of that story** niemand wusste, wie die Geschichte entstanden war; **what are his ~s?** was für eine Herkunft hat er? **b** *(Math)* Ursprung *m*

original [əˈrɪdʒɪnl] **ADJ a** *(= first, earliest)* ursprünglich; **in its ~ form** in seiner ursprünglichen Form; ~ **inhabitants of a country** Ureinwohner *pl* eines Landes; ~ **text** Urtext *m*; ~ **version** *(of book, play)* Urfassung *f*; *(of film, song)* Originalversion *or* -fassung *f*; ~ **edition** Originalausgabe *f*; **in the ~ German** im deutschen Originaltext **b** *(= not imitative) painting* original; *idea, writer, play* originell; ~ **research** eigene Forschung; ~ **document** *(Jur)* Originaldokument *nt* **c** *(= unconventional, eccentric) character, person* originell **N a** Original *nt*; *(of model)* Vorlage *f* **b** *(= eccentric person)* Original *nt*

original costs PL Herstellungs- *or* Gestehungskosten *pl*, Selbstkosten *pl*

originality [əˌrɪdʒɪˈnælɪtɪ] N Originalität *f*

originally [əˈrɪdʒənəlɪ] ADV **a** ursprünglich **b** *(= in an original way)* originell

original: **original packaging** N Originalverpackung *f*; **original sin** N die Erbsünde

originate [əˈrɪdʒɪneɪt] **VT** hervorbringen; *policy, company* ins Leben rufen; *product* erfinden; **who ~d the idea?** von wem stammt die Idee? **VI a** entstehen; **the legend ~d in ...** die Legende ist in *(+dat)* ... entstanden *or* hat ihren Ursprung in *(+dat)* ...; **to ~ from a country** aus einem Land stammen; **to ~ from** *or* **with sb** von jdm stammen; **the company ~d as a family concern** die Firma war ursprünglich *or* anfänglich ein Familienbetrieb **b** *(US: bus, train etc)* ausgehen *(in* von)

origination costs [əˌrɪdʒɪˈneɪʃənkɒsts] PL = **original costs**

originator [əˈrɪdʒɪneɪtəʳ] N *(of plan, idea)* Urheber(in) *m(f)*; *(of company)* Gründer(in) *m(f)*; *(of product)* Erfinder(in) *m(f)*

oriole [ˈɔːrɪəʊl] N Pirol *m*

Orkney Islands [ˈɔːknɪˈaɪləndz], **Orkneys** [ˈɔːknɪz] PL Orkneyinseln *pl*

Orlon® [ˈɔːlɒn] N Orlon® *nt*

ormolu [ˈɔːməʊluː] **N** *(= alloy)* Messing *nt*; *(= decoration)* Messingverzierungen *pl*; *(= mountings)* Messingbeschläge *pl* **ADJ** aus Messing

ornament [ˈɔːnəmənt] **N** **a** *(= decorative object)* Schmuckgegenstand *m*, Verzierung *f*; *(on mantelpiece etc)* Ziergegenstand *m*; *(fig)* Zierde *f* *(to +gen)*; **his secretary is just an ~** seine Sekretärin ist nur zur Verzierung *or* Dekoration da; **she has the house full of ~s** sie hat das Haus voller Nippes *(pej)* *or* Ziergegenstände; **altar ~s** *(Eccl)* Altarschmuck *m* **b** *no pl (= ornamentation)* Ornamente *pl*; *(= decorative articles, on clothes etc)* Verzierungen *pl*, Zierrat *m (geh)*; **by way of ~, for ~** zur Verzierung **c** *(Mus)* Verzierung *f*, Ornament *nt* [ˈɔːnəment] **VT** verzieren; *room* ausschmücken

ornamental [ˌɔːnəˈmentl] ADJ dekorativ; *detail* schmückend, zierend; **for ~ purposes** zur Dekoration; **to be purely ~** zur Verzierung *or* Zierde (da) sein; **wives were only expected to look ~** Ehefrauen hatten nur zur Dekoration da zu sein; **~ object** *or* **piece** Zier- *or* Schmuckgegenstand *m*, Zierat *m (geh)*; **~ garden/pond** Ziergarten *m*/-teich *m*; **~ plant** Zierpflanze *f*

ornamentation [ˌɔːnəmenˈteɪʃən] N **a** *(= ornamenting)* Verzieren *nt*, Verzierung *f*; *(of room)* Ausschmücken *nt*, Ausschmückung *f* **b** *(= ornamental detail)* Verzierungen *pl*, Zierrat *m (geh)*; *(Art, Archit)* Ornamentik *f*; *(= ornaments: in room etc)* Schmuck *m*

ornate [ɔːˈneɪt] ADJ kunstvoll; *(of larger objects)* prunkvoll; *decoration* aufwendig, aufwändig; *music* ornamentreich; *description* reich ausgeschmückt, umständlich *(pej)*; *language, style* umständlich *(pej)*, überladen *(pej)*, reich

ornately [ɔːˈneɪtlɪ] ADV kunstvoll; *describe* mit beredten Worten, umständlich *(pej)*; *written* in reicher Sprache

ornateness [ɔːˈneɪtnɪs] N Verzierungsreichtum *m*; *(of baroque church, palace etc)* Prunk *m*, Prachtentfaltung *f*; *(of music)* ornamentaler Reichtum; *(of style)* Reichtum *m*; *(of description)* Wortreichtum *m*, Umständlichkeit *f (pej)*; *(of decoration)* Reichtum *m*, Aufwendigkeit *f*, Aufwändigkeit *f*

ornithological [ˌɔːnɪθəˈlɒdʒɪkəl] ADJ ornithologisch, vogelkundlich

ornithologist [ˌɔːnɪˈθɒlədʒɪst] N Ornithologe *m*, Ornithologin *f*, Vogelkundler(in) *m(f)*

ornithology [ˌɔːnɪˈθɒlədʒɪ] N Ornithologie *f*, Vogelkunde *f*

orphan [ˈɔːfən] **N** Waise *f*, Waisenkind *nt*; **the accident left him an ~** der Unfall machte ihn zur Waise *or* zum Waisenkind; **like ~ Annie** *(inf)* wie bestellt und nicht abgeholt **ADJ** Waisen-; **~ child** Waisenkind *nt* **VT** zur Waise machen; **to be ~ed** zur Waise werden; **he was ~ed by the war** er ist (eine) Kriegswaise; **he was ~ed at the age of three** er wurde Waise, als er drei Jahre alt war

orphanage [ˈɔːfənɪdʒ] N Waisenhaus *nt*

Orpheus [ˈɔːfjuːs] N *(Myth)* Orpheus *m*

orthodontic [ˌɔːθəʊˈdɒntɪk] ADJ kieferorthopädisch

orthodontics [ˌɔːθəʊˈdɒntɪks] N *sing* Kieferorthopädie *f*

orthodontist [ˌɔːθəʊˈdɒntɪst] N Kieferorthopäde *m*/-orthopädin *f*

orthodox [ˈɔːθədɒks] ADJ **a** *(Rel)* orthodox; **the Orthodox (Eastern) Church** die orthodoxe (Ost)kirche **b** *(fig)* konventionell; *view, method, approach etc* orthodox

orthodoxy [ˈɔːθədɒksɪ] N **a** Orthodoxie *f* **b** *(fig)* Konventionalität *f*; *(of view, method, approach etc)* Orthodoxie *f* **c** *(= orthodox belief, practice etc)* orthodoxe Konvention

orthographic(al) [ˌɔːθəˈgræfɪk(əl)] ADJ orthografisch

orthography [ɔːˈθɒgrəfɪ] N Rechtschreibung *f*, Orthografie *f*

orthopaedic, *(US)* **orthopedic** [ˌɔːθəʊˈpiːdɪk] ADJ orthopädisch; **~ bed** orthopädisches Bett; **~ surgeon** orthopädischer Chirurg, orthopädische Chirurgin

orthopaedics, *(US)* **orthopedics** [ˌɔːθəʊˈpiːdɪks] N *sing* Orthopädie *f*

orthopaedist, *(US)* **orthopedist** [ɔːˈθəʊˈpiːdɪst] N Orthopäde *m*, Orthopädin *f*

orthoptic [ɔːˈθɒptɪk] ADJ *(Med)* normalsichtig; **~ exercises** mechanische Sehübungen

OS **a** *abbr of* **ordinary seaman** **b** *abbr of* **Ordnance Survey** **c** *abbr of* **outsize**

Oscar [ˈɒskəʳ] N *(Film)* Oscar *m*; **Dustin Hoffman in his ~-winning performance** Dustin Hoffman in der Rolle, für die er den Oscar bekam

oscillate [ˈɒsɪleɪt] VI *(Phys)* oszillieren, schwingen; *(compass needle etc)* schwanken; *(rapidly)* zittern; *(fig)* schwanken; **the needle ~d violently** die Nadel schlug stark aus

oscillating [ˈɒsɪleɪtɪŋ] ADJ **a** *(Phys)* schwingend; *needle* ausschlagend; *(rapidly)* zitternd **b** *(fig)* schwankend

oscillation [ˌɒsɪˈleɪʃən] N *(Phys)* Oszillation *f*, Schwingung *f*; *(of compass needle etc)* Schwanken *nt*; *(rapid)* Zittern *nt*; *(= individual movement etc)* Schwankung *f*

oscillator [ˈɒsɪleɪtəʳ] N Oszillator *m*

oscillograph [əˈsɪləgræf] N Oszillograf *m*

oscilloscope [əˈsɪləskəʊp] N Oszilloskop *nt*

OSHA *(US) abbr of* **Occupational Safety and Health Administration** Arbeitsschutzbehörde *f*

osier [ˈəʊzɪəʳ] **N** Korbweide *f*; *(= twig)* Weidenrute *or* -gerte *f* **ATTR** Weiden-; **~ basket** Weidenkorb *m*; **~ chair** Korbstuhl *m*

osmium [ˈɒzmɪəm] N Osmium *nt*

osmosis [ɒzˈməʊsɪs] N Osmose *f*

osmotic [ɒzˈmɒtɪk] ADJ osmotisch

osprey [ˈɒspreɪ] N Fischadler *m*

osseous [ˈɒsɪəs] ADJ knöchern

ossification [ˌɒsɪfɪˈkeɪʃən] N Verknöcherung *f*, Ossifikation *f (spec)*

ossify [ˈɒsɪfaɪ] **VT** *(lit)* verknöchern lassen; *(fig)* erstarren lassen; *mind* unbeweglich machen; **to be ossified** *(lit)* verknöchert sein; *(fig)* erstarrt sein; *(mind)* unbeweglich sein; **to become ossified** *(fig)* erstarren; *(mind)* unbeweglich werden **VI** *(lit)* verknöchern; *(fig)* erstarren; *(mind)* unbeweglich werden

ossuary [ˈɒsjʊərɪ] N Ossarium *nt*; *(= building also)* Beinhaus *nt*

Ostend [ɒˈstend] N Ostende *nt*

ostensible ADJ, **ostensibly** ADV [ɒˈstensəbl, -ɪ] angeblich

ostentation [ˌɒstenˈteɪʃən] N **a** *(= pretentious display) (of wealth etc)* Pomp *m*; *(of skills etc)* Großtuerei *f* **b** *(= obviousness)* aufdringliche *or* penetrante Deutlichkeit; **with ~** demonstrativ, ostentativ; **without ~** betont unauffällig

ostentatious [ˌɒstenˈteɪʃəs] ADJ **a** *(= pretentious)* pompös, protzig *(inf)* **b** *(= conspicuous)* ostentativ, betont auffällig

ostentatiously [ˌɒstenˈteɪʃəslɪ] ADV **a** *(= pretentiously)* pompös, protzig *(inf)*; *live* pompös, in Pomp, auf großem Fuße **b** *(= conspicuously)* ostentativ, betont auffällig

ostentatiousness [ˌɒstenˈteɪʃəsnɪs] N = **ostentation**

osteoarthritis [ˈɒstɪəʊɑːˈθraɪtɪs] N Arthrose *f*

osteopath [ˈɒstɪəpæθ] N Osteopath(in) *m(f)*

osteopathy [ˌɒstɪˈɒpəθɪ] N Osteopathologie *f*

ostler [ˈɒsləʳ] N *(Hist)* Stallknecht *m*

ostracism [ˈɒstrəsɪzəm] N Ächtung *f*

ostracize [ˈɒstrəsaɪz] VT ächten; *(Hist)* verbannen

ostrich [ˈɒstrɪtʃ] N Strauß *m*; **~ policy** Vogel-Strauß-Politik *f*

OT *abbr of* **Old Testament** A. T. *nt*

OTC *abbr of* **over the counter**; **~ medicines** rezeptfreie Medikamente *pl*

other [ˈʌðəʳ] **ADJ** **a** andere(r, s); **~ people** andere (Leute); **some ~ people will come later** später kommen noch ein paar; **there were 6 ~ people there as well** es waren auch noch 6 andere (Leute) da; **do you have any ~ questions?** haben Sie sonst noch Fragen?; **he had no ~ questions** er hatte sonst keine Fragen; **he could be no ~ than strict** er konnte nicht anders als streng sein, er konnte nur streng sein; **the man was none ~ than my father** der Mann war niemand anders als mein Vater; **the ~ day** neulich; **the ~ world** das Jenseits, jene andere Welt *(liter)*; **some ~ time** *(in future)* ein andermal; *(in past)* ein anderes Mal; **~ people's property** fremdes Eigentum; **to see how the ~ half lives** sehen, wie andere leben

b **every ~ ...** *(= alternate)* jede(r, s) zweite ...

c **~ than** *(= except)* außer *(+dat)*; *(= different to)* anders als

d **some time or ~** irgendwann (einmal); **some writer/house** *etc* **or ~** irgend so ein *or* irgendein Schriftsteller/Haus *etc*

PRON andere(r, s); **he doesn't like hurting ~s** er mag niemanden verletzen, er mag niemandem wehtun; **there are 6 ~s** da sind noch 6 (andere); **are there any ~s there?** sind noch andere *or* sonst noch welche da?; **there were no ~s there** es waren sonst keine da; **something/someone or ~** irgendetwas/-jemand; **one or ~ of them will come** einer (von ihnen) wird kommen; **can you tell one from the ~?** kannst du sie auseinanderhalten?; **he fancied a bit of the ~** *(inf)* ihm war nach ein bisschen - na ja, du weißt schon *(inf)*, er wollte ein bisschen bumsen *(inf)* → **each, one**

ADV **he could do no ~ (than come)** er konnte nicht anders (als kommen), er konnte nichts anderes tun (als kommen); **I've never seen her ~ than with her husband** ich habe sie immer nur mit ihrem Mann gesehen; **somehow or ~** irgendwie, auf die eine oder andere Weise; **somewhere or ~** irgendwo

other-directed [ˈʌðədaɪˈrektɪd] ADJ fremdbestimmt

otherness [ˈʌðənɪs] N Anderssein *nt*, Andersartigkeit *f*

other ranks PL *(Brit Mil)* *Angehörige der britischen Streitkräfte unterhalb des Offiziersrangs*

otherwise [ˈʌðəwaɪz] ✪ 2.3 **ADV** **a** *(= in a different way)* anders; **I am ~ engaged** *(form)* ich bin anderweitig beschäftigt; **except where ~ stated** *(form)* sofern nicht anders angegeben; **Richard I, ~ (known as) the Lionheart** Richard I., auch bekannt als Löwenherz, Richard I. oder auch Löwenherz; **you seem to think ~** Sie scheinen anderer Meinung zu sein **b** *(= in other respects)* sonst, ansonsten, im Übrigen **CONJ** *(= or else)* sonst, andernfalls **ADJ** *pred* anders; **poems tragic and ~** tragische und andere Gedichte

otherworldliness [ˌʌðəˈwɜːldlɪnɪs] N *(of person, attitude)* Weltferne *f*; *(of expression)* Entrücktheit *f*

otherworldly [ˌʌðəˈwɜːldlɪ] ADJ *attitude, person* weltfern; *smile, expression* entrückt

otiose [ˈəʊʃɪəʊs] ADJ *(liter)* müßig *(geh)*

OTT *(inf) abbr of* **over the top**

otter [ˈɒtəʳ] N Otter *m*

Ottoman [ˈɒtəmən] **ADJ** osmanisch, ottomanisch *(rare)* **N** Osmane *m*, Osmanin *f*, Ottomane *m (rare)*, Ottomanin *f (rare)*

ottoman [ˈɒtəmən] N Polstertruhe *f*

OU *(Brit) abbr of* **Open University**

ouch [aʊtʃ] INTERJ autsch

ought¹ [ɔːt] ✪ 1.1, 2.2 VB AUX **a** *(indicating moral obligation)* **I ~ to do it** ich sollte *or* müsste es tun; **he ~ to have come** er hätte kommen sollen *or* müssen; **this ~ to have been done** das hätte man tun sollen *or* müssen; **~ I to go too? – yes, you ~ (to)/no, you ~n't (to)** sollte *or* müsste ich auch (hin)gehen? – ja doch/nein, das sollen Sie nicht; **he thought he ~ to tell you/you ~ to know** er meinte, er sollte Ihnen das sagen/Sie sollten das wissen; **people have come who ~ not to have done** es sind Leute gekommen, die nicht hätten kommen sollen; **~n't you to have left by now?** hätten Sie nicht schon gehen müssen?; **cars are parked where they ~ not to be** Autos sind an Stellen geparkt, wo sie nicht hingehören; **he behaved just as he ~ (to have)** *(= was well-behaved)* er hat sich völlig korrekt benommen; *(= did the right thing)* er hat sich völlig richtig verhalten

b *(indicating what is right, advisable, desirable)* **you ~ to see that film** den Film sollten Sie sehen; **you ~ to have seen his face** sein Gesicht hätten Sie sehen müssen; **she ~ to have been a teacher** sie hätte Lehrerin werden sollen

c *(indicating probability)* **he ~ to win the race** er müsste (eigentlich) das Rennen gewinnen; **come at six, that ~ to be early enough** komm (mal) um sechs, das sollte *or* müsste früh genug sein; **that ~ to do** das dürfte wohl *or* müsste reichen; **he ~ to be here soon** er müsste bald hier sein; **he ~ to have left by now** er müsste inzwischen gegangen sein; **… and I ~ to know!** … und ich muss es doch wissen!

ought² N = **aught**

ouija (board) ['wi:dʒə('bɔ:d)] N *Buchstabenbrett für spiritistische Sitzungen*

ounce [aʊns] N Unze *f*; **there's not an ~ of truth in it** daran ist kein Fünkchen Wahrheit; **if he had an ~ of sense** wenn er nur einen Funken *or* für fünf Pfennig *(inf)* Verstand hätte

our ['aʊə'] POSS ADJ unser; **these are ~ own make** die stellen wir selbst her; **Our Father** *(in prayer)* Vater unser; **the Our Father** das Vaterunser *or* Unservater *(Sw)* → *also* **my POSS ADJ**

ours ['aʊəz] POSS PRON unsere(r, s); **~ not to reason why(, ~ but to do or die)** *(prov)* das wissen die Götter *(inf)*, es ist nicht an uns, nach dem Warum zu fragen → *also* **mine¹**

ourself [ˌaʊə'self] PERS PRON *(form)* (wir) selbst

ourselves [ˌaʊə'selvz] PERS PRON *(dir, indir obj +prep)* uns; *(emph)* selbst → *also* **myself**

oust [aʊst] VT *(= get, drive out)* herausbekommen; *government* absetzen; *politician, colleague etc* ausbooten *(inf)*, absägen *(inf)*; *heckler, anglicisms* entfernen; *rivals* ausschalten; *(= take place of)* verdrängen; **to ~ sb from office/his position** jdn aus seinem Amt/seiner Stellung entfernen *or (by intrigue)* hinausmanövrieren; **to ~ sb from power** jdn von der Macht verdrängen

out [aʊt] ADV **a** *(= not in container, car etc)* außen; *(= not in building, room)* draußen; *(indicating motion) (seen from inside)* hinaus, raus *(inf)*; *(seen from outside)* heraus, raus *(inf)*; **to be ~** weg sein; *(when visitors come)* nicht da sein; **they're ~ in the garden** sie sind draußen im Garten; **they're ~ playing** sie spielen draußen; **they are ~ fishing/shopping** sie sind zum Fischen/Einkaufen (gegangen), sie sind fischen/einkaufen; **he's ~ in his car** er ist mit dem Auto unterwegs; **she was ~ all night** sie war die ganze Nacht weg; **it's cold ~ here/there** es ist kalt hier/da *or* dort draußen; **~ you go!** hinaus *or* raus *(inf)* mit dir!; **~!** raus (hier)! *(inf)*; **~ with him!** hinaus *or* raus *(inf)* mit ihm!; **~ it goes!** hinaus damit, raus damit *(inf)*; **everybody ~!** alle Mann *or* alles raus! *(inf)*; **he likes to be ~ and about** er ist gern unterwegs; **at weekends I like to be ~ and about** an den Wochenenden will ich (immer) raus; **we had a day ~ at the beach/in London** wir haben einen Tag am Meer/in London verbracht; **we had a day ~ at the shops** wir haben einen Einkaufsbummel gemacht; **the journey ~** die Hinreise; *(seen from destination)* die Herfahrt; **the goods were damaged on the journey ~** die Waren sind auf dem Transport beschädigt worden; **the book is ~** *(from library)* das Buch ist ausgeliehen *or* unterwegs *(inf)*; **the Socialists are ~** die Sozialisten sind nicht mehr an der Regierung; **the workers are ~** *(= on strike)* die Arbeiter streiken *or* sind im Ausstand; **school is ~** die Schule ist aus; **the tide is ~** es ist Ebbe; **the chicks should be ~ tomorrow** die Küken sollten bis morgen heraus sein

b *(indicating distance)* **when he was ~ in Persia** als er in Persien war; **to go ~ to China** nach China fahren; **~ in the Far East** im Fernen Osten; **~ here in Australia** hier in Australien; **Wilton Street? isn't that ~ your way?** Wilton Street? ist das nicht da (hinten) bei euch in der Gegend?; **the boat was ten miles ~** das Schiff war zehn Meilen weit draußen; **five days ~ from Liverpool** *(Naut)* fünf Tage nach dem Auslaufen aus Liverpool; **five miles ~ from shore** fünf Meilen von der Küste weg, fünf Meilen vor der Küste

c **to be ~** *(sun)* (he)raus *or* draußen sein; *(stars, moon)* am Himmel stehen *(geh)*, da sein; *(flowers)* blühen

d *(= in existence)* **the worst newspaper/best car ~** die schlechteste Zeitung, die/das beste Auto, das es zur Zeit gibt, die schlechteste Zeitung/das beste Auto überhaupt; **to be ~** *(= be published)* herausgekommen sein; **when will it be ~?** wann kommt es heraus?; **there's a warrant ~ for him** *or* **for his arrest** es besteht Haftbefehl gegen ihn

e *(= not in prison)* **to be ~** draußen sein; *(seen from outside also)* (he)raus sein; **to come ~** (he)rauskommen

f *(= in the open, known)* **their secret was ~** ihr Geheimnis war bekannt geworden *or* herausgekommen; **it's ~ now** jetzt ist es heraus; **the results are ~** die Ergebnisse sind (he)raus; **the truth will ~** die Wahrheit will heraus; **~ with it!** heraus damit!, heraus mit der Sprache!

g *(= to or at an end)* **before the day/month is/was ~** vor Ende des Tages/Monats, noch am selben Tag/im selben Monat

h *(light, fire)* aus

i *(= not in fashion)* aus der Mode, passé, out *(inf)*

j *(Sport, ball)* aus; *(player)* aus(geschlagen), out

k *(= out of the question, not permissible)* ausgeschlossen, nicht drin *(inf)*

l *(= worn out)* **the jacket is ~ at the elbows** die Jacke ist an den Ellbogen durch

m *(indicating error)* **he was ~ in his calculations, his calculations were ~** er lag mit seinen Berechnungen daneben *(inf) or* falsch, er hatte sich in seinen Berechnungen geirrt; **not far ~!** beinah(e) (richtig)!; **you're not far ~** Sie haben es fast (getroffen); **you're far** *or* **way ~!** weit gefehlt! *(geh)*, da hast du dich völlig vertan *(inf)*; **you're a little bit ~ there** das stimmt nicht ganz; **we were £5/20% ~** wir hatten uns um £ 5/20% verrechnet *or* vertan *(inf)*; **that's £5/20% ~** das stimmt um £ 5/20% nicht; **the post isn't quite vertical yet, it's still a bit ~** der Pfahl ist noch nicht ganz senkrecht, er ist noch etwas schief; **my clock is 20 minutes ~** meine Uhr geht 20 Minuten falsch *or* verkehrt

n *(indicating loudness, clearness)* **speak ~ (loud)** sprechen Sie laut/lauter; **they shouted ~ (loud)** sie riefen laut (und vernehmlich)

o *(indicating purpose)* **to be ~ for sth** auf etw *(acc)* aus sein; **to be ~ for a good time** sich amüsieren wollen; **to be ~ for trouble** Streit suchen; **she was ~ to pass the exam** sie war (fest) entschlossen, die Prüfung zu bestehen; **he's ~ for all he can get** er will haben, was er nur bekommen kann; **he's ~ to get her** er ist hinter ihr her; **he's just ~ to make money** er ist nur auf Geld aus, ihm geht es nur um Geld; **he was always ~ to make money** er wollte immer das große Geld machen; **she's ~ to find a husband** sie ist auf der Suche nach einem Mann

p *(= unconscious)* **to be ~** bewusstlos *or* weg *(inf)* sein; *(= drunk)* weg *or* hinüber sein *(inf)*; *(= asleep)* weg *(inf) or* eingeschlafen sein; **she went straight ~** sie war sofort weg *(inf)*

q *(dirt, stain etc)* (he)raus

r **~ and away** weitaus, mit Abstand

N **a** → **in**

b *(esp US inf: = way out)* Hintertür(chen *nt*) *f*

PREP aus *(+dat)*; **to go ~ the door/window** zur Tür/zum Fenster hinausgehen; **from ~ the wood** *(poet)* aus dem Walde heraus → *also* **out of**

VT *homosexual* outen

out- PREF *with vbs* **to ~dance** *etc* **sb** jdn im Tanzen *etc* übertreffen, besser als jd tanzen *etc*

outact [ˌaʊt'ækt] VT an die Wand spielen

out-and-out ['aʊtən'aʊt] ADJ *liar, lie* ausgemacht; *fool* vollkommen, ausgemacht; *racist, fascist* eingefleischt; *winner, success* überragend; *defeat* völlig, total; **he is an ~ revolutionary/conservative** er ist ein Revolutionär durch und durch/ein Erzkonservativer; **it's an ~ disgrace** das ist eine bodenlose Schande

outargue [ˌaʊt'ɑ:gju:] VT in der Diskussion überlegen sein *(+dat)*, argumentativ überlegen sein *(+dat) (geh)*

outback ['aʊtbæk] *(in Australia)* N **the ~** das Hinterland ATTR **an ~ farm** eine Farm im Hinterland

out: **outbalance** [ˌaʊtə'bæləns] VT überwiegen, übertreffen; **outbid** *pret, ptp* **outbid** VT überbieten; **outboard** ADJ Außenbord-; **~ motor** Außenbordmotor *m* N Außenborder *m (inf)*; **outbound** ADJ *ship* auslaufend, ausfahrend; **~ flight/journey** Hinflug *m*/-reise *f*; **outbox** VT *sb* besser boxen als; **for once he was completely ~ed** zum ersten Mal ließ ihn seine Technik völlig im Stich; **he was ~ed by the younger man** der jüngere Boxer war ihm (technisch) überlegen

outbreak ['aʊtbreɪk] N *(of war, hostility, disease)* Ausbruch *m*; **a recent ~ of fire caused …** ein Brand verursachte kürzlich …; **if there should be an ~ of fire** wenn ein Brand *or* Feuer ausbricht; **at the ~ of war** bei Kriegsausbruch

outbuilding ['aʊtbɪldɪŋ] N Nebengebäude *nt*

outburst ['aʊtbɜ:st] N *(of joy, anger)* Ausbruch *m*; **~ of temper** *or* **anger** Wutanfall *m*; **~ of feeling** Gefühlsausbruch *m*; **and to what do we owe that little ~?** und warum dieser kleine Gefühlsausbruch, wenn ich mal fragen darf?

outcast ['aʊtkɑ:st] N Ausgestoßene(r) *mf*; **social ~** Außenseiter(in) *m(f)* der Gesellschaft; **he was treated as an ~** er wurde zum Außenseiter gestempelt; **one of the party's ~s** einer, den die Partei verstoßen hat ADJ ausgestoßen, verstoßen

outclass [ˌaʊt'klɑ:s] VT voraus *or* überlegen sein *(+dat)*, in den Schatten stellen

outcome ['aʊtkʌm] N Ergebnis *nt*, Resultat *nt*; **what was the ~ of your meeting?** was ist bei eurem Treffen herausgekommen?; **what was the ~?** was ist dabei herausgekommen?; **I don't know whether there'll be any immediate ~** ich weiß nicht, ob es unmittelbar zu einem Ergebnis führen wird

outcrop ['aʊtkrɒp] N **a** *(Geol)* **an ~ (of rock)** eine Felsnase **b** *(fig: of riots etc)* (plötzlicher) Ausbruch

outcry ['aʊtkraɪ] N Aufschrei *m* der Empörung *(against* über *+acc)*; *(= public protest)* Protestwelle *f (against* gegen); **to cause an ~ against sb/sth** zu lautstarkem Protest gegen jdn/etw führen; **to raise an ~ against sb/sth** gegen jdn/etw lautstarken Protest erheben; **there was a general ~ about the increase in taxes** eine Welle des Protests erhob sich wegen der Steuererhöhung

out: **outdated** ADJ *idea, theory* überholt; *technology, equipment, method, word, style, custom* veraltet; *image, concept, practice* überkommen; **outdid** *pret of* **outdo**; **outdistance** VT hinter sich *(dat)* lassen, abhängen *(inf)*; **Y was ~d by X** Y fiel hinter X *(dat)* zurück, Y wurde von X abgehängt *(inf)*

outdo [ˌaʊt'du:] *pret* **outdid** [ˌaʊt'dɪd] *ptp* **outdone** [ˌaʊt'dʌn] VT übertreffen, überragen, überbieten *(sb in sth* jdn an etw *dat)*; **he can ~ him in every sport** er ist ihm in jeder Sportart überlegen; **but Jimmy was not to be ~ne** aber Jimmy wollte da nicht zurückstehen

outdoor ['aʊtdɔ:'] ADJ *activities, recreation, work, use, tennis court* im Freien; **~ sports** Sports im Freien ausgeübte Sportarten *pl*; **~ café** Café *nt* im Freien; *(in street)* Straßencafé *nt*; **~ clothes**

Kleidung *f* für draußen; ~ **shoes** Straßenschuhe *pl*; ~ **market** Markt *m* im Freien; *(in street)* Straßenmarkt *m*; ~ **games** Freiluftspiele *pl*, Spiele *pl* für draußen *or* im Freien; ~ **living** Leben *nt* in freier Natur; **the ~ life** das Leben im Freien; **to lead an ~ life** viel im Freien sein; ~ **swimming pool** Freibad *nt*

outdoors [ˈaʊtˈdɔːz] ADV *live, play, sleep* draußen, im Freien; **to go ~** nach draußen gehen, rausgehen *(inf)*; **go ~ and play** geh draußen spielen N **the great ~** *(hum)* die freie Natur

outdoor: **outdoor shot** N *(Film)* Außenaufnahme *f*; **outdoor type** N sportlicher Typ

outer [ˈaʊtəʳ] ADJ *attr* äußere(r, s); ~ **harbour** Außen- *or* Vorhafen *m*; ~ **office** *(= reception area)* Vorzimmer *nt*; ~ **man** *(= appearance)* äußere Erscheinung, Äußere(s) *nt*; **the ~ world** die Außenwelt; **the ~ reaches of the solar system** die Weiten *pl* des Sonnensystems

outer: **outer door** N Außentür *f*; **outer garments** PL Oberbekleidung *f*, Überkleidung *f*; **Outer Hebrides** PL Äußere Hebriden *pl*; **Outer London** N die Peripherie Londons; **Outer Mongolia** N die Äußere Mongolei

outermost [ˈaʊtəməʊst] ADJ äußerste(r, s)

outer space N der Weltraum

out: **outfall** N *(of drain, sewer)* Ausfluss *m* ATTR Ausfluss-, Abfluss-; ~ **pipe** Ausfluss- *or* Abflussrohr *nt*; **outfield** N *(Sport) (= place)* Außenfeld *nt*; *(= people)* Außenfeldspieler *pl*; **outfielder** N *(Baseball, Cricket)* Außenfeldspieler(in) *m(f)*; **outfight** *pret, ptp* **outfought** VT besser kämpfen als; *(= defeat)* bezwingen

outfit [ˈaʊtfɪt] N **a** *(= clothes)* Kleidung *f*, Kleider *pl*; *(Fashion)* Ensemble *nt*; *(= fancy dress)* Kostüm *nt*; *(= uniform)* Uniform *f*; *(of scout)* Kluft *f*; **is that a new ~ you're wearing?** hast du dich neu eingekleidet?; **she has so many ~s** sie hat so viel anzuziehen; **her ~s include ...** ihre Garderobe reicht von ... **b** *(= equipment)* Ausrüstung *f* **c** *(inf: = organization)* Laden *m (inf)*, Verein *m (inf)*; *(Mil)* Einheit *f*, Truppe *f*

outfitter [ˈaʊtfɪtəʳ] N *(of ships)* Ausrüster *m*; **gentlemen's ~'s** Herrenausstatter *m*; **sports ~'s** Sport(artikel)geschäft *nt*

out: **outflank** VT **a** *(Mil) enemy* umfassen, von der Flanke/den Flanken angreifen; **~ing movement** Umfassungsangriff *m or* -bewegung *f* **b** *(fig: = outwit)* überlisten; **outflow** N *(of water etc) (= act)* Abfließen *nt*, Ausfluss *m*; *(of lava)* Ausfließen *nt*; *(= amount)* Ausfluss *m*, Auswurf *m*; *(of gas)* Ausströmen *nt*; *(= amount)* Ausströmungsmenge *f*; *(= amount)* Ausflussmenge *f*; *(of money)* Abfließen *nt*; *(= amount)* Abfluss *m*; *(of refugees)* Strom *m*; **outfly** *pret* **outflew**, *ptp* **outflown** VT (fliegerisch) überlegen sein *(sb/sth* jdm/etw); **outfought** *pret, ptp of* **outfight**; **outfox** VT überlisten, austricksen *(inf)*; **outgeneral** VT taktisch überlegen sein *(+dat)*; **outgo** N *(US)* Ausgabe(n) *f(pl)*

outgoing [ˌaʊtˈgəʊɪŋ] ADJ **a** *tenant* ausziehend; *office holder* scheidend; *train, boat* hinausfahrend; *flight* hinausgehend; *(Telec) cable* wegführend, hinausführend; *call* abgehend; ~ **tide** ablaufendes Wasser, Ebbe *f*; **the ~ flight for New York** der Flug nach New York **b** *personality* aus sich herausgehend, kontaktfreudig PL **~s** Ausgaben *pl*

outgrow [ˌaʊtˈgrəʊ] *pret* **outgrew** [ˌaʊtˈgruː] *ptp* **outgrown** [ˌaʊtˈgrəʊn] VT **a** *clothes* herauswachsen aus; **they outgrew their apartment** die Wohnung ist zu klein für sie geworden **b** *habit* entwachsen *(+dat)*, hinauswachsen über *(+acc)*; *opinion* sich hinausentwickeln über *(+acc)*; **he has ~n such childish pastimes** über solche Kindereien ist er hinaus **c** *(= grow taller than) (tree)* hinauswachsen über *(+acc)*; *(person)* über den Kopf wachsen *(+dat)*

outgrowth [ˈaʊtgrəʊθ] N *(= offshoot)* Auswuchs *m*; *(fig)* Folge *f*

out: **out-Herod** VT **to ~ Herod** dem Teufel Konkurrenz machen; **outhouse** [ˈaʊthaʊs] N Seitengebäude *nt*

outing [ˈaʊtɪŋ] N **a** Ausflug *m*; **school/firm's ~** Schul-/Betriebsausflug *m*; **to go on an ~** einen Ausflug machen **b** *(of homosexual)* Outing *nt*, Outen *nt*

outlandish [ˌaʊtˈlændɪʃ] ADJ absonderlich, sonderbar; *behaviour also* befremdend, befremdlich; *prose, style, description etc* eigenwillig; *name, clothes, appearance, colour combination etc* ausgefallen; *prices* haarsträubend; *theory* obskur

outlandishly [ˌaʊtˈlændɪʃlɪ] ADV sonderbar, absonderlich; *decorated, portrayed* eigenwillig; *expensive* haarsträubend

outlandishness [ˌaʊtˈlændɪʃnɪs] N Absonderlichkeit *f*, Sonderbarkeit *f*; *(of prose, style, description)* Eigenwilligkeit *f*; *(of name, colours, clothes, appearance etc)* Ausgefallenheit *f*; *(of theory)* Obskürität *f*

outlast [ˌaʊtˈlɑːst] VT *(person) (= live longer)* überleben; *(= endure longer)* länger aus- *or* durchhalten als; *(thing)* länger halten als; *(idea etc)* überdauern, sich länger halten als

outlaw [ˈaʊtlɔː] N Geächtete(r) *mf*; *(in Western etc)* Bandit *m*; **to declare sb an ~** jdn ächten VT ächten; *newspaper, action etc* für ungesetzlich erklären, verbieten

outlawry [ˈaʊtlɔːrɪ] N Ächtung *f*; *(= defiance)* Gesetzlosigkeit *f*

outlay [ˈaʊtleɪ] N (Kosten)aufwand *m*; *(recurring, continuous)* Kosten *pl*; **the initial ~** die anfänglichen Aufwendungen; **capital ~** Kapitalaufwand *m*; **to recoup one's ~** seine Auslagen wieder hereinholen *or* -bekommen; *(business)* die Unkosten hereinwirtschaften

outlet [ˈaʊtlet] N **a** *(for water etc)* Abfluss *m*, Auslass *m*; *(for steam etc)* Abzug *m*; *(of river)* Ausfluss *m* **b** *(Comm)* Absatzmöglichkeit *f or* -markt *m*; *(= merchant)* Abnehmer(in) *m(f)*; *(= shop)* Verkaufsstelle *f* **c** *(fig) (for talents etc)* Betätigungsmöglichkeit *f*; *(for emotion)* Ventil *nt* ATTR *(Tech)* Ausfluss-, Abfluss-; ~ **pipe** Ausfluss- *or* Abflussrohr *nt*; ~ **valve** Auslassventil *nt*

outlet store N *(esp US)* Factoryoutlet-Laden *m*, Fabrikverkauf *m*

outline [ˈaʊtlaɪn] N **a** *(of objects)* Umriss *m*; *(= line itself)* Umrisslinie *f*; *(= silhouette)* Silhouette *f*; *(of face)* Züge *pl*; **he drew the ~ of a head** er zeichnete einen Kopf im Umriss **b** *(fig: = summary)* Grundriss *m*, Abriss *m*; **in (broad) ~** in großen *or* groben Zügen; **just give (me) the broad ~s** umreißen *or* skizzieren Sie es (mir) grob; **~s of botany** Abriss *m or* Grundriss *m or* Grundzüge *pl* der Botanik **c** *(Shorthand)* Kürzel *nt*, Sigel *nt*, Sigle *nt* ATTR ~ **drawing** Umrisszeichnung *f* VT **a** *(= draw outer edge of)* umreißen, den Umriss *or* die Umrisse zeichnen *(+gen)*; **the mountain was ~d against the sky** die Umrisse des Berges zeichneten sich gegen den Himmel ab; **she stood there ~d against the sunset** ihre Silhouette zeichnete sich gegen die untergehende Sonne ab **b** *(= give summary of)* umreißen, skizzieren

outline view N *(Comput)* Gliederungsansicht *f*

outlive [ˌaʊtˈlɪv] VT **a** *(= live longer than) person* überleben; *century* überdauern; **to have ~d one's day** nicht mehr der/die sein, der/die man einmal war; **to have ~d one's/its usefulness** ausgedient haben; *(method, system)* sich überlebt haben **b** *(= come safely through) storm etc* überstehen; *disgrace etc* sich reinigen (können) von *(geh)*, frei werden von

outlook [ˈaʊtlʊk] N **a** *(= view)* (Aus)blick *m*, Aussicht *f* (*over* über *+acc*, *on to* auf *+acc*) **b** *(= prospects)* (Zukunfts)aussichten *pl*; *(Met)* Aussichten *pl*; **what's the ~ for the mining industry?** wie sind die (Zukunfts)aussichten im Bergbau? **c** *(= mental attitude)* Einstellung *f*; **his ~ (up)on life** seine Lebensauffassung, seine Einstellung zum Leben; **what's his ~ on the matter?** wie steht er zu der Sache?; **his broad ~** sein weiter Horizont; **narrow ~** beschränkter Horizont, (geistige) Beschränktheit; **if you adopt such a narrow ~** wenn Sie die Dinge so eng sehen

out: **outlying** ADJ *(= distant)* entlegen, abgelegen; *(= outside the town boundary)* umliegend; ~ **district** *(of town)* Außenbezirk *m*; ~ **suburbs** Außenbezirke *pl*, äußere Vororte *pl*; **outmanoeuvre**, *(US)* **outmaneuver** VT *(fig)* ausmanövrieren; *(in rivalry)* ausstechen; **outmatch** VT übertreffen, überlegen sein *(+dat)*; **Y was ~ed by X** Y konnte gegen X nichts ausrichten; **outmoded** ADJ unzeitgemäß, altmodisch; *design etc also* antiquiert; *technology etc also* überholt, veraltet; **outmost** ADJ äußerste(r, s); *regions etc also* entlegenste(r, s) N **at the ~** äußerstenfalls, im äußersten Falle

outnumber [ˌaʊtˈnʌmbəʳ] VT in der Mehrzahl sein gegenüber; *(in fight etc also)* zahlenmäßig überlegen sein *(+dat)*; **we were ~ed (by them)** wir waren (ihnen gegenüber) in der Minderzahl *or* Minderheit, wir waren (ihnen) zahlenmäßig unterlegen; **we were ~ed five to one** sie waren fünfmal so viele wie wir, wir waren (ihnen) zahlenmäßig fünffach unterlegen

out of PREP **a** *(= outside, away from) (position)* nicht in *(+dat)*, außerhalb *(+gen)*; *(motion)* aus *(+dat)*; *(fig)* außer *(+dat)*; **I'll be ~ town all week** ich werde die ganze Woche (über) nicht in der Stadt sein; **to go/be ~ the country** außer Landes gehen/sein; **he was ~ the room at the time** er war zu dem Zeitpunkt nicht im Zimmer; **he walked ~ the room** er ging aus dem Zimmer (hinaus); **he went ~ the door** er ging zur Tür hinaus; **as soon as he was ~ the door** sobald er draußen war *or* zur Tür hinaus war; **to look ~ the window** aus dem Fenster sehen, zum Fenster hinaussehen; **I saw him ~ the window** ich sah ihn durchs Fenster; **to keep ~ the sun** nicht in die Sonne gehen; ~ **danger/sight** außer Gefahr/Sicht; **get ~ my sight!** geh mir aus den Augen!; **he's ~ the tournament** er ist aus dem Turnier ausgeschieden; **he feels ~ it** *(inf)* er kommt sich *(dat)* ausgeschlossen vor, er fühlt sich ausgeschlossen; **to be ~ it** *(Brit sl: = drunk)* besoffen *or* dicht sein *(inf)*; **they were 150 miles ~ Hamburg** *(Naut)* sie waren 150 Meilen von Hamburg weg *or* vor Hamburg; **three days ~ port** drei Tage nach dem Auslaufen aus dem Hafen/vor dem Einlaufen in den Hafen; **he lives 10 miles ~ London** er wohnt 10 Meilen außerhalb Londons; **you're well ~ it** *(inf)* so ist es besser für dich **b** *(cause, motive)* aus *(+dat)*; ~ **curiosity** aus Neugier **c** *(indicating origins or source)* aus *(+dat)*; **to drink ~ a glass** aus einem Glas trinken; **made ~ silver** aus Silber (gemacht); **a filly ~ the same mare** ein Fohlen *nt* von derselben Stute **d** *(= from among)* von *(+dat)*; **in seven cases ~ ten** in sieben von zehn Fällen; **one ~ every four smokers** einer von vier Rauchern; **he picked one ~ the pile** er nahm einen aus dem Stapel (heraus) **e** *(= without)* ~ **breath** außer Atem; **we are ~ money/bread** wir haben kein Geld/Brot mehr, das Geld/Brot ist alle *(inf)*

out: **out-of-bounds** ADJ ~ **park** Park, dessen Betreten verboten ist *(to* für); ~ **area** Sperrgebiet *nt*; **out-of-court** ADJ *settlement* außergerichtlich; **out-of-date** ADJ *attr*, **out of date** ADJ *pred* **a** *methods, technology, ideas* überholt, veraltet; *clothes, records* altmodisch, unmodern; *customs* veraltet; **you're out of date** Sie sind nicht auf dem Laufenden **b** *(= expired) ticket* abgelaufen; *food, medicine* mit abgelaufenem Verfallsdatum; **out-of-doors** ADV = **outdoors** ADV; **out of office reply** N *(Comput)* Abwesenheitsnotiz *f*; **out of place** ADJ *pred*, **out-of-place** ADJ *attr remark etc* unangebracht, deplatziert; **out-of-pocket** ADJ *attr*, **out of pocket** ADJ *pred (Brit)* ~ **expenses** Barauslagen *pl*; **to be out of pocket** drauflegen, draufzahlen; **I was £5 out of pocket** ich habe £ 5 aus eigener Tasche bezahlt; **I'm still £2 out of pocket** ich habe immer noch £ 2 zu wenig; **out-of-the-way** ADJ *attr*, **out of the way** ADJ *pred (= remote) spot* abgelegen, aus der

Welt; *(= unusual) theory* ungewöhnlich; *(= not commonly known) facts* wenig bekannt; **out-of--towner** N *(esp US)* Auswärtige(r) *mf*; **outpace** VT schneller sein als; **outpatient** N ambulanter Patient, ambulante Patientin; **~s' (department)** Ambulanz *f*; **~s' clinic** Poliklinik *f*; **outperform** VT ausstechen *(inf)*; **outplacement** ['aʊt,pleɪsmənt] N *(Econ)* Outplacement *nt*; **outplay** VT *(Sport)* besser spielen als, überlegen sein *(+dat)*; **we were completely ~ed (by them)** wir konnten (gegen sie) absolut nichts ausrichten, sie waren uns haushoch überlegen; **outpoint** VT auspunkten; **outpost** N *(Mil, fig)* Vorposten *m*; **outpouring** N *often pl* Erguss *m (fig)*

output ['aʊtpʊt] N *(of machine, factory, person) (= act)* Produktion *f*; *(= quantity also)* Ausstoß *m*, Output *m or nt*; *(= rate of output also)* (Produktions)leistung *f*, Output *m or nt*; *(= quantity in agriculture also)* Ertrag *m*; *(Elec)* Leistung *f*; *(= output terminal)* Ausgang *m*; *(= capacity of amplifier)* (Ausgangs)leistung *f*; *(of mine)* Förderung *f*; *(= quantity)* Fördermenge *f*, Förderung *f*; *(= rate of output)* Förderleistung, Förderung *f*; *(= of computer)* Ausgabe *f*, Output *m or nt*; **effective ~ of a machine** Nutzleistung *f* einer Maschine; **this factory has an ~ of 600 radios a day** diese Fabrik produziert täglich 600 Radios

output data N *usu with sing (Comput)* Ausgabedaten *pl*

output device N *(Comput)* Ausgabegerät *nt*

outrage ['aʊtreɪdʒ] N **a** *(= wicked, violent deed)* Untat *f*; *(cruel)* Gräueltat *f*; *(by police, demonstrators etc)* Ausschreitung *f*; **bomb ~** verbrecherischer Bombenanschlag; **an ~ against the State** ein schändliches *or* ruchloses *(liter)* Verbrechen gegen den Staat
b *(= indecency, injustice)* Skandal *m*; **it's an ~ to waste food** es ist ein Skandal *or* Frevel, Essen verkommen zu lassen; **an ~ against humanity** ein Verbrechen *nt* gegen die Menschlichkeit; **an ~ to common decency** eine empörende Verletzung des allgemeinen Anstandsgefühls; **an ~ against public morality** ein empörender Verstoß gegen die guten Sitten *or* die öffentliche Moral
c *(= sense of outrage)* Empörung *f (at* über *+acc)*, Entrüstung *f (at* über *+acc)*; **he reacted with (a sense of) ~** er war empört *or* entrüstet
VT [aʊt'reɪdʒ] *morals, conventions* ins Gesicht schlagen *(+dat)*, Hohn sprechen *(+dat)*, hohnsprechen *(+dat) (geh)*; *sense of decency* beleidigen; *ideals* mit Füßen treten; *person* empören, entrüsten; **public opinion was ~d by this cruelty/injustice** die öffentliche Meinung war über diese Grausamkeit/Ungerechtigkeit empört; **he deliberately set out to ~ his critics** er hatte es darauf angelegt, seine Kritiker zu schockieren

outraged ['aʊtreɪdʒd] ADJ empört *(at, about* über *+acc)*

outrageous [aʊt'reɪdʒəs] ADJ **a** *(= cruel, violent)* gräulich, verabscheuenswürdig; **murder, rape, and other ~ deeds** Mord, Vergewaltigung und andere Untaten
b *remark, story, price, claim, behaviour* unerhört; *demand, insolence, lie, arrogance etc* unerhört, unverschämt; *nonsense* haarsträubend; *language* entsetzlich, unflätig; *charge, defamation etc* ungeheuerlich; *clothes, make-up etc* ausgefallen, unmöglich *(inf)*; *(= indecent)* geschmacklos; *complexity, selfishness* unglaublich, unerhört; **~ colour** Schockfarbe *f*; **he's ~!** er ist unmöglich!; **it's absolutely ~ that …** es ist einfach unerhört, dass …

outrageously [aʊt'reɪdʒəslɪ] ADV *expensive* unerhört; *flirt* unverschämt; *behave* unerhört, unmöglich; *lie* schamlos; *exaggerate also* masslos; *made-up also, dressed* unmöglich *(inf)*; **he suggested/demanded quite ~ that …** er machte den unerhörten Vorschlag/er stellte die unerhörte Forderung, dass …; **an ~ low neckline** ein schamlos tiefer Ausschnitt; **he's ~ over the top** er ist total ausgefallen; **~ funny** zum Schreien komisch

out: **outran** *pret of* **outrun**; **outrange** VT eine größere Reichweite haben als; **we were ~d** die anderen hatten/der Feind *etc* hatte eine größere Reichweite; **outrank** VT *(Mil)* rangmäßig stehen über *(+dat)*; **he was ~ed** er war rangniedriger

outré ['u:treɪ] ADJ überspannt, extravagant

out: **outride** *pret* **outrode** **outridden** VT besser reiten als; *(on bike)* besser fahren als; *(= outdistance)* davonreiten/-fahren *(+dat)*; **he was completely outridden** er konnte absolut nicht mithalten; **he can't be outridden** mit ihm kann keiner mithalten; **outrider** ['aʊtraɪdəʳ] N *(on motorcycle)* Kradbegleiter(in) *m(f)*; **outrigger** N *(Naut)* Ausleger *m*; *(= boat)* Auslegerboot *nt*

outright [aʊt'raɪt] ADV **a** *(= entirely) reject* rundweg; *own* vollständig; **to buy sth ~** etw komplett kaufen; *(= not on HP)* den ganzen Preis für etw sofort bezahlen; **to win ~** einen klaren Sieg davontragen
b *(= at once) kill* sofort, auf der Stelle, gleich; **he was killed ~** er war sofort tot; **he felled him ~** er streckte ihn mit einem einzigen Schlag zu Boden
c *(= openly)* geradeheraus, unumwunden, ohne Umschweife
ADJ ['aʊtraɪt] **a** *(= complete) deception, lie* rein, glatt *(inf)*; *nonsense, ban, victory* total, absolut; *disaster, loss* völlig, vollkommen, total; *refusal, denial* total, absolut, glatt *(inf)*; *majority* absolut; *hostility, condemnation* offen, unverhohlen; *support* uneingeschränkt; *opponent* eingefleischt; *winner* klar; *defeat, error* gründlich, ausgesprochen, absolut; *independence* vollkommen; **that's ~ arrogance/impertinence** das ist die reine Arroganz/Unverschämtheit; **that's ~ deception/selfishness** das ist reiner *or* glatter *(inf)* Betrug/reiner Egoismus
b *(Comm: = full)* **~ sale/purchase** Verkauf *m*/Kauf *m* gegen sofortige Zahlung der Gesamtsumme; **~ owner** Volleigentümer(in) *m(f)*; **~ ownership** Volleigentum *nt*
c *(= open) person* offen

out: **outrode** *pret of* **outride**; **outrun** *pret* **outran**, *ptp* **outrun** VT schneller laufen als; *(= outdistance)* davonlaufen *(+dat)*; *(fig)* übersteigen; **the white horse outran the rest of the field** der Schimmel ließ das übrige Feld hinter sich *(dat)*; **outset** N Beginn *m*, Anfang *m*; **at the ~** zu *or* am Anfang; **from the ~** von Anfang an, von Anbeginn *(geh)*; **let me make it quite clear at the ~ that …** lassen Sie mich von vornherein klarstellen, dass …; **outshine** *pret, ptp* **outshone** VT überstrahlen *(geh)*, heller sein als; *(fig)* in den Schatten stellen

outside ['aʊt'saɪd] N **a** *(of house, car, object)* Außenseite *f*; **the ~ of the car is green** das Auto ist (von) außen grün; **the ~ of the post** *(Ftbl)* der Außenpfosten; **to open the door from the ~** die Tür von außen öffnen; **they were smuggled in from the ~** sie wurden von draußen eingeschmuggelt; **to stay on the ~ of a group** sich in einer Gruppe im Hintergrund halten; **people on the ~ (of society)** Menschen außerhalb der Gesellschaft; **to overtake on the ~** *(Brit)* außen überholen; **judging from the ~** *(fig)* wenn man es als Außenstehender beurteilt
b *(= extreme limit)* **at the (very) ~** im äußersten Falle, äußerstenfalls
ADJ **a** *(= external)* Außen-, äußere(r, s); *consultant, investor, examiner, opinion* extern; **an ~ broadcast** eine nicht im Studio produzierte Sendung; **an ~ broadcast from Wimbledon** eine Sendung aus Wimbledon; **~ call** *(Telec)* externer Anruf; **to get some ~ help** Hilfe von außen holen; **~ influences** äußere Einflüsse, Einflüsse von außen; **~ seat** *(in a row)* Außensitz *m*, Platz *m* am Gang; **~ work** freie Mitarbeit; **I'm doing ~ work on the dictionary** ich arbeite freiberuflich am Wörterbuch mit
b *price* äußerste(r, s); **at an ~ estimate** maximal
c *(= very unlikely)* **an ~ chance** eine kleine Chance
ADV *(= on the outer side)* außen; *(of house, room, vehicle)* draußen; **to be ~** draußen sein; **to go ~** nach draußen gehen; **seen from ~** von außen gesehen; **put the cat ~** bring die Katze raus *(inf) or* nach draußen; **I feel ~ it all** ich komme mir so ausgeschlossen vor
PREP *(also* **outside of***)* **a** *(= on the outer side of)* außerhalb *(+gen)*; **~ California** außerhalb Kaliforniens; **~ London** außerhalb von London; **visitors from ~ the area** Besucher *pl* von außerhalb; **to be ~ sth** außerhalb einer Sache sein; **to go ~ sth** aus etw gehen; **he went ~ the house** er ging aus dem/vors/hinters Haus, er ging nach draußen; **the noise was coming from ~ the house** der Lärm kam von draußen; **he is waiting ~ the door** er wartet vor der Tür; **the car ~ the house** das Auto vorm Haus
b *(= beyond limits of)* außerhalb *(+gen)*; **it is ~ our agreement** es geht über unsere Vereinbarung hinaus; **~ the Festival** außerhalb der Festspiele; **this falls ~ the scope of …** das geht über den Rahmen *(+gen)* … hinaus; **to marry ~ one's religion** eine konfessionsverschiedene Ehe eingehen; **babies born ~ marriage** außerehelich geborene Kinder *pl*; **sex ~ marriage** Sex *m* außerhalb der Ehe; **you'll have to do it ~ office hours** Sie müssen das nach Büroschluss erledigen
c *(= apart from)* außer *(+dat)*, abgesehen von *(+dat)*

outside: **outside aerial** N *(Brit)* Außenantenne *f*; **outside half** N *(Rugby)* äußerer Halb(-spieler); **outside lane** N Überholspur *f*; **outside left** N *(Ftbl, Hockey)* Linksaußenspieler(in) *m(f)*; **outside line** N *(Tel)* Amtsanschluss *m*

outsider [,aʊt'saɪdəʳ] N Außenseiter(in) *m(f)*, Outsider *m*

outside: **outside right** N *(Ftbl, Hockey)* Rechtsaußenspieler(in) *m(f)*; **outside temperature** N Außentemperatur *f*; **outside toilet** N Außentoilette *f*; **outside wall** N Außenwand *f*; **outside world** N Außenwelt *f*

out: **outsize** ADJ **a** übergroß; **~ clothes** Kleidung *f* in Übergröße, Übergrößen *pl*; **the ~ department** die Abteilung für Übergrößen **b** *(inf: = enormous)* riesig; **outskirts** PL *(of town)* Außen- *or* Randgebiete *pl*, Stadtrand *m*; *(of wood)* Rand *m*; **outsleep** *pret, ptp* **outslept** VT verschlafen; **outsmart** VT *(inf)* überlisten, austricksen *(inf)*

outsource ['aʊtsɔ:s] VT *(Econ) work* outsourcen, außer Haus geben, auslagern

outsourcing ['aʊtsɔ:sɪŋ] N *(Econ)* Auslagerung *f*, Outsourcing *nt*

outspoken [,aʊt'spəʊkən] ADJ *person, criticism, speech, book* freimütig; *attack, remark* direkt; *answer* freimütig, unverblümt; **he is ~** er nimmt kein Blatt vor den Mund; **there was no need for you to be so ~** so deutlich hättest du nicht zu sein brauchen

outspokenly [,aʊt'spəʊkənlɪ] ADV geradeheraus, unverblümt; *answer, write also* freimütig; *remark also* direkt

outspokenness [,aʊt'spəʊkənnɪs] N *(of person, criticism, speech, book)* Freimütigkeit *f*; *(of attack, remark)* Direktheit *f*; *(of answer)* Unverblümtheit *f*

outspread ['aʊtspred] *vb: pret, ptp* **outspread** ADJ ausgebreitet VT ausbreiten

outstanding [,aʊt'stændɪŋ] ADJ **a** *(= exceptional)* hervorragend; *talent, beauty, brilliance* außerordentlich, überragend; **of ~ ability** hervorragend *or* außerordentlich begabt; **work of ~ excellence** ganz ausgezeichnete Arbeit; **of ~ importance** von höchster Bedeutung; **area of ~ natural beauty** *(Brit)* Naturschutzgebiet *nt* (von besonderer Schönheit)
b *(= prominent, conspicuous) event* bemerkenswert; *detail* auffallend; *feature* hervorstechend, auffallend
c *(Comm, Fin) business* unerledigt; *amount, account, bill, interest* ausstehend; **a lot of work is still ~** viel Arbeit ist noch unerledigt; **are there any problems still ~?** gibt es noch irgendwelche ungeklärten Probleme?; **~ debts** Außenstände *pl*

outstandingly [ˌaʊtˈstændɪŋlɪ] ADV hervorragend; *good, beautiful, successful* außergewöhnlich; **the party did ~ well in the elections** die Partei hat in den Wahlen außergewöhnlich gut abgeschnitten

out: **outstation** N Vorposten *m*; **outstay** VT länger bleiben als; **I don't want to ~ my welcome** ich will eure Gastfreundschaft nicht überbeanspruchen *or* nicht zu lange in Anspruch nehmen; **outstretched** ADJ *body* ausgestreckt; *arms also* ausgebreitet; **outstrip** VT **a** *(Sport)* überholen **b** *(fig)* übertreffen (*in* an +*dat*); **outswim** *pret* **outswam**, *ptp* **outswum** VT **to ~ sb** jdm davonschwimmen; **outtake** N *für die endgültige Fassung nicht verwendete, herausgeschnittene Filmsequenz*, Outtake *m (spec)*; **out tray** N Ablage *f* für Ausgänge; **outvote** VT überstimmen

outward [ˈaʊtwəd] ADJ **a** *(= of or on the outside) appearance, form* äußere(r, s); *beauty* äußerlich; **he put on an ~ show of confidence** er gab sich den Anstrich von Selbstsicherheit **b** *(= going out) movement* nach außen führend *or* gehend; *freight* ausgehend; **the ~ flow of traffic** der Verkehr(sstrom) aus der Stadt heraus; **~ journey/voyage** Hinreise *f*; **~ flight** Hinflug *m*; **~ investment** Auslandsinvestitionen *pl* ADV nach außen; **the door opens ~** die Tür geht nach außen auf; **~ bound** *(ship)* auslaufend (*from* von, *for* mit Bestimmung, mit Kurs auf +*acc*); **Outward Bound course** Abenteuerkurs *m*

outward-looking [ˈaʊtwədˌlʊkɪŋ] ADJ *person, organization, country* aufgeschlossen; *attitude, approach* nach vorne gerichtet, aufgeschlossen; *policy* offen

outwardly [ˈaʊtwədlɪ] ADV nach außen hin

outwards [ˈaʊtwədz] ADV nach außen; **the journey ~** die Hinreise

out: **outwear** *pret* **outwore**, *ptp* **outworn** VT **a** *(= last longer than)* überdauern, länger halten als **b** *(= wear out) clothes* abtragen → *also* **outworn**; **outweigh** VT überwiegen, mehr Gewicht haben als; **outwit** VT überlisten; *(in card games etc)* austricksen *(inf)*; **outwork** N *(Mil)* Außenwerk *nt*; **outworker** N **a** *(away from the office/factory)* Außenarbeiter(in) *m(f)* **b** *(= homeworker)* Heimarbeiter(in) *m(f)*; **outworn** ADJ *idea, subject, expression* abgedroschen, abgenutzt; *custom, doctrine* veraltet

ouzo [ˈuːzəʊ] N Ouzo *m*

ova [ˈəʊvə] *pl of* **ovum**

oval [ˈəʊvəl] ADJ oval; **~-shaped** oval N Oval *nt*

Oval Office N *(US)* Oval Office *nt*, *Büro des US-Präsidenten*

ovarian [əʊˈveərɪən] ADJ **a** *(Anat)* des Eierstocks/der Eierstöcke; **~ cyst** Zyste *f* im Eierstock **b** *(Bot)* des Fruchtknotens

ovary [ˈəʊvərɪ] N **a** *(Anat)* Eierstock *m* **b** *(Bot)* Fruchtknoten *m*

ovation [əʊˈveɪʃən] N Ovation *f*, stürmischer Beifall; **to give sb an ~** jdm eine Ovation darbringen, jdm stürmischen Beifall zollen; **to get an ~** stürmischen Beifall ernten → **standing**

oven [ˈʌvn] N *(Cook)* (Back)ofen *m*; *(Tech) (for drying)* (Trocken)ofen *m*; *(for baking pottery etc)* (Brenn)ofen *m*; **to put sth in the ~** etw in den Ofen tun *or* stecken; **put it in the ~ for two hours** backen Sie es zwei Stunden; *pottery* brennen Sie es zwei Stunden; **to cook in a hot** *or* **quick/moderate/slow ~** bei starker/mittlerer/schwacher Hitze backen; **it's like an ~ in here** hier ist ja der reinste Backofen

oven: **ovenable** [ˈʌvnəbl] ADJ *dish* ofenfertig; **oven cleaner** N Ofenreiniger *m*; **oven cloth** N Topflappen *m*; **oven door** N Ofentür *f*, Ofenklappe *f*; **oven glove** N *(Brit)* Topfhandschuh *m*; **ovenproof** ADJ *dish* feuerfest, hitzebeständig; **oven-ready** ADJ bratfertig; **oven-to-table-ware** N feuerfestes Geschirr; **ovenware** N feuerfeste Formen *pl*

over [ˈəʊvəʳ] PREP **a** *(indicating motion)* über (+*acc*); **he spread the blanket ~ the bed** er breitete die Decke über das Bett; **he spilled coffee ~ it** er goss Kaffee darüber, er vergoss Kaffee darauf; **to hit sb ~ the head** jdm auf den Kopf schlagen

b *(indicating position: = above, on top of)* über (+*dat*); **if you hang the picture ~ the desk** wenn du das Bild über dem Schreibtisch aufhängst *or* über den Schreibtisch hängst; **bent ~ one's books** über die Bücher gebeugt

c *(= on the other side of)* über (+*dat*); *(= to the other side of)* über (+*acc*); **to look ~ the wall** über die Mauer schauen; **the noise came from ~ the wall** der Lärm kam von der anderen Seite der Mauer; **it's ~ the page** es ist auf der nächsten Seite; **I looked ~ my shoulder** ich sah mir über meine Schulter; **he looked ~ my shoulder** er sah über die Schulter; **she has to keep looking ~ her shoulder** *(fig)* sie ist verängstigt; **the house ~ the road** das Haus gegenüber; **the family from ~ the road** die Familie von gegenüber; **it's just ~ the road from us** das ist von uns (aus) nur über die Straße; **the bridge ~ the river** die Brücke über den Fluss; **we're ~ the main obstacles now** wir haben jetzt die größten Hindernisse hinter uns *(dat)*; **when they were ~ the river** als sie über den Fluss hinüber waren; **they're all safely ~ the first fence** sie sind alle sicher über die erste Hürde gekommen

d *(= in or across every part of)* in (+*dat*); **it was raining ~ London** es regnete in (ganz) London; **they came from all ~ England** sie kamen aus allen Teilen Englands *or* aus ganz England; **I'll show you ~ the house** ich zeige Ihnen das Haus; **you've got ink all ~ you/your hands** Sie/Ihre Hände sind ganz voller Tinte; **a smile spread ~ her face** ein Lächeln breitete sich auf ihrem Gesicht aus; **to be all ~ sb** *(inf)* ein Mordstheater um jdn machen *(inf)*

e *(= superior to)* über (+*dat*); **to have authority ~ sb** Autorität über jdn haben; **he has no control ~ his urges/his staff** er hat seine Triebe/seine Angestellten nicht unter Kontrolle; **he was promoted ~ me** er wurde über mich befördert; **we were all ~ them** *(inf)* wir waren ihnen haushoch überlegen

f *(= more than, longer than)* über (+*acc*); **~ and above that** darüber hinaus; **~ and above the expenses** über die Ausgaben hinaus; **that was well ~ a year ago** das ist gut ein Jahr her, das war vor gut einem Jahr; **she will not live ~ the winter** sie wird den Winter nicht überleben

g *(in expressions of time)* über (+*acc*); *(= during)* während (+*gen*), in (+*dat*); **can we stay ~ the weekend?** können wir übers Wochenende bleiben?; **~ Christmas** über Weihnachten; **~ the summer** den Sommer über; **~ the summer we have been trying ...** während des Sommers haben wir versucht ...; **~ the (past) years I've come to realize ...** im Laufe der (letzten) Jahre ist mir klar geworden ...; **he has mellowed ~ the years** er ist mit den Jahren milder geworden; **the visits were spread ~ several months** die Besuche verteilten sich über mehrere Monate

h **they talked ~ a cup of coffee** sie unterhielten sich bei einer Tasse Kaffee; **the speeches were made ~ coffee** die Reden wurden beim Kaffee gehalten; **let's discuss that ~ dinner/a beer** besprechen wir das beim Essen/bei einem Bier; **they'll be a long time ~ it** sie werden dazu lange brauchen; **he nodded off ~ his work** er nickte über seiner Arbeit ein; **to get stuck ~ a difficulty** bei einer Schwierigkeit stecken bleiben

i **he told me ~ the phone** er hat es mir am Telefon gesagt; **I heard it ~ the radio** ich habe es im Radio gehört; **a voice came ~ the intercom** eine Stimme kam über die Sprechanlage

j *(= about)* über (+*acc*); **it's not worth arguing ~** es lohnt (sich) nicht, darüber zu streiten; **that's nothing for you to get upset ~** darüber brauchst du dich nicht aufzuregen

k **what is 7 ~ 3?** wie viel ist 7 durch 3?; **blood pressure of 150 ~ 120** Blutdruck *m* von 150 zu 120

ADV **a** *(= across) (away from speaker)* hinüber; *(towards speaker)* herüber; *(= on the other side)* drüben; **they swam ~ to us** sie schwammen zu uns herüber; **he took the fruit ~ to his mother** er brachte das Obst zu seiner Mutter hinüber; **when the first man is ~ the second starts to climb/swim** wenn der Erste drüben angekommen ist, klettert/schwimmt der Zweite los; **come ~ tonight** kommen Sie heute Abend vorbei; **I just thought I'd come ~** ich dachte, ich komme mal rüber *(inf)*; **he is ~ here/there** er ist hier/dort drüben; **~ to you!** Sie sind daran; **and now ~ to our reporter in Belfast** und nun schalten wir zu unserem Reporter in Belfast um; **and now ~ to Paris where ...** und nun (schalten wir um) nach Paris, wo ...; **he has gone ~ to America** er ist nach Amerika gefahren; **~ in America** drüben in Amerika; **he drove us ~ to the other side of town** er fuhr uns ans andere Ende der Stadt; **he went ~ to the enemy** er lief zum Feind über

b **famous the world ~** in der ganzen Welt berühmt; **I've been looking for it all ~** ich habe überall danach gesucht; **I am aching all ~** mir tut alles weh; **you've got dirt all ~** Sie sind voller Schmutz, Sie sind ganz schmutzig; **he was shaking all ~** er zitterte am ganzen Leib; **I'm wet all ~** ich bin völlig nass; **he was black all ~** er war von oben bis unten schwarz; **the dog licked him all ~** der Hund leckte ihn von oben bis unten ab; **that's Fred all ~** das ist typisch (für) Fred; **it happens all ~** das gibt es überall

c *(indicating movement from one side to another, from upright position)* **to turn an object ~ (and ~)** einen Gegenstand (immer wieder) herumdrehen; **he hit her and ~ she went** er schlug sie, und sie fiel um

d *(= ended) film, first act, operation, fight etc* zu Ende; *romance, summer* vorbei, zu Ende; **the rain is ~** der Regen hat aufgehört; **the pain will soon be ~** der Schmerz wird bald vorbei sein; **the danger was ~** die Gefahr war vorüber, es bestand keine Gefahr mehr; **when all this is ~** wenn das alles vorbei ist; **it's all ~ with him** es ist Schluss *or* aus mit ihm; **it's all ~ between us** es ist aus zwischen uns

e *(indicating repetition)* **he counted them ~ again** *(Brit) or* **~** *(US)* er zählte sie noch einmal; **to start (all) ~ again** *(Brit) or* **~** *(US)* noch einmal (ganz) von vorn anfangen; **~ and ~ (again)** immer (und immer) wieder, wieder und wieder; **he did it five times ~** er hat es fünfmal wiederholt; **must I say everything twice ~!** muss ich denn immer alles zweimal sagen!

f *(= excessively)* übermäßig, allzu; **he has not done it ~ well** er hat es nicht gerade übermäßig gut gemacht; **he is not ~ healthy** er ist nicht allzu gesund; **there's not ~ much left** es ist nicht allzu viel übrig

g *(= remaining)* übrig; **there was no/a lot of meat (left) ~** es war kein Fleisch mehr übrig/viel Fleisch übrig; **7 into 22 goes 3 and 1 ~** 22 durch 7 ist 3, Rest 1; **6 feet and a little ~** 6 Fuß und ein bisschen

h *(= more)* **children of 8 and ~** Kinder ab 8; **all results of 5.3 and ~** alle Ergebnisse ab 5,3 *or* von 5,3 und darüber; **if it takes three hours or ~** wenn es drei oder mehr Stunden dauert

i *(Telec)* **come in, please, ~** bitte kommen, over; **~ and out** Ende der Durchsage; *(Aviat)* over and out

N *(Cricket) 6 aufeinanderfolgende Würfe*

over- PREF über-, Über-; **overabundance** N Überfülle *f* (*of* von); **overabundant** ADJ überreichlich, sehr reichlich; **to have an ~ supply of sth** überreichlich mit etw versorgt sein; **overachieve** VI leistungsorientiert sein; **a society which encourages people to ~** ein Gesellschaftssystem, das vom Menschen immer größere Leistungen fordert; **overachiever** N leistungsorientierter Mensch; **a chronic ~** ein typischer Erfolgsmensch; **overact** *(Theat)* VT *role* übertreiben, übertrieben gestalten VI übertreiben *(also fig)*, chargieren; **overactive** ADJ überaktiv, zu aktiv; **~ thyroid** *(Med)* Schilddrüsenüberfunktion *f*

overage[1] [ˌəʊvərˈeɪdʒ] ADJ zu alt

overage² ['əʊvərɪdʒ] N (US) a (Comm) Überschuss *m* b (mobile phone) **~s** *über die Freiminuten hinaus zu zahlende Telefonminuten*

overall¹ [,əʊvər'ɔːl] ADJ a gesamt, Gesamt-; **~ width/length** Gesamtbreite *f*/-länge *f*; **~ dimensions** (Aut) Außenmaße *pl*; **~ direction** Gesamtleitung *f*; **~ majority** absolute Mehrheit; **~ winner** Gesamtsieger(in) *m(f)*; **he is the ~ leader** (Sport) er führt in der Gesamtwertung; **Labour gained ~ control** Labour erlangte die vollständige Kontrolle
b (= general) allgemein; **there's been an ~ improvement recently in his work/health** sein Gesundheitszustand hat sich/seine Leistungen haben sich in letzter Zeit allgemein verbessert; **the ~ effect of this was to …** dies hatte das Endergebnis, dass …
ADV a insgesamt; **what does it measure ~?** wie sind die Gesamtmaße?; **he came second ~** (Sport) er belegte in der Gesamtwertung den zweiten Platz
b (= in general, on the whole) im Großen und Ganzen

overall² ['əʊvərɔːl] N (Brit) Kittel *m*; (for women also) Kittelschürze *f*; (for children) Kittelchen *nt*

overalls ['əʊvərɔːlz] PL Overall *m*, Arbeitsanzug *m*; (US: = dungarees) Latzhose *f*

over: **overambitious** ADJ überehrgeizig, zu ehrgeizig; **overanxiety** N übersteigerte Angst; **overanxious** ADJ übertrieben besorgt; (on particular occasion) übermäßig aufgeregt, übermäßig nervös; **he's ~ to please** er überschlägt sich, um zu gefallen; **I'm not exactly ~ to go** ich bin nicht gerade scharf darauf, zu gehen

overarching ['əʊvər'ɑːtʃɪŋ] ADJ allumfassend

over: **overarm** ADJ, ADV (Sport) *throw* mit gestrecktem (erhobenem) Arm; *serve* über Kopf; **~ stroke** (Swimming) Kraulschlag *m*; **overate** *pret of* **overeat**; **overawe** VT (= intimidate) einschüchtern; (= impress) überwältigen, tief beeindrucken; **overbalance** VI (person, object) aus dem Gleichgewicht kommen, Übergewicht bekommen, das Gleichgewicht verlieren VT *object* umwerfen, umstoßen; *boat* kippen; *person* aus dem Gleichgewicht bringen

overbearing [,əʊvə'beərɪŋ] ADJ herrisch; *arrogance* anmaßend

overbearingly [,əʊvə'beərɪŋlɪ] ADV herrisch; **so ~ arrogant** von einer derartig anmaßenden Arroganz

over: **overbid** *pret, ptp* **overbid** VT a (at auction) überbieten b (Cards) überreizen; **to ~ one's hand** zu hoch reizen VI a (at auction) mehr bieten, ein höheres Angebot machen b (Cards) überreizen;; **overblouse** N Überbluse *f*; **overblow** *pret* **overblew**, *ptp* **overblown** VT (Mus) überblasen; **overblown** ADJ a *flower* verblühend b *prose, rhetoric* geschwollen, schwülstig, hochtrabend c (Mus) *note* überblasen

overboard ['əʊvəbɔːd] ADV a (Naut) über Bord; **to fall ~** über Bord gehen *or* fallen; **man ~!** Mann über Bord!; **to throw sb/sth ~** jdn/etw über Bord werfen; **to throw sth ~** (fig) etw verwerfen b (fig inf) **to go ~** übers Ziel hinausschießen, zu weit gehen, es übertreiben; **to go ~ for** *or* **about sb** von jdm ganz hingerissen sein, Feuer und Flamme für jdn sein (inf); **there's no need to go ~ (about it)** übertreib es nicht, kein Grund zum Übertreiben

over: **overbold** ADJ *person, action* verwegen; **overbook** VI zu viele Buchungen vornehmen VT zu viele Buchungen vornehmen für; **overburden** VT (lit) überladen; (fig) überlasten; **overbuy** *pret, ptp* **overbought** VI zu viel kaufen, über Bedarf einkaufen; **overcall** (Cards) VT überbieten N höheres Gebot; **overcame** *pret of* **overcome**; **overcapacity** N Überkapazität *f*; **overcapitalize** VT überkapitalisieren; **overcareful** ADJ übervorsichtig; **overcast** ADJ a *weather* bedeckt; *sky* bewölkt, bedeckt; **it's getting rather ~** es zieht sich zu b (Sew) *stitch* überwendlich; **~ seam** überwendliche Naht; **overcautious** ADJ übervorsichtig, übertrieben vorsichtig; **overcautiousness** N übertriebene Vorsicht

overcharge [,əʊvə'tʃɑːdʒ] VT a *person* zu viel berechnen (+dat) *or* abverlangen (+dat) (for für); **you've been ~d** man hat dir zu viel berechnet; **they ~d me by £2** sie haben mir £ 2 zu viel berechnet b *electric circuit* überlasten c (with detail, emotion) *painting, style* überladen VI zu viel verlangen (for für); **to ~ on a bill** zu viel berechnen *or* anrechnen

overcoat ['əʊvəkəʊt] N Mantel *m*, Überzieher *m*

overcome [,əʊvə'kʌm] *pret* **overcame** [,əʊvə'keɪm] *ptp* **overcome** VT *enemy* überwältigen, bezwingen; *bad habit* sich (dat) abgewöhnen; *shyness, nerves, difficulty, anger, obstacle etc* überwinden; *temptation* widerstehen (+dat), bezwingen; *disappointment* hinwegkommen über (+acc); **he was ~ by the fumes** die giftigen Gase machten ihn bewusstlos; **sleep overcame him** der Schlaf übermannte ihn; **he was ~ by grief/by emotion** Schmerz/Rührung übermannte ihn; **he was ~ by remorse/(a feeling of) despair** Reue *f*/(ein Gefühl *nt* der) Verzweiflung *f* überkam ihn; **~ with fear** von Furcht ergriffen *or* übermannt; **~ (with emotion)** ergriffen, gerührt VI siegen, siegreich sein; **we shall ~** wir werden siegen

over: **overcompensate** VI **to ~ for sth** etw überkompensieren; **overcompensation** N Überkompensation *f*; **overconfidence** N a (= extreme self-assurance) übersteigertes Selbstvertrauen *or* Selbstbewusstsein b (= over-optimism) zu großer Optimismus c (= excessive trust) blindes Vertrauen (in in +acc); **overconfident** ADJ a (= extremely self-assured) übertrieben selbstsicher *or* selbstbewusst b (= too optimistic) zu optimistisch; **he was ~ of success** er war sich (dat) seines Erfolges zu sicher c (= excessively trustful) blind vertrauend (in auf +acc); **you are ~ in him** Sie haben zu großes Vertrauen in ihn; **overconsumption** N zu starker Verbrauch (of an +dat); **overcook** VT verbraten; (= boil too long) verkochen; **overcorrect** VT überkorrigieren ADJ überkorrekt; **overcritical** ADJ zu kritisch; **overcrop** VT (Agr) *land* Raubbau treiben mit, zugrunde wirtschaften; **overcrowd** VT überladen; *bus etc also, room (with people)* überfüllen; **overcrowded** ADJ (with things) überfüllt; *town also* übervölkert; (= overpopulated) überbevölkert; **overcrowding** N (of bus, room, flat, classroom) Überfüllung *f*; (of town) Überbevölkerung *f*; **overdependent** ADJ zu abhängig (on von); **overdeveloped** ADJ überentwickelt

overdo [,əʊvə'duː] *pret* **overdid** [,əʊvə'dɪd] *ptp* **overdone** VT a (= exaggerate) übertreiben; **you are ~ing it** *or* **things** (= going too far) Sie übertreiben, Sie gehen zu weit; (= tiring yourself) Sie übernehmen *or* überlasten sich; **don't ~ the drink/sympathy** übertreibe es nicht mit dem Trinken/Mitleid; **she rather overdid the loving wife (bit)** (inf) sie hat die liebevolle Ehefrau etwas zu dick aufgetragen; **gin? – please, but don't ~ the tonic** Gin? – ja bitte, aber nicht zu viel Tonic; **I'm afraid you've rather ~ne it with the garlic** ich fürchte, du hast es mit dem Knoblauch etwas zu gut gemeint
b (= cook too long) verbraten; (= boil too long) verkochen

over: **overdone** ADJ a (= exaggerated) übertrieben b (= cooked too long) verbraten; (= boiled too long) verkocht; **overdose** N (lit) Überdosis *f*; (fig) Zuviel *nt* (of an +dat); **he died of an ~ of sleeping pills/a drug** er starb an einer Überdosis Schlaftabletten/Drogen VI eine Überdosis nehmen; **to ~ on heroin** eine Überdosis Heroin nehmen; **to ~ on sun** zu viel Sonne bekommen; **to ~ on TV** zu viel fernsehen VT überdosieren; **overdraft** N Kontoüberziehung *f*; **my bank manager wouldn't let me have a bigger ~** der Direktor meiner Bank wollte mir ein weiteres Überziehen meines Kontos nicht gestatten; **to have an ~ of £100** (= be in debt) sein Konto um £ 100 überzogen haben; (= have an overdraft facility) einen Überziehungskredit von £ 100 haben; **I've still got an ~** mein Konto ist immer noch überzogen; **overdraft facility** N Überziehungs- *or* Dispositionskredit *m*; **overdramatize** VT (fig) überdramatisieren; **overdraw** *pret* **overdrew**, *ptp* **overdrawn** VT *one's account* überziehen; **overdrawn** [əʊvə'drɔːn] ADJ (Fin: = in the red) *account* überzogen; **she is ~** sie hat ihr Bankkonto überzogen; **I'm always ~ at the end of the month** mein Konto ist am Ende des Monats immer überzogen; **to be £100 ~, to be ~ by £100** sein Konto um £ 100 überzogen haben → also **overdraw**; **overdress** [,əʊvə'dres] VI (sich) übertrieben *or* zu fein kleiden VT **to be ~ed** zu vornehm *or* elegant angezogen sein; **do you think I'm ~ed?** was meinst du, bin ich zu elegant angezogen? N ['əʊvədres] Überkleid *nt*; **overdrive** N (Aut) Schnellgang *m*, Schongang *m*; **overdue** ADJ a (= late) *book, change, visit* überfällig; *sum of money, salary* fällig; **long ~** schon seit Langem fällig; **~ interest** Zinsrückstände *pl*; **he is ~** er müsste schon lange da sein; **the US market is ~ for changes** am US-Markt sind Veränderungen überfällig b (inf: = late according to biological cycle) *baby, period* überfällig; **overeager** ADJ übereifrig; **he was ~ to impress** er war (zu) sehr darauf aus, Eindruck zu machen; **he was ~ to start** er konnte den Start kaum abwarten; **they're not exactly ~ to learn** sie sind nicht gerade übermäßig lernbegierig; **overeagerness** N Übereifer *m*; **overeat** *pret* **overate**, *ptp* **overeaten** VI zu viel essen, sich überessen; **overeating** N Überessen *nt*; **over-egg** VT (Brit inf fig) **to ~ the pudding** übertreiben; **overelaborate** ADJ *design, style* manieriert, gekünstelt; *excuse, plan, scheme* (viel zu) umständlich, zu ausgeklügelt; *hairstyle, dress* überladen; **overemphasis** N Überbetonung *f*; **an ~ on money** eine Überbewertung des Geldes; **overemphasize** VT überbetonen; **one cannot ~ the importance of this** man kann nicht genug betonen, wie wichtig das ist; **overemployed** ADJ (beruflich) überfordert; **overenthusiastic** ADJ übertrieben begeistert; **not ~** nicht gerade hingerissen; **she wasn't exactly ~** ihre Begeisterung hielt sich in Grenzen; **overestimate** ✪ 26.1 [,əʊvər'estɪmeɪt] VT überschätzen, zu hoch veranschlagen N [,əʊvər'estɪmɪt] (of price) Überbewertung *f*, zu hohe Schätzung; **overexcite** VT zu sehr aufregen; **overexcited** ADJ *person* überreizt, zu aufgeregt; *children* aufgedreht, zu aufgeregt; **overexcitement** N Überreiztheit *f*, zu starke Aufregung; (of children) Aufgedrehtheit *f*; **overexercise** VT übertrainieren VI übermäßig viel trainieren; **the dangers of overexercising** die Gefahren übermäßigen Trainings; **overexert** VT überanstrengen; **overexertion** N Überanstrengung *f*; **overexploit** VT *land etc* Raubbau treiben (sth an +dat/mit); **overexpose** VT (to sunlight, radiation) zu stark aussetzen (to dat); (Phot) überbelichten; **overexposure** N (Phot) Überbelichtung *f*; (in media etc: of topic) Überbehandlung *f*; **the President's image is suffering from ~ (in the media)** das Image des Präsidenten leidet darunter, dass er zu oft in den Medien erscheint; **overextended** ADJ (= overstretched) *person* überlastet; **the company was ~ and faced bankruptcy** die Firma hatte sich übernommen und stand vor dem Bankrott; **overfamiliar** ADJ **to be ~ with sb** etwas zu vertraulich *or* intim mit jdm sein; (= too pally also) plumpvertraulich mit jdm sein; **I'm not ~ with their methods** ich bin nicht allzu vertraut mit ihren Methoden; **overfeed** *pret, ptp* **overfed** VT überfüttern; **overfill** VT überfüllen, zu voll machen; **overfish** VT *the sea etc* überfischen; **overfishing** N Überfischung *f*; **overflew** *pret of* **overfly**; **overflight** N Überflug *m*

overflow ['əʊvəfləʊ] N a (= act) Überlaufen *nt*
b (= amount) Übergelaufene(s) *nt*, Übergeflossene(s) *nt*
c (= outlet) Überlauf *m*

d (= *excess: of people*) Überschuss *m* (*of* an *+dat*)
VT [ˌəʊvəˈfləʊ] *area* überschwemmen; *container, tank* überlaufen lassen; **the river has ~ed its banks** der Fluss ist über die Ufer getreten
VI [ˌəʊvəˈfləʊ] **a** (*liquid, river etc*) überlaufen, überfließen; (*container*) überlaufen; (*room, vehicle*) zum Platzen gefüllt sein, überfüllt sein (*with* mit); **full to ~ing** (*bowl, cup*) bis oben hin voll, zum Überlaufen voll; *room* überfüllt, zu voll; **the crowd at the meeting ~ed into the street** die Leute bei der Versammlung standen bis auf die Straße; **you'll have to open the doors and let the people ~ into the grounds** man wird die Türen öffnen müssen, damit die Leute in die Gartenanlagen ausweichen können
b (*fig*: = *be full of*) überfließen (*with* von); **his heart was ~ing with love** sein Herz lief *or* floss über vor Liebe

over: **overflow meeting** N Parallelversammlung *f*; **overflow pipe** N Überlaufrohr *nt*; **overfly** *pret* **overflew**, *ptp* **overflown** VT **a** (= *fly over*) *town* überfliegen **b** (= *fly beyond*) *runway, airport* hinausfliegen über (*+acc*); **overfond** ADJ **to be ~ of sth/of doing sth** etw nur zu gern haben/tun; **I'm not exactly ~ of …** ich bin nicht gerade begeistert von …; **overfull** ADJ übervoll (*with* von, mit); **overgarment** N Oberbekleidungsstück *nt*; **~s** Oberbekleidung *f*; **overgenerous** ADJ zu *or* übertrieben großzügig; **she was ~ in her praise** sie geizte nicht mit Lob, sie spendete überreichliches Lob; **he gave me an ~ helping** er überhäufte meinen Teller; **overground** (*Transport*) ADJ oberirdisch ADV oberirdisch; **overgrow** *pret* **overgrew**, *ptp* **overgrown** VT *path, garden, wall* überwachsen, überwuchern; **overgrown** ADJ **a** überwachsen, überwuchert (*with* von); (= *untrimmed*) *hedge, grass* ungeschnitten **b** *child* aufgeschossen, zu groß; **he's just an ~ schoolboy** er ist ein großes Kind; **you're just an ~ baby** du bist der reinste Säugling; **at forty-five, she still looked like an ~ schoolgirl** mit fünfundvierzig sah sie immer noch wie ein zu groß geratenes Schulmädchen aus; **overhand** ADJ, ADV (*Sport*) = **overarm**; **overhand knot** N (*Naut*) einfacher Knoten; **overhang** [ˌəʊvəˈhæŋ] *vb: pret, ptp* **overhung** VT hängen über (*+acc*); (= *project over*: *rocks, balcony*) hinausragen über (*+acc*), vorstehen über (*+acc*) N [ˈəʊvəhæŋ] (*of rock, building*) Überhang *m*; (*Archit*) Überkragung *f*; **overhanging** ADJ *cliff, wall* überhängend; **overhasty** ADJ voreilig, übereilt; **am I being ~?** bin ich da zu voreilig?; **overhaul** [ˈəʊvəhɔːl] N Überholung *f*, Überholen *nt*; (*inf, of patient*) Generalüberholung *f* (*inf*); **the machine needs an ~** die Maschine muss überholt werden VT [ˌəʊvəˈhɔːl] **a** *engine* überholen; *plans* revidieren, überprüfen; (*inf*) *patient* gründlich untersuchen **b** (= *pass*) überholen; (= *catch up*) einholen

overhead[1] [ˌəʊvəˈhed] ADV oben; (= *in the sky: position*) am Himmel, in der Luft; **the people ~** (= *above us*) die Leute über uns; (= *above them*) die Leute darüber; **a plane flew ~** ein Flugzeug flog über uns *etc* (*acc*) (hinweg) ADJ [ˈəʊvəhed] **~ compartment** Gepäckfach *nt*; **~ railway** (*Brit*) Hochbahn *f*; **~ kick** (*Ftbl*) Fallrückzieher *m*; **~ lighting** Deckenbeleuchtung *f*; **~ travelling crane** Laufkran *m*; **~ volley** (*Sport*) Hochball *m*

overhead[2] [ˈəʊvəhed] (*Comm*) ADJ **~ charges** *or* **costs** *or* **expenses** allgemeine Unkosten *pl* N (*US*) = **overheads**

overhead: **overhead bin** N (*Aviat*) Gepäckfach *nt* über den Sitzen; **overhead cable** N Überlandleitung *f*; (*high voltage*) Hochspannungsleitung *f*; (*Rail*) Oberleitung *f*; **overhead cam(shaft)** N oben liegende Nockenwelle; **overhead projector** N Overheadprojektor *m*

overheads [ˈəʊvəhedz] PL (*Brit*) allgemeine Unkosten *pl*; **company ~** allgemeine Geschäftskosten *or* Betriebs(un)kosten *pl*

overhead: **overhead transparency** N (Overhead)folie *f*; **overhead-valve engine** N oben gesteuerter Motor; **overhead valves** PL oben gesteuerte Ventile *pl*

overhear [ˌəʊvəˈhɪəʳ] *pret, ptp* **overheard** [ˌəʊvəˈhɜːd] VT zufällig mit anhören, zufällig mitbekommen; **we don't want him to ~ us** wir wollen nicht, dass er uns zuhören kann *or* dass er mitbekommt, was wir sagen; **I ~d them plotting** ich hörte zufällig, wie sie etwas ausheckten; **things you ~ in bars** Dinge, die man in Bars so mit anhört *or* mitbekommt; **the other day he was ~d to say that …** neulich hat ihn jemand sagen hören, dass …; **he was being ~d** jemand hörte mit

over: **overheat** VT *engine* überhitzen; *room* überheizen VI (*engine*) heiß laufen; (*fig: economy*) sich überhitzen; **overheated** ADJ **a** heiß gelaufen; *room* überheizt; **to become** *or* **get ~** (*person*) einen Hitzschlag erleiden **b** *discussion* erhitzt; *economy, market* überhitzt **c** (= *exaggerated*) **~ prose** überhitzte Prosa; **overhung** *pret, ptp of* **overhang**; **overimpressed** ADJ **I'm not ~ with him** er imponiert mir nicht besonders, von dem halte ich nicht besonders viel; **I'm not ~ with his work** ich bin nicht gerade von seiner Arbeit begeistert, seine Arbeit haut mich nicht vom Hocker (*inf*)

overindulge [ˈəʊvərɪnˈdʌldʒ] VT **a** *person* zu nachsichtig sein mit, zu viel durchgehen lassen (*+dat*) **b** *fantasies, passion etc* allzu freien Lauf lassen (*+dat*) VI zu viel genießen; (*as regards eating also*) Völlerei betreiben; **I ~d at the party** ich habe auf der Party ein bisschen zu viel des Guten gehabt; **to ~ in wine** zu viel Wein trinken

overindulgence [ˈəʊvərɪnˈdʌldʒəns] N **a** allzu große Nachsicht *or* Nachgiebigkeit (*of sb* jdm gegenüber) **b** (*as regards eating*) Völlerei *f*; **~ in wine** übermäßiger Weingenuss; **~ in cigarettes** zu starkes Rauchen; **the author's regrettable ~ in the use of metaphor** die bedauerlicherweise ungezügelte Vorliebe dieses Autors für Metaphern

overindulgent [ˈəʊvərɪnˈdʌldʒənt] ADJ *parent* zu nachsichtig, zu gutmütig (*to(wards) sb* jdm gegenüber, mit jdm); **should I have another or would that be ~?** soll ich mir noch einen nehmen oder wäre das des Guten zu viel?

overjoyed [ˌəʊvəˈdʒɔɪd] ADJ überglücklich, äußerst erfreut (*at, by, with* über *+acc*); **to be ~ to see sb** überglücklich sein, jdn zu sehen; **she was ~ with the present** sie war überglücklich über das Geschenk; **not exactly ~** nicht gerade erfreut

over: **overkill** N (*Mil*) Overkill *m*; (*fig*: = *getting rid of too much etc*) Rundumschlag *m*, Kahlschlag *m*; **repainting the whole room would definitely be ~** das ganze Zimmer neu zu streichen wäre des Guten zu viel *or* wäre übertrieben; **overladen** ADJ (*lit, fig*) überladen (*with* mit); *lorry, circuit also* überlastet; **overlaid** *pret, ptp of* **overlay**; **overland** ADJ *journey* auf dem Landweg; **~ route** Route *f* auf dem Landweg ADV *travel etc* über Land, auf dem Landweg

overlap [ˈəʊvəlæp] N Überschneidung *f*; (*spatial*) Überlappung *f*; (*of concepts*) teilweise Entsprechung *or* Deckung; **3 inches' ~** 3 Zoll Überlapp(ung); **there is an ~ of two days between our exams** unsere Prüfungen überschneiden sich um zwei Tage
VI [ˌəʊvəˈlæp] **a** (*tiles, boards*) einander überdecken, überlappen; (*teeth*) übereinanderstehen; **made of ~ping planks** aus (einander) überlappenden Brettern
b (*visits, dates, responsibilities*) sich überschneiden; (*ideas, concepts, plans, work areas*) sich teilweise decken
VT [ˌəʊvəˈlæp] **a** *part* gehen über (*+acc*), liegen über (*+dat*); (*person*) überlappen; **the tiles ~ each other** die Dachziegel überlappen sich *or* liegen übereinander
b *holiday, visit etc* sich überschneiden mit; *idea etc* sich teilweise decken mit

over: **overlay** *vb: pret, ptp* **overlaid** [ˌəʊvəˈleɪ] VT überziehen; (*with metal*) belegen; *wall* verkleiden N [ˈəʊvəleɪ] Überzug *m*; (*metal*) Auflage *f*; (*on map*) Auflegemaske *f*; (*Typ*) Zurichtung *f*, Zurichtebogen *m*; (*for fridge etc*) Verkleidung *f*; **overleaf** ADV umseitig; **the illustration ~** die umseitige Abbildung; **see ~** siehe umseitig; **overlie** VT bedecken; **overload** N Übergewicht *nt*, zu große Last, Überbelastung *f*; (*Elec*) Überlast *f* VT überladen; *car, lorry, animal also* überlasten; (*Elec, Mech*) überlasten; **overlong** ADJ überlang ADV zu lang

overlook [ˌəʊvəˈlʊk] VT **a** (= *have view onto*) überblicken; **we had a room ~ing the park** wir hatten ein Zimmer mit Blick auf den Park; **the castle ~s the whole town** vom Schloss aus hat man Aussicht auf die ganze Stadt; **the garden is not ~ed** niemand kann in den Garten hineinsehen **b** (= *fail to notice*) *detail* übersehen, nicht bemerken; **it is easy to ~** man übersieht es leicht **c** (= *ignore*) *mistake* hinwegsehen über (*+acc*), durchgehen lassen; **I am prepared to ~ it this time** diesmal will ich noch ein Auge zudrücken

over: **overlord** N (*Hist*) Oberherr *m*; **overlordship** N (*Hist*) Oberherrschaft *f*

overly [ˈəʊvəlɪ] ADV übermäßig, allzu

over: **overmanned** ADJ **to be ~** eine zu große Belegschaft haben; **overmanning** N zu große Belegschaft(en *pl*); **overmantel** N (*Archit*) Kaminaufsatz *or* -aufbau *m*; **overmotivated** ADJ übermotiviert; **overmuch** ADV zu viel, übermäßig; **they're not paid ~** sie bekommen nicht übermäßig viel bezahlt ADJ zu viel; **he didn't show ~ enthusiasm** seine Begeisterung hielt sich in Grenzen; **overnice** ADJ *distinction* spitzfindig, zu genau

overnight [ˈəʊvəˈnaɪt] ADV **a** über Nacht; **we drove ~** wir sind die Nacht durchgefahren; **to stay ~ (with sb)** (bei jdm) übernachten, (bei jdm) über Nacht bleiben
b (*fig*) von heute auf morgen, über Nacht; **the place had changed ~** der Ort hatte sich über Nacht verändert
ADJ **a** Nacht-; **~ accommodation** Übernachtungsmöglichkeit *f*; **including ~ accommodation the cost is £50** die Kosten betragen £ 50 inklusive Übernachtung; **~ train** Nachtzug *m*
b (*fig*: = *sudden*) ganz plötzlich; **an ~ success** ein Blitzerfolg *m*; **she became an ~ star** sie wurde über Nacht zum Star; **the play was an ~ success** das Stück wurde über Nacht ein Erfolg

overnight: **overnight bag** N Reisetasche *f*; **overnight case** N kleine Reisetasche (*für eine einzelne Übernachtung*); **overnight stay** N Übernachtung *f*

over: **overpaid** *pret, ptp of* **overpay**; **overparticular** ADJ zu genau, pingelig (*inf*); **he's not ~ about what he eats** er ist nicht wählerisch *or* pingelig (*inf*), was (das) Essen angeht; **he wasn't ~ about filling in his expenses form correctly** er nahm es mit dem Ausfüllen seines Spesenantrages nicht zu *or* so genau; **overpass** N (*Mot, Rail*) Überführung *f*; **overpay** *pret, ptp* **overpaid** VT überbezahlen, zu viel bezahlen (*+dat*); **he was overpaid by about £5** man hat ihm etwa £ 5 zu viel bezahlt; **overpayment** N (= *act*) Überbezahlung *f*; (= *amount*) zu viel bezahlter Betrag; **overpeople** VT *country* übervölkern; **overphysical** ADJ (*Sport*) **to be ~** den körperlichen Einsatz übertreiben; **overplay** VT (= *overact*) übertrieben darstellen *or* spielen; **to ~ one's hand** (*fig*) es übertreiben, den Bogen überspannen; **overplus** N (*esp US*) Überschuss *m*, Mehr *nt* (*of* an *+dat*); **overpopulated** ADJ überbevölkert; **overpopulation** N Überbevölkerung *f*

overpower [ˌəʊvəˈpaʊəʳ] VT **a** *person, team, player* überwältigen, bezwingen **b** (*emotion, heat*) überwältigen, übermannen **c** (*Mech*) **to be ~ed** übermotorisiert sein

overpowering [ˌəʊvəˈpaʊərɪŋ] ADJ überwältigend; *smell* penetrant; *colour, decoration, perfume, person* aufdringlich; *heat* glühend; **I felt an ~**

desire ... ich fühlte den unwiderstehlichen Drang, ...; **he's a bit ~ at times** seine Art kann einem manchmal zu viel werden

over: **overpraise** VT übertrieben *or* zu sehr loben; **overprice** VT einen zu hohen Preis verlangen für; **if the public will pay for it then it's not ~d** wenn es die Leute bezahlen, dann ist der Preis nicht zu hoch angesetzt; **at £50 it's ~d** £ 50 ist zu viel dafür; **overprint** VT **a** *stamp, text* überdrucken; *(Phot)* überkopieren **b** *(= print too many copies of)* in zu großer Auflage drucken N *(on stamp)* Überdruck *m*; **overproduce** VI überproduzieren, zu viel produzieren; **overproduction** N Überproduktion *f*; **overproportionate** ADJ überproportional; **overprotect** VT *child* überbehüten, zu sehr behüten; **overprotective** ADJ *parent* überängstlich; **overqualified** ADJ *(for job)* überqualifiziert; **overran** *pret of* **overrun**; **overrate** VT überschätzen; *book, play, system etc also* überbewerten; **to be ~d** überschätzt werden; **overreach** VI sich übernehmen; **overreact** VI übertrieben reagieren (*to* auf *+acc*); **overreaction** N übertriebene Reaktion (*to* auf *+acc*)

override [ˌəʊvəˈraɪd] *pret* **overrode** [ˌəʊvəˈrəʊd] *ptp* **overridden** [ˌəʊvəˈrɪdn] VT **a** *(= disregard)* sich hinwegsetzen über *(+acc)* **b** *(= prevail over, cancel out) order, decision, ruling* aufheben, außer Kraft setzen; *objection* ablehnen; **I'm afraid I'll have to ~ you there, said the chairman** da muss ich leider gegen Sie entscheiden, sagte der Vorsitzende **c** *horse* müde reiten **d** *(teeth)* gehen über *(+acc)*

overriding [ˌəʊvəˈraɪdɪŋ] ADJ *principle* vorrangig, wichtigste(r, s); *priority* vordringlich; *desire* dringendste(r, s); **matters of ~ importance** äußerst bedeutende Angelegenheiten; **my ~ ambition is to ...** mein allergrößter Ehrgeiz ist es, zu ...; **her ~ concern was to ...** es ging ihr vor allem darum, zu ...; **~ clause** *(Jur)* Aufhebungsklausel *f*

over: **overripe** ADJ überreif; **overrode** *pret of* **override**

overrule [ˌəʊvəˈruːl] VT ablehnen; *claim also* nicht anerkennen; *objection also* zurückweisen; *verdict, decision* aufheben; **his objection was ~d** sein Einspruch wurde abgewiesen; **we were ~d** unser Vorschlag/unsere Entscheidung *etc* wurde abgelehnt; **he was ~d by the majority** er wurde überstimmt

overrun [ˌəʊvəˈrʌn] *pret* **overran** [ˌəʊvəˈræn] *ptp* **overrun** VT **a** *(weeds)* überwuchern, überwachsen; **the town was ~ by tourists** die Stadt war von Touristen überlaufen; **the house was ~ by mice** das Haus war voller Mäuse
b *(troops etc: = invade) country, district* einfallen in *(+dat)*, herfallen über *(+acc)*; *enemy position* überrennen
c *(= go past) mark* hinauslaufen über *(+acc)*; *(Rail) signal* überfahren; *(train) platform* hinausfahren über *(+acc)*; *(plane) runway* hinausrollen über *(+acc)*
d *(= go beyond) time* überziehen, überschreiten; **the TV documentary overran its time** die Fernsehdokumentation überzog
e *(= overflow) banks* überfluten
VI **a** *(in time: speaker, concert etc)* überziehen; **his speech overran by ten minutes** seine Rede dauerte zehn Minuten zu lang
b *(costs)* überziehen

oversaw [ˌəʊvəˈsɔː] *pret of* **oversee**

overseas [ˈəʊvəˈsiːz] ADJ **a** *(= beyond the sea)* in Übersee *pred*; *country, market* überseeisch, in Übersee; *telegram* nach/aus Übersee; **our ~ office** unsere Zweigstelle in Übersee; **an ~ visitor** ein Besucher *m* aus Übersee
b *(= abroad)* ausländisch, im Ausland; *student, investment* ausländisch; **in ~ countries** im Ausland; **an ~ visitor** ein Besucher *m* aus dem Ausland, ein ausländischer Besucher; **~ trip** Auslandsreise *f*; **he won his first ~ cap this year** er hat dieses Jahr zum ersten Mal bei einem Auswärtsspiel in der Nationalmannschaft gespielt
ADV **to be/work ~** in Übersee/im Ausland sein/arbeiten; **to go ~** nach Übersee/ins Ausland gehen; **to be sent ~** nach Übersee/ins Ausland geschickt werden; **from ~** aus Übersee/dem Ausland

overseas: **overseas aid** N Entwicklungshilfe *f*; **Overseas Development** N *(Brit Pol)* ≈ Entwicklungshilfe *f*; **Minister for ~** ≈ Entwicklungshilfeminister(in) *m(f)*; **~ Administration/Agency** ≈ Entwicklungshilfeministerium *nt*; **overseas trade** N Überseehandel *m*

over: **oversee** *pret* **oversaw**, *ptp* **overseen** VT *(= supervise) person, work* beaufsichtigen, überwachen; **overseer** N Aufseher(in) *m(f)*; *(= foreman)* Vorarbeiter(in) *m(f)*; *(in coal mine)* Steiger *m*; **oversell** *pret, ptp* **oversold** VT **a** *(= sell too many)* **to ~ sth** von etw mehr verkaufen, als geliefert werden kann; *concert, match etc* für etw zu viele Karten verkaufen **b** *(= promote too much)* zu viel Reklame machen für; **to ~ oneself** sich zu gut verkaufen VI *(= sell too many)* mehr verkaufen, als geliefert werden kann; *(for concert, match etc)* zu viele Karten verkaufen; **oversensitive** ADJ überempfindlich; **oversew** *pret* **oversewed**, *ptp* **oversewed** *or* **oversewn** VT umnähen; **oversexed** ADJ **to be ~** einen übermäßig starken Sexualtrieb haben; **you're ~!** du bist unersättlich; **overshadow** VT *(lit, fig)* überschatten; **overshoe** N Überschuh *m*

overshoot [ˌəʊvəˈʃuːt] *pret, ptp* **overshot** [ˌəʊvəˈʃɒt] VT *target, runway* hinausschießen über *(+acc)*; *production target etc* übertreffen; **the golfer overshot the green** der Golfer schlug (den Ball) über das Grün hinaus; **to ~ the mark** *(lit, fig)* übers Ziel hinausschießen VI *(plane)* durchstarten

oversight [ˈəʊvəsaɪt] N **a** Versehen *nt*; **by** *or* **through an ~** aus Versehen **b** *(= supervision)* Aufsicht *f*, Beaufsichtigung *f*; **~ system** Überwachungssystem *nt*

over: **oversimplification** N (zu) grobe Vereinfachung; **oversimplify** VT zu sehr vereinfachen, zu einfach darstellen; **oversize(d)** ADJ übergroß; **~ classes** zu große Klassen *pl*; **oversleep** *pret, ptp* **overslept** VI verschlafen; **oversold** *pret, ptp of* **oversell**; **overspecialization** N Überspezialisierung *f*; **overspend** [əʊvəˈspend] *vb: pret, ptp* **overspent** VI zu viel ausgeben; **we've overspent by £10** wir haben £ 10 zu viel ausgegeben; **~ing city councils** Stadträte *pl* mit zu hoher Ausgabenpolitik VT überschreiten N [ˈəʊvəspend] zu hohe Ausgaben *pl*; **overspending** N zu hohe Ausgaben *pl*; **overspill** *(Brit)* [ˈəʊvəˌspɪl] N Bevölkerungsüberschuss *m*; **~ town** Trabantenstadt *f* VI [ˌəʊvəˈspɪl] = **overflow VI a**; **overstaffed** ADJ überbesetzt; **this office is ~** dieses Büro hat zu viel Personal; **overstaffing** N Personalüberschuss *m*; **~ problems** Probleme aufgrund *or* auf Grund von Personalüberschuss; **overstate** VT *facts, case* übertreiben, übertrieben darstellen; **overstatement** N Übertreibung *f*, übertriebene Darstellung; **this is a bit of an ~** das ist leicht übertrieben; **overstay** VT = **outstay**; **oversteer** N Übersteuern *nt* VI übersteuern; **overstep** VT überschreiten; **to ~ the mark** zu weit gehen

overstock [ˌəʊvəˈstɒk] VT *farm, pond* zu hoch bestücken; **the farm/pond is ~ed** der Hof/der Teich hat einen zu großen Vieh-/Fischbestand; **the shop is ~ed** der Laden hat zu große Bestände VI *(shop)* zu große (Lager)bestände haben, zu viel lagern; *(farm)* zu große (Vieh)bestände haben

overstrain [ˌəʊvəˈstreɪn] VT *horse, person* überanstrengen, überfordern; *metal* überbelasten; *resources, strength, theory* überbeanspruchen; **to ~ oneself** sich übernehmen, sich überanstrengen; **don't ~ yourself** *(iro)* übernimm dich bloß nicht

overstretch [əʊvəˈstretʃ] VT **a** *(lit) muscles, legs* überdehnen **b** *(fig) resources, budget, finances* zu sehr belasten; *abilities* überfordern; **to ~ oneself** sich übernehmen VI *(lit, person)* die Muskeln überdehnen; *(muscles, legs)* sich überdehnen

over: **overstrung** ADJ **a** *person* überspannt **b** *piano* kreuzsaitig; **oversubscribe** VT *(Fin)* überzeichnen; **the zoo outing was ~d** zu viele (Leute) hatten sich für den Ausflug in den Zoo angemeldet; **oversupply** VT überbeliefern N Überangebot *nt* (*of* an *+dat*), Überversorgung *f* (*of* mit)

overt [əʊˈvɜːt] ADJ *behaviour, campaign, operation, sexuality* offen; *hostility* unverhohlen

overtake [ˌəʊvəˈteɪk] *pret* **overtook** [ˌəʊvəˈtʊk] *ptp* **overtaken** [ˌəʊvəˈteɪkən] VT **a** *competitor, rival* einholen; *(esp Brit: = pass) runner, car etc* überholen **b** *(= take by surprise) (storm, night)* überraschen; *(fate)* ereilen *(geh)*; **~n by fear** von Furcht befallen; **we were ~n by events, events have ~n us** wir waren auf die Entwicklung der Dinge nicht gefasst VI *(esp Brit)* überholen

overtaking [ˌəʊvəˈteɪkɪŋ] N *(esp Brit)* Überholen *nt*

over: **overtax** VT **a** *(fig) person, heart* überlasten, überfordern; **to ~ one's strength** sich übernehmen **b** *(lit: = tax too heavily)* übermäßig besteuern; **overtechnical** ADJ zu fachspezifisch; *(regarding technology)* zu technisch; **over-the-counter** ADJ *drugs* nicht rezeptpflichtig; *sale* offen; *(St Ex) securities, transactions* außerbörslich; **~ market** *(St Ex)* Freiverkehr *m*, Freiverkehrsmarkt *m*; **overthrow** *vb: pret* **overthrew**, *ptp* **overthrown** N [ˈəʊvəˌθrəʊ] **a** Sieg *m* (*of* über *+acc*); *(= being overthrown)* Niederlage *f*; *(of dictator, government, empire)* Sturz *m*; *(of country)* Eroberung *f* **b** *(Cricket)* zu weiter Wurf VT [ˌəʊvəˈθrəʊ] *(= defeat) enemy* besiegen; *government, dictator, general* stürzen, zu Fall bringen; *plans* umstoßen; *country* erobern

overtime [ˈəʊvətaɪm] N **a** Überstunden *pl*; **I am on ~** *or* **doing ~** ich mache Überstunden; **he did four hours' ~** er hat vier (Stunden) Überstunden gemacht
b *(US Sport)* Verlängerung *f*; **we had to play ~** es gab eine Verlängerung
ADV **to work ~** Überstunden machen; **my imagination was working ~** *(inf)* meine Fantasie *or* Phantasie lief auf Hochtouren *(inf)*; **his liver's been working ~ to keep up with all this alcohol** *(inf)* seine Leber musste sich ganz schön ranhalten *(inf) or* lief auf Hochtouren *(inf)*, um all den Alkohol zu verkraften; **we shall have to work ~ to regain the advantage we have lost** *(fig)* wir müssen uns mächtig ranhalten, wenn wir den verlorenen Vorsprung wieder wettmachen wollen *(inf)*
VT [ˌəʊvəˈtaɪm] *(Phot)* überbelichten; **the programme planners ~d the symphony** die Programmgestalter hatten zu viel Zeit für die Sinfonie *or* Symphonie eingeplant

overtime: **overtime ban** N Überstundensperre *f*; **overtime pay** N Überstundenlohn *m*; **overtime rates** PL Überstundentarif *m*

overtired [ˌəʊvəˈtaɪəd] ADJ übermüdet

overtly [əʊˈvɜːtlɪ] ADV offen

overtone [ˈəʊvətəʊn] N **a** *(Mus)* Oberton *m* **b** *(fig)* Unterton *m*; **political ~s** politische Untertöne *pl*; **what are the precise ~s of this word?** was klingt bei diesem Wort alles mit?

over: **overtook** *pret of* **overtake**; **overtop** VT überragen; **overtrain** VTI zu viel *or* zu hart trainieren; **~ed** übertrainiert; **overtrick** N *(Cards)* überzähliger Stich; **overtrump** VT übertrumpfen

overture [ˈəʊvətjʊə] N **a** *(Mus)* Ouvertüre *f* **b** *usu pl (= approach)* Annäherungsversuch *m*; **to make ~s to sb** Annäherungsversuche bei jdm machen; **peace ~s** Friedensannäherungen *pl*

overturn [ˌəʊvəˈtɜːn] VT **a** *(lit)* umkippen, umwerfen; *(= capsize) boat* zum Kentern bringen, umkippen; **the ship rocked violently ~ing chairs and tables** das Schiff schwankte so heftig, dass Tische und Stühle umkippten **b** *(fig) regime* stürzen; *philosophy, world view* umstürzen; *law, ban, conviction* aufheben VI *(chair)* umkippen; *(boat also)* kentern N [ˈəʊvətɜːn] *(of govern-*

ment) Sturz *m*; *(of world view etc)* Umsturz *m*; *(of law, ban, conviction)* Aufhebung *f*

over: **overtype** VT *(Comput)* *text* überschreiben; **overuse** [ˌəʊvəˈjuːs] N übermäßiger *or* zu häufiger Gebrauch VT [ˌəʊvəˈjuːz] übermäßig oft *or* zu häufig gebrauchen; **overvalue** VT *goods* zu hoch schätzen; *idea, object, person* überbewerten; **overview** N Überblick *m* *(of* über *+acc)*

overweening [ˌəʊvəˈwiːnɪŋ] ADJ überheblich, anmaßend; *arrogance, pride, ambition* maßlos

overweight [ˈəʊvəˈweɪt] ADJ *thing* zu schwer; *person also* übergewichtig; **to be five kilos ~** *(person, box etc)* fünf Kilo Übergewicht haben; **~ luggage** Übergepäck *nt*; **you're ~** Sie haben Übergewicht N Übergewicht *nt*

overwhelm [ˌəʊvəˈwelm] VT **a** *(= overpower: strong feelings)* überwältigen; **he was ~ed when they gave him the present** er war zutiefst gerührt, als sie ihm das Geschenk gaben; **Venice ~ed me** ich fand Venedig überwältigend; **to be ~ed with joy/grief** von Freude/Trauer überwältigt sein; **you ~ me!** *(iro)* da bin ich aber sprachlos!
b *(= ruin, crush) enemy* überwältigen; *country* besiegen; *(Sport) defence* überrennen
c *(= submerge) (water)* überschwemmen, überfluten; *(earth, lava)* verschütten, begraben
d *(fig) (with favours, praise)* überschütten, überhäufen; *(with questions)* bestürmen; *(with work)* überhäufen

overwhelming [ˌəʊvəˈwelmɪŋ] ADJ überwältigend; *desire, power* unwiderstehlich; *misfortune* erschütternd; **~ evidence** erdrückende Beweise *pl*; **an ~ majority** eine überwältigende Mehrheit; **they won despite ~ odds** sie gewannen obwohl ihre Chancen sehr schlecht standen

overwhelmingly [ˌəʊvəˈwelmɪŋlɪ] ADV **a** *(= extremely)* **he was quite ~ friendly** er war umwerfend freundlich; **he began to feel ~ anxious** er begann, sich unwahrscheinlich ängstlich zu fühlen **b** *(= predominantly) approve, reject, support* mit überwältigender Mehrheit; *white, positive* größtenteils; **they voted ~ for it** sie haben mit überwältigender Mehrheit dafür gestimmt

over: **overwind** *pret, ptp* **overwound** VT *watch* überdrehen; **overwinter** VTI überwintern; **overwork** N Überarbeitung *f*, Arbeitsüberlastung *f*; **he is ill from ~** er hat sich krank gearbeitet VT *horse etc* schinden; *person* überanstrengen; *image, idea, theme etc* überstrapazieren; **to ~ oneself** sich überarbeiten VI sich überarbeiten; **overworked** ADJ überarbeitet, überlastet; *(Sport) defence etc* überlastet, überfordert; **overwrite** *pret* **overwrote**, *ptp* **overwritten** VTI *(Comput)* überschreiben; **overwrite mode** N *(Comput)* Überschreibmodus *m*; **overwritten** ADJ *(= too flowery etc)* zu blumig (geschrieben); *(= too strong)* zu stark formuliert; *(= too rhetorical)* zu schwülstig

overwrought [ˌəʊvəˈrɔːt] ADJ **a** *person* überreizt **b** *(= too elaborate) style* überfeinert, verkünstelt

overzealous [ˌəʊvəˈzeləs] ADJ übereifrig

Ovid [ˈɒvɪd] N Ovid *m*

oviduct [ˈəʊvɪdʌkt] N Eileiter *m*

oviform [ˈəʊvɪfɔːm] ADJ *(form)* eiförmig

oviparous [əʊˈvɪpərəs] ADJ Eier legend, ovipar *(spec)*

ovipositor [ˌəʊvɪˈpɒzɪtəʳ] N Legebohrer *m*, Legestachel *m*

ovoid [ˈəʊvɔɪd] ADJ eiförmig, ovoid

ovulate [ˈɒvjʊleɪt] VI ovulieren

ovulation [ˌɒvjʊˈleɪʃən] N Eisprung *m*, Ovulation *f*

ovule [ˈɒvjuːl] N *(Zool)* Ovulum *nt*, Ei *nt*; *(Bot)* Samenanlage *f*

ovum [ˈəʊvəm] N *pl* **ova** Eizelle *f*, Ovum *nt*

owe [əʊ] VT **a** *money* schulden, schuldig sein *(sb sth, sth to sb* jdm etw); **can I ~ you the rest?** kann ich dir den Rest schuldig bleiben?; **I ~ him a meal** ich bin ihm noch ein Essen schuldig, ich schulde ihm noch ein Essen; **how much do I ~ you?** *(in shop etc)* was bin ich schuldig?
b *reverence, obedience, loyalty* schulden, schuldig sein *(to sb* jdm); *allegiance* schulden *(to sb* jdm)
c *(= be under an obligation for)* verdanken *(sth to sb* jdm etw); **I ~ my life to him** ich verdanke ihm mein Leben; **to what do I ~ the honour** *(Brit) or* **honor** *(US)* **of your visit?** *(iro)* und was verschafft mir die Ehre Ihres Besuches?; **we ~ it to them that we are alive today** wir haben es ihnen zu verdanken, dass wir heute noch leben; **you ~ it to yourself to keep fit** du bist es dir schuldig, fit zu bleiben; **we ~ nothing to him, we ~ him nothing** wir sind ihm (gar) nichts schuldig; **I think you ~ me an explanation** ich glaube, du bist mir eine Erklärung schuldig
VI **to ~ sb for sth** jdm Geld für etw schulden; **can I ~ you for the rest?** kann ich Ihnen den Rest schuldig bleiben?; **I still ~ him for the meal** ich muss ihm das Essen noch bezahlen

owing [ˈəʊɪŋ] ✪ 17.1, 21.4 ADJ unbezahlt; **the amount ~ on the house** die Schulden, die auf dem Haus liegen; **how much is still ~?** wie viel steht noch aus?; **a lot of money is ~ to me** man schuldet mir viel Geld; **the money still ~ to us** *(Comm)* die Außenstände *pl*; **to pay what is ~** den ausstehenden Betrag bezahlen PREP **~ to** wegen *(+gen or (inf) +dat)*, infolge *(+gen)*; **~ to the circumstances** umständehalber; **~ to his being foreign** weil er Ausländer ist; **and it's all ~ to him that we succeeded** und unser Erfolg ist ihm allein zuzuschreiben

owl [aʊl] N Eule *f*; **wise old ~** weise Eule

owlet [ˈaʊlɪt] N junge Eule

owlish [ˈaʊlɪʃ] ADJ **the glasses gave him a somewhat ~ look** die Brille ließ ihn ein wenig eulenhaft erscheinen; **his ~ face** sein Eulengesicht *nt*

owlishly [ˈaʊlɪʃlɪ] ADV *look, stare* wie eine Eule

own[1] [əʊn] VT **a** *(= possess)* besitzen, haben; **who ~s that?** wem gehört das?; **we used to rent the house, now we ~ it** wir hatten das Haus vorher gemietet, jetzt gehört es uns; **he looks as if he ~s the place** er sieht so aus, als wäre er hier zu Hause; **the tourists behaved as if they ~ed the hotel** die Touristen benahmen sich, als gehöre das Hotel ihnen; **you don't ~ me, she said** ich bin nicht dein Privateigentum, sagte sie
b *(= admit)* zugeben, zugestehen; *(= recognize)* anerkennen; **he ~ed that the claim was reasonable** er erkannte die Forderung als gerechtfertigt an, er gab zu, dass die Forderung gerechtfertigt war; **to ~ a child** *(Jur)* ein Kind (als seines) anerkennen
VI **to ~ to sth** etw eingestehen; *to debts* etw anerkennen; **he ~ed to having done it** er gestand, es getan zu haben; **he didn't ~ to having done it** er hat nicht zugegeben, dass er es getan hat

▸ **own up** VI es zugeben; **come on, own up** (nun) gib schon zu; **to own up to sth** etw zugeben; **he owned up to stealing the money** er gab zu *or* er gestand, das Geld gestohlen zu haben

own[2] ADJ *attr* eigen; **his ~ car** sein eigenes Auto; **one's ~ car** ein eigenes Auto; **he's his ~ man** er geht seinen eigenen Weg; **he likes beauty for its ~ sake** er liebt die Schönheit um ihrer selbst willen; **he does (all) his ~ cooking** er kocht für sich selbst; **thank you, I'm quite capable of finding my ~ way out** danke, ich finde sehr gut alleine hinaus; **my ~ one is smaller** meine(r, s) ist kleiner; **my ~ one** *(liter, hum: = beloved)* mein Einziger, meine Einzige; **~ resources** *(Fin)* Eigenmittel *pl*
PRON **a that's my ~** das ist mein Eigenes; **those are my ~** die gehören mir; **my ~ is bigger** meine(r, s) ist größer; **to make sth one's ~** sich *(dat)* etw zu eigen machen; **my time is my ~** ich kann mit meiner Zeit machen, was ich will; **I can scarcely call my time my ~** ich kann kaum sagen, dass ich über meine Zeit frei verfügen kann; **his ideas were his ~** die Ideen stammten von ihm selbst; **I'd like a little house to call my ~** ich würde gern ein kleines Häuschen mein Eigen nennen; **a house of one's ~** ein eigenes Haus; **I have money of my ~** ich habe selbst Geld; **it has a beauty all its ~** *or* **of its ~** es hat eine ganz eigene *or* eigenartige Schönheit; **for reasons of his ~** aus irgendwelchen Gründen; **he gave me one of his ~** er gab mir eins von seinen (eigenen)
b *(in phrases)* **can I have it for my (very) ~?** darf ich das ganz für mich allein behalten?; **to get one's ~ back on sb** *(esp Brit)* es jdm heimzahlen; **he was determined to get his ~ back** *(esp Brit)* er war entschlossen, sich zu revanchieren; **(all) on one's ~** (ganz) allein; *(= without help also)* selbst; **on its ~** von selbst, von allein; **if I can get him on his ~** wenn ich ihn allein erwische; **the goalkeeper came into his ~ with a series of brilliant saves** der Torwart zeigte sich von seiner besten Seite, als er eine Reihe von Bällen geradezu fantastisch abwehrte

own brand N Hausmarke *f*

own-brand [ˈəʊnˌbrænd] ADJ **~ label** Hausmarke *f*

owner [ˈəʊnəʳ] N Besitzer(in) *m(f)*, Eigentümer(in) *m(f)*; *(of shop, factory, firm etc)* Inhaber(in) *m(f)*; *(of dogs, car, slaves)* Halter(in) *m(f)*; **who's the ~ of this umbrella?** wem gehört dieser Schirm?; **at ~'s risk** auf eigene Gefahr

owner: **owner-driver** N *Fahrzeughalter, der sein eigenes Auto fährt*; **owner-editor** N Redakteur(in) *m(f)* im eigenen Hause; **ownerless** ADJ herrenlos; **owner-occupancy** N **there's a growing level of ~** immer mehr Häuser/Wohnungen werden eigengenutzt *or* befinden sich im Besitz der Bewohner; **owner-occupied** ADJ *house* vom Besitzer bewohnt, eigengenutzt; **owner-occupier** N Bewohner(in) *m(f)* im eigenen Haus, Eigennutzer(in) *m(f)* *(form)*

ownership [ˈəʊnəʃɪp] N Besitz *m*; **to establish the ~ of sth** den Besitzer einer Sache *(gen)* feststellen; **there are doubts as to the ~ of the property** es ist nicht klar, wer der Eigentümer dieses Grundstücks ist; **under his ~ the business flourished** das Geschäft blühte in der Zeit, als es sich in seinem Besitz befand; **under new ~** unter neuer Leitung; **since we've been under new ~** seit der Eigentümer gewechselt hat; **this certifies your ~ of …** das weist Sie als Eigentümer von … aus

own goal N *(lit, fig)* Eigentor *nt*; **to score an ~** *(lit, fig)* ein Eigentor schießen

ownsome [ˈəʊnsəm] N **on one's ~** *(inf)* mutterseelenallein

owt [aʊt] PRON *(N Engl)* = **anything PRON**

ox [ɒks] N *pl* **-en** Ochse *m*; **as strong as an ox** bärenstark

oxalic acid [ɒkˈsælɪkˈæsɪd] N Oxalsäure *f*

oxbow lake [ˈɒksbəʊˈleɪk] N toter Flussarm

Oxbridge [ˈɒksbrɪdʒ] N Oxford und/oder Cambridge ADJ *people* der Universität *(gen)* Oxford oder Cambridge

ox cart N Ochsenkarren *m*

oxen [ˈɒksən] *pl of* **ox**

ox-eyed [ˈɒksaɪd] ADJ kuhäugig

oxeye daisy [ˈɒksˌaɪˈdeɪzɪ] N Margerite *f*

Oxfam [ˈɒksfæm] N *abbr of* **Oxford Committee for Famine Relief a** *britische karitative Vereinigung zur Hungerhilfe* **b** *(also* **Oxfam shop)** *Gebrauchtwarenladen, dessen Verkaufserlös der Hungerhilfe zugutekommt,* ≈ Eine-Welt-Laden *m*

> **OXFAM**
>
> **Oxfam (Oxford Committee for Famine Relief)** ist ein eingetragener gemeinnütziger Verein, der für seine Spendenaktionen bekannt ist. Mit den Hilfsgeldern werden Projekte in der Dritten Welt finanziert. **Oxfam** fördert den Einsatz von einfachen, grundlegenden Technologien und erneuerbaren heimischen Ressourcen. **Oxfam** betreibt eine er-

folgreiche Kette von Wohltätigkeitsläden, in denen Kleidung und andere Waren aus zweiter Hand sowie kunsthandwerkliche Produkte aus den Oxfam-Werkstätten und Kooperativen der Dritten Welt verkauft werden.

Oxford ['ɒksfəd] N Oxford *nt*; **my brother is at ~** mein Bruder studiert in Oxford

oxford ['ɒksfəd] N = **Oxford shoe**

Oxford: **Oxford bags** PL sehr weite Hosen *pl*; **Oxford blue** N *Mitglied eines Oxforder Studentensportklubs, das für die Universität angetreten ist*; **Oxford English** N Oxford-Englisch *nt*; **Oxford shoe** N geschnürter Halbschuh

oxidation [ˌɒksɪ'deɪʃən] N *(Chem)* Oxidation *f*

oxide ['ɒksaɪd] N *(Chem)* Oxid *nt*

oxidize ['ɒksɪdaɪz] VTI oxidieren

oxidizing agent ['ɒksɪdaɪzɪŋˌeɪdʒənt] N *(Chem)* Oxidationsmittel *nt*, Oxidans *nt (spec)*

oxlip ['ɒkslɪp] N *(Bot)* hohe *or* weiße Schlüsselblume

Oxon ['ɒksən] **a** *abbr of* **Oxfordshire** **b** *abbr of* **Oxoniensis** der Universität Oxford

Oxonian [ɒk'səʊnɪən] **N** Oxfordstudent(in) *m(f)* **ADJ** der Oxforder Universität angehörend

ox: **oxtail** N Ochsenschwanz *m*; **oxtail soup** [ˌɒksteɪl'suːp] N Ochsenschwanzsuppe *f*

oxyacetylene ['ɒksɪə'setɪliːn] ADJ **~ burner** *or* **lamp** *or* **torch** Schweißbrenner *m*; **~ welding** Autogenschweißen *nt*

oxygen ['ɒksɪdʒən] N Sauerstoff *m*; **the ~ of publicity** *(fig)* öffentlichkeitswirksame Auftritte *pl*

oxygenate [ɒk'sɪdʒəneɪt] VT oxygenieren, mit Sauerstoff behandeln *or* anreichern

oxygenation [ˌɒksɪdʒə'neɪʃən] N Oxygenierung *f*, Anreicherung *or* Behandlung *f* mit Sauerstoff

oxygen: **oxygen bottle**, **oxygen cylinder** N Sauerstoffflasche *f*; **oxygen mask** N Sauerstoff- *or* Atemmaske *f*; **oxygen tank** N Sauerstoffbehälter *m*; **oxygen tent** N Sauerstoffzelt *nt*

oxymoron [ˌɒksɪ'mɔːrɒn] N Oxymoron *nt*

oyez ['əʊjez] INTERJ *(old)* Achtung, Achtung

oyster ['ɔɪstəʳ] N Auster *f*; **the world's his ~** die Welt steht ihm offen; **to shut up** *or* **clam up like an ~** kein Wort mehr sagen

oyster: **oyster bank**, **oyster bed** N Austernbank *f*; **oyster-breeding** N Austernzucht *f*; **oystercatcher** N *(Orn)* Austernfischer *m*; **oyster cracker** N *(US)* Kräcker *m*; **oyster farm** N Austernpark *m*; **oyster mushroom** N Austernpilz *m*; **oyster shell** N Austernschale *f*

oz *abbr of* **ounce(s)**

ozalid ['ɒzəlɪd] N *(Typ)* Blaukopie *f*

ozone ['əʊzəʊn] N Ozon *nt*

ozone alert N Ozonalarm *m*

ozone-depleting ['əʊzəʊndɪˌpliːtɪŋ] ADJ *gas* die Ozonschicht abbauend

ozone: **ozone depletion** N Ozonabbau *m*, Abnahme *f* der Ozonschicht; **ozone-friendly** ADJ *spray etc* ohne Treibgas *pred*, FCKW-frei; **ozone hole** N Ozonloch *nt*; **ozone layer** N Ozonschicht *f*; **a hole in the ~** ein Ozonloch *nt*; **ozone levels** PL Ozonwerte *pl*; **ozone-safe** ADJ = **ozone-friendly**; **ozone shield** N Ozonschicht *f*

P

P, p [piː] N P *nt*, p *nt*; **to mind one's P's and Q's** *(inf)* sich anständig benehmen

p a *abbr of* **page** S. b *abbr of* **penny, pence**

> **P45**
>
> P45 nennt sich eine Bescheinigung, die Arbeitnehmern in Großbritannien am Ende ihres Beschäftigungsverhältnisses vom Arbeitgeber ausgehändigt wird. Darauf sind die Gesamtsumme des Einkommens sowie die Steuer- und Sozialversicherungsbeiträge des Arbeitnehmers im laufenden Steuerjahr aufgeführt. Bei Aufnahme eines neuen Beschäftigungsverhältnisses muss die Karte dem neuen Arbeitgeber übergeben werden.
> „To get one's P45" wird oft als Umschreibung dafür genommen, dass jemand von seinem Arbeitgeber entlassen wird, auch wenn das genau genommen nicht ganz korrekt ist; ein Beispiel: „He is perilously close to getting his P45 if his players let him down again today" – „Er steht gefährlich knapp davor, seine Papiere zu bekommen, wenn ihn seine Spieler heute wieder im Stich lassen."

PA a *abbr of* **Press Association** b *abbr of* **personal assistant** c *abbr of* **public address (system)**

pa [pɑː] N *(inf)* Papa *m*, Papi *m*, Vati *m (all inf)*

p.a. *abbr of* **per annum**

PAC *(US) abbr of* **political action committee**

pace¹ [ˈpeɪsɪ] PREP ohne … *(dat)* nahetreten zu wollen

pace² [peɪs] N a *(= step)* Schritt *m*; *(of horse)* Gangart *f*; *(lifting both legs on same side)* Passgang *m*; **twelve ~s away** zwölf Schritt(e) entfernt; **at 20 ~s** auf 20 Schritte Entfernung; **to put a horse through its ~s** ein Pferd alle Gangarten machen lassen; **to put sb/a new car through his/its ~s** *(fig)* jdn/ein neues Auto auf Herz und Nieren prüfen; **to go through** *or* **show one's ~s** zeigen, was man draufhat *(inf)*
b *(= speed)* Tempo *nt*; **the more leisurely ~ of life in those days** das geruhsamere Leben damals; **at a good** *or* **smart ~** recht schnell; **at an incredible ~** unglaublich schnell, mit *or* in unglaublichem Tempo; **at a slow ~** langsam; **to learn at one's own ~** in seinem eigenen Tempo lernen; **to keep ~** Schritt halten; *(in discussing)* mitkommen; **I can't keep ~ with events** ich komme mit den Ereignissen nicht mehr mit; **to make** *or* **set the ~** das Tempo angeben; **to quicken one's ~** seinen Schritt beschleunigen; *(working)* sein Tempo beschleunigen; **to speed up the ~ of reforms** das Tempo der Reformen erhöhen; **I'm getting old, I can't stand the ~ any more** *(inf)* ich werde alt, ich kann nicht mehr mithalten; **the change of ~ in the narrative** der Tempowechsel in der Erzählung; **he has a good change of ~** *(runner)* er kann sein Tempo gut beschleunigen
VT a *(= measure) floor, room* mit Schritten ausmessen
b *(in anxiety etc)* auf und ab gehen *or* schreiten in *(+dat)*
c *competitor* das Tempo angeben *(+dat)*
d *horse* im Passgang gehen lassen
VI a **to ~ around** hin und her laufen; **to ~ up and down** auf und ab gehen *or* schreiten; **to ~ round the room** im Zimmer umhergehen
b *(horse)* im Passgang gehen

▶ **pace off** *or* **out** VT *sep distance* ausschreiten, mit Schritten ausmessen *or* abmessen

pace bowler N *(Cricket)* Pace Bowler *m*, *Werfer, der die Bälle sehr schnell wirft*

-paced [peɪst] ADJ *suf* **fast-paced** flott, schwungvoll; **well-paced** schnell

pace lap N *(Motor sport)* Aufwärmrunde *f*

pacemaker [ˈpeɪsmeɪkəʳ] N *(Med)* Schrittmacher *m (Sport)* = **pacesetter**

pacer [ˈpeɪsəʳ] N = **pacesetter**

pacesetter [ˈpeɪssetəʳ] N *(Sport)* Tempomacher(in) *m(f)*

pachyderm [ˈpækɪdɜːm] N Dickhäuter *m*

Pacific [pəˈsɪfɪk] N **the ~ (Ocean)** der Pazifische *or* Stille Ozean, der Pazifik; **the ~ islands** die pazifischen Inseln; **a ~ island** eine Insel im Pazifik

pacific [pəˈsɪfɪk] ADJ *people, nation* friedliebend, friedfertig

pacifically [pəˈsɪfɪkəlɪ] ADV *live* in Frieden; *say* besänftigend

pacification [ˌpæsɪfɪˈkeɪʃən] N Versöhnung *f*; *(of area)* Befriedung *f*; **attempts at ~** Friedensbemühungen *pl*

Pacific Standard Time N pazifische Zeit

pacifier [ˈpæsɪfaɪəʳ] N a *(= peacemaker)* Friedensstifter(in) *m(f)* b *(US: for baby)* Schnuller *m*

pacifism [ˈpæsɪfɪzəm] N Pazifismus *m*

pacifist [ˈpæsɪfɪst] ADJ pazifistisch N Pazifist(in) *m(f)*

pacifistic [ˈpæsɪfɪstɪk] ADJ pazifistisch

pacify [ˈpæsɪfaɪ] VT *baby* beruhigen; *warring countries* miteinander aussöhnen; *area* befrieden; *critics* besänftigen; **just to ~ the unions** nur damit die Gewerkschaften stillhalten

pack [pæk] N a *(= bundle)* Bündel *nt*; *(on animal)* Last *f*; *(= rucksack)* Rucksack *m*; *(Mil)* Gepäck *nt no pl*, Tornister *m (dated)*
b *(= packet: for cereal, washing powder, frozen food)* Paket *nt*; *(esp US: of cigarettes)* Packung *f*, Schachtel *f*; **a ~ of six** ein Sechserpack *m*
c *(Hunt)* Meute *f*
d *(of wolves, cubs)* Rudel *nt*; *(of submarines)* Gruppe *f*
e *(pej: = group)* Horde *f*, Meute *f*; **to stay ahead of the ~** *(fig)* der Konkurrenz *(dat)* immer um eine Nasenlänge voraus sein; **a ~ of thieves** eine Diebesbande; **he told us a ~ of lies** er tischte uns einen Sack voll Lügen auf; **it's all a ~ of lies** es ist alles erlogen
f *(of cards)* (Karten)spiel *nt*; **52 cards make a ~** ein Blatt *nt* besteht aus 52 Karten
g *(Rugby)* Stürmer *pl*
h *(Med, Cosmetics)* Packung *f*
i *(of ice)* Scholle *f*
VT a *crate, container etc* vollpacken; *fish, meat in tin etc* abpacken; **~ed in dozens** im Dutzend abgepackt
b *case, trunk* packen; *things in case, clothes etc* einpacken
c *(= wrap, put into parcel)* einpacken; **it comes ~ed in polythene** es ist in Cellophan *or* Zellophan verpackt
d *(= crowd, cram)* packen; *articles* stopfen, packen; **the box was ~ed full of explosives** die Kiste war voll mit Sprengstoff; **the crowds that ~ed the stadium** die Menschenmassen, die sich im Stadium drängten; **he ~ed the committee with his own supporters** er füllte das Komitee mit seinen eigenen Anhängern; **the comedy was playing to ~ed houses** die Komödie lief vor ausverkauften Häusern; **to be ~ed** *(= full)* gerammelt voll sein *(inf)*; **the bus/square was ~ed solid** der Bus/der Platz war rappelvoll *(inf)*; **all this information is ~ed into one chapter** all diese Informationen sind in einem Kapitel zusammengedrängt; **a weekend ~ed with excitement** ein Wochenende voller aufregender Erlebnisse; **a speech ~ed with jokes** eine mit Witzen gespickte Rede; **a thrill-~ed film** ein packender Film; **the coast is ~ed with tourists** an der Küste wimmelt es von Touristen
e *(= make firm) soil etc* festdrücken; **the snow on the path was ~ed hard** der Schnee auf dem Weg war festgetrampelt
f *jury* mit den eigenen Leuten besetzen
g *(US inf: = carry) gun* tragen, dabei haben; **to ~ one's lunch** sich *(dat)* sein Mittagessen mitnehmen
h *(inf)* **to ~ a (heavy) punch** *(person)* kräftig zuschlagen; **he ~s a nasty left** er hat *or* schlägt eine ganz gemeine Linke *(inf)*; **the film ~s a real punch** *(fig)* der Film ist total spannend
i *leak, pipe* (zu)stopfen
j *(Comput) data* komprimieren, packen *(inf)*
VI a *(items)* passen; **that won't all ~ into one suitcase** das passt *or* geht nicht alles in einen Koffer; **it ~s (in) nicely** es lässt sich gut verpacken; **the boxes are designed to ~ into this container** die Kästen sind so gemacht, dass sie in diesen Behälter hineingehen
b *(person)* packen; **I'm still ~ing** ich bin noch beim Packen
c *(= crowd)* **the crowds ~ed into the stadium** die Menge drängte sich in das Stadion; **we can't all ~ into one car** wir können uns nicht alle in ein Auto zwängen; **they ~ed around the president** sie belagerten *or* umringten den Präsidenten
d *(= become firm)* fest werden; **the snow had ~ed round the wheels** an den Rädern klebte eine feste Schneeschicht
e *(inf)* **to send sb ~ing** jdn kurz abfertigen; **he sent her ~ing** er hat sie in die Wüste geschickt *(inf)*; **what should I do with my drunken husband? – I'd send him ~ing** was soll ich mit meinem Trunkenbold von Mann machen? – ich würde ihn vor die Tür setzen

▶ **pack away** VT *sep* a *clothes, boxes etc* wegpacken; **pack your toys away before you go out** räum deine Spielsachen weg, bevor du rausgehst; **I've packed all your books away in the attic** ich habe alle deine Bücher auf den Boden geräumt; **he packed the deck chairs away for the winter** er räumte die Liegestühle für den Winter weg b *(inf)* **he can really pack it away** *(food)* er kann ganz schön was verdrücken *(inf) or* verputzen *(inf)* VI **the bed packs away into a cupboard** man kann das Bett in einem Schrank verschwinden lassen

▶ **pack down** VI *(Rugby)* ein Gedränge *nt* bilden

▶ **pack in** VT *sep* a *clothes etc* einpacken b *people* hineinpferchen in (+*acc*); **we can't pack any more in here** *(people)* hier geht *or* passt keiner mehr rein; *(things)* hier geht *or* passt nichts mehr rein
c *(inf: play, actor etc)* in Scharen anziehen; **this film is really packing them in** dieser Film zieht die Leute in Scharen an
d *(Brit inf) (= give up) job* hinschmeißen *(inf)*; *girlfriend* sausen lassen *(inf)*; *(= stop) noise* aufhören mit; *(= stop) work, activity* Schluss *or* Feierabend *(inf)* machen mit; **a footballer should know when it's time to pack it in** ein Fußballspieler sollte wissen, wann es Zeit ist, Schluss zu machen *or* aufzuhören; **to pack it all in** Schluss machen; **pack it in!** hör auf!, lass es gut sein!; *(job)* schmeiß die Sache hin!
VI a *(= crowd in)* sich hineindrängen; **we all packed into his car** wir zwängten uns alle in sein Auto
b *(Brit inf: = stop working) (engine)* seinen Geist aufgeben *(hum)*; *(person)* zusammenpacken, Feierabend machen *(inf)*

▶ **pack off** VT *sep* **she packed them off to bed/school** sie schickte sie ins Bett/in die Schule

▶ **pack out** VT *sep usu pass* **to be packed out** *(hall, theatre etc)* gerammelt voll sein *(inf)*, überfüllt sein

▶ **pack up** VT *sep clothes etc* zusammenpacken
VI a *(= prepare luggage)* packen; **he just packed up and left** er packte seine Sachen und ging b *(Brit inf: = stop working) (engine)* seinen Geist aufgeben *(hum)*; *(person)* Feierabend machen *(inf)* c **the tent packs up easily** das Zelt lässt sich gut verpacken

package [ˈpækɪdʒ] N a *(= parcel, esp US: = packet)* Paket *nt*; *(of cardboard)* Schachtel *f* b *(esp Comm: = group, set)* Paket *nt*, Bündel *nt*; **software ~** Softwarepaket *nt* c *(hum inf: = genitals)* Gehänge *nt (inf)*; **he's hot a nice ~** er hat ein großes Gehänge *(inf) or* eine Mördergurke *(sl)* VT a *goods* verpacken b *(in order to enhance sales)* präsentieren

package: **package deal** N Pauschalangebot *nt*; **package holiday** N Pauschalreise *f*; **package insert** [ˈpækɪdʒˌɪnsɜːt] N *(of medicine etc)* Packungsbeilage *f*

packager [ˈpækɪdʒəʳ] N Produktionsfirma *f*; *(for books)* Redaktionsbüro *nt*

package: **package store** N *(US)* Spirituosenhandlung *f*; **package tour** N Pauschalreise *f*

packaging [ˈpækɪdʒɪŋ] N a *(= material)* Verpackung *f*; **this is where they do the ~** hier werden die Sachen verpackt b *(= presentation of product)* Präsentation *f*; **the public don't buy the product, they buy the ~** die Leute kaufen nicht das Produkt, sondern die Verpackung; **~ industry** Verpackungsindustrie *f* c *(= act)* Verpacken *nt*

pack: **pack animal** N Packtier *nt*, Lasttier *nt*; **pack drill** N Strafexerzieren *nt* in gefechtsmäßiger Ausrüstung

packed lunch [pæktˈlʌntʃ] N *(Brit)* Lunchpaket *nt*

packer [ˈpækəʳ] N Packer(in) *m(f)*; **he's a very untidy ~** er packt sehr unordentlich

packet [ˈpækɪt] N a *(esp Brit)* Paket *nt*; *(of cigarettes)* Päckchen *nt*, Schachtel *f*, Packung *f*; *(= small box)* Schachtel *f* b *(Naut)* Paketboot *nt* c *(Brit inf: = lot of money)* **to make a ~** ein Schweinegeld verdienen *(inf)*; **that must have cost a ~** das muss ein Heidengeld gekostet haben *(inf)*

packet: **packet boat** N Paketboot *nt*; **packet soup** N *(esp Brit)* Tütensuppe *f*; **packet switching** N *(Telec, Comput)* Paketvermittlung *f*

pack: **packhorse** N Packpferd *nt*; **I'm not your ~!** ich bin nicht dein Packesel!; **pack ice** N Packeis *nt*

packing [ˈpækɪŋ] N a *(= act) (in suitcases)* Packen *nt*; *(in factories etc)* Verpackung *f*; **to do one's ~** packen b *(= material)* Verpackung *f*; *(for leak)* Dichtung *f*

packing: **packing case** N Kiste *f*; **packing house** N *(US)* Abpackbetrieb *m*; **packing list** N *(Comm)* Packliste *f*; **packing plant** N *(US)* = **packing house**

pack: **pack rat** N Buschschwanzratte *f*; **packsack** [ˈpæksæk] N *(US)* Rucksack *m*; **packsaddle** N Packsattel *m*; **packthread** N Zwirn *m*; **pack train** N Tragtierkolonne *f*

pact [pækt] N Pakt *m*; **to make a ~ with sb** mit jdm einen Pakt schließen

pad[1] [pæd] VI **to ~ about** *(Brit) or* **around** umhertapsen; **to ~ along** entlangtrotten; **the panther ~ded up and down** der Pant(h)er trottete auf und ab; **the tiger ~ded off into the bushes** der Tiger trottete ins Gebüsch

pad[2] N a *(= stuffing) (for comfort etc)* Polster *nt*; *(for protection)* Schützer *m*; *(in bra)* Einlage *f*; *(= brake pad etc)* Belag *m*; *(esp US: = sanitary pad)* Damenbinde *f* b *(of paper)* Block *m*; *(of blotting paper)* Schreibunterlage *f* c *(for inking)* Stempelkissen *nt* d *(of animal's foot)* Ballen *m* e *(= launch pad)* (Abschuss)rampe *f* f *(inf: = room, home)* Bude *f (inf)*; **at your ~** in deiner Bude, bei dir VT *shoulders etc* polstern

▶ **pad out** VT *sep* a *shoulders* polstern b *(fig) article, essay etc* auffüllen; *speech* ausdehnen, strecken

padded [ˈpædɪd] ADJ a *shoulders, armour, bra* wattiert; *dashboard, seat* gepolstert; **~ envelope** gefütterter (Brief)umschlag b *(euph: = fat)* gut gepolstert

padded bra N Push-up-BH *m*

padded cell N Gummizelle *f*

padding [ˈpædɪŋ] N a *(= material)* Polsterung *f* b *(fig: in essay etc)* Füllwerk *nt*, Füllsel *pl*

paddle [ˈpædl] N a *(= oar)* Paddel *nt* b *(= blade of wheel)* Schaufel *f*; *(= wheel)* Schaufelrad *nt* c *(for mixing)* Rührschaufel *f* d **Grandpa still enjoys a ~** Opa plan(t)scht noch gern durchs Wasser; **to go for a ~, to have a ~** durchs Wasser waten e *(in table tennis)* Schläger *m* VT a *boat* paddeln b **to ~ one's feet in the water** mit den Füßen im Wasser plan(t)schen; **~ your feet and you'll stay afloat** du musst mit den Füßen paddeln, dann gehst du nicht unter c *(US: = spank)* verhauen, versohlen *(inf)* VI a *(in boat)* paddeln b *(with feet, swimming)* paddeln c *(= walk in shallow water)* waten

paddle: **paddle boat** N Raddampfer *m*; *(small, on pond)* Paddelboot *nt*; **paddle box** N Radkasten *m*; **paddle steamer** N Raddampfer *m*; **paddle wheel** N Schaufelrad *nt*

paddling pool [ˈpædlɪŋˌpuːl] N *(Brit)* Plan(t)schbecken *nt*

paddock [ˈpædək] N *(= field)* Koppel *f*; *(of racecourse)* Sattelplatz *m*; *(Motor Racing)* Fahrerlager *nt*

Paddy [ˈpædɪ] N *(inf)* Paddy *m (Spitzname der Iren)*

paddy[1] [ˈpædɪ] N a *(= rice)* ungeschälter Reis b *(also* **paddy field***)* Reisfeld *nt*

paddy[2] N *(Brit inf)* Koller *m (inf)*; **to get into a ~** einen Koller kriegen *(inf)*; **to be in a ~** einen Koller haben *(inf)*

paddy wagon N *(US inf)* grüne Minna *(inf)*

paddywhack [ˈpædɪwæk] N *(inf)* a = **paddy**[2] b *(= spank)* Klaps *m*

padlock [ˈpædlɒk] N Vorhängeschloss *nt* VT (mit einem Vorhängeschloss) verschließen

padre [ˈpɑːdrɪ] N *(Mil)* Feldkaplan *m*, Feldgeistliche(r) *m*; **yes, ~** ja, Herr Kaplan

paean [ˈpiːən] N Lobrede *f*

paediatric, *(US)* **pediatric** [ˌpiːdɪˈætrɪk] ADJ Kinder-, pädiatrisch *(spec)*

paediatric clinic, *(US)* **pediatric clinic** N Kinderklinik *f*

paediatrician, *(US)* **pediatrician** [ˌpiːdɪəˈtrɪʃən] N Kinderarzt *m*/-ärztin *f*, Pädiater *m (spec)*

paediatric nurse, *(US)* **pediatric nurse** N Kinderkrankenschwester *f*

paediatrics, *(US)* **pediatrics** [ˌpiːdɪˈætrɪks] N Kinderheilkunde *f*, Pädiatrie *f (spec)*

paedological, *(US)* **pedological** [ˌpiːdəˈlɒdʒɪkəl] ADJ pädologisch

paedology, *(US)* **pedology** [ˌpiːˈdɒlədʒɪ] N Pädologie *f*

paedophile, *(US)* **pedophile** [ˈpiːdəfaɪl] N Pädophile(r) *mf*; **~ ring** Pädophilenring *m*

paedophilia, *(US)* **pedophilia** [ˌpiːdəʊˈfɪlɪə] N Pädophilie *f*

paedophiliac, *(US)* **pedophiliac** [ˌpiːdəˈfɪlɪæk] N Pädophile(r) *mf* ADJ pädophil

paella [paɪˈelə] N *(Cook)* Paella *f*

pagan [ˈpeɪgən] ADJ heidnisch N Heide *m*, Heidin *f*

paganism [ˈpeɪgənɪzəm] N Heidentum *nt*

page[1] [peɪdʒ] N *(also* **pageboy***)* Page *m* VT **to ~ sb** jdn ausrufen lassen; **paging Mr Cousin** Herr Cousin, bitte!

page[2] N a Seite *f*; **on ~ 14** auf Seite 14; **write on both sides of the ~** beschreiben Sie beide Seiten; **to be on the same ~** *(US: = in agreement)* auf der gleichen Wellenlänge liegen; **the sports ~s** die Sportseiten *pl* b **a glorious ~ of English history** ein Ruhmesblatt *nt* in der Geschichte Englands; **to go down in the ~s of history** in die Geschichte *or* die Annalen der Geschichte eingehen VT *(Typ)* paginieren, mit Seitenzahlen versehen

pageant [ˈpædʒənt] N *(= show)* historische Aufführung, Historienspiel *nt*; *(= procession)* Festzug *m*; **Christmas ~** Weihnachtsspiel *nt*; **a ~ of Elizabethan times** *(= series of theatrical tableaux etc)* eine historische Darstellung des Elisabethanischen Zeitalters; *(= procession)* ein Festzug *m or* festlicher Umzug im Stil des Elisabethanischen Zeitalters; **the whole ~ of life** die breite Fülle des Lebens

pageantry [ˈpædʒəntrɪ] N Prunk *m*, Gepränge *nt*; **all the ~ of history** die ganze Pracht der Geschichte; **the coronation was celebrated with great ~** die Krönung wurde sehr prunkvoll *or* mit großem Prunk gefeiert

page: **page border** N *(Comput)* Seitenränder *pl*; **pageboy** N a Page *m*; *(Brit: = attendant at wedding) Junge, der bei der Hochzeitszeremonie assistiert* b *(= hairstyle)* Pagenkopf *m*; **page break** N *(Comput)* Seitenumbruch *or* -wechsel *m*; **page description language** N *(Comput)* Seitenbeschreibungssprache *f*; **page layout** N *(Comput)* Seitenlayout *nt*; **page make-up** N *(Typ)* Umbruch *m*; **page number** N Seitenzahl *f*; **page preview** N *(Comput)* Seitenansicht *f*; **page printer** N *(Comput)* Seitendrucker *m*; **page proof** N Korrekturfahne *f*

pager [ˈpeɪdʒəʳ] N *(Telec)* Funkempfänger *m*, Pieper *m (inf)*

> **PAGE THREE**
>
> Lange Jahre befand sich auf der dritten Seite der „Sun", Großbritanniens größter Boulevardzeitung, eine seitenfüllende Oben-ohne-Fotografie einer knackigen jungen Frau, das sogenannte **page three girl**. Jetzt wird der Begriff **page three** allgemein für Oben-ohne-Fotos auch in anderen Boulevardblättern verwendet. Über die **page three** entzweien sich die Gemüter. Die einen sehen darin eine Form von Pornografie, die den Status der Frau erniedrigt, für andere ist sie nur eine harmlose Preisung weiblicher Schönheit.

page-turner N a *(inf: = book)* spannendes Buch b *(person) jd, der Noten umblättert*

paginate [ˈpædʒɪneɪt] VT paginieren

pagination [ˌpædʒɪˈneɪʃən] N Paginierung *f*

pagoda [pəˈgəʊdə] N Pagode *f*

paid [peɪd] *pret, ptp of* **pay** ADJ a *official, work* bezahlt; **a highly ~ job** ein hoch bezahlter Posten; **a highly ~ manager** ein hoch bezahlter Manager, eine hoch bezahlte Managerin; **~ leave**

bezahlter Urlaub **b** *(esp Brit)* **to put ~ to sth** etw zunichtemachen; **that's put ~ to my weekend** damit ist mein Wochenende geplatzt *or* gestorben *(inf)*; **that's put ~ to him** damit ist für ihn der Ofen aus *(inf)*, das wars dann wohl für ihn *(inf)* **N** **the low/well ~** die Gering-/Gutverdienenden *pl*

paid-up ['peɪd'ʌp] ADJ *share* eingezahlt; **500 ~ members** 500 zahlende Mitglieder; **fully ~ member** Mitglied *nt* ohne Beitragsrückstände; **is he fully ~?** hat er alle Beiträge bezahlt?; **to make an insurance policy ~** eine Versicherung beitragsfrei stellen

pail [peɪl] N Eimer *m*; *(child's)* Eimerchen *nt*

pailful ['peɪlfʊl] N Eimer *m*

paillasse ['pælɪæs] N Strohsack *m*

pain [peɪn] **N** **a** Schmerz *m*; **is the ~ still there?** hast du noch Schmerzen?; **where is the ~ exactly?** wo tut es denn genau weh?; **this will help the ~** das ist gut gegen die Schmerzen; **to be in ~** Schmerzen haben; **you can't just leave him in ~** du kannst ihn nicht einfach leiden lassen; **he screamed in ~** er schrie vor Schmerzen; **do insects feel ~?** können Insekten Schmerz empfinden?; **a sharp ~** ein stechender Schmerz; **stomach/chest ~s** Magen-/ /Brustschmerzen *pl*; **my ankle has been giving** *or* **causing me a lot of ~** mein Knöchel tut mir sehr weh; **I felt a ~ in my leg** mein Bein tat mir weh, ich hatte Schmerzen im Bein; **to put sb out of his ~** jdn von seinen Schmerzen erlösen

b *(mental)* Qualen *pl*; **the ~ of parting** der Abschiedsschmerz; **Werther: a soul in ~** Werther: eine gequälte Seele; **being so totally ignored like that was a source of great ~ to her** so vollkommen ignoriert zu werden, war für sie sehr schmerzlich; **he suffered great mental ~** er litt Seelenqualen; **the decision caused me a lot of ~** die Entscheidung war sehr schmerzlich für mich; **a look of ~ came over his face** sein Gesicht nahm einen schmerzlichen Ausdruck an; **no ~, no gain** ohne Fleiß kein Preis *(Prov)*

c **pains** PL *(= efforts)* Mühe *f*; **to be at (great) ~s to do sth** sich *(dat)* (große) Mühe geben, etw zu tun; **to take ~s over sth** sich *(dat)* Mühe mit etw geben; **to take ~s to do sth** sich *(dat)* Mühe geben, etw zu tun; **great ~s have been taken to ...** besondere Mühe wurde darauf verwendet ...; **she takes great ~s with her appearance** sie verwendet sehr viel Sorgfalt auf ihr Äußeres; **all he got for his ~s was a curt refusal** zum Dank für seine Mühe wurde er schroff abgewiesen; **see what you get for your ~s!** das hast du nun für deine Mühe!

d *(= penalty)* **on** *or* **under ~ of death** bei Todesstrafe, bei Strafe des Todes *(old)*, unter Androhung der Todesstrafe

e *(inf: also* **pain in the neck** *or* **arse** *Brit sl)* **to be a (real) ~** einem auf den Wecker *(inf)* or Sack *(sl)* gehen; **this job is getting to be a ~** dieser Job geht mir langsam auf den Wecker *(inf)* or Sack *(sl)*

VT *(mentally)* schmerzen; **it ~s me to see their ignorance** ihre Unwissenheit tut schon weh; **his laziness ~ed his parents** mit seiner Faulheit bereitete er seinen Eltern *(dat)* großen Kummer; **it ~s me to have to tell you this but ...** es schmerzt mich, Ihnen dies mitteilen zu müssen, aber ...

pain: **pain barrier** N Schmerzgrenze *f*; **to go through the ~** trotz Schmerzen weitermachen *or* durchhalten; **pain clinic** N Schmerzklinik *f*

pained [peɪnd] ADJ *expression, voice* schmerzerfüllt; **to look ~** schmerzerfüllt aussehen

painful ['peɪnfʊl] ADJ **a** *(physically) injury* schmerzhaft; **is it ~?** tut es weh?; **it's ~ to the touch** es tut weh, wenn man es berührt; **my arm was becoming ~** mein Arm fing an zu schmerzen; **my boots are still ~** meine Stiefel drücken immer noch

b *(= unpleasant, distressing) task, decision, feeling, subject, fact* schmerzlich; *process, reminder, memory, experience* schmerzlich, schmerzhaft; *lesson* schmerzhaft; **it was ~ to admit that ...** es war schmerzlich zuzugeben, dass...; **it is my ~ duty to tell you that ...** ich habe die traurige Pflicht, Ihnen mitteilen zu müssen, dass ...; **~ to behold** ein qualvoller Anblick

c *(inf: = terrible)* peinlich; **~, isn't it?** das tut weh, was?; **I went to the party but it was really ~** *(= boring)* ich war auf der Party, aber es war zum Sterben langweilig; *(= embarrassing)* ich war auf der Party, eine äußerst peinliche Angelegenheit; **she gave a ~ performance** ihre Vorführung war mehr als peinlich

d *(= laborious)* schmerzlich; **it was a long and ~ process** es war ein langer und schmerzlicher Prozess

painfully ['peɪnfəlɪ] ADV **a** *(physically)* schmerzhaft; *move, walk* unter Schmerzen; **~ swollen** schmerzhaft angeschwollen; **he dragged himself ~ along** er quälte sich mühsam weiter

b *(fig) learn, understand* schmerzlich; **Eleanor thought ~ of Eric** der Gedanke an Eric schmerzte Eleanor

c *(= very)* schrecklich; *thin* furchtbar; *slow* schmerzlich; **it was ~ obvious** es war nicht zu übersehen; **he was being ~ overpolite** es war peinlich, wie betont höflich er sich benahm; **he became ~ aware that ...** ihm wurde schmerzlich bewusst, dass ...

d *(= laboriously)* unter großen Anstrengungen; **the convict could scarcely write but had ~ scrawled out a statement** der Häftling konnte kaum schreiben, hatte aber unter großen Anstrengungen eine Erklärung hingekritzelt

pain: **painkiller** N schmerzstillendes Mittel; **painkilling** ADJ *drug* schmerzstillend

painless ['peɪnlɪs] ADJ schmerzlos; **I promise you the interview will be quite ~** *(inf)* ich versichere Ihnen, dass das Interview kurz und schmerzlos wird *(inf)*; **a procedure which makes paying completely ~** *(inf)* ein Verfahren, bei dem Sie von der Bezahlung überhaupt nichts merken; **don't worry, it's quite ~** *(inf)* keine Angst, es tut gar nicht weh

painlessly ['peɪnlɪslɪ] ADV schmerzlos

painstaking ['peɪnz,teɪkɪŋ] ADJ *person, piece of work* sorgfältig; **with ~ accuracy** mit peinlicher Genauigkeit

painstakingly ['peɪnz,teɪkɪŋlɪ] ADV sorgfältig, gewissenhaft; **one has to be so ~ precise** man muss äußerst genau sein

paint [peɪnt] **N** **a** Farbe *f*; *(on car, furniture)* Lack *m*; *(= make-up)* Schminke *f*; **there's too much ~ on your face** *(= make-up)* du hast zu viel Farbe im Gesicht, du bist zu stark angemalt *(inf)*

b **paints** PL Farben *pl*; **box of ~s** Farb- *or* Malkasten *m*

c *(US: = piebald horse)* Schecke *m*

VT **a** *wall, fence etc* streichen; *car* lackieren; *door* streichen, lackieren; **to ~ one's face** *(with make-up)* sich anmalen *(inf)*; *(Theat)* sich schminken; **to ~ one's lips** sich *(dat)* die Lippen anmalen; **to ~ the town red** *(inf)* die Stadt unsicher machen *(inf)*; **to ~ oneself/sb into a corner** *(fig)* sich selbst/jdn in die Enge treiben

b *picture, person* malen; **he ~ed a very convincing picture of life on the moon** er zeichnete ein sehr überzeugendes Bild vom Leben auf dem Mond → **black ADJ d**

VI malen; *(= decorate)* (an)streichen

▸ **paint in** VT *sep (= add)* dazumalen; *(= fill in)* ausmalen

▸ **paint on** VT *sep* aufmalen

▸ **paint out** *or* **over** VT *sep* übermalen; *(on wall)* überstreichen

▸ **paint up** VT *sep building* neu *or* frisch anstreichen; *face* anmalen; **she gets all painted up on a Friday night** freitags abends legt sie immer ihre Kriegsbemalung an *(inf)*

paint: **paintball** N *Kriegsspiel, bei dem mit Farbpatronen geschossen wird*; **paintbox** N Farb- *or* Malkasten *m*; **paintbrush** N Pinsel *m*

painted woman ['peɪntɪd'wʊmən] N Flittchen *nt (inf)*

painter[1] ['peɪntə'] N *(Art)* Maler(in) *m(f)*; *(= decorator also)* Anstreicher(in) *m(f)*

painter[2] N *(Naut)* Fangleine *f*

painterly ['peɪntəlɪ] ADJ malerisch; **his ~ talents** seine Begabung als Maler; **Magritte's prosaic ~ style** Magrittes prosaischer Malstil; **a ~ effect** ein gemalter Effekt

pain therapy N Schmerztherapie *f*

pain threshold N Schmerzschwelle *f or* -grenze *f*

painting ['peɪntɪŋ] N **a** *(= picture)* Bild *nt*, Gemälde *nt* **b** *no pl (Art)* Malerei *f* **c** *no pl (of flat etc)* Anstreichen *nt*

paint: **paint pot** N Farbtopf *m*; **paint remover** N Abbeizmittel *nt*; **paint roller** N Farbrolle *f*; **paint shop** N *(Ind)* Lackiererei *f*; **paint spray(er)** N Spritzpistole *f*; **paint stripper** N Abbeizmittel *nt*; **paintwork** N *(on car etc)* Lack *m*; *(on wall, furniture)* Anstrich *m*

pair [pɛə'] **N** **a** *(of gloves, shoes, people)* Paar *nt*; *(of animals, cards)* Pärchen *nt*; *(hum sl: = breasts)* Vorbau *m (inf)*, Dinger *pl (sl)*; **these socks are not a ~** diese beiden Socken gehören nicht zusammen; **a ~ of scissors** eine Schere; **six ~s of scissors** sechs Scheren; **a new ~** *(of trousers)* eine neue (Hose); *(of shoes)* (ein Paar) neue; **I've lost my scissors, could I borrow your ~?** ich habe meine Schere verloren, kannst du mir deine leihen?; **I've only got one ~ of hands** ich habe auch nur zwei Hände; **he has a useful ~ of hands** *(boxer)* er ist ein guter Boxer; **to be** *or* **have a safe ~ of hands** zuverlässig sein; **a huge ~ of eyes** ein riesiges Augenpaar; **she has a great ~ of legs** sie hat tolle Beine *(inf)*; **in ~s** paarweise; *hunt, arrive, go out* zu zweit; *be seated* in Zweiergruppen; **they're a ~ of rascals** das sind vielleicht zwei Lausejungen; **what a ~ of fools we are!** wir (beide) sind vielleicht dumm!; **you're a fine ~ you are!** *(iro)* ihr seid mir (vielleicht) ein sauberes Pärchen *(iro)*

b **pairs** SING OR PL **the ~s** *(Skating)* Paarlauf *m*; *(Rowing)* Zweier *m*; **in the ~s** im Paarlauf/ Zweier

VT in Paaren *or* paarweise anordnen; **I was ~ed with Bob for the next round** in der nächsten Runde musste ich mit Bob ein Paar bilden; **to be ~ed against sb** gegen jdn spielen

▸ **pair off** VT *sep* in Zweiergruppen einteilen; **to pair sb off with sb** *(= find boyfriend etc for)* jdn mit jdm zusammenbringen *or* verkuppeln *(inf)*; **she was paired off with Jean in the tournament** sie wurde beim Turnier mit Jean zusammengebracht; **pair off each word with its opposite** ordnen Sie jedem Wort den jeweiligen Gegensatz zu **VI** Paare bilden *(with* mit); **all the people at the party had paired off** bei der Party hatten alle Pärchen gebildet; **Marcel paired off with Emma** Marcel und Emma wurden ein Pärchen

pairing ['pɛərɪŋ] N **a** Paarung *f* **b** *(Parl) Absprache zwischen Regierungs- und Oppositionsabgeordneten, an einer Abstimmung nicht teilzunehmen, um die Mehrheitsverhältnisse nicht zu verändern*, Pairing *nt*

pair-skating ['pɛə,skeɪtɪŋ] N Paarlaufen *nt*

paisley ['peɪzlɪ] **N** türkisches Muster **ADJ** *pattern* türkisch; *shirt* türkisch gemustert

pajamas [pə'dʒɑːməz] PL *(US)* = **pyjamas**

Paki ['pækɪ] *(pej inf)* **N** *(= person)* Pakistani *mf* **ADJ** *shop etc* pakistanisch

Pakistan [,pɑːkɪs'tɑːn] N Pakistan *nt*

Pakistani [,pɑːkɪs'tɑːnɪ] **ADJ** pakistanisch **N** Pakistani *mf*, Pakistaner(in) *m(f)*

pal [pæl] N *(inf)* Kumpel *m (inf)*; **OK, let's be ~s again** na gut, vertragen wir uns wieder!; **be a ~!** sei so nett!; **help me with this, there's a ~** sei doch so nett und hilf mir dabei

▸ **pal up** VI *(inf)* sich anfreunden *(with* mit)

palace ['pælɪs] N *(lit, fig)* Palast *m*; **bishop's ~** bischöfliches Palais, bischöfliche Residenz; **royal ~** (Königs)schloss *nt*; **the PM was summoned**

to the ~ der Premierminister wurde zur Königin/zum König bestellt

palace: **palace grounds** PL Schlossgelände *nt*; **palace guard** N Schlosswache *f*; **palace revolution** N *(lit, fig)* Palastrevolution *f*; **palace wall** N Schlossmauer *f*

paladin ['pælədɪn] N Paladin *m*

palaeo- ['pælɪəʊ-] PREF = **paleo-**

palanquin [ˌpælən'kiːn] N Sänfte *f*

palatability [ˌpælətə'bɪlɪtɪ] N a Schmackhaftigkeit *f* b *(fig)* Attraktivität *f*

palatable ['pælətəbl] ADJ a genießbar; *food also* schmackhaft (*to* für); **to make sth ~** *(Cook)* etw geschmacklich verfeinern b *(fig) experience* attraktiv; **to some the truth is not always ~** manchen Leuten schmeckt die Wahrheit nicht immer; **to make sth ~ to sb** jdm etw schmackhaft machen

palatably ['pælətəblɪ] ADV schmackhaft; *(fig also)* attraktiv

palatal ['pælətl] ADJ Gaumen-; *(Phon)* palatal; **~ muscle** Gaumenmuskel *m* N *(Phon)* Palatal(-laut) *m*

palatalize ['pælətəlaɪz] *(Phon)* VT palatalisieren; **the "t" is ~d** das „t" wird im vorderen Gaumen gebildet VI palatalisieren

palate ['pælɪt] N *(lit)* Gaumen *m*; **to have a sensitive ~** einen empfindlichen Gaumen haben; **to have no ~ for sth** *(fig)* keinen Sinn für etw haben

palatial [pə'leɪʃəl] ADJ *(= spacious)* palastartig; *(= luxurious)* luxuriös, prunkvoll, feudal *(hum inf)*

palatially [pə'leɪʃəlɪ] ADV luxuriös, prunkvoll, feudal *(hum inf)*

palatinate [pə'lætɪnɪt] N Pfalz *f*

palatine ['pælətaɪn] N *(also* **count palatine***)* Pfalzgraf *m*

palaver [pə'lɑːvə'] N *(inf)* a *(= fuss and bother)* Umstand *m*, Theater *nt (inf)* b *(= conference)* Palaver *nt*

pale¹ [peɪl] ADJ *(+er)* a *colour, complexion, material* blass; *face* blass; *(implying unhealthy etc)* bleich, fahl; *light* blass, bleich, fahl; **she has ~ gold hair** sie hat rötlich blondes Haar; **~ green/orange** *etc* blass- *or* zartgrün/-orange *etc*; **to go** *or* **turn ~ with fear** vor Schreck bleich *or* blass werden; **but a ~ imitation of the real thing** nur ein Abklatsch *m* des Originals b *(= faint) moon, sun* fahl
VI *(person)* erbleichen, blass *or* bleich werden; *(paper etc)* verblassen; **to ~ with fear** vor Angst erblassen; **but X ~s beside Y** neben Y verblasst X direkt; **to ~ into insignificance** zur Bedeutungslosigkeit herabsinken; **to ~ (into insignificance) beside** *or* **alongside sth** neben etw *(dat)* bedeutungslos sein

pale² N *(= stake)* Pfahl *m*; **those last few remarks were quite beyond the ~** diese letzten Bemerkungen haben eindeutig die Grenzen überschritten; **he is now regarded as beyond the ~** man betrachtet ihn jetzt als indiskutabel

pale: **pale ale** N *(Brit)* helleres Dunkelbier; **paleface** N Bleichgesicht *nt*; **pale-faced** ADJ bleich, blass

palely ['peɪllɪ] ADV *shine, lit* schwach, matt

paleness ['peɪlnɪs] N Blässe *f*

paleo- [ˌpælɪəʊ-] PREF paläo-, Paläo-; **paleoanthropology** Paläoanthropologie *f*

paleography [ˌpælɪ'ɒgrəfɪ] N Paläografie *f*

paleolithic [ˌpælɪəʊ'lɪθɪk] ADJ paläolithisch, altsteinzeitlich

paleontology [ˌpælɪɒn'tɒlədʒɪ] N Paläontologie *f*

Paleozoic [ˌpælɪəʊ'zəʊɪk] ADJ paläozoisch

Palestine ['pælɪstaɪn] N Palästina *nt*

Palestinian [ˌpælə'stɪnɪən] ADJ palästinensisch; **he is ~** er ist Palästinenser N Palästinenser(in) *m(f)*

palette ['pælɪt] N Palette *f*

palette knife N Palettenmesser *nt*

palfrey ['pɔːlfrɪ] N Zelter *m*

palimony ['pælɪmənɪ] N *(esp US inf)* Unterhaltszahlung *f (bei der Auflösung einer Ehe ohne Trauschein)*

palimpsest ['pælɪmpsest] N Palimpsest *m*

palindrome ['pælɪndrəʊm] N Palindrom *nt*

paling ['peɪlɪŋ] N *(= stake)* Zaunpfahl *m*; *(= fence)* Lattenzaun *m*; *(bigger)* Palisadenzaun *m*

palisade [ˌpælɪ'seɪd] N a Palisade *f* b **palisades** PL *(US)* Steilufer *nt* VT einpfählen

pall¹ [pɔːl] N a *(over coffin)* Bahrtuch *nt*, Sargtuch *nt*; **a ~ of smoke** *(fig) (= covering)* eine Dunstglocke; *(rising in air)* eine Rauchwolke; **her death cast a ~ over the celebrations** *(fig)* ihr Tod trübte die Stimmung auf der Feier b *(Eccl)* Pallium *nt*

pall² VI an Reiz verlieren (*on sb* für jdn)

palladium [pə'leɪdɪəm] N *(Chem)* Palladium *nt*

pallbearer ['pɔːlˌbeərə'] N Sargträger(in) *m(f)*

pallet ['pælɪt] N *(= bed)* Pritsche *f*; *(for storage)* Palette *f*

palletization [ˌpælɪtaɪ'zeɪʃən] N Palettisierung *f*

palliasse ['pælɪæs] N Strohsack *m*

palliate ['pælɪeɪt] VT *(form)* a *disease* lindern b *offence, seriousness of situation (= make less serious)* mildern; *(= make seem less serious)* beschönigen

palliative ['pælɪətɪv] *(form)* ADJ *drug, remedy, effect* lindernd; *explanation* beschönigend N Linderungsmittel *nt*, Palliativ(um) *nt*

palliatory ['pælɪətərɪ] *(form)* ADJ = **palliative ADJ**

pallid ['pælɪd] ADJ blass, fahl; *(= unhealthy looking)* bleich, fahl

pallor ['pælə'] N Blässe *f*, Fahlheit *f*

pally ['pælɪ] ADJ *(+er) (Brit inf)* **they're very ~** sie sind dicke Freunde *(inf)*; **to be ~ with sb** mit jdm gut Freund sein; **to get ~ with sb** sich mit jdm anfreunden; **he immediately tried to get ~ with the boss** er versuchte sofort, sich beim Chef anzubiedern

palm¹ [pɑːm] N *(Bot)* Palme *f*; **to carry off** *or* **bear the ~** die Siegespalme erringen, siegen

palm² N *(Anat)* Handteller *m*, Handfläche *f*; *(of glove)* Innenfläche *f*; **the magician had concealed the ball in the ~ of his hand** der Zauberkünstler hielt den Ball in der hohlen Hand versteckt; **he had the audience in the ~ of his hand** er hielt das Publikum ganz in seinem Bann; **to grease sb's ~** *(fig)* jdn schmieren *(inf)*; **to read sb's ~** jdm aus der Hand lesen
VT a *card* im Ärmel verstecken b **the goalie just managed to ~ the ball over the crossbar** der Torwart schaffte es gerade noch, den Ball mit der Handfläche über die Querlatte zu lenken

▶ **palm off** VT *sep (inf) rubbish, goods* andrehen (*on(to) sb* jdm) *(inf)*; *person (with explanation)* abspeisen *(inf)*; **they palmed him off on me** sie haben ihn mir aufgehalst *(inf)*

palmcorder ['pɑːmkɔːdə'] N Palmcorder *m*

palmetto [pæl'metəʊ] N Palmetto *f*

palmist ['pɑːmɪst] N Handliniendeuter(in) *m(f)*, Handleser(in) *m(f)*

palmistry ['pɑːmɪstrɪ] N Handliniendeutung *f*, Handlesekunst *f*

palm: **palm leaf** N Palmwedel *m*; **palm oil** N Palmöl *nt*; **Palm Sunday** N Palmsonntag *m*; **palmtop** ['pɑːmtɒp] N *(Comput)* Palmtop *m*; **palm tree** N Palme *f*; **palm wine** N Palmwein *m*

palmy ['pɑːmɪ] ADJ *(+er) days* glücklich, unbeschwert

palomino [ˌpælə'miːnəʊ] N Palomino *nt*

palpable ['pælpəbl] ADJ a greifbar; *(Med)* tastbar, palpabel *(spec)* b *(= clear) lie, error* offensichtlich; *nonsense* vollkommen; *injustice* grob

palpably ['pælpəblɪ] ADV *(= clearly)* eindeutig; *(= tangibly)* spürbar; **the scene was ~ intense to watch** man konnte die Spannung in dieser Szene regelrecht spüren

palpate [pæl'peɪt] VT *(Med)* palpieren

palpitate ['pælpɪteɪt] VI *(heart)* heftig klopfen; *(= tremble)* zittern

palpitation [ˌpælpɪ'teɪʃən] N *(of heart)* Herzklopfen *nt*; *(= trembling)* Zittern *nt*; **to have ~s** Herzklopfen haben

palsgrave ['pɔːlzgreɪv] N *(Hist)* Pfalzgraf *m*

palsgravine ['pɔːlzgrəviːn] N *(Hist)* Pfalzgräfin *f*

palsied ['pɔːlzɪd] ADJ gelähmt

palsy ['pɔːlzɪ] N Lähmung *f*; **sick of the ~** *(hum inf)* krank; *(Bibl)* gelähmt → **cerebral**

palsy-walsy ['pælzɪ'wælzɪ] ADJ *(hum inf)* **they are all ~ again** sie sind wieder ein Herz und eine Seele → *also* **pally**

paltriness ['pɔːltrɪnɪs] N Armseligkeit *f*, Schäbigkeit *f*; *(of reason)* Unbedeutendheit *f*, Geringfügigkeit *f*

paltry ['pɔːltrɪ] ADJ armselig, schäbig; **for a few ~ pounds** für ein paar lumpige *or* armselige Pfund; **he gave some ~ excuse** er brachte irgendeine armselige Entschuldigung hervor

pampas ['pæmpəs] PL Pampas *pl*

pampas grass N Pampasgras *nt*

pamper ['pæmpə'] VT verwöhnen; *child also* verhätscheln, verzärteln; *dog* verhätscheln; **why don't you ~ yourself and buy the de luxe edition?** warum gönnst du dir nicht mal etwas und kaufst die Luxusausgabe?

pamphlet ['pæmflɪt] N *(= informative brochure)* Broschüre *f*; *(literary)* Druckschrift *f*; *(political, handed out in street)* Flugblatt *nt*, Flugschrift *f*

pamphleteer [ˌpæmflɪ'tɪə'] N Verfasser(in) *m(f)* von Druckschriften/Flugblättern

pan¹ [pæn] N a *(Cook)* Pfanne *f*; *(= saucepan)* Topf *m* b *(of scales)* Waagschale *f*; *(for gold etc)* Goldpfanne *f*; *(of lavatory)* Becken *nt* c *(in ground)* Mulde *f* VT a *gold* waschen b *(US) fish* braten c *(inf: = slate) new play etc* verreißen VI **to ~ for gold** Gold waschen

▶ **pan out** VI *(inf)* sich entwickeln; **it didn't pan out** es hat nicht geklappt *(inf)*; **if it pans out as we hope** wenns so wird, wie wir es uns erhoffen

pan² *(Film)* N (Kamera)schwenk *m* VI panoramieren; **a ~ning shot** ein Schwenk; **the camera ~ned along the wall** die Kamera fuhr langsam die Mauer ab; **the camera ~ned in to the group in the centre** die Kamera schwenkte auf die Gruppe in der Mitte ein VT **they ~ned the camera across the whole scene** sie fuhren mit der Kamera die ganze Szene ab

pan- PREF pan-, Pan-

panacea [ˌpænə'sɪə] N Allheilmittel *nt*; **there's no universal ~ for ...** es gibt kein Allheilmittel für ...

panache [pə'næʃ] N Schwung *m*, Elan *m*; **she dresses with ~** sie kleidet sich sehr extravagant

Pan-African ['pæn'æfrɪkən] ADJ panafrikanisch

Pan-Africanism ['pæn'æfrɪkənɪzəm] N Panafrikanismus *m*

Panama [ˌpænə'mɑː] N Panama *nt*; **~ Canal** Panamakanal *m*

panama (hat) N Panamahut *m*

Panamanian [ˌpænə'meɪnɪən] ADJ panamaisch N Panamaer(in) *m(f)*, Panamese *m*, Panamesin *f*

Pan-American ['pænə'merɪkən] ADJ panamerikanisch

Pan-Americanism ['pænə'merɪkənɪzəm] N Panamerikanismus *m*

Pan-Arabic ['pæn'ærəbɪk] ADJ panarabisch

Pan-Arabism ['pæn'ærəbɪzəm] N Panarabismus *m*

panatella [ˌpænə'telə] N (dünne, lange) Zigarre *f*

pancake ['pænkeɪk] N Pfannkuchen *m*; **~ landing** Bauchlandung *f*; **~ roll** ≈ Frühlingsrolle *f* VI *(aeroplane)* eine Bauchlandung machen

Pancake Day N *(Brit)* Fastnachtsdienstag *m*

panchromatic ['pænkrəʊ'mætɪk] ADJ panchromatisch

pancreas ['pæŋkrıəs] N Bauchspeicheldrüse *f*, Pankreas *nt*

pancreatic [,pæŋkrı'ætık] ADJ der Bauchspeicheldrüse; ~ **cancer** Bauchspeicheldrüsenkrebs *m*

panda ['pændə] N Panda *m*, Katzenbär *m*

panda car N *(Brit)* (Funk)streifenwagen *m*

pandemic [pæn'demık] **N** Pandemie *f (geh)* **ADJ** pandemisch; ~ **disease** Seuche *f*

pandemonium [,pændı'məʊnıəm] N Chaos *nt*; **at this there was** ~ *or* ~ **broke out** daraufhin brach ein Chaos aus *or* die Hölle los; **scenes of** ~ chaotische Szenen *pl*; **judging by the** ~ **coming from the classroom** dem Höllenlärm in der Klasse nach zu urteilen

pander ['pændə'] **N** *(rare)* Kuppler(in) *m(f)* **VI** nachgeben *(to +dat)*, eingehen *(to* auf *+acc)*; **to** ~ **to sb's whims** jds Launen *(acc)* befriedigen wollen; **to** ~ **to sb's ego** jdm um den Bart gehen; **this is ~ing to the public's basest instincts** damit wird an die niedrigsten Instinkte der Öffentlichkeit appelliert

Pandora's box [pæn'dɔ:rəz'bɒks] N Büchse *f* der Pandora

p and p *abbr of* **post(age) and packing**

pane [peın] N **a** Glasscheibe *f* **b** *(Comput)* Fensterausschnitt *m*

panegyric [,pænı'dʒırık] N Lobrede *f*, Panegyrikus *m (Liter)*

panel ['pænl] **N** **a** *(= piece of wood)* Platte *f*, Tafel *f*; *(in wainscoting, ceiling, door)* Feld *nt*; *(Sew)* Streifen *m*, Einsatz *m*; *(Art)* Tafel *f*; *(= painting)* Tafelbild *nt*; *(= part of a plane's wing, fuselage)* Verschalungs(bau)teil *nt*; *(= part of bodywork of a car)* Karosserieteil *nt*; **door** ~ *(on car)* Türblech *nt*; **wing** ~ *(on plane)* Tragfläche *f*
b *(of instruments, switches)* Schalttafel *f*; **instrument** ~ Armaturenbrett *nt*; *(on machine)* Kontrolltafel *f*
c *(Jur, = list of names)* Geschworenenliste *f*; *(Brit, Med)* ≈ Liste *f* der Kassenärzte
d *(of interviewers etc)* Gremium *nt*; *(in discussion)* Diskussionsrunde *f*; *(in quiz)* Rateteam *nt*; **a** ~ **of experts** ein Sachverständigengremium *nt*; **on the** ~ **tonight we have ...** als Teilnehmer der Diskussionsrunde/des Rateteams begrüßen wir heute Abend ...; **a** ~ **of judges** eine Jury
VT *wall, ceiling* täfeln, paneelieren

panel: **panel beater** N Autoschlosser(in) *m(f)*; **panel-beating** N *(= repair work)* Ausbeulen *nt*; **panel discussion** N Podiumsdiskussion *f*; **panel doctor** N Kassenarzt *m*, Kassenärztin *f*; **panel game** N Ratespiel *nt*

panelled, *(US)* **paneled** ['pænld] ADJ *room, wall, door* paneeliert; **to be** ~ **in** *or* **with sth** mit etw paneeliert sein

panel lighting N indirekte Beleuchtung

panelling, *(US)* **paneling** ['pænəlıŋ] N Täfelung *f*, Paneel *nt*; *(to conceal radiator etc, of plane)* Verschalung *f*

panellist, *(US)* **panelist** ['pænəlıst] N Diskussionsteilnehmer(in) *m(f)*

panel: **panel pin** N Stift *m*; **panel saw** Laubsäge *f*; **panel truck** N *(US)* Lieferwagen *m*

Pan-European ADJ paneuropäisch

pang [pæŋ] N ~ **of conscience** Gewissensbisse *pl*; **I felt a** ~ **of conscience** ich hatte Gewissensbisse; **a** ~ **of jealousy** ein Eifersuchtsanfall *m*; **a** ~ **of regret** ein Anfall *m* von Bedauern; **~s of hunger** quälender Hunger; **~s of childbirth** *(old)* Geburtswehen *pl*

pan: **panhandle** *(US)* **N** Pfannenstiel *m*; *(= shape of land)* Zipfel *m* **VI** *(US inf)* die Leute anhauen *(inf)*; **panhandler** N *(US inf)* Bettler(in) *m(f)*, Schnorrer(in) *m(f) (inf)*

panic ['pænık] *vb: pret, ptp* **panicked** **N** Panik *f*; ~ **on the stock exchange** Börsenpanik *f*; **in a (blind)** ~ in (heller) Panik; **to flee in** ~ panikartig die Flucht ergreifen; **a** ~ **reaction** eine Kurzschlussreaktion; **the country was thrown into a (state of)** ~ das Land wurde von Panik erfasst; ~ **buying/selling** *(esp St Ex)* Panikkäufe *pl*/-verkäufe *pl*; *(of goods also)* Hamsterkäufe *pl*/Angstverkäufe *pl*; **to hit the** ~ **button** *(fig inf: = panic)* in Panik geraten, durchdrehen *(inf)*
VI in Panik geraten; **don't** ~ nur keine Panik!
VT Panik auslösen unter *(+dat)*; **to** ~ **sb into doing sth** jdn veranlassen, etw überstürzt zu tun

panic attack N *(Psych)* Panikanfall *m*; **to have a** ~ einen Panikanfall bekommen

panicky ['pænıkı] ADJ *person* überängstlich; *voice* panisch; *measure, behaviour* panikartig; **to feel** ~ panische Angst haben; **I get this** ~ **feeling whenever ...** ich werde immer nervös *or* gerate immer in Panik, wenn ...; **to get** ~ in Panik geraten; **don't get** ~**!** keine Panik!, dreh bloß nicht durch! *(inf)*; ~ **reaction** Kurzschlussreaktion *f*

panic: **panic-mongering** ['pænık,mʌŋgərıŋ] N *(pej)* Panikmache *f (pej)*; **panic-stricken** ['pænık,strıkən], **panic-struck** ['pænıkstrʌk] ADJ von panischem Schrecken ergriffen; *look* panisch

panjandrum [pæn'dʒændrəm] N *(hum, pej)* Wichtigtuer(in) *m(f) (pej)*

pannier ['pænıə'] N Korb *m*; *(on motor-cycle etc)* Satteltasche *f*; *(for mule etc)* Tragkorb *m*

panoplied ['pænəplıd] ADJ *knight* in Rüstung

panoply ['pænəplı] N *(= armour)* Rüstung *f*; *(= covering)* Baldachin *m*; *(fig liter)* Dach *nt*; *(= array)* Palette *f*, Spektrum *nt*; **beneath the oak's** ~ **of leaves** unter dem Blätterdach der Eiche; **the** ~ **of the sky/of stars** das Himmels-/Sternenzelt *(liter)*

panorama [,pænə'rɑ:mə] N *(= view, also fig: of life etc)* Panorama *nt (of +gen)*; *(= survey)* Übersicht *f (of* über *+acc)*

panoramic [,pænə'ræmık] ADJ Panorama-; ~ **shot** *(Phot)* Panoramaaufnahme *f*; ~ **sight** *(Mil)* Rundblickzielfernrohr *nt*; ~ **window** Panoramafenster *nt*

panoramic view N Panoramablick *m*; **a** ~ **of the hills** ein Blick *m* auf das Bergpanorama

panpipes ['pænpaıps] PL Panflöte *f*

pansy ['pænzı] N **a** *(Bot)* Stiefmütterchen *nt* **b** *(Brit pej: = homosexual)* Schwuchtel *f (pej inf)*

pant [pænt] **N** Atemstoß *m* **VI** **a** *(person)* keuchen; *(dog)* hecheln; **to be ~ing for a drink** nach etwas zu trinken lechzen; **he was ~ing for breath** er schnappte nach Luft *(inf)*, er rang nach Atem **b** *(inf: = desire)* lechzen *(for* nach*)*; **to be ~ing to do sth** danach lechzen *or* darauf brennen, etw zu tun **VT** *(also* **pant out***)* *message* hervorstoßen

pantaloon [,pæntə'lu:n] N *(Theat)* Hanswurst *m*

pantaloons [,pæntə'lu:nz] PL *(Hist)* Pantalons *pl*

pantechnicon [pæn'teknıkən] N *(Brit)* Möbelwagen *m*

pantheism ['pænθi:ızəm] N Pantheismus *m*

pantheist ['pænθi:ıst] N Pantheist(in) *m(f)*

pantheistic [,pænθi:'ıstık] ADJ pantheistisch

pantheon ['pænθıən] N Pantheon *nt*

panther ['pænθə'] N Pant(h)er *m*

panties ['pæntız] PL *(for children)* Höschen *nt*; *(for women also)* (Damen)slip *m*; **a pair of** ~ ein Höschen *nt*/ein Slip *m*

pantile ['pæntaıl] N Dachpfanne *f*

panto ['pæntəʊ] N *(Brit inf)* = **pantomime a**

pantograph ['pæntəgrɑ:f] N Pantograf *m*

pantomime ['pæntəmaım] N **a** *(in GB)* ≈ Weihnachtsmärchen *nt*; **what a ~!** *(inf)* was für ein Theater! *(inf)*; **the government should abandon this** ~ **of secrecy** die Regierung sollte endlich diese Posse der Geheimhaltung beenden **b** *(= mime)* Pantomime *f*

PANTOMIME

Eine **pantomime**, oder kurz **panto**, hat mit der deutschen Form von Pantomime wenig gemein. Es handelt sich dabei vielmehr um ein normalerweise zur Weihnachtszeit aufgeführtes Märchenspiel für die ganze Familie. Die Handlung basiert auf einer bekannten Geschichte, wie z. B. Aschenputtel oder Aladin. Häufig ist die Mithilfe des Publikums, vor allem der Kinder, gefordert. Für die größeren Zuschauer werden Scherze zum aktuellen Zeitgeschehen eingebaut. Außerdem gehören dazu Musik, Slapsticks sowie aufwendige Kostüme und Dekorationen. Die männlichen und weiblichen Hauptrollen werden gern Vertretern des jeweils anderen Geschlechts übertragen, wobei bei den bekannteren Aufführungen Prominente die Rollen übernehmen.

pantomime: **pantomime dame** N *(Brit) Figur einer grotesken, alten Dame im Weihnachsstück, meist von einem Mann gespielt*; **pantomime horse** N *(Brit) von zwei Schauspielern in einem Kostüm gespieltes, komisches Pferd, meist im Weihnachtsstück*

pantry ['pæntrı] N Speisekammer *f*

pants [pænts] PL *(esp US: = trousers)* Hose *f*; *(Brit: = underpants)* Unterhose *f*; **a pair of** ~ eine Hose/Unterhose; **to beat the** ~ **off sb** *(inf)* es jdm ordentlich zeigen; **to charm the** ~ **off sb** *(inf)* jdm um den Bart gehen; **to wear the** ~ *(US fig)* die Hosen anhaben *(inf)*; **to be caught with one's** ~ **down** *(fig)* auf frischer Tat ertappt werden *(inf)*; **to be** ~ *(Brit sl: = awful)* beknackt *or* beschissen sein *(sl)*

pant: **pantskirt** ['pæntskɜ:t] N *(esp US)* Hosenrock *m*

panty: **pantsuit** ['pæntsu:t] N *(US)* Hosenanzug *m*

panty ['pæntı]: **panty girdle** N Miederhöschen *nt*; **pantyhose** N *(US)* Strumpfhose *f*; **panty-liner** N Slipeinlage *f*; **pantywaist** N *(dated US sl)* Schwächling *m*, Memme *f (inf)*

pap [pæp] N *(= food)* Brei *m*

papa [pə'pɑ:] N *(dated inf)* Papa *m*

papacy ['peıpəsı] N Papsttum *nt*; **during the** ~ **of ...** während der Amtszeit des Papstes ..., unter Papst ...

papadum, **papadam** ['pæpədəm] N = **poppadom**

papal ['peıpəl] ADJ päpstlich

Papal States PL *(Hist)* Kirchenstaat *m*

Papanicolaou smear [,pæpə'nıkəlu:-], **Papanicolaou test** N *(esp US Med: = cervical smear)* Papanicolaou-Abstrich *m or* -Test *m*

paparazzo [,pæpə'rætsəʊ] *pl* **paparazzi** [,pæpə'rætsı] N Paparazzo *m*, Fotojäger *m*

papaya [pə'paıə] N Papayabaum *f*; *(= fruit)* Papaya *f*

paper ['peıpə'] **N** **a** *(= material)* Papier *nt*; **a piece of** ~ ein Stück *nt* Papier; **a sheet of** ~ ein Blatt *nt* Papier; **a writer who finds it hard to commit himself to** ~ ein Schriftsteller, der nur zögernd etwas zu Papier bringt; **to get** *or* **put sth down on** ~ etw schriftlich festhalten; **can we get your acceptance down on ~?** können wir Ihre Einwilligung schriftlich haben?; **on** ~ **they're the best firm** auf dem Papier ist das die beste Firma; **it's not worth the** ~ **it's written on** das ist schade ums Papier, auf dem es steht; **the walls are like** ~ die Wände sind wie Pappe
b *(= newspaper)* Zeitung *f*; **to write to the ~s about sth** Leserbriefe/einen Leserbrief über etw *(acc)* schreiben; **he's/his name is always in the ~s** er/sein Name steht ständig in der Zeitung
c **papers** **PL** *(= identity papers)* Papiere *pl*
d **papers** **PL** *(= writings, documents)* Papiere *pl*; **private ~s** private Unterlagen *pl*
e *(= set of questions in exam)* Testbogen *m*; *(= exam) (Univ)* Klausur *f*; *(Sch)* Arbeit *f*; **to do a good** ~ **in maths** eine gute Mathematikklausur/-arbeit schreiben
f *(academic)* Referat *nt*, Paper *nt (inf)*; **he's going to give** *or* **read a** ~ **to the society** er wird vor der Gesellschaft ein Referat halten
g *(= wallpaper)* Tapete *f*

h *(Parl)* **a white ~** ein Weißbuch *nt*
i *(= packet)* **a ~ of pins** ein Päckchen *nt* Stecknadeln
VT *wall, room* tapezieren

▶ **paper over** VT *sep* überkleben; **to paper over the cracks** *(fig)* die Risse übertünchen; *(= cover up mistakes)* die Fehler übertünchen

paper *in cpds* Papier-; **paperback** N Taschenbuch *nt*, Paperback *nt (inf)*; **paperback** *in cpds* Taschenbuch-; **~ edition** Taschenbuchausgabe *f*; **~ book** Taschenbuch *nt*; **paper bag** N Papiertüte *f*; **they couldn't fight/play their way out of a (wet) ~** *(hum)* sie sind zu (überhaupt) nichts zu gebrauchen; **paper bank** N Altpapiercontainer *m*; **paper-bound** N *book* broschiert; **paperboy** N Zeitungsjunge *m*; **paper chain** N Girlande *f*; **paper chase** N Schnitzeljagd *f*; **paperclip** N Büroklammer *f*; **paper cup** N Pappbecher *m*; **paper feed** N *(Comput)* Papiervorschub *m*; **paper format** N *(Comput)* Papierformat *nt*; **paper girl** N Zeitungsmädchen *nt*; **paper handkerchief** N Papiertaschentuch *nt*, ≈ Tempo(taschen)tuch® *nt*; **paper handling** N *(Comput, of printer)* Papierführung *f*; **paperhanger** N Tapezierer(in) *m(f)*; **paperhanging** N Tapezieren *nt*; **paper jam** N *(of printer etc)* Papierstau *m*; **paper-knife** N Brieföffner *m*; **paper lantern** N Lampion *m*; **paperless** ADJ papierlos; **~ office** papierloses Büro; **paper mill** N Papierfabrik *f*, Papiermühle *f*; **paper money** N Papiergeld *nt*; **paper napkin** N Papierserviette *f*; **paper plate** N Pappteller *m*; **paper profit** N rechnerischer Gewinn; **paper round** N **to have** *or* **do a ~** Zeitungen austragen; **paper shop** N *(Brit)* Zeitungsladen *m*; **paper size** N Papierformat *nt*; **paper source** N *(of printer etc)* Papierzufuhr *f*; **paper tape** N Lochstreifen *m*; **paper-thin** ADJ *slice* hauchdünn; *(fig) wall* hauchdünn, hellhörig; **a ~ majority** eine hauchdünne Mehrheit; **paper tiger** N Papiertiger *m*; **paper tissue** N Papiertuch *nt*; **paper trail** N *(US)* belastende Unterlagen *pl*; **investigations found a ~ of documents** Nachforschungen brachten belastende Dokumente zutage; **paper tray** N *(Comput, for printer etc)* Papierschacht *m*; **paperweight** N Briefbeschwerer *m*; **paperwork** N Schreibarbeit *f*

papery ['peɪpərɪ] ADJ *plaster, pastry* bröckelig, krümelig; *skin* pergamenten

papier mâché ['pæpɪeɪ'mæʃeɪ] N Pappmaché *nt*, Pappmaschee *nt* ADJ aus Pappmaché

papism ['peɪpɪzəm] N *(pej)* Papismus *m*

papist ['peɪpɪst] N *(pej)* Papist(in) *m(f)*

papistry ['peɪpɪstrɪ] N *(pej)* Papismus *m*

papoose [pə'puːs] N Indianerbaby *nt*; *(= carrier for American Indian baby)* Winkelbrettwiege *f*; *(= carrier for baby)* Tragegestell *nt*

pappadam, pappadum ['pæpədəm] N = **poppadom**

pappy ['pæpɪ] N *(US inf)* Papi *m (inf)*

paprika ['pæprɪkə] N Paprika *m*

Pap smear ['pæpsmɪə'], **Pap test** ['pæptest] N *(esp US Med: = cervical smear)* Pap-Test *m*

Papua ['pæpjʊə] N Papua *nt*

Papuan ['pæpjʊən] ADJ papuanisch N **a** Papua *mf* **b** *(Ling)* Papuasprache *f*

Papua New Guinea N Papua-Neuguinea *nt*

papyrus [pə'paɪərəs] N *pl* **papyri** [pə'paɪəraɪ] *(= plant)* Papyrusstaude *f*, Papyrus *m*; *(= paper)* Papyrus *m*; *(= scroll)* Papyrusrolle *f*, Papyrus *m*

par [pɑː'] N **a** *(Fin)* Nennwert *m*; **to be above/below ~** über/unter pari *or* dem Nennwert stehen; **at ~** zum Nennwert, al pari
b to be on a ~ with sb/sth sich mit jdm/etw messen können; **this objection is on a ~ with Harry's** dieser Einwand liegt auf der gleichen Ebene wie Harrys; **he's nowhere near on a ~ with her** er kann ihr nicht das Wasser reichen; **culturally, the two countries are on a ~** *or* **can be put on a ~** in kultureller Hinsicht sind die beiden Länder miteinander vergleichbar; **this puts him on a ~ with the champion** dadurch hat er mit dem Meister gleichgezogen; **an above-~ performance** eine überdurchschnittliche Leistung
c below ~ *(fig)* unter Niveau; **I'm feeling physically/mentally below** *or* **under ~** ich fühle mich körperlich/seelisch nicht auf der Höhe; **I'm not feeling quite up to ~ today** ich bin heute nicht ganz auf dem Damm *(inf)* or Posten *(inf)*
d *(Golf)* Par *nt*; **~ three** Par 3; **a ~-five hole** ein Par-5-Loch *nt*; **to go round in six under/over ~** sechs Schläge unter/über Par spielen; **that's ~ for the course for him** *(fig inf)* das kann man von ihm erwarten

par, para ['pærə] *abbr of* **paragraph** Abschn.

parable ['pærəbl] N Parabel *f*, Gleichnis *nt*

parabola [pə'ræbələ] N *(Math)* Parabel *f*

parabolic [ˌpærə'bɒlɪk] ADJ **a** Parabol-; *curve* parabelförmig; **~ mirror** Parabolspiegel *m* **b** *(Liter)* gleichnishaft

parabrake ['pærəbreɪk] N *(Aviat, Motor sport)* Bremsschirm *m*

paracetamol [ˌpærə'siːtəmɒl] N Schmerztablette *f*

parachute ['pærəʃuːt] N Fallschirm *m*; **by ~** mit dem Fallschirm; **~ training** Übung *f* im Fallschirmspringen VT *troops* mit dem Fallschirm absetzen; *supplies* abwerfen; **to ~ food to sb** für jdn Lebensmittel abwerfen VI *(also* **parachute down)** (mit dem Fallschirm) abspringen; **they ~d into the wrong zone** sie sprangen über dem falschen Gebiet ab; **to ~ to safety** sich mit dem Fallschirm retten

▶ **parachute in** VT *sep troops* mit dem Fallschirm absetzen; *supplies* abwerfen VI (mit dem Fallschirm) abspringen

parachute: **parachute brake** N Bremsfallschirm *m*; **parachute drop** N *(by person)* (Fallschirm)absprung *m*; *(of supplies)* (Fallschirm)abwurf *m*; **there was a ~ of ten men** zehn Leute sprangen (mit dem Fallschirm) ab; **they got a ~ of medical supplies** medizinische Versorgungsmittel wurden (mit dem Fallschirm) für sie abgeworfen; **parachute jump** N Absprung *m* (mit dem Fallschirm); **parachute regiment** N Fallschirmjägertruppe *f*

parachutist ['pærəʃuːtɪst] N Fallschirmspringer(in) *m(f)*

parade [pə'reɪd] N **a** *(= procession)* Umzug *m*; *(Mil, of boy scouts, circus)* Parade *f*; *(political)* Demonstration *f*; *(fig: = long series)* (lange) Reihe; **church ~** Prozession *f*; **to be on ~** *(Mil)* eine Parade abhalten; **the regiment on ~** das Regiment bei der Parade; **in the school procession you'll be on ~ in front of the public** bei der Schulparade sieht dich alle Welt
b *(= public walk)* Promenade *f*
c *(= fashion parade)* Modenschau *f*
d *(= display)* Parade *f*; *(of wealth etc)* Zurschaustellung *f*
e *(US Mil) (= review)* Truppeninspektion *f*; *(= ground)* Truppenübungsplatz *m*, Exerzierplatz *m*
f *(= shopping parade)* Reihe *f* Geschäfte *or* Läden
VT **a** *troops* auf- *or* vorbeimarschieren lassen; *military might* demonstrieren; *placards* vor sich her tragen
b *(= show off)* zur Schau stellen
VI *(Mil)* auf- *or* vorbeimarschieren; *(political party)* eine Demonstration veranstalten; **the strikers ~d through the town** die Streikenden zogen durch die Stadt; **she ~d up and down with the hat on** sie stolzierte mit ihrem Hut auf und ab

parade ground N Truppenübungsplatz *m*, Exerzierplatz *m*

paradigm ['pærədaɪm] N Musterbeispiel *nt*; *(Gram)* Paradigma *nt*; **~ shift** *(Pol)* Paradigmenwechsel *m*

paradigmatic [ˌpærədɪg'mætɪk] ADJ beispielhaft, paradigmatisch

paradise ['pærədaɪs] N *(lit, fig)* Paradies *nt*; **a shopper's ~** ein Einkaufsparadies *nt*; **an architect's ~** ein Paradies *nt* für Architekten; **living there must be ~ compared with this place** dort zu leben muss geradezu paradiesisch sein verglichen mit hier; **~, she sighed** himmlisch, seufzte sie; **an earthly ~** ein Paradies auf Erden; **I'm in ~** ich bin im Paradies; **~!** wie im Paradies!, paradiesisch!

paradisiac(al) [ˌpærə'dɪzɪək(əl)] ADJ paradiesisch

paradox ['pærədɒks] N Paradox *nt*, Paradoxon *nt (liter)*; **life/he is full of ~es** das Leben/er steckt voller Widersprüche

paradoxical [ˌpærə'dɒksɪkəl] ADJ paradox; *person* widersprüchlich

paradoxically [ˌpærə'dɒksɪkəlɪ] ADV paradoxerweise; *worded* paradox

paraffin ['pærəfɪn] N *(Brit: = oil, US: = wax)* Paraffin *nt*

paraffin: **paraffin lamp** N Paraffinlampe *f*; **paraffin oil** N *(Brit)* Paraffinöl *nt*; **paraffin stove** N *(Brit)* Paraffinofen *m*; **paraffin wax** N Paraffin *nt*

paraglider ['pærəˌglaɪdə'] N **a** *(= person)* Paraglider(in) *m(f)* **b** *(= object)* Paraglider *m*

paragliding ['pærəglaɪdɪŋ] N Gleitschirmfliegen *nt*, Paragliding *nt*

paragon ['pærəgən] N Muster *nt*; **a ~ of virtue** ein Muster *nt* an Tugendhaftigkeit, ein Ausbund *m* an Tugend *(hum)*

paragraph ['pærəgrɑːf] N **a** Absatz *m*, Abschnitt *m*; **"new ~"** „(neuer) Absatz"; **~ mark** *(Comput)* Absatzmarke *f*, Absatzzeichen *nt* **b** *(= brief article)* Notiz *f* VT (in Abschnitte) gliedern, aufgliedern

Paraguay ['pærəgwaɪ] N Paraguay *nt*

Paraguayan [ˌpærə'gwaɪən] ADJ paraguayisch N Paraguayer(in) *m(f)*

parakeet ['pærəkiːt] N Sittich *m*

paraldehyde [pə'rældɪhaɪd] N Paraldehyd *nt*

paralegal ['pærəˌliːgəl] *(esp US)* N Rechtsassistent(in) *m(f)* ADJ **~ assistant** Rechtsassistent(in) *m(f)*; **~ secretary** Sekretär(in) und Rechtsassistent(in) *m(f)*

parallax ['pærəlæks] N Parallaxe *f*

parallel ['pærəlel] ADJ **a** *lines, streets* parallel; *(Comput)* parallel; **at this point the road and river are ~** an dieser Stelle verlaufen Straße und Fluss parallel (zueinander); **~ to** *or* **with** parallel zu *or* mit; **to lie ~ to** *or* **with sth** parallel zu etw liegen; **in a ~ direction** parallel; **~ connection** *(Elec)* Parallelschaltung *f*; **~ interface** *(Comput)* Parallelschnittstelle *f*; **~ market** *(Econ)* Parallelmarkt *m*; **~ printer** Paralleldrucker *m*
b *(fig) career, development* vergleichbar, parallel verlaufend; *universe, talks, process* parallel; **a ~ case** ein Parallelfall *m*, ein vergleichbarer Fall; **the two systems developed along ~ lines** die Entwicklung der beiden Systeme verlief vergleichbar; **he argues along ~ lines to me** er argumentiert ähnlich wie ich
ADV **to run ~** *(roads, careers)* parallel verlaufen *(to sth* zu etw); **to ski ~** Parallelslalom fahren
N **a** *(Geometry)* Parallele *f*
b *(Geog)* Breitenkreis *m*; **the 49th ~** der 49. Breitengrad
c *(Elec)* **connected in ~** parallel geschaltet
d *(fig)* Parallele *f*; **without ~** ohne Parallele; **it has no ~** es gibt dazu keine Parallele; **to draw a ~ between X and Y** eine Parallele zwischen X und Y ziehen; **in ~ with** parallel mit
VT *(fig)* gleichen *(+dat)*; **a case ~led only by ...** ein Fall, zu dem es nur eine einzige Parallele gibt, nämlich ...; **it is ~led by ...** es ist vergleichbar mit ...

parallel bars PL *(Sport)* Barren *m*

parallel import N *(Econ)* Parallelimport *m*

parallelism ['pærəlelɪzəm] N *(of lines)* Parallelität *f*; *(of cases also)* Ähnlichkeit *f*

parallelogram [ˌpærə'leləʊgræm] N Parallelogramm *nt*

parallel processing N *(Comput)* Parallelverarbeitung *f*

parallel turn N *(Ski)* Parallelschwung *m*

Paralympic [,pærə'lɪmpɪk] **ADJ** paralympisch; ~ **Games** Paralympische Spiele *pl* **N Paralympics PL** Paralympics *pl (inf)*, Paralympische Spiele *pl*, Behindertenolympiade *f*

paralysis [pə'ræləsɪs] N *pl* **paralyses** [pə'rælɪsiːz] Lähmung *f*, Paralyse *f*; *(of industry etc)* Lahmlegung *f*; **creeping** ~ progressive Paralyse

paralytic [,pærə'lɪtɪk] **ADJ a** paralytisch **b** *(Brit inf: = very drunk)* voll dicht *(sl)*, hacke(zu) *(inf)* **N** Paralytiker(in) *m(f)*, Gelähmte(r) *mf*

paralyze ['pærəlaɪz] VT **a** *(lit) person, legs* lähmen, paralysieren *(spec)* **b** *(fig) industry, economy* lahmlegen; *traffic* zum Erliegen bringen, lahmlegen

paralyzed ['pærəlaɪzd] ADJ **a** *(lit) person, legs* gelähmt; **he was left partially** ~ er behielt teilweise Lähmungen zurück; **to be ~ in both legs** in beiden Beinen gelähmt sein; ~ **from the neck/waist down** vom Hals/von der Hüfte abwärts gelähmt **b** *(fig)* **to be ~ with fear/shock/fright** vor Angst/Schock/Schreck (wie) gelähmt sein; **to be ~ by guilt** von Schuldgefühlen gepeinigt werden

paralyzing ['pærəlaɪzɪŋ] ADJ **a** *(lit)* **a ~ injury/disease** eine Verletzung/Krankheit, die Lähmungen verursacht **b** *(fig) fear, jealousy, shyness* lähmend

paramedic [,pærə'medɪk] N Sanitäter(in) *m(f)*; *(in hospital)* medizinisch-technischer Assistent, medizinisch-technische Assistentin

parameter [pə'ræmɪtə'] N **a** *(Math, Comput)* Parameter *m* **b parameters** PL *(= framework, limits)* Rahmen *m*; **to define** *or* **establish** *or* **set the ~s of** *or* **for sth** die Parameter für etw festsetzen; **to fall within the ~s of sth** sich im Rahmen von etw bewegen *or* halten

paramilitary [,pærə'mɪlɪtərɪ] ADJ paramilitärisch

paramount ['pærəmaʊnt] ADJ Haupt-; **to be ~** Priorität haben; **our ~ aim** unser Hauptziel *nt*; **of ~ importance** von größter *or* höchster Wichtigkeit; **the interests of the child must be ~** den Interessen des Kindes muss Priorität eingeräumt werden

paramountcy ['pærəmaʊntsɪ] N größte Bedeutung

paramour ['pærəmʊə'] N *(old)* Liebhaber *m*, Buhle *mf (old)*; *(hum) (= man)* Hausfreund *m (hum)*; *(= woman)* Geliebte *f*

paranoia [,pærə'nɔɪə] N Paranoia *f*; *(inf)* Verfolgungswahn *m*; **this ~ which stops nations trusting each other** dieses krankhafte Misstrauen, das die Völker voneinander trennt

paranoiac [,pærə'nɔɪɪk] **N** Paranoiker(in) *m(f)* **ADJ** paranoisch

paranoid ['pærənɔɪd] ADJ paranoid; **or am I just being ~?** oder bilde ich mir das nur ein?; **aren't you being rather ~?** du scheinst unter Wahnvorstellungen zu leiden; **to be ~ about sth** von etw Wahnvorstellungen haben; **she's getting ~ about what other people think of her** die Angst vor dem, was andere von ihr denken, wird bei ihr langsam zur Manie; ~ **schizophrenia** paranoide Schizophrenie

paranormal [,pærə'nɔːməl] **ADJ** paranormal **N the** ~ das Paranormale

parapet ['pærəpɪt] N *(on rampart, of bridge)* Brüstung *f*; *(of well)* (Brunnen)wand *f*; **to put one's head above the ~** *(fig)* sich in die Schusslinie begeben; **to keep one's head below the ~** *(fig)* sich bedeckt halten

paraphernalia [,pærəfə'neɪlɪə] PL Brimborium *nt*, Drum und Dran *nt*

paraphrase ['pærəfreɪz] **N** Umschreibung *f*, Paraphrase *f (geh)* **VT** umschreiben, paraphrasieren *(geh)*

paraplegia [,pærə'pliːdʒə] N doppelseitige Lähmung

paraplegic [,pærə'pliːdʒɪk] **ADJ** doppelseitig gelähmt, paraplegisch *(spec)* **N** Paraplegiker(in) *m(f) (spec)*

parapsychology [,pærəsaɪ'kɒlədʒɪ] N Parapsychologie *f*

paras ['pærəz] PL *(Brit inf)* Fallschirmjäger *pl*

parasailing ['pærə,seɪlɪŋ] N Gleitsegeln *nt*

parascending ['pærə,sendɪŋ] N Paragliding *nt (bei dem der Start mit Hilfe eines Schnellboots erfolgt)*

parasite ['pærəsaɪt] N *(lit)* Parasit *m*, Schmarotzer *m*; *(fig)* Schmarotzer(in) *m(f)*

parasitic(al) [,pærə'sɪtɪk(əl)] ADJ parasitisch, parasitär *(also fig)*; **to be ~ (up)on sth** von etw schmarotzen; **parasitic insect/plant** Parasit *m*, Schmarotzer *m*

parasitology [,pærəsɪ'tɒlədʒɪ] N Parasitologie *f*

parasol ['pærəsɒl] N Sonnenschirm *m*, Parasol *m (dated)*

paratactic [,pærə'tæktɪk] N *(Ling) clause, phrase* parataktisch, nebenordnend

paratrooper ['pærətruːpə'] N Fallschirmjäger(in) *m(f)*

paratroops ['pærətruːps] PL *(= soldiers)* Fallschirmjäger *pl*; *(= division also)* Fallschirmjägertruppe *f*

paratyphoid ['pærə'taɪfɔɪd] N Paratyphus *m*

parboil ['pɑːbɔɪl] VT vorkochen, halb gar kochen

parcel ['pɑːsl] N **a** *(esp Brit)* Paket *nt*; **to do sth up in a ~** etw als Paket packen; ~ **post** Paketpost *f*; **to send sth (by) ~ post** etw als Paket schicken **b a ~ of land** ein Stück *nt* Land → **part N a**

▶ **parcel out** VT *sep land, inheritance* aufteilen; *business, tasks* delegieren

▶ **parcel up** VT *sep* als Paket verpacken

parcel bomb N *(Brit)* Paketbombe *f*

parcel delivery N Paketzustellung *f*

parcel(s) office N *(Brit Rail)* Paketstelle *f*

parcels counter N Paketschalter *m*, Paketannahme *f*

parch [pɑːtʃ] VT ausdörren, austrocknen

parched [pɑːtʃt] ADJ *lips, throat* ausgetrocknet; *land also* verdorrt; **I'm ~** ich habe furchtbaren Durst

parchment ['pɑːtʃmənt] N Pergament *nt*

pard [pɑːd] N *(obs: = leopard)* Leopard *m*

pardner ['pɑːdnə'] N *(US inf hum)* Partner(in) *m(f)*, Kumpel *m (inf)*

pardon ['pɑːdn] **N a** *(Jur)* Begnadigung *f*; **there will be no ~ for deserters** für Fahnenflüchtige gibt es keinen Pardon; **to grant sb a ~** jdn begnadigen; **general ~** Amnestie *f*
b to beg sb's ~ jdn um Verzeihung bitten; **I beg your ~, but could you ...?** verzeihen *or* entschuldigen Sie bitte, könnten Sie ...?; **I beg your ~!** erlauben Sie mal!, ich muss doch sehr bitten!; **(beg) ~?** *(Brit)* **I beg your ~?** *(Brit)* bitte?, wie bitte?; **I beg your ~, beg ~** *(apology)* verzeihen *or* entschuldigen Sie, Verzeihung, Entschuldigung; **a thousand ~s!** ich bitte tausendmal um Verzeihung *or* Entschuldigung!; **we beg the reader's ~ for ...** wir bitten den Leser für ... um Nachsicht
VT a *(Jur)* begnadigen
b *(= forgive)* verzeihen, vergeben *(sb* jdm, *sth* etw); **to ~ sb sth** jdm etw verzeihen *or* vergeben; **~ me, but could you ...?** entschuldigen *or* verzeihen Sie bitte, könnten Sie ...?; **~ me!** Entschuldigung!, Verzeihung!; **~ me?** *(US)* bitte?, wie bitte?; **~ my mentioning it** entschuldigen *or* verzeihen Sie bitte, dass ich das erwähne; **~ me for asking!** *(iro)* entschuldige bitte, dass ich es gewagt habe zu fragen! *(iro)*; **~ my French!** *(hum)* wenn ich den Ausdruck mal benutzen darf

pardonable ['pɑːdnəbl] ADJ *offence* entschuldbar; *weakness, mistake also* verzeihlich

pardonably ['pɑːdnəblɪ] ADV **he was ~ angry** sein Ärger war verständlich; **and ~ so** und das war verständlich

pare [pɛə'] VT **a** *nails* schneiden; *fruit, stick* schälen; **she ~d the skin off the apple** sie schälte den Apfel **b** *(fig) spending, budget* zurückschneiden; **~d to the bone** auf das Allernotwendigste zurückgeschnitten

▶ **pare back** VT *sep budget, costs, prices* zurückschneiden

▶ **pare down** VT *sep (fig) expenses* einschränken; *personnel* einsparen; **to pare sth down to the minimum** etw auf ein Minimum beschränken

parent ['pɛərənt] **N a** Elternteil *m*; **~s** Eltern *pl*; **the duties of a ~** die elterlichen Pflichten; **his father was his favourite ~** von seinen Eltern hatte er seinen Vater am liebsten **b** *(fig)* Vorläufer *m*; **the Copernican theory is the ~ of modern astronomy** die moderne Astronomie geht auf die Lehren des Kopernikus zurück **ATTR ~ birds** Vogeleltern *pl*; **~ plant** Mutterpflanze *f*; **~ ship** *(Space)* Mutterschiff *nt*

parentage ['pɛərəntɪdʒ] N Herkunft *f*; **of humble/uncertain ~** von einfacher/ungewisser Herkunft; **children of racially mixed ~** gemischtrassige Kinder *pl*

parental [pə'rentl] ADJ *care, guidance etc* elterlich *attr*; **~ choice** Wahlfreiheit *f* der Eltern, elterliche Wahl; **the ~ home** das Elternhaus; **~ leave** Elternzeit *f*

parent company N Muttergesellschaft *f*

parent folder N *(Comput)* übergeordneter Ordner

parenthesis [pə'renθɪsɪs] N *pl* **parentheses** [pə'renθɪsiːz] Klammer(zeichen *nt*) *f*, Parenthese *f*; *(= words, statement)* Einschub *m*, Parenthese *f*; **in parentheses** in (runden) Klammern; **could I just say in ~ that ...** darf ich vielleicht einflechten, dass ...

parenthetical [,pærən'θetɪk(əl)] ADJ beiläufig; **could I make one ~ comment?** darf ich eine Bemerkung einflechten?

parenthetically [,pærən'θetɪkəlɪ] ADV nebenbei, beiläufig

parenthood ['pɛərənthʊd] N Elternschaft *f*; **the joys of ~** die Vater-/Mutterfreuden *pl*; **the idea of ~ frightened her** sie schrak zurück vor dem Gedanken, Mutter zu sein

parenting ['pɛərəntɪŋ] N Kindererziehung *f*

parent power N Mitbestimmung *f* der Eltern

parent's evening N *(Sch)* Elternabend *m*

parent teacher association N *(Sch)* Lehrer- und Elternverband *m*

parer ['pɛərə'] N *(= apple-/fruit-parer)* Schälmesser *nt*

par excellence [,pɑːr'eksəlɑ̃ːns] ADV par excellence

parhelion [pɑː'hiːlɪən] N *(Astron)* Nebensonne *f*

pariah [pə'raɪə] N *(lit)* Paria *m*; *(fig also)* Ausgestoßene(r) *mf*

parietal [pə'raɪɪtl] ADJ *(Anat)* parietal; **~ bone** Scheitelbein *nt*

pari mutuel [,pærɪ'mjuːtʊəl] N *Wettsystem, bei dem der gesamte Einsatz abzüglich der Verwaltungskosten prozentual an die Gewinner verteilt wird*

paring: **paring gouge** ['pɛərɪŋ,gaʊdʒ] N *(Tech)* Hohlbeitel *m*; **paring knife** ['pɛərɪŋ,naɪf] N Schälmesser *nt*

parings ['pɛərɪŋz] PL *(of nails)* abgeschnittene Fingernägel *pl*; *(of apple)* Schalen *pl*

pari passu ['pærɪ'pæsuː] ADV gleichlaufend, synchron

Paris ['pærɪs] N Paris *nt*

parish ['pærɪʃ] N Gemeinde *f*; *(= district also)* Pfarrbezirk *m*, Pfarre *f*, Pfarrei *f*

parish: **parish church** N Pfarrkirche *f*; **parish clerk** N *Verwaltungsangestellte(r) des Gemeinderates*; **parish council** N Gemeinderat *m*

parishioner [pə'rɪʃənə'] N Gemeinde(mit)glied *nt*

parish: **parish priest** N Pfarrer *m*; **parish pump politics** N Kirchturmpolitik *f*; **parish register** N Kirchenbuch *nt*, Kirchenregister *nt*

Parisian [pə'rɪzɪən] **ADJ** Pariser *inv*; **she is ~** sie ist Pariserin **N** Pariser(in) *m(f)*

parity [ˈpærɪtɪ] N **a** *(= equality)* Gleichstellung *f*; *(of opportunities)* Gleichheit *f*; **~ of treatment** Gleichstellung *f*; **~ of pay** Lohngleichheit *f* **b** *(= equivalence)* Übereinstimmung *f*; **by ~ of reasoning** mit den gleichen Argumenten **c** *(Fin, Sci)* Parität *f*; **the ~ of the dollar** die Dollarparität **d** *(US Agr)* Preisparität *f* **e** *(Comput)* Parität *f*; **odd/even** ~ ungerade/gerade Parität

park [pɑːk] **N** **a** Park *m*; **national ~** Nationalpark *m*
b *(Brit Sport: = field)* (Sport)platz *m*
c *(US: = car park)* Parkplatz *m*
d *(Mil)* Arsenal *nt*
e *(Aut)* **to put/leave a car in ~** das Getriebe in Parkstellung bringen/lassen
VT **a** *car* parken; *bicycle* abstellen; **a ~ed car** ein parkendes Auto; **there's been a car ~ed outside for days** draußen parkt schon seit Tagen ein Auto; **he was very badly ~ed** er hatte miserabel geparkt
b *(inf: = put) luggage etc* abstellen; **he ~ed himself right in front of the fire** er pflanzte sich direkt vor den Kamin *(inf)*; **we ~ed the children with the neighbours** wir haben die Kinder bei den Nachbarn abgegeben *or* gelassen; **find somewhere to ~ your backside** *(hum)* such dir was, wo du dich platzen kannst *(hum)*
c *(Comput) hard disk* parken
VI parken; **there was nowhere to ~** es gab nirgendwo einen Parkplatz; **to find a place to ~** einen Parkplatz finden; *(in line of cars)* eine Parklücke finden

parka [ˈpɑːkə] N Parka *m*

park-and-ride [ˌpɑːkənˈraɪd] N Park-and-Ride-System *nt*

park bench N Parkbank *f*

parking [ˈpɑːkɪŋ] N Parken *nt*; **women are usually good at ~** Frauen sind gewöhnlich gut im Einparken; **there's no ~ on this street** in dieser Straße ist Parken verboten *or* ist Parkverbot; **there's plenty of ~** es gibt genug Parkplätze; **"no ~"** „Parken verboten"; **"good ~ facilities"** „gute Parkmöglichkeiten"; **"parking for 50 cars"** „50 (Park)plätze"

parking: **parking attendant** N Parkplatzwächter(in) *m(f)*; **parking bay** N Parkbucht *f*; **parking brake** N *(US Aut)* Handbremse *f*; **parking disk** N Parkscheibe *f*; **parking fine** N Geldbuße *f* (für Parkvergehen); **parking garage** N *(US)* Parkhaus *nt*; **parking level** N *(in multi-storey car park)* Parkdeck *nt*; **parking lot** N *(US)* Parkplatz *m*; **parking meter** N Parkuhr *f*; **parking offender** N Parksünder(in) *m(f)*; **parking orbit** N *(Space)* Parkbahn *f*; **parking place** N *(for single vehicle)* Parkplatz *m*; **parking space** N *(for single vehicle)* Parkplatz *m*, Abstellfläche *f*; **parking ticket** N Strafzettel *m*, Knöllchen *nt (inf)*

Parkinson's (disease) [ˈpɑːkɪnsənz(dɪˈziːz)] N parkinsonsche Krankheit

park: **park keeper** N Parkwächter(in) *m(f)*; **parkland** N Grünland *nt*; **park ranger**, **park warden** N *(in national park)* Nationalparkwächter(in) *m(f)*, Aufseher(in) *m(f)* in einem Nationalpark; *(in forest)* Förster(in) *m(f)*; *(in game reserve)* Wildhüter(in) *m(f)*; **parkway** N *(US)* Allee *f*

parky [ˈpɑːkɪ] ADJ *(+er) (Brit inf)* kühl, frisch; **(it's a bit) ~ today** ganz schön kühl heute

parlance [ˈpɑːləns] N **in common/modern ~** im allgemeinen/modernen Sprachgebrauch; **in technical/legal ~** in der Fachsprache/Rechtssprache

parley [ˈpɑːlɪ] **N** Verhandlungen *pl* **VI** verhandeln

parliament [ˈpɑːləmənt] N Parlament *nt*; **to get into ~** ins Parlament kommen; **to open ~** das Parlament eröffnen; **~ reconvenes in the early autumn** das Parlament tritt Anfang Herbst wieder zusammen; **the German ~** der Bundestag; **the Swiss ~** die Bundesversammlung; **the Austrian ~** der Nationalrat

parliamentarian [ˌpɑːləmenˈtɛərɪən] N Parlamentarier(in) *m(f)*

parliamentarianism [ˌpɑːləmenˈtɛərɪənɪzəm] N Parlamentarismus *m*

parliamentary [ˌpɑːləˈmentərɪ] ADJ parlamentarisch; **the ~ Labour Party** die Parlamentsfraktion der Labour Party; **~ debates** Parlamentsdebatten *pl*; **~ seat** Parlamentssitz *m*

parliamentary: **parliamentary agent** N Parlamentsbeauftragte(r) *mf*; **parliamentary candidate** N Parlamentskandidat(in) *m(f)*; **parliamentary election** N Parlamentswahlen *pl*; **parliamentary private secretary** N *(Brit)* Abgeordnete(r), der/die einem Minister zuarbeitet; **parliamentary privilege** N parlamentarische Sonderrechte *pl*; *(= immunity)* parlamentarische Immunität

parlor car N *(US)* Salonwagen *m*

parlour, *(US)* **parlor** [ˈpɑːləʳ] N **a** *(in house)* Salon *m* **b** *(= beauty parlour, massage parlour etc)* Salon *m*; **ice-cream ~** Eisdiele *f*

parlour: **parlour game** N Gesellschaftsspiel *nt*; **parlourmaid** N *(Brit)* Dienstmädchen *nt*

parlous [ˈpɑːləs] ADJ *(old, liter)* **to be in a ~ state** sich in einem prekären Zustand befinden

Parma ham [ˈpɑːməˈhæm] N Parmaschinken *m*

Parmesan [ˌpɑːmɪˈzæn] N Parmesan *m*

Parnassus [pɑːˈnæsəs] N **Mount ~** der Parnass

parochial [pəˈrəʊkɪəl] ADJ **a** *(Eccl)* Pfarr-; **~ ministry** Pfarramt *nt*; **the ~ duties of a priest** die Aufgaben eines Gemeindepfarrers; **the ~ boundaries** die Grenzen des Pfarrbezirks; **~ school** *(US)* Konfessionsschule *f* **b** *(fig) attitude, person* engstirnig; *mind, ideas* beschränkt; **he's so ~ in his outlook** er hat einen sehr beschränkten Gesichtskreis

parochialism [pəˈrəʊkɪəlɪzəm] N *(fig)* Engstirnigkeit *f*

parodist [ˈpærədɪst] N Parodist(in) *m(f)*

parody [ˈpærədɪ] **N** **a** Parodie *f (of* auf *+acc)* **b** *(= travesty)* Abklatsch *m*; **a ~ of justice** eine Parodie auf die Gerechtigkeit **VT** parodieren

parole [pəˈrəʊl] **N** **a** *(Jur)* Bewährung *f*; *(= temporary release)* Strafunterbrechung *f*, Kurzurlaub *m*; **to be released on ~** bedingt aus der Haft entlassen werden; **to let sb out on ~** jdn auf Bewährung entlassen; *(temporarily)* jdm Strafunterbrechung *or* Kurzurlaub gewähren; **to be on ~** unter Bewährung stehen; *(temporarily)* auf Kurzurlaub sein; **he's on six months' ~** er hat sechs Monate Bewährung(sfrist); **to break one's ~** den Kurzurlaub zur Flucht benutzen **b** *(Mil)* Parole *f* **VT** *prisoner* auf Bewährung entlassen; *(temporarily)* Strafunterbrechung *or* Kurzurlaub gewähren *(+dat)*

paroxysm [ˈpærəksɪzəm] N Anfall *m*; **~ of grief** Verzweiflungsanfall *m*; **to be seized by a ~ of rage** einen Wutanfall bekommen; **~s of laughter** ein Lachkrampf *m*

parquet [ˈpɑːkeɪ] N **a** Parkett *nt*; **~ floor** Parkettboden *m* **b** *(US Theat)* Parkett *nt*; **~ circle** Parkett *nt*

parquetry [ˈpɑːkɪtrɪ] N Mosaikparkett *nt*

parricide [ˈpærɪsaɪd] N *(= act)* Vater-/Muttermord *m*; *(= person)* Vater-/Muttermörder(in) *m(f)*

parrot [ˈpærət] **N** Papagei *m*; **he felt as sick as a ~** *(Brit inf)* ihm war kotzübel *(inf)*; **he was as sick as a ~** *(Brit inf: = vomited)* er kotzte wie ein Reiher *(inf)* **VT** (wie ein Papagei) nachplappern *(sb* jdm)

parrot: **parrot cry** N *(fig)* populäres Schlagwort; **parrot disease** N Papageienkrankheit *f*; **parrot-fashion** ADV **to repeat sth ~** etw wie ein Papagei nachplappern; **he learned the poem ~** er lernte das Gedicht stur auswendig; **parrot fever** N Papageienkrankheit *f*; **parrotfish** N Papageifisch *m*; **parrot-like** ADJ papageienhaft; **this ~ way of learning** dies sture Auswendiglernen; **parrot phrase** N = **parrot cry**

parry [ˈpærɪ] **N** *(Fencing, fig)* Parade *f*; *(Boxing)* Abwehr *f* **VT** *(Fencing, fig)* parieren; *(Boxing) blow* abwehren; *ball, shot* abwehren **VI** *(Fencing)* parieren; *(Boxing, Ftbl)* abwehren

parse [pɑːz] **VT** grammatisch analysieren *(Ling, Comput)* parsen **VI** analysieren; **this sentence doesn't ~ very easily** die Struktur dieses Satzes ist nicht leicht zu analysieren

parser [ˈpɑːsəʳ] N *(Comput)* Parser *m*

parsimonious [ˌpɑːsɪˈməʊnɪəs] ADJ geizig

parsimoniously [ˌpɑːsɪˈməʊnɪəslɪ] ADV geizig; **he ~ refused to lend me any money at all** er war zu geizig, mir auch nur einen einzigen Cent zu leihen

parsimony [ˈpɑːsɪmənɪ] N Geiz *m*

parsing [ˈpɑːsɪŋ] N *(Gram)* Syntaxanalyse *f*; *(Comput)* Parsing *nt*

parsley [ˈpɑːslɪ] N Petersilie *f*

parsnip [ˈpɑːsnɪp] N Pastinak *m*, Pastinake *f*

parson [ˈpɑːsn] N Pfarrer *m*, Pastor *m*, Pfaffe *m (pej)*; **~'s nose** Bürzel *m*, Sterz *m*

parsonage [ˈpɑːsənɪdʒ] N Pfarrhaus *nt*

Parsons table [ˈpɑːsnzˈteɪbl] N *(US)* Tisch *m* aus Plastik

part [pɑːt] **N** **a** *(= portion, fragment)* Teil *m*; **5 ~s of sand to 1 of cement** 5 Teile Sand auf ein(en) Teil Zement; **it's 3 ~s gone** drei Viertel sind schon weg; **the stupid ~ of it is that ...** das Dumme daran ist, dass ...; **you haven't heard the best ~ yet** ihr habt ja das Beste noch gar nicht gehört; **the book is good in ~s** teilweise *or* streckenweise ist das Buch gut; **in ~** teilweise, zum Teil; **the greater ~ of it/of the work is done** der größte Teil davon/der Arbeit ist fertig; **it is in large ~ finished/true** das ist zum großen Teil erledigt/wahr; **a ~ of the country/city I don't know** eine Gegend, die ich nicht kenne; **this is in great ~ due to ...** das liegt größtenteils *or* vor allem an *(+dat)* ...; **during the darkest ~ of the night** in tiefster Nacht; **I kept ~ of it for myself** ich habe einen Teil davon für mich behalten; **I lost ~ of the manuscript** ich habe einen Teil des Manuskripts verloren; **that's ~ of the truth** das ist ein Teil der Wahrheit; **for the most ~** zum größten Teil; **her performance was for the most ~ well executed** ihre Leistung war im Großen und Ganzen gelungen; **in the latter ~ of the year** gegen Ende des Jahres; **the remaining ~ of our holidays** der Rest unseres Urlaubs; **~ of him wanted to call her, ~ of him wanted to forget about her** ein Teil von ihm wollte sie anrufen, ein anderer sie vergessen; **she's become (a) ~ of me** sie ist ein Teil von mir geworden; **it's all ~ of growing up** das gehört alles zum Erwachsenwerden dazu; **to be ~ and parcel of sth** fester Bestandteil einer Sache *(gen)* sein; **it is ~ and parcel of the job** das gehört zu der Arbeit dazu; **are transport costs included? – yes, they're all ~ and parcel of the scheme** sind die Transportkosten enthalten? – ja, es ist alles inbegriffen
b *(Mech, of kit etc)* Teil *nt*; **spare ~** Ersatzteil *nt*; **moving ~s** bewegliche Teile *pl*
c *(Gram)* **~ of speech** Wortart *f*; **principal ~s of a verb** Stammformen *pl*
d *(of series)* Folge *f*; *(of serial)* Fortsetzung *f*; *(of encyclopaedia etc)* Lieferung *f*; **end of ~ one** *(TV)* Ende des ersten Teils
e *(= share, role)* (An)teil *m*, Rolle *f*; *(Theat)* Rolle *f*, Part *m (geh)*; **to play one's ~** *(fig)* seinen Beitrag leisten; **to take ~ in sth** an etw *(dat)* teilnehmen, bei etw *(dat)* mitmachen, sich an etw *(dat)* beteiligen; **who is taking ~?** wer macht mit?, wer ist dabei?; **he's taking ~ in the play** er spielt in dem Stück mit; **in the ~ of Lear** in der Rolle des Lear; **he looks the ~** *(Theat)* die Rolle passt zu ihm; *(fig)* so sieht (d)er auch aus; **to play a ~** *(Theat, fig)* eine Rolle spielen; **to play no ~ in sth** *(person)* nicht an etw *(dat)* beteiligt sein; **we want no ~ of it** wir wollen damit nichts zu tun haben; **he's just playing a ~** *(fig)* der tut nur so
f *(Mus)* Stimme *f*, Part *m*; **the soprano ~** der Sopranpart, die Sopranstimme; **the piano ~** der Klavierpart, die Klavierstimme; **to sing in ~s** mehrstimmig singen
g **parts** **PL** *(= region)* Gegend *f*; **from all ~s** überallher, von überall her; **in** *or* **around these**

~s hier in der Gegend, in dieser Gegend; **in foreign ~s** in der Fremde, in fremden Ländern; **what ~s are you from?** aus welcher Gegend sind Sie?; **he's not from these ~s** er ist nicht aus dieser Gegend *or* nicht von hier
h *(= side)* Seite *f*; **to take sb's ~** sich auf jds Seite *(acc)* stellen, für jdn Partei ergreifen; **for my ~** was mich betrifft, meinerseits; **a miscalculation on my ~** eine Fehlkalkulation meinerseits; **on the ~ of** vonseiten *(+gen)*, von Seiten *(+gen)*, seitens *(+gen)*
i **to take sth in good ~** etw nicht übel nehmen
j **a man of ~s** ein vielseitiges Talent; **a man of many ~s** ein vielseitiger Mensch
k *(US: in hair)* Scheitel *m*
l **parts** PL *(= male genitals)* Geschlechtsteile *pl*
ADV teils, teilweise; **is it X or Y? – ~ one and ~ the other** ist es X oder Y? – teils (das eine), teils (das andere); **it is ~ iron and ~ copper** es ist teils aus Eisen, teils aus Kupfer; **it was ~ eaten** es war halb aufgegessen; **he's ~ French, ~ Scottish and ~ Latvian** er ist teils Franzose, teils Schotte und teils Lette
VT **a** *(= divide)* teilen; *hair* scheiteln; *curtain* zur Seite schieben; *legs* aufmachen; *lips* öffnen; **the police tried to ~ the crowd** *(= make path through)* die Polizei versuchte, eine Gasse durch die Menge zu bahnen
b *(= separate)* trennen; **to ~ sb from sb/sth** jdn von jdm/etw trennen; **till death us do ~** bis dass der Tod uns scheidet; **she's not easily ~ed from her money** sie trennt sich nicht gern von ihrem Geld; **to ~ company** sich trennen; **to ~ company with sb/sth** sich von jdm/etw trennen; *(in opinion)* mit jdm nicht gleicher Meinung sein; **on that issue, I must ~ company with you** in dem Punkt gehen unsere Meinungen auseinander
VI **a** *(= divide)* sich teilen; *(curtains)* sich öffnen; **her lips ~ed in a smile** ihre Lippen öffneten sich zu einem Lächeln
b *(= separate) (people)* sich trennen; *(things)* sich lösen, abgehen; **to ~ from** *or* **with sb** sich von jdm trennen; **we ~ed friends** wir gingen als Freunde auseinander, wir schieden als Freunde *(geh)*; **to ~ with sth** sich von etw trennen; **to ~ with money** Geld ausgeben *or* lockermachen *(inf)*; **to ~ from this life** *(liter)* aus diesem Leben scheiden *(geh)*

partake [pɑːˈteɪk] *pret* **partook**, *ptp* **partaken** [pɑːˈteɪkn] VI *(form)* **a** **to ~ of** *(food, drink)* zu sich *(+dat)* nehmen; **will you ~ of a glass of sherry?** darf ich Ihnen ein Glas Sherry anbieten?; **will** *or* **do you ~?** *(form, hum)* darf *or* kann ich Ihnen etwas anbieten? **b** *(= share in)* **to ~ of an experience** an einer Erfahrung *(dat)* teilhaben, jds Erfahrung *(acc)* teilen **c** **to ~ of a quality** eine Eigenschaft an sich *(dat)* haben; **to a certain extent he ~s of his father's arrogance** er hat etwas von der Arroganz seines Vaters **d** **to ~ in sth** *(in activity)* an etw *(dat)* teilnehmen

parterre [pɑːˈtɛəʳ] N *(US)* Parterre *nt*

part exchange N **to offer/take sth in ~** etw in Zahlung geben/nehmen

parthenogenesis [ˈpɑːθɪnəʊˈdʒenɪsɪs] N Parthenogenese *f*, Jungfernzeugung *f*

Parthian shot [ˈpɑːθɪənˈʃɒt] N zum Abschied fallen gelassene spitze Bemerkung

partial [ˈpɑːʃəl] ADJ **a** *(= not complete)* Teil-, partiell *(geh)*, teilweise; *paralysis, eclipse* teilweise, partiell; **a ~ success** ein Teilerfolg *m*, ein teilweiser Erfolg; **to make a ~ recovery** eine teilweise Erholung *or* Genesung durchmachen; **to give sth ~ support** eine Sache teilweise unterstützen; **to reach a ~ agreement** teilweise Übereinstimmung erzielen
b *(= biased)* voreingenommen; *judgement* parteiisch
c **to be ~ to sth** eine Vorliebe *or* Schwäche für etw haben; **after a while I became rather ~ to it** nach einiger Zeit hatte ich eine ziemliche Vorliebe dafür entwickelt; **to be ~ to doing sth** eine Vorliebe *or* Schwäche dafür haben, etw zu tun

partiality [ˌpɑːʃɪˈælɪtɪ] N **a** *(= bias)* Voreingenommenheit *f*; *(of judgement)* Parteilichkeit *f*; **without ~** unvoreingenommen, unparteiisch **b** *(= liking)* Vorliebe *f* *(for* für*)*, Schwäche *f* *(for* für*)*

partially [ˈpɑːʃəlɪ] ADV **a** *(= not completely)* zum Teil, teilweise; **~ deaf** eingeschränkt hörfähig; **~ clothed** halb angezogen, teilweise bekleidet; **~ furnished** teilmöbliert **b** *(= in part)* zum Teil, teils; **~ because ...** zum Teil deswegen, weil ...; **to be ~ to blame for sth** mitschuldig an etw sein **c** *(= with bias)* parteiisch

partially sighted ADJ eingeschränkt sehfähig

participant [pɑːˈtɪsɪpənt] N Teilnehmer(in) *m(f)* *(in +gen*, an *+dat)*; *(in scuffle etc)* Beteiligte(r) *mf* *(in +gen*, an *+dat)*; **the bank will not be a ~ in this project** die Bank wird sich nicht an diesem Vorhaben beteiligen

participate [pɑːˈtɪsɪpeɪt] VI **a** *(= take part)* sich beteiligen, teilnehmen *(in* an *+dat)*; **to ~ in sport** *(Sch)* am Schulsport teilnehmen; **the council was accused of participating in a housing swindle** man beschuldigte die Stadtverwaltung der Beteiligung an einem Bauschwindel; **participating country** *(of EU etc)* Teilnehmerland *nt* **b** *(= share)* beteiligt sein *(in* an *+dat)*; **to ~ in sb's sorrow** an jds Kummer *(dat)* Anteil nehmen

participation [pɑːˌtɪsɪˈpeɪʃən] N Beteiligung *f*; *(in competition etc)* Teilnahme *f*; *(= worker participation)* Mitbestimmung *f*; **~ in the profits** Gewinnbeteiligung *f*

participative [pɑːˈtɪsɪpətɪv] ADJ mitbestimmend; **a genuinely ~ democracy** eine Demokratie, in der es echte Mitbestimmung gibt

participator [pɑːˈtɪsɪpeɪtəʳ] N Teilnehmer(in) *m(f)*

participatory [ˌpɑːtɪsɪˈpeɪtərɪ] ADJ teilnehmend; *(Ind)* auf Mitbestimmung ausgerichtet; **~ democracy** Bürgerdemokratie *f*

participial [ˌpɑːtɪˈsɪpɪəl] ADJ Partizipial-, partizipial; **~ clause** Partizipialsatz *m*

participle [ˈpɑːtɪsɪpl] N Partizip *nt* → **present, past**

particle [ˈpɑːtɪkl] N **a** *(of sand etc)* Teilchen *nt*, Körnchen *nt*; *(Phys)* Teilchen *nt*; *(fig)* Körnchen *nt*; **~ of dust, dust ~** Stäubchen *nt*, Staubkörnchen *nt*, Staubpartikel *nt (spec)*; **food ~s** Nahrungspartikel *pl*; **there's not a ~ of truth in it** darin steckt kein Körnchen Wahrheit **b** *(Gram)* Partikel *f*

particle: **particle accelerator** N Teilchenbeschleuniger *m*; **particle board** N *(US)* Spanplatte *f*

parti-coloured, *(US)* **parti-colored** [ˈpɑːtɪˌkʌləd] ADJ bunt, vielfarbig

particular [pəˈtɪkjʊləʳ] ✪ 6.3, 7.5, 26.2 ADJ **a** *(= as against others)* **this ~ house is very nice** dies (eine) Haus ist sehr hübsch; **it varies according to the ~ case** das ist von Fall zu Fall verschieden; **in this ~ instance** in diesem besonderen Fall; **in certain ~ cases** in einigen besonderen Fällen; **there's a ~ town in France where ...** in Frankreich gibt es eine Stadt, wo ...; **is there any one ~ city you prefer?** bevorzugen Sie eine bestimmte Stadt?
b *(= special)* besondere(r, s); *problem* besondere(r, s), bestimmt; **in ~** besonders, vor allem, insbesondere; **the wine in ~ was excellent** vor allem der Wein war hervorragend; **nothing in ~** nichts Besonderes *or* Bestimmtes; **is there anything in ~ you'd like?** haben Sie einen besonderen Wunsch?; **did you want to speak to anyone in ~?** wollten Sie mit jemand(em) Bestimmtem sprechen?; **I'm not waiting for anyone in ~** ich warte auf niemand Bestimmten; **he's a ~ friend of mine** er ist ein guter Freund von mir; **for no ~ reason** aus keinem besonderen *or* bestimmten Grund; **no ~ reason for sth/for doing sth** kein besonderer Grund für etw/dafür, etw zu tun; **at a ~ time** zu einer bestimmten Zeit; **at that ~ time** zu (genau) diesem Zeitpunkt; **in a ~ way** auf bestimmte Art und Weise; **to be of ~ interest** von besonderem Interesse sein; **to be of ~ concern to sb** jdm ein besonderes Anliegen sein; **with ~ reference to ...** mit besonderem Hinweis auf ... *(acc)*; **to take ~ care to ...** besonders darauf achten, dass ...
c *(= fussy, fastidious)* eigen; *(= choosy)* wählerisch; **he is very ~ about cleanliness/his children's education** er nimmt es mit der Sauberkeit/der Erziehung seiner Kinder sehr genau; **he's ~ about his car** er ist sehr eigen *or* pingelig *(inf)* mit seinem Auto; **I'm ~ about my friends** ich suche mir meine Freunde genau aus; **you can't be too ~** man kann gar nicht wählerisch genug sein; **I'm not too ~ (about it)** es kommt mir nicht so darauf an, mir ist es gleich; **she was most ~ about it** *(= was definite)* sie bestand darauf
N **a** Besondere(s) *nt*; **the ~ and the general** das Besondere und das Allgemeine
b **particulars** PL Einzelheiten *pl*; *(about person)* Personalien *pl*; **in this ~** in diesem Punkt; **correct in every ~** in jedem Punkt richtig; **for further ~s apply to the personnel manager** weitere Auskünfte erteilt der Personalchef; **to go into ~s** ins Detail *or* in Einzelheiten gehen; **to give ~s** Angaben machen; **please give full ~s** bitte genaue Angaben machen

particularism [pəˈtɪkjʊlərɪzəm] N **a** *(Pol)* Partikularismus *m*; *(adherence to one's own aims)* Sonderbestrebungen *pl*; *(of country)* Kleinstaaterei *f* **b** *(Rel)* Lehre *f* von der Gnadenwahl

particularity [pəˌtɪkjʊˈlærɪtɪ] N **a** *(= individuality)* Besonderheit *f* **b** *(= detailedness)* Ausführlichkeit *f* **c** *(= fastidiousness)* Eigenheit *f*

particularize [pəˈtɪkjʊləraɪz] VT spezifizieren, genau angeben VI ins Detail *or* Einzelne gehen; **he did not ~** er nannte keine Einzelheiten

particularly [pəˈtɪkjʊləlɪ] ADV besonders, vor allem; **everybody, but ~ Smith** alle, aber vor allem *or* ganz besonders Smith; **he said most ~ not to do it** er hat ausdrücklich gesagt, dass man das nicht tun soll; **do you want it ~ for tomorrow?** brauchen Sie es unbedingt morgen?; **we are ~ pleased to have with us today ...** wir freuen uns besonders, heute ... bei uns zu haben; **he was not ~ pleased** er war nicht besonders erfreut; **not ~** nicht besonders; **it's important, ~ since time is getting short** es ist wichtig, zumal die Zeit knapp wird

parting [ˈpɑːtɪŋ] N **a** Abschied *m*; **~ is such sweet sorrow** *(prov)* o süßer Abschiedsschmerz!; **after the ~ of the ways** nachdem sich ihre Wege getrennt hatten; **is this the ~ of the ways then?** das ist also das Ende (unserer Beziehung)?; **this meeting was the ~ of the ways for the Leninists and the Trotskyites** seit dieser Tagung sind die Leninisten und Trotzkisten getrennte Wege gegangen
b *(Brit: in hair)* Scheitel *m*
ADJ Abschieds-, abschließend; **a ~ present/kiss** ein Abschiedsgeschenk *nt*/-kuss *m*; **Charles knows all about it already, was her ~ shot** Charles weiß schon alles, schleuderte sie ihm nach; **he made a ~ threat** zum Abschied stieß er eine Drohung aus; **his ~ words** seine Abschiedsworte *pl*

partisan [ˌpɑːtɪˈzæn] ADJ **a** parteiisch *(esp pej)*, parteilich; *person* voreingenommen; *argument* parteiisch, voreingenommen; **~ politics** Parteipolitik *f*; **~ spirit** Partei- *or* Vereinsgeist *m* **b** *(Mil)* Partisanen-; **~ warfare** Partisanenkrieg *m* N **a** Parteigänger(in) *m(f)* **b** *(Mil)* Partisan(in) *m(f)*, Freischärler(in) *m(f)*

partisanship [ˌpɑːtɪˈzænʃɪp] N Parteilichkeit *f*

partition [pɑːˈtɪʃən] N **a** Teilung *f* **b** *(= wall)* Trennwand *f* **c** *(= section)* Abteilung *f* **d** *(Comput)* Partition *f* VT **a** *country* teilen, spalten; *room* aufteilen **b** *(Comput)* partitionieren

▶ **partition off** VT *sep* abteilen, abtrennen

partitioning attack [pɑːˈtɪʃənɪŋəˌtæk] N *illegales Verfahren zum Auslesen von Daten auf* *einer SIM-Karte eines Mobiltelefons*, Partitioning Attack *f*

partitive ['pɑːtɪtɪv] ADJ *(Gram)* partitiv

part load N *(Comm)* Teilladung *f*

partly ['pɑːtlɪ] ADV zum Teil, teilweise, teils

partner ['pɑːtnəʳ] N Partner(in) *m(f)*; *(in limited company also)* Gesellschafter(in) *m(f)*; *(in crime)* Komplize *m*, Komplizin *f*; **they were/became ~s in crime** sie waren/wurden Komplizen; **junior/senior ~** Junior-/Seniorpartner(in) *m(f)* VT **to ~ sb** jds Partner sein; **to be ~ed by sb** jdn zum Partner haben

partnership ['pɑːtnəʃɪp] N **a** Partnerschaft *f*, Gemeinschaft *f*; *(in sport, dancing etc)* Paar *nt*; **we're** *or* **we make a pretty good ~** wir sind ein ziemlich gutes Paar; **a relationship based on ~** eine partnerschaftliche Beziehung; **to do sth in ~ with sb** etw mit jdm gemeinsam *or* in Zusammenarbeit machen **b** *(Comm)* Personengesellschaft *f*; **to enter into a ~** in eine Gesellschaft eintreten; **to go into ~ with sb** mit jdm eine Personengesellschaft gründen; **general ~** offene Handelsgesellschaft; **he left the ~** er ist aus der Gesellschaft ausgeschieden

partook [pɑː'tʊk] *pret of* **partake**

part: **part owner** N Mitbesitzer(in) *m(f)*, Mitinhaber(in) *m(f)*; **part payment** N Teilzahlung *f*

partridge ['pɑːtrɪdʒ] N Rebhuhn *nt*

part: **part song** N *(= song)* mehrstimmiges Lied; *(= genre)* mehrstimmiger Gesang; **part-time** ADJ Teilzeit-; **~ job/worker** Teilzeitarbeit *f*/-arbeiter(in) *m(f)*; **I'm just ~** ich arbeite nur Teilzeit; **on a ~ basis** auf Teilzeitbasis; **~ employee** Teilzeitbeschäftigte(r) *mf* ADV **to work ~** Teilzeit arbeiten; **can I do the job ~?** kann ich (auf) Teilzeit arbeiten?; **she only teaches ~** sie unterrichtet nur stundenweise; **she is studying ~** sie ist Teilzeitstudentin; **part-timer** N Teilzeitbeschäftigte(r) *mf*

parturition [,pɑːtjʊə'rɪʃən] N *(form)* Entbindung *f*

partway [,pɑːt'weɪ] ADV *(inf: = halfway)* halb; **~ through the meal she became suspicious** mitten während des Essens schöpfte sie Verdacht

part work N *(printing)* Partwork *nt*, Lieferungswerk *nt*, Fortsetzungswerk *nt*

party ['pɑːtɪ] ✪ 25.2 N **a** *(Pol)* Partei *f*; **to be a member of the ~** Parteimitglied sein, in der Partei sein *(inf)*
b *(= group)* Gruppe *f*, Gesellschaft *f*; *(Mil)* Kommando *nt*, Trupp *m*; **a ~ of tourists** eine Reisegesellschaft; **we were a ~ of five** wir waren zu fünft; **I was one of the ~** ich war dabei; **to join sb's ~** sich jdm anschließen
c *(= celebration)* Party *f*, Fete *f (inf)*; *(more formal)* Gesellschaft *f*; **to have** *or* **give** *or* **throw** *(inf)* **a ~** eine Party geben *or* machen *or* schmeißen *(inf)*; **at the ~** auf der Party; *(more formal)* bei der Gesellschaft; **what does he bring to the ~?** *(fig)* was steuert er bei?
d *(Jur, fig)* Partei *f*; **a third ~** ein Dritter *m*; **the third ~** der Dritte; **the parties to a dispute** die streitenden Parteien; **to be a ~ to an agreement** einer Übereinkunft *(dat)* zustimmen; **to be a ~ to a crime** an einem Verbrechen beteiligt sein; **were you a ~ to this?** waren Sie daran beteiligt?
e *(inf: = person)* **a ~ by the name of Johnson** ein gewisser Johnson
VI *(inf)* feiern, eine Party machen; **let's go ~ing tonight** *(Brit)* **let's ~ tonight** *(US)* heute Abend machen wir einen drauf *(inf)*

party: **party chair** N *(also* **party chairman/-woman**) Parteivorsitzende(r) *mf*; **party dress** N Partykleid *nt*; **party drug** N Partydroge *f*; **partygoer** N Partygänger(in) *m(f)*, Fetengänger(in) *m(f)*; **party hat** N Partyhut *m*; **party line** N **a** *(Pol)* Parteilinie *f* **b** *(Telec)* Gemeinschaftsanschluss *m*; **party liner** N *(Pol)* linientreues Parteimitglied; **party man** N Gefolgsmann *m*; **party political** ADJ parteipolitisch; **party political broadcast** N parteipolitische Sendung; **party politics** PL Parteipolitik *f*; **party pooper** N *(inf)* Spaßverderber(in) *m(f) (inf)*; **party spirit** N **a** *(Pol)* Parteigeist *m or* -gesinnung *f* **b** *(= party mood)* Partylaune *f*; **to be in the ~** in Partylaune sein; **party spokesperson** N Parteisprecher(in) *m(f)*; **party ticket** N **a** *(Rail)* Gruppenfahrkarte *f* **b** *(US Pol)* (Kandidaten)liste *f* einer Partei

parvenu ['pɑːvənuː] N Emporkömmling *m*, Parvenü *m*

PASCAL ['pæs,kæl] N *(Comput)* PASCAL *nt*

paschal ['pæskəl] ADJ Passah-, Oster-; **~ feast** Passahfest *nt*

Paschal Lamb N Osterlamm *nt*

pas de deux ['pɑːdə'dɜː] N Pas de deux *m*

pasha ['pæʃə] N Pascha *m*

paso doble ['pæsəʊ'dəʊbleɪ] N Paso doble *m*

pass [pɑːs] N **a** *(= permit)* Ausweis *m*; *(Mil etc)* Passierschein *m*; **a free ~** eine Freikarte; *(permanent)* ein Sonderausweis *m*
b *(Brit Univ)* Bestehen *nt* einer Prüfung; **to get a ~ in German** seine Deutschprüfung bestehen; *(lowest level)* seine Deutschprüfung mit „ausreichend" bestehen; **I still need a ~ in physics** ich muss noch einen Abschluss in Physik machen
c *(Geog, Sport)* Pass *m*; *(Ftbl, for shot at goal)* Vorlage *f*
d *(Fencing)* Ausfall *m*
e *(= movement: by conjurer, hypnotist)* Bewegung *f*, Geste *f*; **the conjurer made a few quick ~es with his hand over the top of the hat** der Zauberer fuhr mit der Hand ein paar Mal schnell über dem Hut hin und her; **the text had a special hyphenation ~** der Text wurde eigens in Bezug auf Silbentrennung überprüft
f **things had come to such a ~ that …** die Lage hatte sich so zugespitzt, dass …; **things have come to a pretty ~ when …** so weit ist es schon gekommen, dass …; **this is a pretty ~!** das ist ja eine schöne Bescherung!
g **to make a ~ at sb** bei jdm Annäherungsversuche machen
h *(Aviat)* **the jet made three ~es over the ship** der Düsenjäger flog dreimal über das Schiff; **on its fourth ~ over the area the plane was almost hit** beim vierten Überfliegen des Gebietes wurde das Flugzeug fast getroffen; **the pilot made two ~es over the landing strip before deciding to come down** der Pilot passierte die Landebahn zweimal, ehe er sich zur Landung entschloss
VT **a** *(= move past)* vorbeigehen/-fahren/-fliegen an *(+dat)*; **he ~ed me without even saying hello** er ging ohne zu grüßen an mir vorbei; **the ship ~ed the mouth of the estuary** das Schiff passierte die Flussmündung
b *(= overtake) athlete, car* überholen; **he's ~ed all the other candidates** er hat alle anderen Kandidaten überflügelt
c *(= cross) frontier etc* überschreiten, überqueren, passieren; *deadline* überschreiten; **not a word ~ed her lips** kein Wort kam über ihre Lippen
d *(= reach, hand)* reichen; **they ~ed the photograph around** sie reichten *or* gaben das Foto herum; **~ (me) the salt, please** reich mir doch bitte das Salz!; **he ~ed the hammer up** er reichte den Hammer hinauf; **the characteristics which he ~ed to his son** die Eigenschaften, die er an seinen Sohn weitergab
e **it ~es belief** es ist kaum zu fassen; **it ~es my comprehension that …** es geht über meinen Verstand *or* meine Fassungskraft, dass …; **love which ~es all understanding** Liebe, die jenseits allen Verstehens liegt
f *(Univ etc) exam* bestehen; *candidate* bestehen lassen
g **this film will never ~ the censors** dieser Film kommt nie und nimmer durch die Zensur
h *(= approve) motion* annehmen; *plan* gutheißen, genehmigen; *(Parl)* verabschieden; **the censors will never ~ this film** die Zensur gibt diesen Film bestimmt nicht frei
i *(Sport)* **to ~ the ball to sb** jdm den Ball zuspielen; **you should learn to ~ the ball and not hang on to it** du solltest lernen abzuspielen, statt am Ball zu kleben
j *forged bank notes* weitergeben
k **he ~ed his hand across his forehead** er fuhr sich *(dat)* mit der Hand über die Stirn; **~ the thread through the hole** führen Sie den Faden durch die Öffnung; **he ~ed a chain around the front axle** er legte eine Kette um die Vorderachse
l *(= spend) time* verbringen; **he did it just to ~ the time** er tat das nur, um sich *(dat)* die Zeit zu vertreiben
m *remark* von sich geben; *opinion* abgeben; *(Jur) sentence* verhängen; *judgement* fällen; **to ~ comment (on sth)** einen Kommentar (zu etw) abgeben
n *(= discharge) excrement, blood* absondern, ausscheiden; **to ~ water** Wasser *or* Harn lassen
VI **a** *(= move past)* vorbeigehen/-fahren; **the street was too narrow for the cars to ~** die Straße war so eng, dass die Wagen nicht aneinander vorbeikamen; **we ~ed in the corridor** wir gingen im Korridor aneinander vorbei; **there isn't room for him to ~** es ist so eng, dass er nicht vorbeikommt
b *(= overtake)* überholen
c *(= move, go)* **no letters ~ed between them** sie wechselten keine Briefe; **words ~ed between them** es gab einige Meinungsverschiedenheiten; **what has ~ed between us** was sich zwischen uns zugetragen hat; **a knowing look ~ed between them** sie tauschten wissende Blicke aus; **if you ~ by the grocer's …** wenn du beim Kaufmann vorbeikommst …; **we ~ed by a line of hotels** wir kamen an einer Reihe Hotels vorbei; **the procession ~ed down the street** die Prozession zog die Straße entlang; **the cars ~ down the assembly line** die Autos kommen das Fließband herunter; **as we ~ from feudalism to more open societies** beim Übergang vom Feudalismus zu offeneren Gesellschaftsformen; **as we ~ from youth to old age** mit zunehmendem Alter; **the virus ~es easily from one person to another** der Virus ist leicht von einer Person auf die andere übertragbar; **people were ~ing in and out of the building** die Leute gingen in dem Gebäude ein und aus; **the land has now ~ed into private hands** das Land ist jetzt in Privatbesitz übergegangen; **to ~ into oblivion** in Vergessenheit geraten; **expressions which have ~ed into/out of the language** Redensarten, die in die Sprache eingegangen sind/aus der Sprache verschwunden sind; **to ~ into history/legend** in die Geschichte/Legende eingehen; **to ~ out of sight** außer Sichtweite geraten; **the firm has ~ed out of existence** die Firma hat aufgehört zu bestehen; **he ~ed out of our lives** er ist aus unserem Leben verschwunden; **everything he said just ~ed over my head** was er sagte, war mir alles zu hoch; **we're now ~ing over Paris** wir fliegen jetzt über Paris; **I'll just ~ quickly over the main points again** ich werde jetzt die Hauptpunkte noch einmal kurz durchgehen; **he's ~ing through a difficult period** er macht gerade eine schwere Zeit durch; **the manuscript has ~ed through a lot of hands** das Manuskript ist durch viele Hände gegangen; **the thread ~es through this hole** der Faden geht durch diese Öffnung; **you have to ~ through Berlin** Sie müssen über Berlin fahren; **shall we ~ to the second subject on the agenda?** wollen wir zum zweiten Punkt der Tagesordnung übergehen?; **the crown always ~es to the eldest son** die Krone geht immer auf den ältesten Sohn über; **the area then ~ed under Roman rule** das Gebiet geriet dann unter römische Herrschaft; **he ~ed under the archway** er ging/fuhr durch das Tor
d *(time: also* **pass by**) vergehen; *(deadline)* verfallen
e *(= disappear, end: anger, hope, era etc)* vorübergehen, vorbeigehen; *(storm) (= go over)* vorüberziehen; *(= abate)* sich legen; *(rain)* vorbeigehen; **to let an opportunity ~** eine Gelegenheit verstreichen lassen; **it'll ~** das geht vorüber!

f *(= be acceptable)* gehen; **to let sth ~** etw durchgehen lassen; **let it ~!** vergiss es!, vergessen wirs!; **it'll ~** das geht
g *(= be considered, be accepted)* angesehen werden *(for or as sth* als etw); **this little room has to ~ for an office** dieses kleine Zimmer dient als Büro; **in her day she ~ed for a great beauty** zu ihrer Zeit galt sie als große Schönheit; **she could easily ~ for 25** sie könnte leicht für 25 durchgehen; **or what ~es nowadays for a hat** oder was heute so als Hut betrachtet wird
h *(in exam)* bestehen; **I ~ed!** ich habe bestanden!; **did you ~ in chemistry?** hast du deine Chemieprüfung bestanden?
i *(Sport)* abspielen; **to ~ to sb** jdm zuspielen, an jdn abgeben
j *(Cards)* passen; **(I) ~!** (ich) passe!; **~** *(in quiz etc)* passe!; **I'll ~ on that** da passe ich
k *(old: = happen)* **to come to ~** sich begeben; **and it came to ~ in those days ...** und es begab sich zu jener Zeit ...; **to bring sth to ~** etw bewirken
l *(US euph: = die)* sterben

▶**pass away** VI **a** *(= end)* zu Ende gehen **b** *(euph: = die)* entschlafen, hinscheiden VT *sep hours* sich *(dat)* vertreiben

▶**pass by** VI *(= go past)* vorbeigehen; *(car etc)* vorbeifahren; *(time, months etc)* vergehen; **there was no room for the lorry to pass by** der Lastwagen kam nicht vorbei; **I can't let that pass by without comment** ich kann das nicht kommentarlos durchgehen lassen; **to pass by on the other side** *(fig)* achtlos vorbeigehen VT *sep (= ignore) problems* übergehen; **life has passed her by** das Leben ist an ihr vorübergegangen

▶**pass down** VT *sep* **a** *traditions* weitergeben *(to* an *+acc)*, überliefern *(to +dat)*; *characteristics* weitergeben *(to* an *+acc)*; **passed down by word of mouth** mündlich überliefert **b** *(= transmit)* **the story was passed down through the ranks** die Sache sprach sich (bis) zu den Soldaten durch

▶**pass off** VI **a** *(= take place)* ablaufen, vonstattengehen **b** *(= end)* vorüber- *or* vorbeigehen **c** *(= be taken as)* durchgehen *(as* als); **she could pass off as an Italian** sie würde als Italienerin durchgehen VT *sep* **to pass oneself/sb/sth off as sth** sich/jdn/etw als *or* für etw ausgeben

▶**pass on** VI **a** *(euph: = die)* entschlafen, verscheiden **b** *(= proceed)* übergehen *(to* zu); **right gentlemen, shall we pass on?** gut, meine Herren, wollen wir nun zum nächsten Punkt übergehen? VT *sep* **a** *news, information* weitergeben; *disease* übertragen; **pass it on!** weitersagen!; **take a leaflet and pass them on** nehmen Sie ein Blatt und geben Sie die anderen weiter; **we passed the information on to the police** wir gaben die Informationen an die Polizei weiter **b** *cost, savings* weitergeben, weiterreichen

▶**pass out** VI **a** *(= become unconscious)* in Ohnmacht fallen, umkippen *(inf)*; **he drank till he passed out** er trank bis zum Umfallen **b** *(new officer)* ernannt werden, sein Patent bekommen *(dated)* VT *sep leaflets* austeilen, verteilen

▶**pass over** VT *sep* übergehen; **he's been passed over again** er ist schon wieder übergangen worden; **to pass sth over in silence** etw stillschweigend übergehen VI *(euph: = die)* entschlafen

▶**pass through** VI **I'm only passing through** ich bin nur auf der Durchreise

▶**pass up** VT *sep chance* vorübergehen lassen

passable ['pɑːsəbl] ADJ **a** passierbar; *road etc* befahrbar, passierbar **b** *(= tolerable)* leidlich, passabel

passably ['pɑːsəblɪ] ADV *(+adj)* einigermaßen, leidlich; *(+vb)* ganz passabel; **she sings ~ well** sie singt ganz passabel

passage ['pæsɪdʒ] N **a** *(= transition: from youth to manhood etc)* Übergang *m*; **the ~ of time** der Verlauf *or* Strom *(geh)* der Zeit; **in** *or* **with the ~ of time** mit der Zeit
b *(through country)* Durchfahrt *f*, Durchreise *f*; *(= right of passage)* Durchreise *f*, Transit *m*, Durchreise- *or* Transitgenehmigung *f*; **to grant sb ~ through an area** jdm die Durchreise durch ein Gebiet genehmigen
c *(= voyage)* Überfahrt *f*, Schiffsreise *f*; *(= fare)* Überfahrt *f*, Passage *f* → **work**
d *(Parl: = process)* parlamentarische Behandlung; *(final)* Annahme *f*, Verabschiedung *f*
e *(= corridor)* Gang *m*; **the narrow ~ between Denmark and Sweden** die schmale Durchfahrt zwischen Dänemark und Schweden; **secret ~** Geheimgang *m*; **he forced a ~ through the crowd** er bahnte sich *(dat)* einen Weg durch die Menge
f *(in book)* Passage *f*; *(Mus)* Stück *nt*, Passage *f*; **a ~ from Shakespeare/the Bible** eine Shakespeare-/Bibelstelle

passageway ['pæsɪdʒweɪ] N Durchgang *m*

pass: **passbook** N Sparbuch *nt*; **passcard** N (digitale) Ausweiskarte *(auf der persönliche Daten und Passwörter gespeichert sind)*; *(Internet)* Passcard *f*; **pass degree** N *niedrigster Grad an britischen Universitäten*, „Bestanden"

passé ['pæseɪ] ADJ überholt, passé *(inf)*

passel ['pæsəl] N *(US inf: = group, quantity)* (Un)menge *f*; *(of people also)* Schar *f*

passenger ['pæsɪndʒəʳ] N **a** *(on bus, in taxi)* Fahrgast *m*; *(on train)* Reisende(r) *mf*; *(on ship)* Passagier(in) *m(f)*; *(on plane)* Fluggast *m*, Passagier(in) *m(f)*; *(in car)* Mitfahrer(in) *m(f)*, Beifahrer(in) *m(f)*; *(on motorcycle)* Beifahrer(in) *m(f)* **b** *(inf)* **we can't afford to carry any ~s** *(= incompetent people)* wir können es uns nicht leisten, Leute mit durchzuschleppen; *(= idle people)* wir können uns keine Drückeberger leisten; **he's just a ~ in the team** er wird von den anderen mit durchgeschleppt

passenger: **passenger aircraft** N Passagierflugzeug *nt*; **passenger door** N *(in car)* Beifahrertür *f*; **passenger ferry** N Personenfähre *f*; **passenger jet** N Passagierflugzeug *nt*; **passenger liner** N Passagierschiff *nt*; **passenger list** N Passagierliste *f*; **passenger mile** N *(Aviat)* Flugkilometer *m* je Fluggast; *(Rail)* Bahnkilometer *m* je Reisender; **passenger seat** N *(in car)* Beifahrersitz *m*; **passenger ship** N Passagierschiff *nt*; **passenger train** N Zug *m* im Personenverkehr

passe-partout ['pæspɑːtuː] N Passepartout *nt*

passer-by ['pɑːsə'baɪ] N *pl* **passers-by** Passant(in) *m(f)*, Vorübergehende(r) *mf*

passim ['pæsɪm] ADV passim, verstreut

passing ['pɑːsɪŋ] N **a** *(= going by)* Vorübergehen *nt*; *(of procession)* Passieren *nt*, Vorüberziehen *nt*; **a swirling wind accompanies the ~ of each train** ein wirbelnder Wind begleitet jeden vorbeifahrenden Zug; **with the ~ of time/the years** im Lauf(e) der Zeit/der Jahre; **I would like to mention in ~ that ...** ich möchte beiläufig noch erwähnen, dass ...
b *(= overtaking)* Überholen *nt*
c *(= disappearance)* Niedergang *m*; *(of customs)* Aussterben *nt*; *(euph: = death)* Heimgang *m*; **the ~ of the old year** der Ausklang des alten Jahres
d *(of deadline)* Überschreiten *nt*
e *(= transmission: of information)* Weitergabe *f*
f *(Ftbl)* Ballabgabe *f*
g *(Parl, of bill)* = **passage d**
ADJ **a** *car* vorbeifahrend; *clouds* vorüberziehend; *years* vergehend; **with every** *or* **each ~ day** mit jedem Tag, der vergeht
b *(= casual) glance, thought, interest* flüchtig; *comments* beiläufig; *fancy* flüchtig, vorübergehend; *fashion, fad* vorübergehend; **to make (a) ~ reference to sth** auf etw *(acc)* beiläufig hinweisen; **to bear a ~ resemblance to sb/sth** mit jdn/etw eine flüchtige Ähnlichkeit haben; **to have a ~ acquaintance with sb** jdn flüchtig kennen; **to have a ~ acquaintance with sth** flüchtige Kenntnis von etw haben
ADV *(old: = very)* gar *(old)*, überaus *(liter)*

passing: **passing lane** N *(Mot)* Überholspur *f*; **passing note** N Durchgangston *m*; **passing-out (ceremony)** N *(Mil)* Abschlussfeier *f*; **passing-out parade** N *(Mil)* Abschlussparade *f*; **passing place** N *(on narrow road)* Ausweichstelle *f*; **passing shot** N *(Tennis)* Passierball *m*

passion ['pæʃən] N **a** Leidenschaft *f*; *(= fervour)* Leidenschaftlichkeit *f*; *(= enthusiasm)* Begeisterung *f*, Leidenschaft *f*; **to have a ~ for sth** eine Passion *or* Leidenschaft für etw haben; **her ~ for oysters/all things Greek** ihre Passion *or* ausgeprägte Vorliebe für Austern/alles Griechische; **~s were running high** die Erregung schlug hohe Wellen; **his ~ for the cause** sein leidenschaftliches Engagement für die Sache; **music is a ~ with him** die Musik ist bei ihm eine Leidenschaft; **his ~ is Mozart** Mozart ist seine Passion; **to be in a ~** erregt sein; **to fly into a ~** in Erregung geraten, sich erregen
b *(Rel, Art, Mus)* Passion *f*; **St Matthew Passion** Matthäuspassion *f*

passionate ['pæʃənɪt] ADJ leidenschaftlich; **to be ~ about sth** für etw eine Leidenschaft haben

passionately ['pæʃənɪtlɪ] ADV leidenschaftlich; **oh yes, she said ~** o ja, sagte sie voller Leidenschaft; **she wept ~** sie weinte heiße Tränen; **to be ~ fond of sth** etw unwahrscheinlich gern haben; **to be ~ in love with sb** leidenschaftlich in jdn verliebt sein; **a ~ held belief** eine felsenfeste Überzeugung

passion: **passionflower** N Passionsblume *f*; *(hum inf, as address)* Schatz *m*, Schätzchen *nt*; **passion fruit** N Passionsfrucht *f*; **passionless** ADJ leidenschaftslos; **Passion play** N Passionsspiel *nt*; **Passion Sunday** N (erster) Passionssonntag; *(in Protestant church)* Sonntag *m* Judika; **Passion Week** N Karwoche *f*

passive ['pæsɪv] ADJ **a** passiv; *acceptance* widerspruchslos, widerstandslos **b** *(Gram)* passivisch, passiv, Passiv-; **~ form** Passivform *f* N *(Gram)* Passiv *nt*, Leideform *f*; **in the ~** im Passiv

passively ['pæsɪvlɪ] ADV passiv; *accept* widerstandslos, widerspruchslos; *watch etc* tatenlos

passiveness ['pæsɪvnɪs], **passivity** [pə'sɪvɪtɪ] N Passivität *f*

passive: **passive resistance** N passiver Widerstand; **passive smoker** N Passivraucher(in) *m(f)*, passiver Raucher, passive Raucherin; **passive smoking** N passives Rauchen, Passivrauchen *nt*; **passive vocabulary** N passiver Wortschatz

passkey ['pɑːskiː] N Hauptschlüssel *m*

Passover ['pɑːsəʊvəʳ] N Passah *nt*

passport ['pɑːspɔːt] N (Reise)pass *m*; *(fig)* Schlüssel *m (to* für, zu)

passport: **passport control** N Passkontrolle *f*; **passport holder** N Passinhaber(in) *m(f)*; **are you a British ~?** haben Sie einen britischen Pass?; **passport office** N *(= building, organization)* Passamt *nt*

password ['pɑːswɜːd] N Losungs- *or* Kennwort *nt*, Parole *f*; *(Comput)* Passwort *nt*

past [pɑːst] ADJ **a** frühe(r, s) *attr*, vergangene(r, s) *attr*; **for some time ~** seit einiger Zeit; **in times ~** in früheren *or* vergangenen Zeiten; **it's ~ history now** das gehört jetzt der Vergangenheit an; **all that is now ~** das ist jetzt alles vorüber *or* vorbei; **what's ~ is ~** was vorbei ist, ist vorbei; **in the ~ week** letzte *or* vorige *or* vergangene Woche, in der letzten *or* vergangenen Woche; **~ president** früherer Präsident
b *(Gram)* **~ tense** Vergangenheit *f*, Vergangenheitsform *f*
N **a** Vergangenheit *f*; **to learn the lessons of the ~** die Lehren aus der Vergangenheit ziehen; **in the ~** in der Vergangenheit, früher; **events in the recent ~ have shown that ...** die jüngsten Ereignisse haben gezeigt, dass ...; **to live in the ~** in der Vergangenheit leben; **to be a thing of the ~** der Vergangenheit *(dat)* angehören; **that's all in the ~ now** das ist jetzt alles

Vergangenheit; **a town/woman with a ~** eine Stadt/Frau mit Vergangenheit; **he was believed to have a "past"** man nahm an, dass er kein unbeschriebenes Blatt sei
b *(Gram)* Vergangenheit *f*, Präteritum *nt*; **the verb is in the ~** das Verb steht in der Vergangenheit
PREP **a** *(motion)* an *(+dat)* ... vorbei *or* vorüber; *(position: = beyond)* hinter *(+dat)*, nach *(+dat)*; **just ~ the library** kurz nach *or* hinter der Bücherei; **to run ~ sb** an jdm vorbeilaufen; **he stared straight ~ me** er starrte geradeaus an mir vorbei
b *(time)* nach *(+dat)*; **ten (minutes) ~ three** zehn (Minuten) nach drei; **half ~ four** halb fünf; **a quarter ~ nine** Viertel nach neun; **it's ~ 12** es ist schon nach 12 *or* 12 vorbei; **the trains run at a quarter ~ the hour** die Züge gehen jeweils um Viertel nach; **it's (well) ~ your bedtime** du solltest schon längst im Bett liegen
c *(= beyond)* über *(+acc)*; **~ forty** über vierzig; **the patient is ~ saving** der Patient ist nicht mehr zu retten; **we're ~ caring** es kümmert uns nicht mehr; **to be ~ sth** für etw zu alt sein; **my car is getting ~ it** *(inf)* mein Auto tuts allmählich nicht mehr, mein Auto bringts nicht mehr *(inf)*; **he's ~ it** *(inf)* er ist zu alt, er ist ein bisschen alt (dafür), er bringts nicht mehr *(sl)*; **she's getting a bit ~ it** *(inf)* sie wird allmählich alt; **I wouldn't put it ~ him** *(inf)* ich würde es ihm schon zutrauen
ADV vorbei, vorüber; **to walk ~** vorüber- *or* vorbeigehen; **to run ~** vorbeirennen

pasta [ˈpæstə] N Teigwaren *pl*, Nudeln *pl*

past anterior N *(Gram)* Vorvergangenheit *f*

paste [peɪst] **N** **a** *(for sticking)* Kleister *m*; **wallpaper ~** Tapetenkleister *m*
b **mix to a smooth/firm ~** *(glue etc)* zu einem lockeren/festen Brei anrühren; *(cake mixture etc)* zu einem glatten/festen Teig anrühren
c *(= spread)* Brotaufstrich *m*; *(= tomato paste)* Mark *nt*
d *(jewellery)* Similistein *m*, Strass *m*
VT **a** *(= apply paste to) wallpaper etc* einkleistern, mit Kleister bestreichen; *(= affix)* kleben; *(Comput) text etc* einfügen; **to ~ pictures into a book** Bilder in ein Buch (ein)kleben; **to ~ sth to sth** etw an etw *(acc)* kleben
b *(inf) opponent* fertigmachen *(inf)*; *new play etc* verreißen; **to ~ sb (one)** *(lit)* jdm eins vor den Latz knallen *(sl)*; **to ~ sb** *(= defeat)* jdn in die Pfanne hauen *(inf)*; **to ~ sth** *(fig)* etw verhackstücken *(inf)*

▶ **paste up** VT *sep* aufkleben, ankleben; *(in publishing)* einen Klebeumbruch machen von

pasteboard [ˈpeɪstbɔːd] N Karton *m*, Pappe *f*

pastedown [ˈpeɪstdaʊn] N *(bookbinding)* Vorsatz *m or nt*, Vorsatzblatt *nt*

pastel [ˈpæstl] **N** *(= crayon)* Pastellstift *m*, Pastellkreide *f*; *(= drawing)* Pastellzeichnung *f*, Pastell *nt*; *(= colour)* Pastellton *m* **ADJ** *attr* Pastell-, pastellfarben; **~ colour** *(Brit) or* **color** *(US)* Pastellfarbe *f*, Pastellton *m*; **~ drawing** Pastellzeichnung *f*

paste-up [ˈpeɪstʌp] N Klebeumbruch *m*

pasteurization [ˌpæstəraɪˈzeɪʃən] N Pasteurisierung *f*, Pasteurisation *f*

pasteurize [ˈpæstəraɪz] VT pasteurisieren, keimfrei machen

pastiche [pæˈstiːʃ] N Pastiche *m*; *(= satirical writing)* Persiflage *f*

pastille [ˈpæstɪl] N Pastille *f*

pastime [ˈpɑːstaɪm] N Zeitvertreib *m*

pastiness [ˈpeɪstɪnɪs] N **the ~ of her complexion** ihr blasses *or* kränkliches Aussehen

pasting [ˈpeɪstɪŋ] N *(inf)* **to take a ~ (from sb)** (von jdm) fertiggemacht werden *(inf)*; **to give sb a ~** jdn fertigmachen *(inf)*

past master N erfahrener Könner, erfahrene Könnerin; *(Art, Sport also)* Altmeister(in) *m(f)*; **to be a ~ at doing sth** ein Experte *m*/eine Expertin darin sein, etw zu tun

pastor [ˈpɑːstəˈ] N Pfarrer(in) *m(f)*, Pastor(in) *m(f) (esp N Ger)*

pastoral [ˈpɑːstərəl] **ADJ** **a** *land, farming, life* ländlich; *(Art, Liter, Mus)* pastoral; **Beethoven's Pastoral Symphony** Beethovens Pastorale *f*; **~ poem** Schäfer- *or* Hirtengedicht *nt*; **~ picture** Pastorale *f or nt* **b** *(Eccl)* pastoral, pfarramtlich; *duties, responsibility* seelsorgerisch; **~ staff** Bischofsstab *m*; **~ letter** Hirtenbrief *m* **N** **a** *(Liter, Art, Mus)* Pastorale *f or nt* **b** *(Eccl)* Hirtenbrief *m*

pastoral care N *(Eccl)* Seelsorge *f*

pastorale [ˌpæstəˈrɑːl] N *(Mus)* Pastorale *f*

past: **past participle** N Partizip Perfekt *nt*, zweites Partizip; **past perfect** N Plusquamperfekt *nt*, Vorvergangenheit *f*

pastrami N [pəˈstrɑːmɪ] *geräuchertes, stark gewürztes Rindfleisch*

pastry [ˈpeɪstrɪ] N Teig *m*; *(= cake etc)* Stückchen *nt*; **pastries** *pl* Gebäck *nt* → **Danish pastry**

pastry: **pastry brush** N Backpinsel *m*; **pastry case** N Törtchenform *f*; **pastry chef**, **pastry cook** N Konditor(in) *m(f)*; *(with higher qualification)* Konditormeister(in) *m(f)*

pasturage [ˈpɑːstjʊrɪdʒ] N **a** *(= grass)* Weide *f* **b** *(= right of pasture)* Weiderecht *nt*

pasture [ˈpɑːstʃəˈ] **N** **a** *(= field)* Weide *f*; **to put out to ~** auf die Weide treiben; *(fig inf, employee)* aufs Abstellgleis schieben; **greener ~s** *(fig)* bessere Weidegründe; **to move on to ~s new** *(fig)* sich *(dat)* etwas Neues suchen, sich nach neuen Weidegründen *(geh)* umsehen; **to seek ~s new** *(fig)* nach neuen Weidegründen suchen
b *no pl* (*also* **pasture land**) Weideland *nt*
c *no pl (= food)* Futter *nt* **VT** *animals* weiden lassen **VI** grasen

pasty¹ [ˈpeɪstɪ] ADJ **a** *consistency* zähflüssig **b** *colour* blässlich; *look* blass, kränklich

pasty² [ˈpæstɪ] N *(esp Brit)* Pastete *f*

pasty-faced [ˈpeɪstɪˈfeɪst] ADJ blass- *or* bleichgesichtig

Pat [pæt] N *(sl)* Ire *m*

pat¹ [pæt] N *(of butter)* Portion *f*; **cow ~** Kuhfladen *m*

pat² **ADV** **to know** *or* **have sth off ~** etw wie am Schnürchen *(inf) or* wie aus dem Effeff *(inf)* können; **he knows the rules off ~** er kennt die Regeln in- und auswendig *or* aus dem Effeff *(inf)*; **to learn sth off ~** etw in- und auswendig lernen; **he's always got an answer off ~** er hat immer eine Antwort parat; **to stand ~** keinen Zollbreit nachgeben **ADJ** *answer, explanation* glatt; **somehow his excuses seem a bit ~ to me** er ist mir immer ein bisschen zu schnell mit Ausreden bei der Hand

pat³ **N** Klaps *m*; **he gave his nephew a ~ on the head** er tätschelte seinem Neffen den Kopf; **excellent work, said the teacher, giving her a ~ on the shoulder** hervorragende Arbeit, sagte der Lehrer und klopfte ihr auf die Schulter; **he gave her knee an affectionate ~** er tätschelte ihr liebevoll das Knie; **to give one's horse/the dog a ~** sein Pferd/ seinen Hund tätscheln; *(once)* seinem Pferd/Hund einen Klaps geben; **to give sb/oneself a ~ on the back** *(fig)* jdm/sich selbst auf die Schulter klopfen; **that's a ~ on the back for you** das ist ein Kompliment für dich
VT *(= touch lightly)* tätscheln; *(= hit gently) ball* leicht schlagen; *sand* festklopfen; *face* abtupfen; **to ~ sb/the dog on the head** jdm/dem Hund den Kopf tätscheln; **to ~ sth/one's face dry** etw/sein Gesicht trocken tupfen; **she ~ted a few loose curls into place** sie drückte ein paar Locken an, die sich gelöst hatten; **the sculptor ~ted the plaster into shape** der Bildhauer klopfte den Gips in die richtige Form; **he ~ted aftershave onto his face** er betupfte sein Gesicht mit Rasierwasser; **to ~ sb on the back** *(lit)* jdm auf den Rücken klopfen; **to ~ sb/oneself on the back** *(fig)* jdm/sich selbst auf die Schulter klopfen

▶ **pat down** VT *sep* festklopfen; *hair* festdrücken, andrücken

pat⁴ *abbr of* **patent**

Patagonia [ˌpætəˈgəʊnɪə] N Patagonien *nt*

Patagonian [ˌpætəˈgəʊnɪən] **ADJ** patagonisch **N** Patagonier(in) *m(f)*

patch [pætʃ] **N** **a** *(for mending)* Flicken *m*; *(on new garments)* Flecken *m*; *(= eye patch)* Augenklappe *f*
b **it's/he's not a ~ on ...** *(Brit inf)* das/er ist gar nichts gegen ...
c *(= small area, stain)* Fleck *m*; *(= piece of land)* Stück *nt*; *(= subdivision of garden)* Beet *nt*; *(= part, section)* Stelle *f*; *(of time)* Phase *f*; *(inf, of policeman, prostitute)* Revier *nt*; **a ~ of blue sky** ein Stückchen *nt* blauer Himmel; **purple ~es on the skin** violette Flecke auf der Haut; **~es of colour** Farbtupfer *pl*; **a ~ of oil** ein Ölfleck *m*; **~es of sunlight dappled the floor of the forest** (die) Sonnenstrahlen tanzten auf dem Waldboden; **the cabbage ~** das Kohlbeet; **we drove through a few ~es of rain on our way here** wir hatten auf dem Weg stellenweise Regen; **there were sunny ~es during the day** hin und wieder schien die Sonne; **he's going through a bad** *or* **rough ~ at the moment** ihm gehts im Augenblick nicht sonderlich gut
d *(= contraceptive)* Hormonpflaster *nt*; **are you on the ~?** benutzt du ein Hormonpflaster?
e *(Comput)* Korrekturroutine *f*
VT flicken; **this piece of cloth will just ~ that hole nicely** dieses Stück Stoff ist gerade richtig für das Loch; **a new government was hastily ~ed together** in aller Eile wurde eine neue Regierung zusammengeflickt *or* -gestückelt

▶ **patch up** VT *sep* zusammenflicken; *quarrel* beilegen; **to patch things up temporarily** die Dinge notdürftig zusammenflicken; **they managed to patch up their relationship** sie haben sich schließlich wieder ausgesöhnt; **I want to patch things up between us** ich möchte unsere Beziehung wieder ins Lot bringen

patchiness [ˈpætʃɪnɪs] N *(of work)* Unregelmäßigkeit *f*; *(of knowledge)* Lückenhaftigkeit *f*; *(of film, book, essay etc)* unterschiedliche Qualität

patch: **patch kit** N Flickzeug *nt*; **patch pocket** N aufgesetzte Tasche; **patch-up** N *(inf)* Flickwerk *nt no art*; **patchwork** [ˈpætʃwɜːk] N Patchwork *nt*; **~ quilt** Patchwork- *or* Flickendecke *f*; *(fig)* **a ~ of fields** ein Mosaik *nt* von Feldern

patchy [ˈpætʃɪ] ADJ *(+er)* **a** *work* ungleichmäßig, unterschiedlich; *knowledge, memory, evidence* lückenhaft; **what was the performance like? – ~** wie war die Aufführung? – gemischt; **his second novel however was much patchier** sein zweiter Roman war wesentlicher unausgeglichener; **this is the patchiest production I've seen them do for a long time** eine derart ungleichmäßige Inszenierung habe ich von ihnen lange nicht mehr gesehen; **what's his work like? – ~** wie ist seine Arbeit? – unterschiedlich
b *(lit) material* gefleckt; *beard, grass* licht; **~ fog on the coast** an der Küste stellenweise Nebel; **the ~ appearance of the half rebuilt city** der Eindruck von Flickwerk, den die zur Hälfte neu aufgebaute Stadt vermittelt

pate [peɪt] N Rübe *f (inf)*, Birne *f (inf)*; **bald ~** Platte *f (inf)*, Glatze *f*

pâté [ˈpæteɪ] N Pastete *f*

patella [pəˈtelə] N *(Anat)* Patella *f (spec)*, Kniescheibe *f*

paten [ˈpætən] N *(Eccl)* Patene *f*, Hostienteller *m*

patent [ˈpeɪtənt] **N** Patent *nt*; **~ applied for** *or* **pending** Patent angemeldet; **to take out a ~ on sth** etw *(acc)* patentieren lassen **VT** patentieren lassen; **is it ~ed?** ist das patentrechtlich geschützt? **ADJ** **a** *(= obvious)* offensichtlich **b** *(= patented) invention* patentiert; **he's got his own ~ method of doing it** *(fig)* dafür hat er seine Spezialmethode; **his ~ remedy for hangovers** *(fig)* sein Patent- *or* Spezialrezept gegen Kater

patentable [ˈpeɪtəntəbl] ADJ patentierbar, patentfähig

patent: **patent application** N Patentanmeldung *f*; **patent attorney** N Patentanwalt *m*/-anwältin *f*

patentee [ˌpeɪtənˈtiː] N Patentinhaber(in) *m(f)*

patent: **patent holder** N Patentinhaber(in) *m(f)*; **patent leather** N Lackleder *nt*; **~ shoes** Lackschuhe *pl*

patently [ˈpeɪtəntlɪ] ADV offenkundig, offensichtlich; **~ obvious/clear** ganz offensichtlich/klar; **I would have thought that was ~ obvious** ich würde meinen, das liegt doch auf der Hand

patent: **patent medicine** N patentrechtlich geschütztes Arzneimittel; **Patent Office** N Patentamt *nt*

patentor [ˌpeɪtənˈtɔːˈ] N Patentgeber(in) *m(f)*

pater [ˈpeɪtəˈ] N *(dated Brit inf)* Herr Vater *(dated)*

paterfamilias [ˈpɑːtəfəˈmiːlɪəs] N Familienvater *m*, Paterfamilias *m (geh)*

paternal [pəˈtɜːnl] ADJ väterlich; **my ~ uncle/grandmother** *etc* mein Onkel *m*/meine Großmutter *etc* väterlicherseits

paternalism [pəˈtɜːnəlɪzəm] N Bevormundung *f*

paternalist [pəˈtɜːnəlɪst] N Patriarch *m*

paternalist(ic) [pəˈtɜːnəlɪst, pəˌtɜːnəˈlɪstɪk] ADJ, **paternalistically** [pəˈtɜːnəˈlɪstɪkəlɪ] ADV patriarchalisch

paternally [pəˈtɜːnəlɪ] ADV väterlich

paternity [pəˈtɜːnɪtɪ] N Vaterschaft *f*; **he denied ~ of the child** er bestritt die Vaterschaft an dem Kind

paternity leave N Vaterschaftsurlaub *m*

paternity suit N Vaterschaftsprozess *m*

paternoster [ˈpætəˈnɒstəˈ] N *(= prayer)* Vaterunser *nt*, Paternoster *nt*; *(= paternoster bead)* Vaterunserperle *f*; *(= lift)* Paternoster *m*

path [pɑːθ] N **a** *(lit) (trodden)* Weg *m*, Pfad *m*; *(surfaced)* Weg *m*; *(in field)* Feldweg *m*; **we took a ~ across the fields** wir nahmen den Weg über das Feld **b** *(= trajectory, route)* Bahn *f*; *(of hurricane)* Weg *m* **c** *(fig)* Weg *m*; **the Christian ~** der Weg des Christentums; **the ~ of** *or* **to salvation** der Weg des Heils; **the ~ of virtue** der Pfad der Tugend **d** *(Comput)* Pfad *m*

path-breaking [ˈpɑːθˌbreɪkɪŋ] ADJ *(esp US)* bahnbrechend

pathetic [pəˈθetɪk] ADJ **a** *(= piteous)* mitleiderregend; **the exhausted refugees made a ~ sight** die erschöpften Flüchtlinge boten ein Bild des Jammers; **it was ~ to see** es war ein Bild des Jammers **b** *(= poor)* erbärmlich, jämmerlich; **it's ~** es ist zum Weinen *or* Heulen *(inf)*; **what a ~ bunch they are!** oh, was ist das für ein jämmerlicher Haufen!; **honestly you're ~, can't you even boil an egg?** ehrlich, dich kann man zu nichts brauchen, kannst du nicht einmal ein Ei kochen? **c the ~ fallacy** die Vermenschlichung der Natur

pathetically [pəˈθetɪkəlɪ] ADV **a** *(= piteously)* mitleiderregend; **he limped along ~** es war ein mitleiderregender Anblick, wie er einherhumpelte; **~ thin/weak** erschreckend dünn/schwach

b *slow, stupid, inefficient* erbärmlich; **a ~ inadequate answer** eine äußerst dürftige Antwort; **a ~ weak attempt** ein kläglicher Versuch; **~ incapable** absolut unfähig; **the goalie dived ~ late** es war zum Weinen, wie spät sich der Torwart nach dem Ball warf; **the trains are ~ late** es ist zum Weinen *or* ein Jammer, wie unpünktlich die Züge sind; **it had become ~ obvious that she was ignoring him** es war schon peinlich zu sehen, wie sie ihn ignorierte

path: **pathfinder** N *(lit)* Führer(in) *m(f)*; *(fig: = innovator)* Wegbereiter(in) *m(f)*; **pathless** ADJ weglos; **path name** N *(Comput)* Pfad(name) *m*

pathogen [ˈpæθədʒɪn] N *(Med)* Krankheitserreger *m*

pathogenic [ˌpæθəˈdʒenɪk] ADJ pathogen, krankheitserregend

pathological [ˌpæθəˈlɒdʒɪkəl] ADJ *(lit, fig)* pathologisch, krankhaft; *studies etc* pathologisch

pathologically [ˌpæθəˈlɒdʒɪkəlɪ] ADV *jealous, violent* krankhaft

pathologist [pəˈθɒlədʒɪst] N Pathologe *m*, Pathologin *f*

pathology [pəˈθɒlədʒɪ] N *(science)* Pathologie *f*; **the ~ of a disease** das Krankheitsbild

pathos [ˈpeɪθɒs] N Pathos *nt*

pathway [ˈpɑːθweɪ] N = **path a**

patience [ˈpeɪʃəns] N **a** Geduld *f*; **to have ~/no ~ (with sb/sth)** Geduld/keine Geduld (mit jdm/etw) haben; **to have no ~ with sb/sth** *(fig inf: = dislike)* für jdn/etw nichts übrighaben; **to lose (one's) ~ (with sb/sth)** (mit jdm/etw) die Geduld verlieren; **to try** *or* **test sb's ~** jds Geduld auf die Probe stellen; **~ is a virtue** *(prov)* Geduld ist eine Tugend; **~, ~!** nur Geduld!, immer mit der Ruhe! → **possess b** *(Brit Cards)* Patience *f*; **to play ~** eine Patience legen

patient [ˈpeɪʃənt] ADJ geduldig; **to be ~ with sb/sth** mit jdm/etw geduldig sein; **you must be very ~ about it** du musst sehr viel Geduld haben *or* sehr geduldig sein; **we have been ~ long enough!** unsere Geduld ist erschöpft!; **his years of ~ work paid off** seine jahrelange geduldige Arbeit zahlte sich aus; **~ endurance** zähe Geduld N Patient(in) *m(f)*; **cancer/heart ~** Krebs-/Herzpatient(in) *m(f)*

patiently [ˈpeɪʃəntlɪ] ADV geduldig; **to wait ~** geduldig warten; **a very ~ reconstructed picture of Babylonian life** ein mit Akribie rekonstruiertes Bild babylonischer Lebensweise

patina [ˈpætɪnə] N *(lit, fig)* Patina *f*

patio [ˈpætɪəʊ] N Veranda *f*, Terrasse *f*; *(= inner court)* Innenhof *m*, Patio *m*; **~ door(s)** Terrassentür *f*

patisserie [pəˈtiːsərɪ] N **a** *(= pastry shop)* Konditorei *f* **b** *(= pastries)* Feingebäck *nt*

patois [ˈpætwɑː] N Mundart *f*

patriarch [ˈpeɪtrɪɑːk] N Patriarch *m*

patriarchal [ˌpeɪtrɪˈɑːkəl] ADJ patriarchalisch

patriarchy [ˈpeɪtrɪˈɑːkɪ] N Patriarchat *nt*

patrician [pəˈtrɪʃən] ADJ patrizisch; **the ~ classes** das Patriziertum; **the old ~ houses** die alten Patrizierhäuser N Patrizier(in) *m(f)*

patricide [ˈpætrɪsaɪd] N Vatermord *m*; *(= murderer)* Vatermörder(in) *m(f)*

patrimony [ˈpætrɪmənɪ] N Patrimonium *nt*

patriot [ˈpeɪtrɪət] N Patriot(in) *m(f)*

patriotic ADJ, **patriotically** ADV [ˌpætrɪˈɒtɪk, -əlɪ] patriotisch

patriotism [ˈpætrɪətɪzəm] N Patriotismus *m*, Vaterlandsliebe *f*

patrol [pəˈtrəʊl] N **a** *(= patrolling) (by police)* Streife *f*; *(by aircraft, ship)* Patrouille *f*; *(by watchman etc)* Runde *f*, Rundgang *m*; **the army/navy carry out** *or* **make weekly ~s of the area** das Heer/die Marine patrouilliert das Gebiet wöchentlich; **the army/navy maintain a constant ~** das Heer/die Marine führt ständige Patrouillen durch; **on ~** *(Mil)* auf Patrouille; *(police)* auf Streife; *(guard dogs, squad car, detectives)* im Einsatz

b *(= patrol unit) (Mil)* Patrouille *f*; *(= police patrol)* (Polizei)streife *f*; *(of boy scouts)* Fähnlein *nt*; *(of girl guides)* Gilde *f*

VT *(Mil) district, waters, sky, streets* patrouillieren, patrouillieren in *(+dat)*; *frontier, coast* patrouillieren, patrouillieren vor *(+dat)*; *(policeman, watchman)* seine Runden machen in *(+dat)*; *(police car)* Streife fahren in *(+dat)*; *(guard dogs, gamewarden)* einen Rund- *or* Streifengang *or* eine Runde machen in *(+dat)*; **the frontier is not ~led** die Grenze wird nicht bewacht *or* ist unbewacht

VI *(soldiers, ships, planes)* patrouillieren; *(planes also)* Patrouille fliegen; *(policeman)* seine Streife machen; *(watchman, store detective etc)* seine Runden machen; **to ~ up and down** auf und ab gehen

patrol: **patrol boat** N Patrouillenboot *nt*; **patrol car** N Streifenwagen *m*; **patrol leader** N *(of scouts)* Fähnleinführer *m*; *(of girl guides)* Gildenführerin *f*; **patrolman** N Wächter *m*; *(US: = policeman)* Polizist *m*; **patrol wagon** N *(US)* grüne Minna *(inf)*, Gefangenenwagen *m*; **patrolwoman** N Wächterin *f*; *(US: = policewoman)* Polizistin *f*

patron [ˈpeɪtrən] N *(= customer of shop)* Kunde *m*, Kundin *f*; *(= customer of restaurant, hotel)* Gast *m*; *(of society)* Schirmherr(in) *m(f)*; *(of artist)* Förderer *m*, Förderin *f*, Gönner(in) *m(f)*; *(= patron saint)* Schutzpatron(in) *m(f)*; **~s only** nur für Kunden/Gäste; **~ of the arts** Kunstmäzen(in) *m(f)*; **our ~s** *(of shop)* unsere Kundschaft

patronage [ˈpætrənɪdʒ] N **a** *(= support)* Schirmherrschaft *f*; **under the ~ of ...** unter der Schirmherrschaft von ...; **his lifelong ~ of the arts** seine lebenslange Förderung der Künste

b *(form, of a shop etc)* **we enjoy the ~ of ...** zu unseren Kunden zählen ...; **we thank you for your ~** wir danken Ihnen für Ihr Vertrauen; **the attitude of the new sales assistant caused her to withdraw her ~** das Benehmen des neuen Verkäufers veranlasste sie, dort nicht mehr einzukaufen

c *(= right to appoint to government jobs)* Patronat *nt*; **under (the) ~ of** unter der Schirmherrschaft von

d *(rare: = condescension)* **an air of ~** eine gönnerhafte Miene

patroness [ˈpeɪtrənes] N *(= sponsor)* Gönnerin *f*; **~ of the arts** Kunstmäzenin *f*

patronize [ˈpætrənaɪz] VT **a** *pub, cinema etc* besuchen; **I hope you will continue to ~ our store** ich hoffe, dass Sie uns weiterhin beehren; **it's not a shop I ~** in dem Geschäft kaufe ich nicht; **the shop is well ~d** das Geschäft hat viel Kundschaft **b** *(= treat condescendingly)* gönnerhaft *or* herablassend behandeln, von oben herab behandeln **c** *(= support) the arts etc* unterstützen, fördern

patronizing [ˈpætrənaɪzɪŋ] ADJ gönnerhaft, herablassend; **to be ~ to** *or* **toward(s) sb** jdn herablassend *or* von oben herab behandeln; **there's no need to be so ~** du brauchst gar nicht so herablassend *or* von oben herab zu tun

patronizingly [ˈpætrənaɪzɪŋlɪ] ADV gönnerhaft, herablassend; **a ~ tolerant attitude** herablassende Nachsicht

patron saint [ˌpeɪtrənˈseɪnt] N *(of church etc)* Schutzpatron(in) *m(f)*, Schutzheilige(r) *mf*

patronymic [ˌpætrəˈnɪmɪk] ADJ patronymisch N Patronymikon *nt*, Vatersname *m*

patsy [ˈpætsɪ] N *(US inf) (= scapegoat)* Sündenbock *m*; *(= easy victim)* Leichtgläubige(r) *mf*; *(= weak man)* Schlappschwanz *m (inf)*, Schwächling *m*

patten [ˈpætən] N Stelzenschuh *m*

patter [ˈpætəˈ] N **a** *(of feet)* Getrippel *nt*; *(of rain)* Platschen *nt*; **the ~ of tiny feet** *(fig)* Kindergetrappel *nt* **b** *(of salesman, comedian, conjurer, disc jockey)* Sprüche *pl (inf)*; **to start one's ~** seine Sprüche loslassen; **you'll never pick up a girl unless you're good with the ~** *(inf)* du wirst nie eine Freundin aufreißen, wenn du nicht gut quatschen kannst *(inf)*; **to have a good line in ~** *(of comedian, disc jockey etc)* gute Sprüche draufhaben *or* auf Lager haben *(inf)*; **sales ~** Vertretersprüche *pl* **c** *(inf: = jargon)* Fachjargon *m (inf)* VI *(person, feet)* trippeln; *(rain: also* **patter down***)* platschen

patter-merchant [ˈpætəˌmɜːtʃənt] N *(Brit inf)* Schönredner(in) *m(f)*, Sprücheklopfer(in) *m(f)* *(inf)*

pattern [ˈpætən] N **a** Muster *nt*; **to make a ~** ein Muster bilden

b *(Sew)* Schnitt *m*, Schnittmuster *nt*; *(Knitting)* Strickanleitung *f*

c *(fig: = model)* Vorbild *nt*; **according to a ~** nach einem (festen) Schema; **on the ~ of Albania, on the Albanian ~** nach albanischem Vorbild *or* Muster; **to set a** *or* **the ~ for sth** ein

Muster *or* Vorbild für etw sein
d (*fig: in events, behaviour etc*) Muster *nt*; (*set*) Schema *nt*; (*recurrent*) Regelmäßigkeit *f*; **there's a distinct ~/no ~ to these crimes** in diesen Verbrechen steckt ein bestimmtes Schema/kein Schema; **what ~ can we find in these events?** was verbindet diese Ereignisse?; **the ~ of events leading up to the war** der Ablauf der Ereignisse, die zum Krieg geführt haben; **a certain ~ emerged** es ließ sich ein gewisses Schema *or* Muster erkennen; **behaviour ~s** Verhaltensmuster *pl*; **eating/sleeping ~s** Ess-/Schlafverhalten *nt*; **the natural ~ of life in the wild** die natürlichen Lebensvorgänge in der Wildnis; **the daily ~ of his existence** die tägliche Routine seines Lebens; **to follow the usual/same ~** nach dem üblichen/gleichen Schema verlaufen; **the town's new buildings follow the usual ~ of concrete and glass** die Neubauten der Stadt entsprechen dem üblichen Baustil aus Beton und Glas; **it's the usual ~, the rich get richer and the poor get poorer** es läuft immer nach demselben Muster ab - die Reichen werden reicher und die Armen ärmer
e (*= verb pattern, sentence pattern etc*) Struktur *f*
VT **a** (*esp US: = model*) machen (*on* nach); **this design is ~ed on one I saw in a magazine** die Idee für dieses Muster habe ich aus einer Illustrierten; **many countries ~ their laws on the Roman system** viele Länder orientieren sich bei ihrer Gesetzgebung an dem römischen Vorbild; **to be ~ed on sth** einer Sache (*dat*) nachgebildet sein; (*music, poem, style etc*) einer Sache (*dat*) nachempfunden sein; **to ~ oneself on sb** sich (*dat*) jdn zum Vorbild nehmen; **he ~ed his lifestyle on that of a country squire** er ahmte den Lebensstil eines Landadligen nach
b (*= put patterns on*) mit einem Muster versehen → *also* **patterned**

pattern book N Musterbuch *nt*

patterned [ˈpætənd] ADJ gemustert

pattern matching N (*esp Comput*) Mustervergleich *m*

patty [ˈpætɪ] N (*esp US*) Pastetchen *nt*

paucity [ˈpɔːsɪtɪ] N (*liter*) Mangel *m* (*of* an +*dat*)

Paul [pɔːl] N Paul *m*; (*Bibl*) Paulus *m*

Pauline [ˈpɔːlaɪn] ADJ paulinisch

paunch [pɔːntʃ] N Bauch *m*, Wanst *m*; (*of cow etc*) Pansen *m*

paunchy [ˈpɔːntʃɪ] ADJ (+*er*) dick

pauper [ˈpɔːpəʳ] N Arme(r) *mf*; (*supported by charity*) Almosenempfänger(in) *m(f)*; **~'s grave** Armengrab *nt*

pauperism [ˈpɔːpərɪzəm] N (*lit, fig*) Armut *f*

pauperization [ˌpɔːpəraɪˈzeɪʃən] N Verarmung *f*; (*fig also*) Verkümmerung *f*

pauperize [ˈpɔːpəraɪz] VT arm machen; (*fig*) verkümmern lassen

pause [pɔːz] **N** Pause *f*; **a hesitant ~** ein kurzes Zögern; **an anxious/a pregnant ~** ein ängstliches/vielsagendes Schweigen; **there was a ~ while …** es entstand eine Pause, während …; **to have a ~** (eine) Pause machen; **without (a) ~** ohne Unterbrechung, pausenlos, ununterbrochen; **to give sb ~ (for thought)** (*esp liter*) jdm zu denken geben, jdn nachdenklich stimmen
VI **a** (*= stop for a short while*) stehen bleiben, stoppen (*inf*); (*speaker*) innehalten; **can't we ~ for a bit, I'm exhausted** können wir nicht eine kurze Pause machen, ich bin erschöpft; **he ~d dramatically** er legte eine Kunstpause ein; **~ before you act** überlege erst mal, bevor du etwas tust; **he ~d for breath/for a drink** er machte eine Pause, um Luft zu holen/etwas zu trinken; **to ~ for thought** (zum Nachdenken) innehalten; **he spoke for thirty minutes without once pausing** er sprach eine halbe Stunde ohne eine einzige Pause; **let's ~ here** machen wir hier Pause; **it made him ~** das machte ihn nachdenklich
b (*= dwell on*) **to ~ (up)on sth** auf etw (*acc*) näher eingehen
VT *video, tape etc* anhalten

pave [peɪv] VT befestigen (*in, with* mit); *road, path (with stones also)* pflastern; *floor (with tiles)* fliesen, mit Fliesen auslegen; (*with slabs*) mit Platten auslegen; **to ~ the way for sb/sth** (*fig*) jdm/einer Sache (*dat*) den Weg ebnen; **where the streets are ~d with gold** wo die Straßen mit Gold gepflastert sind, wo das Geld auf der Straße liegt; **the path to hell is ~d with good intentions** (*prov*) der Weg zur Hölle ist mit guten Vorsätzen gepflastert (*prov*); **the paths are ~d in** *or* **with purest marble** die Wege sind mit feinstem Marmor ausgelegt

▶ **pave over** VT *sep* betonieren; (*with slabs*) mit Platten auslegen

pavement [ˈpeɪvmənt] N (*Brit*) Gehsteig *m*, Bürgersteig *m*, Trottoir *nt*; (*US: = paved road*) Straße *f*; (*= material*) Bodenbelag *m*; **to leave the ~** (*US Aut*) von der Straße abkommen; **~ artist** Pflastermaler(in) *m(f)*

pavilion [pəˈvɪlɪən] N Pavillon *m*; (*old: = tent*) Zelt *nt*; (*Brit Sport*) (*= changing pavilion*) Umkleideräume *pl*; (*= clubhouse*) Klubhaus *nt*

paving [ˈpeɪvɪŋ] N Belag *m*; (*US: of road*) Decke *f*; (*= material*) Belag *m*; (*= action*) Pflastern *nt*; **~ stone** (Stein)platte *f*, Pflasterstein *m*; **~ tile** Fliese *f*

pavlova [ˈpævləvə] N (*Cook*) Baiser *nt* Pawlowa

Pavlovian [pævˈləʊvɪən] ADJ pawlowsch *attr*

paw[1] [pɔː] **N** (*of animal*) Pfote *f*; (*of lion, bear*) Pranke *f*, Tatze *f*; (*pej inf: = hand*) Pfote *f* (*inf*); **keep your ~s off!** Pfoten weg! (*inf*) **VT** **a** (*= touch*) tätscheln; (*lion etc*) mit der Pfote *or* Tatze berühren; **to ~ the ground** (*lit*) scharren **b** (*pej inf: = handle*) betatschen (*inf*) **VI** **to ~ at sb/sth** jdn/etw betätscheln *or* betatschen (*inf*)

paw[2] N (*US dial inf*) Pa *m* (*inf*)

pawl [pɔːl] N Sperrklinke *f*

pawn[1] [pɔːn] N (*Chess*) Bauer *m*; (*fig*) Schachfigur *f*

pawn[2] **N** (*= security*) Pfand *nt*; **in ~** verpfändet, versetzt; **to leave** *or* **put sth in ~** etw versetzen *or* auf die Pfandleihe *or* ins Leihhaus bringen; **the company is in ~ to foreigners** das Unternehmen ist an ausländische Kapitalgeber verpfändet **VT** verpfänden, versetzen

pawn: **pawnbroker** N Pfandleiher(in) *m(f)*; **pawnbroker's (shop)**, **pawnshop** N Pfandhaus *nt*, Leihhaus *nt*; **pawn ticket** N Pfandschein *m*, Leihschein *m*

pawpaw [ˈpɔːpɔː] N Papaya *f*

pax [pæks] INTERJ (*Brit*) Friede

pay [peɪ] *vb: pret, ptp* **paid** **N** Lohn *m*; (*of salaried employee*) Gehalt *nt*; (*Mil*) Sold *m*; (*of civil servant*) Gehalt *nt*, Bezüge *pl*, Besoldung *f*; **three months' ~** drei Monatslöhne; (*of salaried employees*) drei Monatsgehälter; **what's the ~ like?** wie ist die Bezahlung?; **it comes out of my ~** es wird mir vom Gehalt/Lohn abgezogen; **to be suspended on half/full ~** bei halben/vollen Bezügen vom Dienst suspendiert sein; **a low-~ country** ein Land mit niedrigen Löhnen, ein Niedriglohnland; **the discussions were about ~** in den Diskussionen ging es um die Löhne/Gehälter; **to be in sb's ~** für jdn arbeiten
VT **a** zahlen; *person, bill, debt, account* bezahlen; *dividend* ausschütten, zahlen; **to ~ sb £10 (for sth)** jdm £ 10 (für etw) zahlen; **to ~ shareholders** Dividenden ausschütten *or* zahlen; **how much is there still to ~?** wie viel steht noch aus?; **to be** *or* **get paid** (*in regular job*) seinen Lohn/sein Gehalt bekommen; **when do I get paid for doing that?** wann bekomme ich mein Geld dafür?, wann werde ich dafür bezahlt?; **savings accounts that ~ 5%** Sparkonten, die 5% Zinsen bringen; **I ~ you to prevent such mistakes** Sie werden schließlich dafür bezahlt, dass solche Fehler nicht vorkommen; **"paid"** (*on bill*) „bezahlt"; **to ~ the price/a high price for sth** den Preis/einen hohen Preis für etw zahlen → **paid**
b (*lit, fig: = be profitable to*) sich lohnen für; (*honesty*) sich auszahlen für; **it doesn't ~ them to work longer hours** es lohnt sich für sie nicht, mehr zu arbeiten; **in future it would ~ you to ask** in Zukunft solltest du besser vorher fragen; **but it paid him in the long run** aber auf die Dauer hat es sich doch ausgezahlt
c **to ~ (sb/a place) a visit** *or* **call, to ~ a visit to** *or* **a call on sb/a place** jdn/einen Ort besuchen; (*more formal*) jdm/einem Ort einen Besuch abstatten; **to ~ a visit to the doctor** den Arzt aufsuchen → **attention, compliment, respect**
VI **a** zahlen; **to ~ on account** auf Rechnung zahlen; **they ~ well for this sort of work** diese Arbeit wird gut bezahlt; **no, no, I'm ~ing** nein, nein, ich (be)zahle; **to ~ for sth** etw bezahlen; **it's already paid for** es ist schon bezahlt; **how much did you ~ for it?** wie viel hast du dafür bezahlt?; **I'd like to know what I'm ~ing for** ich wüsste gern, für was ich eigentlich mein Geld ausgebe; **to ~ for sb** für jdn zahlen; **I'll ~ for you this time** dieses Mal zahle ich; **they paid for her to go to America** sie zahlten ihr die Reise nach Amerika
b (*= be profitable*) sich lohnen; **it's a business that ~s** es ist ein rentables Geschäft; **it will ~ for itself within two years** innerhalb von zwei Jahren wird sich das rentiert haben; **crime doesn't ~** (*prov*) Verbrechen lohnt sich nicht
c (*fig: = suffer*) **to ~ for sth (with sth)** für etw (mit etw) bezahlen; **you'll ~ for that!** dafür wirst du (mir) büßen; **to make sb ~ (for sth)** jdn für etw büßen lassen; **I'll make you ~ for this!** das wirst du mir büßen, das werde ich dir heimzahlen!

▶ **pay back** VT *sep* **a** *money* zurückzahlen; **when do you want me to pay you back?** wann willst du das Geld wiederhaben?; **pay me back when you like** zahls *or* gibs mir zurück, wenn du willst **b** *compliment, visit* erwidern; *insult, trick* sich revanchieren für; **to pay sb back** es jdm heimzahlen

▶ **pay in** **VT** *sep* einzahlen; **to pay money into an account** Geld auf ein Konto einzahlen **VI** einzahlen

▶ **pay off** **VT** *sep workmen* auszahlen; *seamen* abmustern; *debt* abbezahlen, tilgen; *HP* ab(be)zahlen; *mortgage* abtragen; *creditor* befriedigen; **if this happens again we'll have to pay him off** wenn das noch einmal vorkommt, müssen wir ihn entlassen **VI** sich auszahlen

▶ **pay out** **VT** *sep* **a** *money (= spend)* ausgeben; (*= count out*) auszahlen **b** *rope* ablaufen lassen **VI** bezahlen

▶ **pay over** VT *sep* aushändigen

▶ **pay up** **VT** *sep what one owes* zurückzahlen; *subscription* bezahlen; **his account is paid up** er hat alles bezahlt → **paid-up** **VI** zahlen

payable [ˈpeɪəbl] ADJ zahlbar; (*= due*) fällig; **~ to order** zahlbar an Order; **to make a cheque** (*Brit*) *or* **check** (*US*) **~ to sb** einen Scheck auf jdn ausstellen; **~ over three months** zahlbar über einen Zeitraum von drei Monaten

pay: **pay-and-display** ADJ (*Brit*) **~ parking space** *Parkplatz, auf dem der Parkschein sichtbar im Wagen ausgelegt werden muss*; **pay-as-you-earn** ATTR **~ tax system** Lohnsteuerabzugsverfahren *nt*, *Steuersystem, bei dem die Lohnsteuer direkt einbehalten wird*; **pay-as-you-go (mobile phone)** N Handy *nt* mit Guthabenkarte; **pay award** N Lohn-/ /Gehaltserhöhung *f*; **payback** N (*fig*) **a** (*= return*) Ertrag *m*; **to have a big ~** sich rentieren **b** (*= revenge*) Rache *f*; **it's ~ time** die Zeit der Rache ist gekommen; **pay bargaining** N Tarifverhandlungen *pl*; **pay bed** N (*Brit Med*) Privatbett *nt*; **pay bracket** N Lohn-/Gehaltsgruppe *f*; **pay cheque**, (*US*) **paycheck** N Lohn-/Gehaltsscheck *m*; **pay claim** N Lohn-/ /Gehaltsforderung *f*; **payday** N Zahltag *m*; **pay dirt** N abbauwürdiges Erzlager; **to hit** *or* **strike ~** (*fig inf*) auf eine Goldader treffen

PAYE (*Brit*) *abbr of* **pay-as-you-earn**

payee [peɪˈiː] N Zahlungsempfänger(in) *m(f)*

pay envelope N (*US*) Lohntüte *f*

payer ['peɪəʳ] N Zahler(in) *m(f)*; **late/slow ~** säumiger Zahler, säumige Zahlerin; **to be a bad ~** eine schlechte Zahlungsmoral haben

pay: **pay freeze** N Lohnstopp *m*; **pay increase** N Lohn-/Gehaltserhöhung *f*

paying ['peɪɪŋ] ADJ **a** *(= profitable)* rentabel **b** **~ guest** zahlender Gast; **~ patient** Privatpatient(in) *m(f)*

paying-in slip [,peɪɪŋ'ɪn,slɪp] N *(Brit)* Einzahlungsschein *m*

pay: **payload** N Nutzlast *f*; *(of bomber)* Bombenlast *f*; **paymaster** N Zahlmeister(in) *m(f)*; **Paymaster General** *(Brit) für Lohn- und Gehaltszahlungen im öffentlichen Dienst zuständiges Kabinettsmitglied*

payment ['peɪmənt] N *(= paying) (of person)* Bezahlung *f*, Entlohnung *f*; *(of bill, instalment etc)* Bezahlung *f*, Begleichung *f*; *(of debt, mortgage)* Abtragung *f*, Rückzahlung *f*; *(of interest, bank charge etc)* Zahlung *f*; *(= sum paid)* Zahlung *f*; *(fig: = reward)* Belohnung *f*; **three monthly ~s** drei Monatsraten; **in ~ of a debt/bill** in Begleichung einer Schuld/Rechnung; **as** *or* **in ~ for goods/his services** als Bezahlung für *or* von Waren/für seine Dienste; **to accept sth as** *or* **in ~ (for ...)** etw in Begleichung/als Bezahlung (für ...) annehmen; **on ~ of** bei Begleichung/Bezahlung von; **without ~** *(= free)* umsonst; **to make a ~** eine Zahlung leisten; **to make a ~ on sth** eine Rate für etw zahlen; **to present sth for ~** etw zur Zahlung vorlegen; **to stop ~s** die Zahlungen *pl* einstellen; **to stop ~ of a cheque** *(Brit) or* **check** *(US)* einen Scheck sperren

payment card N *(= debit card)* Kreditkarte *f*; *(prepaid)* Guthabenkarte *f*

pay: **pay negotiations** PL = **pay talks**; **payoff** N *(= final payment)* Abschlusszahlung *f*; *(inf: = bribe)* Bestechungsgeld *nt*; *(= final outcome, climax)* Quittung *f*; *(of joke)* Pointe *f*

payola [peɪ'əʊlə] N *(esp US) (= bribery)* Bestechung *f*; *(= bribe)* Schmiergeld *nt*

pay: **payout** N *(in competition)* Preis *m*; *(from insurance)* (Aus)zahlung *f*; **pay packet** N Lohntüte *f*; **pay-per-view** ATTR *television, service* Pay-per-View-; **~ channel** Pay-per-View-Kanal *m* N *(TV)* Pay-per-view-Fernsehen *nt*; **payphone** N Münzfernsprecher *m*; **pay rise** N Lohn-/Gehaltserhöhung *f*; **payroll** N **they have 500 people on the ~** sie haben eine Belegschaft von 500, sie haben 500 Beschäftigte; **a monthly ~ of £75,000** eine monatliche Lohn- und Gehaltssumme von £ 75.000; **pay round** N Tarifrunde *f*; **payslip** N Lohn-/Gehaltsstreifen *m*; **pay station** N *(US)* öffentlicher Fernsprecher; **pay talks** PL Lohnverhandlungen *pl*; *(for profession, area of industry)* Tarifverhandlungen *pl*; **pay television** N = **pay TV**; **pay tone** N *bei öffentlichen Fernsprechern: Ton, der anzeigt, dass Münzen eingeworfen werden müssen*; **pay TV** N Pay-TV *nt*; **paywall** N *(Internet)* Bezahlmauer *f*

PBX *abbr of* **private branch exchange** Nebenstellenanlage *f*

PC *(Brit)* **a** *abbr of* **Police Constable**; **PC Plod** *(inf)* Streifenpolizist(in) *m(f)* **b** *abbr of* **Privy Council** **c** *abbr of* **Privy Councillor** **d** *abbr of* **personal computer** PC *m* **e** *abbr of* **politically correct**

pc **a** *abbr of* **post card** **b** *abbr of* **per cent** **c** *abbr of* **politically correct**

PCA **a** *(Brit) abbr of* **Police Complaints Authority** **b** *abbr of* **Professional Chess Association**

PCB *abbr of* **printed circuit board**

PCI *(Comput) abbr of* **Peripheral Component Interconnect** PCI

pcm *abbr of* **per calendar month** monatl.; **"rent £230 ~"** „Miete £ 230 monatl."

PCP **a** *(Drugs) abbr of* **phencyclidine** PCP *nt* **b** *(Med) abbr of* **pneumocystis carinii pneumonia** PCP *f* **c** *(Chem) abbr of* **pentachlorophenol** PCP *nt*

pcs *abbr of* **pieces**

PD *(US) abbr of* **police department** Polizeiministerium *nt*; *(of city)* Polizeibehörde *f*

pd *abbr of* **paid** bez.

PDA *(Comput) abbr of* **personal digital assistant** PDA *m*

PDQ *(inf) abbr of* **pretty damned quick** verdammt schnell *(inf)*

PDSA *(Brit) abbr of* **People's Dispensary for Sick Animals** *kostenloses Behandlungszentrum für Haustiere*

PDT *(US) abbr of* **Pacific Daylight Time** pazifische Sommerzeit

PE *abbr of* **physical education**

pea [piː] N Erbse *f*; **they are as like as two ~s (in a pod)** sie gleichen sich *(dat)* wie ein Ei dem anderen

peace [piːs] N **a** *(= freedom from war)* Frieden *m*, Friede *m (geh)*; **the Versailles** *etc* **~** der Friede von Versailles *etc*; **a man of ~** ein friedfertiger *or* friedliebender Mensch; **to be at ~ with sb/sth** mit jdm/etw in Frieden leben; **the two countries are now at ~** zwischen den beiden Ländern herrscht jetzt Frieden; **to be at ~ with oneself/the world** mit sich *(dat)* selbst/mit der Welt in Frieden leben; **to make one's ~ with the world** seinen Frieden mit der Welt schließen; **he is at ~** *(euph: = dead)* er ruht in Frieden; **to hold** *or* **keep one's ~** *(dated)* schweigen; **to make (one's) ~ (with sb)** sich (mit jdm) versöhnen *or* aussöhnen; **to make (one's) ~ with oneself** mit sich *(dat)* selbst ins Reine kommen; **to make ~ between ...** Frieden stiften zwischen *(+dat)* ...
b *(Jur)* öffentliche (Ruhe und) Ordnung; **the (King's/Queen's) ~** *(Jur)* die öffentliche Ordnung; **to keep the ~** *(Jur) (demonstrator, citizen)* die öffentliche Ordnung wahren; *(policeman)* die öffentliche Ordnung aufrechterhalten; *(fig)* Frieden bewahren
c *(= tranquillity, quiet)* Ruhe *f*; **~ of mind** innere Ruhe, Seelenfrieden *m*; **the Peace of God** der Friede Gottes, Gottes Friede; **~ and quiet** Ruhe und Frieden; **to give sb some ~** jdn in Ruhe *or* Frieden lassen; **to give sb no ~** jdm keine Ruhe lassen; **to get some/no ~** zur Ruhe/nicht zur Ruhe kommen

peaceable ['piːsəbl] ADJ *settlement, discussion* friedlich; *person, nature also* friedfertig, friedliebend

peaceably ['piːsəblɪ] ADV *settle, discuss* friedlich

peace: **peace campaign** N Friedenskampagne *f*; **peace campaigner** N Friedenskämpfer(in) *m(f)*; **peace conference** N Friedenskonferenz *f*; **Peace Corps** N *(US)* Friedenskorps *nt*; **peace dividend** N Friedensdividende *f*

peaceful ['piːsfʊl] ADJ friedlich; *(= peaceable) nation, person etc* friedfertig, friedliebend; *(= calm, undisturbed) holiday, sleep etc* ruhig; *death* sanft; *use of nuclear power* für friedliche Zwecke; **a ~ transition to independence** die Erlangung der Unabhängigkeit auf friedlichem Wege; **he had a ~ reign** während seiner Regierungszeit herrschte Frieden; **I didn't get a ~ moment all day long** ich bin den ganzen Tag keine Sekunde zur Ruhe gekommen; **to achieve sth by** *or* **through ~ means** etw mit friedlichen Mitteln erlangen; **for ~ purposes** für friedliche Zwecke

peacefully ['piːsfəlɪ] ADV friedlich; **to die ~ (in one's sleep)** sanft sterben *or* entschlafen *(liter)*

peacefulness ['piːsfʊlnɪs] N Friedlichkeit *f*; *(of person, nation)* Friedfertigkeit *f*, Friedensliebe *f*; *(of place, holiday, sleep)* Ruhe *f*; *(of death)* Sanftheit *f*; **the ~ of the demonstration** der friedliche Charakter der Demonstration; **the ~ of a summer's evening** die friedliche Atmosphäre eines Sommerabends

peace: **peace initiative** N Friedensinitiative *f*; **peacekeeper** N Friedenswächter(in) *m(f)*; **peacekeeping** N Friedenssicherung *f* ADJ *role, force* zur Friedenssicherung; **~ troops** Friedenstruppen *pl*; **UN troops have a purely ~ role** die UN-Truppen sind eine reine Friedenstruppe; **a ~ operation** Maßnahmen *pl* zur Sicherung des Friedens; **peace-loving** ADJ friedliebend; **peacemaker** N Friedensstifter(in) *m(f)*; **peacemaking** N Friedensbemühungen *pl* ADJ *role* friedensstiftend; **~ efforts** Friedensbemühungen *pl*; **~ process** Friedensprozess *m*; **peace movement** N Friedensbewegung *f*

peacenik ['piːsnɪk] N *(inf)* Pazifist(in) *m(f)*

peace: **peace offensive** N Friedensoffensive *f*; **peace offering** N Friedensangebot *nt*; *(fig)* Versöhnungsgeschenk *nt*; **peace pipe** N Friedenspfeife *f*; **peace process** N Friedensprozess *m*; **peace studies** PL Friedensforschung *f*; **peace talks** PL Friedensverhandlungen *pl*; **peacetime** N Friedenszeiten *pl* ADJ in Friedenszeiten

peach [piːtʃ] N **a** *(= fruit)* Pfirsich *m*; *(= tree)* Pfirsichbaum *m*; **her complexion is like ~es and cream, she has a ~es-and-cream complexion** sie hat eine Haut wie ein Pfirsich, sie hat eine Pfirsichhaut **b** *(inf)* **she's a ~** sie ist klasse *(inf)*; **it's a ~** das ist prima *or* klasse *or* Spitze *(all inf)*; **a ~ of a girl/dress/film** *etc* ein klasse Mädchen/Kleid/Film *etc (all inf)* **c** *(= colour)* Pfirsichton *m* ADJ pfirsichfarben

peachick ['piːtʃɪk] N junger Pfau

peach Melba ['piːtʃ'melbə] N Pfirsich Melba *m*

peachy ['piːtʃɪ] ADJ **a** *(in colour) complexion* pfirsichfarben, Pfirsich- **b** *(esp US inf: = excellent)* prima

pea: **peacock** N Pfau *m*; *(fig: = man)* Geck *m*; **to strut up and down like a ~** wie ein Pfau einherstolzieren; **peacock-blue** ADJ pfauenblau; **peacock butterfly** N *(Zool)* Tagpfauenauge *nt*; **pea green** N Erbsengrün *nt*; **pea-green** ADJ erbsengrün; **peahen** N Pfauenhenne *f*; **pea jacket** N *(esp US)* Pijacke *f*

peak [piːk] N **a** *(of mountain)* Gipfel *m*; *(of roof)* First *m*; *(= sharp point)* Spitze *f*
b *(of cap)* Schirm *m*
c *(= maximum)* Höhepunkt *m*; *(on graph)* Scheitelpunkt *m*; **he is at the ~ of fitness** er ist in Höchstform *or* Topform *(inf)*; **when his career was at its ~** als er auf dem Höhepunkt seiner Karriere war; **when demand is at its ~** wenn die Nachfrage ihren Höhepunkt erreicht hat *or* am stärksten ist
ADJ *attr power, position* höchste(r, s); **at ~ time** *(TV, Radio)* zur Hauptsendezeit; **~ pressure** Höchstdruck *m*; **~ value** Spitzenwert *m*; **~ voltage** Höchst- *or* Spitzenspannung *f*; **a ~ year for new car sales** ein Rekordjahr *nt* für den Neuwagenabsatz; **in ~ condition** *(athlete)* in Höchstform
VI den Höchststand erreichen; *(athlete: = reach one's best)* seine Spitzenform erreichen; **inflation ~ed at 9%** die Inflationsrate erreichte ihren Höchstwert bei 9%; **to have ~ed** *(= be on the way down)* auf dem absteigenden Ast sein *(inf)*

▶ **peak off** VI zurückgehen

▶ **peak out** VI den Höhepunkt erreichen

peaked [piːkt] ADJ **a** *cap, helmet etc* spitz **b** *person* verhärmt, abgehärmt

peak: **peak-hour** ADJ **~ consumption** Verbrauch *m* in der Hauptbelastungszeit *or* zu Spitzenzeiten; **~ travel costs more** in der Hauptverkehrszeit *or* zu Spitzenzeiten sind die öffentlichen Verkehrsmittel teurer; **measures to reduce ~ traffic** Maßnahmen zur Reduzierung der Belastung in der Hauptverkehrszeit *or* zu Spitzenzeiten; **peak hours** PL *(of traffic)* Hauptverkehrszeit *f*, Stoßzeit *f*; *(Telec, Elec)* Hauptbelastungszeit *f*; **peak rate** N *(Telec)* Höchsttarif *m*; **peak season** N Hochsaison *f*; **peak-time** ADJ *(Brit)* zu Spitzenzeiten; **~ programme** *(TV, Radio)* Programm *nt* zur besten Sendezeit; **~ traffic** Stoßverkehr *m*; **~ train services** Zugverbindungen *pl* während der Hauptbelastungszeit; **peak time** N *(TV etc)* Hauptsendezeit *f*; *(also* **peak times** *pl, of power consumption etc)* Hauptbelastungszeit *f*

peaky ['piːkɪ] ADJ *(+er) (Brit inf) complexion* blass; *face* verhärmt, abgehärmt; *look, child* kränklich; **to look ~** nicht gut aussehen, angeschlagen aussehen *(inf)*

peal [pi:l] N ~ **of bells** *(= sound)* Glockengeläut(e) *nt*, Glockenläuten *nt*; *(= set)* Glockenspiel *nt*; **~s of laughter** schallendes Gelächter; **~ of thunder** Donnerrollen *nt*, Donnerschlag *m* VT läuten VI *(bell)* läuten; *(thunder)* dröhnen

▶ **peal out** VI verhallen; **the bells pealed out over the fields** das Geläut der Glocken verhallte über den Feldern

peanut ['pi:nʌt] N Erdnuss *f*; **~s** *(inf: = not much money)* Kleingeld *nt*, Peanuts *pl (inf)*; **the pay is ~s** die Bezahlung ist miserabel *or* lächerlich *(inf)*; **£2,000? that's ~s these days** £ 2.000? das ist doch ein Klacks *or* das sind doch Peanuts heutzutage *(inf)*; **if you pay ~s, you get monkeys** *(prov)* wer nichts zahlt, kann nichts erwarten

peanut: **peanut butter** N Erdnussbutter *f*; **peanut gallery** N *(US inf)* Olymp *m (inf)*; **peanut oil** N Erdnussöl *nt*

peapod ['pi:pɒd] N Erbsenschote *f*

pear [pɛə'] N Birne *f*; *(= tree)* Birnbaum *m*

pear: **peardrop** N *(= pendant)* tropfenförmiger Anhänger *m*; *(= sweet) hartes Bonbon in Birnenform*; **pear-drop** ['pɛədrɒp] ADJ *earring etc* tropfenförmig

pearl[1] [pɜ:l] N, VT, VI = **purl**

pearl[2] N *(lit, fig)* Perle *f*; *(= mother-of-pearl)* Perlmutt *nt*; *(of sweat etc)* Perle *f*, Tropfen *m*; *(= colour)* Grauweiß *nt*; **~ of wisdom** weiser Spruch; **to cast ~s before swine** *(prov)* Perlen *pl* vor die Säue werfen *(prov)* ADJ Perlen-; *(= pearl-coloured)* grauweiß; **~ necklace** Perlenkette *f*

pearl: **pearl barley** N Perlgraupen *pl*; **pearl-blue** ADJ silberblau; **pearl fisher** N Perlenfischer(in) *m(f)*; **pearl fishing** N Perlenfischerei *f*; **pearl-grey** ADJ silbergrau; **pearl-handled** ADJ perlmuttbesetzt; **pearl oyster** N Perlenauster *f*

pearly ['pɜ:lɪ] ADJ *(+er) (in colour)* perlmuttfarben; **~ buttons** Perlmuttknöpfe *pl*; **a ~ costume** ein Kostüm *nt* mit Perlmuttknöpfen

pearly: **Pearly Gates** PL Himmelstür *f*; **pearly king/queen** N *Straßenverkäufer(in) in London, der/die ein mit Perlmuttknöpfen und bunten Perlen besticktes Kostüm trägt*; **pearly-white** ADJ strahlend weiß; *teeth* perlweiß; *skin, fabric* blütenweiß

pear-shaped ['pɛəʃeɪpt] ADJ birnenförmig; **to be ~** *(woman)* eine birnenförmige Körperform haben; **to go ~** *(Brit fig inf)* völlig danebengehen *(inf)*

peasant ['pezənt] N *(lit)* (armer) Bauer, (arme) Bäuerin; *(pej inf) (= ignoramus)* Banause *m*, Banausin *f*; *(= lout)* Bauer *m*; *(= pleb)* Prolet(in) *m(f)* ADJ *attr* bäuerlich; **~ boy/girl** Bauernjunge *m*/-mädchen *nt*; **~ farmer** (armer) Bauer; **~ labour** Landarbeiterschaft *f*, landwirtschaftliche Arbeitskräfte *pl*; **~ leader** Bauernführer(in) *m(f)*; **~ unrest** Bauernunruhen *pl*; **~ woman** (arme) Bäuerin; **to be from ~ stock** von bäuerlicher Herkunft sein

peasantry ['pezəntrɪ] N Bauernschaft *f*; *(= class, status)* Bauerntum *nt*

pease pudding [pi:z'pʊdɪŋ] N Erbspüree *nt*

pea: **peashooter** N Pusterohr *nt*; **pea soup** N Erbsensuppe *f*; **peasouper** [pi:'su:pə'] N Waschküche *(inf)*, Suppe *(inf) f*

peat [pi:t] N Torf *m*; *(= piece)* Stück *nt* Torf

peat bog N Torfmoor *nt*

peaty ['pi:tɪ] ADJ *(+er)* torfig; *taste* nach Torf

pebble ['pebl] N Kiesel *m*, Kieselstein *m*; *(= rock crystal)* Bergkristall *m*; *(after polishing)* Kieselglas *nt*; **he/she is not the only ~ on the beach** *(inf)* es gibt noch andere

pebble: **pebble dash** N *(Brit)* (Kiesel)rauputz *m*; **pebble glasses** PL Brille *f* mit sehr dicken Gläsern

pebbly ['peblɪ] ADJ steinig

pecan [pɪ'kæn] N *(= nut)* Pecannuss *f*; *(= tree)* Hickory *m*

peccadillo [,pekə'dɪləʊ] N *pl* **-(e)s** kleine Sünde; *(of youth)* Jugendsünde *f*

peccary ['pekərɪ] N Pekari *nt*, Nabelschwein *nt*

peck[1] [pek] N *(= dry measure)* Viertelscheffel *m*

peck[2] [pek] N **a** *(inf: = kiss)* flüchtiger Kuss *m*, Küsschen *nt* **b** **the hen gave him a ~** die Henne hackte nach ihm VT **a** *(bird)* picken **b** *(inf: = kiss)* ein Küsschen *nt* geben *(+dat)* VI picken *(at* nach)

▶ **peck out** VT *sep* aushacken

pecker ['pekə'] N **a** *(Brit inf)* **keep your ~ up!** halt die Ohren steif! *(inf)* **b** *(US sl: = penis)* Schwanz *m (vulg)*

pecking order ['pekɪŋ,ɔ:də'] N *(lit, fig)* Hackordnung *f*

peckish ['pekɪʃ] ADJ *(Brit inf: = hungry)* **I'm (feeling) a bit ~** ich könnte was zwischen die Zähne gebrauchen *(inf)*

Pecksniffian [pek'snɪfɪən] ADJ scheinheilig, heuchlerisch

pecs [peks] PL *(inf) abbr of* **pectorals** Brustmuskeln *pl*

pectic ['pektɪk] ADJ pektisch

pectin ['pektɪn] N Pektin *nt*

pectoral ['pektərəl] ADJ Brust-, pektoral *(spec)*

pectoral fin N Brustflosse *f*

pectoral muscle N Brustmuskel *m*

peculate ['pekjʊleɪt] *(geh)* VI öffentliche Gelder *etc* unterschlagen, Unterschlagungen begehen VT *money, funds etc* veruntreuen, unterschlagen

peculiar [pɪ'kju:lɪə'] ADJ **a** *(= strange)* seltsam, eigenartig; **funny ~** merkwürdig-komisch; **to feel ~** sich komisch *or* seltsam fühlen **b** *(= exclusive, special)* eigentümlich; **to be ~ to sth** *(to period, religion, group)* für etw eigentümlich sein; **a method ~ to her** eine Methode, die nur sie benutzt; **an animal ~ to Africa** ein Tier, das nur in Afrika vorkommt; **his own ~ style** der ihm eigene Stil; **in his own ~ way** auf die ihm eigene Art und Weise

peculiarity [pɪ,kju:lɪ'ærɪtɪ] N **a** *(= strangeness)* Seltsamkeit *f*, Eigenartigkeit *f* **b** *(= unusual feature)* Eigentümlichkeit *f*, Eigenheit *f*, Besonderheit *f*; **it has the ~ that it is** *or* **of being ...** es hat die Besonderheit, ... zu sein

peculiarly [pɪ'kju:lɪəlɪ] ADV **a** *(= strangely)* seltsam, eigenartig **b** *(= exceptionally)* besonders; **a ~ British characteristic** eine typisch britische Eigenart

pecuniary [pɪ'kju:nɪərɪ] ADJ *(form) gain, advantage, problem, difficulties* finanziell; **~ affairs** Gelddinge *pl*, Geldsachen *pl*; **~ resources** Geldmittel *pl*

ped [ped] N *(inf: = pedestrian)* Fußgänger(in) *m(f)*

pedagogic(al) [,pedə'gɒdʒɪk(əl)] ADJ *(form)* pädagogisch

pedagogically [,pedə'gɒdʒɪkəlɪ] ADV *(form)* pädagogisch

pedagogue ['pedəgɒg] N *(= pedant)* Schulmeister(in) *m(f)*; *(form: = teacher)* Pädagoge *m*, Pädagogin *f*

pedagogy ['pedəgɒgɪ] N *(form)* Pädagogik *f*

pedal ['pedl] N Pedal *nt*; *(on waste bin etc)* Trethebel *m*; **to put the ~ to the metal** *(inf)* Vollgas geben VT **he ~led the bicycle up the hill** er strampelte mit dem Fahrrad den Berg hinauf *(inf)*; **he ~led the three miles to the restaurant** er radelte die drei Meilen zur Gaststätte; **he ~led the organ** er trat das Pedal der Orgel VI *(on bicycle)* treten; *(on organ)* das Pedal treten; **he ~led for all he was worth** er trat in die Pedale, er strampelte *(inf)* so sehr er konnte; **to ~ off** (mit dem Rad) wegfahren

pedal: **pedal bin** N *(Brit)* Treteimer *m*; **pedal boat** N Tretboot *nt*; **pedal car** N Tretauto *nt*

pedal(l)o ['pedələʊ] N Tretboot *nt*

pedal pushers ['pedəlpʊʃəz] PL *dreiviertellange Damen-/Mädchenhose*

pedant ['pedənt] N Pedant(in) *m(f)*, Kleinigkeitskrämer(in) *m(f)*

pedantic [pɪ'dæntɪk] ADJ pedantisch; **to be ~ about sth** in Bezug auf etw *(acc)* pedantisch sein

pedantically [pɪ'dæntɪkəlɪ] ADV pedantisch

pedantry ['pedəntrɪ] N Pedanterie *f*

peddle ['pedl] VT feilbieten, verkaufen; *(fig) gossip etc* verbreiten; **to ~ drugs** mit Drogen handeln

peddler ['pedlə'] N *(esp US)* = **pedlar**

pederast ['pedəræst] N Päderast *m*

pederasty ['pedəræstɪ] N Päderastie *f*

pedestal ['pedɪstl] N Sockel *m*; **to put** *or* **set sb (up) on a ~** *(fig)* jdn in den Himmel heben; **to knock sb off his ~** *(fig)* jdn von seinem Sockel stoßen

pedestrian [pɪ'destrɪən] N Fußgänger(in) *m(f)* ADJ **a** *attr (= of pedestrians)* Fußgänger-; **~ lights** Fußgängerampel *f*; **~ precinct** *or (US)* **zone** Fußgängerzone *f*; **at a ~ pace** im Schritttempo **b** *(= prosaic) style etc* schwunglos; *method etc* umständlich

pedestrian crossing N Fußgängerüberweg *m or* -übergang *m*

pedestrianize [pɪ'destrɪənaɪz] VT *street* in eine Fußgängerzone umwandeln

pedi ['pedɪ] N *(inf)* = **pedicure**

pediatric *etc* [,pi:dɪ'ætrɪk] *(US)* = **paediatric** *etc*

pedicab ['pedɪkæb] N Fahrradtaxi *nt*

pedicure ['pedɪkjʊə'] N Pediküre *f*

pedigree ['pedɪgri:] N *(lit, fig)* Stammbaum *m*; *(= document)* Ahnentafel *f*; *(fig)* Geschichte *f* ATTR reinrassig

pedigreed ['pedɪgri:d] ADJ reinrassig

pediment ['pedɪmənt] N Giebeldreieck *nt*

pedlar ['pedlə'] N Hausierer(in) *m(f)*; *(of drugs)* Dealer(in) *m(f) (inf)*

pedology *etc (US)* = **paedology** *etc*

pedometer [pɪ'dɒmɪtə'] N Pedometer *nt*, Schrittzähler *m*

pedophile *etc (US)* = **paedophile** *etc*

pee [pi:] *(inf)* N *(= urine)* Urin *m*, Pipi *nt (baby-talk)*; **to need a ~** pinkeln müssen *(inf)*; **to have a ~** pinkeln *(inf)*; **I'm just going for a ~** ich geh mal eben pinkeln *(inf)* VI **a** *(person, animal)* pinkeln *(inf)* **b** *(hum: = rain, also* **pee down**) pinkeln *(inf)*

peek [pi:k] N kurzer Blick; *(furtive, from under blindfold etc)* verstohlener Blick; **to take** *or* **have a ~** kurz/verstohlen gucken *(at* nach); **may I just have a ~?** darf ich mal kurz sehen *or* gucken?; **to get a ~ at sb/sth** jdn/etw kurz zu sehen bekommen VI gucken *(at* nach)

peekaboo ['pi:kəbu:] N Kuckucksspiel *nt*; **to play ~** kuckuck spielen INTERJ kuckuck

peel [pi:l] N Schale *f* VT schälen → **eye** VI *(wallpaper)* sich lösen; *(paint)* abblättern; *(skin, person)* sich schälen *or* pellen *(inf)*; **the paper was ~ing off the wall** die Tapete löste sich von der Wand

▶ **peel away** VT *sep wallpaper, paint* abziehen, ablösen *(from* von); *wrapper* abstreifen *(from* von); *bark* abschälen *(from* von) VI *(lit, fig)* sich lösen *(from* von)

▶ **peel back** VT *sep cover, wrapping* abziehen

▶ **peel off** VT *sep (+prep obj* von) *sticky tape, wallpaper, paint* abziehen, ablösen; *tree bark* abschälen; *wrapper, dress, glove etc* abstreifen VI **a** = **peel away VI** **b** *(= leave formation)* ausscheren; *(Aviat)* ausscheren, abdrehen

peeler[1] ['pi:lə'] N *(old Brit inf)* Gendarm *m (old)*

peeler[2] ['pi:lə'] N **a** *(= potato peeler)* Schälmesser *nt*, Schäler *m* **b** *(dated US sl: = stripper)* Stripper(in) *m(f) (inf)*

peeling ['pi:lɪŋ] N **a** Abschälen *nt* **b** **peelings** PL Schalen *pl*

peep[1] [pi:p] N *(= sound) (of bird etc)* Piep *m*; *(of horn, whistle, inf, of person)* Ton *m*; **to give a ~** *(bird)* einen Piep von sich geben; *(horn, whistle)* einen Ton von sich geben; **not to give a ~** keinen Pieps von sich geben *(inf)*; **we haven't heard a ~ out of him** wir haben keinen Pieps

von ihm gehört *(inf)*; **one ~ out of you and ...** *(inf)* noch einen Mucks *(inf)* or Pieps *(inf)* und ...; **~! ~!** *(of horn)* tut! tut!; *(of whistle)* tüt! tüt!
VI *(bird etc)* piepen; *(horn, car)* tuten; *(whistle)* pfeifen; *(person: on horn)* tuten; *(on whistle)* pfeifen
VT **I ~ed my horn at him, I ~ed him** *(inf)* ich habe ihn angehupt *(inf)*

peep² N *(= look)* kurzer Blick; *(furtive, when forbidden etc)* verstohlener Blick; **to get a ~ at sth** etw kurz zu sehen bekommen; **to take** or **have a ~ (at sth)** kurz/verstohlen (nach etw) gucken
VT **she ~ed her head out** sie streckte ihren Kopf hervor VI gucken (*at* nach); **to ~ from behind sth** hinter etw *(dat)* hervorschauen; **to ~ over sth** über etw *(acc)* gucken; **to ~ through sth** durch etw gucken or lugen; **no ~ing!, don't ~!** (aber) nicht gucken!

▶ **peep out** VI herausgucken; **the sun peeped out from behind the clouds** die Sonne sah or kam hinter den Wolken hervor

peepers ['pi:pəz] PL *(inf)* Gucker *pl (inf)*

peephole ['pi:phəʊl] N Guckloch *nt*; *(in door also)* Spion *m*

Peeping Tom ['pi:pɪŋ'tɒm] N Spanner *m (inf)*, Voyeur *m*

peep: **peepshow** N Peepshow *f*; **peep-toe** ADJ offen N *(= shoe)* offener Schuh

peer¹ [pɪə'] N **a** *(= noble)* Peer *m*; **~ of the realm** Peer *m* **b** *(= equal)* Gleichrangige(r) *mf*, Peer *m (spec)*; **he was well-liked by his ~s** er war bei seinesgleichen beliebt; **to be tried by one's ~s** von seinesgleichen gerichtet werden; **as a musician he has no ~** or **is without ~** als Musiker sucht er seinesgleichen

peer² VI starren; *(short-sightedly, inquiringly)* schielen; **to ~ (hard) at sb** jdn anstarren/anschielen; **to ~ (hard) at sth** etw anstarren; **the driver ~ed through the fog** der Fahrer versuchte angestrengt, im Nebel etwas zu erkennen; **if you ~ through the mist you can just see ...** wenn es dir gelingt, im Nebel etwas zu erkennen, kannst du gerade noch ... sehen

peerage ['pɪərɪdʒ] N **a** *(= peers)* Adelsstand *m*; *(in GB)* Peers *pl* **b** *(= rank)* Adelsstand *m*, Adelswürde *f*; *(in GB)* Peerage *f*, Peerswürde *f*; **to raise** or **elevate sb to the ~** jdn in den Adelsstand erheben; **to give sb a ~** jdm einen Adelstitel verleihen, jdn adeln; **to get a ~** geadelt werden, einen Adelstitel verliehen bekommen **c** *(= book) das britische Adelsverzeichnis*

peeress ['pɪərɪs] N Peeress *f*

peer group N Peergroup *f*, Alterskohorte *f*

peerless ADJ, **peerlessly** ADV ['pɪəlɪs, -lɪ] einzigartig, unvergleichlich

peer pressure N Gruppen- or Erwartungsdruck *m (vonseiten Gleichaltriger)*

peeve [pi:v] VT *(inf)* ärgern, reizen, fuchsen *(inf)*

peeved [pi:vd] ADJ *(inf)* eingeschnappt, ärgerlich, verärgert; *look* ärgerlich, verärgert

peevish ['pi:vɪʃ] ADJ *(= irritated)* gereizt, mürrisch, brummig; *(= irritable)* reizbar

peevishly ['pi:vɪʃlɪ] ADV gereizt

peevishness ['pi:vɪʃnɪs] N *(= irritation)* Gereiztheit *f*, Brummigkeit *f*; *(= irritability)* Reizbarkeit *f*

peewit ['pi:wɪt] N Kiebitz *m*

peg [peg] N *(= stake)* Pflock *m*; *(= tent peg also)* Hering *m*; *(for pegboard, wood joints, in games)* Stift *m*; *(of musical instrument)* Wirbel *m*; *(Brit: = clothes peg)* (Wäsche)klammer *f*; *(= hook, for mountaineering)* Haken *m*; *(in barrel)* Zapfen *m*, Spund *m*; **off the ~** von der Stange; **a ~ of rum** *etc* ein Gläschen *nt* Rum *etc*; **to take** or **bring sb down a ~ or two** *(inf)* jdm einen Dämpfer geben; **a (convenient) ~ on which to hang one's prejudices** *etc* ein guter Aufhänger für seine Vorurteile *etc*
VT **a** *(= fasten) (with stake)* anpflocken; *(with clothes peg)* anklammern; *(to pegboard)* anheften; *(with tent peg)* festpflocken
b *(= mark out) area* abstecken
c *(fig) prices, wages* festsetzen; **to have sb ~ged (as sth)** *(inf)* jdn (als etw) abstempeln

▶ **peg away** VI *(inf)* nicht locker lassen (*at* mit)

▶ **peg down** VT *sep tent etc* festpflocken

▶ **peg out** VT *sep* **a** *washing* aufhängen; *skins* ausspannen **b** *(= mark out) area* abstecken VI *(Brit sl: = die)* abkratzen *(inf)*, den Löffel abgeben *(inf)*; *(with exhaustion)* umkippen *(inf)*; *(= stop: machine)* verrecken *(inf)*

▶ **peg up** VT *sep washing* aufhängen; *notice* heften (*on* an *+acc*)

Pegasus ['pegəsəs] N Pegasus *m*

pegboard ['pegbɔ:d] N Lochbrett *nt*

peg leg N *(inf) (= person)* Stelzfuß *m*; *(= leg also)* Holzbein *nt*

peignoir ['peɪnwɑ:] N Negligée *nt*, Negligee *nt*

pejorative ADJ, **pejoratively** ADV [pɪ'dʒɒrɪtɪv, -lɪ] pejorativ, abwertend, abschätzig

peke [pi:k] N *(inf)* = **pekin(g)ese**

Pekin(g) [pi:'kɪŋ] N Peking *nt*; **~ man** Pekingmensch *m*

pekin(g)ese [,pi:kɪ'ni:z] N *pl* - *(= dog)* Pekinese *m*

pelerine ['peləri:n] N *(old)* Pelerine *f*, Umhang *m*

pelican ['pelɪkən] N Pelikan *m*

pelican crossing N *(Brit)* Fußgängerüberweg *m (mit Ampel)*

pelisse [pə'li:s] N *(old)* pelzbesetztes Kleid

pellet ['pelɪt] N Kügelchen *nt*; *(for gun)* Schrotkugel *m*; *(Biol: = regurgitated pellet)* Gewölle *nt*

pellicle ['pelɪkəl] N Film *m*; *(Zool: = membrane)* Pellicula *f*

pell-mell ['pel'mel] ADV durcheinander, wie Kraut und Rüben *(inf)*; *(with vbs of motion)* in heillosem Durcheinander

pellucid [pe'lu:sɪd] ADJ *liquid, meaning* klar; *argument also* einleuchtend

pelmet ['pelmɪt] N *(Brit)* Blende *f*; *(of fabric)* Falbel *f*, Querbehang *m*

Peloponnese [,peləpə'ni:z] N Peloponnes *m*

Peloponnesian [,peləpə'ni:zɪən] ADJ peloponnesisch

pelt¹ [pelt] N Pelz *m*, Fell *nt*

pelt² VT **a** *(= throw)* schleudern (*at* nach); **to ~ sb/sth (with sth)** jdn/etw (mit etw) bewerfen **b** *(= beat hard)* verprügeln VI *(inf)* **a** *(= go fast)* pesen *(inf)* **b** **it ~ed (with rain)** es hat nur so geschüttet *(inf)*; **the rain/hail ~ed against the windows** der Regen/Hagel prasselte an or schlug gegen die Fensterscheiben N *(inf)* **a** *(= speed)* **at full ~** volle Pulle *(inf)* **b** *(= blow)* Schlag *m*; **she gave her a good ~ round the ear** sie gab ihr eine kräftige Ohrfeige

▶ **pelt along** VI *(inf)* entlangrasen

▶ **pelt down** VI **it** or **the rain really pelted down** der Regen prasselte nur so herunter; **it's pelting down** es regnet in Strömen

peltry ['peltrɪ] N **a** *(furs collectively)* Rauchwaren *pl*, Pelzwaren *pl* **b** *(= single furs)* Felle *pl*, Häute *pl*

pelvic ['pelvɪk] ADJ Becken-; *complaint, pains* in der Beckengegend; **~ floor muscles** Beckenboden *m*, Beckenbodenmuskulatur *f*; **~ thrust** Hüftschwung *m*

pelvic: **pelvic bone** N Beckenknochen *m*; **pelvic girdle** N Beckengürtel *m*; **pelvic fin** Bauchflosse *f*

pelvis ['pelvɪs] N Becken *nt*

pen¹ [pen] N *(= dip pen)* Feder *f*; *(= fountain pen)* Füllfederhalter *m*, Füller *m*; *(= ball-point pen)* Kugelschreiber *m*, Kuli *m (inf)*; **to put ~ to paper** zur Feder greifen; **the ~ is mightier than the sword** *(prov)* die Feder ist mächtiger als das Schwert VT niederschreiben; *poem etc also* verfassen

pen² N **a** *(for cattle etc)* Pferch *m*; *(for sheep)* Hürde *f*; *(for pigs)* Koben *m*; *(= play pen)* Laufstall *m*, Ställchen *nt*, Laufgitter *nt* **b** *(US inf: = prison)* Bau *m (inf)*, Knast *m (inf)* **c** *(for submarines)* Bunker *m* VT einsperren

▶ **pen in** VT *sep* einsperren; *(fig) car etc* einklemmen, einkeilen

▶ **pen up** VT *sep* einsperren

pen³ N *(= swan)* weiblicher Schwan

penal ['pi:nl] ADJ **a** Straf-; **~ institution** Strafanstalt *f*; **~ law** Strafrecht *nt*; **~ offence** Straftat *f*; **~ policy** Strafrechtspolitik *f*; **~ reform** Strafrechtsreform *f* **b** *(= harsh) rates, taxation* überzogen

penal code N Strafgesetzbuch *nt*

penal colony N Strafkolonie *f*

penalization [,pi:nəlaɪ'zeɪʃən] N **a** *(= punishment)* Bestrafung *f*; *(fig)* Benachteiligung *f* **b** *(= making punishable)* Unter-Strafe-Stellen *nt*

penalize ['pi:nəlaɪz] VT **a** *(= punish, also Sport)* bestrafen **b** *(fig)* benachteiligen; **we are ~d as we don't have a car** wir sind benachteiligt or im Nachteil, weil wir kein Auto haben **c** *(= make punishable)* unter Strafe stellen

penal servitude N Zwangsarbeit *f*

penal system N Strafrecht *nt*

penalty ['penəltɪ] N **a** *(= punishment)* Strafe *f*; *(fig: = disadvantage)* Nachteil *m*; **the ~ (for this) is death** darauf steht die Todesstrafe; **you know the ~** Sie wissen, welche Strafe darauf steht; **"penalty £50"** „bei Zuwiderhandlung wird eine Geldstrafe von £ 50 erhoben"; **to carry the death ~/the ~ of imprisonment** mit dem Tod/mit Gefängnis bestraft werden; **on ~ of £200** bei einer Geldstrafe von £ 200; **to pay the ~** dafür büßen; **that's the ~ you pay for ...** das ist die Strafe dafür, dass ...
b *(Sport)* Strafstoß *m*; *(Ftbl)* Elfmeter *m*; *(Golf, Bridge)* Strafpunkt *m*; **the match was decided on penalties** *(Ftbl)* die Partie wurde durch Elfmeterschießen entschieden

penalty: **penalty area** N Strafraum *m*; **penalty box** N *(Ftbl)* Strafraum *m*; *(Ice Hockey)* Strafbank *f*; **penalty clause** N Strafklausel *f*; **penalty goal** N *(Rugby)* Straftor *nt*; **penalty kick** N Strafstoß *m*; **penalty killer** N *(Ice Hockey)* Penalty-Killer(in) *m(f)*, Unterzahlspezialist(in) *m(f)*; **penalty line** N Strafraumgrenze *f*; **penalty point** N *(Aut, Jur, Sport)* Strafpunkt *m*; **penalty rates** PL *(Auatral inf)* Zulagen *f (für geleistete Überstunden)*; **penalty shoot-out** N *(Ftbl)* Elfmeterschießen *nt*; **penalty shot** N *(Ice hockey)* Strafschuss *m*; *(Golf)* Strafschlag *m*; *(Basketball US)* Freiwurf *m*; **penalty spot** N *(Ftbl)* Elfmeterpunkt *m*; **penalty taker** N *(Ftbl)* Elfmeterschütze *m/*-schützin *f*

penance ['penəns] N *(Rel)* Buße *f*; *(fig)* Strafe *f*; **to do ~** Buße tun; *(fig)* büßen; **as a ~** *(Rel)* als Buße; *(fig)* zur or als Strafe; **to give sb ~** jdm Buße auferlegen

pen-and-ink ['penənd'ɪŋk] ADJ Feder-; **~ drawing** Federzeichnung *f*

pence [pens] N *pl of* **penny** Pence *pl*

penchant ['pɑ̃:ŋʃɑ̃:ŋ] N Schwäche *f* (*for* für), Vorliebe *f* (*for* für)

pencil ['pensl] N Bleistift *m*; *(= eyebrow pencil)* Augenbrauenstift *m*; *(Math, Phys: of lines, rays etc)* Büschel *nt* VT mit Bleistift schreiben/zeichnen *etc*; **~led eyebrows** nachgezogene Augenbrauen *pl* ATTR Bleistift-; *line* mit Bleistift gezogen; **~ sketch** Bleistiftskizze *f*

▶ **pencil in** VT *sep* **a** *eyebrows* aufzeichnen **b** *(= make provisional arrangement with/for)* vorläufig vormerken; **can I pencil you in for Tuesday?** kann ich Sie erst mal für Dienstag vormerken?

pencil: **pencil box** N Federkasten *m*; **pencil case** N Federmäppchen *nt*; **pencil sharpener** N (Bleistift)spitzer *m*; **pencil skirt** N enger Rock

pendant ['pendənt] N Anhänger *m*

pendent ['pendənt] ADJ herabhängend; **~ lamp** Hängelampe *f*

pending ['pendɪŋ] ADJ anstehend; *lawsuit* anhängig; **"pending"** „unerledigt"; **to be ~** *(deci-*

sion etc) noch anstehen; *(trial)* noch anhängig sein; **he knew my examination was ~** er wusste, dass meine Prüfung bevorstand; **four more charges are ~ against her** gegen sie sind noch vier weitere Klagen anhängig; **to leave sth ~** etw nicht weiterverfolgen; **the offer is left ~ until the examination results are known** über das Angebot wird erst entschieden, wenn die Prüfungsergebnisse bekannt sind PREP **~ his arrival/return** bis zu seiner Ankunft/Rückkehr; **~ a decision** bis eine Entscheidung getroffen worden ist

Pendolino® [ˌpendəʊ'liːnəʊ] N *(Rail)* Pendolino® *m*

pendulous ['pendjʊləs] ADJ herabhängend; **~ breasts** *or* **bosom** Hängebrüste *pl*, Hängebusen *m*; **~ cheeks** Hängebacken *pl*

pendulum ['pendjʊləm] N Pendel *nt*; **the ~ has swung back in the opposite direction** *(lit, fig)* das Pendel ist in die entgegengesetzte Richtung ausgeschlagen; **the ~ has swung back in favour** *(Brit) or* **favor** *(US)* **of** *or* **toward(s) …** *(fig)* die Tendenz geht wieder in Richtung *(+gen)* …; **the swing of the ~** *(fig)* die Tendenzwende

penetrable ['penɪtrəbl] ADJ zu durchdringen; **the barely ~ jungle** der fast undurchdringliche Dschungel

penetrate ['penɪtreɪt] VT eindringen in *(+acc)*; *(= go right through) walls etc* durchdringen; *(Mil) enemy lines* durchbrechen; *(Med) vein* durchstechen; *(= infiltrate) party* infiltrieren; *market* eindringen in; **is there anything that will ~ that thick skull of yours?** geht denn auch überhaupt nichts in deinen Schädel rein?; **to ~ sb's disguise** hinter jds Maske *(acc)* schauen VI eindringen; *(= go right through)* durchdringen; **it just didn't ~** *(fig)* das ist mir/ihm *etc* nicht klar geworden; **has that ~d?** hast du/habt ihr das endlich kapiert?

penetrating ['penɪtreɪtɪŋ] ADJ **a** *(= perceptive) gaze* durchdringend; *insight, person* scharfsinnig; *question, analysis* treffend; *interview* tief gehend; **a ~ mind** ein scharfer Verstand **b** *(= piercing) cold* durchdringend; *light* grell; *pain* stechend

penetratingly ['penɪtreɪtɪŋlɪ] ADV *gaze* durchdringend; *comment, analyze* scharfsinnig; *shine* grell; **a ~ accurate analysis** eine messerscharfe Analyse; **a ~ bright light** ein grelles Licht

penetration [ˌpenɪ'treɪʃən] N *(by bullet etc) (= entering)* Eindringen *nt (into in +acc)*; *(= going right through)* Durchdringen *nt (of +gen)*; *(Mil)* Durchbrechen *nt*, Durchbrechung *f*; *(= infiltration: of party, group)* Infiltration *f*; *(during sex)* Eindringen *nt*, Penetration *f*; **the ~ of his gaze** sein durchdringender Blick; **his powers of ~** sein Scharfsinn *m*

penetrative ['penɪtrətɪv] ADJ **a ~ sex** penetrativer Sex **b** = **penetrating a**

pen friend N Brieffreund(in) *m(f)*

penguin ['peŋgwɪn] N Pinguin *m*; **~ suit** *(hum)* Frack *m*, Schwalbenschwanz *m (hum)*

penholder ['penˌhəʊldəʳ] N Federhalter *m*

penicillin [ˌpenɪ'sɪlɪn] N Penizillin *nt*

peninsula [pɪ'nɪnsjʊlə] N Halbinsel *f*

peninsular [pɪ'nɪnsjʊləʳ] ADJ **the Peninsular War** der Krieg auf der Pyrenäenhalbinsel

penis ['piːnɪs] N Penis *m*

penis envy N Penisneid *m*

penitence ['penɪtəns] N Reue *f (also Eccl)*, Zerknirschtheit *f*

penitent ['penɪtənt] ADJ reuig *(also Eccl)*, zerknirscht N Büßer(in) *m(f)*; *(Eccl)* reuiger Sünder, reuige Sünderin

penitential [ˌpenɪ'tenʃəl] ADJ reuevoll, reumütig, reuig; *(Eccl)* Buß-; **a ~ act** eine Bußtat

penitentiary [ˌpenɪ'tenʃərɪ] N *(esp US: = prison)* Strafanstalt *f*, Gefängnis *nt*

penknife ['pennaɪf] N Taschenmesser *nt*

Penn(a) *(dated US) abbr of* **Pennsylvania**

pen name N Pseudonym *nt*, Schriftstellername *m*

pennant ['penənt] N Wimpel *m*

pen nib N Feder *f*

penniless ['penɪlɪs] ADJ mittellos; **to be ~** keinen Cent haben; **her husband died, leaving her ~** ihr Mann starb, und sie stand völlig mittellos *or* ohne einen einzigen Cent da

Pennines ['penaɪnz] PL Pennines *pl*, *Gebirgszug in Nordengland*

pennon ['penən] N = **pennant**

penn'orth ['penəθ] N = **pennyworth**

Pennsylvania [ˌpensɪl'veɪnɪə] N Pennsylvania *nt*

Pennsylvania Dutch N **a** *(Ling)* Pennsylvania-Deutsch *nt* **b** *pl (= people)* Pennsylvania-Deutsche *pl* ADJ pennsylvania-deutsch

Pennsylvanian [ˌpensɪl'veɪnɪən] ADJ pennsylvanisch

penny ['penɪ] N *pl (coins)* **pennies** *or (sum)* **pence** Penny *m*; *(US)* Centstück *nt*; **it costs 50 pence** es kostet 50 Pence; **he hasn't got a ~ (to his name)** er hat keinen Cent (Geld); **in for a ~, in for a pound** *(esp Brit prov)* wennschon, dennschon *(inf)*; *(morally)* wer A sagt muss auch B sagen *(prov)*; **I'm not a ~ the wiser** ich bin genauso klug wie zuvor; **take care of the pennies and the pounds** *(Brit) or* **dollars** *(US)* **will take care of themselves** *(Prov)* spare im Kleinen, dann hast du im Großen; **to count** *or* **watch the pennies** auf den Pfennig sehen; **a ~ for your thoughts** ich möchte deine Gedanken lesen können; **magpies are two** *or* **ten a ~ in this area** Elstern gibt es in dieser Gegend jede Menge; **he keeps turning up like a bad ~** *(inf)* der taucht immer wieder auf *(inf)*; **to spend a ~** *(Brit inf)* austreten, mal eben verschwinden *(inf)*; **the ~ dropped** *(inf)* der Groschen ist gefallen *(inf)* → **pretty, honest**

penny: **penny arcade** N Spielhalle *f*; **Penny Black** N *(= stamp)* Penny Black *f*; **penny-dreadful** N *(dated Brit)* Groschenroman *m*; **penny-farthing** N *(Brit)* Hochrad *nt*; **penny loafer** N *(US)* Slipper *m*, Mokassin *m*; **penny-pinch** VI jeden Cent *or* Pfennig umdrehen; **penny-pincher** ['penɪˌpɪntʃəʳ] N *(pej)* Pfennigfuchser(in) *m(f) (pej)*; **penny-pinching** ADJ knauserig *(inf)*; **pennyweight** N Pennygewicht *nt*; **penny whistle** N Kinderflöte *f*; **penny wise** ADJ **to be ~ and pound foolish** immer am falschen Ende sparen; **pennyworth** N *(dated)* **a ~ of liquorice** für einen Penny Lakritz; **a ~ of common sense** für fünf Cent gesunden Menschenverstand

penologist [piː'nɒlədʒɪst] N Kriminalpädagoge *m*, Kriminalpädagogin *f*

penology [piː'nɒlədʒɪ] N Kriminalpädagogik *f*

pen: **pen pal** N *(inf)* Brieffreund(in) *m(f)*; **pen-pusher** N Schreiberling *m*; **penpushing** N Schreiberei *f*, Schreibkram *m* ADJ Schreib-; **~ work** Schreibarbeit *f*; **~ clerk** Bürohengst *m (inf)*

pension ['penʃən] N Rente *f*; *(for civil servants also)* Pension *f*, Ruhegehalt *nt (form)*; **company ~** betriebliche Altersversorgung; **to be entitled to a ~** Anspruch auf eine Rente *etc* haben, rentenberechtigt/pensionsberechtigt sein; **to be living on a ~** von der Rente *etc* leben; **to get a ~** eine Rente *etc* beziehen

▶ **pension off** VT *sep (Brit inf)* vorzeitig pensionieren

pensionable ['penʃənəbl] ADJ *job* mit Pensionsberechtigung; **this position is ~** diese Stellung berechtigt zu einer Pension/einem Ruhegehalt; **of ~ age** im Renten-/Pensionsalter; **~ salary** *Gehaltsanteil, der zur Berechnung des Rentenversicherungsbeitrages herangezogen wird*

pension book N Rentenausweis *m*

pensioner ['penʃənəʳ] N Rentner(in) *m(f)*; *(= former civil servant also)* Pensionär(in) *m(f)*, Ruhegehaltsempfänger(in) *m(f) (form)*

pension: **pension fund** N Rentenfonds *m*; **pension plan** N Altersversorgungsplan *m*; **pension rights** PL Rentenanspruch *m*; **pension scheme** N Rentenversicherung *f*

pensive ADJ, **pensively** ADV ['pensɪv, -lɪ] nachdenklich; *(= sadly serious)* schwermütig

pensiveness ['pensɪvnɪs] N Nachdenklichkeit *f*; *(sad)* Schwermütigkeit *f*

pentagon ['pentəgən] N Fünfeck *nt*, Pentagon *nt*; **the Pentagon** das Pentagon

pentagonal [pen'tægənl] ADJ fünfeckig

pentagram ['pentəgræm] N Drudenfuß *m*, Pentagramm *nt*

pentahedron [ˌpentə'hiːdrən] N Fünfflächner *m*, Pentaeder *nt*

pentameter [pen'tæmɪtəʳ] N Pentameter *m*

Pentateuch ['pentətjuːk] N die fünf Bücher *pl* Mose, Pentateuch *m*

pentathlete [pen'tæθliːt] N Fünfkämpfer(in) *m(f)*

pentathlon [pen'tæθlən] N Fünfkampf *m*

pentatonic [ˌpentə'tɒnɪk] ADJ pentatonisch; **~ scale** fünfstufige Tonleiter

Pentecost ['pentɪkɒst] N *(Jewish)* Erntefest *nt*; *(Christian)* Pfingsten *nt*

Pentecostal [ˌpentɪ'kɒstl] ADJ Pfingst-; *sect, service, revival* der Pfingstbewegung; **pentecostal church** Pfingstkirche *f*; **pentecostal minister** Pfarrer(in) *m(f)* einer Pfingstkirche

penthouse ['penthaʊs] N *(= apartment)* Penthouse *nt*, Dachterrassenwohnung *f*; *(= roof)* Überdachung *f*

Pentium processor® [ˌpentɪəm'prəʊsesəʳ] N Pentium-Prozessor® *m*

pentop ['pentɒp] N *(= pen-based computer)* Pentop *m*

pent up ADJ *pred*, **pent-up** ['pent'ʌp] ADJ *attr person (with frustration, anger)* geladen *pred*; *(after traumatic experience)* aufgewühlt; *(= nervous, excited)* innerlich angespannt; *emotions, passion, excitement* aufgestaut; *(Econ) demand* rege, lebhaft; **she had been very ~** es hatte sich alles in ihr gestaut; **pent-up feelings** ein Emotionsstau *m*, angestaute Gefühle *pl*

penultimate [pe'nʌltɪmɪt] ADJ vorletzte(r, s)

penumbra [pɪ'nʌmbrə] N *pl* **-s** *or* **-e** [-briː] Halbschatten *m*

penurious [pɪ'njʊərɪəs] ADJ *(liter) (= poor)* arm, armselig; *existence also* karg, dürftig; *(= mean)* geizig, knauserig

penuriously [pɪ'njʊərɪəslɪ] ADV *(liter) live* arm, armselig

penury ['penjʊrɪ] N Armut *f*, Not *f*; **in a state of ~** in Armut

peony ['piːənɪ] N Pfingstrose *f*, Päonie *f (spec)*

people ['piːpl] PL **a** Menschen *pl*; *(not in formal context)* Leute *pl*; **we're concerned with ~** uns geht es um die Menschen; **French ~ are very fond of their food** die Franzosen lieben ihre gute Küche; **that's typical of Edinburgh ~** das ist typisch für (die) Leute aus Edinburgh; **a job where you meet ~** eine Arbeit, wo man mit Menschen *or* Leuten zusammenkommt; **~ who need ~** Menschen, die andere Menschen brauchen; **all the ~ in the world** alle Menschen auf der Welt; **all ~ with red hair** alle Rothaarigen; **some ~ don't like it** manche Leute mögen es nicht; **most ~ in show business** die meisten Leute im Showgeschäft; **aren't ~ funny?** was gibt es doch für seltsame Menschen *or* Leute?; **the ~ you meet!** Menschen *or* Leute gibts!; **why me of all ~?** warum ausgerechnet ich/mich?; **I met Harry of all ~!** ausgerechnet Harry habe ich getroffen!; **of all ~ who do you think I should meet?** stell dir mal vor, wen ich getroffen habe?; **what do you ~ think?** was haltet ihr denn davon?; **poor ~** arme Leute *pl*, Arme *pl*; **blind ~** Blinde *pl*; **disabled ~** Behinderte *pl*; **middle-aged ~** Menschen *pl* mittleren Alters; **old ~** Senioren *pl*; **city ~** Stadtmenschen *pl*; **country ~** Menschen *pl* vom Land, Landleute *pl (dated)*; **some ~!** Leute gibts!; **some ~ have all the luck** manche Leute haben einfach Glück

b *(= inhabitants)* Bevölkerung *f*; **the ~ of Rome/Egypt** *etc* die Bevölkerung von Rom/

Ägypten *etc*; **Madrid has over 5 million ~** Madrid hat über 5 Millionen Einwohner
c *(= one, they)* man; *(= people in general, the neighbours)* die Leute; **~ say that …** man sagt, dass …; **what will ~ think!** was sollen die Leute denken!; **~ in general tend to say …** im Allgemeinen neigt man zu der Behauptung …
d *(= nation, masses, subjects)* Volk *nt*; **the common ~** das einfache Volk, die breite Masse; **a man of the ~** ein Mann *m* des Volkes; **government by the ~ (of the ~)** eine Regierung des Volkes; **the Belgian ~** die Belgier *pl*, das belgische Volk; **People's police/Republic** *etc* Volkspolizei *f*/-republik *f etc*
VT besiedeln; **to be ~d by** bevölkert sein von; **the world seems to be ~d with idiots** die Welt scheint von Idioten bevölkert zu sein

people: **people carrier** N *(Aut)* Großraumlimousine *f*, Van *m*; **people mover** N **a** *(= moving pavement)* Rollband *nt*, Rollsteig *m* **b** *(Aut)* = **people carrier**; **people power** N Basisdemokratie *f*; **People's Dispensary for Sick Animals** N *(Brit) kostenloses Behandlungszentrum für Haustiere*

pep [pep] N *(inf)* Schwung *m*, Elan *m*, Pep *m* *(inf)*

▶ **pep up** VT *sep (inf)* Schwung bringen in *(+acc)*; *food, drink* pikanter machen; *person* munter machen; **pills to pep you up** Aufputschmittel *pl*

pepper ['pepəʳ] **N** Pfeffer *m*; *(= green, red pepper)* Paprika *m*; *(= plant)* Pfefferstrauch *m*; **two ~s** zwei Paprikaschoten **VT** **a** *(lit)* pfeffern **b** *(fig)* **to ~ sth with quotations** etw mit Zitaten spicken; **to ~ sb with shot** jdn mit Kugeln durchlöchern

pepper: **pepper-and-salt** ADJ Pfeffer-und-Salz-; *hair* meliert; **~ pattern** Pfeffer-und-Salz-Muster *nt*; **pepperbox** N *(US)* Pfefferstreuer *m*; **peppercorn** N Pfefferkorn *nt*; **peppercorn rent** N *(= nominal rent)* nominelle *or* symbolische Miete

peppered ['pepəd] ADJ **a** *(Cook)* gepfeffert; **~ mackerel fillets** gepfefferte Makrelenfilets **b** *(fig)* **to be ~ with sth** mit etw übersät sein; *with quotations etc* mit etw gespickt sein; **his hair is ~ with grey** sein Haar ist von grauen Strähnen durchzogen

pepper: **pepper mill** N Pfeffermühle *f*; **peppermint** N Pfefferminz *nt*; *(Bot)* Pfefferminze *f*; **pepper pot** N Pfefferstreuer *m*; **pepper spray** N Pfefferspray *nt*; **pepper steak** N Pfeffersteak *m*

peppery ['pepərɪ] ADJ gepfeffert; *(fig) old man etc* hitzig, hitzköpfig; **it tastes rather ~** es schmeckt stark nach Pfeffer

pep pill N Aufputschpille *f*, Peppille *f* *(inf)*

peppy ['pepɪ] ADJ *(+er) (inf)* peppig *(inf)*

> **PEP RALLY**
>
> Eine **pep rally** ist ein amerikanischer Begriff für ein Treffen von Schülern und Studenten von **high schools**, Colleges oder Universitäten vor einem sportlichen Ereignis, meist einem Football- oder Basketballspiel, auf dem die Stimmung für ihr Team aufgeheizt werden soll. Bei der Kundgebung, die einen Tag oder noch früher vor dem Spiel abgehalten wird, treten Cheerleader auf, die Blaskapelle der Schule spielt, und die Spieler und Trainer halten kurze Ansprachen. Manchmal wird der Begriff auch für politische Kundgebungen oder Firmenversammlungen verwendet, auf denen die Anhänger oder Arbeitnehmer durch öffentliche Belobigung und die Ankündigung neuer Pläne und zukünftiger Erfolge motiviert werden sollen.

pepsin ['pepsɪn] N Pepsin *nt*

pep talk N *(inf)* aufmunternde Worte *pl*; **to give sb a ~** jdm ein paar aufmunternde Worte sagen

peptic ['peptɪk] ADJ peptisch

peptic ulcer N Magengeschwür *nt*

per [pɜːʳ] PREP pro; **£500 ~ annum** £ 500 im *or* pro Jahr; **60 km ~ hour** 60 Stundenkilometer, 60 km pro Stunde *or* in der Stunde; **£2 ~ dozen** das Dutzend für £ 2, £ 2 das Dutzend; **£5 ~ copy** £ 5 pro *or* je Exemplar, £ 5 für jedes Exemplar; **as ~** gemäß *(+dat)*; **~ se** an sich, per se *(geh)* → **usual**

peradventure [ˌpərəd'ventʃəʳ] ADV *(old: = perhaps)* vielleicht; **if/lest ~** falls

perambulate [pə'ræmbjʊleɪt] *(form)* **VT** sich ergehen in *(+dat) (geh)* **VI** sich ergehen *(liter)*

perambulation [pəˌræmbjʊ'leɪʃən] N *(form)* Spaziergang *m*

perambulator ['præmbjʊleɪtəʳ] N *(Brit form)* Kinderwagen *m*

per capita [pə'kæpɪtə] **ADJ** Pro-Kopf-; **~ income** Pro-Kopf-Einkommen *nt* **ADV** pro Kopf; **what is the average wage ~?** wie hoch ist der Durchschnittslohn pro Kopf?

perceivable [pə'siːvəbl] ADJ erkennbar; **barely ~** kaum auszumachen *or* zu erkennen

perceive [pə'siːv] VT wahrnehmen; *(= understand, realize, recognize)* erkennen; **do you ~ anything strange?** fällt Ihnen irgendetwas Ungewöhnliches auf?; **…, which we ~ to be the case** *(form)* …, was wir als zutreffend erkennen; **to ~ oneself as …** sich als … empfinden

perceived [pə'siːvd] ADJ *danger* empfunden; *need* erkannt; *failure, success* wahrnehmbar

per cent, *(US)* **percent** [pə'sent] N Prozent *nt*; **~ sign** *(Typ)* Prozentzeichen *nt*; **what ~?** wie viel Prozent?; **20 ~** 20 Prozent; **a 10 ~ discount** 10 Prozent Rabatt; **a ten ~ increase** eine zehnprozentige Steigerung; **to increase sth by 10 ~** etw um 10 Prozent erhöhen; **to give 100 ~** 100 Prozent geben; **I'm 99 ~ certain that …** ich bin (zu) 99 Prozent sicher, dass …

percentage [pə'sentɪdʒ] **N** **a** Prozentsatz *m*; *(= commission, payment)* Anteil *m*; *(= proportion)* Teil *m*; **a small ~ of the population** ein geringer Teil der Bevölkerung; **expressed as a ~** prozentual *or* in Prozenten ausgedrückt; **what ~?** wie viel Prozent?; **to get a ~ of all sales** prozentual am Umsatz beteiligt sein **b** *(inf: = advantage)* **there's no ~ in it** das bringt nichts *(inf)* **ATTR** prozentual; **on a ~ basis** prozentual, auf Prozentbasis; **~ sign** Prozentzeichen *nt*

percentile [pə'sentaɪl] N Prozent *nt*; **he's in the ninetieth ~ for reading and maths** in Lesen und Rechnen gehört er zu den besten zehn Prozent

perceptible [pə'septəbl] ADJ wahrnehmbar; *improvement, trend, increase etc* spürbar, deutlich; **there was a ~ pause** es trat eine deutliche Pause ein; **his unhappiness was ~ only to his close friends** nur seine engsten Freunde spürten *or* merkten, dass er unglücklich war

perceptibly [pə'septəblɪ] ADV merklich, spürbar; *(to the eye)* wahrnehmbar, sichtbar; **he paled ~** er wurde sichtbar blass

perception [pə'sepʃən] N **a** *no pl* Wahrnehmung *f*; **his colour ~ is impaired** seine Farbwahrnehmung ist beeinträchtigt; **his powers of ~** sein Wahrnehmungsvermögen *nt*
b *(= mental image, conception)* Auffassung *f* (*of* von); **he seems to have a clear ~ of the dilemma I face** er scheint meine schwierige Lage vollauf zu erkennen; **one's ~ of the situation** die eigene Einschätzung der Lage
c *no pl (= perceptiveness)* Einsicht *f*; *(= perceptive remark, observation)* Beobachtung *f*
d *no pl (= act of perceiving) (of object, visible difference)* Wahrnehmung *f*; *(of difficulties, meaning, illogicality etc)* Erkennen *nt*; **his quick ~ of the danger saved us all from death** weil er die Gefahr blitzschnell erkannte, rettete er uns allen das Leben

perceptive [pə'septɪv] ADJ **a** Wahrnehmungs-; **~ ability** Wahrnehmungsvermögen *nt*
b *person (= quick to smell/see/hear)* aufmerksam; *(= quick to understand)* scharfsinnig; *(= penetrating) analysis, speech, study* erkenntnisreich, scharfsinnig; *book, remark* aufschlussreich; **he has the ~ mind of a true artist** er hat das Einfühlungsvermögen eines wahren Künstlers; **very ~ of you!** *(iro)* du merkst aber auch alles! *(iro)*

perceptively [pə'septɪvlɪ] ADV *say, remark, write* scharfsinnig

perceptiveness [pə'septɪvnɪs] N *(of person) (= quickness to see/hear/smell)* Aufmerksamkeit *f*; *(= quick realization)* Scharfsinnigkeit *f*; *(of analysis, speech, study)* Erkenntnisreichtum *m*, Scharfsinnigkeit *f*; *(of argument)* Einsichtigkeit *f*

perceptual [pə'septjʊəl] ADJ ATTR Wahrnehmungs-; **~ skills** Wahrnehmungsfähigkeit *f*; **~ problems** Wahrnehmungsprobleme *pl*

perch¹ [pɜːtʃ] N *(= fish)* Flussbarsch *m*

perch² **N** **a** *(of bird)* Stange *f*; *(in tree)* Ast *m*; *(= hen-roost)* Hühnerstange *f*; *(fig: for person etc)* Hochsitz *m*; **to fall** *or* **drop** *or* **topple off the** *or* **one's ~** *(Brit fig inf)* den Löffel abgeben *(inf)*; **to knock sb off his ~** *(Brit fig)* jdn von seinem hohen Ross herunterholen **b** *(Measure) Längenmaß (5.029 m)* **VT** **to ~ sth on sth** etw auf etw *(acc)* setzen *or (upright)* stellen **VI** *(bird, fig: person)* hocken; *(= alight)* sich niederlassen; **the tower ~es on the edge of the cliff** der Turm thront über dem Rand der Klippe

perchance [pə'tʃɑːns] ADV *(old)* vielleicht

perched [pɜːtʃt] ADJ **a** *(= situated)* **~ on** thronend auf *+dat*; **a village ~ on a hillside/above the lake** ein Dorf, das auf dem Hang/über dem See thront **b** *(= seated)* **to be ~ on sth** auf etw *(dat)* hocken **c** *(= resting)* **with his glasses ~ on the end of his nose** mit der Brille auf der Nasenspitze

percipient [pə'sɪpɪənt] ADJ *(form)* = **perceptive**

percolate ['pɜːkəleɪt] **VT** filtrieren; *coffee* (in einer Kaffeemaschine) zubereiten; **~d coffee** mit der Kaffeemaschine gebrühter Kaffee **VI** *(lit, fig)* durchsickern; **the coffee is just percolating** der Kaffee läuft gerade durch; **the information was starting to ~ through** die Informationen begannen durchzusickern

percolator ['pɜːkəleɪtəʳ] N Kaffeemaschine *f*

percuss [pə'kʌs] VT *(Med)* perkutieren *(spec)*, abklopfen

percussion [pə'kʌʃən] N **a** Perkussion *f* *(also Med)* **b** *(Mus)* Schlagzeug *nt*

percussion: **percussion cap** N Zündhütchen *nt*; **percussion drill** N Schlagbohrmaschine *f*; **percussion instrument** N *(Mus)* Schlaginstrument *nt*

percussionist [pə'kʌʃənɪst] N Schlagzeuger(in) *m(f)*

percussion section N *(Mus)* Schlagzeug *nt*

percussive [pə'kʌsɪv] ADJ perkussorisch *(spec)*

per diem [pɜː'diːem] **ADV** pro Tag **ADJ** pro Tag; **the ~ rate** der Tagessatz **N** *(esp US)* Tagessatz *m*

perdition [pə'dɪʃən] N ewige Verdammnis

peregrination [ˌperɪgrɪ'neɪʃən] N *(liter)* Fahrt *f*

peregrine (falcon) ['perɪgrɪn('fɔːlkən)] N Wanderfalke *m*

peremptorily [pə'remptərɪlɪ] ADV *command, instruct* kategorisch

peremptory [pə'remptərɪ] ADJ *command, instruction* kategorisch; *gesture, voice* gebieterisch; *person* herrisch; **~ challenge** *(US Jur) Ablehnung eines Geschworenen ohne Angabe von Gründen*

perennial [pə'renɪəl] **ADJ** *plant* mehrjährig, perennierend; *(= perpetual, constant)* immer während, ewig; *(= regularly recurring)* immer wiederkehrend; **buying Christmas presents is a ~ problem** der Kauf von Weihnachtsgeschenken ist ein alljährlich wiederkehrendes Problem **N** *(Bot)* perennierende *or* mehrjährige Pflanze

perennially [pə'renɪəlɪ] ADV *(= perpetually, constantly)* ständig; *(= recurrently)* immer wieder

perestroika [pere'strɔɪkə] N Perestroika *f*

perfect ['pɜːfɪkt] **ADJ** **a** perfekt; *wife, husband, teacher, host, relationship* perfekt, vorbildlich; *weather, day, holiday* ideal, perfekt; *(Comm: = not damaged)* einwandfrei; **to be ~ for doing sth** bestens geeignet sein, um etw zu tun; **it was**

the ~ moment es war genau der richtige Augenblick; **that's the ~ hairstyle/woman for you** das ist genau die richtige Frisur/Frau für dich; **his Spanish is far from ~** sein Spanisch ist bei Weitem nicht perfekt; **with ~ self-confidence** mit absolutem Selbstvertrauen; **nobody is ~** niemand ist perfekt *or* vollkommen; **they make a ~ couple** sie sind das perfekte Paar; **in a ~ world** in einer idealen Welt; **he's the ~ gentleman** er ist der perfekte Gentleman; **~ number** *(Math)* vollkommene Zahl
b *(= absolute, utter)* völlig; *fool, nonsense* völlig, ausgemacht; **she's a ~ terror** sie ist einfach schrecklich; **he's a ~ bore** er ist ausgesprochen langweilig; **~ strangers** wildfremde Leute *pl*; **a ~ stranger** ein wildfremder Mensch; **he's a ~ stranger to me** er ist mir völlig fremd; **it's a ~ disgrace** es ist wirklich eine Schande
c *(Gram)* **~ tense** Perfekt *nt*; **~ ending** Endung *f* im Perfekt; **~ form** Vergangenheitsform *f*
d *(Mus) fourth* rein; *cadence* authentisch → **pitch²**
N *(Gram)* Perfekt *nt*; **in the ~** im Perfekt [pəˈfekt]
VT vervollkommnen; *technique, technology, process also* perfektionieren; **to ~ the art of doing sth** die Kunst perfektionieren, etw zu tun

perfectibility [pəˌfektɪˈbɪlɪtɪ] N Vervollkommnungsfähigkeit *f*; *(of technique, technology, process)* Perfektionierbarkeit *f*

perfectible [pəˈfektɪbl] ADJ vervollkommnungsfähig; *technique, technology, process* perfektionierbar

perfection [pəˈfekʃən] N **a** Vollkommenheit *f*, Perfektion *f*; **to do sth to ~** etw perfekt tun
b *(= perfecting)* Vervollkommnung *f*, Perfektionierung *f*; **the ~ of production methods** die Perfektionierung der Produktionsmethoden

perfectionism [pəˈfekʃənɪzəm] N Perfektionismus *m*

perfectionist [pəˈfekʃənɪst] **N** Perfektionist(in) *m(f)* **ADJ** perfektionistisch

perfective [pəˈfektɪv] ADJ *(also Gram)* perfektiv

perfectly [ˈpɜːfɪktlɪ] ADV **a** *(= flawlessly, completely)* perfekt; **he timed his entry ~** er hat seinen Eintritt genau abgepasst; **a ~ finished piece of work** eine wirklich vollendete Arbeit; **the climate suited us ~** das Klima war ideal für uns; **I understand you ~** ich weiß genau, was Sie meinen
b *(= absolutely, utterly)* absolut, vollkommen; **we're ~ happy about it** wir sind damit völlig zufrieden; **a ~ lovely day** ein wirklich herrlicher Tag; **you know ~ well that …** du weißt ganz genau, dass …; **to be ~ honest, …** um ganz ehrlich zu sein, …; **a Lada is a ~ good car** ein Lada ist durchaus ein gutes Auto

perfect rhyme N rührender Reim

perfidious ADJ, **perfidiously** ADV [pɜːˈfɪdɪəs, -lɪ] *(liter)* perfid(e) *(liter)*

perfidiousness [pɜːˈfɪdɪəsnɪs] N = **perfidy**

perfidy [ˈpɜːfɪdɪ] N *(liter)* Perfidie *f (liter)*

perforate [ˈpɜːfəreɪt] **VT** *(with row of holes)* perforieren; *(= pierce once)* durchstechen, lochen; *(Med)* perforieren **VI** *(ulcer)* durchbrechen

perforation [ˌpɜːfəˈreɪʃən] N *(= act)* Perforieren *nt*; *(= row of holes, Med)* Perforation *f*

perforce [pəˈfɔːs] ADV *(old, liter)* notgedrungen

perform [pəˈfɔːm] **VT** *play, concerto* aufführen; *solo, duet* vortragen; *part* spielen; *trick* vorführen; *miracle* vollbringen; *task* verrichten, erfüllen; *duty, function* erfüllen; *operation* durchführen; *ritual, ceremony* vollziehen
VI a *(= appear: orchestra, circus act etc)* auftreten; **to ~ on the violin** Geige spielen
b *(car, machine, football team etc)* leisten; *(examination candidate etc)* abschneiden; **the 2 litre version ~s better** die Zweiliterversion leistet mehr; **the car ~ed excellently in the speed trials** in den Geschwindigkeitsversuchen brachte der Wagen ausgezeichnete Ergebnisse; **the choir ~ed very well** der Chor war sehr gut *or* hat sehr gut gesungen; **this car ~s best between 50 and 60 kmph** dieser Wagen bringt seine optimale Leistung zwischen 50 und 60 Stundenkilometern; **how did he ~?** *(actor, musician)* wie war er?; **how did the car ~?** wie ist der Wagen gelaufen?; **he ~ed brilliantly as Hamlet** er spielte die Rolle des Hamlet brillant; **how does the metal ~ under pressure?** wie verhält sich das Metall unter Druck?; **the shares are ~ing strongly** die Aktien steigen stark; **he couldn't ~** *(euph, sexually)* er konnte nicht
c *(euph: = excrete)* sein Geschäft verrichten

performance [pəˈfɔːməns] N **a** *(esp Theat, of play, opera etc)* Aufführung *f*; *(cinema)* Vorstellung *f*; *(by actor)* Leistung *f*; *(of a part)* Darstellung *f*; **the late ~** die Spätvorstellung; **her ~ as Mother Courage was outstanding** ihre Darstellung der Mutter Courage war hervorragend; **he gave a splendid ~** er hat eine ausgezeichnete Leistung geboten, er hat ausgezeichnet gespielt/gesungen *etc*; **we are going to hear a ~ of Beethoven's 5th** wir werden Beethovens 5. Sinfonie hören
b *(= carrying out) (of function, duty, task)* Erfüllung *f*; *(of operation)* Durchführung *f*; *(of ritual, ceremony)* Vollzug *m*; *(of trick)* Vorführung *f*; *(of miracle)* Vollbringung *f*; *(of play, concerto)* Aufführung *f*; *(of solo, duet)* Vortrag *m*; *(of part)* Darstellung *f*; **in the ~ of his duties** in Ausübung seiner Pflicht; **he died in the ~ of his duty** er starb in Erfüllung seiner Pflicht
c *(= effectiveness) (of machine, vehicle, sportsman etc)* Leistung *f*; *(of examination candidate etc)* Abschneiden *nt*; *(of shares)* Kursentwicklung *f*; **he put up a good ~** er hat sich gut geschlagen *(inf)*; **what was his ~ like in the test?** wie hat er in der Prüfung abgeschnitten?; **the team gave a poor ~** die Mannschaft hat eine schlechte Leistung gezeigt
d *(inf: = to-do, palaver)* Umstand *m*; *(= bad behaviour)* Benehmen *nt*; **what a ~!** was für ein Umstand!, welch ein Benehmen!; **what a ~ to put on in front of all the guests** sich so vor den Gästen zu benehmen!

performance: **performance art** N Performance Art *f*; **performance artist** N Performancekünstler(in) *m(f)*; **performance car** N leistungsstarker Wagen

performative [pəˈfɔːmətɪv] *(Ling)* **N** performativer Ausdruck **ADJ** performativ

performer [pəˈfɔːməʳ] N Künstler(in) *m(f)*

performing [pəˈfɔːmɪŋ] ADJ *animal* dressiert; *artist* darstellend; **the ~ arts** die darstellenden Künste; **~ rights** Aufführungsrechte *pl*

perfume [ˈpɜːfjuːm] **N** *(= substance)* Parfüm *nt*; *(= smell)* Duft *m* **VT** [pəˈfjuːm] parfümieren; **the flowers ~d the air** der Duft der Blumen erfüllte die Luft

perfumed [ˈpɜːfjuːmd] ADJ **a** *(= scented) substance* parfümiert *(with* mit); *handkerchief, envelope* parfümiert **b** *(naturally) flowers, air* duftend; **a sweetly ~ oil** ein süßlich duftendes Öl

perfumer [pɜːˈfjuːməʳ] N *(= maker)* Parfümeur(in) *m(f)*; *(= seller)* Parfümhändler(in) *m(f)*; *(= device)* Parfümzerstäuber *m*

perfumery [pɜːˈfjuːmərɪ] N *(= making perfume)* Parfümherstellung *f*; *(= perfume factory)* Parfümerie *f*; *(= perfumes)* Parfüm *nt*

perfunctorily [pəˈfʌŋktərɪlɪ] ADV flüchtig

perfunctory [pəˈfʌŋktərɪ] ADJ flüchtig, der Form halber; **he said some ~ words of congratulation** er gratulierte mit ein paar flüchtig hingeworfenen Worten

pergola [ˈpɜːgələ] N Pergola *f*, Laube *f*

perhaps [pəˈhæps, præps] ✪ 1.1, 15.3, 26.3 ADV vielleicht; **~ the greatest exponent of the art** der möglicherweise bedeutendste Vertreter dieser Kunst; **~ so** das kann *or* mag sein; **~ not** vielleicht (auch) nicht; **will he make a complete recovery? – ~ not, but we are doing our best** wird er sich ganz erholen? – das vielleicht nicht, aber wir tun unser Bestes; **~ I might keep it for a day or two?** könnte ich es vielleicht *or* eventuell für ein oder zwei Tage behalten?

pericarp [ˈperɪkɑːp] N Perikarp *nt*

perigee [ˈperɪdʒiː] N *(Astron)* Perigäum *nt*, Erdnähe *f*

peril [ˈperɪl] N Gefahr *f*; **he is in great ~** er schwebt in großer Gefahr; **to be in ~ of one's life** in Lebensgefahr sein; **the cliff is in ~ of collapsing** es besteht die Gefahr, dass die Klippen einstürzen; **do it at your (own) ~** auf Ihre eigene Gefahr

perilous [ˈperɪləs] ADJ gefährlich; *situation also* bedrohlich

perilously [ˈperɪləslɪ] ADV gefährlich; **he was clinging ~ to an outcrop of rock** er hing lebensgefährlich an einem Felsvorsprung; **we came ~ close to bankruptcy/the precipice** wir waren dem Bankrott/Abgrund gefährlich nahe; **she came ~ close to falling** sie wäre um ein Haar heruntergefallen

perimeter [pəˈrɪmɪtəʳ] N *(Math)* Umfang *m*, Perimeter *m*; *(Med)* Perimeter *m*; *(of grounds)* Grenze *f*; **~ fence** Umzäunung *f*; **to walk round the ~** um das Gelände herumgehen

perinatal [perɪˈneɪtəl] ADJ *(Med)* perinatal

perineum [perɪˈniːəm] N *(Anat)* Damm *m*, Perineum *nt (spec)*

period [ˈpɪərɪəd] N **a** *(= length of time)* Zeit *f*; *(= age, epoch)* Zeitalter *nt*, Epoche *f*; *(Geol)* Periode *f*; **Picasso's blue ~** Picassos blaue Periode; **for a ~ of eight weeks/two hours** für eine (Zeit)dauer *or* einen Zeitraum von acht Wochen/zwei Stunden; **within a three-month ~** innerhalb von drei Monaten; **for a three-month ~** drei Monate lang; **at that ~ (of my life)** zu diesem Zeitpunkt (in meinem Leben); **a ~ of cold weather** eine Kaltwetterperiode; **the costume *etc* of the ~** die Kleidung *etc* der damaligen Zeit; **a writer of the ~** ein zeitgenössischer Schriftsteller
b *(Sch)* (Schul)stunde *f*; **double ~** Doppelstunde *f*
c *(form: of sentence)* Periode *f*; *(esp US: = full stop)* Punkt *m*; **I don't know anything about American literature ~** *(esp US)* ich habe überhaupt keine Ahnung von amerikanischer Literatur; **I'm not going ~!** *(esp US)* ich gehe nicht, Schluss *or* und damit basta *(inf)!*
d *(= menstruation)* Periode *f*, Monatsblutung *f*, Tage *pl (inf)*; **she missed a ~** sie bekam ihre Periode *etc* nicht
e *(Chem)* Periode *f*

period: **period costume**, **period dress** N zeitgenössische Kostüme *pl*; **period furniture** N antike Möbel *pl*

periodic [ˌpɪərɪˈɒdɪk] ADJ *(= intermittent)* periodisch; *(= regular also)* regelmäßig

periodical [ˌpɪərɪˈɒdɪkəl] **ADJ** = **periodic** **N** Zeitschrift *f*; *(academic also)* Periodikum *nt*

periodically [ˌpɪərɪˈɒdɪkəlɪ] ADV periodisch; *(= regularly also)* regelmäßig

periodicity [ˌpɪərɪəˈdɪsɪtɪ] N *(Chem)* Periodizität *f*

periodic system, **periodic table** N *(Chem)* Periodensystem *nt*

periodontitis [ˌperɪəʊdɒnˈtaɪtɪs] N Wurzelhautentzündung *f*

period: **period pains** PL Menstruationsbeschwerden *pl*; **period piece** N **a** antikes Stück; *(= painting, music etc)* Zeitdokument *nt* **b** *(also* **period play***)* Zeitstück *nt*

peripatetic [ˌperɪpəˈtetɪk] ADJ umherreisend; *existence* rastlos; *teacher* an mehreren Schulen unterrichtend *attr*

peripheral [pəˈrɪfərəl] **ADJ** Rand-; *(Anat)* peripher; *(fig)* nebensächlich, peripher; *(Comput)* Peripherie-; **to be ~ to sth** *(situation, person)* für etw nebensächlich sein; **~ figure** *(= person)* Randfigur *f*; **~ role** Nebenrolle *f*; **~ device** *(Comput)* Peripheriegerät *nt*; **~ vision** peripheres Sehvermögen **N** *(Comput)* Peripheriegerät *nt*; **the ~s** die Peripherie

periphery [pəˈrɪfərɪ] N Peripherie *f*; **young people on the ~ of society** junge Menschen am Rande der Gesellschaft

periphrastic [ˌperɪˈfræstɪk] ADJ periphrastisch

periscope [ˈperɪskəʊp] N Periskop *nt*

perish [ˈperɪʃ] VI a *(liter) (= die)* umkommen, sterben; *(= be destroyed: cities, civilization)* untergehen; **we shall do it or ~ in the attempt** wir werden es machen, koste es, was es wolle; **he ~ed at sea** er fand den Tod auf See; **~ the thought!** *(inf)* Gott behüte *or* bewahre! b *(rubber, leather etc)* verschleißen, brüchig werden; *(food)* verderben, schlecht werden VT *rubber, leather* zerstören, brüchig werden lassen

perishable [ˈperɪʃəbl] ADJ *food* verderblich; **"perishable"** „leicht verderblich" PL **~s** leicht verderbliche Ware(n)

perished [ˈperɪʃt] ADJ *(inf, with cold)* durchgefroren

perisher [ˈperɪʃəʳ] N *(Brit inf)* Teufelsbraten *m (inf)*

perishing [ˈperɪʃɪŋ] ADJ *(Brit inf)* a *(= very cold) room, weather* eisig kalt; **I'm ~** ich geh fast ein vor Kälte *(inf)* b *(= objectionable)* verdammt *(inf)*

peristalsis [ˌperɪˈstælsɪs] N Peristaltik *f*

peristyle [ˈperɪstaɪl] N Peristyl *nt*

peritoneum [ˌperɪtəʊˈniːəm] N Bauchfell *nt*, Peritoneum *nt (spec)*

peritonitis [ˌperɪtəʊˈnaɪtɪs] N Bauchfellentzündung *f*

periwig [ˈperɪwɪg] N *(Hist)* Perücke *f*

periwinkle [ˈperɪˌwɪŋkl] N *(Bot)* Immergrün *nt*; *(Zool)* Strandschnecke *f*

perjure [ˈpɜːdʒəʳ] VR einen Meineid leisten

perjured [ˈpɜːdʒəd] ADJ *evidence, witness* meineidig

perjury [ˈpɜːdʒərɪ] N Meineid *m*; **to commit ~** einen Meineid leisten

perk [pɜːk] N *(= benefit)* Vergünstigung *f*

▶ **perk up** VT *sep* a *(= lift) head* heben; **he perked up his ears** *(dog, person)* er spitzte die Ohren b **to perk sb up** *(= make lively: coffee etc)* jdn aufmöbeln *(inf) or* munter machen; *(= make cheerful: visit, idea etc)* jdn aufheitern; **she perked up her outfit with a bright scarf** sie peppte ihre Kleidung mit einem hellen Schal auf *(inf)* VI *(= liven up: person, party)* munter werden; *(= cheer up)* aufleben; *(= become interested)* hellhörig werden; **his ears perked up** er spitzte seine Ohren

perkily [ˈpɜːkɪlɪ] ADV *(= cheerfully)* munter; *(= cheekily)* kess, keck

perkiness [ˈpɜːkɪnɪs] N *(= cheerfulness)* Lebhaftigkeit *f*; *(= cheekiness)* Keckheit *f*, forsche Art

perky [ˈpɜːkɪ] ADJ *(+er) (= cheerful, bright)* munter; *(= cheeky, pert)* kess, keck

perm¹ [pɜːm] *abbr of* **permanent wave** N Dauerwelle *f*; **to give sb a ~** jdm eine Dauerwelle machen VT **to ~ sb's hair** jdm eine Dauerwelle machen; **she only had the ends ~ed** sie ließ sich *(dat)* nur an den Enden eine Dauerwelle machen VI **my hair doesn't ~ very easily** Dauerwelle hält bei mir sehr schlecht

perm² N *(for football pools) abbr of* **permutation**

permafrost [ˈpɜːməfrɒst] N Dauerfrostboden *m*

permanence [ˈpɜːmənəns], **permanency** [ˈpɜːmənənsɪ] N Dauerhaftigkeit *f*, Permanenz *f*; *(of relationship, marriage, arrangement also, of job)* Beständigkeit *f*; **having bought a flat, she began to feel some degree of ~** nachdem sie sich *(dat)* eine Wohnung gekauft hatte, entwickelte sie ein gewisses Gefühl der Bodenständigkeit

permanent [ˈpɜːmənənt] ADJ a *(= lasting)* ständig, permanent; *arrangement, position, building* fest; *job, relationship, dye, effect, solution* dauerhaft; *damage* bleibend; *agreement* unbefristet; **on a ~ basis** dauerhaft; **to earn oneself a ~ place in history** sich *(dat)* einen bleibenden Platz in der Geschichte verdienen; **the ~ revolution** die permanente Revolution; **I hope this is not going to become ~** ich hoffe, das wird kein Dauerzustand; **~ assets** Anlagevermögen *nt*; **~ capital** Anlagekapital *nt*; **~ feature** fester Bestandteil; **~ fixture** *(lit)* fest installierte Einrichtung; **he is a ~ fixture here** er gehört schon mit zum Inventar; **~ magnet** Permanentmagnet *m*; **~ memory** *(Comput)* Festspeicher *m*; **~ pleats** Dauerfalten *pl*; **~ residence/address** ständiger *or* fester Wohnsitz; **one's ~ teeth** die zweiten Zähne

b *(= constant) supply* permanent; *staff* fest angestellt; *member* ständig; **~ employees** Festangestellte *pl*; **to make sb ~** jdn fest anstellen; **I'm not ~ here** ich bin hier nicht fest angestellt

N *(US)* = **perm¹** N

permanently [ˈpɜːmənəntlɪ] ADV a permanent, ständig; *fixed* fest; *damage* bleibend; *change* ständig; **a ~ depressing effect** eine anhaltend deprimierende Wirkung; **~ employed** fest angestellt; **~ glued together** dauerhaft verbunden; **~ pleated skirt** Rock mit Dauerfalten; **are you living ~ in Frankfurt?** ist Frankfurt Ihr fester *or* ständiger Wohnsitz? b *(= constantly) closed* dauernd; *tired* dauernd, ständig; *angry* ständig

permanent: **Permanent Secretary** N *(Brit Admin)* beamteter Staatssekretär, beamtete Staatssekretärin; **permanent wave** N → **perm** N; **permanent way** N *(Brit)* Bahnkörper *m*

permanganate [pɜːˈmæŋgənɪt] N Permanganat *nt*

permeability [ˌpɜːmɪəˈbɪlɪtɪ] N Durchlässigkeit *f*, Permeabilität *f (geh, Sci)*

permeable [ˈpɜːmɪəbl] ADJ durchlässig, permeabel *(geh, Sci)*

permeate [ˈpɜːmɪeɪt] VT *(lit, fig)* durchdringen VI dringen *(into* in *+acc, through* durch)

permissible [pəˈmɪsɪbl] ADJ a erlaubt *(for sb* jdm); **legally ~** gesetzlich erlaubt; **the maximum ~ levels of radiation** die maximal zulässige Strahlenbelastung b *(= acceptable)* annehmbar

permission [pəˈmɪʃən] ✪ 9.1, 9.2 N Erlaubnis *f*; **with your ~** mit Ihrer Erlaubnis, wenn Sie gestatten; **without ~ from sb** ohne jds Erlaubnis; **to do sth with/by sb's ~** etw mit jds Erlaubnis tun; **to get ~** eine Erlaubnis erhalten; **to get sb's ~** jds Erlaubnis erhalten; **to give ~ (for sth)** etw erlauben, die Erlaubnis (für etw) erteilen; **to give sb ~ (to do sth)** jdm die Erlaubnis geben *or* jdm erlauben(, etw zu tun); **you have my ~ to leave** Sie haben meine Erlaubnis zu gehen; **no ~ is needed** eine Erlaubnis ist nicht erforderlich; **to ask sb's ~, to ask ~ of sb** jdn um Erlaubnis bitten; **to ask ~ for sb to do sth** um Erlaubnis bitten, dass jd etw tun darf; **"by (kind) ~ of ..."** „mit (freundlicher) Genehmigung *(+gen)* ..."

permissive [pəˈmɪsɪv] ADJ nachgiebig, permissiv *(geh)*; *(= tolerant) age, attitude, law, parents, school* freizügig; *(sexually)* freizügig; **it encourages youngsters to be ~** es führt zu allzu großer Freizügigkeit unter Jugendlichen; **the ~ society** die permissive Gesellschaft

permissiveness [pəˈmɪsɪvnɪs] N Nachgiebigkeit *f*, Permissivität *f (geh)*; *(of age, attitude, law, parents, school)* Freizügigkeit *f*; *(sexually)* Freizügigkeit *f*

permit [pəˈmɪt] ✪ 9.1, 9.2, 9.4 VT *sth* erlauben, gestatten; **to ~ sb/oneself to do sth** jdm/sich *(dat)* erlauben, etw zu tun; **is it/am I ~ted to smoke?** darf man/ich rauchen?; **visitors are not ~ted after 10** nach 10 Uhr sind keine Besucher mehr erlaubt; **to ~ oneself sth** sich *(dat)* etw erlauben; **~ me!** gestatten Sie bitte!

VI a **if you (will) ~** wenn Sie gestatten *or* erlauben; **if the weather ~s, weather ~ting** wenn es das Wetter erlaubt *or* zulässt; **if time ~s** wenn es die Zeit zulässt, wenn die Zeit reicht b *(form)* **to ~ of sth** etw zulassen [ˈpɜːmɪt]

N [ˈpɜːmɪt] Genehmigung *f*; **~ holder** Inhaber(in) *m(f)* eines Berechtigungsscheins *or (for parking)* Parkausweises; **"permit holders only"** *(for parking)* „Parken nur mit Parkausweis"

permutation [ˌpɜːmjʊˈteɪʃən] N Permutation *f*

permute [pəˈmjuːt] VT permutieren

pernicious [pɜːˈnɪʃəs] ADJ schädlich; *(Med)* perniziös, bösartig

pernicious anaemia N *(Med)* perniziöse Anämie

pernickety [pəˈnɪkɪtɪ] ADJ *(inf)* pingelig *(inf)*; *(= tricky, delicate) work, point* heikel

perorate [ˈperəreɪt] VI *(liter) (conclude a speech)* eine Rede zusammenfassend abschließen; *(speak at length)* endlose Reden halten, sich auslassen *(inf) (against* über *+acc)*

peroration [ˌperəˈreɪʃən] N *(liter) (= concluding part)* Resümee *nt*, Zusammenfassung *f*; *(= lengthy speech)* endlose Rede

peroxide [pəˈrɒksaɪd] N Peroxid *nt*; **a ~ blonde** *(pej)* eine Wasserstoffblondine; **~ blonde hair** wasserstoffblonde Haare

perp [pɜːp] N *(inf)* = **perpetrator**

perpendicular [ˌpɜːpənˈdɪkjʊləʳ] ADJ a senkrecht *(to* zu); **the wall is not quite ~ to the ceiling** die Mauer steht nicht ganz lotrecht zur Decke; **a ~ cliff** eine senkrecht abfallende Klippe b *(Archit)* perpendikular N Senkrechte *f*; **to drop a ~** ein Lot fällen; **to be out of ~** nicht im Lot sein

perpendicularly [ˌpɜːpənˈdɪkjʊləlɪ] ADV senkrecht

perpetrate [ˈpɜːpɪtreɪt] VT begehen; *crime also* verüben

perpetration [ˌpɜːpɪˈtreɪʃən] N Begehen *nt*, Begehung *f*; *(of crime also)* Verübung *f*

perpetrator [ˈpɜːpɪtreɪtəʳ] N Täter(in) *m(f)*; *(= originator)* Verursacher(in) *m(f)*; **the ~ of this crime** derjenige, der dieses Verbrechen begangen hat

perpetual [pəˈpetjʊəl] ADJ ständig, fortwährend, immer während; *joy* stet; *ice, snow* ewig; **you're a ~ source of amazement to me** ich muss mich immer wieder über dich wundern; **~ motion/motion machine** Perpetuum mobile *nt*

perpetually [pəˈpetjʊəlɪ] ADV ständig

perpetuate [pəˈpetjʊeɪt] VT aufrechterhalten; *memory* bewahren

perpetuation [pəˌpetjʊˈeɪʃən] N Aufrechterhaltung *f*; *(of memory)* Bewahrung *f*; *(of old names etc)* Beibehaltung *f*

perpetuity [ˌpɜːpɪˈtjuːɪtɪ] N *(form)* Ewigkeit *f*; **in ~** auf ewig; *(Jur)* lebenslänglich

perplex [pəˈpleks] VT verblüffen, verdutzen

perplexed ADJ, **perplexedly** ADV [pəˈplekst, -sɪdlɪ] verblüfft, verdutzt, perplex

perplexing [pəˈpleksɪŋ] ADJ verblüffend

perplexingly [pəˈpleksɪŋlɪ] ADV verwirrend; **a ~ difficult problem** ein schwieriges und verwirrendes Problem

perplexity [pəˈpleksɪtɪ] N a Verblüffung *f*; **in some ~** verblüfft, verdutzt, perplex b *(= complexity)* Komplexität *f*; **the perplexities of sth** die Komplexität einer Sache *(gen)*

perquisite [ˈpɜːkwɪzɪt] N *(form)* Vergünstigung *f*

perry [ˈperɪ] N Birnenmost *m*

per se [pɜːˈseɪ] ADV an sich, per se *(geh)*

per second billing [pɜːˌsekəndˈbɪlɪŋ] N *(Telec)* sekundengenaue Abrechnung

persecute [ˈpɜːsɪkjuːt] VT verfolgen

persecution [ˌpɜːsɪˈkjuːʃən] N Verfolgung *f (of* von); **his ~ by the press** seine Verfolgung durch die Presse; **to have a ~ complex** an Verfolgungswahn leiden

persecutional mania [ˌpɜːsɪˈkjuːʃənlˈmeɪnɪə] N *(Psych)* Verfolgungswahn *m*

persecutor [ˈpɜːsɪkjuːtəʳ] N Verfolger(in) *m(f)*

perseverance [ˌpɜːsɪˈvɪərəns] N Ausdauer *f (with* mit), Beharrlichkeit *f (with* bei)

perseverant ADJ, **perseverantly** ADV [ˌpɜːsɪˈvɪərənt, -lɪ] ausdauernd, beharrlich

persevere [ˌpɜːsɪˈvɪəʳ] VI durchhalten; **to ~ in one's studies** mit seinem Studium weitermachen; **he ~d with German** er machte mit Deutsch weiter; **to ~ in** *or* **with one's attempts/**

efforts to do sth unermüdlich weiter versuchen, etw zu tun

persevering ADJ, **perseveringly** ADV [ˌpɜːsɪˈvɪərɪŋ, -lɪ] ausdauernd, beharrlich

Persia [ˈpɜːʃə] N Persien *nt*

Persian [ˈpɜːʃən] ADJ persisch; **the ~ Gulf** der Persische Golf; **~ lamb** *(= animal)* Karakulschaf *nt*; *(= skin, coat)* Persianer *m* N a Perser(in) *m(f)* b *(Ling)* Persisch *nt*

Persian carpet N Perser(teppich) *m*

Persian cat N Perserkatze *f*

persiflage [ˌpɜːsɪˈflɑːʒ] N Persiflage *f*

persimmon [pɜːˈsɪmən] N Persimone *f*; *(= wood)* Persimmon *nt*

persist [pəˈsɪst] VI *(= persevere)* nicht lockerlassen, unbeirrt fortfahren *(with* mit); *(= be tenacious: in belief, demand etc)* beharren, bestehen *(in* auf *+dat)*; *(= last, continue: fog, pain etc)* anhalten, fortdauern; **if you ~ in misbehaving** wenn du dich weiterhin so schlecht benimmst; **if you ~ in coming late** wenn du weiterhin zu spät kommst; **if the rumours still ~** falls sich die Gerüchte halten sollten; **we shall ~ in** *or* **with our efforts** wir werden in unseren Bemühungen nicht nachlassen

persistence [pəˈsɪstəns], **persistency** [pəˈsɪstənsɪ] N *(= tenacity)* Beharrlichkeit *f*, Hartnäckigkeit *f*; *(= perseverance)* Ausdauer *f*; *(of disease)* Hartnäckigkeit *f*; *(of fog, pain etc)* Anhalten *nt*, Fortdauern *nt*; **the ~ of his questioning brought results** sein beharrliches Fragen hat schließlich doch zu etwas geführt; **the ~ of a high temperature** anhaltend hohes Fieber

persistent [pəˈsɪstənt] ADJ *(= tenacious) demands, questions* beharrlich; *person, smell* hartnäckig; *attempts, efforts* ausdauernd; *(= repeated, constant) drinking, drinker* gewohnheitsmäßig; *nagging, lateness, threats* ständig; *report* wiederholt; *rumour, problems* anhaltend; *cheerfulness* gleichbleibend; *(= continuing) rain, illness, pain, noise* anhaltend; *worry* nicht nachlassend; **~ offender** Wiederholungstäter(in) *m(f)*; **despite our ~ warnings ...** obwohl wir sie/ihn *etc* immer wieder gewarnt haben ...; **~ vegetative state** *(Med)* waches Koma, Wachkoma *nt*

persistently [pəˈsɪstəntlɪ] ADV *deny, ask* beharrlich; *claim, argue* hartnäckig; *fail, criticize* ständig; **to ~ break the law** wiederholt das Gesetz brechen; **~ high inflation** anhaltend hohe Inflation; **to be ~ late** ständig spät kommen

persnickety [pəˈsnɪkɪtɪ] ADJ *(US inf)* pingelig *(inf)*; *(= tricky, delicate) work, point* heikel

person [ˈpɜːsn] N a *pl* **people** *or (form)* **-s** *(= human being)* Mensch *m*; *(in official contexts)* Person *f*; **I like him as a ~, but not as a teacher** ich mag ihn als Mensch, aber nicht als Lehrer; **no ~** kein Mensch, niemand; **I know no such ~** so jemanden kenne ich nicht; **any ~** jeder; **a certain ~** ein gewisser Jemand; **~ to ~ call** Gespräch *nt* mit Voranmeldung; **30 p per ~** 30 Pence pro Person; **the murder was committed by ~ or ~s unknown** der Mord wurde von einem oder mehreren unbekannten Tätern verübt; **I'm more of an outdoor/cat ~** ich bin mehr ein Typ *m* für draußen/ein Katzentyp *m*

b *pl* **-s** *(Gram, Jur: = legal person)* Person *f*; **first ~ singular/plural** erste Person Singular/Plural

c *pl* **-s** *(= body, physical presence)* Körper *m*; *(= appearance)* Äußere(s) *nt*; **in ~** persönlich; **in the ~ of** in Gestalt *(+gen)*; **crime against the ~** Vergehen *nt* gegen die Person; **on** *or* **about one's ~** bei sich

-person SUF *in Berufsbezeichnungen etc als neutralere Form anstelle von „-man"*; **chairperson** Vorsitzende(r) *mf*; **salesperson** Verkäufer(in) *m(f)*

persona [pɜːˈsəʊnə] N *pl* **-e** *(Psych)* Persona *f*; **~ grata** *(Jur)* Persona grata *f*; **~ non grata** *(Jur, fig)* Persona non grata *f*

personable [ˈpɜːsnəbl] ADJ von angenehmer Erscheinung

personae [pɜːˈsəʊniː] *pl of* **persona**

personage [ˈpɜːsənɪdʒ] N Persönlichkeit *f*

personal [ˈpɜːsənl] ADJ a persönlich; **he gave several ~ performances to promote his new record** er trat mehrmals persönlich auf, um für seine neue Platte zu werben; **to make a ~ appearance** persönlich erscheinen; **the ~ touch** der persönliche Touch; **~ freshness** *or* **cleanliness/hygiene** Körperfrische *f*/-pflege *f*; **it's nothing ~, I just don't think you're the right person** nicht, dass ich etwas gegen Sie persönlich hätte, Sie sind nur nicht der/die Richtige; **I have no ~ knowledge of it** mir (persönlich) ist nichts davon bekannt; **~ call** Privatgespräch *nt*; **~ effects** persönliches Eigentum; **~ friend** persönlicher Freund, persönliche Freundin; **~ identification number** persönliche Identifikationsnummer, Geheimzahl *f (inf)*; **~ stationery** Briefpapier *nt* mit persönlichem Briefkopf

b *(= private) problems* persönlich; **her ~ life** ihr Privatleben *nt*; **"personal"** *(on letter)* „privat"

c *(= rude) insult, remark* persönlich; **don't get ~** nun werden Sie mal nicht persönlich

N *(US Press: = advert)* Privatanzeige *f*

personal: **personal ad** N *(inf)* private Kleinanzeige; **personal allowance** N *(for tax purposes)* persönlicher Freibetrag; **personal assistant** N persönlicher Assistent, persönliche Assistentin; *(= secretary)* Chefsekretär(in) *m(f)*; **personal best** N *(Sport)* persönliche Bestleistung; **to set a new ~** *(Sport)* eine neue persönliche Bestleistung aufstellen; **personal chair** N *(Brit Univ) Lehrstelle, die aufgrund außergewöhnlicher Leistungen des Inhabers eingerichtet wurde*; **personal column** N Familienanzeigen *pl*; **personal computer** N Personal Computer *m*, PC *m*; **personal digital assistant** N *(Comput)* PDA *m*, Taschencomputer *m*; **personal hygiene** N Körperpflege *f*; **personal insurance** N Privatversicherung *f*

personality [ˌpɜːsəˈnælɪtɪ] N a *(= character, person)* Persönlichkeit *f*; **~ development** Persönlichkeitsentfaltung *f* b *(= personal remark)* **let's keep personalities out of this** lassen wir persönliche Dinge aus dem Spiel

personality cult N Personenkult *m*

personality disorder N Persönlichkeitsstörung *f*

personalize [ˈpɜːsənəlaɪz] VT a *(= make more personal)* persönlicher gestalten; *(= put initials etc on) diary, calculator, shirt* eine persönliche *or* individuelle Note geben *(+dat)*; **~d letterhead** persönliches *or* individuelles Briefpapier; **~d number plates = vanity plates** b *(= treat as personal issue)* personalisieren

personal loan N Personaldarlehen *nt*, Privatdarlehen *nt*

personally [ˈpɜːsənəlɪ] ✪ 6.1 ADV persönlich; **~, I think that ...** ich persönlich bin der Meinung, dass ...; **I like him ~, but not as an employer** ich mag ihn als Mensch, aber nicht als Arbeitgeber; **to be ~ responsible (for sth)** persönlich (für etw) verantwortlich sein; **to hold sb ~ responsible** jdn persönlich verantwortlich machen; **to be ~ involved** persönlich *or* selbst beteiligt sein; **to take sth ~** etw persönlich nehmen

personal: **personal organizer** N Terminplaner *m*, Zeitplaner *m*; *(electronic also)* elektronisches Notizbuch; **personal pronoun** N *(Gram)* Personalpronomen *nt*, persönliches Fürwort; **personal property** N persönliches Eigentum, Privateigentum *nt*; **personal space** N persönlicher Freiraum; **to invade sb's ~** jdm zu nahe kommen; **personal stereo** N Walkman® *m*; **personal trainer** N privater Fitnesstrainer, private Fitnesstrainerin

personalty [ˈpɜːsnltɪ] N *(Jur)* bewegliches Vermögen

personal video recorder N digitaler Videorekorder *(mit individuell einstellbaren Funktionen)*

personification [pɜːˌsɒnɪfɪˈkeɪʃən] N Verkörperung *f*, Personifizierung *f*; **he is the ~ of good taste** er ist der personifizierte gute Geschmack

personify [pɜːˈsɒnɪfaɪ] VT personifizieren; *(= be the personification of also)* verkörpern; **he is evil personified** er ist das personifizierte Böse *or* das Böse in Person

personnel [ˌpɜːsəˈnel] N *sing or pl* a Personal *nt*; *(on plane)* Besatzung *f*; *(on ship)* Besatzung *f*, Mannschaft *f*; *(Mil)* Leute *pl*; **this firm employs 800 ~** diese Firma beschäftigt 800 Leute; **with a larger ~** mit mehr Personal b *(= personnel department)* die Personalabteilung; *(= personnel work)* Personalarbeit *f* ATTR Personal-; **~ agency** Personalagentur *f*; **~ carrier** *(Mil)* Mannschaftstransportwagen *m*/-transportflugzeug *nt*

personnel: **personnel management** N Personalführung *f*; **personnel manager** N Personalchef(in) *m(f)*; **personnel officer** N Personalleiter(in) *m(f)*

perspective [pəˈspektɪv] N *(lit)* Perspektive *f*; *(fig also)* Blickwinkel *m*; **to get a different ~ on a problem** ein Problem aus einer anderen Perspektive *or* aus einem anderen Blickwinkel sehen; **in ~** *(Art)* perspektivisch; **the foreground isn't in ~** der Vordergrund ist perspektivisch nicht richtig; **try to keep/get things in ~** versuchen Sie, nüchtern und sachlich zu bleiben/das nüchtern und sachlich zu sehen; **to get sth out of ~** *(lit: artist etc)* etw perspektivisch verzerren; *(fig)* etw verzerrt sehen; **in historical ~** aus historischer Sicht; **to see things in their proper** *or* **true ~** die Dinge so sehen, wie sie sind; **to see things from a different ~** die Dinge aus einem anderen Blickwinkel betrachten

Perspex® [ˈpɜːspeks] N Acrylglas *nt*, Akrylglas *nt*

perspicacious [ˌpɜːspɪˈkeɪʃəs] ADJ *person, remark etc* scharfsinnig; *decision* weitsichtig

perspicacity [ˌpɜːspɪˈkæsɪtɪ] N Scharfsinn *m*, Scharfblick *m*; *(of decision)* Weitsicht *f*

perspicuity [ˌpɜːspɪˈkjuːɪtɪ] N Klarheit *f*; *(= clearness: of expression, statement also)* Verständlichkeit *f*

perspicuous [ˌpəˈspɪkjʊəs] ADJ einleuchtend; *(= clear) expression, statement* klar, verständlich

perspiration [ˌpɜːspəˈreɪʃən] N *(= perspiring)* Schwitzen *nt*, Transpiration *f (geh)*; *(= sweat)* Schweiß *m*; **the ~ was dripping off him, he was dripping with ~** ihm lief der Schweiß in Strömen herunter; **beads of ~** Schweißperlen *pl*

perspire [pəˈspaɪəʳ] VI schwitzen, transpirieren *(geh)*

persuadable [pəˈsweɪdəbl] ADJ **he may be ~** *(= amenable)* vielleicht lässt er sich überreden, vielleicht ist er zu überreden; *(= convincible)* vielleicht lässt er sich überzeugen, vielleicht ist er zu überzeugen

persuade [pəˈsweɪd] VT überreden; *(= convince)* überzeugen; **to ~ sb to do sth** jdn überreden, etw zu tun; **to ~ sb into doing sth** jdn dazu überreden, etw zu tun; **to ~ sb out of sth** jdm etw ausreden; **to ~ sb out of doing sth** jdn dazu überreden, etw nicht zu tun; **to ~ oneself/sb of sth** sich selbst/jdn von etw überzeugen; **to ~ sb of the need for sth** jdn von der Notwendigkeit einer Sache überzeugen; **to ~ sb of the need to do sth** jdn von der Notwendigkeit überzeugen, etw zu tun; **to ~ sb that ...** jdn davon überzeugen, dass ...; **I am ~d that ...** ich bin überzeugt, dass ...; **she is easily ~d** sie ist leicht zu überreden/überzeugen; **he doesn't take much persuading** ihn braucht man nicht lange zu überreden

persuader [pəˈsweɪdəʳ] N Überredungskünstler(in) *m(f)*; **the hidden ~s** die geheimen Verführer

persuasible [pəˈsweɪzəbl] ADJ = **persuadable**

persuasion [pəˈsweɪʒən] N a *(= persuading)* Überredung *f*; **advertising uses many subtle means of ~** die Werbung arbeitet mit vielen subtilen Überzeugungsmechanismen; **her powers of ~** ihre Überredungskünste; **she tried every possible means of ~ to get him to agree** sie setzte ihre ganze Überredungskunst ein, um seine Zustimmung zu erlangen; **I don't need much ~ to stop working** man braucht mich

nicht lange zu überreden, damit ich aufhöre zu arbeiten
b *(= persuasiveness)* Überzeugungskraft *f*
c *(= belief)* Überzeugung *f*; *(= sect, denomination)* Glaube *m*, Glaubensrichtung *f*; **I am not of that ~** *(= don't believe that)* davon bin ich nicht überzeugt; *(= don't belong to that sect)* ich gehöre nicht diesem Glauben an; **and others of that ~** und andere, die dieser Überzeugung anhängen; **to be of left-wing ~, to have left-wing ~s** linke Ansichten haben

persuasive [pəˈsweɪsɪv] ADJ *salesman, voice* beredsam; *arguments etc* überzeugend; **he can be very ~** er kann einen gut überreden; *(= convincing)* er kann einen leicht überzeugen; **I had to be very ~** ich musste meine ganze Überredungskunst aufwenden; **her ~ powers** ihre Überredungskünste *pl*

persuasively [pəˈsweɪsɪvlɪ] ADV *argue etc* überzeugend; **..., he said ~** ..., versuchte er sie/ihn *etc* zu überreden

persuasiveness [pəˈsweɪsɪvnɪs] N *(of person, salesman etc)* Überredungskunst *f*, Beredsamkeit *f*; *(of argument etc)* Überzeugungskraft *f*

pert [pɜːt] ADJ *(+er)* keck, kess; *(= impudent)* keck; **a ~ little smile** ein kesses *or* freches Lächeln

pertain [pɜːˈteɪn] VI **to ~ to sth** etw betreffen; *(= belong to: land etc)* zu etw gehören; **all documents ~ing to the case** alle den Fall betreffenden Dokumente; **and other matters ~ing to it** und andere damit verbundene Fragen; **of or ~ing to sth** etw betreffend

pertinacious [ˌpɜːtɪˈneɪʃəs] ADJ *(= persevering)* beharrlich, ausdauernd; *(= tenacious, stubborn)* hartnäckig

pertinacity [ˌpɜːtɪˈnæsɪtɪ] N *(= perseverance)* Beharrlichkeit *f*, Ausdauer *f*; *(= stubbornness)* Hartnäckigkeit *f*

pertinence [ˈpɜːtɪnəns] N Relevanz *f* *(to* für); *(of information)* Sachdienlichkeit *f*

pertinent [ˈpɜːtɪnənt] ADJ relevant *(to* für); *information* sachdienlich

pertinently [ˈpɜːtɪnəntlɪ] ADV passend, völlig richtig; **he asked very ~ whether ...** er stellte zu Recht die Frage, ob ...

pertly [ˈpɜːtlɪ] ADV keck, kess; *(= impudently)* keck

pertness [ˈpɜːtnɪs] N Keckheit *f*, Kessheit *f*; *(= impudence)* Keckheit *f*

perturb [pəˈtɜːb] VT beunruhigen

perturbation [ˌpɜːtɜːˈbeɪʃən] N *(= state)* Unruhe *f*; *(= act)* Beunruhigung *f*; **to be in (a state of) ~** ziemlich in Unruhe sein

perturbed [pəˈtɜːbd] ADJ beunruhigt

perturbing ADJ, **perturbingly** ADV [pəˈtɜːbɪŋ, -lɪ] beunruhigend

Peru [pəˈruː] N Peru *nt*

perusal [pəˈruːzəl] N Lektüre *f*; *(careful)* sorgfältige Durchsicht, Prüfung *f*; **after a brief ~ of the newspaper he ...** nachdem er kurz einen Blick in die Zeitung geworfen hatte ...

peruse [pəˈruːz] VT (durch)lesen; *(carefully)* sorgfältig durchsehen, prüfen

Peruvian [pəˈruːvɪən] ADJ peruanisch N Peruaner(in) *m(f)*

pervade [pɜːˈveɪd] VT erfüllen; *(smell also)* durchziehen; *(light)* durchfluten; **his writing is ~d with dialect expressions** seine Bücher sind voller Dialektausdrücke; **the universities are ~d with subversive elements** die Universitäten sind mit subversiven Elementen durchsetzt

pervading [pɜːˈveɪdɪŋ] ADJ durchdringend

pervasive [pɜːˈveɪsɪv] ADJ *smell etc* durchdringend; *influence, feeling, ideas* um sich greifend

pervasively [pɜːˈveɪsɪvlɪ] ADV durchdringend; **to spread ~** *(smell etc)* sich überall ausbreiten *(through* in *+dat)*; *(ideas, mood etc also)* um sich greifen *(through* in *+dat)*

pervasiveness [pɜːˈveɪsɪvnɪs] N *(of smell etc)* durchdringender Charakter; *(of influence, feeling, ideas)* um sich greifender Charakter

perverse [pəˈvɜːs] ADJ *(= contrary) idea* abwegig; *(= perverted)* pervers, widernatürlich; **it would be ~ to refuse** es wäre unsinnig abzulehnen

perversely [pəˈvɜːslɪ] ADV *(= paradoxically)* paradoxerweise; *think, believe, decide* abwegigerweise; **~, when the day of her departure came, she wanted to stay** als der Abreisetag gekommen war, wollte sie paradoxerweise noch bleiben; **~ enjoyable** auf perverse Art und Weise unterhaltsam; **do you have to be so ~ different?** musst du denn immer um jeden Preis anders sein?; **he is really ~ old-fashioned** er ist wirklich hoffnungslos altmodisch; **the translation still sounds ~ French** die Übersetzung klingt noch immer penetrant französisch

perverseness [pəˈvɜːsnɪs] N *(of idea)* Abwegigkeit *f*; *(= perverted nature)* Perversität *f*, Widernatürlichkeit *f*

perversion [pəˈvɜːʃən] N **a** *(esp sexual, Psych)* Perversion *f*; *(no pl: = act of perverting)* Pervertierung *f* **b** *(Rel)* Fehlglaube *m*; *(no pl: = act)* Irreleitung *f* **c** *(= distortion: of truth etc)* Verzerrung *f*

perversity [pəˈvɜːsɪtɪ] N *(= perverted nature)* Perversität *f*, Widernatürlichkeit *f*

pervert [pəˈvɜːt] VT *(= deprave) person, mind* verderben, pervertieren; *(Rel) believer* irreleiten; *(= change, distort) truth, sb's words* verzerren; **to ~ the course of justice** *(Jur)* die Rechtsfindung behindern; *(by official)* das Recht beugen [ˈpɜːvɜːt] N Perverse(r) *mf*

perverted [pəˈvɜːtɪd] ADJ *mind, person* verdorben, pervertiert; *phone call* pervers

pervious [ˈpɜːvɪəs] ADJ *(lit)* durchlässig; *(fig)* zugänglich *(to* für); **chalk is ~ (to water)** Kalk ist wasserdurchlässig

perviousness [ˈpɜːvɪəsnɪs] N *(lit)* Durchlässigkeit *f*; *(fig)* Zugänglichkeit *f* *(to* für)

peseta [pəˈseɪtə] N Peseta *f*

pesky [ˈpeskɪ] ADJ *(+er) (esp US inf)* nervtötend *(inf)*

pessary [ˈpesərɪ] N *(= contraceptive)* Pessar *nt*; *(= suppository)* Zäpfchen *nt*, Suppositorium *nt* *(spec)*

pessimism [ˈpesɪmɪzəm] N Pessimismus *m*, Schwarzseherei *f*

pessimist [ˈpesɪmɪst] N Pessimist(in) *m(f)*, Schwarzseher(in) *m(f)*

pessimistic [ˌpesɪˈmɪstɪk] ADJ pessimistisch; **I'm rather ~ about it** da bin ich ziemlich pessimistisch, da sehe ich ziemlich schwarz *(inf)*; **I'm ~ about our chances of success** ich bin pessimistisch, was unsere Erfolgschancen angeht, ich sehe schwarz für unsere Erfolgschancen *(inf)*

pessimistically [ˌpesɪˈmɪstɪkəlɪ] ADV pessimistisch

pest [pest] N **a** *(Zool)* Schädling *m*; **~ control** Schädlingsbekämpfung *f* **b** *(fig) (= person)* Nervensäge *f*; *(= thing)* Plage *f*; **sex ~** (lästige) Sexbestie **c** *(obs: = plague)* Pest *f*, Pestilenz *f* *(old)*

pester [ˈpestəʳ] VT belästigen; *(= keep on at: with requests etc)* plagen; **to ~ the life out of sb** jdm keine Ruhe lassen; **she ~ed me for the book** sie ließ mir keine Ruhe wegen des Buches; **to ~ sb to do sth** jdn bedrängen, etw zu tun

pesticide [ˈpestɪsaɪd] N Schädlingsbekämpfungsmittel *nt*, Pestizid *nt (spec)*

pestiferous [peˈstɪfərəs] ADJ verpestet; *(inf: = annoying)* lästig

pestilence [ˈpestɪləns] N *(old, liter)* Pest *f*, Pestilenz *f (old)*

pestilent [ˈpestɪlənt], **pestilential** [ˌpestɪˈlenʃəl] ADJ pesterfüllt; *(fig: = pernicious)* schädlich, verderblich; *(inf: = loathsome)* ekelhaft; **a ~ disease** eine Seuche

pestle [ˈpesl] N Stößel *m*

pet[1] [pet] ADJ *attr* **a** **~ animal** Haustier *nt*; **a ~ lion** ein zahmer Löwe; **her two ~ dogs** ihre beiden Hunde
b *(= favourite)* Lieblings-; **~ idea/theory** Lieblingsidee/-theorie *f*; **~ pupil** Lieblingsschüler(in) *m(f)*; **a ~ name** ein Kosename *m* → **hate N b**
N **a** *(= animal)* Haustier *nt*
b *(= favourite)* Liebling *m*; **teacher's ~** Lehrers Liebling *m or* Schätzchen *nt (inf)*; *(as derogatory name)* Streber(in) *m(f)*
c *(inf: = dear)* Schatz *m*; **yes, (my) ~** ja, (mein) Schatz; **he's rather a ~** er ist wirklich lieb *or* ein Schatz
VT *animal* streicheln; *child also* liebkosen; *(fig: = spoil)* (ver)hätscheln
VI *(sexually)* Petting machen

pet[2] N *(dated inf, = huff)* Verstimmung *f*; **to be in/fly into a ~** verstimmt *or* gekränkt sein/werden

PET *(Med) abbr of* **positron emission tomography** PET *nt*

petal [ˈpetl] N Blütenblatt *nt*; **settle ~!** *(Brit inf: = calm down)* beruhige dich, jetzt komm mal runter *(inf)*

petard [peˈtɑːd] N Petarde *f* → **hoist**

PET bottle N PET-Flasche *f*

pet dander allergy N Haustierallergie *f*

Pete [piːt] N **for ~'s** *or* **pete's sake** *(inf)* um Himmels willen

Peter [ˈpiːtəʳ] N Peter *m*; *(= apostle)* Petrus *m*; **Saint ~** Sankt Peter, der Heilige Petrus; **to rob ~ to pay Paul** ein Loch mit dem anderen zustopfen; **he is a real ~ Pan** er will einfach nicht erwachsen werden; **he's the ~ Pan of show business** er ist der ewig junge Showstar; **~ Pan collar** Bubikragen *m*

▶ **peter out** VI langsam zu Ende gehen; *(mineral vein)* versiegen; *(river)* versickern; *(song, noise)* verhallen; *(interest)* sich verlieren, sich totlaufen; *(excitement)* sich legen; *(plan)* im Sande verlaufen

peterman [ˈpiːtəmən] N *pl* **-men** [-mən] *(sl)* Schränker *m (sl)*, Panzerknacker *m (inf)*

petersham [ˈpiːtəʃəm] N *(= ribbon)* Seidenripsband *nt*

pet food N Tierfutter *nt*

petiole [ˈpetɪəʊl] N Stängel *m*

petit bourgeois [ˈpetɪˈbʊəʒwɑː] N Kleinbürger(in) *m(f)* ADJ kleinbürgerlich

petite [pəˈtiːt] ADJ *woman, girl* zierlich

petite bourgeoisie [petɪˌbʊəʒwɑːˈziː] N Kleinbürgertum *nt*

petit four [ˈpetɪˈfɔːr] N *pl* **-s -s** Petit Four *nt*

petition [pəˈtɪʃən] N **a** *(= list of signatures)* Unterschriftenliste *f*; **to get up a ~ (for/against sth)** Unterschriften (für/gegen etw) sammeln
b *(= request)* Gesuch *nt*, Bittschrift *f*, Petition *f*; **~ for clemency** Gnadengesuch *nt*
c *(Jur)* **~ for divorce** Scheidungsantrag *m*; **a ~ for** *or* **in bankruptcy** ein Konkursantrag *m*
VT *person, authorities (= request, entreat)* ersuchen *(for* um); *(= hand petition to)* eine Unterschriftenliste vorlegen *(+dat)*; **to ~ the court** das Gericht anrufen
VI **a** *(= hand in petition)* eine Unterschriftenliste einreichen
b *(Jur)* **to ~ for divorce** die Scheidung einreichen; **to ~ for bankruptcy** das Konkursverfahren eröffnen

petitioner [pəˈtɪʃənəʳ] N Bittsteller(in) *m(f)*; *(Jur)* Kläger(in) *m(f)*

petit jury [ˌpetɪˈdʒʊərɪ] N ≈ Geschworene *pl*

petit larceny [ˌpetɪˈlɑːsənɪ] N einfacher Diebstahl

petit mal [ˌpətiːˈmæl] N *(Med)* Petit Mal *nt*

petit point [ˌpətiːˈpwɛ̃] N Petit point *nt*

petits pois [ˌpətiːˈpwɑː] PL *(form)* Petits Pois *pl*

pet passport N *(Brit)* Tierpass *m*

Petrarch [ˈpetrɑːk] N Petrarca *m*

petrel [ˈpetrəl] N Sturmvogel *m*

Petri dish [ˈpetrɪˌdɪʃ] N Petrischale *f*

petrifaction [ˌpetrɪˈfækʃən], **petrification** [ˌpetrɪfɪˈkeɪʃən] N Versteinerung *f*, Petrifikation *f*

petrified ['petrɪfaɪd] ADJ **a** *(lit)* versteinert; **as though ~** wie erstarrt **b** *(fig)* **I was ~ (with fear)** ich war starr vor Schrecken; **she is ~ of spiders** sie hat panische Angst vor Spinnen; **to be ~ of doing sth** panische Angst davor haben, etw zu tun

petrify ['petrɪfaɪ] VT **a** *(lit)* versteinern **b** *(= frighten)* **he really petrifies me** er jagt mir schreckliche Angst ein; **a ~ing experience** ein schreckliches Erlebnis; **to be petrified by sth** sich panisch vor etw fürchten VI versteinern

petrochemical ['petrəʊ'kemɪkəl] N petrochemisches Erzeugnis ADJ petrochemisch

petrochemistry [ˌpetrəʊ'kemɪstrɪ] N Petrochemie *f*

petrodollar ['petrəʊdɒlə'] N Petrodollar *m*

petrol ['petrəl] N *(Brit)* Benzin *nt*

petrol *in cpds* Benzin-; **petrol bomb** N Benzinbombe *f*, Molotowcocktail *m*; **petrol can** N Reservekanister *m*; **petrol cap** N Tankdeckel *m*

petroleum [pɪ'trəʊlɪəm] N Petroleum *nt*

petroleum: **petroleum ether** N Petroläther *m*; **petroleum jelly** N Vaselin *nt*, Vaseline *f*; **petroleum refinery** N Erdölraffinerie *f*

petrol gauge N Benzinuhr *f*

petrology [pɪ'trɒlɪdʒɪ] N Gesteinskunde *f*, Petrologie *f*

petrol: **petrol pump** N *(in engine)* Benzinpumpe *f*; *(at garage)* Zapfsäule *f*; **petrol station** N Tankstelle *f*; **petrol tank** N Benzintank *m*; **petrol tanker** N (Benzin)tankwagen *m*

petticoat ['petɪkəʊt] N Unterrock *m*; *(stiffened)* Petticoat *m*; **~ government** Weiberherrschaft *f*, Weiberregiment *nt*

pettifogging ['petɪfɒgɪŋ] ADJ *objections* kleinlich; *details* belanglos; *person* pedantisch

pettiness ['petɪnɪs] N **a** *(= trivial nature)* Unbedeutendheit *f*, Belanglosigkeit *f*, Unwichtigkeit *f*; *(of excuse)* Billigkeit *f*; *(of crime)* Geringfügigkeit *f* **b** *(= small-mindedness)* Kleinlichkeit *f*; *(of remark)* spitzer Charakter

petting ['petɪŋ] N Petting *nt*; **heavy ~** Heavy Petting *nt*

petting zoo N *(US)* Streichelzoo *m*

pettish ADJ, **pettishly** ADV ['petɪʃ, -lɪ] bockig *(inf)*

pettishness ['petɪʃnɪs] N bockige Art *(inf)*

petty ['petɪ] ADJ *(+er)* **a** *(= trivial)* unbedeutend, belanglos, unwichtig; *excuse* billig; *crime* geringfügig **b** *(= small-minded)* kleinlich; *(= spiteful) remark* spitz; **you're being very ~ about it** du bist sehr kleinlich **c** *(= minor) chieftain etc* untergeordnet; *(pej) official* unbedeutend, untergeordnet; **the ~ wars of the time** die Kleinkriege jener Zeit

petty: **petty average** N *(Naut Jur)* Teilschaden *m*, kleine Havarie; **petty bourgeois** N, ADJ = **petit bourgeois**; **petty bourgeoisie** N = **petite bourgeoisie**; **petty cash** N Portokasse *f*; **petty crime** N **a** no pl *(= illegal activities)* Kleinkriminalität *f* **b** *(= illegal act)* Vergehen *nt*, Bagatelldelikt *nt*; **petty jury** N ≈ Geschworene *pl*; **petty larceny** N einfacher Diebstahl; **petty-minded** ADJ kleinlich; **petty officer** N Fähnrich *m* zur See; **petty theft** N einfacher Diebstahl

petulance ['petjʊləns], **petulancy** ['petjʊlənsɪ] N verdrießliche Art; *(of child)* bockige Art *(inf)*

petulant ['petjʊlənt] ADJ verdrießlich; *child* bockig *(inf)*

petulantly ['petjʊləntlɪ] ADV verdrießlich; *(used of child)* bockig *(inf)*

petunia [pɪ'tju:nɪə] N Petunie *f*

pew [pju:] N *(Eccl)* (Kirchen)bank *f*; *(hum: = chair)* Platz *m*; **take a ~!** *(hum)* lass dich nieder! *(hum)*

pewit ['pi:wɪt] N = **peewit**

pewter ['pju:tə'] N *(= alloy)* Zinn *nt*; *(= vessel)* Zinnbecher *m*; *(= articles)* Zinn(geschirr) *nt*

peyote [peɪ'əʊtɪ] N Peyotl *m*

PFI *(Brit Pol) abbr of* **Private Finance Initiative**

PG *(Brit) abbr of* **parental guidance** *Klassifikation für Kinofilme, welche Kinder nur in Begleitung Erwachsener sehen dürfen*

PGA *abbr of* **Professional Golfers' Association** PGA *f*

PGCE *(Brit) abbr of* **Postgraduate Certificate of Education**

pH [pi:'eɪtʃ] N = **pH-value**

phalanx ['fælæŋks] N *pl* **-es** *or* **phalanges** [fæ'lændʒi:z] **a** *(Anat)* Finger-/Zehenglied *nt*, Phalanx *f (spec)* **b** *(= body of people, troops)* Phalanx *f*

phalli ['fælaɪ] *pl of* **phallus**

phallic ['fælɪk] ADJ phallisch; **~ symbol** Phallussymbol *nt*

phallus ['fæləs] N *pl* **-es** *or* **phalli** Phallus *m*

phantasm ['fæntæzəm], **phantasma** [fæn'tæzmə] N *pl* **phantasmata** Phantasma *nt*

phantasmagoria [ˌfæntæzmə'gɔ:rɪə] N Phantasmagorie *f*

phantasmagoric(al) [ˌfæntæzmə'gɒrɪk(əl)] ADJ phantasmagorisch

phantasmal [fæn'tæzməl] ADJ imaginär

phantasmata [fæn'tæzmətə] *pl of* **phantasm, phantasma**

phantasy N = **fantasy**

phantom ['fæntəm] N Phantom *nt*; *(= ghost: esp of particular person)* Geist *m*; **~s of the imagination** Fantasiegebilde *pl*, Phantasiegebilde *pl* ADJ *attr (= imagined)* eingebildet; *(= mysterious)* Phantom-; **a ~ child/knight** *etc* der Geist eines Kindes/Ritters *etc*; **~ limb pains** Phantomschmerzen *pl*; **~ company** Briefkastenfirma *f*; **~ withdrawal** *(from cash dispenser)* falsche *or* irrtümliche Abbuchung, Falschbelastung *f*

phantom pregnancy N eingebildete Schwangerschaft

Pharaoh ['feərəʊ] N Pharao *m*; **the tombs of the ~s** die Pharaonengräber *pl*

Pharaonic [feə'reɪɒnɪk] ADJ pharaonisch

Pharisaic(al) [ˌfærɪ'seɪk(əl)] ADJ **a** pharisäisch **b** **pharisaic(al)** *(fig)* pharisäerhaft

Pharisee ['færɪsi:] N *(fig: also* **pharisee***)* Pharisäer(in) *m(f)*

pharmaceutical [ˌfɑ:mə'sju:tɪkəl] ADJ pharmazeutisch N *usu pl* Arzneimittel *nt*; **the ~ industry** die Pharmaindustrie; **~(s) company** Pharmaunternehmen *nt*

pharmaceutics [ˌfɑ:mə'sju:tɪks] N *sing* = **pharmacy a**

pharmacist ['fɑ:məsɪst] N Apotheker(in) *m(f)*; *(in research)* Pharmazeut(in) *m(f)*

pharmacological [ˌfɑ:məkə'lɒdʒɪkəl] ADJ pharmakologisch

pharmacologist [ˌfɑ:mə'kɒlədʒɪst] N Pharmakologe *m*, Pharmakologin *f*

pharmacology [ˌfɑ:mə'kɒlədʒɪ] N Pharmakologie *f*

pharmacopoeia [ˌfɑ:məkə'pi:ə] N Pharmakopöe *f (spec)*, amtliches Arzneibuch

pharmacy ['fɑ:məsɪ] N **a** *(= science)* Pharmazie *f* **b** *(esp US: = shop)* Apotheke *f*

pharyngeal [fə'rɪndʒɪəl], **pharyngal** [fə'rɪŋgəl] ADJ Rachen-; **~ cancer** Rachenkrebs *m*

pharyngitis [ˌfærɪn'dʒaɪtɪs] N Rachenkatarr(h) *m*, Pharyngitis *f (spec)*

pharynx ['færɪŋks] N Rachen *m*, Pharynx *f (spec)*

phase [feɪz] N Phase *f*; *(of construction, project, history also)* Abschnitt *m*; *(of illness)* Stadium *nt*; **in ~** *(Tech, Elec)* phasengleich, in Phase; *(fig)* koordiniert; **out of ~** *(Tech, Elec)* phasenverschoben; *(fig)* unkoordiniert; **a passing ~** ein vorübergehender Zustand; **he's just going through a ~** das ist nur so eine Phase bei ihm; **he's out of ~ with the times** er ist nicht im Gleichklang mit seiner Zeit VT **a** *(= introduce gradually) plan, change-over, withdrawal* schrittweise durchführen **b** *(= coordinate, fit to one another) starting times, production stages, traffic lights* aufeinander abstimmen; *machines etc* gleichschalten, synchronisieren; **the traffic lights are not ~d here** hier gibt es keine grüne Welle; **a ~d withdrawal of troops** ein schrittweiser Truppenabzug **c** *(Mus inf)* einen Halleffekt herstellen bei, phasen

► **phase in** VT *sep* allmählich einführen

► **phase out** VT *sep* auslaufen lassen

phase: **phase-down** N stufenweise Verringerung, stufenweiser Abbau; **phase modulation** N *(Elec)* Phasenmodulation *f*; **phase-out** N stufenweiser Abbau, stufenweise Außerkraftsetzung

phasing ['feɪzɪŋ] N **a** Synchronisierung *f*, Gleichschaltung *f* **b** *(Mus inf)* Erzeugung *f* eines Halleffekts, Phasen *nt*

phat [fæt] ADJ *(sl)* abgefahren *(sl)*, geil *(sl)*, fett *(sl)*

phatic ['fætɪk] ADJ *(liter)* phatisch

pH-balanced [pi:'eɪtʃˌbælənst] ADJ *(Chem)* pH-neutral

PhD N Doktor *m*, Dr.; **~ thesis** Doktorarbeit *f*; **to do one's ~** seinen Doktor machen, promovieren; **to get one's ~** den Doktor bekommen; **he has a ~ in English** er hat in Anglistik promoviert; **John Smith ~** Dr. John Smith

pheasant ['feznt] N Fasan *m*

phencyclidine [fen'sɪklɪˌdi:n] N Phencyclidin *nt*

phenix ['fi:nɪks] N *(US)* = **phoenix**

phenobarbitone [ˌfi:nəʊ'bɑ:bɪtəʊn], **phenobarbital** [ˌfi:nəʊ'bɑ:bɪtəl] N Phenobarbital *nt*

phenol ['fi:nɒl] N Phenol *nt*

phenomena [fɪ'nɒmɪnə] *pl of* **phenomenon**

phenomenal [fɪ'nɒmɪnl] ADJ **a** phänomenal, sagenhaft *(inf)*; *person, beauty, figure* fabelhaft; *boredom, heat* unglaublich; **at a ~ rate** in phänomenalem Tempo **b** *(Philos)* **the ~ world** die Erscheinungswelt

phenomenalism [fɪ'nɒmɪnəlɪzəm] N Phänomenalismus *m*

phenomenally [fɪ'nɒmɪnəlɪ] ADV außerordentlich; *bad, boring etc* unglaublich

phenomenology [fɪˌnɒmɪ'nɒlədʒɪ] N Phänomenologie *f*

phenomenon [fɪ'nɒmɪnən] N *pl* **phenomena** Phänomen *nt*

phenotype ['fi:nəʊtaɪp] N Phänotyp(us) *m*

phew [fju:] INTERJ Mensch, puh

pH-factor [pi:'eɪtʃfæktə'] N *(Chem)* pH-Wert *m*

phial ['faɪəl] N Fläschchen *nt*; *(for serum)* Ampulle *f*

> **PHI BETA KAPPA**
>
> **Phi Beta Kappa** ist die älteste und renommierteste landesweite Studentenverbindung der USA, die 1776 für College- und Universitätsstudenten mit herausragenden Leistungen gegründet wurde. Der Name besteht aus den griechischen Anfangsbuchstaben des Mottos der Verbindung: „philosophia biou kybernetes" - „Philosophie, der Führer des Lebens". Die Mitglieder werden in ihrem dritten oder vierten Studienjahr aufgenommen und werden dann auch **Phi Beta Kappa** oder „Phi Beta Kappa student" genannt.

Phil *(US) abbr of* **Philadelphia**

Philadelphia lawyer [fɪləˌdelfɪə'lɔ:jə'] N *(esp US inf)* gerissener Anwalt/Jurist, gerissene Anwältin/Juristin

philander [fɪ'lændə'] VI tändeln *(liter)*

philanderer [fɪ'lændərə'] N Schwerenöter *m*

philandering [fɪ'lændərɪŋ] N Liebeleien *pl* ADJ **her ~ husband** ihr zu Seitensprüngen neigender Mann

philanthropic(al) [ˌfɪlən'θrɒpɪk(əl)] ADJ menschenfreundlich; *person also, organization* philanthropisch *(geh)*

philanthropically [ˌfɪlənˈθrɒpɪkəlɪ] ADV menschenfreundlich

philanthropist [fɪˈlænθrəpɪst] N Menschenfreund(in) *m(f)*, Philanthrop(in) *m(f)* *(geh)*

philanthropy [fɪˈlænθrəpɪ] N Menschenfreundlichkeit *f*, Philanthropie *f* *(geh)*

philatelic [ˌfɪləˈtelɪk] ADJ philatelistisch

philatelist [fɪˈlætəlɪst] N Philatelist(in) *m(f)*, Briefmarkensammler(in) *m(f)*

philately [fɪˈlætəlɪ] N Philatelie *f*, Briefmarkenkunde *f*

-phile [-faɪl] SUF N -phile(r) *mf*, -freund(in) *m(f)*; **Anglophile** Anglophile(r) *mf*, Englandfreund(in) *m(f)* ADJ -phil, -freundlich; **Francophile** frankophil, frankreich- *or* franzosenfreundlich

philharmonic [ˌfɪlɑːˈmɒnɪk] ADJ philharmonisch; **~ hall/society** Philharmonie *f* N **Philharmonic** Philharmonie *f*

Philip [ˈfɪlɪp] N Philipp *m*; *(Bibl)* Philippus *m*

Philippians [fɪˈlɪpɪənz] N *sing (Bibl)* Philipper *pl*

philippic [fɪˈlɪpɪk] N *(lit, fig)* Philippika *f*

Philippine [ˈfɪlɪpiːn] ADJ philippinisch

Philippines [ˈfɪlɪpiːnz] PL Philippinen *pl*

philistine [ˈfɪlɪstaɪn] ADJ *(fig)* kulturlos, philisterhaft *(geh)*; **tell that ~ friend of yours …** sag deinem Freund, diesem Banausen … N **a** *(lit)* **Philistine** Philister(in) *m(f)* **b** *(fig)* Banause *m*, Banausin *f*, Philister(in) *m(f)* *(geh)*

philistinism [ˈfɪlɪstɪnɪzəm] N Banausentum *nt*

Phillips® [ˈfɪlɪps]: **Phillips screw** N Kreuzschraube *f*; **Phillips screwdriver** N Kreuzschlitzschraubenzieher *m* *or* -schraubendreher *m*

philological [ˌfɪləˈlɒdʒɪkəl] ADJ philologisch

philologist [fɪˈlɒlədʒɪst] N Philologe *m*, Philologin *f*

philology [fɪˈlɒlədʒɪ] N Philologie *f*

philosopher [fɪˈlɒsəfəʳ] N Philosoph(in) *m(f)*

philosopher's stone [fɪˌlɒsəfəzˈstəʊn] N Stein *m* der Weisen

philosophic(al) [ˌfɪləˈsɒfɪk(əl)] ADJ philosophisch; *(fig also)* gelassen; **to be philosophical about sth** etw philosophisch betrachten

philosophically [ˌfɪləˈsɒfɪkəlɪ] ADV philosophisch; *(fig also)* gelassen; **his ideas are ~ naïve** philosophisch betrachtet sind seine Gedanken naiv; **~ speaking, …** (rein) theoretisch gesehen, …

philosophize [fɪˈlɒsəfaɪz] VI philosophieren *(about, on* über *+acc)*

philosophy [fɪˈlɒsəfɪ] N Philosophie *f*; **~ of life** Lebensphilosophie *f*; **that's my ~** das ist meine Philosophie *or* Einstellung; **~ of education** Erziehungsphilosophie *f*

philtre, *(US)* **philter** [ˈfɪltəʳ] N Zaubertrank *m*; *(= love philtre)* Liebestrank *m*

phishing [ˈfɪʃɪŋ] N *(Internet)* Phishing *nt*

phiz [fɪz] N *(dated Brit sl)* Visage *f* *(inf)*

phlebitis [flɪˈbaɪtɪs] N Venenentzündung *f*, Phlebitis *f* *(spec)*

phlegm [flem] N *(= mucus)* Schleim *m*; *(obs: = humour)* Phlegma *nt*; *(fig) (= coolness)* Gemütsruhe *f*, stoische Ruhe; *(= stolidness)* Trägheit *f*, Schwerfälligkeit *f*, Phlegma *nt*

phlegmatic [flegˈmætɪk] ADJ *(= cool)* seelenruhig, stoisch; *(= stolid)* träge, schwerfällig, phlegmatisch

pH-level [piːˈeɪtʃlevl] N *(Chem)* pH-Wert *m*

phlox [flɒks] N Phlox *m*

-phobe [-fəʊb] N *suf* -phobe(r) *mf*, -feind(in) *m(f)*; **Anglophobe** Anglophobe(r) *mf*, Englandfeind(in) *m(f)*

phobia [ˈfəʊbɪə] N Phobie *f*; **she has a ~ about it** sie hat krankhafte Angst davor

-phobic [-ˈfəʊbɪk] ADJ *suf* -phob, -feindlich; **Anglophobic** anglophob, englandfeindlich

Phoenicia [fəˈniːʃə] N Phönizien *nt*

Phoenician [fəˈniːʃən] ADJ phönizisch N Phönizier(in) *m(f)*

phoenix, *(US)* **phenix** [ˈfiːnɪks] N *(Myth)* Phönix *m*; **like a ~ from the ashes** wie ein Phönix aus der Asche

phoenix-like, *(US)* **phenix-like** [ˈfiːnɪkslaɪk] ADJ wie ein Phönix, dem Phönix gleich ADV wie ein Phönix; **to rise ~ from the ashes** wie ein Phönix aus der Asche (auf)steigen

phone[1] [fəʊn] ✪ 27.4 N Telefon *nt*; **to be on the ~** *(= be a subscriber)* Telefon haben; *(= be speaking)* am Telefon sein; **I'll give you a ~** *(inf)* ich ruf dich an VT *person* anrufen; *message* telefonisch übermitteln VI anrufen, telefonieren → *also* **telephone**

▶ **phone back** VT *sep* zurückrufen VI zurückrufen

▶ **phone in** VI anrufen VT *sep* telefonisch übermitteln

▶ **phone up** VI anrufen, telefonieren VT *sep* anrufen

phone[2] N *(Ling)* Phon *nt*

phone: **phone bill** N Telefonrechnung *f*; **phone book** N Telefonbuch *nt*; **phone booth** N **a** *(in station, hotel etc)* Fernsprechhaube *f* **b** *(US: = call box)* Telefonzelle *f*; **phonecard** N Telefonkarte *f*; **phone dialer** N *(Comput: program)* Wählhilfe(programm *nt*) *f*; **phone-in** N *Rundfunkprogramm, an dem sich Hörer per Telefon beteiligen können*, Phone-in *nt*

phoneme [ˈfəʊniːm] N Phonem *nt*

phonemic [fəʊˈniːmɪk] ADJ phonemisch

phone number N Telefonnummer *f*

phone tapping [ˈfəʊnˌtæpɪŋ] N Abhören *nt* von Telefonen; **new measures to stop ~** neue Maßnahmen zum Abhörschutz

phonetic ADJ, **phonetically** ADV [fəʊˈnetɪk, -əlɪ] phonetisch

phonetician [ˌfɒnɪˈtɪʃən] N Phonetiker(in) *m(f)*

phonetics [fəʊˈnetɪks] N **a** *sing (= subject)* Phonetik *f* **b** *pl (= phonetic script)* Lautschrift *f*, phonetische Umschrift

phoney [ˈfəʊnɪ] *(inf)* ADJ **a** *(= fake, pretentious)* unecht; *excuse, deal, peace* faul *(inf)*; *name, accent* falsch; *passport, money* gefälscht; *story, report* erfunden; **a ~ doctor** ein Scharlatan *m*; **a ~ policeman** ein zwielichtiger Polizist; **a ~ company** eine Schwindelfirma; **a ~ war** kein echter Krieg; **he's so ~** der ist doch nicht echt *(inf)*; **there's something ~ about it** da ist was faul dran *(inf)*
b *(= insincere) person* falsch; *emotion* unecht, vorgetäuscht
N *(= thing)* Fälschung *f*; *(= banknote also)* Blüte *f* *(inf)*; *(= bogus policeman etc)* Schwindler(in) *m(f)*; *(= doctor)* Scharlatan *m*; *(= pretentious person)* Angeber(in) *m(f)*

phonic [ˈfɒnɪk] ADJ phonisch

phonograph [ˈfəʊnəgrɑːf] N *(old, US)* Phonograph *m*

phonological [ˌfəʊnəˈlɒdʒɪkəl] ADJ phonologisch

phonology [fəʊˈnɒlədʒɪ] N *(= science)* Phonologie *f*; *(= system)* Lautsystem *nt*

phonometry [fəʊˈnɒmɪtrɪ] N *(acoustics)* Phonometrie *f*

phony ADJ, N *(US inf)* = **phoney**

phooey [ˈfuːɪ] INTERJ *(scorn)* pah, bah; *(disgust)* pfui

phosphate [ˈfɒsfeɪt] N *(Chem)* Phosphat *nt*; *(Agr: = fertilizer)* Phosphatdünger *m*

phosphate-free ADJ phosphatfrei

phosphide [ˈfɒsfaɪd] N Phosphid *nt*

phosphor [ˈfɒsfəʳ] N Phosphor *m*

phosphoresce [ˌfɒsfəˈres] VI phosphoreszieren

phosphorescence [ˌfɒsfəˈresns] N Phosphoreszenz *f*

phosphorescent [ˌfɒsfəˈresnt] ADJ phosphoreszierend

phosphoric [fɒsˈfɒrɪk] ADJ phosphorig

phosphorous [ˈfɒsfərəs] ADJ phosphorsauer

phosphorus [ˈfɒsfərəs] N Phosphor *m*

photo [ˈfəʊtəʊ] N Foto *nt*, Photo *nt*, Aufnahme *f* → *also* **photograph**

photo: **photo booth** N Passfotoautomat® *m*; **photo call** N Fototermin *m*; **photocell** N Fotozelle *f*; **photocompose** VT *(esp US Typ)* lichtsetzen, fotosetzen; **photocomposition** N *(Typ)* Lichtsatz *m*, Filmsatz *m*; **photocopier** N (Foto)kopierer *m*, (Foto)kopiergerät *nt*; **photocopy** N Fotokopie *f* VT fotokopieren VI **this won't ~** das lässt sich nicht fotokopieren; **photoelectric** ADJ fotoelektrisch; **photoelectric cell** N Fotozelle *f*; **photoelectron** N Fotoelektron *nt*; **photoengraving** N *(= process)* Klischieren *nt*; *(= plate)* Klischee *nt*; **photo finish** N Fotofinish *nt*; **Photofit®** N *(also* **Photofit picture**) Phantombild *nt*; **photoflash** N Blitzlicht *nt*; **~ lamp** Blitzgerät *nt*; **photoflood (lamp)** N Jupiterlampe *f*

photogenic [ˌfəʊtəʊˈdʒenɪk] ADJ fotogen

photograph [ˈfəʊtəgræf] N Fotografie *f*, Aufnahme *f*; **to take a ~ (of sb/sth)** (jdn/etw) fotografieren, eine Aufnahme *or* ein Bild (von jdm/etw) machen; **she takes a good ~** *(= is photogenic)* sie ist fotogen; **this camera takes good ~s** diese Kamera macht gute Aufnahmen *or* Bilder *or* Fotos; **~ album** Fotoalbum *nt* VT fotografieren, knipsen *(inf)*; **"photographed by John Mayne"** „Foto/Fotos: John Mayne" VI **to ~ well** sich gut fotografieren lassen; **she doesn't ~ well** sie ist nicht sehr fotogen

photographer [fəˈtɒgrəfəʳ] N Fotograf(in) *m(f)*

photographic [ˌfəʊtəˈgræfɪk] ADJ *film* für Fotos; *plate, library, studio, evidence, record* fotografisch; *style of painting, art* naturgetreu; **~ agency** Fotoagentur *f*; **~ magazine** Fotomagazin *nt*

photographically [ˌfəʊtəˈgræfɪkəlɪ] ADV fotografisch; **to record sth ~** etw im Bild festhalten

photographic memory N fotografisches Gedächtnis

photography [fəˈtɒgrəfɪ] N Fotografie *f*; *(in film, book etc)* Fotografien *pl*, Aufnahmen *pl*, Bilder *pl*; **his ~ is marvellous** seine Fotografien *etc* sind hervorragend

photogravure [ˈfəʊtəʊgrəˈvjʊəʳ] N Fotogravüre *f*, Heliogravüre *f*

photo: **photojournalism** N Fotojournalismus *m*; **photojournalist** N Fotojournalist(in) *m(f)*, Bildjournalist(in) *m(f)*; **photomechanical** ADJ fotomechanisch

photometer [fəʊˈtɒmɪtəʳ] N Fotometer *nt*

photomontage [ˈfəʊtəʊmɒnˈtɑːʒ] N Fotomontage *f*

photon [ˈfəʊtɒn] N Photon *nt*

photo: **photo opportunity** N Fototermin *m*; **photosensitive** ADJ lichtempfindlich; **photosensitize** VT lichtempfindlich machen; **photo session** N Fotosession *f*; **photoset** VT *(Typ)* im Lichtsatz herstellen; **photosetting** N Lichtsatz *m*; **Photostat®** N, VTI = **photocopy**; **photosynthesis** N Fotosynthese *f*; **phototelegraphy** N Bildtelegrafie *f*; **phototropic** ADJ fototrop(isch); **phototropism** N Fototropismus *m*; **phototypesetting** N *(esp US Typ)* Lichtsatz *m*, Fotosatz *m*

phrasal [ˈfreɪzəl] ADJ im Satz

phrasal verb N Phrasal Verb *nt*, *Verb mit bestimmter Präposition oder bestimmtem Adverb*

phrase [freɪz] N **a** *(Gram)* Phrase *f*, Satzglied *nt or* -teil *m*; *(in spoken language)* Phrase *f*; **noun/verb ~** Nominal-/Verbalphrase *f* **b** *(= mode of expression)* Ausdruck *m*; *(= set expression)* Redewendung *f*; **in a ~** kurz gesagt → **set 2 d, turn 1 b c** *(Mus)* Phrase *f* VT **a** *(= express)* formulieren; *criticism, suggestion* ausdrücken, formulieren **b** *(Mus)* phrasieren

phrase: **phrase book** N Sprachführer *m*; **phrase marker** N *(Ling)* P-Marker *m*, Formationsmarker *m*; **phrasemonger** N *(pej)* Phrasendrescher(in) *m(f)*

phraseology [ˌfreɪzɪˈɒlədʒɪ] N Ausdrucksweise *f*; *(of letter etc)* Diktion *f*; *(= jargon)* Jargon *m*

phrase structure grammar N *(Ling)* Phrasenstrukturgrammatik *f*

phrasing [ˈfreɪzɪŋ] N *(= act)* Formulierung *f*; *(= style)* Ausdrucksweise *f*, Stil *m*; *(Mus)* Phrasierung *f*

phrenetic ADJ = **frenetic**

phrenologist [frɪˈnɒlədʒɪst] N Phrenologe *m*, Phrenologin *f*

phrenology [frɪˈnɒlədʒɪ] N Phrenologie *f*

phthisis [ˈθaɪsɪs] N Schwindsucht *f*, (Lungen)tuberkulose *f*

phut [fʌt] *(inf)* **N** Puff *m* **ADV** **to go ~** *(= make noise)* puff machen; *(= break down)* kaputtgehen *(inf)*; *(plans etc)* platzen *(inf)*

pH-value [piːˈeɪtʃvæljuː] N pH-Wert *m*

phylum [ˈfaɪləm] N *pl* **phyla** [ˈfaɪlə] *(Biol)* Stamm *m*

physalis [faɪˈseɪlɪs] N *(Bot)* Kapstachelbeere *f*, Physalis *f*

physic [ˈfɪzɪk] N *(obs)* Arznei *f*; *(cathartic)* Purgativ *nt*

physical [ˈfɪzɪkəl] **ADJ** **a** *(= of the body)* körperlich; *abuse, violence, punishment, discomfort* physisch, körperlich; *check-up* ärztlich; *(= not psychological)* physisch; **you don't take/get enough ~ exercise** Sie bewegen sich nicht genug; **he's very ~** *(inf)* er ist sehr sinnlich; **play got too ~** *(Sport inf)* das Spiel wurde zu ruppig *or* rabiat *(inf)*; **the ~ force of the impact** die Wucht des Aufpralls; **we don't actually need your ~ presence** Ihre persönliche Anwesenheit ist nicht unbedingt nötig
b *(= sexual) love, relationship* körperlich
c *(= material)* physisch, körperlich; *size* physisch; *world* fassbar
d *(= of physics) laws, properties* physikalisch; **it's a ~ impossibility** es ist ein Ding der Unmöglichkeit
e *(= natural) environment* physisch, real; *conditions* physisch
f *(= actual) possession* physisch, leibhaftig
N ärztliche Untersuchung; *(Mil)* Musterung *f*

physical: **physical chemistry** N physikalische Chemie; **physical education** N *(abbr* **PE**) Sport *m*, Leibesübungen *pl (form)*; **physical education college** N Sporthochschule *f*, Sportakademie *f*; **physical education teacher** N Sportlehrer(in) *m(f)*; **physical fitness** N körperliche Fitness *f*, physische Fitness *f*; **physical geography** N physische *or* physikalische Geografie, Physiogeografie *f*; **physical jerks** PL *(inf)* Gymnastik *f*

physically [ˈfɪzɪkəlɪ] ADV **a** körperlich, physisch; *restrain, separate* körperlich; *(Sci)* physikalisch; **to be ~ sick** sich übergeben; **to be ~ capable/incapable of (doing) sth** körperlich *or* physisch imstande *or* im Stande/außerstand *or* außer Stande sein, etw zu tun; **~ impossible** praktisch unmöglich; **the substance changed ~** die Substanz ging in einen anderen Zustand über; **the journey is ~ dangerous** die Reise ist gefährlich für Leib und Leben; **you don't have to be there ~** Ihre persönliche Anwesenheit ist nicht erforderlich; **they removed him ~ from the meeting** sie haben ihn mit Gewalt aus der Versammlung entfernt
b *(emph: = actually)* **as long as is ~ possible** so lange wie nur irgend möglich

physical: **physical science** N Naturwissenschaft *f*; **physical therapist** N *(US Med)* Physiotherapeut(in) *m(f)*; **physical therapy** N *(US Med)* Physiotherapie *f*; **physical training** N *(abbr* **PT**) = **physical education**

physician [fɪˈzɪʃən] N Arzt *m*, Ärztin *f*

physicist [ˈfɪzɪsɪst] N Physiker(in) *m(f)*

physics [ˈfɪzɪks] N *(sing: = subject)* Physik *f*; **the ~ of this are quite complex** die physikalischen Zusammenhänge sind hierbei ziemlich komplex

physio [ˈfɪzɪəʊ] N *(esp Brit inf)* Physiotherapeut(in) *m(f)*

physiognomy [ˌfɪzɪˈɒnəmɪ] N *(= face)* Physiognomie *f*; *(= study)* Physiognomik *f*; *(fig)* äußere Erscheinung, Aussehen *nt*; **the ~ of the Labour Party** das Gesicht der Labour Party

physiological [ˌfɪzɪəˈlɒdʒɪkəl] ADJ physiologisch

physiologist [ˌfɪzɪˈɒlədʒɪst] N Physiologe *m*, Physiologin *f*

physiology [ˌfɪzɪˈɒlədʒɪ] N Physiologie *f*

physiotherapeutic [ˈfɪzɪəˌθerəˈpjuːtɪk] ADJ physiotherapeutisch

physiotherapist [ˌfɪzɪəˈθerəpɪst] N Physiotherapeut(in) *m(f)*

physiotherapy [ˌfɪzɪəˈθerəpɪ] N Physiotherapie *f*, physikalische Therapie

physique [fɪˈziːk] N Körperbau *m*, Statur *f*; **to be small in ~** von kleiner Statur sein

PI *abbr of* **private investigator** Privatdetektiv(in) *m(f)*

pi [paɪ] N *(Math)* Pi *nt*

pianissimo [pɪəˈnɪsɪˌməʊ] *(Mus)* **ADV** pianissimo, sehr leise; **to play ~** pianissimo spielen **ADJ** pianissimo *inv*, sehr leise; **the ~ section** das Pianissimo

pianist [ˈpɪənɪst] N Klavierspieler(in) *m(f)*; *(= concert pianist)* Pianist(in) *m(f)*

piano [ˈpjænəʊ] **N** *(upright)* Klavier *nt*, Piano *nt* *(geh, old)*; *(= grand piano)* Flügel *m*; **who was at** *or* **on the ~?** wer war am Klavier? [ˈpjɑːnəʊ] **ADV** *(Mus)* piano, leise [ˈpjɑːnəʊ] **ADJ** piano, leise; **the ~ section** das Piano

piano: **piano accordion** N Pianoakkordeon *nt*; **piano concerto** N Klavierkonzert *nt*; **pianoforte** [ˈpjænəʊˈfɔːtɪ] N *(form)* Pianoforte *nt*; **piano keys** PL Klaviertasten *pl*

Pianola® [pɪəˈnəʊlə] N Pianola *nt*

piano: **piano lesson** N Klavierstunde *f*; **piano music** N Klaviermusik *f*; **piano player** N Klavierspieler(in) *m(f)*; **piano recital** N Klavierkonzert *nt*; **piano stool** N Klavierhocker *m*; **piano teacher** N Klavierlehrer(in) *m(f)*; **piano tuner** N Klavierstimmer(in) *m(f)*; **piano wire** N Klaviersaitendraht *m*

piazza [pɪˈætsə] N Piazza *f*, (Markt)platz *m*; *(US: = veranda)* (überdachte) Veranda

pic [pɪk] N *(inf: = photo)* Foto *nt*

picaresque [ˌpɪkəˈresk] ADJ pikaresk; **~ novel** Schelmenroman *m*, pikaresker Roman

picayune [ˌpɪkəˈjuːn], **picayunish** [-ɪʃ] ADJ *(US inf: = paltry)* gering, minimal; *(= petty)* kleinlich

piccalilli [ˈpɪkəˌlɪlɪ] N Piccalilli *pl*

piccaninny [ˌpɪkəˈnɪnɪ] N *(neg!)* Negerkind *nt* *(neg!)*

piccolo [ˈpɪkələʊ] N Pikkoloflöte *f*

pick [pɪk] **N** **a** *(= pickaxe)* Spitzhacke *f*, Picke *f*, Pickel *m*; *(Mountaineering)* Eispickel *m*; *(= toothpick)* Zahnstocher *m*
b *(esp US: = plectrum)* Plektron *nt*, Plektrum *nt*
c *(= choice)* **she could have her ~ of any man in the room** sie könnte jeden Mann im Raum haben; **to have first ~** die erste Wahl haben; **take your ~!** such dir etwas/einen etc aus!
d *(= best)* Beste(s) *nt* → **bunch**
VT **a** *(= choose)* (aus)wählen; **to ~ a team** eine Mannschaft aufstellen; **to ~ sb to do sth** jdn auswählen, etw zu tun; **he has been ~ed for England** er ist für England aufgestellt worden; **to ~ sides** wählen; **to ~ a winner** *(lit)* den Sieger erraten; *(fig)* das große Los ziehen; **a handful of ~ed men** *(Mil)* ein paar ausgewählte Soldaten; **to ~ one's words** seine Worte mit Bedacht wählen; **to ~ one's time** den richtigen Zeitpunkt wählen; **you really ~ your times, don't you?** *(iro)* du suchst dir aber auch immer den günstigsten Augenblick aus! *(iro)*; **to ~ one's way** seinen Weg suchen; **to ~ one's way through sth** seinen Weg durch etw finden; **he knows how to ~ 'em** *(inf)* er hat den richtigen Riecher *(inf)*; **you do ~ 'em** *(iro)* du gerätst auch immer an den Falschen
b *(= pull bits off, make holes in) jumper, blanket etc* zupfen an *(+dat)*; *spot, scab* kratzen an *(+dat)*; *hole (with fingers, instrument)* bohren; *(with beak)* picken, hacken; **to ~ one's nose** sich *(+dat)* in der Nase bohren; **to ~ one's teeth** sich *(dat)* in den Zähnen herumstochern; **to ~ a lock** ein Schloss knacken; **to ~ a bone** *(with fingers)* einen Knochen abzupfen; *(with teeth, beak)* einen Knochen abnagen; **to ~ sth to pieces** *(lit)* etw zerzupfen; *(fig)* kein gutes Haar an etw *(dat)* lassen, etw verreißen; **to ~ holes in sth** *(fig)* etw bemäkeln; *in argument, theory* etw in ein paar Punkten widerlegen; **to ~ a fight** *or* **quarrel (with sb)** (mit jdm) einen Streit vom Zaun brechen; **to ~ pockets** sich als Taschendieb betätigen; **he's very good at ~ing pockets** er ist ein sehr geschickter Taschendieb; **to ~ sb's pocket** jdn bestehlen; **to ~ sb's brains (about sth)** jdn (nach etw) ausfragen → **bone N a**
c *(= pluck) flowers, fruit* pflücken; *(= pick out and remove) fleas, splinter etc* entfernen (from von)
d *(US: = pluck) chicken etc* rupfen
e *(esp US) strings* zupfen, anreißen; *banjo* zupfen
f *(= peck up) corn etc* picken
VI **a** *(= choose)* wählen, aussuchen; **to ~ and choose** wählerisch sein
b *(esp US: on guitar etc)* zupfen

▶ **pick at** VI *+prep obj* **a** **to pick at one's food** im Essen herumstochern, am Essen herumpicken **b** *(inf: = criticize)* **to pick at sb/sth** auf jdm/etw herumhacken

▶ **pick off** VT *sep* **a** *(= remove) fluff etc* wegzupfen; *(= pluck) fruit* pflücken; *nail polish* abschälen; **the crew were picked off by helicopter** die Mannschaft wurde von einem Hubschrauber aufgenommen **b** *(= shoot)* abschießen, abknallen *(inf)*

▶ **pick on** VI *+prep obj (esp Brit) (= choose)* aussuchen; *(= victimize)* herumhacken auf *(+dat)*; **why pick on me?** *(inf)* warum gerade ich?; **pick on somebody your own size!** *(inf)* leg dich doch mit einem Gleichstarken an! *(inf)*; **stop picking on me!** hack nicht ständig auf mir herum!

▶ **pick out** VT *sep* **a** *(= choose)* aussuchen, auswählen; **to pick out a few examples** um ein paar Beispiele herauszugreifen **b** *(= remove) bad apples etc* heraussuchen, auslesen **c** *(= see, distinguish) person, familiar face* ausmachen, entdecken; **the spotlight picked out the leading dancer** der Scheinwerfer wurde auf den Haupttänzer gerichtet **d** *(= highlight)* hervorheben (*in, with* durch) **e** *(Mus)* **to pick out a tune (on the piano)** eine Melodie (auf dem Klavier) improvisieren; **he picked out a few notes** er spielte ein paar Takte

▶ **pick over** *or* **through** VI *+prep obj* durchsehen, untersuchen; **it's no good picking over the past** es hat keinen Sinn, über der Vergangenheit zu brüten

▶ **pick up** **VT** *sep* **a** *(= take up)* aufheben; *(= lift momentarily)* hochheben; *stitch* aufnehmen; **to pick up a child in one's arms** ein Kind auf den Arm nehmen; **pick up your feet when you walk!** heb deine Füße (beim Gehen)!; **to pick oneself up** aufstehen; **as soon as he picks up a book** sobald er ein Buch in die Hand nimmt; **it's the sort of book you can pick up when you have a free minute** das ist so ein Buch, das man mal zwischendurch lesen kann; **to pick up the phone** (den Hörer) abnehmen; **you just have to pick up the phone** du brauchst nur anzurufen; **to pick up the bill** *(= pay)* die Rechnung bezahlen; **to pick up a story** mit einer Geschichte fortfahren; **to pick up the pieces** *(lit, fig)* die Scherben aufsammeln *or* zusammensuchen; **to pick up the thread of a lecture** den Faden (eines Vortrags) wiederfinden; **to pick up the threads of one's life** die Scherben seines Lebens wieder zusammenkitten; **the interviewer picked up this reference and ...** der Interviewer nahm diese Bemerkung auf *or* knüpfte an diese Bemerkung an und ...
b *(= get)* holen; *(= buy)* bekommen; *(= acquire) habit* sich *(dat)* angewöhnen; *news, gossip* aufschnappen; *illness* sich *(dat)* holen *or* zuzie-

hen; *(= earn)* verdienen; *medal* bekommen, erhalten; **to pick sth up at a sale** etw im Ausverkauf erwischen; **to pick up speed** schneller werden; **you never know what you'll pick up** *(= what illness etc)* man weiß nie, was man sich *(dat)* da holen *or* zuziehen kann; **he picked up a few extra points** er hat ein paar Extrapunkte gemacht; **he picked up a reputation as a womanizer** er geriet in den Ruf eines Frauenhelden
c *(= learn) skill etc* sich *(dat)* aneignen; *language* lernen; *accent, word* aufschnappen; *information, tips etc* herausbekommen; *idea* aufgreifen; **you'll soon pick it up** du wirst das schnell lernen; **where did you pick up that idea?** wo hast du denn die Idee her?
d *(= collect) person, goods* abholen; **I'll come and pick you up** ich hole dich ab, ich komme dich abholen
e *(bus etc) passengers* aufnehmen; *(in car)* mitnehmen
f *(= rescue: helicopter, lifeboat)* bergen
g *(= arrest, catch) wanted man, criminal* schnappen *(inf)*; **they picked him up for questioning** sie haben ihn geholt, um ihn zu vernehmen
h *(inf) girl* aufgabeln *(inf)*; **she got picked up at a party** die ist auf einer Party (von einem) abgeschleppt *or* aufgegabelt worden *(inf)*
i *(= find) road* finden; **to pick up the trail** *(Hunt, fig)* die Fährte *or* Spur aufnehmen
j *(Rad) station* hereinbekommen, (rein)kriegen *(inf)*; *message* empfangen, auffangen; *(= see) beacon etc* ausmachen, sichten; *(on radar)* ausmachen; *(record stylus) sound* aufnehmen; **the surface was clearly picked up by the satellite's cameras** das Bild der Oberfläche wurde von den Satellitenkameras deutlich übermittelt; **we picked up a rabbit in the car headlights** wir sahen ein Kaninchen im Scheinwerferlicht
k *(Brit: = correct, put right)* korrigieren; **he picked me up on my bad grammar** er wies auf meine schlechte Grammatik hin; **he picked me up for mispronouncing it** er hat meine falsche Aussprache korrigiert
l *(= restore to health)* wieder auf die Beine stellen
m *(= spot, identify) mistakes* finden
n *(US inf: = tidy) room* auf Vordermann bringen *(inf)*
VI **a** *(= improve)* besser werden; *(appetite)* zunehmen; *(currency)* sich erholen; *(business: after slump)* sich erholen; *(engine)* rund laufen; *(= accelerate)* schneller werden
b *(= continue)* weitermachen; **to pick up where one left off** da weitermachen, wo man aufgehört hat
c *(inf)* **to pick up with sb** *(= get to know)* jds Bekanntschaft machen; **he has picked up with a rather strange crowd** er hat mit merkwürdigen Leuten Umgang; **to pick up on a point** einen Punkt aufgreifen

pickaback ['pɪkəbæk] N, ADV = **piggyback**

pick-and-mix N, ADJ = **pick 'n' mix**

pickaninny N *(US)* = **piccaninny**

pickaxe, *(US)* **pickax** ['pɪkæks] N Spitzhacke *f*, Picke *f*

picker ['pɪkəʳ] N *(of fruit etc)* Pflücker(in) *m(f)*

picket ['pɪkɪt] **N** **a** *(of strikers)* Streikposten *m*; **to mount a ~ (at** *or* **on a gate)** (an *or* bei einem Tor) Streikposten aufstellen **b** *(Mil)* Feldposten *m*, Vorposten *m* **c** *(= stake)* Pfahl *m*; **~ fence** Palisade *f*, Palisadenzaun *m* **VT** *factory* Streikposten aufstellen vor *(+dat)*; *(demonstrators etc)* demonstrieren vor *(+dat)* **VI** Streikposten aufstellen; **he is ~ing at the front entrance** er ist Streikposten am Vordereingang

picket: **picket boat** N *(of port police)* Patrouillenboot *nt*; **picket duty** N Streikpostendienst *m*; **to be on ~** Streikposten sein

picketer ['pɪkɪtəʳ] N Streikposten *m*

picketing ['pɪkɪtɪŋ] N Aufstellen *nt* von Streikposten; **there was no ~** es wurden keine Streikposten aufgestellt; **the ~ of the factory went on for six months** es standen sechs Monate lang Streikposten vor dem Betrieb

picket line N Streikpostenkette *f*; **to cross a ~** eine Streikpostenkette durchbrechen

picking ['pɪkɪŋ] N **a** *(= amount of fruit picked)* Ernte *f* **b** **pickings** PL Ausbeute *f*; *(= stolen goods)* Beute *f*; **most office workers regard pens as legitimate ~s** die meisten Büroangestellten sehen es als ihr Recht an, Kulis mitgehen zu lassen *(inf)* *or* einzustecken; **she went along to see if there were any ~s** sie ging hin, um zu sehen, ob es für sie was zu holen gab; **there are rich ~s to be had** da gibt es reiche Beute; **easy ~s for thieves** leichte Beute für Diebe

pickle ['pɪkl] **N** **a** *(= food)* Pickles *pl* **b** *(= solution) (= brine)* Salzlake *f*, Pökel *m*; *(= vinegar)* Essigsoße *f*; *(for leather, wood)* Beize *f*; *(Med, Sci)* Nasspräparat *nt* **c** *(inf: = predicament)* Klemme *f (inf)*; **he was in a bit of a ~** er steckte in einer Klemme *(inf)*, er saß in der Tinte *(inf)*; **to get (oneself) into a ~** in ein Kuddelmuddel geraten *(inf)*; **what a ~!** so eine verzwickte Lage! **VT** einlegen; *(Med, Sci)* konservieren

pickled ['pɪkld] ADJ **a** eingelegt **b** *pred (inf: = drunk)* besoffen *(inf)*, alkoholisiert *(inf)*

pick: **picklock** N *(= tool)* Dietrich *m*; *(= thief)* Einbrecher(in) *m(f)*; **pick-me-up** N *(= drink)* Muntermacher *m*, Stärkung *f*; *(= holiday etc)* Erholung *f*; **we stopped off at the pub for a ~** wir sind auf ein Gläschen *or* einen Schluck in die Kneipe gegangen; **hearing that was a real ~** das hat mir richtig Auftrieb gegeben

pick 'n' mix [ˌpɪkn'mɪks] **N** *(= sweets etc, fig)* bunte Mischung **ADJ** *approach, selection, collection* bunt gemischt, bunt zusammengewürfelt; *morality, politics* verschiedenste Elemente vereinend

pickpocket ['pɪkˌpɒkɪt] N Taschendieb(in) *m(f)*

pick-up ['pɪkʌp] N **a** Tonabnehmer *m*; **~ arm** Tonarm *m*
b *(also* **pick-up truck***)* Kleinlieferwagen *m*, Kleintransporter *m*
c *(inf: = acquaintance)* Bekanntschaft *f*; **with his latest ~** mit seiner neusten Errungenschaft; **he's just looking for a ~** er will nur eine aufreißen *(inf)*
d *(= collection)* Abholen *nt*; **he was late for the ~** er kam zu spät zum Treffpunkt; **the mail van makes 3 ~s a day** der Postwagen kommt dreimal täglich(, um die Post abzuholen); **the bus makes four ~s** der Bus hält viermal(, um Leute aufzunehmen); **~ point** *(for excursion)* Sammelstelle *f*, Treffpunkt *m*; *(on regular basis)* Haltestelle *f*
e *(= improvement)* Verbesserung *f*; *(= increase)* Ansteigen *nt*
f *(= acceleration)* Beschleunigung *f*

picky ['pɪkɪ] ADJ *(+er) (inf)* pingelig *(inf)*; *eater* wählerisch

picnic ['pɪknɪk] *vb: pret, ptp* **picnicked** **N** Picknick *nt*; **to have a ~** picknicken; **to go for** *or* **on a ~** ein Picknick veranstalten *or* machen; **a ~ lunch** ein Picknick *nt*; **it was no ~** *(fig inf)* es war kein Honiglecken **VI** picknicken, ein Picknick machen; **we went ~king every Sunday** wir machten jeden Sonntag ein Picknick

picnic basket, **picnic hamper** N Picknickkorb *m*

picnicker ['pɪknɪkəʳ] N jd, der picknickt *or* der ein Picknick macht; **the ~s left all their rubbish behind them** die Ausflügler ließen ihre Abfälle liegen

picnic: **picnic site** N Rastplatz *m*; **picnic table** N Campingtisch *m*

pics [pɪks] PL *abbr of* **pictures** *(Brit inf)* = **picture N c**

Pict [pɪkt] N Pikte *m*, Piktin *f*

Pictish ['pɪktɪʃ] **ADJ** piktisch **N** *(Ling)* Piktisch *nt*

pictogram ['pɪktəgræm], **pictograph** ['pɪktəgrɑːf] N Piktogramm *nt*

pictorial [pɪk'tɔːrɪəl] **ADJ** *calendar* bebildert; *magazine also* illustriert; *impact* bildlich; *language, description* bildhaft; **~ dictionary** Bildwörterbuch *nt*; **to keep a ~ record of sth** etw im Bild festhalten **N** *(= magazine)* Illustrierte *f*; *(= stamp)* Sondermarke *f*

pictorially [pɪk'tɔːrɪəlɪ] ADV *(= in pictures)* in Bildern, bildlich; *describe* bildhaft

picture ['pɪktʃəʳ] **N** **a** Bild *nt*; *(Art) (= painting)* Gemälde *nt*, Bild *nt*; *(= drawing)* Zeichnung *f*; **(as) pretty as a ~** bildschön
b *(TV)* Bild *nt*
c *(Film)* Film *m*; **the ~s** *(Brit)* das Kino; **to go to the ~s** *(Brit)* ins Kino gehen; **what's on at the ~s?** *(Brit)* was gibts im Kino?
d *(= mental image)* Vorstellung *f*, Bild *nt*; **these figures give the general ~** diese Zahlen geben ein allgemeines Bild; **have you got the general ~?** wissen Sie jetzt ungefähr Bescheid?; **to give you a ~ of what life is like here** damit Sie sich *(dat)* ein Bild vom Leben hier machen können; **to form a ~ of sth** sich *(dat)* ein Bild von etw machen; **the other side of the ~** die Kehrseite der Medaille; **to be in the ~** im Bilde sein; **to put sb in the ~** jdn ins Bild setzen; **to be left out of the ~** *(= be kept in the dark)* nicht informiert werden; **I get the ~** *(inf)* ich habs begriffen *or* kapiert *(inf)*; **I'm beginning to get the ~** *(inf)* ich fange an zu begreifen *or* kapieren *(inf)*; **he/that no longer comes into the ~** er/das spielt keine Rolle mehr
e *(= sight)* Bild *nt*; *(beautiful)* Traum *m*, Bild *nt*; **his face was a ~** sein Gesicht war ein Bild für die Götter *(inf)*; **she looked a ~** sie war bildschön *or* traumhaft schön; **the garden is a ~** der Garten ist eine Pracht
f *(= embodiment)* Bild *nt*, Verkörperung *f*; *(= spitting image)* Abbild *nt*, Ebenbild *nt*; **she looked** *or* **was the ~ of happiness/health** sie sah wie das Glück/die Gesundheit in Person aus; **she looked** *or* **was the ~ of misery** sie war ein Bild des Elends
VT **a** *(= imagine)* sich *(dat)* vorstellen; **to ~ sth to oneself** sich *(dat)* etw vorstellen
b *(= describe)* beschreiben, darstellen
c *(by drawing, painting)* darstellen; *(in book)* abbilden

picture: **picture book** N Bildband *m*; *(for children)* Bilderbuch *nt*; **picture card** N Bild(karte *f*) *nt*; **picture composition** N *(Art)* Bildkomposition *f*; **picture desk** N *(Press)* Bildredaktion *f*; **picture editor** N *(Press)* Bildredakteur(in) *m(f)*; **picture frame** N Bilderrahmen *m*; **picture gallery** N Gemäldegalerie *f*; **picturegoer** N *(Brit)* Kinogänger(in) *m(f)*, Kinobesucher(in) *m(f)*; **picture hat** N Florentiner(hut) *m*; **picture house** N *(dated Brit)* = **picture palace**; **picture-in-picture** N *(TV, Comput)* Bild-in-Bild *nt*; **picture library** N Bildarchiv *nt*; **picture messaging** N *(Telec)* Picture Messaging *nt*; **picture palace** N *(dated Brit)* Lichtspielhaus *nt (old)*, Lichtspieltheater *nt*; **picture paper** N *(Brit)* Illustrierte *f*; **picture postcard** N Ansichts(post)karte *f*; **picture puzzle** N **a** Vexierbild *nt* **b** Bilderrätsel *nt*; **picture quality** N *(TV etc)* Bildqualität *f*; **picture rail** N Bilderleiste *f*; **picture researcher** N Bildbeschaffer(in) *m(f)*, Pictureresearcher(in) *m(f)*; **picture search** N *(on video)* Bildsuchlauf *m*

picturesque [ˌpɪktʃə'resk] ADJ malerisch, pittoresk *(geh)*; *(fig) description* anschaulich, bildhaft

picturesquely [ˌpɪktʃə'resklɪ] ADV malerisch, pittoresk *(geh)*; *(fig) describe* anschaulich, bildhaft; **a place ~ known as Devil's Dyke** ein Ort mit dem malerischen Namen Devils Dyke

picturesqueness [ˌpɪktʃə'resknɪs] N Malerische(s) *nt*; *(fig: of account, language)* Bildhaftigkeit *f*, Anschaulichkeit *f*

picture: **picture tube** N Bildröhre *f*; **picture window** N Aussichtsfenster *nt*; **picture writing** N Bilderschrift *f*

piddle ['pɪdl] *(inf)* **N** Pipi *nt (inf)*; **to do a ~** pinkeln *(inf)* **VI** **a** *(person, animal)* pinkeln *(inf)*; *(esp child)* Pipi machen *(inf)* **b** **to ~ around** herummachen

piddling ['pɪdlɪŋ] ADJ *(inf)* lächerlich

pidgin ['pɪdʒɪn] N Mischsprache *f*

pidgin English N Pidgin-English *nt*

pie [paɪ] N Pastete *f*; *(sweet)* Obstkuchen *m*; *(individual)* Tortelett *nt*; **that's all ~ in the sky** *(inf)* das sind nur verrückte Ideen; **as nice/sweet as ~** *(inf)* superfreundlich *(inf)*; **as easy as ~** *(inf)* kinderleicht; **she's got a finger in every ~** *(fig inf)* sie hat überall ihre Finger drin *(inf)*

piebald ['paɪbɔːld] ADJ scheckig N Schecke *mf*

piece [piːs] N **a** Stück *nt*; *(= part, member of a set)* Teil *nt*; *(= component part)* Einzelteil *nt*; *(= fragment: of glass, pottery etc)* Scherbe *f*; *(in draughts etc)* Stein *m*; *(in chess)* Figur *f*; *(Press: = article)* Artikel *m*; *(Mil)* Geschütz *nt*; *(= firearm)* Waffe *f*; *(= coin)* Münze *f*; **a 50p ~** ein 50-Pence-Stück, eine 50-Pence-Münze; **a ~ of cake/land/paper** ein Stück *nt* Kuchen/Land/Papier; **a ~ of furniture/luggage/clothing** ein Möbel-/ /Gepäck-/Kleidungsstück *nt*; **a seven-~ band** eine siebenköpfige Band; **a 30-~ dinner service** ein dreißigteiliges Speiseservice; **a ~ of news** eine Nachricht; **a ~ of information** eine Information; **a ~ of advice** ein Rat *m*; **a ~ of luck** ein Glücksfall *m*; **by a ~ of good luck** glücklicherweise; **a ~ of nonsense** Unsinn *m*; **a ~ of work** eine Arbeit; **~ by ~** Stück für Stück; **to be sold by the ~** stückweise verkauft werden; **to take sth to ~s** etw in seine Einzelteile zerlegen; **to come to ~s** *(collapsible furniture etc)* sich auseinandernehmen *or* zerlegen lassen; **to come** *or* **fall to ~s** *(broken chair, old book etc)* auseinanderfallen; *(glass, pottery)* zerbrechen; **to be in ~s** *(= taken apart)* (in Einzelteile) zerlegt sein; *(= broken: vase etc)* in Scherben sein, zerbrochen sein; **to smash sth to ~s** etw kaputt schlagen; **he tore the letter (in)to ~s** er zerriss den Brief (in Stücke *or* Fetzen); **he tore me to ~s during the debate** er zerriss mich förmlich während der Debatte; **to put together the ~s of a mystery** die einzelnen Teile eines Rätsels zusammenfügen; **he said his ~ very nicely** *(poem etc)* er hat das sehr nett vorgetragen; **to recite a ~** etwas aufsagen; **a piano ~** ein Klavierstück *nt*; **down the road a ~** *(US inf)* ein Stückchen die Straße runter *(inf)* → **bit² N a**

b *(phrases)* **to go to ~s** *(= crack up)* durchdrehen *(inf)*; *(= lose grip)* die Kontrolle verlieren; *(sportsman, team)* abbauen *(inf)*; **he's going to ~s** mit ihm gehts bergab; **his confidence is shot to ~s** *(inf)* sein Selbstvertrauen ist am Boden *or* völlig zerstört; **all in one ~** *(= intact)* heil, unversehrt; **are you still in one ~ after your trip?** hast du deine Reise heil überstanden?; **it's all of a ~ with his usual behaviour** so benimmt er sich immer; **his behaviour is all of a ~** sein Verhalten ist konsequent; **to give sb a ~ of one's mind** jdm gehörig *or* ordentlich die Meinung sagen; **he got a ~ of my mind** ich habe ihm meine Meinung gesagt, ich habe ihm Bescheid gestoßen *(inf)*; **to say one's ~** seine Meinung sagen

c *(inf: = woman)* Tussi *f (sl)*

▶**piece together** VT *sep (lit)* zusammenstückeln; *(fig)* sich *(dat)* zusammenreimen; *evidence* zusammenfügen; **to piece together a mystery** die einzelnen Teile eines Rätsels zusammenfügen; **police are trying to piece together his last hours** die Polizei versucht, seine letzten Stunden zu rekonstruieren

pièce de résistance ['pjːesdəˈreɪzɪːˌstɑ̃ŋs] N Krönung *f*; **and now the** *or* **my ~** und nun die Krönung!

piece: **piece goods** PL *(Sew)* Meterware *f*, Schnittware *f*; **piecemeal** ADV Stück für Stück, stückweise; *(= haphazardly)* kunterbunt durcheinander ADJ stückweise; *(= haphazard)* wenig systematisch; **in ~ fashion** auf unsystematische Weise; **piece rate** N Akkordlohnsatz *m*; **piece to camera** N *(TV)* Szene *f* direkt in die Kamera; **to do a ~** in die Kamera sprechen; **piece wages** PL Akkordlohn *m*, Stücklohn *m*; **piecework** N Akkordarbeit *f*; **to be on ~** im Akkord arbeiten; **pieceworker** N Akkordarbeiter(in) *m(f)*

pie: **pie chart** N Kreisdiagramm *nt*; **piecrust** N Teigdecke *f*

pied [paɪd] ADJ gescheckt, gefleckt; **the Pied Piper of Hamelin** der Rattenfänger von Hameln

pied-à-terre [ˌpɪeɪdɑːˈtɛəʳ] N Zweitwohnung *f*

pie dish N Pastetenform *f*

piedmont ['piːdmɒnt] N **a** *(Geol)* Piedmontfläche *f* **b** *(Geog, Region of Italy)* Piemont *nt*

pie-dog ['paɪdɒg] N *(Brit)* streunender Hundebastard

pied wagtail N Trauerbachstelze *f*

pie: **pie-eater** N *(Austral inf: = nonentity)* Null *f (inf)*; **pie-eyed** ['paɪˈaɪd] ADJ *(inf)* blau (wie ein Veilchen) *(inf)*; **pie-flinging** ['paɪˌflɪŋɪŋ] N *(inf: in films)* Tortenschlacht *f (inf)*

pier [pɪəʳ] N **a** Pier *m or f*; *(= landing place)* Anlegestelle *f*, Pier *m or f* **b** *(of bridge etc)* Pfeiler *m*

pierce [pɪəs] VT durchstechen; *(knife, spear)* durchstoßen, durchbohren; *(bullet)* durchbohren; *(fig: sound, coldness etc)* durchdringen; **to ~ a hole in sth** etw durchstechen; **to have** *or* **get one's ears/nose ~d** sich *(dat)* die Ohren/Nase durchstechen lassen; **to ~ sth through (and through)** *(lit, fig)* etw durchbohren; **the news ~d him to the heart** die Nachricht traf ihn bis ins Herz

pierced [pɪəst] ADJ *object* durchstochen; *nose, nipple* gepierct; **to have ~ ears** Löcher in den Ohrläppchen haben

piercer ['pɪəsəʳ] N *(= body piercer)* Piercer(in) *m(f)*

piercing ['pɪəsɪŋ] ADJ **a** durchdringend; *cold, wind also* schneidend; *stare* stechend, durchdringend; *sarcasm* beißend; *wit* scharf; **~ blue eyes** durchdringende blaue Augen **b** *(liter, = painful)* durchdringend N *(= body piercing)* Piercing *nt*

piercingly ['pɪəsɪŋlɪ] ADV **a** *scream, look at* durchdringend **b** *(liter: = painfully)* scharf, schneidend

pierrot ['pɪərəʊ] N Pierrot *m*

pietà [ˌpɪeˈtɑː] N Pieta *f*, Pietà *f*

pietism ['paɪətɪzəm] N **a** **Pietism** der Pietismus **b** *(= piety)* Pietät *f*, Frömmigkeit *f*; *(pej)* Frömmelei *f*

pietist ['paɪətɪst] N Pietist(in) *m(f)*; *(= pious person)* frommer Mensch; *(pej)* Frömmler(in) *m(f)*

pietistic [ˌpaɪəˈtɪstɪk] ADJ *(pej)* frömmelnd

piety ['paɪətɪ] N **a** Pietät *f*, Frömmigkeit *f*; **filial ~** Respekt *m* gegenüber den Eltern **b** **pieties** PL *(pej)* Frömmeleien *pl (pej)*

piffle ['pɪfl] N *(inf)* Quatsch *m (inf)*, Schnickschnack *m (inf)*

piffling ['pɪflɪŋ] ADJ *(inf)* lächerlich

pig [pɪg] N **a** Schwein *nt*; **to buy a ~ in a poke** *(prov)* die Katze im Sack kaufen; **~s might fly** *(Brit prov)* wers glaubt, wird selig; **they were living like ~s** sie haben wie die Schweine gehaust; **as happy as a ~ in muck** *(inf)* *or* **shit** *(sl)* voll gut drauf *(inf)*; **in a ~'s eye** *(US inf)* du spinnst wohl! *(inf)*

b *(inf: = person) (dirty, nasty)* Schwein *nt*, Sau *f (inf)*; *(greedy)* Vielfraß *m (inf)*; **to make a ~ of oneself** sich *(dat)* den Bauch vollschlagen *(inf)*, kräftig zulangen

c *(inf: = awkward thing)* fieses Ding *(inf)*

d *(sl: = policeman)* Bulle *m (sl)*

e *(Metal) (= ingot)* Massel *f*; *(= mould)* Kokille *f*

VT **to ~ it** *(inf)* hausen

VR **to ~ oneself** *(inf)* sich vollstopfen *(inf)*

▶**pig out** VI *(inf)* sich vollstopfen *(inf)*

pigeon ['pɪdʒən] N **a** Taube *f* **b** *(inf)* **that's not my ~** das ist nicht mein Bier *(inf)*

pigeon: **pigeon breast** N *(Brit Med)* Hühnerbrust *f*; **pigeon-breasted** ADJ *(Brit Med)* hühnerbrüstig; **pigeon fancier** N Taubenzüchter(in) *m(f)*; **pigeon-hearted** ['pɪdʒənˈhɑːtɪd] ADJ feige, ängstlich; **pigeonhole** N *(in desk etc)* Fach *nt*; **to put people in ~s** *(fig)* Menschen (in Kategorien) einordnen, Leute abstempeln VT *(lit)* (in Fächer) einordnen; *(fig: = categorize)* einordnen, ein- *or* aufteilen; **pigeon house, pigeon loft** N Taubenschlag *m*; **pigeon-livered** ['pɪdʒənˈlɪvəd] ADJ ängstlich, feige; **pigeon post** N Brieftaubenpost *f*; **pigeon-toed** ADJ, ADV mit einwärtsgerichteten Fußspitzen; **he is/walks ~** er geht über den großen Onkel *(inf)*

pig farmer N Schweinezüchter(in) *m(f)*

piggery ['pɪgərɪ] N **a** Schweinefarm *f*, Schweinemästerei *f* **b** *(inf, = gluttony)* Völlerei *f*

piggish ['pɪgɪʃ] ADJ **a** *eyes, face* Schweins- **b** *(= greedy)* gefräßig; *person* verfressen *(inf)*, gefräßig; *appetite* unmäßig, kannibalisch; *(= dirty)* saumäßig *(inf)*; *(= nasty)* fies *(inf)*, schweinisch *(inf)*; *(= stubborn)* fies *(inf)*

piggy ['pɪgɪ] N *(baby-talk)* Schweinchen *nt* ADJ *(+er)* **a** *attr* Schweins-; **~ eyes** Schweinsaugen *pl* **b** *(inf: = greedy)* verfressen *(inf)*

piggyback ['pɪgɪbæk] N **to give sb a ~** jdn huckepack nehmen; **the little girl wanted a ~** das kleine Mädchen wollte huckepack getragen werden ADV *(US Rail, also Comput)* huckepack *inv* VI **to ~ on sth** *(fig)* etw (zu seinem Vorteil) ausnutzen

piggy bank N Sparschwein *nt*

pig-headed ['pɪgˈhedɪd] ADJ stur; **that was a ~ thing to do** so was von stur *(inf)*

pig-headedly ['pɪgˈhedɪdlɪ] ADV stur

pig-headedness ['pɪgˈhedɪdnɪs] N Sturheit *f*

pig: **pig in the middle** N *(Brit) Spiel, bei dem ein zwischen zwei anderen stehender Spieler einen Ball, den diese sich zuwerfen, zu fangen versucht* **I'm just ~ on this project** *(inf)* ich stehe bei diesem Projekt nur hilflos dabei *or* in der Mitte; **pig iron** N Roheisen *nt*; **pig Latin** N *kindliche Geheimsprache durch Anfügen von Silben*

piglet ['pɪglɪt], **pigling** ['pɪglɪŋ] N Ferkel *nt*

pigman ['pɪgmən] N *pl* **-men** [-mən] Schweinehirt(e) *m*

pigment ['pɪgmənt] N Pigment *nt*

pigmentation [ˌpɪgmənˈteɪʃən] N Pigmentierung *f*

pigmy N = **pygmy**

pig: **pigpen** N *(US)* = **pigsty**; **pig's ear** N **to make a ~ of sth** *(Brit inf)* etw vermasseln *(inf)*; **pigskin** N **a** Schweinsleder *nt* **b** *(US inf: = football)* Pille *f (inf)*, Leder *nt (inf)*; **pigsty** N Schweinestall *m*; *(fig also)* Saustall *m (inf)*; **pigswill** N Schweinefutter *nt*; *(fig) (= coffee, soup etc)* Spülwasser *nt (inf)*; *(= porridge etc)* Schweinefraß *m (inf)*; **pigtail** N Zopf *m*; **pigwoman** N Schweinehirtin *f*

pike¹ [paɪk] N *(= weapon)* Pike *f*, Spieß *m*

pike² N *(= fish)* Hecht *m*

pike³ N *(US inf: = toll-road)* Mautstraße *f*; *(= barrier)* Mautschranke *f*

pikeperch ['paɪkpɜːtʃ] N *(Zool)* Hechtbarsch *m*, Zander *m*

piker ['paɪkəʳ] N *(pej)* **a** *(US sl: = cautious gambler)* vorsichtige(r) Spieler(in) **b** *(US sl: = miser)* Geizhals *m* **c** *(Austral sl: = shirker)* Drückeberger(in) *m(f) (pej)*, Memme *f (pej)*, Faulenzer(in) *m(f) (pej)*

pikestaff ['paɪkstɑːf] N **as plain as a ~** sonnenklar

pilaf ['piːlæf] N = **pilau**

pilaster [pɪˈlæstəʳ] N Pilaster *m*, Halbpfeiler *m*

Pilates [pɪˈlɑːtiːz] N *(= fitness programme)* Pilates *nt*

pilau [pɪˈlaʊ] N *(also* **pilau rice***)* Pilaw *nt*

pilchard ['pɪltʃəd] N Sardine *f*

pile¹ [paɪl] N **a** *(= heap)* Stapel *m*, Stoß *m*; **to put things in a ~** etw (auf)stapeln; **her things lay** *or* **were in a ~** ihre Sachen lagen auf einem Haufen; **he made a ~ of the books** er stapelte die Bücher aufeinander; **at the bottom/top of the ~** *(fig)* untenan/obenauf

b *(inf: = large amount)* Haufen *m*, Menge *f*, Masse *f*; **a great ~ of work** eine Menge *or* Mas-

se *(inf)* Arbeit; **~s of money/trouble/food** eine *or* jede Menge *(inf)* Geld/Ärger/Essen; **a ~ of things to do** massenhaft zu tun *(inf)*
c *(inf: = fortune)* Vermögen *nt*; **to make a ~** einen Haufen Geld verdienen; **to make one's ~** sein Vermögen machen
d *(= funeral pile)* Scheiterhaufen *m*
e *(liter, hum, = building)* ehrwürdiges Gebäude
f *(= atomic pile)* Atommeiler *m*
VT stapeln; **a table ~d high with books** ein Tisch mit Stapeln von Büchern; **the sideboard was ~d high with presents** auf der Anrichte stapelten sich die Geschenke

▶**pile in** VI *(inf)* (*-to* in *+acc*) hineindrängen; *(= get in)* einsteigen; **pile in!** immer herein! VT *sep* einladen (*-to* in *+acc*)

▶**pile off** VI *(inf)* hinausdrängen *(prep obj* aus)

▶**pile on** VI *(inf)* hineindrängen (*-to* in *+acc*) VT *sep (lit)* aufhäufen (*-to* auf *+acc*); **she piled rice on(to) my plate** sie häufte Reis auf meinen Teller; **he's piling work on(to) his staff** er überhäuft seine Leute mit Arbeit; **they are really piling on the pressure** sie setzen uns/euch *etc* ganz gehörig unter Druck; **to pile on weight** *or* **the pounds** Gewicht *nt*/Pfunde *pl* ansetzen; **to pile on the agony** *(inf)* dick auftragen *(inf)*; **to pile it on** *(inf)* dick auftragen *(inf)*

▶**pile out** VI *(inf)* hinausdrängen (*of* aus)

▶**pile up** VI a *(lit, fig)* sich (an)sammeln *or* anhäufen; *(traffic)* sich stauen; *(snow, work)* sich (auf)türmen *or* anhäufen; *(reasons)* sich häufen; *(evidence)* sich verdichten; *(points)* sich ansammeln; **he let the work pile up** die Arbeit türmte sich auf
b *(= crash)* aufeinander auffahren
VT *sep* a *(= stack up)* (auf)stapeln; *money* horten; *(fig) debts* anhäufen; *evidence* sammeln; **her hair was piled up on top of her head** sie trug ihre Haare hoch aufgetürmt; **to pile the fire up (with logs/coal)** (Holz/Kohle) nachlegen; **he's piling up trouble for himself** er handelt sich *(dat)* Ärger ein
b *(inf, = crash) car* kaputt fahren

pile² N *(= post)* Pfahl *m*

pile³ N *(of carpet, cloth)* Flor *m*

pile: **pile bridge** N (Pfahl)jochbrücke *f*; **pile-driver** N Ramme *f*; **pile dwelling** N Pfahlbau *m*

piles [paɪlz] PL Hämorr(ho)iden *pl*

pile-up [ˈpaɪlʌp] N *(= car crash)* (Massen)karambolage *f*, Massenzusammenstoß *m*

pilfer [ˈpɪlfəʳ] VT stehlen, klauen *(inf)*; **a lot of ~ing goes on in the office** im Büro wird viel geklaut *(inf)* VI stehlen, klauen *(inf)*

pilferage [ˈpɪlfərɪdʒ] N Diebstähle *pl (in kleinem Rahmen)*, Beraubung *f (Insur)*

pilferer [ˈpɪlfərəʳ] N Dieb(in) *m(f)*, Langfinger *m (inf)*

pilgrim [ˈpɪlgrɪm] N Pilger(in) *m(f)*; **the Pilgrim Fathers** die Pilgerväter *pl*

> **PILGRIM FATHERS**
> Die **Pilgrim Fathers**, die Pilgerväter, waren eine Gruppe von Puritanern, die 1620 England verließen, um der religiösen Verfolgung zu entgehen. Sie segelten in einem Schiff namens „Mayflower" über den Atlantik und gründeten New Plymouth in Neuengland, das im heutigen Bundesstaat Massachusetts liegt, wo sie sich ansiedelten. Damit begann die britische Kolonisierung Amerikas. Die **Pilgrim Fathers** gelten als die Gründerväter der Vereinigten Staaten, und jedes Jahr wird am Thanksgiving Day wieder ihre erste Ernte gefeiert. → THANKSGIVING

pilgrimage [ˈpɪlgrɪmɪdʒ] N Wallfahrt *f*, Pilgerfahrt *f*; **to go on** *or* **make a ~** pilgern, wallfahren, eine Pilger- *or* Wallfahrt machen; **in our ~ through this life** *(liter)* auf unserem langen Weg *or* unserer langen Reise durch dieses Leben

piling [ˈpaɪlɪŋ] N *(= posts)* Pfähle *pl*

pill [pɪl] N a Tablette *f*; **the ~** die Pille; **to be/go on the ~** die Pille nehmen → **bitter ADJ** a
b *(sl, = ball)* Pille *f (sl)*

pillage [ˈpɪlɪdʒ] N *(= act)* Plünderung *f*; *(= booty)* Beute *f* VTI plündern

pillar [ˈpɪləʳ] N Säule *f*; **~ of salt** Salzsäule *f*; **~ of smoke** Rauchsäule *f*; **the Pillars of Hercules** die Säulen *pl* des Herkules; **a ~ of society/the community** eine Säule *or* Stütze der Gesellschaft/der Gemeinschaft; **from ~ to post** *(Brit)* von Pontius zu Pilatus

pillar box [ˈpɪləbɒks] N *(Brit)* Briefkasten *m*; **pillar-box red** knallrot

pillbox [ˈpɪlbɒks] N a *(Med)* Pillenschachtel *f* b *(Mil)* Bunker *m* c *(also* **pillbox hat**) Pagenkäppi *nt*; *(for women)* Pillbox *f*

pillion [ˈpɪljən] N a *(on motorbike)* Soziussitz *m*; **~ passenger** Sozius *m*, Beifahrer(in) *m(f)*
b *(Hist)* Damensattel *m* ADV **to ride ~** auf dem Sozius- *or* Beifahrersitz mitfahren; *(on horse)* hinter dem Sattel sitzen

pillock [ˈpɪlək] N *(Brit inf pej)* Blödmann *m (pej)*, Schwachkopf *m (pej)*

pillory [ˈpɪlərɪ] N *(Hist)* Pranger *m*; **to be in the ~** am Pranger stehen VT *(fig)* anprangern

pillow [ˈpɪləʊ] N (Kopf)kissen *nt* VT betten

pillow: **pillowcase** N (Kopf)kissenbezug *m*; **pillow fight** N Kissenschlacht *f*; **pillow lace** N Klöppel-/Kissenspitzen *pl*; **pillow lava** N *(Geol)* Kissenlava *f*; **pillowslip** N = **pillowcase**; **pillow talk** N Bettgeflüster *nt*

pill popper N *(inf)* Tablettensüchtige(r) *mf*

pilot [ˈpaɪlət] N a *(Aviat)* Pilot(in) *m(f)*, Flugzeugführer(in) *m(f)*; **~'s licence** Flugschein *m*, Flugzeugführererlaubnis *f (form)* b *(Naut)* Lotse *m*, Lotsin *f* c *(= pilot light)* Zündflamme *f* d *(US: on train)* Schienenräumer *m* e *(TV)* **~ (episode)** Pilotfilm *m* VT *plane* führen, fliegen; *ship* lotsen; *(fig)* führen, leiten

pilot: **pilot beam** N *(Tech)* Leitstrahl *f*; **pilot boat** N Lotsenboot *nt*; **pilot experiment** N *(Tech, Sci)* Pilotversuch *m*, Modellversuch *m*; **pilot fish** N Lotsen- *or* Pilotfisch *m*; **pilot flag** N Lotsenrufflagge *f*; **pilot house** N Ruderhaus *nt*, Steuerhaus *nt*; **pilot lamp** N Kontrolllampe *f*; **pilotless** ADJ führerlos; **pilot light** N Zündflamme *f*; *(for monitoring)* Kontrolllampe *f*; **pilot officer** N *(Brit Aviat)* Leutnant *m*; **pilot plant** N a *(= experimental plant)* Pilot-/Versuchsanlage *f* b *(= model company)* Musterbetrieb *m*; **pilot scheme** N Pilotprojekt *nt*; **pilot study** N Pilotstudie *f*, Musterstudie *f*; **pilot test** N *(Tech, Sci)* Pilotversuch *m*, Modellversuch *m*

Pilsener [ˈpɪlsənəʳ], **Pilsner** [ˈpɪlsnəʳ] N *(beer)* Pils(e)ner *nt*

pimento [pɪˈmentəʊ] N a Paprikaschote *f* b *(= allspice)* Piment *m or nt*, Nelkenpfeffer *m*; *(= tree)* Pimentbaum *m*

pimiento [pɪˈmjentəʊ] N rote Paprikaschote

pimp¹ [pɪmp] N Zuhälter *m* VI Zuhälter sein; **to ~ for sb** für jdn den Zuhälter machen

pimp² N *(Austral sl pej)* Spitzel *m (pej)*, Informant(in) *m(f)*

pimpernel [ˈpɪmpənel] N *(Bot: also* **scarlet pimpernel**) (Acker)gauchheil *m*

pimple [ˈpɪmpl] N Pickel *m*, Pustel *f*; **to get ~s** Pickel bekommen; **her face breaks out in ~s** sie bekommt Pickel im Gesicht

pimply [ˈpɪmplɪ] ADJ *(+er)* pickelig

PIN [pɪn] N *abbr of* **personal identification number** PIN *f*; *(also* **PIN number**) PIN-Nummer *f*, Geheimnummer *f*

pin [pɪn] N a *(Sew)* Stecknadel *f*; *(= tie pin, hatpin, on brooch, hair pin)* Nadel *f*; *(Mech)* Bolzen *m*, Stift *m*; *(= small nail)* Stift *m*; *(in grenade)* Sicherungsstift *m*; *(Med)* Stift *m*, Nagel *m*; *(Elec, of plug)* Pol *m*; *(Comput) (on connector)* Pin *m*, Kontaktstift *m*; *(on printhead)* Nadel *f*; **a two-~ plug** ein zweipoliger Stecker; **~s and needles** *sing or pl* ein Kribbeln *nt*; **I've got ~s and needles in my foot** mir ist der Fuß eingeschlafen; **to be on ~s and needles** wie auf (glühenden) Kohlen sitzen; **like a new ~** blitzsauber, funkelnagelneu; **neat as a (new) ~** wie aus dem Ei gepellt; **for two ~s I'd pack up and go** *(inf)* es fehlt nicht mehr viel, dann gehe ich; **I don't care a ~** *(dated inf)* es ist mir völlig egal *or* schnuppe *(inf)*; **you could have heard a ~ drop** man hätte eine Stecknadel fallen hören können
b *(esp US) (= brooch)* Brosche *f*, Schmucknadel *f*; *(= badge: also* **lapel pin, fraternity pin**) Anstecknadel *f*, Abzeichen *nt*
c *(Golf)* Flaggenstock *m*; *(Bowling)* Kegel *m*
d **pins** PL *(esp Brit inf: = legs)* Gestell *nt (inf)*; **he wasn't very steady on his ~s** er war etwas wackelig auf den Beinen; **to be quick on one's ~s** gut zu Fuß sein
VT a *dress* stecken; **to ~ sth to sth** etw an etw *(acc)* heften; **to ~ papers together** Blätter zusammenheften; **the bone had to be ~ned in place** der Knochen musste genagelt werden; **she ~ned her hair back** sie hatte ihr Haar hinten zusammengesteckt
b *(fig)* **to ~ sb to the ground/against a wall** jdn an den Boden/an eine Wand pressen; **to ~ sb's arms to his side** jdm die Arme an den Körper pressen; **to ~ sb's arm behind his back** jdm den Arm auf den Rücken drehen; **to ~ one's hopes/faith on sb/sth** seine Hoffnungen/sein Vertrauen auf jdn/etw setzen; **you shouldn't ~ everything on one chance** Sie sollten nicht alles auf eine Karte setzen; **to ~ back one's ears** die Ohren spitzen *(inf)*
c *(inf: = accuse of)* **to ~ sth on sb** jdm etw anhängen; **to ~ the blame (for sth) on sb** jdm die Schuld (an etw *(dat)*) anhängen *(inf)*
d *(US inf)* **to be ~ned** verlobt sein; **to get ~ned** sich verloben

▶**pin down** VT *sep* a *(= fix down: with pins)* an- *or* festheften; *(= hold, weight down)* beschweren, niederhalten; *(= trap: rockfall etc)* einklemmen; **he pinned him down on the canvas** er drückte ihn auf die Matte; **two of the gang pinned him down** zwei aus der Bande drückten ihn zu Boden; **our troops were pinned down by heavy artillery fire** unsere Truppen wurden durch heftiges Artilleriefeuer festgehalten
b *(fig)* **to pin sb down** jdn festnageln *or* festlegen; **he wouldn't be pinned down to any particular date** er ließ sich nicht auf ein bestimmtes Datum festnageln *or* festlegen; **he's a difficult man to pin down** man kann ihn nur schwer dazu bringen, sich festzulegen; **I've seen him/it somewhere before but I can't pin him/it down** ich habe ihn/es schon mal irgendwo gesehen, kann ihn/es aber nicht einordnen; **we can't pin down the source of the rumours** wir können die Quelle der Gerüchte nicht lokalisieren; **it's not easy to pin down the precise cause of this** es ist nicht leicht, die genaue Ursache dafür festzustellen; **there's something odd here, but I can't pin it down** irgendetwas ist hier merkwürdig, aber ich kann nicht genau sagen, was

▶**pin up** VT *sep notice* anheften; *hair* aufstecken, hochstecken; *hem, dress, sleeves* stecken

pina colada [ˌpiːnəkəˈlɑːdə] N Pina Colada *m*

pinafore [ˈpɪnəfɔːʳ] N *(= overall: for children)* Kinderkittel *m*; *(= apron)* Schürze *f*, Kittel *m*; **~ dress** *(Brit)* Trägerkleid *nt*

pinball [ˈpɪnbɔːl] N Flipper *m*; **to have a game of ~** Flipper spielen, flippern; **~ machine** Flipper *m*

pince-nez [ˈpɪnsneɪ] N Kneifer *m*, Pincenez *nt (old)*

pincer movement [ˈpɪnsə-] N *(Mil, fig)* Zangenbewegung *f*

pincers [ˈpɪnsəz] PL a Kneifzange *f*, Beißzange *f*; **a pair of ~** eine Kneifzange, eine Beißzange b *(Zool)* Schere *f*, Zange *f*

pinch [pɪntʃ] N a *(with fingers)* Kneifen *nt no pl*, Zwicken *nt no pl*; **to give sb a ~ on the arm** jdn in den Arm kneifen *or* zwicken
b *(= small quantity)* Quäntchen *nt*; *(Cook)* Prise *f*; **a ~ of snuff** eine Prise Schnupftabak
c *(= pressure)* **to feel the ~** die schlechte Lage zu spüren bekommen; **I'm feeling the ~ a bit at the moment** ich bin im Augenblick ziemlich

knapp bei Kasse *(inf)*; **if it comes to the ~** wenn es zum Schlimmsten *or* Äußersten kommt; **at** *(Brit) or* **in** *(US)* **a ~** zur Not

VT **a** *(with fingers)* kneifen, zwicken; *(with implement: = squeeze) end of wire etc* zusammendrücken, zusammenklemmen; *(shoe)* drücken; **to ~ sb's bottom** jdn in den Hintern kneifen; **to ~ oneself** sich kneifen; **to ~ one's finger in the door** sich *(dat)* den Finger in der Tür (ein)klemmen

b *(Brit inf: = steal)* klauen, stibitzen, mopsen *(all inf)*; **don't let anyone ~ my seat** pass auf, dass mir niemand den Platz wegnimmt; **he ~ed Johnny's girlfriend** er hat Johnny *(dat)* die Freundin ausgespannt *(inf)*; **he ~ed that idea from Shaw** die Idee hat er bei Shaw geklaut *(inf)*; **I had my car ~ed** mein Auto ist geklaut worden *(inf)*

c *(inf, = arrest)* schnappen *(inf)*, erwischen

VI **a** *(shoe, also fig)* drücken

b **to ~ and scrape** sich einschränken

▶ **pinch back** *or* **off** VT *sep bud* abknipsen

pinchbeck [ˈpɪntʃbek] **N** *(lit, fig)* Talmi *nt* **ADJ** *jewels* aus Talmi

pinched [ˈpɪntʃt] **ADJ** **a** verhärmt; *(from cold)* verfroren; *(from fatigue)* erschöpft **b** *(inf, = short)* **to be ~ for money** knapp bei Kasse sein *(inf)*; **to be ~ for time** keine Zeit haben

pin cherry **N** *(Bot)* Amerikanische Weichselkirsche

pinch-hit [ˈpɪntʃhɪt] **VI** *(US)* Ersatzspieler sein; *(fig)* einspringen

pinch hitter [ˈpɪntʃˌhɪtəˈ] **N** *(US)* Ersatzspieler(in) *m(f)*; *(fig)* Ersatz *m*

pinchpenny [ˈpɪntʃˌpenɪ] **ADJ** knauserig, pfennigfuchserisch

pin: **pin curl** **N** Löckchen *nt*; **pincushion** [pɪnˌkʊʃən] **N** Nadelkissen *nt*

pine[1] [paɪn] **N** Kiefer *f*

pine[2] **VI** **a** **to ~ for sb/sth** sich nach jdm/etw sehnen *or* verzehren **b** *(= pine away, be sad)* sich vor Kummer verzehren

▶ **pine away** **VI** *(from grief)* sich (vor Kummer) verzehren, vor Gram vergehen; *(from disease)* (dahin)siechen; *(of animal, plant)* eingehen; **she pined away and died** sie starb an gebrochenem Herzen; **the dog just pined away and died** der Hund ging langsam ein

pineal gland [ˈpɪnɪəl-] **N** Zirbeldrüse *f*, Epiphyse *f (spec)*

pineapple [ˈpaɪnˌæpl] **N** Ananas *f*; **~ chunks** Ananasstücke *pl*; **~ juice** Ananassaft *m*

pine: **pine cone** **N** Kiefernzapfen *m*; **pine forest** **N** Kiefernwald *m*; **pine marten** **N** Baummarder *m*; **pine needle** **N** Kiefernnadel *f*; **pine tree** **N** Kiefer *f*; **pine wood** **N** Kiefernwald *m*; *(= material)* Kiefernholz *nt*

ping [pɪŋ] **N** *(of bell)* Klingeln *nt*; *(of bullet)* Peng *nt*; **to make a ~** *(sonar, lift bell etc)* klingeln; **the stone made a ~ as it hit the glass** der Stein machte klick, als er auf das Glas traf **VI** *(bell)* klingeln; *(bullet)* peng machen

ping pong [ˈpɪŋpɒŋ] **N** Pingpong *nt*; **~ ball** Pingpongball *m*

pin: **pinhead** **N** (Steck)nadelkopf *m*; *(inf: = stupid person)* Holzkopf *m (inf)*, Strohkopf *m (inf)*; **pinheaded** **ADJ** *(inf)* schwachköpfig *(inf)*, blöd(e) *(inf)*; **pin holder** **N** Blumenigel *m*; **pinhole** **N** Loch *nt*; **pinhole camera** **N** Lochkamera *f*, Camera obscura *f*

pinion [ˈpɪnjən] **N** **a** *(Mech)* Ritzel *nt*, Treibrad *nt* **b** *(poet, = wing)* Fittich *m (poet)*, Schwinge *f (poet)* **c** *(Orn)* Flügelspitze *f* **VT** **to ~ sb to the ground/against the wall** jdn zu Boden/gegen eine Wand drücken

pink[1] [pɪŋk] **N** **a** *(= colour)* Rosa *nt*; *(= hunting pink)* Rot *nt* **b** *(= plant)* Gartennelke *f* **c** *(Brit)* **to be in the ~ (of health)** vor Gesundheit strotzen; **I'm in the ~** mir gehts prächtig; **to feel in the ~** sich bestens fühlen; **in the ~ of condition** in Top- *or* Hochform **ADJ** **a** *(= colour)* rosa *inv*, rosarot, rosafarben; *cheeks, face* rosig; **to go** *or* **turn ~** erröten; **to see ~ elephants** *or* **mice** *(inf)* weiße Mäuse sehen *(inf)*; **the ~ pound** *(inf)* die Kaufkraft der Homosexuellen **b** *(Pol inf)* rot angehaucht

pink[2] **VT** **a** *(Sew)* mit der Zickzackschere schneiden **b** *(= nick)* streifen

pink[3] **VI** *(Aut)* klopfen

pink-collar **ADJ** *attr* Frauen-; **~ jobs** typische Frauenberufe *pl*

pinkeye [ˈpɪŋkaɪ] **N** *(inf)* Bindehautentzündung *f*

pink gin **N** Pink Gin *m*

pinkie [ˈpɪŋkɪ] **N** *(Scot, US: inf)* kleiner Finger

pinking shears [ˈpɪŋkɪŋʃɪəz] **PL** Zickzackschere *f*

pinkish [ˈpɪŋkɪʃ] **ADJ** rötlich; **~ white** blassrosa

pinko [ˈpɪŋkəʊ] **N** *(Pol pej inf)* roter Bruder *(inf)*, rote Schwester *(inf)*

pink slip **N** *(US inf)* Entlassungspapiere *pl*

> **PINK SLIP**
>
> In den USA ist **pink slip** der umgangssprachliche Ausdruck für das Schreiben, mit dem ein Arbeitgeber seinem Angestellten die Kündigung mitteilt. Der Begriff stammt aus den Zwanzigerjahren, als ein rosafarbener Durchschlag mit der Kündigung in die Lohntüte gesteckt wurde. Es gibt davon auch eine verbale („they pink-slipped him") und eine adjektivische („a pink-slipped worker") Form.

pink-slip **VT** *(US inf)* entlassen; **to ~ sb** jdm den blauen Brief schicken *(inf)*; **to be ~ped** den blauen Brief bekommen

pin money **N** Taschengeld *nt*, Nadelgeld *nt (old)*

pinnace [ˈpɪnɪs] **N** Pinasse *f*

pinnacle [ˈpɪnəkl] **N** *(Archit)* Fiale *f*; *(of rock, mountain)* Gipfel *m*, Spitze *f*; *(fig)* Gipfel *m*, Höhepunkt *m*

pinnate [ˈpɪneɪt] **ADJ** *(Bot)* gefiedert

PIN number **N** = **PIN**

pinny [ˈpɪnɪ] **N** *(Brit inf)* Schürze *f*

pinoc(h)le [ˈpiːnʌkəl] **N** *(Cards)* Binokel *nt*

pin: **pinpoint** **N** Punkt *m*; **the buildings were mere ~s on the horizon** die Gebäude zeichneten sich wie Stecknadelköpfe am Horizont ab; **a ~ of light** ein Lichtpunkt *m*; **~ bombing** Punktzielbombardement *nt* **VT** *(= locate)* genau an- *or* aufzeigen; *(= define, identify)* genau feststellen *or* -legen; **pinprick** **N** Nadelstich *m*; *(fig)* Kleinigkeit *f*; **pin-sharp** **ADJ** *photo* gestochen scharf; **pinstripe** **N** *(= stripe)* Nadelstreifen *m*; *(= cloth)* Tuch *nt* mit Nadelstreifen; *(= pinstripe suit)* Nadelstreifenanzug *m*; **pin-striped** **ADJ** Nadelstreifen-; **~ suit** Nadelstreifenanzug *m*

pint [paɪnt] **N** **a** *(= measure)* Pint *nt* **b** *(esp Brit: = quantity) (of milk)* Tüte *f*; *(= bottle)* Flasche *f*; *(of beer)* Halbe *f*, Glas *nt* Bier; **to have a ~** ein Bier trinken; **to go (out) for a ~** auf ein Bier ausgehen; **he likes a ~** er hebt ganz gern mal einen *(inf)*; **she's had a few ~s** *(inf)* sie hat ein paar intus *(inf)*; **a good ~** ein gutes Bier

pinta [ˈpaɪntə] **N** *(Brit inf)* halber Liter Milch

pin table **N** Flipper *m*

pint mug [ˈpaɪntˈmʌɡ] **N** Humpen *m (der ein Pint fasst)*

pinto [ˈpɪntəʊ] *(US)* **ADJ** *horse* scheckig **N** Schecke *mf*

pinto bean **N** Pintobohne *f*

pint-size(d) [ˈpaɪntsaɪz(d)] **ADJ** *(inf)* stöpselig *(inf)*, knirpsig *(inf)*; **a ~ boxer** ein Knirps *m* von einem Boxer; **a ~ company** eine Zwergfirma

pin: **pin tuck** **N** Biese *f*; **pin-up** **N** *(= picture)* Pin-up-Foto *nt*; *(= woman)* Pin-up-Girl *nt*; *(= man)* Idol *nt*; **pin-up girl** **N** Pin-up-Girl *nt*; **pinwheel** **N** *(= firework)* Feuerrad *nt*; *(US: = toy)* Windrädchen *nt*

Pinyin [ˈpɪnˈjɪn] **N** Pinyin(umschrift *f*) *nt*

piolet [ˈpiːəleɪ] **N** *(Mountaineering)* Eispickel *m*

pioneer [ˌpaɪəˈnɪəˈ] **N** *(Mil)* Pionier *m*; *(fig)* Pionier(in) *m(f)*, Wegbereiter(in) *m(f)* **ADJ** *attr* → **pioneering** **VT** *way* vorbereiten, bahnen; *(fig)* Pionierarbeit *f* leisten für; **to ~ the use of sth** *(= use for the first time)* etw zum ersten Mal anwenden; **the firm which ~ed its technical development** die Firma, die die technische Pionierarbeit dafür geleistet hat **VI** Pionierarbeit *or* Vorarbeit leisten, den Weg bahnen

pioneering [ˌpaɪəˈnɪərɪŋ] **ADJ** *attr method, research* wegbereitend; **~ spirit** Pioniergeist *m*; **~ work** Pionierarbeit *f*; **the pride they take in their ~ ancestors** der Stolz auf ihre Vorfahren, die Pioniere; **in the ~ days of radio** in den Kindertagen des Radios

pious [ˈpaɪəs] **ADJ** **a** *(= devout)* fromm; *(pej also)* frömmlerisch **b** *(pej: = hypocritical) person, words* unaufrichtig, falsch; **a ~ hope** ein frommer Wunsch

piously [ˈpaɪəslɪ] **ADV** fromm

piousness [ˈpaɪəsnɪs] **N** Frömmigkeit *f*; *(pej also)* Frömmelei *f*

pip[1] [pɪp] **N** **a** *(Bot)* Kern *m* **b** *(on card, dice)* Auge *nt*; *(Brit Mil inf)* Stern *m*; *(on radar screen)* Pip *m*, Echozeichen *nt* **c** *(Rad, Telec)* das Zeitzeichen; *(in public telephone)* das Tut-Tut-Tut; **at the third ~ it will be ...** beim dritten Ton des Zeitzeichens ist es ...; **put more money in when you hear the ~s** bitte Geld nachwerfen, sobald das Zeichen ertönt

pip[2] **N** *(Vet)* Pips *m*; **to give sb the ~** *(Brit inf)* jdn aufregen *(inf)*

pip[3] **VT** *(Brit inf)* knapp besiegen *or* schlagen; **to ~ sb at** *or* **to the post** *(in race)* jdn um Haaresbreite schlagen; *(fig)* jdm um Haaresbreite zuvorkommen; *(in getting orders etc)* jdm etw vor der Nase wegschnappen; **I was ~ped at** *or* **to the post again** *(fig)* da war mir wieder jemand zuvorgekommen; **he was ~ped for second place by Moore** er wurde von Moore nur knapp vom zweiten Platz verdrängt

pipe [paɪp] **N** **a** *(= tube: for water, gas, sewage)* Rohr *nt*, Leitung *f*; *(= fuel pipe, for steam)* Leitung *f*; *(in body)* Röhre *f*

b *(Mus)* Flöte *f*; *(= fife, of organ, boatswain's)* Pfeife *f*; **~s** *(= bagpipes)* Dudelsack *m*; **~s of Pan** Panflöte *f*

c *(for smoking)* Pfeife *f*; **~ of peace** Friedenspfeife; **to smoke a ~** Pfeife rauchen; **put that in your ~ and smoke it!** *(inf)* steck dir das hinter den Spiegel! *(inf)*

VT **a** *water, oil etc* in Rohren leiten; *music, broadcast* ausstrahlen; **water has to be ~d in from the next state** Wasser muss in Rohrleitungen aus dem Nachbarstaat herangeschafft werden; **~d music** *(pej)* Musikberieselung *f (inf)*

b *(Mus) tune* flöten, pfeifen; *(= sing in high voice)* krähen; *(= speak in high voice)* piepsen; *(Naut)* pfeifen; **to ~ sb aboard** jdn mit Pfeifensignal an Bord begrüßen *or* empfangen; **he was even ~d to the gallows** selbst zum Galgen wurde er mit Dudelsackmusik geleitet

c *(Cook)* spritzen; *cake* mit Spritzguss verzieren; *(Sew)* paspelieren, paspeln

VI *(Mus)* flöten, (die) Flöte spielen; *(bird)* pfeifen; *(young bird: anxiously)* piep(s)en

▶ **pipe down** **VI** *(inf) (= be less noisy)* die Luft anhalten *(inf)*, ruhig sein; *(= become less confident)* (ganz) klein werden *(inf)*

▶ **pipe up** **VI** *(inf) (person)* den Mund aufmachen, sich melden; **suddenly a little voice piped up** plötzlich machte sich ein Stimmchen bemerkbar; **then he piped up with another objection** dann kam er mit noch einem Einwand

pipe: **pipe band** **N** Dudelsackkapelle *f*; **pipe bomb** **N** Rohrbombe *f*; **pipe burst** **N** Rohrbruch *m*; **pipe clamp** **N** *(Tech)* Rohrschelle *f*; **pipeclay** **N** *(for making pipes)* Pfeifenton *m*; **pipe cleaner** **N** Pfeifenreiniger *m*; **pipe clip** **N** *(Tech)* Rohrschelle *f*; **pipe dream** **N** Hirngespinst *nt*; **that's just a ~** das ist ja wohl nur ein frommer Wunsch; **pipe-layer** **N** Rohrleitungs(ver)leger(in) *m(f)*, Rohrleitungsmonteur(in) *m(f)*; **pipe-laying** **N** Verlegen *nt* von Rohrleitungen; **pipeline** **N** (Rohr)leitung *f*;

(for oil, gas also) Pipeline *f*; **to be in the ~** *(fig)* in Vorbereitung sein; **the pay rise hasn't come through yet but it's in the ~** die Lohnerhöhung ist noch nicht durch, steht aber kurz bevor; **we've got a few changes in the ~** wir müssen auf einige Änderungen gefasst sein

piper ['paɪpəʳ] N Flötenspieler(in) *m(f)*; *(on fife)* Pfeifer(in) *m(f)*; *(on bagpipes)* Dudelsackpfeifer(in) *m(f)*; **to pay the ~** *(fig)* die Kosten tragen, für die Kosten aufkommen; **he who pays the ~ calls the tune** *(Prov)* wer bezahlt, darf auch bestimmen

pipe: **pipe rack** N Pfeifenständer *m*; **pipe smoker** N Pfeifenraucher(in) *m(f)*; **pipe tobacco** N Pfeifentabak *m*; **pipe tool** N *(for pipe-smokers)* Pfeifenbesteck *nt*

pipette [pɪ'pet] N Pipette *f*, Saugröhrchen *nt*

pipe: **pipework** ['paɪpwɜːk] N Rohre *pl*; **pipe wrench** N *(Tech)* Rohrzange *f*

piping ['paɪpɪŋ] N a *(= pipework)* Rohrleitungssystem *nt*; *(= pipe)* Rohrleitung *f* b *(Sew)* Paspelierung *f*; *(on furniture)* Kordel *f*; *(Cook)* Spritzgussverzierung *f* c *(Mus)* Flötenspiel *nt*; *(on bagpipes)* Dudelsackpfeifen *nt* ADJ *voice* piepsend ADV **~ hot** kochend heiß

piping bag N Spritzbeutel *m*

pipistrelle [ˌpɪpɪ'strel] N Zwergfledermaus *f*

pipit ['pɪpɪt] N Pieper *m*

pippin ['pɪpɪn] N Cox *m*

pipsqueak ['pɪpskwiːk] N *(inf)* Winzling *m (inf)*

piquancy ['piːkənsɪ] N Pikantheit *f*, Würze *f*; *(fig)* Pikanterie *f*

piquant ['piːkənt] ADJ *(lit, fig)* pikant

pique [piːk] N Groll *m*, Vergrämtheit *f*; **he resigned in a fit of ~** er kündigte, weil er vergrämt war; **you needn't have a fit of ~ just because ...** du brauchst nicht gleich pikiert *or* beleidigt zu sein, nur weil ...; **to do sth out of ~** etw aus Groll *(dat)* tun; **to be in a ~ with sb** *(old)* gegen jdn einen Groll hegen VT *(= offend, wound)* kränken, verletzen; **to be ~d at** *or* **by sth** über jdn/etw *(acc)* ungehalten *or* pikiert sein VR **to ~ oneself on sth** sich *(dat)* viel auf etw *(acc)* einbilden

piqué ['piːkeɪ] N Pikee *m*, Piqué *m*

piracy ['paɪərəsɪ] N Seeräuberei *f*, Piraterie *f*; *(of book etc)* Raubdruck *m*; *(of record)* Raubpressung *f*; **an act of ~** Seeräuberei *f*, Piraterie *f*

piranha (fish) [pɪ'rɑːnjə(fɪʃ)] N Piranha *m*

pirate ['paɪərɪt] N Seeräuber(in) *m(f)*, Pirat(in) *m(f)*; *(= pirate ship)* Seeräuberschiff *nt*, Piratenschiff *nt*; (*also* **pirate cab**) nicht konzessioniertes Taxi VT *book* einen Raubdruck herstellen von; *invention, idea* stehlen; **a ~d copy of the record** eine Raubpressung; **~d edition** Raubdruck *m*

pirate copy N Raubkopie *f*

pirate radio N *(Brit)* Piratensender *m*

piratical [paɪ'rætɪkəl] ADJ seeräuberisch, piratenhaft

pirogue [pɪ'rəʊg] N *(= dug-out canoe)* Einbaum *m*, Piragua *f*

pirouette [ˌpɪrʊ'et] N Pirouette *f* VI Pirouetten drehen, pirouettieren

Pisces ['paɪsiːz] PL Fische *pl*; **I'm (a) ~** ich bin Fisch

pisciculture ['pɪsɪkʌltʃəʳ] N *(spec)* Fischzucht *f*

pishogue [pɪ'ʃəʊg] N *(Irish)* Hexerei *f*

piss [pɪs] *(sl)* N *(= urine)* Pisse *f (vulg)*; **to have** *or* **take a ~** pissen *(vulg)*; **to go for a ~** pissen gehen *(vulg)*; **to take the ~ out of sb/sth** *(Brit sl)* jdn/etw verarschen *(inf)* VI pissen *(inf)*; **it's ~ing with rain** *(inf)* es pisst *(sl)* VT pissen *(sl)* VR sich bepissen *(vulg)*; **we ~ed ourselves (laughing)** wir haben uns bepisst *(sl)*

▸ **piss about** *or* **around** VI *(Brit inf)* herummachen *(inf)*

▸ **piss down** VI *(Brit inf)* **it's pissing down** es pisst *(sl)*

▸ **piss off** VI *(esp Brit sl)* sich verpissen *(sl)*; **piss off!** *(= go away)* verpiss dich! *(sl)*; *(= don't be stupid)* du kannst mich mal *(inf)* VT *(esp Brit inf)* ankotzen *(sl)*; **to be pissed off with sb/sth** von jdm/etw die Schnauze voll haben *(inf)*; **I'm so pissed off** ich bin total angenervt *(inf)*; **he pisses me off** der kotzt mich total an *(inf)*

piss artist N *(inf)* *(= drunk)* Säufer(in) *m(f)*; *(= boaster)* Großmaul *nt (inf)*; *(= incompetent)* Niete *f (inf)*; *(= silly bastard)* Arschloch *nt (vulg)*

pissed [pɪst] ADJ *(inf)* a *(Brit: = drunk)* stockbesoffen *(inf)*, dicht *(sl)*; **I want to get ~ tonight** heute Abend besaufe ich mich *(inf) or* geb ich mir die Kante *(sl)* b *(US: = angry)* stocksauer *(inf)*; **I'm so ~** ich bin total sauer *or* angenervt *(inf)*

piss: **pisshead** N *(Brit inf)* Saufkopf *m (sl)*; **piss-poor** ADJ *(inf) job, performance* hundsmiserabel *(inf)*; **piss-take** N *(Brit sl)* Verarschung *f (inf)*; **piss-up** N *(Brit sl)* Saufgelage *nt (inf)*; **he couldn't organize a ~ in a brewery** er ist dümmer als die Polizei erlaubt *(inf)*

pistachio [pɪ'stɑːʃɪəʊ] N Pistazie *f* ADJ *(colour)* pistazienfarben

piste [piːst] N *(Ski)* Piste *f*

pistil ['pɪstɪl] N Stempel *m*, Pistill *nt (spec)*

pistol ['pɪstl] N Pistole *f*; **~ shot** Pistolenschuss *m*; *(= person)* Pistolenschütze *m*/-schützin *f*; **to hold a ~ to sb's head** *(fig)* jdm die Pistole auf die Brust setzen; **~-grip camera** Kamera *f* mit Handgriff

pistol-whip ['pɪstəlwɪp] VT *(US)* mit einer Pistole ein paar überziehen *(+dat) (inf)*

piston ['pɪstən] N Kolben *m*; **~ stroke** Kolbenhub *m*

piston: **piston engine** N Kolbenmotor *m*; **piston ring** N Kolbenring *m*; **piston rod** N Pleuel- *or* Kolbenstange *f*

pit[1] [pɪt] N a *(= hole)* Grube *f*; *(Brit: = coal mine)* Zeche *f*, Grube *f*; *(= quarry)* Steinbruch *m*; *(= trap)* Fallgrube *f*; *(in zoo etc)* Grube *f*; *(for cock-fighting)* (Kampf)arena *f*; *(of stomach)* Magengrube *f*; **to have a sinking feeling in the ~ of one's stomach** ein ungutes Gefühl in der Magengegend haben; **it makes me feel sick to the ~ of my stomach** da kommt mir die Galle hoch; **to go down the ~** Bergmann *or* Bergarbeiter werden; **he works down the ~(s)** er arbeitet unter Tage; **the ~** *(= hell)* die Hölle → **bottomless**

b *(Aut, in garage)* Grube *f*; *(Sport)* *(for long jump)* Sprunggrube *f*; *(for high jump)* Sprunghügel *m*; **the ~s** *(Motor Racing)* die Box; **to make a ~ stop** einen Boxenstopp machen

c *(Theat)* *(Brit: usu pl: for audience)* Parkett *nt*; *(= orchestra pit)* Orchestergraben *m or* -versenkung *f or* -raum *m*

d *(US St Ex)* Börsensaal *m*

e *(= scar)* *(on ceramics)* Vertiefung *f*; *(on skin)* Narbe *f*

f **the ~s** *(inf: = very bad)* das Allerletzte

g *(inf: = bed)* Falle *f (inf)*

VT a **the surface of the moon is ~ted with small craters** die Mondoberfläche ist mit kleinen Kratern übersät; **where the meteorites have ~ted the surface** wo die Meteoriten Einschläge hinterlassen haben; **his face was ~ted with smallpox scars** sein Gesicht war voller Pockennarben; **the underside of the car was ~ted with rust holes** die Unterseite des Wagens war mit Rostlöchern übersät; **a ~ted road surface** eine mit Schlaglöchern übersäte Fahrbahn

b **to ~ one's strength/wits against sb/sth** seine Kraft/seinen Verstand an jdm/etw messen; **to ~ oneself against sb** den Kampf gegen jdn aufnehmen; **in the next round A is ~ted against B** in der nächsten Runde stehen sich A und B gegenüber; **they are clearly ~ting their new model against ours** mit ihrem neuen Modell nehmen sie offensichtlich den Kampf gegen uns auf

pit[2] *(US)* N Stein *m* VT entsteinen

pita (bread) ['pɪtə] N *(US)* = **pitta (bread)**

pitapat ['pɪtə'pæt] ADV *(of heart)* poch poch, klopf klopf; *(of feet)* tapp tapp; **to go ~** *(heart)* pochen, klopfen N *(of rain, heart)* Klopfen *nt*; *(of feet)* Getrappel *nt*, Getrippel *nt*

pit babe N *(inf)* Boxenluder *nt*

pit bull terrier N Pitbullterrier *m*

pitch[1] [pɪtʃ] N Pech *nt*; **as black as ~** pechschwarz

pitch[2] N a *(= throw)* Wurf *m*; **he threw a good ~** *(Baseball)* ihm gelang ein guter Wurf

b *(Naut)* Stampfen *nt*

c *(esp Brit Sport)* Platz *m*, Feld *nt*

d *(Brit: for doing one's business, in market, outside theatre etc)* Stand *m*; *(fig: = usual place: on beach etc)* Platz *m*; **keep off my ~!** *(fig)* komm mir nicht ins Gehege! → **queer**

e *(inf: = sales pitch)* *(= long talk)* Sermon *m (inf)*; *(= technique)* Verkaufstaktik *f*, Masche *f (inf)*; **to make a ~ for sth** etw anpreisen; **he gave us his ~ about the need to change our policy** er hielt uns (wieder einmal) einen Vortrag über die Notwendigkeit, unsere Politik zu ändern

f *(Phon, also of note)* Tonhöhe *f*; *(of instrument)* Tonlage *f*; *(of voice)* Stimmlage *f*; **to have perfect ~** das absolute Gehör haben; **their speaking voices are similar in ~** ihre Stimmlagen sind ähnlich

g *(= angle, slope: of roof)* Schräge *f*, Neigung *f*; *(of propeller)* Steigung *f*; **the roofs have a steep ~** die Dächer sind sehr steil; **the floor was sloping at a precarious ~** der Boden neigte sich gefährlich

h *(fig: = degree)* **he roused the mob to such a ~ that ...** er brachte die Massen so sehr auf, dass ...; **the tension/their frustration had reached such a ~ that ...** die Spannung/ihre Frustration hatte einen derartigen Grad erreicht, dass ...; **matters had reached such a ~ that ...** die Sache hatte sich derart zugespitzt, dass ...; **at its highest ~** auf dem Höhepunkt *or* Gipfel; **we can't keep on working at this ~ much longer** wir können dieses Arbeitstempo nicht mehr lange durchhalten → **fever b**

i *(US inf)* **what's the ~?** wie siehts aus?, was liegt an? *(inf)*, was geht? *(sl)*

VT a *(= throw) hay* gabeln; *ball* werfen; **he was ~ed from** *or* **off his horse** er wurde vom Pferd geworfen; **he was ~ed through the windscreen** er wurde durch die Windschutzscheibe geschleudert; **as soon as he got the job he was ~ed into a departmental battle** kaum hatte er die Stelle, wurde er schon in einen Abteilungskrieg verwickelt

b *(Mus) song* anstimmen; *note (= give)* angeben; *(= hit)* treffen; *instrument* stimmen; *(inf: by DJ)* pitchen; **she ~ed her voice higher** sie sprach mit einer höheren Stimme

c *(fig)* **to ~ one's aspirations too high** seine Erwartungen *or* Hoffnungen zu hoch stecken; **the prices of these cars are ~ed extremely competitively** diese Autos haben sehr attraktive Preise; **the production must be ~ed at the right level for London audiences** das Stück muss auf das Niveau des Londoner Publikums abgestimmt werden; **she ~ed the plan to business leaders** sie machte ihren Plan führenden Geschäftsleuten schmackhaft; **that's ~ing it rather strong** das ist ein bisschen übertrieben; **to ~ sb a story** *(inf)* jdm eine Geschichte *or* ein Märchen auftischen *(inf)*

d *(= put up) camp, tent* aufschlagen; *stand* aufstellen

e *(Baseball) ball* werfen; **he ~ed the first two innings** er spielte *or* machte in den ersten beiden Runden den Werfer

VI a *(= fall)* fallen, stürzen; **to ~ forward** vornüberfallen; **he ~ed off his horse** er fiel kopfüber vom Pferd; **he ~ed forward as the bus braked** er fiel nach vorn, als der Bus bremste

b *(Naut)* stampfen; *(Aviat)* absacken; **the ship ~ed and rolled** das Schiff stampfte und rollte

c *(Baseball)* werfen; **he's in there ~ing** *(US fig inf)* er schuftet wie ein Ochse *(inf)*

▸ **pitch for** VI *+prep obj* anpreisen

▶**pitch in** VT *sep* hineinwerfen *or* -schleudern VI *(inf)* einspringen; **if we all pitch in and help** wenn wir alle einspringen; **so we all pitched in together** also packten wir alle mit an

▶**pitch into** VI *+prep obj (= attack)* herfallen über *(+acc)*; *food also, work* sich hermachen über *(+acc)*; *(= criticize)* heruntermachen *(inf)* VT *sep* **to pitch sb into fame/gloom** jdn berühmt/traurig machen

▶**pitch on** VI *+prep obj (inf: = choose)* herauspicken *(inf)*

▶**pitch out** VT *sep (lit, fig)* hinauswerfen; *(= get rid of)* wegwerfen; **he was pitched out when the car crashed** beim Unfall wurde er aus dem Wagen geschleudert

pitch: **pitch accent** N *(Phon)* musikalischer (Ton)akzent; **pitch angle** N Steigungswinkel *m*; **pitch-black** ADJ pechschwarz; **pitch-blende** N Pechblende *f*; **pitch-dark** ADJ pechschwarz N (tiefe) Finsternis

pitched [pɪtʃt] ADJ **a** ~ **roof** Sattel- *or* Giebeldach *nt* **b** *battle* offen

pitcher¹ ['pɪtʃəʳ] N *(esp US)* Krug *m*; *(two-handled)* Henkelkrug *m*

pitcher² N *(Baseball)* Werfer(in) *m(f)*

pitchfork N Heugabel *f*; *(for manure)* Mistgabel *f* VT gabeln; *(fig)* hineinwerfen

pitching ['pɪtʃɪŋ] N *(Mus inf: by DJ)* Pitchen *nt*

pitch: **pitch invasion** N Sturm *m* auf das Spielfeld; **pitch pine** N Pechkiefer *f*; **pitch pipe** N *(Mus)* Stimmpfeife *f*

pit disaster N *(Min)* Grubenunglück *nt*

piteous ['pɪtɪəs] ADJ mitleiderregend; *sounds* kläglich

piteously ['pɪtɪəslɪ] ADV mitleiderregend; *cry etc also* kläglich

pitfall ['pɪtfɔːl] N *(fig)* Falle *f*, Fallstrick *m*; **"Pitfalls of English"** „Hauptschwierigkeiten der englischen Sprache"

pith [pɪθ] N *(Bot)* Mark *nt*; *(of orange, lemon etc)* weiße Haut; *(fig: = core)* Kern *m*, Wesentliche(s) *nt*; **remarks of ~ (and moment)** bedeutungsschwere Äußerungen

pithead ['pɪthed] N Übertageanlagen *pl*; **at the ~** über Tage; **~ ballot** Abstimmung *f* der Bergarbeiter

pith hat, **pith helmet** N Tropenhelm *m*

pithily ['pɪθɪlɪ] ADV prägnant, kernig, markig

pithiness ['pɪθɪnɪs] N *(fig)* Prägnanz *f*, Markigkeit *f*

pithy ['pɪθɪ] ADJ *(+er)* *(Bot)* reich an Mark; *oranges etc* dickschalig; *(fig)* prägnant, markig; **~ remarks** Kraftsprüche *pl*

pitiable ['pɪtɪəbl] ADJ mitleiderregend, bemitleidenswert

pitiably ['pɪtɪəblɪ] ADV *(= pitifully)* erbärmlich, jämmerlich; **her dowry is ~ small** ihre Mitgift ist jämmerlich, sie hat nur eine klägliche Mitgift; **he found her lying on the bed, crying ~** er fand sie auf dem Bett, jämmerlich weinend

pitiful ['pɪtɪfʊl] ADJ **a** *(= moving to pity) sight, story* mitleiderregend; *person* bemitleidenswert, bedauernswert; *cry, whimper* jämmerlich; **to be in a ~ state** in einem erbärmlichen Zustand sein **b** *(= poor, wretched)* erbärmlich, jämmerlich, kläglich; **what a ~ little wretch you are** was bist du doch für ein erbärmlicher kleiner Schuft

pitifully ['pɪtɪfəlɪ] ADV **a** jämmerlich, erbärmlich; *look, say, complain* mitleiderregend; **it was ~ obvious that ...** es war schon qualvoll offensichtlich, dass ... **b** *(= woefully) inadequate* erbärmlich, schmerzlich

pitiless ['pɪtɪlɪs] ADJ mitleidlos; *person also, sun, glare* unbarmherzig; *cruelty also* gnadenlos, erbarmungslos

pitilessly ['pɪtɪlɪslɪ] ADV mitleidlos; *cruel* gnadenlos, erbarmungslos

pitman ['pɪtmən] N *pl* **-men** [-mən] *(Brit)* Bergmann *m*, Kumpel *m (inf)*

piton ['piːtɒn] N *(Mountaineering)* Felshaken *m*

pit: **pit pony** N Grubenpony *nt*; **pit prop** N Grubenstempel *m*

pits [pɪts] PL → **pit¹ N f**

pitta (bread) ['piːtə] N ≈ Fladenbrot *nt*

pittance ['pɪtəns] N Hungerlohn *m*

pitter-patter ['pɪtə'pætəʳ] N *(of rain)* Klatschen *nt*; *(of feet)* Getrappel *nt*, Getrippel *nt* ADV **her heart went ~** ihr Herz klopfte *or* pochte VI *(rain)* platschen, klatschen; *(= run)* trappeln, trippeln

pituitary (gland) [pɪ'tjʊɪtrɪ(,glænd)] N Hirnanhangdrüse *f*

pit worker N *(Brit)* Grubenarbeiter(in) *m(f)*

pity ['pɪtɪ] ✪ 26.3 N **a** Mitleid *nt*, Mitgefühl *nt*, Erbarmen *nt*; **for ~'s sake!** Erbarmen!; *(less seriously)* um Himmels willen!; **to have** *or* **take ~ on sb, to feel ~ for sb** mit jdm Mitleid haben; **but the king took ~ on him and spared his life** aber der König hatte Erbarmen mit ihm und schonte sein Leben; **have you no ~?** hast du kein Mitleid?; **to do sth out of ~ (for sb)** etw aus Mitleid (mit jdm) tun; **to feel no ~** kein Mitgefühl *etc* haben, kein Mitleid fühlen; **to move sb to ~** jds Mitleid *(acc)* erregen **b** *(= cause of regret)* **(what a) ~!** (wie) schade!; **what a ~ he can't come** (wie) schade, dass er nicht kommen kann; **it's a ~ about the lack of tickets** es ist schade, dass es nicht genug Eintrittskarten gibt; **more's the ~!** leider; **and I won't be able to attend, more's the ~** und ich kann leider nicht teilnehmen; **it is a ~ that ...** es ist schade, dass ...; **the ~ of it was that ...** das Traurige daran war, dass ...; **it's a great ~** es ist sehr schade, es ist jammerschade; *(more formally)* es ist sehr bedauerlich; **it would be a ~ if he lost** *or* **were to lose this job** es wäre bedauerlich, wenn er seine Arbeit verlieren sollte; **it would be a ~ to waste this opportunity** es wäre bedauerlich, diese Gelegenheit ungenutzt verstreichen zu lassen VT bemitleiden, bedauern; *(contemptuously)* bedauern; **all I can say is that I ~ you** ich kann nur sagen, du tust mir leid

pitying ADJ, **pityingly** ADV ['pɪtɪɪŋ, -lɪ] mitleidig; *glance also* bedauernd; *(with contempt)* verächtlich

pivot ['pɪvət] *vb: pret, ptp* **pivoted** N Lagerzapfen *m*, Drehzapfen *m*; *(Mil)* Flügelmann *m*; *(fig)* Dreh- und Angelpunkt *m*; **~ bearing** Zapfenlager *nt* VT drehbar lagern; **he ~ed it on his hand** er ließ es auf seiner Hand kreiseln VI sich drehen; **to ~ on sth** *(fig)* sich um etw drehen

pivotal ['pɪvətl] ADJ *(fig)* zentral

pivot: **pivot bridge** N *(Tech)* Drehbrücke *f*; **pivot tooth** N *(Med)* Stiftzahn *m*

pixel ['pɪksl] N *(Comput)* Pixel *nt*

pixelate ['pɪksəleɪt] VT *(TV etc)* unkenntlich machen *(durch Vergrößern der Bildpunkte)*

pixie, **pixy** ['pɪksɪ] N Elf *m*, Elfin *f*; **~ hat** *or* **hood** Rotkäppchenmütze *f*

pixilated ['pɪksɪleɪtɪd] ADJ *(hum inf) (= crazy, eccentric)* überspannt, überkandidelt *(inf)*; *(= drunk)* angeheitert *(inf)*

pizazz [pɪ'zæz] N = **pzazz**

pizza ['piːtsə] N Pizza *f*

pizzazz [pɪ'zæz] N = **pzazz**

pizzeria [,piːtsə'riːə] N Pizzeria *f*

pizzicato [,pɪtsɪ'kɑːtəʊ] *(Mus)* ADV pizzicato ADJ pizzicato; **the ~ section** das Pizzicato N Pizzicato *nt*

pizzle ['pɪzl] N Ochsenziemer *m*

pkt *abbr of* **packet** Pckg.

pl *abbr of* **plural** Pl.

Pl *abbr of* **Place** Pl., **placable** ADJ

placably ADV ['plækəbl, -ɪ] versöhnlich, nachgiebig

placard ['plækɑːd] N Plakat *nt*; *(at demonstrations also)* Transparent *nt* VT plakatieren; **to ~ a wall with posters** eine Wand mit Plakaten bekleben

placate [plə'keɪt] VT besänftigen, beschwichtigen

placatory [plə'keɪtərɪ] ADJ beschwichtigend, besänftigend; *gesture also* versöhnlich; **he held out a ~ hand** er streckte seine Hand zur Versöhnung aus

place [pleɪs]

1 NOUN	2 TRANSITIVE VERB

1 – NOUN

a general Platz *m*, Stelle *f*; **this is the place where he was born** hier *or* an dieser Stelle wurde er geboren; **do the spoons have a special place?** haben die Löffel einen bestimmten Platz?; **water is coming through in several places** an mehreren Stellen kommt Wasser durch; **from place to place** von einem Ort zum anderen; **in another place** woanders; **bed is the best place for him** im Bett ist er am besten aufgehoben; **we found a good place to watch the procession from** wir fanden einen Platz, von dem wir den Umzug gut sehen konnten; **in the right/wrong place** an der richtigen/falschen Stelle; **some/any place** irgendwo; **a poor man with no place to go** ein armer Mann, der nicht weiß, wohin; **this is no place for you/children** das ist nichts *or* kein Platz für dich/für Kinder; **there is no place for the unsuccessful in our society** für Erfolglose ist in unserer Gesellschaft kein Platz; **your place is by his side** dein Platz ist an seiner Seite; **it was the last place I expected to find him** da hätte ich ihn zuletzt *or* am wenigsten vermutet; **this isn't the place to discuss politics** dies ist nicht der Ort, um über Politik zu sprechen; **to laugh in the right places** an den richtigen Stellen lachen; **I can't be in two places at once!** ich kann doch nicht an zwei Stellen gleichzeitig sein; **she likes to have a place for everything and everything in its place** sie hält sehr auf Ordnung und achtet darauf, dass alles an seinem Platz liegt

b = geographical location = district Gegend *f*; *(= country)* Land *nt*; *(= building)* Gebäude *nt*; *(= town)* Ort *m*; **there's nothing to do in the evenings in this place** hier kann man abends nichts unternehmen; **Sweden's a great place** Schweden ist ein tolles Land; **they're building a new place out in the suburbs** sie bauen ein neues Gebäude am Stadtrand; **a little place at the seaside** *(= village)* ein kleiner Ort am Meer; *(= house)* ein Häuschen *nt* am Meer

c = home Haus *nt*, Wohnung *f*; **come round to my place some time** besuch mich mal, komm doch mal vorbei; **let's go back to my place** lass uns zu mir gehen; **I've never been to his place** ich bin noch nie bei ihm gewesen; **where's your place?** wo wohnst du?; **at Peter's place** bei Peter; **your place or mine?** *(hum inf)* gehen wir zu dir oder zu mir?

d in book etc Stelle *f*; **to find one's place** die richtige Stelle finden; **to keep one's place** sich *(dat)* die richtige Stelle markieren; **to lose one's place** die Seite verblättern; *(on page)* die Zeile verlieren

e = seat, position *at table, in team, school, hospital* Platz *m*; *(at university)* Studienplatz *m*; *(= job)* Stelle *f*; **to lay an extra place for sb** ein zusätzliches Gedeck für jdn auflegen; **to take one's place (at table)** Platz nehmen; **take your places for a square dance!** Aufstellung zur Quadrille, bitte!; **places for 500 students** 500 Studienplätze; **to give up one's place** *(in a queue)* jdm den Vortritt lassen; **to lose one's place** *(in a queue)* sich wieder hinten anstellen müssen; **if I were in your place** an Ihrer Stelle, wenn ich an Ihrer Stelle wäre; **put yourself in my place** versetzen Sie sich in meine Lage; **to take the place of sb/sth** jdn/etw ersetzen, jds Platz *or* den Platz von jdm/etw einnehmen

f in hierarchy Rang *m*, Stellung *f*; **people in high places** Leute in hohen Positionen; **to know one's place** wissen, was sich (für einen) gehört; **of course I'm not criticizing you, I know my place!** *(hum)* ich kritisiere dich selbstverständlich nicht, das steht mir gar nicht zu; **it's not my place to comment/tell him what to do** es steht mir nicht zu, einen Kommentar abzugeben/ihm zu sagen, was er tun soll; **to keep** *or* **put sb in his place** jdn in seine Schranken weisen; **that put him in his place!** das hat ihn erst mal zum Schweigen gebracht, da hab ichs/hat ers *etc* ihm gezeigt *(inf)*

g [in exam, competition] Platz *m*, Stelle *f*; **Lunt won, with Moore in second place** Lunt hat gewonnen, an zweiter Stelle *or* auf dem zweiten Platz lag Moore; **to win first place** Erste(r, s) sein; **to take second place to sth** einer Sache *(dat)* gegenüber zweitrangig sein

h [Sport] Platzierung *f*; **to get a place** eine Platzierung erreichen, einen der ersten drei Plätze belegen; **to back a horse for a place** auf Platz wetten, eine Platzwette abschließen

i [in street names] Platz *m*

j [Math] Stelle *f*; **to work sth out to three decimal places** etw auf drei Stellen nach dem Komma berechnen

k [set structures]

♦ **place of** + *noun* **place of amusement** Vergnügungsstätte *f*; **place of birth** Geburtsort *m*; **place of residence** Wohnort *m*; **place of business** *or* **work** Arbeitsstelle *f*

♦ **in places** stellenweise; **the snow was up to a metre deep in places** der Schnee lag stellenweise bis zu einem Meter hoch

♦ **in place everything was in place** alles war an seiner Stelle; **make sure the wire/screw is properly in place** achten Sie darauf, dass der Draht/die Schraube richtig sitzt; **the legislation is already in place** die gesetzlichen Regelungen gelten schon

♦ **out of place to be out of place** *(= in the wrong place)* nicht an der richtigen Stelle sein; *(= untidy)* in Unordnung sein; *(fig, remark)* unangebracht *or* deplatziert sein; *(person)* fehl am Platz *or* deplatziert sein; **to look out of place** fehl am Platz *or* deplatziert wirken; **to feel out of place** sich fehl am Platz *or* deplatziert fühlen; **not a hair out of place** tipptopp frisiert *(inf)*

♦ **all over the place** *(= everywhere)* überall; **she's all over the place** *(inf: = disorganized)* sie ist total chaotisch *(inf)*

♦ **in place of** statt *(+gen)*; **McCormack played in goal in place of Miller** McCormack stand anstelle von Miller im Tor

♦ **to fall into place** Gestalt annehmen

♦ **in the first place** *(= firstly)* erstens; **in the first place ..., in the second place ...** erstens ..., zweitens ...; **she shouldn't have been there in the first place** *(= anyway)* sie hätte überhaupt nicht *or* erst gar nicht dort sein sollen

♦ **to take place** stattfinden; **the meeting will take place on Monday** das Treffen findet am Montag statt

♦ **to go places** *(= travel)* Ausflüge machen, herumreisen; **he's going places** *(fig inf)* er bringts zu was *(inf)*

♦ **to give place to sth** einer Sache *(dat)* Platz machen

2 – TRANSITIVE VERB

a [= put] setzen, stellen; *(= lay down)* legen; *person at table etc* setzen; *guards* aufstellen; *shot (with gun)* anbringen; *(Ftbl, Tennis)* platzieren; *troops* in Stellung bringen; *announcement (in paper)* inserieren *(in* in *+dat)*; *advertisement* setzen *(in* in *+acc)*; **the magician placed one hand over the other** der Zauberer legte eine Hand über die andere; **she slowly placed one foot in front of the other** sie setzte langsam einen Fuß vor den anderen; **he placed the cue ball right behind the black** er setzte die Spielkugel direkt hinter die schwarze Kugel; **he placed a gun to my head** er setzte mir eine Pistole an den Kopf; **she placed a finger on her lips** sie legte den Finger auf die Lippen; **the vase was precariously placed** die Vase stand an einer gefährlichen Stelle; **to place a matter before sb** jdm eine Angelegenheit vorlegen; **I shall place the matter in the hands of a lawyer** ich werde die Angelegenheit einem Rechtsanwalt übergeben; **to place a strain on sth** etw belasten; **this placed him under a lot of pressure** dadurch geriet er stark unter Druck; **to place confidence/trust in sb/sth** Vertrauen in jdn/etw setzen; **to be placed** *(shop, town, house etc)* liegen; **how are you placed for time/money?** wie sieht es mit deiner Zeit/deinem Geld aus?

♦ **well/better placed we are well placed for the shops** was Einkaufsmöglichkeiten angeht, wohnen wir günstig; **Liverpool are well placed in the league** Liverpool liegt gut in der Tabelle; **they were well placed to observe the whole battle** sie hatten einen günstigen Platz, von dem sie die ganze Schlacht verfolgen konnten; **we are well placed now to finish the job by next year** wir stehen jetzt so gut da, dass wir die Arbeit im nächsten Jahr fertigstellen können; **with the extra staff we are better placed now than we were last month** mit dem zusätzlichen Personal stehen wir jetzt besser da als vor einem Monat; **he is well placed** *(to get hold of things)* er sitzt an der Quelle; **he is well placed to get information** er kommt leicht an Informationen

b [= rank] stellen; **to place local interests above** *or* **before** *or* **over those of central government** kommunale Interessen über die der Zentralregierung stellen; **that should be placed first** das sollte an erster Stelle stehen; **where do you place love on your list of priorities?** an welcher Stelle steht die Liebe für dich?; **the German runner was placed third** der deutsche Läufer belegte den dritten Platz *or* wurde Dritter; **to be placed** *(Sport)* sich platzieren

c [= identify context of] einordnen; **in which school would you place this painting?** welcher Schule würden Sie dieses Gemälde zuordnen?; **I don't know, it's very difficult to place** ich weiß es nicht, es ist sehr schwer einzuordnen; **I can't quite place him/his accent** ich kann ihn/seinen Akzent nicht einordnen; **historians place the book in the 5th century AD** Historiker datieren das Buch auf das 5. Jahrhundert

d [Comm] *goods* absetzen; *order* erteilen *(with sb* jdm); *contract* abschließen *(with sb* mit jdm); **who did you place the computer typesetting job with?** wem haben Sie den Auftrag für den Computersatz erteilt?; **this is the last time we place any work with you** das ist das letzte Mal, dass wir Ihnen einen Auftrag erteilt haben

e [money] *(= deposit)* deponieren; *(= invest)* investieren; **to place money at sb's credit** jdm eine Geldsumme gutschreiben

f [phone call] anmelden

g [= find job for] unterbringen *(with* bei)

---

placebo [plə'siːbəʊ] **N** *(Med)* Placebo *nt*

placebo effect N Placeboeffekt *m*

place: **place card N** Tischkarte *f*; **placeholder N** *(Comput, Math)* Platzhalter *m*; **place kick N** Platztritt *m*; **placeman N** *(pej)* Strohmann *m*; **place mat N** Set *nt*

placement ['pleɪsmənt] **N a** *(= act: of social worker, teacher etc)* Platzierung *f*; *(= finding job for)* Vermittlung *f* **b** *(Brit) (= period: of trainee)* Praktikum *nt*; **I'm here on a six-month ~** *(for in-service training etc)* ich bin hier für sechs Monate zur Weiterbildung; *(on secondment)* ich bin für sechs Monate hierhin überwiesen worden

place name N Ortsname *m*

placenta [plə'sentə] **N** Plazenta *f*

placer mining N *(in rivers)* Goldwaschen *nt*

place setting N Gedeck *nt*

placid ['plæsɪd] **ADJ** ruhig; *person also* gelassen; *disposition* friedfertig; *smile* still; *scene* beschaulich, friedvoll

placidity [plə'sɪdɪtɪ] **N** Ruhe *f*; *(of person also)* Gelassenheit *f*; *(of disposition)* Friedfertigkeit *f*; *(of smile)* Stille *f*

placidly ['plæsɪdlɪ] **ADV** ruhig, friedlich; *speak* bedächtig

placings ['pleɪsɪŋz] **PL** Platzierungen *pl*

placket ['plækɪt] **N** Schlitz *m*

plagiarism ['pleɪdʒjərɪzəm] **N** Plagiat *nt*

plagiarist ['pleɪdʒjərɪst] **N** Plagiator(in) *m(f)*

plagiarize ['pleɪdʒjəraɪz] **VT** *book, idea* plagiieren

plague [pleɪg] **N** *(Med)* Seuche *f*; *(Bibl, fig)* Plage *f*; **the ~** die Pest; **to avoid sb/sth like the ~** jdn/etw wie die Pest meiden; **we're suffering from a ~ of crime** wir leiden unter einer wahren Flut an Verbrechen; **a ~ of reporters descended on the town** eine Horde von Reportern suchte die Stadt heim; **a ~ on him!** *(old)* die Pest möge über ihn kommen! *(old)*

VT plagen; **to ~ the life out of sb** jdn (bis aufs Blut) quälen, jdm das Leben schwer machen; **to be ~d by doubts/injury** von Zweifeln/Verletzungen geplagt werden; **to be ~d by bad luck** vom Pech verfolgt werden; **to ~ sb with questions** jdn ständig mit Fragen belästigen

plaice [pleɪs] **N** *no pl* Scholle *f*

plaid [plæd] **N** Plaid *nt*; **~ skirt** karierter Rock

plain [pleɪn] **ADJ** *(+er)* **a** klar; *(= obvious)* offensichtlich, klar; *tracks, differences* deutlich; **it is ~ to see that ...** es ist offensichtlich, dass ...; **it's as ~ as the nose on your face** *(inf)* das sieht doch ein Blinder (mit Krückstock) *(inf)*; **(as) ~ as day** sonnenklar; **to make sth ~ to sb** jdm etw klarmachen *or* klar zu verstehen geben; **the reason is ~ to see** der Grund ist leicht einzusehen; **I'd like to make it quite ~ that ...** ich möchte gern klarstellen, dass ...; **did I make myself** *or* **my meaning ~?** habe ich mich klar ausgedrückt?; **to make one's view ~** seine Meinung klar zum Ausdruck bringen

b *(= frank, straightforward) question, answer* klar; *truth* schlicht; *statement* klar, deutlich; **~ dealing** Redlichkeit *f*; **to be ~ with sb** jdm gegenüber offen *or* direkt sein; **in ~ language** *or* **English** unmissverständlich, auf gut Deutsch; **in ~ language** *or* **English, the answer is no** um es klar *or* auf gut Deutsch zu sagen: die Antwort ist nein; **it was ~ sailing** es ging glatt (über die Bühne) *(inf)*; **it won't all be ~ sailing** es wird gar nicht so einfach sein; **from now on it'll be ~ sailing** von jetzt an geht es ganz einfach

c *(= simple, with nothing added)* einfach; *dress, design, living* schlicht, einfach; *cooking, food* (gut)bürgerlich; *cook* einfach, gutbürgerlich; *water* klar; *paper* unliniert; *envelope* einfach; *colour* einheitlich; *cigarette* filterlos, ohne Filter; **in a ~ colour** *(Brit) or* **color** *(US)* einfarbig, uni *pred*; **under ~ cover** in neutraler Verpackung; *(= in envelope)* in neutralem Umschlag; **he's a ~ Mr** er ist einfach Herr Sowieso; **he used to be ~ Mr X** früher war er einfach *or* schlicht Herr X

d *(= sheer)* rein; *nonsense etc* rein, völlig, blank *(inf)*; **it's just ~ common sense** das ist einfach gesunder Menschenverstand

e *(= not beautiful) person, appearance, face* unattraktiv; **she really is so ~** sie ist recht unansehnlich; **~ Jane** unattraktives *or* unansehnliches Mädchen; **she's a real ~ Jane** sie ist nicht gerade hübsch *or* eine Schönheit

ADV a *(inf: = simply, completely)* (ganz) einfach; **~ stupid/wrong** einfach dumm/falsch

b I can't put it ~er than that deutlicher kann ich es nicht sagen

N a *(Geog)* Ebene *f*, Flachland *nt*; **the ~s** das Flachland, die Ebene; *(in North America)* die Prärie

b *(Knitting)* rechte Masche

plain: **plain chocolate N** *(Brit)* (Zart)bitterschokolade *f*; **plain clothes PL in ~** in Zivil **ADJ plain-clothes** in Zivil; **a plain-clothes policeman** ein Polizist *m* in Zivil; **plainclothesman N** *pl* **-men** Polizist *m* in Zivil, Zivile(r) *m (inf)*; **plain flour N** Mehl *nt (ohne beigemischtes Backpulver)*

plainly ['pleɪnlɪ] **ADV a** *(= clearly)* eindeutig; *explain, remember, visible* klar, deutlich; **~, these new techniques are impractical** es ist ganz klar, dass diese neuen Verfahren unpraktisch sind **b** *(= frankly)* offen, direkt **c** *(= simply, unsophisticatedly)* einfach

plainness ['pleɪnnɪs] N **a** *(= frankness, straightforwardness)* Direktheit *f*, Offenheit *f* **b** *(= simplicity)* Einfachheit *f* **c** *(= lack of beauty)* Unansehnlichkeit *f*

Plain People PL *(US) Sammelbegriff for Mitglieder christlicher Glaubensgruppen wie den Amish, die bewusst einfach leben*

plainsman ['pleɪnzmən] N *pl* **-men** [-mən] Flachländer *m*

plain: **plainsong** N Cantus planus *m*, gregorianischer Gesang; **plain speaking** N Offenheit *f*; **some/a bit of ~** ein paar offene Worte; **plain-spoken** ADJ offen, direkt; *criticism also* unverhohlen; **to be ~** sagen, was man denkt

plaint [pleɪnt] N *(liter)* **a** *(= complaint)* Wehklage *f (geh)* **b** *(= cry)* Gejammer *nt*; **the moans and ~s of their children** das Gequäke und Gejammer ihrer Kinder

plaintiff ['pleɪntɪf] N Kläger(in) *m(f)*

plaintive ['pleɪntɪv] ADJ klagend; *voice etc also* wehleidig *(pej)*; *song etc also* schwermütig, elegisch *(geh)*; *look etc* leidend; **the letter ended on a ~ note** der Brief schloss mit einer Klage

plaintively ['pleɪntɪvlɪ] ADV *say, ask* klagend

plait [plæt] N *(esp Brit)* Zopf *m*; **she wears her hair in ~s** sie trägt Zöpfe VT flechten

plan [plæn] ✪ 8.1, 8.2, 25.2 N **a** *(= scheme)* Plan *m*; *(Pol, Econ)* Programm *nt*, Plan *m*; **~ of action** *(Mil, fig)* Aktionsprogramm *nt*; **~ of campaign** *(Mil)* Strategie *f*; **the ~ is to meet at six** es ist geplant, sich um sechs zu treffen; **so, what's the ~?** was ist also geplant?; **the best ~ is to tell him first** am besten sagt man es ihm zuerst; **to make ~s (for sth)** Pläne (für etw) machen, (etw) planen; **to have great ~s for sb** mit jdm Großes vorhaben, große Pläne mit jdm haben; **what ~s do you have for the holidays/your son?** welche Pläne haben Sie für den Urlaub/Ihren Sohn?; **have you any ~s for tonight?** hast du (für) heute Abend (schon) etwas vor?; **according to ~** planmäßig, wie vorgesehen, programmgemäß
b *(= diagram)* Plan *m*; *(for novel etc also)* Entwurf *m*; *(for essay, speech)* Konzept *nt*; *(= town plan)* Stadtplan *m*
VT **a** *(= arrange)* planen; *programme etc* erstellen
b *(= intend)* vorhaben; **we weren't ~ning to** wir hatten es nicht vor; **she's ~ning a career in law** sie will ins Justizwesen gehen; **this development was not ~ned** diese Entwicklung war nicht eingeplant
c *(= design)* planen; *buildings etc* planen, entwerfen
VI planen; **to ~ for sth** sich einstellen auf *(+acc)*, rechnen mit; **to ~ months ahead** (auf) Monate vorausplanen

▶ **plan on** VI *+prep obj* **a** *(= intend)* **to plan on a trip to London** vorhaben, eine Reise nach London zu machen; **I'm planning on a hot bath and an early night** ich beabsichtige, ein heißes Bad zu nehmen und früh ins Bett zu gehen; **to plan on doing sth** vorhaben, etw zu tun; **she plans on staying in London** sie hat vor, in London zu bleiben
b *(= foresee)* **to plan on sth** mit etwas rechnen; **he hadn't planned on the bad weather** er hatte nicht mit dem schlechten Wetter gerechnet; **I hadn't planned on being paid for my help** ich hatte nicht damit gerechnet, für meine Hilfe bezahlt zu werden

▶ **plan out** VT *sep* in Einzelheiten planen

plane[1] [pleɪn] N *(also* **plane tree***)* Platane *f*

plane[2] ADJ eben *(also Math)*; *surface also* plan N **a** *(Math)* Ebene *f* **b** *(= aeroplane)* Flugzeug *nt*; **to go by ~, to take a ~** fliegen **c** *(= tool)* Hobel *m* **d** *(fig)* Ebene *f*; *(intellectual)* Niveau *nt*; *(= social plane)* Schicht *f*; **he lives on a different ~** er lebt in anderen Sphären; **a higher ~ of consciousness** eine höhere Bewusstseinsebene VT hobeln; **to ~ sth down** etw abhobeln, etw glatt hobeln VI *(bird, glider, speedboat)* gleiten

plane chart N *(Naut)* Plankarte *f*

planeload ['pleɪnləʊd] N Flugzeugladung *f*

plane geometry N *(Math)* Planimetrie *f*

planet ['plænɪt] N Planet *m*

planetarium [ˌplænɪ'tɛərɪəm] N Planetarium *nt*

planetary ['plænɪtərɪ] ADJ planetarisch, Planeten-; *travel* zu anderen Planeten; **~ system** Planetensystem *nt*; **the laws of ~ motion** die Gesetze *pl* der Planetenbewegung

planetoid ['plænɪtɔɪd] N *(Astron)* Planetoid *m*

plangent ['plændʒənt] ADJ *(liter)* getragen, klagend

planify ['plænɪfaɪ] VTI *(esp US inf)* systematisch planen

planimetry [plæ'nɪmɪtrɪ] N *(Math)* Planimetrie *f*

plank [plæŋk] N **a** Brett *nt*; *(Naut)* Planke *f* → **walk b** *(Pol)* Schwerpunkt *m*; **the main ~ of their argument is that …** ihr Argument stützt sich vor allem darauf, dass … VT *(inf)* = **plonk**[1]

planking ['plæŋkɪŋ] N Beplankung *f*, Planken *pl*

plankton ['plæŋktən] N Plankton *nt*

planless ADJ, **planlessly** ADV ['plænlɪs, -lɪ] planlos

planned [plænd] ADJ geplant

planned: **planned economy** N Planwirtschaft *f*; **planned obsolescence** N geplanter Verschleiß; **planned promotion** N Regelbeförderung *f*

planner ['plænəʳ] N Planer(in) *m(f)*

planning ['plænɪŋ] N Planung *f*

planning *in cpds* Planungs-; **~ commission** Planungsausschuss *m*; **~ permission** Baugenehmigung *f*

plant [plɑːnt] N **a** *(Bot)* Pflanze *f*; **rare/tropical ~s** seltene/tropische Gewächse *pl*
b *no pl (= equipment)* Anlagen *pl*; *(= equipment and buildings)* Produktionsanlage *f*; *(US: of school, bank)* Einrichtungen *pl*; *(= factory)* Werk *nt*; **~-hire** Baumaschinenvermietung *f*; **"heavy ~ crossing"** „Baustellenverkehr"
c *(inf: = frame-up) eingeschmuggelter Gegenstand etc, der jdn kompromittieren soll*, Komplott *nt*
ATTR Pflanzen-; **~ life** Pflanzenwelt *f*
VT **a** *plants, trees* pflanzen, ein- *or* anpflanzen; *field* bepflanzen; **to ~ a field with turnips/wheat** auf einem Feld Rüben anbauen *or* anpflanzen/Weizen anbauen *or* säen
b *(= place in position)* setzen; *bomb* legen; *kiss* drücken; *fist* pflanzen *(inf)*; *(in the ground) stick* stecken; *flag* pflanzen; **to ~ sth in sb's mind** jdm etw in den Kopf setzen, jdn auf etw *(acc)* bringen; **a policeman was ~ed at each entrance** an jedem Eingang wurde ein Polizist aufgestellt *or* postiert; **he ~ed himself right in front of the fire** *(inf)* er pflanzte sich genau vor dem Kamin auf *(inf)*; **she ~ed the children in the hall** sie stellte die Kinder im Flur ab *(inf)*; **to ~ one on sb's chin** *(inf)* jdm einen Kinnhaken geben; **to ~ one's feet** *(lit)* die Füße aufsetzen
c *(inf) incriminating evidence, stolen goods etc* manipulieren, praktizieren; *(in sb's car, home)* schmuggeln; *informer, spy etc* (ein)schleusen; **to ~ sth on sb** *(inf)* jdm etw unterjubeln *(inf)*, jdm etw in die Tasche praktizieren

▶ **plant out** VT *sep* auspflanzen

plantain ['plæntɪn] N **a** *(Bot)* Plantainbanane *f* **b** *(= weed)* Wegerich *m*

plantation [plæn'teɪʃən] N Plantage *f*, Pflanzung *f*; *(of trees)* Schonung *f*, Anpflanzung *f*

planter ['plɑːntəʳ] N Pflanzer(in) *m(f)*; *(= plantation owner also)* Plantagenbesitzer(in) *m(f)*; *(= machine)* Pflanzmaschine *f*; *(= seed planter)* Sämaschine *f*; *(= plant pot)* Übertopf *m*

plant kingdom N Pflanzenreich *nt*

plantlet ['plɑːntlɪt] N Pflänzchen *nt*

plant pot N *(esp Brit)* Blumentopf *m*

plaque [plæk] N **a** Plakette *f*; *(on building etc)* Tafel *f* **b** *(Med)* Belag *m*; *(on teeth)* (Zahn)belag *m*

plash [plæʃ] *(liter)* N *(of water, rain)* Plätschern *nt*; *(of oars)* Platschen *nt* VI *(water, rain)* plätschern; *(oars)* platschen

plasm ['plæzəm], **plasma** ['plæzmə] N Plasma *nt*

plasma ['plæzmə]: **plasma screen** N *(TV etc)* Plasmabildschirm *m*; **plasma TV** N Plasmafernseher *m*

plaster ['plɑːstəʳ] N **a** *(Build)* (Ver)putz *m*
b *(Art, Med: also* **plaster of Paris***)* Gips *m*; *(Brit Med: = plaster cast)* Gipsverband *m*; **to have one's leg in ~** das Bein in Gips haben
c *(Brit: = sticking plaster)* Pflaster *nt*
VT **a** *(Build) wall* verputzen; **to ~ over a hole** ein Loch zugipsen
b *(inf: = cover)* vollkleistern; **to ~ a wall with posters** eine Wand mit Plakaten vollkleistern *or* bepflastern *(inf)*; **his picture was ~ed all over the newspapers** sein Bild war in allen Zeitungen; **to ~ one's face with make-up** sein Gesicht mit Make-up vollkleistern *(inf)*; **~ed with mud** schlammbedeckt; **he ~ed down his wet hair with his hands** er klatschte sich das nasse Haar mit den Händen an

plaster: **plaster bandage** N *(Med)* Gipsbinde *f*; **plasterboard** N Gipskarton(platten *pl*) *m*; **a sheet of ~** eine Gipskartonplatte; **plaster cast** N *(= model, statue)* Gipsform *f*; *(of footprint etc)* Gipsabdruck *m*; *(Med)* Gipsverband *m*

plastered ['plɑːstəd] ADJ *pred (inf)* voll *(inf)*; **to get ~** sich vollaufen lassen *(inf)*

plasterer ['plɑːstərəʳ] N Gipser(in) *m(f)*, Stuckateur(in) *m(f)*

plastering ['plɑːstərɪŋ] N **a** *(= plasterwork)* Verputz *m*, Bewurf *m*; *(action)* Verputzen *nt* **b** *(= stucco)* Stuck *m*, Stuckarbeit *f*, Stuckatur *f* **c** *(= application of plaster)* Gipsen *nt*; *(Med)* Eingipsen *nt*

plastic ['plæstɪk] N **a** Plastik *nt*; **~s** Kunststoffe *pl* **b** *(inf: = credit cards)* Kreditkarten *pl*, Plastikkarten *pl (inf)* ADJ **a** *(= made of plastic)* Plastik-, aus Plastik; *(pej inf) person* synthetisch; *smile* aufgesetzt, gekünstelt; *pub* steril; **~ bottle** Plastikflasche *f*; **~ food** *(pej inf)* Plastikessen *nt (inf)* **b** *(= flexible)* formbar *(also fig)*, modellierbar *(also fig)*, plastisch; **the ~ arts** die gestaltenden Künste **c** *(Med)* plastisch

plastic: **plastic bag** N Plastiktüte *f*; **plastic bomb** N Plastikbombe *f*; **plastic bullet** N Plastikgeschoss *nt*; **plastic explosive** N Plastiksprengstoff *m*

Plasticine® ['plæstɪsiːn] N *(Brit)* ≈ Plastilin® *nt*

plasticity [plæ'stɪsɪtɪ] N Formbarkeit *f*, Modellierbarkeit *f*

plastic: **plastic money** N *(inf)* Plastikgeld *nt*; **plastics industry** N Kunststoffindustrie *f*; **plastic surgeon** N plastischer Chirurg; **plastic surgery** N plastische Chirurgie; *(= cosmetic operation)* Schönheitsoperation *f*; **he had to have ~** er musste sich einer Gesichtsoperation unterziehen; **she decided to have ~ on her nose** sie entschloss sich zu einer Schönheitsoperation an ihrer Nase

plate [pleɪt] N **a** *(= flat dish, plateful, collection plate)* Teller *m*; *(= warming plate)* Platte *f*; **~ supper** *(US)* Tellergericht *nt*; **a dinner at 45 dollars a ~** *(US)* ein Essen für *or* zu 45 Dollar pro Person; **cold ~** kalte Platte; **to have sth handed to one on a ~** *(Brit fig inf)* etw auf einem Tablett serviert bekommen *(inf)*; **to have enough/a lot on one's ~** *(fig inf)* genug/viel am Hals haben *(inf)*
b *(= gold, silver)* Silber und Gold *nt*; *(= tableware)* Tafelsilber/-gold *nt*; *(= plated metal)* vergoldetes/versilbertes Metall; *(= plated articles, jewellery)* Doublé *nt*, plattierte Ware, Doublee *nt*; **a piece of ~** ein Stück *or* Gegenstand aus Gold/Silber *etc*; *(= plated article)* ein vergoldeter/versilberter *etc* Gegenstand; **it's only ~** es ist bloß *or* nur vergoldet/versilbert *etc*
c *(Tech, Phot, Typ)* Platte *f*; *(= name plate, number plate)* Schild *nt*
d *(= illustration)* Tafel *f*
e *(= dental plate)* (Gaumen)platte *f*
f *(Racing)* Cup *m*, Pokal *m*; *(= race)* Cup- *or*

Pokalrennen *nt*
g *(Baseball: = home plate)* Gummiplatte *f*
VT *ship* beplanken; *(with armour-plating)* panzern; **to ~ sth with gold/silver/nickel** etw vergolden/versilbern/vernickeln

plateau ['plætəʊ] N *pl* **-s** *or* **-x** *(Geog)* Plateau *nt*, Hochebene *f*; **the rising prices have reached a ~** die Preise steigen nicht mehr und haben sich eingependelt

plateful ['pleɪtfʊl] N Teller *m*; **two ~s of salad** zwei Teller (voll) Salat

plate: **plate glass** N Tafelglas *nt*; **plateholder** N *(Phot)* Plattenkassette *f*; **plate iron** N *(Tech)* Eisenblech *nt*, Walzeisen *nt*; **platelayer** N *(Brit Rail)* Streckenarbeiter(in) *m(f)*

platelet ['pleɪtlɪt] N *(Physiol)* Plättchen *nt*

platen ['plætən] N *(of typewriter, printer)* Walze *f*

plate: **plate rack** N *(Brit)* Geschirrständer *m*; **plate tectonics** N *sing (Geol)* Plattentektonik *f*; **plate warmer** N Warmhalteplatte *f*

platform ['plætfɔːm] N **a** Plattform *f*; *(= stage)* Podium *nt*, Bühne *f* **b** *(Rail)* Bahnsteig *m* **c** *(Pol)* Plattform *f*

platform: **platform crane** N *(Tech)* Laufkran *m*; **platform party** N Podiumsgäste *pl*; **platform shoe** N Plateauschuh *m*; **platform sole** N Plateausohle *f*; **platform ticket** N Bahnsteigkarte *f*

plating ['pleɪtɪŋ] N *(= act) (with gold)* Vergolden *nt*, Vergoldung *f*; *(with silver)* Versilbern *nt*, Versilberung *f*; *(with nickel)* Vernickeln *nt*, Vernickelung *f*; *(= material)* Auflage *f*; *(on ship)* Beplankung *f*, Außenhaut *f*; *(= armour-plating)* Panzerung *f*

platinum ['plætɪnəm] N Platin *nt*; **a ~ blonde** eine Platinblonde

platinum disc N Platinplatte *f*

platitude ['plætɪtjuːd] N *(pej)* Platitüde *f*, Plattheit *f*

platitudinize [ˌplætɪ'tjuːdɪnaɪz] VI *(pej)* sich in Gemeinplätzen ergehen *(geh)*

platitudinous [ˌplætɪ'tjuːdɪnəs] ADJ *(pej)* banal; *speech also* platt

Plato ['pleɪtəʊ] N Plato(n) *m*

Platonic [plə'tɒnɪk] ADJ *philosophy* Platonisch

platonic [plə'tɒnɪk] ADJ *love, friendship* platonisch

platoon [plə'tuːn] N *(Mil)* Zug *m*

platter ['plætə'] N Teller *m*; *(= wooden platter also)* Brett *nt*; *(= serving dish)* Platte *f*; *(inf: = record)* Platte *f*; **to have sth handed to one on a (silver) ~** *(fig)* etw auf einem (silbernen) Tablett serviert bekommen; **to demand sb's head on a ~** *(fig)* jds Kopf verlangen

platypus ['plætɪpəs] N Schnabeltier *nt*

plaudit ['plɔːdɪt] N *usu pl (liter)* Ovation *f (usu pl)*, Huldigung *f (geh)*; **the headmaster's ~s made him blush** die Lobeshymnen des Direktors ließen ihn erröten

plausibility [ˌplɔːzə'bɪlɪtɪ] N Plausibilität *f*; *(of story, excuse also)* Glaubwürdigkeit *f*; *(of liar)* Geschicktheit *f*; *(of manner, person)* überzeugende Art

plausible ['plɔːzəbl] ADJ plausibel; *argument also* einleuchtend; *story, excuse also* glaubwürdig, glaubhaft; *liar* gut, geschickt; *manner, person* überzeugend

plausibly ['plɔːzəblɪ] ADV plausibel; *argue also* einleuchtend; *lie, present one's excuses* geschickt; *tell a story, act a part* auf überzeugende Art, überzeugend

play [pleɪ] **N** **a** *(= amusement, gambling)* Spiel *nt*; **to be at ~** beim Spielen sein; **to do/say sth in ~** etw aus Spaß tun/sagen; **~ on words** Wortspiel *nt*; **children at ~** spielende Kinder; **children learn through ~** Kinder lernen beim Spiel; **he lost £800 in a few hours' ~** er hat beim Spiel innerhalb von ein paar Stunden £ 800 verloren
b *(Sport)* Spiel *nt*; **to abandon ~** das Spiel abbrechen; **because of bad weather ~ was impossible** es konnte wegen schlechten Wetters nicht gespielt werden; **in a clever piece of ~, in a clever ~** *(US)* in einem klugen Schachzug; **there was some exciting ~ toward(s) the end** gegen Ende gab es einige spannende (Spiel)szenen; **to be in ~/out of ~** *(ball)* im Spiel/im Aus sein; **to kick the ball out of ~** den Ball aus *or* ins Aus schießen
c *(Tech, Mech)* Spiel *nt*; **1 mm (of) ~** 1 mm Spiel
d *(Theat)* (Theater)stück *nt*; *(Rad)* Hörspiel *nt*; *(TV)* Fernsehspiel *nt*; **the ~s of Shakespeare** Shakespeares Dramen
e *(fig: = moving patterns)* Spiel *nt*
f *(fig phrases)* **to come into ~** ins Spiel kommen; **to give full ~ to one's imagination** seiner Fantasie *or* Phantasie *(dat)* freien Lauf lassen; **the game allows the child's imagination (to be given) full ~** das Spiel gestattet die freie Entfaltung der kindlichen Fantasie; **to bring** *or* **call sth into ~** etw aufbieten *or* einsetzen; **the ~ of opposing forces** das Widerspiel der Kräfte; **the free ~ of market forces** das freie Spiel der Marktkräfte; **to make great ~ of sth** *(Brit)* viel Aufhebens von etw machen; **to make great ~ of doing sth** *(Brit)* viel Wind darum machen, etw zu tun; **to make a ~ for sb** sich um jdn bemühen; **to make a ~ for sth** es auf etw *(acc)* abgesehen haben
VT **a** *game, card, ball, position* spielen; *player* aufstellen, einsetzen; **to ~ sb (at a game)** gegen jdn (ein Spiel) spielen; **to ~ ball (with sb)** (mit jdm) mitspielen; **to ~ shop** (Kaufmanns)laden spielen, Kaufmann spielen; **to ~ a joke on sb** jdm einen Streich spielen; **to ~ a mean/dirty trick on sb** jdn auf gemeine/schmutzige Art hereinlegen; **to ~ the company game** sich in der Firma profilieren wollen; **they're all ~ing the game** die machen doch alle mit → **card**[1], **game**[1], **market**, **hell** *etc*
b *(Theat, fig) part* spielen; *(= perform in) town* spielen in *(+dat)*; **to ~ it safe** auf Nummer sicher gehen *(inf)*; **to ~ it cautious/clever** vorsichtig/klug vorgehen; **to ~ the fool** den Clown spielen, herumblödeln *(inf)*; **he was ~ing the jealous lover** er spielte den eifersüchtigen Liebhaber → **cool ADJ d**
c *instrument, record, tune* spielen; **to ~ the piano** Klavier spielen; **to ~ sth through/over** etw durchspielen
d *(= direct) lights, jet of water* richten
e *(Fishing)* drillen
VI **a** *(esp child)* spielen; **to go out to ~** rausgehen und spielen; **run away and ~!** geh spielen!; **can Johnny come out to ~?** darf Johnny zum Spielen rauskommen?; **he wouldn't ~** *(fig inf)* er wollte nicht mitspielen *(inf)*
b *(Sport, at game, = gamble)* spielen; **England ~s against Scotland next week** England spielt nächste Woche gegen Schottland; **he ~s for Celtic** er spielt für Celtic; **to ~ at mothers and fathers/cowboys and Indians** Vater und Mutter/Cowboy und Indianer spielen; **to ~ at being a fireman** Feuerwehrmann spielen; **he was ~ing at being angry** seine Wut war gespielt; **~!** Anspiel!; **to ~ in defence** in der Abwehr spielen; **to ~ in goal** im Tor stehen; **he's just ~ing at it** er tut nur so; **what are you ~ing at?** *(inf)* was soll (denn) das? *(inf)*; **to ~ for money** um Geld spielen; **to ~ for time** *(fig)* Zeit gewinnen wollen; **to ~ into sb's hands** *(fig)* jdm in die Hände spielen; **to ~ to one's strengths** seine Stärken ausspielen
c *(Mus)* spielen; **to ~ to sb** jdm vorspielen
d *(= move about, form patterns) (sun, light, water)* spielen; *(fountain)* tanzen; **a smile ~ed on his lips** ein Lächeln spielte um seine Lippen; **the firemen's hoses ~ed on the flames** die Schläuche der Feuerwehrmänner waren auf die Flammen gerichtet; **the searchlights ~ed over the roofs** die Suchscheinwerfer strichen über die Dächer
e *(Theat) (= act)* spielen; *(= be performed)* gespielt werden
f *(Sport: ground, pitch)* sich bespielen lassen; **the pitch ~s well/badly** auf dem Platz spielt es sich gut/schlecht

▶ **play about** *(Brit) or* **around** VI spielen; **I wish he'd stop playing around and settle down to a steady job** ich wollte, er würde mit dem ständigen Hin und Her aufhören und sich eine feste Arbeit suchen; **to play around with sth** mit etw (herum)spielen; **to play about** *or* **around with an idea** mit einer Idee spielen; **to play around with sb/sb's feelings** mit jdm/mit jds Gefühlen spielen; **he's been playing around (with another woman)** er hat mit einer anderen Frau herumgemacht *(inf)*

▶ **play along** **VI** mitspielen; **he played along with the system** er arrangierte sich mit dem System; **to play along with a suggestion** auf einen Vorschlag eingehen; *(= pretend)* auf einen Vorschlag scheinbar eingehen; **to play along with sb** jdm zustimmen **VT** *always separate* hinters Licht führen, ein falsches Spiel spielen mit; *(in order to gain time)* hinhalten

▶ **play back** VT *sep tape recording* abspielen; **the conversation was played back to us** man spielte uns *(dat)* das Gespräch vor

▶ **play down** VT *sep* herunterspielen

▶ **play in** VT *sep (= with music)* musikalisch begrüßen

▶ **play off** **VT** *sep* **to play X off against Y** X gegen Y ausspielen; **he was playing them off against each other** er spielte sie gegeneinander aus **VI** *(Sport)* um die Entscheidung spielen

▶ **play on** **VI** weiterspielen **VI** *+prep obj (also* **play upon***) (= exploit) sb's fears, feelings, good nature* geschickt ausnutzen; *(= emphasize) difficulties, similarities* herausstreichen; **the hours of waiting played on my nerves** das stundenlange Warten zermürbte mich; **the author is playing on words** der Autor macht Wortspiele/ein Wortspiel

▶ **play out** VT *sep* **a** *(Theat) scene (= enact)* darstellen; *(= finish acting)* zu Ende spielen *(also fig)*; **their romance was played out against a background of civil war** ihre Romanze spielte sich vor dem Hintergrund des Bürgerkrieges ab
b *(esp pass: = use up) mine* ausbeuten; **to play out (the) time** die Zeit herumbringen; *(Sport also)* auf Zeit spielen, Zeit schinden *(pej)*; **a played-out joke** *(inf)* ein abgedroschener Witz; **a played-out theory** *(inf)* eine überstrapazierte Theorie; **I was completely played out after the game** *(inf)* nach dem Spiel war ich völlig geschafft *(inf)*
c *(Mus)* mit Musik hinausgeleiten; **the organ played them out** das Spiel der Orgel geleitete sie hinaus

▶ **play through** VI *+prep obj a few bars etc* durchspielen

▶ **play up** **VI** **a** *(= play louder)* lauter spielen **b** *(Sport inf: = play better)* aufdrehen *(inf)*, (richtig) loslegen *(inf)*; **play up!** vor!, ran! **c** *(Brit inf: = cause trouble: car, injury, child)* Schwierigkeiten machen, verrücktspielen *(inf)* **d** *(inf: = flatter)* **to play up to sb** jdn umschmeicheln **VT** *sep (inf)* **a** *(= cause trouble to)* **to play sb up** jdm Schwierigkeiten machen; *(child, injury also)* jdn piesacken *(inf)* **b** *(= exaggerate)* hochspielen

▶ **play upon** VI *+prep obj* = **play on VI** *+prep obj*

▶ **play with** VI *+prep obj* **to play with the idea of doing sth** mit dem Gedanken spielen, etw zu tun; **we don't have much time/money to play with** wir haben zeitlich/finanziell nicht viel Spielraum; **we don't have that many alternatives to play with** so viele Alternativen haben wir nicht zur Verfügung; **to play with oneself** an sich *(dat)* herumfummeln

playa ['plaɪə] N *(Geol)* Playa *f*, Salztonebene *f*

playable ['pleɪəbl] ADJ *pitch* bespielbar; *ball* zu spielen *pred*

play: **play-act** VI *(dated Theat)* schauspielern; *(fig also)* Theater spielen; **play-acting** N *(dated Theat)* Schauspielerei *f*; *(fig also)* Theater(spiel) *nt*; **play-actor** N *(dated Theat)* Mime *m (old, geh)*, Mimin *f (old, geh)*, Schauspieler(in) *m(f) (also fig)*; **playback** N *(= switch, recording)*

Wiedergabe *f*; *(= playing-back also)* Abspielen *nt*; **the producer asked for a ~** der Produzent bat um eine Wiedergabe *or* ein Playback; **they listened to the ~ of their conversation** sie hörten sich *(dat)* die Aufnahme ihres Gespräches an; **playbill** N *(= poster)* Theaterplakat *nt*; *(US: = programme)* Theaterprogramm *nt*; **playboy** N Playboy *m*; **playclothes** PL *(US)* Sport-/Freizeitkleidung *f*; **play console** N *(Comput)* Spiel(e)konsole *f*

player ['pleɪə'] N **a** *(Sport, Mus)* Spieler(in) *m(f)*; *(Theat)* Schauspieler(in) *m(f)*; **one of the main** *or* **major ~s in …** *(fig)* einer der Hauptakteure in … *(+dat)* **b** *(inf: = ladies' man)* Aufreißer(typ) *m (inf)*

player piano N automatisches Klavier

playfellow ['pleɪfeləʊ] N *(Brit)* Spielkamerad(in) *m(f)*

playful ['pleɪfʊl] ADJ neckisch; *remark, smile, look also* schelmisch; *child, animal* verspielt, munter; **the dog is in a ~ mood/just being ~** der Hund will spielen/spielt nur; **the boss is in a ~ mood today** der Chef ist heute zu Späßen aufgelegt; **to do sth in a ~ way** etw zum Scherz *or* aus Spaß tun; **she gave Philip's hand a ~ squeeze** sie drückte spielerisch Philips Hand; **in a ~ tone** in einem spielerischen Ton

playfully ['pleɪfəlɪ] ADV neckisch; *remark, smile, look also* schelmisch; **to do/say sth ~** etw zum Scherz tun/sagen; **he grasped her wrist ~** er ergriff spielerisch ihr Handgelenk

playfulness ['pleɪfʊlnɪs] N *(of child, animal)* Verspieltheit *f*; *(of adult)* Ausgelassenheit *f*, Lustigkeit *f*; **there was a touch of ~ in his manner as he replied** in der Art, wie er antwortete, lag etwas leicht Neckisches *or* Schelmisches

play: **playgoer** N Theaterbesucher(in) *m(f)*; **playground** N Spielplatz *m*; *(Sch)* (Schul)hof *m*; *(fig)* Tummelplatz *m*, Spielwiese *f*; **playgroup** N Spielgruppe *f*; **playhouse** N **a** *(= children's house)* Spielhaus *nt*; *(US: = doll's house)* Puppenstube *f* **b** *(Theat)* Schaubühne *f* *(dated)*, Schauspielhaus *nt*

playing ['pleɪɪŋ]: **playing card** N Spielkarte *f*; **playing field** N Sportplatz *m*; **the school ~s** der Schulsportplatz; **playing method** N *(Sport)* Spielweise *f*; **playing time** N *(Sport)* Spielzeit *f*

playlet ['pleɪlɪt] N Spiel *nt*, Stück *nt*

play: **playlist** N *(Rad) CDs, Platten etc, die von einem Radiosender gespielt werden*; **artists who don't often make it on to the ~s of radio stations** Künstler, die nicht oft im Radio gespielt werden; **playmaker** N *(Sport)* Spielmacher(in) *m(f)*; **playmate** N Spielkamerad(in) *m(f)*; **play-off** N Entscheidungsspiel *nt*, Play-off *nt*; *(= extra time)* Verlängerung *f*; **play park** N Spielplatz *m*; **playpen** N Laufstall *m*, Laufgitter *nt*; **playroom** N Spielzimmer *nt*; **playschool** N *(esp Brit)* Kindergarten *m*; **playsuit** N Kombination *f* mit kurzer Hose, Spielanzug *m*; **plaything** N *(lit, fig)* Spielzeug *nt*; **playtime** N Zeit *f* zum Spielen; *(Sch)* große Pause; **playwear** N *(US)* Sport-/Freizeitkleidung *f*

playwright ['pleɪraɪt] N Dramatiker(in) *m(f)*; *(contemporary also)* Stückeschreiber(in) *m(f)*

plaza ['plɑːzə] N Piazza *f*; *(US: = shopping complex)* Einkaufszentrum *or* -center *nt*

plc *(Brit) abbr of* **public limited company** ≈ AG *f*

plea [pliː] N **a** Bitte *f*; *(= general appeal)* Appell *m*; **to make a ~ for sth** zu etw aufrufen; **to make a ~ for mercy/leniency** um Gnade/Milde bitten **b** *(= excuse)* Begründung *f*; **on the ~ of illness/ill health** aus Krankheitsgründen/gesundheitlichen Gründen **c** *(Jur)* Plädoyer *nt*; **to enter a ~ of guilty** sich schuldig bekennen; **to enter a ~ of not guilty** seine Unschuld erklären; **to enter a ~ of insanity** auf Zurechnungsunfähigkeit plädieren; **he put forward** *or* **he made a ~ of self-defence** er machte Notwehr geltend, er berief sich auf Notwehr

plea: **plea bargain**, **plea agreement** N *Verhandlung zwischen der Anklagevertretung und dem Verteidiger, um eine mildere Strafe zu erwirken, indem sich der Angeklagte für schuldig erklärt*; **plea-bargain** VI *verhandeln zwischen der Anklagevertretung und dem Verteidiger, um eine mildere Strafe zu erwirken, indem sich der Angeklagte für schuldig erklärt*; **plea bargaining** N = **plea bargain**

pleach [pliːtʃ] VT *branches* (zu einer Hecke) verflechten; *hedge* durch Verflechten der Zweige ausbessern

plead [pliːd] *pret, ptp* **pleaded** *or* *(Scot, US)* **pled**
VT **a** *(= argue)* vertreten; **to ~ sb's case** *(Jur)* **to ~ the case for sb** *(Jur)* jdn vertreten; **to ~ the case for the defence** *(Jur)* die Verteidigung vertreten; **to ~ the case for sth** *(fig)* sich für etw einsetzen; **to ~ sb's cause** *(fig)* jds Sache vertreten, für jds Sache eintreten
b *(as excuse) ignorance, insanity* sich berufen auf *(+acc)*
VI **a** *(= beg)* bitten, nachsuchen *(for* um); **to ~ with sb to do sth** jdn bitten *or* ersuchen *(geh)*, etw zu tun; **to ~ with sb for sth** *(= beg)* jdn um etw bitten *or* ersuchen *(geh)*
b *(Jur, counsel)* das Plädoyer halten; **to ~ guilty/not guilty** sich schuldig/nicht schuldig bekennen; **how do you ~?** bekennen Sie sich schuldig?; **to ~ for sth** *(fig)* für etw plädieren

pleading ['pliːdɪŋ] **N** Bitten *nt*; *(Jur)* Plädoyer *nt* **ADJ** *look, voice* flehend

pleadingly ['pliːdɪŋlɪ] ADV flehend

pleasant ['pleznt] ADJ *aroma, taste* angenehm; *surprise also, news* erfreulich; *person also, face* nett; *manner also, smile* freundlich; *building* gefällig; **to make oneself ~ to sb** jdn ein wenig unterhalten

pleasantly ['plezntlɪ] ADV angenehm; *smile, greet, speak etc* freundlich; **~ decorated** nett *or* hübsch eingerichtet; **the room is ~ light and airy** das Zimmer ist angenehm hell und luftig; **to be ~ surprised** angenehm überrascht sein

pleasantness ['plezntnɪs] N Freundlichkeit *f*; *(of news, surprise)* Erfreulichkeit *f*; **the ~ of her manner** ihre freundliche Art; **the ~ of her face** ihr nettes Gesicht

pleasantry ['plezntrɪ] N *(= joking remark)* Scherz *m*; *(= polite remark)* Höflichkeit *f*, Nettigkeit *f*

pleasa(u)nce ['plezəns] N *(old)* Lustgarten *m (old)*

please [pliːz] ✪ 4 **INTERJ** bitte; **(yes,) ~** *(acceptance)* (ja,) bitte; *(enthusiastic)* oh ja, gerne; **~ pass the salt, pass the salt, ~** würden Sie mir bitte das Salz reichen?; **may I? – ~ do!** darf ich? – bitte sehr!
VI **a** **if you ~** *(form, in request)* wenn ich darum bitten darf; **do it now, if you ~** *(angrily)* aber sofort, wenn es recht ist *or* wenn ich bitten darf!; **and then, if you ~, he tried …** und dann, stell dir vor, versuchte er …; **(just) as you ~** ganz wie du willst, wie es Ihnen beliebt *(form)*; **bold as you ~, he entered the room** frech wie Oskar kam er ins Zimmer *(inf)*; **to do as one ~s** machen *or* tun, was man will, machen *or* tun, was einem gefällt
b *(= cause satisfaction)* gefallen; **eager to ~** darum bemüht, alles richtig zu machen; *(servant)* darum bemüht, jeden Wunsch zu erfüllen; **a gift that is sure to ~** ein Geschenk, das sicher gefällt; **we aim to ~** wir wollen, dass Sie zufrieden sind
VT **a** *(= give pleasure to)* eine Freude machen *(+dat)*; *(= satisfy)* zufriedenstellen; *(= do as sb wants)* gefallen *(+dat)*, gefällig sein *(+dat)*; **the gift/idea ~d him** das Geschenk/die Idee hat ihm gefallen; **just to ~ you** nur dir zuliebe; **it ~s me to see him so happy** es freut mich, dass er so glücklich ist; **well do it then if it ~s you** tus doch, wenn es dir Spaß macht; **you can't ~ everybody** man kann es nicht allen recht machen; **there's no pleasing him** er ist nie zufrieden; **he is easily ~d** *or* **easy to ~** er ist leicht zufriedenzustellen; **to be hard to ~** schwer zufriedenzustellen sein → **pleased**
b *(iro, form: = be the will of)* belieben *(+dat) (iro, form)*; **it ~d him to order that …** er beliebte anzuordnen, dass … *(form)*; **may it ~ Your Honour** *(Jur)* mit Erlaubnis des Herrn Vorsitzenden; **if it ~s God** wenn es Gott gefällt; **~ God he will recover** gebe Gott, dass er wieder gesund wird; **he will return safely, ~ God!** er wird wohlbehalten zurückkehren, das gebe Gott!
VR **to ~ oneself** tun, was einem gefällt; **~ yourself!** wie Sie wollen!; **you can ~ yourself about where you sit** es ist Ihnen überlassen, wo Sie sitzen; **he has only himself to ~** er braucht auf keinen Menschen irgendwelche Rücksichten zu nehmen
N Bitte *nt*; **without so much as a ~** ohne auch nur, bitte zu sagen

pleased [pliːzd] ✪ 9.2, 19.3, 20.2, 25.2 ADJ *(= happy) expression* freudig; *(= satisfied)* zufrieden; **to be ~ (about sth)** sich (über etw *acc*) freuen; **I'm ~ to hear that …** es freut mich zu hören, dass …; **~ to meet you** *or* **to make your acquaintance** angenehm *(form)*, freut mich; **I'm ~ to be able to announce that …** ich freue mich, mitteilen zu können, dass …; **we are ~ to inform you that …** wir freuen uns, Ihnen mitteilen zu können, dass …; **to be ~ at sth** über etw *(acc)* erfreut sein; **to be ~ with sb/sth** mit jdm/etw zufrieden sein; **~ with oneself** mit sich selbst zufrieden, selbstgefällig *(pej)*; **that's nothing to be ~ about** das ist aber gar nicht gut; **I was only too ~ to help** es war mir wirklich eine Freude zu helfen; **they will be only too ~ to let someone else take the risk** es wird ihnen nur zu recht sein, jemand anders das Risiko tragen zu lassen

pleasing ['pliːzɪŋ] ADJ angenehm; *sight* erfreulich; **to be ~ to the eye** ein netter Anblick sein; **to be ~ to the ear** sich angenehm anhören

pleasingly ['pliːzɪŋlɪ] ADV angenehm; **a ~ laid-out garden** ein hübsch angelegter Garten

pleasurable ['pleʒərəbl] ADJ angenehm; *anticipation* freudig

pleasurably ['pleʒərəblɪ] ADV freudig, angenehm; **he had often ~ anticipated this moment** er hatte oft voller Vorfreude diesem Augenblick entgegengesehen

pleasure ['pleʒə'] ✪ 3.2 N **a** *(= satisfaction, happiness)* Freude *f*; **it's a ~, (my) ~** gern (geschehen)!; **with ~** sehr gerne, mit Vergnügen *(form)*; **the ~ is all mine** *(form)* das Vergnügen ist ganz meinerseits *(form)*; **it's my very great ~ …** es ist mir ein großes Vergnügen, …; **it gives me great ~ to be here** *(form)* es ist mir eine große Freude, hier zu sein; **it would give me great ~ to …** es wäre mir ein Vergnügen, zu …; **if it gives you ~** wenn es dir Vergnügen bereitet; **I have much ~ in informing you that …** ich freue mich (sehr), Ihnen mitteilen zu können, dass …; **to have the ~ of doing sth** das Vergnügen haben, etw zu tun; **to do sth for ~** etw zum Vergnügen tun; **he finds ~ in books** er hat Freude an Büchern; **he gets a lot of ~ out of his hobby** er hat viel Freude *or* Spaß an seinem Hobby; **to get ~ from** *or* **out of doing sth** Spaß daran haben, etw zu tun; **he seems to take ~ in annoying me** es scheint ihm Vergnügen zu bereiten, mich zu ärgern; **but don't think I'll take ~ in it** aber glaub nicht, dass mir das Spaß macht; **may I have the ~?** *(form)* darf ich (um den nächsten Tanz) bitten? *(form)*; **will you do me the ~ of dining with me?** *(form)* machen Sie mir das Vergnügen, mit mir zu speisen? *(form)*; **Mrs X requests the ~ of Mr Y's company** *(form)* Frau X gibt sich die Ehre, Herrn Y einzuladen *(form)*; **Mr Y has great ~ in accepting …** *(form)* Herr Y nimmt … mit dem größten Vergnügen an *(form)*
b *(= amusement)* Vergnügen *nt*; **is it business or ~?** (ist es) geschäftlich oder zum Vergnügen?
c *(= source of pleasure)* Vergnügen *nt*; **it's a ~ to meet you** es freut mich, Sie kennenzulernen; **it's a ~ to work with him** es ist ein Vergnügen, mit ihm zusammenzuarbeiten; **he's a ~ to teach** es ist ein Vergnügen, ihn zu unterrichten; **the ~s of country life** die Freuden des

Landlebens; **all the ~s of London** alle Vergnügungen Londons; **she has very few ~s in life** sie hat nicht viele Freuden im Leben
d *(iro, form: = will)* Wunsch *m*; **at (one's) ~** nach Belieben, nach Gutdünken; **to await sb's ~** abwarten, was jd zu tun geruht; **during Her Majesty's ~** *(Jur)* auf unbestimmte Zeit

pleasure *in cpds* Vergnügungs-; **pleasure boat** N **a** Vergnügungsdampfer *m or* -schiff *nt*, Ausflugsdampfer *m or* -schiff *nt* **b** *(= yacht etc)* Hobbyboot *nt*; **pleasure craft** N Hobbyboot *nt*; **pleasure cruise** N Vergnügungsfahrt *f*, Kreuzfahrt *f*; **pleasure ground** N Parkanlage *f*; *(= fairground)* Vergnügungspark *m*; **pleasure-loving** ADJ lebenslustig, leichtlebig *(pej)*; **pleasure principle** N *(Psych)* Lustprinzip *nt*; **pleasure-seeker** N Vergnügungshungrige(r) *mf*; **pleasure-seeking** ADJ vergnügungshungrig; **pleasure trip** N Vergnügungsausflug *m or* -reise *f*

pleat [pli:t] **N** Falte *f* **VT** fälteln

pleated ['pli:tɪd] ADJ gefältelt, Falten-; **~ skirt** Faltenrock *m*

pleather ['pleðəʳ] N *(US)* *Plastik, das wie Leder aussieht*

pleb [pleb] N *(Brit pej inf)* Plebejer(in) *m(f)* *(pej)*, Prolet(in) *m(f)* *(pej inf)*; **the ~s** die Proleten *pl* *(pej inf)*, der Plebs *(pej)*

plebby ['plebɪ] ADJ *(pej inf)* primitiv

plebeian [plɪ'bi:ən] **ADJ** plebejisch **N** Plebejer(in) *m(f)*

plebiscite ['plebɪsɪt] N Plebiszit *nt*, Volksentscheid *m*

plectrum ['plektrəm] N Plektron *nt*, Plektrum *nt*

pled [pled] *(US, Scot) pret, ptp of* **plead**

pledge [pledʒ] **N** **a** *(in pawnshop, of love)* Pfand *nt*; *(= promise)* Versprechen *nt*, Zusicherung *f*; **I give you my ~** ich gebe dir mein Wort; **we have given them a ~ of aid** wir haben versprochen, ihnen zu helfen; **as a ~ of** als Zeichen *(+gen)*; **under (the) ~ of secrecy** unter dem Siegel der Verschwiegenheit; **election ~s** Wahlversprechen *pl*; **to sign** *or* **take the ~** *(lit)* sich schriftlich zur Abstinenz verpflichten; *(hum inf)* dem Alkohol abschwören *(usu hum)*
b *(form: = toast)* Toast *m*, Trinkspruch *m*; **to drink a ~ to sb/sth** einen Toast *etc* auf jdn/etw ausbringen
VT **a** *(= give as security, pawn)* verpfänden
b *(= promise)* versprechen, zusichern; **to ~ one's word** sein Wort geben *or* verpfänden; **to ~ support for sb/sth** jdm/einer Sache seine Unterstützung zusichern; **I am ~d to secrecy** ich bin zum Schweigen verpflichtet; **he ~d me to secrecy** er verpflichtete mich zum Schweigen; **to ~ (one's) allegiance to sb/sth** jdm/einer Sache Treue schwören *or* geloben
c *(form: = toast)* einen Trinkspruch ausbringen auf *(+acc)*
VR **to ~ oneself to do sth** geloben *or* sich verpflichten, etw zu tun

> **PLEDGE OF ALLEGIANCE**
>
> Die **Pledge of Allegiance**, ursprünglich 1892 geschrieben, wird jeden Tag von amerikanischen Schulkindern, besonders in der Grundschule, aufgesagt. Sie stellen sich dazu vor der amerikanischen Flagge auf, legen die rechte Hand aufs Herz und sprechen die folgenden Worte: „I pledge allegiance to the flag of the United States of America and to the Republic for which it stands, one nation under God, indivisible, with liberty and justice for all." Besonders die Traditionalisten halten an diesem Brauch fest, den sie als einen Kernpunkt des amerikanischen Patriotismus ansehen.

Pleiades ['plaɪədi:z] PL Plejaden *pl*

Pleistocene ['plaɪstəʊsi:n] **N** Pleistozän *nt* **ADJ** pleistozän, Pleistozän-; **~ period** Pleistozänzeit *f*

plenary ['pli:nərɪ] ADJ Plenar-, Voll-; **~ session** Plenarsitzung *f*, Vollversammlung *f*; **~ powers** unbeschränkte Vollmachten *pl*

plenipotentiary [ˌplenɪpə'tenʃərɪ] **N** (General)bevollmächtigte(r) *mf* **ADJ** *ambassador* (general)bevollmächtigt; **~ powers** Generalvollmachten *pl*

plenitude ['plenɪtju:d] N *(liter)* Fülle *f*

plenteous ['plentɪəs] ADJ *(liter)* = **plentiful**

plentiful ['plentɪfʊl] ADJ reichlich; *commodities, gold, minerals etc* reichlich *or* im Überfluss vorhanden; *hair* voll; **to be in ~ supply** reichlich *or* im Überfluss vorhanden sein

plentifully ['plentɪfəlɪ] ADV reichlich

plenty ['plentɪ] **N** **a** eine Menge; **land of ~** Land des Überflusses; **times of ~** Zeiten *pl* des Überflusses, fette Jahre *pl* *(Bibl)*; **in ~** im Überfluss; **three kilos will be ~** drei Kilo sind reichlich; **there's ~ here for six** es gibt mehr als genug für sechs; **that's ~, thanks!** danke, das ist reichlich; **you've already had ~** du hast schon reichlich gehabt; **I met him once, and that was ~!** ich habe ihn nur einmal getroffen und das hat mir gereicht!; **to see ~ of sb** jdn oft sehen; **there had been ~ going on** es war einiges los gewesen; **there's ~ to do** es gibt viel zu tun; **I've got ~ to do** ich habe viel zu tun; **have I got problems? I've got ~** ob ich Probleme habe? mehr als genug!; **there's ~ more where that came from** davon gibt es genug; **take ~** nimm dir *or* bedien dich reichlich; **there are still ~ left** es sind immer noch eine ganze Menge da
b **~ of** viel, eine Menge; **~ of time/milk** viel Zeit/Milch, eine Menge Zeit/Milch; **~ of eggs/reasons** viele Eier/Gründe, eine Menge Eier/Gründe; **there is no longer ~ of oil** Öl ist nicht mehr im Überfluss vorhanden; **he's certainly got ~ of nerve** der hat vielleicht Nerven! *(inf)*; **a country with ~ of natural resources** ein Land mit umfangreichen Bodenschätzen; **has everyone got ~ of potatoes?** hat jeder reichlich Kartoffeln?; **there will be ~ of things to drink** es gibt dort ausreichend zu trinken; **he had been given ~ of warning** er ist genügend oft gewarnt worden; **we arrived in ~ of time to get a good seat** wir kamen so rechtzeitig, dass wir einen guten Platz kriegten; **don't worry, there's ~ of time** keine Angst, es ist noch genug *or* viel Zeit; **take ~ of exercise** Sie müssen viel Sport treiben
ADJ *(US inf)* reichlich; **~ bananas** reichlich Bananen
ADV *(esp US inf)* **~ big (enough)** groß genug; **he's ~ mean** er ist ziemlich brutal; **he was ~ rude to her** er war ziemlich grob zu ihr; **it rained ~** es hat viel geregnet; **sure, I like it ~** sicher, ich mag das sehr

plenum ['pli:nəm] N Plenum *nt*, Vollversammlung *f*

pleonasm ['pli:ənæzəm] N Pleonasmus *m*

pleonastic [pli:ə'næstɪk] ADJ pleonastisch

plethora ['pleθərə] N *(form)* Fülle *f*

pleurisy ['plʊərɪsɪ] N Brustfellentzündung *f*, Pleuritis *f* *(spec)*

plexus ['pleksəs] N Plexus *m*; *(of nerves also)* Nervengeflecht *nt*; *(of blood vessels also)* Gefäßgeflecht *nt*

pliability [ˌplaɪə'bɪlɪtɪ] N Biegsamkeit *f*; *(of leather)* Geschmeidigkeit *f*; *(of character, mind, person)* Formbarkeit *f*; *(= docility)* Fügsamkeit *f*

pliable ['plaɪəbl], **pliant** ['plaɪənt] ADJ biegsam; *leather* geschmeidig; *character, mind, person* formbar; *(= docile)* fügsam

plied [plaɪd] *pret, ptp of* **ply²**

pliers ['plaɪəz] PL *(also* **pair of pliers***)* (Kombi)zange *f*

plight¹ [plaɪt] VT *(liter)* **to ~ one's word** sein (Ehren)wort geben; **to ~ one's troth (to sb)** *(old, hum)* (jdm) die Ehe versprechen

plight² N Not *f*, Elend *nt*; *(of currency, economy etc)* Verfall *m*; **to be in a sorry ~** in einem traurigen Zustand sein; **the country's economic ~** die wirtschaftliche Misere des Landes

plimsole ['plɪmsəl], **plimsoll** ['plɪmsəl] N *(Brit)* Turnschuh *m*

Plimsoll line, Plimsoll mark N Höchstlademarke *f*

plinth [plɪnθ] N Sockel *m*, Fußplatte *f*, Plinthe *f* *(spec)*

Pliocene ['plaɪəʊsi:n] **N** Pliozän *nt* **ADJ** pliozän

plipper ['plɪpəʳ] N *(esp US)* elektronische Fernbedienung *(für Autotüren, Alarmanlagen etc)*

PLO *abbr of* **Palestine Liberation Organization** PLO *f*

plod [plɒd] **N** Trott *m*, Zockeltrab *m* *(inf)*; **a steady ~** ein gleichmäßiger Trott **VI** **a** *(= trudge)* trotten, zockeln *(inf)*; **to ~ up a hill** einen Hügel hinaufstapfen; **to ~ along** *or* **on** weiterstapfen; **to ~ in/out** herein-/hinausstapfen
b *(fig: in work etc)* sich abmühen *or* abplagen *or* herumquälen; **to ~ away at sth** sich mit etw abmühen *etc*; **to ~ on** sich weiterkämpfen, sich durchkämpfen; **I've already ~ded through 200 pages of this document** ich habe mich schon durch 200 Seiten dieses Dokuments gekämpft

plodder ['plɒdəʳ] N zäher Arbeiter, zähe Arbeiterin

plodding ['plɒdɪŋ] ADJ *walk* schwerfällig, mühsam; *student, worker* hart arbeitend *attr*; *research* langwierig, mühsam

plonk¹ [plɒŋk] **N** *(= noise)* Bums *m* **ADV** *fall, land* bums, peng; **~ in the middle** genau in die/in der Mitte **VT** *(inf: also* **plonk down***)* *(= drop, put down)* hinwerfen, hinschmeißen *(inf)*; *(= bang down)* hinknallen *(inf)*, hinhauen *(inf)*; **to ~ oneself (down)** sich hinwerfen, sich hinpflanzen *(inf)*; **he ~ed himself down in a chair** er warf sich in einen Sessel, er ließ sich in einen Sessel fallen; **just ~ yourself down somewhere** hau dich einfach irgendwo hin *(inf)*

plonk² N *(Brit inf: = wine)* (billiger) Wein, Gesöff *nt* *(hum, pej)*

plonker ['plɒŋkəʳ] N *(Brit inf)* **a** *(= stupid person)* Niete *f* **b** *(= penis)* Pimmel *m* *(inf)*

plook [plu:k] N *(Scot inf: = pimple, zit)* Pickel *m*

plop [plɒp] **N** Plumps *m*; *(in water)* Platsch *m* **ADV** **it fell** *or* **went ~ into the water** es fiel mit einem Platsch ins Wasser **VI** **a** *(= make a plopping sound)* platschen **b** *(inf: = fall)* plumpsen *(inf)* **VT** *(inf: = put down)* hinlegen

plosive ['pləʊsɪv] **ADJ** Verschluss-, explosiv; **~ sound** Verschlusslaut *m* **N** Verschlusslaut *m*, Explosivlaut *m*, Explosivum *nt* *(spec)*

plot [plɒt] **N** **a** *(Agr)* Stück *nt* Land; *(= bed: in garden)* Beet *nt*; *(= building plot)* Grundstück *nt*; *(= allotment)* Parzelle *f*; *(in graveyard)* Grabstelle *f*; **a ~ of land** ein Stück *nt* Land; **a ~ of lettuces** ein Salatbeet *nt*; *(larger)* ein Salatfeld *nt*
b *(US: = diagram, chart, of estate)* Plan *m*; *(of building)* Grundriss *m*
c *(= conspiracy)* Verschwörung *f*, Komplott *nt* → **thicken VI b**
d *(Liter, Theat)* Handlung *f*, Plot *m* *(spec)*; **to lose the ~** *(fig inf)* den Überblick verlieren; **you've lost the ~** *(fig inf)* bei dir ist echt alles verloren *(inf)*
VT **a** *(= plan)* planen, aushecken *(inf)*; **what are you ~ting now?** was heckst du nun schon wieder aus? *(inf)*; **they ~ted to kill him** sie planten gemeinsam, ihn zu töten
b *position, course* feststellen; *(= draw on map)* einzeichnen; *(Math, Med) curve* aufzeichnen
VI sich verschwören; **to ~ against sb** sich gegen jdn verschwören, gegen jdn ein Komplott schmieden

plotless ['plɒtlɪs] ADJ handlungslos, ohne Handlung; **the film is riveting but almost ~** der Film ist faszinierend, hat aber fast keine Handlung

plotter¹ ['plɒtəʳ] N Verschwörer(in) *m(f)*

plotter² N *(Comput)* Plotter *m*

plotting ['plɒtɪŋ] N Verschwörertum *nt*

plotting board, plotting table N Zeichentisch *m*

plough, *(US)* **plow** [plaʊ] N Pflug *m*; **the Plough** *(Astron)* der Wagen; **under the ~** unter dem Pflug; **to put one's hand to the ~** *(fig)* sich in die Riemen legen VT a *(Agr)* pflügen, umpflügen; *furrow* ziehen; **to ~ a lonely furrow** *(fig)* allein auf weiter Flur stehen b *(Brit Univ dated sl)* reinreißen *(inf)*, durchfallen lassen VI a pflügen b *(Brit Univ dated sl)* durchrasseln *(inf)*

▶ **plough back** VT *sep (Agr)* unterpflügen; *(Comm) profits* wieder (hinein)stecken, reinvestieren *(into* in *+acc)*

▶ **plough in** VT *sep manure, crop etc* unterpflügen

▶ **plough into** VI *+prep obj car etc* hineinrasen in *(+acc)* VT SEP *money* reinstecken in *(+acc) (inf)*

▶ **plough through** VI *+prep obj* a **the ship ploughed through the heavy seas** das Schiff pflügte sich durch die schwere See; **we had to plough through the snow** wir mussten uns durch den Schnee kämpfen; **the car ploughed straight through our garden fence** der Wagen brach geradewegs durch unseren Gartenzaun
b *(inf)* **to plough through a novel** *etc* sich durch einen Roman *etc* durchackern *(inf) or* hindurchquälen
VT *sep* a **the ship ploughed its way through the waves** das Schiff pflügte sich durch die Wellen; **we ploughed our way through the long grass** wir bahnten uns unseren Weg durch das hohe Gras
b *(inf)* **to plough one's way through a novel** *etc* sich durch einen Roman *etc* durchackern *(inf)*

▶ **plough up** VT *sep field* umpflügen; *(= uncover)* beim Pflügen zutage *or* zu Tage bringen; *(= uproot) tree* roden; **the lorries had completely ploughed up the village green** die Lastwagen hatten den Dorfanger vollkommen zerpflügt; **the train ploughed up the track for 40 metres** der Zug riss 40 Meter Schienen aus ihrer Verankerung

plough, *(US)* **plow**: **ploughboy** N Pflüger *m*; **ploughhorse** N Ackergaul *m*

ploughing, *(US)* **plowing** [ˈplaʊɪŋ] N Pflügen *nt*; **the ~ back of profits into the company** die Reinvestierung von Gewinnen in die Firma

plough, *(US)* **plow**: **ploughland** N Ackerland *nt*; **ploughman** N Pflüger *m*; **ploughman's lunch** N *(Brit)* Käse und Brot als Imbiss; **ploughshare** N Pflugschar *f*; **to turn** *or* **beat swords into ~s** *(fig)* Schwerter zu Pflugscharen machen

plover [ˈplʌvəʳ] N Regenpfeifer *m*; *(= lapwing)* Kiebitz *m*

plow *etc (US)* = **plough** *etc*

ploy [plɔɪ] N *(= stratagem)* Trick *m*

PLP *(Brit) abbr of* **Parliamentary Labour Party** Parlamentsfraktion *f* der Labour Partei

pls *abbr of* **please** b.

pluck [plʌk] N a *(= courage)* Schneid *m (inf)*, Mut *m*
b *(of animal)* Innereien *pl*
VT a *fruit, flower* pflücken; *chicken* rupfen; *guitar, eyebrows* zupfen; **to ~ (at) sb's sleeve** jdn am Ärmel zupfen; **he ~ed a stray hair off his coat** er zupfte sich *(dat)* ein Haar vom Mantel; **she was ~ed from obscurity to become a film star** sie wurde von einer Unbekannten zum Filmstar gemacht; **his rescuers had ~ed him from the jaws of death** seine Retter hatten ihn den Klauen des Todes entrissen; **he was ~ed to safety** er wurde in Sicherheit gebracht; **to ~ sth out of the air** etw aus der Luft greifen; **to ~ up (one's) courage** all seinen Mut zusammennehmen
b *(also* **pluck out***) hair, feather* auszupfen; **if thy right eye offend thee ~ it out** *(Bibl)* wenn dir dein rechtes Auge zum Ärgernis wird, so reiß es aus
VI **to ~ at sth** an etw *(dat)* (herum)zupfen

plucked instrument [ˈplʌktˈɪnstrʊmənt] N *(Mus)* Zupfinstrument *nt*

pluckily [ˈplʌkɪlɪ] ADV tapfer, mutig

pluckiness [ˈplʌkɪnɪs] N Unerschrockenheit *f*, Schneid *m (inf)*

plucky [ˈplʌkɪ] ADJ *(+er) person* tapfer, mutig; *smile* tapfer; *little pony, action* mutig

plug [plʌg] N a *(= stopper)* Stöpsel *m*; *(for stopping a leak)* Propfen *m*; *(in barrel)* Spund *m*; **a ~ of cotton wool** ein Wattebausch *m*; **to pull the ~** *(in lavatory)* die Spülung ziehen; **to pull the ~ on sb/sth** *(fig inf)* jdm/einer Sache den Boden unter den Füßen wegziehen
b *(Elec)* Stecker *m*; *(incorrect: = socket)* Steckdose *f*; *(Aut: = spark plug)* (Zünd)kerze *f*
c *(inf: piece of publicity)* Schleichwerbung *f no pl*; **to give sb/sth a ~** für jdn/etw Werbung machen
d *(of tobacco)* Scheibe *f*; *(for chewing)* Priem *m*
e *(Geol)* Vulkanstotzen *m*
f *(US: = fireplug)* Hydrant *m*
g *(inf: = punch)* **to take a ~ at sb** jdm eine verpassen *or* runterhauen *(inf)*
VT a *(= stop) hole, gap, crevice, leak* verstopfen, zustopfen; *barrel* (ver)spunden; *tooth* plombieren; **the doctor ~ged the wound with cotton wool** der Arzt stillte die Blutung mit Watte; **to ~ one's ears** sich *(dat)* die Ohren zuhalten; *(with cotton wool etc)* sich *(dat)* etwas in die Ohren stopfen; **to ~ the gaps in the tax laws** die Lücken im Steuergesetz schließen
b *(= insert)* stecken; **~ the TV into the socket, please** steck bitte den Stecker vom Fernseher in die Steckdose; **an old rag had been ~ged into the hole** man hatte einen alten Lappen in das Loch gestopft
c *(inf: = publicize)* Schleichwerbung machen für
d *(inf: = push, put forward) idea* hausieren gehen mit
e *(inf: = shoot)* **to ~ sb in the head/stomach** *etc* jdm ein Loch in den Kopf/Bauch *etc* schießen; **they ~ged him full of lead** sie pumpten ihn mit Blei voll *(inf)*
f *(inf: = punch)* eine verpassen *(+dat) (inf)*

▶ **plug away** VI *(inf)* ackern *(inf)*; **to plug away at sth** sich mit etw abrackern *or* herumschlagen *(inf)*; **keep plugging away** (nur) nicht lockerlassen

▶ **plug in** VT *sep TV, heater etc* hineinstecken, einstöpseln, anschließen; **to be plugged in** angeschlossen sein VI sich anschließen lassen; **where does the TV plug in?** wo wird der Fernseher angeschlossen?; **plug in, then switch on** schließen Sie das Gerät an und schalten Sie es dann ein

▶ **plug into** VI *+prep obj ideas* aufnehmen

▶ **plug up** VT *sep gap, hole, leak etc* verstopfen, zustopfen; *crack* zuspachteln, verspachteln

plug: **plug-and-play** ATTR *(Comput) technology* Plug-and-Play-; **plug hat** N *(old US sl)* Angströhre *f (dated hum)*; **plughole** N *(Brit)* Abflussloch *nt*, Abfluss *m*; **to go down the ~** *(fig inf)* kaputtgehen *(inf)*; **plug-in** ADJ *(Elec)* anschließbar; **~ unit** Steckeinheit *f* N *(Comput)* Plug-in *nt*, Zusatzsoftware *f*; **plug tobacco** N Kautabak *m*; **plug-ugly** *(inf)* N Schlägertyp *m (inf)*, Rabauke *m (inf)* ADJ potthässlich *(inf)*

plum [plʌm] N a *(= fruit, tree)* Pflaume *f*; *(= Victoria plum, dark blue)* Zwetsch(g)e *f*; **to speak with a ~ in one's mouth** *(Brit fig inf)* sprechen, als hätte man eine heiße Kartoffel im Mund
b *(= colour)* Pflaumenblau *nt* c *(fig inf: = good job)* **a real ~ (of a job)** ein Bombenjob *m (inf)* ADJ *attr* a *(inf) job, position* Bomben- *(inf)*, Mords- *(inf)* b *(colour)* pflaumenblau

plumage [ˈpluːmɪdʒ] N Gefieder *nt*, Federkleid *nt (liter)*

plumb [plʌm] N *(= plumbline)* Lot *nt*, Senkblei *nt*;; *(Naut also)* Bleilot *nt* **out of ~** nicht im Lot; **true to ~** *(Tech)* lotrecht
ADV a lotrecht, senkrecht
b *(inf) (= completely)* total *(inf)*, komplett *(inf)*; *(= exactly)* genau; **~ in the middle** (haar)genau in der Mitte; **it hit him ~ on the nose** es traf ihn genau *or* mitten auf die Nase
VT a *ocean, depth* (aus)loten
b *(fig) mystery etc* ergründen; **to ~ the depths of despair** die tiefste Verzweiflung erleben; **this song ~s the depths of bad taste** dieses Lied übertrifft alles bisher Dagewesene *or* da Gewesene an schlechtem Geschmack; **to ~ new depths** einen neuen Tiefstand erreichen; **a look that ~ed his very soul** ein Blick, der in die Tiefen seiner Seele drang
c *(= connect plumbing in) building* Klempnerarbeiten ausführen an *(+dat)*

▶ **plumb in** VT *sep (Brit) washing machine etc* anschließen

plumbago [plʌmˈbeɪgəʊ] N Grafit *m*, Graphit *m*

plumb bob N Lot *nt*, Senkblei *nt*

plumber [ˈplʌməʳ] N Installateur(in) *m(f)*, Klempner(in) *m(f)*

plumbiferous [plʌmˈbɪfərəs] ADJ bleihaltig, Blei führend

plumbing [ˈplʌmɪŋ] N a *(= work)* Installieren *nt*; **he decided to learn ~** er beschloss, Installateur *or* Klempner zu werden; **he does all his own ~** er macht alle Installations- *or* Klempnerarbeiten selbst b *(= fittings)* Rohre *pl*, Leitungen *pl*, Installationen *pl*; *(= bathroom fittings)* sanitäre Anlagen *pl*; **to inspect the ~** *(hum)* die Lokalitäten aufsuchen *(hum)*

plumb: **plumb line** N Lot *nt*, Senkblei *nt*; **plumb rule** N Lotwaage *f*

plum duff [ˈplʌmˈdʌf] N Plumpudding *m*

plume [pluːm] N Feder *f*; *(on helmet)* Federbusch *m*; **~ of smoke** Rauchwolke *f*, Rauchfahne *f*; **a ~ of water** eine Wasserfontäne; **in borrowed ~s** mit fremden Federn geschmückt VR a *(bird)* sich putzen b **to ~ oneself on sth** auf etw *(acc)* stolz sein wie ein Pfau

plumed [pluːmd] ADJ *helmet etc* federgeschmückt, mit Federschmuck; **the peacock with its magnificently ~ tail** der Pfau mit seinem prächtigen Schwanzgefieder

plummet [ˈplʌmɪt] N a *(= weight)* Senkblei *nt*; *(Fishing)* Grundsucher *m* b *(= falling) (Econ)* Sturz *m*; *(of bird, plane)* Sturzflug *m* VI *(bird, plane etc)* hinunterstürzen; *(Econ) (sales figures etc)* stark zurückgehen; *(currency, shares etc)* fallen, absacken; **the pound has ~ted to EUR 1.40** das Pfund ist auf EUR 1,40 gefallen *or* abgesackt; **he has ~ted again to the depths of despair** er ist wieder in tiefster Verzweiflung

plummeting [ˈplʌmɪtɪŋ] ADJ *prices, profits, sales* fallend; *popularity also* schwindend; *temperatures also* abnehmend

plummy [ˈplʌmɪ] ADJ *(+er) (Brit)* a *(inf) job* Bomben- *(inf)*, Mords- *(inf)* b *voice* vornehm-sonor

plump [plʌmp] ADJ *(+er)* a rundlich, mollig, pummelig; *legs etc* stämmig; *face* rundlich, pausbäckig, voll; *chicken etc* gut genährt, fleischig; *fish* fett; *fruit* prall; **~ cheeks** Pausbacken *pl*
b *phrasing, reply* direkt, unverblümt
ADV **to fall ~ onto sth** mit einem Plumps auf etw *(acc)* fallen
VT a *(= drop)* fallen lassen; *(= throw)* werfen; *(angrily, noisily)* knallen *(inf)*; **to ~ sth down** etw hinfallen lassen/hinwerfen/hinknallen *(inf)*; **she ~ed herself down in the armchair** sie ließ sich in den Sessel fallen; **he had ~ed himself in the best chair** er hatte sich im besten Sessel breitgemacht *(inf)*
b *(also* **plump up***) cushion, pillow* aufschütteln
VI *(= fall)* fallen; **to ~ down onto a chair** auf einen Stuhl fallen *or* plumpsen *(inf)*

▶ **plump for** VI *+prep obj* sich entscheiden für

▶ **plump out** VI *(person)* (Gewicht) ansetzen

▶ **plump up** VT *sep cushion, pillow* aufschütteln; *chicken* mästen

plumply [ˈplʌmplɪ] ADV plump

plumpness [ˈplʌmpnɪs] N Rundlichkeit *f*, Molligkeit *f*, Pummeligkeit *f*; *(of legs etc)* Stämmigkeit *f*; *(of face)* Pausbäckigkeit *f*; *(of chicken)*

Wohlgenährtheit *f*; **the ~ of her cheeks** ihre Pausbäckigkeit

plum: **plum pudding** N Plumpudding *m*; **plum tomato** N Eiertomate *f*, italienische Tomate; **plum tree** N Pflaumenbaum *m*; *(= Victoria plum tree)* Zwetsch(g)enbaum *m*

plunder ['plʌndəʳ] N a *(= act) (of place)* Plünderung *f*; *(of things)* Raub *m* b *(= loot)* Beute *f* VT *place* plündern *(also hum)*; *(completely)* ausplündern; *people* ausplündern; *thing* rauben VI plündern

plunderer ['plʌndərəʳ] N Plünderer *m*, Plünderin *f*

plundering ['plʌndərɪŋ] N *(of place)* Plünderung *f*, Plündern *nt*; *(of things)* Raub *m*

plunge [plʌndʒ] VT a *(= thrust)* stecken; *(into water etc)* tauchen; **he ~d the knife into his victim's back** er jagte seinem Opfer das Messer in den Rücken; **to ~ one's hand into sth** seine Hand tief in etw *(acc)* (hinein)stecken; **he ~d his hands into his pockets** er vergrub seine Hände in den Taschen
b *(fig)* **to ~ the country into war/debt** das Land in einen Krieg/in Schulden stürzen; **the room was ~d into darkness** das Zimmer war in Dunkelheit getaucht; **we were ~d into darkness** tiefe Dunkelheit umfing uns; **he was ~d into despair by the news** die Nachricht stürzte ihn in tiefe Verzweiflung
VI a *(= dive)* tauchen; *(goalkeeper)* sich werfen, hechten
b *(= rush: esp downward)* stürzen; **to ~ down the stairs** die Treppe hinunterstürzen; **to ~ to one's death** zu Tode stürzen; **he ~d into/through the crowd** er stürzte sich in/wühlte sich durch die Massen; **the road ~d down the hill** die Straße fiel steil ab
c *(share prices, currency etc)* stürzen, stark fallen; **sales have ~d by 24%** die Verkaufszahlen sind um 24% gefallen
d *(fig) (into debate, studies, preparations, debt)* sich stürzen *(into* in *+acc)*; *(into recession)* stürzen *(into* in *+acc)*
e *(= dip) (horse)* bocken; *(ship)* stampfen
f *(neckline)* fallen; **the dress ~s at the back** das Kleid ist hinten tief ausgeschnitten
g *(= speculate rashly)* sich verspekulieren
VR *(into studies, job etc)* sich stürzen *(into* in *+acc)*
N a *(= dive)* (Kopf)sprung *m*, Köpper *m* *(inf)*; *(of goalkeeper)* Hechtsprung *m*; **to take the ~** *(fig inf)* den Sprung wagen
b *(= downward movement)* Sturz *m*
c *(fig: into debt, despair etc, of shares, currency etc)* Sturz *m*; **a downward ~** ein Absturz *m*; **his ~ into debt began when his business collapsed** nach dem Bankrott seines Geschäftes stürzte er sich in Schulden; **shares took a ~ after the government's announcement** nach der Ankündigung der Regierung kam es zu einem Kurssturz; **a ~ in the value of the pound** ein Kurssturz *m* des Pfunds
d *(= rash investment)* Fehlspekulation *f*

► **plunge in** VT *sep knife* hineinjagen; *hand* hineinstecken; *(into water)* hineintauchen; **he was plunged straight in (at the deep end)** *(fig)* er musste gleich richtig ran *(inf)*, er musste gleich voll einsteigen *(inf)* VI *(= dive)* hineinspringen

plunge pool N Tauchbecken *nt*

plunger ['plʌndʒəʳ] N a *(= piston)* Tauchkolben *m* b *(for clearing drain)* Sauger *m* c *(= speculator)* Spekulant(in) *m(f)*

plunging ['plʌndʒɪŋ] ADJ a *neckline, back* tief ausgeschnitten; **her deeply ~ neckline** der tiefe Ausschnitt ihres Kleides b *(= decreasing) cost, currency, prices* stark fallend

plunk[1] [plʌŋk] VT *banjo* zupfen

plunk[2] N, ADV, VT = **plonk**[1]

pluperfect ['pluː'pɜːfɪkt] N Vorvergangenheit *f*, Plusquamperfekt *nt* ADJ in der Vorvergangenheit, im Plusquamperfekt; **~ tense** Vorvergangenheit *f*, Plusquamperfekt *nt*

plural ['plʊərəl] ADJ a *(Gram)* Plural-, Mehrzahl-; **~ ending** Plural- *or* Mehrzahlendung *f*
b *(= diverse, pluralistic) society, system* pluralistisch N Plural *m*, Mehrzahl *f*; **in the ~** im Plural, in der Mehrzahl

pluralism ['plʊərəlɪzəm] N Pluralismus *m*

pluralist ['plʊərəlɪst] ADJ *(= mixed) society, system, values* pluralistisch N Pluralist(in) *m(f)*

pluralistic [ˌplʊərə'lɪstɪk] ADJ pluralistisch

plurality [plʊə'rælɪtɪ] N a Vielfalt *f*, Mannigfaltigkeit *f*; *(Sociol)* Pluralität *f* b *(US Pol)* (Stimmen)vorsprung *m*

plural voting N Pluralwahlrecht *nt*, Mehrstimmenwahlrecht *nt*

plus [plʌs] PREP *(= added to, increased by)* plus *(+dat)*; *(= together with)* und (außerdem); **the day's takings were ~ £100** die Tageseinnahmen lagen um £ 100 höher; **~ or minus 10%** plus minus 10%
ADJ a *(Math, Elec, fig)* **a ~ figure** eine positive Zahl; **the ~ terminal** der Pluspol; **a ~ factor** ein Pluspunkt *m*; **on the ~ side** auf der Habenseite; **~ 10 degrees** 10 Grad plus *or* über Null
b *(= more than)* **he got B ~ in the exam** ≈ er hat in der Prüfung eine Zwei plus bekommen; **50 pages/hours ~ a week** mehr als *or* über 50 Seiten/Stunden pro Woche; **she has personality ~** sie hat ein gewinnendes Wesen
N *(= sign)* Pluszeichen *nt*; *(= positive factor)* Pluspunkt *m*; *(= extra)* Plus *nt*; **if after all the deductions you still finish up with a ~** wenn dir nach allen Abzügen noch etwas übrig bleibt

plus fours [plʌs'fɔːz] PL Knickerbocker *pl*

plush [plʌʃ] N Plüsch *m* ADJ *(+er)* a Plüsch-; **~ curtains** Plüschvorhänge *pl* b *(inf: = luxurious)* feudal *(inf)*, elegant, vornehm; **a ~ hotel/restaurant** ein Nobelhotel/-restaurant *nt (inf)*

plushly ['plʌʃlɪ] ADV nobel, elegant; **a ~ appointed room** ein elegant ausgestatteter Raum

plushy ['plʌʃɪ] ADJ *(+er) (inf)* = **plush ADJ b**

plus-one N *(inf)* Begleitung *(form)*, *jemand, der zu einem sozialen Ereignis als Begleitung mitgenommen wird*; **she was her ~ for the party** sie war auf der Party ihre Begleitung

plus sign N *(Math, Elec)* Pluszeichen *nt*

Plutarch ['pluːtɑːk] N Plutarch *m*

Pluto ['pluːtəʊ] N *(Myth)* Pluto *m*, Pluton *m*; *(Astron)* Pluto *m*

plutocracy [pluː'tɒkrəsɪ] N Plutokratie *f*

plutocrat ['pluːtəʊkræt] N Plutokrat(in) *m(f)*

plutocratic [ˌpluːtəʊ'krætɪk] ADJ plutokratisch

plutonium [pluː'təʊnɪəm] N Plutonium *nt*

pluvial ['pluːvɪəl] ADJ *(form)* Regen-; **~ erosion** Erosion *f* durch Regen, Regenerosion *f*

pluviometer [ˌpluːvɪ'ɒmɪtəʳ] N Regen- *or* Niederschlagsmesser *m*, Pluviometer *nt*

ply[1] [plaɪ] N **three-~** *(wood)* dreischichtig; *tissues* dreilagig; **three-~ wool** Dreifachwolle *f*, dreifädige Wolle; **what ~ is this wool?** wievielfach ist diese Wolle?, wie viele Fäden hat diese Wolle?

ply[2] VT a *(= work with, use) tool, brush etc* gebrauchen, umgehen mit, führen; *(= work busily with) tool, brush etc* fleißig führen *or* umgehen mit b *(= work at) trade* ausüben, betreiben, nachgehen *(+dat)* c *(ships) sea, river, route* befahren d **to ~ sb with questions** jdn mit Fragen überhäufen; **to ~ sb with drink(s)** jdn immer wieder zum Trinken auffordern; **she kept her guests well plied with drinks** sie sorgte dafür, dass ihren Gästen die Getränke nicht ausgingen VI *(ship)* **to ~ between** verkehren zwischen; **to ~ for hire** seine Dienste anbieten

plywood ['plaɪwʊd] N Sperrholz *nt*

PM *(Brit inf) abbr of* **Prime Minister**

pm *abbr of* **post meridiem**; **at 5 pm** um 5 Uhr nachmittags, um 17 Uhr; **at 9 pm** um 9 Uhr abends, um 21 Uhr; **the 3pm train** der 15-Uhr-Zug

PMS [piːem'es] N *abbr of* **pre-menstrual syndrome** PMS *nt*

PMT [piːem'tiː] N *(Brit)* a *abbr of* **pre-menstrual tension** b *abbr of* **photomechanical transfer**

pneumatic [njuː'mætɪk] ADJ a Druckluft-; **~ valve** Druckluftventil *nt* b *(inf) young lady* vollbusig *(inf)*; *breasts* prall

pneumatically [njuː'mætɪkəlɪ] ADV mit *or* durch Druck- *or* Pressluft; **a ~ operated drill** ein pressluftbetriebener Bohrer

pneumatic: **pneumatic brake** N Druckluftbremse *f*; **pneumatic drill** N Pressluftbohrer *m*; **pneumatic hammer** N Presslufthammer *m*; **pneumatic tyre** N Luftreifen *m*

pneumonia [njuː'məʊnɪə] N Lungenentzündung *f*

PO a *abbr of* **post office** PA b *abbr of* **postal order**

po [pəʊ] N *(inf)* (Nacht)topf *m*, Pott *m (inf)*

POA *(Brit) abbr of* **Prison Officers' Association** Verband *m* der Justizvollzugsbeamten

poach[1] [pəʊtʃ] VT *egg* pochieren; *fish* (blau) dünsten; **~ed egg** pochiertes *or* verlorenes Ei; *(in poacher)* ≈ Ei *nt* im Glas

poach[2] VT unerlaubt fangen, schwarzfangen *(inf)*; *(fig) idea* stehlen; *members, customers* abwerben VI a *(lit)* wildern *(for* auf *+acc)*; **to ~ for salmon** Lachs ohne Berechtigung fangen *or* schwarzfangen *(inf)* b *(fig)* **to ~ (on sb's territory)** *(in sport)* jdm ins Gehege *or* in die Quere kommen; *(in work also)* jdm ins Handwerk pfuschen

poacher[1] ['pəʊtʃəʳ] N Wilderer *m*, Wilderin *f*; *(of game also)* Wilddieb(in) *m(f)*; **it's a case of ~ turned gamekeeper for the new Arsenal manager** *(Brit)* der neue Manager von Arsenal ist ein zum Paulus gewordener Saulus

poacher[2] N *(for eggs)* Pochierpfanne *f*

poaching ['pəʊtʃɪŋ] N Wildern *nt*, Wilderei *f*

pock [pɒk] N *(= pustule)* Pocke *f*, Blatter *f*; *(= mark)* Pocken- *or* Blatternarbe *f*

pocket ['pɒkɪt] N a *(in garment)* Tasche *f*; **take your hands out of your ~s!** nimm die Hände aus der Tasche!; **to have sb/sth in one's ~** *(fig)* jdn/etw in der Tasche haben *(inf)*; **to be in sb's ~** *(fig)* jdm hörig sein; **money burns a hole in his ~** er gibt sein Geld immer schnell aus; **to live in each other's** *or* **one another's ~s** *(fig)* unzertrennlich sein
b *(= receptacle) (in suitcase, file etc)* Fach *nt*; *(in book cover: for map etc)* Tasche *f*; *(Baseball)* Tasche *f*; *(Billiards)* Loch *nt*
c *(= resources)* Geldbeutel *m*; **to be a drain on one's ~** jds Geldbeutel strapazieren *(inf)*; **that hit his ~** das hat seinen Geldbeutel ganz schön strapaziert *(inf)*; **I was £100 in ~ after the sale** nach dem Verkauf war ich um £ 100 reicher; **to pay for sth out of one's own ~** etw aus der eigenen Tasche bezahlen; **to put one's hand in one's ~** tief in die Tasche greifen; **to have deep ~s** *(fig)* großzügig sein; **investors with deep ~s** *(fig)* großzügige Investoren *pl* → **out-of-pocket**
d *(= restricted area, space)* Gebiet *nt*; *(smaller)* Einsprengsel *nt*; **~ of resistance** Widerstandsnest *nt*; **~ of unemployment** Gebiet *nt* mit hoher Arbeitslosigkeit; **~ of infection** Ansteckungsgebiet *nt*; **a ~ of ore** ein Einschluss *m* von Erz
e *(Aviat: = air pocket)* Luftloch *nt*
ADJ *(= for the pocket)* Taschen-; **~ diary** Taschenkalender *m*; **~ dictionary** Taschenwörterbuch *nt*
VT a *(= put in one's pocket)* einstecken; **to ~ one's pride** seinen Stolz überwinden
b *(= gain) money, prize, award* kassieren; *(= misappropriate)* einstecken *(inf)*, einsacken *(inf)*; **the treasurer ~ed the club funds** der Schatzmeister hat die Vereinsgelder in die eigene Tasche gesteckt
c *(Billiards)* ins Loch bringen, einlochen
d *(US Pol) durch Veto aufschieben*

pocket: **pocket battleship** N Westentaschenkreuzer *m*; **pocket billiards** N *sing* a *(US)* Poolbillard *nt* b *(hum sl)* Taschenbillard *(sl) nt*; **pocketbook** N a *(= notebook)* Notizbuch *nt* b *(esp US: = wallet)* Brieftasche *f* c *(US: = handbag)* Handtasche *f*; **pocket borough** N *(Brit Hist) vor 1832 ein Wahlbe-*

zirk, der sich praktisch in den Händen einer Person oder Familie befand; **pocket calculator** N Taschenrechner *m*; **pocket camera** N *(Phot)* Pocketkamera *f*

pocketful ['pɒkɪtfʊl] N **a ~** eine Tasche voll

pocket: **pocket handkerchief** N Taschentuch *nt*; **a ~(-sized) garden** ein Garten *m* im Westentaschenformat; **pocketknife** N Taschenmesser *nt*; **pocket money** N *(esp Brit)* Taschengeld *nt*; **pocket-size(d)** ADJ *book* im Taschenformat; *person* winzig; *garden* im Westentaschenformat; **~ camera/TV** Miniaturkamera *f*/-fernseher *m*; **pocket veto** N *(US Pol)* *Verzögerung der Gesetzesverabschiedung durch aufschiebendes Veto des Präsidenten*

pock: **pockmark** N Pocken- *or* Blatternarbe *f*; **pockmarked** ADJ *face* pockennarbig; *surface* narbig; **the ~ surface of the moon** die mit Kratern übersäte Oberfläche des Mondes; **~ with bullet holes** mit Einschüssen übersät

pod [pɒd] **N** *(Bot)* Hülse *f*; *(of peas also)* Schote *f*; *(Aviat) (for missiles etc)* Magazin *nt*; *(for jet engine)* Gehäuse *nt* **VT** *peas* enthülsen, auslösen

podginess ['pɒdʒɪnɪs] N molliges Aussehen, dickliche Figur

podgy ['pɒdʒɪ] ADJ *(+er)* *(Brit inf)* rundlich, pummelig; *face* schwammig; **~ fingers** Wurstfinger *pl*; **~ face** Mondgesicht *nt (inf)*

podiatrist [pɒ'di:ətrɪst] N *(esp US)* Fußspezialist(in) *m(f)*

podiatry [pɒ'di:ətrɪ] N *(esp US)* Lehre *f* von den Fußkrankheiten; *(= treatment)* Fußpflege *f*

podium ['pəʊdɪəm] N Podest *nt*

Podunk ['pəʊdʌŋk] N *(US pej: = backwater, boring provincial town)* Krähwinkel *nt (pej)*

poem ['pəʊɪm] N Gedicht *nt*; **epic ~** Epos *nt*

poesy ['pəʊɪzɪ] N *(form: = poetry)* Lyrik *f*, Poesie *f (old)*

poet ['pəʊɪt] N Dichter *m*, Poet *m (old)* → **poet laureate**

poetaster [,pəʊɪ'tæstə'] N *(pej)* Poetaster *m*, Dichterling *m*

poetess ['pəʊɪtes] N Dichterin *f*, Poetin *f (old)*

poetic [pəʊ'etɪk] ADJ poetisch; *talent, ability also* dichterisch; *place, charm* stimmungsvoll, malerisch; **~ beauty** *(visual)* malerische Schönheit; *(of thought, scene in play etc)* poetische Schönheit; **he's not at all ~** er hat überhaupt keinen Sinn für Poesie; **he became ~** er wurde poetisch *or* lyrisch

poetical [pəʊ'etɪkəl] ADJ = **poetic**

poetically [pəʊ'etɪkəlɪ] ADV *describe, write, named* poetisch; **very ~ put** sehr poetisch ausgedrückt; **~ gifted** dichterisch begabt

poetic justice N poetische Gerechtigkeit

poetic licence N dichterische Freiheit

poetics [pəʊ'etɪks] N *sing* Poetik *f*

poet laureate ['pəʊɪt'lɔ:rɪɪt] N Hofdichter(in) *m(f)*, Poeta laureatus *m*

poetry ['pəʊɪtrɪ] N **a** Dichtung *f*; *(not epic also)* Lyrik *f*; **to write ~** Gedichte schreiben, dichten; **the rules of ~** die Regeln der Versdichtung; **~ reading** Dichterlesung *f* **b** *(fig)* Poesie *f*; **the dancing was ~ in motion** der Tanz war in Bewegung umgesetzte Poesie; **the sunset was sheer ~** der Sonnenuntergang war reinste Poesie

po-faced ['pəʊfeɪst] ADJ *(inf: = disapproving)* grimmig, mürrisch; **a ~ woman** *(= ugly)* eine Schrulle *(inf)*

pogo ['pəʊgəʊ] **N** *(Mus)* Pogo *m* **VI** *(= dance)* Pogo tanzen

pogo stick ['pəʊgəʊstɪk] N Springstock *m*

pogrom ['pɒgrəm] N Pogrom *nt*

poignancy ['pɔɪnjənsɪ] N Ergreifende(s) *nt*; *(of look, memories)* Wehmut *f*; *(of distress, regret)* Schmerzlichkeit *f*; **the ~ of his message** die Wehmut, die in seinen Worten lag; **he writes with great ~** er schreibt sehr ergreifend

poignant ['pɔɪnjənt] ADJ ergreifend; *memories, look* wehmütig; *distress, regret* schmerzlich

poignantly ['pɔɪnjəntlɪ] ADV *describe, illustrate* ergreifend; **old memories stirred ~ within her** alte Erinnerungen rührten sich wehmütig in ihr; **~ beautiful** auf wehmütige Art schön

poinsettia [pɔɪn'setɪə] N Weihnachtsstern *m*, Poinsettia *f (spec)*

point [pɔɪnt]

⊙ 15.2, 20.7, 26

1 NOUN	4 INTRANSITIVE VERB
2 PLURAL NOUN	5 PHRASAL VERBS
3 TRANSITIVE VERB	

1 – NOUN

a [= sharp end] *of chin, needle* Spitze *f*; *(of a star)* Zacke *f*; *(of antler)* (Geweih)ende *nt*, (Geweih)spitze *f*; **at the point of a gun/sword** mit vorgehaltener Pistole/vorgehaltenem Schwert; **things look different at the point of a gun** alles sieht ein bisschen anders aus, wenn einem jemand die Pistole auf die Brust setzt → **fine**

b [= marker] *on scale, compass* Punkt *m*; *(on thermometer)* Grad *m*; **from all points (of the compass)** aus allen (Himmels)richtungen

♦ **up to a point** bis zu einem gewissen Grad *or* Punkt

c [= unit, score] *in test, competition, St Ex etc* Punkt *m*; **points for/against** Plus-/Minuspunkte *pl*; **points decision** Entscheidung *f* nach Punkten; **points win** Punktsieg *m*, Sieg *m* nach Punkten; **to win on points** nach Punkten gewinnen; **points system** Punktesystem *nt*

d [= dot, punctuation mark] *Typ, Geometry* Punkt *m*; *(in Hebrew texts)* Vokalzeichen *nt*; **(nought) point seven (0.7)** null Komma sieben (0,7)

e [= place, time] Punkt *m*, Stelle *f*; **the northernmost point of Scotland** der nördlichste Punkt Schottlands; **the train stops at Slough and all points east** der Zug hält in Slough und allen Orten östlich davon; **at this point** *(spatially)* an dieser Stelle, an diesem Punkt; *(in time) (= then)* in diesem Augenblick; *(= now)* jetzt; **from that point on they were friends** von da an waren sie Freunde; **at what point ...?** an welcher Stelle ...?; **at no point** nie; **at no point in the book** nirgends in dem Buch, an keiner Stelle des Buches; **they provoked him to the point where he lost his temper** sie reizten ihn so lange, bis er die Geduld verlor

♦ **point of** + *NOUN* **point of entry** *(over border)* Ort *m* der Einreise; **point of departure** *(lit, fig)* Ausgangspunkt *m*; **to be at the point of death** am Rande *or* an der Schwelle des Todes stehen; **severe to the point of cruelty** streng bis an die Grenze der Grausamkeit; **to reach the point of no return** *(fig)* den Punkt erreichen, von dem an es kein Zurück gibt; **point of view** Standpunkt *m*, Gesichtspunkt *m*; **from my point of view** von meinem Standpunkt aus, aus meiner Perspektive *or* Sicht; **from the point of view of productivity** von der Produktivität her gesehen

♦ **point of** + *-ing* **to be on the point of doing sth** im Begriff sein, etw zu tun; **he was on the point of telling me the story when ...** er wollte mir gerade die Geschichte erzählen, als ...; **he had reached the point of resigning** er war nahe daran, zu resignieren; **she was indulgent to the point of spoiling the child** sie war nachgiebig in einem Maße, das schon in Verwöhnung des Kindes umschlug

f [= matter, question] Punkt *m*; **on this point we are agreed** in diesem Punkt stimmen wir überein; **the point at issue** der strittige Punkt; **a 12-point plan** ein Zwölfpunkteplan *m*; **a useful point** ein nützlicher Hinweis; **point by point** Punkt für Punkt; **a point by point comparison** ein Vergleich Punkt für Punkt; **my point was ...** was ich sagen wollte, war ...; **you have a point there** darin mögen Sie recht haben, da ist etwas dran *(inf)*; **he may have a point, you know** da kann er recht haben, weißt du; **can I put that same point another way?** kann ich das noch einmal anders formulieren?; **would you put that point more succinctly?** können Sie das etwas knapper fassen?; **to gain** *or* **carry one's point** sich durchsetzen

♦ **to make a/one's point** ein/sein Argument *nt* anbringen *or* vorbringen; **he made the point that ...** er betonte, dass ...; **you've made your point!** wissen wir ja schon!, das hast du ja schon gesagt!; **the chairman gave him just 30 seconds to make his point** der Vorsitzende gab ihm nur 30 Sekunden, um sein Argument zu erläutern; **he makes his points very clearly** er bringt seine Argumente sehr klar vor; **what point are you trying to make?** worauf wollen Sie hinaus?; **if I may make another point** wenn ich noch auf einen weiteren Punkt aufmerksam machen darf

♦ **to take the/sb's point** **I take your point, point taken** ich akzeptiere, was Sie sagen; *(in exasperation)* ich habe schon begriffen; **do you take my point?** verstehst du mich?

♦ **point of** + *NOUN* **a point of detail** eine Einzelfrage; **a point of interest** ein interessanter Punkt; **a point of law** eine Rechtsfrage; **a point of principle** eine grundsätzliche Frage → **honour, order**

g [= crux, main issue] **the point is that ...** es ist nämlich so ..., die Sache ist die, dass ...; **that's the whole point** das ist es ja gerade; **that's the whole point of doing it this way** gerade darum machen wir das so; **but the pound has been devalued – that's the whole point, your mark is worth more!** aber das Pfund wurde doch abgewertet – genau! deshalb ist die Mark jetzt mehr wert; **the point of the joke/story** die Pointe; **that's not the point** darum geht es nicht; **his remarks are very much to the point** seine Bemerkungen sind sehr sachbezogen

♦ **to get** *or* **see the point** verstehen, worum es geht; **do you see the point of what I'm saying?** weißt du, worauf ich hinauswill?

♦ **to miss the point** nicht verstehen, worum es geht; **he missed the point of what I was saying** er hat nicht begriffen, worauf ich hinauswollte

♦ **to come to the point** zur Sache kommen; **when it comes to the point** wenn es darauf ankommt

♦ **to keep** *or* **stick to the point** beim Thema bleiben

♦ **beside the point** unerheblich, irrelevant; **I'm afraid that's beside the point** das ist nicht relevant, das gehört nicht hierher

♦ **a case in point** ein einschlägiger Fall; **the case in point** der zur Debatte stehende Punkt

♦ **to make a point of doing sth** Wert darauf legen, etw zu tun; **he made a special point of being early** er legte besonderen Wert darauf, früh da zu sein; **we make a point of stressing colloquial usage** wir legen besonderen Nachdruck auf die Umgangssprache

h [= purpose, use] Zweck *m*, Sinn *m*; **there's no point in staying** es hat keinen Zweck *or* Sinn zu bleiben; **I don't see the point of carrying on/changing our system now** ich sehe keinen Sinn darin, weiterzumachen/unser System jetzt zu ändern; **what's the point?** was solls?; **I just don't see the point of it** *or* **any point in it** das sehe ich überhaupt nicht ein, ich sehe überhaupt keinen Sinn darin; **the point of this is ...** Sinn und Zweck ist davon ...; **what's the point of trying?** wozu (es) versuchen?; **he doesn't understand the point of doing this** er versteht nicht, weswegen wir/sie *etc* das machen; **the news gave point to his arguments** die Nachrichten verliehen seinen Argumenten Nachdruck *or* Gewicht; **life has lost its point** das Leben hat jeden Sinn *or* all seinen Sinn verloren

i [= characteristic] **good/bad points** gute/schlechte Seiten *pl*; **he has his good points** er hat auch gute Seiten *or* seine guten Seiten; **the points to look for when buying a new car** die Punkte *or* Dinge, auf die man beim Kauf eines neuen Wagens achten muss

j [Elec] *(Brit)* Steckdose *f*

2 – points PLURAL NOUN

a Aut Unterbrecherkontakte *pl*
b Ballet Spitzen *pl*; **to dance on points** Spitzentanz *m* machen, auf den Spitzen tanzen
c Rail *Brit* Weichen *pl*

3 – TRANSITIVE VERB

a = aim, direct *gun, telescope etc* richten (*at* auf *+acc*); **he pointed his stick in the direction of the house** er zeigte *or* wies mit dem Stock auf das Haus; **he pointed his boat upstream** er drehte sein Boot stromaufwärts; **they pointed the drunk off in the right direction** sie schickten den Betrunkenen in die richtige Richtung → **finger**
b = mark, show zeigen; **to point the way** *(lit, fig)* den Weg weisen; **that really pointed the moral** das bewies, wie recht wir/sie *etc* hatten; **he used the decline in the company's profits to point the moral that ...** er nahm das Absinken der Firmengewinne zum Anlass zu betonen, dass ...
c toes strecken
d Build *wall, brickwork* verfugen, ausfugen
e = punctuate *text* interpunktieren; *Hebrew* vokalisieren; *psalm* mit Deklarationszeichen versehen
f Hunt *game* anzeigen

4 – INTRANSITIVE VERB

a with finger etc zeigen, deuten (*at, to* auf *+acc*); **it's rude to point (at strangers)** es ist unhöflich, mit dem Finger (auf Fremde) zu zeigen; **don't point!** zeig nicht mit dem Finger!; **he pointed toward(s) the house/back towards the house** er zeigte *or* deutete zum Haus/zurück zum Haus; **the compass needle points (to the) north** die Kompassnadel zeigt *or* weist nach Norden
b = indicate *facts, events* hinweisen, hindeuten (*to* auf *+acc*); (*person*: *= point out*) hinweisen; **everything points that way** alles weist in diese Richtung; **the problems which you have pointed to in your paper** die Probleme, auf die du in deinem Aufsatz hingewiesen hast *or* die du in deinem Aufsatz aufgezeigt hast; **the poet doesn't state, he points in certain directions** der Dichter trifft keine Feststellungen, er deutet bestimmte Richtungen an; **all the signs point to success** alle Zeichen stehen auf Erfolg; **all the signs point to economic recovery** alles deutet *or* weist auf eine Erholung der Wirtschaft hin
c = be aimed *gun, vehicle etc* gerichtet sein; (*= face, be situated*: *building, valley*) liegen; **with his gun pointed** *or* **pointing right at me, he said ...** die Pistole direkt auf mich gerichtet, sagte er ...; **the wheels aren't pointing in the same direction** die Räder zeigen nicht in dieselbe Richtung; **in which direction is it pointing?** in welche Richtung zeigt es?
d Hunt (vor)stehen

5 – PHRASAL VERBS

► **point out** VT *sep* **a** *(= show)* zeigen auf *(+acc)*; **to point sth out to sb** jdn auf etw hinweisen, jdn auf etw aufmerksam machen; **could you point him out to me?** kannst du mir zeigen, wer er ist?; **I'll point him out** ich zeige ihn dir; **the guide pointed out the most interesting paintings** der Führer machte auf die interessantesten Gemälde aufmerksam
b *(= mention)* **to point sth out (to sb)** (jdn) auf etw *(acc)* aufmerksam machen, (jdn) auf etw *(acc)* hinweisen; **may I point out that ...?** darf ich darauf aufmerksam machen *or* darauf hinweisen, dass ...?; **thank you for pointing that out to me** vielen Dank, dass Sie mich darauf aufmerksam gemacht haben

► **point up** VT *sep (= emphasize)* unterstreichen, betonen; *(= make clear)* veranschaulichen, verdeutlichen

point-blank [ˈpɔɪntˈblæŋk] ADJ direkt; *refusal* glatt; **at** *or* **from ~ range** aus kürzester Entfernung *or* Distanz; **a ~ shot** *(from gun, Ftbl)* ein Schuss *m* aus kürzester Distanz *or* Entfernung
ADV *fire* aus kürzester Distanz *or* Entfernung; *ask* rundheraus; **to ask sb ~** jdn geradeheraus fragen; **he refused ~ to help** er weigerte sich rundweg *or* er lehnte es rundheraus ab zu helfen

pointed [ˈpɔɪntɪd] ADJ **a** *(= sharp) stick, roof, chin, nose, shoes* spitz; *window, arch* spitzbogig; **a stick with a sharply ~ end** ein Stock mit sehr spitzem Ende; **the ~ windows in the old church** die Spitzbogenfenster in der alten Kirche **b** *(= incisive) wit, criticism* scharf **c** *(= obvious in intention) remark, comment* scharf, spitz; *reference* unverblümt; *question* gezielt; *look* spitz; *absence, gesture, departure* ostentativ; **her ~ lack of interest in my problems** ihr ostentatives *or* betontes Desinteresse an meinen Problemen; **that was rather ~** das war ziemlich deutlich

pointedly [ˈpɔɪntɪdlɪ] ADV *speak, comment, look* spitz; *refer* unverblümt; *leave, stay away etc* ostentativ

pointer [ˈpɔɪntəʳ] N **a** *(= indicator)* Zeiger *m*; **(mouse) ~** *(Comput)* Mauszeiger *m* **b** *(= stick)* Zeigestock *m* **c** *(= dog)* Pointer *m*, Vorstehhund *m* **d** *(fig: = hint)* Hinweis *m*, Fingerzeig *m*, Tip *m*; **he gave me some ~s on how to behave** er gab mir ein paar Hinweise, wie ich mich benehmen sollte **e** *(esp Brit fig: = indication)* Anzeichen *nt*, Hinweis *m*; **a ~ to a possible solution** ein Hinweis auf eine mögliche Lösung

pointer: **pointer speed** N *(of mouse pointer)* Zeigergeschwindigkeit *f*; **pointer trail** N *(of mouse pointer)* Maus(zeiger)spur *f*

pointillism [ˈpwæntɪlɪzəm] N Pointillismus *m*

pointillist [ˈpwæntɪlɪst] N Pointillist(in) *m(f)*
ADJ pointillistisch

pointing [ˈpɔɪntɪŋ] N *(Build) (= act)* Ausfugung *f*; *(= material)* Fugenmörtel *m*; **the ~ on these old buildings needs to be restored** das Mauerwerk dieser alten Gebäude muss neu verfugt *or* ausgefugt werden

pointing device N *(Comput: = mouse, touchpad, stylus, etc)* Zeigegerät*nt*

pointless [ˈpɔɪntlɪs] ADJ sinnlos; **it is ~ to go** es ist sinnlos zu gehen; **it is ~ her going** *or* **for her to go** es ist sinnlos, dass sie geht; **a ~ exercise** eine sinnlose Angelegenheit

pointlessly [ˈpɔɪntlɪslɪ] ADV sinnlos

pointlessness [ˈpɔɪntlɪsnɪs] N Sinnlosigkeit *f*

point of presence N *(Telec, Comput)* Einwahlknoten *m*

point of sale N *(Comm)* Verkaufsstelle *f*

point-of-sale [ˌpɔɪntəvˈseɪl] ADJ *attr advertising* an der Verkaufsstelle

point(s) duty N Verkehrsdienst *m*

pointsman [ˈpɔɪntsmən] N *pl* **-men** [-mən] *(Brit Rail)* Weichensteller *m*

point source N *(Phys)* Punktquelle *f*, punktförmige Lichtquelle

point-to-point [ˌpɔɪnttəˈpɔɪnt] N *(also* **point-to-point race***)* Geländejagdrennen *nt*

pointy [ˈpɔɪntɪ] ADJ *attr (+er)* spitz

pointy-headed [ˌpɔɪntɪˈhedɪd] ADJ *(US pej sl)* abgehoben *(pej inf)*

poise [pɔɪz] N **a** *(= carriage: of head, body)* Haltung *f*; *(= grace)* Grazie *f*; **the ~ of her head** ihre Kopfhaltung; **the graceful ~ of the dancer's body** die Grazie *or* graziöse Haltung der Tänzerin/des Tänzers
b *(= composure)* Gelassenheit *f*; *(= self-possession)* Selbstsicherheit *f*; **a woman of great ~ and charm** eine Frau voller Selbstsicherheit und Charme; **her ~ as a hostess** ihre Sicherheit als Gastgeberin; **to recover** *or* **regain one's ~** seine Selbstbeherrschung wiedererlangen; **he lacks ~** ihm fehlt die Gelassenheit
VT **a** *(= balance, hold balanced)* balancieren; **he ~d the knife ready to strike** er hielt das Messer so, dass er jederzeit zustechen konnte; **she ~d her pen over her notebook** sie hielt den Kugelschreiber schreibbereit über ihrem Notizblock; **the tiger ~d itself to spring** der Tiger machte sich sprungbereit
b *(in passive)* **to be/hang ~d** *(bird, rock, sword)* schweben; **the diver was ~d on the edge of the pool** der Taucher stand sprungbereit auf dem Beckenrand; **the tiger was ~d ready to spring** der Tiger lauerte sprungbereit; **we sat ~d on the edge of our chairs** wir balancierten auf den Stuhlkanten → *also* **poised a, b**
VI (für einen Moment) unbeweglich bleiben; *(bird, helicopter)* schweben; **he ~d for a second on the edge of the pool** er verharrte einen Augenblick am Beckenrand

poised [pɔɪzd] ADJ **a** *(= suspended) hand* erhoben; *object* bereit; **a waitress approached us, pencil and pad ~** die Bedienung näherte sich uns, Stift und Block bereithaltend
b *(= ready)* bereit; **to be ~ to do sth** bereit sein, etw zu tun; **to be ~ for sth** für etw bereit sein; **the enemy are ~ to attack** der Feind steht angriffsbereit; **he was ~ to become champion** er war auf dem besten Weg, die Meisterschaft zu gewinnen; **they sat in the hall, ~ for departure** sie saßen abfahrtbereit in der Halle; **to be ~ between peace and war** am Rande des Krieges stehen; **to be ~ on the brink of sth** dicht vor etw *(dat)* *or* am Rande von etw stehen; **a bright young man ~ on the brink of success** ein intelligenter junger Mann an der Schwelle zum Erfolg
c *(= self-possessed)* gelassen, selbstsicher; **she was ~ and diplomatic on the telephone** am Telefon war sie selbstsicher und diplomatisch

poison [ˈpɔɪzn] N *(lit, fig)* Gift *nt*; **what's your ~?** *(inf)* **name your ~** *(inf)* was willst du trinken?; **to hate sb like ~** jdn glühend *or* wie die Pest *(inf)* hassen → **meat a** VT **a** *(lit)* vergiften; *atmosphere, rivers* verpesten; **it won't ~ you** *(inf)* das wird dich nicht umbringen *(inf)* **b** *(fig)* vergiften; *marriage* zerrütten; **to ~ sb's mind against sb** jdn gegen jdn aufstacheln

poisoned [ˈpɔɪznd] ADJ **a** *food, arrow* vergiftet; **a ~ chalice** *(esp Brit fig)* ein bitterer Kelch **b** *(= contaminated) air, water, soil* vergiftet **c** *(Med: = infected)* infiziert

poisoner [ˈpɔɪznəʳ] N Giftmörder(in) *m(f)*

poison: **poison fang** N *(of snake)* Giftzahn *m*; **poison gas** N Giftgas *nt*; **poison gland** N *(Zool)* Giftdrüse *f*

poisoning [ˈpɔɪznɪŋ] N *(lit, fig)* Vergiftung *f*; **the gradual ~ of the atmosphere by ...** die zunehmende Luftverpestung durch ...; **to die of ~** an einer Vergiftung sterben

poison: **poison ivy** N kletternder Giftsumach, Giftefeu *m*; **poison oak** N *(Bot)* Giftsumach *m*

poisonous [ˈpɔɪznəs] ADJ **a** giftig; **~ mushroom** Giftpilz *m*; **~ snake** Giftschlange *f*; **whisky on top of beer, that's absolutely ~** *(inf)* Whisky auf Bier, das ist tödlich *(inf)* **b** *(fig) literature, doctrine* zersetzend; *remark etc* giftig; **~ propaganda** Hetzpropaganda *f*; **she has a ~ tongue** sie hat eine giftige Zunge; **he's a ~ individual** er ist ein richtiger Giftzwerg; **a long-standing and ~ dispute** ein lang währender und zerrüttender Streit **c** **~ stuff** *(inf: usu hum)* Teufelszeug *nt*

poison: **poison-pen letter** N anonymer Brief; **poison pill** N *(Fin) zum Schutz gegen ein unerwünschtes Übernahmeangebot eingesetzte Maßnahmen, die im Falle der Übernahme zu einem Wertverlust der Firma führen*; **poison sumach** N *(Bot)* Giftsumach *m*

poke¹ [pəʊk] N *(dial, Scot)* Beutel *m*, Sack *m* *(dial)*; *(plastic, paper)* Tüte *f* → **pig**

poke² N **a** *(= jab)* Stoß *m*, Schubs *m (inf)*; **to give sb/sth a ~** *(with stick)* jdn/etw stoßen; *(with finger)* jdn/etw stupsen; **I got a ~ in the eye from his umbrella** er stieß mir den Regenschirm ins Auge; **it's better than a ~ in the eye (with a sharp stick)** *(inf)* es ist besser als gar nichts
b *(US inf: = punch)* Schlag *m*; **~ on the nose** Nasenstüber *m*
c *(vulg: = act of intercourse)* Vögeln *nt (inf)*; **to have a ~** vögeln *(inf)*, ficken *(vulg)*
VT **a** *(= jab) (with stick)* stoßen; *(with finger)* stupsen; **to ~ the fire** das Feuer schüren, im

Feuer stochern; **he ~d the ground with his stick** er stieß mit seinem Stock auf den Boden; **he accidentally ~d me in the eye** er hat mir aus Versehen ins Auge gestoßen

b *(US inf: = punch)* hauen *(inf)*; **to ~ sb on the nose** jdn auf die Nase hauen *or* schlagen

c *(= thrust)* **to ~ one's head/finger/a stick** *etc* **into sth** seinen Kopf/Finger/einen Stock *etc* in etw *(acc)* stecken; **he ~d his head round the door/out of the window** er streckte seinen Kopf durch die Tür/aus dem Fenster

d *(vulg: = have sex with)* vögeln *(inf)*, ficken *(vulg)*

e *(= make by poking) hole* bohren; **to ~ holes in sb's story** jds Geschichte zerpflücken

VI **his elbows were poking through his sleeves** an seinen Ärmeln kamen schon die Ellenbogen durch; **to ~ at sth** *(testing)* etw prüfen; *(searching)* in etw *(dat)* stochern; **he ~d at me with his finger** *(touching)* er stupste mich; *(not touching)* er stieß mit dem Finger nach mir; **the doctor ~d at his ribs** der Arzt tastete seine Rippen ab; **she ~d at her food with a fork** sie stocherte mit einer Gabel in ihrem Essen herum; **well, if you will go poking into things that don't concern you …** na ja, wenn du deine Nase ständig in Dinge steckst, die dich nichts angehen …

▶ **poke about** *(Brit) or* **around** VI **a** *(= prod)* herumstochern **b** *(inf: = nose about)* stöbern, schnüffeln *(inf)* **c** *+prep obj (inf: = wander about)* (herum)bummeln; **we spent a pleasant day poking around the shops** wir haben einen netten Tag mit Geschäftebummeln verbracht

▶ **poke in** VT *sep* hineinstecken *or* -strecken; **he poked his head in through the window** er steckte *or* streckte seinen Kopf zum Fenster herein; **I'll just poke my head in and say hello** *(inf)* ich will nur schnell vorbeischauen und Guten *or* guten Tag sagen

▶ **poke out** **VI** vorstehen; **the tortoise had its head poking out of its shell** die Schildkröte hatte ihren Kopf aus dem Panzer gestreckt; **a handkerchief was poking out of his top pocket** ein Taschentuch schaute *or* guckte aus seiner Brusttasche hervor **VT** *sep* **a** *(= extend)* hinausstrecken **b** *(= remove by poking)* **he poked the dirt out with his fingers** er pulte *(inf) or* kratzte den Schmutz mit den Fingern heraus; **to poke sb's eye out** jdm ein Auge ausstechen

▶ **poke up** VT *sep fire* schüren; **he poked his finger up his nose** er bohrte mit dem Finger in der Nase

poke bonnet N Kiepenhut *m*, Schute *f*

poker[1] ['pəʊkə'] N *(for fire)* Schürhaken *m*, Feuerhaken *m*

poker[2] N *(Cards)* Poker *nt*

poker: **poker dice** N **a** *(= single dice)* Pokerwürfel *m*; *(= set of five)* Pokerwürfel *pl* **b** *no pl (= game)* Würfelpoker *nt or m*; **poker face** N Pokergesicht *nt*, Pokerface *nt*; **poker-faced** ADJ mit einem Pokergesicht *or* Pokerface; *(= bored)* mit unbewegter Miene; **pokerwork** N *(Brit)* Brandmalerei *f*

pokeweed ['pəʊkwi:d] N *(US)* Kermesbeere *f*

poky ['pəʊkɪ] ADJ *(+er) (pej) room, house* winzig; **it's so ~ in here** es ist so eng hier

pol [pɒl] N *(US inf: = politician)* Politiker(in) *m(f)*

Polack ['pəʊlæk] N *(pej)* Polack(e) *m (pej)*, Polackin *f (pej)*

Poland ['pəʊlənd] N Polen *nt*

polar ['pəʊlə'] ADJ **a** Polar-, polar; **~ expedition** Polarexpedition *f* **b** *(= opposite)* polar

polar bear N Polarbär *m*, Eisbär *m*

polar circle N Polarkreis *m*

polarity [pəʊ'lærɪtɪ] N *(Phys, fig)* Polarität *f*

polarization [,pəʊləraɪ'zeɪʃən] N *(Phys)* Polarisation *f*; *(fig)* Polarisierung *f*

polarize ['pəʊləraɪz] **VT** polarisieren **VI** sich polarisieren

Polaroid® ['pəʊlərɔɪd] N *(= camera)* Polaroidkamera® *f*, Sofortbildkamera *f*; *(= photograph)* Sofortbild *nt*

polder ['pəʊldə'] N Polder *m*

Pole [pəʊl] N Pole *m*, Polin *f*

pole[1] [pəʊl] **N** **a** Stange *f*; *(= flagpole, telegraph pole)* Mast *m*, Stange *f*; *(of cart)* Deichsel *f*; *(= ski-pole)* Stock *m*; *(for vaulting)* Stab *m*; *(for punting)* Stange *f*, Stake *f (spec)*; **to be up the ~** *(Brit inf)* eine Schraube locker haben *(inf)*; **to drive sb up the ~** *(inf)* jdn die Wände hochtreiben *(inf)*; **I wouldn't touch it/him with a ten-foot ~** *(US inf)* von so etwas/so jemandem lasse ich die Finger *(inf)*; *(because disgusting, unpleasant)* das/den würde ich noch nicht mal mit der Kneifzange anfassen *(inf)* **b** *(Measure: old)* Rute *f (old)* **VT** *punt* staken

pole[2] N *(Geog, Astron, Elec)* Pol *m*; **they are ~s apart** sie *(acc)* trennen Welten, Welten liegen zwischen ihnen; **at opposite ~s of sth** *(fig)* an entgegengesetzten Enden einer Sache *(gen)*

pole: **poleaxe**, *(US)* **poleax** **N** **a** *(Mil)* Streitaxt *f* **b** *(for slaughtering)* Schlachtbeil *nt* **VT** **a** *(Mil)* (mit der Streitaxt) niederschlagen *or* umhauen; *(fig)* verblüffen **b** *animal* (mit dem Schlachtbeil) töten; **polecat** N Iltis *m*; *(US)* Skunk *m*, Stinktier *nt*; **pole jump** N *(US)* = **pole vault**

polemic [pɒ'lemɪk] **ADJ** polemisch **N** Polemik *f*

polemical [pɒ'lemɪkəl] ADJ polemisch

polemicist [pɒ'lemɪsɪst] N Polemiker(in) *m(f)*

polemicize [pɒ'lemɪsaɪz] VI polemisieren *(against* gegen)

polemics [pɒ'lemɪks] N *sing* Polemik *f*

pole: **pole position** N **a** *(Motor Racing)* Poleposition *f*; **to be** *or* **start in ~** aus der Poleposition starten **b** *(fig)* günstige Ausgangsposition; **to be in ~** in einer günstigen Ausgangsposition sein; **pole star** N Polarstern *m*; **pole vault** **N** *(= event)* Stabhochsprung *m*; *(= one jump)* Sprung *m* mit dem Stab **VI** stabhochspringen; **pole-vaulter** N Stabhochspringer(in) *m(f)*; **pole-vaulting** N Stabhochspringen *nt*, Stabhochsprung *m*

police [pə'li:s] **N** *(+sing vb, = institution, +pl vb, = policemen)* Polizei *f*; **to join the ~** zur Polizei gehen; **he is in** *or* **a member of the ~** er ist bei der Polizei; **all ~ leave was cancelled** allen Polizisten wurde der Urlaub gesperrt; **hundreds of ~** hunderte *or* Hunderte von Polizisten; **extra ~ were called in** es wurden zusätzliche Polizeikräfte angefordert; **three ~ were injured** drei Polizeibeamte *or* Polizisten wurden verletzt

VT *road, frontier, territory* kontrollieren; *agreement, pop concert* überwachen, kontrollieren; **to ~ the peace** den Frieden überwachen; **a heavily ~d area** ein Gebiet *nt* mit hoher Polizeidichte

police: **police car** N Polizeiwagen *m*; **police constable** N *(Brit)* Polizist(in) *m(f)*, Wachtmeister(in) *m(f) (form)*; **police court** N ≈ Polizeigericht *nt*; **police dog** N Polizeihund *m*; **police escort** N Polizeieskorte *f*; **police force** N Polizei *f*; **one of the best-equipped ~s in the world** eine der bestausgestatteten Polizeitruppen der Welt; **police headquarters** N *sing or pl* Polizeipräsidium *nt*; **policeman** N Polizist *m*; **police message** N *(Rad)* Durchsage *f* der Polizei; **police officer** N Polizeibeamte(r) *mf*; **police presence** N Polizeiaufgebot *nt*; **police protection** N Polizeischutz *m*; **police record** N Vorstrafen *pl*; **to have a ~** vorbestraft sein; **police state** N Polizeistaat *m*; **police station** N (Polizei)wache *f or* -revier *nt*; **police supervision** N Polizeiaufsicht *f*; **policewoman** N Polizistin *f*; **police work** N Polizeiarbeit *f*; *(= investigation)* polizeiliche Nachforschungen *pl*

policing [pə'li:sɪŋ] N *(of road, frontier, territory)* Kontrolle *f*; *(of agreement, pop concert also)* Überwachung *f*; **new ~ policies for sports events** neue polizeiliche Richtlinien bei Sportveranstaltungen

policy[1] ['pɒlɪsɪ] N **a** Politik *f no pl*; *(of business)* Geschäfts- *or* Firmenpolitik *f (on* bei), Praktiken *pl (pej) (on* in Bezug auf *+acc)*; *(of team, football manager: = tactics)* Taktik *f*; *(= principle)* Grundsatz *m*; **social and economic ~** Wirtschafts- und Sozialpolitik *f*; **our ~ on immigration/recruitment** unsere Einwanderungs-/ /Einstellungspolitik; **what is company ~ on this matter?** wie sieht die Geschäfts- *or* Firmenpolitik in diesem Falle aus?; **the newspaper followed a ~ of attacking the church** die Zeitung verfolgte eine kirchenfeindliche Linie *or* Politik; **a ~ of restricting immigration** eine Politik zur Einschränkung der Einwanderung; **a matter of ~** eine Grundsatzfrage; **~ decision** Grundsatzentscheidung *f*; **~ statement** Grundsatzerklärung *f*; **your ~ should always be to give people a second chance** du solltest es dir zum Grundsatz machen, Menschen eine zweite Chance zu geben; **my ~ is to wait and see** meine Devise heißt abwarten; **it's our ~ to cater for the mid-twenties** wir wenden uns mit unserer Firmenpolitik an die Mittzwanziger; **our ~ is one of expansion** wir verfolgen eine expansionsorientierte Geschäftspolitik

b *(= prudence, a prudent procedure)* Taktik *f*; **~ demands that the government compromise** die Regierung muss aus taktischen Gründen Kompromisse eingehen; **it was good/bad ~** das war (taktisch) klug/unklug

policy[2] N *(also* **insurance policy**) (Versicherungs)police *f*, Versicherungsschein *m*; **to take out a ~** eine Versicherung abschließen

policy: **policy document** N Grundsatzpapier *nt*, Grundsatzprogramm *nt*; **policyholder** N Versicherungsnehmer(in) *m(f)*; **policy-maker** N Parteiideologe *m*/-ideologin *f*; **policy-making** **N** Treffen *nt* von Grundsatzentscheidungen **ADJ** *body, process, role* grundsatzpolitisch; **policy paper** N = **policy document**; **policy unit** N *(Brit Pol)* Richtlinienkommission *f*

polio ['pəʊlɪəʊ] N Polio *f*, Kinderlähmung *f*; **~ vaccine** Impfstoff *m* gegen Kinderlähmung; **~ victim** Opfer *nt* der Kinderlähmung, Polioopfer *nt*

poliomyelitis ['pəʊlɪəʊmaɪə'laɪtɪs] N *(form)* Poliomyelitis *f (spec)*, Kinderlähmung *f*

Polish ['pəʊlɪʃ] **ADJ** polnisch; **~ Corridor** Polnischer Korridor **N** *(Ling)* Polnisch *nt*

polish ['pɒlɪʃ] **N** **a** *(= material) (= shoe polish)* Creme *f*; *(= floor polish)* Bohnerwachs *nt*; *(= furniture polish)* Politur *f*; *(= metal polish)* Poliermittel *nt*; *(= nail polish)* Lack *m*

b *(= act)* **to give sth a ~** etw polieren; *shoes, silver also* etw putzen; *floor* etw bohnern; **my shoes need a ~** meine Schuhe müssen geputzt werden

c *(= polished state, shine)* Glanz *m*; *(of furniture)* Politur *f*; **high ~** Hochglanz *m*, starker Glanz; **there was a high ~ on the floor** der Fußboden war stark gebohnert; **to put a ~ on sth** etw zum Glänzen bringen, Glanz auf etw *(acc)* bringen; **water will take the ~ off** Wasser nimmt den Glanz/greift die Politur an

d *(fig: = refinement) (of person, style, manners)* Schliff *m*; *(of performance)* Brillanz *f*; **he lacks ~** ihm fehlt der Schliff/die Brillanz; **his style lacks ~** an seinem Stil muss noch gearbeitet werden

VT **a** *(lit)* polieren; *silver, shoes* putzen, polieren; *floor* bohnern

b *(fig) person, performance* den letzten Schliff geben *(+dat)*; *manner, style* polieren *(inf)*, verfeinern

▶ **polish off** VT *sep (inf) food* verdrücken *(inf)*, verputzen *(inf)*; *drink* wegputzen *(inf)*; *work* wegschaffen *(inf)*, erledigen; *opponent, competitor* abfertigen, abservieren *(inf)*

▶ **polish up** **VT** *sep* **a** *shoes, floor, silver etc* polieren, auf Hochglanz bringen **b** *(fig: = improve) style* aufpolieren, verfeinern; *work* überarbeiten; *one's French etc* aufpolieren *(inf)*; **you'd better polish up your ideas** *(inf)* du solltest dich besser auf den Hosenboden setzen *(inf)* **VI** sich polieren lassen

polished ['pɒlɪʃt] ADJ **a** *surface, furniture* poliert, glänzend; *ornaments* poliert; *floor* gebohnert; *stone, glass* geschliffen; **his highly ~ shoes**

seine blank geputzten Schuhe **b** *style etc* verfeinert; *performance, performer* brillant; *language* geschliffen; *image* makellos, sauber **c** *manners* geschliffen; *(= refined, suave) person* gewandt

polisher [ˈpɒlɪʃəʳ] N *(= person)* Schleifer(in) *m(f)*; *(= machine)* Schleif-/Polier-/Bohnermaschine *f*

politainmenmt [pɒlɪˈteɪnmənt] N *(US Film, TV)* *als Unterhaltung vermittelte politische Inhalte*, Politainment *nt*

polite [pəˈlaɪt] ADJ *(+er)* **a** höflich; **it wouldn't be ~** es wäre unhöflich; **to be ~ to sb** höflich zu jdm sein; **be ~ about her cooking** mach ein paar höfliche Bemerkungen über ihre Kochkunst; **when I said it was good I was just being ~** als ich sagte, es sei gut, wollte ich nur höflich sein; **there's no need to be ~ about it if you don't like it** du kannst es ruhig sagen, wenn es dir nicht gefällt; **~ conversation** höfliche Konversation; **we sat around making ~ conversation** wir saßen zusammen und machten Konversation **b** *society* fein

politely [pəˈlaɪtlɪ] ADV höflich

politeness [pəˈlaɪtnɪs] N Höflichkeit *f*

politic [ˈpɒlɪtɪk] ADJ **a** klug; **it would be ~ to apologize** es wäre (taktisch) klug, sich zu entschuldigen; **he tended to do what was ~ rather than that which was proper** er machte eher (das), was klug *or* günstig war, als das, was recht gewesen wäre **b** **the body ~** das Staatswesen, das staatliche Gemeinwesen

political [pəˈlɪtɪkəl] ADJ politisch; **~ action committee** *(US)* politische Aktionsgruppe

political: **political analyst** N politischer Analyst, politische Analystin; **political asylum** N politisches Asyl; **to ask for** *or* **seek ~** um politisches Asyl bitten *or* ersuchen, politisches Asyl beantragen; **he was granted/refused ~** ihm wurde politisches Asyl gewährt/nicht gewährt; **political commentator** N politischer Analytiker, politische Analytikerin; **political correctness** N politische Korrektheit; **our society's obsession with ~** die Besessenheit unserer Gesellschaft, politisch korrekt zu sein; **political economy** N Volkswirtschaft *f*; **political geography** N politische Geografie

politically [pəˈlɪtɪkəlɪ] ADV *aware, expedient* politisch; **~ speaking** im politischen Sinne

politically correct ADJ politisch korrekt

> **POLITICALLY CORRECT**
>
> Die Woge der politischen Korrektheit entstand wie so vieles andere in den Vereinigten Staaten und hat sich mittlerweile auf der ganzen Welt ausgebreitet. Ursprünglich wollte man vermeiden, dass über ethnische Minderheiten, Frauen, Behinderte, Homosexuelle und benachteiligte Bevölkerungsgruppen in Worten gesprochen wird, die sie herabsetzen oder beleidigen. Wer überzeugt **politically correct**, oder auch kurz **PC**, ist, hält sich für den Verfechter einer Weltanschauung, in der all die Werte infrage gestellt werden, die die westliche Gesellschaft im Laufe der Jahrhunderte dem Rest der Welt aufgezwungen hat. Heute wird der Ausdruck **politically correct** überwiegend als Schimpfwort von den Gegnern dieser „liberalen" Ansichten gebraucht. Hier einige Beispiele für politisch korrekte Ausdrucksweise: **Native American** statt **Red Indian**, **visually impaired** statt **blind** und **vertically challenged** statt **short**.

politically incorrect ADJ politisch inkorrekt *or* nicht korrekt

political: **political party** N politische Partei; **political prisoner** N politischer Gefangener, politische Gefangene; **political science** N Politologie *f*; **political scientist** N Politologe *m*, Politologin *f*, Politikwissenschaftler(in) *m(f)*

politician [ˌpɒlɪˈtɪʃən] N Politiker(in) *m(f)*

politicization [pəˌlɪtɪsaɪˈzeɪʃən] N Politisierung *f*

politicize [pəˈlɪtɪsaɪz] VT politisieren

politick [ˈpɒlɪtɪk] *(usu pej)* **VI** politisieren, sich politisch betätigen **VT** **to ~ a bill through parliament** durch seinen politischen Einsatz erreichen, dass ein Gesetz im Parlament verabschiedet wird

politicking [pəˈlɪtɪkɪŋ] N *(pej)* politische Aktivitäten *pl*

politico [pəˈlɪtɪkəʊ] N *(esp US pej)* Politiker(in) *m(f)*

politico- PREF politisch-; **~military** politisch-militärisch

politics [ˈpɒlɪtɪks] N **a** *(+pl vb) (Pol)* Politik *f*; *(= views)* politische Ansichten *pl*; **what are his ~?** welche politischen Ansichten hat er? **b** *(+sing or pl vb) (= political affairs, idea)* Politik *f*; **to be in ~** in der Politik sein; **to go into ~** in die Politik gehen; **to talk ~** über Politik *(acc)* reden; **to study ~** Politik studieren; **interested in ~** politisch interessiert; **to play ~** *(pej)* große Politik spielen *(pej)*; **office ~** Bürorangeleien *pl*; **sexual ~** Rangeleien *pl* zwischen den Geschlechtern

polity [ˈpɒlɪtɪ] N *(= form of government)* politische Ordnung, Staats- *or* Regierungsform *f*; *(= politically organized society)* Staat(swesen *nt*) *m*, Gemeinwesen *nt*; *(= management of public affairs)* Staatsverwaltung *f*

polka [ˈpɒlkə] N Polka *f*

polka dot **N** Tupfen *m* **ADJ** getupft, gepunktet

poll [pəʊl] **N** **a** *(Pol) (= voting)* Abstimmung *f*; *(= election)* Wahl *f*; **a ~ was taken among the villagers** unter den Dorfbewohnern wurde abgestimmt; **to head the ~** bei der Wahl führen; **~ of ~s** ≈ Politbarometer *nt*
b *(= total of votes cast)* Wahlbeteiligung *f*; *(for individual candidate)* Stimmenanteil *m*; **there was an 84% ~** die Wahlbeteiligung betrug 84%; **they got 34% of the ~** sie bekamen 34% der Stimmen
c **~s** *(= voting place)* Wahllokale *pl*; *(= election)* Wahl *f*; **to go to the ~s** wählen gehen, zur Wahl gehen; **a crushing defeat at the ~s** eine vernichtende Niederlage bei den Wahlen, eine vernichtende Wahlniederlage; **a photograph of X at the ~s** ein Foto von X bei der Stimmabgabe
d *(= opinion poll)* Umfrage *f*; **a telephone ~** eine telefonische Abstimmung; **to take a ~ (of 3,000 people)** (3000 Personen) abstimmen lassen
e *(old: = head, esp back of head)* Schädel *m*
VT **a** *votes* erhalten, auf sich *(acc)* vereinigen
b *(in opinion poll)* befragen; **40% of those ~ed supported the Government** 40% der Befragten waren für die Regierung
c *horns, trees* stutzen; **~ed cattle** Rinder mit gestutzten Hörnern
d *(Comput, Internet)* pollen
VI **a** **he ~ed badly (in the election)** er erhielt bei der Wahl wenige Stimmen, er schnitt bei der Wahl schlecht ab; **the nationalists ~ed well** die Nationalisten erhielten bei der Wahl viele Stimmen, die Nationalisten schnitten bei der Wahl gut ab
b *(Comput, Internet)* pollen

pollard [ˈpɒləd] **N** *(= tree)* gekappter Baum **VT** kappen

pollee [pəʊˈliː] N *(esp US, at opinion poll)* Befragte(r) *mf*

pollen [ˈpɒlən] N Blütenstaub *m*, Pollen *m*

pollen basket N Höschen *nt*, Hose *f*

pollen count N Pollenwerte *pl*, Pollenzahl *f*; **a high ~** starker Pollenflug

pollinate [ˈpɒlɪneɪt] VT bestäuben

pollination [ˌpɒlɪˈneɪʃən] N Bestäubung *f*

pollinator [ˈpɒlɪneɪtəʳ] N *(Zool)* Bestäuber *m*

polling [ˈpəʊlɪŋ] N **a** Stimmabgabe *f*, Wahl *f*; **~ will be on Thursday** die Wahl ist am Donnerstag; **~ has been heavy** die Wahlbeteiligung war (sehr) hoch *or* stark; **the ~ was extremely low** die Wahlbeteiligung war äußerst gering **b** *(Comput, Internet)* Polling *nt*

polling: **polling booth** N Wahlkabine *f*, Wahlzelle *f*; **polling card** N Wahlausweis *m*; **polling day** N *(esp Brit)* Wahltag *m*; **polling station** N *(Brit)* Wahllokal *nt*

polliwog [ˈpɒlɪwɒg] N *(US)* Kaulquappe *f*

pollster [ˈpəʊlstəʳ] N Meinungsforscher(in) *m(f)*

poll tax N Kopfsteuer *f*

pollutant [pəˈluːtənt] N Schadstoff *m*

pollute [pəˈluːt] VT *environment* verschmutzen; *river, atmosphere etc also* verunreinigen; *atmosphere also* verpesten *(pej)*; *(fig) mind, morals* verderben, korrumpieren

polluter [pəˈluːtəʳ] N Umweltverschmutzer(in) *m(f)*; **the pulluter pays principle** das Verursacherprinzip

pollution [pəˈluːʃən] N *(of environment)* Umweltverschmutzung *f*, Verschmutzung *f*; *(of atmosphere)* Verunreinigung *f*; *(of rivers)* Verunreinigung *f*, Verpestung *f (pej)*; *(fig)* Korrumpierung *f*; **the fight against ~** der Kampf gegen die Umweltverschmutzung; **~ level** Grad *m* der Umweltverschmutzung; *(of air, water)* Schadstoffbelastung *f*

poll watcher N Wahlbeobachter(in) *m(f)*

polly [ˈpɒlɪ] N **a** *(inf: = parrot)* zahmer Papagei **b** *(Austral inf: = politician)* Politiker(in) *m(f)*

pollywog N = **polliwog**

polo [ˈpəʊləʊ] N Polo *nt*

polonaise [ˌpɒləˈneɪz] N Polonaise *f*, Polonäse *f*

polo neck *(Brit)* **N** Rollkragen *m*; *(= sweater)* Rollkragenpullover *m* **ADJ** Rollkragen-; **~ sweater** Rollkragenpullover *m*

polonium [pəˈləʊnɪəm] N *(Chem)* Polonium *nt*

poltergeist [ˈpɒltəgaɪst] N Poltergeist *m*, Klopfgeist *m*

poltroon [pɒlˈtruːn] N *(liter)* feiger Wicht, Memme *f*

poly [ˈpɒlɪ] **a** *(Brit) abbr of* **polytechnic** **b** *abbr of* **polythene**; **~ bag** Plastetüte *f*, Plastiktüte *f*

polyandrous [ˌpɒlɪˈændrəs] ADJ Vielmännerei betreibend, polyandrisch *(spec)*; *(Bot)* polyadelphisch

polyandry [ˈpɒlɪændrɪ] N Vielmännerei *f*, Polyandrie *f (form)*

polyanthus [ˌpɒlɪˈænθəs] N *(= primrose)* Gartenprimel *f*; *(= narcissus)* Tazette *f*

polychromatic [ˌpɒlɪkrəʊˈmætɪk] ADJ polychrom

polyclinic [ˈpɒlɪklɪnɪk] N Poliklinik *f*

polyester [ˌpɒlɪˈestəʳ] N Polyester *m*

polyethylene [ˌpɒlɪˈeθəliːn] N Polyäthylen *nt*

polygamist [pɒˈlɪgəmɪst] N Polygamist(in) *m(f)*

polygamous [pɒˈlɪgəməs] ADJ polygam

polygamy [pɒˈlɪgəmɪ] N Polygamie *f*, Vielehe *f*, Vielweiberei *f*

polyglot [ˈpɒlɪglɒt] **ADJ** polyglott, vielsprachig **N** *(= person)* Polyglotte(r) *mf*

polygon [ˈpɒlɪgən] N Polygon *nt*, Vieleck *nt*

polygonal [pɒˈlɪgənl] ADJ polygonal, vieleckig

polygraph [ˈpɒlɪgrɑːf] N *(US: = lie detector)* Lügendetektor *m*

polyhedron [ˌpɒlɪˈhiːdrən] N Polyeder *nt*, Vielflächner *m*

polymath [ˈpɒlɪmæθ] N Mensch *m* mit vielseitigem Wissen

polymer [ˈpɒlɪməʳ] N Polymer *nt*

polymeric [ˌpɒlɪˈmerɪk] ADJ polymer

polymerization [ˌpɒlɪməraɪˈzeɪʃən] N Polymerisation *f*

polymorphic [ˌpɒlɪˈmɔːfɪk] ADJ polymorph, vielgestaltig

polymorphism [ˌpɒlɪˈmɔːfɪzəm] N Polymorphismus *m*

Polynesia [ˌpɒlɪˈniːzɪə] N Polynesien *nt*

Polynesian [ˌpɒlɪˈniːzɪən] **ADJ** polynesisch **N** **a** Polynesier(in) *m(f)* **b** *(Ling)* Polynesisch *nt*

polynomial [ˌpɒlɪˈnəʊmɪəl] ADJ polynomisch N Polynom *nt*

polyp [ˈpɒlɪp] N Polyp *m*

polyphonic [ˌpɒlɪˈfɒnɪk] ADJ *(Mus)* polyfon

polyphonist [pəˈlɪfənɪst] N *(Mus)* Polyfoniker(in) *m(f)*, Kontrapunktiker(in) *m(f)*

polyphony [pəˈlɪfənɪ] N *(Mus)* Polyfonie *f*

polypropylene [ˌpɒlɪˈprɒpɪliːn] N Polypropylen *nt*

polypus [ˈpɒlɪpəs] N Polyp *m*

polysemous [pɒˈlɪsəməs] ADJ polysem

polystyrene [ˌpɒlɪˈstaɪriːn] N Polystyrol *nt*; *(extended also)* Styropor® *nt* ADJ Polystyrol-/Styropor-; **~ cup** Styroporbecher *m*

polysyllabic [ˌpɒlɪsɪˈlæbɪk] ADJ viel- *or* mehrsilbig

polysyllable [ˈpɒlɪˌsɪləbl] N Polysyllabum *nt (spec)*, vielsilbiges Wort

polytechnic [ˌpɒlɪˈteknɪk] N *(Brit)* ≈ Polytechnikum *nt*; *(degree-awarding)* technische Hochschule, TH *f*

polytheism [ˈpɒlɪθiːɪzəm] N Polytheismus *m*

polytheistic [ˌpɒlɪθiːˈɪstɪk] ADJ polytheistisch

polythene [ˈpɒlɪθiːn] N *(Brit)* Polyäthylen *nt*; *(in everyday language)* Plastik *nt*; **~ bag** Plastiktüte *f*

polyunsaturated fats [ˌpɒlɪʌnˈsætʃəreɪtɪdˈfæts], **polyunsaturates** [ˌpɒlɪʌnˈsætʃʊrɪts] PL mehrfach ungesättigte Fettsäuren *pl*

polyurethane [ˌpɒlɪˈjʊərɪθeɪn] N Polyurethan *nt*

polyvalent [pəˈlɪvələnt] ADJ mehrwertig, polyvalent

pom¹ [pɒm] N *(Austral inf)* Engländer(in) *m(f)*, Tommy *m (dated inf)*

pom² N *(inf)* = **Pomeranian N b**

pomade [pəˈmɑːd] N Pomade *f* VT mit Pomade einreiben

pomander [pəʊˈmændəʳ] N Duftkugel *f*

pomegranate [ˈpɒməˌgrænɪt] N Granatapfel *m*; *(= tree)* Granatapfelbaum *m*, Granatbaum *m*

pomelo [ˈpɒmɪləʊ] N *(esp US)* Grapefruit *f*, Pampelmuse *f*

Pomerania [ˌpɒməˈreɪnɪə] N Pommern *nt*

Pomeranian [ˌpɒməˈreɪnɪən] ADJ pommer(i)sch N a Pommer(in) *m(f)* b *(= dog)* Spitz *m*

pommel [ˈpʌml] N *(on sword)* Knauf *m*; *(on saddle)* Knopf *m* VT = **pummel**

pommy [ˈpɒmɪ] N *(Austral inf)* Engländer(in) *m(f)*, Tommy *m (dated inf)*; **~ bastard** Scheißengländer *m (inf)*

pomp [pɒmp] N Pomp *m*, Prunk *m*, Gepränge *nt*; **~ and circumstance** Pomp und Prunk *m*

pompadour [ˈpɒmpədʊəʳ] N *(Hist)* Pompadourfrisur *f*

Pompeian [pɒmˈpeɪən] ADJ pompej(an)isch N Pompej(an)er(in) *m(f)*

Pompeii [pɒmˈpeɪiː] N Pompe(j)i *nt*

Pompey [ˈpɒmpɪ] N Pompejus *m*

pompom [ˈpɒmpɒm] N a *(= gun)* automatische Flugzeugabwehrkanone b *(on hat etc)* Troddel *f*, Bommel *f (dial)*

pomposity [pɒmˈpɒsɪtɪ] N *(of person)* Aufgeblasenheit *f*, Wichtigtuerei *f*; *(of attitude, behaviour also, phrase)* Gespreiztheit *f*; *(of language, letter, remark)* Schwülstigkeit *f*, Bombast *m*

pompous [ˈpɒmpəs] ADJ a *person* aufgeblasen, wichtigtuerisch; *attitude, behaviour also, phrase* gespreizt; *language, letter, remark* schwülstig, bombastisch; **don't be so ~** tu nicht so aufgeblasen, sei nicht so wichtigtuerisch b *(= magnificent) building* grandios, bombastisch; *occasion* grandios

pompously [ˈpɒmpəslɪ] ADV *write, speak* schwülstig, bombastisch; *behave* aufgeblasen, wichtigtuerisch

'pon [pɒn] PREP *(old, poet) contr of* **upon**

ponce [pɒns] *(Brit inf)* N *(= pimp)* Loddel *m (inf)*, Lude *m (sl)*; *(pej: = homosexual)* Tunte *f (inf)* VI **to ~ for sb** jds Zuhälter sein

▶ **ponce about** *or* **around** VI *(Brit inf)* herumtänzeln

poncho [ˈpɒntʃəʊ] N Poncho *m*

poncy [ˈpɒnsɪ] ADJ (+er) *(Brit inf)* a *(= flashy)* eingebildet b *(pej: = homosexual)* schwul *(inf)*; *(= affected) walk, actor* tuntig *(inf)*

pond [pɒnd] N Teich *m*; **the ~** *(inf: = Atlantic)* der große Teich *(hum)*; **~ life** Pflanzen- und Tierleben in Teichen

ponder [ˈpɒndəʳ] VT nachdenken über (+acc); *possibilities, consequences etc* erwägen, bedenken VI nachdenken *(on, over* über +acc)

pondering ADJ, **ponderingly** ADV [ˈpɒndərɪŋ, -lɪ] nachdenklich, grüblerisch

ponderous [ˈpɒndərəs] ADJ a *(= laboured, clumsy) person, movement, steps* schwerfällig; *(= heavy)* massiv b *(= too serious) book* gewichtig; *joke* schwerfällig

ponderously [ˈpɒndərəslɪ] ADV schwerfällig; *(= seriously) formal* gewichtig, gravitätisch

ponderousness [ˈpɒndərəsnɪs] N Schwerfälligkeit *f*; *(= heaviness)* Schwere *f*, Gewichtigkeit *f*

pondweed [ˈpɒndwiːd] N Laichkrautgewächs *nt*

pone [pəʊn] N *(US)* Maisbrot *nt*

pong [pɒŋ] *(Brit inf)* N Gestank *m*, Mief *m (inf)*; **there's a bit of a ~ in here** hier stinkts *or* miefts *(inf)* VI stinken, miefen *(inf)*

poniard [ˈpɒnjəd] N *(liter, old)* Dolch *m*

pontiff [ˈpɒntɪf] N Pontifex *m*; *(= pope also)* Papst *m*

pontifical [pɒnˈtɪfɪkəl] ADJ a *(lit)* pontifikal; *(= papal)* päpstlich; **~ robes** Pontifikalien *pl*; *(of pope)* päpstliche Gewänder *pl*; **~ duties** Pontifikalien *pl*; *(of pope)* päpstliche Pflichten *pl*; **~ office** Pontifikat *nt* b *(fig)* päpstlich

pontifically [pɒnˈtɪfɪkəlɪ] ADV *(fig)* päpstlich

Pontifical Mass N Pontifikalamt *nt*

pontificate N [pɒnˈtɪfɪkɪt] Pontifikat *nt* VI [pɒnˈtɪfɪkeɪt] *(fig)* dozieren; **I wish you wouldn't ~ to me** ich wünschte, du würdest nicht in diesem belehrenden Ton mit mir reden

Pontius Pilate [ˈpɒnʃəsˈpaɪlət] N Pontius Pilatus *m*

pontoon¹ [pɒnˈtuːn] N Ponton *m*; **~ bridge** Pontonbrücke *f*

pontoon² N *(Brit Cards)* 17 und 4 *nt*

pony [ˈpəʊnɪ] N a Pony *nt* b *(Brit sl)* 25 Pfund c *(US sl: = crib)* Spickzettel *m* d *(US inf: = small glass)* Gläschen *nt*

pony: **pony express** N Ponyexpress *m*; **ponytail** N Pferdeschwanz *m*; **she was wearing her hair in a ~** sie trug einen Pferdeschwanz; **pony trekking** N Ponyreiten *nt*; **a ~ holiday** ein Ponyreiturlaub *m*

poo [puː] N VI *(baby-talk)* = **pooh N VI**

pooch [puːtʃ] N *(inf)* Hündchen *nt*

poodle [ˈpuːdl] N Pudel *m*

poof [pʊf] N *(dated Brit pej inf)* Warme(r) *m (dated inf)*, Schwule(r) *m (inf)*

poof juice N *(Brit sl: = sweet drink)* Schwulensaft *m (sl)*

poofter [ˈpʊftəʳ] N = **poof**

poofy [ˈpʊfɪ] ADJ (+er) *(Brit pej inf)* schwul *(inf)*; *clothes, colour, actor* tuntig *(inf)*, tuntenhaft *(inf)*

pooh [puː] INTERJ *(bad smell)* puh, pfui; *(disdain)* pah, bah N *(baby-talk)* Aa *nt (baby-talk)*; **to do a ~** Aa machen *(baby-talk)* VI *(baby-talk)* Aa machen *(baby-talk)*

pooh-pooh [ˈpuːˈpuː] VT verächtlich abtun

pool¹ [puːl] N a Teich *m*, Tümpel *m*; *(underground)* See *m*
b *(of rain)* Pfütze *f*; *(of spilled liquid)* Lache *f*; **a ~ of blood** eine Blutlache; **~s of sunlight/shade** sonnige/schattige Stellen
c *(in river)* Loch *nt*
d *(artificial)* Teich *m*; *(= swimming pool)* (Schwimm)becken *nt*; *(in private garden, hotel)* Swimmingpool *m*, Schwimmbecken *nt*; *(= swimming baths)* Schwimmbad *nt*; **to go to the (swimming) ~** ins Schwimmbad gehen; **an Olympic ~ should measure ...** ein olympisches Wettkampfbecken muss ... groß sein; **in the kiddies' ~** im Kinderbecken; **we spent every afternoon down at the ~** wir verbrachten jeden Nachmittag im Schwimmbad; **she was sitting at the edge of the ~** sie saß am Beckenrand

pool² N a *(= common fund)* (gemeinsame) Kasse; **each player put £10 in the ~** jeder Spieler gab £10 in die Kasse; **the ~ stood at £40** es waren £ 40 in der Kasse
b *(= supply, source) (= typing pool)* Schreibzentrale *f*; *(= car pool)* Fahrbereitschaft *f*; *(= car-sharing)* Fahrgemeinschaft *f*; **a ~ of labour** *(Brit)* *or* **labor** *(US)* ein Bestand *m* an Arbeitskräften, eine Arbeitskraftreserve; **the Prime Minister's ~ of advisers** der Beraterstab des Premierministers; **among them they have a great ~ of experience/ideas** zusammen verfügen sie über eine Menge Erfahrung/Ideen
c **pools** PL *(Brit)* **the ~s** *(= football pools)* Toto *m or nt*; **to do the ~s** Toto spielen; **to win the ~s** im Toto gewinnen; **he won £1000 on the ~s** er hat £ 1000 im Toto gewonnen
d *(= form of snooker)* Poolbillard *nt*
e *(Comm)* Interessengemeinschaft *f*; *(US: = monopoly, trust)* Pool *m*, Kartell *nt*
VT *resources, savings* zusammenlegen; *efforts* vereinen *(geh)*; **if we ~ our efforts we'll get the work done sooner** mit vereinten Kräften werden wir schneller mit der Arbeit fertig (werden)

pool: **pool attendant** N Bademeister(in) *m(f)*; **pool hall** N Billardzimmer *nt*; **pool room** N a *(= pool hall)* Billardzimmer *nt* b *(= betting shop)* Wettannahmestelle *f*

pools coupon N *(for football pools)* Tippschein *m*

pool table N Billardtisch *m*

poop¹ [puːp] N Hütte *f*, Poop *f*

poop² VT *(inf: = exhaust)* schlauchen *(inf)*; **to be ~ed (out)** geschlaucht *or* fertig sein *(inf)*

poop³ N *(US inf, pej)* Trottel *m (pej)*, Einfaltspinsel *f (pej)*

poop⁴ VI *(inf: = defecate)* ein großes Geschäft machen *(inf)*, Aa machen *(baby-talk)*

poop deck N Hütten- *or* Poopdeck *nt*

poo-poo [ˈpuːˈpuː] N *(baby-talk: = excreta)* Aa *nt (baby-talk)*

poor [pʊəʳ] ADJ (+er) a arm; **to get** *or* **become ~er** ärmer werden, verarmen; **he was now one thousand pounds (the) ~er** er war nun um eintausend Pfund ärmer; **a ~ little rich girl** ein armes reiches Mädchen; **~ whites** *arme weiße Bevölkerung im Süden der USA*; **a country ~ in natural resources** ein an Bodenschätzen armes Land; **to be ~ in nutrients** arm an Nährstoffen sein; **it's the ~ man's Mercedes/Monte Carlo** *(inf)* das ist der Mercedes/das Monte Carlo des kleinen Mannes *(inf)*; **~ relation** *(fig)* Sorgenkind *nt*
b *(= not good)* schlecht; *(= meagre)* mangelhaft; *health, effort, performance, excuse* schlecht, schwach; *sense of responsibility, leadership* schwach; *soil* mager, schlecht; *quality* schlecht, minderwertig; **a ~ joke** *(= weak)* ein schwacher Witz; *(= in bad taste)* ein geschmackloser Witz; **to show sb/sth in a ~ light** jdn/etw in einem schlechten Licht darstellen; **to get** *or* **become ~er** *(eyesight, hearing, weather)* schlechter werden, sich verschlechtern; **she was a very ~ swimmer** sie war ein sehr schlechter Schwimmer; **he is a ~ traveller/flier** er verträgt Reisen/Flugreisen nicht gut; **a ~ friend you are!** du bist mir ein schöner Freund!; **fruit wines are a ~ substitute for grape wine** Obstwein ist nur ein armseliger Ersatz für Wein aus Trauben; **a ~ imitation of sth** eine schlechte *or* minderwertige Nachahmung von etw; **a ~ chance of success** schlechte Erfolgsaussichten *pl*; **we had a ~ time of it last night** gestern Abend lief auch alles schief *(inf)*; **only £55? that's pretty ~, isn't it?** nur £ 55? das ist aber ziemlich wenig!; **that's ~ consolation** das ist ein schwacher Trost; **it's a ~ thing for Britain if ...** es ist schlecht für Großbritannien, wenn ...; **it will**

be a ~ day for the world when … es wird ein schwarzer Tag für die Welt sein, wenn …; **this is a pretty ~ state of affairs** das sieht aber gar nicht gut aus; **it's very ~ of them not to have replied** es ist sehr unhöflich, dass sie uns *etc (dat)* nicht geantwortet haben; **he has a very ~ grasp of the subject** er beherrscht das Fach sehr schlecht; **he showed a ~ grasp of the facts** er zeigte wenig Verständnis für die Fakten; **he is a ~ hand at public speaking** in der Öffentlichkeit zu sprechen liegt ihm nicht; **she was always ~ at languages** sie war immer schlecht *or* schwach in Sprachen; **hospitals are ~ at collecting information** Krankenhäuser sind schlecht im Sammeln von Informationen
c *(= pitiful, pitiable)* arm; **you ~ (old) chap** *(inf)* du armer Kerl *(inf)*; **~ you!** du Ärmste(r)!; **she's all alone, ~ woman** sie ist ganz allein, die arme Frau; **~ things, they look cold** die Ärmsten, ihnen scheint kalt zu sein; **~ miserable creature that he is …** armseliger Kerl *or* Tropf *(inf)*, der er ist …; **in my ~ opinion** *(iro)* meiner bescheidenen *or* unmaßgeblichen Meinung nach *(iro)*; **it fell to my ~ self to …** es blieb meiner Wenigkeit *(dat)* überlassen, zu … *(iro)*
PL the ~ die Armen *pl*

poor: poor box N Armen- *or* Almosenbüchse *f*; **poorhouse** N *(old)* Armenhaus *nt (old)*; **poor laws** PL Armengesetze *pl*

poorly ['pʊəlɪ] **ADV a** arm; *dressed, furnished* ärmlich; **~ off** schlecht gestellt; **her husband left her very ~ off** ihr Mann ließ sie in sehr ärmlichen Verhältnissen zurück
b *(= badly)* schlecht; *(= inadequately) supported, understood* schlecht, unzureichend; **~-attended** schlecht besucht; **~-designed** schlecht konstruiert, nicht genügend durchdacht; **~-educated** ohne (ausreichende) Schulbildung; **~-equipped** schlecht ausgerüstet; **~-lit** schlecht *or* schwach beleuchtet; **~-paid** schlecht bezahlt; **~-trained** schlecht ausgebildet, ungeschult; **~-ventilated** schlecht gelüftet; **to do ~ (at sth)** (in etw *dat*) schwach *or* schlecht abschneiden; **we're rather ~ off for staff/new ideas** wir haben einen ziemlichen Mangel an Personal/neuen Ideen
ADJ *pred (Brit: = ill)* schlecht, krank, elend; **to be** *or* **feel ~** sich schlecht *etc* fühlen

poorness ['pʊənɪs] N **a** *(= lack of money)* Armut *f* **b** *(= lack of quality)* Dürftigkeit *f*, Mangelhaftigkeit *f*; *(of soil)* Magerkeit *f*, Unergiebigkeit *f*; *(of effort, excuse, harvest, performance)* Dürftigkeit *f*; *(of quality)* Minderwertigkeit *f*; *(of weather, memory, health, eyesight)* Unzulänglichkeit *f*; *(of leadership)* Schwäche *f*

poor-spirited ['pʊə'spɪrɪtɪd] ADJ *person* ängstlich

poor white trash N *(US inf, pej)* weißer Pöbel

poove [pu:v] N = **poof(ter)**

POP, PoP [pɔp] *(Telec, Internet) abbr of* **point of presence** Einwahlknoten *m*

pop¹ [pɒp] N *(esp US inf) (= father)* Papa *m (inf)*; *(= elderly man)* Opa *m (hum inf)*

pop² N *(= pop music)* Popmusik *f*, Pop *m*

pop³ **N a** *(= sound)* Knall *m*; **the toy gun went off with a ~** peng, ging die Spielzeugpistole los; **the faint ~ of a stud unfastening** das leise „Popp" eines aufspringenden Druckknopfs
b *(inf: = shot)* Schuss *m*; **to have** *or* **take a ~ at sb/sth** auf jdn/etw *(acc)* ballern *(inf)*; *(= criticize)* einen Seitenhieb gegen jdn/etw führen, auf jdn/etw losgehen; **to have** *or* **take a ~ at sth** *(fig: = try)* einen Versuch wagen mit etw, sich an etw versuchen
c *(= fizzy drink)* Brause *f*, Limo *f (inf)*
d *(dated inf: = pawn)* **in ~** verpfändet, versetzt
e *(inf: = each)* **the drinks go for £3.50 a ~** jedes Getränk kostet £ 3,50
ADV to go ~ *(cork)* knallen, hochgehen *(inf)*; *(balloon)* platzen; *(ears)* mit einem Knacken aufgehen *or (when going down)* zugehen; **~!** peng!
VT a *balloon, corn* zum Platzen bringen; **to ~ corn** Popcorn machen
b *(inf: = put)* stecken; **to ~ a letter into the postbox** *(Brit) or* **mailbox** *(US)* einen Brief einwerfen *or* einschmeißen *(inf)*; **he ~ped his head round the door** er streckte den Kopf durch die Tür; **to ~ a jacket/hat on** sich *(dat)* ein Jackett überziehen/einen Hut aufsetzen; **to ~ one's clogs** *(Brit hum inf)* das Zeitliche segnen *(inf)*; **to ~ the question** einen (Heirats)antrag machen; **to ~ one's cork** *(inf)* sich begeistern
c *(dated inf: = pawn)* versetzen
d *(inf) pills* schlucken *(inf)*
VI a *(inf)* **a** *(= go pop, burst) (cork)* knallen; *(balloon)* platzen; *(seed pods, buttons, popcorn)* aufplatzen; *(ears)* knacken; **his eyes were ~ping out of his head** ihm gingen die Augen über, ihm fielen fast die Augen aus dem Kopf *(inf)*; **suddenly her blouse ~ped open** plötzlich platzte *or* sprang ihre Bluse auf
b *(= go quickly or suddenly)* **to ~ along/down to the baker's** schnell zum Bäcker laufen; **I'll just ~ upstairs** ich laufe mal eben nach oben; **~ across/over/round and see me sometime** komm doch mal auf einen Sprung bei mir vorbei *(inf)*; **I thought I'd just ~ down to London for the weekend** ich dachte, ich fahr mal eben übers Wochenende nach London

▶ **pop at** VI +*prep obj (inf: = shoot at)* ballern auf *(+acc) (inf)*

▶ **pop back** *(inf)* **VT** *sep* (schnell) zurücktun *(inf)*; **pop the lid back on the box** klapp den Deckel wieder auf die Schachtel; **pop it back in(to) the box** tu es wieder in die Schachtel **VI** schnell zurücklaufen; **she popped back for her book** sie lief zurück, um ihr Buch zu holen

▶ **pop in** *(inf)* **VT** *sep* hineintun; **to pop sth in (-to) sth** etw in etw *(acc)* stecken *or* werfen *(inf)* **VI** *(= visit)* auf einen Sprung vorbeikommen *(inf)*; **to pop in for a short chat** auf einen kleinen Schwatz hereinschauen *(inf)*; **she kept popping in and out** sie lief dauernd rein und raus; **we just popped into the pub for a quickie** wir gingen kurz in die Kneipe, um einen zu heben *(inf)*; **just pop in any time you're passing** komm doch mal vorbei, wenn du in der Gegend bist *(inf)*

▶ **pop off** VI *(Brit inf)* **a** *(= die suddenly)* den Löffel abgeben *(sl)* **b** *(= go off)* verschwinden *(inf)* (*to* nach); **do you fancy popping off to Spain for a week?** wie wärs, wollen wir für eine Woche nach Spanien verschwinden?

▶ **pop out** VI *(inf)* **a** *(= go out)* (schnell) rausgehen *(inf)*; *(spring, rabbit)* herausspringen (*of* aus); **he has just popped out for a beer** er ist schnell auf ein Bierchen gegangen *(inf)*; **he has just popped out to buy a paper/to the shops** er ist schnell eine Zeitung kaufen gegangen/zum Einkaufen gegangen **b** *(eyes)* vorquellen; **his eyes were popping out (with amazement)** vor Staunen fielen ihm fast die Augen aus dem Kopf *(inf)*

▶ **pop up** *(inf)* **VT** *sep* **a** *(= put up) head* hochstrecken **b** *(= bring up)* schnell raufbringen *(inf)* **VI a** *(= appear suddenly)* auftauchen; *(head, toast)* hochschießen *(inf)*; *(figures in illustrations)* sich aufstellen **b** *(= come up)* (mal eben) raufkommen *(inf)*; *(= go up)* (mal eben) raufgehen *(inf)*; **do you feel like popping up to my place?** hast du Lust, mal eben zu mir raufzukommen? *(inf)* **c** *(Comput, window, menu)* aufpoppen *(inf)*, sich öffnen

pop⁴ *abbr of* **population**

pop: pop art N Pop-Art *f*; **pop concert** N Popkonzert *nt*; **popcorn** N Popcorn *nt*

Pope [pəʊp] N Papst *m*

Popemobile, popemobile ['pəʊpməʊˌbi:l] N *(inf)* Papamobil *nt (inf)*

popery ['pəʊpərɪ] N *(pej)* Pfaffentum *nt*; **no ~!** Pfaffen raus!

pop: popeyed ADJ *person* glotzäugig; *(fig)* mit Glotzaugen; **pop festival** N Popfestival *nt*; **pop group** N Popgruppe *f*; **popgun** N Spielzeugpistole *f*; **pop icon** N Popikone *f*, Popidol *nt*

popinjay ['pɒpɪndʒeɪ] N *(old)* Geck *m*, Laffe *m*

popish ['pəʊpɪʃ] ADJ *(pej)* papistisch

poplar ['pɒplə'] N Pappel *f*

poplin ['pɒplɪn] N Popeline *f*; **~ dress** Popelinekleid *nt*

pop: pop music N Popmusik *f*; **popover** N *(US) stark aufgehender hefiger Eierkuchen*

poppa ['pɒpə] N *(US inf)* Papa *m (inf)*

poppadom, poppadum ['pɒpədəm] N *großes, dünnes, rundes, knusprig gebratenes Teigstück als Beilage zu indischen Gerichten*

popper ['pɒpə'] N *(Brit inf: = press-stud)* Druckknopf *m*

poppet ['pɒpɪt] N *(inf)* Schatz *m*; *(inf)* Schätzchen *nt*

poppy ['pɒpɪ] N Mohn *m*

poppycock ['pɒpɪkɒk] N *(dated inf)* Unsinn *m*, Blödsinn *m (inf)*

Poppy Day N *(Brit)* ≈ Volkstrauertag *m (in Germany)*

> **POPPY DAY**
>
> **Poppy Day** ist der volkstümliche Name für den **Remembrance Day**, den zweiten Sonntag im November, an dem in Großbritannien der Toten beider Weltkriege gedacht wird. Der Name geht auf den Brauch zurück, in der Zeit vor diesem Tag Papiermohnblumen zu verkaufen, um Spendengelder für die Unterstützung von Kriegsveteranen und ihren Familien zu sammeln.

poppy seed N Mohn *m*; **poppy-seed cake** Mohnkuchen *m*

pops [pɒps] N *(esp US inf)* Paps *m (inf)*

pop shop N *(dated inf)* Pfandhaus *nt*

Popsicle® ['pɒpsɪkl] N *(US)* Eis *nt* am Stiel

pop: pop singer N Popsänger(in) *m(f)*; **pop socks** PL Kniestrümpfe *pl*; **pop song** N Popsong *m*; **pop star** N Popstar *m*

popsy ['pɒpsɪ] N *(dated sl)* Biene *f (dated inf)*, Puppe *f (dated inf)*

populace ['pɒpjʊlɪs] N Bevölkerung *f*; *(= masses)* breite Öffentlichkeit; **the ~ of Rome** das Volk von Rom, die Bürger von Rom

popular ['pɒpjʊlə'] ADJ **a** *(= well-liked)* beliebt (*with* bei); *(with the public)* populär, beliebt (*with* bei); *decision, measure* populär; **I know I won't be ~ if I decide that, but …** ich weiß, dass ich mich nicht gerade beliebt mache, wenn ich so entscheide, aber …; **he's not the most ~ of men at the moment** er ist im Augenblick nicht gerade einer der Beliebtesten *or (with the public also)* Populärsten; **he was a very ~ choice** seine Wahl fand großen Anklang
b *(= suitable for the general public)* populär; *music* leicht; *prices* erschwinglich; *lectures, journal* populärwissenschaftlich; *television, entertainer* populär, beliebt; *newspaper* weitverbreitet; **~ appeal** Massenappeal *m*; **~ edition** Volksausgabe *f*; **~ newspaper** Boulevardblatt *nt*; **~ science** Populärwissenschaft *f*; **~ theatre** Volkstheater *nt*, Boulevardtheater *nt*; **a series of ~ concerts** eine Reihe volkstümlicher Konzerte
c *(= widespread) belief, fallacy, conviction, discontent, myth* weitverbreitet, weit verbreitet; **~ remedy** Hausmittel *nt*; **contrary to ~ belief** *or* **opinion** entgegen der landläufigen Annahme *or* Meinung; **fruit teas are becoming increasingly ~** Früchtetees erfreuen sich zunehmender Beliebtheit; **it's ~ to despise politicians these days** es gehört heutzutage zum guten Ton, sich über Politiker abfällig zu äußern
d *(Pol) (= of or for the people) government, approval, consent, support* des Volkes; *(= democratic, public) vote* öffentlich, allgemein; *referendum* öffentlich, offen, allgemein; *demand* groß, allgemein; *democracy* allgemein; **~ uprising** Volksaufstand *m*; **~ movement** Volksbewegung *f*; **~ mandate** Mandat *nt*; **he isn't the ~ idea of a great leader** er entspricht nicht gerade der gängigen Vorstellung von einem großen Führer; **to rule by ~ consent** mit Zustimmung der Allgemeinheit regieren; **by ~ request** auf allgemeinen Wunsch

popular culture N Popkultur *f*
popular front N Volksfront *f*
popularity [ˌpɒpjʊˈlærɪtɪ] N Beliebtheit *f*; *(with the public also)* Popularität *f* *(with* bei); **he'd do anything to win ~** er würde alles tun, um sich beliebt zu machen; **he'd never win a ~ contest!** er ist nicht gerade beliebt; **the sport is growing/declining in ~** dieser Sport wird immer populärer/verliert immer mehr an Popularität
popularity rating N Beliebtheitsquote *f*; **to do well in the ~s** bei Meinungsumfragen eine hohe Beliebtheitsquote erzielen
popularization [ˌpɒpjʊləraɪˈzeɪʃən] N Popularisierung *f*; *(= act also)* allgemeine Verbreitung; **a ~ of Hamlet** eine Volksfassung des Hamlet
popularize [ˈpɒpjʊləraɪz] VT **a** *(= make well--liked)* populär machen, zum Durchbruch verhelfen *(+dat)* **b** *(= make understandable) science* popularisieren, unter das Volk bringen *(inf)*; *ideas* zum Durchbruch verhelfen *(+dat)*, popularisieren
popularizer [ˈpɒpjʊləraɪzəʳ] N **he is a great ~ of political/scientific ideas** er macht politische/wissenschaftliche Ideen auch der breiten Masse zugänglich
popularly [ˈpɒpjʊləlɪ] ADV **a** allgemein; **he is ~ believed** *or* **held** *or* **thought to be a rich man** nach allgemeiner Ansicht ist er ein reicher Mann; **to be ~ known as sb/sth** allgemeinhin als jd/etw bekannt sein; **~ supposed to be sb/sth** allgemeinhin als jd/etw gelten; **to be ~ considered (as** *or* **to be) sb/sth** allgemeinhin *or* weithin als jd/etw betrachtet werden, allgemeinhin *or* weithin für jdn/etw gehalten werden **b** *(= democratically, publicly) elected, supported* vom Volk, öffentlich
popular press N Boulevardpresse *f*, Regenbogenpresse *f*
populate [ˈpɒpjʊleɪt] VT *(= inhabit)* bevölkern; *(= colonize)* besiedeln; **~d by** bevölkert von; **this area is ~d mainly by immigrants** in diesem Stadtteil leben *or* wohnen hauptsächlich Einwanderer; **densely ~d areas** dicht besiedelte Gebiete *pl*; **densely ~d cities** dicht bevölkerte Städte *pl*
population [ˌpɒpjʊˈleɪʃən] N *(of region, country)* Bevölkerung *f*; *(of village, town)* Bewohner *pl*, Einwohner *pl*; *(= colonization)* Besiedlung *f*; *(= number of inhabitants)* Bevölkerungszahl *f*; **the ~ explosion** die Bevölkerungsexplosion; **the growing black ~ of London** die wachsende Zahl von Schwarzen in London
population: **population density** N Bevölkerungsdichte *f*; **population statistics** PL Bevölkerungsstatistik *f*
populism [ˈpɒpjʊlɪzəm] N Populismus *m*
populist [ˈpɒpjʊlɪst] **N** Populist(in) *m(f)* **ADJ** populistisch
populous [ˈpɒpjʊləs] ADJ *country* dicht besiedelt; *town, area also* mit vielen Einwohnern, einwohnerstark
pop-up [ˈpɒpʌp] **ADJ** *toaster* automatisch; *book, picture* Hochklapp- *(inf)*; **~ menu** *(Comput)* Pop--up-Menü *nt*; **~ window** *(Comput)* Pop-up-Fenster *nt* **N** *(Comput)* Popup(-Menü) *nt*
pop valve N *(Tech)* Sicherheitsventil *nt*
porage [ˈpɒrɪdʒ] N = **porridge**
porcelain [ˈpɔːsəlɪn] **N** Porzellan *nt* **ADJ** Porzellan-; **~ doll** Porzellanpuppe *f*
porch [pɔːtʃ] N *(of house)* Vorbau *m*, Vordach *nt*; *(US)* Veranda *f*; *(of church)* Vorhalle *f*, Portal *nt*
porcine [ˈpɔːsaɪn] ADJ *(= pig-like)* schweineartig; *(= of pigs)* Schweine-; **... are members of the ~ family** ... gehören zur Familie der Schweine *or* zu den Schweineartigen
porcupine [ˈpɔːkjʊpaɪn] N Stachelschwein *nt*
porcupine fish N Igelfisch *m*
pore [pɔːʳ] N Pore *f*; **in/from every ~** *(fig)* aus allen Poren
▶ **pore over** VI +*prep obj* *(= scrutinize)* genau studieren; *(= meditate)* nachdenken *or* nachgrübeln über *(+acc)*; **to pore over one's books** über seinen Büchern hocken
pork [pɔːk] N **a** Schweinefleisch *nt* **b** *(US sl)* *von der Regierung aus politischen Gründen gewährte finanzielle Vergünstigungen oder Stellen*
pork: **pork barrel** N *(US inf)* *Geldzuwendungen der Regierung an örtliche Verwaltungsstellen, um deren Unterstützung zu gewinnen*; **pork belly** N *(Cook)* Schweinebauch *m*; **pork butcher** N Schweinemetzger *m*; **pork chop** N Schweine- *or* Schweinskotelett *nt*
porker [ˈpɔːkəʳ] N Mastschwein *nt*
pork: **pork pie** N Schweinefleischpastete *f*; **pork pie hat** N *runder, niedriger Filzhut*; **pork sausage** N Schweinswurst *f*
porky[1] [ˈpɔːkɪ] *(inf)* **ADJ** *(+er)* *(= fat)* fett **N** Schwindelei *f*
porky[2] N *(US inf)* Stachelschwein *nt*
porn [pɔːn] *(inf)* **N** Pornografie *f*; **soft ~** weicher Porno, Softporno *m*; **hard ~** harter Porno; **hardcore ~** Hardcorepornografie *f*; **child ~** Kinderpornografie *f* **ADJ** *magazine, film, video* pornografisch; **~ actor** Pornodarsteller *m*; **~ shop** Pornoladen *m* *(inf)*
pornographic ADJ, **pornographically** ADV [ˌpɔːnəˈgræfɪk, -əlɪ] pornografisch
pornography [pɔːˈnɒgrəfɪ] N Pornografie *f*
porosity [pɔːˈrɒsɪtɪ] N *(of rocks, substance)* Porosität *f*; *(of skin)* Porigkeit *f*
porous [ˈpɔːrəs] ADJ **a** *rock, substance* porös; *skin* porig **b** *border, defence* durchlässig
porousness [ˈpɔːrəsnɪs] N = **porosity**
porphyry [ˈpɔːfɪrɪ] N Porphyr *m*
porpoise [ˈpɔːpəs] N Tümmler *m*
porridge [ˈpɒrɪdʒ] N *(esp Brit)* Porridge *m*, Haferbrei *m*; **~ oats** Haferflocken *pl*
port[1] [pɔːt] N **a** *(= harbour)* Hafen *m*; **naval ~** Kriegshafen *m*; **to come/put into ~** in den Hafen einlaufen; **~ of call** Hafen *m*, Halt *m*; **to make ~** den/einen Hafen anlaufen; **~ authority** Hafenamt *nt*, Hafenbehörde *f*; **~ dues** Hafengelder *pl*; **any ~ in a storm** *(prov)* in der Not frisst der Teufel Fliegen *(Prov)*; **the yen is the safest ~ in the current economic storm** der Yen ist in der gegenwärtigen Wirtschaftskrise der sicherste Hafen **b** *(= city or town with a port)* Hafen *m*, Hafenstadt *f*
port[2] N **a** *(Naut, Aviat: = porthole)* Bullauge *nt* **b** *(Naut, for cargo)* (Lade)luke *f* **c** *(Tech)* Durchlass *m* **d** *(Comput)* Anschluss *m*, Port *m*
port[3] **N** *(Naut, Aviat: = left side)* Backbord *m*; **land to ~!** Land an Backbord! **ADJ** *cabin, deck* auf der Backbordseite; **~ side** Backbordseite *f*; **on the ~ bow** Backbord voraus **VT** *(Naut)* **to ~ the helm** nach Backbord drehen
port[4] N *(also* **port wine)** Portwein *m*
port[5] *(Mil)* **N to hold the rifle at ~** das Gewehr (schräg nach links) vor dem Körper halten **VT** *arms* schräg nach links vor dem Körper halten; **~ arms!** ≈ präsentiert das Gewehr!
portability [ˌpɔːtəˈbɪlɪtɪ] N Tragbarkeit *f*
portable [ˈpɔːtəbl] **ADJ** **a** *computer, sound system* tragbar; *generator, toilets* tragbar, mobil; *medical equipment* tragbar, transportierbar, mobil; **easily ~** leicht zu tragen; **~ radio** Kofferradio *nt*; **~ television** Portable *nt*, tragbarer Fernseher; **~ (tele)phone** Mobiltelefon *nt* **b** *pension* übertragbar; *(Comput) software* portierbar *(spec)*; *language* übertragbar **N** *(computer, TV)* Portable *nt*; tragbarer Computer
portage [ˈpɔːtɪdʒ] N *(Comm)* *(= act)* Transport *m*, Beförderung *f*; *(= cost)* Rollgeld *nt*, Transportkosten *pl*, Beförderungsentgelt *nt*
Portakabin® [ˈpɔːtəˌkæbɪn] N Container *m*; *(used as accommodation also)* Wohncontainer *m*; *(used as office also)* Bürocontainer *m*
portal [ˈpɔːtl] N *(liter)* Portal *nt*, Pforte *f* *(geh)*, Tor *nt*; *(Comput)* Portal *nt*
Portaloo® [ˈpɔːtəluː] N *(Brit)* Mobiltoilette *f*
portal site N *(Internet)* Portal *nt*, Startseite *f*
portal vein N Pfortader *f*
portcullis [pɔːtˈkʌlɪs] N Fallgitter *nt*, Fallgatter *nt*
porte-cochère [ˌpɔːtkɒˈʃɛəʳ] N Wagenauffahrt *f*
portend [pɔːˈtend] VT *(form)* bedeuten, hindeuten auf *(+acc)*; **what does this ~?** was hat das zu bedeuten?
portent [ˈpɔːtent] N Zeichen *nt*, Omen *nt* *(geh)* *(of* für); **a matter of great ~ for us all** eine Angelegenheit (von) großer Tragweite für uns alle; **a ~ of things to come** ein Vorgeschmack *m* auf das, was noch bevorsteht; **to be a ~ of sth** etw ahnen lassen
portentous [pɔːˈtentəs] ADJ **a** *(= ominous)* unheilschwanger **b** *(= grave)* gewichtig; *(= pompous)* bombastisch **c** *(= marvellous)* gewaltig
portentously [pɔːˈtentəslɪ] ADV **a** *(= ominously)* unheilschwanger **b** *(= pompously) say* gewichtig; **he cleared his throat ~** er räusperte sich gewichtig
porter[1] [ˈpɔːtəʳ] N *(of office etc)* Pförtner(in) *m(f)*, Portier *m*, Portiersfrau *f*; *(= hospital porter)* Assistent(in) *m(f)*; *(at hotel)* Portier *m*, Portiersfrau *f*; *(Rail, at airport)* Gepäckträger(in) *m(f)*; *(= Sherpa etc)* (Lasten)träger(in) *m(f)*; *(US Rail)* Schlafwagenschaffner(in) *m(f)*; **~'s lodge** Pförtnerloge *f*
porter[2] N *(= beer)* Porter *m or nt*
porterage [ˈpɔːtərɪdʒ] N *(= charge)* Trägerlohn *m*
porterhouse steak [ˈpɔːtəhausˈsteɪk] N Porterhouse Steak *nt*
portfolio [pɔːtˈfəʊlɪəʊ] N **a** (Akten)mappe *f* **b** *(Pol: = office)* Portefeuille *nt* *(form)*, Geschäftsbereich *m*; **minister without ~** Minister ohne Portefeuille *(form)* *or* Geschäftsbereich **c** *(Fin)* Portefeuille *nt* **d** *(of artist, designer)* Kollektion *f*; *(Comm: = range of products)* Kollektion *f*
porthole [ˈpɔːthəʊl] N Bullauge *nt*
portico [ˈpɔːtɪkəʊ] N Portikus *m*
portion [ˈpɔːʃən] N **a** *(= piece, part)* Teil *m*; *(of ticket)* Abschnitt *m*; **your/my ~** dein/mein Anteil *m* **b** *(of food)* Portion *f* **c** *(old, form, = marriage portion)* Mitgift *f*, Heiratsgut *nt* *(old)* **d** *(liter: = fate)* Los *nt*, Schicksal *nt*
▶ **portion out** VT *sep* aufteilen, verteilen *(among* unter *+acc)*
portliness [ˈpɔːtlɪnɪs] N Beleibtheit *f*, Korpulenz *f*
portly [ˈpɔːtlɪ] ADJ *(+er)* beleibt, korpulent
portmanteau [pɔːtˈmæntəʊ] N *pl* **-s** *or* **-x** Handkoffer *m*
portmanteau word N Kombinationsform *f*
Porto Rico [ˈpɔːtəʊˈriːkəʊ] N = **Puerto Rico**
portrait [ˈpɔːtrɪt] N **a** *(also in words)* Porträt *nt*; **to have one's ~ painted** sich malen lassen; **to sit for one's ~** für sein Porträt sitzen; **to paint a ~ of sb** jdn porträtieren **b** *(printing format)* Hochformat *nt*
portraitist [ˈpɔːtrɪtɪst] N Porträtist(in) *m(f)*
portrait: **portrait painter** N Porträtmaler(in) *m(f)*; **portrait photographer** N Porträtfotograf(in) *m(f)*; **portrait photography** N Porträtfotografie *f*
portraiture [ˈpɔːtrɪtʃəʳ] N *(= portrait)* Porträt *nt*; *(= portraits collectively)* Porträts *pl*; *(= art of portraiture)* *(painting)* Porträtmalerei *f*; *(Phot)* Porträtfotografie *f*
portray [pɔːˈtreɪ] VT darstellen; *(= paint also)* malen
portrayal [pɔːˈtreɪəl] N Darstellung *f*; *(= description also)* Schilderung *f*
Portugal [ˈpɔːtjʊgəl] N Portugal *nt*
Portuguese [ˌpɔːtjʊˈgiːz] **ADJ** portugiesisch; **he is ~** er ist Portugiese **N** Portugiese *m*, Portugiesin *f*; *(Ling)* Portugiesisch *nt*
Portuguese man-of-war N Staats- *or* Röhrenqualle *f*, Portugiesische Galeere *f*
pose [pəʊz] **N** **a** *(= position, attitude)* Haltung *f*; *(of model, also pej)* Pose *f*, Haltung *f*; **to take**

up a ~ *(model)* eine Pose *or* Haltung einnehmen; **to hold a ~** eine Pose *or* Haltung beibehalten; **to strike a (dramatic) ~** sich (dramatisch) in Positur werfen; **she's always striking ~s** sie benimmt sich immer so theatralisch
b *(= affectation)* Pose *f*, Gehabe *nt*; *(= façade)* Fassade *f*
VT **a** *(= position) model* aufstellen
b *(= put forward) question, problem* vortragen; **the question ~d by his speech** die in seiner Rede aufgeworfene Frage
c *(= formulate) question, problem* formulieren
d *(= constitute, present) difficulties, problem* aufwerfen; *threat* darstellen; **this could ~ a health risk** das könnte eine Gesundheitsgefährdung darstellen
VI **a** *(= model)* posieren, Modell sitzen/stehen; **to ~ (in the) nude** für einen Akt posieren *or* Modell sitzen/stehen; **to ~ for photographs** für Fotografien posieren
b *(= attitudinize)* posieren, sich in Pose werfen
c *(= present oneself as)* **to ~ as** sich ausgeben als

posed [pəʊzd] ADJ *photo* gestellt

Poseidon [pə'saɪdən] N Poseidon *m*

poser ['pəʊzə'] N **a** *(= person)* Angeber(in) *m(f)* **b** *(inf: = difficult problem or question)* harte Nuss *(inf)*

posh [pɒʃ] *(inf)* ADJ *(+er)* piekfein *(inf)*, vornehm; *neighbourhood, hotel, wedding also* nobel; *friends* vornehm, fein; *occasion* vornehm, elegant ADV *(+er)* **to talk ~** mit vornehmem Akzent sprechen VT **to ~ sth up** *(inf)* etw verschönern *(inf)*

poshly ['pɒʃlɪ] ADJ piekfein *(inf)*, vornehm; *talk* vornehm

poshness ['pɒʃnɪs] N Feinheit *f*, Vornehmheit *f*; *(of accent)* Vornehmheit *f*, Distinguierte(s) *nt*

posing pouch N *knappe Herrenbadehose*

posit ['pɒzɪt] N *(= claim)* Postulat *nt*, Grundannahme *f* VT **a** *(rare: = put down)* absetzen **b** *(= claim)* postulieren; *hypothesis* aufstellen

position [pə'zɪʃən] ✪ 12.3, 19.1 N **a** *(= location, place where sb/sth is, of person)* Platz *m*; *(of object)* Stelle *f*, Platz *m*; *(of microphone, statue, wardrobe, plant etc)* Standort *m*; *(of spotlight, table, in picture, painting)* Anordnung *f*; *(of town, house etc)* Lage *f*; *(of plane, ship, Sport: = starting position, Ftbl etc)* Position *f*; *(Mil: = strategic site)* Stellung *f*; **to be in/out of ~** an der richtigen/falschen Stelle sein; **the actors were in ~ on the stage** die Schauspieler hatten ihre Plätze auf der Bühne eingenommen; **to jockey** *or* **jostle for ~** *(lit)* um eine gute Ausgangsposition kämpfen; *(fig)* um eine gute Position rangeln; **the ~ of the fireplace isn't very good** der Kamin hat keinen sehr günstigen Platz; **what ~ do you play?** auf *or* in welcher Position spielst du?; **his ~ is full-back/goalkeeper** er spielt Außenverteidiger/Torwart
b *(= posture, way of standing, sitting etc)* Haltung *f*; *(in love-making, Art: of model)* Stellung *f*; *(Ballet)* Position *f*; **in a sitting ~** sitzend; **in a reclining ~** zurückgelehnt
c *(in class, league etc)* Platz *m*; **after the third lap he was in fourth ~** nach der dritten Runde lag er auf dem vierten Platz *or* war er Vierter; **to finish in third ~** Dritter werden, auf dem dritten Platz landen *(inf)*
d *(= social, professional standing)* Stellung *f*, Position *f*; **a man of ~** eine hochgestellte Persönlichkeit
e *(= job)* Stelle *f*; **he has a high ~ in the Ministry of Defence** er bekleidet eine hohe Stellung *or* Position im Verteidigungsministerium; **a ~ of trust** eine Vertrauensstellung; **to be in a ~ of power** eine Machtposition innehaben
f *(fig: = situation, circumstance)* Lage *f*; **to be in a ~ to do sth** in der Lage sein, etw zu tun; **what is the ~ regarding ...?** wie sieht es mit ... aus?; **I'm not in a ~ to say anything about that** ich kann dazu nichts sagen; **my ~ is that I don't have the qualifications/money** mir geht es so, dass mir die Qualifikation/das Geld fehlt
g *(fig: = point of view, attitude)* Standpunkt *m*, Haltung *f*, Einstellung *f*; **what is the government's ~ on ...?** welchen Standpunkt vertritt die Regierung zu ...?; **to take (up) a ~ on sth** eine Haltung zu einer Sache einnehmen
VT **a** *(= place in position) microphone, ladder, guards* aufstellen; *soldiers, policemen* postieren; *(artist, photographer etc)* platzieren; *(Comput) cursor* positionieren, platzieren; **he ~ed himself where he could see her** er stellte *or (seated)* setzte sich so, dass er sie sehen konnte; **he has ~ed himself as a moderate** er hat sich als (ein) Gemäßigter etabliert
b *(in marketing) product* positionieren

position: **position finder** N *(Aviat, Naut, Tech)* Ortungsgerät *nt*; **position paper** N *(Pol)* Positionspapier *nt*

positive ['pɒzɪtɪv] ADJ **a** *(Math, Phot, Elec, Gram)* positiv; **~ pole** Pluspol *m*; **the ~ degree** *(Gram)* der Positiv
b *(= affirmative, constructive) result, answer, attitude* positiv; *criticism, suggestion* konstruktiv; **he is a very ~ person** er hat eine sehr positive Einstellung zum Leben; **on the ~ side** auf der positiven Seite; **to take ~ action** positive Schritte unternehmen; **~ thinking** positive Haltung, positives Denken
c *(= definite) person, tone of voice* bestimmt; *instructions* streng; *evidence, answer* definitiv, eindeutig; *rule* fest; **that is ~ proof** *or* **proof ~** das ist der sichere *or* eindeutige Beweis; **to be ~ that ...** sicher sein, dass ..., definitiv wissen, dass ...; **to be ~ about** *or* **of sth** sich *(dat)* einer Sache *(gen)* absolut sicher sein; **to make a ~ identification** *or* **ID** *(Police)* eindeutig identifizieren, die Identität eindeutig feststellen; **this may even do some ~ good** damit tut man vielleicht sogar etwas wirklich *or* richtig Gutes; **are you sure you don't want her address? – ~** bist du sicher, dass du nicht ihre Adresse willst? – absolut *or* ganz bestimmt
d *(= real, downright)* **this is a ~ miracle/crime/disgrace** das ist wirklich ein Wunder/Verbrechen/eine Schande; **he's a ~ genius/menace** er ist wirklich ein Genie/Ärgernis, er ist ein wahres Genie/wirkliches Ärgernis
N **a** *(Phot)* Positiv *nt*; *(Gram)* Positiv *m*; *(Elec)* Pluspol *m*; *(Math)* positive Zahl
b *(= advantage)* Positive(s) *nt*; **the ~s far outweigh the negatives** das Positive wiegt viel schwerer als das Negative, das Positive gleicht das Negative mehr als aus
ADV **a** *(Med)* **to test ~** einen positiven Befund haben; **to show ~ (for sth)** einen positiven Befund (auf etw) zeigen
b to think ~ positiv denken

positive discrimination N *(Brit)* positive Diskriminierung

positive feedback N positives Feedback, positive Reaktion; *(Elec)* Rückkopplung *f*; **to give sb ~ (about sb/sth)** jdm eine positive Rückmeldung (zu jdm/etw) geben; **to get ~ (about sb/sth)** eine positive Rückmeldung (zu jdm/etw) erhalten

positively ['pɒzɪtɪvlɪ] ADV **a** *(= affirmatively, constructively, also Sci)* positiv
b *(= decisively)* bestimmt; *(= definitely, indisputably) prove* definitiv, eindeutig; *(= conclusively) identify* eindeutig, bestimmt, definitiv; **to test ~ for drugs** positiv auf Drogen getestet werden; **I ~ forbid it** ich verbiete es absolut *or* definitiv
c *(= really, absolutely)* wirklich, echt *(inf)*; *(emph: = actively)* eindeutig, bestimmt; **she ~ glowed with pride** sie strahlte regelrecht vor Stolz; **Jane doesn't mind being photographed, she ~ loves it** Jane hat nichts dagegen, fotografiert zu werden, im Gegenteil, sie hat es sehr gern *or* sie hat es eindeutig sehr gern
d *(Elec, Phys) charged* positiv; **~ charged terminal** Plus-Klemme *f*

positiveness ['pɒzɪtɪvnɪs] N **a** *(= constructiveness)* Positive(s) *nt*; **I was reassured by the ~ of his attitude** ich wurde durch seine positive Haltung bestärkt **b** *(= certainty)* Überzeugung *f*; *(of voice)* Bestimmtheit *f*; *(of evidence)* Überzeugungskraft *f*; **her ~ that he was innocent** die Überzeugung, mit der sie an seine Unschuld glaubte

positive: **positive sign** N *(Math)* Pluszeichen *nt*, positives Vorzeichen; **positive stress** N positiver Stress, Eustress *m*; **positive vetting** N Sicherheitsüberprüfung *f*

positivism ['pɒzɪtɪvɪzəm] N Positivismus *m*

positivist ['pɒzɪtɪvɪst] ADJ positivistisch N Positivist(in) *m(f)*

positivistic ADJ, **positivistically** ADV [pɒzɪtɪ'vɪstɪk, -əlɪ] positivistisch

positron ['pɒzɪtrɒn] N Positron *nt*

poss [pɒs] *abbr of* **possible, possibly** mögl.

posse ['pɒsɪ] N *(US: = sheriff's posse)* Aufgebot *nt*; *(fig)* Gruppe *f*, Schar *f*; *(of youths, criminals)* Gang *f*, Bande *f*; **~ of searchers** Suchtrupp *m*

possess [pə'zes] VT besitzen; *(form) foreign language, facts* verfügen über *(+acc)*; **to be ~ed of sth** *(form)* über etw *(acc)* verfügen; **it ~es many advantages** es hat viele Vorteile; **to be ~ed by demons** von Dämonen besessen sein; **to be ~ed by the urge to do sth** von dem Drang besessen sein, etw tun zu müssen; **like a man/woman ~ed** wie ein Besessener/eine Besessene; **to fight like one ~ed** wie ein Besessener kämpfen; **whatever ~ed you to do that?** was ist bloß in Sie gefahren, so etwas zu tun?; **to ~ one's soul in patience** *(form)* sich in Geduld fassen

possession [pə'zeʃən] N **a** *(= ownership)* Besitz *m*; *(Sport: of ball)* Ballbesitz *m*; *(fig: = control) (of feelings, oneself)* Kontrolle *f*; **to have sth in one's ~** etw in seinem Besitz haben; **to have/take ~ of sth** etw in Besitz haben/nehmen; **to come into/get ~ of sth** in den Besitz von etw gelangen/kommen; **to get/have ~ of the ball** in Ballbesitz gelangen/sein; **to be in ~ of sth** im Besitz von etw sein; **I'm in full ~ of the facts** ich verfüge über alle Tatsachen; **he put me in ~ of the information I required** er lieferte *or* verschaffte mir die Informationen, die ich benötigte; **according to the information in my ~** nach den mir zur Verfügung stehenden Informationen; **to be in ~ of a house** ein Haus in Besitz haben; **to take ~ of a house** ein Haus in Besitz nehmen; **~ is nine points of the law** *(prov)* das Recht steht auf der Seite der Besitzenden
b *(by demons)* Besessenheit *f*
c *(= thing possessed)* Besitz *m no pl*; *(= territory)* Besitzung *f*; **all his ~s** sein gesamter Besitz, seine gesamten Besitztümer

possession order N *(Brit Jur)* Räumungsbefehl *m*

possessive [pə'zesɪv] ADJ *(towards belongings)* eigen; *mother, boyfriend, love, manner etc* besitzergreifend; *streak* besitzergreifend, habgierig; **to be ~ about sth** seine Besitzansprüche auf etw *(acc)* betonen; **to be ~ toward(s) sb** an jdn Besitzansprüche stellen N *(Gram: = pronoun, adjective)* Possessiv(um) *nt*

possessive case N *(Gram)* Genitiv *m*, zweiter Fall

possessively [pə'zesɪvlɪ] ADV *(about things)* eigen; *(towards people)* besitzergreifend

possessiveness [pə'zesɪvnɪs] N eigene Art *(about* mit*)*; *(towards people)* besitzergreifende Art *(towards* gegenüber*)*

possessive pronoun N *(Gram)* besitzanzeigendes Fürwort, Possessivpronomen *nt*

possessor [pə'zesə'] N Besitzer(in) *m(f)*; **to be the proud ~ of sth** der stolze Besitzer von etw sein

posset ['pɒsɪt] N **a** *heiße Milch mit Bier oder Wein und Gewürzen* **b** *(of baby)* erbrochene Milch

possibility [ˌpɒsə'bɪlɪtɪ] ✪ 15.2, 26.3 N Möglichkeit *f*; **there's not much ~ of success/of his** *or* **him being successful** die Aussichten auf Erfolg/darauf, dass er Erfolg hat, sind nicht sehr groß; **within the realms** *or* **bounds of ~** im Bereich des Möglichen; **it's not beyond the realms** *or* **bounds of ~** es ist durchaus im Bereich des Möglichen; **do you by any ~ happen to know ...?** wissen Sie zufällig ...?; **the ~ of doing sth** die Möglichkeit *or* Chance, etw zu tun; **it's a distinct ~ that ...** es besteht eindeutig die Möglichkeit, dass ...; **he is a ~ for the job** er kommt für die Stelle infrage *or* in Frage *or* in Betracht; **there is some** *or* **a ~ that ...** es besteht die Möglichkeit, dass ...; **a job with real possibilities** eine Stelle mit echten Möglichkeiten *or* Chancen; **he/that has possibilities** in ihm/darin stecken Möglichkeiten

possible ['pɒsəbl] ✪ 9.1, 15.3, 19.4, 26.3 ADJ möglich; **anything is ~** möglich ist alles; **as soon/often/far as ~** so bald/oft/weit wie möglich; **as quickly as ~** so rasch *or* schnell wie möglich; **the best/worst/quickest ~ ...** der/die/das bestmögliche/schlechtestmögliche/schnellstmögliche ...; **if (at all) ~** falls (irgend) möglich; **it's just ~ that I'll see you before then** eventuell sehe ich dich vorher noch; **it's just ~, I suppose** es ist unwahrscheinlich, aber möglich; **there is no ~ excuse for his behaviour** für sein Verhalten gibt es absolut keine Entschuldigung; **the only ~ choice, the only choice ~** die einzig mögliche Wahl; **it will be ~ for you to return the same day** es besteht *or* Sie haben die Möglichkeit, am selben Tag zurückzukommen; **to make sth ~** etw ermöglichen, etw möglich machen; **to make it ~ for sb to do sth** es jdm ermöglichen, etw zu tun; **where ~** wo möglich; **wherever ~** wo immer möglich, wo immer es möglich ist
N Möglichkeit *f*; **a long list of ~s for the job** eine lange Liste möglicher Kandidaten für die Stelle; **the ~s played the probables** *(Sport)* die möglichen Kandidaten spielten gegen die wahrscheinlichen (Kandidaten); **he is a ~ for the English team** er kommt für die englische Mannschaft infrage *or* in Frage; **the first three houses were all ~s** die ersten drei Häuser kamen alle infrage *or* in Frage

possibly ['pɒsəblɪ] ✪ 12.3, 16.3, 26.3 ADV **a** **not ~** unmöglich; **I can't ~ stay indoors all weekend** ich kann unmöglich das ganze Wochenende in der Wohnung sitzen; **nobody could ~ tell the difference** es war unmöglich, einen Unterschied zu erkennen; **that can't ~ be true** das kann unmöglich wahr sein; **can that ~ be true?** kann das (vielleicht doch) stimmen?; **very** *or* **quite ~** absolut *or* durchaus möglich; **how could I ~ have come?** wie hätte ich denn kommen können?; **how could he ~ have known that?** wie konnte er das nur wissen?; **he did all he ~ could** er tat, was er nur konnte; **I have made myself as comfortable as I ~ can** ich habe es mir so bequem wie möglich gemacht; **if I ~ can** wenn ich irgend kann; **I couldn't ~ ...** *(polite formula)* ich kann unmöglich ...
b *(= perhaps)* vielleicht, möglicherweise; **~ not** vielleicht nicht, möglicherweise nicht

possum ['pɒsəm] N Opossum *nt*, Beutelratte *f*; **to play ~** *(sleeping)* sich schlafend stellen; *(dead)* sich tot stellen

post¹ [pəʊst] N *(= pole, doorpost etc)* Pfosten *m*; *(= lamp post)* Pfahl *m*; *(= telegraph post)* Mast *m*; **a wooden ~** ein Holzpfosten *or* -pfahl *m*; **a metal ~** ein Metallpfosten *m*; **starting/winning** *or* **finishing ~** Start-/Zielpfosten *m*; **the horses were at the ~** die Pferde standen am Start; **he was left at the ~** sie ließen ihn stehen → **deaf**
VT **a** *(= display: also* **post up***)* anschlagen; **"post no bills"** „Plakate ankleben verboten"; **to ~ a wall with advertisements** eine Wand plakatieren *or* mit Werbeplakaten bekleben
b *(= announce) concert etc* durch Anschlag bekannt machen; *gains, profits* veröffentlichen; **to ~ a reward** eine Belohnung ausschreiben; **to be ~ed (as) missing** als vermisst gemeldet sein

post² ✪ 19.1, 19.4 N **a** *(Brit: = job)* Stelle *f*, Posten *m*; **to look for/take up a ~** eine Stelle suchen/antreten; **to hold a ~** eine Stelle innehaben
b *(esp Mil: = place of duty)* Posten *m*; **at one's ~** auf seinem Posten; **to die at one's ~** im Dienst sterben
c *(Mil: = camp, station)* Posten *m*; **a frontier** *or* **border ~** ein Grenzposten *m*; **a chain of ~s along the border** eine Postenkette entlang der Grenze; **~ exchange** *(abbr* **PX***)* *(US) von der Regierung betriebener Versorgungsladen für Truppenangehörige*; **to return to the ~** zur Garnison zurückkehren; **to leave the ~** die Garnison verlassen; **most of the officers live on the ~** die meisten Offiziere leben in der Garnison; **the whole ~ fell sick** die ganze Garnison wurde krank
d *(Brit Mil: = bugle call)* **first ~** Wecksignal *nt*; **last ~** Zapfenstreich *m*
e *(= trading post)* Handelsniederlassung *f*
VT **a** *(= position)* postieren; *sentry, guard* postieren, aufstellen
b *(= send, assign)* versetzen; *(Mil)* abkommandieren; **to be ~ed to a battalion/an embassy/a ship** zu einem Bataillon/an eine Botschaft/auf ein Schiff versetzt *or (Mil)* abkommandiert werden; **he has been ~ed away** er ist versetzt *or (Mil)* abkommandiert worden

post³ N **a** *(Brit: = mail)* Post® *f*; **by ~** mit der Post®, auf dem Postweg *(form)*; **it's in the ~** es ist unterwegs *or* in der Post; **to drop sth in the ~** etw (in den Briefkasten) einwerfen; *(= in post office)* etw zur Post® bringen; **to catch the ~** *(letter)* noch mit der Post mitkommen; *(person)* rechtzeitig zur Leerung kommen; **to miss the ~** *(letter)* nicht mehr mit der Post mitkommen; *(person)* die Leerung verpassen; **there is no ~ today** *(= no delivery)* heute kommt keine Post, heute wird keine Post ausgetragen; *(= no letters)* heute ist keine Post (für uns) gekommen; **has the ~ been?** war die Post® schon da?
b *(Hist)* Post *f*; **to travel ~** mit der Post(kutsche) reisen
VT **a** *(Brit: = put in the post)* aufgeben; *(in letterbox)* einwerfen, einstecken; *(= send by post)* mit der Post® schicken; *(Comput)* abschicken; **I ~ed it to you on Monday** ich habe es am Montag an Sie abgeschickt
b *(= inform)* **to keep sb ~ed** jdn auf dem Laufenden halten
c *(= enter in ledger: also* **post up***)* eintragen *(to* in *+acc)*; **all transactions must be ~ed (up) weekly** alle Geschäftsvorgänge müssen wöchentlich verbucht werden
VI *(old: = travel by post)* mit der Post(kutsche) reisen

▶ **post off** VT *sep* abschicken

post- [pəʊst-] PREF nach-; *(esp with words derived from Latin or Greek)* post-; **postcommunist** post- *or* nachkommunistisch; **~traumatic** posttraumatisch

postage ['pəʊstɪdʒ] N Porto *nt*, Postgebühr *f (form)*; **~ and packing** *(abbr* **p&p***)* Porto und Verpackung; **what is the ~ to Germany?** wie hoch ist das Porto nach Deutschland?

postage: **postage meter** N *(US)* Frankiermaschine *f*; **postage paid** ADJ portofrei; *envelope* frankiert, freigemacht ADV portofrei; **postage rate** N Porto *nt*, Postgebühr *f (form)*; **postage stamp** N Briefmarke *f*, Postwertzeichen *nt (form)*; **what she knows about children would fit on the back of a ~** ihre Kenntnisse über Kinder sind verschwindend gering

postal ['pəʊstl] ADJ Post-, postalisch *(form)*; **~ charges** Postgebühren *pl* N *(US inf)* = **postal card**

postal: **postal area** N Zustellbereich *m (form)*, Postbezirk *m*; **postal ballot** N Briefwahl *f*; **postal card** N *(US) (= letter card) Postkarte mit aufgedruckter Briefmarke für offizielle Zwecke (= postcard)* Postkarte *f*; *(with picture)* Ansichtskarte *f*; **postal code** N *(Brit)* Postleitzahl *f*; **postal district** N *(of main sorting office)* ≈ Postort *m (form)*; *(of local sorting office)* ≈ Postzustellbereich *m (form)*; **postal order** N *(Brit)* ≈ Postanweisung *f*, *Geldgutschein, der bei der Post® gekauft und eingelöst wird*; **postal service** N Postdienst *m*; **postal tuition** N Fernunterricht *m*; **postal vote** N **to have a ~** per Briefwahl wählen; **postal worker** N Postbeamte(r) *m*, Postbeamtin *f*, Postbedienstete(r) *mf*, Postler(in) *m(f) (inf)*

post: **postbag** N *(Brit)* Postsack *m*; **postbox** N *(Brit)* Briefkasten *m*; **postcard** N Postkarte *f*; **(picture) ~** Ansichtskarte *f*; **post chaise** N *(Hist)* Postkutsche *f*; **postclassical** ADJ nachklassisch; **post code** N *(Brit)* Postleitzahl *f*

> **POST CODE**
>
> Der britische **post code** setzt sich aus zwei Gruppen mit jeweils drei Elementen zusammen, normalerweise ein oder zwei Buchstaben plus eine Zahl, danach eine Zahl und zwei Buchstaben: z.B. EH9 2HZ. Die erste Gruppe bezieht sich auf die Region, wobei in diesem Fall „EH" für die Gegend um Edinburgh und „9" für einen bestimmten Bezirk darin steht. Die zweite Gruppe bezeichnet einen bestimmten Straßenabschnitt in dieser Gegend.

post: **postdate** VT **a** *cheque etc* vordatieren **b** *(= be later than)* später datieren als *(+nom)*; **postdoctoral** ADJ nach der *or* im Anschluss an die Promotion; **postedit** VTI *(Comput etc) text etc*nachbearbeiten

poster ['pəʊstəʳ] N *(advertising)* Plakat *nt*; *(for decoration also)* Poster *nt*; **~ colour** *or* **paint** Plakatfarbe *f*, Plakafarbe® *f*

poste restante ['pəʊst'restɑ̃:nt] *(Brit)* N Aufbewahrungsstelle *f* für postlagernde Sendungen ADJ *address, facility* für postlagernde Sendungen ADV postlagernd

posterior [pɒ'stɪərɪəʳ] ADJ *(form)* hintere(r, s); *(in time)* spätere(r, s); **to be ~ to sth** hinter etw *(dat)* liegen; *(in time)* nach etw *(dat)* kommen, auf etw *(acc)* folgen N *(hum)* Allerwerteste(r) *m (hum)*

posterity [pɒ'sterɪtɪ] N die Nachwelt; **they videoed it for ~** sie haben es für die Nachwelt auf Video aufgenommen

postern ['pəʊstɜ:n] N *(old)* Seitenpforte *f*, Nebenpforte *f*

post: **post-free** ADJ, ADV portofrei, gebührenfrei; **postglacial** ADJ postglazial, nacheiszeitlich; **postgrad** ['pəʊst'græd] N ADJ *(Brit inf)* = **postgraduate**; **postgraduate** N *jd, der seine Studien nach dem ersten akademischen Grad weiterführt*, Postgraduierte(r) *mf* ADJ *work, studies, research* weiterführend, postgradual; **~ course** Anschlusskurs *m*; **~ degree** zweiter akademischer Abschluss *or* Grad; **~ diploma/scholarship** Postgraduiertendiplom *nt*/-stipendium *nt*; **~ student** Postgraduierte(r) *mf*; **posthaste** ADV schnellstens, auf dem schnellsten Wege; **post horn** N Posthorn *nt*; **post house** N *(Hist)* Posthalterei *f*

posthumous ['pɒstjʊməs] ADJ post(h)um; *child* nachgeboren

posthumously ['pɒstjʊməslɪ] ADV post(h)um

postie ['pəʊstɪ] N *(Scot, Austral: inf)* Briefträger(in) *m(f)*

postil(l)ion [pə'stɪlɪən] N Reiter(in) *m(f)* des Sattelpferdes

postimpressionism ['pəʊstɪm'preʃənɪzəm] N Nachimpressionismus *m*

postimpressionist ['pəʊstɪm'preʃənɪst] ADJ nachimpressionistisch N Nachimpressionist(in) *m(f)*

postindustrial [,pəʊstɪn'dʌstrɪəl] ADJ post- *or* nachindustriell

posting¹ ['pəʊstɪŋ] N *(= transfer, assignment)* Versetzung *f*; *(Mil also)* Abkommandierung *f*; **he's got a new ~** er ist wieder versetzt/abkommandiert worden; **I've been given an overseas ~ to Japan** ich bin auf einen Auslandsposten nach Japan versetzt worden

posting² N *(on Internet forum)* Posting *nt*

Post-it® ['pəʊstɪt], **Post-it note®** N Haftnotiz *f*

postlude ['pəʊstlu:d] N Nachspiel *nt*

post: **postman** N (Brit) Briefträger m, Postbote m; **postman's knock** N Kinderspiel, bei dem für einen Brief mit einem Kuss bezahlt wird; **postmark** N Poststempel m; **date as ~** Datum nt des Poststempels VT (ab)stempeln; **the letter is ~ed "Birmingham"** der Brief ist in Birmingham abgestempelt; **postmaster** N (Brit) Postmeister m; **postmaster general** N pl **postmasters general** ≈ Postminister(in) m(f); **postmeridian** ADJ (form) nachmittäglich; **post meridiem** ['pəʊstmə'rɪdɪəm] ADV (form) nachmittags; **postmistress** N (Brit) Postmeisterin f; **postmodern** ADJ postmodern; **postmodernism** N a (= style) Postmoderne f b (= era) Postmodernismus m; **postmodernist** N Postmodernist(in) m(f) ADJ postmodernistisch; **postmortem** [,pəʊst'mɔːtəm] N a (also **postmortem examination**) Obduktion f, Autopsie f, Leichenöffnung f b (fig) nachträgliche Erörterung; **to hold** or **have a ~ on sth** etw hinterher erörtern; **postnatal** ADJ nach der Geburt, postnatal (spec); **post office** N Postamt nt; **the Post Office** (= institution) die Post®; **~ box** (abbr **PO Box**) Postfach nt; **~ worker** Postarbeiter(in) m(f); **he has £2000 in ~ savings** or **in the Post Office Savings Bank** (Brit) er hat £ 2000 auf dem Postsparbuch; **postoperative** ADJ postoperativ; **post-paid** ADJ portofrei; envelope frankiert, freigemacht ADV portofrei; **to reply ~** mit freigemachter Postkarte/freigemachtem Briefumschlag antworten; **postpartum** [,pəʊst'pɑːtəm] ADJ post partum, postpartal; **~ depression** Postpartum-Depression f

postpone [pəʊst'pəʊn] VT a aufschieben, hinausschieben; (for specified period) verschieben; **it has been ~d till Tuesday** es ist auf Dienstag verschoben worden; **you mustn't ~ answering a day longer** Sie dürfen die Antwort keinen Tag länger hinausschieben b (Gram form) nachstellen

postponement [pəʊst'pəʊnmənt] N (= act) Verschiebung f; (= result) Aufschub m

post: **postposition** N (Gram) Nachstellung f; (= part of speech) Postposition f; **postpositive** ADJ (Gram) nachgestellt; **postprandial** [,pəʊst'prændɪəl] ADJ (hum) nach dem Essen; **~ walk** Verdauungsspaziergang m; **post road** N (Hist) Poststraße f; **postscript(um)** N (abbr **PS**) (to letter) Postskriptum nt; (to book, article etc) Nachwort nt; (fig: to affair) Nachspiel nt; **he added a postscript** (fig: in speech) er fügte noch eine Bemerkung hinzu

postulant ['pɒstjʊlənt] N (Rel) Postulant(in) m(f)

postulate ['pɒstjʊlɪt] N Postulat nt ['pɒstjʊleɪt] VT postulieren; theory aufstellen

postulation [,pɒstjʊ'leɪʃən] N (= act) Postulieren nt; (= theory) Postulat nt

postural ['pɒstjərəl] ADJ Haltungs-; **~ exercises** Haltungsübungen pl; **children can develop bad ~ habits** Kinder können sich eine schlechte Haltung angewöhnen

posture ['pɒstʃə'] N (lit, fig) Haltung f; (pej) Pose f; **she has very poor ~** sie hat eine sehr schlechte Haltung; **in the ~ of** in der Pose (+gen) VI sich in Positur or Pose werfen; **is he merely posturing (because of the election)?** ist das nur eine (Wahl)pose seinerseits?

post-war ADJ Nachkriegs-; event also in der Nachkriegszeit; **~ era** Nachkriegszeit f; **of the ~ era** aus der Nachkriegszeit; **~ London** das London der Nachkriegszeit

postwoman N (esp Brit) Briefträgerin f, Postbotin f

posy ['pəʊzɪ] N Sträußchen nt

pot [pɒt] N a Topf m; (= teapot, coffee pot) Kanne f; (dated: = tankard) Krug m; (= lobster pot) Korb m; (= chimneypot) Kaminaufsatz m; **~s and pans** Töpfe und Pfannen; **a pint ~** ≈ ein Humpen m; **to keep the ~ boiling** (= earn living) dafür sorgen, dass der Schornstein raucht (inf); (= keep sth going) den Betrieb aufrechterhalten; **that's (a case of) the ~ calling the kettle black** (prov) ein Esel schimpft den anderen Langohr (prov); **to go to ~** (inf) (person, business) auf den Hund kommen (inf); (plan, arrangement) ins Wasser fallen (inf)
b (inf: = large amount) **to have ~s of money/time** massenhaft (inf) or jede Menge (inf) Geld/Zeit haben
c (inf: = important person) **a big ~** ein hohes Tier (inf)
d (inf: = marijuana) Pot nt (sl)
e (Cards: = pool) Topf m, Pott m
f (inf: = prize, cup) Topf m (inf)
g (= potshot) Schuss m aufs Geratewohl
h (inf: = potbelly) Spitzbauch m
VT a meat einmachen, einkochen; jam einfüllen
b plant eintopfen
c (= shoot) game schießen
d (Billiards) ball einlochen
e (inf) baby auf den Topf setzen
VI a **to ~ at** schießen auf (+acc)
b (inf: = make pottery) töpfern (inf)

potable ['pəʊtəbl] ADJ (esp US form) trinkbar

potage ['pəʊtɪdʒ] N (Cook) dicke Suppe (mit Rahm)

potash ['pɒtæʃ] N Pottasche f, Kaliumkarbonat nt

potassic [pə'tæsɪk] ADJ (Chem) Kalium-, Kali-

potassium [pə'tæsɪəm] N Kalium nt

potassium cyanide N Kaliumzyanid nt, Zyankali nt

potassium nitrate N Kaliumnitrat nt, Kalisalpeter m

potations [pəʊ'teɪʃənz] PL (liter) Zecherei f

potato [pə'teɪtəʊ] N pl **-es** Kartoffel f → **hot potato**

potato: **potato beetle**, (esp US) **potato bug** N Kartoffelkäfer m; **potato blight** N Kartoffelfäule f/-krankheit f; **potato chip** N a (esp US) = **potato crisp** b (Brit: = chip) Pomme frite m; **potato crisp** N (Brit) Kartoffelchip m; **potato masher** N Kartoffelstampfer m; **potato peeler** N Kartoffelschäler m; **potato rot** N Kartoffelfäule f/-krankheit f; **potato salad** N Kartoffelsalat m; **potato soup** N Kartoffelsuppe f

pot: **potbellied** ['pɒt'belɪd] ADJ person spitzbäuchig; (through hunger) blähbäuchig; **~ pig** Hängebauchschwein nt; **~ stove** Kanonenofen m; **potbelly** N (= stomach) (from overeating) Spitzbauch m; (from malnutrition) Blähbauch m; (= stove) Kanonenofen m; **potboiler** N rein kommerzielles Werk; **pot-bound** ADJ plant eingewachsen; **pot cheese** ADJ (US) = **cottage cheese**

poteen [pɒ'tiːn, pɒ'tʃiːn] N illegal destillierter irischer Whisky

potency ['pəʊtənsɪ] N (of drink, drug, charm etc) Stärke f; (of argument, reason etc) Durchschlagskraft f; (of weapon, combination, image) Schlagkraft f; (of man) Potenz f

potent ['pəʊtənt] ADJ drink, drug, charm, motive etc stark; argument, reason etc durchschlagend; weapon, combination, image stark, mächtig, durchschlagend; reminder stark, beeindruckend; man potent; ruler mächtig

potentate ['pəʊtənteɪt] N Potentat m

potential [pəʊ'tenʃəl] ADJ (also Phys) potenziell, potentiell
N Potenzial nt, Potential nt (also Elec, Math, Phys); **the ~ for growth** Wachstumspotenzial nt, Wachstumspotential nt; **to have ~** ausbaufähig sein (inf); **he shows quite a bit of ~** es steckt einiges in ihm; **to achieve** or **fulfil** or **realize one's ~** die Grenze seiner Möglichkeiten erreichen or erfüllen or verwirklichen; **to do sth to one's full ~** etw bis an die Grenzen seiner Möglichkeiten tun; **to have great ~ (as/for)** große Möglichkeiten bergen (als/für); **to have the ~ for sth** das Potenzial or Potential für etw haben; **to have the ~ to do sth** das Potenzial or Potential haben, um etw zu tun; **to have no/little ~** kein/kaum Potenzial or Potential haben; **creative ~** kreatives Potenzial or Potential, kreative Möglichkeiten pl; **military ~** militärisches Potenzial or Potential; **employment ~** Arbeitsmöglichkeiten pl; **management ~** Möglichkeiten pl im Management; **she has management ~** sie hat das Zeug zur Managerin; **commercial ~** kommerzielle Möglichkeiten pl

potential difference N (Phys, Elec) potenzieller or potentieller Unterschied

potential energy N (Phys) potenzielle or potentielle Energie

potentiality [pəʊ,tenʃɪ'ælɪtɪ] N Möglichkeit f

potentially [pəʊ'tenʃəlɪ] ✪ 15.3 ADV potenziell, potentiell; **~, these problems are very serious** diese Probleme könnten sich als gravierend herausstellen

potentiometer [pəʊ,tenʃɪ'ɒmɪtə'] N (Tech) Potenziometer nt, Potentiometer nt

potful ['pɒtfʊl] N Topf m; (of coffee, tea) Kanne f

pothead ['pɒthed] N (inf) Kiffer(in) m(f) (inf)

pother ['pɒðə'] N (old) Aufruhr m, Wirbel m; **to make a ~ about sth** wegen etw (ein) Theater machen

pot: **potherb** N Küchenkraut nt; **potholder** N (US) Topflappen m; **pothole** N a (in road) Schlagloch nt b (Geol) Höhle f; **potholed** ADJ voller Schlaglöcher; **workmen are already beginning to mend the ~ roads** Arbeiter haben schon damit begonnen, die Schlaglöcher in den Straßen auszubessern; **potholer** N Höhlenforscher(in) m(f); **potholing** N Höhlenforschung f; **pothook** N a (for pot) Kesselhaken m b (in writing) Krakel m; **pothunter** N a (Sport) unwaidmännischer Jäger b (for prizes) Pokalsammler(in) m(f)

potion ['pəʊʃən] N Trank m

pot: **pot luck** N **to take ~** nehmen, was es gerade gibt; **we took ~ and went to the nearest pub** wir gingen aufs Geratewohl in die nächste Kneipe; **potluck dinner** N (esp US) großes Abendessen, bei dem sich alle Anwesenden selbst mitgebrachte Speisen teilen; **potpie** N (US) in einer Auflaufform gebackene Pastete; **pot plant** N Topfpflanze f

potpourri [pəʊ'pʊərɪ] N a (lit) Duftsträußchen nt b (fig: = mixture, medley) (kunter)bunte Mischung; (of music) Potpourri nt

pot: **pot roast** N Schmorbraten m VT schmoren; **potsherd** N (Archeol) Scherbe f; **pot shot** N Schuss m aufs Geratewohl; **to take a ~ at sb/sth** aufs Geratewohl auf jdn/etw schießen; (fig inf: = criticize) jdn/etw herunterputzen (inf)

potted ['pɒtɪd] ADJ a meat eingemacht; fish eingelegt; **~ flower/plant/palm** Topfblume f/-pflanze f/-palme f b (= shortened) history, biography gekürzt, zusammengefasst; **he gave me a ~ version of the film** er erzählte mir in kurzen Worten, wovon der Film handelte

potter[1] ['pɒtə'] N Töpfer(in) m(f); **~'s clay** Töpferton m; **~'s wheel** Töpferscheibe f

potter[2], (US also) **putter** ['pʌtə'] VI (= do little jobs) herumwerkeln; (= wander aimlessly) herumschlendern; **she ~s away in the kitchen for hours** sie hantiert stundenlang in der Küche herum; **to ~ round the house** im Haus herumwerkeln; **to ~ round the shops** einen Geschäftebummel machen; **to ~ along the road** (car, driver) dahinzuckeln; **we ~ along quite happily** wir leben recht zufrieden vor uns hin

potterer ['pɒtərə'] N Trödelheini m, Trödelsuse f

pottery ['pɒtərɪ] N (= workshop, craft) Töpferei f; (= pots) Töpferwaren pl, Tonwaren pl; (glazed) Keramik f; (= archaeological remains) Tonscherben pl

potting ['pɒtɪŋ]: **potting compost** N Pflanzerde f; **potting shed** N Schuppen m

potty[1] ['pɒtɪ] N Töpfchen nt; **~-trained** (Brit) sauber

potty[2] ADJ (+er) (Brit inf: = mad) verrückt; **to go ~** verrückt werden, durchdrehen; **to drive sb ~** jdn zum Wahnsinn treiben; **to be ~ about sth**

(about hobby etc) ganz verrückt nach etw sein; **he's ~ about her** er ist verrückt nach ihr

pouch [paʊtʃ] N Beutel *m*; *(under eyes)* (Tränen)sack *m*; *(of pelican, hamster)* Tasche *f*; *(Mil)* (Patronen)tasche *f*; *(Hist: for gunpowder)* (Pulver)beutel *m*; *(esp US: = mail pouch)* Postsack *m*

pouf(fe) [pu:f] N **a** *(= seat)* Puff *m* **b** *(Brit inf)* = **poof(ter)**

poult [pəʊlt] N *(Farming)* **a** *(= chicken)* junges Huhn **b** *(= turkey)* junger Truthahn **c** *(= pheasant)* junger Fasan

poulterer [ˈpəʊltərəʳ] N *(Brit)* Geflügelhändler(in) *m(f)*; **~'s (shop)** Geflügelhandlung *f*

poultice [ˈpəʊltɪs] N Umschlag *m*, Wickel *m*; *(for boil)* Zugpflaster *nt* VT einen Umschlag *or* Wickel machen um; *boil* ein Zugpflaster kleben auf *(+acc)*

poultry [ˈpəʊltrɪ] N Geflügel *nt*

poultry: **poultry farm** N Geflügelfarm *f*; **poultry farmer** N Geflügelzüchter(in) *m(f)*; **poultry farming** N Geflügelzucht *f*; **poultry house** N Hühnerhaus *nt*; **poultryman** N *(esp US) (= farmer)* Geflügelzüchter(in) *m(f)*; *(= dealer)* Geflügelhändler(in) *m(f)*

pounce [paʊns] N Sprung *m*, Satz *m*; *(= swoop) (by bird)* Angriff *m*; *(by police)* Zugriff *m* VI *(cat, lion etc)* einen Satz machen; *(bird)* niederstoßen; *(fig)* zuschlagen; **to ~ on sb/sth** *(lit, fig)* sich auf jdn/etw stürzen; **the tiger ~d on its prey** der Tiger stürzte sich auf seine Beute; **the police ~d on him** die Polizei griff sich *(dat)* ihn

pound¹ [paʊnd] N **a** *(= weight)* ≈ Pfund *nt*; **two ~s of apples** zwei Pfund Äpfel; **by the ~** pfundweise; **he is making sure he gets his ~ of flesh** er sorgt dafür, dass er bekommt, was ihm zusteht **b** *(= money)* Pfund *nt*; **one ~ sterling** ein Pfund *nt* Sterling; **five ~s** fünf Pfund; **a five-~ note** eine Fünfpfundnote, ein Fünfpfundschein *m* → **penny**

pound² VT **a** *(= hammer, strike)* hämmern; *earth, paving slabs* feststampfen; *meat* klopfen; *dough* kneten, schlagen; *piano, typewriter* hämmern auf *(+dat)*; *table* hämmern auf *(+acc)*; *door, wall* hämmern gegen; *(waves, sea) ship* schlagen gegen; *(guns, shells, bombs)* ununterbrochen beschießen; *(troops, artillery)* unter Beschuss haben; **to ~ the streets** *(= jog)* durch die Straßen joggen; **the boxer ~ed his opponent with his fists** der Boxer hämmerte mit den Fäusten auf seinen Gegner ein; **the ship was ~ed by the waves** die Wellen schlugen gegen das Schiff; **the old-style policeman ~ing his beat** der Polizist alten Stils, der seine Runde abmarschiert

b *(= pulverize) corn etc* (zer)stampfen; *drugs, spices* zerstoßen; **to ~ sth to pieces** etw klein stampfen; **the guns ~ed the walls to pieces** die Kanonen zertrümmerten die Mauern; **the waves ~ed the boat to pieces** die Wellen zertrümmerten das Boot

VI **a** *(= beat)* hämmern; *(heart)* (wild) pochen; *(waves, sea)* schlagen (*on, against* gegen); *(drums)* dröhnen; *(engine, steamer, hooves)* stampfen; **he ~ed at *or* on the door/on the table** er hämmerte an *or* gegen die Tür/auf den Tisch

b *(= run heavily)* stampfen; *(= walk heavily, stamp)* stapfen; **the sound of ~ing feet** das Geräusch stampfender Füße; **the messenger ~ed up to me and handed me a telegram** der Bote stampfte auf mich zu und übergab mir ein Telegramm

▶ **pound away** VI hämmern; *(music, drums, guns)* dröhnen; **our guns were pounding away at the enemy position** wir hatten die feindliche Stellung unter anhaltendem Beschuss; **he was pounding away at the typewriter** er hämmerte auf der Schreibmaschine herum

▶ **pound down** VT *sep earth, rocks* feststampfen; **to pound sth down to a powder** etw pulverisieren

▶ **pound out** VT *sep* **to pound out a tune** eine Melodie herunterhämmern

pound³ N *(for stray dogs)* städtischer Hundezwinger; *(esp Brit: for cars)* Abstellplatz *m (für amtlich abgeschleppte Fahrzeuge)*

poundage [ˈpaʊndɪdʒ] N **a** *auf Pfundbasis berechnete Gebühr oder Abgabe* **b** *(= weight)* Gewicht *nt* (in Pfund)

pound cake N *(esp US) reichhaltiger Früchtekuchen*

-pounder [-ˈpaʊndəʳ] N *suf* -pfünder *m*; **quarter-pounder** Viertelpfünder *m*

pound foolish ADJ → **penny wise**

pounding [ˈpaʊndɪŋ] N **a** Hämmern *nt*; *(of heart)* Pochen *nt*; *(of music, drums)* Dröhnen *nt*; *(of waves, sea)* Schlagen *nt*; *(of engine, steamer, pile-driver, hooves, feet etc)* Stampfen *nt*; *(of guns, shells, bombs)* Bombardement *nt*; **the ship took a ~ from the waves** das Schiff wurde von den Wellen stark mitgenommen; **the city took a ~ last night** gestern Nacht wurde die Stadt schwer bombardiert; **his theory took a ~ from the critics** seine Theorie wurde von den Kritikern scharf angegriffen; **our team took quite a ~ on Saturday** unsere Mannschaft hat am Samstag eine ziemliche Schlappe einstecken müssen *(inf)*; **he took a ~ in the fight** er musste in dem Kampf einige Schläge einstecken

b *(of corn etc)* Zerstampfen *nt*; *(of drugs)* Zerstoßen *nt*

ADJ *heart* trommelnd, klopfend; *feet* trommelnd; *hooves, drums* donnernd, trommelnd; *headache* pochend; *waves* donnernd, aufschlagend

pound sign N *(Typ)* Pfundzeichen *nt*

pour [pɔːʳ] VT *liquid* gießen; *large amount also, sugar, rice etc* schütten; *drink* eingießen, einschenken; **to ~ sth for sb** jdm etw eingießen *or* einschenken; **she looks as if she's been ~ed into that dress!** *(inf)* das Kleid sitzt wie angegossen *(inf)*; **to ~ money into a project/men into a war** Geld in ein Projekt/Männer in einen Krieg pumpen *(inf)*; **he ~ed all his ideas into one book** alle seine Gedanken flossen in ein Buch

VI **a** *(lit, fig)* strömen; **the sweat ~ed off him** der Schweiß floss in Strömen an ihm herunter; **books are ~ing off the presses** Bücher werden in Massen ausgestoßen; **cars ~ed off the ferry** Autokolonnen rollten von der Fähre

b *(= rain)* **it's ~ing (with rain)** es gießt (in Strömen), es schüttet *(inf)*; **the rain ~ed down** es regnete *or* goss in Strömen → **rain**

c *(= pour out tea, coffee etc)* eingießen, einschenken; *(US: = act as hostess)* als Gastgeberin fungieren

d **this jug doesn't ~ well** dieser Krug gießt nicht gut

▶ **pour away** VT *sep* weggießen

▶ **pour forth** VI, VT *sep* = **pour out VI VT b, c**

▶ **pour in** VI hereinströmen; *(donations, protests)* in Strömen eintreffen VT *sep money, men* hineinpumpen *(inf)*

▶ **pour out** VI herausströmen (*of* aus); *(smoke also)* hervorquellen (*of* aus); *(words)* heraussprudeln (*of* aus) VT *sep* **a** *liquid* ausgießen; *(in large quantities) sugar, rice etc* ausschütten; *drink* eingießen, einschenken; **he poured out two glasses of wine** er goss zwei Gläser Wein ein **b** *(factories, schools) cars, students* ausstoßen **c** *(fig) feelings, troubles, story* sich *(dat)* von der Seele reden; **to pour out one's thanks** sich überströmend bedanken; **to pour out one's heart (to sb)** (jdm) sein Herz ausschütten

pouring [ˈpɔːrɪŋ] ADJ **~ rain** strömender Regen; **a ~ wet day** ein völlig verregneter Tag; **~ cream** Sahne *f*

pout¹ [paʊt] N **a** *(= facial expression)* Schmollmund *m* **b** *(= sulking fit)* Schmollen *nt*; **to have a ~** schmollen VI **a** *(with lips)* einen Schmollmund machen, einen Flunsch *or* eine Schnute ziehen *(inf)* **b** *(= sulk)* schmollen VT *lips* schürzen; *(sulkingly)* zu einem Schmollmund *or* Schmollen verziehen

pout² N *(= kind of cod)* Schellfisch *m*

poverty [ˈpɒvətɪ] N Armut *f*; **~ of ideas/information** Ideen-/Informationsarmut *f*; **to be above/below/on the ~ line** oberhalb/unterhalb/an der Armutsgrenze leben

poverty: **poverty level** N Ausmaß *nt* an Armut; **poverty factor** N *(Sociol)* (Grad *m* der) Armut *f*; **poverty risk** N *(Sociol)* Armutsrisiko *nt*; **poverty-stricken** [ˈpɒvətɪstrɪkən] ADJ Not leidend; *conditions* kümmerlich; **to be ~** Armut leiden; *(hum inf)* am Hungertuch nagen *(hum)*; **poverty trap** N *Situation, wobei (vermehrte) Einkünfte zu einer Verringerung/zum Wegfall von Sozialleistungen führen*, Armutsfalle *f*

POW *abbr of* **prisoner of war**

powder [ˈpaʊdəʳ] N Pulver *nt*; *(= face, talcum powder etc)* Puder *m*; *(= dust)* Staub *m*; **to grind sth to (a) ~** etw pulverig *or* zu Pulver mahlen; **to reduce sth to (a) ~** etw zu Pulver machen

VT **a** *milk* pulverisieren; *sugar* stoßen; *chalk* zermahlen **b** *(= apply powder to) face, body, oneself* pudern; **to ~ one's nose** *(lit)* sich *(dat)* die Nase pudern; *(euph)* kurz verschwinden *(euph)*; **the trees were ~ed with snow** die Bäume waren mit Schnee überzuckert VI *(= crumble)* (zu Staub) zerfallen; **the cement had ~ed away** der Mörtel war zu Staub zerfallen

powder: **powder blue** ADJ taubenblau N Taubenblau *nt*; **powder compact** N Puderdose *f*

powdered [ˈpaʊdəd] ADJ **a** *(= covered with powder) face, wig* gepudert **b** *(= in powder form) coffee* löslich; *egg* pulverisiert; **~ chalk** Kreidepulver *nt*; **~ sugar** *(US)* Puderzucker *m*, Staubzucker *m (Aus)*

powdered milk N Milchpulver *nt*

powder horn N Pulverhorn *nt*

powdering [ˈpaʊdərɪŋ] N *(liter)* **there was a thin ~ of snow on the grass** auf dem Gras lag eine dünne Schneeschicht wie Puderzucker

powder: **powder keg** N *(lit, fig)* Pulverfass *nt*; **powder magazine** N Pulvermagazin *nt*, Pulverkammer *f*; **powder monkey** N *(Mil Hist)* Pulverjunge *m*; *(= explosives man)* Sprengmeister *m*; **powder puff** N Puderquaste *f*; **powder room** N Damentoilette *f*; **powder snow** N Pulverschnee *m*

powdery [ˈpaʊdərɪ] ADJ **a** *(= like powder)* pulvrig **b** *(= crumbly)* bröckelig; *bones* morsch **c** *(= covered with powder)* gepudert

power [ˈpaʊəʳ] N **a** *no pl (= physical strength)* Kraft *f*; *(= force: of blow, explosion etc)* Stärke *f*, Gewalt *f*, Wucht *f*; *(fig: of argument etc)* Überzeugungskraft *f*; **the ~ of love/logic/tradition** die Macht der Liebe/Logik/Tradition; **earning ~** mögliche Verdiensthöhe; **purchasing** *or* **spending ~** Kaufkraft *f*

b *(= faculty, ability: of hearing, imagination)* Vermögen *nt no pl*; **his ~s of hearing** sein Hörvermögen *nt*; **mental/hypnotic ~s** geistige/hypnotische Kräfte *pl*; **to weaken their ~(s) of resistance** um ihre Widerstandskraft zu schwächen

c *(= capacity, ability to help etc)* Macht *f*; **he did all in his ~ to help them** er tat (alles), was in seiner Macht *or* in seinen Kräften stand, um ihnen zu helfen; **it's beyond my ~** *or* **not within my ~ to …** es steht nicht in meiner Macht, zu …

d *(no pl: = sphere or strength of influence, authority)* Macht *f*; *(Jur, parental)* Gewalt *f*; *(usu pl: = thing one has authority to do)* Befugnis *f*; **he has the ~ to act** er ist handlungsberechtigt; **the ~ of the police/of the law** die Macht der Polizei/des Gesetzes; **to be in sb's ~** in jds Gewalt *(dat)* sein; **that does not fall within my ~(s)** das fällt nicht in meinen Machtbereich; **that is beyond *or* outside my ~(s)** das überschreitet meine Befugnisse; **~ of attorney** *(Jur)* (Handlungs)vollmacht *f*; **the party now in ~** die Partei, die im Augenblick an der Macht ist; **to fall from ~** abgesetzt werden; **to come into ~** an die Macht kommen; **they have no ~ over economic matters** in Wirtschaftsfragen haben sie keine Befugnisse; **I have no ~ over her** ich habe keine Gewalt über sie; **he has been given full ~(s) to make all decisions** man hat ihm volle Entscheidungsgewalt übertragen; **that man has no ~ over his destiny** dass der Mensch keine Gewalt über sein Schicksal hat; **"student/worker ~"** „Macht den Studenten/Arbeitern"

e *(= person or institution having authority)* Autorität *f*, Machtfaktor *m*; **to be the ~ behind the scenes/throne** die graue Eminenz sein; **the ~s that be** *(inf)* die da oben *(inf)*; **the ~s of darkness/evil** die Mächte der Finsternis/des Bösen

f *(= nation)* Macht *f*; **a four-~ conference** eine Viermächtekonferenz; **a naval ~** eine Seemacht

g *(= source of energy: nuclear, electric power etc)* Energie *f*; *(of water, steam)* Energie *f*, Kraft *f*; **~ on/off** *(technical device)* ein-/ausschalten; **the ship made port under her own ~** das Schiff lief mit eigener Kraft in den Hafen ein; **they cut off the ~** *(= electricity)* sie haben den Strom abgestellt

h *(of engine, machine, loudspeakers, transmitter)* Leistung *f*; *(of microscope, lens, sun's rays, drug, chemical)* Stärke *f*; **the ~ of suggestion** die Wirkung *or* Wirkkraft des Unterschwelligen; **a low-power microscope** ein schwaches Mikroskop; **a 10-power magnification** eine 10fache Vergrößerung; **microwave on full ~ for one minute** eine Minute bei voller Leistung in der Mikrowelle erhitzen

i *(Math)* Potenz *f*; **to the ~ (of) 2** hoch 2, in der 2. Potenz; **to raise 2 to the ~ (of) 5** 2 mit 5 potenzieren

j *(inf: = a lot of)* **a ~ of help** eine wertvolle *or* große Hilfe; **that did me a ~ of good** das hat mir unheimlich gutgetan *(inf)*

VT *(engine)* antreiben; *(fuel)* betreiben; **~ed by electricity/by jet engines** mit Elektro-/Düsenantrieb; **as he ~s his way down the straight** wie er die Gerade entlangbraust; **he ~ed the ball into the net** er schoss den Ball mit Wucht ins Netz

VI *(runner, racing car)* rasen; **he ~ed away from the rest of the field** er raste dem übrigen Feld davon; **the swimmer ~ed through the water** der Schwimmer wuchtete durch das Wasser; **we're ~ing through the work now** unsere Arbeit geht jetzt mit Riesenschritten voran

▶ **power down** VI *(engine, turbine)* zum Stillstand kommen

▶ **power up** **VT** *sep* starten **VI** starten

power: **power amplifier** N *(Tech)* Endverstärker *m*; **power-assisted** ADJ *(Aut, Tech)* Servo-; **~ steering** Servolenkung *f*; **power base** N Machtbasis *f*; **powerboat** N Rennboot *nt*; **power brakes** PL Servobremsen *pl*; **power broker** N *(esp US Pol)* Drahtzieher(in) *m(f)* *(inf)*; **power cable** N Stromkabel *nt*; **power consumption** N Strom- *or* Energieverbrauch *m*; **power cut** N Stromsperre *f*; *(accidental)* Stromausfall *m*; **power demand** N Strom- *or* Energiebedarf *m*; **power dive** N *(Aviat)* (Voll-gas)sturzflug *m*; **power-dive** VI *(Aviat)* einen Sturzflug machen; **power dressing** N Karrierelook *m*; **power drill** N Bohrmaschine *f*; **power-driven** ADJ mit Motorantrieb; **power failure** N Stromausfall *m*

powerful [ˈpaʊəfʊl] ADJ **a** *(= influential) government, person* mächtig, einflussreich

b *(= strong) boxer, engine, drug, emotions, computer, evidence, influence, message* stark; *swimmer* kraftvoll, stark; *build, arm, kick, light* kräftig; *stroke, punch, detergent* kraftvoll; *bomb* stark, zerstörerisch, von großer Durchschlagskraft; *earthquake, storm* stark, massiv; *smell* massiv, überwältigend; *voice* kräftig, kraftvoll

c *(fig) speaker, actor* mitreißend; *music, film, performance* ausdrucksvoll, mitreißend; *argument* durchschlagend, massiv *(inf)*; *salesman* überzeugend

d **a ~ lot of** *(dial)* ganz schön viel *(inf)*, gehörig viel *(inf)*

powerfully [ˈpaʊəfəlɪ] ADV **a** *(= strongly) influence* mächtig, gewaltig, stark; *reinforce* massiv, gewaltig; *moving* mächtig, stark; *erotic* stark; **a ~ addictive drug** eine stark Sucht erregende Droge; **the room smelled ~ of cats** der Katzengeruch in dem Raum war überwältigend; **~ built** kräftig gebaut **b** *(fig) speak* kraftvoll; *describe, act* mitreißend, kraftvoll; *argue* massiv *(inf)*; **~ written** mitreißend geschrieben; **I was ~ affected by the book** das Buch hat mich mächtig *(inf) or* stark beeindruckt

power: **power glider** N *(Aviat)* Motorsegler *m*; **powerhouse** [ˈpaʊəhaʊs] N **a** *(lit)* = **power station b** *(fig)* treibende Kraft *(behind* hinter *+dat)*; **he's a real ~** er ist ein äußerst dynamischer Mensch; **she's an intellectual ~** sie hat eine erstaunliche intellektuelle Kapazität; **he's a ~ of new ideas** er hat einen unerschöpflichen Vorrat an neuen Ideen; **powerless** ADJ *(physically) punch, body* kraftlos; *(as regards ability to act) committee, person* machtlos; **to be ~ to resist** nicht die Kraft haben, zu widerstehen; **the government is ~ to deal with inflation** die Regierung steht der Inflation machtlos gegenüber; **we are ~ to help you** es steht nicht in unserer Macht, Ihnen zu helfen, wir sind machtlos(, Ihnen zu helfen); **power-lifting** N Powerlifting *nt*, Kraftdreikampf *m*; **power line** N *(Elec)* **a** *(for heavy current)* Starkstromleitung *f* **b** *(on pylons or poles)* Überlandleitung *f*; **power lock** N *(Aut)* Zentralverriegelung *f*; **power loom** N Webmaschine *f*; **power lunch** N Geschäftsessen *nt* unter Führungskräften; **power mower** N Motorrasenmäher *m*; *(electric)* Elektrorasenmäher *m*; **power outage** [ˈpaʊər,aʊtɪdʒ] N Stromsperre *f*; *(accidental)* Stromausfall *m*; **power pack** N *(Elec)* Netzteil *nt*; *(inf: = engine)* Motor *m*, Kraftpaket *nt (inf)*; **power plant** N **a** = **power station b** *(= engine)* Motor *m*;; **power play** N **a** *(Ice Hockey)* Powerplay *nt*, Übermachtsspiel *nt* **b** *(fig) (= attack)* Powerplay *nt*; *(= struggle)* Kraftprobe *f*; **power point** N *(Elec)* Steckdose *f*; **power politics** PL Machtpolitik *f*; **power saw** N Motorsäge *f*; *(electric)* Elektrosäge *f*; **power sharing** N *(Pol)* Machtteilung *f*; **power-sharing** ADJ *(Pol) executive* mit Machtteilung *pred*; **~ agreement** Machtteilungsabkommen *nt*; **power station** N Kraftwerk *nt*, Elektrizitätswerk *nt*; **power steering** N *(Aut)* Servolenkung *f*; **power structure** N Machtstruktur *f*; **power struggle** N Machtkampf *m*; **power supply** N *(Elec)* Stromversorgung *f*; **power surge** N *(Elec)* Überspannung *f*; **power tool** N Elektrowerkzeug *nt*; **power-up** N Start *m*; **power walking** N Walking *nt*, Walken *nt*; **power worker** N Elektrizitätsarbeiter(in) *m(f)*

powwow [ˈpaʊwaʊ] N *(of Native Americans)* Versammlung *f*; *(with Native Americans)* indianische Verhandlungen *pl*; *(inf)* Besprechung *f*; *(to solve problem)* Kriegsrat *m (hum)*; **a family ~** ein Familienrat *m*

pox [pɒks] N *(old) (= smallpox)* Pocken *pl*, Blattern *pl*; *(= syphilis)* Syphilis *f*; **a ~ on ...!** *(old)* zur Hölle mit ...!

pp **a** *abbr of* **pages** S. **b** *abbr of* **per procurationem** *(= on behalf of)* pp., ppa.

PPE *abbr of* **Philosophy, Politics and Economics**

ppm *abbr of* **parts per million**

pppn *abbr of* **per person per night** pro Person pro Nacht

PPS **a** *(Brit) abbr of* **parliamentary private secretary** **b** *abbr of* **post postscriptum** PPS *nt*

PPV *abbr of* **pay-per-view**

PR [piːˈɑːˈ] N **a** *abbr of* **proportional representation** **b** *abbr of* **public relations** PR *f*; **PR agency** PR-Agentur *f*; **PR man** PR-Mann *m*; **PR woman** PR-Frau *f*; **PR work** PR-Arbeit *f*, Öffentlichkeitsarbeit *f*

pr *abbr of* **pair**

practicability [,præktɪkəˈbɪlɪtɪ] N Durchführbarkeit *f*, Praktikabilität *f (rare)*; *(of road)* Befahrbarkeit *f*

practicable [ˈpræktɪkəbl] ADJ durchführbar, praktikabel; *road* befahrbar

practicably [ˈpræktɪkəblɪ] ADV **if it can ~ be done** falls (es) durchführbar (ist)

practical [ˈpræktɪkəl] ADJ **a** praktisch; *person* praktisch (veranlagt); **to have a ~ mind** praktisch denken; **his ideas have no ~ application** seine Ideen sind nicht praxisnah *or* sind praktisch nicht anwendbar; **for (all) ~ purposes** in der Praxis; **to be of no ~ use** ohne (jeden) praktischen Nutzen sein **b** *(= handy)* praktisch; **they are both very ~ about the house** sie sind beide sehr geschickt *or* praktisch in allem, was in einem Haus anfällt **c** *(= virtual)* **it was a ~ certainty** es war praktisch eine Gewissheit

practicality [,præktɪˈkælɪtɪ] N **a** *no pl (of person)* praktische Veranlagung **b** *no pl (of scheme etc)* Durchführbarkeit *f*; **your solution shows/lacks ~** Ihre Lösung ist praxisnah/praxisfremd **c** *(= practical detail)* praktisches Detail

practical: **practical joke** N Streich *m*; **practical joker** N Witzbold *m (inf)*

practically [ˈpræktɪkəlɪ] ADV *(all senses)* praktisch; **~ speaking** konkret gesagt; **~ minded** praktisch veranlagt

practical nurse N *(US)* ≈ Hilfsschwester *f*

practice [ˈpræktɪs] **N** **a** *(= habit, custom) (of individual)* Gewohnheit *f*, Angewohnheit *f*; *(of group, in country)* Brauch *m*, Sitte *f*; *(= bad habit)* Unsitte *f*; *(in business)* Verfahrensweise, Praktik *f*; **he opposes the ~ of pubs being open on Sundays** er ist dagegen, dass Lokale am Sonntag geöffnet sind; **this is normal business ~** das ist im Geschäftsleben so üblich; **as is my (usual) ~** wie es meine Gewohnheit ist; **to make a ~ of doing sth, to make it a ~ to do sth** es sich *(dat)* zur Gewohnheit machen, etw zu tun; **Christian ~ dictates ...** das christliche Brauchtum verlangt ...; **it is the ~ of this Court to ...** es ist an diesem Gericht üblich, zu ...; **that's common ~** das ist allgemeine Praxis, das ist allgemein üblich

b *(= exercise, training)* Übung *f*; *(= rehearsal, trial run)* Probe *f*; *(Sport)* Training *nt*; *(= practice game)* Trainingsspiel *nt*; **~ makes perfect** *(Prov)* Übung macht den Meister *(Prov)*; **Michael Schuhmacher had the fastest time in ~** Michael Schuhmacher fuhr im Training die schnellste Zeit; **this piece of music needs a lot of ~** für dieses (Musik)stück muss man viel üben; **you should do 10 minutes' ~ each day** du solltest täglich 10 Minuten (lang) üben; **to be out of ~** aus der Übung sein; **that was just a ~ run** das war nur mal zur Probe; **to have a ~ session** üben; *(= rehearse)* Probe haben; *(Sport)* trainieren; **the first ~ session** die erste Übung/Probe/das erste Training

c *(= doing, as opposed to theory)* Praxis *f*; **in ~** in der Praxis; **that won't work in ~** das lässt sich praktisch nicht durchführen; **to put one's ideas into ~** seine Ideen in die Praxis umsetzen

d *(of doctor, lawyer etc)* Praxis *f*; **he returned to the ~ of law/medicine** er praktizierte wieder als Rechtsanwalt/Arzt; **to go into** *or* **set up in ~** eine Praxis aufmachen *or* eröffnen, sich als Arzt/Rechtsanwalt *etc* niederlassen; **he's not in ~ any more** er praktiziert nicht mehr; **to retire from ~** sich aus der Praxis zurückziehen; **a large legal ~** eine große Rechtsanwaltspraxis

VTI *(US)* = **practise**

practice room N *(of musician etc)* Übungsraum *m*

practice teacher N *(US Sch)* Referendar(in) *m(f)*

practise, *(US)* **practice** [ˈpræktɪs] **VT** **a** *thrift, patience etc* üben; *self-denial, Christian charity, torture* praktizieren; **to ~ what one preaches** *(prov)* seine Lehren in die Tat umsetzen

b *(in order to acquire skill)* üben; *song, chorus* proben; **to ~ the violin** Geige üben; **to ~ the high jump/one's golf swing** Hochsprung/seinen Schlag im Golf üben *or* trainieren; **to ~ doing sth** etw üben; **I'm practising my German on him** ich probiere mein Deutsch an ihm aus

c *(= follow, exercise) profession, religion* ausüben, praktizieren; **to ~ law/medicine** als Anwalt/Arzt praktizieren; **all a writer wants is peace to ~ his art** alles, was ein Schriftsteller braucht, ist Ruhe, um sich seiner Kunst widmen zu können

VI **a** *(in order to acquire skill)* üben

b *(lawyer, doctor etc)* praktizieren; **to ~ at the Bar** als Anwalt bei Gericht praktizieren

practised, *(US)* **practiced** ['præktɪst] ADJ geübt; *politician, marksman, liar also* erfahren; *performance also* professionell; **with a ~ eye/hand** mit geübtem Auge/geübter Hand; **he's ~ in getting his own way** er hat Übung darin, seinen Willen durchzusetzen; **with ~ skill** gekonnt

practising, *(US)* **practicing** ['præktɪsɪŋ] ADJ *lawyer, doctor, homosexual* praktizierend; *Christian also, socialist* aktiv; *teacher* im Beruf stehend, seinen Beruf ausübend

practitioner [præk'tɪʃənə'] N *(of method)* Benutzer(in) *m(f)*, Anwender(in) *m(f)*; *(= medical practitioner)* praktischer Arzt, praktische Ärztin; *(= dental practitioner)* Zahnarzt *m*/-ärztin *f*; *(= legal practitioner)* Rechtsanwalt *m*/-anwältin *f*; **~s of this profession** diejenigen, die diesen Beruf ausüben; **he is a ~ of Zen Buddhism** er ist ein Anhänger des Zen-Buddhismus → **general practitioner**

praesidium [prɪ'sɪdɪəm] N = **presidium**

praetor ['pri:tə'] N Prätor *m*

praetorian guard [prɪ'tɔ:rɪən'gɑ:d] N **a** *(Hist)* **the Praetorian Guard** *(= body)* die Prätorianergarde **b** *(fig: = loyal group)* Prätorianergarde *f*, Prätorianer *pl*; **that ~ of foreigners around the President** die ausländischen Prätorianer in der Umgebung des Präsidenten

pragmatic ADJ, **pragmatically** ADV [præg'mætɪk, -əlɪ] pragmatisch

pragmatism ['prægmətɪzəm] N Pragmatismus *m*

pragmatist ['prægmətɪst] N Pragmatiker(in) *m(f)*

Prague [prɑ:g] N Prag *nt*

prairie ['prɛərɪ] N Grassteppe *f*; *(in North America)* Prärie *f*

prairie: **prairie chicken** N *(US)* Präriehuhn *nt*; **prairie dog** N Präriehund *m*; **prairie oyster** N Prärieauster *f*; **prairie schooner** N Planwagen *m*; **prairie wolf** N Präriewolf *m*

praise [preɪz] VT loben; *(to others, in worship also)* preisen *(geh)*, rühmen *(geh)*; **to ~ sb for having done sth** jdn dafür loben, etw getan zu haben; **to ~ the virtues of sth** die Vorzüge einer Sache *(gen)* loben *or* preisen *(geh)*; **~ God!** gelobt sei Gott!

N Lob *nt no pl*; **a hymn of ~** eine Lobeshymne; **a poem in ~ of beer** ein Loblied *nt* auf das Bier; **he spoke/made a speech in ~ of their efforts** er sprach lobend von ihren Bemühungen/hielt eine Lobrede auf ihre Bemühungen; **to win ~** *(person)* Lob ernten; *(efforts)* Lob einbringen; **to give ~ (to sb)** (jdn) loben; **to be loud** *or* **warm in one's ~ (of sth)** voll des Lobes (für etw) sein; **I have nothing but ~ for him** ich kann ihn nur loben; **he's beyond ~** er ist über jedes *or* alles Lob erhaben; **all ~ to him** alle Achtung!; **~ indeed!** *(also iro)* ein hohes Lob; **~ from him is ~ indeed** Lob aus seinem Mund will etwas heißen; **~ be to God!** *(in church)* gelobt sei der Herr!; **~(s) be!** Gott sei Dank! → **sing**

praiseworthiness ['preɪz,wɜ:ðɪnɪs] N *(of attempt, effort)* Löblichkeit *f*; **I don't doubt his ~/the ~ of his motives** ich zweifle nicht an seinen lobenswerten Absichten/daran, dass seine Motive lobenswert sind

praiseworthy ['preɪz,wɜ:ðɪ] ADJ lobenswert

praline ['prɑ:li:n] N Praline *f* mit Nuss-Karamellfüllung

pram [præm] N *(Brit)* Kinderwagen *m*; *(dolls')* Puppenwagen *m*

prance [prɑ:ns] VI *(horse)* tänzeln; *(person) (= jump around)* herumhüpfen *or* -tanzen; *(= walk gaily, mince)* tänzeln; **she was prancing about with nothing on** sie lief nackt durch die Gegend; **to ~ in/out** *(person)* herein-/hinausspazieren

prandial ['prændɪəl] ADJ *(form, often hum)* Essens-, Tisch-

prang [præŋ] *(esp Brit inf)* N *(= crash)* Bums *m (inf)*; *(of plane)* Bruchlandung *f* INTERJ krach VT **a** *(= crash) car* ramponieren *(inf)*, lädieren; *plane* eine Bruchlandung machen **b** *(= bomb)* zerbomben, zusammenbomben *(inf)*

prank [præŋk] N Streich *m*; *(harmless also)* Ulk *m*; **to play a ~ on sb** jdm einen Streich spielen; *(harmless also)* einen Ulk mit jdm machen

prankish ['præŋkɪʃ] ADJ *person* zu Streichen aufgelegt *or* bereit; *behaviour, act* schelmisch

prankster ['præŋkstə'] N Schelm(in) *m(f)*

praseodymium [,preɪzɪəʊ'dɪmɪəm] N *(Chem)* Praseodym *nt*

prat [præt] N *(Brit inf: = idiot)* Trottel *m (inf)*

prate [preɪt] VI faseln, schwafeln

pratfall ['prætfɔ:l] N *(esp US inf)* Sturz auf den Hintern *(inf)*; *(fig)* Bauchlandung *f (fig)*; **to take a ~** *(also fig)* auf den Hintern fallen

prating ['preɪtɪŋ] N Gefasel *nt*, Geschwafel *nt* ADJ faselnd, schwafelnd

prattle ['prætl] N Geplapper *nt* VI plappern

prattler ['prætlə'] N *(pej: = chatterbox)* Plappermaul *nt*

prawn [prɔ:n] N Garnele *f*

prawn cocktail N Krabbencocktail *m*

prawn crackers PL Krabbenchips *pl*

pray [preɪ] VI **a** *(= say prayers)* beten; **let us ~** lasset uns beten; **to ~ for sb/sth** für jdn/um etw beten; **to ~ for sth** *(= want it badly)* stark auf etw *(acc)* hoffen

b *(old, liter)* **~ take a seat** bitte, nehmen Sie doch Platz, wollen Sie bitte Platz nehmen?; **what good is that, ~ (tell)?** was hilft das, wenn ich mir die Frage gestatten darf?

VT *(old, liter)* inständig bitten, ersuchen *(geh)*; **I ~ you tell me** *(old)* bitte, erzählen Sie mir doch; *(stronger)* ich bitte Sie inständig, erzählen Sie mir doch; **and what is that, I ~ you?** und was ist das, wenn ich mir die Frage gestatten darf?; **they ~ed the king for mercy** sie flehten den König um Gnade an *(geh)*

prayer [prɛə'] N Gebet *nt*; *(= service, prayer meeting)* Andacht *f*; **to say one's ~s** beten, seine Gebete verrichten *(geh)*; **to be at ~** beim Gebet sein; **he will lead our ~s** er wird uns im Gebet führen; **a ~ for peace** ein Gebet für den Frieden; **a life of ~** ein Leben im Gebet; **Evening Prayer** Abendandacht *f*; **we attended Morning Prayer** wir besuchten die Morgenandacht; **we have ~s every morning** wir haben jeden Morgen eine Andacht; **family ~s** Hausandacht *f*; **the Book of Common Prayer** *das Gebetbuch der anglikanischen Kirche*; **my one ~ is that ...** ich bete nur, dass ...

prayer: **prayer beads** PL Gebetsperlen *pl*; **prayer book** N Gebetbuch *nt*; **prayer mat** N Gebetsteppich *m*; **prayer meeting** N Gebetsstunde *f*; **prayer rug** N = **prayer mat**; **prayer shawl** N Gebetsmantel *m*; **prayer wheel** N Gebetsmühle *f*

praying mantis ['preɪɪŋ'mæntɪs] N Gottesanbeterin *f*

pre- [pri:-] PREF vor-; *(esp with words derived from Latin or Greek)* prä-; **preschool** vorschulisch; **prefascist** präfaschistisch; **at ~1980 prices** zu Preisen von vor 1980

preach [pri:tʃ] VT predigen; *(fig) advantages etc* propagieren; **to ~ a sermon** *(lit, fig)* eine Predigt halten; **to ~ the gospel** das Evangelium verkünden VI *(= give a sermon, be moralistic)* predigen; **who is ~ing today?** wer predigt heute?, wer hält heute die Predigt?; **to ~ to/at sb** jdm eine Predigt halten; **to ~ to the converted** *(prov)* offene Türen einrennen

preacher ['pri:tʃə'] N Prediger(in) *m(f)*; *(fig: = moralizer)* Moralprediger(in) *m(f)*; **all these ~s of détente** alle diese Entspannungsprediger

preachify ['pri:tʃɪfaɪ] VI *(pej inf)* predigen, moralisieren

preaching ['pri:tʃɪŋ] N *(lit, fig) (= act)* Predigen *nt*; *(= sermon)* Predigt *f*

preachy ['pri:tʃɪ] ADJ *(inf)* moralisierend

preadolescent [,pri:ædə'lesənt] ADJ vorpubertär

preamble [pri:'æmbl] N Einleitung *f*; *(of book)* Vorwort *nt*; *(Jur)* Präambel *f*

preamplifier [pri:'æmplɪ,faɪə'], **preamp** *(inf)* [pri:'æmp] N Vorverstärker *m*

prearrange ['pri:ə'reɪndʒ] VT im voraus vereinbaren

prearranged ['pri:ə'reɪndʒd], **pre-arranged** ADJ *(= predetermined) meeting, sign* im Voraus verabredet; *route, location* im Voraus bestimmt *or* festgelegt

prebend ['prebənd] N *(form) (= stipend)* Pfründe *f*, Präbende *f*; *(= person)* Pfründner *m*, Pfründeninhaber *m*, Präbendar(ius) *m*

prebendary ['prebəndərɪ] N Pfründner *m*, Pfründeninhaber *m*, Präbendar(ius) *m*

Pre-Cambrian [pri:'kæmbrɪən] ADJ präkambrisch

precarious [prɪ'kɛərɪəs] ADJ unsicher; *situation also, relationship* prekär; *theory, assertion* anfechtbar; *position* unsicher, schwankend; *balance* unsicher, schwankend, instabil; *peace* gefährdet, instabil, unsicher; **at a ~ angle** in einem gefährlich aussehenden Winkel; **that cup/that shelf looks somewhat ~** die Tasse/das Regal sieht ziemlich gefährlich aus

precariously [prɪ'kɛərɪəslɪ] ADV *cling, dangle* unsicher; **to be ~ balanced** *(lit, fig)* auf der Kippe stehen; **with a cup ~ balanced on the end of his nose** eine Tasse auf der Nase balancierend; **~ perched on the edge of the table** gefährlich nahe am Tischrand; **he lived rather ~ from his work as a photographer** er verdiente einen ziemlich unsicheren Lebensunterhalt als Fotograf

precast [pri:'kɑ:st] *vb: pret, ptp* **precast** VT vorfertigen ADJ vorgefertigt; **~ concrete** Fertig(teil)beton *m*

precaution [prɪ'kɔ:ʃən] N Sicherheitsmaßnahme *f*, (Sicherheits)vorkehrung *f*, Vorsichtsmaßnahme *f*; **security ~s** Sicherheitsmaßnahmen *or* -vorkehrungen *pl*; **fire ~s** Brandschutzmaßnahmen *pl*; **to take ~s against sth** Vorsichtsmaßnahmen *pl* gegen etw treffen; **do you take ~s?** *(euph: = use contraception)* nimmst *or* machst du (irgend)etwas?; **to take the ~ of doing sth** vorsichtshalber *or* sicherheitshalber etw tun

precautionary [prɪ'kɔ:ʃənərɪ] ADJ Vorsichts-, Sicherheits-, vorbeugend; **~ measure** Vorsichts- *or* Sicherheitsmaßnahme *f*; **it's purely ~** es ist eine reine *or* nur eine Vorsichtsmaßnahme

precede [prɪ'si:d] VT *(in order, time)* vorangehen *(+dat)*; *(in importance)* gehen vor *(+dat)*; *(in rank)* stehen über *(+dat)*; **for the month preceding this** den (ganzen) Monat davor; **to ~ a lecture with a joke** einem Vortrag einen Witz vorausschicken

precedence ['presɪdəns] N *(of person)* vorrangige Stellung *(over* gegenüber); *(of problem etc)* Vorrang *m (over* vor *+dat)*; **to take** *or* **have ~ over sb/sth** vor jdm/etw Vorrang haben; **to give ~ to sb/sth** jdm/einer Sache Vorrang geben; **the guests entered the hall in order of ~** die Gäste betraten die Halle in der Reihenfolge ihres (gesellschaftlichen) Rangs; **dukes have ~ over barons** Herzöge stehen im Rang höher als Barone

precedent ['presɪdənt] N Präzedenzfall *m*; *(Jur also)* Präjudiz *nt*; **according to ~** nach den bisherigen Fällen; **against all the ~s** entgegen allen früheren Fällen; **without ~** noch nie da gewesen; **to establish** *or* **create** *or* **set a ~** einen Präzedenzfall schaffen; **to break with ~** dem Präzedenzfall nicht mehr folgen; **is there any ~ for this?** ist der Fall schon einmal da gewesen?; **there is no ~ for this decision** diese Entscheidung kann sich nicht an einem vergleichbaren Fall ausrichten

preceding [prɪ'si:dɪŋ] ADJ *time, month etc* vorangegangen; *page, example also* vorhergehend

precensor [,pri:'sensə'] VT *newspaper article etc* vorzensieren, einer Vorzensur unterwerfen *(geh)*

precentor [prɪˈsentəʳ] N Vorsänger(in) *m(f)*, Präzentor(in) *m(f) (spec)*

precept [ˈpriːsept] N Grundsatz *m*, Prinzip *nt*

preceptor [prɪˈseptəʳ] N *(old, form)* Lehrer *m*, Präzeptor *m (old)*

precession [prɪˈseʃən] N Präzession *f*; **~ of the equinoxes** *(Astron)* Präzession *f* der Äquinoktien

pre-Christian [priːˈkrɪstɪən] ADJ vorchristlich

precinct [ˈpriːsɪŋkt] N **a** *(Brit) (= pedestrian precinct)* Fußgängerzone *f*; *(= shopping precinct)* Geschäfts- *or* Einkaufsviertel *nt*; *(US) (= police precinct)* Revier *nt*; *(= voting precinct)* Bezirk *m* **b** **precincts** PL *(= grounds, premises)* Gelände *nt*, Areal *nt*; *(= environs)* Umgebung *f*; *(of cathedral)* Domfreiheit *f*

preciosity [ˌpresɪˈɒsɪtɪ] N Pretiosität *f*, Preziosität *f*

precious [ˈpreʃəs] ADJ **a** *(= costly)* wertvoll, kostbar
b *(= rare) commodity* kostbar, wertvoll
c *(= treasured)* wertvoll; *(iro)* hochverehrt, heiß geliebt; **my ~ (one)!** mein Schatz!; **I have very ~ memories of that time/of him** ich habe Erinnerungen an diese Zeit/an ihn, die mir sehr wertvoll *or* teuer *(geh)* sind; **the loss of our ~ daughter** der Verlust unserer heiß geliebten Tochter
d *(pej: = mannered, affected) language, humour etc* pretiös, preziös; *person* geziert, geschraubt; *style* geziert, gekünstelt
ADV *(inf)* **~ little/few** herzlich wenig/wenige *(inf)*; **~ little else** herzlich wenig sonst; **I had ~ little choice** ich hatte keine große Wahl

precious metal N Edelmetall *nt*

precious stone N Edelstein *m*

precipice [ˈpresɪpɪs] N *(lit, fig)* Abgrund *m*

precipitance [prɪˈsɪpɪtəns], **precipitancy** [prɪˈsɪpɪtənsɪ] N *(= hastiness)* Hast *f*, Eile *f*; *(= over-hastiness)* Voreiligkeit *f*, Überstürztheit *f*, Überstürzung *f*

precipitant [prɪˈsɪpɪtənt] N (Aus)fällungsmittel *nt* ADJ = **precipitate ADJ**

precipitate [prəˈsɪpɪtɪt] N *(Met)* Niederschlag *m*; *(Chem also)* Präzipitat *nt (spec)* ADJ *(= hasty)* hastig, eilig; *(= over-hasty)* übereilt, voreilig, überstürzt [prɪˈsɪpɪteɪt] VT **a** *(= hurl)* schleudern; *(downwards)* hinunter- *or* hinabschleudern; *(fig)* stürzen **b** *(= hasten)* beschleunigen **c** *(Chem)* (aus)fällen; *(Met)* niederschlagen VI *(Chem)* ausfallen; *(Met)* sich niederschlagen

precipitately [prɪˈsɪpɪtɪtlɪ] ADV *(= hastily)* hastig, eilig; *(= over-hastily)* übereilt, voreilig, überstürzt

precipitation [prɪˌsɪpɪˈteɪʃən] N **a** *(Met)* Niederschlag *m* **b** *(= haste)* Hast *f*, Eile *f*; *(= over-hastiness)* Übereile *f*, Übereiltheit *f*, Überstürztheit *f*

precipitous [prɪˈsɪpɪtəs] ADJ **a** *(= steep)* steil **b** *(= hasty)* überstürzt

precipitously [prɪˈsɪpɪtəslɪ] ADV **a** *(= steeply)* steil; **to fall away ~** *(ground etc)* senkrecht *or* jäh abfallen **b** *(= hastily)* überstürzt

précis [ˈpreɪsiː] N Zusammenfassung *f*; *(Sch)* Inhaltsangabe *f*

precise [prɪˈsaɪs] ADJ **a** genau; *answer, description also* präzise; **at that ~ moment** genau in dem Augenblick; **this was the ~ amount I needed** das war genau *or* exakt der Betrag, den ich brauchte; **please be more ~** drücken Sie sich bitte etwas genauer *or* deutlicher aus; **but was it this ~ colour?** aber war es genau diese Farbe?; **18, to be ~** 18, um genau zu sein; **or, to be more ~, …** oder, um es genauer zu sagen, …; **in that ~ voice of hers** präzise *or* exakt, wie sie nun einmal spricht; **these ~ British accents** die akzentuierte Aussprache der Briten
b *(= meticulous) worker* exakt, genau, präzise

precisely [prɪˈsaɪslɪ] ADV genau; *answer, describe, work also* präzise; *use instrument* exakt; **at ~ 7 o'clock, at 7 o'clock ~** Punkt 7 Uhr, genau um 7 Uhr; **what ~ do you mean/want?** was meinen/wollen Sie eigentlich genau?; **but it is ~ because the money supply is …** aber gerade deshalb, weil das Kapital … ist; **that is ~ why I don't want it** genau deshalb will ich es nicht; **~ nothing** gar nichts; **or more ~ …** oder genauer …

preciseness [prɪˈsaɪsnɪs] N Genauigkeit *f*, Exaktheit *f*

precision [prɪˈsɪʒən] N Genauigkeit *f*; *(of work, movement also)* Präzision *f*

precision: **precision bombing** N gezielter Bombenabwurf; **precision-engineered** ADJ präzisionsgefertigt; **precision engineering** N Präzisionstechnik *f*; **precision instrument** N Präzisionsinstrument *nt*; **precision-made** ADJ präzisionsgefertigt; **precision tool** N Präzisionswerkzeug *nt*; **precision work** N Präzisionsarbeit *f*

preclassical [priːˈklæsɪkəl] ADJ vorklassisch

preclinical [priːˈklɪnɪkəl] ADJ *(Med) Studium* vorklinisch

preclude [prɪˈkluːd] VT *possibility* ausschließen; **to ~ sb from doing sth** jdn daran hindern, etw zu tun; **to ~ sth happening** die Möglichkeit ausschließen, dass etw geschieht

preclusion [prɪˈkluːʒən] N **a** *(of possibility)* Ausschließung *f*, Ausschluss *m* **b** *(= prevention)* Verhinderung *f*

precocious [prɪˈkəʊʃəs] ADJ *interest, teenager, behaviour* frühreif; *way of speaking* altklug; *talent, development* frühreif, früh entwickelt; **at a ~ age** im frühen Alter

precociously [prɪˈkəʊʃəslɪ] ADV frühreif; *talk* altklug; **a ~ articulate child** ein erstaunlich beredsames *or* wortgewandtes Kind, ein Kind von altkluger Beredsamkeit; **~ talented** früh begabt; **~ dressed** auf alt angezogen *(inf)*

precociousness [prɪˈkəʊʃəsnɪs], **precocity** [prɪˈkɒsɪtɪ] N *(of child, behaviour)* Frühreife *f*; *(of way of speaking)* Altklugheit *f*

precognition [ˌpriːkɒɡˈnɪʃən] N *(Psych)* Präkognition *f*; *(= knowledge)* vorherige Kenntnis, vorheriges Wissen

preconceived [ˌpriːkənˈsiːvd] ADJ *opinion, idea* vorgefasst; **to have ~ ideas about sth** eine vorgefasste Meinung zu etw haben

preconception [ˌpriːkənˈsepʃən] N vorgefasste Meinung

precondemn [ˌpriːkənˈdem] VT vorverurteilen

precondition [ˌpriːkənˈdɪʃən] N (Vor)bedingung *f*, Voraussetzung *f*; **to make sth a ~** etw zur Voraussetzung *or* Bedingung machen

precook [priːˈkʊk] VT vorkochen

precursor [priːˈkɜːsəʳ] N Vorläufer(in) *m(f)*; *(= herald: of event etc)* Vorbote *m*, Vorbotin *f*; *(in office)* (Amts)vorgänger(in) *m(f)*

precursory [priːˈkɜːsərɪ] ADJ einleitend

predate [ˌpriːˈdeɪt] VT *(= precede)* zeitlich vorangehen *(+dat)*; *cheque, letter* zurückdatieren

predator [ˈpredətəʳ] N *(= animal)* Raubtier *nt*; *(= person)* Plünderer *m*, Plünderin *f*; **the main ~s of the gazelle** die Hauptfeinde der Gazelle

predatory [ˈpredətərɪ] ADJ **a** *(= involving killing) attack, tribe, behaviour* räuberisch; **~ animal** Raubtier *nt*; **~ instinct** Raubtierinstinkt *m* **b** *(financially etc) person, behaviour* raubtierhaft **c** *(sexually) person* raubtierhaft; **he has a ~ attitude toward(s) all the girls in the office** er betrachtet alle Mädchen im Büro als Freiwild

predecease [ˌpriːdɪˈsiːs] VT **to ~ sb** vor jdm sterben

predecessor [ˈpriːdɪsesəʳ] N *(= person)* Vorgänger(in) *m(f)*; *(= thing)* Vorläufer(in) *m(f)*; **our ~s** *(= ancestors)* unsere Ahnen *or* Vorfahren *pl*; **his latest book is certainly better than its ~s** sein neuestes Buch ist zweifellos besser als seine vorherigen

predefine [ˌpriːdɪˈfaɪn] VT vorher abgrenzen *or* bestimmen

predestination [priːˌdestɪˈneɪʃən] N Vorherbestimmung *f*, Prädestination *f*

predestine [priːˈdestɪn] VT vorherbestimmen, prädestinieren; *person* prädestinieren

predetermination [ˈpriːdɪˌtɜːmɪˈneɪʃən] N *(Philos)* Prädetermination *f*; *(of course of events, sb's future etc)* Vorherbestimmung *f*

predetermine [ˌpriːdɪˈtɜːmɪn] VT *course of events, sb's future etc* vorherbestimmen; *(Philos)* prädeterminieren; *(= fix in advance) price, date etc* vorher *or* im Voraus festlegen *or* festsetzen; *(= ascertain in advance) costs* vorher ermitteln

predetermined [ˌpriːdɪˈtɜːmɪnd] ADJ *(= prearranged) outcome* verabredet, im Voraus festgelegt; *size* vorgegeben; *position* vorherbestimmt; **for a ~ period** für einen vorherbestimmten Zeitabschnitt; **at ~ times** zu (vorher) festgesetzten Zeiten

predicable [ˈpredɪkəbl] ADJ **to be ~ of sth** von etw ausgesagt *or* behauptet werden können

predicament [prɪˈdɪkəmənt] N Zwangslage *f*, Dilemma *nt*; **to be in a ~** in einem Dilemma *or* in einer Zwangslage sein

predicate [ˈpredɪkɪt] N *(Gram)* Prädikat *nt*, Satzaussage *f*; *(Logic)* Aussage *f*; **~ noun** prädikatives Substantiv, Prädikativ(um) *nt* [ˈpredɪkeɪt] VT *(= imply, connote)* aussagen; *(= assert, state)* behaupten; **to ~ sth on sth** *(= base)* etw auf etw *(dat)* gründen; **to ~ sth of sth** *(= assert as quality of)* etw von etw behaupten

predicative ADJ, **predicatively** ADV [prɪˈdɪkətɪv, -lɪ] prädikativ

predict [prɪˈdɪkt] VT vorher- *or* voraussagen, prophezeien

predictability [prəˌdɪktəˈbɪlɪtɪ] N Vorhersagbarkeit *f*

predictable [prɪˈdɪktəbl] ADJ *event, reaction* vorher- *or* voraussagbar; *person* durchschaubar; **to be ~** vorher- *or* voraussagbar sein, vorher- *or* vorauszusagen sein; **that was ~!** das war vorherzusehen!; **you're so ~** man weiß doch genau, wie Sie reagieren; **with ~ consequences** mit vorhersehbaren *or* voraussagbaren Folgen; **to follow a ~ pattern** einem vorhersehbaren *or* voraussagbaren Muster folgen

predictably [prɪˈdɪktəblɪ] ADV *react* vorher- *or* voraussagbar; **~ (enough), he was late** wie vorauszusehen, kam er zu spät

prediction [prɪˈdɪkʃən] N Prophezeiung *f*, Voraussage *f*

predictive [prɪˈdɪktɪv] ADJ *(form: = prophetic) power, value, test* vorausdeutend, vorhersagend; **to be ~ of sth** ein Vorzeichen für etw sein, etw anzeigen

predictor [prɪˈdɪktəʳ] N *(= indication)* Anzeichen *nt* (of für); **opinion polls are an unreliable ~ of election outcomes** Umfragen können Wahlergebnisse nicht zuverlässig voraussagen

predigest [ˌpriːdaɪˈdʒest] VT vorverdauen; *(artificially, chemically)* aufschließen; *(fig)* vorkauen

predilection [ˌpriːdɪˈlekʃən] N Vorliebe *f*, Faible *nt* *(for* für)

predispose [ˌpriːdɪˈspəʊz] VT geneigt machen; *(Med)* prädisponieren, anfällig machen *(to* für); **to ~ sb toward(s) sb/sth** jdn für jdn/etw einnehmen; **it ~s me to believe that …** das führt mich zu der Annahme, dass …; **people are ~d to behave in certain ways** die Menschen sind so veranlagt, sich in einer bestimmten Weise zu verhalten; **I'm not ~d to help him** ich bin nicht geneigt, ihm zu helfen

predisposition [ˌpriːdɪspəˈzɪʃən] N *(= tendency, inclination)* Neigung *f (to* zu); *(Med)* Prädisposition *f (to* für), Anfälligkeit *f (to* für); **he has a natural ~ to violence** er hat eine natürliche Veranlagung zur Gewalttätigkeit

predominance [prɪˈdɒmɪnəns] N *(= control)* Vorherrschaft *f*, Vormachtstellung *f*; *(= prevalence)* Überwiegen *nt*; **the ~ of women in the office** die weibliche Überzahl im Büro

predominant [prɪˈdɒmɪnənt] ADJ *(= most prevalent) idea, theory* vorherrschend; *(= dominating) person, animal* beherrschend; **to be ~ in sth** überwiegend in etw sein; **those things which are ~ in your life** die Dinge, die in Ihrem Leben von größter Bedeutung sind; **he was the ~ member of the group** er war in der Gruppe tonangebend

predominantly [prɪˈdɒmɪnəntlɪ] ADV überwiegend

predominate [prɪˈdɒmɪneɪt] VI **a** *(in numbers)* vorherrschen **b** *(in influence etc)* überwiegen; **Good will always ~ over Evil** das Gute wird immer über das Böse siegen; **if you allow any one individual to ~ (over the others)** wenn man einem einzigen gestattet, die anderen zu beherrschen

predominately [prɪˈdɒmɪnɪtlɪ] ADV *(= largely, mainly)* überwiegend

pre-eclampsia [ˌpriːɪˈklæmpsɪə] N *(Med)* Präeklampsie *f (spec)*

pre-election [ˌpriːɪˈlekʃən] ADJ *poll, campaign, rally* vor der Wahl (durchgeführt); **~ atmosphere** Wahlkampfatmosphäre *f*; **~ promise** Wahlversprechen *nt*

pre-eminence [priːˈemɪnəns] N überragende Bedeutung

pre-eminent [priːˈemɪnənt] ADJ herausragend, überragend

pre-eminently [priːˈemɪnəntlɪ] ADV hauptsächlich, vor allem, in erster Linie; *(= excellently)* hervorragend

pre-empt [priːˈempt] VT zuvorkommen *(+dat)*; *(Bridge) seinen Gegenspielern durch eine schwer zu überbietende Ansage zuvorkommen* **his decision to leave was ~ed by his dismissal** die Entlassung kam seinem Entschluss wegzugehen zuvor

pre-emption [priːˈempʃən] N Zuvorkommen *nt*

pre-emptive [priːˈemptɪv] ADJ präventiv, Präventiv-; **~ attack** Präventivschlag *m*; **~ bid** *(Bridge) Ansage, die durch ihre Höhe weitere Ansagen erschwert*

preen [priːn] VT *feathers* putzen VI *(bird)* sich putzen VR **to ~ oneself** *(bird)* sich putzen; *(person) (= be smug)* sich brüsten (*on* mit); *(= dress up)* sich herausputzen, sich aufputzen

pre-exist [ˌpriːɪɡˈzɪst] VI *(= exist beforehand)* vorher existieren, vorher vorhanden sein; *(= exist in previous life)* präexistieren

pre-existence [ˌpriːɪɡˈzɪstəns] N *(no pl: = existing before)* vorherige Existenz, vorheriges Vorhandensein; *(= previous life)* früheres Leben *or* Dasein, Präexistenz *f*

pre-existent [ˌpriːɪɡˈzɪstənt] ADJ *(= existing before)* vorher vorhanden *or* existent; *(= of an earlier life)* präexistent

prefab [ˈpriːfæb] N Fertighaus *nt*

prefabricate [ˌpriːˈfæbrɪkeɪt] VT vorfertigen

prefabricated [ˌpriːˈfæbrɪkeɪtɪd] ADJ vorgefertigt, Fertig-; **~ building** Fertighaus *nt*

prefabrication [priːˌfæbrɪˈkeɪʃən] N Vorfertigung *f*

preface [ˈprefɪs] N Vorwort *nt*; *(of speech)* Vorrede *f* VT einleiten; *book* mit einem Vorwort versehen

prefaded [ˈpriːfeɪdɪd] ADJ *denims* gebleicht, bleached *pred*

prefatory [ˈprefətərɪ] ADJ einleitend

prefect [ˈpriːfekt] N Präfekt(in) *m(f)*; *(Brit Sch)* Aufsichtsschüler(in) *m(f)*; **form ~** *(Sch)* ≈ Klassensprecher(in) *m(f)*

prefecture [ˈpriːfektjʊəˈ] N Präfektur *f*

prefer [prɪˈfɜːˈ] ✪ 5.2, 7.1, 7.4, 26.3 VT **a** *(= like better)* vorziehen (*to dat*), lieber mögen (*to* als); *applicant, solution* vorziehen, bevorzugen; *(= be more fond of) person* lieber haben (*to* als); **he ~s coffee to tea** er trinkt lieber Kaffee als Tee; **he ~s blondes/hot countries** er bevorzugt Blondinen/warme Länder; **I ~ it that way** es ist mir lieber so; **which (of them) do you ~?** *(of people)* wen ziehen Sie vor?; *(emotionally)* wen mögen *or* haben Sie lieber?; *(of things)* welche(n, s) ziehen Sie vor *or* finden Sie besser?; *(= find more pleasing)* welche(r, s) gefällt Ihnen besser?; **I'd ~ something less ornate** ich hätte lieber etwas Schlichteres; **to ~ to do sth** etw lieber tun, es vorziehen, etw zu tun; **I ~ to resign rather than …** eher kündige ich, als dass …; **I ~ walking (to cycling)** ich gehe lieber zu Fuß(, als mit dem Fahrrad zu fahren); **I ~ flying** ich fliege lieber; **I ~ not to say** ich sage es lieber nicht; **would you ~ me to drive?** soll ich lieber fahren?; **I would ~ you to do it today** *or* **that you did it today** mir wäre es lieber, wenn Sie es heute täten

b *(Jur)* **to ~ charges (against sb)** (gegen jdn) klagen, Klage (gegen jdn) einreichen *or* erheben

c *(esp Eccl: = promote)* befördern; **the bishop was ~red to the archbishopric of York** dem Bischof wurde die Würde eines Erzbischofs von York verliehen

preferable [ˈprefərəbl] ADJ **X is ~ to Y** X ist Y *(dat)* vorzuziehen; **anything would be ~ to sharing a flat with Sophie** alles wäre besser, als mit Sophie zusammen wohnen zu müssen; **death is ~ to dishonour** lieber tot als ehrlos; **it is ~ to use vegetable oil for cooking** zum Kochen eignet sich pflanzliches Öl besser *or* am besten, zum Kochen ist pflanzliches Öl vorzuziehen; **it would be ~ to do it that way** es wäre besser, es so zu machen; **to find sth ~** etw vorziehen, einer Sache *(dat)* den Vorzug geben; **infinitely ~** hundertmal besser *or* lieber

preferably [ˈprefərəblɪ] ADV am liebsten; **tea or coffee? – coffee, ~** Tee oder Kaffee? – lieber Kaffee; **but ~ not Tuesday** aber, wenn möglich, nicht Dienstag

preference [ˈprefərəns] ✪ 7.4, 7.5 N **a** *(= greater liking)* Vorliebe *f*; **for ~** lieber; **to have a ~ for sth** eine Vorliebe für etw haben, etw bevorzugen; **my ~ is for country life** ich ziehe das Leben auf dem Land vor; **I drink coffee in ~ to tea** ich trinke lieber Kaffee als Tee

b *(= thing preferred)* **what is your ~?** was wäre Ihnen am liebsten?; **just state your ~** nennen Sie einfach Ihre Wünsche; **I have no ~** mir ist das eigentlich gleich; **what are your ~s as regards food?** was essen Sie am liebsten?

c *(= greater favour)* Vorzug *m*; **to show ~ for sb** jdn bevorzugen; **to give ~ to sb/sth** jdn/etw bevorzugen, jdm/etw den Vorzug geben (*over* gegenüber); **to give certain imports ~** Vorzugs- *or* Präferenzzölle auf bestimmte Einfuhrartikel gewähren

preference shares [ˈprefərənsˈʃeəz] PL *(Brit Fin)* Vorzugsaktien *pl*

preferential [ˌprefəˈrenʃəl] ADJ bevorzugt, Sonder-; **~ rate** Sonderpreis *m*; **to give sb ~ treatment** jdn bevorzugt behandeln; **to get** *or* **receive ~ treatment** eine Vorzugsbehandlung genießen *or* bekommen; **~ trade** *(Comm)* Präferenz- *or* Vorzugshandel *m*; **~ trade agreement** Vereinbarung *f* über Präferenzhandel *or* Vorzugshandel; **~ trade area** präferenzielle *or* präferentielle *or* vorzugsweise Handelszone; **~ trading status** präferenzieller *or* präferentieller *or* bevorzugter Handelsstatus; **~ tariff** *(Comm)* Präferenz- *or* Vorzugszoll *m*; **~ ballot** *(Pol)* Präferenzwahl *f*; **~ voting** *(Pol)* Präferenzwahlsystem *nt*

preferentially [ˌprefəˈrenʃəlɪ] ADV *treat etc* bevorzugt

preferment [prɪˈfɜːmənt] N **a** *(esp Eccl: = promotion)* Beförderung *f* **b** *(Jur)* **~ of charges** Klageerhebung *f*

preferred [prɪˈfɜːd] ADJ *creditor* bevorrechtigt

preferred stock N *(US Fin)* Vorzugsaktien *pl*

prefigure [priːˈfɪɡəˈ] VT *(= indicate)* anzeigen, ankündigen; *(= imagine beforehand)* sich *(dat)* ausmalen

prefix [ˈpriːfɪks] N *(Gram)* Vorsilbe *f*, Präfix *nt*; *(= title)* Namensvorsatz *m*; *(in code)* Vorsatz *m*; *(Telec)* Vorwahl *f* VT [priːˈfɪks] *(Gram)* präfigieren, mit einer Vorsilbe *or* einem Präfix versehen; *name* mit einem Namensvorsatz versehen; *number (with code)* voranstellen *(+dat)*, voransetzen *(+dat)*; **words ~ed by "un"** Wörter mit der Vorsilbe *or* dem Präfix „un"

preflight [ˈpriːˈflaɪt] ADJ *attr* **~ checks/instructions** Kontrollen *pl*/Anweisungen *pl* vor dem Flug

preform [priːˈfɔːm] VT vorformen

prefrontal [ˌpriːˈfrʌntl] ADJ des Stirnbeins

preggers [ˈpreɡəz] ADJ *pred (esp Brit inf)* schwanger

pregnancy [ˈpreɡnənsɪ] N Schwangerschaft *f*; *(of animal)* Trächtigkeit *f*; *(fig) (of remarks etc)* Bedeutungsgehalt *m*; *(of silence, pause)* Bedeutungsschwere *f*, Bedeutungsgeladenheit *f*

pregnancy test N Schwangerschaftsuntersuchung *f*, Schwangerschaftstest *m*

pregnant [ˈpreɡnənt] ADJ **a** *woman* schwanger; *animal* trächtig, tragend; **3 months ~** im vierten Monat schwanger; **she is ~ with her first child** sie ist zum ersten Mal schwanger; **Gill was ~ by her new boyfriend** Gill war von ihrem neuen Freund schwanger; **to become** *or* **get ~** *(woman)* schwanger werden **b** *(fig) remark, silence, pause* bedeutungsvoll *or* -schwer *or* -geladen; **~ with meaning** bedeutungsvoll *or* -geladen *or* -schwanger *(iro)*; **~ with consequences** folgenschwer

preheat [priːˈhiːt] VT vorheizen

prehensile [prɪˈhensaɪl] ADJ Greif-; **~ tail** Greifschwanz *m*

prehistoric [ˌpriːhɪˈstɒrɪk] ADJ **a** prähistorisch, vorgeschichtlich **b** *(fig)* mittelalterlich, uralt; **it is based on almost ~ technology** es basiert auf geradezu mittelalterlicher Technologie

prehistory [ˌpriːˈhɪstərɪ] N Vorgeschichte *f*

pre-ignition [ˌpriːɪɡˈnɪʃən] N Frühzündung *f*

pre-industrial [ˌpriːɪnˈdʌstrɪəl] ADJ vorindustriell

prejudge [priːˈdʒʌdʒ] VT *case, issue, person* im voraus beurteilen; *(negatively) person* im Voraus verurteilen

prejudice [ˈpredʒʊdɪs] N **a** *(= biased opinion)* Vorurteil *nt*; **his ~ against …** seine Voreingenommenheit gegen …; **that's pure ~** das ist reine Voreingenommenheit; **the newspaper report was full of ~ against …** der Zeitungsbericht steckte voller Vorurteile gegen …; **to have a ~ against sb/sth** ein Vorurteil *nt* gegen jdn/etw haben, gegen jdn/etw voreingenommen sein; **racial ~** Rassenvorurteile *pl*; **colour ~** Vorurteile *pl* gegen Andersfarbige *or* aufgrund *or* auf Grund der Hautfarbe

b *(esp Jur: = detriment, injury)* Schaden *m*; **to the ~ of sb** *(form)* zu jds Schaden; **to the ~ of sth** *(form)* unter Beeinträchtigung einer Sache *(gen)*; **without ~** *(Jur)* ohne Verbindlichkeit *or* Obligo; **without ~ to one's rights** ohne sich *(dat)* selbst zu schaden; **without ~ to any claim** *(Jur)* ohne Beeinträchtigung *or* unbeschadet irgendwelcher Ansprüche

VT **a** *(= bias)* einnehmen, beeinflussen → *also* **prejudiced**

b *(= injure)* gefährden; *chances* beeinträchtigen, gefährden

prejudiced [ˈpredʒʊdɪst] ADJ *person* voreingenommen (*against* gegen); *opinion* vorgefasst; *judge* befangen; **to be ~ in favour of sb/sth** für jdn/etw voreingenommen sein; **to be racially ~** Rassenvorurteile haben

prejudicial [ˌpredʒʊˈdɪʃəl] ADJ abträglich (*to sth* einer Sache *dat*); **to be ~ to a cause** einer Sache *(dat)* schaden; **to be ~ to sb's interests** jds Chancen gefährden

prelacy [ˈpreləsɪ] N *(= office)* Prälatur *f*; *(= bishops etc)* geistliche Würdenträger *pl*; *(= system)* Kirchenhierarchie *f*

prelate [ˈprelɪt] N Prälat *m*

preliminary [prɪˈlɪmɪnərɪ] ADJ *remarks, chapter* einleitend; *steps, measures* vorbereitend; *report, results, tests* vorläufig; *stage* früh; **~ negotiations** Vorverhandlungen *pl*; **~ investigation** Voruntersuchung *f*; **~ contacts** erste Kontakte; **~ round** Vorrunde *f*

N Einleitung *f* (*to* zu); *(= preparatory measure)* Vorbereitung *f*, vorbereitende Maßnahme; *(Sport)* Vorspiel *nt*; **preliminaries** Präliminarien *pl* (*geh, Jur*); (*for speech*) einführende *or* einleitende Worte; (*Sport*) Vorrunde *f*; **the preliminaries are complete, now the actual work can begin** die Vorarbeit ist getan, jetzt kann die eigentliche Arbeit anfangen; **all the preliminaries to sth** alles, was einer Sache (*dat*) vorausgeht; **let's dispense with the preliminaries** kommen wir gleich zur Sache; **as a ~** als Vorarbeit, als Vorbereitung

preliminary hearing N (*Jur*) Voruntersuchung *f*

Preliminary Scholastic Aptitude Test N (*US Sch, Univ*) *Eignungstest vor Aufnahme in eine Universität*

prelims [ˈpriːlɪmz] PL **a** (*Sch, Univ*) Vorprüfung *f* **b** (*in book*) Vorbemerkungen *pl*

preloaded [priːˈləʊdɪd] ADJ (*Comput*) *program etc* vorinstalliert

prelude [ˈpreljuːd] **N** Vorspiel *nt*; (*Mus*: = *introduction to fugue*) Präludium *nt*; (*fig*) Auftakt *m* **VT** einleiten, den Auftakt (*+gen*) bilden

prem [prem] N (*inf*: = *premature baby*) Frühchen *nt* (*inf*)

premarital [priːˈmærɪtl] ADJ vorehelich

premature [ˈpremətʃʊəˈ] ADJ *baldness, birth, arrival* vorzeitig; *labour, death, retirement* frühzeitig, vorzeitig; *decision, action* verfrüht; **you were a little ~** da waren Sie ein wenig voreilig; **the baby was three weeks ~** das Baby wurde drei Wochen zu früh geboren; **it is ~ to talk of sanctions** es ist voreilig *or* verfrüht, von Sanktionen zu sprechen; **~ baby** Frühgeburt *f*; **~ ejaculation** vorzeitiger Samenerguss; **~ retirement** Vorruhestand *m*

prematurely [ˈpremətʃʊəlɪ] ADV *bald* vorzeitig; *aged, middle-aged, menopausal* frühzeitig, vorzeitig; *decide* verfrüht; *act* voreilig; **he was born ~** er war eine Frühgeburt; **to die ~** früh sterben

premed [priːˈmed] N (*inf*) **a** = **premedication** **b** (*US*) (*person*) *Medizinstudent, der auf das Medizinstudium vorbereitende Einführungskurse besucht* (*class*) *vorbereitender medizinischer Einführungskurs*

premedic [priːˈmedɪk] ADJ (*inf*: = *premedical student*) Student im vorklinischen Studium

premedical [priːˈmedɪkl] ADJ (*US*) *course* auf das (eigentliche) Medizinstudium vorbereitend *attr*

premedication [priːˌmedɪˈkeɪʃən] N Beruhigungsspritze *f* (*vor Anästhesie*)

premeditate [priːˈmedɪteɪt] VT vorsätzlich planen

premeditated [priːˈmedɪteɪtɪd] ADJ vorsätzlich

premeditation [priːˌmedɪˈteɪʃən] N Vorsatz *m*

premenstrual [priːˈmenstrʊəl] ADJ prämenstruell, vor der Menstruation auftretend

premenstrual syndrome, premenstrual tension N (*esp Brit*) prämenstruelles Syndrom, prämenstruelle Phase

premier [ˈpremɪəˈ] **ADJ** führend **N** Premier *m*, Premierminister(in) *m(f)*

Premier Division N (*Ftbl, in Scotland*) = **Premier League**

première [ˈpremɪεəˈ] **N** Premiere *f*; (*first ever also*) Uraufführung *f*; (*in particular place also*) Erstaufführung *f* **VT** uraufführen, erstaufführen

Premier League N (*Ftbl*) erste Liga

Premiership [ˈpremɪəʃɪp] N (*Ftbl*) erste Liga

premiership N (= *period*) Amtsperiode *or* -zeit *f* als Premierminister(in); (= *office*) Amt *nt* des Premierministers/der Premierministerin

premise [ˈpremɪs] **N** **a** (*esp Logic*) Prämisse *f* (*spec*), Voraussetzung *f* **b premises** **PL** (*of school, factory*) Gelände *nt*; (= *building*) Gebäude *nt*; (= *shop*) Räumlichkeiten *pl*; (*form*: = *house*) Besitz *m*, Anwesen *nt*; **licensed ~s** Schankort *m*; **business ~s** Geschäftsräume *pl*; **to use as business ~s** geschäftlich nutzen; **drinking is not allowed in** *or* **on these ~s** es ist nicht erlaubt, hier Alkohol zu trinken; **will you escort him off the ~s?** würden Sie ihn bitte hinausbegleiten?; **he was asked to leave the ~s** man forderte ihn auf, das Gelände *etc* zu verlassen; **get off my ~s** verlassen Sie sofort mein Land *or* Grundstück! **VT to be ~d on sth** (*form*) auf etw (*dat*) basieren

premiss N = **premise a**

premium [ˈpriːmɪəm] **N** (= *bonus, additional sum*) Bonus *m*, Prämie *f*; (= *surcharge*) Zuschlag *m*; (= *insurance premium*) Prämie *f*; (*St Ex*) Aufgeld *nt*, Agio *nt*; **~ bond** (*Brit*) Los- *or* Lotterieanleihe *f*; **to sell sth at a ~** etw über seinem Wert verkaufen; **to be at a ~** (*St Ex*) über pari stehen; (*fig*) hoch im Kurs stehen; **to place** *or* **put a (high) ~ on sth** (*fig*) etw hoch einschätzen *or* bewerten
ADJ **a** (= *top-quality*) *goods, brand* erstklassig; **~ petrol** (*Brit*) *or* **gas** (*US*) Super *nt*, Superbenzin *nt*
b (= *inflated*) **~ price** Höchstpreis *m*; **callers are charged a ~ rate of 48p a minute** Anrufern wird der Höchsttarif von 48 Pence pro Minute berechnet

premium-rate [ˈpriːmɪəmˌreɪt] ADJ (*Telec*) *call* zum Höchsttarif; **~ telephone numbers** Telefonnummern *pl*, die man zum Höchsttarif anrufen kann; **~ services** Leistungen *pl*, für die man den Höchsttarif bezahlen muss

premolar [priːˈməʊləˈ] N vorderer Backenzahn

premonition [ˌpriːməˈnɪʃən] N (= *presentiment*) (böse *or* schlechte) Vorahnung, (böses *or* schlechtes) Vorgefühl; (= *forewarning*) Vorwarnung *f*

premonitory [prɪˈmɒnɪtə rɪ] ADJ warnend

prenatal [priːˈneɪtl] ADJ pränatal, vor der Geburt

prenuptial [priːˈnʌpʃəl] ADJ vor der Hochzeit

prenuptial agreement N vorehelicher Vertrag

preoccupation [priːˌɒkjʊˈpeɪʃən] N **his face had a look of ~** seinem Gesicht sah man an, dass ihn etwas beschäftigte; **her ~ with her appearance** ihre ständige Sorge um ihr Äußeres; **her ~ with making money was such that ...** sie war so sehr mit dem Geldverdienen beschäftigt, dass ...; **that was his main ~** das war sein Hauptanliegen

preoccupied [priːˈɒkjʊpaɪd] ADJ *look, tone of voice, smile* gedankenverloren; **to be ~ with sth** nur an etw (*acc*) denken, sich ganz auf etw (*acc*) konzentrieren; **he has been (looking) rather ~ recently** er sieht in letzter Zeit so aus, als beschäftige ihn etwas; **he was too ~ to notice her** er war zu sehr mit anderen Dingen beschäftigt, um sie zu bemerken

preoccupy [priːˈɒkjʊpaɪ] VT (stark) beschäftigen

pre-op [ˈpriːˈɒp] ADJ (*inf*) vor der Operation, präoperativ; **~ medication** vor der Operation verabreichte Medikamente *pl*

preordain [ˈpriːɔːˈdeɪn] VT vorherbestimmen

prep [prep] (*inf*) N (*Brit Sch*) (= *homework*) Hausaufgaben *pl*, Hausarbeit *f*; (= *homework period*) Lernstunde *f*

prepackaged [priːˈpækɪdʒd], **prepacked** [priːˈpækt] ADJ abgepackt

prepaid [priːˈpeɪd] *ptp of* **prepay** ADJ *postage, goods* vorausbezahlt; *envelope* vorfrankiert, freigemacht; **reply ~ envelope** (*Comm*) frankierter Rückumschlag; **~ mobile phone** Handy *nt* (*mit im Voraus entrichteter Grundgebühr*)

preparation [ˌprepəˈreɪʃən] N **a** (= *preparing*) Vorbereitung *f*; (*of meal, medicine etc*) Zubereitung *f*; **in ~ for sth** als Vorbereitung für etw; **to be in ~** in Vorbereitung sein **b** (= *preparatory measure*) Vorbereitung *f*; **~s for war/a journey** Kriegs-/Reisevorbereitungen *pl*; **to make ~s** Vorbereitungen treffen **c** (*Med, Sci*) Präparat *nt*; **beauty ~s** Schönheitspräparate *pl*; **a ~ of herbs** (*Med*) ein Kräuterpräparat *nt*; (*Cook*) eine Kräutermischung **d** = **prep**

preparatory [prɪˈpærətərɪ] ADJ **a** *step, measure, talks, plan* vorbereitend; **~ work** Vorbereitungsarbeit *f*; **the ~ arrangements** die Vorbereitungen *pl* **b** (*Sch*) **~ education** Erziehung *f* *or* Ausbildung *f* in Vorbereitungsschulen; **~ student** (*US*) *Schüler(in) einer privaten Vorbereitungsschule für die Hochschule* **c talks were held ~ to the summit conference** es wurden Gespräche geführt, um die Gipfelkonferenz vorzubereiten; **he cleared his throat ~ to speaking** er räusperte sich vorbereitend *or* er räusperte sich, bevor er zum Sprechen ansetzte

preparatory school N (*Brit*) *private Schule für Kinder von 7 bis 13 Jahren zur Vorbereitung auf weiterführende private Schule* (*US*) *private weiterführende Schule zur Vorbereitung auf die Universität*

> **PREPARATORY SCHOOL**
>
> In Großbritannien ist eine **preparatory school** oder auch **prep school** eine private Grundschule für Kinder im Alter von 7 bis 13 Jahren, in der die Schülerinnen und Schüler auf eine private weiterführende Schule vorbereitet werden sollen, und das sowohl in schulischer wie auch in gesellschaftlicher Hinsicht. Die Institute sind meist nach Geschlechtern getrennt und haben jeweils eigene Schuluniformen, auf deren Tragen streng geachtet wird.
>
> In den USA dagegen ist eine **preparatory school** eine private weiterführende Schule, die die Schülerinnen und Schüler auf das College oder die Universität vorbereiten soll. Wie in Großbritannien, so wird auch in den USA die **preparatory school** mit gesellschaftlicher Exklusivität, Privilegiertheit und Reichtum verbunden.
>
> **Preppy**, Substantiv wie Adjektiv, bezieht sich auf eine Schülerin oder einen Schüler einer **prep school** in den USA oder auf das traditionellerweise damit verbundene Erscheinungsbild: nett, sauber, adrett, unauffällig und konservativ.

prepare [prɪˈpεəˈ] **VT** vorbereiten (*sb for sth* jdn auf etw *acc*, *sth for sth* etw für etw); *meal, medicine* zubereiten; *guest room* zurechtmachen, fertig machen; (*Sci*) präparieren; *data* aufbereiten; **~ yourself for a shock!** mach dich auf einen Schock gefasst!; **we ~d ourselves for a long wait** wir machten uns auf eine lange Wartezeit gefasst; **to ~ the ground for sth** den Boden für etw bereiten **VI to ~ for sth** sich auf etw (*acc*) vorbereiten; **the country is preparing for war** das Land trifft Kriegsvorbereitungen; **to ~ to do sth** Anstalten machen, etw zu tun

prepared [prɪˈpεəd] ADJ **a** (*also* **ready prepared**) vorbereitet; **~ meal** Fertiggericht *nt* **b** (= *in a state of readiness*) vorbereitet (*for* auf *+acc*); **I wasn't ~ for that!** darauf war ich nicht vorbereitet *or* gefasst; **to be ~ for the worst** auf das Schlimmste vorbereitet sein; **I wasn't ~ for him to do that** ich war nicht darauf vorbereitet, dass er das tut; **the country is ~ for war** das Land ist kriegsbereit *or* bereit zum Krieg; **are you ~ for your journey?** sind Sie reisefertig?; **"be ~"** „allzeit bereit" **c** (= *willing*) **to be ~ to do sth** bereit sein, etw zu tun

preparedness [prɪˈpεərɪdnɪs] N (= *readiness*) Vorbereitetsein *nt* (*for* auf *+acc*); (*for untoward events*) Gefasstsein *nt* (*for* auf *+acc*); (= *willingness*) Bereitschaft *f*; **lack of ~** mangelnde Vorbereitung (*for* auf *+acc*); **~ for war** Kriegsbereitschaft *f*; (*of army*) Einsatzbereitschaft *f*

prepay [priːˈpeɪ] *pret, ptp* **prepaid** VT im Voraus bezahlen

prepayment [priːˈpeɪmənt] N Vorauszahlung *f*

preponderance [prɪˈpɒndərəns] N Übergewicht *nt*; (*in number also*) Überwiegen *nt*

preponderant [prɪˈpɒndərənt] ADJ überwiegend

preponderantly [prɪˈpɒndərəntlɪ] ADV überwiegend, mehrheitlich

preponderate [prɪˈpɒndəreɪt] VI überwiegen

preposition [ˌprepəˈzɪʃən] N Präposition *f*, Verhältniswort *nt*

prepositional [ˌprepəˈzɪʃənl] ADJ präpositional; **~ phrase** Präpositionalphrase *f*

prepossess [ˌpriːpəˈzes] VT einnehmen (*in sb's favour* für jdn)

prepossessing [ˌpriːpəˈzesɪŋ] ADJ einnehmend, anziehend

preposterous [prɪˈpɒstərəs] ADJ grotesk, absurd; **you're being ~** das ist ja grotesk; **it is ~ to suggest that …** es ist absurd vorzuschlagen, dass …

preposterously [prɪˈpɒstərəslɪ] ADV grotesk; **he suggested, quite ~ …** er machte den grotesken *or* absurden Vorschlag …; **it took a ~ long time** es dauerte absurd lange

preposterousness [prɪˈpɒstərəsnɪs] N Absurdität *f*

preppie, preppy [ˈprepɪ] ADJ adrett, popperhaft (*esp pej*)

preprinted [ˈpriːˈprɪntɪd] ADJ vorgedruckt

preprogram [ˈpriːˈprəʊgræm] VT vorprogrammieren; **~med** vorprogrammiert

pre-release (version) [ˌpriːrɪˈliːs] N Vorabversion *f*

prep school N = **preparatory school**

prepublication [ˌpriːpʌblɪˈkeɪʃən] ADJ *attr* vor der Veröffentlichung

prepuce [ˈpriːpjuːs] N Vorhaut *f*, Präputium *nt* (*spec*)

prequel [ˈpriːkwəl] N (*Film*) *Film, der die Vorgeschichte eines bereits erfolgreich gelaufenen Films erzählt*

pre-Raphaelite [priːˈræfəlaɪt] ADJ präraffaelitisch N Präraffaelit *m*

prerecord [ˌpriːrɪˈkɔːd] VT vorher aufzeichnen; **~ed cassette** bespielte Kassette

prerequisite [ˌpriːˈrekwɪzɪt] N (Grund)voraussetzung *f*, Vorbedingung *f* ADJ erforderlich, notwendig

prerogative [prɪˈrɒgətɪv] N Vorrecht *nt*, Prärogativ *nt* (*geh*); **that's a woman's ~** das ist das Vorrecht einer Frau

Pres *abbr of* **president** Präs.

presage [ˈpresɪdʒ] N (*= omen*) Vorzeichen *nt*, Anzeichen *nt*, Vorbote *m*; (*= feeling*) Vorahnung *f* VT ankünd(ig)en, andeuten

Presbyterian [ˌprezbɪˈtɪərɪən] ADJ presbyterianisch N Presbyterianer(in) *m(f)*

presbytery [ˈprezbɪtərɪ] N (*= priest's house*) (katholisches) Pfarrhaus; (*part of church*) Presbyterium *nt*

preschool [ˈpriːˈskuːl] ADJ *attr* vorschulisch; **a child of ~ age** ein Kind *nt* im Vorschulalter; **~ children** Kinder *pl* im Vorschulalter; **~ education** Vorschulerziehung *f*; **~ years** Vorschuljahre *pl*

preschooler [ˈpriːˈskuːləʳ] N Vorschulkind *nt*

preschooling [ˈpriːˈskuːlɪŋ] N Vorschulerziehung *f*

prescience [ˈpresɪəns] N vorheriges Wissen, vorherige Kenntnis, Vorherwissen *nt*

prescore [ˌpriːˈskɔːʳ] VT (*Film, TV*) vorsynchronisieren

prescribable [prɪˈskraɪbəbl] ADJ *medicine* verschreibungs- *or* rezeptpflichtig

prescribe [prɪˈskraɪb] VT **a** (*= order, lay down*) vorschreiben; **~d reading** Pflichtlektüre *f* **b** (*Med, fig*) verschreiben, verordnen (*sth for sb* jdm etw); **the ~d dose/punishment** die verordnete Dosis/Strafe VI (*= lay down rules*) Vorschriften machen

prescription [prɪˈskrɪpʃən] N **a** (*Med*) Rezept *nt*; (*act of prescribing*) Verschreiben *nt*, Verordnen *nt*; **to make up** *or* **fill** (*US*) **a ~** eine Medizin zubereiten; **on ~** auf Rezept; **only available on ~** rezeptpflichtig, nur auf Rezept erhältlich **b** (*= regulation*) Vorschrift *f*

prescription charge N Rezeptgebühr *f*

prescription drugs PL verschreibungspflichtige Medikamente *pl*

prescriptive [prɪˈskrɪptɪv] ADJ normativ; **to be ~** Vorschriften machen

prescriptivism [prɪˈskrɪptɪvɪzəm] N Präskriptivismus *m*

presealed [ˈpriːˈsiːld] ADJ versiegelt; *containers etc* plombiert

preseason [ˈpriːˈsiːzn] ADJ (*Sport*) *match, training* vor der Saison; (*in tourism*) Vorsaison-; **~ rates** Vorsaisonpreise *pl*

preselect [ˌpriːsɪˈlekt] VT vorher auswählen; *gear* vorwählen

presence [ˈprezns] N **a** Gegenwart *f*, Anwesenheit *f*; **in sb's ~, in the ~ of sb** in jds (*dat*) Gegenwart *or* Anwesenheit, in Gegenwart *or* im Beisein von jdm; **he was admitted to the king's ~** er wurde zum König vorgelassen; **your ~ is requested** Sie sind eingeladen; **your ~ is required** Ihre Anwesenheit ist erforderlich; **to make one's ~ felt** sich bemerkbar machen; **in the ~ of danger** im Angesicht der Gefahr; **there is a strong German ~ in the 1500 metres** die Deutschen sind beim 1500-Meter-Lauf stark vertreten **b** **a military/police ~** Militär-/Polizeipräsenz *f* **c** (*= bearing, dignity*) Auftreten *nt*, Haltung *f*; (*of actor: also* **stage presence**) Ausstrahlung *f* **d** **they felt a ghostly/an invisible ~** sie spürten, dass etwas Geisterhaftes/Unsichtbares anwesend war

presence of mind N Geistesgegenwart *f*

present¹ [ˈpreznt] ADJ **a** (*= in attendance*) anwesend; **to be ~** anwesend sein; **he was ever ~ in her thoughts** er war in ihren Gedanken immer gegenwärtig; **to be ~ at sth** bei etw (anwesend) sein; **~ company excepted** Anwesende ausgenommen; **all those ~** alle Anwesenden; **all ~ and correct** alle anwesend **b** (*= existing in sth*) vorhanden; **gases ~ in the atmosphere** in der Atmosphäre vorhandene Gase; **carbon is ~ in organic matter** Kohlenstoff ist in organischen Stoffen enthalten; **a quality ~ in all great men** eine Eigenschaft, die man bei allen großen Männern findet **c** **at the ~ time** gegenwärtig, derzeitig, augenblicklich; *year, season etc* laufend; *century* gegenwärtig, jetzig; (*= at the present moment or time*) zum gegenwärtigen *or* jetzigen Zeitpunkt; **the ~ day** (*= nowadays*) heutzutage; **of the ~ day** heutig, modern; **till** *or* **to** *or* **until the ~ day** bis zum heutigen Tag, bis auf den heutigen Tag; **in the ~ circumstances** unter den gegenwärtigen *or* gegebenen Umständen; **in the ~ case** im vorliegenden Fall; **the ~ writer** (*form*) der Autor des hier vorliegenden Werkes **d** (*Gram*) **in the ~ tense** in der Gegenwart, im Präsens; **~ participle** Partizip *nt* Präsens, Mittelwort *nt* der Gegenwart; **~ perfect (tense)** zweite Vergangenheit, Perfekt *nt* N **a** Gegenwart *f*; **at ~** zur Zeit, im Moment *or* Augenblick, derzeit; **up to the ~** bislang, bis jetzt; **there's no time like the ~** (*prov*) was du heute kannst besorgen, das verschiebe nicht auf morgen (*Prov*); **to live for the ~** ganz in der Gegenwart *or* im Hier und Heute leben; **that will be all for the ~** das ist vorläufig *or* einstweilen alles **b** (*Gram*) Gegenwart *f*, Präsens *nt*; **~ continuous/simple** erweitertes/einfaches Präsens, aktuelles/generelles Präsens

present² N (*= gift*) Geschenk *nt*; **to make sb a ~ of sth** jdm etw schenken (*also fig*), jdm etw zum Geschenk machen (*form*); **I got it** *or* **was given it as a ~** das habe ich geschenkt bekommen VT [prɪˈzent] **a** (*= hand over formally*) *medal, prize etc* übergeben, überreichen; (*= give as a gift*) *art collection, book etc* schenken, zum Geschenk machen (*form*); **to ~ sb with sth, to ~ sth to sb** jdm etw übergeben *or* überreichen; (*as a gift*) jdm etw schenken; **they ~ed us with a hefty bill** sie präsentierten *or* überreichten uns (*dat*) eine gesalzene Rechnung; **she ~ed him with a son** sie schenkte ihm einen Sohn **b** (*= put forward*) vorlegen; *cheque (for payment)* präsentieren; *proof* vorlegen, erbringen (*of sth* für etw); *proposal* vorlegen, unterbreiten; **she asked me to ~ her apologies/compliments** (*form*) sie bat mich, ihre Entschuldigung/Komplimente weiterzuleiten; **please ~ my apologies to your mother** (*form*) bitte entschuldigen Sie mich bei Ihrer Mutter; **his report ~s the matter in another light** sein Bericht zeigt die Angelegenheit in anderem Licht *or* stellt die Angelegenheit in anderem Licht dar **c** (*= offer, provide*) *target, view, opportunity* bieten; **to ~ a brave face to the world** sich (*dat*) nichts anmerken lassen; **his action ~ed us with a problem** seine Tat stellte uns vor ein Problem; **he ~ed the appearance of normality** nach außen hin wirkte er ganz normal **d** (*Rad, TV*) präsentieren; (*Theat*) zeigen, aufführen; (*commentator*) moderieren; **~ing, in the blue corner …** in der blauen Ecke des Rings … **e** (*= introduce*) vorstellen; **to ~ Mr X to Miss Y** Herrn X Fräulein Y (*dat*) vorstellen; **may I ~ Mr X?** (*form*) erlauben Sie mir, Herrn X vorzustellen (*form*); **to be ~ed at Court** bei Hof eingeführt werden **f** (*= point*) *gun etc* richten, zielen (*at* auf +*acc*); **~ arms!** (*Mil*) präsentiert das Gewehr! VR [prɪˈzent] (*opportunity, problem etc*) sich ergeben; **how you ~ yourself is very important** es ist sehr wichtig, wie man sich präsentiert; **to ~ oneself as a candidate** sich aufstellen lassen; **to ~ oneself for an exam** sich zu einer Prüfung anmelden; **he was asked to ~ himself for interview** er wurde gebeten, zu einem Vorstellungsgespräch zu erscheinen; **to ~ oneself at an ideal moment** im idealen Augenblick erscheinen

presentable [prɪˈzentəbl] ADJ *clothes, room* präsentabel, vorzeigbar; *food* akzeptabel, in Ordnung; **to be ~** (*person*) sich sehen lassen können; **to look ~** (*person*) akzeptabel aussehen, präsentabel aussehen; **it's not very ~** damit kann man sich nicht gut sehen lassen; **to make sth ~** etw so herrichten, dass man es zeigen kann; **to make oneself ~** sich zurechtmachen; **you're not ~ enough to go** du siehst nicht akzeptabel genug aus, um dorthin zu gehen

presentably [prɪˈzentəblɪ] ADV annehmbar, akzeptabel; **you have to be ~ dressed to get into that bar** man muss angemessen angezogen sein, wenn man in diese Bar will

presentation [ˌprezənˈteɪʃən] N **a** (*of gift etc*) Überreichung *f*; (*of prize, medal*) Verleihung *f*; (*= ceremony*) Verleihung(szeremonie) *f*; (*= gift*) Geschenk *nt*; **to make the ~** die Preise/Auszeichnungen *etc* verleihen; **to make sb a ~** jdm ein Geschenk überreichen **b** (*= act of presenting*) (*of report, voucher, cheque etc*) Vorlage, Präsentation *f*; (*of petition*) Überreichung *f*; (*Jur, of case, evidence*) Darlegung *f*; **on ~ of a certificate** gegen Vorlage einer Bescheinigung (*gen*) **c** (*= manner of presenting*) Darbietung *f*, Präsentation *f* **d** (*Theat*) Inszenierung *f*; (*TV, Rad*) Produktion *f*; (*= announcing, commentary*) Moderation *f* **e** (*Med, at birth*) Lage *f*

presentation copy N Dedikationsexemplar *nt*

present-day [ˈprezntˈdeɪ] ADJ *attr morality, problems, fashions* heutig; **~ Britain** das heutige Großbritannien

presenter [prɪˈzentəʳ] N **a** (*of cheque*) Überbringer(in) *m(f)*; **the ~ of the prize was a child** der Preis wurde von einem Kind überreicht **b** (*esp Brit: TV, Rad*) Moderator(in) *m(f)*

presentiment [prɪˈzentɪmənt] N (Vor)ahnung *f*, Vorgefühl *nt*; **to have a ~ of sth** eine Vorahnung von etw haben; **to have a ~ that …** das Gefühl haben, dass …

presently [ˈprezntlɪ] ADV **a** (*= soon*) bald; (*= shortly afterwards*) bald, bald darauf **b** (*= at present*) zurzeit, derzeit, gegenwärtig

preservation [ˌprezəˈveɪʃən] N **a** (*= maintaining*) (*of custom, building, manuscript*) Erhaltung *f*; (*of peace*) Wahrung *f*, Erhaltung *f*; (*of dignity*) Wahrung *f*; (*of memory, reputation*) Aufrechterhaltung *f*, Wahrung *f* **b** (*to prevent decay*) Konservierung *f*; (*of specimens*) Präservierung *f*; **to be in a good state of ~** gut erhalten sein

preservation order N *(Brit)* **to put a ~ on sth** etw unter Denkmalschutz stellen

preservation society N *(for buildings)* Denkmalschutzverband *m*; *(for nature)* Landschaftsschutzverband *m*

preservative [prɪˈzɜːvətɪv] ADJ Konservierungs-; **~ chemical** Konservierungsmittel *nt* N Konservierungsmittel *nt*

preserve [prɪˈzɜːv] VT **a** *(= keep intact, maintain) customs, building, position, eyesight, manuscript* erhalten; *peace* wahren, erhalten; *dignity, appearances* wahren; *memory, reputation* aufrechterhalten, wahren; *sense of humour, silence* bewahren
b *(= keep from decay)* konservieren; *specimens etc* präservieren; *leather, wood* schützen
c *(Cook)* einmachen, einkochen; *(= pickle)* einlegen; **preserving jar** Weckglas® *nt*, Einmachglas *nt*
d *(= keep from harm, save)* bewahren; **may God ~ you!** Gott behüte dich!; **to ~ sb from sth** jdn vor etw *(dat)* schützen *or* bewahren; **heaven** *or* **the saints ~ me from that!** *(iro)* der Himmel möge mich damit verschonen *or* möge mir das ersparen!
e *(Hunt) game, fish* schützen, hegen; **~d fishing/river/wood** unter Schutz stehende Fische/stehender Fluss/Wald
N **a** **preserves** PL *(Cook)* Eingemachtes *nt*; **peach ~(s)** eingemachte Pfirsiche *pl*; *(= jam)* Pfirsichmarmelade *f*
b *(= special domain)* Ressort *nt*; **this was once the ~ of the wealthy** dies war einst eine Domäne der Reichen; **to poach on sb's ~(s)** jdm ins Handwerk pfuschen; **game ~** *(Hunt)* Jagd *f*, Jagdrevier *nt*

preserved [prɪˈzɜːvd] ADJ **a** *food* konserviert; *(in jars)* eingekocht, eingeweckt, eingemacht; *(= pickled)* eingelegt **b** *(= conserved)* präserviert, erhalten; **well-~** *(building, village, fossil)* gut präserviert, gut erhalten; **he is well-~** *(hum)* er hat sich gut gehalten *(hum)*

preserver [prɪˈzɜːvəʳ] N Retter(in) *m(f)*

preset [priːˈset] *pret, ptp* **preset** VT vorher einstellen

preshave (lotion) [ˈpriːʃeɪv(ˌləʊʃən)] N Preshave-Lotion *f*

preshrink [priːˈʃrɪŋk] *pret* **preshrank** [priːˈʃræŋk] *ptp* **preshrunk** [priːˈʃrʌŋk] VT vorwaschen

preside [prɪˈzaɪd] VI *(at meeting etc)* den Vorsitz haben *or* führen (*at* bei); *(at meal)* den Vorsitz haben (*at* bei); **to ~ over an organization** *etc* eine Organisation *etc* leiten

presidency [ˈprezɪdənsɪ] N Präsidentschaft *f*; *(esp US: of company)* Aufsichtsratsvorsitz *m*; *(US Univ)* Rektorat *nt*

president [ˈprezɪdənt] N Präsident(in) *m(f)*; *(esp US: of company)* Aufsichtsratsvorsitzende(r) *mf*; *(US Univ)* Rektor(in) *m(f)*

president elect [ˌprezɪdəntɪˈlekt] N gewählter Präsident/gewählte Präsidentin *(vor Amtsantritt)*

presidential [ˌprezɪˈdenʃəl] ADJ *(Pol) decree, decision, spokesman* des Präsidenten; **~ debate** Präsidentschaftsdebatte *f*; **~ guard** Wache *f* des Präsidenten; **~ palace** Präsidentenpalast *m*; **his ~ duties** seine Pflichten als Präsident

presidential *(Pol)*: **presidential adviser** N Berater(in) *m(f)* des Präsidenten; **presidential campaign** N Präsidentschaftskampagne *f*; **presidential candidate** N Präsidentschaftskandidat(in) *m(f)*; **presidential election** N Präsidentenwahl *f*; **presidential primary** N Vorwahl *f* für die Präsidentschaft; **presidential year** N Jahr *nt* der Präsidentschaft, Jahr *nt* als Präsident

President's Day [ˈprezɪdəntsˌdeɪ] N *(US) Feiertag am dritten Montag im Februar zum Gedenken an die Geburtstage der Präsidenten Lincoln und Washington*

presidium [prɪˈsɪdɪəm] N (Partei)präsidium *nt*

press [pres] N **a** *(= machine: trouser press, flower press)* Presse *f*; *(= racket press)* Spanner *m*
b *(Typ)* (Drucker)presse *f*; *(= publishing firm)* Verlag *m*; **to go to ~** in Druck gehen; **to be in the ~** im Druck sein
c *(= newspapers, journalists)* Presse *f*; **the daily/sporting ~** die Tages-/Sportpresse; **the weekly ~** die Wochenzeitungen *pl*; **to get a good/bad ~** eine gute/schlechte Presse bekommen
d *(= squeeze, push)* Druck *m*; **to give sth a ~** etw drücken; *(= iron) dress etc* etw bügeln
e *(dial, US: = cupboard)* Wandschrank *m*
f *(= crush)* Gedränge *nt*; **a ~ of people** eine Menschenmenge
g *(Weightlifting)* Drücken *nt*
VT **a** *(= push, squeeze)* drücken (*to* an *+acc*); *button, doorbell, knob, brake pedal* drücken auf *(+acc)*; *clutch, piano pedal* treten; *grapes, fruit* (aus)pressen; *flowers* pressen; **to ~ the accelerator** Gas geben; **to ~ the trigger (of a gun)** abdrücken, den Abzug betätigen; **the shoe ~es my foot here** der Schuh drückt (mich) hier; **to ~ and hold down** *mouse button* gedrückt halten
b *(= iron) clothes* bügeln
c *(= urge, persuade)* drängen; *(= harass, importune)* bedrängen, unter Druck setzen; *(= insist on) claim, argument* bestehen auf *(+dat)*; **to ~ sb hard** jdm (hart) zusetzen; **he didn't need much ~ing** man brauchte ihn nicht lange zu drängen; **to ~ sb for an answer** auf jds Antwort *(acc)* drängen; **to ~ the point** darauf beharren *or* herumreiten *(inf)*; **to ~ home an advantage** einen Vorteil ausnutzen, sich *(dat)* einen Vorteil zunutze *or* zu Nutze machen; **to ~ home an attack** einen Angriff energisch vortragen; **to ~ money/one's views on sb** jdm Geld/seine Ansichten aufdrängen; **to be ~ed for money** in Geldnot sein; **to be ~ed for time** unter Zeitdruck stehen, in Zeitnot sein; **to ~ sb/sth into service** jdn/etw einspannen
d *machine part, record etc* pressen; **~ed steel** gepresster Stahl, Pressstahl *m*
VI **a** *(lit, fig: = bear down, exert pressure)* drücken; **to ~ (down) on sb** *(debts, troubles)* schwer auf jdm lasten
b *(= urge, agitate)* drängen; **to ~ for sth** auf etw *(acc)* drängen; **time ~es** die Zeit drängt
c *(= move, push)* sich drängen; **crowds ~ed round him** Massen drängten sich um ihn; **to ~ ahead** *or* **forward (with sth)** *(fig)* (mit etw) weitermachen; *(with plans)* etw weiterführen

▶ **press on** VI weitermachen; *(with journey)* weiterfahren

▶ **press out** VT *sep juice* auspressen; *pop-out models etc* herausdrücken

press: **press agency** N Presseagentur *f*; **press agent** N Presseagent(in) *m(f)*; **Press Association** N *(Brit)* Presseagentur *f*; **press attaché** N Presseattaché *m*; **press baron** N Pressezar *m*; **press box** N Pressetribüne *f*; **press-button** N = **push-button**; **press campaign** N Pressekampagne *f or* -feldzug *m*; **press card** N Presseausweis *m*; **press centre**, *(US)* **press center** N Pressezentrum *nt*; **press clipping** N Presseausschnitt *m*; *(from newspaper)* Zeitungsausschnitt *m*; **Press Complaints Commission** N *(Brit)* Presseaufsichtsrat *m*; **press conference** N Pressekonferenz *f*; **press corps** N **the ~** die akkreditierten Journalisten *pl*; **press coverage** N Berichterstattung *f* in der Presse *(über ein bestimmtes Thema)*; **press cutting** N *(esp Brit)* Presseausschnitt *m*; *(from newspaper)* Zeitungsausschnitt *m*; **press gallery** N *(esp Jur, Parl)* Pressetribüne *f*; **press gang** N *(Hist) (for navy)* Presspatrouille *f*; *(for army)* Werber *pl* VT *(esp Brit inf)* dazu drängen; **to press-gang sb into (doing) sth** jdn drängen, etw zu tun

pressing [ˈpresɪŋ] ADJ **a** *(= urgent) issue* brennend, dringend; *task* dringend **b** *(= insistent) requests* nachdrücklich; **he was very ~ in his invitation** er drängte mir *etc* seine Einladung richtig auf N *(= records issued at one time)* Auflage *f*; *(= copy of record)* Pressung *f*

press: **press kit** N Pressemappe *f*; **press lord** N = **press baron**; **pressman** N **a** *(esp Brit: = reporter)* Zeitungsmann *m*, Pressemann *m* **b** *(Typ)* Drucker *m*; **pressmark** N Signatur *f*; **press office** N Pressestelle *f*; **press officer** N Pressesprecher(in) *m(f)*

pressor [ˈpresəʳ] ADJ *attr (Med)* blutdruckerhöhend

press: **press photographer** N Pressefotograf(in) *m(f)*; **press reception** N Presseempfang *m*; **press release** N Pressemitteilung *f or* -verlautbarung *f*; **press report** N Pressebericht *m*; **press representative** N Pressevertreter(in) *m(f)*; **pressroom** N Druckerei *f*, (Druck)maschinensaal *m*; **press spokesman** N Pressesprecher *m*; **press spokesperson** N Pressesprecher(in) *m(f)*; **press spokeswoman** N Pressesprecherin *f*; **press stud** N *(Brit)* Druckknopf *m*; **press-up** N *(Brit)* Liegestütz *m*

pressure [ˈpreʃəʳ] N **a** Druck *m (also Phys, Met)*; **at high/full ~** *(lit, fig)* unter Hochdruck; **oil ~** Öldruck *m*
b *(= compulsion, influence)* Druck *m*, Zwang *m*; **parental ~** Druck vonseiten *or* von Seiten der Eltern; **social ~s** gesellschaftliche Zwänge *pl*; **to do sth under ~** etw unter Druck *or* Zwang tun; **to be/come under ~ to do sth** unter Druck *(dat)* stehen/geraten, etw zu tun; **to be under ~ from sb (to do sth)** von jdm gedrängt werden(, etw zu tun); **to put ~ on sb** jdn unter Druck *(dat)* setzen; **to put the ~ on** *(inf)* Druck dahintermachen *(inf)*, Dampf machen *(inf)*
c *(= urgent demands, stress)* Druck *m no pl*, Stress *m no pl*; **~ of work prevents me** Arbeitsüberlastung hindert mich daran; **the ~ of events** der Druck der Ereignisse; **business ~s** geschäftliche Belastungen *pl*; **the ~s of modern life** die Belastungen *pl or* der Stress des modernen Lebens; **the ~s of meeting deadlines** der Stress, Termine einzuhalten; **he works better under ~** er arbeitet besser unter Druck; **to be subjected to ~, to be under ~** unter Druck *(dat)* stehen *or* sein
VT = **pressurize b**

pressure: **pressure cabin** N *(Aviat)* Überdruckkabine *f*; **pressure-cook** VT mit Dampf kochen; **pressure cooker** N Druckkochtopf *m*, Schnellkochtopf *m*; **pressure gauge** N Manometer *nt*, Druckmesser *m*; **pressure group** N Pressuregroup *f*; **pressure point** N *(Anat)* Druckpunkt *m*; **pressure suit** N *(Aviat)* Druckanzug *m*

pressurization [ˌpreʃəraɪˈzeɪʃən] N Druckausgleich *m*

pressurize [ˈpreʃəraɪz] VT **a** *cabin, spacesuit* auf Normaldruck halten; **the cabin is only ~d when ...** der Druckausgleich in der Kabine wird erst hergestellt, wenn ... **b** *(= pressure) sb* unter Druck setzen; **to ~ sb into doing sth** jdn so unter Druck setzen, dass er schließlich etw tut; **I refuse to be ~d into agreeing** ich lasse mir meine Zustimmung nicht abpressen; **she refused to be ~d into going** sie ließ sich nicht zwingen zu gehen

pressurized [ˈpreʃəraɪzd] ADJ **a** *aircraft, container* mit Druckausgleich; **~ chamber** Druckkammer *f* **b** *(= compressed) water, gas* komprimiert, verdichtet, gepresst **c** *(fig)* unter Druck; **to feel ~** sich unter Druck (gesetzt) fühlen; **to feel ~ into sth** sich zu etw gedrängt fühlen; **to feel ~ into doing sth** sich dazu gedrängt fühlen, etw zu tun

pressurized cabin N Druckkabine *f*

pressurized-water reactor [ˈpreʃəraɪzdˈwɔːtəriːˈæktəʳ] N Druckwasserreaktor *m*

presswoman [ˈpresˌwʊmən] N **a** *(esp Brit: = reporter)* Zeitungsfrau *f*, Pressefrau *f* **b** *(Typ)* Druckerin *f*

Prestel® [ˈprestel] N *(Brit Telec)* ≈ Bildschirmtext *m*

prestidigitation [ˈprestɪˌdɪdʒɪˈteɪʃən] N *(form)* Fingerfertigkeit *f*, Geschicklichkeit *f*

prestidigitator [ˌprestɪˈdɪdʒɪteɪtəʳ] N *(form)* Taschenspieler(in) *m(f)*

prestige [preˈstiːʒ] N Prestige *nt*; **~ value** Prestigewert *m*

prestigious [preˈstɪdʒəs] ADJ Prestige-; **a ~ job** ein Prestigeberuf *m*; **to be (very) ~** (einen hohen) Prestigewert haben

presto [ˈprestəʊ] ADV → **hey**

prestressed [ˈpriːstrest] ADJ vorgespannt; **~ concrete** Spannbeton *m*

presumable [prɪˈzjuːməbl] ADJ vermutlich

presumably [prɪˈzjuːməblɪ] ADV vermutlich; **he is ~ very rich, is he?** ich nehme an, er ist sehr reich, oder?, vermutlich ist er sehr reich, nicht wahr?; **~ he'll come later** er wird voraussichtlich später kommen, vermutlich wird er später kommen

presume [prɪˈzjuːm] VT **a** *(= suppose)* annehmen, vermuten; *sb's death* unterstellen *(form)*; **~d dead** mutmaßlich verstorben; **to be ~d innocent** als unschuldig gelten; **he is ~d to be living in Spain** es wird vermutet, dass er in Spanien lebt
b *(= venture)* **to ~ to do sth** sich *(dat)* erlauben *or* sich *(dat)* herausnehmen *or* sich erdreisten, etw zu tun
VI **a** *(= suppose)* annehmen, vermuten; **Dr Livingstone, I ~** Dr. Livingstone, wie ich annehme; **it was his decision, I ~** ich nehme an *or* vermute, das war seine Entscheidung; **I ~ not** ich glaube nein
b *(= take liberties, be presumptuous)* **I didn't want to ~** ich wollte nicht aufdringlich sein; **you ~ too much** Sie sind wirklich vermessen; **to ~ on** *or* **upon sth** etw überbeanspruchen

presumedly [prɪˈzjuːmɪdlɪ] ADV vermutlich, mutmaßlich

presumption [prɪˈzʌmpʃən] N **a** *(= assumption)* Annahme *f*, Vermutung *f*; **the ~ is that …** es wird angenommen *or* man vermutet, dass …; **~ of death/innocence** Todes-/Unschuldvermutung *f* **b** *(= boldness, arrogance)* Unverschämtheit *f*, Dreistigkeit *f*; *(in connection with one's abilities)* Überheblichkeit *f*, Anmaßung *f*, Vermessenheit *f (geh)*

presumptive [prɪˈzʌmptɪv] ADJ **a** *(Jur)* **~ evidence** Indizien(beweis *m*) *pl*; **~ case** Indizienprozess *m* **b** *(= likely)* **heir ~** mutmaßlicher Erbe

presumptuous [prɪˈzʌmptjʊəs] ADJ *person, remark* anmaßend, unverschämt, dreist; *(in connection with one's abilities)* überheblich, anmaßend, vermessen *(geh)*; *behaviour* anmaßend, unverschämt; *idea* anmaßend, vermessen, großspurig; **it would be ~ of me to …** es wäre eine Anmaßung von mir, zu …

presumptuously [prɪˈzʌmptjʊəslɪ] ADV **I had assumed, somewhat ~, that …** es war vielleicht vermessen, aber ich hatte angenommen, dass …

presumptuousness [prɪˈzʌmptjʊəsnɪs] N *(of person, remark)* Unverschämtheit *f*, Dreistigkeit *f*; *(in connection with one's abilities)* Überheblichkeit *f*, Anmaßung *f*, Vermessenheit *f (geh)*; *(of behaviour)* Unverschämtheit *f*

presuppose [ˌpriːsəˈpəʊz] VT voraussetzen; *(= require also)* zur Voraussetzung haben

presupposition [ˌpriːsʌpəˈzɪʃən] N Voraussetzung *f*

pre-tax [priːˈtæks] ADJ unversteuert, vor Besteuerung

pre-teen [ˈpriːˈtiːn] ADJ im Kindesalter

pretence, *(US)* **pretense** [prɪˈtens] N **a** *(= make-believe story)* erfundene Geschichte; *(= make-believe person)* erfundene Gestalt; **he didn't really shoot me, it was just ~** er hat nicht auf mich geschossen, er hat nur so getan; **we soon saw through his ~ of being a foreigner** wir durchschauten bald, dass er nur vorspiegelte *or* vorgab, Ausländer zu sein; **to make a ~ of doing sth** so tun, als ob man etw tut; **he made not even the slightest ~ of being interested** er gab sich *(dat)* nicht einmal den Anschein des Interesses; **this constant ~ that all is well** die ständige Vorspiegelung, dass alles in Ordnung ist; **to maintain a ~ of democracy** den (An)schein einer Demokratie wahren; **it's all a ~** das ist alles nur gespielt *or* Mache *(inf)*
b *(= feigning, insincerity)* Heuchelei *f*, Verstellung *f*; **his coolness is just (a) ~** seine Kühle ist nur gespielt; **his ~ of normality** seine vorgespiegelte Normalität; **he made a ~ of friendship** er heuchelte Freundschaft, er gab Freundschaft vor; **let's stop all this ~** hören wir mit der Heuchelei auf, hören wir auf, uns *(dat)* etwas vorzumachen; **he is incapable of ~** er kann sich nicht verstellen
c *(= affectation)* Unnatürlichkeit *f*, Geziertheit *f*
d **to make no ~ to sth** keinen Anspruch auf etw *(acc)* erheben
e *(= pretext, excuse)* Vorwand *m*; **on** *or* **under the ~ of doing sth** unter dem Vorwand, etw zu tun → **false ADJ a**

pretend [prɪˈtend] VT **a** *(= make believe)* so tun, als ob; *(= feign)* vortäuschen, vorgeben; **to ~ to be interested** so tun, als ob man interessiert wäre; **to ~ to be sick/to have a cold** eine Krankheit/Erkältung vortäuschen *or* vorschützen; **to ~ to be asleep** sich schlafend stellen
b *(= claim)* **I don't ~ to …** ich behaupte nicht, dass ich …
VI **a** *(= make believe)* so tun, als ob; *(= keep up facade)* sich verstellen; **he is only ~ing** er tut nur so (als ob); **let's stop ~ing** hören wir auf, uns *(dat)* etwas vorzumachen
b *(= lay claim)* **to ~ to sth** auf etw *(acc)* Anspruch erheben
ADJ *(inf, child language)* Spiel-; **~ money** Spielgeld *nt*; **~ gun** Spielzeuggewehr *nt*; **it's just ~** *(story etc)* das ist nur Spaß *(inf)*

pretended [prɪˈtendɪd] ADJ vorgetäuscht, angeblich, vorgeblich

pretender [prɪˈtendəʳ] N *(to throne)* Prätendent(in) *m(f)* *(to* auf *+acc)*

pretense N *(US)* = **pretence**

pretension [prɪˈtenʃən] N **a** *(= claim)* Anspruch *m*; *(social, cultural)* Ambition *f*; **he makes no ~(s) to originality** er beansprucht keineswegs, originell zu sein **b** *(= ostentation)* Prahlerei *f*, Protzerei *f (pej inf)*; *(= affectation)* Anmaßung *f*

pretentious [prɪˈtenʃəs] ADJ *(= pretending to be important)* anmaßend; *speech, style, book* hochtrabend, hochgestochen; *(= ostentatious)* angeberisch, protzig *(inf)*, großkotzig *(inf)*; *house, restaurant, décor* pompös, bombastisch

pretentiously [prɪˈtenʃəslɪ] ADV *say, describe* hochtrabend; *decorated* pompös, protzig *(inf)*

pretentiousness [prɪˈtenʃəsnɪs] N *(= self-importance)* Anmaßung *f*; *(of speech, style, book)* Hochgestochenheit *f*; *(= ostentatiousness)* Angeberei *f*, Protzigkeit *f (inf)*, Großkotzigkeit *f (inf)*; *(of house, restaurant, décor)* Pomp *m*, Bombast *m*

preter- [ˈpriːtəʳ-] PREF über-; **preterhuman** übernatürlich

preterite, *(esp US)* **preterit** [ˈpretərɪt] ADJ *verb* im Imperfekt; *(in English)* im Präteritum; **~ form** Imperfekt-/Präteritumsform *f*; **the ~ tense** das Imperfekt, das Präteritum N Imperfekt *nt*, Präteritum *nt*; **in the ~** im Imperfekt/Präteritum

preternatural [ˌpriːtəˈnætʃrəl] ADJ **a** *(= supernatural)* übernatürlich **b** *(= abnormal, exceptional)* außergewöhnlich

preternaturally [ˌpriːtəˈnætʃrəlɪ] ADV übernatürlich, außergewöhnlich, unheimlich; **it was suddenly ~ quiet** plötzlich war es unheimlich still

pretext [ˈpriːtekst] N Vorwand *m*; **on** *or* **under the ~ of doing sth** unter dem Vorwand, etw zu tun

pretorian guard [prɪˈtɔːrɪənˈgɑːd] ADJ *(US)* = **praetorian guard**

pretrial [ˌpriːˈtraɪəl] ADJ *(Jur)* vor der Hauptverhandlung

prettify [ˈprɪtɪfaɪ] VT verschönern

prettily [ˈprɪtɪlɪ] ADV nett; *dress also* hübsch; *(= charmingly)* reizend, hübsch

prettiness [ˈprɪtɪnɪs] N *(= pretty appearance)* hübsches Aussehen; *(of place)* Schönheit *f*; *(= charm) (of woman)* Anmut *f*, Schönheit *f*; *(of manners, compliment etc)* Artigkeit *f*; **the ~ of her hair/face** ihr hübsches Haar/Gesicht

pretty [ˈprɪtɪ] ADJ *(+er)* **a** hübsch, nett; *manners, compliment, speech* artig; **to be ~** *(also pej: man)* hübsch sein; **a ~ man** *(pej)* ein Schönling *m*; **to make oneself ~** sich hübsch machen; **I'm not just a ~ face!** *(inf)* ich bin gar nicht so dumm (wie ich aussehe) *(inf)*; **she's not just a ~ face!** *(inf)* sie hat auch Köpfchen!; **~ Polly!** *(to parrot)* Lora, Lora!; **it wasn't ~** das war alles andere als schön; **it wasn't a ~ sight** das war kein schöner Anblick; **~-~** *(inf)* niedlich
b *(inf)* hübsch, schön *(inf)*; *price, sum* hübsch, stolz; **it'll cost a ~ penny** das wird eine schöne Stange Geld kosten *(inf)*; **a ~ state of affairs** eine schöne Geschichte; **a ~ mess we're in!** da sitzen wir ganz schön in der Tinte! *(inf)*; **say ~ please** sag mal schön bitte
ADV *(= rather)* ziemlich; *good also* ganz; *(= very also)* ganz schön *(inf)*, ganz hübsch *(inf)*; **~ damn** *or* **damned good/quick** verdammt gut/schnell *(inf)*, ganz schön gut/schnell; **~ nearly** *or* **well finished** so gut wie *or* so ziemlich fertig *(inf)*; **how's your job/the patient? – ~ much the same** was macht die Arbeit/der Patient? – so ziemlich wie immer/immer noch so ziemlich gleich
N **my ~** mein Sternchen
VT *(inf)* **to ~ up** schön machen, verschönern

pretzel [ˈpretsl] N Brezel *f*

prevail [prɪˈveɪl] VI **a** *(= gain mastery)* sich durchsetzen *(over, against* gegenüber) **b** *(conditions, wind etc)* vorherrschen; *(= be widespread: customs)* weitverbreitet sein **c** *(= persuade)* **to ~ (up)on sb to do sth** jdn dazu bewegen *or* bringen, etw zu tun

prevailing [prɪˈveɪlɪŋ] ADJ **a** *(= current) fashion, conditions* derzeitig, derzeit herrschend, aktuell; *opinion* aktuell, (vor)herrschend; **the ~ wisdom** die vorherrschende *or* derzeitige Überzeugung **b** *wind* vorherrschend

prevalence [ˈprevələns] N *(= widespread occurrence)* Vorherrschen *nt*, weite Verbreitung; *(of crime, disease)* Häufigkeit *f*; *(of fashion, style)* Beliebtheit *f*

prevalent [ˈprevələnt] ADJ *(= widespread)* vorherrschend, weitverbreitet, weit verbreitet; *opinion, attitude* geläufig, weitverbreitet, weit verbreitet; *custom, disease* weitverbreitet, weit verbreitet; *conditions, situation* herrschend; *fashions, style* beliebt; **that is very ~ these days** das ist heutzutage häufig anzutreffen

prevaricate [prɪˈværɪkeɪt] VI Ausflüchte machen

prevarication [prɪˌværɪˈkeɪʃən] N Ausflucht *f*; *(= prevaricating)* Ausflüchte *pl*, Ausweichmanöver *pl*

prevaricator [prɪˈværɪkeɪtəʳ] N Ausweichtaktiker(in) *m(f)*

prevent [prɪˈvent] ✪ 26.3 VT *sth* verhindern, verhüten; *(through preventive measures)* vorbeugen *(+dat)*; **to ~ sb (from) doing sth** jdn daran hindern *or* davon abhalten, etw zu tun; **the gate is there to ~ them from falling down the stairs** das Gitter ist dazu da, dass sie nicht die Treppe hinunterfallen; **to ~ sb from coming** jdn am Kommen hindern; **there is nothing to ~ me** nichts kann mich daran hindern *or* davon abhalten; **to ~ sth (from) happening** verhindern, dass etw geschieht

preventable [prɪˈventəbl] ADJ vermeidbar, verhütbar

prevention [prɪˈvenʃən] N Verhinderung *f*, Verhütung *f*; *(through preventive measures)* Vorbeugung *f* *(of* gegen); **~ is better than cure** vorbeugen ist besser als heilen; **society for the ~ of cruelty to animals** ≈ Tierschutzverein *m*; **society for the ~ of cruelty to children** Kinderschutzbund *m*; **fire ~** Feuerschutz *m*

preventive [prɪˈventɪv] ADJ *action, measure* vorbeugend, präventiv; **to be ~** zur Vorbeugung dienen; ~ **detention** *(Brit Jur)* Vorbeugehaft *f*; *(of habitual criminal)* Sicherungsverwahrung *f*; ~ **war** Präventivkrieg *m* **N** *(= preventive measure)* Präventivmaßnahme *f*; *(Med)* vorbeugendes Mittel, Präventiv *nt*; **as a ~** als Vorbeugung

preventive medicine N vorbeugende Medizin, Präventivmedizin *f*

preview ['pri:vju:] **N** **a** *(of play, film)* Vorpremiere *f*; *(of exhibition)* Vorbesichtigung *f*; **to give sb a ~ of sth** *(fig)* jdm eine Vorschau auf etw *(acc)* geben **b** *(Film, TV: = trailer)* Vorschau *f* (of auf *+acc*) **c** *(Comput)* Seitenansicht *f* **VT** *(= view beforehand)* vorher ansehen; *(= show beforehand) film* vorher aufführen; *paintings, fashions* vorher zeigen

previous ['pri:vɪəs] ADJ **a** *(= immediately preceding)* vorherig; *page, day* vorhergehend; *year* vorangegangen; *(with indef art)* früher; **the ~ page/day/year** die Seite/der Tag/das Jahr davor; **the/a ~ holder of the title** der vorherige/ein früherer Titelträger; **in ~ years** in früheren Jahren, früher; **he's already been the target of two ~ attacks** er war schon das Opfer von zwei früheren Angriffen; **in a ~ incarnation** *or* **life** in einem früheren Leben; *(fig)* früher im Leben; **from a ~ relationship** aus einer früheren Beziehung; **he beat his ~ best** *(Sport)* er hat seine bisherige Höchstleistung überboten; **have you made any ~ applications?** haben Sie sich davor *or* früher schon einmal beworben?; **on a ~ occasion** zuvor, bei einer früheren Gelegenheit; **I have a ~ engagement** ich habe schon einen Termin; **no ~ experience necessary** Vorkenntnisse (sind) nicht erforderlich; ~ **conviction** *(Jur)* Vorstrafe *f*; **to have a ~ conviction** vorbestraft sein; ~ **owner** Vorbesitzer(in) *m(f)*
b *(dated inf: = premature)* vorschnell, voreilig; **this seems somewhat ~** das scheint etwas voreilig *or* verfrüht
c ~ **to** vor *(+dat)*; ~ **to going out** bevor ich/er *etc* ausging

previously ['pri:vɪəslɪ] ADV vorher, früher; ~ **I had very little time to cook** früher hatte ich nur sehr wenig Zeit zum Kochen; **he'd arrived three hours ~** er war drei Stunden zuvor angekommen; ~ **unreleased/unpublished** bislang *or* bisher unveröffentlicht; ~ **unknown** bislang *or* bisher unbekannt

pre-vocational [,pri:vəʊ'keɪʃənl] ADJ vorberuflich; ~ **training** Berufsschulausbildung *f*

pre-war ['pri:'wɔ:'] ADJ Vorkriegs-; **the ~ years** die Vorkriegsjahre *pl*

prewash ['pri:wɒʃ] N *(on washing machine)* Vorwaschgang *m*

prey [preɪ] **N** *(lit, fig)* Beute *f*; *(= animal also)* Beutetier *nt*; **beast of ~** Raubtier *nt*; **bird of ~** Raubvogel *m*; **to be/fall ~ to sb/sth** *(lit)* eine Beute von jdm/etw werden; *(fig)* ein Opfer von jdm/etw werden; **she was (a) ~ to anxiety** sie war leicht in Angst zu versetzen; **she was (a) ~ to illness** sie wurde leicht krank **VI** **to ~ (up)on** *(animals)* Beute machen auf *(+acc)*; *(pirates, thieves)* (aus)plündern; *(swindler etc)* als Opfer aussuchen; *(doubts)* nagen an *(+dat)*; *(anxiety)* quälen; **it ~ed (up)on his mind** es ließ ihn nicht los, der Gedanke daran quälte ihn

prezzie ['prezɪ] N *(Brit inf: = present)* Geschenk *nt*

price [praɪs] **N** **a** Preis *m*; **the ~ of coffee/cars** die Kaffee-/Autopreise *pl*; **~s and incomes policy** Lohn-Preis-Politik *f*; **to go up** *or* **rise/to go down** *or* **fall in ~** teurer/billiger werden, im Preis steigen/fallen; **they range in ~ from £10 to £30** die Preise dafür bewegen sich zwischen £ 10 und £ 30; **what is the ~ of that?** was kostet das?; **is that the final ~?** bleibt es bei dem Preis?; **at a ~ of ...** zum Preis(e) von ...; **at a ~** zum entsprechenden Preis, wenn man genug dafür hinlegt *(inf)*; **at a reduced ~** verbilligt, zu herabgesetztem *or* reduziertem Preis *(form)*; **if the ~ is right** wenn der Preis stimmt; **ask him for a ~ for the job** frag ihn (mal), was das kostet
b *(fig)* Preis *m*; **everybody has his ~** jeder hat seinen Preis; **the ~ of victory/freedom/fame** der Preis des Sieges/der Freiheit/des Ruhms *or* für den Sieg/die Freiheit/den Ruhm; **but at what ~!** aber zu welchem Preis!; **at any ~** um jeden Preis; **not at any ~** um keinen Preis; **at the ~ of losing his health and his family** auf Kosten seiner Gesundheit und seiner Familie; **it's too big a ~ to pay** das ist ein zu hoher Preis; **but what ~ honour?** wie kann man Ehre bezahlen?
c *(= value, valuation)* **a diamond of great ~** ein sehr wertvoller Diamant; **to put a ~ on sth** einen Preis für etw nennen; **but what ~ do you put on freedom?** aber wie ließe sich die Freiheit mit Gold aufwiegen?; **to be beyond/without ~** nicht mit Geld zu bezahlen *or* mit Gold aufzuwiegen sein
d *(= reward)* Preis *m*; **to put a ~ on sb's head** eine Belohnung auf jds Kopf *(acc)* aussetzen; **to have a ~ on one's head** steckbrieflich gesucht werden
e *(Betting: = odds)* Quote *f*; **what ~ are they giving on that horse?** wie stehen die Wetten für das Pferd?; **the horse had a starting ~ of 3 to 1** das Pferd wurde vor dem Start mit 3:1 gewettet; **what ~ our being able to ...?** *(inf)* wetten, dass wir ... können?; **what ~ freedom/workers' solidarity now?** *(inf)* wie steht es jetzt mit der Freiheit/der Solidarität der Arbeiter?
VT *(= fix price of)* den Preis festsetzen von; *(= put price label on)* auszeichnen (at mit); *(= ask price of)* nach dem Preis fragen von; *(fig: = estimate value of)* schätzen; **it was ~d at £5** *(= marked £5)* es war mit £ 5 ausgezeichnet; *(= cost £5)* es kostete £ 5; **tickets ~d at £20** Karten zum Preis von £ 20; **reasonably ~d** angemessen im Preis; **~d too high/low** zu teuer/billig; **to ~ one's goods/oneself out of the market** seine Waren/sich selbst durch zu hohe Preise konkurrenzunfähig machen; **to ~ sb out of the market** jdn durch niedrigere Preise vom Markt verdrängen

▸ **price down** VT *sep* heruntersetzen, herabsetzen

▸ **price up** VT *sep* heraufsetzen, teurer machen

price: **price agreement** N Preisvereinbarung *f*, Preisabsprache *f*; **price bracket** N = **price range**; **price ceiling** N Preis(ober)grenze *f*; **price control** N Preiskontrolle *f*; **price-controlled** ADJ preisgebunden; **price cut** N Preissenkung *f*; **price cutter** N Preisbrecher(in) *m(f)*; **price cutting** N (starke) Preissenkungen *pl*; **price-earnings ratio** N *(of shares)* Kurs-Gewinn-Verhältnis *nt*; **price fixing** N Preisfestlegung *f*; **price freeze** N Preisstopp *m*; **price gouging** ['praɪs,gaʊdʒɪŋ] N Preiswucherei *f*, Abzockerei *f (inf)*; **price increase** N Preisanstieg *m*, Preiserhöhung *f*; **price index** N Preisindex *m*; **price leader** N *(Econ)* Preisführer(in) *m(f)*

priceless ['praɪslɪs] ADJ unschätzbar, von unschätzbarem Wert; *(inf: = amusing) joke, film* köstlich; *person* unbezahlbar; **Amy, you are ~!** *(inf: = amusing)* Amy, du bist wirklich zum Totlachen

price: **price level** N Preisniveau *nt*; **price limit** N Preisgrenze *f*; **price list** N Preisliste *f*; **price-maintained** ADJ preisgebunden; **price range** N Preisklasse *f*; **price rigging** N Preisabsprachen *pl*; **price ring** N Preiskartell *nt*; **price rise** N Preiserhöhung *f*; **price saving** N Preisersparnis *f*; **price structure** N Preisgefüge *nt*; **price support** N *(US)* Subvention *f*, Preisstützung *f*; **price tag, price ticket** N Preisschild *nt*; **price war** N Preiskrieg *m*

pricey ['praɪsɪ] ADJ *(inf)* kostspielig; **that's a bit ~!** das ist ein bisschen happig *(inf)*

pricing policy ['praɪsɪŋ,pɒlɪsɪ] N Preispolitik *f*

prick [prɪk] **N** **a** *(= puncture, pricking sensation)* Stich *m*; **to give sb/oneself a ~** jdn/sich stechen; ~ **of conscience** Gewissensbisse *pl*
b *(sl: = penis)* Schwanz *m (sl)*
c *(sl: = person)* Arsch *m (vulg)*, Arschloch *nt (vulg)*
VT **a** *(= puncture) oneself, sb* stechen; *balloon* durchstechen; *blister* aufstechen; *outline* (durch Löcher) markieren; **to ~ holes in sth** Löcher in etw stechen; **to ~ one's finger (with sth)** sich *(dat)* (mit etw) in den Finger stechen; **to ~ one's finger (on sth)** sich *(dat)* (an etw *dat*) den Finger stechen; **to ~ the bubble of sth** *(fig)* etw in sich zusammenfallen lassen; **his conscience ~ed him** er bekam *or* hatte Gewissensbisse; **it/she ~ed his conscience** es/sie bereitete ihm Gewissensbisse; **tears ~ed his eyes** *(liter)* er fühlte die Tränen kommen
b **to ~ one's ears** die Ohren spitzen → *also* **prick up VT**
VI *(thorn, injection etc)* stechen; *(eyes)* brennen

▸ **prick out** VT *sep* **a** *seedlings* pflanzen, setzen, pikieren *(spec)* **b** *(= mark) pattern, shape, design* punktieren; *(with marking wheel)* ausrädeln

▸ **prick up** **VI** **her/its ears pricked up** sie/es spitzte die Ohren **VT** *sep* **to prick up its/one's ears** *(lit, fig)* die Ohren spitzen

pricking ['prɪkɪŋ] N *(= sensation)* Stechen *nt*

prickle ['prɪkl] **N** **a** *(= sharp point)* Stachel *m*; *(on plants)* Dorn *m*, Stachel *m* **b** *(= sensation)* Stechen *nt*; *(caused by wool, beard etc)* Kratzen *nt*; *(= tingle, also fig)* Prickeln *nt* **VI** stechen; *(wool, beard)* kratzen; *(= tingle, also fig)* prickeln

prickleback N *(fish)* Stichling *m*

prickly ['prɪklɪ] ADJ *(+er)* **a** *plant, fish, animal* stach(e)lig; *beard, material* kratzig; *sensation* stechend; *(= tingling)* prickelnd *(also fig)* **b** *(fig) person* bissig; *woman also* kratzbürstig *(inf)*; **as ~ as a hedgehog** stachelig wie ein Igel **c** *(= sore) eyes* schmerzend, gereizt

prickly: **prickly ash** N *(Bot)* Stachelesche *f*; **prickly heat** N Hitzepocken *pl*; **prickly pear** N *(= plant)* Feigenkaktus *m*; *(= fruit)* Kaktusfeige *f*

prick: **prick-tease** ['prɪkti:z] *(sl)* **VI** **she's always prick-teasing** sie geilt die Männer auf und lässt sie dann abblitzen *(sl)* **VT** aufgeilen und dann abblitzen lassen *(sl)*; **prick-teaser, prick-tease** N *(sl)* **she's just a ~** sie geilt die Männer nur auf *(sl)*

pricy ['praɪsɪ] ADJ = **pricey**

pride [praɪd] **N** **a** Stolz *m*; *(= arrogance)* Hochmut *m*; **to have too much ~ to do sth** zu stolz sein, um etw zu tun; **to take (a) ~ in sth** auf etw *(acc)* stolz sein; **to take (a) ~ in one's appearance** Wert auf sein Äußeres legen; **to be a (great) source of ~ to sb** jdn mit (großem) Stolz erfüllen; **her ~ and joy** ihr ganzer Stolz; **the ~ of the army** der Stolz der Armee; **to have** *or* **take ~ of place** den Ehrenplatz einnehmen; **~ comes before a fall** *(prov)* Hochmut kommt vor dem Fall *(Prov)*
b *(of lions)* Rudel *nt*
VR **to ~ oneself on sth** sich einer Sache *(gen)* rühmen; **I ~ myself on being an expert in this field** ich darf wohl behaupten, mich auf diesem Gebiet auszukennen; **he ~s himself on the succinctness of his prose** er rühmt sich des knappen Stils seiner Prosa

prie-dieu ['pri:djɜ:] N Betpult *nt*

priest [pri:st] N Priester(in) *m(f)*, Geistliche(r) *mf*

priestess ['pri:stɪs] N Priesterin *f*

priest: **priest-hole** N verborgener Winkel *(in dem verfolgte Priester versteckt wurden)*; **priesthood** ['pri:sthʊd] N Priestertum *nt*; *(= priests collectively)* Priesterschaft *f*; **to enter the ~** Priester werden

priestly ['pri:stlɪ] ADJ priesterlich; ~ **robes** Priestergewand *nt*

priest-ridden ['pri:st,rɪdn] ADJ klerikalistisch

prig [prɪg] N *(= goody-goody)* Tugendlamm *nt (inf)*; *(= boy also)* Musterknabe *m*; *(= snob)* Schnösel *m (inf)*; **don't be such a ~** tu doch nicht so

priggish ['prɪgɪʃ] ADJ tugendhaft; *(= snobbish)* hochnäsig

priggishness ['prɪgɪʃnɪs] N tugendhaftes Getue, Tugendhaftigkeit *f*; *(= snobbishness)* Hochnäsigkeit *f*

prim [prɪm] ADJ *(+er)* **a** *(also* **prim and proper***)* etepetete *pred (inf)*; *woman, manner* steif, prüde; *mouth, expression* verkniffen; *(= prudish)* prüde **b** *(= neat) clothes* sittsam, züchtig; *house* untadelig, mustergültig; *furnishings* steif; *(= demure) person* sittsam, züchtig

prima ballerina [ˈpriːməˌbæləˈriːnə] N Primaballerina *f*

primacy [ˈpraɪməsɪ] N **a** *(= supremacy)* Vorrang *m*; *(= position)* Vorrangstellung *f* **b** *(Eccl)* Primat *nt or m*

prima donna [ˈpriːməˈdɒnə] N *(lit, fig)* Primadonna *f*

primaeval ADJ = **primeval**

prima facie [ˈpraɪməˈfeɪʃɪ] ADV allem Anschein nach ADJ ~ **evidence** glaubhafter Beweis; **the police have a ~ case** die Polizei hat genügend Beweise; **a ~ case of ...** auf den ersten Blick ein Fall von ...

primal [ˈpraɪməl] ADJ ursprünglich, Ur-; ~ **scream** Urschrei *m*

primarily [ˈpraɪmərɪlɪ] ADV hauptsächlich, in erster Linie

primary [ˈpraɪmərɪ] ADJ *(= chief, main)* Haupt-, wesentlich, primär *(form)*; **that is our ~ concern** das ist unser Hauptanliegen *or* unsere Hauptsorge; **of ~ importance** von größter Bedeutung, von äußerster Wichtigkeit; **the ~ meaning of a word** die Grundbedeutung eines Wortes; ~ **source of income** Haupteinnahmequelle *f*; **at ~ level** *(Brit Sch)* in der Grundschule, auf Grundschulniveau N **a** *(= colour)* Grundfarbe *f* **b** *(esp Brit: = primary school)* Grundschule *f* **c** *(US: = election)* (innerparteiliche) Vorwahl

primary: **primary care** N *(Med)* Gesundheitsfürsorge *f* auf kommunaler Ebene; **primary cell** N Primärzelle *f*; **primary colour**, *(US)* **primary color** N Grundfarbe *f*; **primary education** N Grundschul(aus)bildung *f*; **primary election** N *(US)* (innerparteiliche) Vorwahl; **primary feather** N Handschwinge *f*; **primary industry** N Grund(stoff)industrie *f*; *(agriculture etc)* Urindustrie *f*, primäre Industrie *(form)*; *(= main industry)* Hauptindustrie *f*; **primary institution** N Ureinrichtung *f*; **primary producer** N Lieferant(in) *m(f)* von Rohmaterial; **primary product** N Primärprodukt *nt*; *(= main product)* Hauptprodukt *nt*; **primary school** N *(esp Brit)* Grundschule *f*; **primary school teacher** N *(esp Brit)* Grundschullehrer(in) *m(f)*; **primary stress** N Hauptton *m*; **primary teacher** N *(esp Brit)* Grundschullehrer(in) *m(f)*; **primary winding** N Primärwindung *f*

primate [ˈpraɪmɪt] N **a** *(Zool)* Primat *m* **b** *(Eccl)* Primas *m*; **Primate of England/all England** Erzbischof von York/Canterbury

prime [praɪm] ADJ **a** *(= major, chief)* Haupt-, wesentlich; *target, objective* hauptsächlich, oberste(r, s), höchste(r, s); *candidate* erste(r, s); *cause* hauptsächlich, häufigste(r, s); *requirement* erste(r, s), oberste(r, s); ~ **suspect** Hauptverdächtige(r) *mf*; **of ~ importance** von größter Bedeutung, von äußerster Wichtigkeit; **my ~ concern** mein Hauptanliegen *nt*; **she was a ~ favourite** sie war eine hohe Favoritin
b *(= excellent)* erstklassig, beste(r, s); *example* erstklassig; **in ~ condition** *(meat, fruit etc)* von hervorragender Qualität; *athlete, car etc* in erstklassiger *or* hervorragender Verfassung; ~ **cut** Stück *nt* bester Qualität ~ **example**Paradebeispiel *nt*,klassisches Beispiel
N **a** *(= full vigour)* **in the ~ of life** in der Blüte seiner Jahre; **he is in his ~** er ist im besten Alter *or* in den besten Jahren; *(singer, artist)* er ist an seinem Höhepunkt angelangt; **he was cut down in his ~** er wurde in der Blüte seiner Jahre dahingerafft; **he is past his ~** er ist über sein bestes Alter *or* seine besten Jahre hinaus; *(singer, artist)* er hat seine beste Zeit hinter sich; **this city is past its ~** diese Stadt hat auch schon bessere Zeiten gesehen
b *(Math)* Primzahl *f*
c *(Eccl: also* **Prime***)* Prim *f*
VT **a** *gun* schussfertig machen; *bomb* scharf machen; *pump* vorpumpen; *carburettor* Anlasskraftstoff einspritzen in *(+acc)*
b *surface (for painting)* grundieren
c *(with advice, information)* instruieren
d *person (with drink)* alkoholisieren, unter Alkohol setzen

prime costs PL *(Comm)* Selbstkosten *pl*, Gestehungskosten *pl*

primed [praɪmd] ADJ **a** *person* präpariert, vorbereitet, instruiert, gerüstet; **to be ~ for the interview/game** für das Interview/Spiel gut gerüstet sein; ~ **to do sth** gut vorbereitet *or* gerüstet, etw zu tun **b** *(= drunk) person* angetrunken, alkoholisiert, unter Alkohol; ~ **with drink** unter Alkohol gesetzt; **well ~** gut geölt *(inf)* **c** *(= prepared) surface* grundiert, präpariert, vorbereitet **d** *bomb, gun* präpariert

prime: **prime factor** N *(Math)* Primfaktor *m*; **prime meridian** N Nullmeridian *m*; **prime minister** N Ministerpräsident(in) *m(f)*, Premierminister(in) *m(f)*; **prime ministerial** ADJ des Premierministers, der Premierministerin; **prime ministership** N Amt *nt* des Premierministers; **during her ~** während ihrer Amtszeit als Premierministerin; **prime mover** N *(Phys, Tech)* Zugmaschine *f*; *(Philos)* bewegende Kraft, Triebfeder *f*; *(fig: = person)* treibende Kraft; **prime number** N *(Math)* Primzahl *f*

primer [ˈpraɪməʳ] N **a** *(= paint)* Grundierfarbe *f*, Grundierung *f*; *(= coat)* Grundierung *f*, Grundieranstrich *m* **b** *(esp Sch: = book)* Elementarbuch *nt*, Anfangslehrbuch *nt*, Fibel *f* **c** *(= explosive)* Zündhütchen *nt*, Treibladungszünder *m*

prime: **prime rate** N *(Econ, Fin)* Prime Rate *f*, Vorzugszins *nt*; **prime ribs** PL Hochrippen *pl*; **prime time** N Hauptsendezeit *f*

primeval [praɪˈmiːvəl] ADJ urzeitlich, Ur-; ~ **soup** Ursuppe *f*; ~ **slime** Urschleim *m*; ~ **forest** Urwald *m*; ~ **instinct** Urinstinkt *m*

primitive [ˈprɪmɪtɪv] ADJ primitiv; *(Art)* naiv N *(Art) (= artist)* Naive(r) *mf*; *(= work)* naives Werk

primitivism [ˈprɪmɪtɪvɪzəm] N *(Art)* naive Kunst N *(Art) (= artist)* Naive(r) *mf*; *(= work)* naives Werk

primly [ˈprɪmlɪ] ADV *(= demurely)* sittsam, züchtig, überkorrekt; *(= prudishly)* prüde; **she was sitting ~ sipping tea** sie saß steif und vornehm da und nippte an ihrem Tee

primness [ˈprɪmnɪs] N *(= demureness)* Sittsamkeit *f*, Züchtigkeit *f*; *(= prudishness)* Prüderie *f*

primogenitor [ˌpraɪməʊˈdʒenɪtəʳ] N *(= ancestor)* Ahn(e) *m*, Vorfahr *m*; *(= first ancestor)* Urahn(e) *m*, Stammvater *m*

primogeniture [ˌpraɪməʊˈdʒenɪtʃəʳ] N Erstgeburt *f*; **law of ~** Erstgeburtsrecht *nt*

primordial [praɪˈmɔːdɪəl] ADJ primordial *(spec)*, ursprünglich; ~ **slime** Urschleim *m*

primp [prɪmp] VT zurechtmachen; *hair also* richten; **to ~ oneself (up)** sich fein machen, sich schniegeln VI sich zurechtmachen

primrose [ˈprɪmrəʊz] N *(Bot)* Erdschlüsselblume *f*; *(= colour)* Blassgelb *nt* ADJ blassgelb; **the ~ path** *(fig)* der Rosenpfad

primula [ˈprɪmjʊlə] N Primel *f*

Primus (stove)® [ˈpraɪməs(ˌstəʊv)] N Primuskocher *m*

prince [prɪns] N *(= king's son)* Prinz *m*; *(= ruler)* Fürst *m*; **Prince Charming** *(in fairy story)* der Königssohn; *(fig)* der Märchenprinz; **the Prince of Darkness** der Fürst der Finsternis; **the Prince of Peace** der Friedensfürst; **a ~ among men** eine herausragende Erscheinung; **he is ~ of architects/architecture** *(liter)* er ist einer der herausragendsten Architekten

prince consort N Prinzgemahl *m*

princedom [ˈprɪnsdəm] N *(old)* Fürstentum *nt*

princeling [ˈprɪnslɪŋ] N *(old, liter)* Prinzchen *nt*

princely [ˈprɪnslɪ] ADJ *(lit, fig)* fürstlich

prince regent N Prinzregent *m*

princess [prɪnˈses] N Prinzessin *f*; *(= wife of ruler)* Fürstin *f*

Princess Royal N *(Brit) Titel einer der Töchter des regierenden Monarchen*

principal [ˈprɪnsɪpəl] ADJ Haupt-, hauptsächlich; **the ~ cities of China** die wichtigsten Städte Chinas; **my ~ concern** mein Hauptanliegen *nt*; ~ **person** Hauptperson *f*; ~ **teacher** Rektor(in) *m(f)*; ~ **horn in the Philharmonic Orchestra** erster Hornist/erste Hornistin der Philharmoniker N **a** *(of school, college)* Rektor(in) *m(f)*; *(in play)* Hauptperson *f*; *(in duel)* Duellant *m* **b** *(Fin, of investment)* Kapitalsumme *f*; *(of debt)* Kreditsumme *f* **c** *(esp Jur: = client)* Klient(in) *m(f)*, Mandant(in) *m(f)*

principal boy N *(Theat) jugendliche Hauptrolle in britischen Weihnachtsrevuen, die traditionsgemäß von einem Mädchen gespielt wird*

principality [ˌprɪnsɪˈpælɪtɪ] N Fürstentum *nt*

principally [ˈprɪnsɪpəlɪ] ADV vornehmlich, in erster Linie

principal parts PL *(Gram: of verb)* Stammformen *pl*

principle [ˈprɪnsɪpl] N **a** Prinzip *nt*; **to go back to first ~s** zu den Grundlagen zurückgehen **b** *(= moral precept)* Prinzip *nt*, Grundsatz *m*; *(no pl: = integrity)* Prinzipien *pl*, Grundsätze *pl*; **in/on ~** im/aus Prinzip, prinzipiell; **a man of ~(s)** ein Mensch mit *or* von Prinzipien *or* Grundsätzen; **it's against my ~s** es geht gegen meine Prinzipien; **it's a matter of ~, it's the ~ of the thing** es geht dabei ums Prinzip; **I'm doing it for reasons of ~** ich tue das aus Prinzip **c** *(= basic element)* Element *nt*

principled [ˈprɪnsɪpld] ADJ *man, statesman* mit Prinzipien *or* Grundsätzen, prinzipientreu; **high-~** mit hohen Prinzipien *or* Grundsätzen; **to take a ~ stand** seinen Prinzipien treu bleiben; **on ~ grounds** aus prinzipiellen Gründen

prink [prɪŋk] VTI = **primp**

print [prɪnt] N **a** *(= typeface, characters)* Schrift *f*; *(= printed matter)* Gedruckte(s) *nt*; **out of ~** vergriffen; **in ~** gedruckt; **to be in ~ again** wieder erhältlich sein; **to see sth in cold ~** etw schwarz auf weiß sehen; **he'll never get into ~** er wird nie etwas veröffentlichen; **don't let that get into ~** das darf nicht erscheinen; **in large** *or* **big ~** in Großdruck → *also* **small print**
b *(= picture)* Druck *m*
c *(Phot)* Abzug *m*, Kopie *f*; *(of cinema film)* Kopie *f*
d *(= fabric)* bedruckter Stoff; *(= cotton print)* Kattun *m*; *(= dress)* bedrucktes Kleid; *(of cotton)* Kattunkleid *nt*
e *(= impression: of foot, hand etc)* Abdruck *m*; **a thumb/paw ~** ein Daumen-/Pfotenabdruck *m*; **to take sb's ~s** *(police)* von jdm Fingerabdrücke machen *or* nehmen
VT **a** *book, design, money* drucken; *(Comput)* (aus)drucken; *fabric* bedrucken; ~ **to file** *(Comput)* Ausdruck in Datei
b *(= publish) story, picture* veröffentlichen
c *(= write in block letters)* in Druckschrift schreiben; **to ~ sth in large letters** etw in Großbuchstaben schreiben
d *(Phot)* abziehen
e hoof marks ~ed in the sand Hufabdrücke *pl* im Sand
VI **a** *(printer, printing machine)* drucken; **ready to ~** *(book)* druckfertig; *machine* druckbereit; **the book is ~ing now** das Buch ist gerade im Druck
b *(= write in block letters)* in Druckschrift schreiben

▶ **print off** VT *sep (Typ)* drucken; *(Phot)* abziehen

▶ **print out** VT *sep (Comput)* ausdrucken; **print out the results, please** würden Sie bitte die Ergebnisse ausdrucken lassen

printable [ˈprɪntəbl] ADJ druckfähig; *photograph* abzugsfähig, reproduzierbar

print: **print area** N *(Comput)* Druckbereich *m*; **print drum** N *(Comput)* Drucktrommel *f*

printed [ˈprɪntɪd] ADJ Druck-, gedruckt; *(= written in capitals)* in Großbuchstaben; *fabric* bedruckt; ~ matter/papers Büchersendung *f*; the ~ word das gedruckte Wort; the ~ book das gedruckte *or* veröffentlichte Buch; the ~ page die gedruckte Seite; in ~ form in gedruckter Form; ~ circuit gedruckte Schaltung; ~ circuit board Leiterplatte *f*

printer [ˈprɪntəˈ] N Drucker *m*; the text has gone to the ~ der Text ist in Druck gegangen

printer driver N *(Comput)* Druckertreiber *m*

printer's [ˈprɪntəz]: **printer's devil** N Setzerjunge *m*; **printer's error** N Druckfehler *m*; **printer's ink** N Druckerschwärze *f*

printer queue N *(Comput)* Druckerwarteschlange *f*

printery [ˈprɪntərɪ] N Druckerei *f*

print head N *(Comput)* Druckkopf *m*

printing [ˈprɪntɪŋ] N **a** *(= process)* Drucken *nt* **b** *(= unjoined writing)* Druckschrift *f*; *(= characters, print)* Schrift *f* **c** *(= quantity printed)* Auflage *f*

printing: **printing block** N *(Typ)* Druckform *f*, Klischee *nt*; **printing frame** N Kopierrahmen *m*; **printing ink** N Druckerschwärze *f*; **printing office** N (Buch)druckerei *f*; **printing order** N *(Comput)* Druckreihenfolge *f*; **printing paper** N Druckerpapier *nt*, Kopierpapier *nt*; **printing press** N Druckerpresse *f*; **printing works** N *sing or pl* Druckerei *f*

print: **print job** N *(Comput)* Druckauftrag *m*; **print journalist** N Journalist(in) *m(f)* in den Printmedien; **print list** N *(Comput)* Druckliste *f*; **printmaker** [ˈprɪntˌmeɪkəˈ] N *(= artist)* Grafiker(in) *m(f)*; *(= manufacturer)* Druckhersteller(in) *m(f)*; **printmaking** N Grafik *f*; **print media** PL Print- *or* Druckmedien *pl*; **print menu** N *(Comput)* Druckmenü *nt*; **print-out** N *(Comput)* Ausdruck *m*; **print preview** N *(Comput)* Druckvorschau *f*; **print quality** N *(Comput)* Druckqualität *f*; **print queue** N *(Comput)* Druckerwarteschlange *f*; **print range** N *(Comput)* Druckbereich *m*; **print run** N Auflage *f*; **print seller** N Grafikhändler(in) *m(f)*; **print shop** N Grafikhandlung *f*; *(in printing works)* Druckmaschinensaal *m*; **print speed** N *(Comput)* Druckgeschwindigkeit *f*; **print-through paper** N *(Comput)* Durchschlagpapier *nt*; **printwheel** [ˈprɪntwheel] N *(Comput)* Typenrad *nt*

prion [ˈpraɪɒn] N Prion *nt*; ~ protein Prion-Protein *nt*

prior[1] [ˈpraɪəˈ] ADJ **a** *knowledge, agreement* vorherig; *(= earlier)* früher; without ~ warning ohne vorherige Warnung, ohne Vorwarnung; ~ claim Vorrecht *nt (to* auf *+acc)*; a ~ engagement eine vorher getroffene Verabredung **b** *(= stronger) obligation* vorrangig **c** ~ to sth vor etw *(dat)*; ~ to this/that zuvor; ~ to going out bevor ich/er *etc* ausging

prior[2] N *(Eccl)* Prior *m*

prioress [ˈpraɪərɪs] N Priorin *f*

prioritization [praɪˌɒrɪtaɪˈzeɪʃən] N **a** *(= arranging in order of priority)* Ordnung *f* nach Priorität **b** *(= making a priority)* ~ of these issues was a mistake es war falsch, diesen Dingen Priorität einzuräumen

prioritize [praɪˈɒrɪtaɪz] VT **a** *(= arrange in order of priority)* der Priorität nach ordnen **b** *(= make a priority)* Priorität einräumen *(+dat)*

priority [praɪˈɒrɪtɪ] N Vorrang *m*, Priorität *f*; *(= thing having precedence)* vorrangige Sache *or* Angelegenheit; a top ~ eine Sache *or* Angelegenheit (von) äußerster Dringlichkeit *or* höchster Priorität; what is your top ~? was steht bei Ihnen an erster Stelle?; it must be given top ~ das muss vorrangig behandelt werden; to have ~ Vorrang *or* Priorität haben; to give ~ to sth etw vorrangig behandeln, einer Sache *(dat)* Priorität geben; in strict order of ~ ganz nach Dringlichkeit; we must get our priorities right wir müssen unsere Prioritäten richtig setzen; you've got your priorities all wrong du weißt ja nicht, was wirklich wichtig ist; you should get your priorities right du solltest deine Prioritäten finden; high/low on the list of priorities *or* the ~ list oben/unten auf der Prioritätenliste

priority: **priority share** N *(Fin)* Vorzugsaktie *f*; **priority treatment** N Vorzugsbehandlung *f*; to get ~ bevorzugt behandelt werden

priory [ˈpraɪərɪ] N Priorat *nt*; *(in church names)* ≈ Münster *nt*

prise, *(US)* **prize** [praɪz] VT to ~ sth open etw aufbrechen; to ~ the lid up/off den Deckel auf-/abbekommen; to ~ sth out (of sth) etw aus etw herausbekommen; to ~ a secret out of sb jdm ein Geheimnis entlocken

prism [ˈprɪzəm] N Prisma *nt*

prismatic [prɪzˈmætɪk] ADJ prismatisch; *(= multi-coloured)* in den Farben des Spektrums; ~ colour Spektralfarbe *f*

prison [ˈprɪzn] **N** *(lit, fig)* Gefängnis *nt*; to be in ~ im Gefängnis sein *or* sitzen; to go to ~ for 5 years für *or* auf 5 Jahre ins Gefängnis gehen *or* wandern *(inf)*; to send sb to ~ jdn ins Gefängnis schicken, jdn zu einer Freiheitsstrafe verurteilen **ATTR** Gefängnis-

prison: **prison bitch** N *(US inf)* to make sb one's ~ jdn zu seinem Sklaven/seiner Sklavin machen, jdn ausnutzen *or* für sich arbeiten lassen; **prison breach**, **prison breaking** N Gefängnisausbruch *m*, Ausbruch *m* aus dem Gefängnis; **prison camp** N Gefangenenlager *nt*

prisoner [ˈprɪznəˈ] N **a** *(lit, fig)* Gefangene(r) *mf*; to hold *or* keep sb ~ jdn gefangen halten; to take sb ~ jdn gefangen nehmen; to take no ~s *(fig)* keine Gefangenen machen; ~ of war Kriegsgefangene(r) *mf*; ~ of war camp (Kriegs)gefangenenlager *nt* **b** *(Jur: under arrest)* Festgenommene(r) *mf*; *(facing charge, at the bar)* Angeklagte(r) *mf*

prison: **prison guard** N *(US)* = **prison officer**; **prison life** N das Leben im Gefängnis; **prison officer** N *(Brit)* Gefängniswärter(in) *or* -aufseher(in) *m(f)*; **prison system** N Strafvollzugssystem *nt*; **prison visitor** N Gefangenenbetreuer(in) *m(f)*

prissy [ˈprɪsɪ] ADJ *(pej)* zimperlich; *dress, hairstyle* brav

pristine [ˈprɪstaɪn] ADJ *(= in unspoilt state) beauty* unberührt, ursprünglich; *condition* tadellos, makellos; *(= original)* urtümlich, ursprünglich

prithee [ˈprɪðiː] INTERJ *(obs)* bitte

privacy [ˈprɪvəsɪ, ˈpraɪvəsɪ] N Privatleben *nt*; there is no ~ in these flats in diesen Wohnungen kann man kein Privatleben führen; in an open-plan office one has no ~ in einem Großraumbüro hat man keinen privaten Bereich; in the ~ of one's own home im eigenen Heim; in the strictest ~ *(meeting, preparations)* unter strengster Geheimhaltung

private [ˈpraɪvɪt] **ADJ** **a** privat; *(= personal) letter, reasons* persönlich, privat; *(= confidential) matter, affair* vertraulich; *conversation, meeting, interview* privat, vertraulich; *(= secluded) place* abgelegen; *dining room* separat; *(= not public) funeral, wedding* im engsten Kreis; *hearing, sitting* nicht öffentlich, nichtöffentlich; they were sharing a ~ joke sie fanden irgend etwas lustig; it's just a ~ joke between us das ist ein Privatwitz von uns; no ~ jokes! lass uns auch mitlachen!; ~ and confidential streng vertraulich; he acted in a ~ capacity er handelte als Privatperson; they wanted to be ~ sie wollten allein *or* für sich sein; to keep sth ~ etw für sich behalten; his ~ life sein Privatleben *nt*; in his ~ thoughts in seinen ganz persönlichen Gedanken

b ~ branch exchange *(Brit Telec)* Nebenstellenanlage *f*; ~ car Privatwagen *m*; ~ citizen Privatperson *f*; ~ education Ausbildung *f* in Privatschulen; ~ health insurance private Krankenversicherung; ~ individual Einzelne(r) *mf*; ~ law Privatrecht *nt*; ~ limited company ≈ Aktiengesellschaft *f (die nicht an der Börse notiert ist)*; ~ means Privatvermögen *nt*; ~ pupil Privatschüler(in) *m(f)*; ~ soldier *(Mil)* gemeiner *or* einfacher Soldat; ~ treatment Privatbehandlung *f*; ~ tutor Privatlehrer(in) *m(f)*; ~ ward Privatabteilung *or* -station *f*

c *(= withdrawn, reserved) person* reserviert, zurückhaltend

N **a** *(Mil)* Gefreite(r) *mf*; Private X der Gefreite X; *(in address)* Gefreiter X; ~ first class *(US)* Obergefreite(r) *mf*

b privates **PL** *(= genitals)* Geschlechtsteile *pl*

c in ~ privat; *(Jur)* unter Ausschluss der Öffentlichkeit; we must talk in ~ wir müssen das unter uns besprechen

private: **private company** N Privatgesellschaft *f*; **private detective** N Privatdetektiv(in) *m(f)*; **private enterprise** N Privatunternehmen *nt*; *(= free enterprise)* freies Unternehmertum

privateer [ˌpraɪvəˈtɪəˈ] N *(= ship)* Freibeuter *m*, Kaperschiff *nt*; *(= crew member)* Freibeuter *m*, Kaperer *m*

private: **private eye** N *(inf)* Privatdetektiv(in) *m(f)*, Schnüffler(in) *m(f) (pej inf)*; **Private Finance Initiative** N *(Brit Pol) Regierungsprogramm zur Privatfinanzierung öffentlicher Projekte*; **private hotel** N Privathotel *nt*; **private investigator** N Privatdetektiv(in) *m(f)*

privately [ˈpraɪvɪtlɪ] ADV **a** *(= not publicly)* privat; may I speak to you ~? kann ich Sie privat sprechen *or* unter vier Augen sprechen?; the meeting was held ~ das Treffen wurde in kleinem Kreis *or* Rahmen abgehalten; a ~ owned company ein Unternehmen in Privatbesitz; he is being ~ educated er wird privat erzogen; she is having the operation ~ sie lässt sich auf eigene Kosten operieren; I sold/bought my car ~ ich habe meinen Wagen privat verkauft/privat *or* von Privat gekauft

b *(= secretly, personally, unofficially)* persönlich; I have been told ~ that ... mir wurde vertraulich mitgeteilt, dass ...; ~ I think that ... ich persönlich glaube, dass ...; but ~ he was very upset doch innerlich war er sehr aufgebracht

private: **private member** N *(Brit Parl)* Abgeordnete(r) *mf (der/die nicht der Regierung angehört)*; ~'s bill Gesetzesinitiative *f* eines Abgeordneten; **private parts** PL *(= genitals)* Geschlechtsteile *pl* → *also* **private N b**; **private patient** N Privatpatient(in) *m(f)*; **private pension scheme** N Privatrente *f*; **private practice** N *(Brit)* Privatpraxis *f*; he is in ~ er hat Privatpatienten; **private property** N Privateigentum *nt*; **private prosecution** N *(Jur)* Zivilklage *f*; **private school** N Privatschule *f*; **private secretary** N Privatsekretär(in) *m(f)*; **private sector** N privater Sektor; **private-sector company** N Unternehmen *nt* des privaten Sektors, privatwirtschaftliches Unternehmen; **private tuition** N Privatunterricht *m*; **private view** N Vorabbesichtigung *f*

privation [praɪˈveɪʃən] N **a** *(= state)* Armut *f*, Not *f*; a life of ~ ein Leben in Armut *or* Not **b** *(= hardship)* Entbehrung *f*, Einschränkung *f*; to suffer many ~s viele Entbehrungen erleiden; wartime ~s die Entbehrungen *pl* der Kriegszeit

privatization [ˌpraɪvətaɪˈzeɪʃən] N Privatisierung *f*

privatize [ˈpraɪvətaɪz] VT privatisieren

privet [ˈprɪvɪt] N (gemeiner) Liguster; ~ hedge Ligusterhecke *f*

privilege [ˈprɪvɪlɪdʒ] **N** **a** *(= prerogative)* Privileg *nt*, Sonderrecht *nt*; *(= honour)* Ehre *f*; *(Parl)* Immunität *f*; it's a lady's ~ es ist das Vorrecht einer Dame **b** *(Comput)* Zugriffsrecht *nt* **VT** privilegieren, bevorrechtigen

privileged [ˈprɪvɪlɪdʒd] **ADJ** **a** *person, classes* privilegiert; *(Parl) speech* der Immunität unterliegend *attr*; *claim, debt* bevorrechtigt; for a ~ few für wenige Privilegierte, für eine kleine Gruppe von Privilegierten; to be ~ to do sth das Privileg genießen, etw zu tun; I was ~ to meet him ich hatte das Privileg *or* die Ehre, ihm vorgestellt zu werden; in a ~ position in einer privilegierten Position; ~ stock Vorzugsaktien *pl*

b *(= secret) information* vertraulich
c *(Jur) document* vertraulich; ~ **communication** vertrauliche Mitteilung
N **the** ~ *pl (= elite)* die Privilegierten

privily ['prɪvɪlɪ] **ADV** *(old)* insgeheim, im Geheimen

privy ['prɪvɪ] **ADJ** **to be ~ to sth** in etw *(acc)* eingeweiht sein **N** Abort *m*, Abtritt *m*

Privy: **Privy Council** **N** Geheimer Rat; **Privy Councillor**, *(US)* **Privy Councilor** **N** Geheimrat *m*, Geheimrätin *f*; **Privy Purse** **N** Privatschatulle *f*

prize[1] [praɪz] **N** **a** Preis *m*; *(in lottery)* Gewinn *m*, Preis *m*; **the glittering ~s of the pop world** der Flimmerglanz der Popwelt; **(there are) no ~s for guessing** *(inf)* dreimal darfst du raten
b *(Naut: = captured ship)* Prise *f (old)*
ADJ **a** *(= awarded a prize) entry, essay, sheep* preisgekrönt; ~ **idiot** *(inf)* Vollidiot(in) *m(f) (inf)*
b *(= awarded as a prize)* ~ **trophy** Siegestrophäe *f*; ~ **cup** (Sieger)pokal *m*; ~ **medal** (Sieger)medaille *f*
c *(= offering a prize)* ~ **competition** Preisausschreiben *nt*
VT (hoch) schätzen; **to ~ sth highly** etw sehr *or* hoch schätzen; **to ~ sth above sth** etw über *or* vor etw *(acc)* stellen; **~d possession** wertvollster Besitz, wertvollstes Stück; *(of museum etc)* Glanzstück *nt*, Paradestück *nt*

prize[2] **VT** *(US)* = **prise**

prize: **prize day** **N** *(Sch)* (Tag *m* der) Preisverleihung *f*; **prize draw** **N** Lotterie *f*, Tombola *f*; **prizefight** ['praɪzfaɪt] **N** Profi- *or* Berufsboxkampf *m*; **prizefighter** ['praɪzfaɪtəʳ] **N** Profi- *or* Berufsboxer(in) *m(f)*; **prizefighting** ['praɪzfaɪtɪŋ] **N** Profi- *or* Berufsboxkampf *m*; **prize-giving** **N** *(Sch)* Preisverleihung *or* -verteilung *f*; **prize list** **N** *(in lottery, competition)* Gewinnerliste *f*; **prize money** **N** **a** *(= cash prize)* Geld- *or* Barpreis *m*; *(Boxing)* (Sieges)prämie *f*; *(in competition)* Gewinn *m* **b** *(old Naut)* Prisengeld *nt*; **prize ring** **N** *(Boxing)* Ring *m*; **prizewinner** **N** (Preis)gewinner(in) *m(f)*; **prizewinning** **ADJ** *entry, novel* preisgekrönt; ~ **ticket** Gewinnlos *nt*

PRO *abbr of* **public relations officer**

pro[1] [prəʊ] **N** *(inf)* Profi *m*

pro[2] **N** *(inf: = prostitute)* Nutte *f (inf)*

pro[3] **PREP** *(= in favour of)* für **N** **the ~s and cons** das Für und Wider, das Pro und Kontra

pro- **PREF** pro-, Pro-; **~European** proeuropäisch

proactive [prəʊ'æktɪv] **ADJ** proaktiv

pro-am ['prəʊ'æm] **ADJ** ~ **golf tournament** *Golfturnier, bei dem Profis gegen (prominente) Amateure spielen*

prob [prɒb] **N** *(inf)* Problem *nt*; **no ~s** passt schon, kein Problem

probabilistic [ˌprɒbəbə'lɪstɪk] **ADJ** *(esp Philos)* probabilistisch; **these are all ~ models** dies sind alles wahrscheinliche Modelle

probability [ˌprɒbə'bɪlɪtɪ] ✪ 15.2 **N** Wahrscheinlichkeit *f*; **in all ~** aller Wahrscheinlichkeit nach, höchstwahrscheinlich; **the ~ of sth** die Wahrscheinlichkeit einer Sache *(gen)*; **what's the ~ of that happening?** wie groß ist die Wahrscheinlichkeit, dass das geschieht?; **the ~ is that he will leave** wahrscheinlich wird er weggehen

probable ['prɒbəbl] ✪ 15.2 **ADJ** wahrscheinlich

probable cause **N** *(US Jur)* hinreichender (Tat)verdacht

probably ['prɒbəblɪ] ✪ 15.2, 16.2 **ADV** wahrscheinlich; **very ~, but ...** sehr wahrscheinlich, aber ...; **most ~, more ~ than not** höchstwahrscheinlich; **~ not** wahrscheinlich nicht

probate ['prəʊbɪt] **N** *(= examination)* gerichtliche Testamentsbestätigung; *(= will)* beglaubigte Testamentsabschrift; **grant of ~** Erbscheinerteilung *f*

probate court **N** Nachlassgericht *nt*

probation [prə'beɪʃən] **N** **a** *(Jur)* Bewährung *f*; **to put sb on ~ (for a year)** jdm (ein Jahr) Bewährung geben; **to be on ~** auf Bewährung sein, Bewährung haben **b** *(of employee)* Probe *f*; *(= probation period)* Probezeit *f*; *(Rel)* Noviziat *nt*

probational [prə'beɪʃənl] **ADJ** Probe-; ~ **period** Probezeit *f*

probationary [prə'beɪʃnərɪ] **ADJ** Probe-; ~ **period** Probezeit *f*; *(Jur)* Bewährungsfrist *f*

probationer [prə'beɪʃnəʳ] **N** *(Jur)* auf Bewährung Freigelassene(r) *mf*; *(Med)* Lernschwester *f*; *(Rel)* Novize *m*, Novizin *f*

probation officer **N** Bewährungshelfer(in) *m(f)*

probe [prəʊb] **N** **a** *(= device)* Sonde *f* **b** *(= investigation)* Untersuchung *f (into +gen)*; **a police ~ revealed ...** Nachforschungen der Polizei ergaben ... **VT** untersuchen; *(esp with device)* sondieren; *space, sb's past, subconscious, private life* erforschen; *mystery* ergründen, erforschen **VI** suchen, forschen *(for* nach); *(Med)* untersuchen *(for* auf *+acc)*; *(= inquire)* forschen, bohren *(for* nach); **to ~ into a wound** eine Wunde mit der Sonde untersuchen; **to ~ into sb's private life/sb's past** in jds Privatleben/Vergangenheit *(dat)* herumschnüffeln

probing ['prəʊbɪŋ] **N** Untersuchung *f*; *(esp with device)* Sondierung *f*, Sondieren *nt*; **all this ~ into people's private affairs** dieses Herumschnüffeln in den privaten Angelegenheiten der Leute **ADJ** *question, study, fingers* prüfend

probity ['prəʊbɪtɪ] **N** *(form)* Redlichkeit *f*, Integrität *f (geh)*

problem ['prɒbləm] ✪ 26.1 **N** Problem *nt*; *(Math: as school exercise)* Aufgabe *f*; *(= problematic area)* Problematik *f*; **what's the ~?** wo fehlt's?; **he's got a drink(ing) ~** er trinkt (zu viel); **to have no ~ with sth** kein Problem *or* keine Schwierigkeiten mit etw haben, etw nicht problematisch finden; **I had no ~ in getting the money** ich habe das Geld ohne Schwierigkeiten bekommen; **no ~!** *(inf)* kein Problem!; **the whole ~ of modernization** die ganze Modernisierungsproblematik; ~ **area** Problembereich *m*

problematic(al) [ˌprɒblə'mætɪk(əl)] **ADJ** problematisch

problem: **problem child** **N** Problemkind *nt*; **problem family** **N** Problemfamilie *f*; **problem-oriented** **ADJ** *(Comput)* problemorientiert; **problem page** **N** Problemseite *f*; **problem play** **N** Problemstück *nt*; **problem-solving** **N** Problemlösung *f*; ~ **skills** Problemlösungsfähigkeit *f*

proboscis [prəʊ'bɒsɪs] **N** *(Zool, hum inf)* Rüssel *m*

procedural [prə'siːdjʊrəl] **ADJ** verfahrenstechnisch; *(Jur)* verfahrensrechtlich **N** **(police)** ~ *(= novel)* Kriminalroman *m*; *(= film)* Kriminalfilm *m*

procedure [prə'siːdʒəʳ] **N** Verfahren *nt*; **parliamentary/legal ~** parlamentarisches/gerichtliches Verfahren; **what would be the correct ~ in such a case?** wie geht man in einem solchen Falle vor?, wie verfährt man in einem solchen Falle?; **business ~** geschäftliche Verfahrensweise; **rules of ~** Vorschriften *pl*; **questions of ~** verfahrenstechnische *or (Jur)* verfahrensrechtliche Fragen *pl*; **~-oriented** *(Comput)* prozedurorientiert

proceed [prə'siːd] **VI** **a** *(form: = go)* **vehicles must ~ with caution** vorsichtig fahren!; **I was ~ing along the High Street** ich ging die High Street entlang; **please ~ to gate 3** begeben Sie sich zum Flugsteig 3
b *(form: = go on) (person)* weitergehen; *(vehicle, by vehicle)* weiterfahren; **we then ~ed to London** wir fuhren dann nach London weiter, wir begaben uns dann nach London *(geh)*; **to ~ on one's way** seinen Weg fortsetzen
c *(= carry on, continue)* fortfahren; **can we now ~ to the next item on the agenda?** können wir jetzt zum nächsten Punkt der Tagesordnung übergehen?; **they ~ed with their plan** sie führten ihren Plan weiter; *(= start)* sie gingen nach ihrem Plan vor; **to ~ about one's business** *(form)* seinen Geschäften *(dat)* nachgehen *(geh)*; **~ with your work** fahren Sie mit Ihrer Arbeit fort; **the text ~s as follows** der Text lautet dann wie folgt; **everything is ~ing smoothly** alles läuft bestens; **negotiations are ~ing well** die Verhandlungen kommen gut voran; **you may ~** *(= speak)* Sie haben das Wort; **I would like to make a statement – ~** ich möchte eine Aussage machen – bitte!
d *(= set about sth)* vorgehen; **how does one ~ in such cases?** wie verfährt man in solchen Fällen?, wie geht man in solchen Fällen vor?; **to ~ on the assumption that ...** von der Voraussetzung ausgehen, dass ...
e *(= originate)* **to ~ from** kommen von; *(fig)* herrühren von; **all life ~s from the sea** alles Leben kommt aus dem Meer
f *(Jur)* **to ~ against sb** gegen jdn gerichtlich vorgehen; **to ~ with a case** einen Prozess anstrengen
VT **now, he ~ed** nun, fuhr er fort; **to ~ to do sth** (dann) etw tun

proceeding [prə'siːdɪŋ] **N** **a** *(= action, course of action)* Vorgehen *nt*; **our best/safest way of ~ would be to ask him** am besten/sichersten wäre es, wenn wir ihn fragten **b** **proceedings** **PL** *(= function)* Veranstaltung *f* **c** **proceedings** **PL** *(esp Jur)* Verfahren *nt*; **court ~s** Gerichtsverhandlung *f*; **to take/start ~s against sb** gegen jdn gerichtlich vorgehen; **to take legal ~s** ein Gerichtsverfahren *or* einen Prozess anstrengen; **to start divorce ~s** die Scheidung einreichen **d** **proceedings** **PL** *(= record, written minutes etc)* Protokoll *nt*; *(= published report)* Tätigkeitsbericht *m*

proceeds ['prəʊsiːdz] **PL** *(= yield)* Ertrag *m*; *(from sale, bazaar, raffle)* Erlös *m*; *(= takings)* Einnahmen *pl*

process[1] ['prəʊses] **N** **a** Prozess *m*; **the ~es of the law** der Gesetzesweg; **the ~ of time will ...** die Zeit wird ...; **in the ~ of time** im Laufe der Zeit, mit der Zeit; **in the ~** dabei; **in the ~ of learning** beim Lernen; **in the ~ of construction** im Bau; **to be in the ~ of doing sth** dabei sein, etw zu tun
b *(= specific method, technique)* Verfahren *nt*; *(Ind)* Prozess *m*, Verfahren *nt*
c *(Jur)* Prozess *m*, Verfahren *nt*; **to serve a ~ on sb** jdn vorladen
d *(Biol)* vorstehender Teil; **a ~ of a bone/of the jaw** ein Knochen-/Kiefernvorsprung *m*
VT *(= treat) raw materials, data, information, waste* verarbeiten; *food* konservieren; *milk* sterilisieren; *application, loan, wood* bearbeiten; *film* entwickeln; *(= deal with) applicants, people* abfertigen

process[2] [prə'ses] **VI** *(Brit: = go in procession)* ziehen, schreiten

processed cheese ['prəʊsest'tʃiːz], *(US)* **process cheese** **N** Schmelzkäse *m*

processed peas ['prəʊsest'piːz] **PL** Dosenerbsen *pl*

process engineering **N** Prozess- *or* Verfahrenstechnik *f*

processing ['prəʊsesɪŋ] **N** *(of raw materials, data, information, waste)* Verarbeitung *f*; *(of food)* Konservierung *f*; *(of milk)* Sterilisierung *f*; *(of application, loan, wood)* Bearbeitung *f*; *(of film)* Entwicklung *f*; *(of applicants, people)* Abfertigung *f*

processing: **processing language** **N** *(Comput)* Prozesssprache *f*; **processing plant** **N** Aufbereitungsanlage *f*; **processing speed** **N** *(Comput)* Verarbeitungsgeschwindigkeit *f*; **processing unit** **N** *(Comput)* Prozessor *m*

procession [prə'seʃən] **N** *(organized)* Umzug *m*; *(solemn)* Prozession *f*; *(= line of people, cars etc)* Reihe *f*, Schlange *f*; **funeral/carnival ~** Trauer-/Karnevalszug *m*; **to go** *or* **walk in ~** einen Umzug/eine Prozession machen

processional [prə'seʃənl] *(Eccl)* **N** *(= hymn)* Prozessionshymne *f*, Prozessionslied *nt*; (=

book) Prozessionsbuch *nt* ADJ Prozessions-; *pace* gemessen

processor ['prəʊsesəʳ] N *(Comput)* Prozessor *m;* *(= food processor)* Küchenmaschine *f*

process printing N *(Typ)* Vierfarbendruck *m*

process-server N *(Jur)* Zustellungsbeamte(r) *m*/-beamtin *f*

pro-choice [prəʊ'tʃɔɪs] ADJ *group, organization* für Abtreibung *pred;* ~ **movement** Bewegung *f* der Abtreibungsbefürworter

pro-choicer [ˌprəʊ'tʃɔɪsəʳ] N *(inf)* Abtreibungsbefürworter(in) *m(f)*

proclaim [prə'kleɪm] VT **a** *(= announce)* erklären; *revolution* ausrufen; **to ~ sb king** jdn zum König erklären *or* ausrufen *or* proklamieren; **the day had been ~ed a holiday** der Tag war zum Feiertag erklärt worden; **it was ~ed a success** es wurde zu einem Erfolg erklärt **b** *(= reveal)* verraten, beweisen VR **to ~ oneself king** sich zum König erklären

proclamation [ˌprɒklə'meɪʃən] N **a** *(= act) (of war)* Erklärung *f; (of laws, measures)* Verkündung *f; (of state of emergency)* Ausrufung *f;* **after his ~ as Emperor** nach seiner Proklamation zum Kaiser **b** *(= thing proclaimed)* Erklärung *f*, Proklamation *f*

proclivity [prə'klɪvɪtɪ] N Schwäche *f (for* für), Vorliebe *f (for* für)

proconsul [ˌprəʊ'kɒnsəl] N Prokonsul(in) *m(f)*

procrastinate [prəʊ'kræstɪneɪt] VI zögern, zaudern; **he always ~s** er schiebt die Dinge immer vor sich *(dat)* her

procrastination [prəʊˌkræstɪ'neɪʃən] N Zögern *nt*, Zaudern *nt;* ~ **won't solve your problems** durch Aufschieben lösen sich Ihre Probleme nicht

procrastinator [prəʊ'kræstɪneɪtəʳ] N Zögerer *m*, Zögerin *f*, Zauderer *m*, Zauderin *f*

procreate ['prəʊkrɪeɪt] VI zeugen, sich fortpflanzen VT zeugen, hervorbringen

procreation [ˌprəʊkrɪ'eɪʃən] N Zeugung *f*, Fortpflanzung *f; (of species)* Fortpflanzung *f*

Procrustean [prəʊ'krʌstɪən] ADJ unnachgiebig, starr; ~ **bed** Prokrustesbett *nt*

proctor ['prɒktəʳ] N *(Jur)* Prokurator(in) *m(f); (Univ)* Proktor(in) *m(f); (US: = supervisor)* (Prüfungs)aufsicht *f*

proctoscope ['prɒktəskəʊp] N *(Med)* Proktoskop *nt*

procurable [prə'kjʊərəbl] ADJ erhältlich, zu beschaffen *pred*

procurator ['prɒkjʊreɪtəʳ] N *(Hist)* Prokurator *m; (Jur. = agent also)* Bevollmächtigte(r) *mf*

procurator fiscal N *(Scot Jur)* ≈ Staatsanwalt *m*, ≈ Staatsanwältin *f*

procure [prə'kjʊəʳ] VT **a** *(= obtain)* beschaffen, sich *(dat)* verschaffen *or* beschaffen, besorgen; *(= bring about)* bewirken, herbeiführen; **to ~ sth for sb/oneself** jdm/sich etw beschaffen *or* besorgen, etw für jdn/sich beschaffen *or* besorgen; **to ~ sb's release** jds Freilassung bewirken *or* erreichen **b** *(for prostitution)* beschaffen *(for sb* jdm) VI Kuppelei betreiben

procurement [prə'kjʊəmənt] N Beschaffung *f; (of release)* Bewirkung *f; (of prostitutes)* Beschaffung *f*

procurer [prə'kjʊərəʳ] N *(= pimp)* Zuhälter *m*, Kuppler *m*

procuress [prə'kjʊərɪs] N Kupplerin *f*

procuring [prə'kjʊərɪŋ] N *(for prostitution)* Zuhälterei *f*

Prod [prɒd] N *(Ir, Scot: pej sl)* Protestant(in) *m(f)*

prod [prɒd] N **a** *(lit)* Stoß *m*, Knuff *m (inf)*, Puff *m (inf);* **to give sb a ~** jdm einen Stoß *etc* versetzen; **a ~ in the ribs** ein Rippenstoß *m*

b *(fig)* Ansporn *m*, Anstoß *m*, Schubs *m (inf);* **to give sb a ~** jdn anstoßen

VT **a** *(lit)* stoßen, knuffen *(inf)*, puffen *(inf);* **he ~ded the donkey (on) with his stick** er trieb den Esel mit seinem Stock vorwärts; **he ~ded the hay with his stick** er stach mit seinem Stock ins Heu; **..., he said, ~ding the map with his finger** ..., sagte er und stieß mit dem Finger auf die Karte

b *(fig)* anspornen, anstacheln *(into sth* zu etw); **to ~ sb into action** jdm einen Stoß geben VI stoßen; **he ~ded at the picture with his finger** er stieß mit dem Finger auf das Bild; **he ~ded at the cows with his stick** er trieb die Kühe mit seinem Stock an; **he doesn't need any ~ding** man braucht ihn nicht anzuspornen

Proddie ['prɒdɪ] N = **Prod**

prodigal ['prɒdɪgəl] ADJ verschwenderisch; **to be ~ of sth** verschwenderisch mit etw umgehen; **the ~ son** *(Bibl, fig)* der verlorene Sohn N Verschwender(in) *m(f)*

prodigality [ˌprɒdɪ'gælɪtɪ] N *(liter)* Verschwendungssucht *f; (= lavishness)* Fülle *f*, Üppigkeit *f*

prodigious [prə'dɪdʒəs] ADJ *(= vast)* ungeheuer, außerordentlich; *(= marvellous)* erstaunlich, wunderbar

prodigiously [prə'dɪdʒəslɪ] ADV *drink* ungeheuer viel; *eat* üppig, ungeheuer viel; *talented, gifted, successful* außerordentlich

prodigy ['prɒdɪdʒɪ] N Wunder *nt;* **child** *or* **infant ~** Wunderkind *nt*

produce ['prɒdju:s] N *no pl (Agr)* Produkt(e *pl*), Erzeugnis(se) *nt(pl);* **Italian ~, ~ of Italy** italienisches Erzeugnis; **the ~ of the soil** die Bodenprodukte *or* -erzeugnisse *pl*

VT [prə'dju:s] **a** *(= yield)* produzieren; *(Ind)* produzieren, herstellen; *electricity, energy, heat* erzeugen; *crop* abwerfen; *coal* fördern, produzieren; *(= create) book, article, essay* schreiben; *painting, sculpture* anfertigen; *ideas, novel etc, masterpiece* hervorbringen; *interest, return on capital* bringen, abwerfen; *meal* machen, herstellen; **the sort of environment that ~s criminal types** das Milieu, das Kriminelle hervorbringt; **to ~ offspring** Junge bekommen; *(hum: people)* Nachwuchs bekommen; **to be well ~d** gut gemacht sein; *(goods also)* gut gearbeitet sein; **hopefully he can ~ the goods** *(fig inf)* hoffentlich bringt er es auch *(inf)*

b *(= bring forward, show) gift, wallet etc* hervorholen *(from, out of* aus); *pistol* ziehen *(from, out of* aus); *proof, evidence* liefern, beibringen; *results* liefern; *effect* erzielen; *witness* beibringen; *ticket, documents* vorzeigen; **she managed to ~ something special for dinner** es gelang ihr, zum Abendessen etwas Besonderes auf den Tisch zu bringen; **I can't ~ it out of thin air** ich kann es doch nicht aus dem Nichts hervorzaubern *or* aus dem Ärmel schütteln *(inf);* **if we don't ~ results soon** wenn wir nicht bald Ergebnisse vorweisen können; **he ~d an incredible backhand** ihm gelang ein unglaublicher Rückhandschlag; **he ~d a sudden burst of speed** er rannte plötzlich kurz los

c *play* inszenieren; *film* produzieren; **who's producing you?** wer ist Ihr Regisseur?

d *(= cause) famine, bitterness, impression, interest etc* hervorrufen; *spark* erzeugen

e *(Math) line* verlängern

VI [prə'dju:s] **a** *(Theat)* das/ein Stück inszenieren; *(Film)* den/einen Film produzieren

b *(factory, mine)* produzieren; *(land)* Ertrag bringen; *(tree)* tragen; **this cow hasn't ~d for years** *(produced calf)* diese Kuh hat jahrelang nicht mehr gekalbt; *(produced milk)* diese Kuh hat jahrelang keine Milch mehr gegeben; **when is she going to ~?** *(hum)* wann ist es denn so weit?; **it's about time that you ~d** *(hum)* es wird bald Zeit, dass ihr mal an Nachwuchs denkt

producer [prə'dju:səʳ] N Produzent(in) *m(f); (Ind also)* Hersteller(in) *m(f); (Theat)* Regisseur(in) *m(f); (Film, TV, Rad)* Produzent(in) *m(f);* ~ **goods** Produktionsgüter *pl*

-producing [-prə'dju:sɪŋ] ADJ *suf* erzeugend, produzierend; **oil-producing country** Öl erzeugendes *or* produzierendes Land, Ölland *nt;* **coal-producing countries** Kohleförderländer *pl;* **wine-producing area** Weinregion *f*

product ['prɒdʌkt] N Produkt *nt*, Erzeugnis *nt;* *(fig: = result, also Math, Chem)* Produkt *nt;* **food ~s** Nahrungsmittel *pl;* ~ **placement** Produktplacement *nt*

production [prə'dʌkʃən] N **a** Produktion *f; (Ind)* Produktion *f*, Herstellung *f; (of electricity, energy, heat)* Erzeugung *f; (of crop)* Anbau *m; (of coal)* Förderung *f*, Produktion *f; (of book, article, essay)* Schreiben *nt; (of painting, sculpture)* Anfertigung *f; (of ideas, novel etc, masterpiece)* Hervorbringung *f;* **to put sth into ~** die Herstellung *or* Produktion von etw aufnehmen; **when the new car goes into ~** wenn der neue Wagen in die Produktion *or* Herstellung geht; **when we go into ~ (with this new model)** wenn wir (mit diesem neuen Modell) in die Produktion *or* Herstellung gehen; **is it still in ~?** wird das noch hergestellt?; **to take sth out of ~** etw aus der Produktion nehmen

b *(= output)* Produktion *f*

c *(= bringing forward, showing) (of ticket, documents)* Vorzeigen *nt; (of proof, evidence)* Lieferung *f*, Beibringung *f; (of witness)* Beibringung *f;* **on ~ of this ticket** gegen Vorlage dieser Eintrittskarte

d *(of play)* Inszenierung *f; (of film)* Produktion *f;* **there's no need to make a ~ (number) (out) of it** *(inf)* es ist nicht notwendig, daraus eine Staatsaffäre zu machen *(inf)*

production: **production capacity** N Produktionskapazität *f;* **production car** N *(Aut)* Serienwagen *m;* **production company** N *(TV, Video, also Theat)* Produktionsgesellschaft *f;* **production control** N Fertigungskontrolle *f;* **production costs** PL Produktions- *or* Herstellungskosten *pl;* **production department** N *(of publishing company etc)* Herstellungsabteilung *f;* **production director** N *(Radio, TV)* Sendeleiter(in) *m(f);* **production engineer** N Betriebsingenieur(in) *m(f);* **production line** N Fließband *nt*, Fertigungsstraße *f;* **production manager** N Produktionsleiter(in) *m(f);* **production method** N Produktions- *or* Herstellungsverfahren *nt;* **production model** N *(of car)* Serienmodell *nt;* **production planning** N Produktions-/Fertigungsplanung *f;* **production platform** N *(for oil)* Förderplattform *f;* **production site** N Produktionsstätte *f*

productive [prə'dʌktɪv] ADJ produktiv; *mind also* schöpferisch; *land* ertragreich, fruchtbar; *well, mine* ergiebig, ertragreich; *business, shop* rentabel; **to be ~ of sth** etw einbringen; **to lead a ~ life** ein reiches *or* aktives Leben führen; **I don't think it would be very ~ to argue with him** ich halte es nicht für sehr lohnenswert, mit ihm zu streiten *(inf)*

productively [prə'dʌktɪvlɪ] ADV produktiv

productivity [ˌprɒdʌk'tɪvɪtɪ] N Produktivität *f; (of land)* Fruchtbarkeit *f*, Ergiebigkeit *f; (of well, mine)* Ergiebigkeit *f; (of business, shop)* Rentabilität *f*

productivity: **productivity agreement** N Produktivitätsvereinbarung *f;* **productivity bonus** N Leistungszulage *f;* **productivity incentive** N Leistungsanreiz *m*

product liability N *(Jur)* Produkthaftung *f*

proem ['prəʊem] N Einleitung *f*

prof [prɒf] N *(inf)* Prof *m (inf)*

profanation [ˌprɒfə'neɪʃən] N Entweihung *f*, Profanierung *f*

profane [prə'feɪn] ADJ **a** *(= irreverent, sacrilegious)* (gottes)lästerlich; **don't be ~** lästere nicht; **to use ~ language** gotteslästerlich fluchen, lästern; **a ~ expression** eine Gotteslästerung **b** *(= secular)* weltlich, profan VT entweihen, profanieren

profanity [prə'fænɪtɪ] N **a** *(= sacrilegious nature)* Gotteslästerlichkeit *f* **b** *(= act, utterance)* (Gottes)lästerung *f* **c** *(= secular nature)* Weltlichkeit *f*, Profanität *f*

profess [prə'fes] VT **a** *faith, belief etc* sich bekennen zu

b *(= claim to have) interest, enthusiasm, distaste* bekunden; *belief, disbelief* kundtun; *weakness, ignorance* zugeben; **to ~ to love sb/sth** seine Liebe zu jdm/etw bekennen; **to ~ to hate sb/sth** sich dazu bekennen, jdn/etw zu hassen; **she ~es to be 25/a good driver** sie behauptet, 25/eine gute Fahrerin zu sein; **I don't ~ to …** ich behaupte nicht, zu …

VR **to ~ oneself satisfied** seine Zufriedenheit bekunden (*with* über *+acc*); **the judge ~ed himself satisfied that this was so** der Richter fand den Sachverhalt als hinlänglich erwiesen; **to ~ oneself unable/willing to do sth** sich außerstande *or* außer Stande sehen/sich bereit erklären, etw zu tun

professed [prəˈfest] **ADJ** erklärt; (*pej*: = *purported*) angeblich; **a ~ nun/monk** (*Eccl*) eine Nonne, die/ein Mönch, der die Gelübde abgelegt hat; **to be a ~ Christian** sich zum christlichen Glauben bekennen; **he is a ~ coward** er gibt zu, ein Feigling zu sein; **a ~ love of sth** eine erklärte Liebe zu etw

professedly [prəˈfesɪdlɪ] **ADV** zugegebenermaßen; (*pej*: = *purportedly*) angeblich

profession [prəˈfeʃən] **N** **a** (= *occupation*) Beruf *m*; **the medical/teaching ~** der Arzt-/Lehrberuf; **by ~** von Beruf; **the ~s** die gehobenen Berufe; **the oldest ~ in the world** (*hum*) das älteste Gewerbe der Welt

b (= *members of the profession*) **the medical ~** die Ärzteschaft; **the architectural ~** die Architekten *pl*; **the whole ~ was outraged** der gesamte Berufsstand war empört

c (= *declaration, also Eccl*) Gelübde *nt*; **~ of faith** Glaubensbekenntnis *nt*; **a ~ of love** eine Liebeserklärung; **a ~ of contempt** eine Missfallensäußerung; **a ~ of loyalty** ein Treuegelöbnis *nt*; **the ~ of Christianity** das Bekenntnis zum Christentum; **he is, by his own ~, …** nach eigenem Bekunden ist er …

professional [prəˈfeʃənl] **ADJ** **a** Berufs-, beruflich; *opinion* fachmännisch, fachlich; *football, tennis* professionell; **their ~ ability** ihre beruflichen Fähigkeiten; **~ army/soldier** Berufsarmee *m*/-soldat(in) *m(f)*; **his ~ life** sein Berufsleben; **our relationship is purely ~** unsere Beziehung ist rein geschäftlich(er Natur); **a ~ thief** ein professioneller Dieb; **~ criminal** Berufsverbrecher(in) *m(f)*; **~ rioter** Krawalltourist(in) *m(f)*; **we need your ~ help here** hier brauchen wir Ihre fachmännische Hilfe; **he's now doing it on a ~ basis** er macht das jetzt hauptberuflich; **in his ~ capacity as a doctor** in seiner Eigenschaft als Arzt; **to be a ~ singer/author** *etc* von Beruf Sänger/Schriftsteller *etc* sein; **"flat to let to quiet ~ gentleman"** „Wohnung zu vermieten an ruhigen gut situierten Herrn"; **the pub is used mainly by ~ men** das Lokal wird hauptsächlich von Angehörigen der gehobenen Berufe besucht; **the ~ classes** die gehobenen Berufe, die höheren Berufsstände (*dated*); **to seek/take ~ advice** fachmännischen Rat suchen/einholen; **it's not our ~ practice** es gehört nicht zu unseren geschäftlichen Gepflogenheiten; **to turn** *or* **go ~** Profi werden

b (= *skilled, competent*) *piece of work etc* fachmännisch, fachgemäß, fachgerecht; *worker, person* gewissenhaft; *company, approach* professionell; (= *expert*) *performance* kompetent, sachkundig, professionell; **he didn't make a very ~ job of that** er hat das nicht sehr fachmännisch erledigt; **he handled the matter in a very ~ manner** er hat die Angelegenheit in sehr kompetenter Weise gehandhabt; **that's not a very ~ attitude to your work** das ist doch nicht die richtige Einstellung (zu Ihrem Beruf); **it's not up to ~ standards** es entspricht nicht fachlichen Normen; **a typed letter looks more ~** ein maschine(n)geschriebener Brief sieht professioneller aus

c (*inf*) *worrier, moaner* notorisch, gewohnheitsmäßig

N Profi *m*

professional: **professional footballer** **N** Berufsfußballer(in) *m(f)*; **professional foul** **N** absichtliches Foul; **Professional Golfers' Association** **N** Professional Golfers' Association *f, Verband professioneller Golfspieler*

professionalism [prəˈfeʃnəlɪzəm] **N** Professionalismus *m*; (*of job, piece of work*) Perfektion *f*; (*Sport*) Profitum *nt*

professionally [prəˈfeʃnəlɪ] **ADV** beruflich; (= *in accomplished manner*) fachmännisch; **he sings/dances ~** er singt/tanzt von Berufs wegen *or* beruflich, er ist ein professioneller Sänger/Tänzer; **now he plays ~** jetzt ist er Berufsspieler *or* Profi; **he is ~ recognized as the best …** er ist in Fachkreisen als der beste … bekannt; **X, ~ known as Y** (*of artist, musician etc*) X, unter dem Künstlernamen Y bekannt; (*of writer*) X, unter dem Pseudonym Y bekannt; **to know sb ~** jdn beruflich kennen; **they acted most ~ in refusing to …** dass sie … ablehnten, zeugte von hohem Berufsethos

professor [prəˈfesəʳ] **N** **a** Professor(in) *m(f)*; (*US*: = *lecturer of highest rank*) Dozent(in) *m(f)*; **the ~s** die Professorenschaft **b** (*of a faith*) Bekenner(in) *m(f)*

professorial [ˌprɒfəˈsɔːrɪəl] **ADJ** (*of a professor*) eines Professors; (= *professorlike*) wie ein Professor, professoral (*pej*)

professorship [prəˈfesəʃɪp] **N** Professur *f*, Lehrstuhl *m*

proffer [ˈprɒfəʳ] **VT** *arm, gift, drink* anbieten; *apologies, thanks etc* aussprechen; *remark* machen; *suggestion* vorbringen

proficiency [prəˈfɪʃənsɪ] **N** **her ~ at teaching/as a secretary** ihre Tüchtigkeit als Lehrerin/Sekretärin; **his ~ in English** seine Englischkenntnisse; **her ~ in translating/accountancy** ihr Können als Übersetzerin/Buchhalterin; **his ~ with figures** sein Können im Umgang mit Zahlen; **level of ~** Leistungsstand *m*; **~ test** Leistungstest *m*

proficient [prəˈfɪʃənt] **ADJ** tüchtig, fähig; **he is just about ~ in German** seine Deutschkenntnisse reichen gerade aus; **how long would it take to become ~ in Japanese?** wie lange würde es dauern, bis man Japanisch beherrscht?

profile [ˈprəʊfaɪl] **N** Profil *nt*; (= *picture, photograph*) Profilbild *nt*, Seitenansicht *f*; (= *biographical profile*) Porträt *nt*; (*Tech*: = *section*) (*vertical*) Längsschnitt *m*; (*horizontal*) Querschnitt *m*; **in ~** (*person, head*) im Profil; **to keep a low ~** sich zurückhalten **VT** (= *draw a profile of*) (*pictorially*) im Profil darstellen; (*biographically*) porträtieren; (*Tech*) im Längs- *or* Querschnitt zeichnen *or* darstellen

profiler [ˈprəʊfaɪləʳ] **N** **a** (*Police, Psych*) Profilfahnder(in) *m(f)*, Profiler(in) *m(f)* **b** (*Tech*: = *profiling machine*) Profilfräsmaschine *f*

profit [ˈprɒfɪt] **N** **a** (*Comm*) Gewinn *m*, Profit *m* (*also pej*); **there's not much (of a) ~ in this business** dieses Geschäft wirft kaum Gewinn *or* Profit ab; **~ and loss account** Gewinn-und-Verlustrechnung *f*; **to make a ~ (out of** *or* **on sth)** (mit etw) einen Profit *or* Gewinn machen, (mit etw) ein Geschäft machen; **to show** *or* **yield a ~** einen Gewinn *or* Profit verzeichnen; **to sell sth at a ~** etw mit Gewinn verkaufen; **the business is now running at a ~** das Geschäft wirft jetzt Gewinn *or* Profit ab, das Geschäft rentiert sich jetzt; **I'm not doing it for ~** ich tue das nicht, um damit Geld zu verdienen; **a with-~s policy** (*Insur*) eine Police mit Gewinnbeteiligung

b (*fig*) Nutzen *m*, Vorteil *m*; **to turn sth to ~** Nutzen aus etw ziehen; **you might well learn something to your ~** Sie können etwas lernen, was Ihnen von Nutzen *or* Vorteil ist

VT (*liter*) nutzen, nützen (*sb* jdm), von Nutzen sein (*sb* für jdn); **what does it ~ a man if …** was nützt es dem Menschen, wenn …

VI (= *gain*) profitieren (*by, from* von), Nutzen *or* Gewinn ziehen (*by, from* aus)

profitability [ˌprɒfɪtəˈbɪlɪtɪ] **N** Rentabilität *f*, Einträglichkeit *f*

profitability study **N** Rentabilitäts- *or* Wirtschaftlichkeitsstudie *f*

profitable [ˈprɒfɪtəbl] **ADJ** (*Comm*) gewinn- *or* profitbringend, Gewinn *or* Profit bringend, rentabel, profitabel; (*fig*: = *beneficial*) nützlich, vorteilhaft; **could you not find a more ~ way of spending your time?** kannst du nichts Besseres mit deiner Zeit anfangen?

profitably [ˈprɒfɪtəblɪ] **ADV** (*Comm*) *sell, trade* gewinn- *or* profitbringend, Gewinn *or* Profit bringend, rentabel, profitabel; (*fig*: = *beneficially*) nützlich, vorteilhaft; **you could ~ spend a couple of hours reading a book** es käme dir sehr zugute, wenn du ein paar Stunden mit Lesen verbringen würdest; **there was little I could ~ do sitting at my desk** von meinem Schreibtisch aus konnte ich nur wenig Sinnvolles *or* Nützliches tun

profit centre, (*US*) **profit center** **N** Profit-center *nt*

profiteer [ˌprɒfɪˈtɪəʳ] **N** Profitmacher(in), Profitjäger(in) *m(f)*, Profitgeier *m*; **war ~** Kriegsgewinnler(in) *m(f)* **VI** sich bereichern

profiteering [ˌprɒfɪˈtɪərɪŋ] **N** Wucherei *f*, Wucher *m*

profiterole [prəˈfɪtərəʊl] **N** Profiterol(e) *nt*, *kleiner Windbeutel mit süßer oder pikanter Füllung*

profitless [ˈprɒfɪtlɪs] **ADJ** **a** (*Comm*) unrentabel **b** *discussion, exercise* zwecklos

profitlessly [ˈprɒfɪtlɪslɪ] **ADV** **a** (*Comm*) ohne Gewinn **b** *argue* zwecklos

profit: **profit-making** **ADJ** *organization* rentabel; (= *profit-orientated*) auf Gewinn gerichtet; **profit margin** **N** Gewinnspanne *f*; **profit motive** **N** Gewinnstreben *nt*; **profit-seeking** **ADJ** gewinnorientiert; **profit-sharing** **N** Gewinnbeteiligung *f*; **~ scheme** Gewinnbeteiligungsplan *m*

profligacy [ˈprɒflɪgəsɪ] **N** (= *dissoluteness*) Lasterhaftigkeit *f*, Verworfenheit *f*; (= *extravagance*) Verschwendungssucht *f*; (= *an extravagance*) Verschwendung *f*

profligate [ˈprɒflɪgɪt] **ADJ** (= *dissolute*) lasterhaft, verworfen; (= *extravagant*) verschwenderisch **N** (= *roué*) Leichtfuß *m*, Liederjan *m* (*inf*); (= *prodigal*) Verschwender(in) *m(f)*

pro forma (invoice) [ˌprəʊˈfɔːmə(ˈɪnvɔɪs)] **N** Pro-forma-Rechnung *f*

profound [prəˈfaʊnd] **ADJ** **a** *sleep, sigh, sorrow, love, concern, depression* tief; *thought, idea, art* tiefsinnig, tief schürfend, tiefgründig; *experience* tief gehend, im Innersten ergreifend; *book* gehaltvoll, profund (*geh*); *thinker, knowledge* profund (*geh*), tief gehend; *regret* tief gehend; *hatred, mistrust, difference, belief, respect, ignorance* tief sitzend; *effect, influence, implications* tief greifend, weittragend, weit tragend; *problem* tief sitzend, tief gehend; *indifference* vollkommen, völlig; *interest* stark; *changes* tief greifend; **you're very ~ today** (*also iro*) du bist heute sehr tiefsinnig; **that's very ~** (*also iro*) das ist sehr tiefsinnig

b *deafness* vollkommen; *clinical shock, unconsciousness* tief

profoundly [prəˈfaʊndlɪ] **ADV** *different* zutiefst; **~ sad** tieftraurig; **~ deaf** vollkommen taub; **~ significant** äußerst bedeutsam; **~ indifferent** völlig *or* vollkommen gleichgültig; **…, he said ~** …, sagte er tiefsinnig; **to be ~ ignorant of sth** überhaupt keine Ahnung von etw haben

profundity [prəˈfʌndɪtɪ] **N** **a** *no pl* Tiefe *f*; (*of thought, thinker, book etc*) Tiefgründigkeit *f*, Tiefsinnigkeit *f*; (*of knowledge*) Gründlichkeit *f* **b** (= *profound remark*) Tiefsinnigkeit *f*

profuse [prəˈfjuːs] **ADJ** *vegetation* üppig; *bleeding* stark; *thanks, praise* überschwänglich; *apologies* überreichlich; *vomiting* heftig, stark; **to be ~ in one's thanks** sich überschwänglich bedanken; **to be ~ in one's apologies** sich vielmals entschuldigen; **he was ~ in his praise** er geizte nicht mit seinem Lob; **where flowers grow in ~ abundance** wo Blumen in üppiger *or* verschwenderischer Fülle wachsen

profusely [prəˈfjuːslɪ] **ADV** *grow* üppig; *bleed* stark; *thank, praise* überschwänglich; *sweat* heftig, stark; **he apologized ~** er entschuldigte sich vielmals, er bat vielmals um Entschuldigung; **~ illustrated** reich illustriert

profusion [prəˈfjuːʒən] N Überfülle *f*, verschwenderische Fülle; **trees in ~** Bäume in Hülle und Fülle; **his painting was a wild ~ of reds and blues** sein Gemälde war eine Orgie in Rot und Blau

progenitor [prəʊˈdʒenɪtəˈ] N *(form)* Vorfahr(in) *m(f)*, Ahn *m*, Ahne *f*; *(fig)* Vorläufer *m*

progenitrix [prəʊˈdʒenɪtrɪks] N *(form)* Vorfahrin *f*, Ahne *f*

progeny [ˈprɒdʒɪnɪ] N Nachkommen *pl*, Nachkommenschaft *f*

progesterone [prəʊˈdʒestəˌrəʊn] N Progesteron *nt*, Gelbkörperhormon *nt*

prognosis [prɒgˈnəʊsɪs] N *pl* **prognoses** [prɒgˈnəʊsiːz] Prognose *f*, Vorhersage *f*, Voraussage *f*

prognostic [prɒgˈnɒstɪk] ADJ *(form)* prognostisch

prognosticate [prɒgˈnɒstɪkeɪt] VI *(often hum)* Prognosen stellen, Vorhersagen machen VT prognostizieren

prognostication [prɒgˌnɒstɪˈkeɪʃən] N Prognose *f*, Vorhersage *f*, Voraussage *f*

program [ˈprəʊgræm] N a *(Comput)* Programm *nt*, Anwendung *f* b *(US)* = **programme** N VT a *computer* programmieren b *(fig) person* vorprogrammieren

program: **program error** N *(Comput)* Programmfehler *m*; **program group** N *(Comput)* Programmgruppe *f*

programmable [ˈprəʊgræməbl] ADJ *computer, device, oven etc* programmierbar

programme, *(US)* **program** [ˈprəʊgræm] N Programm *nt*; *(Rad, TV also)* Sendung *f*; **we've got a very heavy ~ of meetings** wir haben sehr viele Besprechungen auf unserem Programm; **what's the ~ for tomorrow?** was steht für morgen auf dem Programm?; **what's on the other ~?** was gibt es *or* läuft im anderen Programm?; **our ~s for this evening** das Programm des heutigen Abends VT programmieren; **~d course** programmierter Unterricht; **~d learning** programmiertes Lernen

programme, *(US)* **program**: **programme-maker**, *(US)* **program-maker** N *(TV, Rad)* Programmmacher(in) *m(f)*; **programme music** N Programmmusik *f*; **programme notes** PL Programmhinweise *pl*; **programme planner** N *(TV)* Programmplaner(in) *m(f)*

programmer [ˈprəʊgræməˈ] N Programmierer(in) *m(f)*

programme seller N *(in theatre etc)* Programmverkäufer(in) *m(f)*

programming [ˈprəʊgræmɪŋ] N Programmieren *nt*; **~ language** Programmiersprache *f*

progress [ˈprəʊgres] N a *no pl (= movement forwards)* Fortschreiten *nt*, Vorwärtskommen *nt*; *(Mil)* Vorrücken *nt*, Vordringen *nt*; **we made slow ~ through the mud** wir kamen im Schlamm nur langsam vorwärts; **they made good ~ across the open country** sie kamen im offenen Gelände gut vorwärts
b *no pl (= advance)* Fortschritt *m*; *(Comput)* (Verarbeitungs)status *m*; **the ~ of events** der Gang der Ereignisse; **to make (good/slow) ~** (gute/langsame) Fortschritte machen; **I want to see some ~!** ich möchte Fortschritte sehen!
c **in ~** im Gange; **in full ~** in vollem Gange; **"silence please, meeting in ~"** „Sitzung! Ruhe bitte"; **the work still in ~** die noch zu erledigende Arbeit
d *(obs: = journey)* Reise *f*
VI [prəˈgres] a *(= move, go forward)* sich vorwärtsbewegen, vorwärtsschreiten; **we ~ed slowly across the ice** wir bewegten uns langsam über das Eis vorwärts; **by the third day the enemy/expedition had ~ed as far as …** am dritten Tag war der Feind bis … vorgerückt *or* vorgedrungen/die Expedition bis … vorgedrungen *or* gekommen
b *(in time)* **as the work ~es** mit dem Fortschreiten der Arbeit; **as the game ~ed** im Laufe des Spiels; **while negotiations were actually ~ing** während die Verhandlungen im Gange waren
c *(= improve, make progress: student, patient)* Fortschritte machen; **how far have you ~ed since our last meeting?** wie weit sind Sie seit unserer letzten Sitzung gekommen?; **investigations are ~ing well** die Untersuchungen kommen gut voran *or* machen gute Fortschritte; **we are, in fact, ~ing toward(s) a solution** wir nähern uns jetzt einer Lösung; **that civilization is constantly ~ing (toward(s) a state of perfection)** dass sich die Zivilisation ständig (auf einen Zustand der Perfektion hin) weiterentwickelt; **that mankind is ~ing toward(s) some goal** dass sich die Menschheit auf ein Ziel zubewegt
d *(through hierarchy etc)* **as you ~ through the ranks** bei Ihrem Aufstieg durch die Ränge; **the employee ~es upwards through the company hierarchy** der Angestellte macht seinen Weg durch die Firmenhierarchie
VT [prəˈgres] *(esp Comm) matters etc* weiterverfolgen

progression [prəˈgreʃən] N Folge *f*; *(Math)* Reihe *f*, Progression *f*; *(Mus)* Sequenz *f*; *(= development)* Entwicklung *f*; *(in taxation)* Progression *f*; *(of discount rates etc)* Staffelung *f*; **sales have shown a continuous ~** im Absatz wurde eine stete Aufwärtsentwicklung verzeichnet; **his ~ from a junior clerk to managing director** sein Aufstieg vom kleinen Angestellten zum Direktor; **is there a natural ~ from marijuana to heroin?** ist das Umsteigen von Marihuana auf Heroin zwangsläufig?; **a ~ of …** eine Folge *or* Reihe von …

progressional ADJ [prəˈgreʃənl] *development* fortschreitend; *examinations* aufeinanderfolgend, im Schwierigkeitsgrad ansteigend; *training, development* kontinuierlich (verlaufend *or* weitergehend)

progressive [prəˈgresɪv] ADJ a *(= increasing)* zunehmend; *disease etc* fortschreitend; *action* allmählich steigernd, fortschreitend; *paralysis, taxation* progressiv; **~ form/tense** *(Gram)* Verlaufsform *f* b *(= favouring progress)* progressiv, fortschrittlich; *(Mus)* progressiv N *(= person)* Progressive(r) *mf*

progressive jazz N progressiver Jazz

progressively [prəˈgresɪvlɪ] ADV zunehmend; **he is becoming ~ more addicted** er wird zunehmend *or* immer abhängiger

progressiveness [prəˈgresɪvnɪs] N Fortschrittlichkeit *f*, Progressivität *f*

progressive party N *(Pol)* fortschrittliche Partei, Fortschrittspartei *f*

progress report N Fortschrittsbericht *m*

prohibit [prəˈhɪbɪt] VT a *(= forbid)* verbieten, untersagen; **to ~ sb from doing sth** jdm verbieten *or* untersagen, etw zu tun; **his health ~s him from swimming** sein Gesundheitszustand verbietet (es) ihm zu schwimmen; **"smoking ~ed"** „Rauchen verboten" b *(= prevent)* verhindern; **to ~ sth being done** verhindern, dass etw geschieht; **to ~ sb from doing sth** jdn daran hindern, etw zu tun

prohibited substance [prəˈhɪbɪtɪdˈsʌbstəns] N verbotene Substanz

prohibition [ˌprəʊɪˈbɪʃən] N a Verbot *nt*; **the ~ of alcohol** das Alkoholverbot b **(the) Prohibition** *(US Hist)* die Prohibition; **the Prohibition era** *(US Hist)* die Prohibitionszeit

prohibitionism [ˌprəʊɪˈbɪʃənɪzəm] N Prohibition *f*

prohibitionist [ˌprəʊɪˈbɪʃənɪst] N Prohibitionist(in) *m(f)*

prohibitive [prəˈhɪbɪtɪv] ADJ a *tax* prohibitiv; **~ duty** Sperrzoll *m*; **~ laws** Verbotsgesetze *pl*; **~ signs** Verbotsschilder *pl*; **~ rules** Verbote *pl* b *price, cost* unerschwinglich; **the costs of producing this model have become ~** die Kosten für die Herstellung dieses Modells sind untragbar geworden

prohibitively [prəˈhɪbɪtɪvlɪ] ADV *(= extremely)* ungeheuerlich; **~ expensive** unerschwinglich (teuer)

prohibitory [prəˈhɪbɪtərɪ] ADJ = **prohibitive a**

project¹ [ˈprɒdʒekt] N Projekt *nt*; *(= scheme)* Unternehmen *nt*, Vorhaben *nt*; *(Sch, Univ)* Referat *nt*; *(in primary school)* Arbeit *f*; **~ engineer** Projektingenieur(in) *m(f)*

project² [prəˈdʒekt] VT a *film, map* projizieren; **to ~ oneself/one's personality** sich selbst/seine eigene Person zur Geltung bringen; **to ~ one's emotions onto somebody else** seine Emotionen auf einen anderen projizieren; **to ~ one's voice** seine Stimme zum Tragen bringen; **to ~ one's voice to the back of the hall** seine Stimme so erheben, dass sie auch im hinteren Teil des Saals zu hören ist; **in order to ~ an adequate picture of our country** um ein angemessenes Bild unseres Landes zu vermitteln
b *plan* (voraus)planen; *costs* überschlagen; *figures* projizieren; *(esp in elections)* hochrechnen
c *(Math) line* verlängern; *solid* projizieren
d *(= propel)* abschießen; **to ~ a missile into space** eine Rakete in den Weltraum schießen
e *(= cause to jut) part of building etc* vorspringen lassen
VI a *(= jut out)* hervorragen *(from* aus); **the upper storey ~s over the road** das obere Stockwerk ragt über die Straße
b *(Psych)* projizieren, von sich auf andere schließen
c *(with one's voice: actor/singer)* **you'll have to ~ more than that, we can't hear you at the back** Sie müssen lauter singen/sprechen, wir können Sie hier hinten nicht hören

projectile [prəˈdʒektaɪl] N (Wurf)geschoss *nt*, (Wurf)geschoß *nt (Aus)*; *(Mil)* Geschoss *nt*, Geschoß *nt (Aus)*, Projektil *nt (spec)*

projection [prəˈdʒekʃən] N a *(of films, guilt feelings, map)* Projektion *f* b *(= protrusion, overhang, ledge etc)* Vorsprung *m*, Überhang *m* c *(= extension: of line)* Verlängerung *f* d *(= prediction, estimate)* (Voraus)planung *f*; *(of cost)* Überschlagung *f*; *(of figures, esp in elections)* Hochrechnung *f*

projection booth N Vorführraum *m*

projectionist [prəˈdʒekʃnɪst] N Filmvorführer(in) *m(f)*

projection room N Vorführraum *m*

projective [prəˈdʒektɪv] ADJ a **~ geometry** Projektionsgeometrie *f* b *(Psych)* projizierend

project management N Projektmanagement *nt*

project manager N Projektleiter(in) *m(f)*, Projektmanager(in) *m(f)*

projector [prəˈdʒektəˈ] N *(Film)* Projektor *m*, Vorführgerät *nt*

prolapse [ˈprəʊlæps] N *(Med)* Vorfall *m*, Prolaps *m (spec)*

prole [prəʊl] N *(esp Brit pej inf)* Prolet(in) *m(f)* *(inf)*

proletarian [ˌprəʊləˈtɛərɪən] ADJ proletarisch N Proletarier(in) *m(f)*

proletariat [ˌprəʊləˈtɛərɪət] N Proletariat *nt*

pro-life [ˌprəʊˈlaɪf] ADJ *group, organization* gegen Abtreibung *pred*; **~ movement** Antiabtreibungsbewegung *f*

pro-lifer [ˌprəʊˈlaɪfəˈ] N *(inf)* Abtreibungsgegner(in) *m(f)*

proliferate [prəˈlɪfəreɪt] VI *(number)* sich stark erhöhen; *(ideas)* um sich greifen; *(insects, animals)* sich stark vermehren; *(weeds, cells)* wuchern, sich rasch ausbreiten

proliferation [prəˌlɪfəˈreɪʃən] N *(in numbers)* starke Erhöhung; *(of animals)* zahlreiche Vermehrung; *(of nuclear weapons)* Weitergabe *f*; *(of ideas)* Ausbreitung *f*, Umsichgreifen *nt*; *(of weeds)* Wuchern *nt*

prolific [prəˈlɪfɪk] ADJ a *(= productive)* fruchtbar; *writer also* sehr produktiv; *scorer* erfolgreich b *(= producing young) person* fruchtbar c *(= abundant)* zahlreich, üppig

prolix [ˈprəʊlɪks] ADJ weitschweifig

prolixity [prəʊˈlɪksɪtɪ] N Weitschweifigkeit *f*

prolly [ˈprɒlɪ] ADV *(sl)* wahrscheinlich

prologue, *(US)* **prolog** [ˈprəʊlɒg] N Prolog *m*; *(of book)* Vorwort *nt*; *(fig)* Vorspiel *nt*

prolong [prəˈlɒŋ] VT verlängern; *(unpleasantly) process, pain* hinauszögern; *(Fin) draft* prolongieren; **to ~ the agony** *(fig)* das Leiden verlängern

prolongation [ˌprəʊlɒŋˈgeɪʃən] N Verlängerung *f*; *(unpleasant: of process, pain)* Hinauszögern *nt*; *(Fin, of draft)* Prolongation *f*, Prolongierung *f*

prolonged-action [prəˈlɒŋdˈækʃən] ADJ *(Pharm) medicine* mit Langzeitwirkung *pred*

PROM [prɒm] N *(Comput) abbr of* **Programmable Read Only Memory** PROM *m*

prom [prɒm] N *(inf) (Brit: = promenade)* (Strand)promenade *f*; *(Brit: = concert)* Konzert *nt (in gelockertem Rahmen)*; *(US: = ball)* Studenten-/ /Schülerball *m*

> **PROM**
>
> In Großbritannien versteht man unter einem **prom** (Kurzform von **promenade concert**) ein klassisches Musikkonzert, bei dem ein Großteil des Publikums im Parkett Stehplätze hat. Die bekanntesten **proms** sind die Konzerte, die jeden Sommer in der Londoner Royal Albert Hall abgehalten werden. Der Abschlussabend, „Last Night of the Proms", ist ein ganz besonderes Ereignis, das ganz im Zeichen des Patriotismus steht und im Singen von „Land of Hope and Glory" gipfelt.
> In den USA und Kanada dagegen ist ein **prom** ein Ball für die Schüler und Studenten von Highschools oder Colleges. Ein ganz besonders wichtiges gesellschaftliches Ereignis ist der **senior prom** zum Abschluss der Highschool-Zeit. Zu diesen Bällen geht man normalerweise in Begleitung und in formeller Kleidung.

promenade [ˌprɒmɪˈnɑːd] **N** (= *stroll: also in dancing*) Promenade *f*; *(esp Brit: = esplanade)* (Strand)promenade *f*; *(US: = ball)* Studenten-/ /Schülerball *m*; **~ concert** *(Brit)* Konzert *nt (in gelockertem Rahmen)*; **~ deck** *(Brit)* Promenadendeck *nt* **VT** *(= stroll through)* promenieren in *(+dat)*; *avenue* entlangpromenieren; *(= stroll with)* spazieren führen; *(in dance)* eine Promenade machen mit **VI** *(= stroll)* promenieren; *(in dance)* eine Promenade machen

promenader [ˌprɒmɪˈnɑːdəˈ] N **a** *(= walker)* Spaziergänger(in) *m(f)* **b** *(Brit: in concert)* Stehplatzbesucher(in) *m(f)*; **Promenader** Besucher(in) *m(f)* der Londoner Prom-Konzerte

Promethean [prəˈmiːθɪən] ADJ *(liter)* prometheisch *(liter)*

Prometheus [prəˈmiːθjuːs] N Prometheus *m*

promethium [prəʊˈmiːθɪəm] N *(Chem)* Promethium *nt*

prominence [ˈprɒmɪnəns] N **a** *no pl* **the ~ of his cheekbones/eyes** seine ausgeprägten Wangenknochen/Augen; **because of the ~ of the castle in the middle of the city** wegen der exponierten Lage des Schlosses inmitten der Stadt
b *(of ideas, beliefs)* Beliebtheit *f*; *(of writer, politician etc)* Bekanntheit *f*; **the undisputed ~ of his position as ...** seine unbestritten führende Position als ...; **if you give too much ~ to any one particular aspect** wenn Sie einen bestimmten Aspekt zu sehr in den Vordergrund stellen; **to bring sb/sth (in)to ~** *(= attract attention to)* jdn/etw herausstellen *or* in den Vordergrund rücken; *(= make famous)* jdn/etw berühmt machen; **he came** *or* **rose to ~ in the Cuba affair** er wurde durch die Kuba-Affäre bekannt
c *(= prominent part)* Vorsprung *m*

prominent [ˈprɒmɪnənt] ADJ **a** *(= jutting out) cheekbones, teeth* vorstehend *attr*; *crag* vorspringend *attr*; **to be ~** vorstehen, vorspringen
b *(= conspicuous) markings* auffällig; *feature, characteristic* hervorstechend, auffallend; *position* hervorragend, herausragend, prominent; **put it in a ~ position** stellen Sie es deutlich sichtbar hin; **the castle occupies a ~ position on the hill** das Schloss hat eine exponierte Lage auf dem Hügel
c *(= leading) role* führend; *(= large, significant)* wichtig
d *(= well-known) personality, publisher* prominent; **she is ~ in London society** sie ist ein bekanntes Mitglied der Londoner Gesellschaft

prominently [ˈprɒmɪnəntlɪ] ADV *display, place* deutlich sichtbar; **he figured ~ in the case** er spielte in dem Fall eine bedeutende Rolle; **the murder was ~ reported in the press** in der Presse wurde ausführlich über den Mordfall berichtet, der Mordfall füllte die Schlagzeilen

promiscuity [ˌprɒmɪˈskjuːɪtɪ] N **a** Promiskuität *f*, häufiger Partnerwechsel **b** *(liter: = confusion)* Wirrwarr *m*

promiscuous [prəˈmɪskjʊəs] ADJ **a** *(sexually)* promisk, promiskuitiv *(spec)*; **to be ~** häufig den Partner wechseln; **~ behaviour** häufiger Partnerwechsel **b** *(liter)* wirr

promiscuously [prəˈmɪskjʊəslɪ] ADV *(sexually)* promisk, promiskuitiv *(spec)*

promise [ˈprɒmɪs] **N a** *(= pledge)* Versprechen *nt*; **their ~ of help** ihr Versprechen zu helfen; **~ of marriage** Eheversprechen *nt*; **under ~ of** *(form)* mit dem Versprechen *(+gen)*; **is that a ~?** ganz bestimmt?; **to make sb a ~** jdm ein Versprechen geben *or* machen; **make me one ~** versprich mir eins; **I'm not making any ~s** versprechen kann ich nichts; **to hold** *or* **keep sb to his ~** jdn an sein Versprechen binden; **~s, ~s!** Versprechen, nichts als Versprechen!
b *(= hope, prospect)* Hoffnung *f*, Aussicht *f*; **a young woman of ~** eine vielversprechende junge Frau; **to hold out a** *or* **the ~ of sth to sb** jdm Hoffnungen auf etw *(acc)* machen; **to show ~** zu den besten Hoffnungen berechtigen; **she had a ~ of passion in her eyes** ihre Augen verrieten Leidenschaft
VT *(= pledge)* versprechen; *(= forecast, augur)* hindeuten auf *(+acc)*; **to ~ (sb) to do sth** (jdm) versprechen, etw zu tun; **to ~ sb sth, to ~ sth to sb** jdm etw versprechen; **to ~ sb the earth** jdm das Blaue vom Himmel herunter versprechen; **~ me one thing** versprich mir eins; **to be ~d to sb** *(dated)* jdm versprochen sein *(old)*; **I'm not promising anything but ...** ich will nichts versprechen, aber ...; **I won't do it again, I ~ you** ich werde es nie wieder tun, das verspreche ich Ihnen; **you'll regret this, I ~ you** ich verspreche dir, das wirst du bereuen; **this ~s trouble** das sieht nach Ärger aus; **this ~s better things to come** das lässt auf Besseres hoffen; **it ~d to be another scorching day** der Tag versprach wieder heiß zu werden; **the Promised Land** *(Bibl, fig)* das Gelobte Land
VI a *(= pledge)* versprechen; **(do you) ~?** versprichst du es?; **~!** *(= will you promise)* versprichs mir, ehrlich?; *(= I promise)* ehrlich!; **I'll try, but I'm not promising** ich werde es versuchen, aber ich kann nichts versprechen; **but you ~d!** aber du hast es doch versprochen!
b to ~ well vielversprechend sein
VR to ~ oneself sth sich *(dat)* etw versprechen; **I've ~d myself never to do it again** ich habe mir geschworen, dass ich das nicht noch einmal mache

promising [ˈprɒmɪsɪŋ] ADJ vielversprechend; **that sounds ~** das klingt vielversprechend; **so far the signs are not ~** bislang sind die Anzeichen nicht vielversprechend

promisingly [ˈprɒmɪsɪŋlɪ] ADV vielversprechend

promissory note [ˈprɒmɪsərɪˈnəʊt] N Schuldschein *m*

prommer, **Prommer** [ˈprɒmə] N *(inf)* Besucher(in) *m(f)* der Londoner Prom-Konzerte

promo [ˈprəʊməʊ] N *(inf: = promotional video)* Werbevideo *nt*

promontory [ˈprɒməntrɪ] N Vorgebirge *nt*, Kap *nt*

promote [prəˈməʊt] VT **a** *(in rank)* befördern; **he has been ~d (to) colonel** *or* **to the rank of colonel** er ist zum Obersten befördert worden; **our team was ~d** *(Ftbl)* unsere Mannschaft ist aufgestiegen **b** *(= foster)* fördern; *(Parl) bill* sich einsetzen für **c** *(= organize, put on) conference, race meeting, boxing match etc* veranstalten **d** *(= advertise)* werben für; *(= put on the market)* auf den Markt bringen; **the new model has been widely ~d in the media** für das neue Modell ist in den Medien intensiv geworben worden *or* Werbung gemacht worden

promoter [prəˈməʊtəˈ] N *(Sport, of beauty contest etc)* Promoter *m*, Veranstalter *m*; *(of company)* Promoter *m*; **sales ~** Verkaufsleiter(in) *m(f)*, Salespromoter(in) *m(f) (Comm)*

promotion [prəˈməʊʃən] N **a** *(in rank)* Beförderung *f*; *(of football team)* Aufstieg *m*; **to get** *or* **win ~** befördert werden; *(football team)* aufsteigen **b** *(= fostering)* Förderung *f*; *(Parl: of bill)* Einsatz *m* (of für) **c** *(= organization: of conference etc)* Veranstaltung *f* **d** *(= advertising)* Werbung *f* (of für); *(= advertising campaign)* Werbekampagne *f*; *(= marketing)* Einführung *f* auf dem Markt; **Rochas are doing a special ~ in the store this week** wir haben diese Woche eine Rochas-Werbekampagne im Warenhaus

prompt [prɒmpt] **ADJ** *(+er)* prompt; *action* unverzüglich, sofortig; **he is always very ~ with such things** solche Dinge erledigt er immer prompt *or* sofort; **he is always very ~** *(= on time)* er ist immer sehr pünktlich; **~ to do sth** *(= quick)* prompt *or* rasch *or* schnell dabei, etw zu tun; **the company was ~ in its response to these accusations** die Firma hat prompt auf diese Vorwürfe reagiert
ADV at 6 o'clock ~ pünktlich um 6 Uhr, Punkt 6 Uhr
VT a *(= motivate)* veranlassen (*to* zu); **to ~ sb to do sth** jdn (dazu) veranlassen, etw zu tun; **what ~ed you to do it?** was hat Sie dazu veranlasst?; **he was ~ed purely by a desire to help** sein Beweggrund war einzig und allein der Wunsch zu helfen; **in the hope that this might ~ a discussion** in der Hoffnung, dass das eine Diskussion in Gang setzen wird; **he didn't need any ~ing to ask her** man brauchte ihn nicht darum zu bitten, sie zu fragen; **he's a bit lazy, he needs a little ~ing** er ist ein bisschen faul, man muss ihm manchmal auf die Sprünge helfen; **I'll do it myself, I don't need you to ~ me** ich mache das schon selbst, du brauchst mich nicht erst zu ermahnen; **he doesn't need any ~ing, he's cheeky enough as it is** er braucht keine Ermunterung, er ist auch so schon frech genug
b *(= evoke) memories, feelings* wecken; *conclusion* nahelegen; **it ~s the thought that ...** es drängt einem den Gedanken auf, dass ...
c *(= help with speech)* vorsagen (*sb* jdm); *(Theat)* soufflieren (*sb* jdm); **he recited the whole poem without any ~ing** er sagte das ganze Gedicht auf, ohne dass ihm jemand (etwas) vorsagen musste; **the teacher had to keep ~ing him** der Lehrer musste ihm immer wieder Hilfestellung geben; **he forgot his speech and had to be ~ed** er hatte seine Rede vergessen, so dass *or* sodass man ihm mit Stichworten auf die Sprünge helfen musste
VI *(Theat)* soufflieren
N a *(Theat)* **he needed a ~** ihm musste souffliert werden; **he couldn't hear the ~** er hörte die Souffleuse nicht; **to give sb a ~** jdm weiterhelfen; *(Theat)* jdm soufflieren
b *(= reminder, encouragement)* **to give sb a ~** jdm einen Schubs geben *(inf)*, jdn anstoßen; **we have to give our debtors the occasional ~** wir müssen uns bei unseren Schuldnern hin und wieder in Erinnerung bringen
c *(Comput)* Prompt *m*, Eingabeaufforderung *f*

prompt: **prompt book** N *(Theat)* Soufflierbuch *nt*; **prompt box** N *(Theat)* Souffleurkasten *m*; **prompt copy** N *(Theat)* Rollenheft *nt*

prompter [ˈprɒmptəˈ] N Souffleur *m*, Souffleuse *f*; *(= tele-prompter)* Teleprompter *m*

prompting [ˈprɒmptɪŋ] N **a** *(Theat)* Soufflieren *nt* **b the ~s of conscience/the heart** die Stimme des Gewissens/Herzens

promptitude [ˈprɒmptɪtjuːd] N = **promptness**

promptly ['prɒmptlɪ] ADV **a** prompt; **of course he ~ forgot it all** er hat natürlich prompt alles vergessen; **they left ~ at 6** sie gingen pünktlich um 6 Uhr *or* Punkt 6 Uhr; **when you receive orders you must obey them ~** wenn Sie Anweisungen erhalten, müssen Sie sie auf der Stelle befolgen; **she sat down and ~ fell asleep** sie setzte sich hin und schlief auf der Stelle *or* prompt ein **b** *(= without further ado)* **she ~ gave him a left hook** sie versetzte ihm unverzüglich einen linken Haken

promptness ['prɒmptnɪs] N Promptheit *f*; **the fire brigade's ~** der prompte Einsatz der Feuerwehr

prompt note N *(Comm)* Ermahnung *f*

promulgate ['prɒməlgeɪt] VT verbreiten; *law* verkünden

promulgation [,prɒməl'geɪʃən] N Verbreitung *f*; *(of law)* Verkündung *f*

prone [prəʊn] ADJ **a** *(= lying)* **to be** *or* **lie ~** auf dem Bauch liegen; **in a ~ position** in Bauchlage **b** *(= liable)* **to be ~ to sth** zu etw neigen; **to be ~ to do sth** dazu neigen, etw zu tun

proneness ['prəʊnnɪs] N Neigung *f* (*to* zu)

prong [prɒŋ] **N a** *(of fork)* Zacke *f*, Zinke *f*; *(of antler)* Sprosse *f*, Ende *nt* **b** *(fig) (of argument)* Punkt *m*; *(of policy, strategy)* Element *nt*; *(of attack)* (Angriffs)spitze *f* **VT** aufspießen

pronged [prɒŋd] ADJ zackig, gezinkt

-pronged [-prɒŋd] ADJ *suf fork* -zackig, -zinkig; **three-pronged** dreizackig, dreizinkig; **a three-pronged attack** ein Angriff mit drei Spitzen; **a two-pronged approach** eine zweigleisige Vorgehensweise

pronominal [prəʊ'nɒmɪnl] ADJ pronominal

pronoun ['prəʊnaʊn] N Fürwort *nt*, Pronomen *nt*

pronounce [prə'naʊns] **VT a** *word etc* aussprechen; **I find Russian hard to ~** ich finde die russische Aussprache schwierig; **the "p" isn't ~d** das „p" wird nicht ausgesprochen **b** *(= declare)* erklären für; **the doctors ~d him unfit for work** die Ärzte erklärten ihn für arbeitsunfähig; **to ~ oneself in favour of/against sth** sich für/gegen etw aussprechen; **to ~ sentence** das Urteil verkünden **VI to ~ in favour of/against sth** sich für/gegen etw aussprechen; **to ~ on sth** zu etw Stellung nehmen

pronounceable [prə'naʊnsəbl] ADJ aussprechbar

pronounced [prə'naʊnst] ADJ *(= marked)* ausgesprochen; *accent* ausgeprägt, stark, schwer; *flavour* ausgeprägt, stark; *hipbones* ausgeprägt; *improvement, deterioration* deutlich; *views* prononciert; **he has a ~ limp** er hinkt sehr stark

pronouncedly [prə'naʊnsɪdlɪ, -stlɪ] ADV *(= really)* ausgesprochen; **~ good** ausgesprochen gut

pronouncement [prə'naʊnsmənt] N Erklärung *f*; *(Jur, of sentence)* Verkündung *f*; **to make a ~** eine Erklärung abgeben

pronto ['prɒntəʊ] ADV *(inf)* fix *(inf)*; **do it ~** aber dalli! *(inf)*

pronunciation [prə,nʌnsɪ'eɪʃən] N Aussprache *f*

proof [pru:f] **N a** Beweis *m* (*of* für); **you'll need more ~ than that** die Beweise reichen nicht aus; **as ~ of** als *or* zum Beweis für; **to put sth to the ~** etw auf die Probe stellen; *(Tech)* etw erproben; **that is ~ that ...** das ist der Beweis dafür, dass ...; **to give** *or* **show ~ of sth** etw nachweisen, den Nachweis für etw liefern; **can you give us any ~ of that?** können Sie (uns) dafür Beweise liefern?; **show me your ~** beweisen Sie (mir) das; **what ~ is there that he meant it?** und was beweist, dass er es ernst gemeint hat?; **~ of purchase** *(= receipt)* Kaufbeleg *m*

b *(= test, trial)* Probe *f*; **withstanding these conditions is the ~ of a good paint** es ist der Beweis für die Qualität einer Farbe, wenn sie solchen Bedingungen standhält; **the ~ of the pudding is in the eating** *(Prov)* Probieren *or* probieren geht über Studieren *or* studieren *(Prov)*

c *(Typ)* (Korrektur)fahne *f*; *(Phot)* Probeabzug *m*

d *(of alcohol)* Alkoholgehalt *m*; **70% ~** ≈ 40 Vol-%

ADJ *(= resistant)* **to be ~ against fire/bullets** feuersicher/kugelsicher sein; **to be ~ against water** wasserdicht sein; **~ against inflation** inflationssicher

VT a *(against water)* imprägnieren

b *(Typ) (= make proof)* einen Korrekturabzug herstellen; *(= read proof)* Korrektur lesen

proof: proofread ['pru:fri:d] **VI** Korrektur lesen **VT** Korrektur lesen; **proofreader** ['pru:f-,ri:də'] N Korrektor(in) *m(f)*; **proofreading** ['pru:f,ri:dɪŋ] N Korrekturlesen *nt*; **at the ~ stage** im Korrekturstadium; **proof sheet** N *(Typ)* Korrekturfahne *f*/-bogen *m*; *(= trial print)* Probedruck *m*/-abzug *m*

prop¹ [prɒp] **N** *(lit)* Stütze *f*; *(fig also)* Halt *m* **VT to ~ the door open** die Tür offen halten; **to ~ oneself/sth against sth** sich/etw gegen etw lehnen → **prop up**

▶ **prop up** VT *sep* **a** *(= rest, lean)* **to prop oneself/sth up against sth** sich/etw gegen etw lehnen **b** *(= support)* stützen; *tunnel, wall* abstützen; *engine* aufbocken; *(fig) régime, company, the pound* stützen; *organization* unterstützen; **to prop oneself up on sth** sich auf etw *(acc)* stützen; **he spends most of his time propping up the bar** *(inf)* er hängt die meiste Zeit an der Bar

prop² N *(inf: = propeller)* Propeller *m*; **~ shaft** = **propeller shaft**; → **propeller**

prop³ N *(Theat inf)* = **property d**

prop⁴ *abbr of* **proprietor**

propaedeutic [,prəʊpi:'dju:tɪk] N *(form)* Propädeutik *f*

propaganda [,prɒpə'gændə] N Propaganda *f*; **~ machine** Propagandamaschinerie *f*

propagandist [,prɒpə'gændɪst] **N** Propagandist(in) *m(f)*; **a tireless ~ for penal reform** ein unermüdlicher Verfechter der Strafrechtsreform **ADJ** propagandistisch

propagate ['prɒpəgeɪt] **VT a** *(= reproduce)* fortpflanzen **b** *(= disseminate)* verbreiten; *views* verbreiten, propagieren **c** *(Phys) sound, waves* fortpflanzen **d** *(Hort) plant* vermehren **VI** sich fortpflanzen *or* vermehren; *(views)* sich aus- *or* verbreiten

propagation [,prɒpə'geɪʃən] N *(= reproduction)* Fortpflanzung *f*; *(Hort: of plants)* Vermehrung *f*; *(= dissemination)* Verbreitung *f*; *(of views)* Verbreitung *f*, Propagierung *f*

propane ['prəʊpeɪn] N Propan *nt*

propel [prə'pel] VT antreiben; *(fuel)* betreiben; **~led along by the wind** vom Wind getrieben; **~led by greed** von Habgier getrieben; **he was ~led through the window** er wurde aus dem Fenster geworfen

propellant, propellent [prə'pelənt] **N** Treibstoff *m*; *(in spray can)* Treibgas *nt* **ADJ** treibend

propeller [prə'pelə'] N Propeller *m*; **~ blade** *(Aviat)* Luftschrauben-/Propellerblatt *nt*; *(Naut)* Schraubenflügel *m*; **~ shaft** Antriebswelle *f*; *(Aut)* Kardanwelle *f*; *(Naut)* Schraubenwelle *f*

propelling: propelling force N *(lit, fig)* Triebkraft *f*; **propelling pencil** N Drehbleistift *m*

propensity [prə'pensɪtɪ] N Hang *m*, Neigung *f* (*to* zu); **to have a ~ for sth** einen Hang zu etw haben; **to have a ~ to do sth** *or* **for doing sth** dazu neigen, etw zu tun, die Neigung *or* den Hang haben, etw zu tun

proper ['prɒpə'] **ADJ a** *(= actual)* eigentlich; **physics ~** die eigentliche Physik; **in the ~ sense of the word** in der eigentlichen Bedeutung des Wortes; **is that a ~ policeman's helmet?** ist das ein richtiger Polizeihelm?; **he's never had a ~ job** er hat noch nie einen richtigen Job gehabt; **he's not a ~ electrician** er ist kein richtiger Elektriker; **not in Berlin ~** nicht in Berlin selbst

b *(inf) (= real) fool etc* richtig; *(= thorough) beating* gehörig, anständig *(inf)*, tüchtig *(inf)*; **we got a ~ beating** *(team etc)* wir sind ganz schön geschlagen worden *(inf)*

c *(= fitting, suitable)* richtig; **in ~ condition** in ordnungsgemäßem Zustand; **in the ~ way** richtig; **as you think ~** wie Sie es für richtig halten; **it's only right and ~** es ist nur recht und billig; **to do the ~ thing** das tun, was sich gehört; **the ~ thing to do would be to apologize** es gehört sich eigentlich, dass man sich entschuldigt; **don't touch the injured man unless you know the ~ thing to do** lassen Sie den Verletzten liegen, solange Sie nicht genau wissen, was man machen muss; **it wasn't really the ~ thing to say** es war ziemlich unpassend, das zu sagen; **we considered** *or* **thought it only ~ to ...** wir dachten, es gehört sich einfach zu ...

d *(= seemly)* anständig; **what is ~** was sich gehört; **it is not ~ for you to ...** es gehört sich nicht, dass Sie ...

e *(= prim and proper)* korrekt

f *(= peculiar, characteristic)* **~ to** angestammt *(+dat)*, angehörig *(+dat)*; **a species ~ to the Galapagos** eine Gattung, die den Galapagosinseln angestammt ist; **~ to the species** der Art eigen, arteigen

ADV a *(dial) cruel, poorly* richtig *(inf)*

b *(incorrect usage) behave* anständig; *talk* richtig

proper fraction N echter Bruch

properly ['prɒpəlɪ] ADV **a** *(= correctly)* richtig; **~ speaking** genau genommen, streng genommen; **Holland, more ~ called the Netherlands** Holland, eigentlich *or* richtiger die Niederlande; **Irish is ~ called Gaelic** Irisch heißt korrekt Gälisch **b** *(= in seemly fashion)* anständig; **to conduct oneself ~** sich korrekt verhalten; **she very ~ refused** sie hat sich zu Recht geweigert **c** *(= justifiably)* zu Recht **d** *(inf: = really, thoroughly)* ganz schön *(inf)*

proper name, proper noun N Eigenname *m*

propertied ['prɒpətɪd] ADJ besitzend; *person* begütert; **the ~ classes** die besitzenden Schichten, das Besitzbürgertum

property ['prɒpətɪ] N **a** *(= characteristic, Philos, Comput)* Eigenschaft *f*; **it has healing properties** es besitzt heilende Kräfte

b *(= thing owned)* Eigentum *nt*; **government/company ~** Eigentum *nt* der Regierung/Firma, Regierungs-/Firmeneigentum *nt*; **that's my ~** das gehört mir; **common ~** *(lit)* gemeinsames Eigentum; *(fig)* Gemeingut *nt*; **~ is theft** Eigentum ist Diebstahl; **to become the ~ of sb** in jds Eigentum *(acc)* übergehen; **a man of ~** ein begüterter Mann

c *(= building)* Haus *nt*, Wohnung *f*; *(= office)* Gebäude *nt*; *(= land)* Besitztum *nt*; *(= estate)* Besitz *m*; **this house is a very valuable ~** dieses Haus ist ein sehr wertvoller Besitz; **invest your money in ~** legen Sie Ihr Geld in Immobilien an; **~ in London is dearer** die Preise auf dem Londoner Immobilienmarkt sind höher

d *(Theat)* Requisit *nt*

property: property assets PL Vermögenswerte *pl*; **property consultant** N Vermögensberater(in) *m(f)*; **property developer** N Häusermakler(in) *m(f)*; **property giant** N Baulöwe *m*/-löwin *f (inf)*; **property man** N *(Theat)* Requisiteur *m*; **property manager, property master** N *(Theat)* Requisiteur(in) *m(f)*; **property market** N Immobilienmarkt *m*; **property mistress** N *(Theat)* Requisiteurin *f*; **property owner** N Haus- und Grundbesitzer(in) *m(f)*; **property speculation** N Immobilienspekulation *f*; **property speculator** N Immobilienspekulant(in) *m(f)*; **property tax** N Vermögenssteuer *f*

prophecy ['prɒfɪsɪ] N Prophezeiung *f*; **one skilled in the ~ of the future** jemand, der zukünftige Ereignisse vorhersagen kann *or* der die Gabe der Prophetie hat

prophesy ['prɒfɪsaɪ] **VT** prophezeien **VI** Prophezeiungen machen

prophet ['prɒfɪt] N Prophet(in) *m(f)*; **~ of doom** Unheilsverkünder(in) *m(f)*, Unheilsprophet(in) *m(f)*

prophetess [ˈprɒfɪtɪs] N Prophetin *f*

prophetic ADJ, **prophetically** ADV [prəˈfetɪk, -əlɪ] prophetisch

prophylactic [ˌprɒfɪˈlæktɪk] **ADJ** prophylaktisch, vorbeugend **N** Prophylaktikum *nt*; *(= contraceptive)* Präservativ *nt*

prophylaxis [ˌprɒfɪˈlæksɪs] N Prophylaxe *f*

propinquity [prəˈpɪŋkwɪtɪ] N *(form)* Nähe *f* (*to* zu); *(in time)* zeitliche Nähe (*to* zu); *(of relationship)* nahe Verwandtschaft (*to* mit)

propitiate [prəˈpɪʃɪeɪt] VT *(liter)* versöhnlich stimmen, besänftigen

propitiation [prəˌpɪʃɪˈeɪʃən] N *(liter)* Versöhnung *f*, Besänftigung *f*; **as ~ for, in ~ of** als Sühne für

propitiatory [prəˈpɪʃɪətərɪ] ADJ versöhnend, besänftigend; *mood* versöhnlich

propitious ADJ, **propitiously** ADV [prəˈpɪʃəs, -lɪ] günstig (*to, for* für)

propjet [ˈprɒpdʒet] N = **turboprop**

propman [ˈprɒpmæn, -mən] N *(Theat)* Requisiteur(in) *m(f)*

proponent [prəˈpəʊnənt] N Befürworter(in) *m(f)*

proportion [prəˈpɔːʃən] **N** **a** *(= ratio, relationship in number)* Verhältnis *nt* (*of x to y* zwischen x und y); *(= relationship in size, Art)* Proportionen *pl*; **~s** *(= size)* Ausmaß *nt*; *(of building)* Ausmaße *pl*; *(relative to one another, Art: of building etc)* Proportionen *pl*; **to be in/out of ~ (to one another)** *(in number)* im richtigen/nicht im richtigen Verhältnis zueinanderstehen; *(in size, Art)* in den Proportionen stimmen/nicht stimmen; *(in time, effort etc)* im richtigen/in keinem Verhältnis zueinanderstehen; **to be in/out of ~ to** *or* **with sth** im Verhältnis/in keinem Verhältnis zu etw stehen; *(in size, Art)* in den Proportionen zu etw passen/nicht zu etw passen; **in ~ to what she earns her contributions are very small** im Verhältnis zu dem, was sie verdient, ist ihr Beitrag äußerst bescheiden; **in direct/inverse ~ to sth** in direktem/umgekehrtem Verhältnis zu etw; *(Math)* direkt/indirekt proportional zu etw; **to get sth in ~** *(Art)* etw proportional richtig darstellen; *(fig)* etw objektiv betrachten; **he has got the arms out of ~** er hat die Arme proportional falsch dargestellt; **he has let it all get out of ~** *(fig)* er hat den Blick für die Proportionen verloren; **it's out of all ~!** das geht über jedes Maß hinaus!; **sense of ~** *(lit, fig)* Sinn *m* für Proportionen; **in due ~** in angemessenem Verhältnis; **in ~ as** in dem Maße wie; **a man of huge ~s** ein Koloss von einem Mann; **he admired her ample ~s** er bewunderte ihre üppigen Formen; **a room of good ~s** ein Zimmer mit guter Raumaufteilung
b *(= part, amount)* Teil *m*; **a certain ~ of the population** ein bestimmter Teil der Bevölkerung; **the ~ of drinkers in our society is rising constantly** der Anteil der Trinker in unserer Gesellschaft nimmt ständig zu; **what ~ of the industry is in private hands?** wie groß ist der Anteil der Industrie, der sich in Privathand befindet?; **a ~ of the industry is in private hands** ein Teil der Industrie befindet sich in Privathand
VT **you haven't ~ed the head properly** Sie haben den Kopf proportional falsch dargestellt; **he ~ed the building beautifully** er hat das Gebäude wunderbar ausgewogen gestaltet; **a realistically ~ed model** ein maßstabgetreues Modell; **a nicely ~ed woman** eine wohlproportionierte Frau

proportional [prəˈpɔːʃənl] ADJ proportional (*to* zu); *share, distribution also* anteilmäßig (*to* zu)

proportionality [prəˌpɔːʃəˈnælɪtɪ] N Proportionalität *f*; *(of means)* Verhältnismäßigkeit *f*

proportionally [prəˈpɔːʃnəlɪ] ADV proportional; *share, distribute also* anteilmäßig; *more, less* entsprechend; *elect* durch Verhältnis- *or* Proportionalwahl

proportional: **proportional printing** N *(Typ, Printing)* Proportionaldruck *m*; **proportional representation** N *(Pol)* Verhältniswahlrecht *nt*; **proportional spacing** N *(Typ, Printing)* Proportionalschrift *f*; **proportional voting** N *(Pol)* Verhältniswahlrecht *nt*

proportionate [prəˈpɔːʃnɪt] ADJ proportional; *share also* anteil(s)mäßig; **to be/not to be ~ to sth** im Verhältnis/in keinem Verhältnis zu etw stehen

proportionately [prəˈpɔːʃnɪtlɪ] ADV proportional; *share, distribute also* anteil(s)mäßig; *more, less* entsprechend

proposal [prəˈpəʊzl] N **a** Vorschlag *m* (*on, about* zu); *(= proposal of marriage)* (Heirats)antrag *m*; **to make sb a ~** jdm einen Vorschlag/(Heirats)antrag machen **b** *(= act of proposing) (of toast)* Ausbringen *nt*; *(of motion)* Einbringen *nt*; **his ~ of this plan surprised his colleagues** dass er den Vorschlag zu diesem Plan machte, überraschte seine Kollegen; **his ~ of John as chairman was expected** dass er John zum Vorsitzenden vorschlägt, war erwartet worden

propose [prəˈpəʊz] ✪ 8.1, 8.3 **VT** **a** *(= suggest)* vorschlagen; *motion* stellen, einbringen; **to ~ marriage to sb** jdm einen (Heirats)antrag machen; **I ~ leaving now** *or* **that we leave now** ich schlage vor, wir gehen jetzt *or* dass wir jetzt gehen; **to ~ sb's health** einen Toast auf jdn ausbringen → **toast**[2]
b *(= have in mind)* beabsichtigen, vorhaben; **I don't ~ having any more to do with it/him** ich will nichts mehr damit/mit ihm zu tun haben; **but I don't ~ to** ich habe aber nicht die Absicht; **how do you ~ to pay for it?** wie wollen Sie das bezahlen?; **and just how do you ~ we pay for all that?** können Sie uns denn auch verraten, wie wir das alles bezahlen sollen?
VI **a** *(= offer marriage)* einen (Heirats)antrag machen (*to* +*dat*)
b **man ~s, God disposes** *(Prov)* der Mensch denkt, Gott lenkt *(Prov)*

proposer [prəˈpəʊzəʳ] N *(in debate)* Antragsteller(in) *m(f)*; **if you want to stand for the committee you'll have to find a ~** wenn Sie sich in den Ausschuss wählen lassen wollen, müssen Sie jemanden finden, der Sie vorschlägt

proposition [ˌprɒpəˈzɪʃən] **N** **a** *(= statement)* Aussage *f*; *(Philos, Logic)* Satz *m*; *(Math)* (Lehr)satz *m* **b** *(= proposal)* Vorschlag *m*; *(= argument)* These *f*; **a paying ~** ein lohnendes Geschäft **c** *(= person or thing to be dealt with) (= objective)* Unternehmen *nt*; *(= opponent)* Fall *m*; *(= prospect)* Aussicht *f* **d** *(pej: = improper proposition)* unsittlicher Antrag **VT** **he ~ed me** er hat mich gefragt, ob ich mit ihm schlafen würde

propound [prəˈpaʊnd] VT darlegen

proprietary [prəˈpraɪətərɪ] ADJ *class* besitzend; *attitude, manner* besitzergreifend; **~ rights** Besitzrecht *nt*; **~ article/name** Markenartikel/-name *m*; **~ drug** Markenpräparat *nt*; **the author has rather strong ~ feelings about his work** der Autor sieht sein Werk als persönlichen Besitz an

proprietary article N Markenartikel *m*

proprietary name N Markenname *m*

proprietor [prəˈpraɪətəʳ] N *(of pub, hotel, patent)* Inhaber(in) *m(f)*; *(of house, newspaper)* Besitzer(in) *m(f)*

proprietorship [prəˈpraɪətəʃɪp] N → **proprietor**; **under his ~** während er der Inhaber/Besitzer war

proprietress [prəˈpraɪətrɪs] N *(of pub, hotel)* Inhaberin *f*; *(of newspaper)* Besitzerin *f*

propriety [prəˈpraɪətɪ] N *(= correctness)* Korrektheit *f*, Richtigkeit *f*; *(= decency)* Anstand *m*; *(of clothing)* Gesellschaftsfähigkeit *f*, Züchtigkeit *f (liter)*; **some countries still have doubts about the ~ of bikinis** in manchen Ländern werden Bikinis noch als anstößig betrachtet; **~ of conduct** korrektes Verhalten; **breach of ~** Verstoß *m* gegen die guten Sitten; **the proprieties** die Regeln *pl* des Anstands

props [prɒps] PL *(Theat)* Requisiten *pl*

propulsion [prəˈpʌlʃən] N Antrieb *m*

pro rata [ˈprəʊˈrɑːtə] ADJ, ADV anteil(s)mäßig; **on a ~ basis** auf einer proportionalen Basis

prorate [ˈprəʊreɪt] VT *(US)* anteil(s)mäßig aufteilen *or* verteilen

prorogation [ˌprəʊrəˈgeɪʃən] N Vertagung *f*

prorogue [prəˈrəʊg] **VT** vertagen **VI** sich vertagen

prosaic [prəʊˈzeɪɪk] ADJ *task, explanation, job, name* prosaisch; *approach, message* nüchtern; *life, joke* alltäglich

prosaically [prəʊˈzeɪɪkəlɪ] ADV *say, explain* prosaisch; *approach* nüchtern

proscenium [prəʊˈsiːnɪəm] N *pl* **proscenia** [prəʊˈsiːnɪə] (*also* **proscenium arch**) Proszenium *nt*; **~ stage** Bühne *f* mit Vorbühne

proscribe [prəʊˈskraɪb] VT *(= forbid)* verbieten; *(= outlaw)* ächten; *(= banish, exile)* verbannen

proscription [prəʊˈskrɪpʃən] N Verbot *nt*; *(= ostracism)* Ächtung *f*; *(= banishment)* Verbannung *f*

prose [prəʊz] N Prosa *f*; *(= writing, style)* Stil *m*; *(Sch, Univ: = translation text)* Übersetzung *f* in die Fremdsprache, Hinübersetzung *f*

prose composition N Prosa *f*

prosecutable [ˈprɒsɪkjuːtəbl] ADJ strafbar

prosecute [ˈprɒsɪkjuːt] **VT** **a** *person* strafrechtlich verfolgen *or* belangen (*for* wegen); **prosecuting counsel** *or* **attorney** *(US)* Staatsanwalt *m*/-anwältin *f*; **"trespassers will be ~d"** „widerrechtliches Betreten wird strafrechtlich verfolgt" **b** *(form: = carry on) inquiry, campaign etc* durchführen; *claim* weiterverfolgen **VI** Anzeige erstatten, gerichtlich vorgehen; **"shoplifting – we always ~"** „jeder Ladendiebstahl wird angezeigt *or* strafrechtlich verfolgt"; **Mr Jones, prosecuting, said ...** Herr Jones, der Vertreter der Anklage, sagte ...

prosecution [ˌprɒsɪˈkjuːʃən] N **a** *(Jur: = act of prosecuting)* strafrechtliche Verfolgung; *(in court: = case, side)* Anklage *f* (*for* wegen); **(the) counsel for the ~** die Anklage(vertretung), der Vertreter/die Vertreterin der Anklage; **witness for the ~** Zeuge *m*/Zeugin *f* der Anklage, Belastungszeuge *m*/-zeugin *f* **b** *(form: = carrying on) (of inquiry, campaign etc)* Durchführung *f*; *(of claim)* Weiterverfolgung *f*

prosecutor [ˈprɒsɪkjuːtəʳ] N Ankläger(in) *m(f)*

proselyte [ˈprɒsɪlaɪt] N Neubekehrte(r) *mf*, Proselyt(in) *m(f)*

proselytize [ˈprɒsɪlɪtaɪz] **VT** bekehren **VI** Leute bekehren

prose: **prose poem** N Prosagedicht *nt*; **prose style** N Stil *m*; **prose writer** N Prosaschriftsteller(in) *m(f)*; **prose writing** N Prosadichtung *f*

prosodic [prəˈsɒdɪk] ADJ prosodisch

prosody [ˈprɒsədɪ] N Verslehre *f*

prospect [ˈprɒspekt] **N** **a** *(= outlook, chance)* Aussicht *f* (*of* auf +*acc*); **what a ~!** *(iro)* das sind ja schöne Aussichten!; **he has no ~s** er hat keine Zukunft; **a job with no ~s** eine Stelle ohne Zukunft; **to face the ~ of sth** mit etw rechnen müssen; **to hold out the ~ of sth** etw in Aussicht stellen; **to have sth in ~** etw in Aussicht haben
b *(= person, thing)* **he's not much of a ~ for her** er hat ihr nicht viel zu bieten; **I think this product would be a good ~** ich glaube, dieses Produkt ist sehr aussichtsreich; **Manchester is a good ~ for the cup** Manchester ist ein aussichtsreicher Kandidat für den Pokal; **a likely ~ as a customer/candidate** ein aussichtsreicher Kunde/Kandidat; **a likely ~ as a husband** ein Mann, der als Ehemann infrage *or* in Frage kommt; **he's a good ~ for the team** *(could benefit it)* mit ihm hat die Mannschaft gute Aussichten
c *(old, form: = view)* Aussicht *f* (*of* auf +*acc*); *(= painting)* Ansicht *f* (*of* von)
d *(Min)* Schürfstelle *f*
VT [prəˈspekt] *(Min)* nach Bodenschätzen suchen in (+*dat*)
VI [prəˈspekt] *(Min)* nach Bodenschätzen suchen; **to ~ for gold** nach Gold suchen

prospecting [prəˈspektɪŋ] N *(Min)* Suche *f* nach Bodenschätzen

prospective [prəˈspektɪv] ADJ *attr (= likely to happen) journey, return* voraussichtlich; *(= future) son-in-law, owner* zukünftig; *buyer* interessiert; **~ candidate** Kandidat(in) *m(f)*; **all the ~ cases** alle infrage *or* in Frage kommenden Fälle; **~ earnings** voraussichtliche Einkünfte *pl*

prospector [prəˈspektəʳ] N Prospektor *m (spec)*, Gold-/Erz-/Ölsucher(in) *m(f)*

prospectus [prəˈspektəs] N Prospekt *m*; *(Sch, Univ)* Lehrprogramm *nt*

prosper [ˈprɒspəʳ] VI *(town, country, crime)* gedeihen, blühen; *(financially)* florieren, blühen; *(plan)* erfolgreich sein; **how's he ~ing these days?** wie geht es ihm?

prosperity [prɒsˈperɪtɪ] N Wohlstand *m*, Reichtum *m*; *(of business)* Prosperität *f*

prosperous [ˈprɒspərəs] ADJ *person* wohlhabend, reich; *business* gut gehend, florierend; *economy* florierend, blühend; *(liter) wind* gut; **those were ~ times/years** das waren Zeiten/Jahre des Wohlstands; **he had a ~ look about him** er sah wohlhabend aus

prosperously [ˈprɒspərəslɪ] ADV *live* im Wohlstand

prostaglandin [ˌprɒstəˈglændɪn] N Prostaglandin *nt*

prostate (gland) [ˈprɒsteɪt(ˌglænd)] N Prostata *f*, Vorsteherdrüse *f*

prosthesis [prɒsˈθiːsɪs] N *(spec)* Prothese *f*

prostitute [ˈprɒstɪtjuːt] N Prostituierte(r) *mf* VT *(lit)* prostituieren; *one's talents, honour, ideals* verkaufen VR sich prostituieren; *(fig also)* sich verkaufen

prostitution [ˌprɒstɪˈtjuːʃən] N *(lit, fig)* Prostitution *f*; *(of one's talents, honour, ideals)* Verkaufen *nt*

prostrate [ˈprɒstreɪt] ADJ ausgestreckt; **he was found ~ on the floor** man fand ihn ausgestreckt am Boden liegend; **the servants lay ~ at their master's feet** die Diener lagen demütig *or* unterwürfig zu Füßen ihres Herrn; **~ with grief** vor Gram gebrochen; **she was ~ with exhaustion** sie brach fast zusammen vor Erschöpfung VT [prɒˈstreɪt] *usu pass (lit)* zu Boden werfen; *(fig) (with fatigue)* erschöpfen, mitnehmen; *(with shock)* zusammenbrechen lassen, niederschmettern; **to be ~d by an illness** einer Krankheit *(dat)* zum Opfer gefallen sein; **to be ~d with grief** vor Gram gebrochen sein VR [prɒˈstreɪt] sich niederwerfen *(before* vor *+dat)*

prostration [prɒˈstreɪʃən] N *(lit)* Fußfall *m*; *(fig: = exhaustion)* Erschöpfung *f*

prosy [ˈprəʊzɪ] ADJ *(+er) (= boring)* redselig; *(= over-literary)* schwülstig

Prot *abbr of* **Protestant** ≈ ev.

protactinium [ˌprəʊtækˈtɪnɪəm] N *(Chem)* Protaktinium *nt*

protagonist [prəʊˈtægənɪst] N *(esp Liter)* Protagonist(in) *m(f)*; *(= champion, supporter)* Verfechter(in) *m(f)*

protean [ˈprəʊtɪən] ADJ *(liter)* proteisch *(liter)*

protect [prəˈtekt] VT schützen *(against* gegen, *from* vor *+dat)*; *(person, animal) sb, young* beschützen *(against* gegen, *from* vor *+dat)*; *one's interests, rights* schützen, wahren; *(Comput) cell etc* schützen; **don't try to ~ the culprit** versuchen Sie nicht, den Schuldigen zu decken VI schützen *(against* vor *+dat)*

protected species [prəˌtektɪdˈspiːʃiːz] N geschützte Art

protection [prəˈtekʃən] N **a** Schutz *m (against* gegen, *from* vor *+dat)*; *(of interests, rights)* Wahrung *f*; **to be under sb's ~** unter jds Schutz *(dat)* stehen **b** *(also* **protection money**) Schutzgeld *nt*

protection: **protection error** N *(Comput)* Schutzverletzung *f*; **protection factor** N *(of sun lotion)* Lichtschutzfaktor *m*; **protection fault** N *(Comput)* Schutzverletzung *f*

protectionism [prəˈtekʃənɪzəm] N Protektionismus *m*

protectionist [prəˈtekʃənɪst] ADJ protektionistisch N Protektionist(in) *m(f)*

protection racket N organisiertes Erpresserunwesen, (organisierte) Schutzgelderpressung

protective [prəˈtektɪv] ADJ **a** Schutz-; *attitude, gesture* beschützend; *equipment, layer, covering* schützend; **~ instinct** Beschützerinstinkt *m*; **the mother is very ~ toward(s) her children** die Mutter ist sehr fürsorglich ihren Kindern gegenüber; **some parents can be too ~** manche Eltern sind übermäßig besorgt **b** *(Econ) system* protektionistisch; **~ duty** Schutzzoll *m*

protective: **protective clothing** N Schutzkleidung *f*, Schutzbekleidung *f*; **protective colouring**, *(US)* **protective coloring** N Tarnfarbe *f*, Schutzfarbe *f*; **protective custody** N Schutzhaft *f*

protectively [prəˈtektɪvlɪ] ADV schützend; *(with regard to people)* beschützend; **don't be frightened, he said ~** hab keine Angst, sagte er in beschützendem Ton

protective tariff N *(Econ)* Schutzzoll *m*, Schutzgebühr *f*

protector [prəˈtektəʳ] N **a** *(= defender)* Beschützer(in) *m(f)* **b** *(= protective wear)* Schutz *m*

protectorate [prəˈtektərɪt] N Protektorat *nt*

protectory [prəˈtektərɪ] N (Kinder)fürsorgeheim *nt*

protectress [prəˈtektrɪs] N Beschützerin *f*

protégé, protégée [ˈprɒtəʒeɪ] N Protegé *m*, Schützling *m*

protein [ˈprəʊtiːn] N Eiweiß *nt*, Protein *nt*; **a high-~ diet** eine eiweißreiche *or* stark proteinhaltige Kost

pro tem [ˈprəʊˈtem] *abbr of* **pro tempore** zurzeit, zzt.; **on a ~ basis** auf vorrübergehender Basis

protest [ˈprəʊtest] ✪ 12.2, 14 N Protest *m*; *(= demonstration)* Protestkundgebung *f*; **under ~** unter Protest; **in ~** aus Protest; **to make a/one's ~** Protest *or* Widerspruch erheben; **letter of ~, ~ letter** Protestschreiben *nt* VI [prəʊˈtest] *(against, about* gegen) protestieren; *(= demonstrate)* demonstrieren; **the ~ing scream of the brakes** das gequälte Aufkreischen der Bremsen VT [prəʊˈtest] **a** *innocence* beteuern **b** *(= dispute) decision* protestieren gegen, Protest *or* Einspruch erheben gegen; **it's mine, he ~ed** das gehört mir, protestierte er

Protestant [ˈprɒtɪstənt] ADJ protestantisch; *(esp in Germany)* evangelisch N Protestant(in) *m(f)*, Evangelische(r) *mf*

Protestantism [ˈprɒtɪstəntɪzəm] N Protestantismus *m*

protestation [ˌprɒteˈsteɪʃən] N **a** *(of love, loyalty etc)* Beteuerung *f* **b** *(= protest)* Protest *m*

protester [prəˈtestəʳ] N Protestierende(r) *mf*; *(in demonstration)* Demonstrant(in) *m(f)*

protest march N Protestmarsch *m*

protest vote N Proteststimme *f*

proto- [ˈprəʊtəʊ-] PREF **a** *(Chem, Biol)* proto-, Proto-; **protolysis** Protolyse *f* **b** *(Ling)* ur-, Ur-; **protolanguage** Ursprache *f*

protocol [ˈprəʊtəkɒl] N Protokoll *nt (also Comput)*

protohistory [ˌprəʊtəʊˈhɪstərɪ] N *(Hist)* Urgeschichte *f*

proton [ˈprəʊtɒn] N Proton *nt*

protoplasm [ˈprəʊtəʊplæzəm] N Protoplasma *nt*

protoplast [ˈprəʊtəʊplæst] N *(Bot)* Protoplast *m*

prototype [ˈprəʊtəʊtaɪp] N Prototyp *m*

prototypical [ˌprəʊtəʊˈtɪpɪkəl] ADJ *(= typical)* typisch

protozoan [ˈprəʊtəʊzəʊən] ADJ einzellig N Protozoon *nt (spec)*, Urtierchen *nt*

protozoic [ˈprəʊtəʊzəʊɪk] ADJ einzellig

protract [prəˈtrækt] VT hinausziehen, in die Länge ziehen; *illness* verlängern; *decision* hinauszögern

protracted [prəˈtræktɪd] ADJ *illness* langwierig; *discussion, debate, negotiations also* sich hinziehend *attr*; *description* lang gezogen; *absence, dispute* längere(r, s)

protraction [prəˈtrækʃən] N **that can only lead to the ~ of the discussion/illness** das kann nur dazu führen, dass sich die Diskussion/Krankheit hinzieht

protractor [prəˈtræktəʳ] N *(Math)* Winkelmesser *m*

protrude [prəˈtruːd] VI *(out of, from* aus) vorstehen; *(ears)* abstehen; *(eyes)* vortreten VT hervorstrecken, herausstrecken

protruding [prəˈtruːdɪŋ] ADJ vorstehend; *rock, ledge* vorstehend, herausragend; *ears* abstehend; *eyes* vortretend; *forehead, chin* vorspringend; *stomach* vorstehend, vorspringend; *teeth* vorstehend; *ribs* hervorstehend, hervortretend

protrusion [prəˈtruːʒən] N **a** *(= protruding object)* Vorsprung *m* **b** *(= protruding) (of rock, buttress, teeth etc)* Vorstehen *nt*; *(of forehead, chin)* Vorspringen *nt*; *(of eyes)* Vortreten *nt*

protrusive [prəˈtruːsɪv] ADJ = **protruding**

protuberance [prəˈtjuːbərəns] N *(= bulge)* Beule *f*; *(of stomach)* Vorstehen *nt*; *(of eyes)* Vortreten *nt*

protuberant [prəˈtjuːbərənt] ADJ vorstehend; *eyes* vortretend

proud [praʊd] ADJ **a** *person, expression* stolz *(of* auf *+acc)*; **it made his parents feel very ~** das erfüllte seine Eltern mit Stolz; **to be the ~ owner** *or* **possessor of sth** der stolze Eigentümer *or* Besitzer von etw sein; **as ~ as a peacock** eitel wie ein Pfau, stolz wie ein Hahn; **~ boast** stolze Behauptung; **a ~ day for …** ein stolzer Tag für …; **~ history** stolze Geschichte; **a ~ moment** ein stolzer Moment; **to be ~ that …** stolz (darauf) sein, dass …; **to be ~ to do sth** stolz darauf sein, etw zu tun; **I hope you're ~ of yourself** *(iro)* ich hoffe, du bist stolz auf dich; **that's nothing to be ~ of** das ist nichts, worauf man stolz sein kann
b *(dated Brit: = projecting)* **to be** *or* **stand ~** *(nail etc)* herausragen, hervorragen; *(Typ: character)* erhaben sein; **~ flesh** wildes Fleisch
c *(liter: = high, noble)* stolz
ADV **to do sb/oneself ~** jdn/sich verwöhnen

proudly [ˈpraʊdlɪ] ADV stolz

provable [ˈpruːvəbl] ADJ *hypothesis, story, law* beweisbar; *guilt, innocence also* nachweisbar

prove [pruːv] ✪ 26.1 *pret* **proved**, *ptp* **proved** *or* **proven** VT **a** *(= verify)* beweisen; *will* beglaubigen; **he ~d that she did it** er bewies *or* er wies nach, dass sie das getan hat; **to ~ sb innocent** *or* **sb's innocence** jds Unschuld beweisen *or* nachweisen; **to ~ something against sb** jdm etwas nachweisen; **whether his judgement was right remains to be ~d** *or* **~n** es muss sich erst noch erweisen, ob seine Beurteilung zutrifft; **it all goes to ~ that …** das beweist mal wieder, dass …; **he was ~d right in the end** er hat schließlich doch recht behalten
b *(= test out, put to the proof) rifle, aircraft etc* erproben; *one's worth, courage* unter Beweis stellen, beweisen; **he did it just to ~ a point** er tat es nur der Sache wegen
c *(Cook) dough* gehen lassen
VI **a** *(Cook: dough)* gehen
b *(= turn out)* **to ~ (to be) hot/useful** *etc* sich als heiß/nützlich *etc* erweisen; **if it ~s otherwise** wenn sich das Gegenteil herausstellt
VR **a** *(= show one's value, courage etc)* sich bewähren
b to ~ oneself innocent/indispensable *etc* sich als unschuldig/unentbehrlich *etc* erweisen

proven [ˈpruːvən] *ptp of* **prove** [ˈprəʊvən] ADJ bewährt; **not ~** *(Scot Jur)* unbewiesen

provenance [ˈprɒvɪnəns] N Herkunft *f*, Ursprung *m*; **country of ~** Herkunfts- *or* Ursprungsland *nt*

provender [ˈprɒvɪndəʳ] N Futter *nt*

proverb ['prɒvɜːb] N Sprichwort *nt*; (the Book of) Proverbs die Sprüche *pl*

proverbial [prə'vɜːbɪəl] ADJ *(lit, fig)* sprichwörtlich

proverbially [prə'vɜːbɪəlɪ] ADV *(lit) express* in Form eines Sprichworts; *(fig)* sprichwörtlich; the weather there is ~ unreliable das Wetter dort ist sprichwörtlich wechselhaft; prevention is ~ better than cure wie das Sprichwort sagt, Vorsicht ist besser als Nachsicht

provide [prə'vaɪd] VT a *(= make available)* zur Verfügung stellen; *(agency) personnel* vermitteln; *money* bereitstellen; *(= lay on, as part of service) chairs, materials, food etc* (zur Verfügung) stellen; *(= see to, bring along) food, records etc* sorgen für; *(= produce, give) ideas, specialist knowledge, electricity* liefern; *light, shade* spenden, geben; *privacy* sorgen für, schaffen; *topic of conversation* sorgen für, liefern; X ~d the money and Y (~d) the expertise X stellte das Geld bereit und Y lieferte das Fachwissen; a local band ~d the music eine örtliche Kapelle sorgte für die Musik; candidates must ~ their own pens die Kandidaten müssen ihr Schreibgerät selbst stellen

b to ~ sth for sb etw für jdn stellen; *(= make available)* jdm etw zur Verfügung stellen; *(= find, supply: agency etc)* jdm etw besorgen; to ~ food and clothes for one's family für Nahrung und Kleidung seiner Familie sorgen; I can't ~ enough food for everyone ich kann nicht genug Essen für alle stellen; it ~s a certain amount of privacy/shade for the inhabitants es gibt den Bewohnern eine gewisse Abgeschlossenheit/etwas Schatten; they ~ a restroom/bus for their workers sie stellen einen Ruheraum/Bus für ihre Arbeiter

c to ~ sb with sth *(with food, clothing etc)* jdn mit etw versorgen; *(= equip)* jdn mit etw versehen *or* ausstatten; *with excuse, idea, answer* jdm etw geben *or* liefern; *with opportunity, information* jdm etw verschaffen *or* geben *or* liefern; the job ~d him with a good salary/with the necessary experience die Stelle verschaffte ihm genug Geld/die nötige Erfahrung; this ~d the school with enough money to build a gymnasium dadurch hatte die Schule genügend Geld zur Verfügung, um eine Turnhalle zu bauen

d *(= stipulate: clause, agreement)* vorsehen; unless otherwise ~d sofern nichts Gegenteiliges bestimmt ist → provided (that), providing (that)

VI the Lord will ~ *(prov)* der Herr wirds schon geben; a husband who ~s well ein Ehemann, der gut für seine Familie/Frau sorgt

VR to ~ oneself with sth sich mit etw ausstatten; to ~ oneself with a good excuse sich *(dat)* eine gute Entschuldigung zurechtlegen

▶ **provide against** VI *+prep obj* vorsorgen für, Vorsorge *or* Vorkehrungen treffen für; the law provides against such abuses das Gesetz schützt vor solchem Missbrauch

▶ **provide for** VI *+prep obj* a *family etc* versorgen, sorgen für, Sorge tragen für; he made sure that his family would be well provided for er stellte sicher, dass seine Familie gut versorgt war *or* dass für seine Familie gut gesorgt war

b the law/treaty provides for penalties against abuses bei Missbrauch sieht das Gesetz/der Vertrag Strafe vor; as provided for in the 1970 contract wie in dem Vertrag von 1970 vorgesehen; we provided for all emergencies wir haben für alle Notfälle vorgesorgt; we have provided for an increase in costs of 25% wir haben eine Kostensteigerung von 25% einkalkuliert

provided (that) [prə'vaɪdɪd('ðæt)] CONJ vorausgesetzt(, dass), gesetzt den Fall(, dass)

providence ['prɒvɪdəns] N a *(= fate)* die Vorsehung b *(dated: = prudent thriftiness)* Vorsorge *f*

provident ['prɒvɪdənt] ADJ vorsorglich, vorsorgend, vorausschauend; ~ fund Unterstützungskasse *f*; ~ society *private Altersversicherung*

providential [,prɒvɪ'denʃəl] ADJ a God's ~ care die göttliche Vorsehung b *(= lucky)* glücklich; to be ~ (ein) Glück sein

providentially [,prɒvɪ'denʃəlɪ] ADV *(= luckily)* glücklicherweise; it happened almost ~ das war gleichsam eine Fügung (des Schicksals)

providently ['prɒvɪdəntlɪ] ADV vorsorglich, vorsorgend, vorausschauend

provider [prə'vaɪdə'] N a *(Econ)* Lieferant(in) *m(f)* b *(Internet)* Provider *m*, Anbieter *m* c *(for family)* Ernährer(in) *m(f)*

providing (that) [prə'vaɪdɪŋ('ðæt)] CONJ vorausgesetzt(, dass), gesetzt den Fall(, dass)

province ['prɒvɪns] N a Provinz *f* b provinces PL the ~s die Provinz c *(fig: = area of knowledge, activity etc)* Gebiet *nt*, Bereich *m*; it's not (within) my ~ das fällt nicht in meinen Bereich *or* mein Gebiet; it's outside the ~ of science es liegt außerhalb des wissenschaftlichen Gebiets *or* Bereichs d *(= area of authority)* Kompetenzbereich *m*; that's not my ~ dafür bin ich nicht zuständig

provincial [prə'vɪnʃəl] ADJ Provinz-; *custom, accent* ländlich; *(pej)* provinzlerisch; ~ capital Provinzhauptstadt *f*; ~ narrowness Engstirnigkeit *f*; the World War did not affect daily life in ~ France der Weltkrieg hatte keinen Einfluss auf den Alltag in den ländlichen Teilen Frankreichs N Provinzbewohner(in) *m(f)*; *(pej)* Provinzler(in) *m(f)*

provincialism [prə'vɪnʃəlɪzəm] N Provinzialismus *m*

provincialize [prə'vɪnʃəlaɪz] VT to ~ sth etw provinziell machen, etw *dat* einen provinzlerischen Charakter geben

proving ground ['pruːvɪŋ,graʊnd] N *(for theory)* Versuchsfeld *nt*; *(= situation: for sb, sb's abilities)* Bewährungsprobe *f*; Belfast was his ~ Belfast war für ihn die Bewährungsprobe

provision [prə'vɪʒən] N a *(= act of supplying) (for others)* Bereitstellung *f*; *(for one's own team, expedition etc)* Beschaffung *f*; *(of food, gas, water etc)* Versorgung *f* (of mit, *to sb* jds)

b *(= supply)* Vorrat *m* (of an *+dat*); we had an ample ~ of reference books/houses *etc* uns *(dat)* standen genügend Nachschlagewerke/Häuser *etc* zur Verfügung

c ~s *pl (= food)* Lebensmittel *pl*; *(Mil: for journey, expedition)* Verpflegung *f*, Proviant *m*; ~s ship Versorgungsschiff *nt*

d *(= allowance)* Berücksichtigung *f*; *(= arrangement)* Vorkehrung *f*; *(= stipulation)* Bestimmung *f*; with the ~ that ... mit dem Vorbehalt *or* der Bedingung, dass ...; is there no ~ for such cases in the legislation? sind solche Fälle im Gesetz nicht berücksichtigt *or* vorgesehen?; there's no ~ for later additions spätere Erweiterungen sind nicht vorgesehen; to make ~ for sb/one's family/the future für jdn/für seine Familie/für die Zukunft Vorsorge *or* Vorkehrungen treffen; to make ~ for sth etw vorsehen; *(in legislation, rules also)* etw berücksichtigen; *(for margin of error etc)* etw einkalkulieren; the council made ~ for recreation die Stadt hat Freizeiteinrichtungen geschaffen; to make (a) ~ against sth gegen etw Vorkehrungen treffen

VT die Verpflegung liefern für; *expedition* verproviantieren; *troops* (mit Proviant) beliefern *or* versorgen

provisional [prə'vɪʒənl] ADJ provisorisch; *measures, solution also, offer, acceptance, decision, legislation* vorläufig; ~ driving licence *(Brit)* vorläufige Fahrerlaubnis für Fahrschüler; to be in ~ 4th place *(Sport etc)* vorläufig auf dem vierten Platz liegen; the ~ IRA die provisorische irisch-republikanische Armee N *(Ir Pol)* the Provisionals *Mitglieder der provisorischen irisch-republikanischen Armee*

provisionally [prə'vɪʒnəlɪ] ADV vorläufig; *appoint also* provisorisch; ~ titled ... mit dem vorläufigen Titel *or* Arbeitstitel ..., vorläufig ... benannt

proviso [prə'vaɪzəʊ] N *(= condition)* Vorbehalt *m*, Bedingung *f*; *(= clause)* Vorbehaltsklausel *f*; with the ~ that ... unter der Bedingung, dass ...

provisorily [prə'vaɪzərɪlɪ] ADV a *(= with a proviso)* mit Vorbehalt, bedingt b *(= tentatively)* provisorisch, vorläufig

provisory [prə'vaɪzərɪ] ADJ a *(= with a proviso)* vorbehaltlich; a ~ clause eine Vorbehaltsklausel b = provisional ADJ

Provo ['prəʊvəʊ] N *(Ir Pol)* = provisional N

provocation [,prɒvə'keɪʃən] N Provokation *f*, Herausforderung *f*; what ~ was there for you to hit him? was hat dich dazu provoziert, ihn zu schlagen?; he acted under ~ er wurde dazu provoziert *or* herausgefordert; his deliberate ~ of a quarrel seine bewusste Herbeiführung eines Streits; to suffer great ~ sehr stark provoziert werden; at the slightest ~ bei der geringsten Provokation *or* Herausforderung; he hit me without any ~ er hat mich geschlagen, ohne dass ich ihn dazu provoziert hätte

provocative [prə'vɒkətɪv] ADJ a *(= thought-provoking)* provozierend, provokatorisch; *film, discussion* anregend, kontrovers; he's just trying to be ~ er versucht nur zu provozieren b *(= erotic, seductive) dress* provozierend; *remark* herausfordernd; *pose, manner, behaviour* aufreizend, herausfordernd, provozierend

provocatively [prə'vɒkətɪvlɪ] ADV a provozierend, provokatorisch; ~ entitled ... mit dem provokativen Titel ... b *(= erotically, seductively) say, behave* herausfordernd; *dress* provozierend; ~ dressed aufreizend gekleidet; she smiled ~ sie lächelte aufreizend

provoke [prə'vəʊk] VT *sb* provozieren, reizen, herausfordern; *animal* reizen; *reaction, anger, criticism, dismay, smile* hervorrufen; *lust, pity* erwecken, erregen; *reply, dispute* provozieren; *discussion, revolt, showdown* herbeiführen, auslösen; to ~ a quarrel *or* an argument *(person)* Streit suchen; *(action)* zu einem Streit führen; to ~ sb into doing sth *or* to do sth jdn dazu bringen, dass er etw tut; *(= taunt)* jdn dazu treiben *or* so provozieren, dass er etw tut

provoking [prə'vəʊkɪŋ] ADJ provozierend; *(= annoying) fact, circumstance* ärgerlich; how very ~! wie ärgerlich!

provokingly [prə'vəʊkɪŋlɪ] ADV provozierend

provost ['prɒvəst] N a *(Scot)* Bürgermeister(in) *m(f)* b *(Univ)* ≈ Dekan(in) *m(f)* c *(Eccl)* Propst *m*

provost marshal [prə'vəʊst'mɑːʃəl] N Kommandeur(in) *m(f)* der Militärpolizei

prow [praʊ] N Bug *m*

prowess ['praʊɪs] N *(= skill)* Fähigkeiten *pl*, Können *nt*; *(= courage)* Tapferkeit *f*; his (sexual) ~ seine Potenz, seine Manneskraft

prowl [praʊl] N Streifzug *m*; to be on the ~ *(cat, lion, burglar)* auf Streifzug sein; *(headmaster, boss)* herumschleichen; *(police car)* auf Streife sein; *(inf: for pick-up)* auf Frauen-/Männerjagd sein VT durchstreifen VI *(also* prowl about *or* around) herumstreichen; *(boss, headmaster)* herumschleichen; he ~ed round the house er schlich im Haus

prowl car N *(US)* Streifenwagen *m*

prowler ['praʊlə'] N Herumtreiber(in) *m(f)*; *(= peeping Tom)* Spanner *m (inf)*; he heard a ~ outside er hörte, wie draußen jemand herumschlich

prox [prɒks] *abbr of* proximo

proximate ['prɒksɪmɪt] ADJ a *(= next)* nächste(r, s), folgende(r, s), sich unmittelbar anschließend, unmittelbar; ~ cause unmittelbare Ursache b *(= close, very near)* nahe liegend c *(= forthcoming, imminent)* kurz bevorstehend d *(= approximate)* annähernd, ungefähr; ~ estimate ungefähre Schätzung; ~ analysis *(Chem)* quantitative Analyse

proximity [prɒk'sɪmɪtɪ] N Nähe *f*; in ~ to in der Nähe *(+gen)*; in close ~ to in unmittelbarer Nähe *(+gen)*; ~ in time zeitliche Nähe

proximo ['prɒksɪməʊ] ADV *(Comm)* (des) nächsten Monats

proxy ['prɒksɪ] N *(= power, document)* (Handlungs)vollmacht *f*; *(= person)* Stellvertreter(in) *m(f)*; **by ~** durch einen Stellvertreter; **to be married by ~** ferngetraut werden

proxy vote N stellvertretend abgegebene Stimme

Prozac® ['prəʊzæk] N Prozac® *nt*

prude [pru:d] N **to be a ~** prüde sein; **only ~s would object to that** nur prüde Leute würden sich daran stoßen

prudence ['pru:dəns] N *(of person)* Umsicht *f*; *(of measure, action, decision)* Klugheit *f*; *(of answer)* Überlegtheit *f*; **simple ~ should have made you stop** der gesunde Menschenverstand hätte Sie davon abbringen müssen

prudent ['pru:dənt] ADJ *person* umsichtig; *measure, action, decision* klug; *answer* wohlüberlegt; **I thought it ~ to change the subject** ich hielt es für klüger, das Thema zu wechseln; **how ~!** sehr klug *or* weise!; **that was the ~ thing to do** es war klug, das zu tun

prudential [pru:'denʃəl] ADJ *(geh)* **a** → **prudent** **b** *(= sensible)* verständig **c** *(= expert, competent)* sachverständig; **~ committee** *(US)* beratender Ausschuss

prudently ['pru:dəntlɪ] ADV wohlweislich; *act* umsichtig; *answer* überlegt

prudery ['pru:dərɪ] N Prüderie *f*

prudish ['pru:dɪʃ] ADJ prüde; *clothes* sittsam, züchtig

prudishly ['pru:dɪʃlɪ] ADV *say, behave* prüde; *dress* sittsam, züchtig; **they ~ cut out all the swearwords** prüde wie sie sind, haben sie alle Kraftausdrücke gestrichen

prudishness ['pru:dɪʃnɪs] N *(= prudish behaviour)* Prüderie *f*; *(= prudish nature)* prüde Art; *(of clothes)* Sittsamkeit *f*

prune¹ [pru:n] N Backpflaume *f*

prune² VT *(also* **prune down***)* beschneiden, stutzen; *hedge* schneiden, zurechtstutzen; *(fig) expenditure* kürzen; *workforce* reduzieren; *firm* schrumpfen lassen; *book, essay* zusammenstreichen, kürzen; **to ~ away** ab- *or* wegschneiden; *unnecessary details etc* wegstreichen; **to ~ superfluous matter from an essay** einen Aufsatz straffen

pruners ['pru:nəz] PL Gartenschere *f*, Rebschere *f*

pruning ['pru:nɪŋ] N Beschneiden *nt*, Stutzen *nt*; *(of hedge)* Schneiden *nt*, Zurechtstutzen *nt*; *(fig) (of expenditure)* Kürzung *f*; *(of workforce)* Reduzierung *f*; *(of firm)* Schrumpfung *f*; *(of book, essay)* Zusammenstreichen *nt*, Kürzung *f*; **the tree needs ~** der Baum muss beschnitten *or* gestutzt werden

pruning: **pruning hook** N Rebmesser *nt*; **pruning knife** N Gartenmesser *nt*, Hippe *f*; **pruning shears** PL Gartenschere *f*, Rebschere *f*

prurience ['prʊərɪəns] N Anzüglichkeit *f*; *(of person)* Lüsternheit *f*

prurient ['prʊərɪənt] ADJ anzüglich; *person* lüstern

Prussia ['prʌʃə] N Preußen *nt*

Prussian ['prʌʃən] ADJ preußisch; **~ blue** preußischblau N **a** Preuße *m*, Preußin *f* **b** *(Ling)* Preußisch *nt*; **Old ~** Altpreußisch *nt*

prussic acid [,prʌsɪk'æsɪd] N Blausäure *f*

pry¹ [praɪ] VI neugierig sein; *(in drawers etc)* (herum)schnüffeln *(in* in *+dat)*; **I don't mean to ~, but …** es geht mich ja nichts an, aber …; **to ~ into sb's affairs** seine Nase in jds Angelegenheiten *(acc)* stecken; **to ~ into sb's secrets** jds Geheimnisse ausspionieren wollen; **to ~ around** herumschnüffeln

pry² VT *(US)* = **prise**

prying ['praɪɪŋ] ADJ neugierig

PS *abbr of* **postscript** PS

psalm [sɑ:m] N Psalm *m*; **(the Book of) Psalms** der Psalter; **~ book** Psalmenbuch *nt*

psalmist ['sɑ:mɪst] N Psalmist *m*

psalmody ['sælmədɪ] N Psalmodie *f*

psalter ['sɔ:ltəʳ] N Psalter *m*

psaltery ['sɔ:ltərɪ] N Psalterium *nt*

PSAT N *(US: Sch, Univ) abbr of* **Preliminary Scholastic Aptitude Test** *Eignungstest vor Aufnahme in eine Universität* → *also* **SAT**

PSBR *(Brit) abbr of* **public sector borrowing requirement**

psephological [,sefə'lɒdʒɪkəl] ADJ Wahlforschungs-; **~ study** Wahlforschungsstudie *f*

psephologist [se'fɒlədʒɪst] N Wahlforscher(in) *m(f)*, Psephologe *m*, Psephologin *f*

psephology [se'fɒlədʒɪ] N Wahlforschung *f*

pseud [sju:d] *(Brit inf)* N Möchtegern *m (inf)*; **you ~!** du Angeber(in)! ADJ *book, film* auf intellektuell gemacht *(inf)*, gewollt; *views, ideas* hochgestochen; *décor, pub etc* auf schick gemacht *(inf)*; *person* affektiert, pseudointellektuell

pseudo ['sju:dəʊ] *(inf)* ADJ **a** = **pseud ADJ** **b** *(= pretended)* unecht; *affection, simplicity* aufgesetzt; **~ revolutionary/intellectual** Pseudorevolutionär(in) *m(f)*/-intellektuelle(r) *mf* N = **pseud N**

pseudo- PREF Pseudo-, pseudo; **~scientific** pseudowissenschaftlich

pseudonym ['sju:dənɪm] N Pseudonym *nt*

pseudopregnancy [,sju:dəʊ'pregnənsɪ] N *(Med)* Scheinschwangerschaft *f*

pseudy ['sju:dɪ] ADJ *(+er) (inf)* = **pseud ADJ**

pshaw [pʃɔ:] INTERJ *(dated)* pah

psi [psaɪ] N *no pl* **a** *(= letter)* Psi *nt* **b** *(= psychic phenomena)* Psi *nt*

psittacosis [,psɪtə'kəʊsɪs] N Papageienkrankheit *f*, Psittakose *f (spec)*

psoriasis [sɒ'raɪəsɪs] N Schuppenflechte *f*, Psoriasis *f (spec)*

PST *(US) abbr of* **Pacific Standard Time** pazifische Zeit

Psyche ['saɪkɪ] N *(Myth)* Psyche *f*

psych [saɪk] VT *(inf)* **a** *(psychoanalyst)* analysieren **b** *(= understand, get taped)* **to ~ sb (out), to get sb ~ed (out)** jdn durchschauen

► **psych out** VT *sep (inf)* psychologisch fertigmachen *(inf)* VI *(= freak out)* ausflippen *(inf)*

► **psych up** VT *sep (inf)* hochputschen *(inf)*; **to psych oneself up, to get oneself psyched up** sich hochputschen *(inf)*; **he was all psyched up for the match** er hatte sich für das Spiel so richtig hochgeputscht *(inf)*

psyche ['saɪkɪ] N Psyche *f*

psychedelic [,saɪkɪ'delɪk] ADJ psychedelisch; *drugs also* bewusstseinserweiternd

psychiatric [,saɪkɪ'ætrɪk] ADJ psychiatrisch; *illness, problem* psychisch; **~ hospital** psychiatrische Klinik; **~ nurse** Psychiatrieschwester *f*, psychiatrisch ausgebildete Krankenschwester; **~ unit** psychiatrische Abteilung; **~ ward** Psychiatrie *f*

psychiatrist [saɪ'kaɪətrɪst] N Psychiater(in) *m(f)*

psychiatry [saɪ'kaɪətrɪ] N Psychiatrie *f*

psychic ['saɪkɪk] ADJ **a** übersinnlich; *powers* übernatürlich; **~ research** Parapsychologie *f*; **she is ~** sie besitzt übernatürliche Kräfte *or* übersinnliche Wahrnehmung; **you must be ~!** Sie müssen hellsehen können! **b** *(Psych: = mental)* psychisch; **~ healer** Geistheiler(in) *m(f)* N Mensch *m* mit übernatürlichen Kräften *or* übersinnlicher Wahrnehmung

psychical ['saɪkɪkəl] ADJ → **psychic ADJ**

psycho ['saɪkəʊ] N *(inf)* Verrückte(r) *mf*

psychoanalyse, *(US)* **psychoanalyze** [,saɪkəʊ'ænəlaɪz] VT psychoanalytisch behandeln, psychoanalysieren

psychoanalysis [,saɪkəʊə'nælɪsɪs] N Psychoanalyse *f*

psychoanalyst [,saɪkəʊ'ænəlɪst] N Psychoanalytiker(in) *m(f)*

psychoanalytic [,saɪkəʊænə'lɪtɪk] ADJ psychoanalytisch

psychobabble ['saɪkəʊ,bæbl] N *(inf)* Psychogeschwätz *nt*

psychodynamic [,saɪkəʊdaɪ'næmɪk] ADJ psychodynamisch

psychodynamics [,saɪkəʊdaɪ'næmɪks] N *sing* Psychodynamik *f*

psychogenic [,saɪkəʊ'dʒenɪk] ADJ *disease, complaint* psychogen, seelisch bedingt

psychokinesis [,saɪkəʊkaɪ'ni:sɪs] N *no pl (Parapsychology)* Psychokinese *f*

psycholinguistic [,saɪkəʊlɪŋ'gwɪstɪk] ADJ psycholinguistisch

psycholinguistics [,saɪkəʊlɪŋ'gwɪstɪks] N *sing* Psycholinguistik *f*

psychological [,saɪkə'lɒdʒɪkəl] ADJ *(= mental)* psychisch; *(= concerning psychology)* psychologisch; **the ~ moment** der psychologisch günstige Augenblick; **~ terror** Psychoterror *m*; **he's not really ill, it's all ~** er ist nicht wirklich krank, das ist alles psychisch bedingt

psychologically [,saɪkə'lɒdʒɪkəlɪ] ADV *(= mentally)* psychisch; *(= concerning psychology)* psychologisch; **he is ~ very unstable** er ist psychisch sehr unausgeglichen; **~ speaking** psychologisch ausgedrückt; **to be ~ prepared for sth** psychisch auf etw vorbereitet sein

psychological: **psychological make-up** N Psyche *f*; **psychological profile** N psychologisches Profil; **psychological profiling** N Ausfertigung *f* eines psychologischen Profils; **psychological thriller** N *(Film, Liter)* psychologischer Thriller, Psychothriller *m*; **psychological warfare** N psychologische Kriegführung

psychologist [saɪ'kɒlədʒɪst] N Psychologe *m*, Psychologin *f*

psychology [saɪ'kɒlədʒɪ] N *(= science)* Psychologie *f*; *(= make-up)* Psyche *f*; **it's all a matter of ~** *(inf)* das ist alles eine Frage der Psychologie

psychometrics [,saɪkəʊ'metrɪks] N *sing* = **psychometry**

psychometry [saɪ'kɒmɪtrɪ] N Psychometrie *f*

psychopath ['saɪkəʊpæθ] N Psychopath(in) *m(f)*

psychopathic [,saɪkəʊ'pæθɪk] ADJ psychopathisch

psychopathy [saɪ'kɒpəθɪ] N *(= Med)* Psychopathie *f*, Geisteskrankheit *f*/-störung *f*

psychosexual [,saɪkəʊ'seksjʊəl] ADJ psychosexuell

psychosis [saɪ'kəʊsɪs] N *pl* **psychoses** [saɪ'kəʊsi:z] Psychose *f*

psychosocial [,saɪkəʊ'səʊʃəl] ADJ psychosozial

psychosociological [,saɪkəʊ,səʊsɪə'lɒdʒɪkəl] ADJ psychosoziologisch

psychosomatic [,saɪkəʊsəʊ'mætɪk] ADJ psychosomatisch; **~ medicine** Psychosomatik *f*, psychosomatische Medizin

psychotherapeutic ADJ, **psychotherapeutically** ADV ['saɪkəʊ,θerə'pju:tɪk, -klɪ] psychotherapeutisch

psychotherapist [,saɪkəʊ'θerəpɪst] N Psychotherapeut(in) *m(f)*

psychotherapy [,saɪkəʊ'θerəpɪ] N Psychotherapie *f*

psychotic [saɪ'kɒtɪk] ADJ psychotisch; **~ illness** Psychose *f* N Psychotiker(in) *m(f)*

psychotropic [,saɪkəʊ'trɒpɪk] ADJ *drug* psychotrop

PT *(old) abbr of* **physical training**

pt *abbr of* **part, pint, payment, point**

PTA *abbr of* **parent-teacher association** Lehrer-Eltern-Ausschuss *m*

ptarmigan ['tɑ:mɪgən] N Schneehuhn *nt*

Pte *(Mil) abbr of* **Private**

pterodactyl [,terəʊ'dæktɪl] N Pterodaktylus *m*

pto *abbr of* **please turn over** bitte wenden, b.w.

Ptolemaic [,tɒlə'meɪɪk] ADJ ptolemäisch; **~ system** ptolemäisches Weltbild *or* (Welt)system

Ptolemy ['tɒləmɪ] N *(astronomer)* Ptolemäus *m*; *(king)* Ptolemaios *m*; *(dynasty)* Ptolemäer *pl*

ptomaine ['təʊmeɪn] N Leichengift *nt*, Ptomain *nt (spec)*

ptomaine poisoning ['təʊmeɪn'pɔɪznɪŋ] N Leichenvergiftung *f*

pub [pʌb] N *(esp Brit)* Kneipe *f (inf)*, Wirtschaft *f*, Lokal *nt*; *(in the country)* Gasthaus *nt*, Wirtshaus *nt*; **let's go to the ~** komm, wir gehen einen trinken *or* wir gehen in die Kneipe *(inf)*; **~ grub/lunch** *in Trinkgaststätten servierter Imbiss*

PUB

Ein pub (Kurzform von **public house**) ist ein Lokal, in dem Wein, Bier, Spirituosen und alkoholfreie Getränke an alle Personen über 18 ausgeschenkt werden. In den Pubs kann man aber nicht nur trinken, sondern sie spielen auch eine bedeutsame Rolle im britischen Gesellschaftsleben. Spiele wie Poolbillard, Darts oder Domino stehen oft zur freien Verfügung. In vielen Pubs werden - allerdings meist nur mittags - Mahlzeiten angeboten, und einige verfügen über eigene Räumlichkeiten oder Biergärten für Familien mit Kindern. Normalerweise sind Pubs von 11 bis 23 Uhr geöffnet, doch werden die Öffnungszeiten jetzt vielfach flexibler gehandhabt.
Einige Pubs sind im Besitz großer Brauereigesellschaften und verkaufen nur eigene Produkte; andere, die sogenannten **free houses**, sind im Privatbesitz und bieten eine große Palette verschiedener Biere an → BEER

pub. *abbr of* **published** herausgegeben, erschienen

pub crawl ['pʌbkrɔːl] N *(esp Brit inf)* Kneipenbummel *m (inf)*; **to go on a ~** einen Kneipenbummel machen *(inf)*, einen Zug durch die Gemeinde machen *(hum inf)*; **we're off on a ~** wir machen die Kneipen unsicher

pube [pjuːb] N *(inf)* **a** *(US)* Pubertierende(r) *mf*; *(= youth)* Jugendliche(r) *mf* **b** *(= pubic hair)* Schamhaar *nt*

puberty ['pjuːbətɪ] N die Pubertät; **to reach the age of ~** ins Pubertätsalter *or* in die Pubertät kommen

pubes ['pjuːbiːz] *pl of* **pubis**

pubescence [pjuː'besəns] N die Pubertät

pubescent [pjuː'besənt] ADJ pubertierend

pubic ['pjuːbɪk] ADJ Scham-; **~ hair** Schamhaar *nt*

pubis ['pjuːbɪs] N *pl* **pubes** Schambein *nt*

public ['pʌblɪk] ADJ *support, pressure, subsidy* öffentlich; *official* öffentlich, staatlich; **to be ~ knowledge** allgemein bekannt sein; **to become ~** publik werden; **at ~ expense** aus öffentlichen Mitteln; **~ pressure** Druck *m* der Öffentlichkeit; **it's rather ~ here** es ist nicht gerade privat hier; **it's a bit too ~ here** hier sind (mir) zu viele Leute; **he is a ~ figure** *or* **person** er ist eine Persönlichkeit des öffentlichen Lebens; **in the ~ eye** im Blickpunkt der Öffentlichkeit; **to make sth ~** etw bekannt geben, etw publik machen; *(officially)* etw öffentlich bekannt machen; **in the ~ interest** im öffentlichen Interesse; **to create ~ awareness** öffentliches Interesse wecken; **to go ~** *(Comm)* in eine Aktiengesellschaft umgewandelt werden
N *sing or pl* Öffentlichkeit *f*; **in ~** in der Öffentlichkeit; *speak also, agree, admit* öffentlich; **our/their** *etc* **~** unser/ihr *etc* Publikum; **the (general) ~** die (breite) Öffentlichkeit; **the viewing ~** das Fernsehpublikum, die Zuschauer *pl*; **the reading/sporting ~** die lesende/sportinteressierte Öffentlichkeit; **the racing ~** die Freunde *pl* des Rennsports; **the great American/British ~** *(iro)* die breite amerikanische/britische Öffentlichkeit

public access channel N öffentlicher Fernsehkanal

PUBLIC ACCESS TELEVISION

Public access television in den USA besteht aus einer Reihe nicht kommerzieller Kabelkanäle, die Programmen von Wohlfahrtsverbänden und anderen gemeinnützigen Vereinen der ortsansässigen Bevölkerung vorbehalten sind. Dazu gehören auch Sendungen von Schulen, Freizeit-Entertainern oder sogar rassistischen Gruppierungen. **Public access television** wurde geschaffen, um lokalen Interessen ein Forum zu bieten und um die Vorherrschaft einiger weniger Lizenzinhaber zu vermeiden. Durch den **Cable Act** von 1984 können die Besitzer von Kabelkanälen durch die Kommunen verpflichtet werden, einen öffentlichen Kabelkanal mit Studio, technischer Ausrüstung und dazugehörigem Personal einzurichten.

public: **public accountant** N *(US)* Wirtschaftsprüfer(in) *m(f)*; **Public Accounts Committee** N *(Brit)* Haushaltsausschuss *m*; **public address system** N Lautsprecheranlage *f*

publican ['pʌblɪkən] N **a** *(Brit)* Gastwirt(in) *m(f)* **b** *(Hist: = tax collector)* Zöllner *m*

public: **public analyst** N Analytiker(in) *m(f)* in der Öffentlichkeitsarbeit; **public assistance** N *(US)* staatliche Fürsorge

publication [,pʌblɪ'keɪʃən] N Veröffentlichung *f*, Publikation *f (geh)*; **when's ~?** wann erscheint das Buch?

publication date N Erscheinungsdatum *nt*, Datum *nt* der Veröffentlichung

public: **public bar** N *(Brit)* ≈ Ausschank *m*, Schänke *f*, Schenke *f*; **public building** N öffentliches Gebäude; **public company** N Aktiengesellschaft *f*; **public convenience** N *(Brit)* öffentliche Toilette; **public corporation** N öffentlich-rechtliche Körperschaft; **public debt** N *(esp US)* Verschuldung *f* der öffentlichen Hand; *(= national debt)* Staatsverschuldung *f*; **public defender** N *(US)* Pflichtverteidiger(in) *m(f)*; **public domain** N **a** *(= land)* Domäne *f* **b** *(= unpatented status)* **this book/invention will soon become ~** das Copyright für dieses Buch/das Patent für diese Erfindung läuft bald ab; **to be in the ~** *(= not private property)* allgemein zugänglich sein; *(= generally known)* allgemein bekannt sein; **public enemy** N Staatsfeind(in) *m(f)*; **he is ~ number one** er ist Staatsfeind Nr. 1; **public enterprise** N öffentliches Unternehmertum; **public examination** N öffentliche Prüfung, der Öffentlichkeit zugängliche Prüfung; **public gallery** N *(in parliament, courtroom)* Besuchertribüne *f*, Besucherplätze *pl*; **public health** N *(= health of the public)* die allgemeine *or* öffentliche Gesundheit, die Volksgesundheit; *(= health care)* das (öffentliche) Gesundheitswesen; **a danger to ~** eine Gefahr für die Volksgesundheit; **public health service** N staatliche Gesundheitsfürsorge; **public holiday** N gesetzlicher Feiertag; **public house** N *(Brit form)* Gaststätte *f*; **public housing** N *(US)* Sozialwohnungen *pl*; **public housing project** N *(US)* sozialer Wohnungsbau; **public inquiry** N öffentliche Untersuchung

publicist ['pʌblɪsɪst] N Publizist(in) *m(f)*

publicity [pʌb'lɪsɪtɪ] N **a** Publicity *f* **b** *(Comm: = advertising, advertisements)* Werbung *f*, Reklame *f*; **we must generate more ~ for this product** wir müssen mehr Werbung für dieses Produkt treiben

publicity: **publicity agency** N Publicity-Agentur *f*; *(Comm)* Werbeagentur *f*; **publicity agent** N Publicitymanager(in) *m(f)*; **publicity campaign** N Publicitykampagne *f*; *(Comm)* Werbekampagne *f*; **publicity department** N Publicity-Abteilung *f*; *(Comm)* Werbeabteilung *f*; **publicity film** N Publicity-Film *m*; *(Comm)* Werbefilm *m*; **publicity gimmick** N Publicity-Gag *m (inf)*; *(Comm)* Werbegag *m (inf)*; **publicity material** N Publicitymaterial *nt*; *(Comm)* Werbematerial *nt*; **publicity-shy** ADJ öffentlichkeitsscheu; **publicity stunt** N Werbegag *m*; **publicity tour** N Werbetour *f*; **to be on a ~** auf Werbetour sein

publicize ['pʌblɪsaɪz] VT **a** *(= make public)* bekannt machen, an die Öffentlichkeit bringen; **I don't want this ~d** ich möchte nicht, dass das publik wird; **I don't ~ the fact** ich will das nicht an die große Glocke hängen *(inf)* **b** *(= get publicity for) film, author, product* Werbung *or* Reklame *or* Publicity machen für; **it has been well ~d** es hat viel Publicity bekommen, dafür ist viel Werbung *or* Reklame gemacht worden

public: **public law** N öffentliches Recht; **Public Lending Right** N Verleihrecht *nt*, Anspruch *m* auf Leihbücherei-Tantiemen; **public life** N öffentliches Leben; **public limited company** N *(Brit)* Aktiengesellschaft *f*

publicly ['pʌblɪklɪ] ADV öffentlich; **~ funded** durch öffentliche Mittel finanziert; **~ accountable** der Öffentlichkeit verantwortlich; **this factory is ~ owned** diese Fabrik ist gesellschaftliches Eigentum; **~ quoted company** ≈ Aktiengesellschaft *f*

public: **public money** N öffentliche Gelder *pl*; **public nuisance** N öffentliches Ärgernis; **to cause a ~** öffentliches Ärgernis erregen; **public opinion** N die öffentliche Meinung; **public opinion poll** N Meinungsumfrage *f*; **public ownership** N staatlicher Besitz; **under** *or* **in ~** in staatlichem Besitz; **to take sth (back) into ~** etw (wieder) verstaatlichen, etw (wieder) in Staatsbesitz überführen; **public property** N **a** *(= land etc)* öffentliches Eigentum, Gemeineigentum *nt* **b** *(fig)* **to be ~** *(person)* im Rampenlicht der Öffentlichkeit stehen; *(private life)* Allgemeingut sein; **intimate aspects of her personal life had been made ~** intime Aspekte ihres Privatlebens waren allgemein bekannt geworden; **public prosecutor** N Staatsanwalt *m*/-anwältin *f*; **public prosecutor's office** N Staatsanwaltschaft *f*; **public purse** N Staatskasse *f*, Staatssäckel *m (inf)*; **Public Record(s) Office** N *(Brit)* Nationalarchiv *nt*, ≈ Bundeszentralarchiv *nt (Ger)*; **public relations** N *pl or sing* Public Relations *pl*, Öffentlichkeitsarbeit *f*; **public relations officer** N Öffentlichkeitsarbeiter(in) *m(f)*; **public room** N Gemeinschaftsraum *m*, öffentlich *or* allgemein zugänglicher Raum; **public school** N *(Brit)* Privatschule *f*, Public School *f*; *(US)* staatliche Schule; **public schoolboy** N *(Brit)* Schüler *m* einer Privatschule; **public schoolgirl** N *(Brit)* Schülerin *f* einer Privatschule; **public sector** N öffentlicher Sektor ADJ *attr* des öffentlichen Sektors; **~ borrowing** Anleihe *f* des öffentlichen Sektors, staatliche Kreditaufnahme; **~ borrowing requirement** Kreditbedarf *m* der öffentlichen Hand; **public securities** N *(Fin)* Staatspapiere *pl*; **public servant** N Arbeitnehmer(in) *m(f)* im öffentlichen Dienst; **public service** N *(Civil Service)* öffentlicher Dienst; *(facility: = water, transport etc)* öffentlicher Dienstleistungsbetrieb; *(= benefit)* Dienst *m* an der Allgemeinheit; **public service broadcasting** N *(Rad)* ≈ öffentlich-rechtlicher Rundfunk; *(TV)* ≈ öffentlich-rechtliches Fernsehen; **public-service television** N ≈ öffentlich-rechtliches Fernsehen; **public service vehicle** N öffentliches Verkehrsmittel; **public speaker** N Redner(in) *m(f)*; **public speaking** N Redenhalten *nt*; **a course in ~** ein Rednerlehrgang *m*; **I'm no good at ~** ich kann nicht in der Öffentlichkeit reden; **public spending** N Ausgaben *pl* der öffentlichen Hand; **public spirit** N Gemeinsinn *m*; **public-spirited** ADJ *act, attitude* gemeinsinnig *(geh)*, von Gemeinschaftssinn zeugend *attr*; **it's not very ~ of them to ...** es spricht nicht gerade für ihren Gemeinschaftssinn, dass sie ...; **public television** N *(US)* öffentliches Fernsehen; **public transport** N öffentlicher Nahverkehr, öffentliche Verkehrsmittel *pl*; **by ~** mit öffentlichen Verkehrsmitteln; **public utility** N öffentlicher Versorgungsbetrieb; **public works** PL staatliche Bauvorhaben *pl*

publish [ˈpʌblɪʃ] **VT** **a** *(= issue)* veröffentlichen; *book, magazine etc* veröffentlichen, herausbringen; **~ed by Collins** bei Collins erschienen; **"published monthly"** „erscheint monatlich"; **"just ~ed"** „neu erschienen"; **"to be ~ed shortly"** „erscheint in Kürze"; **who ~es that book?** in welchem Verlag ist das Buch erschienen?; **they ~ novels** sie verlegen Romane
b *(= make public) news, banns* veröffentlichen, bekannt geben; *decree* herausgeben; *will* eröffnen; **to ~ sth abroad** *(fig)* etw überall herumerzählen
VI **when are we going to ~?** *(book)* wann bringen wir das Buch heraus?; *(research)* wann veröffentlichen *or* publizieren wir die Arbeit?; **he used to ~ with Collins** er hat seine Bücher früher bei Collins herausgebracht *or* veröffentlicht

publisher [ˈpʌblɪʃəˈ] **N** *(= person)* Verleger(in) *m(f)*; *(= firm: also* **publishers***)* Verlag *m*; **who are your ~s?** wer ist Ihr Verleger?

publishing [ˈpʌblɪʃɪŋ] **N** *(= trade)* das Verlagswesen; **~ company** *or* **house** Verlagshaus *nt*; **the decline of children's book ~** der Rückgang bei den Kinderbüchern

publishing business **N** *(= trade)* Verlagsgeschäft *nt*, Verlagsbuchhandel *m*; *(= company)* Verlagshaus *nt*, Verlag *m*

puce [pjuːs] **N** Braunrot *nt* **ADJ** braunrot; *(fig: with rage, shame)* rot

puck¹ [pʌk] **N** *(= goblin)* Kobold *m*, Puck *m*

puck² **N** *(Sport)* Puck *m*

pucker [ˈpʌkəˈ] **N** *(in cloth)* Fältchen *nt* **VT** *(also* **pucker up***) one's lips, mouth* verziehen; *(for kissing)* spitzen; *one's brow* runzeln; *material* Falten machen in *(+acc)* **VI** *(also* **pucker up***)* *(lips)* sich verziehen; *(to be kissed)* sich spitzen; *(brow)* sich runzeln; *(material)* Falten werfen

puckered [ˈpʌkəd] **ADJ** *lips* gespitzt, geschürzt; *brow* gefurcht; *skin* zusammengezogen, höckerig; *scar* hervortretend; *seam* wellig, gewellt

puckish **ADJ**, **puckishly** **ADV** [ˈpʌkɪʃ, -lɪ] koboldhaft

pud [pʊd] **N** *(Brit inf)* = **pudding**

pudding [ˈpʊdɪŋ] **N** *(Brit)* **a** *(= dessert)* Nachspeise *f*; *(= crème caramel, instant whip etc)* Pudding *m*; **what's for ~?** was gibt es als Nachspeise *or* Nachtisch? **b** *(savoury: = meat in suet)* ≈ (Fleisch)pastete *f*; **black ~** ≈ Blutwurst *f*; **white ~** ≈ Presssack *m* **c** *(inf) (= idiot)* Knallkopp *m (inf)*; *(= fatty)* Dickerchen *nt*

pudding: **pudding basin** **N** Puddingform *f*; **pudding-basin haircut** **N** Topfschnitt *m (inf)*; **pudding club** **N** **to be in the ~** *(inf)* einen dicken Bauch haben *(inf)*; **pudding-face** **N** *(inf)* Vollmondgesicht *nt (inf)*; **pudding-head** **N** *(inf)* Knallkopp *m (inf)*; **pudding stone** **N** Puddingstein *m*

puddle [ˈpʌdl] **N** Pfütze *f (also euph)*

pudendum [pjuːˈdendəm] **N** *pl* **pudenda** [pjuːˈdendə] **a** *(of woman)* Vulva *f* **b** **pudenda** **PL** *(of either sex)* primäre Geschlechtsmerkmale *pl*, Scham *f (geh)*

pudgy [ˈpʌdʒɪ] **ADJ** *(+er)* = **podgy**

pueblo [ˈpwebləʊ] **N** **a** *(= American Indian settlement)* Pueblo *m* **b** *(= town in Spanish-speaking America)* (Klein)stadt *f*

puerile [ˈpjʊəraɪl] **ADJ** infantil

puerility [pjʊəˈrɪlɪtɪ] **N** Infantilität *f*

puerperal fever [pjuːˈɜːpərəlˈfiːvəˈ] **N** Kindbettfieber *nt*, Puerperalfieber *nt (spec)*

Puerto Rican [ˈpwɜːtəʊˈriːkən] **ADJ** puerto-ricanisch **N** *(= person)* Puerto-Ricaner(in) *m(f)*

Puerto Rico [ˈpwɜːtəʊˈriːkəʊ] **N** Puerto Rico *nt*

puff [pʌf] **N** **a** *(of breathing, of engine)* Schnaufen *nt no pl*; *(of horse)* Schnauben *nt no pl*; *(inf: = breath)* Puste *f (inf)*; *(on cigarette etc)* Zug *m (at, of* an *+dat)*; **a ~ of air/wind** ein Luft-/ /Windstoß *m*; **a ~ of smoke** eine Rauchwolke; **our hopes vanished in a ~ of smoke** unsere Hoffnungen lösten sich in nichts auf; **he blew out the candles with** *or* **in one ~** er blies die Kerzen auf einmal aus; **to be out of ~** *(Brit inf)* außer Puste sein *(inf)*
b *(= powder puff)* Quaste *f*
c *(Cook)* **cream ~** Windbeutel *m*; **jam ~** Blätterteigteilchen *nt* mit Marmelade
VT **a** *smoke* ausstoßen; *(person)* blasen; *cigarette, cigar* paffen *(inf)*; **to ~ sth away** etw wegblasen; **stop ~ing smoke in my face** blas mir nicht dauernd den Rauch ins Gesicht
b *(Sew)* bauschen; **~ed sleeves** Puffärmel *pl*
c *(Cook)* **to ~ rice** Puffreis *m* herstellen
VI *(person, train)* schnaufen; *(horse)* schnauben; *(wind)* blasen; *(chimney, smoke)* qualmen; **he was ~ing and panting** er pustete und schnaufte; **the train ~ed into the station** der Zug fuhr schnaufend in den Bahnhof ein; **to ~ (away) at** *or* **on a cigar** an einer Zigarre paffen

▸ **puff out** **VT** *sep* **a** *(= expand) chest* herausstrecken, herausdrücken; *cheeks* aufblasen; *feathers* (auf)plustern; *sail* blähen **b** *(= emit) air, smoke* ausstoßen; *words* hervorstoßen **c** *(= blow out)* auspusten **d** *(inf) always separate (= make out of breath)* außer Puste bringen *(inf)*

▸ **puff up** **VT** *sep* **a** *feathers* (auf)plustern; *(= blow up)* aufblasen **b** *(fig)* **to be puffed up** aufgeblasen sein; **to be puffed up with pride** ganz aufgeblasen sein; **to puff oneself up** sich aufblasen **VI** **a** *(= swell: eyes, face etc)* anschwellen **b** **he came puffing up (to me)** er kam angeschnauft

puff: **puff adder** **N** Puffotter *f*; **puffball** [ˈpʌfbɔːl] **N** *(Bot)* Bovist *m*

puffed [pʌft] **ADJ** *(inf)* außer Puste *(inf)*

puffed-up [ˈpʌftˈʌp] **ADJ** *face* aufgedunsen

puffer [ˈpʌfəˈ] **N** *(baby-talk: = train)* Puffpuff *f (baby-talk)*

puffin [ˈpʌfɪn] **N** Papageientaucher *m*, Lund *m*

puffin crossing **N** *(Brit; for pedestrians)* sensorgesteuerter Ampelübergang

puffiness [ˈpʌfɪnɪs] **N** Verschwollenheit *f*

puff: **puff pastry**, *(US)* **puff paste** **N** Blätterteig *m*; **puff-puff** **N** *(baby-talk) (= train)* Puffpuff *f (baby-talk)*; *(= sound)* Puffpuff *nt*; **puff sleeve** **N** Puffärmel *m*

puffy [ˈpʌfɪ] **ADJ** *(+er)* **a** *(= swollen)* geschwollen; *face, eyes also* verschwollen; *(from crying)* verquollen **b** *(= voluminous) cloud* bauschig; **~ sleeve** Puffärmel *m*

pug [pʌg] **N** *(also* **pug dog***)* Mops *m*

pugilism [ˈpjuːdʒɪlɪzəm] **N** *(form)* Faustkampf *m*

pugilist [ˈpjuːdʒɪlɪst] **N** *(form)* Faustkämpfer(in) *m(f)*

pugnacious [pʌgˈneɪʃəs] **ADJ** kampfeslustig; *(verbally)* streitsüchtig; *expression, remark* herausfordernd; *support, defence* hartnäckig; *campaign* aggressiv

pugnaciously [pʌgˈneɪʃəslɪ] **ADV** *behave* kampf(es)lustig; *(verbally)* streitsüchtig; *say, remark* herausfordernd; *support, defend* hartnäckig

pugnacity [pʌgˈnæsɪtɪ] **N** Kampfeslust *f*; *(verbal)* Streitsüchtigkeit *f*; *(of expression, remark)* Herausforderung *f (of* in *+dat)*; *(of support, defence)* Hartnäckigkeit *f*; *(of campaign)* Aggressivität *f*; **the ~ of his approach** die Aggressivität seiner Vorgehensweise

pug: **pug nose** **N** Knollennase *f*; **pug-nosed** **ADJ** knollennasig

puke [pjuːk] *(sl)* **VI** kotzen *(inf)*, spucken *(inf)*; **to ~ all over sth** *(inf)* etw vollkotzen *(sl)*; **he makes me ~** er kotzt mich an *(sl)* **VT** kotzen *(inf)*, spucken *(inf)* **N** Kotze *f (vulg)*

▸ **puke up** **VI** *(inf)* kotzen *(sl)*, spucken *(inf)*

pukey [ˈpjuːkɪ] **ADJ** *(inf) colour* kackig *(sl)*, eklig *(inf)*

pukka, **pucka** [ˈpʌkə] **ADJ** *(inf) (= genuine)* echt; *(= proper)* anständig *(inf)*; *(= excellent)* eins a *(inf)*, erstklassig; *(= posh, upper-class)* vornehm; **~ sahib** Gentleman *m*

pulchritude [ˈpʌlkrɪtjuːd] **N** *(liter)* Schönheit *f*

PULITZER PRIZES

Die Pulitzer-Preise sind die renommiertesten Auszeichnungen, die seit 1917 jedes Jahr in den USA für herausragende Leistungen in Journalismus, Literatur, Drama und Musikkomposition vergeben werden. In den vierzehn Kategorien im Bereich Journalismus werden Preise z. B. für Reportagen oder Kritiken vergeben. Im Bereich Literatur gibt es sechs Kategorien, darunter Belletristik, Lyrik und Drama. Die Auszeichnungen sind nach dem amerikanischen Pressemagnaten Joseph Pulitzer (1847 - 1911) benannt, der das Preisgeld in seinem Testament stiftete.

pull [pʊl] **N** **a** *(= tug)* Ziehen *nt*; *(short)* Ruck *m*; *(lit, fig: = attraction)* Anziehungskraft *f*; *(of current)* Sog *m*; **he gave her/the rope a ~** er zog sie/am Seil; **I felt a ~ at my sleeve** ich spürte, wie mich jemand am Ärmel zog; **the ~ of family ties brought him home again** familiäre Bande zogen ihn wieder nach Hause; **to be on the ~** *(Brit inf)* auf Mädchen/Männer aus sein
b *(= uphill journey)* Anstieg *m*
c *(inf: = influence)* Beziehungen *pl (with* zu*)*; **she has some ~ with the manager** sie kann beim Chef was erreichen *(inf)*; **he has ~ in the right places** er hat an den richtigen Stellen seine Leute sitzen
d *(at pipe, beer)* Zug *m*; **he took a ~ at his cigar** er zog an seiner Zigarre; **he took a ~ at his glass** er nahm einen Schluck aus seinem Glas
e *(Typ: = proof)* Abzug *m*
VT **a** *(= draw, drag)* ziehen; **he ~ed the dog behind him** er zog den Hund hinter sich *(dat)* her; **to ~ a door shut** eine Tür zuziehen; **he ~ed her toward(s) him** er zog sie an sich *(acc)*
b *(= tug) handle, rope, bell* ziehen an *(+dat)*; *boat* rudern; **he ~ed her hair** er zog sie an den Haaren; **to ~ sth to pieces** *(lit)* etw zerreißen, etw in Stücke reißen; *(fig: = criticize)* etw verreißen; **to ~ sb's leg** *(fig inf)* jdn auf den Arm nehmen *(inf)*; **~ the other one(, it's got bells on)** *(Brit inf)* das glaubst du ja selber nicht!, das kannst du deiner Großmutter erzählen! *(inf)*; **she was the one ~ing the strings** sie war es, die alle Fäden in der Hand hielt; **to ~ rank (on sb)** (jdm gegenüber) den Vorgesetzten herauskehren; **to ~ one's punches** *(fig)* sich zurückhalten; **when it came to criticizing other people he didn't ~ his** *or* **any punches** wenn es darum ging, andere zu kritisieren, zog er ganz schön vom Leder *(inf)*
c *(= extract, draw out) tooth, cork* (heraus)ziehen; *gun, knife* ziehen; *weeds, lettuce* herausziehen; *beer* zapfen; **to ~ a gun on sb** jdn mit der Pistole bedrohen
d *(= strain) muscle* sich *(dat)* zerren; *(= tear) thread*, ziehen
e *(= attract) crowd* anziehen; *(Brit inf: sexually)* rumkriegen *(inf)*; **Tim ~ed last night** Tim hat gestern Nacht eine Frau vernascht *(inf)*; *(= had sex)* Tim hatte gestern Nacht Sex; **a sports car always ~s the girls** *(inf)* mit einem Sportwagen kommt man leichter an die Mädchen ran *(inf)*
f *(inf: = carry out, do) deal* durchziehen *(inf)*; *(criminal) job* drehen *(inf)*; **what are you trying to ~?** *(inf)* was heckst du wieder aus? *(inf)*; **to ~ a stunt** Geschichten machen
g *(= cancel) TV programme, concert etc* absagen
h *(Typ)* **to ~ a proof** einen Abzug machen
i *(Golf, Cricket, Baseball)* verziehen, *auf die der Schlaghand entgegengesetzte Seite schlagen*
VI **a** *(= draw)* ziehen *(on, at* an *+dat)*; **to ~ to the left/right** *(car, brakes)* nach links/rechts ziehen; **the car/engine isn't ~ing very well** der Wagen/Motor zieht nicht richtig; **to ~ on one's cigarette** an seiner Zigarette ziehen; **to ~ for sb/sth** *(US inf)* jdn/etw unterstützen
b *(= move: train, car etc)* fahren; **the car ~ed into the driveway** der Wagen fuhr in die Einfahrt; **he ~ed across to the left-hand lane** er wechselte auf die linke Spur über; **he ~ed into the next lay-by** er fuhr auf den nächsten Halteplatz; **he ~ed into the kerb/the side of the road** er fuhr an den Bordstein heran/an den Straßenrand; **to ~ alongside** seitlich heranfahren; *(Naut)* längsseits kommen; **to ~ off the road** am Straßenrand anhalten; **the oarsmen ~ed for** *or* **toward(s) the shore** die Ruderer

hielten auf das Ufer zu
c *(Brit inf: sexually)* jemanden rumkriegen *(inf)*

▶ **pull about** *(Brit)* or **around** VT *sep (= handle roughly) toy etc* herumzerren; *person* herumzerren an *(+dat)*

▶ **pull ahead** VI *(in race, poll, contest)* Vorsprung gewinnen; **to pull ahead of sb/sth** *(in race etc)* einen Vorsprung vor jdm/etw gewinnen; *(in poll, contest)* jdm/einer Sache *(dat)* davonziehen

▶ **pull apart** **VT** *sep* **a** *(= separate)* auseinanderziehen; *sheets of paper, fighting people* trennen; *radio etc* auseinandernehmen **b** *(fig inf) (= search thoroughly)* auseinandernehmen *(inf)*; *(= criticize)* verreißen **VI** *(through design)* sich auseinandernehmen lassen; *(= break)* auseinandergehen

▶ **pull away** **VT** *sep* wegziehen; **she pulled it away from him** sie zog es von ihm weg; *(from his hands)* sie zog es ihm aus den Händen **VI** *(= move off)* wegfahren; *(ship)* ablegen; **the car/runner pulled away from the others** der Wagen/Läufer setzte sich (von den anderen) ab

▶ **pull back** **VT** *sep* zurückziehen **VI** *(lit)* sich zurückziehen; **to pull back (from doing sth)** *(fig)* einen Rückzieher machen (und etw nicht tun) *(inf)*; **he pulled back from confrontation** er zog sich aus der Konfrontation zurück

▶ **pull down** **VT** *sep* **a** *(= move down)* herunterziehen; **he pulled his hat down over his eyes** er zog sich *(dat)* den Hut über die Augen **b** *(= demolish) buildings* abreißen **c** *(= weaken, make worse) (illness) person* mitnehmen; *(exam, question) marks* herunterdrücken; *(failure, adverse conditions) company etc* mitnehmen; *profits, results* herunterdrücken; **this bad mark pulled you down** diese schlechte Zensur hat deinen Notenschnitt (herunter)gedrückt **d** *(US inf: = earn)* reinholen *(inf)*, machen *(inf)* **VI** *(blind etc)* sich herunterziehen lassen

▶ **pull in** **VT** *sep* **a** *claws, rope, stomach etc* einziehen; *(into room, swimming pool etc)* hineinziehen; **to pull sb/sth in(to) sth** jdn/etw in etw *(acc)* ziehen **b** *(= rein in) horse* zügeln **c** *(= attract) crowds* anziehen; **to ~ the punters** *(Brit inf)* Kundschaft anlocken **d** *(inf: = earn)* kassieren *(inf)* **e** *(inf: = take into custody)* einkassieren *(inf)* **VI** **a** *(claws)* sich einziehen lassen **b** *(into station, harbour, pier)* einfahren, einlaufen *(into in +acc)*; *(into garage, driveway)* hineinfahren *(into in +acc)*; *(= stop, park)* anhalten

▶ **pull off** VT *sep* **a** *wrapping paper* abziehen; *cover* abnehmen; *(violently)* abreißen; *clothes, pullover, shoes* ausziehen; *gloves, tights* ausziehen, abstreifen; **he pulled his clothes off and jumped into the water** er riss sich *(dat)* die Kleider vom Leib und sprang ins Wasser; **he quickly pulled his/her coat off** er zog sich/ihr schnell den Mantel aus **b** *(inf: = succeed in)* schaffen *(inf)*; *deal, coup* zuwege bringen *(inf)*; *order* an Land ziehen *(inf)*; *bank job, burglary* drehen *(inf)*

▶ **pull on** VT *sep coat etc* sich *(dat)* überziehen; *hat* aufsetzen

▶ **pull out** **VT** *sep* **a** *(= extract) (of* aus) herausziehen; *tooth* ziehen; *page* heraustrennen; **to be pulling one's hair out** *(fig)* sich *(dat)* die Haare ausreißen; **to pull the rug out from under sb** *(fig)* jdm den Boden unter den Füßen wegziehen; **to pull a rabbit out of the hat** *(fig)* etwas aus dem Hut ziehen
b *(= elongate) table, dough* ausziehen
c *(= withdraw)* zurückziehen; *troops* abziehen
VI **a** *(= come out, become detached)* sich herausziehen lassen; *(pages)* sich heraustrennen lassen
b *(= elongate)* sich ausziehen lassen
c *(= withdraw)* aussteigen (of aus) *(inf)*; *(troops)* abziehen
d *(= leave: train etc)* herausfahren (of aus); **to pull out of recession** *(economy)* aus der Rezession kommen
e *(= move on)* herausfahren; **the car/driver pulled out from behind the lorry** der Wagen/Fahrer scherte hinter dem Lastwagen aus; **the boat pulled out into midstream** das Boot fuhr in die Flussmitte hinaus

▶ **pull over** **VT** *sep* **a** *(= move over)* herüberziehen *(prep obj* über *+acc)* **b** *(= topple)* umreißen; **he pulled the whole bookcase over on top of him** er hat das ganze Bücherregal mit sich gerissen **c** *(= move over)* **the police pulled him over** die Polizei stoppte ihn am Straßenrand **VI** *(car, driver)* zur Seite fahren

▶ **pull round** *(esp Brit)* **VT** **a** *sep (= turn round)* herumdrehen **b** *(= bring back to consciousness)* wieder zu sich bringen; *(= help recover)* durchbringen **VI** *(= regain consciousness)* wieder zu sich kommen; *(= recover)* durchkommen

▶ **pull through** **VT** *sep (lit)* durchziehen; *(fig: = help recover, help succeed)* durchbringen; **to pull sb/sth through sth** *(lit)* jdn/etw durch etw ziehen; **to pull sb through a difficult period** jdm helfen, eine schwierige Zeit zu überstehen **VI** *(fig: = recover)* durchkommen; **to pull through sth** *(fig)* etw überstehen

▶ **pull together** **VI** *(lit)* gemeinsam ziehen; *(= row jointly)* im gleichen Takt rudern; *(fig: = cooperate)* an einem *or* am gleichen Strang ziehen **VT** *sep (fig) political party, members of family etc* zusammenschweißen; *novel etc* in einen Zusammenhang bringen; **let me now pull together the threads of my argument** lassen Sie mich nunmehr meine Argumentation zusammenfassen **VR** sich zusammenreißen

▶ **pull under** VT *sep swimmer* nach unten ziehen

▶ **pull up** **VT** *sep* **a** *(= raise by pulling)* hochziehen → **sock**[1]
b *(= uproot)* herausreißen; **to pull up one's roots, to pull up stakes** *(esp US)* alles aufgeben
c *(= move closer) chair* heranrücken
d *(= stop)* anhalten
e *(Brit: = reprimand) (for behaviour)* zurechtweisen; *(for pronunciation, grammar)* korrigieren; **he pulled me up about that** er hat mich deswegen zurechtgewiesen/korrigiert
f *(= improve) marks* verbessern; **that good mark pulled you up a bit** durch diese gute Note hast du ein wenig aufgeholt
VI **a** *(= stop)* anhalten
b *(= improve one's position)* aufholen; **to pull up with sb/sth** jdn/etw einholen, mit jdm/etw gleichziehen *(inf)*

pull: **pullback** N *(Mil)* Abzug *m*; **pull cord** N Zugleine *f*/-schnur *f*; **pull date** N *(US: = eat-by date)* (Mindest)haltbarkeitsdatum *nt*; **pull-down** [ˈpʊldaʊn] ADJ *bed* Klapp-; **~ seat** Klappsitz *m*; **~ menu** *(Comput)* Pull-down-Menü *nt*

pullet [ˈpʊlɪt] N junges Huhn, Hühnchen *nt*

pulley [ˈpʊlɪ] N *(= wheel)* Rolle *f*; *(= block)* Flaschenzug *m*; *(= hospital apparatus)* Streckapparat *m*

pull-in [ˈpʊlɪn] N *(Brit) (= lay-by)* Halteplatz *m*; *(= café)* Raststätte *f*

Pullman® [ˈpʊlmən] N *(= Pullman car)* Pullmanwagen *m*; *(= Pullman train)* Pullman® *m*

pull: **pull-out** **N** **a** *(= withdrawal)* Abzug *m* **b** *(= supplement)* heraustrennbarer Teil **ATTR** *supplement* heraustrennbar; *table leaf, seat* ausziehbar; **pullover** N Pullover *m*; **pull switch** N *(Elec)* Zugschalter *m*; **pull-up** N *(Sport)* Klimmzug *m*

pulmonary [ˈpʌlmənərɪ] ADJ Lungen-; **~ disease** Lungenkrankheit *f*; **~ hospital** Lungenklinik *f*

pulmonary artery N Lungenarterie *f*

pulp [pʌlp] **N** **a** *(= soft mass, paper pulp, wood pulp)* Brei *m*; **to reduce sth to ~** etw in Brei auflösen; *wood etc (for paper)* etw zu einem Brei verarbeiten; **to beat sb to a ~** *(inf)* jdn zu Brei schlagen *(inf)*, Matsch aus jdm machen *(sl)*; **crushed to (a) ~** zu Brei zerquetscht **b** *(of plant stem)* Mark *nt*; *(of fruit, vegetable)* Fruchtfleisch *nt*; *(of tooth)* Zahnmark *nt*, Pulpa *f (spec)* **c** *(pej: also* **pulp magazine***)* Schundmagazin *nt* **VT** *fruit, vegetables* zerdrücken; *paper, book* einstampfen; *wood* zu Brei verarbeiten

pulpboard [ˈpʌlpbɔːd] N Zellstoffpappe *f*

pulpit [ˈpʊlpɪt] N Kanzel *f*

pulpy [ˈpʌlpɪ] ADJ *(+er)* **a** breiig **b** *(inf: = trashy) book* trivial, billig; *newspaper* billig, minderwertig; **~ magazine** Schundmagazin *nt*, Schundblatt *nt*

pulsar [ˈpʌlsəˈ] N Pulsar *m*

pulsate [pʌlˈseɪt] VI *(lit, fig)* pulsieren; *(head, heart)* klopfen, pochen; *(voice, building)* beben; *(music)* rhythmisch klingen; **the whole school ~d with excitement** die ganze Schule fieberte vor Aufregung; **the whole town was pulsating with life** die ganze Stadt war von pulsierendem Leben erfüllt

pulsation [pʌlˈseɪʃən] N *(= pulsating)* Pulsieren *nt*; *(of head, heart)* Klopfen *nt*, Pochen *nt*; *(one beat)* Schwingung *f*; *(of heart, in artery)* Schlag *m*

pulse[1] [pʌls] **N** *(Anat)* Puls *m*; *(Phys)* Impuls *m*; *(fig: of drums, music)* Rhythmus *m*; **~ beat** Pulsschlag *m*; **to feel** *or* **take sb's ~** jdm den Puls fühlen; **he felt the ~ of life in his veins** er spürte, wie das Leben in seinen Adern pulsierte; **he still has** *or* **keeps his finger on the ~ of economic affairs** er hat in Wirtschaftsfragen immer noch den Finger am Puls der Zeit **VI** pulsieren; *(machines)* stampfen

pulse[2] N *(Bot, Cook)* Hülsenfrucht *f*

pulse rate N *(Anat)* Pulszahl *f*, Puls *m*

pulverization [ˌpʌlvəraɪˈzeɪʃən] N Pulverisierung *f*

pulverize [ˈpʌlvəraɪz] VT pulverisieren; *(fig inf) (= beat up)* Kleinholz machen aus *(inf)*; *(= defeat)* fertigmachen *(inf)*

puma [ˈpjuːmə] N Puma *m*

pumice (stone) [ˈpʌmɪs(ˌstəʊn)] N Bimsstein *m*

pummel [ˈpʌml] VT eintrommeln auf *(+acc)*

pump[1] [pʌmp] **N** Pumpe *f*
VT pumpen; *stomach* auspumpen; *pedal* mehrmals treten; **to ~ oil/water out of sth** Öl/Wasser aus etw (heraus)pumpen; **to ~ sth dry** etw leer pumpen; **to ~ bullets into sb** jdn mit Blei vollpumpen *(inf)*; **to ~ sb full of drugs** jdn mit Drogen vollpumpen; **he ~ed my arm up and down** er riss meinen Arm wie einen Pumpenschwengel auf und ab; **to ~ money into sth** Geld in etw *(acc)* hineinpumpen; **to ~ sb (for information)** jdn aushorchen *or* löchern *(inf)*; **to ~ information out of sb** Informationen aus jdm herausholen; **to ~ iron** *(inf)* Gewichte stemmen
VI **a** pumpen; *(water, blood)* herausschießen; **the piston ~ed up and down** der Kolben ging auf und ab
b *(Brit: music, rhythm)* hämmern, stampfen; **she likes to drive with the music ~ing** sie dreht die Musik im Auto gern voll auf
c *(Brit sl: = have sex)* poppen *(sl)*

▶ **pump in** VT *sep (lit, fig)* hineinpumpen

▶ **pump out** VT *sep liquid, air* herauspumpen; *boat, cellar* auspumpen, leer pumpen; *stomach* auspumpen

▶ **pump up** VT *sep* **a** *(= inflate) tyre etc* aufpumpen; *prices, profits* hochtreiben **b** *liquid* hochpumpen **c** *(Brit inf: = turn up) music* lauter stellen; **pump up the tunes!** dreh lauter!

pump[2] N *(= dancing shoe)* Lackschuh *m*; *(= ballet shoe)* Ballettschuh *m*; *(esp Brit: = gym shoe)* Turnschuh *m*; *(US: = court shoe)* Pumps *m*

pump-action shotgun N Pump-Gun *f*

pump attendant N Tankwart(in) *m(f)*

pumpernickel [ˈpʌmpənɪkl] N Pumpernickel *m*

pumping station [ˈpʌmpɪŋˌsteɪʃən] N Pumpwerk *nt*, Pumpstation *f*; *(on a pipeline)* Förderpumpe *f*

pumpkin [ˈpʌmpkɪn] N Kürbis *m*

pump: **pump priming** [ˈpʌmpˌpraɪmɪŋ] N *(fig)* Ankurbelung *f* der Wirtschaft; **pump room** [ˈpʌmpruːm] N Trinkhalle *f*, Brunnenhaus *nt*

pun [pʌn] **N** Wortspiel *nt* **VI** Wortspiele machen

Punch [pʌntʃ] N *(Brit)* Kasper *m*, Kasperle *nt*; **~ and Judy show** Kasper(le)theater *nt*; **to be (as) pleased as ~** *(inf)* sich wie ein Schneekönig freuen *(inf)*

punch[1] [pʌntʃ] N a *(= blow)* Schlag *m* b *no pl (fig: = vigour)* Schwung *m* → **pack, pull** VT boxen; **I wanted to ~ his face** *or* **~ him in the face when he said that** als er das sagte, hätte ich ihn *or* ihm am liebsten ins Gesicht geschlagen; **to ~ the air** die geballte Faust nach oben strecken VI boxen

punch[2] N *(for punching holes)* Locher *m*; *(in tickets)* Lochzange *f*; *(in leather)* Lochstanzer *m*; *(for stamping metal, leather etc)* Prägestempel *m* VT *ticket etc* lochen; *leather, metal* stanzen; *holes* stechen, stanzen; *(= stamp) metal, pattern* prägen; *(US) cattle* hüten; **to ~ the card** *(of time clock)* die Stechkarte stempeln

▶ **punch in** VT *sep* a **I'll punch your face in** *(inf)* ich hau dir eine in die Fresse *(vulg) or* aufs Maul *(inf)* b *(Comput) data* tasten, tippen *(inf)*

▶ **punch out** VT *sep* ausstechen, ausstanzen; *pattern etc* prägen

punch[3] N *(= drink)* Bowle *f*; *(hot)* Punsch *m*

punch: **punchbag** N Sandsack *m*; **punchball** N Punchingball *m*; *(round)* Lederball *m*; **punchbowl** N Bowle *f*; **punch card** N Lochkarte *f*; **punch-drunk** ADJ *(Boxing)* benommen; *(fig)* durcheinander *pred*

Punchinello [pʌntʃɪˈneləʊ] N Pulcinella *f*; *(= clown)* Hanswurst *m*

punching: **punching bag** [ˈpʌntʃɪŋ,bæg] N *(US)* = **punchbag**; **punching power** [ˈpʌntʃɪŋ,paʊəˈ] *(Boxing)* Schlagkraft *f*

punch: **punch line** N Pointe *f*; **punch operator** N Locher(in) *m(f)*; **punch power** N *(Boxing)* Schlagkraft *f*; **punch tape** N Lochstreifen *m*; **punch-up** N *(Brit inf)* Schlägerei *f*

punchy [ˈpʌntʃɪ] ADJ *(+er) (inf)* a *sentence, speech etc* schwungvoll *(inf)* b *(Boxing)* benommen; *(fig: = confused)* benommen, durcheinander *pred*

punctilious [pʌŋkˈtɪlɪəs] ADJ *(regarding etiquette)* korrekt; *(= scrupulous, fastidious)* sehr *or* peinlich genau; **she is always ~ about arriving in time** sie nimmt es mit der Pünktlichkeit sehr genau; **he is always ~ about writing to thank his host** er achtet immer darauf, dass er sich bei seinem Gastgeber schriftlich bedankt

punctiliously [pʌŋkˈtɪlɪəslɪ] ADV korrekt; *(= scrupulously, fastidiously) (+vb)* peinlich genau; *(+adj)* peinlich; *correct* höchst; **he was ~ polite to his mother-in-law** er war äußerst korrekt gegenüber seiner Schwiegermutter

punctiliousness [pʌŋkˈtɪlɪəsnɪs] N peinliche Genauigkeit *or* Korrektheit

punctual [ˈpʌŋktjʊəl] ADJ pünktlich; **to be ~** pünktlich kommen

punctuality [,pʌŋktjʊˈælɪtɪ] N Pünktlichkeit *f*

punctually [ˈpʌŋktjʊəlɪ] ADV pünktlich

punctuate [ˈpʌŋktjʊeɪt] VT a *(Gram)* mit Satzzeichen versehen, interpunktieren b *(= intersperse)* unterbrechen; **he ~d his talk with jokes** er spickte seine Rede mit Witzen; **a long happy life, ~d with** *or* **by short spells of sadness** ein langes glückliches Leben, das zeitweise von traurigen Augenblicken überschattet war c *(= emphasize)* betonen VI Satzzeichen setzen

punctuation [,pʌŋktjʊˈeɪʃən] N Zeichensetzung *f*, Interpunktion *f*; **~ mark** Satzzeichen *nt*, Interpunktionszeichen *nt*

puncture [ˈpʌŋktʃəˈ] N *(in tyre, balloon etc)* Loch *nt*; *(in skin)* (Ein)stich *m*; *(= flat tyre)* Reifenpanne *f*, Platte(r) *m (inf)* VT stechen in *(+acc)*; *membrane* durchstechen; *blister* aufstechen; *tyre, balloon* Löcher/ein Loch machen in *(+acc)*; *pride* einen Stich versetzen *(+dat)*; **a ~d lung** eine perforierte Lunge VI *(tyre)* einen Platten haben *(inf)*; *(balloon)* platzen; **my front tyre ~d** ich hatte einen Platten am Vorderrad

puncture: **puncture needle** N *(Med)* Punktionsnadel *f*; **punctureproof** [ˈpʌŋktʃə,pruːf] ADJ *tyre* nagel-/pannensicher; *(Elec)* durchschlagsicher

pundit [ˈpʌndɪt] N *(lit)* Pandit *m*; *(fig)* Experte *m*, Expertin *f*

pungency [ˈpʌndʒənsɪ] N *(lit, fig)* Schärfe *f*

pungent [ˈpʌndʒənt] ADJ *(lit, fig)* scharf; *smell also* stechend, durchdringend; **to have a ~ style of writing** eine spitze *or* scharfe Feder führen

pungently [ˈpʌndʒəntlɪ] ADV *(lit, fig)* scharf; *smell also* stechend, durchdringend

Punic [ˈpjuːnɪk] ADJ punisch; **the ~ Wars** die Punischen Kriege

puniness [ˈpjuːnɪnɪs] N Schwächlichkeit *f*, Mickerigkeit *f (pej)*

punish [ˈpʌnɪʃ] VT a *person* bestrafen, strafen *(geh)*; *offence* bestrafen; **he was ~ed by a fine** er wurde mit einer Geldstrafe belegt; **he has been ~ed enough** er ist genug bestraft worden; *(= has suffered enough)* er ist gestraft genug; **our team was ~ed for making that mistake** unsere Mannschaft musste für diesen Fehler büßen; **the other team ~ed us for that mistake** die andere Mannschaft ließ uns für diesen Fehler büßen b *(fig inf: = drive hard, treat roughly)* strapazieren; *horses, oneself* schinden; *opponent* vorführen *(inf)*, zusetzen *(+dat)*

punishable [ˈpʌnɪʃəbl] ADJ strafbar; **this offence** *(Brit) or* **offense** *(US)* **is ~ by 2 years' imprisonment** dieses Verbrechen wird mit 2 Jahren Gefängnis bestraft; **it is a ~ offence** *(Brit) or* **offense** *(US)* es ist strafbar

punishing [ˈpʌnɪʃɪŋ] ADJ *blow* hart; *routine, pace* strapaziös, tödlich; *workload* strapaziös, erdrückend; **to get** *or* **take some ~ treatment** *(cars, furniture)* strapaziert werden; *(Sport)* vorgeführt werden *(inf)*, eins aufs Dach bekommen *(inf)* N **to take a ~** *(inf: team, boxer etc)* vorgeführt werden *(inf)*; **he got a real ~ from his opponent** *(inf)* er wurde von seinem Gegner regelrecht vorgeführt *(inf)*; **his self-confidence took a ~** sein Selbstbewusstsein litt darunter *or* bekam einen Knacks *(inf)*

punishment [ˈpʌnɪʃmənt] N a *(= penalty)* Strafe *f*; *(= punishing)* Bestrafung *f*; **you know the ~ for such offences** Sie wissen, welche Strafe darauf steht; **to take one's ~** seine Strafe akzeptieren; **~ beating** Bestrafungsaktion *f* b *(fig inf)* **to take a lot of ~** *(car, furniture etc)* stark strapaziert werden; *(Sport)* vorgeführt werden *(inf)*

punitive [ˈpjuːnɪtɪv] ADJ Straf-; *sanctions* strafend; *strike* vergeltend; *(fig) taxation, fines etc* extrem (hoch); **~ expedition** Strafexpedition *f*; **~ measures** Strafmaßnahmen *pl*; **~ sentence** Strafurteil *nt*; **to take ~ action against sb** eine Strafaktion gegen jdn führen

punitive damages PL *(Jur)* Schadensersatz *m*

Punjab [ˈpʌndʒɑːb] N **the ~** das Pandschab

Punjabi [pʌnˈdʒɑːbɪ] ADJ *state, capital* des Pandschab, pandschabisch N a Pandschabi *mf* b *(Ling)* Pandschabi *nt*

punk [pʌŋk] N a *(= person: also* **punk rocker***)* Punker(in), Punkrocker(in) *m(f)*; *(= music: also* **punk rock***)* → **punk rock** *(= culture)* Punk *m* b *(US inf: = hoodlum)* Ganove *m (inf)* c *(dated inf: = nonsense)* Stuss *m (inf)* ADJ Punk-

punk rock N Punkrock *m*

punnet [ˈpʌnɪt] N *(Brit)* Körbchen *nt*

punster [ˈpʌnstəˈ] N **he is a brilliant ~** er versteht es hervorragend, Wortspiele zu machen

punt[1] [pʌnt] *(esp Brit)* N *(= boat)* Stechkahn *m*, Stocherkahn *m* VI staken, stochern; *(= go by punt)* im Stechkahn fahren; **to go ~ing** Stechkahn fahren VT staken; *(= take by punt)* im Stechkahn fahren

punt[2] N Schuss *m* (aus der Hand); **he gave the ball a ~** er schoss den Ball aus der Hand VT **to ~ the ball** den Ball aus der Hand schießen; **he ~ed the ball back** er schoss den Ball zurück VI *(Rugby)* den Ball aus der Hand schießen

punt[3] N *(= bet)* Wette *f*; *(= gamble)* Spiel *nt* VI wetten, spielen

punt[4] [pʊnt] N *(= Irish currency)* Punt *nt*, irisches Pfund

punter[1] [ˈpʌntəˈ] N *(= boater)* Stechkahnfahrer(in) *m(f)*

punter[2] N a *(Brit inf) (= better)* Wetter(in) *m(f)*; *(= gambler)* Spieler(in) *m(f)* b *(esp Brit inf: = customer etc)* Kunde *m*, Kundin *f*; *(of prostitute)* Freier *m (inf)*; **the average ~** Otto Normalverbraucher

puny [ˈpjuːnɪ] ADJ *(+er) (= weak) person* schwächlich, mick(e)rig *(pej)*; *effort* kläglich; *resources* kläglich, winzig

PUP N *(Brit) abbr of* **Progressive Unionist Party**

pup [pʌp] N a Junge(s) *nt*; **in ~** *(bitch)* trächtig; **she's still a ~** sie ist noch jung *or* klein; **to be sold a ~** *(fig inf)* übers Ohr gehauen werden *(inf)* b *(pej, = youth)* = **puppy b** VI werfen

pupa [ˈpjuːpə] N *pl* **-e** [ˈpjuːpiː] Puppe *f*

pupate [ˈpjuːpeɪt] VI sich verpuppen

pupil[1] [ˈpjuːpl] N *(Sch, fig)* Schüler(in) *m(f)*

pupil[2] N *(Anat)* Pupille *f*

puppet [ˈpʌpɪt] N Puppe *f*; *(= glove puppet)* Handpuppe *f*; *(= string puppet, also fig)* Marionette *f*

puppeteer [pʌpɪˈtɪəˈ] N Puppenspieler(in) *m(f)*

puppet: **puppet government** N Marionettenregierung *f*; **puppet régime** N Marionettenregime *nt*

puppetry [ˈpʌpɪtrɪ] N das Puppenspiel

puppet: **puppet show** N Puppenspiel *nt*; *(with string puppets also)* Marionettentheater *nt*; **puppet state** N Marionettenstaat *m*

puppy [ˈpʌpɪ] N a *(= young dog)* junger *or* kleiner Hund, Hündchen *nt*, Welpe *m*; **when he was still a ~** als er noch jung *or* klein war b **puppies** *(Brit inf: = breasts)* Titten *pl (inf)*, Möpse *pl (inf)*

puppy: **puppy dog** N Hundchen *nt*; **puppy farm** N Hundezucht *f (wo junge Rassehunde zum Weiterverkauf an Tierhandlungen gezüchtet werden)*; **puppy fat** N *(Brit)* Babyspeck *m*; **puppy love** N Schwärmerei *f*

pup tent N *(US Mil)* Zweimannzelt *nt*

purblind [ˈpɜːblaɪnd] ADJ *(liter) (lit)* halb blind; *(fig)* blind, borniert, dumm

purblindness [ˈpɜːblaɪndnɪs] ADJ *(liter) (lit)* Halbblindheit; *(fig)* Blindheit *f*, Borniertheit *f*, Dummheit *f*

purchasable [ˈpɜːtʃəsəbl] ADJ käuflich (zu erwerben *geh*)

purchase [ˈpɜːtʃɪs] N a Kauf *m*; *(of furniture, machine, flat, car)* Kauf *m*, Anschaffung *f*; **to make a ~** einen Kauf tätigen, eine Anschaffung machen b *(= grip)* Halt *m*; **he couldn't get a ~ on the wet rope** er konnte an dem nassen Seil keinen Halt finden VT *(= buy)* kaufen, erwerben *(geh)*, erstehen *(geh)*; *(fig) success, victory* erkaufen

purchase: **purchase account** N *(Comm)* Wareneingangskonto *nt*; **purchase money** N Kaufgeld *nt*; **purchase order** N Auftragsbestätigung *f*; **purchase price** N Kaufpreis *m*

purchaser [ˈpɜːtʃɪsəˈ] N Käufer(in) *m(f)*

purchase tax N *(Brit) nach dem Großhandelspreis berechnete Kaufsteuer*

purchasing [ˈpɜːtʃɪsɪŋ]: **purchasing agent** N *(Comm)* Einkäufer(in) *m(f)*; **purchasing association** N *(Comm)* Einkaufsgenossenschaft *f*; **purchasing power** N Kaufkraft *f*

purdah [ˈpɜːdə] N *Vorhang vor den Frauengemächern im Islam und Hinduismus*, Purdah *f*; **a woman in ~** *(lit)* eine Frau, die von (fremden) Männern ferngehalten wird; **he keeps his wife (like a woman) in ~** er hält seine Frau von allem fern

pure [pjʊəˈ] ADJ *(+er)* a rein; *motive* ehrlich, lauter *(geh)*; *(= utter) madness, nonsense etc also* reinste(r, s); **she stared at him in ~ disbelief** sie starrte ihn ganz ungläubig an; **by ~ chance**

durch puren Zufall, rein zufällig; **malice ~ and simple** reine Bosheit; **a ~ wool dress** ein Kleid aus reiner Wolle, ein reinwollenes Kleid; **blessed are the ~ in heart** *(Bibl)* selig, die reinen Herzens sind **b** *(= theoretical) chemistry* rein, theoretisch; *maths, research, science* rein

pureblood ['pjʊəblʌd], **purebred** ['pjʊəbred] **ADJ** reinrassig **N** reinrassiges Pferd *etc*

purée ['pjʊəreɪ] **N** Püree *nt*, Brei *m*; **tomato ~** Tomatenmark *nt* **VT** pürieren

purely ['pjʊəlɪ] **ADV** rein; **~ and simply** schlicht und einfach

pure-minded ['pjʊə'maɪndɪd] **ADJ** unverdorben

pureness ['pjʊənɪs] **N** = **purity**

purgation [pɜː'geɪʃən] **N** *(liter)* Reinigung *f*; *(of sin, guilt)* Buße *f*; *(form, of bowels)* Entleerung *f*

purgative ['pɜːgətɪv] **ADJ** *(Med)* abführend, purgativ *(spec)*; *(fig liter)* läuternd *(geh)* **N** Abführmittel *nt*, Purgativ *nt (spec)*

purgatorial [,pɜːgə'tɔːrɪəl] **ADJ** **a** *(Rel) concept* des Fegefeuers; *time* im Fegefeuer; **~ fire** Fegefeuer *nt* **b** *(fig)* höllisch

purgatory ['pɜːgətərɪ] **N** **a** *(Rel)* das Fegefeuer **b** *(fig: = state)* die Hölle

purge [pɜːdʒ] **N** **a** *(Med)* (starkes) Abführmittel **b** *(Pol etc)* Säuberung(saktion) *f*; **a ~ of all radical elements in the party** eine Säuberung der Partei von allen radikalen Elementen **VT** reinigen; *body* entschlacken; *guilt, offence, sin* büßen; *(Pol etc) party, organization* säubern (*of* von); *traitor, member* eliminieren (*from* aus); **to ~ the bowels** den Darm entleeren

purification [,pjʊərɪfɪ'keɪʃən] **N** Reinigung *f*

purification plant **N** *(of factory)* Kläranlage *f*

purifier ['pjʊərɪfaɪə'] **N** Reinigungsanlage *f*; *(= air-freshener)* Luftreiniger *m*

purify ['pjʊərɪfaɪ] **VT** reinigen

purism ['pjʊərɪzəm] **N** Purismus *m*

purist ['pjʊərɪst] **N** Purist(in) *m(f)*

puristic **ADJ**, **puristically** **ADV** [pjʊə'rɪstɪk, -lɪ] puristisch

puritan ['pjʊərɪtən] *(Rel: also* **Puritan***)* **ADJ** puritanisch **N** Puritaner(in) *m(f)*

puritanical [,pjʊərɪ'tænɪkəl] **ADJ** puritanisch

puritanism ['pjʊərɪtənɪzəm] **N** *(Rel: also* **Puritanism***)* Puritanismus *m*

purity ['pjʊərɪtɪ] **N** Reinheit *f*; *(of motives)* Lauterkeit *f (geh)*, Ehrlichkeit *f*

purl [pɜːl] **N** linke Masche; **is the next row (in) ~?** ist die nächste Reihe links? **VT** links stricken; **~ two** zwei links **VI** links stricken

purlieus ['pɜːljuːz] **PL** *(liter)* Umgebung *f*

purloin [pɜː'lɔɪn] **VT** *(form, hum)* entwenden *(form, hum)*

purloiner [pɜː'lɔɪnə'] **N** *(form, hum)* Dieb(in) *m(f)*

purple ['pɜːpl] **ADJ** violett, lila; *face* dunkelrot, hochrot; *(pej) prose, passage* hochgestochen, hochtrabend; **to go ~ (in the face)** hochrot werden *or* anlaufen *(inf)* **N** **a** *(= colour)* Violett *nt*, Lila *nt* **b** *(fig)* **the ~** *(= nobility)* der Adel; *(= bishops)* der Kardinalsstand; **to be born to the ~** von königlichem Geblüt sein; **to be raised to the ~** den Kardinalspurpur anlegen

purple heart **N** **a** *(esp Brit inf)* Amphetamintablette *f* **b** *(US)* **Purple Heart** Purpurherz *nt*, Verwundetenabzeichen *nt*

purplish ['pɜːplɪʃ] **ADJ** leicht violett *or* lila

purport **N** ['pɜːpət] Tenor *m* **VT** [pɜː'pɔːt] **a** *(= convey, mean)* hindeuten auf *(+acc)* **b** *(= profess, claim)* **to ~ to be/do sth** *(person)* vorgeben, etw zu sein/tun; *(object)* etw sein/tun sollen; **he is ~ed to be a spy** es wird behauptet, er sei ein Spion; **the law is ~ed to be in the public interest** das Gesetz soll dem Interesse der Öffentlichkeit dienen

purpose ['pɜːpəs] **N** **a** *(= intention)* Absicht *f*; *(= result aimed at, set goal)* Zweck *m*; **on ~** mit Absicht, absichtlich; **what was your ~ in doing this?** was haben Sie damit beabsichtigt?, was war Ihre Absicht dabei?; **he did it for** *or* **with the ~ of improving his image** er tat es in der Absicht *or* mit dem Ziel, sein Image zu verbessern; **he's a man with a ~ in life** er ist ein Mensch mit einem Lebensziel; **a novel with a ~** ein Roman, der einen Zweck erfüllen soll; **to answer** *or* **serve sb's ~(s)** jds Zweck(en) entsprechen *or* dienen; **his activities seem to lack ~** seine Aktivitäten scheinen nicht zweckgerichtet zu sein; **for our ~s** für unsere Zwecke; **for the ~s of this meeting** zum Zweck dieser Konferenz; **for all practical ~s** in der Praxis; **to the ~** relevant; **to some/good/little ~** mit einigem/gutem/wenig Erfolg; **to no ~** ohne Erfolg **b** *no pl (= resolution, determination)* Entschlossenheit *f*; **strength of ~** Entschlusskraft *f*, Entschlossenheit *f*; **sense of ~** Zielbewusstsein *nt*; *(of nation)* Ziel *nt*, Zielvorstellungen *pl*; **to have a sense of ~** zielbewusst sein; **to have no sense of ~** kein Zielbewusstsein *or* kein Ziel haben **VT** *(liter)* beabsichtigen; **to ~ to do sth** etw zu tun gedenken

purpose-built ['pɜːpəs'bɪlt] **ADJ** *(esp Brit)* speziell angefertigt, Spezial-; *construction* speziell gebaut; **~ vehicle** Spezialfahrzeug *nt*

purposeful **ADJ**, **purposefully** **ADV** ['pɜːpəsfʊl, -fəlɪ] entschlossen; *activity, life* sinnvoll

purposefulness ['pɜːpəsfʊlnɪs] **N** Entschlossenheit *f*

purposeless ['pɜːpəslɪs] **ADJ** sinnlos; *person* ziellos

purposely ['pɜːpəslɪ] **ADV** bewusst, absichtlich

purpose-trained ['pɜːpəs'treɪnd] **ADJ** *(esp Brit) troops etc* mit Spezialausbildung *pred*, Spezial-

purposive ['pɜːpəsɪv] **ADJ** *remark, statement, action, behaviour* gezielt; **the ~ use of scientific progress** der gezielte Einsatz des wissenschaftlichen Fortschritts; **to be ~** einen Zweck verfolgen

purr [pɜː'] **VI** *(cat, fig: person)* schnurren; *(engine)* surren **VT** *(= say)* säuseln **N** Schnurren *nt no pl*, Surren *nt no pl*

purse [pɜːs] **N** **a** *(for money)* Portemonnaie *nt*, Geldbeutel *m (dial)*, Geldbörse *f (form)*; **to hold the ~ strings** *(Brit fig)* über die Finanzen bestimmen, die Finanzen in der Hand haben; **the government decided to loosen the ~ strings for defence** die Regierung beschloss, mehr Geld für die Verteidigung auszugeben; **her husband spent too much, so she decided to tighten the ~ strings** ihr Mann gab zu viel Geld aus, also beschloss sie, ihn kurzzuhalten **b** *(US: = handbag)* Handtasche *f* **c** *(= funds)* Gelder *pl*; **that's beyond my ~** das übersteigt meine Finanzen *(inf)* → **public purse** **d** *(= sum of money) (as prize)* Preisgeld *nt*; *(as gift) (to widow, refugee etc)* (Geld)spende *f*; *(on retirement)* Geldgeschenk *nt* **VT** **to ~ one's lips/mouth (up)** einen Schmollmund machen

purser ['pɜːsə'] **N** Zahlmeister(in) *m(f)*

purse snatcher **N** *(US inf)* Handtaschendieb(in) *m(f)*

pursuance [pə'sjuːəns] **N** *(form) (of plan)* Verfolgung *f*; *(of instruction)* Ausführung *f*; *(of duties)* Erfüllung *f*

pursuant [pə'sjuːənt] **ADJ** *(form)* **~ to** gemäß *(+dat)*, entsprechend *(+dat)*; **~ to our agreement** unserem Abkommen gemäß *or* entsprechend

pursue [pə'sjuː] **VT** **a** *(= follow)* verfolgen; *girl, film star etc* nachlaufen *(+dat)*, verfolgen; *(= strive for) pleasure, success* nachjagen *(+dat)*, aus sein auf *(+acc)*; *happiness* streben nach; **bad luck seems to ~ him** er scheint vom Pech verfolgt zu sein **b** *(= carry on) train of thought, course of action, idea* verfolgen; *inquiry* durchführen; *profession, studies* nachgehen *(+dat)*; *subject* weiterführen

pursuer [pə'sjuːə'] **N** Verfolger(in) *m(f)*

pursuit [pə'sjuːt] **N** **a** *(= act of pursuing) (of person)* Verfolgung *f* (*of* +*gen*), Jagd *f* (*of* auf +*acc*); *(of knowledge)* Streben *nt* (*of* nach), Trachten *nt* (*of* nach); *(of pleasure)* Jagd *f* (*of* nach); *(of happiness)* Streben *nt* (*of* nach); **he set off in ~ (of her)** er rannte/fuhr (ihr) hinterher; **to go in ~ of sb/sth** sich auf die Jagd nach jdm/etw machen; **hot ~** *(Mil)* Nacheile *f*; **in hot ~ of sb** hart auf jds Fersen *(dat)*; **to set off/be in hot ~ of sb/sth** jdm/einer Sache nachjagen; **in hot ~ of the thief** in wilder Jagd auf den Dieb; **in (the) ~ of his goal** in Verfolgung seines Ziels; **Kissinger's ~ of peace** Kissingers Friedensbemühungen *pl* **b** *(= occupation)* Beschäftigung *f*; *(= hobby, pastime)* Freizeitbeschäftigung *f*, Zeitvertreib *m*; **his literary ~s** seine Beschäftigung mit der Literatur **c** *(Sport: also* **pursuit race***)* Verfolgungsrennen *nt*

pursuit plane **N** Jagdflugzeug *nt*

purulence ['pjʊərʊləns], **purulency** ['pjʊərʊlənsɪ] **N** Eitern *nt*; *(= pus)* Eiter *m*

purulent ['pjʊərʊlənt] **ADJ** eitrig; **to become ~** eitern

purvey [pɜː'veɪ] **VT** *(form) (= sell)* verkaufen; **to ~ sth to sb** *(= supply)* jdm etw liefern; *food also* jdn mit etw beliefern; *information also* jdn mit etw versorgen

purveyance [pɜː'veɪəns] **N** *(form: = sale)* Verkauf *m*; **the ~ of food to the Navy** die Lieferung von Lebensmitteln an die Marine

purveyor [pɜː'veɪə'] **N** *(form) (= seller)* Händler(in) *m(f)*; *(= supplier)* Lieferant *m*

purview ['pɜːvjuː] **N** *(form)* Rahmen *m*; *(of department)* Aufgabenbereich *m*, Ressort *nt*; **to come within/lie outside the ~ of an inquiry** noch/nicht mehr im Rahmen einer Untersuchung liegen

pus [pʌs] **N** Eiter *m*

push [pʊʃ] **N** **a** Schubs *m (inf)*; *(short)* Stoß *m*; *(in childbirth)* Drücken *nt no pl*; **to give sb/sth a ~** jdn/etw schieben, jdm/einer Sache einen Stoß versetzen; **to give a car a ~** einen Wagen anschieben; **he needs a little ~ now and then** *(fig)* den muss man mal ab und zu in die Rippen stoßen *(inf)*; **to get the ~** *(Brit inf) (employee)* (raus)fliegen *(inf)* (*from* aus); *(boyfriend)* den Laufpass kriegen *(inf)*; **to give sb the ~** *(Brit inf, employee)* jdn rausschmeißen *(inf)*; *boyfriend* jdm den Laufpass geben *(inf)* **b** *(= effort)* Anstrengung *f*; *(= sales push)* Kampagne *f*, Aktion *f*; *(Mil: = offensive)* Offensive *f*; **to make a ~** sich ranhalten *(inf)*, Dampf machen *(inf)*; *(Mil)* eine Offensive starten; **let's make a ~ to get it finished** halten wir uns ran, damit wir fertig werden *(inf)*; **to have a ~ on sales** eine Verkaufskampagne führen **c** *(= drive, aggression)* Durchsetzungsvermögen *nt* **d** *(inf)* **at a ~** notfalls, im Notfall; **if/when it comes to the ~** wenn es darauf ankommt; **if/when ~ comes to shove** wenn der schlimmste Fall eintritt **VT** **a** *(= shove, move by pushing)* schieben; *(quickly, violently)* stoßen, schubsen *(inf)*; *(= press) button, controls* drücken; **to ~ a door open/shut** eine Tür auf-/zuschieben; *(quickly, violently)* eine Tür auf-/zustoßen; **he ~ed the book into my hand** er drückte mir das Buch in die Hand; **to ~ a car to get it started** einen Wagen anschieben; **he ~ed his way through the crowd** er drängte sich durch die Menge; **he ~ed the thought to the back of his mind** er schob den Gedanken beiseite; **he ~ed the ball over the bar** *(Sport)* er hat den Ball über die Latte gestoßen **b** *(fig) views, claims, interests* durchzusetzen versuchen; *candidate* die Werbetrommel rühren für; *export side* intensiv fördern; *product* propagieren, massiv Werbung machen für, puschen *(inf)*, puschen *(inf)*; *drugs* schieben, pushen *(inf)*; **to ~ home one's advantage** seinen Vorteil ausnützen; **the speaker ~ed home his points** der Sprecher machte nachdrücklich seinen Standpunkt klar; **don't ~ your luck** treibs nicht zu weit!; **he's ~ing his luck trying to do that** er legt es wirklich darauf an, wenn er das versucht; **he must be ~ing 70** *(inf)* er muss auf die

70 zugehen
c (*fig: = put pressure on*) drängen, drängeln (*inf*); *athlete, pupil, employee* antreiben; **to ~ sb into doing sth** jdn dazu treiben, etw zu tun; **to ~ sb to do sth** jdn dazu drängen, etw zu tun; **to ~ sb for payment** jdn zum Zahlen drängen; **don't ~ him so hard to make a decision** drängen *or* drängeln (*inf*) Sie ihn nicht zu sehr zu einer Entscheidung; **they ~ed him to the limits** sie trieben ihn bis an seine Grenzen; **that's ~ing it a bit** (*inf*) das ist ein bisschen übertrieben; **to be ~ed (for time)** (*inf*) mit der Zeit knapp dran sein, unter Zeitdruck stehen; **to be ~ed (for money)** (*inf*) knapp bei Kasse sein (*inf*); **to ~ oneself hard** sich schinden; **~ it!** (*US inf*) leg dich ins Zeug! (*inf*)

VI **a** (*= shove*) schieben; (*quickly, violently*) stoßen; (*= press, also in childbirth*) drücken; (*in a crowd*) drängen, drängeln (*inf*); (*= press onward*) sich (vorwärts)kämpfen; (*fig: = be ambitious, assert oneself*) kämpfen; (*= apply pressure*) drängen, drängeln (*inf*); **"push"** (*on door*) „drücken"; (*on bell*) „klingeln"; **~ harder!** fester schieben/stoßen/drücken!; **he ~es too much** (*fig*) er ist zu aggressiv

b **this door ~es (open)** bei dieser Tür muss man drücken

▸ **push about** VT *sep* (*Brit*) = **push around**

▸ **push across** VT *sep* = **push over a**

▸ **push ahead** VI sich ranhalten (*inf*), voranmachen (*inf*); **to push ahead with one's plans** seine Pläne vorantreiben

▸ **push along** **VT** *sep wheelbarrow etc* vor sich (*dat*) her schieben; (*fig: = speed up*) *work etc* voranbringen, vorantreiben; **to push things along** (*fig*) die Dinge vorantreiben **VI** (*inf*) sich auf den Weg *or* auf die Socken machen (*inf*)

▸ **push around** VT *sep* **a** (*lit*) herumschieben; (*quickly, violently*) herumstoßen **b** (*fig inf: = bully*) *child* herumschubsen; *adult* herumkommandieren

▸ **push aside** VT *sep* zur Seite schieben*or* beiseiteschieben; (*quickly, violently*) zur Seite stoßen *or* beiseitestoßen; (*fig*) *problems, suggestions* einfach abtun; *rival* zur Seite drängen

▸ **push away** VT *sep* wegschieben; (*quickly*) wegstoßen

▸ **push back** VT *sep people* zurückdrängen; (*with one push*) zurückstoßen; *curtains, cover, lock of hair* zurückschieben; **to push back the boundaries (of sth)** die Grenzen (einer Sache) zurückdrängen

▸ **push by** VI = **push past**

▸ **push down** **VT** *sep* **a** (*= press down*) nach unten drücken **b** (*= knock over*) umstoßen; *fence* niederreißen **VI** (*= press down*) hinunterdrücken, nach unten drücken; (*in childbirth*) pressen

▸ **push for** VI +*prep obj* drängen auf (+*acc*)

▸ **push forward** **VI** **a** (*Mil*) vorwärtsdrängen **b** = **push ahead** **VT** *sep* (*lit*) nach vorn schieben; (*fig*) *claim* geltend machen; *ideas* hervorheben, herausstellen; *sb, oneself* in den Vordergrund schieben

▸ **push in** **VT** *sep* **a** hineinschieben; (*quickly, violently*) hineinstoßen; **to push sb/sth in(to) sth** jdn/etw in etw (*acc*) schieben/stoßen; **to push one's way in** sich hineindrängen **b** (*= break*) *window, sides of box* eindrücken **VI** (*lit: in queue, into room etc*) sich hineindrängen *or* -drängeln (*inf*); (*fig: = interfere*) sich dazwischendrängen, sich reindrängen (*inf*); **he pushed into the queue** er drängelte sich (in der Schlange) vor

▸ **push off** **VT** *sep* **a** hinunterschieben; (*quickly, violently*) hinunterstoßen; *lid, cap* wegdrücken; **to push sb off sth** jdn von etw schieben/stoßen; **to push sth off sth** etw von etw schieben/stoßen/drücken; **I was pushed off the pavement** ich wurde vom Bürgersteig gedrängt **b** *boat* abstoßen **VI** **a** (*in boat*) abstoßen **b** (*Brit inf: = leave*) abhauen (*inf*); **push off!** mach 'ne Fliege! (*sl*), hau *or* zieh ab! (*inf*) **c** **the top just pushes off** der Deckel lässt sich einfach wegdrücken

▸ **push on** **VI** (*with journey*) weiterfahren; (*walking*) weitergehen; (*with job*) weitermachen **VT** *sep* **a** *top, lid* festdrücken; **he pushed the lid on(to) the jar** er drückte den Deckel auf das Glas **b** (*fig: = urge on*) antreiben; (*= incite*) anstacheln

▸ **push out** **VT** *sep* **a** (*lit*) hinausschieben; (*quickly, violently*) hinausstoßen; **to push sb/sth out of sth** jdn/etw aus etw schieben/stoßen; **to push one's way out (of sth)** sich (aus etw) hinausdrängen → **boat N a** **b** (*fig*) *employee, government, member of group* hinausdrängen; **to push sb out of sth** jdn aus etw drängen **c** (*Bot*) *root, shoots* treiben **VI** (*Bot: roots, shoots*) treiben

▸ **push over** VT *sep* **a** (*= pass over, move over*) hinüberschieben; (*quickly, violently*) hinüberstoßen; **to push sb/sth over sth** jdn/etw über etw (*acc*) schieben/stoßen **b** (*= knock over*) umwerfen

▸ **push past** VI sich vorbeischieben (*prep obj* an +*dat*); (*= move violently*) sich vorbeidrängen (*prep obj* an +*dat*)

▸ **push through** **VT** *sep* **a** (*= shove through*) durchschieben; (*quickly, violently*) durchstoßen; **to push sb/sth through sth** jdn/etw durch etw schieben/stoßen; **to push one's way through** sich durchdrängen; **she pushed her way through the crowd** sie drängte sich durch die Menge **b** (*= get done quickly*) *bill, decision* durchpeitschen (*inf*); *business* durchziehen (*inf*) **VI** (*through crowd*) sich durchschieben; (*more violently*) sich durchdrängen; (*new shoots*) sich herausschieben; **he pushed through the crowd** er schob/drängte sich durch die Menge

▸ **push to** VT *always separate door* anlehnen

▸ **push up** VT *sep* **a** (*lit*) hinaufschieben; (*quickly, violently*) hinaufstoßen; *window* hochschieben/-stoßen → **daisy** **b** (*fig: = raise, increase*) hochtreiben, hochdrücken

push: **pushback** N (*Aviat*) Zurückstoßen *nt*, Zurückschieben *nt*; **to be ready for ~** startklar sein; **pushball** N (*esp US*) Pushball *m*; **pushbar** N Riegel *m*; **push-bike** N (*dated Brit*) Fahrrad *nt*; **push-button** N Drucktaste *f*, Druckknopf *m*; **~ controls** Druckknopfsteuerung *f*; **~ radio** Radio *nt* mit Drucktasten; **~ telephone** Tastentelefon *nt*; **~ warfare** Krieg *m* auf Knopfdruck; **pushcart** [ˈpʊʃkɑːt] N (Hand)karren *m*; **pushchair** N (*Brit*) Sportwagen *m*

pusher [ˈpʊʃəˈ] N **a** (*inf*) (*of drugs*) Pusher(in) *m(f)* (*inf*); (*small-time*) Dealer(in) *m(f)* (*inf*) **b** (*= ambitious person*) **he's a ~** er setzt sich durch

pusher barge, **pusher tug** N (*inland navigation*) Schubschiff *nt*

pushiness [ˈpʊʃɪnɪs] N (*inf*) penetrante Art (*pej*)

pushing [ˈpʊʃɪŋ] (*inf*) ADJ penetrant (*pej*)

push: **push-off** [ˈpʊʃɔf] N (*inf*) Anfang *m*, Start *m*; **pushover** [ˈpʊʃəʊvəˈ] N (*inf*) (*= job etc*) Kinderspiel *nt*; (*= match also*) Geschenk *nt* (*inf*); (*= person*) leichtes Opfer; **he's a ~ for a pretty face** bei einem hübschen Gesicht wird er schwach; **pushpin** [ˈpʊʃpɪn] N (*esp US*) Pin-Nagel *m*; **push-pull** ADJ (*Elec*) Gegentakt-; **~ circuit** Gegentaktschaltung *f*; **pushrod** N (*Mech*) Stößelstange *f*; **push-start** **VT** *car* anschieben **N** **to give a car a ~** ein Auto anschieben; **push-up** N (*US*) Liegestütz *m*; **push-up bra** N Push-up-BH *m*

pushy [ˈpʊʃɪ] ADJ (+*er*) (*inf*) penetrant (*pej*)

pusillanimity [ˌpjuːsɪləˈnɪmɪtɪ] N (*liter*) Unbeherztheit *f*, Feigheit *f*

pusillanimous [ˌpjuːsɪˈlænɪməs] ADJ (*liter*) unbeherzt, feige

puss [pʊs] N (*inf*) Mieze *f* (*inf*), Muschi *f* (*inf*); **~, ~!** Miez, Miez!; **Puss in Boots** der Gestiefelte Kater; **she's a sly ~** (*inf*) sie ist ein schlaues Ding (*inf*)

pussy [ˈpʊsɪ] N **a** (*= cat*) Mieze *f* (*inf*), Muschi *f* (*inf*) **b** (*sl: = female genitals*) Muschi *f* (*inf*) **c** (*esp US inf: = weakling*) Schlappschwanz *m* (*inf*), Weichei *nt* (*inf*)

pussy: **pussycat** [ˈpʊsɪkæt] N (*baby-talk*) Miezekatze *f* (*baby-talk*); **pussyfoot** VI (*inf*) **a** (*= move cautiously*) auf Zehenspitzen tappen, auf Samtpfoten schleichen **b** (*= act cautiously*) **to ~ (about *or* around sth)** (um etw) wie die Katze um den heißen Brei schleichen (*inf*); **pussyfooting** (*inf*) **ADJ** übervorsichtig **N** **I'm fed up with his ~** ich habe es satt, wie er immer wie die Katze um den heißen Brei schleicht; **pussy willow** N Salweide *f*

pustule [ˈpʌstjuːl] N Pustel *f*, Eiterpickel *m*

put[1] [pʊt] *vb: pret, ptp* **put** **N** (*Sport*) Stoß *m* **VT** **to ~ the shot** kugelstoßen; **~ting the shot** Kugelstoßen *nt*

put[2] [pʊt]

pret, ptp **put** [pʊt]

1 TRANSITIVE VERB	3 PHRASAL VERBS
2 INTRANSITIVE VERB	

For combinations of *put* with adverbs and prepositions, e.g. *put in, put on, put up etc.*, see also the phrasal verbs section.

1 – TRANSITIVE VERB

a [= place] stellen, setzen; (*= lay down*) legen; (*= push in*) stecken; **you've put the picture too high up** du hast das Bild zu hoch (auf)gehängt; **put it there!** (*concluding deal*) abgemacht!; (*congratulatory*) gratuliere!; **I didn't know where to put myself** ich wusste gar nicht, wo ich hingucken sollte

♦ **to put + across they put a plank across the stream** sie legten ein Brett über den Bach

♦ **to put + down he put the corpse down the well** er warf die Leiche in den Brunnen

♦ **to put + in to put sth in a drawer** etw in eine Schublade tun *or* legen; **he put his hand in his pocket** er steckte die Hand in die Tasche; **he put his toe in the water** er steckte seinen Zeh ins Wasser; **put the dog in the kitchen** tu *or* steck den Hund in die Küche; **to put milk/sugar in one's coffee** Milch/Zucker in den Kaffee tun *or* geben; **to put the ball in the net** (*Ftbl*) den Ball ins Netz setzen; (*Tennis*) den Ball ins Netz schlagen; **to put a child in a home** ein Kind in ein Heim stecken; **I would put complete confidence in him** ich würde mein volles Vertrauen auf ihn *or* in ihn setzen; **to put sb in possession of the facts** jdn über den Stand der Dinge unterrichten; **to put sb in a good/bad mood** jdn fröhlich/missmutig stimmen; **that puts him in another category** das stuft ihn in eine andere Klasse ein

♦ **to put + into to put a lot of time into sth** viel Zeit auf etw (*acc*) verwenden *or* in etw (*acc*) stecken; **to put a lot of effort into one's work** viel Mühe in seine Arbeit stecken; **she has put a lot into her marriage** sie hat eine Menge in ihre Ehe gesteckt *or* investiert; **to put money into sth** (sein) Geld in etw (*acc*) stecken; **to put a text into Greek** einen Text ins Griechische übersetzen; **to put a verb into the past tense** ein Verb in die Vergangenheit setzen

♦ **to put + on put the lid on the box** tu *or* mach den Deckel auf die Schachtel; **he put some more coal on the fire** er legte Kohle nach; **he put his hat on his head** er setzte sich (*dat*) den Hut auf; **he put his hand/head on my shoulder** er legte seine Hand/seinen Kopf auf meine Schulter; **her aunt put her on the train** ihre Tante setzte sie in den Zug; **to put men on the moon** Menschen auf den Mond bringen; **he put four men on the job** er setzte (für diese Arbeit) vier Leute ein; **to put a patch on sth** einen Flicken auf etw (*acc*) setzen; **to put money on a horse** auf ein Pferd setzen; **he put £10 on the favourite** er setzte £ 10 auf den Favoriten; **I'm putting my money on him** ich setzte auf ihn; **I'm putting my money on him to get the job** ich gehe jede Wette ein, dass er die Stelle bekommt; **to put a value of £100 on sth** den Wert einer Sache (*gen*) auf £ 100 schätzen; **I put the children on their**

best behaviour ich habe den Kindern eingeschärft, sich ja gut zu benehmen

♦ **to put + over/under he put his rucksack over the fence** er setzte seinen Rucksack über den Zaun; **he put the ball over the wall** er schoss den Ball über die Mauer; **to put one's hand over one's/sb's mouth** sich/jdm die Hand vor den Mund halten; **they put someone over/under him in the office** im Büro haben sie jemanden über ihn gesetzt/ihm jemanden unterstellt; **he was put under the care of a nurse** er wurde in die Obhut einer Krankenschwester gegeben

♦ **to put + (a)round he put his head (a)round the door** er steckte den Kopf zur Tür herein

♦ **to put + through to put one's fist through a window** mit der Faust ein Fenster einschlagen; **to put a bullet through sb's head** jdm eine Kugel durch den Kopf schießen

♦ **to put + to he put his lips to my ear and whispered ...** er kam ganz dicht und flüsterte mir ins Ohr ...; **to put a glass to one's lips** ein Glas zum Mund(e) führen; **she put the shell to her ear** sie hielt (sich *dat*) die Muschel ans Ohr; **to put the children to bed** die Kinder ins Bett bringen; **to put a poem to music** ein Gedicht vertonen; **to put sb to great expense** jdm große Ausgaben verursachen; **I don't want to be put to a lot of expense** ich möchte nicht, dass mir damit große Ausgaben entstehen; **to be put to a lot of inconvenience over sth** mit etw viele Unannehmlichkeiten haben; **to put a horse to a fence** mit einem Pferd ein Hindernis angehen *or* anreiten; **to put a heifer to a bull** die Kuh mit dem Bullen zusammenbringen *or* -führen

♦ **to put + toward(s) we'll each put £5 toward(s) the cost of it** jeder von uns gibt £ 5 (zum Betrag) dazu

♦ **to put sb to do** *or* **doing sth** jdn abordnen, etw zu tun; **they put her to work on the new project** ihr wurde das neue Projekt als Arbeitsbereich zugewiesen

♦ **to stay put** liegen/stehen/hängen *etc* bleiben; *(hair)* halten; *(person, = not move)* sich nicht von der Stelle rühren; *(= not stand up)* sitzen bleiben; **just stay put!** bleib, wo du bist!

b [= write] schreiben; *comma, line* machen; *(= draw)* zeichnen, malen; **to put one's signature to a document** seine Unterschrift unter ein Schriftstück setzen; **put your name here** schreiben *or* setzen Sie Ihren Namen hierhin; **to put a cross/tick against sb's name** jds Namen ankreuzen/abhaken; **he put it in his next novel** er brachte das in seinem nächsten Roman

c [= put forward] *case, question, proposal* vorbringen; **to put a matter before a committee** eine Angelegenheit vor einen Ausschuss bringen; **to put the arguments for and against sth** das Für und Wider von etw *(dat)* aufzählen; **to put sth on the agenda** etw auf die Tagesordnung setzen; **to put a question/suggestion to sb** jdm eine Frage stellen/einen Vorschlag unterbreiten

♦ **to put it to sb (that ...)** *(= suggest)* **I put it to you that ...** ich behaupte, dass ...; **it was put to me that ...** es wurde mir nahegelegt, dass ...; **I put it to him that this might not fit in with his theory** ich gab ihm zu bedenken, dass dies vielleicht nicht in seine Theorie passen würde; **you might put it to him that a contribution would be welcome** du könntest ihm nahelegen, dass ein Beitrag erwünscht wäre; **how will you put it to him?** wie wirst du es ihm beibringen?

d [= express] ausdrücken, sagen; **the compliment was eloquently put** das Kompliment war gewandt formuliert

♦ **to put it... that's one way of putting it** so kann mans auch sagen; **as he would put it** wie er sich ausdrücken würde; **as Shakespeare puts it** wie Shakespeare es ausdrückt; **put it so as not to offend her** formulieren Sie es so, dass Sie sie nicht beleidigen; **how shall I put it?** wie soll ich (es) sagen?; **if I may put it so** wenn ich das so sagen darf, wenn ich mich (mal) so ausdrücken darf; **to put it bluntly** um es klipp und klar zu sagen

e [= rate] schätzen *(at* auf *+acc)*

♦ **to put sth above/amongst/before sth I put him above Tennyson** ich schätze ihn höher ein als Tennyson; **I wouldn't put him amongst the greatest poets** ich würde ihn nicht zu den größten Dichtern zählen; **he puts money before his family's happiness** er stellt Geld über das Glück seiner Familie

2 – INTRANSITIVE VERB

♦ **to put to sea** *(Naut)* in See stechen

3 – PHRASAL VERBS

▶ **put about** *(esp Brit)* **VT** *sep* **a** *(= circulate) news, rumour* verbreiten, in Umlauf bringen; **he put it about that ...** er verbreitete (das Gerücht), dass ...; **he's been putting himself about a lot lately** *(inf)* er hat sich in letzter Zeit ganz schön in Szene gesetzt **b** *(Naut)* **to put a ship about** den Kurs (eines Schiffes) ändern **VI** *(Naut)* den Kurs ändern

▶ **put across** **VT** *sep* **a** *(= communicate) ideas* verständlich machen *(to sb* jdm), klar zum Ausdruck bringen; *knowledge* vermitteln *(to sb* jdm); *(= promote)* an den Mann bringen *(inf)*; **to put a product across to the public** ein Produkt an den Mann bringen *(inf)*; **to put oneself across** den richtigen Eindruck von sich geben **b** *(inf: = play a trick)* **to put one across sb** jdn anführen; **he's just trying to put one across (you)** er will dich nur anführen

▶ **put aside** **VT** *sep* **a** *book, knitting etc* beiseitelegen **b** *(= save for later use)* auf die Seite legen, beiseite- *or* zurücklegen; *(in shop)* zurücklegen **c** *(fig: = forget, abandon)* ablegen, über Bord werfen *(inf)*; *anger, grief, animosity* begraben; *thought* aufgeben; *differences* vergessen

▶ **put away** **VT** *sep* **a** *(in usual place)* einräumen; *toys* aufräumen; *(= tidy away)* wegräumen; **put that money away in your bag** steck das Geld in deine Tasche; **put that money away!** steck das Geld weg!; **to put the car away** das Auto wegstellen **b** *(= save)* zurücklegen **c** *(inf: = consume)* schaffen *(inf)*; **he can certainly put it away!** *(food)* der kann was verdrücken! *(inf)*; *(drink)* der kann was schlucken! *(inf)* **d** *(= lock up: in prison, mental home)* einsperren **e** *(= put to sleep) pet* einschläfern

▶ **put back** **VT** *sep* **a** *(= replace)* → **put 1 a** zurückstellen *or* -setzen/-legen/-stecken **b** *(esp Brit: = postpone) meeting, date* verschieben; *(= set back) plans, production* zurückwerfen; *(= readjust) watch etc* zurückstellen; **to be put back a class** eine Klasse zurückgestuft werden → **clock** **VI** *(Naut, = go back)* zurückkehren *(to* nach)

▶ **put by** **VT** *sep (Brit)* zurücklegen, auf die hohe Kante legen; **I've got a few pounds put by** ich habe ein paar Pfund auf der hohen Kante

▶ **put down** ✪ 17.2 **VT** *sep* **a** *(= set down) object* → **put 1 a** wegstellen *or* -setzen/-legen; *surface* verlegen; **put it down on the floor** stellen *or* setzen Sie es auf den Boden; **I simply couldn't put that book down** ich konnte das Buch einfach nicht aus der Hand legen; **to put down the phone** (den Hörer) auflegen → **foot N b**

b *(= lower) umbrella* zumachen, zuklappen; *aerial* einschieben; *car roof* zurückklappen; *lid* zuklappen

c *passenger* absetzen

d *(= land)* landen

e *(= crush) rebellion* niederschlagen; *rebels* niederwerfen; *crime* besiegen; *prostitution, gambling, drinking* unterdrücken; *rumour* zum Verstummen bringen; *critic, heckler* zum Schweigen bringen; *(= reject, humiliate)* demütigen

f *(= pay)* anzahlen; *deposit* machen

g *(= store)* einlagern

h *(esp Brit: = destroy) pet* einschläfern; *injured horse etc* den Gnadenschuss geben *(+dat)*; *rats, vermin* vernichten

i *(= write down)* niederschreiben, aufschreiben; *(on form, in register)* angeben; *(Parl) motion, resolution* vorlegen, einbringen; **to put one's name down for sth** sich *or* seinen Namen (in eine Liste) für etw eintragen; **to put one's son down for Eton** seinen Sohn für Eton anmelden; **you can put me down for £10** für mich können Sie £ 10 eintragen; **put it down to my account/my husband's account** schreiben Sie es mir/meinem Mann an; **put it down under sundries/on expenses** schreiben Sie es unter Verschiedenes auf/als Spesen an → **paper N a, name**

j *(= classify)* halten *(as* für); **I'd put her down as about 30** ich würde sie auf etwa 30 schätzen

k *(= attribute)* zurückführen *(to* auf *+acc)*, zuschreiben *(to dat)*

VI *(Aviat)* landen, niedergehen

▶ **put forth** **VI** *+prep obj buds, shoots* hervorbringen; *plan, claim* vorbringen; *effort* unternehmen

▶ **put forward** **VT** *sep* **a** *(= propose) idea, suggestion, plan* vorbringen; *person (for job etc)* vorschlagen; *(as candidate)* aufstellen; *(= nominate)* vorschlagen; **he put himself/his name forward for the job** er hat sich für den Posten angeboten **b** *(esp Brit: = advance) date, meeting* vorverlegen *(to* auf *+acc)*; *schedule* voranbringen, weiterbringen *(by* um); *watch etc* vorstellen → **clock**

▶ **put in** **VT** *sep* **a** *(= place in)* → **put 1 a** hineinstellen *or* -setzen/-legen/-stecken; *(= pack)* einpacken; **he opened the drawer and put his hand in** er öffnete die Schublade und fuhr *or* griff mit der Hand hinein; **I'll just put the car in** ich stelle eben den Wagen weg

b *(= insert in book, speech etc)* einsetzen, einfügen; *(= add)* hinzufügen, dazusagen

c *(= interpose) remark* einfügen

d *(= enter) application, protest, claim* einreichen; **to put in a plea of not guilty** auf „nicht schuldig" plädieren; **to put one's name in for sth** sich um etw bewerben; *for evening classes, exam* sich für etw anmelden; **to put sb in for an exam/a race** jdn für eine Prüfung/für ein Rennen anmelden; **to put sb in for an award** jdn für eine Ehrung vorschlagen; **to put the car in for a service** das Auto zur Wartung (in die Werkstatt) bringen

e *(= install) central heating, car radio* einbauen

f *(= employ) night watchman* einsetzen; *(= elect) political party* an die Regierung bringen, ranbringen *(inf)*

g *(Sport, = send in) player* hereinnehmen; *team to bat* (als Innenmannschaft) hereinschicken

h *(= devote, expend) time* zubringen, verbringen *(with* mit), verwenden *(with* auf); **we have a couple of hours to put in at Heathrow** wir müssen uns in Heathrow ein paar Stunden die Zeit vertreiben; **to put in an hour at the piano** eine Stunde Klavier spielen; **to put in an hour's painting** eine Stunde lang malen; **could you put in a few hours' work at the weekend?** könnten Sie am Wochenende ein paar Stunden Arbeit einschieben?; **he put in a lot of hard work on the project** er hat eine Menge harter Arbeit in das Projekt gesteckt; **he always puts in a good day's work** er schafft jeden Tag ein ordentliches Arbeitspensum

VI **a** **to put in for sth** *(for job)* sich um etw bewerben; *for leave, rise, house also* etw beantragen

b *(Naut: = enter port)* **to put in at a port** in einen Hafen einlaufen; *(= call at)* einen Hafen anlaufen; **to put in to Bremen/harbour** in Bremen/in den Hafen einlaufen; **to put in for supplies** einen Hafen anlaufen, um die Vorräte aufzufüllen

▶ **put inside** **VT** *sep (inf, in prison)* einsperren *(inf)*

▶ **put off** ✪ 7.3 **VT** *sep* **a** *(= set down) passengers* aussteigen lassen *(prep obj* aus); *(forcibly)* hinauswerfen *(prep obj* aus); **the conductor put us off at the theatre** der Schaffner sagte uns *(dat)* am Theater Bescheid, dass wir aussteigen müssten; **we asked to be put off at the theatre** wir baten darum, uns *(dat)* am Theater Bescheid zu sagen

b *(= lay aside) uniform* ablegen, ausziehen; *responsibilities, worries* ablegen

c (= *postpone, delay*) *match, appointment etc* verschieben; *decision* aufschieben; *sth unpleasant* hinauszögern; **it's too late to put our visitors off** es ist zu spät, die Besucher (wieder) auszuladen; **to put sth off till later** etw auf später verschieben; **to put sth off for 10 days/until January** etw um 10 Tage aufschieben/auf Januar verschieben

d (= *make excuses to, be evasive with*) *questioner, boyfriend, creditor* hinhalten; **he's not easily put off** er lässt sich nicht so leicht beirren; **I won't be put off any longer** ich lasse mich nicht länger hinhalten

e (= *discourage*) die Lust nehmen *or* verderben *(+dat)*; **to put sb off sth** jdm etw verleiden, jdm die Lust an etw *(dat)* nehmen; **don't let his rudeness put you off** störe dich nicht an seiner Flegelhaftigkeit; **are you trying to put me off?** versuchst du, mir das mieszumachen *(inf)* *or* mir das zu verleiden?; **I've been put off the idea** diese Idee ist mir verleidet worden; **to put sb off doing sth** jdn davon abbringen *or (person also)* es jdm ausreden, etw zu tun

f (= *distract*) ablenken (*prep obj* von); **to put sb off the track** jdn von der Fährte abbringen; **he is easily put off his game** er lässt sich leicht vom Spiel ablenken; **I'd like to watch you if it won't put you off** ich würde dir gern zusehen, wenn es dich nicht stört

g (= *switch off*) *light, TV, heater* ausmachen, ausschalten; *power, motor* abstellen

▶ **put on** VT *sep* **a** *coat, shoes etc* anziehen; *hat* (sich *dat*) aufsetzen; *make-up* auftragen, auflegen; (*fig: = assume*) *accent, manners* annehmen; *facade, front* aufsetzen, vortäuschen; **to put on one's make-up** sich schminken; **to put on an air of innocence** eine unschuldige Miene aufsetzen; **his sorrow is put on** sein Kummer ist bloß Schau *(inf)*; **to put it on** *(inf)* so tun(, als ob); **to put sb on** *(inf)* jdn verkohlen *(inf)* → **front**

b (= *increase, add*) **to put on weight** zunehmen; **to put on a few pounds** ein paar Pfund zunehmen; **to put on speed** schneller fahren, beschleunigen; **he put on fifty runs** *(Cricket)* er erhöhte (das Gesamtergebnis) um fünfzig Punkte; **ten pence was put on the price of petrol** *(Brit) or* **gas** *(US)* der Benzinpreis wurde um zehn Pence erhöht; **he saw I wanted it and promptly put another £10 on (the price)** er sah, dass ich es haben wollte, und hat gleich noch einmal £ 10 aufgeschlagen; **he's been putting it on a bit** (= *gaining weight*) er hat ganz schön zugenommen

c *play* aufführen; *party* geben; *exhibition* veranstalten; *film* vorführen; *train, bus* einsetzen; *food (on menu)* auf die Speisekarte setzen; *(fig) act, show* abziehen *(inf)*; **Sobers was put on to bowl** Sobers wurde als Werfer eingesetzt; **he put on quite a show of being angry** er tat so, als wäre er wütend; **she put on a display of temper** sie inszenierte einen Wutanfall

d (*on telephone*) **to put sb on to sb** jdn mit jdm verbinden; **would you put him on?** könnten Sie ihn mir geben?

e (= *switch on*) *light, TV* anmachen, einschalten; **to put the kettle/dinner on** das Wasser/das Essen aufsetzen *or* aufstellen

f *watch etc* vorstellen → **clock**

g to put sb on to sth (= *inform about*) jdm etw vermitteln; **to put sb on to a plumber/garage** *etc* jdm einen Installateur/eine Reparaturwerkstatt *etc* empfehlen; **he put me on to a first-rate dentist** durch ihn bin ich an einen erstklassigen Zahnarzt gekommen; **what put you on to it?** was hat dich darauf gebracht?; **to put the police on to sb** die Polizei auf jds Spur bringen; **to put sb on to a winner/good thing** *etc* jdm einen heißen *(inf) or* todsicheren Tipp geben

▶ **put out** VT *sep* **a** (= *place outside*) *rubbish etc* hinausbringen; *cat, drunk* vor die Tür setzen; **to put the washing out (to dry)** die Wäsche (zum Trocknen) raushängen; **to be put out** (= *asked to leave*) vor die Tür gesetzt werden; **to be put out of a restaurant** aus einem Restaurant herausgeworfen werden; **to put sb out of business** jdn aus dem Markt drängen; **that goal put them out of the competition** mit diesem Tor waren sie aus dem Wettbewerb ausgeschieden; **she could not put him out of her mind** er ging ihr nicht aus dem Sinn; **to put sb's eyes out** jdm die Augen ausstechen → **grass**

b (= *stretch out, push out*) *hand, foot* ausstrecken; *tongue, head* herausstrecken; **to put one's head out of the window** den Kopf zum Fenster hinausstrecken → **feeler**

c (= *sprout*) *leaves, roots* hervorbringen, treiben

d *cards, dishes, cutlery* auflegen; *chessmen etc* aufstellen

e (= *farm out*) *work* weggeben, vergeben (*to* an *+acc*)

f (= *bring out, circulate*) *pamphlet, book* herausbringen; *propaganda* machen; *statement* abgeben; *message, appeal* durchgeben; *description* bekannt geben; (*on TV, radio*) *programme* bringen, senden

g (= *generate*) *kilowatts etc* abgeben; *horsepower* leisten

h (= *extinguish*) *fire, light, candle* ausmachen, löschen

i (= *make unconscious*) bewusstlos machen, betäuben; (*boxer*) k. o. schlagen

j (= *discontent, vex*) **to be put out (by sth)** (über etw *acc*) verärgert *or* ungehalten sein; **nothing seems to put her out** sie scheint sich über nichts zu ärgern

k (= *inconvenience*) **to put sb out** jdm Umstände bereiten *or* machen; **to put oneself out (for sb)** sich *(dat)* (wegen jdm) Umstände machen

l (= *dislocate*) *knee, shoulder* ausrenken; (*more severely*) auskugeln; *back* verrenken → **nose**

m (= *make inaccurate*) *instruments* ungenau machen; (*fig*) *calculations, figures* verfälschen

n to put money out at interest/at 12% Geld für Zinsen/zu 12% (Zinsen) verleihen

VI (*Naut: = set sail*) auslaufen; **to put out to sea** in See stechen; **to put out of port/from Bremen** aus dem Hafen/von Bremen auslaufen

▶ **put over** VT *sep* **a** = **put across b** (*esp US: = postpone*) verschieben (*to, until* auf *+acc*)

▶ **put through** VT *sep* **a** *plan, reform, proposal, bill* durchbringen; (*+prep obj*) bringen durch; *claim* weiterleiten; *deal* tätigen

b *+prep obj* (= *cause to undergo*) durchmachen lassen; **to put sb through a test/an exam** jdn einem Test/einer Prüfung unterziehen; **he has put his family through a lot (of suffering)** seine Familie hat seinetwegen viel durchgemacht; **his guilty conscience put him through hell** sein schlechtes Gewissen machte ihm das Leben zur Hölle; **to put sb through university** jdn durch die Universität bringen; **they really put him through it!** *(inf)* den haben sie vielleicht durch die Mangel gedreht! *(inf)* → **mill, pace[2] N a**

c (= *connect by telephone*) *person* verbinden (*to* mit); *call* durchstellen (*to* zu); **to put a call through to Beirut** ein Gespräch nach Beirut vermitteln *or (caller)* anmelden

▶ **put together** VT *sep* **a** (= *put in same room, cage etc*) zusammentun; (= *seat together*) zusammensetzen; **he's better than all the others put together** er ist besser als alle anderen zusammen → **head 1 c b** (= *assemble*) zusammensetzen; *furniture, machine* zusammenbauen *or* -setzen; *book, essay, menu* zusammenstellen; (*Jur*) *case* zusammenstellen; *collection, evidence, facts* zusammentragen → **two**

▶ **put under** VT *sep* (*doctor*) betäuben

▶ **put up** VT *sep* **a** (= *raise, lift up*) *hand* hochheben; *car window* zumachen; *umbrella* aufklappen; *hair* hochstecken; *collar* hochschlagen, hochklappen; **put 'em up!** *(inf)* (*hands in surrender*) Hände hoch!; (*fists to fight*) na, mach schon! → **back N a, foot N a, wind[1] N a**

b (= *hoist*) *flag, sail* hissen, aufziehen

c (= *fasten up*) *picture, decorations, poster, curtains* aufhängen; *notice* anbringen

d (= *erect*) *building, fence, barrier* errichten; *ladder, scaffolding* aufstellen; *tent* aufschlagen

e (= *send up*) *missile, space probe* hochschießen

f (= *increase*) *numbers, sales, prices, demands* erhöhen; *rent* erhöhen, heraufsetzen; *sb's temperature, blood pressure* hochtreiben

g (= *propose*) *person (for job etc)* vorschlagen; (*as candidate*) aufstellen; (= *nominate*) vorschlagen; **he put himself up for the job** er hat sich für den Posten angeboten

h (= *offer*) **to put sth up for sale/auction** etw zum Verkauf anbieten/zur Versteigerung geben; **to put one's child up for adoption** sein Kind zur Adoption freigeben; **to put up resistance (to sb)** (jdm) Widerstand leisten, sich (gegen jdn) wehren → **fight N a, struggle, performance**

i (= *feign*) *facade* vortäuschen

j (= *give accommodation to*) unterbringen

k (= *provide*) *capital* bereitstellen; *reward* aussetzen

l to put sb up to sth jdn zu etw anstiften

VI **a** (= *stay*) wohnen; (*for one night*) übernachten

b to put up for election sich zur Wahl stellen

c put up or shut up! (*lit*) Geld her oder Maul halten! *(inf)*; (*fig*) Butter bei die Fische! *(inf)*

▶ **put upon** VI *+prep obj* (= *impose on*) ausnutzen; **I won't be put upon any longer** ich lasse mich nicht länger ausnutzen

▶ **put up with** VI *+prep obj* sich abfinden mit; **I won't put up with that** das lasse ich mir nicht gefallen

put and call (option) N (*St Ex*) Stellagegeschäft *nt*

putative ['pju:tətɪv] ADJ (*form*) vermutlich; *father, culprit* mutmaßlich

put: **put-down** N (= *snub*) Abfuhr *f*; **putoff** ['pʊtɒf] N *(inf)* faule Ausrede *(inf)*; **put-on** *(inf)* ADJ unecht, vorgetäuscht, aufgesetzt; *smile also* falsch N Bluff *m*, Schau *f* *(inf)*; **it's just a ~** das ist nur Schau *or* (ein) Bluff; **put option** N (*St Ex*) Verkaufsoption *f*, Rückprämiengeschäft *nt*

put-put ['pʌtpʌt] N (= *sound*) Tuckern *nt* VI tuckern

putrefaction [ˌpju:trɪ'fækʃən] N Verwesung *f*

putrefy ['pju:trɪfaɪ] VI verwesen

putrescent [pju:'tresnt] ADJ (*form*) verwesend

putrid ['pju:trɪd] ADJ verfault; *smell* faulig; (*fig: = corrupt*) zersetzt; (*inf: = horrible*) grässlich, ekelhaft; **the rubbish had become ~** der Abfall war verfault

putsch [pʊtʃ] N Putsch *m*

putt [pʌt] N Schlag *m (mit dem man einlocht)*; **he needed a long ~ at the 5th hole** am 5. Loch musste er aus großem Abstand einlochen VTI putten, einlochen

puttee, putty ['pʌtɪ] N (Wickel)gamasche *f*

putter[1] ['pʌtə'] N (= *golf club*) Putter *m*; **he's a good ~** er kann gut einlochen

putter[2] (*US*) VI = **potter**

putting ['pʌtɪŋ] N Putten *nt*, Einlochen *nt*; (*as game*) Putten *nt*

putting green N (*Golf*) kleiner Rasenplatz zum Putten; (= *green*) Grün *nt*

putty[1] ['pʌtɪ] N Kitt *m*; **he was ~ in her hands** er war Wachs in ihren Händen VT kitten

putty[2] N = **puttee**

putty knife N Spachtel *m*

put: **put-up** ADJ *(inf)* **a ~ job** (*Brit inf*) ein abgekartetes Spiel; **put-upon** ADJ *(inf)* ausgenutzt; **she had a rather ~ air** sie guckte so, als fiele ihr ein Zacken aus der Krone; **put-you-up** N (*Brit inf*) Schlafcouch *f*

putz [pʌts] N (*US*) **a** (*inf: = person*) Dussel *m* *(inf)* **b** (*vulg: = penis*) Schwanz *m* *(sl)*

puzzle ['pʌzl] N **a** (= *wordgame etc*) Rätsel *nt*; (= *toy*) Geduldsspiel *nt*; (= *jigsaw*) Puzzle(spiel) *nt*; **books of ~s** *or* **~ books for children** Rätselbücher *pl* für Kinder **b** *(= mystery)* Rätsel *nt*; **it's a ~ to me** es ist mir ein Rätsel **VT** **a** *(= baffle)* verblüffen; **to be ~d about sth** sich über etw *(acc)* im Unklaren sein; **the authorities are ~d** die Behörden stehen vor einem Rätsel **b** **to ~ sth out** etw (her)austüfteln **VI** **to ~ about** *or* **over sth** sich *(dat)* über etw *(acc)* den Kopf zerbrechen

puzzled ['pʌzld] ADJ *look, frown* verdutzt, verblüfft; *person* verwirrt, verblüfft; **to be ~ why ...** verwundert *or* verdutzt sein, dass ...; **she was ~ why he didn't phone** sie wunderte sich, dass er nicht anrief

puzzle-headed ['pʌzl'hedɪd] ADJ *person* wirr, konfus

puzzlement ['pʌzlmənt] N Verblüffung *f*, Verwirrung *f*; **the look of ~ on her face** die Verwirrung in ihrem Gesicht

puzzler ['pʌzlə'] N *(= problem)* harter Brocken *(inf)*

puzzling ['pʌzlɪŋ] ADJ rätselhaft; *story, mechanism, attitude, question* verwirrend; **to be ~ to sb** jdm rätselhaft sein; **the ~ thing is that ...** das Verblüffende an der Sache ist, dass ...

PVC *abbr of* **polyvinyl chloride** PVC *nt*

PVR *abbr of* **personal video recorder**

PVS **a** *abbr of* **persistent vegetative state** **b** *abbr of* **postviral syndrome**

Pvt *(US Mil) abbr of* **Private**

PX *(US) abbr of* **Post Exchange**

pye-dog ['paɪdɔg] N *(Brit)* streunender Hundebastard

pygmy, pigmy ['pɪgmɪ] **N** **a** **Pygmy** Pygmäe *m* **b** *(= small person, also fig)* Zwerg *m* **ADJ** **a** **Pygmy** Pygmäen-; **Pygmy tribe** Pygmäenvolk *nt* **b** Zwerg-; **~ goat** Zwergziege *f*

pyjama, *(US)* **pajama** [pə'dʒɑːmə] ADJ *attr* Schlafanzug-, Pyjama-; **~ jacket** Schlafanzug- *or* Pyjamajacke *f*; **~ party** Pyjamaparty *f*

pyjamas, *(US)* **pajamas** [pə'dʒɑːməz] PL Schlafanzug *m*, Pyjama *m*

pylon ['paɪlən] N Mast *m*

pyramid ['pɪrəmɪd] N Pyramide *f*

pyramidal [pɪ'ræmɪdl] ADJ pyramidenförmig *or* -artig

pyramid selling N ≈ Schneeballsystem *nt*

pyre ['paɪə'] N Scheiterhaufen *m (zum Verbrennen von Leichen)*

Pyrenean [pɪrə'niːən] ADJ pyrenäisch; **~ mountain dog** Pyrenäenhund *m*

Pyrenees [pɪrə'niːz] PL Pyrenäen *pl*

pyretotherapy [paɪ,retəʊ'θerəpɪ] N *(Med)* Fiebertherapie *f*

Pyrex® ['paɪreks] N Hartglas *nt*, ≈ Jenaer Glas® *nt*

pyrite(s) ['paɪraɪt(s)] N Eisen- *or* Schwefelkies *m*, Pyrit *m*

pyroclastic [,paɪərəʊ'klæstɪk] ADJ *(Geol) rocks* pyroklastisch; **~ flow** pyroklastischer Strom

pyrolysis [paɪ'rɔlɪsɪs] N *(Chem)* Pyrolyse *f*

pyromania [,paɪrəʊ'meɪnɪə] N Pyromanie *f*

pyromaniac [,paɪərəʊ'meɪnɪæk] N Pyromane *m*, Pyromanin *f*

pyrotechnic [,paɪərəʊ'teknɪk] ADJ *(lit)* pyrotechnisch; *(fig)* brillant

pyrotechnics [,paɪrəʊ'teknɪks] N *sing* Pyrotechnik *f*; *(pl: = display)* Feuerwerk *nt*; **a display of ~** *(lit, fig)* ein Feuerwerk *nt*

Pyrrhic ['pɪrɪk] ADJ **~ victory** Pyrrhussieg *m*

Pythagoras [paɪ'θægərəs] N Pythagoras *m*

Pythagoras' theorem N der Satz des Pythagoras

Pythagorean [paɪ,θægə'rɪən] ADJ pythagoräisch

python ['paɪθən] N Python *m*, Pythonschlange *f*

pyx [pɪks] N Hostienkelch *m*; *(for sick communion)* Bursa *f*

pzazz [pzæz] N Flair *nt*, Pfiff *m (inf)*

Q

Q, q [kjuː] N Q *nt*, q *nt* → **P**

Qatar [kæˈtɑːˈ] N Katar *nt*

QC *(Brit) abbr of* **Queen's Counsel**

QED *abbr of* **quod erat demonstrandum** q.e.d.

qt *abbr of* **quart**

q.t. [ˌkjuːˈtiː] N **on the ~** *(Brit inf)* heimlich

Q-tip® [ˈkjuːtɪp] N *(US)* Q-tip® *m*

qtr *abbr of* **quarter**

qua [kwɑː] ADV als

quack[1] [kwæk] N Schnattern *nt no pl*, Quaken *nt no pl*; **~-quack** *(baby-talk)* Entchen *nt* VI *(duck)* schnattern, quaken, quak machen *(inf)*; **what? she ~ed** was?, quakte sie

quack[2] N *(also* **quack doctor***)* Quacksalber *m*, Kurpfuscher *m*; *(hum: = doctor)* Doktor *m*, Medizinmann *m (hum)* ADJ *attr* Kurpfuscher-; **~ methods** Kurpfuschermethoden *pl*; **~ remedy** Mittelchen *nt*

quackery [ˈkwækərɪ] N Quacksalberei *f*, Kurpfuscherei *f*

quad [kwɒd] N **a** *abbr of* **quadrangle** Hof *m* **b** *abbr of* **quadruplet** Vierling *m* **c** *(Typ) abbr of* **quadrat** Quadrat *nt*, Blockade *f*; **em ~** Geviert *nt*; **en ~** Halbgeviert *nt* **d** *(Comput) abbr of* **quadruple**; **~ density** Vierfachdichte *f*

quad (ATV), quad bike N *(= four-wheeler)* Quad *nt*, vierrädriges Motorrad

Quadragesima [ˌkwɒdrəˈdʒesɪmə] N Quadragesima *f*

quadrangle [ˈkwɒdræŋgl] N **a** *(Math)* Viereck *nt* **b** *(Archit)* (viereckiger) (Innen)hof

quadrangular [kwɒˈdræŋgjʊləˈ] ADJ viereckig

quadrant [ˈkwɒdrənt] N Quadrant *m*

quadraphonic [ˌkwɒdrəˈfɒnɪk] ADJ quadrofonisch, quadrophonisch

quadrat [ˈkwɒdrət] N *(Typ)* = **quad c**

quadratic [kwɒˈdrætɪk] ADJ *(Math)* quadratisch

quadrature [ˈkwɒdrətʃəˈ] N *(Math, Astron)* Quadratur *f*

quadrilateral [ˌkwɒdrɪˈlætərəl] ADJ *(Math)* vierseitig N Viereck *nt*

quadrille [kwəˈdrɪl] N Quadrille *f*

quadrillion [kwəˈdrɪljən] N *(Brit)* Quadrillion *f*; *(US)* Billiarde *f*

quadrinomial [ˌkwɒdrɪˈnəʊmɪəl] ADJ viergliedrig, vierteilig

quadripartite [ˈkwɒdrɪˈpɑːtaɪt] ADJ *(Pol, form)* Vierer-; **~ talks** Vierergespräche *pl*; **~ agreement** Viermächteabkommen *nt*; **the ~ division of Berlin** die Teilung Berlins in vier Sektoren

quadriplegia [ˌkwɒdrɪˈpliːdʒə] N Tetraplegie *f*

quadriplegic [ˌkwɒdrɪˈpliːdʒɪk] ADJ tetraplegisch N Tetraplegiker(in) *m(f)*

quadroon [kwɒˈdruːn] N Viertelschwarze(r) *mf*, Viertelneger(in) *m(f) (neg!)*, Terzerone *m (spec)*, Terzeronin *f (spec)*

quadrophonic [ˌkwɒdrəˈfɒnɪk] ADJ quadrofonisch, quadrophonisch

quadruped [ˈkwɒdrʊped] N Vierfüß(l)er *m* ADJ vierfüßig

quadruple [ˈkwɒdrʊpl] ADJ vierfach; *(Mus)* Vierer-; **~ time** *(Mus)* Vierertakt *m* N Vierfache(s) *nt* VT vervierfachen VI sich vervierfachen

quadruplet [kwɒˈdruːplɪt] N *(= child)* Vierling *m*

quadruplicate [kwɒˈdruːplɪkɪt] ADJ vierfach N **in ~** in vierfacher Ausfertigung

quaff [kwɒf] *(old, hum)* VT trinken, schlürfen *(hum)* VI zechen *(old, hum)*; *(= take a swig)* schlucken

quaffable [ˈkwɒfəbl] ADJ *wine* süffig

quagmire [ˈkwægmaɪəˈ] N Sumpf *m*, Morast *m*; *(fig) (of vice etc)* Morast *m*; *(= difficult situation)* Schlamassel *m (inf)*; **the paths were reduced to a ~** die Wege waren völlig aufgeweicht *or* matschig; **he was bogged down in a ~ of tiny details** er hatte sich in einem Wust von kleinen Einzelheiten festgebissen

quail[1] [kweɪl] VI (vor Angst) zittern *or* beben *(before* vor *+dat)*

quail[2] N *(Orn)* Wachtel *f*; **~s' eggs** Wachteleier *pl*

quaint [kweɪnt] ADJ *(+er)* *(= picturesque) cottage, village, scene* malerisch, idyllisch; *(= charmingly old-fashioned) pub, custom, expression* urig, reizend; *(= pleasantly odd) idea* kurios, schnurrig, putzig; *nickname* originell; *person, way of speaking* drollig; **how ~ to live in such an old house** das ist ja urig, in so einem alten Haus zu wohnen; **what a thought, my dear, how ~!** nein so was, meine Liebe, wie originell!

quaintly [ˈkweɪntlɪ] ADV **a** *(= picturesquely)* malerisch, idyllisch; *decorated, finished* malerisch, urig **b** *written* schnurrig; *dressed* putzig; *nicknamed* originell; *old-fashioned* schnurrig, kurios, skurril; **their little daughter got up and danced so ~ that ...** ihr Töchterchen ist aufgestanden und hat so drollig getanzt, dass ...

quaintness [ˈkweɪntnɪs] N **a** *(= picturesque nature)* malerischer *or* idyllischer Anblick; *(= old-fashioned charm: of pub, custom, expression)* Urigkeit *f* **b** *(= oddness) (of idea)* Kuriosität *f*, Schnurrigkeit *f*, Putzigkeit *f*; *(of nickname)* Originalität *f*; *(of person, way of speaking)* Drolligkeit *f*

quake [kweɪk] VI zittern, beben *(with* vor *+dat)*; *(earth, rafters etc)* beben, erzittern N **a** *(inf: = earthquake)* (Erd)beben *nt* **b** *(of rafters etc)* Beben *nt*

quakeproof [ˈkweɪkpruːf] *(inf)* ADJ *building etc* erdbebensicher VT erdbebensicher machen

Quaker [ˈkweɪkəˈ] N Quäker(in) *m(f)*; **~ school** Quäkerschule *f*, von Quäkern geleitete Schule; **~ meeting** Treffen *nt* der Quäker; **~ family** Quäkerfamilie *f*

Quakerism [ˈkweɪkərɪzəm] N Quäkertum *nt*

quaking grass [ˈkweɪkɪŋˌgrɑːs] N Zittergras *nt*

quaky ADJ, **quakily** ADV [ˈkweɪkɪ, -lɪ] zitternd, zitt(e)rig

qualification [ˌkwɒlɪfɪˈkeɪʃən] N **a** *(on paper)* Qualifikation *f*; *(= document itself)* Zeugnis *nt*; *(= skill, ability, suitable quality)* Voraussetzung *f*; **what ~s do you have for this job?** welche Qualifikationen haben Sie für diese Stelle?; **English ~s are not recognized by Scottish schools** englische Zeugnisse werden von schottischen Schulen nicht anerkannt; **the only ~ needed is patience/is a knowledge of French** die einzige Voraussetzung ist Geduld/sind Französischkenntnisse **b** *(= act of qualifying)* Abschluss *m* von jds Ausbildung; **after his ~ as a doctor/an insurance broker** nachdem er seine Ausbildung als Arzt/Versicherungsagent abgeschlossen hatte; **prior to his ~** vor Abschluss seines Studiums **c** *(Sport)* Qualifikation *f* **d** *(= prerequisite)* Voraussetzung *f* **e** *(= limitation)* Einschränkung *f*, Vorbehalt *m*; *(= modification)* Modifikation *f*; **to accept a plan with/without ~(s)** einen Plan unter Vorbehalt/vorbehaltlos billigen **f** *(Gram)* nähere Bestimmung

qualified [ˈkwɒlɪfaɪd] ADJ **a** *(= having training)* ausgebildet; *(= with degree)* Diplom-; **~ engineer/interpreter** Diplomingenieur(in)/-dolmetscher(in) *m(f)*; **highly ~** hoch qualifiziert; **to be ~ to do sth** qualifiziert sein, etw zu tun; **to be fully ~** eine abgeschlossene Ausbildung haben; **~ to practise** *(doctor, lawyer)* zugelassen; **he is/is not ~ to teach** er besitzt die/keine Lehrbefähigung; **he was not ~ for the job** ihm fehlte die Qualifikation für die Stelle; **to be well ~ for sth** für etw hoch qualifiziert *or* gut geeignet sein; **he is fully ~** er ist voll ausgebildet; **now that you are ~** nachdem Sie nun Ihre Ausbildung abgeschlossen haben; **she's better ~ than any other candidate** sie ist besser qualifiziert als die anderen Kandidaten *or* als jeder andere Kandidat **b** *(= able, entitled)* berechtigt; *voter* berechtigt, zugelassen; **to be ~ to vote** wahlberechtigt sein; **I'm not ~ to speak for her** ich bin nicht kompetent, in ihrem Namen zu sprechen; **what makes you think you're ~ to judge her?** mit welchem Recht meinen Sie, sie beurteilen zu können? **c** *(= limited) praise, approval* bedingt, nicht uneingeschränkt; **we're only prepared to make a ~ statement about ...** wir können uns nur bedingt *or* mit Einschränkungen zu ... äußern; **in a ~ sense** mit Einschränkungen; **a ~ success** kein voller Erfolg; **a ~ yes** ein Ja *nt* mit Einschränkungen, ein bedingtes Ja; **~ acceptance** *(Comm)* bedingte Annahme

qualifier [ˈkwɒlɪfaɪəˈ] N **a** *(Sport: = person having qualified)* Qualifikant(in) *m(f)* **b** *(Sport: = qualifying match etc)* Qualifikationsspiel *nt*, Ausscheidungskampf *m* **c** *(Gram)* näher bestimmendes Wort

qualify [ˈkwɒlɪfaɪ] VT **a** *(= make competent)* qualifizieren; *(= make legally entitled)* berechtigen, das Recht geben *(+dat)*; **to ~ sb to do sth** *(= entitle)* jdn berechtigen, etw zu tun; **his experience qualifies him to make these decisions** aufgrund *or* auf Grund seiner Erfahrung ist er qualifiziert *or* kompetent, diese Entscheidungen zu treffen; **this qualifies him for promotion** dadurch kommt er für eine Beförderung in Betracht **b** *(= limit) statement, criticism* einschränken; *(= change slightly) opinion, remark* modifizieren, relativieren **c** *(Gram)* charakterisieren, näher bestimmen; **the adjective qualifies the noun** das Adjektiv bestimmt das Substantiv näher **d** *(= describe)* bezeichnen, klassifizieren VI **a** *(= acquire degree etc)* seine Ausbildung abschließen, sich qualifizieren; **to ~ as a lawyer/doctor** sein juristisches/medizinisches

Staatsexamen machen; **to ~ as a teacher** die Lehrbefähigung erhalten; **to ~ as an officer** das Offizierspatent erwerben; **your salary increases when you ~** Sie bekommen nach bestandener Prüfung ein höheres Gehalt
b *(Sport, in competition)* sich qualifizieren *(for* für); **those who pass the first round of tests ~ for the final interviews** diejenigen, die die erste Testreihe erfolgreich bearbeiten, kommen in die engere und letzte Auswahl
c *(= fulfil required conditions)* infrage *or* in Frage kommen *(for* für); **does he ~ for admission to the club?** erfüllt er die Bedingungen für die Aufnahme in den Klub?; **he hardly qualifies as a poet** er kann kaum als Dichter angesehen werden

qualifying ['kwɒlɪfaɪɪŋ] ADJ **a** *adjective* erläuternd **b** *(Sport)* Qualifikations-; **~ game** *or* **match** Qualifikations- *or* Vorrundenspiel *nt*; **~ examination** Auswahlprüfung *f*; **~ group** Qualifikations- *or* Vorrundengruppe *f*

qualitative ADJ, **qualitatively** ADV ['kwɒlɪtətɪv, -lɪ] qualitativ

quality ['kwɒlɪtɪ] N **a** *(= degree of goodness)* Qualität *f*; *(Comm, categorized)* Güteklasse *f*, Qualität *f*; *(of justice, education etc)* (hoher) Stand; **of the best ~** von bester Qualität; **of good/poor ~** von guter/schlechter Qualität, qualitativ gut/schlecht; **~ matters more than quantity** Qualität geht vor Quantität; **they vary in ~** sie sind qualitativ verschieden; **the excellent ~ of her mind** ihr hervorragender Verstand; **~ of life** Lebensqualität *f*; **~!** *(Brit inf: = great)* super gemacht! *(inf)*
b *(= characteristics: of person, thing)* Eigenschaft *f*; **he has the ~ of great patience** er hat viel *or* große Geduld, er ist sehr geduldig
c *(= nature)* Art *f*; **because of the unique ~ of the relationship** da es eine einzigartige Beziehung war
d *(of voice, sound)* Klangfarbe *f*; *(Ling)* Qualität *f*; *(of colour)* Farbqualität *f*
e *(old, hum, = high rank)* vornehmer Stand; **the ~** die Oberschicht, die vornehme Welt; **people of ~** Leute *pl* von Rang und Namen; **a lady of ~** eine vornehme Dame
f the qualities *(Brit: = newspapers)* die seriösen Zeitungen *pl*
ATTR **a** Qualitäts-; **~ goods** Qualitätsware *f*; **~ mark** Gütezeichen *nt*
b *(inf: = good)* erstklassig *(inf)*; *newspaper* angesehen, seriös; **the ~ press** *(Brit)* die seriöse Presse

quality: **quality control** N Qualitätskontrolle *f*; **quality controller** N *(Ind)* Qualitätskontrolleur(in) *m(f)*; **quality management** N *(Econ)* Qualitätsmanagement *nt*; **quality time** N intensiv genutzte Zeit; **today I spent some ~ with my children** heute habe ich mich einige Zeit den Kindern gewidmet

qualm [kwɑːm] N **a** *(= doubt, scruple)* Skrupel *m*, Bedenken *nt*; **I would feel** *or* **have no ~s about killing that dog** ich würde keine Bedenken *or* Skrupel haben, den Hund zu töten; **without the slightest ~** ohne die geringsten Skrupel *or* Bedenken; **without a ~** ohne jeden Skrupel; **~s of conscience** Gewissensbisse *pl*; **he suddenly had ~s about it** ihn überkamen plötzlich Skrupel *or* Bedenken **b** *(= misgiving)* Bedenken *nt*; **I had some ~s about his future** ich hatte mancherlei Bedenken hinsichtlich seiner Zukunft **c** *(old: = nausea)* Übelkeit *f*

qualmish ADJ, **qualmishly** ADV ['kwɑːmɪʃ, -lɪ] voller Skrupel; *person* immer wieder von Skrupeln geplagt

quandary ['kwɒndərɪ] N Verlegenheit *f*, Dilemma *nt*; **what a ~ he was in!** was für ein Dilemma!; **he was in a ~ as to** *or* **about what to do** er wusste nicht, was er tun sollte; **to put sb in a ~** jdn in Verlegenheit *or* in eine missliche Lage bringen

quango ['kwæŋgəʊ] N *(Brit) abbr of* **quasi-autonomous nongovernmental organization** *regierungsunabhängige Kommission*

> **QUANGO**
>
> Der Begriff **quango** (ein Akronym en aus **quasi-autonomous nongovernmental organization**) kam in den Siebzigerjahren in Großbritannien auf, als man eine Bezeichnung für Organisationen wie **Equal Opportunities Commission** oder **Race Relations Board** finden musste, die von der Regierung eingerichtet werden, aber keiner Regierungsbehörde unterstellt sind. Einige **quangos** üben Regierungsfunktionen aus, andere dagegen haben nur beratende Funktion. Kritisiert wird mittlerweile die Praxis, zahlreiche Bereiche aus der Verantwortlichkeit der Regierung in **quangos** auszulagern, die der Öffentlichkeit gegenüber nicht rechenschaftspflichtig sind.

quanta ['kwɒntə] *pl of* **quantum**

quantification [ˌkwɒntɪfɪ'keɪʃən] N Quantifizierung *f*

quantifier ['kwɒntɪfaɪə'] N *(Logic)* Quantor *m*

quantify ['kwɒntɪfaɪ] VT quantifizieren *(form)*, in Zahlen ausdrücken

quantitative ADJ, **quantitatively** ADV ['kwɒntɪtətɪv, -lɪ] quantitativ; *restrictions, controls* quantitativ, mengenmäßig; **in ~ terms** rein quantitativ *or* mengenmäßig betrachtet

quantity ['kwɒntɪtɪ] N **a** Quantität *f*; *(= amount)* Menge *f*; *(= proportion)* Anteil *m* *(of* an *+dat)*, Quantum *nt*; **to prefer ~ to quality** Quantität der Qualität vorziehen; **in ~, in large quantities** in großen Mengen; **what ~ did you order?** welche Menge haben Sie bestellt?; **a tiny ~ of poison** eine kleine Menge Gift; **what ~ of yeast was used?** wie viel Hefe wurde benutzt?; **the ~ of meat in these sausages is very small** der Fleischanteil in diesen Würsten ist sehr klein; **in equal quantities** zu gleichen Mengen *or* Teilen
b *often pl (= large amount or number)* Unmenge *f*; **quantities of books/beer** Unmengen von Büchern/Bier
c *(Math, Phys, fig)* Größe *f*
d *(Poet, Phon)* Quantität *f*

quantity: **quantity mark** N Quantitätszeichen *nt*; **quantity surveyor** N Baukostenkalkulator(in) *m(f)*

quantum ['kwɒntəm] N *pl* **quanta** *(Phys)* Quant *nt*; **the quality of life cannot be measured as a ~** Lebensqualität kann nicht in Zahlen ausgedrückt werden; **the ~ of satisfaction** das (Aus)maß an Zufriedenheit

quantum: **quantum jump**, **quantum leap** N *(Phys)* Quantensprung *m*; *(fig)* Riesenschritt *m*; **quantum mechanics** N *sing* Quantenmechanik *f*; **quantum number** N Quantenzahl *f*; **quantum physics** N *sing* Quantenphysik *f*; **quantum theory** N Quantentheorie *f*

quarantine ['kwɒrəntiːn] N Quarantäne *f*; **to be in ~** in Quarantäne sein; *(ship)* unter Quarantäne liegen; **to put sb in ~** jdn unter Quarantäne stellen ATTR Quarantäne-; **~ period** Quarantänezeit *f* VT *person, animal, ship, area* unter Quarantäne stellen

quark[1] [kwɑːk] N *(Phys)* Quark *nt*

quark[2] N *(= cheese)* Quark *m*

quarrel[1] ['kwɒrəl] N *(in window)* rautenförmiges Fensterglas

quarrel[2] N **a** Streit *m*; *(= dispute)* Auseinandersetzung *f*; **they have had a ~** sie haben Streit gehabt, sie haben sich gestritten; **let's not have a ~ about it** wir wollen uns nicht darüber streiten; **to start** *or* **pick a ~** einen Streit anfangen *(with* mit)
b *(cause for complaint)* Einwand *m* *(with* gegen); **I have no ~ with him** ich habe nichts gegen ihn
VI **a** *(= have a dispute)* sich streiten *(with* mit, *about, over* über *+acc)*; *(more trivially)* sich zanken; **to ~ over sth** sich über etw *(acc)* streiten; *(over inheritance)* sich wegen *or* um etw streiten; **to ~ over a girl** sich wegen eines Mädchens *or* um ein Mädchen streiten
b *(= find fault)* etwas auszusetzen haben *(with* an *+dat)*; **you can't ~ with that** daran kann man doch nichts aussetzen

quarrelling, *(US)* **quarreling** ['kwɒrəlɪŋ] N Streiterei *f*

quarrelsome ['kwɒrəlsəm] ADJ streitsüchtig; *woman also* zänkisch

quarrelsomeness ['kwɒrəlsəmnɪs] N Streitsucht *f*

quarrier ['kwɒrɪə'] N = **quarryman**

quarry[1] ['kwɒrɪ] N **a** Steinbruch *m*; **sandstone/slate** *etc* **~** Sandstein-/Schieferbruch *etc*
b *(fig)* Fundgrube *f* VT brechen, hauen VI Steine brechen *or* hauen; **to ~ for sth** etw hauen *or* brechen; *(fig)* nach etw suchen

▶ **quarry out** VT *sep block* heraushauen *or* -brechen

quarry[2] N **a** Beute *f* **b** *(fig: = thing)* Ziel *nt*; *(= person)* Opfer *nt*

quarryman ['kwɒrɪmən] N *pl* **-men** [-mən] Steinbrucharbeiter *m*, Steinhauer *m*

quart[1] [kwɔːt] N *(Measure)* Quart *nt*; **to try to put a ~ into a pint pot** *(fig)* Unmögliches versuchen

quart[2] N **a** *(Fencing)* Quart *f* **b** *(Cards)* Viersequenz *f*, Quart *f*; **~ major** Quartmajor *f*

quarter ['kwɔːtə'] N **a** *(= fourth part)* Viertel *nt*; **to divide sth into ~s** etw in vier Teile teilen; **the bottle was a ~/three-~s full** die Flasche war zu einem Viertel/zu drei Vierteln gefüllt, die Flasche war viertel/drei viertel voll; **a ~ (of a pound) of tea** ein Viertel(pfund) Tee; **a mile and a ~** eineinviertel Meilen; **a ~ of a mile** eine Viertelmeile; **it was a ~ as big as the other one** es war ein Viertel so groß wie das andere; **for a ~ (of) the price, for ~ the price** zu einem Viertel des Preises
b *(in expressions of time)* Viertel *nt*; **a ~ of an hour** eine Viertelstunde; **a ~ to seven, a ~ of seven** *(US)* (ein) Viertel vor sieben, drei viertel sieben *(dial)*; **a ~ past six, a ~ after six** *(US)* (ein) Viertel nach sechs, viertel sieben *(dial)*; **it's just on the ~** es ist gerade Viertel; **the clock strikes the ~s** die Uhr schlägt alle Viertelstunde; **the clock has just struck the ~** die Uhr hat eben Viertel *or* die Viertelstunde geschlagen; **an hour and a ~** eineinviertel Stunden, fünf viertel Stunden
c *(= fourth of year)* Vierteljahr *nt*, Quartal *nt*; **paid by the ~** vierteljährlich bezahlt; **a ~'s rent** die Miete für ein Quartal
d *(US)* Vierteldollar *m*, 25-Cent-Stück *nt*
e *(= district in town)* Viertel *nt*
f *(= area)* **he has travelled in every ~ of the globe** er hat schon alle Ecken der Welt bereist; **they came from all ~s of the earth** sie kamen aus allen Teilen der Welt; **in these ~s** in dieser Gegend
g *(= direction)* (Himmels)richtung *f*; **they came from all ~s** sie kamen aus allen Himmelsrichtungen
h *(Naut: = direction of wind)* Richtung *f*; **what ~ is the wind in?** aus welcher Richtung kommt der Wind?
i *(= side)* Seite *f*; *(= place)* Stelle *f*; **he won't get help from that ~** von dieser Seite wird er keine Hilfe bekommen; **in high ~s** höheren Orts; **in various ~s** an verschiedenen Stellen; **at close ~s** in der Nähe; *(= from nearby)* aus der Nähe; **they were unaccustomed to fighting at close ~s** sie waren nicht an den Nahkampf gewöhnt
j quarters PL *(= lodgings)* Quartier *nt (also Mil)*, Unterkunft *f*; **to take up one's ~s** *(Mil)* sein Quartier beziehen; **to be confined to ~s** *(Mil)* Stubenarrest haben
k *(Naut, for battle)* Posten *m*; **to take up one's ~s** Posten beziehen
l *(Naut, = part of ship)* Achterschiff *nt*; **on the port ~** backbord; **on the starboard ~** steuerbord
m *(= mercy in battle)* Schonung *f*, Pardon *m*; **to give ~** Schonung *or* Pardon gewähren; **he gave no ~** er kannte kein Pardon; **no ~ was asked for and none given** es wurde auf beiden

Seiten schonungslos gekämpft
n *(Her)* Wappenfeld *nt*
o *(of moon)* Viertel *nt*
p *(Sport, of match)* (Spiel)viertel *nt*
q *(Measure)* ≈ Viertelzentner *m*
ADJ Viertel-; **~ pound/mile** Viertelpfund *nt*/-meile *f*; **the/a ~ part** das/ein Viertel
VT a *(= cut into four)* vierteln; *beef, horse* (in vier Teile) zerlegen; *traitor's body* vierteilen
b *(= lodge)* unterbringen, einquartieren *(also Mil)* (on bei)

quarter: **quarterback** ['kwɔːtəbæk] **N** *(US)* **a** *(Ftbl)* Quarterback *m* **b** *(= chief coordinator etc)* Leiter(in) *m(f)*; **quarter day N** Quartalstag *m*; **quarterdeck N** *(Naut)* Achterdeck *nt*, Quarterdeck *nt*; **quarterfinal** [ˌkwɔːtə'faɪnl] **N** Viertelfinalspiel *nt*; **quarterfinalist** [ˌkwɔːtə'faɪnlɪst] **N** Teilnehmer(in) *m(f)* am Viertelfinale; **quarter horse N** *(breed of horse)* Quarter Horse *nt*; **quarter-hour N** Viertelstunde *f* **ADJ a** *(lasting 15 minutes)* viertelstündig **b** *(every 15 minutes)* viertelstündlich; **quarter-hourly ADJ, ADV** viertelstündlich

quartering ['kwɔːtərɪŋ] **N a** Vierteln *nt*; *(= division into four also)* Teilung *f* in vier Teile; *(of beef, horse)* Zerlegen *nt*; *(of traitor's body)* Vierteilen *nt* **b** *(Mil)* Einquartierung *f* **c** *(Her)* Einteilung *f* in vier Felder

quarterlight ['kwɔːtəlaɪt] **N** *(Brit)* Dreieckfenster *nt*; *(openable)* Ausstellfenster *nt*

quarterly ['kwɔːtəlɪ] **ADJ** vierteljährlich **N** Vierteljahresschrift *f* **ADV** vierteljährlich, alle Vierteljahre

quartermaster ['kwɔːtəˌmɑːstə'] **N a** *(Mil)* Quartiermeister *m* **b** *(Navy)* Steuermannsmaat *m*; **~'s store** Versorgungslager *nt*

Quartermaster General N Generalquartiermeister *m*

quarter: **quarter note N** *(US Mus)* Viertel(note *f*) *nt*; **quarter-note ADJ ~ rest** Viertelpause *f*; **quarter-pounder N** *(Cook)* Viertelpfünder *m*; **quarter sessions PL** vierteljährliche Gerichtssitzungen *pl*; **quarterstaff N** *(Hist)* Schlagstock *m*; **quarter tone N** Vierteltonintervall *nt*

quartet(te) [kwɔː'tet] **N** *(Mus: = foursome)* Quartett *nt*

quarto ['kwɔːtəʊ] **N** *(Typ)* Quart(format) *nt* **ATTR** *paper, volume* in Quart

quartz ['kwɔːts] **N** Quarz *m*; **~ (iodine) lamp** Quarzlampe *f*

quartz: **quartz clock N** Quarzuhr *f*; **quartz crystal N** Quarzkristall *m*

quartzite ['kwɔːtsaɪt] **N** Quarzfels *m*

quartz watch N Quarzuhr *f*

quasar ['kweɪzɑː'] **N** Quasar *m*

quash [kwɒʃ] **VT a** *(Jur) verdict* aufheben, annullieren **b** *rebellion* unterdrücken; *suggestion, objection* ablehnen

quasi- ['kwɑːzɪ-] **PREF** quasi-, quasi; **~religious** quasireligiös; **acting in a ~managerial role** quasi als Manager handelnd

quatercentenary [ˌkwætəsen'tiːnərɪ] **N** *(also* **quatercentenary celebrations***)* Vierhundertjahrfeier *f*; *(= anniversary)* vierhundertster Jahrestag

quaternary [kwə'tɜːnərɪ] **ADJ** *(Geol)* quartär; *(Chem)* quaternär, aus vier Teilen bestehend **N** *(Geol)* Quartär *nt*

quatrain ['kwɒtreɪn] **N** Vierzeiler *m*

quaver ['kweɪvə'] **N a** *(esp Brit Mus)* Achtel(note *f*) *nt*; **~ rest** Achtelpause *f* **b** *(in voice)* Beben *nt*, Zittern *nt*; **with a ~ in her voice** mit bebender *or* zitternder Stimme **VI** *(voice)* beben, zittern; *(Mus)* tremolieren **VT** mit bebender *or* zitternder Stimme sagen

quavering ['kweɪvərɪŋ], **quavery** ['kweɪvərɪ] **ADJ** *voice* bebend, zitternd; *notes* tremolierend

quay [kiː] **N** Kai *m*; **alongside the ~** am Kai

quayside ['kiːsaɪd] **N** Kai *m*; **the ~ bars** die Hafenkneipen *pl*

queasiness ['kwiːzɪnɪs] **N** Übelkeit *f*

queasy ['kwiːzɪ] **ADJ** *(+er) stomach* gereizt; **I feel ~** mir ist (leicht) übel; **it makes me ~** da wird mir übel; **don't do it if you feel ~ about it** wenn dir nicht wohl dabei ist, dann tus doch nicht; **a ~ feeling** *(unwell)* ein Gefühl *nt* der Übelkeit, ein Übelkeitsgefühl *nt*; **I had a ~ feeling about the whole thing** ich hatte ein ungutes Gefühl bei der ganzen Sache

Quebec [kwɪ'bek] **N** Quebec *nt*

Quebec(k)er [kwɪ'bekə'] **N** Quebecer(in) *m(f)*

queen [kwiːn] **N a** *(also fig)* Königin *f*; **she was ~ to George V** sie war die Gemahlin von Georg V.; **~ of the May** Maikönigin *f* **b** *(= bee, ant etc)* Königin *f* **c** *(Cards)* Dame *f*; **~ of spades** Pikdame **d** *(Chess)* Dame *f*; **~'s bishop/pawn** Damenläufer/-bauer *m* **e** *(inf: = homosexual)* Tunte *f (inf)* **VT a** *(Chess)* in eine Dame verwandeln *or* umwandeln **b** *(inf)* **to ~ it** die große Dame spielen; **to ~ it over sb** jdn herumkommandieren *(inf)* **VI** *(Chess)* sich in eine Dame verwandeln

queen: **Queen-Anne ADJ** *style, furniture, building* Queen-Anne-; **~ style furniture** Möbel *pl* im Queen-Anne-Stil; **queen bee N** Bienenkönigin *f*; **she's the ~ round here** *(fig inf)* sie ist hier die Nummer eins *(inf)*; **queen cake N** kleiner Rosinenkuchen; **queen consort N** Königin *f*, Gemahlin *f* des Königs; **queen dowager N** Königinwitwe *f*

queenhood ['kwiːnhʊd] **N** Rang *m* einer Königin

queenly ['kwiːnlɪ] **ADJ** königlich; *rule also* der Königin

queen: **queen mother N** Königinmutter *f*; **Queen's Bench N** Oberster Gerichtshof

Queensberry rules ['kwiːnzbərɪ'ruːlz] **PL** Queensberry-Regeln *pl*

queen's: **Queen's Counsel N** *(Brit)* Kronanwalt *m*/-anwältin *f*, Anwalt *m*/Anwältin *f* der Krone, ≈ Staatsanwalt *m*/-anwältin *f*; *(as title)* Justizrat *m*/-rätin *f*; **queen's English N** englische Hochsprache; **don't you understand the ~?** verstehst du denn kein Englisch?; **queen's evidence N to turn ~** *(Brit)* als Kronzeuge auftreten; **Queen's Guide N** Pfadfinderin *f* mit den höchsten Auszeichnungen

queen-size bed ['kwiːnsaɪz'bed] **N** *ca. 1,50 m breites Doppelbett*

queen's: **queen's peace N to keep the ~** sich ordnungsgemäß verhalten; **a breach of the ~** öffentliche Ruhestörung; **Queen's Scout N** Pfadfinder *m* mit den höchsten Auszeichnungen; **queen's shilling N to take the ~** *(old)* des Königs Rock anziehen *(obs)*; **Queen's Speech N** Thronrede *f*

> **QUEEN'S SPEECH, KING'S SPEECH**
>
> Die **Queen's Speech** (bzw. die **King's Speech**) ist die Rede, die der britische Monarch jedes Jahr zur feierlichen Parlamentseröffnung im Oberhaus vor den versammelten Parlamentsmitgliedern beider Häuser verliest. Sie wird vom Premierminister in Zusammenarbeit mit seinem Kabinett erstellt und enthält die Regierungserklärung für das kommende Jahr sowie Einzelheiten über geplante Gesetzesänderungen. In der Rede, die sowohl im Radio wie auch im Fernsehen direkt übertragen wird, bezieht sich der Monarch aus Tradition immer noch auf „My government".

queer [kwɪə'] **ADJ** *(+er)* **a** *(= strange)* eigenartig, seltsam, komisch; *(= eccentric)* komisch, kauzig; *(inf: = mentally unbalanced)* nicht ganz richtig (im Kopf) *(inf)*; **a ~-sounding name** ein komischer Name; **he's a bit ~ in the head** *(inf)* er ist nicht ganz richtig im Kopf *(inf)*; **doesn't it feel ~ being the only woman?** kommst du dir nicht komisch vor als einzige Frau?
b *(= causing suspicion)* verdächtig, nicht ganz hasenrein *(inf)*; **there's something ~ about it** da ist etwas faul dran *(inf)*
c *(inf) (= unwell)* unwohl; *(= peculiar) feeling* komisch; **I feel ~** *(= unwell)* mir ist nicht gut; *(= peculiar)* mir ist ganz komisch *(inf)*; **I came over all ~** mir wurde ganz anders *(inf) or* komisch *(inf)*
d *(pej inf: = homosexual)* schwul *(inf)*
N *(pej inf: = homosexual)* Schwule(r) *mf (inf)*
VT *(inf: = spoil)* versauen *(inf)*, vermasseln *(inf)*; **to ~ sb's pitch** *(inf)* jdm einen Strich durch die Rechnung machen

queer-bashing ['kwɪəˌbæʃɪŋ] **N** *(Brit pej inf)* Überfälle *pl* auf Schwule

queerly ['kwɪəlɪ] **ADV** eigenartig, seltsam, komisch

queerness ['kwɪənɪs] **N a** Eigenartigkeit *f*, Merkwürdigkeit *f*, Seltsamkeit *f* **b** *(pej inf: = homosexuality)* Schwulheit *f (inf)*

Queer Street N *(Brit inf)* **to be in ~** pleite *or* blank sein *(inf)*; **we'll really be in ~ if that happens** wenn das passiert, sind wir wirklich in Schwulitäten *(inf)*

quell [kwel] **VT** *fear* bezwingen; *passion* bändigen, zügeln; *riot* unterdrücken, niederschlagen; *anxieties* überwinden

quench [kwentʃ] **VT** *flames, fire, thirst* löschen; *(liter) desire* stillen; *enthusiasm* dämpfen

quenchless ['kwentʃlɪs] **ADJ** *(liter) flames* unlöschbar; *curiosity* unstillbar

quenelle [kə'nel] **N** *(Cook) (of meat)* Fleischklößchen *nt*; *(of fish)* Fischklößchen *nt*

quern [kwɜːn] **N** Hand- *or* Drehmühle *f*; *(Archeol)* Mahlstein *m*

querulous ['kwerʊləs] **ADJ** nörglerisch, missmutig; **a ~ person** ein Querulant *m*, eine Querulantin

querulously ['kwerʊləslɪ] **ADV** nörglerisch, missmutig

query ['kwɪərɪ] **N a** *(= question)* Frage *f*; **there was a note of ~ in his voice** seine Stimme hatte einen fragenden Unterton; **that raises a ~ as to whether …** das wirft die Frage auf, ob …; **that raises a ~ about …** das wirft die Frage *(+gen)* … auf
b *(Typ)* Fragezeichen *nt*
c *(Comput)* Abfrage *f*; **~ language** Abfragesprache *f*
VT a *(= express doubt about)* bezweifeln; *statement, motives* infrage *or* in Frage stellen; *bill, item, invoice* reklamieren; **I'm not ~ing your right to do that but …** ich bezweifle ja nicht, dass Sie dazu berechtigt sind, aber …; **£500! I'd ~ that if I were you** £ 500! da würde ich an Ihrer Stelle reklamieren; **I ~ whether …** ich bezweifle, ob …
b *(= check)* **to ~ sth with sb** etw mit jdm abklären
c *(with a question mark)* mit einem Fragezeichen versehen
d *(Comput) database* abfragen

quest [kwest] **N** *(= search)* Suche *f (for* nach*)*; *(for knowledge, happiness etc)* Streben *nt (for* nach*)*; **to go in ~ of sth** *(old, liter)* sich auf die Suche nach etw machen **VI a** *(old, liter: = seek)* suchen *(for* nach*)*; **to ~ for riches/truth** nach Reichtümern/der Wahrheit streben **b** *(Hunt)* die Beute aufspüren

question ['kwestʃən] ✪ 8.3, 12.3, 16.3, 26.1, 26.3 **N a** *(Gram etc)* Frage *f (to* an *+acc)*; *(Parl)* (An)frage *f (to* an *+acc)*; **to ask sb a ~** jdm eine Frage stellen; **don't ask so many ~s** frag nicht so viel; **they'll buy anything, no ~s asked** sie kaufen alles und stellen keine dummen Fragen; **what a ~ (to ask)!** was für eine Frage!; **(that's a) good ~!** (das ist eine) gute Frage!; **let me put the ~ another way** ich werde die Frage anders formulieren
b *no pl (= doubt)* Zweifel *m*, Frage *f*; **beyond (all) ~, without ~** ohne Frage, ohne (jeden) Zweifel; **his honesty is beyond ~** seine Ehrlichkeit steht außer Zweifel *or* Frage; **there is no ~ but that he has gone** *(form)* es besteht kein Zweifel darüber, er ist fort; **your sincerity is not in ~** niemand zweifelt an Ihrer Aufrichtigkeit; **to call sth into ~** etw infrage *or* in Frage stellen

c (= *matter*) Frage *f*; **that's another ~ altogether** das ist etwas völlig anderes; **that's not the ~** darum geht es nicht; **the German ~** die deutsche Frage; **it's simply a ~ of time** das ist einfach eine Frage der Zeit; **it's not just a ~ of money** es ist nicht nur eine Geldfrage *or* eine Frage des Geldes; **if it's only a ~ of whether ...** wenn es nur darum geht (*inf*) *or* sich darum handelt, ob ...

d no pl (= *possibility, likelihood*) **there is some ~ of whether ...** es ist ziemlich fraglich, ob ...; **there's no ~ of that happening** es steht außer Diskussion *or* es kann keine Rede davon sein, dass das passiert; **there's no ~ of a strike** von einem Streik kann keine Rede sein; **that's out of the ~** das kommt nicht infrage *or* in Frage; **the person/matter in ~** die fragliche *or* infrage *or* in Frage stehende Person/Angelegenheit

VT a (= *ask questions of*) fragen (*about* nach); (*police etc*) befragen, vernehmen, verhören (*about* zu); (*examiner*) prüfen (*on* über +*acc*); **my father started ~ing me about where I'd been** mein Vater fing an, mich auszufragen, wo ich gewesen war; **they were ~ed by the immigration authorities** ihnen wurden von der Einwanderungsbehörde viele Fragen gestellt; **I don't like being ~ed, she said** ich mag diese Verhöre nicht, sagte sie

b (= *express doubt about*) bezweifeln, zweifeln an (+*dat*); (= *dispute, challenge*) infrage *or* in Frage stellen; **they ~ whether it's worth it** sie bezweifeln, dass es der Mühe wert ist; **but I'm not ~ing that!** das bezweifle *or* bestreite ich ja nicht; **he ~ed her inclusion on the committee** er äußerte Bedenken gegen ihre Aufnahme in den Ausschuss

questionable ['kwestʃənəbl] ✪ 26.3 ADJ a (= *suspect*) fragwürdig; **of ~ morals** von zweifelhaftem moralischem Standard; **in ~ taste** geschmacklos b (= *open to doubt*) *statement, figures* fraglich; *advantage* zweifelhaft; **of ~ value** von fragwürdigem Wert

questionary ['kwestʃənərɪ] N (*esp Med*) Fragebogen *m*

questioner ['kwestʃənəʳ] N Fragesteller(in) *m(f)*, Frager(in) *m(f)*

questioning ['kwestʃənɪŋ] ADJ a *nature* neugierig, interrogativ, kritisch, in Zweifel ziehend; **to have a ~ mind** eine kritische Haltung haben, seiner Natur nach den Dingen auf den Grund gehen b (= *doubting*) *look* fragend N (*by parents, husband*) Verhör *nt*; (*by police also*) Vernehmung *f*; (*of candidate*) Befragung *f*; **after hours of ~ by the immigration authorities** nach stundenlanger Befragung durch die Einwanderungsbehörde; **they brought him in for ~** sie holten ihn, um ihn zu vernehmen

questioningly ['kwestʃənɪŋlɪ] ADV fragend

question: **question mark** N Fragezeichen *nt*; **to put a ~ over sth** etw infrage *or* in Frage stellen; **question master** N Quizmaster *m*

questionnaire [ˌkwestʃə'neəʳ] N Fragebogen *m*

question: **question tag** N (*Ling*) Frageanhängsel *nt*; **question time** N Zeit *f* für Fragen; (*Brit Parl*) Fragestunde *f*

queue [kjuː] N a (*Brit: of people, cars*) Schlange *f*; Warteschlange *f* (*also Comput*); **to form a ~** eine Schlange bilden; **to stand in a ~** Schlange stehen, anstehen; **to join the ~** sich (hinten) anstellen; **a ~ of cars** eine Autoschlange; **a long ~ of people** eine lange Schlange

b (*old: = pigtail*) Zopf *m*

VI (*Brit: also* **queue up**) Schlange stehen; (*people also*) anstehen; (= *form a queue*) eine Schlange bilden; (*people*) sich anstellen; **they were queuing outside the cinema** sie standen vor dem Kino Schlange; **we ~d for an hour** wir haben eine Stunde angestanden; **they were queuing for the bus** sie standen an der Bushaltestelle Schlange; **they were queuing for bread** sie standen nach Brot an; **people are queuing up to ...** (*fig*) die Leute schlagen sich darum, zu ...

queue: **queue-jump** VI (*Brit*) sich vordrängе(l)n; (*Mot*) aus einer Kolonne ausscheren und überholen; **queue-jumper** N (*Brit*) *jd, der sich vordräng(el)t* (*Mot*) Kolonnenspringer(in) *m(f)*; **the ~s were booed** die, die sich vordräng(el)ten, wurden ausgebuht; **queue-jumping** ['kjuːdʒʌmpɪŋ] N (*Brit*) Vordränge(l)n *nt*; (*Mot*) Kolonnenspringen *nt*; **hey you, no ~!** he, Vordränge(l)n gibts nicht! (*inf*)

quibble ['kwɪbl] VI (= *be petty-minded*) kleinlich sein (*over, about* wegen); (= *argue with sb*) sich herumstreiten (*over, about* wegen); **to ~ over details** auf Einzelheiten herumreiten; **he ~d about the design** er krittelte am Design herum; **they weren't arguing, just quibbling** sie diskutierten nicht, sondern stritten sich nur über Spitzfindigkeiten

N **these aren't really serious criticisms at all, just ~s** das ist doch keine ernsthafte Kritik, das sind doch nur Spitzfindigkeiten *or* Haarspaltereien; **I've got a few ~s about her work/the design** ich habe ein paar Kleinigkeiten an ihrer Arbeit/am Design auszusetzen; **I hope you don't think this is a ~, but ...** ich hoffe, Sie halten mich nicht für kleinlich, aber ...

quibbler ['kwɪbləʳ] N (= *petty critic*) Krittler(in) *m(f)*, Kritikaster *m* (*pej*); (= *hair-splitter*) Wortklauber(in) *m(f)*, Haarspalter(in) *m(f)*

quibbling ['kwɪblɪŋ] ADJ (= *petty*) *person* kleinlich; (= *hair-splitting*) *person, details, argument* spitzfindig N kleinliches Getue (*inf*); (= *petty criticism*) Krittelei *f*; (= *hair-splitting*) Haarspalterei *f*, Wortklauberei *f*; **all this ~ about details** dieses Herumreiten auf Einzelheiten

quiche [kiːʃ] N Quiche *f*

quick [kwɪk] ADJ (+*er*) a (= *rapid*) schnell; *answer* schnell, prompt; **be ~!** mach schnell!; (*on telephone etc*) fass dich kurz!; **come on, ~, ~!** komm, schnell, schnell *or* zack, zack (*inf*)!; **and be ~ about it** aber ein bisschen dalli (*inf*); **you were/he was ~** das ist ja schnell gegangen, das war ja schnell; **he's a ~ worker** er ist von der schnellen Truppe, er arbeitet schnell; **he was the ~est to be promoted** er wurde am schnellsten befördert; **he was too ~ for me** (*in speech*) das ging mir zu schnell; (*in escaping*) er war zu schnell für mich; **~ march!** (*Mil*) im Eilschritt, marsch!; **it's ~er by train** mit dem Zug geht es schneller; **to be ~ to do sth** etw ganz schnell tun; **he is ~ to criticize other people** er ist mit seiner Kritik schnell bei der Hand; **he is ~ to anger** er wird leicht zornig; **the ~est way to the station** der schnellste Weg zum Bahnhof; **what's the ~est way to the station?** wie komme ich am schnellsten zum Bahnhof?; **what's the ~est way to finish it?** wie werde ich am schnellsten damit fertig?

b (= *short, quickly done*) *kiss* flüchtig; *speech, synopsis* kurz; *rest* klein, kurz; **let me have a ~ look** lass mich mal schnell *or* kurz sehen; **we had a ~ meal** wir haben schnell etwas gegessen; **let's go for a ~ drive** komm, wir machen eine kleine Spritztour; **he took a ~ swig of whisky** er trank schnell einen Schluck Whisky; **to have a ~ chat (with sb)** (mit jdm) ein paar Worte wechseln; **could I have a ~ word?** könnte ich Sie mal kurz sprechen?; **could I have a ~ try?** darf ich mal schnell *or* kurz versuchen?; **I'll just write him a ~ note** ich schreibe ihm schnell mal *or* mal kurz; **I grabbed a ~ sleep** ich legte mich kurz hin; **time for a ~ beer** genügend Zeit, um schnell ein Bierchen zu trinken; **a ~ one** eine(r, s) auf die Schnelle (*inf*); (*question*) eine kurze Frage

c (= *lively, quick to understand*) *mind* wach; *person* schnell von Begriff (*inf*); *child* aufgeweckt; *temper* hitzig, heftig; *eye, ear* scharf; **the ~er children soon get bored** die Kinder, die schneller begreifen *or* die eine schnellere Auffassungsgabe haben, langweilen sich bald; **he is ~ at figures** er kann schnell rechnen; **to be ~ at doing sth** fix dabei sein, etw zu tun; **he's very ~** er begreift *or* kapiert (*inf*) schnell; **he's too ~ for me** mit ihm komme ich nicht mit; **~, isn't he?** (*in repartee*) der ist aber schlagfertig

N a (*Anat*) empfindliches Fleisch (*besonders unter den Fingernägeln*); **to bite one's nails to the ~** die Nägel bis zum Fleisch abkauen; **to be cut to the ~** (*Brit*) tief getroffen sein; **to cut sb to the ~** (*Brit*) jdn zutiefst verletzen

b pl (*liter*) **the ~ and the dead** die Lebenden und die Toten

ADV (+*er*) schnell

quick: **quick-acting** ADJ *medicine* schnell wirkend *attr*; *person* schnell handelnd; **quickbeam** ['kwɪkbiːm] N (*Bot*) Vogelbeerbaum *m*, Eberesche *f*; **quick-change artist** N (*Theat*) Verwandlungskünstler(in) *m(f)*; **quick-drying** ADJ *paint, concrete* schnell trocknend

quicken ['kwɪkən] VT a (*also* **quicken up**) beschleunigen b (*liter: = make more lively*) *feelings* erhöhen; *imagination* beflügeln (*geh*), anregen VI a (*also* **quicken up**) schneller werden, sich beschleunigen; **the pace ~ed** das Tempo nahm zu b (*liter, hope, interest*) wachsen; (*foetus*) sich bewegen

quick: **quick-fire questions** PL Fragen *pl* wie aus der Maschinenpistole; **quick-firing** ADJ (*Mil*) schnell feuernd; **quick fix** N Schnelllösung *f*; **quick-freeze** VT *food* einfrieren, einfrosten; **quick-frozen** ADJ Gefrier-, tiefgekühlt; **~ vegetables** Gefriergemüse *nt*

quickie ['kwɪkɪ] N (*inf*) (= *drink*) eine(r, s) auf die Schnelle (*inf*); (= *question*) kurze Frage; (= *sex*) Quickie *m* (*inf*); **the meeting has to be a ~** mit der Besprechung müssen wirs kurz machen (*inf*)

quicklime ['kwɪklaɪm] N ungelöschter Kalk

quickly ['kwɪklɪ] ADV schnell; **as ~ as I can** so schnell (wie) ich kann

quick motion N Schnellgang *m*; **in ~** (*Film*) im Zeitraffer

quickness ['kwɪknɪs] N a (= *speed*) Schnelligkeit *f*; **his ~ to appreciate the problem** die Schnelligkeit, mit der er das Problem erfasst hat b (= *intelligence*) schnelle Auffassungsgabe; **~ of mind** Fähigkeit *f*, schnell zu denken; **~ of eye** schnelle Auffassungsgabe; **~ of temper** heftiges *or* aufbrausendes Temperament

quick: **quicksand** N Treibsand *m*; **quickset hedge** N Hecke *f*; (= *hawthorn*) Weißdornhecke *f*; **quick-setting** ADJ *glue etc* schnell trocknend *attr*; *cement* schnell bindend *attr*; **quicksilver** N Quecksilber *nt* ADJ *attr* (*fig liter*) quecksilbrig, lebhaft; **quickstep** N Quickstepp *m*; **quick-tempered** ADJ hitzig, leicht erregbar; **to be ~** leicht aufbrausen; **quickthorn** N Rotdorn *m*; **quick time** N (*US Mil*) *Marsch im Normaltempo*; **quick-witted** ADJ geistesgegenwärtig; *answer* schlagfertig; **the more ~ candidates** die Kandidaten mit einer schnelleren Auffassungsgabe; **quick-wittedness** N Geistesgegenwart *f*, Schlagfertigkeit *f*, schnelle Auffassungsgabe

quid[1] [kwɪd] N *pl* - (*Brit inf*) Pfund *nt*; **20 ~** 20 Eier (*sl*); **to be ~s in** auf sein Geld kommen (*inf*)

quid[2] N (= *tobacco*) Priem *m*

quiddity ['kwɪdɪtɪ] N a (*Philos*) Quiddität *f* (*spec*), Wesen *nt* b (*liter: = quibble*) Spitzfindigkeit *f*

quid pro quo ['kwɪdprəʊ'kwəʊ] N Gegenleistung *f*

quiescence [kwɪ'esns] N Ruhe *f*, Stille *f*

quiescent [kwɪ'esnt] ADJ ruhig, still

quiet ['kwaɪət] ADJ (+*er*) a (= *silent*) still; *neighbours, person* ruhig, still; *engine* ruhig; *footsteps, music, car, voice* leise; **at night when the office is ~** nachts, wenn im Büro alles still ist; **double-glazing makes the house ~er** durch Doppelfenster wird das Haus ruhiger; **she was as ~ as a mouse** sie war mucksmäuschenstill (*inf*); **(be) ~!** Ruhe!; **to keep ~** (= *not speak*) still sein; (= *not make noise*) leise sein; **keep ~!** sei still!; **keep this ~** behalts für dich; **can't you keep your dog ~?** können Sie nicht zusehen, dass ihr Hund still ist?; **that book should keep him ~ for a while** das Buch sollte ihn eine Weile beschäftigt halten, mit dem Buch sollte er eine Weile zu tun haben; **to keep ~ about sth** über etw (*acc*) nichts sagen; **you've kept very ~ about it** du hast ja nicht viel darüber verlauten

lassen; **to go ~** still werden; *(music etc)* leise werden; **could you make the class ~ for a minute?** könnten Sie die Klasse für eine Minute zur Ruhe bringen?; **turn the volume down ~** dreh die Lautstärke zurück; **I can't make the radio any ~er** ich kann das Radio nicht (noch) leiser stellen
b *(= peaceful)* ruhig; *evening* geruhsam, ruhig; *conscience* gut, ruhig; *smile* leise; **this town is too ~ for me** die Stadt ist mir zu ruhig; **things are very ~ at the moment** im Augenblick ist nicht viel los; **business is ~** das Geschäft ist ruhig; **to have a ~ mind** beruhigt sein; **he had a ~ sleep** er hat ruhig geschlafen; **the patient had a ~ night** der Patient verbrachte eine ruhige *or* ungestörte Nacht; **to lead a ~ life** ein ruhiges Leben führen; **all ~ on the western front** im Westen nichts Neues; **yesterday everything was ~ on the Syrian border** gestern herrschte Ruhe *or* war alles ruhig an der syrischen Grenze; **I was just sitting there having a ~ drink** ich saß da und habe in aller Ruhe mein Bier *etc* getrunken
c *(= gentle) face, character* sanft; *child* ruhig; *horse* brav, gutwillig; *irony* leise
d *(= unpretentious, simple) dress, tie, colour* dezent; *style* einfach, schlicht; *elegance* schlicht; *wedding, dinner, funeral* im kleinen Rahmen
e *(= not overt) hatred, envy, despair* still; *resentment* heimlich; **I'll have a ~ word with him** ich werde mal ein Wörtchen (im Vertrauen) mit ihm reden; **could we have a ~ word together some time?** könnten wir uns mal unter vier Augen unterhalten?; **I caught him having a ~ drink** ich habe ihn dabei erwischt, wie er heimlich getrunken hat; **they had a ~ laugh over it** sie haben im Stillen darüber gelacht; **he kept the matter ~** er behielt die Sache für sich; **keep it ~** behalte es für dich
f *(= unobtrusive, confidential) dinner* ruhig, im kleinen Kreis; *negotiation* besonnen, vertraulich; *diplomacy* besonnen; **there are grounds for ~ optimism** zurückhaltender Optimismus scheint angebracht *or* am Platz
N Ruhe *f*; **a period of ~** eine Zeit der Stille; **in the ~ of the night** in der Stille der Nacht; **on the ~** heimlich; **he left on the ~** er ist still und heimlich weggegangen → **peace**
VT = **quieten**
VI *(US: = become quiet)* nachlassen, erlahmen, erlöschen; **his sobs ~ed** sein Schluchzen ließ nach

quieten ['kwaɪətn] **VT** *(Brit)* **a** *sb* zum Schweigen bringen; *noisy class, dog* zur Ruhe bringen; *crying baby* beruhigen; *engine* ruhiger machen **b** *(= make calm) person, conscience* beruhigen; *suspicion, fear* zerstreuen

▶ **quieten down** *(Brit)* **VI** *(= become silent)* leiser werden; *(= become calm)* sich beruhigen; *(after wild youth)* ruhiger werden; **quieten down, boys!** ein bisschen ruhiger, Jungens!; **things have quietened down a lot** es ist viel ruhiger geworden **VT** *sep person* beruhigen; *engine* ruhiger machen; **to quieten things down** *(situation)* die Lage beruhigen

quietism ['kwaɪɪtɪzəm] **N** Quietismus *m*

quietist ['kwaɪɪtɪst] **N** Quietist(in) *m(f)* **ADJ** quietistisch

quietly ['kwaɪətlɪ] **ADV** *(= making little noise)* leise; *(= peacefully, making little fuss)* ruhig; *(= secretly)* still und heimlich; *dressed* dezent; *(= placidly)* still; **to live ~** ruhig *or* zurückgezogen leben; **he's very ~ spoken** er spricht sehr leise; **a very ~ spoken young man** ein sehr ruhiger junger Mann; **to be ~ confident** insgeheim sehr sicher sein; **I can only think how happy I am, how ~ content** ich kann mich nur glücklich und zutiefst zufrieden schätzen; **I was sitting here ~ sipping my wine** ich saß da und trank in aller Ruhe meinen Wein; **he sat down and ~ died** er setzte sich hin und starb in aller Stille; **he refused to go ~** er weigerte sich, unauffällig zu gehen; **are you going to come ~?** *(said by policeman)* kommen Sie widerstandslos mit?, kommen Sie ohne Widerstand zu leisten mit?; **he slipped off ~** er machte sich in aller Stille davon *(inf)*; **they got married very ~** sie haben im kleinen Rahmen geheiratet; **and all the time he was ~ writing a novel about us** und die ganze Zeit hat er still und heimlich einen Roman über uns geschrieben

quietness ['kwaɪətnɪs] **N** **a** *(= lack of noise)* Stille *f*; *(of engine, car)* Geräuscharmut *f*; *(of footsteps etc)* Geräuschlosigkeit *f*, Lautlosigkeit *f*; *(of person)* stille Art; **the ~ of her voice** ihre leise Stimme; **then with the sudden ~ of the music ...** und dann, als die Musik plötzlich leise wurde ... **b** *(= peacefulness)* Ruhe *f* **c** *(of tie, colour)* Dezentheit *f*; *(of style)* Schlichtheit *f*

quietude ['kwaɪətju:d] **N** *(liter)* Ruhe *f*, Friede(n) *m*

quietus [kwaɪ'i:təs] **N** *(old, liter)* Todesstoß *m*; **to give sb his/sth its ~** jdm/einer Sache den Todesstoß versetzen; **he found his ~** er schied von hinnen *(liter)*

quiff [kwɪf] **N** *(esp Brit)* Stirnlocke *f*, Tolle *f*

quill [kwɪl] **N** **a** *(= feather)* Feder *f*; *(= feather stem)* Federkiel *m* **b** *(also* **quill-pen**) Federkiel *m*, Feder *f* **c** *(of porcupine)* Stachel *m*

quilt [kwɪlt] **N** *(= continental quilt)* Steppdecke *f*; *(unstitched)* Federbett *nt*; *(= bedspread)* Bettdecke *f* **VT** absteppen; *(with padding)* wattieren; **~ed jacket** Steppjacke *f*

quilting ['kwɪltɪŋ] **N** **a** *(= process)* (Ab)steppen *nt*, Wattieren *nt* **b** *(= material)* Steppstoff *m*

quim [kwɪm] **N** *(Brit sl)* Möse *f (vulg)*

quin [kwɪn] **N** *(Brit) abbr of* **quintuplet** Fünfling *m*

quince [kwɪns] **N** *(= fruit, tree)* Quitte *f*; **~ jelly** Quittengelee *nt*

quincentenary [ˌkwɪnsen'ti:nərɪ] **N** fünfhundertster Jahrestag; *(also* **quincentenary celebrations**) Fünfhundertjahrfeier *f*

quinine [kwɪ'ni:n] **N** Chinin *nt*

Quinquagesima [ˌkwɪŋkwə'dʒesɪmə] **N** Quinquagesima *f*

quinquennia [kwɪŋ'kwenɪə] *pl of* **quinquennium**

quinquennial [kwɪŋ'kwenɪəl] **ADJ** alle fünf Jahre (stattfindend); *(= lasting five years)* fünfjährig

quinquennium [kwɪŋ'kwenɪəm] **N** *pl* **quinquennia** *(form)* Jahrfünft *nt*

quinsy ['kwɪnzɪ] **N** *(old)* Mandelentzündung *f*

quint[1] [kwɪnt] **N** *(US) abbr of* **quintuplet** Fünfling *m*

quint[2] **N** *(Mus)* Quint(e) *f*

quintessence [kwɪn'tesns] **N** *(Philos, fig)* Quintessenz *f*; *(= embodiment)* Inbegriff *m*

quintessential [ˌkwɪntɪ'senʃəl] **ADJ** *(liter)* fundamental *(geh)*; **the ~ English gentleman** der Inbegriff des englischen Gentleman; **an instance of his ~ bad taste** ein Beispiel für seinen von Grund auf schlechten Geschmack; **the ~ Catholicism of his whole attitude** seine fundamental *(geh) or* durch und durch katholische Haltung

quintessentially [ˌkwɪntɪ'senʃəlɪ] **ADV** *(liter)* durch und durch; **they are ~ different** sie sind fundamental *(geh) or* von Grund auf verschieden; **this is ~ Bach** das ist Bach reinsten Wassers

quintet(te) [kwɪn'tet] **N** *(Mus: = group of five)* Quintett *nt*

quintillion [kwɪn'tɪljən] **N** *(Brit)* Quintillion *f*; *(US)* Trillion *f*

quintuple ['kwɪntjʊpl] **ADJ** fünffach **N** Fünffache(s) *nt* **VT** verfünffachen **VI** sich verfünffachen

quintuplet [kwɪn'tju:plɪt] **N** Fünfling *m*

quip [kwɪp] **N** witzige *or* geistreiche Bemerkung **VTI** witzeln

quipster ['kwɪpstə'] **N** Spaßvogel *m*

quire[1] ['kwaɪə'] **N** **a** *(= 24 sheets)* 24 Bogen Papier **b** *(= folded, unbound sheets)* Bogen *m*

quire[2] **N** *(obs)* = **choir**

quirk [kw3:k] **N** Schrulle *f*, Marotte *f*; *(of nature, fate)* Laune *f*; **by a strange ~ of fate** durch eine Laune des Schicksals

quirkiness ['kw3:kɪnɪs] **N** Schrulligkeit *f*

quirky ['kw3:kɪ] **ADJ** *(+er) person, character* schrullig

quirt [kw3:t] **N** *(US)* geflochtene Reitpeitsche

quisling ['kwɪzlɪŋ] **N** Quisling *m*

quit [kwɪt] *vb: pret, ptp* **quitted** *or* **quit** **VT** **a** *(= leave) town, army* verlassen; *this life* scheiden aus; *(= give up) job* aufgeben, kündigen; **I've given her notice to ~ the flat** *(form)* ich habe ihr die Wohnung gekündigt; **I've had notice to ~ the flat** *(form)* mir ist (die Wohnung) gekündigt worden; **the dog would not ~ his prey** *(liter)* der Hund wollte nicht von seiner Beute ablassen *(liter)*
b *(inf: = stop)* aufhören mit; **to ~ doing sth** aufhören, etw zu tun; **~ it!** hör (damit) auf!; **to ~ work** mit der Arbeit aufhören
c *(Comput) job, program* beenden, verlassen, aussteigen aus *(inf)*
VI **a** *(= leave one's job)* kündigen
b *(= go away)* weg- *or* fortgehen; **notice to ~** Kündigung *f*; **they gave me notice to ~** sie haben mir gekündigt
c *(= accept defeat)* aufgeben; **she doesn't ~ easily** sie gibt nicht so leicht *or* schnell auf
d *(Comput)* das Programm *etc* verlassen, beenden, aussteigen *(inf)*
ADJ **~ of** los *or* frei von, ledig *(+gen) (geh)*; **we are ~ of him** wir sind ihn los

quite [kwaɪt] **ADV** **a** *(= entirely)* ganz; *(emph)* völlig; **I am ~ happy where I am** ich fühle mich hier ganz wohl; **it's ~ impossible to do that** das ist völlig *or* gänzlich unmöglich; **you're being ~ impossible** du bist einfach unmöglich; **are you ~ finished?** bist du jetzt fertig?; **when you're ~ ready ...** *(iro)* wenn du dann fertig bist ...; **he's ~ grown up now** er ist jetzt schon richtig erwachsen; **I ~ agree with you** ich stimme völlig mit Ihnen überein; **he ~ understands that he must go** er sieht es durchaus *or* völlig ein, dass er gehen muss; **he has ~ recovered** er ist völlig *or* ganz wiederhergestellt; **that's ~ another matter** das ist doch etwas ganz anderes; **he said it in ~ another tone** er sagte es in einem ganz anderen Ton; **that's ~ enough for me** das reicht wirklich; **that's ~ enough of that** das reicht jetzt aber; **it was ~ some time ago** es war vor einiger Zeit; **not ~** nicht ganz; **you weren't ~ early/tall enough** Sie waren ein bisschen zu spät dran/zu klein; **I don't ~ see what he means** ich verstehe nicht ganz, was er meint; **you don't ~ understand** Sie verstehen mich anscheinend nicht richtig; **that's not ~ your colour** das ist nicht ganz die richtige Farbe für Sie; **he's not ~ the James Bond type** er ist nicht gerade der James-Bond-Typ; **it was not ~ midnight** es war noch nicht ganz Mitternacht; **sorry! – that's ~ all right** entschuldige! – das macht nichts; **I'm ~ all right, thanks** danke, mir gehts gut; **thank you – that's ~ all right** danke – bitte schön; **it's ~ all right, thank you, I can manage alone** das geht schon, danke, ich komme alleine zurecht; **~ (so)!** genau!, sehr richtig!, ganz recht!; **~ the thing** *(inf)* ganz große Mode
b *(= to some degree)* ziemlich; **~ likely/unlikely** sehr wahrscheinlich/unwahrscheinlich; **he's had ~ a lot to drink** er hat ziemlich viel *or* ganz schön viel *(inf)* getrunken; **~ a few people** ziemlich viele Leute; **he is ~ a good singer** er ist ein ziemlich guter Sänger; **I ~ like this painting** dieses Bild gefällt mir ganz gut; **yes, I'd ~ like to** ja, eigentlich ganz gern
c *(= really, truly)* wirklich; **she was a ~ beautiful girl** sie war wirklich eine Schönheit; **she's ~ a girl/friend** *etc* sie ist ein tolles Mädchen/eine tolle Freundin *etc*; **it's ~ delightful** es ist entzückend, es ist einfach wunderbar; **it was ~ a shock** es war ein ziemlicher *or* ganz schöner *(inf)* Schock; **it was ~ a disappointment/change** es war eine ziemliche *or* ganz schöne *(inf)* Enttäuschung/Veränderung; **that's ~ some bruise/car** *(inf)* das ist vielleicht ein blauer Fleck/ein Auto *(inf)*; **it was ~ a party** das war vielleicht eine Party! *(inf)*; **it was ~ an experience** das war schon ein Erlebnis; **he's ~ the gentleman**

now er ist jetzt ganz der feine Herr; **he's ~ a hero now** jetzt ist er ein richtiger Held; **~ the little party-goer, aren't we?** *(inf)* du bist wohl so eine richtige kleine Partynudel, wie? *(inf)*; **he's ~ a comedian, isn't he?** er ist ja sehr komisch

quits [kwɪts] ADJ quitt; **to be ~ with sb** mit jdm quitt sein; **shall we call it ~?** *(= agree to stop)* lassen wirs (dabei bewenden)?; *(when owing money)* sind wir quitt? → **double**

quittance ['kwɪtəns] N Schuldenerlass *m*

quitter ['kwɪtəʳ] N *(inf)* **he's not a ~** er gibt nicht so leicht auf

quiver¹ ['kwɪvəʳ] **VI** zittern; *(person also)* beben *(with* vor *+dat)*; *(wings)* flattern; *(lips, eyelids, heart)* zucken; *(flesh)* wabbeln **N** Zittern *nt*; Beben *nt*; Flattern *nt*; Zucken *nt*; Wabbeln *nt*

quiver² N Köcher *m*

quiverful ['kwɪvəfʊl] N *(of arrows)* Köchervoll *m*

qui vive [ˌkiːˈviːv] N **on the ~** auf dem Quivive *(dated)*, auf der Hut

quixotic [kwɪk'sɒtɪk] ADJ *behaviour, gesture etc* edelmütig, ritterlich; *ideals* schwärmerisch, idealistisch; **a foolish ~ act** eine Donquichotterie; **don't you find that a little ~?** finden Sie das nicht etwas versponnen?

quixotically [kwɪk'sɒtɪkəlɪ] ADV *behave* edelmütig, ritterlich

quiz [kwɪz] **N a** Quiz *nt* **b** *(US Sch inf)* Prüfung *f* **VT a** *(= question closely)* ausfragen *(about* über *+acc)* **b** *(US Sch inf)* abfragen, prüfen **c** *(obs: = stare at impudently)* mustern, beäugen **d** *(obs: = mock)* necken *(geh)*

quiz: **quizmaster** N Quizmaster *m*; **quiz programme**, *(US)* **quiz program** N Quizsendung *f*; **quiz show** N Quiz *nt*

quizzical ['kwɪzɪkəl] ADJ **a** *(= knowing, shrewd) air, look* fragend; *smile* zweifelnd; *face* wissend, gewitzt **b** *(= odd)* eigenartig, drollig

quizzically ['kwɪzɪkəlɪ] ADV *look* fragend; *smile* zweifelnd

quodlibet ['kwɒdlɪbet] N *(Mus)* Quodlibet *nt*, (Lieder)potpourri *nt*

quoin [kwɔɪn] N **a** *(= outer corner of wall)* Ecke *f*; *(= cornerstone)* Eckstein *m* **b** *(Typ)* Schließzeug *nt*

quoit [kwɔɪt] N Wurfring *m*

quoits [kwɔɪts] N *sing* Wurfringspiel *nt*; **to play ~** Wurfring spielen

quondam ['kwɒndæm] ADJ *(liter)* ehemalig, früher; **his ~ wife** weiland seine Gattin *(obs)*

Quonset (hut)® ['kwɒnsɪt('hʌt)] N *(US)* Nissenhütte *f*

quorate ['kwɔːreɪt] ADJ *(form)* **to be ~** ein Quorum haben

quorum ['kwɔːrəm] N Quorum *nt*; **to make a ~** ein Quorum haben, beschlussfähig sein

quota ['kwəʊtə] N **a** *(of work)* Pensum *nt* **b** *(= permitted amount)* Quantum *nt*; *(= share allotted)* Anteil *m*; *(of goods)* Kontingent *nt*; **to fix** *or* **impose a ~ on sth** etw kontingentieren; **the ~ of immigrants allowed into the country** die zugelassene Einwanderungsquote; **import ~** Einfuhrkontingent *nt*

quotability [ˌkwəʊtə'bɪlɪtɪ] N Zitierbarkeit *f*; **something with a little more ~ for the headlines** ein Zitat, das sich besser als Schlagzeile eignet

quotable ['kwəʊtəbl] ADJ zitierbar, zitierfähig; **a highly ~ author** ein gern zitierter Autor; **~ quips from his speech** geistreiche Bemerkungen aus seiner Rede, die sich als Zitate eignen

quota refugee N *(Pol)* Kontingentflüchtling *m*

quota system N Quotensystem *nt or* -regelung *f*

quotation [kwəʊ'teɪʃən] N **a** *(= passage cited)* Zitat *nt*; *(act)* Zitieren *nt*; **dictionary of ~s** Zitatenlexikon *nt*; **a ~ from Shakespeare** ein Shakespearezitat *nt*; **a ~ from the Bible** ein Bibelzitat *nt*; **a two-bar ~ from Bach** zwei Takte, die von Bach übernommen sind **b** *(Fin: = statement of price)* (Börsen- *or* Kurs)notierung *f* **c** *(Comm: = estimate)* (Preis)angebot *nt*; *(for building work etc)* Kostenvoranschlag *m*; **to get a ~** einen Kostenvoranschlag einholen

quotation marks PL Anführungszeichen *pl*, Anführungsstriche *pl*; **open/close ~** Anführungsstriche unten/oben; **single/double ~** einfache/doppelte Anführungszeichen; **to put a word in ~** ein Wort in Anführungszeichen *or* -striche setzen

quote [kwəʊt] ✪ 26.2 **VT a** *author, text* zitieren; **you can ~ me (on that)** Sie können das ruhig wörtlich wiedergeben; **please don't ~ me on this, but ...** *(= this isn't authoritative)* ich kann mich nicht hundertprozentig dafür verbürgen, aber ...; *(= don't repeat it)* bitte wiederholen Sie nicht, was ich jetzt sage, aber ...; **he was ~d as saying that ...** er soll gesagt haben, dass ...; **~ ... end ~** *or* **unquote** Zitat Anfang ... Zitat Ende; **and the ~(, unquote) liberals** und die Liberalen in Anführungszeichen
b *(= cite)* anführen; **to ~ sb/sth as an example** jdn/etw als Beispiel anführen
c *(Comm) price* nennen; *reference number* angeben; **how much did they ~ you for that?** wie viel haben sie dafür verlangt?, wie viel wollten sie dafür haben?
d *(St Ex)* notieren; **the shares are ~d at £2** die Aktien werden mit £ 2 notiert
VI a *(from person, text)* zitieren; **to ~ from an author** einen Schriftsteller zitieren, aus dem Werk eines Schriftstellers zitieren; **... and I ~** ... und ich zitiere
b *(Comm)* ein (Preis)angebot machen; *(building firm etc)* einen Kostenvoranschlag machen; **we asked six companies to ~** wir baten sechs Firmen um Preisangaben
N a *(from author, politician)* Zitat *nt*; **a two-bar ~ from Bach** zwei von Bach übernommene Takte
b quotes PL Anführungszeichen *pl*, Gänsefüßchen *pl (inf)*; **in ~s** in Anführungszeichen; **smart ~s** *(Comput)* typografische Anführungszeichen
c *(Comm)* Preis *m*; *(= estimate)* Kostenvoranschlag *m*

quoth [kwəʊθ] DEFECTIVE VB *(obs, hum)* sagte, sprach *(liter)*

quotidian [kwəʊ'tɪdɪən] ADJ *(form: = daily)* täglich; **the ~ lives of the people** der Alltag der Menschen

quotient ['kwəʊʃənt] N *(Math)* Quotient *m*

qv *abbr of* **quod vide** s.d.

qwerty keyboard ['kwɜːtɪ'kiːbɔːd] N Qwertytastatur *f*

R

R, r [ɑː'] N R *nt*, r *nt*; **three Rs** *(= reading, writing and arithmetic)* Lesen, Schreiben und Rechnen *(die drei grundlegenden Fähigkeiten eines gebildeten Menschen)*

R **a** *abbr of* **river** **b** *(US Film) abbr of* **restricted** für Jugendliche nicht geeignet

r *abbr of* **right** r.

RA *abbr of* **Royal Academy**

rabbet ['ræbɪt] N *(= notch)* Nut *f*; *(= joint)* Nutnaht *f*

rabbi ['ræbaɪ] N Rabbiner *m*; *(as title)* Rabbi *m*

rabbinical [rə'bɪnɪkəl] ADJ rabbinisch

rabbit ['ræbɪt] **N** Kaninchen *nt*; *(= fur also)* Kanin *nt (spec)*; **to behave like a ~ caught in the headlights** ängstlich und überrascht handeln **VI** **a** **to go ~ing** Kaninchen jagen, auf Kaninchenjagd gehen **b** *(Brit inf: also* **rabbit on**) quasseln, schwafeln, sülzen *(all inf)*

rabbit *in cpds* Kaninchen-; **rabbit burrow, rabbit hole** N Kaninchenbau *m*; **rabbit hutch** N Kaninchenstall *m*; **rabbit punch** N Nacken- *or* Genickschlag *m*; **rabbit warren** N **a** Gänge *pl* des Kaninchenbaus **b** *(fig: = maze)* Labyrinth *nt*

rabble ['ræbl] N *(= disorderly crowd)* lärmende Menge, lärmender Haufen *(inf)*; *(pej: = lower classes)* Pöbel *m*

rabble: **rabble-rouser** N Hetzer(in), Volksverhetzer(in) *m(f)*; **rabble-rousing** **N** Hetze *f*, Volksverhetzung *f* **ADJ** (auf)hetzerisch

Rabelaisian [,ræbə'leɪzɪən] ADJ **a** *(of Rabelais)* des Rabelais **b** *(= like Rabelais)* im Stile Rabelais'

rabid ['ræbɪd] ADJ **a** *(Vet)* tollwütig **b** *(= fanatical)* fanatisch; *reformer, hatred* fanatisch, wild

rabidness ['ræbɪdnɪs] N *(= fanaticism)* Fanatismus *m*; *(of reformer, hatred)* Wildheit *f*

rabies ['reɪbiːz] N Tollwut *f*

RAC *abbr of* **Royal Automobile Club**

raccoon N = **racoon**

race¹ [reɪs] **N** **a** Rennen *nt*; *(on foot)* Rennen *nt*, (Wett)lauf *m*; *(swimming)* Wettschwimmen *nt*; **100 metres ~** 100-Meter-Lauf *m*; **to run a ~ (against sb)** (mit jdm um die Wette) laufen; **to go to the ~s** zum Pferderennen gehen; **a day at the ~s** ein Tag auf der Pferderennbahn; **we were at the ~s yesterday** wir waren gestern beim Pferderennen; **the ~ for the Democratic nomination/the White House** das Rennen um die Nominierung des demokratischen Kandidaten/die amerikanische Präsidentschaft; **it was a ~ to get the work finished** es war eine Hetze, die Arbeit fertig zu machen; **a ~ against time** *or* **the clock** ein Wettlauf *m* mit der Zeit *or* gegen die Uhr; **his ~ is run** *(fig)* er ist erledigt *(inf)*

b *(= swift current)* Strömung *f*; *(= mill race)* Gerinne *nt*

c *(liter: of sun, moon)* Lauf *m*

VT **a** *(= compete with)* um die Wette laufen/reiten/fahren/schwimmen *etc* mit; *(Sport)* laufen/reiten/fahren/schwimmen *etc* gegen; **I'll ~ you to school** ich mache mit dir ein Wettrennen bis zur Schule; **the car was racing the train** das Auto fuhr mit dem Zug um die Wette

b *engine* hochjagen

c *(Sport) car* ins Rennen schicken; *horse* laufen *or* rennen lassen

VI **a** *(= compete)* laufen/reiten/fahren/schwimmen *etc*; **to ~ with** *or* **against sb** gegen jdn laufen *etc*, mit jdm um die Wette laufen *etc*; **we're racing against time (to get this finished)** wir arbeiten gegen die Uhr(, um fertig zu werden); **he ~s at Newmarket** er lässt seine Pferde in Newmarket laufen

b *(= rush)* rasen, jagen; *(on foot)* rennen, rasen; *(with work)* hetzen; **to ~ about** herumrasen/-rennen *etc*; **to ~ after sb/sth** hinter jdm/etw herhetzen *or* herjagen; **to ~ to get sth finished** Dampf machen, um etw fertig zu bekommen *(inf)*; **he ~d through his work** er jagte durch sein Arbeitspensum; **to ~ ahead with one's plans/work** *etc* seine Pläne/Arbeit *etc* vorantreiben; **the project is racing ahead** die Arbeit am Projekt geht mit Riesenschritten voran; **clouds ~d across the sky** Wolken jagten über den Himmel; **memories of the past ~d through her mind** Erinnerungen an die Vergangenheit jagten ihr durch den Kopf

c *(engine)* durchdrehen; *(pulse)* jagen, fliegen; *(heart)* rasen; *(thoughts, mind)* jagen

race² N **a** *(= ethnic group, species)* Rasse *f*; **of mixed ~** gemischtrassig; **of noble ~** *(person)* edler Herkunft *or* Abstammung; *(horse)* (von) edler Rasse; **~ is causing a problem in this town** es gibt Rassenprobleme in dieser Stadt **b** *(fig: of authors, poets etc)* Kaste *f*

race: **raceboat** N *(Sport)* Rennboot *nt*; **racecard** N Rennprogramm *nt*; **race conflict** N Rassenkonflikt *m*; **racecourse** N *(Brit)* Rennbahn *f*; **racegoer** N *(esp Brit)* Rennbesucher(in) *m(f)*; **race hatred** N Rassenhass *m*; **racehorse** N Rennpferd *nt*; **race meeting** N *(esp Brit)* Rennveranstaltung *f*

racer ['reɪsə'] N Rennfahrer(in) *m(f)*; *(= car)* Rennwagen *m*; *(= bicycle)* Rennrad *nt*; *(= yacht)* Rennjacht *f*; *(= horse)* Rennpferd *nt*

race: **race relations** N **a** *pl* Beziehungen *pl* zwischen den Rassen **b** *sing (= subject)* Rassenintegration *f*; **Race Relations Board** N *(Brit)* Amt *nt* für Rassenfragen; **race riot** N Rassenkrawall *m usu pl*; **racetrack** N Rennbahn *f*; **race walker** N *(Sport)* Geher(in) *m(f)*; **race walking** N *(Sport)* Gehen *nt*

rachitic [rə'kɪtɪk] ADJ *(Med)* rachitisch

rachitis [rə'kaɪtɪs] N *(Med)* Rachitis *f*

Rachmanism ['rækmænɪzəm] N *(Brit)* Mietwucher *m*

racial ['reɪʃəl] ADJ rassisch, Rassen-; *pride* auf die Rasse; **~ discrimination** Rassendiskriminierung *f*; **~ equality** Rassengleichheit *f*; **~ minority** rassische Minderheit; **~ prejudice** Rassenvorurteil *nt*; **~ violence** rassistische Gewalt; **to promote ~ harmony** das harmonische Zusammenleben der verschiedenen Rassen fördern; **to do sth on ~ grounds** etw aus rassistischen Gründen tun; **to vote along ~ lines** entsprechend der Rassenzugehörigkeit wählen

racial harassment N rassistisch motivierte Schikanierung

racialism ['reɪʃəlɪzəm] N *(esp Brit)* Rassismus *m*

racialist ['reɪʃəlɪst] **N** Rassist(in) *m(f)* **ADJ** rassistisch

racially ['reɪʃəlɪ] ADV *offensive, sensitive* in Bezug auf die Rasse; *abused* aufgrund *or* auf Grund seiner Rasse, in Bezug auf die Rasse; *diverse* multikulturell; *pure* rassisch; **he is ~ bias(s)ed** er hat Rassenvorurteile; **to be of ~ mixed parentage** gemischtrassige Eltern haben; **~ mixed marriage** gemischtrassige Ehe; **the schools were ~ integrated** die Schulen waren multikulturell; **~ superior** rassenmäßig überlegen; **to be ~ motivated** *(riots etc)* rassistisch motiviert sein; **a ~ motivated attack** ein ausländerfeindlicher Überfall *or* Angriff

racily ['reɪsɪlɪ] ADV *write* schwungvoll, feurig

raciness ['reɪsɪnɪs] N *(of speech, style, play)* Schwung *m*, Feuer *nt*; *(= risqué nature)* Gewagtheit *f*

racing ['reɪsɪŋ] N *(= horse-racing)* Pferderennsport *m*, Pferderennen *nt*; *(= motor racing)* Motorrennen *nt*; **he often goes ~** er geht oft zu Pferderennen/Motorrennen; *(= participates)* er nimmt oft an Pferderennen/Motorrennen teil

racing *in cpds* Renn-; **racing bicycle** N Rennrad *nt*; **racing car** N Rennwagen *m*; **racing certainty** N *(Brit fig)* absolute Sicherheit; **it's a ~ that ...** es ist absolut sicher, dass ...; **racing colours** PL Rennfarben *pl*; **racing cyclist** N Radrennfahrer(in) *m(f)*; **racing driver** N Rennfahrer(in) *m(f)*; **racing man** N Anhänger *m* des Pferderennsports; **racing pigeon** N Brieftaube *f*; **racing stable** N Rennstall *m*; **racing tyres** PL Rennreifen *pl*; **racing world** N Welt *f* des Rennsports; **racing yacht** N Rennjacht *f*

racism ['reɪsɪzəm] N Rassismus *nt*

racist ['reɪsɪst] **N** Rassist(in) *m(f)* **ADJ** rassistisch

rack¹ [ræk] **N** **a** *(for hats, toast, pipes etc)* Ständer *m*; *(for bottles, plates)* Gestell *nt*, Ständer *m*; *(= shelves)* Regal *nt*; *(= luggage rack)* Gepäcknetz *nt*; *(on car, bicycle)* Gepäckträger *m*; *(for fodder)* Raufe *f*

b *(US Billiards)* Rahmen *m*

c **to put sb on the ~** *(lit, fig)* jdn auf die Folter spannen; **to be on the ~** *(fig)* Folterqualen leiden

d *(US sl)* **she has a nice ~** sie hat viel Holz vor der Hütte *(inf)*

VT **a** *(to cause pain, also fig)* quälen, plagen; **~ed with pain/by remorse** von Schmerz/Gewissensbissen gequält *or* geplagt

b **to ~ one's brains** sich *(dat)* den Kopf zerbrechen, sich *(dat)* den Kopf *or* das Hirn zermartern *(inf)*

c *(Hist)* auf die Folter spannen, auf der Folter strecken

▶ **rack up** VT *sep* einbringen, hereinholen; **to rack up £200,000 in sales** £ 200 000 aus Verkäufen hereinholen; **to rack up 61% of the vote** 61% der Stimmen auf sich *(dat)* vereinen

rack² N **to go to ~ and ruin** *(person)* verkommen, vor die Hunde gehen *(inf)*; *(country, economy)* herunterkommen, vor die Hunde gehen *(inf)*; *(building)* verfallen, in Schutt und Asche zerfallen

rack³ VT *wine, beer* abfüllen

rack-and-pinion steering ['rækən'pɪnjən,stɪːrɪŋ] N *(Aut)* Zahnstangenlenkung *f*

rack car N *(US Rail)* Doppelstockwagen *m (für Autotransport)*

racket¹ [ˈrækɪt] N *(Sport: for tennis etc)* Schläger *m*

racket² N **a** *(= uproar)* Krach *m*, Lärm *m*, Krawall *m (inf)*; **to make a ~** Krach *etc* machen **b** *(inf: = dishonest business)* Schwindelgeschäft *nt (inf)*, Gaunerei *f (inf)*; *(making excessive profit)* Wucher *m*; **the drugs ~** das Drogengeschäft; **to be in on a ~** bei einer Gaunerei mitmischen *(inf)* **c** *(inf: = business, job)* Job *m (inf)*; **what's his ~?** was macht er? *(inf)*; **what ~ are you in?** was ist Ihr Job? *(inf)*

racketeer [ˌrækɪˈtɪəʳ] N Gauner(in) *m(f) (inf)*; *(in serious crime)* Gangster(in) *m(f)*; *(making excessive profit)* Halsabschneider(in) *m(f) (inf)*

racketeering [ˌrækɪˈtɪərɪŋ] N Gaunereien *pl (inf)*; *(= organized crime)* organisiertes Verbrechen; *(= excessive profit-making)* Beutelschneiderei *f (inf)*; **drugs ~** Drogenhandel *m*, Drogenschieberei *f (inf)*

racket press N Spanner *m*

racking [ˈrækɪŋ] ADJ *attr pain* rasend, entsetzlich; *cough* fürchterlich, quälend; *sob* entsetzlich, fürchterlich

rack: **rack railway** N Zahnradbahn *f*; **rack-rent** N Wuchermiete *f*; **rack wheel** N *(Tech)* Zahnrad *nt*

raclette [rəˈklet] N *(Cook)* Raclette *f or nt*

raconteur [ˌrækɒnˈtɜːʳ] N Erzähler(in) *m(f)* von Anekdoten

racoon, **raccoon** [rəˈkuːn] N Waschbär *m*

racquet [ˈrækɪt] N *(Brit)* = **racket¹**

racquetball [ˈrækɪtˌbɔːl] N *no pl* Racquetball *m*

racy [ˈreɪsɪ] ADJ *(+er)* **a** *speech, style, play* schwungvoll, feurig; *(= risqué)* gewagt **b** *wine* feurig **c** *(inf) car* rasant

RADA [ˈrɑːdə] *abbr of* **Royal Academy of Dramatic Art**

radar [ˈreɪdɑːʳ] N Radar *nt or m*

radar *in cpds* Radar-; **radar beacon** N Radarbake *f*, Radarfunkfeuer *nt*; **radar operator** N Bediener(in) *m(f)* eines/des Radargerätes; **radar scanner** N Rundsuchradargerät *nt*; **radar station** N Radarstation *f*; **radar trap** N Radarfalle *f*

raddle [ˈrædl] N Rötel *m*, Roteisenstein *m* VT *sheep* (mit Rötel) zeichnen

radial [ˈreɪdɪəl] ADJ *(Tech)* radial; *beams, bars, lines also* strahlenförmig; *(Anat)* Speichen- N Gürtelreifen *m*

radial: **radial artery** N Speichenschlagader *f*; **radial engine** N Sternmotor *m*; **radial(-ply) tyre** N Gürtelreifen *m*; **radial velocity** N Radialgeschwindigkeit *f*

radiance [ˈreɪdɪəns] N *(of sun, smile)* Strahlen *nt*; *(of colours also)* Leuchten *nt*

radian measure [ˈreɪdɪənˌmeʒəʳ] N *(Math)* Bogenmaß *nt*

radiant [ˈreɪdɪənt] ADJ **a** *sun* strahlend; *colours* leuchtend; *(fig) person, beauty, smile* strahlend (*with* vor +*dat*); *face* leuchtend, strahlend; **to be ~ with health** vor Gesundheit strotzen; **to be ~ with joy** vor Freude strahlen; **~ optimism** blendender *or* strahlender Optimismus **b** *(Phys)* Strahlungs-; *energy* strahlend, ausstrahlend; *heater* strahlend, ausstrahlend, wärmend N *(Phys, Math, Astron)* Strahl *m*

radiant heat N Strahlungswärme *f*

radiantly [ˈreɪdɪəntlɪ] ADV **a** *happy* strahlend **b** *(liter) shine* blendend, hell

radiate [ˈreɪdɪeɪt] VI **a** Strahlen aussenden; *(= emit heat)* Wärme ausstrahlen; *(heat, light, energy)* ausgestrahlt werden **b** *(lines, roads)* strahlenförmig ausgehen (*from* von) VT *heat, light* ausstrahlen; *electric waves, energy also* abstrahlen; *(fig) happiness, health, love* (förmlich) ausstrahlen

radiation [ˌreɪdɪˈeɪʃən] N *(of heat etc)* (Aus)strahlung *f*; *(= rays)* radioaktive Strahlung; **contaminated by** *or* **with ~** verstrahlt, strahlenverseucht; **exposure to ~** Strahlenbelastung *f*; **~ level** Strahlenbelastung *f*; **~ therapy** *or* **treatment** Strahlenbehandlung *f*; **~ damage/injuries** Strahlenschäden *pl*

radiation sickness N Strahlenkrankheit *f*

radiator [ˈreɪdɪeɪtəʳ] N *(for heating)* Heizkörper *m*, Radiator *m*; *(Aut)* Kühler *m*; **~ cap** Kühlerverschlussdeckel *m*; **~ grill** Kühlergrill *m*; **~ mascot** Kühlerfigur *f*

radiator coil N *(Tech)* Kühlschlange *f*

radical [ˈrædɪkəl] ADJ **a** *(= basic)* fundamental, Grund-; *difference, error* fundamental; *(= extreme) change, reform* radikal, grundlegend; *rethinking, re-examination* total; *measures* einschneidend, radikal; *reduction* radikal, fundamental, rigoros **b** *(Pol) person, organization, idea* radikal; *attitude* radikal, rigoros; **to effect a ~ cure** eine Radikalkur machen; **~ surgery** Radikalchirurgie *f* **c** *(Math)* Wurzel-; **a ~ expression** eine Wurzel **d** *(Bot) leaves* bodenständig N *(Pol)* Radikale(r) *mf*; *(Math, Gram)* Wurzel *f*; *(in Chinese)* Radikal *m*; *(Chem)* Radikal *nt*

radical: **radical fundamentalist** ADJ radikalfundamentalistisch; **radical Islamic** ADJ radikalislamisch

radicalism [ˈrædɪkəlɪzəm] N *(Pol)* Radikalismus *m*

radically [ˈrædɪkəlɪ] ADV *change, differ, improve* radikal, grundlegend; **there's something ~ wrong with this** hier stimmt etwas ganz und gar nicht

radical sign N *(Math)* Wurzelzeichen *nt*

radicchio [rəˈdɪkɪəʊ] N *(variety of chicory)* Radicchio *m*

radices [ˈreɪdɪsiːz] *pl of* **radix**

radicle [ˈrædɪkl] N *(Bot)* Keimwurzel *f*; *(= small root)* Würzelchen *nt*; *(Chem)* Radikal *nt*

radii [ˈreɪdɪaɪ] *pl of* **radius**

radio [ˈreɪdɪəʊ] N **a** Rundfunk *m*; *(also* **radio set***)* Radio *nt*; **to listen to the ~** Radio hören; **to hear sth on the ~** etw im Radio hören; **the programmes on the ~** die Radioprogramme *pl*; **he was on the ~ yesterday** er kam gestern im Radio **b** *(in taxi etc)* Funkgerät *nt*; **over the/by ~** über *or* per Funk; **to talk over the ~** über Funk sprechen; **they don't have (a) ~** sie haben keinen Funk VT *person* per *or* über Funk verständigen; *message, one's position* funken, durchgeben; **to ~ that all is well** funken *or* über Funk durchgeben, dass alles in Ordnung ist VI **to ~ for help** per Funk einen Hilferuf durchgeben

radio: **radioactive** ADJ radioaktiv; **radioactively** ADV radioaktiv; **~ contaminated** radioaktiv verseucht *or* verstrahlt; **radioactive waste** N radioaktiver Müll; **radioactivity** N Radioaktivität *f*; **radio alarm (clock)** N Radiowecker *m*; **radio amateur** N Funkamateur(in) *m(f)*; **radio announcer** N Rundfunkansager(in) *m(f)*, Rundfunksprecher(in) *m(f)*; **radio astronomy** N Radioastronomie *f*; **radio beacon** N *(Aviat, Naut)* Funkfeuer *nt*, Funkbake *f*; **radio beam** N Funkleitstrahl *m*; **radio broadcast** N Radiosendung *f*; **radio button** N *(Comput)* Optionsschaltfläche *f*, Optionsfeld *nt*; **radio cab** N Funktaxi *nt*; **radiocarbon dating** N Radiokarbonmethode *f*, Kohlenstoffdatierung *f*; **radio cassette recorder** N *(Brit)* Radiorekorder *m*; **radio communication** N Funkverbindung *f*; **radio compass** N Radiokompass *m*; **radio contact** N Funkkontakt *m*; **radio control** N Funksteuerung *f*; **radio-controlled** ADJ ferngesteuert, ferngelenkt; **radio direction finding** N Funkpeilung *f*; **radio engineer** N Rundfunktechniker(in) *m(f)*; **radio frequency** N Radiofrequenz *f*

radiogram [ˈreɪdɪəʊɡræm] N **a** *(= apparatus)* Musiktruhe *f* **b** *(= message)* Funkspruch *m* **c** = **radiograph**

radiograph [ˈreɪdɪəʊɡrɑːf] N Radiogramm *nt*; *(= X-ray)* Röntgenogramm *nt*, Röntgenbild *nt*

radiographer [ˌreɪdɪˈɒɡrəfəʳ] N Röntgenassistent(in) *m(f)*

radiography [ˌreɪdɪˈɒɡrəfɪ] N Röntgenografie *f*

radio: **radio ham** N Funkamateur(in) *m(f)*; **radioisotope** N Radioisotop *nt*

radiolarian [ˌreɪdɪəʊˈleərɪən] N *(Zool)* Strahlentierchen *nt*, Radiolarie *f (spec)*

radio link N Funkverbindung *f*

radiological [ˌreɪdɪəʊˈlɒdʒɪkəl] ADJ radiologisch

radiologist [ˌreɪdɪˈɒlədʒɪst] N Röntgenologe *m*, Röntgenologin *f*

radiology [ˌreɪdɪˈɒlədʒɪ] N Radiologie *f*; *(X-ray also)* Röntgenologie *f*

radio: **radio marker** N *(Aviat)* Markierungs-/ /Funk-/Anflugbake *f*; **radio mast** N Funkmast *m*; **radio message** N Funkmeldung *f*/-spruch *m*; **radio operator** N (Bord)funker(in) *m(f)*; **radiopager** [ˌreɪdɪəʊˈpeɪdʒəʳ] N Funkrufempfänger *m*, Piepser *m (inf)*; **radiopaging** [ˌreɪdɪəʊˈpeɪdʒɪŋ] N Funkruf *m*

radio play N Hörspiel *nt*

radio programme N Radio- *or* Rundfunkprogramm *nt*

radioscopy [ˌreɪdɪˈɒskəpɪ] N Radioskopie *f*; *(Med)* Röntgenuntersuchung *f*

radio: **radio set** N Radioapparat *m*, Rundfunkgerät *nt*; **radio silence** N *(Mil)* Funkstille *f*; **radio station** N Rundfunkstation *f*; **radio taxi** N Funktaxi *nt*; **radiotelephone** N Funksprechgerät *nt*; **radiotelephony** N Sprechfunk *m*; **radio telescope** N Radioteleskop *nt*; **radiotherapy** N Strahlen- *or* Röntgentherapie *f*; **radio truck** *(US)*, **radio van** *(Brit)* N Funk- *or* Übertragungswagen *m*; **radio wave** N Radiowelle *f*

radish [ˈrædɪʃ] N *(small red variety)* Radieschen *nt*; *(all other varieties)* Rettich *m*

radium [ˈreɪdɪəm] N Radium *nt*; **~ therapy** *or* **treatment** *(Med)* Radiumtherapie *f*

radius [ˈreɪdɪəs] N *pl* **radii** **a** *(Math)* Radius *m*, Halbmesser *m*; *(of ship, aircraft)* Aktionsradius *m*, Wirkungsbereich *m*; **within a 6 km ~ (of Hamburg)** in einem Umkreis von 6 km (von Hamburg) **b** *(Anat)* Speiche *f*

radix [ˈreɪdɪks] N *pl* **radices** *(Math)* Grundzahl *f*

radome [ˈreɪdəʊm] N *(Tech)* Radom *nt*, Radarkuppel *f*; *(at tip of aircraft)* Radarbug *m*/-nase *f*

radon [ˈreɪdɒn] N *(Chem)* Radon *nt*

RAF *abbr of* **Royal Air Force** königliche (britische) Luftwaffe

raffia [ˈræfɪə] N *(= plant)* Raphia(palme) *f*; *(= fibre)* Raphiabast *m*; *(for handicraft, garden)* Bast *m*; **~ work** Bastarbeit *f*; **~ table mat** Bastuntersetzer *m*

raffish [ˈræfɪʃ] ADJ *appearance* flott, verwegen; *person* flott, verwegen, schnittig; *place, behaviour* verwegen, zwielichtig

raffle [ˈræfl] N Tombola *f*, Verlosung *f* VT *(also* **raffle off***)* verlosen

raffle ticket N Los *nt*

raft [rɑːft] N Floß *nt*

rafter [ˈrɑːftəʳ] N (Dach)sparren *m*

rafting [ˈrɑːftɪŋ] N *(Sport)* Rafting *nt*; **to go ~** Raften gehen

rag¹ [ræɡ] N **a** Lumpen *m*, Fetzen *m*; *(for cleaning)* Lappen *m*, Lumpen *m*; *(for paper)* Lumpen *pl*, Hadern *pl*; *(inf: = shirt, dress)* Fetzen *m (inf)*; **~s** Lumpen *pl*; *(inf: = clothes)* Klamotten *pl (inf)*; **in ~s** zerlumpt, abgerissen; **~s and tatters** abgerissene Lumpen *pl*; **to go from ~s to riches** *(by luck)* vom armen Schlucker zum reichen Mann/zur reichen Frau werden; *(by work)* vom Tellerwäscher zum Millionär werden; **to feel like a wet ~** *(inf)* total ausgelaugt sein *(inf)*; **to lose one's ~** *(inf)* in die Luft gehen *(inf)* → **red rag** **b** *(pej inf: = newspaper)* Käseblatt *nt*

rag² N *(Brit inf)* *(= joke)* Jux *m (inf)*; **for a ~** aus Jux *(inf)*; **~ week** *(Univ) Woche, in der Studenten durch Aufführungen Geld für Wohltätigkeitszwecke sammeln* VT **a** *(= tease)* aufziehen, foppen **b** *(Brit: = play a trick on)* **to ~ sb** jdm einen Streich spielen, einen Jux mit jdm machen *(inf)*

raga [ˈrɑːɡə] N *(Mus)* Raga *m*

ragamuffin ['rægə,mʌfɪn] N Vogelscheuche *f* *(inf)*; *(boy)* Bengel *m*; *(girl)* Göre *f*; **you little ~** du kleiner Fratz

rag: **rag-and-bone man** N *(Brit)* Lumpenhändler *m*, Lumpensammler *m*; **ragbag** N Lumpensack *m*; *(woman)* Schlampe *f*; *(fig)* Sammelsurium *nt (inf)*; **rag doll** N Flickenpuppe *f*

rage [reɪdʒ] **N** Wut *f*, Zorn *m*; *(of storm)* Toben *nt*, Rasen *nt*; **to be in a ~** wütend sein, toben; **to fly into a ~** einen Wutanfall bekommen; **fit of ~** Wutanfall *m*; **to send sb into a ~** jdn wütend *or (stronger)* rasend machen; **to be (all) the ~** *(inf)* der letzte Schrei sein *(inf)*, voll angesagt sein *(inf)* **VI** toben, rasen; *(sea, war, debate)* toben; **to ~ against sb/sth** gegen jdn/etw wettern

ragged ['rægɪd] ADJ *person, clothes* zerlumpt, abgerissen; *beard, hair* zottig, strähnig; *animal's coat* zottig; *coastline, rocks, hole* zerklüftet; *wound* schartig, zerfetzt; *edge, cuff* ausgefranst; *(fig) performance, singing* stümperhaft; **to run sb ~** *(inf: = exhaust)* jdn fertigmachen *(inf)*; **to run oneself ~** *(inf)* sich selbst ganz fertig- *or* kaputtmachen *or* fix und fertig machen *(inf)*; **on the ~ edge** *(US fig)* gefährlich nah am Rande (des Abgrunds); **~ right** *(Typ)* Flattersatz *m*; **to set sth ~ left/right** *(Typ)* etw rechts-/linksbündig setzen

raggedly ['rægɪdlɪ] ADV **a** *(= in torn clothes) dress* abgerissen, zerlumpt **b** *(= unevenly)* stotternd, unregelmäßig

ragged robin N Kuckucklichtnelke *f*, Kuckucksnelke *f*

raggle-taggle [,rægl'tægl] ADJ *gipsy* zerlumpt; *army, group* zusammengewürfelt

raging ['reɪdʒɪŋ] **ADJ** *person* wütend; *fever* heftig, sehr hoch; *temperature* sehr hoch; *thirst* brennend; *pain, toothache* rasend; *storm, sea, wind* tobend; *inflation* galoppierend; *debate* hitzig, wütend, heftig; *nationalist, feminist* radikal, extrem, heftig; *nationalism, feminism* radikal, extrem; **he was ~** er tobte; **to be in a ~ temper** eine fürchterliche Laune haben; **to be ~ mad** *(inf)* eine Stinkwut haben *(inf)*; **a ~ success** ein überwältigender Erfolg **N** *(of person, storm)* Toben *nt*, Rasen *nt*; *(of sea)* Toben *nt*

raglan ['ræglən] **ADJ** Raglan-; **~ sleeve** Raglanärmel *m* **N** *(= coat)* Raglan(mantel) *m*

ragman N = **rag-and-bone man**

ragout ['rægu:] N *(Cook)* Ragout *nt*

rag: **rag rug** N Flickenteppich *m*; **ragtag and bobtail** N Hinz und Kunz *(+pl or sing vb)*; **the ~ of society** Krethi und Plethi *(+pl or sing vb)*; **ragtime** N Ragtime *m*; **rag trade** N *(inf)* Kleiderbranche *f*; **ragweed** N *(Bot)* beifußblättrige Ambrosia; **ragwort** N *(Bot)* Jakobskraut *nt*

raid [reɪd] **N** Überfall *m*; *(Mil also)* Angriff *m*; *(= air raid)* Luftangriff *m*; *(= police raid)* Razzia *f*; *(by thieves)* Einbruch *m* **VT** **a** *(lit)* überfallen; *(police)* eine Razzia durchführen in *(+dat)*; *(thieves)* einbrechen in *(+acc)* **b** *(fig hum)* plündern

raider ['reɪdə'] N *(= bandit)* Gangster(in) *m(f)*; *(= thief)* Einbrecher(in) *m(f)*; *(in bank)* Bankräuber(in) *m(f)*; *(= ship)* Kaperschiff *nt*; *(= plane)* Überfallflugzeug *nt*

rail[1] [reɪl] **N** **a** *(on bridge, stairs etc)* Geländer *nt*; *(Naut)* Reling *f*; *(= curtain rail)* Schiene *f*; *(= towel rail)* Handtuchhalter *m*; *(= altar rail)* Kommunionbank *f*; **~s** *(= fence)* Umzäunung *f* **b** *(for train, tram)* Schiene *f*, Gleis *nt*; **to go off the ~s** *(lit)* entgleisen; *(Brit fig) (morally)* auf die schiefe Bahn geraten; *(mentally)* zu spinnen anfangen *(inf)*; **the project is back on the ~s** *(fig)* das Projekt verläuft wieder nach Plan **c** *(= rail travel, railway)* die (Eisen)bahn; **to travel by ~** mit der Bahn fahren **VT** *goods* per *or* mit der Bahn verschicken *or* senden

▶ **rail in** VT *sep* einzäunen

▶ **rail off** VT *sep* abzäunen; **railed off from the road** gegen die Straße abgezäunt

rail[2] VI **to ~ at sb/sth** jdn/etw beschimpfen; **to ~ against sb/sth** über jdn/etw schimpfen

rail *in cpds* Bahn-; **railcar** N Triebwagen *m*; **railcard** N *(Brit Rail)* ≈ BahnCard® *f*; *(for young people also)* ≈ Juniorenpass *m*, ≈ Bahncard® *f (für Junioren)*; *(for families also)* ≈ Familienpass *m*, ≈ Bahncard® *f (für Familien)*; *(for senior citizens also)* ≈ Seniorenpass *m*, ≈ Bahncard® *f (für Senioren)*; **rail company** N Bahngesellschaft *f*; **railhead** N Endbahnhof *m*; *(= end of track)* Gleisende *nt*

railing ['reɪlɪŋ] N *(= rail)* Geländer *nt*; *(Naut)* Reling *f*; *(= fence: also* **railings***)* Zaun *m*

raillery ['reɪlərɪ] N Neckerei *f*, Stichelei *f*, gutmütiger Spott

railroad ['reɪlrəʊd] **N** *(US)* (Eisen)bahn *f* **VT** **a** *(US) goods* per *or* mit der Bahn befördern **b** *(inf)* **to ~ a bill** eine Gesetzesvorlage durchpeitschen; **to ~ sb into doing sth** jdn dazu hetzen, etw zu tun

railroad car N *(US)* Eisenbahnwaggon *m*/-wagen *m*

railroader ['reɪlrəʊdə'] N *(US)* Eisenbahner(in) *m(f)*

rail: **rail strike** N Bahnstreik *m*; **rail traffic** N Bahnverkehr *m*

railway ['reɪlweɪ] N *(Brit)* (Eisen)bahn *f*; *(= track)* Gleis *nt*

railway *(Brit)*: **railway carriage** N Eisenbahnwagen *m*; **railway crossing** N Bahnübergang *m*; **railway engine** N Lokomotive *f*; **railway engineering** N Bahntechnik *f*, Bahnbautechnik *f*; **railway guide** N Kursbuch *nt*; **railway line** N (Eisen)bahnlinie *f*; *(= track)* Gleis *nt*; **railwayman** N Eisenbahner *m*; **railway network** N Bahnnetz *nt*; **railway porter** N Gepäckträger(in) *m(f)*; **railway station** N Bahnhof *m*; **railwaywoman** N Eisenbahnerin *f*

railworker ['reɪlwɜ:kə'] N Bahnarbeiter(in) *m(f)*

raiment ['reɪmənt] N *(liter)* Gewand *nt (liter)*

rain [reɪn] **N** **a** Regen *m*; **in the ~** im Regen; **(come) ~ or shine** *(lit)* ob es regnet oder schneit; *(fig)* was auch geschieht; **the ~s** die Regenzeit → **right** **b** *(fig: of arrows, bullets, blows)* Hagel *m* **VI** *impers (lit, fig)* regnen; **it is ~ing** es regnet; **it never ~s but it pours** *(Brit prov)* **when it ~s, it pours** *(US prov)* ein Unglück kommt selten allein *(prov)*; **to ~ on sb's parade** *(US fig)* jdm in die Suppe spucken *(inf)* **VT** **to ~ blows on sb** einen Hagel von Schlägen auf jdn niedergehen lassen **VT** *impers* **it's ~ing cats and dogs** *(inf)* es gießt wie aus Kübeln, es schüttet nur so *(inf)*

▶ **rain down** VI *(blows etc)* niederprasseln *(upon* auf *+acc)*

▶ **rain off**, *(US)* **rain out** VT *sep* **to be rained off** wegen Regen nicht stattfinden; *(= abandoned)* wegen Regen abgebrochen werden

rain *in cpds* Regen-; **rain belt** N Regenzone *f*

rainbow ['reɪnbəʊ] N Regenbogen *m*; **a dress (in) all the colours of the ~** ein Kleid in allen Regenbogenfarben; **a pot of gold at the end of the ~** ein Wunschtraum *m*

rainbow: **rainbow coalition** N Regenbogenkoalition *f*; **rainbow family** N Regenbogenfamilie *f*; **rainbow flag** N Regenbogenflagge *f or* -fahne *f*; **rainbow trout** N Regenbogenforelle *f*

rain: **rain check** N *(esp US)* **I'll take a ~ on that** *(fig inf)* das verschiebe ich auf ein andermal; **rain cloud** N Regenwolke *f*; **raincoat** N Regenmantel *m*; **rain dance** N Regentanz *m*; **raindrop** N Regentropfen *m*; **rainfall** N Niederschlag *m*; **rain forest** N Regenwald *m*; **rain gauge** N Regenmesser *m*; **rain hood** N Regenhaube *f*; *(of anorak etc)* Kapuze *f*

raininess ['reɪnɪnɪs] N regnerisches Wetter, Regenwetter *nt*; *(of season, area)* Neigung *f* zu regnerischem Wetter

rain: **rainless** ADJ niederschlagsfrei *(Met)*, ohne Regen, regenfrei; **rainout** N *(US Sport)* wegen Regens abgesagtes Spiel *nt*; **rainproof** **ADJ** wasserfest, wasserdicht **VT** imprägnieren; **rain-sodden** ['reɪn,sɒdn] ADJ *soil* aufgeweicht; **rainstorm** N schwere Regenfälle *pl*; **rainswept** ['reɪnswept] ADJ *attr* regengepeitscht; *evening* regnerisch; **raintight** ['reɪntaɪt] ADJ wasserfest, wasserdicht; **rainwater** N Regenwasser *nt*; **rainwear** N Regenkleidung *f*

rainy ['reɪnɪ] ADJ *(+er)* regnerisch, Regen-; *day also* verregnet; *area also* regenreich; **~ season** Regenzeit *f*; **a ~ spell** ein regnerischer Abschnitt; **to keep** *or* **save sth for a ~ day** *(fig)* etw für schlechte Zeiten zurücklegen *or* aufheben

raise [reɪz] ✪ 26.1, 26.3 **VT** **a** *(= lift) object, arm, head* heben; *blinds, eyebrow* hochziehen; *(Theat) curtain* hochziehen; *(Naut) anchor* lichten; *sunken ship* heben; *(Med) blister* bilden; **to ~ one's hat to sb** *(lit, fig)* den Hut vor jdm ziehen *or* lüften; **to ~ one's glass to sb** jdm zutrinken; **to ~ one's fist to sb** jdm mit der Faust drohen; **to ~ one's hand against sb** die Hand gegen jdn erheben; **to ~ one's eyes to heaven** die Augen zum Himmel erheben; **to ~ the pitch** *(Mus)* eine höhere Tonlage wählen; **to ~ the dead** die Toten wieder zum Leben erwecken *or* auferstehen lassen; **to ~ sb from the dead** jdn von den Toten erwecken; **to ~ one's voice** lauter sprechen; *(= get angry)* laut werden; **not a voice was ~d in protest** nicht eine Stimme des Protests wurde laut; **to ~ sb's/one's hopes** jdm/sich Hoffnung machen; **to ~ the people to revolt** das Volk zur Revolution aufhetzen; **to ~ the roof** *(fig) (with noise)* das Haus zum Beben bringen; *(with approval)* in Begeisterungsstürme ausbrechen; *(with anger)* fürchterlich toben; **the Opposition ~d the roof at the Government's proposals** die Opposition buhte gewaltig, als sie die Vorschläge der Regierung hörte → **eyebrow, toast**

b *(in height) (by* um*) wall, ceiling* erhöhen; *level* anheben

c *(= increase) (to* auf *+acc)* erhöhen; *price* erhöhen, anheben; *limit, standard* anheben, heraufsetzen; **to ~ the stakes** den Einsatz erhöhen; **to ~ the tone** das Niveau heben; **England has to ~ its game** das Spielniveau der englischen Mannschaft muss sich verbessern

d *(= promote)* (er)heben *(to* in *+acc)* → **peerage**

e *(= build, erect) statue, building* errichten

f *(= create, evoke) problem, difficulty* schaffen, aufwerfen; *question* aufwerfen, vorbringen; *objection* erheben; *suspicion, hope* (er)wecken; *spirits, ghosts* (herauf)beschwören; *mutiny* anzetteln; **to ~ a cheer** *(in others)* Beifall ernten; *(oneself)* Beifall spenden; **to ~ a smile** *(in others)* ein Lächeln hervorrufen; *(oneself)* lächeln; **to ~ a protest** protestieren; **to ~ hell** *(inf)* einen Höllenspektakel machen *(inf)*

g *(= grow, breed) children* aufziehen, großziehen; *animals* aufziehen; *crops* anbauen; **to ~ a family** Kinder großziehen

h *(= get together) army* auf die Beine stellen, aufstellen; *taxes* erheben; *funds, money* aufbringen, auftreiben; *loan, mortgage* aufnehmen

i *(= end) siege, embargo* aufheben, beenden

j *(Cards)* erhöhen; **I'll ~ you 6** *(Poker)* ich erhöhe um 6

k *(Telec: = contact)* Funkkontakt *m* aufnehmen mit

l *(Math)* **to ~ a number to the power of 2/3** *etc* eine Zahl in die zweite/dritte *etc* Potenz erheben

N **a** *(esp US) (in salary)* Gehaltserhöhung *f*; *(in wages)* Lohnerhöhung *f*

b *(Cards)* Erhöhung *f*

▶ **raise up** VT *sep* heben; **he raised himself up on his elbow** er stützte sich auf den Ellbogen

raised [reɪzd] ADJ *arm* angehoben; *voice* erhoben, laut; **~ type** *(Typ)* erhabener Druck → **eyebrow**

raisin ['reɪzən] N Rosine *f*

raj [rɑ:dʒ] N Herrschaft *f* eines Radscha; **the British Raj** die britische Oberherrschaft in Indien

rajah ['rɑ:dʒə] N Radscha *m*

rake[1] [reɪk] N *(= garden rake, croupier's rake)* Harke *f*, Rechen *m (dial)*; *(for grate)* Kaminrechen *m*; *(for furnace)* Ofenkrücke *f* VT **a** *garden, hay, leaves* harken, rechen *(dial)*; *grate* säubern; *fire* ausräumen; **to ~ sb/sth over the coals** *(US fig)* jdn/etw ordentlich runterputzen *(inf)* **b** *(machine gun, searchlight)* bestreichen **c** *(liter, nails, branches)* kratzen VI *(= search)* **to ~ around** *or* **about** (herum)wühlen, (herum)stöbern; **to ~ through old papers** in alten Papieren wühlen *or* stöbern

▶ **rake in** VT *sep (inf) money* kassieren *(inf)*; **he's raking it in** er scheffelt das Geld nur so

▶ **rake out** VT *sep fire* ausräumen; *(inf) information* auskundschaften, herausfinden

▶ **rake over** VT *sep earth, plot* harken; *(fig) past* durchwühlen; **to rake over the coals** *or* **ashes** *(esp Brit fig)* alte Wunden wieder öffnen

▶ **rake up** VT *sep* **a** *leaves* zusammenharken **b** *(fig) people, things, money* auftreiben *(inf)* **c** *fire* schüren; *(fig) quarrel* schüren; *memories, grievance* aufwärmen; **to rake up the past** in der Vergangenheit wühlen

rake[2] N *(= person)* Lebemann *m*, Schwerenöter *m*

rake[3] N *(Naut, of mast)* schiefe Stellung, Neigung *f*; *(of stage, seating)* Neigung *f*; *(Aviat, of wing)* Anstellwinkel *m*; *(Aut, of seat)* verstellbare Rückenlehne VI *(Naut)* sich neigen; *(Theat)* ansteigen

rake-off ['reɪkɒf] N *(inf)* (Gewinn)anteil *m*, Prozente *pl (inf)*

rakish[1] ['reɪkɪʃ] ADJ *person, appearance* flott, verwegen; *life* verwegen, flott, ausschweifend; **to wear one's hat at a ~ angle** den Hut verwegen aufgesetzt haben

rakish[2] ADJ *(Naut)* schnittig

rakishly ['reɪkɪʃlɪ] ADV flott, verwegen; *behave* verwegen; **…, he said ~** …, sagte er verwegen

rally[1] ['rælɪ] N **a** *(= gathering)* (Massen)versammlung *f*; *(with speaker)* Kundgebung *f*; *(of troops)* (Ver)sammlung *f*; *(Aut)* Rallye *f*; **electoral ~** Wahlversammlung *f*; **peace ~** Friedenskundgebung *f*; **youth ~** Jugendtreffen *nt* **b** *(in health, spirits)* Erholung *f* **c** *(Tennis etc)* Ballwechsel *m* **d** *(St Ex)* Erholung *f*
VT *troops, supporters* (ver)sammeln, zusammenrufen; **to ~ one's strength** all seine Kräfte sammeln *or* zusammennehmen; **~ing call** *or* **cry** Slogan *m*
VI **a** *(sick person)* Fortschritte machen; *(St Ex)* sich erholen
b *(troops, people)* sich sammeln, sich versammeln; **~ing point** Sammelplatz *m*; **to ~ to the support of sb** *(fig)* jdm in Scharen zu Hilfe eilen
c *(Aut)* **to go ~ing** Rallyes/eine Rallye fahren *or* machen; **to enjoy ~ing** gern Rallyes fahren

▶ **rally (a)round** VI *+prep obj leader* sich scharen um; *person in distress* sich annehmen *(+gen)* VI sich seiner/ihrer *etc* annehmen

rally[2] VT *(obs: = tease)* necken, hänseln

rallycross ['rælɪkrɒs] N *no pl* Rallyecross *nt*, Rallye-Cross *nt*

rally driver N Rallyefahrer(in) *m(f)*

rallying point ['rælɪɪŋ,pɔɪnt] N Sammelpunkt *m*/-platz *m*

ralph [rælf] *(US sl)* VI *(= vomit)* sich erbrechen, kotzen *(inf)* N *(= food thrown up)* Kotze *f (inf)*

RAM [ræm] N *(Comput) abbr of* **random access memory** RAM *m or nt*; **1 megabyte of ~** 1 Megabyte RAM

ram [ræm] N **a** *(= animal)* Widder *m*, Schafbock *m*; **the Ram** *(Astrol)* der Widder
b *(Tech)* Ramme *f*, Rammbär *m*, Rammbock *m*; *(of hydraulic press)* Stoßheber *m*, hydraulischer Widder
c *(Mil)* = **battering ram**
d *(inf: = man)* Rammler *m (inf)*
VT **a** *(= push) stick, post, umbrella* stoßen; *(with great force)* rammen; *(= pack)* zwängen; *(Tech) pile* rammen; **to ~ cotton wool in(to) one's ears** sich *(dat)* Watte in die Ohren stopfen; **to ~ a charge home** *(Mil)* laden; *(Min)* eine Sprengladung anbringen; **to ~ home a message** eine Botschaft an den Mann bringen; **to ~ sth down sb's throat** *(inf)* jdm etw eintrichtern *(inf)*
b *(= crash into) ship, car* rammen; **the car ~med a lamppost** das Auto prallte gegen einen Laternenpfahl

▶ **ram down** VT *sep earth* feststampfen; *(Tech) pile* einrammen; **his hat was rammed down over his ears** sein Hut war fest über beide Ohren gezogen

▶ **ram in** VT *sep* hineinstoßen; *(with great force)* hineinrammen

Ramadan [,ræmə'dæn] N der Ramadan

ramble ['ræmbl] N Streifzug *m*; *(esp Brit: = hike)* Wanderung *f*; **to go for** *or* **on a ~** einen Streifzug/eine Wanderung machen VI **a** *(= wander about)* Streifzüge/einen Streifzug machen; *(esp Brit: = go on hike)* wandern **b** *(in speech: old person)* unzusammenhängendes Zeug reden, faseln *(inf)*; *(pej: also* **ramble on**) schwafeln *(inf)*, vom Hundertsten ins Tausendste kommen **c** *(Hort)* ranken, klettern

rambler ['ræmblə'] N **a** *(esp Brit) (= person)* Spaziergänger(in) *m(f)*; *(= member of club)* Wanderer *m*, Wanderin *f*, Wanderfreund(in) *m(f)* **b** *(also* **rambler rose**) Kletterrose *f*

rambling ['ræmblɪŋ] ADJ **a** *speech, writing* weitschweifig, umständlich; *old person* faselnd *(inf)*, schwafelnd *(inf)*; *building, town, garden* weitläufig **b** *plant* rankend, kletternd; **~ rose** Kletterrose *f* **c ~ club/society** *(esp Brit)* Wanderklub *m*/-verein *m* N **a** *(= wandering about)* Streifzüge *pl*; *(esp Brit: = hiking)* Wandern *nt*; **to go ~** wandern gehen, wandern **b** *(in speech: also* **ramblings**) Gefasel *nt (inf)*, Geschwafel *nt (inf)*

Rambo ['ræmbəʊ] N *(inf)* Rambo *m (inf)*

rambunctious ADJ, **rambunctiously** ADV [ræm'bʌŋkʃəs, -lɪ] *(esp US inf) (= exuberant and noisy)* laut, lärmend; *(= boisterous)* übermütig, ausgelassen, wild

RAM chip N *(Comput)* RAM-Chip *m*

ramekin ['ræmɪkɪn] N *(Cook)* **a** kleiner Käseauflauf **b** *(also* **ramekin dish**) Auflaufförmchen *nt*

ramification [,ræmɪfɪ'keɪʃən] N *(lit)* Verzweigung *f*; *(smaller)* Verästelung *f*; *(of arteries)* Verästelung *f*, Geäst *nt*; **the ~s of this matter are several** *(form)* dies ist eine sehr verzweigte Angelegenheit; **the race question and its many ~s** die Rassenfrage und die damit verbundenen Probleme

ramified ['ræmɪfaɪd] ADJ *(lit, fig)* verzweigt; *(more intricate)* verästelt

ramify ['ræmɪfaɪ] VI *(lit, fig)* sich verzweigen; **the problem ramifies into several areas** das Problem greift in verschiedene Bereiche über

ramjet (engine) ['ræmdʒet('endʒɪn)] N Staustrahltriebwerk *nt*, Ramjet *nt*

rammer ['ræmə'] N Ramme *f*

ramp [ræmp] N Rampe *f*; *(= hydraulic ramp)* Hebebühne *f*; *(Aviat: also* **approach** *or* **boarding ramp**) Gangway *f*; **"(beware** *or* **caution) ~"** *(on road sign)* „Vorsicht Rampe *or* unebene Fahrbahn"

rampage [ræm'peɪdʒ] N **to be/go on the ~** randalieren; *(= looting)* auf Raubzug sein/gehen *(= be angry)* (herum)toben/einen Wutanfall bekommen; VI *(also* **rampage about** *or* **around**) herumwüten; *(angrily)* herumtoben

rampancy ['ræmpənsɪ] N *(of plants, growth)* Üppigkeit *f*, Wuchern *nt*; *(of evil, corruption)* wilde(s) Wuchern

rampant ['ræmpənt] ADJ **a** *(= unrestrained) plants, growth* üppig, wuchernd *attr*; *heresy, evil, social injustice etc* wild wuchernd *attr*; *inflation* wuchernd, galloppierend; *corruption* wuchernd, überhandnehmend, zügellos, ungezügelt; *crime* um sich greifend, blühend; **the ~ growth of** das Wuchern *(+gen)*; **to be ~** (wild) wuchern; **heart disease is ~ in my family** Herzkrankheiten liegen bei uns in der Familie; **to run ~** *(condition)* um sich greifen; *(person)* unbeaufsichtigt herumlaufen **b** *(Her)* (drohend) aufgerichtet; **lion ~** aufgerichteter Löwe

rampart ['ræmpɑːt] N Wall *m*; *(fig: = defence)* Schutzwall *m*

ram raid N *(Brit)* Rammbockeinbruch *m*, Einbruch *m* nach dem Rammbockprinzip

ram-raid ['ræmreɪd] VT *(Brit)* mit dem Auto einbrechen in *(+acc)*

ramrod ['ræmrɒd] N Ladestock *m*; **he's sitting there as stiff** *or* **straight as a ~** er sitzt da, als hätte er einen Besenstiel verschluckt ADJ stocksteif; **he is tall and thin, with a ~ posture** er ist groß und dünn, mit einer Haltung wie ein Ladestock ADV stocksteif; **~ straight** stocksteif, gerade *or* aufrecht wie ein Ladestock

ramshackle ['ræm,ʃækl] ADJ *building* morsch, baufällig; *car* klapprig, altersschwach; *group, movement* schlecht organisiert

ramsons ['ræmzənz, 'ræmsənz] N *(usu with sing vb, Bot)* Bärlauch *m*

ran [ræn] *pret of* **run**

ranch [rɑːntʃ] N Ranch *f*, Viehfarm *f*; **~ hand** Farmhelfer(in) *m(f)*; **~ house** *(on ranch)* Farmhaus *nt*; **~(-style) house** *(US)* Bungalow *m* VI Viehwirtschaft treiben

rancher ['rɑːntʃə'] N Rancher(in) *m(f)*, Viehzüchter(in) *m(f)*

rancid ['rænsɪd] ADJ ranzig

rancidity [ræn'sɪdɪtɪ], **rancidness** ['rænsɪdnɪs] N Ranzigkeit *f*

rancor N *(US)* = **rancour**

rancorous ['ræŋkərəs] ADJ *tone* bitter; *attack* bösartig

rancour, *(US)* **rancor** ['ræŋkə'] N *(of tone)* Bitterkeit *f*, Verbitterung *f*; *(of attack)* Boshaftigkeit *f*

rand [rænd] N *(= monetary unit)* Rand *m*

randan ['ræn,dæn] N *(Brit inf)* **to be out on the ~** eine Sause machen *(inf)*; *(= rowdy behaviour)* auf den Putz hauen *(inf)*, Remmidemmi machen *(inf)*

R & B [ɑːrən'biː] N *(Mus) abbr of* **Rhythm and Blues** R & B *m*

R & D [ɑːrən'diː] N *abbr of* **research and development** Forschung und Entwicklung *f*

randiness ['rændɪnɪs] N *(Brit)* Geilheit *f*

random ['rændəm] N **at ~** *(speak, walk, drive)* aufs Geratewohl; *shoot, drop bombs* ziellos; *take* wahllos; **to hit out at ~** ziellos um sich schlagen; **to talk at ~** ins Blaue hineinreden; **a few examples chosen** *or* **taken at ~** ein paar willkürlich gewählte Beispiele; **he just said anything at ~** er hat einfach irgendetwas gesagt, er hat einfach drauflosgeredet; **I (just) chose one at ~** ich wählte einfach irgendeine (Beliebige) ADJ *selection* willkürlich; *sequence* zufällig; **killed by a ~ bullet** von einer verirrten Kugel getötet; **~ breath/drug test** Stichprobe *f* auf Alkohol im Atem/auf Drogen

random access N *(Comput)* wahlfreier Zugriff

random access memory N *(Comput)* Direktzugriffsspeicher *m*

randomize ['rændəmaɪz] VTI *(Statistics)* randomisieren, eine zufällige Auswahl treffen *(sth aus)*

randomly ['rændəmlɪ] ADV *(= haphazardly)* wahllos, willkürlich

random: random number N Zufallszahl *f*; **random sample** N Stichprobe *f*; **random sampling** N Stichproben *pl*

R & R [,ɑːrən'ɑː'] *(US Mil) abbr of* **rest and recreation**

randy ['rændɪ] ADJ *(+er) (Brit)* scharf *(inf)*, geil; **you ~ old devil** du alter Lustmolch *(inf)*

rang [ræŋ] *pret of* **ring**[2]

range [reɪndʒ] N **a** *(= scope, distance covered) (of missile, telescope)* Reichweite *f*; *(of gun)* Reichweite *f*, Schussweite *f*; *(of vehicle)* Fahrbereich *m*; *(of plane)* Flugbereich *m*; **at a ~ of** auf eine Entfernung von; **at close** *or* **short/long ~**

auf kurze/große Entfernung; **to find the ~** *(Mil)* das Visier einstellen; **to be out of ~** außer Reichweite sein; *(of telescope)* außer Sichtweite sein; *(of gun)* außer Schussweite sein; **within shouting ~** in Hörweite; **within (firing) ~** in Schussweite; **~ of vision** Gesichtsfeld *nt*
b *(= spread, selection)* Reihe *f*; *(of goods)* Sortiment *nt*, Reihe *f*; *(of colours)* Skala *f*; *(of patterns, sizes, models)* Angebot *nt*, Auswahl *f* *(of an +dat)*; *(of interest, abilities)* Palette *f*; **a wide ~** eine große Auswahl; **in this price ~** in dieser Preisklasse *or* Preislage; **in this temperature ~** in diesem Temperaturbereich; **out of/within my price ~** außerhalb/innerhalb meiner (finanziellen) Möglichkeiten *or* meiner Preisklasse; **what sort of price ~ were you thinking of?** an welche Preislage haben Sie gedacht?; **a ~ of prices/temperatures/clients** unterschiedliche Preise *pl*/Temperaturen *pl*/Klienten *pl*; **models available in a whole ~ of prices** Modelle in unterschiedlichen Preislagen erhältlich; **we have the whole ~ of models/prices** wir führen sämtliche Modelle/Waren in allen Preislagen; **we cater for the whole ~ of customers** wir sind auf alle Kundenkreise eingestellt; **his ~ of knowledge is very limited** sein Wissen ist sehr beschränkt
c *(Mus) (of instruments)* (Ton)umfang *m*; *(of voice)* (Stimm)umfang *m*
d *(= domain, sphere)* Kompetenz *f*; *(of influence)* (Einfluss)bereich *m*; **this is outside the ~ of the department/the committee** dies liegt außerhalb der Kompetenz dieser Abteilung/dieses Komitees; **this is outside the ~ of his experience** dies liegt außerhalb seiner Erfahrung
e *(also* **shooting range***)* *(Mil)* Schießplatz *m*; *(= rifle range)* Schießstand *m*; *(at fair)* Schießbude *f*
f *(= cooking stove)* Koch- *or* Küchenherd *m*
g *(= row)* Reihe *f*; *(= mountain range)* Kette *f*
h *(US: = grazing land)* Freiland *nt*, Weideland *nt*; **~ cattle** Freilandvieh *nt*
VT a *(= place in a row)* aufstellen; *objects* aufstellen, anordnen; **they ~d themselves along the pavement** sie stellten sich am Bürgersteig entlang auf; **to ~ oneself with sb** *(fig)* sich auf jds Seite *(acc)* stellen
b *(= classify) person* zählen *(among, with* zu)
c *(= roam over)* durchstreifen, durchziehen; **to ~ the seas** die Meere befahren
d *(= direct) gun, telescope* ausrichten *(on* auf *+acc)*
e *(US) cattle* grasen lassen
f *(Comput)* **~d left/right** links-/rechtsbündig
VI a *(= extend)* **to ~ (from ... to)** gehen (von ... bis); *(temperature, value)* liegen (zwischen ... und); **the discussion ~d from the president to the hot-water system** die Diskussion umfasste alles, vom Präsidenten bis zum Heißwassersystem; **his interests ~ from skiing to chess** seine Interessen reichen vom Skifahren bis zum Schachspielen; **the conversation ~d over a number of subjects** die Unterhaltung kreiste um eine ganze Reihe von Themen; **his knowledge ~s over a wide field** er hat ein sehr umfangreiches Wissen; **the search ~d over the whole country** die Suche erstreckte sich auf das ganze Land
b *(= roam)* streifen; **to ~ over the area** im Gebiet umherstreifen

rangefinder ['reɪndʒ'faɪndə'] **N** Entfernungsmesser *m*

rangeland ['reɪndʒlænd] **N** *(US)* offenes Weideland

ranger ['reɪndʒə'] **N a** *(of forest etc)* Förster(in), Aufseher(in) *m(f)* **b** *(US) (= mounted patrolman)* Ranger *m*; *(= commando)* Überfallkommando *nt* **c** *(Brit)* **~ (scout)/(guide)** Ranger *m*

Rangoon [ræŋ'gu:n] **N** Rangun *nt*

rangy ['reɪndʒɪ] **ADJ** *(+er)* langglied(e)rig

rani ['rɑ:nɪ] **N** Rani *f*

rank[1] [ræŋk] **N a** *(Mil: = grade)* Rang *m*; **officer of high ~** hoher Offizier; **to reach the ~ of general** den Rang eines Generals erlangen → **pull**
b *(= class, status)* Stand *m*, Schicht *f*; **people of all ~s** Leute *pl* aller Stände; **a person of ~** eine hochgestellte Persönlichkeit; **a singer of the first ~** ein erstklassiger Sänger
c *(= row)* Reihe *f*; *(Brit: = taxi rank)* Taxistand *m*; **the taxi at the head of the ~** das erste Taxi in der Reihe
d *(Mil: = formation)* Glied *nt*; **to break ~(s)** aus dem Glied treten; **to keep ~(s)** in Reih und Glied stehen; **to serve in the ~s** gemeiner Soldat sein; **the ~s, other ~s** *(Brit)* die Mannschaften und die Unteroffiziere; **the ~ and file** *(Mil)* die Mannschaft; **the ~ and file of the party/union** die Basis der Partei/Gewerkschaft, die einfachen Partei-/Gewerkschaftsmitglieder; **the ~ and file workers** die einfachen Arbeiter; **to rise from the ~s** aus dem Mannschaftsstand zum Offizier aufsteigen; *(fig)* sich hocharbeiten; **to reduce sb to the ~s** jdn degradieren → **close[2]**
e *(Mus)* Register *nt*
VT *(= class, consider)* **to ~ sb among the best** jdn zu den Besten zählen; **where would you ~ Napoleon among the world's statesmen?** wie würden Sie Napoleon als Staatsmann einordnen *or* einstufen?
VI to ~ among zählen zu; **to ~ above/below sb** bedeutender/weniger bedeutend als jd sein; *(athlete)* leistungsmäßig über/unter jdm liegen; *(officer)* rangmäßig über/unter jdm stehen; **to ~ high among the world's statesmen** einer der großen Staatsmänner sein; **he ~s high among her friends** er hat eine Sonderstellung unter ihren Freunden; **it ~s with the best films of the decade** es zählt zu den besten Filmen des Jahrzehnts; **he ~s as a great composer** er gilt als großer Komponist; **to ~ 6th** den 6. Rang *or* Platz belegen

rank[2] **ADJ** *(+er)* **a** *plants* üppig; *grass* verwildert; **~ with weeds** von Unkraut überwuchert; **to grow ~** wuchern **b** *(= offensive) smell* übel; *dustbin, drain* stinkend *attr*; *fat* ranzig; *person* derb, vulgär; **to be ~** *(dustbin, drains)* stinken; *(breath)* stinken, übel riechend sein **c** *attr (= utter) disgrace* wahr; *injustice* schreiend; *nonsense, insolence* rein; *outsider, amateur* richtig, absolut, ausgesprochen

ranker ['ræŋkə'] **N** *(Mil) (= soldier)* einfacher *or* gemeiner Soldat; *(= officer)* *aus dem Mannschaftsstand aufgestiegener Offizier*

ranking officer ['ræŋkɪŋ'ɒfɪsə'] **N** ranghöchster/ranghöherer Offizier

rankings ['ræŋkɪŋz] **PL** *(Sport)* **the ~** die Platzierungen *pl*

rankle ['ræŋkl] **VI to ~ (with sb)** jdn wurmen

rankness ['ræŋknɪs] **N a** *(of plants)* Üppigkeit *f*; *(of grass)* Verwildertheit *f*; *(of soil)* Überwucherung *f* **b** *(of smell)* Übelkeit *f*; *(of dustbin, drain)* Gestank *m*, Stinken *nt*; *(of person)* Derbheit *f*, Vulgarität *f*

ransack ['rænsæk] **VT** *(= search) room, cupboards* durchwühlen; *(= pillage) house* plündern; *town, region* herfallen über *(+acc)*

ransom ['rænsəm] **N** Lösegeld *nt*; *(= rescue)* Auslösung *f*; *(= release)* Freilassung *f*; *(Rel)* Erlösung *f*; **to hold sb to** *(Brit) or* **for** *(US)* **~** *(lit)* jdn als Geisel halten; *(fig)* jdn erpressen → **king** **VT** *(= buy free)* auslösen, Lösegeld bezahlen für; *(= set free)* gegen Lösegeld freilassen; *(Rel)* erlösen

ransom demand **N** Lösegeldforderung *f*

ransom note **N** Erpresserbrief *m*

rant [rænt] **VI** *(emotionally, angrily)* eine Schimpfkanonade loslassen *(inf)*; *(= talk nonsense)* irres Zeug reden *(inf)*; **to ~ (and rave)** *(= be angry)* herumschimpfen; **to ~ (and rave) at sb** mit jdm schimpfen; **what's he ~ing (on) about?** worüber lässt er sich denn da aus? *(inf)* **N** Schimpfkanonade *f (inf)*

ranting ['ræntɪŋ] **N** *(= outburst)* Geschimpfe *nt*; *(= incoherent talk)* irres Zeug **ADJ** pathetisch

ranunculus [rə'nʌŋkjʊləs] **N** *(= garden flower)* Ranunkel *f*

rap[1] [ræp] **N** *(= noise, blow)* Klopfen *nt no pl*; **there was a ~ at** *or* **on the door** es hat geklopft; **to give sb a ~ on the knuckles** *(lit, fig)* jdm auf die Finger klopfen; **he got a ~ on the knuckles for that** *(lit, fig)* dafür hat er eins auf die Finger bekommen *(inf)*; **to take the ~** *(inf)* die Schuld zugeschoben kriegen *(inf)*; **to take the ~ for sb** *(inf)* für jdn den Kopf hinhalten *(inf)*; **I don't care a ~** *(inf)* das ist mir piepe *(inf)*; **to beat the ~** *(US inf)* (von der Anklage) freigesprochen werden
VT a *table* klopfen auf *(+acc)*; *window* klopfen an *(+acc)*; **to ~ sb's knuckles, to ~ sb over the knuckles** *(lit, fig)* jdm auf die Finger klopfen
b *(= criticize)* kritisieren
VI klopfen; **to ~ at** *or* **on the door/window** an die Tür/ans Fenster klopfen

▶ **rap out** **VT** *sep* **a** *(= say curtly) oath, order* ausstoßen **b** *(Spiritualism) message* klopfen

rap[2] *(Mus)* **N** Rap *m* **VI** rappen

rapacious **ADJ**, **rapaciously** **ADV** [rə'peɪʃəs, -lɪ] habgierig

rapacity [rə'pæsɪtɪ] **N** Habgier *f*

rape[1] [reɪp] **N** Vergewaltigung *f*, Notzucht *f* *(Jur)*; **~ crisis centre** Beratungszentrum *nt (für Frauen, die Opfer einer Vergewaltigung geworden sind)* **VT** vergewaltigen, notzüchtigen *(Jur)*

rape[2] **N** *(= plant)* Raps *m*

rape[3] **N** *(= grape pulp)* Trester *pl*

rape oil **N** Rapsöl *nt*

rapeseed ['reɪpsi:d] **N** Rapssamen *m*

rap group **N** *(US inf)* Diskussionsgruppe *f*

rapid ['ræpɪd] **ADJ** schnell; *action, movement also* rasch; *improvement, change, spread also* rapide; *decline, rise* rapide, steil; *smile* kurz; *loss of heat* plötzlich; *river, waterfall* reißend; *slope, descent* steil **N rapids PL** *(Geog)* Stromschnellen *pl*; **to ride** *or* **run the ~s** die Stromschnellen hinunterfahren

rapid: **rapid deployment force**, **rapid reaction force** **N** *(Mil)* schnelle Eingreiftruppe; **rapid eye movement sleep** **N** REM-Phase *f*; **rapid fire** **N** *(Mil)* Schnellfeuer *nt*; **~ of questions** *(fig)* Feuerwerk *nt* von Fragen; **rapid-fire** **ADJ** *attr (esp US)* **~ gun** Schnellfeuergewehr *nt*; **~ questions** Fragen wie aus dem Schnellfeuergewehr

rapidity [rə'pɪdɪtɪ] **N** Schnelligkeit *f*; *(of action, movement also)* Raschheit *f*; *(of improvement, change, spread also)* Rapidheit *f*; *(of decline, rise)* Steilheit *f*

rapidly ['ræpɪdlɪ] **ADV** schnell; *act, move also* rasch; *improve, change, spread also* rapide; *decline, rise* rapide, steil

rapid transit system **N** Schnellbahnsystem *nt*

rapier ['reɪpɪə'] **N** Rapier *nt*; **~ thrust** *(lit)* Stoß *m* mit dem Rapier; *(fig) (= remark)* Hieb *m*; *(= retort)* Parade *f*; **~ wit** Schlagfertigkeit *f*

rapine ['ræpaɪn] **N** *(liter)* Plünderung *f*

rapist ['reɪpɪst] **N** Vergewaltiger *m*

rappel [ræ'pel] **VI, N** *(US)* = **abseil**

rapper ['ræpə'] **N** *(Mus)* Rapper(in) *m(f)*

rapping ['ræpɪŋ] **N a** Klopfen *nt* **b** *(Mus)* Rappen *nt*

rapport [ræ'pɔ:'] **N the ~ I have with my father** das enge Verhältnis zwischen mir und meinem Vater; **I envied them the obvious ~ that they had** ich beneidete sie um ihr offensichtlich enges Verhältnis zueinander; **in ~ with sb/oneself** in Harmonie mit jdm/sich *(dat)* selbst; **they are in ~ with each other** sie harmonieren gut (miteinander)

rapprochement [ræ'prɒʃmɑ̃:ŋ] **N** Annäherung *f*

rapscallion [ræp'skælɪən] **N** *(old, hum)* Halunke *m*, Gauner *m*

rap sheet **N** *(US sl)* Strafregister *nt*; **to have a ~** vorbestraft sein

rapt [ræpt] **ADJ** *interest* gespannt; *attention* atemlos, höchste(r, s); *person* gebannt, gespannt, hingerissen; *audience* hingerissen, gespannt, in

Bann geschlagen; *look, smile* verzückt; ~ **with concentration** atemlos vor Konzentration; ~ **in contemplation/in thought** in Betrachtungen/Gedanken versunken

raptor [ˈræptəʳ] N *(Zool)* Raubvogel *m*

rapture [ˈræptʃəʳ] N *(= delight)* Entzücken *nt*; *(= ecstasy)* Verzückung *f*; **to be in ~s** entzückt sein *(over* über *+acc, about* von); **she was in ~s when she heard he was returning** sie war außer sich vor Freude, als sie hörte, dass er zurückkommt; **to go into ~s (about sb/sth)** (über jdn/etw) ins Schwärmen geraten; **to send sb into ~s** jdn in Entzücken versetzen

rapturous [ˈræptʃərəs] ADJ *reception* stürmisch, begeistert; *exclamation* entzückt; *look* verzückt, hingerissen; ~ **applause** Beifallstürme *pl*

rapturously [ˈræptʃərəslɪ] ADV *applaud, receive* stürmisch, begeistert; *exclaim* entzückt; *look* verzückt, hingerissen

rare [rɛəʳ] ADJ *(+er)* **a** *(= uncommon)* selten, rar; *occurrence* selten; **with very ~ exceptions** mit sehr wenigen Ausnahmen; **it's ~ for her to come** sie kommt nur selten; **that ~ bird, the man who remembers birthdays** dieser weiße Rabe *or* Ausnahmefall, ein Mann der sich Geburtstage merkt; **on the ~ occasions when he spoke** bei den seltenen Gelegenheiten, bei denen er sprach
b *atmosphere* dünn; *earths* selten
c *meat* roh; *steak* blutig, englisch
d *(inf: = great)* irrsinnig *(inf)*; **a person of ~ kindness** ein selten freundlicher Mensch *(inf)*; **kind to a ~ degree** selten freundlich; **to have a ~ old time** sich selten gut amüsieren

rarebit [ˈrɛəbɪt] N → **Welsh rarebit**

rarefaction [ˌrɛərɪˈfækʃən] N Dünne *f*; *(fig)* Exklusivität *f*

rarefied [ˈrɛərɪfaɪd] ADJ *atmosphere, air* dünn; *(fig)* exklusiv

rarefy [ˈrɛərɪfaɪ] VT *air, atmosphere* verdünnen, dünn werden lassen; *(fig)* exklusiv machen VI *(air)* dünn werden

rare gas N Edelgas *nt*

rarely [ˈrɛəlɪ] ADV selten

rareness [ˈrɛənɪs] N **a** *(= scarcity)* Seltenheit *f*, Rarheit *f*; *(of occurrence)* Seltenheit *f* **b** *(of steak)* Rohheit *f*

raring [ˈrɛərɪŋ] ADJ **to be ~ to go** *(inf)* in den Startlöchern sein

rarity [ˈrɛərɪtɪ] N Seltenheit *f*; *(= rare occurrence also)* Rarität *f*

rascal [ˈrɑːskəl] N Gauner *m*; *(= child)* Schlingel *m*, Frechdachs *m*; *(old: = scoundrel)* Schurke *m*

rascally [ˈrɑːskəlɪ] ADJ *(old, liter) trick* schändlich, schimpflich *(old, liter)*; *person* schurkisch; **a ~ fellow** ein Schurke *m*

rash¹ [ræʃ] N **a** *(Med)* Ausschlag *m*; **to come out** *or* **break out in a ~** einen Ausschlag bekommen **b** *(= series)* Serie *f*, Abfolge *f*; **a ~ of burglaries** eine Einbruchsserie

rash² ADJ *(+er) person* unbesonnen; *act also* voreilig, überstürzt; *thoughts* voreilig; *promise, words, decision* voreilig, vorschnell; **it was ~ of him to promise that** es war etwas voreilig von ihm, das zu versprechen; **don't do anything ~** tu ja nichts Übereiltes *or* Überstürztes, nur nichts übereilen *or* überstürzen; **in a ~ moment** in einem unbedachten *or* unbesonnen Moment

rasher [ˈræʃəʳ] N Streifen *m*; ~ **of bacon** Speckstreifen *m*

rashly [ˈræʃlɪ] ADV *act* voreilig, überstürzt; *promise, decide* voreilig, vorschnell

rashness [ˈræʃnɪs] N *(of person)* Unbesonnenheit *f*; *(of action)* Voreiligkeit *f*, Überstürztheit *f*; *(of promise, decision)* Voreiligkeit *f*

rasp [rɑːsp] N *(= tool)* Raspel *f*; *(= noise)* Kratzen *nt no pl*; *(of cough, when breathing)* Keuchen *nt no pl* VT **a** *(Tech)* raspeln, feilen; **to ~ sth away** etw wegraspeln *or* abfeilen **b** *(= say: also* **rasp out**) *insults* krächzen; *orders* schnarren VI kratzen; *(breath)* rasseln → *also* **rasping**

raspberry [ˈrɑːzbərɪ] N Himbeere *f*; *(= plant: also* **raspberry bush** *or* **cane**) Himbeerstrauch *m*; **to blow a ~ (at sth)** *(inf)* (über etw) verächtlich schnauben; **to get a ~ (from sb)** *(inf)* (von jdm) nur ein verächtliches Schnauben ernten; **"new proposals get ~ from electorate"** *(inf)* „Wähler erteilen neuen Vorschlägen eine Abfuhr" ADJ Himbeer-; *(colour)* himbeerrot; ~ **jam** Himbeermarmelade *f*

rasper [ˈrɑːspəʳ] N *(Tech)* Raspel *f*, Grobfeile *f*; *(Cook)* Raspel *f*, Reibeisen *nt*

rasping [ˈrɑːspɪŋ] ADJ *(= sound)* kratzend; *voice* kratzig *(inf)*, krächzend; *cough* keuchend; *breath* rasselnd, keuchend N *(= sound)* Kratzen *nt*; *(of voice)* Krächzen *nt*, Gekrächze *nt*

raspy [rɑːspɪ] ADJ *(= hoarse) tone* krächzend; *voice* heiser

Rasta [ˈræstə] N Rasta *m*

Rastafarian [ræstəˈfeərɪən] N Rastafari *m*, Rastafarier(in) *m(f)* ADJ der Rastafaris

raster [ˈræstəʳ] N Raster *m or nt*

rat [ræt] N *(Zool)* Ratte *f*; *(pej inf: = person)* elender Verräter *(inf)*; **he's a dirty ~** *(inf)* er ist ein dreckiges *or* gemeines Schwein *(inf)*; **you ~!** du Hund! *(inf)*; **~s!** *(inf) (annoyance)* Mist! *(inf)*; *(rejection)* Quatsch! *(inf)* → **smell** VI **a to ~ on sb** *(inf) (= desert)* jdn sitzen lassen *(inf)*; *(= inform on)* jdn verpfeifen *(inf)*; **to ~ on sth** *(inf: = renege on)* etw nicht einhalten **b to go ~ting** auf Rattenfang gehen

ratable ADJ = **rateable**

rat *in cpds* Ratten-

rat-arsed ADJ *(Brit sl: = drunk)* stockbesoffen *(inf)*; **to get ~** sich zuschütten *(inf)*

rat-a-tat [ˌrætəˈtæt], **rat-a-tat-tat** N Rattern; **the continual ~ of machine-gun fire** das kontinuierliche Rattern von Maschinengewehren ADV ratternd

ratatouille [ˌrætəˈtwiː] N Ratatouille *f*

ratbag N *(Brit pej inf)* Schrulle *f (inf)*

rat-catcher N Rattenfänger(in) *m(f)*

rat-catching N Rattenfang *m*

ratchet [ˈrætʃɪt] N Ratsche *f*; ~ **wheel** Sperrrad *nt*; **it is one more ~ in the cycle of violence that exists here** das ist eine weitere Drehung der Spirale der Gewalt, die hier existiert

▶ **ratchet up** *(esp US)* VI zunehmen VT SEP anheizen *(inf)*; *pressure* verschärfen; *interest rates, rent* anheben

rate¹ [reɪt] N **a** *(= ratio, proportion, frequency)* Rate *f*; *(= speed)* Tempo *nt*; **the failure ~ on this course** die Durchfallrate *or* -quote bei diesem Kurs; **the failure ~ for small businesses** die Zahl der Konkurse bei Kleinunternehmen; **at the** *or* **a ~ of 100 litres** *(Brit) or* **liters** *(US)* **an hour/14 feet per minute** (in einem Tempo von) 100 Liter pro Stunde/14 Fuß pro Minute; ~ **of climb** *(Aviat)* Steigleistung *f*; ~ **of consumption** Verbrauch *m*; ~ **of flow** *(of water, electricity)* Fluss *m*; **pulse ~** Puls *m*; **at a great** *or* **terrific** *(inf)* **~, at a ~ of knots** *(inf)* in irrsinnigem Tempo *(inf)*; *(move also)* mit hundert Sachen *(inf)*; **if you continue at this ~** *(lit, fig)* wenn du so weitermachst, wenn du in diesem Tempo weitermachst; **at his ~ of working** bei seinem Arbeitstempo; **at the ~ you're going you'll be dead before long** wenn du so weitermachst, bist du bald unter der Erde; **at any ~** auf jeden Fall; **at that ~, I suppose I'll have to agree** wenn das so ist, muss ich wohl zustimmen
b *(Comm, Fin)* Satz *m*; *(St Ex)* Kurs *m*; ~ **of exchange** Wechselkurs *m*; **what's the ~ at the moment?** wie steht der Kurs momentan?; **what's the ~ of pay?** wie hoch ist der Satz (für die Bezahlung)?; ~ **of interest** Zinssatz *m*; ~ **of taxation** Steuersatz *m*; ~ **of pay for overtime** Satz *m* für Überstunden; **postage/advertising/insurance ~s** Post-/Werbe-/Versicherungsgebühren *pl*; **there is a reduced ~ for children** Kinderermäßigung wird gewährt; **basic salary ~** Grundgehaltssatz *m*; **to pay sb at the ~ of £10 per hour** jdm einen Stundenlohn von £ 10 bezahlen
c rates PL *(dated Brit: = municipal tax)* Gemeindesteuern *pl*, Kommunal- und Staatssteuern *pl*; **~s and taxes** Kommunal- und Staatssteuern *pl*; **~(s) office** Gemeindesteueramt *nt* → **water rate**
VT **a** *(= estimate value or worth of)* (ein)schätzen; **to ~ sb/sth among ...** jdn/etw zu ... zählen *or* rechnen; **how does he ~ that film?** was hält er von dem Film?; **to ~ sb/sth as sth** jdn/etw für etw halten; **he is generally ~d as a great statesman** er gilt allgemein als großer Staatsmann; **to ~ sb/sth highly** jdn/etw hoch einschätzen; **Shearer was ~d at £1,000,000** Shearers Preis wurde auf £ 1.000.000 geschätzt
b *(Brit Local Government)* veranlagen; **a shop ~d at £1,000 per annum** ein Laden, dessen steuerbarer Wert £ 1.000 pro Jahr ist
c *(= deserve)* verdienen; **does this hotel ~ 3 stars?** verdient dieses Hotel 3 Sterne?; **I think he ~s a pass (mark)** ich finde, seine Leistung kann man mit „ausreichend" oder besser bewerten
d *(inf: = think highly of)* gut finden *(inf)*; **I really/don't really ~ him** ich finde ihn wirklich gut/mag ihn nicht besonders
VI *(= be classed)* **to ~ as ...** gelten als ...; **to ~ among ...** zählen zu ...; **reading does not ~ highly among young people** vom Lesen halten die jungen Leute nicht viel

rate² VT *(liter)* = **berate**

rateable, **ratable** [ˈreɪtəbl] ADJ *(Brit) property* steuerpflichtig, steuerbar

rateable value N *(Brit)* steuerbarer Wert

rate-cap [ˈreɪtkæp] VT *(Brit dated)* **the council was ~ped** dem Stadtrat wurde eine Höchstsatz für die Kommunalsteuer auferlegt

rate-capping [ˈreɪtˌkæpɪŋ] N *(Brit dated) Festlegung eines Kommunalsteuer-Höchstsatzes durch die Zentralregierung*

rated [ˈreɪtɪd] ADJ **a** *(Brit) property* kommunalsteuerpflichtig **b** *(Tech)* Nenn-; ~ **output/power** Nennleistung *f*

ratepayer [ˈreɪtˌpeɪəʳ] N *(Brit dated)* Steuerzahler(in) *m(f) (von Kommunalsteuern)*

rate rebate N *(Brit dated)* Kommunalsteuer-Rückerstattung *f*

ratfink [ˈrætfɪnk] N *(dated US sl)* Arschloch *nt (sl)*; *(= informer)* Spitzel *m*

rather [ˈrɑːðəʳ] ✪ 6.3, 7.4, 8.3, 26.1, 26.3 ADV
a *(= for preference)* lieber; **~ than wait, he went away** er ging lieber, als dass er wartete; **I would ~ have the blue dress** ich hätte lieber das blaue Kleid; **I would ~ be happy than rich** ich wäre lieber glücklich als reich; **I would ~ you came yourself** mir wäre es lieber, Sie kämen selbst; **I'd ~ not** lieber nicht; **I'd ~ not go** ich würde lieber nicht gehen; **I'd ~ die!** eher sterbe ich!; **he expected me to phone ~ than (to) write** er erwartete eher einen Anruf als einen Brief von mir; **it would be better to phone ~ than (to) write** es wäre besser zu telefonieren als zu schreiben
b *(= more accurately)* vielmehr; **he is, or ~ was, a soldier** er ist, beziehungsweise *or* vielmehr war, Soldat; **a car, or ~ an old banger** ein Auto, genauer gesagt eine alte Kiste
c *(= to a considerable degree)* ziemlich; *(= somewhat, slightly)* etwas; **he's a ~ clever person** *or* **~ a clever person** er ist ziemlich klug; **he felt ~ better** er fühlte sich bedeutend wohler; **it's ~ more difficult than you think** es ist um einiges schwieriger, als du denkst; **it's ~ too difficult for me** es ist etwas zu schwierig für mich; **she's ~ an idiot/a killjoy** sie ist reichlich doof/ein richtiger Spielverderber; **I ~ think he's wrong** ich glaube fast, er hat unrecht; **I've ~ got the impression ...** ich habe ganz den Eindruck, ...; **~!** *(inf)* und ob! *(inf)*, klar! *(inf)*

raticide [ˈrætɪsaɪd] N *(spec)* Rattengift *nt*

ratification [ˌrætɪfɪˈkeɪʃən] N Ratifizierung *f*

ratify [ˈrætɪfaɪ] VT ratifizieren

rating¹ [ˈreɪtɪŋ] N **a** *(= assessment)* (Ein)schätzung *f*; *(Brit, of house)* Veranlagung *f*; **what's your ~ of his abilities?** wie schätzen Sie seine Fähigkeiten ein?

b *(= class, category, Sport: of yacht, car)* Klasse *f*; *(Fin: also* **credit rating***)* Kreditfähigkeit *f*; *(Elec)* Leistung *f*; *(of petrol: also* **octane rating***)* Oktanzahl *f*; **what's his ~?** wie wird er eingestuft?; **he has attained world-class ~** er hat Weltklasse(format) erreicht; **the popularity ~ of a TV programme** die Zuschauerzahlen eines Fernsehprogramms; **the government's low ~ in the opinion polls** die niedrigen Werte der Regierung in den Meinungsumfragen; **security ~** Sicherheitseinstufung *f*; **voltage ~** Grenzspannung *f*; **high/low ~s** *(TV)* hohe/niedrige Werte *pl*; **to boost ~s** *(TV)* die Werte stark verbessern; **the ~s war/battle** *(TV)* der Krieg/Kampf um die Einschaltquoten; **~s hit** *(TV)* Quotenhit *m*
c *(Naut) (= rank)* Rang *m*; *(= sailor)* Matrose *m*

rating² N *(= scolding)* Schelte *f*

ratio [ˈreɪʃɪəʊ] N Verhältnis *nt*; **the ~ of men to women** das Verhältnis von Männern zu Frauen; **in the** *or* **a ~ of 100 to 1** im Verhältnis 100 zu 1 *(written: 100:1)*; **inverse ~** umgekehrtes Verhältnis; **in inverse ~ to** *(Math)* umgekehrt proportional zu

ratiocinate [ˌrætɪˈɒsɪneɪt] VI *(form)* reflektieren

ration [ˈræʃən, *(US)* ˈreɪʃən] **N** Ration *f*; *(fig)* Quantum *nt*; **~s** *(= food)* Rationen *pl*; **to put sb on short ~s** jdn auf halbe Ration setzen; **~ book** Bezugsscheinbuch *nt*; **~ card** *or* **coupon** *(Brit)* Bezugsschein *m*; *(for food)* ≈ Lebensmittelkarte *f*/-marke *f*
VT *goods, food* rationieren; *(state, government also)* bewirtschaften; **there is a sugar shortage, so it's being ~ed** Zucker ist knapp und wird daher rationiert; **he was ~ed to 1 kg** ihm wurde nur 1 kg erlaubt; **I'm going to ~ you to one biscuit a day** ich werde dich kurzhalten, du bekommst nur einen Keks pro Tag; **he ~ed himself to five cigarettes a day** er erlaubte sich *(dat)* nur fünf Zigaretten pro Tag

▸ **ration out** VT *sep* zuteilen

rational [ˈræʃənl] ADJ **a** *(= having reason) creature, person* vernunftbegabt, rational **b** *(= sensible, reasonable) person, action, thinking* vernünftig, rational; *activity, solution* vernünftig, sinnvoll; *(Med: = lucid, sane) person* bei klarem Verstand; **it was the only ~ thing to do** es war das einzig Vernünftige **c** *(Math)* rational

rationale [ˌræʃəˈnɑːl] N Gründe *pl*; **it lacks any ~** das entbehrt jeglicher Begründung

rationalism [ˈræʃnəlɪzəm] N Rationalismus *m*

rationalist [ˈræʃnəlɪst] N Rationalist(in) *m(f)*

rationalistic [ˌræʃnəˈlɪstɪk] ADJ rationalistisch

rationality [ˌræʃəˈnælɪtɪ] N *(of person, action, thinking)* Vernünftigkeit *f*, Rationalität *f*; *(of activity, solution)* Vernünftigkeit *f*; *(Med)* klarer Verstand

rationalization [ˌræʃnəlaɪˈzeɪʃən] N Rationalisierung *f*; *(of problem)* vernünftige Betrachtung

rationalize [ˈræʃnəlaɪz] **VT** **a** *event, conduct etc* rationalisieren; *problem* vernünftig sehen *or* betrachten **b** *(= organize efficiently) industry, production, work* rationalisieren **c** *(Math)* in eine rationale Gleichung umändern **VI** rationalisieren

rationally [ˈræʃnəlɪ] ADV *act, behave, think* vernünftig, rational; *(Med)* bei klarem Verstand; **~ (speaking), it should be possible to do it** rational gesehen sollte es möglich sein

rationing [ˈræʃənɪŋ] N *(of goods, food)* Rationierung *f*; *(by state, government also)* Bewirtschaftung *f*

ratline, ratlin [ˈrætlɪn] N *(Naut)* Webeleine *f*

rat: ratpack N *(Brit pej inf)* Journalistenmeute *f (pej inf)*; **rat poison** N Rattengift *nt*; **rat race** N ständiger Konkurrenzkampf; **rat run** N *(Brit inf)* Schleichweg *m (inf)*; **drivers were using the area as a ~** die Gegend wurde von Autofahrern als Schleichweg *(inf)* genutzt; **rats' tails** PL *(pej)* Zotteln *pl (pej)*; *(inf: = bunches)* Rattenschwänze *pl (inf)*; **her hair was** *or* **hung in ~** *(pej)* ihr Haar war zottelig *or* hing zottelig herunter

rattan [ræˈtæn] N *(= plant)* Rotangpalme *f*; *(= cane)* Rattan *nt*, Peddigrohr *nt*

ratted [ˈrætɪd] ADJ *(Brit inf)* stockbesoffen *(inf)*

ratter [ˈrætəʳ] N *(= dog or cat)* Rattenfänger *m*

rattle [ˈrætl] **VI** klappern; *(chains)* rasseln, klirren; *(bottles)* klirren; *(gunfire)* knattern; *(drums)* schlagen; *(hailstones)* prasseln; *(rattlesnake)* klappern; **to ~ at the door** an der Tür rütteln; **there's something rattling** da klappert etwas; **to ~ along/away** *(vehicle)* entlang-/davonrattern; **they ~d through the village** sie ratterten durch das Dorf
VT **a** *box, dice, keys* schütteln; *bottles, cans* zusammenschlagen; *chains* rasseln mit; *windows* rütteln an *(+dat)*; **to ~ sb's cage** *(inf)* jdn verärgern
b *(inf: = alarm) person* durcheinanderbringen; **don't get ~d!** reg dich nicht auf!; **she was ~d by the news, the news ~d her** die Nachricht hat ihr einen Schock versetzt
N **a** *(= sound)* Klappern *nt no pl*; *(of chains)* Rasseln *nt no pl*, Klirren *nt no pl*; *(of bottles)* Klirren *nt no pl*; *(of gunfire)* Knattern *nt no pl*; *(of drums)* Schlagen *nt no pl*; *(of hailstones)* Prasseln *nt no pl*; *(of rattlesnake)* Klappern *nt no pl*; *(Med: also* **death rattle***)* Todesröcheln *nt*
b *(child's)* Rassel *f*; *(sports fan's)* Schnarre *f*

▸ **rattle around** VI *(fig: in house etc)* herumgeistern *(inf)*

▸ **rattle down** VI herunterprasseln, herunterhageln

▸ **rattle off** VT *sep poem, joke, list* herunterrasseln *(inf)*; *win* hinlegen *(inf)*

▸ **rattle on** VI *(inf)* (unentwegt) quasseln *(inf)* *(about* über *+acc)*

▸ **rattle through** VI *+prep obj speech etc* herunterrasseln; *work, music* rasen durch

rattlebrain [ˈrætlbreɪn] N *(inf)* Spatzenhirn *nt (inf)*

rattler [ˈrætləʳ] N *(US inf)* Klapperschlange *f*

rattle: rattlesnake [ˈrætlsneɪk] N Klapperschlange *f*; **rattletrap** N *(hum inf)* Klapperkiste *f (hum inf)*

rattling [ˈrætlɪŋ] **N** *(= sound)* Klappern *nt*; *(of chains)* Rasseln *nt*, Klirren *nt*; *(of bottles)* Klirren *nt*; *(of gunfire)* Knattern *nt*; *(of drums)* Schlagen *nt*; *(of hailstones)* Prasseln *nt* **ADJ** klappernd; *chains* rasselnd, klirrend; *bottles* klirrend; *gunfire* knatternd; *drums* schlagend; *hailstones* prasselnd; **a ~ noise** ein Klappern *nt*/Rasseln *nt etc* **ADV** **~ good** *(dated inf)* verdammt gut *(inf)*

rattrap, rat trap [ˈrættræp] N Rattenfalle *f*

ratty [ˈrætɪ] ADJ *(+er) (inf)* **a** *(Brit: = irritable)* gereizt **b** *(US: = run-down)* verlottert *(inf)*

raucous [ˈrɔːkəs] ADJ *voice, laughter, shouts* rau, heiser; *crowd* lärmend; *party, music* laut, lärmend; *bird cry* heiser, rau

raucously [ˈrɔːkəslɪ] ADV *laugh, shout* rau, heiser; *sing* mit rauer *or* heiserer Stimme

raucousness [ˈrɔːkəsnɪs] N *(of voice, laughter)* Rauheit *f*, Heiserkeit *f*; *(of crowd)* Rauheit *f*, Barschheit *f*; *(of party, music)* Rauheit *f*

raunchy [ˈrɔːntʃɪ] ADJ *(+er) (inf) person* sexy; *film, scene* erotisch, aufreizend; *novel* erotisch; *clothing* aufreizend, sexy

ravage [ˈrævɪdʒ] **N** *(of war)* verheerendes Wüten *no pl*; *(of disease)* Wüten *nt no pl*, Zerstörung *f* (of durch); **~s** *(of war)* Verheerung *f* (of durch); *(of disease)* Zerstörung *f* (of durch); **the ~s of time** die Spuren *pl* der Zeit; **a face marked by the ~s of time** ein von der Zeit schwer gezeichnetes Gesicht **VT** *(= ruin)* verwüsten, verheeren; *(= plunder)* plündern; **~d by disease** von Krankheit schwer gezeichnet

rave [reɪv] **VI** *(= be delirious)* fantasieren, phantasieren, delirieren *(spec)*; *(= talk wildly)* fantasieren, phantasieren, spinnen *(inf)*; *(= speak furiously)* toben; *(inf: = speak, write enthusiastically)* schwärmen (*about, over* von); *(liter) (storm)* toben; *(wind)* brausen; *(sea)* toben; **to ~ against sb/sth** gegen jdn/etw wettern; **he ~d at the children for breaking the window** er donnerte die Kinder wegen der eingeworfenen Fensterscheibe an → **rant**
N **a** *(Brit inf)* Rave *m (sl)*
b *(inf: = praise)* Schwärmerei *f*; **to have a ~ about sth** von etw schwärmen, von etw ganz weg sein *(inf)*; **the play got a ~ review** *(inf)* das Stück bekam eine glänzende *or* begeisterte Kritik
c *(inf: = fashion)* **it's all the ~** das ist große Mode

rave culture N *(Mus)* Ravekultur *f*

ravel [ˈrævəl] **VT** **a** *(= disentangle)* = **ravel out** **VT** **b** *(old: = entangle)* verwirren **VI** *(= become tangled)* sich verwirren; *(= fray)* ausfransen

▸ **ravel out** **VI** ausfransen; *(rope)* faserig werden **VT** *sep material* ausfransen; *threads* entwirren; *knitting* auftrennen, aufziehen; *(fig) difficulty* klären

raven [ˈreɪvən] N Rabe *m*; **~-black** rabenschwarz

raven-haired [ˈreɪvənˈhɛəd] ADJ mit rabenschwarzem Haar

ravening [ˈrævənɪŋ] ADJ beutehungrig, räuberisch

ravenous [ˈrævənəs] ADJ *animal* ausgehungert; *person also* heißhungrig; *appetite, hunger* gewaltig; **I'm ~** ich habe einen Bärenhunger *(inf)*

ravenously [ˈrævənəslɪ] ADV *eat* wie ein Wolf; *look* ausgehungert; **to be ~ hungry** *(animal)* ausgehungert sein; *(person also)* einen Bärenhunger haben *(inf)*

raver [ˈreɪvəʳ] N **a** *(Brit inf)* Raver(in) *m(f)* **b** *(dated Brit sl)* flotte Biene *(dated inf)*; **she's a real little ~** sie führt ein flottes Leben

rave-up [ˈreɪvʌp] N *(dated Brit sl: = party)* Fete *f (inf)*, tolle Party *(inf)*

ravine [rəˈviːn] N Schlucht *f*, Klamm *f*

raving [ˈreɪvɪŋ] **ADJ** **a** *(= frenzied)* wahnsinnig, verrückt; *(= delirious)* im Delirium, fantasierend *attr*, phantasierend *attr*; **his ~ fantasies** seine verrückten Fantastereien *or* Phantastereien; **a ~ lunatic** *(inf)* ein kompletter Idiot *(inf)* **b** *(inf: = remarkable) success* toll *(inf)*; *beauty* hinreißend **ADV** **~ mad** *(inf)* total verrückt *(inf)*; **to go ~ mad** *(inf)* total verrückt werden *(inf)* **N** **~(s)** Fantasien *pl*, Phantasien *pl*

ravioli [ˌrævɪˈəʊlɪ] N Ravioli *pl*

ravish [ˈrævɪʃ] VT **a** *(= delight)* hinreißen **b** *(old, liter: = rape)* schänden *(geh)*; *(obs: = abduct)* rauben

ravisher [ˈrævɪʃəʳ] N *(old, liter)* Schänder *m (geh)*

ravishing [ˈrævɪʃɪŋ] ADJ *woman, sight* atemberaubend; *beauty also, meal* hinreißend

ravishingly [ˈrævɪʃɪŋlɪ] ADV *beautiful* hinreißend, atemberaubend; *dressed, decorated* atemberaubend schön

ravishment [ˈrævɪʃmənt] N **a** *(= delight)* atemloses Staunen, Hingerissenheit *f* **b** *(old, liter: = rape)* Schändung *f (geh)*; *(obs: = abduction)* Raub *m*

raw [rɔː] **ADJ** *(+er)* **a** *(= uncooked) meat, food* roh; *(= unprocessed)* roh, Roh-; *alcohol* rein, unvermischt; *cloth* ungewalkt; *leather* ungegerbt; *cotton* roh, naturbelassen, unbehandelt; *rubber* roh; *sewage* ungeklärt; **~ sugar** Rohzucker *m*; **~ brick** Rohziegel *m*; **~ edge** *(of cloth etc)* ungesäumte Kante; **~ spirits** reiner Alkohol; **it's a ~ deal** *(inf)* das ist eine Gemeinheit *(inf)*; **to give sb a ~ deal** *(inf)* jdn benachteiligen, jdn unfair behandeln; **to get a ~ deal** schlecht wegkommen *(inf)*; **the old get a ~ deal from the state** *(inf)* alte Leute werden vom Staat stiefmütterlich behandelt
b *(= naked, pure, basic) emotion* nackt, unverfälscht; *energy* ursprünglich, impulsiv, nackt; *talent* ungeschliffen, elementar; *ambition, statistics* nackt; *courage* elementar, unverfälscht; *facts* nackt, unverfälscht, ungeschönt; **~ data** *(Comput)* unaufbereitete Daten *pl*; **~ score** *(US Sch)* bloße Punktergebnisse *or* Punkte *pl*
c *(= inexperienced) troops, recruit* neu, unerfahren
d *(= sore) wound* offen; *skin* wund; *nerves* empfindlich; **red and ~** gerötet und wund; **to touch**

a ~ nerve *(fig)* einen wunden Punkt berühren, einen rohen *or* offen liegenden Nerv berühren
e *(= frank) account* ungeschönt, ungeschliffen, ungemildert
f *(Met) climate, wind, air* rau; *night* rau, stürmisch
g *(esp US: = coarse) humour, story, person* derb; *colour* grell
N a to touch *or* **get sb on the ~** *(Brit)* bei jdm einen wunden Punkt berühren
b in the ~ *(inf: = naked)* im Naturzustand; **life/nature in the ~** die raue Seite des Lebens/der Natur

raw: **rawboned** ADJ mager, knochig; **rawhide** ['rɔːhaɪd] N *(= leather)* ungegerbtes Leder; *(= whip)* Lederpeitsche *f*

Rawlplug® ['rɔːlplʌg] N Dübel *m*

rawlplug ['rɔːlplʌg] VT dübeln *(to* an *+acc)*

raw material N Rohmaterial *nt*

rawness ['rɔːnɪs] N **a** *(of meat, food)* Rohheit *f* **b** *(= lack of experience)* Unerfahrenheit *f* **c** *(= soreness)* Wundheit *f* **d** *(of weather)* Rauheit *f* **e** *(esp US: = coarseness)* Derbheit *f*

raw recruit N *(fig)* blutiger Anfänger *(inf)*, blutige Anfängerin *(inf)*

raw silk N Rohseide *f*

ray[1] [reɪ] N **a** Strahl *m*; **a ~ of hope** ein Hoffnungsschimmer *or* -strahl *m*; **a ~ of sunshine** *(fig)* ein kleiner Trost **b** *(of fish)* Flossenstrahl *m*; *(of starfish)* Arm *m*

ray[2] N *(= fish)* Rochen *m*

ray gun N Strahlenpistole *f*

rayon ['reɪɒn] **N** Viskose *f*, Reyon *nt* **ADJ** aus Viskose *or* Reyon; **~ fibre** Viskose- *or* Reyonfaser *f*

raze [reɪz] VT zerstören; *(Mil)* schleifen; **to ~ sth to the ground** etw dem Erdboden gleichmachen

razor ['reɪzəʳ] N Rasierapparat *m*; *(cutthroat)* Rasiermesser *nt*; **electric ~** Elektrorasierer *m*; **~'s edge** *(fig)* = **razor edge b**

razor: **razorback** N *(Zool)* Finnwal *m*; **razorbill** N *(Zool)* Tordalk *m*; **razor blade** N Rasierklinge *f*; **razor cut** N Messerschnitt *m*; **razor-cut** VT mit dem Messer schneiden; **razor edge** N **a** *(= mountain ridge)* Grat *m* **b** *(fig)* **we are living on a ~** wir stehen vor einem Abgrund; **razor-sharp** ADJ *knife* scharf (wie ein Rasiermesser); *teeth* rasiermesserscharf; *(fig) person* sehr scharfsinnig; *mind, wit* messerscharf; **razor wire** N Bandstacheldraht *m*, Natodraht *m (inf)*

razz [ræz] VT *(US inf)* aufziehen *(inf)*, verhohnepiepeln *(inf)*

razzle ['ræzl] N *(inf)* **to go on/be out on the ~** eine Sause machen *(dated inf)*

razzle-dazzle ['ræzl'dæzl], **razzmatazz** ['ræzmə'tæz] N *(esp Brit inf)* Rummel *m*, Trubel *m*

RC *abbr of* **Roman Catholic** r.-k.

RCP *(Brit) abbr of* **Royal College of Physicians** Königlicher Ärzteverband

r-coloured, *(US)* **r-colored** ['ɑːˌkʌləd] ADJ *(Ling) vowels* mit R-Färbung

RCS *(Brit) abbr of* **Royal College of Surgeons** Königlicher Chirurgenverband

Rd *abbr of* **Road** Str.

RDA *abbr of* **recommended daily allowance**

RE *(Brit) abbr of* **Religious Education**

re[1] [reɪ] N *(Mus)* re *nt*

re[2] [riː] PREP *(Admin, Comm etc: = referring to)* betreffs *(+gen)*, bezüglich *(+gen)*; *(Jur: also* **in re***)* in Sachen gegen; **re your letter of 16th June** Betr(eff): Ihr Brief vom 16. Juni

reach [riːtʃ] **N a** *(= act of reaching)* **to make a ~ for sth** nach etw greifen
b *(denoting accessibility)* **within/out of sb's ~** in/außer jds Reichweite *(dat)*, in/außer Reichweite für jdn; **within arm's ~** in greifbarer Nähe; **put it out of the children's ~** *or* **out of the ~ of the children** stellen Sie es so, dass Kinder es nicht erreichen können; **keep out of ~ of children** von Kindern fernhalten; **cars are within everyone's ~ nowadays** Autos sind heute für jeden erschwinglich; **mountains within easy ~** Berge, die leicht erreichbar sind; **within easy ~ of the sea** in unmittelbarer Nähe des Meers; **this town is within easy ~ of London for a day trip** man kann von dieser Stadt aus gut Tagesflüge nach London machen; **I keep it within easy ~** ich habe es in greifbarer Nähe; **she was beyond (the) ~ of help** für sie kam jede Hilfe zu spät; **this subject is beyond his ~** dieses Thema geht über seinen Horizont *(inf)*
c *(= distance one can reach)* Reichweite *f*; *(Boxing)* Aktionsradius *m*; **a long ~** lange Arme *pl*, ein großer Aktionsradius
d *(= sphere of action, influence)* Einflussbereich *m*; **beyond the ~ of the law** außerhalb des Gesetzes
e *(= stretch)* **~es** *(of beach, river)* Strecke *f*; *(of canal)* Wasserhaltung *f*; *(of woodland)* Gebiet *nt*; **the upper ~es of the Rhine** der Oberfluss des Rheins
VT a *(= arrive at)* erreichen; *point* ankommen an *(+dat)*; *town, country* ankommen in *(+dat)*; *perfection* erlangen; *agreement, understanding* erzielen, kommen zu; *conclusion* kommen *or* gelangen zu; **we ~ed London at 3pm** wir kamen um 15 Uhr in London an; **when we ~ed him he was dead** als wir zu ihm kamen, war er tot; **to ~ the terrace you have to cross the garden** um auf die Terrasse zu kommen, muss man durch den Garten gehen; **to ~ page 50** bis Seite 50 kommen; **to ~ school age/the age of 50** das Schulalter/die 50 erreichen; **this advertisement is geared to ~ a younger audience** diese Werbung soll junge Leute ansprechen; **you can ~ me at my hotel** Sie erreichen mich in meinem Hotel; **to ~ the final of the Davis Cup** das Finale des Davis-Cups erreichen
b *(= stretch to get or touch)* **to be able to ~ sth** an etw *(acc)* (heran)reichen können, bis zu etw langen können *(inf)*; **can you ~ it?** kommen Sie dran?; **can you ~ the ceiling?** kannst du bis an die Decke reichen *or* langen? *(inf)*
c *(= come up to, go down to)* reichen *or* gehen bis zu; **he ~es her shoulder** er reicht *or* geht ihr bis zur Schulter
d *(inf: = get and give)* langen *(inf)*, reichen; **~ me (over) that book** reiche *or* lang *(inf)* mir das Buch (herüber)
e *(US Jur) witness* bestechen
VI a *(to, as far as* bis*)* *(territory etc)* sich erstrecken, gehen, reichen; *(voice, sound)* tragen
b *(= stretch out hand or arm)* greifen; **to ~ for sth** nach etw greifen *or* langen *(inf)*; **~ for the sky!** *(US)* Hände hoch!; **to ~ for the moon** *or* **stars** *(fig)* nach den Sternen greifen
c can you ~? kommen Sie dran?

▶ **reach across** VI hinübergreifen *or* -langen *(inf)*

▶ **reach back** VI *(in time)* zurückreichen, zurückgehen *(to* bis*)*

▶ **reach down** **VI** *(clothes, curtains, hair etc)* herunterreichen *(to* bis*)*; *(person)* hinuntergreifen *or* -langen *(inf)* *(for* nach*)* **VT** *sep* herunterreichen

▶ **reach out** **VT** *sep* **he reached out his hand to take the book** er streckte die Hand aus, um das Buch zu nehmen; **he reached out his hand for the cup** er griff nach der Tasse **VI** die Hand/Hände ausstrecken; **to reach out for sth** nach etw greifen *or* langen *(inf)*; **he reached out to grasp the door handle** er griff *or* langte *(inf)* nach dem Türgriff; **she reached out and slapped him** sie holte aus und haute ihm eine runter *(inf)*

▶ **reach over** VI = **reach across**

▶ **reach up** **VI a** *(water, level etc)* (herauf)reichen *or* -gehen *(to* bis*)* **b** *(person)* hinaufgreifen *(for* nach*)* **VT** *sep (inf)* heraufreichen

reachable ['riːtʃəbl] ADJ erreichbar

reach-me-down ['riːtʃmɪˌdaʊn] N *(inf)* = **hand-me-down**

react [riː'ækt] VI **a** *(= respond, Chem, Phys)* reagieren *(to* auf *+acc)*; **slow to ~** *(Chem)* reaktionsträge; **she was slow to ~ to my offer** sie reagierte nur langsam auf mein Angebot; **to ~ against** negativ reagieren auf *(+acc)* **b** *(= have an effect)* wirken *(on, upon* auf *+acc)*

reaction [riː'ækʃən] N **a** *(= response, Chem, Phys)* Reaktion *f* *(to* auf *+acc, against* gegen*)*; **what was his ~ to your suggestion?** wie hat er auf Ihren Vorschlag reagiert?, wie war seine Reaktion auf Ihren Vorschlag?; **a ~ against feminism** eine Absage an den Feminismus; **action and ~** Wirkung und Gegenwirkung **b** *(Pol)* Reaktion *f*; **forces of ~** reaktionäre Kräfte *pl* **c** *(Mil)* Gegenschlag *m* **d** *(St Ex)* Umschwung *m*, Rückgang *m*

reactionary [riː'ækʃənrɪ], **reactionist** [riː'ækʃənɪst] **ADJ** reaktionär **N** Reaktionär(in) *m(f)*

reaction time N Reaktionszeit *f*

reactivate [riː'æktɪveɪt] VT reaktivieren

reactive [riː'æktɪv] ADJ *(Chem, Phys)* reaktiv

reactor [riː'æktəʳ] N *(Phys)* Reaktor *m*; *(Chem also)* Reaktionsapparat *m*; *(Elec)* Blindwiderstand *m*

reactor: **reactor block** N Reaktorblock *m*; **reactor core** N Reaktorkern *m*; **reactor safety** N Reaktorsicherheit *f*

read[1] [riːd] *vb: pret, ptp* **read** [red] **VT a** *(also Comput)* lesen; *(to sb)* vorlesen *(to* +*dat)*; **do you ~ music?** können Sie Noten lesen?; **I ~ him to sleep** ich las ihm vor, bis er einschlief; **~ my lips!** *(inf)* höre meine Worte!; **to take sth as ~** *(fig)* *(= as self-evident)* etw als selbstverständlich voraussetzen; *(= as agreed)* etw für abgemacht halten; **they took the minutes as ~** *(in meeting)* sie setzten das Protokoll als bekannt voraus; **for "meet" ~ "met"** anstelle *or* an Stelle von „meet" soll „met" stehen
b *(= interpret) thoughts, feelings* lesen; *dream* deuten; *words* verstehen; *person* einschätzen können; **to ~ sb's thoughts/mind** jds Gedanken lesen; **to ~ sb's palm** jdm aus der Hand lesen; **to ~ the tea leaves** ≈ aus dem Kaffeesatz lesen; **these words can be ~ in several ways** diese Wörter können unterschiedlich verstanden werden; **to ~ something into a text** etwas in einen Text (hinein)lesen; **don't ~ too much into his words** interpretieren Sie nicht zu viel in seine Worte hinein
c *(Brit Univ form: = study)* studieren
d *thermometer, barometer etc* sehen auf *(+acc)*, ablesen; **to ~ a meter** einen Zähler(stand) ablesen
e *(meter)* (an)zeigen, stehen auf *(+dat)*; *(flight etc instruments)* anzeigen; **the thermometer ~s 37°** das Thermometer steht auf *or* zeigt 37°
f *(Telec)* verstehen; **do you ~ me?** *(Telec)* können Sie mich verstehen?; *(fig)* haben Sie mich verstanden?
VI a *(= read books etc)* lesen; *(to sb)* vorlesen *(to* +*dat)*; **she ~s well** sie liest gut; *(learner, beginner)* sie kann schon gut lesen; **to ~ aloud** *or* **out loud** laut lesen; **to ~ to oneself** für sich lesen; **he likes being ~ to** er lässt sich *(dat)* gern vorlesen; **will you ~ to me, Mummy?** Mutti, liest du mir etwas vor?
b *(= convey impression when read)* **this paragraph ~s/doesn't ~ well** dieser Abschnitt liest sich gut/nicht gut; **this ~s like an official report/a translation** das klingt wie ein offizieller Bericht/eine Übersetzung; **that's how it ~s to me** so verstehe ich das
c *(= have wording)* lauten; **the letter ~s as follows** der Brief geht so *or* lautet folgendermaßen
d *(Brit Univ form: = study)* **to ~ for an examination** sich auf eine Prüfung vorbereiten → **bar**[1]
N she enjoys a good ~ sie liest gern; **this book is quite a good ~** das Buch liest sich gut

▶ **read back** VT *sep shorthand* lesen; *one's notes etc* noch einmal lesen; *(to sb)* noch einmal vorlesen

▶ **read in** VT *sep (Comput) text, data* einlesen

▶ **read off** VT *sep* ablesen; *(without pause)* herunterlesen

►**read on** VI weiterlesen

►**read out** VT *sep* vorlesen; *instrument readings* ablesen

►**read over** *or* **through** VT *sep* durchlesen

►**read up** VT *sep* nachlesen über (+*acc*), sich informieren über (+*acc*) VI nachlesen, sich informieren (*on* über +*acc*)

read² [red] *pret, ptp of* **read¹** ADJ **he is well/not very well** ~ er ist sehr/wenig belesen

readability [,ri:də'bɪlɪtɪ] N (= *legibility, of handwriting etc*) Leserlichkeit *f*, Lesbarkeit *f*; (= *reading enjoyment*) Lesevergnügen *nt*; (= *comprehensibility, of book etc*) Lesbarkeit *f*

readable ['ri:dəbl] ADJ (= *legible*) *handwriting* lesbar; (= *worth reading*) *book etc* lesenswert; **not very** ~ (= *illegible*) schlecht lesbar; (= *not worth reading*) nicht besonders lesenswert

readdress [,ri:ə'dres] VT **a** *letter, parcel* umadressieren **b** *problem* erneut ansprechen

reader ['ri:də'] N **a** Leser(in) *m(f)*; **publisher's** ~ Lektor(in) *m(f)* **b** (*Brit Univ*) ≈ Dozent(in) *m(f)* **c** (= *schoolbook*) Lesebuch *nt*; (*to teach reading*) Fibel *f*; (= *foreign language text*) Text *m*, Lektüre *f*; (= *anthology*) Sammelband *m*; **a** ~ **in the Classics** eine Klassikersammlung; **"first French ~"** „Französisches Lesebuch für Anfänger"

readership ['ri:dəʃɪp] N **a** (*of newspaper, magazine*) Leserschaft *f*, Leser *pl*; **a big** *or* **wide** ~ eine große Leserschaft; **a** ~ **of millions** Millionen Leser **b** (*Brit Univ*) ≈ Dozentur *f*

read head N (*Comput*) Lesekopf *m*

readies ['redɪz] PL (*Brit inf*: = *ready cash*) Bare(s) *nt* (*inf*); **the** ~ das Bare (*inf*); **that'll cost you 100 in** ~ das kostet dich 100 bar auf die Hand (*inf*) *or* Kralle (*sl*); **I don't have the** ~ ich hab nicht die Kohle (*inf*)

readily ['redɪlɪ] ADV bereitwillig; (= *easily*) leicht; ~ **to hand** griffbereit; ~ **available** leicht erhältlich; ~ **accessible** leicht zugänglich; ~ **apparent** offensichtlich, leicht ersichtlich

readiness ['redɪnɪs] N **a** Bereitschaft *f*; ~ **for war** Kriegsbereitschaft *f*; **to be (kept) in** ~ **(for sth)** (für etw) bereitgehalten werden; **his** ~ **to help** seine Hilfsbereitschaft **b** (= *ease*) Leichtigkeit *f*

reading ['ri:dɪŋ] N **a** (= *action*) Lesen *nt*
b (= *reading matter*) Lektüre *f*; **this book makes (for) very interesting** ~ dieses Buch ist sehr interessant zu lesen; **have you any light ~?** haben Sie eine leichte Lektüre?
c (= *recital, excerpt*) Lesung *f*; **play** ~ Lesen *nt* mit verteilten Rollen
d (= *interpretation*) Interpretation *f*, Verständnis *nt*
e (= *variant*) Version *f*
f (*from meter*) Thermometer-/Barometer-/ /Zählerstand *etc m*; (*on flight etc instruments*) Anzeige *f*; (*in scientific experiment*) Messwert *m*; **to take a** ~ den Thermometerstand *etc*/die Anzeige/den Messwert ablesen; **the** ~ **is …** das Thermometer *etc* steht auf …; die Anzeige/der Messwert ist …
g (*Parl, of bill*) Lesung *f*; **the Senate gave the bill its first/a second** ~ der Senat beriet das Gesetz in erster/zweiter Lesung
h (= *knowledge*) Belesenheit *f*; **a man of wide** ~ ein sehr belesener Mann

reading: **reading age** N **a low/high** ~ ein hohes/junges Lesalter; **a** ~ **of 7** die Lesefähigkeit eines 7-Jährigen; **reading book** N Lesebuch *nt*; **reading desk** N (Lese)tisch *m*; **reading glass** N Lupe *f*; **reading glasses** PL Lesebrille *f*; **reading head** N (*Comput*) Lesekopf *m*; **reading knowledge** N **to have a** ~ **of Spanish** Spanisch lesen können; **reading lamp** N Leselampe *f*; **reading list** N Leseliste *f*; **reading matter** N Lesestoff *m*; **reading public** N Leserschaft *f*, Leser *pl*; **reading room** N Lesesaal *m*; **reading speed** N (*of child, Comput*) Lesegeschwindigkeit *f*

readjust [,ri:ə'dʒʌst] VT *instrument, mechanism* neu einstellen; (= *correct*) nachstellen; *prices, salary* anpassen, neu regeln; *opinion* korrigieren VI sich neu *or* wieder anpassen (*to* an +*acc*), sich neu *or* wieder einstellen (*to* auf +*acc*)

readjustment [,ri:ə'dʒʌstmənt] N (*of instrument, mechanism*) Neueinstellung *f*; (= *correction*) Nachstellung *f*; (*of prices, salary*) Anpassung *f*, Neuregelung *f*; (*of opinion*) Korrektur *f*; (*of person*) Wiederanpassung *f*

read: **read-me file** N (*Comput*) Infodatei *f*; **read-only** ADJ *attr* (*Comput*) *file* schreibgeschützt; **read only memory** N (*Comput*) (Nur)lesespeicher *m*, Festwertspeicher *m*; **readout** N (*Comput etc*) Anzeige *f*; **read-through** N (*Theat etc*) Leseprobe *f*; **read-write head** N (*Comput*) Schreib-/Lesekopf *m*; **read-write memory** N (*Comput*) Schreib-/Lesespeicher *m*

ready ['redɪ] ADJ **a** (= *prepared*) *person, thing* bereit, fertig; *answer, excuse* parat, vorformuliert; (= *finished, cooked etc*) fertig; ~ **to leave** abmarschbereit; (*for journey*) abfahrtbereit, reisefertig; ~ **to use** *or* **for use** gebrauchsfertig; ~ **to serve** tischfertig; ~ **for battle** kampfbereit; ~ **for action** bereit zum Angriff, klar zum Angriff *or* Gefecht; ~ **for anything** zu allem bereit; **dinner is** ~ das Essen ist fertig; **"dinner's ~"** „essen kommen", „zum Essen"; **are you ~ to go?** sind Sie so weit?, kann es losgehen? (*inf*); **are you ~ to push?** alles fertig zum Schieben?; **are you ~ to take the weight?** können Sie das Gewicht jetzt übernehmen?; **are you ~ to order?** sind Sie so weit?, möchten Sie jetzt bestellen?; **well, I think we're** ~ ich glaube, wir sind so weit; **I'm not quite ~ yet** ich bin noch nicht ganz fertig; **everything is ~ for his visit** alles ist auf *or* für seinen Besuch vorbereitet; **the final treaty will be ~ for signing tomorrow** der endgültige Vertrag wird morgen zum Unterzeichnen fertig sein *or* bereitliegen; **flight 211 is now ~ for boarding** Flug 211 ist jetzt zum Einsteigen bereit; **the doctor's ~ for you now** der Doktor kann Sie jetzt sehen; **I'm ~ for him!** ich warte nur auf ihn, er soll nur kommen; **to be ~ with an excuse** eine Entschuldigung bereithaben *or* -halten; **to get (oneself)** ~ sich fertig machen; **to get ~ to go out/play tennis** sich zum Ausgehen/Tennisspielen fertig machen; **to get ~ for sth** sich auf etw (*acc*) vorbereiten; **get ~ for it!** (*before blow etc*) Achtung!, pass auf!; (*before momentous news*) mach dich auf was gefasst (*inf*); **to get** *or* **make sth** ~ etw fertig machen, etw bereitmachen; *room, bed, breakfast etc* etw vorbereiten; **to get sth/sb ~ (for sth/to do sth)** etw/jdn vorbereiten *or* fertig machen (für etw/zum Tun von etw); **to make ~ (for sth/to do sth)** sich fertig machen (für etw/ zum Tun von etw); **we were all ~ to sleep** (*expressing need*) wir brauchten alle Schlaf, wir waren alle kurz davor, einzuschlafen; ~ **and waiting** startbereit; ~ **when you are** ich bin bereit *or* startbereit; ~ **about!** (*Naut*) klar zum Wenden!; **~, steady, go!** (*Brit*) Achtung *or* auf die Plätze, fertig, los!
b (= *quick*) *explanation* fertig, zur Hand *pred*; *smile* rasch, schnell; *supply* griffbereit, zur Hand *pred*; *market* schnell; *availability* schnell, griffbereit, zur Hand; ~ **to do sth** (= *willing*) bereit, etw zu tun; (= *quick*) schnell dabei, etw zu tun; **he's always ~ to find fault** er ist immer schnell dabei, wenn es gilt, Fehler zu finden; **they are only too ~ to let us do all the work** sie sind nur allzu bereit *or* immer gern bereit, die ganze Arbeit uns zu überlassen; **don't be so ~ to criticize** kritisieren Sie doch nicht so schnell; **I'm ~ to believe it** ich möchte das fast glauben; **he was ~ to cry** er war den Tränen nahe; **he's always ~ with an answer** er ist mit einer Antwort immer schnell bei der Hand; **~, willing and able (to do sth)** bereit, fertig und willens(, etw zu tun)
c (= *prompt*) *reply* prompt; *wit* schlagfertig; **to have a ~ tongue** schlagfertig sein
d (= *available*) ~ **money** jederzeit verfügbares Geld; ~ **cash** Bargeld *nt*; **to pay in ~ cash** auf die Hand bezahlen; ~ **to hand** zur Hand; **"now ~"** „jetzt zu haben"
e (= *practical*) *solution* sauber; (= *competent*) *speaker* gewandt; **to have a ~ sale** (*Comm*) guten Absatz finden

N **a at the ~** (*Mil*) **to come to the ~** das Gewehr in Anschlag nehmen; mit dem Gewehr im Anschlag; (*fig*) marsch-/fahrbereit *etc*; **with his pen at the ~** mit gezücktem Federhalter **b** (= *money*) **the ~** (*inf*) das nötige Kleingeld (*inf*) → *also* **readies**

VT (*form*: = *prepare*) *object* vorbereiten, fertig machen; **to ~ oneself to do sth** sich vorbereiten, etw zu tun *or* sich vorbereiten für etw

VI (*form*) **to ~ for sth** auf dem Weg *or* unterwegs sein zu etw; **to ~ to do sth** im Begriff sein *or* stehen, etw zu tun, drauf und dran sein, etw zu tun

ready: **ready-cooked** ADJ vorgekocht; **ready-cut** ADJ zugeschnitten; **ready-furnished** ADJ fertig eingerichtet; **ready-made** ADJ **a** *curtains* fertig; *meal* vorgekocht; *answer, ideas* vorgefertigt; ~ **clothes** Konfektionskleidung *f* **b** (= *convenient*) *replacement* nahtlos, übergangslos; *topic* jederzeit verfügbar, immer zur Hand; *family* komplett; ~ **solution** Patentlösung *f* ADV komplett; **you can buy your greenhouse ~** Sie können Ihr Glashaus schon fertig zusammengesetzt *or* zusammengebaut kaufen, Sie können ein komplett fertiges Glashaus kaufen; **ready meal** N Fertiggericht *nt*; **ready-mix** ADJ *attr* (*Cook*) aus einer Packung, aus der Packung; **ready-mixed** ADJ vorgemischt; ~ **concrete** Fertigzement *m*; **ready-prepared** ADJ vorbereitet, im Voraus zubereitet; **ready reckoner** N Rechentabelle *f*; **ready-to-eat** ADJ tafelfertig, essfertig; ~ **frozen meals** tiefgefrorene Fertiggerichte; **ready-to-serve** ADJ tischfertig; **ready-to-wear** ADJ *attr*, **ready to wear** ADJ *pred* Konfektions-, von der Stange (*inf*); ~ **dress** Konfektionskleid *nt*; **ready-witted** ADJ *person* aufgeweckt, schlagfertig

reaffirm [,ri:ə'fɜ:m] VT **a** (= *assert again*) wieder *or* erneut versichern, beteuern **b** (= *strengthen, reconfirm*) *suspicion, doubts* bestätigen; *principles, wish* bestärken

reaffirmation [,ri:æfə'meɪʃən] N **a** (= *assertion*) erneute Versicherung *f* **b** (= *confirmation*) Bestätigung *f*, Bestärkung *f*

reafforest [,ri:ə'fɒrɪst] VT wieder aufforsten

reafforestation ['ri:ə,fɒrɪs'teɪʃən] N (*esp Brit*) Wiederaufforstung *f*

reagent [ri:'eɪdʒənt] N (*Chem*) Reagens *nt*

real [rɪəl] ADJ **a** (= *genuine*) *gold, flowers, silk etc, sympathy, joy, desire* echt; *need, improvement* echt, wirklich; (*as opposed to substitute*) richtig; *name* richtig; (= *true, as opposed to apparent*) *owner, boss, reason, purpose, state of affairs* wirklich, tatsächlich, eigentlich; (= *not imaginary*) *creature, object, life, world* wirklich, real (*esp Philos*); (*Phys, Math*) reell; (*Econ*) real; **you can touch it, it's ~** das können Sie anfassen, es ist wirklich da; **was the unicorn ever a ~ creature?** gab es das Einhorn je wirklich *or* tatsächlich?; **in ~ life** im wirklichen Leben; **he has no ~ power** er hat keine wirkliche Macht; **his grief was very ~** sein Schmerz war echt, er empfand seinen Schmerz zutiefst; **the danger was very ~** das war eine ganz reale Gefahr; **it's the ~ thing** *or* **McCoy, this whisky!** dieser Whisky ist der echte; **"real leather"** echt Leder; **it's not the ~ thing** das ist nicht das Wahre; (= *not genuine*) das ist nicht echt; **climbing this hill isn't much when you've done the ~ thing** dieser Hügel ist gar nichts, wenn man schon einmal richtig geklettert hat; **she wanted to see the ~ Africa** sie wollte das wirkliche Afrika *or* das tiefe Afrika erleben; **the ~ question is…** die wirkliche Frage ist …, der Kern der Frage ist …; **to keep in touch with the ~ world** auf dem Boden der Tatsachen bleiben, nicht die Berührung mit dem wirklichen Leben verlieren; **Real Presence** (*Rel*) Realpräsenz *f*; **get ~!** (*inf*) wach auf!
b (= *proper, complete*) richtig; *sportsman, gentleman, coward* richtig, echt; *champion, friend, friendship* wahr, echt; *threat* echt, wirklich; *idiot, disaster* komplett; **it's a ~ miracle** das ist wirk-

lich *or* echt *(inf)* ein Wunder, das ist wirklich ein wahres Wunder; **it's a ~ shame** es ist wirklich schade, es ist jammerschade; **he doesn't know what ~ contentment/family life is** er weiß ja nicht, was Zufriedenheit/Familienleben wirklich ist; **that's what I call a ~ car** das nenne ich ein Auto; **that's a ~ racket** das ist wirklich ein Schwindel; **I'm in ~ trouble** ich bin in großen Schwierigkeiten; **to make ~ money** wirklich viel Geld verdienen, das große Geld verdienen *or* machen *(inf)*

c *(Fin: = net, overall) income, cost* wirklich, tatsächlich; *interest rate* effektiv; **in ~ terms** effektiv; **this increase is equivalent in ~ terms to …** dieser Anstieg entspricht effektiv …

ADV *(esp US inf)* echt *(inf)*, wirklich; **~ soon** wirklich bald; **we had a ~ good laugh** wir haben so gelacht

N a for ~ wirklich, echt *(inf)*; **is that invitation for ~?** ist die Einladung ernst gemeint?; **he's not for ~** *(= not sincere)* er meint es nicht wirklich; *(= not genuine)* er ist nicht echt; **is this for ~ or is it another practice?** ist das echt *(inf) or* Ernst oder schon wieder eine Übung?

b *(Philos)* **the ~** das Reale, die Wirklichkeit

real: **real ale** N Real Ale *nt*; **real coffee** N Bohnenkaffee *m*; **real estate** N Immobilien *pl*; **~ developer** *(US)* Immobilienhändler(in) *m(f)*; **~ agent** *(US)* Grundstücks- *or* Immobilienmakler(in) *m(f)*; **~ office** *(US)* Immobilienbüro *nt*; **~ register** *(US)* Grundbuch *nt*

realism [ˈrɪəlɪzəm] N Realismus *m*

realist [ˈrɪəlɪst] N Realist(in) *m(f)*

realistic [rɪəˈlɪstɪk] ADJ realistisch; *painting also* naturgetreu

realistically [rɪəˈlɪstɪkəlɪ] ADV *hope for* realistisch, realistischerweise; **it just isn't ~ possible** es ist realistisch gesehen nicht möglich, es ist einfach unrealistisch; **~, he had little chance of winning** realistisch gesehen hatte er kaum eine Chance zu gewinnen; **~ speaking** realistisch gesehen *or* gesagt

reality [riːˈælɪtɪ] ✪ 26.3 N **a** Wirklichkeit *f*, Realität *f*; **to become ~** sich verwirklichen; **(the) ~ is somewhat different** die Wirklichkeit *or* Realität sieht etwas anders aus; **in ~** *(= in fact)* in Wirklichkeit; *(= actually)* eigentlich; **to bring sb back to ~** jdn auf den Boden der Tatsachen zurückbringen; **the realities of the situation** der wirkliche Sachverhalt **b** *(= trueness to life)* Naturtreue *f*

reality: **reality check** N *(inf)* Augenöffner *m* *(inf)*; **to give sb a ~** jdm die Augen öffnen; **he needs a ~** man muss ihn mit der Realität konfrontieren, er muss sich mit der Realität auseinandersetzen; **reality show** N Reality-TV--Show *f*; **reality TV** N Reality TV *nt*; **~ show** = **reality show**

realizable [ˈrɪəlaɪzəbl] ADJ *assets* realisierbar, zu verflüssigen *pred*; *hope, plan* realisierbar, zu verwirklichen *pred*; *wealth* realisierbar

realization [ˌrɪəlaɪˈzeɪʃən] N **a** *(of assets)* Realisation *f*, Verflüssigung *f*; *(of hope, plan)* Realisierung *f*, Verwirklichung *f*; *(of potential)* Verwirklichung *f* **b** *(= awareness)* Erkenntnis *f*

realize [ˈrɪəlaɪz] VT **a** *(= become aware of)* erkennen, sich *(dat)* klar werden *(+gen)*, sich *(dat)* bewusst werden *(+gen)*; *(= be aware of)* sich *(dat)* klar sein über *(+acc)*, sich *(dat)* bewusst sein *(+gen)*; *(= appreciate, understand)* begreifen; *(= notice)* (be)merken; *(= discover)* feststellen; **does he ~ the problems?** sind ihm die Probleme bewusst *or* klar?; **he had not fully ~d that she was dead** es war ihm nicht voll bewusst, dass sie tot war; **I ~d what he meant** mir wurde klar *or* ich begriff, was er meinte; **I ~d how he had done it** ich erkannte *or* mir wurde klar, wie er es gemacht hatte; **I hadn't ~d you were going away** mir war nicht klar, dass Sie weggehen; **I've just ~d I won't be here** mir ist eben aufgegangen *or* klar geworden, dass ich dann nicht hier sein werde; **when will you ~ you can't …?** wann werden Sie endlich begreifen, dass Sie nicht … können?; **I hadn't ~d how late it was** ich habe gar nicht gemerkt, wie spät es war; **he didn't ~ she was cheating him** er merkte nicht, dass sie ihn betrog; **when the parents ~d their child was deaf** als die Eltern (be)merkten *or* feststellten, dass ihr Kind taub war; **I ~d I didn't have any money on me** ich stellte fest, dass ich kein Geld dabei hatte; **I made her ~ that I was right** ich machte ihr klar, dass ich recht hatte; **you couldn't be expected to ~ that** das konnten Sie nicht wissen; **yes, I ~ that** ja, das ist mir klar *or* bewusst; **yes, I ~ that I was wrong** ja, ich sehe ein, dass ich unrecht hatte

b *hope, plan* verwirklichen, realisieren; *potential* verwirklichen

c *(Fin) assets* realisieren, verflüssigen; *price* bringen, erzielen; *interest* abwerfen, erbringen; *(goods)* einbringen; **how much did you ~ on your Rembrandt?** wie viel hat Ihr Rembrandt (ein)gebracht?

VI didn't you ~? war Ihnen das nicht klar?; *(= notice)* haben Sie das nicht gemerkt?; **I've just ~d** das ist mir eben klar geworden; *(= noticed)* das habe ich eben gemerkt; **I should have ~d** das hätte ich wissen müssen; **I thought you'd never ~** ich dachte, Sie merken es nie; **he'll never ~** *(= notice)* das wird er nie merken

real-life ADJ *situation* alltäglich, lebensecht, tatsächlich; *event* real, tatsächlich, wirklich; *person* wirklich, real; *story* wirklich, wahr

reallocate [riˈæləʊkeɪt] VT umverteilen, neu verteilen *or* zuteilen

reallocation [ˌriːæləʊˈkeɪʃən] N Umverteilung *f*, Neuverteilung *f*

really [ˈrɪəlɪ] ADV **a** *(= in reality)* wirklich, tatsächlich; **I ~ don't know what to think** ich weiß wirklich *or* tatsächlich nicht, was ich davon halten soll; **I don't ~ know what I'm going to do** ich weiß eigentlich nicht, was ich machen werde; **I don't ~ think so** das glaube ich eigentlich nicht; **well yes, I ~ think we should** ich finde eigentlich schon, dass wir das tun sollten; **before he ~ knew/understood** bevor er richtig *or* wirklich wusste/verstand; **~ and truly** wirklich

b *(intensifier)* wirklich, echt *(inf)*; *glad, disappointed* wirklich, richtig, echt *(inf)*; **he ~ is an idiot** er ist wirklich *or* echt *(inf)* ein Idiot; **you ~ must visit Paris** Sie müssen wirklich Paris besuchen; **I ~ must say …** ich muss schon sagen …

INTERJ *(in doubt, disbelief, surprise)* wirklich, tatsächlich; *(in protest, indignation)* also wirklich!; **not ~!** ach wirklich?

realm [relm] N *(liter: = kingdom)* Königreich *nt*; *(fig)* Reich *nt*; **within the ~s of possibility** im Bereich des Möglichen

real: **real number** N reelle Zahl; **real property** N *(US)* Grundbesitz *m*; **real tennis** N Ballhaustennis *nt*; **real time** N *(Comput)* Echtzeit *f*; **real-time clock** N *(Comput)* Echtzeituhr *f*; **real-time processing** N *(Comput)* Echtzeitverarbeitung *f*

realtor [ˈrɪəltɔː] N *(US)* Grundstücksmakler(in) *m(f)*

realty [ˈrɪəltɪ] N *no pl (Jur)* Immobilien *pl*

ream [riːm] N *(of paper)* (altes) Ries; **he always writes ~s** *(inf)* er schreibt immer ganze Bände *(inf)*

reanimate [riːˈænɪmeɪt] VT *(Med, form) patient, person* wiederbeleben; *(fig) party, conversation also* neu beleben

reanimation [ˌriːænɪˈmeɪʃən] N *(Med)* Wiederbelebung *f*; *(fig: of party, conversation also)* Neubelebung *f*

reap [riːp] VT **a** *corn (= cut)* schneiden, mähen; *(= harvest)* ernten; *field* abernten **b** *(fig) profit* ernten; *reward* bekommen; **to ~ the fruit of one's labours** die Früchte seiner Arbeit ernten; **to ~ a rich harvest** eine reiche Ernte einbringen; **to ~ what one has sown** ernten, was man gesät hat → **sow**[1] VI schneiden, mähen; *(person)* ernten

reaper [ˈriːpəˈ] N *(= person)* Schnitter(in) *m(f)*; *(= machine)* Mähbinder *m*; **the Reaper** *(fig: = death)* der Schnitter

reaping [ˈriːpɪŋ] N *(of corn) (= cutting)* Schneiden *nt*, Mähen *nt*; *(= harvesting)* Ernten *nt*; *(of field)* Abernten *nt*

reaping: **reaping hook** N Sichel *f*; **reaping machine** N Mähbinder *m*

reappear [ˌriːəˈpɪəˈ] VI wieder erscheinen; *(person, sun also)* sich wieder zeigen; *(character in novel)* wieder auftauchen

reappearance [ˌriːəˈpɪərəns] N Wiedererscheinen *nt*; *(of character in novel)* Wiederauftauchen *nt*

reappoint [ˌriːəˈpɔɪnt] VT *(to a job)* wieder einstellen *(to als)*; *(to a post)* wieder ernennen *(to zu)*

reappointment [ˌriːəˈpɔɪntmənt] N *(to a job)* Wiedereinstellung *f*; *(to a post)* Wiederernennung *f*

reapportion [ˌriːəˈpɔːʃən] VT *money, food, land* neu aufteilen; *duties* neu zuteilen

reappraisal [ˌriːəˈpreɪzəl] N *(of situation, problem)* Neubeurteilung *f*; *(of author, film etc also)* Neubewertung *f*

reappraise [ˌriːəˈpreɪz] VT *situation, problem* von Neuem beurteilen; *author, film etc also* neu bewerten

rear[1] [rɪəˈ] N **a** *(= back part)* hinterer Teil; *(inf: = buttocks)* Hintern *m (inf)*; **in** *or* **at the ~** hinten *(of in +dat)*; **to be situated at/to(wards) the ~ of the plane** hinten im Flugzeug/am hinteren Ende des Flugzeugs sein; **at** *or* **to the ~ of the building** *(outside)* hinter dem Haus; *(inside)* hinten im Haus; **go to the ~ of the house** *(behind the house)* geh hinter das Haus; *(inside the house)* geh nach hinten; **from the ~** von hinten

b *(Mil)* Schwanz *m* (der Truppe); **to attack an army in the ~** eine Armee im Rücken angreifen; **to bring up the ~** *(lit, fig)* die Nachhut bilden

ADJ a Hinter-, hintere(r, s)

b *(Aut)* Heck-; **~ building** Rückgebäude *nt*; **~ door** hintere Tür; **~ engine** Heckmotor *m*; **~ lights** Rücklichter *pl*; **~ wheel** Hinterrad *nt*; **~ window** Heckfenster *nt*; **~ windscreen** Heckscheibe *f*

rear[2] VT **a** *(esp Brit) animals, family* großziehen, aufziehen **b to ~ its head** *(animal)* den Kopf zurückwerfen; *(snake)* sich aufstellen; **violence/racism ~ed its ugly head (again)** die Gewalt/der Rassismus kam (wieder) zum Vorschein; **sex ~s its ugly head** der Trieb meldet sich VI *(horse: also* **rear up***)* sich aufbäumen

rear: **rear admiral** N Konteradmiral *m*; **rear end** N hinteres Ende; *(Aut)* Heck *nt*; *(fig, hum: = buttocks)* Hintern *m (inf)*, Hinterteil *nt (inf)*; **rear-end** VT *(esp US Mot)* auffahren *(sb/sth* auf *+acc)*; **rear-end collision** N *(Mot)*, **rear-ender** [ˌrɪərˈendəˈ] N *(esp US inf Mot)* Auffahrunfall *m*; **rear-engined** ADJ *(Aut)* mit Heckmotor, heckmotorig; **rearguard** N *(Mil)* Nachhut *f*; **rearguard action** N Nachhutgefecht *nt*; **rear gunner** N *(Mil)* Heckschütze *m*/-schützin *f*

rearm [ˌriːˈɑːm] VT *country* wieder bewaffnen; *forces, troops* neu ausrüsten *or* ausstatten VI wieder aufrüsten, neue Ausrüstung anschaffen, sich neu ausrüsten

rearmament [ˌriːˈɑːməmənt] N *(of country)* Wiederbewaffnung *f*, Wiederaufrüstung *f*; *(of forces, troops)* Neuausrüstung *f*, Neuausstattung *f*

rearmost [ˈrɪəməʊst] ADJ hinterste(r, s)

rear: **rear-mounted engine** N *(Aut)* Heckmotor *m*; **rear projection** N *(Film, Theat)* Rückprojektion *f*

rearrange [ˌriːəˈreɪndʒ] VT *furniture, system* umstellen; *plans also, layout, formation, order, ideas* ändern; *appointment, meeting* neu abmachen

rearrangement [ˌriːəˈreɪndʒmənt] N *(of furniture, system)* Umstellung *f*; *(of plans, layout, formation, order, ideas)* Änderung *f*; *(of appointment, meeting)* Neuabmachung *f*

rear spoiler N *(Aut)* Heckspoiler *m*

rear-view mirror [ˈrɪəˌvjuːˈmɪrəʳ] N Rückspiegel *m*

rearward [ˈrɪəwəd] ADJ *part* hintere(r, s); *position* am Ende; *movement* nach hinten, rückwärtig ADV (*also* **rearwards**) rückwärts

rear-wheel drive [ˈrɪəˌwiːlˈdraɪv] N Heckantrieb *m*

reason [ˈriːzn] ✪ 16.1, 17.1, 17.2, 26.3 N a (= *cause, justification*) Grund *m* (*for* für); **~ for living** *or* **being** Grund *m* zum Leben; **my ~ for going, the ~ for my going** (der Grund,) weshalb ich gehe/gegangen bin; **to give sb ~ for complaint** jdm Anlass *or* Grund zu Klagen geben; **the police had no ~ to interfere** die Polizei hatte keinen Grund einzugreifen; *(but did)* die Polizei hat ohne Grund eingegriffen; **what's the ~ for this celebration?** aus welchem Anlass wird hier gefeiert?; **I want to know the ~ why** ich möchte wissen, weshalb; **and that's the ~ why …** und deshalb …; **and that's the ~ why!** und das ist der Grund dafür!; **I have (good) ~/every ~ to believe that …** ich habe (guten) Grund/allen Grund anzunehmen, dass …; **there is ~ to believe that …** es gibt Gründe zu glauben, dass …; **there is every ~ to believe …** es spricht alles dafür …; **for that very ~** eben deswegen; **with (good) ~** mit gutem Grund, mit Recht; **without any ~** ohne jeden Grund *or* Anlass, grundlos; **for no ~ at all** ohne ersichtlichen Grund; **for no particular/apparent ~** ohne einen bestimmten/ersichtlichen Grund; **why did you do that? – no particular ~** warum haben Sie das gemacht? – einfach nur so; **for no other ~ than that …** aus keinem anderen Grund, als dass …; **for some ~ (or (an)other)** aus irgendeinem Grund; **for ~s best known to himself/myself** aus unerfindlichen/bestimmten Gründen; **all the more ~ for doing it** *or* **to do it** umso mehr Grund, das zu tun; **by ~ of** wegen *(+gen)*; **for ~s of State this was never disclosed** die Staatsräson machte die Geheimhaltung erforderlich

b *no pl* (= *mental faculty*) Verstand *m*; **to lose one's ~** den Verstand verlieren; **to reach the age of ~** verständig werden; **the Age of Reason** *(Hist)* das Zeitalter der Vernunft

c *no pl* (= *common sense*) Vernunft *f*; **the voice of ~** die Stimme der Vernunft; **to listen to ~** auf die Stimme der Vernunft hören; **he won't listen to ~** er lässt sich *(dat)* nichts sagen; **he's beyond ~** ihm ist mit Vernunft nicht beizukommen; **that stands to ~** das ist logisch; **we'll do anything within ~ to …** wir tun alles, was in unserer Macht steht, um zu …; **you can have anything within ~** Sie können alles haben, solange es sich in Grenzen hält

VI a (= *think logically*) vernünftig *or* logisch denken; **the ability to ~** logisches Denkvermögen

b (= *argue*) **to ~ (with sb)** vernünftig mit jdm reden; **there's no ~ing with him** mit ihm kann man nicht vernünftig reden

VT a **to ~ sb out of sth** jdm etw ausreden; **to ~ sb into sth** jdn zu etw überreden; **to ~ why/what …** sich *(dat)* klarmachen, warum/was …; **ours is not to ~ why** es steht uns nicht an zu fragen, warum; **he ~ed that if we hurried we could get there by 6 o'clock** er argumentierte, dass wir um 6.00 Uhr dort ankommen könnten, wenn wir uns beeilen würden, er rechnete vor, dass wir bis 6.00 Uhr dort sein könnten

b (*also* **reason out**) (= *deduce*) schließen, folgern; *(verbally)* argumentieren; (= *work out*) *problem* durchdenken

▸ **reason out** VT SEP = **reason VT b**

reasonable [ˈriːznəbl] ADJ a vernünftig; *chance* reell; *claim* berechtigt; *amount* angemessen; (= *acceptable*) *excuse, offer* akzeptabel, angemessen; **be ~!** sei vernünftig; **vegetables are ~ (in price) just now** Gemüse ist momentan preiswert; **to be ~ about sth** angemessen reagieren auf etw, vernünftig sein in einer Sache *(dat)*; **to use ~ force** *(Jur)* angemessene Gewalt anwenden; **~ grounds** *(Jur)* zureichende Gründe *pl*; **~ doubt** berechtigter Zweifel; **beyond (all) ~ doubt** ohne (jeden) Zweifel; **guilty beyond (all) ~ doubt** *(Jur)* hinreichend schuldig; **within a ~ time** innerhalb eines angemessenen Zeitraums; **it would be ~ to assume that …** man könnte durchaus annehmen, dass …

b (= *quite good*) ordentlich, ganz gut; **his work was only ~** seine Arbeit war nur einigermaßen (gut); **with a ~ amount of luck** mit einigem Glück

reasonableness [ˈriːznəblnɪs] N Vernünftigkeit *f*; *(of claim)* Berechtigung *f*; *(of amount)* Angemessenheit *f*

reasonably [ˈriːznəblɪ] ADV a *behave, act, think* vernünftig; **one could ~ think/argue that …** man könnte durchaus annehmen/anführen, dass …; **~ priced** preiswert b (= *quite, fairly*) ziemlich, ganz

reasoned [ˈriːznd] ADJ *argument, approach* durchdacht; *discussion* vernunftgeleitet, vernünftig; *explanation* wohlbegründet, durchdacht; **~ thought** Vernunftdenken *nt*

reasoning [ˈriːznɪŋ] N logisches Denken; (= *arguing*) Argumentation *f*; **I don't follow your ~** ich kann Ihrem Gedankengang *or* Ihrer Argumentation nicht folgen; **this (piece of) ~ is faulty** das Argument ist falsch; **his ~ is all wrong** er argumentiert ganz falsch, seine Argumente sind falsch

reassemble [ˌriːəˈsembl] VT a *people, troops* wieder versammeln b *tool, car, machine* wieder zusammenbauen VI sich wieder versammeln; *(troops)* sich wieder sammeln

reassert [ˌriːəˈsɜːt] VT mit Nachdruck behaupten; **to ~ oneself** seine Autorität wieder geltend machen; **his old habits ~ed themselves** seine alten Gewohnheiten kamen wieder durch

reassess [ˌriːəˈses] VT neu überdenken; *proposals, advantages* neu abwägen; *(for taxation)* neu veranlagen; *damages* neu schätzen

reassume [ˌriːəˈsjuːm] VT *work* wieder aufnehmen; *office* wieder übernehmen

reassurance [ˌriːəˈʃʊərəns] N a (= *feeling of security*) Beruhigung *f*; **to give sb ~** jdn beruhigen; **a mother's presence gives a child the ~ it needs** die Gegenwart der Mutter gibt dem Kind das nötige Gefühl der Sicherheit b (= *renewed confirmation*) Bestätigung *f*; **despite his ~(s)** trotz seiner Versicherungen; *(of lover etc)* trotz seiner Beteuerungen c = **reinsurance**

reassure [ˌriːəˈʃʊəʳ] VT a (= *relieve sb's mind*) beruhigen; (= *give feeling of security to*) das Gefühl der Sicherheit geben *(+dat)* b *(verbally)* versichern *(+dat)*; *(lover)* beteuern *(+dat)*; **to ~ sb of sth** jdm etw versichern/beteuern; **she needs to be constantly ~d that her work is adequate** man muss ihr ständig versichern *or* bestätigen, dass ihre Arbeit gut genug ist c = **reinsure**

reassuring [ˌriːəˈʃʊərɪŋ] ADJ beruhigend; **they had been ~ about the technical problems** sie waren hinsichtlich der technischen Schwierigkeiten zuversichtlich gewesen, sie hatten sich beruhigend über die technischen Schwierigkeiten geäußert; **it is ~ to know that …** es ist beruhigend zu wissen, dass …

reassuringly [ˌriːəˈʃʊərɪŋlɪ] ADV *say, simple* beruhigend; *familiar* beruhigend, tröstlich

reawaken [ˌriːəˈweɪkən] VT *person* wiedererwecken; *love, passion, interest* neu erwecken VI wieder aufwachen; *(interest, love, passion)* wieder aufleben, wieder erwachen

reawakening [ˌriːəˈweɪknɪŋ] N *(of person)* Wiedererwachen *nt*; *(of ideas, interest also)* Wiederaufleben *nt*

rebarbative [rɪˈbɑːbətɪv] ADJ *(form)* abstoßend

rebate [ˈriːbeɪt] N (= *discount*) Rabatt *m*, (Preis)nachlass *m*; (= *money back*) Rückvergütung *f*, Rückzahlung *f*

rebel [ˈrebl] N Rebell(in) *m(f)*, Aufrührer(in) *m(f)*; *(by nature)* Rebell(in) *m(f)* ADJ *attr* rebellisch; *forces, troops also* aufständisch VI [rɪˈbel] rebellieren; *(troops, forces also)* sich erheben

rebellion [rɪˈbeljən] N Rebellion *f*, Aufstand *m*; **to rise (up) in ~** einen Aufstand machen, sich erheben

rebellious [rɪˈbeljəs] ADJ *soldiers, peasants etc* rebellisch, aufrührerisch; *child, nature* rebellisch, widerspenstig

rebelliously [rɪˈbeljəslɪ] ADV *say* rebellisch, aufmüpfig; *act* rebellisch

rebelliousness [rɪˈbeljəsnɪs] N *(of troops, subordinates etc)* Rebellion *f*; (= *nature*: *of child etc*) Widerspenstigkeit *f*

rebirth [ˌriːˈbɜːθ] N Wiedergeburt *f*; *(of desire)* Wiederaufflackern *nt*

rebirthing [ˌriːˈbɜːθɪŋ] N Rebirthing *nt*

reboot [ˌriːˈbuːt] VTI *(Comput)* neu starten, rebooten

rebore [ˌriːˈbɔːʳ] VT wieder bohren; *hole* noch einmal bohren; *(Aut) engine* ausbohren [ˈriːˌbɔːʳ] N *(Aut)* **this engine needs a ~** der Motor muss ausgebohrt werden

reborn [ˌriːˈbɔːn] ADJ **to be ~** wiedergeboren werden; **to be ~ in** *(fig)* weiterleben in *(+dat)*; **to feel ~** sich wie neugeboren fühlen

rebound [rɪˈbaʊnd] VI *(ball, bullet)* zurückprallen, abprallen (*against, off* von); **your methods will ~ on you** Ihre Methoden werden auf Sie zurückfallen N [ˈriːbaʊnd] *(of ball, bullet)* Rückprall *m*; *(Baseball)* Rebound *m*; **to hit a ball on the ~** den zurück- *or* abgeprallten Ball schlagen; **she married him on the ~** sie heiratete ihn, um sich über einen anderen hinwegzutrösten

rebrand [rɪˈbrænd] VT *product* ein neues Markenimage geben *(+dat)*

rebranding [rɪˈbrændɪŋ] N **the ~ of a company** der Versuch, einer Firma ein neues Image zu geben

rebroadcast [ˌriːˈbrɔːdkɑːst] N Wiederholung(ssendung) *f* VT wiederholen, noch einmal senden

rebuff [rɪˈbʌf] N Abfuhr *f*, kurze Zurückweisung; **to suffer a ~** zurück- *or* abgewiesen werden, eine Abfuhr bekommen; *(from opposite sex)* einen Korb bekommen *(inf)* VT zurückweisen *or* abweisen, einen Korb geben *(+dat) (inf)*

rebuild [ˌriːˈbɪld] VT a (= *restore*) *house, wall* wieder aufbauen; *(fig) society, relationship* wiederherstellen; *country* wieder aufbauen; **to ~ one's life** sein Leben wieder aufbauen; **doctors worked to ~ his face** die Ärzte versuchten, sein Gesicht wiederherzustellen b (= *convert*) *house* umbauen; *society* umorganisieren

rebuilding [ˌriːˈbɪldɪŋ] N (= *restoration*: *of house, wall*) Wiederaufbau *m*; (*fig*: *of society, relationship*) Wiederherstellung *f*

rebuke [rɪˈbjuːk] N Verweis *m*, Tadel *m* VT zurechtweisen (*for* wegen), tadeln (*for* für); **to ~ sb for having spoken unkindly** jdn dafür tadeln, dass er so unfreundlich gesprochen hat

rebukingly [rɪˈbjuːkɪŋlɪ] ADV tadelnd

rebus [ˈriːbəs] N Bilderrätsel *nt*, Rebus *m or nt*

rebut [rɪˈbʌt] VT *argument, contention* widerlegen; *charges, allegations* entkräften

rebuttal [rɪˈbʌtl] N *(of argument, contention)* Widerlegung *f*; *(of charges, allegations)* Entkräftung *f*

rec *abbr of* **recommended** empf.

recalcitrance [rɪˈkælsɪtrəns] N Aufsässigkeit *f*

recalcitrant [rɪˈkælsɪtrənt] ADJ aufsässig

recall [rɪˈkɔːl] VT a (= *summon back*) zurückrufen; *ambassador* abberufen; *library book* zurückfordern; *(Fin) capital* zurückfordern, einziehen; **Ferguson was ~ed to the Scotland squad** Ferguson wurde in die schottische Mannschaft zurückberufen; **this music ~s the past** diese Musik ruft die Vergangenheit zurück; **to ~ sb to life** jdn ins Leben zurückrufen; **her voice ~ed him to the present** ihre Stimme brachte ihn in die Wirklichkeit zurück

b (= *remember*) sich erinnern an *(+acc)*, sich entsinnen *(+gen)*; **I cannot ~ meeting him** *or* **having met him** ich kann mich nicht daran erinnern, dass ich ihn kennengelernt habe; **as I ~**

... soweit ich mich erinnere ...
c *(Comput) file* wieder aufrufen
N a *(= summoning back)* Rückruf *m*; *(of ambassador)* Abberufung *f*; *(of library book)* Rückforderung *f*, Einmahnung *f*; *(Fin, of capital)* Einzug *m*; **to sound the ~** *(Mil)* zum Rückzug blasen; **this book is on ~** das Buch wird zurückgefordert; **~ slip** Aufforderung *f* zur Rückgabe eines/des Buches; **beyond ~** für immer vorbei; **lost/gone beyond ~** für immer verloren/gegangen sein
b *(= remembrance)* **powers of ~** Erinnerungsvermögen *nt*

recant [rɪ'kænt] **VT** *religious belief* widerrufen; *statement also* zurücknehmen **VI** widerrufen

recantation [,riːkæn'teɪʃən] **N** *(of religious belief)* Widerruf *m*; *(of statement also)* Zurücknahme *f*

recap¹ ['riːkæp] *(inf)* **N** kurze Zusammenfassung; **can we have a quick ~?** können wir kurz rekapitulieren *or* zusammenfassen? **VTI** rekapitulieren, kurz zusammenfassen

recap² [,riː'kæp] *(US Aut)* **N** runderneuerter Reifen **VT** runderneuern

recapitulate [,riːkə'pɪtjʊleɪt] **VT** rekapitulieren, kurz zusammenfassen; *(Mus) theme* wieder aufnehmen **VI** rekapitulieren, kurz zusammenfassen; *(Mus)* eine Reprise bringen

recapitulation ['riːkə,pɪtjʊ'leɪʃən] **N** Rekapitulation *f*, kurze Zusammenfassung; *(Mus)* Reprise *f*

recapture [,riː'kæptʃə'] **VT** *animal* wieder einfangen; *prisoner* wieder ergreifen; *town, territory* wiedererobern; *(esp Sport) title etc* wiedergewinnen, wiedererlangen; *(fig) atmosphere, emotion, period* wieder wach werden lassen; **they ~d the spark that had originally united them** sie entzündeten den Funken, der einst da war, noch einmal; **to ~ the initiative** die Initiative wieder ergreifen **N** *(of animal)* Wiedereinfangen *nt*; *(of prisoner)* Wiederergreifung *f*; *(of town, territory)* Wiedereroberung *f*; *(esp Sport: of title etc)* Wiedererlangung *f*

recast [,riː'kɑːst] **VT a** *(Metal)* neu gießen, umgießen **b** *play, film* eine neue Besetzung wählen für; *parts, roles* umbesetzen, neu besetzen **c** *(= rewrite)* umformen **N** *(Metal)* Neuguss *m*, Umguss *m*

recce ['rekɪ] **N, VI** *(dated Brit Mil sl)* *abbr of* **reconnaissance, reconnoitre**

recd *abbr of* **received** erh.

recede [rɪ'siːd] **VI a** *(tide)* zurückgehen; *(fig)* sich entfernen; *(hope)* schwinden; **to ~ into the distance** in der Ferne verschwinden; **all hope is receding** jegliche Hoffnung schwindet **b if untreated, the gums ~** ohne Behandlung bildet sich das Zahnfleisch zurück; **his forehead ~s a bit** er hat eine leicht fliehende Stirn; **his hair is receding** er hat eine leichte Stirnglatze → *also* **receding c** *(price)* zurückgehen **d to ~ from** *(opinion, view etc)* abgehen von, aufgeben

receding [rɪ'siːdɪŋ] **ADJ** *chin, forehead* fliehend; *hairline* zurückweichend; *hair* zurückweichend, dünn; **~ gums** Zahnfleischschwund *m*

receipt [rɪ'siːt] ✪ 20.5 **N a** *no pl* Empfang *m*; *(Comm)* Empfang *m*, Erhalt *m*, Eingang *m*; **on ~ of your remittance/the goods, we shall be pleased to ...** nach Empfang *etc* Ihrer Zahlung/der Waren werden wir gerne ...; **to pay on ~ (of the goods)** bei Empfang *etc* (der Waren) bezahlen; **I am in ~ of** *(on letter)* ich bin im Besitz *(+gen)*; **~ stamp** Empfangsstempel *m*
b *(Brit: = paper)* Quittung *f*, Beleg *m*; *(= receipt of posting)* Einlieferungsschein *m* **c** *(Comm, Fin: = money taken)* **~s** Einnahmen *pl*, Einkünfte *pl* **VT** *bill* quittieren

receipt book **N** Quittungsbuch *nt*

receiptor [rɪ'siːtə'] **N** *(esp US)* Empfänger(in) *m(f)*

receivable [rɪ'siːvəbl] **ADJ** *(Jur)* zulässig; **accounts ~** *(Comm)* Außenstände *pl*; **bills ~** *(Comm)* Wechselforderungen *pl*

receive [rɪ'siːv] **VT a** *(= get)* bekommen, erhalten; *punch* (ab)bekommen; *refusal, setback* erfahren; *impression* gewinnen, bekommen; *recognition* finden; *(esp Brit Jur) stolen goods* Hehlerei *f* (be)treiben mit; *(Tennis) ball, service* zurückschlagen; *sacrament* empfangen; **to ~ nothing but praise** nichts als Belobigungen hören; **he ~d nothing worse than a few bruises** er bekam nur ein paar blaue Flecke ab; **"received with thanks"** *(Comm)* „dankend erhalten"; **~d opinion** die allgemeine Meinung
b *offer, proposal, news, new play etc, person (into group, the Church)* aufnehmen; **to ~ a warm welcome** herzlich empfangen werden; **given the welcome we ~d ...** so, wie wir empfangen worden sind, ...; **to ~ sb into one's family** jdn in seine Familie aufnehmen; **the play was well ~d** das Stück wurde gut aufgenommen
c *(Telec, Rad, TV)* empfangen; **are you receiving me?** hören Sie mich?
VI a *(form)* (Besuch) empfangen; **Mrs X ~s on Mondays** Frau X empfängt an Montagen
b *(Jur)* Hehlerei *f* treiben
c *(Tennis)* rückschlagen; **Borg to ~** Rückschläger Borg
d *(Telec)* empfangen

received pronunciation [rɪ'siːvdprə,nʌnsɪ'eɪʃən] **N** hochsprachliche Aussprache

receiver [rɪ'siːvə'] ✪ 27.3 **N a** *(of letter, goods)* Empfänger(in) *m(f)*; *(esp Brit Jur: of stolen property)* Hehler(in) *m(f)* **b** *(Fin, Jur)* **official ~** Konkursverwalter(in) *m(f)*; **to call in the ~** Konkurs anmelden **c** *(Telec)* Hörer *m*; **~ rest** Gabel *f* **d** *(Rad)* Empfänger *m* **e** *(Tennis)* Rückschläger(in) *m(f)*

receivership [rɪ'siːvəʃɪp] **N to go into ~** in Konkurs gehen

receiving [rɪ'siːvɪŋ] **N** *(esp Brit Jur: of stolen property)* Hehlerei *f*

receiving: **receiving end** **N** *(inf)* **to be on the ~ (of it)/of sth** derjenige sein, der es/etw abkriegt *(inf)*; **receiving line** **N** *(US)* Empfangskomitee *nt*; **receiving set** **N** Empfangsgerät *nt*

recency ['riːsənsɪ] **N** Neuheit *f*

recension [rɪ'senʃən] **N** Rezension *f*

recent ['riːsənt] **ADJ** kürzlich; *event, development, closure* jüngste(r, s), neueste(r, s); *news* neueste(r, s), letzte(r, s); *acquaintance, invention, edition, addition* neu; **the ~ improvement** die vor Kurzem eingetretene Verbesserung; **their ~ loss** ihr vor Kurzem erlittener Verlust; **a ~ decision** eine Entscheidung, die erst vor Kurzem gefallen ist; **a ~ publication** eine Neuveröffentlichung; **his most ~ book** sein neuestes Buch; **he is a ~ acquaintance of mine** ich kenne ihn erst seit Kurzem; **his ~ arrival** seine Ankunft vor Kurzem; **her ~ trip** ihre erst kurz zurückliegende Reise; **he is a ~ arrival** er ist erst vor Kurzem angekommen, er ist erst kurz hier; **in the ~ past** in jüngerer *or* jüngster Zeit *(geh)*, erst vor Kurzem; **in ~ years** in den letzten Jahren; **in ~ times** in letzter *or* jüngster *(geh)* Zeit; **of ~ date** neueren Datums; **in ~ history** in der jüngsten Vergangenheit; **~ developments** jüngste Entwicklungen, Entwicklungen in jüngster Zeit

recently ['riːsəntlɪ] **ADV** *(= a short while ago)* vor Kurzem, kürzlich; *(= the other day also)* neulich; *(= during the last few days or weeks)* in letzter Zeit; **~ he has been doing it differently** seit Kurzem macht er das anders; **as ~ as** erst; **quite ~** erst vor Kurzem, erst kürzlich; **until (quite) ~** (noch) bis vor Kurzem; **he lived there until as ~ as last year** er hat bis letztes Jahr noch dort gelebt

receptacle [rɪ'septəkl] **N** Behälter *m*

reception [rɪ'sepʃən] ✪ 13 **N a** *no pl (= receiving, welcome: of person)* Empfang *m*; *(into group, of play, book etc)* Aufnahme *f*; **the play met with** *or* **had a very favourable ~** das Stück fand gute Aufnahme, das Stück wurde gut aufgenommen; **what sort of ~ did you get?** wie sind Sie empfangen *or* aufgenommen worden?; **to give sb a warm/chilly ~** jdm einen herzlichen/kühlen Empfang bereiten, jdn herzlich/kühl empfangen; **~ camp** Aufnahmelager *nt* **b** *(= party, ceremony)* Empfang *m* **c** *(esp Brit: in hotel etc)* der Empfang; **at/to ~** am/zum Empfang **d** *(Rad, TV)* Empfang *m* **e** *(Brit Sch: also* **reception class***)* Anfängerklasse *f*

reception: **reception area** **N** Empfangsbereich *m*; **reception centre**, *(US)* **reception center** **N** Durchgangslager *nt*; **reception committee** **N** Empfangskomitee *nt*; **reception desk** **N** Empfang *m*, Rezeption *f*

receptionist [rɪ'sepʃənɪst] **N** *(in hotel)* Empfangschef *m*, Empfangsdame *f*; *(with firm)* Herr *m*/Dame *f* am Empfang, Empfangssekretärin *f*; *(at airport)* Bodenhostess *f*; *(at doctor's, dentist's etc)* Frau *f* *or* Herr *m* an der Anmeldung

reception room **N** *(Brit)* Wohnzimmer *nt*; *(in hotel)* Aufenthaltsraum *m*

receptive [rɪ'septɪv] **ADJ** *person, mind, market* aufnahmefähig; *audience* empfänglich; **~ to** empfänglich für; **to fall on ~ ears** auf offene Ohren treffen

receptiveness [rɪ'septɪvnɪs], **receptivity** [,riːsep'tɪvɪtɪ] **N** *(of person, mind, market)* Aufnahmefähigkeit *f*; *(of audience)* Empfänglichkeit *f*; **~ to** Empfänglichkeit *f* für

receptor [rɪ'septə'] **N a** *(= nerve)* Reizempfänger *m*, Rezeptor *m* **b** *(Rad)* Empfänger *m*

recess [rɪ'ses] **N a** *(= cessation) (of Parliament)* (Sitzungs)pause *f*; *(of law courts)* Ferien *pl*; *(US Sch)* Pause *f* **b** *(= alcove)* Nische *f* **c** *(= secret place)* Winkel *m*; **in the (deepest) ~es of his mind** in den (tiefsten) Tiefen seines Geistes **VT** *(= set back)* in eine/die Nische stellen; *cupboard, cooker* einbauen; *windows* vertiefen; *lighting* versenken; *(= make a recess in) wall etc* eine Nische machen in *(+acc)*, vertiefen

recession [rɪ'seʃən] **N a** *no pl (receding)* Zurückweichen *f*, Rückgang *m*; *(Eccl)* Auszug *m* **b** *(Econ)* Rezession *f*, (wirtschaftlicher) Rückgang

recessional [rɪ'seʃənl] *(Eccl)* **N** Schlusshymne *f* *(die während des Auszugs gesungen wird)* **ADJ ~ hymn** Schlusshymne *f*

recessive [rɪ'sesɪv] **ADJ** zurückweichend; *(Econ, Biol)* rezessiv

recharge [,riː'tʃɑːdʒ] **VT** *battery* aufladen; *gun* neu *or* wieder laden, nachladen; **to ~ one's batteries** *(fig)* auftanken **VI** sich wieder aufladen; **it ~s automatically** es lädt sich automatisch (wieder) auf

rechargeable [,riː'tʃɑːdʒəbl] **ADJ** *battery* wiederaufladbar

recheck [,riː'tʃek] **VT** nochmals prüfen *or* kontrollieren

recherché [rə'ʃɛəʃeɪ] **ADJ** gewählt; *book, subject* ausgefallen; *expression* gesucht

rechristen [,riː'krɪsən] **VT** umtaufen; **it was ~ed Leningrad** es wurde in Leningrad umbenannt *or* umgetauft

recidivism [rɪ'sɪdɪvɪzəm] **N** Rückfälligkeit *f*

recidivist [rɪ'sɪdɪvɪst] **N** Rückfällige(r) *mf* **ADJ** rückfällig

recipe ['resɪpɪ] **N** Rezept *nt*; *(fig also)* Geheimnis *nt*; **that's a ~ for disaster** das führt mit Sicherheit in die Katastrophe; **a ~ for success** ein Erfolgsrezept *nt*

recipient [rɪ'sɪpɪənt] **N** Empfänger(in) *m(f)*; **Susan, as the ~ of his attentions** Susan, der seine Aufmerksamkeiten galten

reciprocal [rɪ'sɪprəkəl] **ADJ** *(= mutual)* gegenseitig; *agreement* gegenseitig, wechselseitig, wechselwirksam; *measures* gegenseitig, im Gegenzug *pred*; *visit* gegenseitig, untereinander *pred*; *(= done in return)* als Gegenleistung; *(Gram, Math)* reziprok; **the ~ relationship between these two phenomena** die Wechselbeziehung zwischen diesen zwei Phänomenen; **~ trade** Handel *m* untereinander **N** *(Math)* reziproker Wert, Reziproke *nt*

reciprocally [rɪ'sɪprəkəlɪ] **ADV** *admire, help* gegenseitig; *trade, correspond* untereinander, miteinander; *(Gram)* reziprok

reciprocate [rɪ'sɪprəkeɪt] **VT a** *smiles, wishes* erwidern; *help, kindness* erwidern, sich revanchieren für **b** *(Tech)* hin- und herbewegen; *piston* auf- und abbewegen **VI** **a** *(= reply)* sich revanchieren; **she ~d by throwing the saucepan at him** sie wiederum warf ihm den Topf nach **b** *(Tech)* hin- und hergehen; *(piston)* auf- und abgehen

reciprocating engine [rɪ'sɪprəkeɪtɪŋ'endʒɪn] N Kolbenmotor *m*

reciprocation [rɪˌsɪprə'keɪʃən] N **a** *(of help, kindness)* Erwiderung *f (of +gen)*, Revanche *f (of* für) **b** *(Tech)* Hin und Her *nt; (of pistons)* Auf und Ab *nt*

reciprocity [ˌresɪ'prɒsɪtɪ] N *(of feelings, kindness etc)* Gegenseitigkeit *f; (of favours)* Austausch *m; (Pol)* Gegenseitigkeit *f*, Reziprozität *f (form)*

recital [rɪ'saɪtl] N **a** *(of music, poetry)* Vortrag *m; (= piano recital etc)* Konzert *nt;* **song ~** Matinee *f*, Liederabend *m* **b** *(= account)* Schilderung *f; (of details)* Aufführung *f*, Aufzählung *f*

recitation [ˌresɪ'teɪʃən] N Vortrag *m;* **to give a ~ of sth** etw vortragen

recitative [ˌresɪtə'tiːv] N Rezitativ *nt*

recite [rɪ'saɪt] **VT** **a** *poetry* vortragen, rezitieren **b** *facts* hersagen; *details* aufzählen **VI** vortragen, rezitieren

reckless ['reklɪs] ADJ *person, behaviour* leichtsinnig; *driver, driving* rücksichtslos; *speed* gefährlich; *attempt* gewagt; *disregard* leichtsinnig; **~ of the danger** *(liter)* ungeachtet der Gefahr *(liter);* **with ~ abandon** im selbstvergessenen Leichtsinn, mit risikofroher Hingabe

recklessly ['reklɪslɪ] ADV *behave, disregard* leichtsinnig; *drive* rücksichtslos; *attempt* gewagt

recklessness ['reklɪsnɪs] N *(of person)* Leichtsinn *m; (of behaviour)* Leichtsinnigkeit *f; (of driver, driving)* Rücksichtslosigkeit *f; (of attempt)* Gewagtheit *f*

reckon ['rekən] **VT** **a** *(= calculate) time, numbers, points, costs, area* ausrechnen, berechnen; **he ~ed the cost to be £40.51** er berechnete die Kosten auf £ 40,51

b *(= judge)* rechnen, zählen *(among* zu); **she is ~ed (to be) a beautiful woman** sie gilt als schöne Frau

c *(= think, suppose)* glauben; *(= estimate)* schätzen; **what do you ~?** was meinen Sie?; **I ~ we can start** ich glaube, wir können anfangen; **I ~ he must be about forty** ich schätze, er müsste so um die vierzig sein; **he ~s himself to be one of the best …** er hält sich für einen der besten …

d *(sl) (= like)* gut finden *(inf); (= think likely to succeed)* große Chancen geben *(+dat)*

VI *(= calculate)* rechnen; **~ing from tomorrow** ab morgen gerechnet

▶ **reckon in** VT SEP einbeziehen, berücksichtigen

▶ **reckon on** VI *+prep obj* rechnen *or* zählen auf *(+acc);* **you can reckon on 30** Sie können mit 30 rechnen; **I was reckoning on doing that tomorrow** ich wollte das morgen machen; **I wasn't reckoning on having to do that** ich habe nicht damit gerechnet, dass ich das tun muss

▶ **reckon up** **VT** *sep* zusammenrechnen **VI** abrechnen *(with* mit)

▶ **reckon with** VI *+prep obj* rechnen mit; **if you insult him you'll have the whole family to reckon with** wenn Sie ihn beleidigen, müssen Sie mit der ganzen Familie rechnen; **he's a person to be reckoned with** er ist jemand, mit dem man rechnen muss

▶ **reckon without** VI *+prep obj* nicht rechnen mit; **he reckoned without the fact that …** er hatte nicht damit gerechnet, dass …; **you must reckon without my being there to help you** du musst damit rechnen, dass ich nicht da bin(, um dir zu helfen)

reckoner ['rekənə'] N = **ready reckoner**

reckoning ['rekənɪŋ] N **a** *(= calculation)* (Be)rechnung *f; (old: = bill, account)* Rechnung *f;* **to be out in one's ~** sich ziemlich verrechnet haben; **the day of ~** der Tag der Abrechnung; **in your ~** Ihrer Meinung *or* Schätzung nach **b** *(Naut)* = **dead reckoning**

reclaim [rɪ'kleɪm] **VT** **a** *land* gewinnen; *(by irrigation etc)* kultivieren; **to ~ land from the sea** dem Meer Land abringen **b** *(liter) person* abbringen *(from* von) **c** *(from waste)* wiedergewinnen, regenerieren *(from* aus) **d** *(= demand or ask back) rights, privileges, tax* zurückverlangen; *lost item, baggage* abholen; **a campaign to ~ the streets** eine Kampagne für sichere Straßen **N** **a** **past** *or* **beyond ~** rettungslos *or* für immer verloren **b** **baggage** *or* **luggage ~** Gepäckausgabe *f*

reclaimable [rɪ'kleɪməbl] ADJ *land* nutzbar; *by-products* regenerierbar; *money, tax* rückverlangbar

reclamation [ˌreklə'meɪʃən] N **a** *(of land)* Gewinnung *f; (by irrigation etc)* Kultivierung *f* **b** *(= recovery: of rights, privileges)* Rückgewinnung *f*

recline [rɪ'klaɪn] **VT** *arm* zurücklegen *(on* auf *+acc); head also* zurücklehnen *(on* an *+acc); seat* zurückstellen **VI** *(person)* zurückliegen; *(seat)* sich verstellen lassen; **she was reclining on the sofa** sie ruhte auf dem Sofa; **reclining in his bath** im Bade liegend; **reclining figure** *(Art)* Liegende(r) *mf*

recliner [rɪ'klaɪnə'] N Ruhesessel *m*

reclining chair [rɪ'klaɪnɪŋ'tʃeə'] N Ruhesessel *m*

reclining seat [rɪ'klaɪnɪŋ'siːt] N verstellbarer Sitz; *(in car, on boat)* Liegesitz *m*

recluse [rɪ'kluːs] N Einsiedler(in) *m(f)*

recognition [ˌrekəg'nɪʃən] N **a** *(= acknowledgement, also Pol)* Anerkennung *f;* **in ~ of** in Anerkennung *(+gen);* **his ~ of these facts** dass er diese Tatsachen akzeptierte; **to gain/receive ~** Anerkennung finden **b** *(= identification)* Erkennen *nt;* **the baby's ~ of its mother/mother's voice** dass das Baby seine Mutter/die Stimme seiner Mutter erkennt; **he/it has changed beyond** *or* **out of all ~** er/es ist nicht wiederzuerkennen

recognizable ['rekəgnaɪzəbl] ADJ erkennbar; **you're scarcely ~ with that beard** Sie sind mit dem Bart kaum zu erkennen; **Poland is no longer ~ as the country I knew in 1940** Polen ist nicht mehr das Land, das ich 1940 kannte

recognizably ['rekəgnaɪzəblɪ] ADV *(= perceptibly)* offensichtlich, erkennbar

recognizance [rɪ'kɒgnɪzəns] N *(Jur)* Verpflichtung *f; (for debt)* Anerkenntnis *f; (= sum of money)* Sicherheitsleistung *f;* **to be released on one's own ~** auf eigene Gefahr entlassen werden

recognizant [rɪ'kɒgnɪzənt] ADJ *(form)* **to be ~ of sth** etw anerkennen

recognize ['rekəgnaɪz] VT **a** *(= know again) person, town, face, voice etc* wiedererkennen; *(= identify)* erkennen *(by* an *+dat);* **you wouldn't ~ him/the house** *etc* Sie würden ihn/das Haus *etc* nicht wiedererkennen; **do you ~ this tune?** erkennen Sie die Melodie?; **I wouldn't have ~d him in that disguise** ich hätte ihn in der Verkleidung nicht erkannt

b *(= acknowledge, also Pol)* anerkennen *(as, to be* als); **she doesn't ~ me any more when she goes past** sie kennt mich nicht mehr, wenn sie mich trifft; **he doesn't even ~ my existence** er nimmt mich nicht einmal zur Kenntnis

c *(= be aware)* erkennen; *(= be prepared to admit)* zugeben, eingestehen; **you must ~ what is necessary** Sie müssen erkennen, was notwendig ist; **I ~ that I am not particularly intelligent** ich gebe zu, dass ich nicht besonders intelligent bin

d *(US: = let speak)* das Wort erteilen *(+dat,* an *+acc)*

recognized ['rekəgnaɪzd] ADJ anerkannt

recognizedly ['rekəgnaɪzɪdlɪ] ADV anerkanntermaßen

recoil [rɪ'kɔɪl] **VI** **a** *(person) (from* vor *+dat)* zurückweichen; *(in fear)* zurückschrecken; *(in disgust)* zurückschaudern; **he ~ed from (the idea of) doing it** ihm graute davor, das zu tun **b** *(gun)* zurückstoßen; *(spring)* zurückschnellen; **the gun will ~** das Gewehr hat einen Rückstoß **c** *(fig: actions)* **to ~ on sb** auf jdn zurückfallen, sich an jdm rächen **N** ['riːkɔɪl] *(of gun)* Rückstoß *m; (of spring)* Zurückschnellen *nt no pl*

recollect [ˌrekə'lekt] **VT** sich erinnern an *(+acc)*, sich entsinnen *(+gen)* **VI** sich erinnern, sich entsinnen; **as far as I can ~** soweit ich mich erinnern kann

recollection [ˌrekə'lekʃən] N *(= memory)* Erinnerung *f (of* an *+acc);* **to the best of my ~** soweit ich mich erinnern kann; **his ~ of it is vague** er erinnert sich nur vage daran; **I have some/no ~ of it** ich kann mich schwach/nicht daran erinnern

recommence [ˌriːkə'mens] VTI wieder beginnen

recommend [ˌrekə'mend] ✪ 2.1, 19.4 VT **a** *(= advise, speak well of)* empfehlen *(as* als); **what do you ~ for a cough?** was empfehlen *or* raten Sie gegen Husten?; **to ~ sb/sth to sb** jdm jdn/etw empfehlen; **to ~ doing sth** empfehlen, etw zu tun; **it is not to be ~ed** es ist nicht zu empfehlen; **to come highly ~ed** wärmstens empfohlen sein; **~ed speed** Richtgeschwindigkeit *f;* **~ed reading** empfohlene Lektüre; **~ed daily allowance** *or* **amount** empfohlene Tagesdosis *or* Tagesmenge

b *(= make acceptable)* sprechen für; **she has much/little to ~ her** es spricht sehr viel/wenig für sie; **his manners do little to ~ him** seine Manieren sind nicht gerade eine Empfehlung für ihn; **this book has little/a great deal to ~ it** das Buch ist nicht gerade empfehlenswert/sehr empfehlenswert

c *(old, liter: = entrust) child, one's soul* empfehlen *(to sb* jdm)

recommendable [ˌrekə'mendəbl] ADJ empfehlenswert; *course of action, measures also* ratsam; **it is not a ~ wine** dieser Wein ist nicht zu empfehlen

recommendation [ˌrekəmen'deɪʃən] N Empfehlung *f;* **on the ~ of** auf Empfehlung von; **to make a ~** jemanden/etwas empfehlen; **letter of ~** Empfehlung *f*, Empfehlungsschreiben *nt*

recommendatory [ˌrekə'mendətərɪ] ADJ empfehlend

recommended price [ˌrekə'mendɪd'praɪs] N unverbindlicher Richtpreis

recompense ['rekəmpens] **N** **a** *(= reward)* Belohnung *f;* **as a ~** als *or* zur Belohnung; **in ~ for** als Belohnung für **b** *(Jur, fig)* Entschädigung *f; (of loss)* Wiedergutmachung *f* **VT** **a** *(= reward)* belohnen **b** *(Jur, fig: = repay) person* entschädigen; *damage, loss* wiedergutmachen

recompose [ˌriːkəm'pəʊz] VT **a** *(= rewrite)* umschreiben **b** *(= calm)* **to ~ oneself** sich wieder beruhigen

reconcilable ['rekənsaɪləbl] ADJ *people* versöhnbar; *ideas, opinions* miteinander vereinbar

reconcile ['rekənsaɪl] VT **a** *people* versöhnen, aussöhnen; *differences* beilegen; *dispute* schlichten; **they became** *or* **were ~d** sie versöhnten sich, sie söhnten sich aus

b *(= make compatible) facts, ideas, theories, principles* miteinander in Einklang bringen, miteinander vereinbaren; **to ~ sth with sth** etw mit etw in Einklang bringen, etw mit etw vereinbaren; **these ideas cannot be ~d with the plans** diese Ideen sind mit den Plänen unvereinbar; **how do you ~ that with the fact that you said no last week?** wie lässt sich das damit vereinbaren, dass Sie letzte Woche nein *or* Nein gesagt haben?

c *(= make accept)* **to ~ sb to sth** jdn mit etw versöhnen; **to ~ oneself to sth, to become ~d to sth** sich mit etw abfinden; **what ~d him to it was …** was ihn damit versöhnte, war …

reconciliation [ˌrekənˌsɪlɪ'eɪʃən] N *(of persons)* Versöhnung *f*, Aussöhnung *f; (of opinions, principles)* Vereinbarung *f*, Versöhnung *f (esp Philos); (of differences)* Beilegung *f*

reconciliatory [ˌrekən'sɪlɪətərɪ] ADJ versöhnlich, Versöhnungs-

recondite [rɪˈkɒndaɪt] ADJ abstrus

recondition [ˌriːkənˈdɪʃən] VT generalüberholen; **a ~ed engine** ein Austauschmotor *m*

reconnaissance [rɪˈkɒnɪsəns] N *(Aviat, Mil)* Aufklärung *f*; **~ mission** Aufklärungseinsatz *m*; **to be on ~** bei einem Aufklärungseinsatz sein

reconnaissance: **reconnaissance flight** N Aufklärungsflug *m*; **reconnaissance patrol** N Spähtrupp *m*; **reconnaissance plane** N Aufklärer *m*, Aufklärungsflugzeug *nt*

reconnoitre, *(US)* **reconnoiter** [ˌrekəˈnɔɪtəʳ] **VT** *(Aviat, Mil) region* auskundschaften, erkunden, aufklären **VI** das Gelände erkunden *or* aufklären

reconquer [ˌriːˈkɒŋkəʳ] VT *town, territory* zurückerobern; *enemy* erneut *or* wieder besiegen

reconquest [ˌriːˈkɒŋkwest] N *(of town, territory)* Zurückeroberung *f*; *(of enemy)* erneuter Sieg *(of* über *+acc)*

reconsider [ˌriːkənˈsɪdəʳ] **VT** *decision, judgement* noch einmal überdenken; *(= change)* revidieren; *facts* neu erwägen; *(Jur) case* wieder aufnehmen; **to ~ one's position** seine Position überdenken; **won't you ~ your decision and come?** wollen Sie es sich *(dat)* nicht überlegen und doch kommen?; **I have ~ed my decision, I'd rather not accept** ich habe es mir noch einmal überlegt, ich lehne lieber ab **VI** **ask him to ~** sagen Sie ihm, er soll es sich *(dat)* noch einmal überlegen; **there's still time to ~** es ist noch nicht zu spät, seine Meinung zu ändern *or* es sich anders zu überlegen

reconsideration [ˈriːkənˌsɪdəˈreɪʃən] N *(of decision, judgement)* Überdenken *nt*; *(of facts)* erneute Erwägung; *(Jur, of case)* Wiederaufnahme *f*; **after ~, he decided …** nach einiger Überlegung entschied er …

reconstitute [ˌriːˈkɒnstɪtjuːt] VT **a** *assembly, committee* neu einrichten, rekonstituieren *(form)*; *(= reconstruct)* wiederherstellen **b** *food* aus einem Konzentrat zubereiten; *solution* in Wasser auflösen

reconstitution [ˈriːˌkɒnstɪˈtjuːʃən] N **a** *(of assembly, committee)* Rekonstitution *f (form)* **b** *(of food)* Zubereitung *f* aus einem Konzentrat; *(of solution)* Auflösen *nt* in Wasser

reconstruct [ˌriːkənˈstrʌkt] VT rekonstruieren; *cities, building* wieder aufbauen; **to ~ one's life** (im Leben) noch einmal von vorn anfangen

reconstruction [ˌriːkənˈstrʌkʃən] N Rekonstruktion *f*; *(of city, building)* Wiederaufbau *m*

reconstructive [ˌriːkənˈstrʌktɪv] ADJ *(Med)* wiederherstellend; **~ surgery** Wiederherstellungschirurgie *f*

reconvene [ˌriːkənˈviːn] *(form)* **VI** *(parliament etc)* wieder zusammenkommen *or* -treten **VT** *committee, council etc* wieder einberufen

record [rɪˈkɔːd] **VT** **a** *facts, story, events (diarist, person)* aufzeichnen; *(documents, diary etc)* dokumentieren; *(in register)* eintragen; *(= keep minutes of)* protokollieren; *one's thoughts, feelings etc* festhalten, niederschreiben; *protest, disapproval* zum Ausdruck bringen; **these facts are not ~ed anywhere** diese Tatsachen sind nirgends festgehalten; **it's not ~ed anywhere** das ist nirgends dokumentiert *or* belegt; **to ~ sth photographically** etw im Bild festhalten; **to ~ one's vote** seine Stimme abgeben; **to ~ a verdict of accidental death** auf Tod durch Unfall befinden; **history ~s that …** es ist geschichtlich dokumentiert, dass …; **the author ~s that …** der Verfasser berichtet, dass …

b *(thermometer, meter etc)* verzeichnen, registrieren; *(needle)* aufzeichnen, registrieren

c *(on tape, cassette etc)* aufnehmen, aufzeichnen; *(person)* aufnehmen

d *CD, DVD* brennen

VI (Tonband)aufnahmen machen; **he is ~ing at 5 o'clock** er hat um 5 Uhr eine Aufnahme; **his voice does not ~ well** seine Stimme lässt sich nicht gut aufnehmen; **the tape ~er won't ~** das Tonbandgerät nimmt nicht auf

N [ˈrekɔːd] **a** *(= account)* Aufzeichnung *f*; *(of attendance)* Liste *f*; *(of meeting)* Protokoll *nt*; *(= official document)* Unterlage *f*, Akte *f*; *(lit, fig: of the past, of civilization)* Dokument *nt*; **(public) ~s** im Staatsarchiv gelagerte Urkunden; **a photographic ~** eine Bilddokumentation; **it's nice to have a photographic ~ of one's holidays** es ist nett, den Urlaub im Bild festgehalten zu haben; **to keep a ~ of sth** über etw *(acc)* Buch führen; *(official, registrar)* etw registrieren; *(historian, chronicler)* etw aufzeichnen; **to keep a personal ~ of sth** sich *(dat)* etw notieren; **it is on ~ that …** es gibt Belege dafür, dass …; *(in files)* es ist aktenkundig, dass …; **there is no similar example on ~** es ist kein ähnliches Beispiel bekannt; **I'm prepared to go on ~ as saying that …** ich stehe zu der Behauptung, dass …; **he's on ~ as having said …** es ist belegt, dass er gesagt hat, …; **last night the PM went on ~ as saying …** gestern Abend hat sich der Premier dahin gehend geäußert, dass …; **to put sth on ~** etw schriftlich festhalten; **there is no ~ of his having said it** es ist nirgends belegt, dass er es gesagt hat; **to put** *or* **set the ~ straight** für klare Verhältnisse sorgen; **just to set the ~ straight** nur damit Klarheit herrscht; **for the ~** der Ordnung halber; *(= for the minutes)* zur Mitschrift; **this is strictly off the ~** dies ist nur inoffizell; **(strictly) off the ~ he did come** ganz im Vertrauen: er ist doch gekommen

b *(= police record)* Vorstrafen *pl*; **~s** *(= files)* Strafregister *nt*; **he's got a ~** er ist vorbestraft; **~ of previous convictions** Vorstrafen *pl*; **he's got a clean ~, he hasn't got a ~** er ist nicht vorbestraft

c *(= history)* Vorgeschichte *f*; *(= achievements)* Leistungen *pl*; **to have an excellent ~** ausgezeichnete Leistungen vorweisen können; **the team with the best ~** die Mannschaft mit den besten Leistungen; **with a ~ like yours you should be able to handle this job** mit Ihren Voraussetzungen müssten Sie sich in dieser Stelle leicht zurechtfinden; **he has a good ~ of service** er ist ein verdienter Mitarbeiter; **service ~** *(Mil)* militärisches Führungszeugnis; **his attendance ~ is bad** er fehlt oft; **his past ~** seine bisherigen Leistungen; **to have a good school ~** ein guter Schüler/eine guter Schülerin sein; **to have a good safety ~** in Bezug auf Sicherheit einen guten Ruf haben; **to have a dubious ~ as far as sth is concerned** in Bezug auf etw *(acc)* einen zweifelhaften Ruf haben; **he's got quite a ~** *(= has done bad things)* er hat so einiges auf dem Kerbholz; **he left a splendid ~ of achievements behind him** er hat sehr viel geleistet; **to spoil one's ~** es sich *(dat)* verderben, sich *(dat)* ein Minus einhandeln *(inf)*; **I've been looking at your ~, Jones** ich habe mir Ihre Akte angesehen, Jones

d *(Mus)* (Schall)platte *f*; *(= recording) (of voice, music etc)* Aufnahme *f*; *(of programme, speech)* Aufzeichnung *f*, Aufnahme *f*; **to make** *or* **cut a ~** eine Schallplatte machen

e *(Sport, fig)* Rekord *m*; **to beat** *or* **break the ~** den Rekord brechen; **to hold the ~** den Rekord halten *or* innehaben; **long-jump ~** Weitsprungrekord, Rekord im Weitsprung; **~ amount** Rekordbetrag *m*; **~ time** Rekordzeit *f*; **~ result** Rekordergebnis *nt*

f *(on seismograph etc)* Aufzeichnung *f*, Registrierung *f*

g *(Comput, in database)* Datensatz *m*

recordable [rɪˈkɔːdəbl] ADJ *music etc* für eine Aufnahme geeignet; *CD, DVD* beschreibbar

record [ˈrekɔːd]: **record album** N Plattenalbum *nt*; **record breaker** N *(Sport)* Rekordbrecher(in) *m(f)*; **record-breaking** ADJ *(Sport, fig)* rekordbrechend, Rekord-; **a ~ achievement** eine Rekordleistung; **record cabinet** N Plattenschrank *m*; **record card** N Karteikarte *f*; **record changer** N Plattenwechsler *m*; **record company** N Plattenfirma *f*; **record dealer** N Schallplattenhändler(in) *m(f)*; **record deck** N Plattenspieler *m*

recorded [rɪˈkɔːdɪd] ADJ **a** *music, programme* aufgezeichnet; **a ~ programme** *(Brit) or* **program** *(US)* eine Aufzeichnung; **~ message** Ansage *f*, Bandansage *f* **b** *fact, occurrence* schriftlich belegt; *crime* angezeigt, gemeldet; **in all ~ history** seit unserer Geschichtsschreibung

recorded delivery N *(Brit)* eingeschriebene Sendung, Einschreiben *nt*; **by ~** *or* **post** *(Brit)* per Einschreiben

recorder [rɪˈkɔːdəʳ] N **a** *(= apparatus)* Registriergerät *nt*; **cassette ~** Kassettenrekorder *m*; **tape ~** Tonbandgerät *nt* **b** *(Mus)* Blockflöte *f* **c** *(of official facts)* Berichterstatter(in) *m(f)*; *(= historian)* Chronist(in) *m(f)* **d** *(Brit Jur) nebenher als Richter tätiger Rechtsanwalt*

record holder N *(Sport)* Rekordhalter(in) *m(f)*, Rekordinhaber(in) *m(f)*

recording [rɪˈkɔːdɪŋ] N *(of sound)* Aufnahme *f*; *(of programme)* Aufzeichnung *f*

recording: **Recording Angel** N *Engel, der gute und böse Taten aufschreibt*; **recording artist** N Musiker(in) *m(f)*, der/die Schallplattenaufnahmen macht, Plattensänger(in) *m(f)*; **recording equipment** N Aufnahmegeräte *pl*; **recording session** N Aufnahme *f*; **recording studio** N Aufnahmestudio *nt*; **recording tape** N Tonband *nt*; **recording van** N *(Rad, TV)* Aufnahmewagen *m*

record library N Plattenverleih *m*; *(= collection)* Plattensammlung *f*

record player N Plattenspieler *m*

record token N Plattengutschein *m*

recount [rɪˈkaʊnt] VT *(= relate)* erzählen, wiedergeben

re-count [ˌriːˈkaʊnt] **VT** nachzählen **N** [ˈriːˌkaʊnt] *(of votes)* Nachzählung *f*

recoup [rɪˈkuːp] VT **a** *(= make good) money, amount* wieder einbringen *or* hereinbekommen; *losses* wiedergutmachen, wettmachen **b** *(= reimburse)* entschädigen; **to ~ oneself** sich entschädigen **c** *(Jur)* einbehalten

recourse [rɪˈkɔːs] N Zuflucht *f*; **to have ~ to sb** sich an jdn wenden; **to have ~ to sth** Zuflucht zu etw nehmen; **without ~ to his books** ohne seine Bücher zu konsultieren; **without ~** *(Fin)* ohne Regress

recover [rɪˈkʌvəʳ] **VT** *sth lost* wiederfinden; *one's appetite, balance also* wiedergewinnen; *sth lent* zurückbekommen; *health* wiedererlangen; *goods, property, lost territory* zurückgewinnen, zurückbekommen; *(police) stolen/missing goods* sicherstellen; *body, space capsule, wreck* bergen; *(Ind etc) materials* gewinnen; *debt* eintreiben, beitreiben; *(Jur) damages* Ersatz erhalten für; *losses* wiedergutmachen; *expenses* decken, wieder einholen; *(Comput) file* wiederherstellen; **to ~ data** Daten wiederherstellen; **to ~ one's breath/strength** wieder zu Atem/Kräften kommen; **to ~ consciousness** wieder zu Bewusstsein kommen *or* gelangen, das Bewusstsein wiedererlangen *(geh)*; **to ~ one's sight** wieder sehen können; **to ~ land from the sea** dem Meer Land abringen; **to ~ lost ground** *(fig)* aufholen; **to ~ oneself** *or* **one's composure** seine Fassung wiedererlangen; **to be quite ~ed** sich ganz erholt haben

VI **a** *(after shock, accident etc, St Ex, Fin)* sich erholen; *(from illness also)* genesen *(geh)*; *(from falling)* sich fangen; *(regain consciousness)* wieder zu sich kommen

b *(Jur)* (den Prozess) gewinnen

re-cover [ˌriːˈkʌvəʳ] VT *chairs, pillow, umbrella* neu beziehen *or* überziehen; *book* neu einbinden

recoverable [rɪˈkʌvərəbl] ADJ *(Fin) debt* eintreibbar; *losses, damages* ersetzbar; *deposit* zurückzahlbar; *goods* rückgewinnbar, eintreibbar, wiedererlangbar

recovered memory [rɪˌkʌvədˈmeməri] N *(Psych: = thing remembered)* wiedergewonnene Erinnerung

recovery [rɪˈkʌvəri] N **a** *(of sth lost)* Wiederfinden *nt*; *(of one's appetite also)* Wiedergewinnung *f*; *(of sth lent)* Zurückbekommen *nt*; *(of health)* Wiedererlangung *f*; *(of goods, property, lost territory)* Zurückgewinnung *f*; *(of body, space capsule, wreck)* Bergung *f*; *(Ind etc, of materials)* Gewinnung *f*; *(of debt)* Eintreibung *f*; *(Jur, of damages)*

Ersatz *m* (of für); *(of losses)* Wiedergutmachung *f*; *(of expenses)* Deckung *f*
b *(after shock, accident etc, St Ex, Fin)* Erholung *f*; *(from illness also)* Genesung *f (geh)*; *(of consciousness)* Wiedererlangung *f*, Zusichkommen *nt*; *(Jur: = success in lawsuit)* Prozessgewinn *m*; *(Golf)* Schlag *m* vom Rough zum Fairway; **to be on the road** *or* **way to ~** auf dem Weg der Besserung sein; **he is making a good ~** er erholt sich gut; **beyond ~** nicht mehr zu retten; **to make a ~** *(= regain strength etc)* sich erholen; **to be in ~** *(from alcoholism etc)* eine Therapie machen
c *(Comput) (of data)* Wiederherstellung *f*

recovery: **recovery position** N *(Med)* stabile Seitenlage; **to put sb in the ~** jdn in die stabile Seitenlage bringen; **recovery room** N *(in hospital)* Wachstation *f*; **recovery service** N Abschleppdienst *m*; **recovery ship** N Bergungsschiff *nt*; **recovery team** N *(Aviat, Naut)* Bergungsmannschaft *f*, Rettungsmannschaft *f*; **recovery vehicle** N Abschleppwagen *m*

recreant [ˈrekrɪənt] *(liter)* **N** *(= coward)* Memme *f*; *(= traitor)* Verräter(in) *m(f)* **ADJ** *(= cowardly)* memmenhaft; *(= traitorous)* verräterisch

recreate [ˌriːkriːˈeɪt] VT *(= reproduce) atmosphere* wieder schaffen; *scene* nachschaffen; *love, friendship etc* wieder beleben

recreation [ˌrekrɪˈeɪʃən] N **a** *(= leisure)* Erholung *f*, Entspannung *f*; *(= pastime)* Hobby *nt*; **for ~ I go fishing** zur Erholung gehe ich Angeln; **~ centre** *(Brit) or* **center** *(US)* Freizeitzentrum *nt*; **~ facilities** Möglichkeiten *pl* zur Freizeitgestaltung; **~ period** Freistunde *f* **b** *(Sch)* Pause *f*

recreational [ˌrekrɪˈeɪʃənəl] ADJ Freizeit-; **~ facilities** Freizeiteinrichtungen *pl*

recreational: **recreational drug** N Freizeit- *or* Partydroge *f*; **recreational sport** N Freizeitsport *m*; **recreational vehicle** N *(US)* Wohnmobil *nt*, Caravan *m*

recreation ground N Freizeitgelände *nt*

recreation room N Freizeitraum *m*

recreative [ˈrekrɪˌeɪtɪv] ADJ erholsam, entspannend

recriminate [rɪˈkrɪmɪneɪt] VI Gegenbeschuldigungen vorbringen

recrimination [rɪˌkrɪmɪˈneɪʃən] N Gegenbeschuldigung *f*; *(Jur)* Gegenklage *f*; **(mutual) ~s** gegenseitige Beschuldigungen *pl*; **there's no point in all these ~s** es hat keinen Sinn, sich gegenseitig zu beschuldigen

rec room [ˈrekrʊm] N *(US inf) abbr of* **recreation room**

recrudesce [ˌriːkruːˈdes] VI *(form) (wound)* wieder aufbrechen; *(illness)* wieder ausbrechen; *(problems)* wieder beginnen

recruit [rɪˈkruːt] **N** *(Mil)* Rekrut(in) *m(f)* *(to +gen)*; *(to party, club)* neues Mitglied *(to* in *+dat)*; *(to staff)* Neue(r) *mf* *(to* in *+dat)* **VT** *soldier* rekrutieren; *member* werben; *staff* einstellen, anstellen; **to be ~ed from** *(member, staff)* sich rekrutieren aus; **he ~ed me to help** er hat mich dazu herangezogen **VI** *(Mil)* Rekruten ausheben *or* anwerben; *(organization, club)* Mitglieder werben; *(employer)* neue Leute einstellen

recruiter [rɪˈkruːtə/r/] N Personalvermittler(in) *m(f)*

recruiting [rɪˈkruːtɪŋ] N *(of soldiers)* Rekrutierung *f*; *(of members)* Werben *nt*; *(of staff)* Einstellung *f*; **~ office** *(Mil)* Rekrutierungsbüro *nt*; **~ officer** Aushebungsoffizier *m*, Werbeoffizier *m (Hist)*

recruitment [rɪˈkruːtmənt] N *(of soldiers)* Rekrutierung *f*, Aushebung *f*; *(of members)* (An)werbung *f*; *(of staff)* Einstellung *f*

recruitment: **recruitment agency** N Personalagentur *f*; **recruitment consultant** N Personalberater(in) *m(f)*; **recruitment drive** N Anwerbungskampagne *f*; **recruitment process** N Rekrutierungsverfahren *nt*

recta [ˈrektə] *pl of* **rectum**

rectal [ˈrektəl] ADJ rektal *(spec)*, des Mastdarms; **~ passage** Mastdarm *m*

rectangle [ˈrekˌtæŋgl] N Rechteck *nt*

rectangular [rekˈtæŋgjʊləʳ] ADJ rechteckig; *coordinates* rechtwinklig

rectifiable [ˈrektɪfaɪəbl] ADJ **a** korrigierbar; *instrument* richtig einstellbar; *omission* nachholbar **b** *(Chem, Math)* rektifizierbar

rectification [ˌrektɪfɪˈkeɪʃən] N **a** *(= correction)* Korrektur *f*, Verbesserung *f*; *(of statement, situation)* Richtigstellung *f*, Berichtigung *f*; *(of position, anomaly, mistake)* Korrektur *f*; *(of instrument)* richtige Einstellung; *(of omission)* Nachholen *nt*, Wiedergutmachung *f*; *(of problem)* Behebung *f* **b** *(Elec)* Gleichrichtung *f* **c** *(Chem, Math)* Rektifikation *f*

rectifier [ˈrektɪˌfaɪəʳ] N *(Elec)* Gleichrichter *m*

rectify [ˈrektɪfaɪ] VT **a** *(= correct)* korrigieren, verbessern; *statement, situation* richtigstellen, korrigieren; *position, anomaly, mistake* korrigieren; *instrument* richtig einstellen, korrigieren; *omission* nachholen, wiedergutmachen; *problem* beheben **b** *(Elec)* gleichrichten **c** *(Chem, Math)* rektifizieren

rectilineal [ˌrektɪˈlɪnɪəl], **rectilinear** [ˌrektɪˈlɪnɪəʳ] ADJ geradlinig; **in a ~ direction** geradlinig

rectitude [ˈrektɪtjuːd] N Rechtschaffenheit *f*

rector [ˈrektəʳ] N **a** *(Rel)* Pfarrer *m (der Anglikanischen Kirche)* **b** *(Scot) (Sch)* Direktor(in) *m(f)*; *(Univ)* Rektor(in) *m(f)*

rectorship [ˈrektəʃɪp] N **a** *(Rel)* Zeit *f* als Pfarrer **b** *(Scot Sch)* Direktorat *nt*; *(Univ)* Rektorat *nt*

rectory [ˈrektərɪ] N *(= house)* Pfarrhaus *nt*

rectum [ˈrektəm] N *pl* **-s** *or* **recta** Rektum *nt (spec)*, Mastdarm *m*

recumbent [rɪˈkʌmbənt] ADJ *(form)* ruhend *attr*, liegend *attr*; **~ figure** *(Art)* liegende Figur, Liegende(r) *mf*; **~ bicycle** Liegefahrrad *nt*; **to be ~** liegen

recuperate [rɪˈkuːpəreɪt] **VI** sich erholen; *(from illness also)* genesen *(geh)* **VT** *losses* wettmachen, wiedergutmachen

recuperation [rɪˌkuːpəˈreɪʃən] N Erholung *f*; *(from illness also)* Genesung *f (geh)*; *(of losses)* Wiedergutmachung *f*; **after ~, I decided …** nachdem ich mich erholt hatte, entschied ich …; **powers of ~** Heilkräfte *pl*

recuperative [rɪˈkuːpərətɪv] ADJ erholsam; **~ powers** Selbstheilungskräfte *pl*

recur [rɪˈkɜːʳ] VI **a** *(= happen again)* wiederkehren; *(error, event)* sich wiederholen, wieder passieren; *(opportunity)* sich wieder bieten, sich noch einmal bieten; *(problem, symptoms)* wiederkehren, wieder auftreten; *(idea, theme)* wiederauftauchen; *(dream)* wiederkehren **b** *(Math)* sich periodisch wiederholen → **recurring** **c** *(= come to mind again)* wieder einfallen *(to sb* jdm); *(thought, idea)* wieder kommen *(to sb* jdm)

recurrence [rɪˈkʌrəns] N Wiederkehr *f*; *(of error, event)* Wiederholung *f*; *(of problem, symptoms also)* erneutes Auftreten; *(of idea, theme)* Wiederauftauchen *nt*; *(of dream)* Wiederkehr *f*; **let there be no ~ of this** das darf nie wieder vorkommen

recurrent [rɪˈkʌrənt] ADJ **a** *idea, theme, illness, symptom(s), dream, nightmare* (ständig) wiederkehrend *attr*; *error, problem* häufig (vorkommend); *event(s)* sich wiederholend *attr*; *expenses* regelmäßig wiederkehrend **b** *(Anat)* sich zurückziehend

recurring [rɪˈkɜːrɪŋ] ADJ *attr* **a** = **recurrent** **b** *(Math)* **four point nine three ~** vier Komma neun Periode drei

recurring decimal N *(Math)* periodische Dezimalzahl

recusant [ˈrekjʊzənt] ADJ *(Rel Hist)* der/die sich weigert, dem anglikanischen Gottesdienst beizuwohnen; *(fig liter)* renitent

recyclable [ˌriːˈsaɪkləbl] ADJ wiederverwertbar, recycelbar; **~ materials** wiederverwertbare Stoffe *pl*; **~ waste** wiederverwertbare Abfallstoffe *pl*, wiederverwertbarer Müll

recyclate [ˌriːˈsaɪklɪt] N wiedergewonnener Rohstoff

recycle [ˌriːˈsaɪkl] VT *waste, paper etc* wiederverwerten, wiederaufbereiten; **~d paper** Recyclingpapier *nt*; **made from ~d paper** aus Altpapier (hergestellt)

recycle bin N *(Comput)* Papierkorb *m*

recycling [ˌriːˈsaɪklɪŋ] N Wiederaufbereitung *f*, Recycling *nt*

recycling: **recycling bin** N Recyclingbehälter *m*; **recycling centre** N *(Brit)* Wertstoffsammelstelle *f*; **recycling plant** N Wiederaufbereitungsanlage *f*, Recyclingwerk *nt*; **recycling site** N Recycling- *or* Wertstoffhof *m*

red [red] **ADJ** *(also Pol)* rot; **the lights are ~** *(Aut)* es ist rot; **deep ~** tiefrot; **~ as a beetroot** rot wie eine Tomate; **to go ~ in the face** rot anlaufen, einen roten Kopf bekommen; **was my face ~!** da habe ich vielleicht einen roten Kopf bekommen; **she turned ~ with embarrassment** sie wurde rot vor Verlegenheit; **there'll be some ~ faces in the town hall** das wird einigen Leuten im Rathaus sauer aufstoßen *(inf)*; **nature ~ in tooth and claw** grausame Natur; **~ sky at night, shepherds' delight**; **~ sky in the morning, shepherds' warning** *(Prov)* Abendrot verspricht dem Bauern Lohn und Brot, dahingegen Morgenröte verheißt dem Bauern arge Nöte; **better ~ than dead** lieber rot als tot
N *(= colour)* Rot *nt*; *(Pol: = person)* Rote(r) *mf*; *(Billiards)* Karambole *f*, roter Ball; *(Roulette)* Rot *nt*, Rouge *nt*; **to underline mistakes in ~** Fehler rot unterstreichen; **to go through the lights on ~, to go through on ~** bei Rot über die Ampel fahren; **to be (£100) in the ~** (mit £ 100) in den roten Zahlen *or* in den Roten *(inf)* sein; **to go into the ~** in die roten Zahlen kommen; **this pushed the company into the ~** das brachte *or* dadurch kam die Firma in die roten Zahlen; **to get out of the ~** aus den roten Zahlen *or* aus den Roten *(inf)* herauskommen; **to see ~** *(fig)* rotsehen; **~s under the bed** *(Pol pej)* verkappte Kommunisten *pl*, rote Wölfe *pl* im Schafspelz

red: **red admiral** N Admiral *m*; **red alert** N Alarmstufe *f* rot, höchste Alarmbereitschaft; **to be on ~** in höchster Alarmbereitschaft sein; **Red Army** N Rote Armee; **Red Army Faction** N Rote Armee Fraktion *f*; **redbaiting** [ˈredbaɪtɪŋ] N *(US inf)* Kommunistenhetze *f*; **red blood cell** N rotes Blutkörperchen, rote Blutzelle; **red-blooded** ADJ heißblütig; **redbreast** N Rotkehlchen *nt*; **redbrick university** N *(Brit) um die Jahrhundertwende erbaute britische Universität*; **red cabbage** N Rotkohl *m*, Rotkraut *nt (S Ger, Aus)*, Blaukraut *nt (S Ger, Aus)*; **redcap** N *(Brit Mil sl)* Militärpolizist(in) *m(f)*; *(US)* Gepäckträger(in) *m(f)*; *(Orn)* Stieglitz *m*; **red card** N *(Ftbl)* Rote Karte; **to show sb the ~** *(also fig)* jdm die Rote Karte zeigen; **red carpet** N *(lit, fig)* roter Teppich; **a ~ reception** ein Empfang *m* mit rotem Teppich; *(fig also)* ein großer Bahnhof; **to roll out the ~ for sb, to give sb the ~ treatment** *(inf)* den roten Teppich für jdn ausrollen, jdn mit großem Bahnhof empfangen; **red cedar** N Bleistiftzeder *f*, Virginischer Wacholder; **red cell** N *(in blood)* rote Zelle; **red cent** N *(US inf)* **not a ~** *(= nothing)* keinen roten Heller *(inf)*; **Red China** N Rotchina *nt*; **redcoat** N *(Brit Hist)* Rotrock *m (britischer Soldat z.B. im amerikanischen Unabhängigkeitskrieg)*; **red corpuscle** N rotes Blutkörperchen; **Red Crescent** N Roter Halbmond; **Red Cross** **N** Rotes Kreuz **ATTR** Rotkreuz-; **~ hospital** Rotkreuzkrankenhaus *nt*; **Red Cross Society** N (Internationales) Rotes Kreuz; **redcurrant** N *(Brit)* (rote) Johannisbeere; **red deer** N Rothirsch *m*; *(pl)* Rotwild *nt*

redden [ˈredn] **VT** röten; *sky, foliage* rot färben **VI** *(face)* sich röten; *(person)* rot werden; *(sky, foliage)* sich rot färben

reddish [ˈredɪʃ] ADJ rötlich; **~-brown** rotbraun

red duster N *(Naut inf)* = **Red Ensign**

redecorate [ˌriːˈdekəreɪt] VI *(= paper)* neu tapezieren; *(= paint)* neu streichen; **we'll have to ~** wir müssen das Haus/die Wohnung *etc* neu machen *(inf)* VT *(= paper)* neu tapezieren; *(= paint)* neu streichen

redecoration [riːˌdekəˈreɪʃən] N *(action) (= papering)* Neutapezieren *nt*; *(= painting)* Neustreichen *nt*; *(result) (= papering)* neue Tapeten *pl*; *(= painting)* neuer Anstrich

redeem [rɪˈdiːm] VT *pawned object, trading stamps, coupons, bill etc* einlösen *(for* gegen); *promise, obligation* einhalten, erfüllen; *(Fin) debt* abzahlen, löschen; *mortgage* tilgen, abzahlen; *shares* verkaufen; *(US) banknote* wechseln *(for* in *+acc)*; *one's honour, situation* retten; *(Rel) sinner* erlösen; *(= compensate for) failing, fault* wettmachen, ausgleichen; **to ~ oneself** sich reinwaschen; **to ~ sb from sin** jdn von seinen Sünden reinwaschen *or* erlösen

redeemable [rɪˈdiːməbl] ADJ **a** *debt* tilgbar; *pawned object, trading stamps, coupons, bill* einlösbar; **~ against** einlösbar gegen; **~ for cash/goods** gegen Bargeld/Waren einzulösen **b** *(Rel)* erlösbar

Redeemer [rɪˈdiːməʳ] N *(Rel)* Erlöser *m*, Retter *m*, Heiland *m*

redeeming [rɪˈdiːmɪŋ] ADJ *quality* ausgleichend; **~ feature** aussöhnendes Moment; **the only ~ feature of this novel is ...** das Einzige, was einen mit diesem Roman aussöhnt, ist ...

redefine [ˌriːdɪˈfaɪn] VT neu definieren

redeliver [ˌriːdɪˈlɪvəʳ] VT *(= give back)* wieder zurückgeben; *prisoners etc* wieder aushändigen *or* ausliefern

redemption [rɪˈdempʃən] N *(of pawned object, trading stamps, coupons, bill etc)* Einlösung *f*; *(of promise, obligation)* Einhaltung *f*, Erfüllung *f*; *(Fin) (of debt)* Abzahlung *f*, Löschung *f*; *(of mortgage)* Tilgung *f*; *(of shares)* Verkauf *m*; *(US: of banknote)* Wechsel *m*; *(of one's honour, situation)* Rettung *f*; *(Rel)* Erlösung *f*; **beyond** *or* **past ~** *(fig)* nicht mehr zu retten; **~ centre** *(Brit) or* **center** *(US)*) (*(Comm)* Einlösestelle *f*

redemptive [rɪˈdemptɪv] ADJ *(Rel)* erlösend, rettend

Red Ensign N *(Naut) britische Handelsflagge*

redeploy [ˌriːdɪˈplɔɪ] VT *troops* umverlegen; *workers* anders einsetzen; *staff* umsetzen

redeployment [ˌriːdɪˈplɔɪmənt] N *(of troops)* Umverlegung *f*; *(of workers)* Einsatz *m* an einem anderen Arbeitsplatz; *(of staff)* Umsetzung *f*

redevelop [ˌriːdɪˈveləp] VT *building, area* sanieren

redevelopment [ˌriːdɪˈveləpmənt] N Sanierung *f*

redevelopment area N Sanierungsgebiet *nt*

redevelopment costs PL Sanierungskosten *pl*

red: **red eye** N *(Phot) Rotfärbung der Augen auf Blitzlichtfotos*, Rote-Augen-Effekt *m*; **redeye** N *(US sl)* **a** *(= cheap whisky)* Fusel *m (inf)*, schlechter Whisky **b** *(also* **redeye flight**) Übernachtflug *m*; **red-eyed** ADJ mit geröteten *or* roten Augen; **red-faced** ADJ mit rotem Kopf; **Red Flag** N Rote Fahne; **red flag** N *(on beach etc)* rote Warnflagge *or* Signalflagge; **red giant** N *(Astron)* roter Riese *or* Riesenstern; **red grouse** N Rothuhn *nt*; **Red Guard** N Rote Garde; **red-haired** ADJ rothaarig; **red-handed** ADV **to catch sb ~** jdn auf frischer Tat ertappen; *(esp sexually)* jdn in flagranti erwischen *(inf)*; **red hat** N *(Rel, of cardinal)* Kardinalshut *m*; **redhead** N Rothaarige(r) *mf*, Rotschopf *m*; **red-headed** ADJ rothaarig; **red heat** N Rotglut *f*; **to bring iron to ~** Eisen auf Rotglut erhitzen; **red herring** N *(lit)* Räucherhering *m*; *(fig)* Ablenkungsmanöver *nt*; *(in thrillers, historical research)* falsche Spur; **that's a ~** *(= irrelevant)* das führt vom Thema ab; **red-hot** ADJ **a** *(lit)* rot glühend; *(= very hot)* glühend heiß; *(fig) telephone lines* heiß gelaufen; **~ favourite** ganz heißer *or* brandheißer Favorit; **he's a ~ favourite to win the race** er ist der heiße Favorit bei dem Rennen **b** *(fig inf) (= very popular)* heiß *(inf)*; *(= very skilled)* toll *(inf)*; *(= very recent) news* brandaktuell; *(= ardent, burning) person* leidenschaftlich, begeistert; *attitude* glühend, brennend, inständig **c** *(= spicy) chilli* scharf, beißend; **red-hot poker** N *(Bot)* Fackellilie *f*

redial [riːˈdaɪəl] *(Telec)* VTI nochmals wählen N **automatic ~** automatische Wahlwiederholung

red: **Red Indian** N *(neg! dated)* Indianer(in) *m(f)*; **red ink** N *(US: = losses)* finanzielle Verluste *pl*, rote Zahlen *pl*; **to bleed ~** rote Zahlen schreiben

redirect [ˌriːdaɪˈrekt] VT *letter, parcel* umadressieren; *(= forward)* nachsenden; *traffic* umleiten; *attention, efforts, resources* umleiten, umverteilen

rediscounting [ˌriːdɪsˈkaʊntɪŋ] N Rediskontierung *f*

rediscover [ˌriːdɪˈskʌvəʳ] VT wiederentdecken

rediscovery [ˌriːdɪˈskʌvərɪ] N Wiederentdeckung *f*

redistribute [ˌriːdɪˈstrɪbjuːt] VT *wealth* umverteilen, neu verteilen; *(= reallocate) work* neu zuteilen

redistribution [ˌriːdɪstrɪˈbjuːʃən] N *(of wealth)* Umverteilung *f*, Neuverteilung *f*; *(of work)* Neuzuteilung *f*

red: **red lead** N Bleirot *nt*, Bleimennige *f*; **red-letter day** N besonderer Tag, Tag, den man im Kalender rot anstreichen muss; **red light** N *(lit) (= warning light)* rotes Licht; *(= traffic light)* Rotlicht *nt*; **to go through the ~** *(Mot)* bei Rot über die Ampel fahren, die Ampel überfahren *(inf)*; **to see the ~** *(fig)* die Gefahr erkennen; **the red-light district** die Strichgegend, der Strich *(inf)*; *(with nightclubs)* das Rotlichtviertel; **redlining** [ˈredlaɪnɪŋ] N *(US) die Praktik von Banken und Versicherungen, den Bewohnern heruntergekommener Stadtviertel Kredite, Hypotheken und den Abschluss von Versicherungen zu verweigern*; **red man** N *(at street crossing)* rotes Licht; *(as said to children)* rotes Männchen; **red meat** N *Rind-, Lamm- und Rehfleisch*; **red mullet** N (rote) Meeräsche; **redneck** N *(US inf)* Prolet(in) *m(f) (inf)*

redness [ˈrednɪs] N Röte *f*

redo [ˌriːˈduː] VT **a** *(= do again)* noch einmal machen, neu machen; *(Comput: command)* wiederholen; *hair* in Ordnung bringen **b** *(= restore, recover) data* wiederherstellen **c** = **redecorate**

redolence [ˈredəʊləns] N *(liter)* Duft *m*

redolent [ˈredəʊlənt] ADJ *(liter)* duftend; **~ of** *or* **with lavender** nach Lavendel duftend; **to be ~ of the 19th century/my youth** stark an das 19. Jahrhundert/meine Jugend erinnern

redouble [ˌriːˈdʌbl] VT **a** *efforts, zeal etc* verdoppeln; *attacks* verstärken **b** *(Bridge)* rekontrieren VI *(zeal, efforts)* sich verdoppeln; *(attacks)* sich verstärken N *(Bridge)* Rekontra *nt*

redoubt [rɪˈdaʊt] N *(Mil)* Redoute *f*; *(inside a fort)* Kasematte *f*

redoubtable [rɪˈdaʊtəbl] ADJ *(= formidable) task* horrend; *(= to be feared) person, teacher* Respekt gebietend *attr*

redound [rɪˈdaʊnd] VI *(form)* **to ~ to sb's honour/advantage** jdm zur Ehre/zum Vorteil gereichen *(geh)*; **to ~ to sb's credit** jdm hoch angerechnet werden; **to ~ upon** wieder treffen

red: **red pepper** N roter Paprika, rote Paprikaschote; **red pine** N Südkiefer *f*; *(= wood)* Redpine *nt*

redraft [ˌriːˈdrɑːft] N Neuentwurf *m*; *(of speech also)* Neufassung *f*; *(of literary work)* Umschrift *f* VT nochmals *or* neu entwerfen; *literary work* umschreiben

red rag N rotes Tuch; **it's like a ~ to a bull** das wirkt wie ein rotes Tuch

redress [rɪˈdres] VT *one's errors, wrongs* wiedergutmachen, sühnen; *situation* bereinigen; *grievance* beseitigen; *balance* wiederherstellen N *(for errors, wrongs)* Wiedergutmachung *f*; *(for grievance)* Beseitigung *f*; **to seek ~ for** Wiedergutmachung verlangen für; **he set out to seek ~ for these grievances** er wollte zu seinem Recht kommen; **there is no ~** das steht unumstößlich fest; **legal ~** Rechtshilfe *f*; **to have no ~ in law** keinen Rechtsanspruch haben; **but what ~ does a manager have against an employee?** aber welche Wege stehen dem Manager offen, gegen den Arbeitnehmer zu klagen?; **to gain ~** zu seinem Recht kommen

red: **Red Riding Hood** N **(Little) ~** Rotkäppchen *nt*; **red salmon** N Pazifiklachs *m*; **Red Sea** N Rotes Meer; **red setter** N (roter) Setter; **redshank** N *(Orn)* Rotschenkel *m*; **red shift** N Rotverschiebung *f*; **redskin** N *(pej)* Rothaut *f*; **red snapper** N (roter) Schnapper; **red spider mite** N Rote Spinne, Rote Spinnmilbe; **Red Spot** N *(Astron)* roter Punkt; **Red Square** N Roter Platz; **red squirrel** N Eichhörnchen *nt*; **redstart** N *(Orn)* Rotschwanz *m*; **red tape** N *(fig)* Papierkrieg *m (inf)*; *(with authorities also)* Behördenkram *m (inf)*

reduce [rɪˈdjuːs] VT **a** *pressure, weight, swelling, risk, chances* verringern, reduzieren; *speed* reduzieren, verlangsamen; *authority* schwächen; *(= lower) standards, temperatures* herabsetzen, reduzieren; *prices* ermäßigen, herabsetzen, reduzieren; *taxes, costs* senken; *expenses, wages* kürzen; *value* mindern; *(= shorten)* verkürzen; *(in size) width, staff, drawing, photo* verkleinern, reduzieren; *scale of operations* einschränken; *output* drosseln, reduzieren; *(Cook) sauce* einkochen lassen; **to ~ one's weight** abnehmen; **to ~ the strength of a solution** eine Lösung abschwächen; **to ~ speed** *(Mot)* langsamer fahren; **"reduce speed now"** *(Mot)* ≈ langsam; **the facts may all be ~d to four main headings** die Tatsachen können alle auf vier Hauptpunkte reduziert werden; **to be reducing** *(= losing weight)* eine Schlankheitskur machen

b *(in price) goods, item* heruntersetzen, herabsetzen

c *(= change the form of, Chem)* reduzieren; *(Math)* zerlegen *(to* in *+acc)*; **to ~ sth to a powder** etw pulverisieren; **to ~ sth to its parts** etw in seine Einzelteile zerlegen; **to ~ sth to a common denominator** *(Math, fig)* etw auf einen gemeinsamen Nenner bringen; **to ~ an argument to a matter of principle** aus einem Argument eine Frage des Prinzips machen; **it has been ~d to a mere ...** es ist jetzt nur noch ein ...; **it has been ~d to nothing** es ist zu nichts zusammengeschmolzen; **he's ~d to a skeleton** er ist zum Skelett abgemagert; **to ~ sb to silence/despair/tears** jdn zum Schweigen/zur Verzweiflung/zum Weinen bringen; **to ~ sb to begging/to slavery** jdn zum Betteln/zur Sklaverei zwingen; **are we ~d to this!** so weit ist es also gekommen!; **to be ~d to submission** aufgeben müssen

d *(Med) joint* wieder einrenken

VI *(esp US: = slim)* abnehmen; **to be reducing** eine Schlankheitskur machen

reduced [rɪˈdjuːst] ADJ *price, fare* ermäßigt, reduziert; *prices also, goods* herabgesetzt, heruntergesetzt; *scale, version* kleiner; *risk, demand, threat, role* geringer; *circumstances* beschränkt; **the judge gave him a ~ sentence of five years** der Richter verurteilte ihn zu einer verkürzten Haftstrafe von fünf Jahren; **at a ~ price** zu einem ermäßigten *or* reduzierten Preis; **"reduced"** *(on ticket)* „ermäßigt"; **in ~ circumstances** in beschränkten (Lebens)umständen

reduced-emission ADJ *attr car, engine* abgasreduziert

reducer [rɪˈdjuːsəʳ] N *(Phot)* Abschwächer *m*

reducible [rɪˈdjuːsəbl] ADJ *(to* auf *+acc) (Chem, fig)* reduzierbar; *(Math)* zerlegbar; *drawing, scale* verkleinerbar, reduzierbar; *time* verkürzbar; *costs* herabsetzbar; **to be ~ to sth** sich auf etw *(acc)* reduzieren lassen

reducing [rɪˈdjuːsɪŋ]: **reducing agent** N *(Chem)* Reduktionsmittel *nt*; **reducing diet** N Schlankheits-/Abmagerungskur *f*

reduction [rɪˈdʌkʃən] N **a** no pl (in sth etw gen) Reduzierung f, Reduktion f, Verringerung f; (in speed) Reduzierung f, Verlangsamung f; (in authority) Schwächung f; (in standards, temperatures) Herabsetzung f, Reduzierung f; (in prices) Ermäßigung f, Herabsetzung f, Reduzierung f; (in taxes, costs) Senkung f; (in expenses, wages) Kürzung f; (in value) Minderung f; (in size) Verkleinerung f; (= shortening) Verkürzung f; (in output) Drosselung f, Reduzierung f; (in scale of operations) Einschränkung f; (of goods, items) Herabsetzung f; (of fever) Senkung f; (of joint) Wiedereinrenken nt; **to make a ~ on an article** einen Artikel heruntersetzen; **~ for cash** Preisabschlag m bei Barzahlung; **~ of taxes** Steuersenkung f; **~ in rank** Degradierung f
b (to another state, Chem) Reduktion f; (Math) Zerlegung f (to in +acc); **~ of sth to powder/to a pulp** Zermahlung f einer Sache (gen) zu Pulver/zu Brei
c (= amount reduced) (in sth etw gen) (in pressure, temperature, output) Abnahme f, Rückgang m; (of speed) Verlangsamung f; (in size) Verkleinerung f; (in length) Verkürzung f; (in taxes) Nachlass m; (in prices) Ermäßigung f; (Jur. of sentence) Kürzung f; (of swelling) Rückgang m; **to sell (sth) at a ~** etw verbilligt verkaufen, etw zu ermäßigtem Preis verkaufen; **what a ~!** wie billig!; **~ in strength** Nachlassen nt der Kräfte
d (= copy) Verkleinerung f

reductionism [rɪˈdʌkʃənɪzəm] N Reduktionismus m

reductive [rɪˈdʌktɪv] ADJ reduktiv (geh)

redundancy [rɪˈdʌndənsɪ] N **a** Überflüssigkeit f; (of style) Weitschweifigkeit f, Redundanz f (geh) **b** (Brit Ind) Arbeitslosigkeit f; **redundancies** Entlassungen pl; **the recession caused a lot of ~** or **many redundancies** der Konjunkturrückgang brachte viel Arbeitslosigkeit mit sich; **he feared ~** er hatte Angst, seinen Arbeitsplatz zu verlieren

redundancy pay(ment) N (Brit Ind) Abfindung f, Abstandszahlung f

redundant [rɪˈdʌndənt] ADJ **a** überflüssig; land überschüssig; style zu wortreich, redundant (geh); **several ~ buildings have been demolished** mehrere Gebäude, die nicht mehr gebraucht werden, sind abgerissen worden **b** (Brit Ind: = out of work) arbeitslos; **to make sb ~** jdn entlassen, jdn freisetzen; **to become/to be made ~** den Arbeitsplatz verlieren; **he found himself ~** er war plötzlich ohne Arbeitsplatz

reduplicate [rɪˈdjuːplɪkeɪt] VT wiederholen; (Ling) reduplizieren [rɪˈdjuːplɪkɪt] ADJ (Ling) redupliziert

reduplication [rɪˌdjuːplɪˈkeɪʃən] N Wiederholung f; (Ling) Reduplikation f

reduplicative [rɪˈdjuːplɪkətɪv] ADJ (Ling) reduplizierend

red: **red wine** N Rotwein m; **redwing** N Rotdrossel f; **redwood** N Redwood nt

redye [ˌriːˈdaɪ] VT **a** (= dye the same colour) nachfärben **b** (= dye a different colour) umfärben

re-echo [ˌriːˈekəʊ] VI widerhallen VT echoen; **he ~ed his wife's opinion** er war wie das Echo seiner Frau

reed [riːd] N **a** (Bot) Schilf(rohr) nt, Ried nt; **in the ~s** im Schilf or Ried; **a broken ~** (fig) ein schwankendes Rohr **b** (of wind instrument) Rohrblatt nt; (of harmonium) Durchschlagzunge f; (of organ) Zungenpfeife f; **~s** Rohrblattinstrumente pl

reed: **reed basket** N Korb m aus Schilfrohr; **reed bunting** N Rohrammer f; **reed instrument** N Rohrblattinstrument nt

re-edit [ˌriːˈedɪt] VT neu herausgeben; book, text noch einmal redigieren; film, tape neu schneiden

reed: **reed organ** N Harmonium nt; **reed pipe** N Schalmei f; **reed stop** N Zungenregister nt

re-educate [ˌriːˈedjʊkeɪt] VT umerziehen; **to ~ one's body** sich or seinen Körper umgewöhnen

re-education [ˈriːˌedjʊˈkeɪʃən] N Umerziehung f

reed warbler [ˈriːdwɔːbləʳ] N Rohrsänger m

reedy [ˈriːdɪ] ADJ (+er) schilfig; sound näselnd; music schnarrend; voice durchdringend; **~ instrument** Rohrblattinstrument nt

reef¹ [riːf] N **a** (in sea) Riff nt **b** (Min) Ader f, Gang m

reef² N (Naut) Reff nt VT sail reffen

reefer [ˈriːfəʳ] N (= jacket) Seemannsjacke f; (inf: = joint) Joint m (inf)

reef knot N Kreuzknoten m, Weberknoten m

reek [riːk] N Gestank m VI stinken (of nach)

reeky [ˈriːkɪ] ADJ (+er) stinkig, stinkend

reel [riːl] N **a** (of thread, wire etc) Rolle f, Spule f; (of film, magnetic tape) Spule f; (Fishing) (Angel)rolle f
b (= dance) Reel m
VT (Tech) thread aufspulen
VI (person) taumeln; (drunk also) torkeln, schwanken; **he went ~ing down the street** er torkelte or schwankte die Straße hinunter; **the blow made him ~** or **sent him ~ing** er taumelte unter dem Schlag; **my head is ~ing** mir dreht sich der Kopf; **the news made him** or **his mind ~** bei der Nachricht drehte sich ihm alles; **the news left us ~ing in disbelief** die Nachricht verschlug uns einfach die Sprache; **the whole country is still ~ing from the shock** das ganze Land ist noch tief erschüttert von diesem Schock; **economic problems sent markets ~ing** Wirtschaftsprobleme brachten die Börsen ins Wanken

► **reel in** VT sep (Fishing) einrollen; fish einholen; (fig) voters einfangen, an Land ziehen (inf)

► **reel off** VT sep list herunterrasseln (inf); names also herunterspulen (inf); (monotonously) herunterleiern (inf); thread abwickeln, abspulen

► **reel up** VT sep (Fishing) aufrollen, aufspulen

re-elect [ˌriːɪˈlekt] VT wiederwählen

re-election [ˌriːɪˈlekʃən] N Wiederwahl f

re-eligible [ˌriːˈelɪdʒɪbl] ADJ wieder wählbar

reeling [ˈriːlɪŋ] ADJ head brummend (inf)

reel-to-reel [ˈriːltəˈriːl] ADJ **~ (tape recorder)** Tonbandgerät nt, Tonbandmaschine f

re-embark [ˌriːɪmˈbɑːk] VT wieder einschiffen VI sich wieder einschiffen; **to ~ on an enterprise** ein Unternehmen von Neuem beginnen

re-embarkation [ˈriːˌembɑːˈkeɪʃən] N Wiedereinschiffung f

re-emerge [ˌriːɪˈmɜːdʒ] VI (object, swimmer) wieder auftauchen; (facts) (wieder) herauskommen

re-employ [ˌriːɪmˈplɔɪ] VT person wieder einstellen

re-enact [ˌriːɪˈnækt] VT **a** (Jur) wieder in Kraft setzen **b** (= repeat) scene nachspielen; event, crime nachstellen

re-enactment [ˌriːɪˈnæktmənt] N (of law etc) Wiederinkraftsetzung f; (of scene) Nachspiel nt; (of event, crime) Nachstellen nt

re-engage [ˌriːɪnˈgeɪdʒ] VT employee wieder einstellen; (Tech) gear wheels wieder ineinandergreifen lassen; gear wieder einlegen; clutch wieder kommen lassen

re-enlist [ˌriːɪnˈlɪst] VI (Mil) sich wieder melden or verpflichten VT (Mil) neu verpflichten; **to ~ sb's help** jds Hilfe erneut in Anspruch nehmen

re-enter [ˌriːˈentəʳ] VI **a** (= walk in) wieder eintreten; (= drive in) wieder einfahren; (= penetrate: bullet etc) wieder eindringen; (= climb in) wieder einsteigen; (= cross border) wieder einreisen; (ship) wieder einlaufen
b (Theat) wieder auftreten
c (for race, exam etc) sich wieder melden (for zu)
VT **a** room wieder betreten; country wieder einreisen in (+acc); (Space) atmosphere wieder eintreten in (+acc); club etc wieder beitreten (+dat); politics wieder einsteigen in (+acc); society sich wieder eingliedern in (+acc); race sich wieder beteiligen an (+dat)
b name (on list etc) wieder eintragen

re-entrant [ˌriːˈentrənt] N Wiederholungskandidat(in) m(f)

re-entry [ˌriːˈentrɪ] N **a** (also Space) Wiedereintritt m; (into country) Wiedereinreise f (into in +acc); (for exam) Wiederantritt m (for zu); **~ point** (Space) **point of ~** (Space) Wiedereintrittsstelle f; **a ~ into politics** ein Wiedereinstieg m in die Politik; **her ~ into society** ihre Wiedereingliederung in die Gesellschaft **b** (Jur) Wiederinbesitznahme f

re-erect [ˌriːɪˈrekt] VT building, bridge wieder aufbauen; scaffolding also wieder aufstellen

re-establish [ˌriːɪˈstæblɪʃ] VT order wiederherstellen; control wiedererlangen; diplomatic relations, dialogue wieder aufnehmen; custom wieder einführen; **this novel has ~ed him as a best-selling author** mit diesem Roman ist der Autor wieder auf die Bestsellerliste gekommen

re-establishment [ˌriːɪˈstæblɪʃmənt] N (of order) Wiederherstellung f; (of custom) Wiedereinführung f; (of control) Wiedererlangen nt; (of diplomatic relations, dialogue) Wiederaufnahme f; (in a position, office) Wiedereinsetzung f

reeve¹ [riːv] N **a** (Hist) Vogt m **b** (in Canada) ≈ Gemeindevorsteher(in) m(f)

reeve² VT (Naut: = thread) einscheren; (= fasten) festmachen

re-examination [ˈriːɪgˌzæmɪˈneɪʃən] N Überprüfung f, erneute or nochmalige Prüfung; (of role) genaue Überprüfung; (Jur, of witness) erneute or nochmalige Vernehmung

re-examine [ˌriːɪgˈzæmɪn] VT überprüfen, erneut or nochmals prüfen; role nochmals genau ansehen; (Jur) witness erneut or nochmals vernehmen

re-export [ˌriːɪkˈspɔːt] VT wieder ausführen N [riːˈekspɔːt] **goods for ~** Waren pl zur Wiederausfuhr

re-exportation [ˌriːekspɔːˈteɪʃən] N Wiederausfuhr f

ref¹ [ref] N (Sport inf) abbr of **referee** Schiri m (inf)

ref² abbr of **reference (number)**; **~ your letter** mit Bezug auf Ihren Brief; **~ Ms Bright** zur Weiterleitung an Frau Bright

refashion [ˌriːˈfæʃn] VT umgestalten, ummodeln (inf)

refectory [rɪˈfektərɪ] N (in college) Mensa f; (in monastery) Refektorium nt

refer [rɪˈfɜːʳ] VT **a** (= pass) matter, problem weiterleiten (to an +acc); decision übergeben (to sb jdm); **the case was ~red to arbitration** der Fall wurde einem Schiedsgericht übergeben; **it was ~red to us for (a) decision** es wurde uns (dat) zur Entscheidung übergeben; **I ~red him to the manager** ich verwies ihn an den Geschäftsführer; **the patient was ~red for tests** der Patient wurde zu Untersuchungen geschickt; **the doctor ~red him to a specialist** der Arzt überwies ihn an einen Spezialisten or schickte ihn zu einem Spezialisten; **to ~ sb to the article on …** jdn auf den Artikel über (+acc) … verweisen; **to ~ a cheque** (Brit) or **check** (US) **to drawer** (Comm) einen Scheck an den Aussteller zurücksenden
b (Brit Univ) thesis zur Änderung zurückgeben
VI **a** **to ~ to** (= allude to) sprechen von; (= mention also) erwähnen; (words) sich beziehen auf (+acc); **I am not ~ring to you** ich meine nicht Sie; **what can he be ~ring to?** was meint er wohl?, wovon spricht er wohl?; **the letter ~s to you all** der Brief gilt euch allen; **~ring to your letter** (Comm) mit Bezug auf Ihren Brief
b (= apply to) **to ~ to** (orders, rules) gelten für; (criticism, remark) sich beziehen auf (+acc)
c (= consult) **to ~ to** (to notes, book) nachschauen in (+dat), konsultieren (geh); to person sich wenden an (+acc); **you must ~ to the original** Sie müssen aufs Original zurückgreifen

► **refer back** VI **a** (person, remark) sich beziehen (to auf +acc) **b** (= check back, consult again) zurückgehen (to zu) VT sep (= pass back) decision etc zurückgeben (to an +acc); case, mat-

ter zurückverweisen; **he referred me back to you** er hat mich an Sie zurückverwiesen

referee [ˌrefəˈriː] **N** **a** *(Ftbl, Rugby, fig)* Schiedsrichter(in) *m(f)*; *(Boxing)* Ringrichter(in) *m(f)*; *(Judo, Wrestling)* Kampfrichter(in) *m(f)* **b** *(Jur)* Schiedsrichter(in) *m(f)* **c** *(Brit: = person giving a reference)* Referenz *f*; **to be a ~ for sb** jdm als Referenz dienen **VT** *(Sport, fig)* Schiedsrichter(in) sein bei; *match also* (als Schieds-/Ring-/ /Kampfrichter(in)) leiten; *(Ftbl also)* pfeifen *(inf)* **VI** *(Sport, fig)* Schiedsrichter(in) sein, (den) Schiedsrichter/(die) Schiedsrichterin machen *or* spielen *(inf)*; *(Ftbl also)* pfeifen *(inf)*; **who's going to ~?** wer macht den Schiedsrichter?

refereeing [ˌrefəˈriːɪŋ] **N** *(Sport)* Schiedsrichterleistung *f*; *(Boxing)* Ringrichterleistung *f*; **~ is his vocation** er ist zum Schiedsrichter berufen

reference [ˈrefrəns] ✪ 19.2, 19.4 **N** **a** *(= act of mentioning)* Erwähnung *f* *(to sb/sth* jds/einer Sache); *(= allusion, direct)* Bemerkung *f* *(to* über *+acc)*; *(indirect)* Anspielung *f* *(to* auf *+acc)*; **to make (a) ~ to sth** etw erwähnen; **~ to any such delicate issue should be avoided** eine so delikate Sache sollte nicht erwähnt werden; **this was not said with ~ to you** diese Worte waren nicht auf dich gemünzt; **in** *or* **with ~ to** was ... anbetrifft; *(Comm)* bezüglich *(+gen)*; **~ your letter ...** *(Comm)* mit Bezug auf Ihren Brief ... *(form)*; **without ~ to age** ungeachtet des Alters; **without ~ to one's notes** ohne seine Aufzeichnungen zu Hilfe zu nehmen; **keep these details for (future) ~** bewahren Sie diese Einzelheiten als Beleg (für später) auf
b *no pl (= act of passing, of matter, problem)* Weiterleitung *f* *(to* an *+acc)*; *(of decision)* Übergabe *f* *(to* an *+acc)*
c *(= testimonial, also* **references***)* Referenz(en) *f(pl)*, Zeugnis *nt*; **to give sb a good ~** jdm gute Referenzen *or* ein gutes Zeugnis ausstellen; **a banker's ~** eine Bankauskunft *or* -referenz; **I've been asked to give him a ~** man hat mich gebeten, ihm eine Referenz zu geben
d *(= note redirecting reader, in book, on map etc)* Verweis *m*; *(Comm)* Zeichen *nt*; **~ mark** *or* **sign** *(Typ)* Verweiszeichen *nt* → **cross-reference**
e *(= connection)* **to have ~ to** in Beziehung stehen mit *or* zu; **this has no/little ~ to** das steht in keiner/in kaum einer Beziehung zu
f *(= authority, scope: of committee, tribunal)* Zuständigkeitsbereich *m* → **term**
g *(esp US)* = **referee N c**
h *(Comput)* Referenz *f*

reference: **reference book** **N** Nachschlagewerk *nt*; **reference library** **N** Präsenzbibliothek *f*; **reference number** **N** Aktenzeichen *nt*; *(of subscriber etc)* Nummer *f*

referendum [ˌrefəˈrendəm] **N** *pl* **referenda** [ˌrefəˈrendə] Volksentscheid *m*, Referendum *nt*; **to hold a ~** einen Volksentscheid durchführen, ein Referendum abhalten

referential [ˌrefəˈrenʃəl] **ADJ** sich beziehend *(to* auf *+acc)*; **~ mark** Verweiszeichen *nt*

referral [rɪˈfɜːrəl] **N** *(Med: to hospital, specialist etc)* Überweisung *f* *(to* zu); *(Jur: of case)* Verweisung *f* *(to* an *+acc)*; **~ letter, letter of ~** *(Med)* Überweisung *f*

reffing [ˈrefɪŋ] **N** = **refereeing**

refill [ˌriːˈfɪl] **VT** nachfüllen, wieder füllen **N** [ˈriːfɪl] *(for fountain pen, lighter)* Nachfüllpatrone *f*; *(for ballpoint pen)* Nachfüll- *or* Ersatzmine *f*; *(for lipstick)* Nachfüllstift *m*; *(for propelling pencil)* Ersatzmine *f*; *(for notebook)* Nachfüllblätter *pl*; **would you like a ~?** *(inf: = drink)* darf ich nachschenken?; **he wants another ~** er will noch einmal nachgeschenkt haben

refillable [ˌriːˈfɪləbl] **ADJ** nachfüllbar; **~ pack** Nachfüllpackung *f*, Nachfüllpack *m*

refill pack **N** Nachfüllpack *m*, Nachfüllpackung *f*

refinancing [riːfaɪˈnænsɪŋ] **N** Refinanzierung *f*, Neufinanzierung *f*

refine [rɪˈfaɪn] **VT** **a** *metal, oil, sugar* raffinieren **b** *language, manners, taste(s)* verfeinern, kultivieren **c** *techniques, methods* verfeinern, verbessern

▸ **refine upon** **VI** *+prep obj point, detail* näher ausführen; *method* verbessern, verfeinern

refined [rɪˈfaɪnd] **ADJ** **a** *(= processed) metal, oil* raffiniert, rein; *foods* veredelt; **~ sugar** Raffinade *f*; **~ flour** Auszugsmehl *nt*; **~ products** *(St Ex, Econ)* raffinierte/veredelte Produkte *pl*; **~ petroleum products** *(St Ex, Econ)* raffinierte Erdölprodukte *pl* **b** *(= sophisticated) taste* fein; *person, style* fein, vornehm; *model* ausgeklügelt, raffiniert

refinement [rɪˈfaɪnmənt] **N** **a** *no pl (of metal, oil, sugar)* Raffination *f*, Raffinierung *f*, Reinigung *f* **b** *no pl (of person, language, style)* Vornehmheit *f*, Feinheit *f*; **a person of evident ~** ein offensichtlich kultivierter Mensch **c** *(= improvement: in technique, machine etc)* Verfeinerung *f*, Verbesserung *f* *(in sth +gen)*

refinery [rɪˈfaɪnərɪ] **N** *(metal, oil, sugar refinery)* Raffinerie *f*

refit [ˌriːˈfɪt] **VT** *ship* neu ausrüsten; *factory* neu ausstatten **VI** *(ship)* neu ausgerüstet werden **N** [ˈriːfɪt] *(Naut)* Neuausrüstung *f*

refitting [ˌriːˈfɪtɪŋ], **refitment** [ˌriːˈfɪtmənt] **N** = **refit N**

reflate [ˌriːˈfleɪt] **VT** *(Econ)* bewusst inflationieren, ankurbeln **VI** *(economy)* sich beleben, angekurbelt werden; **they decided to ~** man beschloss, die Konjunktur anzukurbeln

reflation [riːˈfleɪʃən] **N** *(Econ)* Reflation *f*, Ankurbelung *f* der Konjunktur

reflationary [riːˈfleɪʃnərɪ] **ADJ** *(Econ)* reflationär

reflect [rɪˈflekt] **VT** **a** *(= cast back) light, image, heat, sound* zurückwerfen, reflektieren; *(surface of water, mirror)* spiegeln, reflektieren; *(fig) views, reality etc* widerspiegeln; **to be ~ed in sth** *(lit, fig)* sich in etw *(dat)* spiegeln; **I saw him/myself ~ed in the mirror** ich sah ihn/mich im Spiegel; **the many difficulties ~ed in his report/attitude** die vielen Schwierigkeiten, die sich in seinem Bericht/seiner Haltung spiegeln; **~ing prism** Spiegelprisma *nt*; **to bask in ~ed glory** sich im Glanze eines anderen sonnen; **to ~ the fact that ...** die Tatsache widerspiegeln, dass ...; **his music ~s his love for her** in seiner Musik spiegelt sich seine Liebe zu ihr wider
b *(= think)* **I ~ed that thus was the way of the world** ich dachte bei mir, dass das eben der Lauf der Welt sei; **do you ever ~ that ...?** denken Sie je darüber nach, dass ...?
VI *(= meditate)* nachdenken, reflektieren *(geh)* *(on, about* über *+acc)*

▸ **reflect (up)on** **VI** *+prep obj* etwas aussagen über *(+acc)*; *person also* ein gutes/schlechtes Licht werfen auf *(+acc)*; *motives, reasons also* in gutem/schlechtem Licht erscheinen lassen; *reputation, sb's honour* sich auswirken auf *(+acc)*; *(unfavourably)* schaden *(+dat)*, ein schlechtes Licht werfen auf *(+acc)*

reflectingly [rɪˈflektɪŋlɪ] **ADV** = **reflectively**

reflecting telescope [rɪˈflektɪŋˈtelɪskəʊp] **N** Spiegelteleskop *nt*

reflection [rɪˈflekʃən] **N** **a** *no pl (= reflecting)* Reflexion *f*; *(by surface of lake, mirror)* Spiegelung *f*; *(fig)* Widerspiegelung *f*
b *(= image)* Spiegelbild *nt*, Reflexion *f*; *(fig)* Widerspiegelung *f*; **to see one's ~ in a mirror** sich im Spiegel sehen; **a pale ~ of ...** ein matter Abglanz ... *(gen)*
c *no pl (= consideration)* Überlegung *f*; *(= contemplation)* Reflexion *f*, Betrachtung *f*; **(up)on ~** wenn ich mir das recht überlege; **on further ~** bei genauerer Überlegung
d *(= thoughts, comments)* **~s on language** Reflexionen *pl* *or* Betrachtungen *pl* über die Sprache
e *(= adverse criticism)* **a ~ on his honour** ein Schatten *m* auf seiner Ehre; **this is a ~ on your taste** das zeigt, wie wenig Geschmack du hast; **this is no ~ on your ability** damit soll gar nichts über Ihr Können gesagt sein
f *(Anat)* Zurückbiegung *f*

reflective [rɪˈflektɪv] **ADJ** **a** *faculty, powers* der Reflexion; *person* nachdenklich; *expression* nachdenklich, grübelnd; **to be in a ~ mood** in einer nachdenklichen Stimmung sein **b** *(Phys etc) surface* reflektierend, spiegelnd; *light* reflektiert; *clothing* reflektierend **c** *(Gram)* = **reflexive** **d** **to be ~ of sth** *(form, = in tune with)* sich in Übereinstimmung mit etw befinden

reflectively [rɪˈflektɪvlɪ] **ADV** *say, speak* überlegt; **he scratched his chin ~** er kratzte sich nachdenklich am Kinn

reflectiveness [rɪˈflektɪvnɪs] **N** *(of person)* Nachdenklichkeit *f*

reflectivity [rɪflekˈtɪvɪtɪ] **N** *(Phys)* Reflexionsvermögen *nt*

reflector [rɪˈflektəˈ] **N** *(on car, cycle)* Rückstrahler *m*; *(= telescope)* Reflektor *m*

reflex [ˈriːfleks] **ADJ** *(Physiol, Psych, Phys, fig)* Reflex-; *(Math) angle* überstumpf; **~ action** *(Physiol, Psych)* Reflexhandlung *f*, Reflex *m*; **~ point** *(Anat)* Reflexzone *f* **N** *(Physiol, Psych, fig)* Reflex *m*; *(Phys, = image)* Reflexion *f* → **condition VT c**

reflex camera **N** *(Phot)* Spiegelreflexkamera *f*

reflexion [rɪˈflekʃən] **N** = **reflection**

reflexive [rɪˈfleksɪv] *(Gram)* **ADJ** reflexiv **N** Reflexiv *nt*

reflexively [rɪˈfleksɪvlɪ] **ADV** *(Gram)* reflexiv

reflexology [ˌriːflekˈsɒlədʒɪ] **N** *(Med)* Reflexologie *f*; *(= practice)* Reflexzonenmassage *f*

refloat [ˌriːˈfləʊt] **VT** *ship (fig) business* wieder flottmachen

reflux [ˈriːflʌks] **N** Rückfluss *m*

reforest [riːˈfɒrɪst] **VT** *(US)* = **reafforest**

reforestation [ˌriːfɒrɪsˈteɪʃən] **N** *(US)* = **reafforestation**

re-form [ˌriːˈfɔːm] **VT** **a** *(= form again)* wieder bilden; *(Mil) ranks, troops* neu formieren **b** *(= give new form to)* umformen, umgestalten *(into* zu) **VI** sich wieder *or* erneut bilden; *(Mil)* sich neu formieren

reform [rɪˈfɔːm] **N** Reform *f*; *(of person)* Besserung *f*; **~ measures** Reformmaßnahmen *pl*; **~ school** *(Brit dated, US)* Besserungsanstalt *f* → **land reform** **VT** *law, institutions, services, spelling system* reformieren; *society also* verbessern; *conduct, person* bessern **VI** *(person)* sich bessern

reformable [rɪˈfɔːməbl] **ADJ** *person, conduct* besserungsfähig

reformat [riːˈfɔːmæt] **VT** *(Comput) disk* neu formatieren

reformation [ˌrefəˈmeɪʃən] **N** *(of person)* Reformierung, Besserung *f*; **the Reformation** die Reformation

reformative [rɪˈfɔːmətɪv] **ADJ** *effect* reformierend; **~ fervour** Reformeifer *m*

reformatory [rɪˈfɔːmətərɪ] **N** Besserungsanstalt *f*

reformed [rɪˈfɔːmd] **ADJ** reformiert; *person also* gewandelt; *alcoholic, communist* ehemalig; *behaviour* gebessert; **he's a ~ character** er hat sich gebessert

reformer [rɪˈfɔːməˈ] **N** *(Pol)* Reformer *m*; *(Rel)* Reformator *m*

reformism [rɪˈfɔːmɪzəm] **N** Reformismus *m*

reformist [rɪˈfɔːmɪst] **N** Reformist *m* **ADJ** reformistisch

refound [ˌriːˈfaʊnd] **VT** *monastery etc* wieder gründen

refract [rɪˈfrækt] **VT** brechen

refracting telescope [rɪˈfræktɪŋˈtelɪskəʊp] **N** Refraktor *m*

refraction [rɪˈfrækʃən] **N** Brechung *f*, Refraktion *f* *(spec)*; **angle of ~** Brechungswinkel *m*

refractive [rɪˈfræktɪv] **ADJ** *material, surface* brechend

refractive index **N** Brechzahl *f*, Brechungsindex *m*

refractor [rɪˈfræktəˈ] **N** **a** *(Phys)* brechendes Medium **b** *(= telescope)* Refraktor *m*

refractoriness [rɪˈfræktərɪnɪs] **N** **a** *(of person)* Eigensinn *m*, störrische Art **b** *(Med)* Hartnäckigkeit *f* **c** *(Chem, Miner)* Hitzebeständigkeit *f*

refractory [rɪˈfræktərɪ] **ADJ** **a** *person* eigensinnig, störrisch **b** *(Med)* hartnäckig **c** *(Chem, Miner)* hitzebeständig

refrain¹ [rɪˈfreɪn] **VI** **please ~!** bitte unterlassen Sie das!; **he ~ed from comment** er enthielt sich eines Kommentars; **they ~ed from such actions** sie sahen von einem solchen Vorgehen ab; **I couldn't ~ from laughing** ich konnte mir das Lachen nicht verkneifen; **kindly ~ from saying that in front of the children** würden Sie das bitte nicht vor den Kindern sagen; **please ~ from smoking** bitte nicht rauchen!

refrain² **N** *(Mus, Poet, fig)* Refrain *m*

refrangible [rɪˈfrændʒəbl] **ADJ** brechbar

refresh [rɪˈfreʃ] **VT** **a** *(drink, bath, sleep, rest)* erfrischen; *(meal)* stärken; **to ~ oneself** *(with drink)* eine Erfrischung zu sich *(dat)* nehmen; *(with a bath)* sich erfrischen; *(with food)* sich stärken; *(with sleep, rest)* sich ausruhen; **to ~ oneself with a glass of beer** zur Erfrischung ein Glas Bier trinken; **to ~ one's memory** sein Gedächtnis auffrischen; **let me ~ your memory** ich will Ihrem Gedächtnis nachhelfen **b** *(Comput: command) display* aktualisieren

refresher [rɪˈfreʃəʳ] **N** **a** *(Brit Jur)* zusätzliches Anwaltshonorar **b** *(inf: = drink)* Erfrischung *f*; **to have a ~** etwas trinken

refresher course [rɪˈfreʃəˈkɔːs] **N** *(Univ etc)* Auffrischungskurs *m*

refreshing ADJ, refreshingly ADV [rɪˈfreʃɪŋ, -lɪ] *(lit, fig)* erfrischend

refreshment [rɪˈfreʃmənt] **N** **a** *(of mind, body)* Erfrischung *f*; *(through food)* Stärkung *f* **b** *(= food, drink)* **(light) ~s** (kleine) Erfrischungen *pl*; **~ tent** Restaurationszelt *nt*; **~ room** Imbissstube *f*; *(= cafeteria)* Cafeteria *f*

refresh rate [rɪˈfreʃˌreɪt] **N** *(Comput, Tech)* *(of screen)* Bildwiederholfrequenz *f*

refried beans [ˌriːfraɪdˈbiːnz] **PL** mexikanisches Bohnengericht *(bei dem die Bohnen gekocht, gebraten, zerstampft und dann noch einmal gebraten werden)*

refrigerant [rɪˈfrɪdʒərənt] **N** Kühlmittel *nt*; *(Med)* kühlendes Mittel; *(= fluid in fridge)* Kältemittel *nt* **ADJ** kühlend

refrigerate [rɪˈfrɪdʒəreɪt] **VT** *(= chill)* kühlen; *(= freeze)* tiefkühlen; **"refrigerate after opening"** „nach dem Öffnen kühl aufbewahren"

refrigeration [rɪˌfrɪdʒəˈreɪʃən] **N** *(= chilling)* Kühlung *f*; *(= freezing)* Tiefkühlung *f*

refrigerating [rɪˈfrɪdʒəreɪtɪŋ]: **refrigerating plant** **N** *(Tech)* Kühlanlage *f*; **refrigerating room** **N** Kühlraum *m*

refrigerator [rɪˈfrɪdʒəreɪtəʳ] **N** Kühlschrank *m*, Eisschrank *m*; *(= room)* Kühlraum *m*

refuel [ˌriːˈfjʊəl] **VTI** auftanken

refuelling, *(US)* **refueling** [ˌriːˈfjʊəlɪŋ] **N** Auftanken *nt*; **~ stop** Zwischenstopp *m* zum Auftanken

refuge [ˈrefjuːdʒ] **N** **a** *(lit, fig)* Zuflucht *f* *(from* vor *(+dat))*; **place of ~** Zufluchtsort *m*; **a ~ for battered women** ein Frauenhaus *nt*; **to seek ~** Zuflucht suchen; **to seek ~ in silence** sich in Schweigen flüchten; **to take ~** Zuflucht nehmen *(in* in *(+dat))*, sich flüchten *(in* in *(+acc))*; **he took ~ in drink and drugs** er nahm Zuflucht zu Alkohol und Drogen; **she found ~ in books** Bücher waren ihre Zuflucht **b** *(for climbers, pedestrians)* Unterstand *m*

refugee [ˌrefjʊˈdʒiː] **N** Flüchtling *m*

refugee camp **N** Flüchtlingslager *nt*

refugee status **N** Flüchtlingsstatus *m*

refulgence [rɪˈfʌldʒəns] **N** *(liter)* Strahlen *nt*

refund [rɪˈfʌnd] **VT** *money* zurückzahlen, zurückerstatten; *expenses* erstatten; *postage* vergüten, zurückerstatten; **to ~ the difference** die Differenz erstatten **N** [ˈriːfʌnd] *(of money)* Rückzahlung *f*, Rückerstattung *f*; *(of expenses)* Erstattung *f*; *(of postage)* Vergütung *f*; **to get a ~ (on sth)** sein Geld (für etw) wiederbekommen; **they wouldn't give me a ~** man wollte mir das Geld nicht zurückgeben; **I'd like a ~ on this blouse, please** ich hätte gern mein Geld für diese Bluse zurück; **we will send (you) a ~** wir senden Ihnen das Geld zurück

refundable [rɪˈfʌndəbl] **ADJ** *money, payment(s)* zurückzahlbar, zurückerstattbar; **these expenses are ~** diese Ausgaben werden erstattet; **postage is ~** das Porto wird vergütet

refurbish [ˌriːˈfɜːbɪʃ] **VT** *image etc* aufarbeiten, aufpolieren; *furniture, house* renovieren

refurnish [ˌriːˈfɜːnɪʃ] **VT** neu möblieren

refusal [rɪˈfjuːzəl] **N** **a** Ablehnung *f*; *(of offer)* Ablehnung *f*, Zurückweisung *f*; *(of food, permission, visa, permit)* Verweigerung *f*; *(to do sth)* Weigerung *f*; **her ~ (of the invitation)** ihre Absage; **to meet with a ~, to get a ~** eine Absage erhalten; **to give (sb) a flat ~** jdm eine glatte Absage erteilen; **to give sb first ~ of sth** jdm etw zuerst *or* als Erstem anbieten; *(with purchase)* jdm das Vorkaufsrecht an etw *(dat)* einräumen; **to have (the) first ~ of sth** etw als Erster angeboten bekommen; **right of first ~** Vorkaufsrecht *nt* **b** *(Showjumping)* Verweigerung *f*

refuse¹ [rɪˈfjuːz] ✪ 9.3, 12.2 **VT** *candidate, proposal, offer* ablehnen; *invitation also* absagen; *(stronger)* abweisen, zurückweisen; *visa, permit, permission, payment* verweigern; **to ~ to do sth** sich weigern, etw zu tun, etw nicht tun wollen; **I ~ to believe it** ich weigere mich, das zu glauben, ich glaube das einfach nicht; **I ~ to be blackmailed** ich lasse mich nicht erpressen; **to be ~d sth** etw nicht bekommen; **he was ~d entry into Germany** ihm wurde die Einreise nach Deutschland verweigert; **he was ~d a visa** ihm wurde das Visum verweigert; **they were ~d permission (to leave)** es wurde ihnen nicht gestattet (wegzugehen); **he ~d food** er verweigerte die Nahrungsaufnahme; **he/his request was ~d** er/seine Bitte wurde abgelehnt; **she ~d him** sie wies ihn ab *or* zurück; **the horse ~d the fence** das Pferd hat am Hindernis verweigert **VI** ablehnen; *(to do sth)* sich weigern

refuse² [ˈrefjuːs] **N** Müll *m*; *(= food waste)* Abfall *m*; **household ~** Haus(halts)müll *m*; **garden ~** Gartenabfälle *pl*

refuse [ˈrefjuːs] *in cpds* Müll-; **refuse bin** **N** Mülleimer *m*; **refuse chute** **N** Müllschlucker *m*; **refuse collection** **N** Müllabfuhr *f*; **refuse collector** **N** Müllwerker(in) *m(f)*, Müllmann *m* *(inf)*; **refuse destructor** **N** Müllvernichtungsanlage *f*; **refuse disposal** **N** Müllbeseitigung *f*; **refuse disposal service** **N** Müllabfuhr *f*; **refuse disposal unit** **N** Müllzerkleinerer *m*; **refuse dump** **N** Müllabladeplatz *m*; **refuse lorry** **N** Müllwagen *m*

refusenik [rɪˈfjuːznɪk] **N** *(inf)* Verweigerer(in) *m(f)*

refuse pit **N** Müllgrube *f*

refuse skip **N** *(Brit)* Müllcontainer *m*

refutable [rɪˈfjuːtəbl] **ADJ** widerlegbar

refutation [ˌrefjʊˈteɪʃən] **N** Widerlegung *f*

refute [rɪˈfjuːt] **VT** widerlegen

-reg [redʒ] **N** *(Brit inf) abbr of* **-registration**; **Y-reg car** Auto *nt* mit dem Zulassungsbuchstaben Y *(wobei der Buchstabe das Jahr der Erstanmeldung angibt)*

reg. [redʒ] **N** *(Brit inf) abbr of* **registration number** amtliches Kennzeichen **ADJ** *abbr of* **registered**; **~ no.** amtl. Kennzeichen

regain [rɪˈgeɪn] **VT** **a** *(= gain back)* wiedererlangen; *lost time* aufholen; *control, confidence, title* wiedergewinnen; *territory* zurückbekommen; **to ~ consciousness** das Bewusstsein wiedererlangen, wieder zu Bewusstsein kommen; **to ~ one's strength** wieder zu Kräften kommen; **to ~ one's health/fitness** wieder gesund/fit werden; **to ~ one's footing** seinen Halt wiederfinden; *(fig)* wieder auf die Beine kommen; **to ~ one's balance** das Gleichgewicht wiederfinden; **to ~ possession of sth** wieder in den Besitz einer Sache *(gen)* gelangen; **to ~ the lead** *(in sport)* wieder in Führung gehen; *(in research etc)* wieder an die Spitze gelangen; **to ~ weight** wieder zunehmen

b *(= reach again) main road/firm ground* wieder gelangen an *(+acc)*/auf *(+acc)*

regal [ˈriːgəl] **ADJ** königlich; *(fig)* hoheitsvoll

regale [rɪˈgeɪl] **VT** *(with food, drink)* verwöhnen; *(with stories)* ergötzen *(geh)*

regalia [rɪˈgeɪlɪə] **PL** Insignien *pl*; **she was in full ~** *(hum)* sie war in großer Gala *or* Aufmachung *(hum)*

regally [ˈriːgəlɪ] **ADV** königlich; *say* hoheitsvoll

regard [rɪˈgɑːd] ✪ 20.5, 21.2 **VT** **a** *(= consider)* betrachten; **to ~ sb/sth as sth** jdn/etw für etw halten, jdn/etw als etw betrachten; **to ~ sb/sth with favour** *(Brit)* *or* **favor** *(US)* jdn/etw wohlwollend betrachten; **to ~ sth with horror** mit Schrecken an etw *(acc)* denken; **to be ~ed as ...** als ... angesehen werden; **he is ~ed as a great poet** er wird als großer Dichter angesehen, er gilt als großer Dichter; **it's not generally ~ed as worth doing** es wird im Allgemeinen angenommen, dass sich das nicht lohnt; **we ~ it as worth doing** wir glauben, dass es sich lohnt(, das zu tun); **we don't ~ it as necessary** wir halten es nicht für notwendig; **she doesn't ~ it as her responsibility** sie betrachtet es nicht als ihre Verantwortung; **to ~ sb/sth highly** *or* **with great esteem** jdn/etw hoch schätzen *or* sehr schätzen; **he is highly ~ed** er ist hoch angesehen; **his work is highly ~ed** seine Arbeit wird sehr geschätzt

b *(= concern)* **as ~s that/my friend/your application** was das/meinen Freund/Ihren Antrag betrifft *or* anbelangt *or* angeht → *also* **regarding**

c *(liter: = look at)* betrachten

d *(= heed)* berücksichtigen; **without ~ing his wishes** ohne Rücksicht auf seine Wünsche

N **a** *(= attention, concern)* Rücksicht *f* *(for* auf *+acc)*; **to have some ~ for sb/sth** auf jdn/etw Rücksicht nehmen; **to show little/no ~ for sb/sth** wenig/keine Rücksichtnahme für jdn/etw zeigen; **with no ~ for his safety** ohne Rücksicht auf seine Sicherheit (zu nehmen); **without ~ to** *or* **for her views** ohne sich um ihre Ansichten zu kümmern; **without ~ to** *or* **for what people might think** ohne sich darum zu kümmern, was die Leute denken mochten

b **in this ~** diesbezüglich *(form)*, in diesem Zusammenhang; **with** *or* **in ~ to** in Bezug auf *(+acc)*

c *(= respect)* Achtung *f*; **to hold sb in high ~** jdn achten *or* sehr schätzen; **to have a great ~ for sb** jdn hoch achten

d **regards** **PL** *(in message)* Gruß *m*; **to send sb one's ~s** jdn grüßen lassen; **give him my ~s** grüßen Sie ihn von mir; **(kindest) ~s, with kind ~s** mit freundlichen Grüßen

e *(liter, = look)* Blick *m*

regardful [rɪˈgɑːdfʊl] **ADJ** *(form)* **~ of (one's) duty** sich *(dat)* seiner Pflicht *(gen)* bewusst, pflichtbewusst; **to be ~ of sb's feelings** jds Gefühle achten *or* respektieren

regarding [rɪˈgɑːdɪŋ] **PREP** in Bezug auf *(+acc)*, bezüglich *(+gen)*

regardless [rɪˈgɑːdlɪs] **ADJ** **~ of** ohne Rücksicht auf *(+acc)*, ungeachtet *(+gen)*; **to do sth ~ of the consequences** etw ohne Rücksicht auf die Folgen tun; **~ of what it costs** egal, was es kostet; **~ of the fact that ...** ungeachtet dessen, dass ... **ADV** trotzdem; **he did it ~** er hat es trotzdem getan

regatta [rɪˈgætə] **N** Regatta *f*

regd *abbr of* **registered** reg.

regency [ˈriːdʒənsɪ] **N** Regentschaft *f*; **the Regency (period)** *(Brit Art etc)* der Regency; **Regency furniture/style** *(Brit Art etc)* Regencymöbel *pl*/-stil *m*

regenerate [rɪˈdʒenəreɪt] **VT** **a** *(= renew, re-create)* erneuern; **to be ~d** sich erneuern, sich neu bilden, sich regenerieren; *(fig: person: by holiday etc)* sich erholen; *(esp Rel)* erneuert werden **b** *(Elec)* rückkoppeln **VI** *(esp Sci)* sich regenerieren **ADJ** [rɪˈdʒenərɪt] regeneriert

regeneration [rɪˌdʒenəˈreɪʃən] N **a** *(= renewal, re-creation)* Erneuerung *f*; *(fig: of person: by holiday etc)* Erholung *f* **b** *(Elec)* Rückkoppelung *f*

regenerative [rɪˈdʒenərətɪv] ADJ **a** *tissue* sich regenerierend; *(esp Rel)* erneuernd; *power, process* regenerativ **b** *(Elec)* positiv rückgekoppelt

regent [ˈriːdʒənt] N Regent(in) *m(f)*; *(US, Univ)* Mitglied *nt* des Universitäts- *or* Schulverwaltungsrats → **prince regent**

reggae [ˈregeɪ] N Reggae *m*

regicide [ˈredʒɪsaɪd] N *(= act)* Königsmord *m*; *(= person)* Königsmörder(in) *m(f)*

regime [reɪˈʒiːm] N **a** *(Pol)* Regime *nt*; **~ change** Führungswechsel *m* **b** *(fig: = management, social system etc)* System *nt* **c** = **regimen**

regimen [ˈredʒɪmen] N *(Med)* Kur *f*

regiment [ˈredʒɪmənt] N *(Mil)* Regiment *nt*; *(fig)* Kompanie *f* [ˈredʒɪment] VT *(fig)* reglementieren

regimental [ˌredʒɪˈmentl] ADJ *(Mil)* Regiments-; **~ commander** Regimentskommandeur *m* N **regimentals** PL *(Mil)* Uniform *f*; *(of a particular regiment)* Regimentsuniform *f*

regimentation [ˌredʒɪmenˈteɪʃən] N *(fig)* Reglementierung *f*

region [ˈriːdʒən] N *(of country)* Gebiet *nt*, Region *f (also TV)*; *(Admin)* Bezirk *m*; *(of body)* Gegend *f*, Region *f*; *(of atmosphere, fig)* Bereich *m*; **the lower ~s** die Unterwelt; *(of charts, football league)* die untere Hälfte; **in the ~ of 5 kg** um die 5 kg

regional [ˈriːdʒənl] ADJ regional; **~ development** Gebietserschließung *f*; **~ television** Regionalfernsehen *nt*

regional council N *(Scot, dated)* ≈ Gemeinderat *m*

regionalism [ˈriːdʒənəlɪzəm] N Regionalismus *m*; *(= division into regions)* Einteilung *f* in Regionen; *(= loyalty)* Lokalpatriotismus *m*; *(= word)* nur regional verwendeter Ausdruck

regionalist [ˈriːdʒənəlɪst] ADJ regionalistisch N Regionalist(in) *m(f)*

regionalize [ˈriːdʒənəlaɪz] VT regionalisieren

register [ˈredʒɪstəˈ] N **a** *(= book)* Register *nt*; *(at school)* Namensliste *f*; *(in hotel)* Gästebuch *nt*; *(of members etc)* Mitgliedsbuch *nt*; **to take the ~** die Namen aufrufen; **~ of births, deaths and marriages** Personenstandsbuch *nt*; **~ of wills** *(US, person)* Testamentsbeamte(r) *m*
b *(Tech, = recording device)* Registriergerät *nt*; *(for controlling airflow)* Klappe *f* → **cash register**
c *(Mus)* Register *nt*; *(= organ stop)* Registerzug *m*
d *(Ling)* (Sprach)ebene *f*, Register *nt (geh)*
e *(Typ)* Register *nt*
VT **a** *(authorities: = record formally)* registrieren; *(in book, files)* eintragen; *fact, figure* erfassen; **he is ~ed (as) disabled/blind** er hat einen Schwerbehinderten-/Sehbehindertenausweis → **registered a**
b *(individual: = have recorded) birth, marriage, death, (Comm) company, trademark* anmelden, eintragen lassen; *vehicle, child at school etc, candidate* anmelden; *student* einschreiben; **to ~ interest** sein Interesse anmelden; **to ~ a protest** Protest anmelden
c *(= indicate) (machine) speed, quantity, rainfall, temperature* registrieren; *(face, expression) happiness, disapproval* zum Ausdruck bringen; **his face ~ed surprise** die Überraschung zeigte sich in seinem Gesichtsausdruck; **he ~ed no emotion** er zeigte keine Gefühlsbewegung
d *(Post) letter* einschreiben → **registered b**
e *(Typ)* in Register bringen
f *(= realize)* registrieren; **I ~ed the fact that he had gone** ich registrierte, dass er gegangen war
VI **a** *(on electoral list etc)* sich eintragen; *(in hotel)* sich anmelden; *(student)* sich einschreiben, sich immatrikulieren; **to ~ with a doctor/dentist** sich bei einem Arzt/Zahnarzt auf die Patientenliste setzen lassen; **to ~ with the police** sich polizeilich melden; **to ~ for a course** sich für einen Kurs anmelden; *(Univ)* einen Kurs belegen
b *(inf: = be understood)* **it hasn't ~ed (with him)** er hat es noch nicht registriert

registered [ˈredʒɪstəd] ADJ **a** *student* eingeschrieben; *voter, company, name* eingetragen; *vehicle* amtlich zugelassen; **~ capital** Grundkapital *nt*, Nominalkapital *nt*; **a Y-~ car** *(Brit)* ein Auto *nt* mit dem Zulassungsbuchstaben Y; **an American-~ ship** ein in Amerika registriertes Schiff; **~ design** Geschmacksmuster *nt* **b** *(Post)* eingeschrieben, Einschreib-; **~ letter** eingeschriebener Brief, Einschreibbrief *m*; **by ~ post** per Einschreiben

registered: **registered charity** N eingetragene wohltätige Organisation; **Registered General Nurse** *(Brit)*, **registered nurse** *(US)* N staatlich geprüfte Krankenschwester, staatlich geprüfter Pfleger; **registered office** N eingetragener (Gesellschafts)sitz; **registered shareholder** N Inhaber(in) *m(f)* von Namensaktien; **Registered Trademark** N eingetragenes Warenzeichen

register office N *(Brit)* = **registry (office)**

register ton N *(Naut)* Registertonne *f*

registrar [ˌredʒɪˈstrɑːˈ] N *(Brit) (Admin)* Standesbeamte(r) *m*/-beamtin *f*; *(Univ)* höchster Verwaltungsbeamter, höchste Verwaltungsbeamtin, ≈ Kanzler(in) *m(f)*; *(Med)* Krankenhausarzt *m*/-ärztin *f*; **to be married by the ~** sich standesamtlich trauen lassen

registrar's office *(Brit Admin)* Standesamt *nt*

registration [ˌredʒɪˈstreɪʃən] N **a** *(by authorities, = formal recording)* Registrierung *f*; *(in books, files)* Eintragung *f*; *(of fact, figure)* Erfassung *f* **b** *(by individual, Comm)* Anmeldung *f*; *(of student)* Einschreibung *f*; **~ fee** Anmeldegebühr *f*; *(for evening class)* Kursgebühr *f*; *(Univ)* Einschreib(e)gebühr *f* **c** *(= indication, by machines)* Registrierung *f*; *(by face, expression)* Ausdruck *m* **d** *(Post, of letter)* Aufgabe *f* als Einschreiben; **~ fee** Einschreibegebühr *f*

registration: **registration document** N *(Brit Aut etc)* Kraftfahrzeugbrief *m*; **registration number** N *(Brit Aut etc)* Kraftfahrzeugkennzeichen *nt*, polizeiliches Kennzeichen; **registration office** N *(Brit)* = **registry (office)**; **registration plate** N *(Aut)* Nummernschild *nt*

registry [ˈredʒɪstrɪ] N **a** Sekretariat *nt*; *(in church)* Sakristei *f*; *(Brit: = registry office)* Standesamt *nt*; **port of ~** Heimathafen *m* **b** *(Comput) (of system files)* Registry*nt*, Registrierung *f*

registry office N *(Brit)* Standesamt *nt*; **to get married in a ~** standesamtlich heiraten

Regius [ˈriːdʒəs] ADJ *(Brit Univ)* **~ professor** *Inhaber eines von einem Monarchen eingerichteten Lehrstuhls*

regorge [rɪˈgɔːdʒ] VT *(form)* erbrechen VI sich ergießen

regress [rɪˈgres] VI *(lit form: = move backwards)* sich rückwärts bewegen; *(fig: society)* sich rückläufig entwickeln; *(Biol, Psych, Med)* sich zurückentwickeln; **he is ~ing into childhood** er fällt wieder ins Kindesalter zurück

regression [rɪˈgreʃən] N *(lit form: = backward movement)* Rückwärtsbewegung *f*; *(fig: of society)* rückläufige Entwicklung; *(Biol, Psych, Med)* Zurückentwicklung *f*; **his ~ into childhood** sein Rückfall *m* in die Kindheit

regressive [rɪˈgresɪv] ADJ regressiv; *trend* rückläufig; *behaviour, decision* rückschrittlich

regret [rɪˈgret] ✪ 12.3, 18.1, 18.2, 20.6 VT bedauern; *one's youth, lost opportunity* nachtrauern *(+dat)*; **I ~ that we will not be coming** ich bedauere, dass wir nicht kommen können; **to ~ the fact that …** (die Tatsache) bedauern, dass …; **I ~ to say that …** ich muss Ihnen leider mitteilen, dass …; **he is very ill, I ~ to say** er ist leider or bedauerlicherweise sehr krank; **we ~ to learn that …** wir hören mit Bedauern, dass …; **we ~ any inconvenience caused** für eventuelle Unannehmlichkeiten bitten wir um Verständnis; **it is to be ~ted that …** es ist bedauerlich, dass …; **you won't ~ it!** Sie werden es nicht bereuen; **this matter is much ~ted** dieser Vorfall hat großes Bedauern ausgelöst
N Bedauern *nt no pl*; **to feel ~ for one's past youth** seiner vergangenen Jugend *(dat)* nachtrauern; **much to my ~** sehr zu meinem Bedauern; **I have no ~s** ich bereue nichts; **please give her my ~s that I cannot come** bitte, sagen Sie ihr, dass ich leider nicht kommen kann; **he sends his ~s** er lässt sich entschuldigen, er muss leider absagen

regretful [rɪˈgretfʊl] ADJ *look, attitude* bedauernd *attr*; **he was extremely ~ (about it)** es tat ihm sehr leid, er bedauerte es sehr; **it is ~ that …** es ist bedauerlich, dass …

regretfully [rɪˈgretfəlɪ] ADV **a** *(= with regret)* mit Bedauern; **very ~ I must announce …** sehr zu meinem Bedauern muss ich bekannt geben, … **b** *(= unfortunately, regrettably)* bedauerlicherweise, leider; **~, nationalism is flourishing in modern Europe** bedauerlicherweise *or* leider gedeiht heute in Europa der Nationalismus

regrettable [rɪˈgretəbl] ✪ 14 ADJ bedauerlich

regrettably [rɪˈgretəblɪ] ADV **a** *(= unfortunately)* bedauerlicherweise, leider **b** *(= very)* bedauerlich; **~ few people came** bedauerlich wenige Leute kamen, leider kamen nur wenige Leute

regroup [ˌriːˈgruːp] VT umgruppieren, neu gruppieren VI sich umgruppieren, sich neu gruppieren

regrouping [ˌriːˈgruːpɪŋ] N Um- *or* Neugruppierung *f*

regt *abbr of* **regiment** Reg.

regular [ˈregjʊləˈ] ADJ **a** *(= at even intervals) service, bus, pulse, reminders* regelmäßig; *footsteps, rhythm* gleichmäßig; *employment* fest, regulär; *way of life, bowel movements* geregelt; **~ flights** regelmäßige Flugverbindungen *pl*; **at ~ intervals** in regelmäßigen Abständen; **on a ~ basis** regelmäßig; **to be in ~ use** regelmäßig benutzt werden; **to be in** *or* **to have ~ contact with sb/sth** mit jdm/etw regelmäßig in Verbindung stehen *or* Kontakt haben; **to be ~ in one's habits** ein geregeltes Leben führen; **to eat ~ meals** regelmäßig essen; **to keep ~ hours** feste Zeiten haben; **his visits are as ~ as clockwork** nach seinen Besuchen kann man die Uhr stellen; **he has a ~ place in the team** er ist ein ordentliches Mannschaftsmitglied; **wanton violence is becoming a ~ feature of urban life** vorsätzliche Gewalt wird immer mehr zum Bestandteil städtischen Lebens; **eating fresh vegetables helps keep you ~** *(Med inf)* frisches Gemüse trägt zu einem regelmäßigen Stuhlgang bei; **I'm quite ~** *(in menstruation)* ich habe eine ziemlich regelmäßige Periode
b *(= habitual) size, price, time* normal; *(Comput) font* Standard-;; *listener, reader* regelmäßig; **our ~ cleaning woman** unsere normale Reinemachefrau; **~ customer** Stammkunde *m*/-kundin *f*; **his ~ pub** *(Brit)* seine Stammkneipe *(inf)*; **to have a ~ partner** einen festen Partner haben; *(in relationship also)* in einer festen Beziehung leben; **it's past his ~ bedtime** es ist nach seiner normalen Schlafenszeit; **would you like ~ or large?** *(esp US)* möchten Sie normal oder extra *or (food also)* eine extragroße Portion?; **~ fries** *(esp US)* eine normale Portion Pommes frites
c *(= symmetrical, Gram)* regelmäßig; *surface* gleichmäßig; *(Geometry)* gleichseitig
d *(= permissible, accepted) action, procedure* richtig; **~ procedure demands that …** der Ordnung halber muss man …; **it is quite ~ to apply in person** es ist ganz in Ordnung, sich persönlich zu bewerben
e *(Mil)* Berufs-, regulär; *(Police) forces, officer* regulär
f *(Rel)* **~ clergy** Ordensgeistlichkeit *f*
g *(esp US: = ordinary)* gewöhnlich; **he's just a ~ guy** er ist ein ganz normaler Typ *(inf)*
h *(inf: = real)* echt *(inf)*; **he's a ~ idiot** er ist ein regelrechter Idiot
N **a** *(Mil)* Berufssoldat(in) *m(f)*, regulärer Soldat, reguläre Soldatin; *(= habitual customer etc)* Stammkunde *m*, Stammkundin *f*; *(in pub, hotel)* Stammgast *m*; **he's one of the ~s on that programme** er ist einer der Stammgäste dieser

Sendung
b *(US, = gasoline)* Normalbenzin *nt*

regular army N Berufsarmee *f*, reguläre Armee

regular gas(oline) N *(US)* Normalbenzin *nt*

regularity [ˌregjʊˈlærɪtɪ] N **a** *(= occurrence at even intervals)* Regelmäßigkeit *f*; *(of rhythm)* Gleichmäßigkeit *f*; *(of employment)* Festheit *f*; *(of way of life, bowel movements)* Geregeltheit *f* **b** *(= symmetry, Gram)* Regelmäßigkeit *f*; *(of surface)* Gleichmäßigkeit *f*; *(Geometry)* Gleichseitigkeit *f* **c** *(= permissibility: of action, procedure)* Richtigkeit *f*

regularize [ˈregjʊləraɪz] VT *breathing, service* regulieren; *situation, relationship* normalisieren; *menstrual period* regeln

regularly [ˈregjʊləlɪ] ADV **a** *(= frequently)* regelmäßig **b** *(= evenly, steadily) breathe, beat* regelmäßig, gleichmäßig **c** *(= at evenly spaced intervals)* in gleichmäßigen Abständen; **huge beeches, planted ~ along the avenue** riesige Buchen, die in gleichmäßigen Abständen die Allee säumen

regulate [ˈregjʊleɪt] VT *(= control)* regulieren; *flow, expenditure also, traffic, lifestyle* regeln; **to ~ the use of sth** den Gebrauch von etw begrenzen

regulation [ˌregjʊˈleɪʃən] **N a** *(= regulating)* Regulierung *f*; *(of flow, expenditure also, traffic, lifestyle)* Regelung *f* **b** *(= rule)* Vorschrift *f*; *(of government etc)* Verordnung *f*, Vorschrift *f*; **the ~s of the society** die Satzung der Gesellschaft; **according to (the) ~s** laut Vorschrift/Satzung; **to be contrary to** *or* **against (the) ~s** gegen die Vorschrift(en)/Satzung verstoßen **c** *(US Sport)* reguläre Spielzeit **ATTR** *boots, dress* vorgeschriebene; **army ~ boots** vorgeschriebene Armeestiefel *pl*

regulative [ˈregjʊlətɪv] ADJ regulativ, regulierend

regulator [ˈregjʊleɪtəˈ] N *(= instrument)* Regler *m*; *(in clock, watch)* Gangregler *m*; *(for manual adjustment)* Rücker *m*

regulatory [regjʊˈleɪtərɪ] ADJ Regulierungs-; **~ authority/body** Regulierungsbehörde *f*/-organ *nt*; **~ control** behördliche Kontrolle; **~ approval** Genehmigung *f* durch die Regulierungsbehörde

Regulo® [ˈregjʊləʊ] N **at ~ 4** auf Gasstufe 4

regurgitate [rɪˈgɜːdʒɪteɪt] VT wieder hochbringen, wieder von sich geben; *(fig) information, facts* wiederkäuen; **the young feed on ~d insects** die Jungen leben von vorverdauten Insekten

regurgitation [rɪˌgɜːdʒɪˈteɪʃən] N Wiederhochbringen *nt*; *(fig: of information, facts)* Wiederkäuen *nt*

rehab [ˈriːˌhæb] *abbr of* **rehabilitation**

rehabilitate [ˌriːəˈbɪlɪteɪt] VT **a** *refugee, troops, the disabled* (in die Gesellschaft) eingliedern; *ex-criminal also* rehabilitieren; *drug addict, alcoholic* therapieren **b** *(= restore position to)* rehabilitieren; *reputation* wiederherstellen

rehabilitation [ˈriːəˌbɪlɪˈteɪʃən] N **a** *(of refugee, troops, the disabled)* Eingliederung *f* in die Gesellschaft; *(of ex-criminal)* Rehabilitation *f*; *(of drug addict, alcoholic)* Therapie *f* **b** *(= restoration of position)* Rehabilitation *f*; *(of reputation)* Wiederherstellung *f*

rehabilitation centre, *(US)* **rehabilitation center** N *(Admin)* Rehabilitationszentrum *nt*

rehash [ˌriːˈhæʃ] **VT** *literary material etc* aufbereiten **N** [ˈriːhæʃ] *(= action)* Aufbereitung *f*; *(= result)* Aufguss *m*

rehear [ˌriːˈhɪəˈ] VT **a** *(= hear again)* erneut anhören **b** *(Jur)* neu verhandeln, sich erneut befassen mit

rehearsal [rɪˈhɜːsəl] N **a** *(Theat, Mus)* Probe *f*; **the play is in ~** das Stück wird geprobt **b** *(= recital: of facts)* Aufzählung *f*

rehearse [rɪˈhɜːs] **VT a** *(Theat, Mus) play, concert* proben; *person* proben lassen; *argument* (wieder) anführen; **to ~ what one is going to say** einüben, was man sagen will **b** *(= recite)* aufzählen **VI** proben

reheat [ˌriːˈhiːt] VT aufwärmen

rehouse [ˌriːˈhaʊz] VT unterbringen

reify [ˈreɪɪfaɪ] VT verdinglichen, reifizieren *(Philos)*

reign [reɪn] **N** *(lit, fig)* Herrschaft *f*; *(of monarch also)* Regentschaft *f*; **in the ~ of ...** während der Herrschaft ... *(+gen)*; **Queen Victoria had a long ~** Königin Viktoria übte eine lange Herrschaft aus; **the Reign of Terror** die Schreckensherrschaft **VI** *(lit, fig)* herrschen *(over* über *+acc)*; **silence ~s** es herrscht Ruhe → **supreme**

reigning [ˈreɪnɪŋ] ADJ *attr* regierend; *champion* amtierend; **the ~ beauty** die Schönheitskönigin

reiki [ˈreɪkɪ] N Reiki *nt*

reimburse [ˌriːɪmˈbɜːs] VT *person* entschädigen; *loss* ersetzen; *expenses, costs* (zurück)erstatten, ersetzen; **to ~ sb for his expenses** jdm die Auslagen zurückerstatten

reimbursement [ˌriːɪmˈbɜːsmənt] N *(of person)* Entschädigung *f*; *(of loss)* Ersatz *m*; *(of expenses, costs)* (Rück)erstattung *f*

reimport [ˌriːɪmˈpɔːt] VT wieder einführen, reimportieren

reimportation [ˌriːɪmpɔːˈteɪʃən] N Wiedereinfuhr *f*

reimpose [ˌriːɪmˈpəʊz] VT *task, conditions* neu aufzwingen *or* auferlegen *(form)* *(on sb* jdm); *sanctions, fine* erneut verhängen *(on* gegen); *one's will, authority* erneut aufzwingen *(on sb* jdm); **to ~ a tax on sth** etw erneut besteuern

rein [reɪn] N *(lit, fig)* Zügel *m*; **~s** *(for child)* Laufgurt *m*; **to hold the ~s** *(lit, fig)* die Zügel *or* das Heft in der Hand haben; **he kept the horse on a long/short ~** er ließ die Zügel lang/hielt die Zügel kurz; **to keep a tight ~ on sb/sth** *(lit, fig)* bei jdm/etw die Zügel kurzhalten; **to give free ~ to sb/sth, to allow** *or* **give sb/sth free ~** *(fig)* jdm/einer Sache freien Lauf lassen; **to give sb free ~ to do sth** jdm freie Hand lassen, etw zu tun

▶ **rein back** **VT** *sep* zügeln **VI** zügeln

▶ **rein in** **VT** *sep horse* zügeln; *(fig) passions also* im Zaum halten; *spending, inflation* in Schranken halten; **to rein the horse in to a trot/canter** das Pferd im Trab/leichten Galopp gehen lassen; **to rein sb/oneself in** jdn/sich zügeln *or* bremsen **VI** zügeln

reincarnate [ˌriːɪnˈkɑːneɪt] **VT** reinkarnieren *(liter)*; **to be ~d** wiedergeboren werden; **the belief that man is ~d (after death)** der Glaube an die Reinkarnation des Menschen *or* an die Wiedergeburt **ADJ** [ˌriːɪnˈkɑːnɪt] wiedergeboren

reincarnation [ˌriːɪnkɑːˈneɪʃən] N die Wiedergeburt, die Reinkarnation

reindeer [ˈreɪndɪəˈ] N *pl* - Ren(tier) *nt*; **Rudolph the red-nosed ~** Rudolf Rotnase *m*

reinforce [ˌriːɪnˈfɔːs] VT *(lit, fig, Psych, Mil)* verstärken; *concrete also* armieren *(spec)*; *sb's demands, belief* stärken, stützen; *evidence, statement* stützen, bestätigen; *opinion* bestätigen; **to ~ sb's decision/determination** jdn in seiner Entscheidung/Absicht bestärken; **to ~ the message** der Botschaft *(dat)* mehr Nachdruck verleihen

reinforced concrete [ˌriːɪnfɔːstˈkɒŋkriːt] N Stahlbeton *m*

reinforcement [ˌriːɪnˈfɔːsmənt] N **a** *no pl (= act) (lit, fig, Psych, Mil)* Verstärkung *f*; *(of concrete also)* Armierung *f*; *(of sb's demands, beliefs)* Stärkung *f*, Stützung *f*; *(of evidence, statement)* Stützung *f*, Bestätigung *f*; *(of opinion)* Bestätigung *f*; **~ troops** *(Mil)* Verstärkungstruppen *pl* **b** *(= thing)* Verstärkung *f*; **~s** *(Mil, fig)* Verstärkung *f*

reinsert [ˌriːɪnˈsɜːt] VT wieder einfügen; *thermometer* wieder einführen; *coin* wieder einwerfen; *filing card* zurückstecken; *needle* wieder einstecken; *zip* wieder einsetzen

reinstate [ˌriːɪnˈsteɪt] VT *person* wieder einstellen *(in* in *(+acc))*; *law and order* wiederherstellen *(in* in *(+dat))*; *death penalty* wieder einführen

reinstatement [ˌriːɪnˈsteɪtmənt] N *(of person)* Wiedereinstellung *f*; *(of law and order)* Wiederherstellung *f*; *(of death penalty)* Wiedereinführung *f*

reinsurance [ˌriːɪnˈʃʊərəns] N Rückversicherung *f*

reinsure [ˌriːɪnˈʃʊəˈ] VT rückversichern; **to ~ one's car** *(with same company)* seine Autoversicherung verlängern

reintegrate [ˌriːˈɪntɪgreɪt] VT wieder eingliedern, wieder *or* erneut integrieren *(into* in *+acc)*

reintegration [ˈriːˌɪntɪˈgreɪʃən] N Wiedereingliederung *f*, Reintegration *f*

reintroduce [ˌriːɪntrəˈdjuːs] VT *measure, death penalty* wieder einführen; *(Parl) bill* erneut vorlegen; *(Zool) species* wieder heimisch machen

reinvent [ˌriːɪnˈvent] VT **to ~ the wheel** das Rad neu erfinden; **to ~ oneself** sich *(dat)* ein neues Image geben

reinvest [ˌriːɪnˈvest] VT reinvestieren

reissue [ˌriːˈɪʃjuː] **VT** *book* neu auflegen; *stamps, recording, coins* neu herausgeben **N** *(of book)* Neuauflage *f*; *(of stamps, recording, coins)* Neuausgabe *f*

reiterate [riːˈɪtəreɪt] VT wiederholen

reiteration [riːˌɪtəˈreɪʃən] N Wiederholung *f*

reiterative [riːˈɪtərətɪv] ADJ *comments* sich wiederholend *attr*; *style* repetitiv

reject [rɪˈdʒekt] **VT a** *damaged goods etc (customer)* ablehnen, zurückweisen; *(maker, producer)* aussortieren, ausscheiden
b *(= turn down) application, request etc* ablehnen; *(stronger)* abweisen, zurückweisen; *candidate (through vote)* durchfallen lassen; *suitor, advances* abweisen, zurückweisen; *offer* ablehnen, ausschlagen; *criticism* zurückweisen; *plea* zurückweisen, abschlagen; *idea, possibility* verwerfen
c *(Med) drug* nicht vertragen, ablehnen; *transplant* abstoßen; *(stomach) food* verweigern
N [ˈriːdʒekt] *(Comm)* Ausschuss *m no pl*; **~ goods** Ausschussware *f*; **although this jacket's a ~ ...** obwohl dieses Jackett zweite Wahl ist, ...; **society's ~s** die Ausgestoßenen *pl*

rejection [rɪˈdʒekʃən] N **a** *(of damaged goods etc, by customer)* Ablehnung *f*, Zurückweisung *f*; *(by maker, producer)* Aussortierung *f*, Ausscheidung *f* **b** *(= turning down, of application, request, offer etc)* Ablehnung *f*; *(stronger)* Abweisung *f*, Zurückweisung *f*; *(of suitor, advances)* Abweisung *f*, Zurückweisung *f*; *(of criticism, plea)* Zurückweisung *f*; *(of idea, possibility)* Verwerfen *nt* **c** *(Med) (of drug)* Ablehnung *f*; *(of transplant)* Abstoßung *f*; *(of food by stomach)* Verweigerung *f*

rejection slip N Absage *f*

reject shop [ˈriːdʒekt-] N *Geschäft für Ausschussware*, Ramschladen *m (inf)*

rejig [riːˈdʒɪg] VT *(Brit: = redo)* neu machen; *system, structures* umkrempeln; *rules, wording* ummodeln *(inf)*

rejoice [rɪˈdʒɔɪs] **VT** *(liter) person* erfreuen **VI** sich freuen; *(= be jubilant)* jubeln; *(Rel)* jauchzen; **they ~d to see peace return to the country** sie jubilierten, dass wieder Frieden ins Land einkehrte; **~ in the Lord!** freut euch im Herrn!; **he ~s in the name of Marmaduke** *(hum)* er erfreut sich des Namens Marmaduke

rejoicing [rɪˈdʒɔɪsɪŋ] N Jubel *m*; **~s** Jubel *m*

rejoin[1] [ˌriːˈdʒɔɪn] VT *person, regiment* sich wieder anschließen *(+dat)*; *party, club* wieder eintreten in *(+acc)*; **to ~ ship** *(Naut)* wieder aufs Schiff kommen; **then we ~ed the motorway** danach fuhren wir wieder auf die Autobahn

rejoin[2] [rɪˈdʒɔɪn] VT *(= reply)* erwidern

rejoinder [rɪˈdʒɔɪndəˈ] N Erwiderung *f*; *(Jur)* Duplik *f*

rejuvenate [rɪˈdʒuːvɪneɪt] VT verjüngen; *(fig)* erfrischen

rekindle [ˌriːˈkɪndl] **VT** *(lit) fire, flame* wieder anzünden; *(fig) passions, love* wieder entzünden *or* entflammen; *tensions, enmities* wieder aufflammen lassen; *hope, interest* wiedererwecken; *debate* wieder entfachen; *affair* wieder aufleben lassen VI *(lit)* wieder aufflackern; *(fig, passion, love also)* wieder entflammen; *(tensions, enmities)* wieder aufflammen; *(hope, interest)* wieder erwachen

relapse [rɪ'læps] N *(Med)* Rückfall *m*, Rückschlag *m*; *(fig, in economy)* Rückschlag *m*; *(into vice, crime)* Rückfall *m* (*into* in *+acc*); **to have a ~** einen Rückfall haben VI *(Med)* einen Rückschlag erleiden; *(economy)* einen Rückschlag erleiden; **to ~ (into crime/vice)** rückfällig werden

Relate [rɪ'leɪt] N *(Brit)* ≈ Eheberatungsstelle *f*

relate [rɪ'leɪt] VT a (= *recount*) *story* erzählen; *details* aufzählen; **strange to ~** so unglaublich es klingt b (= *associate*) in Verbindung *or* Beziehung *or* Zusammenhang bringen (*to, with* mit); **to try to ~ events (to each other)** versuchen, die Dinge im Zusammenhang zu sehen; **it is often difficult to ~ cause and effect** der Zusammenhang zwischen Ursache und Wirkung ist oft schwer zu erkennen VI a (= *refer*) zusammenhängen (*to* mit) b (= *form relationship*) eine Beziehung finden (*to* zu)

related [rɪ'leɪtɪd] ADJ a (*in family*) verwandt (*to* mit); **~ by** *or* **through marriage** angeheiratet, verschwägert; **he is ~ to the president by** *or* **through marriage** er ist durch Heirat mit dem Präsidenten verwandt b (= *connected*) zusammenhängend; *elements, languages, products* verwandt; *issues* (sach)verwandt; **to be ~ to sth** mit etw zusammenhängen, mit etw verwandt sein; **~ topics** verwandte Themen; **the two events are not ~** die beiden Ereignisse hängen nicht miteinander zusammen *or* haben nichts miteinander zu tun; **two closely ~ questions** zwei eng miteinander verknüpfte Fragen; **health-~ problems** gesundheitliche Probleme *pl*; **earnings-~ pensions** einkommensabhängige Renten *pl*

relating [rɪ'leɪtɪŋ] ADJ **~ to** in Zusammenhang mit

relation [rɪ'leɪʃən] N a (= *person*) Verwandte(r) *mf*; **he's a/no ~ (of mine)** er ist/ist nicht mit mir verwandt; **what ~ is she to you?** wie ist sie mit Ihnen verwandt? b (= *relationship*) Beziehung *f*; **to bear a ~ to** in Beziehung stehen zu; **to bear no ~ to** in keinerlei Beziehung stehen zu, keinerlei Beziehung haben zu; **to bear little ~ to** wenig Beziehung haben zu; **in ~ to** (= *as regards*) in Bezug auf (*+acc*); (= *compared with*) im Verhältnis zu c **relations** PL (= *dealings, ties, sexual relations*) Beziehungen *pl*; **to have business ~s with sb** geschäftliche Beziehungen zu jdm haben; **~s are rather strained** die Beziehungen sind etwas gespannt d *no pl* (*of story*) Erzählung *f*; (*of details*) Aufzählung *f*

relational [rɪ'leɪʃənəl] ADJ relational; **~ database** *(Comput)* relationale Datenbank

relationship [rɪ'leɪʃənʃɪp] N a (*in family*) Verwandtschaft *f* (*to* mit); **what is your ~ (to** *or* **with him)?** wie sind Sie (mit ihm) verwandt? b (= *connection: between events etc*) Beziehung *f*, Verbindung *f*; (= *relations*) Verhältnis *nt*, Beziehungen *pl*; (*in business*) Verbindung *f*; **to have a (sexual) ~ with sb** ein Verhältnis *nt* mit jdm haben; **what kind of a ~ do you have with him?** (*is it good or bad?*) wie ist Ihr Verhältnis zu ihm?; (*on what footing?*) in welchem Verhältnis stehen Sie zu ihm?; **to have a good ~ with sb** ein gutes Verhältnis *or* gute Beziehungen zu jdm haben; **they have a good ~** sie haben ein gutes Verhältnis (zueinander); **we have a business ~** wir haben geschäftlich miteinander zu tun; **it is a strictly business ~** es ist eine rein geschäftliche Beziehung

relative ['relətɪv] ADJ a (= *comparative, not absolute, Sci*) relativ; **happiness is ~** Glück ist relativ; **~ to him, she is in a very happy position** verglichen mit ihm ist sie gut dran; **fuel consumption is ~ to speed** der Benzinverbrauch hängt von der Geschwindigkeit ab; **to live in ~ luxury** verhältnismäßig *or* relativ luxuriös leben; **with ~ ease** relativ leicht; **in ~ terms** vergleichsweise, relativ gesehen; **it's all ~** es ist alles relativ b (= *respective*) jeweilig; **the ~ merits of A and B** die jeweiligen Verdienste von A und B c (= *relevant*) **~ to** sich beziehend auf (*+acc*) d *(Gram)* Relativ-; **~ pronoun/clause** Relativpronomen *nt*/-satz *m* e *(Mus) minor, major* parallel N a (= *person*) = **relation a** b (*Gram:* = *clause*) Relativsatz *m*; (= *pronoun*) Relativpronomen *nt*

relatively ['relətɪvlɪ] ADV relativ, verhältnismäßig; **~ speaking** relativ gesehen *or* betrachtet

relativism ['relətɪvɪzəm] N Relativismus *m*

relativist ['relətɪvɪst] N Relativist(in) *m(f)*

relativistic [ˌrelətɪ'vɪstɪk] ADJ relativistisch

relativity [ˌrelə'tɪvɪtɪ] N *(Phys, Philos)* Relativität *f*; **~ theory, the theory of ~** die Relativitätstheorie

relativize ['relətɪvaɪz] VT relativieren

relaunch [rɪ'lɔːntʃ] VT a *(Comm) product* relaunchen, wieder einführen; *business* neu starten b *rocket* erneut starten N ['riːlɔːntʃ] a (*Comm: of product*) Relaunch *m*, Wiedereinführung *f*; (*of business*) Neustart *m*, Neubeginn *m* b (*of rocket*) Zweitstart *m*, Wiederholungsstart *m*

relax [rɪ'læks] VT lockern; *muscles also, person, one's mind* entspannen; *attention, effort* nachlassen in (*+dat*); **to ~ the bowels** *(Med)* den Stuhlgang fördern VI (sich) entspannen; (= *rest*) (sich) ausruhen; (= *calm down*) sich beruhigen; **let's just ~!** ganz ruhig!; **~!** reg dich nicht auf!, immer mit der Ruhe!; **his face ~ed into a smile** sein Gesicht entspannte sich zu einem Lächeln

relaxant [rɪ'læksənt] N *(Med)* Relaxans *nt*

relaxation [ˌriːlæk'seɪʃən] N a (= *act of relaxing sth*) Lockerung *f*; (*of muscles also, person, one's mind*) Entspannung *f*; (*of attention, effort*) Nachlassen *nt* b (= *rest*) Entspannung *f*; (= *recreation*) Erholung *f*, Entspannung *f*; **you need some ~ after work** Sie sollten sich nach der Arbeit entspannen, Sie brauchen ein wenig Erholung nach der Arbeit; **reading is her form of ~** sie entspannt sich durch Lesen

relaxation technique N Entspannungstechnik *f*, Relaxationsmethode *f*

relaxed [rɪ'lækst] ADJ locker; *person, smile, voice* gelöst, entspannt, ruhig; *atmosphere, surroundings* zwanglos, gelöst, gelockert; *throat* angegriffen; **to feel ~** (*physically*) entspannt sein; (*mentally*) sich wohlfühlen; **to stand in a ~ position** in einer zwanglosen Haltung dastehen; **to feel ~ about sth** etw ganz gelassen sehen

relaxing [rɪ'læksɪŋ] ADJ entspannend; *climate* erholsam; **~ music** Musik, die (einen) entspannt

relay ['riːleɪ] N a (*of workers etc*) Ablösung *f*; (*of horses*) frisches Gespann; **to eat in ~s** in Schichten essen b (*Sport, also* **relay race**) Staffel *f*, Staffellauf *m* c *(Rad, TV)* Relais *nt* VT a (*Rad, TV etc*) *programme, signal* (weiter) übertragen b *message* ausrichten (*to sb* jdm); *information, details* weiterleiten (*to sb* an jdm)

re-lay [ˌriː'leɪ] VT *carpet, cable* neu verlegen

release [rɪ'liːs] VT a *animal, person* freilassen; (*from prison*) entlassen; *employee, football player etc* freigeben; (= *rescue*) befreien; (*from obligation, vow*) entbinden, befreien; (*from pain*) erlösen; **to ~ sb from a debt** jdm eine Schuld erlassen; **can you ~ him for a few hours each week?** können Sie ihn für ein paar Stunden pro Woche freistellen?; **to ~ tension** (*emotional*) sich abreagieren; **to ~ one's anger on sb** seinen Ärger an jdm auslassen *or* abreagieren; **to ~ an animal into the wild** ein Tier auswildern b (= *let go of*) loslassen; *handbrake* losmachen, lösen; *(Phot) shutter* auslösen; *bomb* abwerfen; *grip, clasp* lösen; (*police*) *confiscated articles* freigeben; **to ~ the (foot)brake/clutch** den Fuß von der Bremse/Kupplung nehmen, die Kupplung kommen lassen; **to ~ one's hold** *or* **grip (on sth)** (etw) loslassen c (*Comm:* = *issue*) *film, goods* herausbringen; *record* veröffentlichen, herausbringen d (= *make known*) *news, statement* veröffentlichen; *figures also* bekannt geben e (= *emit*) *gas, energy* freisetzen; *smell* ausströmen; (= *let off: into atmosphere*) *pressure, steam* ablassen f *(Jur) property, title* aufgeben, verzichten auf (*+acc*) N a (*of animal, person*) Freilassung *f*; (*from prison*) Entlassung *f*; (*of employee, football player etc*) Freigabe *f*; (= *rescue*) Befreiung *f*; (*from obligation, vow*) Entbindung *f*, Befreiung *f*; (*from pain*) Erlösung *f*; **death was a happy** *or* **welcome ~ for him** der Tod war eine Erlösung für ihn b (= *letting go*) Loslassen *nt*; (*of handbrake*) Lösen *nt*; (*Phot: of shutter*) Auslösen *nt*; (*of bomb*) Abwurf *m*; (= *mechanism*) Auslöser *m* → **shutter** c (*Comm:* = *issuing, of film, goods*) Herausbringen *nt*; (*of record*) Veröffentlichung *f*, Herausbringen *nt*; (= *film*) Film *m*; (= *record*) Platte *f*; **this film is now on general ~** dieser Film ist nun überall zu sehen; **a new ~ from Michael Jackson** eine Neuerscheinung von Michael Jackson; **a new ~ from XYZ Films Inc** ein neuer Film der XYZ Filmgesellschaft d (*of news, statement*) Veröffentlichung *f*; (= *statement*) Verlautbarung *f* e (*of gas, energy*) Freisetzung *f* f (*Jur, of property, title*) Aufgabe *f* (*of* (*+gen*)), Verzicht *m* (*of* auf (*+acc*))

release: **release date** N a (*of film*) Premieren- *or* Erstaufführungstag *m*; (*of record, book*) Erscheinungstag *m* b (*of prisoner*) Entlassungsdatum *nt*; **his first possible ~ is 2007** er kann frühestens 2007 entlassen werden; **release valve** N Entlastungsventil *nt*

relegate ['relɪgeɪt] VT a (*lit, fig:* = *downgrade*) degradieren; *(Sport) team* absteigen lassen (*to* in *+acc*); *old toys, furniture* verbannen (*to* in *+acc*); **to be ~d** *(Sport)* absteigen; **~d to second place** (*fig*) an zweite Stelle abgeschoben *or* verbannt b (= *hand over*) *matter, question* weiterleiten (*to* an *+acc*)

relegation [ˌrelɪ'geɪʃən] N a (*lit, fig:* = *downgrading*) Degradierung *f*; (*Sport: of team*) Abstieg *m*; (*of old toys, furniture etc*) Verbannung *f* (*to* in (*+acc*)) b (= *handing over, of matter, question*) Weiterleitung *f* (*to* an (*+acc*))

relent [rɪ'lent] VI (*person*) nachgeben; (*pace, pain*) nachlassen; (*weather*) sich bessern

relentless [rɪ'lentlɪs] ADJ a (= *uncompromising*) *attitude, opposition, person* unnachgiebig; **to be ~ in doing sth** etw unnachgiebig tun; **to be ~ in one's efforts to do sth** unnachgiebig in seinen Bemühungen sein, etw zu tun b (= *unrelenting*) *pain, cold, growth* nicht nachlassend; *search* unermüdlich; *progress* unaufhaltsam; **the ~ march of technology** der unaufhaltsame Fortschritt der Technik c (= *merciless*) erbarmungslos; *person also* unerbittlich

relentlessly [rɪ'lentlɪslɪ] ADV a (= *uncompromisingly*) *oppose, maintain* unnachgiebig b (= *unrelentingly*) *hurt, rain* unaufhörlich; **to push ~ forward** unaufhaltsam vorwärtsdrängen c (= *mercilessly*) unerbittlich, erbarmungslos

relet [ˌriː'let] VT neu vermieten

relevance ['reləvəns], **relevancy** ['relɪvənsɪ] N Relevanz *f*; **to be of particular ~ (to sb)** (für jdn) besonders relevant sein; **what is the ~ of your question to the problem?** inwiefern ist Ihre Frage für das Problem relevant?; **to have no ~ to sth** irrelevant für *or* bei etw sein

relevant ['reləvənt] ADJ relevant (*to* für); *information, document, page also* entsprechend *attr*; *course, study also* sachbezogen; *authority, person* zuständig; *regulation* maßgeblich, entsprechend *attr*; *time, place* betreffend; *experience* erforderlich, entsprechend *attr*; **that is not ~** das ist nicht relevant; **a course ~ to one's studies** ein studienbezogener Kurs; **a curriculum which is ~ to all pupils** ein Lehrplan, der für alle Schüler relevant ist; **the police are looking for any ~ information** die Polizei bittet um sachdienliche Hinweise; **applicants for the job need three**

years' ~ experience Bewerber für die Stelle benötigen drei Jahre entsprechende (Berufs)-erfahrung

reliability [rɪˌlaɪəˈbɪlɪtɪ] N Zuverlässigkeit *f*; *(of person also)* Verlässlichkeit *f*; *(of firm, company)* Seriosität *f*, Vertrauenswürdigkeit *f*

reliable [rɪˈlaɪəbl] ADJ zuverlässig; *person also* verlässlich; *firm, company* seriös, vertrauenswürdig

reliably [rɪˈlaɪəblɪ] ADV zuverlässig; **I am ~ informed that …** ich weiß aus zuverlässiger Quelle, dass …

reliance [rɪˈlaɪəns] N *(= trust, confidence)* Vertrauen *nt* (*on* auf *(+acc)*); **to place ~ on sb/sth** sich auf jdn/etw *(acc)* verlassen; **his ~ on his memory rather than his notes always gets him into difficulties** er verlässt sich auf sein Gedächtnis statt auf seine Notizen und kommt dadurch immer in Schwierigkeiten

reliant [rɪˈlaɪənt] ADJ *(= dependent)* angewiesen (*on, upon* auf *+acc*) → **self-reliant**

relic [ˈrelɪk] N Überbleibsel *nt*, Relikt *nt*; *(Rel)* Reliquie *f*; **a ~ of** *or* **from the past** ein Überbleibsel *nt* aus vergangener Zeit; **an old ~** *(pej inf, = person)* ein alter Knochen *(inf)*; *(= car/wardrobe etc)* ein vorsintflutlicher Karren/Schrank *etc (pej inf)*

relief [rɪˈliːf] N **a** *(from anxiety, pain)* Erleichterung *f*; **to bring sb ~** *(drug)* jdm Erleichterung verschaffen; *(news)* jdn erleichtern; **that brought him some ~ from his headache** das hat seine Kopfschmerzen etwas gelindert; **that's a ~!** mir fällt ein Stein vom Herzen; **it was a ~ to find it** ich/er *etc* war erleichtert, als ich/er *etc* es fand; **it was a ~ to get out of the office** es war eine Wohltat, aus dem Büro wegzukommen

b *(from monotony, boredom)* Abwechslung *f*; **to provide a little light/comic ~** für eine kleine Abwechslung/für etwas Humor sorgen

c *(= assistance)* Hilfe *f*; **to come to sb's ~** jdm zu Hilfe kommen; **~ was available in the form of blankets and cups of tea** für Decken und heißen Tee war gesorgt; **to send ~ in the form of food to sb** jdm mit Nahrungsmitteln zu Hilfe kommen; **~ of the poor** Armenfürsorge *f*; **to provide ~ for the poor** für die Armen sorgen; **to be on ~** *(US)* Fürsorge bekommen, von der Fürsorge leben

d *(esp Mil: = act of relieving, replacement forces)* Entsatz *m*; *(= substitute)* Ablösung *f*

e *(Art, Geog)* Relief *nt*; *(Typ)* Relief *nt*, Hochdruck *m*; **high/low ~** Hoch-/Flachrelief *nt*; **in ~** erhaben; **to stand out in ~** *(lit)* sich (deutlich) abheben; *(fig)* gegensätzlich sein; **to throw sth into ~** *(lit)* etw (deutlich) hervortreten lassen; *(fig)* etw hervorheben

f *(Jur)* Rechtshilfe *f* (*of* bei)

ATTR **a** *(= aid)* Hilfs-; **the ~ effort** die Hilfsaktion; *(in disaster)* die Rettungsaktion

b *(= replacement) watchman, driver* zur Entlastung; **~ bus/train** Entlastungsbus/-zug *m*

c *(Typ etc)* Relief-; **~ printing** Reliefdruck *m*

relief: **relief agency** N Rettungsorganisation *f*; **relief fund** N Hilfsfonds *m*; **relief map** N Reliefkarte *f*; **relief road** N Entlastungsstraße *f*; **relief supplies** PL Hilfsgüter *pl*; **relief troops** PL Entsatztruppen *pl*; **relief valve** N Ausgleichsventil *nt*; **relief workers** PL Rettungshelfer *pl*; *(in disaster)* Katastrophenhelfer *pl*

relieve [rɪˈliːv] VT **a** *person* erleichtern; *(of pain)* befreien von; **to feel ~d** erleichtert sein; **to be ~d at sth** bei etw erleichtert aufatmen; **he was ~d to learn that** er war erleichtert, als er das hörte; **to ~ sb's mind** jdn beruhigen

b **to ~ sb of sth** *(of burden, pain)* jdn von etw befreien; *of duty, post, command* jdn einer Sache *(gen)* entheben *(geh)*; *of coat, suitcase* jdm etw abnehmen; *(hum) of wallet, purse etc* jdn um etw erleichtern *(hum)*

c *(= mitigate) anxiety* mildern, schwächen; *pain* lindern; *(completely)* stillen; *tension, stress* abbauen; *pressure, symptoms* abschwächen; *monotony (= interrupt)* unterbrechen; *(= liven things up)* beleben; *poverty* erleichtern; *(Med) congestion* abhelfen *(+dat)*; *(completely)* beheben; **to ~ one's feelings** seinen Gefühlen Luft machen; **the black of her dress was ~d by a white collar** das Schwarz ihres Kleides wurde durch einen weißen Kragen etwas aufgelockert; **the new road ~s peak-hour congestion** die neue Straße entlastet den Berufsverkehr; **to ~ oneself** *(euph)* sich erleichtern

d *(= help) stricken country, refugees etc* helfen *(+dat)*

e *(= take over from, also Mil)* ablösen

f *(Mil) town* entsetzen, befreien

religion [rɪˈlɪdʒən] N Religion *f*; *(= set of beliefs)* Glaube(n) *m*; **the Christian ~** der christliche Glaube; **wars of ~** Glaubenskriege *pl*; **her name in ~** ihr Klostername *m*; **to get ~** *(pej inf)* fromm werden; **study of ~** Religionswissenschaft *f*; **it's an absolute ~ with him** *(fig)* **it's his ~** *(fig)* das ist ihm heilig

religiosity [rɪˌlɪdʒɪˈɒsɪtɪ] N Frömmlertum *nt*

religious [rɪˈlɪdʒəs] ADJ **a** religiös; *order* geistlich; **~ freedom/war** Glaubens- *or* Religionsfreiheit *f*/-krieg *m*; **~ education** *or* **instruction** *(Sch)* Religionsunterricht *m*; **~ holiday** kirchlicher Feiertag; **~ leader** Religionsführer(in) *m(f)*; **~ zeal** Glaubenseifer *m* **b** *(= having religious beliefs) person* gläubig; *(= pious)* fromm; **she is a ~ maniac** *or* **lunatic** sie ist eine religiöse Fanatikerin **c** *(fig: = conscientious)* gewissenhaft; *silence* ehrfürchtig N Ordensmann *m*, Ordensfrau *f*; **the Religious** *pl* die Ordensleute *pl*

religiously [rɪˈlɪdʒəslɪ] ADV **a** *live* fromm, gottesfürchtig; *motivated* religiös; **India is a ~ diverse country** in Indien gibt es eine Vielfalt an Religionen **b** *(fig: = conscientiously)* gewissenhaft

religiousness [rɪˈlɪdʒəsnɪs] N *(= piety)* Frömmigkeit *f*; *(fig: = conscientiousness)* Gewissenhaftigkeit *f*

reline [ˌriːˈlaɪn] VT *coat, jacket* neu füttern; *brakes* neu belegen

relinquish [rɪˈlɪŋkwɪʃ] VT **a** *(= give up) hope, habit, plan* aufgeben; *right, possessions, power, post* aufgeben, verzichten auf *(+acc)*; *title* ablegen; **to ~ sth to sb** jdm etw abtreten *or* überlassen **b** *(= let go)* **to ~ one's hold on sb/sth** *(lit, fig)* jdn/etw loslassen; **he ~ed his hold on life** sein Lebenswille erstarb

relinquishment [rɪˈlɪŋkwɪʃmənt] N *(form, of claim, possessions etc)* Verzicht *m* (*of* auf *+acc*)

reliquary [ˈrelɪkwərɪ] N Reliquiar *nt*, Reliquienschrein *m*

relish [ˈrelɪʃ] N **a** *(= enjoyment)* Geschmack *m*, Gefallen *m* (*for* an *+dat*); **to do sth with (great) ~** etw mit (großem) Genuss tun; **he rubbed his hands with ~ at the prospect** er rieb sich *(dat)* beim Gedanken daran genüsslich die Hände; **he ate with (great) ~** er aß mit großem Genuss *or* Appetit; **he had no ~ for such activities** er fand an solchen Dingen keinen Geschmack *or* Gefallen

b *(Cook)* Soße *f*; *(= spiciness)* Würze *f*; *(fig: = charm)* Reiz *m*; **tomato/fruit ~** Tomaten-/Obstchutney *nt*; **hunger is the best ~** *(prov)* Hunger ist der beste Koch *(prov)*; **it had lost all ~ (for me)** *(fig)* das hatte für mich jeglichen Reiz verloren

VT genießen; *food, wine also* sich *(dat)* schmecken lassen; *idea, role, task* großen Gefallen finden an *(+dat)*; **I don't ~ doing that** *(= enjoy)* das ist gar nicht nach meinem Geschmack; *(= look forward to)* darauf freue ich mich überhaupt nicht; **I don't ~ the thought of getting up at 5 a.m** der Gedanke, um 5 Uhr aufzustehen, behagt *or* schmeckt *(inf)* mir gar nicht

relive [ˌriːˈlɪv] VT *life* noch einmal leben; *experience, one's childhood* noch einmal erleben *or* durchleben; *anguish* noch einmal durchleben *or* durchstehen

reload [ˌriːˈləʊd] VT neu beladen; *gun* nachladen, neu laden

relocate [ˌriːləʊˈkeɪt] VT umsiedeln, verlegen VI *(individual)* umziehen; *(company)* den Standort wechseln; **many companies are relocating out of London** viele Firmen verlegen ihren Standort nach außerhalb von London; **we will help you ~** wir helfen Ihnen beim Umzug *or (referring to company)* beim Standortwechsel

relocation [ˌriːləʊˈkeɪʃən] N Umzug *m*; *(of company)* Standortwechsel *m*; *(of refugees etc)* Umsiedlung *f*; **~ allowance** Umzugsbeihilfe *f*

reluctance [rɪˈlʌktəns] N **a** Widerwillen *m*, Abneigung *f*; **to do sth with ~** etw widerwillig *or* ungern tun; **to make a show of ~** sich widerwillig geben **b** *(Phys)* magnetischer Widerstand

reluctant [rɪˈlʌktənt] ADJ unwillig, widerwillig; *admission, consent, praise* widerwillig; **he is ~ to do it** es widerstrebt ihm, es zu tun; **I'm ~ to go, as he may not even be there** ich gehe nur ungern, denn er ist vielleicht nicht einmal da; **he seems ~ to admit it** er scheint es nicht zugeben zu wollen; **he is a ~ soldier/student** er ist nur widerwillig Soldat/Student; **"reluctant sale"** „Notverkauf"

reluctantly [rɪˈlʌktəntlɪ] ADV widerwillig

rely [rɪˈlaɪ] VI **to ~ (up)on sb/sth** sich auf jdn/etw verlassen; *(= be dependent on)* auf jdn/etw angewiesen sein; **she relied on the trains being on time** sie verließ sich darauf, dass die Züge pünktlich waren; **I ~ on him for my income** ich bin finanziell auf ihn angewiesen; **you can ~ (up)on my help** *or* **on me to help you** du kannst dich darauf verlassen, dass ich dir helfe; **she is not to be relied upon** man kann sich nicht auf sie verlassen

REM *abbr of* **rapid eye movement**; **~ sleep** REM-Phase *f*

remain [rɪˈmeɪn] VI **a** *(= be left)* bleiben; *(= be left over)* übrig bleiben; **much ~s to be done** es ist *or* bleibt noch viel zu tun; **nothing ~s to be said** es gibt *or* bleibt nichts mehr zu sagen; **all that ~s (for us) is to accept** wir brauchen jetzt nur noch anzunehmen *or* müssen nur noch zusagen *or* annehmen; *(= have no alternative)* es bleibt uns nichts anderes übrig, als anzunehmen; **all that ~s is for me to wish you every success** ich möchte Ihnen nur noch viel Erfolg wünschen; **all that ~s (for me/us** *etc* **to do) is to lock up** ich brauche/wir brauchen jetzt nur noch abzuschließen; **that ~s to be seen** das wird sich zeigen, das bleibt abzuwarten; **the fact ~s that he is wrong** das ändert nichts an der Tatsache, dass er unrecht hat

b *(= stay)* bleiben; **~ seated!** bleiben Sie sitzen, behalten Sie Platz *(geh)*; **to ~ silent** weiterhin schweigen; **to ~ behind/up** zurück-/aufbleiben; **let things ~ as they are** lassen wir alles so, wie es ist; *(talking to somebody else)* lassen Sie die Dinge so, wie sie sind; **it ~s the same** das bleibt sich gleich; **"I ~ yours faithfully John Smith"** „mit besten Grüßen verbleibe ich Ihr John Smith"

remainder [rɪˈmeɪndəʳ] N **a** Rest *m* *(also Math)*; **the ~** *(= remaining people)* der Rest, die übrigen (Leute); **for the ~ of the week** für den Rest der Woche, für die übrige Woche **b** **remainders** PL *(Comm)* Restbestände *pl*; *(= books)* Restbestände *pl*, Remittenden *pl (spec)* **c** *(Jur)* Erbanwartschaft *f* VT *books* als Remittenden abgeben

remaining [rɪˈmeɪnɪŋ] ADJ übrig, restlich; **the ~ four, the four ~** die übrigen vier, die vier Übrigen; **I have only one ~** ich habe nur noch einen/eine/eins (übrig)

remains [rɪˈmeɪnz] PL *(of meal)* Reste *pl*; *(of fortune, army)* Rest *m*; *(of building)* Überreste *pl*; *(= archaeological remains)* Ruinen *pl*; **his (mortal) ~** seine sterblichen Überreste; **human ~** menschliche Überreste *pl*

remake [ˌriːˈmeɪk] *vb: pret, ptp* **remade** [ˌriːˈmeɪd] VT wieder *or* nochmals machen; *(in new form)* neu machen; **to ~ a film** ein Thema neu verfilmen N [ˈriːmeɪk] *(Film)* Neuverfilmung *f*, Remake *nt (spec)*

remand [rɪˈmɑːnd] VT *(Jur) case* vertagen; **to ~ sb (in custody/on bail)** jdn weiterhin in Untersuchungshaft behalten/unter Kaution halten; **to ~ sb to a higher court** jdm an eine höhere Instanz verweisen; **he was ~ed in custody/on bail** er blieb in Untersuchungshaft/unter Kaution; **the man ~ed in custody** der Untersuchungsgefangene **N** *(of person)* Aufrechterhaltung *f* der Untersuchungshaft/der Erhebung von Kaution (of gegen); *(form, of case)* Vertagung *f*; **to be on ~** in Untersuchungshaft sein; *(= on bail)* auf Kaution freigelassen sein

remand centre, remand home N *(Brit)* Untersuchungsgefängnis *nt* für Jugendliche

remand wing N Flügel *m or* Trakt *m* für Untersuchungsgefangene

remark [rɪ'mɑːk] **N a** *(= comment)* Bemerkung *f*; **I have a few/no ~s to make on that subject** ich habe einiges/nichts zu diesem Thema zu sagen; **to make** *or* **pass unkind ~s about sb/sth** abfällige Bemerkungen über jdn/etw machen; **~s were made** *or* **passed about our absence** man redete über unsere Abwesenheit
b *no pl (= notice)* **worthy of ~** bemerkenswert; **without ~** unbemerkt
VT a *(= say)* bemerken
b *(old, liter, = notice)* bemerken, wahrnehmen
VI to ~ (up)on sth über etw *(acc)* eine Bemerkung machen, sich zu etw äußern; **nobody ~ed on it** niemand hat etwas dazu gesagt; **everybody ~ed on it** alle haben ihre Bemerkungen dazu gemacht

remarkable [rɪ'mɑːkəbl] ADJ *(= notable)* bemerkenswert; *intelligence, talent, wit also* beachtlich; *(= extraordinary)* außergewöhnlich; *(= amazing) escape* wundersam; **to be ~ for sth** sich durch etw auszeichnen

remarkably [rɪ'mɑːkəblɪ] ADV **a** *(= notably)* bemerkenswert; *(= extraordinarily)* außergewöhnlich; **~ similar** bemerkenswert ähnlich; **a type of latex ~ similar to rubber** eine Latexart mit bemerkenswert ähnlichen Eigenschaften wie Gummi; **he looked ~ like his father** er sah seinem Vater bemerkenswert ähnlich; **~ little** erstaunlich wenig **b** *(= amazingly)* bemerkenswerterweise; **the factory had, ~, escaped the bombing** die Fabrik war wundersamerweise *or* wie durch ein Wunder dem Bombenangriff entkommen

remarriage [ˌriː'mærɪdʒ] N Wiederverheiratung *f* (*to* mit)

remarry [ˌriː'mærɪ] VI wieder heiraten

remaster [ˌriː'mɑːstəʳ] VT *recording* remastern

remediable [rɪ'miːdɪəbl] ADJ *situation* rettbar; *fault, defect* behebbar

remedial [rɪ'miːdɪəl] ADJ *attr* Hilfs-; *(Med)* Heil-; **~ action/measures** Hilfsmaßnahmen *pl*; **~ exercises** Heilgymnastik *f*; **~ treatment** *(Med)* Heilbehandlung *f*; **to teach ~ English/reading** einen Förderkurs in Englisch/im Lesen leiten; **~ education** fördernde Erziehung *(für lernschwache Schüler)*; **~ teaching** Förder- *or* Hilfsunterricht *m*; **~ work** *(Sch)* Förderaufgaben *pl*; **~ class** Förderklasse *f*; **~ course** Förderkurs *m*; **she no longer needs ~ help** *(with learning)* sie benötigt keinen Förderunterricht mehr

remedy ['remədɪ] **N** *(Med, fig)* Mittel *nt* (*for* gegen); *(= medication)* Heilmittel *nt* (*for* gegen); *(Jur)* Rechtsmittel *nt*; **the situation is past** *or* **beyond ~** die Lage ist hoffnungslos verloren *or* irreparabel; **unless we can find a ~** wenn wir keinen Ausweg *or* keine Lösung finden **VT** *(Med)* heilen; *(fig) defect, fault, deficiency, problem* beheben; *situation* bessern; *abuse, evil* abhelfen *(+dat)*; **his faults cannot be remedied** man kann ihn nicht von seinen Fehlern heilen; **the situation cannot be remedied** die Lage ist hoffnungslos

remember [rɪ'membəʳ] ✪ 21.2, 26.1, 26.2 **VT**
a *(= recall)* sich erinnern an *(+acc)*; *(= bear in mind)* denken an *(+acc)*; *(= learn) formula, facts, vocabulary* sich *(dat)* merken; **I ~ that he was very tall** ich erinnere mich (daran), dass er sehr groß war; **I ~ her as a beautiful girl** ich habe sie als schönes Mädchen in Erinnerung; **I ~ her as a young girl** *or* **when she was young** ich erinnere mich noch, wie sie als kleines Mädchen war; **we must ~ that he's only a child** wir sollten bedenken *or* daran denken, dass er noch ein Kind ist; **to ~ to do sth** daran denken, etw zu tun; **I ~ doing it** ich erinnere mich daran, dass ich es getan habe; **I can't ~ the word at the moment** das Wort fällt mir im Moment nicht ein; **I've just ~ed his name** mir ist gerade sein Name wieder eingefallen; **don't you ~ me?** erinnern Sie sich nicht an mich?; **here's something to ~ me by** da hast du etwas, das dich (immer) an mich erinnern wird; **do you ~ when ...?** *(reminiscing)* weißt du noch, als ...?; *(asking facts)* weißt du (noch), wann ...?; **I don't ~ a thing about it** ich kann mich überhaupt nicht daran erinnern; *(about lecture, book)* ich weiß nichts mehr davon; **I can never ~ phone numbers** ich kann mir Telefonnummern einfach nicht merken; **we can't always ~ everything** wir können nicht immer an alles denken; **~ where/who you are!** denken Sie daran *or* bedenken Sie, wo/wer Sie sind!; **to ~ sb in one's prayers** jdn in sein Gebet einschließen; **to ~ sb in one's will** jdn in seinem Testament bedenken; **a night to ~** ein unvergesslicher Abend; **an occasion to ~** ein denkwürdiger Anlass; **to get oneself ~ed** sich in Erinnerung bringen; **~ my password** *(Comput: command)* Kennwort speichern
b *(= commemorate) the fallen, a battle* gedenken *(+gen)*
c *(Brit: = give good wishes to)* **~ me to your mother** grüßen Sie Ihre Mutter von mir; **he asks to be ~ed to you** er lässt Sie grüßen
VI sich erinnern; **I can't ~** ich weiß das nicht mehr, ich habs vergessen; **not as far as I ~** soweit ich mich erinnere, nicht!; **if I ~ right(ly)** wenn ich mich recht erinnere *or* entsinne

remembrance [rɪ'membrəns] **N a** Erinnerung *f* (*of* an *+acc*); **in ~ of** zur Erinnerung an *(+acc)*; **I have no ~ of that** ich habe keinerlei Erinnerung daran **b** *(= keepsake)* Andenken *nt* (*of* an *+acc*) **c remembrances** PL *(old, form, = greetings)* Empfehlungen *pl*

Remembrance Day N *(Brit)* ≈ Volkstrauertag *m*

remembrance service N Gedenkgottesdienst *m*

remigration [ˌriːmaɪ'greɪʃən] N Rückwanderung *f*, Rückkehr *f*

remind [rɪ'maɪnd] VT erinnern (*of* an *+acc*); **you are ~ed that ...** wir weisen darauf hin, dass ...; **to ~ sb to do sth** jdn daran erinnern, etw zu tun; **that ~s me!** da(bei) fällt mir was ein

reminder [rɪ'maɪndəʳ] N *(= note, knot etc)* Gedächtnisstütze *f*; **(letter of) ~** *(Comm)* Mahnung *f*; **as a ~ that ...** um dich/ihn *etc* daran zu erinnern, dass ...; **to give sb a ~ to do sth** jdn daran erinnern, etw zu tun; **his presence was a ~ of ...** seine Gegenwart erinnerte mich/dich *etc* an *(+acc)* ...; **a gentle ~** ein zarter Wink; **give him a gentle ~** weis ihn sachte darauf hin

remindful [rɪ'maɪndfʊl] ADJ *(geh)* erinnernd (*of* an *+acc*); **to be ~ of** sich erinnern an *+acc*

reminisce [ˌremɪ'nɪs] VI sich in Erinnerungen ergehen (*about* über *+acc*)

reminiscence [ˌremɪ'nɪsəns] N *(= action)* Zurückgehen *nt* (*of* zu); *(= thought)* Reminiszenz *f*, Erinnerung *f* (*of* an *+acc*)

reminiscent [ˌremɪ'nɪsənt] ✪ 5.1 ADJ **a to be ~ of sth** an etw *(acc)* erinnern; **a style ~ of Shakespeare** ein an Shakespeare erinnernder Stil **b** *(= reminiscing) person* in Erinnerungen versunken *or* vertieft; *smile* erinnernd; *style, chapter* nostalgisch; **to be feeling ~, to be in a ~ mood** in nostalgischer Stimmung sein; **we listened to him speaking, quietly ~** tief in Erinnerungen versunken, hörten wir ihm zu

reminiscently [ˌremɪ'nɪsəntlɪ] ADV *smile, sigh etc* in der Erinnerung; **he talked ~ of the war** er erzählte von seinen Kriegserinnerungen

remiss [rɪ'mɪs] ADJ nachlässig; **he has been ~ in not doing it** es war nachlässig von ihm, das zu unterlassen

remissible [rɪ'mɪsɪbl] ADJ erlässlich, verzeihlich; *(Rel) sin* lässlich

remission [rɪ'mɪʃən] N *(form)* **a** *(= cancelling, pardoning: of debt)* Erlassen *nt*; *(Brit Jur)* (Straf)erlass *m*; *(Rel)* Nachlass *m*; **he got 3 years' ~ for good behaviour** *(Brit)* ihm wurden wegen guter Führung 3 Jahre erlassen **b** *(= sending: of money)* Überweisung *f* **c** *(= postponement)* Verschiebung *f*, Vertagung *f*; *(of motion)* Zurückverweisung *f* **d** *(Jur: = transfer: of case)* Verweisung *f* **e** *(= becoming less)* Nachlassen *nt*; *(Med)* Besserung *f*, Remission *f (spec)*; **to be in ~** *(patient)* sich auf dem Wege der Besserung befinden; *(illness)* abklingen

remissness [rɪ'mɪsnɪs] N Nachlässigkeit *f*

remit¹ [rɪ'mɪt] *(form)* **VT a** *(= cancel, pardon) debt, sentence, sins* erlassen **b** *(= send) money* überweisen **c** *(= postpone)* verschieben, vertagen (*to* auf *+acc*, *till* bis); *motion* zurückverweisen **d** *(Jur, = transfer) case* verweisen (*to* an *+acc*) **VI** *(= become less)* nachlassen

remit² ['riːmɪt] N *(form)* Aufgabe *f*, Auftrag *m*; **that is outside our ~** das liegt außerhalb unseres Aufgabenbereiches

remittal [rɪ'mɪtl] N = **remission b, c**

remittance [rɪ'mɪtəns] N Überweisung *f* (*to* an *+acc*)

remittance advice N Überweisungsbescheid *m*

remittee [rɪmɪ'tiː] N *(Comm)* Überweisungsempfänger(in) *m(f)*

remittent [rɪ'mɪtənt] ADJ *(Med) symptoms* remittierend *(spec)*; **~ fever** Wechselfieber *nt*

remitter [rɪ'mɪtəʳ] N *(= sender)* Überweiser(in) *m(f)*

remix ['riːmɪks] N *(= record)* Remix *m*

remnant ['remnənt] N Rest *m*; *(fig, of splendour, custom)* Überrest *m*; **the ~ of his fortune/~s of his former glory** was von seinem Vermögen/Ruhm übrig geblieben war

remnant day N *(Comm)* Resteverkaufstag *m*

remnant sale N *(Comm)* Resteausverkauf *m*

remodel [ˌriː'mɒdl] VT *(also Art, Tech)* umformen; *nose* richten; *(fig) house, party, public services, society, constitution* umgestalten

remold [ˌriː'məʊld] VT *(US)* = **remould**

remonstrance [rɪ'mɒnstrəns] N Protest *m* (*with* bei)

remonstrant [rɪ'mɒnstrənt] ADJ protestierend

remonstrate ['remənstreɪt] VI protestieren (*against* gegen); **to ~ with sb (about sth)** jdm Vorhaltungen (wegen etw) machen

remonstration [ˌremən'streɪʃən] N Protest *m* (*against* gegen)

remorse [rɪ'mɔːs] N Reue *f* (*at, over* über *+acc*); **he is completely without ~** er zeigt überhaupt keine Reue; **without ~** *(= merciless)* erbarmungslos

remorseful [rɪ'mɔːsfʊl] ADJ reumütig, reuig; **to feel ~** Reue spüren

remorsefully [rɪ'mɔːsfəlɪ] ADV reumütig, reuig

remorsefulness [rɪ'mɔːsfʊlnɪs] N Reue *f*; *(of person also)* Reumütigkeit *f*

remorseless [rɪ'mɔːslɪs] ADJ reu(e)los, ohne Reue; *(fig: = merciless)* unbarmherzig, erbarmungslos

remorselessly [rɪ'mɔːslɪslɪ] ADV reu(e)los, ohne Reue; *(fig: = mercilessly)* erbarmungslos, unbarmherzig, unerbittlich

remorselessness [rɪ'mɔːslɪsnɪs] N Reu(e)losigkeit *f*; *(fig: = mercilessness)* Unbarmherzigkeit *f*

remote [rɪ'məʊt] **ADJ** (+er) **a** *(in place, = distant)* entfernt, fern *(geh) attr*; *(= isolated)* entlegen, abgelegen; *(Comput)* Fern-, Remote-; **in the ~st parts of Africa** in den abgelegensten Teilen Afrikas; **in a ~ spot** an einer entlegenen *or* abgelegenen Stelle; **a village ~ from the world** ein von der Welt abgeschiedenes Dorf
b *(in time) past, future* fern; **~ antiquity** die früheste Antike; **a ~ ancestor** *(= man)* ein Urahn *m*; *(= woman)* eine Urahne

c *(= distanced, removed) relative, descendant, connection, relevance etc* entfernt; **the government's statements seem ~ from the needs of the people** die Aussagen der Regierung scheinen weit von den Bedürfnissen der Bürger entfernt zu sein; **the union leaders have to beware of getting too ~ from their members** die Gewerkschaftsführer müssen aufpassen, sich nicht zu weit von der Basis zu entfernen
d *(= aloof)* unnahbar, unzugänglich
e *(= slight) possibility, resemblance, risk* entfernt; *chance* gering, winzig; **I haven't the ~st idea** ich habe nicht die leiseste Idee; **it could happen, although the odds are ~** das könnte passieren, obwohl es sehr unwahrscheinlich ist
f *(= remote-controlled) handset* zur Fernbedienung
N *(Rad, TV: = remote control)* Fernbedienung *f*

remote: **remote access** N *(Telec, Comput)* Fern- *or* Remotezugriff *m*; **remote control** N Fernsteuerung *f*, Fernlenkung *f*; *(Rad, TV)* Fernbedienung *f*; **remote-control** ADJ *device* zur Fernbedienung; *TV set* mit Fernbedienung; **~ system** Fernbedienungssystem *nt*; **remote-controlled** ADJ *model aeroplane etc* ferngesteuert, ferngelenkt; *gates* fernbedient; **remote data entry** N *(Comput)* Datenfernverarbeitung *f*

remotely [rɪˈməʊtlɪ] ADV **a** *(= vaguely)* **to be ~ connected with sb/sth** entfernt mit jdm/etw zu tun haben; **it's just ~ possible** es ist gerade eben noch möglich; **if it's ~ possible** wenn es auch nur irgend möglich ist; **they're not even ~ similar** sie sind sich nicht im Entferntesten ähnlich; **he didn't say anything ~ interesting** er sagte nichts, was im Entferntesten interessant war; **avoid saying anything ~ likely to upset him** sag nichts, dass ihn im Geringsten aufregen könnte; **I've never seen anything ~ like it** ich habe noch nie irgendetwas Vergleichbares gesehen; **I'm not ~ interested in it/her** ich bin nicht im Geringsten daran/an ihr interessiert
b *(= distantly) situated, related* entfernt
c *(= by remote control)* **to ~ control/detonate sth** etw fernsteuern/fernzünden
d *(= aloofly) say* kühl, abweisend

remoteness [rɪˈməʊtnɪs] N **a** *(in place, = distance)* Ferne *f*; *(= isolation)* Abgelegenheit *f* **b** *(in time)* (weite) Ferne **c** *(= being distanced, removed: of connection, relevance etc)* Entferntheit *f*; **the government's ~ from the people** die Bürgerferne der Regierung; **the government's ~ from the people's needs** die Unwissenheit der Regierung um die Bedürfnisse der Bürger; **his ~ from everyday life** seine Lebensfremdheit **d** *(= aloofness)* Unnahbarkeit *f*, Unzugänglichkeit *f* **e** *(= slightness, of possibility, resemblance, risk)* Entferntheit *f*; *(of chance)* Winzigkeit *f*

remote: **remote pick-up** N *(Comput)* Fernabfrage *f (von Daten)*; **remote sensing** N Fernerkundung *f*; **~ satellite** Fernerkundungssatellit *m*, Radarsatellit *m*

remould, *(US)* **remold** [ˌriːˈməʊld] VT **a** *(Tech) tyre* runderneuern **b** *(fig) society* umgestalten; *team also* ummodeln *(inf)* **N** [ˈriːməʊld] *(= tyre)* runderneuerter Reifen

remount [ˌriːˈmaʊnt] VT **a** *horse, bicycle* wieder besteigen; *ladder* wieder hinaufsteigen *or* -klettern **b** *picture, photo* wieder aufziehen **VI** wieder aufsitzen

removable [rɪˈmuːvəbl] ADJ *cover, attachment* abnehmbar; *trimming* abtrennbar; *lining* abknöpfbar; *stain* entfernbar; *(from container)* herausnehmbar

removal [rɪˈmuːvəl] N **a** *(= taking off, taking away etc)* Entfernung *f*; *(of cover, lid, attachments)* Abnahme *f*, Entfernung *f*; *(of splint, bandage, tie)* Abnahme *f*; *(of clothes)* Ausziehen *nt*; *(of stain)* Entfernung *f*, Beseitigung *f*; *(of buttons, trimmings)* Abtrennung *f*; *(of troops)* Abzug *m*; **his ~ to hospital** seine Einlieferung ins Krankenhaus
b *(= taking out, from container)* Herausnehmen *nt*; *(Med: of lung, kidney)* Entfernung *f*; *(of paragraph, word, item on list)* Streichen *nt*; *(Tech)* Ausbau *m*
c *(= eradication, of threat, abuse, evil, difficulty, problem)* Beseitigung *f*; *(of tax, restrictions)* Aufhebung *f*; *(of objection, obstacle)* Ausräumung *f*; *(of doubt, suspicion, fear)* Zerstreuung *f*; *(euph: = killing)* Beseitigung *f*
d *(form) (= dismissal: of official)* Entfernung *f*
e *(Brit: = move from house)* Umzug *m*; **our ~ to this house/to York** unser Umzug in dieses Haus/nach York; **"Brown & Son, ~s"** „Spedition Brown & Sohn", „Brown & Sohn, Umzüge"

removal *(Brit)*: **removal allowance** N Umzugsbeihilfe *f*; **removal expenses** PL Umzugskosten *pl*; **removal firm** N Spedition *f*; **removal man** N Möbelpacker *m*; **removal van** N Möbelwagen *m*

remove [rɪˈmuːv] VT **a** *(= take off, take away etc)* entfernen; *cover, lid, attachments* abnehmen, entfernen; *splint, bandage, tie* abnehmen; *clothes* ausziehen; *stain* entfernen, beseitigen; *buttons, trimmings* abtrennen; *lining* abknöpfen; *troops* abziehen; *weapons* abnehmen *(from +dat)*; **to ~ sth from sb** jdm etw wegnehmen; **to ~ one's clothes** die Kleider ablegen; **to ~ sb to hospital** jdn ins Krankenhaus einliefern; **to ~ sb to the cells** jdn in die Zelle bringen; **to ~ a child from school** ein Kind von *or* aus der Schule nehmen; **he ~d himself to another room** er begab sich in ein anderes Zimmer
b *(= take out, from container)* herausnehmen *(from* aus); *(Med) lung, kidney* entfernen *(from* aus); *paragraph, word, item on list* streichen; *(Tech)* ausbauen *(from* aus)
c *(= eradicate) threat* beseitigen; *tax, restrictions* aufheben; *objection, obstacle* aus dem Weg schaffen *or* räumen; *difficulty, problem* beseitigen, ein Ende machen *or* setzen *(+dat)*; *doubt, suspicion, fear* zerstreuen; *abuse, evil* abstellen, beseitigen; *(euph: = kill)* beseitigen; **to ~ all obstacles from one's path** *(fig)* alle Hindernisse aus dem Weg räumen
d *(form: = dismiss) official* entfernen
e *(form, to another house)* transportieren
f **to be far ~d from …** weit entfernt sein von …; **a cousin once/twice ~d** ein Cousin *m* ersten/zweiten Grades; **I'm related to him, but several times ~d** *(inf)* ich bin mit ihm verwandt, aber um ein paar Ecken herum *(inf)*
VI *(form, = move house)* **to ~ to London/to larger premises** nach London/in größere Geschäftsräume (um)ziehen
N **a** **to be only a short ~ from …** nicht weit entfernt sein von …; **this is but one ~ from disaster** das kommt einer Katastrophe nahe; **it's a far ~ from …** es ist weit entfernt von …
b *(Brit, Sch)* Klasse *f* für lernschwache Schüler

remover [rɪˈmuːvəˈ] N **a** *(for nail varnish, stains etc)* Entferner *m* **b** *(Brit: = removal man)* Möbelpacker *m*

remunerate [rɪˈmjuːnəreɪt] VT *(= pay)* bezahlen, vergüten; *(= reward)* belohnen

remuneration [rɪˌmjuːnəˈreɪʃən] N Bezahlung *f*, Vergütung *f*; *(= reward)* Belohnung *f*

remunerative [rɪˈmjuːnərətɪv] ADJ lohnend, einträglich

renaissance [rɪˈneɪsɑ̃ːns] N *(liter)* Wiedergeburt *f*; *(of nature)* Wiedererwachen *nt*; **the Renaissance** *(Hist)* die Renaissance; **Renaissance man** der Renaissancemensch; *(fig)* der Humanist; *(= all-rounder)* Allroundtalent *nt*

renal [ˈriːnl] ADJ Nieren-, renal *(spec)*; **~ failure** Nierenversagen *nt*

rename [ˌriːˈneɪm] VT umbenennen *(also Comput)*, umtaufen; **Leningrad was ~d St Petersburg** Leningrad wurde in St. Petersburg umbenannt

renascence [rɪˈnæsns] N = **renaissance**

renascent [rɪˈnæsnt] ADJ *(liter)* wieder erwachend

rend [rend] *pret, ptp* **rent** VT *(liter) cloth* zerreißen; *armour* aufreißen; **to ~ sth from sb/sth** jdm/einer Sache etw entreißen; **a country rent by civil war** ein vom Bürgerkrieg zerrissenes Land; **a cry rent the air** ein Schrei drang durch die Luft; **to ~ sb's heart** jdm das Herz zerreißen

render [ˈrendəˈ] VT **a** *(form: = give) service, help* leisten; *judgement, explanation* abgeben; *homage* erweisen; *decision, verdict* fällen; **~ unto Caesar the things which are Caesar's** *(Bibl, prov)* gebet dem Kaiser, was des Kaisers ist *(Bibl)*; **to ~ thanks to sb/God** jdm/Gott Dank sagen *or* abstatten; **to ~ assistance** Hilfe leisten; **to ~ an account of one's expenditure** Rechenschaft über seine Ausgaben ablegen
b *(Comm)* **to ~ account** Rechnung legen *or* vorlegen; **(to) account ~ed £10** £ 10 laut früherer Rechnung
c *(= interpret, translate)* wiedergeben; *(in writing)* übertragen; *music, poem* vortragen
d *(form: = make)* machen; **his accident ~ed him helpless** der Unfall hat ihn hilflos gemacht
e *(also* **render down)** *fat* auslassen
f *(Build)* verputzen

▶ **render up** VT *sep fortress, prisoner* übergeben

rendering [ˈrendərɪŋ] N **a** Wiedergabe *f*; *(in writing)* Übertragung *f*; *(of piece of music, poem)* Vortrag *m* **b** *(esp Brit, Build)* Putz *m*

rendezvous [ˈrɒndɪvuː] **N** *(= place)* Treffpunkt *m*; *(= agreement to meet)* Rendezvous *nt* **VI** sich treffen *(with* mit)

rendition [renˈdɪʃən] N **a** *(form)* = **rendering** **b** *(of terrorists etc to a foreign state)* Auslieferung *f*, Überstellung *f*

renegade [ˈrenɪgeɪd] **N** Renegat(in) *m(f)*, Abtrünnige(r) *mf* **ADJ** abtrünnig

renege [rɪˈniːg] VI nicht Wort halten; *(Cards)* nicht bedienen; **to ~ on a promise/an agreement** ein Versprechen/eine Übereinkunft brechen

renew [rɪˈnjuː] VT erneuern; *contract, passport etc (authority also)* verlängern; *(holder)* erneuern *or* verlängern lassen; *negotiations, discussions, diplomatic relations, attack, attempts* wieder aufnehmen; *one's strength* wiederherstellen; *fears* wieder wachrufen; *interest* wieder wecken; *supplies* auffrischen; **to ~ a library book** ein Buch verlängern lassen

renewable [rɪˈnjuːəbl] **ADJ** *contract, licence etc* erneuerbar, verlängerbar; *passport, bill of exchange* verlängerbar; *energy, resource* erneuerbar; *(= must be renewed)* zu erneuern/verlängern; **some library books are not ~** einige Bibliotheksbücher können nicht verlängert werden **N** **renewables** **PL** erneuerbare Energiequellen *pl*

renewal [rɪˈnjuːəl] N Erneuerung *f*; *(of contract, passport etc also)* Verlängerung *f*; *(of negotiations, discussions, diplomatic relations, attack, attempts)* Wiederaufnahme *f*; *(of interest)* Wiedererwachen *nt*; *(of one's strength)* Wiederherstellung *f*; *(of supplies)* Auffrischung *f*; **spiritual ~** geistige Erneuerung

renewed [rɪˈnjuːd] ADJ *(= new) fighting* erneut; *interest* erneut, neu; *pressure* erneut, wiederholt; **~ hope** neue Hoffnungen *pl*; **with ~ vigour** *(Brit)* *or* **vigor** *(US)* mit neuer Energie; **with ~ enthusiasm** mit neuem Schwung; **~ efforts** neue Anstrengungen; **~ strength** frische Kraft; **~ courage** frischer Mut; **~ outbreaks of rioting** erneute Krawalle *pl*; **to feel spiritually ~** sich wie ein neuer Mensch fühlen; **to make ~ efforts to do sth** erneute Anstrengungen unternehmen, etw zu tun

rennet [ˈrenɪt] N *(Cook)* Lab *nt*

renounce [rɪˈnaʊns] VT *title, right, violence* verzichten auf *(+acc)*, aufgeben; *terrorism, religion, devil, faith* abschwören *(+dat)*; *(Rel) world* entsagen *(+dat)*; *opinions, cause, treaty* leugnen, abschwören *(+dat)*; *friend* verleugnen; **to ~ the throne** auf den Thron verzichten **VI** *(Cards)* renoncieren

renouncement [rɪˈnaʊnsmənt] N = **renunciation**

renovate [ˈrenəʊveɪt] VT *building* renovieren; *painting, furniture* restaurieren

renovation [ˌrenəʊˈveɪʃən] N *(of building)* Renovierung *f*, Renovation *f*; *(of painting, furniture)* Restaurierung *f*

renown [rɪˈnaʊn] N guter Ruf, Ansehen *nt*; **of great ~** von hohem Ansehen, sehr berühmt; **a wine of ~** ein renommierter Wein

renowned [rɪˈnaʊnd] ADJ berühmt *(for* für)

rent[1] [rent] N *(for house, room)* Miete *f*; *(for farm, factory)* Pacht *f*; **for ~** *(US)* zu vermieten/verpachten/verleihen VT **a** *house, room* mieten; *farm, factory* pachten; *TV, car etc* leihen; *video* sich *(dat)* ausleihen, ausleihen; **we don't own it, we only ~ it** es gehört uns *(dat)* nicht, wir haben es nur gemietet *etc* **b** *(also* **rent out***)* vermieten; verpachten; verleihen; VI *(= rent house, room)* mieten; *(= rent farm, factory)* pachten; *(= rent TV etc)* leasen; *(= rent video)* ausleihen

rent[2] *pret, ptp of* **rend** N *(lit, fig)* Riss *m*; *(in rock)* Spalte *f*

rent-a-car N *(esp US)* **a** *(also* **rent-a-car company** *or* **service***)* Autoverleih *m* **b** *(= hired car)* Leih- *or* Mietwagen *m*

rental [ˈrentl] N *(= amount paid, for house)* Miete *f*; *(for TV, car, boat etc also, video)* Leihgebühr *f*; *(for land)* Pacht *f*; *(= income from rents)* Miet-/ /Pacht-/Leihgebühreinnahmen *pl*; **~ car** Mietwagen *m*; **~ allowance** *(US)* Mietzuschuss *m*; **~ library** *(US)* Leihbücherei *f*

rent: **rent boy** N *(Brit inf)* Strichjunge *m (inf)*, Stricher *m (inf)*; **rent collector** N Mietkassierer(in) *m(f)*; **rent control** N Mietkontrolle *f*, Mieterschutz *m*; **rent-controlled** ADJ bewirtschaftet *(form)*, mit gebundener Miete; **rent-free** ADJ ADV mietfrei; **rent man** N *(inf)* = **rent collector**; **rent rebate** N Mietrückzahlung *f*; *(= reduction)* Mietnachlass *m or* -ermäßigung *f*; **rent review** N Neufestsetzung *f* der Miete; **rent strike** N Mietstreik *m*; **to go on ~, to stage a ~** in den Mietstreik treten; **rent tribunal** N Mieterschiedsgericht *nt*

renumber [ˌriːˈnʌmbəʳ] VT umnummerieren

renunciation [rɪˌnʌnsɪˈeɪʃən] N *(of title, right, violence)* Verzicht *m* (of auf (+acc)), Aufgabe *f*; *(of terrorism)* Aufgabe *f*; *(of religion, devil, faith)* Abschwören *nt*; *(Rel: of world)* Entsagung *f*; *(of opinion, cause, treaty)* Leugnung *f*; *(of friend)* Verleugnung *f*

reoccupy [ˌriːˈɒkjʊpaɪ] VT *post, position* wieder innehaben *or* bekleiden; *house, hotel room etc* wieder belegen

reoffend [ˌriːəˈfend] VI erneut straffällig werden

reopen [ˌriːˈəʊpən] VT wieder öffnen, wieder aufmachen; *school, shop, theatre, fight, hostilities* wieder eröffnen; *debate, discussion, negotiations* wieder aufnehmen; *(Jur) case* wieder aufrollen, wieder aufnehmen VI wieder aufgehen; *(shop, theatre etc)* wieder eröffnen *or* aufmachen; *(school after holidays, negotiations)* wieder beginnen; *(case)* wieder aufgerollt werden; *(wound)* wieder aufgehen

reopening [ˌriːˈəʊpnɪŋ] N *(of shop etc)* Wiedereröffnung *f*; *(of school after holiday)* Wiederbeginn *m*; *(of negotiations, debate, case)* Wiederaufnahme *f*; **the ~ of old wounds** *(fig)* das Aufreißen alter Wunden

reorder [ˌriːˈɔːdəʳ] VT **a** *goods, supplies* nachbestellen; *(because first order is lost etc)* neu bestellen **b** *(= reorganize)* neu ordnen, umordnen; *books, people in a row* umstellen; *appointments* umlegen VI *(= reorder goods, supplies)* nachbestellen; *(because first order is lost etc)* neu bestellen

reorganization [riːˌɔːgənaɪˈzeɪʃən] N Neu- *or* Umorganisation *f*; *(of furniture, books)* Umordnung *f*; *(of work, time)* Neueinteilung *f*; *(of essay)* Neuaufbau *m*; *(of one's life)* Neueinteilung *f*, Umorientierung *f*

reorganize [ˌriːˈɔːgənaɪz] VT neu organisieren, umorganisieren; *furniture, books* umordnen; *work, time* neu einteilen; *essay* neu aufbauen; **to ~ one's life** sich *(dat)* sein Leben anders einteilen, sein Leben umorientieren VI *(Pol)* sich neu organisieren

Rep **a** *abbr of* **Republic** Rep. **b** *abbr of* **Republican** Rep., rep.

rep[1] [rep] N **a** *(Theat) abbr of* **repertory** Repertoire-Theater *nt* **b** *(Comm) abbr of* **representative** Vertreter(in) *m(f)* VI als Vertreter(in) arbeiten

rep[2] N *(Tex)* Rips *m*

repaid [ˌriːˈpeɪd] *pret, ptp of* **repay**

repaint [ˌriːˈpeɪnt] VT neu streichen

repair[1] [rɪˈpɛəʳ] VT *(lit, fig)* reparieren; *tyre also, clothes* flicken; *roof, wall also, road* ausbessern; *(fig) error, wrong, damage* wiedergutmachen; *image, relations* wiederherstellen

N **a** *(lit)* Reparatur *f*; *(of tyre also, clothes)* Flicken *nt*; *(of roof, wall also, road)* Ausbesserung *f*; *(fig: of relationship)* Kitten *nt*; **to be under ~** *(car, ship, machine)* in Reparatur sein; **to put sth in for ~** etw zur Reparatur bringen; **the road is under ~** an der Straße wird gerade gearbeitet; **beyond ~** nicht mehr zu reparieren/zu flicken/ auszubessern; **damaged beyond ~** irreparabel, nicht mehr zu reparieren; **closed for ~s** wegen Reparaturarbeiten geschlossen; **"road ~s"** „Straßenbauarbeiten"; **"repairs while you wait"** „Sofortdienst", „Sofortreparaturen"

b *no pl (= condition)* **to be in good/bad ~** in gutem/schlechtem Zustand sein

repair[2] VI *(liter: = go)* sich begeben *(to* nach)

repairable [rɪˈpɛərəbl] ADJ *(lit, fig)* zu reparieren, reparabel; *tyre also, clothes* zu flicken; *roof, wall also, road* auszubessern *pred*; **is that ~?** lässt sich das reparieren/flicken?

repairer [rɪˈpɛərəʳ] N **watch/shoe ~** Uhr-/Schuhmacher(in) *m(f)*

repair: **repair kit** N Flickzeug *nt*; **repairman** N *(in house)* Handwerker *m*; **repair shop** N Reparaturwerkstatt *m*

repaper [ˌriːˈpeɪpəʳ] VT neu tapezieren

reparable [ˈrepərəbl] ADJ *damage* reparabel, wiedergutzumachen; *loss* ersetzbar

reparation [ˌrepəˈreɪʃən] N *(for damage)* Entschädigung *f*; *(usu pl: after war)* Reparationen *pl*; *(for wrong, misdeed)* Wiedergutmachung *f*; **to make ~ for sth** etw wiedergutmachen

reparative [rɪˈpærətɪv], **reparatory** [rɪˈpærətərɪ] ADJ *payments etc* wiedergutmachend, Entschädigungs-

repartee [ˌrepɑːˈtiː] N Schlagabtausch *m*; *(= retort)* schlagfertige Antwort; **to be good at ~** schlagfertig sein; **renowned for his ~** bekannt für seine Schlagfertigkeit

repartition [ˌriːpɑːˈtɪʃən] N **a** *(= distribution, partition)* Auf- *or* Verteilung *f* **b** *(= new distribution)* Neuverteilung *f* VT (neu) verteilen, aufteilen

repast [rɪˈpɑːst] N *(liter)* Mahl *nt (geh)*

repatriate [ˌriːˈpætrɪeɪt] VT in das Heimatland zurücksenden, repatriieren N [ˌriːˈpætrɪɪt] Repatriierte(r) *mf*

repatriation [ˈriːˌpætrɪˈeɪʃən] N Repatriierung *f*

repay [ˌriːˈpeɪ] *pret, ptp* **repaid** VT *money* zurückzahlen; *expenses* erstatten; *debt* abzahlen; *kindness* vergelten; *visit, compliment* erwidern; **if you lend me £2 I'll ~ it** *or* **you on Saturday** leih mir doch mal 2 Pfund, ich zahle sie dir am Samstag zurück; **I shall ~ my debt to you one day** *(fig)* ich werde es dir eines Tages vergelten *or* lohnen; **to ~ sb for his generosity** sich für jds Großzügigkeit revanchieren; **he repaid their kindness by stealing their camera** zum Dank für ihre Freundlichkeit hat er ihnen die Kamera gestohlen; **to be repaid for one's efforts** für seine Mühen belohnt werden; **how can I ever ~ you?** wie kann ich das jemals wiedergutmachen?; **she wants to ~ his faith in her** sie möchte das Vertrauen, das er in sie gesetzt hat, rechtfertigen

repayable [ˌriːˈpeɪəbl] ADJ rückzahlbar

repayment [ˌriːˈpeɪmənt] N *(of money)* Rückzahlung *f*; *(of effort, kindness)* Lohn *m*; **~s can be spread over 3 years** die Rückzahlung kann über 3 Jahre verteilt werden; **in ~** als Rückzahlung/Lohn

repayment mortgage N Tilgungshypothek *f*

repeal [rɪˈpiːl] VT *law* aufheben N Aufhebung *f*

repeat [rɪˈpiːt] ✪ 27.3 VT wiederholen; *(= tell to sb else)* weitersagen *(to sb* jdm); **to ~ oneself** sich wiederholen; **he wasn't keen to ~ the experience** er war nicht darauf aus, die Erfahrung noch einmal zu machen; **he ~ed his lesson to the teacher** er sagte seine Lektion vor dem Lehrer auf; **to ~ an order** *(Comm)* nachbestellen; **this offer will never be ~ed!** dies ist ein einmaliges Angebot!

VI **a** *(= say again)* wiederholen; **~ after me** sprecht mir nach

b *(Mus)* wiederholen; **~!** *(conductor)* noch einmal!

c **radishes ~ on me** Radieschen stoßen mir auf

d *(gun, clock etc)* repetieren

e *(Math)* periodisch sein

N **a** *(Rad, TV)* Wiederholung *f*

b *(Mus: = section repeated)* Wiederholung *f*; *(= repeat sign)* Wiederholungszeichen *nt*

ADJ **~ business** Nachfolgeaufträge *pl*; **~ customer** Kunde, der/Kundin, die wiederkommt; *(= regular customer)* Stammkunde *m*, Stammkundin *f*

repeated ADJ, **repeatedly** ADV [rɪˈpiːtɪd, -lɪ] wiederholt

repeater [rɪˈpiːtəʳ] N *(= gun)* Repetier- *or* Mehrladegewehr *nt*; *(= watch)* Repetieruhr *f*

repeat function N *(Comput)* Wiederholungsfunktion *f*

repeating [rɪˈpiːtɪŋ] ADJ *(Math)* = **recurring b**

repeat: **repeat mark** N *(Mus)* Wiederholungszeichen *nt*; **repeat offender** N *(Jur)* Wiederholungstäter(in) *m(f)*; **repeat order** N *(Comm)* Nachbestellung *f*; **repeat performance** N *(Theat)* Wiederholungsvorstellung *f*; **he gave a ~** *(fig)* er machte es noch einmal; *(pej)* er machte noch einmal das gleiche Theater *(inf)*; **repeat prescription** N *(Med)* erneut verschriebenes Rezept, Folgerezept *nt*; **repeat sign** N *(Mus)* Wiederholungszeichen *nt*

repel [rɪˈpel] VT **a** *enemy, attack* zurückschlagen; *sb's advances, insects, flies* abwehren; *water* abstoßen **b** *(= disgust)* abstoßen VI *(= disgust)* abstoßen

repellent [rɪˈpelənt] ADJ **a** **~ to water** Wasser abstoßend **b** *(= disgusting)* abstoßend; *sight* widerlich, abstoßend; *smell* ekelerregend, widerlich; **to be ~ to sb** ekelerregend für jdn sein, auf jdn abstoßend wirken; **I find him ~** ich finde ihn abstoßend N *(= insect repellent)* Insektenschutzmittel *nt*

repelling [rɪˈpelɪŋ] ADJ = **repellent ADJ b**

repent [rɪˈpent] VI Reue empfinden *(of* über (+acc)) VT bereuen

repentance [rɪˈpentəns] N Reue *f*

repentant [rɪˈpentənt] ADJ *look, expression* reuig, reuevoll; **he was very ~** es reute ihn sehr; **to feel ~** Reue empfinden; **a ~ sinner** ein reuiger Sünder

repercussion [ˌriːpəˈkʌʃən] N **a** *(= consequence)* Auswirkung *f (on* auf +acc); **~s** *pl (of misbehaviour etc)* Nachspiel *nt*; **that is bound to have ~s** das wird Kreise ziehen; **to have ~s on sth** sich auf etw *(acc)* auswirken **b** *(of shock)* Erschütterung *f*; *(of sounds)* Widerhall *m*

repertoire [ˈrepətwɑːʳ] N *(Theat, Mus)* Repertoire *nt*

repertory [ˈrepətərɪ] N **a** *(also* **repertory theatre***)* Repertoire-Theater *nt*; **to act in ~, to play ~** Repertoire-Stücke spielen; **he was in ~** er spielte an einem Repertoire-Theater **b** *(= songs, plays)* = **repertoire**

repertory company N Repertoire-Ensemble *nt*

repetition [ˌrepɪˈtɪʃən] N Wiederholung *f*; **there are six ~s of the pattern** das Muster wiederholt sich sechsmal

repetitious [ˌrepɪˈtɪʃəs] ADJ sich wiederholend

repetitive [rɪˈpetɪtɪv] ADJ sich dauernd wiederholend; *work also* monoton; **to be ~** sich dauernd wiederholen; **standing in a production line is such ~ work** die Arbeit am Fließband ist äußerst eintönig

repetitive strain injury N Verletzung *f* durch wiederholte Belastung

rephrase [ˌriːˈfreɪz] VT neu formulieren, umformulieren

repine [rɪˈpaɪn] VI *(liter)* hadern *(geh)* *(at, against* mit)

replace [rɪˈpleɪs] VT **a** *(= put back)* zurücksetzen; *(on end, standing up)* zurückstellen; *(on its side, flat)* zurücklegen; **to ~ the receiver** *(Telec)* (den Hörer) auflegen **b** *(= provide or be substitute for) person, thing, ingredient, goods (temporarily)* vertreten; **the boss has ~d Smith with Jones** der Chef hat Smith durch Jones ersetzt **c** *(= renew) components, parts* austauschen, ersetzen **d** *(Comput) text etc* ersetzen

replaceable [rɪˈpleɪsəbl] ADJ *person* ersetzbar, zu ersetzen; *(= renewable) components, parts also* austauschbar

replacement [rɪˈpleɪsmənt] N **a** *(= substituting)* Ersatz *m*; *(by deputy)* Vertretung *f*; **~ cost** *(of equipment)* Wiederbeschaffungskosten *pl*; *(of personnel)* Wiederbesetzungskosten *pl* **b** *(= person or thing)* Ersatz *m*; *(= deputy)* Vertretung *f*; **~ engine** Austauschmotor *m*; **~ part** Ersatzteil *nt* **c** *(= putting back)* Zurücksetzen *nt*; *(on end, standing up)* Zurückstellen *nt*; *(on side, flat)* Zurücklegen *nt*; *(of receiver)* Auflegen *nt*

replant [ˌriːˈplɑːnt] VT *cabbages, trees etc* umpflanzen; *garden, field* neu bepflanzen

replay [ˈriːpleɪ] *(Sport)* N *(= recording)* Wiederholung *f*; *(= match also)* Wiederholungsspiel *nt* → **action replay** [ˌriːˈpleɪ] VT *match, game* wiederholen, nochmals austragen; **to ~ sth in one's mind** sich *(dat)* etw (immer) wieder vor Augen führen

replenish [rɪˈplenɪʃ] VT ergänzen; *(when badly depleted)* wieder auffüllen; *glass* auffüllen; *shelves* nachfüllen

replenishment [rɪˈplenɪʃmənt] N Ergänzung *f*; *(when badly depleted)* Wiederauffüllen *nt*; *(of glass)* Auffüllen *nt*; *(of shelves)* Nachfüllen *nt*

replete [rɪˈpliːt] ADJ *(form)* reichlich versehen *or* ausgestattet *(with* mit); *(= well-fed) person* gesättigt

repletion [rɪˈpliːʃən] N *(form)* Sättigung *f*; **to eat to ~** essen, bis man gesättigt ist

replica [ˈreplɪkə] N *(of painting, statue)* Reproduktion *f*, Kopie *f*; *(of document)* Kopie *f*; *(of ship, building etc)* Nachbildung *f*; **she is a ~ of her sister** sie ist das Ebenbild ihrer Schwester

replicate [ˈreplɪkeɪt] VT *(= copy) work, success* wiederholen

reply [rɪˈplaɪ] ✪ 19.1, 19.4, 27.3, 27.5, 27.7 N *(written)* Antwort *f*; *(spoken also)* Erwiderung *f*; *(esp Comput)* Rückmeldung *f*; **in ~** (als Antwort) darauf; **in ~ to your letter** in Beantwortung Ihres Briefes *(form)*; **~ coupon** Antwortschein *m*; **to send a letter ~ paid** *(Brit)* einen Brief gebührenfrei senden; **~-paid envelope** *(Brit)* freigemachter Briefumschlag, Freiumschlag *m* VT **to ~ (to sb) that ...** (jdm) antworten, dass ... VI *(to sth* auf etw *+acc)* antworten; *(spoken also)* erwidern

reply cardn Antwortkarte *f*

repoint [ˌriːˈpɔɪnt] VT *(Build)* neu verfugen

repointing [ˌriːˈpɔɪntɪŋ] N *(Build)* Neuverfugung *f*

repopulate [ˌriːˈpɒpjʊleɪt] VT *area* neu besiedeln

report [rɪˈpɔːt] N **a** *(= account, statement)* Bericht *m* *(on* über *+acc)*; *(Press, Rad, TV)* Reportage *f*, Bericht *m* *(on* über *+acc)*; **to give a ~ on sth** Bericht über etw *(acc)* erstatten; *(Rad, TV)* eine Reportage über etw *(acc)* machen; **an official ~ on the motor industry** ein Gutachten *nt* über die Autoindustrie; **(school) ~** Zeugnis *nt*; **chairman's ~** Bericht *m* des Vorsitzenden **b** *(= rumour)* **to know sth only by ~** etw nur vom Hörensagen kennen; **there are ~s that ...** es wird gesagt, dass ... **c** *(= reputation)* Ruf *m*; **of good ~** von gutem Ruf **d** *(of gun)* Knall *m*; **with a loud ~** mit lautem Knall

VT **a** *results, findings* berichten über *(+acc)*; *(= announce officially)* melden; *losses* verzeichnen; **to ~ that ...** berichten, dass ...; **to ~ progress** einen Tätigkeitsbericht abgeben; **the papers ~ed the crime as solved** laut Presseberichten ist das Verbrechen aufgeklärt; **he is ~ed as having said ...** er soll gesagt haben ...; **it is ~ed that a prisoner has escaped, a prisoner is ~ed to have escaped** ein Gefangener wird als geflüchtet gemeldet *or* gilt als vermisst; **it is ~ed from the White House that ...** aus dem Weißen Haus wird berichtet *or* gemeldet, dass ... **b** *(to sb* jdm) *(= notify authorities of) accident, crime, suspect, criminal, culprit* melden; *(to police)* melden, anzeigen; *one's position* angeben; **to ~ sb for sth** jdn wegen etw melden; **to ~ sb sick** jdn krankmelden; **to ~ sb missing**jdn als vermisst melden; **~ed missing** als vermisst gemeldet; **nothing to ~** keine besonderen Vorkommnisse!

VI **a** *(= announce oneself)* sich melden; **~ to the director on Monday** melden Sie sich am Montag beim Direktor; **to ~ for duty** sich zum Dienst melden; **to ~ sick** sich krankmelden **b** *(= give a report)* berichten, Bericht erstatten *(on* über *+acc)*; *(= work as journalist)* Reporter(in) *m(f)* sein; **the committee is ready to ~** der Ausschuss hat seinen Bericht fertig; **this is Michael Brown ~ing (from Rome)** *(Rad, TV)* hier spricht Michael Brown (mit einem Bericht aus Rom)

▶ **report back** VI **a** *(= announce one's return)* sich zurückmelden **b** *(= give report)* Bericht erstatten *(to sb* jdm)

▶ **report to** VI *+prep obj (in organization)* unterstellt sein *(+dat)*, unterstehen *(+dat)*; **who do you report to?** wer ist Ihr Vorgesetzter?

reportable [rɪˈpɔːtəbl] ADJ *event* berichtenswert; *(Med) disease* anzeige- *or* meldepflichtig; *capital gains, income etc* steuerpflichtig

reportage [ˌrepɔːˈtɑːʒ] N Reportage *f*; *(= style)* Reporterstil *m*

report card N *(Sch)* Zeugnis(blatt) *nt*

reported [rɪˈpɔːtɪd] ADJ gemeldet

reportedly [rɪˈpɔːtɪdlɪ] ADV angeblich; **several houses were ~ destroyed** wie verlautet, sollen mehrere Häuser zerstört worden sein

reported speech N *(Gram)* indirekte Rede

reporter [rɪˈpɔːtəʳ] N **a** *(Press, Rad, TV)* Reporter(in) *m(f)*, Berichterstatter(in) *m(f)*; *(on the spot)* Korrespondent(in) *m(f)*; **special ~** Sonderberichterstatter(in) *m(f)* **b** *(Jur, Parl, = stenographer)* Stenograf(in) *m(f)*, Gerichtsschreiber(in) *m(f)* *(old)*

reporters' gallery [rɪˈpɔːtəzˈgælərɪ] N *(Jur, Parl)* Pressetribüne *f*

report generator N *(Comput)* Datenbankabfragegenerator *m*

reporting [rɪˈpɔːtɪŋ]: **reporting restrictions** PL *(Brit Jur)* Berichterstattungsbeschränkungen *pl* *(on* in Bezug auf *+acc)*; **~ were not lifted** die Berichterstattungsbeschränkungen wurden nicht aufgehoben; **reporting structure** N Organisationsstruktur *f*

report stage N **the bill has reached the ~** *(Brit Parl)* der Gesetzentwurf kommt nach seiner Beratung im Ausschuss zur Berichterstattung wieder vors Parlament

repose[1] [rɪˈpəʊz] N *(liter. = rest, peace)* Ruhe *f*; *(= composure)* Gelassenheit *f*; **in ~** in Ruhe VI **a** *(form, liter) (= rest, be buried)* ruhen **b** *(= be based)* beruhen *(upon* auf *+dat)*

repose[2] VT *(form, liter) trust, faith* setzen *(in* in *or* auf *+acc)*

repository [rɪˈpɒzɪtərɪ] N *(= warehouse)* Lager *nt*, Magazin *nt*; *(fig, of facts etc)* Quelle *f* *(of* für); *(= book, library)* Fundgrube *f* (of für); *(liter, of secret)* Hüter(in) *m(f)*

repossess [ˌriːpəˈzes] VT wieder in Besitz nehmen

repossession [ˌriːpəˈzeʃən] N Wiederinbesitznahme *f*

repot [ˌriːˈpɒt] VT *plant* umtopfen

repp N = **rep**[2]

reprehend [ˌreprɪˈhend] VT tadeln, rügen

reprehensible [ˌreprɪˈhensɪbl] ADJ verwerflich, tadelnswert

reprehensibly [ˌreprɪˈhensɪblɪ] ADV verwerflich

reprehension [ˌreprɪˈhenʃən] N **a** *no pl (= act)* Tadeln *nt*, Rügen *nt* **b** *(= rebuke)* Tadel *m*, Rüge *f*

represent [ˌreprɪˈzent] VT **a** darstellen; *(= stand for)* stehen für; *(= symbolize)* symbolisieren, darstellen; *opportunity* bedeuten; **he ~s all that is best in ...** er verkörpert das Beste *(+gen)* ... **b** *(= act or speak for, Parl, Jur)* vertreten; **he ~s their firm in London** er vertritt *or* repräsentiert die Firma in London; **many countries were ~ed at the ceremony** viele Länder waren bei der Feier vertreten; **the foreign tourist should never forget that he ~s his country** ein Tourist sollte im Ausland nie vergessen, dass er sein Land repräsentiert **c** *(= declare to be) person, event, risk etc* darstellen *(as* als); *(falsely)* hinstellen *(as* als); **it is exactly as ~ed in the advertisement** es ist genau, wie in der Anzeige dargestellt **d** *(= set forth, explain)* vor Augen führen *(to sb* jdm) **e** *(Theat) character, part* darstellen

re-present [ˌriːprɪˈzent] VT nochmals vorlegen

representation [ˌreprɪzenˈteɪʃən] N **a** *(= representing)* Darstellung *f*; *(= symbolizing)* Symbolisierung *f*; *(= acting or speaking for, Parl, Jur)* Vertretung *f*; *(= declaring to be sb/sth)* Darstellung *f*; *(falsely)* Hinstellung *f* **b** *(= drawing, description, Theat)* Darstellung *f* **c** **representations** PL *(esp Pol: = remonstrations)* Vorstellungen *pl*, Vorhaltungen *pl*; **the ambassador made ~s to the government** der Botschafter wurde bei der Regierung vorstellig

representational [ˌreprɪzenˈteɪʃənəl] ADJ *art, picture* gegenständlich; **in ~ form** symbolisch; **a ~ party of** eine Vertretung *(+gen)*

representational system N *(Pol)* Repräsentativsystem *nt*

representative [ˌreprɪˈzentətɪv] ADJ **a** *(of* für) *(= typical) cross section, sample* repräsentativ; *attitude, game* typisch; *(= symbolic)* symbolisch **b** *(= acting for)* repräsentativ; **a ~ body** eine Vertretung **c** *(Parl) government* repräsentativ, parlamentarisch; **~ assembly** Abgeordnetenversammlung *f* N *(Comm)* Vertreter(in) *m(f)*; *(Jur)* Bevollmächtigte(r), Beauftragte(r) *mf*; *(US Pol)* Abgeordnete(r) *mf*; **authorized ~** Bevollmächtigte(r) *mf* → **house N b**

repress [rɪˈpres] VT *revolt, population, emotions, desires* unterdrücken; *laugh, sneeze* unterdrücken, zurückhalten; *(Psych)* verdrängen

repressed [rɪˈprest] ADJ unterdrückt; *(Psych)* verdrängt

repression [rɪˈpreʃən] N Unterdrückung *f*; *(Psych)* Verdrängung *f*

repressive [rɪˈpresɪv] ADJ repressiv

reprieve [rɪˈpriːv] N *(Jur)* Begnadigung *f*; *(= postponement)* Strafaufschub *m*; *(fig)* Gnadenfrist *f* VT **he was ~d** *(Jur)* er wurde begnadigt; *(= sentence was postponed)* seine Strafe wurde aufgeschoben; **the building/firm has been ~d for a while** das Gebäude/die Firma ist vorerst noch einmal verschont geblieben

reprimand [ˈreprɪmɑːnd] N Tadel *m*; *(official also)* Verweis *m* VT tadeln, maßregeln *(geh)*

reprint [ˌriːˈprɪnt] VT neu auflegen, neu abdrucken, nachdrucken N [ˈriːprɪnt] Neuauflage *f*, Nachdruck *m*

reprisal [rɪˈpraɪzəl] N *(for* gegen) Vergeltungsmaßnahme *f*; *(between companies, countries etc also)* Repressalie *f*; **to take ~s** zu Repressalien greifen; **as a ~ for** als Vergeltung für

reprivatization [ˈriːˌpraɪvətaɪˈzeɪʃən] N *(Econ)* Reprivatisierung *f*

reprivatize [ˌriːˈpraɪvətaɪz] VT *(Econ)* reprivatisieren

repro [ˈreprəʊ] N *(inf) abbr of* **reproduction** Repro *f or nt*

reproach [rɪˈprəʊtʃ] ✪ 26.3 N **a** *(= rebuke)* Vorwurf *m*; **to heap ~es on sb** jdn mit Vorwürfen überhäufen; **a term of ~** ein Vorwurf *m*; **a look of ~** ein vorwurfsvoller Blick; **above** *or* **beyond ~** über jeden Vorwurf erhaben **b** *(= discredit)* **to be a ~ to sb/sth** eine Schande für jdn/etw sein; **to bring ~ (up)on sb/sth** jdn/etw in schlechten Ruf bringen; **to bring ~ (up)on oneself** in schlechten Ruf kommen VT Vorwürfe machen *(+dat)*; **to ~ sb for his mistake** jdm einen Fehler vorwerfen; **to ~ sb for having done sth** jdm Vorwürfe dafür machen, dass er etw getan hat; **he has nothing to ~ himself for** *or* **with** er hat sich *(dat)* nichts vorzuwerfen

reproachful ADJ, **reproachfully** ADV [rɪˈprəʊtʃfʊl, -fəlɪ] vorwurfsvoll

reprobate [ˈreprəʊbeɪt] ADJ *action* ruchlos, verwerflich; *person* verkommen; *(Eccl)* verdammt N verkommenes Subjekt, Gestrauchelte(r) *mf (geh)*; *(Eccl)* Verdammte(r) *mf*

reprobation [ˌreprəʊˈbeɪʃən] N Verdammung *f*

reprocess [ˌriːˈprəʊses] VT wiederverwerten; *sewage, atomic waste, fuel* wiederaufbereiten

reprocessing [ˌriːˈprəʊsesɪŋ] N *(of nuclear waste)* Wiederaufbereitung *f*

reprocessing plant N Wiederaufbereitungsanlage *f*

reproduce [ˌriːprəˈdjuːs] VT **a** *(= copy)* wiedergeben; *(mechanically, electronically)* reproduzieren; *(Typ)* abdrucken **b** *(Biol)* **to ~ its kind** sich *or* seine Art fortpflanzen **c** *(Theat)* play neu inszenieren VI **a** *(Biol)* sich fortpflanzen *or* vermehren **b** *(Typ)* **this picture won't ~ well** dieses Bild lässt sich nicht gut reproduzieren

reproducible [ˌriːprəˈdjuːsɪbəl] ADJ reproduzierbar

reproduction [ˌriːprəˈdʌkʃən] N **a** *(= procreation)* Fortpflanzung *f* **b** *(= copying)* Reproduktion *f*; *(of documents)* Vervielfältigung *f*; **sound ~** Klang- *or* Tonwiedergabe *f*; **this radio has good ~** das Radio gibt den Ton gut wieder **c** *(= copy)* Reproduktion *f*; *(= photo)* Kopie *f*; *(= sound reproduction)* Wiedergabe *f*

reproduction furniture N (moderne) Stilmöbel *pl*

reproductive [ˌriːprəˈdʌktɪv] ADJ Fortpflanzungs-

reproductive organ N Fortpflanzungsorgan *nt*

reproof[1] [ˈriːˈpruːf] VT *garment* frisch *or* neu imprägnieren

reproof[2] [rɪˈpruːf] N Tadel *m*, Rüge *f*

reproval [rɪˈpruːvəl] N **a** *no pl (act)* Tadeln *nt*, Rügen *nt* **b** = **reproof**[2]

reprove [rɪˈpruːv] VT *person, action* tadeln, rügen

reproving ADJ, **reprovingly** ADV [rɪˈpruːvɪŋ, -lɪ] tadelnd

reptile [ˈreptaɪl] N Reptil *nt*, Kriechtier *nt*; *(fig pej)* Kriecher *m (pej)* ADJ Reptilien-, reptilartig; **~ house** Reptilienhaus *nt*; **~ species** Reptilienart *f*

reptilian [repˈtɪlɪən] ADJ reptilartig; *(fig pej)* kriecherisch *(pej)* N Reptil *nt*, Kriechtier *nt*

republic [rɪˈpʌblɪk] N Republik *f*

republican [rɪˈpʌblɪkən] ADJ republikanisch N Republikaner(in) *m(f)*

republicanism [rɪˈpʌblɪkənɪzəm] N Republikanismus *m*

republication [ˈriːˌpʌblɪˈkeɪʃən] N *(of book)* Wieder- *or* Neuveröffentlichung *f*; *(of banns)* erneutes Aushängen

republish [ˌriːˈpʌblɪʃ] VT *book* wieder *or* neu veröffentlichen *or* herausbringen; *banns* wieder aushängen

repudiate [rɪˈpjuːdɪeɪt] VT *person* verstoßen; *authorship, debt, obligation* nicht anerkennen; *accusation, remarks, charge* zurückweisen

repudiation [rɪˌpjuːdɪˈeɪʃən] N *(of person)* Verstoßung *f*; *(of authorship, debt, obligation)* Nichtanerkennung *f*; *(of accusation, remarks, charge)* Zurückweisung *f*

repugnance [rɪˈpʌgnəns] N Widerwille *m*, Abneigung *f (towards, for* gegen)

repugnant [rɪˈpʌgnənt] ADJ widerlich, abstoßend; *(stronger)* ekelerregend; **to be ~ to sb** jdm widerlich sein

repulse [rɪˈpʌls] VT *(Mil) enemy, attack* zurückschlagen, abwehren; *(fig) person, help, offer* abweisen, zurückweisen; **sb is ~d by sth** *(fig)* etw stößt jdn ab, jd findet etw widerwärtig N *(Mil)* Abwehr *f*, Zurückschlagen *nt*; *(fig)* Abweisung *f*, Zurückweisung *f*

repulsion [rɪˈpʌlʃən] N **a** *(= distaste)* Widerwille *m (for* gegen) **b** *(Phys)* Abstoßung *f*

repulsive [rɪˈpʌlsɪv] ADJ **a** *(= loathsome)* abstoßend, widerwärtig; **to be ~ to sb** für jdn abstoßend sein **b** *(Phys) forces* abstoßend, repulsiv

repulsively [rɪˈpʌlsɪvlɪ] ADV abstoßend, widerwärtig; **~ ugly** abstoßend hässlich

repulsiveness [rɪˈpʌlsɪvnɪs] N Widerwärtigkeit *f*

repurchase [ˌriːˈpɜːtʃɪs] N Rückkauf *m* VT zurückkaufen

reputability [ˌrepjʊtəˈbɪlɪtɪ] N Ansehen *nt*; *(of person also)* Ehrbarkeit *f (geh)*; *(of firm)* Seriosität *f*

reputable [ˈrepjʊtəbl] ADJ ehrenhaft; *person* angesehen; *occupation* ordentlich, anständig; *dealer, firm* seriös

reputably [ˈrepjʊtəblɪ] ADV *(= well)* ordentlich; *behave* ehrenhaft; *deal* seriös; **he is ~ established in the business world** er wird in der Geschäftswelt respektiert; **he is now ~ employed as a gardener** er hat jetzt eine seriöse Anstellung als Gärtner

reputation [ˌrepjʊˈteɪʃən] N Ruf *m*, Name *m*; *(= bad reputation)* schlechter Ruf; **what sort of ~ does she have?** wie ist ihr Ruf?; **he has a ~ for being ...** er hat den Ruf, ... zu sein; **to have a ~ for honesty** als ehrlich gelten; **you don't want to get (yourself) a ~, you know** du willst dich doch sicherlich nicht in Verruf bringen; **she was by ~ a good organizer** sie stand in dem Ruf, Organisationstalent zu haben; **to make a ~ for oneself** sich *(dat)* einen Namen machen

repute [rɪˈpjuːt] N Ruf *m*, Ansehen *nt*; **to know sb by ~** von jdm schon viel gehört haben; **to be of high ~** einen guten Ruf genießen; **a restaurant of ~** ein angesehenes Restaurant; **a house of ill ~** ein Haus von zweifelhaftem Ruf; **to be held in low ~** einen schlechten Ruf haben VT *(pass only)* **he is ~d to be ...** man sagt, dass er ... ist; **to be ~d to be rich** als reich gelten; **he is ~d to be the best** er gilt als der Beste, er steht in dem Ruf, der Beste zu sein

reputed [rɪˈpjuːtɪd] ADJ angenommen; **the ~ father** *(Jur)* der vermutliche Vater

reputedly [rɪˈpjuːtɪdlɪ] ADV wie man annimmt; **he is ~ the best player in the world** er gilt als der beste Spieler der Welt

request [rɪˈkwest] ✪ 10.1, 25.1 N Bitte *f*, Wunsch *m*, Ersuchen *nt (geh)*; **at sb's ~** auf jds Bitte *etc*; **on/by ~** auf Wunsch; **no parking by ~** bitte nicht parken; **to make a ~ for sth** um etw bitten; **I have a ~ to make of** *or* **to you** ich habe eine Bitte an Sie, ich muss eine Bitte an Sie richten; **(record) ~s** Plattenwünsche *pl* VT bitten um; *asylum also* nachsuchen um; *(Rad) record* sich *(dat)* wünschen; **to ~ silence** um Ruhe bitten *or* ersuchen *(geh)*; **to ~ sth of** *or* **from sb** jdn um etw bitten *or* ersuchen *(geh)*; **to ~ that ...** bitten, dass ...; **"you are ~ed not to smoke"** „bitte nicht rauchen" → **presence, pleasure**

request: **request programme**, *(US)* **request program** N *(Rad)* Wunschsendung *f*; **request stop** N *(Brit)* Bedarfshaltestelle *f*

requiem [ˈrekwɪem] N Requiem *nt*

requiem mass N Totenmesse *f*

require [rɪˈkwaɪəˈ] ✪ 20.4 VT **a** *(= need)* brauchen, benötigen; *work, action* erfordern; *(= desire)* wünschen, mögen; **I have all I ~** ich habe alles, was ich brauche; **the journey will ~ 3 hours** man braucht *or* benötigt 3 Stunden für die Reise; **it ~s great care** das erfordert große Sorgfalt; **it ~s repairing** es muss repariert werden; **what qualifications are ~d?** welche Qualifikationen werden verlangt *or* sind erforderlich?; **to be ~d to do sth** etw machen *or* tun müssen; **that is not ~d** das ist nicht nötig *or* erforderlich; **if you ~ me** wenn Sie mich benötigen; **if ~d** falls notwendig *or* erforderlich; **when (it is) ~d** auf Wunsch, wenn es gewünscht wird; **as and when ~d** nach Bedarf; **dilute as ~d** nach Bedarf verdünnen **b** *(= order)* verlangen; **to ~ sb to do sth** von jdm verlangen, dass er etw tut; **you are ~d to report to the boss immediately** Sie sollen sich sofort beim Chef melden; **to ~ sth of sb** etw von jdm verlangen; **as ~d by law** den gesetzlichen Bestimmungen gemäß *or* entsprechend

required [rɪˈkwaɪəd] ADJ erforderlich, notwendig; *date* vorgeschrieben; *(= desired)* gewünscht; **the ~ amount** die benötigte Menge

required reading N *(Sch, Univ)* Pflichtlektüre *f*

requirement [rɪˈkwaɪəmənt] N **a** *(= need)* Bedürfnis *nt*, Bedarf *m no pl*; *(= desire)* Wunsch *m*, Anspruch *m*; **to meet sb's ~s** jds Bedürfnisse erfüllen, jds Wünschen *(dat)* entsprechen, jds Ansprüchen *(dat)* gerecht werden; **there isn't enough bread to meet the ~** es ist nicht genügend Brot da, um den Bedarf zu decken **b** *(= condition, thing required)* Erfordernis *nt*; **to fit the ~s** den Erfordernissen entsprechen

requisite [ˈrekwɪzɪt] N Artikel *m*; *(= necessary thing)* Erfordernis *nt*; **travel ~s** Reiseartikel *pl or* -utensilien *pl* ADJ erforderlich, notwendig; **the ~ time** die dazu erforderliche Zeit

requisition [ˌrekwɪˈzɪʃən] N Anforderung *f*; *(= act: of objects)* Requisition *f*; **to make a ~ for sth** etw anfordern VT *sb's services* anfordern; *supplies, food* requirieren; *building* beschlagnahmen, requirieren

requital [rɪˈkwaɪtl] N *(= repayment)* Vergeltung *f*; *(= revenge also)* Rache *f*

requite [rɪˈkwaɪt] VT **a** *(= repay) person* es vergelten *(+dat)*; *action* vergelten; **~d love** erwiderte Liebe **b** *(= avenge) action* vergelten; *person* rächen

reran [ˌriːˈræn] *pret of* **rerun**

reread [ˌriːˈriːd] *pret, ptp* **reread** [ˌriːˈred] VT wieder *or* nochmals lesen

rerecord [ˌriːrɪˈkɔːd] VT *sound recording* überspielen; *(in recording studio)* mischen

reredos [ˈrɪədɒs] N Retabel *nt*

reroute [ˌriːˈruːt] VT *train, bus* umleiten; *electricity etc also* umlenken

rerun [ˌriːˈrʌn] *vb: pret* **reran**, *ptp* **rerun** VT *film* wieder *or* nochmals aufführen; *tape* wieder *or* nochmals abspielen; *race, elections, programme, event* wiederholen N [ˈriːrʌn] *(of film)* Wiederaufführung *f*; *(of tape)* Wiederabspielen *nt*; *(of race, election, programme, event)* Wiederholung *f*

resale [ˈriːseɪl] N Weiterverkauf *m*; **"not for ~"** „nicht zum Weiterverkauf bestimmt"; *(on free sample)* „unverkäufliches Muster"; **~ value** Wiederverkaufswert *m*

resale price maintenance N *(Brit)* Preisbindung *f*

resat [ˌriːˈsæt] *pret, ptp of* **resit**

reschedule [ˌriːˈskedʒʊəl, *(esp Brit)* ˌriːˈʃedjuːl] VT *meeting etc* neu ansetzen *or* festlegen; *date, appointment* verlegen, verschieben *(for* auf *+acc)*; *(Econ, Fin)* die Rückzahlungsmodalitäten ändern für

rescind [rɪˈsɪnd] VT *decision* rückgängig machen, widerrufen; *judgement, contract also* annullieren; *law, act* aufheben

rescission [ˌriːˈsɪʒən] N *(esp Jur, of judgement, law, decision)* Aufhebung *f*, Annullierung *f*; *(of contract etc)* Rücktritt *m* (of von); *(of purchase)* Rückgängigmachung *f*

rescue [ˈreskjuː] **N** *(= saving)* Rettung *f*; *(= freeing)* Errettung *f*, Befreiung *f*; **~ was difficult** die Rettung war schwierig; **to go/come to sb's ~** jdm zu Hilfe kommen; **to the ~!** zu Hilfe!; **it was Bob to the ~** Bob war unsere/seine *etc* Rettung; **~ attempt/operation/party** Rettungsversuch *m*/-aktion *f*/-mannschaft *f* → **air-sea rescue** **VT** *(= save)* retten; *(= free)* erretten, befreien; **you ~d me from a difficult situation** du hast mich aus einer schwierigen Lage gerettet; **the ~d were taken to hospital** die Geretteten wurden ins Krankenhaus gebracht

rescuer [ˈreskjʊəˈ] N *(who saves sb)* Retter(in) *m(f)*; *(who frees sb)* Befreier(in) *m(f)*

rescue services PL Rettungsdienst *m*

rescue worker N Bergungsarbeiter(in) *m(f)*, Rettungsarbeiter(in) *m(f)*

research [rɪˈsɜːtʃ] **N** Forschung *f* *(into, on* über *+acc)*; **a piece of ~** eine Forschungsarbeit; **to do ~** forschen, Forschung betreiben; **to carry out ~ into the effects of sth** Forschungen über die Auswirkungen einer Sache *(gen)* anstellen **VI** forschen, Forschung betreiben; **to ~ into** *or* **on sth** etw erforschen, über etw *(acc)* forschen *or* Forschung betreiben **VT** erforschen, untersuchen; **a well-~ed book** ein Buch, das auf solider Forschungsarbeit beruht; *(journalistic investigation)* ein gut recherchiertes Buch

research *in cpds* Forschungs-; **research assistant** N wissenschaftlicher Assistent, wissenschaftliche Assistentin; **research budget** N Forschungsetat *m*

research centre, research center N Forschungszentrum *nt*

researcher [rɪˈsɜːtʃəˈ] N Forscher(in) *m(f)*

research: research establishment N Forschungsstätte *f*; **research fellow** N *(Univ)* Forschungsstipendiat(in) *m(f)*; **research fellowship** N Forschungsstipendium *nt*; **research student** N *(Univ)* *Student, der Forschungen für einen höheren akademischen Grad betreibt*, ≈ Doktorand(in) *m(f)*; **research worker** N Forscher(in) *m(f)*

reseat [ˌriːˈsiːt] VT **a** *chair* einen neuen Sitz geben *(+dat)*; *trousers* einen neuen Hosenboden anfertigen für **b** *(Tech) valve* neu einschleifen **c** *person* umsetzen; **when everyone was ~ed** *(= had sat down again)* als sich alle wieder gesetzt hatten

resection [riːˈsekʃən] N **a** *(Med)* Resektion *f* **b** *(Surv)* Triangulation *f*

reselect [riːsɪˈlekt] VT *(Pol)* wieder aufstellen

reselection [riːsɪˈlekʃən] N *no pl (Pol)* Wiederaufstellung *f*

resell [ˌriːˈsel] VT weiterverkaufen, wieder verkaufen

reseller [ˌriːˈseləˈ] N Wiederverkäufer(in) *m(f)*

resemblance [rɪˈzembləns] ✪ 5.3 N Ähnlichkeit *f*; **to bear a strong/a faint/no ~ to sb/sth** starke/leichte/keine Ähnlichkeit mit jdm/etw haben; **there's no ~ between them** es besteht keine Ähnlichkeit zwischen ihnen, sie sind sich *(dat)* nicht ähnlich

resemble [rɪˈzembl] VT ähneln, gleichen; **they ~ each other** sie ähneln *or* gleichen sich *(dat)* *or* einander

resent [rɪˈzent] VT *remarks, behaviour* übel nehmen, sich ärgern über *(+acc)*; *person* ein Ressentiment haben gegen; **he ~ed her for the rest of his life** er nahm ihr das sein Leben lang übel; **he ~ed my having** *or* **me for having got the job** er nahm es mir übel, dass ich die Stelle bekommen hatte; **he ~ed the fact that ...** er ärgerte sich darüber, dass ...; **they ~ed the way in which ...** sie ärgerten sich darüber, wie ... *or* auf welche Art und Weise ...; **to ~ sb's success** jdm seinen Erfolg missgönnen; **I ~ that** das gefällt mir nicht; **he may ~ my** *or* **me being here** es könnte ihn ärgern, dass ich hier bin

resentful [rɪˈzentfʊl] ADJ *person, look* verärgert; *(= jealous)* voller Ressentiments (of gegen); **to be ~ at** *or* **about** *or* **of sth/of sb** über etw/jdn verärgert sein, sich über etw/jdn ärgern; **to be ~ of sb's success** jdm seinen Erfolg nicht gönnen; **~ of the criticisms levelled at him** die an ihm geübte Kritik übel nehmend; **he felt ~ about her promotion** er nahm es ihr übel, dass sie befördert worden war; **to feel ~ toward(s) sb for doing sth** es jdm übel nehmen, dass er/sie *etc* etw getan hat; **he felt ~ toward(s) her for not inviting him to the party** er nahm es ihr übel, dass sie ihn nicht zu der Party eingeladen hatte

resentfully [rɪˈzentfəlɪ] ADV *say* ärgerlich; *look* verärgert, wütend; *behave* verärgert

resentment [rɪˈzentmənt] N Ärger *m no pl*, Groll *m no pl* (of über *+acc*)

reservation [ˌrezəˈveɪʃən] N **a** *(= qualification of opinion)* Vorbehalt *m*; *(Philos)* Mentalreservation *f (spec)*; **without ~** ohne Vorbehalt, vorbehaltlos; **with ~s** unter Vorbehalt(en); **to have ~s about sb/sth** Bedenken in Bezug auf jdn/etw haben **b** *(= booking)* Reservierung *f*; **to make a ~ at the hotel/on the boat** ein Zimmer im Hotel/einen Platz auf dem Schiff reservieren lassen; **how many ~s did you make?** für wie viele Personen haben Sie reservieren lassen?; **to have a ~ (for a room)** ein Zimmer reserviert haben **c** *(= area of land)* Reservat *nt*, Reservation *f*; **(central) ~** *(Brit: on motorway)* Mittelstreifen *m*

reservation number N Reservierungsnummer *f*

reservation(s) desk N Reservierungsschalter *m*

reserve [rɪˈzɜːv] ✪ 21.3 **VT** **a** *(= keep)* aufsparen, aufheben; **to ~ judgement/one's decision** mit einem Urteil/seiner Entscheidung zurückhalten; **to ~ the right to do sth** sich *(dat)* (das Recht) vorbehalten, etw zu tun; **to ~ oneself for sth** sich für etw schonen
b *(= book in advance: client)* reservieren lassen; **the lady at the box office ~d 4 seats for us** die Dame an der Kasse hat uns 4 Plätze reserviert; **are you reserving these seats for anyone?** haben Sie diese Plätze für jemanden reserviert?
N **a** *(= store)* *(of* an *+dat)* Reserve *f*, Vorrat *m*; *(Fin)* Reserve *f*; **to have great ~s of energy** große Kraftreserven haben; **cash ~** Barreserve *f*; **world ~s of copper** die Weltkupferreserven *pl*, die Weltreserven *pl* an Kupfer; **to have/keep sth in ~** etw in Reserve haben/halten
b **without ~** ohne Vorbehalt, vorbehaltlos; **with great ~** unter *or* mit starken Vorbehalten
c = **reserve price**
d *(= piece of land)* Reservat *nt*, Reservation *f*
e *(= coolness, reticence)* Reserve *f*, Zurückhaltung *f*; **he treated me with some ~** er behandelte mich etwas reserviert
f *(Mil: = force)* Reserve *f*; *(= soldier)* Soldat(in) *m(f)* der Reserve; **the ~s** die Reserveeinheiten
g *(Sport)* Reservespieler(in) *m(f)*

reserve *in cpds* Reserve-; **reserve currency** N Reservewährung *f*

reserved [rɪˈzɜːvd] ADJ **a** *(= reticent)* zurückhaltend, reserviert (*about* in Bezug auf *+acc*) **b** *room, seat* reserviert, belegt **c** *(Publishing)* **all rights ~** alle Rechte vorbehalten

reservedly [rɪˈzɜːvɪdlɪ] ADV zurückhaltend, reserviert

reserve: reserve fund N Rücklage *f*, Reservefonds *m*; **reserve holdings** PL *(Fin)* Währungsreserven *pl*; **reserve list** N *(Brit Mil)* Reserveliste *f*; **reserve player** N Reservespieler(in) *m(f)*; **reserve price** N *(Brit)* Mindest- *or* Ausrufpreis *m*; **reserve tank** N Reservetank *m*; **reserve team** N Reserve(mannschaft) *f*

reservist [rɪˈzɜːvɪst] N *(Mil)* Reservist(in) *m(f)*

reservoir [ˈrezəvwɑːˈ] N *(lit, for water)* Reservoir *nt*; *(for gas)* Speicher *m*; *(fig, of knowledge, facts, talent etc)* Fundgrube *f*

reset [ˌriːˈset] *pret, ptp* **reset** VT **a** *precious stone* neu (ein)fassen; *watch* neu stellen (*to* auf *+acc*); *(for summer time etc)* umstellen (*for* auf *+acc*); *body clock* umstellen; *dial, gauge* zurückstellen (*to* auf *+acc*); *machine* neu *or* wieder einstellen; *(Comput)* rücksetzen; **~ switch** *or* **button** *(Comput)* Resettaste *f*; *(Typ) text* neu setzen **b** *(Med) limb, bone* wieder einrichten; *dislocated shoulder* wieder einrenken

resettle [ˌriːˈsetl] VT *refugees* umsiedeln; *land* neu *or* wieder besiedeln

resettlement [ˌriːˈsetlmənt] N *(of refugees)* Umsiedlung *f*; *(of land)* Neubesied(e)lung *f*

reshape [ˌriːˈʃeɪp] VT *dough, clay etc* umformen, neu formen; *text* umschreiben; *team* umgestalten; *policy* umstellen; **you can't ~ your body overnight** man kann nicht plötzlich eine andere Figur bekommen; **to ~ itself** *(party)* sich neu formieren

reship [ˌriːˈʃɪp] VT *goods* wieder verschiffen; *(= transfer)* umladen (*to* auf *+acc*)

reshuffle [ˌriːˈʃʌfl] **VT** *cards* neu mischen; *(fig) Cabinet* umbilden; *board of directors* umbilden, umbesetzen **N** *(of cards)* erneutes Mischen; *(fig: of board)* Umbesetzung *f*, Umbildung *f*; **cabinet ~** *(Brit Pol)* Kabinettsumbildung *f*

reside [rɪˈzaɪd] VI **a** *(form: = live)* seinen Wohnsitz haben; *(monarch, ambassador etc)* residieren **b** *(fig form)* **to ~ in sth** in etw *(dat)* liegen; **the power ~s with the President** die Macht liegt *or* ruht beim Präsidenten

residence [ˈrezɪdəns] N **a** *(= house)* Wohnhaus *nt*; *(= hostel: for students, nurses)* Wohnheim *nt*; *(of monarch, ambassador etc)* Residenz *f*; **the President's official ~** der Amtssitz des Präsidenten → **hall**
b *no pl (= stay, living)* **country of ~** Aufenthaltsland *nt*; **place of ~** Wohnort *m*; **after 5 years' ~ in Britain** nach 5 Jahren Aufenthalt in Großbritannien; **to take up ~ in the capital** sich in der Hauptstadt niederlassen; **~ in the country is restricted to nationals** nur Staatsangehörige können im Land Wohnsitz nehmen *(form)*; **to be in ~** *(monarch, governor etc)* anwesend sein; **poet** *etc* **in ~** *(Univ)* ansässiger Dichter *etc*; **the students are now in ~** das Semester hat angefangen

residence permit N Aufenthaltsgenehmigung *f*

residency [ˈrezɪdənsɪ] N **a** *(US)* = **residence b** **b** *(Brit)* Residenz *f* **c** *(of doctor)* Assistenzzeit *f* im Krankenhaus

resident [ˈrezɪdənt] **N** **a** Bewohner(in) *m(f)*; *(in town)* Einwohner(in) *m(f)*; *(of hospital)* Patient(in) *m(f)*; *(of prison)* Insasse *m*, Insassin *f*; *(in hotel)* Gast *m*; **"access restricted to ~s only"** „Anlieger frei"; **"parking for ~s only"** „Parkplatz nur für Mieter"; *(on road)* „Parken nur für Anlieger gestattet"; *(at hotel)* „Parkplatz nur für Gäste"
b *(= doctor)* Anstaltsarzt *m*/-ärztin *f*
ADJ **a** *(in country, town)* wohnhaft; *(= attached to institution)* ansässig, Haus-; *(Comput)* resident; **they are ~ in Germany** sie haben ihren Wohnsitz in Deutschland; **the ~ population** die ansässige Bevölkerung; **are you ~ in the hotel?** sind Sie Hotelgast/Hotelgäste?; **she is our ~ expert on ...** *(hum)* sie ist unsere Expertin vor Ort für ...
b *(Zool) fox, badger etc* ortsansässig; **the ~ population** die ortsansässige Population
c *(fig form)* **to be ~ in sth** = **reside b**

residential [ˌrezɪˈdenʃəl] ADJ *job* im Haus; *college* mit einem Wohnheim verbunden; **~ requirements for voting** Meldevoraussetzungen zur Ausübung des Wahlrechts; **~ accommodation** Unterbringung *f* im Heim; **~ customer** *(for utilities)* Privathaushalt *m*; **~ development** Wohnungsbau *m*; **~ market** Häuser- und Wohnungsmarkt *m*, nichtgewerblicher Immobilienmarkt; **~ mortgage** Hypothek *f* für Wohneigentum; **~ property** Wohngebäude *nt*; **~ street** Wohnstraße *f*

residential: residential area N Wohngebiet *nt*, Wohngegend *f*; **residential care** N Heimpflege *f*; **residential home** N Wohnheim *nt*; *(= superior home)* Wohnstift *nt*

residents association N *(of area)* Bürgerinitiative *f*

residual [rɪˈzɪdjʊəl] ADJ restlich; *(Chem)* rückständig; ~ **soil** *(Geol)* Alluvialboden *m*; *(by erosion)* Verwitterungsboden *m*; ~ **risk** Restrisiko *nt*; ~ **income** *(Brit)* Nettoeinkommen *nt*; ~ **current device** *(Elec)* Unterbrecher *m*, Trennschalter *m* N ~**s** *(= royalties)* Wiederholungsgage *f*

residuary [rɪˈzɪdjʊərɪ] ADJ restlich; *(Chem)* rückständig

residue [ˈrezɪdjuː] N a Rest *m*; *(Chem)* Rückstand *m* b *(Jur)* Nachlass *m (nach Abzug sämtlicher Verbindlichkeiten)*

residuum [rɪˈzɪdjʊəm] N *(Chem)* Rückstand *m*, Residuum *nt*

resign [rɪˈzaɪn] VT a *(= give up) office, post* zurücktreten von, abgeben; *claim, rights* aufgeben, verzichten auf *(+acc)*; **to ~ one's commission** *(Mil)* seinen Abschied nehmen
b **to ~ oneself to sth** sich mit etw abfinden; **to ~ oneself to doing sth** sich damit abfinden, etw zu tun → *also* **resigned**
VI *(from public appointment, committee)* zurücktreten; *(employee)* kündigen; *(civil servant, clergyman)* sein Amt niederlegen; *(teacher)* aus dem Dienst ausscheiden; **to ~ from office** sein Amt niederlegen; **he ~ed from (his job with) "The Times"** er hat (seine Stelle) bei der „Times" gekündigt; **the Prime Minister was forced to ~** der Premierminister wurde zum Rücktritt gezwungen; **to ~ to the inevitable** sich in das Unvermeidliche fügen

resignation [ˌrezɪgˈneɪʃən] N a *(from public appointment, committee)* Rücktritt *m*; *(of employee)* Kündigung *f*; *(of civil servant, clergyman)* Amtsniederlegung *f*; *(of teacher)* Ausscheiden *nt* aus dem Dienst; **to hand in** *or* **tender** *(form)* **one's ~** seinen Rücktritt/seine Kündigung einreichen/sein Amt niederlegen/aus dem Dienst ausscheiden b *(= mental state)* Resignation *f* *(to* gegenüber *+dat)*, Ergebung *f* *(to* in *+acc)* c *(form, of right, claim etc)* Verzicht *m* (of auf *+acc)*

resigned [rɪˈzaɪnd] ADJ *person* resigniert; **to become ~ to sth** sich mit etw abfinden; **I was ~ to walking, when ...** ich hatte mich schon damit abgefunden, zu Fuß gehen zu müssen, als ...; **to be ~ to one's fate** sich in sein Schicksal ergeben haben; **to give a ~ shrug** resigniert die *or* mit den Achseln zucken

resignedly [rɪˈzaɪnɪdlɪ] ADV resigniert

resilience [rɪˈzɪlɪəns] N a *(of material)* Federn *nt* b *(fig, of person, nature)* Unverwüstlichkeit *f*; *(of economy)* Stabilität *f*

resilient [rɪˈzɪlɪənt] ADJ a *material* federnd *attr*; **to be ~** federn b *(fig) person, nature* unverwüstlich; *economy* nicht krisenanfällig, stabil; *(Comm) performance* robust

resin [ˈrezɪn] N Harz *nt*

resinous [ˈrezɪnəs] ADJ harzig

resist [rɪˈzɪst] VT a *(= oppose)* sich widersetzen *(+dat)*; *arrest, sb's advances, enemy, attack* Widerstand leisten gegen, sich wehren gegen; *demand* sich wehren gegen; *(fig) proposal, change also* sich widersetzen *(+dat)*, sich sträuben *or* wehren gegen
b *temptation, sb, sb's charms, urge, impulse* widerstehen *(+dat)*; **I couldn't ~ (eating) another piece of cake** ich konnte der Versuchung nicht widerstehen, noch ein Stück Kuchen zu essen
c *(wall, door)* standhalten *(+dat)*; **the lock ~ed my attempts at opening it** das Schloss widerstand meinen Versuchen, es zu öffnen; **to ~ corrosion** korrosionsbeständig sein
VI a *(= be opposed)* sich widersetzen; *(faced with arrest, sb's advances, enemy, attack)* Widerstand leisten, sich wehren; *(fig, faced with proposal, change also)* sich sträuben *or* wehren
b *(faced with temptation, sb, sb's charms)* widerstehen
c *(wall, door)* standhalten

resistance [rɪˈzɪstəns] N *(to* gegen) Widerstand *m (also Elec, Phys, Mil)*; *(Med)* Widerstandsfähigkeit *f*, Resistenz *f (geh)*; ~ **to water/heat** Wasser-/Hitzebeständigkeit *f*; **to meet with ~** auf Widerstand stoßen; **to offer no ~ (to sb/sth)** *(to attacker, advances etc)* (jdm/gegen etw) keinen Widerstand leisten; *(to proposals)* sich (jdm/einer Sache) nicht widersetzen; **the (French) Resistance** *(Hist)* die Résistance; **the Resistance movement** *(Hist)* die Résistance → **line**[1], **passive resistance**

resistance fighter N Widerstandskämpfer(in) *m(f)*

resistant [rɪˈzɪstənt] ADJ *material, surface* strapazierfähig; *(Med)* immun *(to* gegen)

resister [rɪˈzɪstəʳ] N Wehrdienstverweigerer *m*

resistor [rɪˈzɪstəʳ] N *(Elec)* Widerstand *m*

resit [ˌriːˈsɪt] *vb: pret, ptp* **resat** *(Brit)* VT *exam* wiederholen VI die Prüfung wiederholen N [ˈriːsɪt] Wiederholung(sprüfung) *f*

resize [ˌriːˈsaɪz] VT *(Comput) window* die Größe *(+gen)* verändern

reskill [ˌriːˈskɪl] *(Ind)* VI umgeschult werden, sich umschulen lassen VT umschulen

resole [ˌriːˈsəʊl] VT neu besohlen

resolute [ˈrezəluːt] ADJ energisch, entschlossen; *answer, refusal* entschieden, bestimmt; **to take ~ action** energisch vorgehen; **to be ~ in sth** entschieden in etw *(dat)* sein; **to be ~ in doing sth** etw mit Entschlossenheit tun

resolutely [ˈrezəluːtlɪ] ADV *resist* entschieden; *refuse, answer also* bestimmt; *stare* entschlossen; *stride* entschlossen, resolut; **to be ~ opposed to sth** entschieden gegen etw sein; **to remain ~ committed to sth** sich weiterhin entschieden *or* entschlossen für etw einsetzen; **to stand ~ against sth** sich entschieden *or* entschlossen gegen etw wehren

resoluteness [ˈrezəluːtnɪs] N Entschlossenheit *f*; *(of refusal, answer)* Entschiedenheit *f*, Bestimmtheit *f*

resolution [ˌrezəˈluːʃən] ✪ 8.1 N a *(= decision)* Beschluss *m*; *(esp Pol)* Resolution *f*; *(governing one's behaviour)* Vorsatz *m*; **good ~s** gute Vorsätze *pl* b *no pl (= resoluteness)* Entschlossenheit *f*, Bestimmtheit *f* c *no pl (= solving: of problem, puzzle)* Lösung *f* d *(Comput)* Auflösung *f* e *(Phys, Mus)* Auflösung *f* *(into* in *+acc)* f *(Med, of swelling)* Rückgang *m*

resolvable [rɪˈzɒlvəbl] ADJ a *problem, conflict, crisis* lösbar; *doubt* zerstreubar; **a dispute/an issue which is not ~** ein Streit *m*, der nicht beigelegt/ein Thema *nt*, das nicht geklärt werden kann b *(into elements)* zerlegbar; *(= convertible)* auflösbar

resolve [rɪˈzɒlv] VT a *problem, conflict, crisis* lösen; *doubt* zerstreuen; *dispute* beilegen; *differences, issue* klären
b *(= decide)* **to ~ that ...** beschließen, dass ...; **to ~ to do sth** beschließen, etw zu tun
c *(= break up: into elements)* zerlegen *(into* in *+acc)*; *(= convert)* auflösen *(also Phys)* *(into* in *+acc)*
d *(Mus) chord, harmony* auflösen *(into* in *+acc)*
e *(Med)* zum Rückgang bringen
VI a *(= decide)* **to ~ (up)on sth** etw beschließen
b *(into* in *+acc) (= break up)* zerfallen; *(= be converted)* sich auflösen
VR *(into* in *+acc)* sich zerlegen lassen; *(= be converted)* sich auflösen
N a *(= decision)* Beschluss *m*; **to make a ~ to do sth** den Beschluss fassen, etw zu tun
b *no pl (= resoluteness)* Entschlossenheit *f*; **to do sth with ~** etw fest entschlossen tun

resolved [rɪˈzɒlvd] ADJ (fest) entschlossen

resolvedly [rɪˈzɒlvɪdlɪ] ADV (fest) entschlossen, entschieden

resonance [ˈrezənəns] N a Resonanz *f*; *(of voice)* voller Klang b *(fig)* **to have ~ for sb** für jdn von Bedeutung sein

resonant [ˈrezənənt] ADJ a *sound* voll; *voice* klangvoll; *laugh* schallend; *room* mit Resonanz; **~ with the sound of singing/a thousand voices** von Gesang/vom Klang von tausend Stimmen erfüllt b *(fig)* **to be ~ of sth** an etw *(acc)* erinnern; **to be ~ with tradition/history** reich an Tradition/Geschichte sein

resonate [ˈrezəneɪt] VI a widerhallen b *(fig)* **to ~ with sth** reich an etw *(dat)* sein; **that ~s with me** das bedeutet mir etwas

resonator [ˈrezəneɪtəʳ] N Resonator *m*

resorb [rɪˈzɔːb] VT resorbieren *(spec)*, (wieder) aufsaugen

resort [rɪˈzɔːt] N a *(= recourse)* Ausweg *m*; *(= thing, action resorted to)* Rettung *f*, Ausweg *m*; **without ~ to violence** ohne Gewaltanwendung; **as a last ~** als Letztes; **in the last ~** im schlimmsten Fall, wenn alle Stricke reißen *(inf)*; **you were my last ~** du warst meine letzte Rettung
b *(= place)* Urlaubsort *m*; **coastal ~** Seebad *nt*; **seaside ~** Seebad *nt*; **summer ~** Sommerurlaubsort *m*; **winter sports ~** Wintersportort *m* → **health resort, holiday resort**
VI a *(= have recourse)* **to ~ to sth** zu etw greifen; **to ~ to sb** sich an jdn wenden; **to ~ to violence** Gewalt anwenden, gewalttätig werden; **to ~ to begging/stealing/swearing** sich aufs Betteln/Stehlen/Fluchen verlegen
b *(= frequent)* **to ~ to a place** häufig an einem Ort verkehren

resound [rɪˈzaʊnd] VI (wider)hallen *(with* von); **my ears were still ~ing with the noise** mir tönten noch die Ohren von dem Lärm; **his name ~ed throughout the land** *(fig)* sein Name war in aller Munde

resounding [rɪˈzaʊndɪŋ] ADJ *noise, shout, thud, crack* widerhallend; *laugh, voice* schallend; *(fig) triumph, victory, failure* gewaltig; *success* durchschlagend; *defeat* haushoch; **~ silence** überwältigende Stille; **the response was a ~ "no"** die Antwort war ein überwältigendes „Nein"

resoundingly [rɪˈzaʊndɪŋlɪ] ADV a *(= convincingly) defeat* vernichtend; **to be ~ defeated** eine vernichtende Niederlage erleiden; **the play was ~ successful** das Stück war ein durchschlagender Erfolg b *(= loudly)* schallend

resource [rɪˈsɔːs] a N **resources** PL *(= wealth, supplies, money etc)* Mittel *pl*, Ressourcen *pl*; **financial ~s** Geldmittel *pl*; **mineral ~s** Bodenschätze *pl*; **natural ~s** Naturschätze *pl*; **human ~s** *(= workforce)* Arbeitskräfte *pl*; **~s in men and materials** Reserven *pl* an Menschen und Material; **he has no inner ~s** er weiß sich *(dat)* nie zu helfen; **he has no ~s against boredom** er weiß sich *(dat)* gegen Langeweile nicht zu helfen; **left to his own ~s** sich *(dat)* selbst überlassen b *(= expedient)* Ausweg *m*, Mittel *nt*; **as a last ~** als letzter Ausweg; **you are my last ~** du bist meine letzte Rettung
VT *(Brit) project* mit den nötigen Mitteln *or* Ressourcen versorgen, finanzieren; *(with personnel)* personell ausstatten

resourced [rɪˈsɔːst] ADJ *(Brit)* **well-~** *(with materials)* gut ausgestattet; *(financially)* ausreichend finanziert; **under-~** *(with materials)* unzureichend ausgestattet; *(financially)* unzureichend finanziert; **the museum has always been under-~ in both staff and finances** das Museum hatte immer schon zu wenig Personal und Geld

resourceful [rɪˈsɔːsfʊl] ADV *person* einfallsreich, findig; *scheme* genial

resourcefully [rɪˈsɔːsfəlɪ] ADV einfallsreich, findig

resourcefulness [rɪˈsɔːsfʊlnɪs] N Einfallsreichtum *m*, Findigkeit *f*; *(of scheme)* Genialität *f*

resourcing [rɪˈsɔːsɪŋ] N *no pl* Verfügbarmachen *nt* von Ressourcen

respect [rɪˈspekt] ✪ 11.3 N a *(= esteem)* Respekt *m*, Achtung *f* *(for* vor *+dat)*; **to have/show ~ for** Respekt *or* Achtung haben/zeigen vor *(+dat)*; *for the law* achten; **I have the highest ~ for his ability** ich halte ihn für außerordentlich fähig; **to behave with ~** sich respektvoll verhalten; **to hold sb in (great) ~** jdn (sehr) achten; **he commands ~** er ist eine Respektsperson *or (public figure)* Respekt gebietende Persönlichkeit; **to command the ~ of the nation** dem

Volk Respekt *or* Achtung abnötigen; **you should have a bit more ~ for his right hook** du solltest etwas mehr auf seinen rechten Haken achten
b *(= consideration)* Rücksicht *f (for* auf *+acc)*; **to treat with ~** *(person)* rücksichtsvoll behandeln; *dangerous person etc* sich in Acht nehmen vor *(+dat)*; *toys, clothes etc* schonend behandeln; **nitroglycerine should be treated with ~** Nitroglyzerin muss mit äußerster Vorsicht behandelt werden; **she has** *or* **shows no ~ for other people's feelings** sie nimmt keine Rücksicht auf die Gefühle anderer; **out of ~ for** aus Rücksicht auf *(+acc)*; **with (due) ~, I still think that ...** bei allem Respekt, meine ich dennoch, dass ...
c *(= reference)* **with ~ to ..., in ~ of ...** was ... anbetrifft, in Bezug auf ... *(+acc)*
d *(= aspect)* Hinsicht *f*, Beziehung *f*; **in some/other ~s** in gewisser/anderer Hinsicht *or* Beziehung; **in many ~s** in vieler Hinsicht; **in this ~** in dieser Hinsicht *or* Beziehung; **in what ~?** in welcher Hinsicht *or* Beziehung?
e respects PL *(= regards)* Empfehlungen *pl (geh)*, Grüße *pl*; **to pay one's ~s to sb** jdm seine Aufwartung machen; **give my ~s to** meine Empfehlung an *(+acc) (geh)*; **to pay one's last ~s to sb** jdm die letzte Ehre erweisen
VT **a** *(= show respect for)* respektieren; *person, customs, the law, privacy, rights* respektieren, achten; *ability* anerkennen; **a ~ed company** eine angesehene Firma
b as ~s ... was ... anbelangt *or* betrifft

respectability [rɪˌspektəˈbɪlɪtɪ] N *(= estimable quality, of person)* Ehrbarkeit *f*; *(of motives also)* Ehrenhaftigkeit *f*; *(= decent quality: of life, district, club)* Anständigkeit *f*; *(= socially approved quality, of person)* Angesehenheit *f*; *(of businessman, hotel)* Seriosität *f*; *(of clothes, behaviour)* Korrektheit *f*, Anständigkeit *f*

respectable [rɪˈspektəbl] ADJ **a** *(= estimable) person* ehrbar; *motives* ehrbar, ehrenhaft; *(= decent) life, district, club* anständig; *(= socially approved) person* angesehen, geachtet; *businessman, hotel* seriös; *clothes, behaviour* korrekt, anständig; **they are very ~ people** sie sind sehr ehrbare Leute; **he was outwardly ~ but ...** er wirkte sehr ehrbar, aber ...; **in ~ society** in guter Gesellschaft; **young people from ~ homes** junge Leute aus gutem Hause; **a perfectly ~ way to earn one's living** eine völlig akzeptable Art und Weise, seinen Lebensunterhalt zu verdienen; **the ~ face of capitalism** das ehrbare Gesicht des Kapitalismus; **that's not ~** das schickt *or* gehört sich nicht
b *(= large) size, income, sum* ansehnlich, beachtlich
c *(= fairly good) advantage* beträchtlich; *score, lead* beachtlich; **a ~ writer** ein ganz ordentlicher Schriftsteller; **she finished a ~ fourth** sie belegte einen beachtlichen *or* respektablen vierten Platz

respectably [rɪˈspektəblɪ] ADV **a** *dress, behave* anständig; **I'm a ~ married man** ich bin ein anständig verheirateter Mann **b** *(= fairly well)* **she finished ~ (in the race)** sie erzielte (im Rennen) ein beachtliches *or* respektables Ergebnis

respecter [rɪˈspektəʳ] N **the law is no ~ of persons** vor dem Gesetz sind alle gleich; **this disease is no ~ of persons** diese Krankheit macht vor niemandem halt; **he is no ~ of persons** er lässt sich von niemandem beeindrucken; **death is no ~ of wealth** der Tod nimmt keine Rücksicht auf Reichtum

respectful [rɪˈspektfʊl] ADJ respektvoll *(towards* gegenüber); **to be ~ of sth** etw respektieren; **to keep a ~ silence** respektvoll schweigen; **to follow sb at a ~ distance** jdm in angemessenem Abstand folgen

respectfully [rɪˈspektfəlɪ] ADV **a** respektvoll **b** *(in letters)* **I remain ~ yours** *or* **yours ~** ich verbleibe mit vorzüglicher Hochachtung Ihr ... *(form)*

respectfulness [rɪˈspektfʊlnɪs] N Respekt *m*; **~ of others** Rücksicht *f* auf andere

respecting [rɪˈspektɪŋ] PREP bezüglich *(+gen)*

respective [rɪˈspektɪv] ADJ jeweilig; **we took our ~ partners/glasses** wir nahmen jeder unseren Partner/unser Glas, wir nahmen unsere jeweiligen Partner/Gläser; **they each have their ~ merits** jeder von ihnen hat seine eigenen Vorteile

respectively [rɪˈspektɪvlɪ] ADV beziehungsweise; **the girls' dresses are green and blue ~** die Mädchen haben grüne beziehungsweise blaue Kleider; **and then allocate the funds ~** und die Mittel dann dementsprechend verteilen

respiration [ˌrespɪˈreɪʃən] N *(Bot, Med)* Atmung *f*

respirator [ˈrespɪreɪtəʳ] N *(Med)* Respirator *m*; *(Mil)* Atemschutzmaske *f*

respiratory [rɪˈspɪrətərɪ] ADJ Atem-, respiratorisch *(spec)*; *infection, disease* der Atemwege; **~ problems** Atembeschwerden *pl*

respiratory: **respiratory failure** N respiratorische Insuffizienz *(spec)*; **respiratory organs** PL Atmungsorgane *pl*; **respiratory system** N Atmungssystem *nt*; **respiratory tract** N Atemwege *pl*

respire [rɪˈspaɪəʳ] VTI *(Med, form)* atmen, respirieren *(spec)*

respite [ˈrespaɪt] N **a** *(= rest)* Ruhepause *f (from* von); *(= easing off)* Nachlassen *nt*; **without (a) ~** ohne Unterbrechung *or* Pause **b** *(= reprieve)* Aufschub *m*

resplendence [rɪˈsplendəns] N *(of person)* Glanz *m*, Strahlen *nt*; *(of clothes)* Pracht *f*

resplendent [rɪˈsplendənt] ADJ *person, face* glänzend, strahlend; *clothes* prächtig; **there he was, ~ in his new uniform** da war er, in seiner funkelnden neuen Uniform; **the stage, ~ in blue and gold** die Bühne in einer Pracht von Gold- und Blautönen

resplendently [rɪˈsplendəntlɪ] ADV prächtig

respond [rɪˈspɒnd] VI **a** *(= reply)* antworten; **to ~ to a question** eine Frage beantworten, auf eine Frage antworten *or* erwidern; **to ~ to a toast** einen Toast erwidern
b *(= show reaction)* *(to* auf *+acc)* reagieren; *(brakes, meter)* reagieren, ansprechen; **to ~ to an appeal** einen Appell beantworten; **to ~ to an appeal for money** einem Spendenaufruf folgen; **they ~ed well to the appeal for money** der Spendenaufruf fand ein großes Echo; **to ~ to a call** einem Ruf folgen; **the patient did not ~ to the treatment/his mother's voice** der Patient sprach auf die Behandlung nicht an/reagierte nicht auf die Stimme seiner Mutter; **the illness ~ed to treatment** die Behandlung schlug an

respondent [rɪˈspɒndənt] N *(Jur)* Scheidungsbeklagte(r) *mf*

responder [rɪˈspɒndəʳ] N *(Radar)* Antwortbake *f*, Responder *m (spec)*

response [rɪˈspɒns] N **a** *(= reply)* Antwort *f*, Erwiderung *f*; **in ~ (to)** als Antwort (auf *+acc*), in Erwiderung *(+gen) (geh)* **b** *(= reaction)* Reaktion *f*; *(esp Comput)* Rückmeldung *f*; **£50,000 was raised in ~ to the radio appeal** auf den Aufruf im Rundfunk hin gingen Spenden in Höhe von 50.000 Pfund ein; **we had hoped for a bigger ~ from the public** wir hatten uns größere Resonanz in der Öffentlichkeit erhofft; **my appeal met with no ~** meine Bitte fand kein Echo *or* keine Resonanz; **to receive a positive ~** eine gute *or* positive Resonanz finden

response mode N *(Comput)* Antwortmodus *m*

response time N *(of machine, police, ambulance etc)* Ansprechzeit *f*

responsibility [rɪˌspɒnsəˈbɪlɪtɪ] ✪ 18.3, 20.6 N **a** *no pl* Verantwortung *f*; **to put** *or* **place the ~ for sth on sb** jdm die Verantwortung für etw übertragen; **to take** *or* **assume (full) ~ (for sth)** die (volle) Verantwortung (für etw) übernehmen; **the management takes no ~ for objects left here** die Firma haftet nicht für liegen gelassene Gegenstände; **that's his ~** dafür ist er verantwortlich; **she's his ~** er hat die Verantwortung für sie; **it's not my ~ to do that** ich bin nicht dafür verantwortlich, das zu tun; **on one's own ~** auf eigene Verantwortung; **sense of ~** Verantwortungsgefühl *nt*; **~ payment** Verantwortlichkeitszuschlag *m*
b *(= duty, burden)* Verpflichtung *f (to* für); **the responsibilities of state** die staatsmännischen Pflichten; **the responsibilities of office** die Dienstpflichten *pl*

responsible [rɪˈspɒnsəbl] ADJ **a** *(denoting cause)* verantwortlich; *(= to blame)* schuld *(for* an *+dat)*; **bad workmanship was ~ for the failure** schlechte Arbeit war an dem Versagen schuld; **what's ~ for the hold-up?** woran liegt die Verzögerung?; **who is ~ for breaking the window?** wer hat das Fenster eingeschlagen?
b *(= liable, answerable)* verantwortlich; **she is not ~ for her actions** sie ist für ihre Handlungen nicht voll verantwortlich; **to be ~ to sb for sth** jdm gegenüber für etw verantwortlich sein; **to be directly ~ to sb** jdm unmittelbar unterstellt sein; **to hold sb ~ for sth** jdn für etw verantwortlich machen; **she is ~ for popularizing the sport** *(her task)* es ist ihre Aufgabe *or* sie ist dafür verantwortlich, die Sportart populärer zu machen; *(her merit)* es ist ihr zu verdanken, dass die Sportart populär geworden ist
c *(= trustworthy) person, attitude* verantwortungsbewusst; *firm* seriös, zuverlässig
d *(= involving responsibility) job* verantwortungsvoll

responsibly [rɪˈspɒnsəblɪ] ADV *act, behave* verantwortungsbewusst; *carry out one's duties* zuverlässig

responsive [rɪˈspɒnsɪv] ADJ **a** *person, audience* interessiert, mitgehend; *steering, brakes, motor* leicht reagierend *or* ansprechend; **to be ~ to sth** auf etw *(acc)* reagieren *or* ansprechen; **to be ~ to sb's needs** auf jds Bedürfnisse eingehen; **to be ~ to antibiotics** auf Antibiotika ansprechen; **he wasn't very ~ when I suggested it to him** er war nicht sehr begeistert, als ich ihm das vorschlug; **the pupils weren't very ~** die Schüler machten nicht richtig mit; **he wasn't very ~** *(to my complaint)* er ging kaum darauf ein
b *(form, = answering) smile, gesture* in Erwiderung; **the dog gave a ~ wag of his tail** der Hund reagierte mit einem Schwanzwedeln

responsiveness [rɪˈspɒnsɪvnɪs] N **because of the tremendous ~ of the audience** weil das Publikum so hervorragend mitging; **a class not noted for its ~** eine Klasse, die dafür bekannt ist, dass sie kaum mitmacht; **the ~ of the government** die Reaktionsfreudigkeit der Regierung; **they have improved the ~ of the steering** es ist ein leichteres Ansprechen der Steuerung erzielt worden; **I was somewhat surprised at their ~ to my suggestion/my needs** ich war über ihre positive Reaktion auf meinen Vorschlag/meine Bedürfnisse einigermaßen überrascht

rest[1] [rest] N **a** *(= relaxation)* Ruhe *f*; *(= pause)* Pause *f*, Unterbrechung *f*; *(in rest cure, on holiday etc)* Erholung *f*; **a day of ~** ein Ruhetag *m*; **to need ~** Ruhe brauchen; **I need a ~** ich muss mich ausruhen; *(= vacation)* ich brauche Urlaub; **to go to the mountains for a ~** zur Erholung in die Berge fahren; **to have** *or* **take a ~** *(= relax)* (sich) ausruhen; *(= pause)* (eine) Pause machen; **she took** *or* **had an hour's ~** *(= relaxation)* sie ruhte sich eine Stunde aus; *(= pause)* sie machte eine Stunde Pause; **take a ~!** mach mal Pause!; **to have a good night's ~** sich ordentlich ausschlafen; **to give one's eyes a ~** seine Augen ausruhen; **to give sb/the horses a ~** jdn/die Pferde ausruhen lassen; **give it a ~!** *(inf)* hör doch auf!
b to be at ~ *(= peaceful)* ruhig sein; *(euph: = dead)* ruhen; **to lay to ~** *(euph)* zur letzten Ruhe betten; **to set at ~** *(fears, doubts)* beschwichtigen; **to put** *or* **set sb's mind at ~** jdn beruhigen; **you can set** *or* **put your mind at ~** Sie können sich beruhigen, Sie können beruhigt sein; **to come to ~** *(ball, car etc)* zum Stillstand kom-

men; *(bird, insect)* sich niederlassen; *(gaze, eyes)* hängen bleiben *(upon* an *+dat)*
c *(= support)* Auflage *f*; *(of telephone)* Gabel *f*; *(Billiards)* Steg *m* → **armrest, footrest**
d *(Mus)* Pause *f*; *(Poet)* Zäsur *f*
VI a *(= lie down, take rest)* ruhen *(geh)*; *(= relax, be still)* sich ausruhen; *(= pause)* Pause machen, eine Pause einlegen; *(on walk, in physical work)* rasten, Pause machen; *(euph: = be buried)* ruhen; **you must ~ for an hour** Sie sollten eine Stunde ausruhen; **she never ~s** sie arbeitet ununterbrochen; **he will not ~ until he discovers the truth** er wird nicht ruhen (und rasten), bis er die Wahrheit gefunden hat; **to ~ easy (in one's bed)** beruhigt schlafen; **to be ~ing** ruhen *(geh)*; *(euph: = out of work)* ohne Engagement sein; **to let a field ~** einen Acker brachliegen lassen; **(the case for) the prosecution ~s** das Plädoyer der Anklage ist abgeschlossen; **to let a matter ~** eine Sache auf sich beruhen lassen; **let the matter ~!** lass es dabei!; **may he ~ in peace** er ruhe in Frieden; **to ~ in the Lord** im Herrn ruhen
b *(= remain: decision, authority, blame, responsibility etc)* liegen *(with* bei*)*; **the matter must not ~ there** man kann die Sache so nicht belassen; **and there the matter ~s for the moment** und damit ist die Sache momentan erledigt; **(you may) ~ assured that …** Sie können versichert sein, dass …
c *(= lean: person, head, ladder)* lehnen *(on* an *+dat, against* gegen*)*; *(= be supported: roof etc)* ruhen *(on* auf *+dat)*; *(fig: eyes, gaze)* ruhen *(on* auf *+dat)*; *(fig: = be based, argument, case)* sich stützen *(on* auf *+acc)*; *(reputation)* beruhen *(on* auf *+dat)*; *(responsibility)* liegen, ruhen *(on* auf *+dat)*; **her elbows were ~ing on the table** ihre Ellbogen waren auf den Tisch gestützt; **her head was ~ing on the table** ihr Kopf lag auf dem Tisch
VT a *one's eyes* ausruhen; *voice* schonen; *horses* ausruhen lassen; **to ~ oneself** sich ausruhen; **to be ~ed** ausgeruht sein; **to feel ~ed** sich ausgeruht fühlen; **(may) God ~ his soul** Gott hab ihn selig!; **to ~ one's case** *(Jur)* das Plädoyer abschließen
b *(= lean) ladder* lehnen *(against* gegen, *on* an *+acc)*; *elbow* stützen *(on* auf *+acc)*; *(fig) theory, suspicions* stützen *(on* auf *+acc)*; **to ~ one's hand on sb's shoulder** jdm die Hand auf die Schulter legen; **to ~ one's head on the table** den Kopf auf den Tisch legen; **he ~ed his head against the wall** er lehnte den Kopf an die Wand

▸ **rest up** VI *(inf)* sich ausruhen

rest² N *(= remainder)* Rest *m*; **the ~ of the money/meal** der Rest des Geldes/Essens, das übrige Geld/Essen; **the ~ of the boys** der Rest der Jungen, die übrigen Jungen; **you go off and the ~ of us will wait here** ihr geht, und der Rest von uns wartet hier; **he was as drunk as the ~ of them** er war so betrunken wie der Rest *or* die übrigen; **she's no different from the ~** sie ist wie alle anderen; **all the ~ of the money** der ganze Rest des Geldes, das ganze übrige Geld; **all the ~ of the books** alle übrigen Bücher; **and all the ~ of it** *(inf)* und so weiter und so fort; **Mary, Jane and all the ~ of them** Mary, Jane und wie sie alle heißen; **for the ~** im Übrigen

restage [ˌriːˈsteɪdʒ] VT *play etc* wieder aufführen; *scene, event* nachstellen, rekonstruieren

restart [ˌriːˈstɑːt] **VT** *job, activity* wieder aufnehmen; *negotiations, career also* wieder beginnen *or* anfangen; *race* neu starten; *game (from beginning)* neu beginnen; *(after interruption)* fortsetzen; *engine, car* wieder anlassen; *machine* wieder anschalten; *computer* neu starten; *economy* wieder ankurbeln; **to ~ work** wieder zu arbeiten anfangen
VI wieder anfangen *or* beginnen; *(race)* von Neuem beginnen; *(game) (from beginning)* neu beginnen; *(after interruption)* fortgesetzt werden; *(machine)* wieder starten; *(computer)* neu starten; *(engine, car)* wieder anspringen
N [ˈriːstɑːt] Neubeginn *m*; *(of activity)* Wiederaufnahme *f*; *(of computer)* Neustart *m*

restate [ˌriːˈsteɪt] VT **a** *(= express again) reasons* wieder *or* erneut nennen; *problem, argument, theory* wieder *or* erneut vortragen; *case, one's position* wieder *or* erneut darstellen; *(Mus) theme* wieder aufnehmen **b** *(= express differently)* umformulieren; *case, one's position* neu darstellen

restatement [ˌriːˈsteɪtmənt] N **a** *(= expressing again, of reasons)* erneute Nennung; *(of problem, argument, theory)* erneuter Vortrag; *(of case, one's position)* erneute Darstellung; *(Mus, of theme)* Wiederaufnahme *f* **b** *(= expressing differently)* Umformulierung *f*; *(of case, one's position)* Neudarstellung *f*

restaurant [ˈrestərɒnt] N Restaurant *nt*, Gaststätte *f*; **~ food/prices** Restaurantessen *nt*/-preise *pl*

restaurant car N *(Brit Rail)* Speisewagen *m*

restaurateur [ˌrestərəˈtɜːʳ] N Gastwirt *m*, Gastronom *m*

rest: **rest cure** N Erholung *f*; *(in bed)* Liegekur *f*; **rest day** N Ruhetag *m*

restful [ˈrestfʊl] ADJ *occupation, pastime etc* erholsam; *atmosphere* gemütlich, entspannend; *lighting* beruhigend; *colour* ruhig; *place* friedlich; **she is very ~ to be with** es ist sehr gemütlich, mit ihr zusammen zu sein

rest home N Altersheim *nt*, Pflegeheim *nt*

resting place [ˈrestɪŋˌpleɪs] N Rastplatz *m*; *(euph: = grave)* Ruhestätte *f*

restitution [ˌrestɪˈtjuːʃən] N **a** *(= giving back)* Rückgabe *f*; *(of money)* Rückerstattung *f*, Rückgabe *f*; **to make ~ of sth** *(form)* etw zurückgeben/zurückerstatten; **~ of conjugal rights** *(Jur)* Wiederherstellung *f* der ehelichen Gemeinschaft **b** *(= reparation)* Schadenersatz *m*, Entschädigung *f*

restive [ˈrestɪv] ADJ **a** *horse (= stubborn)* störrisch; *(= nervous)* unruhig **b** *(= restless) person, manner* rastlos; *tribes* widerspenstig, aufsässig

restiveness [ˈrestɪvnɪs] N **a** *(of horse, = stubbornness)* störrische Art; *(= nervousness)* Unruhe *f* **b** *(= restlessness: of person, manner)* Rastlosigkeit *f*; *(of tribes)* Widerspenstigkeit *f*, Aufsässigkeit *f*

restless [ˈrestlɪs] ADJ *(= unsettled) person, manner, sea, night* unruhig; *mind* ruhelos, unruhig; *energy* rastlos; *(= not wanting to stay in one place)* rastlos; **~ spirit** ruheloser Geist; **the natives are ~** *(hum)* es herrscht Unruhe im Land

restlessly [ˈrestlɪslɪ] ADV *(= in an unsettled manner)* unruhig; *(= not wanting to stay in one place)* rastlos

restlessness [ˈrestlɪsnɪs] N *(= unsettled manner)* Unruhe *f*; *(= not wanting to stay in one place)* Rastlosigkeit *f*

restock [ˌriːˈstɒk] VT *shelves, fridge, bar* wieder auffüllen; *pond* wieder (mit Fischen) besetzen; *farm* den Viehbestand *(+gen)* erneuern

restorable [rɪˈstɔːrəbl] ADJ wiederherstellbar

restoration [ˌrestəˈreɪʃən] N **a** *(= return)* Rückgabe *f (to* an *+acc)*; *(of property)* Rückerstattung *f*, Rückgabe *f (to* an *+acc)*; *(of confidence, order, calm, peace)* Wiederherstellung *f*; *(to office)* Wiedereinsetzung *f (to* in *+acc)* **b the Restoration** *(Hist)* die Restauration **c** *(of monument, work of art)* Restaurierung *f* **d** *(Comput) (of window, file, default etc)* Wiederherstellung *f*

restorative [rɪˈstɔːrətɪv] **ADJ** stärkend **N** Stärkungsmittel *nt*

restore [rɪˈstɔːʳ] VT **a** *sth lost, borrowed, stolen (= give back)* zurückgeben; *(= bring back)* zurückbringen; *confidence, order, calm, peace* wiederherstellen; **to ~ sb's health, to ~ sb to health** jds Gesundheit wiederherstellen, jdn wiederherstellen; **~d to health** wiederhergestellt; **to ~ freedom to sb** jdm die Freiheit wiedergeben; **to ~ sb to life** jdn ins Leben zurückrufen; **to ~ sth to its former condition** etw wiederherstellen; **the brandy ~d my strength** *or* **me** der Weinbrand hat mich wiederhergestellt
b *(to former post)* wieder einsetzen *(to* in *+acc)*; **to ~ sb to the throne** jdn als König(in) wieder einsetzen; **to ~ to power** wieder an die Macht bringen
c *(= repair) building, painting, furniture, text* restaurieren
d *(= recover) (Comput) data, file, default etc* wiederherstellen

restorer [rɪˈstɔːrəʳ] N *(Art)* Restaurator(in) *m(f)* → **hair restorer**

rest period N Erholungspause *f*

restrain [rɪˈstreɪn] VT *person* zurückhalten; *prisoner* mit Gewalt festhalten; *animal, unruly children, madman* bändigen; *radicals* in Schranken halten; *sb's activities, power* einschränken; *emotions, laughter* unterdrücken; **to ~ inflation/prices** die Inflationsrate/Preisentwicklung aufhalten; **to exercise a ~ing influence** etwas mildernd einwirken *(on* auf *+acc)*; **to ~ sb from doing sth** jdn davon abhalten, etw zu tun; **to ~ oneself** sich beherrschen

restrained [rɪˈstreɪnd] ADJ *person, performance, response* zurückhaltend; *emotions* unterdrückt; *manner, words* beherrscht; *tone, voice, colour* verhalten; *criticism* maßvoll, gezügelt; **he was very ~ when he heard the news** er war sehr beherrscht, als er die Nachricht hörte

restraining order [rɪˈstreɪnɪŋ-] N *(Jur)* Verbotsverfügung *f*; **to get a ~ (against sb)** eine gerichtliche (Verbots)verfügung (gegen jdn) erwirken

restraint [rɪˈstreɪnt] N **a** *(= restriction)* Einschränkung *f*, Beschränkung *f*; **without ~** unbeschränkt; *develop* ungehemmt; **to put/keep sb under ~** *(Jur)* jdn in Haft nehmen/behalten
b *(= moderation)* Beherrschung *f*; **to show a lack of ~** wenig Beherrschung zeigen; **he said with great ~ that …** er sagte sehr beherrscht, dass …; **to express oneself without ~** sich zwangslos ausdrücken; **wage ~** Zurückhaltung *f* bei Lohnforderungen **c** *(= head restraint)* Kopfstütze *f*

restrict [rɪˈstrɪkt] VT **a** *(= limit)* beschränken *(to* auf *+acc)*; *freedom, authority also* einschränken; *time, number also* begrenzen *(to* auf *+acc)*; **to ~ sb's movements** jdn in seiner Bewegungsfreiheit einschränken; **all speakers are ~ed to three hours** die Redezeit ist auf drei Stunden beschränkt **b** *(= hinder)* **~ing clothes** beengende Kleidungsstücke

restricted [rɪˈstrɪktɪd] ADJ **a** *(= limited) view* beschränkt, begrenzt; *diet* eingeschränkt; *(Admin, Mil) document, information* geheim; *locality* nur bestimmten Gruppen zugänglich; *admission* begrenzt; **within a ~ area** *(= within limited area)* auf begrenztem Gebiet **b** *(= hindered)* **I feel too ~ in jeans** ich fühle mich in Jeans zu beengt

restricted area N Sperrgebiet *nt*; *(Brit Mot)* Strecke *f* mit Geschwindigkeitsbeschränkung

restriction [rɪˈstrɪkʃən] N *(on sth* etw *gen)* Beschränkung *f*; *(of freedom, authority also)* Einschränkung *f*; *(on time, number also)* Begrenzung *f*; **to place ~s on sth** etw beschränken *or* einschränken; **~s of space** räumliche Beschränktheit; **without ~s** uneingeschränkt; **speed ~** *(Mot)* Geschwindigkeitsbegrenzung *f or* -beschränkung *f*; **price ~** Preisbeschränkung *f*

restrictive [rɪˈstrɪktɪv] ADJ **a** *(= limiting)* restriktiv, einschränkend *attr*; *environment* beengend, restriktiv **b** *(= hindering) clothing* beengend, eng

restrictive practices PL *(Jur, Ind)* wettbewerbsbeschränkende Geschäftspraktiken *pl*

restring [ˌriːˈstrɪŋ] *pret, ptp* **restrung** [ˌriːˈstrʌŋ] VT *instrument* neu besaiten; *bow, racket* neu bespannen; *pearls* neu aufziehen

rest room N *(US)* Toilette *f*

restructure [ˌriːˈstrʌktʃəʳ] VTI *(Comm, Ind)* umstrukturieren

restructuring [ˌriːˈstrʌktʃərɪŋ] N *(Comm, Ind)* Umstrukturierung *f*

rest stop N *(US Aut) (= place)* Rastplatz *m*; *(= break in journey)* Rast *f*

restyle [ˌriːˈstaɪl] VT *(= rearrange, remake)* umgestalten, umarbeiten; *(= realign)* neu ausrichten

result [rɪˈzʌlt] ✪ 17.1 N **a** Folge *f*; **as a ~ he failed** folglich fiel er durch; **as a ~ of this** und folglich; **as a ~ of which he …** was zur Folge hatte, dass er …; **to be the ~ of** resultieren aus **b** *(of election, exam, race, Math etc)* Ergebnis *nt*, Resultat *nt*; *(good result)* Resultat *nt*; **~s** *(of test, experiment)* Werte *pl*; **I want to see ~s** ich möchte einen Erfolg *or* ein Resultat sehen; **to get ~s** *(person)* Erfolg *or* Resultate erzielen; **we had very good ~s with this** wir hatten damit großen Erfolg *or* sehr gute Resultate; **as a ~ of my inquiry** auf meine Anfrage (hin); **what was the ~?** *(Sport)* wie ist es ausgegangen?; **without ~** ergebnislos
VI sich ergeben, resultieren (*from* aus); **from which it ~s that …** woraus folgt, dass …

▶ **result in** VI *+prep obj* führen zu; **this resulted in his being late** das führte dazu, dass er zu spät kam

resultant [rɪˈzʌltənt] ADJ resultierend, sich daraus ergebend N *(Phys)* Resultierende *f*

resume [rɪˈzjuːm] VT **a** *(= restart)* wieder aufnehmen; *activity also* weitermachen mit; *tale, account* wieder aufnehmen, fortfahren in *(+dat)*; *journey* fortsetzen; **to ~ work** die Arbeit wieder aufnehmen; **well?, he ~d** nun?, fuhr er fort **b** *command, possession, role* wieder übernehmen; *name* wieder annehmen; **to ~ one's seat** seinen Platz wieder einnehmen; **to ~ possession of sth** etw wieder in Besitz nehmen **c** *(= sum up)* zusammenfassen VI *(classes, work etc)* wieder beginnen; *(Comput)* (den) Stand-by-Modus beenden

résumé [ˈreɪzjuːmeɪ] N Resümee *nt*, Zusammenfassung *f*; (*US*: *= curriculum vitae*) Lebenslauf *m*

resumption [rɪˈzʌmpʃən] N *(of activity)* Wiederaufnahme *f*; *(of command, possession)* erneute Übernahme; *(of journey)* Fortsetzung *f*; *(of classes)* Wiederbeginn *m*

resurface [ˌriːˈsɜːfɪs] VT *road* neu belegen VI *(diver, submarine, fig)* wieder auftauchen

resurge [rɪˈsɜːdʒ] VT wiederauferstehen; (*fig*: *= flare up again*) wieder erwachen *or* aufleben

resurgence [rɪˈsɜːdʒəns] N Wiederaufleben *nt*

resurgent [rɪˈsɜːdʒənt] ADJ wieder auflebend

resurrect [ˌrezəˈrekt] VT **a** *(lit) person* wiederbeleben; *(Rel)* auferstehen lassen; **to be ~ed** auferstehen **b** *(fig) law* wieder einführen; *ideology, institution* wieder ins Leben rufen; *custom, fashion, style, career* wieder beleben; *custom, fashion, style, career* wieder beleben; *ideas, memories* wieder aufleben lassen; *(inf) old dress etc* ausgraben *(inf)*; **to ~ the past** die Vergangenheit wieder heraufbeschwören

resurrection [ˌrezəˈrekʃən] N **a** *(lit, of person)* Wiederbelebung *f*; **the Resurrection** *(Rel)* die Auferstehung **b** *(fig, of law)* Wiedereinführung *f*; *(of custom, fashion, style)* Wiederbelebung *f*; *(of ideas, memories)* Auflebenlassen *nt*

resuscitate [rɪˈsʌsɪteɪt] VT *(Med)* wiederbeleben; *(fig)* beleben, neue Lebensgeister geben *(+dat)*

resuscitation [rɪˌsʌsɪˈteɪʃən] N *(Med)* Wiederbelebung *f*; *(fig)* Belebung *f*

resuscitator [rɪˈsʌsɪteɪtəˈ] N *(Med)* Sauerstoffapparat *m*

retail [ˈriːteɪl] N Einzelhandel *m*, Kleinhandel *m*, Detailhandel *m (dated)*; **~ and wholesale** Einzel- und Großhandel *m*; **to sell sth by ~** etw im Einzelhandel verkaufen VT **a** *(= sell) goods* im Einzel- *or* Kleinhandel *or* en detail *(dated)* verkaufen **b** *(fig) gossip* weitererzählen VI *(goods)* **to ~ at …** im Einzelhandel … kosten ADV im Einzelhandel; **to sell ~** im Einzelhandel *or* en detail *(dated)* verkaufen

retail *in cpds* Einzelhandels-; **retail banking** N Bankgeschäft *nt*; **retail business** N Einzel- *or* Kleinhandel *m*; *(= shop)* Einzelhandelsgeschäft *nt*; **retail chain** N Einzelhandelskette *f*; **retail dealer** N Einzelhändler(in) *m(f)*, Detailhändler(in) *m(f) (dated)*

retailer [ˈriːteɪləˈ] N Einzelhändler(in) *m(f)*, Kleinhändler(in) *m(f)*

retailing [ˈriːteɪlɪŋ] N der Einzelhandel

retail: **retail outlet** N Einzelhandelsverkaufsstelle *f*; **retail park** N *(Brit)* großes Einkaufszentrum, Shoppingcenter *nt*; **retail price** N Einzelhandelspreis *m*; **retail price index** N Einzelhandelspreisindex *m*; **retail sales** PL Einzelhandelsumsatz *m*; **retail trade** N Einzelhandel *m*

retain [rɪˈteɪn] VT **a** *(= keep)* behalten; *money, possession, person* zurück(be)halten; *custom* beibehalten, bewahren; *urine* zurückhalten; *colour* behalten; *flavour* beibehalten; *moisture* speichern; *(battery) charge* halten; *(dam) water* stauen; **to ~ water** *(soil, body)* Wasser speichern; *(sponge)* Wasser halten; **to ~ control of sth** etw weiterhin in der Gewalt haben; **to ~ power** weiter an der Macht bleiben; **to ~ the use of a limb/one's eyes** ein Glied/seine Augen noch gebrauchen können **b** *(= remember)* sich *(dat)* merken; *(computer) information* speichern **c** *(= engage) lawyer* beauftragen

retainer [rɪˈteɪnəˈ] N **a** (*old*: *= servant*) Faktotum *nt* **b** *(= fee)* Vorschuss *m*

retaining [rɪˈteɪnɪŋ]: **retaining fee** N Vorschuss *m*; **retaining nut** N Befestigungsschraube *f*; **retaining wall** [reˈteɪnɪŋˌwɔːl] N Stützmauer *f*

retake [ˌriːˈteɪk] *vb: pret* **retook**, *ptp* **retaken** [ˌriːˈteɪkən] VT **a** *(Mil) town* zurückerobern; **he was ~n (prisoner)** er wurde wieder gefangen genommen **b** *(Film)* nochmals aufnehmen **c** *(Sport) penalty* wiederholen **d** *exam* wiederholen N [ˈriːteɪk] *(Film)* Neuaufnahme *f*; *(of exam)* Wiederholung(sprüfung) *f*; **we need a ~ of that scene** wir müssen die Szene noch einmal filmen

retaliate [rɪˈtælieɪt] VI Vergeltung üben; *(for bad treatment, insults etc)* sich revanchieren (*against sb* an jdm); *(in battle)* zurückschlagen; *(Sport, in fight, with measures, in argument)* kontern; **he ~d by pointing out that …** er konterte, indem er darauf hinwies, dass …; **he ~d by kicking him on the shins** er hat sich mit einem Tritt gegen das Schienbein revanchiert; **then she ~d by calling him a pig** sie revanchierte sich damit *or* zahlte es ihm damit heim, dass sie ihn ein Schwein nannte; **how will the unions ~?** wie werden die Gewerkschaften kontern?

retaliation [rɪˌtæliˈeɪʃən] N Vergeltung *f*; *(in fight also)* Vergeltungsschlag *m*; *(in argument, diplomacy etc)* Konterschlag *m*; **his ~ was vicious** er hat sich auf üble Weise revanchiert; **in ~** zur Vergeltung; **that's my ~ for what you did to me** das ist meine Revanche für das, was Sie mir angetan haben; **in ~ for your unkindness** um mich für Ihre Unfreundlichkeit zu revanchieren; **policy of ~** Vergeltungspolitik *f*

retaliatory [rɪˈtæliətərɪ] ADJ **~ measures** Vergeltungsmaßnahmen *pl*; **a ~ assassination** ein Vergeltungsmord *m*; **to take ~ action** zurückschlagen; *(Mil)* einen Vergeltungsschlag durchführen

retard [rɪˈtɑːd] VT *development* verlangsamen, verzögern; *explosion* verzögern; *(Aut) ignition* verzögern; *(Biol, Phys)* retardieren N [ˈriːtɑːd] (*pej sl*: *= handicapped person*) Spasti *m (sl)*, Behindi *m (sl)*

retardant [rɪˈtɑːdənt] N *(Chem)* Verzögerungsmittel *nt*

retarded [rɪˈtɑːdɪd] ADJ zurückgeblieben; *growth, progress* verzögert; **mentally ~** geistig zurückgeblieben

retarded ignition N *(Aut)* Spätzündung *f*

retarget [ˌriːˈtɑːgɪt] VT *range of goods etc* neu ausrichten; *space vehicle etc* umdirigieren

retch [retʃ] VI würgen N Würgen *nt*

retching [ˈretʃɪŋ] N Würgerei *f*, Gewürge *nt*

ret(d) *abbr of* **retired** a. D.

retell [ˌriːˈtel] *pret, ptp* **retold** VT wiederholen; *(novelist) old legend* nacherzählen

retention [rɪˈtenʃən] N **a** Beibehaltung *f*; *(of possession)* Zurückhaltung *f*; *(of water)* Speicherung *f*; *(of facts)* Behalten *nt*; *(of information by computer)* Speicherung *f*; *(of lawyer)* Beauftragung *f*; (*Med*: *also* **retention of urine**) Harnverhaltung *f* **b** *(= memory)* Gedächtnis *nt*

retentive [rɪˈtentɪv] ADJ *memory* aufnahmefähig; **he is very ~** er hat ein gutes Gedächtnis; **moisture-~ soil** Boden, der gut Feuchtigkeit speichert

retentiveness [rɪˈtentɪvnɪs] N *(of memory)* Aufnahmefähigkeit *f*; *(of person)* Merkfähigkeit *f*

rethink [ˌriːˈθɪŋk] *vb: pret, ptp* **rethought** [ˌriːˈθɔːt] VT überdenken N [ˈriːˌθɪŋk] *(inf)* Überdenken *nt*; **we'll have to have a ~** wir müssen das noch einmal überdenken

reticence [ˈretɪsəns] N Zurückhaltung *f*

reticent [ˈretɪsənt] ADJ zurückhaltend; **to be ~ about sth** in Bezug auf etw *(acc)* nicht sehr gesprächig sein

reticently [ˈretɪsəntlɪ] ADV zurückhaltend

reticle [ˈretɪkl] N *(Opt)* Messkreuz *nt*

reticulate [rɪˈtɪkjʊlɪt], **reticulated** [rɪˈtɪkjʊleɪtɪd] ADJ netzartig, retikular

retina [ˈretɪnə] N *pl* **-e** *or* **-s** [ˈretɪniː] Netzhaut *f*, Retina *f (spec)*

retinue [ˈretɪnjuː] N Gefolge *nt*

retire [rɪˈtaɪəˈ] VI **a** *(= give up work)* aufhören zu arbeiten; *(civil servant, military officer)* in Pension gehen, sich pensionieren lassen, in den Ruhestand treten; *(self-employed)* sich zur Ruhe setzen; *(soldier)* aus der Armee ausscheiden; *(singer, player etc)* (zu singen/spielen *etc*) aufhören; **to ~ from business** sich zur Ruhe setzen, sich aus dem Geschäftsleben zurückziehen
b *(= withdraw, Mil)* sich zurückziehen; *(Sport)* aufgeben; *(Ftbl, Rugby etc)* vom Feld gehen; *(jury)* sich zurückziehen; **to ~ into one's shell** sich in sein Schneckenhaus verkriechen; **to ~ from public life** sich aus dem öffentlichen Leben zurückziehen
c (*old, form*: *= go to bed*) sich zurückziehen
VT aus Altersgründen entlassen; *civil servant, military officer* pensionieren, in den Ruhestand versetzen; *soldier* verabschieden; *(Fin) bond* aus dem Verkehr ziehen

retired [rɪˈtaɪəd] ADJ **a** *(= no longer working) worker, employee* aus dem Arbeitsleben ausgeschieden *(form)*; *civil servant, military officer* pensioniert, im Ruhestand; *soldier* aus der Armee ausgeschieden; **he is ~** er arbeitet nicht mehr; *(soldier)* er ist nicht mehr in der Armee; **~ people** Leute, die im Ruhestand sind; **a ~ worker/teacher/soldier** ein Rentner/pensionierter Lehrer/ehemaliger Soldat; **"occupation - ~"** „Beruf - Rentner/Pensionär/Veteran" **b** *(= secluded) life* zurückgezogen

retired list N *(Mil)* Liste *f* der aus dem aktiven Dienst Geschiedenen

retiree [ˌrɪtaɪˈriː] N Ruheständler(in) *m(f)*

retirement [rɪˈtaɪəmənt] N **a** *(= stopping work)* Ausscheiden *nt* aus dem Arbeitsleben *(form)*; *(of civil servant, military officer)* Pensionierung *f*; *(of soldier)* Verabschiedung *f*; **~ at 60/65** Altersgrenze *f* bei 60/65; **to announce one's ~** sein Ausscheiden (aus seinem Beruf/seiner Stellung *etc*) ankündigen, sich pensionieren lassen wollen
b *(= period)* **how will you spend your ~?** was tun Sie, wenn Sie einmal nicht mehr arbeiten/wenn Sie pensioniert *or* im Ruhestand sind?; **to come out of ~** wieder zurückkommen
c *(= seclusion)* Zurückgezogenheit *f*; **to live in ~** zurückgezogen leben
d *(Mil)* Rückzug *m*; *(Sport)* Aufgabe *f*; *(Ftbl, Rugby etc)* Abgang *m* vom Spielfeld

retirement: **retirement age** N Renten(eintritts)alter *nt*; *(of civil servant)* Pensionsalter *nt*; **to reach ~** das Renten(eintritts)alter/Pensionsalter erreichen; **retirement benefit** N Altenhilfe *f*; **retirement home** N Seniorenheim *nt*; *(personal)* Alterswohnsitz *m*; **retirement pay** N Altersrente *f*; **retirement pension** N Altersruhegeld *nt (form)*

retiring [rɪˈtaɪərɪŋ] ADJ **a** *(= shy)* zurückhaltend **b** **~ age** Rentenalter *nt*; *(of civil servant)* Pensionsalter *nt*

retold [ˌriːˈtəʊld] *pret, ptp of* **retell**

retook [ˌriːˈtʊk] *pret of* **retake**

retort [rɪˈtɔːt] **N** **a** *(= answer)* scharfe Erwiderung *or* Antwort **b** *(Chem)* Retorte *f*; **~ stand** Retortenhalter *m or* -stand *m* **VT** scharf erwidern, zurückgeben **VI** scharf erwidern

retouch [ˌriːˈtʌtʃ] **VT** *(Art, Phot)* retuschieren

retrace [rɪˈtreɪs] **VT** *past, argumentation* zurückverfolgen; *development also* nachgehen *(+dat)*, nachvollziehen; **to ~ one's path** *or* **steps** denselben Weg zurückgehen

retract [rɪˈtrækt] **VT** **a** *(= withdraw) offer* zurückziehen; *statement* zurücknehmen; *decision* zuücknehmen, rückgängig machen **b** *(= draw back) claws* einziehen; *(Aviat) undercarriage* einziehen **VI** **a** *(= withdraw)* einen Rückzieher machen **b** *(claws, undercarriage)* eingezogen werden

retractable [rɪˈtræktəbl] **ADJ** **a** *offer* zurückziehbar; *statement, decision* zurücknehmbar **b** *claws* einziehbar; *clothes line etc* ausziehbar; *(Aviat) undercarriage* einziehbar

retraction [rɪˈtrækʃən] **N** **a** *(= act, of offer)* Rückzug *m*; *(of statement)* Rücknahme *f*; *(of decision)* Rückgängigmachung *f*; *(= thing retracted)* Rückzieher *m* **b** *(of claws, Aviat, of undercarriage)* Einziehen *nt*

retrain [ˌriːˈtreɪn] **VT** umschulen **VI** umlernen, umgeschult werden, sich umschulen lassen

retraining [ˌriːˈtreɪnɪŋ] **N** Umschulung *f*

retranslate [ˌriːtrænzˈleɪt] **VT** neu übersetzen

retranslation [ˌriːtrænzˈleɪʃən] **N** Neuübersetzung *f*

retransmit [ˌriːtrænzˈmɪt] **VT** weiterübertragen

retread **VT** [ˌriːˈtred] *tyre* die Laufflächen erneuern von **N** [ˈriːˌtred] *(= tyre)* runderneuerter Reifen

retreat [rɪˈtriːt] **N** **a** *(Mil)* Rückzug *m*; **to sound the ~** zum Rückzug blasen; **the army is in ~** die Armee befindet sich *or* ist auf dem Rückzug; **to make** *or* **beat a (hasty** *or* **swift) ~** *(Mil)* (schnell) den Rückzug antreten; *(fig)* (schleunigst) das Feld räumen; **his ~ into silence** seine Zuflucht zum Schweigen
b *(= place)* Zufluchtsort *m*, Zuflucht *f*; *(= hiding place)* Schlupfwinkel *m*; **this is my ~** hierhin ziehe ich mich zurück; **he has gone to his country ~** er hat sich aufs Land zurückgezogen
VI **a** *(Mil)* den Rückzug antreten; *(in fear)* zurückweichen; *(flood, glacier)* zurückgehen, zurückweichen; **to ~ inside oneself** sich in sich selbst zurückziehen
b *(Chess)* zurückziehen
VT *(Chess)* zurückziehen

retrench [rɪˈtrentʃ] **VT** *expenditure* einschränken, kürzen; *personnel* einsparen; *book* kürzen **VI** sich einschränken

▸ **retrench on** **VI** *+prep obj* = **retrench VT**

retrenchment [rɪˈtrentʃmənt] **N** *(of expenditure)* Einschränkung *f*, Kürzung *f*; *(of personnel)* Einsparung *f*

retrial [riːˈtraɪəl] **N** *(Jur)* Wiederaufnahmeverfahren *nt*; **the case may go to a ~** es könnte zu einer Wiederaufnahme des Verfahrens kommen; **he requested a ~** er verlangte die Wiederaufnahme des Verfahrens

retribution [ˌretrɪˈbjuːʃən] **N** Vergeltung *f*; **in ~** als Vergeltung

retributive [rɪˈtrɪbjʊtɪv] **ADJ** Vergeltungs-, vergeltend; *justice* ausgleichend; **~ action** Vergeltungsaktion *f*

retrievable [rɪˈtriːvəbl] **ADJ** **a** *(= recoverable)* zurück-/hervor-/heraus-/herunterholbar; *(= rescuable)* rettbar; *(from wreckage etc)* zu bergen; *material from waste* rückgewinnbar; *(Comput) information, data* abrufbar; *(after a crash)* wiederherstellbar; *honour, position, money, investment* wiedererlangbar **b** *loss, error* wiedergutzumachen *pred*, wiedergutzumachend *attr*; *situation* zu retten

retrieval [rɪˈtriːvəl] **N** **a** *(= recovering)* Zurück-/-/Hervor-/Heraus-/Herunterholen *nt*; *(= rescuing)* Rettung *f*; *(from wreckage etc)* Bergung *f*; *(of material from waste)* Rückgewinnung *f*; *(Comput: of information)* Abfragen *nt*, Abrufen *nt*; *(after a crash)* Wiederherstellen *nt*; *(of honour, position, money, investment)* Wiedererlangen *nt*; *(of loss)* Wiedergutmachen *nt* **b** *(= setting to rights, of error)* Wiedergutmachung *f*; *(of situation)* Rettung *f*; **beyond ~** hoffnungslos **c** *(by dog)* Apportieren *nt*

retrieve [rɪˈtriːv] **VT** **a** *(= recover)* zurück-/hervor-/heraus-/herunterholen; *(= rescue)* retten; *(from wreckage etc)* bergen; *material from waste* zurückgewinnen; *(Comput) information, data* abrufen; *(after a crash)* wiederherstellen; *honour, position, money, investment* wiedererlangen; *loss* wiedergutmachen; **to ~ sth from oblivion** etw der Vergessenheit entreißen **b** *(= set to rights) error* wiedergutmachen; *situation* retten **c** *(dog)* apportieren **VI** *(dog)* apportieren

retriever [rɪˈtriːvəʳ] **N** *(= breed)* Retriever *m*; **he is a good ~** er ist ein guter Apportierhund

retro [ˈretrəʊ] **N** *(= retrorocket)* Bremsrakete *f* **ADJ** **a** *(Mus, Fashion)* Retro-; **~ music** Retromusik *f* **b** *(inf: = outdated)* retro *(inf)*

retro- **PREF** rück-, Rück-

retroactive [ˌretrəʊˈæktɪv] **ADJ** rückwirkend; **a ~ effect** eine Rückwirkung

retroactively [ˌretrəʊˈæktɪvlɪ] **ADV** rückwirkend

retrofit [ˈretrəʊfɪt] **VT** *(= re-equip)* nachträglich ausstatten (*with* mit), nachrüsten (*with* mit); *(= convert)* umrüsten; *building etc* modernisieren **N** *(= re-equipping)* Nachrüstung *f*; *(= conversion)* Umrüstung *f*; *(= modernization)* Modernisierung *f*; *(= fitted equipment)* nachgerüstetes Teil, nachgerüstete Ausstattung

retroflected [ˌretrəʊˈflektɪd] **ADJ** *Zunge etc* zurückgebogen; *(Phon)* retroflex

retrograde [ˈretrəʊgreɪd] **ADJ** rückläufig; *order* umgekehrt; *policy* rückschrittlich; *(Phys, Biol, Astron)* rückläufig, retrograd *(spec)*; **~ step** Rückschritt *m* **VI** *(Biol)* sich zurückentwickeln; *(Astron)* sich retrograd bewegen

retrogress [ˌretrəʊˈgres] **VI** *(= go backwards)* sich rückwärts bewegen; *(= deteriorate)* sich zurückentwickeln

retrogression [ˌretrəʊˈgreʃən] **N** *(= backward movement)* rückläufige Bewegung; *(= deterioration)* Rückentwicklung *f*

retrogressive [ˌretrəʊˈgresɪv] **ADJ** *(= moving backwards)* rückläufig; *(fig) plan, policy* rückschrittlich; *(Biol)* rückläufig; **~ step** Rückschritt *m*

retrorocket [ˈretrəʊˈrɒkɪt] **N** Bremsrakete *f*

retrospect [ˈretrəʊspekt] **N** **in ~, what would you have done differently?** was hätten Sie rückblickend *or* im Rückblick anders gemacht?; **everything looks different in ~** im Nachhinein *or* im Rückblick sieht alles anders aus

retrospection [ˌretrəʊˈspekʃən] **N** Zurückblicken *nt*

retrospective [ˌretrəʊˈspektɪv] **ADJ** *thought* rückblickend; *wisdom* im Nachhinein; *(Admin, Jur)* rückblickend; *pay rise* rückwirkend; **~ effect** Rückwirkung *f*; **a ~ exhibition** eine Retrospektive; **a ~ look (at)** ein Blick *m* zurück (auf *+acc*) **N** Retrospektive *f*

retrospectively [ˌretrəʊˈspektɪvlɪ] **ADV** **a** *act* rückwirkend **b** *(= in retrospect)* rückblickend, im Nachhinein; **to look ~ at sth** auf etw *(acc)* zurückblicken

retrovirus [ˈretrəʊˌvaɪrəs] **N** Retrovirus *nt or m*

retry [riːˈtraɪ] **VT** *(Jur) case* wieder aufnehmen, neu verhandeln; *(Comput)* erneut ausführen, wiederholen

retsina [retˈsiːnə] **N** Retsina *m*

retune [ˈriːtjuːn] **VT** **a** *(Mus)* neu stimmen **b** *engine, video recorder* neu einstellen **N** **the engine needs a ~** der Motor muss neu eingestellt werden

return [rɪˈtɜːn] ✪ 20.3, 21.3, 23.3 **VI** *(come back: person, vehicle)* zurück- *or* wiederkommen, zurück- *or* wiederkehren *(geh)*; *(go back, person)* zurückgehen; *(vehicle)* zurückfahren; *(symptoms, doubts, fears)* wiederkommen, wieder auftreten; *(property: = pass back to)* zurückfallen (*to* an *+acc*); **to ~ to London/the town/the group** nach London/in die Stadt/zur Gruppe zurückkehren; **to ~ to school** wieder in die Schule gehen; **to ~ to (one's) work** *(after short pause)* wieder an seine Arbeit gehen; *(after strike)* die Arbeit wieder aufnehmen; **to ~ to a subject** auf ein Thema zurückkommen; **to ~ to one's old ways** in seine alten Gewohnheiten zurückfallen; **to ~ home** nach Hause kommen/gehen, heimkehren *(geh)*; **his good spirits ~ed** seine gute Laune kehrte wieder; **to ~ to health** wieder gesund werden; **to ~ to dust** wieder zu Staub werden

VT **a** *(= give back) sth borrowed, stolen, lost* zurückgeben (*to sb* jdm); *(= bring or take back)* zurückbringen (*to sb* jdm); *(= put back)* zurücksetzen/-stellen/-legen; *(= send back)* (*to* an *+acc*) *letter etc* zurückschicken *or* -senden; *(= refuse) cheque* nicht einlösen; *ball* zurückschlagen/-werfen; *sound, light* zurückwerfen; *salute, visit, sb's love, compliment* erwidern; **to ~ sb's (phone) call** jdn zurückrufen; **to ~ a/sb's blow** zurückschlagen; **to ~ a book to the shelf/box** ein Buch auf das Regal zurückstellen/in die Kiste zurücklegen; **to ~ goods to the shop** Waren in das Geschäft zurückbringen; **to ~ thanks** *(form)* danksagen, Dank sagen; **to ~ thanks to sb** jdm danksagen *or* Dank sagen; **I hope to ~ your kindness** ich hoffe, dass ich mich einmal bei Ihnen revanchieren kann; **to ~ good for evil** Böses mit Gutem vergelten; **to ~ fire** *(Mil)* das Feuer erwidern; **to ~ hearts** *(Cards)* Herz nachspielen
b *(= reply)* erwidern, zurückgeben
c *(= declare) details of income* angeben; **to ~ a verdict of guilty (on sb)** *(Jur)* (jdn) schuldig sprechen, einen Schuldspruch (gegen jdn) fällen; **to ~ a verdict of murder on sb** *(Jur)* jdn des Mordes für schuldig erklären
d *(Fin) income* einbringen; *profit, interest* abwerfen
e *(Brit Parl) candidate* wählen

N **a** *(= coming/going back, of person, vehicle, seasons)* Rückkehr *f*, Wiederkehr *f (geh)*; *(of illness)* Wiederauftreten *nt*; **on my ~** bei meiner Rückkehr; **~ home** Heimkehr *f*; **~ to school** Schulbeginn *m*; **by ~ (of post)** *(Brit)* postwendend; **~ to work** *(after strike)* Wiederaufnahme *f* der Arbeit; **~ to health** Genesung *f*; **a ~ to one's old habits** ein Rückfall *m* in seine alten Gewohnheiten; **many happy ~s (of the day)!** herzlichen Glückwunsch zum Geburtstag! → **point**
b *(= giving back)* Rückgabe *f*; *(= bringing or taking back)* Zurückbringen *nt*; *(= putting back)* Zurücksetzen/-stellen/-legen *nt*; *(= sending back)* Zurückschicken *nt* or -senden *nt*; *(= refusal: of cheque)* Nichteinlösen *nt*; *(of ball)* Zurückschlagen *nt*/-werfen *nt*; *(of salute, compliment, sb's love)* Erwiderung *f*
c *(Brit: also* **return ticket**) Rückfahrkarte *f*; *(Aviat)* Rückflugticket *nt*
d *(= profit: from investments, shares)* (*on* aus) Einkommen *nt*; *(on capital)* Ertrag *m*, Gewinn *m*; *(= product: from land, mine etc)* Ertrag *m*; **~s** *(= profits)* Gewinn *m*; *(= receipts)* Einkünfte *pl*; **~ on capital** *(Fin)* Kapitalertrag *m*, Rendite *f*
e *(fig: = recompense)* **in ~** dafür; **in ~ for** für; **to do sb a favour** *(Brit)* or **favor** *(US)* **in ~** sich bei jdm für einen Gefallen revanchieren
f *(= act of declaring, of verdict, election results)* Verkündung *f*; *(= report)* Bericht *m*; **the ~ of the jury** ≈ das Urteil der Schöffen; **the (election) ~s** das Wahlergebnis
g *(Brit Parl, of candidate)* Wahl *f* (*to* in *+acc*)
h *(Sport: = game, match)* Rückspiel *nt*; *(= stroke)* Rückschlag *m*; *(Tennis)* Return *m*; *(= throw)* Rückwurf *m*; *(= return pass)* Rückpass *m*; **to make a good ~** den Ball gut zurückschlagen/-werfen
i *(Comm: = returned item)* zurückgebrachte Ware; *(Theat)* zurückgebrachte Karte; *(= book)* Remittende *f*
j *(= carriage return, Comput)* Zeilenendschal-

tung *f*; *(on typewriter)* Rücklauftaste *f*
k *(Comput: = symbol)* Absatzmarke *f*

returnable [rɪˈtɜːnəbl] ADJ zur Rückgabe bestimmt; *(= reusable)* Mehrweg-; **~ bottle** Mehrwegflasche *f*; *(with deposit)* Pfandflasche *f*

return bout N *(Boxing)* Rückkampf *m*

returnee [rɪtɜːˈniː] N *(Pol)* Rückkehrer(in) *m(f)*

returner [rɪˈtɜːnəʳ] N Wiedereinsteiger(in) *m(f)* (ins Berufsleben)

return: **return fare** N *(Brit)* Preis *m* für eine Rückfahrkarte *or (Aviat)* ein Rückflugticket *nt*; **return fight** N *(Boxing)* Rückkampf *m*; **return flight** N *(Brit)* Rückflug *m*; *(both ways)* Hin- und Rückflug *m*; **return game** N *(Sport)* Rückspiel *nt*; **return half** N *(Brit: of ticket)* Abschnitt *m* für die Rückreise

returning: **returning board** [rɪˈtɜːnɪŋ,bɔːd] N *(US Pol)* Wahlausschuss *m*; **returning officer** [rɪˈtɜːnɪŋˈɒfɪsəʳ] N *(Brit Parl)* Wahlleiter(in) *m(f)*

return: **return journey** N *(Brit)* Rückreise *f*; *(both ways)* Hin- und Rückreise *f*; **return key** N *(Comput)* Eingabetaste *f*; **return leg, return match** N *(Brit)* Rückspiel *nt*; **return match** N *(Brit)* Rückspiel *nt*; **return pass** N *(Sport)* Rückpass *m*; **return ticket** N *(Brit)* Rückfahrkarte *f*; *(Aviat)* Rückflugticket *nt*; **return visit** N *(to person)* Gegenbesuch *m*; *(to place)* zweiter Besuch; **to make a ~ (to a place)** (an einen Ort) zurückkehren

reunification [riːˌjuːnɪfɪˈkeɪʃən] N Wiedervereinigung *f*

reunify [ˌriːˈjuːnɪfaɪ] VT wiedervereinigen

reunion [rɪˈjuːnjən] N **a** *(= coming together)* Wiedervereinigung *f* **b** *(= gathering)* Treffen *nt*, Zusammenkunft *f*; **a family/school ~** ein Familien-/Klassentreffen *nt*

reunite [ˌriːjuːˈnaɪt] VT wieder vereinigen; **they were ~d at last** sie waren endlich wieder vereint VI *(countries, parties)* sich wiedervereinigen; *(people)* wieder zusammenkommen

re-up [ˌriːˈʌp] VI *(US Mil inf)* sich weiterverpflichten, sich wieder verpflichten

reusable [ˌriːˈjuːzəbl] ADJ wiederverwendbar, wiederverwertbar; **~ package** Mehrwegverpackung *f*

Rev [rev] *abbr of* **Reverend**

rev [rev] N *abbr of* **revolution** *(Aut)* Umdrehung *f*; **the number of ~s per minute** die Dreh- *or* Tourenzahl pro Minute; **4,000 ~s per minute** 4.000 Umdrehungen *or* Touren *(inf)* pro Minute; **~ counter** Drehzahlmesser *m*, Tourenzähler *m* VI *(driver)* den Motor auf Touren bringen; *(noisily)* den Motor aufheulen lassen; *(engine)* aufheulen VT *engine* aufheulen lassen

▶ **rev up** VI **a** *(Aut)* = **rev VI** **b** *(inf: = prepare)* sich vorbereiten *(for* auf *+acc)* VT *sep* **a** *(Aut) engine* aufheulen lassen **b** *(Ind inf) production* ankurbeln **c to be revved up for sth** *(inf: = eager)* ganz wild auf etw *(acc)* sein

revaluation [riːˌvæljʊˈeɪʃən] N *(Fin)* Aufwertung *f*

revalue [ˌriːˈvæljuː] VT *(Fin)* aufwerten

revamp [ˌriːˈvæmp] VT *(inf) book, play, image* aufmotzen *(inf)*; *company* auf Vordermann bringen *(inf)*; *(Pol) party* auf Vordermann bringen *(inf)*; *house, room* aufmöbeln

revanchist [rɪˈvæntʃɪst] ADJ revanchistisch

reveal [rɪˈviːl] VT **a** *(= make visible)* zum Vorschein bringen; *(= show)* zeigen; **stripping off the wallpaper ~ed an old frieze** unter der Tapete war ein alter Fries zum Vorschein gekommen; **a nightdress that ~ed her slender figure** ein Nachthemd, das ihre schlanke Gestalt abzeichnete; **a neckline that ~ed her bosom** ein Ausschnitt, der ihren Busen freigab
b *(= make known) truth, facts* enthüllen, aufdecken; *one's/sb's identity* zu erkennen geben, enthüllen; *name, details* preisgeben, verraten; *ignorance, knowledge* erkennen lassen; **to ~ the (full) extent of sth** etw völlig *or* in seinem vollen Umfang aufdecken *or* klarmachen; **I cannot ~ to you what he said** ich kann Ihnen nicht verraten, was er gesagt hat; **he ~ed himself as being ...** er verriet sich als ...; *(deliberately)* er gab sich als ... zu erkennen; **he could never ~ his feelings for her** er konnte seine Gefühle für sie nie zeigen; **what does this ~ about the motives of the hero?** was sagt das über die Motive des Helden aus?; **Nixon ~s all** Nixon packt aus *(inf)*; **the doctor did not ~ to him how hopeless his situation was** der Arzt hat ihn nicht darüber aufgeklärt, wie hoffnungslos sein Zustand war
c *(Rel)* offenbaren *(to sb* jdm)

revealed religion [rɪˈviːldrɪˈlɪdʒən] N *(Rel)* Offenbarungsreligion *f*

revealing [rɪˈviːlɪŋ] ADJ **a** aufschlussreich; *insight also* verräterisch **b** *material, skirt etc* viel zeigend; *dress, neckline also* offenherzig *(hum)*

revealingly [rɪˈviːlɪŋli] ADV *say* bezeichnenderweise; **he ~ remarked that he'd never read the book in question** er bemerkte, und das sagt schon einiges, dass er das fragliche Buch nie gelesen habe; **~, 60 per cent of purchasers are women** es ist sehr aufschlussreich *or* es lässt tief blicken, dass 60 Prozent der Käufer Frauen sind

reveille [rɪˈvælɪ] N *(Mil)* Reveille *f*, Wecksignal *nt*; **(the) ~ is at 6** um 6 Uhr ist Wecken

revel [ˈrevl] VI **a** *(= make merry)* feiern **b** *(= delight)* **to ~ in sth** etw in vollen Zügen genießen; **to ~ in doing sth** seine wahre Freude daran haben, etw zu tun; **like it? I ~ in it** gefallen? es macht mir Riesenspaß! N **revels** PL Feiern *nt*

revelation [ˌrevəˈleɪʃən] N Enthüllung *f*; *(Rel)* Offenbarung *f*; **(the book of) Revelations** die Offenbarung (des Johannes); **it was a ~ to me** das hat mir die Augen geöffnet; **what a ~!** unglaublich!

revelatory [ˌrevəˈleɪtərɪ] ADJ aufschlussreich

reveller, *(US)* **reveler** [ˈrevləʳ] N Feiernde(r) *mf*

revelry [ˈrevlrɪ] N *usu pl* Festlichkeit *f*

revenge [rɪˈvendʒ] N Rache *f*; *(Sport)* Revanche *f*; **to take ~ on sb (for sth)** sich an jdm (für etw) rächen; *(Mil etc)* an jdm (für etw) Vergeltung üben; **to get one's ~** sich rächen, seine Rache bekommen; *(Sport)* sich revanchieren; **out of ~** aus Rache; **in ~ for** als Rache für; **~ is sweet** Rache ist süß VT *insult, murder, sb* rächen; **to ~ oneself** *or* **to be ~d (for sth)** sich (für etw) rächen; **to ~ oneself on sb (for sth)** sich (für etw) an jdm rächen

revengeful [rɪˈvendʒfʊl] ADJ rachsüchtig

revengefully [rɪˈvendʒfəlɪ] ADV rachsüchtig; *act* aus Rache

revenger [rɪˈvendʒəʳ] N Rächer(in) *m(f)*

revenue [ˈrevənjuː] N *(of state)* Staatseinkünfte *pl*, öffentliche Einnahmen *pl*; *(= tax revenue)* Steueraufkommen *nt*; *(of individual)* Einnahmen *pl*, Einkünfte *pl*; *(= department)* Finanzbehörde *f*, Fiskus *m* → **Inland Revenue, internal**

revenue: **revenue investigator** N Steuerfahnder(in) *m(f)*; **revenue officer** N Finanzbeamte(r) *m*/-beamtin *f*; **revenue stamp** N *(US)* Steuermarke *f*, Steuerbanderole *f*

reverb [rɪˈvɜːb] N *(= shaking effect)* Hall *m*; *(= echoing effect)* Echo *nt*

reverberant [rɪˈvɜːbərənt] ADJ *acoustics* nach- *or* widerhallend

reverberate [rɪˈvɜːbəreɪt] VI *(sound)* widerhallen, nachhallen; *(light, heat)* zurückstrahlen, reflektieren VT *sound, light, heat* zurückwerfen, reflektieren

reverberation [rɪˌvɜːbəˈreɪʃən] N *(of sound)* Widerhall *m*, Nachhall *m*; *(of light, heat)* Zurückstrahlen *nt*, Reflexion *f*

revere [rɪˈvɪəʳ] VT verehren

reverence [ˈrevərəns] N **a** Ehrfurcht *f*, Reverenz *f (geh)*; *(= veneration)* Verehrung *f (for* für); **to have ~ for sb** jdn verehren; **to bow in ~** sich ehrfürchtig verneigen; **to treat sth with ~** etw ehrfürchtig behandeln; **to show ~** Ehrfurcht zeigen; **to show sb ~** jdm Ehrfurcht bezeigen **b your Reverence** (Euer) Hochwürden **c** *(obs, = bow)* Reverenz *f* VT verehren

reverend [ˈrevərənd] ADJ **the Reverend Robert Martin** ≈ Pfarrer Robert Martin; **the Most Reverend John Smith** Erzbischof John Smith; **the Very Reverend John Smith** Dekan John Smith; **the Right Reverend John Smith** Bischof John Smith; **the Reverend Mother** die Mutter Oberin N *(inf)* ≈ Pfarrer *m*

reverent [ˈrevərənt] ADJ ehrfürchtig, ehrfurchtsvoll

reverential [ˌrevəˈrenʃəl] ADJ *awe, respect* ehrfürchtig; *bow, gesture etc* ehrerbietig; **in ~ tones** ehrfürchtig, ehrerbietig

reverently [ˈrevərəntlɪ] ADV ehrfürchtig, ehrfurchtsvoll

reverie [ˈrevərɪ] N *(liter)* Träumereien *pl*; **he drifted off into a ~** er verfiel ins Träumen

revers [rɪˈvɪəʳ] N *pl* - Revers *nt or m*

reversal [rɪˈvɜːsəl] N **a** *(= turning the other way round, of order, situation, procedure)* Umkehren *nt*; *(of objects, sentences, words)* Umstellen *nt*, Vertauschung *f*; *(of garment)* Wenden *nt*; *(of result)* Umkehren *nt*, Umdrehen *nt* **b** *(of verdict, judgement)* Umstoßung *f*; *(of decree)* Aufhebung *f*; *(of trend, process)* Umkehrung *f*; *(of policy)* Umkrempeln *nt*; *(of decision, surgical operation)* Rückgängigmachen *nt* **c** *(= setback)* Rückschlag *m*; **to suffer a ~** einen Rückschlag erleiden

reverse [rɪˈvɜːs] ADJ **a** *(= opposite)* umgekehrt; *direction also* entgegengesetzt; *(Opt) image* seitenverkehrt; **in ~ order** in umgekehrter Reihenfolge; **in the ~ direction** in umgekehrter Richtung
b ~ motion *or* **action** *(Tech, = backwards)* Rückwärtsbewegung *f*; *(= opposite direction)* entgegengesetzte Bewegung
N **a** *(= opposite)* Gegenteil *nt*; **quite the ~!** ganz im Gegenteil!; **he is the ~ of polite** er ist alles andere als höflich
b *(= back)* Rückseite *f*; *(of cloth)* Rückseite *f*, linke Seite
c *(= setback, loss)* Rückschlag *m*; *(= defeat)* Niederlage *f*; **he suffered a ~ of fortune** sein Glück schlug um; **a ~ of fortune led to his losing all his wealth** sein Glück schlug um, und er verlor all seinen Reichtum
d *(Aut)* Rückwärtsgang *m*; **in ~** im Rückwärtsgang; **to put a/the car into ~** den Rückwärtsgang einlegen; **to go into ~** in den Rückwärtsgang schalten
e to do sth in ~ etw in umgekehrter Reihenfolge tun; **at this point the party's fortunes went into ~** *(fig)* zu diesem Zeitpunkt wendete sich das Schicksal der Partei
f *(on typewriter)* Rückstelltaste *f*; *(on tape recorder)* Rücklauftaste *f*
VT **a** *(= turn the other way round) order, situation, procedure* umkehren; *objects, sentences, words* umstellen, vertauschen; *garment* wenden; *result* umkehren, umdrehen; **to ~ one's direction** eine Kehrtwendung machen; **to ~ the order of sth** etw herumdrehen; **to ~ the charges** *(Brit Telec)* ein R-Gespräch führen; **~-charge call** *(Brit Telec)* R-Gespräch *nt*; **to ~ roles** die Rollen tauschen
b *(= cause to move backwards) moving belt* rückwärtslaufen lassen; **to ~ one's car into the garage/down the hill/into a tree** *(esp Brit)* rückwärts in die Garage fahren *or* setzen/den Berg hinunterfahren/gegen einen Baum fahren
c *verdict, judgement* umstoßen, kassieren; *decree* aufheben; *trend, process* umkehren; *policy* völlig umstellen, umkrempeln; *decision, surgical operation* rückgängig machen; **lowering cholesterol levels can sometimes ~ coronary diseases** ein gesenkter Cholesterinspiegel kann bewirken, dass sich Herzgefäßerkrankungen zurückbilden
VI *(= move backwards) (esp Brit: car, driver)* zurücksetzen; *(dancer)* rückwärtstanzen; *(machine)* rückwärtslaufen; **to ~ into the garage** *(esp Brit)* rückwärts in die Garage fahren

▶ **reverse out** VT *sep (Typ)* invertieren

reverse: **reverse discrimination** N *(US)* positive *or* umgekehrte Diskriminierung; **reverse**

gear N *(Aut)* Rückwärtsgang *m*; **to put a/the car into ~** den Rückwärtsgang einlegen; **reverse racism** N umgekehrter Rassismus; **reverse video** N *(Comput)* invertierte Darstellung

reversibility [rɪˌvɜːsɪˈbɪlɪtɪ] N *(of decision)* Rückgängigmachung *f*; *(of process, Phys, Chem)* Umkehrbarkeit *f*; *(of operation etc)* Reversibilität *f*

reversible [rɪˈvɜːsəbl] ADJ *decision* rückgängig zu machen *pred*, rückgängig zu machend *attr*; *process* umkehrbar, reversibel; *operation, contraception* reversibel; *medical condition* heilbar, reversibel; *(Phys, Chem)* umkehrbar; **is vasectomy ~?** kann eine Sterilisation rückgängig gemacht werden?

reversible cloth N Doubleface *m or nt*

reversible jacket N Wendejacke *f*

reversing light [rɪˈvɜːsɪŋlaɪt] N Rückfahrscheinwerfer *m*

reversion [rɪˈvɜːʃən] N **a** (= *return to former state: of person*) Umkehr *f* (*to* zu); *(to bad state)* Rückfall *m* (*to* in *+acc*); **the ~ of this country to a republic** die Rückverwandlung dieses Landes in eine Republik; **~ to type** *(Biol)* (Arten)rückschlag *m*; **his ~ to type** das erneute Durchbrechen seiner alten Natur **b** *(Jur, of property)* Zurückfallen *nt* (*to* an *+acc*)

reversionary [rɪˈvɜːʃnərɪ] ADJ **a** *(Jur)* anwartschaftlich **b** *(Biol)* atavistisch *(spec)*

revert [rɪˈvɜːt] VI (= *return, to former state*) zurückkehren (*to* zu); *(to bad state)* zurückfallen (*to* in *+acc*); *(to topic)* zurückkommen (*to* auf *+acc*); *(to a dialect etc)* (zurück)verfallen (*to* in *+acc*); *(Jur: property)* zurückfallen (*to* an *+acc*); **he has ~ed back to childhood** er ist wieder ins Kindheitsalter zurückgefallen; **to ~ to type** *(Biol)* in der Art zurückschlagen; **he has ~ed to type** *(fig)* seine alte Natur ist wieder durchgebrochen; **fields ~ing to moorland/woodland** Felder, die wieder versumpfen/wieder zu Wäldern werden

review [rɪˈvjuː] N **a** (= *look back*) Rückblick *m*, Rückschau *f* (*of* auf *+acc*); (= *report*) Überblick *m* (*of* über *+acc*); **I shall keep your case under ~** ich werde Ihren Fall im Auge behalten
b (= *re-examination*) nochmalige Prüfung; **to do a ~ of sth** etw überprüfen; **the agreement comes up for ~** *or* **comes under ~ next year** das Abkommen wird nächstes Jahr nochmals geprüft; **his salary is due for ~ in January** im Januar wird sein Gehalt neu festgesetzt; **there will be a ~ of the situation in 3 months' time** in 3 Monaten wird die Lage noch einmal überprüft
c *(Mil:* = *inspection)* Inspektion *f*; **to hold a ~** eine Inspektion vornehmen
d *(of book, film, play etc)* Kritik *f*, Besprechung *f*, Rezension *f*
e (= *magazine*) Zeitschrift *f*
VT **a** (= *look back at*) *one's life, the past etc* zurückblicken auf *(+acc)*, überdenken
b (= *re-examine*) *situation, case* erneut (über)prüfen
c *(Mil) troops* inspizieren, mustern
d *book, play, film* besprechen, rezensieren
e *(US, before exam)* wiederholen

review body N Untersuchungsausschuss *m*

review copy N *(of book)* Rezensionsexemplar *nt*

reviewer [rɪˈvjuːəʳ] N Kritiker(in) *m(f)*, Rezensent(in) *m(f)*

reviewing stand [rɪˈvjuːɪŋ-] N Ehrentribüne *f*

review panel N = **review body**

revile [rɪˈvaɪl] VT schmähen, verunglimpfen VI **to ~ against sb/sth** gegen jdn/etw schmähen

revisal [rɪˈvaɪzəl] N Nachprüfung *f*, nochmalige Durchsicht; *(Editing)* zweite Korrektur, Revision *f (spec)*

revise [rɪˈvaɪz] VT **a** (= *change*) *opinion, estimate, law* revidieren; **to ~ the constitution** die Verfassung überarbeiten **b** (= *correct*) *proof, text* revidieren, überarbeiten **c** *(Brit:* = *learn up)* wiederholen VI *(Brit)* (den Stoff) wiederholen

revised [rɪˈvaɪzd] ADJ **a** (= *amended*) *version, plan, procedure* überarbeitet, revidiert; *figure, estimate, schedule* revidiert; *offer* neu; **according to a ~ estimate** nach neuen Schätzungen **b** *(Typ) edition* überarbeitet; **the Revised Version** *(Brit)* die Bibelübersetzung *(von 1884)*; **the Revised Standard Version** *(US)* die Bibelübersetzung *(von 1953)*

reviser [rɪˈvaɪzəʳ] N Bearbeiter(in) *m(f)*; *(of translations etc)* Korrektor(in) *m(f)*

revision [rɪˈvɪʒən] N **a** *(of opinion, estimate)* Überholen *nt*, Revidieren *nt* **b** *(of proofs)* Revision *f*, Überarbeitung *f* **c** *(Brit, for exam)* Wiederholung *f* (des Stoffs) **d** (= *revised version*) überarbeitete Ausgabe

revisionism [rɪˈvɪʒənɪzəm] N Revisionismus *m*

revisionist [rɪˈvɪʒənɪst] ADJ revisionistisch N Revisionist(in) *m(f)*

revisit [ˌriːˈvɪzɪt] VT *place, person* wieder *or* nochmals besuchen; *(fig) argument, issue* nochmals zurückkommen auf *(+acc)*

revitalize [ˌriːˈvaɪtəlaɪz] VT neu beleben

revival [rɪˈvaɪvəl] N **a** (= *bringing back, of custom, usage*) Wiedererwecken *nt*, Wiederaufleben lassen *nt*; *(of old ideas, affair)* Wiederaufnehmen *nt*, Wiederaufgreifen *nt*; *(from faint, fatigue)* Wiederbeleben *nt*, Wiederbelebung *f*; *(of play)* Wiederaufnahme *f*; *(of law)* Wiederinkrafttreten *nt*
b (= *coming back, return: of custom, old ideas etc*) Wiederaufleben *nt*; *(from faint, fatigue)* Wiederbelebung *f*; **there has been a ~ of interest in ...** das Interesse an ... ist wieder wach geworden *or* ist wieder erwacht; **the dollar experienced a slight ~** der Dollar verzeichnete wieder einen leichten Aufschwung; **an economic ~** ein wirtschaftlicher Wiederaufschwung
c *(Rel)* Erweckung *f*; **~ meeting** Erweckungsversammlung *f*

revivalism [rɪˈvaɪvəlɪzəm] N *(Rel)* Erweckungsbewegung *f*

revivalist [rɪˈvaɪvəlɪst] ADJ erneuernd; *meeting, spirit, preacher* der Erweckungsbewegung; **~ movement** Erweckungsbewegung *f*; **a ~ rock group** eine Revival-Rockband N Anhänger(in) *m(f)* der Erweckungsbewegung

revive [rɪˈvaɪv] VT *person (from fainting, from fatigue)* (wieder *or* neu) beleben, munter machen *(inf)*; *(from near death)* wiederbeleben; *economy* wieder beleben, wieder ankurbeln; *confidence* neu stärken; *memories* wieder lebendig werden lassen; *fashion, custom, usage, hatred, speculation, fears* wieder aufleben lassen; *friendship, old habit, word* wieder aufgreifen, wieder aufnehmen; *old play, talks, career* wieder aufnehmen; **a glass of brandy will ~ you** ein Glas Weinbrand wird Sie wieder beleben *or* wieder auf die Beine bringen; **to ~ interest in sth** neues Interesse an etw *(dat)* wecken; **to ~ the fortunes of sb/sth** jdm/einer Sache wieder auf die Beine helfen
VI *(person, from fainting)* wieder zu sich kommen; *(from fatigue)* wieder aufleben, wieder munter werden; *(hope, feelings)* wieder aufleben; *(business, trade)* wieder aufblühen

revivify [riːˈvɪvɪfaɪ] VT *person* wiederbeleben, wieder munter machen; (= *restore to life*) wiederbeleben

revocable [ˈrevəkəbl] ADJ widerruflich

revocation [ˌrevəˈkeɪʃən] N *(of law)* Aufhebung *f*; *(of order, promise)* Zurückziehen *nt*; *(of decision)* Widerruf *m*; *(of licence)* Entzug *m*

revoke [rɪˈvəʊk] VT *law* aufheben; *order, promise* zurückziehen; *decision* widerrufen, rückgängig machen; *licence* entziehen VI *(Cards)* nicht Farbe bekennen N *(Cards)* Nichtfarbebekennen *nt*

revolt [rɪˈvəʊlt] N Empörung *f*, Revolte *f*, Aufstand *m*; **to rise (up) in ~** einen Aufstand *or* eine Revolte machen, sich erheben; **to be in ~ (against)** rebellieren (gegen) VI **a** (= *rebel*) *(against* gegen) revoltieren, rebellieren **b** (= *be disgusted*) *(at, against* bei, gegen) *(one's nature, sensibilities)* sich empören; *(stomach)* rebellieren VT abstoßen, anekeln *(inf)*; **I was ~ed by it** es hat mich angeekelt *(inf)* *or* abgestoßen

revolting [rɪˈvəʊltɪŋ] ADJ (= *repulsive, disgusting*) abstoßend; *meal, story* ekelhaft; *(inf:* = *unpleasant) weather, colour, dress* scheußlich, abscheulich; *person* widerlich

revoltingly [rɪˈvəʊltɪŋlɪ] ADV *dirty, ugly* ekelhaft; *sentimental* scheußlich

revolution [ˌrevəˈluːʃən] N **a** *(Pol, fig)* Revolution *f* **b** (= *turn*) *(around own axis)* Umdrehung *f*; *(of planet around sun)* Umlauf *m*; **4,000 ~s per minute** eine Drehzahl von 4.000 pro Minute

revolutionary [ˌrevəˈluːʃnərɪ] ADJ *(lit, fig)* revolutionär; **~ government** Revolutionsregierung *f*; **~ leader** Revolutionsführer(in) *m(f)* N Revolutionär(in) *m(f)*, Revoluzzer(in) *m(f) (pej)*

revolutionize [ˌrevəˈluːʃənaɪz] VT revolutionieren

revolvable [rɪˈvɒlvəbl] ADJ drehbar

revolve [rɪˈvɒlv] VT drehen VI sich drehen; **to ~ on an axis/around the sun** sich um eine Achse/um die Sonne drehen; **he thinks everything ~s around him** *(fig)* er glaubt, alles drehe sich nur um ihn

revolver [rɪˈvɒlvəʳ] N Revolver *m*

revolving [rɪˈvɒlvɪŋ] *in cpds* Dreh-; **revolving chair** N Drehstuhl *m*; **revolving credit** N revolvierender Kredit; **revolving door** N **a** Drehtür *f* **b** *(fig)* **a ~ of highly paid executives** das Personalkarussell bei hoch dotierten Führungsposten; **the ~ between government and the private sector** das Hin und Her zwischen Regierung und privatem Sektor; **the ~ of the justice system** der Drehtüreffekt in der Rechtsprechung; **revolving light** N Rundumleuchte *f*; **revolving pencil** N Drehbleistift *m*; **revolving restaurant** N Drehrestaurant *nt*; **revolving stage** N Drehbühne *f*

revue [rɪˈvjuː] N *(Theat)* Revue *f*; *(satirical)* Kabarett *nt*; **~ artist** Revuestar *m*, Kabarettist(in) *m(f)*

revulsion [rɪˈvʌlʃən] N **a** (= *disgust*) Abscheu *m*, Ekel *m* (*at* vor *+dat*) **b** (= *sudden change*) Umschwung *m*; (= *reaction*) Empörung *f*

reward [rɪˈwɔːd] N Belohnung *f*; (= *money*) Entgelt *nt (form)*; **as a ~ for helping me** als Belohnung für Ihre Hilfe; **EUR 1,000 ~** 1.000 EUR Belohnung; **~ offered for the return of ...** Finderlohn für ...; **the ~s of this job** die Vorzüge dieser Arbeit VT belohnen; **"finder will be ~ed"** „Finderlohn (ist) ausgesetzt"

reward card N *(Econ)* Kundenkarte *f*, Paybackkarte *f*

rewarding [rɪˈwɔːdɪŋ] ADJ *(financially)* lohnend, einträglich; *(mentally, morally) experience* lohnend; *task, work* dankbar; *relationship* bereichernd; **this is a very ~ book/film** es lohnt sich wirklich, dieses Buch zu lesen/diesen Film zu sehen; **bringing up a child is ~** ein Kind großzuziehen ist eine dankbare *or* lohnende Aufgabe

rewind [ˌriːˈwaɪnd] *pret, ptp* **rewound** VT *thread* wieder aufwickeln; *watch* wieder aufziehen; *film, tape, video* zurückspulen; **~ button** Rückspultaste *f*

rewire [ˌriːˈwaɪəʳ] VT neu verkabeln

reword [ˌriːˈwɜːd] VT *explanation, question* umformulieren, anders ausdrücken; *paragraph, sentence also* neu abfassen

rework [ˌriːˈwɜːk] VT (= *use again*) *theme* wieder verarbeiten; (= *revise*) neu fassen; *story* neu bearbeiten; *proposals* neu formulieren

rewound [ˌriːˈwaʊnd] *pret, ptp of* **rewind**

rewrite [ˌriːˈraɪt] *vb: pret* **rewrote** [ˌriːˈrəʊt] *ptp* **rewritten** [ˌriːˈrɪtn] VT (= *write out again*) neu schreiben; (= *recast*) umschreiben; **to ~ history** die Geschichte umschreiben; **to ~ the record books** einen neuen Rekord verzeichnen N [ˈriːˌraɪt] **this is just a ~ of his first novel** dies ist nur ein Neuaufguss *m* seines ersten Romans; **it needs a complete ~** es muss vollständig neu geschrieben werden

RGN *(Brit) abbr of* **Registered General Nurse**

Rh *abbr of* **rhesus** Rh

Rhaeto-Romanic [ˌriːtəʊrəʊˈmænɪk] N Rätoromanisch *nt*

rhapsodic [ræpˈsɒdɪk] ADJ *(Mus)* rhapsodisch; *(fig)* ekstatisch

rhapsodize [ˈræpsədaɪz] VI überschwänglich schwärmen (*over, about* von)

rhapsody [ˈræpsədɪ] N *(Mus)* Rhapsodie *f*; *(fig)* Schwärmerei *f*

rhd *abbr of* **right hand drive**

rhea [ˈriːə] N Nandu *m*, Pampasstrauß *m*

Rhenish [ˈrenɪʃ] ADJ *region, town* rheinisch; ~ **wine** Rheinwein *m*

rhenium [ˈriːnɪəm] N *(Chem)* Rhenium *nt*

rheostat [ˈriːəʊstæt] N Regelwiderstand *m*, Rheostat *m (spec)*

rhesus [ˈriːsəs] N Rhesus *m*

rhesus: **rhesus baby** N Rhesus-geschädigtes Baby; **rhesus factor** N Rhesusfaktor *m*; **rhesus monkey** N Rhesusaffe *m*; **rhesus-negative** ADJ Rhesus negativ; ~ **baby** Baby *nt* mit Rhesus negativ; **rhesus-positive** ADJ Rhesus positiv

rhetoric [ˈretərɪk] N Rhetorik *f*; *(pej)* Phrasendrescherei *f (pej)*

rhetorical [rɪˈtɒrɪkəl] ADJ rhetorisch; *(pej)* phrasenhaft, schwülstig *(pej)*

rhetorically [rɪˈtɒrɪkəlɪ] ADV *(pej)* schwülstig; *ask* rhetorisch

rhetorical question N rhetorische Frage

rhetorician [ˌretəˈrɪʃən] N Rhetoriker(in) *m(f)*; *(pej)* Phrasendrescher(in) *m(f) (pej)*

rheumatic [ruːˈmætɪk] N **a** *(= person)* Rheumatiker(in) *m(f)* **b rheumatics** SING Rheumatismus *m* ADJ *pains* rheumatisch; *joint* rheumakrank

rheumatic fever N rheumatisches Fieber, akuter Rheumatismus

rheumaticky [ruːˈmætɪkɪ] ADJ *(inf: = rheumatic) person* rheumatisch; **only now he realized how ~ he was becoming** er merkte erst jetzt, wie schlimm sein Rheuma geworden war; ~ **hands/fingers** Rheumahände *pl*/-finger *pl*; ~ **ache/pain** Rheumaschmerzen *pl*

rheumatism [ˈruːmətɪzəm] N Rheuma *nt*, Rheumatismus *m*

rheumatoid arthritis [ˈruːmətɔɪdɑːˈθraɪtɪs] N chronischer Rheumatismus, Gelenkrheumatismus *m*

rheumatologist [ˌruːməˈtɒlədʒɪst] N Rheumatologe *m*, Rheumatologin *f*

rheumatology [ˌruːməˈtɒlədʒɪ] N Rheumatologie *f*

rheumy [ˈruːmɪ] ADJ *eyes* wässrig

Rhine [raɪn] N Rhein *m*; ~ **wine** Rheinwein *m*

Rhine: **Rhineland** N Rheinland *nt*; **Rhinelander** [ˈraɪnlændəˈ] N Rheinländer(in) *m(f)*; **rhinestone** N Rheinkiesel *m*

rhino [ˈraɪnəʊ] N *abbr of* **rhinoceros**

rhinoceros [raɪˈnɒsərəs] N Nashorn *nt*, Rhinozeros *nt*

rhinoplasty [ˈraɪnəʊˌplæstɪ] N *(Med)* Nasenkorrektur *f*, Rhinoplastik *f (spec)*

rhizome [ˈraɪzəʊm] N Rhizom *nt*, Wurzelstock *m*

Rhodes [rəʊdz] N Rhodos *nt*; **in ~** auf Rhodos

Rhodesia [rəʊˈdiːʒə] N *(Hist)* Rhodesien *nt*

Rhodesian [rəʊˈdiːʒən] *(Hist)* ADJ rhodesisch N Rhodesier(in) *m(f)*

Rhodian [ˈrəʊdɪən] ADJ rhodisch, (von) der Insel Rhodos N Rhodier(in) *m(f)*

rhodium [ˈrəʊdɪəm] N *(Chem)* Rhodium *nt*

rhododendron [ˌrəʊdəˈdendrən] N Rhododendron *m or nt*

rhomb [rɒm] N Rhombus *m*

rhombic [ˈrɒmbɪk] ADJ rhombisch

rhomboid [ˈrɒmbɔɪd] N Rhomboid *nt* ADJ rhomboid

rhombus [ˈrɒmbəs] N Rhombus *m*

Rhone [rəʊn] N Rhone *f*

rhubarb [ˈruːbɑːb] N Rhabarber *m*; **"rhubarb, ~, ~"** *(Theat, hum)* „Rhabarberhabarberhabarba"

rhyme [raɪm] N **a** *(= rhyming word)* Reim *m*; ~ **scheme** Reimschema *nt*; **without ~ or reason** ohne Sinn und Verstand; **there seems to be no ~ or reason to it, that has no ~ or reason** das hat weder Sinn noch Verstand **b** *(= poem)* Gedicht *nt*; **in ~** in Reimen *or* Versen; **to put into ~** in Reime *or* Verse bringen VT reimen VI **a** *(words)* sich reimen **b** *(pej, = write verse)* reimen, Verse schmieden

rhymester [ˈraɪmstəˈ], **rhymer** [ˈraɪməˈ] N *(pej)* Verseschmied *m (pej)*, Dichterling *m (pej)*

rhyming [ˈraɪmɪŋ] ADJ ~ **couplets** Reimpaare *pl*; ~ **dictionary** Reimwörterbuch *nt*

> **RHYMING SLANG**
>
> **Rhyming slang** ist eine Sonderform des Cockney-Slangs, in dem das gemeinte Wort durch einen Ausdruck ersetzt wird, der sich darauf reimt: z. B. „apples and pears" statt **stairs**. Für Leute, die damit nicht vertraut sind, kann das ziemlich verwirrend werden, vor allem dann, wenn das Reimwort weggelassen wird – so wird „butcher's hook", das für **look** steht, zu „butcher's", wie in „let's take a butcher's". Einige Ausdrücke des „rhyming slang" sind Teil der Umgangssprache geworden, z. B. „use your loaf", wobei **loaf** die Abkürzung von „loaf of bread" ist, das wiederum für **head** steht; kurz gesagt: „streng deinen Grips an" → COCKNEY

rhythm [ˈrɪðəm] N Rhythmus *m*; **the ~ method (of contraception)** die Knaus-Ogino-Methode; ~ **section** *(of band)* Rhythmusgruppe *f*; ~ **and blues** Rhythm-and-Blues *m*

rhythmic(al) [ˈrɪðmɪk(əl)] ADJ rhythmisch; *breathing, pulse* gleichmäßig; **rhythmic gymnastics** rhythmische Gymnastik

rhythmically [ˈrɪðmɪkəlɪ] ADV rhythmisch; *breathe* gleichmäßig

RI *abbr of* **Religious Instruction**

rib [rɪb] N **a** *(Anat, Cook)* Rippe *f*; **to dig** *(esp Brit) or* **poke sb in the ~s** jdn in die Rippen stoßen **b** *(of leaf, ceiling, ship, shell)* Rippe *f*; *(of umbrella)* Speiche *f* **c** *(Knitting)* Rippen *pl*; **in ~** in Rippen VT *(inf: = tease)* necken, foppen

RIBA [ˈriːbə] *abbr of* **Royal Institute of British Architects**

ribald [ˈrɪbəld, ˈraɪbəld] ADJ deftig, zotig *(pej)*; *behaviour* derb; *company* liederlich; ~ **comments** Ferkeleien *pl*

ribaldry [ˈrɪbəldrɪ] N Ferkeleien *pl*, Schweinereien *pl*

riband [ˈrɪbənd] N *(obs)* = **ribbon**

ribbed [rɪbd] ADJ *sole, condom, knitting* gerippt; *shell, ceiling* mit Rippen

ribbon [ˈrɪbən] N **a** *(for hair, dress)* Band *nt*; *(for typewriter)* Farbband *nt*; *(on medal)* Ordensband *nt*; *(fig, narrow strip)* Streifen *m* **b ribbons** PL *(= tatters)* Fetzen *pl*; **to tear sth to ~s** etw zerfetzen *or* zerreißen; *(fig) play etc* etw in der Luft zerreißen

ribbon: **ribbon development** N *(Brit)* Zeilenbauweise *f*; **ribbon saw** N *(Tech)* Bandsäge *f*

rib cage N Brustkorb *m*

riboflavin [ˈraɪbəʊˈfleɪvɪn] N Riboflavin *nt*

ribonucleic acid [ˈraɪbəʊnjuːˈkliːɪkˈæsɪd] N Ribonukleinsäure *f*

rib-tickler N *(hum inf)* **it's a real ~** das ist die reinste Zwerchfellmassage *(inf)*

ribwort [ˈrɪbwɜːt] N Spitzwegerich *m*

rice [raɪs] N Reis *m*

rice *in cpds* Reis-; **ricefield** N Reisfeld *nt*; **rice growing** N Reis(an)bau *m*; **rice-growing** ADJ Reis anbauend; **rice paper** N Reispapier *nt*; **rice pudding** N *(esp Brit)* Milchreis *m*

ricer [ˈraɪsəˈ] N *(esp US Cook)* Kartoffelpresse *f*

rice wine N Reiswein *m*

rich [rɪtʃ] ADJ *(+er)* **a** *(= wealthy)* reich; ~ **and famous** reich und berühmt; **for ~er, for poorer** in guten wie in schlechten Zeiten; **to get ~ quick** schnell zu Reichtum gelangen
b *(= splendid) furniture, decoration, style, clothes* prächtig; *gift* teuer; *banquet* üppig
c *food* schwer; ~ **tea biscuit** ≈ Butterkeks *m*; **a ~ diet** reichhaltige Kost
d *(= fertile) soil* fruchtbar, fett; *land* fruchtbar, reich
e *(= abundant, plentiful)* reich; **seaweed is a ~ source of iodine** Seetang ist eine reiche Jodquelle
f *(= intense) colour* satt; *sound, voice* voll; *wine* schwer; *smell* kräftig, stark
g *(= full, eventful) life* erfüllt; *history, experience* reich; **to be (all) the ~er for sth** durch etw bereichert sein
h *(inf: = amusing)* köstlich; **that's ~!** *(iro)* das ist stark *(inf)*
i *(Aut) mixture* fett
j *(= full of)* **to be ~ in sth** *(in resources etc)* reich an etw *(dat)* sein; ~ **in vitamins/protein** vitamin-/eiweißreich; ~ **in corn/minerals** reich an Getreide/Bodenschätzen; ~ **in detail** sehr detailliert; ~ **in illustrations/examples** mit vielen Abbildungen/Beispielen; **to be ~ in spirit** ein gutes Herz haben; **the air was ~ with the scent of blossom** die Luft war von Blütenduft erfüllt
N **a the ~**
PL die Reichen *pl*; **the ~ and famous** die Reichen und Berühmten *pl*, die Schickeria *f (iro)* **b riches** PL Reichtümer *pl*; **natural ~es** natürliche Reichtümer *pl*

Richard [ˈrɪtʃəd] N Richard *m*; ~ **(the) Lionheart** Richard Löwenherz

richly [ˈrɪtʃlɪ] ADV **a** *(= ornately) dress, decorate* prächtig **b** *(= abundantly) illustrated* reich; **to be ~ endowed with sth** mit etw reich ausgestattet sein **c** *(= strongly) coloured, flavoured* kräftig; *scented* kräftig, intensiv; ~ **rewarding/satisfying** überaus lohnend/befriedigend; **a ~ textured narrative** eine üppig angelegte *or* ausgestattete Erzählung **d** *(= thoroughly)* **he ~ deserves it** er hat es mehr als verdient; **he was ~ rewarded** *(lit)* er wurde reich belohnt; *(fig)* er wurde reichlich belohnt

richness [ˈrɪtʃnɪs] N **a** *(= wealthiness)* Reichtum *m* **b** *(= splendour, of furniture, decoration, style, clothes)* Pracht *f*; *(of banquet)* Üppigkeit *f* **c** *(of food)* Schwere *f*; **the ~ of the food** die reichhaltige Kost **d** *(= fertility: of soil, land)* Fruchtbarkeit *f* **e** *(= intensity, of colour)* Sattheit *f*; *(of wine)* Schwere *f*; *(of smell)* Stärke *f*; **the ~ of his voice** seine volle Stimme **f** *(= fullness, of life)* Erfülltheit *f*; *(of history, experience)* Reichtum *m* **g** *(Aut, of mixture)* Fettheit *f* **h** *(in minerals, vitamins etc)* Reichtum *m (in an +dat)*

Richter scale [ˈrɪktəˈskeɪl] N Richterskala *f*

rick[1] [rɪk] N Schober *m*

rick[2] N, VT = **wrick**

rickets [ˈrɪkɪts] N *sing* Rachitis *f*, die englische Krankheit

rickety [ˈrɪkɪtɪ] ADJ **a** *furniture, stairs etc* wack(e)lig; *vehicle* klapprig **b** *(Med)* rachitisch

rickrack [ˈrɪkræk] N *no pl (US)* Zickzackbordüre *f*

rickshaw [ˈrɪkʃɔː] N Rikscha *f*

ricochet [ˈrɪkəʃeɪ] N Abprall *m* VI abprallen (*off* von); **the stone ~ed off the water** der Stein hüpfte auf dem Wasser

rictus [ˈrɪktəs] N *(Anat, Zool)* Sperrweite *f*

rid [rɪd] *pret, ptp* **rid** *or* **ridded** VT **to ~ of** *(of pests, disease)* befreien von; *of bandits etc* säubern von; **to ~ oneself of sb/sth** jdn/etw loswerden; *of pests also* sich von etw befreien; *of ideas, prejudice etc* sich von etw lösen; **to get ~ of sb/sth** jdn/etw loswerden; **to be ~ of sb/sth** jdn/etw los sein; **get ~ of it** sieh zu, dass du das loswirst; *(= throw it away)* schmeiß es weg *(inf)*; **you are well ~ of him** ein Glück, dass du den los bist

riddance [ˈrɪdəns] N **good ~ (to bad rubbish)!** *(inf)* ein Glück, dass wir das/den *etc* los sind

ridden [ˈrɪdn] *ptp of* **ride** ADJ **angst-~** angsterfüllt; **debt-~** hoch verschuldet; **disease-~** von

Krankheiten befallen; **strife-~** zerstritten; **~ with crime** mit hoher Kriminalität; **~ with intolerance** ohne die leiseste Spur von Toleranz

riddle[1] [ˈrɪdl] N (= *sieve*) (Schüttel)sieb *nt* VT a *soil etc* sieben; *coal* sieben, schütteln b **to ~ sb/sth with bullets** jdn/etw mit Kugeln durchlöchern; **~d with holes** völlig durchlöchert; **~d with woodworm** wurmzerfressen; **~d with cancer/corruption** vom Krebs/von der Korruption zerfressen; **~d with mistakes/contradictions** voller Fehler/Widersprüche

riddle[2] N Rätsel *nt*; **I'll ask you a ~** ich werde Ihnen ein Rätsel aufgeben; **to speak in ~s** in Rätseln sprechen

ride [raɪd] *vb: pret* **rode**, *ptp* **ridden** N a (*in vehicle, on bicycle*) Fahrt *f*; (*on horse*) Ritt *m*; (*for pleasure*) Ausritt *m*; **to go for a ~** eine Fahrt machen; (*on horse*) reiten gehen; **after a hard ~ across country** nach einer langen Überlandfahrt; (*on horse*) nach einem langen Ritt querfeldein; **he gave the child a ~ on his back** er ließ das Kind auf den Schultern reiten; **cycle/car/coach ~** Rad-/Auto-/Busfahrt *f*; **to go for a ~ in the car** mit dem Auto wegfahren, eine Fahrt (mit dem Auto) machen; **I just came along/went along for the ~** (*fig inf*) ich bin nur zum Vergnügen mitgekommen/mitgegangen; **to take sb for a ~** (*in car etc*) mit jdm eine Fahrt machen; (*inf: = deceive*) jdn anschmieren (*inf*); **he gave me a ~ into town in his car** er nahm mich im Auto in die Stadt mit; **it's my first ~ in a limousine/in a train** ich fahre zum ersten Mal in einer Limousine/in einem Zug; **can I have a ~ on your bike?** kann ich mal mit deinem Rad fahren?; **3 ~s on the merry-go-round** 3 Karussellfahrten; **that roller coaster is the scariest ~ I've ever been on** ich habe noch nie so viel Angst gehabt wie bei der Fahrt auf der Achterbahn; **to have a ~ in a helicopter** in einem Hubschrauber fliegen; **we had a ~ in a taxi/train** wir sind in einem Taxi/Zug gefahren; **it's an 80p ~ from the station** ab Bahnhof kostet die Fahrt 80 Pence; **the Ride of the Valkyries** der Ritt der Walküren

b (= *quality of ride*) **this car gives a smooth/bumpy ~** mit diesem Auto fährt es sich sanft/unsanft

c (= *path for horses*) Reitweg *m*

d (*sl: = lay*) **to be a good ~** gut im Bett sein (*inf*)

VI a (*on a horse etc, Sport*) reiten (*on* auf +*dat*); **to go riding** reiten gehen; **the jockey was riding just under 65 kg** der Jockey brachte knapp 65 kg auf die Waage; **Peter Mandelson ~s again!** (*fig hum*) Peter Mandelson ist wieder da!

b (= *go in vehicle, by cycle etc*) fahren; **he was riding on a bicycle** er fuhr mit einem Fahrrad; **to ~ on a bus/in a car/in a train/in a cart** in einem Bus/Wagen/Zug/Schubkarren fahren; **to ~ away** *or* **off/down** weg- *or* davon-/hinunterfahren

c (*fig: = float*) **the seagull ~s on the wind** die Möwe lässt sich vom Wind tragen; **the moon was riding high in the sky** der Mond zog hoch am Himmel dahin; **he's riding high** (*fig*) er schwimmt ganz oben; **he was riding high in public opinion** in der öffentlichen Meinung stand er ganz oben; **to ~ at anchor** (*ship*) vor Anker liegen; **we'll just have to let the matter** *or* **to let things ~ for a while** wir müssen einfach für eine Weile den Dingen ihren Lauf lassen; **... but I'll let it ~** ..., aber ich lasse es vorerst einmal

d (*horse*) **to ~ well** gut laufen

VT a *horse, donkey etc* reiten mit *or* auf (+*dat*), reiten; *bicycle, motorbike* fahren mit, fahren; **I have never ridden a bicycle/a motorbike** ich bin noch nie Rad/Motorrad gefahren; **may I ~ your bike?** darf ich mit deinem Fahrrad fahren?; **he rode his horse away/back** *etc* er ritt mit seinem Pferd weg/zurück *etc*; **he rode him hard** er ritt es scharf; **he rode the horse into the stable** er ritt das Pferd in den Stall; **Jason will be ridden by H. Martin** Jason wird unter H. Martin laufen; **to ~ two horses at the same time** (*fig*) auf zwei Hochzeiten tanzen; **to ~ a race** bei einem Rennen reiten; **to ~ a good race** (bei einem Rennen) gut reiten; **they had ridden 10 km** sie waren 10 km geritten/gefahren; **they had ridden all the way** sie waren den ganzen Weg geritten/gefahren; **he rode the land looking for ...** er durchritt/durchfuhr das ganze Land auf der Suche nach ...; **the birds riding the wind** die Vögel, die sich vom Wind tragen lassen; **the ship rode the waves** das Schiff trieb auf den Wellen; **the surfers rode the waves** die Surfer ritten auf den Wellen; **the party is riding the wave of public support** die Partei nutzt die Gunst der Öffentlichkeit; **witches ~ broomsticks** Hexen reiten auf einem Besen; **to ~ the storm** (*lit, fig*) den Sturm überstehen; **to ~ a horse to death** ein Pferd zu Tode reiten; **to ~ an argument to death** ein Argument totreden → *also* **ridden**

b (*US inf: = torment*) piesacken (*inf*), schikanieren, zusetzen (+*dat*); **don't ~ him too hard** treibts nicht so toll mit ihm

c (*sl: = have sex with*) reiten (*sl*)

▸ **ride about** (*Brit*) *or* **around** VI (*on horse etc*) herumreiten; (*in vehicle, on motorcycle*) herumfahren; (*on bicycle*) herumradeln (*inf*), herumfahren

▸ **ride behind** VI (*on same horse, bicycle*) hinten sitzen; (*on different horse, bicycle*) hinterherreiten, hinterherfahren

▸ **ride down** VT *sep* a (= *trample*) umreiten b (= *catch up with*) einholen

▸ **ride on** VI +*prep obj* (*money, reputation*) hängen an (+*dat*)

▸ **ride out** VT *sep* überstehen; **to ride out the storm** (*lit, fig*) den Sturm überstehen VI (*on horse*) ausreiten, einen Ausritt machen

▸ **ride up** VI a (*horseman*) heranreiten; (*motorcyclist etc*) heranfahren b (*skirt etc*) hochrutschen

rider [ˈraɪdəʳ] N a (= *person, on horse*) Reiter(in) *m(f)*; (*on bicycle, motorcycle*) Fahrer(in) *m(f)* b (= *addition*) Zusatz *m*; (*to document, will etc*) Zusatzklausel *f*; (*to bill*) Allonge *f*; (*to jury's verdict*) zusätzliche Empfehlung; **I'd just like to add one ~ to that** zusätzlich (dazu) möchte ich noch eins sagen

ridge [rɪdʒ] N a (= *raised strip, on fabric, cardboard etc*) Rippe *f*; (*on corrugated iron*) Welle *f*; (*on sand*) Rippelmarke *f*; (*on ploughed land*) Grat *m*; (*in sea: = reef*) Riff *nt*; **a ~ of hills** eine Hügelkette; **a ~ of mountains** ein Höhenzug *m*; **a ~ of high pressure** (*Met*) ein Hochdruckkeil *m* b (*of hills, mountains*) Rücken *m*, Kamm *m*; (*pointed, steep*) Grat *m*; (*of roof*) First *m*; (*of nose*) Rücken *m* VT *rocks, land, sand* zerfurchen

ridge: **ridgepole** N (*of tent*) Firststange *f*; **ridge tent** N Firstzelt *nt*; **ridge tile** N Firstziegel *m*; **ridgeway** N (*Brit*) Gratweg *m*

ridgy [ˈrɪdʒɪ] ADJ *mountain passage etc* grat- *or* kammartig; (= *furrowed*) zerfurcht

ridicule [ˈrɪdɪkjuːl] N Spott *m*; **to hold sb/sth up to ~** sich über jdn/etw lustig machen; **she's an object of ~** alles macht sich über sie lustig; **to become an object of ~** der Lächerlichkeit preisgegeben werden VT verspotten, verlachen

ridiculous [rɪˈdɪkjʊləs] ADJ lächerlich; **don't be ~** red keinen Unsinn; **to make oneself (look) ~** sich lächerlich machen; **to be made to look ~** der Lächerlichkeit preisgegeben werden; **to take sth to ~ extremes** *or* **lengths** etw bis ins Lächerliche *or* bis zur Lächerlichkeit übertreiben; **to go to ~ lengths (to do sth)** großen Aufwand betreiben(, um etw zu tun)

ridiculously [rɪˈdɪkjʊləslɪ] ADV lächerlich; **you're talking ~** du redest dummes Zeug; **~, he blamed himself for the accident** er gab sich lächerlicherweise selbst die Schuld an dem Unfall

ridiculousness [rɪˈdɪkjʊləsnɪs] N Lächerlichkeit *f*

riding [ˈraɪdɪŋ] N Reiten *nt*; **I enjoy ~** ich reite gern

riding *in cpds* Reit-; **riding breeches** PL Reithosen *pl*, Breeches *pl*; **a pair of ~** eine Reithose; **riding crop** N Reitgerte *f*; **riding habit** N Reitkostüm *nt*, Reitkleid *nt*; **riding jacket** N Reitjacke *f*; **riding light** N (*Naut*) Ankerlicht *nt*; **riding master** N Reitlehrer *m*; **riding whip** N Reitpeitsche *f*

Riesling [ˈriːzlɪŋ] N (= *variety of white wine*) Riesling *m*

rife [raɪf] ADJ a (= *widespread*) *disease, corruption* weitverbreitet; **to be ~** grassieren; (*rumour*) umgehen; **rumours** (*Brit*) *or* **rumors** (*US*) **are/speculation is ~ that ...** es geht das Gerücht um/es wird spekuliert, dass ... b (= *full of*) **~ with** voll von, voller +*gen*; **the garden was ~ with weeds** der Garten strotzte vor Unkraut; **countries ~ with Aids** Länder mit einer hohen Aidsrate; **areas ~ with unemployment/violence** Gegenden mit hoher Arbeitslosigkeit/Gewaltkriminalität

riffle [ˈrɪfl] VT (*also* **riffle through**) *pages* blättern durch; *cards* mischen

riffraff [ˈrɪfræf] N Pöbel *m*, Gesindel *nt*

rifle[1] [ˈraɪfl] VT a *town* plündern; (*also* **rifle through**) *sb's pockets, drawer, till, house* durchwühlen b *ball, shot* donnern (*inf*)

rifle[2] N (= *gun*) Gewehr *nt* (*mit gezogenem Lauf*); (*for hunting*) Büchse *f*; **the Rifles** (*Mil*) ≈ die Schützen *pl*

rifle: **rifle association** N Schützenverein *m*; **rifle butt** N Gewehrkolben *m*; **rifle club** N Schützenverein *m*; **rifleman** N (Gewehr)-schütze *m*; **rifle practice** N (*Mil*) Schießübung *f*; **rifle range** N Schießstand *m*; **within ~** in Schussweite (eines Gewehrs); **riflescope** N Zielfernrohr *nt*; **rifle shot** N Gewehrschuss *m*

rift [rɪft] N a Spalt *m* b (*fig: in friendship*) Riss *m*; (*Pol*) Spalt *m*, Riss *m*

rift: **rift saw** N (*Tech*) Gattersäge *f*; **rift valley** N Grabenbruch *m*

rig [rɪg] N a (*Naut*) Takelage *f*, Takelung *f* b (= *oil rig*) (Öl)förderturm *m*; (*offshore*) Ölbohrinsel *f* c (*inf: = outfit: also* **rig-out**) Ausrüstung *f*; **in full ~** in großer Aufmachung, in voller Montur (*inf*) d (*inf: = articulated lorry*) Sattelschlepper *m* VT a (*Naut*) auftakeln b (*fig*) *election, market etc* manipulieren; **to ~ the vote** die Wahlergebnisse manipulieren; **it was ~ged!** das war Manipulation

▸ **rig out** VT *sep* (*inf: = equip*) ausstaffieren (*inf*); (= *dress*) auftakeln (*inf*)

▸ **rig up** VT *sep ship* auftakeln; *equipment* aufbauen; (*fig: = make*) improvisieren; (= *arrange*) arrangieren

rigger [ˈrɪgəʳ] N (*Naut*) Takler *m*

rigging [ˈrɪgɪŋ] N a (*Naut, = action*) Auftakeln *nt*; (*Naut: = ropes*) Tauwerk *nt* b (*inf: = dishonest interference*) Manipulation *f*, Schiebung *f* (*inf*)

right [raɪt] ⊙ 11.1, 13 ADJ a (= *just, fair, morally good*) richtig, recht (*S Ger*); **it isn't ~ to lie** es ist nicht richtig *or* recht zu lügen; **he thought it ~ to warn me** er hielt es für richtig, mich zu warnen; **it seemed only ~ to give him the money** es schien richtig, ihm das Geld zu geben; **it's only ~ (and proper)** es ist nur recht und billig; **it is only ~ to point out that ...** es ist nur recht und billig, wenn man darauf hinweist, dass ...; **to do the ~ thing by sb** sich jdm gegenüber anständig benehmen

b (= *true, correct*) *answer, solution, time, train* richtig; **to be ~** (*person*) recht haben; (*answer, solution*) richtig sein, stimmen; (*clock*) richtig gehen; **what's the ~ time?** wie viel Uhr ist es genau?; **you're quite ~** Sie haben ganz recht; **how ~ you are!** (*inf*) da haben Sie ganz recht; **you were ~ to refuse** *or* **in refusing** Sie hatten recht, als Sie ablehnten; **my guess was ~** ich habe richtig geraten; **let's get it ~ this time!** mach es dieses Mal richtig; (*in reporting facts etc*) sag es dieses Mal richtig; **to put** *or* **set ~** (*error*) korrigieren; *clock* richtig stellen; *situation* wieder in Ordnung bringen; **I tried to put**

things ~ after their quarrel ich versuchte, nach ihrem Streit wieder einzulenken; **to put** *or* **set sb ~** *(= correct)* jdn berichtigen

c *(= proper) clothes, document* richtig; **what's the ~ thing to do in this case?** was tut man da am besten?; **to come at the ~ time** zur rechten Zeit kommen; **to do sth the ~ way** etw richtig machen; **that is the ~ way of looking at it** das ist die richtige Einstellung; **the ~ man for the job** der rechte *or* richtige Mann für die Stelle; **Mr/Miss Right** *(inf)* der/die Richtige *(inf)*; **we will do what is ~ for the country** wir werden tun, was für das Land gut ist; **to know the ~ people** die richtigen Leute kennen

d *(= well)* **the medicine soon put** *or* **set him ~** die Medizin hat ihn schnell wiederhergestellt *or* wieder auf die Beine gebracht; **I don't feel quite ~ today** ich fühle mich heute nicht ganz wohl; **to be as ~ as rain** *(Brit)* kerngesund sein; *(after accident)* keine Schramme abbekommen haben *(inf)*; **to put the engine ~** den Motor reparieren; **the plumber put things ~** der Klempner brachte alles wieder in Ordnung; **to be in one's ~ mind** klar bei Verstand sein; **nobody in their ~ mind would ...** kein vernünftiger Mensch würde ...; **who in their ~ mind would ...?** welcher vernünftige Mensch würde ...?; **he's not ~ in the head** *(inf)* bei ihm stimmts nicht im Oberstübchen *(inf)* → **all right**

e *(phrases)* **~!, ~ oh!** *(Brit inf)* **~ you are!** *(Brit inf)* gut, schön, okay *(inf)*; **~ on!** *(esp US inf)* super! *(sl)*; **that's ~!** *(= correct, true)* das stimmt!; **that's ~, dear, put it on the table** schön, stell es bitte auf den Tisch; **so they came in the end – is that ~?** und so kamen sie schließlich – wirklich?; **~ enough!** (das) stimmt!; **it's a ~ mess in there** *(Brit inf)* das ist vielleicht ein Durcheinander hier *(inf)*; **he's a ~ fool!** *(Brit inf)* er ist wirklich doof *(inf)*; **you're a ~ one** *(Brit inf)* du bist mir der Richtige *(inf)*

f *(= opposite of left)* rechte(r, s); **~ hand** rechte Hand; **I'd give my ~ hand to know the answer** ich würde was drum geben, wenn ich die Antwort wüsste *(inf)*; **on your ~ hand** rechter Hand, rechts

g the ~ side of the material die rechte Seite (des Stoffes)

ADV a *(= straight, directly)* direkt; *(= exactly)* genau; **~ in front/ahead of you** direkt *or* genau vor Ihnen; **go ~ on** gehen/fahren Sie geradeaus weiter; **~ away, ~ off** *(= immediately)* sofort, schnurstracks *(inf)*; **~ off** *(= at the first attempt)* auf Anhieb *(inf)*; **~ now** *(= at this very moment)* in diesem Augenblick; *(= immediately)* sofort; **~ here** genau hier; **~ in the middle** genau *or* direkt in der/die Mitte; **~ at the beginning** gleich am Anfang; **I'll be ~ with you** ich bin gleich da; **it hit me ~ in the face** der Schlag traf mich genau *or* voll ins Gesicht

b *(= completely, all the way)* ganz; **~ round the house** ganz um das Haus herum; *(inside)* durch das ganze Haus; **~ through** *(drive, go)* mitten durch; **rotten ~ through** durch und durch verfault *or (fig)* verdorben

c *(= correctly)* richtig; **to guess ~** richtig raten; **you did ~ to refuse** es war richtig (von Ihnen) abzulehnen; **if everything goes ~** wenn alles klappt *(inf)*; **nothing goes ~ for them** nichts klappt bei ihnen *(inf)*, bei ihnen läuft alles schief *(inf)*; **if I get you ~** *(inf)* wenn ich Sie (da) richtig verstehe; **I'll see you ~** *(inf)* ich werde aufpassen, dass Sie nicht zu kurz kommen *(inf)* → **serve**

d *(old, dial, = very)* sehr; *(Brit)* **the Right Honourable John Smith MP** der Abgeordnete John Smith

e *(= opposite of left)* rechts; **it is ~ of the bridge** es ist rechts von der Brücke; **turn ~** biegen Sie rechts ab; **~, left and centre** *(Brit) or* **center** *(US) (= everywhere)* überall; **to be cheated ~, left and centre** *or* **~ and left** *(inf)* von vorne bis hinten betrogen werden *(inf)*; **to owe money ~, left and centre** *(Brit) or* **center** *(US inf)* bei Gott und der Welt Schulden haben *(inf)*

N a *no pl (moral, legal)* Recht *nt*; **he doesn't know ~ from wrong** er kann Recht und Unrecht nicht auseinanderhalten; **I want to know the ~s and wrongs of it first** ich möchte erst beide Seiten kennenlernen; **to be in the ~** im Recht sein

b *(= entitlement)* Recht *nt*; *(to sth)* (An)recht *nt*, Anspruch *m*; **(to have) a ~ to sth** ein (An)recht *or* einen Anspruch auf etw *(acc)* (haben); **to have a** *or* **the ~ to do sth** ein *or* das Recht haben, etw zu tun; **what ~ have you to say that?** mit welchem Recht sagen Sie das?; **by what ~?** mit welchem Recht?; **he is within his ~s** das ist sein gutes Recht; **by ~s** rechtmäßig, von Rechts wegen; **in one's own ~** selber, selbst; **the divine ~ (of kings)** das Gottesgnadentum → **civil rights**

c rights PL *(Comm)* Rechte *pl*; **to have the (sole) ~s to sth** die (alleinigen) Rechte an etw *(dat)* haben

d to put *or* **set sth to ~s** etw (wieder) in Ordnung bringen; **to put things** *or* **the world to ~s** die Welt verbessern; **to have sb bang** *or* **dead to ~s** *(esp liter: = have evidence against sb)* jdn festgenagelt haben *(inf)*; *(inf) (= understand sb well)* jdn genau kennen; *(= describe sb well)* jdn genau so beschreiben, wie er/sie ist

e *(= not left)* rechte Seite; **to drive on the ~** rechts fahren; **to keep to the ~** sich rechts halten, rechts bleiben; **on my ~** rechts (von mir); **on** *or* **to the ~ of the church** rechts von der Kirche; **the Right** *(Pol)* die Rechte; **those to the ~ of him** *(Pol)* diejenigen, die weiter rechts stehen als er

VT a *(= return to upright position)* aufrichten

b *(= make amends for) wrong* wiedergutmachen

c the problem should ~ itself *(fig)* das Problem müsste sich von selbst lösen

right: **rightabout** [ˈraɪtəbaʊt] N *(Mil)* Kehrtwendung *f*; **right-aligned** ADJ *(Typ)* rechtsbündig; **right angle** N rechter Winkel; **at ~s (to)** rechtwinklig (zu); **right-angled** ADJ rechtwinklig; **right-angled triangle** N rechtwinkliges Dreieck; **right-click** *(Comput)* VI rechts klicken VT rechts klicken auf *(+acc)*

righteous [ˈraɪtʃəs] ADJ **a** rechtschaffen; *(pej)* selbstgerecht *(pej)* **b** *indignation, anger* gerecht N **the ~** *(Bibl)* die Gerechten *pl*

righteously [ˈraɪtʃəslɪ] ADV rechtschaffen

righteousness [ˈraɪtʃəsnɪs] N Rechtschaffenheit *f*

rightful [ˈraɪtfʊl] ADJ **a** *heir, owner, inheritance, role, place* rechtmäßig; **their ~ share** ihr rechtmäßiger Anteil, der ihnen zustehende Anteil **b** *punishment* gerecht

rightfully [ˈraɪtfəlɪ] ADV **a** rechtmäßig; **they must give us what is ~ ours** sie müssen uns geben, was uns rechtmäßig zusteht **b** *punish* gerechterweise

right: **right-hand** ADJ **~ drive** rechtsgesteuert; **~ side** rechte Seite; **right-handed** ADJ *person* rechtshändig; *punch, throw also* mit der rechten Hand ADV rechtshändig; **right-hander** N *(= punch)* Rechte *f*; *(= person)* Rechtshänder(in) *m(f)*; **right-hand man** N rechte Hand

rightie [ˈraɪtɪ] N *(inf)* = **righty**

rightist [ˈraɪtɪst] N *(Pol)* Rechte(r) *mf* ADJ rechtsorientiert

rightly [ˈraɪtlɪ] ✪ 11.1, 13, 26.3 ADV **a** *(= correctly)* richtig; **he said, ~, that ...** er sagte sehr richtig, dass ...; **quite ~** ganz recht; **they are ~ regarded as ...** sie werden zu Recht als ... angesehen; **if I remember ~** wenn ich mich recht erinnere

b *(= justifiably)* mit *or* zu Recht; **~ or wrongly** ob das nun richtig ist oder nicht; **and ~ so** und zwar mit Recht

c *(form, = properly)* richtig; **willpower can achieve great things when ~ applied** richtig eingesetzt, kann Willenskraft große Dinge erreichen

d *(inf: = really)* wirklich; **I can't ~ say** ich kann es wirklich nicht sagen; **I don't ~ know** ich weiß nicht genau

right: **right-minded** ADJ vernünftig; **right-of-centre**, *(US)* **right-of-center** ADJ *(Pol)* Mitte-rechts-; **~ politician** Mitte-rechts-Politiker(in) *m(f)*; **right of way** N *(across property)* Durchgangsrecht *nt*; *(Mot: = priority)* Vorfahrt(srecht *nt*) *f*; **it's his ~** *(Mot)* **he has the ~** *(Mot)* er hat Vorfahrt

rights issue N *(St Ex)* Bezugsrechtsemission *f*

right: **rightsizing** N *(Comm)* Rightsizing *nt*; **right-thinking** ADJ vernünftig; **right-to-lifer** N *(US)* Abtreibungsgegner(in) *m(f)*; **right triangle** N *(US)* rechtwinkliges Dreieck; **right wing** N **a** *(Pol)* rechter Flügel **b the ~** *(Ftbl, Hockey etc)* der rechte Flügel; **he's the ~** er ist (der) Rechtsaußen; **right-wing** ADJ *(Pol) government, party* rechtsgerichtet, rechtsorientiert; *politics, ideas* rechtsgerichtet, rechtslastig *(pej)*; **~ extremist** Rechtsextremist(in) *m(f)*; **~ extremism** Rechtsextremismus *m*; **right-winger** N *(Sport)* Rechtsaußen *m*; *(Pol)* Rechte(r) *mf*

righty [ˈraɪtɪ] N *(inf)* **a** *(Pol)* Rechte(r) *mf* **b** *(esp US: = right-handed person)* Rechtshänder(in) *m(f)*

rigid [ˈrɪdʒɪd] ADJ **a** *(lit) board, material, frame* starr, steif; **~ with fear** starr *or* steif vor Angst; **to be ~ with anger** starr vor Wut sein; **to bore sb ~** jdn zu Tode langweilen; **to be bored ~** sich zu Tode langweilen; **the prison visit had shaken her ~** *(inf)* der Gefängnisbesuch hatte sie umgehauen *(inf)* **b** *(fig) person, character* strikt, streng, stur *(pej)*; *discipline, principles* streng, strikt; *(= intolerant of others)* unbeugsam; *interpretation* genau, stur *(pej)*; *specifications* genau festgelegt, strikt; *system* starr, unbeugsam; *timetable* fest, streng

rigidity [rɪˈdʒɪdɪtɪ] N **a** *(lit)* Starrheit *f*, Steifheit *f* **b** *(fig, of person, character)* Striktheit *f*, Strenge *f*, Sturheit *f (pej)*; *(of discipline, principles)* Strenge *f*, Striktheit *f*; *(= intolerance of others)* Unbeugsamkeit *f*; *(of interpretation)* Genauigkeit *f*, Sturheit *f (pej)*; *(of specifications)* Striktheit *f*; *(of system)* Starrheit *f*, Unbeugsamkeit *f*; *(of timetable)* Festigkeit *f*

rigidly [ˈrɪdʒɪdlɪ] ADV **a** *(lit) stand etc* starr, steif; **to stand ~ to** *or* **at attention** in Habachtstellung sein; **to sit ~ upright** steif aufrecht sitzen **b** *(fig) behave, treat* streng, strikt; *oppose* stur, strikt; *(= intolerantly of others)* unbeugsam

rigmarole [ˈrɪgmərəʊl] N Gelaber *nt*; *(= process)* Gedöns *nt (inf)*; **to go through the whole** *or* **same ~ again** nochmal mit demselben Gelaber/Gedöns anfangen

rigor N *(US)* = **rigour**

rigor mortis [ˈrɪgəˈmɔːtɪs] N die Toten- *or* Leichenstarre

rigorous [ˈrɪgərəs] ADJ **a** *(= strict) person, character, discipline, rule, structure, method* streng, strikt; *measures* rigoros; *(= thorough) book-keeping, work* peinlich genau; *analysis, tests* gründlich; **with ~ precision/accuracy** mit äußerster Präzision/peinlicher Genauigkeit; **they were ~ in controlling expenditure** sie nahmen es mit der Ausgabekontrolle sehr genau; **he was a very ~ teacher** er war ein Lehrer, der es sehr genau nahm; **he is ~ about quality** er ist sehr streng, wenn es um Qualität geht **b** *(= harsh) climate* streng

rigorously [ˈrɪgərəslɪ] ADV *enforce* rigoros; *test* gründlich, streng; *control* streng

rigour, *(US)* **rigor** [ˈrɪgəʳ] N **a** *no pl (= strictness)* Strenge *f*, Striktheit *f*; **the full ~ of the law** die ganze Strenge des Gesetzes **b rigours** PL *(of climate, famine etc)* Unbilden *pl*

rigout [ˈrɪgaʊt] N *(Brit inf)* = **rig N c**

rile [raɪl] VT *(inf)* ärgern, reizen

Riley [ˈraɪlɪ] N **to live the life of ~** *(Brit inf)* leben wie Gott in Frankreich *(inf)*

rill [rɪl] N *(poet)* Bächlein *nt*

rim [rɪm] N *(of cup, bowl)* Rand *m*; *(of hat also)* Krempe *f*; *(of spectacles also)* Fassung *f*; *(of wheel)* Felge *f*, Radkranz *m*

rime[1] [raɪm] N = **rhyme**

rime[2] N *(liter)* (Rauh)reif *m*

rimless [ˈrɪmlɪs] ADJ *spectacles* randlos

rimmed [rɪmd] ADJ mit Rand; *wheel* mit Felge; **gold-~ spectacles** Brille *f* mit Goldfassung *or* -rand; **red-~ eyes** rot geränderte Augen

rind [raɪnd] N *(of cheese)* Rinde *f*; *(of bacon)* Schwarte *f*; *(of fruit)* Schale *f*

rinderpest ['rɪndəpest] N *(Vet)* Rinderpest *f*

ring¹ [rɪŋ] N a Ring *m*; *(for swimmer)* Schwimmring *or* -reifen *m*
b *(= circle)* Ring *m*; *(in tree trunk)* Jahresring *m*; **the ~s of Saturn** die Saturnringe *pl*; **to have (dark) ~s round** *or* **under one's eyes** (dunkle) Ringe unter den Augen haben; **to sit in a ~** im Kreis sitzen; **to run ~s round sb** *(inf)* jdn in die Tasche stecken *(inf)*
c *(= group, Pol)* Gruppe *f*; *(of dealers, spies)* Ring *m*
d *(= enclosure, at circus)* Manege *f*; *(at exhibition)* Ring *m*; *(Horse Racing)* Buchmacherring *m*; *(= boxing ring)* (Box)ring *m*
VT *(= surround)* umringen; *(in game: with hoop)* einen Ring werfen über *(+acc)*; *(= put ring on or round) item on list etc* einkreisen, einen Kreis machen um; *(esp Brit) bird* beringen

ring² *vb: pret* **rang**, *ptp* **rung** N a *(sound)* Klang *m*; *(= ringing) (of bell, alarm bell)* Läuten *nt*; *(of electric bell, alarm clock, phone)* Klingeln *nt*; *(of crystal)* Klang *m*; **there was a ~ at the door** es hat geklingelt *or* geläutet; **to hear a ~ at the door** die Türklingel hören; **give two ~s for the maid** für das Zimmermädchen zweimal läuten
b *(esp Brit Telec)* Anruf *m*; **to give sb a ~** jdn anrufen
c *(fig)* Klang *m*; **his voice had an angry ~ (to it)** seine Stimme klang etwas böse; **that has the** *or* **a ~ of truth (to** *or* **about it)** das klingt sehr wahrscheinlich
d *(= set)* **~ of bells** Glockenspiel *nt*
VI a *(= make sound)* klingen; *(bell, alarm bell)* läuten; *(electric bell)* läuten, klingeln; *(alarm clock, phone)* klingeln; *(= make metallic sound: swords etc)* klirren; *(crystal)* klingen; *(hammers)* schallen; **the (door)bell rang** es hat geläutet *or* geklingelt; **the bell rang for dinner** es hat zum Essen geläutet; **when the bell ~s** wenn es klingelt *or* läutet; **to ~ for sb** (nach) jdm läuten; **to ~ for sth** für etw läuten; **you rang, sir?** (gnädiger Herr,) Sie haben geläutet?; **please ~ for attention** bitte läuten; **to ~ at the door** (an der Tür) klingeln *or* läuten
b *(esp Brit Telec)* anrufen
c *(= sound, resound, words, voice)* tönen, schallen; *(music, singing)* erklingen *(geh)*, tönen; **to ~ false/true** falsch/wahr klingen; **my ears are ~ing** mir klingen die Ohren; **the valley rang with their shouts** das Tal hallte von ihren Rufen wider *(geh)*; **his words are still ~ing in my ears** seine Worte klingen mir noch im Ohr
VT a *bell* läuten; **to ~ the doorbell** (an der Tür) läuten *or* klingeln; **that/his name ~s a bell** *(fig inf)* das/sein Name kommt mir bekannt vor; **he/it ~s my bell** *(US inf)* den/das find ich gut *(inf)*; **to ~ the changes** *(lit: on bells)* (etw) im Wechsel läuten; *(fig)* alle Variationen durchspielen
b *(esp Brit: also* **ring up**) anrufen

▶ **ring back** *(esp Brit)* VT *sep* zurückrufen VI zurückrufen

▶ **ring down** VT *sep* **to ring down the curtain** *(Theat)* den Vorhang niedergehen lassen; **to ring down the curtain on sth** *(fig, on project)* einen Schlussstrich unter etw *(acc)* ziehen; *on era* den Vorhang über etw *(acc)* fallen lassen

▶ **ring in** VI a *(esp Brit Telec)* sich telefonisch melden *(to* in *+dat)* b *(US: = clock in)* (zu Beginn der Arbeit) stempeln *or* stechen VT *sep* **to ring in the New Year** das neue Jahr einläuten

▶ **ring off** VI *(esp Brit Telec)* aufhängen, (den Hörer) auflegen

▶ **ring out** VI a *(bell)* ertönen; *(shot)* knallen; *(= sound above others)* herausklingen b *(US: = clock out)* (am Ende der Arbeit) stempeln *or* stechen VT *sep* **to ring out the Old Year** das alte Jahr ausläuten

▶ **ring up** VT *sep* a *(esp Brit Telec)* anrufen b **to ring up the curtain** *(Theat)* den Vorhang hochgehen lassen c *(cashier)* eintippen; *(Comm) sales, profits* einnehmen

ring: **ring-a-ring-o'-roses** N Ringelreihen *m*; **ring binder** N Ringbuch *nt*; **ringbolt** N Ringbolzen *m*; **ring circuit** N Ringverzweigung *f*; **ringdove** N Ringeltaube *f*

ringer ['rɪŋə'] N a *(= bell-ringer)* Glöckner(in) *m(f)* b **to be a dead ~ for sb** *(inf)* jdm aufs Haar gleichen

ring: **ring exercise** N *(Sport)* Übung *f* an den Ringen; **ring fence** N Umzäunung *f*; **ring-fence** ['rɪŋfens] VT einzäunen; *funding, assets* reservieren; **ring finger** N Ringfinger *m*

ringing ['rɪŋɪŋ] ADJ *bell* läutend; *voice, tone* schallend; *phrases, declaration* leidenschaftlich; *endorsement* klar, eindeutig; **in ~ tones** leidenschaftlich; **~ tone** *(Brit Telec)* Rufzeichen *nt* N a *(of bell)* Läuten *nt*; *(of electric bell also, alarm clock, phone)* Klingeln *nt*; *(in ears)* Klingen *nt*
b *(= bell-ringing)* Glockenläuten *nt*

ringleader ['rɪŋ,li:də'] N Anführer(in) *m(f)*

ringlet ['rɪŋlɪt] N Ringellocke *f*, Korkenzieherlocke *f*

ring: **ringmaster** N Zirkusdirektor *m*; **ring-pull** N *(on can)* Dosenring *m*, Ringpull *m*; **ring-pull can** N Aufreißdose *f*, Ringpulldose *f*; **ring road** N *(Brit)* Umgehung(sstraße) *f*; **ringside** N **at the ~** am Ring; **ringside seat** N *(Boxing)* Ringplatz *m*; *(in circus)* Manegenplatz *m*; **to have a ~** *(fig)* einen Logenplatz haben; **ring spanner** N Ringschlüssel *m*; **ring-tailed** ADJ mit Ringelschwanz; **ring tone, ringtone** N *(Telec)* Klingelton *m*; **ringworm** N Scherpilzflechte *f*

rink [rɪŋk] N Eisbahn *f*; *(= roller-skating rink)* Rollschuhbahn *f*

rinse [rɪns] N a *(= act)* Spülung *f*; **to give sth a ~** *(clothes, hair)* etw spülen; *plates* etw abspülen; *cup, mouth* etw ausspülen; **have a ~** *(said by dentist)* bitte spülen b *(for hair)* Spülung *f*; *(= colorant)* Tönung *f* VT a *clothes, hair* spülen; *plates* abspülen; *cup, mouth, basin* ausspülen; **to ~ one's hands** sich *(dat)* die Hände abspülen; **to ~ the soap off one's hands** sich *(dat)* die Seife von den Händen abspülen b *(= colour with a rinse) hair* tönen

▶ **rinse down** VT *sep car, wall* abspülen

▶ **rinse out** VT *sep* a *hair, tint, colour, soap, cup* ausspülen, auswaschen; **to rinse out one's mouth** sich *(dat)* den Mund ausspülen b *(= wash quickly) clothes* auswaschen

Rio (de Janeiro) ['ri:əʊ(dədʒə'nɪərəʊ)] N Rio (de Janeiro) *nt*

riot ['raɪət] N a *(Pol)* Aufstand *m no pl*, Aufruhr *m no pl*; *(by mob, football fans etc)* Krawall *m*, Ausschreitungen *pl*; *(fig: = wild occasion)* Orgie *f*; **there'll be a ~ if you announce that** wenn Sie das verkünden, gibt es einen Aufstand; **to run ~** *(people)* randalieren; *(vegetation)* wuchern; **his imagination runs ~** seine Fantasie *or* Phantasie geht mit ihm durch; **ivy had run ~ all over the house** Efeu hatte das ganze Haus überwuchert
b **a ~ of colour(s)** *(Brit) or* **color(s)** *(US)* eine Farbenexplosion, eine Farbenorgie; **a ~ of reds and blues** eine Explosion von Rot- und Blautönen; **a ~ of flowers** ein wildes Blumenmeer
c **to be a ~** *(inf)* zum Schießen *or* Schreien sein *(inf)*
VI randalieren; *(= revolt)* einen Aufruhr machen

riot: **riot act** N a *(Hist)* **the Riot Act** die Aufruhrakte b *(fig)* **to read sb the ~** jdm die Leviten lesen; **riot control** N *no pl* Einsatz *m* bei Krawallen; **riot-control** ADJ *equipment etc* für den Einsatz bei Krawallen

rioter ['raɪətə'] N Randalierer(in) *m(f)*; *(= rebel)* Aufrührer(in) *m(f)*

riot gear N Schutzausrüstung *f*

rioting ['raɪətɪŋ] N Krawalle *pl*; *(Pol also)* Aufstände *pl*; **~ in the streets** Straßenkrawalle *or* -schlachten *pl*

riotous ['raɪətəs] ADJ a *person, crowd* randalierend; *living, behaviour, child* wild b *(inf: = wild, exuberant, boisterous)* wild; *(= hilarious)* urkomisch *(inf)*; **we had a ~ time** es ging hoch her *(inf)*; **a ~ success** ein Riesen- *or* Bombenerfolg *(inf) m*; **she burst into ~ laughter** sie brach in wildes Gelächter aus; **a ~ welcome** ein überschwängliches Willkommen

riotously ['raɪətəslɪ] ADV *behave, live* wild; **it was ~ funny** *(inf)* es war zum Schreien *(inf)*

riot: **riot police** N Bereitschaftspolizei *f*; **riot shield** N Schutzschild *m*; **riot squad** N Überfallkommando *nt*

RIP *abbr of* **requiescat** *or* **requiescant in pace** R.I.P.

rip [rɪp] N Riss *m*; *(made by knife etc)* Schlitz *m*
VT a *material, clothes* einen Riss machen in *(+acc)*; *(stronger)* zerreißen; *(= vandalize) pictures etc* zerschlitzen; **you've ~ped your jacket** du hast einen Riss in der Jacke, du hast dir die Jacke zerrissen; **to ~ sth down the middle** etw mitten durchreißen; **to ~ open** aufreißen; *(with knife)* aufschlitzen
b **to ~ one** *(US) inf: (= break wind)* einen (fahren) lassen *(inf)*
VI a *(cloth, garment)* reißen
b *(inf)* **the car ~s along** der Wagen rast dahin; **let her ~!** volle Pulle! *(inf)*; **to let ~** loslegen *(inf)*; **he let ~ (with) a stream of complaints** er hat einen Schwall Beschwerden vom Stapel gelassen *(inf)*; **he let ~ at me** er ist auf mich losgegangen *(inf)*

▶ **rip down** VT *sep* herunterreißen; *old buildings* abreißen

▶ **rip into** VI *+prep obj* a *(bullets etc)* sich bohren in *(+acc)* b *(fig inf: = criticize)* zusammenstauchen *(inf)*

▶ **rip off** VT *sep* a *(lit)* abreißen *(prep obj* von); *clothing* herunterreißen; **he ripped off her dress** er riss ihr das Kleid vom Leib b *(inf) object, goods* mitgehen lassen *(inf)*; *bank, shop, house* ausrauben; *person* abzocken *(inf)*

▶ **rip out** VT *sep* herausreißen *(of* aus)

▶ **rip through** VI *+prep obj (explosion)* erschüttern; *(bullet)* durchbohren

▶ **rip up** VT *sep* zerreißen; *road* aufreißen; *floorboards* herausreißen

riparian [raɪ'pɛərɪən] ADJ *(form)* Ufer-; **~ right** Uferanliegerrecht *nt*

ripcord ['rɪp,kɔ:d] N Reißleine *f*

ripe [raɪp] ADJ *(+er)* a *fruit, cheese, wine* reif; *(Anat) egg* reif, gereift; *(fig) lips* voll
b *(fig: = mature)* reif; **to live to a ~ old age** ein hohes Alter erreichen; **at the ~ old age of eighty** im hohen *or* reifen Alter von achtzig Jahren
c *(= ready)* **to be ~ for sth** für etw reif sein; **to be ~ for the picking** pflückreif sein; **the time is ~ for revolution** die Zeit ist reif für eine Revolution; **the time is ~ to begin afresh** die Zeit ist reif *or* es ist höchste Zeit, neu anzufangen; **when the time is ~** wenn die Zeit dafür reif ist
d *(inf: = pungent) smell* durchdringend
e *(inf, = crude) language* derb

ripen ['raɪpən] VT *(lit, fig)* reifen lassen VI reifen

ripeness ['raɪpnɪs] N Reife *f*

rip-off ['rɪpɒf] N *(inf)* Wucher *m*, Nepp *m (inf)*; *(= cheat)* Schwindel *m*; *(= copy: of film, song etc)* Abklatsch *m*; **it's a ~** das ist Wucher *or* Nepp *(inf)*/Schwindel/nachgemacht *or* ein Abklatsch; **he'd been the victim of a ~** er war ausgenommen worden *(inf)*

riposte [rɪ'pɒst] N *(= retort)* scharfe Antwort, Gegenschlag *m*; *(Fencing)* Riposte *f* VI *(= retort)* scharf erwidern, parieren; *(Fencing)* parieren und eine Riposte bringen

ripped [rɪpt] ADJ *(US inf: = muscular)* muskulös

ripper ['rɪpə'] N *(= murderer)* Frauenmörder *m*

ripping ['rɪpɪŋ] ADJ *(dated Brit inf)* herrlich, wunderbar

ripple ['rɪpl] N a *(in water)* kleine Welle; *(of crops)* sanftes Wogen *no pl*; **little ~s spread out across the water** das Wasser kräuselte sich; **the**

wind blew across the grass in ~s das Gras wogte im Wind **b** *(= noise)* Plätschern *nt*; *(of waves)* Klatschen *nt*; **a ~ of laughter** ein kurzes Lachen; *(girls')* ein perlendes Lachen VI **a** *(= undulate, water)* sich kräuseln; *(crops)* wogen **b** *(= murmur, water)* plätschern; *(waves)* klatschen VT *water* kräuseln; *corn* wogen lassen; *muscles* spielen lassen

ripple: **ripple effect** N *(= knock-on effect)* Nachwirkungen *pl*; **ripple mark** N *(on sand etc)* Rippelmarke *f*

rip: **rip-rap** N *(Build)* Steinbettung *f*, Steinschüttung *f*; **rip-roaring** ADJ *(inf)* sagenhaft *(inf)*; **ripsaw** [ˈrɪpsɔː] N *(Tech)* Spaltsäge *f*; **riptide** N Kabbelung *f*

rise [raɪz] ✪ 17.2 *vb: pret* **rose**, *ptp* **risen** N **a** *(= increase) (in sth* etw *gen) (in temperature, pressure, of tide, river)* Anstieg *m*, Steigen *nt no pl*; *(in number)* Zunahme *f*; *(in prices, bank rate)* Steigerung *f*, Anstieg *m*; *(St Ex)* Aufschwung *m*; **a (pay) ~** *(Brit)* eine Gehaltserhöhung; **prices are on the ~** die Preise steigen; **there has been a ~ in the number of participants** die Zahl der Teilnehmer ist gestiegen; **a ~ in the population** ein Bevölkerungszuwachs *m*
b *(= upward movement, of theatre curtain)* Hochgehen *nt*, Heben *nt*; *(of sun)* Aufgehen *nt*; *(Mus: in pitch)* Erhöhung *f (in +gen)*; *(fig, to fame, power etc)* Aufstieg *m (to* zu*)*; **the ~ of the working classes** der soziale Aufstieg der Arbeiterklasse; **the ~ and fall of an empire** der Aufstieg und Niedergang eines Weltreichs; **to get a ~ out of sb** *(inf)* jdn zur Reaktion bringen; **to take the** *or* **a ~ out of sb** *(dated inf)* jdn auf den Arm nehmen *(inf)*
c *(= small hill)* Erhebung *f*; *(= slope)* Steigung *f*
d *(= origin: of river)* Ursprung *m*; **to give ~ to sth** etw verursachen; *to questions* etw aufwerfen; *to complaints* Anlass zu etw geben; *to speculation* zu etw führen; *to hopes, fears* etw aufkommen lassen
VI **a** *(= get up) (from sitting, lying)* aufstehen, sich erheben *(geh)*, um zu gehen; **to ~ from the table** vom Tisch aufstehen, sich vom Tisch erheben *(geh)*; **to ~ in the saddle** sich im Sattel heben; **he rose from his sickbed to go and see her** er verließ sein Krankenlager, um sie zu sehen; **~ and shine!** *(inf)* raus aus den Federn! *(inf)*; **the horse rose on its hind legs** das Pferd stellte sich auf die Hinterbeine; *(= reared up)* das Pferd bäumte sich auf; **to ~ from the dead** *(liter, Bibl)* von den Toten auferstehen
b *(= go up)* steigen; *(smoke, mist etc)* (auf)steigen, emporsteigen; *(prices, temperature, pressure etc)* (an)steigen *(to* auf *+acc)*; *(balloon, aircraft, bird)* (auf)steigen, sich heben *(geh)*; *(lift)* hochfahren, nach oben fahren; *(theatre curtain)* hochgehen, sich heben; *(sun, moon, bread, dough)* aufgehen; *(wind, storm)* aufkommen, sich erheben; *(voice, in volume)* sich erheben; *(in pitch)* höher werden; *(swimmer, fish)* hochkommen; *(new buildings)* entstehen; *(fig, hopes)* steigen; *(anger)* wachsen, zunehmen; *(stomach)* sich heben; **to ~ to the surface** an die Oberfläche kommen; **the fish are rising well** die Fische beißen gut; **he won't ~ to any of your taunts** er lässt sich von dir nicht reizen; **the idea rose in his mind** ihm kam der Gedanke; **the image rose in his mind** das Bild tauchte vor ihm auf; **I can't ~ to £100** ich kann nicht bis £ 100 gehen; **her spirits rose** ihre Stimmung hob sich; **his voice rose to screaming pitch** seine Stimme wurde kreischend *or* schrill; **to ~ to a crescendo** zu einem Crescendo anschwellen; **the colour** *(Brit)* *or* **color** *(US)* **rose in her cheeks** die Röte stieg ihr ins Gesicht
c *(ground)* ansteigen; *(mountains, hills, castle)* sich erheben; **the mountain ~s to 5,000 feet** der Berg erhebt sich auf 5.000 Fuß; **where the hills ~ against the sky** wo sich die Berge gegen den Himmel abheben
d *(fig, in society, rank)* **to ~ in the world** es zu etwas bringen; **to ~ to fame** Berühmtheit erlangen; **to ~ from nothing** sich aus dem Nichts empor- *or* hocharbeiten; **he rose to be President/a captain** er stieg zum Präsidenten/Kapitän auf → **rank**[1]
e *(= adjourn, assembly)* auseinandergehen; *(meeting)* beendet sein; **the House rose at 2 a.m.** *(Parl)* das Haus beendete die Sitzung um 2 Uhr morgens; **Parliament will ~ on Thursday** das Parlament geht Donnerstag in Ferien
f *(= originate: river)* entspringen
g *(also* **rise up***)* *(= revolt: people)* sich empören, sich erheben; *(= rebel: one's soul etc)* sich empören; **to ~ (up) in protest (at sth)** *(people)* sich protestierend (gegen etw) erheben; **to ~ (up) in anger (at sth)** *(people)* sich (gegen etw) empören; *(soul, inner being etc)* sich (gegen etw) auflehnen/zornig empören

▶ **rise above** VI *+prep obj level of inflation etc* ansteigen um mehr als; *insults etc* erhaben sein über *(+acc)*, stehen über *(+dat)*

▶ **rise up** VI *(person)* aufstehen, sich erheben *(geh)*; *(mountain etc)* sich erheben → *also* **rise VI g**

risen [ˈrɪzn] *ptp of* **rise** ADJ *(Rel)* **the ~ Lord** der Auferstandene; **Jesus Christ is ~!** Christ ist erstanden!

riser [ˈraɪzəʳ] N **a** *(= person)* **to be an early ~** Frühaufsteher(in) *m(f)* sein, früh aufstehen; **to be a late ~** spät aufstehen, ein Langschläfer *m*/eine Langschläferin sein *(inf)* **b** *(of stair)* Setzstufe *f* **c** *(for gas, water etc)* Steigrohr *nt*, Steigleitung *f*

risibility [ˌrɪzɪˈbɪlɪtɪ] N *(liter: = disposition)* Lachlust *f*

risible [ˈrɪzɪbl] ADJ *(liter: = laughable)* lächerlich, lachhaft

rising [ˈraɪzɪŋ] N **a** *(= rebellion)* Erhebung *f*, Aufstand *m*
b *(of sun, star)* Aufgehen *nt*, Aufgang *m*; *(of barometer, prices, river)* (An)steigen *nt*; *(from dead)* Auferstehung *f*; *(of theatre curtain)* Hochgehen *nt*; *(of ground)* Steigung *f*, Anstieg *m*; **the ~ and falling of …** das Auf und Ab *(+gen)* …
c *(= adjournment: of Parliament etc)* Auseinandergehen *nt*
ADJ **a** *sun, star* aufgehend; *tide, barometer* steigend; *(= sloping) ground* ansteigend; **the ~ sap** der aufsteigende Saft
b *(= increasing) prices, inflation, stock market, currency* steigend; *unemployment* steigend, zunehmend; *crime* zunehmend; *wind* aufkommend; *hopes* steigend; *anger, fury* wachsend; **the ~ tide of violence** die zunehmende Welle der Gewalt
c *(fig)* **a ~ young doctor** ein aufstrebender junger Arzt; **a ~ politician** ein kommender Politiker; **the ~ generation** die kommende Generation; **(the) ~ threes/fives** *(Brit Sch)* die knapp Drei-/Fünfjährigen
ADV *(inf)* **she's ~ sixteen** sie ist fast sechzehn

rising damp N Bodenfeuchtigkeit *f*

risk [rɪsk] ✪ 2.3, 16.2 N **a** Risiko *nt*; *(in cpds)* -gefahr *f*; **health/war ~** Gesundheits-/Kriegsgefahr *f*; **~ of infection** Infektionsrisiko *nt*, Ansteckungsgefahr *f*; **to take** *or* **run ~s/a ~** Risiken/ein Risiko eingehen; **to take** *or* **run the ~ of doing sth** das Risiko eingehen, etw zu tun; **you('ll) run the ~ of losing a lot of money** Sie laufen dabei Gefahr, eine Menge Geld zu verlieren; **there is no ~ of his coming** *or* **that he will come** es besteht keine Gefahr, dass er kommt; **at one's own ~** auf eigene Gefahr, auf eigenes Risiko; **goods sent at sender's ~** Warenversand *m* auf Risiko des Senders; **"cars parked at owners' ~"** „Parken auf eigene Gefahr"; **at the ~ of seeming stupid** auf die Gefahr hin, dumm zu scheinen; **at the ~ of his life** unter Einsatz seines Lebens; **children at ~** gefährdete Kinder; **some jobs are at ~** einige Stellen sind gefährdet; **to put sb at ~** jdn gefährden; **to put sth at ~** etw riskieren
b *(Insur)* Risiko *nt*; **fire ~** Feuerrisiko; **he's a bad accident ~** bei ihm besteht ein hohes Unfallrisiko; **to be a good/bad (credit) ~** *(Fin)* eine gute/schlechte Bonität haben → **security risk**
VT **a** *career, future, reputation, savings, life* riskieren, aufs Spiel setzen → **neck**
b *defeat, quarrel, accident* riskieren; *(= venture) criticism, remark* wagen, riskieren; **to ~ sb's wrath** riskieren, dass jd sehr erzürnt ist; **you'll ~ falling/losing your job** Sie riskieren dabei, hinzufallen/Ihre Stelle zu verlieren; **she won't ~ coming today** sie wird es heute nicht riskieren, zu kommen; **I'll ~ it** das riskiere ich, ich lasse es darauf ankommen

risk: **risk capital** N Risikokapital *nt*; **risk factor** N Risikofaktor *m*; **risk group** N Risikogruppe *f*

riskily [ˈrɪskɪlɪ] ADV riskant

riskiness [ˈrɪskɪnɪs] N Riskantheit *f*

risk: **risk management** N Risikomanagement; Absicherung *f* von Risiken; **risk sharing** N Risikoteilung *f*

risky [ˈrɪskɪ] ADJ *(+er)* **a** *enterprise, deed, loan, investment, debt* riskant; **it's ~, it's a ~ business** das ist riskant **b** *joke, story* pikant, gewagt

risotto [rɪˈzɒtəʊ] N Risotto *m*

risqué [ˈriːskeɪ] ADJ pikant, gewagt

rissole [ˈrɪsəʊl] N ≈ Frikadelle *f*

rite [raɪt] N Ritus *m*; **burial ~s** Bestattungsriten *pl*

rite of passage N *(fig)* Übergangsritual *m*, Rites *pl* de passage *(Sociol)*; **a rite(s)-of-passage film** ein Film *m* über das Erwachsenwerden

ritual [ˈrɪtjʊəl] ADJ **a** rituell; **~ abuse** ritueller Missbrauch; **~ murder** Ritualmord *m* **b** *(usu hum: = usual) comments* üblich; *visit* üblich, gewohnheitsmäßig N Ritual *nt*; *(pej also)* Zeremoniell *nt no pl*; **the courtship ~ of frogs** das Paarungsverhalten der Frösche; **he went through the same old ~** *(fig)* er durchlief dasselbe alte Ritual *or* Zeremoniell; **he went through the ~ of checking all the locks** er überprüfte nach dem üblichen Zeremoniell *or* Ritual, ob alles abgeschlossen war

ritualism [ˈrɪtjʊəlɪzəm] N Ritualismus *m*

ritualist [ˈrɪtjʊəlɪst] N Ritualist(in) *m(f)*; *(= expert)* Ritualienforscher(in) *m(f)*

ritualistic [ˌrɪtjʊəˈlɪstɪk] ADJ **a** *(= pre-arranged) remarks* üblich; **he came out with some ~ nonsense about …** er hat den üblichen Blödsinn über … *(acc)* losgelassen *(inf)* **b** *(= ceremonial)* rituell; **~ abuse** ritueller Missbrauch

ritualize [ˈrɪtjʊəlaɪz] VT ritualisieren

ritually [ˈrɪtjʊəlɪ] ADV rituell

ritzy [ˈrɪtsɪ] ADJ *(+er) (inf)* nobel *(inf)*, protzig *(pej inf)*

rival [ˈraɪvəl] N **a** *(= competitor)* Rivale *m*, Rivalin *f (for* um, *to* für*)*; *(in love also)* Nebenbuhler(in) *m(f) (old)*; *(Comm)* Konkurrent(in) *m(f)*
b *(= equal)* **this collection of paintings has few ~s in the world** diese Gemäldesammlung hat in der Welt kaum ihresgleichen
ADJ *groups, fans, leaders* rivalisierend; *claims, plans, attraction* konkurrierend; **~ firm** Konkurrenzfirma *f*; **~ bid** Konkurrenzangebot *nt*; **~ candidate** Gegenkandidat(in) *m(f)*; **~ supporters** *(Sport)* Anhänger(innen) *pl* der gegnerischen Mannschaft
VT *(in love, for affections)* rivalisieren mit; *(Comm)* konkurrieren mit; **he can't ~ her in intelligence** er kann sich mit ihr in Bezug auf Intelligenz nicht messen; **his achievements ~ even yours** seine Leistungen können sich sogar mit deinen messen; **I can't ~ that** da kann ich nicht mithalten; **to ~ sth in significance** einer Sache *(dat)* die Bedeutung streitig machen

rivalry [ˈraɪvəlrɪ] N Rivalität *f*; *(Comm)* Konkurrenzkampf *m*

rive [raɪv] *pret* **rived**, *ptp* **riven** [ˈrɪvn] VT *(old, liter)* spalten; **~n by grief** *(fig)* von Schmerz zerrissen

river [ˈrɪvəʳ] N Fluss *m*; *(major)* Strom *m*; **down ~** fluss-/stromabwärts; **up ~** fluss-/stromaufwärts; **the ~ Rhine** *(Brit)* **the Rhine ~** *(US)* der Rhein; **~s of blood/lava** Blut-/Lavaströme *pl* → **sell**

river *in cpds* Fluss-; **river basin** N Flussbecken *nt*; **riverbed** N Flussbett *nt*; **riverboat** N Ausflugsschiff *nt*; **river fish** N Flussfisch *m*; **river fishing** N Flussangeln *nt*; **river head** N Flussquelle *f*

riverine [ˈrɪvəraɪn] ADJ (*form*: = *of river*) Fluss-; (= *like river*) flussartig; *people* am Fluss wohnend; ~ **estuary** Flussmündung *f*

river: **river mouth** N Flussmündung *f*; **river navigation** N Flussschifffahrt *f*; **river police** N Wasserschutzpolizei *f*; **riverside** N Flussufer *nt*; **on/by the** ~ am Fluss ADJ am Fluss (-ufer); **river traffic** N Flussschiffahrt *f*

rivet [ˈrɪvɪt] N Niete *f* VT (*lit*) nieten; *two things* vernieten; (*fig*) *audience, attention* fesseln; **his eyes were ~ed to the screen** sein Blick war auf die Leinwand geheftet; **it ~ed our attention** das fesselte uns *or* unsere Aufmerksamkeit; **~ed (to the spot) by fear** vor Angst wie festgenagelt; ~ **joint** Nietnaht *f*, Nietung *f*

riveter [ˈrɪvɪtəʳ] N Nieter(in) *m(f)*; (= *tool*) Nietmaschine *f*

riveting [ˈrɪvɪtɪŋ] ADJ (= *gripping*) fesselnd; **the book is a ~ read** das Buch ist spannender *or* fesselnder Lesestoff; **it's ~ stuff** es ist faszinierend

rivet(t)ing [ˈrɪvɪtɪŋ] N Nieten *nt*

Riviera [ˌrɪvɪˈɛərə] N **the (French)/Italian** ~ die französische/italienische Riviera

rivulet [ˈrɪvjʊlɪt] N Flüsschen *nt*, Bach *m*

riyal [rɪˈjɑːl] N (*Saudi Arabian*) saudi-arabischer Riyal; (*Yemeni*) Jemen-Riyal *m*

RM (*Brit*) *abbr of* **Royal Marines**

rm *abbr of* **room** Zim.

RN **a** (*Brit*) *abbr of* **Royal Navy** **b** (*US*) *abbr of* **registered nurse**

RNA *abbr of* **ribonucleic acid** RNS *f*

RNAS (*Brit*) *abbr of* **Royal Naval Air Services**

RNLI (*Brit*) *abbr of* **Royal National Lifeboat Institution** ≈ DLRG *f*

RNR (*Brit*) *abbr of* **Royal Navy Reserve**

RNVR (*Brit*) *abbr of* **Royal Navy Volunteer Reserve**

roach [rəʊtʃ] N Plötze *f*; (*inf*: = *cockroach*) Schabe *f*

road [rəʊd] N **a** Straße *f*; **"road up"** (*Brit*) „Straßenbauarbeiten"; **"road narrows"** „Straßenverengung"; **by ~** (*send sth*) per Spedition; (*travel*) mit dem Bus/Auto *etc*; **she lives across the ~ (from us)** sie wohnt gegenüber (von uns); **my car is off the ~ just now** ich kann mein Auto momentan nicht benutzen; **my car has never been/is never off the ~** mein Auto war noch nie/ist nie in der Werkstatt; **I hope to put the car back on the ~ soon** ich hoffe, das Auto bald wieder fahren zu können; **this vehicle shouldn't be on the ~** das Fahrzeug ist nicht verkehrstüchtig; **he is a danger on the ~** er ist eine Gefahr für den Straßenverkehr; **to take to the ~** sich auf den Weg machen, losfahren; (*as tramp*) Vagabund werden; **to be on the ~** (= *travelling*) unterwegs sein; (*theatre company*) auf Tournee sein; (*car*) fahren; **is this the ~ to London?** geht es hier nach London?; **the London ~** die Straße nach London; **"Westlands/London ~"** „Westlandsstraße/Londoner Straße"; **to have one for the ~** (*inf*) zum Abschluss noch einen trinken; **gentleman of the ~** Vagabund *m*
b (*fig*) Weg *m*; **you're on the right ~** (*lit, fig*) Sie sind auf dem richtigen Weg; **on the ~ to ruin/success** auf dem Weg ins Verderben/zum Erfolg; **somewhere along the ~ he changed his mind** irgendwann hat er seine Meinung geändert; **you're in my ~** (*Brit dial inf*) du bist mir im Weg; **(get) out of the ~!** (*Brit dial inf*) geh weg!; **any ~** (*Brit dial inf*) = **anyhow**
c **roads** PL (*Naut*) Reede *f* **d** (*US*) = **railroad**

> **ROADS**
>
> In Großbritannien und den USA hat man verschiedene Bezeichnungen für die unterschiedlichen Straßentypen.
> In Großbritannien gibt es zwei Arten von Landstraßen: die wichtigeren, die unseren Bundesstraßen entsprechen (man nennt sie auch **trunk roads**), tragen die Bezeichnung **A roads**, die weniger wichtigen sind **B roads**. Einige der **A roads** können mehrere Fahrbahnen für beide Fahrtrichtungen haben: Diese werden dann **dual carriageways** genannt. Der amerikanische Ausdruck dafür ist **divided highway**.
> Die Benutzung des britischen Pendants zu den Autobahnen, die **motorways**, ist kostenlos. In den USA heißt dieser Straßentyp allgemein **superhighway**, allerdings gibt es daneben noch einige ebenfalls gebräuchliche Bezeichnungen: die **interstate highways** verbinden mindestens zwei Staaten miteinander und sind manchmal gebührenfrei, meist kosten sie jedoch Maut, weshalb sie auch **toll roads** oder **turnpikes** heißen; **expressways** befinden sich normalerweise innerhalb oder in der Nähe von Städten; und **freeways** werden so genannt, weil sie gebührenfrei sind.

roadability [ˌrəʊdəˈbɪlɪtɪ] N (*US*: *of car*) Fahreigenschaften *pl*

road *in cpds* Straßen-; **road accident** N Verkehrsunfall *m*; **roadblock** N Straßensperre *f*; **road book** N Straßenatlas *m*; **road conditions** PL Straßenzustand *m*; **road construction** N (*US*) Straßenbau *m*; **road contractor** N Fuhrunternehmer(in) *m(f)*; (= *company*) Fuhrunternehmen *nt*; **road-fund licence** N (*Brit*) ≈ Verkehrssteuer *f*; **road haulage** N (*esp Brit*) Spedition *f*; **road haulier**, (*US*) **road hauler** N Spediteur(in) *m(f)*; (= *company*) Spedition *f*; **road hog** N (*inf*) Verkehrsrowdy *m* (*inf*); **roadholding (ability)** N Straßenlage *f*; (*of tyres*) Griffigkeit *f*; **roadhouse** N Rasthaus *nt*

roadie [ˈrəʊdiː] N (*inf*) Roadie *m* (*inf*)

road: **road improvement** N Straßenausbau *m*; **roadmaking** N Straßenbau *m*; **roadman** N (*inf*) Straßenbauarbeiter *m*; **road manager** N (*of pop group*) Roadmanager(in) *m(f)*; **roadmender** N Straßenbauarbeiter(in) *m(f)*; **road metal** N Straßenschotter *m*; **road movie** N Roadmovie *nt*; **road pricing** N (*Brit*) Straßenbenutzungsgebühren *pl*; **road race** N Straßenrennen *nt*; **road racer** N (= *bicycle*) Rennrad *nt* (*für Straßenrennen*); **road rage** N Aggressivität *f* im Straßenverkehr; **road rager** [ˈrəʊdˌreɪdʒəʳ] N aggressiver Straßenverkehrsteilnehmer, aggressive Straßenverkehrsteilnehmerin; **roadroller** N Straßenwalze *f*; **road safety** N Verkehrssicherheit *f*, Sicherheit *f* im Straßenverkehr; **road salt** N Streusalz *nt*; **road sense** N Verkehrssinn *m*; **road show** N (*Theat*) Tournee *f*; **roadside** N Straßenrand *m*; **along** *or* **by the** ~ am Straßenrand ADJ *stall, toilet, pub* an der Straße; **a ~ bomb** eine Bombe, die im Straßengraben versteckt ist; **~ check** Straßenkontrolle *f*; **~ ditch** Straßengraben *m*; **~ repairs** (*professional*) Sofortdienst *m*; (*done alone*) Reparatur *f* am Straßenrand; **~ shrine** Wegkreuz *nt*; **roadsign** N (Straßen)verkehrszeichen *nt*; **roadstead** N (*Naut*) Reede *f*

roadster [ˈrəʊdstəʳ] N (*old*: = *car*) Vehikel *nt* (*inf*); (= *bicycle*) Drahtesel *m* (*inf*)

road: **roadsweeper** N (= *person*) Straßenkehrer(in) *m(f)*; (= *vehicle*) Straßenkehrmaschine *f*; **road tax** N (*Brit*) Kraftfahrzeugsteuer *f*; **road test** N Straßentest *m*; **road-test** VT Probe fahren; **road toll** N Straßenbenutzungsgebühr *f*, Maut(gebühr) *f*; **road traffic accident** N Verkehrsunfall *m*; **road transport** N Straßengüterverkehr *m*; **road trials** PL (= *road-test*) Straßentest *m*; (= *rally*) Straßenwettbewerb *m*; **road user** N Verkehrsteilnehmer(in) *m(f)*; **roadway** N Fahrbahn *f*; **roadwork** N (*Sport*) Straßentraining *nt*; **roadworks** PL (*Brit*) Straßenbauarbeiten *pl*; **roadworthiness** N (*of car*) Verkehrstüchtigkeit *f*, Verkehrssicherheit *f*; **roadworthy** ADJ verkehrstüchtig, verkehrssicher

roam [rəʊm] VT *streets, countryside* wandern *or* ziehen durch; **to ~ the (seven) seas** die sieben Meere durchkreuzen; **to ~ the streets** (*child, dog*) (in den Straßen) herumstreunen; **to ~ the earth/world** durch die Welt ziehen VI (herum)wandern; (*hum, hands*) wandern, sich verirren

▶ **roam about** (*Brit*) *or* **around** VI herumwandern; (*dogs, looters*) herumstreunen VI +*prep obj* **to roam around the house** durch das Haus wandern; **to roam around the city/the streets** durch die Stadt/die Straßen streifen

roamer [ˈrəʊməʳ] N Vagabund(in) *m(f)*; (= *dog*) Herumstreuner *m*; (= *child*) Stromer *m* (*inf*)

roaming [ˈrəʊmɪŋ] ADJ *person* wandernd; *animal also* herumziehend; (*fig*) *thoughts* schweifend N Herumwandern *nt*; **this life of ~** dieses Vagabundenleben

roan [rəʊn] ADJ *horse* rötlich grau N Rotschimmel *m*

roar [rɔːʳ] VI (*person, crowd, lion, bull*) brüllen (*with* vor +*dat*); (*fire in hearth*) prasseln; (*wind, engine, plane*) heulen; (*sea, waterfall*) tosen; (*thunder, forest fire*) toben; (*gun*) donnern; **to ~ at sb** jdn anbrüllen; **the trucks ~ed past** die Lastwagen donnerten vorbei; **the car ~ed up the street** der Wagen donnerte die Straße hinauf; **he had them ~ing (with laughter)** sie brüllten vor Lachen
VT **a** (*also* **roar out**) *order, song etc* brüllen; **the fans ~ed their approval** die Fans grölten zustimmend
b *engine* aufheulen lassen
N **a** *no pl* (*of person, crowd, lion, bull*) Gebrüll *nt*; (*of fire in hearth*) Prasseln *nt*; (*of wind, engine, plane*) Heulen *nt*; (*of sea, waterfall*) Tosen *nt*; (*of thunder, forest fire*) Toben *nt*; (*of gun, traffic*) Donnern *nt*
b **~s of laughter** brüllendes Gelächter; **the ~s of the crowd/lion** das Brüllen der Menge/des Löwen

roaring [ˈrɔːrɪŋ] ADJ *person, crowd, lion, bull* brüllend; *fire in hearth* prasselnd; *wind, engine, plane* heulend; *sea, waterfall* tosend; *thunder, forest fire* tobend; *gun, traffic, noise* donnernd; **~ drunk** (*inf*) sternhagelvoll (*inf*); **the ~ Twenties** die wilden zwanziger Jahre *or* Zwanzigerjahre; **a ~ success** ein voller Erfolg, ein Bombenerfolg *m* (*inf*); **to do a ~ trade (in sth)** ein Riesengeschäft *nt* (mit etw) machen N = **roar N a**

Roaring Forties PL (*Geog*) **the ~** stürmischer Teil des Ozeans (zwischen dem 39. und 50. Breitengrad)

roast [rəʊst] N Braten *m*; **pork ~** Schweinebraten *m* ADJ *pork, veal* gebraten; *potatoes* in Fett im Backofen gebraten; **~ chicken** Brathähnchen *nt*; **~ beef** Roastbeef *nt*; **we had ~ pork** es gab Schweinebraten VT **a** *meat* braten; *chestnuts, coffee beans, ore* rösten; **to ~ oneself by the fire/in the sun** sich am Feuer/in der Sonne braten lassen; **to be ~ed alive** (*fig*) sich totschwitzen (*inf*); (*by sun*) gebraten werden (*inf*) → *also* **roasting** **b** (*inf*, = *criticize*) ins Gericht gehen mit (*inf*) VI (*meat*) braten; (*inf, person*) irrsinnig schwitzen (*inf*); (*in sun*) in der Sonne braten → *also* **roasting**

roaster [ˈrəʊstəʳ] N (= *oven*) Bratofen *m*, Bratröhre *f*; (= *dish*) Bräter *m*; (= *coffee roaster*) Röstapparat *m*; (*for ore*) Röstofen *m*; (= *chicken*) Brathähnchen *nt*; (= *pig*) Spanferkel *nt*

roasting [ˈrəʊstɪŋ] N **a** (*lit*) Braten *nt* **b** (*inf*: = *criticism*) Verriss *m*; (= *telling-off*) Standpauke *f*; **to give sb a ~** jdn verreißen, jdm eine Standpauke halten ADJ **a** (*inf*: = *hot*) *days, weather* knallheiß (*inf*) **b** (*Cook*) zum Braten; **~ chicken** Brathähnchen *nt*; **~ meat** Bratenfleisch *nt*

roasting: **roasting bag** N Bratschlauch *m*; **roasting tin, roasting tray** N Bräter *m*

rob [rɒb] VT *person* bestehlen; (*more seriously*) berauben; *shop, bank* ausrauben; *orchard* plündern; **to ~ sb of sth** (*lit, fig*) jdn einer Sache (*gen*) berauben (*geh*), jdm etw rauben; (*lit also*) jdm etw stehlen; **I've been ~bed!** ich bin bestohlen worden!; (= *had to pay too much*) ich bin geneppt worden (*inf*); **to ~ the till** (*Brit*) die Ladenkasse ausräumen *or* plündern; **he was ~bed of the pleasure of seeing her** es war ihm nicht vergönnt, sie zu sehen; **the shock ~bed him of speech** er hat vor Schreck die Stimme verloren; (*briefly also*) der Schreck hat ihm die Sprache verschlagen; **our team was ~bed** (*inf*) das ist nicht fair(, wir hätten gewinnen müssen)

robber ['rɒbəʳ] N Räuber(in) *m(f)*

robbery ['rɒbərɪ] N Raub *m no pl*; *(= burglary)* Einbruch *m* (*of* in *+acc*); **~ with violence** *(Jur)* Raubüberfall *m*; **armed ~** bewaffneter Raubüberfall; **at that price it's sheer ~!** *(inf)* das ist der reinste Nepp *(inf)*, das ist reiner Wucher *(inf)*; **the bank ~** der Überfall auf die Bank

robe [rəʊb] N **a** *(= garment, of office)* Robe *f*, Talar *m*; *(for priest)* Rock *m*, Robe *f*; *(for baby)* langes Kleidchen; *(esp US: for house wear)* Morgenrock *m*, Haus- *or* Bademantel *m*; *(obs: = gown)* Kleid *nt*; **he was wearing his ~ of office** er war im Ornat; **ceremonial ~s** Festgewänder *pl*; **christening ~** Taufkleid *nt* **b** *(US: = wrap)* Decke *f* VT *(lit)* ankleiden, die Amtsrobe *or* den Ornat anlegen *(+dat)*; **to ~ sb/sth in sth** *(lit, fig)* jdn/etw in etw *(acc)* kleiden VI *(judge etc)* die Amtsrobe *or* den Ornat anlegen

robin ['rɒbɪn] N Rotkehlchen *nt* → **round robin**

robinia [rə'bɪnɪəʳ] N *(Bot)* Robinie *f*, Scheinakazie *f*

robot ['rəʊbɒt] N Roboter *m*; *(fig also)* Automat *m*; **~ guidance, ~ pilot** Selbststeuerung *f*

robotics [rəʊ'bɒtɪks] N *sing or pl* Robotertechnik *f*, Robotik *f*

robust [rəʊ'bʌst] ADJ **a** *(= strong, solid) person, material, toy, machine* robust, widerstandsfähig; *structure* massiv, stabil; *build* kräftig, robust; *economy* robust, gesund; *economic growth* gesund; *constitution* kräftig; *appetite, humour* gesund, unverwüstlich; **to be in ~ health** sich bester Gesundheit erfreuen
b *(= determined) attitude* entschieden; *speech, style* markig; *defence* stark; **to put up** *or* **to make a ~ defence** *(Brit) or* **defense** *(US)* **of sth** etw energisch verteidigen, für etw energisch eintreten
c *(= vigorous) exercise* hart; **he enjoyed more ~ recreations like rock climbing** er hatte Spaß an etwas aktiveren Sportarten wie Klettern
d *(= intense) flavour* kräftig; *aroma* kräftig, herzhaft; *wine* kernig

robustly ADV **a** *(= strongly, solidly)* robust **b** *(= determinedly)* energisch **c** *flavoured* kräftig, herzhaft

robustness [rəʊ'bʌstnɪs] N **a** *(of person, material, toy, machine)* Robustheit *f*, Widerstandsfähigkeit *f*; *(of structure)* Massivität *f*, Stabilität *f*; *(of build)* Kräftigkeit *f*, Robustheit *f*; *(of economy)* Robustheit *f*, Gesundheit *f*; *(of economic growth)* Gesundheit *f*; *(of constitution)* Kräftigkeit *f* **b** *(of attitude)* Entschiedenheit *f*; *(of speech, style)* Markigkeit *f*; *(of defence)* Stärke *f* **c** *(of wine)* Kernigkeit *f*

rock[1] [rɒk] VT **a** *(= swing)* schaukeln; *(gently: = lull)* wiegen; **to ~ a baby to sleep** ein Baby in den Schlaf wiegen; **~ed by the waves** von den Wellen hin und her geschaukelt
b *(= shake) town* erschüttern, zum Beben bringen; *building* ins Wanken bringen, erschüttern; *ship* hin und her werfen; *(fig inf) person* erschüttern; **to ~ the boat** *(fig)* für Unruhe sorgen
VI **a** *(gently)* schaukeln; **he was ~ing back and forth (in his chair)** er schaukelte (auf seinem Stuhl) vor und zurück
b *(violently, building, tree, post)* schwanken; *(ship)* hin und her geworfen werden; *(ground)* beben; **they ~ed with laughter** sie schüttelten sich *or* bebten vor Lachen
c *(= rock and roll)* rocken
d *(inf: = be exciting, lively) (place)* eine aufregende Atmosphäre haben; *(music, show)* supergut *(inf) or* echt geil *(sl)* sein; **she ~s** sie ist einfach klasse *or* spitze *(inf)*
N *(= pop music)* Rock *m*; *(= dance)* Rock n' Roll *m*; **~-and-roll** Rock and Roll *m*, Rock n' Roll *m*; **to do the ~-and-roll** Rock n' Roll tanzen, rocken

rock[2] N **a** *(= substance)* Stein *m*; *(= rock face)* Fels(en) *m*; *(Geol)* Gestein *nt*; **caves hewn out of the ~** aus dem Fels(en) gehauene Höhlen; **hewn out of solid ~** aus massivem Stein/Fels gehauen; **built on ~** *(lit, fig)* auf Fels gebaut; **porous/volcanic ~** poröses/vulkanisches Gestein; **the study of ~s** Gesteinskunde *f*
b *(large mass)* Fels(en) *m*; *(= boulder also)* Felsbrocken *m*; *(smaller)* (großer) Stein; **the Rock (of Gibraltar)** der Felsen von Gibraltar; **on the Rock** *(inf)* in Gibraltar; **to be caught between a ~ and a hard place** *(fig)* in der Klemme stecken *or* sitzen; **as solid as a ~** *(structure)* massiv wie ein Fels; *firm, marriage* unerschütterlich wie ein Fels; **the ship went on the ~s** das Schiff lief (auf die Felsen) auf; **on the ~s** *(inf: = with ice)* mit Eis; *(marriage etc)* kaputt *(inf)*; *(= broke)* bankrott; **"danger, falling ~s"** „Steinschlaggefahr"
c *(inf: = diamond)* Diamant *m*; **~s** *(= jewels)* Klunker *pl (inf)*
d *no pl (Brit: = sweet)* Zuckerstange *f*
e **to get one's ~s off** *(sl)* seinen Spaß haben *(inf)*

rock: **rock bed** N *(Geol)* Felsengrund *m*; **rock bottom** N der Tiefpunkt; **to be at ~** auf dem Nullpunkt *or* Tiefpunkt sein; **to reach** *or* **hit ~** den Nullpunkt *or* Tiefpunkt erreichen; **this is ~** *(inf)* schlimmer kann es nicht werden; **rock-bottom** ADJ *(inf) interest rates* niedrigste(r, s); **~ prices** Niedrigstpreise *pl*; **rock-bound** ADJ von Felsen umschlossen; **rock bun, rock cake** N ≈ Rosinenhäufchen *nt*; **rock carving** N Felszeichnung *f*; *(= writing)* Felsschrift *f*; *(= action)* Ritzen *nt* in Fels; **rock-climber** N (Felsen)kletterer(in) *m(f)*; **rock climbing** N Klettern *nt* (im Fels); **rock club** N Rockklub *m*, Rockschuppen *m (inf)*; **rock crystal** N Bergkristall *m*

rocker ['rɒkəʳ] N **a** *(of cradle etc)* Kufe *f*; **to be off one's ~** *(inf)* übergeschnappt sein *(inf)*; **to go off one's ~** *(inf)* überschnappen *(inf)* **b** *(sl: = person)* Rocker(in) *m(f)* **c** *(Aut: also* **rocker arm***)* Kipphebel *m*

rockery ['rɒkərɪ] N Steingarten *m*

rocket ['rɒkɪt] N **a** Rakete *f* **b** *(Brit inf: = reprimand)* Anschiss *m (inf)*; **to get a ~** einen Anschiss bekommen *(inf)*; **to give sb a ~** jdm einen Anschiss verpassen *(inf)* VI *(prices)* hochschießen, hochschnellen; **to ~ to fame** über Nacht berühmt werden; *(person also)* kometenhaft aufsteigen; **he went ~ing past my door** *(inf)* er zischte *or* schoss (wie ein geölter Blitz) an meiner Tür vorbei *(inf)*

rocket *in cpds* Raketen-; **rocket attack** N Raketenangriff *m*; **rocket fuel** N Raketentreibstoff *m*; **rocket launcher** N Raketenabschussgerät *nt*; *(on plane)* Raketenwerfer *m*; *(multiple)* Stalinorgel *f*; **rocket projector** N *(Mil)* Raketenwerfer *m*

rocket-propelled ['rɒkɪtprə,peld] ADJ *(Mil)* **~ grenade** Panzerfaust *f*

rocket propulsion N Raketenantrieb *m*

rocket range N Raketenversuchsgelände *nt*; **within ~** mit Raketen zu erreichen

rocketry ['rɒkɪtrɪ] N Raketentechnik *f*; *(= rockets)* Raketen *pl*

rocket: **rocket science** N Raketentechnik *f*; **it's hardly ~** *(inf)* so schwer kann das doch nicht sein; **rocket scientist** N Raketentechniker(in) *m(f)*; **it doesn't take a ~ to ...** *(inf)* man muss kein Genie sein, um zu ...; **rocket ship** N Raketenträger *m*; *(rocket-propelled)* Raketenschiff *nt*; **rocket silo** N Raketensilo *nt*

rock: **rock face** N Felswand *f*; **rock fall** N Steinschlag *m*; **rock garden** N Steingarten *m*; **rock group** N *(Mus)* Rockgruppe *f*

Rockies ['rɒkɪz] PL **the ~** die Rocky Mountains *pl*

rocking ['rɒkɪŋ]: **rocking chair** N Schaukelstuhl *m*; **rocking horse** N Schaukelpferd *nt*

rock: **rock lobster** N *(Zool)* Gemeine Languste; **rock plant** N Steinpflanze *f*; **rock pool** N *Wasserlache, die sich bei Ebbe zwischen Felsen bildet*; **rockrose** N Sonnenröschen *nt*; **rock salmon** N *(Brit)* Dorsch *m*; **rock salt** N Steinsalz *nt*; **rock star** N *(Mus)* Rockstar *m*; **rock-steady** ADJ *hand, camera, gun, car* ganz ruhig; *voice* ganz fest

rocky[1] ['rɒkɪ] ADJ *(= unsteady)* wackelig *(also fig inf)*

rocky[2] ADJ *(+er) mountain, hill* felsig; *road, path* steinig; **~ outcrop** ausstreichendes Gestein *(spec)*

Rocky Mountains PL **the ~** die Rocky Mountains *pl*

rococo [rəʊ'kəʊkəʊ] N Rokoko *nt* ADJ Rokoko-; **~ period** Rokoko *nt*, Rokokozeit *f*

rod [rɒd] N **a** Stab *m*, Stange *f*; *(= switch)* Rute *f*, Gerte *f*; *(in machinery)* Stange *f*; *(for punishment, fishing)* Rute *f*; *(symbol of authority)* Stab *m*; **spare the ~ and spoil the child** *(prov)* wer mit der Rute spart, verzieht das Kind *(prov)*; **~ bacterium** Stäbchenbakterie *f* **b** *(= measure)* ≈ Rute *f (5,5 Yards)* **c** *(dated US sl: = gun)* Schießeisen *nt (hum inf)*

rode [rəʊd] *pret of* **ride**

rodent ['rəʊdənt] N Nagetier *nt*

rodeo ['rəʊdɪəʊ] N Rodeo *nt*

rodomontade [,rɒdəmɒn'teɪd] N *(liter)* Prahlerei *f*, Bramarbasieren *nt (geh)*

roe[1] [rəʊ] N *pl* **-(s)** *(species: also* **roe deer***)* Reh *nt*; **~buck** Rehbock *m*; **~ deer** *(female)* Reh *nt*, Ricke *f (spec)*

roe[2] N *pl* **-** *(of fish)* Rogen *m*; **hard ~** Rogen *m*; **soft ~** Milch *f*; **herring ~** Heringsrogen *m*

roentgen ['rɒntjən] N Röntgen *nt*

rogation [rəʊ'geɪʃən] N *(Eccl: = litany)* Litanei *f*; *(= period: also* **Rogation** *or* **Rogation-tide***)* Bittwoche *f*

Rogation Days PL *(Eccl)* Bitttage *pl*, Rogationstage *pl*

Rogation Sunday N *(Eccl)* (Sonntag *m*) Rogate *no art*

roger ['rɒdʒəʳ] INTERJ **"roger"** „verstanden"

rogue [rəʊg] N **a** *(= scoundrel)* Gauner(in) *m(f)*, Schurke *m*; *(= scamp)* Schlingel *m*; **you little ~!** du kleiner Gauner! **b** *(Zool)* Einzelgänger(in) *m(f)* ADJ **a** *(Zool)* **a ~ male** ein Einzelgänger *m*; **~ elephant** Einzelgänger(elefant) *m* **b** *(= maverick) person* einzelgängerisch; *(= criminal) person, organization* verbrecherisch, skrupellos **c** *(= abnormal, aberrant)* abnormal, entartet; *(Biol, Med) cell* aberrant, entartet; *satellite, rocket* fehlgeleitet; **a ~ firework flew into the crowd** ein fehlgezündeter Feuerwerkskörper flog in die Menge

roguery ['rəʊgərɪ] N *no pl (= wickedness)* Gaunerei *f*, Schurkerei *f*; *(= mischief)* Spitzbüberei *f*

rogues' gallery ['rəʊgz'gælərɪ] N *(Police inf)* Verbrecheralbum *nt*; **they look like a real ~** sie sehen wie Gauner aus

roguish ['rəʊgɪʃ] ADJ spitzbübisch; *(old, = wicked)* schurkisch

roguishly ['rəʊgɪʃlɪ] ADV spitzbübisch; *(old, = wickedly)* schurkisch

roil ['rɔɪl] *(esp US)* VI *(= churn: water)* strudeln VT *(fig)* in Aufruhr bringen; **to ~ the waters** für Unruhe sorgen

roister ['rɔɪstəʳ] VI *(= revel)* herumtollen

roisterer ['rɔɪstərəʳ] N Krawallmacher(in) *m(f)*

role [rəʊl] N *(Theat, fig)* Rolle *f*; **in the ~ of Ophelia** in der Rolle der Ophelia; **~ reversal** *(Psych)* Rollentausch *m*

role: **role model** N *(Psych)* Rollenbild *nt*; **role-playing** N Rollenspiel *nt*; **role swapping** ['rəʊl,swɒpɪŋ] N Rollentausch *m*

roll [rəʊl] N **a** *(of paper, netting, film, hair etc)* Rolle *f*; *(of fabric)* Ballen *m*; *(of banknotes)* Bündel *nt*; *(of butter)* Röllchen *nt*; *(of flesh, fat)* Wulst *m*, Röllchen *nt*; **a ~ of paper** eine Rolle Papier; **a ~ of banknotes** ein Bündel *nt* Banknoten; **he has ~s on his belly** er hat Speckrollen am Bauch
b *(Cook: also* **bread roll***)* Brötchen *nt*; **ham/cheese ~** Schinken-/Käsebrötchen *nt* → **sausage roll** *etc*
c *(= movement) (of sea, waves)* Rollen *nt*; *(of ship)* Schlingern *nt*, Rollen *nt*; *(= somersault, Avi-*

at) Rolle *f*; *(of person's gait)* Schaukeln *nt*, Wiegen *nt*; **to do a ~** eine Rolle machen; **the ship gave a sudden ~** das Schiff schlingerte plötzlich; **the dog was having a ~ on the grass** der Hund wälzte sich im Gras; **to have a ~ in the hay with sb** *(inf)* mit jdm ins Heu gehen *(inf)*; **to be on a ~** *(inf)* eine Glückssträhne haben
d *(= sound, of thunder)* Rollen *nt*; *(of drums)* Wirbel *m*; *(of organ)* Brausen *nt*
e *(= list, register)* Liste *f*, Register *nt*; *(of solicitors)* Anwaltsliste *f*; **we have 60 pupils on our ~** bei uns sind 60 Schüler angemeldet; **to call the ~** die Namensliste verlesen, die Namen aufrufen; **~ of honour** *(Brit)* Ehrenliste *f*; *(= plaque)* Ehrentafel *f*; **to strike sb** *or* **sb's name off the ~** jdn *or* jds Namen von der Liste streichen → **electoral roll**
VI **a** *(person, object)* rollen; *(from side to side: ship)* schlingern; *(presses)* laufen; *(Aviat)* eine Rolle machen; **to ~ over and over** rollen und rollen, kullern und kullern *(inf)*; **the children/stones ~ed down the hill** die Kinder/Steine rollten *or* kugelten *(inf)* den Berg hinunter; **tears were ~ing down her cheeks** Tränen rollten *or* kullerten *(inf)* ihr über die Wangen; **the newspapers were ~ing off the presses** die Zeitungen rollten von den Druckerpressen; **heads will ~!** *(fig)* da werden die Köpfe rollen!; **to keep the show ~ing** *(Theat inf)* die Show in Gang halten; **can you keep the ball** *or* **things ~ing while I'm away?** *(inf)* können Sie den Laden in Schwung halten, solange ich weg bin? *(inf)*; **the dog ~ed in the mud** der Hund wälzte sich im Schlamm; **he's ~ing in money** *or* **in it** *(inf)* er schwimmt im Geld *(inf)*; **the words just ~ed off his tongue** die Worte flossen ihm nur so von den Lippen; **his eyes ~ed** *(during a fit)* er rollte mit den Augen; **to ~ with the punches** *(fig)* sich nicht aus dem Gleis werfen *or* bringen lassen; **he ~s from side to side as he walks** er hat einen schaukelnden Gang
b *(= sound, thunder)* rollen, grollen; *(drum)* wirbeln; *(organ)* brausen; *(echo)* rollen
c *(camera)* laufen
d *(Cine)* **the credits ~ed** der Abspann lief
VT *barrel, hoop, ball, car* rollen; *umbrella* aufrollen; *cigarette* drehen; *pastry, dough* ausrollen; *metal, lawn, road* walzen; **to ~ one's eyes** die Augen rollen *or* verdrehen; **to ~ one's r's** das R rollen; **to ~ sth between one's fingers** etw zwischen den Fingern drehen; **to ~ one's own** *(cigarettes)* sich *(dat)* seine eigenen drehen; **to ~ wool into a ball** Wolle zu einem Knäuel aufwickeln; **the hedgehog ~ed itself into a ball** der Igel rollte sich zu einer Kugel zusammen; **he ~ed himself in a blanket** er wickelte sich in eine Decke; **it has a kitchen and a dining room ~ed into one** es hat eine Küche und Esszimmer in einem → *also* **rolled**

▶ **roll about** *(Brit)* or **around** VI *(balls)* herumrollen *or* -kugeln *(inf)*; *(ship)* schlingern; *(person, dog)* sich herumwälzen, sich wälzen; *(inf, with laughter)* sich kugeln (vor Lachen) *(inf)*

▶ **roll along** **VI** **a** *(ball)* entlang- *or* dahinrollen; **we were rolling along enjoying the countryside** wir rollten dahin und genossen die Landschaft **b** *(inf, = arrive)* aufkreuzen *(inf)*, eintrudeln *(inf)* **VT** *sep* rollen

▶ **roll away** **VI** *(ball, vehicle)* wegrollen; *(clouds, mist)* abziehen **VT** *sep trolley, table* wegrollen

▶ **roll back** **VI** zurückrollen; *(eyes)* nach innen rollen **VT** *sep object, carpet* zurückrollen; *sheet* zurückschlagen; **if only we could roll back the years** wenn wir nur die Uhr zurückdrehen könnten

▶ **roll by** VI *(vehicle, procession)* vorbeirollen; *(clouds)* vorbeiziehen; *(time, years)* dahinziehen

▶ **roll down** **VI** *(ball, person, tears)* hinunterrollen *or* -kugeln *(inf)* **VT** *sep cart* hinunterrollen; *window* herunterlassen

▶ **roll in** **VI** hereinrollen; *(letters, money, contributions, suggestions)* hereinströmen; *(inf, person)* eintrudeln *(inf)* **VT** *sep barrel, trolley* hereinrollen

▶ **roll off** VI **a** *(vehicle, procession)* weg- *or* davonrollen **b** *(= fall off: object, person)* herunterrollen

▶ **roll on** **VI** weiterrollen; *(time)* verfliegen; **roll on the holidays!** *(Brit)* wenn doch nur schon Ferien wären! **VT** *sep stockings* (die Beine) hochrollen

▶ **roll out** **VT** *sep* **a** *barrel* hinausrollen **b** *pastry, dough* ausrollen; *metal* auswalzen **c** *(inf) sentence, verse* produzieren *(inf)* **d** *(= introduce) system in company etc* einführen **VI** hinausrollen

▶ **roll over** **VI** herumrollen; *(vehicle)* umkippen; *(person)* sich umdrehen; **the dog rolled over onto its back** der Hund rollte auf den Rücken **VT** *sep person, animal, object* umdrehen; *patient* auf die andere Seite legen

▶ **roll past** VI = **roll by**

▶ **roll through** *(esp US: = drive through)* **VI** durchrollen *or* -fahren **VI** *+prep obj* rollen *or* fahren durch; *(= ignore)* nicht beachten; **to roll through a stop sign** ein Stoppschild überfahren

▶ **roll up** **VI** **a** *(animal)* sich zusammenrollen *(into* zu) **b** *(inf: = arrive)* antanzen *(inf)* **c** *(at fairground etc)* **roll up!** treten Sie näher! **VT** *sep cloth, paper, map, umbrella* auf- *or* zusammenrollen; *sleeves, trouser legs* hochkrempeln

roll: **rollback** N **a** *(esp US: of tax)* Minderung *f* **b** *(of prices)* Rückgang *m* **c** *(Mil: of troops)* Rückzug *m* **d** *(lit: = rolling back)* Zurückrollen *nt*; **rollbar** N Überrollbügel *m*; **roll call** N *(Sch)* Namensaufruf *m*; *(Mil)* (Anwesenheits)appell *m*; **a ~ of sporting giants** ein Verzeichnis *nt* von Spitzensportlern; **roll collar** N Rollkragen *m*

rolled [rəʊld] ADJ *blanket, paper etc* zusammengerollt; *tobacco* gerollt, gedreht

rolled: **rolled gold** N Dubleegold *nt*; **rolled oats** PL Haferflocken *pl*; **rolled steel** N Walzstahl *m*

roller [ˈrəʊləˈ] N **a** *(for pressing, smoothing)* Rolle *f*; *(= pastry roller)* Nudelholz *nt*; *(for lawn, road, Ind)* Walze *f*; *(= paint roller)* Rolle *f* **b** *(for winding sth round)* Rolle *f*; *(= hair roller)* (Locken)wickler *m*; **to put one's hair in ~s** sich *(dat)* die Haare aufdrehen *or* eindrehen; **with her ~s in** mit Lockenwicklern (im Haar) **c** *(for moving things)* Rolle *f*; *(log-shaped)* Rollklotz *m* **d** *(= wave)* Brecher *m*

rollerball pen [ˌrəʊləbɔːlˈpen] N Tintenroller *m*

roller: **roller bandage** N Rollbinde *f*; **roller bearing** N Rollenlager *nt*; **roller blind** N Springrollo *nt*; **roller coaster** N Achterbahn *f*, Berg-und-Tal-Bahn *f*; **an emotional ~** eine gefühlsmäßige Berg-und-Tal-Fahrt; **roller skate** N Rollschuh *m*; **roller-skate** VI Rollschuh laufen; **he ~d down the street** er lief *or* fuhr mit seinen Rollschuhen die Straße entlang; **roller-skater** N Rollschuhläufer(in) *m(f)*; **roller-skating** N Rollschuhlaufen *nt*; **roller towel** N Rollhandtuch *nt*

rollick [ˈrɒlɪk] VI *(also* **rollick about***)* herumtollen

rollicking [ˈrɒlɪkɪŋ] **ADJ** *person* ausgelassen; *occasion, life* wild; **~ (good) fun** Mordsspaß *m* *(inf)*; **a ~ success** ein Mordserfolg *m* *(inf)*; **to have a ~ time** richtig auf die Pauke hauen *(inf)* **N** *(Brit inf: = telling-off)* **to get a ~** runtergeputzt werden *(inf)*; **to give sb a ~** jdn runterputzen *(inf)*

rolling [ˈrəʊlɪŋ] ADJ **a** *(= swaying) motion* schwankend; *ship* schlingernd; *sea, waves* rollend, wogend; **to have a ~ gait** einen schaukelnden Gang haben; **to be ~ drunk** sturzbetrunken sein *(inf)* **b** *(= undulating) hills* gewellt; *landscape, countryside* wellig, hügelig; *lawns* wellig **c** *(= progressing) plan, programme* kontinuierlich; **three weeks of ~ strikes** dreiwöchige Streikmaßnahmen *pl*; **~ news service** Nachrichtendienst *m* rund um die Uhr

rolling: **rolling mill** N *(= factory)* Walzwerk *nt*; *(= machine)* Walze *f*; **rolling pin** N Nudelholz *nt*, Teigrolle *f*; **rolling stock** N *(Rail)* rollendes Material, Fahrzeuge *pl*; **rolling stone** N **he's a ~** er ist ein unsteter Bursche; **a ~ gathers no moss** *(Prov)* wer rastet, der rostet *(Prov)*; **rolling train** N Walzstraße *f*

roll: **rollmop (herring)** N Rollmops *m*; **rollneck** N Rollkragen *m*; **rollneck(ed)** ADJ Rollkragen-; **~ sweater** Rollkragenpullover *m*; **roll-on** N **a** Elastikschlüpfer *m* **b** *(also* **roll-on deodorant***)* Deoroller *m*; **roll-on/ /roll-off** ADJ Roll-on-roll-off-; **~ ferry** Roll-on-roll-off-Fähre *f*; **roll-out** N **a** *(= presentation of new aircraft)* Roll-out *m*; *(launch of new product)* (Produkt)präsentation *f*, (Produkt)einführung *f* **b** *(of aircraft on runway)* Ausrollen *nt*; **rollover** **N** **a** *(Fin, of loan etc)* Laufzeitverlängerung *f* **b** *(US: cellphone)* Mitnehmen *nt* von nicht vertelefonierten Freiminuten in den Folgemonat **ATTR** *(Brit, in National Lottery)* **~ week** *Woche mit Lotto-Jackpot, da es in der vorhergehenden Woche keinen Hauptgewinner gab*; **~ jackpot** Jackpot *m*; **roll-top** N Rollladen *m*; **roll-top desk** N Rollschreibtisch *m*; **roll-up** N *(Brit inf)* Selbstgedrehte *f*; **to have a ~** sich *(dat)* eine drehen

Rolodex® [ˈrəʊlədeks] N Rolodex® *m*, Rotationskartei *f*

roly-poly [ˈrəʊlɪˈpəʊlɪ] **ADJ** *(inf)* kugelrund, mopsig *(inf)* **N** **a** *(Brit: also* **roly-poly pudding***)* *mit Nierentalg hergestellter Strudel, der gebacken oder im Wasserbad gekocht wird* **b** *(inf: = plump child)* Rollmops *m (inf)*, Pummel *m (inf)* **c** *(inf: = somersault)* Purzelbaum *m (inf)*

ROM [rɒm] N *(Comput) abbr of* **read only memory** ROM *m or nt*

romaine [ˌrəʊˈmeɪn] N *(US)* Romagnasalat *m*, römischer Salat

Roman [ˈrəʊmən] **N** **a** Römer(in) *m(f)* **b** *(Typ: also* **Roman type***)* Magerdruck *m* **ADJ** **a** römisch; **~ times** Römerzeit *f* **b** *(= Roman Catholic)* römisch-katholisch; **the ~ Church** die römische Kirche **c** **roman** *(Typ)* mager; **roman letters** Magerdruck *m*

roman à clef [ˈrəʊmɑ̃ŋæˈkleɪ] N Schlüsselroman *m*

Roman: **Roman alphabet** N römisches Alphabet; **Roman arch** N romanischer Bogen; **Roman calendar** N römischer Kalender; **Roman candle** N Goldrausch *m*; **Roman Catholic** **ADJ** (römisch-)katholisch; **the ~ Church** die (römisch-)katholische Kirche **N** Katholik(in) *m(f)*, (Römisch-)Katholische(r) *mf*; **Roman Catholicism** N römisch-katholischer Glaube

romance [rəʊˈmæns] **N** **a** *(= book)* Fantasie- *or* Phantasieerzählung *f*, Roman *m*; *(= love story)* Liebesgeschichte *f or* -roman *m*; *(= adventure story)* Abenteuerroman *m*; *(= tale of chivalry)* Ritterroman *m*; *(no pl: = romantic fiction)* Liebesromane *pl*; *(fig: = lies)* Märchen *nt*; **it's pure ~** es ist das reinste Märchen
b *(= love affair)* Romanze *f*; **it's quite a ~** das ist eine richtige Liebesgeschichte
c *no pl (= romanticism)* Romantik *f*; **an air of ~ pervaded the village** ein romantischer Zauber umgab das Dorf; **the ~ of foreign lands** der Zauber ferner Länder
d *(Mus)* Romanze *f*
e **Romance** *(= Romance languages)* die romanischen Sprachen *pl*
ADJ **Romance** *(language etc)* romanisch
VI fantasieren, phantasieren, fabulieren
VT eine Romanze haben mit

romancer [rəʊˈmænsəˈ] N *(fig)* Fantast(in) *m(f)*, Phantast(in) *m(f)*

Roman Empire N Römisches Reich

Romanesque [ˌrəʊməˈnesk] ADJ romanisch

Roman holiday N Spaß *m* auf Kosten anderer

Romania [rəʊˈmeɪnɪə] N Rumänien *nt*

Romanian [rəʊˈmeɪnɪən] **ADJ** rumänisch **N** **a** Rumäne *m*, Rumänin *f* **b** *(= language)* Rumänisch *nt*

Romanic [rəʊˈmænɪk] ADJ *language* romanisch

romanize [ˈrəʊmənaɪz] VT *(Hist)* romanisieren; *(Rel)* nach dem Katholizismus ausrichten

Roman: **Roman law** N römisches Recht; **Roman nose** N Römernase *f*; **Roman numeral** N römische Ziffer

Romansh [rəʊˈmænʃ] ADJ romantsch N Romantsch *nt*

romantic [rəʊˈmæntɪk] ADJ *(also Art, Liter, Mus: also* **Romantic***)* romantisch; *person also* romantisch veranlagt; **~ comedy** romantische Komödie; **~ novel** Liebesroman *m*; **the Romantic movement** die Romantik; **they were very good friends but there was no ~ involvement** sie waren sehr enge Freunde, aber sie hatten keine Liebesbeziehung; **he played the ~ lead in several plays** er spielte in mehreren Stücken den romantischen Liebhaber N *(also Art, Liter, Mus: also* **Romantic***)* Romantiker(in) *m(f)*

romantically [rəʊˈmæntɪkəlɪ] ADV romantisch; **to be ~ involved with sb** eine Liebesbeziehung mit jdm haben; **she was ~ linked with ...** ihr wurde eine Beziehung mit ... nachgesagt; **to be ~ inclined** romantisch veranlagt sein; **~, things are looking up** in Liebesdingen geht es aufwärts

romantic fiction N Liebesromane *pl*

romanticism [rəʊˈmæntɪsɪzəm] N *(Art, Liter, Mus: also* **Romanticism***)* Romantik *f*; **his ~** sein romantisches Wesen

romanticist [rəʊˈmæntɪsɪst] N *(Art, Liter, Mus: also* **Romanticist***)* Romantiker(in) *m(f)*

romanticize [rəʊˈmæntɪsaɪz] VT romantisieren, zu romantisch sehen VI fantasieren, phantasieren

romantic love N *(Liter)* romantische Liebe

Romany [ˈrəʊmənɪ] N **a** Roma *mf* **b** *(Ling)* die Zigeunersprache *(neg!)*, Romani *nt* ADJ *language, culture* der Roma; **~ gypsy** Rom *m*, Zigeuner(in) *m(f) (neg!)*

Rome [rəʊm] N Rom *nt*; **when in ~ (do as the Romans do)** *(prov)* ≈ andere Länder, andere Sitten *(Prov)*; **~ wasn't built in a day** *(Prov)* Rom ist auch nicht an einem Tag erbaut worden *(Prov)*; **all roads lead to ~** *(Prov)* viele Wege führen nach Rom *(prov)*; **the Church of ~** die römische Kirche

Romeo [ˈrəʊmɪəʊ] N Romeo *m*; *(fig)* Herzensbrecher *m*; **a Latin ~** ein Papagallo *m (inf)*

Romish [ˈrəʊmɪʃ] ADJ *(pej)* Katholen- *(pej)*, papistisch *(pej)*

romp [rɒmp] N Tollerei *f*; *(hum: = sexual intercourse)* Nümmerchen *nt (inf)*; **the play was just a ~** das Stück war reiner Klamauk; **to have a ~** herumtollen *or* -toben/ein Nümmerchen machen *(inf)* VI **a** *(children, puppies)* herumtollen *or* -toben; **he came ~ing up to me** er kam auf mich zugetollt **b to ~ home** *(= win)* spielend gewinnen; **to ~ away with the title** den Titel einstecken **c to ~ through sth** mit etw spielend fertig werden, etw mit der linken Hand erledigen

rompers [ˈrɒmpəz] PL *(also* **pair of rompers***)* einteiliger Spielanzug

romping ADJ, **rompingly** ADV [ˈrɒmpɪŋ, -lɪ], **rompish** ADJ, **rompishly** ADV [ˈrɒmpɪʃ, -lɪ] *(= lively and boisterous)* ausgelassen, wild

rondeau [ˈrɒndəʊ], **rondel** [ˈrɒndəl] N *(Mus)* Rondeau *nt*; *(Liter also)* Rondel *nt*

rondo [ˈrɒndəʊ] N *(Mus)* Rondo *nt*

Roneo® [ˈrəʊnɪəʊ] VT (mit Matrize) kopieren N Kopie *f*

rood [ru:d] N **a** *(Archit)* Kruzifix *nt* **b** *(Brit: = measure)* Rute *f*, ≈ Viertelmorgen *m*

rood screen [ˈru:dskri:n] N Lettner *m (spec)*

roof [ru:f] N Dach *nt*; *(of car also)* Verdeck *nt*; *(of cave, tunnel)* Gewölbe *nt*; **the ~ of the mouth** der Gaumen; **the ~ of the world** das Dach der Welt; **a ~ of branches** ein Blätterdach *nt*; **without a ~ over one's head** ohne Dach über dem Kopf; **a room in the ~** ein Zimmer *nt* unter dem Dach; **to live under the same ~ as sb** mit jdm unter demselben Dach wohnen; **as long as you live under my ~** solange du deine Beine unter meinen Tisch streckst; **to go through the ~** *(inf, person)* an die Decke gehen *(inf)*; *(prices etc)* untragbar werden → **hit, raise** VT *house* mit einem Dach decken; **flat-/red--ed** mit flachem/rotem Dach

▶ **roof in** *or* **over** VT *sep* überdachen

roofer [ˈru:fəʳ] N Dachdecker(in) *m(f)*

roof: **roof garden** N Dachgarten *m*; **roof guard** N Schneefang *m*

roofing [ˈru:fɪŋ] N Material *nt* zum Dachdecken; *(= action)* Dachdecken *nt*; **~ felt** *(Brit) or* **paper** Dachpappe *f*

roof: **roof lining** N *(in car)* Himmel *m*; **roof rack** N Dach(gepäck)träger *m*; **rooftop** N Dach *nt*; **to shout** *or* **scream sth from the ~s** *(fig)* etw überall herumposaunen *(inf)*, etw an die große Glocke hängen *(inf)*

rook [rʊk] N **a** *(= bird)* Saatkrähe *f* **b** *(= swindler)* Betrüger(in) *m(f)*, Gauner(in) *m(f)* **c** *(Chess)* Turm *m* VT *(= swindle)* übers Ohr hauen *(inf)*, betrügen; **to ~ sb of £5** jdm £ 5 abgaunern VI *(Chess)* mit dem Turm ziehen

rookery [ˈrʊkərɪ] N Kolonie *f*

rookie [ˈrʊkɪ] N *(esp Mil sl)* Grünschnabel *m (inf)*

room [ru:m] N **a** *(in house, building)* Zimmer *nt*, Raum *m (geh)*; *(= public hall, ballroom etc)* Saal *m*; *(= bedroom, also in hotel)* Zimmer *nt*; *(= office)* Büro *nt*; **the whole ~ laughed** alle im Zimmer lachten, der ganze Saal lachte; **"rooms to let"** „Zimmer zu vermieten"; **~ and board** Unterkunft mit Verpflegung; **they used to live in ~s** sie haben früher in möblierten Zimmern gewohnt; **I'll come to your ~s** ich komme in deine Wohnung *or* auf deine Bude *(esp Univ inf)*

b *no pl (= space)* Platz *m*; *(fig)* Spielraum *m*; **is there (enough) ~?** ist da genügend Platz?; **there is ~ for two (people)** es ist genügend Platz für zwei (Leute); **there is no ~ (for you/that box)** es ist nicht genug Platz (für dich/die Kiste); **to make ~ for sb/sth** für jdn/etw Platz machen *or* schaffen; **there is still ~ for hope** es besteht immer noch Hoffnung; **there is little ~ for hope** es besteht wenig Hoffnung; **there is no ~ for doubt** es kann keinen Zweifel geben; **there is ~ for improvement in your work** Ihre Arbeit könnte um einiges besser sein; **~ for manoeuvre** *(Brit) or* **maneuver** *(US)* Spielraum *m*

VI zur Untermiete wohnen; **~ing house** *(esp US)* Mietshaus *nt (mit möblierten Wohnungen)*

room: **room clerk** N *(US)* Empfangschef *m*, Empfangsdame *f*; **room divider** N Raumteiler *m*

-roomed [-ru:md] ADJ *suf* **a 6-roomed house** ein Haus mit 6 Zimmern; **a two-roomed apartment** eine Zweizimmerwohnung

roomer [ˈru:məʳ] N *(US)* Untermieter(in) *m(f)*

roomful [ˈru:mfʊl] N **there was quite a ~** das Zimmer war ganz schön voll; **a ~ of people** ein Zimmer voll(er) Leute

roominess [ˈru:mɪnɪs] N Geräumigkeit *f*; *(of garment)* Weite *f*

room: **roommate** N *(Brit)* Zimmergenosse *m*, Zimmergenossin *f*; *(US: = flatmate)* Mitbewohner(in) *m(f)*; **room service** N Zimmerservice *m*, Etagendienst *m*; **room temperature** N Zimmertemperatur *f*; **wine at ~** Wein mit *or* auf Zimmertemperatur

roomy [ˈru:mɪ] ADJ *(+er)* geräumig; *garment* weit

roost [ru:st] N *(= pole)* Stange *f*; *(= henhouse)* Hühnerhaus *nt or* -stall *m*; **at ~** auf der Stange; **to come home to ~** *(fig)* auf den Urheber zurückfallen → **cock, rule** VI *(= settle)* sich niederlassen; *(= sleep)* auf der Stange schlafen

rooster [ˈru:stəʳ] N Hahn *m*

root [ru:t] N **a** *(of plant, hair, tooth)* Wurzel *f*; **~s** *(fig, of person)* Wurzeln; **by the ~s** mit der Wurzel; **to take ~** *(lit, fig)* Wurzeln schlagen; **her ~s are in Scotland** sie ist in Schottland verwurzelt; **she has no ~s** sie ist nirgends zu Hause; **to put down ~s in a country** in einem Land Fuß fassen; **~ and branch** *(fig)* mit Stumpf und Stiel → **grass-roots, pull up**

b *(fig: = source: of evil, of trouble etc)* Wurzel *f*; **the ~ of the matter** der Kern der Sache; **to get to the ~(s) of the problem** dem Problem auf den Grund gehen; **that is** *or* **lies at the ~ of his behaviour** *(Brit) or* **behavior** *(US)* das ist der eigentliche Grund für sein Benehmen

c *(Math, Ling)* Wurzel *f*; *(of equation)* Lösung *f*; *(Ling: = base form)* Stamm *m* → **cube, square root**

VT *plant* Wurzeln schlagen lassen bei

VI *(plants etc)* Wurzeln schlagen *or* fassen

▶ **root about** *(Brit) or* **around** VI herumwühlen *(for* nach)

▶ **root for** VI *+prep obj team* anfeuern; **to root for sb** jdm die Daumen drücken; *(esp Sport: = cheer on)* jdn anfeuern

▶ **root out** VT *sep* **a** *(lit)* = **root up b** *(fig) (= remove) evil* mit der Wurzel ausreißen; *(= find)* aufspüren, ausgraben *(inf)*

▶ **root up** VT *sep plant* herausreißen; *(= dig up)* ausgraben

root *in cpds* Wurzel-; **root beer** N *(US) Art Limonade*; **root-canal work, root-canal therapy** N *(Dentistry)* Wurzelkanalbehandlung *f*, Zahnwurzelbehandlung *f*; **root cause** N eigentlicher Grund; **root crop** N Wurzelgemüse *nt no pl*; **root directory** N *(Comput)* Stammverzeichnis *nt*

rooted [ˈru:tɪd] ADJ **a** *(= grounded, based)* verwurzelt; **to be ~ in sth** in etw *(dat)* verwurzelt sein **b** *(= embedded)* **(deeply) ~** *(objection, conviction etc)* tief sitzend *attr*, tief verwurzelt **c to be** *or* **stand ~ (to the spot)** *(= immobile, frozen)* wie angewurzelt dastehen

rooter [ˈru:təʳ] N *(esp US inf Sport)* begeisterter Anhänger *or* Fan, begeisterte Anhängerin

rootless [ˈru:tlɪs] ADJ *plant* wurzellos; *(fig) person* ohne Wurzeln; **a ~ existence** ein wurzelloses Leben, ein Leben ohne Wurzeln

root: **root sign** N *(Math)* Wurzelzeichen *nt*; **rootstock** N *(Bot)* Wurzelstock *m*; **root treatment** N *(Dentistry)* Wurzelbehandlung *f*; **root vegetable** N Wurzelgemüse *nt*; **root word** N *(Ling)* Wortwurzel *f*; *(= base form)* Wortstamm *m*

rope [rəʊp] N **a** Seil *nt*; *(Naut)* Tau *nt*; *(of bell)* Glockenstrang *m*; *(= hangman's rope)* Strang *m*, Strick *m*; **a ~ of pearls** eine Perlenschnur; **to give sb more/plenty of ~** *(fig)* jdm mehr/viel Freiheit lassen; **give him enough ~ and he'll hang himself** *(fig)* der dreht sich *(dat)* schon selbst seinen Strick; **I am at the end of my ~** *(US inf) (= annoyed, impatient)* mir reichts *(inf)*; *(= desperate)* ich bin am Ende

b *(Mountaineering)* Seil *nt*; **a ~ of climbers** eine Seilschaft; **to put on the ~s** anseilen; **to be on the ~** angeseilt sein; **there were three of them on the ~** sie waren zu dritt am Seil

c the ~s *(Boxing etc)* die Seile *pl*; **to be on the ~s** *(boxer)* in den Seilen hängen; *(inf)* in der Klemme sein; **to know the ~s** *(inf)* sich auskennen; **to show sb the ~s** *(inf)* jdn in alles einweihen; **to learn the ~s** *(inf)* sich einarbeiten

VT **a** *box, case* verschnüren; **to ~ sb to a tree** jdn an einen Baum binden; **to ~ sb's feet together** jdm die Füße zusammenbinden; **to ~ climbers (together)** Bergsteiger anseilen **b** *(= lasso)* mit dem Lasso fangen

▶ **rope in** VT *sep* **a** *area* (mit einem Seil) abgrenzen; *cattle* mit einem Seil einfrieden **b** *(esp Brit fig)* rankriegen *(inf)*; **how did you get roped into that?** wie bist du denn da reingeraten? *(inf)*; **I don't want to get roped into helping** ich will nicht, dass die mich zum Helfen rankriegen *(inf)*

▶ **rope off** VT *sep area* mit einem Seil abgrenzen

▶ **rope together** VT *sep objects* zusammenbinden; *climbers* aneinanderseilen, anseilen

▶ **rope up** VI *(climbers)* sich anseilen VT *sep* anseilen

rope *in cpds* Seil-; **rope burn** N Reibungsverbrennung *f (beim Umgang mit Seilen)*, Seilbrand *m (spec)*; **rope ladder** N Strickleiter *f*; **rope light** N Flexlicht *nt*; **ropemaker** N Seiler(in) *m(f)*

ropery ['rəʊpərɪ] N Seilerei *f*

rope: **rope sole** N (aus Seil) geflochtene Sohle; **rope-soled** ADJ mit (aus Seil) geflochtener Sohle; **ropewalker** N Seiltänzer(in) *m(f)*

rop(e)y ['rəʊpɪ] ADJ *(+er) (Brit inf: = bad)* miserabel *(inf)*; *(= worn)* mitgenommen; **the engine is a bit ~** der Motor pfeift auf dem letzten Loch *(inf)*

ropeyard ['rəʊpjɑːd] N Seilerei *f*

rosary ['rəʊzərɪ] N *(Rel)* Rosenkranz *m*; **to say the ~** den Rosenkranz beten

rose[1] [rəʊz] *pret of* **rise**

rose[2] **N** **a** Rose *f*; **wild ~** Wildrose *f*; **my life isn't all ~s** *(inf)* ich bin auch nicht auf Rosen gebettet; **life/marriage isn't all ~s** *(inf)* das Leben/die Ehe hat auch seine/ihre Schattenseiten; **an English ~** *(fig)* eine englische Schöne; **everything's coming up ~s** *(inf)* alles ist *or* läuft bestens *(inf)*; **to come up smelling of ~s** *(inf)* gut dastehen; **that will put the ~s back in your cheeks** davon bekommst du wieder etwas Farbe im Gesicht; **under the ~** *(fig liter)* unter dem Siegel der Verschwiegenheit; **the Wars of the Roses** die Rosenkriege *pl*
b *(= nozzle)* Brause *f*; *(= rosette, Archit)* Rosette *f*
c *(= colour)* Rosarot *nt*, Rosenrot *nt*
ADJ rosarot, rosenrot

rosé ['rəʊzeɪ] **ADJ** rosé **N** Rosé *m*

roseate ['rəʊzɪɪt] ADJ *(liter)* rosenfarben

rose *in cpds* Rosen-; **rosebay** N Oleander *m*; **rosebowl** N Rosenpokal *m*; **rosebud** N Rosenknospe *f*; **~ mouth** Rosenmund *m*; **rose-bush** N Rosenstrauch *m*; **rose-coloured**, *(US)* **rose-colored** ADJ rosarot, rosenrot; **to see everything/life through ~ spectacles** *(Brit) or* **rose-colored glasses** *(US)* alles/das Leben durch die rosarote Brille sehen; **rose-cut** ADJ mit Rosetteschliff; **rose garden** N Rosengarten *m*; **rosehip** N Hagebutte *f*; **rosehip syrup** N Hagenbuttensirup *m*

rosemary ['rəʊzmərɪ] N Rosmarin *m*

rose: **rose petal** N Rosen(blüten)blatt *nt*; **rose-pink** **ADJ** rosarot **N** Rosarot *nt*; **rose quartz** N Rosenquarz *m*; **rose-red** ADJ rosenrot; **rosetree** N Rosenstrauch *m*

Rosetta stone [rəʊ'zetə'stəʊn] N Stein *m* von Rosette

rosette [rəʊ'zet] N Rosette *f*

rose: **rosewater** N Rosenwasser *nt*; **rose window** N (Fenster)rosette *f*; **rosewood** N Rosenholz *nt*

Rosicrucian [rəʊzɪ'kruːʃən] **N** Rosenkreu(t)zer *m* **ADJ** der Rosenkreu(t)zer

rosin ['rɒzɪn] **N** Harz *nt*, Kolophonium *nt (esp Mus)* **VT** mit Harz *or* Kolophonium behandeln

ROSPA ['rɒspə] N *(Brit) abbr of* **Royal Society for the Prevention of Accidents** Königliche Gesellschaft für Unfallverhütung

roster ['rɒstə'] N Dienstplan *m* → **duty roster**

rostrum ['rɒstrəm] N *pl* **rostra** ['rɒstrə] Tribüne *f*, Rednerpult *nt*; *(for conductor)* Dirigentenpult *nt*

rosy ['rəʊzɪ] ADJ *(+er)* **a** *(= pink)* rosarot; *complexion, cheeks, face* rosig **b** *(fig: = hopeful) future, situation, view* rosig; **to look ~** *(situation, future)* rosig aussehen; **to paint a ~ picture of sth** etw in den rosigsten Farben ausmalen

rot [rɒt] **N** **a** *(in teeth, plants, wood)* Fäulnis *f no pl*; **to stop the ~** *(lit, fig)* den Fäulnisprozess aufhalten; **then the ~ set in** *(fig)* dann setzte der Fäulnisprozess *or* Verfall ein → **dry rot** **b** *(inf: = rubbish)* Quatsch *m (inf)*, Blödsinn *m (inf)* **VI** *(wood, material, rope)* verrotten, faulen; *(teeth, plant)* verfaulen; *(fig)* verrotten; **to ~ in jail** im Gefängnis verrotten; **let him ~!** *(inf)* soll er doch vor die Hunde gehen! *(inf)* **VT** verfaulen lassen

▶**rot away** VI verfaulen

rota ['rəʊtə] N **a** *(Brit)* Dienstplan *m* **b** *(Eccl)* **Rota** Rota *f*

Rotarian [rəʊ'teərɪən] **ADJ** rotarisch **N** Rotarier(in) *m(f)*

rotary ['rəʊtərɪ] ADJ rotierend, Dreh-; **~ motion** Drehbewegung *f*; **~ iron** Heißmangel *f*

rotary: **Rotary Club** N Rotary Club *m*; **rotary engine** N Umlaufmotor *m*; **rotary plough**, *(US)* **rotary plow** N *(Tech)* **a** *(also* **rotary snow plough**) Schneefräse *f* **b** *(Agr)* Bodenfräse *f*; **rotary printer** N Rotationsdrucker *m*; **rotary (printing) press** N Rotationsmaschine *f*; **rotary pump** N Kreiselpumpe *f*

rotate [rəʊ'teɪt] **VT** **a** *(around axis)* drehen, rotieren lassen; *(Math)* rotieren lassen; *(Comput)* rotieren; *head, body* drehen **b** *crops* im Wechsel anbauen; *work, jobs* turnusmäßig erledigen
VI **a** *(around axis)* sich drehen, rotieren; *(Math)* rotieren **b** *(crops)* im Wechsel angebaut werden; *(people: = take turns)* sich (turnusmäßig) abwechseln

rotating [rəʊ'teɪtɪŋ] ADJ *(= revolving)* rotierend, sich drehend; *crops* im Wechsel angebaut; *presidency* im Turnus wechselnd; **on a ~ basis** in einem gewissen Turnus

rotation [rəʊ'teɪʃən] N **a** *no pl (around axis)* Drehung *f*, Rotation *f (also Math)*; *(of crops)* Wechsel *m*, Rotation *f*; *(= taking turns)* turnusmäßiger Wechsel; **in** *or* **by ~** abwechselnd im Turnus; **~ of crops, crop ~** Fruchtwechsel *m*
b *(= turn)* (Um)drehung *f*, Rotation *f*

rotatory [rəʊ'teɪtərɪ] ADJ **a** rotierend; **~ motion** Drehbewegung *f* **b** *schedule* turnusmäßig; *cultivation* abwechselnd

Rotavator® ['rəʊtəveɪtə'] N *(Brit)* = **Rotovator**

rote [rəʊt] N **by ~** *(learn)* auswendig; *recite, teach* mechanisch

rotgut ['rɒt,gʌt] N *(pej inf)* Fusel *m (inf)*

rotisserie [rəʊ'tɪsərɪ] N *(= spit)* Grillspieß *m*; *(= restaurant)* Rotisserie *f*

rotogravure [,rəʊtəʊgrə'vjʊə'] N Kupferdruck *m*

rotor ['rəʊtə'] N *(Aviat, Elec, Aut)* Rotor *m*

rotor: **rotor arm** N Verteilerfinger *m*; **rotor blade** N Flügelblatt *nt*

Rotovator® ['rəʊtəveɪtə'] N *(Brit)* Bodenfräse *f*

rot-proof ['rɒt,pruːf] ADJ fäulnissicher

rotten ['rɒtn] ADJ **a** *vegetation, egg, tooth* faul; *wood* morsch, faul; *fruit* faul, verdorben; *(fig: = corrupt)* korrupt, verdorben; **~ to the core** *(fig)* durch und durch verdorben; **~ apple** *(fig)* schwarzes Schaf; **there's always one ~ egg (in the basket)** *(fig)* es gibt immer ein schwarzes Schaf
b *(inf: = poor, incompetent)* mies *(inf)*; **she was a ~ driver** sie war eine miserable Fahrerin; **to be ~ at sth** in etw *(dat)* schlecht sein; **I was always ~ at drawing** ich konnte noch nie gut zeichnen
c *(inf: = dreadful, unpleasant)* scheußlich *(inf)*; *weather* mies *(inf)*, scheußlich *(inf)*; **what ~ luck!** so ein Pech!; **it's a ~ business** das ist eine üble Sache; **to have a ~ time** eine schlimme Zeit durchmachen; **what a ~ time you're having** was du zurzeit aber auch alles durchmachen musst! *(inf)*; **isn't it ~ about poor David?** ist das nicht furchtbar mit dem armen David?
d *(inf: = mean)* gemein, eklig; **that was a ~ trick/a ~ thing to do** das war ein übler Trick/eine Gemeinheit; **that's a ~ thing to say** es ist gemein, so etwas zu sagen
e *(inf: = unwell)* elend, mies *(inf)*; **to feel ~** sich elend fühlen; **to look ~** schlecht aussehen
f *(inf: = guilty)* **to feel ~ about doing sth** sich *(dat)* mies vorkommen, etw zu tun *(inf)*
g *(inf: = damned)* verdammt *(inf)*; **you can keep your ~ bike!** du kannst dein verdammtes *or* blödes Fahrrad behalten! *(inf)*
h *(inf)* **to spoil sb (something) ~** jdn nach Strich und Faden verwöhnen *(inf)*; **to fancy sb (something) ~** jdn wahnsinnig gernhaben *(inf)*

rottenness ['rɒtnnɪs] N *(of vegetation, egg, fruit, tooth)* Faulheit *f*; *(of wood)* Morschheit *f*, Faulheit *f*; *(fig: = corruptness)* Korruptheit *f*, Verdorbenheit *f*

rotter ['rɒtə'] N *(dated Brit inf)* Lump *m*

rotting ['rɒtɪŋ] ADJ *meat, food* verfaulend; *wood also* modrig; *carcass, bones also* verwesend; *teeth* faul; *fruit* faulig

rotund [rəʊ'tʌnd] ADJ *person* rund(lich); *object* rund; *speech, literary style* bombastisch, hochtrabend; *voice* voll

rotunda [rəʊ'tʌndə] N Rotunde *f*, Rundbau *m*

rotundity [rəʊ'tʌndɪtɪ] N *(of person)* Rundlichkeit *f*; *(of object)* Rundheit *f*

rouble, *(US)* **ruble** ['ruːbl] N Rubel *m*

roué ['ruːeɪ] N *(dated)* Lebemann *m*

rouge [ruːʒ] **N** Rouge *nt* **VT** **to ~ one's cheeks** Rouge auflegen

rough [rʌf] **ADJ** *(+er)* **a** *(= uneven) ground* uneben; *path, road* uneben, holprig; *surface, skin, hands, cloth* rau; **~ edges** *(fig)* Ecken und Kanten *pl*
b *(= harsh) sound* hart; *voice, tone* rau; *taste, wine* sauer; *words* grob, hart; **to have ~ luck** schweres Pech haben; **to have a ~ tongue** *(fig)* eine scharfe Zunge haben; **he got the ~ side of her tongue** er bekam (von ihr) den Marsch geblasen
c *(= coarse, unrefined) person* ungehobelt; *manners, speech* grob, roh
d *(= violent) person, child* grob, roh; *treatment, handling* grob, hart; *life* wüst; *children's game* wild; *match, sport, work* hart; *neighbourhood, manners, pub* rau; *sea, weather, wind* rau, stürmisch; *sea crossing* stürmisch; **a ~ customer** *(inf)* ein übler Typ *(inf)*; **to be ~ with sb** grob mit jdm umgehen, unsanft mit jdm umspringen *(inf)*; **~ play** *(Sport)* Holzerei *f (inf)*
e *(inf: = unpleasant)* **he had a ~ time (of it)** es ging ihm ziemlich dreckig *(inf)*; **to be in for a ~ time (of it)** harten Zeiten entgegensehen; **the examiners gave him a ~ time** die Prüfer haben ihn ganz schön rangenommen *(inf)*; **to make things ~ for sb** jdm Schwierigkeiten machen; **to be ~ on sb** grob mit jdm umspringen; **it's ~ on him** das ist hart für ihn; **things are ~ just now** die Dinge stehen im Moment schlecht; **to have a ~ ride** es nicht leicht haben; **to get a ~ ride** Schwierigkeiten bekommen; **to give sb a ~ ride** jdm die Hölle heißmachen *(inf)*; **he faces a ~ ride from the media** die Medien werden es ihm nicht leicht machen; **when the going gets ~ …** wenn es hart wird, …
f *(= approximate, rudimentary) plan, calculation, estimate, translation* grob, ungefähr; *workmanship* schludrig; **~ sketch** Faustskizze *f*; **in its ~ state** im Rohzustand; **do your ~ work on the paper provided** macht euer Konzept auf dem dafür bereitgestellten Papier; **at a ~ guess** grob geschätzt; **to give sb a ~ idea** jdm einen groben Anhaltspunkt geben; **to have a ~ idea** eine vage Idee *or* eine ungefähre Ahnung haben
g *(= basic, crude) shelter* notdürftig; *clothes* derb
h *(inf: = unwell)* **to feel ~** sich mies fühlen *(inf)*; **the engine sounds pretty ~** der Motor hört sich nicht gerade gut an
ADV *live* wüst; *play* wild; **to sleep ~** im Freien übernachten
N **a** unwegsames Gelände; *(Golf)* Rau *nt*; **~ or smooth?** *(Sport)* untere oder obere Seite? *(des Schlägers, die durch einen roten Faden gekennzeichnet ist; zum Bestimmen, wer anfängt)*; **she likes a bit of ~** *(Brit inf: sexually)* sie mags gern heftig *(sl)*
b *(= unpleasant aspect)* **to take the ~ with the smooth** das Leben nehmen, wie es kommt
c *(= draft, sketch)* Rohentwurf *m*; **in (the) ~** im Rohzustand; **a diamond in the ~** ein Rohdiamant *m*
d *(= person)* Rowdy *m*, Schläger *m*
VT **to ~ it** *(inf)* primitiv leben

▶**rough out** VT *sep plan, drawing* grob entwerfen

▶**rough up** VT *sep hair* zersausen, verstrubbeln *(inf)*; *(inf) person* zusammenschlagen

roughage ['rʌfɪdʒ] N Ballaststoffe *pl*

rough: **rough-and-ready** ADJ *method, equipment, place* provisorisch; *work* zusammengehauen *(inf)*, zusammengepfuscht *(inf)*; *person* rau (-beinig); *measure, interpretation, attitude* grob; **rough-and-tumble** N *(= play)* Balgerei *f*; *(= fighting)* Keilerei *f*; **after the ~ of life in the navy** nach seinem wilden Leben in der Marine; **rough book** N *(Sch)* Schmierheft *nt*; **roughcast** *vb: pret, ptp* **roughcast** N Rauputz *m* VT rau verputzen; **rough coat** N *(Archit)* Roh- *or* Rauputz *m*; **rough copy** N Konzept *nt*; **rough diamond** N *(lit)* Rohdiamant *m*; **he's a ~** er ist rau, aber herzlich; **rough draft** N Rohentwurf *m*, grober Entwurf; **rough-dry** VT einfach trocknen

roughen ['rʌfn] VT *ground* uneben machen; *skin, cloth* rau machen, rau werden lassen; *surface* aufrauen VI a *(skin)* rau werden b *(sound)* hart werden; *(voice)* rau werden c *(treatment)* hart werden; *(neighbourhood)* verrohen; *(sea, wind, weather)* rau *or* stürmisch werden

rough: **rough-hew** VT *timber* grob behauen; **roughhouse** *(inf)* N Schlägerei *f* VT herumstoßen

roughing ['rʌfɪŋ] N *(Ice hockey)* übertriebene Härte

rough justice N willkürliche Urteile *pl*

roughly ['rʌflɪ] ADV a *(= not gently)* grob, roh; *play* rau; *speak* grob; *answer, order* grob, hart b *(= crudely) make, sew, sketch, chop, slice* grob c *(= approximately)* ungefähr; **~ (speaking)** grob gesagt; **~ half** ungefähr die Hälfte; **~ equal** ungefähr gleich; **~ the same** ungefähr dasselbe; **~ similar** in etwa ähnlich; **to be ~ similar to sth** eine grobe Ähnlichkeit mit etw besitzen; **~ comparable** grob vergleichbar; **~ translated** grob übersetzt

roughneck ['rʌf,nek] N *(inf)* a *(= thug)* Schläger *m* b *(= oil rig worker)* Ölbohrarbeiter(in) *m(f)*

roughness ['rʌfnɪs] N a *(= unevenness, of ground, path, road)* Unebenheit *f*; *(of surface, skin, hands, cloth)* Rauheit *f* b *(= harshness, of sound)* Härte *f*; *(of voice, tone)* Rauheit *f*; *(of wine)* saurer Geschmack; *(of words)* Grobheit *f* c *(= coarseness, of person)* Ungehobeltheit *f*; *(of manners, speech)* Grobheit *f*, Rohheit *f* d *(= violence, of person)* Grobheit *f*, Rohheit *f*; *(of treatment)* Grobheit *f*, Härte *f*; *(of children's game)* Wildheit *f*; *(of match, sport, work)* Härte *f*; *(of neighbourhood, manners, pub)* Rauheit *f*

rough: **rough notebook** N *(Sch)* Schmierheft *nt*; **rough paper** N Konzeptpapier *nt*; **roughrider** N Zureiter(in) *m(f)*; **roughshod** ADV **to ride ~ over sb/sth** rücksichtslos über jdn/etw hinweggehen; **rough-spoken** ADJ **to be ~** sich ungehobelt ausdrücken; **rough stuff** N Schlägereien *pl*, eine Schlägerei; **rough trade** N *(sl) (ohne feste Bindungsabsicht ausgewählter) homosexueller Geschlechtspartner mit grobem oder gewalttätigem Verhalten*

roulette [ru:'let] N Roulett(e) *nt*; **~ table/wheel** Roulettetisch *m*/-scheibe *f* → **Russian roulette**

Roumania *etc* [ru:'meɪnɪə] = **Romania** *etc*

round [raʊnd] ADJ (+*er*) a rund; *(Ling) vowel* gerundet; **~ arch** *(Archit)* Rundbogen *m*; **a ~ dozen** ein rundes Dutzend; **~ figure, ~ number** runde Zahl; **in ~ figures, that will cost 20 million** es kostet rund (gerechnet) *or* runde 20 Millionen

b *(dated) (= unequivocal) oath* kräftig; *(= considerable) sum* rund; *pace* flott; **in ~ terms** klar und deutlich

ADV *(esp Brit)* **there was a wall right ~** *or* **all ~** rings- *or* rundherum war eine Mauer; **you can't get through here, you'll have to go ~** Sie können hier nicht durch, Sie müssen außen herum gehen; **the long way ~** der Umweg, der längere Weg; **that's a long way ~** *(detour)* das ist ein großer Umweg; *(round field, town)* das ist eine ganz schöne Strecke; **for 5 km ~** im Umkreis von 5 km; **~ and ~** *(= in circles, round field etc)* rundherum; *(= all over the place)* überall herum; **I asked him ~ for a drink** ich lud ihn auf ein Glas Wein/Bier *etc* bei mir ein; **I'll be ~ at 8 o'clock** ich werde um 8 Uhr da sein; **spring will soon be ~ again** der Frühling steht bald wieder vor der Tür; **for the second time ~** zum zweiten Mal; **all (the) year ~** das ganze Jahr über *or* hindurch; **all ~** *(lit)* ringsherum; *(esp Brit fig: for everyone)* für alle; **drinks all ~!** *(esp Brit)* eine Runde!; **taking things all ~, taken all ~** insgesamt gesehen, wenn man alles zusammennimmt; **this ought to make life much easier all ~** *(esp Brit)* damit müsste es insgesamt einfacher werden; **a pillar 2 m ~** eine Säule mit 2 m Umfang

PREP a *(esp Brit: of place etc)* um (… herum); **~ the table/fire** um den Tisch/das Feuer (herum); **the ribbon ~ her hat** das Band um ihren Hut; **all ~ the house** *(inside)* im ganzen Haus; *(outside)* um das ganze Haus herum; **~ and ~ the field** rings um das Feld herum; **to go ~ a corner/bend** um eine Ecke/Kurve gehen/fahren *etc*; **if you're ~ this way** wenn Sie in der Gegend sind; **to look** *or* **see ~ a house** sich *(dat)* ein Haus ansehen; **to show sb ~ a town** jdm eine Stadt zeigen, jdn in einer Stadt herumführen; **they went ~ the cafés looking for him** sie gingen in alle Cafés, um nach ihm zu suchen; **to talk ~ a subject** um ein Thema herumreden; **she's 75 cm ~ the waist** um die Taille misst *or* ist sie 75 cm

b *(= approximately)* ungefähr; **~ (about** *(esp Brit)*) **7 o'clock** ungefähr um 7 Uhr; **~ (about** *(esp Brit)*) **£800** um die £ 800

N a *(= circle etc)* Kreis *m*, Ring *m*; *(esp Brit: = slice of bread, meat etc)* Scheibe *f*; **a ~ of toast** *(esp Brit)* eine Scheibe Toast; **a ~ of beef sandwiches** *(esp Brit)* ein belegtes Brot mit Braten, eine Bratenschnitte

b *(= delivery round)* Runde *f*; **~(s)** *(of policeman, watchman, doctor)* Runde *f*; **to do** *or* **make one's ~(s)** seine Runde machen; **to be (out) on one's ~(s)** auf seiner Runde sein; **to go** *or* **make** *or* **do the ~s** *(visiting relatives etc)* die Runde machen; **to do the ~s of the clubs** *etc (inf)* durch die Klubs *etc* ziehen; **he does a paper ~** *(Brit)* er trägt Zeitungen aus; **the daily ~** *(fig)* die tägliche Arbeit, der tägliche Trott *(pej)*; **her life was one long ~ of parties** ihr Leben war eine einzige Folge von Partys

c **to go** *or* **do the ~s** *(story etc)* reihum gehen; **the story went the ~s of the club** die Geschichte ging im ganzen Verein reihum; **this coat has gone the ~s of the family** dieser Mantel ist durch die ganze Familie gegangen

d *(Sport, of election, talks)* Runde *f*; *(Show-jumping)* Durchgang *m*; **a ~ (of drinks)** eine Runde; **a new ~ of negotiations** eine neue Verhandlungsrunde; **~ of ammunition** Ladung *f*; **10 ~s of bullets** 10 Schuss; **a ~ of 5 shots** eine Folge von 5 Schüssen; **a ~ of applause** Applaus *m*

e *(Mus)* Kanon *m*

f **in the ~** *(= as a whole)* insgesamt; **theatre in the ~** Arenatheater *nt*

VT a *(= make round)* runden

b *(= go round) corner, bend* gehen/fahren um; *cape* umfahren, herumfahren um; *obstacle* herumgehen/-fahren um

▶ **round down** VT *sep price, number* abrunden

▶ **round off** VT *sep* a *edges etc* abrunden b *(= complete, perfect) list, series* vollmachen; *speech, sentence, meal* abrunden; *debate, meeting, one's career* beschließen, abschließen; **and now, to round off, I would like to say …** und zum Abschluss möchte ich nun sagen …

▶ **round on** VI +*prep obj (verbally)* anfahren; *(in actions)* herumfahren zu

▶ **round out** VT *sep story etc* runden; *year* abschließen VI sich runden

▶ **round up** VT *sep* a *(= bring together) people* zusammentrommeln *(inf)*; *cattle* zusammentreiben; *criminals* hochnehmen *(inf)*; *facts* zusammentragen b *price, number* aufrunden

▶ **round upon** VI +*prep obj* = **round on**

roundabout ['raʊndəbaʊt] ADJ *answer, question* umständlich; **~ route** Umweg *m*; **we came a ~ way** *or* **by a ~ route** wir sind auf Umwegen gekommen, wir haben einen Umweg gemacht; **he has a ~ way of going about things** er geht sehr umständlich an die Dinge heran; **what a ~ way of doing things!** wie kann man nur so umständlich sein!; **by ~ means** auf Umwegen; **~ phrase** (umständliche) Umschreibung; **she gave a ~ reply** sie antwortete auf Umwegen; **to say sth in a ~ way** etw auf Umwegen sagen N *(Brit, at fair)* Karussell *nt*; *(in children's playground)* Karussell *nt*; *(Mot)* Kreisverkehr *m*

round: **round cell** N *(= battery)* Knopfzelle *f*; **round-cheeked** ['raʊnd'tʃi:kt] ADJ mit runden Backen; **round dance** N Reigen *m*; *(= ballroom dance)* Rundtanz *m*

rounded ['raʊndɪd] ADJ a *(= curved)* rundlich; *edges* abgerundet; *hills* gerundet; *handwriting* rundlich; **(well-)rounded** *(bosom, figure)* wohlgerundet b *(fig: = complete) picture, character, individual, education, flavour* abgerundet; *film, book* in sich geschlossen; **(well-)rounded** *(sentences, style)* abgerundet c **a ~ tablespoon** *(Cook)* ein gehäufter Esslöffel d *(= resonant) tone* rund e *(Ling) vowel* rund

roundel ['raʊndl] N runde (Flugzeug)kokarde

roundelay ['raʊndɪleɪ] N *(Mus)* Lied *nt* mit Refrain

rounder ['raʊndəʳ] N *(Brit Sport)* **to score a ~** einen Lauf machen

rounders ['raʊndəz] N *sing (Brit Sport)* ≈ Schlagball *m*

round: **round-eyed** ADJ großäugig; **round-faced** ADJ rundgesichtig, mit rundem Gesicht; **Roundhead** N *(Brit Hist)* Rundkopf *m*; **roundhouse** N *(esp US Rail)* Lokomotivschuppen *m*

roundly ['raʊndlɪ] ADV *condemn, criticize* rundum; *reject* rundweg, rundheraus; *defeat* klar, eindeutig

round-necked ['raʊnd'nekt] ADJ mit rundem Ausschnitt

roundness ['raʊndnɪs] N Rundheit *f*; *(of sound also)* Vollheit *f*; *(of vowel)* Gerundetheit *f*

round: **round robin** N a *(= petition)* gemeinsamer Antrag *(bei dem die Unterschriften (oft) im Kreis angeordnet sind)* b *(esp US Sport)* Wettkampf *m*, in dem jeder gegen jeden spielt; **round-shouldered** ['raʊnd'ʃəʊldəd] ADJ mit runden Schultern; **to be ~** runde Schultern haben

roundsman ['raʊndzmən] N *pl* **-men** [-mən] *(Brit)* Austräger *m*; **milk ~** Milchmann *m*

round: **Round Table** N *(Hist)* (König Artus') Tafelrunde *f*; **round-table discussion/conference** N Diskussion *f*/Konferenz *f* am runden Tisch; **round-the-clock** ADJ *(Brit)* rund um die Uhr *not attr*; **round towel** N Rollhandtuch *nt*; **round trip** N Rundreise *f*; **round-trip ticket** N *(US)* Rückfahrkarte *f*; *(Aviat)* Hin- und Rückflugticket *nt*; **roundup** N a *(= act, of cattle)* Zusammentreiben *nt*; *(of people)* Zusammentrommeln *nt (inf)*; *(of criminals)* Hochnehmen *nt (inf)*; *(of facts)* Sammlung *f*, Zusammentragen *nt* b *(= group of cattle)* zusammengetriebene Herde; **a round-up of today's news** eine Zusammenfassung der Nachrichten vom Tage c *(US, = rodeo)* Rodeo *nt*; **roundworm** N Fadenwurm *m*

rouse [raʊz] VT a *(from sleep, daydream etc)* wecken b *(= stimulate) person* bewegen; *feeling, admiration, interest* wecken, wachrufen; *hatred, indignation* erregen; *suspicions* erwecken, erregen; **to ~ sb (to anger)** jdn reizen; **to ~ sb to passion** jds Leidenschaft entfachen; **to ~ sb to action** jdn zum Handeln bewegen; **to ~ sb out of his/her apathy** jdn aus seiner Apathie aufrütteln; **to ~ the masses** die Massen aufrütteln; **~ yourself!** raff dich auf! VI *(= waken)* wach werden; *(= become active)* lebendig werden

rousing ['raʊzɪŋ] ADJ *speech, sermon* zündend, mitreißend; *cheers, applause* stürmisch; *music* schwungvoll; *chorus* schallend; *reception* überschwänglich

roust [raʊst] VT (*US, from home, usual place on street: also* **roust out**) vertreiben; (*= call out*) kommen lassen; **to ~ sb out of bed, to ~ sb out** jdn aus dem Bett holen

roustabout [ˈraʊstəbaʊt] N **a** (*US Naut*) (*= deckhand*) Deckhelfer *m*; (*in dock*) Werft- *or* Hafenarbeiter *m* **b** (*US: = unskilled labourer*) Hilfsarbeiter *m* **c** (*Austral*) Helfer *m* beim Scheren

rout¹ [raʊt] **N** **a** (*= defeat*) Schlappe *f*; **to put to ~** in die Flucht schlagen **b** (*Jur, = mob*) Bande *f*, Rotte *f* **VT** (*= defeat*) in die Flucht schlagen

rout² VI (*pig: also* **rout about**) herumwühlen

▶ **rout out** VT *sep* (*= find*) aufstöbern; (*= force out*) (heraus)jagen (*of* aus)

route [ruːt, (*US*) raʊt] **N** **a** Strecke *f*, Route *f*; (*bus service*) Linie *f*; (*fig, in planning etc*) Weg *m*; **shipping ~s** Schifffahrtsstraßen *or* -wege; **air ~s** Flugwege; **what ~ does the 39 bus take?** welche Strecke *or* Route fährt der 39er-Bus?; **we live on a bus ~** wir wohnen an einer Buslinie; **the ~ to the coast goes through Easthampton** der Weg zur Küste führt durch Easthampton; **"all ~s"** (*Mot*) „alle Richtungen"; **~ map** Straßenkarte *f*
b (*Mil*) Marschbefehl *m*; **~ march** Geländemarsch *m*
c (*US: = delivery round*) Runde *f*; **he has a paper ~** er trägt Zeitungen aus
d (*Med, of drug*) Weg *m*
VT *train, coach, bus* legen; *telephone call* leiten; **my baggage was ~d through Amsterdam** mein Gepäck wurde über Amsterdam geschickt; **the train is ~d through Birmingham** der Zug wird durch Birmingham geführt *or* über Birmingham gelegt

router [ˈruːtəʳ] N (*Comput*) Router *m*

routine [ruːˈtiːn] **N** **a** Routine *f* (*also Comput*); **business** *or* **office ~** Büroroutine *f*; **as a matter of ~** routinemäßig
b (*Dancing, Skating*) Figur *f*; (*Gymnastics*) Übung *f*; **he gave me the old ~ about his wife not understanding him** er kam mit der alten Geschichte, dass seine Frau ihn nicht versteht
ADJ Routine-, routinemäßig; **~ duties** tägliche Pflichten *pl*; **~ examination** Routineuntersuchung *f*; **~ flight** Routineflug *m*; **on a ~ basis** routinemäßig; **to be ~ procedure** Routine(sache) sein; **it was quite ~** es war eine reine Formsache; **reports of bloodshed had become almost ~** Berichte über Blutvergießen waren fast zur Gewohnheit geworden *or* waren fast an der Tagesordnung

routinely [ruːˈtiːnlɪ] ADV *use, torture* regelmäßig; *test* routinemäßig; *describe* üblicherweise

routinist [ruːˈtiːnɪst] N Gewohnheitsmensch *m*

roux [ruː] N Mehlschwitze *f*, Einbrenne *f*

rove [rəʊv] **VI** (*person*) umherwandern *or* -ziehen; (*eyes*) umherwandern *or* -schweifen; **to ~ over sth** (*eyes*) über etw (*acc*) schweifen *or* wandern **VT** *countryside, streets* wandern *or* ziehen durch, durchwandern *or* -ziehen

rover [ˈrəʊvəʳ] N **a** (*= wanderer*) Vagabund(in) *m(f)* **b** (*also* **Rover Scout**) Rover *m*

roving [ˈrəʊvɪŋ] **ADJ** (*= itinerant*) *musicians* (herum)ziehend; *gang* vagabundierend; **he has a ~ eye** er riskiert gern ein Auge; **~ life** Vagabundenleben *nt* **N** Vagabundenleben *nt no pl*

roving: roving ambassador N Botschafter(in) *m(f)* für mehrere Vertretungen; **roving commission** N weitläufiges Mandat; (*= travelling*) Reisemandat *nt*; **to have a ~ to do sth** eine umfassende Befugnis haben, etw zu tun; **roving reporter** N Reporter, der ständig unterwegs ist, rasender Reporter (*hum*)

row¹ [rəʊ] N Reihe *f*; (*Comput*) (*of table*) Zeile *f*; **4 failures in a ~** 4 Misserfolge hinter- *or* nacheinander; **arrange them in ~s** stell sie in Reihen auf

row² [rəʊ] **VI** (*in boat*) rudern; **to ~ away/back** weg-/zurückrudern **VT** *boat* rudern; **to ~ sb across** jdn hinüberrudern; **to ~ stroke** Schlagmann sein **N** **I enjoy a ~** ich rudere gern; **to go for a ~** rudern gehen

row³ [raʊ] **N** (*esp Brit inf*) **a** (*= noise*) Lärm *m*, Krach *m* (*inf*); **to make a** *or* **kick up** (*inf*) **a ~** Krach schlagen (*inf*) **b** (*= quarrel*) Streit *m*, Krach *m* (*inf*); **to have a ~ with sb** mit jdm Streit *or* Krach (*inf*) haben; **to start a ~** Streit anfangen **c** (*= scolding*) **to get a ~** Krach bekommen (*inf*); **to give sb a ~** jdn runtermachen (*inf*) **VI** (*= quarrel*) (sich) streiten

rowan [ˈraʊən] N (*= tree*) Eberesche *f*, Vogelbeere *f*; **~ berry** Vogelbeere *f*

rowboat [ˈrəʊˌbəʊt] N (*US*) Ruderboot *nt*

rowdiness [ˈraʊdɪnɪs] N (*= noisiness*) Lärmen *nt*; (*= disorderliness*) rüpelhaftes *or* flegelhaftes Benehmen

rowdy [ˈraʊdɪ] **ADJ** (+*er*) (*= noisy*) laut; *football fans* randalierend; *behaviour* grob, ungehobelt; *event, scene* gewalttätig; *party* ausufernd, chaotisch; **the party got a bit ~** die Party artete in Krawall aus **N** (*Brit*) Krawallmacher *m*; **football rowdies** Fußballrowdys *pl*

rowdyism [ˈraʊdɪɪzəm] N (*Brit*) Rowdytum *nt*

rower [ˈrəʊəʳ] N Ruderer *m*, Ruderin *f*

row house [ˈrəʊˌhaʊs] N (*US*) Reihenhaus *nt*

rowing¹ [ˈrəʊɪŋ] N Rudern *nt*

rowing² [ˈraʊɪŋ] N (*esp Brit: = quarrelling*) Streiterei *f*, Streitereien *pl*

rowing [ˈrəʊɪŋ]: **rowing boat** N (*Brit*) Ruderboot *nt*; **rowing club** N Ruderklub *or* -verein *m*; **rowing machine** N Rudergerät *nt*

rowlock [ˈrɒlək] N (*esp Brit*) Dolle *f*

royal [ˈrɔɪəl] **ADJ** königlich; (*fig also*) fürstlich; **the ~ family** die königliche Familie, die Königsfamilie; **the ~ household** der königliche Haushalt; **~ enclosure** (*on racecourse*) *abgeteilter Zuschauerbereich für die königliche Familie*; **the ~ we** (*usu hum*) der Pluralis Majestatis; **the ~ road to freedom/success** *etc* (*fig*) der sichere Weg zur Freiheit/zum Erfolg *etc*; **he's a ~ pain (in the neck)** (*inf*) er geht einem tierisch auf die Nerven (*inf*) **N** **a** (*inf*) Angehörige(r) *mf* der königlichen Familie **b** (*= stag*) kapitaler Bock

royal: Royal Academy (of Arts) N (*Brit*) *Königliche Akademie (der Künste)*; **Royal Air Force** N (*Brit*) Königliche Luftwaffe; **Royal Assent** N (*Brit*) **to receive** *or* **be given ~** die königliche Genehmigung bekommen; **royal blue** N Königsblau *nt*; **royal-blue** ADJ königsblau; **Royal Canadian Mounted Police** N *kanadische berittene Polizei*; **Royal Commission** N (*Brit*) königliche Untersuchungskommission; **royal correspondent** N Hofkorrespondent(in) *m(f)*; **Royal Engineers** N (*Brit Mil*) Königliches Pionierkorps; **royal flush** N (*Cards*) Royal Flush *m*; **Royal Highness** N **Your/His ~** Eure/Seine Königliche Hoheit

royalism [ˈrɔɪəlɪzəm] N Royalismus *m*, Königstreue *f*

royalist [ˈrɔɪəlɪst] **ADJ** royalistisch, königstreu **N** Royalist(in) *m(f)*, Königstreue(r) *mf*

royal jelly N (*Med*) Gelée royale *nt*

royally [ˈrɔɪəlɪ] ADV **a** königlich; (**right**) **~** (*fig: = lavishly*) fürstlich, königlich **b** (*inf: = totally*) **to get ~ drunk** sich total besaufen (*inf*); **you have messed up ~** da hast du totalen Scheiß gebaut (*inf*)

royal: Royal Mail N (*Brit*) *britischer Postdienst*; **Royal Marines** PL (*Brit*) *britische Marineinfanterie*; **Royal Mint** N (*Brit*) Königliche Münzanstalt; **Royal Navy** (*Brit*) **N** Königliche Marine **ATTR** der Königlichen Marine; **royal palace** N Königspalast *m*; **royal purple** N (*colour*) Purpur *m*; **Royal Society** N (*Brit*) Königliche Gesellschaft

> **ROYAL SHAKESPEARE COMPANY**
>
> Die **Royal Shakespeare Company** (oder auch nur **RSC**) ist ein britisches Theaterensemble, das 1960 in Shakespeares Geburtsort, Stratford-on-Avon, gegründet wurde. Sie hat gegenwärtig zwei Stammhäuser, eines in Stratford und das Barbican in London, und bringt selbstverständlich Stücke von Shakespeare, aber auch andere Klassiker und einige zeitgenössische Werke zur Aufführung. In den letzten Jahren ging die **RSC** jährlich für sechs Monate auf Tournee durch Großbritannien und konnte sich durch die ausgezeichnete Qualität ihrer Inszenierungen einen ausgezeichneten internationalen Ruf erwerben.

royalty [ˈrɔɪəltɪ] N **a** (*= dignity, rank*) das Königtum; (*collectively: = royal persons*) das Königshaus, die königliche Familie; **symbols of ~** Wahrzeichen *pl* der Königswürde; **he's ~** er gehört zur königlichen Familie **b** **royalties** PL (*on* auf +*acc*) (*from book, records*) Tantiemen *pl*; (*from patent*) Patent- *or* Lizenzgebühren *pl*

royal warrant N *königliche Urkunde für Hoflieferanten*

royal-watchers [ˈrɔɪəlˌwɒtʃəz] PL Hofbeobachter *pl*

rozzer [ˈrɒzəʳ] N (*Brit sl*) Bulle *m* (*sl*), Polyp *m* (*dated sl*)

RP *abbr of* **received pronunciation**

RPG (*Mil*) *abbr of* **rocket-propelled grenade**

RPM (*Brit*) *abbr of* **resale price maintenance**

rpm *abbr of* **revolutions per minute** U/min

RR (*US*) *abbr of* **Railroad**

R-rated ADJ (*US*) *film* nicht jugendfrei

RSC (*Brit*) *abbr of* **Royal Shakespeare Company**

RSI *abbr of* **repetitive strain injury**

RSPB (*Brit*) *abbr of* **Royal Society for the Protection of Birds** ≈ Bund *m* für Vogelschutz

RSPCA (*Brit*) *abbr of* **Royal Society for the Prevention of Cruelty to Animals** ≈ Tierschutzverein *m*

RSVP *abbr of* **répondez s'il vous plaît** u. A. w. g.

RTA *abbr of* **road traffic accident** Verkehrsunfall *m*

RTF *abbr of* **rich text format** RTF *nt*

Rt Hon (*Brit*) *abbr of* **Right Honourable**

rub [rʌb] **N** **a** Reiben *nt*; (*with duster etc*) Polieren *nt*; **to give sth a ~** etw reiben; *furniture, shoes, silver* etw polieren; **~-a-dub(-dub)!** (*inf*) rubbel-rubbel! (*inf*)
b (*fig*) **there's the ~!** da liegt der Hase im Pfeffer
VT reiben; (*with towel also*) frottieren; (*= polish*) polieren; (*Art*) *brass, inscription* durchzeichnen; **to ~ lotion into sth/oneself** etw/sich mit einer Lotion einreiben; **to ~ sth with sandpaper** etw (mit Sandpapier) abschmirgeln; **to ~ one's eyes** sich (*dat*) die Augen reiben; **to ~ one's hands (together) (in** *or* **with glee)** sich (*dat*) (vor Freude) die Hände reiben; **to ~ sth dry** etw trocken reiben *or* rubbeln (*inf*); **to ~ noses** (*as greeting*) die Nasen aneinanderreiben; **to ~ sb's nose in sth** (*fig*) jdm etw dauernd unter die Nase reiben *or* halten; **to ~ shoulders** (*esp Brit*) *or* **elbows** (*esp US*) **with all sorts of people** (*fig*) mit allen möglichen Leuten in Berührung kommen; **to ~ sb the wrong way** (*US*) bei jdm anecken → **salt N a**
VI (*thing*) (*against* an +*dat*) reiben; (*collar*) scheuern; **you must have ~bed against some wet paint** da musst du an feuchte Farbe gekommen sein; **the cat ~bed against my legs/the tree** die Katze strich mir um die Beine/scheuerte sich am Baum

▶ **rub along** VI (*Brit inf: = manage*) sich durchschlagen (*inf*); **to rub along (together)** recht und schlecht miteinander auskommen

▶ **rub away** VT *sep* wegreiben

▶ **rub down** VT *sep horse* (*= dry*) abreiben; (*= clean*) striegeln; *person* abrubbeln (*inf*), abfrottieren; *wall, paintwork* (*= clean*) abwaschen; (*= sandpaper*) abschmirgeln

▶ **rub in** VT *sep* **a** *oil, lotion* einreiben (*prep obj, -to* in +*acc*); *butter* hinzureiben **b** (*fig*) *sb's stupidity* herumreiten auf (+*dat*); **he's always rubbing (it) in how rich he is** (*inf*) er reibt es uns/ihnen *etc* immer unter die Nase, wie reich er ist (*inf*); **don't rub it in!** (*= don't keep mentioning*) reite nicht so darauf herum!; (*= don't keep allud-*

ing to) musst du auch noch Salz in die Wunde streuen?

► **rub off** VT *sep dirt* abreiben; *writing* ausradieren; *tape* löschen; *(from blackboard)* aus- *or* wegwischen; *paint, gold-plating* abreiben; *(through wear)* abwetzen VI *(lit, fig)* abgehen; *(through wear also)* sich abwetzen; **to rub off on sb** *(fig)* auf jdn abfärben

► **rub out** VT *sep stain etc* herausreiben; *(with eraser)* ausradieren; *(inf: = kill)* auslöschen VI herausgehen; *(with eraser)* sich ausradieren lassen

► **rub up** VT *sep* **a** *vase, table* blank reiben, (auf)polieren **b to rub sb up the wrong way** *(Brit)* bei jdm anecken VI **the cat rubbed up against my leg** die Katze strich mir um die Beine; **to rub up against all sorts of people** *(esp Brit fig)* mit allen möglichen Leuten in Berührung kommen

rubber¹ [ˈrʌbəˈ] N *(= material)* Gummi *m; (unprocessed, synthetic also)* Kautschuk *m (spec); (Brit: = eraser)* (Radier)gummi *m; (esp US sl: = contraceptive)* Gummi *m (inf);* **~s** *(= shoes)* Turnschuhe *pl; (= overshoes)* (Gummi)überschuhe *pl; (= clothing)* Ölzeug *nt* ADJ Gummi-; **~ goods** Gummiwaren; **is that a ~ cheque** *(Brit) or* **check** *(US)? (inf)* platzt der Scheck? *(inf)*

rubber² N *(Cards)* Rubber *m*, Robber *m*

rubber: rubber band N Gummiband *nt;* **rubber boat** N Schlauchboot *nt;* **rubber boot** N *(US)* Gummistiefel *m;* **rubber bullet** N Gummi(wucht)geschoss *nt;* **rubber coating** N Gummierung *f;* **rubber dinghy** N Schlauchboot *nt*

rubber gloves PL Gummihandschuhe *pl*

rubber goods PL *(euph: = condoms)* Kondome *pl*

rubberize [ˈrʌbəraɪz] VT *(= cover)* mit Gummi überziehen; *(= impregnate)* gummieren

rubber: rubberneck *(esp US inf)* N Gaffer(in) *m(f) (inf)* VI gaffen *(inf);* **rubber plant** N Gummibaum *m;* **rubber plantation** N Kautschukplantage *f;* **rubber stamp** N Stempel *m;* **rubber-stamp** VT *(lit)* stempeln; *(fig inf)* genehmigen; **rubber tree** N Kautschukbaum *m;* **rubber-tyred** [ˈrʌbəˈtaɪəd] ADJ mit Gummireifen

rubbery [ˈrʌbərɪ] ADJ **a** *material, skin* gummiartig; *meat* zäh, wie Gummi *pred; (hum) lips* wulstig **b** *(= weak) legs* gummiweich *(inf)*

rubbing [ˈrʌbɪŋ] N **a** *(= action)* Reiben *nt; (of collar)* Scheuern *nt*, Reiben *nt; (with towel)* Frottieren *nt; (= polishing)* Polieren *nt; (with sandpaper)* Schmirgeln *nt* **b** *(Art)* → **brass rubbing**

rubbing: rubbing alcohol N *(US)* Wundbenzin *nt;* **rubbing varnish** N Schleiflack *m*

rubbish [ˈrʌbɪʃ] *(esp Brit)* N **a** *(= waste material)* Abfall *m*, Abfälle *pl; (= household rubbish, in factory also)* Müll *m; (on building site)* Schutt *m; (fig: = trashy goods, record etc)* Mist *m;* **household ~** Hausmüll *m;* **garden ~** Gartenabfälle *pl;* **most modern furniture is ~** die meisten modernen Möbel sind nichts wert

b *(inf: = nonsense)* Quatsch *m (inf)*, Blödsinn *m;* **don't talk ~!** red keinen Quatsch *or* Blödsinn! *(inf);* **he talked a lot** *or* **a load of ~** er hat eine Menge Blödsinn verzapft *(inf);* **(what a lot of) ~!** (so ein) Quatsch! *(inf);* **this book is ~** das Buch ist Quatsch *(inf)*

ATTR *(inf)* **a** = **rubbishy**

b I'm ~ at it ich bin zu blöd dazu *(inf);* **I'm ~ at doing it** ich krieg das (einfach) nicht hin *(inf)*

VT *(inf) person, idea* runtermachen *(inf)*

rubbish *in cpds (esp Brit)* Müll-; **rubbish bin** N Mülleimer *m;* **rubbish cart** N Müllwagen *m;* **rubbish chute** N Müllschlucker *m;* **rubbish collection** N Müllabfuhr *f;* **rubbish dump** N Müllabladeplatz *m; (in garden: also* **rubbish heap**) Abfallhaufen *m;* **rubbish tip** N Müllabladeplatz *m*

rubbishy [ˈrʌbɪʃɪ] ADJ *(Brit inf) (= worthless) goods* minderwertig, wertlos; *magazine, film* mies *(inf); (= nonsensical) ideas* blödsinnig; **~ shoes** Schuhe, die nichts taugen; **this is ~ stuff** *(article)* das taugt nichts, das ist Mist *(inf); (book, theory)* das ist Quatsch *(inf)*

rubble [ˈrʌbl] N Trümmer *pl; (smaller pieces)* Schutt *m; (Geol)* Geröll *nt*

rubdown [ˈrʌbˈdaʊn] N **to give sb/sth a ~** → **rub down**

rube [ruːb] N *(dated US sl)* (Bauern)tölpel *m*

rubella [ruːˈbelə] N Röteln *pl*

Rubicon [ˈruːbɪkən] N **to cross the ~** den Rubikon überschreiten

rubicund [ˈruːbɪkənd] ADJ rot

rubidium [ruːˈbɪdɪəm] N *(Chem)* Rubidium *nt*

Rubik's cube® [ˈruːbɪksˈkjuːb] N Zauberwürfel *m*

ruble N *(US)* = **rouble**

rubric [ˈruːbrɪk] N *(= heading)* Überschrift; *(Eccl)* (liturgische) Anweisungen *pl; (on exam paper)* Prüfungsanweisungen *pl;* **under the ~ …** in der Rubrik …

ruby [ˈruːbɪ] N *(= stone)* Rubin *m; (colour: also* **ruby red**) Rubinrot *nt* ADJ *(= ruby-coloured) wine, lips* rubinrot; *(= made of rubies)* Rubin-; **~ ring** Rubinring *m*

ruby-red [ˈruːbɪˈred] ADJ rubinrot

ruby wedding (anniversary) N vierzigster Hochzeitstag, Rubinhochzeit *f*

RUC *abbr of* **Royal Ulster Constabulary** *nordirische Polizeibehörde*

ruche [ruːʃ] N Rüsche *f*

ruched [ruːʃt] ADJ Rüschen-, gerüscht; **~ dress** Rüschenkleid *nt;* **~ and edged with lace** mit Rüschen und Spitzenbesatz

ruching [ˈruːʃɪŋ] N Rüschen *pl*

ruck¹ [rʌk] N **a** *(Racing)* Pulk *m;* **the (common) ~** *(fig)* die (breite) Masse; **to get out of the ~** *(fig)* sich von der breiten Masse absetzen **b** *(Rugby)* offenes Gedränge **c** *(Prison sl: = ruckus)* Krawall *m (inf)*

ruck² N *(= wrinkle)* Falte *f*

► **ruck up** VT *sep seam* zusammenziehen; *rug* verschieben; **his shirt is all rucked up** sein Hemd hat sich hochgeschoben VI *(seam)* sich zusammenziehen; *(shirt etc)* sich hochschieben; *(rug)* Falten schlagen

rucksack [ˈrʌksæk] N *(esp Brit)* Rucksack *m*

ruckus [ˈrʌkəs] N *(inf)* Krawall *m*

ruction [ˈrʌkʃən] N *(inf) usu pl (= dispute, scolding)* Krach *m no pl; (= uproar also)* Krawall *m no pl;* **there'll be ~s if you do that** es gibt Krach, wenn du das tust

rudder [ˈrʌdəˈ] N *(Naut, Aviat)* Ruder *nt*

rudderless [ˈrʌdəlɪs] ADJ ohne Ruder; *(fig)* führungslos

ruddiness [ˈrʌdɪnɪs] N Röte *f;* **the ~ of his complexion** seine gesunde Gesichtsfarbe

ruddy [ˈrʌdɪ] ADJ *(+er)* **a** *(= red) face* rot; *complexion* gesund, rot; *sky, glow* rötlich **b** *(Brit inf: = bloody)* verdammt *(inf)* ADV *(Brit inf: = bloody)* verdammt *(inf);* **how could you be so ~ stupid?** wie konntest du nur so verdammt blöd sein? *(inf)*

rude [ruːd] ADJ *(+er)* **a** *(= impolite, bad-mannered)* unhöflich; *(stronger)* unverschämt; *(= rough, uncouth)* grob; **to be ~ to sb** unhöflich zu jdm sein; **it's ~ to stare** es gehört sich nicht, Leute anzustarren, man starrt andere Leute nicht an; **don't be so ~!** so was sagt man/tut man nicht!; **talk about ~!** der/die hat vielleicht einen Ton am Leib! *(inf)*

b *(= obscene, dirty)* unanständig, unflätig *(geh);* **to make a ~ gesture at sb** jdm gegenüber eine anstößige Geste machen; **to make a ~ noise** *(euph)* pup(s)en *(inf)*

c *(= harsh) shock* bös, hart; *blast, weather* wüst, rau; *reminder* unsanft → **awakening**

d *(liter, = crude, primitive)* primitiv; *fare* einfach, schlicht

e *(liter: = vigorous) strength* gewaltig; **he is in ~ health/strength** er strotzt (nur so) vor Gesundheit/Kraft

rudely [ˈruːdlɪ] ADV **a** *(= impolitely)* unhöflich; *(stronger)* unverschämt; *(= roughly, uncouthly)* grob; *push* rüde; **before I was so ~ interrupted** bevor ich so unhöflich unterbrochen wurde **b** *(= obscenely)* unanständig **c** *(= harshly) awaken, remind, shatter* unsanft **d** *(liter, = crudely, primitively)* grob

rudeness [ˈruːdnɪs] N **a** *(= impoliteness)* Unhöflichkeit *f; (stronger)* Unverschämtheit *f; (= roughness, uncouthness)* Grobheit *f* **b** *(= obscenity)* Unanständigkeit *f*, Unflätigkeit *f (geh)* **c** *(= harshness: of shock)* Härte *f*

rudiment [ˈruːdɪmənt] N = **rudiments**

rudiments [ˈruːdɪmənts] PL **a** Anfangsgründe *pl*, Grundlagen *pl* **b** *(Biol)* Rudiment *nt*

rudimentary [ˌruːdɪˈmentərɪ] ADJ *(= basic) principles* elementar; *equipment* primitiv; *language, system* rudimentär; *(Biol)* rudimentär; **~ knowledge** Grundkenntnisse *pl;* **in a ~ way** in einer primitiven Form *or* Art und Weise

rue¹ [ruː] VT *(liter)* bereuen; **to ~ the day that …** den Tag verwünschen, an dem …

rue² N *(Bot)* Raute *f*

rueful [ˈruːfʊl] ADJ *look* reuig, reuevoll; *situation* beklagenswert

ruefully [ˈruːfəlɪ] ADV reuevoll

ruff¹ [rʌf] N **a** *(on dress etc, of bird, animal)* Halskrause *f* **b** *(= bird)* Kampfläufer *m*

ruff² *(Cards)* N Trumpfen *nt* VTI trumpfen, stechen

ruffian [ˈrʌfɪən] N Rüpel *m*, Grobian *m; (violent)* Schläger *m;* **you little ~!** du kleiner Halbstarker!

ruffianism [ˈrʌfɪənɪzəm] N Rohheit *f*, Gewalttätigkeit *f*, Brutalität *f*

ruffle [ˈrʌfl] N *(on dress)* Rüsche *f; (on water)* Kräuseln *nt no pl* VT **a** *(= disturb) hair, feathers* zerzausen; *surface, water* kräuseln; *bedspread, clothes* verkrumpeln *(inf);* **the bird ~d (up) its feathers** der Vogel plusterte sich auf **b** *(fig: = upset, disturb)* aus der Ruhe bringen; *(= annoy)* verärgern, aufbringen; **to ~ sb's calm** jdn aus der Ruhe bringen; **to ~ sb's feathers** jdn aufregen

ruffled [ˈrʌfld] ADJ **a** *(= flustered, perturbed) person* aufgebracht; *feelings* erregt; **to smooth ~ feelings** erregte Gemüter besänftigen; **to smooth sb's ~ feathers** jdn besänftigen, jds erregtes Gemüt besänftigen **b** *(= rumpled, dishevelled) bedclothes* zerwühlt; *hair* zerzaust **c** *shirt, skirt* gekräuselt, gerafft

rug [rʌg] N **a** Teppich *m; (esp rectangular)* Läufer *m; (valuable)* Brücke *f; (bedside)* (Bett)vorleger *m;* **fireside ~** Kaminvorleger *m;* **to pull the ~ from under sb** *(fig)* jdm den Boden unter den Füßen wegziehen **b** *(= blanket)* (Woll)decke *f*

rugby [ˈrʌgbɪ] N *(also* **rugby football**) Rugby *nt;* **~ footballer** Rugbyspieler(in) *m(f)*

rugby: Rugby League N Rugby *nt (mit 13 (Profi)spielern pro Team);* **rugby player** N Rugbyspieler(in) *m(f);* **rugby tackle** N Rugby-Tackling *nt* VT zu Boden bringen; **Rugby Union** N Rugby *nt (mit 15 (Amateur)spielern pro Team)*

rugged [ˈrʌgɪd] ADJ **a** *(= rough, uneven)* rau; *country, landscape also* wild; *cliff, rocks, mountains* zerklüftet; *ground* felsig; *statue* grob **b** *(= tough-looking) man, face, features* markig **c** *(= tough: in character) personality* rau; *breed* zäh, rau; *determination* wild; *resistance* verbissen; **a ~ test** eine harte Prüfung; **~ individualism** rauer *or* knorriger Individualismus; **hill farmers are a ~ breed** Bergbauern sind ein rauer Menschenschlag **d** *(= durable) machine* widerstandsfähig; *clothing* strapazierfähig

ruggedize [ˈrʌgɪdaɪz] VT *(esp US) product etc* (besonders) robust machen; **~d laptop** besonders robuster Laptop

ruggedness [ˈrʌgɪdnɪs] N **a** *(= roughness, unevenness)* Rauheit *f; (of country, landscape also)* Wildheit *f; (of ground)* Felsigkeit *f;* **the ~ of the cliffs** die zerklüfteten Klippen **b** *(= tough appearance: of man, face, features)* Markigkeit *f*

rugger [ˈrʌgəˈ] N *(Brit inf)* = **rugby**

ruin [ˈruːɪn] N **a** *no pl (of thing, person)* Untergang *m; (of event)* Ende *nt; (financial, social)* Ru-

in *m*; **the palace was going to ~** *or* **falling into ~** der Palast verfiel (zur Ruine); **~ stared him in the face** *(financial/social)* er stand vor dem (finanziellen/gesellschaftlichen) Ruin
b *(= cause of ruin)* Ende *nt*; *(of person)* Ruin *m*; **the ~ of my hopes** das Ende meiner Hoffnungen; **it will be the ~ of him** das wird ihn ruinieren; **you will be the ~ of me** du bist mein Ruin
c *(= ruined building)* Ruine *f*; *(fig: = person)* Wrack *nt*; **~s** *(of building)* Ruinen *pl*; *(of reputation, beauty)* Reste *pl*; *(of hopes, career)* Trümmer *pl*; **to be** *or* **lie in ~s** *(lit)* eine Ruine sein; *(fig)* zerstört sein; *(life: financially, socially)* ruiniert sein
VT *(= destroy) building* zerstören; *hopes also* zunichtemachen; *chances, reputation, health, sb's life also* ruinieren; *(financially, socially) person* ruinieren, zugrunde *or* zu Grunde richten; *(= spoil) clothes, event, enjoyment, child, horse* verderben; **they ~ed my birthday party** sie haben (mir) die Geburtstagsfeier verdorben

ruination [ˌruːɪˈneɪʃən] **N** *(of building, hopes)* Zerstörung *f*; *(of reputation, health, sb's life also, of person)* Ruinierung *f*; **to be the ~ of sb** jds Ruin *m* sein

ruined [ˈruːɪnd] **ADJ** **a** *building* in Ruinen *pred*, zerfallen; *city* in Ruinen *pred*; **he visited ~ Warsaw** er besuchte das zerstörte *or* das in Ruinen liegende Warschau **b** *(= wrecked) economy* zugrunde *or* zu Grunde gerichtet, ruiniert; *career* ruiniert **c** *(financially)* ruiniert, erledigt

ruinous [ˈruːɪnəs] **ADJ** *(financially)* ruinös; *price* extrem; **to be in a ~ state** *or* **in ~ condition** *(building)* verfallen *or* baufällig sein

ruinously [ˈruːɪnəslɪ] **ADV** **~ expensive** wahnsinnig teuer *(inf)*

rule [ruːl] **N** **a** *(= regulation)* Regel *f*; *(Sport, Cards)* (Spiel)regel *f*; *(Admin)* Vorschrift *f*, Bestimmung *f*; **the ~s of the game** *(lit, fig)* die Spielregeln; **to play by the ~s** *(lit, fig)* die Spielregeln einhalten; **to bend** *or* **stretch the ~s** es mit den Regeln/Vorschriften nicht so genau nehmen; **running is against the ~s, it's against the ~s to run** Rennen ist nicht erlaubt; **~s and regulations** Regeln und Bestimmungen; **it's a ~ that …** es ist Vorschrift, dass …; **that's the ~ of the road** *(Mot)* das ist im Straßenverkehr üblich; **the Franciscan ~** die Regeln des Franziskanerordens; **to work to ~** Dienst nach Vorschrift machen; **to do sth by ~** etw vorschriftsmäßig tun; **the ~ of three** *(Math)* der Dreisatz; **as a ~ of thumb** als Faustregel; **~ book** Regelheft *nt*, Vorschriftenbuch *nt*; **to throw the ~ book at sb** *(fig)* jdn wegen jeder Kleinigkeit drankriegen *(inf)*
b *(= custom)* Regel *f*; **I make it a ~ to get up early** ich habe es mir zur Regel gemacht, früh aufzustehen; **as a (general) ~** in der Regel; **ties are the ~ at the office** Krawatten sind im Büro die Regel; **violence is the ~ rather than the exception** Gewalt ist eher (die) Regel als (die) Ausnahme
c *(= authority, reign)* Herrschaft *f*; *(= period)* Regierungszeit *f*; **the ~ of law** die Rechtsstaatlichkeit
d *(for measuring)* Metermaß *nt*, Maßstab *m*; **a foot ~** *(1 foot long)* ein (30 cm langes) Lineal; *(showing feet)* ein Maßstab *m* mit Fußeinteilung; **folding ~** Zollstock *m* → **slide rule**
VT **a** *(= govern)* beherrschen, regieren; *(individual)* beherrschen, herrschen über *(+acc)*; *(fig) passions, emotion* beherrschen, zügeln; *person* beherrschen; **to ~ the roost** *(fig)* Herr im Haus sein *(inf)*; **to be ~d by emotions** sich von Gefühlen beherrschen lassen; **if you would only be ~d by what I say** wenn du nur auf mich hören würdest; **I won't be ~d by what he wants** ich richte mich nicht nach seinen Wünschen; **he let his heart ~ his head** er ließ sich von seinem Herzen und nicht von seinem Verstand leiten
b *(Jur, Sport, Admin: = give decision)* entscheiden; **his question was ~d out of order** seine Frage wurde als unzulässig abgewiesen; **the judge ~d the defence out of order** *(Jur)* der Richter rügte die Verteidigung
c *(= draw lines on) paper* linieren; *(= draw) line, margin* ziehen; **~d paper** liniertes Papier
VI **a** *(lit, fig: = reign)* herrschen *(over* über *+acc)*, regieren *(over +acc)*
b *(Fin: = prices)* notieren; **the prices ruling in London** die in London notierten Preise
c *(Jur)* entscheiden *(against* gegen, *in favour of* für, *on* in *+dat)*

▶ **rule off** **VT** *sep* einen Schlussstrich ziehen unter *(+acc)*

▶ **rule out** ✪ 16.3 **VT** *sep word, sentence* einen Strich ziehen durch; *(fig: = exclude, dismiss)* ausschließen

ruler [ˈruːləʳ] **N** **a** *(for measuring)* Lineal *nt* **b** *(= sovereign)* Herrscher(in) *m(f)*

ruling [ˈruːlɪŋ] **ADJ** **a** *(= in power) body, elite* herrschend; **the ~ class** die herrschende Klasse; **the ~ party** die Regierungspartei **b** *(= determining) factor* ausschlaggebend; *passion* vorherrschend; *(= prevalent)* (vor)herrschend; *(Fin, St Ex) prices* notiert; **~ principle** leitendes Prinzip, Leitprinzip *nt* **N** *(Admin, Jur)* Entscheidung *f*; **to get a ~** einen Bescheid erhalten; **to give a ~** eine Entscheidung fällen

rum[1] [rʌm] **N** Rum *m*; **~ toddy** Grog *m*

rum[2] **ADJ** *(dated Brit inf)* komisch *(inf)*; *person also* kauzig; **they're a ~ lot** das sind mir (so) die Rechten *(inf)*

Rumania *etc* [ruːˈmeɪnɪə] = **Romania** *etc*

rumba [ˈrʌmbə] **N** Rumba *m or f*

rumble [ˈrʌmbl] **N** **a** *(of thunder)* Grollen *nt no pl*; *(of cannon)* Donnern *nt no pl*; *(of pipes)* Knacken *nt no pl*; *(of stomach)* Knurren *nt no pl*; *(of train, truck)* Rumpeln *nt no pl*; **his stomach gave a ~** sein Magen knurrte **b** *(inf, = fight)* Schlägerei *f* **VI** *(thunder)* grollen; *(cannon)* donnern; *(pipes)* knacken; *(stomach)* knurren; *(train, truck)* rumpeln; **to ~ past/along/off** vorbei-/entlang-/davonrumpeln **VT** *(Brit inf: = see through) swindle, trick, person* durchschauen; **I soon ~d him** *or* **what he was up to** ich bin ihm bald auf die Schliche gekommen *(inf)*

rumble on **VI** *(Brit: argument, controversy, scandal)* weiterschwelen

rumble: **rumble seat** **N** Notsitz *m*; **rumble strip** **N** *(Mot)* akustische Schwelle

rumbling [ˈrʌmblɪŋ] **N** **a** *(of thunder)* Grollen *nt no pl*; *(of cannon)* Donnern *nt no pl*; *(of stomach)* Knurren *nt no pl*; *(of train, truck)* Rumpeln *nt no pl* **b** **rumblings** **PL** Gerüchte *pl*; **there are ~s that …** man munkelt, dass …

rumbustious [rʌmˈbʌstʃəs] **ADJ** derb

ruminant [ˈruːmɪnənt] **N** Wiederkäuer *m* **ADJ** *(lit)* wiederkäuend; *(fig)* grübelnd

ruminate [ˈruːmɪneɪt] **VI** *(lit)* wiederkäuen; *(fig)* grübeln *(over, about, on* über *+acc)* **VT** wiederkäuen

rumination [ˌruːmɪˈneɪʃən] **N** *(lit)* Wiederkäuen *nt no pl*; *(fig)* Grübeln *nt no pl*

ruminative **ADJ**, **ruminatively** **ADV** [ˈruːmɪnətɪv, -lɪ] *(fig)* grübelnd

rummage [ˈrʌmɪdʒ] **N** **a** **to have a good ~ in sth** etw gründlich durchstöbern *or* durchwühlen; **to have a good ~ around** gründlich herumstöbern *or* herumwühlen **b** *(= jumble)* Ramsch *m* **VI** *(also* **rummage about, rummage around***)* herumstöbern, herumwühlen *(among, in* in *+dat, for* nach)

rummage sale **N** *(US)* Ramschverkauf *m*

rummy [ˈrʌmɪ] **N** *(Cards)* Rommé *nt*, Rommee *nt*

rumour, *(US)* **rumor** [ˈruːməʳ] **N** Gerücht *nt*; **~ has it that …** es geht das Gerücht, dass …; **as ~ has it** wie es Gerüchten zufolge heißt; **there are ~s of war** es gehen Kriegsgerüchte um; **have you heard the ~s?** hast dus schon gehört? **VT** **it is ~ed that …** es geht das Gerücht, dass …; *(through gossip)* man munkelt, dass …; **he is ~ed to be in London** Gerüchten zufolge ist er in London; **he is ~ed to be rich** er soll angeblich reich sein; **his ~ed relationship with a model** die ihm nachgesagte Beziehung zu einem Model

rumour, *(US)* **rumor**: **rumour mill** [ˈruːməˌmɪl] **N** *(inf, pej)* Gerüchteküche *f (inf, pej)*; **rumour-monger** [ˈruːməˌmʌŋgəʳ] **N** Gerüchtemacher(in) *m(f)*, Klatschbase *f (pej)*; **rumour-mongering** [ˈruːməˌmʌŋgərɪŋ] **N** *no pl* Klatscherei *f (pej)*, Verbreitung *f no pl* von Gerüchten

rump [rʌmp] **N** *(of animal)* Hinterbacken *pl*; *(of fowl)* Bürzel *m*; *(inf: of person)* Hinterteil *nt*, Allerwerteste(r) *m (hum)*; **~ steak** Rumpsteak *nt*; **the Rump** *(Brit, Hist)* das Rumpfparlament *(im 17. Jahrhundert in England)*

Rumpelstiltskin [ˈrʌmpəlˌstɪltskɪn] **N** Rumpelstilzchen *nt*

rumple [ˈrʌmpl] **VT** *(also* **rumple up***) clothes, paper* zerknittern; *hair* verwuscheln, zerzausen

rumpled [ˈrʌmpld] **ADJ** *clothes, sheets* zerknittert; *person* unordentlich; *hair* zerzaust

rumply [ˈrʌmplɪ] **ADJ** *clothes, sheets etc* zerknittert

rumpus [ˈrʌmpəs] **N** *(inf: = noise)* Spektakel *nt (inf)*, Krach *m*; *(= quarrel)* Krach *m (inf)*; **to make a ~** *(= make noise)* einen Spektakel *or* Heidenlärm machen *(inf)*; *(= complain)* Krach schlagen *(inf)*; **to kick up a ~** Krach schlagen *(over* wegen); **to have a ~ with sb** sich mit jdm in die Haare geraten

rumpus room **N** *(US)* Spielzimmer *nt*

run [rʌn]

vb: pret **ran**, *ptp* **run**

1 NOUN	3 TRANSITIVE VERB
2 INTRANSITIVE VERB	4 PHRASAL VERBS

1 – NOUN

a [= act of running] Lauf *m (also Cricket, Baseball, Comput)*; **to go for a 2-km run** einen 2-km-Lauf machen; **his run is slower than my walk** ich kann schneller gehen, als er laufen kann; **let the dog have a run** lass den Hund laufen; **he set off at a run** er rannte los; **he took the fence at a run** er nahm die Hürde im Lauf; **to break into a run** zu laufen *or* rennen anfangen; **to take a run at a hurdle** auf eine Hürde loslaufen; **to make a run for it** weglaufen, wegrennen; **he made a run for the door** er lief *or* rannte zur Tür; **he's had a good run** *(= long life)* er hatte ein langes Leben

♦ **on the run** *(from the police etc)* auf der Flucht; **at last we've got them on the run!** endlich haben wir sie in die Flucht geschlagen!; **to keep the enemy on the run** den Feind weiter zur Flucht zwingen; **the house and family keep you on the run** Haus und Familie halten einen ganz schön auf Trab *(inf)*

♦ **a good run for one's money** **we'll give him a good run for his money, he'll have a good run for his money** *(inf, in competition)* wir werden ihn auf Trab halten *(inf)*; **the theory has had a good run for its money** *(inf)* die Theorie hat sich lange gehalten

b [= journey] *in vehicle* Fahrt *f*; *(for pleasure)* Ausflug *m*; **to go for a run in the car** eine Fahrt/einen Ausflug im Auto machen

c [= distance travelled] *in bus, boat, car* Fahrt *f*; *(in plane)* Flug *m*; *(= route)* Strecke *f*; **it's a 30-minute run** es ist eine Fahrt von 30 Minuten; **the boat no longer does that run** das Schiff fährt die Strecke nicht mehr; **the ferries on the Dover-Calais run** die Fähren der Linie Dover-Calais; **the ships on the China run** die Schiffe der China-Linie; **bombing run** Bombenzielanflug *m*

♦ **in the long run** auf die Dauer; **it will be cheaper in the long run** es wird auf die Dauer billiger sein

♦ **in the short run** fürs Nächste; **this could be the best solution in the short run** dies könnte fürs Nächste die beste Lösung sein

d [= use] **to have the run of a place** einen Ort zur freien Verfügung haben; **to give sb the run of one's house** jdm sein Haus überlassen

e [= series] Folge *f*, Reihe *f*, Serie *f*; *(Cards)* Sequenz *f*; *(Theat)* Spielzeit *f*; *(of film)* Laufzeit *f*; **a run on the red** *(Roulette)* eine Serie von roten Zahlen; **when the London run was over** *(Theat)* als das Stück in London abgelaufen war; **the play had a long run** das Stück lief sehr lange; **a run of luck/of bad luck** eine Glücks-/Pechsträhne

f [= great demand] **run on** Ansturm *m* auf (+*acc*); *(St Ex, Fin)* Run *m or* Ansturm *m* auf (+*acc*); **there could be a run on the pound** es könnte einen Run *or* Ansturm auf das Pfund geben

g [= type] **the common run of athletes** der Durchschnittsathlet; **the usual run of illnesses** die normale Serie von Krankheiten

h [= trend] *of market, opinion* Tendenz *f*; *(of events)* Lauf *m*; **the ordinary run of things** der normale Gang der Dinge

i [= track for sledging, skiing] Bahn *f*; **ski run** Abfahrt(sstrecke) *f*

j [= animal enclosure] Gehege *nt*; *(for chickens)* Hühnerhof *m*

k [= diarrhoea] *inf* **the runs** der flotte Otto *(inf)*, die Renneritis *(hum inf)*

l [in stocking] Laufmasche *f*

m [Typ] = *printing run* Auflage *f*

n [Mus] Lauf *m*

2 – INTRANSITIVE VERB

a laufen, rennen; *(in race)* laufen; **to run past/off** vorbei-/davonlaufen *or* -rennen; **she came running out** sie kam herausgelaufen *or* -gerannt; **to run down a slope** einen Abhang hinunterlaufen *or* -rennen; **run!** lauf!; **walk don't run!** du sollst gehen, nicht rennen!; **he's trying to run before he can walk** *(fig)* er sollte erst einmal langsam machen; **to run for the bus** zum Bus laufen *or* rennen; **she ran to meet him** sie lief *or* rannte ihm entgegen; **she ran to help him** sie kam ihm schnell zu Hilfe; **to run in the 100 metres** *(Brit) or* **meters** *(US)* die 100 Meter laufen; **to go running** *(to keep fit)* joggen gehen; **eleven ran** *(Horse Racing)* elf (Pferde) waren am Start; **X, Y, Z also ran** *(Horse Racing)* X, Y, Z waren ebenfalls am Start; **this horse will run in the National** das Pferd startet im National → **also-ran**

b [= flee] davonlaufen, wegrennen; **to run for one's life** um sein Leben laufen *or* rennen; **run for it!** lauft *or* rennt, was ihr könnt!; **go on then, run to mummy!** na, lauf doch schon zu deiner Mutti!

c [= go] *story, words* gehen, lauten; *(tune)* gehen; **the rumour** *(Brit) or* **rumor** *(US)* **ran (a)round the office that ...** im Büro ging das Gerücht um, dass ...; **so the story runs** die Geschichte geht so; **the wording ran as follows** es hieß *or* lautete folgendermaßen; **the lyrics ran through my head** der Text ging mir durch den Kopf; **all the things I have to do keep running through my head** mir geht ständig durch den Kopf, was ich noch alles machen muss; **he ran down the list** er ging die Liste durch; **a shiver ran down her spine** ein Schauer lief ihr über den Rücken; **his eyes/fingers ran over the sculpture** seine Augen/Finger glitten über die Plastik

♦ **to run in the family** in der Familie liegen

d [= stand as candidate] kandidieren, sich aufstellen lassen; **to run for President** *or* **for the Presidency** für die Präsidentschaft kandidieren; **to run against sb** jds Gegenkandidat *m* sein

e [= be] **I'm running a bit late** ich bin ein bisschen spät dran; **all planes/trains are running late** alle Flugzeuge/Züge haben Verspätung; **the project is running late/to schedule** das Projekt hat sich verzögert/geht ganz nach Plan voran; **supplies are running low** die Vorräte sind knapp; **his blood ran cold** das Blut fror ihm in den Adern; **to be running scared** Angst haben → **seed, short, wild, high**

♦ **to run dry** *(river)* austrocknen; *(pen)* leer werden; *(resources, funds)* ausgehen; *(conversation)* verstummen; **he ran dry of ideas** ihm gingen die Ideen aus; **their conversation ran dry** ihnen ging der Gesprächsstoff aus

♦ **to be running at** *(= stand)* betragen; **inflation is running at 20%** die Inflationsrate beträgt 20%; **interest rates are running at record levels/15%** die Zinssätze sind auf Rekordhöhe/stehen auf 15%

f [= slide] *drawer, curtains, rope* laufen, gleiten; *(vehicle)* rollen; **it runs on wheels** es läuft *or* fährt auf Rädern; **money just runs through his fingers** das Geld rinnt ihm (nur so) durch die Finger

g [= flow] *water, tears, tap, nose, butter* laufen; *(ink, river, electric current)* fließen; *(eyes)* tränen; *(sore, abscess)* eitern; *(paint, colour)* zerfließen, ineinanderfließen; *(colour, dye: in washing)* färben; **my shirt has run** mein Hemd hat gefärbt; **a heavy sea was running** die See ging hoch; **where the tide is running strongly** wo die Gezeiten sehr stark sind; **let the water run hot** lass das Wasser laufen, bis es heiß kommt; **your bath is running** dein Badewasser läuft ein

♦ **to be running with** *(= saturated)* **the walls were running with damp** die Wände tropften vor Feuchtigkeit; **running with sweat** schweißüberströmt

♦ **to run into** *(= join)* **where the river runs into the sea** wo der Fluss ins Meer mündet; **the street runs into the square** die Straße mündet auf den Platz

h [= continue, extend] *play, film, contract* laufen; *(Jur: sentence)* laufen; *(Fin: interest rate)* gelten

♦ **to run into** *(with amounts, numbers)* **the expenditure runs into thousands of pounds** die Ausgaben gehen in die tausende *or* Tausende (von Pfund); **the book has run into three editions** das Buch hat schon drei Auflagen erreicht

♦ **to run and run** *(story, production)* noch lange laufen; *(debate)* noch lange fortgesetzt werden

i [= sail] **to run before the wind** vor dem Wind segeln; **to run onto the rocks** (auf die Felsen) auflaufen; **to run into port** in den Hafen einlaufen

j [= provide service] *bus, train etc* fahren, verkehren; **the train doesn't run on Sundays** der Zug fährt sonntags nicht; **no trains run there any more** dorthin gibt es keine Zugverbindung mehr

k [= function] *machine, wheel* laufen; *(factory)* arbeiten; *(fig, ceremony)* laufen; **when the central heating is running** wenn die Zentralheizung angeschaltet ist; **you mustn't leave the engine running** Sie dürfen den Motor nicht laufen lassen; **this model runs on diesel** dieses Auto fährt mit Diesel; **the radio runs off the mains/off batteries** das Radio läuft auf Netz/Batterie; **things are running smoothly** alles läuft glatt

l [= extend in space] *road* gehen, führen; *(mountains)* sich ziehen, sich erstrecken; *(river)* fließen; **he has a scar running across his chest** eine Narbe zieht sich quer über seine Brust; **a wall runs (a)round the garden** um den Garten zieht sich *or* läuft eine Mauer; **the railway line runs for 300 km** die Bahnlinie ist 300 km lang; **this theme runs through all his work** dieses Thema zieht sich durch sein ganzes Werk

m [= unravel] *(stocking)* eine Laufmasche bekommen; *(stitch)* laufen

n [Comput] *software, computer* laufen; **this software doesn't run under the new version** diese Software läuft nicht unter der neuen Version

3 – TRANSITIVE VERB

a [subject: person: distance] laufen, rennen; *race* laufen; **he runs 3 km every day** er läuft jeden Tag 3 km; **the first race will be run at 2 o'clock** das erste Rennen findet um 2 Uhr statt; **to run errands** Botengänge machen; **to run the streets** *(child, dog)* sich auf der Straße herumtreiben; **to run sb/sth a close second** *(fig)* von jdm/etw nur knapp geschlagen werden; **to run sb close** *(Sport, fig)* nur knapp von jdm geschlagen werden → **mile**

b [subject: events, disease, person] **to run its/their course** seinen/ihren Lauf nehmen; **to run a temperature** *or* **a fever** Fieber haben; **he was running a high temperature** er hatte Fieber → **gauntlet**

c [= pursue = hunt] *fox, deer* treiben; *(= make run) person, animal* jagen; **they ran him out of the house** sie jagten ihn aus dem Haus; **to run sb off his feet** *(inf)* jdn ständig auf Trab halten *(inf)*; **to run sb into debt** jdn in Schulden stürzen → **earth, ground**[1]

d [= cause to flow] **to run water into a bath** Wasser in die Badewanne einlaufen lassen; **I'll run you a bath** ich lasse dir ein Bad einlaufen; **he runs his words together** bei ihm fließen alle Wörter ineinander über

e [= transport] *person, thing* fahren, bringen; **I'll run you to the station** ich fahre Sie zum Bahnhof

f [= drive] *vehicle* fahren; **he ran the car into the garage/a tree** er fuhr das Auto in die Garage/gegen einen Baum; **he runs a Rolls** er fährt einen Rolls Royce

g [buses, trains] unterhalten; *extra buses, trains* einsetzen; **this company runs a bus service** diese Firma unterhält einen Busdienst; **they run trains to London every hour** es besteht stündlicher Zugverkehr nach London; **how many machines does this factory run?** wie viele Maschinen laufen in dieser Fabrik?

h [horse] laufen lassen

i [candidate] aufstellen

j [= operate] *machine, engine* betreiben; *computer* laufen lassen; *software* benutzen; *program* ausführen; *(person)* bedienen; **to run a radio off the mains** ein Radio auf Netz laufen lassen; **it would be cheaper to run the heating on gas** es wäre billiger, mit Gas zu heizen; **I can't afford to run a car** ich kann es mir nicht leisten, ein Auto zu unterhalten; **this car is cheap to run** dieses Auto ist billig im Unterhalt; **can you run SuperText 3 on your computer?** läuft SuperText 3 auf deinem Computer?

k [= conduct] *experiment, test* durchführen

l [= be responsible for = manage] *business, hotel* führen, leiten; *shop* führen; *mine* betreiben; *school, organization, newspaper* leiten; *(= organize) course of study, competition* veranstalten, durchführen; *(= be in charge of) course, competition, department, project* leiten; **a well-run hotel** ein gut geführtes Hotel; **he runs a small hotel in the village** er hat ein kleines Hotel im Dorf; **to run a house** einen Haushalt führen; **a house which is easy to run** ein Haus, das leicht in Schuss gehalten werden kann; **I want to run my own life** ich möchte mein eigenes Leben leben; **she's the one who really runs everything** sie ist diejenige, die den Laden schmeißt *(inf)*; **I'm running this show!** *(inf)* ich bestimme, was gemacht wird

m [= smuggle] *guns etc* schmuggeln

n [= move] **to run one's fingers over the piano keys** die Finger über die (Klavier)tasten gleiten lassen; **to run one's finger down a list** mit dem Finger eine Liste durchgehen; **to run one's fingers/a comb through one's hair** sich *(dat)* mit den Fingern/einem Kamm durch die Haare fahren; **to run one's eye over a page** eine Seite überfliegen; **he ran the vacuum cleaner over the carpet** er ging mit dem Staubsauger über den Teppich

o [= put] *rope, road* führen; *piece of elastic, line, ditch* ziehen; *pipe, wires* (ver)legen; *(above ground)* führen; **to run a rope round a tree** ein Seil um einen Baum legen

p [= thrust] **he ran a sword into his side** er stieß ihm das Schwert in die Seite, er durchbohrte ihn mit dem Schwert

q [= publish] *Press article, series* bringen

r [= present] *film* zeigen, bringen; *(Comm) line* verkaufen; **the supermarket is running a new line in exotic fruit** im Supermarkt werden jetzt exotische Früchte angeboten

s [= go through] **to run a red light** eine rote Ampel überfahren

4 – PHRASAL VERBS

▶ **run about** *(Brit) or* **around** VI *(lit, fig)* herumlaufen *or* -rennen; **to run around with sb** sich mit jdm herumtreiben; **I'm not going to run about** *or* **around after you cleaning up** ich putze doch nicht dauernd hinter dir her

▶ **run across** VI **a** *(lit)* hinüberlaufen *or* -rennen **b** *(= go to see)* kurz rüberlaufen *or* -gehen *(to* zu*)* VI +*prep obj (= meet) person* zufällig treffen; *(= find) object, reference* stoßen auf *(+acc)*

▶ **run after** VI **to come running after** hinterherlaufen *or* -rennen VI *+prep obj* nachlaufen *or* -rennen *(+dat)*; **I'm not going to spend the rest of my days running after you!** *(fig)* ich denke gar nicht daran, nur immer für dich da zu sein!

▶ **run along** VI laufen, rennen; *(= go away)* gehen; **run along!** nun geht mal schön!

▶ **run around** VI = **run about**

▶ **run at** VI *+prep obj* zu- *or* loslaufen auf *(+acc)*; *(= attack)* losstürzen auf *(+acc)*

▶ **run away** VI **a** *(child, animal)* weglaufen, wegrennen; *(person)* weglaufen; *(horse)* durchgehen; **to run away from home** von zu Hause weglaufen; **don't run away, I need your advice** *(inf)* gehen Sie nicht weg, ich möchte Sie um Rat fragen; **run away and play!** geht (mal schön) spielen! **b** *(water)* auslaufen

▶ **run away with** VI *+prep obj (= use up) funds, money, resources* verschlucken *(inf)*, verbrauchen; *(= steal) money, object* durchgehen *or* durchbrennen mit *(inf)*; *(Sport etc: = win easily) race, prize* spielend gewinnen; **don't run away with the idea that …** *(fig)* kommen Sie nur nicht auf den Gedanken, dass …; **he lets his imagination/enthusiasm run away with him** seine Fantasie *or* Phantasie/seine Begeisterung geht leicht mit ihm durch

▶ **run back** VI *(lit)* zurücklaufen, zurückrennen; **she'll come running back** sie wird reumütig zurückkommen VT *sep* **a** *person* zurückfahren *or* -bringen **b** *(= rewind) tape, film* zurückspulen

▶ **run down** VI **a** *(lit: person)* hinunterlaufen *or* -rennen **b** *(watch, clock)* ablaufen; *(battery)* leer werden; **to let stocks run down** das Lager leer werden lassen; *(deliberately)* die Vorräte abbauen VT *sep* **a** *(= knock down)* umfahren; *(= run over)* überfahren **b** *(= limit, reduce) factory, shop* (allmählich) auflösen; *department, stocks, staff* abbauen; *battery* zu stark belasten **c** *(= disparage)* schlechtmachen, runtermachen *(inf)* **d** *(= pursue and capture) criminal, stag* zur Strecke bringen; *person* ausfindig machen

▶ **run in** VI *(lit)* hineinlaufen *or* -rennen VT *sep* **a** *car* einfahren **b** *(inf: = arrest)* sich *(dat)* schnappen

▶ **run into** VI *+prep obj (= meet)* zufällig treffen; *(= collide with)* rennen/fahren gegen; **to run into difficulties/trouble** Schwierigkeiten/Ärger bekommen; **to run into problems** auf Probleme stoßen; **to run into danger/debt** in Gefahr/Schulden geraten → *also* **run 2 h**

▶ **run off** VI = **run away VI a** VT *sep* **a** *water* ablassen **b** *(= reproduce) copy* abziehen **c** *(Sport)* **to run off the heats** die Ausscheidungskämpfe durchführen **d** *excess weight* sich *(dat)* ablaufen *or* abrennen

▶ **run on** VI **a** *(lit)* weiterlaufen, weiterrennen **b** *(fig: in speaking)* **he does run on so!** er redet wie ein Buch!; **it ran on for four hours** das zog sich über vier Stunden hin **c** *(letters)* verbunden sein; *(words)* fortlaufend geschrieben sein; *(line of type)* ohne Absatz gedruckt sein **d** *(time)* weitergehen VT *sep letters* verbinden; *words* fortlaufend schreiben; *line of type* ohne Absatz drucken

▶ **run out** VI **a** *(person)* hinauslaufen *or* -rennen; *(rope, chain)* ablaufen; *(liquid)* herauslaufen; *(through leak)* auslaufen **b** *(= come to an end, lease, contract, period of time)* ablaufen; *(money, supplies)* ausgehen, zu Ende gehen; **my patience is slowly running out** mir geht langsam die Geduld aus VT *sep* **a** *rope, chain* abwickeln **b** *(Cricket)* ausschlagen *(während der Schlagmann seinen Lauf macht)*

▶ **run out of** VI *+prep obj* **he ran out of supplies/money/patience** ihm gingen die Vorräte/ging das Geld/die Geduld aus; **she ran out of time** sie hatte keine Zeit mehr; **we're running out of time** wir haben nicht mehr viel Zeit

▶ **run over** VI **a** *(to neighbour etc)* kurz hinüberlaufen *or* hinübergehen *or* rübergehen *(inf)* **b** *(= overflow: liquid, container)* überlaufen **c** *(Rad, TV etc)* **the play ran over by 10 minutes** das Stück hatte 10 Minuten Überlänge; **we're running over** wir überziehen VI *+prep obj story, part in play, details* durchgehen; *text, notes* durchsehen; **I'll run over your part with you** ich gehe Ihre Rolle kurz mit Ihnen durch VT *sep (in vehicle)* überfahren

▶ **run round** VI *(esp Brit)* kurz vorbeigehen; **to run round and see sb** kurz bei jdm vorbeigehen → *also* **run about**

▶ **run through** VI *(lit)* durchlaufen VI *+prep obj* **a** *(= use up) money, fortune* durchbringen **b** *(= rehearse) piece of music, play* durchspielen; *ceremony, part, list* durchgehen **c** = **run over VI** *+prep obj* VT *sep* **to run sb through (with a sword)** jdn (mit einem Schwert) durchbohren

▶ **run to** VI *+prep obj* **a** *(= afford)* **I can't run to a new car** ich kann mir kein neues Auto leisten; **the funds won't run to a party** die Finanzen reichen nicht für eine Party **b** *(= amount to)* **the poem runs to several hundred lines** das Gedicht geht über mehrere hundert Zeilen

▶ **run up** VI *(lit: = climb quickly)* hinauflaufen; *(= approach quickly)* hinlaufen *or* -rennen *(to* zu); **to run up against difficulties** auf Schwierigkeiten stoßen VT *sep* **a** *flag* hissen, hochziehen; **they ran the flag up (the mast)** sie hissten die Fahne **b** *(= incur)* machen; **to run up a bill** eine Rechnung zusammenkommen lassen; **to run up a debt** Schulden machen **c** *(= sew quickly)* schnell zusammennähen

---

run: **runabout** N *(= car)* kleiner Flitzer *(inf)*; *(= boat)* kleines Motorboot; **runaround** N *(inf)* **to give sb the ~** jdn an der Nase herumführen *(inf)*; **to get the ~ (from sb)** (von jdm) an der Nase herumgeführt werden *(inf)*

runaway [ˈrʌnəweɪ] N Ausreißer(in) *m(f)* ADJ **a** *slave* entlaufen; *person, couple, horse* durchgebrannt *(inf)*, ausgerissen; **a ~ car/train** ein Auto/ein Zug, das/der sich selbstständig gemacht hat; **the ~ child** der kleine Ausreißer; **they planned a ~ wedding** sie beschlossen, wegzulaufen und zu heiraten **b** *(fig: = unstoppable) winner* überragend; *inflation* unkontrollierbar; **a ~ success** ein Riesenerfolg *m*, ein voller Erfolg; **the ~ bestseller** der mit Abstand erfolgreichste Bestseller; **he had a ~ victory** er hatte einen sehr leichten Sieg; **she was the ~ winner of the championship** sie gewann die Meisterschaften mit großem Abstand

runback [ˈrʌnbæk] N *(Tennis)* Auslauf *m* hinter der Grundlinie

rundown [ˈrʌndaʊn] N **a** *(of factory, shop)* (allmähliche) Auflösung; *(of department, stock, personnel)* Abbau *m* **b** *(inf: = report)* Bericht *m*, Zusammenfassung *f*; **to give sb a ~ on sth** jdn über etw *(acc)* informieren, jdm einen Bericht über etw *(acc)* geben

run-down [ˌrʌnˈdaʊn] ADJ **a** *(= dilapidated)* heruntergekommen **b** *(= tired)* abgespannt **c** *(= inefficient) industry, service* heruntergekommen; *battery* leer

rune [ruːn] N Rune *f*; **to read the ~s** *(Brit fig)* die Vorzeichen deuten

rung[1] [rʌŋ] *ptp of* **ring**[2]

rung[2] N *(of ladder, also fig)* Sprosse *f*; *(of chair)* Querstab *m*

runic [ˈruːnɪk] ADJ runisch, Runen-; **~ symbol** Runenzeichen *nt*

run-in [ˈrʌnɪn] N *(inf: = argument)* Streit *m*

runner [ˈrʌnəˈ] N **a** *(= athlete)* Läufer(in) *m(f)*; *(= horse)* Rennpferd *nt*; *(= messenger)* Bote *m*, Botin *f*, Laufbursche *m*; *(= smuggler)* Schmuggler(in) *m(f)*; **(Bow Street) Runners** *(Brit, Hist)* ≈ Büttel *pl*; **it's a good ~, this car** *(inf)* das Auto läuft wirklich einwandfrei **b** *(on sledge, skate)* Kufe *f*; *(for curtain)* Vorhangröllchen *nt*; *(for drawer, machine part)* Laufschiene *f* **c** *(= carpet, for table)* Läufer *m* **d** *(Bot)* Ausläufer *m* **e** **to do a ~** *(Brit inf)* die Fliege machen *(sl)*

runner bean N *(Brit)* Stangenbohne *f*

runner-up [ˈrʌnərˈʌp] N Zweite(r), Zweitplatzierte(r) *mf*; **the runners-up** die weiteren Plätze; *(in competition)* die weiteren Gewinner

running [ˈrʌnɪŋ] N **a** Laufen *nt*, Rennen *nt*; **~ style, style of ~** Laufstil *m*; **~ gear** Laufausrüstung *f*; **he started professional ~ eight years ago** er begann seine Laufkarriere vor acht Jahren; **to make the ~** *(lit, fig)* das Rennen machen; **to be in the ~ (for sth)** im Rennen (für etw) liegen; **out of the ~** aus dem Rennen; **to take up the ~** *(lit, fig)* sich an die Spitze setzen **b** *(= functioning: of machine, vehicle)* Laufen *nt* **c** *(= management, of business, hotel)* Führung *f*, Leitung *f*; *(of country, shop)* Führung *f*; *(of mine)* Betrieb *m*; *(of school, organization, newspaper)* Leitung *f*; *(= organization: of course, competition)* Veranstaltung *f*, Durchführung *f*; *(= being in charge: of course, competition, department, project)* Leitung *f* **d** *(= maintenance: of machine)* Unterhaltung *f* **e** *(= smuggling)* Schmuggel *m*
ADJ **a** *(= flowing) water, stream* fließend; *tap, nose* laufend; *eyes* tränend; **~ sore** *(Med)* eiternde Wunde; *(fig)* Eiterbeule *f*; **~ cold** schwerer Schnupfen; **hot and cold ~ water** fließend warmes und kaltes Wasser **b** *(= current) prices* momentan **c** *(Comput) program etc* aktiv
ADV hintereinander; **(for) five days ~** fünf Tage hintereinander; **for the third year ~** im dritten Jahr hintereinander; **sales have fallen for the third year ~** die Verkaufszahlen sind seit drei Jahren rückläufig

running: **running account** N *(Fin)* laufendes Konto; **running battle** N *(Mil) Gefecht, bei dem eine Seite immer weiter zurückgedrängt wird*; *(fig)* Kleinkrieg *m*; **to fight a ~** einen Kleinkrieg führen; **running board** N Trittbrett *nt*; **running commentary** N *(Rad, TV)* fortlaufender Kommentar; **to give sb a ~ (on sth)** *(fig)* jdm fortlaufend Erläuterungen (über etw *acc*) geben; **we don't need a ~** *(inf)* wir brauchen keinen Kommentar; **running costs** PL Betriebskosten *pl*; *(of car)* Unterhaltskosten *pl*; **running expenses** PL laufende Kosten *pl*; **running head** N *(Typ)* Kolumnentitel *m*; **running joke** N **it was a ~ between them** es war ein ständiger Witz bei ihnen; **running jump** N Sprung *m* mit Anlauf; **to take a ~ at sth** mit Anlauf über etw *(acc)* springen; **go and take a ~** *(Brit inf)* du kannst mich gernhaben *(inf)*; **running knot** N Schlaufenknoten *m*; **running light** N *(Naut)* Positionslampe *f*, Fahrlicht *nt*; **running mate** N *(US Pol) Kandidat für die Vizepräsidentschaft*; **running order** N **in ~** betriebsbereit; **running shoe** N Rennschuh *m*; **running speed** N *(Tech)* Umlaufgeschwindigkeit *f*; *(Mot)* Fahrgeschwindigkeit *f*; **running stitch** N *(Sew)* Vorstich *m*, Reihstich *m*; **running tally** N laufende Summe; **running text** N fortlaufender Text; **running time** N *(of film)* Laufzeit *f*; **running title** N = **running head**; **running total** N laufende Summe; **to keep a ~ of sth** *(lit, fig)* etw fortlaufend festhalten; **running track** N Aschenbahn *f*

runny [ˈrʌnɪ] ADJ *(+er) egg, wax* flüssig; *nose* laufend; *eyes* wässerig, tränend; *honey, sauce, consistency* dünnflüssig; **I've got a ~ nose** mir läuft die Nase, meine Nase läuft

run: **runoff** N *(Sport)* Entscheidungslauf *m*, Stechen *nt*; **run-of-the-mill** ADJ durchschnittlich, gewöhnlich; *theme, novel* Feld-Wald-Wiesen- *(inf)*; **run-on (line)** N fortlaufende Zeile; **run-out** N *(Ski)* Auslauf *m*; **run-proof** ADJ *tights etc* laufmaschenfest

runt [rʌnt] N kleinstes Ferkel *(eines Wurfes)*; *(pej)* Wicht *m*; *(despicable)* Fiesling *m (inf)*

run: **run-through** N Durchgehen *nt*; **let's have a final ~** gehen wir das noch einmal durch; **to have a ~ of sth** etw durchgehen; **run-up** N *(Sport)* Anlauf *m*; *(fig)* Vorbereitungszeit *f*; **in the ~ to the election** in der Zeit vor der Wahl; **runway** N *(Aviat)* Start- und Landebahn *f*, Runway *f or m*

rupee [ruːˈpiː] N Rupie *f*

rupture [ˈrʌptʃəˈ] N *(lit, fig)* Bruch *m*; *(Pol, of relations)* Abbruch *m* VT brechen; **to ~ oneself** *(inf)* sich *(dat)* einen Bruch heben *(inf)*; **to ~ a**

muscle sich *(dat)* einen Muskelriss zuziehen **VI** brechen

ruptured [ˈrʌptʃəd] ADJ *tank, pipe* geplatzt; *(Med) organ, tendon* gerissen; *blood vessel* geplatzt

rural [ˈrʊərəl] ADJ **a** *(= of the countryside)* ländlich; *poverty, crime* auf dem Land; **~ land** ländlicher Raum; **~ development programme** *or (US)* **program** ländliches Entwicklungsprogramm; **~ worker** Landarbeiter(in) *m(f)*; **~ doctor** Landarzt *m*/-ärztin *f*; **~ policeman** Dorfpolizist *m*; **~ England** das ländliche England; **Ireland used to be largely a ~ country** Irland war früher hauptsächlich ein Agrarstaat **b** *(= rustic) landscape* bäuerlich; *accent* dörflich

rural: **rural depopulation** N Abwanderung *f* der Landbevölkerung, Landflucht *f*; **rural deprivation** N Strukturschwäche *f* in ländlichen Gebieten; **rural district** N *(Brit Admin)* Landbezirk *m*; **rural life** N Landleben *nt*; **rural planning** N Raumplanung *f* in ländlichen Gebieten; **rural population** N Landbevölkerung *f*

ruse [ruːz] N List *f*

rush[1] [rʌʃ] **N** **a** *(= rapid movement, of crowd)* Andrang *m*, Gedränge *nt*; *(of air)* Stoß *m*; **he was caught in the ~ for the door** die zur Tür drängende Menge riss ihn mit; **they made a ~ for the door** sie drängten zur Tür; **there was a ~ for the empty seats** alles stürzte sich auf die leeren Sitze; **there's been a ~ on these goods** diese Waren sind rasend weggegangen; **we have a ~ on in the office just now** bei uns im Büro herrscht zurzeit Hochbetrieb; **the Christmas ~** der Weihnachtsbetrieb; **we've had a ~ of orders** wir hatten eine Flut von Aufträgen; **there was a ~ of water** Wasser strömte *or* schoss herein/heraus *etc*; **water streamed out in a ~** das Wasser schoss in einem Schwall heraus; **a ~ of blood to the head** Blutandrang *m* im Kopf; **a ~ of panic** eine plötzliche Panik; **a ~ of emotion** eine Gefühlsaufwallung → **gold rush**

b *(= hurry)* Eile *f*; *(stronger)* Hetze *f*, Hast *f*; **the ~ of modern life** die Hetze des modernen Lebens; **to be in a ~** in Eile sein; **I had a ~ to get here on time** ich musste ganz schön hetzen, um rechtzeitig hier zu sein; **I did it in a ~** ich habe es sehr schnell *or* hastig gemacht; **what's (all) the ~?** wozu die Eile/Hetzerei?; **is there any ~ for this?** eilt das?; **it all happened in such a ~** das ging alles so plötzlich

c rushes PL *(Film)* erste Kopie

VI *(= hurry)* eilen; *(stronger)* hetzen, hasten; *(= run)* stürzen; *(wind)* brausen; *(water)* schießen, stürzen; *(= make rushing noise)* rauschen; **they ~ed to help her** sie eilten ihr zu Hilfe; **I ~ed to her side** ich eilte an ihre Seite; **I'm ~ing to finish it** ich beeile mich, es fertig zu machen; **don't ~, take your time** überstürzen Sie nichts, lassen Sie sich Zeit; **you shouldn't just go ~ing into things** Sie sollten die Dinge nicht so überstürzen; **to ~ into marriage** überstürzt heiraten; **to ~ through** *(book)* hastig lesen; *meal* hastig essen; *museum, town* hetzen durch; *work* hastig erledigen; **to ~ past** *(person)* vorbeistürzen; *(vehicle)* vorbeischießen; **to ~ in/out/back** *etc* hinein-/hinaus-/zurückstürzen *or* -stürmen *etc*; **the ambulance ~ed to the scene** der Krankenwagen raste zur Unfallstelle; **to ~ to sb's defence** *(Brit) or* **defense** *(US) (lit, fig)* jdm zur Seite eilen; **to ~ into print** vorzeitig veröffentlichen; **the blood ~ed to his face** das Blut schoss ihm ins Gesicht; **memories ~ed into his mind** Erinnerungen schossen ihm durch den Kopf

VT **a** **to ~ sb to hospital** jdn schnellstens ins Krankenhaus bringen; **they ~ed more troops to the front** sie schickten eilends mehr Truppen an die Front; **they ~ed him out (of the room)** sie brachten ihn eilends aus dem Zimmer; **they ~ed the bill through Parliament** sie peitschten die Gesetzesvorlage durch das Parlament; **to ~ a book into print** ein Buch eilends in Druck geben

b *(= force to hurry)* hetzen, drängen; **don't ~ me!** hetz mich nicht; **he won't be ~ed** er lässt sich nicht drängen *or* treiben; **to be ~ed off one's feet** dauernd auf Trab sein *(inf)*; **to ~ sb off his feet** jdn dauernd auf Trab halten *(inf)*; **to ~ sb into a decision** jdn zu einer hastigen Entscheidung treiben; **to ~ sb into doing sth** jdn dazu treiben, etw überstürzt zu tun

c *(= charge at)* stürmen; *fence* zustürmen auf *(+acc)*; **the mob ~ed the line of policemen** der Mob stürmte auf den Polizeikordon zu; **to ~ one's fences** *(fig)* die Sache überstürzen

d *(= do hurriedly) job, task* hastig machen, schnell machen; *(= do badly)* schludern bei *(pej)*; **you can't ~ this sort of work** für solche Arbeit muss man sich *(dat)* Zeit lassen

e *(inf, = charge exorbitantly)* schröpfen *(inf)*; **what were you ~ed for it?** wie viel haben sie dir dafür abgeknöpft? *(inf)*

▶ **rush about** *(Brit) or* **around** VI herumhasten *or* -hetzen

▶ **rush at** VI *+prep obj* **a** *(lit)* losstürzen auf *(+acc)*, sich stürzen auf *(+acc)* **b** *(fig)* **he tends to rush at things** er neigt dazu, die Dinge überstürzt zu machen

▶ **rush down** VI *(person)* hinuntereilen; *(very fast, also water etc)* hinunterstürzen

▶ **rush out** **VI** hinauseilen; *(very fast)* hinausstürzen; **he rushed out and bought one** er kaufte sofort eines **VT** *sep order* eilends wegschicken; *statement, book* schnell(stens) veröffentlichen; *troops, supplies* eilends hintransportieren

▶ **rush through** VT *sep order* durchjagen; *goods, supplies* eilends durchschleusen; *legislation, bill* durchpeitschen; **they rushed medical supplies through to him** sie schickten eilends Medikamente zu ihm

▶ **rush up** **VI** *(lit)* hinaufeilen; *(very fast)* hinaufstürzen **VT** *sep help, reinforcements* eilends schicken

rush[2] N *(Bot)* Binse *f*; **in the ~es** im Schilf

rushed [rʌʃt] ADJ **a** *(= hurried) meal* hastig; *decision* übereilt **b** *(= busy)* gehetzt

rush: **rush hour(s)** N(PL) Hauptverkehrszeit *f*, Stoßzeit(en) *f(pl)*, Rushhour *f*; **rush-hour traffic** Stoßverkehr *m*; **rush job** N eiliger Auftrag; *(pej: = bad work)* Schluderarbeit *f (inf)*; **can you do a ~ for me?** können Sie das ganz schnell für mich machen?; **rushlight** N aus Binsen und Talg hergestellte Kerze; **rush mat, rush matting** N Binsenmatte *f*; **rush order** N *(Comm)* Eilauftrag *m*

rusk [rʌsk] N Zwieback *m*

russet [ˈrʌsɪt] **N** **a** *(= colour)* gelbliches Rotbraun **b** *(= apple)* Boskop *m* **ADJ** rostfarben

Russia [ˈrʌʃə] N Russland *nt*

Russian [ˈrʌʃən] **ADJ** russisch **N** **a** Russe *m*, Russin *f* **b** *(Ling)* Russisch *nt*; **~ teacher** Russischlehrer(in) *m(f)*

Russian: **Russian doll** N russische Puppe; **Russian dressing** N *pikant gewürzte Mayonnaise mit gehackten Salzgurken*; **Russian Federation** N **the ~** die Russische Föderation; **Russian leather** N Juchten *nt*; **Russian Orthodox** ADJ *(Rel)* russisch-orthodox; **the ~ Church** die russisch-orthodoxe Kirche; **Russian roulette** N russisches Roulette; **Russian salad** N russischer Salat

Russification [ˌrʌsɪfɪˈkeɪʃən] N Russifizierung *f*

Russky [ˈrʌskɪ] *(pej)* **N** Iwan *m*, Russki *m*; **the Russkies** der Iwan **ADJ** russisch

Russo- [ˈrʌsəʊ] PREF russisch-; **~Japanese** russisch-japanisch

rust [rʌst] **N** Rost *m*; *(Bot)* Brand *m*; **covered in ~** völlig verrostet **ADJ** *(also* **rust-coloured***)* rostfarben **VT** *(lit)* rosten lassen **VI** rosten; *(talent)* verkümmern; *(brain, language)* (ein)rosten

▶ **rust in** VI *(screw)* einrosten

▶ **rust over** VI verrosten; **to be rusted over** verrostet sein

▶ **rust through** **VI** durchrosten **VT** *sep* durchrosten lassen

▶ **rust up** VI festrosten

rust: **Rust Belt** N *(US)* **the ~** ≈ das Industriegebiet; **the ~ states of America's industrial heartland** die Staaten in Amerikas industriellem Zentrum; **rust bucket** N *(inf: = car, boat)* Rostlaube *f (inf)*; **rust-coloured**, *(US)* **rust-colored** ADJ rostbraun, rostfarben; **rust converter** N Rostumwandler *m*

rusted [ˈrʌstɪd] ADJ *(esp US)* rostig

rustic [ˈrʌstɪk] **N** Bauer *m*, Bäuerin *f* **ADJ** **a** *(= rural)* bäuerlich; *furniture, style* rustikal; **~ novel** Bauernroman *m* **b** *(pej: = crude)* derb, bäurisch

rusticate [ˈrʌstɪkeɪt] VT **a** *(form, liter: = send to country)* aufs Land schicken; *(= make rustic)* bäurisch machen **b** *(Brit Univ)* vorübergehend von der Universität verweisen

rusticity [rʌsˈtɪsɪtɪ] N Ländlichkeit *f*

rustiness [ˈrʌstɪnɪs] N Rostigkeit *f*; *(fig)* eingerostete Kenntnisse *pl* (of in *+dat*)

rustle [ˈrʌsl] **N** Rascheln *nt*; *(of foliage)* Rauschen *nt* **VI** *(leaves, silk, papers)* rascheln; *(foliage, skirts)* rauschen; **the wind ~d through the leaves** der Wind rauschte in den Blättern; *(on the ground)* der Wind raschelte mit den Blättern **VT** **a** *paper, skirt, leaves on ground etc* rascheln mit; *(wind) leaves on tree* rauschen in *(+dat)* **b** *(= steal) cattle, sheep* klauen *(inf)*

▶ **rustle up** VT *sep (inf) meal* improvisieren *(inf)*; *money* auftreiben; **can you rustle up a cup of coffee?** können Sie eine Tasse Kaffee beschaffen?

rustler [ˈrʌslə'] N *(= cattle thief)* Viehdieb(in) *m(f)*

rustling [ˈrʌslɪŋ] **ADJ** *noise, leaves, paper* raschelnd; *skirt* rauschend **N** **N** **a** *(of leaves, paper)* Rascheln *nt*; *(of material)* Rauschen *nt* **b** *(= cattle theft)* Viehdiebstahl *m*

rust: **rust perforation** N Durchrosten *nt*; **rustproof** [ˈrʌstpruːf] **ADJ** rostfrei **VT** einem Rostschutzverfahren unterziehen; **rustproofing** N *(= substance)* Rostschutzmittel *nt*; *(applied to surface etc)* Rostschutz *m*; **rust resistant** ADJ nicht rostend; **rust-through** N Durchrosten *nt*

rusty [ˈrʌstɪ] ADJ *(+er) (lit)* rostig; *(fig) mind, maths, language* eingerostet; *talent* verkümmert; **I'm a bit ~** ich bin etwas aus der Übung; **to get ~** *(lit)* verrosten; *(fig, person)* aus der Übung kommen; **~ brown** rostbraun

rut[1] [rʌt] *(Zool)* **N** Brunft *f*, Brunst *f* **VI** brunften, brunsten; **~ting call** Brunftschrei *m*; **~ting season** Brunftzeit *f*

rut[2] **N** *(in track, path)* Spur *f*, Furche *f*; *(fig: = routine)* Trott *m (inf)*; **to be in a ~** *(fig)* im Trott sein *(inf)*; **to get into a ~** *(fig)* in einen Trott geraten *(inf)*; **to get out of a ~** *(fig)* aus dem Trott herauskommen *(inf)* **VT** furchen

rutabaga [ˌruːtəˈbeɪgə] N *(US)* Steckrübe *f*

ruthenium [ruːˈθiːnɪəm] N *(Chem)* Ruthenium *nt*

ruthless [ˈruːθlɪs] ADJ *person, deed* rücksichtslos; *cuts, treatment, self-analysis* schonungslos; *irony, sarcasm* unbarmherzig, schonungslos; **you'll have to be ~** man muss hart sein; **to be ~ in doing sth** etw ohne jede Rücksicht tun

ruthlessly [ˈruːθlɪslɪ] ADV *suppress, crush* rücksichtslos; *criticize* schonungslos, unbarmherzig; **a ~ ambitious businessman** ein skrupellos ehrgeiziger Geschäftsmann

ruthlessness [ˈruːθlɪsnɪs] N *(of person, deed)* Rücksichtslosigkeit *f*; *(of cuts, treatment)* Schonungslosigkeit *f*; *(of irony, sarcasm)* Unbarmherzigkeit *f*, Schonungslosigkeit *f*

RV **a** *abbr of* **Revised Version** **b** *abbr of* **recreational vehicle** **c** *abbr of* **rat(e)able value**

Rwanda [rʊˈændə] N Ruanda *nt*

Rwandan [rʊˈændən] **N** Ruander(in) *m(f)* **ADJ** ruandisch

rye [raɪ] N *(= grain)* Roggen *m*; *(US inf)* Roggenwhisky *m*, Rye(whisky) *m*; *(= bread)* Roggenbrot *nt*

rye: **rye bread** N Roggenbrot *nt*; **rye whisk(e)y** N Roggen- *or* Ryewhisky *m*

S

S, s [es] N S *nt*, s *nt*

S a *abbr of* **south** S b *abbr of* **Saint** St c *abbr of* **small**

s *(Brit, old) abbr of* **shilling**

's a **he's** *etc* = **he is/has; what's** = **what is/has/does?** b *(genitive)* **John's book** Johns Buch; **my brother's car** das Auto meines Bruders; **at the Browns'** bei den Browns; **at the butcher's** beim Fleischer c **let's** = **let us**

SA a *abbr of* **South Africa** b *abbr of* **South America** c *abbr of* **South Australia** d *abbr of* **Salvation Army**

sab [sæb] N *(Brit inf)* Jagdsaboteur(in) *m(f) (bei Fuchsjagden)*

Sabbatarian [ˌsæbəˈtɛərɪən] N strenger Befürworter des Sonntagsgebots *or (Jewish)* Sabbatgebots

Sabbath [ˈsæbəθ] N Sabbat *m*; *(non-Jewish)* Sonntag *m* → **witch**

sabbatical [səˈbætɪkəl] ADJ a *(Rel)* Sabbat- b *(Univ)* **he is on ~ leave** er hat akademischen Urlaub *or* Forschungsurlaub N *(Univ)* akademischer Urlaub, Forschungsurlaub *m*; **to have a/be on ~** Forschungsurlaub *or* akademischen Urlaub haben

sabbatical term N *(Univ)* ≈ Forschungssemester *nt*

sabbatical year N a *(Rel)* Sabbatjahr *nt* b *(Univ)* Forschungsjahr *nt*

sabbing [ˈsæbɪŋ] N *(Brit inf)* Jagdsabotage *f (bei Fuchsjagden)*

saber N *(US)* = **sabre**

Sabine [ˈsæbaɪn] ADJ sabinisch N Sabiner(in) *m(f)*

sable [ˈseɪbl] N Zobel *m*; *(= fur)* Zobelfell *nt or* -pelz *m*; *(liter, = colour)* Schwarz *nt* ADJ Zobel-; *(liter, = black)* schwarz; **~ coat** Zobelmantel *m*

sabot [ˈsæbəʊ] N Holzschuh *m*

sabotage [ˈsæbətɑːʒ] N Sabotage *f* VT *(lit, fig)* sabotieren

saboteur [ˌsæbəˈtɜːʳ] N Saboteur(in) *m(f)*

sabre, *(US)* **saber** [ˈseɪbəʳ] N Säbel *m*

sabre, *(US)* **saber**: **sabre cut** N Säbelhiebwunde *f*; *(duelling fraternity)* Schmiss *m*; **sabre-rattler** N Säbelrassler(in) *m(f)*; **sabre-rattling** N Säbelrasseln *nt*; **sabre-toothed tiger** N Säbelzahntiger *m*

sac [sæk] N *(Anat)* Sack *m*; *(= pollen sac)* Staubbeutel *m*

saccharin(e) [ˈsækərɪn] N Sa(c)charin *nt*

saccharine [ˈsækəriːn] ADJ Sa(c)charin-; *(fig liter)* zuckersüß; **~ sweetener** Sa(c)charinsüßstoff *m*

sacerdotal [ˌsæsəˈdəʊtl] ADJ priesterlich

sachet [ˈsæʃeɪ] N Beutel *m*; *(of powder)* Päckchen *nt*; *(of shampoo, cream)* Briefchen *nt*; *(= lavender sachet)* Kissen *nt*

sack¹ [sæk] N a Sack *m*; **2 ~s of coal** 2 Säcke *or* Sack Kohlen; **to buy sth by the ~** etw sackweise *or* in Säcken kaufen; **like a ~ of potatoes** *(fig)* wie ein Mehlsack b *(inf: = dismissal)* Entlassung *f*, Rausschmiss *m (inf)*; **to get the ~** rausgeschmissen werden *(inf)*, rausfliegen *(inf)*; **to give sb the ~** jdn rausschmeißen *(inf)*; **it's the ~ for him** er wird rausgeschmissen *(inf)*, er fliegt raus *(inf)* c *(inf: = bed)* **to hit the ~** sich in die Falle *or* Klappe hauen *(sl)* VT a *(= put in sacks)* einsacken b *(inf: = dismiss)* rausschmeißen *(inf)*, entlassen

sack² N *(= pillage)* Plünderung *f* VT plündern

sack³ N *(old)* Sherry *m*

sackbut [ˈsækbʌt] N *(Hist)* Posaune *f*

sackcloth [ˈsækklɒθ] N Sackleinen *nt*; **in ~ and ashes** in Sack und Asche

sackful [ˈsækfʊl] N Sack *m*; **two ~s of potatoes** zwei Sack Kartoffeln

sacking [ˈsækɪŋ] N a *(= material)* Sackleinen *nt* b *(inf: = dismissal)* Entlassung *f*

sack: **sack race** N *(as contest)* Sackhüpfen *nt*; **sack racing** N Sackhüpfen *nt*

sacral [ˈseɪkrəl] ADJ a *(Rel)* sakral b *(Anat)* Kreuzbein-; **~ vertebrae** Kreuzbeinwirbel *pl*

sacrament [ˈsækrəmənt] N Sakrament *nt*; **the (Blessed** *or* **Holy) Sacrament** das heilige Sakrament; **to receive the Holy Sacrament** die heilige Kommunion *or (Protestant)* das heilige Abendmahl empfangen; **the last ~s** die Sterbesakramente *pl*

sacramental [ˌsækrəˈmentl] ADJ *vows, rites, significance* sakramental; **~ wine** Opferwein *m*

sacred [ˈseɪkrɪd] ADJ a *(= holy)* heilig; *building* sakral; **a statue ~ to Venus** eine der Venus geweihte Statue b *(= religious) art, theme, rite* sakral; *music, poetry* geistlich; **~ and profane** geistlich und weltlich c *(= sacrosanct)* **~ duty** heilige Pflicht; **~ to the memory of ...** zum Gedenken *or* Andenken an *(+acc)* ...; **these memories are ~ to me** diese Erinnerungen sind mir heilig; **she saw motherhood as woman's ~ calling** sie sah Mutterschaft als die heilige Berufung einer jeden Frau an; **is nothing ~?** *(inf)* ist denn nichts mehr heilig?

sacred cow N *(lit, fig)* heilige Kuh

Sacred Heart N Herz *nt* Jesu

sacrifice [ˈsækrɪfaɪs] N *(lit, fig)* Opfer *nt*; *(= thing sacrificed also)* Opfergabe *f*; **to make a ~ of sb/sth** jdn/etw opfern *or* zum Opfer bringen; **to make ~s** *(lit, fig)* Opfer bringen; **what a ~ (to make)!** welch ein Opfer!; **the ~ of quality to speed** wenn Qualität der Geschwindigkeit geopfert wird *or* zum Opfer fällt; **to sell sth at a ~** *(inf)* etw mit Verlust verkaufen VT opfern *(sth to sb* jdm etw)

sacrificial [ˌsækrɪˈfɪʃəl] ADJ Opfer-; **~ rite** Opferritus *m*, Opferritual *nt*

sacrificial lamb N Opferlamm *nt*

sacrilege [ˈsækrɪlɪdʒ] N Sakrileg *nt*; *(fig also)* Frevel *m*; **that would be ~** das wäre ein Sakrileg *or* Frevel

sacrilegious [ˌsækrɪˈlɪdʒəs] ADJ *(lit)* gotteslästerlich, sakrilegisch *(geh)*; *(fig)* frevelhaft, frevlerisch

sacristan [ˈsækrɪstən] N Sakristan(in) *m(f)*

sacristy [ˈsækrɪstɪ] N Sakristei *f*

sacrosanct [ˈsækrəʊˌsæŋkt] ADJ *(lit, fig)* sakrosankt

sacrum [ˈsækrəm] N Kreuzbein *nt*

SAD *(Med) abbr of* **seasonal affective disorder**

sad [sæd] ADJ *(+er)* a traurig; *loss* schmerzlich; *disappointment* schlimm; *mistake, lack* bedauerlich; **to feel ~** traurig sein; **he was ~ to see her go** er war betrübt, dass sie wegging; **it makes me ~ to think that ...** der Gedanke betrübt mich, dass ...; **to be ~ at heart** *(liter)* zutiefst betrübt sein *(geh)*; **he left a ~der and wiser man** er ging betrübt und geläutert weg; **the ~ death of our father** der schmerzliche Verlust unseres Vaters; **how ~ for you!** wie schrecklich für Sie!, wie traurig!; **a ~ state of affairs** eine traurige Sache; **it's a ~ business** es ist eine traurige Angelegenheit; **the ~ fact/truth is that ...** die traurige Wahrheit ist, dass ...; **~ to say, ...** *(= regrettably)* bedauerlicherweise ... b *(inf) (= pathetic)* bedauernswert; *(= unfashionable)* uncool *(inf)*; **what ~ people they must be if they have nothing better to do** was für bedauernswerte Menschen, die nichts Besseres zu tun haben; **she's a ~ case** sie ist ein bedauernswerter Fall; **it's pretty ~ stuff for a writer of his ability** für einen Schriftsteller seines Formats ist das traurig

sadden [ˈsædn] VT betrüben

saddle [ˈsædl] N *(also of hill)* Sattel *m*; *(of meat)* Rücken *m*; **to be in the ~** *(lit)* im Sattel sein; *(fig)* im Sattel sitzen VT a *horse* satteln b *(inf)* **to ~ sb/oneself with sb/sth** jdm/sich jdn/etw aufhalsen *(inf)*; **to ~ sb/oneself with responsibilities** jdm/sich Verantwortung aufbürden; **to ~ sb/oneself with doubts** jdn/sich mit Zweifeln belasten; **to be/have been ~d with sb/sth** jdn/etw auf dem Hals *or* am Hals haben *(inf)*; **how did I get ~d with him?** wie kommt es (nur), dass ich ihn am Hals habe?

▶ **saddle up** VT *sep* aufsatteln VI aufsatteln

saddle: **saddle-backed** ADJ *hill* sattelförmig; *pig, gull* mit sattelförmiger Markierung am Rücken; **saddlebag** [ˈsædlbæg] N Satteltasche *f*; **saddlecloth** N Satteldecke *f*; **saddle horse** N Reitpferd *nt*

saddler [ˈsædləʳ] N Sattler(in) *m(f)*

saddle roof N Satteldach *nt*

saddlery [ˈsædlərɪ] N Sattlerei *f*; *(= articles)* Sattelzeug *nt*

saddle: **saddle shoes** PL *(US) Sportschuhe aus hellem Leder mit andersfarbigen Einsatz*; **saddle soap** N *Seife für die Behandlung von Sätteln*; **saddle sore** N wund gescheuerte Stelle; **saddle-sore** ADJ *person* wund geritten; **to get ~** sich wund reiten

Sadducee [ˈsædjʊsiː] N Sadduzäer *m*

sad: **sad-eyed** ADJ traurig blickend *attr*; **sad-faced** ADJ traurig blickend *attr*, mit traurigem Gesichtsausdruck

sadism [ˈseɪdɪzəm] N Sadismus *m*

sadist [ˈseɪdɪst] N Sadist(in) *m(f)*

sadistic ADJ, **sadistically** ADV [səˈdɪstɪk, -əlɪ] sadistisch

sadly [ˈsædlɪ] ADV a *(= sorrowfully)* traurig; **she will be ~ missed** sie wird (uns/ihnen) allen sehr fehlen b *(= unfortunately)* bedauerlicherweise, leider; **~ (enough) he has ...** bedauerlicherweise hat er ...; **~ for the dolphins, there are no regulations to protect them** leider gibt es keine Bestimmungen zum Schutz der Delfine *or* Delphine c *(= regrettably, woefully)* bedauerlicherweise; **he is ~ lacking in any sensitivity** ihm fehlt absolut jegliches Feingefühl; **the house had been ~ neglected** es war traurig, wie vernachlässigt das Haus war; **to be ~ in need of sth** etw dringend benötigen *or* brauchen; **to be ~ mistaken** sich sehr *or* arg täuschen; **if you think you can hide the truth from us, you are ~ mistaken** wenn du glaubst, dass du uns die Wahrheit verheimlichen kannst, hast du dich sehr getäuscht

sadness ['sædnɪs] N Traurigkeit *f*; **our ~ at his death** unsere Trauer über seinen Tod

sadomasochism [,seɪdəʊ'mæsəʊkɪzəm] N Sadomasochismus *m*

sadomasochist [,seɪdəʊ'mæsəʊkɪst] N Sadomasochist(in) *m(f)*

s.a.e. *abbr of* **stamped addressed envelope**

safari [sə'fɑːrɪ] N Safari *f*; **to be/go on ~** eine Safari machen, auf Safari sein/gehen; **to go on ~ to Kenya** nach Kenia auf Safari fahren; **~ jacket** Safarijacke *f*; **~ park** Safaripark *m*

safarist [sə'fɑːrɪst] N Safariteilnehmer(in) *m(f)*

safe[1] [seɪf] N *(for valuables)* Safe *m or nt*, Panzerschrank *m*, Tresor *m*

safe[2] ADJ *(+er)* **a** *(= not in danger)* sicher; *(= out of danger)* in Sicherheit; *(= not injured)* unverletzt; **to be ~ from sb/sth** vor jdm/etw sicher sein; **no girl is ~ with him** bei ihm ist kein Mädchen sicher; **to keep sth ~** etw sicher aufbewahren; **all the passengers/climbers are ~** alle Passagiere/Bergsteiger sind in Sicherheit *or (not injured)* sind unverletzt; **you're not ~ without a seat belt** es ist gefährlich *or* nicht sicher, ohne Gurt zu fahren; **~ journey!** gute Fahrt/Reise!; **~ journey home!** komm gut nach Hause!; **we've found him – is he ~?** wir haben ihn gefunden! – ist ihm etwas passiert?; **thank God you're ~** Gott sei Dank ist dir nichts passiert; **he was ~ at home all the time** er saß die ganze Zeit wohlbehalten zu Hause; **~ and sound** gesund und wohlbehalten; **the patient is ~ now** der Patient ist jetzt außer Gefahr; **my life's not ~ here** ich bin hier meines Lebens nicht sicher; **your reputation is ~** Ihr Ruf ist nicht in Gefahr; **the secret is ~ with me** bei mir ist das Geheimnis gut aufgehoben; **the thieves are now ~ in prison** die Diebe sind jetzt in sicherem Gewahrsam

b *(= not likely to cause harm, not dangerous, not presenting risks)* ungefährlich; *(= stable, secure) building, roof etc* sicher; **not ~** gefährlich; **this car is not ~ to drive** das Auto ist nicht verkehrssicher; **she is not ~ on the roads** sie ist eine Gefahr im Straßenverkehr; **is this beach ~ for bathing?** kann man an diesem Strand gefahrlos *or* ohne Gefahr baden?; **it is ~ to leave it open/tell him** man kann es unbesorgt *or* ohne Weiteres auflassen/es ihm unbesorgt *or* ohne Weiteres erzählen; **is it ~ to touch that/drive so fast/light a fire?** ist es auch nicht gefährlich, das anzufassen/so schnell zu fahren/ein Feuer anzumachen?; **it is ~ to eat/drink** das kann man gefahrlos essen/trinken; **the dog is ~ with children** der Hund tut Kindern nichts; **it's now ~ to turn off your computer** Sie können den Computer jetzt ausschalten

c *(= secure) place, hiding place* sicher; **in a ~ place** an einem sicheren Ort

d *(= reliable) job, contraceptive, driver* sicher; *mountain guide, method, player* zuverlässig, verlässlich; **~ period** sichere *or* ungefährliche Zeit; **to be** *or* **have a ~ pair of hands** sicher und verlässlich sein; **in ~ hands** in sicheren Händen

e *(= not likely to be/go wrong) investment, theory, choice, option* sicher; *policy* vorsichtig, risikolos; *estimate* realistisch; **~ margin** Spielraum *m*; *(Fin also)* Reserve *f*; **it is ~ to assume** *or* **a ~ assumption that …** man kann mit ziemlicher Sicherheit annehmen, dass …; **it's a ~ guess** es ist so gut wie sicher; **they appointed a ~ man as headmaster** sie bestimmten einen gemäßigten Mann als Rektor; **he plays a ~ game (of tennis)** er spielt (Tennis) auf Sicherheit; **I think it's ~ to say …** ich glaube, man kann wohl *or* ruhig sagen …; **is it ~ to generalize?** kann man das ohne Weiteres verallgemeinern?; **is it ~ to draw that conclusion?** kann man diesen Schluss so ohne Weiteres ziehen?; **to be ~ in the knowledge that …** sich sicher fühlen, dass …; **do you feel ~ just taking on three extra staff?** haben Sie keine Bedenken, wenn Sie nur drei extra Leute einstellen?; **just to be ~** *or* **on the ~ side** um ganz sicher zu sein, um sicherzugehen; **the ~st thing (to do) would be to wait here for her** das Sicherste wäre, hier auf sie zu warten; **it is a ~ bet that …** man kann darauf wetten, dass …; **to follow sb at a ~ distance** jdm in sicherem Abstand folgen; **better ~ than sorry** Vorsicht ist besser als Nachsicht *(Prov)*

f *(= certain)* **he is ~ to win/get the job** er wird sicher gewinnen/die Stelle sicher bekommen

safe: **safe area** N *(Pol)* Sicherheitszone *f*, Schutzzone *f*; **safe-blower**, **safe-breaker** N Schränker(in) *m(f) (sl)*, Safeknacker(in) *m(f) (inf)*; **safe-conduct** N freies *or* sicheres Geleit; *(= document)* Geleitbrief *m*; **safe-cracker** N *(inf)* Schränker(in) *m(f) (sl)*, Safeknacker(in) *m(f) (inf)*; **safe-deposit** N Tresorraum *m*; **safe-deposit box** N Banksafe *m or nt*; **safeguard** N Schutz *m*; **as a ~ against** zum Schutz gegen; **double-check these figures as a ~** überprüfen Sie diese Zahlen zur Sicherheit noch einmal VT schützen *(against* vor *+dat)*; *interests* wahrnehmen VI **to ~ against sth** sich gegen etw absichern; **safe haven** N *(fig)* sicherer Zufluchtsort *or* Hafen; **safe house** N Zufluchtsort *m*; *(police term for house used by terrorists)* konspirative Wohnung; **safe keeping** N sichere Verwahrung; **to give sb sth for ~** jdm etw zur (sicheren) Aufbewahrung geben; **safelight** N *(Phot)* Dunkelkammerlicht *nt*

safely ['seɪflɪ] ADV *(= unharmed) arrive, get home* wohlbehalten, heil; *(= without problems also)* sicher, gut; *(= without running risks)* unbesorgt, gefahrlos; *drive* vorsichtig; *(= solidly, firmly)* sicher, fest; *(= not dangerously)* ungefährlich; **drive ~!** fahr vorsichtig!; **she held the door open until we were all ~ inside** sie hielt die Tür auf, bis wir alle sicher drinnen waren; **we can ~ estimate that …** wir können mit einiger Sicherheit annehmen, dass …; **I think I can ~ say/claim/assume …** ich glaube, ich kann wohl *or* ruhig sagen/behaupten/annehmen …; **I got ~ through the first interview** ich bin gut *or* heil durch das erste Interview gekommen; **the election is now ~ out of the way** die Wahlen haben wir jetzt zum Glück hinter uns; **money ~ deposited in the bank** sicher auf der Bank deponiertes Geld; **~ invested** sicher angelegt; **to put sth away ~** etw an einem sicheren Ort verwahren; **he put it ~ away in a drawer** er verwahrte es sicher in einer Schublade; **put it ~ out of the reach of the children** bringen Sie es vor den Kindern in Sicherheit; **he's ~ locked away in prison** er sitzt hinter Schloss und Riegel; **once the children are ~ tucked up in bed** wenn die Kinder erst mal im Bett sind; **he was ~ tucked up in bed** er lag wohlvermummt im Bett; **you can now ~ turn off your computer** Sie können den Computer jetzt ausschalten

safe mode N *(Comput)* abgesicherter Modus

safeness ['seɪfnɪs] N Sicherheit *f*

safe: **safe passage** N sicheres Geleit; **safe seat** N *(Pol)* ein sicherer Sitz; **safe sex** N Safer Sex *m*

safety ['seɪftɪ] N Sicherheit *f*; **in a place of ~** an einem sicheren Ort; **for ~'s sake** aus Sicherheitsgründen; **for his (own) ~** zu seiner (eigenen) Sicherheit; **to walk the streets in ~** unbehelligt ausgehen; **with complete ~** vollkommen sicher; **I can say with ~ that …** ich kann mit Sicherheit behaupten, dass …; **to play for ~** *(Sport)* auf Sicherheit spielen; *(fig)* sichergehen; **(there's) ~ in numbers** zu mehreren ist man sicherer; **to reach ~** in Sicherheit gelangen; **when we reached the ~ of the opposite bank** als wir sicher das andere Ufer erreicht hatten; **to leap to ~** sich in Sicherheit bringen; **to seek ~ abroad** sich ins Ausland in Sicherheit bringen; **the government must ensure the ~ of nuclear power plants** die Regierung muss die Betriebssicherheit von Atomkraftwerken gewährleisten

safety: **safety belt** N Sicherheitsgurt *m*; **safety binding** N *(Ski)* Sicherheitsbindung *f*; **safety buoy** N *(Naut)* Rettungsboje *f*; **safety car** N *(Motor Racing)* Sicherheitsauto *nt*; **safety catch** N *(on gun)* (Abzugs)sicherung *f*, Sicherungsbügel *m*; **was the ~ on/off?** war das Gewehr gesichert/entsichert?; **safety chain** N Sicherheitskette *f*; **safety curtain** N *(Theat)* eiserner Vorhang; **safety expert** N Sicherheitsexperte *m*, Sicherheitsexpertin *f*; **safety first** N **to opt for ~** der Sicherheit den Vorrang geben; **~ campaign** Unfallverhütungskampagne *f*; **"safety first"** *(as slogan)* „Sicherheit geht vor"; **safety glass** N Sicherheitsglas *nt*; **safety harness** N Sicherheitsgurt *m*; **safety island** N *(US Aut)* Verkehrsinsel *f*; **safety lamp** N Grubenlampe *f*; **safety lock** N Sicherheitsschloss *nt*; **safety margin** N Sicherheitsmarge *f*; **safety match** N Sicherheitszündholz *nt*; **safety measure** N Sicherheitsmaßnahme *f*; **safety net** N Sprung- *or* Sicherheitsnetz *nt*; **safety pin** N Sicherheitsnadel *f*; **safety precaution** N Sicherheitsvorkehrung *f*; **safety razor** N Rasierapparat *m*, Nassrasierer *m (inf)*; **safety rope** N Sicherungsseil *nt*; **safety shot** N *(Snooker)* Safety *m*; **safety standards** PL Sicherheitsnormen *pl*; **safety switch** N *(Elec etc)* Sicherheitsschalter *m*; **safety technology** N Sicherheitstechnik *f*; **safety valve** N Sicherheitsventil *nt*; *(fig)* Ventil *nt*

saffron ['sæfrən] N Safran *m*; *(= colour)* Safrangelb *nt* ADJ Safran-; *(colour)* safrangelb; **~ rice** Safranreis *m*

sag [sæg] N **there's a bit of a ~ in the bed/ceiling** das Bett/die Decke hängt etwas durch; **the ~ of her shoulders** ihre herabhängenden Schultern VI absacken; *(in the middle)* durchhängen; *(shoulders)* herabhängen; *(breasts)* schlaff herunterhängen; *(production, rate)* zurückgehen; *(price, spirit)* sinken; *(conversation)* abflauen; **don't ~, stand up straight** steh nicht so schlaff da *(inf)*, stell dich gerade hin

saga ['sɑːgə] N Saga *f*; *(= novel also)* Generationsroman *m*; *(fig)* Geschichte *f*, Story *f (inf)*

sagacious ADJ, **sagaciously** ADV [sə'geɪʃəs, -lɪ] weise, klug

sagacity [sə'gæsɪtɪ] N Weisheit *f*, Klugheit *f*

sage[1] [seɪdʒ] N Weise(r) *m* ADJ *(+er)* weise

sage[2] N *(Bot)* Salbei *m*

sage green N Graugrün *nt*

sage-green ['seɪdʒ'griːn] ADJ graugrün

sagely ['seɪdʒlɪ] ADV weise

sageness ['seɪdʒnɪs] N Weisheit *f*

sagging ['sægɪŋ] ADJ **a** *ceiling, beam, rope* durchhängend; *armchair* durchgesessen **b** *skin* schlaff; **~ stomach/bosom/cheeks** Hängebauch *m*/-busen *m*/-backen *pl* **c** *(fig) morale* sinkend; **a drink will revive his ~ spirits** ein Drink wird seine Stimmung wieder heben

saggy ['sægɪ] *(+er)* ADJ *mattress* durchgelegen; *sofa* durchgesessen; *garment* ausgebeult; *bottom, breasts* schlaff; **if my breasts got ~** wenn ich einen Hängebusen bekäme; **~ breasts/cheeks** Hängebusen *m*/-backen *pl*

Sagittarian [,sædʒɪ'teərɪən] N Schütze *m* ADJ des Schützen

Sagittarius [,sædʒɪ'teərɪəs] N Schütze *m*; **he's (a) ~** er ist Schütze

sago ['seɪgəʊ] N Sago *m*

Sahara [sə'hɑːrə] N Sahara *f*; **the ~ Desert** die (Wüste) Sahara

sahib ['sɑːhɪb] N Sahib *m*

said [sed] *pret, ptp of* **say** ADJ *(form)* besagt

sail [seɪl] N **a** Segel *nt*; *(of windmill)* Flügel *m*; **under ~** mit aufgezogenen Segeln; **in** *or* **under full ~** mit vollen Segeln; **with all ~s set** mit gesetzten Segeln; **to make ~** *(= hoist)* Segel setzen; **to set** *or* **make ~ (for …)** los- *or* abfahren (nach …); *(with sailing boat)* absegeln (nach …); **he set ~ from Dover** er fuhr von Dover los;

(with sailing boat) er segelte von Dover ab *or* los **b** *(= trip)* Fahrt *f*; **it's 3 days' ~ from here** von hier aus fährt *or (in yacht)* segelt man 3 Tage; **to go for a ~** segeln gehen; **to take sb for a ~** mit jdm segeln gehen; **have you ever had a ~ in his yacht?** sind Sie schon einmal auf seiner Jacht gefahren *or* gesegelt?
c *(= boat)* (Segel)schiff *nt*; *(small)* (Segel)boot *nt*; **20 ~** 20 Schiffe/Boote; **there was not a ~ in sight** kein einziges Schiff war zu sehen
VT *ship* segeln mit; *liner etc* steuern; **they ~ed the ship to Cadiz** sie segelten nach Cadiz; **he ~s his own yacht** er hat eine eigene Jacht; **to ~ the Atlantic** den Atlantik durchkreuzen; **to ~ the seas** die Meere befahren
VI **a** *(Naut)* fahren; *(with yacht)* segeln; **are you flying? – no, ~ing** fliegen Sie? – nein, ich fahre mit dem Schiff; **I went ~ing for a week** ich ging eine Woche segeln; **to ~ round the world** um die Welt segeln, die Erde umsegeln; **to ~ round a headland** eine Landzunge umfahren/umsegeln
b *(= leave) (for* nach) abfahren; *(yacht, in yacht)* absegeln; **passengers ~ing for New York** Passagiere nach New York
c *(fig) (glider, swan etc)* gleiten; *(moon, clouds)* ziehen; *(ball, object)* fliegen; **the plate ~ed past my head** der Teller segelte an meinem Kopf vorbei; **she ~ed past/out of the room** sie rauschte vorbei/aus dem Zimmer *(inf)*; **she ~ed into the room** sie kam ins Zimmer gerauscht *(inf)*; **she ~ed through all her exams** sie schaffte alle Prüfungen spielend *or* mit Leichtigkeit; **the week just ~ed by** *(inf)* die Woche verging wie im Flug

▶ **sail in** VI *(inf: = enter argument)* sich einschalten

▶ **sail into** VI *+prep obj (inf) person* anfahren; *discussion* sich einschalten in *(+acc)*

sail: **sailable** [ˈseɪləbl] ADJ *(Naut)* **a** *canal, river etc* schiffbar, befahrbar **b** *boat* segelfertig; **sailboard** **N** Windsurfbrett *nt* **VI** windsurfen; **sailboarder** N Windsurfer(in) *m(f)*; **sailboarding** N Windsurfen *nt*; **sailboat** N *(US)* Segelboot *nt*; **sailcloth** N Segeltuch *nt*; **sailfish** N Fächerfisch *m*

sailing [ˈseɪlɪŋ] N **a** Segeln *nt*; *(as sport)* Segeln *nt*, Segelsport *m* **b** *(= departure)* **when is the next ~ for Arran?** wann fährt das nächste Schiff nach Arran? → **plain**

sailing: **sailing boat** N *(Brit)* Segelboot *nt*; **sailing date** N Abfahrtstermin *m*; **sailing school** N Segelschule *f*; **sailing ship** N Segelschiff *nt*; **sailing time** N Abfahrtszeit *f*; **sailing vessel** N Segelschiff *nt*; **sailing yacht** [ˈseɪlɪŋˌjɔt] N Segeljacht *f*

sail maker N Segelmacher(in) *m(f)*

sailor [ˈseɪləˈ] N **a** Seemann *m*; *(in navy)* Matrose *m*, Matrosin *f*; *(= sportsman)* Segler(in) *m(f)*; **~ suit** Matrosenanzug *m*; **hello ~** *(hum)* hallo Süßer **b** *(fig)* **to be a good/bad ~** seefest/nicht seefest sein

sailplane [ˈseɪlpleɪn] N Segelflugzeug *nt*

saint [seɪnt] ✪ 23.2 N **a** Heilige(r) *mf* **b** *(before name) (abbr* **St** *[snt])* **St John** der heilige Johannes, Sankt Johannes, St. Johannes; **St Francis** der heilige Franziskus; **St Mark's (Church)** die Markuskirche **c** *(fig)* Heilige(r) *mf*; **she is a ~ to put up with that** sie muss ja eine Engelsgeduld haben, dass sie sich das gefallen lässt

sainted [ˈseɪntɪd] ADJ heiliggesprochen; **my ~ aunt!** *(inf)* heiliger Strohsack! *(inf)*, heiliger Bimbam! *(inf)*

Saint Elmo's fire [sntˈelməʊzˌfaɪəˈ] N *(Met)* Elmsfeuer *nt*

sainthood [ˈseɪnthʊd] N Heiligkeit *f*; **martyrs who were elevated to ~** Märtyrer, die in die Gemeinschaft der Heiligen aufgenommen wurden

saintliness [ˈseɪntlɪnɪs] N Heiligkeit *f*; *(fig pej, of person)* frömmlerisches Wesen; **the ~ of his smile** sein lammfrommes Lächeln

saintly [ˈseɪntlɪ] ADJ *(+er) image, figure, life* heilig; *(fig pej) person* frömmlerisch; *smile* lammfromm; **he stood there with a ~ look on his face** *(lit)* er hatte einen verklärten Gesichtsausdruck; *(iro)* er sah aus, als ob er kein Wässerchen trüben könnte

saint's day [ˈseɪntsdeɪ] N Heiligenfest *nt*, Tag *m* des/der Heiligen; **when is your ~?** wann ist Ihr Namenstag?

Saint Valentine's Day [sntˈvæləntaɪnzˌdeɪ] N Valentinstag *m (14. Februar)*

saith [seθ] *(old)* = **says**

sake¹ [seɪk] N **for the ~ of ...** um *(+gen)* ... willen; **for my ~** meinetwegen; *(= to please me)* mir zuliebe; **for your own ~** dir selbst zuliebe; **for your family's ~** um Ihrer Familie willen, Ihrer Familie wegen; **for the ~ of your career/my health** wegen deiner Karriere/meiner Gesundheit, deiner Karriere/meiner Gesundheit zuliebe; **for heaven's** *or* **Christ's ~!** *(inf)* um Gottes willen!; **for heaven's** *or* **Christ's ~ shut up** *(inf)* nun halt doch endlich die Klappe *(inf)*; **for old times' ~** in Erinnerung an alte Zeiten; **for the ~ of those who ...** für diejenigen, die ...; **for whose ~ is the writer writing, his own or the public's?** für wen schreibt der Schriftsteller, (für) sich selbst oder den Leser?; **I'd do anything for your ~** für dich tue ich alles; *(= to keep you happy)* dir zuliebe tue ich alles; **I did it just for the ~ of having a new experience** ich habe es nur getan, um eine neue Erfahrung zu machen; **and all for the ~ of a few pounds** und alles wegen ein paar Pfund; **to talk for talking's ~** reden, nur damit etwas gesagt wird; **I do the job for its own ~** ich mache die Arbeit um ihrer selbst willen *or* ihrer selbst wegen

sake², **saki** [ˈsɑːkɪ] N *(= drink)* Sake *m*

sal *abbr of* **salary** Geh.

salaam [səˈlɑːm] **N, INTERJ** Salem *m* **VI** sich mit Salem begrüßen

salable *etc* ADJ *(US)* = **saleable** *etc*

salacious [səˈleɪʃəs] ADJ schlüpfrig; *picture* aufreizend; *chuckle* anzüglich

salaciousness [səˈleɪʃəsnɪs] N Schlüpfrigkeit *f*; *(of picture)* aufreizende Darstellung; *(of chuckle)* Anzüglichkeit *f*

salad [ˈsæləd] N Salat *m*

salad: **salad bar** N Salatbüffet *nt*; **salad bowl** N Salatschüssel *f*; **salad cream** N ≈ Mayonnaise *f*, ≈ Majonäse *f*; **salad days** PL unschuldige Jugendtage *pl*; **in the ~ of his youth** als er noch jung und unschuldig war; **salad dressing** N Salatsoße *f*; **lettuce with ~** angemachter Salat; **salad oil** N Salatöl *nt*; **salad spinner** N *(Cook)* Salatschleuder *f*

salamander [ˈsæləˌmændəˈ] N Salamander *m*; *(Myth)* Feuergeist *m*

salami [səˈlɑːmɪ] N Salami *f*

salami tactics PL *(inf)* Salamitaktik *f (inf)*

sal ammoniac [ˌsæləˈməʊnɪæk] N Ammoniumsalz *nt*, Salmiak *m*

salaried [ˈsælərɪd] ADJ **~ post** Angestelltenposten *m*; **~ employee** Gehaltsempfänger(in) *m(f)*; **~ staff** Gehaltsempfänger *pl*

salary [ˈsælərɪ] ✪ 19.2 N Gehalt *nt*; **he earns a good ~** er hat ein gutes Gehalt; **what is his ~?** wie hoch ist sein Gehalt?

salary: **salary account** N Gehaltskonto *nt*; **salary earner** N Gehaltsempfänger(in) *m(f)*; **salary increase** N Gehaltserhöhung *f*; **salary package** N Gehalt *nt (einschließlich Sonderleistungen)*, Gehaltspaket *nt*; **salary range** N Gehaltsrahmen *m*, Gehaltsspanne *f*; **salary scale** N Gehaltsskala *f*

sale [seɪl] N **a** *(= selling)* Verkauf *m*; **for ~** zu verkaufen; **to put sth up for ~** etw zum Verkauf anbieten; **is it up for ~?** steht es zum Verkauf?; **not for ~** nicht verkäuflich; **going cheap for a quick ~** umständehalber billig abzugeben; **to be on ~** verkauft werden; **on ~ at all bookshops** in allen Buchhandlungen erhältlich; **on a ~ or return basis** auf Kommission(sbasis)
b *(instance)* Geschäft *nt*; *(of insurance, bulk order)* Abschluss *m*; **~s** *pl (= turnover)* der Absatz; **how many ~s have you made?** wie viel (Stück) haben Sie verkauft?; *(of insurance etc)* wie viele Abschlüsse haben Sie gemacht?; **we've made no ~ to China** mit China haben wir keine Geschäfte abgeschlossen; **"no ~"** *(on till)* ≈ Nullbon
c **sales** SING *(= department)* Verkaufsabteilung *f* **d** *(at reduced prices)* Rabattaktion *f*, Ausverkauf *m*; *(at end of season)* Schlussverkauf *m*; *(= clearance sale)* Räumungsverkauf *m*; **to go to the ~s** zum Ausverkauf gehen; **they've got a ~ on** da ist eine Rabattaktion; **in the ~, on ~** *(US)* im (Sonder)angebot; **to buy in** *or* **at the ~s** im Ausverkauf kaufen
e *(= auction, selling off)* Auktion *f*; **~ of work** Basar *m*

saleability, *(US)* **salability** [ˈseɪləbɪlɪtɪ] N **to ascertain the ~ of a product** feststellen, wie gut sich ein Produkt verkauft

saleable, *(US)* **salable** [ˈseɪləbl] ADJ *(= marketable)* absatzfähig; *skill* vermarktbar; *artist, idea* gut verkäuflich; *(= in saleable condition)* verkäuflich; **not in a ~ condition** nicht zum Verkauf geeignet

sale: **sale and leaseback** N Verkauf *m* mit Rückmiete; **sale price** N Ausverkaufspreis *m*; **saleroom** N Auktionsraum *m*

sales: **sales check** N Kassenbeleg *m*; **sales clerk** N *(US)* Verkäufer(in) *m(f)*; **sales conference** N Vertreterkonferenz *f*; **sales department** N Verkaufsabteilung *f*; **sales director** N Verkaufsdirektor(in) *m(f)*; **sales drive** N Verkaufskampagne *f*; **sales executive** N Verkaufsleiter(in) *m(f)*; **sales figures** PL Verkaufs- *or* Absatzziffern *pl*; **sales force** N Verkäufer *pl*; *(= sales reps)* Vertreter *pl*; **salesgirl**, **saleslady** N Verkäuferin *f*; **salesman** N Verkäufer *m*; *(= representative)* Vertreter *m*; **sales manager** N Verkaufsleiter(in) *m(f)*

salesmanship [ˈseɪlzmənʃɪp] N Verkaufstechnik *f*

sales: **salespeople** PL Verkaufspersonal *nt*; **salesperson** N Verkäufer(in) *m(f)*; **sales pitch** N Verkaufstechnik *or* -masche *(inf) f*; **to make one's ~** seine Ware anpreisen; *(fig inf)* seine Ideen verkaufen *or* anpreisen; **sales promotion** N Verkaufsförderung *f*; **sales rep** N *(inf)*, **sales representative** N Vertreter(in) *m(f)*; **sales resistance** N Kaufunlust *f*; **to meet (with) ~** auf Absatzschwierigkeiten stoßen; **sales revenue** N Verkaufserlös *m*; **salesroom** N = **saleroom**; **sales slip** N Kassenzettel *m*, Bon *m*; *(received prior to payment)* Kaufbeleg *m*; **sales talk** N Verkaufsgespräch *nt*; **his ~ won me over** die Art, wie er die Ware angepriesen hat, hat mich überzeugt; **that's just ~** er/sie macht nur Reklame; **sales target** N Verkaufsziel *nt*; **sales tax** N *(US)* Verkaufssteuer *f*; **sales volume** N Umsatz *m*; **saleswoman** N Verkäuferin *f*; *(= representative)* Vertreterin *f*

salicylic acid [ˌsælɪsɪlɪkˈæsɪd] N *(Chem)* Salizylsäure *f*

salient [ˈseɪlɪənt] ADJ *(lit)* hervorstehend; *(fig)* hervorstechend; **the ~ points of his argument** die Hauptpunkte *pl* seiner Argumentation

salina [səˈlaɪnə] N Salzsee *m*, Salzpfanne *f*, Salzsumpf *m*

saline [ˈseɪlaɪn] ADJ salzig

saline: **saline drip** N *(Med: = device)* Infusionsapparat *m or* Tropf *m (inf)* mit Kochsalzlösung; *(= liquid)* Kochsalzlösung *f*; **saline solution** N Salzlösung *f*

salinity [səˈlɪnɪtɪ] N Salzigkeit *f*; *(= content)* Salzgehalt *m*

saliva [səˈlaɪvə] N Speichel *m*

salivary gland [səˈlaɪvərɪˈglænd] N Speicheldrüse *f*

salivate [ˈsælɪveɪt] VI Speichel produzieren; *(animal)* geifern; *(old people, baby)* sabbern; *(with lust)* lüstern geifern; **to ~ over sth** *(fig)* von etw schwärmen

salivation [ˌsælɪˈveɪʃən] N Speichelfluss *m*

sallow [ˈsæləʊ] ADJ bleich, teigig; *colour* fahl

sallowness ['sæləʊnɪs] N Blässe *f*, Fahlheit *f*

sally ['sælɪ] **N** Ausbruch *m*; *(of troops)* Ausfall *m*; **to make a ~** *(troops)* einen Ausfall machen; *(fig: verbally)* eine Tirade loslassen; **I made a ~ into town** ich habe einen Trip in die Stadt gemacht **VI** *(old, hum)* **to ~ forth** *(Mil)* einen Ausfall machen; *(= rush out)* hinausstürmen; *(= set out)* sich aufmachen

Sally Army ['sælɪ'ɑːmɪ] N *(Brit inf)* = **Salvation Army**

salmon ['sæmən] **N** *pl* - Lachs *m*, Salm *m*; *(= colour)* Lachs(rosa) *nt* **ADJ** *(colour)* lachs(farben)

salmonella [ˌsælmə'nelə] N *(also* **salmonella poisoning***)* Salmonellenvergiftung *f*

salmon: **salmon leap** N Lachssprung *m*; *(man-made)* Lachsleiter *or* -treppe *f*; **salmon pink** N Lachsrosa *nt*; **salmon-pink** ADJ lachsrosa; **salmon river** N *Fluss in dem Lachse vorkommen*; **salmon trout** N Lachsforelle *f*

salon ['sælɒn] N *(all senses)* Salon *m*

saloon [sə'luːn] N **a** Saal *m*; *(Naut)* Salon *m* **b** *(Brit Aut)* Limousine *f*; *(in motor racing)* Tourenwagen *m* **c** *(US dated) (= bar)* Wirtschaft *f*; *(in Westerns)* Saloon *m*

saloon: **saloon bar** N *(Brit) vornehmerer Teil eines Lokals*; **saloon car** N *(Brit)* Limousine *f*

Salop ['sæləp] *abbr of* **Shropshire**

salopettes [ˌsælə'pets] PL *(Ski)* Lifthose *f*

salsa ['sælsə] N **a** *(Mus)* Salsa *m* **b** *(Cook)* Salsasoße *f*

salsify ['sælsɪfɪ] N Schwarzwurzel *f*

SALT [sɔːlt] *abbr of* **Strategic Arms Limitation Treaty** SALT

salt [sɔːlt] **N** **a** *(Cook, Chem)* Salz *nt*; *(for icy roads)* Streusalz *nt*; **~ of the earth** *(fig)* Salz der Erde; **to be worth one's ~** *(fig)* etwas taugen; **to take sth with a pinch** *(Brit) or* **grain** *(US)* **of ~** *(fig)* etw nicht ganz für bare Münze *or* nicht ganz so wörtlich nehmen; **to rub ~ into sb's wounds** *(fig)* Salz in jds Wunde streuen *or* reiben → **old salt**

b **salts** **PL** *(= smelling salts)* Riechsalz *nt*; *(for bowels)* salinisches Abführmittel; **that drink went through me like a dose of ~s** *(inf)* das Getränk hat mich richtig durchgeputzt *(inf)*; **the new director went through the board like a dose of ~s** *(inf)* der neue Direktor hat im Vorstand mit eisernem Besen ausgekehrt

c *(fig: = zest, flavour)* Würze *f*

ADJ **a** *(= salty) air* salzig; **~ water** Salzwasser *nt*

b *(= salted) butter, meat, fish* gesalzen; **it's very ~** es ist sehr salzig

VT **a** *(= cure)* einsalzen; *(= flavour)* salzen **b** *(= grit) road* mit Salz streuen

► **salt away** VT *sep (inf) money* auf die hohe Kante legen *(inf)*

saltcellar ['sɔːltselə'] N Salzfässchen *nt*; *(= shaker)* Salzstreuer *m*

salted ['sɔːltɪd] ADJ *nuts, butter, meat, fish* gesalzen; **highly ~** stark gesalzen; **lightly** *or* **slightly ~ butter** leicht gesalzene Butter; **~ herrings** Salzheringe *pl*

salt: **salt flats** PL Salztonebene *f*; **salt-free** ADJ salzlos

saltiness ['sɔːltɪnɪs] N Salzigkeit *f*

salt: **salt lake** N Salzsee *m*; **salt lick** N Salzlecke *f*; **salt marsh** N Salzsumpf *m*; **salt mine** N Salzbergwerk *nt*

saltness ['sɔːltnɪs] N Salzigkeit *f*

salt: **saltpan** N Salzpfanne *f*; **saltpetre**, *(US)* **saltpeter** [ˌsɔːlt'piːtə'] N Salpeter *m*; **salt shaker** N Salzstreuer *m*; **salt tax** N Salzsteuer *f*; **salt water** N Salzwasser *nt*; **saltwater** ADJ **~ fish** Meeresfisch *m*; **~ lake** Salzsee *m*; **saltworks** N *sing or pl* Saline *f*

salty ['sɔːltɪ] ADJ *(+er)* **a** salzig; **~ water** Salzwasser *nt* **b** *(dated fig) language* gesalzen; *story* scharf, gesalzen

salubrious [sə'luːbrɪəs] ADJ **a** *(form) air, climate* gesund **b** *(inf) district, friends* ersprießlich; **not a very ~ pub** eine recht zweifelhafte Kneipe

salubriousness [sə'luːbrɪəsnɪs], **salubrity** [sə'luːbrɪtɪ] N Heilsamkeit *f*, Bekömmlichkeit *f*, Zuträglichkeit *f*

salutary ['sæljʊtərɪ] ADJ **a** *(= healthy)* gesund **b** *(= beneficial) advice* nützlich; *experience* heilsam, lehrreich; *effect* günstig; **a ~ reminder that ...** eine heilsame *or* lehrreiche Erinnerung daran, dass ...

salutation [ˌsæljʊ'teɪʃən] N Begrüßung *f*; *(in letters)* Anrede *f*; **he raised his hand in ~** er hob die Hand zum Gruß

salutatorian [səluːtə'tɔːrɪən] N *(US) Student, der die Begrüßungsrede hält*

salutatory [sə'luːtətərɪ] ADJ Begrüßungs-; **~ oration** Begrüßungsansprache *f*

salute [sə'luːt] **N** Gruß *m*; *(of guns)* Salut *m*; **he raised his hand in ~** er hob seine Hand zum Gruß; **to raise one's glass in ~** sein Glas zu einem Toast hochheben; **flags were raised in ~** zur Begrüßung wurden die Fahnen gehisst; **to stand at the ~** salutieren; **a 21-gun ~** 21 Salutschüsse; **to take the ~** die Parade abnehmen; **he gave a smart ~** er salutierte zackig

VT *(Mil) flag etc* grüßen; *person also* salutieren vor *(+dat)*; *(fig liter: = welcome)* begrüßen; *courage* bewundern, den Hut ziehen vor *(+dat)*; **we ~ the glorious dead** wir gedenken der gefallenen Helden

VI *(Mil)* salutieren, grüßen

salutories [sə'luːtərɪz] PL *(US)* Begrüßungsrede *f (bei Semesterabschluss und Zeugnisüberreichung)*

salvage ['sælvɪdʒ] **N** *(= act)* Bergung *f*; *(= objects)* Bergungsgut *nt*; *(= payment)* Bergelohn *m*; *(= proceeds from salvaged goods)* Wert *m* der geretteten Waren **VT** *(from wreck, building)* bergen *(from* aus); *(fig)* retten *(from* von); **to ~ sth from the fire** etw aus den Flammen retten; **to ~ one's pride/reputation** sich *(dat)* seinen Stolz/Ruf erhalten können; **~ what you can** *(lit, fig)* rettet, was ihr retten könnt; **a few happy memories can be ~d from the marriage** ein paar glückliche Erinnerungen können aus den Trümmern der Ehe geborgen werden

salvage: **salvage operation** N Bergungsaktion *f*; *(fig)* Rettungsaktion *f*; **salvage tug** N Bergungsschlepper *m*; **salvage vessel** N Bergungsschiff *nt*

salvation [sæl'veɪʃən] N *(= act of saving)* Rettung *f*; *(= state of being saved also, esp Rel)* Heil *nt*; **he found ~ in the Church** er fand sein Heil in der Kirche; **he found ~ in his work** die Arbeit war seine Rettung; **the path to ~** der Weg des Heils; **you were/that was my ~** du warst/das war meine Rettung; **everyone has to work out his own ~** jeder muss für sein eigenes Heil sorgen

Salvation Army **N** Heilsarmee *f* **ATTR** *hostel, band, meeting* der Heilsarmee

salvationist [sæl'veɪʃənɪst] N Heilsprediger(in) *m(f)*; *(also* **Salvationist**: *= of Salvation Army)* Angehörige(r) *mf* der Heilsarmee

salve[1] [sælv] VT *(liter)* = **salvage**

salve[2] **N** Salbe *f*; *(fig liter)* Balsam *m*; **as a ~ for his conscience** um sein Gewissen zu beruhigen **VT** *(fig) conscience* beruhigen

salver ['sælvə'] N Tablett *nt*

salvo ['sælvəʊ] N *(of guns, fig)* Salve *f*; **a ~ of applause** ein Beifallssturm *m*

sal volatile [ˌsælvə'lætəlɪ] N Riechsalz *nt*

Samaritan [sə'mærɪtən] N Samariter(in) *m(f)*; **good ~** *(lit, fig)* barmherziger Samariter

samarium [sə'meərɪəm] N *(Chem)* Samarium *nt*

samba ['sæmbə] **N** Samba *f or m* **VI** Samba tanzen

sambo ['sæmbəʊ] N *(pej)* Kaffer *m*

same [seɪm] ✪ 5.4, 26.2, 26.3 **ADJ** **the ~ ...** der/die/das gleiche ...; *(= one and the same)* der-/die-/dasselbe; **they were both wearing the ~ dress** sie hatten beide das gleiche Kleid an; **they both live in the ~ house** sie wohnen beide in demselben *or* im selben Haus; **they are all the ~** sie sind alle gleich; **that's the ~ tie as I've got** so eine Krawatte habe ich auch, ich habe die gleiche Krawatte; **she just wasn't the ~ person** sie war ein anderer Mensch; **it's the ~ thing** das ist das Gleiche; **see you tomorrow, ~ time ~ place** bis morgen, gleicher Ort, gleiche Zeit *or* Ort und Zeit wie gehabt; **we sat at the ~ table as usual** wir saßen an unserem üblichen Tisch; **how are you? – ~ as usual** wie gehts? – wie immer; **I've made the ~ mistake myself** den Fehler habe ich auch gemacht, ich habe den gleichen Fehler gemacht; **this ~ person** eben dieser Mensch; *(Jur)* besagte Person; **she was killed with this ~ knife** sie wurde mit eben *or* genau diesem Messer erstochen; **he is the ~ age as his wife** er ist (genau) so alt wie seine Frau; **it happened the ~ day** es ist am gleichen *or* selben Tag passiert; **if you can do the two jobs in the ~ day** wenn sie die beiden Arbeiten an einem Tag erledigen können; **(on) the very ~ day** genau am gleichen Tag; **the ~ old story** *(fig)* die altbekannte Geschichte; **it's the ~ old rubbish every night on TV** *(inf)* es gibt jeden Abend den gleichen Mist im Fernsehen *(inf)*; **~ difference** *(inf)* was ist der Unterschied?; **in the ~ way** (genau) gleich; *(= by the same token)* ebenso → **time**

PRON **a** **the ~** der/die/das Gleiche, der-/die-/dasselbe; **I would do the ~ for you** ich würde das Gleiche für dich tun; **and I would do the ~ again** und ich würde es wieder tun; **he left and I did the ~** er ist gegangen, und ich auch *or* ebenfalls; **they are one and the ~** das ist doch dasselbe; *(people)* das ist doch ein und der-/dieselbe; **the (very) ~** *(form: = yes)* genau; **is he that artist from New Orleans?– the very ~** ist das dieser Künstler aus New Orleans?– genau der; **another drink? – thanks, (the) ~ again** noch etwas zu trinken? – ja bitte, das Gleiche noch mal; **~ again, Joe** und noch einen, Joe; **she's much the ~** sie hat sich kaum geändert; *(in health)* es geht ihr kaum besser; **he will never be the ~ again** er wird niemals mehr derselbe sein; **you're not the ~ any more** du bist nicht mehr der-/dieselbe; **I'm not the ~ as my brother** ich bin nicht so wie mein Bruder; **frozen chicken is not the ~ as fresh** tiefgefrorene Hähnchen sind kein Vergleich zu frischen; **it's always the ~** es ist immer das Gleiche; **it comes** *or* **amounts to the ~** das kommt *or* läuft aufs Gleiche hinaus

b *no art (Comm)* **for repairing chair: £10, for recovering ~: £25** Stuhlreparatur: £ 10, Beziehen: £ 25

c *(in adverbial uses)* **the ~** gleich; **to pay/treat everybody the ~** alle gleich bezahlen/behandeln; **things go on just the ~ (as always)** es ändert sich nichts; **it's not the ~ as before** es ist nicht wie früher; **I don't feel the ~ about it** ich sehe das nicht so; **I used to love you but I don't feel the ~ any more** ich habe dich mal geliebt, aber das ist jetzt anders; **I still feel the ~ about you** an meinen Gefühlen dir gegenüber hat sich nichts geändert; **if it's all the ~ to you** wenn es Ihnen egal ist; **it's all the ~ to me (what you do)** es ist mir egal(, was du tust)

d *(phrases)* **all** *or* **just the ~** *(= nevertheless)* trotzdem; **thanks all the ~** trotzdem vielen Dank; **~ here** ich/wir auch; **~ to you** (danke) gleichfalls; **you're an idiot – ~ to you** du bist ein Idiot – gleichfalls; **I'd have hit him, (the) ~ as you did** *(inf)* ich hätte ihn (an Ihrer Stelle) auch geschlagen; **we left our country the ~ as you did** wir haben unsere Heimat verlassen, wie Sie auch

same-day ['seɪmdeɪ] ADJ *delivery* am gleichen Tag; **~ service** Erledigung *f* am gleichen Tag

sameness ['seɪmnɪs] N Eintönigkeit *f*

same-sex ['seɪmseks] ADJ gleichgeschlechtlich

samey ['seɪmɪ] ADJ *(inf)* eintönig, dasselbe in Grün *(inf)*

Samoa [sə'məʊə] N Samoa *nt*

Samoan [sə'məʊən] ADJ samoanisch N a Samoaner(in) *m(f)* b *(Ling)* Samoanisch *nt*

samovar [ˌsæməʊ'vɑːʳ] N Samowar *m*

sampan ['sæmpæn] N Sampan *m*

sample ['sɑːmpl] N *(= example)* Beispiel *nt* (of für); *(for tasting, fig: of talent, behaviour)* Kostprobe *f*; *(Comm, of cloth etc)* Muster *nt*; *(of commodities, urine, blood etc)* Probe *f*; *(Statistics)* (Zufalls)stichprobe *f*, Sample *nt*; **that's a typical ~ of her cooking** genau so kocht sie immer; **up to ~** *(Comm)* mustergetreu; **a representative ~ of the population** eine repräsentative Auswahl aus der Bevölkerung; **to take ~s of sb's blood** bei jdm Blutproben machen; **to take water ~s** Wasserproben entnehmen
ADJ *attr* Probe-; *(esp Comm)* Muster-; **~ collection** Mustersammlung *f*; **a ~ section of the population** eine Auswahl aus der Bevölkerung
VT a *wine, food* probieren, kosten; *pleasures* kosten; *atmosphere* testen; **to ~ wines** eine Weinprobe machen; **the newspaper has ~d public opinion on this matter** die Zeitung hat die öffentliche Meinung in dieser Frage getestet
b *(Mus)* sampeln, samplen

sample: **sample book** N Musterbuch *nt*; **sample bottle** N Probierflasche *f*; **sample pack** N Probepackung *f*

sampler ['sɑːmpləʳ] N a *(= person)* Probierer(in) *m(f)* b *(Sew)* Stickmustertuch *nt* c *(= record)* Auswahlplatte *f*

sample survey N Stichprobenerhebung *f*

sampling ['sɑːmplɪŋ] N *(of food)* Kostprobe *f*; *(of wine)* Weinprobe *f*; *(Statistics)* Stichprobenverfahren *nt* ATTR *(Statistics)* Stichproben-; **~ error** Fehler *m* im Stichprobenverfahren

Samson ['sæmsn] N *(lit)* Samson *m*; *(fig)* Herkules *m*

Samurai ['sæmjʊraɪ] N Samurai *m* ATTR Samurai-; **~ sword** Samuraischwert *nt*; **~ tradition** Tradition *f* der *or* bei den Samurai; **~ warrior** Samurai-Krieger *m*

sanatorium [ˌsænə'tɔːrɪəm] N *pl* **sanatoria** [ˌsænə'tɔːrɪə] *(Brit)* Sanatorium *nt*

sanctification [ˌsæŋktɪfɪ'keɪʃən] N *(= making holy)* Heiligung *f*; *(= consecrating)* Weihe *f*; *(= making binding: of vows)* Annahme *f*

sanctify ['sæŋktɪfaɪ] VT *(= make holy)* heiligen; *(= give quasi-moral sanction to also)* sanktionieren; *(= consecrate)* weihen; *(= make binding) vows* annehmen; **a custom sanctified by tradition** ein durch die Tradition geheiligter Brauch

sanctimonious [ˌsæŋktɪ'məʊnɪəs] ADJ frömmlerisch; **don't be so ~ about it** tu doch nicht so fromm

sanctimoniously [ˌsæŋktɪ'məʊnɪəslɪ] ADV frömmlerisch

sanctimoniousness [ˌsæŋktɪ'məʊnɪəsnɪs] N frömmlerisches Wesen; **the ~ of his remarks** seine frömmlerischen Bemerkungen

sanction ['sæŋkʃən] N a *(= permission, approval)* Zustimmung *f*; **to give one's ~ to sth** etw sanktionieren, seine Zustimmung zu etw geben; **rituals which have received the ~ of tradition** Rituale, die durch die Tradition sanktioniert sind b *(= enforcing measure)* Sanktion *f*; **to lift the ~s on a country** die Sanktionen gegen ein Land aufheben VT a sanktionieren b *(Pol: = impose sanctions on)* Sanktionen *pl* verhängen gegen

sanctions-busting ['sæŋkʃənzˌbʌstɪŋ] N *(Pol)* Sanktionsbruch *m*

sanctity ['sæŋktɪtɪ] N Heiligkeit *f*; *(of rights)* Unantastbarkeit *f*; **a man of great ~** ein sehr heiliger Mann; **the ~ of (human) life** die Unantastbarkeit des (menschlichen) Lebens

sanctuary ['sæŋktjʊərɪ] N a *(= holy place)* Heiligtum *nt*; *(= altar sanctuary)* Altarraum *m* b *(= refuge)* Zuflucht *f*; **to seek ~ with** Zuflucht suchen bei c *(for animals)* Schutzgebiet *nt*

sanctum ['sæŋktəm] N a *(= holy place)* heiliger Ort b *(fig: = private place)* Allerheiligste(s) *nt*

sand [sænd] N Sand *m no pl*; **to be built on ~** *(fig)* auf Sand gebaut sein; **~s** *(of desert)* Sand *m*; *(= beach)* Sandstrand *m*; **the ~s are running out** *(fig)* die Zeit *or* Uhr läuft ab; **the ~s of time** *(fig)* die Zeit; **the shifting ~s of politics** der politische Flugsand VT *(= smooth)* schmirgeln; *(= sprinkle with sand)* streuen

▶ **sand down** VT *sep* (ab)schmirgeln

sandal ['sændl] N Sandale *f*

sandalled ['sændəld] ADJ **in her ~ feet** in *or* mit Sandalen

sandalwood ['sændlwʊd] N Sandelholz *nt* ATTR Sandelholz-; **~ oil** Sandelholzöl *nt*

sand: **sandbag** N Sandsack *m* VT mit Sandsäcken schützen; **sandbank** N Sandbank *f*; **sandbar** N Sandbank *f*; **sandblast** VT sandstrahlen; **sandblaster** N Sandstrahler *m*; **sandblasting** N Sandstrahlen *nt*; **sandbox** N a *(Rail)* Sandstreuer *m*; *(Metal)* Sandform *f*; *(for playing)* Sandkasten *m* b *(Comput)* Sandbox *f*; **sandboy** N **as happy as a ~** *(Brit inf)* quietschvergnügt *(inf)*; **sand castle** N Sandburg *f*; **sand dune** N Sanddüne *f*

sander ['sændəʳ] N *(= tool)* Rutscher *m*, Vibrationsschleifer *m*

sand: **sand flea** N Strandfloh *m*; *(harmful)* Sandfloh *m*; **sand fly** N Sandfliege *f*; **sand glass** N Sanduhr *f*; **sand hopper** N Sandhüpfer *m*

sandiness ['sændɪnɪs] N Sandigkeit *f*; **noted for the ~ of its beaches** berühmt für seine Sandstrände

S & L *(US Fin) abbr of* **savings and loan association** Spar- und Darlehenskasse *f*

sand: **sandlot** ADJ *(US)* **~ baseball** *auf einem nicht als Spielfeld markierten Gelände und zum Spaß gespielter Baseball*; **sandman** N Sandmann *m*; **sand martin** N Uferschwalbe *f*; **sandpaper** N Sand- *or* Schmirgelpapier *nt* VT schmirgeln; **sandpaper down** VT *sep* abschmirgeln; **sandpiper** N Strandläufer *m*; **sandpit** N a *(= sand quarry)* Sandgrube *f* b *(Brit: in playground)* Sandkasten *m or* -kiste *f* c *(Comput)* Sandbox *f*; **sandshoe** N Stoffschuh *m*; *(for beach)* Strandschuh *m*; **sandstone** N Sandstein *m* ADJ Sandstein-, aus Sandstein; **~ building** Sandsteinbau *m*; **sandstorm** N Sandsturm *m*; **sand table** N *(Mil)* Sandkasten *m*

sandwich ['sænwɪdʒ] N Sandwich *nt*, Doppelschnitte *f or* -stulle *f (N Ger)*; **open ~** belegtes Brot; **he has ~es for lunch** er isst Butterbrote *or* Sandwiches *or* Stullen *(N Ger)* zum Mittagessen; **he's the meat** *or* **filling in the ~** *(Brit inf)* er ist das arme Opfer in der Mitte
VT *(also* **sandwich in***)* hineinzwängen; *car* einkeilen; **to be ~ed between two things/people** *(car, house)* zwischen zwei Dingen/Menschen eingekeilt sein; *(person also, small object)* zwischen zwei Dingen/Menschen eingezwängt sein; **~ed between two slices of bread** zwischen zwei Brotscheiben; **three pieces of wood, ~ed together** drei Stück Holz, die nebeneinandergequetscht sind

sandwich: **sandwich bar** N Snackbar *f*; **sandwich board** N Reklametafel *f*, Sandwich *nt (hum)*; **sandwich cake** N Schichttorte *f*; **sandwich course** N *Ausbildungsgang, bei dem sich Theorie und Praxis abwechseln*; **sandwich man** N Plakatträger *m*, Sandwichmann *m*

sandy ['sændɪ] ADJ (+er) a sandig; **~ beach** Sandstrand *m* b *(colour)* rötlich; *hair* rotblond

sand yacht N Strandsegler *m*

sane [seɪn] ADJ (+er) a *(= mentally healthy) person* normal; *(Med, Psych etc)* geistig gesund; *(Jur)* zurechnungsfähig; *world, society etc* gesund b *(= sensible) advice, policy, system, person, behaviour* vernünftig; **it's simply not ~ to ...** es ist doch verrückt, zu ...; **there is no ~ reason why ...** es gibt keinen vernünftigen Grund, weshalb ...

sang [sæŋ] *pret of* **sing**

sangfroid ['sɑ̃ːŋ'frwɑː] N Gelassenheit *f*, Seelenruhe *f*

sangria [sæŋ'griːə] N Sangria *f*

sanguinary ['sæŋgwɪnərɪ] ADJ *(liter) battle* blutig; *person* blutrünstig; *expression etc* derb; **~ language** *(hum)* ≈ Fäkalsprache *f*

sanguine ['sæŋgwɪn] ADJ a *(= optimistic)* optimistisch; **to have a ~ nature** *or* **disposition** von Natur aus ein Optimist sein; **to be ~ about sth** in Bezug auf etw *(acc)* zuversichtlich sein; **he is ~ about the future of his country** er ist voller Zuversicht was die Zukunft seines Landes betrifft; **I remain ~ about his chances** was seine Chancen betrifft, bin ich noch immer zuversichtlich; **~ that we shall succeed** zuversichtlich, dass wir Erfolg haben werden b **~ complexion** rote *or* gesunde *(euph)* Gesichtsfarbe

sanguinely ['sæŋgwɪnlɪ] ADV optimistisch; *say* zuversichtlich

sanguinity [sæŋ'gwɪnɪtɪ] N Optimismus *m*

sanies ['seɪnɪiːz] N *(Med form)* Jauche *f*

sanitariness ['sænɪtərɪnɪs] N Hygiene *f*; **the ~ of conditions** die hygienischen Zustände; **the ~ of the toilets is not up to standard** bei den Toiletten lässt die Hygiene zu wünschen übrig

sanitarium [ˌsænɪ'tɛərɪəm] N *(US)* = **sanatorium**

sanitary ['sænɪtərɪ] ADJ hygienisch; *arrangements, services, installations* sanitär *attr*; *recommendations* in Bezug auf die Hygiene; *questions* der Hygiene; **~ regulations** Gesundheits- *or* Hygienebestimmungen *pl*

sanitary: **sanitary belt** N Bindengürtel *m*; **sanitary engineer** N *(= expert)* Sanitärtechniker(in) *m(f)*; *(euph: = dustman)* Entsorgungsfachmann *m*/-frau *f*; **sanitary engineering** N Sanitärtechnik *f*; **sanitary inspector** N Gesundheitsaufseher(in) *m(f)*; **sanitary napkin** N *(US)* Damenbinde *f*; **sanitary pad** N Damenbinde *f*; **sanitary protection** N *(= sanitary towels or tampons)* Binden und Tampons *pl*; **sanitary towel** N Damenbinde *f*

sanitation [ˌsænɪ'teɪʃən] N Hygiene *f*; *(= toilets etc)* sanitäre Anlagen *pl*; *(= sewage disposal)* Kanalisation *f*; **the ~ department** das Amt für Stadtreinigung

sanitation man N *pl* **sanitation men**, **sanitation worker** N *(US)* Stadtreiniger *m*, Müllmann *m*

sanitize ['sænɪtaɪz] VT a *(esp US)* keimfrei machen b *novel, film etc* von anstößigen Stellen reinigen *or* säubern

sanity ['sænɪtɪ] N a *(= mental balance)* geistige Gesundheit; *(esp of individual)* gesunder Verstand; *(Jur)* Zurechnungsfähigkeit *f*; **to lose one's ~** den Verstand verlieren; **to doubt sb's ~** an jds Verstand *(dat)* zweifeln; **the line between ~ and insanity** die Grenze zwischen gesundem und krankem Verstand b *(= sensibleness)* Vernünftigkeit *f*; **~ of judgement** ein gesundes Urteilsvermögen; **~ demands that it be done soon** die Vernunft gebietet, es bald zu tun; **to return to ~** Vernunft annehmen

sank [sæŋk] *pret of* **sink**[1]

San Marino [ˌsænmə'riːnəʊ] N San Marino *nt*

sanserif [ˌsɒnse'riːf] N serifenlose Schrift; *(= character)* serifenloser Buchstabe ADJ serifenlos

Sanskrit ['sænskrɪt] ADJ sanskritisch N Sanskrit *nt*

Santa (Claus) ['sæntə('klɔːz)] N der Weihnachtsmann

sap[1] [sæp] N *(Bot)* Saft *m*; *(fig)* Lebenskraft *f*; **the ~ is rising** *(lit)* der Saft steigt; *(fig)* die Triebe erwachen

sap[2] N *(Mil)* Sappe *f* VT a *(Mil)* unterminieren, untergraben b *(fig)* untergraben; *confidence* untergraben, schwächen; **to ~ sb's strength** jdn entkräften, jds Kräfte angreifen; **to ~ sb's energy/enthusiasm** jdm die Energie/Begeisterung nehmen

sap[3] N *(inf)* Trottel *m (inf)*

sapling ['sæplɪŋ] N junger Baum

sapper ['sæpəʳ] N *(Mil)* Pionier *m*

Sapphic ['sæfɪk] ADJ sapphisch

sapphire ['sæfaɪə'] **N** Saphir *m*; *(= colour)* Saphirblau *nt* **ADJ** Saphir-; *(liter) sky* strahlend blau; **~ ring** Saphirring *m*

sappy ['sæpɪ] ADJ **a** *plant etc* saftig, voller Saft; *(fig)* kraftvoll, voller Energie **b** *(esp US = over-sentimental) play, book, film* rührselig; *(inf: = silly, foolish)* einfältig, dämlich

saraband ['særəbænd] N Sarabande *f*

Saracen ['særəsn] **ADJ** sarazenisch, Sarazenen- **N** Sarazene *m*, Sarazenin *f*

Sarajevo [,s[ae]rə'jeɪvəʊ] N Sarajevo *nt*

sarcasm ['sɑːkæzəm] N Sarkasmus *m*

sarcastic [sɑː'kæstɪk] ADJ sarkastisch; **he has a ~ tongue** er hat eine sarkastische Art; **are you being ~?** sind Sie jetzt sarkastisch?, das soll wohl ein Witz sein *(inf)*; **to be ~ about sth** über etw *(acc)* sarkastische Bemerkungen machen

sarcastically [sɑː'kæstɪkəlɪ] ADV sarkastisch

sarcoma [sɑː'kəʊmə] N *pl* **-s** *or* **-ta** [-tə] *(Med)* Sarkom *nt*

sarcophagus [sɑː'kɒfəgəs] N *pl* **sarcophagi** [sɑː'kɒfəgaɪ] Sarkophag *m*

sardine [sɑː'diːn] N Sardine *f*; **packed (in) like ~s** wie die Sardinen

Sardinia [sɑː'dɪnɪə] N Sardinien *nt*

Sardinian [sɑː'dɪnɪən] **ADJ** sardisch, sardinisch **N** Sarde *m*, Sardin *f*, Sardinier(in) *m(f)*

sardonic ADJ, **sardonically** ADV [sɑː'dɒnɪk, -əlɪ] süffisant; *grin, laugh also* sardonisch *(liter)*

sari ['sɑːrɪ] N Sari *m*

sarky ['sɑːkɪ] ADJ *(+er)* *(Brit inf)* sarkastisch

sarnie ['sɑːnɪ] N *(Brit inf)* belegtes Brot, Sandwich *nt*

sarong [sə'rɒŋ] N Sarong *m*

SARS [sɑːz] *(Med)* abbr of **severe acute respiratory syndrome** SARS *nt*, schweres akutes Atemnotsyndrom

sarsaparilla [,sɑːsəpə'rɪlə] N *(= plant)* Sarsaparille *f*; *(= drink) dunkelbraunes Limonadengetränk aus Sarsaparillenwurzeln*

sartorial [sɑː'tɔːrɪəl] ADJ **his ~ elegance** sein elegantes Aussehen, seine elegante Art, sich zu kleiden; **the very last word in ~ elegance** der letzte Schrei in der Herrenmode; **his unusual ~ preferences** seine Vorliebe für ungewöhnliche Kleidung; **~ styles** Herrenmoden *pl*

sartorially [sɑː'tɔːrɪəlɪ] ADV *dressed* elegant, stilvoll

SAS *(Brit)* abbr of **Special Air Service** *Spezialeinheit der britischen Armee*

SASE N *(US)* abbr of **self-addressed stamped envelope** adressierter und frankierter Rückumschlag

sash[1] [sæʃ] N Schärpe *f*

sash[2] N *(= sash window)* Schiebefenster *nt*; *(= cord)* Gewichtsschnur *f*

sashay ['sæʃeɪ] VI *(esp US inf)* stolzieren; **I'll just ~ down to the bar** ich latsche mal eben zur Bar *(inf)*

sash: **sash cord** N Gewichtsschnur *f*; **sash saw** N Schlitzsäge *f*; **sash window** N Schiebefenster *nt*

Sask abbr of **Saskatchewan**

sass [sæs] *(US inf)* **N** Frechheit *f* **VT** frech antworten *(+dat)*

sassafras ['sæsəfræs] N Sassafras *m*

Sassenach ['sæsənæx] *(Scot: pej, hum)* **N** Engländer(in) *m(f)* **ADJ** englisch

sassy ['sæsɪ] ADJ *(+er)* *(US inf)* frech

SAT **a** *(US Sch)* abbr of **scholastic aptitude test** **b** *(Brit Sch)* abbr of **standars assessment task**

> **SAT**
>
> **Scholastic Aptitude Tests** oder auch **SAT** sind Standardprüfungen, die US-Highschool-Schülerinnen und -Schüler ablegen, die ein College oder eine Universität besuchen wollen. Die Schwerpunkte des Examens bewerten die sprachlichen und mathematischen Fähigkeiten der Kandidaten, wobei eine ideale Punktzahl von 1600 erreicht werden kann; die durchschnittlich erreichte Punktzahl liegt bei 900. Die Ergebnisse, die sogenannten „SAT scores", werden dann den Colleges zugesandt, bei denen sich die Studenten bewerben. Für die Aufnahme entscheidend sind neben diesen Ergebnissen auch die allgemeinen schulischen Leistungen auf der Highschool. Der Test war als objektive und unvoreingenommene Bewertungsgrundlage gedacht, es wird aber bemängelt, dass er dem kulturellen Hintergrund von Schülern aus der Mittelklasse entgegenkommt. Der **SAT** kann beliebig oft wiederholt werden, allerdings wird jedes Mal eine Examensgebühr erhoben.

Sat abbr of **Saturday** Sa.

sat [sæt] *pret, ptp of* **sit**

Satan ['seɪtən] N Satan *m*

satanic [sə'tænɪk] ADJ **a** satanisch; **~ abuse** ritueller Missbrauch **b** *(fig)* teuflisch

Satanism ['seɪtənɪzəm] N Satanismus *m*, Satanskult *m*

satay ['sæteɪ] N *Fleischspießchen mit Erdnusssoße*

satchel ['sætʃəl] N Schultasche *f*, Schulranzen *m*

sate [seɪt] VT *(liter) appetite, desires* stillen *(geh)*, befriedigen; **now that he was ~d** nun, da seine Lüste gestillt waren *(geh)*; **a nation ~d with every luxury** ein Volk von jedem erdenklichen Luxus übersättigt; **to ~ oneself** *(with food)* sich sättigen *(on* an *+dat)* *(liter)*; *(sexually)* seine Lust befriedigen

sateen [sæ'tiːn] N Baumwollsatin *m*

satellite ['sætəlaɪt] N Satellit *m*; *(natural also, fig)* Trabant *m*

satellite: **satellite broadcasting** N Satellitenfunk *m*; **satellite country** N Satellitenstaat *m*; **satellite dish** N Parabolantenne *f*, Satellitenschüssel *f*; **satellite radio** N Satellitenradio *nt*; **satellite receiver** N Satellitenempfänger *m*; **satellite state** N Satellitenstaat *m*; **satellite telephone** N Satellitentelefon *nt*; **satellite television** N Satellitenfernsehen *nt*; **satellite town** N Satelliten- *or* Trabantenstadt *f*

satiate ['seɪʃɪeɪt] VT *appetite, desires, lust etc* stillen *(geh)*; *person, animal* sättigen; *(to excess)* übersättigen; **we were ~d with food and drink** wir hatten unseren Hunger und Durst zur Genüge gestillt; **I'm quite ~d** *(liter, hum)* mein Bedarf ist gedeckt *(hum inf)*, ich bin gesättigt *(hum, geh)*

satiation [,seɪʃɪ'eɪʃən] N Befriedigung *f*, Sättigung *f*; *(excessive)* Übersättigung *f*

satiety [sə'taɪətɪ] N Sättigung *f*; **they ate to ~** sie aßen sich satt

satin ['sætɪn] **N** Satin *m* **ADJ** Satin-; *skin* samtig; **~ dress** Satinkleid *nt*

satin: **satin paper** N satiniertes Papier, Atlaspapier *nt*; **satin stitch** N Plattstich *m*; **satinwood** ['sætɪnwʊd] N Satinholz *nt*

satiny ['sætɪnɪ] ADJ seidig; *skin* samtig

satire ['sætaɪə'] N Satire *f* *(on* auf *+acc)*; **the ~ in his voice** die Ironie in seiner Stimme

satirical [sə'tɪrɪkəl] ADJ *literature, film etc* satirisch; *(= mocking, joking)* ironisch

satirically [sə'tɪrɪkəlɪ] ADV satirisch; *(= mockingly, jokingly)* ironisch

satirist ['sætərɪst] N Satiriker(in) *m(f)*

satirize ['sætəraɪz] VT satirisch darstellen *or (written also)* beschreiben; **his novel ~s** *or* **in his novel he ~s contemporary American life** sein Roman ist eine Satire auf die zeitgenössische amerikanische Lebensart

satisfaction [,sætɪs'fækʃən] N **a** *(= act) (of person, needs, creditors, curiosity etc)* Befriedigung *f*; *(of debt)* Begleichung *f*, Tilgung *f*; *(of employer etc)* Zufriedenstellung *f*; *(of ambition)* Verwirklichung *f*; *(of conditions, contract)* Erfüllung *f* **b** Zufriedenheit *f* *(at* mit); **the ~ at** *or* **of having solved a difficult problem** die Genugtuung *or* das befriedigende Gefühl, ein schwieriges Problem gelöst zu haben; **to feel a sense of ~ at sth** Genugtuung über etw *(acc)* empfinden; **at least you have the ~ of seeing him pay** Sie haben wenigstens die Genugtuung, dass er zahlen muss; **she would not give him the ~ of seeing how annoyed she was** sie wollte ihm nicht die Genugtuung geben, ihren Ärger zu sehen; **he did it just for the ~ of seeing her suffer** er tat es nur, um sie leiden zu sehen; **we hope the meal was to your complete ~** wir hoffen, Sie waren mit dem Essen zufrieden *or* das Essen ist zu Ihrer vollen Zufriedenheit ausgefallen *(form)*; **has it been done to your ~?** sind Sie damit zufrieden?, ist es zu Ihrer Zufriedenheit erledigt worden? *(form)*; **if anything in the hotel is not to your ~** sollte irgendetwas im Hotel nicht zu Ihrer Zufriedenheit sein; **our aim, your ~** bei uns ist der Kunde König; **the machine is guaranteed to give complete ~** wir garantieren mit diesem Gerät vollste Zufriedenheit; **it gives me much ~ to introduce ...** es ist mir eine besondere Freude, ... vorstellen zu können; **to get ~ out of sth** Befriedigung in etw *(dat)* finden; *(= find pleasure)* Freude *f* an etw *(dat)* haben; **I can't get any ~** ich bin unbefriedigt; **he gets ~ out of his job** seine Arbeit befriedigt ihn; **I get a lot of ~ out of listening to music** Musik gibt mir viel; **what ~ do you get out of climbing mountains?** was gibt Ihnen das Bergsteigen?; **he proved to my ~ that ...** er hat überzeugend bewiesen, dass ...; **he has shown to the examiners' ~ that ...** der Prüfungsausschuss hat befunden, dass er ...; **she has shown to the court's ~ that ...** sie hat dem Gericht überzeugend dargelegt, dass ... **c** *(= satisfying thing)* **your son's success must be a great ~ to you** der Erfolg Ihres Sohnes muss für Sie sehr befriedigend *or* eine große Freude sein; **one of her greatest ~s comes from her work with children** eines der Dinge, die sie am meisten befriedigt, ist ihre Arbeit mit Kindern; **it is no ~ to me to know that ...** es ist kein Trost (für mich) zu wissen, dass ...; **what ~ is that supposed to be!** das ist ein schwacher Trost **d** *(= redress)* Genugtuung *f*, Satisfaktion *f* *(old)*; **to demand/obtain ~ from sb** Genugtuung *or* Satisfaktion *(old)* von jdm verlangen/erhalten; **to give sb ~** jdm Genugtuung *or* Satisfaktion *(old)* geben

satisfactorily [,sætɪs'fæktərɪlɪ] ADV zufriedenstellend; **does that answer your question ~?** ist damit Ihre Frage hinreichend beantwortet?; **was it done ~?** waren Sie damit zufrieden?; **he is progressing ~** er macht zufriedenstellende Fortschritte *pl*

satisfactory [,sætɪs'fæktərɪ] ADJ befriedigend, zufriedenstellend; *account, completion of contract* zufriedenstellend; *(= only just good enough)* ausreichend, hinlänglich *attr*; *reason* triftig, einleuchtend; *excuse* angemessen, annehmbar; *(in exams)* ausreichend, befriedigend; **to bring sth to a ~ conclusion** etw zufriedenstellend zum Abschluss bringen; **to be in a ~ condition** *(Med)* sich in einem zufriedenstellenden Zustand befinden; **work is proceeding at a ~ pace** die Arbeit geht zufriedenstellend voran; **how ~ do you find the new conditions?** wie sind Sie mit den neuen Verhältnissen zufrieden?; **his work is only just ~** seine Arbeit ist gerade noch annehmbar *or (Sch)* befriedigend; **this is just not ~!** das geht so nicht!; *(= not enough)* das reicht einfach nicht (aus)!; **it's hardly ~ being given only one hour's notice** das geht doch nicht, wenn einem nur eine Stunde vorher Bescheid gesagt wird; **an offer of 8% is simply not ~** ein Angebot von 8% reicht einfach nicht; **your attitude is not ~** Ihre Einstellung lässt zu wünschen übrig

satisfied ['sætɪsfaɪd] ADJ **a** *(= content) person, customer* zufrieden; **to be ~ with sth** mit etw zufrieden sein; **you'll have to be ~ with that** Sie werden sich damit zufriedengeben *or* begnügen *or* bescheiden *(geh)* müssen; **not ~ with that he … damit** noch immer nicht zufrieden, er …; **(are you) ~?** *(iro)* (bist du nun) zufrieden?; **you've really upset her now, I hope you're ~** sie ist ganz außer sich, bist du jetzt zufrieden?; **with a ~ look on his face** mit einem zufriedenen Gesichtsausdruck

b *(= certain, = convinced)* überzeugt; **to be ~ that …** der Überzeugung sein, dass …; **they were not ~ with the answers** sie waren mit den Antworten nicht zufrieden

satisfy ['sætɪsfaɪ] **VT** **a** *(= make contented)* befriedigen; *employer, customers etc* zufriedenstellen; *(meal) person* sättigen; *hunger* stillen; **that won't ~ the boss** damit wird der Chef nicht zufrieden sein; **nothing satisfies him** ihn kann nichts befriedigen; *(= always wants more)* er ist mit nichts zufrieden; **one glass of water didn't ~ him/his thirst** das eine Glas Wasser hat ihm nicht gereicht/hat seinen Durst nicht gelöscht

b *needs, wishes, lust, demand, curiosity, person* befriedigen; *(sexually)* befriedigen; *hunger* stillen; *contract, conditions* erfüllen; *requirements* genügen *(+dat)*; *ambitions* verwirklichen; **to do sth to ~ one's pride** etw nur aus reinem Stolz tun

c *(= convince)* überzeugen; **if you can ~ him that …** wenn Sie ihn davon überzeugen können, dass …; **X has satisfied the examiners that …** der Prüfungsausschuss hat befunden, dass X …; **X has satisfied the examiners in the following subjects** X hat in den folgenden Fächern die Prüfung bestanden

d *(Comm) debt* begleichen, tilgen; *claims* nachkommen *(+dat)*; *creditors* befriedigen

e *(Math) equation* erfüllen

VR **to ~ oneself about sth** sich von etw überzeugen; **to ~ oneself that …** sich davon überzeugen, dass …

VI *(meal)* sättigen; **we aim to ~** wir bemühen uns, allen Wünschen zu entsprechen; **pleasures which no longer ~** Genüsse, die einen nicht mehr befriedigen

satisfying ['sætɪsfaɪɪŋ] **ADJ** befriedigend; *food, meal* sättigend; **a ~ experience** ein befriedigendes Erlebnis; **they had the ~ experience of seeing him fail** es tat ihnen gut, seinen Misserfolg zu erleben; **sounds which are very ~ to the ear** angenehme Klänge *pl*; **a cool ~ beer** ein kühles, durststillendes Bier

satsuma [,sæt'suːmə] **N** Satsuma *f*

saturate ['sætʃəreɪt] **VT** **a** *(with liquid)* (durch)tränken; *(rain)* durchnässen; **I'm ~d** *(inf)* ich bin klatschnass *(inf)*

b *(Chem)* sättigen; **a ~d solution/colour** eine gesättigte Lösung/Farbe

c *(fig) market* sättigen; *airways* auslasten; **this area is ~d with a sense of history** dies ist eine geschichtsträchtige Gegend; **he ~d himself in French literature until the exam was over** er hat sich mit französischer Literatur vollgepfropft, bis die Prüfung vorbei war; **the government ~d the area with troops** die Regierung entsandte massenhaft Truppen in das Gebiet; **the area is ~d with troops** die Gegend wimmelt von Soldaten

saturation [,sætʃə'reɪʃən] **N** Sättigung *f*

saturation: saturation bombing **N** völliges Zerbomben; **saturation point** **N** Sättigungspunkt *m*; *(fig)* Sättigungsgrad *m*; **to have reached ~** seinen Sättigungsgrad erreicht haben

Saturday ['sætədɪ] **N** Samstag *m*, Sonnabend *m* *(esp N Ger)*; **~ draw** *(in lottery)* Samstagsziehung *f* → *also* **Tuesday**

Saturn ['sætən] **N** *(Astron, Myth)* Saturn *m*

saturnalia [,sætə'neɪlɪə] **PL** **a** **Saturnalia** Saturnalien *pl* **b** *(liter: = wild revelry)* wilde Feste *pl*, Freudenfeste *pl*

saturnine ['sætənaɪn] **ADJ** *(liter)* finster, düster

satyr ['sætə'] **N** Satyr *m*

sauce [sɔːs] **N** **a** Soße *f*, Sauce *f*; **white ~** Mehlsoße *f*; **what's ~ for the goose is ~ for the gander** *(Prov)* was dem einen recht ist, ist dem anderen billig *(prov)* **b** *no pl (inf, = cheek)* Frechheit *f*; **none of your ~!** werd bloß nicht frech! *(inf)* **c** *(US inf: = alcohol)* Alk *m (sl)*, Stoff *m (inf)*; **to be on the ~** saufen *(inf)*

sauce: sauce boat **N** Sauciere *f*; **saucebox** **N** *(inf)* Frechdachs *m*

saucepan ['sɔːspən] **N** Kochtopf *m*

saucer ['sɔːsə'] **N** Untertasse *f*

saucily ['sɔːsɪlɪ] **ADV** **a** *(= cheekily)* frech **b** *(= suggestively) say, joke* aufreizend

sauciness ['sɔːsɪnɪs] **N** *no pl* Frechheit *f*

saucy ['sɔːsɪ] **ADJ** *(+er)* **a** *(= cheeky)* frech; **don't be ~!** sei nicht so frech! **b** *(= suggestive) joke, humour* anzüglich, schlüpfrig; *picture, clothes* gewagt, aufreizend; **with her hat at a ~ angle** mit frech *or* keck aufgesetztem Hut

Saudi ['saʊdɪ] **N** *(inf)* = **Saudi Arabia** **ADJ** = **Saudi Arabian ADJ**

Saudi Arabia ['saʊdɪə'reɪbɪə] **N** Saudi-Arabien *nt*

Saudi Arabian ['saʊdɪə'reɪbɪən] **N** Saudi(-Araber) *m*, Saudi-Araberin *f* **ADJ** saudisch, saudiarabisch

Saul [sɔːl] **N** Saul(us) *m*

sault [suː] **N** *(US) (= waterfall)* Wasserfall *m*; *(in river)* Stromschnelle *f*

sauna ['sɔːnə] **N** Sauna *f*; **to have a ~** in die Sauna gehen

saunter ['sɔːntə'] **N** Bummel *m*; **to have a ~ in the park** einen Parkbummel machen, durch den Park schlendern **VI** schlendern; **he ~ed up to me** er schlenderte auf mich zu; **she came ~ing in four hours late** sie tanzte vier Stunden zu spät an *(inf)*; **to ~ out/away** hinaus-/wegschlendern

saunterer ['sɔːntərə] **N** Bummler(in) *m(f)* *(inf)*

saurian ['sɔːrɪən] **N** Echse *f*; *(= dinosaur etc)* Saurier *m*

sausage ['sɒsɪdʒ] **N** **a** Wurst *f*; **you can't judge a ~ by its skin** *(prov)* man kann nicht nach dem Äußeren urteilen; **not a ~** *(Brit inf)* rein gar nichts *(inf)* **b** *(Brit, inf, = silly person)* Dummerchen *nt (inf)*, Schäfchen *nt (inf)*

sausage: sausage dog **N** *(Brit hum)* Dackel *m*; **sausage machine** **N** Wurstfüllmaschine *f*; *(fig hum: = school)* Bildungsfabrik *f*; **sausage meat** **N** Wurstbrät *nt*; **sausage roll** **N** ≈ Bratwurst *f* im Schlafrock

sauté ['səʊteɪ] **ADJ** **~ potatoes** Brat- *or* Röstkartoffeln *pl* **VT** *potatoes* rösten; *(= sear)* (kurz) anbraten

sauterne [səʊ'tɜːn] **N** Sauternes *m*

savable ['seɪvəbl] **ADJ** zu retten *pred*; *goal* haltbar, zu halten *pred*

savage ['sævɪdʒ] **ADJ** wild; *sport, fighter, punch, revenge* brutal; *custom* grausam; *animal* gefährlich; *competition* scharf, brutal *(inf)*; *conflict* schwer, brutal; *war* grausam, brutal; *(= drastic, severe) cuts, measures* rigoros, hart, drastisch; *changes* drastisch; *criticism* schonungslos, brutal *(inf)*; **the ~ people of New Guinea** die Wilden Neuguineas; **to put up a ~ fight** sich wütend *or* grimmig *(geh) or* wild *(inf)* verteidigen, sich verbissen wehren; **with a ~ snap of its jaws the crocodile …** wütend biss das Krokodil …; **the dog became a ~ beast** der Hund wurde zur reißenden Bestie; **the guard dogs are ~** die Wachhunde sind scharf *or* gefährlich; **to make a ~ attack on sb** brutal über jdn herfallen; *(fig)* jdn scharf angreifen; **he has a ~ temper** er ist ein äußerst jähzorniger Mensch; **he is in a ~ temper** er ist fuchsteufelswild *(inf)*; **the critics were really ~ with her new play** die Kritiker haben ihr neues Stück wirklich schonungslos verrissen

N Wilde(r) *mf*

VT **a** *(animal)* anfallen; *(fatally)* zerfleischen

b *(fig: = criticize)* verreißen; *person also* (in der Luft) zerreißen

savagely ['sævɪdʒlɪ] **ADV** *attack, fight, punch* brutal; *bite* gefährlich; *reduce services* drastisch, rigoros; *criticize* schonungslos, brutal *(inf)*; **he glared at her ~** er warf ihr einen wilden Blick zu; **a ~ funny film** ein satirisch-humoriger Film; **the scenery was ~ beautiful** die Landschaft war von einer wilden Schönheit

savageness ['sævɪdʒnɪs] **N** Wildheit *f*; *(of sport, fighter, punch, revenge)* Brutalität *f*; *(of custom, war)* Grausamkeit *f*; *(of animal)* Gefährlichkeit *f*; *(of competition)* Schärfe *f*; *(of conflict)* Schwere *f*, Brutalität *f*; *(= severity, of cuts, measures)* Härte *f*; *(of criticism)* Schonungslosigkeit *f*

savagery ['sævɪdʒərɪ] **N** **a** *(of tribe, people)* Wildheit *f* **b** *(= cruelty)* Grausamkeit *f*; *(of attack)* Brutalität *f*; *(of treatment, prison life, cuts)* brutale Härte; **the savageries committed …** die Grausamkeiten *or* Gräueltaten *pl* …

savanna(h) [sə'vænə] **N** Savanne *f*

save[1] [seɪv] **N** *(Ftbl etc)* Ballabwehr *f*; **what a ~!** eine tolle Parade!; **he made a fantastic ~** er hat den Ball prima abgewehrt *or* gehalten

VT **a** *(= rescue, Rel also)* retten; **to ~ sb from sth** jdn vor etw *(dat)* retten; **to ~ sb from disaster/ruin** jdn vor einer Katastrophe/dem Ruin bewahren *or* retten; **he ~d me from falling/making that mistake** er hat mich davor bewahrt hinzufallen/den Fehler zu machen; **to ~ sth from sth** etw aus etw retten; **his goal ~d the match** sein Tor hat das Spiel gerettet *or* herausgerissen *(inf)*; **to ~ the day** die Rettung sein; **God ~ the Queen** Gott schütze die Königin; **to ~ a building for posterity** ein Gebäude der Nachwelt erhalten; **to be ~d by the bell** *(inf)* gerade noch einmal davonkommen; **to ~ one's neck** *or* **ass** *(US sl) or* **butt** *(US inf)* seinen Kopf retten; **to ~ sb's neck** *or* **ass** *(US sl) or* **butt** *(US inf)* jdn rauspauken *(inf)*, jdn retten

b *(= put by)* aufheben, aufbewahren, aufsparen; *money* sparen; *(= collect) stamps etc* sammeln; **~ some of the cake for me** lass mir etwas Kuchen übrig; **~ me a seat** halte mir einen Platz frei; **~ it for later, I'm busy now** *(inf)* spar dirs für später auf, ich habe jetzt zu tun *(inf)*; **~ it!** *(inf)* spar dir das! *(inf)*; **to ~ the best for last** das Beste bis zum Schluss aufheben

c *(= avoid using up) fuel, time, space, money* sparen; *(= spare) strength, eyes, battery* schonen; *(= save up) strength, fuel etc* aufsparen; **that will ~ you £20 a week** dadurch sparen Sie £ 20 die Woche; **going by plane will ~ you four hours on the train journey** der Flug spart dir vier Stunden Reisezeit im Vergleich zum Zug; **you don't ~ much by taking this short cut** Sie gewinnen nicht viel, wenn Sie diese Abkürzung nehmen; **he's saving himself for the big match** er schont sich für das große Spiel; **he's saving himself for the right woman** er spart sich für die Richtige auf

d *(= prevent) bother, trouble* ersparen; **at least it ~d the rain coming in** es hat wenigstens den Regen abgehalten; **it'll ~ a lot of hard work if we …** es erspart uns *(dat)* sehr viel Mühe, wenn wir …; **it ~d us having to do it again** das hat es uns *(dat)* erspart, es noch einmal machen zu müssen; **I've been ~d a lot of expense** mir blieben *or* mir wurden sehr viel Ausgaben erspart

e *goal* verhindern; *shot, penalty* halten; **well ~d!** gut gehalten!

f *(Comput)* speichern; **to ~ as** speichern unter; **to ~ sth to disk** etw auf Diskette (ab)speichern *or* sichern

VI **a** *(with money)* sparen; **to ~ for sth** für *or* auf etw *(acc)* sparen; **~ as you earn** *(Brit: = savings scheme)* *Sparprogramm, bei dem der monatliche Beitrag unversteuert bleibt*

b *(inf: = keep, food)* sich halten; *(news)* warten können

c *(Comput)* **the file won't ~** die Datei lässt sich nicht sichern *or* abspeichern

▶ **save up** **VI** sparen *(for* für, auf *+acc)* **VT** *sep* *(= not spend)* sparen; *(= not use)* aufheben, aufbewahren; **he's saving himself up for the big match** er schont sich für das große Spiel

save[2] **PREP** außer *+dat* **CONJ** **a** *(old, liter)* es sei denn *(geh)* **b** **~ that** nur dass

saveable **ADJ** = **savable**

saveloy ['sævəlɔɪ] **N** Zervelatwurst *f*

saver ['seɪvəʳ] N **a** Retter(in) *m(f)*; **a ~ of lives** ein Lebensretter *m*, eine Lebensretterin **b** *(with money)* Sparer(in) *m(f)*

-saver N *suf* **it is a time-/money-/space-saver** es spart Zeit/Geld/Platz; **life-saver** Lebensretter(in) *m(f)*

saving ['seɪvɪŋ] ADJ **a** *(= redeeming)* **the one ~ feature of the scheme** das einzig Gute an dem Plan, das Einzige, was für den Plan spricht; **its/his ~ grace** was einen damit/mit ihm versöhnt
b sparsam; **she's not the ~ sort** sie ist nicht gerade sparsam
c ~ clause Sicherheitsklausel *f*, einschränkende Klausel
N **a** *no pl (= rescue, Rel)* Rettung *f*
b *no pl (of money)* Sparen *nt*; **to encourage ~** zum Sparen ermutigen
c *(of cost etc, = act)* Einsparung *f*; *(= amount saved)* Ersparnis *f*; **how much of a ~ is there?** wie viel wird eingespart?; **we must make ~s** wir müssen sparen; **a considerable ~ in time and money** eine beträchtliche Zeit- und Geldersparnis
d savings PL Ersparnisse *pl*; *(in account)* Spareinlagen *pl*; **post-office ~s** Postsparguthaben *nt*
PREP, CONJ = **save²**

-saving ADJ *suf* ... sparend; **time-/energy-saving** zeit-/energiesparend; **life-saving** lebensrettend

savings *in cpds* Spar-; **savings account** N Sparkonto *nt*; **savings bank** N Sparkasse *f*; **savings bond** N *(US Fin)* (staatlicher) Sparbrief; **savings book** N Sparbuch *nt*; **savings certificate** N *(Brit Fin)* Sparbrief *m*; **savings deposit** N Spareinlage *f*; **savings stamp** N *(Brit)* Sparmarke *f*

saviour, *(US)* **savior** ['seɪvjəʳ] N Retter(in) *m(f)*; *(Rel also)* Erlöser *m*, Heiland *m*; **Our Saviour** unser Erlöser

savoir-faire ['sævwɑː'feəʳ] N Gewandtheit *f*; *(in social matters)* gute Umgangsformen *pl*; **it's a question of ~** es ist nur eine Frage, wie man es anfasst

savor *etc (US)* = **savour** *etc*

savory ['seɪvərɪ] N *(Bot)* Bohnenkraut *nt*

savour, *(US)* **savor** ['seɪvəʳ] N **a** Geschmack *m*; **a ~ of garlic** ein Knoblauchgeschmack *m* **b** *(slight trace)* Spur *f*; **there is a ~ of pride in everything he says** in allem, was er sagt, schwingt ein gewisser Stolz mit **c** *(= enjoyable quality)* Reiz *m* VT **a** *(form)* kosten *(geh)*, verkosten *(form)*; *aroma (of food)* riechen **b** *(fig liter)* genießen, auskosten VI **to ~ of sth** *(fig liter)* etw ahnen lassen

savouriness, *(US)* **savoriness** ['seɪvərɪnɪs] N **a** *(= tastiness)* Schmackhaftigkeit *f*; **the ~ of the smells** die leckeren Gerüche **b** *(= spiciness)* Würzigkeit *f*, Pikantheit *f*; **the excessive ~ of all the food** das zu stark gewürzte Essen

savourless, *(US)* **savorless** ['seɪvəlɪs] ADJ geschmacklos

savoury, *(US)* **savory** ['seɪvərɪ] ADJ **a** *(= appetizing)* lecker **b** *(= not sweet)* pikant; **~ omelette** gefülltes Omelett; **~ biscuits** Salzgebäck *nt* **c** *(fig)* angenehm, ersprießlich; **that was not the most ~ adjective to have chosen** das war ja nicht gerade das feinste Adjektiv N *(Brit)* Häppchen *nt*; **would you like a sweet or a ~?** hätten Sie gern etwas Süßes oder etwas Pikantes *or* Salziges?

savoy (cabbage) [sə'vɔɪ('kæbɪdʒ)] N Wirsing(-kohl) *m*

savvy ['sævɪ] *(inf)* N *(= common sense)* Grips *m (inf)*, Köpfchen *nt (inf)*; *(= know-how)* Können *nt*, Know-how *nt*; **he hasn't got much ~** er hat keine Ahnung *(inf) or* keinen Dunst *(inf)*; **show a bit of ~!, use your ~!** streng mal dein Köpfchen *or* deinen Grips an *(inf)* VT kapieren *(inf)*; **~?** kapiert? *(inf)*, kapisko? *(dated sl)*; **no ~** keine Ahnung *(inf)*; *(= don't understand)* kapier ich nicht *(inf)*

saw¹ [sɔː] *pret of* **see¹**

saw² N Spruch *m*, Weisheit *f*

saw³ *vb: pret* **sawed**, *ptp* **sawed** *or* **sawn** N Säge *f*; **musical ~** Singende Säge VT **a** *(lit)* sägen; **to ~ sth through** etw durchsägen; **to ~ sth in two** etw entzweisägen; **~ the wood into smaller logs** zersägen Sie das Holz in kleinere Scheite; **~n timber** *(esp Brit)* Schnittholz *nt* **b he/his arms ~ed the air** er schlug wild um sich, er fuchtelte mit den Armen (durch die Luft) VI **a** *(person, saw)* sägen; *(wood)* sich sägen lassen **b to ~ away at the violin** auf der Geige herumsägen; **to ~ (away) at the meat** am Fleisch herumsäbeln *(inf)*

▶ **saw down** VT *sep* um- *or* absägen

▶ **saw off** VT *sep* absägen

▶ **saw up** VT *sep* zersägen *(into* in *+acc)*

saw: **saw blade** N Sägeblatt *nt*; **sawbones** N *(dated sl)* Medizinmann *m (inf)*; **sawbuck** N *(US)* Sägebock *m*; *(sl: = banknote)* Zehndollarschein *m*; **sawdust** N Sägemehl *nt*; **sawfish** N Sägefisch *m*; **sawhorse** N Sägebock *m*; **sawmill** N Sägewerk *nt*

sawn [sɔːn] *ptp of* **saw³**

sawn-off ['sɔːn'ɒf], *(US)* **sawed-off** ['sɔːd'ɒf] ADJ **~ shotgun** Gewehr *nt* mit abgesägtem Lauf

sawtooth N Sägezahn *m*

sawtoothed [ˌsɔː'tuːθt] ADJ gezähnt

sawyer ['sɔːjəʳ] N Sägewerker(in) *m(f)*

sax [sæks] N *(inf: = saxophone)* Saxofon *nt*

saxhorn ['sækshɔːn] N *(Mus)* Saxhorn *nt*, Saxofon *nt*

saxifrage ['sæksɪfrɪdʒ] N Steinbrech *m*

Saxon ['sæksn] N **a** Sachse *m*, Sächsin *f*; *(Hist)* (Angel)sachse *m*/-sächsin *f* **b** *(Ling)* Sächsisch *nt* ADJ sächsisch; *(Hist)* (angel)sächsisch

Saxony ['sæksənɪ] N Sachsen *nt*

saxophone ['sæksəfəʊn] N Saxofon *nt*, Saxophon *nt*

saxophonist [ˌsæk'sɒfənɪst] N Saxofonist(in) *m(f)*, Saxophonist(in) *m(f)*

say [seɪ]
vb: pret, ptp **said**
➲ 1.1, 3.3, 6.3, 13

1 TRANSITIVE/INTRANSITIVE VERB   2 NOUN

1 – TRANSITIVE/INTRANSITIVE VERB

a sagen; **you can say what you like (about it/me)** Sie können (darüber/über mich) sagen, was Sie wollen; **I never thought I'd hear him say that** ich hätte nie gedacht, dass er das sagen würde; **that's not for him to say** es steht ihm nicht zu, sich darüber zu äußern; *(= to decide)* das kann er nicht entscheiden; **he looks very smart, I'll say that for him** er sieht sehr schick aus, das muss man ihm lassen; **if you see her, say I haven't changed my mind** wenn du sie siehst, sag ihr *or* richte ihr aus, dass ich es mir nicht anders überlegt habe; **I'm not saying it's the best, but ...** ich sage *or* behaupte ja nicht, dass es das Beste ist, aber ...; **though I say it myself** wenn ich das mal selbst sagen darf; **never let it be said that I didn't try** es soll keiner sagen können *or* mir soll keiner nachsagen, ich hätte es nicht versucht; **well, all I can say is ...** na ja, da kann ich nur sagen ...; **it tastes, shall we say, interesting** das schmeckt aber, na, sagen wir mal interessant; **you'd better do it – who says?** tun Sie das lieber – wer sagt das?; **well, what can I say?** na ja, was kann man da sagen?; **what does it mean? – I wouldn't like to say** was bedeutet das? – das kann ich auch nicht sagen; **having said that, I must point out ...** ich muss allerdings darauf hinweisen ...; **so saying, he sat down** und mit den Worten setzte er sich

♦ **to say for oneself he didn't have much to say for himself** er sagte *or* redete nicht viel; *(in defence)* er konnte nicht viel (zu seiner Verteidigung) sagen; **what have you got to say for yourself?** was haben Sie zu Ihrer Verteidigung zu sagen?

♦ **to say so if you don't like it, say so** wenn Sie es nicht mögen, dann sagen Sie es doch; **why didn't you say so?** warum haben Sie das denn nicht gesagt?; **do it this way – if you say so** machen Sie es so – wenn Sie meinen

b [giving instructions] **he said to wait here** er hat gesagt, ich soll/wir sollen *etc* hier warten

c [= announce] melden; **who shall I say?** wen darf ich melden?

d [= recite] *poem* aufsagen; *prayer, text* sprechen; **say after me ...** sprechen Sie mir nach ...

e [= pronounce] aussprechen; **he can't say his r's** er kann kein R aussprechen

f [= indicate] *newspaper, dictionary, clock, horoscope* sagen *(inf)*; *(thermometer)* anzeigen, sagen *(inf)*; *(law, church, Bible, computer)* sagen; **it says in the papers that ...** in den Zeitungen steht, dass ...; **what does the paper/this book/your horoscope** *etc* **say?** was steht in der Zeitung/diesem Buch/deinem Horoskop *etc*?; **the rules say that ...** in den Regeln heißt es, dass ...; **what does the weather forecast say?** wie ist *or* lautet *(form)* der Wetterbericht?; **the weather forecast said that ...** es hieß im Wetterbericht, dass ..., laut Wetterbericht ...; **what does your watch say?** wie spät ist es auf Ihrer Uhr?, was sagt Ihre Uhr? *(inf)*; **did the news say anything about the strike?** kam in den Nachrichten etwas über den Streik?; **they weren't allowed to say anything about it in the papers** sie durften in den Zeitungen nichts darüber schreiben

g [= tell] sagen; **it's hard to say what's wrong** es ist schwer zu sagen, was nicht stimmt; **what does that say about his intentions/the main character?** was sagt das über seine Absichten/die Hauptperson aus?; **that says a lot about his character/state of mind** das lässt tief auf seinen Charakter/Gemütszustand schließen; **these figures say a lot about recent trends** diese Zahlen sind in Bezug auf neuere Tendenzen sehr aufschlussreich; **and that's saying a lot** und das will schon etwas heißen; **that's not saying much** das will nicht viel heißen; **that doesn't say much for him** das spricht nicht für ihn; **that says a lot for him** das spricht für ihn; **there's no saying** das weiß keiner; **there's no saying what might happen** was (dann) passiert, das kann keiner vorhersagen; **there's something/a lot to be said for being based in London** es spricht einiges/viel für ein Zuhause *or (for a firm)* für einen Sitz in London

h [= suppose] **say it takes three men to ...** angenommen, man braucht drei Leute, um zu ...; **if it happens on, say, Wednesday?** wenn es am, sagen wir mal Mittwoch, passiert?

i [in suggestions] **what would you say to a whisky/game of tennis?** wie wärs mit einem Whisky/mit einer Partie Tennis?; **shall we say Tuesday/£50?** sagen wir Dienstag/£ 50?; **what did he say to your plan?** was hat er zu Ihrem Plan gesagt?; **I'll offer £500, what do you say to that?** ich biete £ 500, was meinen Sie dazu?; **what do you say we go now?** *(inf)* wie wärs *or* was hieltest du davon, wenn wir jetzt gingen?, was meinst du, sollen wir jetzt gehen?; **let's try again, what d'you say?** *(inf)* was meinste, versuchen wirs noch mal? *(inf)*; **what do you say?** was meinen Sie?; **I wouldn't say no to a cup of tea** ich hätte nichts gegen eine Tasse Tee; **he never says no to a drink** er schlägt einen Drink nie aus, er sagt nie Nein *or* nein zu einem Drink

j [exclamatory] **well, I must say!** na, ich muss schon sagen!; **I say!** *(dated)* na so was!; *(to attract attention)* hallo!; **I say, thanks awfully, old man!** *(dated)* na dann vielen Dank, altes Haus! *(dated)*; **say, what a great idea!** *(esp US)* Mensch, tolle Idee! *(inf)*; **say, buddy!** *(esp US)* he, Mann! *(inf)*; **I should say so!** das möchte ich doch meinen!; **you don't say!** *(also iro)* nein wirklich?, was du nicht sagst!; **well said!** (ganz) richtig!; **you('ve) said it!** Sie sagen es!; **you can say that again!** das kann man wohl sagen!; **say no more!** ich weiß Bescheid!; **says you!** *(inf)* das meinst auch nur du! *(inf)*; **says**

who? *(inf)* wer sagt das?; **and so say all of us** und wir stimmen alle zu

k set expressions **(it's) easier said than done** das ist leichter gesagt als getan; **no sooner said than done** gesagt, getan; **when all is said and done** letzten Endes; **they say ..., it is said ...** es heißt ...; **he is said to be very rich** er soll sehr reich sein, es heißt, er sei sehr reich; **a building said to have been built by ...** ein Gebäude, das angeblich von ... gebaut wurde *or* das von ... gebaut worden sein soll; **it goes without saying that ...** es versteht sich von selbst, dass ..., es ist selbstverständlich, dass ...; **that goes without saying** das ist selbstverständlich; **that is to say** das heißt; *(correcting also)* beziehungsweise; **that's not to say that ...** das soll nicht heißen, dass ...; **the plan sounded vague, not to say impractical** der Plan klang vage, um nicht zu sagen unpraktisch; **to say nothing of the noise/costs** *etc* von dem Lärm/den Kosten *etc* ganz zu schweigen *or* mal ganz abgesehen; **to say nothing of being ...** davon, dass ich/er *etc* ... ganz zu schweigen *or* mal ganz abgesehen; **enough said!** genug!

2 – NOUN

a = opportunity to speak **let him have his say** lass ihn mal reden *or* seine Meinung äußern; **everyone should be allowed to have his say** jeder sollte seine Meinung äußern dürfen, jeder sollte zu Wort kommen; **you've had your say** Sie haben Ihre Meinung äußern können

b = right to decide etc Mitspracherecht *nt* *(in* bei); **to have no/a say in sth** bei etw nichts/etwas zu sagen haben, bei etw kein/ein Mitspracherecht haben; **I want more say in determining ...** ich möchte mehr Mitspracherecht bei der Entscheidung ... haben; **to have the last** *or* **final say (in sth)** (etw) letztlich entscheiden; *(person also)* das letzte Wort (bei etw) haben

SAYE *(Brit) abbr of* **save as you earn**

sayest ['seɪəst] *(obs) 2nd pers sing of* **say**

saying ['seɪɪŋ] N Redensart *f*; *(= proverb)* Sprichwort *nt*; **as the ~ goes** wie man so sagt, wie es so schön heißt

say-so ['seɪsəʊ] N *(inf: = assertion)* Wort *nt*; *(= authority)* Plazet *nt*; **on whose ~?** wer sagt das? *(inf)*, mit welchem Recht?

s/c *abbr of* **self-contained**

scab [skæb] N **a** *(on cut)* Schorf *m*, Grind *m* **b** *(= scabies)* Krätze *f* **c** *(inf: = strikebreaker)* Streikbrecher(in) *m(f)*; **~ labour** *(Brit) or* **labor** *(US)* Streikbrecher *pl* VI **a** *(inf)* den Streik brechen **b** *(wound)* **to ~ over** Schorf bilden

scabbard ['skæbəd] N Scheide *f*

scabby ['skæbɪ] ADJ *(+er)* **a** *skin, hands* schorfig, grindig; *knees* verschorft **b** *(= having scabies)* räudig **c** *(inf: = dilapidated)* schäbig, oll *(inf)*

scabies ['skeɪbiːz] N Krätze *f*, Skabies *f (spec)*; *(of animal also)* Räude *f*, Schäbe *f*

scabious ['skeɪbɪəs] ADJ *(= having scabies)* räudig

scabrous ['skeɪbrəs] ADJ *(= indecent)* geschmacklos

scaffold ['skæfəld] N *(on building)* Gerüst *nt*; *(for execution)* Schafott *nt*

scaffolder ['skæfəldəʳ] N Gerüstbauer(in) *m(f)*

scaffolding ['skæfəldɪŋ] N Gerüst *nt*; **to put up ~** ein Gerüst aufbauen

scag [skæg] N *(US Drugs sl)* Schnee *m (inf)*

scalawag ['skæləwæg] N *(US)* = **scallywag**

scald [skɔːld] N Verbrühung *f* VT **a** *oneself, skin etc* verbrühen; **he was ~ed to death** er erlitt tödliche Verbrennungen; **like a ~ed cat** *(Brit)* wie von der Tarantel gestochen **b** *instruments, vegetables* abbrühen; *milk* abkochen

scalding ['skɔːldɪŋ] ADJ siedend; *(inf: = very hot)* siedend heiß; *(fig) tears* heiß ADV **~ hot** siedend heiß; *skin, weather* glühend heiß

scale¹ [skeɪl] N *(of fish, snake, skin)* Schuppe *f*; *(of rust)* Flocke *f*; *(of paint)* Plättchen *nt*; *(= kettle scale)* Kesselstein *m no pl*; **to take the ~s from sb's eyes** jdm die Augen öffnen; **the ~s fell from his eyes** es fiel ihm wie Schuppen von den Augen VT **a** *fish* (ab)schuppen **b** **to ~ teeth** den Zahnstein entfernen VI *(also* **scale off)** sich schuppen; *(paint, rust)* abblättern

scale² N **(pair of) ~s** *pl*, **~** *(form)* Waage *f*; **the Scales** *(Astron)* die Waage; **~-pan** Waagschale *f*; **he turns** *or* **tips the ~s at 80 kilos** er bringt 80 Kilo auf die Waage; **the extra votes have tipped** *or* **turned the ~s in favour** *(Brit) or* **favor** *(US)* **of Labour** die zusätzlichen Stimmen gaben den Ausschlag für die Labour Party VI wiegen

scale³ N **a** Skala *f*; *(on thermometer etc)* Skala *f*, Gradeinteilung *f*; *(on ruler)* (Maß)einteilung *f*; *(fig)* Leiter *f*; *(= social scale)* Stufenleiter *f*; *(= list, table)* Tabelle *f*; **~ of charges** Gebührenordnung *f*, Tarife *pl*; **he ranks at the top of the ~ of contemporary violinists** er steht an der Spitze der zeitgenössischen Geiger
b *(= instrument)* Messgerät *nt*
c *(Mus)* Tonleiter *f*; **the ~ of G** die G(-Dur)-Tonleiter
d *(of map etc)* Maßstab *m*; **on a ~ of 5 km to the cm** in einem Maßstab von 5 km zu 1 cm; **what is the ~?** welchen Maßstab hat es?, in welchem Maßstab ist es?; **to be out of ~ (with sth)** im Maßstab nicht (zu etw) passen; **to draw sth to ~** etw maßstabgerecht *or* im Maßstab zeichnen; **(drawn/true) to ~** maßstabgerecht
e *(fig: = size, extent)* Umfang *m*, Ausmaß *nt*; **to entertain on a large/small ~** Feste im größeren/im kleineren Rahmen geben; **large stores buy on a different ~ from small ones** große Kaufhäuser kaufen in ganz anderen Mengen als kleine Geschäfte; **inflation on an unprecedented ~** Inflation von bisher nie gekanntem Ausmaß; **they differ enormously in ~** sie haben völlig verschiedene Größenordnungen; **small/large in ~** von kleinem/großem Umfang; **a house designed on a magnificent ~** ein in großem Stil *or* großzügig angelegtes Haus; **it's similar but on a smaller ~** es ist ähnlich, nur kleiner; **on a national ~** auf nationaler Ebene; **on a commercial ~** gewerbsmäßig

▶ **scale down** VT *sep (lit)* verkleinern; *(fig)* verringern; **a sort of scaled-down Parthenon** eine Art Parthenon im Kleinformat

▶ **scale up** VT *sep (lit)* vergrößern; *(fig)* erhöhen

scale⁴ VT *mountain, wall* erklettern

scale: scale drawing N maßstabgerechte *or* maßstabgetreue Zeichnung; **scale model** N maßstäbliches *or* maßstabgetreues Modell

scalene ['skeɪliːn] ADJ *triangle* ungleichseitig; *cone* schief

scaliness ['skeɪlɪnɪs] N Schuppigkeit *f*

scaling ladder ['skeɪlɪŋ'lædəʳ] N Sturmleiter *f*

scallion ['skælɪən] N *(US)* = **spring onion**

scallop ['skɒləp] N **a** *(Zool)* Kammmuschel *f*, Jakobsmuschel *f (esp Cook)*; **~ shell** *(for cooking)* Muschelschale *f* **b** ['skæləp] *(= loop)* Bogen *m*, bogenförmige Verzierung; *(on linenware)* Feston *m* ['skæləp] VT *(= decorate with loops)* mit Bögen *or* mit einem Bogenrand versehen; *linenware* festonieren

scalloped ['skæləpt] ADJ **a** mit einem Bogenrand; *linenware* festoniert; **~ edge** Bogen-/Festonrand *m* **b** ['skɒləpt] *(Cook)* überbacken

scallywag ['skælɪwæg] N *(Brit inf)* Schlingel *m (inf)*, Strolch *m (inf)*

scalp [skælp] N Kopfhaut *f*; *(= American Indian trophy)* Skalp *m*; *(Sport etc)* Trophäe *f*; **she'll not have my ~ quite so easily** so leicht wird sie mich nicht besiegen; **to be after sb's ~** *(fig)* jdn fertigmachen wollen *(inf)* VT skalpieren; *(hum, barber)* kahl scheren *(hum)*; **you've really been ~ed** *(hum)* du bist wohl die Treppe runtergefallen *(inf)*

scalpel ['skælpəl] N Skalpell *nt*

scaly ['skeɪlɪ] ADJ *(+er)* **a** *skin, creature* schuppig; *walls* abblätternd **b** *kettle, pipe* verkalkt

scam [skæm] N *(inf: = deception)* Betrug *m*, Beschiss *m (inf)*

scamp¹ [skæmp] N *(inf)* Frechdachs *m*, Lausebengel *m (inf)*

scamp² VT *work* pfuschen *or* schludern *(inf)* bei

scamper ['skæmpəʳ] N **they can go for a ~ in the garden** sie können im Garten herumtollen VI *(person, child, puppy)* tollen; *(rabbit)* hoppeln; *(squirrel, mice)* huschen

scampi ['skæmpɪ] PL Scampi *pl*

scan [skæn] VT **a** *(= search with sweeping movement)* schwenken über *(+acc)*; *(person)* seine Augen wandern lassen über *(+acc)*; *newspaper, book* überfliegen; *(= examine closely) horizon* absuchen; *(by radar)* absuchen, abtasten; *luggage* durchleuchten; **to ~ the crowd(s)** seinen Blick über die Menge schweifen lassen; **he ~ned her face for a sign of emotion** er suchte in ihrem Gesicht nach Anzeichen einer Gefühlsregung
b *(Med)* eine Tomografie machen von; *pregnant woman* einen Ultraschall machen bei
c *(TV)* abtasten, rastern
d *(Comput)* (ein)scannen
e *verse* in Versfüße zerlegen
VI *(verse)* das richtige Versmaß haben, sich reimen *(inf)*; **he couldn't make it ~** er konnte es nicht ins richtige Versmaß bringen; **stressed differently so that the line ~s** anders betont, um das richtige Metrum in der Zeile zu bekommen
N *(Med)* Scan *m*; *(in pregnancy)* Ultraschalluntersuchung *f*; *(= picture)* Ultraschallaufnahme *f*

▶ **scan in** VT *sep (Comput) graphics* einbinden, einfügen, einscannen

scandal ['skændl] N **a** Skandal *m*; **the ~ of our overcrowded hospitals** unsere skandalös überfüllten Krankenhäuser; **to cause/create a ~** einen Skandal verursachen; *(amongst neighbours etc)* allgemeines Aufsehen erregen; **it's a ~!** (das ist) ein Skandal!; **it is a ~ that ...** es ist skandalös, dass ... **b** *no pl (= gossip)* Skandalgeschichten *pl*; *(= piece of gossip)* Skandalgeschichte *f*; **the latest ~** der neueste Klatsch

scandalize ['skændəlaɪz] VT schockieren; **she was ~d** sie war entrüstet *or* empört *(by* über *+acc)*

scandal: scandalmonger N Klatschmaul *nt (inf)*, Lästerzunge *f*; **scandalmongering** N Klatschsucht *f*; *(by press)* Skandalsucht *f*

scandalous ['skændələs] ADJ skandalös; **~ talk** böswilliger Klatsch; **a ~ report/tale** eine Skandalgeschichte; **to reach ~ proportions** skandalöse Ausmaße annehmen

scandalously ['skændələslɪ] ADV skandalös; **to speak ~ of sb** böse *or* üble Gerüchte über jdn verbreiten; **her children are ~ neglected** es ist skandalös *or* ein Skandal, wie vernachlässigt ihre Kinder sind

scandal-plagued ['skændəl,pleɪgd] ADJ skandalgeplagt

scandal sheet N *(pej inf)* Skandalblatt *nt (pej)*

Scandinavia [,skændɪ'neɪvɪə] N Skandinavien *nt*

Scandinavian [,skændɪ'neɪvɪən] ADJ skandinavisch N Skandinavier(in) *m(f)*

scanner ['skænəʳ] N *(Rad)* Richtantenne *f*; *(TV)* Bildabtaster *m*; *(Comput: = OCR reader, Med)* Scanner *m*

scanning ['skænɪŋ] N *(Comput, Rad, TV)* Scannen *nt*, Abtastung *f*

scanning line N *(TV)* Rasterlinie *f*

scan rate N *(Comput, TV)* Bildwiederholfrequenz *f*

scansion ['skænʃən] N *(Poet)* metrische Gliederung; *(Sch)* Zerlegung *f* in Versfüße

scant [skænt] ADJ *(+er)* wenig *inv*; *satisfaction, attention, respect also, chance* gering; *success* gering, mager; *supply, grazing, amount* dürftig, spärlich; **to do ~ justice to sth** einer Sache *(dat)* wenig *or* kaum gerecht werden; **to have ~ regard for sth** auf etw *(acc)* wenig Rücksicht nehmen; **to show ~ respect for sth** einer Sache *(dat)* wenig Respekt entgegenbringen, für etw wenig Respekt zeigen; **to pay ~ attention to sth** etw kaum beachten; **a ~ 3 hours** knappe *or* kaum 3 Stunden

scantily ['skæntɪlɪ] ADV spärlich; **~ clad** *or* **dressed** spärlich bekleidet

scantiness ['skæntɪnɪs], **scantness** ['skæntnɪs] N *(of amount, supply, information, knowledge)* Spärlichkeit *f*, Dürftigkeit *f*; *(of piece of clothing)* Knappheit *f*

scanty ['skæntɪ] ADJ *(+er) amount, supply, information, knowledge* spärlich, dürftig; *vegetation, meal also* kärglich; *harvest also* mager; *hair* schütter; *piece of clothing* knapp

scapegoat ['skeɪpgəʊt] **N** Sündenbock *m*; **to be a ~ for sth** für etw der Sündenbock sein; **to use sb/sth as a ~, to make sb/sth one's ~** jdm/einer Sache die Schuld zuschieben **VT** die Schuld zuschieben *(+dat)*

scapula ['skæpjʊlə] N *(Anat)* Schulterblatt *nt*

scar [skɑː'] **N** *(on skin, tree)* Narbe *f*; *(= scratch)* Kratzer *m*; *(= burn)* Brandfleck *m*, Brandloch *nt*; *(fig, emotional)* Wunde *f*; *(on good name)* Makel *m*
VT *furniture* zerkratzen, Brandflecken hinterlassen auf *(+dat)*; *(fig) person* zeichnen; **to ~ the skin/a tree** auf der Haut/an einem Baum Narben/eine Narbe hinterlassen; **he was ~red for life** *(lit)* er behielt bleibende Narben zurück; *(fig)* er war fürs Leben gezeichnet; **her ~red face** ihr narbiges Gesicht; **the table was ~red with cigarette burns** der Tisch war mit Brandlöchern *or* Brandflecken von Zigaretten übersät; **his mind was ~red forever by this tragic occurrence** dieses tragische Ereignis hatte bei ihm tiefe Wunden hinterlassen
VI Narben/eine Narbe hinterlassen

scarab ['skærəb] N Skarabäus *m*

scarce [skɛəs] **ADJ** *(+er) (= in short supply)* knapp; *(= rare)* selten; *jobs* rar; **to make oneself ~** *(inf)* verschwinden *(inf)*, abhauen *(inf)* **ADV** *(old)* = **scarcely**

scarcely ['skɛəslɪ] ADV **a** kaum; **~ anybody** kaum einer *or* jemand; **~ anything** fast *or* beinahe nichts; **~ ever** kaum jemals, fast *or* beinahe nie; **with ~ a sound** fast lautlos; **I ~ know what to say** ich weiß nicht recht, was ich sagen soll; **~ had the car drawn to a halt when ...** das Auto war kaum zum Stehen gekommen, als ... **b** *(= not really)* wohl kaum; **you can ~ expect him to believe that** Sie erwarten doch wohl nicht *or* kaum, dass er das glaubt; **he's ~ the most polite of men** er ist nicht gerade *or* er ist wohl kaum der Höflichste

scarceness ['skɛəsnɪs], **scarcity** ['skɛəsɪtɪ] N *(= shortage)* Knappheit *f*; *(= rarity)* Seltenheit *f*; **because of the scarcity of talent among the singers/pupils** weil so wenige Sänger/Schüler wirklich begabt sind; **his pictures are expensive because of their ~** seine Bilder sind teuer, weil es so wenige davon gibt; **a scarcity of qualified people** ein Mangel *m* an qualifizierten Kräften; **in times of scarcity** in schlechten Zeiten; **there are many scarcities in wartime** in Kriegszeiten ist vieles knapp

scarcity value N Seltenheitswert *m*

scare [skɛə'] **N** *(= fright, shock)* Schreck(en) *m*; *(= general alarm)* Panikstimmung *f*, Hysterie *f* *(about* in Bezug auf *+acc*, wegen); **to give sb a ~** jdm einen Schrecken einjagen; *(= make sb jump also)* jdn erschrecken; **the devaluation ~** die Abwertungshysterie; **to create** *or* **cause a ~** eine Panik auslösen
VT einen Schrecken einjagen *(+dat)*; *(= worry)* Angst machen *(+dat)*; *(= frighten physically) person, animal* erschrecken; *birds* aufschrecken; **to be easily ~d** sehr schreckhaft sein; *(= easily worried)* sich *(dat)* leicht Angst machen lassen; *(= timid) deer etc* sehr scheu sein; **to ~ sb stiff** *or* **to death** *or* **out of his/her wits** *(all inf)* jdn zu Tode erschrecken *(inf)*
VI **I don't ~ easily** ich bekomme nicht so schnell Angst

▶ **scare away** VT *sep* verscheuchen; *people* verjagen

▶ **scare off** VT *sep* **a** = **scare away b** *(= put off)* abschrecken *(prep obj* von)

scare: **scare buying** N Angstkäufe *pl*; **scarecrow** N *(lit, fig)* Vogelscheuche *f*

scared ['skɛəd] ADJ **a** *(= afraid) look, face, voice* ängstlich, verängstigt; **he's a ~ man** er hat Angst; **to be ~ (of sb/sth)** (vor jdm/etw) Angst haben; **to be ~ stiff** *or* **to death** *or* **out of one's wits** *(all inf)* Todesängste ausstehen, fürchterliche Angst haben; **to be ~ to do sth** Angst haben, etw zu tun; **she was too ~ to speak** sie konnte vor Angst nicht sprechen; **she was always too ~ to speak in public** sie getraute sich nie, in der Öffentlichkeit zu sprechen; **he's ~ of telling her the truth** er getraut sich nicht, ihr die Wahrheit zu sagen
b *(= apprehensive)* ängstlich; **to be ~ that ...** Angst haben, dass ..., befürchten, dass ...

scaredy-cat ['skɛədɪ,kæt] N *(inf)* Angsthase *m* *(inf)*

scare: **scarehead** N *(US)* Sensationsschlagzeile *f*; **scaremonger** N *(esp Brit)* Panikmacher(in) *m(f)*; **scaremongering** N *(esp Brit)* Panikmache(rei) *f (inf)*; **scare story** N Schauergeschichte *f*; **scare tactics** PL Panikmache(rei) *f (inf)*, Verängstigungstaktik *f*

scarf [skɑːf] N *pl* **scarves** Schal *m*; *(= neck scarf)* Halstuch *nt*; *(= head scarf)* Kopftuch *nt*; *(round the shoulders)* Schultertuch *nt*; **~ pin** Brosche *f*, Vorstecknadel *f*

scarfskin ['skɑːfskɪn] N *(Anat)* Oberhaut *f*

scarifying ['skɛərɪfaɪɪŋ] ADJ *(inf)* beängstigend; *film* grus(e)lig *(inf)*

scarlatina [,skɑːlə'tiːnə] N Scharlach *m*

scarlet ['skɑːlɪt] **N** Scharlach(rot) *nt* **ADJ** (scharlach)rot, hochrot; **to turn** *or* **go ~** hochrot werden, rot anlaufen *(inf)*; **he was ~ with rage** er war rot *or* knallrot *(inf)* vor Wut; **a ~ woman** *(old, hum)* eine verrufene *or* liederliche Frau

scarlet fever N Scharlach *m*, Scharlachfieber *nt*

scarp [skɑːp] N Abhang *m*

scarper ['skɑːpə'] VI *(Brit inf)* abhauen *(inf)*, verduften *(inf)*

scar tissue N vernarbtes Fleisch

scarves [skɑːvz] *pl of* **scarf**

scary ['skɛərɪ] ADJ *(+er) (inf)* **a** unheimlich; *film* grus(e)lig *(inf)*; **it was pretty ~** da konnte man schon Angst kriegen *(inf)*; **that's a ~ thought** das ist ein beängstigender Gedanke **b** *(= nervous) horse, person* schreckhaft; *(= easily worried)* ängstlich

scat¹ [skæt] INTERJ *(inf)* verschwinde!, verschwindet!

scat² *(Jazz)* **N** Scat *m*, *rhythmisches Singen von Silben anstelle von Worten* **VI** Scat singen

scathing ['skeɪðɪŋ] ADJ bissig; *remark also* schneidend; *attack* scharf, schonungslos; *look* vernichtend; *criticism* beißend, vernichtend; **to be ~** bissige *or* schneidende Bemerkungen *pl* machen *(about* über *+acc)*; **to make a ~ attack on sb/sth** jdn/etw scharf angreifen

scathingly ['skeɪðɪŋlɪ] ADV *answer* mit schneidendem Hohn; *look* vernichtend; *criticize, attack* scharf, schonungslos

scatology [skæ'tɒlədʒɪ] N *(Med)* Koprologie *f* *(spec)*; *(fig)* Fäkalsprache *f*, Skatologie *f (geh)*

scatter ['skætə'] **N** = **scattering**
VT **a** *(= distribute at random)* verstreuen; *seeds, gravel* streuen *(on, onto* auf *+acc)*; *(Phys) light* streuen *(on, onto* auf *+acc)*; *money* verschleudern; *(= not group together)* (unregelmäßig) verteilen; *votes* verteilen *(between* auf *+acc)*; **to ~ sth around** *or* **about** etw überall umherstreuen *or* verstreuen; **to ~ sth with sth** etw mit etw bestreuen; **she knocked the table over, ~ing papers all over the room** sie stieß den Tisch um, und die Papiere flogen durch das ganze Zimmer
b *(= disperse)* auseinandertreiben; *demonstrators, crowd also* zerstreuen → *also* **scattered**
VI sich zerstreuen *(to* in *+acc)*; *(in a hurry, in fear)* auseinanderlaufen

scatter: **scatterbrain** N *(inf)* Schussel *m (inf)*; **scatterbrained** ['skætə,breɪnd] ADJ *(inf)* schuss(e)lig *(inf)*, zerfahren, flatterhaft; **scatter cushion** N (Sofa)kissen *nt*

scattered ['skætəd] ADJ *population* weitverstreut; *objects, villages* verstreut; *trees* einzeln stehend; *clouds, showers, fighting* vereinzelt; **my relatives are ~ all over the country** meine Verwandten sind über das ganze Land verstreut; **the books were ~ (about) all over the room** die Bücher lagen im ganzen Zimmer herum *or* verstreut; **a piano ~ with photographs** ein mit Fotos übersätes Klavier

scatter-gun ['skætəgʌn] **N** Schrotflinte *f* **ADJ** *(fig) approach* auf breiter Ebene, breit gefächert

scattering ['skætərɪŋ] N *(of people)* vereinzeltes Häufchen; *(Phys, of light, waves)* Streuung *f*; **a ~ of books/houses** vereinzelte Bücher *pl*/Häuser *pl*; **a thin ~ of snow on the hillside** dünner Schneefall auf dem Hügel

scatter rug N kleiner Teppich

scattershot ['skætəʃɒt] ADJ oberflächlich; **the money has been spent in a ~ fashion** das Geld ist nach dem Gießkannenprinzip *or* ziemlich willkürlich ausgegeben worden

scatty ['skætɪ] ADJ *(+er) (inf)* **a** *(= scatterbrained)* schusslig *(inf)*, schusselig *(inf)* **b** *(= mad)* verrückt, närrisch *(inf)*

scavenge ['skævɪndʒ] **VT** *(lit, fig)* ergattern; **the scraps are ~d by hungry gulls** hungrige Möwen ergattern *or* holen sich *(dat)* die Essensreste; **the tramp ~d food from the piles of litter** der Landstreicher plünderte die Abfallhaufen **VI** *(lit)* Nahrung suchen; **to ~ for sth** nach etw suchen; **jackals live by scavenging** Schakale leben von Aas; **to ~ in the bins** die Abfalleimer plündern; **he's always scavenging around in scrapyards** er durchstöbert dauernd die Schrottplätze

scavenger ['skævɪndʒə'] N *(= animal)* Aasfresser *m*; *(fig: = person)* Aasgeier *m*

SCE *abbr of* **Scottish Certificate of Education** *höherer Schulabschluss in Schottland*

scenario [sɪ'nɑːrɪəʊ] N Szenar(ium) *nt*; *(fig)* Szenario *nt*

scene [siːn] N **a** *(= place, setting)* Schauplatz *m*; *(of play, novel)* Ort *m* der Handlung; **the ~ of the crime** der Tatort, der Schauplatz des Verbrechens; **the ~ of the battle was a small hill** die Schlacht fand auf einem kleinen Hügel statt; **to set the ~** *(lit, fig)* den Rahmen geben; **the ~ is set in Padua** Ort der Handlung ist Padua, das Stück/der Roman *etc* spielt in Padua; **a change of ~ does you good** ein Tapetenwechsel *m* tut dir gut; **to come** *or* **appear on the ~** auftauchen, auf der Bildfläche erscheinen; **to disappear from the ~** von der Bildfläche verschwinden; **after the accident the police were first on the ~** nach dem Unfall war die Polizei als erste zur Stelle
b *(= description, incident)* Szene *f*
c *(Theat)* Szene *f*; **Act II, ~ i** Akt II, 1. Auftritt *or* Szene
d *(Theat: = scenery)* Bühnenbild *nt*, Kulisse *f*; **the stagehands move the ~s** die Bühnenarbeiter wechseln die Kulissen; **behind the ~s** *(lit, fig)* hinter den Kulissen
e *(= sight)* Anblick *m*; *(= landscape)* Landschaft *f*; *(= tableau)* Szene *f*; **~s of Parisian life** Szenen aus dem Pariser Leben; **favourite** *(Brit) or* **favorite** *(US)* **Glasgow ~s** die beliebtesten Ansichten von Glasgow; **they left behind a ~ of destruction** sie hinterließen eine Stätte der Verwüstung
f *(= fuss, argument)* Szene *f*; **to make a ~** eine Szene machen
g *(inf: = area of activity)* Szene *f*; **the London drug/pop** *etc* **~** die Londoner Drogen-/Popszene *etc*; **on the fashion ~** in der Modewelt; **that's not my ~** da steh ich nicht drauf *(inf)*; **to know the ~** *or* **what the ~ is** wissen, was abgeht *(sl)*; **it's a whole different ~ here** hier sieht alles

ganz anders aus, hier läuft alles ganz anders *(inf)*; **to make the ~** groß herauskommen *(inf)*; **he knew he'd made the ~ when ...** er wusste, dass er es geschafft hatte, als ... *(inf)*

scene: **scene change** N Szenenwechsel *m*; **scene painter** N Bühnen- *or* Kulissenmaler(in) *m(f)*

scenery ['si:nərɪ] N **a** *(= landscape)* Landschaft *f*; **there was no ~ at all to look at** die Landschaft bot überhaupt nichts Sehenswertes; **do you like the ~?** gefällt Ihnen die Gegend?; **I'm tired of all the city ~** ich bin stadtmüde **b** *(Theat)* Bühnendekoration *f*, Kulissen *pl*

scene shifter N Kulissenschieber(in) *m(f)*

scenic ['si:nɪk] ADJ **a** *(= of landscape)* landschaftlich; **~ shots** *(Phot)* Landschaftsaufnahmen *pl* **b** *(= picturesque)* malerisch; **to take the ~ route** die landschaftlich schöne Strecke nehmen; *(hum)* einen kleinen Umweg machen **c** *(= theatrical)* bühnentechnisch; *(Film)* filmtechnisch; **~ effects** *(Theat)* Bühneneffekte *pl*; *(Film)* landschaftliche Effekte *pl*

scenic: **scenic design** N Szenenbild *nt*; **scenic designer** N Szenenbildner(in) *m(f)*; **scenic railway** N Touristenbahnlinie *f (durch landschaftlich schönes Gebiet)*, ≈ Berg- und Tal-Bahn *f*; *(= roller coaster)* Achterbahn *f*; **scenic road**, **scenic route** N landschaftlich schöne Strecke

scent [sent] N **a** *(= smell)* Duft *m*, Geruch *m*; **there was the ~ of danger in the air** es roch nach Gefahr **b** *(= perfume)* Parfüm *nt* **c** *(of animal)* Fährte *f*; **to be on the ~** *(lit, fig)* auf der Fährte *or* Spur sein *(of sb/sth* jdm/einer Sache); **to lose the ~** *(lit, fig)* die Spur *or* Fährte verlieren; **to put** *or* **throw sb off the ~** *(lit, fig)* jdn von der Spur *or* Fährte abbringen *or* ablenken **d** *(= sense of smell)* Geruchssinn *m*; *(fig)* (Spür)nase *f* VT **a** *(= smell, suspect)* wittern **b** *(= perfume)* parfümieren; **roses ~ed the air** der Duft von Rosen erfüllte die Luft

▶ **scent out** VT *sep (lit, fig)* aufspüren; *story* ausfindig machen

scent bottle N Parfümfläschchen *nt*

scented ['sentɪd] ADJ *soap, handkerchief* parfümiert; *flower, garden* duftend; **sweet ~** süß duftend; **~ candle** Duftkerze *f*; **~ oil** Duftöl *nt*

scent: **scent gland** N *(pleasant smell)* Duftdrüse *f*; *(unpleasant smell)* Stinkdrüse *f*; **scentless** ['sentlɪs] ADJ *flower* duftlos, geruchlos; *shampoo etc* geruchsfrei, geruchsneutral; **scent spray** N Parfümzerstäuber *m*

scepter N *(US)* = **sceptre**

sceptic, *(US)* **skeptic** ['skeptɪk] N Skeptiker(in) *m(f)*

sceptical, *(US)* **skeptical** ['skeptɪkəl] ADJ skeptisch; **to be ~ about** *or* **of sth** über etw *(acc)* *or* in Bezug auf etw *(acc)* skeptisch sein; **he was ~ about it** er stand der Sache skeptisch gegenüber, er war skeptisch; **I'm ~ about how necessary this is** ich bin skeptisch *or* ich bezweifle, ob das nötig ist; **to have/adopt a ~ attitude toward(s) sth** eine skeptische Haltung gegenüber etw haben/einnehmen; **to cast a ~ eye on** *or* **over sth** einen skeptischen Blick auf etw *(acc)* werfen

sceptically, *(US)* **skeptically** ['skeptɪkəlɪ] ADV skeptisch

scepticism, *(US)* **skepticism** ['skeptɪsɪzəm] N Skepsis *f* *(about* gegenüber)

sceptre, *(US)* **scepter** ['septə'] N Zepter *nt*

sch *abbr of* **school** Sch.

schedule ['skedʒuəl, *(esp Brit)* 'ʃedju:l] N **a** *(of events)* Programm *nt*; *(of work)* Zeitplan *m*; *(of lessons)* Stundenplan *m*; *(esp US: = timetable)* Fahr-/Flugplan *m*; *(US: = list)* Verzeichnis *nt*; **production ~** Produktionsplan *m*, Fertigungsprogramm *nt*; **building ~** Bauprogramm *nt*; **what's on the ~ for today?** was steht für heute auf dem Programm?; **according to ~** planmäßig; *(work also)* nach Plan; **the train is behind ~** der Zug hat Verspätung; **the bus was on ~** der Bus war pünktlich, der Bus kam fahrplanmäßig an; **the building will be opened on ~** das Gebäude wird wie geplant eröffnet werden; **the work is up to ~** die Arbeit verläuft nach Zeitplan; **the work is ahead of/behind ~** wir/sie *etc* sind (mit der Arbeit) dem Zeitplan voraus/in Verzug *or* im Rückstand; **we are working to a very tight ~** unsere Termine sind sehr eng *(inf)*
b *(= insurance, mortgage schedule)* Urkunde *f*; *(US Jur. = appendix)* Anhang *m*
VT planen; *(= put on programme, timetable)* ansetzen; *(US: = list)* aufführen; **the work is ~d for completion in 3 months** die Arbeit soll (nach dem *or* laut Zeitplan) in 3 Monaten fertig(gestellt) sein; **this is not ~d for this year** das steht für dieses Jahr nicht auf dem Programm; **this building is ~d for demolition** es ist geplant, dieses Gebäude abzureißen; **you are ~d to speak for 20 minutes** für Sie sind 20 Minuten Sprechzeit vorgesehen; **she is ~d to speak tomorrow** ihre Rede ist für morgen geplant *or* angesetzt; **trains/buses to New York will be ~d differently** die Abfahrtszeiten der Züge/Busse nach New York werden geändert; **the plane is ~d to take off at 2 o'clock** planmäßiger Abflug ist 2 Uhr; **the journey is ~d to last 7 hours** die Fahrt soll 7 Stunden dauern; **this stop was not ~d** dieser Aufenthalt war nicht eingeplant

scheduled ['skedʒuəld, *(esp Brit)* 'ʃedju:ld] ADJ vorgesehen, geplant; *departure etc* planmäßig; **to make a ~ stop** einen planmäßigen Halt machen; **on/before the ~ date** zum/vor dem geplanten *or* vorgesehenen Datum; **at the ~ time** zum vorgesehenen Zeitpunkt

scheduled: **scheduled building** N *(Brit Archit)* denkmalgeschütztes *or* unter Denkmalschutz stehendes Gebäude; **scheduled flight** N *(= not charter)* Linienflug *m*; *(= on timetable)* planmäßiger Flug; **scheduled territories** PL *(Brit Fin)* der Sterlingblock

schema ['ski:mə] N *pl* **-ta** ['ski:mətə] Darstellung *f*; *(Philos)* Schema *nt*

schematic ADJ, **schematically** ADV [skɪ'mætɪk, -əlɪ] schematisch

scheme [ski:m] N **a** *(= plan)* Plan *m*, Programm *nt*; *(= project)* Projekt *nt*; *(= insurance scheme)* Programm *nt*; *(= idea)* Idee *f*; **the ~ for the new bypass** das neue Umgehungsstraßenprojekt; **a ~ of work** ein Arbeitsprogramm *nt or* -plan *m*; **savings ~** Sparprogramm *nt*
b *(= plot)* (raffinierter) Plan; *(esp political)* Komplott *nt*; *(at court, in firm etc)* Intrige *f*; **a ~ to overthrow the government** ein Komplott *m* gegen die Regierung, Pläne *pl*, die Regierung zu stürzen; **the CIA's ~s to discredit Castro** die Machenschaften *pl* des CIA, um Castro zu diskreditieren
c *(= arrangement, layout, of town centre etc)* Anlage *f*; *(of room etc)* Einrichtung *f*; **the new road ~** das neue Straßensystem; **rhyme ~** Reimschema *nt*; **it doesn't fit into my ~ of things** es hat keinen Platz in meiner Betrachtungsweise; **in the grand ~ of things** im Ganzen gesehen
d *(Brit: = housing scheme)* Siedlung *f*
VI Pläne schmieden *or* aushecken *(inf)*; *(in firm etc)* intrigieren; **to ~ for sth** auf etw *(acc)* hinarbeiten

schemer ['ski:mə'] N raffinierter Schlawiner; *(in firm etc)* Intrigant(in) *m(f)*, Ränkeschmied(in) *m(f) (geh)*; **my mother's a real ~** meine Mutter schmiedet immer ganz raffinierte Pläne

scheming ['ski:mɪŋ] N raffiniertes Vorgehen, Tricks *pl (inf)*; *(of politicians, businessmen etc)* Machenschaften *pl*, Schliche *pl*; *(at court, in firm etc)* Intrigen *pl*, Ränke *pl (liter)* ADJ *girl, methods, businessman* raffiniert, durchtrieben; *colleague, courtier* intrigant; *politician* gewieft *(inf)*; **what's in your ~ little mind?** was führst du im Schild?; **her ~ mother-in-law** ihre hinterhältige Schwiegermutter

schemozzle [ʃɪ'mɒzl] N *(US inf)* Durcheinander *nt*

Schengen Agreement [ʃeŋənə'gri:mənt] N *(Pol)* Schengener Abkommen *nt*

scherzo ['skɜ:tsəʊ] N Scherzo *nt*

schilling ['ʃɪlɪŋ] N *(Hist)* Schilling *m*

schism ['sɪzəm] N *(Eccl)* Schisma *nt*; *(general also)* Spaltung *f*

schismatic [sɪz'mætɪk] ADJ schismatisch N Schismatiker(in) *m(f)*

schist [ʃɪst] N Schiefer *m*

schizo ['skɪtsəʊ] *(inf)* N *(= schizophrenic)* Schizophrene(r) *mf*; *(= crazy person)* Verrückte(r) *mf (inf)* ADJ *(= schizophrenic)* schizophren; *(= crazy)* verrückt *(inf)*

schizoid ['skɪtsɔɪd] ADJ schizoid N Schizoide(r) *mf*

schizophrenia [,skɪtsəʊ'fri:nɪə] N Schizophrenie *f*

schizophrenic [,skɪtsəʊ'frenɪk] ADJ *person, reaction* schizophren; **he has ~ tendencies** er neigt zur Schizophrenie; **a ~ illness** eine Art Schizophrenie N Schizophrene(r) *mf*

schizophrenically [,skɪtsəʊ'frenɪkəlɪ] ADV schizophren; **a ~ disturbed person** ein Mensch mit Bewusstseinsspaltung

schlemiel, **schlemihl** [ʃlə'mi:l] N *(US inf)* Schlemihl *m*, Pechvogel *m*; *(= awkward person)* Tollpatsch *m (pej)*

schlep, **schlepp** [ʃlep] *(US inf)* VT *(= lug)* schleppen, mit sich (herum)schleppen VI *(= traipse)* latschen *(inf)*, sich schleppen; **to ~ through the traffic** sich durch den Verkehr quälen N **a** *(= strenuous journey)* ermüdende Fahrt *or* Reise; *(on foot)* ermüdender Weg **b** = **schlepper**

schlepper ['ʃlepə'] N *(US inf, pej)* **a** *(= tedious person)* Langweiler(in) *m(f) (pej)* **b** *(= awkward person)* Tollpatsch *m (pej)*, Umstandskrämer(in) *m(f) (inf, pej)* **c** *(= stupid person)* Trottel *m (inf, pej)*

schlock [ʃlɒk] N *(dated esp US sl: = trash)* Mist *m (inf)*, Schund *m*

schlong [ʃlɒŋ] N *(US sl)* Schwanz *m (sl)*

schmal(t)z [ʃmɔ:lts] N *(inf)* Schmalz *m (inf)*

schmal(t)zy ['ʃmɔ:ltsɪ] ADJ *(inf: = slushy)* schmalzig *(inf)*

schmear [ʃmɪə'] N *(US inf)* **a** *(= bribe)* Bestechung *f* **b** **the whole ~** das ganze Drumherum *or* Brimborium *(inf)*

schmo [ʃməʊ] N *(US inf: = fool)* Bekloppte(r) *mf (inf)*, Beknackte(r) *mf (sl)*

schmooze [ʃmu:z] *(esp US inf)* VI plaudern beschwatzen *(inf)* Schwätzchen *nt (inf)*

schmoozer [ʃmu:zə'] N *(esp US inf)* *jd, der andere zum eigenen Vorteil ständig beschwatzt*

schmuck [ʃmʌk] N *(US inf: = fool)* Beknackte(r) *mf (sl)*

schnap(p)s [ʃnæps] N Schnaps *m*

schnitzel ['ʃnɪtsəl] N (Wiener) Schnitzel *nt*

schnorkel ['ʃnɔ:kl] N = **snorkel**

schnozzle ['ʃnɒzəl] N *(esp US inf)* Zinken *m (inf)*

scholar ['skɒlə'] N **a** *(= learned person)* Gelehrte(r) *mf*; **the leading ~s of our time** die führenden Wissenschaftler unserer Zeit; **a famous Shakespeare ~** ein bekannter Shakespearekenner; **I'm no ~** ich bin ja kein Gelehrter **b** *(= student)* Student(in) *m(f)*, Schüler(in) *m(f)* **c** *(= scholarship holder)* Stipendiat(in) *m(f)*

scholarliness ['skɒləlɪnɪs] N *(of person, work)* Gelehrtheit *f*, Gelehrsamkeit *f*; **the ~ of his interests** sein Interesse *nt* an hochgeistigen Dingen; **the ~ of his appearance** sein gelehrtes Aussehen

scholarly ['skɒləlɪ] ADJ wissenschaftlich; *(= learned)* gelehrt; *interests* hochgeistig; **he's not at all ~** er hat keinen Hang zum Hochgeistigen; *(in his approach)* er geht überhaupt nicht wissenschaftlich vor; **his way of life was very ~** er führte das Leben eines Gelehrten

scholarship ['skɒləʃɪp] N **a** *(= learning)* Gelehrsamkeit *f*; **~ flourished during the Renaissance** die Gelehrsamkeit entfaltete sich in der Renaissance zur vollen Blüte **b** *(= money award)* Stipendium *nt*; **to win a ~ to Cambridge**

ein Stipendium für Cambridge bekommen; **on a ~** mit einem Stipendium; **~ holder** Stipendiat(in) *m(f)*

scholastic [skəˈlæstɪk] **ADJ** **a** *(= relative to school)* schulisch, Schul-; *(Univ)* Studien-; **her ~ record** ihre schulischen Leistungen, ihre Schulleistungen; *(Univ)* ihre Studienleistungen; **the ~ profession** der Lehrberuf; **~ aptitude test** *(US) Eignungstest vor der Zulassung zu einem College/einer Universität* → *also* **SAT** **b** *(= relative to scholasticism)* scholastisch

scholasticism [skəˈlæstɪsɪzəm] **N** Scholastik *f*

school[1] [sku:l] **N** **a** Schule *f*; *(US: = college, university)* College *nt*, Universität *f*; **at ~** in der Schule/im College/an der Universität; **to go to ~** in die Schule/ins College/zur Universität gehen; **there's no ~ tomorrow** morgen ist schulfrei *or* keine Schule; **~ of art/dancing, art/dancing ~** Kunst-/Tanzschule *f*; **the ~ of life** die Schule des Lebens; **to be brought up in the ~ of hard knocks** durch bittere *or* schlechte Erfahrungen gelernt haben; **to take sb to ~** *(inf)* es jdm zeigen *(inf)*
b *(Univ: = department)* Fachbereich *m*; *(of medicine, law)* Fakultät *f*; **School of Arabic Studies** Institut *nt* für Arabistik
c *(= group of artists, philosophers etc)* Schule *f*; **Plato and his ~** Platon und seine Schüler (-schaft); **I'm not one of that ~** ich gehöre nicht zu den Leuten, die das meinen; **he adheres to another ~ of thought** er vertritt eine andere Lehrmeinung; **he's a diplomat of the old ~** er ist ein Diplomat der alten Schule
VT lehren; *animal* dressieren; *one's temper* zügeln; **to ~ sb in a technique** jdn eine Technik lehren, jdn in einer Technik unterrichten *or* unterweisen; **he ~ed himself to control his temper** er hatte sich dazu erzogen, sich zu beherrschen

school[2] **N** *(of fish)* Schule *f*; *(of herrings)* Schwarm *m*

school *in cpds* Schul-; **school age** **N** schulpflichtiges Alter, Schulalter *nt*; **is he of ~ yet?** ist er schon schulpflichtig *or* im schulpflichtigen Alter?; **school bag** **N** Schultasche *f*; **school board** **N** *(US)* Schulbehörde *f*; *(Brit)* Schulaufsichtsrat *m*; **school book** **N** Schulbuch *nt*; **schoolboy** **N** Schuljunge *m*, Schüler *m* **ADJ** *attr* Pennäler-, Schuljungen-; **~ prank** Pennäler- *or* Schuljungenstreich *m*; **~ humour** *or (US)* **humor** Pennälerhumor *m*; **schoolchildren** **PL** Schüler *pl*, Schulkinder *pl*; **school days** **PL** Schulzeit *f*; **school dinner** **N** Schulessen *nt*; **school dropout** **N** Schulabbrecher(in) *m(f)*

schooled [sku:ld] **ADJ** **to be ~ in sth** in etw *(dat)* geschult sein; **to be well ~ in sth** sich in etw *(dat)* auskennen

school: **school fees** **PL** Schulgeld *nt*; **schoolgirl** **N** Schulmädchen *nt*, Schülerin *f*; **schoolhouse** **N** *(= teacher's house)* Lehrerhaus *nt*; *(= school)* Schulhaus *nt*

schooling [ˈsku:lɪŋ] **N** *(= education)* Ausbildung *f*; **compulsory ~ was introduced in 1870** 1870 wurde die Schulpflicht eingeführt; **compulsory ~ lasts 11 years** die (gesetzlich) vorgeschriebene Schulzeit dauert 11 Jahre

school: **school-leaver** **N** *(Brit)* Schulabgänger(in) *m(f)*; **school-leaving age** **N** *(Brit)* Schulabgangsalter *nt*, Schulentlassungsalter *nt*; **schoolma'am**, **schoolmarm** **N** *(pej)* Schulmeisterin *f (pej)*; **schoolmaster** **N** *(dated)* Lehrer *m*, Schulmeister *m (dated)*; **village ~** Dorfschulleiter *m*, Dorfschulmeister *m (dated)*; **schoolmate** **N** *(Brit)* Schulkamerad(in) *m(f)*, Schulfreund(in) *m(f)*; **school meals** **PL** Schulessen *nt*; **schoolmistress** **N** *(dated)* Lehrerin *f*, Schulmeisterin *f (dated)*; **school outing** **N** Schulausflug *m*; **school report** **N** Schulzeugnis *nt*; **schoolroom** **N** *(in school)* Klassenzimmer *nt*; *(in private house)* Schulzimmer *nt*; **school run** **N** *(Brit) die Zeit, in der Eltern ihre Kinder am Morgen zur Schule bringen und am Nachmittag wieder abholen*; **he's doing the morning ~ this week** diese Woche bringt er die Kinder am Morgen zur Schule; **school ship** **N** *(Mil Naut)* Schulschiff *nt*

schools inspector [ˈsku:lzɪnˈspektəʳ] **N** Schulinspektor(in) *m(f)*

school: **schoolteacher** **N** Lehrer(in) *m(f)*; **school tie** **N** Schulkrawatte *f* → **old school tie**; **school uniform** **N** Schuluniform *f*; **school yard** **N** Schulhof *m*; **school year** **N** Schuljahr *nt*

schooner [ˈsku:nəʳ] **N** **a** *(= boat)* Schoner *m* **b** *(= sherry glass)* großes Sherryglas; *(US, Austral: = beer schooner)* hohes Bierglas

schtick [ʃtɪk] **N** *(US inf: = routine, act)* Nummer *f (inf)*

schuss [ʃʊs] *(Ski)* **N** Schuss *m* **VI** (im) Schuss fahren

schwa [ʃwɑ:] **N** *(Phon)* Schwa *nt*

sciatic [saɪˈætɪk] **ADJ** Ischias-, ischiadisch *(spec)*; **~ nerve** Ischiasnerv *m*

sciatica [saɪˈætɪkə] **N** Ischias *m or nt*

science [ˈsaɪəns] **N** **a** Wissenschaft *f*; *(= natural science)* Naturwissenschaft *f*; **to study ~** Naturwissenschaften studieren; **a man of ~** ein Wissenschaftler *m*; **things that ~ cannot explain** Dinge, die man nicht naturwissenschaftlich erklären kann; **on the ~ side of the school** im naturwissenschaftlichen Zweig der Schule; **the ~ of cooking** die Kochkunst; **the ~ of life/astrology** die Lehre vom Leben/von den Gestirnen
b *(= systematic knowledge or skill)* Technik *f*; **it wasn't luck that helped me to do it, it was ~!** das war kein Zufall, dass mir das gelungen ist, das war Können; **there's a lot of ~ involved in that** dazu gehört großes Können

science fiction **N** Sciencefiction *f*; **~ novel** Zukunftsroman *m*, Sciencefictionroman *m*

science park **N** Forschungspark *m*

scientific [ˌsaɪənˈtɪfɪk] **ADJ** **a** *(= of natural sciences)* naturwissenschaftlich; *apparatus, equipment* wissenschaftlich; **on a ~ basis** auf wissenschaftlicher Grundlage; **the ~ community** die Wissenschaftlergemeinde; **~ officer** wissenschaftlicher Mitarbeiter, wissenschaftliche Mitarbeiterin; **~ opinion** die Expertenmeinung, die wissenschaftliche Lehrmeinung
b *(= systematic, exact) classification, methods, study* wissenschaftlich; **to be ~ about sth** etw systematisch angehen; **he is a keen but not ~ football player** er ist ein begeisterter, doch technisch schwacher Fußballspieler; **his ~ boxing technique** seine gekonnte Boxtechnik

scientifically [ˌsaɪənˈtɪfɪkəlɪ] **ADV** **a** *(= relating to natural sciences)* naturwissenschaftlich; **~ (speaking), his work is ...** vom wissenschaftlichen Standpunkt aus ist seine Arbeit ...; **~ proven** wissenschaftlich erwiesen; **~ based** auf wissenschaftlicher Basis; **~ trained** wissenschaftlich ausgebildet **b** *(= systematically, exactly)* wissenschaftlich, systematisch; *box, fence etc* technisch gekonnt; **he approaches sport very ~** der Sport wird bei ihm zur Wissenschaft

scientist [ˈsaɪəntɪst] **N** (Natur)wissenschaftler(in) *m(f)*

Scientology® [ˌsaɪənˈtɒlɪdʒɪ] **N** Scientology® *f*

sci-fi [ˈsaɪfaɪ] **N** *(inf)* = **science fiction**

Scillies [ˈsɪlɪz], **Scilly Isles** [ˈsɪlɪˌaɪlz] **PL** Scillyinseln *pl*

scimitar [ˈsɪmɪtəʳ] **N** Krummschwert *nt*

scintillate [ˈsɪntɪleɪt] **VI** *(diamonds, stars)* funkeln; *(fig: person, conversation)* vor Geist sprühen

scintillating [ˈsɪntɪleɪtɪŋ] **ADJ** funkelnd *attr*; *(fig: = witty, lively) wit, humour, performance* sprühend *attr*; *person, speech* vor Geist sprühend *attr*; *(= fascinating) information* faszinierend; **to be ~** funkeln; sprühen; vor Geist sprühen; faszinierend sein; **in ~ form** in Hoch- *or* Glanzform

scintillatingly [ˈsɪntɪleɪtɪŋlɪ] **ADV** **~ funny** brillant komisch

scion [ˈsaɪən] **N** **a** *(Bot)* Schössling *m*; *(for grafting)* (Pfropf)reis *nt* **b** *(form)* Nachkomme *m*, Nachfahr(in) *m(f)*

scissors [ˈsɪzəz] **N** **a** *pl* Schere *f*; **a pair of ~** eine Schere **b** *sing (Sport, also* **scissors jump**) Schersprung *m*; *(also* **scissors hold**) Schere *f*

scissors-and-paste [ˌsɪzəzəndˈpeɪst] **ADJ** *(Brit)* **a ~ job** eine zusammengestückelte Arbeit *(usu pej)*

scissors kick **N** *(Swimming, Ftbl)* Scherenschlag *m*

sclerosis [sklɪˈrəʊsɪs] **N** Sklerose *f* → **multiple sclerosis**

sclerotic [sklɪˈrɒtɪk] **ADJ** *(Med) blood vessel* sklerotisch *(spec)*, verkalkt; *(fig)* verkalkt *(inf)*

scoff[1] [skɒf] **N** verächtliche *or* abschätzige Bemerkung **VI** spotten; **to ~ at sb/sth** jdn/etw verachten; *(verbally)* sich verächtlich *or* abschätzig über jdn/etw äußern

scoff[2] *(Brit inf)* **N** *(= food)* Fressalien *pl (inf)*; *(= eating)* Fresserei *f (inf)* **VT** futtern *(inf)*, in sich *(acc)* hineinstopfen *(inf)*; **she ~ed the lot** sie hat alles verputzt *(inf) or* verdrückt *(inf)*

scoffer [ˈskɒfəʳ] **N** Spötter(in) *m(f)*

scoffing [ˈskɒfɪŋ] **N** Spötterei *f*, verächtliche Bemerkungen *pl* **ADJ** spöttisch, verächtlich

scoffingly [ˈskɒfɪŋlɪ] **ADV** spöttisch, verächtlich

scold [skəʊld] **VT** (aus)schelten, ausschimpfen *(for* wegen); **she ~ed him for coming home late** sie schimpfte ihn aus, weil er so spät heimgekommen war **VI** schimpfen **N** *(= person)* Beißzange *f (inf)*; *(= woman also)* Xanthippe *f (inf)*

scolding [ˈskəʊldɪŋ] **N** Schelte *f no pl*; *(= act)* Schimpferei *f*; **to give sb a ~** jdn ausschimpfen, jdn (aus)schelten

scollop **N** = **scallop N a**

sconce [skɒns] **N** *(with candles)* Wandleuchter *m*; *(electric)* Wandleuchte *f*

scone [skɒn] **N** *(Brit) brötchenartiges Buttergebäck*

scoop [sku:p] **N** **a** *(= instrument)* Schaufel *f*; *(for ice cream, potatoes etc)* Portionierer *m*; *(= ball of ice cream, potato)* Kugel *f*; **in one ~** *(lit, fig)* auf einmal **b** *(inf: = lucky gain)* Fang *m (inf)* **c** *(Press)* Knüller *m (inf)*, Scoop *m (sl)*; **have you heard the latest ~?** weißt du schon das Neueste? **VT** **a** *(with scoop)* schaufeln; *liquid* schöpfen **b** **The Times ~ed the other papers** die Times ist den anderen Zeitungen zuvorgekommen **c** *prize, jackpot, award* gewinnen

▶ **scoop out** **VT** *sep* **a** *(= take out)* herausschaufeln; *liquid* herausschöpfen; **the cat scooped out the goldfish with its paw** die Katze hat den Goldfisch mit ihrer Pfote herausgefischt **b** *(= hollow out) melon, marrow etc* aushöhlen; *hole* graben

▶ **scoop up** **VT** *sep* aufschaufeln; *liquid* aufschöpfen; **she scooped the child/cards/money up** sie raffte das Kind/die Karten/das Geld an sich *(acc)*

scoop: **scoop neck** **N** U-Ausschnitt *m*; **scoop-necked** [ˈsku:pˈnekt] **ADJ** mit U-Ausschnitt

scoot [sku:t] **VI** *(inf: = scram)* abzischen *(inf)*; *(= walk quickly)* rennen; **~ across and get it!** komm rüber und hols dir! *(inf)*

scooter [ˈsku:təʳ] **N** (Tret)roller *m*; *(= motor scooter)* (Motor)roller *m*

scope [skəʊp] **N** **a** *(of topic, idea, investigation)* Umfang *m*; *(of law, measures)* Reichweite *f*; *(of sb's duties, department, tribunal)* Kompetenzbereich *m*; **sth is within the ~ of sth** etw hält sich *or* bleibt im Rahmen einer Sache *(gen)*; **sth is within the ~ of a department** *etc* etw fällt in den Kompetenzbereich einer Abteilung *etc*; **sth is beyond *or* outside the ~ of sth** etw geht über etw *(acc)* hinaus; **that's beyond the ~ of this department** das geht über den Kompetenzbereich dieser Abteilung hinaus; **it's not within the ~ of my authority to allow that** es würde meine Kompetenzen überschreiten, dies zu erlauben; **this project is more limited in ~** dieses

Projekt ist auf einen engeren Rahmen begrenzt; **to be broad in ~** breit angelegt sein
b *(= extent of one's perception, grasp)* Fassungsvermögen *nt*; *(of talents, knowledge)* Umfang *m*; **that job would be beyond my ~** diese Arbeit würde meine Fähigkeiten übersteigen; **that is beyond my ~** *or* **the ~ of my understanding** das übersteigt mein Fassungsvermögen; **that job is within his ~** diese Arbeit liegt im Bereich seiner Fähigkeiten
c *(= opportunity)* Möglichkeit(en) *f(pl)*; *(to develop one's talents)* Entfaltungsmöglichkeit *f*; *(to use one's talents)* Spielraum *m*; **there is ~ for improvement** es könnte noch verbessert werden; **there is ~ for further growth in the tourist industry** die Tourismusindustrie ist noch ausbaufähig *or* hat noch Entwicklungsmöglichkeiten; **there is little ~ for originality** es gibt wenig Spielraum für Originalität; **there is little ~ for reducing our costs** es gibt wenig Spielraum, um die Kosten zu senken; **to give sb ~ to do sth** jdm den nötigen Spielraum geben, etw zu tun; **the job gave him/his imaginative powers full ~** in diesem Beruf konnten sich seine Fähigkeiten/konnte sich seine Fantasie *or* Phantasie frei entfalten
d *(inf)* = **microscope, periscope** *etc*

scorbutic [skɔːˈbjuːtɪk] ADJ skorbutisch

scorch [skɔːtʃ] **N** *(also* **scorch mark***)* verbrannte *or* versengte Stelle, Brandfleck *m* **VT** versengen; **the sun ~ed our faces** die Sonne brannte auf unsere Gesichter **VI** **a** **the sun ~ed down** die Sonne brannte herunter **b** *(= become scorched)* **that dress will ~ easily** das Kleid kann man leicht versengen **c** *(inf: = go fast)* rasen *(inf)*

scorched earth policy [ˌskɔːtʃtˈɜːθˈpɒlɪsɪ] N *(Mil)* Politik *f* der verbrannten Erde

scorcher [ˈskɔːtʃəʳ] N *(inf)* **last summer was a real ~** im letzten Sommer war es wirklich heiß; **phew, what a ~!** das ist vielleicht eine Bullenhitze! *(inf)*; **his goal was quite a ~** das war ein scharfes Tor

scorching [ˈskɔːtʃɪŋ] **ADJ** *(= very hot) sun, iron* glühend heiß; *day, weather* brütend heiß, knallheiß *(inf)*; *heat* sengend; *(inf: = very fast) speed* rasend; *driver* rasant; *(fig: = scathing)* gepfeffert *(inf)*; **to set a ~ pace** *(Sport)* ein rasantes Tempo vorlegen **ADV** **the sun is ~ hot** die Sonne ist glühend heiß

score [skɔːʳ] **N** **a** *(= number of points)* (Punkte)stand *m*; *(of game, Sport)* (Spiel)stand *m*; *(= final score)* Spielergebnis *nt*; **what was your ~ in the test?** wie viele Punkte hast du bei dem Test erreicht *or* gemacht? *(inf)*; **England didn't get a very good ~** England hat nicht sehr gut abgeschnitten; *(in game, test also)* England hat nicht sehr viele Punkte erzielt; *(Ftbl etc also)* England hat nicht sehr viele Tore erzielt *or* geschossen; **the ~ was Rangers 3, Celtic 0** es stand 3:0 für Rangers (gegen Celtic); *(= final score)* Rangers schlug Celtic (mit) 3:0; **there was no ~ at half-time** zur Halbzeit stand es 0:0; **to keep (the) ~** (mit)zählen; *(officially)* Punkte zählen; *(on scoreboard)* Punkte anschreiben; **what's the ~?** wie steht es?; *(fig also)* wie sieht es aus? (*on* mit) *(inf)*; **he doesn't know the ~** *(fig)* er weiß nicht, was gespielt wird *(inf)*; **to make a ~ with sb** *(fig)* jdn stark beeindrucken
b *(= reckoning, grudge)* Rechnung *f*; **what's the ~?** was bin ich schuldig?, wie viel macht das?; **to pay off** *or* **settle old ~s** alte Schulden begleichen; **to have a ~ to settle with sb** mit jdm eine alte Rechnung zu begleichen haben
c *(Mus: = printed music)* Noten *pl*; *(esp of classical music)* Partitur *f*; *(of film, musical)* Musik *f*
d *(= line, cut)* Rille *f*, Kerbe *f*; *(on body)* Kratzer *m*; *(= weal)* Striemen *m*
e *(= 20)* zwanzig; **~s of ...** *(= many)* hunderte *or* Hunderte von ..., jede Menge ... *(inf)*; **a ~ of people** zwanzig Leute; **3 ~ years and 10** *(old)* 70 Jahre; **~s and ~s** hunderte *or* Hunderte, jede Menge *(inf)*; **~s of times** hundertmal, zigmal *(inf)*; **by the ~** massenweise *(inf)*
f *(= reason, ground)* Grund *m*; **on that ~** aus diesem Grund, deshalb
VT **a** *(= win)* erzielen; *marks, points* erzielen, bekommen; *goals* schießen, erzielen; *runs* schaffen; *(Rugby) try* erzielen; *(Golf) hole-in-one* machen; **he ~d an advantage over his opponent** er war gegenüber seinem Gegner im Vorteil; **our last contestant ~d one hundred points** unser letzter Kandidat hat hundert Punkte; **each correct answer ~s five points** jede richtige Antwort zählt fünf Punkte; **to ~ a point off** *or* **over sb** *(fig)* auf jds Kosten *(acc)* glänzen, jdn ausstechen; **to ~ a hit with sb** jdn stark beeindrucken; **that remark ~d a hit** diese Bemerkung hat ins Schwarze getroffen
b *(= groove)* einkerben, Rillen/eine Rille machen in *(+acc)*; *(= mark)* Kratzer/einen Kratzer machen in *(+acc)*; *(Cook) fat, meat etc* einschneiden; **the wall is heavily ~d with lines** die Wand weist tiefe Rillen auf
c *(Mus)* schreiben; **the film was ~d by Michael Nyman** die Musik zu dem Film ist *or* stammt von Michael Nyman
d *(inf) drugs* sich *(dat)* beschaffen
VI **a** *(= win points etc)* einen Punkt erzielen *or* machen *(inf)*; *(Ftbl etc)* ein Tor schießen; **to ~ well/badly** gut/schlecht abschneiden; *(in game, test etc also)* eine gute/keine gute Punktzahl erreichen; *(Ftbl etc also)* viele/wenig Tore schießen; **the batsman didn't ~ off the fast balls** der Schlagmann konnte die schnellen Bälle nicht verwandeln; **that's where he ~s** *(fig)* das ist sein großes Plus
b *(= keep score)* (mit)zählen
c *(inf: sexually)* **did you ~ (with her)?** hast du sie flachgelegt? *(sl)*
d *(inf: = obtain drugs)* sich *(dat)* Stoff beschaffen *(inf)*

▶ **score off** **VT** *sep (= delete)* ausstreichen **VI** *+prep obj* **to score off sb** jdn als dumm hinstellen

▶ **score out** *or* **through** VT *sep* aus- *or* durchstreichen

▶ **score up** VT *sep* anschreiben (*to sb* für jdn); **score it up to me** *(fig)* eins zu null für mich *(inf)*

score: **scoreboard** N Anzeigetafel *f*; *(on TV)* Tabelle *f* der Spielergebnisse; **scorecard** N Spielprotokoll *nt*; *(Golf)* Zählkarte *f*; **score draw** N *(Brit Ftbl)* Unentschieden *nt*; **scorekeeper** N *(= official, Sport)* Anschreiber(in) *m(f)*; *(in quiz etc)* Punktezähler(in) *m(f)*; **who's the ~?** wer zählt (mit)?; **scoreless** ADJ *(Sport: = without goals)* torlos; *(= without runs/points)* ohne dass ein Lauf/Punkt erzielt wurde; **Norway had held Holland to a ~ draw in Rotterdam** in Rotterdam hatte Norwegen gegen Holland null zu null gespielt; **the next six innings were ~** bei den nächsten sechs Innings wurde kein Lauf erzielt

scoreline [ˈskɔːlaɪn] N *(Brit Sport)* Endergebnis *nt*, Endstand *m*

scorer [ˈskɔːrəʳ] N **a** *(Ftbl etc: = player)* Torschütze *m*/-schützin *f*; **to be the top ~** die meisten Punkte machen; *(Ftbl etc)* die meisten Tore schießen; **Chelsea were the highest ~s** Chelsea schoss die meisten Tore; **he is the leading ~ in the competition** er hat die meisten Punkte *or (Ftbl)* Tore im Wettbewerb erzielt
b = **scorekeeper**

score sheet N Spielberichtsbogen *m*, Protokoll *nt*

scoring [ˈskɔːrɪŋ] **N** Erzielen *nt* eines Punktes; *(Ftbl etc)* Torschuss *m*; *(= scorekeeping)* Zählen *nt*; **to open the ~** den ersten Punkt machen; *(Ftbl etc)* das erste Tor schießen; **rules for ~** Regeln über die Zählweise; **so far there has been no ~** *(Ftbl etc)* bis jetzt ist noch kein Tor gefallen; **X did most of the ~** X erzielte die meisten Punkte; *(Ftbl etc)* X schoss die meisten Tore **ADJ** *suf* **a low-/high-~ match** ein Spiel, in dem wenig/viele Punkte/Tore erzielt wurden; **he is Arsenal's top-~ player** er hat die meisten Tore für Arsenal erzielt *or* geschossen, er ist Arsenals Torschützenkönig

scoring: **scoring chance** N *(Sport)* Torchance *f*; **scoring spree** N *(Sport)* Schützenfest *nt (inf)*; **to go on a ~** ein Schützenfest veranstalten *(inf)*

scorn [skɔːn] **N** *(= disdain)* Verachtung *f*; *(verbal also)* Hohn *m*; **to laugh sb/sth to ~** jdn/etw höhnisch verlachen; **to pour** *or* **heap ~ on sb/sth** jdn/etw verächtlich abtun; **to arouse sb's ~** jds Verachtung ernten **VT** *(= treat scornfully)* verachten; *(condescendingly)* verächtlich behandeln; *(= turn down) gift, advice* verschmähen; *idea* mit Verachtung von sich weisen; **to ~ to do sth** es für seiner *(gen)* unwürdig halten, etw zu tun; **to ~ sb as sth** jdn verächtlich als etw abtun

scornful [ˈskɔːnfʊl] ADJ verächtlich; *laughter also, person* spöttisch, höhnisch; **to be ~ of sb/sth** jdn/etw verachten; *(verbally)* jdn/etw verhöhnen; **to be ~ about sb/sth** sich über jdn/etw verächtlich äußern

scornfully [ˈskɔːnfəlɪ] ADV verächtlich; *laugh also* spöttisch, höhnisch

scornfulness [ˈskɔːnfʊlnɪs] N Verachtung *f* (*of* für); **her ~ at the mere mention of his name** ihre verächtliche *or* höhnische Reaktion bei der bloßen Erwähnung seines Namens

Scorpio [ˈskɔːpɪəʊ] N Skorpion *m*; **he's (a) ~** er ist Skorpion

scorpion [ˈskɔːpɪən] N Skorpion *m*

Scot [skɒt] N Schotte *m*, Schottin *f*

Scotch [skɒtʃ] **ADJ** schottisch; **~ terrier** Scotchterrier *m*, Schottischer Terrier **N** **a** *(= Scotch whisky)* Scotch *m* **b** **the ~** *pl* die Schotten *pl*

scotch [skɒtʃ] VT *rumour* aus der Welt schaffen; *idea, plan* unterbinden, einen Riegel vorschieben *(+dat)*; **the rain has ~ed that** der Regen hat uns *(dat)* einen Strich durch die Rechnung gemacht *(inf)*

Scotch: **Scotch broth** N *(Brit) Gemüsesuppe mit Gerstengraupen und Hammelfleischbrühe*; **Scotch egg** N *(Brit) hart gekochtes Ei in Wurstbrät, paniert und ausgebacken*; **Scotch fir** N Föhre *f*, (gemeine) Kiefer; **Scotchman** N = **Scotsman**; **Scotch mist** N feuchter Nebel; **Scotch tape®** N Klebeband *nt*, Klebestreifen *m*, ≈ Tesafilm® *m*; **Scotchwoman** N = **Scotswoman**

scot-free [ˈskɒtˈfriː] ADV ungeschoren; **to get off ~** ungeschoren davonkommen

Scotland [ˈskɒtlənd] N Schottland *nt*

Scots [skɒts] **ADJ** schottisch **N** *(= dialect)* Schottisch *nt*; **the ~** *(= people)* die Schotten *pl*

Scots: **Scots law** N schottisches Recht; **Scotsman** N Schotte *m*; **Scots pine** N Föhre *f*, (gemeine) Kiefer; **Scotswoman** N Schottin *f*

Scotticism [ˈskɒtɪsɪzəm] N schottischer Ausdruck

scotticize [ˈskɒtɪsaɪz] VT schottifizieren, verschotten *(hum)*

Scottie [ˈskɒtɪ] N **a** *(also* **Scottie dog***)* Scotchterrier *m*, Schottischer Terrier **b** *(inf: = Scotsman)* Schotte *m*

Scottish [ˈskɒtɪʃ] **ADJ** schottisch **N** **a** *(= dialect)* Schottisch *nt* **b** **the ~** *pl* die Schotten *pl*

Scottish: **Scottish Nationalism** N schottischer Nationalismus; **Scottish National Party** N *schottische Partei, die sich für die Unabhängigkeit des Landes einsetzt*; **Scottish Office** N **the ~** das Ministerium für schottische Angelegenheiten; **Scottish Parliament** N **the ~** das schottische Parlament; **Scottish Secretary** N *(Brit Pol)* Minister(in) *m(f)* für schottische Angelegenheiten

scoundrel [ˈskaʊndrəl] N *(dated)* Schurke *m*; Bengel *m*

scoundrelly [ˈskaʊndrəlɪ] ADJ *(dated)* schurkisch

scour[1] [ˈskaʊəʳ] **VT** scheuern **N** Scheuern *nt*; **give the pan a good ~** scheuern Sie den Topf gründlich

▶**scour away** *or* **off** VT *sep* abscheuern; *rust* abreiben

▶**scour out** VT *sep pan* ausscheuern; *borehole* durchspülen

scour² VT *area, town, shops* absuchen, abkämmen (*for* nach); *newspaper* durchkämmen (*for* nach)

▶**scour about** (*Brit*) *or* **around** VI herumsuchen (*for* nach)

scourer ['skaʊərəʳ] N Topfkratzer *m*; (= *sponge*) Scheuerschwamm *m*

scourge [skɜːdʒ] N (*lit, fig*) Geißel *f* VT **a** (*lit*) geißeln **b** (*fig,* = *punish*) (be)strafen; (= *devastate*) heimsuchen; (*verbally*) geißeln (*geh*)

scouring pad ['skaʊərɪŋ,pæd] N = **scourer**

Scouse [skaʊs] ADJ Liverpooler N **a** (= *person*) Liverpooler(in) *m(f)* **b** (= *dialect*) Liverpooler Dialekt *m*

Scouser ['skaʊsəʳ] N (*Brit inf*) Liverpooler(in) *m(f)*

scout [skaʊt] N **a** (*Mil:* = *person*) Kundschafter(in) *m(f)*, Späher(in) *m(f)*; (= *ship, plane*) Aufklärer *m*
b (= *reconnaissance*) Erkundung *f*; (*Mil*) Aufklärung *f*; (= *search*) Suche *f*; **to have** *or* **take a ~ (a)round for sth** sich nach etw umsehen
c Scout (= *boy scout*) Pfadfinder *m*; (*US:* = *girl scout*) Pfadfinderin *f*
d (= *football scout etc*) Kundschafter(in) *m(f)*, Spion(in) *m(f)*; (= *talent scout*) Talentsucher(in) *m(f)*
e (*employed by motoring organization*) Pannenhelfer(in) *m(f)*
f (*Brit, Univ*) *Diener für die College-Studenten*
VI erkunden, auskundschaften; **they were ~ing inside enemy territory** sie waren auf Erkundung in feindlichem Gebiet; **to ~ for sth** nach etw Ausschau *or* Umschau halten; **he was ~ing for new talent** er war auf Talentsuche
VT *area, country* erkunden

▶**scout about** (*Brit*) *or* **around** VI sich umsehen (*for* nach)

▶**scout out** VT *sep* aufstöbern; (*Mil*) auskundschaften

scout car N Aufklärungsfahrzeug *nt*; (*heavier*) Aufklärungs- *or* Spähpanzer *m*

scouting ['skaʊtɪŋ] N **a** Erkunden *nt*, Auskundschaften *nt*; (*Mil*) Aufklärung *f*; (= *looking*) Suche *f* (*for* nach); (*for talent*) Talentsuche *f* **b Scouting** (= *scout movement*) Pfadfinderei *f* (*inf*), Pfadfindertum *nt* ADJ *attr* **Scouting** Pfadfinder-; **Scouting organization** Pfadfinderorganisation *f*

scout: **scoutmaster** N Gruppenführer *m*; **scout movement** N Pfadfinderbewegung *f*; **scout troop** N Pfadfindergruppe *f*

scow [skaʊ] N (*Naut*) Prahm *m*

scowl [skaʊl] N unmutiger Ausdruck, finsterer Blick, böses Gesicht; **to give sb a ~** jdn böse ansehen VI ein böses *or* finsteres Gesicht machen; **to ~ at sb** jdn böse ansehen; **what are you ~ing about** *or* **at?** warum machst du so ein böses Gesicht?

scowling ['skaʊlɪŋ] ADJ missmutig

SCR (*Brit Univ*) *abbr of* **senior common room**

scrabble ['skræbl] VI (*also* **scrabble about** (*Brit*) *or* **around**) (herum)tasten; (*among movable objects*) (herum)wühlen; **the hens ~d (around) in the earth** die Hühner wühlten im Boden herum; **his mind ~d for alternatives** er suchte in seinem Hirn nach Alternativen N **Scrabble**® Scrabble® *nt*

scrag [skræg] N (*also* **scrag end**) Hals *m* VT (*sl:* = *kill*) abmurksen (*inf*)

scragginess ['skrægɪnɪs] N Magerkeit *f*; (*of meat*) minderwertige Qualität, Sehnigkeit *f*

scraggly ['skræglɪ] ADJ (+*er*) *beard, hair* zottig, zottelig; *plant* kümmerlich

scraggy ['skrægɪ] ADJ (+*er*) **a** (= *scrawny*) dürr; *meat* minderwertig, sehnig **b** (= *unkempt, scanty*) *hair* zottig, zerfranst; *fur* zottig

scram [skræm] VI (*inf*) abhauen (*inf*); **~!** verschwinde/verschwindet!

scramble ['skræmbl] N **a** (= *climb*) Kletterei *f*; **we went for a ~ in the hills** wir sind in den Bergen herumgeklettert
b (= *mad dash*) Gerangel *nt*, Gedrängel *nt*; **the ~ for the better-paid jobs** die Jagd nach den besser bezahlten Stellen
c (*Motor sport*) Querfeldeinrennen *nt*
VT **a** *pieces, letters* (untereinander) mischen; **this will ~ your brain(s)** das verwirrt dein armes Hirn
b *eggs* verquirlen, verrühren
c (*Telec*) *message* chiffrieren, verschlüsseln; *line* an das Verschlüsselungsgerät anschließen
d (*Mil*) *helicopter, crew* schnell losschicken
VI **a** (= *climb*) klettern; **to ~ out** herausklettern; **he ~d to his feet** er rappelte sich auf (*inf*); **to ~ through a hedge** durch eine Hecke kriechen *or* krabbeln (*inf*); **to ~ up sth** auf etw (*acc*) hinaufklettern *or* hinaufkraxeln (*inf*)
b (= *struggle*) **to ~ for sth** sich um etw balgen *or* raufen; *for ball etc* um etw kämpfen; *for bargains, job, good site* sich um etw drängeln; **to ~ to get sth** sich balgen *or* raufen, um etw zu bekommen; *ball etc* darum kämpfen, etw zu bekommen; *bargains, job, good site* sich drängeln, um etw zu bekommen
c (*Aviat*) einen Soforteinsatz fliegen; **~!** höchste Alarmstufe

scrambled egg(s) [,skræmbld'eg(z)] N(PL) Rührei(er) *nt(pl)*

scrambler ['skræmbləʳ] N **a** (*Telec*) Chiffriergerät *nt* **b** (= *motorcyclist*) Querfeldeinfahrer(in) *m(f)*

scrap¹ [skræp] N **a** (= *small piece*) Stückchen *nt*; (*fig*) bisschen *no pl*; (*of papers, conversation, news*) Fetzen *m*; (*of truth*) Fünkchen *nt*, Spur *f*; (*of poetry*) Fragment *nt*; **there isn't a ~ of food in the house** es ist überhaupt nichts zu essen *or* kein Bissen zu essen im Haus; **his few ~s of German** seine paar Brocken Deutsch; **his few ~s of knowledge** das bisschen Wissen, das er hat; **a few ~s of information** ein paar magere Auskünfte; **it's a ~ of comfort** es ist wenigstens ein kleiner Trost; **not a ~!** nicht die Spur!; **not a ~ of evidence** nicht der geringste Beweis; **he was not a ~ of help** er war überhaupt keine Hilfe, er war nicht die geringste Hilfe
b (*usu pl:* = *leftover*) Rest *m*
c (= *waste material*) Altmaterial *nt*, Altwaren *pl*; (= *metal*) Schrott *m*; (= *paper*) Altpapier *nt*; **these bits are ~** diese Sachen werden nicht mehr gebraucht; **are these notes ~?** können die Notizen weggeworfen werden?; **to sell a ship for ~** ein Schiff als Schrott *or* zum Verschrotten verkaufen; **what is your car worth as ~?** wie hoch ist der Schrottwert Ihres Autos?
VT *car, ship etc* verschrotten; *furniture, clothes* ausrangieren; *idea, plan etc* fallen lassen; *piece of work* wegwerfen; **~ that** (*inf:* = *forget it*) vergiss es!

scrap² (*inf*) N Balgerei *f*; (*verbal*) Streiterei *f*; **to get into** *or* **have a ~ with sb** mit jdm in die Wolle geraten (*inf*) VI sich balgen; (*verbal*) sich streiten

scrap: **scrapbook** ['skræpbʊk] N Sammelalbum *nt*; **scrap car** N Altauto *nt*, Schrottauto *nt*; **scrap dealer** N Altwarenhändler(in) *m(f)*; (*in metal*) Schrotthändler(in), Altmetallhändler(in) *m(f)*

scrape [skreɪp] N **a** (= *act*) **to give sth a ~** (= *make clean or smooth, potatoes, carrots etc*) etw schaben; *plate, wall, shoes* etw abkratzen; *dish, saucepan* etw auskratzen; (= *mark, graze*) *car* etw schrammen; *wall, gatepost* etw streifen; *arm, knee* etw auf- *or* abschürfen
b (= *mark, graze*) Schramme *f*
c (= *sound*) Kratzen *nt*; **the ~ of his feet on the gravel** das Knirschen seiner Füße auf dem Kies
d (*dated:* = *difficulty*) Schwulitäten *pl* (*inf*); **to get into a ~** in Schwulitäten kommen (*inf*); **he gets into one ~ after another** er handelt sich (*dat*) dauernd Ärger ein (*inf*); **to get sb out of a ~** jdm aus der Patsche *or* Klemme helfen (*inf*)
VT **a** (= *make clean or smooth*) *potatoes, carrots etc* schaben; *plate, wall, shoes* abkratzen; *dish, saucepan* auskratzen; **that's really scraping the (bottom of the) barrel** (*fig*) das ist wirklich das Letzte vom Letzten
b (= *mark, graze*) *car* schrammen; *wall, gatepost* streifen; *arm, knee* auf- *or* abschürfen; **the paint was ~d in the crash** der Lack bekam bei dem Unfall Kratzer
c (= *grate against*) kratzen an (+*dat*); **he ~d his bow across the violin** er kratzte mit dem Bogen auf der Geige; **he ~d his nail along the glass** er kratzte mit dem Nagel über das Glas
d (= *make by scraping*) *hole* scharren; **to ~ a living** gerade so sein Auskommen haben; **he ~d a living as a freelance reporter** er hielt sich als freier Reporter gerade so über Wasser (*inf*); **he was trying to ~ (up) an acquaintance with him** er versuchte mit allen Mitteln, seine Bekanntschaft zu machen
VI **a** (= *make clean*) kratzen; **he ~d at the paint for hours** er kratzte stundenlang an der Farbe herum
b (= *rub*) streifen (*against* +*acc*); (= *grate*) kratzen (*against* an +*dat*); **the bird's broken wing ~d along the ground** der gebrochene Flügel des Vogels schleifte am Boden; **as he ~d past me** als er sich an mir vorbeizwängte; **the car just ~d past the gatepost** der Wagen fuhr um Haaresbreite am Torpfosten vorbei → **bow²**
c (= *be economical*) knapsen (*inf*), knausern

▶**scrape along** VI sich schlecht und recht durchschlagen (*inf*) (*on* mit)

▶**scrape away** VI herumkratzen (*at* an +*dat*) VT *sep* abkratzen

▶**scrape by** VI (*lit*) sich vorbeizwängen; (*fig*) sich durchwursteln (*inf*) (*on mit*)

▶**scrape in** VI **he just managed to scrape in** er ist gerade noch hineingerutscht (*inf*)

▶**scrape off** VI sich abkratzen lassen VT *sep* abkratzen (*prep obj* von)

▶**scrape out** VT *sep* auskratzen, ausschaben; *eyes of potato, bad parts* ausschneiden

▶**scrape through** VI (*lit, object*) gerade so durchgehen; (*person*) sich durchzwängen; (*in exam*) durchrutschen (*inf*) VI +*prep obj narrow gap* sich durchzwängen durch; *exam* durchrutschen durch (*inf*)

▶**scrape together** VT *sep leaves* zusammenharken, zusammenrechen; *money* zusammenkratzen; *people* zusammenbringen, organisieren; *support* organisieren

▶**scrape up** VT *sep* (*lit*) aufkratzen, zusammenkratzen; *money* auftreiben (*inf*); *support* organisieren

scraper ['skreɪpəʳ] N (= *tool*) Spachtel *m*; (*at door*) Kratzeisen *nt*

scrap heap N Schrotthaufen *m*; **to be thrown on the ~** (*thing*) zum Schrott geworfen werden; (*person*) zum alten Eisen geworfen werden; (*idea*) über Bord geworfen werden; **to end up on the ~** (*person*) beim alten Eisen landen; **at 55 you're on the ~** mit 55 gehört man zum alten Eisen

scrapings ['skreɪpɪŋz] PL (*of food*) Reste *pl*; (= *potato scrapings*) Schalen *pl*; (= *carrot scrapings*) Schababfälle *pl*, Schabsel *pl*; (= *metal scrapings*) Späne *pl*; **~ of old paint** abgekratzte alte Farbe

scrap: **scrap iron** N Alteisen *nt*; **scrap merchant** N Schrotthändler(in) *m(f)*; **scrap metal** N Schrott *m*, Altmetall *nt*

scrapped car [,skræpt'kɑː] N Altauto *nt*, Schrottauto *nt*

scrappiness ['skræpɪnɪs] N (*of knowledge*) Lückenhaftigkeit *f*; **she apologized for the ~ of the meal** sie entschuldigte sich für das zusammengestoppelte Essen

scrappy ['skræpɪ] ADJ (+*er*) (= *disjointed*) zusammengestückelt, zusammengestoppelt (*inf*); *knowledge* lückenhaft; *football match* orientierungslos; **a ~ goal** ein Zufallstor *nt*

scrapyard ['skræpjɑ:d] N (*esp Brit*) Schrottplatz *m*

scratch [skrætʃ] N a (*= mark*) Kratzer *m*
b (*= act*) **to give a dog a ~** einen Hund kratzen; **to have a ~** sich kratzen; **the dog enjoys a ~** der Hund kratzt sich gern
c (*= sound*) Kratzen *nt no pl*
d **to start from ~** (ganz) von vorn(e) anfangen; (*Sport*) ohne Vorgabe anfangen; **to start sth from ~** etw ganz von vorne anfangen; *business* etw aus dem Nichts aufbauen; **to learn a language/a new trade from ~** eine Sprache/einen neuen Beruf ganz von Anfang an *or* von Grund auf erlernen; **to be** *or* **come up to ~** (*inf*) die Erwartungen erfüllen, den Anforderungen entsprechen; **he/it is not quite up to ~ yet** (*inf*) er/es lässt noch zu wünschen übrig; **to bring sb up to ~** jdn auf Vordermann bringen (*inf*)
ADJ *attr* a *meal* improvisiert; *crew, team* zusammengewürfelt
b (*= with no handicap*) ohne Vorgabe
VT a (*with nail, claw etc*) kratzen; *hole* scharren; (*= leave scratches on*) zerkratzen; **the spots will get worse if you ~ them** die Pickel werden nur schlimmer, wenn du (daran) kratzt; **she ~ed the dog's ear** sie kratzte den Hund am Ohr; **to ~ sth away** etw abkratzen; **we ~ed our names in the wood** wir ritzten unsere Namen ins Holz; **to ~ a living** sich (*dat*) einen kümmerlichen Lebensunterhalt verdienen; **he ~ed a living from the soil** er konnte sich nur mühsam von den Erträgen des Bodens ernähren; **to ~ one's head** (*lit, fig*) sich am Kopf kratzen; **if you ~ my back, I'll ~ yours** (*fig*) eine Hand wäscht die andere; **to ~ the surface of sth** (*fig*) etw oberflächlich berühren
b **to ~ sth through** etw durchstreichen; **to ~ sb/sb's name off a list** jdn/jds Namen von *or* aus einer Liste streichen
c (*Sport etc, = withdraw*) streichen; *horse* zurückziehen
VI a (*= make scratching movement/noise*) kratzen; (*in soil etc*) scharren; (*= scratch oneself*) sich kratzen
b (*= become scratched*) **the new paint will ~ easily/won't ~** die neue Farbe bekommt leicht Kratzer/bekommt keine Kratzer
c (*Mus*) scratchen
d (*Sport*) zurücktreten; **to ~ from** nicht antreten zu

▶ **scratch about** (*Brit*) *or* **around** VI (*lit*) herumscharren; (*fig inf*) sich umtun (*inf*) *or* umsehen (*for* nach)

▶ **scratch out** VT *sep* auskratzen; (*= cross out*) ausstreichen

▶ **scratch together** = **scratch up b**

▶ **scratch up** VT *sep* a (*lit*) ausscharren b (*fig*) *money* zusammenkratzen; *team* zusammenbringen, auftreiben (*inf*)

scratch and sniff, scratch 'n' sniff ADJ **~ card** Duftkarte *f*; **a ~ advertisement for perfume** eine Parfümwerbung mit einer Duftprobe zum Rubbeln

scratchcard ['skrætʃkɑ:d] N (*Brit: for lottery etc*) Rubbellos *nt*

scratchily ['skrætʃɪlɪ] ADV kratzend

scratchiness ['skrætʃɪnɪs] N Kratzen *nt*

scratching ['skrætʃɪŋ] N (*Mus*) Scratchen *nt*, Scratching *nt*

scratch: **scratch line** N (*US, in races*) Startlinie *f*; (*in jumping*) Absprunglinie *f*; (*in throwing*) Abwurflinie *f*; **scratch method** N (*Med: = test*) Skarifikation *f* (*spec*); (*= inoculation*) Ritzmethode *f*; **scratch 'n' sniff** ADJ = **scratch and sniff**; **scratch pad** N (*US Comput*) Notizblock *m*; **scratch paper** N (*US*) Notizpapier *nt*; **scratch-resistant** ADJ kratzfest; **scratch sheet** N (*US Horse Racing inf*) Rennzeitung *f*; **scratch test** N (*Med*) Kutanreaktionstest *m*, Einreibungstest *m*

scratchy ['skrætʃɪ] ADJ (*+er*) *sound, pen* kratzend *attr*; *record* zerkratzt; *feel, sweater* kratzig; **does his beard feel ~?** kratzt sein Bart?; **my old record-player has a rather ~ tone** mein alter Plattenspieler kracht ziemlich

scrawl [skrɔ:l] N Krakelei *f*, Gekrakel *nt* (*inf*); (*= handwriting*) Klaue *f* (*inf*); (*inf: = message*) gekritzelte Nachricht; **the word finished in a ~** das Wort hörte mit einem Krakel auf (*inf*) VT hinschmieren (*inf*), hinkritzeln; **it's been ~ed all over with obscene messages** es war ganz vollgeschmiert mit Obszönitäten VI krakeln (*inf*), schmieren

scrawny ['skrɔ:nɪ] ADJ (*+er*) dürr

scream [skri:m] N a Schrei *m*; (*of saw, tyres*) Kreischen *nt*; (*of engines, siren*) Heulen *nt*; **there were ~s of laughter from the audience** das Publikum kreischte vor Lachen; **to let out** *or* **give a ~** einen Schrei ausstoßen; **a ~ of pain** ein Schmerzensschrei *m*; **a ~ of fear** ein Aufschrei *m*; **the car stopped with a ~ of tyres** das Auto hielt mit kreischenden Reifen an
b (*fig inf*) **to be a ~** zum Schreien sein (*inf*)
VT schreien; *command* brüllen; (*fig, headlines*) ausschreien; **to ~ sth at sb** jdm etw zuschreien; **you idiot, she ~ed at me** du Idiot, schrie sie mich an; **she ~ed insults at him** sie schrie ihm Beleidigungen ins Gesicht; **to ~ one's head off** (*inf*) sich (*dat*) die Lunge aus dem Leib *or* Hals schreien
VI schreien; (*saw, tyres*) kreischen; (*wind, engine, siren*) heulen; **to ~ at sb** jdn anschreien; **to ~ for sth** nach etw schreien; **to ~ in** *or* **with pain** vor Schmerzen schreien; **to ~ with laughter** vor Lachen kreischen; **an ambulance ~ed past** ein Krankenwagen heulte vorbei; **newspaper headlines which ~ at you** (*fig*) Schlagzeilen, die einem entgegenschreien

▶ **scream out** VI aufschreien; **to scream out for sth** (*lit, fig*) nach etw schreien VT *sep* ausschreien; (*person*) hinausschreien; *name* schreien, rufen; *warning* ausstoßen

screaming ['skri:mɪŋ] ADJ (*lit, fig*) schreiend; *saw, tyres* kreischend; *wind, engine, siren* heulend; (*inf, = bold*) *clothes* grell, in schreienden Farben N **~ match** gegenseitige Anbrüllerei (*inf*); **to have a ~ match** sich gegenseitig anbrüllen (*inf*)

screamingly ['skri:mɪŋlɪ] ADV **~ funny** (*inf*) zum Schreien komisch (*inf*)

scree [skri:] N Geröll *nt*; **~ slope** Geröllhalde *f*, Geröllfeld *nt*

screech [skri:tʃ] N Kreischen *nt no pl*; (*of women, tyres, brakes also*) Quietschen *nt no pl*; (*of owl*) Schrei *m*; (*of whistle*) Schrillen *nt no pl*; **the car stopped with a ~ of brakes** das Auto hielt mit quietschenden Bremsen; **to give a ~ of anger/laughter** zornig/vor Lachen kreischen
VT schreien; *high notes* quietschen
VI kreischen; (*women, tyres, brakes also*) quietschen; **to ~ with pain** vor Schmerzen schreien; **to ~ with anger/laughter** zornig/vor Lachen kreischen; **to ~ with delight** vor Vergnügen quietschen; **jet planes ~ing over the housetops** Düsenflugzeuge, die heulend über die Hausdächer fliegen

screech owl N Schleiereule *f*

screed [skri:d] N Roman *m* (*inf*); **to write ~s (and ~s)** (*inf*) ganze Romane schreiben (*inf*)

screen [skri:n] N a (*protective*) Schirm *m*; (*for privacy etc*) Wandschirm *m*; (*as partition*) Trennwand *f*; (*against insects*) Fliegenfenster *nt*; (*against light*) Verdunklungsschutz *m*; (*fig, for protection*) Schutz *m*; (*of trees*) Wand *f*; (*of mist, secrecy*) Schleier *m*; (*of indifference*) Mauer *f*; **~ of smoke** Rauchschleier *m*, Nebelwand *f*; **protected by a ~ of destroyers** durch eine Zerstörerflotte geschützt
b (*Film*) Leinwand *f*; (*TV: = radar screen*) (Bild)schirm *m*; **stars of the ~** Filmstars *pl*; **to write for the ~** für den Film/das Fernsehen schreiben; **they are married off ~ as well as on** sie sind nicht nur im Film, sondern auch in Wirklichkeit *or* im wirklichen Leben verheiratet; **the big ~** die Leinwand; **the small ~** die Mattscheibe
c (*Comput*) Bildschirm *m*; **on ~** auf Bildschirm (*dat*); **to edit/work on ~** am Bildschirm editieren/arbeiten; **to move forward a ~** einen Bildschirm vorrücken
d (*= sieve*) (Gitter)sieb *nt*
e (*in church*) Lettner *m*
f (*Cricket*) = **sightscreen**
VT a (*= hide*) verdecken; (*= protect*) abschirmen; (*fig*) schützen (*from* vor *+dat*), abschirmen (*from* gegen); **to ~ the windows** (*with screen*) einen Schirm vor die Fenster stellen; (*with fabric*) die Fenster verhängen; (*against light*) die Fenster verdunkeln; (*against insects*) Fliegenfenster an den Fenstern anbringen; **to ~ sth from the enemy** etw vor dem Feind tarnen *or* verbergen; **he ~ed his eyes from the sun** er schützte die Augen vor der Sonne
b *TV programme* senden; *film* vorführen; **they gave permission for the conference to be ~ed** sie genehmigten die Vorführung der Filmaufzeichnungen von der Konferenz
c (*= sift*) sieben
d (*= investigate*) *applicants, security risks* überprüfen; *calls* überwachen; (*Med*) untersuchen
VI **to ~ for sth** (*Med*) auf etw (*acc*) untersuchen

▶ **screen off** VT *sep* (durch einen Schirm/Vorhang/eine Wand *etc*) abtrennen

screen: **screen actor** N Filmschauspieler *m*; **screen actress** N Filmschauspielerin *f*; **screen filter** N Bildschirmfilter *m*

screenful ['skri:nfʊl] N (*Comput*) Inhalt *m* einer Bildschirmseite

screening ['skri:nɪŋ] N a (*of film*) Vorführung *f*; (*TV*) Sendung *f* b (*of applicants, security risks*) Überprüfung *f* c (*Med*) Röntgenuntersuchung *f*; (*= tomography*) Computertomografie *f* d (*Aviat*) *Gepäck- und Passagierkontrolle mit Durchleuchtungsgeräten*

screening room N (*Film*) Vorführraum *m*

screen: **screen junkie** N (*inf*) Bildschirmjunkie *m* (*inf*); **screen memory** N (*Psych*) Deckerinnerung *f*; **screen name** N (*Internet*) Nickname *m*; **screenplay** N Drehbuch *nt*; **screenprint** N Siebdruck *m* VT im Siebdruckverfahren drucken; **screen-printing** N Siebdruck *m*, Siebdruckverfahren *nt*; **screensaver** N (*Comput*) Bildschirmschoner *m*; **screenshot** N (*Comput*) Bildschirmausdruck *m*; **screen test** N Probeaufnahmen *pl*; **screen-test** VT Probeaufnahmen machen von; **screenwriter** N Drehbuchautor(in) *m(f)*; **screenwriting** N Drehbuchschreiben *nt*, Verfassen *nt* von Drehbüchern

screw [skru:] N a (*Mech*) Schraube *f*; **he's got a ~ loose** (*inf*) bei dem ist eine Schraube locker (*inf*); **to put** *or* **turn** *or* **tighten the ~s on sb** (*inf*) **to turn the ~ on sb** (*inf*) jdm die Daumenschrauben anlegen; **this is another turn of the ~** das macht es noch schlimmer, das setzt sie/ihn *etc* noch mehr unter Druck
b (*Naut, Aviat*) Schraube *f*, Propeller *m*
c (*= action*) Drehung *f*; **to give sth a ~** an etw (*dat*) drehen
d (*sl: = sexual intercourse*) Nummer *f* (*inf*); **he/she is a good ~** er/sie vögelt gut (*inf*); **to have a ~** vögeln (*inf*), bumsen (*inf*)
e (*Brit inf: = wage*) **he earns a good ~** er verdient ganz schön viel Kohle (*inf*); **that's not a bad ~** bei dem Job stimmt die Kohle (*inf*)
f (*Brit sl: = prison officer*) Schließer(in) *m(f)* (*inf*)
VT a (*using screws*) schrauben (*to* an *+acc*, *onto* auf *+acc*); **he ~ed his head round** er drehte seinen Kopf herum; **she ~ed her handkerchief into a ball** sie knüllte ihr Taschentuch zu einem Knäuel zusammen; **he ~ed his face into a smile** er verzog das Gesicht zu einem Lächeln
b (*inf: = put pressure on*) in die Mangel nehmen (*inf*); **to ~ sb for sth** etw aus jdm herausquetschen (*inf*)
c (*sl: = have intercourse with*) vögeln (*inf*), bumsen (*inf*); **~ you!** (*sl*) leck mich am Arsch! (*vulg*), du kannst mich mal! (*inf*)
d (*inf*) (*= rip off*) abzocken (*inf*); (*= cheat*) bescheißen (*sl*); **we're not out to ~ you for every penny you've got** wir wollen dich nicht abzo-

cken *(inf)*
VI **a** *(= can be screwed)* sich schrauben lassen; *(= fasten with screw)* angeschraubt werden
b *(sl: = have intercourse)* vögeln *(inf)*, bumsen *(inf)*

▶ **screw down** VT *sep* an- *or* festschrauben

▶ **screw in** **VT** *sep* (hin)einschrauben *(prep obj, -to* in *+acc)* **VI** (hin)eingeschraubt werden *(prep obj, -to* in *+acc)*

▶ **screw off** **VT** *sep* abschrauben *(prep obj* von) **VI** abgeschraubt werden *(prep obj* von)

▶ **screw on** **VT** *sep* anschrauben; **to screw sth on(to) sth** etw an etw *(acc)* schrauben; *lid, top* etw auf etw *(acc)* schrauben; **it was screwed on tightly** es war festgeschraubt; *(lid, top)* es war fest zugeschraubt; **to have one's head screwed on (the right way)** *(inf)* ein vernünftiger Mensch sein **VI** aufgeschraubt werden; *(= with screws)* angeschraubt werden

▶ **screw out** **VT** *sep* herausschrauben *(of* aus); **to screw sth out of sb** *(esp Brit inf, money)* etw aus jdm herausquetschen *(inf)*; *concessions* etw aus jdm herauspressen **VI** herausgeschraubt werden

▶ **screw together** **VT** *sep* zusammenschrauben **VI** zusammengeschraubt werden

▶ **screw up** **VT** *sep* **a** *screw, nut* anziehen
b *(= crush) paper, material* zusammenknüllen, zerknüllen
c *eyes* zusammenkneifen; *face* verziehen; **to screw up one's courage** seinen ganzen Mut zusammennehmen; **to screw oneself up to do sth** sich aufraffen, etw zu tun
d *(inf: = spoil)* vermasseln *(inf)*; **he's really screwed things up** er hat da wirklich Scheiße gebaut *(inf)*
e *(inf: = make uptight) sb* neurotisch machen; **he's so screwed up** der hat einen Schaden *(inf)*; **to be screwed up about sth** sich wegen etw ganz verrückt machen; **to get screwed up about sth** sich in etw *(acc)* hineinsteigern
VI *(inf: = make a mess)* Scheiße bauen *(inf)* *(on sth* bei etw)

screw: **screwball** *(esp US inf)* **N** Spinner(in) *m(f) (inf)* **ADJ** hirnverbrannt *(inf)*; **screw cap** N Schraubverschluss *m or* -deckel *m*; *(Tech)* Überwurfmutter *f*; **screwdriver** N Schraubendreher *m*, Schraubenzieher *m (inf)*

screwed [skruːd] ADJ *(Brit inf: = drunk)* voll *(inf)*, hackezu *(sl)*

screw: **screw nut** N *(Tech)* Schraubenmutter *f*; **screw plug** N *(Tech)* Verschlussschraube *f*; **screw top** N Schraubverschluss *m*; **screw-topped** ['skruː,tɒpt] ADJ mit Schraubverschluss; **screw-up** N *(inf: = muddle)* Chaos *nt (inf)*; **it was one big ~** es war das totale Chaos *(inf)*

screwy ['skruːɪ] ADJ *(+er) (inf)* verrückt, bekloppt *(inf)*; *person* komisch, schrullig; **you must be ~!** du bist wohl bekloppt *(inf) or* verrückt!

scribble ['skrɪbl] **N** Gekritzel *nt no pl*; *(= note)* schnell hingekritzelte Nachricht; **covered in ~(s)** vollgekritzelt **VT** hinkritzeln; **to ~ sth on sth** etw auf etw *(acc)* kritzeln; **paper ~d (over) with notes** mit Notizen vollgekritzeltes Papier; **to ~ sth down** etw hinkritzeln **VI** **a** *(= write, draw untidily)* kritzeln; **the children ~d all over the wallpaper** die Kinder haben die ganze Tapete vollgekritzelt **b** *(inf: = write novel etc)* schreiben; **he ~s away all day at his novel** er schreibt den ganzen Tag an seinem Roman herum

scribbler ['skrɪblə'] N *(inf)* Schreiberling *m*

scribbling block ['skrɪblɪŋ,blɒk], **scribbling pad** ['skrɪblɪŋ,pæd] N *(Brit)* Schreibblock *m*, Notizblock *m*

scribe [skraɪb] N Schreiber(in) *m(f)*; *(Bibl)* Schriftgelehrte(r) *m*

scrimmage ['skrɪmɪdʒ] **N** *(US Ftbl)* Gedränge *nt*; *(Rugby)* offenes Gedränge; *(inf: = struggle)* Rangelei *f (inf)*; **a ~ with the police** ein Handgemenge *nt* mit der Polizei **VI** sich drängen

scrimp [skrɪmp] VI sparen, knausern; **to ~ on sth** an etw *(dat)* sparen; **to ~ and save** geizen und sparen

scrimshank ['skrɪmʃæŋk] VI *(Brit Mil sl)* sich drücken *(inf)*

scrimshanker ['skrɪmʃæŋkə'] N *(Brit Mil sl)* Drückeberger(in) *m(f) (inf)*

script [skrɪpt] **N** **a** *(= style of writing)* Schrift *f*; *(= joined writing)* Schreibschrift *f*; *(= handwriting)* Handschrift *f*; *(Typ, = cursive)* Kursivdruck *m* **b** *(Sch, Univ)* (schriftliche) Arbeit **c** *(of play, documentary)* Text *m*; *(= screenplay)* Drehbuch *nt*; *(of talk etc)* (Manu)skript *nt* **VT** *play, documentary* den Text schreiben zu; *screenplay* das Drehbuch schreiben für; *talk etc* das (Manu)skript schreiben für; **a ~ed conversation** ein vorbereitetes Gespräch

script girl N *(Film)* Scriptgirl *nt*

scriptorium [skrɪp'tɔːrɪəm] N *pl* **scriptoria** [skrɪp'tɔːrɪə] Schreibstube *f (eines Klosters)*

scriptural ['skrɪptʃərəl] ADJ Bibel-; **~ text** Bibeltext *m*; **that isn't strictly ~** das entspricht nicht genau der Bibel

scripture ['skrɪptʃə'] N **a** **Scripture, the Scriptures** die (Heilige) Schrift; **the Hindu ~s** die heiligen Schriften *or* Bücher der Hindus **b** *(Sch)* Religion *f*

scriptwriter ['skrɪpt,raɪtə'] N Textautor(in) *m(f)*; *(of screenplay)* Drehbuchautor(in) *m(f)*; *(of talk etc)* Verfasser(in) *m(f)* des (Manu)skripts

scrivener ['skrɪvənə'] N *(Hist)* Schreiber *m*

scrod ['skrɒd] N *(US) junger, kochfertig geschnittener Fisch*

scrofula ['skrɒfjʊlə] N *(dated Med)* Skrofulose *f*, Skrofel *f*

scrofulous ['skrɒfjʊləs] ADJ *(dated Med)* skrofulös; *(depraved)* verkommen

scroll [skrəʊl] **N** **a** Schriftrolle *f*; *(decorative)* Schnörkel *m*; *(= volute, of violin)* Schnecke *f* **b** *(Comput)* Scrollen *nt*, Bildlauf *m* **VI** *(Comput)* scrollen, blättern *(inf)*

▶ **scroll down** **VT** *sep* vorscrollen **VI** vorscrollen, nach unten blättern *(inf)*

▶ **scroll up** **VT** *sep* zurückscrollen **VI** zurückscrollen, nach oben blättern *(inf)*

scrollable ADJ *(Comput)* bildlauffähig, mit Bildlaufleiste (versehen) *f*

scroll bar N *(Comput)* Bildlaufleiste *f*

scroll saw N Laubsäge *f*

scrooch [skruːtʃ] VI *(esp US)* kauern; **to ~ down** sich hinkauern

Scrooge [skruːdʒ] N Geizhals *m*

scrotum ['skrəʊtəm] N Hodensack *m*, Skrotum *nt (spec)*

scrounge [skraʊndʒ] *(inf)* **VI** **a** *(= sponge)* schnorren *(inf)* *(off, from* bei); **he ~d off his parents for years** er lag seinen Eltern jahrelang auf der Tasche *(inf)* **b** *(= hunt)* **to ~ around for sth** nach etw herumsuchen **VT** schnorren *(inf)*, abstauben *(inf)* *(from, off* bei) **N** **to be on the ~** am Schnorren *or* Abstauben sein *(inf)*; **he's always on the ~ for cigarettes** er schnorrt dauernd Zigaretten *(inf)*

scrounger ['skraʊndʒə'] N *(inf)* Schnorrer(in) *m(f) (inf)*

scrounging ['skraʊndʒɪŋ] N *(inf)* Schnorrerei *f (inf)*

scroungy ['skraʊndʒɪ] ADJ *(+er)* *(US inf)* gammelig *(inf)*

scrub[1] [skrʌb] N Gebüsch *nt*, Gestrüpp *nt*; *(also* **scrubland**) Gestrüpp *nt*; *(tropical)* Busch(land *nt*) *m*

scrub[2] **N** Schrubben *nt no pl*; **to give sth a ~/a good ~** etw schrubben/gründlich abschrubben **VT** schrubben, scheuern; *vegetables* putzen; *(inf: = cancel)* abblasen *(inf)*; *idea* abschreiben *(inf)*; **to ~ oneself all over** sich von oben bis unten abschrubben; **to ~ off a dirty mark** einen Schmutzfleck wegschrubben **VI** **to ~ at sth** an etw *(dat)* herumreiben

▶ **scrub down** VT *sep walls, person, oneself* abschrubben

▶ **scrub out** VT *sep pans etc* ausscheuern

▶ **scrub up** VI *(= wash hands)* sich *(dat)* die Hände waschen *or* schrubben *(inf)*

scrubber ['skrʌbə'] N *(Brit inf)* (billiges) Flittchen *(inf)*

scrubbing brush ['skrʌbɪŋ,brʌʃ] *(Brit)*, **scrub brush** *(US)* N Scheuerbürste *f*

scrubby ['skrʌbɪ] ADJ *(+er) bushes, beard* struppig; *grass* buschig; *countryside* mit Buschwerk bewachsen; *chin* stoppelig

scrubland ['skrʌblænd] N → **scrub**

scrubwoman N *(US)* Scheuer- *or* Putzfrau *f*

scruff[1] [skrʌf] N **by the ~ of the neck** am Genick

scruff[2] N *(inf: = scruffy person) (= woman)* Schlampe *f (inf)*; *(= man)* abgerissener Typ *(inf)*

scruffily ['skrʌfɪlɪ] ADV *(inf)* schlampig *(inf)*

scruffiness ['skrʌfɪnɪs] N *(inf, of person)* schlampiges *or* gammeliges Aussehen *(inf)*; *(of city)* verlotterter Zustand *(inf)*

scruffy ['skrʌfɪ] ADJ *(+er) (inf)* gammelig *(inf)*; *person, clothes also* schlampig *(inf)*; *park, city* verlottert *(inf)*, verwahrlost

scrum [skrʌm] N **a** *(Rugby)* Gedränge *nt*; **loose ~** offenes Gedränge; **set ~** Gedränge *nt* **b** *(of reporters, photographers etc)* Gedränge *nt*

scrum half N *(Rugby)* Gedrängehalbspieler(in) *m(f)*

scrummage ['skrʌmɪdʒ] N offenes Gedränge

scrump [skrʌmp] **VT** *apples* stehlen **VI** Äpfel stehlen

scrumptious ['skrʌmpʃəs] ADJ *(inf) meal etc* lecker; *girl* zum Anbeißen *(inf)*

scrumpy ['skrʌmpɪ] N *(Brit)* ≈ Most *m (S Ger, Aus, Sw), starker Cider aus Südwestengland*

scrunch [skrʌntʃ] **N** Knirschen *nt*; **the car came up the snowy road with a ~ of tyres** *(Brit) or* **tires** *(US)* die Reifen des Wagens knirschten auf der schneebedeckten Straße **VT** *nose* rümpfen; **to ~ sth (up) into a ball** etw zusammenknüllen **VI** *(gravel, snow)* knirschen; **his boots ~ed on the gravel** seine Stiefel knirschten auf dem Kies; **they ~ed through the fallen leaves** das Laub raschelte unter ihren Schritten; **he ~ed up his face** er verzog das Gesicht

scrunchie ['skrʌntʃɪ] N *(for hair)* Zopfkranz *m*, Zopfband *nt*

scruple ['skruːpl] **N** Skrupel *m*; **~s** *(= doubts)* (moralische) Bedenken *pl*; **to be without ~** keine Skrupel haben; **to have no ~s about sth** bei einer Sache keine Skrupel haben; **to have no ~s about doing sth** keine Skrupel haben, etw zu tun **VI** **I did not ~ to accept his offer** ich hatte keine Skrupel *or* Bedenken, sein Angebot anzunehmen

scrupulous ['skruːpjʊləs] ADJ *person, organization* gewissenhaft; *honesty, fairness* unbedingt, kompromisslos; *cleanliness* peinlich; *account* (peinlich) genau; **he can't afford to be too ~** er kann sich keine allzu großen Skrupel leisten; **he is not too ~ in his business dealings** er hat keine allzu großen Skrupel bei seinen Geschäften; **she is not too ~ in matters of cleanliness** sie nimmt es mit der Sauberkeit nicht so genau; **to be ~ in doing sth** etw sehr gewissenhaft tun; **to be ~ about sth** mit etw sehr gewissenhaft sein; **the kitchen staff are ~ about hygiene** das Küchenpersonal nimmt es mit der Hygiene sehr genau

scrupulously ['skruːpjʊləslɪ] ADV *(= honestly, conscientiously)* gewissenhaft; *(= honourably) behave* korrekt; *(= meticulously)* sorgfältig; *exact, clean* peinlich; *fair, careful* äußerst; **he's ~ careful about telling the truth** er nimmt es mit der Wahrheit äußerst *or* peinlichst genau; **the old church has been ~ maintained** die alte Kirche ist äußerst sorgfältig instand *or* in Stand gehalten worden

scrupulousness ['skru:pjʊləsnɪs] N *(= honesty, fairness)* Gewissenhaftigkeit *f*; *(= meticulousness)* (peinliche) Genauigkeit

scrutineer [,skru:tɪ'nɪə'] N *(Brit Pol)* Wahlprüfer(in) *m(f)*

scrutinize ['skru:tɪnaɪz] VT *(= examine)* (genau) untersuchen; *(= check)* genau prüfen; *(= stare at)* prüfend ansehen, mustern; **to ~ sth for sth** etw auf etw *(acc)* untersuchen *or* prüfen

scrutiny ['skru:tɪnɪ] N **a** *(= examination)* Untersuchung *f*; *(= checking)* (Über)prüfung *f*; *(of person)* Musterung *f*; *(= stare)* prüfender *or* musternder Blick; **everyone was subject to police ~** jeder wurde einer Überprüfung durch die Polizei unterzogen; **it does not stand up to ~** es hält keiner genauen Untersuchung *or* Prüfung stand **b** *(Pol)* Wahlprüfung *f*

SCSI ['skʌzɪ] *(Comput) abbr of* **Small Computer Systems Interface** SCSI

scuba ['sku:bə] N (Schwimm)tauchgerät *nt*

scuba: **scuba dive** VI tauchen mit Sauerstoffgerät; **scuba diver** N Sporttaucher(in) *m(f)*; **scuba diving** N Sporttauchen *nt*

scud [skʌd] VI flitzen; *(clouds)* jagen

scuff [skʌf] **VT** abwetzen; **don't ~ your feet like that!** schlurf nicht so! **VI** schlurfen; **the children ~ed through the pile of leaves** die Kinder raschelten *or* wateten durch den Laubhaufen **N** **a** *(also* **scuff mark***)* abgewetzte Stelle **b** *(US: = slipper)* Pantolette *f*

scuffle ['skʌfl] **N** *(= skirmish)* Rauferei *f (inf)*, Handgemenge *nt* **VI** *(= have skirmish)* sich raufen; *(= make noise)* poltern; **to ~ with the police** ein Handgemenge mit der Polizei haben

scull [skʌl] **N** *(= oar)* Skull *nt*; *(= boat)* Skullboot *nt* **VT** rudern **VI** rudern, skullen *(spec)*

scullery ['skʌlərɪ] N Spülküche *f*; **~ maid** Küchenmagd *f*

sculpt [skʌlpt] **VT** = **sculpture VT** **VI** bildhauern *(inf)*; **he ~s for a living** er verdient sich *(dat)* seinen Lebensunterhalt als Bildhauer, er lebt vom Bildhauern *(inf)*

sculptor ['skʌlptə'] N Bildhauer(in) *m(f)*

sculptress ['skʌlptrɪs] N Bildhauerin *f*

sculptural ['skʌlptʃərəl] ADJ plastisch; *(= of statues)* bildhauerisch; **the ~ work on the cathedral** die Skulpturenarbeit der Kathedrale; **~ details** plastisch gearbeitete Details *pl*; **the ~ triumphs of Ancient Greece** die Meisterwerke der altgriechischen Bildhauerkunst

sculpture ['skʌlptʃə'] **N** *(= art)* Bildhauerkunst *f*, Skulptur *f*; *(= work)* Bildhauerei *f*; *(= object)* Skulptur *f*, Plastik *f* **VT** formen, arbeiten; *(in stone)* hauen, meißeln; *(in clay etc)* modellieren; **he ~d the tombstone out of marble** er haute den Grabstein in Marmor

sculptured ['skʌlptʃəd] ADJ **a** *(lit)* geformt; *(in stone)* gehauen, gemeißelt; **decorated with ~ flowers** mit plastisch gearbeiteten Blumen verziert **b** *(fig) cheekbones, profile* ausgeprägt, markant

scum [skʌm] N **a** *(on liquid)* Schaum *m*; *(= residue)* Rand *m*; **a pond covered in green ~** ein mit einer grünen Schleimschicht bedeckter Teich; **a greasy ~ floated on the soup** auf der Suppe schwamm eine Fettschicht **b** *(pej inf)* Abschaum *m*; *(= one individual)* Drecksau *f (inf)*; **the ~ of the earth** der Abschaum der Menschheit

scumbag ['skʌmbæg] N *(inf: = man)* Bastard *m (inf)*, Scheißkerl *m (inf)*; *(= woman)* Miststück *nt (inf)*

scupper ['skʌpə'] **N** Speigatt *nt* **VT** **a** *(Naut)* versenken **b** *(Brit inf: = ruin)* zerschlagen; **if he finds out, we'll be ~ed** wenn er das erfährt, sind wir erledigt *(inf)*

scurf [skɜ:f] N Schuppen *pl*

scurrility [skʌ'rɪlɪtɪ] N *(= abusiveness)* Ehrenrührigkeit *f*; *(of person)* verleumderische Art; *(= abusive remark)* Verleumdung *f*, Verunglimpfung *f*; *(= indecency)* Zotigkeit *f*, Unflätigkeit *f*; *(= indecent remark)* zotige *or* unflätige Bemerkung

scurrilous ['skʌrɪləs] ADJ *(= abusive)* verleumderisch; *remark, attack, story also* ehrenrührig; *(= indecent)* unflätig, zotig

scurrilously ['skʌrɪləslɪ] ADV *(= abusively)* verleumderisch; *(= indecently)* unflätig, zotig

scurry ['skʌrɪ] **N** *(= hurry)* Hasten *nt*; *(= sound)* Trippeln *nt*; **there was a ~ to leave the room** alle hatten es eilig, das Zimmer zu verlassen **VI** *(person)* hasten; *(with small steps)* eilig trippeln; *(animals)* huschen; **to ~ along** entlanghasten/-trippeln/-huschen; **they all scurried out of the classroom** sie hatten es alle eilig, aus dem Klassenzimmer zu kommen; **to ~ for shelter** sich *(dat)* eilig einen Unterschlupf suchen; **she scurried through her work** hastig erledigte sie ihre Arbeit

scurvy ['skɜ:vɪ] **N** Skorbut *m* **ADJ** *(obs) knave* schändlich

'scuse [skju:z] VT *(inf)* = **excuse VT**

scut [skʌt] N Stummelschwanz *m*; *(of rabbit also)* Blume *f (Hunt)*; *(of deer also)* Wedel *m (Hunt)*

scutcheon ['skʌtʃən] N = **escutcheon**

scutter ['skʌtə'] N, VI *(Brit inf)* = **scurry**

scuttle¹ ['skʌtl] N *(= coal scuttle)* Kohleneimer *m*

scuttle² VI *(person)* trippeln; *(animals)* hoppeln; *(spiders, crabs etc)* krabbeln; **she/it ~d off in a hurry** sie/es flitzte davon

scuttle³ *(Naut)* **N** Luke *f* **VT** **a** versenken **b** *(fig) treaty, agreement, talks* sprengen; *plans* kaputt machen

scutwork N *(US inf: = tedious work)* langweilige *or* eintönige Arbeit; Drecksarbeit *f (inf)*

scythe [saɪð] **N** Sense *f* **VT** (mit der Sense) mähen; **to ~ people down** Menschen niedermähen **VI** **to ~ through the crowd** durch die Menge pflügen; **the motorway ~s through the city** die Autobahn führt mitten durch die Stadt

Scythia ['sɪθɪə] N Skythien *nt*

SDI *abbr of* **strategic defence initiative** SDI *f*

SDP *(Brit) abbr of* **Social Democratic Party**

SE *abbr of* **south-east** SO

sea [si:] N **a** Meer *nt*, See *f*; **by ~** auf dem Seeweg; **to travel by ~** mit dem Schiff fahren; **a town by** *or* **on the ~** eine Stadt am Meer *or* an der See; **(out) at ~** auf See; **as I looked out to ~** als ich aufs Meer hinausblickte; **to be all at ~** *(fig)* nicht durchblicken *(with* bei*)* *(inf)*; **I'm all at ~ about how to answer this question** ich habe keine Ahnung, wie ich die Frage beantworten soll; **that left him all at ~** er hatte überhaupt keinen Durchblick *(inf)*; **to go to ~** zur See gehen; **to put to ~** in See stechen; **beyond the ~s** *(dated)* überm großen Meer *(old)*, in Übersee **b** *(= state of the sea)* See *f no pl*, Seegang *m*; **heavy/strong ~s** schwere/raue See **c** *(fig)* Meer *nt*; **a ~ of faces** ein Meer von Gesichtern; **a ~ of flames** ein Flammenmeer

sea: **sea air** N Seeluft *f*; **sea anemone** N Seeanemone *f*; **sea animal** N Meerestier *nt*; **sea-based** ADJ *missiles* seegestützt; **sea bathing** N Baden *nt* im Meer; **sea battle** N Seeschlacht *f*; **seabed** N Meeresboden *m*, Meeresgrund *m (geh)*; **sea bird** N Seevogel *m*; **seaboard** N *(US)* Küste *f*; **seaborne** ADJ *attack, landing* von See; *fruit, articles etc* auf dem Seeweg befördert; **~ goods** Seefrachtgüter *pl*; **~ trade** Seehandel *m*; **sea breeze** N Seewind *m*; **sea calf** N Meerkalb *nt*, Seehund *m*; **sea change** N totale Veränderung; **sea coast** N Meeresküste *f*; **sea cow** N Seekuh *f*; **sea cucumber** N Seegurke *f*, Seewalze *f*; **sea defences**, *(US)* **sea defenses** PL Hochwasserschutzmaßnahmen *pl*; **sea dog** N *(inf: = sailor)* Seebär *m*; *(= seal)* Seehund *m*; **sea elephant** N Elefantenrobbe *f*, See-Elefant *m*, Seeelefant *m*; **seafarer** N Seefahrer(in) *m(f)*; **seafaring** **ADJ** *nation, people* seefahrend; *boat* hochseetüchtig; **~ man** Seefahrer *m*; **he has little ~ experience** er hat wenig Erfahrung auf See **N** Seefahrt *f*; **sea fight** N Seegefecht *nt*; **seafish** N See- *or* Meeresfisch *m*; **seafloor** N Meeresboden *m*; **sea fog** N Küstennebel *m*, Seenebel *m*; **seafood** N Meeresfrüchte *pl*; **~ restaurant** Fischrestaurant *nt*; **seafront** N *(= beach)* Strand *m*; *(= promenade)* Strandpromenade *f*; **sea god** N Meer(es)gott *m*; **sea goddess** N Meer(es)göttin *f*; **seagoing** ADJ *boat etc* hochseetüchtig; **~ nation** Seefahrernation *f*; **seagrass** N *(Bot)* Seegras *nt*; **sea green** N Meergrün *nt*; **sea-green** ADJ meergrün; **seagull** N Möwe *f*; **sea horse** N Seepferdchen *nt*; **sea kale** N See- *or* Strandkohl *m*

seal¹ [si:l] **N** *(Zool)* Seehund *m*; *(= sealskin)* Seal *m* **VI** **to go ~ing** auf Seehundfang *or* -jagd gehen; **to go on a ~ing expedition** an einer Seehundjagd teilnehmen

seal² **N** **a** *(= impression in wax etc)* Siegel *nt*; *(against unauthorized opening)* Versiegelung *f*; *(of metal)* Plombe *f*; *(= die)* Stempel *m*; *(= ring)* Siegelring *m*; *(= decorative label)* Aufkleber *m*; **to be under ~** versiegelt sein; **under the ~ of secrecy** unter dem Siegel der Verschwiegenheit; **the ~ of the confessional** das Beichtgeheimnis; **~ of quality** Gütesiegel *nt*; **to put one's** *or* **the ~ of approval on sth** einer Sache *(dat)* seine offizielle Zustimmung geben; **to set one's ~ on sth** *(lit, fig)* unter etw *(acc)* sein Siegel setzen; **this set the ~ on their friendship** das besiegelte ihre Freundschaft; **as a ~ of friendship** zum Zeichen der Freundschaft **b** *(= airtight closure)* Verschluss *m*; *(= washer)* Dichtung *f* **VT** versiegeln; *envelope, parcel also* zukleben; *(with wax)* siegeln; *border* dichtmachen; *area* abriegeln; *(= make air- or watertight) joint, container* abdichten; *porous surface* versiegeln; *(fig: = settle, finalize)* besiegeln; **~ed envelope** verschlossener Briefumschlag; **~ed orders** versiegelte Order; **~ed train** plombierter Zug; **~ the meat before adding the stock** Poren (durch rasches Anbraten) schließen und dann Fleischbrühe hinzufügen; **my lips are ~ed** meine Lippen sind versiegelt; **this ~ed his fate** dadurch war sein Schicksal besiegelt; **to ~ victory** den Sieg besiegeln

▶ **seal in** VT *sep* einschließen; **this process seals all the flavour** *(Brit)* *or* **flavor** *(US)* **in** dieses Verfahren erhält das volle Aroma

▶ **seal off** VT *sep* absperren, abriegeln

▶ **seal up** VT *sep* versiegeln; *parcel, letter* zukleben; *crack, windows* abdichten

sea lane N *(Naut)* Seeweg *m*, Schifffahrtsweg *m*

sealant ['si:lənt] N Dichtungsmittel *nt*

sea: **sea-launched** ['si:,lɔ:nʃt] ADJ *missiles* seegestützt; **sea legs** PL **to get** *or* **find one's ~** *(inf)* standfest werden

sealer¹ ['si:lə'] N *(= boat)* Robbenfänger *m*; *(= person)* Robbenfänger(in) *m(f)*

sealer² N *(= varnish)* (Ver)siegeler *m*

sea level N Meeresspiegel *m*; **above/below ~** über/unter dem Meeresspiegel

sealing ['si:lɪŋ]: **sealing ring** N Dichtungsring *m*; **sealing wax** N Siegelwachs *nt*

sea lion N Seelöwe *m*

seal: **seal ring** N Siegelring *m*; **sealskin** ['si:lskɪn] N Seehundfell *nt*, Seal *m*

Sealyham ['si:lɪəm] N Sealyhamterrier *m*

seam [si:m] **N** **a** Naht *f*; *(= scar)* Narbe *f*; *(Naut)* Fuge *f*; **are my ~s straight?** sitzen meine Nähte gerade?; **to come** *or* **fall apart at the ~s** *(lit, fig)* aus den Nähten gehen; **to be bursting at the ~s** *(lit, fig)* aus allen Nähten platzen *(inf)* **b** *(Geol)* Flöz *nt* **VT** *(= sew, join)* nähen; *(fig: = mark with lines)* durchziehen

seaman ['si:mən] N *pl* **-men** [-mən] Seemann *m*

seaman: **seaman-like** ADJ seemännisch; **seamanship** N Seemannschaft *f*

sea mile N Seemeile *f*

seamless ['si:mlɪs] ADJ **a** *tube, stockings* nahtlos; *cardigan* ohne Nähte **b** *(fig)* **the ~ transition to democracy** der nahtlose Übergang zur Demokratie

seamstress ['semstrɪs] N Näherin *f*

seam welding N Nahtverschweißung *f*

seamy ['si:mɪ] ADJ *(+er) club, bar, person* heruntergekommen; *story, area, past* zwielichtig; *events, details* schmutzig; **the ~ side of life** die Schattenseite des Lebens

séance ['seɪɑ̃:ns] N spiritistische Sitzung, Séance *f*

sea: **seapiece** N *(Painting)* Seestück *nt*; **sea pink** N (gemeine) Grasnelke; **seaplane** N Wasserflugzeug *nt*; **seaport** N Seehafen *m*; **sea power** N Seemacht *f*; **seaquake** N Seebeben *nt*

sear [sɪə'] VT **a** (= *burn: hot metal, water etc*) verbrennen; *(pain)* durchzucken; (*Med*: = *cauterize*) ausbrennen; (*Cook*: = *brown quickly*) rasch anbraten; *(fig)* zutiefst treffen **b** (= *scorch, wither: sun, wind*) ausdörren, austrocknen

search [sɜ:tʃ] **N** (= *hunt: for lost object, missing person etc*) Suche *f* (*for* nach); (= *examination: of cupboard, luggage, suspect etc*) Durchsuchung *f* (*of +gen*); (*esp Jur: of documents*) Nachforschungen *pl* (*of* über *+acc*); *(Comput)* Suchlauf *m*, Suchvorgang *m*; **right of ~** Durchsuchungsrecht *nt*; **to go in ~ of sb/sth** auf die Suche nach jdm/etw gehen; **to carry out a ~ of a house** eine Haus(durch)suchung machen; **I found an interesting book in my ~** bei meiner Suche *or* beim Suchen habe ich ein interessantes Buch gefunden; **to do a ~ for sth** nach etw suchen; **they arranged a ~ for the missing child** sie veranlassten eine Suchaktion nach dem vermissten Kind; **to do a ~ (and replace) for sth** *(Comput)* etw suchen (und ersetzen)

VT (*for* nach) durchsuchen; *archives, records* suchen in (*+dat*), durchforschen; *conscience* erforschen; *memory, sb's face* durchforschen; **to ~ a place for sb/sth** einen Ort nach jdm absuchen/nach etw durch- *or* absuchen; **~ me!** *(inf)* was weiß ich? *(inf)*; **if you ~ your heart ...** wenn Sie Ihr Herz fragen ...

VI *(also Comput)* suchen (*for* nach)

▶ **search about** *(Brit)* or **around** VI herumstöbern (*in* in *+dat*); *(in country etc)* (herum)suchen (*in* in *+dat*)

▶ **search out** VT *sep* heraussuchen; *person* ausfindig machen, aufspüren; *cause* herausfinden

▶ **search through** VI *+prep obj* durchsuchen; *papers, books* durchsehen

search: **search-and-destroy** ADJ *(Mil)* Vernichtungs-; **~ mission** Vernichtungsmission *f*; **search engine** N *(Comput)* Suchmaschine *f*

searcher ['sɜ:tʃə'] N *(Customs etc)* Durchsuchungsbeamte(r) *m*, Durchsuchungsbeamtin *f*; **the ~s** (= *search party*) die Suchmannschaft *f*

search function N *(Comput)* Suchfunktion *f*

searching ADJ ['sɜ:tʃɪŋ] *look* prüfend, forschend; *question* durchdringend, bohrend; *examination, test* gründlich; **his questions became more ~** er stellte tiefer gehende Fragen

searchingly ['sɜ:tʃɪŋlɪ] ADV *look* prüfend, forschend

search: **search item** N *(Comput)* Suchbegriff *m*; **searchlight** N Suchscheinwerfer *m*; **search mode** N *(Comput)* Suchmodus *m*; **search operation** N **a** *(of police)* Fahndung *f* **b** *(Comput)* Suchlauf *m*; **search party** N Suchmannschaft *f*; **search program** N *(Comput)* Suchprogramm *nt*; **search time** N *(Comput)* Suchdauer *f*; **search tuning** N *(Rad)* Sendersuchlauf *m*; **search warrant** N Durchsuchungsbefehl *m*; **search word** N *(Comput)* Suchwort *nt*, Suchbegriff *m*

sea-rescue aircraft N Seerettungsflugzeug *nt*

searing ['sɪərɪŋ] ADJ *heat* glühend; *pain also* scharf; *wind* glühend heiß; *(fig)* (= *painful*) *grief, sense of loss* quälend; (= *forceful*) *indictment, attack* scharf; *documentary* eindringlich

sea: **seascape** N Seestück *nt*; **sea serpent** N Seeschlange *f*; **sea shanty** N Seemannslied *nt*; **seashell** N Muschel(schale) *f*; **seashore** N Strand *m*; **on the ~** am Strand; **the life found on the ~** die Strandflora und -fauna; **seasick** ADJ seekrank; **seasickness** N Seekrankheit *f*; **seaside** **N** **at the ~** am Meer; **to go to the ~** ans Meer fahren **ATTR** See-; *town* am Meer; **~ café** Strandcafé *nt*; **~ holidays** *(Brit)* Ferien *pl* am Meer; **seaside resort** N Seebad *nt*; **sea snake** N *(Zool)* Seeschlange *f*

season ['si:zn] **N** **a** *(of the year)* Jahreszeit *f*; **rainy/monsoon ~** Regen-/Monsunzeit *f*

b (= *social season, sporting season etc*) Saison *f*; **nesting/hunting ~** Brut-/Jagdzeit *f*; **the football ~** die Fußballsaison; **the strawberry ~** die Erdbeerzeit; **strawberries are in ~/out of ~ now** für Erdbeeren ist jetzt die richtige/nicht die richtige Zeit; **their bitch is in ~** ihre Hündin ist läufig; **in and out of ~** andauernd, jahrein (und) jahraus; **to go somewhere out of/in ~** an einen Ort fahren *or* gehen, wenn keine Saison/wenn Saison ist; **at the height of the ~** in der *or* zur Hochsaison; **the height of the London ~** der Höhepunkt der Londoner Saison; **the ~ of good will** (= *Christmas*) die Zeit der Nächstenliebe; **"Season's greetings"** „fröhliche Weihnachten und ein glückliches neues Jahr"; **totally last ~** *(inf)* absolut von gestern *(inf)*

c *(Theat)* Spielzeit *f*; **they did a ~ at La Scala** sie spielten eine Saison lang an der Scala; **for a ~** eine Spielzeit lang; *(TV, Film)* Serie *f*; *(of series)* Staffel *f*; **a Dustin Hoffman ~, a ~ of Dustin Hoffman films** eine Serie von Dustin-Hoffman-Filmen

d *(fig liter)* **in due ~** zu gegebener Zeit; **in good ~** rechtzeitig; **if I might offer a word in ~** wenn ich dazu meinen Rat anbieten darf

VT **a** *food* würzen; (*fig*: = *temper*) durchsetzen **b** *wood* ablagern; (*fig*: = *inure*) *troops* stählen

seasonable ['si:zənəbl] ADJ **a** *dress, weather etc* der Jahreszeit entsprechend *attr*; **to be ~** der Jahreszeit entsprechen **b** (*form*: = *timely*) *advice, rebuke* zur rechten Zeit

seasonal ['si:zənl] ADJ jahreszeitlich bedingt; *(Econ)* Saison-, saisonbedingt; **~ fruit/vegetables** Früchte *pl*/Gemüse *nt* der Saison; **we eat whatever fruit is ~** wir essen das Obst, das gerade auf dem Markt ist

seasonal: **seasonal adjustment** N *(Econ, Pol)* Saisonbereinigung *f*; **seasonal affective disorder** N *(Med)* Winterdepression *f*

seasonally ['si:zənəlɪ] ADV **~ adjusted** *(figures)* saisonbereinigt; **~ available fruit and vegetables** Obst und Gemüse *nt* der Saison

seasonal: **seasonal unemployment** N saisonbedingte Arbeitslosigkeit; **seasonal worker** N Saisonarbeiter(in) *m(f)*

seasoned ['si:znd] ADJ **a** *food* gewürzt **b** *timber* abgelagert **c** (*fig*: = *experienced*) erfahren

seasoning ['si:znɪŋ] N *(Cook)* Gewürz *nt*; *(fig)* Würze *f*

season ticket N *(Rail)* Zeitkarte *f*; *(Theat)* Abonnement *nt*; **~ holder** Inhaber(in) *m(f)* einer Zeitkarte, Abonnent(in) *m(f)*

seat [si:t] **N** **a** (= *place to sit*) (Sitz)platz *m*; (= *actual piece of furniture*) Sitz *m*; (*usu pl*: = *seating*) Sitzgelegenheit *f*; **to have a front ~ at the opera** in der Oper in den vorderen Reihen sitzen; **an aircraft with 250 ~s** ein Flugzeug mit 250 Plätzen *or* Sitzen; **we'll have to borrow some ~s** wir werden uns wohl ein paar Stühle borgen müssen; **we haven't enough ~s** wir haben nicht genügend Sitzgelegenheiten; **to lose one's ~** seinen Platz verlieren *or* loswerden *(inf)*; **will you keep my ~ for me?** würden Sie mir meinen Platz frei halten?; **I've booked two ~s** ich habe zwei Plätze reservieren lassen → **take**

b *(of chair etc)* Sitz *m*, Sitzfläche *f*; *(of trousers)* Hosenboden *m*; (= *buttocks*) Hinterteil *nt*; **he picked him up by the ~ of his pants** er packte ihn beim Hosenboden; **to fly by the ~ of one's pants** (*Aviat sl*) mit dem Hintern fliegen *(inf)*; *(fig)* immer seinem Riecher folgen; **it's a ~-of-the-pants operation** *(inf)* es kommt dabei auf den richtigen Riecher an *(inf)*

c *(on committee, board of company)* Sitz *m*; **a ~ in Parliament** ein Sitz *m* im Parlament, ein Mandat *nt*; **to win a ~** ein Mandat gewinnen; **his ~ is in Devon** sein Wahlkreis *m* ist in Devon

d (= *centre, of government, commerce etc*) Sitz *m*; *(of fire, trouble)* Herd *m*; **~ of emotions** Sitz der Gefühle; **~ of learning** Lehrstätte *f*

e (= *country seat, bishop's seat etc*) Sitz *m*

f *(of rider)* Sitz *m*; **to keep one's ~** im Sattel bleiben; **to lose one's ~** aus dem Sattel fallen

VT **a** *person etc* setzen; **to ~ oneself** sich setzen; **to be ~ed** sitzen; **please be ~ed** bitte, setzen Sie sich; **to remain ~ed** sitzen bleiben

b (= *have sitting room for*) **the car/table/sofa ~s 4** im Auto/am Tisch/auf dem Sofa ist Platz für 4 Personen; **the hall ~s 900** die Halle hat 900 Sitzplätze

c (*Tech*, = *fix in place*) einpassen

VI (*skirt etc*: = *go baggy*) ausbeulen, sich durchsitzen

seat: **seat belt** N Sicherheits- *or* Sitzgurt *m*; **to fasten one's ~, to put one's ~ on** sich anschnallen, seinen Sicherheitsgurt anlegen; **"fasten ~s"** „bitte anschnallen"; **seat belt tensioner** N Gurtstraffer *m*; **seat cover** N *(Aut)* Sitzbezug *m*

-seater [-si:tə'] **SUF N** -sitzer *m*; **two-seater** Zweisitzer *m* **ATTR** -sitzig; **single-seater** *(racing car, plane)* einsitzig

seating ['si:tɪŋ] N Sitzgelegenheiten *pl*, Sitzplätze *pl*; **~ room** Platz *m* zum Sitzen

seating arrangements PL Sitzordnung *f*

seating plan N *(Theat etc)* Sitzplan *m*, Bestuhlungsplan *m*; *(at wedding etc)* Sitzordnung *f*

SEATO ['si:təʊ] *abbr (Hist) of* **South-East Asia Treaty Organization** SEATO *f*

sea: **sea transport** N Seetransport *m*; **sea trip** N Seereise *f*; **sea trout** N Meerforelle *f*; **sea turtle** N Meeresschildkröte *f*; **sea urchin** N Seeigel *m*; **sea view** N Seeblick *m*; **sea wall** N Deich *m*; **seaward** **ADJ** *direction, course* aufs Meer hinaus; **~ wind** Seewind *m*; **the ~ side of the quay** die seewärtige Seite des Kais **ADV** (*also* **seawards**) see- *or* meerwärts; **sea water** N Meer- *or* Seewasser *nt*; **seaway** N (= *route*) Seestraße *f*; (= *waterway*) Wasserweg *m or* -straße *f*; **seaweed** N (Meeres)alge *f*, (See-)tang *m*, Seegras *nt*; **seaworthy** ADJ seetüchtig

sebaceous [sɪ'beɪʃəs] ADJ Talg-

sebaceous glands PL Talgdrüsen *pl*

seborrhoea, *(US)* **seborrhea** [sebə'rɪə] N Seborrhö(e) *f*

sebum ['si:bəm] N Talg *m*

sec [sek] **a** *abbr of* **second(s)** Sek.; **wait a ~** *(inf)* Augenblick *or* Moment mal **b** *abbr of* **secretary**

secant ['si:kənt] N **a** Sekans *m* **b** (= *line*) Sekante *f*

secateurs [,sekə'tɜ:z] PL Gartenschere *f*

secede [sɪ'si:d] VI sich abspalten

secession [sɪ'seʃən] N Abspaltung *f*; *(US Hist)* Sezession *f*

secessionism [sɪ'seʃənɪzəm] N Abspaltungsbestrebungen *pl*

secessionist [sɪ'seʃənɪst] **ADJ** Sezessions-, sezessionistisch; **~ movement** Sezessionsbewegung *f* **N** Sezessionist(in) *m(f)*

seclude [sɪ'klu:d] VT absondern

secluded [sɪ'klu:dɪd] ADJ *spot, house* abgelegen; *life* zurückgezogen, abgeschieden

seclusion [sɪ'klu:ʒən] N (= *act of secluding*) Absondern *nt*, Absonderung *f*; (= *being secluded*) Abgeschlossenheit *f*, Abgeschiedenheit *f*; *(of house, spot)* Abgelegenheit *f*; **in ~ from the world** in Weltabgeschiedenheit

second[1] ['sekənd] **ADJ** zweite(r, s); **the ~ floor** *(Brit)* der zweite Stock; *(US)* der erste Stock; **a ~ Goethe** ein zweiter Goethe; **every ~ house** jedes zweite Haus; **every ~ day/Thursday** jeden zweiten Tag/Donnerstag; **to be ~** Zweite(r, s) sein; **to be ~ to none** unübertroffen *or* unerreicht sein; **to be ~ only to sb/sth** nur von jdm/etw übertroffen werden; **in ~ place** *(Sport etc)* an zweiter Stelle; **to be** *or* **lie in ~ place** auf dem zweiten Platz sein *or* liegen; **to finish in ~ place** den zweiten Platz belegen; **in the ~ place** (= *secondly*) zweitens; **to be ~ in the queue** *(Brit)* *or* **line** *(US)* der/die Zweite in der Schlange sein; **to be ~ in command** *(Mil)* stellvertretender Kommandeur sein; *(fig)* der zweite Mann sein; **~ violin** zweite Geige; **~ tenor** zweiter Tenor; **the ~ teeth** die zweiten *or* bleibenden Zähne, das bleibende Gebiss; **the Müllers' ~ car** der Zweitwagen der Müllers; **England's ~ city** die zweitwichtigste Stadt Englands; **she's like a ~ mother to me** sie ist wie eine Mutter zu mir; **will you have a ~ cup?** möchten Sie noch eine Tasse?; **I won't tell you a ~ time** ich sage dir das kein zweites Mal; **~ time around** beim zweiten Mal; **to give sb a ~ chance** jdm eine zweite *or* noch eine Chance geben; **you won't get a ~ chance** die Möglichkeit kriegst du so schnell nicht wieder *(inf)*; **the ~ thing he did was (to) get himself a drink** als Zweites holte er sich etwas zu trinken → **fiddle, wind[1]**

ADV **a** *(+adj)* zweit-; *(+vb)* an zweiter Stelle; **the ~ largest house** das zweitgrößte Haus; **the ~ most common question** die zweithäufigste Frage, die am zweithäufigsten gestellte Frage; **the speaker against a motion always speaks ~** der Gegenredner spricht immer als Zweiter; **to come/lie ~** *(in race, competition)* Zweite(r) werden/sein; **to go** *or* **travel ~** *(by rail, bus etc)* zweiter Klasse fahren *or* reisen

b *(= secondly)* zweitens

VT *motion, proposal* unterstützen; **I'll ~ that!** *(at meeting)* ich unterstütze das; *(in general)* (genau) meine Meinung

N **a** *(of time, Math, Sci)* Sekunde *f*; *(inf: = short time)* Augenblick *m*; **just a ~!** (einen) Augenblick!; **it won't take a ~** es dauert nicht lange; **I'll only be a ~ (or two)** ich komme gleich; *(= back soon)* ich bin gleich wieder da; **at that very ~** genau in dem Augenblick

b **the ~** *(in order)* der/die/das Zweite; *(in race, class etc)* der/die Zweite; **to come a poor/good ~** einen schlechten/guten zweiten Platz belegen; **to come a poor ~ to sb/sth** erst an zweiter Stelle nach jdm/etw kommen; **Elizabeth the Second** Elizabeth die Zweite

c *(Aut)* **~ (gear)** der zweite Gang; **to put a/the car into ~** den zweiten Gang einlegen; **to drive in ~** im zweiten Gang *or* im Zweiten fahren

d *(Mus: = interval)* Sekunde *f*

e *(Brit Univ: = degree) mittlere Noten bei Abschlussprüfungen*; **he got an upper/a lower ~** ≈ er hat mit Eins bis Zwei/Zwei bis Drei abgeschnitten

f *(Sport, in duel)* Sekundant *m*; **~s out!** Ring frei!

g **seconds** **PL** *(inf: = second helping)* Nachschlag *m (inf)*; **there aren't any ~s** es ist nichts mehr da; **can I have ~s?** kann ich noch etwas nachbekommen?

h *(Comm)* **this is a ~** das ist zweite Wahl; **~s are much cheaper** Waren zweiter Wahl sind viel billiger

second[2] [sɪ'kɒnd] **VT** *(Brit)* abordnen, abstellen

secondarily ['sekəndərɪlɪ] **ADV** in zweiter Linie

secondary ['sekəndərɪ] **ADJ** **a** sekundär; *industry* verarbeitend; *reason* weniger bedeutend; **of ~ importance** von untergeordneter *or* sekundärer Bedeutung; **that was only ~ to our need to save money** das kam erst an zweiter Stelle nach der Notwendigkeit, Geld zu sparen; **~ character** *(Film, Theat)* Nebenfigur *f*

b *(= higher) education* höher; **~ modern (school)** *(dated Brit)* ≈ Realschule *f*; **~ school** höhere Schule; **~ schooling** höhere Schulausbildung; **~ teacher** Lehrer(in) *m(f)* an einer höheren Schule; **subjects taught at ~ level** Unterrichtsfächer *pl* in höheren Schulen

N *(inf: = school)* höhere Schule

secondary: **secondary action** **N** *Streik in nur indirekt beteiligten Firmen*; **secondary cancer** **N** Sekundärkrebs *m*; **secondary colour**, *(US)* **secondary color** **N** Mischfarbe *f*; **secondary feather** **N** Armschwinge *f*; **secondary host** **N** *(Biol)* Zwischenwirt *m*; **secondary infection** **N** Sekundärinfektion *f*; **secondary picketing** **N** *Aufstellung von Streikposten vor nur indirekt beteiligten Firmen*; **secondary road** **N** Nebenstraße *f*; **secondary sex(ual) characteristic** **N** sekundäres Geschlechtsmerkmal; **secondary smoking** **N** Passivrauchen *nt*; **secondary stress** **N** *(Gram)* Nebenton *m*

second: **second ballot** **N** *(Pol)* Stichwahl *f*; **second best** **N** Zweitbeste(r, s); **(the) ~ isn't good enough for him** das Beste ist gerade gut genug für ihn; **I won't settle for ~** ich gebe mich nicht mit dem Zweitbesten zufrieden **ADV** **to come off ~** es nicht so gut haben; *(= come off badly)* den kürzeren ziehen; **second-best** **ADJ** zweitbeste(r, s); **she always felt she was ~** sie hatte immer das Gefühl, zweite Wahl zu sein; **he was always ~ to his older brother** er stand immer im Schatten seines älteren Bruders; **that job was ~ for him** diese Stelle war eine Ausweichlösung für ihn; **second chamber** **N** zweite Kammer; **second childhood** **N** zweite Kindheit; **second class** **N** *(Rail, Post etc)* zweite Klasse; **second-class** **ADJ** **a** *travel, ticket, carriage, mail* zweiter Klasse *pred*; *status, education, treatment* zweitklassig; **~ degree** *(Brit Univ)* = **second[1] N e**; **~ stamp** *Briefmarke für nicht bevorzugt beförderte Briefsendungen*; **~ letter** *nicht bevorzugt beförderter Brief* **b** = **second-rate** **ADV** *travel* zweiter Klasse; **to send sth ~** etw mit nicht bevorzugter Post schicken; **second-class citizen** **N** Bürger(in) *m(f)* zweiter Klasse; **Second Coming** **N** Wiederkunft *f*; **second cousin** **N** Cousin *m*/Cousine *f or* Kusine *f* zweiten Grades; **second-degree** **ADJ** *attr* zweiten Grades; **second-degree burn** **N** Verbrennung *f* zweiten Grades

seconder ['sekəndə'] **N** Befürworter(in) *m(f)*

second: **second-guess** **VT** **a** *(= predict)* vorhersagen, prophezeien; **to ~ sb** vorhersagen, was jd machen/sagen wird **b** *(US: = criticize)* nachträglich *or* im Nachhinein kritisieren; **second-guesser** **N** *(US) jd, der nachträglich kritisiert*, Besserwisser(in) *m(f)*; **second-guessing** **N** **a** *(= predicting)* Voraus- *or* Vorhersagen *nt* **b** *(US: = criticising)* nachträgliches Kritisieren, nachträgliche Kritik; **second hand** **N** *(of watch)* Sekundenzeiger *m*; **second-hand** **ADJ** gebraucht; *clothes* getragen, secondhand *(esp Comm)*; *(fig) information, knowledge* aus zweiter Hand; **a ~ car** ein Gebrauchtwagen *m*; **~ dealer** Gebrauchtwarenhändler(in) *m(f)*; *(for cars)* Gebrauchtwagenhändler(in) *m(f)*; **~ value** Gebrauchtwert *m*; **~ shop** Secondhandshop *nt or* -laden *m*; **~ bookshop** Antiquariat *nt*; **~ market** *(for cars)* Gebrauchtwagenmarkt *m*; **~ smoking** passives Rauchen; **there is a thriving ~ market for this** das ist auch gebraucht sehr gefragt **ADV** gebraucht, aus zweiter Hand; **I only heard it ~** ich habe es nur aus zweiter Hand; **second home** **N** Zweitwohnung *f*; **second language** **N** Zweitsprache *f*; **second lieutenant** **N** Leutnant *m*

secondly ['sekəndlɪ] ✪ 26.2 **ADV** zweitens; *(= secondarily)* an zweiter Stelle, in zweiter Linie

secondment [sɪ'kɒndmənt] **N** *(Brit)* Abordnung *f*; **to be on ~** abgeordnet sein

second: **second mortgage** **N** zweite Hypothek; **to take out a ~** eine zweite Hypothek aufnehmen; **second name** **N** Familienname *m*, Nachname *m*, Zuname *m*; **second nature** **N** zweite Natur; **to become ~ (to sb)** (jdm) in Fleisch und Blut übergehen; **second officer** **N** *(Mil)* zweiter Offizier; **second person** **N** *(Gram)* zweite Person; **the ~ singular/plural** die zweite Person Einzahl/Mehrzahl; **second-rate** **ADJ** *(pej)* zweitklassig, zweitrangig; **second sight** **N** das Zweite Gesicht; **you must have ~** du musst hellsehen können; **second string** **N** **a** *(= second possibility)* zweite Möglichkeit; **history/translation is my ~** ich kann jederzeit auf Geschichte/Übersetzungen als zweite Möglichkeit zurückgreifen; **to have a ~ to one's bow** zwei Eisen im Feuer haben **b** *(esp US Sport) (= player)* Ersatzspieler(in) *m(f)*, Reservespieler(in) *m(f)*; *(= team)* Ersatzmannschaft *f*, Reservemannschaft *f*; **second-string** **ADJ** *(esp US Sport)* Ersatz-, Reserve-; **~ team** Ersatzmannschaft *f*, Reservemannschaft *f*; **second thought** **N** **with hardly** *or* **without a ~** ohne einen weiteren Gedanken, ohne lange *or* weiter darüber nachzudenken; **I didn't give him/it a ~** ich habe an ihn/daran überhaupt keinen Gedanken verschwendet; **to have ~s about sth** sich *(dat)* etw anders überlegen; **on ~s I decided not to** dann habe ich mich doch dagegen entschieden; **on ~s maybe I'd better do it myself** vielleicht mache ich es, genau besehen, doch lieber selbst; **Second World War** **N** **the ~** der Zweite Weltkrieg

secrecy ['siːkrəsɪ] **N** *(of person, = ability to keep secrets)* Verschwiegenheit *f*; *(= secretiveness)* Geheimnistuerei *f*, Heimlichtuerei *f*; *(of event, talks)* Heimlichkeit *f*; **in ~** im Geheimen; **in strict ~** ganz im Geheimen; **there is no ~ about it** das ist kein Geheimnis → **swear**

secret ['siːkrɪt] **ADJ** geheim; *pocket* versteckt; *drinker, admirer, ambition* heimlich; *ballot, vote* geheim; **a ~ door** eine verborgene Tür, eine Geheimtür; **the ~ ingredient** die geheimnisvolle Zutat; *(fig, of success etc)* die Zauberformel; **to keep sth ~ (from sb)** etw (vor jdm) geheim halten; **it's all highly ~** es ist alles streng geheim; **she was a ~ drug addict** sie verheimlichte ihre Drogensucht

N Geheimnis *nt*; **to keep sb/sth a ~ (from sb)** jdn/etw (vor jdm) geheim halten; **to tell sb a ~** jdm ein Geheimnis anvertrauen *or (give away)* verraten; **open ~** offenes Geheimnis; **in ~** im Geheimen; **I told you that in ~** *or* **as a ~** ich habe Ihnen das im Vertrauen erzählt; **they always met in ~** sie trafen sich immer heimlich; *(group etc)* sie hatten immer geheime Versammlungen; **she pretended to hate London, but in ~ she loved the city** sie gab vor, London zu hassen, aber insgeheim liebte sie die Stadt; **to be in on the ~** (in das Geheimnis) eingeweiht sein; **to let sb in on** *or* **into a ~** jdn in ein Geheimnis einweihen; **there's no ~ about it** das ist kein Geheimnis; **it's no ~ that …** es ist kein Geheimnis, dass …; **to keep a ~** ein Geheimnis für sich behalten; **can you keep a ~?** kannst du schweigen?; **to make no ~ of sth** kein Geheimnis *or* keinen Hehl aus etw machen; **the ~ of success** das Erfolgsgeheimnis; **the ~ of being a good teacher** das Geheimnis eines guten Lehrers; **I have no ~s from you** ich habe keine Geheimnisse vor dir

secret agent **N** Geheimagent(in) *m(f)*

secretaire [ˌsekrə'tɛə'] **N** *(Brit)* Sekretär *m*

secretarial [ˌsekrə'tɛərɪəl] **ADJ** *job, qualifications* als Sekretärin/Sekretär; **to do a ~ course** einen Sekretärinnenkurs machen, einen Kurs für Bürofachkräfte machen; **~ work** Sekretariatsarbeit *f*; **~ college** Schule *f* für Bürofachkräfte; **~ staff** Sekretärinnen und Schreibkräfte *pl*; *(of politician)* Stab *m*; **she joined his ~ staff** sie wurde Sekretärin bei ihm; **basic ~ skills** grundlegende Fertigkeiten *pl* als Bürofachkraft

secretarial agency **N** Personalvermittlung *f* für Bürokräfte

secretariat [ˌsekrə'tɛərɪət] **N** Sekretariat *nt*

secretary ['sekrətrɪ] **N** **a** Sekretär(in) *m(f)*; *(of society)* Schriftführer(in) *m(f)*; *(esp US Pol: = minister)* Minister(in) *m(f)*; **~ to the board** Schriftführer(in) *m(f)* **b** *(= desk)* = **secretaire**

secretary: **secretary bird** **N** Sekretär *m*; **secretary-general** **N** *pl* **secretaries-general, secretary-generals** Generalsekretär(in) *m(f)*; **Secretary of State** **N** *(Brit)* Minister(in) *m(f)*; *(US)* Außenminister(in) *m(f)*; **secretaryship** **N** *(= office)* Amt *nt* des Schriftführers; *(= period)* Zeit *f* als Schriftführer

secret code **N** Geheimkode *m*

secrete [sɪ'kriːt] **VT** **a** *(= hide)* verbergen **b** *(Med)* absondern **VI** *(Med)* absondern

secretion [sɪ'kriːʃən] **N** **a** *(= hiding)* Verbergen *nt* **b** *(Med: = act)* Absonderung *f*, Sekretion *f*; *(= substance)* Sekret *nt*

secretive[1] [sɪ'kriːtɪv] **ADJ** *(Med)* sekretorisch

secretive[2] ['siːkrətɪv] **ADJ** *person (by nature)* verschlossen; *(in action)* geheimnistuerisch; *organization* verschwiegen, geheimnistuerisch; *smile,* *behaviour* geheimnisvoll; **to be ~ about sth** mit etw geheimnisvoll tun

secretively ['si:krətɪvlɪ] ADV geheimnisvoll; *(= in secret)* heimlich; **to behave ~** geheimnistuerisch sein

secretiveness ['si:krətɪvnɪs] N *(= character trait)* Verschlossenheit *f*; *(= secretive behaviour)* Geheimnistuerei *f*; **the ~ of his smile/behaviour** sein geheimnisvolles Lächeln/Benehmen

secretly ['si:krətlɪ] ADV *(= in secrecy)* im Geheimen; *meet, marry, film* heimlich; *(= privately)* insgeheim, im Stillen; **he was ~ concerned** insgeheim war er beunruhigt

secretory [sɪ'kri:tərɪ] ADJ *gland etc* sekretorisch

secret: **secret police** N Geheimpolizei *f*; **secret service** N Geheimdienst *m*; **secret society** N Geheimgesellschaft *f*; **secret weapon** N *(lit, fig)* Geheimwaffe *f*

sect [sekt] N Sekte *f*

sectarian [sek'tɛərɪən] ADJ sektiererisch; *differences* konfessionell; **~ loyalties** konfessionelles Zugehörigkeitsgefühl; **~ violence** Gewalttätigkeiten *pl* mit konfessionellem Hintergrund N Sektierer(in) *m(f)*

sectarianism [sek'tɛərɪənɪzəm] N Sektierertum *nt*

section ['sekʃən] N **a** *(= part)* Teil *m*; *(= wing of building)* Trakt *m*; *(of book)* Abschnitt *m*; *(of document, law)* Absatz *m*; *(of motorway etc)* Abschnitt *m*; *(under construction)* Trakt *m*; *(of railway)* Streckenabschnitt *m*; *(of orange)* Stück *nt*; **the brass/string ~ of the orchestra** die Blechbläser *pl*/Streicher *pl* des Orchesters; **the sports ~** *(Press)* der Sportteil; **all ~s of the public** alle Teile der Öffentlichkeit; **the Indian ~ of the community** die Gruppe der Inder in der Gesellschaft
b *(= department, Mil)* Abteilung *f*; *(esp of academy etc)* Sektion *f*
c *(= diagram)* Schnitt *m*; **in ~** im Schnitt; **vertical/longitudinal ~** Quer-/Längsschnitt *m*
d *(= cutting: of rock, Med: of tissue)* Schnitt *m*; *(Med) (= operation)* Sektion *f*; *(= Caesarean section)* Kaiserschnitt *m*; **he took a horizontal ~ of the tissue** er machte einen Horizontalschnitt von dem Gewebe
VT **a** *(= cut to show a section)* einen Schnitt machen durch
b *(= divide into sections)* teilen
c *(Psych)* **to be ~ed** zwangseingewiesen werden

▶ **section off** VT *sep* abteilen; *(= cordon off)* absperren

sectional ['sekʃənl] ADJ **a** *(= in sections) road-building* abschnittsweise; *furniture, pipe, fishing rod* zerlegbar; **~ drawing** Darstellung *f* im Schnitt **b** *differences, rivalries* zwischen den Gruppen; *interests* partikularistisch

sectionalism ['sekʃənəlɪzəm] N Partikularismus *m*

sectionalize ['sekʃənəlaɪz] VI *(= subdivide)* unterteilen; **~d design** gegliederte Bauweise; *(according to different aspects)* nach lokalen Gesichtspunkten/Interessen einteilen

section mark N *(Comput: = symbol)* Paragrafenzeichen *nt*

sector ['sektəʳ] N *(also Comput)* Sektor *m*

sectoral ['sektərəl] ADJ *(Econ)* sektorenspezifisch

secular ['sekjʊləʳ] ADJ weltlich, säkular; *music, art* profan; *court, education* weltlich; *state* säkular; **~ priest** Weltgeistliche(r) *mf*

secularism ['sekjʊlərɪzəm] N Säkularismus *m*; *(of attitude)* Weltlichkeit *f*

secularization [,sekjʊləraɪ'zeɪʃən] N Säkularisation *f*; *(of education, court, Sunday also)* Säkularisierung *f*

secularize ['sekjʊləraɪz] VT säkularisieren

secure [sɪ'kjʊəʳ] ADJ *(+er)* **a** *(= safe)* sicher; *(emotionally)* geborgen; *existence, income* gesichert; **~ in the knowledge that ...** ruhig in dem Bewusstsein, dass ...; **to be ~ against** *or* **from sth** vor etw *(dat)* sicher sein; **to feel ~** sich sicher fühlen; *(emotionally)* sich geborgen fühlen; **to feel ~ about one's future** der Zukunft sicher entgegensehen; **to make sb feel ~** jdm das Gefühl der Sicherheit geben; **to be financially ~** finanziell abgesichert sein; **to be emotionally ~** emotional stabil sein
b *(= fastened) lock, door* gesichert; *(= firm, well-fastened) grip, knot, tile* fest; **is the window ~?** ist das Fenster fest zu?; **is the lid ~?** ist der Deckel fest drauf?; **to make a door/window/rope ~** eine Tür/ein Fenster/ein Seil sichern; **to make a tile ~** einen Ziegel befestigen
c *(= solid) base* sicher, solide; **to have a ~ foothold** *(fig)* festen Fuß gefasst haben; **on ~ ground** auf sicherem Boden
VT **a** *(= fasten, make firm)* festmachen; *(= tie up)* befestigen, festmachen; *window, door* fest zumachen; *(with chain, bolt etc)* sichern; *tile* befestigen; *(= make safe)* sichern *(from, against* gegen), schützen *(from, against* vor *+dat)*
b *(= obtain)* sich *(dat)* sichern; *majority of votes, order* erhalten; *profits, higher prices* erzielen; *share, interest in business* erwerben; *(= buy)* erstehen; *cook, employee* verpflichten; **to ~ sth for sb, to ~ sb sth** jdm etw sichern; **to ~ sb's services** jdn verpflichten; **their troops have now ~d the bridge/the airport** die Truppen haben jetzt die Brücke/den Flugplatz gegen feindliche Angriffe gesichert
c *(= guarantee)* sichern, garantieren; *loan* (ab-)sichern

secure accommodation N Sicherheitsverwahrung *f*

securely [sɪ'kjʊəlɪ] ADV *(= firmly)* fest; *(= safely)* sicher; **the prisoner was kept ~ in his cell** der Gefangene wurde streng gesichert in seiner Zelle gehalten; **~ established** fest etabliert

secureness [sɪ'kjʊənɪs] N **a** *(= safety)* Sicherheit *f*; *(emotional)* Geborgenheit *f* **b** *(of lock, door)* Sicherheit *f*

secure unit N Sicherheitsabteilung *f*

securities market [sɪ'kjʊərɪtɪz'mɑ:kɪt] M *(Fin)* Wertpapiermarkt *m*

security [sɪ'kjʊərɪtɪ] N **a** Sicherheit *f*; *(emotional)* Geborgenheit *f*; *(= security measures)* Sicherheitsvorkehrungen *or* -maßnahmen *pl*; **for ~** zur Sicherheit; **~ of tenure** Kündigungsschutz *m*; **to increase ~** die Sicherheitsmaßnahmen verschärfen *or* verstärken; **airports have tightened their ~** die Flughäfen haben ihre Sicherheitsvorkehrungen verschärft; **in the ~ of one's own home** sicher im eigenen Heim; *(from emotional point of view)* in der Geborgenheit des eigenen Heims
b *(= security department)* Sicherheitsdienst *m*
c *(Fin: = guarantee)* Sicherheit *f*; *(= guarantor)* Bürge *m*, Bürgin *f*; **up to £500 without ~** bis zu £ 500 ohne Sicherheit; **to lend money on ~** Geld gegen Sicherheit leihen; **to stand ~ for sb** für jdn Bürge/Bürgin sein *or* Bürgschaft leisten
d **securities** PL *(Fin)* Effekten *pl*, (Wert)papiere *pl*

security *in cpds* Sicherheits-; **security adviser** N Sicherheitsberater(in) *m(f)*; **security agency** N Sicherheitsdienst *m*; **security blanket** N **a** *(around politicians etc)* Sicherheitsnetz *nt*; **to throw a ~ around sb/sth** jdm/etw mit einem Sicherheitsnetz umgeben **b** *(of child)* Kuscheldecke *f*; **security bond** N *(Fin)* Bürgschaftswechsel *m*; **security camera** N Überwachungskamera *f*; **security check** N Sicherheitskontrolle *f*; **security clearance** N Einstufung *f* als vertrauenswürdig *or* als kein Sicherheitsrisiko; **to have ~** kein Sicherheitsrisiko sein *or* darstellen; **Security Council** N Sicherheitsrat *m*; **security expert** N Sicherheitsexperte *m*, Sicherheitsexpertin *f*; **security firm** N Wach- und Sicherheitsdienst *m*; **security force** N Sicherheitstruppe *f*; *(UN)* Friedenstruppe *f*; **security forces** PL Sicherheitskräfte *pl*; *(UN)* Friedensstreitmacht *f*; **security gap** N Sicherheitslücke *f*; **security guard** N Wache *f*, Wächter(in) *m(f)*; *(for security checks)* Sicherheitsbeamte(r) *m*/-beamtin *f*; **security man** N Wache *f*, Wächter *m*; *(for security checks)* Sicherheitsbeamte(r) *m*; **one of the security men** einer der Sicherheitsleute; **security measure** N Sicherheitsmaßnahme *or* -vorkehrung *f*; **security police** N Sicherheitspolizei *m*; **security precautions** PL Sicherheitsvorkehrungen *pl*; **security risk** N Sicherheitsrisiko *nt*; **security screening** N *(Pol)* Unbedenklichkeitsüberprüfung *f*; **security technology** N Sicherheitstechnik *f*; **security vetting** N Sicherheitsüberprüfung *f*

secy *abbr of* **secretary**

sedan [sɪ'dæn] N **a** *(also* **sedan chair***)* Sänfte *f* **b** *(US Aut)* Limousine *f*

sedate [sɪ'deɪt] ADJ *(+er)* gesetzt; *little girl, colour* ruhig; *furnishings, décor* gediegen; *life* geruhsam; *place* beschaulich; *party* ruhig, gesittet; *speed* gemächlich; *prose* bedächtig; **at a ~ pace** in gemessenem Tempo; **in a ~ manner** ruhig, gemessen VT Beruhigungsmittel geben *(+dat)*, sedieren *(spec)*; **he was heavily ~d** er stand stark unter dem Einfluss von Beruhigungsmitteln

sedately [sɪ'deɪtlɪ] ADV **a** *(= gently)* gemessen, ruhig; **he pulled ~ out of the driveway** er fuhr gemächlich aus der Auffahrt heraus **b** *(= conservatively) dressed, furnished* gediegen

sedateness [sɪ'deɪtnɪs] N Gesetztheit *f*; *(of little girl)* ruhige Art; *(of colour)* ruhiger Ton; *(of furnishings, décor)* Gediegenheit *f*; *(of life)* Geruhsamkeit *f*; *(of place)* Beschaulichkeit *f*; *(of prose)* Bedächtigkeit *f*

sedation [sɪ'deɪʃən] N Beruhigungsmittel *pl*; **to put sb under ~** jdm Beruhigungsmittel geben; **drugs used for ~** Drogen *pl* zur Beruhigung

sedative ['sedətɪv] N Beruhigungsmittel *nt*, Sedativum *nt* *(spec)* ADJ beruhigend, sedativ *(spec)*

sedentariness ['sedntərɪnɪs] N **a** **as a result of the ~ of the job** durch das dauernde Sitzen bei der Arbeit; **the excessive ~ of his daily life** das übermäßige tägliche Sitzen **b** *(of tribe)* Sesshaftigkeit *f*; *(of bird)* Verbleiben *nt* am Nistort

sedentary ['sedntərɪ] ADJ **a** *job, occupation* sitzend *attr*; **to lead a ~ life** sehr viel sitzen; **any job of a ~ nature** jede im Sitzen ausgeübte Tätigkeit **b** *tribe* sesshaft; **~ bird** Standvogel *m*

sedge warbler N Seggenrohrsänger *m*

sedge [sedʒ] N Riedgras *nt*, Segge *f*

sedgy ['sedʒɪ] ADJ **a** *(grown with sedge)* mit Riedgras bewachsen **b** *(= resembling sedge)* riedgrasartig

sediment ['sedɪmənt] N (Boden)satz *m*; *(in river)* Ablagerung *f*; *(in chemical solution)* Niederschlag *m*, Sediment *nt*

sedimentary [,sedɪ'mentərɪ] ADJ sedimentär; **~ rocks** Sedimentgestein *nt*

sedimentation [,sedɪmen'teɪʃən] N Ablagerung *f*, Sedimentation *f*

sedition [sə'dɪʃən] N Aufwiegelung *f*, Verhetzung *f*

seditious [sə'dɪʃəs] ADJ aufrührerisch, aufwieglerisch

seduce [sɪ'dju:s] VT verführen; **to ~ sb into doing sth** jdn zu etw verleiten, jdn dazu verleiten, etw zu tun; **to ~ sb (away) from his duty/a place** jdn seine Pflichten vergessen lassen/von einem Ort weglocken; **to ~ sb (away) from his wife** jdn seiner Frau abspenstig machen

seducer [sɪ'dju:səʳ] N Verführer *m*

seducible [sɪ'dju:sɪbl] ADJ verführbar

seduction [sɪ'dʌkʃən] N Verführung *f*

seductive [sɪ'dʌktɪv] ADJ verführerisch; *salary, offer, suggestion* verlockend

seductively [sɪ'dʌktɪvlɪ] ADV verführerisch; *offer, suggest* verlockend

seductiveness [sɪ'dʌktɪvnɪs] N verführerische Art; **the ~ of the offer** *etc* das verlockende Angebot *etc*

seductress [sɪ'dʌktrɪs] N Verführerin *f*

sedulous ADJ, **sedulously** ADV ['sedjʊləs, -lɪ] unermüdlich, unentwegt

see[1] [siː]
pret **saw**, *ptp* **seen**
✪ 6.1, 6.2, 12.1, 15.2, 26.3

1 TRANSITIVE VERB 3 PHRASAL VERBS
2 INTRANSITIVE VERB

1 – TRANSITIVE VERB

a sehen; **to see sb do sth** sehen, wie jd etw macht; **I've never seen him swim(ming)** ich habe ihn noch nie schwimmen sehen; **he was seen to enter the building** man hat ihn gesehen *or* er wurde gesehen, wie er das Gebäude betrat; **I saw it happen** ich habe gesehen, wie es passiert ist; **I've seen it done three times** das habe ich schon dreimal gesehen; **I wouldn't see you starve** ich würde doch nicht zusehen, wie du verhungerst; **I don't like to see people mistreated** ich kann es nicht sehen, wenn Menschen schlecht behandelt werden; **I wouldn't like to see you unhappy** ich möchte doch nicht, dass du unglücklich bist; **see page 8** siehe Seite 8; **there was nothing to be seen** es war nichts zu sehen; **I don't know what she sees in him** ich weiß nicht, was sie an ihm findet; **we don't see much of them nowadays** wir sehen sie zurzeit nur selten; **I want to see a bit of the world** ich möchte etwas von der Welt sehen *or* kennenlernen; **I'll see him in hell first** *(inf)* ich denke nicht (im Schlaf) daran; **she won't see 40 again** sie ist gut und gern 40; **I/you must be seeing things** ich sehe/du siehst wohl Gespenster!; **I must be seeing things, if it isn't Peter!** ich glaub, ich seh nicht richtig, das ist doch der Peter!; **am I seeing things or is ...?** seh ich richtig, ist das nicht ...?; **I can't see my way to doing that** ich sehe mich nicht in der Lage, das zu tun; **I saw myself obliged to/faced with the need to ...** ich sah mich gezwungen, zu ...; **I suddenly saw myself being cheated** ich sah *or* erkannte plötzlich, dass man mich betrog

b = check nachsehen, gucken *(inf)*; **I'll go and see who it is** ich gehe mal nachsehen *or* ich gucke *(inf)* mal(, wer das ist)

c = go and see *film, show, sights* sich *(dat)* ansehen; **worth seeing** sehenswert

d = visit besuchen; *(on business)* aufsuchen; **to call** *or* **go and see sb** jdn besuchen (gehen); **to see the doctor** zum Arzt gehen; **he is the man you ought to see about this** Sie sollten sich damit an ihn wenden

e = meet, talk to, receive = meet with sehen; *(= have a word with, talk to)* sprechen; *(= receive visit of)* empfangen; **the boss can't see you now, you can't see the boss now** Sie können den Chef jetzt nicht sprechen, Sie können jetzt nicht zum Chef *(inf)*; **the boss/doctor will see you now** der Chef/der Herr Doktor ist jetzt frei; **what did he want to see you about?** weswegen wollte er Sie sprechen?; **I'll have to see my wife about that** das muss ich mit meiner Frau besprechen; **have you seen Personnel yet?** waren Sie schon bei der Personalabteilung?; **the minister saw the Queen yesterday** der Minister war gestern bei der Königin; **the Queen will see the minister tomorrow** die Königin wird den Minister morgen empfangen; **she refused to see us** sie wollte uns nicht empfangen *or* sehen; **there was only one applicant worth seeing** es war nur ein Bewerber dabei, den es sich anzusehen lohnte; **I shall be seeing them for dinner** ich treffe sie beim Abendessen; **see you (soon)!** bis bald!; **be seeing you!, see you later!** bis später!, bis nachher!; **see you on Sunday!** bis Sonntag!

f = have relationship with befreundet sein mit; **I'm not seeing anyone at the moment** ich habe zurzeit keinen Freund/keine Freundin

g = accompany begleiten, bringen; **to see sb to the door** jdn zur Tür bringen

h = find out, know **we'll see if we can help** mal sehen, ob wir helfen können; **we'll soon see who is right** wir werden ja bald sehen, wer recht hat; **that remains to be seen** das wird sich zeigen; **let's just see what happens** wollen wir mal sehen *or* abwarten, was passiert; **I don't see any way I can help** ich sehe nicht, wie ich da helfen kann; **let me see if I can fix up something** ich werde mal sehen, ob sich etwas arrangieren lässt; **let me see if I can't find a better way** mal sehen, ob ich nicht etwas Besseres finden kann

i = visualize sich *(dat)* vorstellen; **I can't** *or* **don't see that working/him winning/myself living there** ich kann mir kaum vorstellen, dass das klappt/dass er gewinnt/dass ich da leben möchte; **I can't see myself in that job** ich glaube nicht, dass das eine Stelle für mich wäre; **can you see him as a father?** kannst du ihn dir als Vater vorstellen?; **he saw himself as a martyr** er sah sich als Märtyrer; **I can see it happening** ich sehe es kommen; **I can't see any chance of that happening** das halte ich für unwahrscheinlich *or* kaum möglich

j = experience erleben; **he lived to see the beginning of a new age** er hat den Anfang eines neuen Zeitalters miterlebt; **now I've seen everything!** ist das denn zu fassen?; **what impudence, I've never seen anything like it!** so eine Frechheit, so etwas habe ich ja noch nie gesehen *or* erlebt!; **it's seen a lot of hard wear** das ist schon sehr strapaziert worden

k = hear, notice sehen; **I see you still haven't done that/he's got married again** wie ich sehe, hast du das immer noch nicht gemacht/hat er wieder geheiratet

l = comprehend = understand verstehen; *(= recognize)* einsehen; *(= realize)* erkennen; **I don't see the importance of doing it/the need for the change** ich verstehe nicht *or* ich sehe nicht ein, warum das unbedingt gemacht werden muss/warum das geändert werden muss; **I can see that it might be a good thing** ich sehe ja ein, dass das eine gute Idee wäre; **I can see I'm going to be busy** ich sehe schon, ich werde viel zu tun haben; **I fail to** *or* **don't see how anyone could ...** ich begreife einfach nicht, wie jemand nur ... kann; **I don't see where the problem is** ich sehe das Problem nicht; **I see from this report that ...** ich ersehe aus diesem Bericht, dass ...; **(do you) see what I mean?** verstehst du(, was ich meine)?; *(= didn't I tell you!)* siehst dus jetzt!; **I see what you mean** ich verstehe, was du meinst; *(= you're quite right)* ja, du hast recht; **to make sb see sth** jdm etw klarmachen; **to make sb see reason** jdn zur Vernunft bringen; **I saw only too clearly that ...** ich erkannte nur zu deutlich, dass ...

m = consider *problem* sehen; **as I see it** so, wie ich das sehe; **this is how I see it** ich sehe das so; **that's how I see it** so sehe ich das jedenfalls; **try to see it my way** versuchen Sie doch einmal, es aus meiner Sicht zu sehen; **I don't see it that way** ich sehe das anders

n = ensure **see that it is done by tomorrow** sieh zu, dass es bis morgen fertig ist; **see that it doesn't happen again** sieh zu *or* pass auf, dass das nicht noch mal passiert; **I'll see you (all) right** *(inf)* ich werd dich nicht vergessen *(inf)*

o Cards **I'll see you** ich halte

2 – INTRANSITIVE VERB

a = have sight sehen

b = look sehen; **let me see, let's see** lassen Sie mich mal sehen; **can you see if I sit here?** können Sie (etwas) sehen, wenn ich hier sitze?; **it was so dark I couldn't see** es war so dunkel, ich konnte nichts sehen; **who was it? – I couldn't/didn't see** wer war das? – ich konnte es nicht sehen; **can you see to read?** ist es Ihnen hell genug zum Lesen?; **as far as the eye can see** so weit das Auge reicht; **see for yourself!** sieh doch selbst!; **now see here!** nun hören Sie mal her!

c = check, find out nachsehen, gucken *(inf)*; **is he there? – I'll see** ist er da? – ich sehe mal nach *or* ich guck mal *(inf)*; **I'll go and see** ich gehe mal nachsehen; **see for yourself!** sieh doch selbst (nach)!; **let me see** lassen Sie mich mal nachsehen

d = discover sehen; **will he come? – we'll soon see** kommt er? – das werden wir bald sehen *or* rausfinden *(inf)*; **what kind of person is she? – you'll soon see for yourself** was für ein Mensch ist sie? – das werden Sie bald selbst sehen *or* feststellen; **you'll see!** du wirst es (schon) noch sehen!

e = understand verstehen; **as far as I can see ...** so wie ich das sehe ...; **it's all over, see?** es ist vorbei, verstehst du?; **it's logical, do you see?** es ist logisch, nicht wahr?; **he's dead, don't you see?** er ist tot, begreifst du das denn nicht?; **as I see from your report** wie ich in Ihrem Bericht lese, wie ich aus Ihrem Bericht ersehe; **it's too late, (you) see** *(explaining)* weißt du, es ist zu spät; *(= I told you so)* siehst du, es ist zu spät!; **(you) see, it's like this** es ist nämlich so; **(you) see, we can't do that** weißt du, das können wir nicht machen; **that's the way he is, (you) see** das ist eben seine Art(, weißt du); **but this still has to be improved, you see** das muss natürlich noch verbessert werden; **and we went out, see, and saw this film, see, and ...** *(dial)* und wir sind weggegangen, weißte *(inf) or* nich *(N Ger) or* gell *(S Ger)*, und haben uns den Film angesehen, weißte *etc*, und ...; **I see!** aha!; *(after explanation)* ach so!; *(to keep conversation going, = I'm with you)* ja; **yes, I see** ja, aha

f = consider **we'll see** (wir werden *or* wollen) mal sehen; **I don't know, I'll have to see** ich weiß nicht, ich muss mal sehen; **will you be there? – I'll see** bist du da? – mal sehen; **he said he'll see** er sagt, er will mal sehen; **let me see, let's see** warten Sie mal, lassen Sie mich mal überlegen

3 – PHRASAL VERBS

▶ **see about** VI +prep obj **a** *(= attend to)* sich kümmern um; **I'll have to see about getting the roof mended** ich muss mich darum kümmern, dass das Dach repariert wird; **he came to see about the TV** er kam, um sich *(dat)* den Fernseher anzusehen; **I've still a few things to see about** ich muss noch ein paar Dinge erledigen; **he came to see about the rent** er ist wegen der Miete gekommen; **we'd better see about going now** wir sehen besser zu, dass wir jetzt gehen
b *(= consider)* **I'll see about it** ich will mal sehen *or* schauen *(esp S Ger)*; **we'll see about that!** *(iro)* das wollen wir mal sehen

▶ **see across** VT *always separate* hinüberbegleiten *or* -bringen *(prep obj* über *+acc)*

▶ **see after** VI +prep obj *(esp US: = attend to)* sich kümmern um

▶ **see in** VI *(= look in)* hineinsehen VT *sep (= show in)* hereinbringen; **to see the New Year in** das neue Jahr begrüßen

▶ **see into** VI +prep obj **a** *house, room* hineinsehen in *(+acc)*; **to see into the future** in die Zukunft sehen *or* schauen; **to see into sb's mind** jds Gedanken lesen **b** *(= investigate)* untersuchen, prüfen, nachgehen *(+dat)*

▶ **see off** VT *sep* **a** *(= bid farewell to)* verabschieden; **are you coming to see me off (at the airport** *etc***)?** kommt ihr mit mir (zum Flughafen *etc*)? **b** *(= chase off)* Beine machen *(+dat) (inf)*; **see him off, boy!** verjag ihn! **c** *(inf: = be better than)* in die Tasche stecken *(inf)*

▶ **see out** VI *(= look out)* hinaussehen; **I can't see out of the window** ich kann nicht zum Fenster hinaussehen VT *sep* **a** *(= show out)* hinausbringen *or* -begleiten (of aus); **I'll see myself out** ich finde (schon) alleine hinaus **b** *(= last to the end of) (coat, car) winter etc* überdauern; *(old man, invalid) wife, year etc* überleben; **will he be fit enough to see out the game?** ist er fit genug, um das Spiel ganz durchzustehen?; **to see the Old Year out** das alte Jahr verabschieden

▶ **see over** *or* **round** *(esp Brit)* VI +prep obj *house etc* sich *(dat)* ansehen

▶ **see through** VI *(lit)* (hin)durchsehen *(prep obj* durch*)* VI +prep obj *(fig: = not be deceived by)* durchschauen; **I can see right through you** ich habe dich durchschaut *or* erkannt VT *always separate* **a** *(= help through difficult time)* beistehen *(+dat)*; **to see sb through a bad time** jdm über eine schwierige Zeit hinweghelfen; **he**

had £100 to see him through the term er hatte £ 100 für das ganze Semester; **I hope £10 will see you through** die £ 10 reichen dir hoffentlich **b** *job* zu Ende bringen; *(Parl) bill* durchbringen

▸ **see to** VI *+prep obj* sich kümmern um; **that cough needs seeing to** um den Husten muss man sich kümmern; **that cough needs seeing to** um den Husten muss man sich kümmern; **see to it that you don't/he doesn't forget** sieh zu, dass du/er das nicht vergisst; **I'll see to it** ich werde mich d(a)rum kümmern; **there's no chance now, the rain has seen to that** es ist aussichtslos, dafür hat der Regen schon gesorgt

▸ **see up** VI *+prep obj (= look up)* hinaufsehen; **I could see up her skirt** ich konnte ihr unter den Rock sehen VT *sep (= show up)* heraufbringen

see² N Bistum *nt*; *(Catholic also)* Diözese *f*; *(Protestant in Germany)* Landeskirche *f*; **Holy See, See of Rome** Heiliger Stuhl

seed [si:d] N **a** *(Bot: = one single)* Samen *m*; *(of grain, poppy, sesame etc)* Korn *nt*; *(within fruit)* (Samen)kern *m*; *(collective)* Samen *pl*; *(for birds)* Körner *pl*; *(= grain)* Saat *f*, Saatgut *nt*; *(liter, = sperm)* Samen *pl*; *(= offspring)* Nachkommen *pl*; *(fig, of unrest, idea etc)* Keim *m* (of zu); **to go** *or* **run to ~** *(vegetables)* schießen; *(flowers)* einen Samenstand bilden; *(fig: person)* herunterkommen; **to sow the ~s of doubt (in sb's mind)** (bei jdm) Zweifel säen *or* den Keim des Zweifels legen; **he sowed the ~ from which ... developed** er hat den Keim gelegt, aus dem sich ... entwickelte; **I don't want to make a detailed proposal, just to sow the ~s** ich möchte keinen konkreten Vorschlag machen, ich möchte nur den Boden dafür bereiten
b *(Sport)* **to be the third ~** als Dritter platziert *or* gesetzt sein; **the number one ~** der/die als Nummer eins Gesetzte
VT **a** *(= sow with seed)* besäen
b *(= extract seeds from)* entkernen
c *(Sport)* setzen, platzieren; **~ed number one** als Nummer eins gesetzt; **~ed players** gesetzte *or* platzierte Spieler
VI *(vegetables)* schießen; *(flowers)* Samen entwickeln
VR **to ~ itself** *(plant)* sich aussäen

seed: **seedbed** N Saatbeet *nt*, Saatbett *nt*; **seed box** N Setzkasten *m*; **seedcake** N Kümmelkuchen *m*; **seedcase** N Samenkapsel *f*; **seed corn** N *(Bot)* Samenkorn *nt*; **they are eating their own ~** *(fig)* sie gehen aus Eingemachte *(inf)*; **seed drill** N Sämaschine *f*

seediness ['si:dɪnɪs] N *(= disreputableness)* Zwielichtigkeit *f*

seed: **seed leaf** N Keimblatt *nt*; **seedless** ['si:dlɪs] ADJ kernlos

seedling ['si:dlɪŋ] N Sämling *m*

seed: **seed pearl** N Staubperle *f*; **seed plant** N Samenpflanze *f*; **seed potato** N Saatkartoffel *f*

seedsman ['si:dzmən] N *pl* **-men** [-mən] Samenhändler *m*

seed: **seedtime** N Saatzeit *f*; **seed tray** N = **seed box**

seedy ['si:dɪ] ADJ *(+er)* **a** *(= disreputable) person, character* zweifelhaft, zwielichtig; *area, place* zwielichtig **b** *(inf: = unwell)* **I feel ~** mir ist flau *(inf)*, mir ist nicht gut; **to look ~** angeschlagen aussehen *(inf)*, nicht gut aussehen

seeing ['si:ɪŋ] N Sehen *nt*; **I'd never have thought it possible but ~ is believing** ich hätte es nie für möglich gehalten, aber ich habe es mit eigenen Augen gesehen; **look, ~ is believing, you can't deny it now** da haben Sie den Beweis vor Augen, jetzt können Sie es nicht mehr abstreiten CONJ **~ (that** *or* **as)** da

Seeing Eye Dog N *(US)* Blindenhund *m*

seek [si:k] *pret, ptp* **sought** VT **a** *(= look for)* suchen; *fame, wealth* erlangen wollen, streben nach; **to ~ sb's advice** jdn um Rat fragen; **the prosecutors are ~ing the death penalty** die Staatsanwaltschaft will die Todesstrafe; **the reason is not far to ~** der Grund liegt auf der Hand; **the quarrel is not of my ~ing** ich habe den Streit nicht gesucht; **~ time** *(Comput)* Zugriffszeit *f* **b** *(liter: = attempt)* suchen *(geh)*; **to ~ to do sth** sich bemühen, etw zu tun; **those who sought his downfall** die(jenigen), die ihn zu Fall bringen wollten

▸ **seek after** VI *+prep obj* **a** *(= look got)* suchen **b** → **sought-after**

▸ **seek for** VI *+prep obj* suchen nach; *reforms, changes* anstreben; **long-sought-for reforms/changes** lang erstrebte Reformen *pl*/Veränderungen *pl*

▸ **seek out** VT *sep* ausfindig machen; *opinion* herausfinden; **seek him out, discover what he thinks** *(liter)* erforschen Sie ihn, finden Sie heraus, was er denkt *(geh)*

seeker ['si:kəʳ] N Suchende(r) *mf*; *(= pursuer)* Verfolger(in) *m(f)*; **to be a ~ of knowledge** auf der Suche nach Wissen *or* Erkenntnis sein; **~ of** *or* **after truth** Wahrheitssucher(in) *m(f)*

seem [si:m] ✪ 6.2, 26.2, 26.3 VI **a** *(= appear)* scheinen; **he ~s (to be) honest/a nice young man** er scheint ehrlich/ein netter junger Mann zu sein; **he ~ed nice enough** er schien ganz nett (zu sein); **he may ~ poor but ...** er mag arm scheinen *or* wirken, aber ...; **he ~s younger than he is** er wirkt jünger, als er ist; **that makes it ~ longer** dadurch wirkt es länger *or* kommt es einem länger vor; **he doesn't ~ (to be) able to concentrate** er scheint sich nicht konzentrieren zu können; **he is not what he ~s (to be)** er ist nicht (das), was er zu sein scheint; **things aren't always what they ~** vieles ist anders, als es aussieht; **I ~ to have heard that before** das habe ich doch schon mal gehört; **what ~s to be the trouble?** worum geht es denn?; *(doctor)* was kann ich für Sie tun?; **there ~s to be no solution** da scheint es keine Lösung zu geben; **it ~s to me that I'll have to do that again** mir scheint, ich muss das noch einmal machen; **he has left, it ~s** er ist anscheinend weggegangen, es scheint, er ist weggegangen; **we are not welcome, it ~s** wir sind anscheinend *or* scheinbar nicht willkommen; **so it ~s** es sieht (ganz) so aus; **he is, so it ~s, ...** er scheint ... zu sein; **it ~s** *or* **would ~ that he is coming after all** es sieht so aus, als ob er doch noch kommt, es scheint, er kommt doch noch; **it doesn't ~ that he'll be coming** es sieht nicht so aus, als ob er kommt; **if it ~s right to you** wenn Sie es für richtig halten; **it ~s** *or* **would ~ (to be) advisable** das scheint ratsam (zu sein); **how does it ~ to you?** was meinen SIE?; **how did she ~ to you?** wie fandst du sie?; **it ~s a shame to leave it unfinished** es ist doch irgendwie *or* eigentlich schade, das nicht fertig zu machen; **it just doesn't ~ right somehow** das ist doch irgendwie nicht richtig; **it would ~ that ...** es scheint fast so, als ob ...; **I can't ~ to do it** ich kann das anscheinend *or* scheinbar *or* irgendwie nicht
b it only ~s like it das kommt einem nur so vor; **I ~ to be floating in space** es kommt mir so vor, als ob ich schweben würde; **it all ~s so unreal to him/me** es kommt ihm/mir alles so unwirklich vor; **I ~ to remember that you had that problem before** es kommt mir so vor, als hätten Sie das Problem schon einmal gehabt

seeming ['si:mɪŋ] ADJ *attr* scheinbar

seemingly ['si:mɪŋlɪ] ADV scheinbar, anscheinend

seemliness ['si:mlɪnɪs] N Schicklichkeit *f*

seemly ['si:mlɪ] ADJ *(+er)* schicklich; **it isn't ~ (for sb to do sth)** es schickt sich nicht (für jdn, etw zu tun)

seen [si:n] *ptp of* **see¹**

seep [si:p] VI sickern; **to ~ through sth** durch etw durchsickern; **to ~ into sth** in etw *(acc)* hineinsickern

▸ **seep away** VI *(water)* versickern; *(strength)* schwinden

seepage ['si:pɪdʒ] N *(out of sth)* Aussickern *nt*; *(through sth)* Durchsickern *nt*; *(into sth)* Hineinsickern *nt*; **there is an excessive amount of ~** *(out of sth)* es läuft zu viel aus; *(into sth)* es dringt zu viel ein; *(Comm)* die Leckage ist zu groß

seer [sɪəʳ] N Seher(in) *m(f)*

seeress ['sɪəres] N Seherin *f*

seersucker ['sɪə,sʌkəʳ] N Krepp *m*, Seersucker *m*

seesaw ['si:sɔ:] N Wippe *f*; *(fig, back and forth)* Hin und Her *nt*; *(up and down)* Auf und Ab *nt* ADJ schaukelnd; **~ changes** ständiges Hin und Her VI wippen; *(fig, emotional states)* auf und ab gehen; *prices, public opinion* schwanken

seethe [si:ð] VI *(= boil)* sieden; *(= surge)* schäumen; *(= be crowded)* wimmeln (*with* von); *(= be angry)* kochen *(inf)*; **to ~ with anger** vor Wut schäumen *or* kochen *(inf)*; **resentment ~d in him** er schäumte innerlich vor Groll; **the crowd ~d forward** die Menge drängte sich vor; **a seething mass of people** eine wogende Menschenmenge

see-through ['si:θru:] ADJ durchsichtig; **~ pack** Klarsichtpackung *f*

segment ['segmənt] N Teil *m*; *(of worm)* Glied *nt*, Segment *nt*; *(of orange)* Stück *nt*, Rippe *f*, Schnitz *m (dial)*; *(of circle)* Abschnitt *m*, Segment *nt* VT [seg'ment] zerlegen, segmentieren VI [seg'ment] sich teilen

segmentation [,segmən'teɪʃən] N Zerlegung *f*, Segmentierung *f*; *(Biol)* Zellteilung *f*

segregate ['segrɪgeɪt] VT *individuals* absondern; *group of population* nach Rassen/Geschlechtern/Konfessionen trennen; *activities, facilities* nach gewissen Gesichtspunkten unterteilen; **to be ~d from sb/sth** von jdm/etw abgesondert sein; **~d** *(racially, church)* nur für Weiße/Schwarze; *school also* mit Rassentrennung; *society* nach Rassen getrennt

segregation [,segrɪ'geɪʃən] N Trennung *f*; **racial/sexual ~** Rassen-/Geschlechtertrennung *f*

segregationist [,segrɪ'geɪʃənɪst] N Befürworter(in) *m(f)* der Rassentrennung

segregative ['segrɪgeɪtɪv] ADJ sich absondernd, Trennungs-

segue ['segweɪ] *(Mus, fig)* VI **to ~ from/into** übergehen *or* überleiten von/in *(+acc)* N Übergang *m*

seine [seɪn] N Wade *f*

seismic ['saɪzmɪk] ADJ seismisch; *(fig) changes, events* kolossal, dramatisch; *forces* ungeheuer; **~ focus** Erdbebenherd *m*

seismograph ['saɪzməgrɑ:f] N Seismograf *m*

seismography [saɪz'mɒgrəfɪ] N Seismologie *f*

seismologist [saɪz'mɒlədʒɪst] N Seismologe *m*, Seismologin *f*

seismology [saɪz'mɒlədʒɪ] N Seismologie *f*, Erdbebenkunde *f*

seize [si:z] VT **a** *(= grasp)* packen, ergreifen; *(as hostage)* nehmen; *(= confiscate)* beschlagnahmen; *passport* einziehen; *ship (authorities)* beschlagnahmen; *(pirates)* kapern; *(= capture) town* einnehmen; *train, building* besetzen; *criminal* fassen; **to ~ sb's arm, to ~ sb by the arm** jdn am Arm packen
b *(fig) (= lay hold of: panic, fear, desire)* packen, ergreifen; *power, leadership* an sich *(acc)* reißen; *(= leap upon) idea, suggestion* aufgreifen; *opportunity, initiative* ergreifen; **to ~ the moment** den günstigen Augenblick wahrnehmen; **to ~ the day** den Tag nutzen; **to ~ control of sth** etw unter Kontrolle bringen
VI = **seize up**

▸ **seize on** *or* **upon** VI *+prep obj* **a** *(= clutch at) idea, offer* sich stürzen auf *(+acc)*; *excuse* beim Schopf packen **b** *(= pick out for criticism)* herausgreifen

▸ **seize up** VI **a** *(engine, brakes)* sich verklemmen **b** *(inf)* **my back seized up** es ist mir in den Rücken gefahren *(inf)*; **she talks so much it's a miracle her jaw doesn't seize up** sie redet so viel, es ist ein Wunder, dass ihr Mundwerk nicht ausleiert *(inf)*

seizure ['siːʒəʳ] N **a** *(= confiscation)* Beschlagnahmung *f*; *(of passport)* Einzug *m*; *(of ship)* Beschlagnahme *f*; *(by pirates)* Kapern *nt*; *(= capture)* Einnahme *f*; *(of train, building)* Besetzung *f* **b** *(Med)* Anfall *m*; *(= apoplexy)* Schlaganfall *m*

seldom ['seldəm] ADV selten; **I ~ go there** ich gehe (nur) selten dorthin; **they are ~ seen** man sieht sie nur selten; **~ have I ...** ich habe selten ...; **~, if ever, does he do that** er tut das nur äußerst selten

select [sɪ'lekt] VT (aus)wählen; *(in buying also)* aussuchen; *(Sport)* auswählen; *(for football match etc)* aufstellen; *(Comput)* markieren; **~ed poems** ausgewählte Gedichte *pl*; **~ all** *(Comput: command)* alles markieren VI (aus)wählen; *(in buying also)* aussuchen; *(Sport)* auswählen; *(for football match etc)* aufstellen ADJ *(= exclusive)* exklusiv; *(= carefully chosen)* auserwählt, auserlesen; **a ~ few** eine kleine Gruppe Auserwählter

select committee N Sonderausschuss *m*

selection [sɪ'lekʃən] N **a** *(= choosing)* (Aus)wahl *f*; *(Biol)* Auslese *f*, Selektion *f* **b** *(= person, thing selected)* Wahl *f*; *(= likely winner)* Tipp *m*; **to make one's ~** seine Wahl treffen; **~s from Rossini** ausgewählte Stücke *pl* von Rossini; **~ commission** Auswahlkommission *f*; **~ committee** Auswahlkommission *f*; *(for exhibition etc)* Jury *f* **c** *(= range, assortment)* Auswahl *f* *(of* an *+dat)* **d** *(Comput)* Markierung *f*, Auswahl *f*

selective [sɪ'lektɪv] ADJ **a** wählerisch; *reader* kritisch, anspruchsvoll; **~ examination** Auslese- *or* Auswahlprüfung *f*; **~ process** Auslese- *or* Auswahlverfahren *nt*; **to be ~ in sth** in etw *(dat)* wählerisch sein; **he was very ~ in buying shoes** er war beim Schuhkauf sehr wählerisch; **we can't treat everything, we have to be ~** wir können nicht alles abhandeln, wir müssen eine Auswahl treffen *or* selektiv vorgehen *or (choose carefully)* wählerisch sein; **a more ~ approach to the available material ...** wenn Sie aus dem vorhandenen Material etwas kritischer auswählen würden ...; **a very ~ admission procedure** ein stark aussiebendes Aufnahmeverfahren; **the computer program has to be made more ~** man sollte mehr Wahlmöglichkeiten in das Computerprogramm einbauen; **~ school** Eliteschule *f*; **~ entry** *(Brit Sch)* **~ admission** *(US Sch)* selektives Aufnahmeverfahren; **~ breeding** *(Agr)* selektive Züchtung, Zuchtwahl *f*; **~ strike** *(Mil)* gezielter Angriff; *(Ind)* Schwerpunktstreik *m* **b** *radio* trennscharf, selektiv

selective attention N *(Psych)* selektives Aufnahmevermögen

selectively [sɪ'lektɪvlɪ] ADV wählerisch; *read also, operate* selektiv; **to read/buy ~** beim Lesen wählerisch/beim Einkaufen kritisch sein; **if you approach the material more ~** wenn Sie das Material besser auswählen *or* selektiver behandeln *(geh)*; **he built up his collection very ~** er wählte bei der Zusammenstellung seiner Sammlung sorgfältig aus

selective memory N selektives Erinnerungsvermögen

selective service N *(US)* Wehrdienst *m*

selectivity [ˌsɪlek'tɪvɪtɪ] N **a** Selektivität *f*; *(of reader, buyer)* kritisches Auswählen; **his collection shows great ~** seine Sammlung ist mit viel Sorgfalt ausgewählt; **to move toward(s) greater ~** ein kritischeres Bewusstsein entwickeln; **to show ~ in one's taste** einen anspruchsvollen Geschmack haben; **it diminishes the degree of ~** es verringert die (Aus)wahlmöglichkeiten *pl* **b** *(of radio)* Trennschärfe *f*, Selektivität *f*

selectman [sɪ'lektmən] N *pl* **-men** [-mən] *(US)* Stadtrat *m*, Stadträtin *f*

selector [sɪ'lektəʳ] N **a** *(Tech)* Wählschalter *m*; *(= lever)* Schaltgriff *m*; *(= knob)* Schaltknopf *m*; *(TV)* Programmtaste *f*; *(Rad)* Stationstaste *f*; *(on record-player)* Geschwindigkeitsregler *m*; *(Aut)* Schalthebel *m* **b** *(Sport) jd, der die Mannschaftsaufstellung vornimmt*

selenium [sɪ'liːnɪəm] N Selen *nt*

self [self] N *pl* **selves** Ich *nt*, Selbst *nt no pl*; *(esp Psych: = side of character)* Seite *f*; **he showed his true ~** er zeigte sein wahres Ich *or* Gesicht; **one's other/better ~** sein anderes/besseres Ich; **my whole ~ revolted at the idea** alles in mir lehnte sich gegen diese Idee auf; **he's quite his old ~ again, he's back to his usual ~** er ist wieder ganz der Alte *(inf)*; **back to her usual cheerful ~** wieder fröhlich wie immer; **to be all ~** *(inf)* **to think of nothing but ~** nur an sich *(acc)* selbst denken; **with no thought of ~** ohne an sich *(acc)* selbst zu denken; **how is your good ~?** wie geht es Ihnen?
PRON *(Comm)* **pay ~** zahlbar an selbst; **a room for wife and ~** ein Zimmer für meine Frau und mich
ADJ *attr lining* aus gleichem Material; **in a ~ colour** in uni

self: **self-abandonment** N (Selbst)aufopferung *f*, bedingungslose Hingabe; *(pej: to desire)* Zügellosigkeit *f*; **self-abasement** N Selbsterniedrigung *f*; **self-abnegation** N Selbstverleugnung *f*; **self-absorbed** ADJ mit sich selbst beschäftigt; **self-abuse** N *(euph)* Selbstbefleckung *f (euph)*; **self-accusation** N Selbstanklage *f*; **self-accusing** ADJ selbstanklagend; **self-acting** ADJ selbsttätig; **self-activating** ADJ *bomb* selbstzündend; **self-addressed** ADJ *envelope* adressiert; **self-addressed stamped envelope** N *(US)* frankierter Rückumschlag; **self-adhesive** ADJ selbstklebend; **self-adjusting** ADJ selbstregulierend *attr*; *brakes* selbstnachstellend *attr*; **to be ~** sich selbst regulieren/nachstellen; **self-admiration** N Selbstbewunderung *f*; **self-advertisement** N Eigenreklame *f*; **self-aggrandizement** N Selbstverherrlichung *f*; **self-appointed** ADJ selbst ernannt; **he is the ~ spokesman of the group** er hat sich selbst zum Sprecher der Gruppe gemacht; **self-approval** N Selbstgefälligkeit *f*; **self-asserting** ADJ sich selbst behauptend; *(pej)* von sich selbst eingenommen; **self-assertion** N Durchsetzungsvermögen *nt*; *(pej)* Überheblichkeit *f*, Eingenommenheit *f* von sich selbst; **self-assertive** ADJ selbstbewusst; *(pej)* von sich selbst eingenommen; **self-assertiveness** ADJ Durchsetzungskraft *f*; *(pej)* Selbstverliebtheit *f*; **self-assessment** N **a** *(= self-judgement)* Selbsteinschätzung *f* **b** *(for tax)* Selbstveranlagung *f*; **self-assurance** N Selbstsicherheit *f*; **self-assured** ADJ selbstsicher; **self-aware** ADJ sich *(dat)* seiner selbst bewusst, selbstbewusst; **self-awareness** N Selbsterkenntnis *f*, Selbstbewusstsein *nt*

self-belief [ˌselfbɪ'liːf] N Glaube *m* an sich *(acc)* selbst

self: **self-cancelling** ADJ *indicator* sich automatisch abschaltend *attr*; **self-catering** *(Brit)* N Selbstversorgung *f*; **to go ~** *(holidaymaker)* Urlaub *m* für Selbstversorger machen; *(hotel owner)* auf Selbstversorger umstellen ADJ für Selbstversorger; **self-censorship** N Selbstzensur *f*; **self-centred**, *(US)* **self-centered** ADJ egozentrisch, ichbezogen; **self-centredness**, *(US)* **self-centeredness** N Egozentrik *f*, Ichbezogenheit *f*; **self-certification** N *(Brit Admin)* Krankmeldung *f* des Arbeitnehmers *(bei kurzer Abwesenheit anstelle eines ärztlichen Attests)*; **self-cleaning** ADJ selbstreinigend; **self-closing** ADJ automatisch schließend, selbstschließend; **self-coloured**, *(US)* **self-colored** ADJ einfarbig, uni; **self-command** N Selbstbeherrschung *f*; **self-complacent** ADJ; **self-complacently** ADV selbstgefällig; **self-composed** ADJ ruhig, gelassen; **self-conceit** N Eingebildetheit *f*; **self-conceited** ADJ; **self-conceitedly** ADV eingebildet, dünkelhaft; **self-confessed** ADJ erklärt *attr*; **self-confidence** N Selbstvertrauen *nt*, Selbstbewusstsein *nt*; **self-confident** ADJ selbstbewusst, selbstsicher; **self-conscious** ADJ befangen, gehemmt; *piece of writing, style etc* bewusst; *(Philos: = self-aware)* selbstbewusst; **she walked to the door in a ~ way** sie wirkte gehemmt *or* verlegen, als sie zur Tür ging; **to be ~ about sth** *(about one's nose, looks etc)* sich *(dat)* einer Sache *(gen)* sehr bewusst sein; **self-consciously** ADV **a** *(= uncomfortably)* verlegen **b** *(= deliberately)* bewusst; **self-consciousness** N Befangenheit *f*, Gehemmtheit *f*; *(of piece of writing, style etc)* Bewusstheit *f*; *(Philos: = self-awareness)* Selbstbewusstsein *nt*; **self-contained** ADJ **a** *person* distanziert; *(= self-sufficient)* selbstgenügsam **b** *flat* separat; *community* unabhängig; *place* in sich geschlossen; *economy* eigenständig; *group* geschlossen; **self-contradictory** ADJ sich *(dat)* selbst widersprechend *attr*; *alibi* widersprüchlich; **his argument is ~** seine Argumente widersprechen sich *(dat)*; **self-control** N Selbstbeherrschung *f*; **self-controlled** ADJ selbstbeherrscht; **self-correcting** ADJ selbstregulierend *attr*; *machine* mit Autokorrekturfunktion; **to be ~** sich selbst regulieren/korrigieren; **self-critical** ADJ selbstkritisch; **self-criticism** N Selbstkritik *f*

self: **self-deceit**, **self-deception** N Selbsttäuschung *f*, Selbstbetrug *m*; **self-defeating** ADJ sinnlos, unsinnig; *argument* sich selbst widerlegend *attr*; **the government's plan was ~** dieser Plan der Regierung hat das Gegenteil erzielt; **a ~ exercise** ein Eigentor *nt*; **self-defence**, *(US)* **self-defense** N Selbstverteidigung *f*; *(Jur)* Notwehr *f*; **to act in ~** in Notwehr handeln; **the noble art of ~** Boxen *nt*; **self-delusion** N Selbsttäuschung *f*; **self-denial** N Selbstzucht *f*; *(Rel)* Selbstverleugnung *f*; **self-denying** ADJ sich selbst einschränkend *attr*; *(Rel)* sich selbst verleugnend *attr*; **to be ~** sich einschränken/verleugnen; **self-deprecating** ADJ *person* bescheiden; *remark* sich selbst herabwürdigend *attr*; **to be ~** *(person)* sich selbst abwerten; **Woody Allen's ~ humour** *(Brit) or* **humor** *(US)* Woody Allens Humor, der seine eigenen Schwächen offenbart; **self-destruct** VI sich selbst zerstören ADJ *attr* **~ button** Knopf *m* zur Selbstzerstörung; **self-destruction** N Selbstzerstörung *f*; *(of person, race)* Selbstmord *m*; **self-destructive** ADJ *behaviour, film star* selbstzerstörerisch; **she has a tendency to be ~** sie hat selbstzerstörerische Neigungen; **self-determination** N Selbstbestimmung *f (also Pol)*; **self-development** N Selbstentfaltung *f*; **self-discipline** N Selbstdisziplin *f*; **self-doubt** N Zweifel *m* an sich *(dat)* selbst; **self-dramatization** N **his tendency toward(s) ~** seine Neigung, sich in Szene zu setzen; **self-drive** ADJ *(Brit) car* für Selbstfahrer; **~ holiday** Ferienreise *f* mit dem eigenen Auto

self: **self-educated** ADJ autodidaktisch; **~ person** Autodidakt(in) *m(f)*; **he is ~** er ist Autodidakt; **self-effacement** N Zurückhaltung *f*; **self-effacing** ADJ zurückhaltend; **self-employed** ADJ selbstständig; *artist* freischaffend; *journalist* freiberuflich; **on a ~ basis** freiberuflich; **self-esteem** N *(= self-respect)* Selbstachtung *f*; *(= conceit)* Selbstüberschätzung *f*; **to have high/low ~** sehr/wenig selbstbewusst sein; **self-evident** ADJ offensichtlich; *(= not needing proof)* selbstverständlich; **we'll need more money – that's ~** wir brauchen mehr Geld – das versteht sich von selbst; **self-evidently** ADV *(= obviously)* offensichtlich; **self-examination** N Selbstprüfung *f*; **self-explanatory** ADJ unmittelbar verständlich; **this word is ~** das Wort erklärt sich selbst; **self-expression** N Selbstdarstellung *f*

self: **self-fertilization** N Selbstbefruchtung *f*; **self-financing** ADJ selbstfinanzierend; **self-flagellation** N Selbstgeißelung *f*; **self-fulfilling** ADJ **a ~ prophecy** eine sich selbst bewahrheitende Voraussage, eine Selffulfilling Prophecy *(Sociol)*; **to be ~** sich selbst bewahrheiten; **self-fulfilment**, *(US)* **self-fulfillment** N Erfüllung *f*; **self-governed** ADJ = **self-governing**; **self-governing** ADJ selbstverwaltet, sich selbst verwaltend *attr*; **to become ~** eine eigene Regierung bekommen; **self-government** N Selbstverwaltung *f*; **self-harming** N Selbstverstümmelung *f*; **self-help** N Selbsthilfe *f*; **she never was one for ~** sie konnte sich noch nie selbst behelfen; **self-image** N Selbstbild *nt*; **self-importance** N Aufgeblasenheit *f*; **self-important** ADJ aufgeblasen; **self-imposed** ADJ selbst auferlegt; **his exile is ~** er hat sich *(dat)* sein Exil selbst auferlegt; **self-improvement** N Weiterbildung *f*; **self-incrimination** N Selbstbezichtigung *f*; **self-induced** ADJ selbstverursacht *attr*; **her miscarriage was ~** sie hat die Fehlgeburt selbst verursacht; **self-induction** N *(Elec)* Selbstinduktion *f*; **self-indulgence** N genießerische Art; *(in eating, drinking)* Maßlosigkeit *f*; **go on, take one, a little ~ never hurt anyone** nehmen Sie doch einen, jeder darf sich doch einmal gehen lassen *or* verwöhnen; **self-indulgent** ADJ genießerisch; *(in eating, drinking)* maßlos; **his columns grew ever more ~** er schrieb seine Spalten immer mehr zum eigenen Vergnügen; **be ~, have another slice** verwöhnen Sie sich, nehmen Sie noch ein Stück; **self-inflicted** ADJ *wounds* sich *(dat)* selbst zugefügt *or* beigebracht *attr*; *task, punishment* sich *(dat)* freiwillig auferlegt; **~ death** Selbstmord *m*; **his wounds are ~** er hat sich *(dat)* die Wunden selbst beigebracht; **self-interest** N *(= selfishness)* Eigennutz *m*; *(= personal advantage)* eigenes Interesse; **in our own ~** in unserem eigenen Interesse; **self-interested** ADJ *(= selfish)* eigennützig, auf sein eigenes Interesse bedacht; **self-invited** ADJ selbst eingeladen *attr*; **he is a ~ guest** er hat sich selbst eingeladen

selfish ['selfɪʃ] ADJ egoistisch, selbstsüchtig; **for ~ reasons** aus selbstsüchtigen Gründen

selfishly ['selfɪʃlɪ] ADV egoistisch, selbstsüchtig; **I was ~ glad that...** ich war egoistischerweise froh, dass ...

selfishness ['selfɪʃnɪs] N Egoismus *m*, Selbstsüchtigkeit *f*

self: **self-justification** N Rechtfertigung *f*; **he saw no reason for ~** er sah keinen Grund, sich zu rechtfertigen; **..., he said in ~** ..., sagte er zu seiner eigenen Rechtfertigung; **self-justifying** ADJ sachlich gerechtfertigt; **self-knowledge** N Selbsterkenntnis *f*; **self-laceration** N *(fig)* Selbstzerfleischung *f*

selfless ['selflɪs] ADJ selbstlos

selflessly ['selflɪslɪ] ADV selbstlos, in selbstloser Weise

selflessness ['selflɪsnɪs] N Selbstlosigkeit *f*

self: **self-loader** N Selbstlader *m*; **self-loading** ADJ **~ gun** Selbstlader *m*; **self-locking** ADJ von selbst schließend *attr*; *attachment* von selbst einrastend *attr*; **~ door** Tür mit Schnappschloss; **self-love** N Eigenliebe *f*, Selbstliebe *f (also Philos)*

self: **self-made** ADJ **~ man** Selfmademan *m*; **he's a ~ millionaire** er hat es aus eigener Kraft zum Millionär gebracht; **self-medication** N Selbstmedikation *f*; **self-mockingly** ADV *say* voller Selbstironie; **self-murder** N Selbstmord *m*; **self-mutilation** N Selbstverstümmelung *f*; **self-neglect** [ˌselfnɪ'glekt] N Vernachlässigung *f* seiner *(gen)* selbst; **as a result of his ~** weil er sich selbst vernachlässigt hat; **self-obsessed** ADJ ichbezogen, selbstsüchtig; **self-opinionated** [ˌselfə'pɪnjəneɪtɪd] ADJ rechthaberisch; *nonsense, drivel* selbstherrlich; **he's too ~ to change his mind** er ist viel zu sehr von sich selbst überzeugt, um seine Meinung zu ändern; **self-opinionatedness** N rechthaberisches und selbstherrliches Wesen; **this stream of ~** dieses selbstherrliche Gerede; **self-parody** N Selbstparodie *f*; **self-perception** N Selbstwahrnehmung *f*; **self-perpetuating** ADJ sich selbst erneuernd *or* erhaltend *attr*; **~ misery** sich ständig fortsetzendes Elend; **the system is ~** das System erhält sich selbst; **self-perpetuation** N Selbstperpetuierung *f*; **self-pity** N Selbstmitleid *nt*; **self-pitying** ADJ selbstbemitleidend; **self-pollination** N Selbstbestäubung *f*; **self-portrait** N Selbstporträt *or* -bildnis *nt*; **self-possessed** ADJ selbstbeherrscht; **self-possession** N Selbstbeherrschung *f*; **self-praise** N Eigenlob *nt*; **self-preservation** N Selbsterhaltung *f*; **the instinct for ~** der Selbsterhaltungstrieb; **self-propagating** ADJ *flower* sich selbst aussäend *attr*; *poverty, bad state of affairs* sich aus sich selbst weiterentwickelnd *attr*; **self-propelled** ADJ selbst angetrieben *attr*, mit Selbstantrieb; **self-publicist** N Selbstanpreiser(in) *m(f)*

self: **self-raising**, *(US)* **self-rising** ADJ *flour* selbsttreibend, *mit bereits beigemischtem Backpulver*; **self-realization** N Selbstverwirklichung *f*; **self-regard** N **a** *(= self-interest)* Eigennutz *m* **b** *(= self-esteem)* Selbstachtung *f*; **self-regulating** ADJ selbstregulierend *attr*; **this system is ~** dieses System reguliert sich selbst; **self-reliance** N Selbstständigkeit *f*; **self-reliant** ADJ selbstständig; **self-reproach** N Selbstvorwurf *m*; **all this ~** diese Selbstvorwürfe *pl*; **self-respect** N Selbstachtung *f*; **have you no ~?** schämen Sie sich gar nicht?; **self-respecting** ADJ anständig; **no ~ person would ...** niemand, der etwas auf sich hält, würde ...; **self-restraint** N Selbstbeherrschung *f*; **self-righteous** ADJ selbstgerecht; **self-righteousness** N Selbstgerechtigkeit *f*; **self-righting** ADJ *boat* sich (von) selbst aufrichtend *attr*; **self-rising** ADJ *(US)* = **self-raising**; **self-rule** N Selbstbestimmung *f*, Selbstverwaltung *f*

self: **self-sacrifice** N Selbstaufopferung *f*; **it should not require too much ~** das sollte kein zu großes Opfer sein; **self-sacrificing** ADJ aufopfernd; **selfsame** ADJ **the ~** genau der/die/das gleiche ..., der-/die-/ dasselbe ...; **on the ~ day** noch am selben Tag; **self-satisfaction** N Selbstzufriedenheit *f*; *(= smugness)* Selbstgefälligkeit *f*; **self-satisfied** ADJ *(= smug)* selbstgefällig, selbstzufrieden; **self-sealing** ADJ *envelope, bag* selbstklebend; *fuel tank* selbstdichtend; **self-seeking** ADJ selbstsüchtig N Selbstsucht *f*; **self-service**, *(esp US)* **self-serve** ADJ Selbstbedienungs-; **~ restaurant** Selbstbedienungsrestaurant *nt*; **the petrol station is now ~** *(Brit)* **the gas station is now self-serve** *(US)* die Tankstelle hat jetzt auf Selbstbedienung umgestellt N Selbstbedienung *f*; **self-slaughter** N *(US Jur)* Selbstmord *m*; **self-starter** N *(Aut)* Selbstanlasser *m*; **self-stick notes** PL Haftnotizen *pl*; **self-styled** ADJ selbst ernannt; **self-sufficiency** N *(of person)* Selbstständigkeit *f*; *(emotional)* Selbstgenügsamkeit *f*; *(of country)* Autarkie *f*; *(of community)* Selbstversorgung *f*; **self-sufficient** ADJ *person* selbstständig; *(emotionally)* selbstgenügsam; *country* autark; **they are ~ in oil** sie können ihren Ölbedarf selbst decken; **a ~ community** eine Gemeinde, die sich selbst versorgen kann; **self-supplier** N Selbstversorger(in) *m(f)*; **self-supporting** ADJ *person* finanziell unabhängig; *structure* freitragend; *chimney* frei stehend; **the club is ~** der Klub trägt sich selbst; **our commune is ~** wir sind in unserer Kommune Selbstversorger; **self-sustaining** ADJ *(Econ) development, growth, economy* nachhaltig

self: **self-tapping screw** N selbstschneidende Schraube, Treibschraube *f*; **self-taught** ADJ *skills* selbst erlernt; **he is ~** er hat sich *(dat)* das selbst beigebracht; *(intellectually)* er hat sich durch Selbstunterricht gebildet; **he's a ~ guitarist** er hat sich *(dat)* das Gitarrespielen selbst beigebracht; **a ~ man** ein Autodidakt *m*; **self-test** N *(of machine)* Selbsttest *m*; **to do a ~** einen Selbsttest durchführen VI *(machine)* einen Selbsttest durchführen; **self-torture** N Selbstquälerei *f*

self: **self-will** N Eigenwilligkeit *f*, Eigensinn *m (pej)*; **self-willed** ADJ eigenwillig, eigensinnig *(pej)*; **self-winding** ADJ **~ clock/watch** Automatikuhr *f*

sell [sel] *vb: pret, ptp* **sold** VT **a** *item, goods* verkaufen (*sb sth, sth to sb* jdm etw, etw an jdn); *insurance policy* abschließen (*to* mit); *(business) goods* verkaufen, absetzen; **I was sold this in Valencia** man hat mir das in Valencia verkauft; **the book sold 3,000 copies** von dem Buch wurden 3.000 Exemplare verkauft; **he could ~ a fridge to an Eskimo** er könnte einem Eskimo einen Eisschrank andrehen *(inf) or* aufschwatzen *(inf)*; **to ~ insurance (for a living)** Versicherungsvertreter(in) *m(f)* sein; **to ~ one's life dearly** sein Leben teuer verkaufen; **he sold himself to the enemy** er hat sich an den Feind verkauft; **to ~ one's body** seinen Körper verkaufen; **to ~ one's soul to sb/sth** jdm/einer Sache seine Seele verschreiben; **modern man has sold his soul** der moderne Mensch hat seine Seele verloren; **what are you ~ing it for?** wie viel verlangen Sie dafür?, wie viel wollen Sie dafür haben?; **I can't remember what I sold it for** ich weiß nicht mehr, für wie viel ich es verkauft habe

b *(= stock)* führen, haben *(inf)*; *(= deal in)* vertreiben

c *(= promote the sale of)* zugkräftig machen, einen guten Absatz verschaffen *(+dat)*; **you need advertising to ~ your product** Sie müssen werben, um Ihr Produkt zu verkaufen *or* abzusetzen; **nothing will ~ this product, it's so bad** das Produkt ist so schlecht, dass es sich nicht verkaufen *or* an den Mann bringen *(inf)* lässt; **she finished up ~ing toothpaste on television** sie warb schließlich im Fernsehen für Zahnpasta

d *(inf: = gain acceptance for)* schmackhaft machen (*to sb* jdm), gewinnen für (*to sb* jdn); *religion* aufschwatzen *(inf)*, verkaufen *(inf)* (*to sb* jdm); **you'll never ~ them that idea** dafür sind sie nicht zu haben; **I know I'll never be able to ~ it to him** ich weiß, dass ich ihn dafür nicht erwärmen kann *or* dass er dafür nicht zu haben ist; **to ~ oneself** *(= put oneself across)* sich profilieren (*to* bei), sich verkaufen (*to* an *+acc*)

e *(inf: = convince of the worth of)* **to ~ sb on sth** jdn von etw überzeugen; **to be sold on sb/sth** von jdm/etw begeistert sein; **how sold is he on the idea?** wie sehr hat es ihm diese Idee angetan? *(inf)*

f *(fig: = betray)* verraten; **to ~ sb down the river** *(inf)* jdn ganz schön verschaukeln *(inf)*

VI *(person)* verkaufen (*to sb* an jdn); *(article)* sich verkaufen (lassen); **his book is ~ing well/won't ~** sein Buch verkauft sich gut/lässt sich nicht verkaufen; **the house sold for £85,000** das Haus wurde für £ 85.000 verkauft; **what are they ~ing at** *or* **for?** wie viel kosten sie?; **the idea didn't ~** *(fig)* die Idee kam nicht an, die Idee fand keinen Anklang

N **a** *(Comm inf: = sales appeal)* Zugkraft *f*, Attraktivität *f*

b *(= selling technique)* Verkaufstaktik *or* -methode *f* → **hard sell, soft sell**

c *(dated inf, = disappointment)* Reinfall *m*, Pleite *f (inf)*

▶ **sell off** VT *sep* verkaufen; *(= get rid of quickly, cheaply)* abstoßen; *(at auction)* versteigern

▶ **sell on** VT *sep* weiterverkaufen (*to* an *+acc*)

▶ **sell out** VT *sep* **a** *(= sell entire stock of)* ausverkaufen; **sorry, sold out** wir sind leider ausverkauft; **we're sold out of ice cream/size 10** wir haben kein Eis/keine Größe 10 mehr, das Eis/Größe 10 ist ausverkauft

b *share, interest* verkaufen, abgeben

c *(inf: = betray)* verraten (*to* an *+acc*)

VI **a** *(= sell entire stock)* alles verkaufen *or* absetzen; **this book/we sold out in two days** das Buch war/wir waren in zwei Tagen ausverkauft

b *(in business)* sein Geschäft/seine Firma/seinen Anteil *etc* verkaufen *or* abstoßen

c *(inf: = betray)* **the union leader sold out to the bosses** der Gewerkschaftsführer verkaufte die Arbeiter an die Bosse *(inf)*; **he sold out to the right wing/the enemy** er hat sich an den rechten Flügel/den Feind verkauft

▶ **sell up** *(esp Brit)* VT *sep* zu Geld machen *(inf)*; *(Fin)* zwangsverkaufen; **he was sold up by his creditors** die Gläubiger ließen seinen Besitz zwangsverkaufen VI sein Haus/seinen Besitz/seine Firma *etc* verkaufen *or* zu Geld machen *(inf)*

sell-by date ['selbaɪˌdeɪt] N ≈ Haltbarkeitsdatum *nt*; **to be past one's ~** *(hum inf)* seine besten Tage hinter sich *(dat)* haben

seller ['selə'] N **a** Verkäufer(in) *m(f)*; **you should take faulty goods back to the ~** du solltest fehlerhafte Ware (zum Händler) zurückbringen **b** *(= thing sold)* **big ~** Verkaufsschlager *m*; **this book is a good/slow ~** das Buch verkauft sich gut/schlecht; **it's the best/worst ~ we've had** das ist der bestgehende/am schlechtesten gehende Artikel, den wir je hatten

sellers' market N **it's a ~ in housing just now** zurzeit bestimmen die Verkäufer die Hauspreise

seller's option N *(St Ex)* Verkaufsoption *f*

selling ['selɪŋ] N Verkauf *m*, Verkaufen *nt*; **they get a special training in ~** sie werden besonders im Verkaufen ausgebildet

selling: **selling point** N Verkaufsanreiz *m*; **selling price** N Verkaufspreis *m*

sell-off ['selɒf] N Verkauf *m*

Sellotape® ['seləʊteɪp] *(Brit)* **N** Klebeband *nt*, Klebestreifen *m*, ≈ Tesafilm® *m* **VT** **to sellotape (down)** mit Tesafilm® festkleben

sell: **sellout** ['selaʊt] N **a** *(inf: = betrayal)* fauler Kompromiss *or* Handel (*to* mit); *(of one's ideals etc)* Ausverkauf *m* (*to* an *+acc*) **b** *(Theat, Sport)* ausverkauftes Haus; **to be a ~** ausverkauft sein **c** *(Comm)* Verkaufsschlager *m*; **sell-through** ADJ *video* Verkaufs-

Seltzer (water) ['seltsə('wɔːtə')] N Selterswasser *nt*

selvage, selvedge ['selvɪdʒ] N Web(e)kante *f*

selves [selvz] *pl of* **self**

semantic ADJ, **semantically** ADV [sɪ'mæntɪk, -əlɪ] semantisch

semanticist [sɪ'mæntɪsɪst] N Semantiker(in) *m(f)*

semantics [sɪ'mæntɪks] N *sing* Semantik *f*; **the discussion got bogged down in ~** die Diskussion blieb in Wortklaubereien stecken; **it's just a question of ~** es ist nur eine Frage der Formulierung *or (interpretation)* Auslegung

semaphore ['seməfɔː'] **N** **a** *(Rail)* Semaphor *nt*, Signalmast *m* **b** *(= system)* Signalsprache *f*, Winken *nt*; **transmitted by ~** durch optische Signale übermittelt; **to learn ~** das Winkeralphabet lernen **VTI** durch Winkzeichen signalisieren

semblance ['sembləns] N *(with def art)* Anschein *m* (*of* von); *(with indef art)* Anflug *m* (*of* von); **without a ~ of a smile** ohne den leisesten Anflug eines Lächelns; **to maintain some ~ of order** den Anschein von Ordnung wahren; **he had the ~ of an experienced lawyer** er erweckte den Anschein eines erfahrenen Anwalts; **I saw in him the ~ of his father** *(liter)* ich konnte in ihm die Ähnlichkeit mit seinem Vater erkennen; **it possessed some ~ of reality** *(liter)* es schien beinahe Wirklichkeit zu sein *(liter)*

semen ['siːmən] N Samenflüssigkeit *f*, Sperma *nt*

semester [sɪ'mestə'] N Semester *nt*

semi ['semɪ] N **a** *(Brit inf)* = **semidetached** **b** *(inf)* = **semifinal** **c** *(US inf)* = **semitrailer**

semi- PREF halb-, Halb-

semi: **semiautomatic** **ADJ** halb automatisch **N** *(= weapon)* halb automatische Waffe; **semibreve** N *(esp Brit)* ganze Note; **semicircle** N Halbkreis *m*; **semicircular** ADJ halbkreisförmig; **~ canal** *(Anat)* Bogengang *m*; **semicolon** N Strichpunkt *m*, Semikolon *nt*; **semiconductor** N Halbleiter *m*; **semiconscious** ADJ halb bewusstlos; **he's only ~, but you can talk to him** er ist zwar noch nicht ganz bei Bewusstsein, Sie können aber mit ihm reden; **semidarkness** N Halbdunkel *nt*; **semi-derelict** [,semɪ'derɪlɪkt] ADJ halb verfallen; **semidetached** *(Brit)* **ADJ** **~ house** Doppelhaushälfte *f* **N** Doppelhaushälfte *f*; **semifinal** N Halb- *or* Semifinalspiel *nt*; **~s** Halb- *or* Semifinale *nt*; **semifinalist** N Teilnehmer(in) *m(f)* am Halbfinale; **semi-finished** ADJ halb fertig, halbfertig; **~ product** Halb(fertig)fabrikat *nt*

seminal ['semɪnl] ADJ **a** **~ fluid** Samenflüssigkeit *f* **b** *(= embryonic)* keimhaft *(geh)*; **to be present in a ~ state** im Keim vorhanden sein **c** *(form: = influential) book, author, text* einflussreich; *ideas* ertragreich; *event* grundlegend; **of ~ importance** von herausragender Bedeutung

seminar ['semɪnɑː'] N Seminar *nt*

seminarian [,semɪ'neərɪən], **seminarist** ['semɪnərɪst] N Seminarist(in) *m(f)*

seminary ['semɪnərɪ] N Priesterseminar *nt*

semiofficial [,semɪə'fɪʃəl] ADJ halbamtlich, halb amtlich, offiziös; *rule* halboffiziell

semiotic [semɪ'ɒtɪk] ADJ semiotisch

semiotics [semɪ'ɒtɪks] N *sing* Semiotik *f*

semi: **semiprecious** ADJ **~ stone** Halbedelstein *m*; **semipro** ['semɪ'prəʊ] N *(inf)* = **semi-professional**; **semiprofessional** **ADJ** **a** *job* überwiegend praktische Kenntnisse erfordernd; *musician etc* nebenberuflich **b** *(esp Sport)* halbprofessionell **N** *(esp Sport)* Halbprofi *m*, Feierabendprofi *m*; **semiquaver** N *(esp Brit)* Sechzehntel(note *f*) *nt*; **semi-retirement** N ≈ Altersteilzeit *f*; **semiskilled** ADJ *worker* angelernt; **~ job** Anlernberuf *m*; **~ labour** *(Brit) or* **labor** *(US)* *(= workforce)* Angelernte *pl*; *(= work)* Arbeit *f* für Angelernte; **semi-skimmed milk** N *(Brit)* Halbfettmilch *f*, teilentrahmte Milch; **semisolid** **ADJ** halbfest **N** halbfeste Substanz; **semisubmersible** N *(= oil rig)* schwimmende Bohrinsel, Halbtaucher *m*

Semite ['siːmaɪt] N Semit *m*, Semitin *f*

Semitic [sɪ'mɪtɪk] ADJ semitisch

semi: **semitone** N Halbton *m*; **semitrailer** N *(Brit)* Sattelschlepper *m*; *(= part)* Sattelauflieger *m*; **semivowel** N Halbvokal *m*

semolina [,semə'liːnə] N Grieß *m*

sempiternal [,sempɪ'tɜːnl] ADJ *(liter)* immerwährend *(liter)*

sempstress ['sempstrɪs] N Näherin *f*

SEN *(Brit) abbr of* **State Enrolled Nurse** *staatlich geprüfte Krankenschwester, staatlich geprüfter Krankenpfleger*

Sen *(US) abbr of* **Senator**

senate ['senɪt] N Senat *m*

senator ['senɪtə'] N Senator(in) *m(f)*; *(as address)* Herr Senator/Frau Senatorin

senatorial [,senə'tɔːrɪəl] ADJ des/eines Senators

send [send] ✪ 20.1, 20.3, 21.1, 21.3 *pret, ptp* **sent** **VT** **a** *(= dispatch)* schicken; *letter, messenger* schicken, senden; *(= send off) letter* abschicken; *(Rad) radio wave* ausstrahlen; *signal, SOS* senden; *(through wires)* übermitteln; *data* senden, übertragen; **the satellite ~s signals (to us)** der Satellit sendet Signale aus/sendet uns Signale; **it ~s the wrong signal** *or* **message** *(fig)* das könnte falsch verstanden werden; **to ~ sb to prison/to his death** jdn ins Gefängnis/in den Tod schicken; **to ~ sb on a course/tour** jdn auf einen *or* zu einem Kurs/auf eine Tour schicken; **to ~ sb to university** jdn studieren lassen; **to ~ sb for sth** jdn nach etw schicken

b **she ~s her love/congratulations/apologies** *etc* sie lässt grüßen/ihre Glückwünsche ausrichten/sich entschuldigen *etc*; **~ him my love/best wishes** grüßen Sie ihn von mir

c *(= propel, make go) arrow, ball* schießen; *(hurl)* schleudern; *(conveyor belt)* leiten, befördern; **he/the explosion sent everything crashing to the ground** er/die Explosion ließ alles krachend zu Boden fallen; **the blow sent him sprawling** der Schlag schleuderte ihn zu Boden; **the fire sent everyone running out of the building** das Feuer ließ alle das Gebäude fluchtartig verlassen; **the blue ball sent the red across the table** die blaue Kugel ließ die rote über den Tisch rollen; **the particle is sent off at an angle** das Teilchen fliegt schräg zur Seite weg; **his speech sent a wave of excitement through the audience** seine Rede ließ eine Woge der Aufregung durch die Zuschauer gehen; **the decision sent shock waves through the motor industry** die Entscheidung hat die Autobranche erschüttert; **the explosion had sent the spaceship off course** die Explosion hatte das Raumschiff vom Kurs abgebracht

d *(= cause to become, cause to go)* **this sent him into a real fury** das machte ihn fürchterlich wütend; **this sent him (off) into fits of laughter** das ließ ihn in einen Lachkrampf ausbrechen; **to ~ prices soaring** die Preise in die Höhe treiben; **to ~ shares soaring** Aktien in die Höhe schnellen lassen

e *(inf)* umhauen; **that tune/he ~s me** der Song/Typ haut mich um *(inf)*, ich bin ganz hin und weg von dem Song/ihm *(sl)* → **sent**

f *(old)* geben; **~ her victorious** möge sie siegreich sein *(liter)*

VI **she sent to say that …** sie ließ sagen *or* ausrichten *or* bestellen, dass …; **the mail-order firm suddenly stopped ~ing** die Versandfirma lieferte plötzlich nicht mehr

▶ **send across** VT *sep* hinüberschicken; *(+prep obj)* schicken über *(+acc)*

▶ **send after** **VT** *sep* **to send sb after sb** jdn jdm nachschicken **VI** *+prep obj* **they sent after him** sie schickten ihm jemanden nach

▶ **send along** VT *sep* (her-/hin)schicken

▶ **send away** **VT** *sep* **a** *(= dispatch)* wegschicken, fortschicken; *letter etc* abschicken; **his parents sent him away to Europe/to school** seine Eltern schickten ihn nach Europa/ins Internat; **to send sth away to be mended** etw zur *or* in die Reparatur geben *or* schicken **b** **I had to send him away without an explanation** ich musste ihn ohne Erklärung weggehen lassen *or* wegschicken **VI** schreiben; **the number of people who sent away when they saw the TV advertisement** die Anzahl von Leuten, die auf die Fernsehreklame hin schrieben; **to send away for sth** etw anfordern

▶ **send back** **VT** *sep* zurückschicken; *food in restaurant* zurückgehen lassen **VI** **to send back for reinforcements** nach Verstärkung schicken, Verstärkung holen lassen

▶ **send down** VT *sep* **a** *temperature, prices* fallen lassen; *(gradually)* senken **b** *(Brit Univ: = expel)* relegieren **c** *prisoner* verurteilen (*for* zu)

▶ **send for** VI *+prep obj* **a** *person* kommen lassen; *doctor, police, priest* rufen; *help* herbeirufen; *reinforcements* herbeibeordern; *food* bringen lassen; *(person in authority) pupil, secretary, minister* zu sich bestellen; **I'll send for you/these books when I want you/them** ich lasse Sie rufen/ich schicke nach den Büchern, wenn ich Sie/sie brauche; **to send for sb to do sth** jdn herbeiholen *or* nach jdm schicken, um etw zu tun; **has the doctor been sent for yet?** ist der Arzt schon gerufen worden? **b** *copy, catalogue* anfordern, sich *(dat)* kommen lassen

▶ **send forth** VT *sep (liter)* aussenden *(geh)*; *blossom* hervorbringen; *smell* verströmen *(geh)*; *heat, light* ausstrahlen

▶ **send in** **VT** *sep* einschicken, einsenden; *person* hereinschicken; *troops* einsetzen **VI** = **send away VI**

▶ **send off** **VT** *sep* **a** *letter, parcel* abschicken **b** *children to school* wegschicken; **he sent his son off to Paris** er schickte seinen Sohn nach Paris **c** = **send away VT b** **d** *(Sport)* vom Platz stellen (*for* wegen); *(Ice hockey)* auf die Strafbank schicken; **he was sent off the pitch** er wurde vom Platz gestellt, er erhielt einen Platzverweis; **send him off, ref!** Platzverweis! **e** *(= see off)* verabschieden **VI** = **send away VI**

▶ **send on** VT *sep* **a** *(= forward) letter* nachschicken; *(= pass on) memo* weiterleiten **b** *(in advance) troops, luggage etc* vorausschicken **c** *substitute* aufs Feld schicken, einsetzen; *actor* auf die Bühne schicken

▶ **send out** VT *sep* **a** *(out of house, room)* hinausschicken (*of* aus); **he sent me out to the post office** er hat mich zur Post® geschickt; **she sent me out to buy a paper** sie hat mich losgeschickt, um eine Zeitung zu kaufen; **the company started sending work out** die Firma hat angefangen, Arbeit außer Haus zu geben **b** *(= emit) rays, radio signals* aussenden; *light,* *heat, radiation* ausstrahlen, abgeben; *smoke* ausstoßen, abgeben **c** *leaflets, invitations, application forms* verschicken

▸**send out for** VI +*prep obj* holen lassen VT *sep* **to send sb out for sth** jdn nach etw schicken

▸**send up** VT *sep* **a** *rocket* hochschießen; *balloon* steigen lassen; *flare* in die Luft schießen; **I sent up a prayer of thanks** ich habe ein Dankgebet zum Himmel geschickt **b** *prices, temperature* hochtreiben, in die Höhe treiben; *pressure* steigen lassen **c** *(= destroy)* in die Luft gehen lassen; **to send sth up in flames** etw in Flammen aufgehen lassen **d** *(Brit inf: = satirize)* verulken *(inf)* **e** *(US inf: = send to prison)* hinter Gitter bringen *(inf)*

sender ['sendəʳ] N Absender(in) *m(f)*; **return to ~** zurück an Absender

send: **sendoff** N Abschied *m*, Verabschiedung *f*; **to give sb a good ~** jdn ganz groß verabschieden *(inf)*; **send-up** N *(Brit inf)* Verulkung *f (inf)*; **to do a ~ of sb/sth** jdn/etw verulken *(inf)*

Senegal [ˌsenɪ'gɔːl] N Senegal *nt*

Senegalese [ˌsenɪgə'liːz] ADJ senegalesisch N Senegalese *m*, Senegalesin *f*

senescence [sɪ'nesəns] N *(form)* Alterungsprozess *m*, Seneszenz *f (spec)*

senescent [sɪ'nesənt] ADJ *(form)* alternd

senile ['siːnaɪl] ADJ *person* senil; *(physically)* altersschwach; **~ decay** Altersabbau *m*; **he must be getting ~** er wird langsam senil *or (physically)* ein richtiger Tattergreis *(inf)*

senile dementia N *(Med)* senile Demenz *(spec)*, Altersschwachsinn *m*

senility [sɪ'nɪlɪtɪ] N Senilität *f*; *(physical)* Altersschwäche *f*

senior ['siːnɪəʳ] ADJ *(in age)* älter; *(in rank)* vorgesetzt, übergeordnet; *(with longer service)* dienstälter; *rank, civil servant* höher; *officer* ranghöher; *position* höher, leitend; *designer, editor, executive, accountant etc* leitend; **at ~ level** *(in sport)* in einer höheren Altersgruppe; **he is ~ to me** *(in age)* er ist älter als ich; *(in rank)* er ist mir übergeordnet; *(in length of service)* er ist *or* arbeitet schon länger hier als ich; **~ section** ältere *or* höhere Altersgruppe; **the ~ management** die Geschäftsleitung; **~ consultant** Chefarzt *m*/-ärztin *f*; **~ pupil** Oberstufenschüler(in) *m(f)*; **my ~ officer** mein Vorgesetzter; **a very ~ officer** ein sehr hoher Offizier; **he's very/not very ~** er hat eine ziemlich hohe/keine sehr hohe Stellung; **can I speak to somebody more ~?** könnte ich bitte jemanden sprechen, der verantwortlich ist?; **J. B. Schwartz, Senior** J. B. Schwartz senior
N *(Sch)* Oberstufenschüler(in) *m(f)*; *(US Univ)* Student(in) *m(f)* im 4./letzten Studienjahr; *(in club etc)* Senior(in) *m(f)*; **he is my ~** *(in age)* er ist älter als ich; *(in rank)* er ist mir übergeordnet; *(in length of service)* er ist *or* arbeitet schon länger hier als ich; **he is two years my ~, he is my ~ by two years** er ist zwei Jahre älter als ich

senior: **senior citizen** N älterer (Mit)bürger, ältere (Mit)bürgerin; **~ rail/bus pass** Seniorenpass *m*; **senior common room** N *(Brit Univ)* Aufenthaltsraum *m* für Dozenten; **senior doctor** N Oberarzt *m*, Oberärztin *f*

seniority [ˌsiːnɪ'ɒrɪtɪ] N *(in age)* (höheres) Alter; *(in rank)* (höhere) Position; *(Mil)* (höherer) Rang; *(in civil service etc)* (höherer) Dienstgrad; *(by length of service)* (längere) Betriebszugehörigkeit; *(in civil service etc)* (höheres) Dienstalter; **promotion on the basis of ~** Beförderung *f* nach Länge der Dienstzeit/Betriebszugehörigkeit

senior: **senior nurse** N Oberschwester *f*; *(male)* Oberpfleger *m*; **senior partner** N Seniorpartner(in) *m(f)*; **senior school**, *(US)* **senior high school** N Oberstufe *f*; **senior service** N *(Brit)* Kriegsmarine *f*

senna ['senə] N *(= drug)* Sennesblätter *pl*; *(= plant)* Sennespflanze *f*

sennight ['senɪt] N *(obs)* Woche *f*

sen(r) *abbr of* **senior** sen.

sensation [sen'seɪʃən] N **a** *(= feeling)* Gefühl *nt*; *(of heat, cold etc)* Empfindung *f*; *(of the external world)* Sinneseindruck *m*; **a/the ~ of falling** das Gefühl zu fallen; **a ~ of fear** ein Gefühl *nt* der Angst, ein Angstgefühl *nt*; **a ~ of hunger** ein Hungergefühl *nt*; **how can one describe the ~ of touching silk?** wie kann man beschreiben, was man beim Berühren von Seide empfindet?; **I felt a ~ of being watched** ich hatte das Gefühl, beobachtet zu werden **b** *(= great success)* Sensation *f*; **to cause** *or* **create a ~** (großes) Aufsehen erregen

sensational [sen'seɪʃənl] ADJ **a** sensationell, aufsehenerregend; *newspaper, film, book* reißerisch aufgemacht, auf Sensation bedacht; *style, writing* reißerisch; *journalist* sensationsgierig *or* -lüstern *(inf)* **b** *(inf: = very good etc)* sagenhaft *(inf)*

sensationalism [sen'seɪʃnəlɪzəm] N *(of paper, reporter etc)* Sensationsmache *f (inf)*; *(of reader)* Sensationsgier *f*; **the cheap ~ of his style** die billige Effekthascherei in seinem Stil

sensationalist [sen'seɪʃnəlɪst] ADJ Sensations-; *style also* sensationslüstern; **~ journalism/story** Sensationsjournalismus *m*/-geschichte *f*

sensationally [sen'seɪʃnəlɪ] ADV **a** *(= dramatically)* sensationell; *write, report* in einem reißerischen Stil **b** *(inf: = amazingly)* sensationell, sagenhaft *(inf)*; **a ~ successful movie** ein sensationell erfolgreicher Film; **our business has improved ~** unser Geschäft hat sich sensationell verbessert

sensation: **sensation-seeker** N sensationslüsterner Mensch; **sensation-seeking** ADJ sensationslüstern

sense [sens] N **a** *(bodily)* Sinn *m*; **~ of hearing** Gehörsinn *m*, Gehör *nt*; **~ of sight** Sehvermögen *nt*; **~ of smell** Geruchssinn *m*; **~ of taste** Geschmack(sinn) *m*; **~ of touch** Tastsinn *m*
b senses PL *(= right mind)* Verstand *m*; **no man in his ~s …** kein einigermaßen vernünftiger Mensch …; **to frighten sb out of his ~s** jdn zu Tode erschrecken; **his ~s were deranged by …** er war durch … völlig verstört; **to bring sb to his ~s** jdn zur Vernunft *or* Besinnung bringen; **to come to one's ~s** zur Vernunft *or* Besinnung kommen, Vernunft annehmen
c *(= feeling)* Gefühl *nt*; **~ of duty** Pflichtbewusstsein *or* -gefühl *nt*; **~ of guilt** Schuldgefühl *nt*; **a ~ of pleasure** *etc* ein Gefühl der Freude *etc*; **a ~ of occasion** das Gefühl, dass etwas Besonderes stattfindet; **he has an exaggerated ~ of his own importance** er nimmt sich selbst übertrieben wichtig; **imbued with a ~ of history** von Geschichte durchtränkt *(liter)*; **there's a ~ of insecurity in the country** im Land herrscht ein Gefühl der Unsicherheit; **a false ~ of security** ein falsches Gefühl der Sicherheit; **these buildings create a ~ of space** diese Gebäude vermitteln den Eindruck von Weite
d *(= instinct, appreciation)* Sinn *m*; **his ~ for what is appropriate** sein Gefühl *nt or* Gespür *nt* dafür, was angebracht ist; **~ of colour** *(Brit) or* **color** *(US)*/**justice** Farben-/Gerechtigkeitssinn *m*
e *(= good sense)* **(common) ~** gesunder Menschenverstand; **haven't you ~ enough** *or* **enough ~ to stop when you're tired?** bist du nicht vernünftig genug aufzuhören, wenn du müde bist?; **he had the (good) ~ to …** er war so vernünftig *or* klug *or* gescheit und …; **you should have had more ~ than to …** du hättest vernünftiger sein sollen und nicht …; **there is no ~ in that** das hat keinen Sinn, es ist zwecklos; **there's a lot of ~ in that** das hat Hand und Fuß, das ist ganz vernünftig; **what's the ~ of** *or* **in doing this?** welchen Sinn hat es denn, das zu tun?; **there is no ~ in doing that** es ist zwecklos *or* sinnlos, das zu tun; **there is no ~ in crying** es hat keinen Sinn zu heulen; **there's some ~ in what he says** was er sagt, ist ganz vernünftig; **there's some ~ in doing that** es wäre ganz vernünftig, das zu tun; **to be full of good ~** grundvernünftig sein; **to talk ~** vernünftig sein; **you're just not talking ~** du bist doch völlig unvernünftig; **now you're talking ~** das lässt sich schon eher hören; **he hasn't the ~ he was born with** er hat nicht für fünf Cent Verstand *(inf)*; **to make sb see ~** jdn zur Vernunft bringen
f to make ~ *(sentence etc)* (einen) Sinn ergeben; *(= be sensible, rational etc)* sinnvoll *or* vernünftig sein, Sinn machen; **it doesn't make ~ doing it that way/spending** *or* **to spend all that money** es ist doch Unsinn *or* unvernünftig, es so zu machen/so viel Geld auszugeben; **why did he decide that? – I don't know, it doesn't make ~** warum hat er das beschlossen? – ich weiß es nicht, es ist mir unverständlich *or* es macht keinen Sinn; **the whole thing fails to make ~ to me** die ganze Sache leuchtet mir nicht ein; **it makes good** *or* **sound ~** das scheint sehr vernünftig; **it makes good financial/political ~ to …** aus finanzieller/politischer Sicht gesehen ist es sehr vernünftig, zu …; **sometimes life just doesn't make ~** manchmal ergibt das Leben einfach keinen Sinn; **her conduct doesn't make ~ to me** ich werde aus ihrem Verhalten nicht schlau *(inf)*; **he/his theory doesn't make ~** er/seine Theorie ist völlig unverständlich; **it all makes ~ now** jetzt wird einem alles klar; **it doesn't make ~, the jewels were there a minute ago** das ist ganz unverständlich, die Juwelen waren doch eben noch da; **to make ~ of sth** etw verstehen, aus etw schlau werden *(inf)*; **you're not making ~** *(in explaining sth, in plans, intentions etc)* das ist doch Unsinn; *(in behaviour, attitude)* ich werde aus Ihnen nicht schlau *(inf)*; **now you're making ~** *(in explaining sth)* jetzt verstehe ich, was Sie meinen; *(in plans, intentions etc)* das ist endlich eine vernünftige Idee
g *(= meaning)* Sinn *m no pl*; **in the full** *or* **true ~ of the word** im wahrsten Sinn des Wortes; **it has three distinct ~s** es hat drei verschiedene Bedeutungen; **in what ~ are you using the word?** in welchem Sinn *or* welcher Bedeutung gebrauchen Sie das Wort?; **he is an amateur in the best ~** er ist Amateur im eigentlichen Sinn des Wortes; **in every ~ of the word** in der vollen Bedeutung des Wortes; **in the usual ~ of the word** im herkömmlichen Sinne des Wortes
h *(= way, respect)* **in a ~** in gewisser Hinsicht, gewissermaßen; **in every ~** in jeder Hinsicht; **in what ~?** inwiefern?; **in one ~ what he claims is true** in gewisser Hinsicht hat er mit seiner Behauptung recht
VT fühlen, spüren; **I could ~ someone there in the dark** ich fühlte *or* spürte, dass da jemand in der Dunkelheit war

sense: **sense datum** N Sinnesdatum *nt*; **sense group** N *(Ling)* Sinngruppe *f*; *(Comput Ling: in SGML- or XML-text)* Bedeutungsgruppe *f*

senseless ['senslɪs] ADJ **a** *(= unconscious)* besinnungslos, bewusstlos; **to knock sb ~** jdn bewusstlos schlagen **b** *(= stupid)* unvernünftig, unsinnig; *(= futile) waste, discussion* sinnlos; **what a ~ thing to do/say** *etc* welch ein Unsinn

senselessly ['senslɪslɪ] ADV *(= pointlessly)* sinnlos; **a ~ cruel act** ein sinnloser Akt der Gewalt

senselessness ['senslɪsnɪs] N *(= stupidity)* Unvernunft *f*, Unsinnigkeit *f*; *(= futility)* Sinnlosigkeit *f*

sense organ N Sinnesorgan *nt*

sensibility [ˌsensɪ'bɪlɪtɪ] N *(to beauty etc)* Empfindsamkeit *f*; *(= artistic sensibility also)* Sensibilität *f*; *(= emotional sensibility, susceptibility to insult)* Empfindlichkeit *f*, Sensibilität *f*; **sensibilities** Zartgefühl *nt*

sensible ['sensəbl] ADJ **a** vernünftig; **be ~ about it** seien Sie vernünftig; **that's the ~ thing to do** das ist vernünftig **b** *(liter: = aware)* **to be ~ of sth** sich *(dat)* einer Sache *(gen)* bewusst sein **c** *(rare: = appreciable)* spürbar, merklich

sensibleness ['sensəblnɪs] N Vernünftigkeit *f*

sensibly ['sensəblɪ] ADV *(= reasonably)* vernünftig; **he very ~ ignored the question** er hat die

Frage vernünftigerweise ignoriert; **~ priced** preisgünstig

sensitive ['sensɪtɪv] ADJ **a** *(emotionally) person* sensibel, empfindsam; *(= easily hurt)* empfindlich; *(= understanding)* einfühlsam; *novel, film, remark* einfühlend; **to be ~ about sth** in Bezug auf etw *(acc)* empfindlich sein; **she is very ~ to criticism/these things** sie reagiert sehr empfindlich auf Kritik/diese Dinge **b** *(physically) instruments, part of body, leaves, plants* empfindlich; *(Phot) emulsion, film* lichtempfindlich; *(= delicate) balance, adjustment* fein; *(fig) topic, issue* heikel, prekär; **~ to heat/light** wärme-/lichtempfindlich; **his wound is ~ to touch** seine Wunde tut weh, wenn man sie berührt; **he has access to some highly ~ information** er hat Zugang zu streng vertraulichen Informationen; **his visit comes at a ~ time** er macht diesen Besuch zu einem schwierigen Zeitpunkt; **just how ~ are these figures?** inwiefern sind diese Zahlen als vertraulich zu behandeln?

sensitively ['sensɪtɪvlɪ] ADV **a** *(= sympathetically)* einfühlsam **b** *(= tastefully)* einfühlsam **c** *(= precisely)* genau; **the markets ~ register changes in consumer demand** der Markt reagiert empfindlich auf Nachfrageveränderungen

sensitiveness ['sensɪtɪvnɪs] N = **sensitivity**

sensitivity [ˌsensɪ'tɪvɪtɪ] N **a** *(emotional)* Sensibilität *f*, Empfindsamkeit *f*; *(= getting easily hurt)* Empfindlichkeit *f*; *(= understanding)* Einfühlsamkeit *f*; *(of novel, film, remark)* Einfühlungsvermögen *nt* **b** *(physical, of instrument, part of body etc)* Empfindlichkeit *f*; *(Phot: of emulsion, film)* Lichtempfindlichkeit *f*; *(= delicacy: of balance, adjustment)* Feinheit *f*; *(fig: of topic, issue)* heikle Natur; **~ to heat/light** Wärme-/Lichtempfindlichkeit *f*; **an issue of great ~** eine sehr heikle Angelegenheit

sensitize ['sensɪtaɪz] VT sensibilisieren

sensor ['sensəʳ] N Sensor *m*; *(non-electronic also)* Fühler *m*

sensorimotor ['sensərɪ'məʊtəʳ] ADJ sensomotorisch

sensory ['sensərɪ] ADJ sensorisch; **~ organ** Sinnesorgan *nt*

sensory deprivation N Reizabschirmung *f*, sensorische Deprivation *(spec)*

sensual ['sensjʊəl] ADJ sinnlich, wollüstig *(pej)*; *person, life also* sinnesfreudig, lustbetont; **~ moments** Augenblicke *pl* der Lust

sensualism ['sensjʊəlɪzəm] N Sinnlichkeit *f*, Wollüstigkeit *f (pej)*; *(Philos)* Sensualismus *m*

sensualist ['sensjʊəlɪst] N Genussmensch *m*, sinnlicher Mensch, Lüstling *m (pej)*; *(Philos)* Sensualist(in) *m(f)*

sensuality [ˌsensjʊ'ælɪtɪ] N Sinnlichkeit *f*, Wollüstigkeit *f (pej)*; *(of person also)* Sinnesfreudigkeit *f*

sensualize ['sensjʊəlaɪz] VT sinnlich machen, versinnlichen

sensually ['sensjʊəlɪ] ADV sinnlich, wollüstig *(pej)*

sensuous ADJ, **sensuously** ADV ['sensjʊəs, -lɪ] sinnlich, sinnenhaft

sensuousness ['sensjʊəsnɪs] N Sinnlichkeit *f*, Sinnenhaftigkeit *f*

sent [sent] *pret, ptp of* **send** ADJ *(inf) look* hingerissen *(inf)*; **he's ~** er ist ganz weg *(inf)*

sentence ['sentəns] N **a** *(Gram)* Satz *m*; **~ structure** Satzbau *m*; *(of particular sentence)* Satzaufbau *m*, Satzstruktur *f* **b** *(Jur)* Strafe *f*; **to be under ~ of death** zum Tode verurteilt sein; **the judge gave him a 6-month ~** der Richter verurteilte ihn zu 6 Monaten Haft; **to pass ~ (on sb)** (über jdn) das Urteil verkünden; *(fig)* jdn verurteilen VT *(Jur)* verurteilen; **he was ~d to life imprisonment** er wurde zu lebenslänglichem Freiheitsentzug verurteilt

sententious ADJ, **sententiously** ADV [sen'tenʃəs, -lɪ] salbungsvoll

sententiousness [sen'tenʃəsnɪs] N **the ~ of the lecture/speaker** der salbungsvolle Vortrag/Redner; **..., he said with great ~** ..., sagte er salbungsvoll

sentience ['sentɪəns] N Empfindungsvermögen *nt*; **the ~ of approaching death** das Vorgefühl des nahenden Todes

sentient ['sentɪənt] ADJ empfindungsfähig

sentiment ['sentɪmənt] N **a** *(= feeling, emotion)* Gefühl *nt* **b** *(= sentimentality)* Sentimentalität *f*, Rührseligkeit *f* **c** *(= opinion)* Ansicht *f*, Meinung *f*; **what are your ~s on this?** was ist Ihre Meinung *or* Ansicht dazu?, wie denken Sie darüber?; **my ~s exactly!** genau meine Ansicht *or* Meinung! **d** *(= thought behind words or deeds)* Gedanke *m*

sentimental [ˌsentɪ'mentl] ADJ sentimental; *person, mood also* gefühlvoll; *novel, song, music also* gefühlsselig, kitschig *(pej)*, schmalzig *(pej)*; *value* gefühlsmäßig; **for ~ reasons** aus Sentimentalität; **to make a ~ visit to a place** einem Ort aus Sentimentalität einen Besuch abstatten; **a certain ~ attachment** eine gewisse gefühlsmäßige Bindung; **~ nonsense** Gefühlsduselei *f*

sentimentalism [ˌsentɪ'mentəlɪzəm] N Sentimentalität *f*

sentimentalist [ˌsentɪ'mentəlɪst] N Gefühlsmensch *m*, sentimentaler Mensch

sentimentality [ˌsentɪmen'tælɪtɪ] N Sentimentalität *f*

sentimentalize [ˌsentɪ'mentəlaɪz] VT sentimental *or* gefühlvoll darstellen VI sentimental sein

sentimentally [ˌsentɪ'mentəlɪ] ADV *important, attached etc* gefühlsmäßig; *say, reminisce* sentimental; *sing, play music* gefühlvoll; *(pej)* sentimental, kitschig *(pej)*, schmalzig *(pej)*

sentinel ['sentɪnl] N **a** Wache *f*; **to stand ~ over sth** *(liter)* über etw *(acc)* wachen *or* Wacht halten **b** *(Comput)* Hinweissymbol *nt*

sentry ['sentrɪ] N Wache *f*, Wachtposten *m*; **to be on ~ duty** auf Wache sein

sentry: **sentry box** N Wachhäuschen *nt*; **sentry go** N *(Mil)* Wachdienst *m*

sep *abbr of* **separate**

sepal ['sepəl] N Kelchblatt *nt*

separability [ˌseprə'bɪlɪtɪ] N Trennbarkeit *f*

separable ['sepərəbl] ADJ trennbar

separate ['seprət] ADJ **a** getrennt, gesondert *(from* von); *organization, unit* gesondert, eigen *attr*; *two organizations, issues, parts* gesondert *attr*, voneinander getrennt, verschieden *attr*; *provisions, regulations* besondere(r, s) *attr*, separat, gesondert *attr*; *beds, rooms, accounts* getrennt; *account, bill, agreement, department* gesondert *attr*, extra *attr inv*; *entrance, toilet, flat* separat; *existence* eigen *attr*; **~ peace** Separat- *or* Sonderfrieden *m*; **~ treaty** Sondervertrag *m*; **that is a ~ question/issue** das ist eine andere Frage, das ist eine Frage für sich; **on two ~ occasions** bei zwei verschiedenen Gelegenheiten; **on a ~ occasion** bei einer anderen Gelegenheit; **there will be ~ discussions on this question** diese Frage wird extra *or* separat *or* gesondert diskutiert; **they live ~ lives** sie gehen getrennte Wege; **a ~ sheet of paper** ein anderes Blatt Papier; *(= additional)* ein gesondertes *or* extra Blatt Papier; **this is quite ~ from his job** das hat mit seinem Beruf nichts zu tun; **to keep two things ~** zwei Dinge nicht zusammentun; *questions, issues* zwei Dinge auseinanderhalten; **always keep your chequebook** *(Brit) or* **checkbook** *(US)* **~ from your card** bewahren Sie Scheckbuch und Scheckkarte immer getrennt auf; **keep this book ~ from the others** halten Sie dieses Buch von den anderen getrennt **b** *(= individual)* einzeln; **all the ~ sections/pieces/units/questions** alle einzelnen Abschnitte/Teile/Einheiten/Fragen; **everybody has a ~ cup/task** jeder hat eine Tasse/Aufgabe für sich *or* seine eigene Tasse/Aufgabe N **separates** PL Röcke, Blusen, Hosen *etc* VT ['sepəreɪt] trennen; *(Chem also)* scheiden; *milk* entrahmen; *(= divide up)* aufteilen *(into* in *+acc)*; **to ~ the good from the bad** die Guten von den Schlechten trennen *or* scheiden; **he can't ~ his private life from his work** er kann Privatleben und Arbeit nicht (voneinander) trennen, er kann das Privatleben nicht von der Arbeit trennen; **he is ~d from his wife** er lebt von seiner Frau getrennt ['sepəreɪt] VI ['sepəreɪt] sich trennen; *(Chem also)* sich scheiden; **it ~s into four parts** es lässt sich in vier Teile auseinandernehmen; *(fig: problem etc)* es zerfällt in vier Teile

▶ **separate out** VT *sep* trennen *(from* von), absondern *(from* von), aussondern VI getrennt werden

separated ['sepəreɪtɪd] ADJ getrennt; *couple* getrennt lebend *attr*; **the couple are ~** das Paar lebt getrennt

separately ['seprətlɪ] ADV getrennt, gesondert, separat; *live* getrennt; *(= singly)* einzeln

separateness ['seprətnɪs] N Getrenntheit *f*, Gesondertheit *f*

separation [ˌsepə'reɪʃən] N Trennung *f*; *(Chem also)* Scheidung *f*; *(of rocket etc)* Abtrennung *f (from* von)

separation allowance N Trennungsentschädigung *f*

separatism ['sepərətɪzəm] N Separatismus *m*

separatist ['sepərətɪst] ADJ separatistisch N Separatist(in) *m(f)*

separator ['sepəreɪtəʳ] N Separator *m*; *(Comput)* Trennzeichen *nt*

sepia ['si:pjə] N Sepia *f* ADJ Sepia-; *(also* **sepia-coloured)** sepia(farben); **~ drawing** Sepiazeichnung *f*

sepoy ['si:pɔɪ] N Sepoy *m*

sepsis ['sepsɪs] N Vereiterung *f*, Sepsis *f (spec)*

Sept *abbr of* **September** Sept.

September [sep'tembəʳ] N September *m*; **the first/tenth of ~** der erste/zehnte September; **on ~ 1st/19th** *(written)*, **on 1st/19th ~** *(written)*, **on the 1st/19th of ~** *(spoken)* am 1./19. September; **~ 3rd, 1990, 3rd ~ 1990** *(on letter)* 3. September 1990; **in ~** im September; **during ~** im September; **every** *or* **each ~** jeden September; **at the beginning/end of ~** Anfang/Ende September; **~ is a pleasant month** der September ist ein angenehmer Monat; **there are 30 days in ~** der September hat 30 Tage ADJ *attr* September-; *weather, mists etc also* septemberlich; **~ issue** *(of magazine etc)* Septemberausgabe *f*

septennial [sep'tenɪəl] ADJ siebenjährig; *(= every seven years)* alle sieben Jahre stattfindend, siebenjährlich

septet, **septette** [sep'tet] N Septett *nt*

septic ['septɪk] ADJ vereitert, septisch; **the wound turned ~** die Wunde eiterte

septicaemia, *(US)* **septicemia** [ˌseptɪ'si:mɪə] N Vergiftung *f* des Blutes, Septikämie *f (spec)*

septic shock N *(Med)* septischer Schock

septic tank N Faulbehälter *m*, Klärbehälter *m*

septuagenarian [ˌseptjʊədʒɪ'neərɪən] ADJ siebzigjährig N Siebzigjährige(r) *mf*; **to be a ~** ein(e) Siebziger(in) sein

Septuagesima [ˌseptjʊə'dʒesɪmə] N Sonntag *m* Septuagesima

septuplet [sep'tju:plɪt] N *(= baby)* Siebenling *m*; *(Mus)* Septole *f*

sepulcher N *(US)* = **sepulchre**

sepulchral [sɪ'pʌlkrəl] ADJ *(liter)* sepulkral *(liter)*; *(fig)* düster; **~ voice/silence** Grabesstimme *f*/-stille *f*; **in a ~ tone** mit Grabesstimme

sepulchre, *(US)* **sepulcher** ['sepəlkəʳ] N Grabstätte *f*; **the Holy Sepulchre** das Heilige Grab

sequel ['si:kwəl] N Folge *f (to* von); *(of book, film)* Fortsetzung *f (to* von); **it had a tragic ~** es hatte ein tragisches Nachspiel

sequence ['si:kwəns] N **a** *(= order)* Folge *f*, Reihenfolge *f*; **~ of tenses/words** Zeiten-/Wortfolge *f*; **in ~** der Reihe nach; **to do sth in logical ~** etw in der logisch richtigen Reihenfolge tun **b** *(= things following)* Reihe *f*, Folge *f*;

(Mus, Cards, Eccl) Sequenz *f*; *(Math)* Reihe *f* **c** *(Film: = dance sequence)* Sequenz *f*

sequencer ['si:kwənsəʳ] N *(Comput)* Ablaufsteuerung *f*, Sequenzer *m*

sequential [sɪ'kwenʃəl] ADJ *(form)* der Reihe nach, in regelmäßiger Folge; *(= following)* folgend; *(Comput)* sequenziell, sequentiell; **to be ~ to sth** auf etw *(acc)* folgen

sequester [sɪ'kwestəʳ] VT **a** *(liter: = isolate)* abkapseln **b** *(Jur)* = **sequestrate**

sequestered [sɪ'kwestəd] ADJ **a** *(liter) village* abgeschieden; *spot* abgelegen; *life* zurückgezogen **b** *(Jur) asset* sequestriert

sequestrate [sɪ'kwestreɪt] VT *(Jur)* sequestrieren

sequestration [ˌsi:kwe'streɪʃən] N *(Jur)* Sequestration *f*; *(in bankruptcy case also)* Zwangsverwaltung *f*

sequin ['si:kwɪn] N Paillette *f*

sequined ['si:kwɪnd] ADJ mit Pailletten besetzt

sequoia [sɪ'kwɔɪə] N Mammutbaum *m*, Sequoie *f*

seraglio [se'rɑ:lɪəʊ] N Serail *nt*

seraph ['serəf] N *pl* **-s** *or* **-im** Seraph *m*

seraphic [sə'ræfɪk] ADJ verklärt, verzückt

seraphim ['serəfɪm] *pl of* **seraph**

Serb [sɜ:b] N Serbe *m*, Serbin *f*

Serbia ['sɜ:bɪə] N Serbien *nt*

Serbian ['sɜ:bɪən] **ADJ** serbisch **N a** Serbe *m*, Serbin *f* **b** *(Ling)* Serbisch *nt*

Serbo-Croat ['sɜ:bəʊ'krəʊæt] N **a** *(Ling)* Serbokroatisch *nt* **b the ~s** *pl (= people)* die Serben und Kroaten

Serbo-Croatian ['sɜ:bəʊkrəʊ'eɪʃən] **ADJ** serbokroatisch **N the Serbo-Croatians PL** die Serben und Kroaten

serenade [ˌserə'neɪd] **N** Serenade *f* **VT** ein Ständchen *nt* bringen *(+dat)*

serenader [ˌserə'neɪdəʳ] N *jd, der ein Ständchen bringt*

serendipity [ˌserən'dɪpɪtɪ] N Spürsinn *m (fig)*, mehr Glück als Verstand

serene [sə'ri:n] ADJ gelassen; *sea* ruhig; *sky* heiter, klar; **His Serene Highness** seine Durchlaucht, Serenissimus

serenely [sə'ri:nlɪ] ADV gelassen; **~ indifferent to the noise** gleichmütig dem Lärm gegenüber; **her face was ~ beautiful** ihr Gesicht war von einer gelassenen Schönheit

serenity [sɪ'renɪtɪ] N Gelassenheit *f*; *(as title: also* **Serenity***)* Durchlaucht *f*

serf [sɜ:f] N Leibeigene(r) *mf*

serfdom ['sɜ:fdəm] N Leibeigenschaft *f*; *(fig)* Knechtschaft *f*

serge [sɜ:dʒ] N Serge *f*

sergeant ['sɑ:dʒənt] N *(Mil)* Feldwebel(in) *m(f)*; *(Police)* Polizeimeister(in) *m(f)*; **~ at arms** *(Hist)* Waffenmeister *m*; *(Brit, Parl)* Exekutivbeamte(r) *m*/-beamtin *f* des Parlaments

sergeant first class N *(US)* Oberfeldwebel(in) *m(f)*

sergeant major N Oberfeldwebel(in) *m(f)*

serg(t) *abbr of* **sergeant**

serial ['sɪərɪəl] **ADJ** Serien-; *radio/TV programme* in Fortsetzungen; *writer* von Fortsetzungsromanen; *(Comput) printer, interface etc* seriell; **published in ~ form** in Fortsetzungen veröffentlicht; **he is a ~ rapist** er ist ein Serientäter, der bereits mehrere Vergewaltigungen begangen hat; **~ drama** *(TV)* (Fernseh)serie *f*; **~ novel/story** Fortsetzungsroman *m*/-geschichte *f*
N *(= novel)* Fortsetzungsroman *m*; *(in periodical)* Serie *f*; *(Rad)* Sendereihe *f* (in Fortsetzungen); *(TV)* Serie *f*; *(spec: = magazine)* (periodisch erscheinende) Zeitschrift; **it was published/broadcast as a ~** es wurde in Fortsetzungen veröffentlicht/gesendet

serialization [ˌsɪərɪəlaɪ'zeɪʃən] N *(Rad, TV)* Sendung *f* in Fortsetzungen; *(in magazines etc)* Fortsetzung(sreihe) *f*; *(= serializing)* Umarbeitung *f* in Fortsetzungen

serialize ['sɪərɪəlaɪz] VT in Fortsetzungen veröffentlichen; *(Rad, TV)* in Fortsetzungen senden; *(= put into serial form)* in Fortsetzungen umarbeiten

serial killer N Serienmörder(in) *m(f)*, Serienkiller(in) *m(f)*

serial killing N Serienmord *m*

serially ['sɪərɪəlɪ] ADV *publish, broadcast* in Fortsetzungen; *(= in order) number* fortlaufend; *(Mus, Comput)* seriell

serial: serial murder N Serienmord *m*; **serial number** N fortlaufende Nummer; *(on manufactured goods)* Fabrikationsnummer *f*; **serial port** N *(Comput)* serielle Schnittstelle; **serial rights** PL Rechte *pl* für die Veröffentlichung in Fortsetzungen

seriatim [ˌsɪərɪ'eɪtɪm] ADV *(form)* der Reihe nach

sericulture [ˌserɪ'kʌltʃəʳ] N Seidenraupenzucht *f*

series ['sɪərɪz] N *pl* **- a** Serie *f*; *(of books, lectures etc also, of films, talks, Math, Mus, Elec)* Reihe *f*; *(of events also, succession of things)* Reihe *f*, Folge *f*; **a ~ of articles** eine Artikelserie *or* -reihe; **in ~** der Reihe nach; *(Elec)* in Reihe; *(Comm)* serienmäßig; *publish* als Serie **b** *(Rad)* Sendereihe *f*; *(TV)* Serie *f*

series-wound ['sɪəri:zˌwaʊnd] ADJ *(Elec)* in Serie *or* Reihe geschaltet

serif ['serɪf] **N** Serife *f* **ADJ** *font* serifenbetont

seriocomic(al) ['sɪərɪəʊ'kɒmɪk(l)] ADJ halb ernst, halb heiter

serious ['sɪərɪəs] ADJ **a** *(= earnest)* ernst; *(= not frivolous)* ernsthaft; *consideration, discussion, conversation, doubts* ernst, ernsthaft; *point, matter, business* ernst; *newspaper, publication, interest* ernsthaft, seriös; *offer, suggestion* ernst gemeint, seriös; *attempt* ernsthaft; *contender* ernst zu nehmend *attr*; **to be ~ about doing sth** etw im Ernst tun wollen; **I'm ~ (about it)** ich meine das ernst, das ist mein Ernst; **I'm deadly ~** es ist mir todernst *(inf)*; **he is ~ about her** er meint es ernst mit ihr; **be ~ about your studies** du musst dein Studium ernst nehmen; **you can't be ~!** das meinst du doch nicht ernst!, das kann nicht dein Ernst sein!; **to give ~ thought** *or* **consideration to sth** sich *(dat)* etw ernsthaft *or* ernstlich überlegen, sich über etw *(acc)* ernsthafte Gedanken machen; **the ~ student of jazz will ...** wer sich ernsthaft mit Jazz beschäftigt, wird ...; **to earn ~ money** *(inf)* das große Geld verdienen
b *(= critical) accident, flooding, deficiencies, loss* schwer; *mistake, injury* schwer, schlimm; *problem* ernst, ernst zu nehmend *attr*; *illness* schwer, ernst; *situation* ernst, schlimm; *patient's condition* ernst, bedenklich; *threat, shortage, lack* ernst, ernstlich; *deterioration* bedenklich; **it's ~** das ist schlimm; **it's getting ~** es wird ernst; **inflation is getting ~** die Inflation nimmt ernste Ausmaße an

Serious Fraud Office N *(Brit) Ermittlungsbehörde für schwere Betrugsfälle*

seriously ['sɪərɪəslɪ] ✪ 12.2, 26.1 ADV **a** *(= earnestly)* ernst; *talk, interested, work* ernsthaft; *(= not jokingly)* im Ernst; **to take sb/sth ~** jdn/etw ernst nehmen; **to take oneself too ~** sich selbst zu wichtig nehmen; **do you ~ want to do that?** wollen Sie das wirklich *or* im Ernst tun?; **~ now/though ...** jetzt mal/aber mal ganz im Ernst ...; **but ~, ...** aber jetzt mal im Ernst ...; **~?** im Ernst?, ernsthaft?; **do you mean that ~?** meinen Sie das ernst?, ist das Ihr Ernst?; **he offered it quite ~** er hat das ernstlich angeboten; **a play that deals ~ with the issue of divorce** ein Stück, das sich auf ernsthafte Weise mit Scheidungsfragen befasst
b *(= critically) wounded, damaged, ill, flooded* schwer; *worried* ernstlich; *deteriorate* bedenklich; *threaten* ernsthaft; **he went ~ wrong** er hat einen schweren Fehler gemacht; **the takeoff went ~ wrong** beim Start ist etwas schlimm danebengegangen; **there is something ~ wrong with that** irgendetwas ist damit überhaupt nicht in Ordnung; **we are ~ short of water** bei uns herrscht schwerer *or* schlimmer Wassermangel

c *(inf: = really)* ehrlich *(inf)*; **~ rich** *(person)* schwerreich; **I was beginning to get ~ annoyed** ich wurde langsam ernsthaft sauer *(inf)*

serious-minded ['sɪərɪəs'maɪndɪd] ADJ seriös, ernsthaft

seriousness ['sɪərɪəsnɪs] N **a** *(= earnestness)* Ernst *m*; *(= lack of frivolity)* Ernsthaftigkeit *f*; *(of consideration, discussion, point, matter etc)* Ernst *m*; *(of newspaper, interest)* Ernsthaftigkeit *f*, Seriosität *f*; *(of offer, suggestion)* Seriosität *f*; **in all ~** ganz im Ernst **b** *(= critical nature, of accident, loss, mistake, injury, illness)* Schwere *f*; *(of problem, situation, patient's condition, threat, shortage)* Ernst *m*; *(of deterioration)* Bedenklichkeit *f*

serjeant ['sɑ:dʒənt] N = **sergeant**

sermon ['sɜ:mən] N *(Eccl)* Predigt *f*; *(= homily)* Moralpredigt *f*; *(= scolding)* Strafpredigt *f*; **the Sermon on the Mount** die Bergpredigt

sermonize ['sɜ:mənaɪz] VI Vorträge halten; *(= reprove)* Moralpredigten halten

serotonin [ˌserə'təʊnɪn] N *(Biol, Med: = hormone)* Serotonin *nt*

serous ['sɪərəs] ADJ serös

serpent ['sɜ:pənt] N **a** *(liter)* Schlange *f (also fig)* **b** *(Mus)* Serpent *nt*

serpentine ['sɜ:pəntaɪn] ADJ *lane, river* gewunden, mit vielen Windungen; *road also* kurvenreich; *garden* verschlungen

Serps [sɜ:ps] N *(Brit) abbr of* **state earnings-related pension scheme** *staatliche Rentenversicherung*

serrated [se'reɪtɪd] ADJ gezackt; *leaves also* gesägt; **~ knife** Sägemesser *nt*

serration [se'reɪʃən] N Zacke *f*; *(= edge)* gezackter Rand; *(on knife)* Sägerand *m*; *(of leaves)* gesägter Rand

serried ['serɪd] ADJ **~ ranks** eng geschlossene Reihen *pl*

serum ['sɪərəm] N Serum *nt*

servant ['sɜ:vənt] N *(lit, fig)* Diener(in) *m(f)*; *(also* **servant girl***)* Dienstmädchen *nt*; *(domestic)* Bedienstete(r) *mf*, Dienstbote *m*/-botin *f*; **to have ~s** Bedienstete *or* Diener haben; **~s' quarters** Gesinderäume *pl (Hist)*, Dienstbotenräume *pl*; **your devoted** *or* **humble** *or* **obedient ~** *(old)* Ihr ergebenster *or* untertänigster Diener *(old)* → **public servant, civil servant**

serve [sɜ:v] **VT a** *(= work for)* dienen *(+dat)*; *(= be of use)* dienlich sein *(+dat)*, nützen *(+dat)*; **he ~d his country/the company well** er hat sich um sein Land/die Firma verdient gemacht; **he has ~d our cause faithfully** er hat sich um unsere Sache verdient gemacht, er hat unserer Sache treue Dienste geleistet; **if my memory ~s me right** wenn ich mich recht erinnere; **to ~ its purpose** seinen Zweck erfüllen; **to ~ sb's purpose** jds Zwecken *(dat)* dienen; **it ~s a variety of purposes** es hat viele verschiedene Verwendungsmöglichkeiten; **it ~s no useful purpose** es hat keinen praktischen Wert; **that will ~ my needs** das ist genau (das), was ich brauche; **this box has ~d us as a table** diese Kiste hat uns *(dat)* als Tisch gedient; **it has ~d us well** es hat uns gute Dienste geleistet; **his knowledge of history ~d him well** seine Geschichtskenntnisse kamen ihm sehr zugute
b *(= work out)* abdienen, ableisten; *term of office* durchlaufen; *apprenticeship* durchmachen; *sentence* verbüßen, absitzen *(inf)*; **when he ~d his term as Prime Minister** während seiner Amtszeit als Premierminister
c *(= supply:) transport, gas etc* versorgen
d *(in shop)* bedienen; **to ~ sb with 5 kilos of potatoes** jdm 5 kg Kartoffeln bringen *or* geben; **are you being ~d?** werden Sie schon bedient?; **I'm being ~d, thank you** danke, ich werde schon bedient *or* ich bekomme schon *(inf)*
e *(esp in restaurant) food, drink* servieren; *(= put on plate)* aufgeben; *guests* bedienen; *(waiter)* bedienen, servieren *(+dat)*; *(= pour drink for)* einschenken *(+dat)*; *wine etc* einschenken; *rations* verteilen (*to* an *+acc*); **dinner is ~d** *(butler)* das Essen *or* es ist aufgetragen; *(host, hostess)* darf ich zu Tisch bitten?; **"serves three"** *(on packet*

etc) „(ergibt) drei Portionen"
f *Mass, Communion* ministrieren bei
g *(Tennis etc) ball* aufschlagen; **he ~d a double fault** er hat einen Doppelfehler gemacht
h *(Jur)* zustellen *(on sb* jdm); **to ~ a summons on sb, to ~ sb with a summons** jdn vor Gericht laden; **the landlord ~d notice (to quit) on his tenants** *(esp Brit)* der Vermieter kündigte den Mietern
i *(old: = treat)* behandeln; **to ~ sb ill** jdm einen schlechten Dienst erweisen, jdm übel mitspielen; **(it) ~s you right!** *(inf)* das geschieht dir (ganz) recht!; **it ~s him right for being so greedy** *(inf)* das geschieht ihm ganz recht, was muss er auch so gierig sein!; **it would have ~d you right if ...** *(inf)* es wäre dir ganz recht geschehen, wenn ...
j *(stallion etc)* decken
VI a *(= do duty)* dienen; **to ~ on the jury** Geschworene(r) *mf* sein; **to ~ on a committee** einem Ausschuss angehören; **to ~ on the council** Ratsmitglied *nt* sein; **to ~ as chairman** das Amt des Vorsitzenden innehaben *or* bekleiden *(form)*
b *(Mil)* dienen
c *(at table)* aufgeben; *(waiter, butler etc)* servieren *(at table* bei Tisch); **is there anyone serving at this table?** bedient hier jemand?
d to ~ as, to ~ for dienen als; **it will ~** das tuts; **it ~s to show/explain ...** das zeigt/erklärt ...; **these facts merely ~ to prove my point** diese Fakten dienen lediglich dazu, mein Argument zu beweisen
e *(Eccl)* ministrieren
f *(Tennis etc)* aufschlagen
N *(Tennis etc)* Aufschlag *m*; **whose ~ is it?** wer hat Aufschlag?

▶**serve out** VT *sep* **a** *food* ausgeben; *rations etc* vergeben, verteilen **b** *(= work out) time in army* ableisten; *apprenticeship* beenden, abschließen; *term of office* ausüben; *sentence* absitzen

▶**serve up** VT *sep* **a** *food* servieren; *rations* verteilen; **you can't serve this stuff up** *(inf)* so etwas kann man doch niemandem vorsetzen! **b** *(inf: = present)* servieren *(inf)*; *excuse* auftischen

server ['sɜːvəʳ] **N a** *(= tray)* Servierbrett *nt* **b** *(= spoon/fork)* Servierlöffel *m*, Vorlegelöffel *m*/-gabel *f*; *(= pie server)* Tortenheber *m*; *(= fish server)* Fischvorlegelöffel *m*; **salad ~s** Salatbesteck *nt* **c** *(Tennis)* Aufschläger(in) *m(f)*; **he's a strong ~** er hat einen guten Aufschlag **d** *(Eccl)* Ministrant(in), Messdiener(in) *m(f)* **e** *(Comput)* Server *m*

servery ['sɜːvərɪ] **N** *(Brit Cook)* Anrichte *f (meist als eigener Raum)*

service ['sɜːvɪs] **N a** Dienst *m*; **his faithful ~** seine treuen Dienste; **~s to one's country/the Queen** *(of soldier etc)* Dienst an seinem Vaterland/für die Königin; **her ~s to industry/the country** *(politician, industrialist)* ihre Verdienste in der Industrie/um das Land; **he died in the ~ of his country** er starb in Pflichterfüllung für sein Vaterland; **he has ten years' ~ behind him** er hat zehn Jahre Dienstzeit hinter sich *(dat)*; **to do sb a ~** jdm einen Dienst erweisen; **to do** *or* **see good ~** gute Dienste leisten; **this box did ~ as a table** diese Kiste hat schon als Tisch gedient; **to be of ~** nützlich sein; **to be of ~ to sb** jdm nützen; **it's of little ~ in an emergency** im Notfall nützt es wenig; **to be at sb's ~** jdm zur Verfügung stehen; *(person also)* jdm zu Diensten stehen; **can I be of ~ to you?** kann ich Ihnen behilflich sein?; **out of ~** außer Betrieb; **to need the ~s of a lawyer** einen Anwalt brauchen, einen Anwalt zuziehen müssen
b *(= operation)* Betrieb *m*; **to be out of ~** außer Betrieb sein; **to bring sth into ~** etw in Betrieb nehmen; **to come into ~** in Betrieb genommen werden; **"this number is not in ~"** *(US Telec)* „kein Anschluss under dieser Nummer"
c *(Mil)* Militärdienst *m*; **to see ~ as a soldier/sailor** beim Militär/in der Marine dienen; **when I was in the ~s** als ich beim Militär war; **the three ~s** die drei Waffengattungen
d *(with adj attr: = branch, department etc)* -dienst *m*; **telephone ~** Telekommunikation *f*; **telephone ~s** *(= utility)* Telekommunikationsdienste *pl*; **BT offers different telephone ~s** BT bietet eine Reihe von (Telekommunikations)-dienstleistungen an; **medical ~(s)** ärztliche Versorgung
e *(to customers)* Service *m*; *(in shop, restaurant etc)* Bedienung *f*
f *(= bus, train, plane service etc)* Bus-/Zug-/ /Flugverbindung *f*; **to increase ~s in rural areas** den Verkehr *or* die Verkehrslage in ländlichen Gebieten verbessern; **there's no ~ to Oban on Sundays** sonntags besteht kein Zug-/Busverkehr nach Oban; **the number 12 (bus) ~** die Linie 12
g *(= domestic service)* Dienst *m*, Stellung *f*; **to be in ~ (with sb)** (bei jdm) in Stellung sein, in jds Dienst *(dat)* stehen; **to go into ~ (with sb)** (bei jdm) in Stellung gehen, in jds Dienst *(acc)* treten
h *(Eccl)* Gottesdienst *m*
i *(of machines)* Wartung *f*; *(Aut: = major service)* Inspektion *f*; **my car is in for/has had a ~** mein Auto wird/wurde gewartet, mein Auto ist/war zur Inspektion
j *(= tea or coffee set)* Service *nt*
k *(Tennis)* Aufschlag *m*; **to lose one's ~** seinen Aufschlag abgeben; **whose ~ is it?** wer hat Aufschlag?
l *(Jur)* Zustellung *f*
m services PL *(commercial)* Dienstleistungen *pl*; *(gas, electricity, water)* Versorgungsnetz *nt*; **all the ~s have been cut off** Gas, Wasser und Strom sind abgestellt worden
n services PL *(Brit Mot)* Tankstelle und Raststätte *f*
VT a *car, machine* warten; **to send a car to be ~d** ein Auto warten lassen; *(major service)* ein Auto zur Inspektion geben
b *area* bedienen; *committee etc* zuarbeiten *(+dat)*; **to ~ sb's needs** jds Bedürfnissen gerecht werden
c *cow, mare* decken
d *(Fin) loan, debt* bedienen

serviceability [ˌsɜːvɪsəˈbɪlɪtɪ] **N** *(= durability)* Strapazierfähigkeit *f*; *(= practicality)* Zweckmäßigkeit *f*; *(= usability)* Brauchbarkeit *f*

serviceable ['sɜːvɪsəbl] **ADJ** *(= durable)* strapazierfähig; *(= practical)* praktisch, zweckmäßig; *(= usable)* brauchbar; *(Tech)* betriebsfähig

serviceableness ['sɜːvɪsəblnɪs] **N** Brauchbarkeit *f*, gute Verwendbarkeit; *(= durability)* Strapazierfähigkeit *f*; *(Tech)* Betriebsfähigkeit *f*

service: **service academy** **N** *(US Mil)* Militärakademie *f*; **service agreement** **N** Wartungsvertrag *m*; **service area** **N** *(Brit)* Tankstelle und Raststätte *f*; **service box** **N** *(Elec)* Hauptanschlusskasten *m*; **service break** **N** *(Tennis)* Break *nt*; **service bus** **N** Linienbus *m*; **service ceiling** **N** *(Aviat)* Dienstgipfelhöhe *f*; **service charge** **N** Bedienung *f*, Bedienungsgeld *nt*; *(of bank)* Bearbeitungsgebühr *f*; **service contract** **N a** Arbeitsvertrag *m* **b** *(= maintenance contract)* Wartungsvertrag *m*; **service court** **N** *(Tennis etc)* Aufschlagfeld *nt*; **service department** **N** Kundendienstabteilung *f*; **service dress** **N** Dienstkleidung *f*; **service elevator** **N** *(esp US)* Lasten- *or* Warenaufzug *m*; **service engineer** **N** Servicemechaniker(in) *m(f)*; **service entrance** **N** Dienstboteneingang *m*; **service family** **N** Familie *f* von Militärpersonal; **service flat** **N** *(Brit)* Appartement *nt* mit vollem Service *(Portier, Hausmeister etc)*; **service game** **N** Aufschlagspiel *nt*; **service hatch** **N** Durchreiche *f*; **service industry** **N** Dienstleistungsbranche *f*; **service life** **N** *(Tech)* Lebensdauer *f*; **service lift** **N** *(Brit)* Lasten- *or* Warenaufzug *m*; **service line** **N** *(Tennis etc)* Aufschlaglinie *f*; **serviceman** **N** Militärangehörige(r) *m*; **service module** **N** *(Space)* Versorgungsmodul *nt*; **service provider** **N** *(Comput)* Serviceprovider *m*; **service road** **N** *(for access)* Zufahrtsstraße *f*; *(for works traffic)* Versorgungsstraße *f*; *(for delivery)* Andienungsstraße *f*; **service sector** **N** *(of economy)* Dienstleistungssektor *m*; **service speed** **N** *(Naut)* Reisegeschwindigkeit *f*; **service station** **N** Tankstelle *f* (mit Reparaturwerkstatt); *(Brit: = service area)* Tankstelle und Raststätte *f*; **service switch** **N** *(Elec)* Hauptschalter *m*; **service tunnel** **N** Versorgungstunnel *m*; **servicewoman** **N** Militärangehörige *f*

servicing ['sɜːvɪsɪŋ] **N a** *(Tech)* Wartung *f*, Pflege *f*; **~ schedule** Wartungsplan *m* **b** *(= supplying)* Versorgung *f*

serviette [ˌsɜːvɪ'et] **N** *(Brit)* Serviette *f*; **~ ring** Serviettenring *m*

servile ['sɜːvaɪl] **ADJ** unterwürfig; *obedience* sklavisch

servility [sɜː'vɪlɪtɪ] **N** Unterwürfigkeit *f*

serving ['sɜːvɪŋ] **ADJ** *politician* amtierend; *(Mil) officer* diensttuend *attr*, im Dienst; *man* im Dienst **N** *(= helping of food)* Portion *f*; **"makes 4 ~s"** *(Cook)* „ergibt 4 Portionen"

serving: **serving bowl** **N** Servierschüssel *f*; **serving dish** **N** Servierplatte *f*; **serving girl** **N** Dienstmädchen *nt*; **serving hatch** **N** Durchreiche *f*; **serving spoon** **N** Vorlegelöffel *m*

servitude ['sɜːvɪtjuːd] **N** Knechtschaft *f*

servo ['sɜːvəʊ] **N** *(inf)* Servomechanismus *m* **ADJ** *attr* Servo-; **~(-assisted) brakes** Servobremsen *pl*; **~mechanism** Servomechanismus *m*; **~ steering** Servolenkung *f*

sesame ['sesəmɪ] **N a** *(Bot)* Sesam *m* **b open ~!** Sesam, öffne dich!; **an open ~** *(fig)* ein Sesam-öffne-dich *nt*

sesame: **sesame oil** **N** Sesamöl *nt*; **sesame seed** **N** Sesamkorn *nt*; **~ roll** Sesambrötchen *nt*

sessile ['sesaɪl] **ADJ** *(Bot)* festgewachsen, sessil *(spec)*

session ['seʃən] **N a** *(= meeting)* Sitzung *f*; *(Jur, Parl: = period)* Sitzungsperiode *f*; *(Parl: = term of office)* Legislaturperiode *f*; **to be in ~** eine Sitzung abhalten; *(Jur, Pol)* tagen; **to go into secret ~** eine Geheimsitzung abhalten; **a ~ of talks/negotiations** Gespräche *pl*/Verhandlungen *pl* → **quarter sessions, court**
b *(with psychiatrist etc: = period devoted to activity)* Sitzung *f*; *(= computer session)* (Arbeits)sitzung *f*; *(at doctor's, dentist's)* Behandlung *f*; *(= discussion, meeting)* Besprechung *f*; **recording ~** Aufnahme *f*; **photo ~** Fotosession *f*; **we're in for a long ~** das wird lange dauern; **I'll have a cleaning ~ tomorrow** *(inf)* morgen werde ich mal ausgiebig putzen *(inf)*
c *(= academic year, Univ)* Studienjahr *nt*; *(Sch)* Schuljahr *nt*; *(= term)* Semester/Trimester *nt*; *(esp Sch)* Halbjahr *nt*; *(= division of course)* Stunde *f*, Sitzung *f (esp Univ)*; **the afternoon ~s begin ...** der Nachmittagsunterricht fängt ... an

session musician **N** Sessionmusiker(in) *m(f)*

sestet [ses'tet] **N** *(Mus)* Sextett *nt*; *(Poet)* Sestine *f*

SET *(Internet) abbr of* **secure electronic transaction** SET *m*

set [set]
vb: pret, ptp **set**

1 NOUN
2 ADJECTIVE
3 TRANSITIVE VERB
4 INTRANSITIVE VERB
5 PHRASAL VERBS

When the verb *set* is part of a fixed combination, eg *to set on fire, to set one's cap at*, look up the other word.

1 – NOUN

a of objects Satz *m*; *(of two)* Paar *nt*; *(of underwear, cutlery, furniture, hairbrushes etc)* Garnitur *f*; *(= tea set etc)* Service *nt*; *(of tablemats etc)* Set *nt*; *(= chess or draughts set etc)* Spiel *nt*; *(= chemistry set etc)* Bastelkasten *m*; *(= painting set)* Malkasten *m*; *(= Meccano ®, construction set)* Baukasten *m*; *(of books, on one subject)* Reihe *f*, Serie *f*; *(by one author)* gesammelte Ausgabe; (=

gift or presentation set) Kassette *f*; *(of rooms)* Zimmerflucht *f*; **a set of tools** Werkzeug *nt*; **a set of teeth** ein Gebiss *nt*; **a complete set of Dickens' novels** eine Gesamtausgabe von Dickens

b [= batch] Reihe *f*; **he had a whole set of questions** er hatte eine ganze Menge *or* Reihe Fragen; **a strange set of ideas** eigenartige Ideen

c [= group of people] Kreis *m*; *(pej)* Bande *f*; *(Brit Sch: = stream)* Kurs *m*; **the literary set** die Literaten *pl*; **the golfing set** die Golffreunde *pl*; **that set of people** dieser Personenkreis; **a nice set of people** nette Leute *pl*

d [Math] Reihe *f*; *(in set theory)* Menge *f*

e [Sport Tennis] Satz *m*; *(Table Tennis)* Spiel *nt*

f [= part of concert] Programmnummer *f*

g [of play] *(Theat)* Bühnenbild *nt*; *(Film)* Szenenaufbau *m*; **to be on the set** bei den Dreharbeiten sein

h [= appliance] *TV, radio etc* Gerät *nt*, Apparat *m*; *(= headset)* Paar *nt*; **set of headphones** Kopfhörer *m*

i [Dancing] Gruppe *f*; **to make up a set** eine Gruppe bilden; **they then move up the set** sie rücken (in der Gruppe) auf

j [= position] *of head, shoulders* Haltung *f*; **the set of sb's mouth** jds Mundstellung *f*

k [= hairset] Frisur *f*, Form *f*; **to have a shampoo and set** sich *(dat)* die Haare waschen und legen lassen

l [of wind] Richtung *f*

m [Hunt] Vorstehen *nt*; **to make a dead set at sb** *(dated, = try to attract)* sich an jdn ranmachen *(inf)*

n [US] = **sett**

2 – ADJECTIVE

a [= likely]

♦ **to be set to he is set to become the new champion** ihm werden die besten Chancen auf den Meistertitel eingeräumt; **the talks are set to continue all week** die Gespräche werden voraussichtlich die ganze Woche über andauern

b [= ready] fertig, bereit

♦ **all set are we all set?** sind wir alle fertig *or* bereit?; **all set?** alles klar?; **to be all set for sth** für etw gerüstet *or* auf etw *(acc)* vorbereitet sein; *(= mentally prepared)* auf etw *(acc)* eingestellt sein; **to be all set to do sth** *(= have made all the arrangements)* sich darauf eingerichtet haben, etw zu tun; *(= mentally prepared)* fest entschlossen *or* drauf und dran sein, etw zu tun; **we're all set to go** wir sind so weit *or* startklar; **with their cameras all set** mit schussbereiten Kameras

c [= rigid] starr; *face* starr, unbeweglich; *expression* feststehend; *forms* starr, fest; *habit, custom* fest; **to be set in one's ways** in seinen Gewohnheiten festgefahren sein

d [= fixed] *time, place* festgesetzt, bestimmt, ausgemacht *(inf)*; **one of my set tasks is ...** eine der mir übertragenen Aufgaben ist es ...; **set hours for studying** feste Zeiten zum Lernen; **his set purpose was to ...** er war fest entschlossen, zu ...; **set menu** Tageskarte *f*; **set lunch/meal** Tagesgericht *nt*; **set speech** Standardrede *f*; **set phrase** feststehender Ausdruck

♦ **set piece** *(in novel, play)* Standardszene *nt*; *(in exam)* Pflichtstück *nt*; *(in football match etc)* Standardsituation *f*; *(= fireworks)* Feuerwerksbild *nt*

e [= prescribed] festgesetzt, fest; *task* bestimmt; *essay topic* vorgegeben, bestimmt; **set book(s)** Pflichtlektüre *f*; **set song** Pflichtstück *nt*

f [= resolved] entschlossen; **to be set on sth** zu etw entschlossen sein; **to be set on doing sth** entschlossen sein, etw zu tun; **to be dead set on sth/doing sth** etw auf Biegen oder Brechen haben/tun wollen; **to be (dead) set against sth/doing sth/sb doing sth** (absolut) gegen etw sein/dagegen sein, etw zu tun/dagegen sein, dass jd etw tut; **she is far too set on getting her own way** sie will immer nur ihren eigenen Kopf durchsetzen

3 – TRANSITIVE VERB

a [= place] stellen; *(on its side, flat)* legen; *(deliberately, carefully)* setzen; **to set the chairs by the window** die Stühle ans Fenster setzen *or* stellen; **he set the stones carefully on top of each other** er setzte *or* legte die Steine vorsichtig aufeinander; **to set the child on his feet** das Kind auf die Beine stellen; **I set him on his way** *(lit)* ich schickte ihn los; *(fig)* ich habe ihm zu einem guten Anfang verholfen; **I set him/his books above all others** ich schätze ihn/seine Bücher höher ein als alle anderen; **to set a value/price on sth** *(lit, fig)* einen Wert/Preis für etw festsetzen; **to set a high value on sth** einer Sache *(dat)* großen Wert beimessen, etw hoch bewerten

♦ **to set free to set sb free** jdn freilassen

♦ **to set right to set sth/things right** etw/die Dinge in Ordnung bringen; **to set sb right (about sth)** jdn (in Bezug auf etw *acc*) berichtigen

♦ **to set straight to set sb straight** jdn berichtigen

b [= cause] **to set sth going/in motion** etw in Gang/Bewegung bringen

♦ **to set sb doing sth** jdn dazu veranlassen, etw zu tun; **that set me thinking** das veranlasste mich nachzudenken

♦ **to set sb to doing** *or* **to do sth** jdn etw tun lassen; **to set oneself to doing** *or* **to do sth** sich daranmachen, etw zu tun

c [= regulate] *timer, controls* einstellen (*at* auf *+acc*); *clock* stellen (*by* nach, *to* auf *+acc*); *trap, snare (lit)* aufstellen; *(fig)* stellen (*for sb* jdm)

d [= prescribe, impose] *target, limit etc* festsetzen, festlegen; *task, question* stellen (*sb* jdm); *homework* aufgeben; *exam, exam questions* zusammenstellen; *book for exam* vorschreiben; **Hamlet has not been set this year** Hamlet steht dieses Jahr nicht auf dem Lehrplan; **to set sb a problem** *(lit)* jdm ein Problem aufgeben; *(fig)* jdn vor ein Problem stellen; **he was set a target** ihm wurde ein Soll vorgeschrieben; **England was set 75 to win** *(Sport)* England brauchte 75 (Punkte), um zu gewinnen

e [= arrange] *time, date* festsetzen, ausmachen *(inf)*, anberaumen *(form)*; *place* bestimmen, ausmachen *(inf)*; **to set the date (of the wedding)** die Hochzeit festsetzen; **the attack was set for midnight** der Angriff war für Mitternacht geplant

f [= establish] *record* aufstellen; *fashion* bestimmen

g [= mount] *gem* fassen (*in* in *+dat*); *piece of jewellery* besetzen (*with* mit); *windowpane* einsetzen (*in* in *+acc*)

h [= embed firmly] einlegen (*in* in *+acc*); *(in ground)* einlassen (*in* in *+acc*); **to set stones in concrete** Steine einzementieren

i [= locate] **to be set in the valley** im Tal liegen; **a house set on a hillside** ein am Berghang gelegenes Haus; **his eyes were set wide apart** er hatte weit auseinanderliegende Augen; **the book is set in Rome** das Buch spielt in Rom; **he set the book in 19th century France/in Rome** er wählte das Frankreich des 19. Jahrhunderts/Rom als Schauplatz für sein Buch; **she set the action in the 16th century/in Vienna** sie verlegte die Handlung ins 16. Jahrhundert/nach Wien

j [= lay with cutlery] *table* decken; **to set places for 14** für 14 decken, 14 Gedecke auflegen

k [= station] *guard* aufstellen; **to set a guard on sb/sth** jdn/etw bewachen lassen

l [= make solid] *jam* fest werden lassen, gelieren lassen; *concrete* hart werden lassen; *dye* fixieren

m [bone] *(Med)* einrichten; *dislocated joint* einrenken

n [hair] legen, eindrehen

o [Typ] setzen, absetzen *(spec)*

p [set expressions] **to set sth to music** etw vertonen; **to set a dog/the police on sb** einen Hund/die Polizei auf jdn ansetzen *or* hetzen

4 – INTRANSITIVE VERB

a [= go down] *sun, moon* untergehen; **his star is setting** *(fig)* sein Stern ist im Sinken

b [= harden] *jelly, cement* hart *or* fest werden; *(jam)* fest werden, gelieren; *(bone)* zusammenwachsen

c [dye] farbbeständig werden

d [Dancing] **to set to one's partner** sich dem Partner zuwenden

e [Hunt] vorstehen

5 – PHRASAL VERBS

▸ **set about** VI *+prep obj* **a** *(= begin)* sich machen an *(+acc)*, anfangen; *(= tackle)* anfassen, anpacken *(inf)*, anstellen *(inf)*; **to set about doing sth** *(= begin)* sich daranmachen, etw zu tun; **how do I set about getting a loan?** wie fasse *or* packe *(inf)* ich es an, um ein Darlehen zu bekommen? **b** *(= attack)* herfallen über *(+acc)*

▸ **set against** VT *sep +prep obj* **a** *(= influence against)* einnehmen gegen; *(= cause trouble between)* Zwietracht säen zwischen *(+dat)*; **to set oneself against sth** sich einer Sache *(dat)* entgegenstellen; **the civil war set friend against friend/father against son** der Bürgerkrieg ließ Freunde/Väter und Söhne zu Feinden werden → *also* **set 2 c b** *(= balance against)* gegenüberstellen *(+dat)*; **his story must be set against the evidence of the police** man muss seine Darstellung den Aussagen der Polizei gegenüberhalten

▸ **set apart** VT *sep* **a** *(= distinguish)* abheben, unterscheiden; **he felt set apart from the other boys** er fühlte, dass er nicht so war wie die anderen Jungen **b** *(= save) money* beiseitelegen, auf die Seite legen; *time* einplanen

▸ **set aside** VT *sep* **a** *newspaper, book etc* zur Seite legen; *work, money* beiseitelegen; *time* einplanen; *land, room* reservieren; *plans* aufschieben; *differences, quarrels, hostilities* beiseiteschieben, begraben; *dislike* vergessen; *mistrust, bitterness* sich frei machen von; *formality* verzichten auf *(+acc)*; *rules, protest* übergehen, außer Acht lassen **b** *(Jur)* aufheben; *will* für nichtig *or* ungültig erklären

▸ **set back** VT *sep* **a** *(= place at a distance)* zurücksetzen; **the house is set back from the road** das Haus liegt etwas von der Straße ab *or* liegt nicht direkt an der Straße **b** *(= retard)* verzögern, behindern; *(by a certain length of time)* zurückwerfen; **the plans have been set back (by) 2 years** die Pläne sind um 2 Jahre zurückgeworfen **c** *(inf: = cost)* kosten; **the dinner set me back £35** das Essen hat mich £ 35 gekostet *or* ärmer gemacht *(inf)*

▸ **set down** VT *sep* **a** *(= put down) suitcase, passenger* absetzen **b** *(in writing)* (schriftlich) niederlegen **c** *(= attribute)* zuschreiben *(to dat)* **d** *(= classify as)* **to set sb/sth down as sth** jdn/etw für etw halten

▸ **set forth** VT *sep (= expound) theory, plan* darlegen VI *(liter)* ausziehen *(old)*

▸ **set in** VI *(= start)* einsetzen; *(panic)* ausbrechen; *(night)* anbrechen; *(Med, gangrene, complications)* sich einstellen; **the rain has set in** es hat sich eingeregnet VT *sep* **a** *(Typ, = indent)* einrücken **b** *(Sew) sleeve* einsetzen; *pocket* einarbeiten *(into* in *+acc)*

▸ **set off** VT *sep* **a** *(= ignite) bomb, firework* losgehen lassen

b *(= start)* führen zu; *speculation, quarrel* auslösen; **that set us all off laughing** das brachte uns *(acc)* alle zum Lachen; **to set sb off on a new line of thought** jdn auf einen neuen Gedanken bringen; **her remark set him off on a story** auf ihre Bemerkung hin erzählte er eine Geschichte; **don't set him off!** lass ihn nur nicht damit anfangen!; **that really set him off** daraufhin legte er richtig los *or* war er nicht mehr zu bremsen *(inf)*

c *(= offset)* **to set sth off against sth** etw einer Sache *(dat)* gegenüberstellen

d *(= enhance)* hervorheben; **to set sth off from sth** etw von etw abheben

VI *(= depart)* sich auf den Weg machen, aufbrechen; *(car, in car)* losfahren; **to set off on a journey** eine Reise antreten; **to set off for Spain** nach Spanien abfahren; **the police set**

off in pursuit die Polizei nahm die Verfolgung auf

▶**set on** VT *sep +prep obj dogs* hetzen *or* ansetzen auf *(+acc)* → **eye** VI *+prep obj* = **set upon**

▶**set out** VT *sep (= display)* ausbreiten; *(= arrange) chess pieces* aufstellen; *printed matter, essay* anordnen, anlegen; *(= state)* darlegen, darstellen VI **a** *(= depart)* = **set off VI b** *(= intend)* beabsichtigen; *(= start)* sich daranmachen

▶**set to** VI *(= start working, fighting)* loslegen *(inf)*; *(= start eating)* reinhauen *(inf)*; **they set to and repaired it** sie machten sich an die Arbeit und reparierten es VI *+prep obj* **to set to work** sich an die Arbeit machen; **to set to work doing** *or* **to do sth** beginnen, etw zu tun

▶**set up** VI *(= establish oneself)* **to set up as a doctor** sich als Arzt niederlassen; **to set up in business** sein eigenes Geschäft aufmachen; **to set up for oneself** sich selbstständig machen

VT *sep* **a** *(= place in position) statue, post* aufstellen; *(= assemble, get ready) tent, stall, apparatus* aufbauen; *(Typ)* einrichten; *(fig: = arrange) meeting* arrangieren, vereinbaren; *robbery* planen, vorbereiten; **to set sth up for sb** etw für jdn vorbereiten

b *(= establish)* gründen; *school, office, system* einrichten; *inquiry* veranlassen, anordnen; *record* aufstellen; **to set sb up in business** jdm zu einem Geschäft verhelfen; **to set sb up in an apartment** jdm eine Wohnung einrichten; **to set sb up as sth** (es) jdm ermöglichen, etw zu werden; **to set oneself up as sth** sich als etw aufspielen; **to be set up for life** für sein ganzes Leben ausgesorgt haben; **to be well set up** sich gutstehen; **to set up camp** die Zelte *or* das Lager aufschlagen; **they've set up home in Glasgow/Spain** sie haben sich in Glasgow/Spanien niedergelassen → **house, shop**

c *(= restore to health)* guttun *(+dat)*; **a weekend at the seaside will set you up again** ein Wochenende am Meer wird dich schon wieder auf die Beine bringen

d *(= raise) cry, protest, cheer* anstimmen; **to set up a commotion** allgemeinen Aufruhr auslösen *or* hervorrufen; *(= make noise)* Krach machen

e *(= cause) infection, reaction* auslösen, verursachen

f *(inf: = frame)* **to set sb up** jdm etwas anhängen; **I've been set up** das will mir einer anhängen *(inf) or* in die Schuhe schieben

g *(inf: = rig)* **the fight had been set up** der Kampf war von vornherein eine abgekartete Sache

▶**set upon** VI *+prep obj* überfallen; *(animal)* anfallen

set: **set-aside** *(Agr)* N **a** *(= taking land out of cultivation)* Flächenstilllegung *f* **b** *(= area of land)* stillgelegte Fläche; **setback** N Rückschlag *m*; **set designer** N *(Theat)* Bühnenbildner(in) *m(f)*; **setdown** N **a** *(fig: = damper)* Dämpfer *m (inf, fig)* **b** *(= dressing-down)* Rüffel *m (inf)*; **set-in** ADJ *sleeve* eingesetzt; *pocket* eingearbeitet; **set-piece specialist** N *(Ftbl)* Freistoß- *or* Eckballspezialist(in) *m(f)*; **set point** N Set- *or* Satzpunkt *m*; **set square** N Zeichendreieck *nt*

sett, *(US)* **set** [set] N *(= badger's den)* Bau *m*

settee [se'tiː] N Couch *f*, Sofa *nt*

setter ['setə'] N **a** *(= typesetter)* Setzer(in) *m(f)* **b** *(= dog)* Setter *m*

set theory N Mengenlehre *f*

setting ['setɪŋ] N **a** *(of sun, moon)* Untergang *m* **b** *(= background, atmosphere)* Rahmen *m*; *(= environment, surroundings)* Umgebung *f*; *(of novel etc)* Schauplatz *m*; **a film with a medieval ~** ein Film, der im Mittelalter spielt **c** *(of jewel)* Fassung *f* **d** *(= place setting)* Gedeck *nt* **e** *(= position on dial etc)* Einstellung *f (also Comput)*; **advanced ~s** erweiterte Einstellungen *pl*; **regional ~s** Ländereinstellungen *pl* **f** *(= musical arrangement)* Vertonung *f* **g** *(Hairdressing)* Legen *nt*

setting lotion N (Haar)festiger *m*

setting-up ['setɪŋ'ʌp] N *(of machine etc)* Aufstellen *nt*, Montage *f*; *(Comput: of program etc)* Installation *f*

setting-up exercises PL *(US Sport)* Gymnastik *f*, gymnastische Übungen *pl*

settle[1] ['setl] N (Wand)bank *f*

settle[2] VT **a** *(= decide)* entscheiden; *(= sort out)* regeln, erledigen; *problem, question, points* klären; *dispute, differences, quarrel* beilegen, schlichten; *doubts* ausräumen, beseitigen; *date, place* vereinbaren, ausmachen *(inf)*; *venue* festlegen *or* -setzen; *deal* abschließen; *price* sich einigen auf *(+acc)*, aushandeln; *terms* aushandeln; **the result of the game was ~d in the first half** das Ergebnis des Spiels stand schon in der ersten Halbzeit fest; **when my future is ~d** wenn sich meine Zukunft entschieden hat; **to ~ one's affairs** seine Angelegenheiten in Ordnung bringen; **to ~ an estate** *(Jur)* die Verteilung des Nachlasses regeln; **to ~ a case out of court** einen Fall außergerichtlich klären; **that's ~d then** das ist also klar *or* geregelt; **that ~s it** damit wäre der Fall (ja wohl) erledigt; *(angry)* jetzt reichts

b *(= pay) bill* begleichen, bezahlen; *account* ausgleichen

c *(= calm) nerves, stomach* beruhigen; **we need rain to ~ the dust** wir brauchen Regen, damit sich der Staub setzt

d *(= place carefully)* legen; *(in upright position)* stellen; *(= make comfortable for sleep etc) child, invalid* versorgen; *pillow* zurechtlegen; **to ~ oneself comfortably in an armchair** es sich *(dat)* in einem Sessel bequem machen; **she ~d her head back against the headrest** sie lehnte ihren Kopf zurück an die Kopfstütze; **to ~ oneself to doing sth** sich daranmachen, etw zu tun; **to ~ one's gaze on sb/sth** seinen Blick auf jdm/etw ruhen lassen

e *(= establish: in house)* unterbringen; **to get one's daughter ~d with a husband** seine Tochter verheiraten *or* unter die Haube bringen *(inf)*

f **to ~ sb into a house/job** jdm helfen, sich häuslich einzurichten/sich in eine Stellung einzugewöhnen; **we'd just ~d the children into a new school** wir hatten die Kinder gerade in einer neuen Schule gut untergebracht → **settle in VT**

g *(= colonize) land* besiedeln; *(= set up) people* ansiedeln

h *(form)* **to ~ money/property on sb** jdm Geld/Besitz überschreiben *or* übertragen; *(in will)* jdm Geld/Besitz vermachen; **to ~ an annuity on sb** für jdn eine Rente aussetzen

i *(inf: = put an end to)* **I'll soon ~ his nonsense** ich werde ihm schon die Flausen austreiben; **I'll soon ~ him** dem werd ichs geben *(inf)*; *(verbally also)* dem werd ich was erzählen *(inf)*; **that ~d him!** da hatte er sein Fett weg *(inf)*

VI **a** *(= put down roots)* sesshaft werden; *(in country, town, profession)* sich niederlassen; *(as settler)* sich ansiedeln; *(in house)* sich häuslich niederlassen, sich einrichten; *(= feel at home)* *(in house, town, country)* sich einleben *(into* in *+dat)*; *(in job, surroundings)* sich eingewöhnen *(into* in *+dat)*; **to ~ into a way of life** sich an einen Lebensstil gewöhnen; **to ~ into a habit** sich *(dat)* etw angewöhnen; **as he ~d into middle age** als er älter und reifer wurde

b *(= become less variable: weather)* beständig werden; **the wind ~d in the east** der Wind kam schließlich aus Osten

c *(= become calm, child, matters, stomach)* sich beruhigen; *(panic, excitement)* sich legen; *(= become less excitable or restless)* zur Ruhe kommen, ruhiger werden; **he couldn't ~ to anything** er konnte sich auf nichts konzentrieren

d *(= come to rest, sit down, person, bird, insect)* sich niederlassen *or* setzen; *(dust)* sich setzen *or* legen; *(= sink slowly, subside, building, walls)* sich senken; *(ground, liquid, sediment, coffee grounds)* sich setzen; *(wine)* sich beruhigen; **to ~ comfortably in an armchair** es sich *(dat)* in einem Sessel gemütlich *or* bequem machen; **the boat ~d in the water** das Boot hörte auf zu schaukeln; **fog/silence ~d over the city** Nebel/Stille legte sich über die Stadt *or* breitete sich über der Stadt aus; **gloom ~d over the meeting** eine bedrückte Stimmung breitete sich in der Versammlung aus → **dust**

e *(Jur)* **to ~ (out of court)** sich vergleichen

f *(= pay)* bezahlen → *also* **settle with**

▶**settle back** VI sich (gemütlich) zurücklehnen

▶**settle down** VI **a** → **settle[2] VI a**; **it's time he settled down** es ist Zeit, dass er ein geregeltes Leben anfängt *or* dass er zur Ruhe kommt; **to marry and settle down** heiraten und sesshaft *or* häuslich werden; **to settle down at school/in a new house** sich an einer Schule/in einem Haus einleben; **to settle down in a new job** sich in einer neuen Stellung eingewöhnen; **he ought to settle down with a steady job** er sollte sich *(dat)* endlich eine feste Stellung suchen; **they have settled down in Spain** sie haben sich in Spanien niedergelassen; **settle down, children!** ruhig, Kinder!

b = **settle[2] VI c**

c **to settle down to work** sich an die Arbeit machen *or* setzen; **to settle down for a chat** sich zu einem Schwatz zusammensetzen; **to settle down for the night** sich schlafen legen; **to settle down to watch TV** es sich *(dat)* vor dem Fernseher gemütlich machen

VT *sep* **a** *(= calm down)* beruhigen

b *baby* hinlegen; *patient* versorgen; **to settle oneself down to work** sich an die Arbeit machen *or* setzen; **to settle oneself down to finish the job** sich daranmachen, die Arbeit fertig zu machen; **the cat settled itself down for the night** die Katze kuschelte sich zum Schlafen zurecht; **the campers settled themselves down for the night** die Zeltenden richteten alles für die Nacht her

▶**settle for** VI *+prep obj* sich zufriedengeben mit; **I'd settle for a diamond necklace** ich wäre schon mit einem Diamanthalsband zufrieden; **I think I'll settle for this one** ich glaube, ich nehme doch das da; **she won't settle for anything less** mit weniger gibt sie sich nicht zufrieden; **he was glad to settle for a bronze medal** er war schon mit einer Bronzemedaille zufrieden

▶**settle in** VI *(in house, town)* sich einleben; *(in job, school)* sich eingewöhnen; **how are you settling in?** haben Sie sich schon eingelebt/eingewöhnt? VT *sep* **to settle sb in** jdm helfen, sich einzuleben/sich einzugewöhnen

▶**settle on** *or* **upon** VI *+prep obj* sich entscheiden für, sich entschließen zu; *(= agree on)* sich einigen auf *(+acc)*

▶**settle up** VI (be)zahlen; **to settle up with sb** *(lit, fig)* mit jdm abrechnen VT *sep bill* bezahlen

▶**settle with** VI *+prep obj (lit, fig)* abrechnen mit VT *sep +prep obj* **a** *debt etc* abrechnen mit; **to settle one's account with sb** *(lit, fig)* mit jdm abrechnen **b** *(= come to agreement with)* **to settle sth with sb** sich mit jdm auf etw *(acc)* einigen

settled ['setld] ADJ *weather* beständig; *way of life* geregelt; *opinions* fest; *procedure* feststehend, festgelegt; **to be ~** in geregelten Verhältnissen leben, etabliert sein; *(in place)* sesshaft sein; *(= have permanent job etc)* festen Fuß gefasst haben; *(in a house)* sich häuslich niedergelassen haben; *(= be less restless)* ruhiger *or* gesetzter sein; **to feel ~** sich wohlfühlen; **I don't feel very ~ at the moment** ich hänge zurzeit in der Luft *(inf)*, ich fühle mich zurzeit verunsichert

settlement ['setlmənt] ✪ 20.7 N **a** *(act, = deciding)* Entscheidung *f*; *(= sorting out)* Regelung *f*, Erledigung *f*; *(of problem, question etc)* Klärung *f*; *(of dispute, differences etc)* Beilegung *f*, Schlichtung *f*; *(of estate)* Regelung *f*; *(of bill, claim)* Bezahlung *f*; *(of account)* Ausgleich *m*; *(= contract, agreement etc)* Übereinkunft *f*, Übereinkommen *nt*; **an out-of-court ~, a ~ out of court** *(Jur)* ein außergerichtlicher Vergleich; **to reach a ~** sich einigen, einen Vergleich treffen; **the terms of the ~** *(Jur)* die Bedingungen des Übereinkom-

mens; **this payment is made in ~ of all claims** mit dieser Zahlung werden alle Forderungen beglichen; **in ~ of our account** zum Ausgleich unseres Kontos; **~ discount** Skonto *nt or m*
b *(= settling of money)* Übertragung *f*, Überschreibung *f* *(on auf +acc)*; *(esp in will)* Vermächtnis *nt*; *(of annuity, income)* Aussetzung *f*; *(= document, agreement)* Schenkungsvertrag *m*; **he receives £10,000 by the ~** auf ihn wurden £ 10.000 übertragen *or* überschrieben, ihm wurden £ 10.000 vermacht
c *(of building)* Senkung *f*; *(of sediment)* Absetzen *nt*
d *(= colony, village)* Siedlung *f*, Niederlassung *f*; *(= act of settling persons)* Ansiedlung *f*; *(= colonization)* Besiedlung *f*
e *(US: also* **settlement house**, *= institution)* Wohlfahrtseinrichtung *f*; *(= building)* Gemeindezentrum *nt*

settlement day N *(Econ)* Abrechnungstag *m*

settler ['setlə'] N Siedler(in) *m(f)*

settling day ['setlɪŋ,deɪ] N *(Econ)* Abrechnungstag *m*

set-to ['settuː] N *(Brit inf)* Krach *m*, Streiterei *f (inf)*; **to have a ~ with sb** sich mit jdm in die Wolle kriegen *(inf)*

set-top box ['settɒp'bɒks] N *(TV)* Digitalreceiver *m*, d-box® *f*

setup ['setʌp] N **a** *(inf: = situation)* Umstände *pl*; *(= way of organizing things)* Organisation *f*, Drum und Dran *nt (inf)*; **it's a funny ~** das sind (vielleicht) komische Zustände!; **what's the ~ here?** wie verhält sich *or* läuft *(inf)* das hier (alles)?; **she didn't quite understand the ~** sie verstand die Sachlage nicht ganz **b** *(= equipment)* Geräte *pl*, Instrumente *pl*; *(Comput)* Setup *nt*; **page ~** Seite einrichten **c** *(US, for drinks)* Zubehör *nt* für Cocktails *etc* **d** *(inf: = rigged contest)* abgekartete Sache

setup CD N *(Comput)* Installations-CD *f*, Setup-CD *f*

setup file N *(Comput)* Einrichtungsdatei *f*, Setupdatei *f*

seven ['sevn] ADJ sieben; **to sail the ~ seas** die sieben Meere befahren; **he's got the ~-year itch** *(inf)* er ist im verflixten siebenten Jahr N Sieben *f* → *also* **six**

sevenfold ['sevnfəʊld] ADJ siebenfach ADV um das Siebenfache

seventeen ['sevn'tiːn] ADJ siebzehn; **17-inch monitor** *(Comput)* 17-Zoll-Monitor *m* N Siebzehn *f* → *also* **sixteen**

seventeenth ['sevn'tiːnθ] ADJ siebzehnte(r, s); **a ~ part** ein Siebzehntel *nt* N *(= fraction)* Siebzehntel *nt*; *(of series)* Siebzehnte(r, s)

seventh ['sevnθ] ADJ siebte(r, s); **a ~ part** ein Siebtel *nt*; **Seventh-Day Adventist** Adventist(in) *m(f)* vom Siebenten Tag N *(= fraction)* Siebtel *nt*; *(in series)* Siebte(r, s); *(Mus, = interval)* Septime *f*; *(= chord)* Septimenakkord *m* → *also* **sixth**

seventhly ['sevnθlɪ] ADV siebtens

seventieth ['sevntɪɪθ] ADJ siebzigste(r, s) N *(= fraction)* Siebzigstel *nt*; *(in series)* Siebzigste(r, s)

seventy ['sevntɪ] ADJ siebzig N Siebzig *f*

seventy-eight [,sevntɪ'eɪt] N Achtundsiebzig *f*; *(= record)* Achtundsiebziger(platte) *f*, 78er-Platte *f*

sever ['sevə'] VT *(= cut through)* durchtrennen; *(violently)* durchschlagen; *(= cut off)* abtrennen; *(violently)* abschlagen; *(fig: = break off) ties* lösen; *relations, links, friendship* abbrechen; *communications* unterbrechen; *(= divide) nation* teilen; **the wires were ~ed in the storm** beim Sturm sind die Leitungen (durch)gerissen; **to ~ sb from sb/sth** jdn von jdm/etw trennen; **to ~ sth from sth** etw von etw abtrennen VI (durch)reißen

several ['sevrəl] ADJ **a** *(= some)* einige, mehrere; *(= different, diverse, various)* verschiedene; **I went with ~ others** ich ging mit einigen *or* ein paar anderen zusammen; **I've seen him ~ times/~ times already** ich habe ihn einige Male gesehen/schon mehrmals *or* mehrere Male gesehen; **there are ~ ways of doing it** das kann man auf mehrere *or* verschiedene Arten machen; **I'll need ~ more** ich brauche noch einige **b** *(dated: = respective)* jeweilig; **they went their ~ ways** jeder ging seinen Weg, sie gingen ihrer Wege *(old)*
PRON einige; **~ of the houses** einige (der) Häuser; **~ of us** einige von uns

severally ['sevrəlɪ] ADV einzeln

severance ['sevərəns] N **a** *(= cutting through)* Durchtrennen *nt*; *(violently)* Durchschlagen *nt*; *(= cutting off)* Abtrennen *nt*; *(violently)* Abschlagen *nt*; *(fig: = breaking off) (of ties)* Lösen *nt*; *(of relations, links, friendship)* Abbruch *m*; *(of communications)* Unterbrechung *f* **b** *(also* **severance package**, *Econ)* Abfindung *f*, Abfindungspaket *nt*

severance pay N Abfindung *f*

severe [sɪ'vɪə'] ADJ *(+er)* **a** *(= grave, grievous) defeat, hardship, damage, pressure* schwer; *illness, injury, blow, loss* schwer, schlimm; *pain* stark, heftig; *problem* schwer, ernsthaft; *consequence* schwerwiegend, schwer wiegend; **to have a ~ cold** eine schwere Erkältung haben
b *(= strict) critic, law, punishment, test* hart; *penalty* schwer(wiegend), schwer (wiegend); *discipline* streng, eisern; *reprimand, criticism* scharf
c *(= harsh) weather* rau; *weather conditions* schwer, schwierig; *winter* streng, hart; *frost, drought* schwer, schlimm; *storm* schwer, stark
d *(= grim, serious) person, manner* streng; *expression* ernst; **to be ~ with sb** streng mit jdm sein; **to be ~ on sb** hart über jdn urteilen
e *(= austere) clothes, appearance, hairstyle, architecture, style* streng

severely [sɪ'vɪəlɪ] ADV **a** *(= gravely, badly) defeat, affect, damage, injure, disabled* schwer; *disrupt, limit* stark; *strain* schwer, äußerst; **a ~ ill child** ein schwer krankes Kind **b** *(= strictly) punish* hart; *criticize, reprimand* scharf; **to be ~ critical of sth** sich äußerst kritisch über etw *(acc)* äußern **c** *(= grimly, seriously)* streng **d** *(= austerely) dress* streng

severeness [sɪ'vɪənɪs] N = **severity**

severity [sɪ'verɪtɪ] N *(= strictness, of person, appearance, style)* Strenge *f*; *(= harshness, of critic, law, winter also, punishment, competition, test)* Härte *f*; *(of criticism)* Schärfe *f*; *(= seriousness, of expression, warning)* Ernst *m*; *(of illness, injury, blow, crime, storm, loss)* Schwere *f*; *(of pain, storm)* Stärke *f*, Heftigkeit *f*; *(of weather)* Rauheit *f*; **the ~ of the cold/drought** die große *or* schwere Kälte/Dürre; **the ~ of the frost** der starke *or* schwere Frost; **severities** Härten *pl*

Seville [sə'vɪl] N Sevilla *nt*

Seville orange N Bitterorange *f*, Pomeranze *f*

sew [səʊ] *pret* **sewed**, *ptp* **sewn** VT nähen; **to ~ sth on/down/together** etw an-/auf-/zusammennähen VI nähen

▶ **sew up** VT *sep* **a** *(lit)* nähen *(also Med)*; *opening* zunähen; **to sew sth up in sth** etw in etw *(acc)* einnähen **b** *(fig)* unter Dach und Fach bringen; **it's all sewn up** es ist unter Dach und Fach; **we've got the game all sewn up** das Spiel ist gelaufen *(inf)*

sewage ['sjuːɪdʒ] N Abwasser *nt*; **~ sludge** Klärschlamm *m*

sewage: **sewage disposal** N Abwasserbeseitigung *f*; **sewage farm** N Rieselfeld *nt*; **sewage works** N *sing or pl* Kläranlage *f*

sewer[1] ['səʊə'] N Näher(in) *m(f)*

sewer[2] ['sjʊə'] N *(= pipe)* Abwasserleitung *f or* -rohr *nt*; *(= main sewer)* Abwasserkanal *m*; *(fig: = smelly place)* Kloake *f*; **~ gas** Faulschlammgas *nt*; **~ rat** Wanderratte *f*; **he has a mind like a ~** *(inf)* er hat eine schmutzige *or* dreckige *(inf)* Fantasie *or* Phantasie

sewerage ['sjʊərɪdʒ] N Kanalisation *f*; *(= service)* Abwasserbeseitigung *f*; *(= sewage)* Abwässer *pl*

sewing ['səʊɪŋ] N *(= activity)* Nähen *nt*; *(= piece of work)* Näharbeit *f*

sewing: **sewing basket** N Nähkorb *m*; **sewing box** N Nähkästchen *nt*; **sewing machine** N Nähmaschine *f*; **sewing needle** N Nähnadel *f*

sewn [səʊn] *ptp of* **sew**

sex [seks] N **a** *(Biol)* Geschlecht *nt*; **what ~ is the baby?** welches Geschlecht hat das Baby? **b** *(= sexuality)* Sexualität *f*, Sex *m*; *(= sexual intercourse)* Sex *m (inf)*, Geschlechtsverkehr *m (form)*; **to teach pupils (about) ~** Schüler aufklären; **to have ~** (Geschlechts)verkehr haben
ADJ *attr* Geschlechts-, Sexual-; **~ hygiene** Sexualhygiene *f*; **~ film/scandal** Sexfilm/-skandal *m* VT das Geschlecht *(+gen)* bestimmen

sexagenarian [,seksədʒɪ'neərɪən] ADJ sechzigjährig; **~ members of the club** Klubmitglieder, die in den Sechzigern sind N Sechzigjährige(r) *mf*; **to be a ~** in den Sechzigern sein

Sexagesima [,seksə'dʒesɪmə] N Sonntag *m* Sexagesima

sex: **sex aid** N sexuelles Hilfsmittel; **sex-and-shopping** ADJ **~ novel** *(Brit) Roman der Trivialliteratur, in dessen Mittelpunkt Sex und Luxusartikel stehen*; **sex appeal** N Sexappeal *m*; **sex change** N Geschlechtsumwandlung *f*; **to have a ~** sich einer Geschlechtsumwandlung unterziehen ATTR **~ operation** (Operation *f* zur) Geschlechtsumwandlung *f*; **sex crime** N Trieb- *or* Sexualverbrechen *nt*; **sex discrimination** N Diskriminierung *f* aufgrund *or* auf Grund des Geschlechts; **sex drive** N Geschlechts- *or* Sexualtrieb *m*

sexed [sekst] ADJ **to be highly ~** einen starken Geschlechtstrieb haben → **oversexed, undersexed**

sex: **sex education** N Sexualerziehung *f*; **sex god** N Sexgott *m*; **sex goddess** N Sexgöttin *f*; **sex hormone** N Geschlechts- *or* Sexualhormon *nt*

sexily ['seksɪlɪ] ADV aufreizend, sexy *(inf)*

sex industry N Sexindustrie *f*

sexism ['seksɪzəm] N Sexismus *m*

sexist ['seksɪst] N Sexist(in) *m(f)* ADJ sexistisch

sex: **sex killing** N Sexualmord *m*; **sex kitten** N *(inf)* Sexkätzchen *nt (inf)*, Sexmieze *f (inf)*; **sexless** ADJ geschlechtslos; **sex life** N Geschlechtsleben *nt*; *(of people also)* Liebesleben *nt*; **sexlinked** ADJ geschlechtsgebunden; **sex maniac** N *(= criminal)* Triebverbrecher(in) *or* -täter(in) *m(f)*; **he/she is a ~** *(inf)* er/sie ist ganz verrückt nach *or* ganz wild auf Sex *(inf)*; **you're a ~** *(inf)* du denkst aber auch nur an Sex; **sex manual** N Sexbuch *nt*; **sex object** N Sex(ual)objekt *nt*, Lustobjekt *nt*; **sex offender** N Sexualtäter(in) *m(f)*

sexologist [sek'sɒlədʒɪst] N Sexologe *m*, Sexologin *f*

sex organ N Geschlechts- *or* Sexualorgan *nt*

sex partner N Sexualpartner(in) *m(f)*

sexpert ['sekspɜːt] N *(hum)* Experte *m*/Expertin *f* in Sachen Sex *(inf)*, Sexperte *m (hum)*, Sexpertin *f (hum)*

sexploit ['seksplɔɪt] N *(hum)* Liebesabenteuer *nt*

sexploitation [,seksplɔɪ'teɪʃən] N Kommerzialisierung *f* des Sex

sex: **sexpot** N *(inf: = woman)* Sexbombe *f (inf)*; **to be a real ~** unheimlich sexy sein *(inf)*; **sex scene** N *(Film, Theat)* Sexszene *f*; **sex shop** N Sexshop *m*, Sexladen *m*; **sex show** N Sexshow *f*; **sex-starved** ADJ *(inf)* sexhungrig; **sex symbol** N Sexsymbol *nt*

sextant ['sekstənt] N Sextant *m*

sextet(te) [seks'tet] N Sextett *nt*

sex therapy N Sexualtherapie *f*

sex therapist N Sexualtherapeut(in) *m(f)*

sextillion [sek'stɪljən] N *(Brit)* Sextillion *f*; *(US)* Trilliarde *f*

sexton ['sekstən] N Küster *m*

sex tourism N Sextourismus *m*

sextuplet [seks'tjuːplɪt] N *(= baby)* Sechsling *m*; *(Mus)* Sextole *f*

sexual ['seksjʊəl] ADJ **a** *performance, preference, violence* sexuell; **~ crime** Sexualdelikt *nt*, Sexualverbrechen *nt*; **his ~ exploits** seine Liebesabenteuer *pl*; **his/her ~ politics** seine/ihre Haltung zu Fragen der Sexualität; **~ services** sexuelle Dienste *pl* **b** *(Physiol)* Sexual-; **~ characteristics** Geschlechtsmerkmale *pl*; **~ cycle** Sexualzyklus *m*; **~ drive** *or* **urge** Geschlechts- *or* Sexualtrieb *m*; **~ maturity** Geschlechtsreife *f*

sexual: **sexual abuse** N sexueller Missbrauch; **sexual equality** N Gleichberechtigung *f* (der Geschlechter); **sexual harassment** N sexuelle Belästigung; **sexual health** N Sexualhygiene *f*; **sexual intercourse** N Geschlechtsverkehr *m*

sexuality [ˌseksjʊˈælɪtɪ] N Sexualität *f*

sexually [ˈseksjʊəlɪ] ADV **a** sexuell; **~ mature** geschlechtsreif; **~ transmitted diseases** durch Geschlechtsverkehr übertragene Krankheiten; **to be ~ harassed** sexuell belästigt werden; **to be ~ attracted to sb** sich zu jdm sexuell hingezogen fühlen **b** *(= according to gender)* **~ segregated groups** nach Geschlechtern getrennte Gruppen

sexual: **sexual offence**, *(US)* **sexual offense** N Sexualstraftat *f*; **sexual organ** N Geschlechts- *or* Sexualorgan *nt*; **sexual orientation** N sexuelle Orientierung; **sexual partner** N Sexual- *or* Intimpartner(in) *m(f)*; **sexual reproduction** N geschlechtliche Vermehrung; **sexual stereotyping** N traditionelle *or* klischeehafte Zuordnung der Geschlechterrollen

sex worker N *(euph)* Prostituierte *f*

sexy [ˈseksɪ] ADJ *(+er)* **a** *(inf) person, clothes* sexy *inv usu pred (inf)*; *smile, pose also* aufreizend; *joke, film* erotisch; **the sexiest girl in the class** das Mädchen in der Klasse, das am meisten Sexappeal hat **b** *(inf: = exciting)* geil *(sl)*

Seychelles [seɪˈʃelz] PL Seychellen *pl*

SF **a** *abbr of* **science fiction** **b** *(Ir Pol) abbr of* **Sinn Féin**

SFO **a** *(Brit) abbr of* **Serious Fraud Office** **b** *(US) abbr of* **San Francisco**

s.g. *abbr of* **specific gravity**

sgraffito [sgræˈfiːtəʊ] N Sgraffito *nt*

sgt *abbr of* **sergeant**

sh [ʃ] INTERJ sch(t)

shabbily [ˈʃæbɪlɪ] ADV *(lit, fig)* schäbig

shabbiness [ˈʃæbɪnɪs] N *(lit, fig)* Schäbigkeit *f*

shabby [ˈʃæbɪ] ADJ *(+er) (lit, fig)* schäbig; **they were ~-genteel** sie gehörten zur verarmten Oberschicht; **that was a ~ trick!** das war ein schäbiger *or* mieser Trick!

shack [ʃæk] N Hütte *f*, Schuppen *m* VI *(inf)* **to ~ up with sb** mit jdm zusammenziehen; **to ~ up together** zusammenziehen

shackle [ˈʃækl] N **a** *usu pl* Kette *f*, Fessel *f* *(also fig)* **b** *(Tech)* Schäkel *m* VT in Ketten legen; **they were ~d together/to the wall** sie waren aneinandergekettet/an die Wand (an)gekettet; **to ~ sb with sth** *(fig)* jdn mit etw belasten; **to be ~d by sth** *(fig)* an etw *(acc)* gebunden sein; **to be ~d with sth** die Belastung einer Sache *(gen)* haben

shad [ʃæd] N Alse *f*

shade [ʃeɪd] N **a** Schatten *m*; **30° in the ~** 30 Grad im Schatten; **to give** *or* **provide ~** Schatten spenden; **the ~s of night** *(liter)* der Schatten der Nacht *(liter)*; **to put sb/sth in the ~** *(fig)* jdn/etw in den Schatten stellen

b *(= lampshade)* (Lampen)schirm *m*; *(= eye shade)* Schild *nt*, Schirm *m*; *(esp US: = blind)* Jalousie *f*; *(= roller blind)* Springrollo *nt*; *(outside house)* Markise *f*; **~s** *(inf: = sunglasses)* Sonnenbrille *f*

c *(of colour)* (Farb)ton *m*; *(fig, of opinion)* Schattierung *f*; *(of meaning)* Nuance *f*; **turquoise is a ~ of blue** Türkis ist ein blauer Farbton; **a brighter ~ of red** ein leuchtenderer Rotton; **a new ~ of lipstick** ein neuer Farbton für Lippenstifte; **~-card** Farb(en)probe *f*; **of all ~s and hues** *(lit)* in den verschiedensten Farben, in allen Schattierungen; *(fig)* aller Schattierungen

d *(= small quantity)* Spur *f*; **it's a ~ long/too long** es ist etwas lang/etwas *or* eine Spur zu lang

e *(liter: = ghost)* Schatten *m*; **the ~s** *(Myth)* die Bewohner *pl* des Schattenreiches; *(= Hades)* das Reich der Schatten, das Schattenreich; **~s of Professor Jones!** *(inf)* wie mich das an Professor Jones erinnert!

VT **a** *(= cast shadow on)* Schatten werfen auf *(+acc)*, beschatten *(geh)*; *(= protect from light, sun)* abschirmen; *lamp, window* abdunkeln; **that part is ~d by a tree** der Teil liegt im Schatten eines Baumes; **to be ~d from the sun** im Schatten liegen *or* sein; *(protected against sun)* vor der Sonne geschützt sein; **he ~d his eyes with his hand** er hielt die Hand vor die Augen(, um nicht geblendet zu werden); **to ~ the truth** die Wahrheit beschönigen

b *(= darken with lines)* schraffieren; *(for artistic effect)* schattieren; **to ~ sth in** etw ausschraffieren; *(= colour in)* etw ausmalen; **to ~ one colour** *(Brit) or* **color** *(US)* **into another** eine Farbe langsam in die andere übergehen lassen

c *(inf) (= narrowly win) game* knapp gewinnen; *(= narrowly defeat) opponent* knapp besiegen

VI *(lit, fig)* übergehen; **to ~ off** allmählich blasser werden; **blue that ~s (off) into black** Blau, das in Schwarz übergeht

shadeless [ˈʃeɪdlɪs] ADJ schattenlos

shadiness [ˈʃeɪdɪnɪs] N Schattigkeit *f*; *(fig)* Zwielichtigkeit *f*

shading [ˈʃeɪdɪŋ] N *(= shaded area)* Schraffierung *f*, Schraffur *f*; *(Art)* Schattierung *f*

shadow [ˈʃædəʊ] N **a** *(lit, fig)* Schatten *m* *(also Med, Art)*; *(= growth of beard)* Anflug *m* von Bartstoppeln; *(fig: = threat)* (Be)drohung *f*; **in the ~** im Schatten; **in the ~s** im Dunkel; **the valley of the ~ of death** das finstere Tal des Todes; **sb lives under the ~ of sth** etw liegt *or* lastet wie ein Schatten auf jdm; **to be in sb's ~** *(fig)* in jds Schatten *(dat)* stehen; **to be afraid of one's own ~** *(fig)* sich vor seinem eigenen Schatten fürchten; **to wear oneself to a ~** sich aufreiben, sich zugrunde *or* zu Grunde richten; **to be just a ~ of one's former self** nur noch ein Schatten seiner selbst sein; **to chase ~s** *(fig)* einem Phantom *or* Schatten nachjagen

b *(= trace)* Spur *f*; **a ~ of hope** ein Hoffnungsschimmer *m*; **without a ~ of a doubt** ohne den geringsten Zweifel

c *(= person following sb)* Schatten *m*; **to put a ~ on sb** jdn beschatten lassen *(inf)*

ATTR *(Brit Pol)* Schatten-; **~ government** Schattenregierung *f*; **~ Foreign Secretary** Schattenaußenminister(in) *m(f)*, Außenminister(in) *m(f)* des Schattenkabinetts

VT **a** *(= darken)* Schatten werfen auf *(+acc)*; *(fig)* überschatten; **the room is ~ed by a high wall** das Zimmer liegt im Schatten einer hohen Mauer

b *(= follow)* beschatten *(inf)*

shadow: **shadow-boxing** N *(lit, fig)* Schattenboxen *nt*; **shadow cabinet** N *(Brit Pol)* Schattenkabinett *nt*; **shadow earnings** PL *(Pol)* Schatteneinkommen *nt*; **shadow mask** N *(Tech)* Lochmaske *f*; **shadow minister** N *(Brit Pol)* Schattenminister(in) *m(f)*; **shadow printing** N *(Comput)* Schattendruck *m*

> **SHADOW CABINET**
>
> Im politischen Leben Großbritanniens spielt das **Shadow Cabinet**, das Schattenkabinett der stärksten Oppositionspartei, eine wichtige Rolle. Jeder Regierungsposten hat seine Entsprechung im Schattenkabinett, so gibt es z. B. einen Schatten-Innenminister, **Shadow Home Secretary**, und einen Schatten-Finanzminister, **Shadow Chancellor**. Die Schattenminister haben die Aufgabe, die Regierungspolitik in ihren jeweiligen Verantwortungsbereichen infrage zu stellen und die Politik ihrer Partei öffentlich zu vertreten → CABINET

shadowy [ˈʃædəʊɪ] ADJ schattig; *(= blurred) outline, form* schattenhaft, verschwommen; *(= vague) thought, fear* unbestimmt, vage; **a ~ figure** *(lit)* eine schemenhafte Gestalt; *(fig)* eine undurchsichtige Gestalt; **the ~ world of espionage** die dunkle Welt der Spionage; **a ~ existence** ein undurchsichtiges Dasein

shady [ˈʃeɪdɪ] ADJ *(+er)* **a** *place* schattig; *tree, hat* Schatten spendend **b** *(inf: = of dubious honesty)* zwielichtig, zweifelhaft; **he has a ~ past** er hat eine dunkle Vergangenheit; **to be on the ~ side of the law** dunkle Geschäfte treiben; **on the ~ side of forty** *(US inf)* vierzig vorbei *(inf)*; **there's something ~ about it** da ist etwas faul dran *(inf)*

shaft [ʃɑːft] N **a** Schaft *m*; *(of tool, golf club etc)* Stiel *m*; *(of cart, carriage)* Deichsel *f*; *(of light)* Strahl *m*; *(Mech)* Welle *f*; *(liter: = arrow)* Pfeil *m*; *(= spear)* Speer *m*; *(fig: = remark)* Spitze *f*; **~s of wit** geistreiche Spitzen *pl*; **the ~s of Cupid** Amors Pfeile *pl* **b** *(of lift, mine etc)* Schacht *m* VT *(sl)* **a** *(= have sex with)* stoßen *(vulg)* **b** *(= trick, cheat)* aufs Kreuz legen *(inf)*

shag[1] [ʃæg] N **a** *(= tobacco)* Shag *m* **b** *(of carpet etc)* Flor *m*; **~-pile carpet** langfloriger Teppich

shag[2] N *(Orn)* Krähenscharbe *f*

shag[3] *(Brit sl)* N *(= intercourse, partner)* Nummer *f* *(inf)*; **to have a ~** eine Nummer machen *(inf)*; **~ buddy** Fickpartner(in) *m(f)* *(vulg)* VT **a** *(= have sex)* bumsen *(inf)* **b** **to be ~ged out** voll am Ende sein *(sl)* VI bumsen *(inf)*

shaggy [ˈʃægɪ] ADJ *(+er)* *(= long-haired)* zottig; *(= unkempt)* zottelig; **~ carpet** zotteliger Teppich

shaggy dog story N *breit gewalzte Geschichte mit schwacher Pointe*

shagreen [ʃæˈgriːn] N Chagrin(leder) *nt*

Shah [ʃɑː] N Schah *m*

shake [ʃeɪk] *vb: pret* **shook**, *ptp* **shaken** N **a** *(= act of shaking)* Schütteln *nt*; **to give a rug a ~** einen Läufer ausschütteln; **give the paint a (good) ~** die Farbe (gut) durchschütteln; **to give sb/oneself a good ~** jdn/sich kräftig schütteln; **with a ~ of her head** mit einem Kopfschütteln; **with a ~ in his voice** mit zitternder Stimme

b *(= milkshake)* Milchshake *m*

c *(inf: = moment)* Minütchen *nt* *(inf)*; **in two ~s (of a lamb's tail)** in zwei Sekunden

d **to be no great ~s** *(inf)* nicht umwerfend sein *(at* in *+dat)*

e **the ~s** *pl (inf)* der Tatterich *(inf)*; *(esp with fear)* das Zittern; **he's got the ~s** er hat einen Tatterich *(inf)*; *(due to alcoholism also)* ihm zittern die Hände, er hat einen Flattermann *(inf)*; *(esp with fear)* er hat das große Zittern *(inf)*; *(esp with cold, emotion)* er zittert am ganzen Körper

VT **a** *person, head, object* schütteln; *building* erschüttern; *cocktail* durchschütteln; **"shake well before using"** „vor Gebrauch gut schütteln"; **to be ~n to pieces** total durchgeschüttelt werden; **she shook the door handle which seemed to have stuck** sie rüttelte an der Türklinke, die zu klemmen schien; **to ~ pepper on a steak** Pfeffer auf ein Steak streuen; **to ~ one's fist at sb** jdm mit der Faust drohen; **to ~ oneself/itself free** sich losmachen; **to ~ hands** sich *(dat)* die Hand geben; *(for longer time, in congratulations etc)* sich *(dat)* die Hand schütteln; **to ~ hands with sb** jdm die Hand geben/schütteln; **I'd like to ~ him by the hand** ihm würde ich gern die Hand schütteln *or* drücken; **English people don't often ~ hands** Engländer geben sich *(dat)* selten die Hand; **~ hands** *(to dog)* (gib) Pfötchen; *(to child)* gib mal die Hand; **to ~ a leg** *(inf, = hurry)* Dampf machen *(inf)*; *(dated: = dance)* das Tanzbein schwingen *(dated)*; **he has more medals than you can ~ a stick at** *(inf)* er hat jede Menge Medaillen *(inf)*

b *(= weaken) faith, foundation of society* erschüttern; *evidence, reputation, courage, resolve* ins Wanken bringen; **to ~ the foundations of sth** die Grundfesten einer Sache *(gen)* erschüttern; **society was ~n to its very core** die Gesellschaft wurde bis in ihre Grundfesten erschüttert

c *(= shock, amaze)* erschüttern; **to ~ the world** die Welt erschüttern; **that shook him!** da war er platt *(inf)*; **it shook me rigid** *(inf)* da war ich schwer geschockt *(inf)*; **it was a nasty accident, he's still rather badly ~n** es war ein schlimmer Unfall, der Schreck sitzt ihm noch in den Knochen; **she was badly ~n by the news** die Nachricht hatte sie sehr mitgenommen *or* erschüttert

d *(inf)* = **shake off**

VI wackeln; *(hand, voice)* zittern; *(earth, voice)* beben; **the whole boat shook as the waves struck it** das ganze Boot wurde vom Aufprall der Wellen erschüttert; **the trees shook in the wind** die Bäume schwankten im Wind; **to ~ like a leaf** zittern wie Espenlaub; **to ~ with fear/cold** vor Angst/Kälte zittern; **he was shaking all over** er zitterte am ganzen Körper; **to ~ with laughter** sich vor Lachen schütteln; **to ~ in one's shoes** *(inf)* das große Zittern kriegen *(inf)*; **~!** *(inf)* **~ on it!** *(inf)* Hand drauf; **~!** *(= me too)* da können wir uns ja die Hand reichen!; **they shook on the deal** sie bekräftigten das Geschäft mit Handschlag; **what's shaking?** *(US) (sl)* was geht ab? *(inf)*

▸ **shake down** **VT** *sep* **a** *fruit* herunterschütteln **b** *(US inf: = extort money from)* ausnehmen *(inf)*; **to shake sb down for 500 dollars** jdn um 500 Dollar erleichtern *(inf)* **c** *(US inf: = search)* absuchen, durchsuchen *(for* nach) **VI** *(inf)* **a** *(= sleep)* kampieren, sein Lager aufschlagen **b** *(= settle, people)* sich eingewöhnen; *(machinery)* sich einlaufen; *(situation)* sich einspielen

▸ **shake off** **VT** *sep dust, snow, pursuer* abschütteln; *visitor, cold, image, illness, feeling* loswerden; **to shake the dust (of a place) off one's feet** *(fig)* den Staub (eines Ortes) von seinen Schuhen schütteln

▸ **shake out** **VT** *sep* **a** *(lit)* herausschütteln; *tablecloth, rug* ausschütteln; **she took off her hat and shook out her long hair** sie nahm den Hut ab und schüttelte sich *(dat)* die langen Haare zurecht **b** *(fig, out of complacency etc)* aufrütteln *(of* aus) **VI** *(Mil, = spread out)* ausschwärmen

▸ **shake up** **VT** *sep* **a** *bottle, liquid* schütteln **b** *(= upset)* erschüttern; **he was badly shaken up by the accident** der Unfall hat ihm einen schweren Schock versetzt; **she's still a bit shaken up** sie ist immer noch ziemlich mitgenommen **c** *management, recruits* auf Zack bringen *(inf)*; *ideas* revidieren; *system* umkrempeln *(inf)*; *country, industry* wachrütteln; **your ideas could do with a bit of shaking up** deine Ansichten müssten auch mal wieder revidiert werden; **to shake things up** die Dinge in Bewegung bringen

shakedown [ˈʃeɪkdaʊn] **N** *(= bed)* Lager *nt*, Notbett *nt*; *(US inf) (= extortion)* Gaunerei *f*; *(= search)* Razzia *f (inf)*, Durchsuchung *f*; **he slept on a ~ in the living room** er hatte sein Lager im Wohnzimmer aufgeschlagen, er kampierte im Wohnzimmer; **to give a room a ~** ein Zimmer *nt* auf den Kopf stellen; **~ cruise** Probefahrt *f*

shaken [ˈʃeɪkən] *ptp of* **shake**

shake-out [ˈʃeɪkaʊt] **N** *(inf)* Gesundschrumpfung *f (inf)*

shaker [ˈʃeɪkəʳ] **N** *(= cocktail shaker)* Mixbecher *m*, Shaker *m*; *(= flour/salt shaker)* Mehl-/Salzstreuer *m*

Shakespearean, **Shakespearian** [ʃeɪkˈspɪərɪən] **ADJ** shakespearesch, shakespearisch; **~ actor** Shakespeare-Schauspieler *m*; **a tragedy of ~ proportions** eine Tragödie, die eines Shakespeare würdig ist *or* wäre **N** Shakespeareforscher(in) *m(f)*

shake-up [ˈʃeɪkʌp] **N** *(inf: = reorganization)* Umbesetzung *f*; **to give a department** *etc* **a good ~** *(= revitalization)* eine Abteilung *etc* auf Zack bringen *(inf)*; *(= reorganization)* eine Abteilung *etc* umbesetzen *or* umorganisieren

shakily [ˈʃeɪkɪlɪ] **ADV** wackelig; *talk, say* mit zitteriger Stimme; *walk* mit wackeligen Schritten; *write, pour etc* zitterig

shakiness [ˈʃeɪkɪnɪs] **N** *(of chair)* Wackeligkeit *f*; *(of evidence)* Fragwürdigkeit *f*, Unsicherheit *f*; *(of voice, hands, writing)* Zitterigkeit *f*; *(of knowledge)* Unsicherheit *f*; *(of sb's French)* Holprigkeit *f*; **the ~ of their position** ihre wackelige Position

shaking [ˈʃeɪkɪŋ] **N** Zittern *nt*; **to give sb/sth a good ~** jdn/etw kräftig schütteln; *(fig)* jdn kräftig treten; **a nasty experience, it gave me a ~** ein unangenehmes Erlebnis, das sitzt mir immer noch in den Knochen

shako [ˈʃækəʊ] **N** Tschako *m*

shaky [ˈʃeɪkɪ] **ADJ** *(+er) chair, position* wackelig; *evidence* fragwürdig, unsicher; *voice, hands, writing* zitt(e)rig; *knowledge* unsicher, wackelig; **in rather ~ French** in ziemlich holprigem Französisch; **to be ~ on one's legs** wackelig auf den Beinen sein; **to feel ~** *(physically)* sich ganz schwach fühlen; *(from nerves)* sich zitt(e)rig fühlen; **I still feel a bit ~ about this theory** diese Theorie sitzt bei mir noch nicht; **to get off to a ~ start** *(fig)* einen unsicheren *or* holprigen Anfang nehmen; **to be on ~ ground** *(fig)* sich auf schwankendem *or* unsicherem Boden bewegen

shale [ʃeɪl] **N** Schiefer *m*

shale oil **N** Schieferöl *nt*

shall [ʃæl] ✪ 3.3 *pret* **should** **MODAL AUX VB** **a** *(future)* **I/we ~** *or* **I'll/we'll go to France this year** ich werde/wir werden dieses Jahr nach Frankreich fahren, ich fahre/wir fahren dieses Jahr nach Frankreich; **~ do** *(inf)* wird gemacht *(inf)*; **no, I ~ not** *or* **I shan't** nein, das werde ich nicht tun *or* das tue ich nicht; **yes, I ~** jawohl, das werde ich tun *or* das tue ich!

b *(determination, obligation)* **you ~ pay for this!** dafür sollst *or* wirst du büßen!; **but I say you ~ do it!** aber ich sage dir, du wirst das machen!; **the directors ~ not be disturbed** *(form)* die Direktoren dürfen nicht gestört werden; **the court ~ rise** das Gericht muss sich erheben; *(command)* erheben Sie sich!; **thou shalt not kill** *(Bibl)* du sollst nicht töten; **the manufacturer ~ deliver …** *(in contracts etc)* der Hersteller liefert …; **I want to go too – and so you ~** ich will auch mitkommen – aber gewiss doch *or (in fairy stories)* es sei!

c *(in questions, suggestions)* **what ~ we do?** was sollen wir machen?, was machen wir?; **let's go in, ~ we?** komm, gehen wir hinein!; **~ I go now?** soll ich jetzt gehen?; **I'll buy 3, ~ I?** soll ich 3 kaufen?, ich kaufe 3, oder?

shallot [ʃəˈlɒt] **N** Schalotte *f*

shallow [ˈʃæləʊ] **ADJ** flach; *water also* seicht; *soil* dünn; *(Physiol) breathing* flach; *(fig)* oberflächlich; *talk, person, novel* seicht, oberflächlich; **in the ~ end of the pool** am flachen *or* niedrigen Ende des Beckens; **his body was buried in a ~ grave** seine Leiche wurde verscharrt **N** **shallows** **PL** seichte *or* flache Stelle (im Wasser), Untiefe *f*

shallowly [ˈʃæləʊlɪ] **ADV** *breathe* flach

shallowness [ˈʃæləʊnɪs] **N** Flachheit *f*; *(of water also)* Seichtheit *f*; *(of soil)* Dünne *f*; *(Physiol: of breathing)* Schwäche *f*; *(fig, of talk, person, novel)* Seichtheit *f*, Oberflächlichkeit *f*

shalom [ʃæˈlɒm] **INTERJ** schalom!

shalt [ʃælt] *(obs) 2nd pers sing of* **shall**

sham [ʃæm] **N** **a** *(= pretence)* Heuchelei *f*; **he's not really sorry, it's all a big ~** es tut ihm nicht wirklich leid, es ist alles nur *or* das ist geheuchelt; **their marriage had become a ~** ihre Ehe war zur Farce geworden *or* bestand nur noch zum Schein; **his life seemed a ~** sein Leben erschien ihm als Lug und Trug; **this diamond is a ~** dieser Diamant ist nicht echt

b *(= person)* Scharlatan *m*; **you don't really feel anything, you big ~!** du empfindest überhaupt nichts, du Heuchler!

ADJ *diamonds, oak etc* unecht, imitiert; *politeness etc* vorgetäuscht, geheuchelt; *person* betrügerisch; **a ~ marriage** eine Scheinehe; **a ~ deal** ein Scheingeschäft *nt*; **a ~ battle** ein Scheingefecht *nt*

VT vortäuschen, vorgeben; *illness also* simulieren; *emotions, sympathy* heucheln

VI so tun; *(esp with illness)* simulieren; *(with feelings)* heucheln; **he's just ~ming** er tut nur so

shamanism [ˈʃæmənɪzəm] **N** Schamanismus *m*

shamble [ˈʃæmbl] **VI** trotten; *(people also)* latschen *(inf)*; **every morning he ~s in half an hour late** er kommt jeden Morgen eine halbe Stunde zu spät angelatscht *(inf)*

shambles [ˈʃæmblz] **N** *sing* heilloses Durcheinander; *(esp of room etc)* Tohuwabohu *nt*; **the room was a ~** im Zimmer herrschte das reinste Tohuwabohu *or* ein heilloses Durcheinander; **the economy/country is in a ~** die Wirtschaft/das Land befindet sich in einem Chaos; **they left the house in a ~** sie hinterließen das Haus wie ein Schlachtfeld; **the game was a ~** das Spiel war das reinste Kuddelmuddel *(inf)*; **he made a ~ of that job** da hat er vielleicht einen Mist gebaut! *(inf)*

shambolic [ʃæmˈbɒlɪk] **ADJ** *(inf)* chaotisch *(inf)*

shame [ʃeɪm] ✪ 14, 18.2 **N** **a** *(= feeling of shame)* Scham *f*; *(= cause of shame)* Schande *f*; **to feel ~ at sth** sich für etw schämen; **he hung his head in ~** er senkte beschämt den Kopf; *(fig)* er schämte sich; **to bring ~ upon sb/oneself** jdm/sich Schande machen; **he is without ~** er hat keinerlei Schamgefühl, ihm fehlt jegliches Schamgefühl; **she is beyond all (sense of) ~** sie hat jegliches Schamgefühl verloren; **she has no ~, dancing around like that** dass sie sich nicht schämt so herumzutanzen; **have you no ~?** schämst du dich (gar) nicht?; **to put sb/sth to ~** *(lit)* jdm/etw Schande machen; *(fig)* jdn/etw in den Schatten stellen; **by working so hard he puts us to ~** er arbeitet so schwer, dass er uns alle beschämt; **to my (eternal) ~** zu meiner (ewigen) Schande; **I'll never forget the ~ of it** ich werde nie vergessen, wie ich mich schämte; **the ~ of it all** die Schande *or* Schmach; **the ~ of it!** was für eine Schande!, diese Schande!; **the street is the ~ of the town** die Straße ist der Schandfleck *or* die Schande dieser Stadt; **for ~!** schäm dich!/schämt euch!; **she didn't! for ~!** nein! sie sollte sich schämen!; **~ on you!** du solltest dich/ihr solltet euch schämen!

b *(= pity)* **it's a ~ you couldn't come** schade, dass du nicht kommen konntest; **it's a (great) ~ we have to leave so early** es ist (so) schade *or* ein Jammer, dass wir schon so früh gehen müssen; **what a ~!** (das ist aber) schade!, wie schade!; **what a ~ he …** schade, dass er …; **nice legs, ~ about the face** *(inf)* hübsche Beine, aber über den Rest schweigen wir lieber → **crying**

VT Schande machen *(+dat)*; *(fig, by excelling)* in den Schatten stellen; **he ~d us by working so hard** er hat uns alle durch sein hartes Arbeiten beschämt; **by giving so much he ~d me into making a bigger contribution** dadurch, dass er so viel gab, fühlte ich mich moralisch gezwungen, mehr zu spenden; **see if you can ~ him into changing his mind** appelliere an sein besseres Ich, dann überlegt er es sich vielleicht anders

shamefaced [ˈʃeɪmˈfeɪst] **ADJ**, **shamefacedly** [ˈʃeɪmˈfeɪsɪdlɪ] **ADV** betreten

shamefacedness [ˈʃeɪmˈfeɪstnɪs] **N** Betretenheit *f*

shameful [ˈʃeɪmfʊl] **ADJ** schändlich; *experience, secret* peinlich; **another ~ day for the pound** noch ein schmachvoller Tag für das Pfund Sterling; **how ~!** was für eine Schande!; **what ~ prices/behaviour!** diese Preise sind/dieses Benehmen ist eine Schande; **there is nothing ~ about it** das ist doch keine Schande

shamefully [ˈʃeɪmfəlɪ] **ADV** schändlich; **he is ~ ignorant** es ist eine Schande, wie wenig er weiß

shamefulness [ˈʃeɪmfʊlnɪs] **N** Ungeheuerlichkeit *f*

shameless [ˈʃeɪmlɪs] **ADJ** schamlos; **are you completely ~?** hast du gar kein Schamgefühl?; **he was quite ~ about it** er schämte sich überhaupt nicht; **he was quite ~ about lying to his parents** er belog seine Eltern schamlos

shamelessly ['ʃeɪmlɪslɪ] ADV schamlos; **a ~ sentimental film** ein unverhohlen sentimentaler Film

shamelessness ['ʃeɪmlɪsnɪs] N Schamlosigkeit *f*

shaming ['ʃeɪmɪŋ] ADJ beschämend

shammer ['ʃæmə'] N Schwindler(in) *m(f)*, Heuchler(in) *m(f)*; *(of illness)* Simulant(in) *m(f)*

shammy (leather) ['ʃæmɪ('leðə')] N Ledertuch *nt*, Fensterleder *nt*

shampoo [ʃæm'pu:] N *(= liquid)* Shampoo *nt*, Schampon *nt*; *(for hair also)* Haarwaschmittel *nt*; *(= act of washing)* Reinigung *f*; *(of hair)* Waschen *nt*; **to give the carpet a ~** den Teppich reinigen *or* schamponieren; **~ and set** Waschen und Legen; **to have a ~ and set** sich *(dat)* die Haare waschen und legen lassen VT *person* die Haare waschen *(+dat)*; *hair* waschen; *dog* das Fell waschen *(+dat)*; *carpet, upholstery* reinigen, schamponieren; **to have one's hair ~ed** sich *(dat)* die Haare waschen lassen

shamrock ['ʃæmrɒk] N Klee *m*; *(= leaf)* Kleeblatt *nt*

shandy ['ʃændɪ] N *(Brit)* Bier *nt* mit Limonade; **lemonade ~** Alsterwasser *nt (N Ger)*, Radlermaß *nt (S Ger)*

shanghai [ʃæŋ'haɪ] VT *(Naut)* schanghaien; **to ~ sb into doing sth** *(fig inf)* jdn zwingen, etw zu tun

shank [ʃæŋk] N **a** *(= part of leg, of person)* Unterschenkel *m*; *(of horse)* Unterarm *m*; *(of beef)* Hachse *f*; **~s** *(inf: = legs)* Hachsen *pl (inf)*; **(to go) on Shanks' pony** auf Schusters Rappen (reiten) **b** *(of anchor, key etc)* Schaft *m*; *(of spoon)* Stiel *m*

shan't [ʃɑ:nt] *contr of* **shall not**; **~!** *(inf)* will nicht! *(inf)*

shantung [ʃæn'tʌŋ] N Schantungseide *f*

shanty[1] ['ʃæntɪ] N *(= hut)* Baracke *f*, Hütte *f*

shanty[2] N *(Mus)* Seemannslied *nt*, Shanty *nt*

shantytown ['ʃæntɪtaʊn] N Slum(vor)stadt *f*, Bidonville *f*

SHAPE [ʃeɪp] *abbr of* **Supreme Headquarters Allied Powers Europe** *Hauptquartier der alliierten Streitkräfte in Europa während des 2. Weltkriegs*

shape [ʃeɪp] N **a** *(= geometrical form, outline)* Form *f*; **what ~ is it?** welche Form hat es?; **it's rectangular** *etc* **in ~** es ist rechteckig *etc*; **that dress hasn't much/has lost its ~** das Kleid hat keine richtige Form/hat seine Form verloren; **she's the right ~ for a model** sie hat die richtige Figur für ein Mannequin; **to hammer metal into ~** Metall zurechthämmern *or* -schlagen; **to knock sth out of ~** etw zerbeulen; **to take ~** *(lit)* Form bekommen; *(fig)* Gestalt *or* Konturen annehmen; **a flowerbed in the ~ of a circle** ein Blumenbeet in der Form eines Kreises; **government action took the ~ of a ban** die Regierung griff mit einem Verbot ein; **help in the ~ of a donation** Hilfe in Form einer Spende; **of all ~s and sizes, of every ~ and size** aller Art, jeder Art, in allen Variationen; **I don't accept gifts in any ~ or form** ich nehme überhaupt keine Geschenke an; **we do not know the ~ of things to come** wir wissen nicht, wie sich die Zukunft gestalten wird; **this may be the ~ of things to come** so könnte das vielleicht in Zukunft sein **b** *(= unidentified figure)* Gestalt *f*; *(= object)* Form *f* **c** *(= guise)* Gestalt *f*; **in human ~** in Menschengestalt, in menschlicher Gestalt **d** *(fig: = order, condition)* **to be in good/bad ~** *(sportsman)* in Form/nicht in Form sein; *(mentally, healthwise)* in guter/schlechter Verfassung sein, gut/schlecht drauf sein *(inf)*; *(things)* in gutem/schlechtem Zustand sein; *(business)* gut/schlecht in Schuss sein *(inf)*, in gutem/schlechtem Zustand sein; **what sort of ~ is your boxer in?** wie fit ist Ihr Boxer?; **to be out of ~** *(physically)* nicht in Form sein; **what sort of ~ was the business in?** in welchem Zustand war das Unternehmen?; **to get sb/a business into ~** jdn/ein Geschäft *or* Unternehmen auf Vordermann bringen *(inf)*; **to get a house into ~** ein Haus in Ordnung bringen; **to get one's affairs into ~** seine Angelegenheiten ordnen **e** *(= mould, for hats)* Hutform *f*; *(for dressmaking)* Schneiderpuppe *f*; *(Cook)* Form *f*; *(for cutting)* Ausstecher *m* **f let's go throw some ~s** *(Brit inf)* gehen wir tanzen
VT *(lit) stone, wood etc* bearbeiten; *clay etc* formen *(into* zu); *(fig) character, ideas* formen, prägen; *future, development, market, one's life* gestalten; **he ~d the wood/stone into the desired form** er verlieh dem Holz/Stein die gewünschte Form; **the factors which ~ one's life** die Faktoren, die das Leben prägen *or* bestimmen; **those who ~ the course of history** die(jenigen), die den Lauf der Geschichte bestimmen; **those who have helped ~ our society** die(jenigen), die unsere Gesellschaft mitgeformt haben; **we must ~ our strategy according to our funds** wir müssen unsere Strategie nach den zur Verfügung stehenden Mitteln ausrichten
VI sich entwickeln

▶ **shape up** VI **to shape up well** sich gut entwickeln, vielversprechend sein; **he is shaping up nicely as a goalkeeper** er ist ein vielversprechender Torwart; **things are shaping up well** es sieht sehr gut aus

shaped [ʃeɪpt] ADJ geformt; **an oddly ~ hat** ein Hut mit einer komischen Form; **~ like a ...** in der Form einer/eines ...

-shaped [-ʃeɪpt] ADJ *suf* -förmig; **egg-/pear--shaped** ei-/birnenförmig

shapeless ['ʃeɪplɪs] ADJ formlos; *(= ugly)* unförmig

shapelessly ['ʃeɪplɪslɪ] ADV unförmig

shapelessness ['ʃeɪplɪsnɪs] N Formlosigkeit *f*; *(= ugliness)* Unförmigkeit *f*

shapeliness ['ʃeɪplɪnɪs] N *(of figure)* Wohlproportioniertheit *f*; *(of legs, bust)* Wohlgeformtheit *f*

shapely ['ʃeɪplɪ] ADJ *(+er) figure, woman* wohlproportioniert; *legs, bust* wohlgeformt; *car* formschön

shard [ʃɑ:d] N (Ton)scherbe *f*

share[1] [ʃɛə'] ✪ 12.1, 26.3 N **a** *(= portion)* Anteil *m (in or of* an *+dat)*; **we want fair ~s for all** wir wollen, dass gerecht geteilt wird; **I want my fair ~** ich will meinen (An)teil, ich will, was mir zusteht; **he didn't get his fair ~** er ist zu kurz gekommen; **I've had more than my fair ~ of bad luck** ich habe mehr (als mein Teil an) Pech gehabt; **I'll give you a ~ in the profits** ich beteilige Sie am Gewinn; **in equal ~s** zu gleichen Teilen; **your ~ is £5** du bekommst £ 5, du musst £ 5 bezahlen; **how much is my ~?** wie groß ist mein Anteil?; **he came in for his full ~ of criticism** er hat sein Teil an Kritik abbekommen; **to fall to sb's ~** *(liter)* jdm zufallen *(liter)*; **to go ~s** *(inf)* teilen; **to bear one's ~ of the cost** seinen Anteil an den Kosten tragen; **to take one's ~ of the proceeds** sich *(dat)* seinen Anteil am Gewinn nehmen; **to take one's ~ of the blame** sich mitschuldig erklären; **to pay one's ~** seinen (An)teil bezahlen; **to do one's ~** sein(en) Teil *or* das Seine tun *or* beitragen; **to have a ~ in sth** an etw *(dat)* beteiligt sein; **I had no ~ in that** damit hatte ich nichts zu tun **b** *(Fin, general)* (Geschäfts)anteil *m*; *(in a public limited company)* Aktie *f*; **to hold ~s in a company** (Geschäfts)anteile *pl*/Aktien *pl* eines Unternehmens besitzen
VT **a** *(= divide)* teilen; *(= have in common also)* gemeinsam haben; *responsibility* gemeinsam tragen; **we ~ the same birthday** wir haben am gleichen Tag Geburtstag; **they ~ a room** sie teilen ein Zimmer, sie haben ein gemeinsames Zimmer; **I do not ~ that view** diese Ansicht teile ich nicht **b** *(Comput) file* gemeinsam nutzen; *(in network)* freigeben
VI **a** teilen; **there was only one room free so we had to ~** es gab nur noch ein freies Zimmer, also mussten wir es uns teilen; **children have to learn to ~** Kinder müssen lernen, mit anderen zu teilen; **to ~ and ~ alike** (brüderlich) mit (den) anderen teilen **b to ~ in sth** sich an etw *(dat)* beteiligen; *in profit* an etw *(dat)* beteiligt werden; *in enthusiasm* etw teilen; *in success, sorrow* an etw *(dat)* Anteil nehmen

▶ **share out** VT *sep* verteilen

share[2] N *(Agr)* (Pflug)schar *f*

share: **share broker** N *(esp Brit)* Effekten- *or* Börsenmakler(in) *m(f)*; **share capital** N Aktienkapital *nt*; **share certificate** N Aktienzertifikat *nt*; **sharecropper** N *(US Agr)* (Farm)-pächter(in) *m(f) (der/die Pacht in Form eines Ernteanteils zahlt)*; **shareholder** N Aktionär(in) *m(f)*; **shareholding** N Beteiligung *f*; **shareholders' meeting** Aktionärsversammlung *f*; **share index** N Aktienindex *m*; **share issue** N *(St Ex)* Aktienemission *f*; **share option** N Aktienoption *f*; **share-out** N Verteilung *f*; *(St Ex)* (Dividenden)ausschüttung *f*

shareware [ɔɔ] N *(Comput, Internet)* Shareware *f*

share warrant N *(Fin)* (auf den Inhaber lautendes) Aktienzertifikat

shark [ʃɑ:k] N **a** Hai(fisch) *m* **b** *(inf: = swindler)* Schlitzohr *nt (inf)*; **loan/property ~** Kredit-/Grundstückshai *m (inf)*

sharp [ʃɑ:p] ADJ *(+er)* **a** *knife, blade etc* scharf; *needle, point etc* spitz **b** *(= clear-cut, not blurred) outline, photo, contrast* scharf; **to come into ~ focus** *(fig inf)* aufs Korn genommen werden **c** *(= observant, keen) eyes, wits, glance, mind* scharf; *nose* gut, empfindlich; *observation, remark* scharfsinnig, schlau; *(= intelligent) person* schlau, gewieft *(inf)*, auf Draht *(inf)*; *child* schlau, aufgeweckt; **that was pretty ~ of you** das war ganz schön schlau *or* clever *(inf)* von dir; **keep a ~ watch for him/the train** pass gut auf, ob du ihn/den Zug siehst **d** *(= sudden, intense) whistle, cry* durchdringend, schrill; *drop in prices* steil; *frost, contrast* scharf; *shower, desire, pain* heftig; *hunger* nagend *(geh)*, groß; **after a short, ~ struggle** nach kurzem, heftigem Kampf; **be ~ about it!** *(inf)* (ein bisschen) dalli! *(inf)*, zack, zack! *(inf)* **e** *(= acute) angle* spitz; *bend, turn by car* scharf **f** *(pej: = cunning) person* gerissen, raffiniert, clever *(inf)*; *trick etc* raffiniert; **~ practice** unsaubere Geschäfte *pl*; **that was a pretty ~ move** das war ein raffinierter Schachzug **g** *(= harsh, fierce) tongue, retort, tone of voice* scharf; *person* schroff; *temper* hitzig **h** *(= acidic, pungent) taste* scharf; *apple* sauer; *wine* herb, sauer *(pej)*; *(fig: = biting) air* schneidend kalt; *wind* beißend **i** *(Mus) note (= too high)* zu hoch; *(= raised a semitone)* (um einen Halbton) erhöht; **you played F natural instead of F ~** du hast f statt fis gespielt; **her voice goes ~ on the higher notes** sie singt die höheren Töne zu hoch **j** *(inf: = stylish) person, clothes* toll *(inf)*, todschick *(inf)*; *piece of driving* clever *(inf)*; **he's a ~ dresser** er zieht sich immer todschick an *(inf)*
ADV *(+er)* **a** *(Mus)* zu hoch **b** *(= punctually)* pünktlich, genau; **at 5 o'clock ~** Punkt 5 Uhr **c look ~!** dalli! *(inf)*, zack, zack! *(inf)*; **if you don't look ~ ...** wenn du nicht schnell machst ...; **to pull up ~** plötzlich anhalten; **to turn ~ left** scharf nach links abbiegen
N *(Mus)* Kreuz *nt*

sharp-edged [ʃɑ:p'edʒd] ADJ *knife, outline etc* scharf; *piece of furniture etc* scharfkantig

sharpen ['ʃɑ:pən] VT **a** *knife* schleifen, schärfen, wetzen; *razor* wetzen; *pencil* spitzen; *(fig) appetite* anregen; *wits* schärfen; *sensation* erhöhen; **to ~ one's claws** *(lit, fig)* seine Krallen wetzen **b** *(Mus, by a semitone)* (um einen Halbton) erhöhen; *(= raise pitch)* höher singen/spielen/stimmen VI **her voice ~ed** *(in fear, anxiety etc)* ihre Stimme wurde schrill

sharp end N **at the ~** *(fig)* in vorderster Front

sharpener ['ʃɑ:pnə'] N Schleifgerät *nt*; *(in rod shape)* Wetzstahl *m*; *(= pencil sharpener)* (Bleistift)spitzer *m*

sharper [ˈʃɑːpəˈ] N Gauner(in) *m(f)*; *(= card sharper)* Falschspieler(in) *m(f)*

sharp: **sharp-eyed** [ʃɑːpˈaɪd] ADJ scharfsichtig; **to be ~** scharfe *or* gute Augen haben; **it was ~ of you to see that** du hast ja Augen wie ein Luchs; **sharp-featured** ADJ mit scharfen (Gesichts)zügen

sharpish [ˈʃɑːpɪʃ] ADV *(Brit inf)* schnell, fix *(inf)*

sharpness [ˈʃɑːpnɪs] N **a** *(of knife, blade etc)* Schärfe *f*; *(of needle, point etc)* Spitzheit *f*
b *(of outline, photo, contrast)* Schärfe *f*
c *(= keenness, of eyes, wits, mind)* Schärfe *f*; *(of nose)* Empfindlichkeit *f*; *(of observation, remark)* Scharfsinnigkeit *f*; *(= intelligence, of person)* Schläue *f*, Gewieftheit *f (inf)*; *(of child)* Aufgewecktheit *f*
d *(= suddenness, intensity, of whistle, cry)* Schrillheit *f*; *(of frost, contrast)* Schärfe *f*; *(of desire, pain)* Heftigkeit *f*; *(of hunger)* Größe *f*; **because of the unexpected ~ of the drop in prices** wegen des unerwartet steilen Preissturzes
e *(= acuteness, of angle)* Spitzheit *f*; *(of bend, turn by car)* Schärfe *f*
f *(pej: = shrewdness)* Gerissenheit *f*, Raffiniertheit *f*, Cleverness *f (inf)*
g *(= fierceness) (of tongue, retort, tone of voice)* Schärfe *f*; *(of person)* Schroffheit *f*; *(of temper)* Hitzigkeit *f*
h *(= acidity, pungency, of taste)* Schärfe *f*; *(of apple)* Säure *f*; *(of wine)* Herbheit *f*; **there is a ~ in the air** es ist sehr frisch

sharp: **sharpshooter** N *(esp US)* Scharfschütze *m*, Scharfschützin *f*; **sharp-sighted** ADJ = sharp-eyed; **sharp-tempered** ADJ hitzig; **sharp-tongued** ADJ scharfzüngig; **sharp--witted** ADJ scharfsinnig

shat [ʃæt] *pret, ptp of* **shit¹**

shatter [ˈʃætəˈ] VT **a** *(lit)* zertrümmern, zerschmettern; *hopes, dreams* zunichtemachen; *nerves* zerrütten; **he hurled a brick at the window, ~ing it into a thousand pieces** er schleuderte einen Ziegel gegen das Fenster, das in tausend Stücke zersplitterte *or* zersprang; **the blast ~ed all the windows** durch die Explosion zersplitterten alle Fensterscheiben; **to ~ sth against a wall** etw gegen eine Wand schmettern; **his hopes were ~ed** seine Hoffnungen hatten sich zerschlagen
b *(Brit fig inf: = exhaust)* erledigen *(inf)*; *(mentally)* mitnehmen; **how are you? – ~ed!** wie gehts? – ich bin total kaputt *or* erledigt *(inf)*; **she was absolutely ~ed by the divorce** die Scheidung hatte sie schwer mitgenommen
c *(Brit inf, = flabbergast)* erschüttern; **I've won the pools? I'm ~ed!** ich habe im Toto gewonnen? ich bin platt! *(inf)*
VI zerbrechen, zerspringen; *(windscreen)* (zer)splittern

shattering [ˈʃætərɪŋ] ADJ **a** *blow* wuchtig, gewaltig; *explosion* gewaltig; *defeat* vernichtend; **it had a ~ effect on the economy** es wirkte sich verheerend auf die Wirtschaft aus
b *(fig inf: = exhausting)* erschöpfend, anstrengend; *(psychologically)* niederschmetternd; **a ~ blow to his ego** ein schwerer Schlag für sein Ich; **I had a ~ day at the office** der Tag im Büro hat mich wahnsinnig geschlaucht *(inf)*, ich bin total erledigt vom Büro *(inf)*; **the divorce was a ~ experience for her** die Scheidung hat sie unheimlich mitgenommen *(inf)*
c *(inf: = flabbergasting) news, realization* erschütternd; *effect* umwerfend *(inf)*; **this new film is a ~ experience** dieser neue Film ist ein umwerfendes Erlebnis *(inf)*; **it must have been absolutely ~ for you to have found out that …** das war bestimmt entsetzlich für Sie, als Sie erfuhren, dass …

shatterproof [ˈʃætəpruːf] ADJ splitterfest *or* -frei

shave [ʃeɪv] *vb: pret* **shaved**, *ptp* **shaved** *or* **shaven**
N Rasur *f*; **to have a ~** sich rasieren; *(at a barber's)* sich rasieren lassen; **this new razor gives you a good ~** dieser neue Rasierapparat rasiert gut; **a close ~** *(lit)* eine glatte Rasur; **to have a close ~** *(fig)* gerade noch davonkommen, mit knapper Not davonkommen, gerade noch Glück haben; **that was a close ~** das war knapp
VT *face, legs* rasieren; *leather* (ab)falzen; *wood* hobeln; *(= graze)* streifen
VI *(person)* sich rasieren; *(razor)* rasieren, schneiden

▶ **shave off** VT *sep beard* sich *(dat)* abrasieren; *sb's beard* abrasieren; *wood* abhobeln; **she has shaved four seconds off the world record** sie hat den Weltrekord um vier Sekunden verbessert

shave foam N *(US)* Rasierschaum *m*

shaven [ˈʃeɪvn] ADJ *head etc* kahl geschoren; **~--headed** kahl geschoren

shaver [ˈʃeɪvəˈ] N **a** *(= razor)* Rasierapparat *m*
b *(inf)* **young ~** junger Bengel *(inf)*; *(as address)* junger Freund

shaver point, *(US)* **shaver outlet** N Steckdose *f* für Rasierapparate

Shavian [ˈʃeɪvɪən] ADJ shawsch

shaving [ˈʃeɪvɪŋ] N **a** Rasieren *nt* **b shavings** PL Späne *pl*

shaving *in cpds* Rasier-; **shaving brush** N Rasierpinsel *m*; **shaving cream** N Rasiercreme *f*; **shaving foam** N Rasierschaum *m*; **shaving gel** N Rasiergel *nt*; **shaving mug** N Rasierschale *f*; **shaving point** N Steckdose *f* für Rasierapparate; **shaving soap**, **shaving stick** N Rasierseife *f*; **shaving tackle** N Rasierzeug *nt*

shawl [ʃɔːl] N *(round shoulders)* (Umhänge)tuch *nt*; *(tailored)* Umhang *m*; *(covering head)* (Kopf)tuch *nt*

she [ʃiː] PRON sie; *(of boats, cars etc)* es; **~ who …** *(liter)* diejenige, die …; **it is ~** *(form)* sie ist es
N Sie *f*

she- PREF weiblich; **~bear** weiblicher Bär, Bärin *f*

s/he PRON *(= he or she)* er/sie

sheading [ˈʃiːdɪŋ] N *(Brit)* Verwaltungsbezirk *m (der Isle of Man)*

sheaf [ʃiːf] N *pl* **sheaves** *(of wheat, corn)* Garbe *f*; *(of arrows etc, papers, notes)* Bündel *nt*

shear [ʃɪəˈ] *pret* **sheared**, *ptp* **shorn** VT *sheep* scheren; *wool* (ab)scheren → **shorn**
VI **a the knife ~s through the metal** das Messer zerschneidet das Metall; **the bird ~ed through the air** der Vogel segelte durch die Luft; **the motorboat ~ed through the water** das Motorboot durchpflügte das Wasser **b** *(Mech: = fracture)* **the metal plate had ~ed** in der Metallplatte hatte sich ein Riss gebildet

▶ **shear off** VT *sep sheep's wool* abscheren; **the ship had its bows shorn off in the collision** beim Zusammenstoß wurde dem Schiff der Bug abrasiert
VI *(= break off)* abbrechen

shearer [ˈʃɪərəˈ] N (Schaf)scherer(in) *m(f)*

shearing [ˈʃɪərɪŋ] N (Schaf)schur *f*; **~s** Schur- *or* Scherwolle *f*

shearing: **shearing machine** N Schermaschine *f*; **shearing time** N Schurzeit *f*, Zeit *f* der Schafschur

shears [ʃɪəz] PL (große) Schere; *(for hedges)* Heckenschere *f*; *(for metal)* Metallschere *f*

shearwater [ˈʃɪəwɔːtəˈ] N Sturmtaucher *m*

sheath [ʃiːθ] N *(for sword etc)* Scheide *f*; *(Bot)* (Blatt)scheide *f*; *(on cable)* Mantel *m*, Armierung *f*; *(= contraceptive)* Gummischutz *m*, Kondom *m or nt*; *(= dress)* Futteralkleid *nt*; **the cat withdrew its claws into their ~s** die Katze zog die Krallen ein; **the wing-sheath of an insect** die Flügeldecke eines Insekts

sheathe [ʃiːð] VT *sword, knife* in die Scheide stecken; *claws* einziehen; *cables* armieren; **to ~ sth in metal** etw mit Metall verkleiden; **she was ~d in a red dress** sie steckte in einem roten Kleid

sheathing [ˈʃiːðɪŋ] N *(on roof, house)* Verkleidung *f*; *(on ship also)* Beschlag *m*; *(with wood)* Verschalung *f*; *(on cables)* Armierung *f*, Bewehrung *f*

sheath knife N Fahrtenmesser *nt*

sheaves [ʃiːvz] *pl of* **sheaf**

shebang [ʃəˈbæŋ] N *(inf)* **the whole ~** die ganze Chose *(inf)*, der ganze Kram *(inf)*

shebeen [ʃɪˈbiːn] N *(Ir)* Kaschemme *f*, Spelunke *f*

shed¹ [ʃed] *pret, ptp* **shed** VT **a** *leaves, hair etc* verlieren; *horns* abwerfen; *clothes* ausziehen, ablegen; **the dancer slowly ~ another layer** die Tänzerin schälte sich langsam aus einer weiteren Hülle; **to ~ its skin** sich häuten; **to ~ its load** *(lorry)* seine Ladung verlieren; **you should ~ a few pounds** Sie sollten ein paar Pfund abnehmen *or* abspecken
b *tears, blood* vergießen; **he ~ his blood** sein Blut floss; *(= died also)* sein Blut wurde vergossen; **why should I ~ my blood?** warum sollte ich Leib und Leben einsetzen?; **I won't ~ any tears over him** ich weine ihm keine Träne nach
c *burden, leader, reputation* loswerden; *cares, ideas* ablegen; *friend* fallen lassen; *jobs* abbauen; **an actress who ~s husbands like a snake ~s skins** eine Schauspielerin, die die Ehemänner wechselt wie andere das Hemd
d *light, perfume* verbreiten; **to ~ light on sth** *(fig)* etw erhellen, Licht auf etw *(acc)* werfen
VI *(dog, cat etc)* sich haaren

shed² N Schuppen *m*; *(industrial also)* Halle *f*; *(= cattle shed)* Stall *m*; *(= night shelter etc)* Unterstand *m* → **watershed**

she'd [ʃiːd] *contr of* **she would, she had**

sheen [ʃiːn] N Glanz *m*

sheep [ʃiːp] N *pl* - *(lit, fig)* Schaf *nt*; **to count ~** Schäfchen zählen; **to separate the ~ from the goats** *(fig)* die Schafe von den Böcken trennen; **to make ~'s eyes at sb** jdn anhimmeln; **you might as well be hanged for a ~ as a lamb** *(prov)* wennschon, dennschon

sheep: **sheep-dip** N Desinfektionsbad *nt* für Schafe; *(for mange)* Räudebad *nt*; **sheepdog** N Hütehund *m*; **sheepdog trials** PL Gehorsamkeits- und Geschicklichkeitsprüfungen *pl* für Hütehunde; **sheep farm** N Schaffarm *f*; **sheep farmer** N Schafzüchter(in) *m(f)*; **sheep farming** N Schafzucht *f*; **sheepfold** N Schafhürde *f*

sheepherder [ˈʃiːpˌhɜːdəˈ] N *(US)* Schäfer(in) *m(f)*

sheepish [ˈʃiːpɪʃ] ADJ verlegen; **I felt a bit ~ about it** das war mir ein bisschen peinlich

sheepishly [ˈʃiːpɪʃlɪ] ADV verlegen

sheep: **sheep run** N Schafweide *f*; **sheepshearer** N *(= person)* Schafscherer(in) *m(f)*; **sheepshearing** N Schafschur *f*; **sheepskin** N **a** Schaffell *nt*; **~ (jacket)** Schaffelljacke *f* **b** *(US inf: = diploma)* Pergament *nt*; **sheepwalk** N *(Brit)* Schafweide *f*

sheer [ʃɪəˈ] ADJ *(+er)* **a** *(= absolute)* rein; *nonsense, madness* rein, glatt; *stupidity* rein, schier; **by ~ force of personality** aufgrund *or* auf Grund seiner Persönlichkeit; **by ~ chance** rein zufällig; **by ~ hard work** durch nichts als harte Arbeit; **the ~ impossibility of doing that** die schiere Unmöglichkeit, das zu tun; **it was ~ hell** es war die (reinste) Hölle *(inf)*
b *(= steep) cliff, drop* steil, jäh *(geh)*; **there is a ~ drop of 200 feet** es fällt 200 Fuß steil *or* senkrecht ab
c *cloth etc* (hauch)dünn, (hauch)zart; **~ nylon stockings** hauchdünne Nylonstrümpfe *pl*
ADV steil, jäh *(geh)*; *(= vertically)* senkrecht
VI *(Naut)* ausscheren

▶ **sheer away** VI **a** *(ship, plane)* ausweichen **b** *(= avoid)* **to sheer away from sb/sth** jdm/einer Sache ausweichen

▶ **sheer off** VI **a** *(ship)* ausscheren **b** *(person: = make off)* sich davonmachen

sheerness [ˈʃɪənɪs] N *(of cliffs)* Steilheit *f*

sheet¹ [ʃiːt] N **a** *(for bed)* (Bett)laken *nt*, Leinor Betttuch *nt*; *(= waterproof sheet)* Gummidecke *f*; *(for covering furniture)* Tuch *nt*; **between the ~s** *(inf)* im Bett *(inf)*; **the furniture was covered with (dust)sheets** die Möbel waren verhängt
b *(of paper, inf: = newspaper)* Blatt *nt*; *(big, as of wrapping paper, stamps etc, Typ)* Bogen *m*; **~ of music** Notenblatt *nt*; **~s** *(Brit sl: = money)* Kohle *f (inf)*

c *(of plywood, metal)* Platte *f*; *(of glass)* Scheibe *f*, Platte *f*; *(= baking sheet)* (Back)blech *nt*; *(Geol)* Schicht *f*; *(of water, ice etc)* Fläche *f*; *(of flame)* Flammenmeer *nt*; **a ~ of ice covered the lake** eine Eisschicht bedeckte den See; **the ~ of water covering the lawn** das Wasser, das auf dem Rasen stand; **the lake, a glasslike ~ of water** der See, eine spiegelblanke Wasserfläche; **a huge ~ of flame engulfed the building** das Gebäude ging in einem Flammenmeer unter; **the rain was coming down in ~s** es regnete in Strömen

d *(Comput: = spreadsheet)* Tabelle *f*

▶ **sheet down** VI *(Brit inf)* **it's sheeting down** *(= raining hard)* es regnet in Strömen; *(snow)* es schneit in dicken Flocken

sheet² N *(Naut: = rope)* Schot *f*, (Segel)leine *f*; **he's three ~s to** *or* **in the wind** *(dated inf)* er ist voll wie eine Strandhaubitze *(dated inf)*

sheet: **sheet anchor** N Notanker *m*; *(fig)* Rettungsanker *m*; **sheet anchor man** N Eckpfeiler *m*; **sheetbend** N Schotstek *m*; **sheet copper** N Kupferblech *nt*; **sheet feed** N *(Comput)* Einzelblatteinzug *m*; **sheet glass** N Flach- *or* Scheibenglas *nt*; **sheet ice** N Glatteis *nt*

sheeting [ˈʃiːtɪŋ] N *(= cloth)* Leinen *nt*; *(= metal etc)* Verkleidung *f*; *(= wood)* Verschalung *f*; **plastic ~** Plastiküberzug *m*

sheet: **sheet iron** N Eisenblech *nt*; **sheet lightning** N Wetterleuchten *nt*; **sheet metal** N Walzblech *nt*; **sheet music** N Notenblätter *pl*

sheik(h) [ʃeɪk] N Scheich *m*

sheik(h)dom [ˈʃeɪkdəm] N Scheichtum *nt*

sheila [ˈʃiːlə] N *(Austral inf)* Biene *f (inf)*, Puppe *f (inf)*

shekel [ˈʃekl] N Sekel *m*, Schekel *m*; **~s** *(inf)* Moneten *pl (dated sl)*

sheldrake [ˈʃeldreɪk] N Brandente *f*

shelf [ʃelf] N *pl* **shelves** **a** Brett *nt*, Bord *nt*; *(for books)* Bücherbrett *or* -bord *nt*; **shelves** *(= unit of furniture)* Regal *nt*; **to buy sth off the ~** etw als Handelsware kaufen; **to be on the ~** *(girl)* eine alte Jungfer sein, sitzen geblieben sein; *(worker)* zum alten Eisen gehören; **she was left on the ~** sie ist eine alte Jungfer geworden, sie ist sitzen geblieben **b** *(= ledge of rock etc, on rock face)* Gesims *nt*, (Fels-)vorsprung *m*; *(under water)* (Felsen)riff *nt*, Felsbank *f*; *(= sandbank)* Sandbank *f*, Untiefe *f*

shelf: **shelf life** N *(lit)* Lagerfähigkeit *f*; *(fig)* Dauer *f*; **to have a long/short ~** *(fig)* sich lange/kurz halten; **shelf mark** N Standortzeichen *nt*; **shelf room** N Platz *m* in den Regalen; **shelf-warmer** N *(hum)* Ladenhüter *m (inf)*

shell [ʃel] **N** **a** *(of egg, nut, mollusc)* Schale *f*; *(on beach)* Muschel *f*; *(of pea etc)* Hülse *f*; *(of snail)* (Schnecken)haus *nt*; *(of tortoise, turtle, insect)* Panzer *m*; *(= pastry shell)* Form *f*; **to come out of one's ~** *(fig)* aus seinem Schneckenhaus kommen, aus sich *(dat)* herausgehen; **to retire into one's ~** *(fig)* sich in sein Schneckenhaus verkriechen; **I'm just an empty ~** *(fig)* ich bin nur noch eine leere Hülse

b *(= frame, of building)* Mauerwerk *nt*, Mauern *pl*; *(unfinished)* Rohbau *m*; *(= ruin)* Gemäuer *nt*, Ruine *f*; *(of car, unfinished)* Karosserie *f*; *(gutted)* Wrack *nt*; *(of ship)* Gerippe *nt*, Rumpf *m*; *(gutted)* Wrack *nt*

c *(Mil)* Granate *f*; *(esp US: = cartridge)* Patrone *f*

d *(= boat)* Rennruderboot *nt*

e *(Comput)* Shell *f*

VT **a** *peas etc* enthülsen; *eggs, nuts* schälen; **~ed prawns** geschälte Garnelen

b *(Mil)* (mit Granaten) beschießen; **the town is still being ~ed** die Stadt steht immer noch unter Beschuss

▶ **shell out** *(inf)* **VT** *sep* blechen *(inf)* **VI** **to shell out for sth** für etw blechen *(inf)*

she'll [ʃiːl] *contr of* **she will, she shall**

shellac [ʃəˈlæk] *vb: pret, ptp* **shellacked** **N** Schellack *m* **VT** **a** *(= varnish)* mit Schellack behandeln **b** *(US sl: = defeat utterly)* fertigmachen *(inf)*; *(= beat)* vermöbeln *(inf)*; **to get a ~king** eins auf die Schnauze kriegen *(inf)*; *(= beating also)* eine Tracht Prügel kriegen

shell: **shell company** N *(Comm)* Firmenmantel *m*; **shellfire** N Granatfeuer *nt*; **shellfish** N Schaltier(e) *nt(pl)*; *(Cook)* Meeresfrüchte *pl*; **shell-hole** N Granattrichter *m*

shelling [ˈʃelɪŋ] N Granatfeuer *nt* (of auf *+acc*)

shell: **shell program** N *(Comput)* Shellprogramm *nt*; **shellproof** ADJ bombensicher; **shell shock** N Kriegsneurose *f*; **shell-shocked** ADJ **to be ~** *(lit)* unter einer Kriegsneurose leiden; *(fig)* verstört sein; **shell suit** N *modischer leichter Jogginganzug*

shelter [ˈʃeltəʳ] **N** *(= protection)* Schutz *m*; *(= place)* Unterstand *m*; *(= air-raid shelter)* (Luftschutz)keller *or* -bunker *m*; *(= bus shelter)* Wartehäuschen *nt*; *(= mountain shelter)* (Berg- *or* Schutz)hütte *f*; *(for the night)* Obdach *nt (liter)*, Unterkunft *f*; **a ~ for homeless people** ein Obdachlosenheim *or* -asyl *nt*; **under the ~ of the rock** im Schutze des Felsens; **when the ship reached ~** als das Schiff eine sichere *or* schützende Stelle erreichte; **to take ~** sich in Sicherheit bringen; *(from rain, hail etc)* sich unterstellen; **to seek ~** Schutz suchen; **to run for ~** Zuflucht suchen; **to give sb ~** jdn beherbergen; **to provide ~ for sb** jdm Schutz bieten; *(= accommodation)* jdn beherbergen; **the peasants offered the guerrillas ~** die Bauern boten den Partisanen Zuflucht

VT schützen *(from* vor *+dat)*; *criminal* verstecken; **to ~ sb from blame** jdn gegen Vorwürfe in Schutz nehmen; **to ~ sb from harm** jdn vor Schaden bewahren; **the police think he's ~ing someone** die Polizei glaubt, dass er jemanden deckt; **parents ~ing their children from harsh reality** Eltern, die ihre Kinder vor der rauen Wirklichkeit behüten

VI **there was nowhere to ~** man konnte nirgends Schutz finden; *(from rain etc)* man konnte sich nirgends unterstellen; **a good place to ~** eine Stelle, wo man gut geschützt ist; **we ~ed in a shop doorway** wir stellten uns in einem Ladeneingang unter; **we ~ed behind the rocks** wir stellten uns zum Schutz hinter die Felsen; **to ~ behind a friend/one's reputation** *(fig)* sich hinter einem Freund/seinem Ansehen verstecken

sheltered [ˈʃeltəd] ADJ *place* geschützt; *life* behütet; **~ from the wind** windgeschützt

sheltered: **sheltered housing** N *(for the elderly)* Wohnungen *pl* für Senioren; *(for the disabled)* Wohnungen *pl* für Behinderte; **sheltered workshop** N beschützende Werkstätte, Behindertenwerkstatt *f*

sheltie, **shelty** [ˈʃeltɪ] N *(= Shetland pony)* Sheltie *nt*; *(= Shetland sheepdog)* Sheltie *m*

shelve [ʃelv] **VI** *(= slope)* abfallen **VT** **a** *room* mit Regalen versehen, Regale einbauen in *(+acc)* **b** *problem* aufschieben; *plan, project* ad acta legen

shelves [ʃelvz] *pl of* **shelf**

shelving [ˈʃelvɪŋ] N Regale *pl*; *(= material also)* Bretter *pl*

shemozzle [ʃɪˈmɒzl] N *(US inf)* = **schemozzle**

shenanigans [ʃəˈnænɪgənz] PL *(inf: = tomfoolery)* Faxen *pl (inf)*, Mumpitz *m (inf)*; *(= goings-on)* Dinger *pl (inf)*, Sachen *pl (inf)*; *(= trickery)* üble Tricks *pl (inf)*, Dinger *pl (inf)*

shepherd [ˈʃepəd] **N** **a** Schäfer *m*, (Schaf)hirt *m*; **the Good Shepherd** der Gute Hirte **b** *(US)* = **German shepherd (dog)** **VT** führen

shepherd: **shepherd boy** N Hütejunge *m*; **shepherd dog** N Schäferhund *m*

shepherdess [ˈʃepədɪs] N Schäferin *f*

shepherd's [ˈʃepədz]: **shepherd's pie** N *Auflauf aus Hackfleisch und Kartoffelbrei*; **shepherd's plaid** N *schwarz-weiß or schwarzweiß karierter Wollstoff*; **shepherd's-purse** N *(Bot)* Hirtentäschel(kraut) *nt*

sherbet [ˈʃɜːbət] N *(= powder)* Brausepulver *nt*; *(= drink)* Brause *f*, Sorbet *m or nt*; *(US: = water ice)* Fruchteis *nt*

sherd [ʃɜːd] N = **shard**

sheriff [ˈʃerɪf] N Sheriff *m*; *(Scot)* Friedensrichter(in) *m(f)*

Sherpa [ˈʃɜːpə] N Sherpa *m*

sherry [ˈʃerɪ] N Sherry *m*

she's [ʃiːz] *contr of* **she is, she has**

Shetland [ˈʃetlənd] N, **Shetland Islands** [ˈʃetləndˈaɪləndz] PL Shetlandinseln *pl*

Shetland pony N Shetlandpony *nt*

Shetlands [ˈʃetləndz] PL Shetlandinseln *pl*

shew [ʃəʊ] VTI *(old) ptp* **shewn** [ʃəʊn] → **show**

shiatsu [ʃiːˈætsuː] N Shiatsu *nt*

shibboleth [ˈʃɪbəleθ] N *(= custom)* Gepflogenheit *f*, Konvention *f*; *(= catchword)* Losung *f*, Parole *f*, Schibboleth *nt (rare, liter)*

shield [ʃiːld] **N** *(Mil, Her)* Schild *m*; *(Zool also)* Panzer *m*; *(= sporting trophy also)* Trophäe *f*; *(on machine)* Schutzschirm *or* -schild *m*; *(= eyeshield, radiation shield)* Schirm *m*; *(fig)* Schutz *m*; **riot ~** Schutzschild *m*; **God is our ~** Gott ist unser Schild **VT** schützen *(sb from sth* jdn vor etw *dat)*; *industry* absichern, abschirmen; **she tried to ~ him from the truth** sie versuchte, ihm die Wahrheit zu ersparen

shift [ʃɪft] **N** **a** *(= change)* Änderung *f*; *(in policy, opinion)* Wandel *m*, Änderung *f*; *(Ling)* Verschiebung *f*; *(Mus)* Lagenwechsel *m*; *(from one place to another)* Verlegung *f*; **a ~ of scene** ein Szenenwechsel *m*; **a ~ in direction** eine Richtungsänderung; **a ~ in public opinion** ein Meinungsumschwung *m* in der Bevölkerung; **a ~ of** *or* **in emphasis** eine Gewichtsverlagerung; **a population ~** eine Bevölkerungsverschiebung; **this shows a ~ away from the government** dies lässt eine für die Regierung ungünstige Tendenz erkennen; **a new ~ toward(s) liberalism** ein neuer Trend zum Liberalismus

b *(Aut: = gear shift)* Schaltung *f*

c *(= period at work, group of workers)* Schicht *f*; **to work (in) ~s** in Schichten arbeiten

d *(= stratagem)* List *f*, Kniff *m*; *(= expedient)* Ausweg *m*; **to make ~ with/without sth** sich mit/ohne etw behelfen

e *(= dress)* Hemdkleid *nt*; *(old: = undergarment)* Hemd *nt*

VT **a** *(= move)* (von der Stelle) bewegen; *screw, nail* loskriegen, rauskriegen; *lid* abkriegen; *cork* rauskriegen; *furniture* verrücken; *head, arm* wegnehmen; *(from one place to another)* verlagern, verschieben; *offices etc* verlegen; *rubble, boulder* wegräumen; **to ~ scenery** Kulissen schieben; **to ~ sb from an opinion** jdn von einer Meinung abbringen; **he stood ~ing his weight from foot to foot** er trat von einem Fuß auf den anderen; **to ~ one's gaze** seinen Blick abwenden; **to ~ the blame onto somebody else** die Verantwortung auf jemand anders schieben; **to ~ sth to another room** etw in ein anderes Zimmer schaffen; **~ the table over to the wall** rück den Tisch an die Wand (rüber)!; **can you ~ your car back a bit?** können Sie ein Stück zurücksetzen?; **they ~ed him to Munich** sie haben ihn nach München versetzt; **we'll ~ all this junk out of the cupboard** wir räumen das ganze Gerümpel aus dem Schrank

b *(inf: = get rid of)* loswerden

c *(US Aut)* **to ~ gears** schalten

d *(inf) food* verputzen *(inf)*; *drink* schlucken *(inf)*

VI **a** *(= move)* sich bewegen; *(ballast, cargo)* sich verlagern; *(scene)* wechseln; *(wind)* umspringen; *(from one's opinion)* abgehen; **he ~ed out of the way** er ging aus dem Weg; **he was ~ing about in his chair** er rutschte auf seinem Stuhl hin und her; **~ over, you're taking up too much room** rück mal rüber, du nimmst zu viel Platz weg!; **he ~ed onto his back** er drehte sich auf den Rücken; **he refused to ~** *(fig)* er war nicht umzustimmen

b *(Aut)* schalten

c *(Brit inf: = move quickly)* flitzen *(inf)*, rasen;

that's really ~ing! das nenne ich Tempo!
d *(= manage)* **to ~ for oneself** sich *(dat)* (selbst) behelfen

shifter ['ʃɪftəʳ] N **a** *(Theat)* Kulissenschieber(in) *m(f)* **b** *(US Aut, bicycle)* Schalthebel *m*

shiftily ['ʃɪftɪlɪ] ADV zwielichtig, nicht ganz sauber *(inf)*; *glance* verstohlen; *reply* ausweichend; *behave* verdächtig

shiftiness ['ʃɪftɪnɪs] N Zwielichtigkeit *f*; *(of person, character also)* Fragwürdigkeit *f*; *(of glance)* Verstohlenheit *f*; *(of reply)* Ausweichen *nt*; **there was a certain ~ in his manner** sein Verhalten hatte etwas Verdächtiges

shifting sands ['ʃɪftɪŋ'sændz] PL **a** *(Geol)* Flugsand *m* **b** *(Naut)* Treibsand *m*

shift key N *(on typewriter)* Umschalttaste *f*; *(Comput)* Shifttaste *f*

shiftless ['ʃɪftlɪs] ADJ träge, energielos

shiftlessness ['ʃɪftlɪsnɪs] N Trägheit *f*, Energielosigkeit *f*

shift: **shift lever** N *(esp US; Aut, bicycle)* Schalthebel *m*; **shift lock** N *(= Comput)* Feststelltaste *f*; *(on typewriter)* Umschaltfeststeller *m*; **shiftwork** N Schichtarbeit *f*; **to do ~** Schicht arbeiten, Schichtarbeit machen; **shiftworker** N Schichtarbeiter(in) *m(f)*

shifty ['ʃɪftɪ] ADJ *(+er)* zwielichtig, nicht ganz sauber *(inf)*; *person, character also* fragwürdig; *glance* verstohlen; *eyes* verschlagen; *reply* ausweichend; **there was something ~ about ...** mit ... war etwas faul *(inf)*; **he has a ~ look in his eye** er hat so einen unsicheren Blick; **a ~ expression came over his face** sein Gesicht nahm einen gerissenen Ausdruck an; **a ~ little man** ein verdächtiger kleiner Kerl

shiitake [ʃiːɪ'tɑːkeɪ] N *pl* **shiitake** *(Bot)* Shitakepilz *m*

Shiite ['ʃiːaɪt] N Schiit(in) *m(f)* ADJ schiitisch

shillelagh [ʃə'leɪlə] N *(Ir)* (Schlehdorn- *or* Eichen)knüppel *m*

shilling ['ʃɪlɪŋ] N *(Brit old, Africa etc)* Shilling *m*

shilly-shally ['ʃɪlɪʃælɪ] VI *(esp Brit inf)* unschlüssig sein; **stop ~ing** lass das Fackeln; **you've shilly-shallied long enough** du hast lange genug gezögert

shimmer ['ʃɪməʳ] N Schimmer *m* VI schimmern

shimmy ['ʃɪmɪ] N Shimmy *m* VI sich schieben; *(= dance the shimmy)* den Shimmy tanzen

shin [ʃɪn] N Schienbein *nt*; *(of meat)* Hachse *f*; **to kick sb on the ~** jdn vors Schienbein treten VI **to ~ up/down** (geschickt) hinauf-/hinunterklettern

shinbone ['ʃɪnbəʊn] N Schienbein *nt*

shindig ['ʃɪndɪg] N *(inf)* Remmidemmi *nt (inf)*

shindy ['ʃɪndɪ] N *(inf)* Radau *m (inf)*; *(= noise also, dispute)* Krach *m (inf)*

shine [ʃaɪn] *vb: pret, ptp* **shone** N Glanz *m*; **to give one's shoes a ~** seine Schuhe polieren *or* blank putzen; **~, sir?** Schuhe putzen, der Herr?; **to have a ~** glänzen; **to put a ~ on sth** etw blank polieren; *(fig)* einer Sache *(dat)* (den richtigen) Glanz geben; **to take the ~ off sth** *(lit, fig)* einer Sache *(dat)* den Glanz nehmen; **she's taken a real ~ to Oxford/my brother** *(inf)* Oxford/mein Bruder hat es ihr wirklich angetan → **rain**

VT **a** *pret, ptp usu* **shined** *(= polish: also* **shine up***)* blank putzen; *shoes* polieren
b *(= direct a light)* **to ~ a light on sth** etw beleuchten; **~ the torch this way!** leuchte einmal hierher!; **don't ~ it in my eyes!** blende mich nicht!

VI **a** *(lit)* leuchten; *(stars, eyes, face)* leuchten, glänzen; *(metal, nose, paint)* glänzen; *(moon, sun, lamp)* scheinen; *(glass)* blitzblank sein; **to ~ like a beacon** *(fig)* wie ein Licht in der Dunkelheit sein *or* leuchten; *(hum: face, nose)* wie ein Lampion leuchten
b *(fig: = excel)* glänzen; **to ~ at/in sth** bei/in etw *(dat)* glänzen; **he doesn't exactly ~ at sports/his work** er ist keine *or* nicht gerade eine Leuchte im Sport/bei der Arbeit

▸ **shine down** VI herabscheinen *(on* auf *+acc)*

▸ **shine out** VI **a** *(light)* **the light shining out from the windows across the lawn** das durch die Fenster auf den Rasen fallende Licht; **a light (suddenly) shone out from the darkness** in der Dunkelheit blitzte (plötzlich) ein Licht auf; **the sun shone out from behind a cloud** die Sonne schien hinter einer Wolke hervor; **he thinks the sun shines out of her arse** *(Brit) or* **ass** *(US) (sl)* für ihn ist sie (einfach) die Größte *(inf)* **b** *(fig, qualities)* **his courage shines out** sein Mut ragt heraus

shiner ['ʃaɪnəʳ] N *(inf: = black eye)* Veilchen *nt (sl)*

shingle¹ ['ʃɪŋgl] N **a** *(= tile)* Schindel *f*; *(US inf: = signboard)* Schild *nt*; **to put up one's ~** *(US)* ein Geschäft eröffnen; *(doctor, lawyer)* sich niederlassen **b** *(= hairstyle)* Herrenschnitt *m*, Bubikopf *m* VT **a** *roof etc* mit Schindeln decken **b** *hair* einen Herrenschnitt *or* Bubikopf machen *(+dat)*

shingle² N *no pl (= pebbles)* Kiesel *m*, Kieselsteine *pl*; *(= shingle beach)* Kiesel(strand) *m*

shingles ['ʃɪŋglz] N *sing (Med)* Gürtelrose *f*

shingly ['ʃɪŋglɪ] ADJ *beach* steinig, voller Kieselsteine

shin guard ['ʃɪngɑːd] N Schienbeinschützer *m*

shininess ['ʃaɪnɪnɪs] N Glanz *m*

shining ['ʃaɪnɪŋ] ADJ *(lit, fig)* leuchtend; *light* strahlend; *metal, paint, hair* glänzend; *car* blitzend, blitzblank; **a ~ light** *(fig)* eine Leuchte; **~ white** leuchtend *or* strahlend weiß; **he's my knight in ~ armour** *(Brit) or* **armor** *(US)* er ist mein Märchenprinz

Shinto ['ʃɪntəʊ] *(Rel)* N Schintoismus *m* ADJ schintoistisch

Shintoism ['ʃɪntəʊɪzəm] N *(Rel)* Schintoismus *m*

shinty ['ʃɪntɪ] N *dem Hockey ähnliches Spiel*

shiny ['ʃaɪnɪ] ADJ *(+er)* glänzend; *elbows, trousers also* blank

ship [ʃɪp] N **a** Schiff *nt*; **the good ~ Venus** die gute Venus; **on board ~** an Bord; **to take ~ (for)** *(liter)* sich einschiffen (nach); **when my ~ comes home** *or* **in** *(fig)* wenn ich das große Los ziehe; **~ of the line** Kriegsschiff *nt*; **~ of the desert** Wüstenschiff *nt*; **the great ~ of state** das Staatsschiff
b *(US inf: = plane)* Maschine *f*; *(= spaceship)* (Raum)schiff *nt*

VT **a** *(= take on board)* an Bord nehmen; *mast* setzen; **to ~ oars** die Riemen einlegen; **to ~ water** leck sein; **we're ~ping water** unser Boot leckt *or* ist leck
b *(= transport)* versenden; *coal, grain etc* verfrachten; *(esp by sea)* verschiffen

VI *(= take employment)* anheuern

▸ **ship off** VT *sep* versenden; *coal, grain etc* verfrachten; *(esp by ship)* verschiffen; **they shipped their sons off to boarding school** sie steckten ihre Söhne ins Internat *(inf)*

▸ **ship out** VT *sep* versenden; *coal, grain etc* verfrachten; **to ship supplies out to sb** jdn (per Schiff) mit Vorräten versorgen

ship: **ship biscuit** N *(US)* Schiffszwieback *m*; **shipboard** N **on ~** an Bord (eines/des Schiffes) ADJ an Bord (eines/des Schiffes); **a ~ romance** eine Romanze auf See; **shipborne aircraft** [ʃɪpbɔːn'ɛəkrɑːft] N *(Naut, Aviat)* Bordflugzeug *nt*; **shipbreaker** N Schiffsverschrotter *m*; **shipbuilder** N Schiffbauer(in) *m(f)*; **a firm of ~s** eine Schiffbaufirma; **shipbuilding** N Schiffbau *m*; **ship canal** N (See)kanal *m*; **ship chandler** N Schiffsausrüster(in) *m(f)*; **shipload** N Schiffsladung *f*; **the tourists were arriving by the ~** *(inf)* ganze Schiffsladungen von Touristen kamen an; **shipmaster** N *(Naut)* (Handels)kapitän *m*; **shipmate** N Schiffskamerad(in) *m(f)*

shipment ['ʃɪpmənt] N Sendung *f*; *(of coal, grain, tractors)* Transport *m*; *(= transporting by sea)* Verschiffung *f*; *(= taking on board)* Verladen *nt*

shipowner ['ʃɪpəʊnəʳ] N Schiffseigner(in) *m(f)*; *(of many ships)* Reeder(in) *m(f)*

shipper ['ʃɪpəʳ] N *(= company)* Speditionsfirma *f*

shipping ['ʃɪpɪŋ] N *no pl* **a** Schifffahrt *f*; *(= ships)* Schiffe *pl*; **the Suez Canal has been reopened to ~** der Suezkanal ist wieder für die Schifffahrt *or* für den Schiffsverkehr geöffnet **b** *(= transportation)* Verschiffung *f*; *(by rail etc)* Versand *m* ADJ *attr* **~ business** Reederei- *or* Schifffahrtsgeschäft *nt*; **~ costs** Frachtkosten *pl*; **~ documents** Versanddokumente *pl*, Warenbegleitpapiere *pl*

shipping: **shipping agent** N Reeder(in) *m(f)*; **shipping case** N Versandkiste *f or* -behälter *m*; **shipping clerk** N Expedient(in) *m(f)*, Angestellte(r) *mf* in der Versandabteilung; **shipping company** N Schifffahrtsgesellschaft *f or* -linie *f*, Reederei *f*; **shipping forecast** N *(Met)* Seewetterbericht *m*; **shipping lane** N Schifffahrtsstraße *f*; **shipping line** N = **shipping company**; **shipping losses** PL Verluste *pl* von *or* an Schiffen; **shipping office** N *(= agent's office)* Büro *nt* einer Reedereivertretung; *(= place where seamen get jobs)* Heuerbüro *nt*; **shipping route** N Schifffahrtslinie *f*

ship's: **ship's articles** PL Heuervertrag *m*, Schiffsartikel *pl*; **ship's biscuit** N Schiffszwieback *m*; **ship's company** N (Schiffs)besatzung *f*; **ship's doctor** N Schiffsarzt *m*/-ärztin *f*; **ship's manifest** M *(for goods)* Ladeverzeichnis *nt*; *(for passengers)* Passagierliste *f*

shipshape ['ʃɪpʃeɪp] ADJ, ADV tipptopp *(inf)*; **to get everything ~** alles tipptopp machen *(inf)*; **we'll soon have you ~ again, said the doctor** *(inf)* Sie werden bald wieder auf dem Damm sein, sagte der Arzt *(inf)*; **~ and Bristol fashion** in bester Ordnung

ship's papers PL Schiffspapiere *pl*

ship: **ship-to-shore radio** N Seefunk *m*; **shipway** N *(= support)* Stapel *m*; *(= ship canal)* (See)kanal *m*, Schifffahrtsweg *m*; **shipwreck** N *(lit, fig)* Schiffbruch *m*; *(fig also)* Scheitern *nt*; **in the ~** bei dem Schiffbruch VT *(lit)* schiffbrüchig werden lassen; *(fig)* zum Scheitern bringen, scheitern lassen; **to be ~ed** *(lit)* schiffbrüchig sein; *(fig)* Schiffbruch erleiden, scheitern; **shipwright** N Schiffbauer(in) *m(f)*; **shipyard** N (Schiffs)werft *f*

shire ['ʃaɪəʳ] N *(Brit old)* Grafschaft *f*

shire horse N Zugpferd *nt*

shirk [ʃɜːk] VT sich drücken vor *(+dat)*, ausweichen *(+dat)* VI sich drücken; **you're ~ing!** du willst dich drücken!

shirker ['ʃɜːkəʳ] N Drückeberger(in) *m(f)*

shirking ['ʃɜːkɪŋ] N Drückebergerei *f*

shirr [ʃɜːʳ] VT kräuseln

shirring ['ʃɜːrɪŋ] N Kräuselarbeit *f*; **~ elastic** Gummizug *m*

shirt [ʃɜːt] N *(men's)* (Ober)hemd *nt*; *(Ftbl)* Hemd *nt*, Trikot *nt*; *(women's)* Hemdbluse *f*; **keep your ~ on** *(Brit inf)* reg dich nicht auf!; **to put one's ~ on a horse** *(inf)* den letzten Cent *or* sein letztes Hemd auf ein Pferd setzen; **to lose one's ~ on a horse** *(inf)* den letzten Cent *or* sein letztes Hemd bei einer Pferdewette verlieren; **I'm putting my ~ on him to get the job** *(inf)* ich gehe jede Wette ein, dass er die Stelle bekommt; **he'd give you the ~ off his back** *(inf)* er würde einem sein letztes Hemd geben; **he'll have the ~ off your back!** *(inf)* er zieht dich aus bis aufs letzte Hemd! *(inf)*

shirt: **shirt collar** N Hemdkragen *m*; **shirt front** N Hemdbrust *f*

shirting ['ʃɜːtɪŋ] N Hemdenstoff *m*

shirtsleeve ADJ hemdsärmelig; **it's real ~ weather now** jetzt kann man wirklich in Hemdsärmeln gehen N **shirtsleeves** PL Hemdsärmel *pl*; **in his/their ~s** in Hemdsärmeln

shirt-tail N Hemd(en)schoß *m*

shirtwaister ['ʃɜːtˌweɪstəʳ], *(US)* **shirtwaist** ['ʃɜːtˌweɪst] N Hemdblusenkleid *nt*

shirty ['ʃɜːtɪ] ADJ *(+er) (esp Brit inf)* sauer *(inf)*, verärgert; *(as characteristic)* griesgrämig *(inf)*; **he got pretty ~ about it** er wurde ganz schön sauer *(inf)*; **now don't get ~ with me!** nun werd nicht gleich sauer! *(inf)*

shit¹ [ʃɪt] *vb: pret, ptp* **shat** *(sl)* N a *(= excrement)* Scheiße *f (vulg)*; **to have/take a ~** scheißen *(vulg)*; **to have the ~s** Dünnschiss haben *(inf)*
b *(= person)* Arschloch *nt (vulg)*
c *(= nonsense)* Scheiße *f (inf)*, Scheiß *m (inf)*; **that film/idea/singer is ~** dieser Film/diese Idee/dieser Sänger ist Scheiße *(inf)*; **don't give me that ~!** erzähl mir nicht solche Scheiße *(inf) or* solchen Scheiß *(inf)!*
d **shits** PL *(= state of fear)* Schiss *m (sl)*, Muffensausen *nt (inf)*; **to have/get the ~s** Schiss *(sl) or* Muffensausen *(inf)* haben/kriegen; **it gives me the ~s** da krieg ich Schiss *(sl)*
e **to be up ~ creek (without a paddle)** bis zum Hals in der Scheiße stecken *(vulg)*; **to be in the ~** *or* **in deep ~** in der Scheiße stecken *(vulg)*; **I don't give a ~** das ist mir scheißegal *(inf)*, das geht mir am Arsch vorbei *(inf)*; **tough ~!** Scheiße auch! *(inf)*
ADJ *attr* Scheiß- *(inf)*, beschissen *(inf)*; **a ~ film** ein Scheißfilm *m (inf)*, ein beschissener Film *(inf)*
VI scheißen *(vulg)*; **to ~ on sb** *(= inform)* jdn verpfeifen *(inf)*; **all offenders will be shat on from a great height** *(hum)* wer nicht spurt, wird unheimlich zusammengeschissen *(inf) or* zur Sau gemacht *(inf)*; **it's time to ~ or get off the pot** *(US fig)* komm endlich zu Potte oder lass es ganz bleiben *(inf)*
VT **you're ~ting me** *(US)* erzähl mir keinen Scheiß *(inf)*; **to ~ bricks** *or* **a brick** sich *(dat)* (vor Angst) in die Hosen scheißen *(vulg)*
VR **to ~ oneself** sich vollscheißen *(vulg)*; *(with fear)* sich *(dat)* vor Angst in die Hosen scheißen *(vulg)*
INTERJ Scheiße *(inf)*

shit² N *(sl: = drugs)* Shit *m (sl)*

shitake [ʃɪ'tɑːkeɪ] N *pl* **-ke** *(Bot)* Shitakepilz *m*

shite [ʃaɪt] N, ADJ VIR, INTERJ *(Brit sl)* = **shit¹**

shit: **shitface** N *(sl)* = **shithead**; **shitfaced** ADJ *(sl) (with alcohol)* stockbesoffen *(inf)*; *(with drugs)* high *(inf)*; **shithead** N *(sl)* Scheißkerl *m (inf)*, Scheißtyp *m (inf)*; **shit-hot** ADJ *(Brit sl: = very good)* geil *(sl)*, krass *(sl)*; **shithouse** N *(sl: = lavatory)* Scheißhaus *nt (sl)*; **this ~ of a country** dieses Scheißland *(inf)*; **shitless** ADJ **to be scared ~** *(sl)* sich *(dat)* vor Angst in die Hosen scheißen *(vulg)*; **shitload** N *(US sl)* Menge *f*; **to be in a ~ of trouble** einen Haufen Ärger haben *(inf)*

shitty ['ʃɪtɪ] ADJ *(+er) (inf)* beschissen *(inf)*; **to feel ~** sich beschissen fühlen *(inf)*

shitwork ['ʃɪtwɜːk] N *no pl (US sl)* Scheißarbeit *f (inf)*

shiver¹ ['ʃɪvə'] N a *(of cold)* Schauer *m*; *(of horror)* Schauder *m*, Schauer *m*; **a ~ of cold** ein kalter Schauer; **a ~ ran down my spine** es lief mir kalt den Rücken hinunter; **a little ~ of fear ran down my spine** ein Angstschauer überlief mich; **the sight sent ~s down my spine** bei dem Anblick lief es mir kalt den Rücken hinunter *or* überlief es mich kalt; **his touch sent ~s down her spine** es durchzuckte sie bei seiner Berührung b *(fig)* **to get the ~s** eine Gänsehaut kriegen; **it gives me the ~s** ich kriege davon eine Gänsehaut VI zittern *(with* vor *+dat)*; *(with fear also)* schaudern

shiver² N Splitter *m*, Scherbe *f* VTI zersplittern, zerbrechen

shivering ['ʃɪvərɪŋ] N Schau(d)er *m*; **~ bout** *or* **fit** Schüttelfrost *m*

shivery ['ʃɪvərɪ] ADJ **to feel ~** frösteln; **the 'flu made him a bit ~** wegen seiner Grippe fröstelte er leicht

shlep [ʃlep] VT, VI, N *(US inf)* = **schlep**

shlepper [ʃlepə'] N *(US inf)* = **schlepper**

shlock [ʃlɒk] N *(dated esp US sl)* = **schlock**

shlong N *(US sl: = penis)* Schwanz *m (sl)*

shmear [ʃmɪə'] N *(US inf)* = **schmear**

shmo [ʃməʊ] N *(US inf)* = **schmo**

shmuck [ʃmʌk] N *(US inf)* = **schmuck**

shoal¹ [ʃəʊl] N *(= shallow place)* Untiefe *f*; *(= sandbank)* Sandbank *f*

shoal² N *(of fish)* Schwarm *m*; **in ~s** *(letters, applications etc)* massenweise, in Massen; *(people)* in hellen Scharen; **~s of letters** Unmengen *pl* von Briefen, eine Briefflut

shoat [ʃəʊt] N *(US: = piglet)* Ferkel *nt*, junges Schwein

shock¹ [ʃɒk] N a *(of explosion, impact)* Wucht *f*; *(of earthquake)* (Erd)stoß *m*
b *(Elec)* Schlag *m*; *(Med)* (Elektro)schock *m*; **to get a ~** einen Schlag bekommen
c *(= emotional disturbance)* Schock *m*, Schlag *m*; *(= state)* Schock(zustand) *m*; **to suffer from ~** einen Schock (erlitten) haben; **to be in (a state of) ~** unter Schock stehen; **the ~ killed him** den Schock hat er nicht überlebt; **rabbits can die of ~** für ein *or* bei einem Kaninchen kann ein Schock tödlich sein; **a feeling of ~ spread through the town** Entsetzen *nt* verbreitete sich in der Stadt; **our feeling is one of ~** wir sind zutiefst bestürzt; **a ~ to one's system** ein Kreislaufschock; **it comes as a ~ to hear that ...** mit Bestürzung höre ich/hören wir, dass ...; **to give sb a ~** jdn erschrecken; **it gave me a nasty ~** es hat mir einen bösen Schreck(en) eingejagt; **to get the ~ of one's life** den Schock seines Lebens kriegen; **I got the ~ of my life when I heard ...** ich dachte, mich trifft der Schlag, als ich hörte ... *(inf)*; **he is in for a ~!** *(inf)* der wird sich wundern *(inf)*
VT *(= affect emotionally)* erschüttern, bestürzen; *(= make indignant)* schockieren, schocken *(inf)*; **to be ~ed by sth** über etw *(acc)* erschüttert *or* bestürzt sein; *(morally)* über etw *(acc)* schockiert *or* geschockt *(inf)* sein; **she is easily ~ed** sie ist leicht *or* schnell schockiert; **he was ~ed when they took his passport away** es hat ihn geschockt, dass man ihm den Pass abgenommen hat *(inf)*; **to ~ sb into doing sth** jdm eine solche Angst einjagen, dass er etw tut; **to ~ sb into action/out of his/her** *etc* **complacency** jdn zum Handeln/aus seiner Selbstzufriedenheit aufrütteln
VI *(film, writer etc)* schockieren, schocken *(inf)*

shock² N *(Agr)* Garbenbündel *nt*, Hocke *f*

shock³ N *(also* **shock of hair***)* (Haar)schopf *m*

shock absorber ['ʃɒkəb,zɔːbə'] N Stoßdämpfer *m*

shocked [ʃɒkt] ADJ erschüttert, bestürzt; *(= indignant, outraged)* schockiert, empört; *(= amazed)* geschockt *(inf)*; **to be ~** *(Med)* unter Schock stehen, in einem Schockzustand sein; **the patient is badly ~** der Patient hat einen schweren Schock (erlitten)

shocker ['ʃɒkə'] N *(inf)* Reißer *m (inf)*, Schocker *m (inf)*; **he told me a ~ about conditions in jail** er erzählte mir eine Schauergeschichte über die Zustände im Gefängnis; **it's a ~** das haut einen um *(inf)*; **I have a ~ of a cold** ich habe eine grausige *(inf) or* entsetzliche Erkältung; **he's a ~** er ist ein ganz Schlimmer *(hum)*

shockheaded ['ʃɒk,hedɪd] ADJ **to be ~** strubbeliges *or* zotteliges Haar haben, ein Struwwelpeter sein *(inf)*

shock-horror ['ʃɒk'hɒrə'] ADJ **~ story** *(Press, hum)* Horrorgeschichte *f*

shocking ['ʃɒkɪŋ] ADJ a *(= outrageous)* schockierend; *(= upsetting) news, report* erschütternd, schockierend; **it may be ~ to the older generation** es mag für die ältere Generation schockierend sein; **the ~ truth** die grausame Wahrheit; **~ pink** knallrosa *(inf)*, pink *(Fashion)* b *(inf: = very bad)* entsetzlich, furchtbar; *state* schockierend; **I'm ~ at spelling** meine Rechtschreibung ist entsetzlich; **what a ~ thing to say/way to behave!** wie kann man bloß so etwas Schreckliches sagen/sich bloß so schrecklich benehmen!; **isn't it ~!** es ist doch furchtbar!

shockingly ['ʃɒkɪŋlɪ] ADV a *(= badly)* schrecklich, furchtbar; **to behave ~ (toward(s) sb)** sich (jdm gegenüber) haarsträubend *or* miserabel benehmen b *(= extremely)* entsetzlich, schrecklich c *(= disturbingly)* erschreckend; **suddenly and ~** auf plötzliche und erschreckende Weise

shock: **shock jock** N *(esp US inf) Radio-Discjockey, der seine kontroversen (meist rechtsradikalen) Ansichten provokativ vertritt*; **shockproof** ADJ stoßfest *or* -sicher; **shock tactics** PL *(Mil)* Stoß- *or* Durchbruchstaktik *f*; *(fig)* Schocktherapie *f*; **shock therapy, shock treatment** N Schocktherapie *or* -behandlung *f*; **shock troops** PL Stoßtruppen *pl*; **shock value** N Schockwirkung *f*; **shock wave** N *(lit)* Druckwelle *f*; *(fig)* Erschütterung *f*, Schock *m no pl*

shod [ʃɒd] *pret, ptp of* **shoe**

shoddily ['ʃɒdɪlɪ] ADV schäbig

shoddiness ['ʃɒdɪnɪs] N Schäbigkeit *f*; *(of work)* Schludrigkeit *f*; *(of goods)* Minderwertigkeit *f*

shoddy ['ʃɒdɪ] ADJ *(+er)* schäbig; *work* schludrig; *goods* minderwertig; *service* schlampig, schluderig; **a ~ attempt** ein schluderiger Versuch N *(= cloth)* Shoddy *nt or m*

shoe [ʃuː] *vb: pret, ptp* **shod** N a Schuh *m*; **I wouldn't like to be in his ~s** ich möchte nicht in seiner Haut stecken; **to put oneself in sb's ~s** sich in jds Lage *(acc)* versetzen; **to step into** *or* **fill sb's ~s** an jds Stelle *(acc)* treten *or* rücken; **where the ~ pinches** *(fig)* wo mich/uns der Schuh drückt; **if the ~ fits(, wear it)** *(US prov)* wem die Jacke passt(, der soll sie sich *(dat)* anziehen)
b *(= horseshoe)* (Huf)eisen *nt*
c *(= brake shoe)* Bremsschuh *m*
d *(for electric power cable)* (Gleit)schuh *m*; *(for mast)* Schuh *m*; *(on sledge)* Beschlag *m*
VT *horse* beschlagen; **to be well-shod** *(of person)* gut beschuht sein *(hum, geh)*

shoe: **shoeblack** N Schuhputzer *m*; **shoebox** N *(lit: for shoes)* Schuhkarton *m*; *(fig: = small flat)* Schuhkarton *m (inf fig)*; **shoebrush** N Schuhbürste *f*; **shoe cream** N Schuhcreme *f*, Schuhkrem(e) *f*; **shoehorn** N Schuhanzieher *m*, Schuhlöffel *m* VT **to ~ oneself/sth into sth** sich/etw in etw *(acc)* zwängen; **shoelace** N Schnürsenkel *m*; **shoe leather** N Schuhleder *nt*; **to wear out one's ~** seine Schuhe auftragen; **save ~ by taking the bus** fahr mit dem Bus und schone deine Schuhsohlen; **shoeless** ADJ ohne Schuhe; **shoemaker** N Schuhmacher(in) *m(f)*, Schuster(in) *m(f)*; **shoemender** N (Flick)schuster(in) *m(f)*; **shoe polish** N Schuhcreme *f*; **shoe repairer** N *(= person)* Schuster(in) *m(f)*; *(= shop)* Schuhreparaturdienst *m*; **shoeshine** N *(US)* Schuh(e)putzen *nt*; **to have a ~** sich *(dat)* die Schuhe putzen lassen; **shoeshine boy** N Schuhputzer *m*; **shoe shop** N Schuhgeschäft *nt*; **shoe size** N Schuhgröße *f*; **what ~ are you?** welche Schuhgröße haben Sie?; **act your age, not your ~** *(inf)* stell dich nicht so kindisch an; **shoestring** N a *(US: = shoelace)* Schnürsenkel *m*, Schnürband *nt* b *(fig)* **to live on a ~** von der Hand in den Mund leben; **the project is run on a ~** das Projekt wird mit ganz wenig Geld finanziert; **shoestring budget** N Minibudget *nt (inf)*; **shoetree** N (Schuh)spanner *m*

shone [ʃɒn] *pret, ptp of* **shine**

shoo [ʃuː] INTERJ sch; *(to dog etc)* pfui; *(to child)* husch VT **to ~ sb away** jdn verscheuchen *or* wegscheuchen; **I ~ed the children into the garden** ich scheuchte die Kinder in den Garten

shoo-in ['ʃuːɪn] N *(US inf)* todsicherer Tipp *(inf)*

shook¹ [ʃʊk] *pret of* **shake**

shook² N *(of corn)* Garbenbündel *nt*, Hocke *f*

shoot [ʃuːt] *vb: pret, ptp* **shot** N a *(Bot)* Trieb *m*; *(esp sprouting from seed, potato etc)* Keim *m*; *(out of ground: of bushes, trees)* Schössling *m*, Schoss *m*; *(= young branch)* Reis *nt*
b *(= shooting party)* Jagdgesellschaft *f*; *(= competition)* (Wett)schießen *nt*; *(= land)* (Jagd)revier *nt*, Jagd *f*
c *(= photographic assignment)* Fotosession *f*
VT a *(Mil etc)* schießen; *bullet, gun* abfeuern
b *person, animal (= hit)* anschießen; *(= wound*

seriously) niederschießen; *(= kill)* erschießen; **to ~ sb dead** jdn erschießen; **he shot himself** er hat sich erschossen; **he shot himself in the foot** er schoss sich *(dat)* in den Fuß; *(fig inf)* er hat ein Eigentor geschossen *(inf)*; **he was shot in the leg** er wurde ins Bein getroffen; **the bird had been shot in the wing** dem Vogel war ein Flügel durchschossen worden; **he was fatally shot in the neck** ihn traf ein tödlicher Genickschuss; **you'll get me shot** *(fig inf)* du bringst mich um Kopf und Kragen *(inf)*; **you'll get shot for doing that!** *(fig inf)* das kann dich Kopf und Kragen kosten! *(inf)*; **people have been shot for less!** *(hum inf)* es sind schon Leute für weniger an den Galgen gekommen! *(inf)*; **it was like ~ing fish in a barrel** es war ein ungleicher Wettkampf
c *(= throw, propel)* schleudern; **to ~ a question at sb** eine Frage auf jdn abfeuern; **to ~ a glance at sb, to ~ sb a glance** jdm einen (schnellen) Blick zuwerfen; **to ~ a line** *(inf)* aufschneiden, sich wichtigtun *(to sb* bei jdm*)*
d **to ~ the bolt** den Riegel vorlegen; **to ~ one's bolt** *(fig)* sein Pulver verschießen; **to ~ the rapids** über die Stromschnellen jagen; **to ~ the lights** eine Ampel (bei Rot) überfahren; **to ~ the breeze** *(inf)* einfach daherreden *(inf)*
e *(Sport)* schießen; *(US sl: = play) craps, pool* spielen; **to ~ dice** würfeln, Würfel spielen
f *(Phot) film, scene* drehen; *snapshot* schießen; *subject* aufnehmen
g *(inf: = inject) drug* drücken *(sl)*
VI **a** *(with gun)* schießen; *(as hunter)* jagen; **to ~ to kill** gezielt schießen; *(police)* einen gezielten Todesschuss/gezielte Todesschüsse abgeben; **don't ~!** nicht schießen!; **stop or I'll ~!** stehen bleiben oder ich schieße!; **to ~ at sb/sth** auf jdn/etw schießen; **to ~ straight** genau schießen; **to ~ wide** danebenschießen; **to ~ from the hip** aus der Hüfte schießen; *(fig: = talk without thinking)* ohne Überlegung daherreden; **~!** *(fig inf: = ask away etc)* schieß los!; **to ~ for the moon** sich *(dat)* Großes vornehmen
b *(= move rapidly)* schießen *(inf)*; **to ~ ahead/into the lead** an die Spitze vorpreschen; **he shot ahead of the other boys in maths** er ließ die anderen Jungen in Mathe weit hinter sich *(dat)*; **the car shot along the track** der Wagen schoss *or* jagte die Piste entlang; **he shot down the stairs** er schoss *or* jagte die Treppe hinunter; **to ~ by** *or* **past** vorbeischießen *or* -jagen; **to ~ in** (he)reingeschossen kommen; **to ~ to fame/stardom** auf einen Schlag berühmt/zum Star werden
c *(Sport)* schießen; **to ~ at goal** aufs Tor schießen
d *(pain)* **the pain shot up his leg** der Schmerz durchzuckte sein Bein; **~ing pains** stechende Schmerzen *pl*
e *(Phot)* knipsen *(inf)*; *(Film)* drehen
f *(inf: = inject drugs)* fixen *(inf)*

▶ **shoot away** **VI** **a** *(= move rapidly)* davonschießen, losjagen **b** *(= shoot continuously)* schießen; **we shot away at them for two hours** wir beschossen sie zwei Stunden lang; **shoot away!** *(fig inf)* schieß los! **VT** *sep* wegschießen

▶ **shoot down** **VT** *sep plane* abschießen; *(fig inf) person* fertigmachen *(inf)*; *suggestion* abschmettern *(inf)*; *argument* in der Luft zerreißen; **the plane was shot down in flames** die Maschine wurde in Brand geschossen und stürzte ab; **his plan was shot down in flames** *(fig)* sein Plan wurde in der Luft zerrissen

▶ **shoot off** **VI** **a** *(= rush off)* davonschießen, losjagen *(inf)* **b** *(sl, = ejaculate)* abspritzen *(sl)* **VT** *sep* abschießen; *gun etc also* abfeuern; **to shoot one's mouth off** *(inf, indiscreetly)* tratschen *(inf)*; *(boastfully)* das Maul aufreißen *(inf)*; **he'll start shooting his mouth off to the police** er wird bei der Polizei anfangen zu quatschen *(inf)*

▶ **shoot out** **VI** *(= emerge swiftly)* herausschießen *(of* aus*)* **VT** *sep* **a** *(= put out swiftly) hand etc* blitzschnell ausstrecken; *tongue etc* hervor- *or* herausschnellen (lassen); *(inf: = eject)* an die Luft setzen *(inf)*, raussetzen *(inf)*; **they were shot out of the car** sie wurden aus dem Auto geschleudert **b** **to shoot it out** sich *(dat)* ein (Feuer)gefecht liefern; **the cowboys shot it out** die Cowboys machten die Sache mit ihren Colts aus *(inf)*; **nobody dared to shoot it out with Bad Jake** keiner wagte es, sich mit Bad Jake zu schießen *(inf)*

▶ **shoot up** **VI** **a** *(hand, prices, temperature)* in die Höhe schnellen; *(= grow rapidly, children, plant)* in die Höhe schießen; *(new towns, buildings etc)* aus dem Boden schießen **b** *(Drugs inf)* sich *(dat)* einen Schuss setzen *(inf)* **VT** *sep* **a** **to shoot up a town** *(inf)* in einer Stadt herumballern *(inf) or* -knallen *(inf)*; **the aerodrome was shot up** das Flugfeld wurde heftig beschossen; **he was badly shot up in the war** er ist im Krieg übel zusammengeschossen worden **b** *(inf) drug* drücken *(sl)*

shooter [ˈʃuːtəʳ] **N** *(inf: = gun)* Knarre *f (sl)*, Kanone *f (sl)*

shooting [ˈʃuːtɪŋ] **N** **a** *(= shots)* Schießen *nt*; *(by artillery)* Feuer *nt*; **was there any ~?** gab es Schießereien?
b *(= murder, execution)* Erschießung *f*; **there was a ~ last night** gestern Nacht ist jemand erschossen worden; **"new outbreak of ~s in Beirut"** „Schießereien in Beirut wieder aufgeflammt"; **the police are investigating the ~** die Polizei untersucht die Schießerei
c *(Sport: Ftbl etc, with guns)* Schießen *nt*
d *(Hunt)* Jagen *nt*, Jagd *f*; *(= shooting rights)* Jagdrecht(e) *nt(pl)*; *(= land)* Jagd *f*, Jagdrevier *nt*; **there is good ~ in Scotland** in Schottland kann man gut jagen; **to go ~** auf die Jagd gehen; **good ~!** Weidmannsheil!
e *(Film)* Drehen *nt*; **~ was interrupted** die Dreharbeiten wurden unterbrochen

shooting: **shooting box** **N** Jagdhütte *f*; **shooting brake** **N** *(dated Aut)* Kombiwagen *m*; **shooting club** **N** Schießklub *m*; **shooting gallery** **N** **a** Schießstand *m*, Schießbude *f* **b** *(sl: = drug users)* Fixertreff *m (inf)*; **shooting iron** **N** *(US inf)* Schießeisen *nt (hum inf)*, Knarre *f (sl)*; **shooting jacket** **N** Jagdrock *m*; **shooting lodge** **N** = **shooting box**; **shooting match** **N** Wett- *or* Preisschießen *nt*; **the whole ~** *(inf)* der ganze Laden *(inf)*; **shooting party** **N** Jagdgesellschaft *f*; **shooting range** **N** Schießplatz *m*; **shooting rights** **PL** Jagdrecht(e) *nt(pl)*; **shooting script** **N** *(Film)* Drehplan *m*; **shooting star** **N** Sternschnuppe *f*; *(fig)* Shootingstar *m*, *(inf)* Senkrechtstarter(in) *m(f)*; **shooting stick** **N** Jagdstuhl *m*; **shooting war** **N** offener *or* heißer Krieg

shoot-out [ˈʃuːtaʊt] **N** **a** Schießerei *f* **b** *(Ftbl: = penalty shoot-out)* Elfmeterschießen *nt*

shop [ʃɒp] **N** **a** *(esp Brit)* Geschäft *nt*, Laden *m*; *(= large store)* Kaufhaus *nt*; **I have to go to the ~s** ich muss einkaufen gehen; **~!** Bedienung!; **to set up ~** ein Geschäft *or* einen Laden eröffnen; **to shut up** *or* **close up ~** zumachen, schließen; **you've come to the wrong ~** *(fig inf)* da sind Sie an der falschen Adresse; **all over the ~** *(Brit inf)* in der ganzen Gegend herum *(inf)*; **to talk ~** über die *or* von der Arbeit reden; *(esp of professional people)* fachsimpeln; **no ~, please!** keine Fachsimpelei, bitte!
b *(= workshop)* Werkstatt *f*; *(= workers)* Arbeiter *pl*, Arbeiterschaft *f*
c *(Brit: = shopping)* **to do one's weekly ~** seinen wöchentlichen Einkauf erledigen
VI einkaufen, Einkäufe machen; **to go ~ping** einkaufen gehen; **we spend Saturday mornings ~ping** samstags vormittags gehen wir einkaufen; **~ at Macfarlane's!** kaufen Sie bei Macfarlane!; **to ~ for fish** Fisch kaufen gehen
VT *(Brit inf)* **to ~ sb (to sb)** jdn (bei jdm) verpfeifen *(inf)*

▶ **shop around** **VI** *(lit, fig)* sich umsehen *(for* nach*)*

shopaholic [ʃɒpəˈhɒlɪk] **N** *(inf)* Einkaufssüchtige(r) *mf (inf)*

shop: **shop assistant** **N** *(esp Brit)* Verkäufer(in) *m(f)*; **shopbreaker** **N** Einbrecher(in) *m(f)*; **shopbreaking** **N** Ladeneinbruch *m*; **shop-fitter** **N** Geschäftsausstatter(in) *m(f)*; **shop-fittings** **PL** Ladeneinrichtungen *pl*; **shop floor** **N** **a** *(= place)* Produktionsstätte *f*; *(for heavier work)* Werkstatt *f*; **the manager's son started off working on the ~** der Sohn des Direktors hat ganz unten in der Fabrik angefangen; **on the ~** in der Werkstatt *etc*, bei *or* unter den Arbeitern **b** *(= workers)* Arbeiter *pl*, Leute *pl* in der Produktion; **shop-floor gossip** Klatsch *m or* Tratsch *m* unter den Arbeitern; **shop front** **N** *(esp Brit)* Ladenfassade *f*; **shop-girl** **N** *(Brit)* Ladenmädchen *nt*; **shopgrifting** [ˈʃɒp,grɪftɪŋ] **N** *(US) die Praxis, etw zu kaufen und innerhalb von 30 Tagen gegen Gelderstattung wieder zurückzugeben*; **shop hours** **PL** *(esp Brit)* Öffnungszeiten *pl*; **shop-in-shop** **N** Shop-in-Shop *m*; **shopkeeper** **N** *(esp Brit)* Ladenbesitzer(in) *m(f)*, Geschäftsinhaber(in) *m(f)*; **a nation of ~s** ein Krämervolk *nt*; **shop-keeping** [ˈʃɒp,kiːpɪŋ] **N** Betrieb *m* eines (Laden)geschäfts; **shoplifter** **N** Ladendieb(in) *m(f)*; **shoplifting** **N** Ladendiebstahl *m*

shopper [ˈʃɒpəʳ] **N** Käufer(in) *m(f)*; **she's a good ~** sie kann gut einkaufen; **the streets were thronged with ~s** in den Straßen drängten sich die Kauflustigen

shopping [ˈʃɒpɪŋ] **N** *(= act)* Einkaufen *nt*; *(= goods bought)* Einkäufe *pl*; **she had her ~ in a plastic bag** sie hatte ihre Einkäufe in einer Plastiktüte; **to do one's ~** einkaufen, Einkäufe machen

shopping: **shopping bag** **N** Einkaufstasche *f*; **shopping basket** **N** Einkaufskorb *m*; **shopping cart** **N** *(US)* = **shopping trolley**; **shopping centre**, *(US)* **shopping center** **N** Einkaufszentrum *nt*; **shopping channel** **N** *(TV)* Shoppingsender *m*; **shopping list** **N** Einkaufszettel *m*; **a ~ of requests/demands** eine (Wunsch)liste von Bitten/Forderungen; **shopping mall** **N** Shoppingcenter *nt*; **shopping precinct** **N** Ladengegend *f*, Ladenbereich *m*; **shopping spree** **N** Einkaufsbummel *m*; **shopping street** **N** Einkaufsstraße *f*; **shopping trolley** **N** *(Brit)* Einkaufswagen *m*

shop: **shopsoiled** **ADJ** *(Brit) clothes, furniture, wallpaper* angestaubt, angeschmutzt; *goods, material* leicht beschädigt; **shop steward** **N** (gewerkschaftlicher) Vertrauensmann *(im Betrieb)*; **shoptalk** **N** Reden *nt* über die Arbeit; *(of professional people also)* Fachsimpelei *f*; **shopwalker** **N** *(Brit)* Aufsichtsperson *f (form)*, Aufsicht *f*; **shop window** **N** *(lit, fig)* Schaufenster *nt*; **shopworn** **ADJ** *goods, furniture etc* leicht beschädigt

shore[1] [ʃɔːʳ] **N** **a** *(= seashore, lake shore)* Ufer *nt*, Gestade *nt (liter)*; *(= beach)* Strand *m*; **these ~s** *(fig)* dieses Land, diese Gestade *pl (liter)*; **he returned to his native ~s** er kehrte zurück zu heimatlichen Gefilden; **a house on the ~s of the lake** ein Haus am Seeufer; **no invader has since set foot on these ~s** seitdem hat kein Eroberer mehr diesen Boden betreten **b** *(= land)* Land *nt*; **on ~** an Land

shore[2] **N** *(Min, Naut)* Stützbalken *m*, Strebe *f* **VT** *(also* **shore up***)* (ab)stützen; *(fig)* stützen

shore: **shore area** **N** Uferzone *f*, Uferregion *f*; **shore dinner** **N** *(US)* Meeresfrüchte *pl*; **shore leave** **N** *(Naut)* Landurlaub *m*; **shoreline** **N** Wasserlinie *f*, Uferlinie *f*; **shore pass** **N** *(Naut)* Landurlaubsschein *m*; **shore patrol** **N** *(US)* Küstenstreife *f*, Küstenpatrouille *f (der US-Marine)*; **shoreward(s)** **ADJ** **~ wind** Seewind *m*; **in a ~ direction** in Richtung Küste *or* Land, landwärts **ADV** landwärts, zum Land (hin)

shoring [ˈʃɔːrɪŋ] **N** **a** *(= supporting beams)* Stützbalken *pl* **b** *(supporting of wall etc)* Abstützen *nt*

shorn [ʃɔːn] *ptp of* **shear** **ADJ** **a** **to be ~ of sth** einer Sache *(gen)* entkleidet sein **b** *sheep* geschoren; *head* (kahl) geschoren; **her ~ locks** ihr kurz geschorenes Haar

short [ʃɔːt] **ADJ** *(+er)* **a** kurz; *steps, person* klein; *waist (of dress)* hoch; **a ~ way off** nicht weit entfernt; **to be ~ in the leg** *(person)* kurze Beine haben; *(trousers)* zu kurz sein; **to be in ~**

trousers in kurzen Hosen herumlaufen; *(fig)* ein kleiner Junge sein; **~ back and sides** kurzer Haarschnitt; **a ~ time ago** vor kurzer Zeit, vor Kurzem; **in a ~ time** *or* **while** in Kürze, in kurzer Zeit; **time is getting/is ~** die Zeit wird/ist knapp; **to take the ~ view** die Sache auf kurze Sicht betrachten; **in ~ order** *(US inf)* sofort; **~ drink** Kurze(r) *m (inf)*, Schnaps *m*

b *(Ling) vowel, syllable* kurz; *(= unstressed)* unbetont

c *(= brief)* kurz; **~ and sweet** schön kurz, kurz und ergreifend *(iro)*; **the ~ answer is that he refused** kurz gesagt, er lehnte ab; **in ~** kurz gesagt; **she's called Pat for ~** sie wird kurz *or* einfach Pat genannt; **Pat is ~ for Patricia** Pat ist die Kurzform von Patricia

d *(= curt) reply* knapp; *(= rude)* barsch, schroff; *manner, person* schroff, kurz angebunden *(inf)*; **to have a ~ temper** unbeherrscht sein; **his ~ temper** seine Unbeherrschtheit; **to be ~ with sb** jdn schroff behandeln, jdm gegenüber kurz angebunden sein *(inf)*

e *(= insufficient)* zu wenig *inv*; *rations* knapp; **to be in ~ supply** knapp sein; *(Comm)* beschränkt lieferbar sein; **to be ~** *(= in short supply)* knapp sein; *(shot, throw)* zu kurz sein, nicht weit genug sein; **we are (five/£3) ~, we are ~ (of five/£3)** wir haben (fünf/£ 3) zu wenig; **it's five/£3 ~** es fehlen fünf/£ 3; **we are seven ~** uns *(dat)* fehlen sieben; **we are ~ of books/staff** wir haben zu wenig Bücher/Personal; **we are not ~ of volunteers** wir haben genug Freiwillige, uns fehlt es nicht an Freiwilligen; **to be ~ of time** wenig Zeit haben; **I'm a bit ~ (of cash)** *(inf)* ich bin etwas knapp bei Kasse *(inf)*; **he's one sandwich ~ of a picnic** *(hum inf)* **he's one** *or* **several cards ~ of a full deck** *(US hum inf)* er hat sie nicht alle beisammen *(inf)*; **we are £2,000 ~/not far ~ of our target** wir liegen £ 2.000/(nur) knapp unter unserem Ziel; **not far** *or* **much ~ of £100** nicht viel weniger als £ 100, beinahe £ 100, knapp unter £ 100; **he is not far ~ of his fiftieth birthday now** er ist jetzt knapp unter fünfzig, ihm fehlt nicht mehr viel bis zu seinem fünfzigsten Geburtstag; **to be ~ on experience/examples** wenig Erfahrung/Beispiele haben; **to give sb ~ change** jdm zu wenig herausgeben *or* zu wenig Wechselgeld geben → **breath, measure**

f *(Fin) sale* ohne Deckung, ungedeckt; *loan, bill* kurzfristig; **~ stock** auf Baisse gekaufte Aktien

g *pastry* mürbe

ADV **a** *(= below the expected amount)* **to fall ~** *(arrow etc)* zu kurz landen; *(shot)* zu kurz sein; *(supplies etc)* nicht ausreichen; **that's where the book falls ~** daran fehlt es dem Buch; **to fall ~ of sth** etw nicht erreichen; *of expectations* etw nicht erfüllen; **it fell 10 feet ~ of the target** es fehlten 10 Fuß zum Ziel, es war 10 Fuß zu kurz; **it falls far ~ of what we require** das bleibt weit hinter unseren Bedürfnissen zurück; *(in quantity)* das bleibt weit unter unseren Bedürfnissen; **production has fallen ~ by 100 tons** die Produktion ist um 100 Tonnen zu niedrig; **to go ~ (of money/food** *etc***)** zu wenig (Geld/zu essen *etc*) haben; **we never went ~** wir hatten immer genügend; **the parents went ~ of food so that the children could eat** die Eltern haben an sich *(dat)* selbst gespart, damit die Kinder zu essen hatten; **they never let the children go ~** sie ließen es den Kindern an nichts fehlen; **we are running ~ (of water/time)** wir haben nicht mehr viel (Wasser/Zeit); **I'm running ~ of ideas** mir gehen die Ideen aus; **my patience is running ~** meine Geduld ist bald zu Ende; **sugar/water is running ~** Zucker/Wasser ist knapp; **to sell sb ~** *(in shop)* jdm zuwenig geben; *(= betray, cheat)* jdn betrügen; **to sell oneself ~** *(inf)* sein Licht unter den Scheffel stellen, sich unter Wert verkaufen; **to sell ~** *(Fin)* ungedeckt *or* ohne Deckung verkaufen

b *(= abruptly, suddenly)* plötzlich, abrupt; **to pull up** *or* **stop ~** *(while driving)* plötzlich *or* abrupt anhalten; *(while walking also)* plötzlich *or* abrupt stehen bleiben; **to stop ~** *(while talking)* plötzlich *or* unvermittelt innehalten; **to stop sb ~** jdn unterbrechen; **to stop sth ~** etw abbrechen; **I'd stop ~ of murder** vor Mord würde ich haltmachen; **he stopped ~ of actually calling me a liar** er ging nicht so weit, mich tatsächlich einen Lügner zu nennen; **to be caught ~** *(inf: = unprepared)* überrascht werden; *(= without money, supplies)* zu knapp (dran) sein; *(= need the toilet)* dringend mal müssen *(inf)*; **to catch sb ~** *(inf)* jdn in einer Verlegenheit antreffen; **to be caught ~ by sth** auf etw *(acc)* nicht vorbereitet sein

c **~ of** *(= except)* außer *(+dat)*; **it is nothing ~ of robbery** das ist glatter Diebstahl; **nothing ~ of a revolution can ...** nur eine Revolution kann ...; **it's little ~ of madness** das grenzt an Wahnsinn; **it's little ~ of murder** das ist ja schon fast Mord; **I don't see what you can do ~ of asking him yourself** ich sehe keine andere Möglichkeit, außer dass Sie ihn selbst fragen; **~ of telling him a lie ...** außer ihn zu belügen ...

N *(= short circuit)* Kurzschluss, Kurze(r) *(inf) m*; *(inf: = short drink)* Kurze(r) *m (inf)*; *(= short film)* Kurzfilm *m*; **to have/get sb by the ~ and curlies** *(Brit inf)* jdn am Wickel haben/kriegen *(inf)* → **long**[2]

VT *(Elec)* kurzschließen

VI *(Elec)* einen Kurzschluss haben

shortage [ˈʃɔːtɪdʒ] **N** *(of goods, objects)* Knappheit *f no pl* (of an *+dat*); *(of people)* Mangel *m no pl* (of an *+dat*); **the housing ~** die Wohnungsknappheit; **a ~ of staff** ein Mangel *m* an Arbeitskräften, ein Personalmangel *m*; **in times of ~** in Zeiten der Knappheit; **there are always ~s** irgendetwas ist immer knapp; **there's no ~ of advice** es fehlt nicht an guten Ratschlägen

short: **short arse** **N** *(Brit sl)* Knirps *m (inf)*; **shortbread** **N** Shortbread *nt*, ≈ Butterkeks *m*; **shortcake** **N** *(Brit: = shortbread)* Butterkeks *m*; *(US: = sponge)* Biskuittörtchen *nt*; **strawberry ~** Erdbeertörtchen *nt*; **short-change** **VT** **to ~ sb** *(lit)* jdm zu wenig Wechselgeld geben, jdm zu wenig herausgeben; *(fig inf)* jdn übers Ohr hauen *(inf)*; **short circuit** **N** Kurzschluss *m*; **short-circuit** **VT** kurzschließen; *(fig: = bypass)* umgehen **VI** einen Kurzschluss haben; **shortcoming** **N** *(esp pl)* Mangel *m*; *(of person)* Fehler *m*; *(of system)* Unzulänglichkeit *f*, Mangel *m*; **short course** **N** *(Swimming)* Kurzbahn *f*; **shortcrust** **N** *(also* **shortcrust pastry***)* Mürbeteig *m*; **shortcut, short cut** **N** **a** Abkürzung *f*; *(fig)* Schnellverfahren *nt*; *(= easy solution)* Patentlösung *f*; **there's no ~ to success** der Erfolg fällt einem nicht in den Schoß **b** *(Comput)* Verknüpfung *f*; *(= shortcut key)* Shortcut *m*, Tastenkombination *f*; **broken ~** ungültige Verknüpfung

shortcut key **N** *(Comput)* Shortcut *m*, Tastenkombination *f*

short-dated **ADJ** *(Fin) stock* kurzfristig; *bonds, gilts* mit kurzer Laufzeit

shorten [ˈʃɔːtn] **VT** **a** *(= make shorter)* verkürzen; *life, name* abkürzen; *dress, rope* kürzer machen, kürzen; *book, programme, letter, syllabus etc* kürzen; *odds* verringern; *sail* reffen **b** *pastry* Fett beigeben *(+dat)* **VI** *(evenings, days)* kürzer werden; *(odds)* sich verringern

shortening [ˈʃɔːtnɪŋ] **N** *(Cook)* (Back)fett *nt*

short: **shortfall** **N** Defizit *nt*; **short-haired** **ADJ** kurzhaarig; **shorthand** **N** Kurzschrift *f*, Stenografie *f*; **in ~** in Kurzschrift; **to write ~** stenografieren; **to take sth down in ~** etw stenografieren; **short-handed** **ADJ** **to be ~** zu wenig Personal haben; **shorthand notebook** **N** Stenoblock *m*; **shorthand notes** **PL** stenografische Notizen *pl*; **shorthand typist** **N** Stenotypist(in) *m(f)*; **shorthand writer** **N** Stenograf(in) *m(f)*; **short haul** **N** Nahtransport *m*; **short-haul jet** **N** Kurzstreckenflugzeug *nt*; **shorthorn** **N** Kurzhornrind *nt*, Shorthorn *nt*; **~ cattle** Kurzhornrinder *pl*

shortie [ˈʃɔːtɪ] **N** **a** *(inf: also* **shortie nightie***)* Shorty *nt*, kurzes Nachthemd **b** = **shorty**

shortish [ˈʃɔːtɪʃ] **ADJ** **a** ziemlich kurz; *person* ziemlich klein **b** *(= scarce)* ziemlich knapp

short: **short list** **N** *(esp Brit)* Auswahlliste *f*; **to be on the ~** in der engeren Wahl sein; **short-list** **VT** *(esp Brit)* **to ~ sb** jdn in die engere Wahl nehmen *or* ziehen; **he has not been ~ed** er ist nicht in die engere Wahl gekommen; **short-lived** **ADJ** *(lit, fig)* kurzlebig; *protests, attempts* nicht lange andauernd; **to be ~** *(success, happiness)* von kurzer Dauer sein

shortly [ˈʃɔːtlɪ] **ADV** **a** *(= soon)* bald, in Kürze; *after, before, afterwards* kurz **b** *(= briefly)* kurz **c** *(= curtly)* barsch

shortness [ˈʃɔːtnɪs] **N** **a** Kürze *f*; *(of person)* Kleinheit *f*; **~ of sight** Kurzsichtigkeit *f*; **~ of breath** Kurzatmigkeit *f* **b** *(= curtness)* Schroffheit *f*, Barschheit *f* **c** *(of supplies, money)* Knappheit *f*

short: **short-order** **ADJ** *(US) cook, waiter* im Schnellimbiss; **~ dishes** Schnellgerichte *pl*; **short pastry** **N** Mürbeteig *m*; **short-range** **ADJ** mit geringer *or* kurzer Reichweite; *walkie-talkie* für den Nahbereich; *(fig) plans* kurzfristig; **~ missile/aircraft** Kurzstreckenrakete *f*/-flugzeug *nt*; **~ weapon** Nahkampfwaffe *f*; **~ weather forecast** Wetterbericht *m* für die nächsten Tage

shorts [ʃɔːts] **PL** **a** *(= short trousers)* Shorts *pl*, kurze Hose(n *pl*) **b** *(esp US: = underpants)* Unterhose *f*

short: **short sharp shock** **N** *(Brit: = punishment) kurze, aber harte Gefängnisstrafe*; **short-sighted** **ADJ**, **short-sightedly** **ADV** *(lit, fig)* kurzsichtig; **short-sightedness** **N** *(lit, fig)* Kurzsichtigkeit *f*; **short ski** **N** Kurzski *m*; **short-sleeved** **ADJ** kurzärmelig; **short-staffed** **ADJ** **to be ~** zu wenig Personal haben; **short-stay** **ADJ** *(Brit)* **~ hospital ward** Kurzzeitstation *f*; **~ car park** Kurzzeitparkplatz *m*; **~ visa** Visum *nt* für einen Kurzaufenthalt; **short-stay parking** **N** *(Brit)* Kurzparken *nt*; **short story** **N** Kurzgeschichte *f*, Shortstory *f*, Short Story *f*, Erzählung *f*; **short-story writer** Autor(in) *m(f)* von Kurzgeschichten; **short-tempered** **ADJ** *(in general)* unbeherrscht; *(in a bad temper)* gereizt; **to be ~ with sb** mit jdm ungeduldig sein; **short-temperedly** **ADV** unbeherrscht; *reply* unwirsch, ungeduldig; **short term** **N** **for the ~** auf kurze Frist gesehen, vorläufig; **plans for the ~** kurzfristige Pläne; **in the ~** auf kurze Sicht; **short-term** **ADJ** kurzfristig; **~ memory** Kurzzeitgedächtnis *nt*; **to take a ~ view** kurzfristig denken; **banks took a ~ view that was harmful to small firms** die kurzsichtige Einstellung der Banken schadete den Kleinunternehmen; **on a ~ basis** kurzfristig **ADV** kurzfristig; **short-term contract** **N** Kurzzeitvertrag *m*; **he was engaged on a ~** er wurde mit Kurzzeitvertrag eingestellt; **short time** **N** Kurzarbeit *f*; **to be on ~, to work ~** kurzarbeiten, Kurzarbeit haben; **short ton** **N** *Tonne von 2000 Pounds = 907,18 kg*; **short-waisted** **ADJ** *person* mit kurzer Taille; *coat* hochtailliert; **to be ~** eine kurze/hohe Taille haben; **short wave** **N** Kurzwelle *f*; **short-wave** **ADJ** *transmission* auf Kurzwelle; **a ~ radio** ein Kurzwellenempfänger *m*; **short-winded** **ADJ** *(= breathless)* kurzatmig

shorty [ˈʃɔːtɪ] **N** *(inf)* Kleine(r) *mf*, Knirps *m (inf)*

shot[1] [ʃɒt] *pret, ptp of* **shoot** **N** **a** *(from gun, bow etc)* Schuss *m*; **to fire** *or* **take a ~ at sb/sth** einen Schuss auf jdn/etw abfeuern *or* abgeben; **a ~ across the bows** *(lit, fig)* ein Schuss *m* vor den Bug; **to exchange ~s** sich *(dat)* einen Schusswechsel liefern; **the first ~s in the election campaign** *(fig)* die ersten scharfen Schüsse im Wahlkampf; **to call the ~s** *(fig)* das Sagen haben *(inf)* → **long shot, parting**

b *(= projectile)* Kugel *f*; *(no pl: = lead shot)* Schrot *m*, Schrotkugeln *pl*

c *(= person)* Schütze *m*, Schützin *f* → **big shot**

d *(= attempt)* Versuch *m*; **at the first ~** auf Anhieb; **to take** *or* **have a ~ (at it)** *(= try)* es (mal) versuchen; *(= guess)* (auf gut Glück) raten; **I had a ~ at water-skiing** ich habe auch mal versucht, Wasserski zu laufen; **it's your ~**

du bist dran; **to give sth one's best ~** *(inf)* sich nach Kräften um etw bemühen
e *(= space shot)* (Raum)flug *m*; *(= launch)* Start *m*
f like a ~ *(inf: = quickly, run away, be off)* wie der Blitz *(inf)*; *do sth, agree* sofort
g *(= injection)* Spritze *f*; *(= immunization)* Impfung *f*; *(of alcohol)* Schuss *m*; **he gave him a ~ of morphine** er gab ihm eine Morphiumspritze; **a ~ of rum** ein Schuss *m* Rum; **Chris is doing** *or* **taking ~s** *(inf)* Chris kippt ganz schön runter *(inf)* *or* kippt Shots in sich rein *(sl)*; **to give a company a ~ in the arm** *(fig)* einer Firma eine Finanzspritze geben
h *(Phot)* Aufnahme *f*; **out of ~** nicht im Bild
i *(Sport, Ftbl, Hockey etc)* Schuss *m*; *(= throw)* Wurf *m*; *(Tennis, Golf)* Schlag *m*; **to take a ~ at goal** aufs Tor schießen
j *(= shot-putting)* **the ~** *(= discipline)* Kugelstoßen *nt*; *(= weight)* die Kugel; **to put the ~** kugelstoßen

shot² ADJ **a** *(= variegated)* durchzogen, durchschossen *(with* mit*)*; *silk* eingeschossen, changierend; **to be ~ through with sth** *(lit, with colour etc)* von etw durchzogen sein; *(fig) with emotion etc* von etw durchdrungen sein; **his hair is ~ through with silver** sein Haar ist von silbernen Strähnen durchzogen **b** *(Brit inf: = rid)* **to be/get ~ of sb/sth** jdn/etw los sein/loswerden **c** *(= destroyed)* **my nerves are totally ~** ich bin mit den Nerven fertig *or* am Ende; **her confidence was ~ to pieces** ihr Vertrauen war völlig zerstört

shot: **shotgun** N Schrotflinte *f*; **shotgun wedding** N Mussheirat *f*; **shot put** N *(= event)* Kugelstoßen *nt*; *(= throw)* Wurf *m*, Stoß *m*; **shot-putter** N Kugelstoßer(in) *m(f)*; **shot tower** N Schrotturm *m*

should [ʃʊd] ✪ 1.1, 2.1, 14, 15.2, 26.1 *pret of* **shall** MODAL AUX VB **a** *(expressing duty, advisability, command)* **I/he ~ do that** ich/er sollte das tun; **you ~n't do that** Sie sollten das nicht tun; **I ~ have done it** ich hätte es tun sollen *or* müssen; **I ~n't have done it** ich hätte es nicht tun sollen *or* dürfen; **all is as it ~ be** alles ist so, wie es sein sollte *or* muss; **which is as it ~ be** und so soll(te) es auch sein; **he ~ know that it's wrong to lie** er sollte *or* müsste wissen, dass man nicht lügen darf; **you really ~ see that film** den Film sollten *or* müssen Sie wirklich sehen; **you ~ have seen his face!** *(inf)* du hättest sein Gesicht sehen sollen!; **~ I go too? – yes you ~** sollte ich auch gehen? – ja, das sollten Sie schon; **was it a good film? – I ~ think it was** war der Film gut? – und ob; **he's coming to apologize – I ~ think so** er will sich entschuldigen – das möchte ich auch meinen *or* hoffen; **... and I ~ know** ... und ich müsste es ja wissen; **how ~ I know?** woher soll ich das wissen?
b *(expressing probability)* **he ~ be there by now** er müsste eigentlich schon da sein; **they ~ arrive tomorrow** sie müssten morgen ankommen; **this ~ be enough** das müsste eigentlich reichen; **why ~ he suspect me?** warum sollte er mich verdächtigen?; **this book ~ help you** dieses Buch wird Ihnen bestimmt helfen; **this ~ be good!** *(inf)* das wird bestimmt gut!
c *(in tentative statements)* **I ~n't like to say** das möchte ich nicht gern sagen; **I ~ hardly have called him an idiot** ich hätte ihn wohl kaum einen Idioten genannt; **I ~ think there were about 40** ich würde schätzen, dass etwa 40 dort waren; **~ I open the window?** soll ich das Fenster aufmachen?; **I ~ like to disagree** da möchte ich widersprechen; **I ~ like to know** ich wüsste gern, ich möchte gern wissen; **I ~ like to apply for the job** ich würde mich gern um die Stelle bewerben; **thanks, I ~ like to** danke, gern
d *(expressing surprise)* **who ~ I see/~ it be but Anne!** und wen sehe ich/und wer wars? Anne!; **why ~ he want to know/do that?** warum will er das wohl wissen/machen?; **why ~ he have done it, if ...?** warum hat er es dann gemacht, wenn ...?
e *(subjunc, conditional)* **I/he ~ go if ...** ich/er würde gehen, wenn ...; **we ~ have come if ...** wir wären gekommen, wenn ...; **it seems unbelievable that he ~ have failed/be so young** es scheint unglaublich, dass er versagt hat/so jung ist; **I don't see why he ~n't have paid by now** ich verstehe nicht, warum er bis jetzt noch nicht bezahlt hat; **if they ~ send for me** wenn *or* falls sie nach mir schicken sollten; **if he ~ come, ~ he come** falls er kommen sollte, sollte er kommen; **~ it not be true** sollte das nicht wahr sein; **I ~n't be surprised if he comes** *or* **came** *or* **were to come** ich wäre nicht *or* keineswegs überrascht, wenn er kommen würde *or* wenn er käme; **I ~n't (do that) if I were you** ich würde das an Ihrer Stelle nicht tun; **I ~n't worry about it** ich würde mir darüber keine Gedanken machen; **it is necessary that he ~ be told** es ist nötig, dass man es ihm sagt; **unless he ~ change his mind** falls er es sich *(dat)* nicht anders überlegt

shoulder [ˈʃəʊldəʳ] **N a** *(of person, animal)* Schulter *f*; *(of bird)* Schultergürtel *m*; *(of meat)* Bug *m*; *(of pork)* Schulter *f*, Schulterstück *nt*; *(of garment)* Schulter(partie) *f*; **to shrug one's ~s** mit den Schultern *or* Achseln zucken; **to have broad ~s** *(lit)* breite Schultern haben; *(fig also)* einen breiten Rücken *or* Buckel *(inf)* haben; **to put one's ~ to the wheel** *(fig)* sich ins Zeug legen; **to cry on sb's ~** sich an jds Brust *(dat)* ausweinen; **a ~ to cry on** jemand, bei dem man sich ausweinen kann; **~ to ~** Schulter an Schulter → **cold, rub, straight**
b *(of mountain)* Schulter *f*; *(of road)* Seitenstreifen *m*, Bankett *nt*; *(US: = hard shoulder)* Seitenstreifen *m*; *(of vase, bottle)* Ausbuchtung *f*
VT a *(lit) load, case, person* schultern, auf die Schulter nehmen; *(fig) responsibilities, blame, task* auf sich *(acc)* nehmen; *expense* tragen; **~ arms!** *(Mil)* das Gewehr über!; **the fans ~ed him off the pitch** die Fans trugen ihn auf den Schultern vom Platz
b *(= push)* (mit der Schulter) stoßen; **to ~ sb aside** *(lit)* jdn zur Seite stoßen; *(fig)* jdn beiseitedrängen; **to ~ one's way through (the crowd)** sich durch die Menge drängen *or* boxen

shoulder: **shoulder bag** N Umhängetasche *f*; **shoulder blade** N Schulterblatt *nt*; **shoulder flash** N *(Mil)* Dienstgradabzeichen *nt*, Schulterstück *nt*; **shoulder-high** ADV schulterhoch; **his hands were raised ~** er hatte seine Hände schulterhoch erhoben; **to carry sb ~** jdn auf den Schultern tragen; **to stand ~ to sb** jdm bis an die Schultern reichen ADJ *pred* schulterhoch, schulterhohe(r, s) *attr*; **shoulder holster** N Schulterholster *nt*; **shoulder-length** ADJ *hair* schulterlang; **shoulder loop** N Dienstgradabzeichen *nt*; **shoulder pad** N Schulterpolster *nt*; **shoulder strap** N *(Mil)* Schulterklappe *f*; *(of dress)* Träger *m*; *(of satchel, bag etc)* (Schulter)riemen *m*

shouldn't [ˈʃʊdnt] *contr of* **should not**

shout [ʃaʊt] **N** Ruf *m*, Schrei *m*; **a ~ of protest** ein Protestruf *m*; **a ~ of joy/pain** ein Freuden-/ /Schmerzensschrei *m*; **~s of applause** Beifallsrufe *pl*; **~s of laughter** Lachsalven *pl*, brüllendes Gelächter; **to give a ~** einen Schrei ausstoßen; **to give sb a ~** jdn rufen; **give me a ~ when you're ready** *(inf)* sag Bescheid, wenn du fertig bist; **his voice rose to a ~** seine Stimme steigerte sich bis zum Brüllen; **it's my ~** *(Brit inf)* *(= turn)* ich bin dran; *(for food, drink)* ich zahle
VT a schreien; *(= call)* rufen; *order* brüllen; *protest, disapproval etc* laut(stark) kundtun; **to ~ abuse at sb** jdn (laut) beschimpfen; **to ~ a warning to sb** jdm eine Warnung zurufen
b *(inf: = buy as treat)* **to ~ sb sth** jdm etw spendieren *(inf)*
VI *(= call out)* rufen; *(very loudly)* schreien; *(angrily, commanding)* brüllen; **to ~ for sb/sth** nach jdm/etw rufen; **she ~ed for Jane to come** sie rief, Jane solle kommen; **to ~ at sb** mit jdm schreien; *(abusively)* jdn anschreien; **don't ~!** schrei nicht (so)!; **to ~ to sb** jdm zurufen; **he ~ed to me to open the door** er rief mir zu, ich sollte die Tür öffnen; **to ~ for help** um Hilfe rufen; **to ~ for joy** einen Freudenschrei ausstoßen; **to ~ with laughter** vor Lachen brüllen; **it was nothing to ~ about** *(inf)* es war nicht umwerfend
VR to ~ oneself hoarse sich heiser schreien

► **shout down** VT *sep person* niederbrüllen; *play* ausbuhen

► **shout out** **VI** einen Schrei ausstoßen; *(in pain, rage, protest)* aufschreien; **to shout out in despair/pain** verzweifelt/vor Schmerz aufschreien, einen Verzweiflungs-/Schmerzensschrei ausstoßen; **shout out when you're ready** ruf, wenn du fertig bist **VT** *sep* ausrufen; *order* brüllen

shouting [ˈʃaʊtɪŋ] N *(= act)* Schreien *nt*; *(= sound)* Geschrei *nt*; **it's all over bar the ~** *(inf)* es ist so gut wie gelaufen *(inf)*

shouting match N **it turned into a ~** sie brüllten sich nur noch gegenseitig an

shove [ʃʌv] **N** Schubs(er) *m (inf)*, Stoß *m*; **to give sb a ~** jdn schubsen *(inf)* *or* stoßen; **to give sth a ~** etw rücken; *door* gegen etw stoßen; *ball* etw anstoßen; *car* etw anschieben; **one more ~** noch einmal schieben, noch einen Ruck
VT a *(= push)* schieben; *(with one short push)* stoßen, schubsen *(inf)*; *(= jostle)* drängen; **stop shoving me** hör auf zu drängeln *or* mich zu schubsen *(inf)*; **to ~ sb against a wall** jdn gegen die Wand drücken; **to ~ sb off the pavement** jdn vom Bürgersteig herunterschubsen *(inf)*, jdn vom Bürgersteig herunterdrängen; **to ~ one's way forward** sich nach vorn durchdrängen; **to ~ a door open** eine Tür aufstoßen
b *(inf: = put)* **to ~ sth on(to) sth** etw auf etw *(acc)* werfen *(inf)*; **to ~ sth in(to)/between sth** etw in etw *(acc)*/zwischen etw *(acc)* stecken; **he ~d his head out of the window** er steckte seinen Kopf aus dem Fenster; **he ~d a book into my hand** er drückte mir ein Buch in die Hand
c ~ it! *(sl)* leck mich! *(inf)*, fick dich! *(vulg)*
VI stoßen; *(to move sth)* schieben; *(= jostle)* drängeln

► **shove about** *(Brit)* *or* **around** VT *sep (inf)* herumstoßen

► **shove away** VT *sep (inf)* wegstoßen, wegschubsen *(inf)*

► **shove back** VT *sep (inf) chair etc* zurückschieben; *sb, plate* zurückstoßen, zurückschubsen *(inf)*; *(= replace)* zurücktun; *(into pocket etc)* wieder hineinstecken

► **shove down** VT *sep (inf: = put)* hinlegen, hinwerfen *(inf)*; *(= write)* hinschmieren *(inf)*, aufschreiben

► **shove off** **VT** *sep (Naut)* vom Ufer abstoßen **VI a** *(in boat)* ablegen **b** *(inf: = leave)* abschieben *(inf)*

► **shove on** VT *sep (inf) coat* anziehen; *hat* aufsetzen; *record* auflegen

► **shove out** VT *sep boat* abstoßen; *person* rausschmeißen *(inf)*; **to shove sb out of office** *(inf)* jdn rausschmeißen *(inf)*

► **shove over** *(inf)* **VT** *sep* rüberwerfen *(inf)*, rüberschmeißen *(inf)* **VI** *(also* **shove up***)* rutschen

shove-halfpenny [ʃʌvˈheɪpnɪ] N *Spiel, bei dem Münzen in auf einer Platte vorgezeichnete Felder gestoßen werden*

shovel [ˈʃʌvl] **N** Schaufel *f*; *(with long handle also)* Schippe *f*; *(on power shovel)* Löffel *m*; *(= power shovel)* Löffelbagger *m*; **a ~ of coal** eine Schaufel Kohle **VT** schaufeln; *coal, snow also* schippen; **to ~ food into one's mouth** *(inf)* Essen in sich *(acc)* hineinschaufeln; **to ~ snow off a path** einen Pfad vom Schnee frei schaufeln

shoveler [ˈʃʌvələʳ] N *(Orn)* Löffelente *f*

shovelful [ˈʃʌvlfʊl] N Schaufel *f*; **a ~ of coal** eine Schaufel Kohle

show [ʃəʊ] ✪ 26.2 *vb: pret* **showed**, *ptp* **shown**
N a *(= display)* **a fine ~ of roses** eine Rosenpracht; **~ of force** Machtdemonstration *f*; **there was a strong ~ of resistance** es gab starken Wi-

derstand; the demonstration was a ~ of sympathy die Demonstration war eine Solidaritätsbekundung; ~ of hands Handzeichen *nt*, Hand(er)heben *nt*
b (= *outward appearance*) Schau *f*; (= *trace*) Spur *f*; (*of hatred, affection*) Kundgebung *f*; it's just for ~ das ist nur zur Schau da; (= *pretence*) das ist nur Schau (*inf*); to do sth for ~ etw tun, um Eindruck zu schinden (*inf*) *or* zu machen; it's all done for ~ das ist alles nur dazu da, um Eindruck zu machen; to make a great ~ of being impressed/overworked/pleased sich (*dat*) ganz den Anschein geben, beeindruckt/überarbeitet/erfreut zu sein; they made a great ~ of their wealth sie protzten mit ihrem Reichtum (*inf*); without any ~ of emotion ohne irgendwelche Gefühle zu zeigen; it was all ~ es war alles nur Schau (*inf*); to be fond of ~ gerne prunken
c (= *exhibition*) Ausstellung *f*; dog/fashion ~ Hunde-/Modenschau *f*; to be on ~ ausgestellt *or* zu sehen sein
d (*Theat*) Aufführung *f*; (*TV, variety or pop show*) Show *f*; (*Rad*) Sendung *f*; (*Film*) Vorstellung *f*; to go to a ~ (*esp Brit: in theatre*) ins Theater gehen; (*US: in movie theater*) ins Kino gehen; the ~ must go on es muss trotz allem weitergehen; on with the ~! anfangen!; (= *continue*) weitermachen!; to stop the ~ (*lit*) die Aufführung unterbrechen; he stopped the ~ with his marvellous medley of old hits (*fig*) der Höhepunkt der Show war sein wunderbares Medley alter Hits → steal
e (*esp Brit inf*) (jolly) good ~! (*dated*) ausgezeichnet!, bravo!; bad ~! (*dated*) schwaches Bild (*inf*); (= *what a pity*) so ein Pech!; to put up a good/poor ~ eine gute/schwache Leistung zeigen; it's a pretty poor ~ when … das ist vielleicht traurig *or* ein schwaches Bild (*inf*), wenn …
f (*inf: = undertaking, organization*) Laden *m* (*inf*); he runs the ~ er schmeißt hier den Laden (*inf*); to give the (whole) ~ away alles verraten
VT **a** (= *display*) zeigen; (*Comput*) anzeigen; (*at exhibition*) ausstellen, zeigen; (= *demonstrate*) *dog* vorführen; *slides, film* zeigen, vorführen; *passport, ticket* vorzeigen; to ~ sb sth, to ~ sth to sb jdm etw zeigen; ~ me how to do it zeigen Sie mir, wie man das macht; it's been ~n on television das kam im Fernsehen; the film was first ~n in 1988 der Film wurde 1988 uraufgeführt; to ~ one's face sich zeigen; he had nothing to ~ for it er hatte am Ende nichts vorzuweisen; he has nothing to ~ for all his effort seine ganze Mühe hat nichts gebracht; I'll ~ him! (*inf*) dem werd ichs zeigen! (*inf*); that ~ed him! (*inf*) dem habe ichs aber gezeigt! (*inf*) → hand, heel[1]
b (= *register*) (an)zeigen; *loss, profit* haben, verzeichnen; *rise in numbers* aufzeigen; (*thermometer, speedometer*) stehen auf (+*dat*); (*calendar*) zeigen; it ~s that … es zeigt, dass …; as ~n in the illustration wie in der Illustration dargestellt; the roads are ~n in red die Straßen sind rot (eingezeichnet); what time does your watch ~? wie spät ist es nach Ihrer Uhr?; the dial will ~ red if … der Zeiger zeigt auf Rot, wenn …
c (= *indicate*) zeigen; (= *prove*) beweisen; *kindness, favour* erweisen; *courage* zeigen, beweisen; *loyalty, taste, tact, intelligence* beweisen; *respect* bezeigen; *proof* erbringen; to ~ one's gratitude sich dankbar zeigen; this ~s him to be a thief das beweist, dass er ein Dieb ist; I hope I have ~n how silly it is ich habe hoffentlich (auf)gezeigt, wie dumm das ist; it all *or* just goes to ~ that … das zeigt doch nur, dass …
d (= *reveal*) zeigen; the housing market is ~ing signs of life auf dem Immobilienmarkt tut *or* rührt sich (wieder) (et)was (*inf*); it ~ed signs of having been used man sah, dass es gebraucht worden war; to ~ signs of wear Abnutzungserscheinungen *pl* aufweisen; to ~ signs of tiredness Ermüdungserscheinungen *pl* zeigen; ~ a leg! (*Brit inf*) raus aus den Federn! (*inf*); he's beginning to ~ his age man sieht ihm allmählich das Alter an; that dress ~s her bra bei dem Kleid sieht man ihren BH; the carpet ~s the dirt auf dem Teppich sieht man den Schmutz
e (= *direct*) zeigen; to ~ sb the way jdm den Weg zeigen; to ~ sb in/out jdn hereinbringen/hinausbringen *or* -begleiten; to ~ sb out of a room jdn hinausbegleiten, jdn aus dem Zimmer begleiten; to ~ sb into a room jdn hereinbringen, jdn ins Zimmer bringen; to ~ sb to his seat/to the door jdn an seinen Platz/an die *or* zur Tür bringen; to ~ sb over *or* (a)round the house jdm das (ganze) Haus zeigen; they were ~n over *or* (a)round the factory ihnen wurde die Fabrik gezeigt, sie wurden in der Fabrik herumgeführt
VI **a** (= *be visible*) zu sehen sein, sichtbar sein; (*petticoat etc*) vorsehen, rausgucken (*inf*); (*film*) gezeigt werden, laufen; (= *exhibit: artist*) ausstellen; the dirt doesn't ~ man sieht den Schmutz nicht; his anger ~ed in his eyes man konnte ihm seinen Ärger von den Augen ablesen; don't let your anger ~ lassen Sie sich (*dat*) den Ärger nicht anmerken!; the tulips are beginning to ~ die Tulpen kommen langsam heraus; the pregnancy *or* she is now beginning to ~ man sieht *or* merkt jetzt allmählich, dass sie schwanger ist; it only ~s when … (= *be visible*) man sieht es nur, wenn …; (= *be noticed*) man merkt es nur, wenn …; to ~ through durchkommen; the house ~s through the gap durch den Spalt kann man das Haus sehen; he didn't ~ (*inf*) er hat sich nicht blicken lassen (*inf*)
b (= *prove*) it just goes to ~! da sieht mans mal wieder!
c (*Horse Racing*) sich platzieren
VR to ~ oneself sich blicken lassen (*inf*); to ~ oneself to be incompetent sich (als) unfähig erweisen; he ~ed himself to be a coward es zeigte sich, dass er ein Feigling war; it ~s itself in his speech das merkt man an seiner Sprache

▶ **show off** **VI** angeben (*to, in front of* vor +*dat*)
VT *sep* **a** (= *flaunt*) *knowledge, medal* angeben mit; *new car, son* vorführen (*to sb* jdm); *wealth* protzen mit (*inf*) **b** (= *enhance*) *beauty, picture* hervorheben; *figure* betonen; to show sth off to its best advantage etw (richtig) zur Geltung bringen; the dress shows her off to great advantage das Kleid ist sehr vorteilhaft für sie

▶ **show up** **VI** **a** (= *be seen*) zu sehen *or* zu erkennen sein; (= *stand out*) hervorstechen; the stain shows up man sieht den Fleck; the tower showed up clearly against the sky der Turm zeichnete sich deutlich gegen den Himmel ab; to show up well/badly (*fig*) eine gute/schlechte Figur machen
b (*inf: = turn up*) auftauchen, sich blicken lassen (*inf*)
VT *sep* **a** (= *highlight*) (deutlich) erkennen lassen; the bright light showed up the faded wallpaper in dem hellen Licht konnte man sehen, wie verblichen die Tapete war
b (= *reveal*) *flaws, bad condition, errors* zum Vorschein bringen; *sb's character, intentions* deutlich zeigen; *impostor* entlarven; *fraud* aufdecken; *person* bloßstellen; my question showed him up to be a liar meine Frage entlarvte ihn als Lügner
c (= *shame*) blamieren; his bad manners show his parents up mit seinen schlechten Manieren blamiert er seine Eltern; he always gets drunk and shows her up er betrinkt sich immer und bringt sie dadurch in eine peinliche Situation; to show oneself up sich blamieren
d (= *direct*) heraufbringen

show: **show bill** N Werbe- *or* Reklameplakat *nt*; **show biz** N (*inf*) = **show business**; **showboat** N (*esp US*) *Dampfer auf dem eine Schauspieltruppe etc Vorstellungen gibt*; **show business** N Showbusiness *nt*, Showgeschäft *nt*; to be in ~ im Showgeschäft (tätig) sein; ~ personalities Persönlichkeiten *pl* aus dem Showgeschäft; **showcase** **N** Schaukasten *m*, Vitrine *f*; (*fig*) Schaufenster *nt* **VT** *sb's work, talents* präsentieren, vorstellen; **showdown** N (*inf*) Kraftprobe *f*, Show-down *m*, Showdown *m* (*inf*); there was a ~ between the two rivals zwischen den Rivalen kam es zur Kraftprobe; to have a ~ with sb sich mit jdm auseinandersetzen

shower [ˈʃaʊəˈ] **N** **a** (*of rain etc*) Schauer *m*; (*of arrows, stones, blows, bullets etc*) Hagel *m*; (*of curses, questions*) Schwall *m*; a ~ of sparks ein Funkenregen *m*; ~ of water Dusche *f*, Wasserstrahl *m*
b (= *shower bath*) Dusche *f*; to take *or* have a ~ (sich) duschen; to send sb to the ~s (*US inf*) (*Sport*) jdn vom Feld schicken; (*fig*) jdn rausschmeißen (*inf*); his bad language earned him a trip to the ~s (*US fig inf*) weil er ständig Kraftausdrücke benutzte, wurde er rausgeschmissen (*inf*)
c (*Brit fig inf*) Blödmänner *pl* (*inf*); what a ~! so ein lausiges Volk! (*inf*)
d (*US inf: = party:*) *Party, auf der jeder ein Geschenk für den Ehrengast mitbringt*; (*for bride-to-be*) ≈ Polterabend *m*; baby ~ *Party vor Geburt eines Babys, auf der jeder ein Geschenk für das Baby mitbringt*
VT to ~ sb with sth, to ~ sth on sb (*curses*) etw auf jdn niederregnen lassen; *blows* etw auf jdn niederprasseln *or* niederhageln lassen; *praise, affection, honours, presents* jdn mit etw überschütten *or* überhäufen; the broken pipe ~ed water on the passers-by das Wasser aus dem kaputten Rohr bespritzte die Passanten; to ~ abuse on sb, to ~ sb with abuse einen Schwall von Beschimpfungen gegen jdn loslassen
VI **a** (= *wash*) duschen, brausen (*dated*)
b (= *descend: also* **shower down**) niedergehen auf (+*acc*)

shower: **shower attachment** N Brauseaufsatz *m*; **shower base** N Duschwanne *f*; **shower bath** N Dusche *f*; **shower cabinet** N Duschkabine *f*; **shower cap** N Duschhaube *f*; **shower cubicle** N = **shower stall**; **shower curtain** N Duschvorhang *m*; **shower gel** N Duschgel *nt*; **showerproof** ADJ regenfest; **shower stall** N Duschkabine *f*

showery [ˈʃaʊərɪ] ADJ regnerisch

show: **show flat** N (*Brit*) Musterwohnung *nt*; **showgirl** N Revuegirl *nt*; **showground** N Ausstellungsgelände *nt*; (*for circus*) Zirkusgelände *nt*; **show home**, **show house** N (*Brit*) Musterhaus *nt*

showily [ˈʃəʊɪlɪ] ADV protzig (*inf*); *furnished also, produced* bombastisch; *behave* theatralisch; ~ dressed aufgeputzt

showiness [ˈʃəʊɪnɪs] N Protzigkeit *f* (*inf*); (*of person*) auffallende Art; (*as regards clothes*) Aufgeputztheit *f*; (*of manner*) theatralische Art; (*of ceremony, décor*) bombastische Art; (*of colour*) Auffälligkeit *f*; (*of production*) Effekthascherei *f*

showing [ˈʃəʊɪŋ] N **a** (= *exhibition*) Ausstellung *f* **b** (= *performance*) Aufführung *f*; (*of film*) Vorstellung *f*; (*of programme*) Ausstrahlung *f* **c** (= *standard of performance*) Leistung *f*; to make a good/poor ~ eine gute/schwache Leistung zeigen; on his present ~ mit seinen jetzigen Leistungen; on present ~ so, wie die Dinge zurzeit stehen **d** on his own ~ nach eigenen Angaben

showing-off [ˈʃəʊɪŋˈɒf] N Angeberei *f*

show: **show-jumper** N Springreiter(in) *m(f)*; **showjumping** N Springen *nt*, Springreiten *nt*

showman [ˈʃəʊmən] N *pl* **-men** [-mən] Showman *m*; (*fig*) Schauspieler *m*

showmanship [ˈʃəʊmənʃɪp] N (*of person*) Talent *nt* für effektvolle Darbietung; (*of act*) effektvolle Darbietung; (*fig*) Talent *nt* sich in Szene zu setzen; he knows nothing about ~ er hat keine Ahnung, wie man etwas effektvoll darbietet *or* in Szene setzt; it's just ~ das ist reine Schau *or* Effekthascherei

shown [ʃəʊn] *ptp of* **show**

show: **show-off** N (*inf*) Angeber(in) *m(f)*; **showpiece** N Schaustück *nt*; (= *fine example*) Paradestück *nt*; **showplace** N (= *tourist attraction*) Sehenswürdigkeit *f*; **showroom** N Ausstellungsraum *m*; in ~ condition in makellosem Zustand; **show stopper** N (*inf*) Publikumshit *m (inf); (fig)* Clou *m* des Abends/der Party *etc*; **show-stopping** ADJ *attr (inf) performance, product* fantastisch, phantastisch *(inf)*; **~ number** Publikumshit *m*; **show tent** N Ausstellungszelt *nt*; **showtime** N *(Theat, TV)* Vorstellungsbeginn *m*; **it's close to ~ now** die Vorstellung fängt gleich an; **show trial** N Schauprozess *m*; **show window** N Schaufenster *nt*, Auslage *f*

showwoman [ˈʃəʊwʊmən] N *pl* **-women** [-wɪmɪn] Showfrau *f*; *(fig)* Schauspielerin *f*

showy [ˈʃəʊɪ] ADJ *(+er)* protzig *(inf)*; *person* auffallend; *(as regards clothes)* protzig angezogen *(inf)*; *manner* theatralisch; *ceremony, décor* bombastisch; *colour* grell, auffällig; *production* bombastisch, auf Schau *(inf)* or Effekte gemacht

shrank [ʃræŋk] *pret of* **shrink**

shrapnel [ˈʃræpnl] N Schrapnell *nt*

shred [ʃred] N *(= scrap)* Fetzen *m*; *(of paper also)* Schnipsel *m*, Schnippel *m (inf)*; *(of vegetable, meat)* Stückchen *nt*; *(fig)* Spur *f*; *(of truth)* Fünkchen *nt*; **~ of cloth** Stoffetzen *m*; **not a ~ of evidence** keinerlei Beweis; **without a ~ of clothing on** splitter(faser)nackt; **to be** *or* **hang in ~s** zerfetzt sein; **her dress hung in ~s** ihr Kleid hing ihr in Fetzen vom Leib; **his reputation was in ~s** sein (guter) Ruf war ruiniert; **to tear sth to ~s** etw total zerreißen, etw in Stücke reißen; *(fig)* etw verreißen; *argument* etw total zerpflücken; **to tear sb to ~s** *(fig)* keinen guten Faden an jdm lassen
VT **a** *food* zerkleinern, schnitzeln; *(= grate) carrots* raspeln; *cabbage* hobeln; *paper* zerstückeln, schnitzeln; *(in shredder)* schreddern; *piece of clothing* zerkleinern
b *(= tear)* in kleine Stücke reißen; *(with claws)* zerfetzen

shredder [ˈʃredəˈ] N **a** Schredder *m*, Shredder *m*, Zerkleinerungsmaschine *f*; *(esp for wastepaper)* Papierwolf *m*, Reißwolf *m* **b** *(= grater)* Reibe *f*; *(in electric mixer)* Gemüseschneider *m*

shredding machine [ˈʃredɪŋməˈʃiːn] N = **shredder**

shrew [ʃruː] N Spitzmaus *f*; *(fig)* Xanthippe *f*; **"The Taming of the Shrew"** *(Liter)* „Der Widerspenstigen Zähmung"

shrewd [ʃruːd] ADJ *(+er) person* gewitzt, klug, clever *(inf)*; *businessman also, plan, move* clever *(inf)*, raffiniert, geschickt; *investment, argument* taktisch geschickt, klug; *assessment, observer* scharf, genau; *smile* verschmitzt, wissend; *eyes* schlau; *mind* scharf; *glance* durchdringend, prüfend; **I can make a ~ guess** ich kann ja mal raten; **that was a ~ guess** das war gut geraten; **I have a ~ idea that …** ich habe so das bestimmte Gefühl, dass …; **I have a ~ idea of what he'll say** ich kann mir gut denken, was er sagen wird; **to be ~ enough to do sth** schlau *or* clever *(inf)* genug sein, etw zu tun; **a ~ judge of character** ein guter Menschenkenner; **to have a ~ suspicion that …** den stillen Verdacht hegen, dass …; **to have a ~ understanding of sth** in Bezug auf etw *(acc)* Durchblick haben

shrewdly [ˈʃruːdlɪ] ADV geschickt, clever *(inf)*; *look* wissend; *observe* klug; **he ~ realized that …** schlauerweise erkannte er, dass …; **he ~ guessed that/what …** er hat gut geraten, dass/was …; **~, he decided …** gewitzt *or* clever *(inf)* wie er ist, hat er beschlossen …; **… he said ~** … sagte er schlau *or* clever *(inf)*

shrewdness [ˈʃruːdnɪs] N *(of person)* Gewitztheit *f*, Klugheit *f*, Cleverness *f (inf)*; *(of businessman also, plan, move)* Raffiniertheit *f*, Geschicktheit *f*; *(of investment, argument)* Klugheit *f*; *(of assessment, observer)* Schärfe *f*, Genauigkeit *f*; *(of guess)* Treffsicherheit *f*

shrewish [ˈʃruːɪʃ] ADJ zänkisch, boshaft, giftig

shrewishly [ˈʃruːɪʃlɪ] ADV giftig

shrewishness [ˈʃruːɪʃnɪs] N Boshaftigkeit *f*, Giftigkeit *f*

shriek [ʃriːk] N (schriller) Schrei; *(of whistle)* schriller Ton; *(of brakes, hinges)* Quietschen *nt no pl*; **a ~ of pain/horror** ein Schmerzens-/ /Schreckensschrei *m*; **~s of laughter** kreischendes Lachen; **to give a ~** einen schrillen Schrei ausstoßen VT kreischen, schreien VI aufschreien; **to ~ at sb** jdn ankreischen; **to ~ with pain/horror** vor Schmerz/Entsetzen schreien; **to ~ with laughter** vor Lachen quietschen; **to ~ out** aufschreien, einen Schrei ausstoßen

shrift [ʃrɪft] N **to give sb/sth short ~** jdn/etw kurz abfertigen

shrike [ʃraɪk] N Würger *m*

shrill [ʃrɪl] ADJ *(+er)* schrill; *criticism, speech* scharf; *demand* lautstark VI schrillen VT kreischen, schrill schreien

shrillness [ˈʃrɪlnɪs] N Schrillheit *f*

shrilly [ˈʃrɪlɪ] ADV schrill; *(fig: = fiercely)* lautstark; **what are you doing?, she demanded ~** was tust du da?, fragte sie mit einer schrillen Stimme

shrimp [ʃrɪmp] N Garnele *f*, Krevette *f*; **that ~ of a child** der kleine Steppke *(inf)* VI **to go ~ing** auf Krevetten- *or* Garnelenfang gehen; **~ing net** Reuse *f (für den Garnelenfang)*

shrine [ʃraɪn] N Schrein *m*; *(= sacred place also)* Heiligtum *nt*; *(= tomb)* Grabstätte *f*; *(= chapel)* Grabkapelle *f*; *(= altar)* Grabaltar *m*; **to worship at sb's ~** *(fig inf)* jdm zu Füßen liegen

shrink [ʃrɪŋk] *vb: pret* **shrank**, *ptp* **shrunk** VT einlaufen lassen; **the fabric is shrunk before it is used** der Stoff wird vor Gebrauch gewaschen, damit er danach nicht mehr einläuft; **to ~ a part on** *(Tech)* ein Teil aufschrumpfen
VI **a** *(= get smaller)* kleiner werden, schrumpfen; *(clothes etc)* einlaufen; *(metal etc)* sich zusammenziehen, schrumpfen; *(wood)* schwinden; *(fig, popularity)* abnehmen, schwinden; *(trade)* zurückgehen; **to ~ away to nothing** auf ein Nichts zusammenschrumpfen
b *(fig: = recoil)* zurückschrecken; **to ~ from doing sth** davor zurückschrecken, etw zu tun; **to ~ from saying sth** sich davor scheuen, etw zu sagen; **to ~ from the truth** vor der Wahrheit die Augen verschließen; **to ~ back** zurückweichen; **to ~ away from sb** vor jdm zurückweichen
N *(inf)* Seelenklempner(in) *m(f) (inf)*, Psychiater(in) *m(f)*

shrinkage [ˈʃrɪŋkɪdʒ] N *(of material, clothes)* Einlaufen *nt*; *(of wood)* Schwund *m*; *(of metal)* Schrumpfung *f*; *(fig: of tourism, economic growth etc)* Schrumpfung *f*, Rückgang *m*; *(Comm)* Schwund *m*, Einbußen *pl*; **there will be ~ with this material** dieser Stoff läuft noch ein

shrinking [ˈʃrɪŋkɪŋ] ADJ **a** *(= decreasing)* schrumpfend, abnehmend **b** *(= shy)* scheu

shrinking violet [ʃrɪŋkɪŋˈvaɪəlɪt] N *(inf: = shy person)* schüchternes Pflänzchen

shrinkproof [ˈʃrɪŋkpruːf], **shrink-resistant** [ˈʃrɪŋkrɪˈzɪstənt] ADJ nicht einlaufend

shrink-wrap [ˈʃrɪŋkræp] VT einschweißen

shrink-wrapping [ˈʃrɪŋkræpɪŋ] N *(= process)* Einschweißen *nt*; *(= material)* Klarsichtfolie *f*

shrive [ʃraɪv] *pret* **shrove**, *ptp* **shriven** VT *(old)* die Beichte abnehmen *(+dat)*

shrivel [ˈʃrɪvl] VT *plants (frost, dryness)* welk werden lassen; *(heat)* austrocknen; *skin, fruit* runzlig werden lassen; *nylon* zusammenschrumpfen lassen VI kleiner werden, schrumpfen; *(balloon, nylon)* zusammenschrumpfen; *(plants)* welk werden; *(through heat)* austrocknen; *(fruit, skin)* runzlig werden → *also* **shrivelled**

▶ **shrivel away** VI zusammenschrumpfen; *(leaves)* verwelken, vertrocknen; *(nylon®)* zusammenschmelzen; *(worries, problems)* sich in Luft auflösen

▶ **shrivel up** VT *sep* = **shrivel** VT VI **a** = **shrivel** VI **b** *(fig)* **I just want to shrivel up when he looks at me like that** wenn er mich so ansieht, möchte ich am liebsten in den Boden versinken; **he just shrivelled up when the boss questioned him** bei den Fragen des Chefs wurde er ganz klein

shrivelled, *(US)* **shriveled** [ˈʃrɪvld] ADJ *(= withered) vegetation* verwelkt, verdorrt; *person* verwelkt; *body part* verrunzelt, runz(e)lig; *fruit* verschrumpelt; **a ~ old lady** eine kleine, vertrocknete alte Dame

shriven [ˈʃrɪvn] *ptp of* **shrive**

shroud [ʃraʊd] N **a** Leichentuch *nt*, Totenhemd *nt* **b** *(fig)* Schleier *m*; **a ~ of smoke** Rauchschwaden *pl*; **a ~ of secrecy** der Schleier eines Geheimnisses **c** **shrouds** PL *(Naut)* Wanten *pl* VT **a** *(lit)* in ein Leichentuch hüllen **b** *(fig)* hüllen; **the whole thing is ~ed in mystery** die ganze Angelegenheit ist von einem Geheimnis umgeben

shrove [ʃrəʊv] *pret of* **shrive**

Shrove Monday [ʃrəʊvˈmʌndɪ] N Rosenmontag *m*

Shrovetide [ˈʃrəʊvtaɪd] N Fastnacht *f (die drei Tage vor Aschermittwoch)*

Shrove Tuesday [ʃrəʊvˈtjuːzdɪ] N Fastnachtsdienstag *m*

shrub [ʃrʌb] N Busch *m*, Strauch *m*

shrubbery [ˈʃrʌbərɪ] N *(= shrub bed)* Strauchrabatte *f*; *(= shrubs)* Büsche *pl*, Sträucher *pl*, Buschwerk *nt*; **the ball got lost in the ~** der Ball ging im Gebüsch verloren

shrubby [ˈʃrʌbɪ] ADJ strauchartig

shrug [ʃrʌg] N Achselzucken *nt no pl*; **to give a ~** mit den Schultern *or* Achseln zucken; **a ~ of despair** ein verzweifeltes Achselzucken VT *shoulders* zucken (mit); **she ~ged herself out of the coat** sie schüttelte ihren Mantel ab

▶ **shrug off** VT *sep* mit einem Achselzucken abtun; *coat* abschütteln; **he simply shrugged the whole affair off** er hat die ganze Sache einfach von sich abgeschüttelt

shrunk [ʃrʌŋk] *ptp of* **shrink**

shrunken [ˈʃrʌŋkən] ADJ (ein)geschrumpft; *old person* geschrumpft; *profits, savings* zusammengeschrumpft

shrunken head N Schrumpfkopf *m*

shtoom [ʃtʊm] ADJ *(inf: = quiet)* **to keep ~ about sth** über etw *(acc)* die Klappe halten *(inf)*

shtuck [ʃtʊk] ADJ *(inf)* angeschmiert *(inf)*; **to be in (dead) ~** angeschmiert sein *(inf)*

shuck [ʃʌk] *(US)* N Schale *f*; *(of corn, peas)* Hülse *f* VT **a** *(= shell)* schälen; *peas* enthülsen **b** *(inf)* **he ~ed his jacket** er warf seine Jacke ab

▶ **shuck off** VT SEP *(US inf) garment* abwerfen, abstreifen; **to shuck off one's clothes** seine Kleidung abstreifen

shucks [ʃʌks] INTERJ *(US)* verflixt, Mist *(inf)*; *(= rubbish)* Unsinn, Quatsch *(inf)*; **~, I'm sorry** Mist!, tut mir leid *(inf)*; **~ to you** *(inf)* bätsch! *(inf)*

shudder [ˈʃʌdəˈ] N Schauer *m*, Schauder *m*; **to give a ~** *(person)* sich schütteln, erschaudern *(geh)*; *(ground)* beben; **she gave a ~ of revulsion** sie schüttelte sich vor Ekel; **the dying man gave a last great ~** ein letztes Zucken lief durch den Körper des Sterbenden; **a ~ ran through her/her body** ein Schauer überlief sie; **she realized with a ~ that …** schaudernd erkannte sie, dass …; **a ~ of fear/cold** ein Angst-/Kälteschauer *m*; **with a ~ of anticipation/pleasure** zitternd *or* bebend vor Erwartung/Freude; **a ~ went through the building as the heavy truck passed by** das Gebäude bebte, als der schwere Lastwagen vorbeifuhr; **with a ~ the old car moved into second gear** der alte Wagen vibrierte, als der zweite Gang eingelegt wurde; **that gives me the ~s** *(inf)* da läufts mir kalt den Buckel runter *(inf)*; **he gives me the ~s** *(inf)* er ist mir unheimlich
VI *(person)* schaudern, schauern; *(house, ground)* beben, zittern; *(car, train)* rütteln, geschüttelt werden; **her whole body was ~ing** sie zitterte am ganzen Körper; **the train ~ed to a halt** der Zug kam rüttelnd zum Stehen; **I ~ to think** mir graut, wenn ich nur daran denke

shudderingly [ˈʃʌdərɪŋlɪ] ADV *(with fear etc)* schaudernd; *(with cold)* zitternd; **the rocket climbed ~ into the sky** die Rakete stieg zitternd zum Himmel auf

shuffle [ˈʃʌfl] N **a** Schlurfen *nt no pl*; **to walk with a ~** schlurfen

b *(= dance)* Shuffle *m*
c *(Cards)* **to give the cards a ~** die Karten mischen
d *(= change round)* Umstellung *f*; *(of jobs)* Umbesetzung *f*; **the latest ~ of the cabinet** die letzte Kabinettsumbildung; **to get lost in the ~** *(people)* in der Menge untergehen; *(things)* verloren gehen
VT **a** **he ~d his feet as he walked** er schlurfte beim Gehen; **he sat there shuffling his feet** er saß da und scharrte mit den Füßen
b *cards* mischen; **he ~d the papers on his desk** er durchwühlte die Papiere auf seinem Schreibtisch
c *(fig: = change round) cabinet* umbilden; *jobs* umbesetzen; **top men are ~d around quite often** die Männer an der Spitze werden oft von einem Ressort ins andere versetzt
VI **a** *(= walk)* schlurfen; **the dancers ~d around on the floor** die Tänzer schoben sich über die Tanzfläche; **he just ~s through life** er lässt sich einfach treiben
b *(Cards)* mischen

▶ **shuffle off** VT *sep skin, dress* abstreifen; *(fig) worries, fear* ablegen; *responsibility* abwälzen, abschieben *(onto* auf *+acc)*; **to shuffle off this mortal coil** *(euph)* die sterbliche Hülle ablegen *or* abstreifen

shuffling ['ʃʌflɪŋ] ADJ *walk, steps, sound* schlurfend; **the ~ movement of a badger** das Watscheln eines Dachses

shun [ʃʌn] VT meiden; *publicity, light* scheuen; **to be ~ned by the world** ausgestoßen sein

'shun [ʃʌn] INTERJ *(Mil)* Achtung

shunt [ʃʌnt] **N** Stoß *m*; *(inf: = car crash)* Crash *m (sl)*; **they gave the wagon a ~ into the siding** sie schoben *or* rangierten den Waggon auf das Abstellgleis; **to give sth a ~** etw anstoßen, einer Sache *(dat)* einen Stoß geben
VT **a** *(Rail)* rangieren, verschieben; **they ~ed the train off the main line** sie schoben den Zug auf ein Nebengleis
b *(inf) person* schieben; *(out of the way)* abschieben; **to ~ sb from one place to another** jdn herumschubsen *(inf)*; **our department then has to ~ the papers back for signing** unsere Abteilung muss die Papiere dann zur Unterschrift zurückverfrachten *(inf)*; **they ~ed him off to boarding school** sie schoben ihn ins Internat ab
c *(inf, = crash) car* einen Unfall bauen mit *(inf)*
VI *(Rail, train)* rangiert *or* verschoben werden; *(person)* rangieren; **a line of trucks ~ed past** eine Reihe Güterwagen schob sich vorbei

shunter ['ʃʌntə'] N *(Brit Rail)* Rangierer *m*

shunting ['ʃʌntɪŋ] N *(Rail)* Rangieren *nt*; **~ engine** Rangierlokomotive *f*

shunting yard N Rangier- *or* Verschiebebahnhof *m*

shush [ʃʊʃ] **INTERJ** pst, sch **VT** beruhigen, zum Schweigen bringen; **the teacher ~ed the excited children** der Lehrer brachte die aufgeregten Kinder mit einem „Pst!" zum Schweigen **VI** still sein; **oh ~, will you!** sei doch still!, pst!

shut [ʃʌt] *vb: pret, ptp* **shut** **VT** **a** *(= close) eyes, door, box etc* zumachen, schließen; *sportsground* schließen; *penknife, book, wallet* zumachen, zuklappen; **they ~ the office at 6** das Büro wird um 18.00 Uhr geschlossen; **the strike ~ the factory for a week** der Streik legte die Fabrik für eine Woche still; **~ your eyes** mach die Augen zu; **to ~ one's ears/eyes to sth** vor etw *(dat)* die Ohren/Augen verschließen; **to ~ one's mind to sth** sich einer Sache *(dat)* verschließen; **he ~ his mind to thoughts of the past** Gedanken an die Vergangenheit schob er weit von sich; **~ your mouth** *or* **face!** *(inf)* **~ it!** *(inf)* halts Maul! *(inf)*
b **to ~ sb/sth in(to) sth** jdn/etw in etw *(dat)* einschließen; **she was ~ in the cellar as a punishment** sie wurde zur Strafe im Keller eingesperrt; **to ~ one's fingers in the door** sich *(dat)* die Finger in der Tür einklemmen
VI *(door, window, box)* schließen, zugehen; *(shop, factory)* schließen, geschlossen werden, zumachen *(inf)*; *(sportsground)* geschlossen werden; *(eyes)* sich schließen; **the suitcase just won't ~** der Koffer will einfach nicht zugehen; **it ~s very easily** es lässt sich ganz leicht schließen *or* zumachen; **when do the shops ~?** wann schließen die Geschäfte?, wann machen die Geschäfte zu? *(inf)*; **the door ~ in the wind** der Wind schlug die Tür zu
ADJ geschlossen, zu *pred (inf)*; **sorry sir, we're ~** wir haben leider geschlossen; **the door swung ~** die Tür schlug zu; **to find the door ~** vor verschlossener Tür stehen; **~ in his dungeon** in seinem Kerker eingeschlossen; **~ in his own little world** abgekapselt in seiner eigenen kleinen Welt; **the ~ mind of a reactionary** die Verbohrtheit eines Reaktionärs; **his mind is ~ to anything new** er verschließt sich allem Neuen

▶ **shut away** VT *sep (= put away)* wegschließen; *(in sth)* einschließen *(in* in *+dat)*; *(= keep locked away) books, papers etc* unter Verschluss halten; *(safely)* verwahren; *persons* verborgen halten; **to keep sb shut away from sth** jdn von etw fernhalten; **he was shut away in a mental hospital** er wurde in eine Nervenklinik gesteckt; **to shut oneself away** sich zurückziehen

▶ **shut down** **VT** *sep shop, factory* zumachen *(inf)*, schließen; *computer, reactor* herunterfahren; *(Comput) Windows® etc* beenden; *reactor* abschalten; *operations* stilllegen; **Heathrow is completely shut down** Heathrow ist vollkommen zu *or* dicht *(inf)* **VI** *(shop, factory etc)* zumachen *(inf)*, schließen; *(reactor)* sich abschalten; *(engine)* sich ausschalten; *(resort)* Betrieb einstellen; **the television service shuts down at midnight** um Mitternacht ist Sendeschluss im Fernsehen

▶ **shut in** VT *sep* einschließen *(also fig)*, einsperren *(inf) (prep obj, -to* in *+dat)*; **close the door and shut the heat in** schließe die Tür, damit die Wärme drinnen bleibt

▶ **shut off** **VT** *sep* **a** *gas, water, electricity* abstellen; *light, engine* ab- *or* ausschalten; *street* (ab)sperren; **the kettle shuts itself off** der Wasserkessel schaltet von selbst ab **b** *(= isolate)* (ab)trennen; **I feel very shut off on this island** ich fühle mich auf dieser Insel sehr abgeschlossen; **I feel shut off from my friends/civilization** ich komme mir von meinen Freunden/der Zivilisation abgeschnitten vor; **to shut oneself off (from sth)** sich abkapseln (von etw) **VI** abschalten; **the heater shuts off automatically** das Heizgerät schaltet (sich) automatisch ab

▶ **shut out** VT *sep* **a** *person, oneself* aussperren *(of* aus*)*; *view* versperren; *light, world* nicht hereinlassen *(of* in *+acc)*; **the child was shut out of the house** das Kind war ausgesperrt; **don't shut the sun out** lass doch die Sonne herein; **draw the curtains to shut out the light** zieh die Vorhänge zu, damit das Licht nicht hereinfällt; **the trees shut out the light** die Bäume nehmen das Licht weg; **she closed the door to shut out the noise/draught** *(Brit)* *or* **draft** *(US)* sie schloss die Tür, damit kein Lärm hereinkam/damit es nicht zog
b *(fig) foreign competition* ausschalten; *memory* loswerden, unterdrücken; *(= censor) foreign news etc* unterdrücken; **I can't shut her out of my life** ich kann sie nicht von meinem Leben ausschließen
c *(US Sport) opponent* nicht zum Zuge kommen lassen; **they shut the opponents out with two hits** sie schalteten ihre Gegner mit zwei Treffern aus; **they shut them out 1-0** sie warfen sie mit 1:0 aus dem Rennen

▶ **shut to** VT *sep* ganz *or* richtig zumachen; *(not quite closed)* anlehnen; **the door wasn't shut to** die Tür war nicht ganz zu

▶ **shut up** **VT** *sep* **a** *house* verschließen → **shop** **b** *(= imprison)* einsperren; **you can't spend your whole life shut up in libraries** Sie können sich doch nicht Ihr ganzes Leben lang in Bibliotheken vergraben **c** *(inf: = silence)* zum Schweigen bringen; **that'll soon shut him up** das wird ihm schon den Mund stopfen *(inf)*; **every time I try to say something she always tries to shut me up** jedes Mal, wenn ich etwas sagen will, fährt sie mir über den Mund **VI** *(inf)* den Mund *or* die Klappe halten *(inf)*; **shut up!** halt die Klappe! *(inf)*; *(= you can't be serious)* das meinst du nicht im Ernst!

shut: **shutdown** N Stilllegung *f*; *(of schools, factory)* Schließung *f*; *(TV, Rad)* Sendeschluss *m*; **shuteye** N *(inf)* Schlaf *m*; **I need some ~** ich brauche etwas Schlaf *or* ein paar Stunden Schlaf; **shut-in** **ADJ** **a** *(US: = confined to the house/bed)* ans Haus/Bett gefesselt **b** **a ~ feeling** ein Gefühl *nt* des Eingeschlossenseins **N** *(US)* **he is a ~** er ist ans Haus/ans Bett gefesselt; **shut-off** **N** *(of gas, water)* Abstellen *nt*; **we regret the temporary water ~ yesterday** wir bedauern, dass wir gestern vorübergehend das Wasser abstellen mussten **ADJ** **a** **a ~ feeling** ein Gefühl des Abgeschlossenseins *or* Abgeschnittenseins **b** **~ switch** *(of electricity, engine)* Hauptschalter *m*; **shut-out** N *(US Sport)* Zu-null-Niederlage *f*, Zu-null-Sieg *m*

shutter ['ʃʌtə'] **N** (Fenster)laden *m*; *(Phot)* Verschluss *m*; **to put up the ~s** *(lit)* die (Fenster)läden zumachen; *(fig)* den Laden dichtmachen *(inf)* **VT** **~ the windows** mach die (Fenster)läden zu

shutterbug ['ʃʌtəbʌg] N *(esp US inf)* Fotonarr *m*/-närrin *f (inf)*

shuttered ['ʃʌtəd] ADJ **a** *(= with shutters) house* mit (Fenster)läden; *door, window* mit Läden **b** *(= with closed shutters) house, room* mit geschlossenen (Fenster)läden; **the people watched from behind ~ windows** die Leute sahen hinter den geschlossenen (Fenster)läden zu **c** *(fig)* **a ~ look** ein verschlossener Blick

shutter release N *(Phot)* Auslöser *m*

shuttle ['ʃʌtl] **N** **a** *(of loom, sewing machine)* Schiffchen *nt* **b** *(= shuttle service)* Pendelverkehr *m*; *(= plane/train etc)* Pendelflugzeug *nt*/-zug *m etc*; *(= space shuttle)* Raumtransporter *m*, Spaceshuttle *m* **c** *(= shuttlecock)* Federball *m*
VT *passengers, goods* hin- und hertransportieren; **to ~ sb around** jdn herumschieben; **the form was ~d around between different departments** das Formular wurde in den verschiedenen Abteilungen herumgereicht **VI** *(people)* pendeln; *(goods)* hin- und hertransportiert werden; *(forms)* herumgereicht werden

shuttle: **shuttle bus** N Shuttlebus *m*, Pendelbus *m*; **shuttlecock** N Federball *m*; **shuttle diplomacy** N Pendeldiplomatie *f*; **shuttle service** N Pendelverkehr *m*

shy[1] [ʃaɪ] **ADJ** *(+er)* **a** schüchtern; *animal* scheu; **don't be ~** nur keine Hemmungen! *(inf)*; **to be ~ of/with sb** Hemmungen vor/gegenüber jdm haben; **to be ~ of** *or* **about doing sth** Hemmungen haben, etw zu tun; **to feel ~** schüchtern sein; **don't be ~ of telling me if there's anything you need** sagen Sie mir ruhig, wenn Sie etwas brauchen; **to make sb ~** jdn verschüchtern → **fight** **b** *(esp US inf: = short)* **we're 3 dollars ~** wir haben 3 Dollar zu wenig; **two days ~ of his 95th birthday** zwei Tage vor seinem 95. Geburtstag **VI** *(horse)* scheuen *(at* vor *+dat)*

▶ **shy away** VI *(horse)* zurückscheuen; *(person)* zurückweichen; **to shy away from sb** vor jdm zurückweichen; **to shy away from sth** vor etw *(dat)* zurückschrecken; **he shies away from accepting responsibility** er scheut sich, Verantwortung zu übernehmen

shy[2] **N** *(= throw)* Wurf *m*; **to have** *or* **take a ~ at sth** nach etw werfen; **to have a ~ at sth** *(fig)* sich an etw *(dat)* versuchen; **I'll have a ~ at it** ich kanns ja mal versuchen; **to have a ~ at doing sth** etw zu tun versuchen **VT** werfen

Shylock ['ʃaɪlɒk] N *(fig: = mean person)* Geizhals *m*; *(dated: = moneylender)* Wucherer *m*, Wucherin *f*

shyly ['ʃaɪlɪ] ADV *smile, say* schüchtern

shyness ['ʃaɪnɪs] N Schüchternheit *f*; *(esp of animals)* Scheu *f*; **his ~ at meeting people** seine Schüchternheit, wenn er andere Leute kennenlernt; **her ~ of strangers** ihre Scheu vor Fremden

shyster [ˈʃaɪstəˈ] N (*US inf*) Gauner(in) *m(f)*; (*= lawyer*) Rechtsverdreher(in) *m(f)* (*inf*)

Siam [saɪˈæm] N Siam *nt*

Siamese [ˌsaɪəˈmiːz] ADJ siamesisch N a Siamese *m*, Siamesin *f* b (*Ling*) Siamesisch *nt* c (*= cat*) Siamkatze *f*, siamesische Katze

Siamese cat N Siamkatze *f*, Siamesische Katze

Siamese twins PL siamesische Zwillinge *pl*

Siberia [saɪˈbɪərɪə] N Sibirien *nt*

Siberian [saɪˈbɪərɪən] ADJ sibirisch N Sibirier(in) *m(f)*, Sibirer(in) *m(f)*

sibilant [ˈsɪbɪlənt] ADJ zischend; *hiss* scharf; **~ sound** (*Phon*) Zischlaut *m* N (*Phon*) Zischlaut *m*

sibling [ˈsɪblɪŋ] N Geschwister *nt* (*form*)

sibyl [ˈsɪbɪl] N (*lit*) Sibylle *f*; (*fig*) Prophetin *f*, Weissagerin *f*

sibylline [ˈsɪbɪlaɪn] ADJ (*lit*) sibyllinisch; (*fig*) prophetisch

sic [sɪk] ADV sic

SIC (*Brit*) *abbr of* **Standard Industrial Classification** ≈ DIN

Sicilian [sɪˈsɪlɪən] ADJ sizilianisch N a Sizilianer(in) *m(f)* b (*Ling*) Sizilianisch *nt*

Sicily [ˈsɪsɪlɪ] N Sizilien *nt*

sick [sɪk] ✪ 7.3 N (*= vomit*) Erbrochene(s) *nt*
ADJ (+*er*) a (*= ill*) krank (*also fig*); **the ~** die Kranken *pl*; **to be (off) ~** (wegen Krankheit) fehlen; **to fall** *or* **take ~, to be taken ~** krank werden; **to go ~** krank werden; **to call in** *or* **phone in** (*esp Brit*) **~** sich (telefonisch) krankmelden; **she's off ~ with tonsillitis** sie ist wegen einer Mandelentzündung krankgeschrieben; **he's as ~ as a parrot** *or* **dog** (*inf*) ihm ist kotzübel (*sl*); **he was ~ at heart** (*liter*) er war von Kummer verzehrt (*liter*)
b (*= vomiting or about to vomit*) **to be ~** brechen, sich übergeben, kotzen (*sl*); (*esp cat, baby, patient*) spucken; **he was ~ all over the carpet** er hat den ganzen Teppich vollgespuckt *or* vollgekotzt (*sl*); **I think I'm going to be ~** ich glaube, ich muss kotzen (*sl*) *or* mich übergeben; **I felt ~** mir war schlecht *or* übel; **to feel ~ to one's stomach** sich im Magen schlecht fühlen; **I get ~ in aeroplanes** im Flugzeug wird mir immer schlecht *or* übel; **that smell/that food makes me ~** bei dem Geruch/von dem Essen wird mir übel *or* schlecht; **to make sb ~** (*fig inf*) jdn (ganz) krank machen (*inf*); **it's enough to make you ~** (*inf*) das reicht, damit einem schlecht wird; **it makes me ~ to think that ...** (*inf*) mir wird schlecht, wenn ich daran denke, dass ...; **it makes you ~ the way he's always right** (*inf*) es ist zum Weinen *or* zum Kotzen (*sl*), dass er immer recht hat; **to be ~ at sth** (*fig: = disgusted*) von etw angewidert sein; (*= upset*) wegen etw geknickt sein; **to feel ~ about sth** (*fig*) von etw angewidert sein; **I am worried ~, I am ~ with worry** mir ist vor Sorge ganz schlecht; **~ with envy** grün vor Neid
c (*inf: = fed up*) **to be ~ of sth/sb** etw/jdn satthaben; **to be ~ of doing sth** es satthaben, etw zu tun; **I'm ~ and tired of it** ich habe davon die Nase (gestrichen) voll (*inf*), ich habe es gründlich satt; **to be ~ and tired of doing sth** es leid sein, etw zu tun; **I'm ~ of the sight of her** ich habe ihren Anblick satt; **I get ~ of listening to her complaining** ich habe es langsam satt, immer ihr Gejammer hören zu müssen
d (*inf*) geschmacklos; *joke* makaber, geschmacklos; *person* abartig, pervers; **~ humour** schwarzer Humor; **he has a ~ mind** er ist abartig; **a comedy about life in Dachau, how ~ can you get!** eine Komödie über das Leben in Dachau, das ist ja schon pervers!

▶ **sick up** VT *sep* erbrechen

sick: **sickbag** N Spucktüte *f*; **sickbay** N Krankenrevier *nt*; **sickbed** N Krankenlager *nt*; **sick building syndrome** N *gesundheitliche Probleme aufgrund eines schlechten Raumklimas*

sicken [ˈsɪkn] VT (*= turn sb's stomach*) anekeln, anwidern; (*= upset greatly*) erschüttern, krank machen (*inf*); (*= disgust*) anwidern; **what they saw in the camp ~ed them** sie waren entsetzt über das, was sie im Lager sahen; **it ~s me the way he treats her** es macht mich krank, wie er sie behandelt (*inf*); **doesn't it ~ you?** das ist doch unerträglich *or* zum Kotzen (*sl*)
VI a (*= feel ill*) **to ~ at sth** sich vor etw (*dat*) ekeln
b (*= become ill*) krank werden; **he's definitely ~ing for something** er wird bestimmt krank; **you must be ~ing for something** (*lit iro*) ist mit dir was nicht in Ordnung?; **he's ~ing for a virus** bei ihm ist ein Virus im Anzug
c **to ~ of sth** einer Sache (*gen*) müde (*geh*) werden *or* sein, etw satthaben

sickener [ˈsɪknəˈ] N (*inf*) a (*thing*) ekelhafte Sache, Brechmittel *nt* (*fig inf*) b (*= obnoxious person*) Ekel *nt* (*fig*)

sickening [ˈsɪknɪŋ] ADJ (*lit*) ekelerregend; *smell, sight also* widerlich; (*= upsetting*) erschütternd; (*= disgusting, annoying*) ekelhaft, zum Kotzen (*sl*); *treatment* abscheulich; *cruelty* widerlich; *delays, price increase* unerträglich; *person* ekelhaft; **his ~ habit of always being right** seine unerträgliche Angewohnheit, immer recht zu haben; **the most ~ thing I've ever seen** das Widerlichste, was ich je gesehen habe; **we're going to be late again – how ~** wir kommen schon wieder zu spät – es ist einfach furchtbar

sickeningly [ˈsɪknɪŋlɪ] ADV (*lit*) ekelerregend; (*fig*) unerträglich; **~ sweet** widerlich süß; **his English is ~ good** es ist schon unerträglich, wie gut sein Englisch ist; **we had all that ~ good weather during the exams** es war richtig gemein, dass wir ausgerechnet während der Prüfungszeit so schönes Wetter hatten; **now it's all ~ obvious** das schreit ja schon zum Himmel (*inf*)

sick headache N ≈ Migräneanfall *m*, ≈ Migräne *f*

sickie [ˈsɪkɪ] N (*Brit, Austral inf*) Krankentag *m*; **to take a ~** einen Tag krankfeiern (*inf*)

sickle [ˈsɪkl] N Sichel *f*

sick leave N **to be on ~** krankgeschrieben sein; **employees are allowed six weeks' ~ per year** Angestellte dürfen insgesamt sechs Wochen pro Jahr wegen Krankheit fehlen; **he has three months' ~ because of his accident** aufgrund *or* auf Grund seines Unfalls hat er drei Monate Genesungsurlaub; **he only gets two weeks' paid ~** im Krankheitsfall wird sein Gehalt nur zwei Wochen (lang) weitergezahlt

sickle-cell anaemia, (*US*) **sickle-cell anemia** [ˈsɪklseləˈniːmɪə] N Sichelzellenanämie *f*

sickliness [ˈsɪklɪnɪs] N (*of person, appearance*) Kränklichkeit *f*; (*of complexion, light*) Blässe *f*; (*of smell, taste, food, sentimentality, colour*) Widerlichkeit *f*, Ekelhaftigkeit *f*; (*of smile*) Mattheit *f*; (*of grin*) Schwachheit *f*

sick list N (*because of illness*) Krankenliste *f*; (*because of injury*) Verletztenliste *f*; **to be on the ~** (*Mil, Sport*) auf der Kranken-/Verletztenliste stehen; **he's off the ~** (*inf*) er ist wieder im Einsatz (*inf*)

sickly [ˈsɪklɪ] ADJ (+*er*) *person, appearance* kränklich; *complexion, light* blass; *smell, taste, food, sentimentality, colour* widerlich, ekelhaft; *smile* matt; *grin* schwach; *climate* ungesund; **~ sweet smell** unangenehm süßer Geruch; **~ sweet smile** übersüßes *or* zuckersüßes Lächeln

sick-making [ˈsɪkmeɪkɪŋ] ADJ (*inf*) grässlich (*inf*)

sickness [ˈsɪknɪs] N (*Med*) Krankheit *f* (*also fig*); (*= nausea*) Übelkeit *f*; (*= vomiting*) Erbrechen *nt*; (*of joke, book, film*) Geschmacklosigkeit *f*; **there is ~ on board** an Bord geht eine Krankheit um; **in ~ and in health** in guten und in schlechten Zeiten *or* Tagen; **the ~ of his mind** seine Abartigkeit

sickness benefit N (*Brit*) Krankengeld *nt*

sick note N (*Brit inf*) Krankmeldung *f*

sicko [ˈsɪkəʊ] (*esp US inf*) N Kranke(r) *mf*, Irre(r) *mf* (*pej*) ADJ *person, group* krank, irr (*pej*)

sick: **sick-out** N (*US Ind*) *geschlossene Krankmeldung der Mitarbeiter einer Firma*; **sick pay** N Gehalts- *or* (*for workers*) Lohnfortzahlung *f* im Krankheitsfall; **sickroom** N Krankenzimmer *nt*; **sick ward** N (*of prison etc*) Krankenabteilung *f or* -station *f*

side [saɪd] N a (*= wall, vertical surface, of car, box, hole, ditch*) Seite *f*; (*of cave, artillery trench, mining shaft, boat, caravan*) Wand *f*; (*of cliff, mountain*) Hang *m*; **the ~s of the hill** die Berghänge *pl*
b (*= flat surface, line: of triangle, cube, coin, paper, material, record*) Seite *f*; **this ~ up!** (*on parcel etc*) oben!; **right/wrong ~** (*of cloth*) rechte/linke Seite; **this pillowcase is right/wrong ~ out** dieser Kopfkissenbezug ist rechts/links (herum)
c (*= edge*) Rand *m*; **at the ~ of the road** am Straßenrand; **the body was found on the far ~ of the wood** die Leiche wurde am anderen Ende des Waldes gefunden; **at** *or* **on the ~ of his plate** auf dem Tellerrand
d (*= not back or front, area to one side*) Seite *f*; **by/at the ~ of sth** seitlich von etw; **the destroyer rammed the ~ of the boat** der Zerstörer rammte das Boot seitlich; **to drive on the left (-hand) ~** auf der linken Straßenseite fahren; **the path goes down the ~ of the house** der Weg führt seitlich am Haus entlang; **it's this/the other ~ of London** (*out of town*) es ist auf dieser/auf der anderen Seite Londons; (*in town*) es ist in diesem Teil/am anderen Ende von London; **the south/respectable ~ of Glasgow** der südliche/vornehme Teil Glasgows; **the debit/credit ~ of an account** die Soll-/Habenseite eines Kontos; **the enemy attacked them on** *or* **from all ~s** der Feind griff sie von allen Seiten an; **this statement was attacked on** *or* **from all ~s** diese Behauptung wurde von allen angegriffen; **he moved over** *or* **stood to one ~** er trat zur Seite; **the car moved to one ~ of the road and stopped** der Wagen fuhr seitlich heran und hielt; **he stood to one ~ and did nothing** (*lit*) er stand daneben und tat nichts; (*fig*) er hielt sich raus; **to put sth on one ~** etw beiseitelegen *or* auf die Seite legen; (*shopkeeper*) etw zurücklegen; **I'll put that issue on** *or* **to one ~** ich werde diese Frage vorerst zurückstellen; **to take sb to** *or* **on one ~** jdn beiseitenehmen; **just this ~ of the boundary** (*lit*) (noch) diesseits der Grenze; (*fig*) gerade an der Grenze; **on the other ~ of the boundary** jenseits der Grenze; **this ~ of Christmas** vor Weihnachten; **just this ~ of legal** (*inf*) am Rande der Legalität; **just this ~ of the line between sanity and madness** gerade an der Grenze zum Wahnsinn; **with one's head on one ~** mit zur Seite geneigtem Kopf; **from ~ to ~** hin und her; **to shake one's head from ~ to ~** den Kopf schütteln
e **to be on the safe ~** sichergehen; **we'll take an extra £50 just to be on the safe ~** wir werden vorsichtshalber *or* für alle Fälle £ 50 mehr mitnehmen; **to get on the right ~ of sb** jdn für sich einnehmen; **to stay on the right ~ of sb** es (sich *dat*) mit jdm nicht verderben; **to get on the wrong ~ of sb** es (sich *dat*) mit jdm verderben; **to be on the right/wrong ~ of 40** noch nicht 40/über 40 sein; **on the right ~ of the law** auf dem Boden des Gesetzes; **only just on the right ~ of the law** an der Grenze der Legalität; **to make a bit (of money) on the ~** (*inf*) sich (*dat*) etwas nebenher *or* nebenbei verdienen (*inf*); **to have a bit on the ~** (*inf*) einen Seitensprung machen; (*for longer*) noch nebenher etwas laufen haben (*inf*); **I'm not going to be your bit on the ~** (*inf*) ich will nicht deine Nebenfrau/dein Nebenmann sein (*inf*)
f (*of person, Anat*) Seite *f*; **~ of bacon** Speckseite *f*; **by sb's ~** neben jdm; **~ by ~** nebeneinander, Seite an Seite; **to stand/sit ~ by ~ with sb** direkt neben jdm stehen/sitzen; **to fight ~ by ~ with sb** Seite an Seite mit jdm kämpfen; **I'll be by your ~** (*fig*) ich werde Ihnen zur Seite stehen; **to hold one's ~s** (*with laughter*) sich

(dat) den Bauch halten (vor Lachen) → **split**
g *(= branch, of family)* Seite *f*; *(of business, school)* Zweig *m*; **the Catholic/intellectual ~ of the family** der katholische Teil/die Intelligenz der Familie; **on one's father's/mother's ~** väterlicher-/mütterlicherseits; **there's French blood on the paternal/maternal ~** von väterlicher/mütterlicher Seite ist französisches Blut da
h *(= aspect)* Seite *f*; **there are always two ~s to every story** alles hat seine zwei Seiten; **let's hear your ~ of the story** erzählen Sie mal Ihre Version (der Geschichte); **the management's ~ of the story was quite different** die Geschichte hörte sich vonseiten *or* von Seiten des Managements ganz anders an; **to hear both ~s of the question** bei einer Frage beide Seiten (an)hören; **the bright/seamy ~ of life** die Sonnen-/Schattenseite des Lebens; **to look on the bright ~** *(= be optimistic)* zuversichtlich sein; *(= look on the positive side)* die positive Seite betrachten; **you don't know his cruel ~** Sie kennen ihn nicht von seiner grausamen Seite
i **(a bit) on the large/high/formal** *etc* **~** etwas groß/hoch/förmlich *etc*; *(for somebody)* etwas zu groß/hoch/förmlich *etc*; **he errs on the ~ of generosity** er ist eher etwas zu großzügig
j *(= team etc, Sport, in quiz)* Mannschaft *f*; *(fig)* Seite *f*; **there are two ~s in the dispute** in dem Streit stehen sich zwei Parteien gegenüber; **the management ~ refused to give in** die Managementseite weigerte sich nachzugeben; **with a few concessions on the government ~** mit einigen Zugeständnissen vonseiten *or* von Seiten der Regierung; **to change ~s** sich auf die andere Seite schlagen; *(Sport)* die Seiten wechseln; **to take ~s** parteiisch sein; **to take ~s with sb** für jdn Partei ergreifen; **he's on our ~** er steht auf unserer Seite; **whose ~ are you on?** *(supporting team)* für wen sind Sie?; *(playing for team)* bei wem spielen Sie mit?; *(in argument)* zu wem halten Sie eigentlich? → **angel**
k *(dated inf: = superiority)* **there's no ~ to him** er sitzt nicht auf dem hohen Ross; **to put on ~** sich aufplustern
ADJ *attr (= on one side)* Seiten-; *(= not main)* Neben-; **~ door** Seiten-/Nebentür *f*; **~ road** Seiten-/Nebenstraße *f*
VI **to ~ with/against sb** Partei für/gegen jdn ergreifen

side: **side airbag** N *(Aut)* Seitenairbag *m*; **side aisle** N *(of church)* Seitenschiff *nt*; **side arm** N an der Seite getragene Waffe; *(= sword etc)* Seitenwaffe *f*; **sideboard** N Anrichte *f*, Sideboard *nt*; **sideboards** *(Brit)*, **sideburns** PL Koteletten *pl*; *(longer)* Backenbart *m*; **sidecar** N Beiwagen *m*; *(esp Sport)* Seitenwagen *m*

-sided [-saɪdɪd] ADJ *suf* -seitig; **one-sided** einseitig; **double-sided** doppelseitig

side: **side dish** N Beilage *f*; **side drum** N kleine Trommel; **side effect** N Nebenwirkung *f*; **side elevation** N Seitenansicht *f*, Seitenriss *m*; **side face** N Seitenansicht *f*, Profil *nt*; **side glance** N *(lit, fig)* Seitenblick *m*; **side horse** N *(apparatus gymnastics)* Seitpferd *nt*; **side impact protection system** N *(Aut)* Seitenaufprallschutz *m*; **side issue** N Randproblem *nt*; **that's just a ~** das ist Nebensache; **sidekick** N *(inf)* Kumpan(in) *m(f)* *(inf)*, Kumpel *m* *(inf)*; *(= assistant)* Handlanger(in) *m(f)* *(pej)*; **the rancher and his ~s** der Farmer und seine Leute; **sidelight** N *(Brit Aut)* Parklicht *nt*, Parkleuchte *f*; *(incorporated in headlight)* Standlicht *nt*; **that was an interesting ~ on his character** das warf ein neues Licht auf seinen Charakter; **sideline** N *(= extra business)* Nebenerwerb *m*; **it's just a ~** das läuft so nebenher *(inf)*; **to do sth as a ~** etw nebenher *or* nebenbei tun **VT** **to be ~d** *(Sport, fig)* aus dem Rennen sein; **sidelines** PL Seitenlinien *pl*; **the trainer sat on the ~** der Trainer saß am Spielfeldrand; **to keep to the ~** *(fig)* im Hintergrund bleiben; **to be** *or* **stand** *or* **sit on the ~** *(fig)* unbeteiligter Außenstehender *or* Zuschauer sein; **sidelong** ADJ **a ~ glance** ein Seitenblick *m*; **to give sb a ~ glance** jdn kurz aus den Augenwinkeln anblicken ADV **to glance ~ at sb** jdn kurz aus den Augenwinkeln anblicken; **side netting** N *(Sport: of goal)* Außennetz *nt*; **side-on** ADJ **~ collision** *or* **crash** Seitenaufprall *m*; **~ view** Seitenansicht *f*; **side order** N *(Cook)* Beilage *f*

sidereal [saɪˈdɪərɪəl] ADJ *(spec)* siderisch

side: **side-saddle** N Damensattel *m* ADV im Damensattel *or* Damensitz ADJ *rider* im Damensattel; **she was a wonderful ~ rider** sie ritt vorzüglich im Damensattel; **side salad** N Salat *m* (als Beilage); **sideshow** N Nebenvorstellung *f*; *(= exhibition)* Sonderausstellung *f*; **sideslip** N *(Aviat)* Slippen *nt*, Seitenrutsch *m*

sidesman [ˈsaɪdzmən] N *pl* **-men** [-mən] ≈ Kirchendiener *m*

side: **side-splitting** ADJ urkomisch, zum Totlachen *(inf)*; **side step** N Schritt *m* zur Seite; *(Dancing)* Seitenschritt *m*; *(Sport)* Ausfallschritt *m*; *(fig: = dodge)* Ausweichmanöver *nt*; **a master of the dribble and ~** ein Meister im Dribbeln und Ausweichen; **sidestep** VT *tackle, punch* (seitwärts) ausweichen *(+dat)*; *person* ausweichen *(+dat)*; *(fig)* ausweichen *(+dat)*, umgehen VI (seitwärts *or* zur Seite) ausweichen; *(fig)* ausweichen, ausweichende Antworten geben; **side street** N Seitenstraße *f*; **sidestroke** N Seitenschwimmen *nt*; **to do the ~** seitenschwimmen; **sideswipe** N Puff *m* *(inf)*; *(fig)* Seitenhieb *m* *(at* gegen); **to take a ~ at sb** *(lit)* jdm einen Puff geben *(inf)*; *(verbally)* jdm einen Seitenhieb versetzen; **side table** N Beistelltisch *m*; **sidetrack** N *(esp US)* = **siding** VT ablenken; **I got ~ed onto something else** ich wurde durch irgendetwas abgelenkt; *(from topic)* ich wurde irgendwie vom Thema abgebracht *or* auf ein anderes Thema gebracht; **she's easily ~ed** sie lässt sich leicht ablenken; **side view** N Seitenansicht *f*; **to have a ~ of sth** etw von der Seite sehen; **I just caught a ~ of her head** ich konnte sie nur kurz im Profil sehen; **sidewalk** N *(US)* Bürgersteig *m*, Gehsteig *m*, Trottoir *nt* *(S Ger)*; **sidewalk artist** N *(US)* Pflastermaler(in) *m(f)*; **sidewalk café** N *(US)* Straßencafé *nt*; **sidewall** N Seitenwand *f*; **sideward** ADJ = **sidewards ADJ**

sidewards [ˈsaɪdwədz] ADJ *(= to one side) movement* zur Seite; *glance* von der Seite; **to give sb/sth a ~ glance** jdn/etw von der Seite ansehen ADV *(= to one side) move* zur Seite, seitwärts; *look at sb* von der Seite

sideways [ˈsaɪdweɪz] ADJ **a** *(= to one side) movement* zur Seite; *glance* von der Seite **b** *(in career)* **the Justice Minister's recent ~ move to education** die kürzliche Versetzung des Justizministers in das Bildungsressort ADV **a** *(= to one side) move* zur Seite, seitwärts; *look at sb* von der Seite; **it goes in ~** es geht seitwärts hinein; **he was knocked ~ by it** *(fig inf)* es hat ihn umgehauen *(inf)* **b** *(= side on) sit* seitlich; **~ on** seitlich *(to sth* zu etw) **c** *(in career)* **to move ~** sich auf gleichem Niveau verändern

side: **sidewheeler** [ˈsaɪd,wiːləʳ] N *(US: = paddle steamer)* Raddampfer *m*; **side wind** N Seitenwind *m*; **side whiskers** PL Backenbart *m*; **sidewinder** N **a** *(US: = blow)* Haken *m* **b** *(= rattlesnake)* Seitenwinder *m*, gehörnte Klapperschlange

sidewise [ˈsaɪdwaɪz] ADJ, ADV = **sidewards**

siding [ˈsaɪdɪŋ] N Rangiergleis *nt*; *(= dead end)* Abstellgleis *nt*

sidle [ˈsaɪdl] VI (sich) schleichen; **to ~ away** (sich) wegschleichen; **he must have ~d off** er muss sich verdrückt haben *(inf)*; **to ~ up to sb** sich an jdn heranschleichen

SIDS [sɪdz] *(Med) abbr of* **sudden infant death syndrome**

siege [siːdʒ] N *(of town)* Belagerung *f*; *(by police)* Umstellung *f*; **to be under ~** belagert werden; *(by police)* umstellt sein; **to lay ~ to a town** eine Stadt belagern; **to lay ~ to a house** ein Haus umstellen; **he attempted to lay ~ to her emotions** er versuchte, ihr Herz zu erobern

siege mentality N Bunkermentalität *f*

sienna [sɪˈenə] N *(= earth)* Sienaerde *f*; *(= colour)* Ockergelb *nt*; **raw ~** Ockergelb *nt*; **burned ~** gebrannte Siena ADJ ockergelb; **raw ~** ockergelb; **burned ~** siena(braun), rotbraun

sierra [sɪˈerə] N Sierra *f*

Sierra Leone [sɪˈerəlɪˈəʊn] N Sierra Leone *f*

siesta [sɪˈestə] N Siesta *f*; **to have** *or* **take a ~** Siesta halten *or* machen

sieve [sɪv] N Sieb *nt*; **to have a memory** *or* **brain like a ~** *(inf)* ein Gedächtnis wie ein Sieb haben *(inf)* VT = **sift VT a**

sift [sɪft] VT **a** *(lit)* sieben; *coal* schütteln; **~ the sugar onto the cake** den Kuchen mit Zucker besieben **b** *(fig: = search)* sichten, durchgehen; *(= separate)* trennen VI *(fig)* sieben; **to ~ through the evidence** das Beweismaterial durchgehen; **a ~ing process** ein Siebeverfahren *nt*

▶ **sift out** VT *sep* **a** *stones, seed, wheat* aussieben **b** *(fig)* herausfinden, herauskristallisieren; *(= eliminate)* absondern; *applicants* aussieben

sifter [ˈsɪftəʳ] N Sieb *nt*

sigh [saɪ] N *(of person)* Seufzer *m*; *(of wind, = murmur)* Säuseln *nt no pl*; *(= moan)* Seufzen *nt no pl (liter)*; **a ~ of relief** ein Seufzer *m* der Erleichterung → **breathe** VI seufzen; *(wind, = murmur)* säuseln; *(= moan)* seufzen *(liter)*; **to ~ with relief** erleichtert aufatmen; **to ~ with pleasure** vor Vergnügen seufzen; **to ~ for sb/sth** sich nach jdm/etw sehnen VT seufzen

sighing [ˈsaɪɪŋ] N *(of person)* Seufzen *nt*; *(of wind, = murmuring)* Säuseln *nt*; *(= moaning)* Seufzen *nt (liter)*

sight [saɪt] N **a** *(= faculty)* Sehvermögen *nt*; **the gift of ~** die Gabe des Sehens; **long/short ~** Weit-/Kurzsichtigkeit *f*; **to have long/short ~** weit-/kurzsichtig sein; **to lose/regain one's ~** sein Augenlicht verlieren/wiedergewinnen; **he has very good ~** er sieht sehr gut; **~ is the most valuable sense** das Auge ist das wertvollste Sinnesorgan
b *(= glimpse, seeing)* **it was my first ~ of Paris** das war das Erste, was ich von Paris gesehen habe; **to hate sb at first ~** *or* **on ~** jdn vom ersten Augenblick an nicht leiden können; **at first ~ I hated him, but then …** zuerst konnte ich ihn gar nicht leiden, aber dann …; **at first ~ it seemed easy** auf den ersten Blick erschien es einfach; **to shoot at** *or* **on ~** sofort schießen; **he played the music by ~** er hat vom Blatt gespielt; **love at first ~** Liebe auf den ersten Blick; **at the ~ of the police they ran away** als sie die Polizei sahen, rannten sie weg; **to know sb by ~** jdn vom Sehen kennen; **to catch ~ of sb/sth** jdn/etw entdecken *or* erblicken; **if I catch ~ of you round here again …** wenn du mir hier noch einmal unter die Augen kommst, …; **don't let me catch ~ of you with her again** ich möchte dich nicht noch einmal mit ihr erwischen; **to get a ~ of sb/sth** jdn/etw zu sehen *or* zu Gesicht bekommen; **we had a glorious ~ of the mountains** wir hatten einen herrlichen Blick auf die Berge; **to lose ~ of sb/sth** *(lit, fig)* jdn/etw aus den Augen verlieren; **don't lose ~ of the fact that …** Sie dürfen nicht außer Acht lassen, dass … → **second sight**
c *(= sth seen)* Anblick *m*; **the ~ of blood/her makes me sick** wenn ich Blut/sie sehe, wird mir übel; **that is the most beautiful ~ I've ever seen** das ist das Schönste, was ich je gesehen habe; **I hate** *or* **can't bear the ~ of him/his greasy hair** ich kann ihn/seine fettigen Haare (einfach) nicht ausstehen; **to be a ~ to see** *or* **behold** ein herrlicher Anblick sein; *(funny)* ein Bild *or* Anblick für die Götter sein *(inf)*; **what a horrible ~!** das sieht ja furchtbar aus!; **it was a ~ for sore eyes** es war eine wahre Augenweide; **you're a ~ for sore eyes** es ist schön, dich zu sehen
d *(inf)* **to be** *or* **look a ~** *(funny)* zum Schreien aussehen *(inf)*; *(horrible)* fürchterlich aussehen; **he looks a ~** der sieht vielleicht aus *(inf)*; **what a ~ you are!** wie siehst du denn aus!

e *(= range of vision)* Sicht *f*; **to be in** *or* **within ~** in Sicht *or* in Sichtweite sein; **land in ~!** Land in Sicht!; **our goal is in ~** unser Ziel ist in greifbare Nähe gerückt; **we are in ~ of victory** unser Sieg liegt in greifbarer Nähe; **we came in ~ of the coast** die Küste kam in Sicht; **at last we were in ~ of land** endlich war Land in Sicht; **to keep sb in ~** jdn im Auge behalten; **to keep out of ~** sich verborgen halten; **to keep sb/sth out of ~** jdn/etw nicht sehen lassen; **keep out of my ~!** lass dich bloß bei mir nicht mehr sehen *or* blicken; **to be out of** *or* **lost to ~** nicht mehr zu sehen sein, außer Sicht sein; **the minute I was out of ~ of the school** sobald ich von der Schule aus nicht mehr zu sehen war; **when he's out of our ~** wenn wir ihn nicht sehen; **somewhere out of ~ a cat was mewing** irgendwo miaute eine (unsichtbare) Katze; **don't let the children out of your ~** lass die Kinder nicht aus den Augen; **darling, I'll never let you out of my ~ again** Schatz, ich lasse dich nie mehr fort; **she dropped out of ~ after her first movie** nach ihrem ersten Film geriet sie in Vergessenheit; **to be lost to ~** nicht mehr zu sehen sein; **out of ~, out of mind** *(Prov)* aus den Augen, aus dem Sinn *(Prov)*
f *(Comm)* **payable at ~** zahlbar bei Sicht; **30 days' ~** 30 Tage nach Sicht; **~ unseen** unbesehen, ohne Besicht *(form)*; **we need to have ~ of the document first** das Dokument muss uns *(dat)* zuerst vorliegen
g *(fig: = opinion)* **in sb's ~** in jds Augen *(dat)*; **in the ~ of God** vor Gott
h *usu pl (of city etc)* Sehenswürdigkeit *f*; **to see the ~s of a town** *etc* eine Stadt *etc* besichtigen
i *(on telescope etc)* Visiereinrichtung *f*; *(on gun)* Visier *nt*; **to set one's ~s too high** *(fig)* seine Ziele zu hoch stecken; **to lower one's ~s** *(fig)* seine Ansprüche herabsetzen *or* herunterschrauben; **to set one's ~s on sth** *(fig)* ein Auge auf etw *(acc)* werfen; **to have sb/sth in** *or* **within one's ~s** *(fig)* jdn/etw im Fadenkreuz haben
j *(= aim, observation)* **to take a ~ with a gun** *etc* **at sth** etw mit einem Gewehr *etc* anvisieren
k *(inf)* **not by a long ~** bei Weitem nicht; **a ~ better/cheaper** einiges besser/billiger; **he's a damn ~ cleverer than you think** er ist ein ganzes Ende gescheiter als du meinst *(inf)*
l *(inf)* **out of ~** sagenhaft *(sl)*, der Wahnsinn *(inf)*
VT **a** *(= see)* sichten *(also Mil)*; *person* ausmachen
b *gun (= provide with sights)* mit Visier versehen; *(= adjust sights)* richten

sight bill, sight draft N Sichtwechsel *m*

sighted ['saɪtɪd] ADJ sehend

-sighted ADJ *suf (Med, fig)* -sichtig; **far-sighted** weitsichtig; **short-sighted** kurzsichtig

sighting ['saɪtɪŋ] N Sichten *nt*; **at the first ~ of land** als zum ersten Mal Land gesichtet wurde; **another ~ of the monster was reported** das Ungeheuer soll erneut gesehen *or* gesichtet worden sein

sightless ['saɪtlɪs] ADJ *person* erblindet, blind; **~ since birth** von Geburt an blind; **worms are completely ~** Würmer haben kein Sehvermögen *(form)*, Würmer können überhaupt nicht sehen; **with ~ eyes** mit blicklosen *(geh) or* toten Augen

sightlessness ['saɪtlɪsnɪs] N Blindheit *f*

sightline ['saɪtlaɪn] N Sicht *f*

sightly ['saɪtlɪ] ADJ ansehnlich

sight: **sight-read** VTI vom Blatt spielen/lesen/singen; **sightscreen** N *(Cricket)* Sichtblende *f* hinter dem Tor; **sightseeing** N Besichtigungen *pl*; **I hate ~** ich hasse Sightseeing; **~ in Ruritania** eine Rundreise durch Ruritanien; *(= list of sights)* Sehenswürdigkeiten *pl* von Ruritanien; **to go ~** auf Besichtigungstour gehen ADJ **~ tour** Rundreise *f*; *(in town)* (Stadt)rundfahrt *f*; **~ tourists** Touristen *pl (auf Besichtigungstour)*; **sightseer** N Tourist(in) *m(f)*; **sight test** N Sehtest *m*

sign [saɪn] N **a** *(with hand etc)* Zeichen *nt*; **he nodded as a ~ of recognition** er nickte zum Zeichen, dass er mich/ihn *etc* erkannt hatte; **to give sb a ~** jdm ein Zeichen geben; **to make a ~ to sb** jdm ein Zeichen machen *or* geben; **he gave** *or* **made me a ~ to stay** er gab mir durch ein Zeichen zu verstehen, ich solle bleiben; **he made a rude ~** er machte eine unverschämte Geste
b (= *indication, Med*) Anzeichen *nt* (*of* für, *+gen*); *(= evidence)* Zeichen *nt* (*of* von, *+gen*); *(= trace)* Spur *f*; **a sure/good/bad ~** ein sicheres/gutes/schlechtes Zeichen; **it's a ~ of the times** es ist ein Zeichen unserer Zeit; **it's a ~ of a true expert** daran erkennt man den wahren Experten; **at the slightest/first ~ of disagreement** beim geringsten/ersten Anzeichen von Uneinigkeit; **there is no ~ of their agreeing** nichts deutet darauf hin, dass sie zustimmen werden; **to show ~s of sth** Anzeichen von etw erkennen lassen; **he shows ~s of doing it** es sieht so aus, als ob er es tun würde; **our guest showed no ~(s) of leaving** unser Gast machte keine Anstalten zu gehen; **the rain showed no ~(s) of stopping** nichts deutete darauf hin, dass der Regen aufhören würde; **he gave no ~ of having heard** er ließ nicht erkennen, ob er es gehört hatte; **he gave no ~ of life** er gab kein Lebenszeichen von sich; **there was no ~ of life in the village** es gab keine Spur *or* kein Anzeichen von Leben im Dorf; **there was no ~ of him/the book anywhere** von ihm/von dem Buch war keine Spur zu sehen; **is there any ~ of him yet?** ist er schon zu sehen?
c *(= road sign, inn sign, shop sign)* Schild *nt*
d *(= written symbol)* Zeichen *nt*; *(= Math)* Vorzeichen *nt*; *(Astron, Astrol)* (Tierkreis)zeichen *nt*
VT **a** **to ~ one's name** unterschreiben; **to ~ one's name in a book** sich in ein Buch eintragen; **he ~s himself J.G. Jones** er unterschreibt mit J. G. Jones
b *letter, contract, cheque* unterschreiben, unterzeichnen *(form)*; *picture, book* signieren; **to ~ the guest book** sich ins Gästebuch eintragen; **to ~ the register** sich eintragen; **~ed and sealed** (unterschrieben und) besiegelt; **~ed, sealed and delivered** unter Dach und Fach, fix und fertig *(inf)*; **~ed copy** handsigniertes Exemplar
c *football player etc* unter Vertrag nehmen, einstellen
d *(= use sign language in) programme, performance* in die Gebärdensprache übersetzen
VI **a** *(= signal)* **to ~ to sb to do sth** jdm ein Zeichen geben, etw zu tun
b *(with signature)* unterschreiben; **Fellows has just ~ed for United** Fellows hat gerade bei United unterschrieben
c *(= use sign language)* die Gebärdensprache benutzen

▸ **sign away** VT *sep* verzichten auf *(+acc)*; **she felt she was signing away her life** sie hatte den Eindruck, ihr Leben abzuschreiben; **I'm not going to sign my life away with a mortgage** ich werde mich nicht ein Leben lang mit einer Hypothek belasten

▸ **sign for** VI *+prep obj* den Empfang *(+gen)* bestätigen

▸ **sign in** VT *sep person* eintragen; **to sign sb in at a club** jdn als Gast in einen Klub mitnehmen VI sich eintragen

▸ **sign off** VI *(Rad, TV)* sich verabschieden; *(in letter)* Schluss machen VI *+prep obj* **to sign off (the dole)** *(Brit)* eine Arbeit aufnehmen

▸ **sign on** VT *sep* = **sign up VT** VI **a** = **sign up VI** **b** *(Brit: for unemployment benefit etc)* **to sign on (for unemployment benefit)** *(= apply)* sich arbeitslos melden; **he's still signing on** er ist immer noch arbeitslos, er bezieht immer noch Arbeitslosenunterstützung **c** *(disc jockey etc)* sich melden VI *+prep obj* **to sign on (the dole)** *(Brit)* sich arbeitslos melden

▸ **sign out** VI sich austragen; **to sign out of a hotel** (aus einem Hotel) abreisen VT *sep* austragen

▸ **sign over** VT *sep* überschreiben (*to sb* jdm)

▸ **sign up** VT *sep (= employ, enlist)* verpflichten; *workers, employees* anstellen; *mercenaries* anwerben; *sailors* anheuern VI sich verpflichten; *(mercenaries)* sich melden (*with* zu); *(employees, players)* unterschreiben; *(sailors)* anheuern; *(for evening class etc)* sich einschreiben

signal[1] ['sɪgnl] N **a** *(= sign)* Zeichen *nt*; *(as part of code)* Signal *nt*; *(= message)* Nachricht *f*; **to give the ~ for sth** das Zeichen/Signal zu etw geben; **to make a ~ to sb** jdm ein Zeichen geben
b *(= apparatus, Rail)* Signal *nt*; **the ~ is at red** das Signal steht auf Rot
c *(Telec)* Signal *nt*
d *(Brit, Mil)* **Signals** ≈ Fernmelder *pl*, *Angehörige der britischen Fernmeldetruppe Royal Corps of Signals*
VT **a** *(= indicate)* anzeigen; *arrival, future event, spring etc* ankündigen; **to ~ sb to do sth** jdm ein Zeichen geben, etw zu tun; **the policeman ~led** *(Brit) or* **~ed** *(US)* **the cars on** der Polizist gab den Autos das Zeichen weiterzufahren; **he ~led** *(Brit) or* **~ed** *(US)* **that he was going to turn left** er zeigte an, dass er (nach) links abbiegen wollte; **the train was ~led** *(Brit) or* **~ed** *(US)* **onto another line** der Zug wurde durch Signale auf ein anderes Gleis gewiesen *or* geleitet; **to ~ one's intention to do sth** anzeigen, dass man vorhat, etw zu tun
b *message* signalisieren
VI ein Zeichen geben; **he ~led** *(Brit) or* **~ed** *(US)* **to the waiter** er winkte dem Ober; **he ~led for his bill** *(Brit)* **he ~ed for the check** *(US)* er winkte zum Zeichen, dass er zahlen wollte; **the driver didn't ~** der Fahrer hat kein Zeichen gegeben *or* hat nicht angezeigt; **the general ~led** *(Brit) or* **~ed** *(US)* **for reinforcements** der General forderte Verstärkung an

signal[2] ADJ *attr (liter) victory, courage* beachtlich, bemerkenswert; *success, contribution* beachtlich; *failure, stupidity* eklatant *(geh)*

signal: **signal box** N Stellwerk *nt*; **signal flag** N Signalflagge *f*

signalize ['sɪgnəlaɪz] VT kennzeichnen

signal lamp N Signallampe *f*

signaller, *(US)* **signaler** ['sɪgnələ'] N *(Mil)* Fernmelder(in) *m(f)*, Funker(in) *m(f)*

signalling, *(US)* **signaling** ['sɪgnəlɪŋ] N *(Mil)* Nachrichtenübermittlung *f*

signally ['sɪgnəlɪ] ADV *(liter) successful, ineffective* bemerkenswert; *stupid* eklatant; **he has ~ failed** er hat eindeutig versagt; **he has ~ failed to provide evidence** er hat es eindeutig nicht geschafft, Beweise vorzulegen

signal: **signalman** N *(Rail)* Stellwerkswärter *m*; *(Mil)* Fernmelder *m*, Funker *m*; **signal-red** ADJ signalrot; **signal tower** N *(US Rail)* Stellwerk *nt*

signatory ['sɪgnətərɪ] ADJ Signatar-; **the ~ countries of an agreement** die Signatarstaaten eines Abkommens N *(= person)* Unterzeichner(in) *m(f)*, Signatar(in) *m(f) (form)*; **the signatories of** *or* **to the EC treaty** die Signatarstaaten des EG-Vertrags

signature ['sɪgnətʃə'] N **a** Unterschrift *f*; *(of artist)* Signatur *f* **b** *(Mus)* Vorzeichnung *f* **c** *(Typ)* Signatur *f*

signature tune N *(Brit)* Erkennungsmelodie *f*

signboard ['saɪnbɔːd] N Schild *nt*; *(= hoarding)* Anschlagtafel *f*

signer ['saɪnə'] N Unterzeichner(in) *m(f)*

signet ring ['sɪgnɪt,rɪŋ] N Siegelring *m*

significance [sɪg'nɪfɪkəns] N Bedeutung *f*; *(of action also)* Tragweite *f*; *(of one special event also)* Wichtigkeit *f*; **what is the ~ of this?** was bedeutet das?, welche Bedeutung hat das?; **of no ~** belanglos, bedeutungslos; **to attach great ~ to sth** einer Sache *(dat)* große Bedeutung beimessen; **he attaches great ~ to us arriving on time** er legt großen Wert darauf, dass wir pünktlich sind

significant [sɪɡˈnɪfɪkənt] ADJ **a** *(= considerable, having consequence)* bedeutend; *(= important)* wichtig; **is it of any ~ interest?** ist das von wesentlichem Interesse?; **to be ~ to** *or* **for sth** eine bedeutende *or* wichtige Rolle in etw *(dat)* spielen; **statistically ~** statistisch signifikant *or* bedeutsam; **politically/historically ~** politisch/historisch bedeutend
b *(= meaningful)* bedeutungsvoll; *look* vielsagend, bedeutsam; *sigh, tone of voice* bedeutungsvoll, bedeutsam; **it is ~ that …** es ist bezeichnend, dass …; **he wondered whether her glance was ~** er fragte sich, ob ihr Blick etwas zu bedeuten habe; **to be ~ of sth** *(liter)* ein (An)zeichen *nt* für etw sein

significantly [sɪɡˈnɪfɪkəntlɪ] ADV **a** *(= considerably)* bedeutend; **it is not ~ different** das ist kaum anders, da besteht kein wesentlicher Unterschied **b** *(= meaningfully)* bedeutungsvoll; *look* vielsagend, bedeutsam; **~, she refused** bezeichnenderweise lehnte sie ab; **he was ~ absent** er fehlte bezeichnenderweise

signification [ˌsɪɡnɪfɪˈkeɪʃən] N **a** *(= meaning)* Sinn *m*, Bedeutung *f* **b** *(= indication)* Bezeichnung *f*; **a ~ of one's intentions** eine Absichtsbekundung *or* -erklärung

signify [ˈsɪɡnɪfaɪ] VT **a** *(= mean)* bedeuten **b** *(= indicate)* andeuten, erkennen lassen VI *(dated)* **it/he doesn't ~** das/er spielt keine Rolle

signing [ˈsaɪnɪŋ] N **a** *(of document)* Unterzeichnen *nt* **b** *(of football player, pop star etc)* Unterverträgnahme *f*; *(= football player, pop star etc)* neu unter Vertrag Genommene(r) *mf* **c** *(= sign language)* Gebärdensprache *f*

sign: **sign language** N Zeichensprache *f*; *(for deaf also)* Gebärdensprache *f*; **sign painter** N Plakat- *or* Schildermaler(in) *m(f)*; **signpost** N Wegweiser *m* VT *way* beschildern; *diversion, special route* ausschildern; **signposting** N Beschilderung *f*; *(of special route, diversion)* Ausschilderung *f*; **signwriter** N Schriften- *or* Schildermaler(in) *m(f)*

Sikh [siːk] N Sikh *mf*

silage [ˈsaɪlɪdʒ] N Silage *f*, Silofutter *nt*

silence [ˈsaɪləns] N Stille *f*; *(= quietness also)* Ruhe *f*; *(= absence of talk also, of letters etc)* Schweigen *nt*; *(on a particular subject)* (Still)schweigen *nt*; **~!** Ruhe!; **in ~** still; *(= not talking also)* schweigend; **there was ~** alles war still; **there was a short ~** es herrschte für kurze Zeit Stille; **the conversation was full of awkward ~s** die Unterhaltung kam immer wieder ins Stocken; **to break the ~** die Stille durchbrechen; **he broke his ~** er brach sein Schweigen; **to observe a minute's** *(Brit) or* **moment's** *(US)* **~** eine Schweige- *or* Gedenkminute einlegen *(in memory of* für)
VT *(lit, fig)* zum Schweigen bringen; **to ~ sb's tongue** jdn zum Schweigen bringen

silencer [ˈsaɪlənsəʳ] N *(on gun, Brit: on car)* Schalldämpfer *m*; *(= whole fitting on car)* Auspufftopf *m*

silent [ˈsaɪlənt] ADJ **a** still; *(= not talking also)* schweigsam; *engine, machine etc (= running quietly)* ruhig; **to fall** *or* **become ~** still werden; *(people also, guns)* verstummen; **to keep** *or* **remain ~** still sein *or* bleiben, sich still verhalten; **be ~!** sei still!; **the guns are ~** die Waffen schweigen; **ovarian cancer is a ~ killer** Eierstockkrebs tötet auf leise *or* unbemerkte Art; **his father was the strong ~ type** sein Vater war ein schweigsamer, willensstarker Typ
b *(= not giving comment)* **to be ~** schweigen; **to be ~ about** *or* **on sth** über etw *(acc)* schweigen *or* Stillschweigen bewahren; **the law is ~ on this point** das Gesetz schweigt zu diesem Punkt; **to keep** *or* **remain ~** nichts sagen, sich nicht äußern; **he kept completely ~ when questioned** er sagte kein einziges Wort *or* überhaupt nichts, als man ihn verhörte; **everyone kept ~** keiner sagte etwas; **you have the right to remain ~** Sie haben das Recht zu schweigen; **to give sb the ~ treatment** jdn mit Schweigen strafen; **a ~ witness** ein stummer Zeuge, eine stumme Zeugin
c *(= quiet, wordless) protest* still; *agreement, disapproval* (still)schweigend *attr*; **~ demonstration** Schweigemarsch *m*
d *(Film)* **~ film** *(esp Brit) or* **movie** *(esp US)* Stummfilm *m*; **the ~ era** die Stummfilmzeit
e *(Ling: = not pronounced)* **~ letter** stummer Buchstabe; **the "k" is ~ in the word "knee"** das Wort „knee" hat ein stummes „k"; **~ "h"** stummes „h"
PL **the silents** *(Brit Film)* die Stummfilme *pl*

silently [ˈsaɪləntlɪ] ADV lautlos; *(= without talking)* schweigend; *(= with little noise)* leise

silent: **silent majority** N **the ~** die schweigende Mehrheit; **silent partner** N *(US Comm)* stiller Teilhaber *or* Gesellschafter; **silent vigil** N Mahnwache *f*

Silesia [saɪˈliːzɪə] N Schlesien *nt*

Silesian [saɪˈliːzɪən] ADJ schlesisch N Schlesier(in) *m(f)*

silhouette [ˌsɪluːˈet] N Silhouette *f*; *(= picture)* Schattenriss *m*, Scherenschnitt *m* VT **to be ~d against sth** sich (als Silhouette) gegen *or* von etw abzeichnen

silica [ˈsɪlɪkə] N Kieselerde *f*

silica gel N Kieselgel *nt*

silicate [ˈsɪlɪkɪt] N Silikat *nt*, Silicat *nt*

siliceous [sɪˈlɪʃəs] ADJ kiesig

silicon [ˈsɪlɪkən] N Silizium *nt*

silicon chip N Siliziumchip *nt*

silicone [ˈsɪlɪkəʊn] N Silikon *nt*; **~ treatment** Silikonbehandlung *f*; **~ (breast) implants** Silikonimplantate *pl*, Silikon(brust)einlagen *pl*

Silicon Valley N Silicon Valley *nt*

silicosis [ˌsɪlɪˈkəʊsɪs] N *(Med)* Staublunge *f*, Silikose *f (spec)*

silk [sɪlk] N **a** Seide *f*; *(= silk dress)* Seidene(s) *nt*, Seidenkleid *nt*; **dressed in beautiful ~s** in herrliche Seidengewänder gekleidet; **dressed in ~s and satins** in Samt und Seide (gekleidet) **b** *(Brit, Jur, = barrister)* Kronanwalt *m*/-anwältin *f*; *(= gown)* Seidengewand *nt*; **to take ~** Kronanwalt werden **c** **silks** PL *(= racing colours)* (Renn)farben *pl* ADJ Seiden-, seiden; **~ tie** Seidenkrawatte *f*; **the dress is ~** das Kleid ist aus Seide; **you can't make a ~ purse out of a sow's ear** *(Prov)* aus einem Ackergaul kann man kein Rennpferd machen *(prov)*

silken [ˈsɪlkən] ADJ *(old: = of silk)* seiden; *(= like silk)* seidig; *manner* glatt; *voice* (bedrohlich) sanft

silk hat N Zylinder *m*

silkiness [ˈsɪlkɪnɪs] N *(= appearance)* seidiger Glanz; *(= feeling)* seidige Weichheit; *(of voice)* Sanftheit *f*; *(of manner)* Glätte *f*

silk: **silk moth** N Seidenspinner *m*; **silk screen** N Seidensieb *nt*; *(also* **silk-screen printing**) Seidensiebdruck *m*; **silk stocking** N Seidenstrumpf *m*; **silk-stocking** ADJ *(US)* vornehm; **silkworm** N Seidenraupe *f*

silky [ˈsɪlkɪ] ADJ *(+er)* seidig; *voice* samtig; *manner* glatt; *movements* weich; **~ smooth/soft** seidenweich

sill [sɪl] N Sims *m or nt*; *(= windowsill)* (Fenster)sims *m or nt*; *(esp of wood)* Fensterbrett *nt*; *(= doorsill)* Schwelle *f (on car)* Türleiste *f*

sillabub N = **syllabub**

silliness [ˈsɪlɪnɪs] N Albernheit *f*; **no ~ while we're out, children!** macht keine Dummheiten, wenn wir nicht da sind!

silly [ˈsɪlɪ] ADJ *(+er)* albern, dumm, doof *(inf)*; **don't be ~** *(= do silly things)* mach keinen Quatsch *(inf)*; *(= say silly things)* red keinen Unsinn; *(= ask silly questions)* frag nicht so dumm; **that was ~ of you, that was a ~ thing to do** das war dumm (von dir); **I've done a ~ thing and come without the key** ich war so dumm, ohne Schlüssel zu kommen, ich Dussel bin ohne Schlüssel gekommen *(inf)*; **it was a ~ thing to say** es war dumm, das zu sagen; **I hope he doesn't do anything ~** ich hoffe, er macht keine Dummheiten; **I know it's ~ to feel jealous** ich weiß, es ist dumm, eifersüchtig zu sein; **he was ~ to resign** es war dumm von ihm zurückzutreten; **I feel ~ in this hat** mit diesem Hut komme ich mir albern *or* lächerlich vor; **to make sb look ~** jdn lächerlich machen; **that remark of yours made him look/left him looking a bit ~** nach dieser Bemerkung von dir stand er ziemlich dumm da; **to knock sb ~** *(inf)* jdn windelweich schlagen *(inf)*; **to laugh oneself ~** *(inf)* sich dumm und dämlich lachen *(inf)*; **to worry sb ~** *(inf)* jdn vor Sorge (ganz) krank machen; **to drink oneself ~** *(inf)* seinen Verstand versaufen *(inf)*; **to be bored ~** *(inf)* zu Tode gelangweilt sein; **to bore sb ~** *(inf)* jdn zu Tode langweilen; **to pay a ~ price for sth** *(inf, high price)* für etw einen sündhaft teuren Preis bezahlen; *(low price)* für etw einen Spottpreis bezahlen; **~ money** *(inf)* Wahnsinnssummen *pl (inf)*
N *(Brit: also* **silly-billy**) Dussel *m (inf)*; **you big ~** du Dummerchen *(inf)*; **don't be such a ~** sei nicht albern

silly season N närrische Zeit; *(Brit Press)* Saure-Gurken-Zeit *f*

silo [ˈsaɪləʊ] N Silo *nt*; *(for missile)* (Raketen)silo *nt*

silt [sɪlt] N Schwemmsand *m*; *(= river mud)* Schlick *m* VT *(also* **silt up**) mit Schlick/Schwemmsand füllen VI *(also* **silt up**) verschlammen

silty [ˈsɪltɪ] ADJ verschlammt, schlammig

Silurian [saɪˈljuːrɪən] ADJ *(Geol)* silurisch

silvan [ˈsɪlvən] ADJ *(liter)* = **sylvan**

silver [ˈsɪlvəʳ] N **a** *(= metal)* Silber *nt* **b** *(= coins)* Silber(geld) *nt*, Silbermünzen *pl*; **£10 in ~** £ 10 in Silber **c** *(= tableware, articles)* Silber *nt* **d** *(= colour)* Silber *nt* ADJ Silber-, silbern; **~ jewellery** *(Brit) or* **jewelry** *(US)* Silberschmuck *m*; **to be born with a ~ spoon in one's mouth** *(prov)* mit einem silbernen Löffel im Mund geboren sein *(prov)* VT *metal, mirror* versilbern; **old age had ~ed his hair** das Alter hatte sein Haar silbergrau werden lassen

silver: **silverbeet** N *(Bot: = Swiss chard)* Mangold *m*; **silver birch** N Weißbirke *f*; **silver disc** N *(Brit Mus)* silberne Schallplatte; **silver fir** N Weiß- *or* Silbertanne *f*; **silverfish** N Silberfischchen *nt*; **silver foil** N *(= kitchen foil)* Alu(minium)folie *f*; *(= silver paper)* Silberpapier *nt*; **silver fox** N Silberfuchs *m*; **silver-grey**, *(US)* **silver-gray** ADJ silbergrau; *hair* silberweiß; **silver-haired** ADJ silberhaarig; **he is ~** er hat silberweißes Haar

silveriness [ˈsɪlvərɪnɪs] N silbriger Schimmer; *(of sound, voice)* silberheller Klang

silver: **silver jubilee** N 25jähriges Jubiläum; **silver lining** N *(fig)* Silberstreifen *f (am Horizont)*, Lichtblick *m (fig)*; **silver medal** N Silbermedaille *f*; **silver medallist**, *(US)* **silver medalist** N *(Sport)* Silbermedaillengewinner(in) *m(f)*; **silver nitrate** N Silbernitrat *nt*; **silver oxide** N Silberoxid *nt*; **silver oxide battery** N Silberoxidbatterie *f*; **silver paper** N Silberpapier *nt*; **silver plate** N *(= plating)* Silberauflage *f*, Versilberung *f*; *(= articles)* versilberte Sachen *pl*; **is that ~?** ist das versilbert?; **silver-plate** VT versilbern; **silver-plating** N Versilberung *f*; *(= layer also)* Silberauflage *f*; **silver screen** N Leinwand *f*; **silver service** N *(in restaurant) Servieren nach allen Regeln der Kunst*; **silverside** N *(Cook) quer geschnittenes Stück aus der Rindskeule*; **silversmith** N Silberschmied(in) *m(f)*; **silversmith's (shop)** N Silberschmiede *f*; **silver standard** N Silberstandard *m*; **silver surfer** N *(inf)* Internetbenutzer(in) *m(f)* in fortgeschrittenem Alter; **silver-tongued** ADJ *(liter)* wort- *or* redegewandt; **silverware** N Silber *nt*, Silberzeug *nt (inf)*; *(in shop also)* Silberwaren *pl*; **silver wedding** N Silberhochzeit *f*

silvery [ˈsɪlvərɪ] ADJ silbern, silbrig; *sound, voice* silberhell; **~ grey** *(Brit) or* **gray** *(US)* silbergrau; **~ white** silberweiß

silviculture [ˈsɪlvɪkʌltʃəʳ] N Waldbau *m*

SIM *(Telec) abbr of* **subscriber identification module** SIM; **~ card** SIM-Karte *f*

simian ['sɪmɪən] ADJ *(form)* der Affen; *appearance* affenartig N Affe *m*

similar ['sɪmɪlə'] ADJ ähnlich *(also Math)*; *amount, size* fast *or* ungefähr gleich; **to be ~ to sb/sth** jdm/einer Sache ähnlich sein; **this is ~ to what happened before** etwas Ähnliches ist schon einmal geschehen; **she and her sister are very ~, she is very ~ to her sister** ihre Schwester und sie sind sich sehr ähnlich, sie ähnelt ihrer Schwester sehr; **to be ~ in appearance to sth** eine ähnliche Erscheinung wie etw haben; **they are very ~ in appearance/character** sie ähneln sich äußerlich/charakterlich sehr; **~ in size** ungefähr *or* fast gleich groß; **to taste ~ to sth** ähnlich wie etw schmecken; **they are of a ~ age** sie sind etwa gleich alt; **in a ~ way** ähnlich; *(= likewise)* genauso, ebenso

similarity [ˌsɪmɪ'lærɪtɪ] N Ähnlichkeit *f* (*to* mit)

similarly ['sɪmɪləlɪ] ADV ähnlich; *(= equally)* genauso, ebenso; **a ~ pained expression** ein ähnlich qualvoller Ausdruck; **~, you could maintain …** genauso gut könnten Sie behaupten …

simile ['sɪmɪlɪ] N Gleichnis *nt*; **his use of ~** sein Gebrauch *m* von Gleichnissen

similitude [sɪ'mɪlɪtjuːd] N *(liter)* Ähnlichkeit *f*

simmer ['sɪmə'] N **to be on the ~** *(Cook)* auf kleiner Flamme kochen; **to keep sth on the ~** *(lit)* etw auf kleiner Flamme kochen lassen; *(fig)* etw nicht zur Ruhe kommen lassen VT auf kleiner Flamme kochen lassen VI auf kleiner Flamme kochen; *(fig, with rage)* kochen *(inf)*; *(with excitement)* fiebern

▶ **simmer down** VI sich beruhigen, sich abregen *(inf)*

simnel cake ['sɪmnlkeɪk] N *(Brit)* marzipanüberzogener Früchtekuchen

simonize ['saɪmənaɪz] VT polieren

simony ['saɪmənɪ] N *(old Eccl)* Simonie *f*

simp [sɪmp] N *(US inf, pej)* Simpel *m (pej)*

simper ['sɪmpə'] N **… she said with a ~** …, sagte sie mit säuselnder Stimme VI *(= smile)* geziert *or* albern lächeln; *(= talk)* säuseln VT säuseln

simpering ['sɪmpərɪŋ] ADJ geziert, albern

simperingly ['sɪmpərɪŋlɪ] ADV geziert, albern; *talk* säuselnd

simple ['sɪmpl] ADJ *(+er)* **a** *(= uncomplicated, easy)* einfach; **the camcorder is ~ to use** der Camcorder ist einfach zu bedienen; **it's as ~ as ABC** es ist kinderleicht; **"chemistry made ~"** „Chemie leicht gemacht"

b *(= plain, not elaborate)* einfach; *decor, dress* schlicht, einfach; **in ~ terms** in einfachen Worten; **in ~ language** in einfacher Sprache; **the ~ fact** *or* **truth is …** es ist einfach so, dass …; **the ~ fact that …** die schlichte Tatsache, dass…; **for the ~ reason that …** aus dem einfachen *or* schlichten Grund, dass …; **it's a ~ matter of money** es ist schlicht und einfach eine Frage des Geldes; **it's a ~ matter of finding adequate finance** es geht ganz einfach darum, angemessene finanzielle Mittel zu finden

c *(= unsophisticated, unworldly)* einfach, schlicht; **I'm a ~ soul** ich bin ein einfacher Mensch; **she likes the ~ life** sie mag das einfache Leben *or* einen einfachen Lebensstil; **the ~ things in** *or* **of life** die einfachen Dinge des Lebens *or* im Leben

d *(= foolish, mentally deficient)* einfältig

e *(Chem, Med, Math, Ling)* einfach; *(Biol, Bot) life form* primitiv, einfach

simple: **simple contract** N *(Jur)* formloser Vertrag; **simple fracture** N *(Med)* einfacher Bruch; **simple interest** N *(Fin)* Kapitalzinsen *pl*; **simple majority** N einfache Mehrheit; **simple-minded** ADJ einfältig; **simple-mindedness** N Einfältigkeit *f*, Einfalt *f*; **Simple Simon** [ˌsɪmpl'saɪmən] N *(= simpleton)* Einfaltspinsel *m (inf pej)*; **simple time** N *(Mus)* gerader Takt

simpleton ['sɪmpltən] N Einfaltspinsel *m*

simplex ['sɪmpleks] N *(Ling)* Simplex *nt*

simplicity [sɪm'plɪsɪtɪ] N **a** Einfachheit *f*; *(= unworldliness, lack of sophistication: of decor, dress)* Schlichtheit *f*, Einfachheit *f*; **it's ~ itself** das ist das Einfachste, das ist die einfachste Sache der Welt **b** *(= foolishness)* Einfalt *f*, Einfältigkeit *f*

simplifiable ['sɪmplɪfaɪəbl] ADJ zu vereinfachend *attr*, zu vereinfachen *pred*, simplifizierbar

simplification [ˌsɪmplɪfɪ'keɪʃən] N Vereinfachung *f*, Simplifizierung *f*

simplified ['sɪmplɪfaɪd] ADJ vereinfacht

simplify ['sɪmplɪfaɪ] VT vereinfachen, simplifizieren

simplistic [sɪm'plɪstɪk] ADJ simpel, simplistisch *(geh)*; **or am I being ~?** oder sehe ich das zu einfach?

simply ['sɪmplɪ] ADV einfach; *(= merely)* nur, bloß; **but you ~ must!** aber du musst einfach!; **to put it ~ …** um es einfach auszudrücken …; **very ~, he was short of money** er war schlicht und einfach knapp bei Kasse; **not ~ … but also …** nicht (einfach) nur …, sondern auch …; **he was known ~ as Jay** er war einfach als Jay bekannt; **he is quite ~ the best** er ist ganz einfach der Beste

simulate ['sɪmjʊleɪt] VT **a** *(= feign)* vortäuschen; *illness* simulieren; **to ~ sth** *(material)* etw imitieren; *(animal, person)* sich als etw tarnen; **~d leather** Lederimitation *f*; **~d sheepskin** falsches Schafsfell **b** *(= reproduce) conditions* simulieren

simulation [ˌsɪmjʊ'leɪʃən] N **a** Vortäuschung *f*; *(= simulated appearance)* Imitation *f*; *(of animals)* Tarnung *f*; **his ~ of pain** seine simulierten Schmerzen **b** *(= reproduction)* Simulation *f*

simulator ['sɪmjʊleɪtə'] N Simulator *m*

simulcast ['sɪməlkɑːst] VT gleichzeitig in Fernsehen und Hörfunk übertragen N gleichzeitige Übertragung in Fernsehen und Hörfunk

simultaneity [ˌsɪməltə'nɪətɪ] N Gleichzeitigkeit *f*, Simultan(e)ität *f (geh)*

simultaneous [ˌsɪməl'teɪnɪəs] ADJ gleichzeitig, simultan *(geh)*; **~ interpreting/translation** Simultandolmetschen *nt*/-übersetzung *f*

simultaneous equation N *(Math)* Simultangleichung *f*

simultaneously [ˌsɪməl'teɪnɪəslɪ] ADV gleichzeitig, zur gleichen Zeit, simultan *(geh)*; **~ with sb/sth** zur gleichen Zeit wie jd/etw

sin [sɪn] N *(Rel, fig)* Sünde *f*; **to live in ~** *(inf)* in wilder Ehe leben; *(Rel)* in Sünde leben; **I've been chosen to organize the office party, for my ~s** *(hum)* man hat mich drangekriegt, ich darf die Büroparty organisieren *(inf)*; **is that your work/family? – yes for my ~s** *(hum)* haben Sie das gemacht/ist das Ihre Familie? – ja, leider; **to cover a multitude of ~s** *(hum)* viele Schandtaten verdecken; **this hat is covering a multitude of ~s, she said** *(hum)* aber fragen Sie bloß nicht, wie es unter dem Hut aussieht!, sagte sie; **isn't it a ~!** ist das nicht unerhört *or* eine Schande?

VI sündigen (*against* gegen, an *+dat*), sich versündigen (*against* an *+dat*); *(against principles, standards etc)* verstoßen (gegen); **he was more ~ned against than ~ning** er hat mehr Unrecht erlitten als begangen

Sinai ['saɪneɪaɪ] N Sinai *m*; **~ Peninsula** Sinaihalbinsel *f*; **Mount ~** der Berg Sinai

sin bin N *(Ice Hockey inf)* Strafbank *f*; **in the ~** auf der Strafbank

since [sɪns] ✪ 21.1 ADV *(= in the meantime)* inzwischen; *(= up to now)* seitdem; **ever ~** seither; **a long time ~, long ~** schon lange; **he died long ~** er ist schon lange tot; **not long ~** erst vor Kurzem; **I've never heard it before or ~** ich habe das weder vorher noch nachher je wieder gehört

PREP seit; **ever ~ 1900** (schon) seit 1900; **he had been living there ~ 1900** er lebte da schon seit 1900; **I've been coming here ~ 1992** ich komme schon seit 1992 hierher; **he left in June, ~ when we have not heard from him** er ging im Juni fort und seitdem haben wir nichts mehr von ihm gehört; **it's a long time ~ then** das ist schon lange her; **how long is it ~ the accident?** wie lange ist der Unfall schon her?; **~ when?** *(inf)* seit wann denn das? *(inf)*

CONJ **a** *(time)* seit(dem); **ever ~ I've known him** seit(dem) ich ihn kenne

b *(= because)* da

sincere [sɪn'sɪə'] ADJ aufrichtig; *person also* offen; *intention also* ernst, ehrlich; **a ~ friend** ein wahrer Freund; **to be ~ about sth** in Bezug auf etw *(acc)* aufrichtig sein; **to be ~ in one's desire to do sth** *or* **in wanting to do sth** den aufrichtigen Wunsch haben, etw zu tun; **it is our ~ hope that …** wir hoffen aufrichtig, dass …

sincerely [sɪn'sɪəlɪ] ADV aufrichtig; *intend also* ernsthaft; **her ~ held religious beliefs** ihre ehrlich *or* aufrichtig gemeinte religiöse Überzeugung; **yours ~** *(Brit)* mit freundlichen Grüßen, hochachtungsvoll *(form)*

sincerity [sɪn'serɪtɪ] N Aufrichtigkeit *f*; *(of person also)* Offenheit *f*; *(of intention also)* Ernsthaftigkeit *f*; **in all ~** in aller Offenheit; **I was acting in all ~ when …** ich habe es ganz aufrichtig *or* ehrlich gemeint, als …

sine [saɪn] N *(Math)* Sinus *m*

sinecure ['saɪnɪkjʊə'] N Pfründe *f*, Sinekure *f* *(geh)*; **this job is no ~!** diese Arbeit ist kein Ruheposten

sine die [ˌsaɪnɪ'daɪiː, 'siːneɪ'diːeɪ] ADV **to adjourn ~** auf unbestimmte Zeit vertagen

sine qua non [ˌsɪnɪkwɑː'nəʊn] N unerlässliche Voraussetzung, Conditio sine qua non *f* (*to, for* für)

sinew ['sɪnjuː] N **a** Sehne *f* **b** **sinews** PL *(fig)* Kräfte *pl*, Stärke *f*

sinewy ['sɪnjʊɪ] ADJ sehnig; *(fig) plant, tree* knorrig; *prose style* kraftvoll, kernig

sinfonia [sɪn'fəʊnɪə] N *(= symphony)* Sinfonie *f*, Symphonie *f*; *(= overture)* Opernsinfonia *f*; *(= orchestra)* Sinfonie- *or* Symphonieorchester *nt*, Sinfoniker *pl*, Symphoniker *pl*

sinfonietta [ˌsɪnfəʊnɪ'etə] N *(= music)* Sinfonietta *f*; *(= orchestra)* kleines Sinfonie- *or* Symphonieorchester

sinful ['sɪnfʊl] ADJ sündig; *person, act, thought also* sündhaft *(geh)*; *waste* sündhaft *(geh)*; **it is ~ to …** es ist eine Sünde, zu …

sinfully ['sɪnfəlɪ] ADV sündig, sündhaft *(geh)*

sinfulness ['sɪnfʊlnɪs] N Sündigkeit *f*, Sündhaftigkeit *f (geh)*

sing [sɪŋ] *vb: pret* **sang**, *ptp* **sung** N **to have a (good) ~** (tüchtig) singen VT **a** *song* singen; **to ~ a child to sleep** ein Kind in den Schlaf singen; **to ~ the praises of sb/sth** ein Loblied auf jdn/etw singen; **to ~ one's own praises** sich selber loben **b** *(poet)* besingen, singen von

VI singen; *(ears)* dröhnen; *(kettle)* summen; **they are ~ing from the same hymn sheet** *or* **song sheet** *(Brit fig)* sie sagen alle das Gleiche *or* dasselbe

▶ **sing along** VI mitsingen

▶ **sing away** VI *(person, bird)* (ununterbrochen) singen; *(kettle)* summen; *(to oneself)* vor sich *(acc)* hin trällern VT *sep troubles* fortsingen

▶ **sing of** VI *+prep obj* singen von *(poet)*, besingen

▶ **sing out** VI **a** *(= sing loudly, person, bird)* laut *or* aus voller Kehle singen; *(voice)* erklingen, tönen; *(kettle)* summen; **come on, sing out, let's hear you** na los, singt mal tüchtig, wir wollen was hören *(inf)*; **their voices sang out through the church** ihr Singen tönte durch die Kirche **b** *(inf: = shout)* schreien *(inf)* VT *sep words, tune* singen, hervorbringen; *(= shout out)* (mit singender Stimme) ausrufen; **to sing one's heart out** sich *(dat)* die Seele aus dem Leib singen

▶ **sing up** VI lauter singen

sing. *abbr of* **singular** Sing.

singable ['sɪŋəbl] ADJ sangbar *(geh)*; **that tune is (not/very) ~** diese Melodie lässt sich (nicht/sehr) gut singen

Singapore [ˌsɪŋɡəˈpɔːʳ] N Singapur *nt*

Singaporean [ˌsɪŋɡəˈpɔːrɪən] ADJ *person, culture* singapurisch; **he is ~** er ist Singapurer N *(= person)* Singapurer(in) *m(f)*

singe [sɪndʒ] VT sengen; *clothes also* versengen; *(slightly)* ansengen; *hairs, eyebrows* absengen VI versengt/angesengt werden, sengen N *(on clothes etc)* versengte/angesengte Stelle; **there's a slight ~ on the sleeve** der Ärmel ist leicht angesengt

singer [ˈsɪŋəʳ] N Sänger(in) *m(f)*

singer-songwriter [ˌsɪŋəˈsɒŋraɪtəʳ] N Liedermacher(in) *m(f)*

Singhalese [ˌsɪŋɡəˈliːz] ADJ singhalesisch; **he is ~** er ist Singhalese N **a** Singhalese *m*, Singhalesin *f* **b** *(Ling)* Singhalesisch *nt*

singing [ˈsɪŋɪŋ] N Singen *nt*; *(of person, bird also)* Gesang *m*; *(in the ears)* Dröhnen *nt*; *(of kettle)* Summen *nt*; **he teaches ~** er gibt Sing- *or* Gesangstunden, er gibt Singen *(inf)*; **do you like my ~?** gefällt dir, wie ich singe?, gefällt dir mein Gesang?

singing: **singing lesson** N Gesangstunde *f*; **singing telegram** N *durch eine Agentur persönlich übermittelter, in Gesangsform vorgetragener Geburtstagsgruß etc*; **singing voice** N Singstimme *f*

single [ˈsɪŋɡl] ADJ **a** *(= one only)* einzige(r, s); **not a ~ one spoke up** nicht ein Einziger äußerte sich dazu; **every ~ day was precious** jeder (einzelne) Tag war kostbar; **I've missed the bus every ~ day this week** diese Woche habe ich jeden Tag den Bus verpasst; **every ~ book I looked at** (aber auch) jedes Buch, das ich mir ansah; **with a ~ voice they cried out for reform** wie mit einer Stimme riefen sie nach Reformen; **not a ~ thing** überhaupt nichts; **the ~ most expensive product** das teuerste Produkt; **in a ~ day** in einem einzigen Tag; **in a ~ gulp** mit einem einzigen Schluck; **in ~ figures** in einstelligen Zahlen

b *(= not double etc)* einzeln; *(Typ)* einfach; *carburettor* einfach; *(Brit) ticket* einfach; **~ pneumonia** einseitige Lungenentzündung; **a ~-tank aqualung** ein Pressluftatmer *m* mit nur einer Sauerstoffflasche

c *(= not married)* unverheiratet, ledig; **marital status? – ~** Familienstand? – ledig; **he was tired of the ~ life** er hatte das Junggesellendasein satt; **~ people** Ledige *pl*, Unverheiratete *pl*; **I'm a ~ man/girl** ich bin ledig; **the ~ homeless** die alleinstehenden Obdachlosen

N **a** *(Cricket)* Schlag *m* für einen Lauf; *(Baseball)* Lauf *m* zum ersten Mal; *(Golf)* Zweier *m*

b *(Brit: = ticket)* Einzelfahrschein *m*, Einzelfahrkarte *f*; *(= room)* Einzelzimmer *nt*; *(= record)* Single *f*; *(= bank note)* Einpfund-/Eindollarschein *m*; **a ~/two ~s to Xanadu** *(Brit)* einmal/zweimal einfach nach Xanadu

c *(= unmarried person)* Single *m*

▶ **single out** VT *sep (= choose)* auswählen; *victim, prey* sich *(dat)* herausgreifen; *(= distinguish, set apart)* herausheben *(from* über *+acc)*; **to single sb out for special attention** jdm besondere Aufmerksamkeit zuteilwerden lassen; **you couldn't single any one pupil out as the best** es wäre unmöglich, einen einzelnen Schüler als den besten hinzustellen

single: **single-action** ADJ *(Mil)* **~ rifle** Einzelfeuergewehr *nt*; **single-barrelled**, *(US)* **single-barreled** [ˌsɪŋɡlˈbærld] ADJ *gun* mit einem Lauf; **single bed** N Einzelbett *nt*; **single-blind** ADJ **~ experiment** *(Pharm, Psych)* Blindversuch *m*; **single-breasted** ADJ *jacket* einreihig; **~ suit** Einreiher *m*; **single-cell(ed)** ADJ *(Biol)* einzellig; **single-chamber** ADJ *(Pol)* Einkammer-; **~ parliament** Einkammerparlament *nt*; **single combat** N Nah- *or* Einzelkampf *m*; *(esp of knights etc)* Kampf *m* Mann gegen Mann, Zweikampf *m*; **single cream** N *(Brit)* Sahne *f (mit geringem Fettgehalt)*; **single currency** N einheitliche Währung, Einheitswährung *f*; **single-decker** N *(Brit)* einstöckiger Omnibus/einstöckige Straßenbahn, Eindecker *m*; **single-density** ADJ *(Comput) disk* mit einfacher Dichte; **singledom** [ˈsɪŋɡldəm] N Singledasein *nt or* -leben *nt*; **single-drive** ADJ *computer* mit Einzellaufwerk; **single-engined** ADJ *plane* einmotorig; **single-entry bookkeeping** N einfache Buchführung; **single European currency** N einheitliche europäische Währung, europäische Einheitswährung; **single European market** N Europäischer Binnenmarkt; **single file** N **in ~** im Gänsemarsch; **single-handed** ADJ (ganz) allein *pred*; *achievement* allein *or* ohne (fremde) Hilfe vollbracht; *arrest* allein *or* ohne (fremde) Hilfe durchgeführt; *struggle* einsam ADV *(also* **single-handedly***)* ohne Hilfe, im Alleingang; **to sail ~ (a)round the world** ganz allein *or* als Einhandsegler(in) um die Welt fahren; **single honours** N *(Brit Univ)* Abschluss *m* in einem Einzelfach; **singlehood** [ˈsɪŋɡlhʊd] N Singledasein *nt or* -leben *nt*; **single-lens reflex (camera)** N (einäugige) Spiegelreflexkamera; **single life** N Singledasein *nt*; **single-line** ADJ eingleisig; *track* einspurig; **single malt (whisky)** N Single Malt (Whisky) *m*; **single-masted** ADJ einmastig; **~ ship** Einmaster *m*; **single-minded** ADJ zielbewusst, zielstrebig, beharrlich; *devotion* unbeirrbar; **his ~ pursuit of money** sein ausschließlich auf Geld gerichtetes Streben; **to be ~ in** *or* **about doing sth** zielstrebig darin sein, etw zu tun; **single-mindedly** ADV zielstrebig; **he was ~ interested in science** er interessierte sich einzig und allein für Naturwissenschaften; **single-mindedness** N Zielstrebigkeit *f*, Beharrlichkeit *f*; *(of devotion)* Unbeirrbarkeit *f*; **single mother** N alleinerziehende Mutter

singleness [ˈsɪŋɡlnɪs] N **~ of purpose** Zielstrebigkeit *f*; **his ~ of purpose caused him to neglect his family** er ging so vollkommen in der Sache auf, dass er seine Familie vernachlässigte

single: **single parent** N Alleinerziehende(r) *mf*, allein Erziehende(r) *mf*; **I as a ~ …** ich als alleinerziehende Mutter/alleinerziehender Vater …; **single-parent** ADJ **a ~ family** eine Familie mit nur einem Elternteil, eine Einelternfamilie; **single parents** PL alleinerziehende Eltern(teile) *pl*; **single-party** ADJ Einparteien-; **~ system** Einparteiensystem *nt*; **single-phase** ADJ einphasig, Einphasen-; **~ power** Einphasenstrom *m*; **single price** N Einheitspreis *m*; **single room** N Einzelzimmer *nt*; **single room supplement** N Einzelzimmerzuschlag *m*

singles [ˈsɪŋɡlz] N *sing or pl (Sport)* Einzel *nt*; **the ~ finals** das Finale im Einzel; **~ is more tiring** Einzel sind anstrengender

singles bar N Singles-Bar *f*

single-seater [ˌsɪŋɡlˈsiːtəʳ] N Einsitzer *m*

single-sex [ˈsɪŋɡlˈseks] ADJ *education* nach Geschlechtern getrennt; **a ~ class** eine reine Jungen-/Mädchenklasse; **a ~ school** eine reine Jungen-/Mädchenschule

singles holiday N *(Brit)* Urlaub *m* für Singles

single-sided [ˈsɪŋɡlˈsaɪdɪd] ADJ *(Comput) disk* einseitig

single-space [ˈsɪŋɡlˈspeɪs] VTI *(Typ, Comput)* mit einzeiligem Abstand schreiben

single-storey, *(US)* **single-story** [ˈsɪŋɡlˈstɔːrɪ] ADJ einstöckig

singlet [ˈsɪŋɡlɪt] N *(Brit Sport)* ärmelloses Trikot; *(= underclothing)* (ärmelloses) Unterhemd, Trikothemd *nt*

singleton [ˈsɪŋɡltən] N *(Cards)* Single *nt (einzige Karte einer Farbe)*

single: **single-tongue** VTI mit einfachem Zungenschlag spielen; **single-tonguing** N der einzelne Zungenschlag; **single-track** ADJ einspurig; *(Rail also)* eingleisig; **to have a ~ mind** nur eine einzige Sache im Kopf haben; **Single Transferable Vote** N *(Pol) modifiziertes Mehrheitswahlrecht, bei dem die Stimme auf einen anderen Kandidaten übertragen wird, falls der gewünschte Kandidat ausscheidet*

singly [ˈsɪŋɡlɪ] ADV einzeln; *(= solely)* einzig, nur

singsong [ˈsɪŋsɒŋ] ADJ **the ~ Welsh accent** der walisische Singsang; **in his ~ voice** mit *or* in seinem Singsang N Liedersingen *nt no indef art, no pl*; **we often have a ~ after a few drinks** nachdem wir etwas getrunken haben, singen wir oft zusammen

singular [ˈsɪŋɡjʊləʳ] ADJ **a** *(Gram)* im Singular, singularisch *(form)*; **a ~ noun** ein Substantiv *nt* im Singular; **~ ending** Singularendung *f*; **~ form** Singular *m* **b** *(= odd)* sonderbar, eigenartig; **how very ~!** das ist aber sehr sonderbar *or* eigenartig! **c** *(= outstanding)* einzigartig, einmalig N Singular *m*; **in the ~** im Singular

singularity [ˌsɪŋɡjʊˈlærɪtɪ] N *(= oddity)* Sonderbarkeit *f*, Eigenartigkeit *f*

singularly [ˈsɪŋɡjʊləlɪ] ADV **a** außerordentlich; *appropriate, unattractive* (ganz) besonders, überaus; **he was ~ unimpressed** er war ganz und gar nicht beeindruckt; **he has ~ failed to achieve this** er ist mit seinem Versuch, dies zu erreichen, vollkommen gescheitert; **hey are ~ lacking in originality** es fehlt ihnen ganz und gar an Originalität **b** *(dated, = strangely)* sonderbar, eigenartig

Sinhalese [sɪnhəˈliːz] ADJ N = **Singhalese**

sinister [ˈsɪnɪstəʳ] ADJ **a** unheimlich; *person, night, scheme* finster, unheimlich; *music, look* düster; *fate* böse; *forces* dunkel; *development, motives* unheilvoll; **a ~ organization** eine in dunkle Machenschaften verwickelte Organisation **b** *(Her)* linke(r, s)

sink[1] [sɪŋk] *pret* **sank**, *ptp* **sunk** VT **a** *ship, object* versenken

b *(fig: = ruin) theory* zerstören; *hopes* zunichtemachen, zerstören; **now we're sunk!** *(inf)* jetzt sind wir geliefert *(inf)*

c *shaft* senken, teufen *(spec)*; *hole* ausheben; **to ~ a post in the ground** einen Pfosten in den Boden einlassen; **they sank a pipe under the riverbed** sie versenkten ein Rohr unter dem Flussbett → **well**[1]

d *(Brit inf) drink* hinunterschütten *(inf)*, hinunterspülen *(inf)*

e *teeth, claws* schlagen; **I'd like to ~ my teeth into a juicy steak** ich möchte in ein saftiges Steak reinbeißen *(inf)*

f *differences* begraben

g **to ~ money into sth** Geld in etw *(acc)* stecken

h *golf ball* einlochen; *billiard ball* in das Loch treiben

i *(= lower) eyes, voice, value of currency* senken; **he sank his head in his hands** er stützte den Kopf auf die Hände

j **to be sunk in thought** in Gedanken versunken sein; **to be sunk in a book** in ein Buch vertieft sein; **sunk in depression/despair** völlig deprimiert/verzweifelt

VI **a** *person, object* untergehen; *(ship)* untergehen, sinken; **to ~ to the bottom** auf den Grund sinken; **he was left to ~ or swim** *(fig)* er war ganz auf sich allein angewiesen; **if I go down I'll make sure you all ~ with me** wenn es mich erwischt, werde ich euch alle mitreißen

b *(= go down, subside)* sinken; *(sun)* versinken; *(voice)* sich senken; *(building, land etc)* sich senken, absinken; **the building is gradually ~ing into the mud** das Gebäude versinkt allmählich im Schlamm; **he sank up to his knees in the mud** er sank bis zu den Knien im Schlamm ein; **to ~ (down) into a chair** in einen Sessel (nieder)sinken; **to ~ back into the cushions** in die Kissen versinken; **the flames sank lower and lower** das Feuer fiel immer mehr in sich zusammen; **the sun sank beneath the horizon** die Sonne versank am Horizont; **the record has sunk to the bottom of the charts** die Platte ist ans Ende der Liste gerutscht; **to ~ to one's knees** auf die Knie sinken; **to ~ out of sight** versinken; **to ~ into a deep sleep/into depression** in tiefen Schlaf/in Depressionen versinken; **my spirits** *or* **my heart sank at the sight of the work** beim Anblick der Arbeit verließ mich der Mut; **the sick man is ~ing fast** der Kranke verfällt zusehends

c (= *deteriorate, lessen*: *output, shares, standards*) sinken; **to ~ into insignificance** zur Bedeutungslosigkeit herabsinken; **to ~ deeper into recession** immer tiefer in die Rezession geraten

▶ **sink away** VI (*seabed, ground*) abfallen

▶ **sink in** VI **a** (*into mud etc*) einsinken (*prep obj, -to* in *+acc*) **b** (*inf*: = *be understood*) kapiert werden (*inf*); **it's only just sunk in that it really did happen** ich kapiere/er kapiert *etc* erst jetzt, dass das tatsächlich passiert ist (*inf*); **can't you get this to sink in?** kannst du das denn nicht in deinen dicken Schädel bekommen?; **repeat each line so that the words sink in** wiederhole jede Zeile, damit dus dir merkst (*inf*) VT *sep stakes, pylons etc* einlassen (*prep obj, -to* in *+acc*)

sink² N Ausguss *m*; (*in kitchen also*) Spülbecken *nt*; **~ unit** Spültisch *m*, Spüle *f*; **~ tidy** Abflusssieb *nt*; **~ of iniquity** Sündenpfuhl *m*, Stätte *f* des Lasters → **kitchen sink**

sinker [ˈsɪŋkəʳ] N (*Fishing*) Senker *m*, Senkgewicht *nt* → **hook N d**

sinking [ˈsɪŋkɪŋ] N (*of ship*) Untergang *m*; (*deliberately*) Versenkung *f*; (*of shaft*) Senken *nt*, Abteufen *nt (spec)*; (*of well*) Bohren *nt* ADJ (*Fin*) *currency* fallend; **a ~ ship** (*lit, fig*) ein sinkendes Schiff; **with (a) ~ heart** schweren Herzens; **he realized with a ~ heart that …** das Herz wurde ihm schwer, als er merkte, dass …; **~ feeling** flaues Gefühl (im Magen) (*inf*); **I got a horrible ~ feeling when I realized …** mir wurde ganz anders, als ich erkannte …

sinking fund N (*Fin*) Tilgungsfonds *m*

sinless [ˈsɪnlɪs] ADJ *person* ohne Sünde, frei von Sünde; *life also* sündenfrei

sinner [ˈsɪnəʳ] N Sünder(in) *m(f)*

Sinn Fein [ʃɪnˈfeɪn] N (*Ir Pol*) Sinn Fein *f*

Sino- [ˈsaɪnəʊ-] PREF chinesisch-, sino- (*form*); **~American** chinesisch-amerikanisch, sinoamerikanisch (*form*)

sinologist [ˌsaɪˈnɒlədʒɪst] N Sinologe *m*, Sinologin *f*

sinology [ˌsaɪˈnɒlədʒɪ] N Sinologie *f*

sinuosity [ˌsɪnjʊˈɒsɪtɪ] N (*liter*) Schlangenbewegungen *pl*; (*of river*) Windungen *pl*; (*fig*) Gewundenheit *f*

sinuous [ˈsɪnjʊəs] ADJ (*lit, fig*) gewunden; *motion of snake* schlängelnd *attr*; *dancing etc* geschmeidig, schlangenartig; **the river follows a ~ course through the trees** der Fluss windet sich *or* schlängelt sich zwischen den Bäumen hindurch

sinuously [ˈsɪnjʊəslɪ] ADV gewunden; *dance etc* geschmeidig, schlangenartig

sinus [ˈsaɪnəs] N (*Anat*) Sinus *m (spec)*; (*in head*) (Nasen-)nebenhöhle *f*, Stirnhöhle *f*

sinusitis [ˌsaɪnəˈsaɪtɪs] N Stirnhöhlenkatarr(h) *m*, Sinusitis *f*

Sioux [suː] N Sioux *mf* ADJ Sioux-, der Sioux; **~ chief** Siouxhäuptling *m*

sip [sɪp] N Schluck *m*; (*very small*) Schlückchen *nt* VT in kleinen Schlucken trinken; (*suspiciously, daintily*) nippen an (*+dat*); (= *savour*) schlürfen VI **to ~ at sth** an etw (*dat*) nippen

siphon [ˈsaɪfən] N Heber *m*; (= *soda siphon*) Siphon *m* VT absaugen; (*into tank*) (mit einem Heber) umfüllen

▶ **siphon off** VT *sep* **a** (*lit*) abziehen, absaugen; *petrol* abzapfen; (*into container*) (mit einem Heber) umfüllen *or* abfüllen **b** (*fig*) *staff, money* abziehen; *profits* abschöpfen

▶ **siphon out** VT *sep liquid* mit einem Heber herausleiten

SIPS *abbr of* **side impact protection system**

sir [sɜːʳ] N **a** (*in direct address*) mein Herr (*form*), Herr X; **no, ~** nein(, Herr X); (*Mil*) nein, Herr Leutnant/General *etc*; **you will apologize, ~!** (*dated*) dafür werden Sie sich entschuldigen (müssen); **Sir** (*to editor of paper*) *not translated*; **Dear Sir (or Madam), …** Sehr geehrte (Damen und) Herren!; **my dear** *or* **good ~!** (*dated*) mein (lieber) Herr! (*dated*) **b** (= *knight etc*) **Sir** Sir *m* **c** (*Sch inf*: = *teacher*) er (*Sch sl*); **please ~!** Herr X!; **I'll tell ~** ich sags ihm

sire [ˈsaɪəʳ] N **a** (*Zool*) Vatertier *nt*, Vater *m*; (= *stallion*) Deck- *or* Zuchthengst *m*, Beschäler *m* (*form*) **b** (*old*: *to monarch etc*) **Sire** Majestät *f*, Sire *m* **c** (*old, poet*: = *father, forebear*) Erzeuger *m*, Ahn *m* VT zeugen; **the horse A, ~d by B** Pferd A, Vater B; **he ~d 49 children** (*hum*) er hat 49 Kinder in die Welt gesetzt

siren [ˈsaɪərən] N (*all senses*) Sirene *f*

siriasis [sɪˈraɪəsɪʃ] N (*Med*) Sonnenstich *m*

sirloin [ˈsɜːlɔɪn] N (*Cook*) Lendenfilet *nt*

sirocco [sɪˈrɒkəʊ] N Schirokko *m*

sirrah [ˈsɪrə] N (*obs*) Bube *m (obs)*

sirup N (*US*) = **syrup**

sis [sɪs] N (*inf*) Schwesterherz *nt (inf)*

sisal [ˈsaɪsəl] N Sisal *m*

siskin [ˈsɪskɪn] N (*Orn*) Zeisig *m*

sissified [ˈsɪsɪfaɪd] ADJ weibisch, wie ein Weib

sissy [ˈsɪsɪ] (*inf*) N Waschlappen *m (inf)*, Memme *f* ADJ **a** weibisch, verweichlicht; **a ~ man** ein Schlappschwanz *m (inf)*, ein Weichei *m (inf)*; **poetry is ~ stuff** Gedichte sind Weiberkram (*inf*) **b** (= *cowardly*) feig(e)

sister [ˈsɪstəʳ] N **a** Schwester *f*; (*in trade union*) Kollegin *f*; (= *ship*) Schwesterschiff *nt*; **to be ~ to** (*form*) *or* **the ~ of sb** jds Schwester sein **b** (= *nun*) (Ordens)schwester *f*; (*before name*) Schwester *f* **c** (*Brit*: = *senior nurse*) Oberschwester *f*

sister *in cpds* Schwester-; **sister city** N (*US*) = **twin town**; **sister company** N Schwesterfirma *f or* -gesellschaft *f*; **sisterhood** [ˈsɪstəhʊd] N **a** Schwesterschaft *f*; **she emphasized the ~ of women all over the world** sie betonte, dass alle Frauen der ganzen Welt Schwestern seien **b** (*Eccl*) Schwesternorden *m* **c** (= *association of women*) Frauenvereinigung *f*; **sister-in-law** N *pl* **sisters-in-law** Schwägerin *f*

sisterly [ˈsɪstəlɪ] ADJ schwesterlich

Sistine [ˈsɪstiːn] ADJ Sixtinisch

Sisyphus [ˈsɪsɪfəs] N Sisyphus *m*

sit [sɪt] *vb: pret, ptp* **sat** VI **a** (= *be sitting*) sitzen (*in/on* in/auf *+dat*); (= *sit down*) sich setzen (*in/on* in/auf *+acc*); **~!** (*to dog*) sitz!; **a place to ~** ein Sitzplatz *m*; **~ by/with me** setz dich zu mir/neben mich; **to ~ for a painter** für einen Maler Modell sitzen; **to ~ for an exam** (*Brit*) eine Prüfung ablegen (*form*) *or* machen; **to ~ on one's hands** (*fig*) untätig zusehen; **to be ~ting pretty** (*fig inf*) gut dastehen (*inf*); **don't just ~ there, do something!** sitz nicht nur tatenlos da (herum), tu (endlich) was! → **still¹**

b (*assembly*) tagen; (= *have a seat*) einen Sitz haben; **he ~s for Liverpool** (*Brit Parl*) er ist der Abgeordnete für Liverpool; **to ~ in parliament/on a committee** einen Sitz im Parlament/in einem Ausschuss haben

c (*object*: = *be placed, rest*) stehen; **the car sat in the garage** das Auto stand in der Garage; **the package is ~ting in the hall** das Päckchen liegt im Flur

d (*bird*: = *hatch*) sitzen, brüten; **the hen is ~ting on two eggs** das Huhn brütet zwei Eier aus, das Huhn sitzt auf zwei Eiern

e (*fig*: *clothes*) sitzen (*on sb* bei jdm)

f **how ~s the wind?** (*liter*) wie steht der Wind?

g (*inf*) = **baby-sit**

h (*esp US*: = *be agreeable, food*) bekömmlich sein; (*idea*) behagen; **this food didn't ~ too well** dieses Essen liegt mir (schwer) im Magen (*inf*)

VT **a** (*also* **sit down**) setzen (*in* in *+acc*, *on* auf *+acc*); (= *place*) *object* stellen; **to ~ a child on one's knee** sich (*dat*) ein Kind auf die Knie setzen; **the table/car ~s 5 people** (= *accommodate*) an dem Tisch/in dem Auto haben 5 Leute Platz

b *horse* sitzen auf (*+dat*); **to ~ a horse well** gut zu Pferde sitzen

c (*Brit*) *examination* ablegen (*form*), machen

VR **to ~ oneself down** sich gemütlich niederlassen *or* hinsetzen; **~ you down** (*dial*) setz dich hin

N **to have a ~** sitzen

▶ **sit about** (*Brit*) *or* **around** VI herumsitzen

▶ **sit back** VI (*lit, fig*) sich zurücklehnen; (*fig*: = *do nothing, not take action*) die Hände in den Schoß legen

▶ **sit by** VI (tatenlos) dasitzen, (tatenlos) herumsitzen

▶ **sit down** VI **a** (*lit*) sich (hin)setzen; **to sit down in a chair** sich auf einen Stuhl setzen **b** (*fig*) **to take sth sitting down** etw einfach hinnehmen

▶ **sit for** VI **a** (*Brit*) *exam* machen **b** (*Brit*) die Prüfung machen für **c** (*Brit, Parl*) *constituency* vertreten, Abgeordnete(in) *m(f)* sein für **d** (*Art*) **to sit for one's portrait** sich porträtieren lassen

▶ **sit in** VI **a** (*demonstrators*) ein Sit-in machen *or* veranstalten **b** (= *take place of*) **to sit in for sb** jdn vertreten **c** (= *attend as visitor*) dabei sein, dabeisitzen (*on sth* bei etw) **d** (= *stay in*) zu Hause *or* im Haus sitzen

▶ **sit on** VI (= *continue sitting*) sitzen bleiben VI *+prep obj* **a** *committee, panel, jury* sitzen in (*+dat*); **I was asked to sit on the committee** man bat mich, Mitglied des Ausschusses zu werden **b** (= *not deal with*) sitzen auf (*+dat*) **c** (*inf*: = *suppress*) *idea, invention, product* unterdrücken, nicht hochkommen lassen; *person* einen Dämpfer aufsetzen (*+dat*) (*inf*); **to get sat on** (= *suppressed*) unterdrückt werden; (= *rebuked*) eins draufkriegen (*inf*)

▶ **sit out** VI draußen sitzen VT *sep* **a** (= *stay to end*) *play, film, meeting* bis zum Schluss *or* Ende (sitzen) bleiben bei, bis zum Schluss *or* Ende durch- *or* aushalten (*pej*); *storm* auf das Ende (*+gen*) warten; *problem* aussitzen; *war* durchstehen; **we'd better sit it out** wir bleiben besser bis zum Ende (hier) **b** *dance* auslassen; **I'll sit this one out** ich setze diesmal aus; **to sit out a round** (*in game*) eine Runde aussetzen

▶ **sit through** VI *+prep obj* durchhalten, aushalten (*pej*)

▶ **sit up** VI **a** (= *be sitting upright*) aufrecht sitzen; (= *action*) sich aufrichten, sich aufsetzen; **to sit up (and beg)** (*dog etc*) Männchen machen (*inf*) **b** (= *sit straight*) aufrecht *or* gerade sitzen; **sit up!** setz dich gerade hin!, sitz gerade!; **to make sb sit up (and take notice)** (*fig inf*) jdn aufhorchen lassen **c** (= *not go to bed*) aufbleiben, aufsitzen (*dated*); **she sat up with the sick child** sie wachte bei dem kranken Kind; **to sit up and wait for sb** aufbleiben und auf jdn warten **d** **to sit up to the table** sich an den Tisch setzen VT *sep* aufrichten, aufsetzen; *doll also, baby* hinsetzen

▶ **sit upon** VI *+prep obj* = **sit on VI** *+prep obj*

sitar [sɪˈtɑːʳ] N Sitar *m*

sitcom [ˈsɪtkɒm] N (*inf*) Situationskomödie *f*, Sitcom *f*

sit-down [ˈsɪtdaʊn] N (*inf*: = *rest*) Verschnaufpause *f (inf)* ADJ *attr* **to stage a ~ strike** einen Sitzstreik abhalten; **a ~ meal** eine richtige Mahlzeit

site [saɪt] N **a** Stelle *f*, Platz *m*; (*Med, of infection*) Stelle *f* **b** (*Archeol*) Stätte *f* **c** (= *building site*) (Bau)gelände *nt*, Baustelle *f*; **missile ~** Raketenbasis *f*; **~ foreman** Polier *m*; **~ office** (Büro *nt* der) Bauleitung *f* **d** (= *camping site*) Campingplatz *m* **e** (*Internet*) = **website** VT legen, anlegen; **to be ~d** liegen, (gelegen) sein; **a badly ~d building** ein ungünstig gelegenes Gebäude

sit-in [ˈsɪtɪn] N Sit-in *nt*; **to hold** *or* **stage a ~** ein Sit-in veranstalten

siting [ˈsaɪtɪŋ] N Legen *nt*; **the ~ of new industries away from London is being encouraged** man fördert die Errichtung neuer Betriebe außerhalb Londons; **the ~ of the buildings here was a mistake** es war ein Fehler, die Gebäude hier zu errichten

sit spin N (*Figure Skating*) Sitzpirouette *f*

sits vac *abbr of* **situations vacant** Stellenangebote *pl*

sitter ['sɪtəʳ] N *(Art)* Modell *nt*; *(= baby-sitter)* Babysitter(in) *m(f)*; *(= bird)* brütender Vogel; *(Sport sl)* todsicherer Ball *(inf)*

sitting ['sɪtɪŋ] ADJ sitzend; *bird* brütend; *conference* tagend, in Sitzung; **to be in a ~ position** aufsitzen; **to get into a ~ position** sich aufsetzen; **there is ~ room only** es gibt nur Sitzplätze N *(of committee, parliament, for portrait)* Sitzung *f*; **they have two ~s for lunch** sie servieren das Mittagessen in zwei Schüben; **the first ~ for lunch is at 12 o'clock** die erste Mittagessenzeit ist um 12 Uhr; **at one** *or* **a single ~** *(fig)* auf einmal

sitting: **sitting duck** N *(fig)* leichte Beute; **sitting member** N *(Brit Parl)* (derzeitiger) Abgeordneter, (derzeitige) Abgeordnete; **sitting room** N *(esp Brit)* *(= lounge)* Wohnzimmer *nt*; *(in guest house etc)* Aufenthaltsraum *m*; **sitting target** N *(lit, fig)* leichte Beute; **sitting tenant** N *(Brit)* (derzeitiger) Mieter, (derzeitige) Mieterin

situate ['sɪtjʊeɪt] VT legen

situated ['sɪtjʊeɪtɪd] ADJ gelegen; *person (financially)* gestellt, situiert *(geh)*; **it is ~ in the High Street** es liegt an der Hauptstraße; **a pleasantly ~ house** ein Haus in angenehmer Lage; **he is well ~ to appreciate the risks** er ist sehr wohl (dazu) in der Lage, die Risiken abzuschätzen

situation [ˌsɪtjʊ'eɪʃən] N **a** *(= state of affairs)* Lage *f*, Situation *f*; *(financial, marital etc)* Lage *f*, Verhältnisse *pl*; *(in play, novel)* Situation *f*; **to save the ~** die Lage *or* Situation retten; **a 2-0 ~** eine 2:0-Situation **b** *(of house etc)* Lage *f* **c** *(= job)* Stelle *f*; **"situations vacant"** *(Brit)* „Stellenangebote"; **"situations wanted"** *(Brit)* „Stellengesuche"

situation comedy N Situationskomödie *f*

Situationism [sɪtjʊ'eɪʃəˌnɪzəm] N *(Philos)* Situationismus *f*

Situationist [sɪtjʊ'eɪʃəˌnɪst] *(Philos)* ADJ situationistisch N Situationist(in) *m(f)*

sit-up ['sɪtʌp] N *(Sport)* Sit-up *m*; **to do ~s** Sit-ups machen

sitz bath ['zɪtsbɑːθ] N Sitzbadewanne *f*

six [sɪks] ADJ sechs; **she is ~ (years old)** sie ist sechs (Jahre alt); **at (the age of) ~** im Alter von sechs Jahren, mit sechs Jahren; **it's ~ (o'clock)** es ist sechs (Uhr); **there are ~ of us** wir sind sechs; **it cost ~ pounds** es kostete sechs Pfund; **~ and a half/quarter** sechseinhalb/-einviertel; **in ~-eight time** *(Mus)* im Sechsachteltakt; **to be ~ foot under** *(hum)* sich *(dat)* die Radieschen von unten besehen *(hum)*; **it's ~ (of one) and half a dozen (of the other)** *(inf)* das ist Jacke wie Hose *(inf)*, das ist gehupft wie gesprungen *(inf)*
N **a** *(Math: = figure, mark, tram)* Sechs *f*; *(= bus)* Sechser *m*; **~ and a half/quarter** Sechseinhalb/-einviertel *f*
b *(Cards, on dice, Golf)* Sechs *f*; *(Cricket)* Sechserschlag *m*; *(= team of six)* Sechsermannschaft *f*; **to divide sth into ~** etw in sechs Teile teilen; **we divided up into ~es** wir teilten uns in Sechsergruppen auf; **they are sold in ~es** sie werden in Sechserpackungen verkauft; **to be at ~es and sevens** *(things)* wie Kraut und Rüben durcheinanderliegen *(inf)*; *(person)* völlig durcheinander sein; **to knock sb for ~** *(Brit inf)* jdn umhauen *(inf)*

six: **Six Counties** PL **the ~** *(Brit) die sechs Grafschaften Nordirlands*; **six-day race** N, **six days** PL *(inf, Cycling etc)* Sechstagerennen *nt*; **sixfold** ADJ sechsfach ADV um das Sechsfache; **six-footer** N **to be a ~** über 1,80 *(gesprochen: einsachtzig)* sein; **six-gun** N *(US inf)* = **six-shooter**; **six hundred** ADJ sechshundert N Sechshundert *f*

sixish ['sɪksɪʃ] ADJ um sechs herum

six: **six million** ADJ, N sechs Millionen; **six-pack** N **a** Sechserpackung *f* **b** *(Brit inf: = muscles)* Waschbrettbauch *m (inf)*; **sixpence** N *(Brit old: = coin)* Sixpencestück *nt*; **sixpenny** ADJ für Sixpence N *(= stamp)* Sixpence-Marke *f*; **six-shooter** N *(US inf)* sechsschüssiger Revolver

sixteen ['sɪks'tiːn] ADJ sechzehn N Sechzehn *f*

sixteenth ['sɪks'tiːnθ] ADJ sechzehnte(r, s); **a ~ part** ein Sechzehntel *nt*; **a ~ note** *(esp US Mus)* eine Sechzehntelnote, ein Sechzehntel *nt* N **a** *(= fraction)* Sechzehntel *nt*; *(in series)* Sechzehnte(r, s) **b** *(= date)* **the ~** der Sechzehnte

sixth [sɪksθ] ADJ sechste(r, s); **a ~ part** ein Sechstel *nt*; **he was** *or* **came ~** er wurde Sechster; **he was ~ from the end/left** er war der Sechste von hinten/von links
N **a** *(= fraction)* Sechstel *nt*; *(in series)* Sechste(r, s); **Charles the Sixth** Karl der Sechste
b *(= date)* **the ~** der Sechste; **on the ~** am Sechsten; **the ~ of September, September the ~** der sechste September
c *(Mus, = interval)* Sexte *f*; *(= chord)* Sextakkord *m*
d *(Brit)* = **sixth form**
ADV **he did it ~** *(= the sixth person to do it)* er hat es als Sechster gemacht; *(= the sixth thing he did)* er hat es als Sechstes *or* an sechster Stelle gemacht

sixth: **sixth form** N *(Brit)* Abschlussklasse *f*, ≈ Prima *f*; **sixth-former** N *(Brit)* Schüler(in) *m(f)* der Abschlussklasse, ≈ Primaner(in) *m(f)*; **sixth grade** N *(US Sch) sechstes Schuljahr (unmittelbar vor Eintritt in die Junior High-school)*

sixthly ['sɪksθlɪ] ADV sechstens, als Sechstes

six thousand ADJ sechstausend N Sechstausend *f*

sixth sense N sechster Sinn

sixtieth ['sɪkstɪɪθ] ADJ sechzigste(r, s); **a ~ part** ein Sechzigstel *nt* N *(= fraction)* Sechzigstel *nt*; *(in series)* Sechzigste(r, s)

sixty ['sɪkstɪ] ADJ sechzig; **~-one** einundsechzig N Sechzig *f*; **the sixties** die sechziger Jahre *or* Sechzigerjahre *pl*; **to be in one's sixties** in den Sechzigern sein; **to be in one's late/early sixties** Ende/Anfang sechzig sein; **~-one** Einundsechzig *f* → *also* **six**

sixty-fourth note [ˌsɪkstɪ'fɔːθ'nəʊt] N *(esp US Mus)* Vierundsechzigstel(note *f*) *nt*

sixty-four thousand dollar question N *(hum)* Hunderttausendmarkfrage *f (hum)*

sixtyish ['sɪkstɪɪʃ] ADJ um die Sechzig *(inf)*, ungefähr sechzig

six: **six-yard box** N *(Ftbl)* Fünfmeterraum *m*; **six-year-old** ADJ sechsjährig *attr*, sechs Jahre alt *pred*; *war* schon sechs Jahre dauernd N Sechsjährige(r) *mf*

sizable ADJ = **sizeable**

size¹ [saɪz] N *(all senses)* Größe *f*; *(of problem, operation also)* Ausmaß *nt*; **collar/hip/waist ~** Kragen-/Hüft-/Taillenweite *f*; **shoe/dress ~** Schuh-/Kleidergröße *f*; **bra ~** BH-Größe *f*; **it's the ~ of a brick** es ist so groß wie ein Ziegelstein; **he's about your ~** er ist ungefähr so groß wie du; **what ~ is it?** wie groß ist es?; *(clothes, shoes, gloves etc)* welche Größe ist es?; **it's quite a ~** es ist ziemlich groß; **it's two ~s too big** es ist zwei Nummern zu groß; **to cut sth to ~** etw auf die richtige Größe zurechtschneiden; **do you want to try it for ~?** möchten Sie es anprobieren, ob es Ihnen passt?; **try this one for ~** *(fig inf)* wie wärs denn damit?; **that's about the ~ of it** *(inf)* ja, so ungefähr kann man es sagen
VT größenmäßig ordnen

▶ **size up** VT *sep* abschätzen; **I can't quite size him up** ich werde aus ihm nicht schlau

size² N (Grundier)leim *m* VT grundieren

sizeable ['saɪzəbl] ADJ ziemlich groß, größer; *car, estate, jewel also* ansehnlich; *sum, problem, difference also* beträchtlich

sizeably ['saɪzəblɪ] ADV beträchtlich

-size(d) [-saɪz(d)] ADJ *suf* -groß; **medium-size(d)** mittelgroß, von mittlerer Größe; **life-size(d)** lebensgroß

sizzle ['sɪzl] VI brutzeln N Brutzeln *nt*, Brutzelei *f*

sizzler ['sɪzləʳ] N *(inf)* glühend heißer Tag

sizzling ['sɪzlɪŋ] ADJ *fat, bacon* brutzelnd; *(inf) temperatures* siedend; *weather* brütend heiß; *performance* erregend ADV **~ hot** kochend heiß; **it was a ~ hot day** *(inf)* es war knallheiß *(inf)*

skag [skæg] *(US sl)* N *(= heroin)* Heroin *nt* VT *(= murder)* (er)morden

skank [skæŋk] N *(US pej sl)* Drecksschlampe *f (sl)*

skanky ['skæŋkɪ] ADJ *(inf)* eklig; *manner* abstoßend

skate¹ [skeɪt] N *(= fish)* Rochen *m*

skate² N *(= shoe)* Schlittschuh *m*; *(= blade)* Kufe *f*; **put** *or* **get your ~s on** *(fig inf)* mach/macht mal ein bisschen dalli! *(inf)* → **ice skate, roller skate** VI eislaufen, Schlittschuh laufen; *(= figure-skate)* Eiskunst laufen; *(= roller-skate)* Rollschuh laufen; **he ~d across the pond** er lief (auf Schlittschuhen) über den Teich; **she ~d up to him** sie lief auf ihn zu; **the next couple to ~** das nächste Paar auf dem Eis

▶ **skate (a)round** *or* **over** VI *+prep obj* links liegen lassen; *difficulty, problem* einfach übergehen

skateboard ['skeɪtbɔːd] N Skateboard *nt*, Rollbrett *nt*

skateboarder ['skeɪtbɔːdəʳ] N Skateboardfahrer(in) *m(f)*

skateboarding ['skeɪtbɔːdɪŋ] N Skateboardfahren *nt*

skateboard park N Skateboardanlage *f*

skatepark ['skeɪtpɑːk] N Skateboardanlage *f*

skater ['skeɪtəʳ] N *(= ice-skater)* Eisläufer(in) *m(f)*, Schlittschuhläufer(in) *m(f)*; *(= figure-skater)* Eiskunstläufer(in) *m(f)*; *(= roller-skater)* Rollschuhläufer(in) *m(f)*

skate sailing N *(Sport)* Eissegeln *nt*

skating ['skeɪtɪŋ] N *(= ice-skating)* Eislauf *m*, Schlittschuhlauf *m*; *(= figure-skating)* Eiskunstlauf *m*; *(= roller-skating)* Rollschuhlauf *m*

skating: **skating exhibition** N *(Sport)* Schaulaufen *nt*; **skating rink** N Eisbahn *f*; *(for roller-skating)* Rollschuhbahn *f*

skedaddle [skɪ'dædl] VI *(inf)* Reißaus nehmen *(inf)*, türmen *(inf)*; **~!** weg mit dir/euch!, verzieh dich/verzieht euch!

skeet shooting ['skiːtʃuːtɪŋ] N *(Sport)* Skeetschießen *nt*, Tontaubenschießen *nt*

skein [skeɪn] N *(of wool etc)* Strang *m*; *(of geese)* Schwarm *m*; *(of evidence, lies etc)* Geflecht *nt*

skeletal ['skelɪtl] ADJ *person* bis aufs Skelett abgemagert; *appearance* wie ein Skelett; *shapes of trees etc* skelettartig; **~ muscles** Skelettmuskulatur *f*; **~ remains** Teile *pl* eines Gerippes; **the ~ system** das Skelett

skeleton ['skelɪtn] N *(lit, fig)* Skelett *nt*; *(esp of ship)* Gerippe *nt*; **a ~ in one's cupboard** *(Brit) or* **closet** *(US)* ein dunkler Punkt (seiner Vergangenheit); *(of public figure)* eine Leiche im Keller ADJ *plan, outline etc* provisorisch

skeleton: **skeleton crew** N Not- *or* Minimalbesatzung *f*; **skeleton key** N Dietrich *m*; **skeleton service** N Notdienst *m*; **skeleton staff** N Notbesetzung *f*

skep [skep] N *(old, = basket)* Korb *m*; *(= bee skep)* Bienenkorb *m*

skeptic *etc (US)* = **sceptic** *etc*

sketch [sketʃ] N *(Art, Liter)* Skizze *f*; *(Mus)* Impression *f*; *(Theat)* Sketch *m*; *(= draft, design also)* Entwurf *m* VT *(lit, fig)* skizzieren VI Skizzen machen

▶ **sketch in** VT *sep (= draw)* (grob) einzeichnen; *(verbally)* umreißen

▶ **sketch out** VT *sep (= draw)* grob skizzieren; *(= outline also)* umreißen

sketch: **sketch block** N Skizzenblock *m*; **sketchbook** ['sketʃbʊk] N Skizzenbuch *nt*

sketchily ['sketʃɪlɪ] ADV flüchtig, oberflächlich

sketchiness ['sketʃɪnɪs] N Flüchtigkeit *f*, Oberflächlichkeit *f*; *(= insufficiency)* Unzulänglichkeit *f*

sketching ['sketʃɪŋ] N *(Art)* Skizzenzeichnen *nt*

sketch map N Kartenskizze *f*

sketch pad N Skizzenblock *m*

sketchy ['sketʃɪ] ADJ *(+er) (= inadequate) knowledge, account* flüchtig, oberflächlich; *outline* skizzenhaft; *(= incomplete) record* bruchstückhaft

skew [skju:] N **on the ~** schief; *(= on the diagonal)* schräg ADJ *(lit, fig)* schief; *(= diagonal)* schräg VT *(= turn round)* umdrehen; *(= make crooked)* krümmen; *(fig: = distort)* verzerren VI **the car ~ed off the road** der Wagen kam von der Straße ab; **the ball ~s to the right** der Ball hat einen Rechtsdrall

skewbald ['skju:bɔ:ld] N Schecke *mf* ADJ scheckig

skewer ['skjʊə'] N Spieß *m* VT aufspießen

skewwhiff, **skewwiff** [skju:'wɪf] ADJ, ADV *(Brit inf)* schief

ski [ski:] N Ski *m*; *(Aviat)* Kufe *f* VI Ski laufen *or* fahren; **they ~ed down the slope** sie fuhren (auf ihren Skiern) den Hang hinunter

ski *in cpds* Ski-; **skibob** N Skibob *m*; **ski boot** N Skistiefel *or* -schuh *m*; **ski circuit**, **ski circus** N Skizirkus *m*

skid [skɪd] N **a** *(= sliding movement: Aut etc)* Schleudern *nt*; **to steer into/against a ~** mit-/ /gegensteuern; **to go into a ~** ins Schleudern geraten *or* kommen; **to correct a ~, to pull out of a ~** das Fahrzeug abfangen *or* wieder in seine Gewalt bekommen; **to stop with a ~** schleudernd zum Stehen kommen
b *(on wheel)* Rolle *f*
c *(= runner)* Gleiter *m*; *(of plane, sledge etc)* Gleitkufe *f*
d skids PL *(fig)* **he was on** *or* **hit the ~s** *(inf)* es ging abwärts mit ihm; **her marriage/career is on the ~s** *(inf)* ihre Ehe/Karriere ist ins Schleudern geraten; **to put the ~s under sb/sb's plans** *(inf)* jdn/jds Pläne zu Fall bringen, jdm die Suppe versalzen *(inf)*
VI *(car, objects)* schleudern; *(person)* ausrutschen; **to ~ across the floor** über den Boden rutschen *or* schlittern; **the car ~ded into a tree** der Wagen schleuderte gegen einen Baum

skid: **skidlid** N *(sl)* Sturzhelm *m*; **skidmark** N Reifenspur *f*; *(from braking)* Bremsspur *f*; **skidpan** N Schleuderstrecke *f*; **skidproof** ADJ *tyre etc* rutschfest; **skid row** N *(esp US inf)* (Kaschemmen- und) Pennergegend *f (inf)*; **to be on** *or* **in ~** heruntergekommen sein; **he ended up in ~** er ist als Penner geendet *(inf)*

skier ['ski:ə'] N Skiläufer(in) *m(f)*, Skifahrer(in) *m(f)*

skiff [skɪf] N Skiff *nt*; *(Sport)* Einer *m*

skiffle ['skɪfl] N Skiffle *m*; **~ group** Skifflegroup *f*

ski-flying ['ski:ˌflaɪɪŋ] N Skifliegen *nt*

skiing ['ski:ɪŋ] N Skilaufen *nt*, Skifahren *nt*; **to go ~** Ski laufen *or* Ski fahren gehen

skiing goggles PL Skibrille *f*

ski: **ski jump** N *(= action)* Skisprung *m*; *(= place)* Sprungschanze *f*; **ski-jumping** N Skispringen *nt*

skilful, *(US)* **skillful** ['skɪlfʊl] ADJ geschickt; *piano-playing etc also* gewandt; *sculpture, painting etc* kunstvoll; *job* fachgerecht

skilfully, *(US)* **skillfully** ['skɪlfəlɪ] ADV geschickt; *play the piano also* gewandt; *paint, sculpt etc* kunstvoll

skilfulness, *(US)* **skillfulness** ['skɪlfʊlnɪs] N = **skill a**

ski lift N Skilift *m*

skill [skɪl] N **a** *no pl (= skilfulness)* Geschick *nt*, Geschicklichkeit *f*; *(of sculptor etc)* Kunst(fertigkeit) *f*; **his ~ at billiards** sein Geschick *nt* beim Billard; **her ~ in persuading people** ihre Fähigkeit, andere zu überreden **b** *(= acquired technique)* Fertigkeit *f*; *(= ability)* Fähigkeit *f*; **to learn new ~s** etwas Neues lernen; **it's a ~ that has to be acquired** so etwas muss gelernt sein

Skillcentre ['skɪlsentə'] N *(Brit) staatliches Ausbildungs- und Umschulungszentrum*

skilled [skɪld] ADJ *(= skilful)* geschickt, gewandt (*at* in *+dat*); *(= trained)* ausgebildet; *(= requiring skill)* fachmännisch; **he's ~ in persuading people** er versteht es, andere zu überreden; **a man ~ in diplomacy** ein geschickter Diplomat

skilled worker N Facharbeiter(in) *m(f)*

skillet ['skɪlɪt] N Bratpfanne *f*

skillful *etc (US)* = **skilful** *etc*

skill shortage N *(Econ)* Mangel *m* an qualifizierten Fachkräften

skim [skɪm] VT **a** *(= remove floating matter)* abschöpfen; *milk* entrahmen; *(fig) profits* absahnen *(inf)*
b *(= pass low over)* streifen *or* streichen über *(+acc)*; *(fig: = touch on)* berühren; **he ~med stones across the water** er ließ Steine übers Wasser hüpfen *or* springen; **he ~med his hat across the room** er schleuderte seinen Hut quer durchs Zimmer; **the book merely ~s the surface of the problem** das Buch berührt das Problem nur an der Oberfläche
c *(= read quickly)* überfliegen
VI *(across, over* über *+acc) (= move quickly)* fliegen; *(aircraft also)* rasch gleiten; *(stones)* springen, hüpfen

▶ **skim off** VT *sep* abschöpfen; *(fig)* absahnen; **to skim the cream off the milk** die Milch entrahmen; **to skim the cream off sth** *(fig)* Geld von etw absahnen *(inf)*

▶ **skim through** VI *+prep obj book etc* überfliegen

skimmed milk [ˌskɪmd'mɪlk], *(US)* **skim milk** N Magermilch *f*

skimmer ['skɪmə'] N **a** Schaumlöffel *m* **b** *(Orn)* Scherenschnabel *m*

skimp [skɪmp] VT *food, material* sparen an *(+dat)*, knausern mit; *work* hudeln bei *(inf)*, nachlässig erledigen; *details* zu kurz kommen lassen VI sparen (*on* an *+dat*), knausern (*on* mit)

skimpily ['skɪmpɪlɪ] ADV dürftig; *live, eat also* kärglich; *dressed* spärlich

skimpy ['skɪmpɪ] ADJ *(+er)* dürftig; *meal also* kärglich; *clothes* knapp

skin [skɪn] N **a** Haut *f*; **to be soaked to the ~** bis auf die Haut nass sein; **he's nothing but ~ and bone(s) nowadays** er ist nur noch Haut und Knochen; **that's no ~ off his nose** *(esp Brit inf)* das braucht ihn nicht zu stören; **that's no ~ off my nose** *(esp Brit inf)* das juckt mich nicht *(inf)*; **to get inside the ~ of a part** *(Theat)* in einer Rolle aufgehen; **all men/women are brothers/sisters under the ~** im Grunde sind alle Menschen gleich; **to save one's own ~** die eigene Haut retten; **to jump out of one's ~** *(inf)* erschreckt hochfahren; **to get under sb's ~** *(inf: = irritate)* jdm auf die Nerven gehen *(inf)*; *(= fascinate, music, voice)* jdm unter die Haut gehen; *(person)* jdn faszinieren; *(= understand)* jdn verstehen; **I've got you under my ~** du hast mirs angetan; **to have a thick/thin ~** *(fig)* ein dickes Fell *(inf)*/eine dünne Haut haben; **by the ~ of one's teeth** *(inf)* mit knapper Not, mit Ach und Krach *(inf)*
b *(= hide)* Haut *f*; *(= fur)* Fell *nt*
c *(= oilskins)* Ölhaut *f*, Ölzeug *nt*
d *(for wine etc)* Schlauch *m*
e *(of fruit etc)* Schale *f*; *(of grape, tomato)* Haut *f*, Schale *f*
f *(on sausage etc)* Haut *f*, Darm *m*
g *(on milk etc)* Haut *f*
h *(for duplicating)* Matrize *f*
i *(= skinhead)* Skin *m*
j *(Drugs inf: = cigarette paper)* Zigarettenpapier *nt (zum Rauchen von Drogen)*
VT **a** *animal* häuten; *fruit* schälen; *grapes, tomatoes* enthäuten; **there's more than one way to ~ a cat** *(inf)* es gibt nicht nur einen Weg; **to ~ sb alive** *(inf)* jdm den Kopf abreißen *(hum inf)* → **eye**
b *(= graze) knee* abschürfen

▶ **skin up** VI *(Drugs inf)* sich *(dat)* einen Joint drehen *(inf)*; **that guy is always skinning up** der Typ kifft ständig *(inf)*

skin: **skin care** N Hautpflege *f*; **skin-deep** ADJ → **beauty**; **skin disease** N Hautkrankheit *f*; **skin-diver** N Sporttaucher(in) *m(f)*; **skin diving** N Sporttauchen *nt*; **skin flick** N *(US inf)* Porno(film) *m*; **skinflint** N *(inf)* Geizkragen *m (inf)*; **skin food** N Nahrung *f* für die Haut

skinful ['skɪnfʊl] N *(Brit inf)* **to have had a ~** einen über den Durst getrunken haben, einen sitzen haben *(inf)*

skin: **skin game** N *(US inf)* Schwindel *m*; **skin graft** N Hauttransplantation *or* -verpflanzung *f*; **skinhead** N Skin(head) *m* ADJ *attr* Skin(head)-; **~ gang** Skin(head)bande *f*; **skinless** ADJ *sausage* ohne Haut *or* Darm; *chicken breast* ohne Haut

-skinned [-skɪnd] ADJ *suf* -häutig; **fair-skinned** hellhäutig; **dark-skinned** dunkelhäutig

skinner ['skɪnə'] N *(removing skins)* Abdecker(in) *m(f)*; *(preparing skins)* Gerber(in) *m(f)*

skinny ['skɪnɪ] ADJ *(+er) (inf) person, legs, arms* dünn; *sweater* eng anliegend *attr*, hauteng N *(US inf: = piece of information)* vertrauliche Information, Insider-Information *f*; **that's the ~ (on that)** das ist der Witz daran *(inf)*, das ist genau der Punkt

skinny: **skinny-dip** VI *(inf)* nackt baden; **skinny dipping** N *(inf)* Nacktbaden *nt*; **to go ~** nackt baden; **skinny-rib** ADJ Rippen-; **~ sweater** Rippenpullover *m*

skin patch N *(Med)* Hautfleck *m*

skint [skɪnt] ADJ *(Brit inf)* **to be ~** pleite *or* blank sein *(inf)*

skin: **skin test** N Hauttest *m*; **skintight** ADJ hauteng

skip[1] [skɪp] N Hüpfer *m*; *(in dancing)* Hüpfschritt *m*; **she gave a little ~ of pleasure** sie machte einen Freudensprung
VI **a** hüpfen; *(with rope)* seilhüpfen, seilspringen; **she came ~ping up to us** sie kam auf uns zugesprungen; **she was ~ping** *(with rope)* sie sprang Seil
b *(= move from subject to subject)* springen
c *(inf: = abscond, flee)* abhauen *(inf)*, türmen *(inf)*
VT **a** *(= omit, miss) school, church etc* schwänzen *(inf)*; *generation, passage, chapter etc* überspringen, auslassen; *(Comput, printer)* überspringen; **my heart ~ped a beat** mein Herzschlag setzte für eine Sekunde aus; **to ~ lunch** das Mittagessen ausfallen lassen; **to ~ bail** *(inf)* die Kaution verfallen lassen *(und nicht vor Gericht erscheinen)*; **~ it!** ist ja auch egal!
b *(US)* **to ~ rope** seilhüpfen, seilspringen
c *(US inf)* **to ~ town** aus der Stadt verschwinden *(inf)*; **to ~ the country** über die Grenze fliehen

▶ **skip about** *(Brit) or* **around** VI *(lit)* herumhüpfen; *(fig: author, speaker)* springen

▶ **skip across** VI *(inf)* rüberspringen *(inf)*; **skip across to the other office** spring doch mal rüber ins andere Büro! *(inf)*

▶ **skip off** VI *(inf)* abhauen *(inf)*

▶ **skip over** VI *(inf)* = **skip across** VI *+prep obj (= pass over)* überspringen

▶ **skip through** VI *+prep obj book* durchblättern

skip[2] N **a** *(Build)* Container *m*, Bauschuttmulde *f (form)*; *(Min)* Förderkorb *m* **b** = **skep**

skip[3] N *(Sport)* Kapitän *m*

ski: **ski pants** PL Skihose *f*; **ski pass** N Skipass *m*; **skiplane** N Flugzeug *nt* mit Schneekufen; **ski pole** N = **ski stick**

skipper ['skɪpə'] N Kapitän(in) *m(f)*; **aye, aye ~!** jawohl, Käpt'n! VT anführen; **the team was ~ed by X** Kapitän(in) der Mannschaft war X

skipping ['skɪpɪŋ] N Seilhüpfen *nt*, Seilspringen *nt*

skipping rope N *(Brit)* Hüpf- *or* Sprungseil *nt*

ski: **ski rack** N Skiträger *m*; **ski resort** N Skiort *m*

skirl [skɜːl] N **the ~ of the bagpipes** das Pfeifen der Dudelsäcke

skirmish [ˈskɜːmɪʃ] N *(Mil)* Gefecht *nt*, Plänkelei *f*; *(= scrap, fig)* Zusammenstoß *m* VI *(Mil)* kämpfen; *(= scrap, also fig)* zusammenstoßen

skirmisher [ˈskɜːmɪʃəʳ] N Kämpfende(r) *mf*

skirt [skɜːt] N **a** Rock *m*; *(of jacket, coat)* Schoß *m* **b** *(inf: = woman)* Braut *f (sl)*; **a bit of ~** eine Braut VT *(also* **skirt around***)* umgehen; *(= encircle)* umgeben

skirting (board) [ˈskɜːtɪŋ(ˌbɔːd)] N *(Brit)* Fußleiste *f*

ski: **ski run** N Skipiste *f*; **ski school** N Skischule *f*; **ski stick** N Skistock *m*; **ski suit** N Skianzug *m*

skit [skɪt] N (satirischer) Sketch *(on* über *+acc)*, Parodie *f (on +gen)*

ski: **ski touring** N Skitouren *nt*; **ski tow** N Schlepplift *m*

skitter [ˈskɪtəʳ] VI rutschen

skittish [ˈskɪtɪʃ] ADJ *(= playful)* übermütig, schelmisch; *(= flirtatious) woman* neckisch, kokett; *(= nervous) horse, investor* unruhig

skittishly [ˈskɪtɪʃlɪ] ADV *(= playfully)* übermütig, schelmisch; *(= flirtatiously: of woman)* neckisch, kokett; *(= nervously: of horse)* unruhig

skittishness [ˈskɪtɪʃnɪs] N *(= playfulness)* Übermütigkeit *f*, Übermut *m*; *(= flirtatiousness: of woman)* Neckereien *pl*; *(= nervousness: of horse)* Unruhe *f*

skittle [ˈskɪtl] N *(Brit)* Kegel *m*; **to play ~s** kegeln; **~ alley** Kegelbahn *f*

skive [skaɪv] *(Brit inf)* N **to be on the ~** blaumachen *(inf)*; *(from school etc)* schwänzen *(inf)*; **to have a good ~** sich *(dat)* einen schönen Tag machen *(inf)*, sich vor der Arbeit drücken VI blaumachen *(inf)*; *(from school etc)* schwänzen *(inf)*

▶ **skive off** VI *(Brit inf)* sich abseilen *(sl)*, sich drücken *(inf)*

skiver [ˈskaɪvəʳ] N *(Brit inf)* fauler Bruder *(inf)*, faule Schwester *(inf)*

skivvy [ˈskɪvɪ] N *(Brit inf)* Dienstmagd *f*

skua [ˈskjuːə] N Skua *f*, Große Raubmöwe

skulduggery [skʌlˈdʌgərɪ] N *(inf)* üble Tricks *pl (inf)*; **a bit of ~** ein übler Trick *(inf)*; **what ~ are you planning?** *(hum)* na, was für Schandtaten hast du denn vor? *(inf)*

skulk [skʌlk] VI *(= move)* schleichen, sich stehlen; *(= lurk)* sich herumdrücken

▶ **skulk off** VI sich davonschleichen, sich davonstehlen

skull [skʌl] N Schädel *m*; **I couldn't get it into his thick ~** *(inf)* das wollte einfach nicht in seinen Schädel *(inf)*; **~ and crossbones** Totenkopf *m*

skullcap [ˈskʌlkæp] N Kipa *f*

skunk [skʌŋk] N **a** Skunk *m*, Stinktier *nt*; *(inf, = person)* Schweinehund **b** *(inf: = marijuana)* Pot *nt (sl)*

sky [skaɪ] N Himmel *m*; **under the open ~** unter freiem Himmel; **in the ~** am Himmel; **the ~'s the limit!** nach oben sind keine Grenzen gesetzt; **out of a clear (blue) ~** aus heiterem Himmel; **to praise sb to the skies** jdn in den Himmel heben, jdn über den grünen Klee loben *(inf)*

sky: **sky advertising** N Luftwerbung *f*; **skybeam** N Skybeamer *m*; **sky blue** N Himmelblau *nt*; **sky-blue** ADJ himmelblau; **skycap** N *(US)* Gepäckträger(in) *m(f)*; **skydiver** N Fallschirmspringer(in) *m(f)*; **skydiving** N Fallschirmspringen *nt*

Skye terrier [ˈskaɪˈterɪəʳ] N Skyeterrier *m*

sky: **sky-high** ADJ **a** *prices* schwindelnd hoch; *confidence* unermesslich **b** *(= tall)* himmelhoch ADV zum Himmel; **mortgage rates went ~** die Hypothekenzinsen stiegen in schwindelerregende Höhen; **to blow a bridge ~** *(inf)* eine Brücke in die Luft sprengen *(inf)*; **to blow a theory ~** *(inf)* eine Theorie zum Einsturz bringen; **skyjack** [ˈskaɪdʒæk] VT entführen N Flugzeugentführung *f*; **skyjacker** N Luftpirat(in) *m(f)*, Flugzeugentführer(in) *m(f)*; **skylark** N Feldlerche *f* VI *(inf, = frolic)* tollen; *(= fool around)* blödeln *(inf)*;; **skylarking** N *(inf)* Tollen *nt*; *(= fooling around)* Blödelei *f (inf)*; **skylight** N Oberlicht *nt*; *(in roof also)* Dachfenster *nt*; **skyline** N *(= horizon)* Horizont *m*; *(of building, hills etc)* Silhouette *f*; *(of city)* Skyline *f*, Silhouette *f*; **sky marshal** N *(esp US Aviat)* Sky-Marshal *m*, *zur Verhinderung von Flugzeugentführungen mitfliegender Sicherheitsbeamter*; **sky park** N *(US)* **a** *(on top of skyscraper) Parkanlage auf dem Dach eines Wolkenkratzers* **b** *(= residential area)* Wohnanlage *f* mit eigenem Flugplatz; **sky pilot** N *(Mil sl)* Schwarzrock *m (inf)*; **skyrocket** N (Feuerwerks)rakete *f* VI *(prices, expenses, blood pressure)* in die Höhe schießen VT in die Höhe schießen lassen; **skyscape** [ˈskaɪskeɪp] N Wolkenlandschaft *f*; **skyscraper** N Wolkenkratzer *m*; **skysurfer** N *(Sport)* Skysurfer(in) *m(f)*; **skysurfing** N *(Sport)* Skysurfen *nt*, Skysurfing *nt*

skyward(s) [ˈskaɪwəd(z)] ADJ zum *or* gen *(geh)* Himmel gerichtet ADV zum *or* gen *(geh)* Himmel

sky: **skyway** N Luftweg *m*; **skywriting** N Himmelsschrift *f*

slab [slæb] N *(of wood etc)* Tafel *f*; *(of stone, concrete etc)* Platte *f*; *(in mortuary)* Tisch *m*; *(= slice)* dicke Scheibe; *(of cake, bread)* großes Stück; *(of chocolate)* Tafel *f*

slack [slæk] ADJ *(+er)* **a** *(= not tight)* locker **b** *(= lazy)* bequem, träge; *student* verbummelt; *(= negligent)* nachlässig, schlampig *(inf)*; **they are very ~ in renewing contracts** das Erneuern der Verträge wird sehr nachlässig gehandhabt; **to be ~ in one's work** in Bezug auf seine Arbeit nachlässig sein
c *(= not busy) (Comm) market* flau; *period, season* ruhig; **business is ~** das Geschäft geht schlecht
d *(= slow) water* träge; *wind* flau
N **a** *(of rope etc)* durchhängendes Teil (des Seils/Segels etc), Lose(s) *nt (spec)*; **to take up the ~ (on a rope/sail)** ein Seil/Segel straffen *or* spannen; **there is too much ~** das Seil/Segel hängt zu sehr durch; **to cut sb some ~** *(fig inf)* mit jdm nachsichtig sein
b *(= coal)* Grus *m*
VI bummeln

▶ **slack off** VI = **slacken off b**

slacken [ˈslækn] VT **a** *(= loosen)* lockern **b** *(= reduce)* vermindern, verringern VI **a** *(= become loose)* sich lockern **b** *(speed)* sich verringern; *(rate of development)* sich verlangsamen; *(wind, demand, market)* abflauen, nachlassen

▶ **slacken off** VI **a** *(= diminish)* nachlassen; *(wind)* abflauen, nachlassen; *(work, trade)* abnehmen **b** *(person, = relax)* nachlassen; *(for health reasons)* sich schonen

▶ **slacken up** VI = **slacken off b**

slackening [ˈslæknɪŋ] N *(= loosening)* Lockern *nt*; *(= reduction)* Abnahme *f*; *(of rate of development, speed)* Verlangsamung *f*; *(of wind, efforts, market)* Abflauen *nt*; **there is no ~ off in the demand** die Nachfrage ist nicht zurückgegangen

slacker [ˈslækəʳ] N Bummelant(in) *m(f)*

slackly [ˈslæklɪ] ADV **a** *(= loosely, floppily)* schlaff; *hold* locker; *hang* schlaff, lose **b** *(= carelessly, sloppily)* schlampig

slackness [ˈslæknɪs] N **a** *(of rope, reins)* Schlaffheit *f*, Durchhängen *nt* **b** *(= laziness)* Bummelei *f*; *(= negligence)* Nachlässigkeit *f*, Schlampigkeit *f (inf)* **c** *(of business, market etc)* Flaute *f*

slacks [slæks] PL Hose *f*

slacksuit [ˈslæksuːt] N *(US)* **a** *(for leisure)* Freizeitanzug *m* **b** *(= pantsuit)* Hosenanzug *m*

slag [slæg] N **a** Schlacke *f* **b** *(Brit sl: = woman)* Schlampe *f (inf)* VT *(Brit inf: = run down)* miesmachen *(inf)*, runtermachen *(inf)*

▶ **slag off** VT *sep (Brit inf: = run down)* miesmachen *(inf)*, runtermachen *(inf)*

slag heap N Schlackenhalde *f*

slain [sleɪn] *ptp of* **slay**

slake [sleɪk] VT **a** *(liter: = quench)* stillen **b** *lime* löschen; **~d lime** gelöschter Kalk, Löschkalk *m*

slalom [ˈslɑːləm] N Slalom *m*

slam [slæm] N **a** *(of door etc)* Zuschlagen *nt*, Zuknallen *nt no pl*; *(of fist etc)* Aufschlagen *nt no pl*; **with a ~** mit voller Wucht
b *(Cards)* Schlemm *m*; **little** *or* **small ~** Kleinschlemm *m* → *also* **grand slam**
VT **a** *(= close violently)* zuschlagen, zuknallen; **to ~ the door** *(lit, fig)* die Tür zuschlagen; **to ~ sth shut** etw zuknallen; **to ~ the door in sb's face** jdm die Tür vor der Nase zumachen; **to ~ home a bolt** einen Riegel vorwerfen
b *(inf: = put, throw etc with force)* knallen *(inf)*; **he ~med his fist into my face** er knallte mir die Faust ins Gesicht *(inf)*; **she ~med her fist on the table** sie knallte mit der Faust auf den Tisch *(inf)*; **to ~ the brakes on** *(inf)* auf die Bremse latschen *(inf)*
c *(inf, = defeat)* vernichtend schlagen, am Boden zerstören
d *(inf: = criticize harshly)* verreißen; *person* herunterputzen *(inf)*, miesmachen *(inf)*
VI **a** *(door, window)* zuschlagen, zuknallen
b **to ~ into/against sth** in etw *(acc)*/gegen etw knallen

▶ **slam down** VT *sep (= put down violently)* hinknallen *(inf)*; *phone* aufknallen *(inf)*; *window* zuknallen; **to slam sth down on the table** etw auf den Tisch knallen

slam dancing N Slamdancing *nt*

slam-dunk [ˈslæmdʌŋk] *(US Basketball)* N Slam Dunk *m* VT *ball* kraftvoll im Korb versenken VI einen Slam Dunk spielen

slammer [ˈslæməʳ] N *(inf: = prison)* Knast *m (inf)*, Bau *m (inf)*

slander [ˈslɑːndəʳ] N Verleumdung *f* VT verleumden

slanderer [ˈslɑːndərəʳ] N Verleumder(in) *m(f)*

slanderous [ˈslɑːndərəs] ADJ verleumderisch

slang [slæŋ] N Slang *m*; *(= army slang, schoolboy slang etc)* Jargon *m*; **street ~** Straßenjargon *m*; **gipsy ~** Zigeunersprache *f (neg!)* ADJ Slang-; **~ expression** Slangausdruck *m* VT *(esp Brit inf)* **to ~ sb** jdn beschimpfen; **to ~ sth** über etw *(acc)* schimpfen

slanging match [ˈslæŋɪŋˌmætʃ] N *(Brit)* Wettschimpfen *nt*; **they were having a ~** sie beschimpften sich um die Wette *(inf)*

slangy ADJ *(+er)*, **slangily** ADV [ˈslæŋɪ, -lɪ] salopp

slant [slɑːnt] N **a** Neigung *f*, Schräge *f*; **to be on a ~** sich neigen, schräg sein; **his handwriting has a definite ~ to the right/left** er schreibt stark nach rechts/links
b *(fig: = bias, leaning)* Tendenz *f*, Neigung *f*; *(of newspaper article)* Anstrich *m*; **these newspapers have a right-wing ~** diese Zeitungen sind rechtsgerichtet *or* haben einen Rechtsdrall; **to put a ~ on sth** etw biegen
c *(Typ: = slash)* Schrägstrich *m*
VT verschieben; *report* färben; **the book is ~ed toward(s) women** das Buch ist auf Frauen ausgerichtet
VI *(road)* sich neigen; **the light ~ed in through the window** das Licht fiel schräg durch das Fenster herein; **her eyes ~ up at the corners** ihre Augen sind schräg gestellt

slanted [ˈslɑːntɪd] ADJ *(fig)* gefärbt

slant-eyed [ˈslɑːntˈaɪd] ADJ *(pej)* schlitzäugig *(pej)*

slanting [ˈslɑːntɪŋ] ADJ schräg

slantways [ˈslɑːntweɪz], **slantwise** [ˈslɑːntwaɪz] ADV quer

slap [slæp] **N** Schlag *m*, Klaps *m*; **to give sb a ~** jdm einen Klaps geben; **a ~ across the face** *(lit)* eine Ohrfeige; **a ~ in the face** *(fig)* ein Schlag *m* ins Gesicht; **to give sb a ~ on the back** jdm (anerkennend) auf den Rücken klopfen; *(fig)* jdn loben; **~ and tickle** *(hum inf)* Balgerei *f (inf)*, Kalberei *f (inf)*; **to give sb a ~ on the wrist** *(fig inf)* jdn zurechtweisen, jdm einem Anpfiff geben *(inf)*; **a £1,000 fine to him is just a ~ on the wrist** eine Geldstrafe von £ 1.000 ist für ihn allenfalls ein kleiner Denkzettel
ADV *(inf)* direkt; **to run ~ into sb/sth** mit jdm/etw zusammenknallen *(inf)*; **~ in the middle of the beach** mitten auf dem Strand
VT **a** *(= hit)* schlagen; **to ~ sb's face, to ~ sb on** *or* **round the face** jdn ohrfeigen, jdm ins Gesicht schlagen, jdm eine runterhauen *(inf)*; **to ~ sb on the back** jdm auf den Rücken klopfen; **to ~ one's knee(s)** sich *(dat)* auf die Schenkel schlagen
b *(= put noisily)* knallen *(on(to)* auf *+acc)*
c *(inf: = put carelessly)* **a piece of cheese ~ped between two slices of bread** ein Stück Käse zwischen zwei Scheiben Brot geklatscht *(inf)*

▶ **slap down** VT *sep (inf)* **a** *(= put down)* hinknallen **b** *(fig)* **to slap sb down** jdm eins aufs Dach *or* auf den Deckel geben *(inf)*; **to be slapped down** eins aufs Dach *or* auf den Deckel bekommen *(inf)*

▶ **slap on** VT *sep (inf)* **a** *(= apply carelessly) paint, make-up* draufklatschen *(inf)* **b** *(= put on top)* draufklatschen *(inf)*; *(fig) tax, money* draufhauen *(inf)*; **to slap an injunction/a fine on sb** jdm eine einstweilige Verfügung/eine Geldstrafe verpassen *(inf)*

slap: **slap-bang** ADV *(esp Brit inf)* mit Karacho *(inf)*; **it was ~ in the middle** es war genau in der Mitte; **to run ~ into sb/sth** mit jdm/etw zusammenknallen *(inf)*; **slapdash** ADJ flüchtig, schludrig *(pej)*; **slaphappy** ADJ *(inf)* unbekümmert; **slaphead** N *(inf)* Glatzkopf *m (inf)*; **slapjack** N *(US)* ≈ Pfannkuchen *m*

slapper ['slæpəʳ] N *(Brit inf)* Flittchen *nt (inf)*

slap: **slapstick** N Klamauk *m (inf)*; **~ comedy** Slapstick *m*; **slap-up meal** N *(Brit inf)* Schlemmermahl *nt (inf)*

slash [slæʃ] **N** **a** *(= action)* Streich *m*; *(= wound)* Schnitt *m*
b *(Sew)* Schlitz *m*; **a black velvet dress with ~es of red silk** ein schwarzes Samtkleid mit roten Seidenschlitzen
c *(Typ, Comput)* Schrägstrich *m*
d *(Brit inf)* **to go for a ~** schiffen gehen *(sl)*; **to have** *or* **take a ~** schiffen *(sl)*
VT **a** *(= cut)* zerfetzen; *face, tyres, throat* aufschlitzen; *undergrowth* abhauen, wegschlagen; *(with sword)* hauen auf *(+acc)*, schlagen; **to ~ sb with a knife** jdn durch Messerstiche verletzen; **to ~ sth to ribbons** etw zerfetzen; **he ~ed the air with his sword** er ließ das Schwert durch die Luft sausen → **wrist**
b *(inf: = reduce drastically) price* radikal herabsetzen; *workforce* drastisch reduzieren; *estimate, budget* zusammenstreichen *(inf)*; **they've really ~ed their prices** sie haben ihre Preise drastisch reduziert; **to ~ the odds** die Chance(n) erheblich reduzieren
c *(Sew)* mit Schlitzen versehen; **~ed sleeves** Schlitzärmel *pl*; **~ed doublet** Schlitzwams *nt*
VI **to ~ at sb/sth** nach jdm/etw schlagen

▶ **slash off** VT *sep* abschlagen; **to slash £500 off the budget** £ 500 aus dem Etat streichen

slash-and-burn [ˌslæʃən'bɜːn] ADJ **~ farming** Brandrodung *f*

slasher film ['slæʃəˌfɪlm], **slasher movie** ['slæʃəˌmuːvɪ] N *(inf) Horrorfilm mit Szenen, in denen Menschen mit Messern, Rasierklingen etc verletzt werden*

slashing ['slæʃɪŋ] ADJ *blow* zerschmetternd; *attack also* scharf; *criticism* vernichtend

slat [slæt] N Leiste *f*; *(wooden also)* Latte *f*; *(in grid etc)* Stab *m*

slate [sleɪt] **N** **a** *(= rock)* Schiefer *m*; *(= roof slate)* Schieferplatte *f*; *(= writing slate)* (Schiefer)tafel *f*; **put it on the ~** *(Brit inf)* schreiben Sie es mir an; **to have a clean ~** *(fig)* eine reine Weste haben, nichts auf dem Kerbholz haben *(inf)*; **to start with a clean ~** *(fig)* einen neuen Anfang machen; **to wipe the ~ clean** *(fig)* reinen Tisch machen
b *(US Pol)* (Kandidaten)liste *f*
ADJ Schiefer-, schief(e)rig; **the roof is ~** das Dach ist aus Schiefer
VT **a** *roof* (mit Schiefer) decken
b *(esp US: = propose)* vorschlagen; *(= schedule)* ansetzen; **it is ~d to start at nine** es ist für neun Uhr angesetzt
c *(Brit inf: = criticize harshly) play, performance* verreißen; *person* zusammenstauchen *(inf)*

slate: **slate-blue** ADJ blaugrau; **slate-coloured** ADJ schiefergrau, schieferfarben; **slate-grey**, *(US)* **slate-gray** ADJ schiefergrau; **slate pencil** N Griffel *m*; **slate quarry** N Schieferbruch *m*

slater ['sleɪtəʳ] N Dachdecker(in) *m(f)*, Schieferdecker(in) *m(f) (rare)*

slate roof N Schieferdach *nt*

slating ['sleɪtɪŋ] N *(Brit inf)* Verriss *m*; **to give sb a ~** jdn zusammenstauchen *(inf)*; **to get a ~** zusammengestaucht werden *(inf)*; *(play, performance etc)* verrissen werden

slatted ['slætɪd] ADJ → **slat** aus Leisten/Latten/Stäben bestehend; **a ~ fence** ein Lattenzaun *m*

slattern ['slætən] N Schlampe *f*

slatternly ['slætənlɪ] ADJ liederlich, schlampig

slaty ['sleɪtɪ] ADJ *material* schief(e)rig; *(in colour)* schieferfarben; **~ blue eyes** graublaue Augen *pl*

slaughter ['slɔːtəʳ] **N** *(of animals)* Schlachten *nt no pl*; *(of persons)* Gemetzel *nt no pl*, Abschlachten *nt no pl (liter)*; **the Slaughter of the Innocents** *(Bibl)* der Mord der Unschuldigen Kinder; **the ~ on the streets** das Töten auf den Straßen **VT** schlachten; *persons (lit)* abschlachten; *(fig)* fertigmachen *(inf)*

slaughterer ['slɔːtərəʳ] N *(lit)* Schlachter(in) *m(f)*; *(fig)* Schlächter(in) *m(f)*

slaughterhouse ['slɔːtəhaʊs] N Schlachthof *m*, Schlachthaus *nt*

Slav [slɑːv] **ADJ** slawisch **N** Slawe *m*, Slawin *f*

slave [sleɪv] **N** Sklave *m*, Sklavin *f*; **to be a ~ to sb/sth** jds Sklave/Sklave von etw sein **VI** sich abplagen, schuften *(inf)*; **to ~ (away) at sth** sich mit etw herumschlagen; **to ~ over a hot stove** (den ganzen Tag) am Herd stehen; **he was slaving over his homework** er schlug sich mit seinen Hausaufgaben herum

slave: **slave-driver** N *(lit, fig)* Sklaventreiber(in) *m(f)*; **slave labour**, *(US)* **slave labor** N **a** *(= work)* Sklavenarbeit *f* **b** *(= work force)* Sklaven *pl*; **he uses ~** seine Leute müssen wie die Sklaven arbeiten; **slave market** N *(Hist)* Sklavenmarkt *m*

slaver[1] ['sleɪvəʳ] N *(= ship)* Sklavenschiff *nt*; *(= person)* Sklavenhändler(in) *m(f)*

slaver[2] ['slævəʳ] **VI** speicheln *(geh)*, geifern; **the dog ~ed at the mouth** der Hund hatte Schaum vor dem Maul; **he began to ~ at the thought of food** bei dem Gedanken ans Essen lief ihm das Wasser im Munde zusammen; **to ~ over sb/sth** nach jdm/etw geifern **N** Speichel *m*, Geifer *m*

slavery ['sleɪvərɪ] N Sklaverei *f*; *(= condition)* Sklavenleben *nt*; *(fig: = addiction)* sklavische Abhängigkeit *(to* von*)*; **she was tired of domestic ~** sie hatte es satt, sich immer im Haushalt abrackern zu müssen

slave: **slave ship** N Sklavenschiff *nt*; **slave trade** N Sklavenhandel *m*; **slave trader** N = **slaver**[1]

slavey ['sleɪvɪ] N *(dated Brit inf)* (Dienst)mädchen *nt*

Slavic ['slɑːvɪk] **ADJ** slawisch **N** das Slawische

slavish ADJ, **slavishly** ADV ['sleɪvɪʃ, -lɪ] sklavisch

slavishness ['sleɪvɪʃnɪs] N sklavische Abhängigkeit; *(= submissiveness)* Unterwürfigkeit *f*; **the ~ with which she imitated him** die sklavische Art, in der sie ihn nachahmte

Slavonian [slə'vəʊnɪən] **ADJ** slawonisch **N** Slawone *m*, Slawonin *f*

Slavonic [slə'vɒnɪk] **ADJ** slawisch **N** das Slawische

slaw [slɔː] N *(US)* Krautsalat *m*

slay [sleɪ] *pret* **slew**, *ptp* **slain** VT erschlagen; *(with gun etc, esp US: = kill)* ermorden; **this will ~ you** *(inf)* da lachst du dich tot! *(inf)*; **he really ~s me** *(inf)* ich könnte mich über ihn totlachen *(inf)*

slayer ['sleɪəʳ] N *(liter)* Mörder(in) *m(f)*, Töter(in) *m(f) (old liter)*

slaying ['sleɪɪŋ] N *(esp US: = murder)* Mord *m*; **an increasing number of ~s** eine Zunahme von Mordfällen

SLD *(Brit Pol) abbr of* **Social and Liberal Democrats**

sleaze [sliːz] N *(inf)* **a** *(= depravity)* Verderbtheit *f*; *(esp Pol: = corruption)* Skandalgeschichten *pl* **b** *(US: = sleazebag)* Dreckskerl *m (inf)*, Schwein *nt (inf)*

sleazebag ['sliːzbæg], **sleazeball** ['sliːzbɔːl] N *(pej inf)* Dreckskerl *m (inf)*

sleazo ['sliːzəʊ] N *(inf: = sleazy person)* schmierige Type *(inf)*

sleazoid ['sliːzɔɪd] *(esp US pej inf)* **ADJ** schmierig *(inf)*, aalglatt *(inf)* **N** schmieriger *or* aalglatter Typ *(inf)*, Widerling *m (inf)*

sleazy ['sliːzɪ] ADJ *(+er) (inf)* schäbig

sledge [sledʒ], *(esp US)* **sled** [sled] **N** Schlitten *m* **VI** Schlitten fahren

sledge(hammer) ['sledʒ(ˌhæməʳ)] N Vorschlaghammer *m*; **to use a sledgehammer to crack a nut** *(fig)* mit Kanonen auf Spatzen schießen

sleek [sliːk] **ADJ** *(+er) hair, fur, animal* geschmeidig, glatt; *(of general appearance)* gepflegt; *car also* schnittig, elegant; *behaviour* aalglatt *(pej)*, glatt **VT** glätten; *(cat)* lecken

sleekness ['sliːknɪs] N *(of hair, fur, animal)* Geschmeidigkeit *f*; *(of general appearance)* Gepflegtheit *f*; *(of car)* Schnittigkeit *f*, Eleganz *f*

sleep [sliːp] *vb: pret, ptp* **slept** **N** **a** Schlaf *m*; **to go to ~** *(person, limb)* einschlafen; **to drop off to ~** *(person)* einschlafen; **I couldn't get to ~ last night** ich konnte letzte Nacht nicht einschlafen; **try and get some ~** versuche, etwas zu schlafen; **to have a ~** (etwas) schlafen; **to have a good night's ~** sich richtig ausschlafen, richtig schlafen; **to put sb to ~** *(person, cocoa etc)* jdn zum Schlafen bringen; *(drug)* jdn einschläfern; **to put an animal to ~** *(euph)* ein Tier einschläfern; **that film sent me to ~** bei dem Film bin ich eingeschlafen; **to walk in one's ~** schlafwandeln; **to talk in one's ~** im Schlaf sprechen
b *(Brit inf: in eyes)* **you've got some ~ (in your eyes)** du hast noch Schlaf in den Augen *(inf)*
VT **a** **to ~ the day away** den ganzen Tag verschlafen; **to ~ the ~ of the just** den Schlaf des Gerechten schlafen; **to ~ the ~ of the dead** *or* **the last ~** den ewigen *or* letzten Schlaf schlafen *(liter)*
b *(= accommodate)* unterbringen; **the house ~s 10** in dem Haus können 10 Leute schlafen *or* übernachten
VI schlafen; **to ~ like a log** *or* **top** *or* **baby** wie ein Klotz *or* wie ein Murmeltier schlafen; **to ~ late** lange schlafen; **to ~ right round the clock** rund um die Uhr schlafen; **the village slept** *(liter)* das Dorf schlief *(geh)*; **you must have been ~ing** *(fig)* da musst du geschlafen haben

▶ **sleep around** VI *(inf)* mit jedem schlafen

▶ **sleep in** VI **a** *(= lie in)* ausschlafen; *(inf: = oversleep)* verschlafen **b** *(= live in)* im Hause wohnen

▶ **sleep off** VT *sep (inf) hangover etc* ausschlafen; **to sleep it off** seinen Rausch ausschlafen; *cold etc* sich gesund schlafen; **to sleep off one's lunch** ein Verdauungsschläfchen *nt* halten

▶**sleep on** VI *(= continue sleeping)* weiterschlafen VI +*prep obj problem etc* überschlafen; **let's sleep on it** schlafen wir erst einmal darüber, überschlafen wir die Sache erst einmal

▶**sleep out** VI **a** *(in open air)* draußen *or* im Freien schlafen **b** *(hotel staff: = live out)* außer Haus wohnen

▶**sleep through** VI durchschlafen VI +*prep obj* weiterschlafen bei; **to sleep through the alarm (clock)** den Wecker verschlafen

▶**sleep together** VI zusammen schlafen

▶**sleep with** VI +*prep obj* schlafen mit

sleep disturbance N Schlafstörung *f*, Einschlaf- *or* Durchschlafstörung *f*

sleeper ['sli:pəʳ] N **a** *(= person)* Schlafende(r) *mf*, Schläfer(in) *m(f)*; **to be a heavy/light ~** einen festen/leichten Schlaf haben **b** *(Brit Rail: = on track)* Schwelle *f* **c** *(Brit Rail: = train)* Schlafwagenzug *m*; *(= coach)* Schlafwagen *m*; *(= berth)* Platz *m* im Schlafwagen; **I've booked a ~** ich habe Schlafwagen gebucht **d** *(esp Brit: = earring) einfacher Ohrring, der das Zuwachsen des Loches im Ohrläppchen verhindern soll* **e** *(= spy)* abgeschalteter Agent, abgeschaltete Agentin **f** *(= terrorist)* Schläfer *m* **g** **sleepers** PL *(US: = child's pyjamas)* einteiliger Schlafanzug

sleepily ['sli:pılı] ADV *ask, smile, blink* verschlafen

sleepiness ['sli:pınıs] N **a** *(= drowsiness)* Müdigkeit *f*, Schläfrigkeit *f* **b** *(fig: of place, atmosphere)* Verschlafenheit *f*

sleeping ['sli:pıŋ] ADJ schlafend; **Sleeping Beauty** Dornröschen *nt* N Schlafen *nt*; **between ~ and waking** zwischen Schlaf und Wachen

sleeping: **sleeping accommodation** N Schlafgelegenheit *f*; **sleeping bag** N Schlafsack *m*; **sleeping car** N Schlafwagen *m*; **sleeping draught**, *(US)* **sleeping draft** N Schlaftrunk *m*; **sleeping partner** N *(Brit)* stiller Teilhaber *or* Gesellschafter; **sleeping pill** N Schlaftablette *f*; **sleeping policeman** N *(= traffic bump)* (fahrdynamische) Schwelle, Bodenschwelle *f*; **sleeping quarters** PL Schlafräume *pl*, Schlafsaal *m*; **sleeping sickness** N Schlafkrankheit *f*; **sleeping tablet** N Schlaftablette *f*

sleepless ['sli:plıs] ADJ schlaflos

sleeplessness ['sli:plısnıs] N Schlaflosigkeit *f*

sleep: **sleepover** N Übernachtung *f (bei Freunden, Bekannten etc)*; **sleepwalk** VI schlafwandeln; **he was ~ing** er hat *or* ist geschlafwandelt; **sleepwalker** N Schlafwandler(in) *m(f)*; **sleepwalking** N Schlafwandeln *nt* ATTR schlafwandlerisch; **sleepwear** ['sli:pwɛəʳ] N Nachtwäsche *f*

sleepy ['sli:pı] ADJ (+er) **a** *(= drowsy) person, voice etc* müde, schläfrig; *(= not yet awake)* verschlafen; **to be/look ~** müde sein/aussehen; **I feel very ~ by midnight** gegen Mitternacht bin ich schon sehr müde **b** *(= inactive) person* lahm *(inf)*, müde; *place, atmosphere* verschlafen; *climate* schläfrig machend; *afternoons* schläfrig

sleepyhead ['sli:pıhed] N *(inf)* Schlafmütze *f (inf)*

sleet [sli:t] N Schneeregen *m* VI **it was ~ing** es gab Schneeregen

sleeve [sli:v] N **a** *(on garment)* Ärmel *m*; **to roll up one's ~s** *(lit)* sich *(dat)* die Ärmel hochkrempeln; *(fig)* die Ärmel aufkrempeln *(inf)*; **to have sth up one's ~** *(fig inf)* etw in petto haben *or* auf Lager haben → **laugh** **b** *(for record, on book)* Hülle *f* **c** *(Tech)* Muffe *f*, Manschette *f*

-sleeved [-sli:vd] ADJ *suf* -ärmelig; **long-sleeved** langärmelig; **short-sleeved** kurzärmelig

sleeveless ['sli:vlıs] ADJ ärmellos

sleigh [sleı] N (Pferde)schlitten *m*; **~ bell** Schlittenglocke *f*; **~ ride** Schlittenfahrt *f*

sleighing ['sleııŋ] N Schlittenfahren *nt*

sleight [slaıt] N **~ of hand** Fingerfertigkeit *f*; **by ~ of hand** durch Taschenspielertricks

slender ['slendəʳ] ADJ schlank; *hand, waist also* schmal; *resources, income* knapp, mager; *chance, hope* schwach, gering; *excuse, profit margin* dürftig, schwach; *lead, majority* knapp, gering

slenderize ['slendəraız] VT *(US)* schlank machen

slenderly ['slendəlı] ADV **~ built** *or* **made** schlank

slenderness ['slendənıs] N Schlankheit *f*; *(of hand, waist also)* Schmalheit *f*; *(fig) (of chance, hope)* Schwäche *f*; *(of excuse)* Dürftigkeit *f*; *(of lead, majority)* Knappheit *f*; **the ~ of his income** sein geringes Einkommen

slept [slept] *pret, ptp of* **sleep**

sleuth [slu:θ] N *(inf)* Spürhund *m (inf)* VI Detektiv spielen

slew[1], *(US)* **slue** [slu:] *(also* **slew round)** VT *crane, lorry* (herum)schwenken; *head* drehen; **to ~ sth to the left** etw nach links schwenken VI (herum)schwenken; **to ~ to the left/right** nach links/rechts schwenken

slew[2], *(US)* **slue** N *(inf)* Haufen *m (inf)*

slew[3] *pret of* **slay**

slewed [slu:d] ADJ *pred (inf)* voll *(inf)*, besoffen *(inf)*; **to get ~** sich vollaufen lassen *(inf)*

slice [slaıs] N **a** *(lit) (of cake, lemon, meat etc)* Scheibe *f*; *(of bread)* Scheibe *f*, Schnitte *f* **b** *(fig: = portion, of population, profits)* Teil *m*; *(of land)* Stück *nt*; **a ~ of life in contemporary Paris** ein Ausschnitt *m* aus dem Leben im heutigen Paris; **a ~ of luck** eine Portion Glück; **that was a ~ of luck!** das war ein glücklicher Zufall **c** *(esp Brit: = food server)* Wender *m*; **cake ~** Tortenheber *m* **d** *(Sport)* angeschnittener Ball; **to put a bit of ~ on the ball** den Ball etwas anschneiden VT **a** *(= cut)* durchschneiden; *bread, meat etc* (in Scheiben) schneiden; **to ~ sth in two** etw durchschneiden, etw in zwei Teile schneiden **b** *ball* (an)schneiden VI **a** *(= cut)* schneiden; **to ~ through sth** etw durchschneiden **b** *(Sport)* schneiden

▶**slice off** VT *sep* **a** abschneiden; **he sliced off the top of his egg** er köpfte sein Ei *(inf)* **b** *money, time* wegnehmen; **he sliced £1000 off the total cost** er hat die Gesamtkosten noch um £ 1000 gesenkt; **he sliced 4 seconds off the world record** er hat den Weltrekord um 4 Sekunden unterboten

▶**slice up** VT *sep* (ganz) in Scheiben schneiden; *bread, meat, sausage also* aufschneiden; *(= divide)* aufteilen

sliced [slaıst] ADJ (in Scheiben) geschnitten; *loaf, bread, sausage* (auf)geschnitten; **he/it is the best thing since ~ bread** *(inf)* so jemanden/etwas hat die Welt schon lange nicht mehr gesehen *(inf)*

slicer ['slaısəʳ] N *(= cheese-slicer, cucumber-slicer etc)* Hobel *m*; *(= machine, = bread-slicer)* Brot(schneide)maschine *f*, Brotschneider *m*; *(= bacon-slicer)* ≈ Wurstschneidemaschine *f*

slick [slık] ADJ (+er) **a** *(often pej: = clever)* gewieft *(inf)*, clever *(inf)*; *answer, solution* glatt; *show, performance, translation, style* glatt, professionell; **a ~ novel** ein glatt *or* professionell geschriebener Roman; **a ~ customer** ein ganz gewiefter Kerl *(inf)* **b** *hair* geschniegelt **c** *(US: = slippery)* glatt, schlüpfrig N **a** *(= oil slick)* (Öl)teppich *m*, Schlick *nt* **b** *(US inf: = glossy)* Hochglanzmagazin *nt* **c** *(= racing tyre)* Slick *m (inf)*

▶**slick back** VT *sep* **to slick one's hair back** sich *(dat)* die Haare anklatschen *(inf)*; **the slicked-back hairstyles of the 50s** die geschniegelten Frisuren der 50er Jahre

slicker ['slıkəʳ] N *(US)* **a** *(= coat)* Regenjacke *f* **b** *(inf, = swindler)* Gauner *m (inf)*, Ganove *m (inf)* **c** → **city slicker**

slickly ['slıklı] ADV *(often pej: = cleverly)* gewieft *(inf)*, clever *(inf)*; *answer, perform, write, translate* glatt

slickness ['slıknıs] N **a** *(often pej: = cleverness)* Gewieftheit *f (inf)*, Cleverness *f (inf)*; *(of performance, style, writing)* Glattheit *f*; **we were impressed by the ~ with which he answered** wir waren davon beeindruckt, wie glatt er antwortete **b** *(of appearance)* geschniegeltes Aussehen

slide [slaıd] *vb: pret, ptp* **slid** [slıd] N **a** *(= place for sliding, chute)* Rutschbahn *f*; *(in playground, for logs etc)* Rutsche *f* **b** *(fig: = fall, drop)* Abfall *m*; **the ~ in share prices** der Preisrutsch bei den Aktien; **his slow ~ into alcoholism** sein langsamer Abstieg zum Alkoholiker **c** *(= landslide)* Rutsch *m*, Rutschung *f (spec)* **d** *(of trombone)* Zug *m*; *(= sequence of notes)* Schleifer *m* **e** *(Tech, = part)* gleitendes Teil, Schlitten *m* **f** *(esp Brit, for hair)* Spange *f* **g** *(Phot)* Dia *nt*, Diapositiv *nt (form)*; *(= microscope slide)* Objektträger *m*; **a lecture with ~s** ein Diavortrag *m*, ein Lichtbildervortrag *m* VT *(= push)* schieben; *(= slip)* gleiten lassen; **he slid the gun into the holster** er ließ den Revolver ins Halfter gleiten; **to ~ the drawer (back) into place** die Schublade (wieder) zurückschieben VI **a** *(= slip)* rutschen; **to ~ down the banisters** das Treppengeländer hinunterrutschen; **suddenly it all slid into place** plötzlich passte alles zusammen **b** *(= move smoothly: machine part etc)* sich schieben lassen; **it slid into its place** es glitt *or* rutschte an die richtige Stelle **c** *(person)* schleichen; **he slid into the room** er kam ins Zimmer geschlichen **d** *(fig)* **the days slid past** die Tage schwanden dahin *(geh)*; **to ~ into bad habits** (allmählich) in schlechte Gewohnheiten verfallen; **to let sth ~** etw schleifen lassen, etw vernachlässigen; **to let things ~** die Dinge laufen *or* schleifen lassen

slide: **slide area** N *Gebiet, in dem es zu Rutschungen kommt*; **"slide area"** *(road sign)* „Vorsicht Erdrutschgefahr"; **slide bar** N *(Tech)* Gleitschiene *f*; **slide control** N Schieberegler *m*

slider ['slaıde/r/] N *(Comput: in dialog box)* Schieberegler *m*

slide: **slide fastener** N *(US)* Reißverschluss *m*; **slide film** N Diafilm *m*; **slide projector** N Diaprojektor *m*; **slide rule** N Rechenschieber *m*; **slide show** N Diavortrag *m*; **slide tackle** N *(Ftbl)* Grätsche *f*

sliding ['slaıdıŋ] ADJ *part* gleitend

sliding: **sliding contact** N *(Elec)* Schleifkontakt *m*; **sliding door** N Schiebetür *f*; **sliding roof** N Schiebedach *nt*; **sliding scale** N gleitende Skala; **sliding seat** N verschiebbarer Sitz, Schiebesitz *m*; *(in rowing boat)* Rollsitz *m*; **sliding tackle** N *(Ftbl)* Grätsche *f*

slight [slaıt] ADJ (+er) **a** *person, build* zierlich; **to be of ~ build** eine schlanke *or* zierliche Figur haben **b** *(= small, trivial)* leicht; *change, possibility* geringfügig; *importance, intelligence* gering; *error* leicht, klein; *problem* klein; *pain* leicht, schwach; *acquaintance* flüchtig; **the wound is only ~** es ist nur eine leichte Verwundung; **the wall's at a ~ angle** die Mauer ist leicht *or* etwas geneigt; **to have a ~ cold** eine leichte Erkältung haben; **to a ~ extent** in geringem Maße; **he showed some ~ optimism** er zeigte gewisse Ansätze von Optimismus; **just the ~est bit short** ein ganz kleines bisschen zu kurz; **it doesn't make the ~est bit of difference** es macht nicht den geringsten *or* mindesten Unterschied; **I wasn't the ~est bit interested** ich war nicht im Geringsten *or* Mindesten *or* mindesten interessiert; **nobody showed the ~est interest** niemand zeigte auch nur das geringste Interesse; **the ~est optimism** das geringfügigste Zeichen von Optimismus; **the ~est criticism/possibility** die geringste Kritik/Möglichkeit; **he is upset by at the ~est thing** er ist wegen jeder kleins-

ten Kleinigkeit gleich verärgert; **I haven't the ~est idea** ich habe nicht die geringste *or* leiseste *(inf)* Ahnung; **I don't have the ~est idea (of) what he's talking about** ich habe nicht die geringste *or* leiseste Ahnung, wovon er redet; **not in the ~est** nicht im Geringsten *or* Mindesten *or* mindesten *(geh)*; **without the ~est difficulty** ohne die kleinste *or* mindeste Schwierigkeit; **without the ~est hint of embarrassment** ohne das geringste Anzeichen von Verlegenheit; **to do sth at the ~est provocation** etw bei der geringsten Provokation tun
N *(= affront)* Affront *m* *(on* gegen); **a ~ on one's/sb's character** eine persönliche Kränkung *or* Beleidigung
VT *(= offend)* kränken, beleidigen; *(= ignore)* ignorieren; **to feel ~ed** gekränkt *or* beleidigt sein

slighting ['slaɪtɪŋ] **ADJ** *(= offensive)* kränkend; *(= disparaging) behaviour* geringschätzig; *remark* abschätzig, abfällig

slightingly ['slaɪtɪŋlɪ] **ADV** *speak* abschätzig, abfällig; *treat* geringschätzig

slightly ['slaɪtlɪ] **ADV** **a** **~ built** *or* **made** *(person)* zierlich **b** *(= to a slight extent)* etwas, ein klein(es) bisschen; *know* flüchtig; *smell* leicht, etwas; **~ injured** leicht verletzt; **he hesitated ever so ~** er zögerte fast unmerklich

slightness ['slaɪtnɪs] **N** **a** *(of person, build)* Zierlichkeit *f* **b** *(= triviality)* Geringfügigkeit *f*; *(of acquaintance)* Flüchtigkeit *f*

slim [slɪm] **ADJ** *(+er)* **a** schlank; *ankle, waist etc* schmal; *volume* schmal, dünn **b** *resources, profits* mager; *excuse, hope* schwach; *chances* gering; *majority* knapp **VI** eine Schlankheitskur machen **VT** schlank(er) machen; *(fig) demands etc* schrumpfen

▶ **slim down** **VT** *sep* **a** *person* abnehmen lassen, schlank(er) machen **b** *(fig) business etc* verschlanken; *budget* kürzen **VI** **a** *(person)* abnehmen, abspecken *(inf)* **b** *(fig, business etc)* verschlanken, abspecken *(inf)*

slim disease **N** *in Afrika gebräuchlicher Ausdruck für Aids*

slimdown ['slɪmdaʊn] **N** *(of company)* Gesundschrumpfung *f*

slime [slaɪm] **N** Schleim *m*; **trail of ~** Schleimspur *f*

slimeball ['slaɪmbɔːl] **N** *(esp US pej inf)* schmierige Type *(inf)*, Ekeltyp *m (pej inf)*

sliminess ['slaɪmɪnɪs] **N** *(of liquid, secretion)* Schleimigkeit *f*; *(of stone, wall)* Glitschigkeit *f*; *(of hands)* Schmierigkeit *f*; *(fig: of person, smile)* Schleimigkeit *f*, Öligkeit *f*

slimline ['slɪmlaɪn] **ADJ** *diary* dünn; *mobile phone* flach; *figure* schlank

slimmer ['slɪmə'] **N** Kalorienzähler(in) *m(f)* *(hum)*; **special meals for ~s** spezielle Gerichte für Leute, die abnehmen wollen

slimming ['slɪmɪŋ] **ADJ** schlank machend *attr*; **crispbread/black is ~** Knäckebrot/schwarz macht schlank; **to be on a ~ diet** eine Schlankheitskur machen; **~ foods** kalorienarme Nahrungsmittel *pl* **N** Abnehmen *nt*; **is ~ really worth it?** lohnt es sich wirklich abzunehmen?

slimming club **N** Diätklub *m*, Schlankheitsklub *m*

slimming pill **N** Schlankheitspille *f*

slimnastics [ɔɔ] **N** **a** *sing (= discipline)* Schlankheitsgymnastik *f* **b** *pl (= exercises)* Schlankheitsgymnastik *f*

slimness ['slɪmnɪs] **N** **a** Schlankheit *f*; *(of ankle, waist etc)* Schmalheit *f*; *(of volume)* Dünne *f* **b** *(of resources, profits)* Magerkeit *f*; *(of majority)* Knappheit *f*; **because of the ~ of their chances** weil ihre Chancen so gering waren

slimy ['slaɪmɪ] **ADJ** *(+er) liquid, secretion* schleimig; *stone, wall* glitschig; *hands* schmierig; *(fig)* schleimig; *smile, person* ölig, schleimig; **~ trail** Schleimspur *m*

sling [slɪŋ] *vb: pret, ptp* **slung** **N** **a** *(Med)* Schlinge *f*; **to have one's arm in a ~** den Arm in der Schlinge tragen
b *(for hoisting)* Schlinge *f*, Schlaufe *f*; *(for rifle)* (Trag)riemen *m*; *(for baby)* (Baby)tragetuch *nt*, (Baby)trageschlinge *f*; **to carry a rifle/baby in a ~** ein Gewehr am Riemen/ein Baby in einer *or* der Schlinge tragen
c *(= weapon)* Schleuder *f*; **~s and arrows** *(fig)* Missgeschicke *pl*
VT **a** *(= throw)* schleudern; *(inf)* schmeißen *(inf)*; **to ~ sth away** etw wegschleudern/wegschmeißen *(inf)*; **to ~ sth over to sb** *(inf)* jdm etw zuschmeißen *(inf)*; **he slung the box onto his back** er warf sich *(dat)* die Kiste auf den Rücken; **to ~ one's hook** *(Brit fig inf)* Leine ziehen *(inf)*
b *(= hoist with a sling)* in einer Schlinge hochziehen
c *(= hang)* aufhängen

▶ **sling out** **VT** *sep (inf)* rausschmeißen *(inf)*

sling: **slingback** **ADJ** **~ shoes** Slingpumps *pl*; *(= sandals)* Sandaletten *pl* **N** **~s** Slings *pl*, Slingpumps *pl*; **sling bag** **N** *(US)* Schultertasche *f*; **slingshot** **N** *(US)* (Stein)schleuder *f*

slink [slɪŋk] *pret, ptp* **slunk** **VI** schleichen; **to ~ away** *or* **off** sich davonschleichen; **to ~ along the wall** sich an der Wand entlangdrücken; **to ~ off with one's tail between one's legs** *(fig inf)* mit eingezogenem Schwanz abziehen *(inf)*

slinky **ADJ** *(+er)*, **slinkily** **ADV** ['slɪŋkɪ, -lɪ] *(inf)* aufreizend; *walk etc also* katzenhaft

slip [slɪp] **N** **a** *(= slide)* **she had a nasty ~** sie ist ausgerutscht und bös gefallen
b *(= mistake)* Ausrutscher *m*, Patzer *m*; **to make a (bad) ~** sich (übel) vertun *(inf)*, einen (ganz schönen) Bock schießen *(inf)*; **a ~ of the pen** ein Flüchtigkeitsfehler *m*; **a ~ of the tongue** ein Versprecher *m*; **it was just a ~ of the pen** da habe ich mich nur verschrieben; **there's many a ~ ('twixt cup and lip)** *(Prov)* man soll den Tag nicht vor dem Abend loben *(Prov)*, zwischen Lipp und Kelchesrand (schwebt der finstern Mächte Hand) *(liter)*
c **to give sb the ~** *(inf: = escape)* jdm entwischen
d *(= pillow slip)* Kissenbezug *m*
e *(= undergarment)* Unterrock *m*; **waist ~** Halbunterrock *m*; **full-length ~** Unterkleid *nt*
f *(of paper)* Zettel *m*; **~s of paper** Zettel *pl*; **withdrawal ~** Auszahlungsschein *m*; **sales ~** Kassenzettel *m*
g *(inf: = person)* **a (mere) ~ of a girl** *(= slightly built)* ein zierliches Persönchen; *(= young)* eine halbe Portion *(inf)*
h *(Hort, for planting)* Steckling *m*; *(for grafting)* Reis *nt*
i *(Cricket, = position/area) Position/Gebiet neben dem Torwächter (= fielder)* Eckmann *m*
j **slips** **PL** *(Theat)* Bühnenloge *f*
k *(Pottery)* geschlämmter Ton
l *(Aviat, = side-slip)* Schlipp *m*
VT **a** *(= move smoothly)* schieben; *(= slide)* gleiten *or* rutschen lassen; **to ~ sth across to sb** jdm etw zuschieben; *(unobtrusively)* jdm etw zuschmuggeln; **she ~ped the dress over her head** sie streifte sich *(dat)* das Kleid über den Kopf; **to ~ one's arm round sb's waist** jdm den Arm um die Taille legen; **to ~ one over on sb** *(inf)* jdn reinlegen *(inf)*; **to ~ sb some money** *(inf)* jdm etwas Geld zustecken *(inf)*
b *(= escape from)* sich losreißen von; **the dog ~ped its lead** der Hund schlüpfte aus seinem Halsband; **the boat had ~ped its moorings** das Boot hatte sich losgerissen; **to ~ anchor** *(Naut)* den Anker kappen *(form)*; **it/his birthday ~ped my mind** *or* **memory** ich habe es/seinen Geburtstag vergessen *or* verschwitzt *(inf)*
c *(= loose)* losmachen; **he ~ped the dog from its chain** er machte den Hund (von der Kette) los
d *(Med)* **to ~ a disc** sich *(dat)* einen Bandscheibenschaden zuziehen; **a ~ped disc** ein Bandscheibenschaden *m*
e *(Aut) clutch* schleifen lassen
f **to ~ a stitch** eine Masche (ungestrickt) abheben
VI **a** *(= slide, person)* (aus)rutschen; *(feet, tyres)* (weg)rutschen; *(= become loose: knot, nut)* sich lösen; *(Aut: clutch)* schleifen; **the knife ~ped** das Messer rutschte ab; **it ~ped from her hand** es rutschte ihr aus der Hand; **the beads ~ped through my fingers** die Perlen glitten durch meine Finger; **money ~s through her fingers** das Geld rinnt ihr (nur so) durch die Finger; **to let sth ~ through one's fingers** sich *(dat)* etw entgehen lassen; **the police let the thief ~ through their fingers** die Polizei ließ sich *(dat)* den Dieb in letzter Minute durch die Finger schlüpfen; **suddenly everything ~ped into place** plötzlich passte alles zusammen
b *(= move quickly)* schlüpfen; *(= move smoothly)* rutschen; **I'll ~ round to the shop** ich spring schnell zum Laden; **the motorcycle ~s through the traffic** das Motorrad schlängelt sich durch den Verkehr
c **to let (it) ~ that ...** fallen lassen, dass ...; **he let ~ an oath** ihm entfuhr ein Fluch; **to let a secret ~** ein Geheimnis ausplaudern; **to let a chance ~** eine Gelegenheit vorübergehen lassen
d *(= decline: standards, morals etc)* fallen; **you're ~ping!** *(inf)* du lässt nach *(inf)*

▶ **slip away** **VI** sich wegschleichen, sich wegstehlen; *(time)* verstreichen, vergehen; *(chances)* (allmählich) schwinden; *(opportunity)* dahinschwinden; **her life was slipping away from her** ihr Leben schwand dahin

▶ **slip back** **VI** **a** *(= return unobtrusively)* unbemerkt zurückgehen; *(quickly)* schnell zurückgehen **b** *(= deteriorate, production)* zurückgehen; *(patient)* einen Rückfall haben

▶ **slip by** **VI** *(= pass unobtrusively, person)* sich vorbeischleichen *or* vorbeischmuggeln *(prep obj* an *+dat)*; *(mistake)* durchgehen; *(years)* verfliegen, nur so dahinschwinden

▶ **slip down** **VI** *(= fall)* ausrutschen, ausgleiten; *(= go down)* hinunterlaufen; **this wine slips down easily** dieser Wein rutscht *or* kullert so schön (die Kehle hinunter) *(inf)*

▶ **slip in** **VI** *(= enter unobtrusively)* (sich) hineinschleichen; *(burglar also, mistake)* sich einschleichen **VT** *sep* **a** **to slip sth into sb's pocket** jdm etw in die Tasche gleiten lassen; **to slip a coin into a slot** eine Münze einwerfen; **she slipped the car into first gear** sie legte den ersten Gang ein **b** *(= mention casually)* einfließen lassen

▶ **slip off** **VI** sich wegschleichen, sich wegstehlen **VT** *sep clothes, shoes* ausziehen, abstreifen

▶ **slip on** **VT** *sep* schlüpfen in *(+acc)*; *dress, gloves also* überstreifen, überziehen; *ring* aufziehen; *lid* drauftun *(prep obj* auf *+acc)*; **he slipped the ring onto her finger** er steckte ihr den Ring an den Finger

▶ **slip out** **VI** **a** *(= leave unobtrusively)* kurz weggehen *or* rausgehen **b** *(= be revealed)* herauskommen; **the secret slipped out** das Geheimnis ist ihm/ihr *etc* herausgerutscht

▶ **slip past** **VI** = **slip by**

▶ **slip up** **VI** *(inf: = err)* sich vertun *(inf)*, (einen) Schnitzer machen *(over, in* bei); **you really slipped up there!** da hast du aber wirklich Murks gemacht *(inf)*; **he usually slips up on spelling** meistens stolpert er über die Rechtschreibung *(inf)*

slip: **slipcase** **N** Schuber *m*; **slipcover** **N** *(esp US)* Schonbezug *m*; **slipknot** **N** Schlippstek *m (spec)*; **slip-ons** **PL** *(also* **slip-on shoes**) Slipper *pl*; **slipover** **N** Pullunder *m*

slippage ['slɪpɪdʒ] **N** **a** *(fig)* Rückstand *m*; **to prevent ~** um Rückstände zu vermeiden **b** *(fig: = delay)* Verzögerung *f* **c** *(lit, fig: drop)* (Ab)sinken *nt*

slipper ['slɪpə'] **N** *(= bedroom slipper)* Pantoffel *m*, Hausschuh *m*; *(= dancing slipper)* Pumps *m*, Slipper *m*

slipperiness ['slɪpərɪnɪs] **N** **a** Schlüpfrigkeit *f*; *(of rope, road, ground, shoes)* Glätte *f*; *(of fish, mud)* Glitschigkeit *f* **b** *(pej inf, of person)* Glätte *f*, aalglatte Art

slippery ['slɪpərɪ] **ADJ** **a** schlüpfrig; *rope, road, ground* glatt, rutschig; *shoes* glatt; *fish, mud* glitschig; **the roads were ~ with ice** die Straßen waren eisglatt; **my hands were ~ with sweat** meine Hände waren ganz glitschig vor lauter Schweiß; **to be on ~ ground** *(fig)* sich auf unsicherem Boden bewegen; **he's on the ~ slope** *(fig)* er ist auf der schiefen Bahn; **it's a ~ slope** *(fig)* das ist ein gefährlicher Weg **b** *(pej inf) person* glatt, windig *(inf)*; **a ~ customer** ein aalglatter Kerl *(inf)*; **he's as ~ as they come** *or* **as an eel** er ist aalglatt

slippy [ˈslɪpɪ] ADJ *(inf)* **a** *(= slippery)* glatt **b** *(esp Brit)* **to look ~** einen Zahn zulegen *(inf)* *(about sth* bei etw*)*; **… and look ~ (about it)!** … und zwar flott *or* ein bisschen dalli! *(inf)*

slip-resistant ADJ *sole, socks etc* rutschfest, rutschsicher

slip road [ˈslɪprəʊd] N *(Brit)* Zufahrtsstraße *f*; *(for entering motorway)* (Autobahn)auffahrt *f*; *(for leaving motorway)* (Autobahn)ausfahrt *f*

slipshod [ˈslɪpʃɒd] ADJ schludrig

slip: **slipsole** [ˈslɪpsəʊl] N *(for shoes)* Einlegesohle *f*; **slipstream** N *(Aviat)* Sog *m*; *(Aut)* Windschatten *m*; **slip-up** N *(inf)* Schnitzer *m*; *(more serious)* Patzer *m*; **there's been a ~ somewhere** da muss irgendetwas schiefgelaufen sein; **slipway** N *(Aut)* Ablaufbahn *f*, Gleitbahn *f*

slit [slɪt] *vb: pret, ptp* **slit** N Schlitz *m*; *(in castle wall also)* Schießscharte *f* VT (auf)schlitzen; **to ~ a sack open** einen Sack aufschlitzen; **to ~ sb's throat** jdm die Kehle aufschlitzen

slit-eyed [ˈslɪtˈaɪd] ADJ *(pej)* schlitzäugig

slither [ˈslɪðəʳ] VI rutschen; *(snake)* gleiten; **to ~ about on the ice** auf dem Eis herumschlittern *or* -rutschen

slit: **slit pocket** N Durchgrifftasche *f*; **slit trench** N Splittergraben *m*

sliver [ˈslɪvəʳ] N *(of wood, glass etc)* Splitter *m*; *(= thin slice)* Scheibchen *nt*

Sloane (Ranger) [ˈsləʊn(ˈreɪndʒəʳ)] N *(dated Brit inf) wohlhabendes (weibliches) Mitglied der gehobenen Mittelklasse*

slob [slɒb] N *(inf)* Drecksau *f (inf)*

slob out VI *(inf)* herumfaulenzen

slobber [ˈslɒbəʳ] N Sabber *m (inf)* VI sabbern, sabbeln *(also fig)*; *(dog)* geifern; **to ~ over sb** *(fig inf)* von jdm schwärmen; *(= kiss)* jdn abküssen; **to ~ over sth** *(fig inf)* etw anschmachten; *(dirty old man etc)* sich an etw *(dat)* aufgeilen *(sl)*

slobbery [ˈslɒbərɪ] ADJ *(inf)* nass; **the newspaper is all ~** die Zeitung ist ganz vollgesabbert *(inf)*

sloe [sləʊ] N *(= fruit)* Schlehe *f*; *(= tree)* Schlehdorn *m*; **~ gin** Schlehdornschnaps *m*

sloe-eyed [ˈsləʊˈaɪd] ADJ *person* dunkeläugig

slog [slɒg] *(inf)* N **a** *(= effort)* Schinderei *f*, Plackerei *f (inf)*; **it's a long ~ to the top of the hill** es ist eine ganz schöne Schinderei *or* Plackerei *(inf)*, bis man oben ist **b** *(= stroke)* wuchtiger Schlag; **to take a ~ at sb/sth** auf jdn/etw (ein)dreschen VT *ball* dreschen *(inf)*; *opponent* hart schlagen *or* treffen VI **a** **to ~ at sth** *(= hit)* auf etw *(acc)* (ein)dreschen *(inf)*; *(= work)* an etw *(dat)* schuften *(inf)*; **to ~ away (at sth)** sich (mit etw) abrackern **b** *(= walk)* **to ~ on/along** sich weiter-/dahinschleppen

slogan [ˈsləʊgən] N Slogan *m*; *(= motto)* Motto *nt*, Wahlspruch *m*; *(political)* Parole *f*, Slogan *m*; **advertising ~** Werbeslogan *m*, Werbespruch *m*

sloganeering [ˌsləʊgəˈnɪərɪŋ] N *Einsatz von Werbe- bzw. Wahlslogans*

slogger [ˈslɒgəʳ] N *(Brit inf)* Arbeitstier *nt (inf)*

slo-mo [ˌsləʊˈməʊ] *(inf) abbr of* **slow motion**

sloop [sluːp] N Slup *f*, Schlup *f*

slop [slɒp] VI **a** *(= spill)* (über)schwappen; **to ~ over (into sth)** überschwappen (in etw *acc*) **b** **to ~ around** *(= splash)* herumschwappen *(inf)*; *(fig inf, in slippers etc)* herumschlurfen VT *(= spill)* verschütten; *(= pour out)* schütten N **a** *(inf: sentimental)* rührseliges Zeug, Schmalz *m* **b** *(= tasteless food: also* **slops***)* Schlabber *m (inf)* **c** *(usu pl, = waste)* Schmutzwasser *nt*, Abwasser *nt*; *(= swill)* Schweinetrank *m*

▶ **slop out** VI *(in prison etc)* den/die Toiletteneimer (aus)leeren

slop basin, **slop bowl** N Abgussschale *f (Teil des Teeservice, in das Teereste gegossen werden)*

slope [sləʊp] N **a** *(= angle)* Neigung *f*; *(esp downwards)* Gefälle *nt*; *(of roof)* Schräge *f* **b** *(= sloping ground)* (Ab)hang *m*; **on a ~** am Hang; **halfway up the ~** auf halber Höhe; **there is a ~ down to the town** es fällt zur Stadt hin ab; **he broke his leg on the (ski) ~s** er hat sich das Bein auf der Piste gebrochen **c** *(Mil)* **with his rifle at the ~** mit geschultertem Gewehr VT neigen, schräg (an)legen; **~ arms!** *(Mil)* schultert Gewehr! VI **a** *(writing)* geneigt sein; *(road, garden, floor, roof, ground)* sich neigen; **the picture is sloping to the left/right** das Bild hängt schief; **his handwriting ~s to the left/backwards** seine Handschrift ist nach links/nach hinten geneigt **b** *(inf: = move casually)* schlendern *(inf)*

▶ **slope away** VI **a** *(ground, roof)* abfallen **b** *(inf: = slip away)* abziehen *(inf)*

▶ **slope down** VI sich neigen, abfallen

▶ **slope off** VI *(inf)* abziehen *(inf)*

▶ **slope up** VI **a** *(road etc)* ansteigen **b** *(inf: person)* herschlendern; **to slope up to sb** auf jdn zuschlendern

sloping [ˈsləʊpɪŋ] ADJ *hill, road (upwards)* ansteigend; *(downwards)* abfallend; *roof, floor* schräg, geneigt; *shoulders* abfallend; *garden, field etc* am Hang; *(= not aligned)* schief

slop pail N Eimer *m* für Schmutzwasser

sloppily [ˈslɒpɪlɪ] ADV *(inf: = carelessly)* schlampig *(inf)*; *work* nachlässig, schlud(e)rig *(inf)*; **to write/talk ~** nachlässig *or* schlampig *(inf)* schreiben/sprechen

sloppiness [ˈslɒpɪnɪs] N *(inf)* **a** *(= carelessness)* Schlampigkeit *f (inf)*; *(of work, writing)* Nachlässigkeit *f*, Schlud(e)rigkeit *f (inf)* **b** *(= sentimentality: of film, book)* Rührseligkeit *f*

slopping out [ˈslɒpɪŋˈaʊt] N *(in prison etc) Ausleeren von Toiletteneimern in Gefängnissen*

sloppy [ˈslɒpɪ] ADJ *(+er) (inf)* **a** *(= careless)* schlampig *(inf)*; *work, writing* nachlässig, schlud(e)rig *(inf)* **b** *(= sentimental)* rührselig; *film, novel also* schmalzig

sloppy joe N **a** *(= pullover)* Schlabberpullover *m (inf)* **b** *(US inf: = burger) Hamburger mit soßenartiger Hackfleisch-Tomaten-Füllung*

slopshop [ˈslɒpʃɒp] N *(pej)* Laden *m* mit billiger Konfektionsware

slosh [slɒʃ] *(inf)* VT **a** *(Brit, = hit) person* eine schmieren *(+dat) (inf)*; *ball* dreschen **b** *(= splash)* klatschen; **don't ~ the milk around** schwapp nicht so mit der Milch herum VI **to ~ (around)** *(liquid)* (herum)schwappen; **to ~ through mud/water** durch Matsch/Wasser waten

sloshed [slɒʃt] ADJ *pred (Brit inf)* blau *(inf)*, voll *(inf)*; **to get ~** sich besaufen *(inf)*

slot [slɒt] N *(= opening)* Schlitz *m*; *(= groove)* Rille *f*; *(Comput)* Slot *m*, Steckplatz *m*; *(for aircraft to land etc: = time slot)* Slot *m*; *(inf: = place)* Plätzchen *nt (inf)*; *(TV)* (gewohnte) Sendezeit; **do we have a ~ for this in our range?** können wir das in unser Programm einbauen?

▶ **slot in** VT *sep* hineinstecken; **to slot sth into sth** etw in etw *(acc)* stecken; **to slot sb/sth in** *(fig: = fit in)* jdn/etw dazwischenschieben; **to slot sb into the firm** jdn in der Firma unterbringen; **to slot in commercials** Werbespots einbauen VI sich einfügen lassen; **suddenly everything slotted into place** plötzlich passte alles zusammen

▶ **slot together** VI *(parts, object)* sich zusammenfügen lassen; *(fig, pieces of mystery etc)* sich zusammenfügen, zusammenpassen VT *sep parts, object* zusammenfügen

sloth [sləʊθ] N **a** *(= laziness)* Trägheit *f*, Faulheit *f* **b** *(Zool)* Faultier *nt*

slothful [ˈsləʊθfʊl] ADJ faul; *person, life also* träge

slothfully [ˈsləʊθfəlɪ] ADV faul

slothfulness [ˈsləʊθfʊlnɪs] N Trägheit *f*, Faulheit *f*

slot machine N Münzautomat *m*; *(for gambling)* Spielautomat *m*

slot meter N Münzzähler *m*

slotted spoon [ˈslɒtɪdˈspuːn] N Schaumlöffel *m*

slouch [slaʊtʃ] N **a** *(= posture)* krumme Haltung; *(of shoulders)* Hängen *nt*; *(= gait)* latschiger Gang *(inf)*; **to walk with a ~** latschen, latschig gehen *(inf)* **b** *(inf: = incompetent or lazy person)* Niete *f (inf)*; **to be no ~ at sth** etw ganz schön gut können *(inf)* VI *(= stand, sit)* herumhängen, sich lümmeln *(inf)*; *(= move)* latschen; **to ~ off** davonzockeln *(inf)*; **he was ~ed over his desk** er hing über seinem Schreibtisch, er war über seinen Schreibtisch gebeugt; **he sat ~ed on a chair** er hing auf einem Stuhl

slouch hat N Schlapphut *m*

slough[1] [slaʊ] N *(liter)* Morast *m*; *(= swamp also)* Sumpf *m (also fig liter)*; **to sink into the Slough of Despond** *(liter)* in tiefe Verzweiflung stürzen *(liter)*

slough[2] [slʌf] N *(Zool)* abgestreifte Haut; *(Med)* Schorf *m* VT *(snake) skin* abstreifen; **it ~s (off) its skin** sie häutet sich

▶ **slough off** VT *sep skin, cells* abstreifen; *habits, cares* abwerfen, abschütteln; *(hum) husband* den Laufpass geben *(+dat)*

Slovak [ˈsləʊvæk] ADJ slowakisch N **a** Slowake *m*, Slowakin *f* **b** *(Ling)* Slowakisch *nt*

Slovakia [sləʊˈvækɪə] N die Slowakei

Slovak Republic N Slowakische Republik, die Slowakei

sloven [ˈslʌvn] N Schlampe *f (pej inf)*; *(= man)* Schlamper *m (inf)*

Slovene [ˈsləʊviːn] ADJ slowenisch N **a** Slowene *m*, Slowenin *f*, Slowenier(in) *m(f)* **b** *(Ling)* Slowenisch *nt*

Slovenia [sləʊˈviːnɪə] N Slowenien *nt*

Slovenian [sləʊˈviːnɪən] ADJ, N = **Slovene**

slovenliness [ˈslʌvnlɪnɪs] N Schlampigkeit *f*; *(of person, work also)* Schlud(e)rigkeit *f (inf)*

slovenly [ˈslʌvnlɪ] ADJ schlud(e)rig *(inf)*, schlampig *(inf)*; *appearance, person also* verlottert *(inf)*

slow [sləʊ] ADJ *(+er)* **a** langsam; **it's ~ work** das braucht seine Zeit; **he's a ~ learner/reader** er lernt/liest langsam; **it was ~ going** es ging nur langsam voran; **to get off to a ~ start** *(race)* schlecht vom Start kommen; *(project)* nur langsam in Gang kommen; **at (a) ~ speed** mit langsamer Geschwindigkeit; **this method is ~ but sure** dieses Verfahren ist langsam, aber sicher; **to be ~ to do sth** sich *(dat)* mit etw Zeit lassen; **to be ~ in doing sth** sich *(dat)* Zeit damit lassen, etw zu tun; **not to be ~ to do sth** *or* **in doing sth** etw prompt erledigen; **he is ~ to make up his mind** er braucht lange, um sich zu entscheiden; **he is ~ to anger** er wird nicht so leicht wütend; **they were ~ to act** sie ließen sich *(dat)* Zeit; **to be (20 minutes) ~** *(clock)* (20 Minuten) nachgehen

b *(= stupid) person* langsam, begriffsstutzig → **uptake**

c *(= dull) person, place, event* langweilig

d *(Comm: = slack)* flau; **business is ~** das Geschäft ist flau *or* geht schlecht

e *(= unhurried)* ruhig; **life there is ~** das Leben dort ist ruhig

f *(= slowing down movement) surface, track, pitch* langsam; *(because of rain etc)* schwer; *(= slow-burning) fire* langsam brennend; **bake in a ~ oven** bei schwacher Hitze backen

ADV *(+er)* langsam; **to go ~** *(driver)* langsam fahren; *(workers)* einen Bummelstreik machen; **~-spoken** langsam sprechend; **"slow"** *(on sign)* „langsam fahren"

VI sich verlangsamen; *(= drive/walk more slowly)*

langsamer fahren/gehen; *(inflation)* abnehmen; **to ~ to a stop/standstill** langsam zum Halten/zum Stillstand kommen

VT verlangsamen; **he ~ed his horse to a walk** er ließ sein Pferd langsamer gehen; **he ~ed his speed to 30 miles an hour** er verminderte seine Geschwindigkeit auf 30 Meilen pro Stunde

▶ **slow down** *or* **up VI** sich verlangsamen; *(= drive/walk more slowly)* langsamer fahren/gehen; *(worker)* langsamer arbeiten; *(inflation)* abnehmen; **if you don't slow down** *or* **up you'll make yourself ill** Sie müssen zurückstecken, sonst werden Sie krank; **my mind has slowed down** ich werde immer langsamer im Denken **VT** *sep (lit)* verlangsamen; *engine* drosseln; *machine* herunterschalten; *(fig) project* verzögern, verlangsamen; **to slow the car down** langsamer fahren; **you just slow me up** *or* **down** du hältst mich nur auf; **we should slow things down** *or* **up** wir sollten etwas langsamer machen *(inf)*

slow: **slow-acting** ADJ *poison* langsam wirkend; *(Tech also)* träge (ansprechend); *medicine, therapy* Langzeit-; **slow-burning** ADJ *candle* langsam herunterbrennend; *fire also* langsam brennend; *(fig) rage, anger* schwelend; **~ stove** Dauerbrandofen *m*; **slowcoach** N *(Brit inf)* Langweiler(in) *m(f)*; *(mentally)* Transuse *f (inf)*; **slow cooker** N Reiskocher *m*; **slowdown** N **a** *(= slowing)* Verlangsamung *f (in, of +gen)* **b** *(US: = go-slow)* Bummelstreik *m*; **slow film** N unempfindlicher Film; **slow food** N *(Cook)* Slow Food *nt*; **slow fuse** N Zündschnur *f*; **slow handclap** N rhythmisches Klatschen *(zum Zeichen des Protests)*; **to give sb the/a ~** durch Klatschen gegen jdn protestieren; **slow lane** N *(Aut)* Kriechspur *f*; **life in the ~** *(fig)* das ruhige *or* gemächliche Leben

slowly [ˈsləʊlɪ] ADV langsam; **~ but surely** langsam aber sicher

slow: **slow march** N Trauermarsch *m*; **slow match** N *(Mil Hist)* Zündschnur *f*, Lunte *f*; **slow motion** N Zeitlupe *f*; **in ~** in Zeitlupe; **slow-motion** ADJ **a ~ shot** eine Einstellung in Zeitlupe; **slow-moving** ADJ sich (nur) langsam bewegend; *traffic* kriechend; *river* langsam fließend; *bureaucracy* träge, schwerfällig; *plot* langatmig; *film* langsam

slowness [ˈsləʊnɪs] N **a** Langsamkeit *f*; **their ~ to act** ihr Zaudern **b** *(= stupidity: of person)* Begriffsstutzigkeit *f*; **~ of mind** Begriffsstutzigkeit *f* **c** *(= inactivity: of party, film, plot)* Lahmheit *f*, Langweiligkeit *f* **d** *(Comm: = slackness)* Flaute *f* **e** *(slowing down movement) (of surface, track, pitch)* Langsamkeit *f*; *(because of rain etc)* Schwere *f*

slow: **slow poison** N schleichendes Gift; **slowpoke** N *(US inf)* = **slowcoach**; **slow puncture** N *(esp Brit)* langsam Luft ablassendes Loch *nt* in einem Reifen; **slow train** N *(Brit)* Personenzug *m*, Bummelzug *m (inf)*; **slow virus** N Slow-Virus *m*; **slow-witted** ADJ begriffsstutzig, schwer von Begriff; **slow-worm** N Blindschleiche *f*

sludge [slʌdʒ] N Schlamm *m*, Matsch *m (inf)*; *(= sediment)* schmieriger Satz

slue N, VTI *(US)* = **slew¹**, **slew²**

slug¹ [slʌg] N Nacktschnecke *f*; **~s and snails** Schnecken *pl* (mit und ohne Gehäuse)

slug² N **a** *(= bullet)* Kugel *f* **b** *(Typ, = piece of metal)* Reglette *f*; *(= line)* (Setzmaschinen)zeile *f* **c** *(inf)* **a ~ of whisky** ein Schluck *m* Whisky

slug³ *(inf: = hit)* **VT** (eine) knallen *(+dat) (inf)* **N** gehöriger *or* tüchtiger Schlag *(inf)*; **to give sb a ~** jdm eine knallen *(inf)*

slugabed [ˈslʌgəbed] N Langschläfer(in) *m(f)*

sluggard [ˈslʌgəd] N Faulpelz *m*

sluggardly [ˈslʌgədlɪ] ADJ faul, träge

slugger [ˈslʌgəˈ] N *(inf)* Schläger(in) *m(f) (inf)*; *(Baseball)* Schmetterer *m*

sluggish [ˈslʌgɪʃ] ADJ *(= indolent, also Med)* träge; *engine, car* lahm, langsam; *temperament* phlegmatisch; *steps* schwerfällig; *river* träge; *business* flau; *market, stock exchange* flau, lustlos

sluggishly [ˈslʌgɪʃlɪ] ADV *move, flow* träge; *walk* schwerfällig; *(Comm)* flau, lustlos

sluggishness [ˈslʌgɪʃnɪs] N *(= indolence, also Med)* Trägheit *f*; *(of engine, car)* Lahmheit *f*; *(of temperament)* Phlegma *nt*; *(of steps, pace)* Schwerfälligkeit *f*; *(of river)* Trägheit *f*; **the ~ of the market** die Flaute am Markt; **the ~ of the business** die geschäftliche Flaute

sluice [sluːs] **N** Schleuse *f*; *(Min)* (Wasch)rinne *f*; **to give the car/wall a ~ down** Wasser über das Auto/gegen die Wand schütten; *(with hose)* das Auto/die Wand abspritzen **VT** *ore* waschen; **to ~ sth (down)** etw abspritzen **VI** **to ~ out** herausschießen

sluice: **sluicegate** [ˈsluːsgeɪt] N Schleusentor *nt*; **sluiceway** N (Schleusen)kanal *m*

slum [slʌm] **N** *(usu pl: = area)* Slum *m*, Elendsviertel *nt*; *(= house)* Elendsquartier *nt*; **to live in the ~s** in den Slums leben **VI** *(also* **go slumming***)* sich unters gemeine Volk mischen **VTI** *(inf: also* **slum it***)* primitiv leben; **we don't often see you (a)round here – I'm ~ming (it)** du lässt dich doch sonst kaum hier sehen! – ich will mich eben mal unters gemeine Volk mischen

slumber [ˈslʌmbəˈ] *(liter)* **N** Schlummer *m (geh)*, Schlaf *m*; **~s** Schlummer *m*, Träume *pl*; *(fig: intellectual etc)* Dornröschenschlaf *m*; **to disturb sb's ~s** jds Schlummer stören **VI** schlummern *(geh)*

slumb(e)rous [ˈslʌmb(ə)rəs] ADJ *(liter: = sleepy)* schläfrig; *(= inducing sleep)* einschläfernd, einlullend

slumber party N *(esp US)* *Party, bei der Jugendliche im Elternhaus eines Teilnehmers feiern und anschließend auch dort schlafen*

slum: **slum children** PL Slumkinder *pl*; **slum clearance** N ≈ (Stadt)sanierung *f*, Beseitigung *f* der Slums; **slum dweller** N Slumbewohner(in) *m(f)*

slummy [ˈslʌmɪ] ADJ *(+er) (inf)* verwahrlost; **~ district** Slumgegend *f*

slump [slʌmp] **N** *(in sth* etw *gen) (in numbers, popularity, morale etc)* (plötzliche) Abnahme; *(in production, sales)* Rückgang *m*; *(= state)* Tiefstand *m*; *(Fin)* Sturz *m*, Baisse *f (spec)*; *(of prices)* plötzliches Absinken; **~ in prices** Preissturz *m* (of bei); **the 1929 Slump** die Weltwirtschaftskrise von 1929

VI **a** *(also* **slump off***, Fin, Comm, prices)* stürzen, fallen; *(sales, production)* plötzlich zurückgehen; *(fig, morale etc)* sinken, fallen **b** *(= sink)* fallen, sinken; **to ~ into a chair** sich in einen Sessel fallen *or* plumpsen *(inf)* lassen; **he was ~ed over the wheel** er war über dem Steuer zusammengesackt; **he was ~ed on the floor** er lag in sich *(dat)* zusammengesunken auf dem Fußboden

slum schools PL Schulen *pl* in den Slums

slung [slʌŋ] *pret, ptp of* **sling**

slunk [slʌŋk] *pret, ptp of* **slink**

slur [slɜːˈ] **N** **a** Makel *m*, Schandfleck *m*; *(= insult)* Beleidigung *f*; **to cast a ~ on sb/sth** jdn/etw in schlechtem Licht erscheinen lassen; *(person)* jdn/etw verunglimpfen; **it is no ~ on him to say that ...** es geht nicht gegen ihn, wenn man sagt, dass ... **b** *(Mus, = mark)* Bindebogen *m*; *(= notes)* Bindung *f* **c** **to speak with a ~** unartikuliert sprechen **VT** **a** *(= pronounce indistinctly)* undeutlich artikulieren; *words, syllable* (halb) verschlucken, verschleifen **b** *(Mus)* binden, gebunden spielen/singen

▶ **slur over** VI *+prep obj* hinweggehen über *(+acc)*

slurp [slɜːp] **VTI** *(inf)* schlürfen **N** Schlürfen *nt*; **to drink sth with a ~** etw schlürfen

slurred [slɜːd] **ADJ** undeutlich; *(Mus) note* gebunden **ADV** *(Mus)* gebunden

slush [slʌʃ] N *(= watery snow)* (Schnee)matsch *m*; *(= mud)* Matsch *m*, Morast *m*; *(inf: = sentimental nonsense)* Kitsch *m*

slush fund N Schmiergelder *pl*, Schmiergeldfonds *m*

slush pile N *(Publishing inf)* *unaufgefordert eingesandte Manuskripte*

slushy [ˈslʌʃɪ] ADJ *(+er) snow* matschig; *mud, path also* morastig; *(inf: = sentimental)* kitschig

slut [slʌt] *(inf)* N (liederliche) Schlampe *(inf)*

sluttish [ˈslʌtɪʃ] ADJ liederlich

sly [slaɪ] **ADJ** *(+er)* **a** *(= cunning)* schlau, gerissen; *person, look also* verschlagen **b** *(= mischievous) look, wink* verschmitzt; *humour* versteckt **N** **on the ~** heimlich, still und leise *(hum)*, ganz heimlich

slyboots [ˈslaɪbuːts] N *pl* **-boots** *(inf)* Schlauberger(in) *m(f) (inf, hum)*

slyly [ˈslaɪlɪ] ADV **a** *(= cunningly)* schlau; *say, look at* listig **b** *(= mischievously) look, wink* verschmitzt

slyness [ˈslaɪnɪs] N **a** *(= cunning)* Schlauheit *f*, Gerissenheit *f*; *(of person, look also)* Verschlagenheit *f* **b** *(= mischievousness: of look)* Verschmitztheit *f*

smack¹ [smæk] **N** *(= taste)* (leichter) Geschmack *(of* nach*)*, Spur *f (of* von*)*; *(= smell)* (leichter) Geruch *(of* nach*)*, Hauch *m (of* von*)*; *(fig)* Spur *f (of* von*)* **VI** **to ~ of** *(= taste)* leicht schmecken nach; *(= smell)* leicht riechen nach; *(fig)* riechen nach

smack² **N** **a** (klatschender) Schlag; *(= slap also)* fester Klaps; *(= sound)* Klatschen *nt*; **to give a child a (hard) ~** einem Kind eine knallen *(inf)*; **you'll get a ~** du fängst gleich eine *(inf)*; **a ~ in the eye** *(fig)* ein Schlag *m* ins Gesicht **b** *(inf: = kiss)* **to give sb a ~ on the cheek** jdn einen Schmatz auf die Backe geben *(inf)*

VT *(= slap)* knallen *(inf)*; **to ~ a child** einem Kind eine runterhauen *(inf)*; **to ~ sb's face** jdn ins Gesicht schlagen; **to ~ one's hands (together)** in die Hände klatschen; **to ~ one's thigh** sich *(dat)* auf den Schenkel klatschen; **I'll ~ your bottom, you'll get a ~ed bottom** ich versohl dir gleich den Hintern! *(inf)*; **to ~ sb in the chops** *(inf)* jdm eins reinsemmeln *(inf)* → **lip**

ADV *(inf)* direkt; **he kissed her ~ on the lips** er gab ihr einen Schmatzer *(inf)*; **she ran ~ into the door** sie rannte rums! gegen die Tür *(inf)*; **~ in front of sth** genau vor etw *(dat)*; **to be ~ in the middle of sth** mittendrin in etw *(dat)* sein; **the office was ~ in the middle of the building site** das Büro befand sich mitten auf der Baustelle; **~ on 4 o'clock** Punkt 4 Uhr

smack³ N *(inf: = heroin)* Heroin *nt*

smack⁴ N *(Naut)* Schmack(e) *f*

smacker [ˈsmækəˈ] N *(inf)* **a** *(= kiss)* Schmatzer *m (inf)* **b** *(= money)* Pfund *nt*; Dollar *m* **c** *(Brit sl: = face)* Fresse *f (vulg)*

smackhead [ˈsmækhed] N *(sl)* Heroinfixer(in) *m(f)*

smacking [ˈsmækɪŋ] N Tracht *f* Prügel; **to give sb a good ~** jdn tüchtig verdreschen *(inf)*

small [smɔːl] **ADJ** *(+er)* **a** klein; *supply, stock* klein, gering; *waist* schmal; *(= not much) reason, desire* wenig, gering; *effort* gering; **~ in size** von geringer Größe, klein; **a ~ number of people** eine geringe Anzahl von Leuten; **the ~est possible number of books** so wenig Bücher wie möglich; **to have a ~ appetite** keinen großen Appetit haben; **it's written with a ~ "e"** es wird mit kleinem „e" geschrieben; **~ shareholder** Kleinaktionär(in) *m(f)*; **no ~ success** ein beachtlicher Erfolg; **to feel ~** *(fig)* sich (ganz) klein (und hässlich) vorkommen; **to look ~** *(fig)* schlecht aussehen *or* dastehen; **he/it made me feel pretty ~** da kam ich mir ziemlich klein vor; **to be of ~ concern to sb** jdn nur wenig betreffen

b *(= unimportant, minor)* klein; *present, sum* klein, bescheiden; *importance, consequence* gering; **a few ~ matters/problems** ein paar Kleinigkeiten; **to be of no ~ consequence** nicht unbeträchtliche Folgen haben; **this is no ~ matter** das ist keine Kleinigkeit; **to help/contribute in a ~ way** bescheidene Hilfe/einen bescheidenen Beitrag leisten; **to start in a ~ way** bescheiden *or* klein anfangen

c *(= quiet) voice* leise; **to say sth in a ~ voice** etw mit leiser Stimme sagen
d *(fig: = mean, petty) person* kleinlich
N a the ~ of the back das Kreuz
b smalls **PL** *(Brit inf)* Unterwäsche *f*
ADV to chop sth up ~ etw klein hacken

small: **small ads** PL *(Brit)* Kleinanzeigen *pl*; **small arms** PL Handfeuerwaffen *pl*; **small beer** N *(old)* Dünnbier *nt*; **he's very ~** *(inf)* er ist ein kleiner Fisch *(inf)*; **small-bore** ADJ kleinkalibrig; **small business** N Kleinunternehmen *nt*; **small businessman** N Kleinunternehmer *m*; **small capitals** PL Kapitälchen *pl*; **small change** N Kleingeld *nt*; **small claims court** N Zivilgericht *nt (für Bagatellfälle)*; **small fry** PL *(= unimportant people)* kleine Fische *pl (inf)*; **smallholder** N Kleinbauer *m*, Kleinbäuerin *f*; **smallholding** N kleiner Landbesitz; **small hours** PL früher Morgen; **in the (wee) ~** in den frühen Morgenstunden; **small intestine** N Dünndarm *m*

smallish ['smɔːlɪʃ] ADJ (eher) kleiner; **he is ~** er ist eher klein; **a ~ number of sth/people** eine geringe Anzahl an etw *(dat)*/von Leuten

small: **small letter** N Kleinbuchstabe *m*; **small-minded** ADJ *person, attitude* engstirnig; **small-mindedness** N Engstirnigkeit *f*

smallness ['smɔːlnɪs] N Kleinheit *f*; *(of sum, present)* Bescheidenheit *f*; *(= pettiness)* Kleinlichkeit *f*

small: **small potatoes** PL *(esp US fig inf)* kleine Fische *pl (inf)*; **smallpox** N Pocken *pl*, Blattern *pl (old)*; **smallpox vaccination** N Pockenimpfung *f*; **small print** N **the ~** das Kleingedruckte; **in ~** klein gedruckt; **small-scale** ADJ *map, model* in verkleinertem Maßstab; *project, study* klein angelegt; *war, conflict* begrenzt; **~ farmers** Kleinbauern *pl*; **~ industry** Kleinindustrie *f*; **~ integration** *(Comput)* niedriger Integrationsgrad; **small screen** N *(TV)* **on the ~** auf dem Bildschirm; **small-sized** ADJ klein; **small talk** N oberflächliche Konversation, Smalltalk *m*, Small Talk *m*; **she has no ~** oberflächliche *or* höfliche Konversation liegt ihr nicht; **to make ~** plaudern, Smalltalk *or* Small Talk machen; **to engage in** *or* **make ~ with sb** höflich mit jdm Konversation machen; **small-time** ADJ *(inf)* mickerig *(inf)*, armselig; *crook* klein; **~ politician/reporter** Schmalspurpolitiker(in) *m(f)*/-reporter(in) *m(f)*; **small-town** ADJ Kleinstadt-, kleinstädtisch; **~ life** Kleinstadtleben *nt*; **~ America** die amerikanische Provinz

> **SMALL TOWN**
>
> In den USA wird mit dem Begriff **small town** jede Ortschaft mit bis zu 10.000 Einwohnern bezeichnet. Das Wort **village** wird in den Vereinigten Staaten für eine Kleinstadt selten verwendet, da der Begriff mit Europa oder auch der Dritten Welt assoziiert wird. Eine **small town** ist in der Vorstellung der Amerikaner normalerweise mit positiven Werten verbunden, wie Freundlichkeit, Ehrlichkeit, Höflichkeit, Nachbarschaftshilfe und Vaterlandsliebe. Allerdings kann **small town** manchmal auch negative Seiten repräsentieren: so versteht man unter „small-town attitudes" vorurteilsbehaftete und engstirnige Ansichten.

smarm [smɑːm] *(Brit inf)* **VT to ~ one's hair down** sich *(dat)* das Haar anklatschen *(inf) or* an den Kopf kleben **VI to ~ up to sb** sich an jdn heranschmeißen *(inf)*; **to ~ one's way into sb's confidence** sich in jds Vertrauen *(acc)* einschleichen **N** Kriecherei *f*

smarmy ['smɑːmɪ] ADJ *(+er) (Brit inf: = greasy)* schmierig; *(= ingratiating)* kriecherisch *(pej)*; *voice* einschmeichelnd

smart [smɑːt] **ADJ** *(+er)* **a** schick; *person, clothes, car* schick, flott; *society* fein; *(= not shabby) appearance* gepflegt; **a ~-looking girl** ein flott aussehendes Mädchen; **a ~-looking garden** ein gepflegter Garten; **the ~ set** die Schickeria *(inf)*; **I want something ~** *(when buying clothes)* ich möchte etwas Schickes
b *(= bright, clever)* clever *(inf)*, schlau, gewitzt; *thief, trick* raffiniert, clever *(inf)*; *(pej) person, answer* superklug, neunmalklug *(pej inf)*; *(Comput, Mil)* intelligent; **that wasn't very ~ (of you)** das war nicht besonders intelligent (von dir); **~ as a whip** *(US inf)* supergescheit *(inf)*, sehr intelligent; **to get ~** *(US inf)* sich am Riemen reißen *(inf)*; *(= get cheeky)* frech kommen *(with +dat)*; **he thinks it's ~ to criticize his parents** er kommt sich toll vor, wenn er seine Eltern kritisiert
c *(= quick)* (blitz)schnell; *pace, work* rasch, flott *(inf)*; *work* schnell, fix *(inf)*; **and look ~ (about it)!** und zwar ein bisschen fix *or* plötzlich! *(inf)*
N Schmerz *m (also fig)*; *(of ointment, from wound also)* Brennen *nt*
VI brennen; **it will make the cut ~** es wird in der Schnittwunde brennen; **to ~ under sth** *(fig)* unter etw *(dat)* leiden; **he is still ~ing after the criticism** die Kritik tut ihm immer noch weh; **to ~ from sth** *(from blow etc)* von etw brennen; *(fig)* unter etw *(dat)* leiden; **to ~ over sth** über etw *(acc)* gekränkt sein

smart: **smart alec(k)** N *(inf)* Schlauberger(in) *m(f) (inf)*, Besserwisser(in) *m(f)*; **smart-alec(k)** ADJ *(inf) remarks* besserwisserisch, superschlau *(inf)*; *child* neunmalklug *(pej inf)*; **smartarse** ['smɑːtɑːs], *(US)* **smartass** ['smɑːtæs] *(sl)* **N** Klugscheißer(in) *m(f) (inf)* **ADJ** klugscheißerisch *(inf)*; **smart bomb** N intelligente Bombe; **smart card** N Chipkarte *f*; **smart drug** N bewusstseinsverändernde Droge

smarten ['smɑːtn] *(also* **smarten up***)* **VT** *house, room* herausputzen; *appearance* (her)richten, aufmöbeln *(inf)*; **to ~ oneself up** *(= dress up)* sich in Schale werfen *(inf)*; *(= generally improve appearance)* mehr Wert auf sein Äußeres legen; **you'd better ~ up your ideas** *(inf)* du solltest dich am Riemen reißen *(inf)* **VI** *(= dress up)* sich in Schale werfen *(inf)*; *(= improve appearance)* sich herausmachen; *(pace)* schneller *or* flotter *(inf)* werden

smartly ['smɑːtlɪ] ADV **a** *(= elegantly)* schick; *dress* schick, flott **b** *(= cleverly)* clever *(inf)*, schlau, gewitzt; *(pej)* superschlau *(inf)*, neunmalklug *(pej inf)* **c** *(= quickly)* (blitz)schnell, fix *(inf)*; *walk* rasch

smart money N *(Fin)* Investitionsgelder *pl*; **the ~ is on him winning** Insider setzen darauf, dass er gewinnt

smartness ['smɑːtnɪs] N **a** *(= elegance, of person, clothes, car)* Schick *m*; *(of appearance)* Gepflegtheit *f* **b** *(= brightness, cleverness)* Cleverness *f (inf)*, Schlauheit *f*, Gewitztheit *f*; *(of thief, trick)* Raffiniertheit *f*; *(pej, of person)* Besserwisserei *f (pej)*; *(of answer)* Vorwitzigkeit *f* **c** *(= quickness)* Schnelligkeit *f*, Fixheit *f (inf)*; *(of pace)* Raschheit *f*

smartphone ['smɑtfəʊn] N *(Telec)* Smartphone *nt*

smarty(-pants) ['smɑːtɪ(,pænts)] N *sing (inf)* Schlaumeier(in) *m(f)*, Schlauberger(in) *m(f) (inf)*

smash [smæʃ] **VT a** *(= break into pieces)* zerschlagen; *window* einschlagen; **I ~ed my glasses** mir ist die Brille kaputtgegangen; **I ~ed my knee** ich habe mir das Knie aufgeschlagen
b *(= defeat or destroy)* zerschlagen; *rebellion, revolution* niederschlagen, zerschlagen; *opponent* zerschmettern; *record* haushoch schlagen; *business* ruinieren
c *(= strike, also Tennis)* schmettern; **he ~ed his fist into his face** er schlug ihm mit der Faust ins Gesicht; **he ~ed him on the nose** er schlug ihm auf die Nase; **he ~ed his way through the mob** er musste sich *(dat)* gewaltsam einen Weg durch den Mob bahnen; **to ~ one's way into a building** gewaltsam in ein Gebäude eindringen
VI a *(= break)* zerschlagen, zerbrechen; **it ~ed into a thousand pieces** es (zer)sprang in tausend Stücke
b *(= crash)* prallen; **the car ~ed into the wall** das Auto krachte gegen die Mauer; **the terrified animal ~ed through the fence** das verängstigte Tier durchbrach das Gatter; **the plane ~ed into the houses** das Flugzeug raste in eine Häusergruppe; **the ship ~ed onto the rocks** das Schiff prallte gegen die Felsen; **the sound of the waves ~ing against the rocks** das Geräusch der gegen die Felsen klatschenden Wellen
N a *(= noise)* Krachen *nt*; *(of waves)* Klatschen *nt*; **there was a ~** es hat gekracht *or (of broken glass)* gescheppert
b *(= collision)* Unfall *m*; *(esp with another vehicle)* Zusammenstoß *m*; **rail ~** Zugunglück *nt*
c *(= blow)* Schlag *m*; *(Tennis)* Smash *m*, Schmetterball *m*
d *(inf: = success: also* **smash hit***)* Riesenhit *m*
ADV *(inf)* mit Karacho *(inf)*

▶ **smash in** VT *sep* einschlagen; **the firemen had to smash their way in** die Feuerwehrleute mussten gewaltsam eindringen; **to smash sb's face in** *(inf)* Hackfleisch aus jdm machen *(inf)*

▶ **smash up VT** *sep* zertrümmern; *face* übel zurichten; *car* kaputt fahren **VI** kaputtgehen; **the capsule completely smashed up on landing** die Kapsel zerschellte bei der Landung

smash-and-grab (raid) [,smæʃən'græb(reɪd)] N Schaufenstereinbruch *m*

smashed [smæʃt] ADJ *pred (inf)* stockbesoffen *(inf)*, hackedicht *(inf)*, total zu *(inf)*; **to get ~ on whisky** sich mit Whisky volllaufen lassen

smasher ['smæʃəʳ] N *(esp Brit inf)* toller Typ *(inf)*; *(= woman also)* Klassefrau *f (inf)*; **to be a ~** eine Wucht *(inf) or* (ganz große) Klasse sein *(inf)*

smash hit N *(inf)* Superhit *m (inf)*; **her new boyfriend was a ~ with her family** ihr neuer Freund kam bei ihrer Familie unwahrscheinlich gut an *(inf)*

smashing ['smæʃɪŋ] ADJ *(esp Brit inf)* klasse *inv*, Klasse *pred*, dufte *(all inf)*; **isn't it ~!** unheimlich dufte! *(inf)*

smash-up ['smæʃʌp] N *(Brit: Aut, Rail)* übler Unfall; *(esp with another vehicle)* Karambolage *f*

smatterer ['smætərəʳ] N Stümperer *m (pej)*, Stümperin *f (pej)*

smattering ['smætərɪŋ] N **a ~ of French** ein paar Brocken Französisch

smear [smɪəʳ] **N** verschmierter Fleck; *(fig)* Beschmutzung *f*, Verleumdung *f*; *(Med)* Abstrich *m*; **he had ~s of blood/grease on his hands** er hatte blut-/fettbeschmierte Hände; **this left a ~ on the institution** das hinterließ einen Fleck auf dem guten Namen der Institution; **he angrily repudiated their ~s** empört wies er ihre Verleumdungen zurück
VT a *grease, ointment* schmieren; *(= spread)* verschmieren; *(= mark, make dirty)* beschmieren; *face, body* einschmieren; **don't ~ the paint** verschmiere die Farbe nicht!
b *(fig) person* verunglimpfen; *sb's reputation, name* beschmutzen, besudeln; *organization* in den Schmutz ziehen
VI *(glass)* verschmieren; *(print)* verschmiert *or* verwischt werden; *(ballpoint pen)* schmieren; *(paint, ink)* verlaufen

smear: **smear campaign** N Verleumdungskampagne *f*; **smear tactics** PL Verleumdungstaktiken *pl*; **smear test** N *(Med)* Abstrich *m*; **smear word** N Schimpfwort *nt*

smeary ['smɪərɪ] ADJ *(+er) glass* verschmiert; *clothes* schmierig; *(= likely to smear) paint, ink* schmierend

smell [smel] *vb: pret, ptp* **smelt** *(esp Brit) or* **smelled N** *(= sense of smell, odour)* Geruch *m*; *(unpleasant also)* Gestank *m*; *(fragrant also)* Duft *m*; **it has a nice ~** es riecht gut *or* angenehm; **there's a funny ~ in here** hier riecht es komisch; **to have** *or* **take a ~ at sth** an etw *(acc)* riechen *or (dog etc)* schnuppern
VT a *(lit)* riechen; **can** *or* **do you ~ burning?** riechst du, dass etwas brennt *or (Cook)* anbrennt?; **first he ~s the wine** zunächst einmal riecht er an dem Wein
b *(fig) danger* wittern; **to ~ trouble** Ärger *or*

Stunk *(inf)* kommen sehen; **to ~ a rat** *(inf)* Lunte *or* den Braten riechen, etw spitzkriegen; **aha, I can ~ a rat** *(inf)* da scheint mir doch etwas faul zu sein!
VI riechen; *(unpleasantly also)* stinken; *(fragrantly also)* duften; **that ~s!** *(lit, fig)* das stinkt!; **to ~ of sth** *(lit, fig)* nach etw riechen; **his breath ~s** er riecht aus dem Mund, er hat Mundgeruch; **can fish ~?** können Fische riechen?

▶**smell out** VT *sep* **a** *rabbit, traitor etc* aufspüren; *plot* aufdecken **b these onions are smelling the house out!** die Zwiebeln verpesten das ganze Haus!

smelling bottle [ˈsmelɪŋˌbɒtl] N Riechfläschchen *nt*

smelling salts [ˈsmelɪŋˌsɔːlts] PL Riechsalz *nt*

smelly [ˈsmelɪ] ADJ *(+er)* übel riechend, stinkend; **it's ~ in here** hier drin stinkt es; **~ cheese** *(inf)* Stinkkäse *m (inf)*; **you've got ~ feet** deine Füße stinken; **come here, ~!** komm her, du kleines Stinktier! *(inf)*

smelt[1] [smelt] *(esp Brit) pret, ptp of* **smell**

smelt[2] VT *ore* schmelzen; *(= refine)* verhütten

smelt[3] N *pl* **-(s)** *(= fish)* Stint *m*

smelter [ˈsmeltəˈ] N *(= furnace)* Schmelzhütte *f*, Schmelzerei *f*; *(= person)* Schmelzer(in) *m(f)*

smidgen, smidgin [ˈsmɪdʒən] N *(inf)* **just a ~ for me** für mich nur ein (klitzekleines *(inf)*) bisschen

smile [smaɪl] **N** Lächeln *nt*; **there was a sarcastic ~ on his face** ein sarkastisches Lächeln ging über sein Gesicht; **to be all ~s** übers ganze Gesicht strahlen; **she gave a little ~** sie lächelte schwach *or* ein bisschen; **to give sb a ~** jdm zulächeln; **come on, give me a ~** lach doch mal!; **take that ~ off your face!** hör auf, so zu grinsen!
VI lächeln; **we tried to make the baby ~** wir versuchten, das Baby zum Lachen zu bringen; **come on, ~** lach mal!; **~ for the camera!** bitte recht freundlich!; **he's always smiling** er lacht immer; **keep smiling!** keep smiling!; **he kept smiling through all his troubles** trotz aller Schwierigkeiten ließ er den Kopf nicht hängen; **to ~ at sb** jdn anlächeln; *(cheerful person)* jdn anlachen; **to ~ at sth** über etw *(acc)* lächeln; **to ~ at danger** der Gefahr *(dat)* ins Gesicht lachen; **to ~ with pleasure/relief** *etc* vor Freude/Erleichterung *etc* strahlen; **fortune ~d on him** *(liter)* ihm lachte das Glück
VT she ~d her thanks sie lächelte dankbar; **he ~d a bitter ~** er lächelte bitter

smiley [ˈsmaɪlɪ] **ADJ a** *face, eyes, person* freundlich **b** *(on computer bulletin boards etc)* **~ badge** Smileybutton *m*; **~ symbol** Smileysymbol *nt* **N** *(on computer bulletin boards etc)* Smiley *nt*

smiling ADJ, **smilingly** ADV [ˈsmaɪlɪŋ, -lɪ] lächelnd

smirch [smɜːtʃ] *(liter)* **N** Schmutz- *or* Schandfleck *m*, Makel *m (geh)* **VT** beflecken *(liter)*, besudeln *(geh)*

smirk [smɜːk] **N** Grinsen *nt* **VI** grinsen, süffisant lächeln

smite [smaɪt] *pret* **smote**, *ptp* **smitten** VT *(old, liter)* schlagen; **he smote off his head** er schlug *or* hieb *(old, liter)* ihm den Kopf ab; **the sound of gunfire smote our ears** der Lärm von Schüssen schlug an unsere Ohren; **and the Lord shall ~ them down** und der Herr wird sie zerschmettern

smith [smɪθ] N Schmied(in) *m(f)*

smithereens [ˌsmɪðəˈriːnz] PL **to smash sth to ~** etw in tausend Stücke schlagen; **in ~** in tausend Stücken

smithery [ˈsmɪθərɪ] N Schmiedekunst *f*, Schmiedehandwerk *nt*; *(= single piece of work)* Schmiedearbeit *f*

> **SMITHSONIAN INSTITUTION**
>
> Die **Smithsonian Institution** ist der weltweit größte Museumskomplex, der sich in Washington, DC befindet und von der US-Regierung als ein Zentrum für Wissenschaft und Künste unterstützt wird. Der amerikanische Kongress gründete das Institut 1846 mit den finanziellen Mitteln, die der englische Wissenschaftler James Smithson den Vereinigten Staaten zur Förderung der Wissenschaften hinterlassen hatte. Mittlerweile umfasst es eine Sammlung von rund 100 Millionen Kunstwerken und anderen Ausstellungsstücken in 14 Museen, wie zum Beispiel dem **National Air and Space Museum**, dem **National Museum of American History**, dem **National Museum of the American Indian**, der **National Gallery of Art** und der **National Portrait Gallery**. Das **Smithsonian** wird im Volksmund auch „the nation's attic" genannt, weil sich dort wie auf einem Speicher alles Mögliche angesammelt. Es hat sogar einen Zoo und führt Forschungen in allen Wissenschaftsbereichen durch.

smithy [ˈsmɪðɪ] N Schmiede *f*

smitten [ˈsmɪtn] *ptp of* **smite** ADJ **to be ~ with the plague** von der Pest heimgesucht werden; **to be ~ with remorse/fear** von Reue/Angst geplagt werden; **to be ~ with pity** von Mitleid ergriffen sein; **he's really ~ with her** *(inf)* er ist wirklich vernarrt in sie; **he's really ~ this time** *(inf)* diesmal hats ihn erwischt *(inf)*; **I've never seen him so ~** *(inf)* ich habe ihn noch nie so vernarrt gesehen; **to be ~ with sth** *(= captivated)* von etw begeistert sein; **do you like it? – I'm not ~ with it** gefällt es dir? – ich bin nicht erpicht darauf

smock [smɒk] **N** Kittel *m*; *(as top)* Hänger *m* **VT** smoken

smocking [ˈsmɒkɪŋ] N Smokarbeit *f*

smog [smɒg] N Smog *m*

smog alert N Smogalarm *m*

smoggy [ˈsmɒgɪ] ADJ *(+er) city, sky, air* versmogt

smoke [sməʊk] **N a** Rauch *m*; **there's no ~ without fire, where there's ~ there's fire** *(prov)* wo Rauch ist, da ist auch Feuer *(prov)*; **to go up in ~** in Rauch (und Flammen) aufgehen; *(fig)* sich in Wohlgefallen auflösen; *(inf: = get angry)* in die Luft gehen *(inf)*; **it's all ~ and mirrors** *(US)* das ist nur Blendwerk
b *(inf: = cigarette etc)* was zu rauchen *(inf)*; **have you got a ~?** hast du was zu rauchen? *(inf)*; **it's a good ~, this tobacco** dieser Tabak raucht sich gut; **~s** Glimmstengel *pl (dated inf)*
c *(= act)* **to have a ~** eine rauchen; **I'm dying for a ~** ich muss unbedingt eine rauchen; **the condemned were allowed a final ~** die Verurteilten durften eine letzte Zigarette rauchen
VT a *tobacco, pipe, cigarette, cannabis* rauchen **b** *bacon, fish etc* räuchern
VI rauchen; *(oil lamp etc)* qualmen; **to ~ like a chimney** wie ein Schlot rauchen; **do you mind if I ~?** stört es (Sie), wenn ich rauche?

▶**smoke out** VT *sep* ausräuchern; *(= fill with smoke)* einräuchern, einnebeln *(inf)*

▶**smoke up** VI *(US sl* kiffen) *sl* **that guy's always smoking up** der Typ kifft ständig *(inf)*

smoke: **smoke alarm** N Rauchmelder *m*; **smoke bomb** N Rauchbombe *f*

smoked [sməʊkt] ADJ *bacon, fish* geräuchert, Räucher-

smoke detector N Rauchmelder *m*

smoke-dried [ˈsməʊkdraɪd] ADJ geräuchert

smoked: **smoked glass** M Rauchglas *nt*; **smoked glasses** PL Gläser *pl* aus Rauchglas; **smoked salmon** N Räucherlachs *m*

smoke: **smoke-filled** [ˈsməʊkfɪld] ADJ *room* verräuchert, verqualmt; **smoke-free** [ˈsməʊkfriː] ADJ *zone* rauchfrei; **smoke hood** N *(on plane)* Sauerstoffmaske *f*

smokeless [ˈsməʊklɪs] ADJ *zone* rauchfrei; *fuel* rauchlos

smoker [ˈsməʊkəˈ] N **a** *(= person)* Raucher(in) *m(f)*; **to be a heavy ~** stark rauchen, starker Raucher sein; **~'s cough** Raucherhusten *m* **b** *(Rail)* Raucherabteil *nt*, Raucher *m* **c** *(= entertainment)* Herrenabend *m*

smoke: **smoke ring** N (Rauch)ring *m*; **smokeroom** N Rauchsalon *m*, Rauchzimmer *nt*; **smoke screen** N Nebelwand *f*, Rauchvorhang *m*; *(fig)* Deckmantel *m*, Vorwand *m*; **a ~ of words** ein Schwall *m* von Worten; **his answer was just a ~** seine Antwort war nur ein Ablenkungsmanöver *nt*; **smoke signal** N Rauchzeichen *nt*; **smokestack** N Schornstein *m*; **~ industries** Schornsteinindustrien *pl*

smoking [ˈsməʊkɪŋ] **ADJ** rauchend **N** Rauchen *nt*; **"no ~"** „Rauchen verboten"

smoking: **smoking compartment**, *(US)* **smoking car** N Raucherabteil *nt*; **smoking gun** N *(esp US fig)* entscheidender Beweis; **smoking jacket** N Rauchjacke *f*, Hausjacke *f*; **smoking room** N Rauchzimmer *nt*

smoko [ˈsməʊkəʊ] N *(Austral inf) (= cigarette break)* Zigarettenpause *f*; *(= coffee break)* Kaffeepause *f*

smoky [ˈsməʊkɪ] ADJ *(+er) chimney, fire* rauchend; *room, atmosphere* verraucht; *(= stained by smoke)* verräuchert; *(= like smoke) flavour* rauchig; *colour* rauchfarben; **~ glass** Rauchglas *nt*

smoky: **smoky bacon** N Räucherschinken *m*; **smoky blue** ADJ rauchblau; **smoky grey**, *(US)* **smoky gray** ADJ rauchgrau

smolder VI *(US)* = **smoulder**

smooch [smuːtʃ] *(inf)* **VI** knutschen *(inf)* **N** Kuss *m*, Bussi *nt (inf)*; **to have a ~** rumknutschen *(inf)*

smoochy [ˈsmuːtʃɪ] ADJ *(+er) (inf) music, record* schmusig *(inf)*, zum Knutschen *(inf)*, romantisch

smooth [smuːð] **ADJ** *(+er)* **a** *(in texture, surface etc)* glatt; *sea* ruhig, glatt; *road, surface* glatt, eben; *outline* sanft; *skin* glatt, weich; *hair* weich; **as ~ as silk** weich wie Seide, seidenweich; **as ~ as glass** spiegelglatt; **worn ~** *(steps)* glatt getreten; *knife* abgeschliffen; *tyre* abgefahren; **this razor gives you a really ~ shave** dieser Apparat rasiert wirklich sanft
b *(in consistency) paste* sämig; *sauce* glatt; **whisk sauce until ~** Soße glatt rühren
c *motion, flight, crossing* ruhig; *flow* gleichmäßig; *gear change* weich, leicht; *takeoff, landing* glatt; *breathing* gleichmäßig; **the car came to a ~ stop** der Wagen kam glatt *or* ruhig zum Stehen; **he is a very ~ driver** er ist ein sehr angenehmer, ruhiger Fahrer; **to ensure a ~ fit** damit es genau passt
d *(= trouble-free) transition, functioning* reibungslos, glatt; *relations* reibungslos; **the bill had a ~ passage through Parliament** der Gesetzentwurf kam glatt durchs Parlament; **we want the move to the new offices to be as ~ as possible** wir wollen, dass der Umzug in die neuen Büroräume so reibungslos wie möglich verläuft
e *(= not harsh in taste) flavour, coffee* mild; *whisky* weich; *beer* süffig
f *style of writing* glatt, flüssig; *tones* sanft; *diction* flüssig, geschliffen; **the ~, relaxing voice of the hypnotist** die sanft beruhigende Stimme des Hypnotiseurs
g *(= polite: often pej) manners* glatt; *person* glatt, aalglatt *(pej)*; *(= unruffled)* kühl, cool *(inf)*; **to be a ~ talker** schönreden können; **he's too ~ to be sincere** er ist bestimmt nicht ehrlich, er redet zu schön; **a ~ operator** ein Schlawiner *m (inf)*
h *(inf) restaurant, furniture, car, person* gepflegt
i *(Tennis)* glatt
N to give sth a ~ etw glatt streichen → **rough N**
VT *surface* glätten, glatt machen; *dress, hair* glätten, glatt streichen; *wood* glatt hobeln; *(fig) feelings* besänftigen, beruhigen; **to ~ one's skirt over one's knees** sich den Rock über den Knien glatt streichen; **to ~ cream into sb's skin** Creme auf jds Haut streichen; **to ~ the way for sb/sth** jdm/einer Sache den Weg ebnen

▶**smooth away** VT *sep* glätten; *(fig) fears* besänftigen

▶ **smooth back** VT *sep hair* zurückstreichen

▶ **smooth down** VT *sep* glatt machen; *feathers, hair, dress* glatt streichen; *(fig) person, feelings* besänftigen VI *(fig)* sich beruhigen

▶ **smooth out** VT *sep (= make smooth) crease, surface* glätten; *(fig) difficulty, differences* ausräumen, aus dem Weg räumen

▶ **smooth over** VT *sep (fig) quarrel* in Ordnung bringen, geradebiegen *(inf)*; **to smooth things over** die Sache geradebiegen *(inf)*

smooth: **smoothbore** ADJ glatt N Gewehr *nt* mit glattem Lauf; **smooth-faced** [ˈsmuːðˈfeɪst] ADJ zarthäutig; *(fig)* scheinheilig

smoothly [ˈsmuːðlɪ] ADV **a** *shave* sanft **b** *land, change gear* weich; *drive* ruhig; *fit* genau; **to run ~** *(engine)* ruhig laufen **c** *(= without problems)* **to go ~** glatt über die Bühne gehen; **to run ~** *(event)* reibungslos verlaufen; **~ running organization** reibungslos laufende Organisation **d** **~ flowing prose** flüssige Prosa; **the music passes ~ from one mood to another** die Musik fließt unmerklich von einer Stimmung in die andere über **e** *talk* schön; *behave* aalglatt *(pej)*; **he handled the situation very ~** er hat die Lage sehr kühl gemeistert

smoothness [ˈsmuːðnɪs] N **a** *(of texture etc)* Glätte *f*; *(of sea)* Ruhe *f*; *(of road, surface)* Ebenheit *f*; *(of skin)* Glätte *f*, Weichheit *f*; **it has the ~ of silk** es ist seidenweich
b *(in consistency) (of paste)* Sämigkeit *f*; *(of sauce)* Glätte *f*
c *(of motion, flight, crossing)* Ruhe *f*; *(of gear change)* Weichheit *f*; *(of takeoff, landing)* Sanftheit *f*; *(of breathing, flow)* Gleichmäßigkeit *f*; *(of fit)* Genauigkeit *f*
d *(= ease: of transition, functioning, relations)* Reibungslosigkeit *f*
e *(in taste, of whisky etc)* Weichheit *f*; *(of coffee)* Milde *f*
f *(of style of writing, diction)* Flüssigkeit *f*; *(of tones)* Sanftheit *f*
g *(pej, of manners, salesman)* Glätte *f*; *(of person)* (aal)glatte Art *(pej)*

smooth: **smooth-running** ADJ *engine, car* ruhig laufend; *convention etc* reibungslos verlaufend; **smooth-shaven** ADJ *man, face* glatt rasiert; **smooth-spoken**, **smooth-tongued** ADJ *(pej)* schönredend *(pej)*, schönrednerisch *(pej)*; **smooth-talk** VT *(pej)* überreden (*into* zu); **to ~ sb into doing sth** jdn dazu überreden etw zu tun

smoothy [ˈsmuːðɪ] N *(inf)* Schönling *m*; *(= smooth talker)* Schönredner *m*; *(pej)* Lackaffe *m* *(inf)*

smorgasbord [ˈsmɔːgəsbɔːd] N *aus vielen Speisen bestehendes kaltes Büfett/Buffet*; **a ~ of** *(fig)* eine Vielzahl *or* große Auswahl an *+dat or* von

smote [sməʊt] *pret of* **smite**

smother [ˈsmʌðəʳ] VT **a** *(= stifle) person, fire, weeds* ersticken; *(fig) criticism, yawn, laughter* unterdrücken; **to ~ sb with affection** jdn mit seiner Liebe erdrücken **b** *(= cover)* bedecken, überschütten; **fruit ~ed in cream** Obst, das in Sahne schwimmt; **~ed in dust** völlig eingestaubt; **she ~ed his face in kisses** sie bedeckte sein Gesicht mit Küssen, sie erstickte ihn fast mit ihren Küssen VI ersticken

smother-love [ˈsmʌðəˌlʌv] N *(inf)* übertriebene Mutterliebe

smoulder, *(US)* **smolder** [ˈsməʊldəʳ] VI *(lit, fig)* glimmen, schwelen; *model, actress etc* Sexappeal *m* ausstrahlen; **his eyes were ~ing with anger** seine Augen glühten vor Zorn; **she was ~ing with rage** der Zorn schwelte in ihr

smouldering, *(US)* **smoldering** [ˈsməʊldərɪŋ] ADJ **a** *fire* schwelend; *embers, cigarette* glimmend **b** *(= suppressed) anger, resentment, hatred* schwelend **c** *(= passionate) eyes* feurig; **a ~ look** ein glühender Blick

SMP *(Brit) abbr of* **Statutory Maternity Pay** gesetzliches Erziehungsgeld

SMS *(Telec) abbr of* **Short Message Service** SMS

smudge [smʌdʒ] N **a** Fleck *m*; *(of ink)* Klecks *m* **b** *(US: = fire)* (qualmendes) Feuer *(gegen Insekten)* VT *ink, lipstick, paint* verwischen; **he had chocolate ~d all over his face** er hatte sich *(dat)* das ganze Gesicht mit Schokolade vollgeschmiert VI verlaufen, verschmieren

smudgy [ˈsmʌdʒɪ] ADJ *(+er)* verschmiert; *outline* verwischt, verschwommen

smug [smʌg] ADJ *(+er)* selbstgefällig; *grin, remark also* süffisant; **~ satisfaction** eitle Selbstzufriedenheit

smuggle [ˈsmʌgl] VT *(lit, fig)* schmuggeln; **to ~ sb/sth in** jdn/etw einschmuggeln, jdn einschleusen; **to ~ sb/sth out** jdn/etw herausschmuggeln, jdn herausschleusen VI schmuggeln

smuggler [ˈsmʌgləʳ] N Schmuggler(in) *m(f)*

smuggling [ˈsmʌglɪŋ] N Schmuggel *m*

smuggling ring N Schmugglerring *m*

smugly [ˈsmʌglɪ] ADV selbstgefällig; *grin, say also* süffisant; **he is ~ self-confident** er ist eitel selbstzufrieden

smugness [ˈsmʌgnɪs] N Selbstgefälligkeit *f*

smut [smʌt] N **a** *(= piece of dirt)* Rußflocke *f*; **there's a ~ on your nose/in your eye** du hast da was an der Nase/im Auge; **~s from the stove** Ruß *m* aus dem Ofen **b** *(fig)* Schmutz *m*; **to talk ~** Schweinereien erzählen **c** *(Bot)* Brand *m*

smuttiness [ˈsmʌtɪnɪs] N *(fig)* Schmutz *m*; *(of joke, language)* Anstößigkeit *f*, Unflätigkeit *f*

smutty [ˈsmʌtɪ] ADJ *(+er) (lit, fig)* schmutzig

snack [snæk] N Kleinigkeit *f* (zu essen), Imbiss *m*; **to have a ~** eine Kleinigkeit essen, einen Imbiss zu sich *(dat)* nehmen; **we just have a ~ for lunch** mittags essen wir nicht viel *or* groß *(inf)*; **too many ~s between meals ...** wenn man zwischen den Mahlzeiten zu viel isst ...

snack bar N Imbissstube *f*

snaffle[1] [ˈsnæfl] N *(also* **snaffle bit**) Trense *f*

snaffle[2] VT *(Brit inf)* sich *(dat)* unter den Nagel reißen *(inf)*

▶ **snaffle up** VT *sep (Brit inf) bargain* wegschnappen *(inf)*

snafu [snæˈfuː] *(US sl)* N Schlamassel *m (inf)* VT total durcheinanderbringen

snag [snæg] N **a** *(= hidden difficulty)* Haken *m*, Schwierigkeit *f*; **there's a ~** die Sache hat einen Haken; **what's the ~?** woran liegt es?, was ist das Problem?; **to run into** *or* **hit a ~** in Schwierigkeiten *(acc)* kommen **b** *(= flaw in clothes etc)* gezogener Faden **c** *(in water)* Baumstumpf *m* (im Wasser) VT sich *(dat)* einen Faden ziehen; **I ~ged my tights** ich habe mir an den Strumpfhosen einen Faden gezogen VI Fäden ziehen

snail [sneɪl] N Schnecke *f*; **edible ~** Weinbergschnecke *f*; **at a ~'s pace** im Schneckentempo

snail lane N *(US Aut)* Kriechspur *f*

snail mail N *(hum)* Schneckenpost *f (inf, im Gegensatz zur elektronischen Post)*

snake [sneɪk] N Schlange *f*; **a ~ in the grass** *(fig: = woman)* eine listige Schlange; *(= man)* ein heimtückischer Kerl VI sich schlängeln

snake: **snakebite** N **a** Schlangenbiss *m* **b** *(= drink) Getränk aus Cidre und Bier*; **snakeboard** N *(Sport)* Snakeboard *nt*, *Skateboard für Slalomfahrten*; **snakeboarding** N *(Sport)* Snakeboarden *nt*, Snakeboarding *nt*; **snake charmer** N Schlangenbeschwörer(in) *m(f)*; **snake fence** N *(esp US)* Scherengitter *nt*; **snake fruit** N Salak *f*, Schlangenhautfrucht *f*; **snakepit** N Schlangengrube *f*; **snakeskin** N Schlangenhaut *f*; *(= leather)* Schlangenleder *nt* ADJ Schlangenleder-, aus Schlangenleder; **~ boots** Schlangenlederstiefel *pl*

snaky [ˈsneɪkɪ] ADJ *windings* schläng(e)lig; *movements* schlangenartig

snap [snæp] N **a** *(= sound)* Schnappen *nt*; *(with fingers)* Schnippen *nt*, Schnalzen *nt*; *(of sth breaking)* Knacken *nt*; *(= click)* Klicken *nt*; *(of whip)* Knall *m*
b *(= fastener)* Druckknopf *m*
c *(Phot)* Schnappschuss *m*
d *(Cards)* ≈ Schnippschnapp *nt*
e *(inf, = vigour)* Schwung *m*; **put a bit of ~ into it** mach ein bisschen zackig! *(inf)*
f *(Brit: = biscuit)* Plätzchen *nt*
g **cold ~** Kälteeinbruch *m*
h *(US inf: = cinch)* **it's a ~** das ist ein Kinderspiel *or* ein Klacks *(inf)*
ADJ **a** *attr* plötzlich, spontan; **~ vote** Blitzabstimmung *f*
b *(US inf: = easy)* kinderleicht
ADV **to go ~** *(= make sound)* schnapp machen; *(sth breaking)* knacken; *(= break)* (knackend) entzweibrechen
INTERJ **I bought a green one – ~!** *(Brit inf)* ich hab mir ein grünes gekauft – ich auch!
VT **a** *fingers* schnipsen *or* schnalzen mit; *whip* knallen mit; **to ~ a book shut** ein Buch zuklappen; **to ~ a purse shut** ein Portemonnaie zuschnappen lassen; **he ~ped the lid down** er ließ den Deckel runterklappen; **to ~ sth into place** etw einschnappen lassen; **to ~ one's fingers at sb/sth** *(fig)* auf jdn/etw pfeifen *(inf)*
b *(= break)* zerbrechen, entzweibrechen; *bone* brechen
c *(also* **snap out**) **to ~ an order** bellend etwas befehlen; **she ~ped a few words at the children** sie pfiff die Kinder an
d *(Phot)* knipsen
VI **a** *(= click)* (zu)schnappen, einschnappen; *(= crack, break)* entzweibrechen, zerbrechen; *(of whip)* knallen; **to ~ shut** zuschnappen; **my patience finally ~ped** dann ist mir aber der Geduldsfaden gerissen
b *(= speak sharply)* bellen *(inf)*, schnappen *(inf)*; **to ~ at sb** jdn anpfeifen *or* anschnauzen *(inf)*; **there's no need to ~** du brauchst nicht gleich so zu schnauzen!
c *(of dog, fish etc, fig)* schnappen (*at* nach)
d **to ~ to attention** zackig Haltung annehmen; **~ to it!** mach 'n bisschen zackig! *(inf)*
e *(inf: = crack up)* durchdrehen *(inf)*; **something ~ped (in him)** da hat (bei ihm) etwas ausgehakt *(inf)*

▶ **snap off** VT *sep (= break off)* abbrechen; *(= bite off)* abbeißen; **to snap sb's head off** *(fig inf)* jdm ins Gesicht springen *(inf)* VI *(= break off)* abbrechen

▶ **snap out** VT *sep* **a** *order* brüllen, bellen **b** **to snap sb out of sth** jdn aus etw herausreißen VI **to snap out of sth** sich aus etw herausreißen, mit etw Schluss machen; **it's time he snapped out of this depression** es wird höchste Zeit, dass er aus dieser Depression rauskommt; **snap out of it!** reiß dich zusammen *or* am Riemen! *(inf)*; *(= cheer up)* Kopf hoch!

▶ **snap up** VT *sep (lit, fig)* wegschnappen

snap: **snap decision** N plötzlicher Entschluss; **snapdragon** [ˈsnæpˌdrægən] N Löwenmaul *nt*; **snap fastener** N Druckknopf *m*; **snap hook** N Karabinerhaken *m*; **snap lock** N Schnappschloss *nt*

snapper [ˈsnæpəʳ] N *(= fish)* Schnapper *m*

snappish [ˈsnæpɪʃ] ADJ *(lit, fig)* bissig

snappishness [ˈsnæpɪʃnɪs] N *(lit, fig)* Bissigkeit *f*

snappy [ˈsnæpɪ] ADJ *(+er)* **a** *(inf: = quick)* flott *(inf)*, zackig *(inf)*; **and be ~ about it!, and make it ~!** und zwar ein bisschen flott *or* dalli! *(inf)* **b** *(lit, fig) dog, person* bissig **c** *(inf) translation* kurz und treffend; *phrase* zündend **d** *(inf: = fashionable)* flott, schick; **he's a ~ dresser** er kleidet sich sehr modebewusst

snap: **snap ring** N Karabinerhaken *m*; **snapshot** [ˈsnæpʃɒt] N Schnappschuss *m*

snare[1] [sneəʳ] N *(lit, fig: = trap)* Falle *f*; *(fig also)* Fallstrick *m* VT *(lit, fig)* (ein)fangen

snare[2] N **a** *(of drum)* Schnarrsaite *f* **b** *(= snare drum)* kleine Trommel

snarl[1] [snɑːl] N Knurren *nt no pl*; **..., he said with a ~** ..., sagte er knurrend VI knurren; **to ~ at sb** jdn anknurren

snarl[2] N *(in wool)* Knoten *m*, verhedderte Stelle VT *wool* verheddern

▶ **snarl up** *(inf)* VT *sep traffic, system* durcheinanderbringen; *plan also* vermasseln *(inf)*; **traffic always gets snarled up at the bridge** an der Brücke ist der Verkehr immer chaotisch; **I got snarled up in a traffic jam** ich bin im Verkehr stecken geblieben VI *(traffic)* chaotische Formen annehmen

snarl-up ['snɑːlʌp] N *(Brit inf, in traffic)* (Verkehrs)chaos *nt*; *(in system, on switchboard etc)* Kuddelmuddel *nt (inf)*; **~s** ein großes Kuddelmuddel *(inf)*; **the ~s at rush-hour periods** das Chaos in den Stoßverkehrszeiten

snatch [snætʃ] N **a** *(= act)* Griff *m* **b** *(Brit inf: = robbery)* Raub *m*; *(= kidnapping)* Entführung *f* **c** *(= snippet)* Stück *nt*, Brocken *m*; *(of conversation)* Fetzen *m*; *(of music)* ein paar Takte; **to do sth in ~es** etw in Etappen tun **d** *(Weightlifting)* Reißen *nt* **e** *(US, sl, = female genitals)* Möse *f (vulg)* VT **a** *(= grab)* greifen; **to ~ sth from sb** jdm etw entreißen; **to ~ hold of sth** nach etw greifen, etw packen; **to ~ sth out of sb's hand** jdm etw aus der Hand reißen **b** *some sleep etc* ergattern; **to ~ a quick meal** schnell etwas essen; **the Ferrari ~ed the lead on the last lap** der Ferrari riss in der letzten Runde die Führung an sich; **to ~ an opportunity** eine Gelegenheit ergreifen *or* beim Schopf packen; **they ~ed a quick kiss** sie gaben sich *(dat)* schnell einen Kuss; **he ~ed a kiss while she wasn't looking** als sie gerade wegsah, stahl er ihr schnell einen Kuss; **to ~ defeat from the jaws of victory** einen sicheren Sieg in eine Niederlage verwandeln; **they ~ed victory from the jaws of defeat with a goal in the last minute** mit einem Tor in der letzten Minute konnten sie aus der Niederlage noch einen Sieg machen **c** *(inf) (= steal) money* klauen *(inf)*; *handbag* aus der Hand reißen; *(= kidnap)* entführen VI greifen (*at* nach); **don't ~!** nicht grapschen! *(inf)*; **to ~ at an opportunity** nach einer Gelegenheit greifen

▶ **snatch away** VT *sep* wegreißen (*sth from sb* jdm etw); **death snatched him away from us** der Tod hat ihn uns *(dat)* entrissen

▶ **snatch up** VT *sep* schnappen; **he snatched up his camera** er schnappte sich *(dat)* seine Kamera; **the mother snatched her child up** die Mutter riss ihr Kind an sich *(acc)*

snatcher ['snætʃəʳ] N *(esp Brit)* Handtaschenräuber(in) *m(f)*; *(esp US)* Kidnapper(in) *m(f)*

snatch squad N *(Brit)* Greifertrupp *m (inf)*

snazzy ADJ *(+er)*, **snazzily** ADV ['snæzɪ, -lɪ] *(dated inf)* flott

sneak [sniːk] N Schleicher(in) *m(f)*; *(dated Brit Sch inf)* Petzer *m*, Petze *f (Sch inf)* VT **he ~ed a cake off the counter** er klaute *or* stibitzte einen Kuchen vom Tresen *(inf)*; **to ~ sth into a room** etw in ein Zimmer schmuggeln; **to ~ a look at sb/sth** auf jdn/etw schielen VI **a to ~ about** herumschleichen; **to ~ away** *or* **off** sich wegschleichen *or* -stehlen; **to ~ in** sich einschleichen; **to ~ past sb** (sich) an jdm vorbeischleichen; **to ~ up on sb** sich an jdn heranschleichen **b** *(dated Brit Sch inf: = tell tales)* petzen *(inf)*; **to ~ on sb** jdn verpetzen *(inf)*

sneakers ['sniːkəz] PL *(esp US)* Freizeitschuhe *pl*, Leisetreter *pl (hum)*, Schleicher *pl (hum)*

sneaking ['sniːkɪŋ] ADJ *attr* geheim *attr*; *suspicion also* leise; **to have a ~ feeling that …** ein schleichendes Gefühl haben, dass …

sneak preview N *(of film etc)* Vorschau *f*; *(of new car etc)* Vorbesichtigung *f*

sneak thief N Langfinger *m (inf)*, Einschleichdieb(in) *m(f)*

sneaky ['sniːkɪ] ADJ *(+er) (pej inf)* gewieft *(inf)*, raffiniert; **there's something ~ about it** da ist was faul dran

sneer [snɪəʳ] N *(= expression)* spöttisches *or* höhnisches Lächeln; *(= remark)* spöttische *or* höhnische Bemerkung VI spotten; *(= look sneering)* spöttisch *or* höhnisch grinsen; **adolescents often ~ at what they cannot understand** Jugendliche spotten oft über das, was sie nicht verstehen können; **to ~ at sb** jdn verhöhnen; *(facially also)* jdn auslachen

sneerer ['snɪərəʳ] N Spötter(in) *m(f)*

sneering ADJ, **sneeringly** ADV ['snɪərɪŋ, -lɪ] höhnisch, spöttisch

sneeze [sniːz] N Nieser *m*; **~s** Niesen *nt* VI niesen; **not to be ~d at** nicht zu verachten; **when America ~s, Britain catches a cold** wenn Amerika niest, bekommt Großbritannien einen Schnupfen

sneezing ['sniːzɪŋ] N Niesen *nt*; **~ fit** Niesanfall *m*

snick [snɪk] N *(= small cut)* Kerbe *f* VT *(with razor)* schneiden; *(with knife)* schnitzen; *(with tweezers)* zupfen; *(Cricket) ball* auf Kante schlagen

snicker ['snɪkəʳ] N, VI = **snigger**

snide [snaɪd] ADJ abfällig

sniff [snɪf] N Schniefen *nt no pl (inf)*; *(disdainful)* Naserümpfen *nt no pl*; *(of dog)* Schnüffeln *nt no pl*; **we never even got a ~ of the money** wir haben das Geld noch nicht mal von Weitem zu sehen bekommen; **have a ~ at this** riech mal hieran; **at the first ~ of danger, he backed out** sobald er Gefahr witterte, zog er sich zurück VT *(= test by smelling)* riechen, schnuppern an *(+dat) (inf)*; *air* riechen, schnuppern; *smelling salts* einziehen; *glue* einatmen, schnüffeln *(inf)*; *drugs* sniffen *(sl)*; *snuff* schnupfen; *(fig: = detect)* wittern, riechen; **the dogs ~ed each other** die Hunde beschnupperten sich; **~ these flowers** riech mal an den Blumen VI *(person)* schniefen *(inf)*; *(dog)* schnüffeln, schnuppern; **to ~ at sth** *(lit)* an etw *(dat)* schnuppern; *(fig)* die Nase über etw *(acc)* rümpfen; **not to be ~ed at** nicht zu verachten

▶ **sniff around** *(inf)* VI *(for information)* herumschnüffeln *(inf)* VI *+prep obj* **a** *room etc* herumschnüffeln in *(+dat) (inf)* **b** *girlfriend etc* herumhängen bei *(inf)*

▶ **sniff out** VT *sep (lit, fig inf)* aufspüren; *crime, plot* aufdecken

▶ **sniff round** VI VI *+prep obj (esp Brit)* = **sniff around**

sniffer dog ['snɪfə,dɒg] N Spürhund *m*

sniffle ['snɪfl] N, VI = **snuffle**

sniffy ['snɪfɪ] ADJ *(+er) (inf: = disdainful)* naserümpfend; *(= put out)* verschnupft, eingeschnappt *(inf)*; **she was rather ~ about the plan** sie hat über den Plan nur die Nase gerümpft

snifter ['snɪftəʳ] N *(dated inf)* Kurze(r) *m (inf)*; **to have a ~** einen Kurzen trinken *or* nehmen *(inf)*

snigger ['snɪgəʳ] N Kichern *nt*, Gekicher *nt*; **to give a ~** loskichern VI kichern (*at, about* wegen)

snip [snɪp] N **a** *(= cut, cutting action)* Schnitt *m*; *(= sound)* Schnipsen *nt no pl*, Klappern *nt no pl* **b** *(of cloth)* Stück *nt*; *(of paper)* Schnipsel *m*, Schnippel *m or nt (inf)*; *(from newspaper)* Ausschnitt *m* **c** *(esp Brit inf: = bargain)* Geschäft *nt*, günstiger Kauf; **at only £2 it's a real ~** für nur £ 2 ist es unheimlich günstig **d** *(US inf: = insignificant person)* Würstchen *nt (pej inf)* VT schnippeln *(inf)*; **to ~ sth off** etw abschnippeln *(inf)* VI **to ~ at** schnippeln an *(+dat) (inf)*

snipe [snaɪp] N *pl* - *(Orn)* Schnepfe *f* VI **to ~ at sb** *(lit, fig)* aus dem Hinterhalt auf jdn schießen

sniper ['snaɪpəʳ] N Heckenschütze *m*/-schützin *f*; **~-fire** Heckenschützenfeuer *nt*

snippet ['snɪpɪt] N Stückchen *nt*; *(of paper also)* Schnipsel *m or nt*; *(of information)* (Bruch)stück *nt*; **~s of (a) conversation** Gesprächsfetzen *pl*

snippy [snɪpɪ] ADJ *(US inf) person, tone* schnippisch, kurz angebunden; **to be in a ~ mood** kurz angebunden sein

snitch [snɪtʃ] *(inf)* VT klauen *(inf)* VI **to ~ on sb** über jdn plaudern *(inf) or* klatschen

snivel ['snɪvl] VI heulen, flennen *(inf)*

sniveller ['snɪvləʳ] N Jammerer *m*

snivelling, *(US)* **sniveling** ['snɪvlɪŋ] ADJ heulend, flennend *(inf)* N Geheul(e) *nt (inf)*, Geflenne *nt (inf)*

snob [snɒb] N Snob *m*; **~ appeal** *or* **value** Snob-appeal *m*

snobbery ['snɒbərɪ] N Snobismus *m*

snobbish ADJ ['snɒbɪʃ] snobistisch, versnobt *(inf)*; *place* für Snobs; **to be ~ about sth** bei etw wählerisch sein

snobbishly ['snɒbɪʃlɪ] ADV snobistisch, versnobt *(inf)*

snobbishness ['snɒbɪʃnɪs] N Snobismus *m*, Versnobtheit *f (inf)*

snobby ['snɒbɪ] ADJ snobistisch; **she's ~** sie ist ein Snob

snog [snɒg] *(Brit inf)* N Knutscherei *f (inf)*; **to have a ~ with sb** mit jdm rumknutschen *(inf)* VI rumknutschen *(inf)* VT abknutschen *(inf)*

snood [snuːd] N Haarnetz *nt*

snook [snuːk] N → **cock VT b**

snooker ['snuːkəʳ] N Snooker *nt* VT **to ~ sb** jdn sperren; **to be ~ed** *(Brit fig inf)* festsitzen *(inf)*; **I've ~ed myself** *(fig inf)* ich habe mich festgefahren

snoop [snuːp] N **a** = **snooper b** *(= act)* **I'll have a ~ around** ich gucke mich mal (ein bisschen) um VI schnüffeln; **to ~ about** *(Brit) or* **around** herumschnüffeln

snooper ['snuːpəʳ] N Schnüffler(in) *m(f)*

snoopy ADJ, **snoopily** ADV ['snuːpɪ, -lɪ] *(inf)* neugierig

snootily ['snuːtɪlɪ] ADV *(inf)* hochnäsig, von oben herab

snooty ['snuːtɪ] ADJ *(+er) (inf)* hochnäsig

snooze [snuːz] N Schläfchen *nt*, Nickerchen *nt*; **to have a ~** ein Schläfchen machen; **~ button** *(on alarm clock)* Schlummertaste *f* VI dösen, ein Nickerchen machen

snore [snɔːʳ] N Schnarchen *nt no pl* VI schnarchen

snorer ['snɔːrəʳ] N Schnarcher(in) *m(f)*

snoring ['snɔːrɪŋ] N Schnarchen *nt*

snorkel ['snɔːkl] N Schnorchel *m* VI schnorcheln; **to go ~ling** schnorcheln gehen

snorkelling, *(US)* **snorkeling** ['snɔːkəlɪŋ] N Schnorcheln *nt*

snort [snɔːt] N Schnauben *nt no pl*; *(of person also)* Prusten *nt no pl*; *(of boar)* Grunzen *nt no pl*; **with a ~ of rage** wutschnaubend; **he gave a ~ of contempt/rage** er schnaubte verächtlich/vor Wut; **to give a ~ of laughter** losprusten VI schnauben; *(person also)* prusten; *(boar)* grunzen VT **a** *(person)* schnauben **b** *drugs* sniffen *(sl)*

snot [snɒt] N *(inf)* Rotz *m (inf)*

snotty ['snɒtɪ] ADJ *(+er) (inf)* **a** *handkerchief* rotzig *(inf)*; *child* rotznäsig *(inf)*; **~ nose** Rotznase *f (inf)* **b** *(fig: = snooty)* rotzig *(inf)*, pampig *(inf)*

snotty-nosed ['snɒtɪ'nəʊzd] ADJ rotznäsig *(inf)*

snout [snaʊt] N **a** *(of animal)* Schnauze *f*; *(of pig also, of insect)* Rüssel *m*; *(inf, of person)* Rüssel *m (inf)*, Zinken *m (inf)* **b** *(sl: = informer)* Spitzel *m* **c** *(Brit, inf, = tobacco)* Knaster *m (inf)*

snow [snəʊ] N **a** Schnee *m*; *(= snowfall)* Schneefall *m*; **new ~** Neuschnee *m*; **the ~s that lie on the plains** der Schnee in der Ebene; **the heavy ~s last winter** die heftigen Schneefälle im letzten Winter; **as white as ~** schneeweiß, blütenweiß; **as pure as the driven ~** engelrein **b** *(TV)* Geflimmer *nt*, Schnee *m* **c** *(sl: = cocaine or heroin)* Schnee *m (inf)* VI schneien

▶ **snow in** VT *sep (usu pass)* **to be** *or* **get snowed in** einschneien; **we are snowed in** wir sind eingeschneit

▶ **snow off** VT *sep (usu pass)* **to be snowed off** wegen Schnee abgesagt werden *or* ausfallen

▶ **snow under** VT *sep (inf, usu pass)* **to be snowed under** *(with work)* reichlich eingedeckt sein; *(with requests)* überhäuft werden

▶ **snow up** VT *sep (usu pass)* = **snow in**

snow: **snowball** N Schneeball *m*; *(= drink)* Snowball *m*; **he doesn't stand a ~'s chance in hell** *(Brit inf)* seine Chancen sind gleich null VT Schneebälle werfen auf *(+acc)* VI eskalieren; **we must take action now otherwise things will ~ and get out of control** wir müssen jetzt etwas unternehmen, sonst wachsen uns die Dinge über den Kopf; **opposition to the referendum just ~ed** die Opposition gegen die Volksabstimmung wuchs lawinenartig an; **snowball effect** N Schneeballeffekt *m*; **snow bank** N *(esp US)* Schneeverwehung *f*, Schneewehe *f*; **snow-blind** ADJ schneeblind; **snow blindness** N Schneeblindheit *f*; **snow-blower** N Schneefräse *f*; **snowboard** ['snəʊbɔːd] N Snowboard *nt* VI snowboarden, Snowboard fahren; **snowboarder** N Snowboarder(in) *m(f)*; **snowboarding** N Snowboarding *nt*, Snowboardfahren *nt*; **snowbound** ADJ eingeschneit; **snow cannon** N *(Ski)* Schneekanone *f*; **snowcapped** ADJ schneebedeckt; **snowcat** N *(Ski)* Pistenwalze *f*; **snow chains** PL Schneeketten *pl*; **snow-clad** *(poet)*, **snow-covered** ADJ verschneit; **snow-cuffs** PL Schneegamaschen *pl*; **snowdrift** N Schneewehe *f*; **snowdrop** N Schneeglöckchen *nt*; **snowfall** N Schneefall *m*; **snowfield** N Schneefeld *nt*; **snowflake** N Schneeflocke *f*; **snow goggles** PL Schneebrille *f*; **snow goose** N Schneegans *f*; **snow guard** N *(on roof)* Schneefang *m*; **snow-in-summer** N *(Bot)* Hornkraut *nt*; **snow job** N *(inf)* freundliches Gerede; **to do a ~ on sb** jdn einzuwickeln versuchen *(inf pej)*; **snow leopard** N Schneeleopard *m*; **snow line** N Schneegrenze *f*; **snowman** N Schneemann *m* → **abominable**; **snowmobile** N Schneemobil *nt*; **snowplough**, *(US)* **snowplow** N *(also Ski)* Schneepflug *m*; **snowshed** N *(US)* Schneedach *nt*; **snowshoe** N Schneeschuh *m*; **snowslide** N *(US)* Schneerutsch *m*; **snowstorm** N Schneesturm *m*; **snowsuit** N gefütterter Overall; **snow tyre**, *(US)* **snow tire** N Winterreifen *m*; **Snow White** N Schneewittchen *nt*; **snow-white** ADJ schneeweiß; *hair, beard also* schlohweiß

snowy ['snəʊɪ] ADJ *(+er)* **a** *weather, region* schneereich; *hills* verschneit; **it was very ~ yesterday** gestern hat es viel geschneit **b** *(= white as snow)* schneeweiß

snowy owl N Schneeeule *f*

SNP *abbr of* **Scottish National Party**

snub [snʌb] N Brüskierung *f*; **to give sb a ~** jdn brüskieren, jdn vor den Kopf stoßen; *subordinate, pupil etc (verbally)* jdm über den Mund fahren; **to get a ~ from sb** von jdm brüskiert *or* vor den Kopf gestoßen werden VT **a** *person* brüskieren, vor den Kopf stoßen; *subordinate, pupil (verbally)* über den Mund fahren *(+dat)*; *suggestion, proposal* kurz abtun; *offer, request, plea* ablehnen; *talks* bewusst fernbleiben *(+dat)* **b** *(= ignore, not greet)* schneiden

snub: **snub nose** N Stupsnase *f*; **snub-nosed** ADJ stumpfnasig; *person also* stupsnasig

snuff [snʌf] N **a** Schnupftabak *m*; **to take ~** schnupfen **b to be/come up to ~** *(dated inf)* mithalten können *(inf)* VT *candle (= extinguish: also* **snuff out***)* auslöschen; *(= trim wick)* putzen, schnäuzen *(old)*; *(fig) revolt* ersticken; *hopes* zunichtemachen, zerschlagen; **to ~ out sb's life** jds Lebenslicht auslöschen; **to ~ it** *(Brit inf: = die)* abkratzen *(sl)*

snuffbox ['snʌfbɒks] N Schnupftabakdose *f*, Tabatiere *f (geh)*

snuffer ['snʌfəʳ] N Kerzenlöscher *m*; **~s** Lichtputzschere *f*

snuffle ['snʌfl] N Schniefen *nt no pl*; **to have the ~s** *(inf)* einen leichten Schnupfen haben VI *(person, animal)* schnüffeln; *(with cold, from crying also)* schniefen *(inf)*

snuff movie N *brutaler (Porno)film, in dem tatsächlich gestorben wird*

snug [snʌg] ADJ *(+er) (= cosy, comfortable)* behaglich, gemütlich; *(= cosy and warm) bed, garment, room etc* mollig warm, behaglich warm; *(= sheltered) spot, harbour* geschützt; *(= close-fitting)* gut sitzend *attr*; *(= tight)* eng; **to be ~ in bed/in one's sleeping bag** es im Bett/Schlafsack mollig *or* behaglich warm haben; **I was as ~ as a bug in a rug** *(Brit inf)* es war urgemütlich; **it is a good ~ fit** es passt gut N *(Brit, in pub)* kleines Nebenzimmer

snuggle ['snʌgl] VI sich schmiegen, sich kuscheln; **to ~ down in bed** sich ins Bett kuscheln; **to ~ up (to sb)** sich (an jdn) anschmiegen *or* ankuscheln; **I like to ~ up with a book** ich mache es mir gern mit einem Buch gemütlich; **to ~ into sb/sth** sich an jdm ankuscheln/in etw *(acc)* einkuscheln; **the cottages ~d in the valley** die Häuschen schmiegten sich ins Tal VT an sich *(acc)* schmiegen

snugly ['snʌglɪ] ADV **a** *(= cosily)* gemütlich, behaglich; **~ tucked in, ~ tucked up (in bed)** mollig warm eingepackt (im Bett) **b** *(= tightly) close* fest; *fit* gut

snugness ['snʌgnɪs] N *(= cosiness, comfort)* Behaglichkeit *f*, Gemütlichkeit *f*; *(= cosiness and warmth)* mollige *or* behagliche Wärme; *(= sheltered nature)* Geschütztheit *f*; *(= closeness of fit: of garment)* guter Sitz

So *abbr of* **south** S

so [səʊ] ADV **a** so; **so much tea** so viel Tee; **so many flies** so viele Fliegen; **he was so stupid (that)** er war so *or* dermaßen *or* derart dumm(, dass); **he's so quick I can't keep up with him** er ist so schnell, dass ich nicht mithalten kann; **not so ... as** nicht so ... wie; **he is not so fast a runner as you** er ist kein so schneller Läufer wie Sie, er kann nicht so schnell laufen wie Sie; **I am not so stupid as to believe that** *or* **that I believe that** so dumm bin ich nicht, dass ich das glaube(n würde); **he was so stupid as to tell her** er war so dumm und hat es ihr gesagt; **would you be so kind as to open the door?** wären Sie bitte so freundlich und würden die Tür öffnen?; **so great a writer as Shakespeare** ein so großer Dichter wie Shakespeare; **he's not been so well recently** in letzter Zeit geht es ihm nicht so sonderlich; **how are things? – not so bad!** wie gehts? – nicht schlecht!; **not so as you'd notice** aber das fällt kaum auf

b *(emphatic) glad, sorry, sure, rich, hurt* so; *pleased, relieved, hope, wish* sehr; *love* so sehr; *hate* so sehr, derart; **that's so true** das ist ja so wahr, das ist wirklich wahr; **I'm so very tired** ich bin ja so müde; **it's not so very difficult** es ist gar nicht so schwer; **it would be so much better/nicer** *etc* es wäre so viel besser/netter *etc*; **so much the better/worse (for sb)** umso besser/schlechter (für jdn); **that's so kind of you** das ist wirklich sehr nett von Ihnen; **I so hope you're right!** ich hoffe (wirklich) sehr, dass Sie recht haben!

c *(replacing longer sentence)* da, es; **I hope so** hoffentlich; *(emphatic)* das hoffe ich doch sehr; **I think so** ich glaube schon; **I never said so** das habe ich nie gesagt; **I told you so** ich habe es dir doch *or* ja gesagt; **I told you so yesterday** das habe ich dir gestern gesagt; **why should I do it? – because I say so** warum muss ich das tun? – weil ich es sage, darum; **I didn't say so** das habe ich nicht gesagt; **can I go/will you do it? – I suppose so** darf ich gehen/machen Sie es? – na ja, meinetwegen; **is that right/can I do it like that? – I suppose so** stimmt das/kann ich es so machen? – ich glaube schon; **so I believe** ja, ich glaube schon; **so I see** ja, das sehe ich; **please, do so** bitte(, tun Sie es ruhig); **perhaps so** vielleicht; **it may be so** es kann schon sein; **so be it** nun gut; **if so** wenn ja; **he said he would finish it this week, and so he did** er hat gesagt, er würde es diese Woche fertig machen und das hat er auch (gemacht); **how** *or* **why so?** wieso *or* warum das?; **or so they say** oder so heißt es jedenfalls; **he's a millionaire, or so he says** er ist Millionär, zumindest *or* jedenfalls behauptet er das; **it is so!** *(contradiction)* doch!; **I can so!** *(contradiction)* und ob (ich das kann)!, doch!; **I didn't say that – you did so** das habe ich nicht gesagt – doch, das hast du (sehr wohl gesagt)!; **you've got the papers? – yes, that's so** haben Sie die Papiere? – jawohl; **that is so** das stimmt; **if that's so** wenn das stimmt; **he's coming by plane – is that so?** er kommt mit dem Flugzeug – ach so, ja?, tatsächlich?; **you're a fool – is that so?** du bist ein Idiot – ach, wirklich?; **... – so it is/I have/he did** *etc* ... – (ja) tatsächlich; **he's a nice chap – so he is** er ist ein netter Kerl – ja, wirklich *or* ja, das ist er auch

d *(= thus, in this way)* so; **perhaps it was better so** vielleicht war es auch besser so; **so it was that ...** so kam es, dass ...; **and so it was** und so war es auch; **by so doing he has ...** dadurch hat er ..., indem er das tat, hat er ...; **bother them! he exclaimed, and so saying walked out** zum Kuckuck! rief er, und damit ging er hinaus; **... and so to bed ...** und dann ins Bett; **and so on** *or* **forth** und so weiter

e *(unspecified amount)* **how high is it? – oh, about so high** *(accompanied by gesture)* wie hoch ist das? – oh, ungefähr so; **so much per head** so viel pro Kopf; **they looked like so many soldiers** sie sahen wie so viele andere Soldaten auch aus; **how long will it take? – a week or so** wie lange dauert das? – ungefähr eine Woche *or* so eine Woche; **50 or so** etwa 50

f *(= likewise)* auch; **so am/would/do/could** *etc* **I** ich auch; **he's wrong and so are you** ihr irrt euch beide; **as A is to B, so D is to E** A verhält sich zu B wie D zu E

g he walked past and didn't so much as look at me er ging vorbei, ohne mich auch nur anzusehen; **he didn't say so much as thank you** er hat nicht einmal danke gesagt; **I haven't so much as a penny** ich habe keinen Cent; **so much for that!** *(inf)* das wärs ja wohl gewesen! *(inf)*; **so much for him** *(inf)* das war ja wohl nichts mit ihm! *(inf)*; **so much for his/her help** schöne Hilfe! *(inf)*; **so much for his ambition to be a doctor/for our new car** aus der Traum vom Arztwerden/vom neuen Auto; **so much for his promises** und er hat solche Versprechungen gemacht → **ever, far ADV d, just**[1], **long**[1] **ADV a, c, quite a**

CONJ **a** *(expressing purpose)* damit; **so (that) you don't have to do it again** damit Sie es nicht noch einmal machen müssen; **we hurried so as not to be late** wir haben uns beeilt, um nicht zu spät zu kommen

b *(expressing result, = therefore)* also; **it rained (and) so we couldn't go out** es regnete, also konnten wir nicht weggehen *or* und deshalb konnten wir nicht weggehen; **he refused to move so (that) finally the police had to carry him away** er weigerte sich wegzugehen, so dass *or* sodass ihn die Polizei schließlich wegtragen musste; **he was standing in the doorway so (that) no-one could get past** er stand in der Tür, sodass *or* so dass niemand vorbeikonnte; **I told him to leave and so he did** ich habe ihm gesagt, er solle gehen und das hat er auch getan; **so I told him he could get lost** *(inf)* da habe ich ihm gesagt, er kann *or* könnte mir den Buckel runterrutschen; **so, far from helping us, he ...** nicht nur, dass er uns nicht geholfen hat, sondern ...; **so you see ...** wie du siehst ...

c *(in questions, exclamations)* also; **so you're Spanish?** Sie sind also Spanier(in)?; **so you're leaving?** Sie gehen also?; **so you lost it, did you?** du hast es also verloren, wie?; **so you did do it!** du hast es also doch gemacht!; **so there you are!** hier steckst du also!; **so what did you do?** und was haben Sie (da) gemacht?; **so (what)?** *(inf)* (na) und?; **so what if you don't do it?** *(inf)* (na) und wenn dus nicht machst?; **I'm not going, so there!** *(inf)* ich geh nicht, fertig, aus!

s. o. *(St Ex) abbr of* **seller's option**

soak [səʊk] VT **a** *(= wet)* durchnässen **b** *(= steep)* einweichen *(in in +dat)*; **to ~ oneself in sth** *(fig)* sich in etw *(acc)* vertiefen **c** *(inf) the rich etc* schröpfen; **to ~ sb for sth** jdn um etw angehen
VI **a** *(= steep)* **leave it to ~** weichen Sie es ein; *(in dye)* lassen Sie die Farbe einziehen; **to ~ in a bath** sich einweichen *(inf)*
b *(= penetrate)* **rain has ~ed through the ceiling** der Regen ist durch die Decke gesickert; **the coffee was ~ing into the carpet** der Kaffee saugte sich in den Teppich
N **a** *(= act of soaking)* **give the washing a good ~** lassen Sie die Wäsche gut einweichen; **the sheets are in ~** die Laken sind eingeweicht; **the garden needs a ~** der Garten muss gründlich bewässert werden; **I had a long ~ in the bath** ich habe lange in der Wanne gelegen
b *(inf: = drunkard)* Schluckbruder *m (inf)*, Säufer(in) *m(f)*

▶ **soak in** VI *(stain, dye etc)* einziehen; **to leave sth to soak in** etw einziehen lassen

▶ **soak off** VT *sep* ablösen VI sich (ab)lösen *(+prep obj* von)

▶ **soak out** VT *sep mark, stain* durch Einweichen entfernen VI beim Einweichen herausgehen

▶ **soak up** VT *sep liquid* aufsaugen; *sunshine* genießen; *alcohol* in sich *(acc)* hineinkippen; *sound, money, resources* schlucken; *(fig) atmosphere* in sich *(acc)* hineinsaugen; *information* aufsaugen

soaked [səʊkt] ADJ **a** *(= drenched) person, garment* durchnässt; **her dress was ~** ihr Kleid war klatschnass *(inf)* or völlig durchnässt; **his T-shirt was ~ in sweat** sein T-Shirt war schweißgetränkt; **to get ~** völlig durchnässt werden; **to be ~ to the skin, to be ~ through** bis auf die Haut nass sein **b** *(fig: = steeped)* **to be ~ in sth** *(person)* in etw *(dat)* ganz aufgehen; *(performance etc)* von etw durchdrungen sein

soaking [ˈsəʊkɪŋ] ADJ *person* klitschnass, patschnass; *object also* triefend ADV **~ wet** triefend nass, klitschnass N *(= steeping)* Einweichen *nt no indef art*; **to get a ~** patschnass werden; **to give sth a ~** etw einweichen

so-and-so [ˈsəʊənsəʊ] N *(inf)* **a** *(= unspecified person)* Soundso *no art*; **~ up at the shop** Herr/Frau Soundso im Laden **b** *(pej)* **he's a real/an old ~** das ist ein gemeiner Kerl; **you old ~** du bist vielleicht einer/eine

soap [səʊp] N **a** *(= substance)* Seife *f* **b** *(= soap opera)* Seifenoper *f (inf)*, Soap *f (inf)* VT einseifen, abseifen

soap: **soapbox** N *(lit: = packing case)* Seifenkiste *f*; *(fig: = platform)* Apfelsinenkiste *f*; *(as cart)* Seifenkiste *f*; **to get up on one's ~** *(fig)* Volksreden *pl* halten; **soapbox derby** N Seifenkistenrennen *nt*; **soapbox evangelist** N Wanderprediger(in) *m(f)*; **soapbox orator** N Volksredner(in) *m(f)*; **soap bubble** N Seifenblase *f*; **soapdish** N Seifenschale *f*; **soap dispenser** N Seifenspender *m*; **soap flakes** PL Seifenflocken *pl*; **soap opera** N *(TV, Rad: inf)* Seifenoper *f (inf)*, Soap-Opera *f (inf)*; **soap powder** N Seifenpulver *nt*; **soapstone** N Speckstein *m*; **soapsuds** PL Seifenschaum *m*

soapy [ˈsəʊpɪ] ADJ *(+er)* **a** *taste, smell* seifig; **~ water** Seifenwasser *nt* **b** *(pej: = sentimental)* rührselig

soar [sɔːˈ] VI **a** *(rise: also* **soar up***)* aufsteigen; **to ~ (up) into the sky** zum Himmel steigen **b** *(fig, building, tower)* hochragen; *(price, cost, profit)* hochschnellen; *(ambition, popularity, reputation, hopes)* einen Aufschwung nehmen; *(morale, spirits)* einen Aufschwung bekommen; **the tower/hill ~ed above the town** der Turm/Hügel ragte über die Stadt hinaus

soaraway [ˈsɔːrəweɪ] ADJ *(inf) success* fantastisch *(inf)*; *career* steil; **~ sales** explosionsartig ansteigende Verkaufszahlen *pl*

soaring [ˈsɔːrɪŋ] ADJ **a** *bird, plane* aufsteigend, in die Luft steigend; *tower* hoch aufragend; *imagination, ideas, ambition* hochfliegend; *popularity, reputation* schnell zunehmend; *prices* in die Höhe schnellend; *inflation* unaufhaltsam; *unemployment* hochschnellend; *pride, hopes* wachsend; **I watched the lark's ~ flight** ich sah, wie sich die Lerche in die Lüfte schwang; **the ~ crime rate** die schnell zunehmende Verbrechensrate **b** *(liter) voice, music* sich erhebend

sob [sɒb] N Schluchzer *m*, Schluchzen *nt no pl*; **to give a ~** (auf)schluchzen; **..., he said with a ~ ...** ..., sagte er schluchzend VI schluchzen *(with* vor *+dat)*; **~, ~** *(inf)* schluchz, schluchz VT schluchzen; **to ~ oneself to sleep** sich in den Schlaf weinen

▶ **sob out** VT *sep information* schluchzend hervorstoßen; *story* schluchzend erzählen; **to sob one's heart out** sich *(dat)* die Seele aus dem Leib weinen

s.o.b. *(esp US sl) abbr of* **son of a bitch**

sobbing [ˈsɒbɪŋ] N Schluchzen *nt* ADJ schluchzend

sober [ˈsəʊbəˈ] ADJ **a** *(= not drunk)* nüchtern; **to be as ~ as a judge** stocknüchtern sein *(inf)* **b** *(= sedate, serious) life, expression, mood, occasion, person* ernst; *(= sensible, moderate) opinion* vernünftig; *assessment, statement, advice, facts* nüchtern **c** *(= not bright or showy)* schlicht, dezent; *colour, suit* gedeckt

▶ **sober down** VI ruhiger werden

▶ **sober up** VT *sep (lit)* nüchtern machen; *(fig)* zur Vernunft bringen VI *(lit)* nüchtern werden; *(fig)* ruhiger werden; *(after laughing, joking etc)* sich beruhigen

sober-headed [ˌsəʊbəˈhedɪd] ADJ nüchtern, vernünftig

sobering [ˈsəʊbərɪŋ] ADJ *effect, experience, thought* ernüchternd

soberly [ˈsəʊbəlɪ] ADV nüchtern; *behave* vernünftig; *dress, furnish* schlicht, dezent

sober-minded [ˌsəʊbəˈmaɪndɪd] ADJ nüchtern, vernünftig

soberness [ˈsəʊbənɪs] N = **sobriety**

sobersides [ˈsəʊbəsaɪdz] N *(dated inf)* Fadian *m (inf)*

sobriety [səˈbraɪɪtɪ] N **a** *(= not being drunk)* Nüchternheit *f*; **she maintained her ~ for 7 years** sie hat 7 Jahre lang nicht getrunken **b** *(= seriousness, sedateness)* Solidität *f*; *(of dress etc)* Schlichtheit *f*, Dezentheit *f*; *(of colour)* Gedecktheit *f*

sobriquet [ˈsəʊbrɪkeɪ], **soubriquet** N Spitzname *m*

sob: **sob sister** N *(esp US inf)* Briefkastentante *f (inf)*; **sob story** N *(inf)* rührselige Geschichte *(inf)*; **sob stuff** N *(inf)* Schmalz *m (inf)*; *(= book, film)* Tränendrüsendrücker *m (inf)*; *(= heartrending tale)* todtraurige Geschichte *(inf)*

Soc *abbr of* **Socialist** Soz.

soc *abbr of* **society** Ges.

so-called [ˌsəʊˈkɔːld] ADJ sogenannt; *(= supposed)* angeblich

soccer [ˈsɒkəˈ] N Fußball *m*; **~ player** *(US)* Fußballer(in) *m(f)*, Fußballspieler(in) *m(f)*

soccer mom N *(US inf) gestresste Frau, die ständig ihre Kinder zu Sportveranstaltungen fahren muss*

sociability [ˌsəʊʃəˈbɪlɪtɪ] N Geselligkeit *f*

sociable [ˈsəʊʃəbl] ADJ *(= gregarious)* gesellig; *(= friendly)* freundlich; **... just to be ~** ..., man möchte sich ja nicht ausschließen; **I'm not feeling very ~ today** mir ist heute nicht nach Geselligkeit (zumute or zu Mute); **they eat together because it's ~** sie essen aus Gründen der Geselligkeit zusammen

sociably [ˈsəʊʃəblɪ] ADV *say* freundlich; **he didn't behave very ~** er war nicht gerade umgänglich

social [ˈsəʊʃəl] ADJ **a** *(= relating to community, = Admin, Pol)* sozial; *structure, development, conditions, evil* gesellschaftlich, sozial; **~ order/system** Gesellschafts- or Sozialordnung *f*/-system *nt*; **~ reform/legislation/policy** Sozialreform *f*/-gesetzgebung *f*/-politik *f*; **to suffer from ~ deprivation** sozial benachteiligt sein; **~ justice** soziale Gerechtigkeit; **~ programme** Sozialprogramm *nt*; **~ research** Sozialforschung *f*; **~ spending** die Sozialausgaben *pl*; **to have a ~ conscience** ein soziales Gewissen haben; **to be a ~ outcast/misfit** ein sozialer Außenseiter/eine soziale Außenseiterin sein; **the norms of ~ behaviour** die gesellschaftlichen Normen *pl*; **~ skills** soziale Fähigkeiten *pl*
b *engagements, pleasures, ambitions, life, equal, superior, event, activities* gesellschaftlich; *visit* privat; *relationship* sozial; *behaviour* in Gesellschaft; *distinctions, advancement, rank, status* sozial, gesellschaftlich; **~ snobbery** Standesdünkel *m*; **to be sb's ~ inferior/superior** gesellschaftlich unter/über jdm stehen; **a room for ~ functions** ein Gesellschaftsraum *m*; *(larger)* ein Saal *m* für Gesellschaften; **there isn't much ~ life around here** hier in der Gegend wird gesellschaftlich nicht viel geboten; **how's your ~ life these days?** *(inf)* und was treibst du so privat? *(inf)*; **a job which leaves no time for one's/a ~ life** ein Beruf, bei dem man keine Freizeit or kein Privatleben hat; **to have an active** or **a good ~ life** ein ausgefülltes Privatleben haben; **to broaden** or **widen one's ~ circle** seinen Bekanntenkreis erweitern; **to be a ~ drinker/smoker** nur in Gesellschaft trinken/rauchen; **a ~ acquaintance** ein Bekannter, eine Bekannte; **this isn't a ~ call** or **visit** dies ist kein privater Besuch; **to have ~ contact with sb** privaten Kontakt mit jdm pflegen
c *(= gregarious) evening, person* gesellig; *(= living in groups) animals, bees, ants etc* gesellig lebend, sozial; **~ gathering** *(form)* geselliges Beisammensein; **man is a ~ animal** der Mensch ist ein Gesellschaftswesen
N geselliger Abend

social: **social administration** N Sozialverwaltung *f*; **social anthropologist** N Sozialanthropologe *m*/-anthropologin *f*; **social anthropology** N Sozialanthropologie *f*; **Social Chapter** N *(Pol)* Sozialcharta *f*; **Social Charter** N *(Pol)* Sozialcharta *f*; **social class** N gesellschaftliche Klasse, Gesellschaftsklasse *f*; **social climber** N Emporkömmling *m (pej)*, sozialer Aufsteiger, soziale Aufsteigerin; **social club** N Verein *m*, Klub *m* für geselliges Beisammensein; **social column** N Gesellschaftsspalte *f*; **social contract** N **the ~** *(Hist)* der Gesellschaftsvertrag; **social democracy** N Sozialdemokratie *f*; **social democrat** N Sozialdemokrat(in) *m(f)*; **social democratic** ADJ sozialdemokratisch **the Social Democratic Party** *(Brit)* die sozialdemokratische Partei; **social disease** N **a** *(euph: = VD)* Geschlechtskrankheit *f* **b** *(caused by social conditions)* Volksseuche *f*; **social engineering** N *(Sociol)* Steuerung *f* des Sozialverhaltens; **social exclusion** N sozialer Ausschluss; **social fund** N Sozialfonds *m*; **social history** N Sozialgeschichte *f*; **social housing** N *(Brit)* Sozialwohnungen *pl*; **social insurance** N Sozialversicherung *f*

socialism [ˈsəʊʃəlɪzəm] N Sozialismus *m*

socialist [ˈsəʊʃəlɪst] ADJ sozialistisch; **the Socialist Republic of ...** die Sozialistische Republik ...; **Socialist Workers' Party** Sozialistische Arbeiterpartei N Sozialist(in) *m(f)*

socialistic [ˌsəʊʃəˈlɪstɪk] ADJ *(esp pej)* sozialistisch angehaucht

socialist realism N *(Art, Liter)* sozialistischer Realismus

socialite [ˈsəʊʃəlaɪt] N *(inf)* Angehörige(r) *mf* der Schickeria or der feinen Gesellschaft; *(= man also)* Salonlöwe *m (inf)*; **a London ~** eine Figur der Londoner Schickeria

socialization [ˌsəʊʃəlaɪˈzeɪʃən] N *(Pol)* Vergesellschaftung *f*, Sozialisierung *f*; *(Sociol, Psych)* Sozialisation *f*

socialize [ˈsəʊʃəlaɪz] VT sozialisieren; *means of production* vergesellschaften VI **to ~ with sb** *(= meet socially)* mit jdm gesellschaftlich verkehren; *(= chat to)* sich mit jdm unterhalten; **I don't ~ much these days** ich komme zurzeit nicht viel unter die Leute; **she ~s a lot** sie hat ein reges gesellschaftliches Leben

socially ['səʊʃəlɪ] ADV **a** *(relating to community)* gesellschaftlich; *deprived, structured etc* sozial; **~ acceptable/unacceptable** gesellschaftlich akzeptabel/unakzeptabel; **~ aware** sozialbewusst, gesellschaftlich bewusst; **~ inferior** gesellschaftlich auf einer niedrigeren Stufe stehend; **~ prominent** gesellschaftlich bedeutend **b** *(as opposed to professionally etc)* gesellschaftlich; *meet* privat; **to mix ~ with sb** privaten Umgang mit jdm haben; **to know sb ~** jdn privat kennen

social: **social media** NPL *(Internet)* soziale Medien *pl*; **social networking** N Social Networking *nt, Pflege von sozialen Kontakten über das Internet*; **social networking site** N soziales Netzwerk; **social partner** N *(Pol)* Sozialpartner *m*; **social realism** N *(Art, Liter)* **a** sozialer Realismus **b** = **socialist realism**; **social science** N Sozialwissenschaft *f*; **social scientist** N Sozialwissenschaftler(in) *m(f)*; **social secretary** N persönlicher Sekretär, persönliche Sekretärin; *(of club)* Veranstaltungsbeauftragte(r) *mf*; **social security** N *(Brit)* Sozialhilfe *f*; *(US)* Sozialversicherungsleistungen *pl*; *(= scheme)* Sozialversicherung *f*; **to be on ~** *(Brit)* Sozialhilfeempfänger(in) sein; *(US)* Sozialversicherungsleistungen erhalten; **~ benefits** Sozialleistungen *pl*; **~ payments** *(Brit)* ≈ Sozialhilfe *f*; *(US)* Sozialversicherungsbezüge *pl*; **~ taxes** Sozialabgaben *pl*; **the ~ budget** der Sozialhaushalt; **~ minister** *(Brit)* Minister(in) *m(f)* für Soziales; **Social Security Administration** *(US)* Sozialversicherungsbehörde *f*; *(= social security office)* Sozialamt *nt*

> **SOCIAL SECURITY NUMBER**
>
> Die **social security number**, die Sozialversicherungsnummer, ist in den USA zu einer wichtigen landesweiten Identifikationshilfe geworden. Sie setzt sich aus neun Zahlen zusammen und war ursprünglich nur bei der Aufnahme eines Beschäftigungsverhältnisses oder für den Bezug von Sozialhilfe nötig. Seit 1987 bekommen Kinder gleich bei der Geburt eine **social security number** zugeteilt. Die Nummer wird auf Bankschecks gedruckt, einige Staaten benutzen sie für den Führerschein und Colleges und Universitäten als Immatrikulationsnummer.

social: **social services** PL Sozialdienste *pl*, soziale Einrichtungen *pl*; **social studies** N *sing or pl* ≈ Gemeinschaftskunde *f*; **social welfare** N soziales Wohl; **~ programme** Sozialfürsorgeprogramm *nt*; **~ system** (soziales) Wohlfahrtssystem; **social work** N Sozialarbeit *f*; **~ training** Sozialhelferausbildung *f*; **social worker** N Sozialarbeiter(in) *m(f)*

societal [sə'saɪətl] ADJ gesellschaftlich

society [sə'saɪətɪ] N **a** *(= social community)* die Gesellschaft; **modern industrial ~** die moderne Industriegesellschaft **b** *(= company)* Gesellschaft *f*; **I enjoy her ~** *(esp liter)* ich bin gerne in ihrer Gesellschaft; **everyone needs human ~** jeder braucht die Gesellschaft anderer Menschen **c** *(= high society)* die Gesellschaft; **London ~** die Londoner Gesellschaft, die gesellschaftlichen Kreise Londons; **to go into ~** in die Gesellschaft eingeführt werden; **the years she spent in ~** die Jahre, die sie in gesellschaftlichen *or* feinen Kreisen verbracht hat **d** *(= club, organization)* Verein *m*; *(learned, Comm)* Gesellschaft *f*; *(debating, history, dramatic etc, Sch)* Arbeitsgemeinschaft *f*; *(Univ)* Klub *m*; **cooperative ~** Genossenschaft *f*; **Society of Jesus** Gesellschaft Jesu

society *in cpds* Gesellschafts-; **society column** N Gesellschaftsspalte *f*; **society gossip** N Gesellschaftsklatsch *m*; **society man** N Mann *m* der Gesellschaft; **society wedding** N Hochzeit *f* in den besseren Kreisen

socio- [,səʊsɪəʊ-] PREF sozio-; **socioeconomic** sozioökonomisch; **socioeconomic grouping** sozioökonomische Gruppe; **sociolinguistic** soziolinguistisch; **sociolinguistics** Soziolinguistik *f*

sociological ADJ [,səʊsɪə'lɒdʒɪkəl] soziologisch

sociologically [,səʊsɪə'lɒdʒɪkəlɪ] ADV soziologisch; **~ speaking** in soziologischer Hinsicht

sociologist [,səʊsɪ'ɒlədʒɪst] N Soziologe *m*, Soziologin *f*

sociology [,səʊsɪ'ɒlədʒɪ] N Soziologie *f*

sociopolitical [,səʊsɪəʊpə'lɪtɪkəl] ADJ sozialpolitisch

sock¹ [sɒk] N Socke *f*, Socken *m (inf)*; *(knee-length)* Kniestrumpf *m*; *(= wind sock)* Wind- *or* Luftsack *m*; **to pull one's ~s up** *(Brit inf)* sich am Riemen reißen *(inf)*; **put a ~ in it!** *(Brit inf)* hör auf damit!; **to work ones ~s off** *(inf)* bis zum Umkippen arbeiten *(inf)*; **this will knock** *or* **blow your ~s off** *(inf)* das wird dich umhauen; **this film knocks the ~s off most other science fiction films** *(inf)* dieser Film stellt die meisten anderen Sciencefictionfilme in den Schatten

sock² N *(inf)* Schlag *m* (mit der Faust); **to give sb a ~ on the jaw/in the eye** jdm eine aufs Kinn/aufs Auge verpassen *(inf)*; **that's a ~ in the eye for her!** *(fig inf)* das hat es ihr ordentlich gegeben! VT *(inf: = hit)* hauen *(inf)*; **~ him one!** knall ihm eine! *(inf)*, hau ihm eine rein! *(inf)*; **he ~ed her right in the eye** er verpasste ihr eine aufs Auge *(inf)*

socket ['sɒkɪt] N **a** *(of eye)* Augenhöhle *f*; *(of joint)* Gelenkpfanne *f*; *(of tooth)* Zahnhöhle *f*; **to pull sb's arm out of its ~** jdm den Arm auskugeln **b** *(Elec)* Steckdose *f*; *(for light bulb)* Fassung *f*; *(Mech)* Sockel *m*, Fassung *f*

socket: **socket joint** N *(Anat, Tech)* Kugelgelenk *nt*; **socket wrench** N *(Tech)* Steckschlüssel *m*

socko ['sɒkəʊ] *(US inf)* N *(= great success)* Bombenerfolg *m (inf)* ADJ *(= great)* bombig *(inf)*

Socrates ['sɒkrəti:z] N Sokrates *m*

Socratic [sɒ'krætɪk] ADJ sokratisch

sod¹ [sɒd] N *(= turf)* Grassode *f*; **beneath the ~** *(liter)* unter dem grünen Rasen *(liter)*

sod² *(Brit inf)* N *(mean, nasty)* Sau *f (inf)*; **the poor ~s** die armen Schweine *(inf)*; **you stupid ~** blöde Sau! *(inf)* VT **~ it!** verdammte Scheiße! *(inf)*; **~ him/you** der kann/du kannst mich mal *(inf) or* mal am Arsch lecken *(vulg)!*

▶ **sod off** VI *(Brit inf)* Leine ziehen *(inf)*; **sod off!** zieh Leine, du Arsch! *(vulg)*

soda ['səʊdə] N **a** *(Chem)* Soda *nt*; *(= sodium oxide)* Natriumoxid *nt*; *(= caustic soda)* Ätznatron *nt* **b** *(= soda water)* Soda(wasser) *nt*; *(US: = sweet fizzy drink)* Limo *f (inf)*, Softdrink *m*

soda: **soda biscuit**, *(US)* **soda cracker** N Kräcker *m*; **soda bread** N *mit Backpulver gebackenes Brot*; **soda crystals** PL (Wasch)soda *nt*; **soda fountain** N *(dated US: serving drinks etc)* Theke *f*; **soda pop** N *(US inf)* Limo *f (inf)*

sod all N *(Brit inf: = nothing)* rein gar nichts; **how much did he give you? – ~ ~** wie viel hat er dir gegeben? – rein gar nichts *(inf)*

soda: **soda siphon** N Siphon *m*; **soda water** N Sodawasser *nt*

sodden ['sɒdn] ADJ durchnäßt, triefnaß; *ground* durchnässt, durchweicht; **to be ~ with drink** sinnlos betrunken sein

sodding ['sɒdɪŋ] *(Brit inf)* ADJ verflucht *(inf)*, Scheiß- *(inf)*; **what a ~ nuisance** verdammte Scheiße *(inf)*; **what the ~ hell is going on?** was zum Teufel geht hier vor? *(inf)* ADV verdammt *(inf)*, verflucht *(inf)*; **I'll ~ murder you if you do that!** verdammt noch mal, ich bring dich um, wenn du das tust! *(inf)*

sodium ['səʊdɪəm] N Natrium *nt*

sodium: **sodium bicarbonate** N Natron *nt*, doppeltkohlensaures Natrium; **sodium carbonate** N Natriumkarbonat *nt*, Soda *nt*; **sodium chloride** N Natriumchlorid *nt*, Kochsalz *nt*; **sodium glutamate** N Natriumglutamat *nt*; **sodium hydroxide** N Natriumhydroxid *nt*, Ätznatron *nt*; **sodium nitrate** N Natriumnitrat *nt*

Sodom ['sɒdəm] N Sodom *nt*; **~ and Gomorrha** Sodom und Gomorr(h)a

sodomite ['sɒdəmaɪt] N *jd, der Analverkehr betreibt*

sodomize ['sɒdəmaɪz] VT sodomisieren

sodomy ['sɒdəmɪ] N Analverkehr *m*

Sod's law [,sɒdz'lɔ:] N *(inf) „Gesetz", demzufolge eine Sache, die schiefgehen kann, auch bestimmt schiefgehen wird*; **after all that it didn't work – that's ~, isn't it?** am Ende hat es noch nicht mal funktioniert – das musste ja so kommen

sofa ['səʊfə] N Sofa *nt*, Couch *f*; **~ bed** Sofabett *nt*, Schlafcouch *f*

soft [sɒft] ADJ *(+er)* **a** weich; *meat* zart; *(pej: = flabby) muscle* schlaff; **a book in ~ covers** ein kartoniertes Buch; **~ cheese** Weichkäse *m*; **~ margarine** ungehärtete Margarine; **~ ice cream** Softeis *nt* **b** *(= smooth) skin* zart; *surface* glatt; *material, velvet* weich; *hair* seidig; **as ~ as silk** *or* **velvet** seiden- *or* samtweich **c** *(= gentle, not harsh)* sanft; *(= subdued) light, sound* gedämpft, sanft; *music* gedämpft; *(= not loud)* leise; *rain, breeze, tap, pressure* leicht; *fold, curve* sanft; *pleat* zart; *line* weich; **a ~ landing** *(lit, fig)* eine weiche Landung **d** *(Ling) consonant* weich **e** *(= weak) character, government* schwach; *treatment* nachsichtig; *(= lenient) teacher, parent* nachsichtig, gutmütig; *judge, sentence, punishment* mild(e); **to be ~ with** *or* **on sb** jdm gegenüber nachgiebig sein; *with children also* jdm alles durchgehen lassen; **to be (too) ~ on sth** (zu) nachgiebig mit etw sein; **to go ~ (on sth)** (einer Sache *(dat)* gegenüber) zu nachgiebig sein; **to have a ~ heart** ein weiches Herz haben; **to be as ~ as shit** *(sl)* ein Weichei sein *(sl)* **f** *(= not tough)* verweichlicht; *liberalism* gemäßigt; **he thinks it's ~ for a boy to play the violin** er hält es für unmännlich, wenn ein Junge Geige spielt; **to make sb ~** jdn verweichlichen; **the ~ left** *(Pol)* die gemäßigte Linke **g** *(= easy) job, life* bequem; **he has a ~ time of it** er hats leicht *or* bequem; **that's a ~ option** das ist der Weg des geringsten Widerstandes **h** *(= kind, warm) smile* warm; **he had another, ~er side to him** er hatte noch eine andere, gefühlvollere Seite **i** *(Econ) currency* weich; *prices* instabil; *stocks, economy, growth* schwach; *market* nachgiebig **j** *drink* alkoholfrei; *drug, pornography* weich; **~ porn film/magazine** weicher Porno; **~ porn actress** Softpornodarstellerin *f* **k** *(Typ, Comput) return, hyphen* weich; **~ fonts** *(for printer)* ladbare Schriften *pl* **l** *(Brit inf: = foolish)* doof *(inf)*, nicht ganz richtig im Kopf *(inf)*; **he's ~ (in the head)** er ist nicht ganz richtig im Kopf *(inf)*; **you must be ~!** du spinnst wohl! *(inf)*; **I must be going ~** ich fange wohl an zu spinnen *(inf)* **m** *(inf: = feeling affection)* **to be ~ on sb** für jdn schwärmen; **to have a ~ spot for sb** eine Schwäche für jdn haben

soft: **softball** N Softball *m*; **soft benefits** PL *(Econ)* nicht-monetäre Leistungen *pl*; **soft-boiled** ADJ *egg* weich (gekocht); **softboot** N *(Sport)* Softboot *m*; **soft centre** N *(= chocolate)* Praline *f (mit Cremefüllung)*; **soft-centred** ADJ mit Cremefüllung; **soft coal** N Stein- *or* Fettkohle *f*; **soft-core** ADJ *pornography* weich; **soft-cover** ADJ **a ~ book** ein Taschenbuch *nt*

soften ['sɒfn] VT weich machen; *water also* enthärten; *light, sound, colour* dämpfen; *effect, sb's anger, reaction, impression, tone* mildern; *outline* weicher machen; *image* weich zeichnen; *voice* sanfter machen; *resistance, opposition, sb's position, stance* schwächen; *demands, impact* abschwächen VI *(material, person, heart)* weich werden; *(voice, look)* sanft werden; *(anger, resistance)* nachlassen; *(outlines)* weicher werden

▶ **soften up** VT sep **a** *(lit)* weich machen **b** *(fig) person, opposition* milde stimmen; *(by flattery etc)* schmeicheln *(+dat)*; *customer* kaufwillig stimmen; *(by bullying)* einschüchtern, weichmachen; *enemy, resistance* zermürben; *enemy position* schwächen; *prisoner* weichmachen VI *(material)* weich werden; *(person, attitude)* nachgiebiger werden; **to soften up on sb** jdm gegenüber nachgiebig *or* schwach werden

softener ['sɒfnəʳ] N Weichmacher *m*; *(for water also)* Enthärtungsmittel *nt*; *(= fabric softener)* Weichspüler *m*, Weichspülmittel *nt*

softening ['sɒfnɪŋ] N **a** *(lit)* Weichmachen *nt*; **~ of the brain** *(Med)* Gehirnerweichung *f* **b** *(fig, of person)* Erweichen *nt*; *(of anger, resistance)* Nachlassen *nt*; **there has been a ~ of his attitude** er ist nachgiebiger geworden

soft: **soft focus** N *(Film, Phot)* Weichzeichnung *f*; **a photo taken in ~** ein Foto mit weichen Kontrasten; **soft-focus lens** N Weichzeichner *m*; **soft-footed** ADJ *tiger, person* auf leisen Sohlen schleichend *attr*; *tread* leise, lautlos; **to be ~** leise gehen; **soft fruit** N *(Brit)* Beerenobst *nt*; **soft furnishings** PL *(Brit) Vorhänge, Teppiche, Kissen etc*; **softhead** N *(inf)* Schwachkopf *m (inf)*; **soft-headed** ADJ *(inf)* doof *(inf)*; **soft-hearted** ADJ weichherzig; **soft-heartedness** N Weichherzigkeit *f*

softie ['sɒftɪ] N *(inf, too tender-hearted)* gutmütiger Trottel *(inf)*; *(sentimental)* sentimentaler Typ *(inf)*; *(effeminate, cowardly)* Schlappschwanz *m (inf)*, Weichling *m (inf)*; **I know I'm an old ~ but ...** ich bin ja ein gutmütiger Typ *or* Mensch, aber ...

softly ['sɒftlɪ] ADV **a** *(= gently, tenderly)* sanft; *(= not loud)* leise; *rain, blow* leicht, sacht; **her hair falls ~ round her shoulders** ihr Haar fällt weich auf die Schultern; **a ~ blowing breeze** ein sanfter *or* schwacher Wind; **~ whipped cream** leicht geschlagene Sahne; **to be ~ spoken** eine angenehme Stimme haben; **~ lit** gedämpft beleuchtet **b** *(= leniently)* nachsichtig

softly-softly [ˌsɒftlɪ'sɒftlɪ] ADJ *(Brit: = careful) approach* vorsichtig; *style* taktvoll ADV sachte; **~ works best** man sollte behutsam vorgehen

softness ['sɒftnɪs] N **a** Weichheit *f*; *(of meat)* Zartheit *f*; *(of muscle)* Schlaffheit *f* **b** *(= smoothness, of skin)* Zartheit *f*; *(of surface)* Glätte *f*; *(of material, velvet)* Weichheit *f*; *(of hair)* Seidigkeit *f* **c** *(= gentleness)* Sanftheit *f*; *(of light)* Gedämpftheit *f*; *(of music)* leiser Klang; *(of rain, breeze, pressure)* Sanftheit *f*, Leichtheit *f* **d** *(Ling, of consonant)* Weichheit *f* **e** *(= weakness, of character, government)* Schwäche *f*; *(of treatment)* Nachsichtigkeit *f*; *(= leniency, of teacher, parent)* Gutmütigkeit *f*; *(of judge, punishment)* Milde *f* **f** *(= ease: of life, job)* Bequemlichkeit *f*

soft: **soft option** N **to take the ~** den Weg des geringsten Widerstands gehen; **soft palate** N weicher Gaumen, Gaumensegel *nt*; **soft pedal** N *(Mus; on piano)* Dämpfer *m*, Pianopedal *nt*; **soft-pedal** VT *(Mus) note, passage* mit Dämpfer spielen; *(fig inf) demands etc* herunterschrauben VI zurückstecken; **soft return** N *(Comput)* weiche Zeilenschaltung; **soft sell** N Softsell *m*, weiche Verkaufstaktik; **he's very good at the ~** er kann die Leute sehr gut auf sanfte Art *or* auf die sanfte Tour *(inf)* überreden; **soft-shelled** ADJ weichschalig; **soft shoulder** N *(of road)* unbefestigtes Bankett; **soft-soap** *(Brit fig)* N Schmeichelei *f* VT einseifen *(inf)*, um den Bart gehen *(+dat)*; **they ~ed him into doing it** sie sind ihm so lange um den Bart gegangen, bis er es getan hat *(inf)*; **soft-spoken** ADJ *person* leise sprechend *attr*; **to be ~** eine angenehme Stimme haben; **soft target** N leichte Beute; *(Mil)* leichtes Ziel; **soft top** N *(esp US Aut)* Cabriolet *nt*; **soft toy** N *(Brit)* Stofftier *nt*; **soft verges** PL *(Brit Aut)* nicht befahrbare Bankette; *(on sign)* Seitenstreifen nicht befahrbar; **software** N Software *f*; **software company** N Softwarehaus *nt*; **software-controlled** ADJ softwaregesteuert; **software package** N Softwarepaket *nt*; **softwood** N Weichholz *nt*

softy N *(inf)* = **softie**

SOGAT ['səʊgæt] *(Brit old) abbr of* **Society of Graphical and Allied Trades** *britische Grafikergewerkschaft*

sogginess ['sɒgɪnɪs] N triefende Nässe; *(of soil)* Aufgeweichtheit *f*; *(of food)* Matschigkeit *f (inf)*; *(of cake, bread)* Klitschigkeit *f*

soggy ['sɒgɪ] ADJ *(+er)* durchnässt, triefnass; *soil, compost* durchweicht; *food, vegetables* matschig *(inf)*; *cake, bread* klitschig; **a ~ mess** eine Matsche

soi-disant [ˌswɑːdiː'zɑːŋ] ADJ sogenannt, angeblich

soigné ['swɑːnjeɪ] ADJ gepflegt, soigniert *(geh)*

soil[1] [sɔɪl] N *(= earth, ground)* Erde *f*, Erdreich *nt*, Boden *m*; **cover it with ~** bedecken Sie es mit Erde; **native/foreign/British ~** heimatlicher/fremder/britischer Boden, heimatliche/fremde/britische Erde; **the ~** *(fig: = farmland)* die Scholle; **a son of the ~** ein mit der Scholle verwachsener Mensch

soil[2] VT *(lit)* beschmutzen, schmutzig machen; *(fig) reputation* beschmutzen, beflecken; *honour* beflecken; *oneself* besudeln; **the baby has ~ed its nappy** das Baby hat eine schmutzige Windel *or* hat in die Windel gemacht; **to ~ one's hands** *(lit, fig)* sich *(dat)* die Hände schmutzig *or* dreckig *(inf)* machen VI schmutzig werden, verschmutzen

soilage ['sɔɪlɪdʒ] N *(Agr)* Grünfutter *nt*

soil conservation N Bodenschutz *m*

soiled [sɔɪld] ADJ schmutzig, verschmutzt; *goods* verschmutzt; *sanitary towel* gebraucht; **~ linen** Schmutzwäsche *f*

soil pipe N Abflussrohr *nt*

soirée ['swɑːreɪ] N *(form)* Soirée *f (geh)*

soixante-neuf [ˌswæsɑːnt'nɜːf] N Neunundsechzig *nt no art*, Soixante-neuf *nt no art*

sojourn ['sɒdʒɜːn] N *(liter)* Aufenthalt *m*; *(= place)* Aufenthaltsort *m* VI (ver)weilen *(liter) (in* in *+dat)*

sojourner ['sɒdʒənəʳ] N *(geh)* Gast *m*, Besucher(in) *m(f)*

solace ['sɒlɪs] N Trost *m* VT trösten

solar ['səʊləʳ] ADJ Sonnen-, Solar-; **~ activity** Sonnenaktivität *f*; **~ calendar** Sonnenkalender *m*; **~ heat** Sonnenwärme *f*; **~ power/radiation** Sonnenkraft *f*/-strahlung *f*; **~ year** Sonnenjahr *nt*

solar: **solar battery** N Sonnen- *or* Solarbatterie *f*; **solar cell** N Solarzelle *f*; **solar collector** N Sonnenkollektor *m*; **solar eclipse** N Sonnenfinsternis *f*; **solar energy** N Sonnenenergie *f*; **solar flare** N Sonneneruption *f*; **solar heating** N Solarheizung *f*

solarium [səʊ'leərɪəm] N *pl* **solaria** [səʊ'leərɪə] Solarium *nt*

solar: **solar panel** N Sonnenkollektor *m*; **solar plexus** N Solarplexus *m (spec)*, Magengrube *f*; **solar-powered** ADJ durch Sonnenenergie angetrieben, mit Sonnenenergie betrieben; **solar power plant** N Solaranlage *f*, Solarkraftwerk *nt*; **solar system** N Sonnensystem *nt*; **solar wind** N Sonnen- *or* Solarwind *m*

sold [səʊld] *pret, ptp of* **sell**

solder ['səʊldəʳ] N Lötmittel *nt*, Lötzinn *nt* VT löten; *(= solder together)* verlöten; **~ed joint** Lötstelle *f*

soldering iron ['səʊldərɪŋaɪən] N Lötkolben *m*

soldier ['səʊldʒəʳ] N **a** Soldat(in) *m(f)*; **~ of fortune** Söldner(in) *m(f)*; **to play (at) ~s** Soldaten *or* Krieg spielen; **old ~** altgedienter Soldat; *(fig)* alter Kämpe; **old ~s never die(, they just fade away)** *(prov)* manche Leute sind nicht totzukriegen *(inf)* **b** *(Zool)* Soldat *m* VI Soldat(in) sein, (in der Armee) dienen; **after 6 years of ~ing** nach 6 Jahren Dienst in der Armee; **tired of ~ing** des Soldatenlebens müde

▶ **soldier on** VI unermüdlich weitermachen; **two of them soldiered on to the top** zwei kämpften sich bis zum Gipfel vor

soldierly ['səʊldʒəlɪ] ADJ soldatisch

soldiery ['səʊldʒərɪ] N Soldaten *pl*, Soldateska *f (pej geh)*

sole[1] [səʊl] N Sohle *f* VT besohlen

sole[2] N *(= fish)* Seezunge *f*

sole[3] ADJ *reason* einzig; *responsibility, owner, ownership* alleinig; *use* ausschließlich; **with the ~ exception of ...** mit alleiniger Ausnahme *+gen* ...; **for the ~ purpose of ...** einzig und allein zu dem Zweck *+gen* ..., zum alleinigen *or* einzigen Zweck *+gen* ...; **he is the ~ remaining candidate** er ist der einzige (noch) verbleibende *or* noch übrige Kandidat; **~ heir** Alleinerbe *m*/-erbin *f*; **their ~ surviving daughter** ihre einzige überlebende Tochter

sole: **sole agency** N Alleinvertretung *f*; **sole agent** N Alleinvertreter(in) *m(f)*; **sole beneficiary** N *(Jur)* Alleinbegünstigte(r) *m(f)*

solecism ['sɒləsɪzəm] N *(linguistic)* Solözismus *m (geh)*, Fehler *m*; *(in behaviour etc)* Fauxpas *m*

-soled [-səʊld] ADJ *suf* mit ... Sohlen; **soft-soled** mit weichen Sohlen; **rubber-soled** mit Gummisohlen

solely ['səʊllɪ] ADV (einzig und) allein, nur; **he is ~ responsible** er allein trägt die Verantwortung, er ist allein verantwortlich; **they are not ~ to blame** man kann ihnen nicht die alleinige Schuld geben; **~ because of this ...** nur *or* allein deswegen ...

solemn ['sɒləm] ADJ feierlich; *face, mood, music also, person, plea, warning* ernst; *architecture* ehrwürdig, erhaben; *promise, duty, oath* heilig; *(= drab) colour* trist; **in a ~ tone** mit feierlicher Stimme; **I give you my ~ word** ich verspreche es hoch und heilig

solemnity [sə'lemnɪtɪ] N Feierlichkeit *f*; *(of face, mood, music also, person, plea, warning)* Ernst *m*; *(of architecture)* Ehrwürdigkeit *f*, Erhabenheit *f*; *(of promise, duty, oath)* heiliger Ernst; *(of colour)* Tristheit *f*; **with great ~** feierlich (und würdig)

solemnization [ˌsɒləmnaɪ'zeɪʃən] N feierlicher Vollzug

solemnize ['sɒləmnaɪz] VT feierlich begehen; *marriage* (feierlich) vollziehen

solemnly ['sɒləmlɪ] ADV feierlich; *walk* gemessenen Schrittes, würdevoll; *look, warn, plead* ernst; *say* ernsthaft; *promise* hoch und heilig; *swear* bei allem, was einem heilig ist; **I do ~ swear to tell the truth** *(Jur)* ich schwöre feierlich, die Wahrheit zu sagen

solenoid ['səʊlənɔɪd] N Magnetspule *f*; **~ switch** Magnetschalter *m*

sole: **sole rights** PL Alleinrechte *pl*; **sole trader** N Einzelunternehmer(in) *m(f)*, Einzelkaufmann *m*/-kauffrau *f*

sol-fa [ˌsɒl'fɑː] N Solmisation *f*

solicit [sə'lɪsɪt] VT *support, money, donations* erbitten, bitten um; *person* anflehen, inständig bitten; *business, sympathy* werben um; *news, advice, help* bitten um; *(prostitute) customers* ansprechen; **to ~ sb for sex** *(prostitute)* jdm Sex anbieten; **to ~ sb for sth** jdn um etw bitten, etw von jdm erbitten; **to ~ custom** um Kunden werben VI *(prostitute)* Kunden anwerben, zur Unzucht auffordern *(form)*

solicitation [səˌlɪsɪ'teɪʃən] N *(form)* Flehen *nt no pl (geh)*

soliciting [sə'lɪsɪtɪŋ] N Aufforderung *f* zur Unzucht

solicitor [sə'lɪsɪtəʳ] N *(Jur, Brit)* Rechtsanwalt *m*/-anwältin *f (der/die normalerweise nicht vor Gericht plädiert)*; *(US)* Justizbeamte(r) *m*/-beamtin *f*; **Solicitor General** *(Brit)* zweiter Kronanwalt, zweite Kronanwältin; *(US)* ≈ Generalstaatsanwalt *m*/-anwältin *f*

solicitous [sə'lɪsɪtəs] ADJ *(form: = concerned)* besorgt *(about* um*)*; *(= eager)* dienstbeflissen; **to be ~ of sb** um jdn besorgt sein

solicitously [sə'lɪsɪtəslɪ] ADV *(form)* besorgt; *(= eagerly)* eifrig

solicitude [sə'lɪsɪtjuːd] N *(form)* Besorgtheit *f*

solid ['sɒlɪd] ADJ **a** *(= firm, not liquid) fuel, food, substance* fest; **~ body** Festkörper *m*; **to be frozen ~** hart gefroren sein; **to be stuck ~** festsitzen; **the pudding is rather ~** der Nachtisch ist ziemlich schwer
b *(= pure, not hollow, not broken) block, gold, oak, rock* massiv; *matter* fest; *crowd, traffic etc* dicht; *stretch, row, line* ununterbrochen; *queue, line of people etc* geschlossen; *layer* dicht, dick; *week* ganz; *(= heavily-built) person* stämmig; **~ ball/tyre** Vollgummiball *m*/-reifen *m*; **the square was packed ~ with cars** die Autos standen dicht an dicht auf dem Platz; **the room was ~ with people** der Raum war mit Leuten vollgedrängt; **the garden was a ~ mass of colour** der Garten war ein einziges Farbenmeer; **they worked for two ~ days** sie haben zwei Tage ununterbrochen gearbeitet, sie haben zwei volle Tage gearbeitet; **we had a week of ~ rain** wir hatten eine Woche lang Dauerregen *m*; **he was 6 ft of ~ muscle** er war fast 2 Meter groß und bestand nur aus Muskeln; **a man of ~ build** ein kräftig *or* massiv gebauter Mann; **a ~ gold bracelet** ein Armband *nt* aus massivem Gold
c *(= stable, secure) bridge, house, car* stabil; *furniture, piece of work, character* solide; *foundations, ground* fest; *business, firm* gesund, solide, reell; *(= worthy) place* respektabel; *(= powerful) grip* kraftvoll; *(= competent) performance* solide; **he's a good ~ worker** er ist ein solider *or* guter Arbeiter; **he's a good ~ sort** er ist ein verlässlicher Kerl; **he is a ~ citizen** er ist ein grundsolider Bürger
d *reason, argument* handfest, stichhaltig; *grounds* gut, fundiert; **it makes ~ good sense** das leuchtet durchaus ein; **~ common sense** gesunder Menschenverstand
e *(= unanimous) vote* einstimmig; *support* voll, geschlossen; **to be ~ on sth** *(accept/reject)* etw einstimmig *or* geschlossen annehmen/ablehnen; **we are ~ behind you/that proposal** wir stehen voll und ganz hinter Ihnen/diesem Vorschlag; **we are ~ for peace** wir sind hundertprozentig für den Frieden; **Newtown is ~ for Labour** Newtown wählt fast ausschließlich Labour
f *(= valuable, substantial) education, knowledge, grounding* solide; *relationship* stabil; *meal* kräftig, nahrhaft
g *(= not hyphenated)* **to be written ~** zusammengeschrieben werden
h *(dated US inf: = excellent)* prima *inv (inf)*
ADV **a** *(= completely)* völlig; **the main streets were jammed ~** die Hauptstraßen waren völlig verstopft; **flights to Israel are booked ~** Flüge nach Israel sind voll *or* total ausgebucht
b *(= without a break)* pausenlos; **for eight hours ~** acht Stunden lang ununterbrochen
N **a** fester Stoff; **~s and liquids** feste und flüssige Stoffe *pl*; *(Sci)* Festkörper und Flüssigkeiten *pl*
b *(Geometry)* Körper *m*
c solids PL *(= food)* feste Nahrung *no pl*; *(= sewage)* Feststoffe *pl*

solidarity [ˌsɒlɪ'dærɪtɪ] N Solidarität *f*

solid: **solid figure** N *(Geometry)* Körper *m*; **solid fuel** N fester Brennstoff; *(for rockets)* Feststoff *m*; **solid geometry** N Raumlehre *f*

solidification [səˌlɪdɪfɪ'keɪʃən] N Festwerden *nt*, Verfestigung *f*; *(of planet, lava etc)* Erstarrung *f*; *(of metal also)* Erhärtung *f*; *(of blood)* Gerinnung *f*; *(fig, of support)* Festigung *f*

solidify [sə'lɪdɪfaɪ] VI fest werden; *(planet, lava etc)* erstarren; *(metal also)* hart werden; *(blood)* gerinnen; *(fig: support)* sich festigen VT fest werden lassen; *lava* erstarren lassen; *metal also* hart werden lassen; *blood* gerinnen lassen; *(fig) support* festigen

solidity [sə'lɪdɪtɪ] N **a** *(of substance)* Festigkeit *f* **b** *(= stability, of bridge, house, car)* Stabilität *f*; *(of furniture also, piece of work, character)* solide Art; *(of foundations)* Festigkeit *f* **c** *(= unanimity, of vote)* Einstimmigkeit *f*; *(of support)* Geschlossenheit *f*

solidly ['sɒlɪdlɪ] ADV **a** *(= firmly) stuck, secured* fest; *(= hard)* hart; **~ built** *(house)* fest *or* solide gebaut; *person* kräftig *or* massiv gebaut; **to be ~ based on sth** fest auf etw *(dat)* beruhen **b** *reasoned, argued* stichhaltig **c** *(= uninterruptedly) work* ununterbrochen **d** *(= unanimously) vote* einstimmig; *support* geschlossen; **to be ~ behind sb/sth** geschlossen hinter jdm/etw stehen **e** *(= thoroughly) Republican, Conservative* durch und durch; **a ~ middle-class neighbourhood** eine durch und durch bürgerliche Nachbarschaft

solid-state [ˌsɒlɪd'steɪt] ADJ Festkörper-; *(Elec)* Halbleiter-; **~ laser** Halbleiterlaser *m*

solid-state physics N Festkörperphysik *f*

soliloquize [sə'lɪləkwaɪz] VI monologisieren; *(= talk to oneself)* Selbstgespräche führen VT zu sich selbst sagen

soliloquy [sə'lɪləkwɪ] N Monolog *m* *(also Theat)*, Zwiegespräch *nt* mit sich selbst

solipsism ['sɒlɪpsɪzəm] N Solipsismus *m*

solipsist ['sɒlɪpsɪst] N Solipsist(in) *m(f)*

solipsistic [ˌsɒlɪp'sɪstɪk] ADJ solipsistisch

solitaire [ˌsɒlɪ'teə'] N *(= game)* Patience *f*; *(= gem)* Solitär *m*

solitariness ['sɒlɪtərɪnɪs] N *(of task)* Einsamkeit *f*; *(of life)* Abgeschiedenheit *f*

solitary ['sɒlɪtərɪ] ADJ **a** *(= alone, secluded) life, person* einsam; *place* abgelegen, einsam; **a few ~ houses** ein paar einzelne *or* vereinzelte Häuser; **to take a ~ walk** allein einen Spaziergang machen; **do you enjoy this ~ life?** gefällt Ihnen das Leben so allein?; **in ~ splendour** in einsamer Pracht; **a ~ person** ein Einzelgänger *m*, eine Einzelgängerin; **I'm not a ~ drinker** ich trinke nicht gern allein; **she ate a ~ dinner** sie nahm ein einsames Mahl
b *(= sole) case, example, goal* einzig; **with the ~ exception of …** mit alleiniger Ausnahme von …; **not a ~ one** kein Einziger
N *(= solitary confinement)* Einzelhaft *f*

solitary confinement N Einzelhaft *f*; **to be put/kept** *or* **held in ~** in Einzelhaft genommen/gehalten werden

solitude ['sɒlɪtjuːd] N Einsamkeit *f*; *(of place also)* Abgelegenheit *f*

solo ['səʊləʊ] N Solo *nt*; **piano ~** Klaviersolo *nt* ADJ Solo-; **a ~ goal** ein im Alleingang geschossenes Tor; **~ album** Soloalbum *nt*; **~ artist** Solokünstler(in) *m(f)*; **~ career** Solokarriere *f*; **~ flight** Solo- *or* Alleinflug *m*; **~ passage** *(Mus)* Solopassage *f*; **~ performance** *(Mus)* Solo *nt*; *(Theat)* Solovorstellung *f* ADV allein; *(Mus)* solo; **to go ~** *(musician etc)* eine Solokarriere einschlagen; **to fly ~** einen Alleinflug machen

soloist ['səʊləʊɪst] N Solist(in) *m(f)*

Solomon ['sɒləmən] N Salomo(n) *m*; **the ~ Islands** die Salomonen *pl*, die Salomon-Inseln *pl*

solstice ['sɒlstɪs] N Sonnenwende *f*, Solstitium *nt (spec)*

solubility [ˌsɒljʊ'bɪlɪtɪ] N **a** Löslichkeit *f* **b** *(of problem)* Lösbarkeit *f*

soluble ['sɒljʊbl] ADJ **a** löslich, auflösbar; **~ in water** wasserlöslich; **fat-~** fettlöslich **b** *problem* lösbar

solution [sə'luːʃən] ✪ 26.3 N **a** Lösung *f* *(to +gen)*; *(of crime)* Aufklärung *f*; **a problem incapable of ~** ein unlösbares Problem **b** *(Chem: = liquid)* Lösung *f*; *(= act)* Auflösen *nt*

solvable ['sɒlvəbl] ADJ = **soluble b**

solve [sɒlv] VT *problem, equation* lösen; *mystery* enträtseln; *crime, murder* aufklären; **that problem remains to be ~d** dieses Problem muss noch geklärt werden

solvency ['sɒlvənsɪ] N *(Fin)* Zahlungsfähigkeit *f*, Solvenz *f*

solvent ['sɒlvənt] ADJ **a** *(Chem)* lösend **b** *(Fin)* zahlungsfähig, solvent N *(Chem)* Lösungsmittel *nt*

solvent: **solvent abuse** N *(Brit form)* Lösungsmittelmissbrauch *m*; **solvent abuser** N *(Brit form)* Schnüffler(in) *m(f) (inf)*

Som *(Brit) abbr of* **Somerset**

Somali [səʊ'mɑːlɪ] ADJ somali; *person, culture, institution* somalisch; **he is ~** er ist Somalier N **a** Somali *mf*, Somalier(in) *m(f)* **b** *(Ling)* Somali *nt*

Somalia [səʊ'mɑːlɪə] N Somalia *nt*

Somaliland [səʊ'mɑːlɪlænd] N Somaliland *nt*

somatic [səʊ'mætɪk] ADJ somatisch

sombre, *(US)* **somber** ['sɒmbə'] ADJ **a** *(= dark)* dunkel; *(= gloomy)* düster **b** *(= grave, serious) prospect* trüb, düster; *message* trüb, traurig; *news* traurig; *face* düster; *person* düster, finster; *music* trist, trauervoll; **in ~ mood** in trüber *or* düsterer Stimmung

sombrely, *(US)* **somberly** ['sɒmbəlɪ] ADV *say* traurig, düster; *watch* finster; *dress* trist

sombreness, *(US)* **somberness** ['sɒmbənɪs] N **a** *(= darkness)* Dunkelheit *f*; *(= gloominess)* Düsterkeit *f* **b** *(of mood)* Trübheit *f*; *(of news)* trauriger Charakter; *(of face)* Düsterkeit *f*; *(of person)* finsteres *or* düsteres Wesen; *(of music)* trauervoller *or* trister Klang

sombrero [sɒm'brɛərəʊ] N Sombrero *m*

some [sʌm] ADJ **a** *(with plural nouns)* einige; *(= a few, emph)* ein paar; *(= any: in "if" clauses, questions)* *meist nicht übersetzt*; **if you have ~ questions** wenn Sie Fragen haben; **did you bring ~ records?** hast du Schallplatten mitgebracht?; **~ records of mine** einige meiner Platten; **would you like ~ more biscuits?** möchten Sie noch (ein paar) Kekse?; **take ~ nuts** nehmen Sie sich *(dat)* doch (ein paar) Nüsse; **~ few people** einige wenige Leute; **~ suggestions, please!** Vorschläge bitte!
b *(with singular nouns)* etwas, *meist nicht übersetzt* *(= a little, emph)* etwas, ein bisschen; **there's ~ ink on your shirt** Sie haben Tinte auf dem Hemd; **would you like ~ cheese?** möchten Sie (etwas) Käse?; **~ more (tea)?** noch etwas (Tee)?; **leave ~ cake for me** lass mir ein bisschen *or* etwas Kuchen übrig; **did she give you ~ money/sugar?** hat sie Ihnen Geld/Zucker gegeben?; **have you got ~ money?** haben Sie Geld?; **it was (of) ~ help** es war eine gewisse Hilfe; **we played ~ golf** wir haben ein bisschen Golf gespielt
c *(= certain, in contrast)* manche(r, s); **~ people say …** manche Leute sagen …; **~ people just don't care** es gibt Leute, denen ist das einfach egal; **there are ~ things you just don't say** es gibt (gewisse *or* manche) Dinge, die man einfach nicht sagt; **~ questions were really difficult** manche (der) Fragen waren wirklich schwierig; **~ work is very rewarding** manche Arbeit ist sehr lohnend; **~ butter is salty** manche Buttersorten sind salzig; **in ~ ways** in gewisser Weise
d *(vague, indeterminate)* irgendein; **~ book/man or other** irgendein Buch/Mann; **~ woman rang up** da hat eine Frau angerufen; **~ woman, whose name I forget …** eine Frau, ich habe ihren Namen vergessen, …; **~ idiot of a driver** irgend so ein Idiot von (einem) Autofahrer; **in ~ way or another** irgendwie; **at ~ place in Africa** irgendwo in Afrika; **or ~ such** oder so etwas Ähnliches; **or ~ such name** oder so ein ähnlicher Name; **(at) ~ time last week** irgendwann letzte Woche; **~ time or other** irgendwann einmal; **~ other time** ein andermal; **~ day** eines Tages; **~ day next week** irgendwann nächste Woche
e *(intensifier)* ziemlich; *(in exclamations)* vielleicht ein *(inf)*; **it took ~ courage** dazu brauchte man schon (einigen) *or* ziemlichen Mut; **(that was) ~ argument/party!** das war vielleicht ein Streit/eine Party! *(inf)*; **that's ~ whisky** das ist vielleicht ein Whisky! *(inf)*; **it's ~ size!** das ist vielleicht ein Ding!; **this might take ~ time** das könnte einige Zeit dauern; **quite ~ time** ganz schön lange *(inf)*, ziemlich lange; **to speak at ~ length** ziemlich lange sprechen; **it's ~ distance from the house** es ist

ziemlich weit vom Haus entfernt

f *(iro)* vielleicht ein *(inf)*; **~ experts!** das sind vielleicht Experten! *(inf)*; **~ help you are/this is** du bist/das ist mir vielleicht eine Hilfe *(inf)*; **~ people!** Leute gibts!

PRON **a** *(= some people)* einige; *(= certain people)* manche; *(in "if" clauses, questions)* welche; **~ ..., others ...** manche ..., andere ...; **~ of my friends** einige *or* manche meiner Freunde; **there are still ~ who will never understand** es gibt immer noch Leute, die das nicht begreifen werden; **~ of them were late** einige kamen zu spät

b *(referring to plural nouns, = a few)* einige; *(= certain ones)* manche; *(in "if" clauses, questions)* welche; **~ of these books** einige dieser Bücher; **~ of them have been sold** einige sind verkauft worden; **I've only seen ~ of the mountains** ich habe nur ein paar von den Bergen gesehen; **they're lovely, try ~** die schmecken gut, probieren Sie mal; **I've still got ~** ich habe noch welche; **he took ~** er hat welche genommen; **tell me if you see ~** sagen Sie mir Bescheid, wenn Sie welche sehen; **would you like ~?** möchten Sie welche?

c *(referring to singular nouns, = a little)* etwas; *(= a certain amount, in contrast)* manches; *(in "if" clauses, questions)* welche(r, s); **here is the milk, if you feel thirsty drink ~** hier ist die Milch, wenn du Durst hast, trinke etwas; **I drank ~ of the milk** ich habe (etwas) von der Milch getrunken; **I drank ~ of the milk but not all** ich habe etwas von der Milch getrunken, aber nicht alles; **have ~!** nehmen Sie sich *(dat)*, bedienen Sie sich; **it's lovely cake, would you like ~?** das ist ein sehr guter Kuchen, möchten Sie welchen?; **try ~ of this cake** probieren Sie doch mal diesen Kuchen; **would you like ~ money/tea? – no, I've got ~** möchten Sie Geld/Tee? – nein, ich habe Geld/ich habe noch; **have you got money? – no, but he has ~** haben Sie Geld? – nein, aber er hat welches; **~ of it had been eaten** einiges (davon) war gegessen worden; **he only believed/read ~ of it** er hat es nur teilweise geglaubt/gelesen; **~ of his speech was excellent** manches *or* einiges in seiner Rede war ausgezeichnet; **~ of his work is good** manches, was er macht, ist gut

d **this is ~ of the oldest rock in the world** dies gehört zum ältesten Gestein der Welt; **~ of the finest poetry in the English language** einige der schönsten Gedichte in der englischen Sprache; **this is ~ of the finest scenery in Scotland** dies ist eine der schönsten Landschaften Schottlands

ADV **a** ungefähr, etwa, circa; **~ 20 people** ungefähr 20 Leute; **~ few difficulties** einige Schwierigkeiten

b *(US inf)* *(= a little)* etwas, ein bisschen; *(= a lot)* viel; **it sure bothered us ~** das hat uns ziemlich zu schaffen gemacht; **he's travelling ~** er fährt schnell; **I really drank ~ last night** ich habe gestern Abend ganz schön was getrunken *(inf)*; **that's going ~** das ist ganz schön schnell *(inf)*

somebody ['sʌmbədɪ] **PRON** jemand; *(dir obj)* jemand(en); *(indir obj)* jemandem; **~ else** jemand anders; **~ or other** irgendjemand; **~ knocked at the door** es klopfte jemand an die Tür; **we need ~ German** wir brauchen einen Deutschen; **everybody needs ~ to talk to** jeder braucht einen, mit dem er sprechen kann; **~ or other** irgendjemand; **you must have seen ~** Sie müssen doch irgendjemand(en) gesehen haben **N** **to be (a) ~** etwas vorstellen, wer *(inf)* *or* jemand sein; **he thinks he's ~ now** er bildet sich *(dat)* ein, er wäre jetzt jemand *or* wer *(inf)*

someday ['sʌmdeɪ] **ADV** eines Tages

somehow ['sʌmhaʊ] **ADV** irgendwie; **it must be done ~ or other** es muss irgendwie gemacht werden; **~ (or other) I never liked him** irgendwie habe ich ihn nie gemocht *or* nie leiden können

someone ['sʌmwʌn] **PRON** = **somebody PRON**

someplace ['sʌmpleɪs] **ADV** *(US inf)* *be* irgendwo; *go* irgendwohin; **~ else** *(be)* woanders; *go* woandershin

somersault ['sʌməsɔːlt] **N** Purzelbaum *m*; *(Sport, fig)* Salto *m*; **to do** *or* **turn a ~** einen Purzelbaum schlagen; *(Sport)* einen Salto machen; *(car)* sich überschlagen, einen Salto machen *(inf)*; *(stomach)* einen Satz machen **VI** *(person)* einen Purzelbaum schlagen; *(Sport)* einen Salto machen; *(car)* sich überschlagen, einen Salto machen *(inf)*; **the car ~ed into a lamppost** das Auto hat sich überschlagen und ist gegen einen Laternenpfahl geprallt

something ['sʌmθɪŋ] **PRON** **a** etwas; **~ nice/unpleasant/serious** *etc* etwas Nettes/Unangenehmes/Ernstes *etc*; **~ or other** irgendetwas, irgendwas; **did you say ~?** hast du (et)was gesagt?; **~ of the kind** so (et)was (Ähnliches); **that's ~ I don't know** das weiß ich nicht; **there's ~ I don't like about him** irgendetwas *or* irgendwas gefällt mir an ihm nicht; **do you want to make ~ of it?** willst du dich mit mir anlegen? *(inf)*; **there's ~ in what you say** an dem, was du sagst, ist (schon) was dran; **well, that's ~** (das ist) immerhin etwas; **he's ~ to do with the Foreign Office** er ist irgendwie beim Außenministerium; **she's called Rachel ~** sie heißt Rachel Soundso *or* Sowieso; **there were thirty ~** es waren etwas über dreißig; **three hundred and ~** dreihundert und ein paar (Zerquetschte *(inf)*); **we left at five ~** wir sind etwas nach fünf gegangen

b *(inf: = something special or unusual)* **it was ~ else** *(esp US)* *or* **quite ~** das war schon toll *(inf)*; **it's quite ~ to be Prime Minister at 44** es will schon was heißen, mit 44 Premierminister zu sein; **what a beautiful dress! that's really ~** so ein schönes Kleid! ganz große Klasse! *(inf)*

c **or ~** *(inf)* oder so (was); **are you drunk or ~?** *(inf)* bist du betrunken oder was? *(inf)*; **she's called Maria or ~ like that** sie heißt Maria oder so ähnlich

N **a little ~** *(= present etc)* eine kleine Aufmerksamkeit, eine Kleinigkeit; **a certain ~** ein gewisses Etwas; **that certain ~ that makes all the difference** das gewisse Etwas, auf das es ankommt

ADV **a** **~ over 200** etwas über 200, etwas mehr als 200; **~ like 200** ungefähr 200, um die 200 herum; **you look ~ like him** du siehst ihm irgendwie ähnlich; **this is ~ like the one I wanted** so (et)was Ähnliches wollte ich haben; **now that's ~ like a rose!** das nenne ich eine Rose!; **another £500, now that's ~ like it** noch £ 500 und wir kommen der Sache schon näher

b **it's ~ of a problem** das ist schon ein Problem; **I feel ~ of a stranger here** ich fühle mich hier irgendwie fremd; **he's ~ of a musician** er ist ein recht guter Musiker; **~ of a surprise** eine ziemliche Überraschung; **~ of a drunkard** ein ziemlicher Säufer

c *(Brit dial)* **they tease her ~ chronic** sie ziehen sie immer ganz furchtbar auf; **the weather was ~ shocking** das Wetter war einfach schrecklich

-something [-sʌmθɪŋ] **SUF** **he's twenty-something** er ist in den Zwanzigern *or* zwischen zwanzig und dreißig; **thirty-somethings** Leute *pl* in den Dreißigern *or* zwischen dreißig und vierzig; **most American twenty-somethings, most twenty-something Americans** die meisten Amerikaner in den Zwanzigern *or* zwischen zwanzig und dreißig

sometime ['sʌmtaɪm] **ADV** irgendwann; **~ or other it will have to be done** irgendwann muss es gemacht werden; **write to me ~ soon** schreib mir (doch) bald (ein)mal; **~ before tomorrow** bis morgen, heute noch; **~ next year** irgendwann nächstes Jahr *or* im nächsten Jahr **ADJ** *attr (form)* ehemalig, früher, einstig

sometimes ['sʌmtaɪmz] **ADV** manchmal

someway ['sʌmweɪ] **ADV** *(US)* irgendwie

somewhat ['sʌmwɒt] **ADV** ein wenig; **more than ~!** mehr als das!, und ob! *(inf)*; **more than ~ disappointed/late** *etc* ganz schön enttäuscht/verspätet *etc*; **the system is ~ less than perfect** das System funktioniert irgendwie nicht ganz; **it was ~ of a mystery** es war irgendwie rätselhaft; **~ of a surprise/disappointment** eine ziemliche *or* arge Überraschung/Enttäuschung; **~ of a drunkard** ein arger Trinker; **~ to my surprise ...** ziemlich überraschend für mich ...

somewhere ['sʌmwɛəʳ] **ADV** **a** *be* irgendwo; *go* irgendwohin; **~ else** irgendwo anders, anderswo, irgendwo anders hin, anderswohin; **to take one's business ~ else** seine Geschäfte woanders machen; **from ~** von irgendwo, irgendwoher; **from ~ else** von irgendwo anders, anderswoher; **I left it ~ or other** ich habe es irgendwo liegen/stehen lassen; **I know ~ where ...** ich weiß, wo ...; **I needed ~ to live in London** ich brauchte irgendwo in London eine Unterkunft; **we just wanted ~ to go after school** wir wollten bloß einen Ort, wo wir nach der Schule eingehen können; **it's about** *or* **around ~** es ist hier irgendwo; **~ about** *or* **around here** irgendwo hier in der Nähe; **~ nice/cheap** irgendwo, wo es nett/billig ist; **the ideal place to go is ~ like New York** am besten fährt man in eine Stadt wie New York; **he went to live in Cumbria or ~ like that** er zog nach Cumbria oder so; **somebody ~ must know where she is** irgendjemand irgendwo muss wissen, wo sie ist; **don't I know you from ~?** kenne ich Sie nicht von irgendwoher?

b *(fig)* **the temperature was ~ about 40° C** die Temperatur betrug ungefähr 40° C *or* war um die 40° *(inf)*; **~ about £50** *or* **in the region of £50** um (die) £ 50 herum; **she is ~ in her fifties** sie muss in den Fünfzigern sein; **~ between midnight and one o'clock** irgendwann zwischen Mitternacht und ein Uhr; **the truth lies ~ in the middle** die Wahrheit liegt irgendwo dazwischen; **~ between 10,000 and 20,000 people** irgendwo zwischen 10.000 und 20.000 Leute; **now we're getting ~** jetzt kommen wir voran

somnambulism [sɒm'næmbjʊlɪzəm] **N** Nacht- *or* Schlafwandeln *nt*, Mondsüchtigkeit *f*, Somnambulismus *m (spec)*

somnambulist [sɒm'næmbjʊlɪst] **N** Nacht- *or* Schlafwandler(in) *m(f)*, Mondsüchtige(r) *mf*, Somnambule *mf (spec)*

somnolence ['sɒmnələns] **N** Schläfrigkeit *f*; **the heavy ~ of this summer's day** die bleierne Schwere dieses Sommertages

somnolent ['sɒmnələnt] **ADJ** **a** *(= sleepy)* schläfrig **b** *(= causing sleep)* einschläfernd

son [sʌn] **N** *(lit, fig)* Sohn *m*; *(as address)* mein Junge; **Son of God/Man** Gottes-/Menschensohn *m*; **the ~s of men** *(liter)* die Menschen; **he's his father's ~** er ist ganz der Vater; **~ of a bitch** *(esp US sl)* Scheißkerl *m (inf)*, Hurensohn *m (vulg)*; *(= thing)* Scheißding *nt (inf)*; **~ of a gun** *(esp US inf)* Schlawiner *m (inf)*

sonant ['səʊnənt] *(Ling, Phon)* **N** Sonant *m*, stimmhafter Laut **ADJ** stimmhaft

sonar ['səʊnɑːʳ] **N** Sonar(gerät) *nt*, Echolot *nt*

sonata [sə'nɑːtə] **N** Sonate *f*

sonata form **N** *(Mus)* Sonatenform *f*

sonatina [ˌsɒnə'tiːnə] **N** *(Mus)* Sonatine *f*

sonde [sɒnd] **N** *(Tech)* Sonde *f*

son et lumière [ˌsɒneɪ'luːmɪɛəʳ] **N** Son et Lumière *nt*

song [sɒŋ] **N** **a** Lied *nt*; *(= modern folk song, blues song)* Song *m*; **give us a ~!** sing uns etwas vor!; **one of Brecht's ~s** ein Brecht-Song *m*; **to burst into ~** ein Lied anstimmen; **~-and-dance act** Gesangs- und Tanznummer *f*; **Song of Songs, Song of Solomon** Lied *nt* der Lieder, Hohelied *nt* Salomos

b *(= singing, bird song)* Gesang *m*

c *(Brit fig inf)* **to make a ~ and dance about sth** eine Haupt- und Staatsaktion aus etw machen *(inf)*; **that's nothing to make a ~ (and dance) about** darauf brauchst du dir/braucht er sich *etc* nichts einzubilden; **to be on ~** *(Brit)* in Hochform sein; **to sell/buy sth for a ~** etw für einen Apfel und ein Ei *or* für ein Butterbrot verkaufen/kaufen; **it was going for a ~** das gab es für einen Apfel und ein Ei

song: **songbird** N Singvogel *m*; **songbook** N Liederbuch *nt*; **song cycle** N Liederzyklus *m*; **songless** ADJ *bird* nicht singend *attr*; **song sheet** N Liedblatt *nt*, Liederzettel *m*; **songsmith** N *(liter)* Texter(in) *m(f)*

songster ['sɒŋstəʳ] N Sänger *m*

songstress ['sɒŋstrɪs] N Sängerin *f*

song: **song thrush** N Singdrossel *f*; **songwriter** N Texter(in) *m(f)* und Komponist(in) *m(f)*; *(of modern ballads)* Liedermacher(in) *m(f)*

sonic ['sɒnɪk] ADJ Schall-

sonic: **sonic barrier** N Schallmauer *f*; **sonic boom** N Überschallknall *m*; **sonic depth finder** N Echolot *nt*

son-in-law ['sʌnɪnlɔː] N *pl* **sons-in-law** Schwiegersohn *m*

sonnet ['sɒnɪt] N Sonett *nt*; **~ form** Sonettform *f*

sonny ['sʌnɪ] N *(inf)* Junge *m*; **~ Jim** *(inf)* mein Junge *m*

sonority [sə'nɒrɪtɪ] N Klangfülle *f*

sonorous ['sɒnərəs] ADJ volltönend, sonor *(geh)*; *language, poem* klangvoll; *snore* laut

sonorously ['sɒnərəslɪ] ADV volltönend, sonor *(geh)*; **the French horns echoing ~ in the background** das volle Echo der Hörner im Hintergrund

sonorousness ['sɒnərəsnɪs] N Klangfülle *f*

sons-in-law *pl of* **son-in-law**

soon [suːn] ADV **a** *(= in a short time from now)* bald; *(= early)* früh; *(= quickly)* schnell; **it will ~ be Christmas** bald ist Weihnachten; **~ after his death** kurz nach seinem Tode; **~ afterwards** kurz *or* bald danach; **how ~ can you be ready?** wann kannst du fertig sein?; **how ~ would you like it back?** wann *or* bis wann möchtest du es wiederhaben?; **we got there too ~** wir kamen zu früh an; **Friday is too ~** Freitag ist zu früh; **all too ~** viel zu schnell; **we were none too ~** wir kamen gerade rechtzeitig; **as ~ as** sobald; **as ~ as possible** so schnell wie möglich; **when can I have it? – as ~ as you like** wann kann ichs kriegen? – wann du willst!; **please reply ~est** bitte antworten Sie schnellstmöglich
b **I would just as ~ not go** *(= prefer not to)* ich würde lieber nicht gehen; *(= don't mind)* es ist mir egal, wenn ich nicht gehe; **I would (just) as ~ you didn't tell him** es wäre mir lieber, wenn du es ihm nicht erzählen würdest

sooner ['suːnəʳ] ADV **a** *(time)* früher, eher; **~ or later** früher oder später; **the ~ the better** je eher *or* früher, desto besser; **no ~ had we arrived than ...** wir waren gerade *or* kaum angekommen, da ...; **in 5 years or at his death, whichever is the ~** in 5 Jahren bzw. bei seinem Tode, je nachdem, was früher eintrifft; **no ~ said than done** gesagt, getan **b** *(preference)* lieber; **I would ~ not do it** ich würde es lieber nicht tun; **which would you ~?** was möchtest du lieber?

soot [sʊt] N Ruß *m*; **black as ~** rußschwarz

sooth [suːθ] N **in ~** *(obs, liter)* wahrlich *(obs)*

soothe [suːð] VT beruhigen; *pain* lindern, mildern VI beruhigen; *(= relieve pain)* lindern; **an ointment which ~s** eine schmerzlindernde Salbe

soothing ['suːðɪŋ] ADJ beruhigend, besänftigend; *(= pain-relieving)* schmerzlindernd; *massage* wohltuend; *bath* entspannend; **he put a ~ hand on my shoulder** er legte mir beruhigend *or* besänftigend die Hand auf die Schulter

soothingly ['suːðɪŋlɪ] ADV *say, whisper* beruhigend, besänftigend; **she rubbed his bruised arm ~** sie rieb ihm den Arm, um den Schmerz zu lindern; **the old house was ~ familiar** das alte Haus war auf beruhigende Weise vertraut

soothsayer ['suːθseɪəʳ] N *(old)* Wahrsager(in) *m(f)*

soothsaying ['suːθseɪɪŋ] N *(old)* Wahrsagerei *f*

sooty ['sʊtɪ] ADJ *(+er)* rußig; **buildings covered with a ~ deposit** mit einer Rußschicht bedeckte Gebäude; **a dull ~ black** ein trübes, rußfarbenes Schwarz; **~ particles** Rußpartikel *pl*

sop [sɒp] N **a** *(= food)* eingetunktes Brotstück **b** *(to pacify)* Beschwichtigungsmittel *nt*; **they're just offering you that as a ~ to keep you quiet** die bieten euch das nur an, damit ihr ruhig bleibt; **as a ~ to his conscience** als Trostpflaster für sein (schlechtes) Gewissen

▶ **sop up** VT *sep gravy etc* aufnehmen

sophism ['sɒfɪzəm] N Sophismus *m*

sophist ['sɒfɪst] N Sophist(in) *m(f)*

sophistic(al) [sə'fɪstɪk(əl)] ADJ sophistisch

sophisticate [sə'fɪstɪkɪt] N **the ~s who haunt the fashionable restaurants** die Schickeria, die sich in den richtigen Restaurants zeigt

sophisticated [sə'fɪstɪkeɪtɪd] ADJ **a** *(= worldly, cultivated)* kultiviert; *cabaret act, audience* anspruchsvoll, niveauvoll; *restaurant* niveauvoll; *hairdo* gepflegt, elegant; *dress* raffiniert, schick; **she's a very ~ young lady considering she's only twelve** für eine Zwölfjährige ist sie schon sehr weit; **she thinks she looks more ~ with a cigarette holder** sie glaubt, mit einer Zigarettenspitze mehr darzustellen
b *(= complex, advanced)* hoch entwickelt; *techniques* raffiniert; *method* durchdacht; *device* ausgeklügelt
c *(= subtle, refined)* subtil; *prose, style, discussion* anspruchsvoll; *plan* ausgeklügelt, raffiniert; *system, approach* differenziert, komplex; *mind* differenziert; **the conversation was too ~ for me** mir war die Unterhaltung zu hochgestochen; **politically ~** politisch anspruchsvoll

sophistication [sə,fɪstɪ'keɪʃən] N **a** *(= worldliness)* Kultiviertheit *f*; *(of manners, taste also)* Feinheit *f*; *(of cabaret act, audience)* hohes Niveau; *(of person, restaurant also)* Gepflegtheit *f*, Eleganz *f*; *(of dress)* Raffiniertheit *f*, Schick *m*
b *(= complexity)* hoher Entwicklungsstand *or* -grad; *(of techniques)* Raffiniertheit *f*; *(of method)* Durchdachtheit *f*; *(of device)* Ausgeklügeltheit *f*
c *(= subtlety, refinement)* Subtilität *f*; *(of mind)* Differenziertheit *f*; *(of prose, style)* hohe Ansprüche *pl*; *(of discussion)* hohes Niveau; *(of plan)* Ausgeklügeltheit *f*, Raffiniertheit *f*; *(of system, approach)* Komplexheit *f*

sophistry ['sɒfɪstrɪ] N Sophisterei *f*

Sophocles ['sɒfəkliːz] N Sophokles *m*

sophomore ['sɒfəmɔːʳ] N *(US)* *Student(in) im zweiten Jahr*

soporific [,sɒpə'rɪfɪk] ADJ einschläfernd N *(= drug)* Schlafmittel *nt*

sopping ['sɒpɪŋ] ADJ *(also* **sopping wet***)* durchnässt, triefend; *person* klitschnass

soppy ['sɒpɪ] ADJ *(Brit inf)* *(= sentimental) book, song* schmalzig *(inf)*; *person* sentimental; *look* schmachtend; *(= effeminate)* weibisch

soprano [sə'prɑːnəʊ] N Sopran *m*; *(= person also)* Sopranist(in) *m(f)*; *(= voice also)* Sopranstimme *f*; *(= part)* Sopranpartie *f*, Sopran *m*; **to sing ~** Sopran singen ADJ Sopran-; **~ saxophone** Sopransaxofon *or* -saxophon *nt* ADV im Sopran

s. o. r. *(Comm) abbr of* **sale or return**

Sorb [sɔːb] N Sorbe *m*, Sorbin *f*

sorbet ['sɔːbeɪ] N Sorbet *nt or m*, Fruchteis *nt*; **lemon ~** Zitronensorbet *nt or m*

sorbic acid [,sɔːbɪk'æsɪd] N *(Chem)* Sorbinsäure *f*

sorcerer ['sɔːsərəʳ] N Hexenmeister *m*, Hexer *m*

sorceress ['sɔːsəres] N Hexe *f*

sorcery ['sɔːsərɪ] N Hexerei *f*

sordid ['sɔːdɪd] ADJ eklig; *place, room also* verkommen, heruntergekommen; *motive* schmutzig, niedrig, gemein; *conditions, life, story* elend, erbärmlich; *crime* gemein; *affair* schmutzig; **he considers it ~ to discuss money** er hält es für unfein, über Geld zu sprechen; **spare me the ~ details** erspar mir die schmutzigen Einzelheiten

sordidness ['sɔːdɪdnɪs] N Ekligkeit *f*; *(of place, room also)* Verkommenheit *f*; *(of motive)* Schmutzigkeit *f*, Niedrigkeit *f*, Gemeinheit *f*; *(of conditions, life, story)* Elend *nt*, Erbärmlichkeit *f*; *(of crime)* Gemeinheit *f*; *(of affair)* Schmutzigkeit *f*

sore [sɔːʳ] ADJ *(+er)* **a** *(= hurting)* weh, schlimm *(inf)*; *(= inflamed)* wund, entzündet; **to have a ~ throat** Halsschmerzen haben; **my eyes are ~** mir tun die Augen weh; **my wrist feels ~** mein Handgelenk schmerzt *(geh) or* tut weh; **to have ~ muscles** Muskelkater haben; **to have a ~ head** *(esp US, Scot)* Kopfschmerzen haben; **I've got ~ feet after all that walking** meine Füße tun nach all dem Wandern weh; **I'm ~ all over** mir tut alles weh; **where are you ~?** wo tut es (dir/Ihnen) weh?, was tut (dir/Ihnen) weh?; **to be ~ at heart** *(liter)* betrübt sein *(geh)*; **her heart was ~** *(liter)* ihr war weh ums Herz *(liter)*
b *(fig)* **a ~ point** ein wunder Punkt; **a ~ subject** ein heikles Thema
c *(esp US inf: = angry, upset)* verärgert, sauer *(inf)* *(about sth* über etw *acc, at sb* über jdn*)*; **now don't get ~ at me** werd doch nicht gleich sauer! *(inf)*
d *(= great)* **to be in ~ need of sth** etw unbedingt *or* dringend brauchen; **in ~ distress** *(liter)* in arger Not *(liter)*
ADV *(obs, = greatly)* arg *(old)*, gar sehr *(obs)*; **and when they saw the angel they were ~ afraid** *(Bibl)* und als sie den Engel sahen, fürchteten sie sich sehr
N *(Med)* wunde Stelle; *(caused by friction)* wunde *or* wund gescheuerte Stelle; **open ~** offene Wunde; **to open old ~s** *(fig)* alte Wunden öffnen

sorehead ['sɔːhed] N *(US inf)* Brummbär *m (inf)*

sorely ['sɔːlɪ] ADV *tempted* sehr, arg *(S Ger, Aus, Sw)*; *needed* dringend; *missed* schmerzlich; *(liter) afflicted, troubled, offended* zutiefst; *wounded* schwer; **he has been ~ tested** *or* **tried** seine Geduld wurde auf eine sehr harte Probe gestellt; **to be ~ lacking** bedauerlicherweise fehlen

soreness ['sɔːnɪs] N **a** *(= ache)* Schmerz *m*; *(= rawness)* Wundsein *nt* **b** *(inf, = anger)* Verärgerung *f (at* über *+acc)*

sorghum ['sɔːgəm] N Sorghum *nt*

sororicide [sə'rɒrɪsaɪd] N Schwestermord *m*; *(= person)* Schwestermörder(in) *m(f)*

sorority [sə'rɒrɪtɪ] N *(US Univ)* Studentinnenvereinigung *f*

SORORITY/FRATERNITY

An vielen amerikanischen Colleges und Universitäten gibt es Studentenverbindungen, für Frauen **sororities**, für Männer **fraternities**. Mitglied kann man nur nach persönlicher Einladung werden. Die Hauptaktivitäten bestehen aus Freizeitveranstaltungen wie Partys, aber auch Spendenaktionen für gemeinnützige Zwecke oder Veranstaltungen, mit denen das Prestige der eigenen Verbindung angehoben werden soll. Die **sororities** und **fraternities** haben normalerweise einen Namen, der sich aus zwei oder drei Buchstaben des griechischen Alphabets zusammensetzt: z. B. „Kappa Kappa Gamma sorority" oder „Sigma Chi fraternity". Heutzutage stehen die Verbindungen in dem Ruch, elitär und diskriminierend zu sein. Außerdem werden die geheimen Aufnahmeriten kritisiert, bei denen die Kandidaten verschiedenen seelischen und körperlichen Prüfungen, dem sogenannten **hazing**, unterworfen werden.

sorrel ['sɒrəl] N **a** *(Bot)* Großer Sauerampfer; *(= wood-sorrel)* Sauerklee *m* **b** *(= horse)* Fuchs *m* ADJ *horse* rotbraun

sorrow ['sɒrəʊ] ✪ 24.4 N *(no pl: = sadness)* Traurigkeit *f*; *(no pl: = grief)* Trauer *f*, Kummer *m*; *(= trouble, care)* Sorge *f*, Kümmernis *f*; *(= affliction, suffering)* Leiden *nt*; **more in ~ than in anger** eher aus Betrübnis als aus Zorn; **to my (great) ~** zu meinem größten Kummer; **this**

was a matter of real ~ to me das hat mir großen Kummer bereitet; **a feeling of ~** ein Gefühl von Traurigkeit, ein wehes Gefühl *(liter)*; **to drown one's ~s** seine Sorgen ertränken; **the ~s of their race** die Leiden ihres Volkes
VI sich grämen *(geh)* *(at, over, for* über *+acc)*

sorrowful ADJ, **sorrowfully** ADV ['sɒrəʊ fʊl, -fəlɪ] traurig

sorry ['sɒrɪ] ✪ 18.1, 18.2 ADJ *(+er)* **a** *pred (= sad)* traurig; **I was ~ to hear that** es tat mir leid, das zu hören *or* das hören zu müssen; **we were ~ to hear about your mother's death** es tat uns leid, dass deine Mutter gestorben ist; **he wasn't in the least bit ~ to hear the news** es war ihm egal, was passiert war; **I can't say I'm ~ he lost** es tut mir wirklich nicht leid, dass er verloren hat; **I'm not ~ I did it** es tut mir nicht leid, es getan zu haben; **this work is no good, I'm ~ to say** diese Arbeit taugt nichts, das muss ich leider sagen; **to be** *or* **feel ~ for sb/oneself** jdn/sich selbst bemitleiden; **I feel ~ for the child** das Kind tut mir leid; **I feel ~ for him having to ...** es tut mir leid, dass er ... muss; **I'm only ~ I didn't do it sooner** es tut mir nur leid, dass ich es nicht eher getan habe; **don't feel ~ for me, I don't need your pity!** du brauchst mich nicht zu bedauern, kein Mitleid, bitte!; **you'll be ~ (for this)!** das wird dir noch leidtun!
b *(in apologizing, = repentant)* **~!** Entschuldigung!, Verzeihung!; **I'm/he's ~** es tut mir/ihm leid; **I'm so ~!** entschuldige(n Sie) bitte!; **can you lend me £5? – ~** kannst du mir £ 5 leihen? – bedaure, leider nicht; **~?** *(= pardon)* wie bitte?; **he's from England, ~ Scotland** er ist aus England, nein, Entschuldigung, aus Schottland; **to say ~ (to sb for sth)** sich (bei jdm für etw) entschuldigen; **I'm ~ to hurt you** es tut mir leid, dass ich dir wehtun muss; **I'm ~ but ...** (es) tut mir leid, aber ...; **I'm ~ about that vase/your dog** es tut mir leid um die Vase/um Ihren Hund; **I'm ~ about Thursday, but I can't make it** es tut mir leid mit Donnerstag, aber ich kann nicht; **I'm ~ about (what happened on) Thursday** es tut mir leid wegen Donnerstag
c *(= pitiful) condition, plight* traurig; *sight, figure* jämmerlich, traurig; *excuse* faul; **to be in a ~ state** *(person)* in einer jämmerlichen Verfassung sein; *(object)* in einem jämmerlichen Zustand sein

sort [sɔːt] N **a** *(= kind)* Art *f*; *(= species, type, model)* Sorte *f*, Art *f*; **a ~ of** eine Art *(+nom)*, so ein/eine; **this ~ of house** diese Art Haus, so ein Haus; **an odd ~ of novel** ein komischer Roman; **I felt a ~ of shame** ich schämte mich irgendwie; **a silly ~ of smile** so ein albernes Grinsen; **I have a ~ of idea that ...** ich habe das *or* so ein Gefühl, dass ...; **what ~ of** was für ein; **what ~ of (a) man is he?** was für ein Mensch ist er?; **he's not the ~ of man to do that** er ist nicht der Mensch, der das täte; **this ~ of thing** so etwas; **all ~s of things** alles Mögliche; **people of all ~s** alle möglichen Leute; **he's a painter of a ~** *or* **of ~s** er ist Maler, sozusagen; **it's coffee of a ~** *or* **of ~s** das ist Kaffee oder so etwas Ähnliches; **something of the ~** (irgend) so (et)was; **he's some ~ of administrator** er hat irgendwie in der Verwaltung zu tun; **he's got some ~ of job with ...** er hat irgendeinen Job bei ...; **nothing of the ~!** von wegen!; **you'll do nothing of the ~!** von wegen!, das wirst du schön bleiben lassen!; **that's the ~ of person I am** ich bin nun mal so!; **I'm not that ~ of girl** ich bin nicht so eine
b *(= person)* **he's a good ~** er ist ein prima Kerl; **she sounds a good ~** sie scheint in Ordnung zu sein; **he's not my ~** er ist nicht mein Typ; **I don't trust his ~** solchen Leuten traue ich nicht; **I know your ~** euch Brüder kenn ich! *(inf)*; **your ~ never did any good** du und deinesgleichen, ihr habt noch nie etwas zustande gebracht; **it takes all ~s (to make a world)** es gibt so 'ne und solche
c to be out of ~s *(Brit)* nicht ganz auf der Höhe *or* auf dem Damm *(inf)* sein
d *(Comput)* Sortieren *nt*, Sortiervorgang *m*; **to do a ~** sortieren
ADV **~ of** *(inf)* irgendwie; **it's ~ of heavy** es ist irgendwie schwer *(inf)*; **is it tiring? – ~ of** ist das anstrengend? – irgendwie schon; **it's ~ of finished** es ist eigentlich schon fertig; **aren't you pleased? – ~ of** freust du dich nicht? – doch, eigentlich schon; **is this how he did it? – well, ~ of** hat er das so gemacht? – ja, so ungefähr
VT **a** *(also Comput)* sortieren; **to ~ the ripe tomatoes from the unripe ones** die reifen und die unreifen Tomaten aussortieren; **to ~ sth on sth** *(Comput)* etw nach etw sortieren
b *(= solve, organize)* **to get sth ~ed** etw auf die Reihe bekommen; **everything is now ~ed** es ist jetzt alles (wieder) in Ordnung
VI **a to ~ through sth** etw durchsehen
b *(Comput)* sortieren

▶ **sort out** VT *sep* **a** *(= arrange)* sortieren, ordnen; *(= select)* aussortieren, aussuchen; **to sort sth out from sth** etw von etw trennen; **to sort red apples out from green ones** rote und grüne Äpfel aussortieren
b *(= straighten out) muddle* in Ordnung bringen; *problem* lösen; *situation* klären; **the problem will sort itself out** das Problem wird sich von selbst lösen *or* erledigen; **to sort oneself out** zur Ruhe kommen, sich *(dat)* über sich *(acc)* selbst klar werden; **you must come and visit us once we've sorted ourselves out** wenn wir uns erst mal richtig eingerichtet haben, musst du uns unbedingt besuchen
c *(esp Brit inf)* **to sort sb out** sich *(dat)* jdn vorknöpfen *(inf)*

sorta ['sɔːtə] ADV *(inf)* = **sort of**, → **sort** ADV

sort code N *(Banking)* Bankleitzahl *f*

sorter ['sɔːtəʳ] N *(= person)* Sortierer(in) *m(f)*; *(= machine)* Sortiermaschine *f*; *(Post: = person)* Briefverteiler(in) *m(f)*

sort field N *(Comput)* Sortierfeld *nt*

sortie ['sɔːtɪ] N *(Mil)* Ausfall *m*; *(Aviat)* (Einzel)einsatz *m*, Feindflug *m*; **a ~ into town/banking** ein Ausflug *or* Abstecher *m* in die Stadt/ins Bankwesen

sorting office ['sɔːtɪŋˌɒfɪs] N *(Brit)* Sortierstelle *f*

sorting order N *(esp Comput)* Sortierreihenfolge *f*

sort key N *(Comput)* Sortierschlüssel *m*

sort run N *(Comput)* Sortierlauf *m*

SOS N SOS *nt*; **to radio an ~** SOS funken

so-so ['səʊ'səʊ] ADJ PRED, ADV *(inf)* soso, so la la

sot [sɒt] N *(pej)* Säufer *m*, Trunkenbold *m* *(dated)*

sottish ['sɒtɪʃ] ADJ dem Trunk ergeben; *grin* benebelt

sotto voce ['sɒtəʊ'vəʊtʃɪ] ADV leise; *(= conspiratorially)* mit unterdrückter Stimme; *(Mus)* sotto voce

sou [suː] N *(inf)* **I haven't a ~** ich habe keinen Cent

sou' [saʊ] *(Naut) abbr of* **south**

soubrette [suː'bret] N *(dated)* Soubrette *f* *(dated)*

soubriquet ['suːbrɪkeɪ] N = **sobriquet**

Soudanese ADJ, N = **Sudanese**

sou'easter [saʊ'iːstəʳ] N *(Naut: = wind)* Südost(-wind) *m*

soufflé ['suːfleɪ] N Soufflé *nt*, Soufflee *nt*

sough [saʊ] *(liter)* N Rauschen *nt* VI *(wind)* rauschen

sought [sɔːt] *pret, ptp of* **seek**

sought-after ['sɔːtɑːftəʳ] ADJ begehrt; **much ~** viel begehrt; *rare object* gesucht

soul [səʊl] N **a** Seele *f*; **upon my ~!** *(dated)* **(God) bless my ~!** meiner Treu *(dated)*, na so was!; **All Souls' Day** Allerheiligen *nt*; **God rest his ~!** Gott hab ihn selig! → **body a**
b *(= inner being)* Innerste(s), Wesen *nt*; **he may not be a brilliant intellect, but he has a beautiful ~** er ist vielleicht kein großer Geist, aber er hat innere Werte; **he loved her with all his ~** er liebte sie von ganzem Herzen; **he loved her with all his heart and with all his ~** er liebte sie mit jeder Faser seines Herzens; **the priest urged them to search their ~s** der Priester drängte sie, ihr Gewissen zu erforschen; **a little humility is good for the ~** ein bisschen Bescheidenheit tut der Seele gut; **the ~ of the city has been destroyed by modernization** durch die Modernisierung ist die Stadt in ihrem innersten Wesen zerstört worden; **to have a ~ above sth** über etw *(acc)* hoch erhaben sein; **the music lacks ~** der Musik fehlt echter Ausdruck; **poetry is the ~ of civilization** die Dichtkunst ist die Seele der Zivilisation
c *(= finer feelings)* Herz *nt*, Gefühl *nt*; **complete lack of ~** vollkommene Gefühllosigkeit; **a musician of considerable technical skill, but lacking ~** ein Musiker von beachtlichem technischem Können, aber ohne echtes Gefühl; **you've got to have ~** *(US sl)* du musst Feeling haben *(inf)*; **~ brother** Bruder *m*; **~ sister** Schwester *f*; **he's a ~ brother** er ist einer von uns
d *(= person)* Seele *f*; **3,000 ~s** 3.000 Seelen *(geh)*; **poor ~!** *(inf)* Ärmste(r)!; **how is she, the wee ~?** wie gehts denn unsrer Kleinen?; **he's a good ~** er ist ein guter Mensch; **she's a kind** *or* **kindly ~** sie ist eine gute Seele; **she's a simple ~** sie hat ein schlichtes Gemüt; **not a ~** keine Menschenseele; **there wasn't a living ~ about** keine Menschenseele war zu sehen; **the ship was lost with all ~s** das Schiff ging mit (der ganzen Besatzung und) allen Passagieren unter
e he's the ~ of generosity/discretion er ist die Großzügigkeit/Diskretion in Person
f *(Mus)* Soul *m*

soul-destroying ['səʊldɪˌstrɔɪɪŋ] ADJ geisttötend; *factory work etc* nervtötend

soulful ['səʊlfʊl] ADJ *look* seelenvoll; *person, song* gefühlvoll; *eyes* ausdrucksstark

soulfully ['səʊlfəlɪ] ADV *sing, write* gefühlvoll; *look* voll Gefühl

soulless ['səʊllɪs] ADJ *person* seelenlos; *work also* eintönig; *place* gottverlassen; *system* herzlos, seelenlos; *music* eintönig; *eyes* leer; *existence* eintönig, öde

soul: **soul mate** N Seelenfreund(in) *m(f)*; **soul music** N Soul *m*, Soulmusik *f*; **soul-searching** N Gewissensprüfung *f*; **soul-stirring** ADJ *speech, music* bewegend

sound[1] [saʊnd] ADJ *(+er)* **a** *(= in good condition) person, animal, tree, constitution, lungs* gesund; *condition, building, chassis* einwandfrei; **to be as ~ as a bell** kerngesund sein; **to be ~ in wind and limb** gesund und munter sein; **to be of ~ mind** *(esp Jur)* bei klarem Verstand sein, im Vollbesitz seiner geistigen Kräfte sein *(Jur)*; **the windows were broken, but the frames were ~** die Fensterscheiben waren zerbrochen, aber die Rahmen waren heil
b *(= valid, good, dependable)* solide; *argument, analysis* fundiert, solide; *economy, currency* stabil; *person, goalkeeper* verlässlich, in Ordnung *pred* *(inf)*; *idea* gesund, vernünftig; *basis* solide; *move* vernünftig; *advice* wertvoll, vernünftig; **he's ~ on financial policy** er hat gründliche Kenntnisse in der Finanzpolitik; **a ~ scholar** ein ernst zu nehmender Gelehrter; **that's ~ sense** das ist vernünftig
c *(= thorough)* gründlich, solide; *beating* gehörig; *defeat* vernichtend
d *(Jur) decision* rechtmäßig; *claim* berechtigt
e *(= deep) sleep* tief, fest; **I'm a very ~ sleeper** ich schlafe sehr tief *or* fest, ich habe einen gesunden Schlaf
ADV *(+er)* **to be ~ asleep** fest schlafen; **I shall sleep the ~er for it** ich werde nur umso besser schlafen

sound[2] N **a** *(= noise)* Geräusch *nt*; *(Ling)* Laut *m*; *(Phys)* Schall *m*; *(Mus, of instruments)* Klang *m*; *(verbal, TV, Rad, Film)* Ton *m*; *(of band etc)* Sound *m*; **don't make a ~** still!; **the speed of ~** (die) Schallgeschwindigkeit; **within ~ of** in Hörweite *(+gen)*; **to the ~(s) of the national anthem** zu den Klängen der Nationalhymne;

French has a soft ~ die französische Sprache hat einen weichen Klang; **would you still recognize the ~ of Karin's voice?** würdest du Karins Stimme immer noch erkennen?; **not a ~ was to be heard** man hörte keinen Ton;**~s** *(Comput)* akustische Signale *pl*; **the ~(s) of laughter** Gelächter *nt*; **we heard the ~ of voices on the terrace** wir hörten Stimmen auf der Terrasse; **vowel ~** Vokallaut *m*; **~ and fury** leerer Schall
b *(= impression)* **I don't like the ~ of it** das klingt gar nicht gut; **from the ~ of it he had a hard time** es hört sich so an *or* es klingt, als sei es ihm schlecht gegangen; **his remarks had a familiar ~** seine Bemerkungen klangen vertraut
VT a *(= produce sound from)* **~ your horn** hupen!; **the trumpeter ~ed a high note** der Trompeter spielte einen hohen Ton; **to ~ the alarm** Alarm schlagen; *(mechanism)* die Alarmanlage auslösen; **to ~ the retreat** zum Rückzug blasen; **to ~ the "r" in "cover"** das „r" in „cover" aussprechen; **his speech ~ed a note of warning** in seiner Rede klang eine Warnung an; **I think we need to ~ a note of warning** ich finde, wir sollten eine vorsichtige Warnung aussprechen
b *(= test by tapping, Med)* abklopfen
VI a *(= emit sound)* erklingen, ertönen; **feet ~ed in the corridor** im Flur waren Schritte zu hören; **a gun ~ed a long way off** in der Ferne hörte man einen Schuss
b *(= give aural impression)* klingen, sich anhören; **it ~s hollow** es klingt hohl; **the children ~ happy** es hört sich so an, als ob die Kinder Spaß haben; **he ~s angry** es hört sich so an, als wäre er wütend; **he ~ed depressed on the phone** am Telefon klang er deprimiert; **he ~s French (to me)** er hört sich (für mich) wie ein Franzose an
c *(= seem)* sich anhören; **that ~s very odd** das hört sich sehr seltsam an; **he ~s like a nice man** er scheint ein netter Mensch zu sein; **it ~s like a sensible idea** das klingt ganz vernünftig; **how does it ~ to you?** wie findest du das?

▶ **sound off** VI *(inf)* sich verbreiten *or* auslassen (*about* über *+acc*); **don't listen to him, he's just sounding off** hör nicht auf ihn, er spielt sich nur auf!

sound[3] VT *(Naut)* loten, ausloten; *(Met)* messen; **~ing line** Lot *nt*, Senkblei *nt*; **~ing balloon** Versuchs- *or* Registrierballon *m*

▶ **sound out** VT *sep person* aushorchen, ausfragen; *intentions, opinions* herausfinden, herausbekommen; **to sound sb out about** *or* **on sth** bei jdm in Bezug auf etw *(acc)* vorfühlen

sound[4] N *(Geog)* Meerenge *f*, Sund *m*

sound: **sound-absorbing** ['saʊndəb,sɔːbɪŋ] ADJ schalldämpfend *or* -schluckend; **sound archives** PL Tonarchiv *nt*; **sound barrier** N Schallmauer *f*; **sound bite** N Soundclip *m*, Tonclip *m*; **soundboard** N *(Comput)* Soundkarte *f* **a** = **sounding board a**; **soundbox** N *(Mus)* Schallkörper *m*, Schallkasten *m*; **sound card** N *(Comput)* Soundkarte *f*; **sound check** N *(Mus)* Soundcheck *m*; **sound effects** PL Toneffekte *pl*; **sound engineer** N Toningenieur(in) *m(f)*; **sound film** N Tonfilm *m*; **sound hole** N Schallloch *nt*

sounding ['saʊndɪŋ] N *(Naut)* Loten *nt*, Peilung *f*; **to take ~s** *(lit)* Lotungen vornehmen; *(fig)* sondieren

sounding board ['saʊndɪŋ,bɔːd] N **a** *(on instrument)* Resonanzboden *m*; *(over platform etc)* Schalldeckel *m* **b** *(fig)* Resonanzboden *m*; **he used the committee as a ~ for his ideas** er benutzte den Ausschuss, um die Wirkung seiner Vorschläge zu sondieren

sound insulation N Schalldämmung *f*

soundless ['saʊndlɪs] ADJ lautlos

soundlessly ['saʊndlɪslɪ] ADV *(= silently) move* geräuschlos; *weep* lautlos; *laugh* tonlos; *(= inaudibly)* unhörbar

soundly ['saʊndlɪ] ADV *built, made* solide; *argue, reason, invest, play also* vernünftig; *thrash* tüchtig, gehörig; *defeat* vernichtend; *condemn* rundum; *train* gründlich; *based* fest; **our team was ~ beaten** unsere Mannschaft wurde eindeutig *or* klar geschlagen; **to sleep ~** (tief und) fest schlafen

sound motion picture N *(US)* Tonfilm *m*

soundness ['saʊndnɪs] N **a** *(= good condition)* gesunder Zustand; *(of building, chassis)* guter Zustand **b** *(= validity, dependability)* Solidität *f*; *(of argument, analysis)* Fundiertheit *f*, Solidität *f*; *(of economy, currency)* Stabilität *f*; *(of idea, advice, move, policy)* Vernünftigkeit *f*; *(of person, goalkeeper)* Verlässlichkeit *f* **c** *(= thoroughness)* Gründlichkeit *f*, Solidität *f* **d** *(Jur, of decision, claim)* Rechtmäßigkeit *f* **e** *(of sleep)* Tiefe *f*

sound: **sound pollution** N Umweltverschmutzung *f* durch Lärm, Lärmbelästigung *f*; **soundproof** ADJ schalldicht; **~ barrier** Lärmschutzwall *m* VT schalldicht machen, schalldämmen; **soundproofing** N Schallisolierung *f*; **sound quality** N Tonqualität *f*; **sound recorder** N *(Comput)* Audiorekorder *m*; **sound recording** N Tonaufnahme *f*, Tonaufzeichnung *f*; **sound scheme** N *(Comput)* Audioschema *nt*; **sound shift** N Lautverschiebung *f*; **sound technician** N *(Radio, TV)* Tontechniker(in) *m(f)*; **soundtrack** N Tonspur *f*; *(= sound, recording)* Ton *m*, Filmmusik *f*; **sound wave** N Schallwelle *f*

soup [suːp] N Suppe *f*; **to be in the ~** *(inf)* in der Tinte *or* Patsche sitzen *(inf)*

▶ **soup up** VT *sep (inf) car, engine* (hoch)frisieren *(inf)*

soupçon ['suːpsɔ̃ːŋ] N *(of spice etc)* Spur *f*; *(of irony etc)* Anflug *m*; *(of melancholy)* Hauch *m*, Spur *f*; **sauce? – just a ~** Soße? – (ja bitte, nur) ganz wenig

soup: **soup kitchen** N Volksküche *f*; *(for disaster area etc)* Feldküche *f*; **soup plate** N Suppenteller *m*, tiefer Teller; **soup spoon** N Suppenlöffel *m*; **soup tureen** N Suppenterrine *f*

sour ['saʊə'] ADJ (+er) **a** *fruit, soil* sauer; *wine, vinegar* säuerlich; **whisky ~** *(esp US)* Whisky mit Zitrone
b *(= bad) milk* sauer; *smell* streng, säuerlich; **to go** *or* **turn ~** *(lit)* sauer werden; **to go** *or* **turn ~ (on sb)** *(fig, relationship, marriage)* jdn anöden; *(plan, investment)* sich als Fehlschlag erweisen; **things began to turn ~** die Dinge begannen einen negativen Verlauf zu nehmen
c *(fig) person, expression* verdrießlich, griesgrämig; *remark* bissig; **he's feeling ~ about being demoted** er ist über seine Absetzung verbittert; **it's just ~ grapes** die Trauben sind zu sauer *or* hängen zu hoch; **it sounds like ~ grapes to me** das kennt man: die Trauben sind zu sauer *or* hängen zu hoch
VT *milk* sauer *or* dick werden lassen; *soil* sauer *or* kalkarm machen; *(fig) person* verdrießlich *or* griesgrämig machen; *relationship, atmosphere* vergiften; *success* verderben
VI *(milk)* sauer *or* dick werden; *(soil)* sauer *or* kalkarm werden; *(fig, person)* verbittern, griesgrämig werden; *(atmosphere, mood, relationship)* sich verschlechtern

source [sɔːs] N *(of river, light, information)* Quelle *f (also Comput)*; *(of troubles, problems etc)* Ursache *f*, Ursprung *m*; **a ~ of vitamin C** eine Vitamin-C-Quelle *f*; **they tried to trace the ~ of the gas leak** sie versuchten, das Leck in der Gasleitung ausfindig zu machen; **he is a ~ of embarrassment to us** er bringt uns ständig in Verlegenheit; **~ of supply** Bezugsquelle *f*; **to have its ~ in sth** seine Ursache *or* seinen Ursprung in etw *(dat)* haben; **I have it from a good ~ that ...** ich habe es aus sicherer Quelle, dass ...; **at ~** *(tax)* unmittelbar, direkt; **these rumours must be stopped at ~** diese Gerüchte darf man gar nicht erst aufkommen lassen; **~s** *(in book etc)* Quellen *pl*, Literaturangaben *pl*; **from reliable ~s** aus zuverlässiger Quelle
VT *(Comm)* beschaffen; **furniture ~d from all over the world** Möbel aus der ganzen Welt

source: **source application** N *(Comput)* Quellanwendung *f*; **sourcebook** N Quellenwerk *nt*, Quellensammlung *f*; **source code** N *(Comput)* Quellcode *m*; **source drive** N *(Comput)* Quelllaufwerk *nt*; **source file** N *(Comput)* Quelldatei *f*, Ursprungsdatei *f*; **source language** N Ausgangssprache *f*; **source material** N Quellenmaterial *nt*; **source program** N *(Comput)* Quellprogramm *nt*

sourdough ['saʊədəʊ] N Sauerteig *m*

sour(ed) cream [,saʊə(d)'kriːm] N saure Sahne, Sauerrahm *m*

sour-faced ['saʊəfeɪst] ADJ *(inf)* vergrätzt *(inf)*

sourly ['saʊəlɪ] ADV *(fig)* verdrießlich, griesgrämig

sourness ['saʊənɪs] N *(of lemon, milk)* saurer Geschmack; *(of wine, vinegar also, of smell)* Säuerlichkeit *f*; *(of soil)* saure Beschaffenheit; *(fig, of person, expression)* Verdrießlichkeit *f*, Griesgrämigkeit *f*, Verbitterung *f*; *(of remark)* Bissigkeit *f*

sourpuss ['saʊəpʊs] N *(inf)* Miesepeter *m (inf)*

sousaphone ['suːzəfəʊn] N Sousafon *nt*, Sousaphon *nt*

souse [saʊs] VT **a** *(= cover with water etc)* nass machen; *fire* löschen; **he ~d himself with water** er übergoss sich mit Wasser **b** *(= pickle) fish* einlegen, marinieren **c** **to be ~d** *(inf)* sternhagelvoll sein *(inf)*; **to get ~d** *(inf)* sich volllaufen lassen *(inf)*

soutane [suː'tæn] N *(Eccl)* Soutane *f*

south [saʊθ] N Süden *m*; **in the ~ of** im Süden *+gen*; **to the ~ of** im Süden *or* südlich von; **from the ~** aus dem Süden; *(wind)* aus Süden; **to veer to the ~** in südliche Richtung *or* nach Süden drehen; **the wind is in the ~** es ist Südwind; **the South of France** Südfrankreich *nt*; **which way is ~?** in welcher Richtung ist Süden?; **down ~** *(be, live)* unten im Süden; *go* runter in den Süden
ADJ südlich; *(in names)* Süd-; **South German** süddeutsch; **~ London** Süd-London *nt*; **South Wales** Südwales *nt*; **the MP for Coventry South** der Abgeordnete für (den Wahlkreis) Coventry Süd
ADV im Süden; *(= towards the south)* nach Süden, gen Süden *(liter)*, südwärts *(liter, Naut)*; *(Met)* in südliche Richtung; **to be further ~** weiter südlich sein; **~ of** südlich *or* im Süden von; **~ of one million** *(US fig)* weniger als eine Million

south *in cpds* Süd-; **South Africa** N Südafrika *nt*; **South African** ADJ südafrikanisch; **he's ~** er ist Südafrikaner N Südafrikaner(in) *m(f)*; **South America** N Südamerika *nt*; **South American** ADJ südamerikanisch; **he's ~** er ist Südamerikaner N Südamerikaner(in) *m(f)*; **South Atlantic** N Südatlantik *m*; **South Australia** N Südaustralien *nt*; **southbound** ADJ (in) Richtung Süden; **South Carolina** N Südkarolina *nt*, South Carolina *nt*; **South Dakota** N Süddakota *nt*, South Dakota *nt*; **southeast** N Südosten *m*, Südost *m (esp Naut)*; **from the ~** aus dem Südosten; *(wind)* von Südosten; **in the ~** im Südosten ADJ südöstlich; *(in names)* Südost-; **~ wind** Südost (-wind) *m*, Wind *m* aus Südost *or* südöstlicher Richtung; **~ London** Südostlondon *nt* ADV nach Südosten; **~ of** südöstlich von; **Southeast Asia** N Südostasien *nt*; **southeaster** N *(esp Naut)* Südostwind *m*, Südost *m*; **southeasterly** ADJ *direction* südöstlich; *wind also* aus Südost N *(= wind)* Südostwind *m*; **southeastern** ADJ südöstlich, im Südosten; **~ England** Südostengland *nt*; **southeastward(s)** ADV nach Südosten

southerly ['sʌðəlɪ] ADJ südlich; *course also* nach Süden; *wind* aus Süden *or* südlicher Richtung ADV nach Süden, südwärts *(esp Naut)* N Südwind *m*

southern ['sʌðən] ADJ südlich; *(in names)* Süd-; *(= Mediterranean)* südländisch; **~ people** Südländer *pl*; **a ~ belle** eine Schönheit aus dem Süden; **Southern Africa** das südliche Afrika; **Southern Europe** Südeuropa *nt*; **Southern England** Südengland *nt*; **Southern States** *(US)* Südstaaten *pl*

Southern Cross N Kreuz *nt* des Südens

southerner ['sʌðənə'] N Bewohner(in) *m(f)* des Südens, Südengländer(in) *m(f)*/-deutsche(r) *mf etc; (from the Mediterranean)* Südländer(in) *m(f); (US)* Südstaatler(in) *m(f)*

Southern Ireland N *(Pol)* (Süd)irland *nt, die Republik Irland*

southern lights PL Südlicht *nt*

southernmost [ˈsʌðənməʊst] ADJ südlichste(r, s)

south: **south-facing** ADJ *wall, window* nach Süden gerichtet; *garden* nach Süden gelegen; **~ slope** Südhang *m*; **South Korea** N Südkorea *nt*; **South Korean** ADJ südkoreanisch N Südkoreaner(in) *m(f)*; **South Pacific** N Südpazifik *m*; **southpaw** N *(Boxing)* Linkshänder(in), Rechtsausleger(in) *m(f)*; **South Pole** N Südpol *m*; **South Sea Islands** PL Südseeinseln *pl*; **South Seas** PL Südsee *f*; **south-south-east** N Südsüdosten *m*, Südsüdost *m (esp Naut)* ADJ südsüdöstlich ADV nach Südsüdost(en); **south-south-west** N Südsüdwesten *m*, Südsüdwest *m (esp Naut)* ADJ südsüdwestlich ADV nach Südsüdwest(en); **~ of** südsüdwestlich von; **South Vietnam** N Südvietnam *nt*; **southward(s)** ADJ südlich ADV nach Süden, südwärts; **southwest** N Südwesten *m*, Südwest *m (esp Naut)*; **in the ~** im Südwesten; **from the ~** aus dem Südwesten; *(wind)* von Südwesten ADJ Südwest-, südwestlich; **~ wind** Südwestwind *m* ADV nach Südwest(en); **~ of** südwestlich von; **South West Africa** N Südwestafrika *nt*; **southwester** N *(esp Naut)* Südwest(wind) *m*; **southwesterly** ADJ *direction* südwestlich; *wind also* aus Südwest N Südwestwind *m*; **southwestern** ADJ südwestlich, im Südwesten; **southwestward(s)** ADV nach Südwesten; **South Yorkshire** N Süd-Yorkshire *nt*

souvenir [ˌsuːvəˈnɪəˈ] N Andenken *nt*, Souvenir *nt (of an +acc)*

sou'wester [saʊˈwestəˈ] N **a** *(= hat)* Südwester *m* **b** *(Naut: = wind)* Südwest(wind) *m*

sovereign [ˈsɒvrɪn] N *(= monarch)* Souverän *m*, Herrscher(in) *m(f)*; *(Brit, old: = coin)* 20-Shilling-Münze *f* ADJ **a** *(= supreme)* höchste(r, s), oberste(r, s); *state, power* souverän; *contempt* tiefste(r, s), äußerste(r, s); **the ~ power of the Pope** die Oberhoheit des Papstes; **our ~ Lord the King** *(old)* unser gnädiger Herr, der König **b a ~ remedy** *(lit, fig)* ein Allheilmittel *nt (for gegen)* **c** *(Fin)* **~ debt** Staatsschulden *pl*; **~ lending** staatliche Kreditaufnahme

sovereignty [ˈsɒvrəntɪ] N Oberhoheit *f*, Oberherrschaft *f*; *(= right of self-determination)* Souveränität *f*; **the ~ of papal decrees** die unumschränkte Gültigkeit der päpstlichen Erlasse

soviet [ˈsəʊvɪət] N Sowjet *m*; **the Soviets** *(= people)* die Sowjets; **the Supreme Soviet** der Oberste Sowjet ADJ *attr* sowjetisch, Sowjet-; **~ power** Sowjetmacht *f*; **~ citizen** Sowjetbürger(in) *m(f)*

sovietize [ˈsəʊvɪətaɪz] VT sowjetisieren

Sovietologist [ˌsəʊvɪəˈtɒlədʒɪst] N Sowjetologe *m*, Sowjetologin *f*

Soviet: **Soviet Republic** N Sowjetrepublik *f*; **Soviet Russia** N Sowjetrussland *nt*; **Soviet Union** N Sowjetunion *f*

sow¹ [səʊ] *pret* **sowed**, *ptp* **sown** *or* **sowed** VT **a** *corn, plants* säen; *seed* aussäen; *(Mil) mine* legen; **to ~ the garden with grass** im Garten Gras (aus)säen; **this field has been ~n with barley** auf diesem Feld ist Gerste gesät; **to ~ mines in a strait** eine Meerenge verminen **b** *(fig)* **to ~ (the seeds of) hatred/discord** Hass/Zwietracht säen; **to ~ (the seeds of) anarchy** zur Anarchie anstiften; **to ~ the wind and reap the whirlwind** *(prov)* wer Wind sät, wird Sturm ernten *(Prov)*; **as you ~ so shall you reap** *(prov)* was der Mensch säet, das wird er ernten *(Prov)* → **seed**

sow² [saʊ] N **a** *(= pig)* Sau *f*; *(of wild boar)* (Wild)sau *f*; *(of badger)* Dächsin *f* **b** *(Tech, = block of iron)* Massel f; *(= channel)* Masselgraben *m*

sower [ˈsəʊəˈ] N *(= person)* Säer(in) *m(f)*, Sämann *m*; *(= machine)* Sämaschine *f*; **a ~ of doubt** ein Mensch, der Zweifel verbreitet

sowing [ˈsəʊɪŋ] N *(= action)* (Aus)säen *nt*, Aussaat *f*; *(= quantity sown)* Saat *f*; **the ~ of a field** die Aussaat auf einem Feld

sown [səʊn] *ptp of* **sow¹**

sox [sɒks] *pl (US Comm inf)* = **socks**

soya [ˈsɔɪə], **soy** [sɔɪ] N Soja *f*; **~ flour** Sojamehl *nt*

soya: **soya bean** N Sojabohne *f*; **soya milk** N Sojamilch *f*; **soya sauce** N Sojasoße *f*

soybean [ˈsɔɪbiːn] N *(US)* = **soya bean**

soybean sprouts PL Sojasprossen *pl*, Sojabohnenkeimlinge *pl*

sozzled [ˈsɒzld] ADJ *(Brit inf)* **to be ~** einen sitzen haben *(inf)*; **to get ~** beschwipst werden

SP *abbr of* **starting price a** *(Horse Racing)* Starterquote *f* **b** *(inf: = information)* **what's the SP on him?** was erzählt man sich so über ihn?; **to give sb the SP on sb/sth** jdm Infos über jdn/etw geben *(inf)*

spa [spɑː] N *(= town)* (Heil- *or* Mineral)bad *nt*, Kurort *m*; *(= spring)* (Heil- *or* Mineral)quelle *f*

space [speɪs] N **a** Raum *m (also Phys)*; *(= outer space)* der Weltraum, das Weltall; **time and ~** Zeit und Raum; **to stare** *or* **gaze into ~** ins Leere starren; **to give sb some ~** *(fig)* jdm Freiraum gewähren → **outer space**

b *no pl (= room)* Platz *m*, Raum *m*; *(Typ, between letters)* Spatien *pl*; *(between lines)* Durchschuss *m*; **to take up a lot of ~** viel Platz wegnehmen *or* einnehmen; **to clear/leave some ~ for sb/sth** für jdn/etw Platz schaffen/lassen; **to buy/sell ~** *(Press)* Platz für Anzeigen kaufen/verkaufen; *(TV)* Sendezeit kaufen/verkaufen; **parking ~** Platz *m* zum Parken

c *(= gap, empty area)* Platz *m no art*; *(between objects, words, lines)* Zwischenraum *m*; *(= parking space)* Lücke *f*; *(Typ, Comput)* Leerschlag *m*, Leerzeichen *nt*; **to leave a ~ for sb/sth** für jdn/etw Platz lassen; **there was a (blank) ~ at the end of the document** am Ende des Dokuments war Platz gelassen; **please answer in the ~ provided** bitte an der dafür vorgesehenen Stelle beantworten; **to leave an empty ~ in a room** eine Lücke in einem Zimmer hinterlassen; **indent the line a few ~s** rücken Sie die Zeile ein paar Stellen ein; **the wide open ~s** das weite, offene Land

d *(Typ: = piece of metal, between words)* Spatienkeil *m*; *(between lines)* Reglette *f*

e *(of time)* Zeitraum *m*; **in a short ~ of time** in kurzer Zeit; **in the ~ of one hour/three generations** innerhalb einer Stunde/von drei Generationen

VT *(also* **space out***)* in Abständen verteilen; *chairs also* in Abständen aufstellen; *seedlings also* in Abständen setzen; *visits* verteilen; *words* Zwischenraum *or* Abstand lassen zwischen *(+dat)*; *(Typ)* spatiieren *(spec)*; **~ them out more, ~ them further out** *or* **further apart** lassen Sie etwas mehr Zwischenraum *or* Abstand (dazwischen); **well ~d-out houses** genügend weit auseinander gebaute Häuser; **houses ~d (out) along the road** Häuser, die sich entlang der Straße verteilen; **to ~ payments** nach und nach zahlen; **to ~ the children (out)** *(when planning a family)* in vernünftigen (Zeit)abständen Kinder bekommen → **spaced out**

space *in cpds* (Welt)raum-; **space age** N (Welt)raumzeitalter *nt*; **space-age** ADJ *attr* des Raumzeitalters; **space bar** N *(Typ)* Leertaste *f*; **space blanket** N Rettungsdecke *f*, (Alu)isoliermatte *f*; **space-borne** ADJ **a** (Welt)raum-; **~ satellite** Weltraumsatellit *m* **b** *(= via satellite)* über Satellit, Satelliten-; **~ television** Satellitenfernsehen *nt*; **space cadet** N *(US inf)* **to be a ~** ständig zugedröhnt *or* auf dem Trip sein *(inf)*; **space capsule** N (Welt)raumkapsel *f*; **space carrier** N Raumtransporter *m*; **space character** N *(Comput, Typ)* Leerzeichen *nt*, Zwischenraumzeichen *nt*; **spacecraft** N Raumfahrzeug *nt*; *(unmanned)* Raumkörper *m*; **space debris** N Weltraummüll *m*

spaced out [ˌspeɪstˈaʊt] ADJ *(inf: = confused etc)* geistig weggetreten *(inf)*; *(= on drugs)* high *(inf)*

space: **space fiction** N Zukunftsromane *pl* über den Weltraum; **space flight** N Weltraumflug *m*; **space heater** N *(esp US)* Heizgerät *nt*; **space helmet** N Astronautenhelm *m*; **Space Invaders®** N SING Space Invaders *pl*; **space key** N *(Typ)* Leertaste *f*; **space lab(oratory)** N Weltraumlabor *nt*; **spaceman** N (Welt)raumfahrer *m*; **space module** N Weltraummodul *nt*; **space platform** N Raumstation *f*; **spaceport** N Raumflugzentrum *nt*; **space probe** N Raumsonde *f*; **space programme**, *(US)* **space program** N Raumfahrtprogramm *nt*

spacer [ˈspeɪsəˈ] N = **space bar**

space: **space race** N Wettlauf *m* im All; **space rocket** N Weltraumrakete *f*; **space-saving** ADJ *equipment, gadget* platzsparend; *furniture also* Raum sparend; **space science** N Raumforschung *f*; **space scientist** N Raumforscher(in) *m(f)*; **space-seller** N *(Press)* Anzeigenakquisiteur(in) *m(f)*; *(TV)* Werbungspromoter(in) *m(f)*; **spaceship** N Raumschiff *nt*; **space shot** N *(= launching)* Abschuss *m* eines Raumfahrzeugs/-körpers; *(= flight)* Raumflug *m*; **space shuttle** N Raumfähre *f*; **space sickness** N Weltraumkrankheit *f*; **space station** N (Welt)raumstation *f*; **spacesuit** N Raumanzug *m*; **space-time (continuum)** N Raum-Zeit-Kontinuum *nt*; **space travel** N die Raumfahrt; **space vehicle** N Raumfahrzeug *nt*; **space walk** N Weltraumspaziergang *m* VI im Weltraum spazieren gehen; **spacewoman** N (Welt)raumfahrerin *f*; **space writer** N *(Press)* Korrespondent(in) *m(f) (der/die nach der Länge seiner/ihrer Artikel bezahlt wird)*

spacey [ˈspeɪsɪ] ADJ *(inf)* spacig *(inf)*; *music also* trancehaft, sphärisch; *person also* ausgeflippt *(inf)*

spacing [ˈspeɪsɪŋ] N Abstände *pl*; *(between two objects)* Abstand *m*; *(also* **spacing out***)* Verteilung *f*; *(of payments)* Verteilung *f* über längere Zeit; **single/double ~** *(Typ)* einzeiliger/zweizeiliger Abstand

spacious [ˈspeɪʃəs] ADJ geräumig; *garden, park* weitläufig

spaciousness [ˈspeɪʃəsnɪs] N Geräumigkeit *f*; *(of garden, park)* Weitläufigkeit *f*

spacy [ˈspeɪsɪ] ADJ = **spacey**

spade [speɪd] N **a** *(= tool)* Spaten *m*; *(= children's spade)* Schaufel *f*; **to call a ~ a ~** *(Brit prov)* das Kind beim Namen nennen *(Prov)* **b** *(Cards)* Pik *nt*; **the Queen/two of Spades** die Pikdame/Pikzwei; **to play in ~s** Pik spielen; **~s are trumps** Pik ist Trumpf **c** *(pej sl)* Nigger *m (pej sl)*

spadeful [ˈspeɪdfʊl] N **a ~ of earth** ein Spaten *m or* eine Schaufel (voll) Erde; **by the ~** spaten- *or* schaufelweise

spadework [ˈspeɪdwɜːk] N *(fig)* Vorarbeit *f*

spag bol [ˌspægˈbɒl] N *(Brit inf)* Spag(h)etti *pl* Bolognese

spaghetti [spəˈgetɪ] N Spag(h)etti *pl*; *(fig inf: = cabling)* Kabelgewirr *nt*, Kabelsalat *m (inf)*

spaghetti: **spaghetti bolognaise** N Spag(h)etti *pl* Bolognese; **spaghetti junction** N *(inf)* Autobahnknoten(punkt) *m*; **spaghetti western** N *(inf)* Italowestern *m*

Spain [speɪn] N Spanien *nt*

spake [speɪk] *(obs) pret of* **speak**

Spam® [spæm] N Frühstücksfleisch *nt*

spam *(Internet)* N (E-Mail-)Spam *m*; *(= single e-mail)* Spam-Mail *f* VT (zu)spammen *(sl)*, mit Werbung bombardieren *(inf) or* zumüllen *(sl)*

spam *(Internet)*: **spam filter** N Spam-Filter *m*; **spam mail** N Spam-(E-)Mail *f*

spamming [ˈspæmɪŋ] N *(Internet)* Spamming *nt (sl)*, Bombardierung *f* mit Werbung *(inf)*

span¹ [spæn] N **a** *(of hand)* Spanne *f*; *(= wingspan, of bridge etc)* Spannweite *f*; *(= arch of bridge)* (Brücken)bogen *m*; **a single-span bridge** eine eingespannte Bogenbrücke **b** *(= time span)* Zeitspanne *f*, Zeitraum *m*; *(of memory)* Gedächtnisspanne *f*; *(of attention)*

Konzentrationsspanne *f*; *(= range)* Umfang *m*; **for a ~ of several months** einige Monate lang; **the whole ~ of world affairs** die Weltpolitik in ihrer ganzen Spannweite
c *(of oxen)* Gespann *nt*
d *(old: = measurement)* Spanne *f*
VT *(rope, rainbow)* sich spannen über *(+acc)*; *(bridge also)* überspannen; *(plank)* führen über *(+acc)*; *years, globe, world* umspannen; *(= encircle)* umfassen; *(in time)* sich erstrecken über *(+acc)*, umfassen

span² *(old) pret of* **spin**

spangle ['spæŋgl] **N** Paillette *f* **VT** mit Pailletten besetzen; **~d with stars/flowers** mit Sternen/Blumen übersät

Spanglish ['spæŋglɪʃ] **N** *Mischung aus Spanisch und Englisch*

spangly ['spæŋglɪ] **ADJ** paillettenbesetzt

Spaniard ['spænjəd] **N** Spanier(in) *m(f)*

spaniel ['spænjəl] **N** Spaniel *m*

Spanish ['spænɪʃ] **ADJ** spanisch; **he is ~** er ist Spanier; **she is ~** sie ist Spanierin **N a the ~** die Spanier *pl* **b** *(Ling)* Spanisch *nt*

Spanish: **Spanish America** **N** *die spanischsprachigen Länder Mittel- und Südamerikas*; **Spanish-American** **N** spanischsprachiger Lateinamerikaner, spanischsprachige Lateinamerikanerin **ADJ** spanisch-amerikanisch; **Spanish chestnut** **N** Edelkastanie *f*; **Spanish Civil War** **N the ~** der Spanische Bürgerkrieg; **Spanish fly** **N** *no pl* Spanische Fliege; **Spanish guitar** **N** spanische Gitarre; **Spanish Main** **N** Karibik *f*; **Spanish moss** **N** *(US)* Spanisches Moos, Greisenbart *m*; **Spanish omelette** **N** Omelett *nt* mit Piment, Paprika und Tomaten; **Spanish onion** **N** Gemüsezwiebel *f*

spank [spæŋk] **N** Klaps *m*; **to give sb a ~** jdm einen Klaps geben; *(= spanking)* jdm den Hintern versohlen **VT** versohlen; **to ~ sb's bottom** jdm den Hintern versohlen **VI to ~ along** dahinjagen, dahinrasen

spanker ['spæŋkəʳ] **N a** *(Naut: = sail)* Besan *m* **b** *(dated inf: = horse)* Renner *m*; **a real ~** *(= blow)* ein Schlag, der nicht von Pappe war *(inf)*

spanking ['spæŋkɪŋ] **N** Tracht *f* Prügel; **to give sb a ~** jdm eine Tracht Prügel verpassen, jdm den Hintern versohlen **ADJ a** *(= brisk) pace* scharf, schnell; **at a ~ pace** in schnellem Tempo **b** *(= splendid)* **in ~ condition** in hervorragendem Zustand **ADV** *(dated inf: = exceedingly)* **~ new** funkelnagelneu; **~ clean** blitzsauber

spanner ['spænəʳ] **N** *(Brit)* Schraubenschlüssel *m*; **to put** *or* **throw a ~ in the works** *(fig)* jdm Knüppel *or* einen Knüppel zwischen die Beine werfen; **that's a real ~ in the works** das ist wirklich ein Hemmschuh

span roof **N** Satteldach *nt*

spar¹ [spɑːʳ] **N** *(Naut)* Rundholz *nt*

spar² **VI** *(Boxing)* sparren, ein Sparring *nt* machen; *(fig)* sich kabbeln *(inf)* *(about* um)

spar³ **N** *(Miner)* Spat *m*

spare [speəʳ] **ADJ a** den/die/das man nicht braucht, übrig *pred*; *(= surplus)* überzählig, übrig *pred*; **~ bed** Gästebett *nt*; **have you any ~ string?, have you any string ~?** kannst du mir (einen) Bindfaden geben?, hast du (einen) Bindfaden für mich?; **I can give you a racket/pencil, I have a ~ one** ich kann dir einen Schläger/Bleistift geben, ich habe noch einen *or* ich habe einen übrig; **take a ~ pen in case that one doesn't work** nehmen Sie noch einen Füller mit, falls dieser nicht funktioniert; **take some ~ clothes** nehmen Sie Kleider zum Wechseln mit; **it's all the ~ cash I have** mehr Bargeld habe ich nicht übrig; **if you have any ~ cash** wenn Sie Geld übrig haben; **should you have any ~ time** *or* **a ~ minute** sollten Sie Zeit (übrig) haben; **when you have a few ~ minutes** *or* **a few minutes ~** wenn Sie mal ein paar freie Minuten haben *or* ein paar Minuten übrig haben; **we have two ~ seats** wir haben zwei Plätze übrig; **I still have one ~ place in the car** ich habe noch einen Platz im Auto (frei); **there are two seats (going) ~** es sind noch zwei Plätze frei
b *(= thin)* hager; *(= meagre)* dürftig
c to drive sb ~ *(inf)* jdn wahnsinnig machen *(inf)*; **to go ~** durchdrehen *(inf)*, wild werden *(inf)*
N Ersatzteil *nt*; *(= tyre)* Reserverad *nt*
VT a *usu neg (= grudge, use sparingly)* sparen mit; *expense, pains, effort* scheuen; **don't ~ the horses** *(hum)* steig aufs Gas *(inf)*; **we must ~ no effort in trying to finish this job** wir dürfen keine Mühe scheuen, um diese Arbeit zu erledigen; **there was no expense ~d in building this hotel** beim Bau dieses Hotels ist an nichts gespart worden *or* hat man keine Kosten gescheut; **no expense ~d** es wurden keine Kosten gescheut; **she doesn't ~ herself** sie schont sich nicht; **~ the rod and spoil the child** *(prov)* wer mit der Rute spart, verzieht das Kind *(Prov)*
b *(= give) money etc* übrig haben; *space, room* frei haben; *time* (übrig) haben; **to ~ sb sth** jdm etw überlassen *or* geben; *money* jdm etw geben; **can you ~ the time to do it?** haben Sie Zeit, das zu machen?; **I can ~ you five minutes** ich habe fünf Minuten Zeit für Sie (übrig); **can you ~ a penny for a poor old man?** haben Sie einen Groschen für einen armen alten Mann?; **there is none to ~** es ist keine(r, s) übrig; **to have sth to ~** etw übrig haben; **there's enough and to ~** es ist mehr als genug da; **to have a few minutes/hours to ~** ein paar Minuten/Stunden Zeit haben; **I got to the theatre/airport with two minutes to ~** ich war zwei Minuten vor Beginn der Vorstellung im Theater/vor Abflug am Flughafen
c *(= do without) person, object* entbehren, verzichten auf *(+acc)*; **I can't ~ him/it** ich kann ihn/es nicht entbehren, ich kann auf ihn/es nicht verzichten, ich brauche ihn/es unbedingt; **can you ~ this for a moment?** brauchst du das gerade?, kannst du das im Moment entbehren?; **if you can ~ it** wenn Sie es nicht brauchen; **to ~ a thought for sb/sth** an jdn/etw denken
d *(= show mercy to)* verschonen; *(= refrain from upsetting) sb, sb's feelings* schonen; **the fire ~d nothing** nichts blieb vom Feuer verschont; **the soldiers ~d no-one** die Soldaten verschonten keinen; **if we're ~d** wenn wir (dann) noch leben; **to ~ sb's life** jds Leben verschonen
e *(= save)* **to ~ sb/oneself sth** jdm/sich etw ersparen; **~ me the gory details** verschone mich mit den grausigen Einzelheiten; **to ~ him any embarrassment** um ihn nicht in Verlegenheit zu bringen; **he has been ~d the ordeal of seeing her again** es blieb ihm erspart, sie noch einmal sehen zu müssen

sparely ['speəlɪ] **ADV ~ built** schlank gebaut

spare: **spare part** **N** Ersatzteil *nt*; **spare-part surgery** **N** *(inf)* Ersatzteilchirurgie *f* *(inf)*; **sparerib** **N** Rippchen *nt*, Spare Rib *no art*; **spare room** **N** Gästezimmer *nt*; **spare time** **N** *(= leisure time)* Freizeit *f*; **spare tyre**, *(US)* **spare tire** **N** Ersatzreifen *m*; *(fig inf)* Rettungsring *m (hum inf)*; **spare wheel** **N** *(esp Brit)* Ersatzrad *nt*

sparing ['speərɪŋ] **ADJ** sparsam; **to be ~ with one's time** mit seiner Zeit geizen *or* knausern; **to be ~ in one's praise** mit Lob geizen; **to be ~ of words** nicht viel sagen, wortkarg sein

sparingly ['speərɪŋlɪ] **ADV** sparsam; *spend, drink, eat* in Maßen; **to use sth ~** mit etw sparsam umgehen; **these plants should be watered more ~** diese Pflanzen sollten mäßiger gegossen werden

spark [spɑːk] **N a** *(from fire, Elec)* Funke *m*; *(fig: = glimmer)* Fünkchen *nt*, Funke(n) *m*; **not a ~ of life** kein Fünkchen Leben, kein Lebensfunke; **a ~ of interest** ein Fünkchen *or* Funke(n) Interesse; **a few ~s of wit toward(s) the end of the speech** ein paar geistreiche Bemerkungen am Ende der Rede; **when the ~s start to fly** *(fig)* wenn die Funken anfangen zu fliegen
b *(dated inf, = person)* Stutzer *m (dated)*; **a bright ~** *(iro)* ein Intelligenzbolzen *m (iro)*; *(clumsy)* ein Tollpatsch *m*
VT *(also* **spark off***)* entzünden; *explosion* verursachen; *(fig)* auslösen; *quarrel* entfachen; *interest, enthusiasm* wecken; **to ~ a fire** ein Feuer entzünden *or* entfachen; *(by accident)* ein Feuer auslösen *or* verursachen
VI Funken sprühen; *(Elec)* zünden

spark: **spark coil** **N** Zündspule *f*; **spark gap** **N** Funkenstrecke *f*

sparking plug ['spɑːkɪŋplʌg] **N** Zündkerze *f*

sparkle ['spɑːkl] **N** Funkeln *nt*, Glitzern *nt*; *(of eyes)* Funkeln *nt*; **he has no ~, he lacks ~** ihm fehlt der (rechte) Schwung **VI** funkeln, glitzern; *(eyes)* blitzen, funkeln *(with* vor *+dat)*; *(fig: person)* vor Leben(sfreude) sprühen; *(with intelligence, wit etc)* brillieren; **her eyes ~d with excitement** ihre Augen blitzten vor Erregung; **she was so happy she really ~d** sie sprühte geradezu vor Glück; **his conversation ~d (with wit)** seine Unterhaltung sprühte vor Geist

sparkler ['spɑːkləʳ] **N a** *(= firework)* Wunderkerze *f* **b** *(inf: = diamond)* Klunker *m (inf)*

sparkling ['spɑːklɪŋ] **ADJ** *lights* glänzend, funkelnd; *eyes* funkelnd; *wit* sprühend; *(= lively) person* vor Leben sprühend; *(= scintillating) performance* brilliant; *(= witty) person, speech, conversation* vor Geist sprühend; *(= bubbling) lemonade etc* perlend; *wine* perlend, moussierend; *cider* kohlensäurehaltig; **~ (mineral) water** Mineralwasser *nt* mit Kohlensäure, Selterswasser *nt*; **~ wine** *(as type)* Schaumwein *m*, Sekt *m*; *(= slightly sparkling)* Perlwein *m*; **in ~ form** in glänzender Form; **the car was ~ (clean)** das Auto blitzte vor Sauberkeit
ADV funkelnd, blitzend; **~ clean floors and walls** blitzsaubere Fußböden und Wände

sparkly ['spɑːklɪ] **ADJ** *(inf)* funkelnd; **her eyes were ~** ihre Augen funkelten

spark plug **N** Zündkerze *f*

sparring ['spɑːrɪŋ]: **sparring match** **N** *(lit)* Sparringkampf *m*; *(fig)* (Wort)geplänkel *nt*, Wortgefecht *nt*; **sparring partner** **N** *(lit)* Sparringpartner(in) *m(f)*; *(fig also)* Kontrahent(in) *m(f)*

sparrow ['spærəʊ] **N** Sperling *m*, Spatz *m*; **house ~** Haussperling *m*

sparrowgrass ['spærəʊgrɑːs] **N** *(inf)* Spargel *m*

sparrowhawk ['spærəʊhɔːk] **N** *(European)* Sperber *m*; *(N American)* amerikanischer Falke

sparse [spɑːs] **ADJ** spärlich; *covering, vegetation also* dünn; *hair* dünn, schütter; *furnishings, data, resources* dürftig

sparsely ['spɑːslɪ] **ADV** spärlich; *wooded also, populated* dünn; *furnished also* dürftig; **a hillside ~ covered with trees** ein Hang mit spärlichem Baumwuchs

sparseness ['spɑːsnɪs] **N** Spärlichkeit *f*; *(of furnishings also)* Dürftigkeit *f*; *(of population)* geringe Dichte

Sparta ['spɑːtə] **N** Sparta *nt*

Spartan ['spɑːtən] **ADJ** *(fig: also* **spartan***)* spartanisch **N** Spartaner(in) *m(f)*

spasm ['spæzəm] **N** *(Med)* Krampf *m*, Spasmus *m (spec)*; *(of asthma, coughing, fig)* Anfall *m*; **~s of coughing** krampfartige Hustenanfälle *pl*; **there was a ~ of activity** es entwickelte sich fieberhafte Aktivität; **they play well in ~s** sie spielen ab und zu ganz gut

spasmodic [spæz'mɒdɪk] **ADJ** *(Med)* krampfartig, spasmisch, spasmodisch *(spec)*; *(fig: = occasional)* sporadisch; *growth* schubweise; **his generosity was ~** er hatte Phasen *or* Anfälle von Großzügigkeit

spasmodically [spæz'mɒdɪkəlɪ] **ADV** *(Med)* krampfartig; *(fig)* sporadisch, hin und wieder; *grow* in Schüben, schubweise

spastic ['spæstɪk] **ADJ** spastisch; *(pej sl)* schwach *(inf)* **N** Spastiker(in) *m(f)*

spasticity [spæ'stɪsɪtɪ] **N** spastische Lähmung

spat[1] [spæt] **N** *(of oyster etc)* Muschellaich *m* **VI** *(oyster etc)* laichen

spat[2] **N** Halbgamasche *f*

spat[3] **N** *(inf: = quarrel)* Knatsch *m (inf)*, Krach *m (inf)* **VI** *(US inf: = quarrel)* zanken, streiten

spat[4] *pret, ptp of* **spit**[1]

spate [speɪt] **N** *(of river)* Hochwasser *nt; (fig, of letters, orders etc)* Flut *f; (of burglaries, accidents)* Serie *f; (of words, abuse)* Schwall *m;* **the river is in (full) ~** der Fluss führt Hochwasser; **a ~ of words** ein Wortschwall *m;* **a ~ of excited talk** aufgeregtes Stimmengewirr

spatial **ADJ**, **spatially** **ADV** ['speɪʃəl, -ɪ] räumlich

spatiotemporal [ˌspeɪʃɪəʊ'tempərəl] **ADJ** räumlich-zeitlich

spatter ['spætəʳ] **VT** bespritzen; **to ~ water over sb, to ~ sb with water** jdn nass spritzen; **a wall ~ed with blood** eine blutbespritzte Wand **VI** **to ~ over sth** etw vollspritzen; **it ~ed all over the room** es verspritzte im ganzen Zimmer; **the rain ~ed (down) on the roof** der Regen klatschte aufs Dach **N** *(= mark)* Spritzer *pl; (= sound: of rain)* Klatschen *nt;* **a ~ of rain** ein paar Tropfen Regen; **a ~ of applause** kurzer Beifall

spatula ['spætjʊlə] **N** Spachtel *m; (Med)* Spatel *m*

spavin ['spævɪn] **N** Spat *m*

spavined ['spævɪnd] **ADJ** *horse* spatkrank

spawn [spɔːn] **N** **a** *(of fish, shellfish, frogs)* Laich *m* **b** *(of mushrooms)* Fadengeflecht *nt* **VI** laichen **VT** *(fig)* hervorbringen, erzeugen; **bad living conditions ~ crime** schlechte Wohnverhältnisse sind Brutstätten des Verbrechens

spawning ['spɔːnɪŋ] **N** Laichen *nt* **ADJ** **a** *fish* laichend, Laich-; **~ time** Laichzeit *f* **b** *(= sprawling)* sich stark ausbreitend *or* vermehrend

spawning ground ['spɔːnɪŋgraʊnd] **N** Laichplatz *m*

spay [speɪ] **VT** *cat, dog* sterilisieren

SPCA *abbr of* **Society for the Prevention of Cruelty to Animals** ≈ Tierschutzverein *m*

speak [spiːk] *pret* **spoke** *or (obs)* **spake**, *ptp* **spoken** *or (obs)* **spoke** **VT** **a** *(= utter)* sagen; *one's thoughts* aussprechen, äußern; *one's lines* aufsagen; **to ~ one's mind** seine Meinung sagen; **nobody spoke a word** niemand sagte ein Wort, keiner sagte etwas; **his eyes spoke his love** sein Blick verriet seine Liebe → **volume**

b *language* sprechen; **English spoken here** man spricht Englisch

VI **a** *(= talk, be on speaking terms)* sprechen, reden *(about* über *+acc,* von*); (= converse)* reden, sich unterhalten *(with* mit*); (fig, guns, drums)* sprechen, ertönen; **to ~ to** *or* **with sb** mit jdm sprechen *or* reden; **did you ~?** haben Sie etwas gesagt?; **to ~ in a whisper** flüstern; **~, don't shout** nun schreien Sie doch nicht (so)!; **they don't ~ (to one another)** sie reden *or* sprechen nicht miteinander; **I'm not ~ing to you** mit dir rede *or* spreche ich nicht mehr; **she never spoke to me again** seitdem hat sie nie wieder mit mir geredet *or* gesprochen; **to ~ to oneself** Selbstgespräche führen; **I'll ~ to him about it** *(euph: = admonish)* ich werde ein Wörtchen mit ihm reden; **I'll have to ~ to my lawyer about it** das muss ich mit meinem Anwalt besprechen; **~ when you're spoken to** antworte, wenn man mit dir redet *or* spricht; **servants should only ~ when spoken to** Diener sollten nur dann etwas sagen, wenn man sie anspricht; **I don't know him to ~ to** ich kenne ihn nicht näher; **music ~s directly to the soul** Musik spricht die Seele an; **~ing of dictionaries ...** da *or* wo wir gerade von Wörterbüchern sprechen ..., apropos Wörterbücher ...; **not to ~ of ...** ganz zu schweigen von ...; **it's nothing to ~ of** es ist nicht weiter erwähnenswert, es ist nichts weiter; **no money/trees** *etc* **to ~ of** so gut wie kein Geld/keine Bäume *etc;* **to ~ ill of sb/sth** über jdn/etw schlecht reden; **to ~ well of sb/sth** jdn/etw loben, (nur) Gutes über jdn/etw sagen; **he is well spoken of** er genießt große Achtung; **so to ~** sozusagen, eigentlich; **roughly ~ing** grob gesagt; **strictly ~ing** genau genommen; **legally/biologically ~ing** rechtlich/biologisch gesehen; **generally ~ing** im Allgemeinen; **~ing personally ...** wenn Sie mich fragen ..., was mich betrifft ...; **~ing as a member of the club I have ...** als Mitglied des Vereins habe ich ...; **to ~ down to sb** jdn von oben herab behandeln

b *(= make a speech)* reden *(on* zu*)*, sprechen *(on* zu*); (= give one's opinion)* sich äußern *(on, to* zu*);* **to ~ in public** in der Öffentlichkeit reden; **to ~ in the debate** in der Debatte das Wort ergreifen; **to ask sb to ~** jdm das Wort erteilen; **Mr X will ~ next** als Nächster hat Herr X das Wort; **then Geoffrey rose to ~** dann stand Geoffrey auf, um das Wort zu ergreifen

c *(Telec)* **~ing!** am Apparat!; **Jones ~ing!** (hier) Jones!; **who is that ~ing?** wer ist da, bitte?; *(on extension phone, in office)* wer ist am Apparat?

d *(fig: = suggest)* zeugen *(of* von*);* **their appearance ~s of poverty** ihre Erscheinung verrät Armut *or* zeugt von Armut

N *suf* **Euro-~** Eurojargon *m*

▶ **speak against** **VI** *+prep obj (in debate)* sprechen gegen, sich aussprechen gegen; *(= criticize)* etwas sagen gegen, kritisieren

▶ **speak for** **VI** *+prep obj* **a** *(in debate)* unterstützen

b **to speak for sb** *(= on behalf of)* in jds Namen *(dat)* sprechen; *(= in favour of)* ein gutes Wort für jdn einlegen; **he speaks for the miners/delegation** er ist der Sprecher der Bergleute/Abordnung; **I know I speak for all of us** ich bin sicher, dass ich im Namen aller spreche; **speaking for myself ...** was mich angeht ...; **let her speak for herself** lass sie selbst reden; **speak for yourself!** *(= I don't agree)* das meinst auch nur du!; *(= don't include me)* du vielleicht!; **I can speak for his honesty** ich kann mich für seine Ehrlichkeit verbürgen; **that speaks well for him** das spricht für ihn; **to speak well/badly for sth** ein Beweis *m*/nicht gerade ein Beweis *m* für etw sein

c **to speak for itself** *(= be obvious)* für sich sprechen, alles sagen

d **to be spoken for** *(dated: girl)* versprochen sein *(old)*, vergeben sein *(hum);* **the chair had already been spoken for** *(hum)* der Stuhl war schon reserviert; **that's already spoken for** *(hum)* das ist schon vergeben

▶ **speak to** **VI** sprechen über *(+acc);* **to speak to the topic of ...** über das Thema ... sprechen; **to speak to a subject** sich zu einem Thema äußern

▶ **speak out** **VI** *(audibly)* deutlich sprechen; *(= give one's opinion)* seine Meinung deutlich vertreten; **to speak out in favour of sth** für etw eintreten; **to speak out against sth** sich gegen etw aussprechen

▶ **speak up** **VI** **a** *(= raise one's voice)* lauter sprechen *or* reden; *(= talk loudly)* laut (und verständlich) sprechen *or* reden; **speak up!** sprich lauter!; **if you want anything speak up** sag, wenn du etwas willst **b** *(fig)* seine Meinung sagen *or* äußern; **don't be afraid to speak up** sagen Sie ruhig Ihre Meinung, äußern Sie sich ruhig; **to speak up for sb/sth** für jdn/etw eintreten; **what's wrong? speak up!** was ist los? heraus mit der Sprache!

speakeasy ['spiːkiːzɪ] **N** *(US)* Mondscheinkneipe *f (inf, Lokal, in dem während der Prohibition Alkohol ausgeschenkt wurde)*

speaker ['spiːkəʳ] **N** **a** *(of language)* Sprecher *m;* **all ~s of German, all German ~s** alle, die Deutsch sprechen, alle Deutsch Sprechenden; *(esp native speakers)* alle Deutschsprachigen **b** Sprecher(in) *m(f); (in lecture, = public speaker)* Redner(in) *m(f);* **the last** *or* **previous ~** der Vorredner; **our ~ today is ...** der heutige Referent ist ...; **he's a good/poor ~** er ist ein guter/schlechter Redner **c** *(= loudspeaker)* Lautsprecher *m; (on hi-fi etc)* Box *f* **d** *(Parl)* **Speaker** Sprecher(in) *m(f);* **Mr Speaker** ≈ Herr Präsident

> **SPEAKER/SPEAKER OF THE HOUSE**
>
> Im britischen Parlamentssystem hat der **Speaker** die Aufgabe, im **House of Commons** die Ordnung aufrechtzuerhalten und zu garantieren, dass alle Mitglieder die Geschäftsordnung befolgen. Der **Speaker**, der nicht Mitglied der Regierungspartei sein muss, wird zur Eröffnung eines neuen Parlaments gewählt. Sobald er oder sie im Amt ist, spricht der **Speaker** nur noch in seiner offiziellen Funktion und muss absolut unparteiisch sein. Die Parlamentsmitglieder beginnen ihre Reden stets mit „Mister/Madam Speaker". In den Vereinigten Staaten ist der **Speaker of the House** der Vorsitzende des Repräsentantenhauses, der zudem der Vorsitzende der Partei ist, die die Mehrheit stellt. Er ist selbst Mitglied des **House of Representatives** und wird von seiner eigenen Partei gewählt. Er ist nicht nur für die Einhaltung der Geschäftsordnung zuständig, sondern fungiert zugleich als Sprecher seiner Partei. Der **Speaker of the House** steht direkt nach dem Vizepräsidenten in der Präsidentennachfolge.

speaker phone, **speakerphone** **N** *(Telec)* Freisprechanlage *f*

speaking ['spiːkɪŋ] **N** *(= act of speaking)* Sprechen *nt; (= speeches)* Reden *pl;* **the art of ~** die Redekunst **ADJ** *attr doll* sprechend, Mama- *(inf); (fig) likeness* verblüffend; **to be within ~ distance** nahe genug sein, dass man sich verständigen kann; **I have a ~ engagement later today** ich muss heute noch eine Rede halten

-speaking **ADJ** *suf* -sprechend; *(with native language also)* -sprachig; **English-speaking** Englisch sprechend, englischsprachig

speaking: **speaking clock** **N** *(Brit)* telefonische Zeitansage; **speaking part**, **speaking role** **N** *(Film, Theat)* Sprechrolle *f;* **speaking terms** **PL** **to be on ~ with sb** mit jdm sprechen *or* reden; **speaking trumpet** **N** *(old)* Hörrohr *nt;* **speaking tube** **N** Sprachrohr *nt;* **speaking voice** **N** Sprechstimme *f*

spear [spɪəʳ] **N** Speer *m; (= leaf)* Lanzettenblatt *nt; (of grass)* Halm *m; (of grain)* Keim *m;* **broccoli ~s** Brokkoliköpfe *pl;* **asparagus ~s** Stangen *pl* Spargel **VT** aufspießen; *(= wound, kill)* durchbohren; *(= catch with spear)* mit Speeren fangen; **he ~ed him through the arm** er durchbohrte ihm den Arm; **he ~ed the meat with his fork** er spießte das Fleisch auf die Gabel

spear: **spear carrier** **N** **a** *(Theat)* Statist(in) *m(f)* **b** *(pej = henchman)* Handlanger(in) *m(f) (pej);* **spearhead** **N** **a** *(of spear)* Speerspitze *f; (Mil)* Angriffsspitze *f* **b** *(fig: = thing)* Bahnbrecher *m (of* für*); (= person)* Bahnbrecher(in) *m(f) (of* für*)* **VT** *(lit, fig)* anführen; **spearman** **N** Speerträger *m;* **spearmint** **N** *(= plant, flavour)* Grüne Minze; **~ chewing gum** Spearmintkaugummi *m*

spec [spek] **N** *(inf)* **on ~** auf Verdacht, auf gut Glück

special ['speʃəl] **ADJ** **a** besondere(r, s); *(= specific) purpose, use, person, date* bestimmt, speziell; *(= exceptional) friend, favour, occasion* speziell; **I have no ~ person in mind** ich habe eigentlich an niemanden Bestimmtes gedacht; **in this one ~ instance** in diesem einen Fall; **take ~ care of it** passen Sie besonders gut darauf auf; **nothing ~** nichts Besonderes; **he expects ~ treatment** er will besonders behandelt werden, er will eine Extrawurst gebraten haben *(inf);* **this is rather a ~ day for me** heute ist ein ganz besonderer Tag für mich; **he uses the word in a ~ way** er gebraucht das Wort in einer speziellen Bedeutung; **he's a very ~ person to her, he's very ~ to her** er bedeutet ihr sehr viel; **you're extra ~!** *(inf)* du bist was ganz Besonderes! *(inf);* **what's so ~ about her/the house?** was ist denn an ihr/an dem Haus so besonders?; **what's so ~ about that?** na und? *(inf)*, das ist doch nichts Besonderes!; **I do that my own ~ way** ich mache das ganz auf meine (eigene)

Weise; **everyone has his ~ place** jeder hat seinen eigenen Platz; **to feel ~** sich als etwas ganz Besonderes vorkommen; **make him feel ~** seien Sie besonders nett zu ihm
b *(= out of the ordinary)* Sonder-, besondere(r, s); **~ permission** Sondererlaubnis *f*; **~ legislation** Sondergesetzgebung *f*; **~ feature** *(Press)* Sonderartikel *m*
c *(= specialized)* speziell, Spezial-; **~ subject** Spezialfach *nt*
d *(inf, = separate) place, book etc* gesondert
N **a** *(= constable)* Hilfspolizist(in) *m(f)*
b *(TV, Rad)* Sonderprogramm *nt*; *(Press: = edition)* Sonder- *or* Extraausgabe *f*
c *(= train)* Sonderzug *m*
d *(Cook)* Tagesgericht *nt*; **chef's ~** Spezialität *f* des Küchenchefs
e *(pej inf: = person)* **you're such a ~** du bist ja SO blöd! *(inf)*

special: **special agent** N *(= spy)* Agent(in) *m(f)*; **special bargain** N *(Comm)* Sonderangebot *nt*, Schnäppchen *nt (inf)*; **Special Branch** N *(Brit)* Sicherheitspolizei *f*, Sicherheitsdienst *m*; **special case** N *(also Jur)* Sonderfall *m*; **special character** N *(Comput)* Sonderzeichen *nt*; **special code** N *(Comput)* Sonderzeichen *nt*; **special constable** N Hilfspolizist(in) *m(f)*; **special correspondent** N *(Press)* Sonderberichterstatter(in) *m(f)*; **special delivery** N Eilzustellung *f*; **a special-delivery letter** ein Eilbrief *m*; **by ~** durch Eilzustellung, per Eilboten *(inf)*; **special drawing rights** PL Sonderziehungsrechte *pl*; **special edition** N Sonderausgabe *f*; **special effects** PL *(Film)* Spezialeffekte *pl*; **special envoy** N Sondergesandte(r) *mf*; **special investigator** N Sonderbeauftragte(r) *mf*, Untersuchungsbeamte(r) *m*/-beamtin *f*

specialism [ˈspeʃəlɪzəm] N *(= specializing)* Spezialisierung *f*; *(= special subject)* Spezialgebiet *nt*

specialist [ˈspeʃəlɪst] **N** Spezialist(in) *m(f)*, Fachmann *m*, Fachfrau *f* *(in* für); *(Med)* Facharzt *m*/-ärztin *f*; **a ~ in tropical diseases** ein Facharzt *or* Spezialist für Tropenkrankheiten **ADJ** *attr* Fach-; **~ dictionary** Fach- *or* Spezialwörterbuch *nt*; **it's ~ work** dazu braucht man einen Fachmann

specialist knowledge N Fachwissen *nt*

speciality [ˌspeʃɪˈælɪtɪ], *(US)* **specialty** [ˈspeʃəltɪ] N Spezialität *f*; *(= subject also)* Spezialgebiet *nt*; **to make a ~ of sth** sich auf etw *(acc)* spezialisieren; **to make a ~ of doing sth** sich darauf spezialisieren, etw zu tun; **a ~ of the house** eine Spezialität des Hauses

specialization [ˌspeʃəlaɪˈzeɪʃən] N Spezialisierung *f* *(in* auf *+acc)*; *(= special subject)* Spezialgebiet *nt*

specialize [ˈspeʃəlaɪz] **VI** sich spezialisieren *(in* auf *+acc)*; **we ~ in …** wir haben uns auf … *(acc)* spezialisiert **VT** **the species/tail has been ~d** die Art/der Schwanz hat sich gesondert entwickelt

specialized [ˈspeʃəlaɪzd] ADJ spezialisiert; **a ~ knowledge of biology** Fachkenntnisse *pl* in Biologie

special licence N *(Brit)* (Ehe)dispens *f* *(des Erzbischofs von Canterbury)*

specially [ˈspeʃəlɪ] ADV besonders; *(= specifically)* extra; *(= for a particular purpose)* speziell, extra; **a ~ difficult task** eine besonders schwierige Aufgabe; **I had it ~ made** ich habe es extra machen lassen; **we asked for it ~** wir haben extra darum gebeten; **he brought it ~ for me** er hat es extra *or* eigens für mich gebracht; **they were all pretty girls, ~ the two sisters** die Mädchen waren alle hübsch, besonders *or* insbesondere die beiden Schwestern; **we would ~ like to see the orchard** wir würden besonders gern den Obstgarten sehen; **don't go to the post office ~/~ for me** gehen Sie deswegen/meinetwegen nicht extra zur Post®

special: **special messenger** N Expressbote *m*/-botin *f*; *(Mil)* Kurier(in) *m(f)*; **special needs** PL *(Brit)* **children with ~, ~ children** behinderte Kinder *pl*, Kinder *pl* mit Behinderungen; **~ teacher** Behindertenlehrer(in) *m(f)*, Sonderschullehrer(in) *m(f)*; **special offer** N Sonderangebot *nt*; **special pleading** N *(Jur)* Beibringung *f* neuen Beweismaterials; *(fig)* Berufung *f* auf einen Sonderfall; **special prosecutor** N *(US)* Sonderstaatsanwalt *m*/-anwältin *f*; **special relationship** N *(Pol)* besondere Beziehungen *pl* *(with* mit); **special school** N *(Brit)* Sonderschule *f*; *(for physically handicapped)* Behindertenschule *f*

specialty [ˈspeʃəltɪ] N *(US)* = **speciality**

special waste N Sondermüll *m*; **~ dump** Sondermülldeponie *f*

specie [ˈspiːʃiː] N *no pl* Hartgeld *nt*, Münzgeld *nt*

species [ˈspiːʃiːz] N *pl* - Art *f*; *(Biol also)* Spezies *f*; **the human ~** der Mensch

specific [spəˈsɪfɪk] **ADJ** **a** *(= definite)* bestimmt, speziell; *(= precise) statement, instructions* genau; *example* ganz bestimmt; **9.3, to be ~** 9,3, um genau zu sein; **can you be a bit more ~?** können Sie sich etwas genauer äußern?; **to be ~ about sth** sich spezifisch zu etw äußern; **he was quite ~ on that point** er hat sich zu diesem Punkt recht spezifisch geäußert; **nothing ~** nichts Spezielles
b **to be ~ to sb/sth** *(= peculiar)* auf jdn/etw zutreffen
c *(Biol, Chem, Phys, Med)* spezifisch
N **a** *(old Med)* Spezifikum *nt*
b **specifics** **PL** nähere *or* genauere Einzelheiten *pl*; **to get down to ~s** zu den Einzelheiten kommen

-specific [spəˈsɪfɪk] ADJ *suf* -spezifisch; **country-specific** landesspezifisch; **job-specific** berufsspezifisch, berufsbezogen

specifically [spəˈsɪfɪkəlɪ] ADV *warn, order, state, mention* ausdrücklich; *(= specially) designed, request* speziell; *(= precisely)* genau; *(= in particular)* im Besonderen; **~, we need three** wir brauchen genau drei; **can you define that more ~?** können Sie das etwas genauer definieren?

specification [ˌspesɪfɪˈkeɪʃən] N **a** *(= specifying)* Angabe *f*; **his ideas need more ~** seine Ideen müssen noch genauer ausgeführt werden
b *(= detailed statement, of requirements)* genaue Angabe, Aufstellung *f*; *(for patent)* (genaue) Beschreibung; *(= design, for car, machine)* (detaillierter) Entwurf; *(for building)* Bauplan *m*; **~s** *pl* genaue Angaben *pl*; *(of car, machine)* technische Daten *or* Angaben *pl*; *(of new building)* Raum- und Materialangaben *pl*, Baubeschreibung *f*; **the new ~ includes …** *(= model)* die neue Ausführung hat auch …
c *(= stipulation)* Bedingung *f*; *(for building)* Vorschrift *f*

specific: **specific character** N *(Biol)* Artmerkmal *nt*; **specific gravity** N *(Chem, Phys)* spezifisches Gewicht, Wichte *f*; **specific heat** N *(Chem, Phys)* spezifische Wärme

specified [ˈspesəfaɪd] ADJ *(= particular) amount, number* bestimmt; *period* vorgeschrieben; *price* vorgegeben; **at a ~ time** zu einer bestimmten Zeit; **~ risk material** BSE-Risikomaterial *nt*

specify [ˈspesɪfaɪ] **VT** angeben; *(= list individually or in detail)* spezifizieren, (einzeln) aufführen; *(= stipulate)* vorschreiben; *(blueprint, contract etc)* vorsehen; **in the specified order** in der angegebenen *or* vorgeschriebenen Reihenfolge; **a specified period of time** ein bestimmter Zeitabschnitt; **to ~ how to do sth** genauer *or* näher ausführen, wie etw gemacht werden soll **VI** genaue Angaben machen; **unless otherwise specified** wenn nicht anders angegeben

specimen [ˈspesɪmɪn] **N** Exemplar *nt*; *(of urine, blood etc)* Probe *f*; *(= sample)* Muster *nt*; **a beautiful** *or* **fine ~** ein Prachtexemplar *nt*; **if that's a ~ of your work** wenn das eine Probe deines Könnens ist; **you're a pretty poor ~** *(inf)* du hast ja nicht viel zu bieten *(inf)* **ADJ** *attr* Probe-; **~ page** Probeseite *f*; **a ~ copy** ein Beleg- *or* Probeexemplar *nt*; **a ~ signature** eine Unterschriftenprobe

specious [ˈspiːʃəs] ADJ *argument, proposal, logic* vordergründig bestechend; *excuse* fadenscheinig; *claim* unfundiert, fadenscheinig; *charm, phrases* leer; *nonsense* hohl

speciousness [ˈspiːʃəsnɪs] N *(of argument)* Vordergründigkeit *f*; *(of excuse)* Fadenscheinigkeit *f*; *(of claim)* Unfundiertheit *f*

speck [spek] **N** Fleck *m*; *(of blood, paint, mud also)* Spritzer *m*; *(of dust)* Körnchen *nt*; *(of soot)* Flocke *f*, Flöckchen *nt*; *(of gold, colour etc)* Sprenkel *m*; *(= small portion, of drink etc)* Tropfen *m*, Tröpfchen *nt*; *(of sugar, butter)* kleines bisschen; *(fig, of truth, confidence)* Fünkchen *nt*, Quäntchen *nt*; **a ~ on the horizon** ein Punkt *m* or Pünktchen *nt* am Horizont **VT** **to be ~ed with black** schwarze Fleckchen haben; *(bird, eyes etc)* schwarz gesprenkelt sein; **his face was ~ed with dirt** er hatte Schmutzflecken im Gesicht; **to be ~ed with blood** blutbespritzt sein

speckle [ˈspekl] **N** Sprenkel *m*, Tupfer *m*, Tupfen *m* **VT** sprenkeln; **to be ~d with sth** mit etw gesprenkelt sein; **to be ~d with brown** braun gesprenkelt sein

speckless ADJ, **specklessly** ADV [ˈspeklɪs, -lɪ] fleckenlos, sauber, rein

specs [speks] PL **a** *(inf)* Brille *f* **b** *abbr of* **specifications**

spectacle [ˈspektəkl] N **a** *(= show)* Schauspiel *nt*; **a sad ~** ein trauriger Anblick; **to make a ~ of oneself** unangenehm auffallen **b** **spectacles** PL *(also* **pair of spectacles***)* Brille *f*

spectacle case N Brillenetui *or* -futteral *nt*

spectacled [ˈspektəkld] ADJ bebrillt; *(Zool)* brillenähnlich gezeichnet

spectacular [spekˈtækjʊləʳ] **ADJ** sensationell; *improvement, success also* spektakulär; *scenery* atemberaubend; *sight* sensationell, atemberaubend; *failure* spektakulär **N** *(Theat)* Show *f*

spectacularly [spekˈtækjʊləlɪ] ADV **a** *(= stunningly)* überwältigend **b** *(= dramatically) successful* sensationell; *improve, fail also* spektakulär; *good, bad* unglaublich; **he was ~ wrong** er hat einen Riesenfehler gemacht; **to do ~ well/badly** unglaublich gut/schlecht abschneiden

spectate [spekˈteɪt] VI *(inf: esp Sport)* zuschauen *(at* bei)

spectator [spekˈteɪtəʳ] N Zuschauer(in) *m(f)*

spectator sport N Publikumssport *m*

specter N *(US)* = **spectre**

spectogram [ˈspektəʊgræm] N Spektogramm *nt*

spectra [ˈspektrə] *pl of* **spectrum**

spectral [ˈspektrəl] ADJ **a** *(of ghosts)* geisterhaft, gespenstisch **b** *(of the spectrum)* spektral, Spektral-; **~ colour** Spektralfarbe *f*

spectre, *(US)* **specter** [ˈspektəʳ] N Gespenst *nt*; *(fig)* (Schreck)gespenst *nt*; **the ~ of a woman in white** die Erscheinung einer Frau in Weiß

spectrograph [ˈspektrəʊgræf] N Spektrograph *m*

spectroscope [ˈspektrəʊskəʊp] N Spektroskop *nt*

spectroscopic [ˌspektrəʊˈskɒpɪk] ADJ spektroskopisch

spectroscopic analysis N Spektralanalyse *f*

spectrum [ˈspektrəm] N *pl* **spectra** Spektrum *nt*; *(fig: = range also)* Palette *f*, Skala *f*; **~ analysis** Spektralanalyse *f*

specula [ˈspekjʊlə] *pl of* **speculum**

speculate [ˈspekjʊleɪt] VI **a** *(= meditate, ponder)* (nach)grübeln, nachdenken *(on* über *+acc)*; *(= conjecture)* Vermutungen anstellen, spekulieren *(about, on* über *+acc)*; **I ~ that …** ich vermute, dass … **b** *(Fin)* spekulieren *(in* mit, *on* an *+dat)*

speculation [ˌspekjʊˈleɪʃən] N *(all senses)* Spekulation *f* *(on* über *+acc)*; *(= guesswork also)* Vermutung *f*; **it is the subject of much ~** darüber sind viele Spekulationen *or* Vermutungen angestellt worden; **it's pure ~** das ist reine Vermutung

speculative ['spekjʊlətɪv] ADJ **a** spekulativ *(esp Philos)*; *approach, suggestions, ideas* rein theoretisch; *expression, look* grüblerisch **b** *(Fin)* Spekulations-; **~ gain** Spekulationsgewinn *m*; **~ builder** Bauspekulant(in) *m(f)*; **~ building** Bauspekulation *f*; **~ investor** Investitionsspekulant(in) *m(f)*; **a ~ venture** ein Spekulationsvorhaben *nt*

speculatively ['spekjʊlətɪvlɪ] ADV **a** spekulativ, theoretisch; *look, say* grüblerisch **b** *(= tentatively)* vorsichtig **c** *(Fin)* spekulativ; **to invest ~ in sth** mit etw spekulieren

speculator ['spekjʊleɪtəʳ] N *(also Fin)* Spekulant(in) *m(f)*

speculum ['spekjʊləm] N *pl* **specula** *(Med)* Spekulum *nt*; *(in telescope)* Metallspiegel *m*

sped [sped] *pret, ptp of* **speed**

speech [spiːtʃ] N **a** *no pl (= faculty of speech)* Sprache *f*; *(= act of speaking)* Sprechen *nt*; *(= manner of speaking)* Sprechweise *f*; **to be slow of ~** langsam sprechen; **his ~ was very indistinct** er sprach sehr undeutlich; **he expresses himself better in ~ than in writing** er drückt sich mündlich besser aus als schriftlich; **to burst into ~** in einen Redeschwall ausbrechen; **to lose/recover the power of ~** die Sprache verlieren/zurückgewinnen; **~ is silver, silence is golden** *(prov)* Reden ist Silber, Schweigen ist Gold *(Prov)*; **freedom of ~** Redefreiheit *f*
b *(= language)* Sprache *f*; **in dockers' ~** in der Sprache der Hafenarbeiter
c *(= oration, Theat)* Rede *f* *(on, about* über *+acc)*; *(in court)* Plädoyer *nt*; **to give** *or* **make a ~** eine Rede halten; **the actor had three ~es** der Schauspieler hat dreimal gesprochen; **the chairman invited ~es from the floor** der Vorsitzende forderte das Publikum zu Meinungsäußerungen auf; **the ~ from the throne** die Thronrede
d *(Brit Gram)* **direct/indirect** *or* **reported ~** direkte/indirekte Rede → **figure, part**
e *(US: Sch, Univ: = study of speech)* Sprechkunde *f*

speech: **speech act** N Sprechakt *m*; **speech bubble** N *(in comic, cartoon)* Sprechblase *f*; **speech community** N Sprachgemeinschaft *f*; **speech day** N *(Brit)* Schulfeier *f*; **speech defect** N Sprachfehler *m*

speechify ['spiːtʃɪfaɪ] VI salbadern, Volksreden halten

speechifying ['spiːtʃɪfaɪɪŋ] N Volksreden *pl*, Schwätzerei *f*

speechless ['spiːtʃlɪs] ADJ **a** *(= at a loss for words)* sprachlos *(with* vor); *anger* stumm; **everybody was ~ at this** darüber waren alle völlig sprachlos; **his remark left me ~** seine Bemerkung machte mich sprachlos *or* verschlug mir die Sprache; **she stared at him in ~ disbelief** sie starrte ihn sprachlos vor Verblüffung an **b** *(lit: = dumb)* stumm; **to be ~** nicht sprechen können

speechlessly ['spiːtʃlɪslɪ] ADV wortlos; *(from surprise, shock etc)* sprachlos

speechlessness ['spiːtʃlɪsnɪs] N **a** Sprachlosigkeit *f* **b** *(lit)* Stummheit *f*; *(= loss of speech)* Sprachverlust *m*

speech: **speechmaking** N *(= making speeches)* Redenhalten *nt*; *(pej: = speechifying)* Schwätzerei *f*, Gelabere *nt (inf)*; **speech organ** N Sprechwerkzeug *nt*; **speech pattern** N Sprechmuster *nt*; **speech recognition** N Spracherkennung *f*; **~ software** Spracherkennungssoftware *f*; **speech sound** N Sprachlaut *m*; **speech synthesizer** N Sprachsynthesizer *m*; **speech therapist** N Sprachtherapeut(in) *m(f)*, Logopäde *m*, Logopädin *f*; **speech therapy** N Sprachtherapie *f*, Logopädie *f*; *(= treatment)* logopädische Behandlung; **speech writer** N Ghostwriter(in) *m(f) (inf)*, Redenschreiber(in) *m(f)*

speed [spiːd] *vb: pret, ptp* **sped** *or* **speeded** N **a** Geschwindigkeit *f*; *(= esp fast speed)* Schnelligkeit *f*; *(of moving object or person)* Tempo *nt*, Geschwindigkeit *f*; **at ~** äußerst schnell; **at high/low ~** mit hoher/niedriger Geschwindigkeit; **at full** *or* **top ~** mit Höchstgeschwindigkeit; **at a ~ of 50 mph** mit einer Geschwindigkeit *or* einem Tempo von 50 Meilen pro Stunde; **the ~ of light/sound** die Licht-/Schallgeschwindigkeit; **at the ~ of light** mit Lichtgeschwindigkeit; **walking ~** Schritttempo *nt*; **to pick up** *or* **gather ~** beschleunigen, schneller werden; *(fig, development)* sich beschleunigen; *(person)* schneller werden; **to lose ~** (an) Geschwindigkeit verlieren; **to be up to ~** *(inf: = informed)* auf dem neuesten Stand sein; **to bring a factory/system up to ~** eine Fabrik/ein System auf den neuesten Stand bringen; **to bring sb up to ~** *(inf)* jdn auf den neuesten Stand bringen; **what ~ were you doing?** wie schnell sind Sie gefahren?; **her typing/shorthand ~ is good** sie kann schnell Maschine schreiben/stenografieren; **what is her typing/shorthand ~?** wie viele Anschläge/Silben (pro Minute) schreibt sie?; **with all possible ~** so schnell wie möglich; **with such ~** so schnell; **full ~ ahead!** *(Naut)* volle Kraft voraus!
b *(Aut, Tech: = gear)* Gang *m*; **three-~ bicycle** Fahrrad mit Dreigangschaltung; **a three-speed gear** ein Dreiganggetriebe *nt*
c *(Phot: = film speed)* Lichtempfindlichkeit *f*; *(= shutter speed)* Belichtungszeit *f*
d *(inf: = drug)* Speed *nt (sl)*
VT **to ~ sb on his way** *(person)* jdn verabschieden; *(iro)* jdn hinauskomplimentieren; *(good wishes etc)* jdn auf seinem Weg begleiten; **if you fetch the visitors' coats it may ~ them on their way** wenn du die Mäntel der Gäste holst, machen sie sich vielleicht auf den Weg; **God ~ you!** *(old)* Gott (sei) mit dir! *(old)*
VI **a** *pret, ptp* **sped** *(= move quickly)* jagen, flitzen; *(arrow)* sausen, flitzen; **the years sped by** die Jahre verflogen *or* vergingen wie im Fluge; **God ~** *(old)* Gott mit dir *(old)*
b *pret, ptp* **speeded** *(Aut: = exceed speed limit)* zu schnell fahren, die Geschwindigkeitsbegrenzung überschreiten

▶ **speed along** *pret, ptp* **speeded** *or* **sped along** VT *sep work etc* beschleunigen; *person* antreiben; **to speed things along** die Dinge vorantreiben VI entlangjagen *or* -flitzen *(+prep obj +acc)*; *(work)* vorangehen

▶ **speed off** *pret, ptp* **speeded** *or* **sped off** VI davonjagen; *(car also)* davonbrausen; *(person also)* davonflitzen

▶ **speed up** *pret, ptp* **speeded up** VI *(car, driver etc)* beschleunigen; *(person)* Tempo zulegen, schneller machen; *(work, production etc)* schneller werden; **their pace speeded up** ihr Tempo wurde schneller; **with practice you'll speed up** wenn du erst mehr Übung hast, wirst du schneller VT *sep* beschleunigen; *person* antreiben, auf Trab bringen *(inf)*; **that speeded me up** das hat mir Antrieb gegeben; **tell her to speed up that coffee** *(inf)* sag ihr, sie soll sich mit dem Kaffee beeilen

speed: **speedboat** N Renn- *or* Schnellboot *nt*; **speed bump** N Fahrbahnschwelle *f*, Aufpflasterung *f (form)*; **speed camera** N *(Police)* Blitzgerät *nt*; **speed cop** N *(inf)* weiße Maus *(inf)*, Verkehrsbulle *m (inf)*; **speed counter** N *(esp Aut)* Drehzahlmesser *m*

speed dial *(esp US Telec)* N Kurzwahl *f* ADJ *attr* Kurzwahl-; **~ button** Kurzwahltaste *f*

speed dialling N *(esp US Telec)* Kurzwahl *f*

speeder ['spiːdəʳ] N Temposünder(in) *m(f) (inf)*, Raser(in) *m(f) (inf)*

speed freak N **a** *(inf)* Geschwindigkeitsfreak *m (inf)* **b** *(Drugs inf)* Speedabhängige(r) *m(f) (sl)*

speed hump N = **speed bump**

speedily ['spiːdɪlɪ] ADV schnell; *reply, return* prompt

speediness ['spiːdɪnɪs] N Schnelligkeit *f*

speeding ['spiːdɪŋ] N Geschwindigkeitsüberschreitung *f*; **to get a ~ fine** eine Geldstrafe wegen Geschwindigkeitsüberschreitung bekommen

speed: **speed limit** N Geschwindigkeitsbegrenzung *f*; **a 30 mph ~** eine Geschwindigkeitsbegrenzung von 50 km/h; **speed merchant** N *(inf)* Raser *m (inf)*; **Nicholas is a real ~** Nicholas fährt wie der Henker *(inf)*

speedo ['spiːdəʊ] N *(Brit inf)* Tacho *m (inf)*

speedometer [spɪ'dɒmɪtəʳ] N Geschwindigkeitsmesser *m*, Tachometer *m*

speed: **speed ramp** N *(Mot)* Bodenschwelle *f*; **speed-read** VTI diagonal lesen, querlesen; **speed skater** N Eisschnellläufer(in) *m(f)*; **speed skating** N Eisschnelllauf *m*

speedster ['spiːdstəʳ] N *(inf: = car)* Flitzer *m*; *(= person)* Raser(in) *m(f) (inf)*

speed: **speed table** N *(US Mot)* Bodenschwelle *f*; **speed trap** N Radarfalle *f (inf)*; **speed-up** N *(inf)* schnelleres Tempo *(inf)* *(in* bei), Beschleunigung *f (in +gen)*; *(in research)* Vorantreiben *nt (in +gen)*; *(in rate of inflation)* Steigerung *f (in +gen)*; **speedway** N **a** *(Sport)* Speedwayrennen *nt*; *(= track)* Speedwaybahn *f* **b** *(US: = racetrack)* Rennstrecke *f*; *(= expressway)* Schnellstraße *f*; **speedwell** N *(Bot)* Ehrenpreis *m or nt*, Veronika *f*; **speedwriting** N Schnellschreiben *nt*

speedy ['spiːdɪ] ADJ *(+er)* schnell; *answer, service also* prompt; *remedy* schnell wirkend; **we wish Joan a ~ recovery** wir wünschen Joan eine rasche Genesung; **to bring sth to a ~ conclusion** etw schnell zu Ende bringen; **to bring a ~ end to sth** etw schnell beenden

speleologist [ˌspiːlɪ'ɒlədʒɪst] N Höhlenkundler(in) *m(f)*

speleology [ˌspiːlɪ'ɒlədʒɪ] N Höhlenkunde *f*, Speläologie *f (spec)*

spell[1] [spel] N *(lit, fig)* Zauber *m*; *(= incantation)* Zauberspruch *m*; **to be under a ~** *(lit)* unter einem Zauber stehen, verzaubert *or* verhext sein; *(fig)* wie verzaubert sein; **to put a ~ on sb, to cast a ~ on** *or* **over sb, to put sb under a ~** *(lit)* jdn verzaubern *or* verhexen; *(fig)* jdn in seinen Bann ziehen, jdn verzaubern; **to be under sb's ~** *(fig)* in jds Bann *(dat)* stehen; **to break the ~** *(lit, fig)* den Bann brechen, den Zauber lösen

spell[2] N *(= period)* Weile *f*, Weilchen *nt*; **for a ~** eine Weile, eine Zeit lang; **cold/hot ~** Kälte-/Hitzewelle *f*; **dizzy ~** Schwächeanfall *m*; **a short ~ of sunny weather** eine kurze Schönwetterperiode; **we had** *or* **spent a ~ in Chile** wir hielten uns eine Zeit lang in Chile auf; **to do a ~ on the assembly line/as a waitress** sich kurzzeitig am Fließband/als Serviererin betätigen; **he did** *or* **had a ~ in prison** er hat eine Zeit lang (im Gefängnis) gesessen; **to take a ~ at the wheel** eine Zeit lang *or* ein Weilchen das Steuer übernehmen; **they're going through a bad ~** sie machen eine schwierige Zeit durch

spell[3] *pret, ptp* **spelt** *(esp Brit) or* **spelled** VI *(in writing)* (orthografisch) richtig schreiben; *(aloud)* buchstabieren; **she can't ~** sie kann keine Rechtschreibung; **children should learn to ~** Kinder sollten richtig schreiben lernen
VT **a** *(in writing)* schreiben; *(aloud)* buchstabieren; **how do you ~ "onyx"?** wie schreibt man „Onyx"?; **how do you ~ your name?** wie schreibt sich Ihr Name?, wie schreiben Sie sich?; **what do these letters ~?** welches Wort ergeben diese Buchstaben? **b** *(= denote)* bedeuten; **it ~s disaster (for us)** das bedeutet Unglück (für uns)

▶ **spell out** VT *sep (= spell aloud)* buchstabieren; *(= read slowly)* entziffern; *(= explain)* verdeutlichen, klarmachen; **to spell sth out for sb** jdm etw klarmachen; **he needs everything spelled out to him** man muss ihm alles überdeutlich machen; **do I have to spell it out for you?** *(inf)* muss ich noch deutlicher werden?

spellbinder ['spelbaɪndəʳ] N fesselnder Redner/Sänger *etc*, fesselnde Rednerin/Sängerin *etc*; *(= film)* fesselnder Film, Knüller *m (inf)*; **to be a ~** das Publikum fesseln

spellbinding ['spelbaɪndɪŋ] ADJ fesselnd

spellbound ['spelbaʊnd] ADJ, ADV *(fig)* wie verzaubert, gebannt; *(lit) princess, castle* verzaubert;

to hold sb ~ jdn fesseln; *(person also)* jdn in seinen Bann schlagen

spell: **spell-check** *(Comput)* N Rechtschreibprüfung *f* VT die Rechtschreibung *(+gen)* prüfen; **spellchecker** N *(Comput)* Rechtschreibprüfung *f*

speller [ˈspeləʳ] N **to be a good/bad ~** in Rechtschreibung gut/schlecht sein

spelling [ˈspelɪŋ] N Rechtschreibung *f*, Orthografie *f*; *(of a word)* Schreibweise *f*; *(= activity)* Rechtschreiben *nt*; *(Sch: = lesson)* Rechtschreibeunterricht *m*; **the correct ~ is …** die richtige Schreibweise ist …

spelling: **spelling bee** N *(Sch)* Buchstabierwettbewerb *m*; **spelling book** N Fibel *f*; **spelling check** N *(Comput)* Rechtschreibprüfung *f*; **spelling mistake** N (Recht)schreibfehler *m*, orthografischer Fehler; **spelling pronunciation** N buchstabengetreue Aussprache

spelt¹ [spelt] N *(Bot)* Spelz(weizen) *m*, Dinkel *m*

spelt² *(esp Brit) pret, ptp of* **spell³**

spelunker [spɪˈlʌŋkəʳ] N Hobbyhöhlenforscher(in) *m(f)*

spend [spend] *pret, ptp* **spent** VT **a** *(= use) money* ausgeben *(on* für); *energy, strength* verbrauchen; *time* brauchen; **I've spent all my strength** ich habe meine ganze Kraft aufgebraucht; **we spent a lot of time in useless discussion** wir haben sehr viel Zeit mit nutzlosen Diskussionen vertan; **I've spent three hours on this job** ich habe drei Stunden für diese Arbeit gebraucht; **time well spent** sinnvoll genutzte Zeit
b *(= pass) time, holiday, evening etc* verbringen; **he ~s all his spare time on his car/with his friends** er verbringt jede freie Minute an seinem Auto/mit seinen Freunden; **I spent the night with her/in a hotel** ich habe bei ihr/in einem Hotel übernachtet; **I ~ my weekends sleeping** ich verschlafe meine Wochenenden; **he ~s his time reading** er verbringt seine Zeit mit Lesen
c to ~ money/time/effort on sth *(= devote to)* Geld/Zeit/Mühe für etw aufbringen *or* in etw *(acc)* investieren; **I spent a lot of effort on that** das hat mich viel Mühe gekostet
d *(= exhaust)* **to have spent itself** *(anger, fury)* sich erschöpft *or* gelegt haben; **the storm had spent itself** *or* **its fury** der Sturm hatte sich ausgetobt *or* gelegt → *also* **spent**
VI Geld ausgeben; **he was ~ing somewhat too freely** er gab das Geld mit vollen Händen aus

spendaholic [ˌspendəˈhɒlɪk] N *(inf)* Kaufsüchtige(r) *mf*

spender [ˈspendəʳ] N **he is a big/free ~** bei ihm sitzt das Geld locker; **the Arabs are the big ~s nowadays** heutzutage haben die Araber das große Geld; **the last of the big ~s** *(iro)* ein echter Großkapitalist *(hum)*

spending [ˈspendɪŋ] N *no pl* Ausgaben *pl*; **government ~ cuts** Kürzungen *pl* im Etat

spending: **spending money** N Taschengeld *nt*; **spending power** N Kaufkraft *f*; **spending spree** N Großeinkauf *m*; **to go on a ~** groß einkaufen gehen

spendthrift [ˈspendθrɪft] ADJ verschwenderisch N Verschwender(in) *m(f)*

spent [spent] *pret, ptp of* **spend** ADJ *ammunition, cartridge, match* verbraucht; *bullets also* verschossen; *person* erschöpft; **to be/look ~** erschöpft sein/aussehen; *(= prematurely aged)* müde und verbraucht sein/aussehen; **as a poet he was ~ at 25** mit 25 war seine dichterische Schaffenskraft verbraucht; **to be a ~ force** nichts mehr zu sagen haben; *(movement)* sich totgelaufen haben; *(ideology)* keine Zugkraft mehr haben; **they collapsed, their energy ~** ihre ganze Energie verbraucht, brachen sie zusammen; **he held her down until her fury was ~** er hielt sie fest, bis ihre Wut erschöpft war

sperm [spɜːm] N Samenfaden *m*, Spermatozoon *nt*, Spermium *nt*; *(= fluid)* Samenflüssigkeit *f*, Sperma *nt*

spermaceti [ˌspɜːməˈsetɪ] N Spermazet *nt*, Walrat *nt*

spermary [ˈspɜːmərɪ] N *(Anat)* Keimdrüse *f*

spermatic [spɜːˈmætɪk] ADJ Samen-

spermatic cord N Samenstrang *m*

spermatozoon [ˌspɜːmætəʊˈzəʊɒn] N *pl* **spermatozoa** [ˌspɜːmætəˈzəʊə] Spermatozoon *nt*, Spermium *nt*

sperm bank N Samenbank *f*

sperm cell N Samenzelle *f*

sperm count N Spermienzahl *f*

spermicidal [ˌspɜːmɪˈsaɪdəl] ADJ spermizid

spermicide [ˈspɜːmɪsaɪd] N Spermizid *nt*

sperm: **sperm oil** N Walratöl *nt*; **sperm whale** N Pottwal *m*

spew [spjuː] VI **a** *(inf: = vomit)* brechen, spucken; **it makes me ~** *(fig)* es kotzt mich an *(sl)*
b *(= flow: also* **spew forth** *(form) or* **out***)* sich ergießen *(geh)*; *(esp liquid)* hervorsprudeln
VT **a** *(also* **spew up***) (inf: = vomit)* erbrechen, ausspucken; *blood* spucken, speien **b** *(fig: also* **spew out***) flames* spucken, speien; *lava* auswerfen, spucken; *waste water etc* ablassen; **the popular press ~s (out) lies** die Boulevardpresse überschüttet ihre Leser mit Lügen

sphagnum [ˈsfægnəm] N Torf- *or* Bleichmoos *nt*

sphere [sfɪəʳ] N **a** Kugel *f*; *(= heavenly sphere)* Gestirn *nt (geh)*; *(old Astron)* Sphäre *f (old)*; **the celestial ~** *(poet)* das Himmelszelt *(poet)*; **to be a ~** kugelförmig sein **b** *(fig)* Sphäre *f*, Welt *f*; *(of person, personal experience)* Bereich *m*; *(of knowledge etc)* Gebiet *nt*, Feld *nt*; *(= social etc circle)* Kreis *m*; **in the ~ of politics** in der Welt der Politik; **his ~ of interest/influence** sein Interessen-/Einflussbereich; **~ of activity** *(= job, specialism)* Wirkungskreis *m*; **that's outside my ~** das geht über meinen Horizont; *(= not my responsibility)* das ist nicht mein Gebiet

spherical [ˈsferɪkəl] ADJ *(in shape)* kugelförmig, (kugel)rund; *(Math, Astron)* sphärisch

sphericity [sfəˈrɪsɪtɪ] N Kugelform *f or* -gestalt *f*

spheroid [ˈsfɪərɔɪd] N *(Geometry)* Rotationsellipsoid *nt*

sphincter [ˈsfɪŋktəʳ] N *(Anat)* Schließmuskel *m*, Sphinkter *m (spec)*

sphinx [sfɪŋks] N Sphinx *f*

sphinxlike [ˈsfɪŋkslaɪk] ADJ sphinxhaft

spice [spaɪs] N **a** Gewürz *nt*; **~ rack** Gewürzbord *or* -regal *nt*; **~ trade** Gewürzhandel *m*; **mixed ~** Gewürzmischung *f* **b** *(fig)* Würze *f*; *(= trace: of irony, humour)* Anflug *m*, Hauch *m*; **the ~ of life** die Würze des Lebens; **stories with some ~** pikante Geschichten *pl* VT *(lit, fig)* würzen

spiced [spaɪst] ADJ *(Cook) savoury dish* würzig; *sweet dish* aromatisch; **~ wine** Glühwein *m*; **highly ~** pikant (gewürzt); **delicately ~** delikat gewürzt

spiciness [ˈspaɪsɪnɪs] N *(= quality)* Würzigkeit *f*, Würze *f*; *(= taste)* Würze *f*; *(fig)* Pikanterie *f*; **because of its ~** weil das so stark gewürzt ist

spick-and-span [ˌspɪkənˈspæn] ADJ *house etc* blitzsauber, tipptopp in Ordnung *pred*; **to look ~** *(person)* wie aus dem Ei gepellt aussehen; *(house)* blitzsauber sein

spicy [ˈspaɪsɪ] ADJ *(+er)* würzig; *sauce, food also* stark gewürzt; *(fig) story etc* pikant; *language* kräftig

spider [ˈspaɪdəʳ] N **a** Spinne *f*; **~'s web** Spinnwebe *f*, Spinnengewebe *nt*, Spinnennetz *nt* **b** *(inf, = wheelbrace)* Kreuzschlüssel *m* **c** *(for roofrack)* elastisches Befestigungsband

spider: **spider crab** N Spinnenkrabbe *f or* -krebs *m*; **spiderman** N *(inf)* **a** *(= building worker)* Gerüstbauer *m* **b** *(= steeplejack)* Schornsteinarbeiter *m*; **spider monkey** N Klammeraffe *m*; **spider plant** N Grünlilie *f*; **spider veins** N *(Med inf)* Besenreiser *pl (inf)*, Besenreißer *pl (inf)*; **spiderweb** N *(US)* Spinnwebe *f*, Spinnengewebe *nt*, Spinnennetz *nt*

spidery [ˈspaɪdərɪ] ADJ *writing* krakelig; *outline, drawing, pattern* fein, spinnwebartig; *limbs etc* spinnenhaft

spiel [ʃpiːl] N *(inf)* Sermon *m (inf)*, Blabla *nt (inf)*; *(= tall story, excuse)* Geschichte *f (inf)*

spiffing [ˈspɪfɪŋ] ADJ *(dated inf)* famos *(dated inf)*

spigot [ˈspɪgət] N *(on cask)* Spund *m*, Zapfen *m*; *(in tap)* Abschlusskörper *m*; *(US: = faucet)* Hahn *m*

spike [spaɪk] N **a** *(on wall, railing, helmet etc)* Spitze *f*; *(= nail)* Nagel *m*; *(on plant)* Stachel *m*; *(on shoe, tyre etc)* Spike *m*; *(for receipts, wastepaper etc)* Dorn *m*; **~ heel** Pfennigabsatz *m* → *also* **spikes**
b *(Bot)* Ähre *f*
c *(Elec)* Spannungsspitze *f*
d *(= hair)* (Igel)schnitt *m*
VT **a** *(lit: = pierce)* aufspießen; *(with weapon)* durchbohren
b *(fig: = frustrate) rumours* den Boden entziehen *(+dat)*; *plans* ruinieren; **the editor ~d the story** *(Press)* der Redakteur ließ die Story in einer Schublade verschwinden; **to ~ sb's guns** *(Brit inf)* jdm den Wind aus den Segeln nehmen
c *(= lace) drink* einen Schuss zusetzen *(+dat)*; **~d with rum** mit einem Schuss Rum

spiked [spaɪkt] ADJ *shoe* mit Spikes; *stick* mit Dornen versehen; *railings* mit Spitzen; *drink* mit Schuss; **~ hair** Igel(schnitt) *m*; **~ helmet** Pickelhaube *f*

spikes [spaɪks] PL *(inf: = running shoes)* Spikes *pl*

spiky [ˈspaɪkɪ] ADJ *(+er)* **a** *(= having spikes) railings, top of wall* mit Metallspitzen; *bush, animal* stach(e)lig; *branch* dornig **b** *(= like spikes) grass* spitz, stach(e)lig; *flower* mit spitzen Blütenblättern; *plant* spitzblättrig; *leaf* spitz; *hair* hochstehend; *writing* steil **c** *(fig) person* empfindlich, leicht eingeschnappt *(inf)*

spilehole [ˈspaɪlhəʊl] N *(of barrel)* Spundloch *nt*

spill¹ [spɪl] *vb: pret, ptp* **spilt** *(esp Brit) or* **spilled**
N **a** *(= spilled liquid etc)* Lache *f*; **oil ~** Ölkatastrophe *f*
b *(= fall)* Sturz *m*; **to have a ~** stürzen
VT **a** *(= water, sand, salt etc)* verschütten; **to ~ sb's blood** jds Blut vergießen; **to ~ the beans** alles ausplaudern, plaudern; **to ~ the beans about sth** etw ausplaudern
b *(horse)* abwerfen; **the lorry ~ed its load onto the road** die Ladung fiel vom Lastwagen herunter auf die Straße
VI verschüttet werden; *(large quantity)* sich ergießen; *(tears)* strömen, laufen; *(fig: people)* strömen; **the milk ~ed all over the carpet** die Milch war auf dem ganzen Teppich verschüttet; **light ~ed into the room** Licht strömte ins Zimmer; **light ~ed under the door** Licht drang durch den Türspalt herein

▶ **spill out** VI *(of* aus) *(liquid)* herausschwappen; *(grain)* herausrieseln; *(money, jewels)* herausfallen; *(fig: people)* (heraus)strömen; **clothes were spilling out of the drawer** Kleidungsstücke quollen aus der Schublade hervor VT *sep* ausschütten; *(by accident)* verschütten

▶ **spill over** VI *(liquid)* überlaufen; *(grain etc, assembly)* überquellen; *(fig, population)* sich ausbreiten *(into* auf *+acc)*; *(meeting)* sich hinziehen *(into* bis in *+acc)*

spill² N *(of wood)* (Kien)span *m*; *(of paper)* Fidibus *m*

spillage [ˈspɪlɪdʒ] N *(act)* Verschütten *nt*; *(= quantity)* verschüttete Menge, Spillage *f (Comm)*

spillikin [ˈspɪlɪkɪn] N **a** *(old: = spill)* Kienspan *m* **b** **spillikins** PL *(= game)* Mikado *nt*

spillover [ˈspɪləʊvəʳ] N Überschuss *m*

spillway [ˈspɪlweɪ] N Überlaufrinne *f*

spilt [spɪlt] *(esp Brit) pret, ptp of* **spill¹**

spin [spɪn] *vb: pret* **spun** *or (old)* **span**, *ptp* **spun**
N **a** *(= revolution)* Drehung *f*; *(= washing machine programme)* Schleudern *nt no pl*; **to give**

sth a ~ etw (schnell) drehen; *spinning top* etw treiben; *(in washing machine etc)* etw schleudern; **to be in a (flat) ~** *(Brit fig inf)* am Rotieren *or* Durchdrehen sein *(inf)* *(about* wegen); **to send sb/sth into a (flat) ~** *(Brit fig inf)* jdn/etw zum Rotieren bringen *(inf)*
b *(on ball)* Dreh *m*, Drall *m*; *(Billiards)* Effet *m*; **to put ~ on the ball** dem Ball einen Drall/Effet geben; *(with racquet)* den Ball anschneiden
c *(inf: = interpretation)* **to put a new/different** *etc* **~ on sth** etw neu/anders *etc* interpretieren
d *(Aviat)* Trudeln *nt no pl*; **to go into a ~** zu trudeln anfangen
e *(dated: = trip)* **to go for a ~** eine Spritztour machen
VT a *(person, spider)* spinnen; **to ~ a web of deceit** ein Lügengewebe spinnen → **yarn**
b *(= turn) wheel* drehen; *(fast)* herumwirbeln; *top* tanzen lassen, treiben; *(in washing machine)* schleudern; *(= toss) ball, coin* (hoch)werfen; *(Sport) ball* einen Drall/Effet geben *(+dat)*; *(with racquet)* (an)schneiden; **he's just ~ning his wheels** *(US fig inf)* er tritt nur Wasser *(inf)*
VI a *(person)* spinnen
b *(= revolve)* sich drehen; *(fast)* (herum)wirbeln; *(plane etc)* trudeln; *(in washing machine)* schleudern; **to ~ round and round** sich im Kreis drehen; *(dancer)* im Kreis herumwirbeln; **the ball spun into the air/past him** der Ball flog wirbelnd in die Luft/an ihm vorbei; **the car spun out of control** der Wagen begann, sich unkontrollierbar zu drehen; **to send sb/sth ~ning** jdn/etw umwerfen; **my head is ~ning** mir dreht sich alles; **the wine makes my head ~** von dem Wein dreht sich mir alles; **the noise made his head ~** ihm schwirrte der Kopf von dem Lärm

▶ **spin along** VI *(= move quickly)* (dahin)rasen, (dahin)sausen

▶ **spin (a)round** **VI** *(= revolve)* sich drehen; *(very fast)* (herum)wirbeln; *(in surprise)* herumwirbeln, herumfahren **VT** *sep* (schnell) drehen; *(very fast)* herumwirbeln

▶ **spin out** VT *sep (inf) money, food* strecken *(inf)*; *holiday, meeting* in die Länge ziehen; *story* ausspinnen

spina bifida [ˌspaɪnəˈbɪfɪdə] **N** offene Wirbelsäule, Spina bifida *f (spec)* **ADJ** *attr baby* mit einer offenen Wirbelsäule

spinach [ˈspɪnɪtʃ] N Spinat *m*

spinal [ˈspaɪnl] ADJ Rücken-, Rückgrat-, spinal *(spec)*; **~ injury** Rückgratverletzung *f*

spinal: **spinal column** N Wirbelsäule *f*; **spinal cord** N Rückenmark *nt*; **spinal fluid** N Rückenmark(s)flüssigkeit *f*; **spinal marrow** N Rückenmark *nt*; **spinal meningitis** N Spinalmeningitis *f*

spin box N *(Comput)* Drehfeld *nt*

spin bowler N *(Cricket)* *Werfer, der dem Ball einen Drall gibt*

spindle [ˈspɪndl] N *(for spinning, Mech)* Spindel *f*

spindleshanks [ˈspɪndlʃæŋks] N *(inf)* **a** *pl (= legs)* Streichholzbeine *pl (inf)*, Stelzen *pl (inf)* **b** *sing (= person)* Langbein *nt (inf)*

spindly [ˈspɪndlɪ] ADJ *(+er) legs, arms, plant* spindeldürr *(inf)*; *chairs* zierlich

spin: **spin doctor** N *(Pol inf)* PR-Berater(in) *m(f)*; *(press spokesperson)* (schönrednerischer) Pressesprecher, (schönrednerische) Pressesprecherin; **spin-drier** N *(Brit)* (Wäsche)schleuder *f*; **spindrift** N Gischt *f*; **spin-dry** VTI schleudern; **spin-dryer** N = **spin-drier**

spine [spaɪn] N **a** *(Anat)* Rückgrat *nt*; *(of book)* (Buch)rücken *m*; *(of mountain range)* (Gebirgs)grat *m* **b** *(= spike)* Stachel *m*; *(of plant)* Dorn *m*, Stachel *m*

spine: **spine-chiller** N *(inf)* Gruselgeschichte *f*, Gruselfilm *m*; **spine-chilling** [ˈspaɪntʃɪlɪŋ] ADJ *(inf)* schaurig, gruselig; *noise also* unheimlich

spineless [ˈspaɪnlɪs] ADJ **a** *(Anat)* wirbellos; *(fig) person* ohne Rückgrat; *compromise, refusal* feige; **don't be so ~** beweisen Sie mal, dass Sie Rückgrat haben! **b** *(Zool)* stachellos; *(Bot)* dornenlos, stachellos

spinelessly [ˈspaɪnlɪslɪ] ADV *(fig)* feige

spinet [spɪˈnet] N **a** Spinett *nt* **b** *(US)* Kleinklavier *nt*

spine-tingling [ˈspaɪntɪŋglɪŋ] ADJ *(= frightening)* schaurig, schaudererregend; *(= moving)* ergreifend

spinnaker [ˈspɪnəkəˈ] N *(Naut)* Spinnaker *m*

spinner [ˈspɪnəˈ] N **a** *(of cloth)* Spinner(in) *m(f)* **b** *(inf)* = **spin-drier** **c** *(Fishing)* Spinnköder *m* **d** *(Cricket)* *Werfer, der den Bällen einen Drall gibt*

spinney [ˈspɪnɪ] N *(Brit)* Dickicht *nt*

spinning [ˈspɪnɪŋ] N Spinnen *nt*

spinning *in cpds* Spinn-; **spinning jenny** N Jennymaschine *f*; **spinning mill** N Spinnerei *f*; **spinning top** N Kreisel *m*; **spinning wheel** N Spinnrad *nt*; **spinning works** N *sing or pl* Spinnerei *f*, Spinnstofffabrik *f*

spin-off [ˈspɪnɒf] N *(= side-product)* Nebenprodukt *nt*; **~ effect** Folgewirkung *f*

spinster [ˈspɪnstəˈ] N Unverheiratete *f*, Ledige *f*; *(pej)* alte Jungfer *(pej)*; **Mary Jones, ~** die ledige Mary Jones; **to be a ~** unverheiratet *or* ledig *or* eine alte Jungfer *(pej)* sein

spinsterhood [ˈspɪnstəhʊd] N *(old)* Ehelosigkeit *f*, Jungfernstand *m (old)*; **she preferred ~** sie wollte lieber unverheiratet bleiben

spinsterish [ˈspɪnstərɪʃ] ADJ *(pej)* altjüngferlich *(pej)*

spiny [ˈspaɪnɪ] ADJ *(+er)* stach(e)lig; *plant also* dornig; **~ lobster** *(Zool)* Languste *f*, Stachelhummer *m*

spiracle [ˈspɪrəkl] N *(of shark, ray etc)* Atemloch *nt*; *(of insect also)* Stigma *nt (spec)*; *(of whale, dolphin)* Spritzloch *nt*

spiral [ˈspaɪərəl] **ADJ** spiralförmig, spiralig; *shell also* gewunden; *spring* Spiral-; *movement, descent* in Spiralen; **a ~ curve** eine Spirale; **~ nebula** Spiralnebel *m* **N** *(lit, fig)* Spirale *f*; **price/inflationary ~** Preis-/Inflationsspirale *f* **VI** *(also* **spiral up***)* sich (hoch)winden; *(smoke also, missile etc)* spiralförmig *or* in einer Spirale aufsteigen; *(prices)* (nach oben) klettern

▶ **spiral down** VI spiralförmig *or* in einer Spirale herunterkommen; *(staircase also)* sich abwärtswinden

spirally [ˈspaɪərəlɪ] ADV in einer Spirale, spiralförmig

spiral staircase N Wendeltreppe *f*

spirant [ˈspaɪərənt] N *(Ling, Phon)* Spirans *m*, Spirant *m*, Reibelaut *m*

spire [spaɪəˈ] N *(of church)* Turmspitze *f*, Turm *m*

spired [ˈspaɪəd] ADJ spitz (zulaufend), zugespitzt; *church* mit Spitzturm

spirit [ˈspɪrɪt] **N a** *(= soul)* Geist *m*; **the life of the ~** das Seelenleben; **he was troubled in ~** *(liter)* etwas lastete auf seiner Seele *(geh)*; **I'll be with you in ~** im Geiste werde ich bei euch sein; **the ~ is willing (but the flesh is weak)** der Geist ist willig(, aber das Fleisch ist schwach)
b *(= supernatural being, ghost)* Geist *m*
c *(= leading person, of age, movement etc)* Geist *m*; *(of party, enterprise)* Kopf *m*
d *no pl (= courage)* Mut *m*, Schneid *m*; *(= vitality, enthusiasm)* Elan *m*, Schwung *m*; **a man of ~** *(= courageous)* ein mutiger Mensch; **a horse with plenty of ~** ein feuriges Pferd; **to break sb's ~** jdn brechen, jds Mut brechen; **to sing with ~** mit Inbrunst singen; **to reply with ~** mutig antworten; **to put ~ into sth** Leben in eine Sache bringen
e *(= mental attitude: of country, group of people, doctrine, reform etc)* Geist *m*; *(= mood)* Stimmung *f*; **Christmas ~** *(Rel)* weihnachtlicher Geist; *(= mood)* weihnachtliche Stimmung; **a ~ of optimism/rebellion** eine optimistische/rebellische Stimmung; **to do sth in a ~ of optimism/humility** etw voll Optimismus/voller Demut tun; **in a ~ of forgiveness/revenge** aus einer vergebenden/rachsüchtigen Stimmung heraus; **Christian ~** Christlichkeit *f*; **the ~ of the age** der Zeitgeist; **he has the right ~** er hat die richtige Einstellung; **to enter into the ~ of sth** bei etw mitmachen *or* dabei sein; **when the ~ moves him** wenn es ihn überkommt; **that's the ~!** *(inf)* so ists recht! *(inf)*
f *no pl (= intention)* Geist *m*; **the ~ of the law** der Geist *or* Sinn des Gesetzes; **to take sth in the right/wrong ~** etw richtig/falsch auffassen; **to take sth in the ~ in which it was intended** etw so nehmen, wie es gemeint war; **the ~ in which it is done** wie es getan wird
g spirits PL *(= state of mind)* Stimmung *f*, Laune *f*; *(= courage)* Mut *m*; **to be in high ~s** bester Laune sein; **to be in good/low ~s** guter/schlechter Laune sein; **to be out of ~s** niedergeschlagen sein; **to keep up one's ~s** den Mut nicht verlieren; **my ~s rose** ich bekam (neuen) Mut; **her ~s fell** ihr sank der Mut; **to raise** *or* **lift sb's ~s** jdn aufmuntern; **to revive sb's ~s** jds Lebensgeister wiedererwecken
h spirits PL *(= alcohol)* Branntwein *m*, Spirituosen *pl*, geistige Getränke *pl*
i *(Chem)* Spiritus *m*; **~s of ammonia** Salmiakgeist *m*; **~(s) of turpentine** Terpentinöl *nt*
VT to ~ sb/sth away *or* **off** jdn/etw verschwinden lassen *or* wegzaubern; **to ~ sb out of a room** *etc* jdn aus einem Zimmer *etc* wegzaubern

spirited [ˈspɪrɪtɪd] ADJ temperamentvoll; *horse also* feurig; *book, performance* lebendig; *(= courageous) person, reply, attack, attempt etc* beherzt, mutig; **to make a ~ defence of sth** etw mutig verteidigen

spiritedly [ˈspɪrɪtɪdlɪ] ADV *say* beherzt; *defend* mutig

spiritedness [ˈspɪrɪtɪdnɪs] N Temperament *nt*; *(of horse also)* Feurigkeit *f*; *(of performance)* Lebendigkeit *f*; *(= courage) (of person, reply, attempt etc)* Beherztheit *f*, Mut *m*; *(of defence)* Mut *m*

spirit gum N Mastix(gummi) *m*

spiritism [ˈspɪrɪtɪzəm] N Spiritismus *m*

spiritistic ADJ, **spiritistically** ADV [ˌspɪrɪˈtɪstɪk, -əlɪ] spiritistisch

spirit lamp N Petroleumlampe *f*

spiritless ADJ *person, performance, book* saft- und kraftlos; *agreement, acceptance, reply* lustlos; *animal* brav, lahm *(inf)*

spirit level N Wasserwaage *f*

spirit rapping [ˈspɪrɪtˌræpɪŋ] N Geisterklopfen *nt (in spiritistischer Sitzung)*

spirit stove N Spirituskocher *m*

spiritual [ˈspɪrɪtjʊəl] **ADJ** geistig; *person* spirituell; *expression* vergeistigt; *(Eccl)* geistlich; **~ life** Seelenleben *nt*; **my ~ home** meine geistige Heimat; **Lords ~** geistliche Lords (im Oberhaus); **the ~ world** die spirituelle Welt **N** *(Mus)* Spiritual *nt*

spiritualism [ˈspɪrɪtjʊəlɪzəm] N Spiritismus *m*

spiritualist [ˈspɪrɪtjʊəlɪst] N Spiritist(in) *m(f)*

spirituality [ˌspɪrɪtjʊˈælɪtɪ] N Geistigkeit *f*

spiritually [ˈspɪrɪtjʊəlɪ] ADV geistig; **~, he is …** in geistiger Hinsicht ist er …

spirituous [ˈspɪrɪtjʊəs] ADJ *(form)* alkoholisch, spirituos *(rare)*

spit[1] [spɪt] *vb: pret, ptp* **spat** **N a** *(= action)* (Aus)spucken *nt*; *(= saliva)* Spucke *f*; **there was just a ~ of rain** es tröpfelte nur; **to give sth a bit of ~ and polish** *(inf)* etw wienern *(inf)*; **it needs a bit of ~ and polish** *(inf)* es müsste einmal tüchtig gewienert werden *(inf)*; **a ~ and sawdust club** *(Brit inf)* eine (echte) Spelunke
b *(inf: = image)* = **spitting image**
VT spucken, speien *(geh)*
VI spucken, speien *(geh)*; *(fat)* spritzen; *(fire)* zischen; *(person: verbally, cat)* fauchen, zischen; **to ~ at sb** jdn anspucken, jdn anspeien *(geh)*, jdn anfauchen, jdn anzischen; **to ~ in sb's face/eye** jdm ins Gesicht spucken; *(fig)* auf jdn pfeifen *(inf)*; **it is ~ting (with rain)** *(Brit)* es tröpfelt; **she's ~ting in the wind if she thinks that'll work** *(inf)* da hat sie sich verrechnet, wenn sie denkt, dass das funktionieren wird; **fighting the system is like ~ting in the wind** *(inf)* gegen das System anzukämpfen hat sowieso keine Wirkung

▶ **spit out** VT *sep* ausspucken, ausspeien *(geh)*; *words* ausstoßen; **spit it out!** *(fig inf)* spucks aus! *(inf)*, heraus mit der Sprache!

spit² N a *(Cook)* (Brat)spieß *m*; **on the ~** am Spieß b *(of land)* Landzunge *f* VT *meat* (auf)spießen

spite [spaɪt] ✪ 26.2 N a *(= ill will)* Boshaftigkeit *f*, Gehässigkeit *f*; **to do sth out of ~** etw aus reiner Boshaftigkeit tun b **in ~ of** *(= despite)* trotz *(+gen)*; **it was a success/we went in ~ of him** dennoch war es ein Erfolg/gingen wir hin; **he did it in ~ of himself** er konnte nicht anders; **in ~ of the fact that he …** obwohl er …; **in ~ of that I'll still go** ich gehe trotzdem VT ärgern; **she just does it to ~ me** sie tut es nur mir zum Trotz, sie tut es nur, um mich zu ärgern

spiteful [ˈspaɪtfʊl] ADJ boshaft, gemein; *(= gloating also)* schadenfroh, gehässig

spitefully [ˈspaɪtfəlɪ] ADV boshaft, gemein; *(= gloatingly)* gehässig; **~ she told him …** voll Bosheit erzählte sie ihm …; *(= gloatingly)* voll Schadenfreude erzählte sie ihm …

spitefulness [ˈspaɪtfʊlnɪs] N Boshaftigkeit *f*, Gemeinheit *f*; *(= gloating)* Schadenfreude *f*, Gehässigkeit *f*

spitfire [ˈspɪtfaɪəʳ] N Feuer speiender Drache; *(= woman also)* Giftnudel *f (inf)*

spitroast [ˈspɪtrəʊst] VT am Spieß braten; **with ~ pieces of lamb** mit Lammstücken vom Spieß

Spitsbergen [ˈspɪtsˌbɜːgən] N Spitzbergen *nt*

spitting: **spitting distance** N *(inf)* **to be within ~ of a place** nur einen Steinwurf von einem Ort entfernt sein; **spitting image** N *(inf)* Ebenbild *nt*; **to be the ~ of sb** jdm wie aus dem Gesicht geschnitten sein, jdm zum Verwechseln ähnlich sehen; **spitting snake** N Ringelhalskobra *f*, Ringelhalsotter *f*

spittle [ˈspɪtl] N Speichel *m*, Spucke *f*

spittoon [spɪˈtuːn] N Spucknapf *m*

spiv [spɪv] N *(Brit inf)* schmieriger Typ *(inf)*

spivvy [ˈspɪvɪ] ADJ *(Brit inf) person* schmierig *(inf)*; *tie, suit etc* ordinär

splash [splæʃ] N a *(= spray)* Spritzen *nt no pl*; *(= noise)* Platschen *nt no pl*, Platscher *m (inf)*; **he dived in with a ~** es spritzte/platschte, als er hineinsprang; **it made a ~ as it hit the water** das Wasser spritzte nach allen Seiten, als es hineinfiel; *(noise)* es fiel platschend ins Wasser; **to make a ~** *(fig)* Furore machen; *(news)* wie eine Bombe einschlagen; *(book)* einschlagen
b *(= sth splashed)* Spritzer *m*; *(esp in drink etc)* Schuss *m*; *(of colour, light)* Tupfen *m*; *(= patch)* Fleck *m*; **~es of paint** Farbspritzer *pl*
VT a *water etc* spritzen; *(= pour)* gießen; *person, object* bespritzen; **to ~ sb with water, to ~ water over sb** jdn mit Wasser bespritzen; **to ~ paint on sth** etw mit Farbe bespritzen; *(with brush)* Farbe auf etw *(acc)* klatschen *(inf)*; **to ~ one's way through a stream** platschend einen Bach durchqueren
b *(Press inf) story* groß rausbringen *(inf)*; **the story was ~ed all over the papers** die Geschichte wurde in allen Zeitungen groß rausgebracht *(inf)*
VI *(liquid)* spritzen; *(rain, waves)* klatschen; *(tears)* tropfen; *(when diving, walking etc)* platschen; *(when playing)* plan(t)schen

▶ **splash about** *(Brit)* or **around** VI herumspritzen; *(in water)* herumplan(t)schen; *(while walking)* herumplatschen VT *sep water* herumspritzen mit; *(fig inf) money* um sich werfen mit *(inf)*; *story* groß aufziehen *or* rausbringen *(inf)*

▶ **splash down** VI a *(Space)* wassern b *(rain)* herunterrinnen *(prep obj* an *+dat)*

▶ **splash out** VI *(Brit inf)* tüchtig in die Tasche greifen *(inf)*; *(on reception, giving presents etc)* sich nicht lumpen lassen *(inf)*; **to splash out on sth** sich *(dat)* etw spendieren *(inf)*

▶ **splash up** VT *sep* spritzen VI *(water, mud)* aufspritzen

splash: **splashback**, **splashboard** N Spritzschutz *m*; **splashdown** N *(Space)* Wasserung *f*; **splash guard** N *(US Aut)* Schmutzfänger *m*; **splash water** N *(Tech)* Schwall- *or* Spritzwasser *nt*

splashy [ˈsplæʃɪ] ADJ *(US inf)* protzig, auffällig

splat [splæt] N Platschen *nt* ADV **to go ~ into sth** gegen etw platschen

splatter [ˈsplætəʳ] N Spritzen *nt no pl*; *(of rain)* Prasseln *nt no pl*; *(= sth splattered)* Fleck *m*; *(of ink, paint etc)* Klecks *m*; *(Art, = splatter technique)* Spritztechnik *f* VI spritzen; *(ink, paint also)* klecksen; *(rain)* prasseln VT bespritzen; *(with ink, paint etc)* beklecksen; **to ~ sb with mud, to ~ mud over sb** jdn mit Schlamm bespritzen

splay [spleɪ] VT a *(= spread out) legs, fingers, toes* spreizen; *feet* nach außen stellen; **the wheels are ~ed** die Räder stehen nach außen, die Räder haben negativen Sturz b *(Tech) pipe* weiten; *window frame* ausschrägen VI nach außen gehen; *(pillars also)* sich nach außen biegen; *(window frame)* ausgeschrägt sein; **he was ~ed out on the ground** er lag auf der Erde und hatte alle viere von sich gestreckt N *(Archit)* Ausschrägung *f*

splay: **splayfoot** N nach außen gestellter Fuß; **splayfooted** ADJ mit nach außen gestellten Füßen; **to be ~** nach außen gehen

spleen [spliːn] N *(Anat)* Milz *f*; *(fig)* Zorn *m*, Rage *f* → **vent VT**

splendid [ˈsplendɪd] ADJ a *(= excellent)* hervorragend; *rider etc, chance, idea, amusement* glänzend, ausgezeichnet; **(that's simply) ~!** (das ist ja) ausgezeichnet! b *(= magnificent) clothes, sunset, music* herrlich; *occasion, scale, villain* großartig

splendidly [ˈsplendɪdlɪ] ADV a *(= magnificently) dressed* prächtig; *restored* herrlich b *(= excellently)* hervorragend, glänzend, ausgezeichnet; **everything is going ~** alles klappt wunderbar c *(= outrageously)* unerhört; **he is ~ arrogant** er ist unerhört arrogant

splendidness [ˈsplendɪdnɪs] N a *(= magnificence)* Glanz *m*, Pracht *f* b *(= excellence)* Großartigkeit *f*

splendiferous [splenˈdɪfərəs] ADJ *(dated inf)* fabelhaft

splendour, *(US)* **splendor** [ˈsplendəʳ] N Pracht *f no pl*; *(of music, achievement)* Großartigkeit *f*; **the ~s of the Roman Empire** der Glanz *or* die Pracht des Römischen Reiches

splenetic [splɪˈnetɪk] ADJ a *(Anat)* Milz-; **~ cell** Milzzelle *f* b *(liter: = peevish)* unwirsch; **his ~ outbursts** seine Galligkeit

splice [splaɪs] N Verbindung *f*; *(of ropes also)* Spleiß *m (spec)*; *(of tapes, film also)* Klebung *f*; *(of wood also)* Fuge *f* VT *ropes* spleißen *(spec)*; *tapes, film* (zusammen)kleben; *pieces of wood etc* verfugen; **to ~ sth together** etw zusammenfügen; **to get ~d** *(inf)* sich verehelichen *(hum)*

splicer [ˈsplaɪsəʳ] N *(for films)* Klebepresse *f*

spliff [splɪf] N *(inf: = joint)* Joint *m (inf)*

splint [splɪnt] N Schiene *f*; **to put a ~ on sb/sth** jdn/etw schienen; **to be in ~s** geschient sein VT schienen

splinter [ˈsplɪntəʳ] N Splitter *m* VT (zer)splittern; *(with axe) wood* zerhacken; *(fig) party* spalten VI (zer)splittern; *(fig: party)* sich spalten; **to ~ off** absplittern; *(fig)* sich abspalten

splinter: **splinter group** N Splittergruppe *f*; **splinter party** N *(Pol)* Splitterpartei *f*; **splinterproof** ADJ splitterfrei

splintery [ˈsplɪntərɪ] ADJ splitt(e)rig

split [splɪt] *vb: pret, ptp* **split** N a Riss *m (in* in *+dat)*; *(esp in wall, rock, wood)* Spalt *m (in* in *+dat)*
b *(fig: = division)* Bruch *m (in* in *+dat)*, Entzweiung *f (+gen)*; *(Pol, Eccl)* Spaltung *f (in +gen)*; **there is a ~ in the party over …** die Partei ist in der Frage *(+gen)* … gespalten; **there is a three-way ~ in the party over …** die Partei zerfällt in der Frage *(+gen)* … in drei Lager, die Partei ist in der Frage *(+gen)* … dreigeteilt; **a three-way ~ of the profits** eine Drittelung des Gewinns; **I want my ~** *(inf)* ich will meinen Schnitt *(inf)*
c *(= distinction: in meaning)* Aufteilung *f*
d *pl* **the ~s** Spagat *m*; **to do the ~s** (einen) Spagat machen
e *(inf: = sweet)* *(also* **banana split***)* (Bananen)split *m*; **jam/cream ~** *mit Marmelade/Sahne gefülltes Gebäckstück*
f *(esp US: = bottle)* kleine Flasche
g *(Comput) (of window)* Teilung *f*; **remove ~** Teilung aufheben
ADJ gespalten *(on, over* in *+dat)*; *(Comput) screen* geteilt
VT a *(= cleave)* (zer)teilen; *wood, atom* spalten; *stone* zerbrechen; *fabric, garment* zerreißen, zerschlitzen; *seam* aufplatzen lassen; **the sea had ~ the ship in two** in dem Sturm zerbrach das Schiff in zwei Teile; **I ~ the seam** die Naht ist (auf)geplatzt; **to ~ hairs** *(inf)* Haarspalterei treiben *(inf)*; **to ~ one's sides (laughing)** *(inf)* vor Lachen fast platzen *(inf)*; **to ~ sth open** etw aufbrechen; **his lip had been ~ open** seine Lippe war aufgeplatzt; **he ~ his head open** when he fell er hat sich *(dat)* beim Fallen den Kopf aufgeschlagen
b *(= divide)* spalten; *(Comput) screen, window* teilen; *(= share) work, costs, roles etc* (sich *dat*) teilen; **to ~ sth into three parts** etw in drei Teile aufteilen; **to ~ the vote** die Abstimmung zum Scheitern bringen; **a party ~ three ways** eine in drei Lager gespaltene Partei; **to ~ one's vote** *or (US)* **ticket** panaschieren; **they ~ the profit three ways** sie haben den Gewinn gedrittelt *or* in drei Teile geteilt; **to ~ the difference** *(fig: in argument etc)* sich auf halbem Wege einigen; *(lit, with money etc)* sich *(dat)* die Differenz teilen
VI a *(wood, stone)* (entzwei)brechen; *(hair)* sich spalten; *(trousers, seam etc)* platzen; *(fabric)* zerreißen; *(ship)* auseinanderbrechen; **to ~ open** aufplatzen, aufbrechen; **to ~ at the seams** *(lit)* an den Nähten aufplatzen; *(fig)* aus allen *or* den Nähten platzen; **my head is ~ting** *(fig)* mir platzt der Kopf
b *(= divide)* sich teilen; *(people)* sich aufteilen; *(Pol, Eccl)* sich spalten *(on, over* wegen)
c *(inf: = leave)* abhauen *(inf)*
d *(Brit inf, = tell tales)* **to ~ on sb** jdn verpfeifen *(inf)*

▶ **split off** VT *sep* abtrennen *(prep obj* von); *(with axe also)* abspalten *(prep obj* von); *(= break)* abbrechen *(prep obj* von) VI abbrechen; *(rock also)* sich lösen; *(fig)* sich trennen *(from* von)

▶ **split up** VT *sep money, work* (auf)teilen; *meanings* aufteilen; *party, organization* spalten; *meeting* ein Ende machen *(+dat)*; *two people* trennen; *crowd* zerstreuen VI zerbrechen; *(= divide)* sich teilen; *(meeting, crowd)* sich spalten; *(partners)* sich voneinander trennen; **he split up with her** er hat mit ihr Schluss gemacht

split: **split decision** N *(Boxing)* nicht einstimmige Entscheidung; **split ends** PL gespaltene Haarspitzen *pl*, Spliss *m*; **split infinitive** N *(Gram)* getrennter Infinitiv; **split-level** ADJ *(Archit)* mit versetzten Geschossen; **split peas** PL getrocknete (halbe) Erbsen *pl*; **split-pea soup** N Erbsensuppe *f*; **split personality** N *(Psych)* gespaltene Persönlichkeit; **split pin** N *(= cotter pin)* Splint *m*; *(on envelope)* Musterklammer *f*; **split screen** N *(Comput)* geteilter Bildschirm; **split second** N Bruchteil *m* einer Sekunde; **in a ~** in Sekundenschnelle; **split-second** ADJ **~ timing** Abstimmung *f* auf die Sekunde; *(of actor)* Gefühl *nt* für den richtigen Moment; **split time** N *(Sport)* Zwischenzeit *f*

splitting [ˈsplɪtɪŋ] N Zerteilung *f*; *(of wood)* Spalten *nt*; **the ~ of the atom** die Kernspaltung ADJ *headache* rasend, heftig; **there was a ~ sound** *(of wood)* es klang, als ob etwas zerbräche; *(of cloth)* es klang, als ob etwas zerrisse

split-up [ˈsplɪtʌp] N *(of friends)* Bruch *m (of* zwischen *+dat)*; *(of partners)* Trennung *f (of +gen)*; *(of party)* Spaltung *f (of +gen)*

splodge [splɒdʒ], *(US)* **splotch** [splɒtʃ] N Fleck *m*, Klecks *m*; *(of cream etc)* Klacks *m* VT clothes bespritzen; (with paint, ink also) beklecksen; mud spritzen; paint klecksen

splodgy ['splɒdʒɪ], **splotchy** ['splɒtʃɪ] ADJ fleckig, schmutzig

splurge [splɜːdʒ] N (inf: = shopping spree) Kauforgie f (pej inf); **to go on a ~** groß einkaufen gehen; **a big ~ on publicity** eine groß aufgemachte Werbekampagne; **we had a big ~ on the reception** unser Empfang war ein Riesentamtam (inf)

▶ **splurge (out) on** VI +prep obj (inf) sich in Unkosten stürzen mit

splutter ['splʌtəʳ] N (of engine) Stottern nt; (of fire) Zischen nt; (while talking) Prusten nt no pl
VI (person, = spit) prusten, spucken; (= stutter) stottern; (engine) stottern; (fire, lamp, fat) zischen; (sausages) brutzeln, zischen; **to ~ with indignation** vor Entrüstung prusten VT (her-vor)stoßen; **that's not true, he ~ed** das ist nicht wahr, platzte er los

spoil [spɔɪl] vb: pret, ptp **spoilt** (Brit) or **spoiled**
N usu pl Beute f no pl; (fig: = profits also) Gewinn m; **the ~s of war** die Kriegsbeute; **~s of office** Vergünstigungen pl im Amt
VT a (= ruin, detract from) verderben; town, looks etc verschandeln; peace of mind zerstören; life ruinieren; (Brit) ballot papers ungültig machen; **to ~ the party** (fig) ein Spaßverderber sein; **to ~ sb's fun** jdm den Spaß verderben; **it ~ed our evening** das hat uns (dat) den Abend verdorben; **if you eat now you'll ~ your lunch** wenn du jetzt etwas isst, verdirbst du dir den Appetit fürs Mittagessen; **~ed ballot papers** (Brit) ungültige Stimmzettel pl
b person verwöhnen; children verwöhnen, verziehen; **to ~ sb for sth** (inf) jdn für etw verderben; **to be ~ed for choice** eine übergroße Auswahl haben, die Qual der Wahl haben
VI a (food) verderben
b **to be ~ing for trouble/a fight** Ärger/Streit suchen

spoilage ['spɔɪlɪdʒ] N (Comm) verdorbene Ware, Verderb m (von Waren); (Printing) Makulatur f

spoiler ['spɔɪləʳ] N a (Aut, Aviat) Spoiler m b (= person) Spielverderber(in) m(f); (Press) Publikation, die zur gleichen Zeit wie ein Konkurrenzprodukt erscheint

spoilsman ['spɔɪlzmən] N pl **-men** [-mən] (US Pol) a (= supporter) Befürworter(in) m(f) der Ämterpatronage b (= profiteer) Profiteur(in) m(f) der Ämterpatronage

spoilsport ['spɔɪlspɔːt] N (inf) Spielverderber(in) m(f) (inf)

spoils system ['spɔɪlzˌsɪstəm] N (US Pol) Ämterpatronage f, Filzokratie f (inf)

spoilt [spɔɪlt] (Brit) pret, ptp of **spoil** ADJ child verwöhnt, verzogen; meal verdorben; ballot papers ungültig

spoke[1] [spəʊk] N Speiche f; **to put a ~ in sb's wheel** (Brit inf) jdm Knüppel zwischen die Beine werfen (inf)

spoke[2] pret of **speak**

spoken ['spəʊkən] ptp of **speak** ADJ language gesprochen; **his ~ English is better than ...** er spricht Englisch besser als ...; **~-voice record** Sprechplatte f; **the ~ word** das gesprochene Wort

spokeshave ['spəʊkʃeɪv] N Schabhobel m, Speichenhobel m

spokesman ['spəʊksmən] N pl **-men** [-mən] Sprecher m; **to act as (a) ~ for a group** als Sprecher einer Gruppe auftreten

spokesperson ['spəʊkspɜːsən] N Sprecher(in) m(f)

spokeswoman ['spəʊkswʊmən] N pl **-women** [-wɪmɪn] Sprecherin f

spoliation [ˌspəʊlɪ'eɪʃən] N (liter) Plünderung f

spondee ['spɒndiː] N Spondeus m

spondulicks, **spondulix** [spɒn'duːlɪks] PL (hum inf) Piepen pl (inf)

sponge [spʌndʒ] N a (also Zool) Schwamm m; **contraceptive ~** (empfängnisverhütendes) Schwämmchen nt → **throw in** b (= sponging) **to give sth a ~** (floor) etw wischen; car etw waschen; walls etw abwaschen; table etw abwischen c (Cook, also **sponge cake**) Rührkuchen m; (fatless) Biskuit(kuchen) m; (= sponge mixture) Rührteig m, Biskuitmasse f; **jam ~** Biskuit(kuchen) mit Marmeladenfüllung VT a (= clean) abwischen; wound abtupfen b (inf: = scrounge) schnorren (inf) (from bei)

▶ **sponge down** VT sep person (schnell) waschen; walls also abwaschen; horse abreiben

▶ **sponge off** VT sep stain, liquid abwischen

▶ **sponge off** or **on** VI +prep obj (inf) **to sponge off** or **on sb** jdm auf der Tasche liegen (inf)

▶ **sponge out** VT sep (= remove) stain herausreiben, herausmachen; (= clean out) drawer auswaschen; wound austupfen

▶ **sponge up** VT sep aufwischen

sponge: **sponge bag** N (Brit) Waschbeutel m, Kulturbeutel m; **sponge bath** N (esp US) **to give sb a ~** jdn (gründlich) waschen; **sponge cake** N Rührkuchen m; (fatless) Biskuit(kuchen) m; **sponge-down** N kurze Wäsche; **to give sb/sth a ~** jdn/etw kurz abwaschen; **sponge pudding** N Mehlpudding m

sponger ['spʌndʒəʳ] N (inf) Schmarotzer(in) m(f), Schnorrer(in) m(f) (inf)

sponginess ['spʌndʒɪnɪs] N Nachgiebigkeit f, Weichheit f; (of pudding) Lockerheit f; (of skin etc) Schwammigkeit f

spongy ['spʌndʒɪ] ADJ (+er) nachgiebig, weich; (= light) pudding locker; skin etc schwammig

sponsor ['spɒnsəʳ] N a Förderer m, Förderin f; (for membership) Bürge m, Bürgin f; (for event) Schirmherr(in) m(f); (Rad, TV, Sport etc) Geldgeber(in) m(f), Sponsor(in) m(f); (for fund-raising) Spender(in) m(f); (Parl, of bill) Befürworter(in) m(f); **to stand ~ for sb** jdn fördern, für jdn bürgen
b (= godparent) Pate m, Patin f; **to stand ~ for a child** Pate/Patin eines Kindes sein
VT a unterstützen; (financially) fördern, unterstützen, sponsern; event sponsern, die Schirmherrschaft übernehmen (+gen); future member bürgen für; membership, bill befürworten, empfehlen; (Rad, TV) programme sponsern; (Sport) event sponsern; **he ~ed him (at) 5p a mile** (Brit) er verpflichtete sich, ihm 5 Pence pro Meile zu geben
b (as godparent) die Patenschaft (+gen) übernehmen

sponsored ['spɒnsəd] ADJ (Brit: for charity etc) walk, silence etc gesponsert

sponsorial [spɒn'sɔːrɪəl] ADJ Paten-

sponsorship ['spɒnsəʃɪp] N a Unterstützung f; (financial also) Förderung f, Sponsern nt; (of future member) Bürgschaft f; (of membership, bill) Befürwortung f, Empfehlung f; (Rad, TV: of programme) Finanzierung f; (Sport, of event) Finanzierung f; **he got into the club under my ~** durch or auf meine Empfehlung kam er in den Klub b Patenschaft f

spontaneity [ˌspɒntə'neɪətɪ] N Spontaneität f; (of style) Ungezwungenheit f

spontaneous [spɒn'teɪnɪəs] ADJ spontan; style ungezwungen

spontaneous: **spontaneous abortion** N spontaner Abort; **spontaneous combustion** N Selbstentzündung f; **spontaneous generation** Urzeugung f, Abiogenese f (spec)

spontaneously [spɒn'teɪnɪəslɪ] ADV spontan; (= voluntarily also) von sich aus, von selbst; **to combust ~** sich selbst entzünden

spontaneous remission N (Med) Spontanheilung f

spoof [spuːf] (inf) N a (= parody) Parodie f (of auf +acc) b (= hoax) Ulk m (inf), (April)scherz m (inf) ADJ attr poem, programme etc parodiert; version verballhornt VT (= parody) novel parodieren; poem also verballhornen

spook [spuːk] (inf) N a Gespenst nt b (US: = spy) Spion(in) m(f) VT (esp US: = frighten) einen Schrecken einjagen (+dat)

spooky ['spuːkɪ] ADJ (+er) (inf) a gespenstisch, gruselig (inf) b (= strange) sonderbar; **it was really ~** das war wirklich ein sonderbares or eigenartiges Gefühl; **to bear a ~ resemblance to sb/sth** eine unheimliche Ähnlichkeit mit jdm/etw haben

spool [spuːl] N (Phot, on sewing machine) Spule f; (on fishing line) Rolle f; (for thread) (Garn)rolle f; (of thread) Rolle f VT (Comput) file spulen; **to ~ a print job** einen Druckauftrag in die Warteschlange stellen

spooler ['spuːləʳ] N (Comput) (Drucker)spooler m

spoon [spuːn] N Löffel m → **silver** VT löffeln VI (dated inf) schmusen, poussieren (dated inf)

▶ **spoon out** VT sep (löffelweise) ausschöpfen

▶ **spoon up** VT sep löffeln; (= eat up) auslöffeln; spillage auflöffeln

spoon: **spoon bait** N (Angling) Blinker m; **spoonbill** ['spuːnbɪl] N Löffler m, Löffelreiher m; **spoon chisel** N (Tech) Hohlmeißel m

spoonerism ['spuːnərɪzəm] N lustiger Versprecher

spoon-feed ['spuːnfiːd] pret, ptp **spoon-fed** ['spuːnfed] VT baby, invalid füttern; (fig: = do thinking for) gängeln; (= supply with) füttern (inf)

spoonful ['spuːnfʊl] N Löffel m; **a ~ of soup** ein Löffel Suppe

sporadic [spə'rædɪk] ADJ sporadisch; (= occasional also) gelegentlich; **we heard ~ gunfire** wir hörten gelegentlich Schüsse

sporadically [spə'rædɪkəlɪ] ADV sporadisch; (= occasionally also) gelegentlich; **snow fell ~** es fiel vereinzelt Schnee

spore [spɔːʳ] N Spore f

sporran ['spɒrən] N Felltasche f (über dem Schottenrock getragen)

sport [spɔːt] N a (= games collectively) Sport m no pl; (= type of sport) Sportart f; **to be good at ~(s)** gut im Sport sein, sportlich sein; **tennis is my ~** Tennis ist mein Lieblingssport; **the ~ of kings** der königliche Sport, der Pferderennsport; **to offer good ~** gute Jagd-/Angelmöglichkeiten pl bieten; **outdoor ~s** Sport m im Freien; **indoor ~s** Hallensport m
b **sports** PL (also **sports meeting**) Sportveranstaltung f
c (= amusement) Spaß m; **to do sth in ~** etw zum Spaß tun; **it was great ~** es hat großen Spaß gemacht; **to say sth in ~** etw aus or im or zum Spaß sagen; **to make ~ of sb/sth** (old) sich über jdn/etw lustig machen
d (inf: = person) feiner or anständiger Kerl (inf); (Austral) Junge m; **to be a (good) ~** alles mitmachen; **they are such good ~s** mit ihnen kann man Pferde stehlen (inf); **he's a good ~, he doesn't mind losing** er ist kein Spielverderber, er macht sich nichts daraus, wenn er verliert; **be a ~!** sei kein Spielverderber!, sei nicht so! (inf)
e (Biol, Zool) Spielart f, Abart f
VT tie, dress anhaben; (= show off) ring etc protzen mit; black eye, pink etc hair, beard herumlaufen mit (inf)
VI (= frolic) (herum)tollen; (kitten) (herum)spielen
ADJ attr (US) = **sports**

sport car N (US) Sportwagen m

sport coat N = **sports jacket**

sporting ['spɔːtɪŋ] ADJ a person, interests sportlich; **~ events** Wettkämpfe pl; **~ gods** Sportidole pl; **~ goods** Sportartikel pl; **~ gun** Sportwaffe f; **~ injury** Sportverletzung f; **~ organization** Sportverband m; **a great ~ man** ein großer Sportsmann; **~ editor** (US) Sportredakteur(in) m(f); **the ~ world** die Welt des Sports
b (= sportsmanlike) sportlich; (fig) offer, solution fair; (= decent) anständig; **it's ~ of you to ...** es ist anständig von dir, zu ...; **to give sb a ~ chance** jdm eine faire Chance geben; **there is a ~ chance that ...** die Chancen stehen nicht schlecht, dass ...; **to have a ~ chance of win-**

ning eine faire Siegchance haben; ~ **spirit** Sportsgeist *m*

sportingly [ˈspɔːtɪŋlɪ] ADV fair; *(= decently)* anständig; **he ~ gave him a start** er gab ihm fairerweise einen Vorsprung

sportive ADJ, **sportively** ADV [ˈspɔːtɪv, -lɪ] *(liter)* fidel, launig *(liter)*

sports [spɔːts], *(US also)* **sport** *in cpds* Sport-; **sports bar** N *(esp US)* Sportkneipe *f (inf)*, Kneipe *f* mit Sportübertragungen; **sports bra** N Sport-BH *m*; **sports car** N Sportwagen *m*; **sportscast** N Sportübertragung *or* -sendung *f*; **sports centre**, *(US)* **sports center** N Sportzentrum *nt*; **sports commentator**, *(esp US)* **sportscaster** N Sportreporter(in) *m(f)*, (Sport)kommentator(in) *m(f)*; **sports coat** N = **sports jacket**; **sports day** N *(Brit)* (Schul)-sportfest *nt*; **sports department** N Sportabteilung *f*; **sports drink** N Sportgetränk *nt*; **sports field**, **sports ground** N *(Brit)* Sportplatz *m*; **sports jacket** N Sportjackett *nt*, Sakko *m or nt*; **sportsman** [-mən] N *(= player)* Sportler *m*; *(= hunter)* Jäger *m*; ~ **of the year** Sportler *m* des Jahres; **sportsmanlike** [-mənlaɪk] ADJ sportlich; *(fig) behaviour, act etc* fair; **sportsmanship** [-mənʃɪp] N *(= skill)* Sportlichkeit *f*; *(= fairness also)* sportliches Verhalten, Fairness *f*; **sports medicine** N Sportmedizin *f*; **sports page** N Sportseite *f*; **sportsperson** N Sportler(in) *m(f)*; **sports programme**, *(US)* **sports program** N Sportprogramm *nt*; **sports section** N *(of newspaper)* Sportteil *m*; **sportswear** N *(for sport)* Sportkleidung *f*; *(= leisure wear)* Freizeitkleidung *f*; **sportswoman** N Sportlerin *f*; ~ **of the year** Sportlerin *f* des Jahres; **sports writer** N Sportjournalist(in) *m(f)*

sport utility vehicle N Sport-utility-Fahrzeug *nt*, Geländewagen *m*

sporty [ˈspɔːtɪ] ADJ *(+er) (inf)* **a** *person* sportbegeistert, sportlich; *clothes, car* sportlich **b** *(= jaunty)* flott

spot [spɒt] **N** **a** *(= dot)* Tupfen *m*, Punkt *m*; *(on dice)* Punkt *m*; *(Zool, Bot)* Fleck *m*, Punkt *m*; *(= stain) (on fruit)* Fleck *m*; *(fig, on reputation, good name)* Makel *m (on* an *+dat)*; **a dress with ~s** ein getupftes *or* gepunktetes Kleid; **~s of blood/grease** Blut-/Fettflecken *pl*; **~s of ink** Tintenkleckse *or* -flecke *pl*; **to knock ~s off sb/sth** *(fig inf)* jdn/etw in den Schatten stellen; **to see ~s before one's eyes** Sternchen sehen; **without a ~ (or stain)** *(fig liter)* makellos

b *(Med etc)* Fleck *m*; *(= pimple)* Pickel *m*; *(= place)* Stelle *f*; **to break out** *or* **come out in ~s** Flecken/Pickel bekommen

c *(= place)* Stelle *f*; *(= point)* Punkt *m*; **this is the ~ where Rizzio was murdered** an dieser Stelle *or* hier ist Rizzio ermordet worden; **a pleasant ~** ein schönes Fleckchen *(inf)*; **on the ~** *(= at the scene)* an Ort und Stelle; *(= at once)* auf der Stelle, sofort; **our man on the ~** unser Mann am Ort (des Geschehens) *or* vor Ort; **on-the-~ investigation** *(= at the scene)* Untersuchung *f* an Ort und Stelle; *(= immediate)* sofortige Untersuchung; **an on-the-~ report** ein Bericht vom Ort des Geschehens; **an on-the-~ fine** eine sofort *or* auf der Stelle zu bezahlende Geldstrafe

d *(Brit inf: = small quantity)* **a/the ~ of** ein/das bisschen; **we had a ~ of rain/a few ~s of rain** wir hatten ein paar Tropfen Regen; **there was a ~ of trouble/bother** es gab etwas Ärger; **we're in a ~ of bother** wir haben Schwierigkeiten; **why don't you do a ~ of work?** warum arbeiten Sie nicht mal ein bisschen?; **after a ~ of bother** nach einigen Schwierigkeiten; **would you like a ~ of lunch?** möchten Sie eine Kleinigkeit zu Mittag essen?

e *(fig: = characteristic)* Punkt *m*, Stelle *f*; **weak ~** schwache Stelle

f *(= difficulty)* Klemme *f*; **to be in a (tight) ~** in der Klemme sitzen *(inf)*, in Schwulitäten sein *(inf)*; **to put sb in a** *or* **on the ~** jdn in Verlegenheit *or* Schwulitäten *(inf)* bringen

g *(in show)* Nummer *f*; *(Rad, TV)* (ein paar Minuten) Sendezeit *f*; *(for advertisement)* Werbespot *m*; *(= announcement)* Kurzmeldung *f*; **he's got a ~ on that show** er tritt in dieser Show auf; **a three-minute TV ~** drei Minuten Sendezeit im Fernsehen, ein dreiminütiger Werbespot im Fernsehen

h **spots** **PL** *(Comm)* Lokowaren *pl (spec)*, sofort lieferbare Waren *pl*

i *(Billiards, on table)* Marke *f*; *(also* **spot ball***)* Spielball *m*

j *(esp Theat, inf: = spotlight)* Scheinwerfer *m*

VT **a** *(= notice, see)* entdecken, sehen; *(= pick out) signs, difference, opportunity* erkennen; *trends, talent, gap* entdecken; *mistake, bargain* finden; *(Mil: = pinpoint)* ausmachen; **to ~ a winner** *(lit, fig)* richtig tippen *(inf)*

b *(= stain)* bespritzen

c *(Billiards) ball* auf die Marke(n) setzen

VI **a** *(Brit)* **it's ~ting (with rain)** es tröpfelt

b *(= stain)* Flecken bekommen, schmutzen

spot: **spot business** N *(Comm)* Lokogeschäft *nt*; **spot cash** N sofortige Bezahlung; **for ~** gegen sofortige Bezahlung; **spot check** N Stichprobe *f*; **spot-check** VT stichprobenweise untersuchen *(for* auf *+acc)*; *motorists* Stichproben machen bei *(for* in Bezug auf *+acc)*; **spot fine** N Bußgeld *nt (das sofort an Ort und Stelle bezahlt werden muss)*; **spot goods** PL sofort lieferbare Waren *pl*, Lokowaren *pl (spec)*; **spot height** N Höhenangabe *f*

spotless [ˈspɒtlɪs] ADJ *person, house, clothes* tadellos *or* makellos sauber, pikobello *(inf)*; *(fig) reputation* makellos, untadelig; ~ **white** strahlend weiß

spotlessly [ˈspɒtlɪslɪ] ADV ~ **clean** blitzsauber

spotlessness [ˈspɒtlɪsnɪs] N *(of person, house etc)* tadellose *or* makellose Sauberkeit; *(fig, of reputation)* Makellosigkeit *f*, Untadeligkeit *f*

spot: **spotlight** *vb: pret, ptp* **spotlighted** **N** *(= lamp, in TV studio etc)* Scheinwerfer *m*; *(small, in room etc)* Spot *m*, Strahler *m*; *(= light)* Scheinwerferlicht *nt*, Rampenlicht *nt (also fig)*; *(on car etc)* Suchscheinwerfer *m*; **to be in the ~** *(lit)* im Scheinwerferlicht *or* Rampenlicht stehen; *(fig)* im Rampenlicht der Öffentlichkeit stehen; **to turn the ~ on sb/sth** *(lit)* die Scheinwerfer auf jdn/etw richten; *(fig)* die Aufmerksamkeit auf jdn/etw lenken; **to come under the ~** *(fig)* ins Rampenlicht der Öffentlichkeit geraten **VT** anstrahlen; *(fig)* aufmerksam machen auf *(+acc)*; **spot market** N Spotmarkt *m*, Kassamarkt *m*; **spot news** N Kurznachrichten *pl*; **spot-on** ADJ *(Brit inf) answer, analysis* exakt, haarscharf richtig *(inf)*; **~!** richtig!, genau!; **his guess was ~** er hat es haarscharf getroffen; **spot price** N *(St Ex)* Kassapreis *m*; **spot remover** N Fleck(en)entferner *m*; **spot survey** N Stichprobenuntersuchung *f*

spotted [ˈspɒtɪd] ADJ gefleckt; *(= with dots)* getüpfelt; *material* getüpfelt, getupft; *(= marked, stained)* fleckig; **~ with brown** braun gefleckt; **blue material ~ with white** blauer Stoff mit weißen Tupfen; **~ with blood** blutbespritzt; **~ with paint/mould** mit Farb-/Schimmelflecken

spotted: **spotted dick** N *(Brit)* ≈ Kochpudding *m* mit Rosinen; **spotted flycatcher** N *(Orn)* Grauer Fliegenschnäpper; **spotted hyena** N Tüpfelhyäne *f*

spotter [ˈspɒtəʳ] N **a** *(Aviat: also* **spotter plane***)* Aufklärer *m* → **train spotter** **b** *(US inf: = detective)* Detektiv(in) *m(f)*

spot test N Stichprobe *f*

spottiness [ˈspɒtɪnɪs] N *(Med)* Fleckigkeit *f*, Flecken *pl*, fleckige Haut; *(= pimples)* Pickeligkeit *f (inf)*, Pickel *pl*, pickelige Haut

spotty [ˈspɒtɪ] ADJ *(+er) (= stained)* fleckig; *(Med)* fleckig, voller Flecken; *(= pimply)* pick(e)lig, voller Pickel

spot-weld [ˈspɒtweld] VTI punktschweißen

spousal [spaʊzl] ADJ *(esp US)* ehelich

spouse [spaʊs] N *(form)* Gatte *m*, Gattin *f*

spout [spaʊt] **N** **a** Ausguss *m*, Tülle *f*; *(on teapot, cup)* Schnabel *m*, Ausguss *m*; *(on gargoyle, guttering)* Speirohr *nt*; *(on pump, tap)* Ausflussrohr *nt*; *(on pipe)* Ausfluss *m*; *(on watering can)* Rohr *nt*; **up the ~** *(Brit inf: plans, building, schedule etc)* im Eimer *(inf)*; **she's up the ~** *(Brit inf: = pregnant)* sie hat 'nen dicken Bauch *(inf)*

b *(of whale: also* **spout-hole***)* Spritzloch *nt*, Atemloch *nt*

c *(= jet of water etc)* Fontäne *f*; *(Met: = water spout)* Wasserhose *f*

VT **a** *(= gush, fountain etc)* (heraus)spritzen; *(whale)* ausstoßen, spritzen; *(volcano, gargoyle)* speien

b *(inf: = declaim) poetry, speeches* vom Stapel lassen *(inf)*, loslassen *(at sb* auf jdn) *(inf)*; *words* hervorsprudeln; *figures* herunterrasseln *(inf)*; *nonsense* von sich geben

VI **a** *(water, fountain etc, whale)* spritzen *(from* aus); *(gargoyle)* speien; **to ~ out (of sth)** (aus etw) hervorspritzen; *(lava)* (aus etw) ausgespien werden; **to ~ up (from sth)** (aus etw) hochspritzen *or* herausschießen

b *(fig inf: = declaim)* palavern *(inf)*, salbadern *(pej)*; **to ~ (forth) about sth** über etw *(acc)* salbadern

sprain [spreɪn] **N** Verstauchung *f* **VT** verstauchen; **to ~ one's wrist/ankle** sich *(dat)* das Handgelenk/den Fuß verstauchen

sprang [spræŋ] *pret of* **spring**

sprat [spræt] N Sprotte *f*; **to set** *or* **use a ~ to catch a mackerel** *(prov)* mit der Wurst nach der Speckseite werfen *(Prov)*

sprawl [sprɔːl] **N** *(= posture)* Lümmeln *nt no pl (inf)*, Flegeln *nt no pl (inf)*; *(= mass: of buildings, town etc)* Ausbreitung *f*; **urban ~** wild wuchernde Ausbreitung des Stadtgebietes; **in the urban ~** in der riesigen Stadtlandschaft

VI *(person, = fall)* der Länge nach hinfallen; *(= lounge)* (herum)lümmeln *(inf)*, sich hinflegeln; *(plant, town)* (wild) wuchern; **he was ~ing (out) on the floor** er lag ausgestreckt auf dem Fußboden; **she was ~ing in a chair** sie hatte sich in einem Sessel breitgemacht; **to send sb ~ing** jdn zu Boden werfen, jdn der Länge nach umwerfen

VT **to be ~ed over sth/on sth** *(body)* ausgestreckt auf etw *(dat)* liegen; **his legs were ~ed over the arm of the chair** seine Beine hingen zwanglos über der Sessellehne

sprawling [ˈsprɔːlɪŋ] ADJ **a** *city, suburbs* wild wuchernd; *house* großflächig; *grounds* ausgedehnt; *figure* hingeflegelt; *body* ausgestreckt; *handwriting* riesig **b** *novel* ausufernd

spray[1] [spreɪ] N *(= bouquet)* Strauß *m*; *(= buttonhole)* Ansteckblume *f*

spray[2] **N** **a** Sprühnebel *m*, Sprühregen *m*; *(of sea)* Gischt *m*; **the ~ from the lorries makes it difficult to see** die Lastwagen spritzen so, dass man kaum etwas sehen kann

b *(= implement)* Sprühdose *f*, Sprühflasche *f*; *(= insecticide spray, for irrigation)* Spritze *f*, Sprühgerät *nt*; *(= scent spray)* Zerstäuber *m*; *(on shower)* Brause *f*, Duschkopf *m*

c *(= preparation, Med, hairspray etc)* Spray *m or nt*

d *(= act of spraying)* (Be)sprühen *nt*; **to give sth a ~** etw besprühen; *(with paint, insecticide)* etw spritzen; *(with hairspray etc)* etw sprayen

VT *plants, insects etc* besprühen; *garden, crops (with paint, insecticide)* spritzen; *hair* sprayen; *room* aussprühen; *bullets* regnen lassen; *water, paint, foam* sprühen, spritzen; *champagne* verspritzen; *graffiti* sprühen; *perfume* zerstäuben, (ver)sprühen; **to ~ insecticide on plants** Pflanzen (mit Insektenmittel) spritzen; **to ~ sth with water/bullets** etw mit Wasser besprühen/mit Kugeln übersäen

VI sprühen; *(water, mud)* spritzen; **to ~ out** heraussprühen/-spritzen; **to ~ against sth** gegen etw spritzen

spray: **spray artist** N Sprayer(in) *m(f)*; **spray can** N Sprühdose *f*

sprayer [ˈspreɪəʳ] N = **spray**[2] **N b**

spray: **spray gun** N Spritzpistole *f*; **spray-on** [ˈspreɪɒn] ADJ **a** *(lit)* zum Aufsprühen; **~ furniture polish** Möbelpolitur *f* zum Aufsprühen **b** *(hum inf) jeans, dress etc* knalleng; **spray-**

paint ['spreɪpeɪnt] VT sprühen (*on* auf *+acc*, an *+acc*)

spread [spred] *vb: pret, ptp* **spread** N **a** *(of wings)* Spannweite *f*, Flügelspanne *f*; *(= range, of marks)* Verteilung *f*, Streuung *f*; *(of prices)* Spanne *f*; *(of ideas, interests)* Spektrum *nt*; *(= distribution: of wealth)* Verteilung *f*; *(= scope: of theory, ideas)* Umfang *m*; **middle-age ~** Fülligkeit *f*, Altersspeck *m (inf)*; **Gerry's beginning to suffer from middle-age ~** Gerry setzt langsam Speck an *(inf)*
b *(= growth)* Ausbreitung *f*, Verbreitung *f*; *(spatial)* Ausdehnung *f*; **the ~ of nuclear weapons** die zunehmende Verbreitung von Atomwaffen
c *(inf, of food etc)* Festessen *nt*, Festschmaus *m*; **that was an excellent ~** das war prima, was du *etc* da aufgetischt hast
d *(= cover)* Decke *f*
e *(for bread)* (Brot)aufstrich *m*; **anchovy ~** Sardellenpaste *f*; **cheese ~** Streichkäse *m*
f *(Press, Typ: = two pages)* Doppelseite *f*; **a full-page/double ~** ein ganz-/zweiseitiger Bericht; *(= advertisement)* eine ganz-/zweiseitige Anzeige; **a picture ~** ein ganzseitiger Bildbericht; **the centre ~ of a paper** die Mittelseite einer Zeitung
VT **a** *(= open or lay out: also* **spread out***) rug, nets, hay, wings, arms* ausbreiten; *fan* öffnen; *goods* ausbreiten, auslegen; *hands, legs* spreizen; **the peacock ~ its tail** der Pfau schlug ein Rad; **he was lying with his arms and legs ~ out** er lag mit ausgestreckten Armen und Beinen da; **the fields were ~ (out) below us** die Felder breiteten sich unter uns aus; **the view which was ~ (out) before us** die Sicht, die sich uns bot; **the yacht ~ its sails** die Segel des Bootes blähten sich
b *bread, canvas, surface* bestreichen; *butter, paint etc* (ver- *or* auf)streichen; *table* decken; **~ the paint evenly** verteilen Sie die Farbe gleichmäßig; **he ~ the plaster over the wall** er verstrich den Gips auf der Wand; **to ~ a cloth/blanket over sth** ein Tuch/eine Decke über etw *(acc)* breiten; **the table was ~ with food** der Tisch war reichlich *or* üppig gedeckt
c *(= distribute: also* **spread out***) forces, writing, objects, payments, risk* verteilen; *sand, fertilizer, muck* streuen; *(in time)* verteilen *(over* über *+acc)*; **our resources are ~ very thin** unsere Mittel sind maximal beansprucht
d *(= disseminate) news, knowledge, panic, disease, smell* verbreiten; *rumour* ausstreuen, verbreiten; **I'll ~ the news to everyone in the office** ich werde es allen im Büro mitteilen
VI **a** *(= extend, spatially)* sich erstrecken, sich ausdehnen *(over, across* über *+acc)*; *(with movement, weeds, liquid, fire, smile, industry)* sich ausbreiten *(over, across* über *+acc)*; *(towns, settlements)* sich ausdehnen; *(knowledge, fear etc, smell)* sich verbreiten; *(disease, trouble, fire)* sich verbreiten, um sich greifen; **the course ~s over four months** der Kurs erstreckt sich über vier Monate; **to ~ to sth** etw erreichen; *(disease etc)* auf etw *(acc)* übergreifen; **to ~ into sth** sich in etw *(acc)* erstrecken; *(in time)* sich bis in etw *(acc)* erstrecken; **under the ~ing trees** unter den ausladenden Bäumen; **he's worried about his ~ing stomach** *(inf)* er macht sich Sorgen, weil er in die Breite geht *(inf)* → **wildfire**
b *(butter etc)* sich streichen *or* schmieren *(inf)* lassen
VR **to ~ oneself** *(physically)* sich ausstrecken; *(= spread one's things)* sich ausbreiten; *(in speech, writing)* sich verbreiten

▶ **spread about** *(Brit) or* **around** VT *sep news, rumours, disease* verbreiten, unters Volk bringen *(inf)*; *toys, seeds etc* verstreuen

▶ **spread out** VT *sep* = **spread VT a, c** VI **a** *(countryside etc)* sich ausdehnen **b** *(troops, runners)* sich verteilen

spread-eagle ['spred,i:gl] VT **to be** *or* **lie ~d** mit ausgestreckten Armen und Beinen daliegen, alle viere von sich *(dat)* strecken *(inf)*; **the policeman outlined the ~d body** der Polizist zeichnete die Umrisse des ausgestreckt daliegenden Toten

spreader ['spredəʳ] N **a** Spachtel *m*; *(for butter etc)* Messer *nt* **b** *(Agr: = muck spreader)* (Stall)miststreuer *m*

spreadsheet ['spredʃi:t] N *(Comput)* Tabellenkalkulation *f*, Spreadsheet *nt*; *(= software)* Tabellenkalkulations- *or* Spreadsheetprogramm *nt*

spree [spri:] N **spending** *or* **shopping ~** Großeinkauf *m*; **drinking/gambling ~** Zech-/Spieltour *f (inf)*; **killing ~** *(of gunman)* Amoklauf *m*; **to go/be on a ~** *(drinking)* eine Zechtour machen; *(spending)* groß einkaufen gehen/groß einkaufen

sprig [sprɪg] N Zweig *m*; **embroidered with ~s of heather** mit Heidekrautzweigen bestickt

sprightliness ['spraɪtlɪnɪs] N *(of person, tune)* Munterkeit *f*, Lebhaftigkeit *f*; *(of old person)* Rüstigkeit *f*; *(of walk, dance)* Schwung *m*

sprightly ['spraɪtlɪ] ADJ *(+er) person, tune* munter, lebhaft; *old person* rüstig; *walk, dance* schwungvoll

spring [sprɪŋ] *vb: pret* **sprang** *or (US)* **sprung**, *ptp* **sprung** N **a** *(lit, fig liter: = source)* Quelle *f*; **~s** *(fig liter: = origins)* Ursprung *m*
b *(= season)* Frühling *m*, Frühjahr *nt*, Lenz *m (poet)*; **in (the) ~** im Frühling, im Frühjahr; **~ is in the air** der Frühling liegt in der Luft, der Lenz hält seinen Einzug *(poet)*; **in the ~ of his life** im Frühling seines Lebens, im Lenz des Lebens *(poet)*
c *(= leap)* Sprung *m*, Satz *m*; **to make a ~ at sb/sth** sich auf jdn/etw stürzen
d *(Mech)* Feder *f*; *(in mattress, seat etc)* (Sprung)feder *f*; **~s** *(Aut)* Federung *f*
e *no pl (= bounciness, of chair)* Federung *f*; *(of wood, grass etc)* Nachgiebigkeit *f*, Elastizität *f*; **to walk with a ~ in one's step** mit federnden Schritten gehen; **the news put an extra ~ in his step** die Nachricht beflügelte seine Schritte
ADJ *attr* **a** *(seasonal)* Frühlings-; **a ~ day** ein Frühlingstag *m*
b *(= with springs)* gefedert; **~ mattress** Federkernmatratze *f*
VT **a** *(= leap over)* überspringen, springen über *(+acc)*
b *(= put springs in)* federn
c *(= cause to operate)* auslösen; *mine* explodieren lassen; *lock, mousetrap etc* zuschnappen lassen; **to ~ a leak** *(pipe)* (plötzlich) undicht werden; *(ship)* (plötzlich) ein Leck bekommen; **to ~ sth on sb** *(fig, idea, decision)* jdn mit etw konfrontieren; **to ~ a piece of news on sb** jdn mit einer Neuigkeit überraschen; **to ~ a surprise on sb** jdn völlig überraschen
d *(inf, = free)* rausholen *(inf)*
VI **a** *(= leap)* springen; *(= be activated)* ausgelöst werden; *(mousetrap)* zuschnappen; **to ~ at sb** jdn anspringen; **to ~ out at sb** auf jdn lospringen; **to ~ open** aufspringen; **to be poised to ~** *(lit, fig)* sprungbereit sein; **to ~ into the saddle** sich in den Sattel schwingen; **to ~ to one's feet** aufspringen; **to ~ out of bed** aus dem Bett hüpfen; **tears sprang to her eyes** ihr schossen die Tränen in die Augen; **his hand sprang to his gun** er griff (schnell) zur Waffe; **an oath sprang to his lips** ein Fluch drängte sich auf seine Lippen *(geh)*; **to ~ into action** aktiv werden; *(police, fire brigade etc)* in Aktion treten; **to ~ to attention** *(Mil)* Haltung annehmen; **to ~ to arms** zu den Waffen eilen; **to ~ into view** plötzlich in Sicht kommen; **to ~ to mind** einem einfallen; **to ~ to sb's aid/defence** jdm zu Hilfe eilen; **he sprang to fame** er wurde plötzlich berühmt; **to ~ (in)to life** (plötzlich) lebendig werden; **the debate sprang (in)to life** es kam plötzlich Leben in die Debatte
b *(= issue: also* **spring forth***, liter, water, blood)* (hervor)quellen *(from* aus*)*; *(fire, sparks)* sprühen *(from* aus*)*; *(shoot)* (hervor)sprießen *(from* aus*)*; *(from family etc)* abstammen *(from* von*)*; *(fig, idea)* entstehen *(from* aus*)*; *(interest, irritability etc)* herrühren *(from* von*)*; **where did you ~ from?** *(inf)* wo kommst du denn her?; **to ~ into existence** (plötzlich *or* rasch) entstehen

▶ **spring back** VI *(person)* zurückspringen; *(in fear)* zurückschrecken; *(object)* zurückschnellen

▶ **spring up** VI *(plant)* hervorsprießen; *(weeds)* aus dem Boden schießen; *(person)* hoch- *or* aufspringen; *(wind)* aufkommen; *(building, settlement)* aus dem Boden schießen; *(fig, suspicion, friendship)* erwachen, (plötzlich) entstehen; *(firm, magazine)* entstehen; *(problem, rumour)* auftauchen

spring: **spring balance** N Federwaage *f*; **spring binder** N Klemmhefter *m*; **springboard** N *(lit, fig)* Sprungbrett *nt*

springbok ['sprɪŋbɒk] N Springbock *m*

spring: **spring chicken** N Stubenküken *nt*; **he's no ~** *(fig inf)* er ist nicht mehr feucht hinter den Ohren *(inf)*; **spring-clean** VT gründlich putzen; **to ~ a house** (in einem Haus) Frühjahrsputz machen VI Frühjahrsputz machen; **spring-cleaning** N Frühjahrsputz *m*

springer (spaniel) ['sprɪŋəʳ-] N Springerspaniel *m*

spring fever N **a** *(= energetic feeling)* Frühlingsgefühle *pl*; **it must be ~!** das muss der Frühling sein!, es muss am Frühling liegen!
b *(= lassitude)* Frühjahrsmüdigkeit *f*

springform ['sprɪŋfɔ:m] N *(also* **springform pan***, Cook)* Springform *f*

springiness ['sprɪŋɪnɪs] N Elastizität *f*; *(of turf, wood, grass, track also)* Nachgiebigkeit *f*; *(of springboard also)* Sprungkraft *f*; *(of bed)* Federung *f*; **the ~ of his step** sein federnder Gang

spring: **springless** ADJ ungefedert; **spring-like** ADJ frühlingshaft; **spring-loaded** ADJ mit einer Sprungfeder; **to be ~** eine Sprungfeder haben; **spring mattress** N Federkernmatratze *f*; **spring onion** N *(Brit)* Frühlingszwiebel *f*; **spring roll** N Frühlingsrolle *f*; **spring tide** N Springflut *f*; **springtide** N *(poet: = springtime)* Lenz *m (poet)*; **springtime** N Frühlingszeit *f*, Frühjahr *nt*; *(fig)* Frühling *m*, Lenz *m (poet)*; **spring water** N Quellwasser *nt*; **spring wheat** N Sommerweizen *m*

springy ['sprɪŋɪ] ADJ *(+er) step* federnd; *plank, turf, grass also* nachgiebig, elastisch; *rubber, wood, plastic etc, hair* elastisch; *bed* weich gefedert

sprinkle ['sprɪŋkl] VT *water* sprenkeln, sprengen; *lawn, plant* besprengen; *(with holy water)* besprengen; *salt, dust, sugar etc* streuen; *dish, cake* bestreuen; **a lawn ~d with daisies** ein mit Gänseblümchen durchzogener Rasen; **his hair was ~d with grey** sein Haar war grau meliert; **churches/pubs are ~d throughout the town** man findet Kirchen/Gasthäuser über die ganze Stadt verstreut; **~d with quotations** mit Zitaten durchsetzt N *(of liquid, vinegar)* ein paar Spritzer; *(of salt etc)* Prise *f*

sprinkler ['sprɪŋkləʳ] N **a** *(Hort, Agr)* Berieselungsapparat *m*, Sprinkler *m*; *(in garden also)* (Rasen)sprenger *m*; *(for firefighting)* Sprinkler *m*; *(on watering can etc)* Sprenger *m*, Gießkannenkopf *m*; *(on shower)* Brause *f*; *(= sugar sprinkler)* Streudose *f*, Streuer *m* **b** *(Eccl)* Weihwasserwedel *m*

sprinkler: **sprinkler head** N Sprinkler *m*; *(on watering can)* Sprenger *m*, Gießkannenkopf *m*; *(on shower)* Brause *f*; **sprinkler system** N Berieselungsanlage *f*; *(for firefighting also)* Sprinkleranlage *f*

sprinkling ['sprɪŋklɪŋ] N *(of rain, dew etc)* ein paar Tropfen; *(of sugar etc)* Prise *f*; *(fig, of humour, comedy etc)* Anflug *m*; *(of common sense)* Spur *f*; **there was a ~ of grey in his hair** ein paar graue Fäden durchzogen sein Haar; **there was a ~ of young people** es waren ein paar vereinzelte junge Leute da; **a ~ of freckles** ein paar Sommersprossen; **to give sth a ~** *(with water)* etw besprengen *or* besprenkeln

sprinkling can N *(US)* Gießkanne *f*

sprint [sprɪnt] N Lauf *m*; *(= race)* Sprint *m*; *(= burst of speed)* Spurt *m*, Sprint *m*; **the 100-m ~**

der 100-m-Lauf; **she made a ~ for the bus** sie sprintete *or* spurtete zum Bus; **a ~ finish** ein Endspurt *m*; **he has a good ~ finish** er legt einen guten Endspurt vor **VI** *(in race)* sprinten; *(= dash)* rennen

sprinter ['sprɪntəʳ] **N** Kurzstreckenläufer(in) *m(f)*, Sprinter(in) *m(f)*

sprit [sprɪt] **N** Spriet *nt*

sprite [spraɪt] **N** Elf *m*, Elfe *f*; Kobold *m* *(also Comput: icon)*; **water/wood ~** Wasser-/Waldgeist *m*

spritsail ['sprɪtsəl] **N** Sprietsegel *nt*

spritzer ['sprɪtsəʳ] **N** (Wein)schorle *f*, Gespritzte(r) *m*

sprocket ['sprɒkɪt] **N** **a** *(= tooth)* Zahn *m* **b** *(= sprocket wheel)* Kettenrad *nt*; *(on bicycle)* Kettenzahnrad *nt*, Zahnkranz *m*; *(Film)* Greifer *m*; *(on printer etc)* Stachelrad *nt*

sprog [sprɒg] *(Brit inf)* **N** **a** *(= baby, child)* Balg *nt (pej inf)*, Gör *nt (inf)*; **how are the ~s?** was macht der Nachwuchs? *(inf)* **b** *(Mil)* Rekrut(in) *m(f)*

sprout [spraʊt] **N** **a** *(= shoot, of plant)* Trieb *m*; *(of tree also)* Schössling *m*, Trieb *m*; *(from seed)* Keim *m*
b *(= Brussels sprout)* (Rosenkohl)röschen *nt*; **~s** *pl* Rosenkohl *m*
VT *leaves, buds, shoots etc* treiben; *horns etc* entwickeln; *seeds, wheat etc* keimen lassen; *(inf) beard* sich *(dat)* wachsen lassen; **the town is ~ing new buildings** in der Stadt sprießen neue Gebäude hervor; **he suddenly started ~ing hairs on his chest** er bekam plötzlich Haare auf der Brust
VI **a** *(= grow)* wachsen, sprießen; *(seed, wheat etc)* keimen; *(potatoes, trees etc)* Triebe *pl* bekommen
b *(lit, fig: also* **sprout up***)* *(plants)* emporschießen, sprießen; *(new sects, new buildings)* wie die Pilze aus dem Boden schießen

spruce[1] [spru:s] **N** *(also* **spruce fir***)* Fichte *f*

spruce[2] **ADJ** *(+er) person* proper, gepflegt; *men's clothes* flott, schmuck *(dated)*; *women, children, women's clothes, appearance* adrett; *building* schmuck; *lawn, flower beds* gepflegt; **he was looking very ~** er sah geschniegelt und gebügelt aus

▶ **spruce up** **VT** *sep child* herausputzen; *house, garden* auf Vordermann bringen *(inf)*; *image* aufpolieren; **to spruce oneself up** *(in general)* sein Äußeres pflegen; *(= get dressed up)* sich in Schale werfen; *(woman)* sich schönmachen; **he looks much better now that he has spruced himself up** so gepflegt sieht er wesentlich besser aus; **all spruced up** *(children, men)* geschniegelt und gestriegelt; *(women)* schön zurechtgemacht; *(house)* auf Hochglanz

sprucely ['spru:slɪ] **ADV** *dressed (man)* flott, schmuck *(dated)*; *(woman, child)* adrett; *painted, decorated etc* schmuck; *laid out* sauber und ordentlich; **~ kept gardens** gepflegte Gärten

spruceness ['spru:snɪs] **N** *(of person, appearance)* Gepflegtheit *f*

sprung [sprʌŋ] *ptp of* **spring** **ADJ** gefedert; **a well-~ mattress** eine gut gefederte Matratze

spry [spraɪ] **ADJ** rüstig

SPUC *(Brit) abbr of* **Society for the Protection of the Unborn Child** *Gesellschaft zum Schutz des ungeborenen Lebens*

spud [spʌd] **N** *(inf: = potato)* Kartoffel *f*; **~-bashing** *(Brit Mil sl)* Küchendienst *m*

spume [spju:m] **N** *(liter)* Gischt *m*

spun [spʌn] *pret, ptp of* **spin** **ADJ** *gold, silver, silk* gesponnen; **~ sugar** *(= candyfloss)* Zuckerwatte *f*

spunk [spʌŋk] **N** **a** *(inf)* Mumm *m (inf)*, Courage *f* **b** *(vulg: = semen)* Saft *m (sl)*

spunky ['spʌŋkɪ] **ADJ** *(+er) (inf)* couragiert

spur [spɜ:ʳ] **N** **a** Sporn *m*; *(fig)* Ansporn *m*, Antrieb *m* (to für); **he urged the horse on with his ~s** er gab dem Pferd die Sporen; **to win** *or* **earn one's ~s** *(fig)* sich *(dat)* die Sporen verdienen; **this might act as a ~ to the players** das könnte ein Ansporn für die Spieler sein; **this was a new ~ to his ambition** das gab seinem Ehrgeiz neuen Antrieb *or* Ansporn
b **on the ~ of the moment** ganz spontan; **a ~-of-the-moment decision** ein spontaner Entschluss
c *(Geog)* Vorsprung *m*
d *(Zool)* Sporn *m*
e *(Rail)* Nebengleis *nt*, Rangiergleis *nt*
VT **a** *horse* die Sporen geben *(+dat)*
b *(= urge on: also* **spur on***)* (vorwärts)treiben, vorantreiben; *(fig)* anspornen; **~red (on) by greed/ambition** von Habgier/vom Ehrgeiz getrieben
VI *(also* **spur on***)* galoppieren

spurge [spɜ:dʒ] **N** *(Bot)* Wolfsmilch *f*; **~ laurel** Lorbeerseidelbast *m*

spurious ['spjʊərɪəs] **ADJ** *claim, claimant* unberechtigt; *document, account* falsch; *anger, interest, affection* nicht echt; *argument* fadenscheinig; **on the ~ grounds that ...** mit der fadenscheinigen Begründung, dass ...

spuriousness ['spjʊərɪəsnɪs] **N** *(of claim, claimant)* mangelnde Berechtigung; *(of document, account)* Falschheit *f*; *(of anger, interest, affection)* mangelnde Echtheit; *(of argument)* Fadenscheinigkeit *f*

spurn [spɜ:n] **VT** verschmähen; *advice also* missachten

spurned [spɜ:nd] **ADJ** *offer, gift* zurückgewiesen; *love* verschmäht; **spurner lover** verschmähter Liebhaber, verschmähte Liebhaberin

spurred [spɜ:d] **ADJ** gespornt

spurt [spɜ:t] **N** **a** *(= flow)* Strahl *m*; **~s of flame** Stichflammen **b** *(= burst of speed)* Spurt *m*; **a final ~** *(lit, fig)* ein Endspurt *m*; **to put a ~ on** *(lit, fig)* einen Spurt vorlegen; **there was a ~ of activity** es brach plötzliche Aktivität aus; **in a sudden ~ of energy** in einer plötzlichen Energieanwandlung; **to work in ~s** (nur) sporadisch arbeiten **VI** **a** *(= gush: also* **spurt out***)* (heraus)spritzen *(from* aus*)* **b** *(= run)* spurten **VT** **the wound ~ed blood** aus der Wunde spritzte Blut; **the pipe ~ed water** aus dem Rohr spritzte das Wasser

spur: spur track **N** *(Rail)* Nebengleis *nt*, Rangiergleis *nt*; **spur wheel** **N** Stirnrad *nt*

Sputnik ['spʊtnɪk] **N** Sputnik *m*

sputter ['spʌtəʳ] **VI** zischen; *(in frying pan)* brutzeln; *(fat)* spritzen; *(engine)* stottern; *(in speech)* sich ereifern *(about* über *+acc)*; **he was ~ing with rage** er geiferte (vor Zorn); **the candle ~ed out** die Kerze ging flackernd aus; **to ~ to a halt** *(lit, fig)* stotternd zum Stillstand kommen

sputum ['spju:təm] **N** *(Med)* Auswurf *m*, Sputum *nt (spec)*

spy [spaɪ] **N** Spion(in) *m(f)*; *(= police spy)* Spitzel *m*; **~ in the cab** *(inf: = tachograph)* Fahrtenschreiber *m* **VT** sehen, erspähen *(geh)*; **finally I spied him coming** endlich sah ich ihn kommen; **I ~ with my little eye something ...** ≈ ich sehe was, was du nicht siehst, und ... **VI** spionieren, Spionage treiben; **to ~ into sth** in etw *(dat)* herumspionieren; **to ~ on sb** jdn bespitzeln; *on neighbours* jdm nachspionieren; **I Spy** *(= game)* ≈ ich sehe was, was du nicht siehst

▶ **spy out** **VT** *sep* ausfindig machen; **to spy out the land** *(Mil)* die Gegend auskundschaften; *(fig)* die Lage peilen

spy: spy case **N** Spionagefall *m*; **spycatcher** **N** *(inf)* Geheimdienstler(in) *m(f) (inf)*; **spy film** **N** Agentenfilm *m*; **spy glass** **N** Fernglas *nt*; **spy hole** **N** Guckloch *nt*, Spion *m*; **spy master** **N** Chefagent *m*, Agentenführer *m*; **spy movie** **N** *(esp US)* Agentenfilm *m*; **spy plane** **N** Spionageflugzeug *nt*; **spy ring** **N** Spionagering *m*, Agentenring *m*; **spy satellite** **N** Spionagesatellit *m*; **spy story** **N** Spionagegeschichte *f*; **spyware** **N** *(Comput)* Spionagesoftware *f*

Sq *abbr of* **Square**

sq *abbr of* **square**; **sq m** qm, m²

squab [skwɒb] **N** **a** *(Orn)* Jungtaube *f* **b** *(Aut)* Bank *f*

squabble ['skwɒbl] **N** Zank *m*, Streit *m*; **~s** Zankereien *pl*, Streitigkeiten *pl* **VI** (sich) zanken, (sich) streiten *(about, over* um)

squabbler ['skwɒbləʳ] **N** Streithammel *m (inf)*

squabbling ['skwɒblɪŋ] **N** Zankerei *f*, Streiterei *f*

squad [skwɒd] **N** *(Mil)* Korporalschaft *f*; *(= special unit of police etc)* Kommando *nt*; *(= police department)* Dezernat *nt*; *(of workmen)* Trupp *m*; *(Sport, fig)* Mannschaft *f*

squad car **N** *(US)* Streifenwagen *m*

squaddie ['skwɒdɪ] **N** *(Brit inf: = private soldier)* Gefreite(r) *mf*; **the pub was full of ~s** die Kneipe war voller Soldaten

squadron ['skwɒdrən] **N** *(of cavalry)* Schwadron *f*; *(Aviat)* Staffel *f*; *(Naut)* Geschwader *nt*

squadron leader **N** *(Brit Aviat)* Luftwaffenmajor(in) *m(f)*

squalid ['skwɒlɪd] **ADJ** *room, house* schmutzig und verwahrlost; *existence, conditions* elend, erbärmlich; *motive, manoeuvres, deed, idea etc* gemein, niederträchtig; *experience* übel; *dispute, gossip* entwürdigend; *affair* schmutzig

squalidly ['skwɒlɪdlɪ] **ADV** *live* in elenden *or* erbärmlichen Verhältnissen; *behave, treat sb* gemein, niederträchtig

squall [skwɔ:l] **N** **a** *(= storm)* Bö(e) *f*; *(fig)* Gewitter *nt*, Sturm *m*; **there are ~s ahead** *(fig)* wir gehen stürmischen Zeiten entgegen **b** *(= cry)* Schrei *m* **VI** schreien

squally ['skwɔ:lɪ] **ADJ** *(+er)* stürmisch; *wind also* böig

squalor ['skwɒləʳ] **N** Schmutz *m*; *(= moral squalor)* Verkommenheit *f*; **the ~ of the conditions** die elenden *or* erbärmlichen Verhältnisse; **to live in ~** in unbeschreiblichen Zuständen leben

squander ['skwɒndəʳ] **VT** verschwenden, vergeuden *(on* an *+acc)*; *opportunity* vertun

square [skwɛəʳ] **N** **a** *(= shape, Geometry, on graph paper)* Quadrat *nt*; **a 6 metre ~** 6 Meter im Quadrat
b *(piece of material, paper etc) (= perfect square)* Quadrat *nt*; *(= rectangle)* Viereck *nt*; *(on chessboard etc)* Feld *nt*; *(on paper)* Kästchen *nt*, Karo *nt*; *(in crossword)* Kästchen *nt*; *(= check on material etc)* Karo *nt*; *(= head square)* Kopftuch *nt*; **form yourselves into a ~** stellen Sie sich im Viereck auf; **cut it in ~s** schneiden Sie es quadratisch *or* in Quadrate zu; **to go back to ~ one** *(fig)* **to start (again) from ~ one** *(fig)* noch einmal von vorne anfangen; **we're back to ~ one** jetzt sind wir wieder da, wo wir angefangen haben
c *(in town)* Platz *m*; *(US: of houses)* Block *m*; *(Mil: = barrack square)* (Kasernen)platz *m*
d *(Math)* Quadrat(zahl *f*) *nt*; **the ~ of 3 is 9** 3 hoch 2 *or* 3 (im) Quadrat ist 9
e *(Tech)* Winkelmaß *nt*; *(= set square)* Zeichendreieck *nt*; *(= T-square)* Reißschiene *f*; **to be on the ~** *(fig inf, = above board)* in Ordnung sein
f *(Mil, = battle formation)* Karree *nt*
g *(inf: = conventional person)* Spießer(in) *m(f) (inf)*; **to be a ~** von (vor)gestern sein
ADJ *(+er)* **a** *(in shape)* quadratisch; *picture, lawn etc* viereckig, quadratisch; *nib* viereckig; *block of wood etc* vierkantig; **to be a ~ peg in a round hole** am falschen Platz sein
b *(= forming right angle) angle* recht; *corner* rechtwinklig; *shoulder* eckig; *chin, jaw* kantig, eckig; *build* vierschrötig; **~ bracket** eckige Klammer
c *(Math)* Quadrat-; **3 ~ kilometres** 3 Quadratkilometer; **3 metres ~** 3 Meter im Quadrat; **there wasn't a ~ inch of space left** es war kein Zentimeter Platz mehr
d *attr (= complete) meal* anständig, ordentlich
e *(= fair) deal* gerecht, fair; *dealings, game, person* ehrlich; **to give sb a ~ deal** jdn gerecht *or* fair behandeln; **to get a ~ deal** fair behandelt werden; **I'll be ~ with you** ich will ehrlich *or* offen mit dir sein
f *(fig: = even)* **to be ~** *(accounts etc)* in Ordnung sein; **to get ~ with sb** mit jdm abrechnen;

we are (all) ~ *(Sport)* wir stehen beide/alle gleich; *(fig)* jetzt sind wir quitt; **he wanted to be ~ with his creditors** er wollte mit seinen Gläubigern im Reinen sein; **we can start again all ~** wir sind wieder quitt

g *(inf: = conventional)* überholt, verstaubt; *person, ideas* spießig *(inf)*; **he's ~** er ist von (vor)gestern; **be there or be ~!** das kann man sich nicht entgehen lassen!

ADV *(+er)* **a** *(= at right angles)* rechtwinklig; **~ with sth** im rechten Winkel *or* senkrecht zu etw

b *(= directly)* direkt, genau; **to hit sb ~ in the chest** jdn voll in die Brust treffen; **to look sb ~ in the eye** jdm direkt in die Augen schauen; **to be ~ in the middle of sth** mitten in etw *(dat)* drin sein; **he kissed her ~ on the mouth** er küsste sie direkt auf den Mund

c *(= parallel)* **to stand ~** gerade stehen; **he turned to face me ~ on** er wandte sich mir voll zu; **to be ~ with** *or* **to sth** parallel zu etw ausgerichtet sein

d *(= honestly)* ehrlich, fair → **fair**[1]

VT **a** *(= make square)* quadratisch machen; *(= make a right angle)* rechtwinklig machen; **to ~ one's shoulders** die Schultern straffen; **to ~ a block of wood** *(= cut square)* einen Holzklotz vierkantig zuschneiden; **to try to ~ the circle** die Quadratur des Kreises versuchen; **he ~d the ball to Gascoigne** er spielte einen Querpass auf Gascoigne; **to ~ a match** in einem Spiel gleichziehen

b *(Math) number* quadrieren; **3 ~d is 9** 3 hoch 2 *or* 3 (im) Quadrat ist 9

c *(= adjust) debts* begleichen; *creditors* abrechnen mit; *(= reconcile)* in Einklang bringen; **to ~ one's accounts** abrechnen *(with* mit); **to ~ sth with one's conscience** etw mit seinem Gewissen vereinbaren *or* in Einklang bringen; **I'll ~ it with the porter** *(inf)* ich mache das mit dem Portier ab *(inf)*

d *(inf, = bribe)* schmieren *(inf)*

VI übereinstimmen

▸ **square off** **VT** *sep* **a** *(= make square) corner* rechtwinklig machen **b** *(= draw squares on)* in Quadrate einteilen **VI** *(esp US)* in Kampfstellung gehen, Kampfstellung annehmen

▸ **square up** **VI** **a** *(boxers, fighters)* in Kampfstellung gehen, Kampfstellung annehmen; **to square up to sb** sich vor jdm aufpflanzen *(inf)*; *(boxer)* vor jdm in Kampfstellung gehen; *(fig)* jdm die Stirn bieten; **to square up to sth** sich einer Sache *(dat)* stellen **b** *(lit, fig: = settle)* abrechnen

square: **square-bashing** N *(Brit Mil sl)* Drill *m*; **square bracket** N eckige Klammer; **square-built** ADJ *woman* stämmig *or* breit gebaut; *man* vierschrötig; *house* quadratisch gebaut; **square-cut** ADJ *(in a perfect square)* quadratisch; *(= rectangular)* rechteckig

squared [skwɛəd] ADJ *paper* kariert

square: **square dance** N Squaredance *m*; **squarehead** ['skwɛəhed] N *(US inf)* **a** *(= stupid person)* Holzkopf *m (pej)* **b** *(pej: = person of Germanic or Scandinavian origin)* Quadratschädel *m (pej)*; **square-jawed** ADJ mit kantigem Kinn; **square knot** N *(US)* Kreuzknoten *m*

squarely ['skwɛəlɪ] ADV **a** *(= directly)* direkt, genau; *(fig: = firmly)* fest; **to hit sb ~ in the stomach** jdn voll in den Magen treffen; **~ in the middle of sth** genau in der Mitte von etw; **to place the blame for sth ~ on sb** jdm voll und ganz die Schuld an etw *(dat)* geben; **to face sb/sth ~** jdm/einer Sache tapfer entgegentreten; **we must face this ~** wir müssen dieser Sache *(dat)* (fest) ins Auge sehen **b** *(= honestly)* ehrlich; *(= fairly)* gerecht, fair; **to deal ~ with sb** jdn gerecht *or* fair behandeln **c** **~ built** stämmig *or* breit gebaut

square: **square measure** N Flächenmaß *nt*; **square number** N Quadratzahl *f*; **square-rigged** ADJ voll getakelt; **square-rigger** N *(Naut)* Rahsegler *m*; **square root** N Quadratwurzel *f*, zweite Wurzel; **to work out the ~ of sth** die zweite Wurzel *or* Quadratwurzel aus etw ziehen; **square sail** N Rahsegel *nt*; **square shooter** N *(US inf)* ehrlicher Kerl *(inf)*; **square-shouldered** ADJ mit eckigen Schultern; **square-toed** ADJ *shoes* mit breiter Kappe

squash[1] [skwɒʃ] **N** **a** *(Brit: = fruit concentrate)* Fruchtsaftkonzentrat *nt*, Squash *nt*; *(= drink)* Fruchtsaft *m*; **a glass of orange ~** ein Glas Orangensaft

b *(= crush)* Gedränge *nt*; **it's a bit of a ~** es ist ziemlich eng

VT **a** *(also* **squash up***)* zerdrücken, zerquetschen; *box etc* zusammendrücken; **to be ~ed to a pulp** zu Brei gequetscht *or* zerquetscht werden; **my hat was ~ed flat** *or* **in** mein Hut war völlig zerdrückt

b *(fig) (inf: = silence, = quash) protest, argument, proposal* vom Tisch fegen *(inf)*; *hopes* vernichten; **I felt completely ~ed** ich kam mir ganz klein und hässlich vor *(inf)*

c *(= squeeze)* quetschen; **to ~ sb in** jdn einquetschen; **to ~ sth in** etw hineinquetschen; **to be ~ed up against sb** gegen jdn gequetscht *or* gepresst werden; **to be ~ed together** eng zusammengepresst *or* -gequetscht sein

VI **a** *(= get squashed)* zerdrückt *or* zerquetscht werden

b *(= squeeze)* sich quetschen; **to ~ in** sich hinein-/hereinquetschen; **could you ~ up?** könnt ihr etwas zusammenrücken?; *(one person)* kannst du dich etwas kleiner machen?

squash[2] N *(Sport: also* **squash rackets** *or (esp US)* **racquets***)* Squash *nt*; **~ courts** *pl* Squashhalle *f*

squash[3] N *no pl (US)* (Pâtisson)kürbis *m*

squash court N Squashplatz *m*

squasher ['skwɔʃə'] N Squasher(in) *m(f)*

squash racket, *(esp US)* **squash racquet** N Squash-Schläger *m*

squashy ['skwɒʃɪ] ADJ *(+er)* matschig; *cushion* weich

squat [skwɒt] **ADJ** *(+er)* gedrungen, kompakt; *chair* niedrig; *figure, person* gedrungen **VI** **a** *(person)* hocken, kauern; *(animal)* hocken **b** *(also* **squat down***)* sich (hin)hocken *or* (hin)kauern **c** *(on land)* sich (illegal) ansiedeln; **to ~ (in a house)** ein Haus besetzt haben, sich in einem Haus eingenistet haben *(inf)*; **they are not tenants, they're just ~ting** das sind keine Mieter, das sind Hausbesetzer **N** *(inf: = place)* Unterschlupf *m (für Hausbesetzer)*; **after their ~ in that house ...** nachdem sie sich in dem Haus eingenistet hatten ... *(inf)*, nachdem sie das Haus als Unterschlupf benutzt hatten ...

squatter ['skwɒtə'] N *(on land)* Squatter(in) *m(f)*, illegaler Siedler, illegale Siedlerin; *(in house)* Hausbesetzer(in) *m(f)*

squat thrust N Stützstrecke *f*

squat toilet N Stehtoilette *f*

squaw [skwɔː] N *(neg!)* Squaw *f*

squawk [skwɔːk] **N** heiserer Schrei; *(fig inf: = complaint)* Protest *m*; **he let out a ~** er kreischte auf; **the ~s of the hens** das aufgeregte Gackern der Hühner **VI** *(bird, person)* schreien, kreischen; *(fig inf: = complain)* protestieren

squeak [skwiːk] **N** *(of hinge, wheel etc, shoe, pen)* Quietschen *nt no pl*; *(of person)* Quiekser *m*; *(of small animal)* Quieken *nt no pl*; *(of mouse, bird)* Piepsen *nt no pl*; *(fig inf: = sound)* Pieps *m (inf)*, Mucks *m (inf)*; **she gave a ~ of delight** sie quiekste entzückt; **to give a ~ of protest** schwach protestieren; **the door opened with a ~** die Tür ging quietschend auf **VI** *(door, hinge, shoes etc)* quietschen; *(person)* quieksen; *(small animal)* quieken, quieksen; *(mouse, bird)* piepsen **VT** quieksen

▸ **squeak by** *or* **through** **VI** *(inf: = narrowly succeed)* gerade so durchkommen *(inf)*

squeaky ['skwiːkɪ] ADJ *(+er)* quietschend; *voice* piepsig

squeaky-clean [ˌskwiːkɪ'kliːn] ADJ *(inf)* absolut sauber *(inf)*, blitzsauber *(inf)*; **the ~ brigade** die Saubermänner *pl (inf)*

squeal ['skwiːl] **N** Schrei *m*; *(of person, tyre, brakes)* Kreischen *nt no pl*; *(of protest)* (Auf)schrei *m*; *(of pig)* Quieken *nt no pl*; **with a ~ of brakes/tyres** mit kreischenden Bremsen/Reifen; **a ~ of pain** ein Schmerzensschrei *m*; **~s of protest** Protestgeschrei *nt*; **~s/a ~ of laughter** schrilles Gelächter

VI **a** *(= screech) (person)* schreien, kreischen; *(brakes, tyres)* kreischen, quietschen; *(pig, puppy)* quieksen; *(fig inf)* jammern; **to ~ in pain** vor Schmerz aufheulen *or* kreischen; **to ~ with delight** vor Wonne quietschen; **to ~ with laughter** laut auflachen; **to ~ for sb** nach jdm schreien; **to ~ for help** um Hilfe schreien

b *(inf: = confess, inform, criminal)* singen *(inf)* *(to* bei); *(schoolboy etc)* petzen *(inf)* *(to* bei)

VT schreien, kreischen

squeamish ['skwiːmɪʃ] ADJ *person (= easily nauseated)* empfindlich, heikel *(dial)*; *(= easily shocked)* zartbesaitet, empfindlich; **I felt a bit ~** *(= sick)* mir war leicht übel; **it gave me a ~ feeling in my stomach** mein Magen revoltierte; **I felt a bit ~ about telling him the bad news** mir war gar nicht wohl dabei, dass ich ihm die schlechte Nachricht mitteilen musste; **I'm not ~** *(= not easily nauseated)* mir wird nicht so schnell schlecht *or* übel; *(= not easily shocked)* ich bin nicht so zartbesaitet *or* empfindlich; *(= not nervous about unpleasant things)* ich bin ja nicht zimperlich; **don't be so ~** sei nicht so zimperlich; **this book is not for the ~** das Buch ist nichts für zarte Gemüter

squeamishness ['skwiːmɪʃnɪs] N *(= nausea)* Übelkeit *f*; *(= disgust)* Ekel *m*; *(= prudishness)* Zimperlichkeit *f*; **his ~ when he sees blood** die Übelkeit, die ihn beim Anblick von Blut überkommt; **you have to overcome your ~** *(= prudishness, reluctance)* Sie dürfen nicht so zimperlich sein; *(= disgust)* Sie müssen Ihren Ekel überwinden

squeegee ['skwiːdʒiː] N (Gummi)wischer *m*; *(Phot)* Rollenquetscher *m*

squeegee merchant N *(inf) jd, der unaufgefordert die Scheiben von vor Ampeln etc wartenden Autos putzt*

squeeze [skwiːz] **N** **a** *(= act of squeezing)* Drücken *nt no pl*, Pressen *nt no pl*; *(= hug)* Umarmung *f*; *(of hand)* Händedruck *m*; *(in bus etc)* Gedränge *nt*; **to give sth a ~** etw drücken, etw pressen; *lemon, sponge* etw ausdrücken; **to give sb a ~** jdn an sich *(acc)* drücken; **to give sb's hand a ~** jdm die Hand drücken; **it was a tight ~** es war fürchterlich eng; **getting into that dress was a bit of a ~** es war nicht so leicht, mich in das Kleid zu zwängen

b *(= amount)* Spritzer *m*; **put a ~ of toothpaste on the brush** drücken Sie etwas Zahnpasta auf die Bürste

c *(= credit squeeze)* Kreditbeschränkung *f*

d **to put the ~ on sb** *(inf)* jdm die Daumenschrauben ansetzen *(inf)*

e *(inf: = romantic partner)* Freund *m*, Freundin *f*

VT drücken; *sponge, tube* ausdrücken; *orange* auspressen, ausquetschen; *(= squash) person, hand* einquetschen; *(fig: = restrict) person, economy, business etc* unter Druck setzen; *profits, costs* drücken; **to ~ one's eyes shut** die Augen fest zudrücken; **to ~ clothes into a case** Kleider in einen Koffer zwängen; **to ~ liquid out of** *or* **from sth** Flüssigkeit aus etw (heraus)pressen; **to ~ out water/juice** Wasser/Saft herauspressen *(from* aus); **he ~d the trigger** er drückte ab; **to ~ out a tear** eine Träne zerdrücken; **to ~ sth dry** *(lit)* etw auswringen; *(fig)* das Letzte aus etw herausholen; **to ~ sb dry** *(fig)* jdn ausbluten; **to ~ money/information** *etc* **out of sb** Geld/Informationen *etc* aus jdm herausquetschen; **to ~ the rich** die Reichen schröpfen; **to be ~d to death** erdrückt werden; **I'll see if we can ~ you in** vielleicht können wir Sie noch unterbringen; **we'll ~ another song in before the interval** wir schaffen vor der Pause noch ein Lied

VI **you should be able to ~ through** wenn du dich kleinmachst, kommst du durch; **to ~ in/**

out sich hinein-/hinausdrängen; **to ~ past sb** sich an jdm vorbeidrücken; **to ~ onto the bus** sich in den Bus hineinzwängen; **to ~ through a crowd/hole** sich durch eine Menge/ein Loch zwängen; **to ~ (through) underneath a fence** sich unter einem Zaun durchzwängen; **you'll have to ~ up a bit** Sie müssen ein bisschen zusammenrücken

squeeze: **squeeze-bottle** ['skwi:z,bɒtl] N (Plastik)spritzflasche *f*; **squeeze-box** ['skwi:zbɒks] N *(inf)* Quetschkommode *f (inf)*

squeezer ['skwi:zə'] N Presse *f*

squeezy ['skwi:zɪ] ADJ *(+er) (inf)* nachgiebig

squelch [skweltʃ] **N** quatschendes Geräusch *(inf)*; **I heard the ~ of his footsteps in the mud** ich hörte, wie er quatschend *(inf) or* platschend durch den Schlamm lief; **the tomato hit the floor with a ~** die Tomate schlug mit einem satten Platsch auf den Boden auf **VT** **a** **to ~ one's way through sth** durch etw p(l)atschen **b** *(inf: speculation, protest)* unterdrücken **VI** patschen, platschen; *(shoes, mud)* quatschen

squib [skwɪb] N *(= firework)* Knallfrosch *m* → **damp**

squid [skwɪd] N Tintenfisch *m*

squiffy ['skwɪfɪ] ADJ *(+er) (Brit inf)* angesäuselt *(inf)*

squiggle ['skwɪgl] **N** Schnörkel *m* **VT** **to ~ a line under sth** eine Wellenlinie unter etw *(acc)* machen

squiggly ['skwɪglɪ] ADJ *(+er)* schnörkelig; **~ tail** Ringelschwanz *m*

squillion ['skwɪlɪən] N *(inf)* Myriade *f usu pl*, Abermillionen *pl*; **~s of pounds** Abermillionen Pfund

squinch [skwɪntʃ] *(US)* **VT** *eyes* zusammenkneifen **VI** blinzeln, die Augen zusammenkneifen

squint [skwɪnt] **N** **a** *(Med)* Schielen *nt no pl*; **to have a ~** leicht schielen; **he has a terrible ~ in his left eye** er schielt furchtbar auf dem linken Auge **b** *(inf: = look)* Blick *m*; *(= sidelong glance)* Seitenblick *m*; **to have** *or* **take a ~ at sb/sth** einen Blick auf jdn/etw werfen; *(obliquely)* jdn/etw von der Seite ansehen, nach jdm/etw schielen **VI** schielen; *(in strong light etc)* blinzeln; **to ~ at sb/sth** nach jdm/etw schielen; *(quickly)* einen kurzen Blick auf jdn/etw werfen **ADJ** *(= crooked)* schief

squint-eyed [,skwɪnt'aɪd] ADJ *person* schielend *attr*; **to be ~** schielen

squire ['skwaɪə'] **N** **a** *(esp Brit: = landowner)* Gutsherr *m*, ≈ Junker *m (Hist)*; **right, ~** *(Brit inf)* jawohl, der Herr *(dated)*, in Ordnung, Chef *(inf)*; **the ~ of the manor** der Herr des Gutes **b** *(Hist, = knight's attendant)* Knappe *m* **c** *(dated, = escort)* Kavalier *m (dated)* **VT** *(dated)* begleiten, eskortieren *(dated)*

squirearchy ['skwaɪərɑ:kɪ] N Gutsbesitzer *pl*, ≈ Landjunkertum *nt (Hist)*

squirm [skwɜ:m] **N** Winden *nt*; **to give a ~** sich winden **VI** sich winden; *(in distaste)* schaudern; *(with embarrassment)* sich (drehen und) winden; *(from discomfort)* hin und her rutschen; **blood/that joke makes me ~** bei Blut/diesem Witz dreht sich in mir alles herum

squirrel ['skwɪrəl] **N** Eichhörnchen *nt* **ADJ** *attr* Eichhörnchen-; **~ fur** Eichhörnchenpelz *m*

squirt [skwɜ:t] **N** **a** Spritzer *m* **b** *(= implement)* Spritze *f* **c** *(pej inf: = person)* Fatzke *m (inf)*; *(small)* Pimpf *m (inf)* **VT** *liquid* spritzen; *object, person* bespritzen; **to ~ water at sb, to ~ sb with water** jdn mit Wasser bespritzen **VI** spritzen

squirt gun N *(US)* Spritzpistole *f*, Wasserpistole *f*

squish [skwɪʃ] VT *(inf)* zermatschen *(inf)*

squishy ['skwɪʃɪ] ADJ *(+er) (inf)* matschig *(inf)*

squit [skwɪt] N *(Brit inf)* **a** *(= small or insignificant person)* kleiner Scheißer *(inf)* **b** *(= diarrhoea)* **the ~s** *(sl)* die Scheißerei *(sl)*, Durchfall *m*

Sr *abbr of* **senior** sen., Sr

SRC *(Brit) abbr of* **Students' Representative Council**

Sri Lanka [,sri:'læŋkə] N Sri Lanka *nt*

Sri Lankan [,sri:'læŋkən] **ADJ** sri-lankisch; **he/she is ~** er/sie ist aus Sri Lanka **N** Sri-Lanker(in) *m(f)*, Sri Lanker(in) *m(f)*

SRM *abbr of* **specified risk material**

SRN *(Brit) abbr of* **State Registered Nurse**

SS *abbr of* **steamship**

SSE *abbr of* **south-south-east** SSO

SSP *(Brit) abbr of* **statutory sick pay**

SST N *(US) abbr of* **supersonic transport** Überschallflugzeug *nt*

SSW *abbr of* **south-south-west** SSW

st *(Brit) abbr of* **stone(s)**

St. **a** *abbr of* **Street** Str. **b** *abbr of* **Saint** hl., St. **c** *abbr of* **Strait**

stab [stæb] **N** **a** *(with knife etc, wound, of pain)* Stich *m*; **~ wound** Stichwunde *f*; **to feel a ~ of pain** einen stechenden Schmerz empfinden; **to feel a ~ of guilt** ein schlechtes Gewissen haben, Gewissensbisse haben; **she felt a ~ of jealousy** plötzlich durchfuhr sie Eifersucht; **he felt a ~ of alarm/panic** plötzlich bekam er Angst/verspürte er Panik; **he felt a ~ of pity** das Mitleid schnitt ihm in die Seele; **a ~ in the back** *(fig)* ein Dolchstoß *m*

b *(inf: = try)* Versuch *m*; **to have a ~ at sth** etw probieren

VT *person* einen Stich versetzen *(+dat)*; *(several times)* einstechen auf *(+acc)*; *(= wound seriously)* niederstechen; *food* durchstechen; **to ~ sb (to death)** jdn erstechen; *(with dagger also)* jdn erdolchen; **to ~ sb with a knife, to ~ a knife into sb** jdn mit einem Messerstich/mit Messerstichen verletzen; **he ~bed his penknife into the desk** er stach sein Taschenmesser in den Tisch; **he was ~bed through the arm/heart** der Stich traf ihn am Arm/ins Herz; **to ~ a knife into sth** ein Messer in etw *(acc)* hineinstoßen; **to ~ a fork into sth** mit einer Gabel in etw *(acc)* hineinstechen; **to ~ sb in the back** *(lit)* jdm in den Rücken stechen; *(fig)* jdm in den Rücken fallen; **he ~bed the air with his finger** er fuchtelte in der Luft herum *(inf)*

VI **to ~ at sb/sth** *(with knife etc)* nach jdm/etw stechen; *(with finger)* auf jdn/etw zeigen

stabbing ['stæbɪŋ] **N** Messerstecherei *f* **ADJ** *pain* stechend; *fear, memory* durchdringend; **~ incident** Messerstecherei *f*

stability [stə'bɪlɪtɪ] N Stabilität *f*; *(of relationship also, of job)* Beständigkeit *f*; **(mental) ~** (seelische) Ausgeglichenheit

stability-oriented ADJ *policy* stabilitätsorientiert

stabilization [,steɪbəlaɪ'zeɪʃən] N Stabilisierung *f*

stabilize ['steɪbəlaɪz] **VT** *(Fin, Naut, Aviat)* stabilisieren **VI** sich stabilisieren

stabilizer ['steɪbəlaɪzə'] N *(Naut, Chem)* Stabilisator *m*; *(Aviat)* Stabilisierungsfläche *f*; *(US Aviat)* Höhenflosse *f*; *(on bicycle)* Stützrad *nt*

stable¹ ['steɪbl] ADJ *(+er)* stabil; *ladder, structure also* sicher; *relationship also, job* beständig, dauerhaft; *character* gefestigt; *(Psych, Med) condition, blood pressure* stabil; *weight* konstant; **mentally ~** ausgeglichen, innerlich gefestigt

stable² **N** *(= building)* Stall *m*; *(= group of racehorses)* (Renn)stall *m*; **riding ~s** Reitstall *m*; **to be out of the same ~** *(fig)* aus dem gleichen Stall stammen; **to close** *or* **shut** *or* **lock the ~ door after the horse has bolted** *(prov)* den Brunnen erst zudecken, wenn das Kind hineingefallen ist *(prov)* **VT** *(= put in stable)* in den Stall bringen; *(= keep in stable)* im Stall halten; **he ~s his horses with the trainer** seine Pferde stehen im Stall des Trainers

stable: **stableboy** N Stallbursche *m*; **stable companion** N = **stablemate**; **stable door** N quer geteilte Tür; **stablelad** *(Brit)*, **stableman** N Stallbursche *m*; **stablemate** N *(= horse)* Pferd *nt* aus demselben Stall

stabling ['steɪblɪŋ] N Stallungen *pl*, Ställe *pl*

stab wound N Stichwunde *f*

staccato [stə'kɑ:təʊ] ADJ, ADV *(Mus)* staccato, stakkato; *(fig)* abgehackt

stack [stæk] **N** **a** *(= pile)* Haufen *m*; *(neatly piled)* Stoß *m*, Stapel *m*; *(Comput)* Stapel *m*, Stack *m*; *(of rifles)* Pyramide *f*; **to be in the ~** *(Aviat)* kreisen, Warteschleifen *pl* ziehen *(over* über *+dat)*

b *(inf: = lots)* Haufen *m (inf)*; **~s** jede Menge *(inf)*; **~s of time/helpers** jede Menge *(inf)* Zeit/Hilfskräfte

c *(in library: also* **stacks***)* Magazin *nt*

d = **chimney stack, smokestack**

e *(Geol)* Felssäule *f*

VT **a** *(= pile up)* stapeln *(also Comput)*; *shelves* einräumen; **to ~ up** aufstapeln

b *(Aviat)* **incoming planes had to be ~ed** ankommende Maschinen mussten kreisen *or* Warteschleifen ziehen

c *(US Cards)* packen, *beim Mischen betrügen*; **the cards** *or* **odds are ~ed against us** *(fig)* wir haben keine großen Chancen

VI sich stapeln lassen; **~ing chairs** Stühle, die sich (gut) stapeln lassen

stacked [stækt] ADJ *(inf)* **to be (well) ~** einen großen *or* üppigen Vorbau haben *(inf)*, Holz vor der Hütte haben *(inf)*

stacker ['stækə'] N *(for printer)* Ablage *f*

stack fault ['stæk,fɔ:lt] N *(Comput)* Stapelfehler *m*

stacking box ['stækɪŋ,bɒks] N Stapelbox *f*

stadium ['steɪdɪəm] N *pl* **-s** *or* **stadia** ['steɪdɪə] Stadion *nt*

staff [stɑ:f] **N** **a** *(= personnel)* Personal *nt*; *(Sch, Univ)* Kollegium *nt*, Lehrkörper *m (form)*; *(of one department, on one project)* Mitarbeiterstab *m*; **all the ~ support this idea** die ganze Belegschaft *or (Sch, Univ)* das ganze Kollegium unterstützt diesen Vorschlag; **we have a large ~** wir haben viel Personal/ein großes Kollegium/einen großen Mitarbeiterstab; **we don't have enough ~ to complete the project** wir haben nicht genügend Mitarbeiter, um das Projekt zu beenden; **editorial ~** Redaktion *f*, Redaktionsstab *m*; **administrative ~** Verwaltungsstab *m*, Verwaltungspersonal *nt*; **a member of ~** ein Mitarbeiter *m*, eine Mitarbeiterin; *(Sch)* ein Kollege *m*, eine Kollegin; **my fellow members of ~** meine Kollegen; **we have 30 women on the ~** bei uns sind 30 Frauen angestellt; **to be on the ~** zum Personal/Kollegium/Mitarbeiterstab gehören; **are you ~?** *(inf)* arbeiten Sie hier?; **he joined the** *or* **our ~ in 1996** er arbeitet seit 1996 bei uns; **he has left our ~** er arbeitet nicht mehr hier

b *pl* **-s** *or (old)* **staves** *(= stick, symbol of authority)* Stab *m*; *(= flagstaff)* Stock *m*; *(fig liter: = support)* Stütze *f*; **~ of office** Amtsstab *m*; **the ~ of life** das wichtigste Nahrungsmittel

c *(Mil: = general staff)* Stab *m*

d *pl* **staves** *(Mus)* Notenlinien *pl*, Notensystem *nt*

VT *department* Mitarbeiter finden für; *hospital, shop, hotel* mit Personal besetzen, Personal finden für; *school* mit Lehrpersonal besetzen; **the kitchens are ~ed by foreigners** das Küchenpersonal besteht aus Ausländern

staff: **staff association** N ≈ Betriebsrat *m*; **staff canteen** N (Betriebs)kantine *f*; **staff college** N Generalstabsakademie *f*

staffed [stɑ:ft] ADJ *hospital, hotel* mit Personal besetzt; *railway station* bemannt; **to be well ~** gut besetzt sein, ausreichend Personal haben

staffer ['stɑ:fə'] N *(esp US)* Mitarbeiter(in) *m(f)*

staffing ['stɑ:fɪŋ] N Stellenbesetzung *f*

staffing: **staffing costs** PL Personalkosten *pl*; **staffing problem** N Problem *nt* mit der Stellenbesetzung

staff: **staff notation** N Notenschrift *f*; **staff nurse** N *(Brit)* (voll)ausgebildete Krankenschwester, Vollschwester *f (inf)*; **staff officer** N Stabsoffizier(in) *m(f)*; **staff problem** N Personalproblem *nt*; **staffroom** N Lehrerzimmer *nt*; **staff training** N betriebliche Ausbildung

stag [stæg] **N** **a** (*Zool*: = *deer*) Hirsch *m*; (= *male animal*) Bock *m*, Bulle *m* **b** (*Brit, Fin*) Spekulant(in) *m(f)* (*der/die junge Aktien aufkauft*) **c** (*inf*) Mann, der solo ist (*inf*) **ADJ** *film, weekend etc* für Männer **ADV** **to go ~** solo ausgehen (*inf*)

stag beetle N Hirschkäfer *m*

stage [steɪdʒ] **N** **a** (*Theat, fig*) Bühne *f*; **the ~** (= *profession*) das Theater, die Bühne; **to be on/go on/leave the ~** (*as career*) beim Theater sein/zum Theater gehen/das Theater verlassen; **to go on ~** (*actor*) die Bühne betreten; (*play*) anfangen; **to come off ~, to leave the ~** von der Bühne abtreten; **to put a play on the ~** ein Stück aufführen *or* auf die Bühne bringen; **to write for the ~** Theater- *or* Bühnenstücke schreiben; **to adapt a novel for the ~** einen Roman fürs Theater bearbeiten; **to hold** *or* **dominate the ~** (*lit, fig*) die Szene beherrschen; **the ~ was set** (*lit*) das Bühnenbild war aufgebaut; (*fig*) alles war vorbereitet; **to set the ~ for sth** (*fig*) den Weg für etw bereiten; **the ~ was set for a confrontation** die Situation war reif für eine Auseinandersetzung
b (= *platform in hall*) Podium *nt*
c (= *period*) Stadium *nt*; (*of process, operation, development*) Phase *f*; **at this ~ such a thing is impossible** zum gegenwärtigen Zeitpunkt ist das unmöglich; **at this ~ in the negotiations** an diesem Punkt der Verhandlungen; **at this ~ in the game** (*fig*) zu diesem Zeitpunkt; **in the early/final ~(s)** im Anfangs-/Endstadium; **at an early ~ in its history** ganz zu Anfang seiner Geschichte; **what ~ is your thesis at?** wie weit sind Sie mit Ihrer Dissertation?; **I'm at the talking ~ with the club** ich befinde mich mit dem Klub gerade in Gesprächen; **we have reached a ~ where …** wir sind an einem Punkt angelangt, wo …; **to go through a difficult ~** eine schwierige Phase durchmachen; **to be at the experimental ~** im Versuchsstadium sein
d (= *part of journey, race etc*) Abschnitt *m*, Etappe *f*; (= *fare stage*) Teilstrecke *f*, Fahrzone *f*; (= *actual bus stop*) Zahlgrenze *f*; **in** *or* **by (easy) ~s** (*lit*) etappenweise; (*fig also*) Schritt für Schritt
e (= *section of rocket*) Stufe *f*; **a three-stage rocket** eine dreistufige Rakete
f (*old inf*, = *stagecoach*) Postkutsche *f*
VT *play* aufführen, auf die Bühne bringen; *competition, event* durchführen; *accident, scene, coup* inszenieren; *welcome* arrangieren; *demonstration, strike, protest etc* veranstalten; **to ~ a recovery** sich erholen; **to ~ a comeback** sein Come-back *or* Comeback machen; **the play is ~d in the 19th century** das Stück spielt im 19. Jahrhundert; **~ed reading** Bühnenlesung *f*, dramatische Lesung

stage: **stage box** N Bühnen- *or* Prosceniumsloge *f*; **stage career** N Bühnen- *or* Theaterkarriere *f*; **stagecoach** N Postkutsche *f*; **stagecraft** N dramaturgisches Können; (*of actor*) schauspielerisches Können; **stage design** N Bühnenbild *f*; **stage designer** N Bühnenbildner(in) *m(f)*; **stage direction** N Bühnen- *or* Regieanweisung *f*; **stage director** N Regisseur(in) *m(f)*; **stage-dive** VI (*rock musician etc*) von der Bühne ins Publikum springen; **stage door** N Bühneneingang *m*; **stage effect** N Bühneneffekt *m*; **stage fright** N Lampenfieber *nt*; **to have an attack of ~** Lampenfieber haben; **stage hand** N Bühnenarbeiter(in) *m(f)*; **stage-manage** VT (*lit*) Inspizient sein bei; (*fig*) *demonstration, argument* inszenieren; **stage manager** N Inspizient(in) *m(f)*; **stage name** N Künstlername *m*; **stage play** N Bühnenstück *nt*

stager ['steɪdʒəʳ] N **old ~** alter Hase (*inf*)

stage: **stage race** N (*Cycling*) Etappenrennen *nt*; **stage rights** PL Aufführungs- *or* Bühnenrechte *pl*; **stage set** N Bühnenbild *nt*; **stage setting** N Bühnenbild *nt*; **stage-struck** ADJ theaterbesessen; **to be ~** unbedingt zum Theater wollen; **stage whisper** N Bühnenflüstern *nt*; **to say sth in a ~** etw hörbar flüstern; **stage win** N (*Cycling*) Etappensieg *f*

stagey ADJ = **stagy**

stagflation [stæg'fleɪʃən] N (*Econ*) Stagflation *f*

stagger ['stægəʳ] **VI** schwanken, taumeln; (*because of illness, weakness*) wanken; (*drunkenly*) torkeln; **he was ~ing along the street** er taumelte die Straße entlang
VT **a** (*fig*: = *amaze*: *news etc*) den Atem verschlagen (*+dat*), umhauen (*inf*); **he was ~ed to hear of his promotion** die Nachricht von seiner Beförderung verschlug ihm die Sprache *or* haute ihn um (*inf*); **you ~ me!** da bin ich aber platt! (*inf*)
b *hours, holidays* staffeln, stufen; *seats, spokes* versetzt anordnen, versetzen
N **a** Taumeln *nt*; **to give a ~** taumeln, schwanken; **with a ~** taumelnd, schwankend
b **staggers** *sing or pl* (*Vet*) (Dumm)koller *m*

staggered ['stægəd] ADJ **a** (= *amazed*) verblüfft, platt (*inf*) **b** *working hours etc* gestaffelt, gestuft; **they work ~ hours** ihre Arbeitszeit ist gestaffelt; **a ~ junction** eine Kreuzung mit versetzt angeordneten Straßen; **a ~ start** ein versetzter Start; (*in time*) ein zeitlich gestaffelter Start

staggering ['stægərɪŋ] ADJ **a** **to be a ~ blow (to sb/sth)** ein harter *or* schwerer Schlag (für jdn/etw) sein **b** (= *amazing*) atemberaubend, umwerfend

staggeringly ['stægərɪŋlɪ] ADV (= *amazingly*) umwerfend, erstaunlich; *beautiful, successful* umwerfend; **~ high prices** unglaublich hohe Preise

stag: **staghound** N Jagdhund *m* (*für die Hirschjagd*); **stag hunt, stag hunting** N Hirschjagd *f*

stagily ['steɪdʒɪlɪ] ADV *dressed, made up* auffallend

staginess ['steɪdʒɪnɪs] N auffällige Art

staging ['steɪdʒɪŋ] N **a** (= *production*) Inszenieren *nt*; (= *scenery etc*) Inszenierung *f* **b** (= *stage*) Bühne *f*

staging area N (*esp Mil, of troops*) Bereitstellungsraum *m*; (= *assembly point*) Auffangsraum *m*

stagnancy ['stægnənsɪ] N Stagnieren *nt*; (*of trade also*) Stagnation *f*, Stocken *nt*

stagnant ['stægnənt] ADJ (= *still, not moving*) *air, water* (still)stehend *attr*, gestaut; (= *foul, stale*) *water* abgestanden; *air* verbraucht; *trade* stagnierend, stockend; *mind* träge; **the economy/market is ~** die Wirtschaft/der Markt stagniert

stagnate [stæg'neɪt] VI (= *not circulate*) stagnieren; (= *become foul, water*) abstehen; (*air*) verbraucht werden; (*trade*) stagnieren, stocken; (*person*) verdummen; (*mind*) einrosten

stagnation [stæg'neɪʃən] N Stagnieren *nt*; (*of trade also*) Stagnation *f*, Stocken *nt*; (*of air*) Stau *m*; (*of person*) Verdummung *f*; (*of mind*) Verlangsamung *f*

stag: **stag night** N Saufabend *m* (*inf*) des Bräutigams mit seinen Kumpeln (*am Vorabend der Hochzeit*); **stag party** N **a** Herrenabend *m* **b** = **stag night**

stagy ['steɪdʒɪ] ADJ (+*er*) theatralisch; *appearance* auffallend

staid [steɪd] ADJ (+*er*) seriös, gesetzt; *community* respektabel; *place, product* seriös; *colour* gedeckt

staidly ['steɪdlɪ] ADV gesetzt; *dressed* gedeckt

staidness ['steɪdnɪs] N Gesetztheit *f*

stain [steɪn] **N** **a** (*lit*) Fleck *m*; (*fig*) Makel *m*; **a blood ~** ein Blutfleck *m*; **a grease ~** ein Fettfleck *m*; **a mud ~** ein Schlammspritzer *m*; **~ remover** Fleckenentferner *m*; **without a ~ on his character** ohne (einen) Makel **b** (= *colorant*) (Ein)färbemittel *nt*; (= *woodstain*) Beize *f* **VT** beflecken; (= *colour*) einfärben; (*with woodstain*) beizen **VI** **a** (= *leave a stain*) Flecken hinterlassen **b** (= *become stained*) fleckig werden, Flecken bekommen

stained [steɪnd] ADJ *fingers, teeth* gefärbt; *clothes, floor* fleckig, befleckt (*geh*); *glass* bunt, bemalt; *reputation* befleckt; **~-glass window** Buntglasfenster *nt*, farbiges Glasfenster; **~ with blood** blutbefleckt; **the white shirt was ~ crimson with blood** das weiße Hemd hatte dunkelrote Blutflecken

staining ['steɪnɪŋ] N **a** (= *change in colour*) (Ver)färbung *f*; (= *soiling*) Verschmutzung *f* **b** (*esp Tech*: = *dyeing*) Färben *nt*; (*of wood*) Beizen *nt*

stainless ['steɪnlɪs] ADJ **a** *character* tadellos **b** (= *rust-resistant*) rostfrei

stainless steel N rostfreier (Edel)stahl; **"stainless steel"** „rostfrei"; **~ cutlery** rostfreies Besteck

stair [steəʳ] N **a** (= *step*) Stufe *f* **b** *usu pl* (= *stairway*) Treppe *f*; **at the top of the ~s** oben an der Treppe; **below ~s** (*Brit, dated*) beim (Haus)personal → **flight**[1]

stair: **stair carpet** N Treppenläufer *m*; **staircase** N Treppe *f*; **stair climber** N (*in fitness centre*) Stepper *m*; **stair lift** N Treppenlift *m*; **stair rod** N Teppichstab *m*; **stairway** N Treppe *f*; **stairwell** N Treppenhaus *nt*

stake [steɪk] **N** **a** (= *post*) Pfosten *m*, Pfahl *m*; (*for vampires*) Pfahl *m*; (*for plant*) Stange *f*; (*for animal*) Pflock *m* → **pull up**
b (= *place of execution*) Scheiterhaufen *m*; **to die at the ~** auf dem Scheiterhaufen sterben, verbrannt werden; **he was ready to go to the ~** *or* **be burned at the ~ for his principles** er war bereit, sich für seine Prinzipien ans Kreuz nageln zu lassen
c (= *bet*) Einsatz *m*; (= *financial interest*) Anteil *m*; **to be at ~** auf dem Spiel stehen; **he has a lot at ~** er hat viel zu verlieren; **to have a ~ in sth** (*in business*) einen Anteil an etw (*dat*) haben; *in the future* von etw betroffen werden; **he has a big ~ in the success of the plan** für ihn hängt viel vom Erfolg des Planes ab; **that's precisely the issue at ~** genau darum geht es; **the issue at ~ is not …** es steht nicht zur Debatte, ob …
d **stakes** **PL** (= *prize*) Gewinn *m*; **the Newmarket ~s** der Große Preis von Newmarket; **to raise the ~s** (*lit, fig*) den Einsatz erhöhen
VT **a** *animal* anpflocken
b (*also* **stake up**) *plant* hochbinden; *fence* abstützen
c (= *bet, risk*) setzen (*on* auf +*acc*); (*esp US*: = *back financially*) finanziell unterstützen; **to ~ one's life on sth** seine Hand für etw ins Feuer legen; **to ~ one's reputation on sth** sein Wort für etw verpfänden; **to ~ a/one's claim to sth** sich (*dat*) ein Anrecht auf etw (*acc*) sichern

▶ **stake off** *or* **out** VT *sep land* abstecken

▶ **stake out** VT *sep place* umstellen; *person* überwachen

stakeholder ['steɪkhəʊldəʳ] N Teilhaber(in) *m(f)*

stakeholder society N Teilhabergesellschaft *f*

stakeout ['steɪkaʊt] N Überwachung *f*

stalactite ['stæləktaɪt] N Stalaktit *m*

stalagmite ['stæləgmaɪt] N Stalagmit *m*

stale [steɪl] ADJ (+*er*) **a** (= *old, musty*) alt; *cake* trocken; *bread, biscuit* altbacken; (*in smell*) muffig; *water, beer, wine* abgestanden, schal; *air* verbraucht; *cigarette smoke* kalt; **to go ~** (*food*) verderben; **to smell ~** muffig riechen **b** (*fig*) *news* veraltet; *joke* abgedroschen; *idea* abgegriffen; *athlete, pianist etc* ausgepumpt, verbraucht; **to be ~** (*person*) alles nur noch routinemäßig machen; **to become ~** (*relationship*) an Reiz verlieren; (*situation*) langweilig werden; **I'm getting ~** ich mache langsam alles nur noch routinemäßig; **don't let yourself get ~** pass auf, dass du nicht in Routine verfällst

stalemate ['steɪlmeɪt] **N** (*Chess*) Patt *nt*; (*fig*) Patt(situation *f*) *nt*, Sackgasse *f*; **to reach ~** (*lit*) ein Patt erreichen; (*fig*) in eine Sackgasse geraten; **to end in (a) ~** (*lit*) mit (einem) Patt enden, patt enden; (*fig*) in einer Sackgasse enden **VT** (*Chess*) patt setzen; (*fig*) mattsetzen; *negotiations* zum Stillstand bringen

staleness ['steɪlnɪs] N **a** *(lit, of beer, water etc)* Schalheit *f*, Abgestandenheit *f*; *(of bread, biscuit)* Altbackenheit *f*; *(of taste, smell)* Muffigkeit *f*; **the ~ of the air made them sleepy** die verbrauchte Luft machte sie schläfrig **b** *(fig, of joke)* Abgedroschenheit *f*; **the ~ of the news** die veraltete Nachricht; **he practised to the point of ~** er übte, bis er langsam alles nur noch routinemäßig machte

stalk¹ [stɔːk] VT *game* sich anpirschen an *(+acc)*; *(animal)* beschleichen, sich heranschleichen an *(+acc)*; *person* sich anschleichen an *(+acc)*; *(= harass)* belästigen, verfolgen; **he's ~ing his former girlfriend** er stellt seiner Ex-Freundin nach; **evil ~ed the streets** *(liter)* das Böse ging in den Straßen um VI **a** *(= walk haughtily)* stolzieren **b** *(Hunt)* pirschen; **to go ~ing** auf die Pirsch gehen

stalk² N *(of plant, leaf)* Stiel *m*; *(= cabbage stalk)* Strunk *m*; **his eyes came out on ~s** *(inf)* er bekam Stielaugen *(inf)*

stalker ['stɔːkəʳ] N **a** *(Hunt)* Pirschjäger(in) *m(f)* **b** *(= pursuer) jd, der die ständige Nähe zu einer von ihm verehrten (meist prominenten) Person sucht oder sie mit Anrufen, Briefen etc belästigt*

stalking ['stɔːkɪŋ] N **a** *(Hunt)* Pirschjagd *f* **b** *(Jur) das Verfolgen und Belästigen einer (meist prominenten) Person*

stalking-horse ['stɔːkɪŋ,hɔːs] N *(fig: = person)* Strohmann *m*/-frau *f*; *(= pretext)* Vorwand *m*

stall [stɔːl] N **a** *(in stable)* Box *f*, Bucht *f*; *(old, = stable)* Stall *m*
b *(at market etc)* Stand *m*
c stalls PL *(Brit: Theat, Film)* Parkett *nt*; **in the ~s** im Parkett
d *(Eccl)* Kirchenstuhl *m*; **~s** Chorgestühl *nt*
e *(Aviat)* überzogener Flug; **to do a ~ turn** *(Aviat)* ein Flugzeug auffangen und neu starten
VT **a** *horse, cow* einstellen
b *(Aut)* abwürgen; *(Aviat)* überziehen
c *(also* **stall off***)* *person* hinhalten; *decision, process, bill* hinauszögern; *talks* verzögern
VI **a** *(engine)* absterben; *(Aviat)* überziehen
b *(= delay)* Zeit schinden *(inf)*; **stop ~ing!** hören Sie auf auszuweichen *or* drum herumzureden *(inf)!*; **to ~ over a decision** eine Entscheidung hinauszögern; **to ~ for time** versuchen, Zeit zu gewinnen *or* zu schinden *(inf)*

stall-feed ['stɔːlfiːd] VT *cattle etc* in Boxen mästen

stalling speed N *(Aviat)* kritische Geschwindigkeit

stallion ['stæljən] N Hengst *m*; *(for breeding)* Zuchthengst *m*

stalwart ['stɔːlwət] ADJ **a** *(in spirit)* treu, unentwegt; *supporter* treu, getreu; *belief* unerschütterlich **b** *(in build)* kräftig, robust N *(= supporter)* (getreuer) Anhänger; **the party leader and his ~s** der Parteichef und seine Getreuen

stalwartly ['stɔːlwətlɪ] ADV *fight, oppose* tapfer, unentwegt; *support* treu; *believe* unerschütterlich; *built* kräftig

stamen ['steɪmən] N Staubgefäß *nt*

stamina ['stæmɪnə] N Stehvermögen *nt*, Durchhaltevermögen *nt*

stammer ['stæməʳ] N Stottern *nt*; **to speak with a ~** stottern; **he has a bad ~** er stottert stark VT *(also* **stammer out***)* stammeln VI stottern; **to start ~ing** ins Stottern geraten

stammerer ['stæmərəʳ] N Stotterer *m*, Stotterin *f*

stammering ['stæmərɪŋ] N *(act)* Stottern *nt*, Stammeln *nt*; *(= stammered speech)* Gestotter(e) *nt*, Gestammel(e) *nt*

stammeringly ['stæmərɪŋlɪ] ADV stammelnd, stotternd

stamp [stæmp] N **a** *(= postage stamp)* (Brief)marke *f*, (Post)wertzeichen *nt (form)*; *(= insurance stamp, revenue stamp etc)* Marke *f*; *(= trading stamp)* (Rabatt)marke *f*; *(= charity stamp, airmail stamp, sticker)* Aufkleber *m*; **to collect (postage) ~s** Briefmarken *pl* sammeln; **to save (trading) ~s** Rabattmarken sammeln
b *(= rubber stamp, die, impression)* Stempel *m*
c *(fig)* **a man of his ~** ein Mann seines Schlags; **to bear the ~ of the expert/of authenticity** den Stempel des Experten/die Züge der Echtheit tragen
VT **a to ~ one's foot** (mit dem Fuß) (auf)stampfen; **he ~ed the turf back into place** er stampfte die Sode wieder an ihrem Platz fest
b *(= put postage stamp on)* freimachen, frankieren; **a ~ed addressed envelope** ein frankierter Rückumschlag
c *paper, document etc (with rubber stamp)* stempeln; *(with embossing machine)* prägen; *name, pattern* aufstempeln, aufprägen (*on* auf *+acc*); *(fig)* ausweisen (*as* als)
VI *(= walk)* sta(m)pfen, trampeln; *(disapprovingly, in dancing)* (mit dem Fuß) (auf)stampfen; *(horse)* aufstampfen; **he was ~ing about the house** er trampelte im Haus herum; **to ~ in/out** hinein-/hinausstapfen; **you ~ed on my foot** Sie haben mir auf den Fuß getreten

▶ **stamp on** VT *sep pattern, design* aufprägen; **to stamp a pattern on sth** auf etw *(acc)* ein Muster (auf)prägen; **to be stamped on sb's memory** sich jdm eingeprägt haben; **the new leader has stamped his personality on the party** der neue Vorsitzende hat der Partei seine Persönlichkeit aufgeprägt *or* seinen Stempel aufgedrückt; **to stamp one's authority on sth** einer Sache *(dat)* seine Autorität aufzwingen VI *+prep obj (= put one's foot on)* treten auf *(+acc)*; *(fig)* im Keim ersticken; **to stamp on the brakes** *(lit)* auf die Bremse treten; *(fig)* die Notbremse ziehen

▶ **stamp out** VT *sep* **a** *fire* austreten; *(fig: = eradicate) epidemic, crime, practice* ausrotten; *opposition* unterdrücken, zunichtemachen; *trouble* niederschlagen; *rebels* unschädlich machen **b** *(= punch or cut out) pattern, shape* ausstanzen **c** *rhythm* (mit)stampfen VI heraustrampeln, heraussta(m)pfen

stamp: **stamp album** N Briefmarkenalbum *nt*; **stamp collecting** N Briefmarkensammeln *nt*; **stamp collection** N Briefmarkensammlung *f*; **stamp collector** N Briefmarkensammler(in) *m(f)*; **stamp dealer** N Briefmarkenhändler(in) *m(f)*; **stamp duty** N *(Brit)* (Stempel)gebühr *f*

stampede [stæm'piːd] N *(of horses, cattle)* wilde Flucht; *(of people)* Massenandrang *m*, Massenansturm *m* (*on* auf *+acc*); *(to escape)* wilde *or* panikartige Flucht; **the exodus turned into a ~** der Exodus geriet zur Panik VT *cattle, horses, crowd* in (wilde *or* helle) Panik versetzen; **to ~ sb into doing sth** *(fig)* jdn dazu drängen, etw zu tun; **let's not be ~d** *(fig)* wir wollen uns nicht kopfscheu machen lassen VI durchgehen; *(crowd)* losstürmen (*for* auf *+acc*)

stamping ground ['stæmpɪŋ,graʊnd] N = **stomping ground**

stamp machine N Briefmarkenautomat *m*

stance [stæns] N *(= posture, Sport)* Haltung *f*; *(= mental attitude also)* Einstellung *f*; *(Cricket, Golf etc also)* Stand *m*; **to take up a ~** *(lit)* in Stellung gehen; *(fig)* eine Haltung einnehmen

stand [stænd] ✪ 7.3 *vb: pret, ptp* **stood** N **a** *(= position)* Platz *m*, Standort *m*; *(fig)* Standpunkt *m*, Einstellung *f* (*on* zu); **my ~ is that …** ich stehe auf dem Standpunkt, dass …, ich vertrete die Einstellung, dass …; **to take a ~ (on a matter)** (zu einer Angelegenheit) eine Einstellung vertreten; **to take a firm ~** einen festen Standpunkt vertreten (*on* zu)
b *(Mil: = resistance)* Widerstand *m*; *(= battle)* Gefecht *nt*; **to make a ~** *(lit, fig)* sich widersetzen, Widerstand leisten; **that was their last ~** das war ihr letztes Gefecht
c *(= taxi stand)* Stand *m*
d *(Brit Theat)* Gastspiel *nt*; *(of pop group etc)* Konzert *nt*
e *(= furniture, lamp stand, music stand)* Ständer *m*
f *(= market stall etc)* Stand *m*
g *(= band stand)* Podium *nt*
h *(Brit Sport)* Tribüne *f*; *(US Jur)* Zeugenstand *m*; **(we sat) in the ~** (wir saßen) auf der Tribüne; **to take the ~** *(Jur)* in den Zeugenstand treten
i *(esp US: Forest)* (Baum)bestand *m*
VT **a** *(= place)* stellen → **stead, head**
b *(= withstand) pressure, close examination etc (= object)* standhalten *(+dat)*; *(person)* gewachsen sein *(+dat)*; *test* bestehen; *climate* vertragen; *heat, noise* ertragen, aushalten; *loss, cost* verkraften; **the wall could ~ another coat of paint** *(inf)* die Wand könnte noch einen Anstrich vertragen
c *(inf: = put up with) person, noise, interruptions etc* aushalten; **I can't ~ him/it** *(= don't like)* ich kann ihn/das nicht ausstehen; **I can't ~ being kept waiting** ich kann es nicht leiden *or* ausstehen, wenn man mich warten lässt; **I can't ~ it any longer** ich halte das nicht mehr (länger) aus
d *(Brit inf: = treat)* **to ~ sb a drink/a meal** jdm einen Drink/ein Essen spendieren
e to ~ trial vor Gericht stehen (*for* wegen)
VI **a** *(= be upright)* stehen; *(= get up)* aufstehen; **all ~!** alles aufstehen!; **don't just ~ there(, do something)!** stehen Sie nicht nur (dumm) rum, tun Sie was! *(inf)*; **to ~ still** still stehen; **we stood talking** wir standen da und unterhielten uns; **~ and deliver!** *(old, hum)* anhalten, her mit dem Zeug! *(inf)* → **attention, ease**
b *(= measure, person)* groß sein; *(tree etc)* hoch sein
c *(= be situated)* stehen; **it has stood there for 600 years** es steht da schon seit 600 Jahren
d *(= remain unchanged)* stehen; *(fig)* bestehen (bleiben)
e to ~ as a candidate kandidieren → *also* **stand for a**
f *(= continue to be valid, offer, argument, promise)* gelten; *(objection, contract)* gültig bleiben; *(decision, record, account)* stehen; **the theory ~s or falls by** *or* **on this** damit steht und fällt die Theorie
g *(= be at a certain level, thermometer, record)* stehen (*at* auf *+dat*); *(sales)* liegen (*at* bei)
h *(fig: = be in a position)* **we ~ to lose/gain a lot** wir können sehr viel verlieren/gewinnen; **he ~s to make a lot of money** er wird wohl eine Menge Geld (dabei) verdienen; **what do we ~ to gain by it?** was springt für uns dabei heraus? *(inf)*, was bringt uns *(dat)* das ein?
i *(fig: = be placed)* **how do we ~?** wie stehen wir?; **I'd like to know where I ~ (with him)** ich möchte wissen, woran ich (bei ihm) bin; **where do you ~ with him?** wie stehen Sie sich mit ihm?; **where do you ~ on this issue?** welchen Standpunkt vertreten Sie in dieser Frage?; **as things ~** nach Lage der Dinge; **as it ~s** so wie die Sache aussieht; **to ~ alone** *(= be best)* unerreicht sein; **to ~ accused of sth** einer Sache *(gen)* angeklagt sein
j *(fig: = be, continue to be)* **to ~ firm** *or* **fast** festbleiben; **to ~ ready** sich bereithalten; **to ~ in need of help** Hilfe brauchen; **to ~ together** zusammenhalten; **to ~ (as) security for sb** für jdn bürgen; **nothing now ~s between us** es steht nichts mehr zwischen uns
k to leave sb/sth ~ing *(Brit inf)* jdn/etw in den Schatten stellen

▶ **stand about** *(Brit)* or **around** VI herumstehen

▶ **stand apart** VI *(lit)* abseitsstehen; *(fig)* sich fernhalten; **to stand apart from the others** abseitsstehen

▶ **stand aside** VI *(lit)* zur Seite treten; *(fig: = withdraw)* zurücktreten; *(= play no part)* (tatenlos) danebenstehen

▶ **stand back** VI *(= move back)* zurücktreten; *(= be situated at a distance)* zurückstehen, abliegen, zurückliegen; *(fig: = distance oneself)* Abstand nehmen; *(= play no part)* (tatenlos) danebenstehen; **to stand back and do nothing** tatenlos zusehen

▶ **stand by** VI **a** *(= remain uninvolved)* (unbeteiligt) danebenstehen; **to stand by and do nothing** tatenlos zusehen **b** *(= be on alert)*

sich bereithalten; **to stand by for further news** auf weitere Nachrichten warten **VI** +*prep obj* **to stand by a promise/sb** ein Versprechen/zu jdm halten

▸**stand down** VI **a** (= *retire, withdraw*) zurücktreten **b** (*Jur*) den Zeugenstand verlassen **c** (*Mil*) aufgelöst werden

▸**stand for** VI +*prep obj* **a** (= *be candidate for*) kandidieren für, sich zur Wahl stellen für; **to stand for Labour** für Labour kandidieren; **to stand for (the post of) chairman** für den Posten des Vorsitzenden kandidieren; **to stand for election** (in einer Wahl) kandidieren, sich zur Wahl stellen; **to stand for re-election** sich zur Wiederwahl stellen; **to stand for election to sth** für etw kandidieren; **she is standing for election to Parliament** sie kandidiert in den Parlamentswahlen **b** (= *be abbreviation for, represent*) stehen für, bedeuten **c** (= *put up with*) hinnehmen, sich (*dat*) gefallen lassen

▸**stand in** VI einspringen

▸**stand off** VI (*Naut*) seewärts anliegen

▸**stand out** VI **a** (= *project*) hervorstehen; (*land, balcony*) herausragen **b** (= *contrast, be noticeable*) hervorstechen, auffallen; **to stand out against sth** sich gegen etw *or* von etw abheben; **to stand out from the others** hervorstechen, auffallen **c** (= *hold out*) **to stand out against sth** weiterhin gegen etw Widerstand leisten; **to stand out for sth** auf etw (*acc*) bestehen

▸**stand over** **VI** (*work, project*) liegen bleiben; **to let sth stand over** etw liegen lassen **VI** +*prep obj* (= *supervise*) auf die Finger sehen (+*dat*); **I can't work with you standing over me** ich kann nicht arbeiten, wenn du mir (dauernd) über die Schulter siehst

▸**stand to** VI (*Mil*) in Bereitschaft *or* in Waffen stehen

▸**stand up** **VI** **a** (= *get up*) aufstehen; (= *be standing*) stehen; **stand up straight!** stell dich gerade hin; **to stand up and be counted** sich zu seiner Meinung *or* seinen Überzeugungen bekennen **b** (= *be valid, argument*) überzeugen; (*Jur*) bestehen **c** **to stand up for sb/sth** für jdn/etw eintreten; **to stand up to sth** (*to test, pressure, object*) einer Sache (*dat*) standhalten; (*person*) einer Sache (*dat*) gewachsen sein; *to hard wear* etw vertragen *or* aushalten; **to stand up to sb** sich jdm gegenüber behaupten **VT** *sep* **a** (= *put upright*) hinstellen **b** (*inf*) *boyfriend, sb* versetzen

stand-alone ['stændələʊn] N (*Comput*) eigenständiges Gerät, Stand-alone-Gerät *nt*

standard ['stændəd] **N** **a** (= *average, established norm*) Norm *f*; (= *criterion*) Maßstab *m*; (*usu pl*: = *moral standards*) (sittliche) Maßstäbe *pl*; **to set a good ~** Maßstäbe setzen; **to be above/below ~** über/unter der Norm sein *or* liegen; **to be up to ~** den Anforderungen genügen; **his (moral) ~s are abysmally low** er hat eine erschreckend niedere Moral; **to conform to society's ~s** den Wertvorstellungen der Gesellschaft entsprechen; **he sets himself very high ~s** er stellt hohe Anforderungen an sich (*acc*) selbst; **by any ~(s)** egal, welche Maßstäbe man anlegt; **by today's ~(s)** aus heutiger Sicht **b** (= *degree, level*) Niveau *nt*; **~ of living** Lebensstandard *m*; **~ of culture** kulturelles Niveau; **first-year university ~** Wissensstand *m* des ersten Studienjahrs; **of high/low ~** von hohem/niedrigem Niveau **c** (*Measurement*) (Maß)einheit *f*, Standard *m*; (= *monetary standard*) (Währungs)standard *m*; **these coins don't contain enough silver to conform to the monetary ~** diese Münzen enthalten weniger Silber, als dem Münzfuß entspräche **d** (= *flag*) Flagge *f*, Fahne *f*; (*on car*) Stander *m*; (= *royal standard*) (königliche) Standarte **e** (= *pole*) Mast *m* **f** (*Hort*) (Hoch)stamm *m*; **~ rose** Stammrose *f* **g** (= *piece of popular music*) Klassiker *m* **ADJ** **a** (= *usual, customary*) üblich; (*Comm*) Standard-, (handels)üblich; (= *average*) *performance, work* durchschnittlich; (= *widely referred to*) Standard-; **~ model** Standardmodell *nt*; **~ weight** Normalgewicht *nt*; **such requirements are not ~** solche Forderungen sind nicht die Norm *or* Regel; **to be ~ practice** üblich sein **b** (*Ling*) (allgemein) gebräuchlich; **~ English** korrektes Englisch; **~ German** Hochdeutsch *nt*; **that word is hardly ~** dieses Wort ist ziemlich ungebräuchlich

standard: **standard assessment task** N (*Brit Sch*) *standardisierter schulischer Test in einem Kernfach*; **standard-bearer** N Fahnenträger(in) *m(f)*; (*fig also*) Bannerträger(in) *m(f)* (*old*); **standard button** N (*Comput*) Standardschaltfläche *f*; **standard class** N (*Rail*) zweite Klasse; **standard deviation** N Standardabweichung *f*; **standard format** N (*Comput*) Standardformat *nt*; **Standard Grade** N (*Scot Sch*) ≈ Realschulabschluss *m*; **standard-issue** ADJ zur Standardausrüstung gehörend; (*Mil*) standardmäßig; **to be standard issue** Standardausführung sein; **a ~ shirt** (= *ordinary*) ein ganz normales Hemd, ein Nullachtfünfzehnhemd *nt* (*pej inf*)

standardization [ˌstændədaɪ'zeɪʃən] N (*of education, style, approach*) Vereinheitlichung *f*; (*of format, sizes*) Normung *f*, Standardisierung *f*

standardize ['stændədaɪz] **VT** *education, style, approach* vereinheitlichen; *format, sizes etc* normen, standardisieren **VI** **to ~ on sth** etw standardmäßig verwenden

standard: **standard lamp** N Stehlampe *f*; **standard letter** N Formbrief *m*; **standard pronunciation** N Standardaussprache *f*; **standard software** N Standardsoftware *f*; **standard time** N Standardzeit *f*

standby ['stændbaɪ] **N** **a** (= *person*) Ersatz *m*, Ersatzperson *f*; (*Sport*) Ersatz- *or* Auswechselspieler(in) *m(f)*; (= *thing*) Reserve *f*; (*Aviat*: = *plane*) Entlastungsflugzeug *nt*; (= *ticket*) Stand-by-Ticket *nt*; (= *passenger*) Passagier, der mit einem Stand-by-Ticket reist **b** (= *state of readiness*) **on ~** in Bereitschaft; (= *ready for action*) in Einsatzbereitschaft; **to be on 24-hour ~** 24 Stunden Bereitschaftsdienst haben **c** (*Tech*) Stand-by-Modus *m*, Stand-by *nt* **ADJ** *attr* (*Mil, Sport*) Reserve-, Ersatz-; **~ plane** Entlastungsflugzeug *nt*; **~ player** Ersatz- *or* Reservespieler(in) *m(f)*; **~ ticket** Stand-by-Ticket *nt*

standby mode N (*Tech*) Stand-by-Modus *m*

stand-down ['stænddaʊn] N **a** (*Mil*) Feuerpause *f* **b** (*in firm etc*: = *work stoppage*) (vorübergehende) Arbeitseinstellung *f* *or* -niederlegung *f*

standee [stæn'diː] N (*esp US*) *jd, der steht oder einen Stehplatz hat*

stand-in ['stændɪn] N (*Film, Theat*) Ersatz *m*

standing ['stændɪŋ] **N** **a** (*social*) Rang *m*, (gesellschaftliche) Stellung; (*professional*) Position *f*; (*financial*) (finanzielle) Verhältnisse *pl*; (= *repute*) Ruf *m*, Ansehen *nt*; **of high ~** von hohem Rang; (= *repute*) von hohem Ansehen; **a man of some ~** ein angesehener Mann; **what is his ~ locally?** was hält man in der Gegend von ihm?; **to be in good ~ with sb** gute Beziehungen zu jdm haben **b** (= *duration*) Dauer *f*; **a treaty of only six months' ~** ein Vertrag, der erst seit sechs Monaten besteht; **her husband of five years' ~** ihr Mann, mit dem sie seit fünf Jahren verheiratet ist; **of long ~** alt, langjährig; *relationship, agreement etc also* von langer Dauer **ADJ** *attr* **a** (= *established, permanent*) ständig; *rule, custom* bestehend; *army* stehend; **it's a ~ joke** das ist schon zu einem Witz geworden; **the ~ orders of an association** die Geschäftsordnung einer Gesellschaft **b** (= *from a standstill*) aus dem Stand; (= *erect*) *corn* auf dem Halm (stehend); **~ ticket** Stehplatzkarte *f*; **~ room only** nur Stehplätze; **to give sb a ~ ovation** jdm eine stehende Ovation darbringen; **to receive a ~ ovation** eine stehende Ovation erhalten, stürmischen Beifall ernten

standing: **standing charge** N Grundgebühr *f*, Grundpreis *m*; **standing committee** N ständiger Ausschuss; **standing order** N (*Brit Fin*) Dauerauftrag *m*; **to pay sth by ~** etw per Dauerauftrag bezahlen; **standing start** N (*Sport*) stehender Start; **from a ~** mit stehendem Start; **standing stone** N Menhir *m*; **circle of ~s** Steinkreis *m*

stand: **standoff** N (= *stalemate*) Patt *nt*, Pattsituation *f*; **standoffish** ADJ, **standoffishly** ADV [ˌstænd'ɒfɪʃ, -lɪ] (*inf*) distanziert; **standoffishness** N (*inf*) Distanziertheit *f*; **standpipe** N Steigrohr *nt*; **standpoint** N Standpunkt *m*; **from the ~ of the teacher** vom Standpunkt des Lehrers (aus) gesehen; **standstill** N Stillstand *m*; **to be at a ~** (*plane, train*) stehen; (*machines, traffic*) stillstehen; (*trade, factory, production*) ruhen; **to bring production to a ~** die Produktion lahmlegen *or* zum Erliegen bringen; **to come to a ~** (*person*) stehen bleiben, anhalten; (*vehicle*) zum Stehen kommen, anhalten; (*traffic, machines*) zum Stillstand kommen; (*industry etc*) zum Erliegen kommen; **stand-up** **ADJ** *attr meal* im Stehen; **~ buffet** Stehbüffet *nt*; **~ collar** Stehkragen *m*; **~ comedian** Bühnenkomiker(in) *m(f)*, Alleinunterhalter(in) *m(f)*; **~ comedy** Stand-up Comedy *f*; **~ fight** Schlägerei *f* **N** (*inf*) (= *comedy*) Stand-up Comedy *f*; (= *comedian*) Bühnenkomiker(in) *m(f)*, Alleinunterhalter(in) *m(f)*

stank [stæŋk] *pret of* **stink**

stannic ['stænɪk] ADJ Zinn-

stannic sulphide N Zinnsulfid *nt*

stanza ['stænzə] N Strophe *f*

staple[1] ['steɪpl] **N** Klammer *f*; (*for paper*) Heftklammer *f* **VT** heften; **to ~ sth together** etw zusammenheften

staple[2] **ADJ** Haupt-; **~ diet** Grund- *or* Hauptnahrung *f*; **~ subject** Hauptthema *nt* **N** **a** (= *main product*) Hauptartikel *m*; (= *main element*) Ausgangsmaterial *nt*; (= *main food*) Hauptnahrungsmittel *nt* **b** (*of cotton*) Rohbaumwolle *f*; (*of wool*) Rohwolle *f*

staple gun N Tacker *m*

stapler ['steɪpləʳ] N Heftgerät *nt*

star [stɑːʳ] **N** **a** Stern *m*; (= *asterisk, Sch*) Sternchen *nt*; **Star of David** Davidsstern *m*; **the Stars and Stripes** das Sternenbanner; **to be born under a lucky ~** unter einem glücklichen Stern geboren sein; **you can thank your lucky ~s that ...** Sie können von Glück sagen, dass ...; **it's (all) in the ~s** es steht (alles) in den Sternen; **to see ~s** Sterne sehen; **to have ~s in one's eyes** sich (*dat*) optimistische Hoffnungen machen; **a three-star general** (*US, Mil*) ein Dreisternegeneral *m* **b** (= *person*) Star *m* **ADJ** *attr* Haupt-; **~ attraction** Hauptattraktion *f*; **~ performer/player** Star *m* **VT** **a** (= *mark with stars*) mit einem Stern/mit Sternen versehen; (*fig*, = *scatter*) übersäen **b** (*Film etc*) **to ~ sb** (*film*) jdn in der Hauptrolle zeigen; **a film ~ring Greta Garbo** ein Film mit Greta Garbo (in der Hauptrolle); **~ring ...** in der Hauptrolle/den Hauptrollen ... **VI** (*Film etc*) die Hauptrolle spielen *or* haben

star: **star billing** N **to get ~** auf Plakaten groß herausgestellt werden; **starboard** ['stɑːbəd] **N** Steuerbord *nt*; **to ~** (*direction*) (nach) Steuerbord; (*place*) (in) Steuerbord **ADJ** Steuerbord-; **~ side** Steuerbordseite *f* **ADV** (nach) Steuerbord; **star boat** N (*Naut*) Starboot *nt*; **starburst** N (*liter*) Sternregen *m*

starch [stɑːtʃ] **N** Stärke *f*; **low in ~** stärkearm **VT** stärken

starchily ['stɑːtʃɪlɪ] ADV (*fig*) steif

starchiness ['stɑːtʃɪnɪs] N (*fig*) Steifheit *f*, Förmlichkeit *f*

starch-reduced [ˌstɑːtʃrɪ'djuːst] ADJ stärkereduziert

starchy ['stɑːtʃɪ] ADJ (+*er*) stärkehaltig; (*fig*) steif

star cloud N *(Astron)* Sternnebel *m*

star-crossed ['stɑ:krɒst] ADJ **they were ~ lovers** ihre Liebe stand unter einem Unstern

stardom ['stɑ:dəm] N Berühmtheit *f*, Ruhm *m*; **where he hoped to find ~** wo er hoffte, ein Star zu werden

stardust ['stɑ:dʌst] N **a** *(Astron)* Sternnebel *m* **b** *(= naively romantic quality)* **there was ~ in her eyes** in ihrem Blick lag etwas Naiv-Romantisches **c** *(= charisma)* Ausstrahlung *f* eines Stars

stare [stɛə'] N (starrer) Blick; **the village idiot looked at me with a vacant ~** der Dorftrottel sah mich mit stierem Blick an; **to give sb a ~** jdn anstarren

VT **the answer was staring us in the face** die Antwort lag klar auf der Hand; **to ~ death/defeat in the face** dem Tod/der Niederlage ins Auge blicken; **defeat was staring us in the face** wir blickten der Niederlage ins Auge

VI *(vacantly etc)* (vor sich hin) starren; *(cow, madman)* stieren, glotzen *(inf)*; *(in surprise)* große Augen machen; *(eyes)* weit aufgerissen sein; **he ~d in disbelief** er starrte ungläubig; **it's rude to ~** es ist unhöflich, andere Leute anzustarren; **to ~ at sb/sth** jdn/etw anstarren; *(cow, madman also)* jdn/etw anstieren *or* anglotzen *(inf)*; **don't ~ (at me)!** starr (mich) nicht so (an)!; **to ~ at sb in horror/amusement/disbelief** *etc* jdn entsetzt/verblüfft/ungläubig *etc* anstarren; **to ~ after sb** jdm nachstarren *or* hinterherstarren

▶ **stare down** *or* **out** VT *sep* **they were trying to stare each other down** *or* **out** sie versuchten, sich so lange gegenseitig anzustarren, bis einer aufgab; **I bet I can stare you down** *or* **out** wetten, dass du zuerst wegguckst *(inf)*; **the teacher just sat there and stared him down** *or* **out** der Lehrer saß da und fixierte ihn

starer N Gaffer(in) *m(f)* *(inf)*

star: **starfish** N Seestern *m*; **stargazer** N *(hum inf)* Sterngucker(in) *m(f)* *(hum inf)*

staring ['stɛərɪŋ] ADJ starrend *attr*; **~ eyes** starrer Blick

stark [stɑ:k] ADJ *(+er) realism, contrast, ignorance, poverty, warning* krass; *reality, truth, terror, fact* nackt; *clothing, simplicity* schlicht; *madness* rein, schier, hell; *reminder, message also* überdeutlich; *choice, silhouette* hart; *landscape, cliffs, branches* nackt, kahl; *light bulb* grell; *colour* eintönig; *(= glaring)* grell; *black* trist; *white* nackt; **in ~ terms** in harten Worten, unverblümt ADV **~ raving** *or* **staring mad** *(inf)* total verrückt *(inf)*; **~ naked** splitter(faser)nackt *(inf)*

starkers ['stɑ:kəz] ADJ *pred (Brit inf)* splitter(faser)nackt *(inf)*; *children also* nackig *(inf)*

starkly ['stɑ:klɪ] ADV *lit* grell; *described* krass, schonungslos; *different, apparent* vollkommen; **~ dressed in black** in tristes Schwarz gekleidet; **trees ~ silhouetted against the winter sky** Bäume, die sich hart gegen den Winterhimmel abhoben; **to contrast ~ with sth** *(fig)* sich krass von etw unterscheiden; **to be ~ exposed** schonungslos aufgedeckt sein; **a ~ beautiful region** eine karge und zugleich schöne Gegend

starkness ['stɑ:knɪs] N *(of clothing)* Schlichtheit *f*; *(of colour)* Eintönigkeit *f*; *(glaring)* Grellheit *f*; *(of truth, contrast)* Härte *f*, Krassheit *f*; *(of landscape)* Nacktheit *f*, Kahlheit *f*

starless ['stɑ:lɪs] ADJ sternenlos

starlet ['stɑ:lɪt] N (Film)sternchen *nt*, Starlet *nt*

starlight ['stɑ:laɪt] N Sternenlicht *nt*

starling ['stɑ:lɪŋ] N Star *m*

star: **starlit** ADJ *sky, night* stern(en)klar; *woods, hills* von Sternen beschienen; **star part** N Hauptrolle *f*; **star prize** N *(in competition)* Hauptpreis *m*

starred [stɑ:d] ADJ mit (einem) Sternchen bezeichnet

starriness ['stɑ:rɪnɪs] N *(of night, sky)* Stern(en)klarheit *f*; *(of eyes)* Leuchten *nt*, Strahlen *nt*

star role N = **star part**

starry ['stɑ:rɪ] ADJ *(+er) night* stern(en)klar; *eyes* strahlend, leuchtend; **~ sky** Sternenhimmel *m*

starry-eyed [,stɑ:rɪ'aɪd] ADJ *idealist* romantisch, blauäugig; *(= naively trusting)* arglos, blauäugig; **to go all ~** glänzende Augen kriegen

star: **star shell** N Leuchtkugel *f*, Leuchtgeschoss *nt*; **star sign** N Sternzeichen *nt*; **star-spangled** ['stɑ:spæŋgld] ADJ *(liter) sky* stern(en)übersät *(liter)*; **star-spangled banner** N **The Star-spangled Banner** das Sternenbanner; **starstruck** ADJ überwältigt; *(= fascinated by famous names)* starbegeistert; **star-studded** ['stɑ:stʌdɪd] ADJ **a** *(liter) night* sternenklar, voller Sterne; *sky* sternenklar, sternenübersät *(liter)* **b** *(fig)* **~ cast/audience** Starbesetzung *f*/-publikum *nt*; **star system** N **a** *(Astron)* Sternsystem *nt* **b** *(Film)* **the ~** *Engagement bekannter Schauspieler, um den Erfolg durchschnittlicher Filme zu garantieren*

START [stɑ:t] *abbr of* **Strategic Arms Reduction Treaty** START(-Vertrag) *m*

start[1] [stɑ:t] N **to give a ~** zusammenfahren; *(= start up)* aufschrecken; *(horse)* scheuen; **to give sb a ~** jdn erschrecken, jdm einen Schreck(en) einjagen; **to wake with a ~** aus dem Schlaf hochschrecken; **he looked up with a ~** er blickte erschreckt hoch → **fit**[2]

VI **a** *(= jump nervously)* zusammenfahren; *(= start up)* aufschrecken; **to ~ from one's chair** aus dem Stuhl hochfahren; **to ~ out of one's sleep** aus dem Schlaf hochschrecken **b** **tears ~ed to his eyes** Tränen traten ihm in die Augen; **his eyes were ~ing out of his head** die Augen traten ihm fast aus dem Kopf

VT *pheasant etc* aufscheuchen *(from* aus)

start[2] ✪ 20.4, 26.1 N **a** *(= beginning)* Beginn *m*, Anfang *m*; *(= departure)* Aufbruch *m*; *(of race etc)* Start *m*; *(of rumour, trouble, journey)* Ausgangspunkt *m*; **at the ~** am Anfang, zu Beginn; *(Sport)* am Start; **for a ~** *(= to begin with)* fürs Erste; *(= firstly)* zunächst einmal; **from the ~** von Anfang an; **from ~ to finish** von Anfang bis Ende, von vorn bis hinten *(inf)*; **to get off to a good** *or* **flying ~** gut vom Start wegkommen; *(fig)* einen glänzenden Start haben; **to get off to a bad ~** schlecht vom Start wegkommen; *(fig)* einen schlechten Start haben; **to get sb off to a good ~** jdm einen guten Start verschaffen; **to get sth off to a good ~** etw gut anlaufen lassen; **to give sb a (good) ~ in life** jdm eine (gute) Starthilfe geben; **the review gave the book a good ~** die Rezension war eine gute Starthilfe für das Buch; **to make a ~ (on sth)** (mit etw) anfangen; **to make an early ~** frühzeitig aufbrechen; **to make a ~ for home** sich auf den Heimweg machen; **to make a new ~ (in life)** (noch einmal) von vorn anfangen

b *(= advantage, Sport)* Vorsprung *m* *(over* vor *+dat)*

VT **a** *(= begin)* anfangen mit; *argument, career, new life, negotiations* beginnen, anfangen; *new job, journey* antreten; **to ~ work** anfangen zu arbeiten; **he ~ed life as a miner** er hat als Bergmann angefangen; **don't ~ that again!** fang nicht schon wieder (damit) an!; **to ~ smoking** das Rauchen *or* mit dem Rauchen anfangen; **he ~ed coming late** er fing an, zu spät zu kommen; **you ~ed it!** du hast angefangen!

b *(runners)* starten zu; *(= cause to begin) runners, race* starten; *rumour* in Umlauf setzen; *conversation* anfangen, anknüpfen; *fight* anfangen; *war* anfangen, auslösen; *blaze, collapse, chain reaction* auslösen; *coal fire etc* anzünden; *(arsonist)* legen; *(= found) enterprise, newspaper* gründen, starten *(inf)*; **to ~ sb thinking** jdn nachdenklich machen; **to ~ sb on a subject** jdn auf ein Thema bringen; **to ~ sb in business/on a career** jdm zu einem Start im Geschäftsleben/zu einer Karriere verhelfen; **the discovery ~ed a new line of research** mit der Entdeckung kam eine neue Forschungsrichtung in Gang; **I don't want to ~ anything but …** ich will keinen Streit anfangen, aber …; **just to ~ you getting used to it** nur damit Sie sich erst mal daran gewöhnen; **as soon as she ~ed the baby** *(inf)* sobald sich das Baby angekündigt hatte; **when she wore the first miniskirt she didn't realize what she was ~ing** als sie den ersten Minirock trug, war ihr nicht bewusst, was sie damit auslösen würde; **look what you've ~ed now!** da hast du was Schönes angefangen! *(inf)*

c *car, computer* starten; *engine* anlassen, starten; *clock* in Gang setzen; *machine, motor* starten, anwerfen

d **to ~ a horse in a race** eine Nennung für ein Pferd abgeben

VI *(= begin)* anfangen, beginnen; *(car, engine)* anspringen, starten; *(plane)* starten; *(= move off)* anfahren; *(bus, train)* abfahren; *(boat)* ablegen; *(rumour)* in Umlauf kommen; *(violins, cellos etc)* einsetzen; **~ing from Tuesday** ab Dienstag; **to ~ for home** (nach Hause) aufbrechen, sich auf den Heimweg machen; **to ~ for work** zur Arbeit gehen/fahren; **to ~ for London** nach London losfahren; **to ~ (off) with** *(= firstly)* erstens, erst einmal; *(= at the beginning)* zunächst; **what shall we have to ~ (off) with?** was nehmen wir als Vorspeise?; **I'd like soup to ~ (off) with** ich möchte erst mal eine Suppe; **to ~ after sb** jdn verfolgen; **to get ~ed** anfangen; *(on journey)* aufbrechen; **he finds it difficult to get ~ed in the morning** er kommt morgens nur schwer in Schwung *or* Gang; **to ~ on a task/journey/the food** sich an eine Aufgabe/auf eine Reise/ans Essen machen; **to ~ talking** *or* **to talk** zu sprechen beginnen *or* anfangen; **he ~ed by saying …** er sagte zunächst …; **don't you ~!** fang du nicht auch noch an!; **(are you) ~ing?** *(Brit sl)* willst du mich anmachen? *(inf)*; *(= provoke)* willst du mich provozieren?

▶ **start back** VI sich auf den Rückweg machen; **we started back for home** wir machten uns auf den Heimweg; **the rocket started back to earth** die Rakete trat die Rückreise zur Erde an

▶ **start in** VI *(inf)* **a** *(= begin to scold)* loslegen *(inf)*, vom Leder ziehen *(inf)* *(on sb* gegen jdn) **b** **to start in on sth** sich an etw *(acc)* machen

▶ **start off** VI *(= begin)* anfangen; *(= begin moving: person)* losgehen; *(on journey)* aufbrechen; *(= run)* loslaufen; *(= drive)* losfahren; *(esp Sport)* starten; *(= begin talking etc)* anfangen, loslegen *(inf)* *(on* mit); **to start off with** = **start**[2] **VI**

VT *sep sth* anfangen; **to start sb off (talking)** jdm das Stichwort geben; **to start the baby off (crying)** das Baby zum Schreien bringen; **whatever you do, don't start her off** sieh bloß zu, dass sie nicht damit anfängt; **that started the dog off (barking)** da fing der Hund an zu bellen; **to start sb off on sth** jdn auf etw *(acc)* bringen; **a few stamps to start you off** ein paar Briefmarken für den Anfang; **I'll play a few bars to start you off** ich spiele ein paar Takte, um Sie einzustimmen

▶ **start out** VI *(= begin)* (zunächst) beginnen *or* anfangen; *(= begin a journey)* aufbrechen *(for* nach); **we started out on a long journey** wir machten uns auf eine lange Reise; **I'm starting out on a new career** ich fange eine neue Berufslaufbahn an; **we started out with great hopes for the future** wir hatten mit großen Zukunftshoffnungen begonnen

▶ **start over** VI *(esp US)* noch (ein)mal von vorn anfangen

▶ **start up** VI **a** *(= move suddenly)* **a rabbit started up out of the undergrowth** ein Kaninchen schoss aus dem Unterholz hervor

b *(= begin) (music etc)* anfangen; *(machine)* angehen *(inf)*, in Gang kommen; *(computer)* starten; *(motor)* anspringen; *(siren)* losheulen; **when I started up in business** als ich als Geschäftsmann anfing; **he started up by himself when he was 21** er machte sich mit 21 selbstständig; **my computer won't start up** mein Computer lässt sich nicht hochfahren

VT *sep* **a** *(= cause to function)* anmachen *(inf)*, in Gang bringen; *engine also* anlassen, starten; *machine also* anwerfen; *computer* hochfahren, booten

b *(= begin)* eröffnen; *business also* anfangen;

conversation anfangen, anknüpfen; *(amongst other people)* in Gang bringen

starter ['stɑːtəʳ] N **a** *(Sport)* Starter(in) *m(f) (also horse)*; *(= competitor)* Teilnehmer(in) *m(f)*; **to be under ~'s orders** auf das Startkommando warten; *(fig)* in den Startblöcken sitzen **b** *(Aut etc: = self-starter)* Starter *m*, Anlasser *m* **c** *(inf: = person)* **to be a late ~** ein Spätzünder *m* sein *(inf)*; *(child)* ein Spätentwickler *m* sein; **to be a late ~ with girls** ein Spätzünder *m* sein, was Mädchen betrifft *(inf)*; **he was a late ~ in the presidential race** er beteiligte sich erst spät an den Präsidentschaftswahlen; **she is a slow ~ in the morning** sie kommt morgens nur langsam in Schwung **d** *(Brit inf: = first course)* Vorspeise *f* **e for ~s** *(inf)* für den Anfang *(inf)*

starter: **starter home** N *Immobilienobjekt für Erstkäufer*; **starter kit** N Starterkit *nt*, Startset *nt*; **starter model** N Einstiegsmodell *nt*; **starter pack** N *(Comm)* Erstausstattung *f*, Startpaket *nt*

starting ['stɑːtɪŋ] *in cpds (Sport)* Start-; **starting block** N Startblock *m*; **to be fast/slow off the ~s** schnell/langsam aus den Startblöcken wegkommen; **starting gate** N Startmaschine *f*; **starting grid** N Start(platz) *m*; **starting gun** N Startpistole *f*; **starting handle** N Anlasserkurbel *f*; **starting point** N *(lit, fig)* Ausgangspunkt *m*; **starting post** N Startpflock *m*; **starting price** N *(Horse Racing)* letzter Kurs vor dem Start; **starting signal** N Startzeichen *nt*; **starting stalls** PL *(Brit: horse racing)* Startmaschine *f*

startle ['stɑːtl] VT erschrecken; *animal also* aufschrecken; **I was ~d to see how old he looked** ich stellte entsetzt fest, wie alt er aussah VI **she ~s easily** sie ist sehr schreckhaft

startling ['stɑːtlɪŋ] ADJ *news, clarity, revelation* überraschend; *(= bad)* alarmierend, bestürzend; *coincidence, resemblance, contrast, change* erstaunlich; *colour, originality* aufregend, erregend; *dress, blue* aufregend; *discovery, claim, success, results* aufregend, sensationell

startlingly ['stɑːtlɪŋlɪ] ADV *simple, alike* überraschend; *dressed, beautiful* aufregend; *different* verblüffend; **nothing ~ new/original** nichts besonders *or* allzu Neues/Originelles

start menu N *(Comput)* Startmenü *nt*

start-up ['stɑːtʌp] N *(of machine, new business)* Start *m*, *(Comput also)* Hochfahren *nt*; **100 new ~s a week** *(= new businesses)* 100 Neugründungen pro Woche; **~ costs** *(of business, project)* Startkosten *pl*; **Start-Up scheme** *(Brit) Existenzgründungsprogramm für Arbeitslose*

star turn N *(esp Brit)* Sensation *f*, Hauptattraktion *f*

starvation [stɑː'veɪʃən] N *(act)* Hungern *nt*; *(of besieged people)* Aushungern *nt*; *(= condition)* Hunger *m*; **to die of ~** verhungern, hungers *or* den Hungertod sterben *(geh)*; **to live on a ~ diet** Hunger leiden; **the prisoners were kept on a ~ diet for months** man ließ die Gefangenen monatelang fast verhungern; **to go on a ~ diet** *(hum)* eine Hungerkur machen; **~ wages** Hungerlohn *m*, Hungerlöhne *pl*

starve [stɑːv] VT **a** *(= deprive of food)* hungern lassen; *(also* **starve out***)* aushungern; *(= kill: also* **starve to death***)* verhungern lassen, hungers sterben lassen *(geh)*; **to ~ oneself** hungern; **to ~ a town into surrender** eine Stadt durch Aushungern zur Kapitulation zwingen; **I'm ~d** *(inf)* ich hab 'nen Mordshunger *(inf)*; **he ~d his way through college** er hat sich *(dat)* das Studium vom Mund abgespart **b** *(fig)* **to ~ sb of sth** jdm etw vorenthalten *or* verweigern; **to be ~d of oxygen** Sauerstoffmangel haben; **to be ~d of capital/graduates** an akutem Kapital-/Akademikermangel leiden; **to be ~d of affection** zu wenig Zuneigung erfahren, an Liebesentzug leiden VI hungern; *(= die: also* **starve to death***)* verhungern; **I'm starving** *(inf)* ich hab 'nen Mordshunger *(inf)*; **you must be starving!** du musst doch halb verhungert sein! *(inf)*; **to ~ for sth** *(fig)* nach etw hungern

▶ **starve out** VT *sep garrison etc* aushungern

starveling ['stɑːvlɪŋ] N *(dated)* Hungerleider *m*

starving ['stɑːvɪŋ] ADJ *(lit)* hungernd *attr*; *(fig)* hungrig

Star Wars N *sing* Sternenkrieg *m*, Krieg *m* der Sterne

stash [stæʃ] VT *(inf: also* **stash away***)* bunkern *(sl)*; *money* beiseiteschaffen

stasis ['steɪsɪs] N Stauung *f*, Stase *f (spec)*; *(Liter)* Stillstand *m*

state [steɪt] N **a** *(= condition)* Zustand *m*; **~ of health/mind/war/siege** Gesundheits-/Geistes-/ /Kriegs-/Belagerungszustand *m*; **married/single ~** Ehe-/Ledigenstand *m*; **to be in a ~ of weightlessness** sich im Zustand der Schwerelosigkeit befinden; **the ~ of the nation** die Lage der Nation; **the present ~ of the economy** die gegenwärtige Wirtschaftslage; **in a liquid/solid ~** in flüssigem/festem Zustand; **where animals live in their natural ~** wo Tiere im Naturzustand leben; **in a good/bad ~** in gutem/ schlechtem Zustand; **he's in no (fit) ~ to do that** er ist auf gar keinen Fall in der Verfassung, das zu tun; **what a ~ of affairs!** was sind das für Zustände!; **look at the ~ of your hands!** guck dir bloß mal deine Hände an!; **my papers are in such a ~!** meine Papiere sind in einem furchtbaren Durcheinander!; **the room was in a terrible ~** im Zimmer herrschte ein fürchterliches Durcheinander **b** *(inf: = anxiety)* **to get into a ~ (about sth)** *(inf)* wegen etw durchdrehen *(inf)*; **to be in a terrible ~** *(inf)* in heller Aufregung *or* ganz durchgedreht *(inf)* sein **c** *(= rank)* Stand *m*, Rang *m*; **~ of bishop** Bischofswürde *f* **d** *(= pomp)* Aufwand *m*, Pomp *m*; **to be received in great ~** mit großem Staat empfangen werden; **to travel in ~** aufwendig *or* aufwändig *or* pompös reisen; **to lie in ~** (feierlich) aufgebahrt sein **e** *(Pol)* Staat *m*; *(= federal state)* (Bundes)staat *m*; *(in Germany, Austria)* (Bundes)land *nt*; **the States** die (Vereinigten) Staaten; **the State of Florida** der Staat Florida; **a ~ within a ~** ein Staat im Staate; **affairs of ~** Staatsangelegenheiten *pl*

VT darlegen, vortragen; *name, price, amount* nennen, angeben; *preference, purpose* angeben; *opposition, intention* anmelden; **to ~ that ...** feststellen *or* erklären, dass ...; **to ~ one's case** seine Sache vortragen; **it must be clearly ~d in the records ...** es muss aus den Akten einwandfrei hervorgehen, ...; **to ~ the case for the prosecution** *(Jur)* die Anklage vortragen; **the theme is ~d in the first few bars** das Thema wird in den ersten paar Takten vorgestellt; **unless otherwise ~d** wenn nicht anders angegeben; **as ~d in my letter I ...** wie in meinem Brief erwähnt, ... ich ...

state *in cpds* Staats-; *control, industry* staatlich; *(US etc)* des Bundes- *or* Einzelstaates, bundesstaatlich; **state-aided** ADJ staatlich gefördert; **state apartment** N Prunksaal *m*; **state bank** N Staatsbank *f*; **statecraft** N die Staatskunst

stated ['steɪtɪd] ADJ **a** *(= declared) sum, date* angegeben, genannt; *limits* bestimmt **b** *(= fixed, regular) times, amount* fest(gesetzt); **at the ~ intervals** in den festgelegten Abständen; **on the ~ date** zum festgesetzten Termin

state: **State Department** N *(US)* Außenministerium *nt*; **state education** N staatliche Erziehung; *(= system)* staatliches Erziehungs- *or* Bildungswesen; **state-funded** ADJ staatlich finanziert; **state funding** N staatliche Finanzierung; **state funeral** N Staatsbegräbnis *nt*

statehood ['steɪthʊd] N Eigenstaatlichkeit *f*; **to achieve ~** ein eigener *or* selbstständiger Staat werden; **when was Alaska granted ~?** wann wurde Alaska zum Bundesstaat erklärt?

state: **statehouse** N *(US)* Parlamentsgebäude *nt*, Kapitol *nt*; **stateless** ADJ staatenlos; **~ person** Staatenlose(r) *mf*; **statelessness** N Staatenlosigkeit *f*

statelet ['steɪtlɪt] N *(Pol)* Splitterstaat *m*

stateliness ['steɪtlɪnɪs] N *(of person, bearing)* Würde *f*; *(of pace, walk)* Gemessenheit *f*; *(of palace)* Pracht *f*

stately ['steɪtlɪ] ADJ *(+er) person, bearing* würdevoll; *progress* gemessen; *palace, tree* prächtig; **~ home** herrschaftliches Anwesen, Schloss *nt*

statement ['steɪtmənt] N **a** *(= putting forward: of thesis etc)* Darstellung *f*; *(of problem)* Darlegung *f*; **a clear ~ of the facts** eine klare Feststellung der Tatsachen **b** *(= that said)* Feststellung *f*; *(= claim)* Behauptung *f*; *(Mus, of theme)* Vorstellen *nt*; *(= official, Government statement)* Erklärung *f*, Stellungnahme *f*; *(in court, to police)* Aussage *f*; *(written)* Protokoll *nt*, Aussage *f*; **to make a ~ to the press** eine Presseerklärung abgeben **c** *(Philos)* Behauptung *f*, These *f*; *(Logic)* Satz *m*; *(Gram)* Feststellung *f* **d** *(Fin)* Rechnung *f*; *(also* **bank statement***)* Kontoauszug *m*

VT *(= assess)* **to ~ a child** Lernschwierigkeiten bei einem Kind offiziell feststellen; **~ed children** Kinder, bei denen offiziell eine Lernschwäche festgestellt wurde

state: **state occasion** N Staatsanlass *m*, Staatsfeierlichkeit *f*; **state-of-the-art** [,steɪtəvðiː'ɑːt] ADJ hochmodern, dem neuesten Stand der Technik entsprechend *attr*; **to be ~** dem neuesten Stand der Technik entsprechen; **~ technology** Spitzentechnologie *f*

> **STATE OF THE UNION ADDRESS**
>
> **State of the Union address** ist eine Rede, die der US-Präsident jeden Januar im Kongress hält und in der er seine Sicht zur Lage der Nation und seine Pläne für die Zukunft darlegt. Da die Rede landesweit von den Medien übertragen wird, richtet sich der Präsident in seiner Rede sowohl an das amerikanische Volk als auch an die Kongressmitglieder. Die Tradition der Regierungserklärung im Kongress kurz nach dessen Zusammentreten am 3. Januar erwuchs aus einer in der Verfassung verankerten Forderung, wonach der Präsident dem Kongress Informationen über die Lage der Nation **(information on the State of the Union)** geben muss.

state: **state-owned** ADJ staatseigen; **State Registered Nurse** N *(Brit)* staatlich anerkannte Krankenschwester, staatlich anerkannter Krankenpfleger; **stateroom** N *(Naut)* Kabine *f*; *(US Rail)* Privat(schlafwagen)abteil *nt*; **state school** N *(Brit)* öffentliche Schule; **state secret** N Staatsgeheimnis *nt*; **state's evidence** N *(US)* Aussage *f* eines Kronzeugen; **to turn ~** als Kronzeuge auftreten; **stateside** *(US inf)* ADJ in den Staaten *(inf)*; *newspaper* aus den Staaten *(inf)* ADV nach Hause, nachhause *(Aus, Sw)*; **when I'm back ~ ...** wenn ich wieder zu Hause in den Staaten bin, ...

statesman ['steɪtsmən] N *pl* **-men** [-mən] Staatsmann *m*

statesmanlike ['steɪtsmənlaɪk], **statesmanly** ['steɪtsmənlɪ] ADJ staatsmännisch

statesmanship ['steɪtsmənʃɪp] N Staatskunst *f*; **act of ~** staatsmännische Handlungsweise *f*

> **STATES' RIGHTS**
>
> **States' Rights** nennt man in den USA eine Doktrin, die den einzelnen Bundesstaaten Sonderrechte gegenüber der Bundesregierung einräumt. Dazu gehören z. B. das Aufbringen von Geldmitteln, das Verabschieden von Gesetzen und die Kontrolle über das Bildungswesen. Der zehnte Verfassungszusatz besagt, dass Rechte, die durch die Verfassung nicht an die Bundesregierung übertragen wurden, „den Staaten, beziehungsweise dem

Volk vorbehalten sind". Die Auslegung dieses Satzes ist jedoch sehr umstritten und wird immer mehr zugunsten des Bundes ausgehöhlt. Mit den **States' Rights** wurde die Abspaltung der Südstaaten vor dem Bürgerkrieg begründet. In den 50er-Jahren wurde dieser Begriff im Süden als Vorwand gegen die Rassenintegration benutzt. In letzter Zeit besinnt man sich landesweit wieder auf diese Rechte, da das Misstrauen gegen die Bundesregierung wegen deren wachsender Befugnisse und Ausgaben immer mehr zunimmt.

stateswoman ['steɪtswʊmən] N *pl* **-women** Staatsmännin *f*

state: **state trooper** N *(US)* Staatspolizist(in) *m(f)*; **state visit** N Staatsbesuch *m*; **statewide** ADJ *(US)* im ganzen Bundesstaat, landesweit

static ['stætɪk] ADJ **a** *(Phys)* statisch; **~ electricity** Reibungselektrizität *f*, statische Aufladung **b** *(= not moving or changing)* konstant; *(= stationary)* feststehend *attr*; *condition, society* statisch; **if the development of a civilization remains ~ ...** wenn eine Kultur sich nicht mehr weiterentwickelt, ...; **their relationship became ~** ihre Beziehung stagnierte, ihre Beziehung trat auf der Stelle N *(Phys)* Reibungselektrizität *f*; *(Rad also)* atmosphärische Störungen *pl*

statics ['stætɪks] N *sing* Statik *f*

station ['steɪʃən] N **a** Station *f*; *(= police station, fire station)* Wache *f*; *(= space station)* (Raum)station *f*; *(US: = gas station)* Tankstelle *f* → **workstation**
b *(= railway station, bus station)* Bahnhof *m*; *(= stop)* Station *f*
c *(Mil: = post)* Stellung *f*, Posten *m*; **border ~** Grenzstellung *f*; **naval ~** Flottenstützpunkt *m*
d *(esp Austral: = ranch)* Farm *f*; **sheep/cattle ~** Schaf-/Rinderzuchtfarm *f*; **~ hand** Farmgehilfe *m*/-gehilfin *f*
e *(Rad, TV)* Sender *m*, Sendestation *f*; *(= channel)* Sender *m*
f *(= position)* Platz *m*; **to take up (one's) ~** sich (auf)stellen, seinen Platz einnehmen; **the Stations of the Cross** die Stationen *pl* des Kreuzwegs
g *(= rank)* Stand *m*, Rang *m*; **~ in life** Stellung *f* (im Leben), Rang *m*; **to marry below/above one's ~** nicht standesgemäß/über seinem Stand heiraten; **he has got ideas above his ~** er hat Ideen, die jemandem aus seinem Stand gar nicht zukommen
VT (auf)stellen, postieren; *(Mil)* stationieren; *bicycle, train* abstellen

station agent N *(US)* = **stationmaster**

stationary ['steɪʃənərɪ] ADJ *(= not moving) car* parkend *attr*, haltend *attr*; *(= not movable)* fest (stehend *attr*); *(Space, Comput etc)* stationär; **to be ~** *(vehicles)* stehen; *(traffic, fig)* stillstehen; **to remain ~** sich nicht bewegen; *(traffic)* stillstehen

station break N *(US Radio, TV)* Pausenzeichen *nt*

stationer ['steɪʃənəʳ] N Schreibwarenhändler(in) *m(f)*; **~'s (shop)** Schreibwarenhandlung *f*

stationery ['steɪʃənərɪ] N *(= notepaper)* Briefpapier *nt*; *(= writing materials)* Schreibwaren *pl*; **office ~** Büromaterial *nt*

station: **station house** N *(US Police)* (Polizei)wache *f*, (Polizei)revier *nt*; **stationmaster** N Bahnhofsvorsteher(in), Stationsvorsteher(in) *(dated) m(f)*; **station police** N Bahnpolizei *f*; **station selector** N *(Rad)* Sendereinstellung *f*; **station wagon** N *(US)* Kombi(wagen) *m*

statist ['steɪtɪst] ADJ *(Pol)* staatlich

statistic [stə'tɪstɪk] N Statistik *f*

statistical [stə'tɪstɪkəl] ADJ statistisch

statistically [stə'tɪstɪkəlɪ] ADV statistisch; **~ speaking** statistisch gesehen

statistician [ˌstætɪ'stɪʃən] N Statistiker(in) *m(f)*

statistics [stə'tɪstɪks] N **a** *sing* Statistik *f* **b** *pl* *(= data)* Statistiken *pl* → **vital statistics**

stator ['steɪtəʳ] N *(Elec)* Stator *m*

statuary ['stætjʊərɪ] *(form)* ADJ statuarisch *(geh)*; **~ art** Plastik *f* N *(Art)* Plastik *f*, Bildhauerei *f*; *(= statues)* Plastiken *pl*, Statuen *pl*

statue ['stætjuː] N Statue *f*, Standbild *nt*; **Statue of Liberty** Freiheitsstatue *f*

statuesque [ˌstætjʊ'esk] ADJ standbildhaft, statuesk *(liter)*; **a woman with ~ looks** eine Frau von klassischer Schönheit

statuette [ˌstætjʊ'et] N Statuette *f*

stature ['stætʃəʳ] N **a** Wuchs *m*; *(esp of man)* Statur *f*; **of short ~** von kleinem Wuchs **b** *(fig)* Format *nt*

status ['steɪtəs] N Stellung *f*; *(= legal status, social status also)* Status *m*; *(Comput)* Status *m*; **equal ~** Gleichstellung *f*; **marital ~** Familienstand *m*; **many people who merely desire ~** viele Menschen, die bloß nach Prestige streben; **unsupported statements have no ~ in law** unbewiesene Behauptungen sind rechtlich irrelevant; **the idea that possession brings ~** die Vorstellung, dass Besitz das Prestige erhöht

status: **status bar** N *(Comput)* Statusleiste *f*; **status-conscious** ADJ statusbewusst; **status inquiry** N **a** *(Comput)* Statusabfrage *f* **b** *(Fin)* Anfrage *f* zur Kreditwürdigkeit; **status line** N *(Comput)* Statuszeile *f*

status quo [ˌsteɪtəs'kwəʊ] N Status quo *m*

status: **status report** N Zwischenbericht *m*; **status symbol** N Statussymbol *nt*

statute ['stætjuːt] N Gesetz *nt*; *(of organization)* Satzung *f*, Statut *nt*; **by ~** gesetzlich, statutarisch, satzungsgemäß

statute: **statute-barred** ['stætjuːtbɑːd] ADJ *(US Jur)* verjährt; **statute book** N *(esp Brit)* Gesetzbuch *nt*; **to put sth on the ~** etw zum Gesetz machen *or* erheben; **to be on the ~** geltendes Recht sein; **statute law** N Gesetzesrecht *nt*, Statute Law *nt*; **statute mile** N britische Meile

statutorily ['stætjʊtərəlɪ] ADV *(= legally)* gesetzlich; **broadcasting needs to be regulated ~** Rundfunk und Fernsehen müssen gesetzlich geregelt werden; **refugee families are ~ homeless** Flüchtlingsfamilien sind rechtlich gesehen heimatlos

statutory ['stætjʊtərɪ] ADJ gesetzlich; *holiday also, quarantine* gesetzlich vorgeschrieben; *(in organization)* satzungsgemäß, statutarisch; *right* verbrieft; *punishment* (vom Gesetz) vorgesehen; **~ maternity pay** *(Brit)* gesetzliches Erziehungsgeld; **~ nuisance** Ruhestörung *f*; **~ sick pay** *(Brit)* gesetzlich festgelegtes Krankengeld; **this is ~** das ist Gesetz

statutory rape N *(US)* Unzucht *f* mit Minderjährigen

staunch[1] [stɔːntʃ] ADJ (+er) *ally, friend* unerschütterlich; *Catholic, loyalist etc* überzeugt; *member, supporter* ergeben, getreu; *support* standhaft; **to be ~ in one's belief** fest *or* unerschütterlich im Glauben sein

staunch[2] VT *flow* stauen; *bleeding* stillen; **to ~ a wound** die Blutung einer Wunde stillen

staunchly ['stɔːntʃlɪ] ADV treu, standhaft; *oppose* entschieden; *defend* standhaft; *Catholic* streng

staunchness ['stɔːntʃnɪs] N *(of Catholic, loyalist)* Überzeugtheit *f*; *(of member, supporter)* Treue *f*; *(of support)* Unerschütterlichkeit *f*

stave [steɪv] N **a** *(of barrel)* (Fass)daube *f*; *(= rung)* (Leiter)sprosse *f*; *(= stick)* Knüppel *m*, Knüttel *m (old)* **b** *(Mus: = staff)* Notenlinien *pl* **c** *(Liter, = stanza)* Strophe *f*, Vers *m*

▶ **stave in** *pret, ptp* **staved** *or* **stove in** VT *sep* eindrücken; *head* einschlagen VI eingedrückt werden

▶ **stave off** VT *sep* **a** *attack* zurückschlagen; *threat, crisis, cold* abwehren; *defeat, disaster, bankruptcy* abwenden; *hunger, boredom* lindern **b** *(= delay) person* hinhalten; *crisis, day* hinausschieben

stave rhyme N *(Poet)* Stabreim *m*

staves [steɪvz] *pl of* **staff N b**

stay[1] [steɪ] N **a** Aufenthalt *m*; **come for a longer ~ next year** komm nächstes Jahr für länger; **a short ~ in hospital** ein kurzer Krankenhausaufenthalt
b *(Jur)* Aussetzung *f*; **~ of execution** Aussetzung *f*, Vollstreckungsaufschub *m*; *(fig)* Galgenfrist *f*; *(of death penalty)* Hinrichtungsaufschub *m*
VT **a** *(old, liter, = stop)* Einhalt gebieten *(+dat) (geh)*; *hunger* stillen; **to ~ one's/sb's hand** sich/jdn zurückhalten
b *(Jur) order, sentence* aussetzen
c **to ~ the course** *(lit, fig)* durchhalten
d **to ~ the night (with sb/in a hotel)** (bei jdm/in einem Hotel) übernachten
VI **a** *(= remain)* bleiben; **to ~ for** *or* **to supper** zum Abendessen bleiben; **to have come to ~** *(fashion etc)* sich halten; **is unemployment here to ~?** ist die Arbeitslosigkeit nun ein Dauerzustand?; **if it ~s fine** wenn es schön bleibt; **if he can ~ with the others** wenn er mit den anderen mithalten kann; **~ with it!** nicht aufgeben! → **put**[2]
b *(= reside)* wohnen; *(at youth hostel etc)* übernachten; **to ~ at a hotel** im Hotel wohnen *or* übernachten; **I ~ed in Italy for a few weeks** ich habe mich ein paar Wochen in Italien aufgehalten; **when I/Goethe was ~ing in Italy** als ich/Goethe in Italien war *or* weilte *(liter)*; **where are you ~ing?** wo wohnen Sie?; **he is ~ing at Chequers for the weekend** er verbringt das Wochenende in Chequers; **he went to ~ in the country for a while** er ist für einige Zeit aufs Land gefahren; **we would ~ at a different resort each year** wir waren jedes Jahr an einem anderen Urlaubsort; **it's a nice place to ~ in the summer** dort kann man gut den Sommer verbringen; **my brother came to ~ for a week** mein Bruder ist für eine Woche gekommen; **my brother came to ~** mein Bruder ist zu Besuch gekommen
c *(old, = wait)* **~!** stehen bleiben!; **~, wanderer!** halt inne, Wanderer! *(old, liter)*

▶ **stay away** VI *(from* von) wegbleiben; *(from person)* sich fernhalten; **to stay away from a girl** von einem Mädchen die Finger lassen; **he can't stay away from the pub** *(esp Brit)* ihn zieht es immer wieder in die Kneipe *(inf)*

▶ **stay behind** VI zurückbleiben; *(Sch, as punishment)* nachsitzen; **I stayed behind after the party** ich blieb nach der Party noch da

▶ **stay down** VI *(= keep down)* unten bleiben; *(Sch)* wiederholen; **nothing I eat stays down** alles, was ich esse, kommt wieder hoch

▶ **stay in** VI *(at home)* zu Hause bleiben; *(in position, in book etc)* drinbleiben; *(Sch)* nachsitzen; **he had to stay in as a punishment** *(at home)* er kriegte zur Strafe Stubenarrest *or* Hausarrest

▶ **stay off** VI **a** *(rain)* ausbleiben **b** *(from work etc)* zu Hause bleiben VI *+prep obj* **a** *(= not go on)* nicht betreten **b** **to stay off work/school** nicht zur Arbeit/Schule gehen; **to stay off the bottle** *(inf)* die Flasche nicht anrühren *(inf)*

▶ **stay on** VI *(lid etc)* draufbleiben; *(light)* anbleiben; *(people)* (noch) bleiben; **he stayed on for another year** er blieb noch ein Jahr; **to stay on at school** (in der Schule) weitermachen; **to stay on as manager** (weiterhin) Geschäftsführer bleiben

▶ **stay out** VI draußen bleiben; *(esp Brit: on strike)* weiterstreiken; *(= not come home)* wegbleiben; **to stay out of sth** sich aus etw heraushalten; **he never managed to stay out of trouble** er war dauernd in Schwierigkeiten; **you stay out of this!** halt du dich da raus!

▶ **stay up** VI **a** *(person)* aufbleiben; **don't stay up for me!** bleib nicht meinetwegen auf! **b** *(tent, fence, pole)* stehen bleiben; *(picture, decorations)* hängen bleiben; *(swimmer)* oben bleiben; *(roof)* draufbleiben; **his trousers won't stay up** seine Hosen rutschen immer **c** *(at university)* (an der Uni) bleiben **d** **he's still staying up with the front runners** er liegt immer noch auf gleicher Höhe mit den Läufern an der Spitze

stay² N **a** *(= guy-rope)* Stütztau *nt*, Halteseil *nt*; *(Naut)* Stag *nt*; **the ~ of one's old age** *(fig)* die Stütze seines Alters **b** **stays** *pl (old: = corsets)* Korsett *nt*

stay-at-home [ˈsteɪəthəʊm] N Stubenhocker(in) *m(f)* ADJ *attr* stubenhockerisch

stayer [ˈsteɪəʳ] N *(= horse)* Steher *m*; *(= person)* beständiger *or* ausdauernder Mensch

staying power [ˈsteɪɪŋˌpaʊəʳ] N Stehvermögen *nt*, Durchhaltevermögen *nt*, Ausdauer *f*

stay-in strike [ˈsteɪɪnˌstraɪk] N *(Brit)* Sitzstreik *m*

St Bernard [sənt'bɜːnəd] N Bernhardiner *m*

STD **a** *(Brit Telec) abbr of* **subscriber trunk dialling** der Selbstwählferndienst; **~ code** Vorwahl(nummer) *f* **b** *abbr of* **sexually transmitted disease** Geschlechtskrankheit *f*; **~ clinic** Sprechstunde *f*/Praxis *f* für Geschlechtskrankheiten

stead [sted] N **in his ~** an seiner Stelle *or* statt *(liter, form)*; **to stand sb in good ~** jdm zugute- *or* zustattenkommen

steadfast [ˈstedfəst] ADJ fest; *look also* unverwandt; *person also* standhaft, unerschütterlich; *refusal also* standhaft; *belief also* unerschütterlich; **to remain ~ in faith** in seinem Glauben nicht schwanken; **the sky was a ~ blue** *(poet)* der Himmel war von einem wolkenlosen Blau

steadfastly [ˈstedfəstlɪ] ADV fest; *look* unverwandt; *adhere, refuse* standhaft, unerschütterlich; **to be ~ loyal to sb** jdm unerschütterlich treu sein; **to ~ maintain one's innocence** unerschütterlich auf seiner Unschuld beharren; **to remain ~ at one's post** beharrlich auf seinem Posten bleiben

steadfastness [ˈstedfəstnɪs] N Festigkeit *f*; *(of look also)* Unverwandtheit *f*; *(of person also)* Standhaftigkeit *f*, Unerschütterlichkeit *f*; *(of refusal also)* Standhaftigkeit *f*; *(of belief also)* Unerschütterlichkeit *f*

Steadicam® [ˈstedɪkæm] N *(Film)* Steadicam® *nt*

steadily [ˈstedɪlɪ] ADV **a** *(= firmly)* ruhig; *balanced* fest; *gaze* fest, unverwandt **b** *(= constantly)* ständig; *rain* ununterbrochen; **the atmosphere in the country is getting ~ more tense** die Stimmung im Land wird immer gespannter **c** *(= reliably)* zuverlässig, solide **d** *(= regularly)* gleichmäßig, regelmäßig

steadiness [ˈstedɪnɪs] N *(= stability)* Festigkeit *f*; *(of hand, eye)* Ruhe *f*; *(= regularity)* Stetigkeit *f*; *(of gaze)* Unverwandtheit *f*; *(of character)* Zuverlässigkeit *f*, Solidität *f*

steady [ˈstedɪ] ADJ *(+er)* **a** *(= firm, not wobbling) hand, nerves, eye* ruhig; *gaze* fest, unverwandt; *(= composed) voice* fest; **with a ~ hand** mit ruhiger Hand; **~ on one's legs/feet** fest *or* sicher auf den Beinen; **to hold sth ~** etw ruhig halten; *ladder* etw festhalten; **the chair is not very ~** der Stuhl ist wacklig

b *(= constant) wind, progress, demand etc* ständig, stet *(geh)*; *drizzle* ununterbrochen; *temperature* beständig; *income* geregelt; **at a ~ pace** in gleichmäßigem Tempo; **at a ~ 70** ständig mit 70

c *(= reliable, regular) worker* zuverlässig, solide; **he plays a ~ game** er ist ein zuverlässiger Spieler

d *job, boyfriend* fest

ADV **~!** *(= carefully, gently)* vorsichtig!; *(Naut)* Kurs halten!; **~ (on)!**, **~ the buffs!** immer mit der Ruhe! *(inf)*, sachte! *(inf)*; **to go ~ (with sb)** *(inf)* mit jdm (fest) gehen *(inf)*; **they're going ~** *(inf)* sie gehen fest miteinander, sie sind fest zusammen

N *(inf)* fester Freund *(inf)*, feste Freundin *(inf)*

VT *plane, boat* wieder ins Gleichgewicht bringen; *(= stabilize) nerves, person* beruhigen; *(in character)* ausgleichen; **to ~ oneself** festen Halt finden; **she had a ~ing influence on him** durch ihren Einfluss wurde er ausgeglichener

VI sich beruhigen; *(person, voice)* ruhig(er) werden; **her breathing steadied** ihr Atem wurde ruhiger

steady-going [ˈstedɪˌgəʊɪŋ] ADJ gleichbleibend, beständig, ausgeglichen; *service to a good cause etc* unerschütterlich; *family man etc* solide, gesetzt

steady-state theory [ˌstedɪ'steɪtθɪərɪ] N *(Phys)* Gleichgewichtstheorie *f*

steak [steɪk] N Steak *nt*; *(of fish)* Filet *nt*; **a ham/bacon ~** eine Scheibe gebackener Schinken/Speck; **~ and kidney pie** Fleischpastete *f* mit Nieren; **~ dinner** Steakmenü *nt*

steak: **steakhouse** [ˈsteɪkhaʊs] N Steakhouse *nt*; **steak knife** N Steakmesser *nt*; **steak tartare** N Tatarbeefsteak *nt*

steal [stiːl] *vb: pret* **stole**, *ptp* **stolen** VT *object, idea, kiss, heart* stehlen; **to ~ sth from sb** jdm etw stehlen; **to ~ sb's girlfriend** jdm die Freundin ausspannen *(inf)*; **to ~ the show** die Schau stehlen; **to ~ the limelight from sb** jdm die Schau stehlen; **to ~ sb's thunder** jdm den Wind aus den Segeln nehmen; **Labour have stolen the Tories' clothes** Labour hat sich der Politik der Tories bemächtigt; **the baby stole all the attention** das Kind zog die ganze Aufmerksamkeit auf sich; **to ~ a glance at sb** verstohlen zu jdm hinschauen

VI **a** *(= thieve)* stehlen

b *(= move quietly etc)* sich stehlen, (sich) schleichen; **to ~ away** *or* **off** sich weg- *or* davonstehlen; **to ~ into a room** sich in ein Zimmer stehlen; **to ~ up on sb** sich an jdn heranschleichen; **old age was ~ing up on her** das Alter machte sich allmählich bei ihr bemerkbar; **the mood/feeling which was ~ing over the country** die Stimmung, die sich allmählich im Land verbreitete; **he could feel happiness ~ing over him** er fühlte, wie ihn ein Glücksgefühl überkam; **to ~ home** *(Baseball)* ungehindert zur Ausgangsbase vorrücken

N *(US inf: = bargain)* Geschenk *nt (inf)*; **a total ~** ein echtes Schnäppchen *(inf)*; **it's a ~!** das ist (ja) geschenkt! *(inf)*

stealth [stelθ] N List *f*; *(of fox also)* Schläue *f*; **by ~** durch List

Stealth bomber N *(Aviat)* Tarn(kappen)bomber *m*, Stealthbomber *m*

stealthily [ˈstelθɪlɪ] ADV verstohlen

stealthiness [ˈstelθɪnɪs] N Verstohlenheit *f*

stealthy [ˈstelθɪ] ADJ *(+er)* verstohlen; *footsteps* verhalten

steam [stiːm] N Dampf *m*; *(from swamp also)* Dunst *m*; **driven by ~** dampfgetrieben; **full ~ ahead** *(Naut)* volle Kraft voraus; *(fig)* mit Volldampf voraus; **to get** *or* **pick up ~** *(lit)* feuern, Dampf aufmachen *(dated)*; *(fig)* in Schwung kommen; **to let off ~** *(lit, fig)* Dampf ablassen; **to run out of ~** *(lit)* Dampf verlieren; *(fig)* Schwung verlieren; **he ran out of ~** ihm ist die Puste ausgegangen *(inf)*; **the ship went on under its own ~** das Schiff fuhr mit eigener Kraft weiter; **under one's own ~** *(fig)* allein, ohne Hilfe

VT dämpfen; *food also* dünsten; **to ~ open an envelope** einen Briefumschlag über Dampf öffnen; **~ed pudding** Kochpudding *m*

VI **a** *(= give off steam)* dampfen

b *(= move)* dampfen; **we were ~ing along at 12 knots** wir fuhren mit 12 Knoten; **the ship ~ed into the harbour** das Schiff kam in den Hafen gefahren; **the ship ~ed out** das Schiff dampfte ab; **the runner came ~ing round the last bend** *(inf)* der Läufer kam mit Volldampf um die letzte Kurve *(inf)*

▶ **steam ahead** VI *(inf, project, work)* gut vorankommen

▶ **steam off** VT *sep stamp, label* über Dampf ablösen; *excess flab* sich *(dat)* abschwitzen VI abfahren; *(train also)* losdampfen

▶ **steam over** VI *(window)* beschlagen

▶ **steam up** VT *sep window* beschlagen lassen; **to be (all) steamed up** (ganz) beschlagen sein; *(fig inf)* (ganz) aufgeregt sein; **to get (all) steamed up** (ganz) beschlagen; *(fig inf)* sich aufregen, hochgehen *(inf)*; **look at you, all steamed up about nothing** deine ganze Aufregung war umsonst VI beschlagen

steam: **steam blower** N *(Tech)* Dampf(strahl)gebläse *nt*, Dampfstrahler *m*; **steamboat** N Dampfschiff *nt*, Dampfer *m*; **steam-driven** ADJ mit Dampfantrieb, dampfgetrieben; **steam engine** N Dampflok *f*; *(stationary)* Dampfmaschine *f*

steamer [ˈstiːməʳ] N *(= ship)* Dampfer *m*; *(Cook)* Dampf(koch)topf *m*

steam: **steam fitter** N Heizungsinstallateur(in) *m(f)*; **steam gauge**, *(US)* **steam gage** N *(Tech)* Dampfdruckmesser *m*; **steam hammer** N Dampfhammer *m*; **steam heating** N Dampfheizung *f*

steaming [ˈstiːmɪŋ] ADJ *(inf)* **a** *(= angry) person, letter* wütend **b** *(Scot, = drunk)* voll *(inf)*, breit *(inf)*

steam: **steam iron** N Dampfbügeleisen *nt*; **steam radio** N *(hum)* Dampfradio *nt (hum)*; **steamroller** N Dampfwalze *f* VT *road* glatt walzen; *(fig) person* überfahren; **they ~ed their way into the next round** sie bahnten sich unaufhaltsam den Weg in die nächste Runde; **to ~ a bill through parliament** *(fig)* ein Gesetz im Parlament durchpeitschen ADJ **~ tactics** Holzhammermethode *f (inf)*; **steam room** N Saunaraum *m*; *(in Turkish bath)* Dampfraum *m*; **steamship** N Dampfschiff *nt*, Dampfer *m*; **steamship company** N Dampfschifffahrtsgesellschaft *f*; **steamship line** N Schifffahrtslinie *f*, Dampferlinie *f*; **steam-shovel** N Löffelbagger *m*; **steam turbine** N Dampfturbine *f*

steamy [ˈstiːmɪ] ADJ *(+er)* dampfig, dunstig; *jungle, swamp* dunstig; *room, atmosphere* dampfig, voll Dampf; *window, mirror* beschlagen; *(fig) affair, novel* heiß; **it is so ~ in here** hier ist vielleicht ein Dampf!

stearin [ˈstɪərɪn] N Stearin *nt*

steed [stiːd] N *(liter)* Ross *nt*

steel [stiːl] N Stahl *m*; *(= sharpener)* Wetzstahl *m*; *(for striking spark)* Feuerstahl *m*; **he felt cold ~ between his ribs** er spürte den kalten Stahl zwischen den Rippen; **a man of ~** ein stahlharter Mann; **as hard as ~** stahlhart, so hart wie Stahl → **nerve**

ADJ *attr* Stahl-; **~ manufacture** Stahlproduktion *f*

VT **to ~ oneself** sich wappnen *(for* gegen); *(physically)* sich stählen *(for* für); **to ~ oneself to do sth** allen Mut zusammennehmen, um etw zu tun; **to ~ oneself against sth** sich gegen etw hart machen *or* verhärten; **he ~ed his troops for the battle** er machte seiner Truppe Mut für den Kampf; *(physically)* er stählte seine Truppe für den Kampf

steel *in cpds* Stahl-, stahl-; **steel band** N Steelband *f*; **steel cable** N Stahlseil *nt*; **steel-clad** ADJ stahlgepanzert; **steel girder** N *(Tech)* Stahlträger *m*; **steel grey**, *(US)* **steel gray** N Stahlgrau *nt* ADJ stahlgrau; **steel guitar** N Hawaiigitarre *f*; **steel helmet** N *(Mil)* Stahlhelm *m*; **steel mill** N Stahlwalzwerk *nt*; **steel-plated** ADJ mit Stahlüberzug; *(for protection)* stahlgepanzert; **steel wool** N Stahlwolle *f*; **steel worker** N (Eisen- und) Stahlarbeiter(in) *m(f)*; **steelworks** N *sing or pl* Stahlwerk *nt*

steely [ˈstiːlɪ] ADJ *(+er) grip* stahlhart; *smile, expression* hart; *gaze* hart, stählern; *eyes* stählern; *determination* eisern, ehern; *(= grim) person* knallhart; **~ blue/grey** stahlblau/-grau

steelyard [ˈstiːljɑːd] N Handwaage *f*

steely-eyed [ˈstiːlɪˌaɪd] ADJ mit hartem *or* stählernem Blick

steep¹ [stiːp] ADJ *(+er)* **a** steil; *fall* tief; **it's a ~ climb** es geht steil hinauf; **there's been a ~ drop in the value of the pound** das Pfund ist stark gefallen **b** *(fig inf) demand, price* unverschämt; *bill* gepfeffert *(inf)*, gesalzen *(inf)*; **that's pretty ~!** das ist allerhand!; **it seems a bit ~ that …** es ist ein starkes Stück, dass …

steep² VT **a** *(in liquid)* eintauchen; *(in marinade, dye)* ziehen lassen; *dried food, washing* einweichen **b** *(fig)* **to be ~ed in sth** von etw durchdrungen sein; **~ed in history** geschichtsträchtig; **~ed in vice/prejudice** durch und durch verdorben/voreingenommen; **a scholar ~ed in the classics** ein Gelehrter, der sich in die Klassiker versenkt hat **VI** **to leave sth to ~** etw einweichen; *(in marinade, dye)* etw ziehen lassen

steepen ['stiːpən] **VT** steiler machen **VI** *(slope)* steiler werden; *(ground)* ansteigen; *(fig)* *slump* zunehmen

steeple ['stiːpl] **N** Kirchturm *m*

steeple: **steeplechase** **N** *(for horses)* Jagdrennen *nt*, Hindernisrennen *nt*; *(for runners)* Hindernislauf *m*; **steeplechaser** **N** *(= horse)* Steepler *m*; *(= jockey)* Reiter(in) *m(f)* in einem Jagdrennen; *(= runner)* Hindernisläufer(in) *m(f)*; **steeplejack** **N** Turmarbeiter(in) *m(f)*

steeply ['stiːplɪ] **ADV** steil

steepness ['stiːpnɪs] **N** **a** Steile *f*, Steilheit *f* **b** *(fig inf)* Unverschämtheit *f*

steer[1] [stɪəʳ] **VT** *(lit, fig)* lenken; *car also, ship* steuern; *person also* lotsen; **to ~ a steady course** *(lit, fig)* einen geraden Kurs steuern; **to ~ a course through sth** *(lit, fig)* durch etw hindurchsteuern; **this car is easy to ~** der Wagen lässt sich leicht lenken **VI** *(in car)* lenken; *(in ship)* steuern; **to ~ due north** Kurs nach Norden halten; **~ left a bit** lenken *or* *(in ship)* steuern Sie etwas nach links; **to ~ for sth** auf etw *(acc)* zuhalten; *(Naut)* etw ansteuern, auf etw *(acc)* Kurs halten; *(fig)* auf etw *(acc)* zusteuern → **clear**

steer[2] **N** junger Ochse

steerage ['stɪərɪdʒ] **N** Zwischendeck *nt*

steerageway ['stɪərɪdʒweɪ] **N** Steuerkraft *f*

steering ['stɪərɪŋ] **N** *(in car etc)* Lenkung *f*; *(Naut)* Steuerung *f*

steering: **steering column** **N** Lenksäule *f*; **steering-column lock** **N** *(Aut)* Lenkerschloss *nt*; **steering committee** **N** Lenkungsausschuss *m*; **steering gear** **N** *(of plane)* Leitwerk *nt*; *(of boat)* Ruderanlage *f*; **steering lock** **N** Lenkradschloss *nt*; **steering wheel** **N** Steuer(rad) *nt*; *(of car also)* Lenkrad *nt*; **steering-wheel lock** **N** *(Aut)* Lenkradschloss *nt*

steersman ['stɪəzmən] **N** *pl* **-men** [-mən] Steuermann *m*

stein [ʃtaɪn] **N** Maßkrug *m*

stele ['stiːlɪ] **N** *(Archeol)* Stele *f*

stellar ['steləʳ] **ADJ** stellar

stem [stem] ✪ 17.2 **N** **a** *(of plant)* Stiel *m*; *(of woody plant, shrub)* Stamm *m*; *(of grain)* Halm *m*; *(fig, of family tree)* Hauptlinie *f*, Hauptzweig *m*

b *(of glass)* Stiel *m*; *(of pipe)* Hals *m*; (*Mus*: *of note*) (Noten)hals *m*; *(in watch)* Welle *f*; *(of thermometer)* Röhre *f*

c *(of word)* Stamm *m*

d *(Naut)* Vordersteven *m*; **from ~ to stern** von vorne bis achtern

VT *(= check, stop)* aufhalten; *flow of sth, tide, flood, losses, exodus also* eindämmen; *bleeding, decline also* zum Stillstand bringen; *inflation also, flow of words* Einhalt gebieten *(+dat)*

VI **to ~ from sth** *(= result from)* von etw kommen, von etw herrühren; *(= have as origin)* aus etw (her)stammen, auf etw *(acc)* zurückgehen; **what does this increase in inflation ~ from?** welche Ursachen hat diese Zunahme der Inflation?

stem: **stem cell** **N** *(Biol, Med)* Stammzelle *f*; **~ research** Stammzellenforschung *f*

stem christie [stem'krɪstɪ] **N** *(Ski)* Kristianiaschwung *m*

stem ginger **N** kandierter Ingwer

stemmed [stemd] **ADJ** Stiel-; **~ glass** Stielglas *nt*

stem parallel **N** *(Ski)* (ausgestemmter) Parallelschwung

stem turn **N** Stemmbogen *m*

stench [stentʃ] **N** Gestank *m*; **~ trap** Geruchsverschluss *m*

stencil ['stensl] **N** Schablone *f*; (*Printing*: *for duplicating*) Matrize *f* **VT** mit Schablonen zeichnen; *(Printing)* auf Matrize schreiben

sten gun ['stengʌn] **N** *(Mil)* leichtes Maschinengewehr

steno ['stenəʊ] **N** *(US inf)* = **stenographer, stenography**

stenographer [ste'nɒgrəfəʳ] **N** *(US form)* Stenograf(in) *m(f)*

stenography [ste'nɒgrəfɪ] **N** *(form)* Stenografie *f*

stentorian [sten'tɔːrɪən] **ADJ** schallend; *voice* Stentor- *(geh)*

step [step] **N** **a** *(= pace, in dancing)* Schritt *m*; **to take a ~** einen Schritt machen; **~ by ~** *(lit, fig)* Schritt für Schritt; **we followed his ~s in the snow** wir folgten seinen Fußstapfen im Schnee; **he watched my every ~** *(fig)* er beobachtete mich auf Schritt und Tritt; **to watch one's ~** achtgeben; *(fig also)* sich vorsehen; **to be** *or* **stay one ~ ahead of sb** *(fig)* jdm einen Schritt voraussein

b **to be in ~** *(lit)* im Gleichschritt *or* Tritt sein (*with* mit); *(in dancing)* im Takt sein (*with* mit); *(fig)* im Gleichklang sein (*with* mit); **to be out of ~** *(lit)* nicht im Tritt *or* im gleichen Schritt sein (*with* mit); *(in dancing)* nicht im gleichen Takt sein (*with* wie); *(fig)* nicht im Gleichklang sein (*with* mit); **to get out of ~** *(lit)* aus dem Schritt *or* Tritt kommen; *(in dancing)* aus dem Takt kommen; *(fig)* von der gemeinsamen Linie abkommen; **to keep in ~** *(lit)* Tritt halten; *(fig)* Schritt halten; **to break ~** *(lit)* aus dem Tritt kommen; *(fig)* aus dem Schritt kommen; **to fall into ~** *(lit)* in Gleichschritt fallen (*with* mit); *(fig)* in den gleichen Takt kommen (*with* wie)

c (*Brit*: *= distance*) **it's (quite) a good ~ (to the village)** es ist ein ziemlich weiter Weg (bis zum Dorf), es ist ziemlich weit (bis zum Dorf); **it's only a few ~s** es sind nur ein paar Schritte

d *(= move)* Schritt *m*; *(= measure)* Maßnahme *f*, Schritt *m*; **the first ~ is to form a committee** als Erstes muss ein Ausschuss gebildet werden; **it's a great ~ forward** es ist ein großer Schritt nach vorn; **that would be a ~ back/in the right direction for him** das wäre für ihn ein Rückschritt/ein Schritt in die richtige Richtung; **one can't take a single ~ without having to consult somebody** man kann (rein) gar nichts unternehmen, ohne fragen zu müssen; **to take ~s to do sth** Maßnahmen ergreifen, (um) etw zu tun; **to take legal ~s** gerichtlich vorgehen

e *(in process, experiment)* Abschnitt *m*, Stufe *f*; *(in learning, course)* Stufe *f*, Lernschritt *m*

f *(= stair, fig, in scale, hierarchy)* Stufe *f*; **~s** *(outdoors)* Treppe *f*; **mind the ~** Vorsicht Stufe

g **steps** **PL** (*Brit*: *= stepladder*: *also* **pair of steps**) Tritt- *or* Stufenleiter *f*

h *(= step aerobics)* Steppaerobic *nt*

VT **a** *(old) dance* tanzen

b *(= arrange in steps)* terrassenförmig anlegen, abstufen

c **~ two paces to the left** treten Sie zwei Schritte nach links

VI gehen; **to ~ into/out of sth** *(house, room, puddle)* in etw *(acc)*/aus etw treten; *train, dress* in etw *(acc)*/aus etw steigen; **to ~ on(to) sth** *(plane, train)* in etw *(acc)* steigen; *platform, ladder* auf etw *(acc)* steigen; **to ~ on sth** *(object, toy)* auf etw *(acc)* treten; **he ~ped on my foot** er ist mir auf den Fuß getreten; **to ~ over sb/sth** über jdn/etw steigen; **please mind where you ~** geben Sie acht, wo Sie hintreten; **~ this way, please** hier entlang, bitte!; **he ~ped into the road** er trat auf die Straße; **he ~ped into his father's job/shoes** er übernahm die Stelle seines Vaters; **to ~ into sb's boots** *(Brit Sport)* in jds Fußstapfen treten; **to ~ on board** an Bord gehen; **to ~ inside** hineintreten; **to ~ outside** hinaustreten; *(for fight)* (mal eben) vor die Tür gehen; **~ on it!** mach mal ein bisschen (schneller)! *(inf)*; *(in car)* gib Gas!

▶ **step aside** **VI** **a** *(lit)* zur Seite treten **b** *(fig)* Platz machen; **to step aside to make way for sb** jdm Platz machen

▶ **step back** **VI** **a** *(lit)* zurücktreten **b** *(fig)* **to step back from sth** von etw Abstand gewinnen; **let us step back into the 18th century** versetzen wir uns einmal ins 18. Jahrhundert zurück

▶ **step down** **VI** **a** *(lit)* hinabsteigen **b** *(fig)* **to step down for sb** *or* **in favour of sb** jdm Platz machen, zu jds Gunsten zurücktreten; **he decided to step down and not stand for the presidency** er beschloss, seine Kandidatur für das Amt des Präsidenten zurückzuziehen **c** *(= resign)* zurücktreten; **to step down as president/chairman** vom Amt des Präsidenten/Vorsitzenden zurücktreten

▶ **step forward** **VI** vortreten; *(fig)* sich melden

▶ **step in** **VI** **a** *(lit)* eintreten (*-to, +prep obj* in *+acc*); **she suddenly stepped into a totally new world** sie fand sich plötzlich in einer ganz neuen Welt wieder **b** *(fig)* eingreifen, einschreiten; *(interferingly)* dazwischenkommen

▶ **step off** **VI** *+prep obj (off bus, plane, boat)* aussteigen (*prep obj* aus); **to step off the pavement** vom Bürgersteig treten; **step off!** (*US sl*) verpiss dich! *sl*

▶ **step out** **VT** *sep (= measure)* abschreiten **VI** **a** *(= go out)* hinausgehen **b** *(= walk briskly)* zügig *or* schnell gehen, forsch ausschreiten *(liter)*; *(= speed up)* schneller gehen **c** **to be stepping out with sb** *(dated)* mit jdm gehen

▶ **step up** **VT** *sep* steigern; *efforts also, security, campaign, search, criticism, support, activities* verstärken; *pressure also, demands, volume, numbers, pace* erhöhen; *fight* steigern; **to step up a gear** *(fig)* eine Stufe höherschalten **VI** **a** *(= come forward)* vortreten; **to step up to sb** auf jdn zugehen/zukommen; **step up, ladies and gentlemen** treten Sie näher, meine Damen und Herren; **he stepped up onto the stage** er trat auf die Bühne; **he stepped up another rung** er stieg eine Sprosse höher **b** *(= increase)* zunehmen; *(rate, pressure)* ansteigen

step- **PREF** Stief-; **stepbrother** Stiefbruder *m*; **stepchild** Stiefkind *nt*; **stepdaughter** Stieftochter *f*; **stepfather** Stiefvater *m*; **stepmother** Stiefmutter *f*

step aerobics **N** *sing* Steppaerobic *nt*

stepbrother **N** Stiefbruder *m*

step-by-step ['stepbaɪ'step] **ADJ** schrittweise

stepdad **N** *(inf)* Stiefvater *m*

stepdaughter **N** Stieftochter *f*

step-down ['stepdaʊn] **ADJ** *(Elec)* heruntertransformierend

stepfather **N** Stiefvater *m*

Stephen ['stiːvn] **N** Stephan *m*

stepladder ['step,lædəʳ] **N** Stufenleiter *f*, Trittleiter *f*

step machine **N** *(in fitness centre)* Stepper *m*

stepmother, **stepmum** *(Brit inf)* **N** Stiefmutter *f*

step-off ['stepɒf] **N** Steilabhang *m*

steppe [step] **N** Steppe *f*

stepper motor ['stepə,məʊtəʳ] **N** Schrittmotor *m*

stepping stone ['stepɪŋ,stəʊn] **N** (Tritt)stein *m*; *(fig)* Sprungbrett *nt*

step pyramid **N** Stufenpyramide *f*

stepsister **N** Stiefschwester *f*

stepson ['stepsʌn] **N** Stiefsohn *m*

step-up ['stepʌp] **N** (*inf*: *= increase*) Anstieg *m*, Zunahme *f* *(in +gen)* **ADJ** *(Elec)* herauftransformierend;

stepwise ['stepwaɪz] **ADJ**, **ADV** schritt- *or* stufenweise

stereo ['sterɪəʊ] **N** Stereo *nt*; *(= record-player)* Stereoanlage *f*; **in ~** in Stereo; **on the ~** auf einem Stereogerät **ADJ** Stereo-; **~ unit** Stereoanlage *f*

stereophonic [ˌsterɪəʊ'fɒnɪk] ADJ stereofon, stereophon

stereophony [ˌsterɪ'ɒfənɪ] N Stereofonie *f*, Stereophonie *f*, Raumklang *m*

stereoscope ['sterɪəʊˌskəʊp] N Stereoskop *nt*

stereoscopic [ˌsterɪəʊ'skɒpɪk] ADJ stereoskopisch

stereotype ['sterɪəˌtaɪp] N **a** *(fig)* Klischee (-vorstellung *f*), Stereotyp *nt*; *(= stereotype character)* stereotype Figur; **the ~ of the Englishman** der typische Engländer **b** *(Typ, = plate)* Stereotypplatte *f*; *(= process)* Plattendruck *m* ATTR stereotyp; *ideas, thinking also* klischeehaft VT **a** *(fig) character* klischeehaft zeichnen *or* darstellen; **the plot of the Western has become ~d** die Handlung des Western ist zu einem Klischee geworden; **I don't like being ~d** ich lasse mich nicht gern in ein Klischee zwängen **b** *(Typ)* stereotypieren

stereotyped ['sterɪəˌtaɪpt] ADJ = **stereotype ATTR**

stereotypical [ˌstɪərɪə'tɪpɪkl] ADJ stereotyp

sterile ['steraɪl] ADJ **a** *animal, soil* unfruchtbar; *person* steril, unfruchtbar; *(fig: = fruitless)* ergebnislos, unfruchtbar **b** *(= germ-free)* steril, keimfrei; *(fig)* steril

sterility [ste'rɪlɪtɪ] N **a** *(of animal, soil)* Unfruchtbarkeit *f*; *(of person also)* Sterilität *f*; *(fig: = fruitlessness also)* Ergebnislosigkeit *f* **b** *(= absence of contamination, fig)* Sterilität *f*

sterilization [ˌsterɪlaɪ'zeɪʃən] N Sterilisierung *f*, Sterilisation *f*

sterilize ['sterɪlaɪz] VT *person, instruments* sterilisieren

sterilizer ['sterɪlaɪzə'] N *(for instruments)* Sterilisator *m*

sterling ['stɜːlɪŋ] ADJ **a** *(Fin)* Sterling-; **in pounds ~** in Pfund Sterling **b** *(fig)* gediegen; *character* lauter **c ~ cutlery** Silberbesteck *nt* N **a** *no art (= money)* das Pfund Sterling, das englische Pfund; **in ~** in Pfund Sterling **b** *(= silver)* (Sterling)silber *nt* ADJ *attr* aus (Sterling)-silber

sterling area N Sterlinggebiet *nt*, Sterlingblock *m*

sterling silver N Sterlingsilber *nt*

stern¹ [stɜːn] N *(Naut)* Heck *nt*; **the ~ of the ship** das Achterschiff

stern² ADJ *(+er) (= strict)* streng; *words also, character, warning* ernst; *(= tough) test* hart; *opposition* stark, hart; **with a ~ face** mit strenger Miene; **made of ~er stuff** aus härterem Holz geschnitzt

sternly ['stɜːnlɪ] ADV **a** *(= severely) say, rebuke* ernsthaft; *look* streng; *warn* ernst; **a ~ worded statement** eine streng formulierte Aussage; **to deal ~ with sb/sth** streng mit jdm/etw umgehen **b** *(= firmly) forbid* streng; *oppose, resist* eisern

sternmost ['stɜːnməʊst] ADJ achterste(r, s)

sternness ['stɜːnnɪs] N Strenge *f*; *(of words, character, warning also)* Ernst *m*;

sternum ['stɜːnəm] N Brustbein *nt*, Sternum *nt* *(spec)*

sternway ['stɜːnweɪ] N *(Naut)* Heckfahrt *f*

sternwheeler ['stɜːnˌwiːlə'] N Heckraddampfer *m*

steroid ['stɪərɔɪd] N Steroid *nt*

stertorous ['stɜːtərəs] ADJ *(liter) breathing* röchelnd, rasselnd

stet [stet] *(Typ)* INTERJ stehen lassen *(Punkte unter falscher Korrektur)* VT die Korrektur *(+gen)* rückgängig machen

stethoscope ['steθəskəʊp] N Stethoskop *nt*

Stetson® ['stetsən] N Stetson® *m*, Texashut *m*

stevedore ['stiːvɪdɔː'] N Stauer *m*, Schauermann *m*

Steven ['stiːvn] N Stefan *m*

stew [stjuː] N **a** Eintopf *m* → **Irish stew b** *(inf)* **to be in a ~ (over sth)** (über etw *(acc)* or wegen etw) (ganz) aufgeregt sein **c** *(obs, = brothel)* Bordell *nt* VT **a** *meat* schmoren; *fruit* dünsten; **~ed apples** Apfelkompott *nt*; **the tea was ~ed** der Tee war bitter geworden **b to be ~ed** *(inf: = drunk)* voll sein *(inf)*; **to get ~ed** sich volllaufen lassen *(inf)* VI *(meat)* schmoren; *(fruit)* dünsten; *(inf: tea)* bitter werden; **to let sb ~** *or* **to leave sb to ~ (in his/her own juice)** jdn (im eigenen Saft) schmoren lassen

steward ['stjuːəd] N Steward *m*; *(on estate etc)* Verwalter(in) *m(f)*; *(at dance, meeting)* Ordner(in) *m(f)*; *(= bouncer)* Türsteher(in) *m(f)*; *(= shop steward)* (gewerkschaftlicher) Vertrauensmann *(im Betrieb)*

stewardess [ˌstjuːə'des] N Stewardess *f*

stewardship ['stjuːədʃɪp] N Verwaltung *f*; *(= rank, duties)* Verwalteramt *nt*

stewing ['stjuːɪŋ]: **stewing pan** N Kasserolle *f*, Bratentopf *m*; **stewing steak** ['stjuːɪŋˌsteɪk] N *(Brit)* Rindfleisch *nt* für Eintopf

stewpot N Schmortopf *m*

St. Ex. *abbr of* **Stock Exchange**

STI *abbr of* **sexually transmitted infection** Geschlechtskrankheit *f*

stick¹ [stɪk] N **a** Stock *m*; *(= twig)* Zweig *m*; *(= conductor's baton)* Taktstock *m*; *(= hockey stick)* Schläger *m*; *(= drumstick)* Schlegel *m*; **it was used as a ~ to beat us with** *(fig)* es wurde gegen uns verwendet; **he might try to use the vote as a ~ to beat striking coal miners with** vielleicht versucht er, die Abstimmung als Peitsche gegen die streikenden Bergarbeiter einzusetzen; **to give sb the ~, to take the ~ to sb** jdm eine Tracht Prügel geben; **to give sb/sth some/a lot of ~** *(Brit inf: = criticize)* jdn/etw heruntermachen *(inf)* or herunterputzen *(inf)*; **to take (a lot of) ~** *(Brit inf)* viel einstecken (müssen); **just a few ~s of furniture** nur ein paar Möbelstücke; **to carry a big ~** *(fig)* Macht haben; **they adopted the policy of the big ~** sie holten den großen Knüppel raus *(inf)*; **to get hold of the wrong end of the ~** *(fig inf)* etw falsch verstehen → **carrot**

b *(of sealing wax, celery, rhubarb, dynamite)* Stange *f*; *(of chalk, shaving soap)* Stück *nt*; *(Aviat: = joystick)* Steuerknüppel *m*; *(of bombs)* Bombenladung *f* für Reihenabwurf; *(Typ)* Winkelhaken *m*; **a ~ deodorant** *(Brit)* **a deodorant ~, a ~ of deodorant** ein Deostift *m*; **a ~ of rock** eine Zuckerstange

c *(Brit inf: = person)* Kerl *m (inf)*; **he's/she's a funny old ~** er/sie ist ein komischer Kauz; **he's/she's such a dry old ~** er/sie ist ein solcher Stockfisch

d the ~s *(Horse Racing inf)* die Hürden *pl*

e in the ~s *(= backwoods)* in der hintersten *or* finsteren Provinz

VT *plants* stützen

stick² *pret, ptp* **stuck** VT **a** *(with glue etc)* kleben; **to ~ a stamp on sth** eine Briefmarke auf etw *(acc)* kleben; **please ~ the posters to the walls with pins** bitte die Poster mit Stecknadeln an den Wänden befestigen; **is this glue strong enough to ~ it?** wird dieser Klebstoff das halten?; **to ~ the blame on sb** jdm die Schuld zuschieben

b *(= pin)* stecken; **he stuck a badge on his lapel** er steckte sich *(dat)* ein Abzeichen ans Revers; **he stuck a badge on her** er steckte ihr ein Abzeichen an

c *(= jab) knife, sword etc* stoßen; **he stuck a knife into her arm** er stieß ihr ein Messer in den Arm; **he stuck a pin into his finger** *(accidentally)* er hat sich *(dat)* mit einer Nadel in den Finger gestochen → *also* **stick in**

d *pig* (ab)stechen; **he stuck him with his bayonet** er spießte ihn mit dem Bajonett auf

e *(inf: = place, put)* tun *(inf)*; *(esp in sth)* stecken *(inf)*; **~ it on the shelf** tus ins *or* aufs Regal; **he stuck his head round the corner** er steckte seinen Kopf um die Ecke; **to ~ one's hat on** sich *(dat)* den Hut aufsetzen; **he stuck a drink in my hand and a record on the turntable** er drückte mir ein Glas in die Hand und legte eine Platte auf; **you know where you can ~ that** *(inf)* du kannst mich am Arsch lecken! *(vulg)*; **I'll tell him where he can ~ his job!** *(inf)* den Job kann er sich *(dat)* sonst wohin stecken *(inf)*

f *(= decorate: with pearls)* besetzen

g *(Brit inf: = tolerate)* aushalten; *pace, pressure of work* durchhalten; **I can't ~ him/that** ich kann ihn/das nicht ausstehen *(inf)*; **I can't ~ it any longer!** ich halte das nicht mehr (länger) aus!

h to ~ sb with sth *(inf) (= lumber)* jdm etw aufladen *or* aufhalsen *(inf)*; *(with bill)* jdm etw andrehen

VI **a** *(glue, burr etc)* kleben *(to* an *+dat)*; **to make a charge ~** genügend Beweismaterial haben; **you'll never make it ~!** damit kommen Sie nie durch!; **how do they hope to make the charge ~?** wie wollen sie das (je) beweisen?; **the name seems to have stuck** der Name scheint ihm/ihr geblieben zu sein

b *(= become caught, wedged etc)* stecken bleiben; *(drawer, window)* klemmen; **the word "please" seems to ~ in her throat** sie scheint das Wort „bitte" nicht über die Lippen bringen zu können → **stuck**

c *(sth pointed)* stecken *(in* in *+dat)*; **it stuck in my foot** das ist mir im Fuß stecken geblieben

d *(Cards)* halten

e *(= project)* **his toes are ~ing through his socks** seine Zehen kommen durch die Socken; **we could see Manfred's head ~ing over the wall** wir sahen Manfreds Kopf über die Mauer gucken *(inf)*; **a narrow finger of land ~ing into German territory** ein schmaler Landstreifen, der in deutsches Gebiet hineinragt

f *(= stay)* bleiben; *(slander)* haften bleiben; **to ~ in sb's mind** jdm im Gedächtnis bleiben; **to make sth ~ in one's mind** sich *(dat)* etw einprägen; **a teacher must be able to make things ~** der Lehrer muss den Stoff so bringen, dass er haften bleibt

▶ **stick around** VI *(inf)* dableiben; **stick around!** warts ab!; **he decided to stick around Bonn** er beschloss, noch in Bonn zu bleiben

▶ **stick at** VI *+prep obj* **a** *(= persist)* bleiben an *(+dat) (inf)*; **to stick at it** dranbleiben *(inf)* **b** *(= stop at)* zurückschrecken vor *(+dat)*; **he will stick at nothing** er macht vor nichts halt

▶ **stick by** VI *+prep obj sb* halten zu; *promise* stehen zu; *rules, principles* sich halten an

▶ **stick down** VT *sep* **a** *(= glue)* ankleben; *envelope* zukleben **b** *(inf: = put down)* abstellen; *(= write down)* aufschreiben

▶ **stick in** VT *sep* **a** *(= glue) stamps etc* einkleben; **to stick stamps in(to) an album** Briefmarken in ein Album kleben **b** *(= put in)* hineinstecken; *knife etc* hineinstechen; **to stick sth in(to) sth** etw in etw *(acc)* stecken; *(= prick) knife, pin etc* mit etw in etw *(acc)* stechen; **he stuck his knife in(to) the table** er stieß das Messer in den Tisch; **she stuck a knife in(to) him** sie stieß ihm ein Messer in den Leib VI *(knife, arrow)* stecken (bleiben)

▶ **stick on** VT *sep* **a** *label, cover* aufkleben *(prep obj* auf *+acc)* **b** *(= add) money* draufschlagen; *(+prep obj)* aufschlagen auf *(+acc)* VI **a** *(label etc)* kleben, haften *(prep obj* an *+dat)* **b** *(inf: on horse)* oben bleiben; **to stick on the horse** auf dem Pferd bleiben

▶ **stick out** VI vorstehen *(of* aus*)*; *(ears, hair)* abstehen; *(fig: = be noticeable)* auffallen; **his head was sticking out of the turret** sein Kopf sah aus dem Turm vor VT *sep* **a** herausstrecken **b** *(= not give up)* durchhalten; **I decided to stick it out a bit longer** ich beschloss, noch ein bisschen länger durchzuhalten

▶ **stick out for** VI *+prep obj* sich starkmachen für

▶ **stick to** VI *+prep obj* **a** *(= adhere to)* bleiben bei; *(= remain faithful to) principles etc* treu bleiben *(+dat)*; *(= follow) rules, timetable, plan, policy, diet* sich halten an *(+acc)* **b the photographers stuck to her wherever she went** die Fotografen hefteten sich ihr überall an die Fersen **c** *(= persist with) task* bleiben an *(+dat)*; **to stick to one's knitting** *(fig)* bei seinem Leisten bleiben

▸**stick together** VI zusammenkleben; (*fig: partners etc*) zusammenhalten

▸**stick up** VT *sep* **a** (*with tape etc*) zukleben **b** (*inf: = raise*) **stick 'em up!** Hände hoch!; **stick up your hand if you want to go** Hand hoch, wer gehen will; **three pupils stuck up their hands** drei Schüler meldeten sich **c** (*inf, = rob*) *bank* überfallen **d** (*inf*) **she just stuck up her nose and marched off** sie stolzierte erhobenen Hauptes weg; **don't stick your nose up at my cooking** rümpf bloß nicht die Nase über meine Kochkünste VI (*nail etc*) vorstehen; (*hair*) abstehen; (*collar*) hochstehen

▸**stick up for** VI +*prep obj sb, one's principles* eintreten für; **to stick up for oneself** sich behaupten

▸**stick with** VI +*prep obj* bleiben bei; (*= remain loyal to*) halten zu; *the leaders* mithalten mit

stick: **stick celery** N Stangensellerie *m*; **stick control** N (*Aviat*) Knüppelsteuerung *f*

sticker ['stɪkəʳ] N **a** (*= label*) Aufkleber *m*; (*= price sticker*) Klebeschildchen *nt* **b** (*inf, = determined person*) **he's a ~** er ist zäh

stick figure N Strichmännchen *nt*

stickiness ['stɪkɪnɪs] N (*lit*) Klebrigkeit *f*; (*of atmosphere, weather*) Schwüle *f*; (*of air*) Stickigkeit *f*; **the ~ of the situation** die heikle Situation

sticking ['stɪkɪŋ]: **sticking plaster** N (*Brit*) Heftpflaster *nt*; **sticking point** N **the main ~ (in the discussion) was …** der kontroverseste Punkt (in der Diskussion) war …

stick insect N Gespenstheuschrecke *f*

stick-in-the-mud ['stɪkɪnðə,mʌd] (*inf*) N Muffel *m* (*inf*) ADJ rückständig; *parents etc also* muffelig (*inf*)

stickleback ['stɪklbæk] N Stichling *m*

stickler ['stɪkləʳ] N **to be a ~ for sth** es mit etw peinlich genau nehmen

stick: **stick-on** ADJ zum Aufkleben; **~ label** Klebeetikett *nt*; **stick-out** (*US inf*) ADJ herausragend, Star- N Star *m* (*among* unter +*dat*); **stick pin** N (*US*) Krawattennadel *f*; **stick-to-it-ive** [stɪk'tuːɪtɪv] ADJ (*US inf*) zäh, hartnäckig; **stick-to-it-ive-ness** [stɪk'tuːɪtɪvnɪs] N (*US inf*) Zähigkeit *f*, Hartnäckigkeit *f*; **stickum** ['stɪkəm] N (*US inf*) Klebstoff *m*, Kleister *m*; **stick-up** N (*inf*) Überfall *m*

sticky ['stɪkɪ] ADJ (+*er*) **a** klebrig; *paint* feucht; *atmosphere, weather* schwül; *air* stickig; (*= sweaty*) *hands* feucht, verschwitzt; **I'm all hot and ~** ich bin total verschwitzt; **to have ~ eyes** verklebte Augen haben; **to be ~ with blood/sweat** blut-/schweißverklebt sein; **~ bun** ≈ Krapfen *m*; **~ label** Klebeetikett *nt*; **~ note** Haftnotiz *f*; **~ tape** (*Brit*) Klebeband *nt* **b** (*fig inf*) *problem, person* schwierig; *situation, moment* heikel; **he was a bit ~ about it** er hat dabei Schwierigkeiten gemacht; **we had a ~ time in the discussion** wir hatten in der Diskussion ein paar heikle Augenblicke; **to go through a ~ patch** eine schwere Zeit durchmachen; **to find the going ~** sich schwertun; **to come to a ~ end** ein böses Ende nehmen; **to be** *or* **to bat on a ~ wicket** in der Klemme sein; **he's got ~ fingers** (*Brit fig*) er hat lange Finger (*inf*)

stiff [stɪf] ADJ (+*er*) **a** steif; *corpse* starr, steif; *brush, bristles* hart; *dough, paste* fest **b** *resistance, drink, dose* stark; *fight* zäh, hart; *sentence, challenge, competition* hart; *opposition* stark, heftig; *breeze* steif; *climb, test* schwierig; *examination, task* schwer, schwierig; *penalty, punishment* schwer; *price, demand* hoch; **that's a bit ~** das ist ganz schön happig (*inf*) **c** *door, lock, drawer* klemmend **d** **to be ~ with cold** steif gefroren sein; **to go ~ with terror** in Angststarre verfallen; **to be (as) ~ as a board** *or* **poker** steif wie ein Brett sein **e** *smile* kühl; *bow, person, manner, atmosphere* steif ADV steif N (*inf*) Leiche *f*

stiff: **stiff arm** N (*US*) **to give sb the ~** jdn mit ausgestrecktem Arm wegstoßen; **stiff-arm** VT (*US*) **to ~ sb** jdn mit ausgestrecktem Arm wegstoßen

stiffen ['stɪfn] (*also* **stiffen up**) VT steif machen; *shirt etc* stärken, steifen; (*disease*) *limb* steif werden lassen; *resistance etc* verstärken VI steif werden; (*fig: resistance*) sich verhärten; (*breeze*) auffrischen; **when I said this she ~ed (up)** als ich das sagte, wurde sie ganz starr

stiffener ['stɪfnəʳ] N (*for collar*) Kragenstäbchen *nt*; (*= starch etc*) Stärke *f*

stiffening ['stɪfnɪŋ] N Einlage *f*

stiffly ['stɪflɪ] ADV steif; *starched* kräftig

stiff-necked [,stɪf'nekt] ADJ (*fig*) halsstarrig

stiffness ['stɪfnɪs] N **a** Steifheit *f*; (*of corpse also*) Starre *f*; (*of brush*) Härte *f*; (*of dough, paste*) Festigkeit *f* **b** (*of resistance, opposition, dose*) Stärke *f*; (*of fight*) Zähigkeit *f*; (*of sentence, challenge, competition*) Härte *f*; (*of breeze*) Steifheit *f*; (*of climb, test, task*) Schwierigkeit *f*; (*of penalty, punishment*) Schwere *f*; (*of price, demand*) Höhe *f* **c** (*of door, lock, drawer*) Klemmen *nt* **d** (*of person, bow, manner*) Steifheit *f*

stifle ['staɪfl] VT (*= suffocate*) ersticken; (*fig*) *laugh, cough also, rage, opposition* unterdrücken; **the heat nearly ~d them** sie sind fast umgekommen vor Hitze VI ersticken

stifling ['staɪflɪŋ] ADJ **a** *fumes, smoke* erstickend; *heat* drückend; **it's ~ in here** es ist ja zum Ersticken hier drin (*inf*) **b** (*fig*) beengend; *situation* erdrückend; *atmosphere* stickig

stigma ['stɪgmə] N **a** *pl* **-s** (*= mark of shame*) Brandmal *nt*, Stigma *nt* **b** *pl* **-ta** [stɪg'mɑːtə] Wundmal *nt*; (*Rel*) Stigmatisierung *f* **c** *pl* **-s** (*Bot*) Narbe *f*, Stigma *nt*

stigmatize ['stɪgmətaɪz] VT **a** (*Rel*) stigmatisieren **b** **to ~ sb as sth** jdn als etw brandmarken

stile [staɪl] N (Zaun)übertritt *m*

stiletto [stɪ'letəʊ] N (*esp Brit*) **a** (*= knife*) Stilett *nt* **b** (*also* **stiletto heel**) Bleistift- *or* Pfennigabsatz *m*, Stilettoabsatz *m* **c** (*also* **stiletto-heeled shoe**) Schuh *m* mit Bleistift- *or* Pfennigabsatz

still[1] [stɪl] ADJ, ADV (+*er*) **a** (*= motionless*) bewegungslos; *person* bewegungs- *or* reglos; *sea, waters* ruhig; **to keep ~** stillhalten, sich nicht bewegen; **to hold sth ~** etw ruhig *or* still halten; **to be ~** (*vehicle, measuring needle etc*) stillstehen; **to lie ~** still *or* reglos daliegen; **to stand/sit ~** still stehen/sitzen; **my heart stood ~** mir stockte das Herz; **time stood ~** die Zeit stand still; **his hands were never ~** seine Hände ruhten nie; **~ waters run deep** (*Prov*) stille Wasser sind tief (*Prov*) **b** (*= quiet, calm*) still; **be ~!** (*US*) sei still!; **a ~ small voice** ein leises Stimmchen ADJ *wine* nicht moussierend; *drink* ohne Kohlensäure; **a ~ photograph** ein Standfoto *nt* N **a** Stille *f*; **in the ~ of the night** in der nächtlichen Stille, in der Stille der Nacht **b** (*Film*) Standfoto *nt*; **~(s) photographer** Fotograf(in) *m(f)* VT (*liter: = calm*) beruhigen; *anger* besänftigen; *sounds* zum Verstummen bringen; *passion, pain* abklingen lassen, stillen; **to ~ sb's fears** jdm die Furcht nehmen VI sich legen; **the roar of the crowd ~ed to a murmur** der Lärm der Menge legte sich zu einem Murmeln

still[2] ADV **a** (*temporal*) noch; (*for emphasis, in exasperation, used on its own*) immer noch; (*in negative sentences*) noch immer, immer noch; (*= now as in the past*) nach wie vor; **is he ~ coming?** kommt er noch?; **she is ~ in the office** sie ist noch im Büro; (*with emphasis*) sie ist immer noch im Büro; **do you mean you ~ don't believe me?** willst du damit sagen, dass du mir immer noch nicht *or* noch immer nicht glaubst?; **it ~ hasn't come** es ist immer noch nicht gekommen; **I will ~ be here** ich werde noch da sein; **will you ~ be here at 6?** bist du um 6 noch da?; **the results have ~ to be published** die Ergebnisse müssen (erst) noch veröffentlicht werden; **the problems were ~ to come** die Probleme sollten erst noch kommen; **there are ten weeks ~ to go** es bleiben noch zehn Wochen; **there will ~ be objections, no matter …** es wird nach wie vor Einwände geben, egal … **b** (*esp US inf: also* **still and all**: *= nevertheless, all the same*) trotzdem; **~, it was worth it** es hat sich trotzdem gelohnt; **~, he's not a bad person** na ja, er ist eigentlich kein schlechter Mensch; **~, he is my brother** er ist trotz allem mein Bruder; **rich but ~ not happy** reich und doch nicht glücklich; **~, at least we didn't lose anything** na ja, wir haben wenigstens nichts dabei verloren; **~, what can you expect?** was kann man auch anderes erwarten? **c** (*with comp*) noch; **~ better** noch besser; **better ~, do it this way** oder noch besser, mach es so; **~ more (so) because …** und umso mehr, als …, und umso mehr, weil …; **more seriously ~** *or* **~ more serious is …** noch ernster ist …; **worse ~, …** schlimmer noch, … CONJ (und) dennoch

still[3] N Destillierapparat *m*; (*= small distillery*) Brennerei *f*

still: **stillbirth** N Totgeburt *f*; **stillborn** ADJ (*lit, fig*) tot geboren; **the child was ~** das Kind war eine Totgeburt, das Kind kam tot zur Welt; **still hunt** N **a** (*Hunt*) Pirschjagd *f* **b** (*US inf fig*) heimliche Jagd (*for* auf +*acc*); **still life** N *pl* **still lifes** Stillleben *nt*; **still-life** ADJ *attr* **a ~ picture/composition** ein Stillleben *nt*

stillness ['stɪlnɪs] N **a** (*= motionlessness*) Unbewegtheit *f*; (*of person*) Reglosigkeit *f* **b** (*= quietness*) Stille *f*, Ruhe *f*

still room N (*= pantry*) Vorratskammer *f*

stilt [stɪlt] N Stelze *f*; (*Archit*) Pfahl *m*; **a house built on ~s** ein Pfahlbau *m*

stilted ADJ, **stiltedly** ADV ['stɪltɪd, -lɪ] gestelzt, gespreizt

stiltedness ['stɪltɪdnɪs] N Gestelztheit *f*, Gespreiztheit *f*

Stilton® ['stɪltən] N Stilton *m*

stimulant ['stɪmjʊlənt] N Stimulans *nt*, Anregungsmittel *nt*; (*fig*) Ansporn *m* ADJ anregend, belebend

stimulate ['stɪmjʊleɪt] VT **a** (*= excite*) *body, circulation, mind* anregen; (*cold shower, coffee etc*) *sb* beleben; (*Med*) stimulieren; *nerve* reizen; (*sexually*) erregen, stimulieren; (*fig*) *person* animieren, anspornen; (*mentally, intellectually*) stimulieren; *sb's interest* erregen; **to ~ sb to do sth** jdn anspornen *or* dazu animieren, etw zu tun; **to ~ sb into activity** jdn aktiv werden lassen **b** (*= increase*) *economy, sales etc* ankurbeln; *growth, production, market* stimulieren; (*= incite*) *response* hervorrufen; *criticism* anregen zu; **to ~ investments** Investitionen anlocken

stimulating ['stɪmjʊleɪtɪŋ] ADJ anregend; *drug also* stimulierend; *bath, shower, walk, music* belebend; *prospect* ermunternd, animierend, beflügelnd; *experience* (*physically*) erfrischend, ermunternd; (*mentally*) stimulierend; **intellectually ~** intellektuell anregend *or* stimulierend; **visually ~** visuell anregend; **sexually ~** sexuell erregend

stimulation [,stɪmjʊ'leɪʃən] N **a** (*act, physical, mental*) Anregung *f*; (*from shower, walk etc*) belebende Wirkung; (*Med*) Stimulation *f*; (*sexual*) Stimulieren *nt*, Erregen *nt*; (*= state*) Angeregtheit *f*, Erregung *f*; (*sexual*) Erregung *f*; (*fig: = incentive*) Anreiz *m*, Ansporn *m*; (*intellectual*) Stimulation *f* **b** (*of economy, sales etc*) Ankurbelung *f* (*to* +*gen*); (*of criticism*) Anregung *f* (*of* zu); (*of response*) Hervorrufen *nt*

stimulative ['stɪmjʊlətɪv] ADJ anregend, belebend; (*esp Physiol*) stimulierend; **to have a ~ effect on the economy** konjunkturbelebend wirken

stimulus ['stɪmjʊləs] N *pl* **stimuli** ['stɪmjʊlaɪ] Anreiz *m*, Ansporn *m*; (*= inspiration*) Anregung *f*, Stimulus *m*; (*Physiol*) Reiz *m*; (*Psych*) Stimulus *m*; **it gave the trade new ~** das hat dem Handel neuen Aufschwung gegeben

stimy VT = **stymie**

sting [stɪŋ] vb: pret, ptp **stung** N a (Zool, Bot: = organ, of insect) Stachel *m*; (of jellyfish) Brennfaden *m*; (of nettle) Brennhaar *nt*
b (of insect: = act, wound) Stich *m*; (of nettle, jellyfish, = act) Brennen *nt*; (= wound) Quaddel *f*
c (= pain, from needle etc) Stechen *nt*, stechender Schmerz; (of antiseptic, ointment, from nettle etc) Brennen *nt*; (of whip) brennender Schmerz; **there might be a bit of a ~** das brennt jetzt vielleicht ein bisschen; **we felt the ~ of the hail on our faces** wir spürten den Hagel wie Nadeln im Gesicht
d (fig, of remark, irony) Stachel *m*; (of attack, criticism etc) Schärfe *f*; **a ~ of remorse** Gewissensbisse *pl*; **to take the ~ out of sth** etw entschärfen; (out of remark, criticism also) einer Sache *(dat)* den Stachel nehmen; **to have a ~ in its tail** (story, film) ein unerwartet fatales Ende nehmen; (remark) gesalzen sein; **death, where now thy ~?** Tod, wo ist dein Stachel?
VT a (insect) stechen; (jellyfish) verbrennen; **she was stung by the nettles** sie hat sich an den Nesseln verbrannt
b **the hail stung our faces** der Hagel stach uns wie mit Nadeln im Gesicht
c (comments, sarcasm etc) treffen, schmerzen; (remorse, conscience) quälen; **he was stung by their insults** ihre Beleidigungen haben ihn sehr getroffen *or* geschmerzt; **to ~ sb into doing sth** jdn antreiben, etw zu tun; **he was stung into replying** er ließ sich dazu hinreißen zu antworten; **to ~ sb into action** jdn aktiv werden lassen
d (inf) **to ~ sb for sth** jdn bei etw ausnehmen *(inf)* *or* schröpfen *(inf)*; **could I ~ you for a fiver?** kann ich dir einen Fünfer abknöpfen? *(inf)*
VI a (insect) stechen; (nettle, jellyfish etc) brennen; (= burn: eyes, cut, ointment etc) brennen; **smoke makes your eyes ~** Rauch brennt in den Augen
b (hail etc) wie mit Nadeln stechen
c (comments, sarcasm etc) schmerzen

stingaree [ˈstɪŋəriː] N (US, Austral) Stachelrochen *m*

stinger [ˈstɪŋəʳ] N a (= cocktail) Stinger *m* b (US: = insect) stechendes Insekt c (US inf: = remark) Stichelei *f*, Spitze *f*

stingily [ˈstɪndʒɪlɪ] ADV (inf) knauserig *(inf)*, knickerig *(inf)*; **he ~ donated a mere 20p** knauserig *or* knickerig, wie er ist, hat er nur 20 Pence gespendet *(inf)*

stinginess [ˈstɪndʒɪnɪs] N (inf, of person, government) Geiz *m*, Knauserigkeit *f (inf)*, Knickerigkeit *f (inf)*; (of sum, portion, donation) Schäbigkeit *f*, Popeligkeit *f (inf)*

stinging [ˈstɪŋɪŋ] ADJ a pain, sensation, blow stechend; cut, slap, ointment brennend; rain peitschend; wind scharf b (fig) comment stechend, schneidend; attack scharf N (= sensation) Stechen *nt*

stinging nettle N Brennnessel *f*

stingray [ˈstɪŋreɪ] N Stachelrochen *m*

stingy [ˈstɪndʒɪ] ADJ (+er) (inf) person, government geizig, knauserig *(inf)*, knickerig *(inf)*; sum, portion, donation schäbig, popelig *(inf)*; **to be ~ with sth** mit etw knausern

stink [stɪŋk] vb: pret **stank**, ptp **stunk** N a (lit: = unpleasant smell) Gestank *m* (of nach); (fig, of corruption etc) (Ge)ruch *m* b (inf: = fuss, scandal) Knatsch *(inf)*, Stunk *(inf) m*; **to kick up** *or* **make a ~** Stunk machen *(inf)* VI a (lit: = smell unpleasant) stinken; **it ~s in here** hier (drin) stinkts; **it ~s to high heaven** das stinkt zum Himmel *(inf)* b (fig inf: = be bad) sauschlecht *or* miserabel sein *(inf)*; **the idea ~s** das ist eine sauschlechte *or* miserable Idee *(inf)*; **the whole business ~s** die ganze Sache stinkt *(inf)*

▶ **stink out** VT sep (Brit) a (inf) room verstänkern *(inf)* b fox etc ausräuchern

▶ **stink up** VT sep (US inf) room verstänkern *(inf)*

stink bomb N Stinkbombe *f*

stinker [ˈstɪŋkəʳ] N (inf: = person) Ekel *nt*, Fiesling *m (inf)*; (= problem, question) harter Brocken, harte Nuss; (= letter) gesalzener *or* geharnischter Brief; **that problem/meeting was a ~** das war ein ganz verzwicktes *(inf)* Problem/eine äußerst schwierige Besprechung

stinking [ˈstɪŋkɪŋ] ADJ a (lit) stinkend b (inf) beschissen *(inf)*; **you can keep your ~ money!** du kannst dein Scheißgeld behalten! *(inf)*; **I've got a ~ cold** ich habe eine Mordserkältung ADV (inf) **~ rich** (Brit) stinkreich *(inf)*

stinko [ˈstɪŋkəʊ] ADJ (inf: = extremely drunk) sturzbesoffen *(inf)*

stinky [ˈstɪŋkɪ] ADJ (+er) (inf: = smelly) stinkend

stint [stɪnt] N a (= allotted amount of work) Arbeit *f*, Aufgabe *f*; (= share) Anteil *m*, Teil *nt or m* (of an *+dat*); **to do one's ~** (= daily work) seine Arbeit leisten *or* tun; (= one's share) sein(en) Teil beitragen *or* tun; **a 2-hour ~** eine 2-Stunden Schicht; **he did a five-year ~ on the oil rigs** er hat fünf Jahre auf Ölplattformen gearbeitet; **my ~ was from 3 to 6/lasted two hours** ich war von 3 bis 6/zwei Stunden lang dran; **he has done his ~ of washing up** er hat seinen (An)teil am Abwaschen geleistet; **would you like to do a ~ at the wheel?** wie wärs, wenn du auch mal fahren würdest?; **that was a long ~** das hat vielleicht lange gedauert!; **I've finished my ~ for today** für heute habe ich genug getan; **he does a ~ in the gym/at the computer every day** er betätigt sich jeden Tag eine Weile in der Turnhalle/am Computer
b **without ~** ohne Einschränkung
VT sparen mit, knausern mit; **to ~ sb of sth** jdm gegenüber mit etw knausern; of praise, reward jdm etw vorenthalten; **to ~ oneself (of sth)** sich (mit etw) einschränken
VI **to ~ on sth** mit etw sparen *or* knausern

stipend [ˈstaɪpend] N (esp Brit: for official, clergyman) Gehalt *nt*; (US: for student) Stipendium *nt*

stipendiary [staɪˈpendɪərɪ] ADJ official, magistrate, duty nicht ehrenamtlich; **~ allowance** Gehalt *nt*, Bezüge *pl*

stipple [ˈstɪpl] VT picture in der Tupfentechnik malen; paint tupfen, in Tupfen auftragen VI die Tupfentechnik anwenden N Tupfen *pl*; (= technique) Tupfentechnik *f*

stipulate [ˈstɪpjʊleɪt] VT a (= make a condition) zur Auflage machen, verlangen b delivery date, amount, price festsetzen; size, quantity vorschreiben, festsetzen; conditions stellen, fordern, stipulieren *(geh)*

stipulation [ˌstɪpjʊˈleɪʃən] N a (= condition) Auflage *f*; **with** *or* **on the ~ that ...** unter der Bedingung *or* mit der Auflage, dass ... b (= act of stipulating, of delivery date, amount, price, size, quantity) Festsetzung *f*; (of conditions) Stellen *nt*, Fordern *nt*, Stipulation *f (geh)*

stipulator [ˈstɪpjʊleɪtəʳ] N (Jur) Vertragspartei *f*, Kontrahent(in) *m(f)*

stir [stɜːʳ] N a (lit) Rühren *nt*; **to give sth a ~** etw rühren; tea etc etw umrühren
b (fig: = excitement) Aufruhr *m*; **to cause** *or* **create a ~** Aufsehen erregen
VT a tea, paint, soup umrühren; cake mixture rühren; **~ sugar into the mixture** den Zucker darunterrühren; **he sat there thoughtfully ~ring his tea** er saß da und rührte gedankenverloren in seinem Tee; **to ~ the pot** (fig) die Sache am Kochen halten
b (= move) bewegen; limbs rühren; water, waves kräuseln; **come on, ~ yourself, we're late** *(inf)* komm, beweg dich, wir sind ohnehin schon spät dran; **if you want to pass the exam you'd better ~ yourself** wenn du die Prüfung bestehen willst, solltest du dich besser ranhalten *(inf)*
c (fig) emotions aufwühlen; passion, controversy, memories wachrufen; imagination anregen; curiosity anstacheln, erregen; blood in Wallung versetzen; (= incite) person anstacheln; (= move) person, heart rühren, bewegen; **to ~ sb to do sth** jdn bewegen, etw zu tun; (= incite) jdn dazu anstacheln, etw zu tun; **to ~ sb into action** jdn zum Handeln bewegen; **to ~ sb to pity** an jds Herz *(acc)* rühren, jds Mitleid erregen; **we were all ~red by the speech** wir waren alle von der Rede tief bewegt
VI a (= move) sich regen; (person) sich rühren, sich regen; (leaves, curtains, animal etc) sich bewegen; (emotion, anger etc) wach werden; (pity, love) sich rühren, wach werden
b (inf, through gossip etc) stänkern *(inf)*; **he's always ~ring** er muss immer stänkern *(inf)*

▶ **stir up** VT sep a liquid, mixture umrühren; cream rühren, schlagen; mud aufwühlen b (fig) curiosity, attention, anger, controversy erregen; memories, the past wachrufen; opposition, discord entfachen, erzeugen; hatred schüren; revolution, revolt anzetteln; mob aufstacheln; lazy person aufrütteln; **to stir up trouble** Unruhe stiften; **to stir sb up to do sth** jdn dazu anstacheln, etw zu tun; **that'll stir things up** das kann heiter werden!; **he's always trying to stir things up among the workers** er versucht immer, die Arbeiter aufzuhetzen

stir-fry [ˈstɜːˌfraɪ] N Pfannengericht *nt* VT (unter Rühren) kurz anbraten

stirrer [ˈstɜːrəʳ] N (Brit inf: = gossipmonger etc) Stänkerer *m*, Stänkerin *f (inf)*; (= troublemaker) Scharfmacher(in) *m(f) (inf)*, Agitator(in) *m(f)*

stirring [ˈstɜːrɪŋ] ADJ speech, music, scene, poetry bewegend; (stronger) aufwühlend; victory bewegend; days, times bewegt N (= development) **a ~ of interest** ein sich regendes Interesse; **there were ~s of unease/discontent** Unbehagen/Unzufriedenheit machte sich breit; **the first ~s of sth** die ersten Anzeichen *pl* von etw

stirrup [ˈstɪrəp] N Steigbügel *m (also Anat)*

stirrup: **stirrup cup** N Abschiedstrunk *m*; **stirrup pump** N Handspritze *f*

stitch [stɪtʃ] N a Stich *m*; (in knitting etc) Masche *f*; (= kind of stitch, in knitting etc) Muster *nt*; (in embroidery) Stichart *f*; **to put a few ~es in sth** etw mit ein paar Stichen nähen; **to put ~es in a wound** eine Wunde nähen; **he had to have ~es** er musste genäht werden; **he needed ~es in his arm** sein Arm musste genäht werden; **to have the ~es taken out** die Fäden gezogen bekommen; **a ~ in time saves nine** *(Prov)* was du heute kannst besorgen, das verschiebe nicht auf morgen *(Prov)*
b (inf: = piece of clothing) **she hadn't a ~ on** sie war splitter(faser)nackt *(inf)*; **I haven't a ~ to wear** ich habe überhaupt nichts anzuziehen
c (= pain) Seitenstiche *pl*
d **to be in ~es** (inf, from laughing) sich schieflachen *(inf)*; **the story had us all in ~es** wir haben uns alle darüber schiefgelacht *(inf)*; **he had us all in ~es** er brachte uns alle furchtbar zum Lachen *(inf)*
VT (Sew, Med) nähen; book (zusammen)heften, broschieren; (= mend) hole, tear zunähen, stopfen; (= embroider) sticken
VI nähen (at an *+dat*); (= embroider) sticken (at an *+dat*)

▶ **stitch down** VT sep festnähen

▶ **stitch on** VT sep aufnähen; button annähen

▶ **stitch up** VT sep a seam, wound, patient nähen; (= mend) hole etc zunähen, stopfen; (= sew up) hem hochnähen b (Brit inf: = frame) **I've been stitched up** man hat mich reingelegt *(inf)*; (= something has been foisted on me) man hat mir das untergejubelt *(inf)* c (Brit inf) agreement zusammenstoppeln *(inf)*

stitching [ˈstɪtʃɪŋ] N (= seam) Naht *f*; (ornamental) Zierstiche *pl*, Ziernaht *f*; (= embroidery) Stickerei *f*; (of book) Broschur *f*

stitching: **stitching machine** N Stepp- *or* Heftmaschine *f*; **stitching needle** N Heft- *or* Stücknadel *f*

stitch-up [ˈstɪtʃʌp] N (Brit inf) abgekartete Sache

stoat [stəʊt] N Wiesel *nt*

stock [stɒk] N a (= supply) Vorrat *m* (of an *+dat*); (Comm) Bestand *m* (of an *+dat*); **~ of knowledge** Wissensschatz *m*; **~ of information** Informationsmaterial *nt*; **to lay in a ~ of wood/**

candles *etc* sich *(dat)* einen Holz-/Kerzenvorrat *etc* anlegen; **to have sth in ~** etw vorrätig haben; **to be in ~/out of ~** vorrätig/nicht vorrätig sein; **to keep sth in ~** etw auf Vorrat haben; **to get sth from ~** etw vom Lager holen; **to take ~** *(Comm)* Inventur machen; *(fig)* Bilanz ziehen; **to take ~ of sb** jdn abschätzen; **to take ~ of sth** *(of situation, prospects)* sich *(dat)* klar werden über etw *(acc)*; *of one's life* Bilanz aus etw ziehen; **surplus ~** Überschuss *m*; **the ~ was auctioned** die Bestände wurden versteigert
b *(= livestock)* Viehbestand *m*; **some good ~** schönes Vieh
c *(Cook)* Brühe *f*
d *(Fin: = capital raised by company)* Aktienkapital *nt*; *(= shares held by investor)* Anteil *m*; *(= government stock)* Staatsanleihe *f*; **to have** *or* **hold ~ in oil companies** Ölaktien haben; **~s and shares** (Aktien und) Wertpapiere *pl*, Effekten *pl*
e *(Hort, of tree, plant)* Stamm *m*; *(of vine, rose)* Stock *m*; *(for grafting onto)* Wildling *m*, Unterlage *f*; *(for supplying grafts)* das Edelreis liefernde Pflanze
f *(Bot)* Levkoje *f*
g *(= tribe, race etc)* Stamm *m*; *(= descent)* Abstammung *f*, Herkunft *f*; *(Ling)* (Sprach)familie *f*, (Sprach)gruppe *f*; **to be** *or* **come of good ~** guter Herkunft sein; **to be from good farming ~** aus einer alten Bauernfamilie stammen
h *(= handle)* Griff *m*; *(of rifle)* Schaft *m*
i **to be on the ~s** *(ship)* im Bau sein; *(book etc)* in Arbeit sein
j **stocks** PL *(Hist: for punishment)* Stock *m*
k *(= neckcloth)* Halsbinde *f*
l *(Rail)* rollendes Material
m *(US Theat)* **to play in summer ~** bei den Sommeraufführungen mitwirken; **this play is in their ~** dieses Stück gehört zu ihrem Repertoire
ADJ *attr (Comm, fig)* Standard-; **~ size** Standardgröße *f*; **~ response** Standardantwort *f*
VT **a** *(shop etc) goods* führen
b *(= provide with stock) cupboard* füllen; *shop, library* ausstatten; *pond, river* (mit Fischen) besetzen; *farm* mit einem Viehbestand versehen

▶ **stock up** VI sich eindecken *(on* mit); *(squirrel etc)* einen Vorrat anlegen; **I must stock up on rice, I've almost run out** mein Reis ist fast alle, ich muss meinen Vorrat auffüllen VT *sep shop, larder etc* auffüllen; *library* anreichern; *farm* den Viehbestand *(+gen)* vergrößern; *lake, river* den Fischbestand vergrößern in *(+dat)*

stockade [stɒˈkeɪd] N *(= fence)* Palisade *f*; *(= area)* Einfriedung *f*, Umzäunung *f*

stock: **stockbreeder** N Viehzüchter(in) *m(f)*; **stockbreeding** N Viehzucht *f*; **stockbroker** N Börsenmakler(in) *m(f)*; **the ~ belt** *(Brit)* ≈ die reichen Villenvororte *pl*; **stockbroking** N Effektenhandel *m*, Wertpapierhandel *m*; **stock car** N **a** *(for racing)* Stockcar *m (frisierter, verstärkter Serienwagen)* **b** *(US Rail: = cattle truck)* Viehwag(g)on *m*, Viehwagen *m*; **stock-car racing** N Stockcarrennen *nt*; **stock certificate** N *(esp US; Econ, Fin)* Aktienzertifikat *nt*; **stock character** N *(Theat)* Typ *m* (im Rollenfach); **stock company** N **a** *(Fin)* Aktiengesellschaft *f* **b** *(US Theat)* Repertoiretheater *nt*; **stock corporation** N *(esp US; Econ)* **a** *(= incorporated company)* Kapitalgesellschaft *f* **b** *(= public company)* Aktiengesellschaft *f*; **stock cube** N Brüh- *or* Suppenwürfel *m*; **stock dividend** N *(esp US; Econ, Fin)* Dividende *f* in Form von Gratisaktien; **stock exchange** N Börse *f*; **stock farmer** N Viehhalter(in) *m(f)*; **stock farming** N Viehzucht *f*, Viehhaltung *f*; **stockfish** N Stockfisch *m*; **stockholder** N *(US)* Aktionär(in) *m(f)*; **stockholding** N **a** *(Comm: = storage)* Lagerhaltung *f*; *(= stock stored)* Lagerbestand *m* **b** *usu pl (Fin)* Aktienbestand *m*

stockily [ˈstɒkɪlɪ] ADV **~ built** stämmig

stockiness [ˈstɒkɪnɪs] N Stämmigkeit *f*

stockinet(te) [ˌstɒkɪˈnet] N (Baumwoll)trikot *m*

stocking [ˈstɒkɪŋ] N Strumpf *m*; *(knee-length)* Kniestrumpf *m*; *(of horse)* Fessel *f*; **in one's ~(ed) feet** in Strümpfen

stocking: **stocking filler** N kleines Geschenk *(für den Weihnachtsstrumpf)*; **stocking mask** N Strumpfmaske *f*; **stocking stitch** N glatt rechts gestricktes Muster; **in ~** glatt rechts gestrickt

stock in trade [ˌstɒkɪnˈtreɪd] N *(= tools, materials, also fig)* Handwerkszeug *nt*; **that joke is part of his ~** den Witz hat er ständig auf Lager

stockist [ˈstɒkɪst] N *(Brit)* (Fach)händler(in) *m(f)*; *(= shop)* Fachgeschäft *nt*

stock: **stockjobber** N *(Brit)* Börsenhändler(in) *m(f)*; *(US pej)* Börsenspekulant(in) *m(f)*; **stock list** N **a** *(Comm)* Warenliste *f* **b** *(Fin)* Börsenzettel *m*; **stockman** N **a** *(US, Austral)* Viehzüchter *m*; *(= farmhand)* Farmarbeiter *m* **b** *(US, in shop etc)* Lagerist *m*, Lagerverwalter *m*; **stock market** N Börsenmarkt *m*, Börse *f*; **stock option** N *(esp US; Econ)* Aktienbezugsrecht *nt (für Betriebsangehörige)*; **stockpile** N Vorrat *m* (of an *+dat*); *(of weapons)* Lager *nt*; **the nuclear ~** das Atomwaffenlager, das Kernwaffenarsenal VT Vorräte an *(+dat)* … anlegen; *(pej)* horten; **to ~ weapons** Waffenlager *or* Waffenarsenale anlegen; **stockpiling** [ˈstɒkˌpaɪlɪŋ] N Vorratsbildung *f*; **stock play** N *(Theat)* gängiges Repertoirestück; **stock room** N Lagerraum *m*, Lager *nt*; **stock-still** ADJ, ADV **to be/stand ~** stockstill sein/stehen; **stock swap** N *(Fin)* Aktientausch *m*; **stocktaking** N Inventur *f*; *(fig)* Bestandsaufnahme *f*; **stocktaking sale** N Ausverkauf *m* wegen Inventur, ≈ Jahresschlussverkauf *m*; **stock warrant** N *(esp US Fin)* (auf den Inhaber lautendes) Aktienzertifikat

stocky [ˈstɒkɪ] ADJ *(+er)* stämmig

stockyard [ˈstɒkjɑːd] N Viehhof *m*, Schlachthof *m*

stodge [stɒdʒ] N *(inf)* Pampe *f (inf)*

stodgy [ˈstɒdʒɪ] ADJ *(+er) food* pampig *(inf)*, schwer; *style* schwerfällig; *subject* trocken; *book* schwer verdaulich; *person* langweilig, fad

stog [stɒg] N *(sl: = cigarette)* Kippe *f (inf)*, Ziggi *f (inf)*

stog(e)y, stogie [ˈstəʊgɪ] N *(US inf: = cigar)* Zigarillo *nt*

Stoic [ˈstəʊɪk] *(Philos)* N Stoiker *m* ADJ stoisch

stoic [ˈstəʊɪk] N Stoiker(in) *m(f)* ADJ stoisch

stoical ADJ, **stoically** ADV [ˈstəʊɪkəl, -ɪ] stoisch

Stoicism [ˈstəʊɪsɪzəm] N *(Philos)* Stoizismus *m*

stoicism [ˈstəʊɪsɪzəm] N *(fig)* Stoizismus *m*, stoische Ruhe, Gleichmut *m*

stoke [stəʊk] VT *furnace* (be)heizen, beschicken *(spec)*; *fire* schüren; *(fig) inflation, fears, conflict, speculation* anheizen, schüren

▶ **stoke up** VT *sep furnace* (be)heizen, beschicken *(spec)*; *fire* schüren; *(fig) conflict, pressure, inflation, violence* anheizen, schüren VI *(= eat)* sich satt essen *(on* an *+dat)*; *(= drink)* tanken *(inf)*

stoke: **stokehold** N *(Naut)* Heizraum *m*; **stokehole** N **a** *(Naut)* Heizraum *m* **b** *(in furnace)* Schürloch *nt*

stoker [ˈstəʊkəʳ] N Heizer(in) *m(f)*; *(= device)* Beschickungsanlage *f*

stole[1] [stəʊl] N Stola *f*

stole[2] *pret of* **steal**

stolen [ˈstəʊlən] *ptp of* **steal** ADJ gestohlen; *pleasures* heimlich; **~ goods** gestohlene Waren *pl*, Diebesgut *nt*; **to receive ~ goods** Hehler *m* sein; **he was charged with receiving ~ goods** er wurde wegen Hehlerei angeklagt *or* der Hehlerei bezichtigt

stolid [ˈstɒlɪd] ADJ *person* phlegmatisch, stur *(pej)*; *indifference* stumpf; *determination, silence* beharrlich, stur *(pej)*

stolidly [ˈstɒlɪdlɪ] ADV phlegmatisch, stur *(pej)*; *remain silent, work* beharrlich, stur *(pej)*; **he is ~ British** er ist durch und durch ein Brite

stolidness [ˈstɒlɪdnɪs] N *(of person)* Phlegma *nt*, Sturheit *f (pej)*; **the ~ of his manner** sein Phlegma *nt*, seine sture Art *(pej)*

stoma [ˈstəʊmə] N *pl* **-ta** *(Bot)* Stoma *nt (spec)*

stomach [ˈstʌmək] N *(= abdomen)* Magen *m*; *(= belly, paunch)* Bauch *m*; *(fig: = appetite)* Lust *f* (for auf *+acc*), Interesse *nt* (for an *+dat*); **to lie on one's ~** auf dem Bauch liegen; **hold your ~ in** zieh den Bauch ein!; **to have a pain in one's ~** Magen-/Bauchschmerzen haben; **to hit sb in the ~** jdn in die Magengrube/Bauchgegend schlagen *or (bullet etc)* treffen; **on an empty ~** *(drink, take medicine etc)* auf leeren *or* nüchternen Magen; **on an empty/full ~** *(swim, drive etc)* mit leerem *or* nüchternem/vollem Magen; **an army marches on its ~** *(prov)* mit leerem Magen kann man nichts Ordentliches zustande *or* zu Stande bringen; **I feel sick to my ~** *(fig)* mir ist speiübel; **I have no ~ for that** das ist mir zuwider; *(for party, journey etc)* mir ist nicht danach (zumute); **he doesn't have the ~ for it** *(= guts)* dazu hat er nicht den Mumm *(inf)*; **to have a strong ~** eine guten Magen haben
VT *(inf) behaviour, rudeness, cruelty* vertragen; *person, film, music etc* ausstehen

stomach *in cpds* Magen-; **stomach ache** N Magenschmerzen *pl*; **stomach pump** N Magenpumpe *f*; **stomach trouble** N Magenbeschwerden *pl*; **stomach upset** N Magenverstimmung *f*

stomata [stəʊˈmɑːtə] *pl of* **stoma**

stomp [stɒmp] VI stapfen

stomping ground [ˈstɒmpɪŋˌgraʊnd] N Gefilde *nt usu pl*; **his old ~s** seine alten Jagdgründe *pl*; **we were far from our usual ~** wir waren weit entfernt von unseren heimatlichen Gefilden; **it is a favourite ~ for collectors** es ist ein beliebter Tummelplatz für Sammler; **it's the ~ of a lot of students** es ist ein beliebter Studententreff

stone [stəʊn] N **a** Stein *m*; **a heart of ~** ein Herz aus Stein; **a ~'s throw from the station** nur einen Steinwurf *or* Katzensprung vom Bahnhof entfernt; **to leave no ~ unturned** nichts unversucht lassen; **to have a ~ in one's kidney/gall bladder** einen Nieren-/Gallenstein haben; **to be set** *or* **cast** *or* **carved in ~** *(fig)* in Stein gemeißelt sein
b *(Brit: = weight) britische Gewichtseinheit = 6,35 kg*
ADJ Stein-, aus Stein; **~ building** Steinbau *m*
VT **a** *(= throw stones at)* mit Steinen bewerfen; *(= kill)* steinigen; **~ the crows!** *(Brit, inf)* jetzt brat mir einer einen Storch! *(inf)*
b *(esp Brit) fruit* entsteinen
c *(inf)* **to be ~d (out of one's mind)** total zu sein *(inf)*

stone: **Stone Age** N Steinzeit *f*; **stone-blind** ADJ stockblind *(inf)*; **stone-broke** ADJ *(US inf)* = **stony-broke**; **stone circle** N *(Brit)* Steinkreis *m*; **stone coal** N *(Miner)* Anthrazit *m*; **stone-cold** ADJ eiskalt ADV **~ sober** stocknüchtern *(inf)*; **stone crusher** N *(Tech)* Steinbrechmaschine *f*; **stone-dead** ADJ mausetot *(inf)*; **to kill sb/sth ~** jdm/einer Sache den Garaus machen *(inf)*; **stone-deaf** ADJ stocktaub *(inf)*; **stone erosion** N *(Build)* Steinfraß *m*; **stone fruit** N Steinfrucht *f*; *(as collective)* Steinobst *nt*; **stone marten** N *(Zool)* Stein- *or* Hausmarder *m*; **stonemason** N Steinmetz *m*; **stone pit**, **stone quarry** N Steinbruch *m*; **stoner** [ˈstəʊnəʳ] N *(inf)* Kiffer(in) *m(f)*; **stonewall** VI *(fig, esp Parl)* obstruieren; *(in answering questions)* ausweichen; *(Sport)* mauern *(sl)*; **stonewaller** [ˌstəʊnˈwɔːləʳ] N *(Pol)* Obstruktionspolitiker(in) *m(f)*; **stoneware** N Steingut *nt* ADJ *attr* aus Steingut; **stonewashed** ADJ *jeans* stone-washed; **stonework** N Mauerwerk *nt*

stonily [ˈstəʊnɪlɪ] ADV *(fig)* mit steinerner Miene, starr

stoniness [ˈstəʊnɪnɪs] N *(of ground etc)* Steinigkeit *f*; *(fig, of look etc)* Versteinertheit *f*

stoning [ˈstəʊnɪŋ] N Steinigen *nt*, Steinigung *f*

stonking ['stɒŋkɪŋ] *(dated Brit inf)* **ADJ** irre gut *(dated inf)* **ADV** irre *(dated inf)*; **to have a ~ good time** sich irre gut amüsieren *(sl)*

stony ['stəʊnɪ] **ADJ** *(+er) ground, beach* steinig; *texture* steinartig; *(fig) glance, silence* steinern; *person, welcome* kalt; *face* undurchdringlich

stony: **stony-broke** **ADJ** *(Brit inf)* völlig abgebrannt *(inf)*, total blank *or* pleite *(inf)*; **stony-faced** ['stəʊnɪ'feɪst] **ADJ** *(= solemn)* ernst; *(= impassive)* mit steinerner Miene; **stony-hearted** **ADJ** kaltherzig

stood [stʊd] *pret, ptp of* **stand**

stooge [stu:dʒ] **N** *(inf)* Handlanger(in) *m(f)*; *(= comedian's stooge)* Stichwortgeber(in) *m(f)*

stook [stu:k] **N** Hocke *f*

stool [stu:l] **N** **a** *(= seat)* Hocker *m*; *(= milking stool)* Schemel *m*; *(folding)* Stuhl *m*; **to fall between two ~s** sich zwischen zwei Stühle setzen; *(= be neither one thing nor the other)* weder dem einen noch dem anderen gerecht werden
b *(esp Med: = faeces)* Stuhl *m*

stool pigeon **N** **a** *(lit, fig: = decoy)* Lockvogel *m* **b** *(inf: = informer)* Spitzel *m (inf)*

stoop[1] [stu:p] **N** Gebeugtheit *f*; *(= deformity)* krummer Rücken, Buckel *m*; **to walk with a ~** gebeugt gehen; **to have a ~** einen Buckel *or* einen krummen Rücken haben **VT** beugen; *head (to avoid sth)* einziehen **VI** sich beugen *or* neigen (*over* über *+acc*); *(also* **stoop down***)* sich bücken; *(= have a stoop, walk with a stoop)* gebeugt gehen; **~ing shoulders** krumme Schultern *pl*; **to ~ to sth** *(fig)* sich zu etw herablassen *or* hergeben; **to ~ to doing sth** *(fig)* sich dazu herablassen *or* hergeben, etw zu tun

stoop[2] **N** *(US)* Treppe *f*

stooping ['stu:pɪŋ] **ADJ** gebückt, gebeugt, krumm

stop [stɒp] **N** **a** *(= act of stopping)* Halt *m*, Stoppen *nt*; **the signal is at ~** das Signal steht auf Halt *or* Stop; **to bring sth to a ~** *(lit)* etw anhalten *or* stoppen, etw zum Stehen bringen; *traffic* etw zum Erliegen bringen; *(fig) project, meeting, development* einer Sache *(dat)* ein Ende machen; *conversation* etw verstummen lassen; **to come to a ~** *(car, machine)* anhalten, stoppen; *(traffic)* stocken; *(fig, meeting, rain)* aufhören; *(research, project)* eingestellt werden; *(conversation)* verstummen; **to come to a dead/sudden ~** *(vehicle)* abrupt anhalten *or* stoppen; *(traffic)* völlig/plötzlich zum Erliegen kommen; *(rain)* ganz plötzlich aufhören; *(research, project, meeting)* ein Ende *nt*/ein abruptes Ende finden; *(conversation)* völlig/abrupt verstummen; **when the aircraft has come to a complete ~** wenn die Maschine völlig zum Stillstand gekommen ist; **to make a ~** *(bus, train, tram)* (an)halten; *(plane, ship)* (Zwischen)station machen; **to put a ~ to sth** einer Sache *(dat)* einen Riegel vorschieben
b *(= stay)* Aufenthalt *m*; *(= break)* Pause *f*; *(Aviat, for refuelling etc)* Zwischenlandung *f*; **to have a ~ for coffee** eine Kaffeepause machen; **to have a ~** haltmachen; **we had** *or* **made three ~s** wir haben dreimal haltgemacht; **to work for eight hours without a ~** acht Stunden ohne Unterbrechung arbeiten
c *(= stopping place)* Station *f*; *(for bus, tram, train)* Haltestelle *f*; *(for ship)* Anlegestelle *f*; *(for plane)* Landeplatz *m*
d *(Brit: = punctuation mark)* Punkt *m*
e *(Mus, of wind instruments)* (Griff)loch *nt*; *(on organ: also* **stopknob***)* Registerzug *m*; *(= organ pipe)* Register *nt*; **to pull out all the ~s** *(fig)* alle Register ziehen
f *(= stopper, for door, window)* Sperre *f*; *(on typewriter)* Feststelltaste *f*
g *(Phot: = f number)* Blende *f*
h *(Phon)* Verschlusslaut *m*; *(= glottal stop)* Knacklaut *m*
VT **a** *(= stop when moving) person, vehicle, clock* anhalten; *ball* stoppen; *engine, machine etc* abstellen; *blow* abblocken, auffangen; *(= stop from going away, from moving on) runaway, thief etc* aufhalten; *attack, enemy, progress* aufhalten, hemmen; *traffic (= hold up)* aufhalten; *(= bring to complete standstill)* zum Stehen *or* Erliegen bringen; *(policeman)* anhalten; *(= keep out) noise, light* abfangen, auffangen; **~ thief!** haltet den Dieb!; **to ~ a bullet** *(be shot)* eine Kugel verpasst kriegen *(inf)*; **to ~ sb dead** *or* **in his tracks** jdn urplötzlich anhalten lassen; *(in conversation)* jdn plötzlich verstummen lassen
b *(= stop from continuing) activity, rumour, threat, crime* ein Ende machen *or* setzen *(+dat)*; *nonsense, noise* unterbinden; *match, conversation, work* beenden; *development* aufhalten; *(temporarily)* unterbrechen; *flow of blood* stillen, unterbinden; *progress, inflation* aufhalten, hemmen; *speaker, speech* unterbrechen; *production* zum Stillstand bringen; *(temporarily)* unterbrechen; **he was talking and talking, we just couldn't ~ him** er redete und redete, und wir konnten ihn nicht dazu bringen, endlich aufzuhören; **the referee ~ped play** der Schiedsrichter hat das Spiel abgebrochen; *(temporarily)* der Schiedsrichter hat das Spiel unterbrechen lassen; **this will ~ the pain** das hilft gegen die Schmerzen
c *(= cease)* aufhören mit; **to ~ doing sth** aufhören, etw zu tun, etw nicht mehr tun; **she never ~s talking** sie redet ununterbrochen *or* in einer Tour *(inf)*; **to ~ smoking** mit dem Rauchen aufhören; *(temporarily)* das Rauchen einstellen; **I'm trying to ~ smoking** ich versuche, das Rauchen aufzugeben *or* nicht mehr zu rauchen; **~ saying that** nun sag das doch nicht immer; **~ it!** lass das!, hör auf!; **I just can't ~ it** ich kann es nicht lassen
d *(= suspend)* stoppen; *payments, production, fighting* einstellen; *leave, cheque, water supply, wages* sperren; *privileges* unterbinden; *subsidy, allowances, grant etc* streichen; *battle, negotiations, proceedings* abbrechen; *(= cancel) subscription* kündigen; *(temporarily) delivery, newspaper* abbestellen; **the money was ~ped out of his wages** *(Brit)* das Geld wurde von seinem Lohn einbehalten
e *(= prevent from happening) sth* verhindern; *(= prevent from doing) sb* abhalten; **to ~ oneself** sich beherrschen, sich bremsen *(inf)*; **can't you ~ him?** können Sie ihn nicht davon abhalten?; **there's no ~ping him** *(inf)* er ist nicht zu bremsen *(inf)*; **there's nothing ~ping you** *or* **to ~ you** es hindert Sie nichts, es hält Sie nichts zurück
f *(in participial construction)* **to ~ sb (from) doing sth** jdn davon abhalten *or (physically)* daran hindern, etw zu tun; *(= put a stop to)* dafür sorgen, dass jd etw nicht mehr tut *or* dass jd aufhört, etw zu tun; **to ~ sth (from) happening** *(= prevent, put a stop to)* (es) verhindern, dass etw geschieht; **that will ~ it (from) hurting** *(= prevent)* dann wird es nicht wehtun; *(= put a stop to)* dann wird es nicht mehr wehtun; **how can we ~ the baby (from) crying?** *(= prevent)* was können wir tun, damit das Baby nicht schreit?; **that'll ~ the gas (from) escaping/the pipe (from) leaking** das wird verhindern, dass Gas entweicht/das Rohr leckt; **to ~ the thief (from) escaping** den Dieb an der Flucht hindern; **it will ~ you from worrying** dann brauchen Sie sich *(dat)* keine Sorgen zu machen; **to ~ oneself from doing sth** sich zurückhalten und etw nicht tun
g *(= block)* verstopfen; *(with cork, bung, cement etc)* zustopfen (*with* mit); *(= fill) tooth* plombieren, füllen; *(fig) gap* füllen, stopfen; *leak of information* stopfen; *(Mus) string* greifen; *finger hole* zuhalten; **to ~ one's ears with cotton wool/one's fingers** sich *(dat)* Watte/die Finger in die Ohren stecken
VI **a** *(= halt)* anhalten; *(train, car)* (an)halten, stoppen; *(traveller, driver, hiker)* haltmachen; *(pedestrian, clock, watch)* stehen bleiben; *(engine, machine)* nicht mehr laufen; **~ right there!** halt!, stopp!; **we ~ped for a drink at the pub** wir machten in der Kneipe Station, um etwas zu trinken; **to ~ at nothing (to do sth)** *(fig)* vor nichts haltmachen(, um etw zu tun); **to ~ dead** *or* **in one's tracks** plötzlich *or* abrupt *or* auf der Stelle stehen bleiben → **short**
b *(= finish, cease)* aufhören; *(heart)* aufhören zu schlagen, stehen bleiben; *(production, payments, delivery)* eingestellt werden; *(programme, show, match, film)* zu Ende sein; **to ~ doing sth** aufhören, etw zu tun, mit etw aufhören; **ask him to ~** sag ihm, er soll aufhören; **he ~ped in mid sentence** er brach mitten im Satz ab; **I will not ~ until I find him/convince you** ich gebe keine Ruhe, bis ich ihn gefunden habe/dich überzeugt habe; **if you had ~ped to think** wenn du nur einen Augenblick nachgedacht hättest; **~ to think before you speak** erst denken, dann reden; **he never knows when** *or* **where to ~** er weiß nicht, wann er aufhören muss *or* Schluss machen muss
c *(Brit inf: = stay)* bleiben (*at* in *+dat*, *with* bei); **to ~ for** *or* **to supper** zum Abendessen bleiben

▶ **stop behind** **VI** *(inf)* (noch) dableiben, länger bleiben; *(Sch, as punishment)* nachsitzen

▶ **stop by** **VI** kurz vorbeikommen *or* vorbeischauen; **to stop by sb's house** bei jdm hereinschauen *(inf)*

▶ **stop down** **VI** *(Phot)* abblenden, eine niedrigere Blende einstellen

▶ **stop in** **VI** *(Brit inf)* drinbleiben *(inf)*; *(Sch, as punishment)* nachsitzen, dableiben

▶ **stop off** **VI** (kurz) haltmachen (*at sb's place* bei jdm); *(on travels also)* Zwischenstation machen (*at* in *+dat*); **let's stop off and pick up a pizza on the way home** lass uns kurz auf dem Heimweg eine Pizza mitnehmen

▶ **stop on** **VI** *(Brit inf)* (noch) dableiben, länger bleiben; **to stop on at school** in der Schule weitermachen

▶ **stop out** **VI** *(inf)* wegbleiben, streiken

▶ **stop over** **VI** kurz haltmachen; *(on travels)* Zwischenstation machen (*in* in *+dat*); *(Aviat)* zwischenlanden

▶ **stop up** **VT** *sep* verstopfen; *crack, hole also* zustopfen **VI** **a** *(inf, = stay up)* aufbleiben **b** *(Phot)* eine größere Blende einstellen

stop: **stop-and-go traffic** [ˌstɒpəŋgəʊ'træfɪk] **N** Stop-and-go-Verkehr *m*; **stop bit** **N** *(Comput)* Stoppbit *nt*; **stop button** **N** Halteknopf *m*; **stopcock** **N** Absperrhahn *m*; **stopgap** **N** *(= thing)* Notbehelf *m*; *(= scheme)* Notlösung *f*; *(= person)* Lückenbüßer(in) *m(f)*; **stopgap measure** **N** Überbrückungsmaßnahme *f*; **stop-go** **ADJ** *attr* **~ policies** Politik *f* des ewigen Hin und Her; **stoplight** **N** *(= brakelight)* Bremslicht *nt*, Stopplicht *nt*; *(esp US: = traffic light)* rotes Licht; **stop-loss order** ['stɒplɒs-ˌɔ:də'] **N** *(St Ex)* Stop-loss-Auftrag *m*; **stop-motion camera** ['stɒpˌməʊʃənˌkæmərə] **N** Zeitrafferkamera *f*; **stopover** **N** Zwischenstation *f*; *(Aviat)* Zwischenlandung *f*; **to have** *or* **make a ~** Zwischenstation/Zwischenlandung machen; **stopover ticket** **N** *(Aviat)* Rundreiseticket *nt*

stoppage ['stɒpɪdʒ] **N** **a** *(in work, game)* Unterbrechung *f*; *(in traffic)* Stockung *f*; *(in production etc, temporary, because of mechanical problems)* Unterbrechung *f*; *(for longer time, because of strike etc)* Stopp *m*; *(= strike)* Streik *m*; **~ of work** Arbeitsniederlegung *f* **b** *(of pay, leave, cheque)* Sperrung *f*; *(of delivery, supplies etc)* Stopp *m*; *(= deduction)* Abzug *m* **c** *(= blockage)* Verstopfung *f*, Stau *m*

stop payment **N** *(Fin: for cheques etc)* Zahlungssperre *f*

stopper ['stɒpə'] **N** *(= plug)* Stöpsel *m*; *(= cork also)* Pfropfen *m* **VT** verstöpseln

stopping ['stɒpɪŋ] **N** **~ and starting** *(in driving)* stückchenweises Vorwärtskommen, Stop-and-go-Verkehr *m*; *(in work)* ständige Unterbrechungen *pl*

stopping: **stopping place** **N** *(of bus, train etc)* Haltestelle *f*; **this is an ideal ~** das ist ein idealer Platz zum Haltmachen; **stopping train** **N** *(esp Brit)* Personenzug *m*

stop: **stop press** **N** *(esp Brit: = space)* Spalte *f* für letzte Meldungen; *(= news)* letzte Meldungen *pl*; **stop sign** **N** Stoppschild *nt*; **stopwatch** **N** Stoppuhr *f*

storable ['stɔ:rəbl] **ADJ** *goods etc* lagerfähig, Lager- **N** lagerfähige Ware

storage ['stɔːrɪdʒ] N *(of goods, food)* Lagerung *f*; *(of books, documents, in household)* Aufbewahrung *f*; *(of water, electricity, data)* Speicherung *f*, Speichern *nt*; *(= cost)* Lagergeld *nt*; **to put sth into ~** etw unterstellen, etw (ein)lagern → **cold storage**

storage: **storage battery** N Akkumulator *m*; **storage capacity** N *(of computer)* Speicherkapazität *f*; **storage charge** N Lagergeld *nt*; **storage density** N *(Comput)* Speicherdichte *f*; **storage device** N *(Comput)* Speichereinheit *f*; **storage disk** N *(Comput)* Speicherplatte *f*; **storage heater** N (Nachtstrom)speicherofen *m*; **storage problems** PL Lagerungsprobleme *pl*; *(in house)* Probleme *pl* mit der Aufbewahrung, Platzmangel *m*; **storage space** N Lagerraum *m*; *(in house)* Schränke und Abstellräume *pl*; **storage tank** N Vorratstank *m*

store [stɔːˈ] N **a** *(= stock)* Vorrat *m* (of an +*dat*); *(fig)* Fülle *f*, Schatz *m*, Reichtum *m* (of an +*dat*); **~s** *pl (= supplies)* Vorräte *pl*, Bestände *pl*; **to lay in a ~ of food/coal** einen Lebensmittel-/Kohlenvorrat anlegen; **to have** *or* **keep sth in ~** etw lagern, einen Vorrat von etw haben; *(in shop)* etw auf Lager *or* etw vorrätig haben; **to be in ~ for sb** jdm bevorstehen, auf jdn warten; **to have a surprise in ~ for sb** für jdn eine Überraschung auf Lager haben; **that's a treat in ~ (for you)** da habt ihr noch was Schönes vor euch, das ist etwas, worauf ihr euch freuen könnt; **what has the future in ~ for us?** was wird uns *(dat)* die Zukunft bringen?; **to set great/little ~ by sth** viel/wenig von etw halten, einer Sache *(dat)* viel/wenig Bedeutung beimessen; **a vast ~ of knowledge** ein großer Wissensschatz
b *(= place)* Lager *nt*; **he is** *or* **works in the ~s** er ist im Lager tätig; **to put one's furniture in ~** seine Möbel unterstellen *or* (ein)lagern
c *(Comput)* (Daten)speicher *m*
d *(= large shop, book store)* Geschäft *nt*; *(= department store)* Kaufhaus *nt*, Warenhaus *nt*; *(esp US: = shop)* Laden *m*
ADJ *attr (US) clothes* von der Stange; *bread* aus der Fabrik
VT lagern; *documents* aufbewahren; *furniture* unterstellen; *(in depository)* einlagern; *information, electricity, heat, energy* speichern; *(in one's memory)* sich *(dat)* merken; *(= equip, supply) larder etc* auffüllen; **the cellar can ~ enough coal for the winter** der Keller hat genügend Platz für die Winterkohle; **to ~ sth away** etw verwahren; **squirrels ~ away nuts for the winter** Eichhörnchen legen einen Vorrat von Nüssen für den Winter an; **to ~ sth up** einen Vorrat an etw *(dat)* anlegen; *(fig)* etw anstauen; *surprise* etw auf Lager haben; **to ~ up trouble for sb/oneself** jdm/sich Ärger bereiten; **hatred ~d up over years** jahrelang angestauter Hass
VI *(fruit, vegetables)* sich lagern *or* aufbewahren lassen

store: **store card** N Kundenkreditkarte *f*; **store detective** N Kaufhausdetektiv(in) *m(f)*; **storefront** ['stɔːfrʌnt] N *(esp US)* **a** Ladenfront *f* **b** *(Internet)* Storefront *f*; **storehouse** N Lager(haus) *nt*; *(fig)* Fundgrube *f*, Schatzkammer *f*; **storekeeper** N *(in storehouse)* Lagerverwalter(in) *m(f)*, Lagerist(in) *m(f)*; *(esp US: = shopkeeper)* Ladenbesitzer(in) *m(f)*, Geschäftsinhaber(in) *m(f)*; **storeman** N Lagerverwalter *m*, Lagerist *m*; *(esp US: = shopkeeper)* Ladenbesitzer *m*; **storeroom** N Lagerraum *m*; *(for food)* Vorratskammer *f*

storey, *(esp US)* **story** ['stɔːrɪ] N *pl* **-s** *or (US)* **stories** Stock(werk *nt*) *m*, Etage *f*; **a nine-~ building** ein neunstöckiges Gebäude, ein Gebäude mit neun Stockwerken *or* Etagen; **on the second ~** im zweiten Stock(werk), auf der zweiten Etage; *(US)* im ersten Stock(werk), auf der ersten Etage; **he fell from the third-~ window** er fiel aus dem Fenster des dritten *or (US)* zweiten Stock(werk)s *or* der dritten *or (US)* zweiten Etage

-storeyed, *(esp US)* **-storied** [-'stɔːrɪd] ADJ *suf* -stöckig; **an eight-storeyed building** ein achtstöckiges Gebäude

stork [stɔːk] N Storch *m*

storm [stɔːm] N **a** Unwetter *nt*; *(= thunderstorm)* Gewitter *nt*; *(= strong wind)* Sturm *m*; **there is a ~ blowing** es stürmt; **come in out of the ~** kommen Sie herein ins Trockene; **to brave the ~** dem Unwetter/Gewitter/Sturm trotzen; *(fig)* das Gewitter über sich *(acc)* ergehen lassen; **a ~ in a teacup** *(Brit fig)* ein Sturm im Wasserglas
b *(fig, of abuse, insults)* Flut *f* (of von); *(of applause, indignation, criticism)* Sturm *m* (of +*gen*); *(of blows, arrows, missiles)* Hagel *m* (of von); *(= outcry)* Aufruhr *m*; **~ of protest** Proteststurm *m*; **~ and stress** Sturm und Drang *m*
c **to take sth/sb by ~** *(Mil, fig)* etw/jdn im Sturm erobern
VT stürmen
VI **a** *(= talk angrily)* toben, wüten (*at* gegen); **he ~ed on for an hour about the government** er schimpfte eine Stunde lang wütend über die Regierung
b *(= move violently)* stürmen; **to ~ out of/into a room** aus einem/in ein Zimmer stürmen
c *(esp US Met)* stürmen

storm: **storm-beaten** ADJ *sea* sturmgepeitscht; **stormbound** ADJ vom Sturm aufgehalten; **storm centre**, *(US)* **storm center** N Sturmzentrum *nt*; *(fig)* Unruheherd *m*; **storm cloud** N *(lit, fig)* Gewitterwolke *f*; **storm cone** N Sturmkegel *m*; **storm door** N äußere Windfangtür; **storm force** N Windstärke *f*; **storm-force** ADJ *wind* mit Sturmstärke wehend

stormily ['stɔːmɪlɪ] ADV *(lit, fig)* stürmisch; *protest, reply, answer, react* hitzig, heftig

storminess ['stɔːmɪnɪs] N *(of reaction, temper)* Heftigkeit *f*; **the ~ of the weather** das stürmische Wetter; **the ~ of his reception** sein stürmischer Empfang

storming ['stɔːmɪŋ] ADJ *(inf: = impressive) performance, comeback* stürmisch

storm: **storm lantern** N Sturmlaterne *f*; **storm-lashed** ['stɔːmlæʃt] ADJ *sea* sturmgepeitscht; **storm petrel** N Sturmschwalbe *f*; **stormproof** ADJ sturmsicher; **storm signal** N Sturmsignal *nt*; **storm-tossed** ADJ *(liter)* sturmgepeitscht *(liter)*; **storm trooper** N *(NS)* SA-Mann *m*; **storm troopers** PL (Sonder)einsatzkommando *nt*; **storm troops** PL Sturmtruppe *f*; **storm warning** N Sturmwarnung *f*; **storm window** N äußeres Doppelfenster

stormy ['stɔːmɪ] ADJ (+*er*) *(lit, fig)* stürmisch; *discussion also, temper* hitzig; *protests* heftig; **he has a ~ temper** er ist jähzornig; **~ waters** *(fig)* turbulente Zeiten *pl*

stormy petrel N Sturmschwalbe *f*; *(fig)* Unglücksbote *m*/-botin *f*

story[1] ['stɔːrɪ] N **a** *(= tale)* Geschichte *f*; *(esp Liter)* Erzählung *f*; *(= joke)* Witz *m*; **it's a long ~** das ist eine lange Geschichte; **the ~ of her life** ihre Lebensgeschichte; **that's the ~ of my life** *(inf)* das plagt mich mein ganzes Leben lang! *(inf)*; *(said as a response)* wem sagen Sie das! *(inf)*; **that's another ~** das ist eine andere Geschichte; **the ~ goes that …** man erzählt sich, dass …; **his ~ is that …** er behauptet, dass …; **according to your ~** dir zufolge; **I've heard his (side of the) ~** ich habe seine Version gehört; **the full ~ still has to be told** die ganze Wahrheit muss noch ans Licht kommen; **that's not the whole ~** das ist nicht die ganze Wahrheit; **your school marks tell their own ~** deine Zeugnisnoten sprechen für sich; **to cut a long ~ short** um es kurz zu machen, kurz und gut; **it's the (same) old ~** es ist das alte Lied; **but it's a different ~ now** aber jetzt sieht die Sache anders aus
b *(Press: = event)* Geschichte *f*; *(= newspaper story)* Artikel *m*; **it'll make a good ~** das gibt einen guten Artikel
c *(= plot)* Handlung *f*
d *(inf: = lie)* Märchen *nt*; **to tell stories** Märchen erzählen

story[2] N *(US)* = **storey**

story: **storyboard** N *(TV, Film)* Storyboard *nt*; **storybook** N Geschichtenbuch *nt* ADJ *attr castles, romance etc* märchenhaft; **~ ending** Ende *nt* wie im Märchen, Happy End *nt*, Happyend *nt*; **story line** N Handlung *f*; **storyteller** N **a** *(= narrator)* Geschichtenerzähler(in) *m(f)* **b** *(inf, = liar)* Lügenbold *m*; **storytelling** N *no pl (spoken)* Geschichtenerzählen *nt*; *(written)* Erzählkunst *f*

stoup [stuːp] N *(Eccl)* Weihwasserbecken *nt*

stout [staʊt] ADJ (+*er*) **a** *(= corpulent) man* untersetzt, korpulent; *woman* füllig; **to get** *or* **grow ~** untersetzter/fülliger werden **b** *(= strong) stick, horse etc* kräftig; *door, rope, wall, gate* stark; *shoes* fest; *coat* dick **c** *(= brave) heart* tapfer; *person* beherzt; *fellow, resistance* beherzt, tapfer, mannhaft *(liter)*; *refusal, denial* entschieden; *belief* fest; *defence* hartnäckig; *opposition* zäh; *support* solide; **~ fellow!** *(dated inf)* tapferer Kerl! *(dated inf)*; **with ~ heart** tapferen Herzens N *(Brit)* Stout *m*, *dunkles, obergäriges Bier (= sweet stout)* Malzbier *nt*

stouthearted ADJ, **stoutheartedly** ADV [ˌstaʊt'hɑːtɪd, -lɪ] tapfer, unerschrocken, mannhaft *(liter)*

stoutish ['staʊtɪʃ] ADJ *person etc* ziemlich dick, korpulent *(geh, euph)*

stoutly ['staʊtlɪ] ADV *(= strongly) made* solide; *(= resolutely) resist, defend, fight* tapfer, beherzt, mannhaft *(liter)*; *believe, maintain* fest, steif und fest *(pej)*; *resist, refuse, deny* entschieden; **~ built** *(person)* stämmig, kräftig (gebaut); *wall, door* stark, kräftig; *house* solide gebaut; **~ Catholic** *etc* gut katholisch *etc*

stoutness ['staʊtnɪs] N **a** *(= corpulence)* Untersetztheit *f*, Korpulenz *f*; *(of woman)* Fülligkeit *f* **b** *(= sturdiness, of stick, horse)* Kräftigkeit *f*; *(of door, rope, wall, gate)* Stärke *f*; *(of shoes)* Festigkeit *f* **c** *(= resoluteness, of heart)* Tapferkeit *f*; *(of resistance also)* Beherztheit *f*, Mannhaftigkeit *f (liter)*; *(of refusal, denial)* Entschiedenheit *f*; *(of belief)* Festigkeit *f*

stove [stəʊv] N Ofen *m*; *(for cooking)* Herd *m*; **electric/gas ~** Elektro-/Gasherd *m*

stove: **stove enamel** N Einbrennlack *m*; **stovepipe** N Ofenrohr *nt*; **stovepipe hat** N *(inf)* Angströhre *f (inf)*, Zylinder *m*

stow [stəʊ] VT **a** *(Naut) cargo* verladen, (ver)stauen; *ship* (be)laden **b** *(= put away: also* **stow away***)* verstauen (*in* in +*dat*); **he ~ed the money (away) behind the clock** er versteckte das Geld hinter der Uhr **c** *(inf, = desist)* **~ it!** hör auf!

▸ **stow away** VI als blinder Passagier fahren

stowage ['stəʊɪdʒ] N *(= stowing)* (Be)laden *nt*, Stauen *nt*; *(= space)* Stauraum *m*; *(= charge)* Staugeld *nt*, Staugebühr *f*

stowaway ['stəʊəweɪ] N blinder Passagier

strabismus [strə'bɪzməs] N *(Med)* Schielen *nt*

straddle ['strædl] VT *(standing)* breitbeinig *or* mit gespreizten Beinen stehen über (+*dat*); *(sitting)* rittlings sitzen auf (+*dat*); *(jumping)* grätschen über (+*acc*); *(fig) differences* überbrücken; *two continents, border* überspannen; *periods* gehen über; **he ~d the fence/horse** *etc* er saß rittlings auf dem Zaun/Pferd *etc*; **to ~ the border/river** sich über beide Seiten der Grenze/beide Ufer des Flusses erstrecken; **to ~ an issue** *(US inf)* in einer Frage zwischen zwei Lagern schwanken N *(Sport)* Grätsche *f*; *(in high jump)* Schersprung *m*

strafe [streɪf] VT unter Beschuss nehmen; *(with shells also)* mit Granaten bewerfen; *(with bombs)* bombardieren

straggle ['strægl] VI **a** *(= spread untidily, houses, trees)* verstreut liegen; *(hair)* (unordentlich) hängen; *(plant)* (in die Länge) wuchern, in die Höhe schießen; **the town ~s on for miles** die Stadt zieht sich über Meilen hin **b** **to ~ behind** zurückbleiben, hinterherzockeln *(inf)*; **to ~ behind the leader** in weitem Abstand hinter dem Führer zurückbleiben *or* hinterherzockeln *(inf)*; **to ~ along the road** die Straße entlangbummeln *or* -zockeln *(inf)*; **to ~ in/out** vereinzelt kommen/gehen; **stop straggling** bleibt beieinander

straggler [ˈstræglə˞] N Nachzügler(in) *m(f)*

straggling [ˈstræglɪŋ] ADJ **a** *children, cattle etc* weit verteilt; *group of people* ungeordnet; *(= straggling behind)* zurückgeblieben, hinterherzottelnd *(inf)*; *village* sich lang hinziehend; *houses* zerstreut liegend; *group, row of houses* auseinandergezogen **b** *(inf: also* **straggly**) *hair* unordentlich, zottig; *beard* zottig; *plant* hochgeschossen; *handwriting* krakelig

straight [streɪt] ADJ *(+er)* **a** gerade; *shot, pass* direkt; *stance, posture* aufrecht; *hair* glatt; *skirt, trousers* gerade geschnitten; **your tie isn't ~** deine Krawatte sitzt schief; **the picture isn't ~** das Bild hängt schief; **your hem isn't ~** dein Saum ist nicht gerade; **to pull sth ~** etw gerade ziehen; **is my hat on ~?** sitzt mein Hut gerade?; **please put the picture ~** bitte hängen Sie das Bild gerade hin; **hold yourself ~** gerade!; **as ~ as a die** *(Brit)* kerzengerade; *road* schnurgerade; *(= honest)* grundehrlich; **to keep a ~ face, to keep one's face ~** ernst bleiben, das Gesicht nicht verziehen; **with a ~ face** ohne die Miene zu verziehen; **~ left/right** *(Boxing)* gerade Linke/Rechte

b *(= clear) thinking* klar; **to get things ~ in one's mind** sich *(dat)* der Dinge klar werden

c *(= frank) answer, talking, question* offen, direkt; *piece of advice* offen, ehrlich; *denial, refusal* direkt, ohne Umschweife; *(= honest) person, dealings* ehrlich; **to be ~ with sb** offen und ehrlich zu jdm sein; **to keep sb ~** dafür sorgen, dass jd ehrlich bleibt *or* nicht auf die schiefe Bahn gerät *(inf)*; **to play a ~ bat** *(Brit fig)* ein faires Spiel spielen; **~ arrow** *(US inf)* biederer Mensch; *(= man also)* Biedermann *m (inf)*

d *(= plain, straightforward) drink* pur; *(Pol) fight* direkt; *yes or no, choice, exam pass* einfach; **~ A's** glatte Einsen *pl*; **she's a ~ A student** sie hat alles Einsen; **to vote the ~ ticket** *(US Pol)* seine Stimme einer einzigen Partei *(dat)* geben; **he's a ~ Democrat** er ist ein hundertprozentiger Demokrat; **to have a ~ choice between …** nur die Wahl zwischen … haben

e *(= continuous)* ununterbrochen; **for the third ~ day** *(US)* drei Tage ohne Unterbrechung; **the ~ line of succession to the throne** die Thronfolge in der direkten Linie; **our team had ten ~ wins** unsere Mannschaft gewann zehnmal hintereinander *or* in ununterbrochener Folge; **in ~ sets/games** *(win)* ohne Satz-/Spielverlust; *(lose)* ohne Satz-/Spielgewinn, in aufeinanderfolgenden Sätzen/Spielen

f *(Theat) production* konventionell; *actor* ernsthaft; **a ~ play** ein reines Drama

g *pred (in order) house, room* ordentlich; *paperwork* in Ordnung; **to be (all) ~** in Ordnung sein; *(fig: = clarified also)* (völlig) geklärt sein; **now we're ~** jetzt haben wir die Sache geklärt; *(= tidy)* jetzt ist alles in Ordnung; **to put things ~** *(= tidy)* alles in Ordnung bringen; *(= clarify)* alles klären; **let's get this ~** das wollen wir mal klarstellen; **and get this ~** und damit wir uns richtig verstehen; **to put or set sb ~ about sth** jdm etw klarmachen; **if I give you a fiver, then we'll be ~** *(inf)* wenn ich dir einen Fünfer gebe, sind wir quitt

h *(inf: = heterosexual)* hetero *(inf)*; *(= conventional)* etabliert, spießig *(pej)*

i *(Drugs inf)* clean *(inf)*; **I've been ~ for three years now** ich bin jetzt seit drei Jahren clean *(inf)*

ADV **a** *hold, walk, fly, shoot, grow* gerade; *sit up, stand up* aufrecht, gerade; *hit* genau; *leap at, aim for* direkt; *above* genau, direkt; *across* direkt; **~ through sth** glatt durch etw; **he came ~ at me** er kam direkt *or* geradewegs auf mich zu; **it went ~ up in the air** es flog senkrecht in die Luft; **to look ~ ahead** geradeaus sehen; **the town lay ~ ahead of us** die Stadt lag direkt *or* genau vor uns; **the airport is ~ ahead** der Flughafen ist geradeaus; **go ~ ahead with your plan** führen Sie Ihren Plan wie vorgesehen durch; **to drive ~ on** geradeaus weiterfahren; **he drove ~ into a tree** er fuhr direkt *or* voll *(inf)* gegen einen Baum; **the arrow went ~ to the target** der Pfeil traf genau ins Ziel; **to go ~** *(criminal)* keine krummen Sachen (mehr) machen *(inf)*

b *(= directly)* direkt; **I went ~ home** ich ging direkt *or* sofort nach Hause; **to look sb ~ in the eye** jdm direkt *or* genau in die Augen sehen

c *(= immediately)* sofort; **~ after this** sofort *or* unmittelbar danach; **~ away** *or* **off** sofort, gleich, auf der Stelle; **he said ~ off that …** er sagte ohne Umschweife *or* sofort, dass …; **to come ~ to the point** sofort *or* gleich zur Sache kommen

d *(= clearly) think, see* klar

e *(= frankly)* offen, rundheraus, ohne Umschweife; **I'll give it to you ~, you're fired** ich sage es Ihnen rundheraus *or* ohne Umschweife, Sie sind entlassen; **~ out** *(inf)* unverblümt *(inf)*, rundheraus; **to give** *or* **tell sb sth/it ~ from the shoulder** jdm etw/es jdm unverblümt *or* ohne Umschweife sagen; **~ up, I got fifty quid for it** *(inf)* echt, ich habe fünfzig Pfund dafür gekriegt *(inf)*; **I got fifty quid for it – ~ up?** *(inf)* ich habe fünfzig Pfund dafür gekriegt – echt? *(inf)*

f *(Theat) play, produce* konventionell

g *drink* pur

N **a** *(= straight part) (on race track)* Gerade *f*; *(on road, Rail)* gerade Strecke; **the final ~** die Zielgerade; **in the ~** auf der Geraden; **the ~ and narrow** der Pfad der Tugend; **to keep sb on the ~ and narrow** dafür sorgen, dass jd ehrlich bleibt *or* nicht auf die schiefe Bahn gerät; **to stay on** *or* **keep to the ~ and narrow** auf dem Pfad der Tugend bleiben

b *(= straight line)* Gerade *f*; **to cut sth on the ~** etw gerade (ab)schneiden; *cloth* etw am Faden(lauf) entlang schneiden

c *(inf: = heterosexual)* Hetero *m (inf)*

straight: **straight angle** N gestreckter Winkel, Winkel *m* von 180°; **straight arrow** N *(US inf fig)* grundanständiger Kerl; **straightaway** *(US)* N Gerade *f*; *(on road, Rail)* gerade Strecke ADV = **straight** ADV **c**; **straight edge** N Lineal *nt*

straighten [ˈstreɪtn] VT **a** *(= make straight) back, legs etc* gerade machen; *picture* gerade hinhängen; *road, river* begradigen; *hat* gerade aufsetzen; *tablecloth, sheet, rope, clothes, tie* gerade ziehen; *wire* gerade biegen; *one's shoulders* straffen; *hair* glätten **b** *(= tidy)* in Ordnung bringen VI *(road, plant etc)* gerade werden; *(hair)* glatt werden; *(person)* sich aufrichten VR **to ~ oneself** sich aufrichten

▸ **straighten out** VT *sep* **a** *(= make straight) legs etc* gerade machen; *road* begradigen; *wire* gerade biegen; *rope* gerade ziehen; *hair* glätten **b** *(= put right) problem, situation* klären; *one's ideas* ordnen; *one's affairs, the economy* in Ordnung bringen; *misunderstanding* (auf)klären; *person (by discipline)* auf die richtige Bahn bringen; **to straighten oneself out** ins richtige Gleis kommen; **the problem will soon straighten itself out** das Problem wird sich bald von selbst erledigen; **to straighten things out** die Sache geradebiegen *or* in Ordnung bringen; *(= clarify)* Klarheit in die Sache bringen

VI *(road etc)* gerade werden; *(hair)* glatt werden

▸ **straighten up** VI sich aufrichten VT *sep* **a** *(= make straight)* gerade machen; *papers* ordentlich hinlegen; *picture* gerade hinhängen; *hat* gerade aufsetzen; *lines* begradigen; **to straighten oneself up** sich aufrichten **b** *(= tidy)* in Ordnung bringen, aufräumen

straight: **straight-faced** [ˈstreɪtˈfeɪst] ADV ohne die Miene zu verziehen ADJ **to be ~** keine Miene verziehen; **straight flush** N *(Cards)* Straightflush *m*; **straightforward** ADJ *(= honest) person* aufrichtig; *explanation, look also* offen, freimütig; *(= simple) question, problem, situation, choice* einfach; *process* unkompliziert; *instructions* einfach, verständlich; **I'm a ~ soldier** ich bin ein einfacher Soldat; **straightforwardly** ADV *answer* offen, freimütig; *behave* aufrichtig; **everything went ~** alles verlief nach Plan; **straightforwardness** N *(= frankness, of person)* Aufrichtigkeit *f*; *(of explanation, look also)* Offenheit *f*, Freimütigkeit *f*; *(= simplicity: of question, problem, situation, choice)* Einfachheit *f*; *(of process)* Unkompliziertheit *f*; *(of instructions)* Einfachheit *f*, Verständlichkeit *f*; **straight-from-the-shoulder** [ˌstreɪtfrəmðəˈʃəʊldə˞] ADJ *remark etc* unverblümt; **straight-laced** ADJ = **strait-laced**; **straight man** N *(Theat) Stichwortgeber für einen Komiker*; **straight-out** ADJ *(esp US inf) resentment, threat* unverblümt *(inf)*, offen; *opposition also* kompromisslos; *refusal, murder* glatt *(inf)*; **he's a ~ Democrat** er ist durch und durch Demokrat ADV *(inf)* unverblümt *(inf)*, rundheraus; **straight run** N *(Cards)* Sequenz *f*; **straightway** ADV *(liter)* sogleich *(liter)*

strain[1] [streɪn] N **a** *(Mech)* Belastung *f*, Beanspruchung *f*; *(on rope, arch)* Spannung *f*, Belastung *f*; *(on beams, floor)* Druck *m*; **the ~ on a rope** die Seilspannung; **can you take some of the ~?** können Sie mal mit festhalten/mit ziehen?; **to put a (great) ~ on sth** etw (stark) belasten; **to show signs of ~** Zeichen *pl* von Überlastung *or* Überbeanspruchung zeigen; **to take the ~ off sth** etw entlasten

b *(fig, mental, economic etc)* Belastung *f* (on für); *(= effort)* Anstrengung *f*; *(= pressure, of job etc also)* Beanspruchung *f* (of durch); *(of responsibility)* Last *f*; **to be under a lot of ~** großen Belastungen ausgesetzt sein; **to suffer from (nervous) ~** (nervlich) überlastet sein, im Stress sein; **I find her/it a bit of a ~** ich finde sie/das ziemlich anstrengend; **to put a (great) ~ on sb/sth** jdn/etw stark belasten; **to put too great a ~ on sb/sth** jdn/etw überlasten; **to show signs of ~** Zeichen *pl* von Überlastung *or* Überanstrengung zeigen; **to take the ~ off sb/sth** jdn/etw entlasten; **the ~ of six hours at the wheel** die Anstrengung, sechs Stunden am Steuer zu sitzen

c *(= muscle-strain)* (Muskel)zerrung *f*; *(on eyes, heart etc)* Überanstrengung *f* (on *+gen*); **back ~** überanstrengter Rücken

d strains PL *(of instrument, tune)* Klänge *pl*; **to the ~s of** zu den Klängen *(+gen)*

VT **a** *(= stretch)* spannen

b *(= put strain on) rope, beams, relationship, faith, budget* belasten; *nerves, patience, resources* strapazieren; *(= put too much strain on)* überlasten; *meaning, word* dehnen; **it ~s my nerves** das zerrt an meinen Nerven; **to ~ one's ears/eyes to …** angestrengt lauschen/gucken, um zu …; **to ~ every nerve** jeden Nerv anspannen; **to ~ oneself** sich anstrengen; *(excessively)* sich überanstrengen; **don't ~ yourself!** *(iro inf)* überanstrenge dich bloß nicht!, reiß dir bloß kein Bein aus! *(inf)*

c *(Med) muscle* zerren; *ankle, arm, neck* verrenken; *back, eyes, voice* anstrengen, strapazieren; *(excessively)* überanstrengen; *heart* belasten; *(excessively)* überlasten

d *(= filter)* (durch)sieben, (durch)seihen; *(= pour water off) vegetables* abgießen; **to ~ off water** Wasser abgießen; **to ~ out solids** feste Stoffe aussieben

VI *(= exert effort)* sich anstrengen, sich abmühen; *(= pull)* zerren, ziehen; *(fig: = strive)* sich bemühen, streben; **to ~ to do sth** sich anstrengen *or* abmühen, etw zu tun; **to ~ at sth** sich mit etw abmühen; *(= pull)* an etw *(dat)* zerren *or* ziehen; **to ~ at the leash** *(dog)* an der Leine zerren; *(fig)* aufmucken, aufmüpfig werden *(inf)*; **to ~ after sth** nach etw streben, sich um etw bemühen; **to ~ against sb** sich an jdn drücken; **to ~ against sth** sich gegen etw stemmen; **to ~ at a gnat and swallow a camel** *(prov)* Mücken seihen und Kamele verschlucken

strain[2] N **a** *(= streak)* Hang *m*, Zug *m*; *(hereditary)* Veranlagung *f*; **a ~ of madness** eine Veranlagung zum Wahnsinn **b** *(= style)* Anflug *m*; **there is a humorous ~ in his writing** seine Schriften haben einen humorvollen Anflug *or* Zug **c** *(= breed, of animal)* Rasse *f*; *(of plants)* Sorte *f*; *(of virus etc)* Art *f*

strained [streɪnd] ADJ **a** *(= unnatural) expression, performance, style* unnatürlich, gekünstelt; *laugh, smile, conversation* gezwungen; *economic situation, relationship* angespannt; *meeting* steif;

voice, relations, atmosphere, nerves (an)gespannt; **he looked rather ~** er sah ziemlich abgespannt aus **b** *liquids* durchgesiebt, durchgeseiht; *solids* ausgesiebt; *vegetables* abgegossen **c** *muscle* gezerrt; *back, eyes* überanstrengt, strapaziert; **to have a ~ ankle** sich *(dat)* den Knöchel verrenkt haben

strainer ['streɪnəʳ] N **a** *(Cook)* Sieb *nt* **b** *(Tech)* Filter *m*

strait [streɪt] N **a** *(Geog)* Meerenge *f*, Straße *f*; **the ~s of Dover/Gibraltar** die Straße von Dover/Gibraltar **b** **straits** PL *(fig)* Nöte *pl*, Schwierigkeiten *pl*; **to be in dire** *or* **desperate ~s** in großen Nöten sein, in einer ernsten Notlage sein

straitened ['streɪtnd] ADJ *means* beschränkt; *circumstances also* bescheiden, dürftig; **in these ~ times** in diesen harten Zeiten

strait: **straitjacket** N *(lit, fig)* Zwangsjacke *f*; **strait-laced** [,streɪt'leɪst] ADJ prüde, puritanisch, spießig *(inf)*

strand[1] [strænd] **N** *(liter, = beach)* Gestade *nt (liter)* **VT** *ship, fish* stranden lassen; *person (in place)* verschlagen, geraten lassen; *(without money, help etc)* seinem Schicksal überlassen; **to be ~ed** *(ship, fish, shipwrecked person)* gestrandet sein; **to be (left) ~ed** *(person)* festsitzen; *(without money also)* auf dem Trockenen sitzen *(inf)*; **to leave sb ~ed** jdn seinem Schicksal überlassen

strand[2] N Strang *m*; *(of hair)* Strähne *f*; *(of thread, wool)* Faden *m*; *(fig, in melody etc)* Melodienfolge *f*; *(in story)* Handlungsfaden *m*; **a three-~ necklace** eine dreireihige Halskette

strange [streɪndʒ] ADJ *(+er)* **a** seltsam, sonderbar, merkwürdig; **to think/find it ~ that ...** es seltsam finden, dass ...; **~ as it may seem ...** so seltsam es auch scheinen mag, ...; **for some ~ reason** aus irgendeinem unerfindlichen *or* seltsamen Grund; **the ~ thing is (that) ...** das Seltsame ist, dass...; **he told me the ~st story** er erzählte mir eine sehr seltsame *etc* Geschichte; **by a ~ chance** *or* **coincidence** durch einen seltsamen Zufall; **~ to say** so seltsam es klingen mag; **I feel a bit ~** *(= odd)* mir ist etwas seltsam **b** *(= unfamiliar) country, surroundings, bed* fremd; *(= unusual, unaccustomed) work, activity* nicht vertraut, ungewohnt; **don't talk to ~ men** sprich nicht mit fremden Männern; **I felt rather ~ at first** zuerst fühlte ich mich ziemlich fremd; **I feel ~ in a skirt** ich komme mir in einem Rock komisch vor *(inf)*; **to be ~ to sb** jdm fremd *or* unbekannt sein; **the boys are ~ to the school** die Schule ist den Jungen noch nicht vertraut *or* noch fremd

strangely ['streɪndʒlɪ] ADV *(= oddly)* seltsam, sonderbar, merkwürdig; *act, behave also* komisch *(inf)*; **~ enough** seltsamerweise, sonderbarerweise, merkwürdigerweise; **to be ~ reminiscent of sb/sth** seltsam an jdn/etw erinnern; **~ named** seltsam benannt

strangeness ['streɪndʒnɪs] N **a** *(= oddness)* Seltsamkeit *f*, Merkwürdigkeit *f* **b** *(= unfamiliarity)* Fremdheit *f*; *(of work, activity)* Ungewohntheit *f*

stranger ['streɪndʒəʳ] N Fremde(r) *mf*; **he's a complete ~ to me** ich kenne ihn überhaupt nicht; **I'm a ~ here myself** ich bin selbst fremd hier; **he is no ~ to London** er kennt sich in London aus; **he is no ~ to misfortune** Leid ist ihm nicht fremd; **to be a ~ to this kind of work** mit dieser Art von Arbeit nicht vertraut sein; **hullo, ~!** *(inf)* hallo, lange nicht gesehen; **you're quite a ~ here** *(inf)* man kennt dich ja gar nicht mehr; **the little ~** *(hum)* der kleine Neuankömmling

Strangers' Gallery N *(Brit Parl)* Besuchergalerie *f*

strangle ['stræŋgl] VT *(= murder)* erwürgen, erdrosseln, strangulieren *(form)*; *(fig) cry, economy, originality* ersticken; *protests* abwürgen, ersticken; **this collar is strangling me** *(inf)* dieser Kragen schnürt mir den Hals zu *or* ein

strangled ['stræŋgld] ADJ *voice, sound, laugh, cry* erstickt; **in a ~ voice** mit erstickter Stimme

stranglehold ['stræŋgl,həʊld] N *(lit)* Würgegriff *m*, Manschette *f*; *(fig)* absolute Machtposition *(on gegenüber)*; **they have a ~ on us** *(fig)* sie haben uns in der Zange

strangler ['stræŋgləʳ] N Würger(in) *m(f)*

strangling ['stræŋglɪŋ] N **a** *(= murder)* Mord *m* durch Erwürgen **b** *(= act of strangling)* Erwürgen *nt*, Erdrosseln *nt*; *(fig)* Ersticken *nt*

strangulate ['stræŋgjʊleɪt] VT *(Med)* abschnüren, abbinden

strangulation [,stræŋgjʊ'leɪʃən] N **a** *(= being strangled)* Ersticken *nt*; *(= act of strangling)* Erwürgen *nt*, Erdrosseln *nt*; **death was due to ~** der Tod trat durch Ersticken ein **b** *(Med)* Abschnürung *f*, Abbindung *f*

strap [stræp] **N** Riemen *m*; *(esp for safety)* Gurt *m*; *(in bus etc)* Schlaufe *f*, Lasche *f*; *(on ski pants etc)* Steg *m*; *(= watch strap)* Band *nt*; *(= shoulder strap)* Träger *m*; **to give sb the ~** jdn verprügeln, jdn züchtigen

VT **a** *(= fasten with strap)* festschnallen (*to* an *+dat*); **to ~ sth onto sth** etw auf etw *(acc)* schnallen; **he ~ped on his rucksack** er schnallte (sich *dat*) den Rucksack auf; **to ~ sb/sth down** jdn/etw festschnallen; **to ~ on one's watch** sich *(dat)* die Uhr umbinden; **to ~ on one's belt** sich *(dat)* den Gürtel umschnallen; **to ~ sb/oneself in** *(in car, plane)* jdn/sich anschnallen

b *(Med: also* **strap up***)* bandagieren; *dressing* festkleben

c *(= punish) person* verprügeln, züchtigen

d *(inf)* **to be ~ped (for cash)** *(= broke)* pleite *or* blank sein *(inf)*

strap: **strap-hang** VI *(inf)* **I had to ~** ich musste stehen; **straphanger** N *(inf: = commuter)* Pendler(in) *m(f)*; **straphanging** N *(inf: = commuting)* Pendeln *nt*; **strapless** ADJ trägerlos, schulterfrei; **strapline** N *(Press)* Schlagzeile *f*

strapping ['stræpɪŋ] ADJ *(inf)* stramm; *woman also* drall

strappy ['stræpɪ] ADJ *(inf)* **~ sandals** Riemchensandalen *pl*; **~ dress** Kleid *nt* mit Spag(h)ettiträgern; **~ top** Oberteil *or* Top *nt* mit Spag(h)ettiträgern

Strasbourg ['stræzbɜːg] N Straßburg *nt*

strata ['strɑːtə] *pl of* **stratum**

stratagem ['strætɪdʒəm] N *(Mil)* Kriegslist *f*; *(= artifice)* List *f*

strategic [strə'tiːdʒɪk] ADJ strategisch; *(= strategically important)* strategisch wichtig; *(fig)* taktisch, strategisch; **to put sth in a ~ position** etw in eine strategisch günstige Position bringen

strategically [strə'tiːdʒɪkəlɪ] ADV strategisch; *(fig also)* taktisch; **to be ~ placed** eine strategisch günstige Stellung haben; **a few ~ placed plants will brighten up any room** ein paar Pflanzen an der richtigen Stelle machen jedes Zimmer freundlicher; **~, his move was a mistake** strategisch gesehen war das falsch

strategist ['strætɪdʒɪst] N Stratege *m*, Strategin *f*; *(fig also)* Taktiker(in) *m(f)*

strategy ['strætɪdʒɪ] N **a** *(Mil)* Strategie *f*; *(Sport, fig)* Taktik *f*, Strategie *f* **b** *(= art of strategy, Mil)* Kriegskunst *f*; *(fig)* Taktieren *nt*

stratification [,strætɪfɪ'keɪʃən] N *(lit, fig)* Schichtung *f*; *(= stratifying also)* Schichtenbildung *f*; *(Geol)* Stratifikation *f*

stratified ['strætɪfaɪd] ADJ *(Geol)* geschichtet, schichtförmig; **~ rock** Schichtgestein *nt*

stratify ['strætɪfaɪ] **VT** schichten; *(Geol also)* stratifizieren; **a highly stratified society** eine vielschichtige Gesellschaft **VI** *(Geol)* Schichten bilden, sich aufschichten; *(fig)* Schichten herausbilden, in Schichten zerfallen

stratosphere ['strætəʊsfɪəʳ] N Stratosphäre *f*; **to send sth into the ~** *(fig)* etw astronomisch ansteigen lassen

stratospheric [,strætəʊ'sferɪk] ADJ stratosphärisch

stratum ['strɑːtəm] N *pl* **strata** *(Geol, fig)* Schicht *f*

stratus ['strɑːtəs] N *(Met)* Stratus *m*, Schichtwolke *f*

straw [strɔː] **N** **a** *(= stalk)* Strohhalm *m*; *(collectively)* Stroh *nt no pl*; **it's the last ~, it's the ~ that breaks the camel's back** *(prov)* das ist der letzte Tropfen, der das Fass zum Überlaufen bringt *(prov)*; **that's the last** *or* **final ~!** *(inf)* das ist der Gipfel! *(inf)*; **it's a ~ in the wind** das ist ein Vorzeichen; **to clutch** *or* **grasp at ~s** sich an einen Strohhalm klammern; **to draw the short ~** den kürzeren ziehen; **man of ~** Strohmann *m*; *(in politics)* Marionette *f*; *(= set-up opponent)* Scheingegner(in) *m(f)* → **drowning**

b *(= drinking straw)* Trink- *or* Strohhalm *m*

ADJ *attr* Stroh-; *basket* aus Stroh; **~ mat** Strohmatte *f*

straw bale N Strohballen *m*

strawberry ['strɔːbərɪ] N *(= plant, fruit)* Erdbeere *f*

strawberry *in cpds* Erdbeer-; **strawberry blonde** **N** Rotblonde(r) *mf*; **she's a ~** sie hat rotblondes Haar **ADJ** rotblond; **strawberry jam** N Erdbeermarmelade *f*; **strawberry mark** N (rotes) Muttermal

straw: **straw boss** N *(US inf)* Pro-forma-Vorgesetzte(r) *mf*; **straw-coloured**, *(US)* **straw-colored** ADJ strohfarben, strohfarbig; *hair* strohblond; **straw hat** N Strohhut *m*; **straw man** N Strohmann *m*; *(in politics)* Marionette *f*; *(= set-up opponent)* Scheingegner(in) *m(f)*; **straw mattress** N Strohsack *m*; **straw poll, straw vote** N Probeabstimmung *f*; *(in election)* Wählerbefragung *f*

stray [streɪ] **VI** *(also* **stray away***)* sich verirren, abirren; *(also* **stray about***)* (umher)streunen; *(fig: thoughts, speaker)* abschweifen; **to ~ (away) from sth** *(lit, fig)* von etw abkommen; **to ~ from a path** von einem Weg abkommen; **to ~ from the path of virtue** vom rechten Weg *or* vom Pfad der Tugend abkommen; **the cattle ~ed into the road** die Rinder haben sich auf die Straße verirrt; **they ~ed into the enemy camp** sie verirrten sich ins feindliche Lager

ADJ *child, bullet, cattle* verirrt; *cat, dog etc* streunend *attr*; *(= ownerless)* herrenlos; *(= isolated) remarks, houses, cases, hairs* vereinzelt; *(= single) remark, success* einzeln; *(= occasional)* gelegentlich; *thoughts* flüchtig

N **a** *(= dog, cat)* streunendes Tier; *(ownerless)* herrenloses Tier; **that cat's a ~** das ist eine herrenlose Katze → **waif**

b **strays** **PL** *(Rad)* (atmosphärische) Störungen *pl*

streak [striːk] **N** Streifen *m*; *(of light)* Strahl *m*; *(fig: = trace)* Spur *f*; *(of jealousy, meanness etc)* Zug *m*; *(of madness, humour)* Anflug *m*; **~s** *(in hair)* Strähnchen *pl*, Strähnen *pl*; **~ of lightning** Blitz(strahl) *m*; **there was a ~ of blood on his arm** eine Blutspur zog sich über seinen Arm; **there is a ~ of Spanish blood in her** sie hat spanisches Blut in den Adern; **his lucky ~** seine Glückssträhne; **a winning/losing ~** eine Glücks-/Pechsträhne; **he's got a mean ~** er hat einen gemeinen Zug (an sich *(dat)*); **he went past like a ~ (of lightning)** er sauste vorbei wie der Blitz

VT streifen; **to be ~ed** gestreift sein; **the sky was ~ed with red** der Himmel hatte rote Streifen; **to have one's hair ~ed** sich *(dat)* Streifen ins Haar färben lassen; **hair ~ed with blonde/grey** Haar mit blonden/grauen Strähnen; **~ed with dirt** schmutzverschmiert; **~ed with tears** tränenverschmiert; **rock ~ed with quartz** von Quarzadern durchzogener Stein

VI **a** *(lightning)* zucken; *(inf: = move quickly)* flitzen *(inf)*; **to ~ along/past** entlang-/vorbeiflitzen *(inf)*

b *(= run naked)* blitzen, flitzen

streaker ['striːkəʳ] N Blitzer(in) *m(f)*, Flitzer(in) *m(f)*

streaky ['striːkɪ] ADJ *(+er) glass, face* verschmiert; *window, mirror* streifig; *pattern* gestreift; *hair* strähnig; **~ bacon** *(Brit)* durchwachsener Speck

stream [striːm] **N** **a** *(= small river)* Bach *m*, Flüsschen *nt*; *(= current)* Strömung *f*; **to go with/against the ~** *(lit, fig)* mit dem/gegen den Strom schwimmen
b *(= flow, of liquid, air, people, cars)* Strom *m*; *(of light, tears)* Flut *f*; *(of words, excuses, abuse)* Schwall *m*, Flut *f*; **~ of consciousness** *(Liter)* Bewusstseinsstrom *m*
c *(Brit Sch)* Leistungsgruppe *f*
d *(Tech)* **to be/come on ~** *(oil well)* in Betrieb sein/genommen werden; *(oil)* fließen/zu fließen anfangen
VT **a** *(liter)* **the walls ~ed water** von den Wänden rann das Wasser; **his face ~ed blood** Blut rann *or* strömte ihm übers Gesicht
b *(Brit Sch)* in (Leistungs)gruppen einteilen
VI **a** *(= flow, liquid)* strömen, fließen, rinnen; *(eyes: because of cold, gas etc)* tränen; *(air, sunlight)* strömen, fluten; *(people, cars etc)* strömen; **the wound was ~ing with blood** Blut strömte *or* rann aus der Wunde; **the walls were ~ing with water** die Wände trieften vor Nässe; **her eyes were/face was ~ing with tears** Tränen strömten ihr aus den Augen/übers Gesicht; **his nose was ~ing** *(Brit)* seine Nase lief
b *(= wave: flag, hair)* wehen

▶ **stream down** **VI** *(liquid)* in Strömen fließen; *(+prep obj)* herunterströmen; *(cars)* in Strömen herunterfahren; *(hair)* wallend herunterfallen *(prep obj* über *+acc)*; **the rain was streaming down** es regnete in Strömen; **tears streamed down her face** Tränen rannen *or* strömten *or* liefen über ihr Gesicht

▶ **stream in** **VI** hereinströmen

▶ **stream out** **VI** hinausströmen *(of* aus*)*; *(liquid also)* herausfließen *(of* aus*)*; **her hair streamed out behind her** ihre Haare wehten nach hinten

▶ **stream past** **VI** vorbeiströmen *(prep obj* an *+dat)*; *(cars)* in Strömen vorbeifahren *(prep obj* an *+dat)*; **the cars kept streaming past** der Strom der Autos brach nicht ab

streamer [ˈstriːməʳ] **N** **a** *(= flag)* Banner *nt*; *(made of paper)* Papier- *or* Luftschlange *f*; *(made of cloth, as decoration)* Band *nt*; **~ of smoke** Rauchfahne *f*; **~ headline** *(US)* Balkenüberschrift *f* **b** *(also* **data streamer***: for data storage)* Streamer *m*, Streamer-Tape *nt*

stream feed **N** *(on photocopier)* automatischer Papiereinzug

streaming [ˈstriːmɪŋ] **N** *(Brit Sch)* Einteilung *f* in Leistungsgruppen **ADJ** *nose, windows* triefend; *eyes also* tränend; **I have a ~ cold** *(Brit)* ich habe einen fürchterlichen Schnupfen

streamlet [ˈstriːmlət] **N** *(poet)* Bächlein *nt*, Rinnsal *nt (liter)*

streamline [ˈstriːmlaɪn] **VT** *racing car, aeroplane* windschlüpfig machen, Stromlinienform geben *(+dat)*; *(fig)* rationalisieren

streamlined [ˈstriːmlaɪnd] **ADJ** *wing* windschlüpfig; *car, plane also* stromlinienförmig; *(fig)* rationalisiert

street [striːt] **N** **a** Straße *f*; **in** *or* **on the ~** auf der Straße; **to live in** *or* **on a ~** in einer Straße wohnen; **the man/woman in the ~** *(fig)* der Mann/die Frau auf der Straße; **it's right up my ~** *(Brit fig inf)* das ist genau mein Fall *(inf)*; **to be ~s ahead of sb** *(fig inf)* jdm haushoch überlegen sein *(inf)*; **~s apart** *(fig)* grundverschieden; **he's not in the same ~ as her** *(fig inf)* zwischen ihm und ihr ist ein himmelweiter Unterschied *(inf)*; **to take to the ~s** *(demonstrators)* auf die Straße gehen; **to go on the ~s** *(inf)* auf den Strich gehen *(inf)*; **a woman of the ~s** ein Mädchen *nt* von der Straße, ein Straßenmädchen *nt* → **man**
b *(inf: = residents)* Straße *f*

street *in cpds* Straßen-; **street Arab** **N** *(Brit dated liter)* Gassenkind *nt*; **streetball** **N** Streetball *nt*; **street battle** **N** Straßenschlacht *f*; **streetcar** **N** *(US)* Straßenbahn *f*; **street circuit** **N** *(Sport, for race)* Straßenkurs *m*, Stadtkurs *m*; **street cleaner** **N** *(esp US)* Straßenkehrer(in) *m(f)*, Straßenfeger(in) *m(f)*; **street collection** **N** Straßensammlung *f*; **street cred** *(Brit inf)*, **street credibility** **N** Glaubwürdigkeit *f*; **as an undercover agent in the Bronx you need ~** als Geheimagent in der Bronx muss man sich dem Milieu anpassen können; **this jacket does nothing for my ~** dieses Jackett versaut mein ganzes Image *(inf)*; **street crime** **N** Straßenkriminalität *f*; **street door** **N** Tür *f* zur Straße hin; **street fighter** **N** Straßenkämpfer(in) *m(f)*; **street fighting** **N** Straßenkämpfe *pl*; **street furniture** **N** *(= benches, road signs, cycle stands etc)* Stadtmöbel *pl*, urbanes Mobiliar; **street lamp** **N** Straßenlaterne *f*; **street level** **N** **at ~** zu ebener Erde; **street life** **N** *(inf)* Leben *nt* auf der Straße; **street light** **N** Straßenlaterne *f*; **street lighting** **N** Straßenbeleuchtung *f*; **street map** **N** Stadtplan *m*, Straßenplan *m*; **street market** **N** Straßenmarkt *m*; **street musician** **N** Straßenmusikant(in) *m(f)*; **street party** **N** Straßenfest *nt*; **street people** **PL** Obdachlose *pl*; **street plan** **N** Straßen- *or* Stadtplan *m*; **street smart** **ADJ** *(esp US inf: = streetwise)* gewieft *(inf)*, clever *(inf)*; **street sweeper** **N** *(= person)* Straßenkehrer(in) *m(f)* *or* -feger(in) *m(f)*; *(= machine)* Kehrmaschine *f*; **street theatre**, *(US)* **street theater** **N** Straßentheater *nt*; **street urchin** **N** Straßen- *or* Gassenjunge *m*; **street vendor** **N** Straßenverkäufer(in) *m(f)*; **streetwalker** **N** Prostituierte *f*, Straßenmädchen *nt*; **streetwise** **ADJ** gewieft *(inf)*, clever *(inf)*; **streetworker** **N** Streetworker(in) *m(f)*

strength [streŋθ] **N** **a** *(lit, fig)* Stärke *f*; *(of person, feelings)* Kraft *f*; *(of table, bolt, nail, wall)* Stabilität *f*; *(of material, character)* Stärke *f*, Festigkeit *f*; *(of conviction, shoes)* Festigkeit *f*; *(of views)* Überzeugtheit *f*; *(of imagination)* Lebhaftigkeit *f*; *(of reason, argument, evidence)* Überzeugungskraft *f*; *(of plea, protest)* Eindringlichkeit *f*; *(of letter)* geharnischte *or* starke Ausdrucksweise; *(of measure)* Drastik *f*; **~ of character/will** *or* **mind** Charakter-/Willensstärke *f*; **to increase in** *or* **gain ~** stärker werden; **on the ~ of sth** aufgrund einer Sache *(gen)*; **he decided to be a writer on the ~ of selling one short story** er beschloss, Schriftsteller zu werden, nachdem er eine einzige Kurzgeschichte verkauft hatte; **his ~ failed him** seine Kräfte versagten, ihn verließen die Kräfte; **to be beyond sb's ~** über jds Kräfte *(acc)* gehen; **to save one's ~** mit seinen Kräften haushalten *or* Haus halten; **you don't know your own ~!** du weißt gar nicht, wie stark du bist!; **to argue from a position of ~** von einer starken Position aus argumentieren; **to go from ~ to ~** einen Erfolg nach dem anderen erzielen *or* haben; **he was a great ~ to me** er war mir eine große Stütze
b *(= health, of constitution)* Robustheit *f*, Kräftigkeit *f*; *(of eyes, heart)* Stärke *f*; **the patient is recovering his ~** der Patient kommt wieder zu Kräften; **when she has her ~ back** wenn sie wieder bei Kräften ist
c *(of colour)* Kräftigkeit *f*, Intensität *f*; *(of acid, bleach)* Stärke *f*; *(of diluted solution)* Konzentration *f*
d *(= numbers)* (An)zahl *f*; *(Mil)* Stärke *f*; **to be at full ~** vollzählig sein; **to bring sth up to ~** etw vollzählig machen; **to be up to/below** *or* **under ~** (die) volle Stärke/nicht die volle Stärke haben; **to turn out in ~** in großer Zahl kommen, zahlreich erscheinen; **the police were there in ~** ein starkes Polizeiaufgebot war da
e *(of currency)* Stärke *f*; *(of market prices)* Stabilität *f*; *(of economy)* Gesundheit *f*

strengthen [ˈstreŋθən] **VT** stärken; *material, shoes, building, grip, resolve also* verstärken; *eyesight* verbessern; *muscles, patient* stärken, kräftigen; *person (lit)* Kraft geben *(+dat)*; *(fig)* bestärken; *currency, market* festigen; *effect* vergrößern; **to ~ sb's hand** *(fig)* jdn bestärken *or* ermutigen; **this only ~ed her determination** das bestärkte sie nur in ihrem Entschluss **VI** stärker werden; *(wind, desire also)* sich verstärken; **the ~ing economy** die sich verbessernde Wirtschaftslage

strenuous [ˈstrenjʊəs] **ADJ** **a** *(= exhausting)* anstrengend; *march, game* anstrengend, ermüdend
b *(= energetic) attempt, supporter, support* unermüdlich, energisch; *attack, effort, denial* hartnäckig; *opposition, conflict, protest* heftig

strenuously [ˈstrenjʊəslɪ] **ADV** **a** *exercise* anstrengend **b** *(= vigorously) deny* entschieden; *oppose* energisch, entschieden; *object* nachdrücklich

strep throat [ˈstrepˈθrəʊt] **N** *(esp US inf)* Halsentzündung *f*

streptococcus [ˌstreptəʊˈkɒkəs] **N** *pl* **streptococci** [ˌstreptəʊˈkɒksaɪ] Streptokokkus *m*

stress [stres] ✪ 26.3 **N** **a** *(= strain)* Belastung *f*, Stress *m*; *(Med)* Überlastung *f*, Stress *m*; **the ~es and strains of modern life** die Belastungen *or* der Stress des heutigen Lebens; **times of ~** Krisenzeiten *pl*, Zeiten *pl* großer Belastung; **to be under ~** großen Belastungen ausgesetzt sein; *(as regards work)* unter Stress stehen, im Stress sein; **to put sb under great ~** jdn großen Belastungen aussetzen; **to break down under ~/the ~** unter Stress *or* bei Belastung/unter dem Stress *or* unter der Belastung zusammenbrechen
b *(= accent)* Betonung *f*, Ton *m*; *(fig: = emphasis)* Akzent *m*, (Haupt)gewicht *nt*; **to put** *or* **lay (great) ~ on sth** großen Wert auf etw *(acc)* legen, einer Sache *(dat)* großes Gewicht beimessen; *fact, detail* etw (besonders) betonen
c *(Mech)* Belastung *f*; *(= pressure)* Druck *m*; *(= tension)* Spannung *f*; **the ~ acting on the metal** die Belastung, der das Metall ausgesetzt ist
VT **a** *(lit, fig: = emphasize)* betonen; *innocence* beteuern; *good manners, subject* großen Wert legen auf *(+acc)*; *fact, detail* hervorheben, betonen
b *(Mech)* belasten, beanspruchen

stress ball **N** (Anti)stressball *m*

stressed [strest] **ADJ** **a** *syllable, word* betont **b** *(= under stress) person* gestresst, über(be)lastet

stressed out **ADJ** gestresst; **what are you getting so ~ about?** worüber regst du dich so auf? *(inf)*

stress fracture **N** Spannungsriss *m*

stress-free **ADJ** stressfrei

stressful [ˈstresfʊl] **ADJ** anstrengend, stressig; **a ~ situation** eine angespannte Lage

stress mark **N** Akzent *m*, Betonungszeichen *nt*

stretch [stretʃ] **N** **a** *(= act of stretching)* Strecken *nt*, Dehnen *nt*; **to have a ~** sich strecken *or* dehnen; *(person also)* sich recken; **to be at full ~** *(lit: material)* bis zum Äußersten gedehnt sein; *(fig, person)* mit aller Kraft arbeiten; *(factory etc)* auf Hochtouren arbeiten *(inf)*; *(engine, production, work)* auf Hochtouren laufen; **by no ~ of the imagination** beim besten Willen nicht; **not by a long ~** bei Weitem nicht
b *(= elasticity)* Elastizität *f*, Dehnbarkeit *f*; **a fabric with plenty of ~** ein stark dehnbares *or* sehr elastisches Material; **there's not much ~ left in this elastic** das Gummi ist ziemlich ausgeleiert
c *(= expanse, of road etc)* Strecke *f*, Stück *nt*; *(on racecourse)* Gerade *f*; *(of wood, river, countryside etc)* Stück *nt*; *(of journey)* Abschnitt *m*, Teil *m*; **a straight ~ of road** eine gerade Strecke; **that ~ of water is called …** dieser Gewässerlauf heißt …; **in that ~ of the river** in dem Teil des Flusses; **for a long ~** über eine weite Strecke
d *(= stretch of time)* Zeit *f*, Zeitraum *m*, Zeitspanne *f*; **for a long ~ of time** für (eine) lange Zeit, lange Zeit; **for hours at a ~** stundenlang; **three days at a ~** drei Tage an einem Stück *or* ohne Unterbrechung; **to do a ~** *(inf, in prison)* im Knast sein *(inf)*
ADJ *attr* dehnbar, elastisch; **~ trousers** Stretchhose *f*
VT **a** *(= extend, lengthen)* strecken; *(= widen) jumper, gloves also, elastic, shoes* dehnen; *(= spread) wings, blanket etc* ausbreiten; *(= tighten) rope, canvas* spannen; **to become ~ed** ausleiern; **a curtain was ~ed across the room** ein Vorhang war quer durchs Zimmer gezogen; **she ~ed a**

tarpaulin over the woodpile sie breitete eine Plane über den Holzstoß; **to ~ sth tight** etw straffen, etw straff ziehen; *cover* etw stramm ziehen; **to ~ one's legs** *(= go for a walk)* sich *(dat)* die Beine vertreten *(inf)*; **to ~ one's neck** den Hals recken
b *(= make go further) meal, money* strecken; *(= use fully) resources* voll (aus)nutzen; *credit* voll beanspruchen; *athlete, student etc* fordern; *one's abilities* bis zum Äußersten fordern; **to ~ one's imagination** seine Fantasie anstrengen; **to ~ sb/sth to the limit(s)** jdn/etw bis zum äußersten belasten; **to be fully ~ed** *(esp Brit, person)* voll ausgelastet sein; **he ~ed his lead to 10 points** er baute seinen Vorsprung auf 10 Punkte aus
c *(= strain) meaning, word* äußerst weit fassen; *truth, law, rules* es nicht so genau nehmen mit; **this clause/law could be ~ed to allow …** diese Klausel/dieses Gesetz könnte so weit gedehnt werden, dass sie/es … zulässt; **to ~ a point** ein Auge zudrücken, großzügig sein; **that's ~ing it too far/a bit (far)** das geht zu weit/fast zu weit
VI *(after sleep etc)* sich strecken; *(= be elastic)* sich dehnen, dehnbar sein; *(= extend: time, area, authority, influence)* sich erstrecken *(to* bis, *over* über *+acc)*; *(= be enough: food, money, material)* reichen *(to* für*)*; *(= become looser)* weiter werden; *(= become longer)* länger werden; **the rope won't ~ to that post** das Seil reicht nicht bis zu dem Pfosten (hinüber); **to ~ to reach sth** sich recken, um etw zu erreichen; **he ~ed across and touched her cheek** er reichte herüber und berührte ihre Wange; **to ~ back to** zurückreichen bis; **the fields ~ed away into the distance** die Felder dehnten sich bis in die Ferne aus; **the years ~ed (out) ahead of him** die Jahre dehnten sich vor ihm aus; **a life of misery ~ed (out) before her** vor ihr breitete sich ein Leben voll Kummer und Leid aus; **the protests ~ed into their second week** die Proteste dauerten bereits die zweite Woche an; **I can't ~ to that** so viel kann ich mir nicht erlauben; **our funds won't ~ to that** das lassen unsere Finanzen nicht zu
VR **a** *(after sleep etc)* sich strecken
b *(= strain oneself)* sich verausgaben; **if only he'd ~ himself a little** wenn er sich nur etwas anstrengen würde

▸ **stretch out** VT *sep arms, wings, blanket* ausbreiten; *leg, hand* ausstrecken; *foot* vorstrecken; *rope* spannen; *meeting, discussion, essay, story* ausdehnen; **to stretch oneself out (on the ground)** sich auf den Boden legen VI sich strecken; *(inf: = lie down)* sich hinlegen; *(countryside)* sich ausbreiten; *(in time)* sich erstrecken, sich hinziehen *(over* über *+acc)*; **her arm stretched out** sie streckte den Arm aus; **he stretched out on the bed** er legte sich (ausgestreckt) aufs Bett

stretcher [ˈstretʃəʳ] N **a** *(Med)* (Trag)bahre *f*
b *(for shoes, gloves)* Spanner *m*; *(Art, for canvas)* Rahmen *m*

▸ **stretcher off** VT *sep* auf einer (Trag)bahre wegtragen *or* abtransportieren

stretcher: **stretcher-bearer** N Krankenträger(in) *m(f)*; **stretcher case** N Kranke(r) *mf*/Verletzte(r) *mf*, der/die nicht gehen kann; *(Mil)* Schwerverwundete(r) *mf*, schwer Verwundete(r) *mf*; **by the time I've finished this work I'll be a ~** *(hum)* bis ich diese Arbeit fertig habe, bin ich krankenhausreif *(inf)*; **stretcher party** N Team *nt* von Krankenträgern

stretch: **stretch limo** *(inf)*, **stretch limousine** N Großraumlimousine *f*; **stretch mark** N Dehnungsstreifen *m*; *(in pregnancy)* Schwangerschaftsstreifen *m or* -narbe *f*; **stretch nylon** N Stretchnylon *nt*, Helanca® *nt*; *(esp for ski pants)* Lastex *nt*

stretchy [ˈstretʃɪ] ADJ *(+er)* elastisch, dehnbar

strew [struː] *pret* **strewed**, *ptp* **strewed** *or* **strewn** [struːn] VT *(= scatter)* verstreuen; *flowers, gravel, sand* streuen; *(= cover with) floor etc* bestreuen; **to ~ one's clothes around (the room)** seine Kleider im Zimmer verstreuen; **dresses were ~n about the room** Kleider lagen im ganzen Zimmer verstreut herum; **the floor was ~n with …** … lagen überall auf dem Boden verstreut

strewth [struːθ] INTERJ *(inf)* = **struth**

striated [straɪˈeɪtɪd] ADJ *(form: = striped)* gestreift; *(= furrowed)* gefurcht; *(Geol)* mit Schliffen *or* Schrammen

striation [straɪˈeɪʃən] N *(form: = stripes)* Streifen *pl*; *(= furrows)* Furchen *pl*, Furchung *f*; *(Geol)* Schliffe *pl*, Schrammen *pl*

stricken [ˈstrɪkən] *(old) ptp of* **strike** ADJ *(liter: = wounded)* verwundet; *(= afflicted)* leidgeprüft, schwer geprüft; *(with grief)* schmerzerfüllt, gramgebeugt *(liter)*; *(= ill)* leidend *(geh)*; *ship, plane* in Not; *(= horrified) person* wie vom Blitz getroffen *or* vom Donner gerührt; *expression* niedergeschlagen; **~ with guilt/fear** *etc* von Schuld/Angst *etc* erfüllt, von Angst ergriffen; **~ in years** hochbetagt *(geh)*; **to be ~ by** *or* **with illness** leidend sein *(geh)*; **to be ~ with blindness** mit Blindheit geschlagen sein *(geh)*; **to be ~ by drought/famine** von Dürre/Hungersnot geplagt *or* heimgesucht werden

-stricken ADJ *suf (with emotion)* -erfüllt; *(by catastrophe)* von … heimgesucht; **grief-stricken** schmerzerfüllt; **panic-stricken** von Panik ergriffen

strict [strɪkt] ADJ *(+er)* **a** *(= stern, severe) law, parent, principles, judge etc* streng; *order, ban, discipline* strikt, streng; *obedience* absolut, strikt; *Catholic* strenggläubig; **they're very ~ about timekeeping** es wird streng auf Pünktlichkeit geachtet
b *(= precise)* streng; *accuracy, neutrality, secrecy* absolut, streng; *translation, meaning* genau; **in the ~ sense of the word** genau genommen; **in ~ confidence** streng vertraulich; **in (the) ~est confidence** in strengster Vertraulichkeit, strengstens vertraulich; **there is a ~ time limit on that** das ist zeitlich genau begrenzt; **in ~ order of precedence** streng nach Rangordnung

strictly [ˈstrɪktlɪ] ADV **a** streng; **smoking is ~ forbidden** Rauchen ist streng *or* strengstens verboten
b *(= precisely)* genau; *(= absolutely)* absolut, streng; **to be ~ accurate** um ganz genau zu sein; **our relationship was ~ business** unser Verhältnis war rein geschäftlich; **~ in confidence** ganz im Vertrauen; **~ personal** privat; **~ confidential** streng vertraulich; **"strictly private"** „streng vertraulich"; **~ speaking** genau genommen; **not ~ true** nicht ganz richtig; **~ between ourselves/between you and me** ganz unter uns; **unless ~ necessary** wenn nicht unbedingt erforderlich; **fox-hunting is ~ for the rich** Fuchsjagden sind ausschließlich etwas für reiche Leute; **the car park is ~ for the use of residents** der Parkplatz ist ausschließlich für Anwohner vorgesehen

strictness [ˈstrɪktnɪs] N **a** Strenge *f*; *(of order, discipline)* Striktheit *f*, Strenge *f* **b** *(= preciseness)* Genauigkeit *f*

stricture [ˈstrɪktʃəʳ] N **a** *usu pl (form: = criticism)* (scharfe) Kritik *no pl*; **to make** *or* **pass ~s upon sb** jdn (scharf) kritisieren **b** *(Med)* Verengung *f*, Striktur *f (spec)*

stride [straɪd] *vb: pret* **strode**, *ptp* **stridden** [ˈstrɪdn] N *(= step)* Schritt *m*; *(= gait also)* Gang *m*; *(fig)* Fortschritt *m*; **to get into** *or* **hit one's ~** *(fig)* in Schwung *or* in Fahrt kommen; **to take sth in one's ~** *(Brit) or* **in ~** *(US)* mit etw spielend fertig werden; *exam, interview* etw spielend schaffen; **to put sb off his/her ~** jdn aus dem Konzept bringen; **he took everything in his ~** es schien alles spurlos an ihm vorübergegangen zu sein
VI schreiten *(geh)*, mit großen Schritten gehen; **to ~ along** ausschreiten *(geh)*; **to ~ away** *or* **off** sich mit schnellen Schritten entfernen, davonschreiten *(geh)*; **to ~ up to sb** (mit großen Schritten) auf jdn zugehen, auf jdn zuschreiten *(geh)*; **to ~ up and down** auf- und abgehen *or* -schreiten *(geh)*

stridency [ˈstraɪdənsɪ] N *(of sound, voice)* Schrillheit *f*, Durchdringlichkeit *f*; *(of colour)* Grellheit *f*; *(of person)* Streitbarkeit *f*; *(of protest, criticism, tone)* Schärfe *f*; *(of demand)* Stärke *f*

strident [ˈstraɪdənt] ADJ *sound, voice* schrill, durchdringend; *colour* grell; *person* streitbar; *criticism, tone* scharf; *demand, protest, nationalism, attack* lautstark

stridently [ˈstraɪdəntlɪ] ADV *talk etc* schrill, durchdringend; *object, protest* scharf, lautstark; *demand, behave* lautstark; **a ~ anti-American approach** eine scharf antiamerikanische Haltung

strife [straɪf] N Unmut *m (geh)*, Unfriede *m*; *(in family, between friends)* Zwietracht *f (geh)*; **party ~** Zwietracht *f (geh) or* Zwistigkeiten *pl* in der Partei; **internal ~** innere Kämpfe *pl*; **civil/industrial ~** Auseinandersetzungen *pl* in der Bevölkerung/Industrie; **to cease from ~** *(liter)* allen Zwist begraben *(geh)*

strife-torn [ˈstraɪftɔːn], **strife-ridden** [ˈstraɪfrɪdn] ADJ *country* konfliktgeschüttelt; *party* zerstritten

strike [straɪk] *vb: pret* **struck**, *ptp* **struck** *or (old)* **stricken** N **a** Streik *m*, Ausstand *m*; **official/unofficial ~** offizieller/wilder Streik; **to be on ~** streiken, im Ausstand sein; **to be on official/unofficial ~** offiziell/wild streiken; **to come out on ~, to go on ~** in den Streik *or* Ausstand treten; **to bring sb out on ~** jdn zum Streik veranlassen → **hunger strike**
b *(= discovery of oil, gold etc)* Fund *m*; **a big oil ~** ein großer Ölfund; **to make a ~** fündig werden; **a lucky ~** ein Treffer *m*, ein Glücksfall *m*
c *(Baseball)* verfehlter Schlag; *(Tenpin Bowling)* Strike *m*, alle zehne; **to get a ~** alle zehne werfen, abräumen *(inf)*; **to have the ~** *(Cricket)* schlagen; **three ~s and you're out** wenn du den Ball dreimal verfehlst, bist du draußen; **it/she has two ~s against it/her** *(esp US inf)* es/sie hat zwei Nachteile
d *(Fishing)* **he got three ~s** drei haben angebissen
e *(Mil: = attack)* Angriff *m*
f *(= act of striking)* Schlag *m*
VT **a** *(= hit)* schlagen; *door* schlagen an *or* gegen *(+acc)*; *nail, table* schlagen auf *(+acc)*; *metal, hot iron etc* hämmern; *(stone, blow, bullet etc)* treffen; *(snake)* beißen; *(pain)* durchzucken, durchfahren; *(misfortune, disaster)* treffen; *(disease)* befallen; **to ~ one's fist on the table, to ~ the table with one's fist** mit der Faust auf den Tisch schlagen; **to ~ sb/sth a blow** jdm/einer Sache einen Schlag versetzen; **who struck the first blow?** wer hat zuerst (zu)geschlagen?; **to ~ a blow for sth** *(fig)* eine Lanze für etw brechen; **to ~ a blow (at sth)** *(fig)* einen Schlag (gegen etw) führen; **to be struck by lightning** vom Blitz getroffen werden; **he struck his forehead in surprise** er schlug sich *(dat)* überrascht an die Stirn; **to ~ 38 (per minute)** 38 Ruderschläge (pro Minute) machen
b *(= collide with, meet, person)* stoßen gegen; *(spade)* stoßen auf *(+acc)*; *(car)* fahren gegen; *ground* aufschlagen *or* auftreffen auf *(+acc)*; *(ship)* auflaufen auf *(+acc)*; *(sound, light) ears, eyes* treffen; *(lightning) person* treffen; *tree* einschlagen in *(+acc)*, treffen; **to ~ one's head against sth** mit dem Kopf gegen etw stoßen, sich *(dat)* den Kopf an etw *(acc)* stoßen; **to ~ problems** *(fig)* in Schwierigkeiten geraten; **a terrible sight struck my eyes** plötzlich sah ich etwas Schreckliches
c *(= sound) instrument* zu spielen anfangen; *string, chord, note* anschlagen; *(clock)* schlagen; **to ~ the keys** *(of piano, typewriter)* in die Tasten greifen; **to ~ the hour** die volle Stunde schlagen; **to ~ 4** 4 schlagen; **that struck a familiar note** das kam mir/ihm *etc* bekannt vor → **note**
d *(Hort) cutting* schneiden; *(plant) roots* schlagen
e *(= occur to)* in den Sinn kommen *(+dat)*; **to ~ sb as cold/unlikely** *etc* jdm kalt/unwahrscheinlich *etc* vorkommen; **that ~s me as a good idea** das kommt mir sehr vernünftig vor; **has it ever struck you that …?** *(= occurred to you)* haben Sie je daran gedacht, dass …?; *(= have you noticed)* ist Ihnen je aufgefallen, dass …?; **it ~s me that …** *(= I have the impression)* ich

habe den Eindruck, dass ...; *(= I am noticing)* mir fällt auf, dass ...; **it struck me how ...** *(= occurred to me)* mir ging plötzlich auf, wie ...; *(= I noticed)* mir fiel auf, wie ...; **the funny side of it struck me later** erst später ging mir auf, wie lustig das war; **a thought struck me** mir kam plötzlich ein Gedanke

f *(= impress)* beeindrucken; **to be struck by sth** von etw beeindruckt sein; **how does it ~ you?** wie finden Sie das?, was halten Sie davon?; **how does she ~ you?** welchen Eindruck haben Sie von ihr?; **she struck me as being very competent** sie machte auf mich einen sehr fähigen Eindruck → *also* **struck**

g *(= produce, make) coin, medal* prägen; *(fig) agreement, truce* sich einigen auf *(+acc)*, aushandeln; *pose* einnehmen; **to ~ a light** Feuer machen; **to ~ a match** ein Streichholz anzünden; **to ~ sparks** Funken schlagen; **to be struck blind/deaf/dumb** blind/taub/stumm werden, mit Blindheit/Taubheit/Stummheit geschlagen werden *(geh)*; **to ~ fear** *or* **terror into sb/sb's heart** jdn mit Angst *or* Schrecken erfüllen; **~ a light!** *(inf)* ach du grüne Neune! *(inf)*, hast du da noch Töne! *(inf)*

h *(= find) gold, oil, correct path* finden, stoßen auf *(+acc)*; **to ~ it rich** das große Geld machen; **to ~ gold** *(fig)* auf eine Goldgrube stoßen → **oil**

i *(= make) path* hauen

j *(= take down) camp, tent* abbrechen; *(Naut) flag, sail* einholen, streichen; *mast* kappen, umlegen; *(Theat) set* abbauen

k *(= remove)* streichen; **to be struck** *or (US)* **stricken from a list/the record** von einer Liste/aus dem Protokoll gestrichen werden

VI a *(= hit)* treffen; *(lightning)* einschlagen; *(snake)* zubeißen; *(tiger)* die Beute schlagen; *(attack, Mil etc)* zuschlagen, angreifen; *(disease)* zuschlagen; *(panic)* ausbrechen; **to ~ against sth** gegen etw stoßen; **to ~ at sb/sth** *(lit)* nach jdm/etw schlagen; *(fig: at democracy, existence)* an etw *(dat)* rütteln; **they struck at his weakest point** sie trafen ihn an seinem wundesten Punkt; **to ~ at the roots of sth** etw an der Wurzel treffen; **to be/come within striking distance of sth** einer Sache *(dat)* nahe sein; **to put sb within striking distance of sth** jdn in Reichweite von etw bringen; **to come within striking distance of doing sth** nahe daran sein, etw zu tun; **they were within striking distance of success** der Erfolg war für sie in greifbarer Nähe; **the snake struck at me** die Schlange fuhr auf mich los → **home, iron**

b *(clock)* schlagen; **when midnight ~s** wenn es Mitternacht schlägt

c *(workers)* streiken

d *(match)* zünden, angehen

e *(Naut, = run aground)* auflaufen *(on* auf *+acc)*

f *(Fishing)* anbeißen

g inspiration struck er/sie *etc* hatte eine Eingebung; **to ~ on a new idea** eine neue Idee haben, auf eine neue Idee kommen

h *(= take root)* Wurzeln schlagen

i *(= go in a certain direction)* **to ~ across country** querfeldein gehen; **to ~ into the woods** sich in die Wälder schlagen; **the sun struck through the mist** die Sonne brach durch den Dunst

▶ **strike back** VI zurückschlagen; *(fig also)* sich wehren, sich zur Wehr setzen; **to strike back at sb** jds Angriff *(acc)* erwidern; *(fig)* sich gegen jdn wehren *or* zur Wehr setzen VT *sep* zurückschlagen

▶ **strike down** VT *sep* niederschlagen; *(God) enemies* vernichten; *(fig)* zu Fall bringen; *(US) law* abschaffen; **to be struck down** niedergeschlagen werden; *(by illness)* getroffen werden; *(by blow)* zu Boden gestreckt werden; **he was struck down in his prime** er wurde in seiner Blüte dahingerafft

▶ **strike off** VT *sep* **a** *(= cut off)* abschlagen **b** *(= remove) (from list)* (aus)streichen; *solicitor* die Lizenz entziehen *(+dat)*; *doctor* die Zulassung entziehen *(+dat)*; *(from price)* abziehen *(prep obj* von); **to be struck off** *(Brit Med, Jur)* die Zulassung verlieren **c** *(= print)* drucken; **to strike off a proof** einen Bürstenabzug machen VI *(= set off)* sich auf den Weg machen; *(road etc also)* abbiegen

▶ **strike out** VI **a** *(= hit out)* schlagen; **to strike out wildly** *or* **blindly** wild um sich schlagen; **to strike out at sb** *(lit, fig)* jdn angreifen **b** *(= change direction)* zuhalten *(for, towards* auf *+acc)*; *(= set out)* sich aufmachen, losziehen *(inf) (for* zu); **to strike out for home** sich auf den Heimweg machen; **to strike out on one's own** *(lit)* allein losziehen; *(fig)* eigene Wege gehen; **to strike out in a new direction** *(fig)* neue Wege gehen **c** *(Baseball)* „aus" sein; *(US fig inf)* nicht durchkommen VT *sep* (aus)streichen; **to strike sth out of the record** etw aus dem Protokoll streichen

▶ **strike through** VT *sep* durchstreichen

▶ **strike up** VI *(band etc)* einsetzen, anfangen (zu spielen) VT *insep* **a** *(band) tune* anstimmen; **strike up the band!** Musik! **b** *friendship* schließen, anknüpfen; *conversation, relationship* anfangen

strike: **strike action** N Streikmaßnahmen *pl*; **strike ballot** N Urabstimmung *f*; **strike-bound** ADJ bestreikt, vom Streik betroffen; **strikebreaker** N Streikbrecher(in) *m(f)*; **strikebreaking** N Streikbruch *m*; **strike call** N Aufruf *m* zum Streik; **strike force** N *(Mil)* Kampftruppe *f*; **strike fund** N Streikkasse *f*; **strike leader** N Streikführer(in) *m(f)*

strikeout ADJ *(Comput: typeface)* durchgestrichen

strike: **strike pay** N Streikgeld *nt*; **strike-prone** ADJ streikanfällig

striker ['straɪkəʳ] N **a** *(= worker)* Streikende(r), Ausständige(r) *mf* **b** *(Ftbl)* Stürmer(in) *m(f)*

striking ['straɪkɪŋ] ADJ **a** *(= arresting) contrast, colour, resemblance etc* auffallend, bemerkenswert; *difference* verblüffend, erstaunlich; *person* bemerkenswert; *looks* umwerfend; *appearance, beauty* eindrucksvoll; **a ~ example of sth** ein hervorragendes Beispiel für etw **b** *attr worker* streikend **c** *attr clock* mit Schlagwerk; **the ~ clock keeps me awake** das Schlagen der Uhr lässt mich nicht schlafen; **~ mechanism** Schlagwerk *nt*

striking distance N *(of missile etc)* Reichweite *f*

strikingly ['straɪkɪŋlɪ] ADV *similar, evident, bold* auffallend; *different* unübersehbar; *attractive* bemerkenswert; *modern* verblüffend; *demonstrate* unmissverständlich; *contrast* deutlich; **more ~, ...** was noch mehr ins Auge fällt ist, dass ...

Strimmer® ['strɪməʳ] N Rasentrimmer *m*

strine [straɪn] N *(hum inf) australisches Englisch*

string [strɪŋ] *vb: pret, ptp* **strung** N **a** *(pl rare: = cord)* Schnur *f*, Kordel *f*, Bindfaden *m*; *(on apron etc)* Band *nt*; *(on anorak, belt)* Kordel *f*; *(of puppet)* Faden *m*, Schnur *f*, Draht *m*; **to have sb on a ~** *(fig inf)* jdn am Gängelband haben *(inf)*; **to pull ~s** *(fig)* Fäden ziehen, Beziehungen spielen lassen; **without ~s, with no ~s attached** ohne Bedingungen; **a relationship with no ~s attached** eine völlig lockere Beziehung; **he wants a girlfriend but no ~s attached** er möchte eine Freundin, will sich aber in keiner Weise gebunden fühlen

b *(= row, of beads, onions etc)* Schnur *f*; *(of racehorses etc)* Reihe *f*; *(of people)* Schlange *f*; *(of vehicles)* Kette *f*, Schlange *f*; *(fig: = series)* Reihe *f*; *(of lies, curses)* Haufen *m*, Serie *f*

c *(of musical instrument, tennis racquet etc)* Saite *f*; *(of bow)* Sehne *f*; **a twelve-~ guitar** eine zwölfsaitige Gitarre; **to have two ~s** *or* **a second ~ to one's bow** zwei Eisen im Feuer haben → **second string a**

d strings PL *(= instruments)* **the ~s** die Streichinstrumente *pl*; *(= players)* die Streicher *pl*; **he plays in the ~s** er ist Streicher, er gehört zu den Streichern

e *(Bot)* Faden *m*

f *(Comput: of characters)* Zeichenfolge *f*

VT **a** *(= put on string)* aufreihen, auffädeln, aufziehen

b *violin etc, tennis racquet* (mit Saiten) bespannen, besaiten; *bow* spannen → **highly strung**

c *beans* abfasern, (die) Fäden *(+gen)* abziehen

d *(= space out)* aufreihen; **they strung lights in the trees** sie haben Lampen in die Bäume gehängt

▶ **string along** *(inf)* VT *sep* **to string sb along** jdn hinhalten VI *(= go along, play along with)* sich anschließen *(with +dat)*

▶ **string out** VI sich verteilen; **the children strung out behind the teacher** die Kinder gingen in weiten Abständen hinter dem Lehrer her VT *sep lanterns, washing* aufhängen; *guards, posts* verteilen

▶ **string together** VT *sep words, sentences* aneinanderreihen; **she can't even string two sentences together** sie bringt keinen vernünftigen Satz zusammen; **she can't string her thoughts together coherently** sie ist unfähig, zusammenhängend zu denken

▶ **string up** VT *sep* **a** *(= suspend with string)* aufhängen; *(inf: = hang)* aufknüpfen *(inf)* **b** → **strung-up**

string: **string bag** N *(esp Brit)* Einkaufsnetz *nt*; **string band** N Streichorchester *nt*; **string bass** N Kontrabass *m*; **string bean** N *(esp US: = bean)* grüne Bohne; *(fig: = person)* Bohnenstange *f (hum inf)*

stringed [strɪŋd] ADJ **~ instrument** Saiteninstrument *nt*; *(played with bow also)* Streichinstrument *nt*

stringency ['strɪndʒənsɪ] N *(of standards, law, reforms, discipline)* Strenge *f*; *(of rules, testing, training etc also)* Härte *f*; *(of measures)* Härte *f*, Schärfe *f*; **economic ~** strenge Sparmaßnahmen *pl*

stringent ['strɪndʒənt] ADJ *standards, laws, discipline, reforms* streng; *rules, testing, training etc also* hart; *measures* hart, scharf; *market* gedrückt; **~ economies** strenge Sparmaßnahmen *pl*; **they have to practise ~ economy** sie müssen eisern sparen

stringently ['strɪndʒəntlɪ] ADV *control* streng; *enforce, train also* hart; *deal with* energisch; *economize* eisern

stringer ['strɪŋəʳ] N *(Press sl)* Lokalreporter(in) *m(f)*

string: **string instrument** N Saiteninstrument *nt*; *(played with bow also)* Streichinstrument *nt*; **string player** N Streicher(in) *m(f)*; **string-puller** N Drahtzieher *m*; **string-pulling** N Spielenlassen *nt* von Beziehungen; **string quartet** N Streichquartett *nt*; **string tanga** N *(Fashion)* Stringtanga *m*, String *m*; **string tie** N schmale Krawatte; **string vest** N Netzhemd *nt*

stringy ['strɪŋɪ] ADJ *(+er) meat* sehnig, zäh, faserig; *vegetable* faserig, voller Fäden; *person* sehnig; *plant, seaweed, root* lang und dünn; *hair* strähnig

strip [strɪp] N **a** *(= narrow piece)* Streifen *m*; *(of metal)* Band *nt* → **comic strip, tear off**

b *(Brit Sport)* Trikot *nt*, Dress *m*

c *(US: = main street)* Hauptgeschäftsstraße *f*

d *(inf: = airstrip)* Start-und-Lande-Bahn *f*, Piste *(inf) f*

e *(inf: = striptease)* **to do a ~** strippen *(inf)*

VT **a** *(= remove clothes etc from) person* ausziehen; *bed* abziehen; *wall (= remove paint from)* abkratzen; *(= remove paper from)* die Tapeten abziehen von; *floor* abziehen, abschleifen; *paint* abbeizen; *wallpaper* abziehen; *(= remove contents from)* ausräumen; **to ~ sb naked** *or* **to the skin** jdn bis auf die Haut ausziehen, jdn nackt ausziehen; **to ~ a house of its contents** ein Haus ausräumen; **to ~ a room of all its pictures** alle Bilder aus einem Zimmer entfernen; **to ~ sth from** *or* **off sth** etw von etw entfernen; **to ~ a tree of fruit** einen Baum abernten; **the wind ~ped the leaves from** *or* **off the trees** der Wind wehte die Blätter von den Bäumen; **to ~ the bark from the trees** Bäume schälen *or* entrinden; **~ped of sth** ohne etw; **~ped of official**

language, this means ... in einfachen Worten heißt das ...
b *(fig: = deprive of)* berauben *(of +gen)*; **he was ~ped of his titles** seine Titel wurden ihm aberkannt
c *(Tech) (= damage) gear* kaputt machen *(inf)*, beschädigen; *screw* überdrehen; *(= dismantle) engine, car, gun* auseinandernehmen, zerlegen; **to ~ the thread (off a screw)** eine Schraube überdrehen
VI *(= remove clothes)* sich ausziehen; *(at doctor's)* sich frei machen; *(= perform striptease)* strippen *(inf)*; **to ~ naked** sich bis auf die Haut ausziehen, sich ganz ausziehen; **to ~ to the waist** den Oberkörper frei machen; **~ped to the waist** mit nacktem Oberkörper

▶ **strip away** VT SEP *layer of dirt, turf, bark* ablösen, abziehen; *(fig) pretence, hypocrisy* abwerfen, über Bord werfen *(inf)*

▶ **strip down** **VT** *sep engine* auseinandernehmen, zerlegen **VI** **to strip down to one's underwear** sich bis auf die Unterwäsche ausziehen

▶ **strip off** **VT** *sep clothes* ausziehen; *berries, leaves* abmachen *(prep obj* von); *(wind)* herunterwehen *(prep obj* von); *paper* abziehen *(prep obj* von); *buttons, ornaments* entfernen, abmachen *(prep obj* von); *fruit skin, bark* abschälen, ablösen *(prep obj* von); **to strip off the leaves** die Blätter vom Zweig entfernen **VI** **a** *(= take one's clothes off)* sich ausziehen; *(at doctor's)* sich frei machen; *(in striptease)* strippen *(inf)* **b** *(bark)* sich abschälen lassen; *(paper)* sich abziehen lassen

strip: **strip cartoon** N *(Brit)* Comic(strip) *m*; **strip club** N Stripteaseklub *m*; **strip cropping** N *(Agr)* Streifenpflanzung *f*

stripe [straɪp] N **a** Streifen *m* **b** *(Mil)* (Ärmel)streifen *m*, Winkel *m*; **to gain** *or* **get/lose one's ~s** befördert/degradiert werden **c** *(old: = stroke)* Schlag *m*, Hieb *m* **d** *(US: = kind, of politics)* Färbung *f*, Richtung *f*; *(of character, opinion)* Art *f*, Schlag *m* **e** **stripes** PL *(US inf: = prison uniform)* Sträflingsanzug *m (inf)*

striped [straɪpt] ADJ gestreift; **~ with ...** mit ... Streifen; **to be ~ with grey** graue Streifen haben, grau gestreift sein

strip: **strip farming** N *(Agr)* Streifenpflanzung *f*, Streifenflurwirtschaft *f*; **strip light** N *(esp Brit)* Neonröhre *f*; **strip lighting** N *(esp Brit)* Neonlicht *nt or* -beleuchtung *f*

stripling ['strɪplɪŋ] N *(liter)* Bürschchen *nt*; *(pej also)* Grünschnabel *m*

strip: **strip mall** N *(US)* Einkaufsmeile *f*; **strip mill** N Walzwerk *nt*; **strip mine** N *(US)* Tagebau *m*; **strip mining** N *(US)* Abbau *m* über Tage

strippagram ['strɪpəgræm] N *durch eine Angestellte einer Agentur persönlich übermittelter Geburtstagsgruß etc mit Striptease*

stripped-down ['strɪptdaʊn] ADJ *car etc* ohne Extras *pred*

stripper ['strɪpəʳ] N **a** *(= performer)* Stripperin *f*, Stripteasetänzerin *f*; **male ~** Stripper *m*, Stripteasetänzer *m* **b** *(= tool)* Abisolierer *m*; *(= machine)* Schälmaschine *f*, Abstreifer *m* **c** *(= paint stripper)* Farbentferner *m*; *(= wallpaper stripper)* Tapetenlöser *m*

strip: **strip poker** N Strippoker *nt*; **strip-search** **N** Leibesvisitation *f* **VT** einer Leibesvisitation *(dat)* unterziehen; **he was ~ed** er musste sich einer Leibesvisitation unterziehen; **strip show** N Strip(tease)show *f*, Striptease *m or nt*; **striptease** **N** Striptease *m or nt*; **to do a ~** strippen *(inf)*, einen Striptease machen **ADJ** *attr* Striptease-; **~ act** Stripteasenummer *f*

stripy ['straɪpɪ] ADJ *(+er) (inf)* gestreift

strive [straɪv] *pret* **strove**, *ptp* **striven** ['strɪvn] VI *(= exert oneself)* sich bemühen; *(= fight)* kämpfen; **to ~ to do sth** bestrebt *or* bemüht sein, etw zu tun; **to ~ for** *or (old)* **after sth** etw anstreben, nach etw streben; **to ~ against sth** gegen etw (an)kämpfen; **to ~ with sb/sth** mit jdm/etw ringen *or* kämpfen

strobe [strəʊb] **ADJ** stroboskopisch **N** stroboskopische Beleuchtung

strobe light N Stroboskoplicht *nt*

stroboscope ['strəʊbəskəʊp] N Stroboskop *nt*

stroboscopic [ˌstrəʊbəʊ'skɒpɪk] ADJ stroboskopisch

strode [strəʊd] *pret of* **stride**

stroke [strəʊk] **N** **a** *(= blow)* Schlag *m*, Hieb *m*; **a ~ of lightning** ein Blitz(schlag) *m*
b *(Cricket, Golf, Rowing, Tennis)* Schlag *m*; *(Billiards)* Stoß *m*; *(Swimming: = movement)* Zug *m*; *(= type of stroke)* Stil *m*; **~ rate** *(Rowing)* Schlagzahl *f*; **they are rowing (at) a fast ~** sie rudern mit hoher Schlagzahl; **to put sb off his ~** *(fig)* jdn aus dem Takt *or* Konzept bringen
c *(Rowing: = person)* Schlagmann *m*
d *(of pen, brush etc)* Strich *m*; *(fig, of work)* Schlag *m*; *(in diplomacy, business)* Schachzug *m*; **he doesn't do a ~ (of work)** er tut keinen Schlag *(inf)*, er rührt keinen Finger *(inf)*; **a ~ of genius** ein genialer Einfall; **a ~ of luck** ein Glücksfall *m*; **we had a ~ of luck** wir hatten Glück; **with one ~ of the pen** *(lit, fig)* mit einem Federstrich; **at a** *or* **one ~** mit einem Schlag
e *(of clock)* Schlag *m*; **on the ~ of twelve** Punkt zwölf (Uhr)
f *(of piston)* Hub *m*; **two-stroke engine** Zweitaktmotor *m*
g *(Med)* Schlag *m*; **to have a ~** einen Schlag (-anfall) bekommen
h *(= caress)* Streicheln *nt no pl*; **to give sb/sth a ~** jdn/etw streicheln; **with gentle ~s** mit sanftem Streicheln; **different ~s for different folks** *(esp US inf)* jedem Tierchen sein Pläsierchen *(hum inf)*
VT **a** *cat, hand, hair, face* streicheln; **he ~d his chin** er strich sich *(dat)* übers Kinn; **to ~ one's hair down** sich *(dat)* das Haar glatt streichen
b **to ~ a boat (to victory)** als Schlagmann (ein Boot zum Sieg) rudern

stroke play N *(Golf)* Zählspiel *nt*; **stroke-play tournament** Zählspielturnier *nt*

stroll [strəʊl] **N** Spaziergang *m*, Bummel *m*; **to go for** *or* **have** *or* **take a ~** einen Spaziergang *or* Bummel machen
VI spazieren, bummeln; **to ~ along/around** herumspazieren *or* -bummeln *or* -schlendern; **to ~ along the road** die Straße entlangspazieren *or* -bummeln *or* -schlendern; **to ~ around the house** um das Haus herumspazieren; **to ~ around the town** durch die Stadt bummeln; **to ~ up to sb** auf jdn zuschlendern; **to ~ in(to the room)** (ins Zimmer) hineinspazieren *or* -schlendern; **to ~ out (of the room)** (aus dem Zimmer) herausspazieren *or* -schlendern; **to ~ up and down (the road)** die Straße auf und ab spazieren *or* bummeln *or* schlendern

stroller ['strəʊləʳ] N **a** *(= walker)* Spaziergänger(in) *m(f)* **b** *(esp US: = pushchair)* Sportwagen *m*

strolling ['strəʊlɪŋ] ADJ *attr actor, minstrel* fahrend

strong [strɒŋ] **ADJ** *(+er)* **a** stark; *(physically) person, material, kick, hands* kräftig, stark; *grip, voice* kräftig; *table, bolt, nail, wall* stabil, solide; *shoes* fest; *(= strongly marked) features* ausgeprägt; **you need a ~ stomach to be a nurse** als Krankenschwester muss man allerhand verkraften können
b *(= healthy)* kräftig; *person, constitution* robust, kräftig; *teeth, eyes, eyesight, heart, nerves* gut; **when you're ~ again** wenn Sie wieder bei Kräften sind; **he's getting ~er every day** er wird mit jedem Tag wieder kräftiger
c *(= powerful, effective)* stark; *character, convictions, views* fest; *country* mächtig; *candidate, case* aussichtsreich; *influence, temptation* groß, stark; *reason, argument, evidence* überzeugend; *protest, plea* energisch; *measure* drastisch; *letter* geharnischt, in starken Worten abgefasst; *(Liter) plot, sequence, passage, performance* gut, stark *(inf)*; **to have ~ feelings/views about sth** in Bezug auf etw *(acc)* stark engagiert sein; **I didn't know you had such ~ feelings about it** ich habe nicht gewusst, dass Ihnen so viel daran liegt *or* dass Ihnen das so viel bedeutet; *(against it)* ich habe nicht gewusst, dass Sie so dagegen sind; **she has very ~ feelings about him** sie hat sehr viel für ihn übrig; *(as candidate etc)* sie hält sehr viel von ihm; *(against him)* sie ist vollkommen gegen ihn; **to have ~ feelings for** *or* **about sth** eine starke Bindung an etw *(acc)* haben; **we need a ~ hand to fight crime** wir müssen das Verbrechen mit starker Hand bekämpfen; **his ~ point** seine Stärke; **to protest in ~ terms** energisch protestieren; **I had a ~ sense of déjà-vu** ich hatte ganz den Eindruck, das schon einmal gesehen zu haben; **there is a ~ possibility that ...** es ist überaus wahrscheinlich, dass ...
d *(in numbers)* stark; **a group 20 ~** eine 20 Mann starke Gruppe
e *(= capable)* gut, stark *(inf)*; **he is ~ in/on sth** etw ist seine Stärke *or* starke Seite
f *(= enthusiastic, committed)* begeistert; *supporter, Catholic, socialist* überzeugt; *belief, faith* unerschütterlich, stark; **he's very ~ for Smith** *(inf)* er ist (ein) Smith-Fan *(inf)*
g *food* deftig; *smell, perfume etc* stark; *(= pungent, unpleasant) smell, taste* streng; *(of butter)* ranzig; *colour, light* kräftig; *acid, bleach* stark; *solution* konzentriert; **a ~ drink** ein harter Drink
h *accent, verb, rhyme* stark; *syllable etc* betont
i *(Fin) market, economy* gesund; *price* stabil; *currency* stark
ADV *(+er)* **a** *(inf)* **to be going ~** *(old person, thing)* gut in Schuss sein *(inf)*; *(runner)* gut in Form sein; *(party, rehearsals)* in Schwung sein *(inf)*; **that's (coming it) a bit ~!** das ist ein starkes Stück!; **he pitched it pretty ~** *(inf)* er drückte sich ziemlich drastisch aus
b *(Fin)* in einer starken Position

strong: **strong-arm** *(inf)* **ADJ** *tactics etc* brutal; **~ man** Schläger *m* **VT** *(esp US: = beat up)* zusammenschlagen; *(= intimidate)* unter Druck setzen; **they were ~ed into paying** sie wurden so unter Druck gesetzt, dass sie zahlten; **strongbox** N (Geld)kassette *f*; **strong breeze** N *(Met)* starke Winde *pl*, Windstärke 6; **strong gale** N *(Met)* Windstärke 9; **stronghold** N *(= castle, fortress)* Festung *f*; *(= town etc)* Stützpunkt *m*; *(fig)* Hochburg *f*

strongly ['strɒŋlɪ] ADV **a** *(physically)* stark; *kick, grip, shine* kräftig; *fight, attack* heftig; *built* solide, stabil; *(person)* kräftig; *marked* stark
b *(mentally) influence, suspect, tempt, interest* stark; *desire* sehr; *believe* fest; **to feel ~ about sb/sth** → **strong ADJ c**
c *(= powerfully)* stark; *protest, defend* heftig, energisch; *plead* inständig; *support* kräftig; *sense* zutiefst; *answer, worded* in starken Worten; **~ anti-American** stark antiamerikanisch; **he spoke ~ against it** er sprach sich entschieden dagegen aus; **I ~ advise you ...** ich möchte Ihnen dringend(st) raten ...; **I feel very ~ that ...** ich vertrete entschieden die Meinung, dass ...; **he is a man with ~ held views** er ist ein Mann mit sehr festen Ansichten; **to be ~ recommended** besonders *or* nachdrücklich empfohlen werden; **to be ~ in favour of sth** etw sehr *or* stark befürworten; **to be ~ opposed to** *or* **against sth** etw scharf ablehnen; **to be ~ critical of sb/sth** eine sehr kritische Haltung gegenüber jdm/etw haben; **to react ~ to sth** heftig auf etw *(acc)* reagieren
d *(= markedly)* **her accent sounded ~ northern** sie hatte einen auffallend norddeutschen/-englischen *etc* Akzent; **vegetables featured ~ on the menu** auf der Speisekarte war Gemüse besonders stark vertreten; **to smell/taste ~ of sth** stark nach etw riechen/schmecken

strongman ['strɒŋmæn] N *pl* **-men** [-men] *(lit, fig)* starker Mann

strong-minded ADJ, **strong-mindedly** ADV [ˌstrɒŋ'maɪndɪd, -lɪ] willensstark

strong-mindedness [ˌstrɒŋ'maɪndɪdnɪs] N Willensstärke *f*

strong: **strong point** N Stärke *f*; **strongroom** N Tresorraum *m*, Stahlkammer *f*; **strong-willed** [ˌstrɒŋ'wɪld] ADJ willensstark, entschlossen; *(pej)* eigensinnig, trotzig

strontium ['strɒntɪəm] N Strontium *nt*

strop [strɒp] N Streichriemen *m* VT abziehen

strophe ['strəʊfɪ] N Strophe *f*

stroppiness ['strɒpɪnɪs] N *(Brit inf)* Fuchtigkeit *f (inf)*; *(of answer, children)* Pampigkeit *f (inf)*; *(of bouncer etc)* Aggressivität *f*; *(of official)* Sturheit *f*

stroppy ['strɒpɪ] ADJ *(+er) (Brit inf)* fuchtig *(inf)*; *answer, children* pampig *(inf)*; *bouncer etc* aggressiv; *(= obstinate) official* stur; **to be ~ about doing sth** fuchtig/pampig sein, weil man etw tun soll *(inf)*; **don't get ~ with me** *(= aggressive)* werd jetzt nicht pampig *(inf)*; *(= obstinate, uncooperative)* mach nicht so auf stur *(inf)*

strove [strəʊv] *pret of* **strive**

struck [strʌk] *pret, ptp of* **strike** ADJ **a** *pred* **to be ~ with sb/sth** *(= impressed)* von jdm/etw begeistert *or* angetan sein; **I wasn't very ~ with him** er hat keinen großen Eindruck auf mich gemacht; **to be ~ on sb/sth** *(= keen)* auf jdn/etw stehen *(inf)*, auf jdn/etw versessen sein **b** *attr (US: = striking) workers* streikend; *factory, employers* vom Streik betroffen, bestreikt

structural ['strʌktʃərəl] ADJ **a** strukturell, Struktur-; *(of building) alterations, damage, requirements* baulich; **~ material** Baumaterial *nt*; **~ part** Bauteil *nt*; **the bridge suffered ~ damage** die Struktur der Brücke wurde beschädigt **b** *(= weight-bearing) wall, beam* tragend **c** *(fig, = essential)* essenziell, essentiell, notwendig

structural: **structural analysis** N *(Gram)* Strukturanalyse *f*; **structural change** N Strukturwandel *m*; **structural crisis** N Strukturkrise *f*; **structural defect** N Konstruktionsfehler *m*; **structural engineer** N Konstrukteur(in) *m(f)*; **structural engineering** N Bautechnik *f*; **structural fault** N Konstruktionsfehler *m*; **structural formula** N *(Chem)* Strukturformel *f*

structuralism ['strʌktʃərəlɪzəm] N der Strukturalismus

structuralist ['strʌktʃərəlɪst] N Strukturalist(in) *m(f)* ADJ *attr* strukturalistisch

structurally ['strʌktʃərəlɪ] ADV strukturell; **~ the novel is excellent** vom Aufbau her ist der Roman ausgezeichnet; **~ sound** sicher; **the building is ~ unsound** das Gebäude weist bautechnische Mängel auf; **~ the building is in good condition** was das rein Bauliche betrifft, ist das Haus in gutem Zustand; **~ weak** strukturschwach

structural: **structural steel** N Konstruktionsstahl *m*; **structural survey** N Bauzustandsgutachten *nt*; **structural unemployment** N strukturelle Arbeitslosigkeit

structure ['strʌktʃəʳ] N **a** *(= organization)* Struktur *f*; *(Liter)* Aufbau *m*; *(Tech, of bridge, car etc)* Konstruktion *f*; **bone ~** Knochenbau *m* **b** *(= thing constructed)* Konstruktion *f* VT strukturieren; *essay, argument* aufbauen, gliedern; *layout, life* gestalten

structured ['strʌktʃəd] ADJ *programme* strukturiert; *approach* durchdacht; *essay* sorgfältig gegliedert; *society* durchorganisiert, strukturiert; **highly ~** *(society)* stark gegliedert; *novel etc* sorgfältig (auf)gebaut *or* gegliedert

strudel ['ʃtru:dl] N *(esp US)* Strudel *m*

struggle ['strʌgl] N *(lit, fig)* Kampf *m* (*for* um); *(fig: = effort)* Anstrengung *f*; **without a ~** kampflos; **to put up a ~** sich wehren; **the ~ for survival/existence** der Überlebens-/Daseinskampf; **the ~ to feed her seven children** der Kampf, ihre sieben Kinder zu ernähren; **the ~ to find somewhere to live** der Kampf *or* die Schwierigkeiten, bis man eine Wohnung gefunden hat; **it is/was a ~** es ist/war mühsam; **she finds life a ~** sie findet das Leben mühsam; **I had a ~ to persuade him** es war gar nicht einfach, ihn zu überreden

VI **a** *(= contend)* kämpfen; *(in self-defence)* sich wehren; *(= writhe)* sich winden; *(financially)* in Schwierigkeiten sein, krebsen *(inf)*; *(fig: = strive)* sich sehr bemühen *or* anstrengen, sich abmühen; **the police were struggling with the burglar** zwischen der Polizei und dem Einbrecher gab es ein Handgemenge; **to ~ to do sth** sich sehr anstrengen, etw zu tun; **to ~ for sth** um etw kämpfen, sich um etw bemühen; **to ~ against sb/sth** gegen jdn/etw kämpfen; **to ~ with sb** mit jdm kämpfen; **to ~ with sth** *(with problem, difficulty, question)* sich mit etw herumschlagen; *with injury, mortgage, debts, feelings* mit etw zu kämpfen haben; *with doubts, one's conscience* mit etw ringen; *with luggage, language, subject, homework, words* sich mit etw abmühen; **to ~ with life** es im Leben nicht leicht haben; **this firm/team/family is struggling** diese Firma/Mannschaft/Familie hat (schwer) zu kämpfen; **are you struggling?** hast du Schwierigkeiten?; **can you manage? – I'm struggling** schaffst dus? – mit Müh und Not; **he was struggling to make ends meet** er hatte seine liebe Not durchzukommen

b *(= move with difficulty)* sich quälen; **to ~ to one's feet** mühsam aufstehen *or* auf die Beine kommen, sich aufrappeln *(inf)*; **to ~ to get up** sich hochquälen; **he ~d through the tiny window** er zwängte sich durch das kleine Fenster; **to ~ on** *(lit)* sich weiterkämpfen; *(fig)* weiterkämpfen; **to ~ along/through** *(lit, fig)* sich durchschlagen *or* -kämpfen

struggling ['strʌglɪŋ] ADJ *artist, musician, actor* am Hungertuch nagend *attr*

strum [strʌm] VT *tune, chord* klimpern; *guitar* klimpern auf *(+dat)*; **to ~ out a song** ein Liedchen klimpern VI klimpern (*on* auf *+dat*)

strumpet ['strʌmpɪt] N *(old)* Hure *f*, Dirne *f*

strung [strʌŋ] *pret, ptp of* **string**

strung-up [,strʌŋ'ʌp] ADJ **to be ~** nervös *or* gespannt sein (*about sth* wegen etw)

strut[1] [strʌt] VI stolzieren; **to ~ about (the yard)** (auf dem Hof) herumstolzieren; **to ~ past** vorbeistolzieren VT **to ~ one's stuff** *(inf)* zeigen, was man drauf hat; *(sexually)* zeigen, was man hat N angeberischer Gang, Stolzieren *nt*; **to walk with a ~** stolzieren

strut[2] N *(horizontal)* Strebe *f*; *(sloping also)* Stütze *f*; *(vertical)* Pfeiler *m*

struth [stru:θ] INTERJ *(Brit inf)* heiliger Strohsack *(inf)*

strychnine ['strɪkni:n] N Strychnin *nt*

stub [stʌb] N *(of candle, pencil, tail)* Stummel *m*; *(of cigarette also)* Kippe *f*; *(of cheque, ticket)* Abschnitt *m*; *(of tree)* Stumpf *m* VT **to ~ one's toe (on *or* against sth)** sich *(dat)* den Zeh (an etw *dat*) stoßen, mit dem Zeh an *or* gegen etw *(acc)* stoßen; **to ~ out a cigarette** eine Zigarette ausdrücken

stub axle N Achszapfen *m*

stubble ['stʌbl] N *no pl* Stoppeln *pl*; **a field of ~** ein Stoppelfeld *nt*

stubbly ['stʌblɪ] ADJ *(+er)* Stoppel-; *face* stoppelig; **~ beard** Stoppelbart *m*; **~ field** Stoppelfeld *nt*

stubborn ['stʌbən] ADJ **a** *(= obstinate) person, insistence* stur; *animal, child* störrisch; **to be ~ about sth** stur auf etw *(dat)* beharren; **she has a ~ streak** sie kann sehr stur sein **b** *(= persistent) refusal, resistance, campaign, stain etc* hartnäckig; **in ~ silence** stur schweigend **c** *lock, material* widerspenstig; *weeds, cough* hartnäckig

stubbornly ['stʌbənlɪ] ADV **a** *refuse* stur; *insist* störrisch; *say* trotzig, starrköpfig **b** *(= persistently)* hartnäckig; **interest rates have remained ~ high** die Zinsen sind unbeirrt hoch geblieben

stubbornness ['stʌbənnɪs] N **a** *(= obstinacy, of person)* Sturheit *f*; *(of animal, child)* störrische Art **b** *(of refusal, resistance)* Hartnäckigkeit *f* **c** *(of lock)* Widerspenstigkeit *f*; *(of cough)* Hartnäckigkeit *f*

stubby ['stʌbɪ] ADJ *(+er) revolver etc* kurz; *tail* stummelig; *pencil, vase* kurz und dick; *person* gedrungen, stämmig, untersetzt; *legs* kurz und stämmig; **~ fingers** Wurstfinger *pl (inf)*; **~ wings** Stummelflügel *pl*

stucco ['stʌkəʊ] N *pl* **-(e)s** Stuck *m*; *(also* **stucco work***)* Stuckarbeit *f*, Stukkatur *f* ADJ *attr* Stuck-; **~ ceiling** Stuckdecke *f* VT mit Stuck verzieren

stuck [stʌk] *pret, ptp of* **stick**[2] ADJ **a** *(= baffled)* (*on, over* mit) **to be ~** nicht klarkommen, nicht zurechtkommen; **to get ~** nicht weiterkommen; **I was really ~** ich war total aufgeschmissen *(inf)*

b *(= wedged)* **to be ~** *(door etc)* verkeilt sein; **to get ~** stecken bleiben

c *(= trapped, stranded)* **to be ~** festsitzen; **to be ~ in a traffic jam** im Stau festsitzen

d *(inf)* **he/she is ~ for sth** es fehlt ihm/ihr an etw *(dat)*, ihm/ihr fehlt etw; **I'm a bit ~ for cash** ich bin ein bisschen knapp bei Kasse; **he wasn't exactly ~ for something to say** man kann nicht gerade sagen, dass ihm der Gesprächsstoff fehlte; **to be ~ for sb** jdn dringend brauchen

e *(Brit inf)* **to get ~ into sb** jdn richtig in die Mangel nehmen *(inf)*; **to get ~ into sth** sich in etw *(acc)* richtig reinknien *(inf)*; **Stephen got ~ into his steak** Stephen nahm sein Steak in Angriff; **get ~ in!** schlagt zu! *(inf)*

f *(inf, = infatuated)* **to be ~ on sb** in jdn verknallt sein *(inf)*

g *(inf)* **to be ~ with sb/sth** mit jdm/etw dasitzen, jdn/etw am Hals haben *(inf)*

h **to squeal like a ~ pig** wie am Spieß schreien

stuck-up [,stʌk'ʌp] ADJ *(inf) person, attitude, voice* hochnäsig; **she's ~** sie ist eine hochnäsige Ziege *(inf)*; **to be ~ about sth** sich *(dat)* viel auf etw *(acc)* einbilden

stud[1] [stʌd] N **a** *(= nail)* Beschlagnagel *m*; *(decorative)* Ziernagel *m*; *(Brit: on boots)* Stollen *m*; **reflector ~** Katzenauge *nt* **b** *(= collar stud)* Kragenknopf *m* **c** *(= earring)* Ohrstecker *m* VT *(usu pass)* übersäen; *(with jewels)* (dicht) besetzen; **their family tree is ~ded with generals** in ihrem Stammbaum wimmelt es von Generälen

stud[2] N (= *group of horses, for breeding*) Gestüt *nt*, Zucht *f*; *(for racing etc)* Stall *m*; *(= stallion)* (Zucht)hengst *m*; *(inf: = man)* Hengst *m (inf)*; **the stallion is at ~** der Hengst wird zur Zucht benutzt; **to put to ~** zu Zuchtzwecken verwenden

studbook ['stʌdbʊk] N Gestüt- *or* Zuchtbuch *nt*

student ['stju:dənt] N *(Univ)* Student(in) *m(f)*, Studierende(r) *mf*; *(esp US, at school, night school)* Schüler(in) *m(f)*; **he is a ~ of French life/human nature** er studiert die französische Lebensart/die menschliche Natur; **he is a ~ of French** *or* **a French ~** *(Univ)* er studiert Französisch; *(Sch)* er lernt Französisch; **medical/law ~s** Medizin-/Jurastudenten *pl* ADJ *attr* Studenten-; *activities, protest movement* studentisch; **~ driver** *(US)* Fahrschüler(in) *m(f)*; **~ nurse** Krankenpflegeschüler(in) *m(f)*

student: **student body** N Studentenschaft *f*; **student card** N Studentenausweis *m*; **student loan** N Studentendarlehen *nt*; **studentship** N *(Brit: = grant)* Stipendium *nt*; **student(s') union** N *(Brit)* **a** *(= organization) Studentenorganisation an britischen Universitäten, die sich um soziale Belange der Studenten kümmert (esp political)* Studentenbund *m* **b** *(= building)* Gebäude *nt* der Student(s') Union/des Studentenbundes; **student teacher** N Referendar(in) *m(f)*; **student unrest** N Studentenunruhen *pl*

stud: **stud farm** N Gestüt *nt*; **stud horse** N Zuchthengst *m*

studied ['stʌdɪd] *pret, ptp of* **study** ADJ *(= carefully considered) reply* (gut) durchdacht, wohlüberlegt; *simplicity* bewusst, ausgesucht; *prose, style* kunstvoll; *(= deliberate)* berechnet; *calm, politeness* gewollt; *insult* beabsichtigt, bewusst; *avoidance* sorgfältig; *pose* einstudiert; *elegance* gekünstelt; *voice* gewählt; **to maintain a ~ silence** wohlüberlegt schweigen

studio ['stju:dɪəʊ] N *(all senses)* Studio *nt*; *(of painter, photographer also)* Atelier *nt*; *(= broadcasting studio also)* Senderaum *m*

studio: **studio apartment** N Studiowohnung *f*; **studio audience** N Publikum *nt* im Studio; **studio couch** N Schlafcouch *f*; **studio flat** N *(Brit)* = **studio apartment**

studious ['stju:dɪəs] ADJ *person* fleißig, eifrig; *life, habits, appearance* gelehrsam; *turn of mind* lernbegierig; *attention, piece of work, research* gewissenhaft, sorgfältig; *avoidance* gezielt, sorgsam; *politeness* bewusst; *effort* eifrig, beflissen *(geh)*; **a ~ atmosphere** eine eifrige Lernatmosphäre

studiously ['stju:dɪəslɪ] ADV fleißig, eifrig; *(= painstakingly)* sorgsam, sorgfältig; *polite* bewusst; *avoid* gezielt, sorgsam; *(= deliberately)* absichtlich, bewusst; **to remain ~ neutral** sorgsam auf Neutralität bedacht sein

studiousness ['stju:dɪəsnɪs] N *(of person)* Lerneifer *m*, Fleiß *m*

study ['stʌdɪ] ✪ 26.2 **N** **a** *(= studying, branch of study, esp Univ)* Studium *nt*; *(at school)* Lernen *nt*; *(of situation, evidence, case)* Untersuchung *f*; *(of nature)* Beobachtung *f*; **the ~ of cancer** die Krebsforschung; **the ~ of Chinese** das Chinesischstudium; **African studies** *(Univ)* afrikanische Sprache und Kultur, Afrikanistik *f*; **modern French studies** französische Sprache und Landeskunde; **to make a ~ of sth** etw untersuchen; *(academic)* etw studieren; **to spend one's time in ~** seine Zeit mit Studieren/Lernen verbringen; **fond of ~** lernbegierig; **during my studies** während meines Studiums; **his face was a ~** *(inf)* sein Gesicht war sehenswert
b *(= piece of work)* Studie *f* (of über *+acc*); *(Art, Phot)* Studie *f* (of *+gen*); *(Liter, Sociol)* Untersuchung *f* (of über *+acc*); *(Mus)* Etüde *f*
c *(= room)* Arbeits- *or* Studierzimmer *nt*
VT studieren; *(Sch)* lernen; *nature also, stars* beobachten; *author, particular tune, text etc* sich befassen mit; *(= research into)* erforschen; *(= examine)* untersuchen; *clue, evidence* prüfen, untersuchen
VI studieren; *(esp Sch)* lernen; **to ~ to be a teacher/doctor** ein Lehrerstudium/Medizinstudium machen; **to ~ for an exam** sich auf eine Prüfung vorbereiten, für eine Prüfung lernen; **to ~ under sb** bei jdm studieren

study: **study group** N Arbeitsgruppe *or* -gemeinschaft *f*; **study hall** N Studien- *or* Lesesaal *m*; **study tour** N Informationsreise *f*; **study visit** N Studienreise *f*

stuff [stʌf] **N** **a** Zeug *nt*; **black/sweet** *etc* **~** schwarzes/süßes *etc* Zeug; **the ~ that dreams are made of** der Stoff, aus dem die Träume sind; **the ~ of tragedy** echte Tragik; **show him what kind of ~ you're made of** zeig ihm, aus welchem Holz du geschnitzt bist; **there was a lot of rough ~** es ging ziemlich rau zu; **there is some good ~ in that book** in dem Buch stecken ein paar gute Sachen; **it's poor/good ~** das ist schlecht/gut; **this book is strong ~** das Buch ist starker Tobak; **this tea is strong ~** der Tee ist ziemlich stark; **I can't read his ~** ich kann sein Zeug nicht lesen; **his later ~ is less original** seine späteren Sachen sind weniger originell; **he brought me some ~ to read/to pass the time** er hat mir etwas zum Lesen/zur Unterhaltung mitgebracht; **books and ~** Bücher und so *(inf)*; **and ~ like that** und so was *(inf)*; **all that ~ about how he wants to help us** all das Gerede, dass er uns helfen will; **~ and nonsense** Quatsch *m (inf)*, Blödsinn *m*; **all this ~ about Father Christmas** *(inf)* all der Quatsch vom Weihnachtsmann *(inf)*
b *(inf)* **she's a nice bit of ~** die ist nicht ohne *(inf)*; **a drop of the hard ~** ein Schluck von dem scharfen Zeug; **that's the ~!** so ists richtig!, weiter so!; **to do one's ~** seine Nummer abziehen *(inf)*; **go on, do your ~!** nun mach mal *or* doch! *(inf)*; **he did his ~ well** er hat seine Sache gut gemacht; **to know one's ~** wissen, wovon man redet, sich auskennen → **hot stuff**
c *(= possessions)* Zeug *nt*, Sachen *pl*
d *(inf: = drugs)* Stoff *m (inf)*
e *(old: = cloth)* Material *nt*, Stoff *m*
VT **a** *(= fill) container, room, person* vollstopfen; *hole* zustopfen, verstopfen; *contents, object, books* (hinein)stopfen *(into* in *+acc)*; *(into envelope)* stecken *(into* in *+acc)*; **to ~ sb with food** jdn mit Essen vollstopfen, jdn mästen *(inf)*; **to ~ one's face** *(inf)* sich vollstopfen *(inf)*; **I'm ~ed** *(inf: with food)* ich bin total voll *(inf)*; **to ~ sth away** etw wegstecken; **he ~ed it away in his pocket** er stopfte es in seine Tasche; **he ~ed some money into my hand** er drückte mir Geld in die Hand; **to ~ one's fingers into one's ears** sich *(dat)* die Finger in die Ohren stecken; **to be ~ed up (with a cold)** verschnupft sein, eine verstopfte Nase haben; **my nose is ~ed up** ich habe eine verstopfte Nase
b *(Cook)* füllen
c *cushion etc* füllen; *toy* ausstopfen; *(in taxidermy)* ausstopfen; **a ~ed toy** ein Stofftier *nt*
d *(Brit inf)* **~ it** *(= be quiet)* halts Maul! *(inf)*, Schnauze! *(inf)*; **get ~ed!** du kannst mich mal *(inf)*!; **I told him to ~ it** *or* **to get ~ed** ich habe ihm gesagt, er kann mich mal *(inf)*; **you can ~ your job** *etc* du kannst deinen blöden Job *etc* behalten *(inf)*; **~ him!** der kann mich mal! *(inf)*; **~ the tax reform!** ich scheiß auf die Steuerreform! *(sl)*
VI *(inf: = eat)* sich vollstopfen *(inf)*
VR **to ~ oneself (with food/on cakes)** sich (mit Essen/Kuchen) vollstopfen *(inf)*

stuffed shirt ['stʌft'ʃɜ:t] N *(inf)* Stockfisch *m (inf)*

stuffily ['stʌfɪlɪ] ADV *(= narrow-mindedly)* spießig; *(= prudishly)* prüde; *(= stiffly)* steif, gezwungen; *(= dully)* langweilig

stuffiness ['stʌfɪnɪs] N **a** *(of room, atmosphere)* Stickigkeit *f*, Dumpfheit *f* **b** *(of person, = narrow-mindedness)* Spießigkeit *f*; *(= prudishness)* Prüderie *f*, Zimperlichkeit *f*

stuffing ['stʌfɪŋ] N *(of pillow, quilt, Cook)* Füllung *f*; *(of furniture)* Polstermaterial *nt*; *(in taxidermy, toys)* Füllmaterial *nt*, Stopfmaterial *nt*; **to knock the ~ out of sb** *(inf)* jdn fertigmachen *(inf)*, jdn schaffen *(inf)*

stuffy ['stʌfɪ] ADJ *(+er)* **a** *room, atmosphere* stickig, dumpf; **it's a bit ~ in here** es ist etwas stickig hier drinnen **b** *(= narrow-minded)* spießig; *(= prudish)* prüde, zimperlich **c** *(= stiff)* steif; *atmosphere* gezwungen, steif; *(= dull)* langweilig, öde, fad **d** *(= blocked) nose* verstopft

stultify ['stʌltɪfaɪ] **VT** lähmen; *mind, person* verkümmern *or* verdummen lassen; **to become stultified** verkümmern, verdummen **VI** verkümmern, verdummen

stultifying ['stʌltɪfaɪɪŋ] ADJ lähmend; *boredom, inactivity also* abstumpfend; **to have a ~ effect on sb** jdn verkümmern lassen

stumble ['stʌmbl] **N** Stolpern *nt no pl, no indef art*; *(in speech etc)* Stocken *nt no pl, no indef art* **VI** *(lit, fig)* stolpern; *(in speech)* stocken; **to ~ against sth** gegen etw stoßen; **to ~ on sth** *(lit)* über etw *(acc)* stolpern; *(fig)* auf etw *(acc)* stoßen; **he ~d through a waltz/his speech** stockend *or* holperig spielte er einen Walzer/hielt er seine Rede

stumbling block ['stʌmblɪŋblɒk] N *(fig)* Hürde *f*, Hindernis *nt*, Problem *nt*; **to be a ~ to sth** einer Sache *(dat)* im Weg stehen

stumer ['stju:məʳ] N *(Brit inf)* **a** *(= counterfeit)* Fälschung *f* **b** *(= cheque)* wertloser Scheck **c** *(= failure)* Misserfolg *m*

stump [stʌmp] **N** **a** *(of tree, limb, tooth)* Stumpf *m*; *(of candle, pencil, tail, cigar)* Stummel *m*; *(Cricket)* Stab *m*; **to stir one's ~s** *(inf)* sich rühren, sich regen
b *(US Pol: = platform)* Rednertribüne *f*; **~ speaker** Wahlredner(in) *m(f)*; **to go out on the ~s** (öffentlich *or* vor Ort) als Redner auftreten
VT **a** *(Cricket)* ausschalten *(durch Umwerfen der Stäbe)*
b *(fig inf)* **you've got me ~ed** da bin ich überfragt; **I'm ~ed by that problem, that problem's got me ~ed** ich bin mit meiner Weisheit *or* meinem Latein am Ende *(inf)*; **to be ~ed for an answer** um eine Antwort verlegen sein
c *(US Pol)* **to ~ the country** Wahl(kampf)reisen durch das Land machen
VI *(inf)* stapfen; **to ~ along/about** entlang-/herumstapfen

▶ **stump up** *(Brit inf)* **VT** *insep* springen lassen *(inf)*, lockermachen *(inf)* **VI** blechen *(inf)* *(for sth* für etw)

stumpy ['stʌmpɪ] ADJ *(+er) pencil, candle* stummelig *(inf)*, kurz; *person* stämmig, untersetzt; *tree* klein und gedrungen; *legs* kurz; *building* gedrungen; **a ~ tail** ein Stummelschwanz *m*

stun [stʌn] VT *(= make unconscious)* betäuben; *(noise also: = daze)* benommen machen; *(fig: = shock)* fassungslos machen; *(= amaze)* erstaunen, verblüffen; **he was ~ned by the news** *(bad news)* er war über die Nachricht fassungslos *or* wie gelähmt; *(good news)* die Nachricht hat ihn überwältigt; **he was ~ned by his good fortune** er war sprachlos über sein Glück

stun bullet N Wuchtgeschoss *nt*

stung [stʌŋ] *pret, ptp of* **sting**

stun grenade N Blendgranate *f*

stun gun N Elektroschocker *m*

stunk [stʌŋk] *ptp of* **stink**

stunned [stʌnd] ADJ *(= unconscious)* betäubt; *(= dazed)* benommen; *(fig: = shocked)* fassungslos; *(= amazed)* sprachlos; **there was a ~ silence** benommenes Schweigen breitete sich aus; **I sat in ~ silence/disbelief** ich saß sprachlos/fassungslos da

stunner ['stʌnəʳ] N *(inf: = thing)* Wucht *f (inf)*; *(= woman)* tolle Frau, tolles Weib *(inf)*; *(= man)* toller Mann *or* Kerl *(inf)*

stunning ['stʌnɪŋ] ADJ *(lit) blow* wuchtig, betäubend; *(fig) news, victory* fantastisch, phantastisch, toll *(inf)*; *dress, girl, effect, view, display, looks* atemberaubend; *defeat, shock* überwältigend

stunningly ['stʌnɪŋlɪ] ADV atemberaubend, fantastisch, phantastisch; *beautiful* überwältigend; *simple* erstaunlich

stunt[1] [stʌnt] N Kunststück *nt*, Nummer *f*; *(= publicity stunt, trick)* Gag *m*; *(Aviat)* Kunststück *nt*; *(Film)* Stunt *m*; **to do ~s** *(= be stuntman)* ein Stuntman sein, doubeln; **he does most of his own ~s** gefährliche Szenen spielt er meist selbst

stunt[2] VT *(lit, fig) growth, development* hemmen; *trees, mind etc* verkümmern lassen

stunt double N *(Film)* Double *nt*

stunted ['stʌntɪd] ADJ *plant, mind* verkümmert; *child* unterentwickelt; **the ~ growth of these trees** die verkümmerten Bäume; **his ~ growth** seine Verwachsenheit; **~ development** Unterentwicklung *f*

stunt: **stunt flying** N Kunstflug *m*; **stunt kite** N Drachen *m (mit dem Flugmanöver vorgeführt werden können)*; **stuntman** N Stuntman *m*, Double *nt*; **stuntwoman** N Stuntwoman *nt*, Double *nt*

stupefaction [ˌstju:pɪ'fækʃən] N Verblüffung *f*; **he looked at me in ~** er sah mich verblüfft *or* voller Verblüffung an

stupefy ['stju:pɪfaɪ] VT benommen machen; *(fig: = amaze, surprise)* verblüffen; **to be stupefied by drink** vom Alkohol benommen sein

stupefying ['stju:pɪfaɪɪŋ] ADJ betäubend; *(fig: = amazing)* verblüffend

stupendous [stju:'pendəs] ADJ fantastisch, phantastisch; *effort* enorm

stupendously [stju:'pendəslɪ] ADV fantastisch, phantastisch; *hard* enorm; *boring* ungeheuer

stupid ['stju:pɪd] **ADJ** **a** dumm; *(= foolish also, boring, wretched)* blöd(e) *(inf)*; **don't be ~** sei nicht so blöd *(inf)*; **I've done a ~ thing** ich habe etwas ganz Dummes *or* Blödes *(inf)* gemacht; **you ~ idiot!** du blöder Idiot!; **you ~ little man!** Sie Blödmann! *(inf)*; **take that ~ look off your face** guck nicht so dumm *or* blöd *(inf)*!; **that was ~ of you** das war dumm (von dir); **that was a ~ thing to do** das war dumm; **it was ~ of me (to say anything)** es war blöd von mir (etwas zu sagen); **I was ~ to do that** es war dumm von mir, das zu tun; **you would be ~ to**

move to London du wärst ja dumm *or* blöd *(inf)*, wenn du nach London ziehen würdest; **to make sb look** ~ jdn blamieren; **to be so** ~ *or* **to be** ~ **enough as to do sth** dumm genug sein, etw zu tun; **it is the ~est thing I've ever done/heard** das ist das Dümmste, was ich jemals getan/gehört habe
b *(= stupefied)* benommen, benebelt; **to drink oneself** ~ sich sinnlos betrinken; **the blow knocked him** ~ der Schlag hat ihn völlig benebelt; **to be** ~ **with tiredness** ganz benommen vor lauter Müdigkeit sein; **to bore sb** ~ jdn zu Tode langweilen; **to laugh oneself** ~ sich dumm und dämlich lachen *(inf)*
ADV *(inf)* **to talk** ~ Quatsch reden *(inf)*; **to act** ~ sich dumm stellen
N *(inf, = person)* Blödmann *m (inf)*, Dummkopf *m (inf)*

stupidity [stjuːˈpɪdɪtɪ] **N** Dummheit *f*; *(= silliness also)* Blödheit *f (inf)*

stupidly [ˈstjuːpɪdlɪ] **ADV** *(= unintelligently)* dumm; *(= foolishly also)* blöd *(inf)*; *say* dummerweise; *stare* dumm; *grin* albern; ~ **I'd forgotten my keys** dummerweise hatte ich meine Schlüssel vergessen; **he** ~ **refused** er war so dumm *or* blöd *(inf)* abzulehnen; **he had told the boss several** ~ **obvious lies** er hatte dem Chef einige dummdreiste Lügen erzählt

stupor [ˈstjuːpəʳ] **N** Benommenheit *f*; **he lay/sat there in a** ~ er lag/saß benommen *or* apathisch *or* teilnahmslos da; **to be in a drunken** ~ sinnlos betrunken *or* im Vollrausch sein

sturdily [ˈstɜːdɪlɪ] **ADV** **a** stabil; ~ **built** *(person)* kräftig *or* stämmig gebaut; *chair, ship etc* stabil gebaut **b** *(fig)* unerschütterlich, standhaft; *say* resolut, bestimmt; *independent* unerschütterlich

sturdiness [ˈstɜːdɪnɪs] **N** **a** *(of person, body, plant)* Kräftigkeit *f*, Stämmigkeit *f*; *(of material)* Robustheit *f*; *(of building, ship, car)* Stabilität *f* **b** *(fig, of opposition)* Unerschütterlichkeit *f*, Standhaftigkeit *f*

sturdy [ˈstɜːdɪ] **ADJ** *(+er)* **a** *person, body, plant* kräftig, stämmig; *material* robust; *building, ship, car* stabil; ~ **shoes** festes Schuhwerk *nt* **b** *(fig) opposition* unerschütterlich, standhaft

sturgeon [ˈstɜːdʒən] **N** Stör *m*

stutter [ˈstʌtəʳ] **N** *(of person, engine)* Stottern *nt no pl*; *(of guns)* Trommeln *nt*; **he has a bad** ~ er stottert sehr; **to say sth with a** ~ etw stotternd sagen, etw stottern **VI** **a** stottern; **he was ~ing with embarrassment** er stotterte vor Verlegenheit; **she ~ed out an apology** sie entschuldigte sich stotternd **b** *(= advance slowly)* **to** ~ **on/along** entlangstottern; *(fig, reform)* sich dahinquälen **VT** stottern; **she ~ed an apology** sie entschuldigte sich stotternd

stutterer [ˈstʌtərəʳ] **N** Stotterer *m*, Stotterin *f*

stuttering [ˈstʌtərɪŋ] **N** Stottern *nt*

sty [staɪ] **N** *(lit, fig)* Schweinestall *m*

sty(e) [staɪ] **N** *(Med)* Gerstenkorn *nt*

Stygian [ˈstɪdʒɪən] **ADJ** *(liter) gloom, darkness* stygisch *(liter)*

style [staɪl] **N** **a** *(Art, Mus, Liter, personal etc)* Stil *m*; ~ **of painting** Malstil *m*; **the** ~ **of his writing** sein Stil *m*; ~ **of life** Lebensstil *m*; ~ **of management** Führungsstil *m*; **a poem in the Romantic** ~ ein Gedicht *nt* im Stil der Romantik; **he won in fine** ~ er gewann souverän *or* überlegen; **in his own inimitable** ~ *(iro)* in seiner unnachahmlichen Art *or* Manier, auf die ihm typische Art; **that house is not my** ~ so ein Haus ist nicht mein Stil; **hillwalking is not his** ~ Bergwanderungen liegen ihm nicht; **that's the** ~ *(inf)* so ists richtig
b *(= elegance)* Stil *m*; **the man has (real)** ~ der Mann hat Klasse *or* Format; **in** ~ stilvoll; **to do things in** ~ alles im großen Stil tun; **to celebrate in** ~ groß feiern; **to get married in** ~ eine Hochzeit großen Stils *or* im großen Stil feiern
c *(= sort, type)* Art *f*; **a new** ~ **of house/car** *etc* ein neuer Haus-/Autotyp *etc*; **just the** ~ **of car I like** ein Auto, wie es mir gefällt
d *(Fashion)* Stil *m no pl*, Mode *f*; *(= cut)* Schnitt *m*; *(= hairstyle)* Frisur *f*; **these coats are available in two ~s** diese Mäntel gibt es in zwei verschiedenen Schnittarten *or* Macharten; **I want something in that** ~ ich hätte gern etwas in der Art *or* in dem Stil; **all the latest ~s** die neue(ste) Mode, Mode im neue(ste)n Stil; **the latest ~s in shoes** die neue(ste)n Schuhmoden
e *(= style of address)* Anrede *f*; *(= title)* Titel *m*
f *(Bot)* Griffel *m*
VT **a** *(= designate)* nennen
b *(= design)* entwerfen; *interior etc* gestalten; *hair* stylen; **a smartly ~d dress** ein elegant geschnittenes Kleid; **it is ~d for comfort, not elegance** es ist auf Bequemlichkeit und nicht Eleganz zugeschnitten

-style [staɪl] **ADJ** *suf* nach … Art, auf *(+acc)* … Art; **American-style fried chicken** Brathähnchen nach amerikanischer Art; **cowboy-style** auf Cowboyart, nach Art der Cowboys; **Swedish-style furniture/design** Möbel/Design im schwedischen Stil; **Western-style democracy** Demokratie nach westlichem Vorbild; **to dress 1920s-style** sich im Stil der zwanziger Jahre *or* Zwanzigerjahre kleiden; **the old-style cricketer** der Cricketspieler der alten Schule

stylebook [ˈstaɪlbʊk] **N** *(Typ)* Stilvorschriften *pl*; *(Fashion)* Modeheft *nt*; *(for hairstyles)* Frisurenheft *nt*

style sheet **N** *(Comput, Typ)* ≈ Formatvorlage *f*; *(Editing)* Stilblatt *nt*

styli [ˈstaɪlaɪ] *pl of* **stylus**

styling [ˈstaɪlɪŋ] **N** *(of car etc)* Design *nt*; *(of dress)* Machart *f*, Schnitt *m*; *(of hair)* Schnitt *m*; ~ **mousse** Schaumfestiger *m*

stylish [ˈstaɪlɪʃ] **ADJ** **a** *(= elegant)* stylish; *car, hotel also, district* vornehm; *furnishings, film, performer, design* stilvoll; *performance* kunstvoll; *wedding* großen Stils; *way of life* großartig, im großen Stil **b** *(= fashionable) clothes* modisch

stylishly [ˈstaɪlɪʃlɪ] **ADV** **a** *(= elegantly)* elegant; *furnished* stilvoll; *live* im großen Stil; *travel* mit allem Komfort **b** *(= fashionably) dress* modisch

stylishness [ˈstaɪlɪʃnɪs] **N** **a** *(= elegance) (of person)* Eleganz *f*; *(of car, hotel, district also)* Vornehmheit *f*; *(of furnishings)* stilvolle Art; *(of wedding etc)* groß angelegter Stil **b** *(= fashionableness)* modische Finesse

stylist [ˈstaɪlɪst] **N** **a** *(Fashion)* Modeschöpfer(in) *m(f)*, Modestylist(in) *m(f)*; *(= hair stylist)* Friseur *m*, Friseuse *f*, Coiffeur *m (geh)*, Coiffeuse *f (geh)* **b** *(Liter, Sport)* Stilist(in) *m(f)*

stylistic [staɪˈlɪstɪk] **ADJ** stilistisch; ~ **device** Stilmittel *nt*

stylistically [staɪˈlɪstɪkəlɪ] **ADV** *radical, surprising, conventional* stilistisch; **~, it lacks polish** stilistisch gesehen *or* vom Stil her fehlt es am letzten Schliff

stylistics [staɪˈlɪstɪks] **N** *sing* Stilistik *f*

stylite [ˈstaɪlaɪt] **N** Säulenheilige(r) *m*, Stylit *m (spec)*

stylize [ˈstaɪlaɪz] **VT** stilisieren

stylized [ˈstaɪlaɪzd] **ADJ** *picture, performance, design* stilisiert; *gesture* abstrakt, stilisiert

stylus [ˈstaɪləs] **N** **a** *pl* **styli** *(on record player)* Nadel *f* **b** *(= writing instrument)* Griffel *m*, Stilus *m (Hist)* **c** *(Comput: for PDAs etc)* (Eingabe)stift *m*

stymie [ˈstaɪmɪ] **VT** *(fig inf)* mattsetzen *(inf)*; **to be ~d** aufgeschmissen sein *(inf)*

styptic [ˈstɪptɪk] **N** blutstillendes Mittel **ADJ** *effect* blutstillend

styptic pencil **N** Blutstillstift *m*

Styria [ˈstɪrɪə] **N** *(part of Austria)* Steiermark *f*

Styrofoam® [ˈstaɪərəfəʊm] **N** *(US)* ≈ Styropor® *nt*

Suabian [ˈsweɪbɪən] **ADJ, N** = **Swabian**

suave **ADJ**, **suavely** **ADV** [swɑːv, -lɪ] weltmännisch, aalglatt *(pej)*

suaveness [ˈswɑːvnɪs] **N** = **suavity**

suavity [ˈswɑːvɪtɪ] **N** Gewandtheit *f*, aalglatte Art *(pej)*

sub [sʌb] *abbr* **a** *of* **sub-edit** *of* **sub-editor** **b** *of* **submarine** **c** *of* **subscription** **d** *of* **substitute**

sub- **PREF** *(= under, subordinate, inferior)* Unter-, unter-; *(esp with foreign words)* Sub-, sub-; **subgroup** Untergruppe *f*; **subalpine** subalpin

subagency [ˈsʌbˌeɪdʒənsɪ] **N** **a** *(Comm etc)* Unteragentur *f*; *(US)* Nebenstelle *f* **b** *(Jur)* Nebenvollmacht *f*

subaltern [ˈsʌbltən] **N** *(Brit, Mil)* Subalternoffizier(in) *m(f)*

sub: **subaqua** [sʌbˈækwə] **ADJ** *attr* unter Wasser; ~ **club** Taucherklub *m*; **subaquatic** [ˌsʌbəˈkwætɪk] **ADJ** Unterwasser-; **subarctic** **ADJ** subarktisch; **subatomic** **ADJ** *particle* subatomar; **subbasement** **N** Kellergeschoss *nt*, Kellergeschoß *nt (Aus, Sw)*; **subcategory** **N** Subkategorie *f*, Untergruppe *f*; **subclass** **N** Unterabteilung *f*; **subclassify** **VTI** unterteilen; **subcommittee** **N** Unterausschuss *m*; **subcompact** **N** *(US Aut)* Kleinstwagen *m*; **subconscious** **ADJ** unterbewusst **N** **the** ~ das Unterbewusstsein; **in his** ~ im Unterbewusstsein; **subconsciously** **ADV** im Unterbewusstsein; **subcontinent** **N** Subkontinent *m*; **subcontract** **VT** (vertraglich) weitervergeben *(to* an *+acc)* **N** Nebenvertrag *m*, Untervertrag *m*; **subcontractor** **N** Unterkontrahent(in) *m(f)*, Subunternehmer(in) *m(f)*; **subculture** **N** Subkultur *f*; **subcutaneous** **ADJ** subkutan; **subdirectory** **N** *(Comput)* Unterverzeichnis *nt*; **subdivide** **VT** unterteilen **VI** sich aufteilen; **subdivision** **N** *(= act)* Unterteilung *f*; *(= subgroup)* Unterabteilung *f*; **subdominant** **N** Subdominante *f* **ADJ** ~ **chord** Subdominantakkord *m*

subdue [səbˈdjuː] **VT** *rebels, country* unterwerfen; *enemy also* besiegen; *rioters* überwältigen; *demonstrations* niederschlagen; *(fig) anger, desire* unterdrücken, zähmen; *noise, light, high spirits* dämpfen; *animals, children* bändigen; *pain* lindern; *wilderness* zähmen

subdued [səbˈdjuːd] **ADJ** *(= quiet) colour, lighting, voice, response* gedämpft; *manner, person* ruhig, still; *mood, atmosphere* gedrückt; *(= submissive) voice, manner, person* fügsam, gehorsam, gefügig; *(= repressed) feelings, excitement* unterdrückt; **lunch was a** ~ **affair** die Stimmung während des Mittagessens war gedrückt

sub: **subedit** **VTI** *(esp Brit)* redigieren; **subeditor** **N** *(esp Brit)* Redakteur(in) *m(f)*; **subentry** **N** *(Book-keeping)* Nebenposten *m*; **subfamily** **N** *(esp Biol)* Unterfamilie *f*; **subfolder** **N** *(Comput)* untergeordneter Ordner; **sub-frame** **N** *(of car)* Zwischenrahmen *m*, Nebenrahmen *m*; **subgrade** **N** *(of road etc)* Unterbau *m*; **subhead** *(inf)*, **subheading** **N** Untertitel *m*; **subhuman** **ADJ** *treatment, person* unmenschlich; **they were treated as if they were** ~ sie wurden behandelt, als seien sie Untermenschen

subject [ˈsʌbdʒɪkt] ✪ 26.2 **N** **a** *(Pol)* Staatsbürger(in) *m(f)*; *(of king etc)* Untertan *m*, Untertanin *f*
b *(Gram)* Subjekt *nt*, Satzgegenstand *m*
c *(= topic, Mus)* Thema *nt*; **the** ~ **of the picture is …** das Thema *or* Sujet *(geh)* des Bildes ist …; **he paints urban ~s** er malt städtische Motive; **to change the** ~ das Thema wechseln; **on the** ~ **of …** zum Thema *(+gen)* …; **while we're on the** ~ da wir gerade beim Thema sind; **while we're on the** ~ **of mushrooms** wo wir gerade von Pilzen reden, apropos Pilze; **that's off the** ~ das gehört nicht zum Thema
d *(= discipline, Sch, Univ)* Fach *nt*; *(= specialist subject)* (Spezial)gebiet *nt*
e *(= reason)* Grund *m*, Anlass *m* *(for* zu)
f *(= object)* Gegenstand *m* *(of +gen)*; *(in experiment, = person)* Versuchsperson *f*, Versuchsobjekt *nt*; *(= animal)* Versuchstier *nt*, Versuchsobjekt *nt*; *(esp Med, for treatment)* Typ *m*; **he is the** ~ **of much criticism** er wird stark kritisiert, er ist Gegenstand häufiger Kritik; **he's a good** ~ **for treatment by hypnosis** er lässt sich gut hypnotisch behandeln; **the survey team asked 100 ~s** die Meinungsforscher befragten 100 Perso-

nen
g *(Philos: = ego)* Subjekt *nt*, Ich *nt*
h *(Phot)* Objekt *nt*
ADJ **a** *(= conquered)* unterworfen
b ~ **to** *(= under the control of)* unterworfen *(+dat)*; **provinces ~ to foreign rule** Provinzen *pl* unter Fremdherrschaft; **to be ~ to sth** *(to law, constant change, sb's will)* einer Sache *(dat)* unterworfen sein; *to illness* für etw anfällig sein; *to consent, approval* von etw abhängig sein; **northbound trains are ~ to delays** bei Zügen in Richtung Norden muss mit Verspätung gerechnet werden; **prices/opening times are ~ to change** *or* **alteration without notice** Preisänderungen/Änderungen der Öffnungszeiten sind vorbehalten; **all these plans are ~ to last minute changes** all diese Pläne können in letzter Minute geändert werden; **~ to flooding** überschwemmungsgefährdet; **to be ~ to taxation** besteuert werden; **~ to correction** vorbehaltlich Änderungen; **all offers are ~ to availability** alle Angebote nur so weit verfügbar; **~ to confirmation in writing** vorausgesetzt, es wird schriftlich bestätigt; **~ to certain conditions** unter bestimmten Bedingungen
VT [səb'dʒekt] **a** *(= subjugate)* unterwerfen; *terrorists, guerrillas* zerschlagen
b **to ~ sb to sth** *(to questioning, analysis, treatment)* jdn einer Sache *(dat)* unterziehen; *to test also* jdn einer Sache *(dat)* unterwerfen; *to torture, suffering, heat, ridicule, criticism* jdn einer Sache *(dat)* aussetzen; **to ~ sb to insults** jdn beschimpfen; **to ~ sb to criticism** jdn unter Kritik nehmen, jdn kritisieren
VR [səb'dʒekt] **to ~ oneself to sth** *(to insults, suffering)* etw hinnehmen; *(to criticism, ridicule)* sich einer Sache *(dat)* aussetzen; *(to examination, test, questioning)* sich einer Sache *(dat)* unterziehen

subject: **subject catalogue** N Schlagwortkatalog *m*; **subject heading** N Überschrift *f*; *(in index)* Rubrik *f*; **subject index** N Sachregister *nt*

subjection [səb'dʒekʃən] N **a** *(= state)* Abhängigkeit *f*; **to keep a people in ~** ein Volk unterdrücken **b** *(= act)* Unterwerfung *f*; *(of terrorists, guerrillas etc)* Zerschlagung *f* **c** **the ~ of sb to sth** → **subject VT**

subjective [səb'dʒektɪv] ADJ **a** subjektiv **b** *(Gram)* ~ **case** Nominativ *m*

subjectively [səb'dʒektɪvlɪ] ADV subjektiv

subjectivism [səb'dʒektɪvɪzəm] N Subjektivismus *m*

subjectivity [ˌsʌbdʒek'tɪvɪtɪ] N Subjektivität *f*

subject matter ['sʌbdʒɪktmætəʳ] N *(= theme)* Stoff *m*; *(= content)* Inhalt *m*

subjoin [ˌsʌb'dʒɔɪn] VT hinzufügen *(to dat)*, beilegen *(to gen)*, beifügen *(to dat)*

sub judice [ˌsʌb'dʒu:dɪsɪ] ADJ *(Jur)* **to be ~** verhandelt werden

subjugate ['sʌbdʒʊgeɪt] VT unterwerfen

subjugation [ˌsʌbdʒʊ'geɪʃən] N Unterwerfung *f*

subjunctive [səb'dʒʌŋktɪv] ADJ konjunktivisch; **the ~ verb/mood/form** der Konjunktiv **N** *(= mood, verb)* Konjunktiv *m*

sub: **sublease** **N** *(= contract, on farm etc)* Unterpachtvertrag *m* *(on* für); *(on house etc)* Untermietvertrag *m* *(on* für); **they have a ~ on that house** das Haus ist an sie untervermietet worden **VT** *land* unter- *or* weiterverpachten *(to* an *+acc)*; *house* unter- *or* weitervermieten *(to* an *+acc)*; **she has ~d the flat from the tenants** sie hat die Wohnung in Untermiete; **sublessee** [ˌsʌble'si:] N *(of house)* Untermieter(in) *m(f)*; *(of land)* Unterpächter(in) *m(f)*; **sublessor** [ˌsʌble'sɔ:] N *(of house)* Untervermieter(in) *m(f)*; *(of land)* Unterverpächter(in) *m(f)*; **sublet** *pret, ptp* **sublet** **VT** *house, room* unter- *or* weitervermieten *(to* an *+acc)* **VI** untervermieten; **subletting** N Untervermietung *f*; **sublieutenant** N *(esp Brit)* Leutnant *m* zur See

sublimate ['sʌblɪmeɪt] **N** *(Chem)* Sublimat *nt* **VT** *(Chem, Psych)* sublimieren

sublimation [ˌsʌblɪ'meɪʃən] N Sublimierung *f*

sublime [sə'blaɪm] ADJ **a** *poetry, beauty, scenery, thoughts, feelings* erhaben; *achievement, courage, genius also* überragend; **that's going from the ~ to the ridiculous** *(inf)* das nenne ich tief sinken *(inf)* **b** *(iro: = extreme) ignorance* vollendet; *impertinence, confidence* unglaublich; *indifference, contempt* herablassend **c** *(inf: = delightful)* reizend

sublimely [sə'blaɪmlɪ] ADV erhaben; *unaware, ignorant* ergreifend *(iro)*, vollkommen; *foolish, drunk, simple* unglaublich; **~ beautiful** von erhabener Schönheit; **~ romantic** von erhabener Romantik; **a ~ contented expression on his face** ein überglücklicher Gesichtsausdruck; **~ contemptuous/indifferent, he ...** mit souveräner Verachtung/Gleichgültigkeit ... er ...

subliminal [ˌsʌb'lɪmɪnl] ADJ *(Psych)* unterschwellig

subliminal advertising N Schleichwerbung *f*

subliminal message N unterschwellige *or* an das Unterbewusstsein gerichtete Botschaft

sublimity [sə'blɪmɪtɪ] N *(liter)* Erhabenheit *f*

submachine gun [ˌsʌbmə'ʃi:ngʌn] N Maschinenpistole *f*

submarginal [ˌsʌb'mɑ:dʒɪnl] ADJ *(Agr) land* nicht (mehr) rentabel

submarine ['sʌbməˌri:n] **N** **a** Unterseeboot *nt*, U-Boot *nt* **b** *(US inf: = sandwich)* Jumbosandwich *nt (inf)* **ADJ** *life, equipment, cable* unterseeisch, submarin; **~ base** U-Boot-Stützpunkt *m*

submariner [sʌb'mærɪnəʳ] N U-Boot-Fahrer(in) *m(f)*

submenu ['sʌbˌmenju:] N *(Comput)* Untermenü *nt*

submerge [səb'mɜ:dʒ] **VT** untertauchen; *(= flood)* überschwemmen; **to ~ sth in water** etw in Wasser (ein)tauchen; **to ~ oneself in sth** *(fig)* ganz in etw *(acc)* versinken **VI** *(diver, submarine)* tauchen

submerged [səb'mɜ:dʒd] ADJ *rocks* unter Wasser; *wreck* gesunken; *city* versunken; *(Pol: = underprivileged)* unterdrückt; *(Psych)* verdrängt; **to be half ~** halb versunken sein; **the house was completely ~** das Haus stand völlig unter Wasser; **she is ~ in work** sie erstickt in Arbeit

submersible [səb'mɜ:səbl] **ADJ** versenkbar; *submarine* tauchfähig **N** Tauchboot *nt*

submersion [səb'mɜ:ʃən] N Untertauchen *nt*; *(of submarine)* Tauchen *nt*; *(by flood)* Überschwemmung *f*; **~ in liquid** Eintauchen *nt* in Flüssigkeit; **prolonged ~ in water** langes Liegen im Wasser

submission [səb'mɪʃən] N **a** *(= yielding)* Unterwerfung *f (to* unter *+acc)*; *(= submissiveness)* Gehorsam *m*; *(Sport)* Aufgabe *f*; **to force sb into ~** jdn zwingen, sich zu ergeben; **to starve sb into ~** jdn aushungern **b** *(= presentation)* Eingabe *f*; *(= documents submitted)* Vorlage *f*; **to make a ~ to sb** jdm eine Vorlage machen *or* unterbreiten; **his ~ to the appeals tribunal** seine Berufung **c** *(= contention)* Einwurf *m* *(to* gegenüber); **it is our ~ that ...** wir behaupten, dass ...

submissive [səb'mɪsɪv] ADJ demütig, gehorsam, unterwürfig *(pej)* *(to* gegenüber); **~ to authority** autoritätsgläubig

submissively [səb'mɪsɪvlɪ] ADV *bow, kneel* demütig; *behave* unterwürfig

submissiveness [səb'mɪsɪvnɪs] N Demut *f*, Gehorsam *m*, Unterwürfigkeit *f (pej)* *(to* gegenüber)

submit [səb'mɪt] **VT** **a** *(= put forward)* vorlegen *(to +dat)*; *application, claim etc* einreichen *(to* bei); **to be ~ted to ...** zur Vorlage bei ...; **to ~ that ...** *(esp Jur)* behaupten, dass ...; **to ~ an entry to a competition** *(= participate)* an einem Wettbewerb teilnehmen
b *(= refer)* verweisen *(to* an *+acc)*; **to ~ sth to scrutiny/tests** *etc* etw einer Prüfung/Tests *(dat)* *etc* unterziehen; **to ~ sth to heat/cold** *etc* etw der Hitze/Kälte *(dat)* *etc* aussetzen
VI *(= yield)* sich beugen, nachgeben; *(Mil)* sich ergeben *(to +dat)*; *(Sport)* aufgeben; **to ~ to sth** *(to sb's orders, judgement, God's will)* sich einer Sache *(dat)* beugen *or* unterwerfen; *to inspection* sich einer Sache *(dat)* unterziehen; *to indignity* sich *(dat)* etw gefallen lassen, etw erdulden; *to demands, pressure* einer Sache *(dat)* nachgeben; **to ~ to blackmail/questioning** sich erpressen/verhören lassen
VR **to ~ oneself to sth** *(to examination, operation, questioning etc)* sich einer Sache *(dat)* unterziehen

subnet ['sʌbˌnet] N *(Comput)* Teilnetz *nt*

subnormal [ˌsʌb'nɔ:məl] ADJ *intelligence, temperature* unterdurchschnittlich; *person* minderbegabt; *(inf)* schwachsinnig; **educationally ~** lernbehindert; **mentally ~** minderbemittelt

subordinate [sə'bɔ:dnɪt] **ADJ** *officer* rangniedriger; *rank, position, importance, role* untergeordnet; **to be ~ to sb/sth** jdm/einer Sache untergeordnet sein; **to be ~ in importance to** weniger wichtig sein als; **~ in rank** rangniedriger *(to* als) **N** Untergebene(r) *mf* [sə'bɔ:dɪneɪt] **VT** unterordnen *(to dat)*

subordinate clause N *(Gram)* Nebensatz *m*

subordinating conjunction [səˌbɔ:dɪneɪtɪŋkən'dʒʌŋkʃən] N *(Gram)* unterordnende Konjunktion

subordination [səˌbɔ:dɪ'neɪʃən] N *(= subjection)* Unterordnung *f (to* unter *+acc)*

suborn [sʌ'bɔ:n] VT *(Jur) witness* beeinflussen

subplot ['sʌbˌplɒt] N Nebenhandlung *f*

subpoena [sə'pi:nə] *(Jur)* **N** Vorladung *f*; **to serve a ~ on sb** jdn vorladen **VT** *witness* vorladen; *documents* unter Strafandrohung verlangen *or* fordern; **he was ~ed to give evidence** er wurde als Zeuge vorgeladen

sub: **subpolar** ADJ subpolar; **sub-postmaster/-postmistress** N *(Brit)* Poststellenleiter(in) *m(f)*; **sub-post office** N *(Brit)* Poststelle *f*; **sub rosa** [ˌsʌb'rəʊzə] *(form)* **ADJ** geheim, sub rosa *(geh)* **ADV** im Geheimen, sub rosa *(geh)*; **subroutine** N *(Comput)* Unterroutine *f*, Unterprogramm *nt*

subscribe [səb'skraɪb] ✪ 12.1 **VT** *money* zeichnen *(form)*; *(to appeal)* spenden *(to* für); **to ~ one's signature** *or* **name to a document** *(form)* ein Dokument (unter)zeichnen
VI **a** *(= contribute, promise to contribute)* spenden, geben *(to +dat)*; **to ~ to an appeal** sich an einer Spendenaktion beteiligen; **to ~ for a book** ein Buch vorbestellen; **to ~ for shares in a company** Aktien einer Gesellschaft zeichnen
b *(to e-mail list)* sich anmelden; **to ~ to a magazine** *etc* eine Zeitschrift *etc* abonnieren
c *(= support)* **to ~ to sth** *(to proposal)* etw gutheißen, etw billigen; *to opinion, theory* sich einer Sache *(dat)* anschließen

subscriber [səb'skraɪbəʳ] N *(to paper)* Abonnent(in) *m(f)*; *(to fund)* Spender(in) *m(f)*, Zeichner(in) *m(f)* *(form)*; *(Telec)* Teilnehmer(in) *m(f)*; *(to opinion)* Befürworter(in) *m(f)*; *(of shares)* Zeichner(in) *m(f)*; **~ trunk dialling** *(Brit)* der Selbstwählferndienst

subscript ['sʌbskrɪpt] *(Typ)* **ADJ** *character, number* tiefgestellt **N** tiefgestelltes Zeichen

subscription [səb'skrɪpʃən] N Subskription *f* *(form)*, Zeichnung *f* *(form)*; *(= money subscribed)* Beitrag *m*; *(to newspaper, concert etc)* Abonnement *nt* *(to +gen)*; **to take out a ~ to sth** etw abonnieren; **to pay one's ~ (to a club)** seinen (Vereins)beitrag bezahlen; **by public ~** mit Hilfe von *or* durch Spenden; **by ~** durch Subskription(en) *f(pl)*

subscription rate N Abonnements- *or* Bezugspreis *m*

subsection ['sʌbˌsekʃən] N Unterabteilung *f*; *(Jur)* Paragraf *m*

subsequent ['sʌbsɪkwənt] ADJ (nach)folgend, anschließend; *(in time)* später, anschließend; **~ to** *(form)* im Anschluss an *(+acc)*

subsequently ['sʌbsɪkwəntlɪ] ADV *(= afterwards)* später, anschließend; *alter, add etc also* nachträglich; *(= from that time)* von da an

subserve [səb'sɜːv] VT *(form)* dienen *(+dat)*, dienlich *or* förderlich sein *(+dat) (form)*

subservience [səb'sɜːvɪəns] N *(pej)* Unterwürfigkeit *f (to* gegenüber); *(form)* Unterworfenheit *f (to* unter *+acc)*

subservient [səb'sɜːvɪənt] ADJ *(pej)* unterwürfig *(to* gegenüber); *(form)* unterworfen *(to +dat)*

subserviently [səb'sɜːvɪəntlɪ] ADV unterwürfig

subset ['sʌbset] N *(Math)* Teilmenge *f*

subside [səb'saɪd] VI **a** *(flood, river)* sinken; *(land, building, road)* sich senken, absacken *(inf)*; **the lorry ~d into the mud** der Lastwagen sank im Schlamm ein; **to ~ into a chair** auf einen Stuhl sinken **b** *(storm, wind)* abflauen, nachlassen, sich legen; *(anger, excitement, laughter, noise)* nachlassen, abklingen; *(fever)* sinken

subsidence [səb'saɪdəns] N Senkung *f*, Absacken *nt (inf)*; **there's a lot of ~ in the area** in der Gegend senkt sich das Erdreich; **"danger: ~"** „Achtung: Bodensenkung"; **we can't get a mortgage because of the ~** wir bekommen keine Hypothek, weil sich das Gelände senkt

subsidiarity [sʌb,sɪdɪ'ærɪtɪ] N *(Pol)* Subsidiarität *f*; *(principle)* Subsidiaritätsprinzip *nt*

subsidiary [səb'sɪdɪərɪ] ADJ untergeordnet; *question* zusätzlich; *importance* nebensächlich; **~ role** Nebenrolle *f*; **~ subject** Nebenfach *nt*; **~ company** Tochtergesellschaft *f*; **to be ~ to sth** einer Sache *(dat)* untergeordnet sein N Tochtergesellschaft *f*

subsidization [,sʌbsɪdaɪ'zeɪʃən] N Subventionierung *f*

subsidize ['sʌbsɪdaɪz] VT *company etc* subventionieren; *housing* finanziell unterstützen; *(inf) sb's habits* subventionieren; *person* unterstützen

subsidized ['sʌbsɪdaɪzd] ADJ *prices, food, exports* subventioniert; *housing* finanziell unterstützt

subsidy ['sʌbsɪdɪ] N Subvention *f*, Zuschuss *m*; **there is a ~ on butter** Butter wird subventioniert *or* bezuschusst; **rent ~** Wohnungsbeihilfe *f*; **housing subsidies** *(for building, renovation etc)* Wohnungsbaubeihilfen *pl*

subsist [səb'sɪst] VI *(form)* sich ernähren, leben *(on* von)

subsistence [səb'sɪstəns] N *(= living)* Leben *nt (on* von); *(= means of subsistence)* Existenz *f*, (Lebens)unterhalt *m*; **~ on £11 is impossible** es ist unmöglich, von £ 11 zu leben; **rice is their chief means of ~** sie ernähren sich hauptsächlich von Reis

subsistence: **subsistence allowance** N Unterhaltszuschuss *m*; **subsistence farmer** N Bauer, der nur für den Eigenbedarf anbaut; **subsistence farming** N Ackerbau *m* für den Eigenbedarf, Subsistenzwirtschaft *f*; **subsistence level** N Existenzminimum *nt*; **at ~** auf dem Existenzminimum; **subsistence wage** N Minimallohn *m*

sub: **subsoil** N Untergrund *m*; **subsonic** ADJ Unterschall-; **~ speed** Unterschallgeschwindigkeit *f*; **subspecies** N Unterart *f*, Subspezies *f*

substance ['sʌbstəns] N **a** Substanz *f*, Materie *f*, Stoff *m*; **what is this ~?** was ist das für eine Substanz?; **he rubbed a yellow ~ on the wound** er strich eine gelbe Masse auf die Wunde **b** *no pl (= subject matter)* Substanz *f*, Gehalt *m*; *(= essence)* Kern *m*; **in ~** im Wesentlichen; **I agree with the ~ of his proposals** im Wesentlichen stimme ich seinen Vorschlägen zu **c** *no pl (= weight, importance)* Gewicht *nt*; **the book lacks ~** das Buch hat keine Substanz; **there is some ~ in his claim** seine Behauptung ist nicht unfundiert **d** *no pl* **a man of ~** ein vermögender Mann

substance abuse N Drogen- und Alkoholmissbrauch *m*

substandard [,sʌb'stændəd] ADJ *work, goods* minderwertig; *quality also, housing* unzulänglich; *worker* unterdurchschnittlich; *(Ling)* nicht korrekt

substantial [səb'stænʃəl] ADJ **a** *person, cloth* kräftig; *furniture, building, firm* solide; *rope* stark; *book* umfangreich; *meal, dish* reichhaltig **b** *(= considerable) income, loss, gain, amount* beträchtlich, erheblich; *part, majority, contribution, improvement* wesentlich, bedeutend; *(= rich) landowner, businessman* vermögend, kapitalkräftig **c** *(= weighty, important)* bedeutend; *proof, argument* überzeugend, stichhaltig; *difference* wesentlich, bedeutend; **to be in ~ agreement** im Wesentlichen übereinstimmen **d** *(= real, material)* körperlich, wesenhaft

substantially [səb'stænʃəlɪ] ADV **a** *(= solidly)* solide; *(= considerably)* erheblich, beträchtlich, wesentlich; **~ built** *(house)* solide gebaut; *person* kräftig gebaut **b** *(= essentially, basically)* im Wesentlichen; **to remain ~ unchanged** größtenteils *or* im Wesentlichen unverändert bleiben

substantiate [səb'stænʃɪeɪt] VT erhärten, untermauern

substantiation [səb,stænʃɪ'eɪʃən] N Erhärtung *f*, Untermauerung *f*; **as yet this theory lacks ~** diese Theorie ist bisher noch nicht erhärtet; **in ~ of** zur Erhärtung *(+gen)*

substantival [,sʌbstən'taɪvəl] ADJ *(Gram)* substantivisch

substantive ['sʌbstəntɪv] ADJ **a** *evidence, argument* überzeugend, stichhaltig **b** *(= considerable) contribution, improvement* beträchtlich, wesentlich, bedeutend **c** **~ motion** endgültige Formulierung des Antrags **d** *(Gram)* = **substantival** N *(Gram)* Substantiv *nt*, Hauptwort *nt*

substantivize ['sʌbstəntɪ,vaɪz] VT substantivieren

substation ['sʌb,steɪʃən] N *(Elec)* Umspann(ungs)werk *nt*

substitute ['sʌbstɪtjuːt] N Ersatz *m no pl*; *(= representative also)* Vertretung *f*; *(Sport)* Ersatzspieler(in) *m(f)*, Auswechselspieler(in) *m(f)*; **to find a ~ for sb** für jdn Ersatz finden; **to use sth as a ~** etw als Ersatz benutzen; **substitutes' bench** *(Sport)* Auswechsel- *or* Ersatzbank *f*; **coffee ~** Kaffee-Ersatz *m*; **various coffee ~s** verschiedene Sorten Kaffee-Ersatz; **there's no ~ for ...** es gibt keinen Ersatz für ..., ... kann man durch nichts ersetzen

ADJ *attr* Ersatz-; **~ drug** Ersatzdroge *f*

VT **to ~ A for B** B durch A ersetzen; *(Sport also)* B gegen A austauschen *or* auswechseln; **~ 3 for X** setze für X 3 ein, substituiere 3 für X

VI **to ~ for sb** jdn vertreten, für jdn einspringen; **to ~ for sth** etw ersetzen

substitute teacher N *(US)* Aushilfslehrer(in) *m(f)*

substitution [,sʌbstɪ'tjuːʃən] N Ersetzen *nt (of X for Y* von Y durch X); *(Sport)* Austausch *m (of X for Y* von Y gegen X); *(Math)* Substitution *f*, Einsetzen *nt (of X for Y* von X für Y); **the ~ of margarine for butter** der Gebrauch von Margarine statt Butter; **to make a ~** *(Sport)* (einen Spieler) auswechseln

substrate ['sʌbstreɪt] N *(Chem)* Substrat *nt*

substratum ['sʌb,strɑːtəm] N *pl* **substrata** ['sʌb,strɑːtə] Substrat *nt*; *(Geol)* Untergrund *m*; *(Sociol)* Substratum *nt*

substructure ['sʌb,strʌktʃə'] N Unterbau *m*; *(fig also)* Grundlage *f*; *(Build)* Fundament *nt*; *(of bridge)* Widerlager *nt*

subsume [səb'sjuːm] VT **to ~ sth under sth** etw unter etw *(dat)* zusammenfassen *or* subsumieren *(geh)*

subsystem ['sʌbsɪstəm] N Untersystem *nt*

subteen ['sʌb'tiːn] N *(esp US)* Kind *nt*

sub-teenage ['sʌb'tiːneɪdʒ] ADJ *attr (esp US) drinking etc* von Kindern; *fans* im Kindesalter

subtenancy [,sʌb'tenənsɪ] N **during his ~ of the flat/farm** während er Untermieter in der Wohnung/Unterpächter des Bauernhofes war

subtenant [,sʌb'tenənt] N *(of flat etc)* Untermieter(in) *m(f)*; *(of land)* Unterpächter(in) *m(f)*

subtend [səb'tend] VT gegenüberliegen *(+dat)*

subterfuge ['sʌbtəfjuːdʒ] N *(= trickery)* Täuschung *f*, List *f*; *(= trick)* Trick *m*, List *f*; **to resort to ~** zu einer List greifen; **to be incapable of ~** (zu) keiner Falschheit *or* List fähig sein

subterranean [,sʌbtə'reɪnɪən] ADJ unterirdisch; *(fig) force, power* verborgen

subterraneous ADJ, **subterraneously** ADV [,sʌbtə'reɪnɪəs, -lɪ] = **subterranean**

subtext ['sʌbtekst] N **the ~** das eigentlich Gemeinte

subtitle ['sʌbtaɪtl] N Untertitel *m (also Film)* VT *film* mit Untertiteln versehen; *book etc* einen Untertitel geben *(+dat)*; **the film is ~d in English** der Film hat englische Untertitel; **the book is ~d ...** das Buch hat den Untertitel ...

subtle ['sʌtl] ADJ **a** *(= delicate, gentle)* fein; *irony, distinction* fein, subtil *(geh)*; *perfume, flavour* zart, fein; *hint, allusion* zart, leise; *charm* leise, unaufdringlich **b** *(= ingenious, not obvious) remark, argument, point* scharfsinnig, spitzfindig; *problem* subtil; *pressure* sanft; *design, construction, proof* raffiniert, fein ausgedacht *or* ausgetüftelt *(inf)*; **he has a very ~ mind** er ist ein sehr subtiler Denker *(geh)*; **be ~ about it** gehen Sie mit Zartgefühl vor **c** *(= quick at seeing fine distinctions) observer, critic* aufmerksam, subtil *(geh)*

subtlety ['sʌtltɪ] N **a** *(= delicacy)* Feinheit *f*; *(of irony, distinction also)* Subtilität *f (geh)*; *(of perfume, flavour also, hint, allusion)* Zartheit *f*; *(of charm)* Unaufdringlichkeit *f*

b *(= sophistication, of remark, argument, point)* Scharfsinn(igkeit *f*) *m*, Spitzfindigkeit *f*; *(of problem)* Subtilität *f*; *(of design, construction, proof)* Raffiniertheit *f*; **his methods lack ~** seinen Methoden fehlt (die) Finesse *or* Subtilität *(geh)*; **the subtleties of the novel** die Feinheiten *pl* des Romans; **~ is wasted on him** feine Andeutungen nützen bei ihm nichts

c *(= discriminative powers, of observer, critic)* Aufmerksamkeit *f*, Subtilität *f (geh)*

subtly ['sʌtlɪ] ADV fein; *flavoured also* delikat; *argue, reply* scharfsinnig, subtil *(geh)*; *analyse, think* scharfsinnig; *(= slightly) change* geringfügig; *(= indirectly) imply* unterschwellig, indirekt; *achieve one's ends* auf raffinierte Weise; **~ different** auf subtile Weise verschieden *or* unterschiedlich; **he ~ suggested** er schlug geschickt vor; **it's just very ~ wrong** es ist schwer zu fassen, was falsch daran ist

subtotal ['sʌbtəʊtl] N Zwischen- *or* Teilsumme *f*

subtract [səb'trækt] VTI abziehen, subtrahieren *(from* von)

subtraction [səb'trækʃən] N Subtraktion *f*; *(= act also)* Abziehen *nt*

subtrahend ['sʌbtrə,hend] N *(Math, form)* Subtrahend *m*

subtropical [,sʌb'trɒpɪkəl] ADJ subtropisch

subtropics [,sʌb'trɒpɪks] PL Subtropen *pl*

subtype ['sʌbtaɪp] N Unterart *f*

suburb ['sʌbɜːb] N Vorort *m*; **in the ~s** am Stadtrand

suburban [sə'bɜːbən] ADJ *area, community* vorstädtisch; *(pej)* spießig, kleinbürgerlich; **the area is becoming increasingly ~** die Gegend nimmt immer mehr vorstädtischen Charakter an; **~ line** *(Rail)* Vorortbahn *f*; **~ street** Vorortstraße *f*; **in ~ London** in Londons Vorstädten; **~ sprawl** Vorstädte *pl*

suburbanite [sə'bɜːbənaɪt] N Vorstädter(in) *m(f)*, Vorstadtbewohner(in) *m(f)*

suburbia [sə'bɜːbɪə] N *(usu pej)* die Vororte *pl*; **to live in ~** am Stadtrand wohnen; **that's typical of ~!** typisch Spießbürger!

subvention [səb'venʃən] N Subvention *f*

subversion [səb'vɜːʃən] N *no pl* Subversion *f*; *(of rights, freedom etc)* Untergrabung *f*, Unterminierung *f*; **the US was accused of ~ in Chile** die USA wurden subversiver *or* umstürzlerischer Tätigkeiten in Chile beschuldigt; **~ is rife in the army** die Armee ist voll(er) subversiver Elemente

subversive [səb'vɜːsɪv] ADJ subversiv, umstürzlerisch; **~ elements** subversive Elemente *or* Kräfte *pl* N Umstürzler(in) *m(f)*, Subversive(r) *mf*

subvert [səbˈvɜːt] VT *government* zu stürzen versuchen; *faith, morals etc* untergraben, unterminieren; *constitution, state authority, socialism* unterwandern; *person* zum Umsturz anstacheln

subway [ˈsʌbweɪ] N Unterführung *f*; *(for cars also)* Tunnel *m*; *(esp US Rail)* U-Bahn *f*

subzero [ˌsʌbˈzɪərəʊ] ADJ *temperature* unter null, unter dem Nullpunkt

succeed [səkˈsiːd] VI **a** *(= be successful, person)* erfolgreich sein, Erfolg haben; *(plan etc)* gelingen, erfolgreich sein; **to ~ in business/in a plan** geschäftlich/mit einem Plan erfolgreich sein; **I ~ed in doing it** es gelang mir, es zu tun; **you'll only ~ in making things worse** damit erreichst du nur, dass alles noch schlimmer wird; **nothing ~s like success** *(prov)* nichts ist so erfolgreich wie der Erfolg; **if at first you don't ~(, try, try, try again)** *(Prov)* wirf die Flinte nicht gleich ins Korn *(prov)*
b *(= come next)* **to ~ to an office** in einem Amt nachfolgen; **he ~ed to his father's position** er wurde (der) Nachfolger seines Vaters, er trat die Nachfolge seines Vaters an *(geh)*; **to ~ to the throne** die Thronfolge antreten; **there ~ed a period of peace** *(form)* es folgte eine Zeit des Friedens
VT *(= come after, take the place of)* folgen *(+dat)*, folgen auf *(+acc)*; *(person also)* Nachfolger(in) *m(f)* werden *+gen*; **to ~ sb in a post/in office** jds Nachfolger werden, jds Stelle/Amt *(acc)* übernehmen; **who ~ed James I?** wer kam nach *or* folgte auf Jakob I.?

succeeding [səkˈsiːdɪŋ] ADJ folgend; **~ generations** spätere *or* nachfolgende Generationen *pl*

success [səkˈses] ✪ 23.5 N Erfolg *m*; **without ~** ohne Erfolg, erfolglos; **wishing you every ~ in your exams** mit besten Wünschen für eine erfolgreiche Prüfung; **to make a ~ of sth** mit *or* bei etw Erfolg haben, mit *or* bei etw erfolgreich sein; **they made a ~ of their marriage** ihre Ehe war ein Erfolg; **to be a ~ with sb** bei jdm ankommen; **the new car is not a ~** das neue Auto ist nicht gerade ein (durchschlagender) Erfolg; **the plan was a ~** der Plan war erfolgreich *or* ein voller Erfolg; **to meet with ~** Erfolg haben, erfolgreich sein; **~ story** Erfolgsstory *f*; *(= person)* Erfolg *m*

successful [səkˈsesfʊl] ADJ erfolgreich; **to reach a ~ conclusion** zu einem erfolgreichen Abschluss kommen; **after ~ completion** nach erfolgreicher Beendigung; **to be ~** erfolgreich sein, Erfolg haben *(in* mit, bei); **to be entirely ~** ein voller Erfolg sein; **I was ~ in doing it** es gelang mir, es zu tun; **to be ~ in one's efforts** mit seinen Bemühungen Erfolg haben; **to be ~ at doing sth** etw erfolgreich tun; **unfortunately your application has not been ~** Ihre Bewerbung war leider nicht erfolgreich; **to be ~ as a doctor** ein erfolgreicher Arzt sein

successfully [səkˈsesfəlɪ] ADV erfolgreich, mit Erfolg

succession [səkˈseʃən] N **a** Folge *f*, Serie *f*; *(with no intervening period)* (Aufeinander)folge *f*, Kette *f*; **a ~ of visitors** eine Kette *or* Serie von Besuchern; **life is a ~ of joys and sorrows** das Leben ist ein steter Wechsel von Kummer und Freude; **in ~** nacheinander, hintereinander; **in quick** *or* **rapid ~** in rascher Folge, schnell hintereinander
b *(to post)* Nachfolge *f*; *(to throne)* Thronfolge *f*; *(to title, estate)* Erbfolge *f*; **his ~ to the office** seine Amtsübernahme; **his ~ to the title** seine Übernahme des Titels; **her ~ to the throne** ihre Thronbesteigung; **in ~ to sb** als jds Nachfolger(in) *m(f)*, in jds Nachfolge *(dat)* *(geh)*; **fourth in (line of) ~ to the throne** an vierter Stelle in der Thronfolge → **apostolic**

succession state N Nachfolgestaat *m*

successive [səkˈsesɪv] ADJ aufeinanderfolgend *attr*; **four ~ days** vier Tage nacheinander *or* hintereinander, vier aufeinanderfolgende Tage; **on four ~ days** an vier aufeinanderfolgenden Tagen; **for the third ~ time** zum dritten Mal hintereinander; **he was sacked from three ~ jobs** er wurde nacheinander *or* hintereinander aus drei verschiedenen Stellen hinausgeworfen

successively [səkˈsesɪvlɪ] ADV nacheinander, hintereinander; **~ higher levels of unemployment** sukzessiv höhere Arbeitslosenraten

successor [səkˈsesəʳ] N Nachfolger(in) *m(f)* *(to +gen)*; *(to throne)* Thronfolger(in) *m(f)*

succinct [səkˈsɪŋkt] ADJ knapp, kurz und bündig *pred*

succinctly [səkˈsɪŋktlɪ] ADV kurz und bündig, in kurzen *or* knappen Worten *or* Zügen; *write* in knappem *or* gedrängtem Stil; **as he very ~ put it** wie er so treffend bemerkte

succinctness [səkˈsɪŋktnɪs] N Knappheit *f*, Kürze *f*; **with great ~** kurz und bündig, in kurzen Worten; *write* in knappem Stil

succour, *(US)* **succor** [ˈsʌkəʳ] *(liter)* N Beistand *m* VT beistehen *(+dat)*

succotash [ˈsʌkətæʃ] N *(US Cook)* Mais-Bohnen--Eintopf *m*

succubus [ˈsʌkjʊbəs] N *pl* **succubi** [ˈsʌkjʊbaɪ] Sukkubus *m*

succulence [ˈsʌkjʊləns] N Saftigkeit *f*

succulent [ˈsʌkjʊlənt] ADJ *peach, steak* saftig; *(Bot) plant, stem* fleischig, sukkulent *(spec)* N *(Bot)* Fettpflanze *f*, Sukkulente *f (spec)*

succumb [səˈkʌm] VI erliegen *(to +dat)*; *(to threats)* sich beugen *(to +dat)*

such [sʌtʃ] ADJ **a** *(= of that kind)* solche(r, s); **~ a person** so *or* solch ein Mensch, ein solcher Mensch; **~ a book** so ein Buch, ein solches Buch; **~ people/books** solche Leute/Bücher; **many/few/all ~ people/books** viele/wenige/all solche Leute/Bücher; **all ~ books are very expensive** solche Bücher sind sehr teuer; **do you have ~ a book?** haben Sie so ein Buch?; **~ a thing** so etwas, so was *(inf)*; **have you got ~ a thing as ...?** haben Sie so etwas wie ...?; **there's ~ a thing as divorce** es gibt so etwas wie eine Scheidung; **I said no ~ thing** das habe ich nie gesagt; **no ~ thing** nichts dergleichen; **I'll/you'll do no ~ thing** ich werde mich/du wirst dich hüten; **there's no ~ thing as a unicorn** so etwas wie ein Einhorn gibt es nicht; **... or some ~ idea** ... oder so etwas, ... oder so was in der Richtung *(inf)*, ... oder so ähnlich; **... or some ~ name/place** ... oder so (ähnlich); **he was ~ a one/just ~ another** er war einer von ihnen/auch (so) einer; **in ~ a case** in einem solchen Fall; **men/books ~ as these, men/books as these** Männer/Bücher wie diese, solche Männer/Bücher; **writers ~ as Agatha Christie, ~ writers as Agatha Christie** (solche) Schriftsteller wie Agatha Christie; **he's not ~ a fool as you think** er ist nicht so dumm, wie Sie denken; **I'm not ~ a fool as to believe that** *or* **that I'd believe that** ich bin nicht so dumm *or* kein solcher Dummkopf, dass ich das glaube; **~ people as attended** die(jenigen), die anwesend waren; **I'll give you ~ books/money as I have** was ich an Büchern/Geld habe, gebe ich Ihnen
b *(= so much, so great etc)* **he's ~ a liar** er ist so *or* solch ein Lügner, er ist ein derartiger *or* solcher Lügner; **he did it in ~ a way that ...** er machte es so, dass ...; **~ wealth!** welch (ein) Reichtum!; **~ beauty!** welche Schönheit!; **he's always in ~ a hurry** er hat es immer so eilig
c *pred* **his surprise was ~ that ..., ~ was his surprise that ...** seine Überraschung war so groß, dass ..., er war so überrascht, dass ...; **his manner was ~ that ...** er benahm sich so, dass ...; **her speech was ~ that ...** ihre Rede war so gehalten, dass ...
d → **such-and-such**
ADV so, solch *(geh)*; **nobody else makes ~ a good cup of tea as you** niemand kocht so guten Tee wie du; **it's ~ a long time ago** es ist so lange her
PRON **rabbits and hares and ~** Kaninchen, Hasen und dergleichen; **~ being the case ...** in diesem Fall ...; **~ was not my intention** dies war nicht meine Absicht; **~ is not the case** dies ist nicht der Fall; **~ is life!** so ist das Leben!; **those and ~ as those** *(hum inf)* die oberen zehntausend *(hum)*; **may all ~ perish!** mögen sie alle verderben!; **as ~** an sich; **~ as?** (wie) zum Beispiel?; **~ as it is** so, wie es nun mal ist; **the food, ~ as there was of it ...** das Essen, so weit vorhanden ..., was an Essen da war, ...; **I'll give you ~ as I have** ich gebe Ihnen, was ich habe

such-and-such [ˈsʌtʃənˈsʌtʃ] *(inf)* ADJ **~ a time/town** die und die Zeit/Stadt N Soundso *nt*

suchlike [ˈsʌtʃˌlaɪk] *(inf)* ADJ solche PRON dergleichen

suck [sʌk] N **to have a ~** *(at straw)* saugen, ziehen *(at* an *+dat)*; *(at lemonade etc)* nuckeln *(inf)*, ziehen *(at* an *+dat)*; *(at lollipop)* lutschen *(at* an *+dat)*; **to give ~ (to a baby)** *(old)* (ein Baby) stillen
VT saugen; *breast, straw* saugen an *(+dat)*; *sweet, pastille* lutschen; *lollipop* lutschen an *(+dat)*; *thumb* lutschen *or* nuckeln *(inf)* an *(+dat)*; **to ~ one's teeth** an den Zähnen saugen; **to ~ the juice out of sth** den Saft aus etw heraussaugen; **to ~ sb's blood** *(lit)* jdm das Blut aussaugen; *(fig)* jdn bis aufs Blut aussaugen; **to ~ sb dry** *(fig)* jdn bis aufs Blut aussaugen; **go and teach your grandmother to ~ eggs** *(prov)* da will das Ei wieder klüger sein als die Henne *(prov)*; **~ it and see** *(fig)* Probieren geht über Studieren *(Prov)*
VI **a** *(at* an *+dat)* saugen; *(at dummy)* nuckeln *(inf)*; *(at lollipop)* lutschen; *(at thumb)* lutschen, nuckeln *(inf)*; *(at pipe, through straw)* ziehen; **he always makes a ~ing noise with his soup** er schlürft seine Suppe immer
b *(US inf: = be very bad)* **this city ~s** diese Stadt ist echt Scheiße *(inf)*

▸ **suck down** VT *sep* hinunterziehen

▸ **suck in** VT *sep liquid, dust* aufsaugen; *air (ventilator)* ansaugen; *(person)* in tiefen Zügen einatmen; *cheeks, stomach* einziehen; *(fig) knowledge, facts* (in sich *acc*) aufsaugen; *imports* anlocken

▸ **suck off** VT *sep (vulg)* **to suck sb off** jdm einen (ab)lutschen *(vulg)*

▸ **suck under** VT *sep* hinunterziehen; *(completely)* verschlingen

▸ **suck up** VT *sep liquid, dust* aufsaugen; **the child sucked up his milk** das Kind trank seine Milch (mit einem Strohhalm) aus VI *(inf)* **to suck up to sb** vor jdm kriechen

sucker [ˈsʌkəʳ] N **a** *(= rubber sucker, Zool)* Saugnapf *m*; *(Bot)* unterirdischer Ausläufer; *(on creeper)* Häkchen *nt* **b** *(US inf: = lollipop)* Lutscher *m*; **all-day ~** Dauerlutscher *m* **c** *(inf: = fool)* Trottel *m (inf)*; **to be a ~ for sth** (immer) auf etw *(acc)* hereinfallen; *(= be partial to)* eine Schwäche für etw haben; **to be had for a ~** zum Narren gehalten werden, für dumm verkauft werden; **he's looking for some ~ who'll lend him £200** er sucht einen Dummen, der ihm £ 200 leiht

sucker punch N *(Boxing, fig inf)* Überraschungsschlag *m*

sucking: **sucking calf** [ˈsʌkɪŋˌkɑːf] N Milchkalb *nt*; **sucking pig** [ˈsʌkɪŋˌpɪg] N Spanferkel *nt*

suckle [ˈsʌkl] VT *child* stillen; *animal* säugen VI saugen, trinken

suckling [ˈsʌklɪŋ] N *(old)* Säugling *m*; *(= animal)* Jungtier *nt*; **out of the mouths of babes and ~s** *(Bibl)* aus dem Mund von Kindern und Säuglingen; *(fig)* Kindermund tut Wahrheit kund *(Prov)*

suckling pig N Spanferkel *nt*

sucky [ˈsʌkɪ] ADJ *(US sl)* beschissen *(inf)*

sucrose [ˈsuːkrəʊz] N Sa(c)charose *f*, pflanzlicher Zucker

suction [ˈsʌkʃən] N Saugwirkung *f*; *(caused by air or water currents)* Sog *m*

suction pad N Saugnapf *m*

suction pump N Saugpumpe *f*

Sudan [sʊˈdɑːn] N **(the) ~** der Sudan

Sudanese [ˌsuːdəˈniːz] ADJ sudanesisch, sudanisch; **he is ~** er ist Sudanese N Sudanese *m*, Sudanesin *f*

sudden [ˈsʌdn] ADJ plötzlich; *movement also* jäh, abrupt; *drop, silence also* jäh; *(= unexpected) bend, change of direction* unerwartet; **there was a ~ bend** da war plötzlich eine Kurve, da war eine unerwartete Kurve; **this is all so ~** das kommt alles so plötzlich N **all of a ~** (ganz) plötzlich, urplötzlich *(inf)*

sudden: **sudden death** N *(Ftbl: at end of drawn game)* Sudden Death *m*, *Spielverlängerung bis zum entscheidenden Tor*; **sudden-death (overtime)** *(US Sport)* Sudden Death *m*, *Spielverlängerung bis zum entscheidenden Punktgewinn*; **sudden-death (play-off)** *(Sport)* Ausscheidungsrunde *f*; **sudden infant death syndrome** N *(Med)* plötzlicher Kindstod

suddenly [ˈsʌdnlɪ] ADV plötzlich, auf einmal; *move also* jäh, abrupt; **he had died ~ of a heart attack** er war ganz plötzlich an einem Herzanfall gestorben

suddenness [ˈsʌdnnɪs] N Plötzlichkeit *f*; *(of movement also)* Jähheit *f*, Abruptheit *f*

Sudetenland [suːˈdeɪtənˌlænd] N Sudetenland *nt*

sudorific [ˌsjuːdəˈrɪfɪk] *(Med, Pharm)* ADJ schweißtreibend N schweißtreibendes Mittel

suds [sʌdz] PL Seifenwasser *nt or* -lauge *f*; *(= lather)* (Seifen)schaum *m*; *(US inf: = beer)* Bölkstoff *m (sl)*

sudser [ˈsʌdzəʳ] N *(esp US inf)* **a** *(= soap opera)* Seifenoper *f* **b** *(Film: = tear-jerker)* Schmachtfetzen *m (inf)*

sudsy [ˈsʌdzɪ] ADJ Seifen-; **~ water** Seifenwasser *nt*

sue [suː] VT **a** *(Jur)* verklagen, (gerichtlich) belangen; **to ~ sb for sth** jdn auf etw *(acc) or* wegen etw verklagen; **to ~ sb for divorce** gegen jdn die Scheidung einreichen; **to ~ sb for damages** jdn auf Schadenersatz verklagen; **I'll ~ you for every penny you've got** ich werde (vor Gericht) den letzten Cent aus dir herausholen **b** *(liter, = ask)* bitten, anflehen *(for* um) VI **a** *(Jur)* klagen, einen Prozess anstrengen, Klage erheben; **to ~ for divorce** die Scheidung einreichen **b** *(liter)* **to ~ for peace** um Frieden bitten

suede [sweɪd] N Wildleder *nt*; *(soft, fine also)* Velours(leder) *nt* ADJ Wildleder-, aus Wildleder; *(of finer quality also)* Velours(leder)-, aus Velours(leder); **~ boots** Wildleder-/Velours(leder)stiefel *pl*

suet [ˈsʊɪt] N Nierenfett *nt*, Nierentalg *m*; **~ pudding** *(sweet) im Wasserbad gekochte Süßspeise, zu der Nierenfett verwendet wird (savoury) mit Nierenfett zubereitete Pastete*

Suetonius [swiːˈtəʊnɪəs] N Sueton(ius) *m*

suety [ˈsuːɪtɪ] ADJ talgig

Suez [ˈsuːɪz] N Sues *nt*, Suez *nt*

Suez Canal N Sueskanal *m*, Suezkanal *m*

suffer [ˈsʌfəʳ] VT **a** *(= undergo, be subjected to) pain, injuries, heart attack, loss, setback, damage, hardship* erleiden; *hunger* leiden; *headache, stress, effects etc* leiden unter *or* an *(+dat)*; *shock* haben; **to ~ defeat/death** eine Niederlage/den Tod *(geh)* erleiden; **the pound ~ed further losses** das Pfund musste weitere Einbußen hinnehmen; **she ~ed quite a blow** sie hat einen Schicksalsschlag erlitten; **her popularity ~ed a decline** ihre Beliebtheit hat gelitten **b** *(= tolerate)* dulden, ertragen; **he doesn't ~ fools gladly** Dummheit ist ihm ein Gräuel **c** *(liter: = allow)* zulassen, dulden; **to ~ sth to be done** zulassen *or* dulden, dass etw geschieht; **~ the little children to come unto me** *(Bibl)* lasset die Kindlein zu mir kommen *(Bibl)* VI *(physically, mentally, fig)* leiden *(from* unter *+dat, from illness* an *+dat)*; *(as punishment, in hell etc)* büßen; **he was ~ing from shock** er hatte einen Schock (erlitten); **your health/work will ~** deine Gesundheit/Arbeit wird darunter leiden; **the runners are clearly ~ing in this heat** die Hitze macht den Läufern sichtlich zu schaffen; **the regiment ~ed badly** das Regiment erlitt schwere Verluste; **the town ~ed badly in the raids** die Stadt wurde bei den Luftangriffen schwer in Mitleidenschaft gezogen; **how I ~ed!** was ich alles durchgemacht habe!; **to ~ for one's sins** für seine Sünden büßen; **you'll ~ for this!** das wirst du büßen!; **we will see that you don't ~ from the changes** wir werden zusehen, dass Ihnen aus den Umstellungen keine Nachteile entstehen

sufferable [ˈsʌfərəbl] ADJ erträglich

sufferance [ˈsʌfərəns] N Duldung *f*; **on ~** (nur *or* stillschweigend) geduldet; **he's allowed to sleep here on ~ only** es wird nur geduldet, dass er hier schläft

sufferer [ˈsʌfərəʳ] N *(Med)* Leidende(r) *mf (from* an *+dat)*; **diabetes ~s, ~s from diabetes** Diabeteskranke *pl*, an Diabetes Leidende *pl*; **he's been a ~ from arthritis for several years** er leidet seit mehreren Jahren an Arthritis; **the ~s from the earthquake** die Erdbebenopfer *pl*; **my fellow ~s at the concert** meine Leidensgenossen bei dem Konzert

suffering [ˈsʌfərɪŋ] N Leiden *nt*; *(= hardship, deprivation)* Leid *nt no pl*

suffice [səˈfaɪs] *(form)* VI genügen, (aus)reichen VT genügen *(+dat) (geh)*; *sb also* zufriedenstellen; **~ it to say ...** es reicht wohl, wenn ich sage, ...

sufficiency [səˈfɪʃənsɪ] N *(= adequacy)* Hinlänglichkeit *f*; **to have a ~** genügend haben

sufficient [səˈfɪʃənt] ADJ genügend, ausreichend, genug *inv*; *maturity, temperature* genügend *attr*, ausreichend; *reason, condition, explanation, translation* hinreichend; *funds* ausreichend, hinreichend; *evidence* ausreichend; **is that ~ reason for his dismissal?** ist das Grund genug *or* ein ausreichender Grund, ihn zu entlassen?; **to be ~** genügen, ausreichen, genug sein; **thank you, that's ~** danke, das genügt *or* reicht; **I think you have drunk quite ~** ich glaube, Sie haben genug getrunken; **we haven't got ~ to live on** wir haben nicht genug zum Leben; **~ unto the day (is the evil thereof)** *(Prov)* der morgige Tag wird für sich selber sorgen

sufficiently [səˈfɪʃəntlɪ] ADV genug; **~ good/warm** *etc* gut/warm *etc* genug *pred*, genügend *or* ausreichend gut/warm *etc*; **a ~ large number** eine ausreichend große Anzahl

suffix [ˈsʌfɪks] N *(Ling)* Suffix *nt*, Nachsilbe *f*; *(in code etc)* Zusatz *m* VT anfügen, anhängen *(to* an *+acc)*

suffocate [ˈsʌfəkeɪt] VT *(lit, fig)* ersticken; **his obsessive jealousy/he is suffocating me** seine krankhafte Eifersucht/er erdrückt mich; **he felt ~d in that environment** er hatte das Gefühl, in dieser Umgebung zu ersticken; **he was ~d by the smoke** er erstickte am Rauch VI *(lit, fig)* ersticken

suffocating [ˈsʌfəkeɪtɪŋ] ADJ *(lit)* erstickend *attr*; *heat* drückend *attr*, brütend *attr*; *room* stickig; *(fig) relationship, atmosphere* erdrückend *attr*; **it's ~ in here** es ist stickig hier drinnen, hier erstickt man fast; **intellectually ~** geisttötend

suffocation [ˌsʌfəˈkeɪʃən] N *(lit, fig)* Ersticken *nt*

suffragan [ˈsʌfrəgən] ADJ Suffragan-; **~ bishop** Suffraganbischof *m* N Suffragan(bischof) *m*

suffrage [ˈsʌfrɪdʒ] N Wahl- *or* Stimmrecht *nt*; *(form: = vote)* Stimme *f*; **universal ~** das allgemeine Wahlrecht; **female ~** das Frauenstimmrecht

suffragette [ˌsʌfrəˈdʒet] N Suffragette *f*

suffuse [səˈfjuːz] VT erfüllen; *(light)* durchfluten; **~d with light** in Licht getaucht, lichtdurchflutet *(geh)*; **eyes ~d with tears** Augen voller Tränen, tränenerfüllte Augen; **a blush ~d her face** eine Röte überzog ihr Gesicht

sugar [ˈʃʊgəʳ] N **a** Zucker *m* **b** *(inf: = term of affection)* (meine) Süße, (mein) Süßer, Schätzchen *nt (all inf)* VT zuckern, süßen; *(fig) criticism etc* versüßen, mildern; **to ~ the pill** die bittere Pille versüßen

sugar *in cpds* Zucker-; **sugar basin** N Zuckerdose *f*; **sugar beet** N Zuckerrübe *f*; **sugar bowl** N Zuckerdose *f*; **sugar candy** N Kandis(zucker) *m*; *(US: = sweet)* Bonbon *nt or m*; **sugar cane** N Zuckerrohr *nt*; **sugar-coated** ADJ mit Zucker überzogen; **sugar-coating** N **a** *(Cook)* Zuckerguss *m* **b** *(fig)* Beschönigen *nt*, Beschönigung *f*; **sugar cube** N Zuckerwürfel *m*; **sugar daddy** N *(inf)* **she's looking for a ~** sie sucht einen alten Knacker, der sie aushält *(inf)*; **sugar diabetes** N Zuckerkrankheit *f*, Diabetes *m (spec)*, Zucker *m (inf)*

sugared [ˈʃʊgəd] ADJ gezuckert; *words* (honig)süß; **~ almonds** Zuckermandeln *pl*

sugar: **sugar-free** ADJ ohne Zucker; **sugar loaf** N Zuckerhut *m*; **Sugar Loaf Mountain** der Zuckerhut; **sugar maple** N Zuckerahorn *m*; **sugarplum** N Bonbon *nt or m*, Süßigkeit *f*; **~ fairy** Zuckerfee *f*; **sugar shaker** N Zuckerstreuer *m*; **sugar tongs** PL Zuckerzange *f*

sugary [ˈʃʊgərɪ] ADJ *taste* süß; *(= full of sugar)* zuckerig; *(fig pej) style, music, sentiment etc* süßlich; *film* zuckersüß

suggest [səˈdʒest] ✪ 1.1, 1.2 VT **a** *(= propose) candidate, place, idea etc* vorschlagen; **I ~ that we go, I ~ going** ich schlage vor, zu gehen *or* (dass) wir gehen; **what do you ~ we do?** was schlagen Sie vor?; **are you ~ing I should tell a deliberate lie?** soll das heißen, dass ich bewusst lügen soll?; **I am ~ing nothing of the kind** das habe ich nicht gesagt **b** *(= put forward for consideration) explanation, theory* nahelegen, vorbringen; **I ~ (to you) that ...** *(esp Jur)* ich möchte (Ihnen) nahelegen, dass ... **c** *(= insinuate, hint at)* andeuten; *(unpleasantly)* unterstellen; **what are you trying to ~?** worauf wollen Sie hinaus?, was wollen Sie damit sagen?; **I'm not trying to ~ that he's lying** ich will damit nicht unterstellen *or* sagen, dass er lügt **d** *(= indicate, facts, data, sb's action)* andeuten, hindeuten auf *(+acc)*; *(= evoke, music, poem)* denken lassen an *(+acc)*; *(symbolism, colours)* andeuten; **it certainly ~s complicity** das deutet zweifellos auf Mittäterschaft hin; **the symptoms would ~ an operation** die Symptome lassen eine Operation angeraten erscheinen **e** *(Psych)* **to ~ sth to sb** jdm etw suggerieren VR *(idea, thought, plan)* sich aufdrängen, sich anbieten

suggestibility [səˌdʒestɪˈbɪlɪtɪ] N Beeinflussbarkeit *f*

suggestible [səˈdʒestɪbl] ADJ *person* beeinflussbar

suggestion [səˈdʒestʃən] ✪ 1.1, 1.2 N **a** *(= proposal, recommendation)* Vorschlag *m*, Anregung *f*; **my ~ is that ...** mein Vorschlag lautet ..., ich schlage vor, dass ...; **following your ~** auf Ihren Vorschlag *or* Ihre Anregung hin; **Rome was your ~** Rom war deine Idee; **John was his ~ as candidate** er schlug John als Kandidaten vor; **I'm open to ~s** Vorschläge sind *or* jeder Vorschlag ist willkommen **b** *(= theory, explanation)* Vermutung *f*; **he made the ~ that ...** er äußerte die Vermutung, dass ...; **that theory was Professor Higgins' ~** die Theorie stammt von Professor Higgins **c** *(= insinuation, hint)* Andeutung *f*, Anspielung *f*; *(unpleasant)* Unterstellung *f*; **I resent that ~** ich weise diese Unterstellung zurück; **there is no ~ that he was involved** *(= nobody is suggesting it)* niemand deutet an *or* unterstellt, dass er beteiligt war; *(= no indication)* es gibt keinen Hinweis darauf *or* Anhaltspunkt dafür, dass er beteiligt war **d** *(= trace)* Spur *f*; **with a ~ of irony in his voice** mit einer Spur *or* einem Anflug von Ironie in der Stimme **e** *(= impression)* Eindruck *m*, Vorstellung *f*; **to create a ~ of depth** um den Eindruck von Tiefe zu erwecken **f** *(also* **indecent suggestion***)* unsittlicher

Antrag
g (Psych) Suggestion *f*

suggestions box N Kasten *m* für Verbesserungsvorschläge, Kummerkasten *m (inf)*

suggestive [sə'dʒestɪv] ADJ **a** **to be ~ of sth** an etw *(acc)* denken lassen, auf etw *(acc)* hindeuten; *(= create impression of)* den Eindruck von etw erwecken *or* vermitteln; *(= be indicative of)* auf etw *(acc)* hindeuten **b** *(Psych)* suggestiv **c** *(= indecent) joke, remark etc* zweideutig, anzüglich; *movements, gesture, clothing* aufreizend; **sexually ~** sexuell aufreizend

suggestively [sə'dʒestɪvlɪ] ADV vielsagend, anzüglich; *move, dance* aufreizend

suggestiveness [sə'dʒestɪvnɪs] N Zweideutigkeit *f*, Anzüglichkeit *f*; **the ~ of her dancing** ihr aufreizendes Tanzen

suicidal [ˌsʊɪ'saɪdl] ADJ selbstmörderisch; **she was ~** sie war selbstmordgefährdet; **to have ~ tendencies** zum Selbstmord neigen; **I feel ~ this morning** ich möchte heute Morgen am liebsten sterben; **it would be ~ (for them) to do that** *(fig)* es wäre glatter Selbstmord (für sie), das zu tun

suicide ['sʊɪsaɪd] N Selbstmord *m*, Freitod *m (euph)*, Suizid *m (spec)*; *(= person)* Selbstmörder(in) *m(f)*; **to commit ~** Selbstmord begehen; **to try to commit ~** einen Selbstmordversuch unternehmen; **to contemplate ~** sich mit Selbstmordgedanken tragen; **~ squad** Selbstmordkommando *nt*

suicide: suicide attack N Selbstmordanschlag *m*; **suicide attacker** N Selbstmordattentäter(in) *m(f)*; **suicide attempt, suicide bid** N Selbstmord- *or* Suizidversuch *m*; **suicide bomber** N Selbstmordattentäter(in) *m(f)*; **suicide bombing** N Selbstmordanschlag *m*; **suicide note** N Abschiedsbrief *m*; **suicide pact** N Selbstmordabkommen *nt*

sui generis [ˌsuːaɪ'dʒenərɪs] ADJ sui generis *(geh)*, einzig(artig)

suit [suːt] ✪ 7.4, 11.3 N **a** Anzug *m*; *(woman's)* Kostüm *nt*; **~ of clothes** Garnitur *f* (Kleider); **they bought him a new ~ of clothes** sie kleideten ihn von Kopf bis Fuß neu ein; **~ of armour** Rüstung *f*
b *(Jur)* Prozess *m*, Verfahren *nt*; **to bring a ~ (against sb for sth)** (wegen etw gegen jdn) Klage erheben *or* einen Prozess anstrengen; **he lost his ~** er hat seinen Prozess verloren
c *(Cards)* Farbe *f*; **short ~** kurze Farbe; **long/strong ~** lange/starke Farbe; *(fig)* starke Seite, Stärke *f*; **to follow ~** *(lit)* Farbe bedienen; *(fig)* jds Beispiel *(dat)* folgen
d *(inf: = business executive)* Businessman *m*, Businessfrau *f*
e *(old, liter, in marriage)* Werbung *f*; **to press one's ~** seiner Werbung *(dat)* Nachdruck verleihen
f *(form, = request)* Anliegen *nt (form)*, Bitte *f*; **to press one's ~** seinem Anliegen *or* seiner Bitte Nachdruck verleihen
VT **a** *(= be convenient, pleasing to, arrangement, date, price)* passen *(+dat)*; *(climate, food)* bekommen *(+dat)*; *(occupation, job)* gefallen *(+dat)*; **~s me!** *(inf)* ist mir recht *(inf)*, mir solls recht sein *(inf)*; **that ~s me fine!** *(inf)* das ist mir recht; **that would ~ me nicely** *(time, arrangement)* das würde mir gut (in den Kram *(inf)*) passen; *(house, job etc)* das wäre genau das Richtige für mich; **when would it ~ you to come?** wann würde es Ihnen passen?, wann wäre es Ihnen recht?; **I know what ~s me best** ich weiß, was für mich das Beste ist
b **to be ~ed for/to** *(= be suitable, right for)* geeignet sein für; **he is very well ~ed to the job** er eignet sich sehr gut für die Stelle; **he is not ~ed to be a doctor** er eignet sich nicht zum Arzt; **they are well ~ed (to each other)** sie passen gut zusammen
c *(clothes, hairstyle)* (gut) stehen *(+dat)*, passen zu; **you ~ a beard/fringe** ein Bart/Pony steht dir gut; **such behaviour hardly ~s you** so ein Benehmen steht dir nicht an
d *(= adapt)* anpassen *(to +dat)*; **to ~ one's style to the audience** sich dem Publikumsgeschmack anpassen, sich nach dem Publikum richten; **~ing the action to the word he ...** er setzte seine Worte in die Tat um und ...
e *(= please)* gefallen *(+dat)*, zufriedenstellen; **you can't ~ everybody** man kann es nicht jedem recht machen; **we try to ~ every taste** wir versuchen, etwas für jeden Geschmack zu finden *or* jedem Geschmack gerecht zu werden
VR **he ~s himself** er tut, was er will *or* was ihm passt; **you can ~ yourself whether you come or not** du kannst kommen oder nicht, ganz wie du willst; **~ yourself!** wie du willst!, mach, was du willst!; **I like to be able to ~ myself** ich möchte gern tun und lassen können, was ich will
VI *(= be suitable)* passen

suitability [ˌsuːtə'bɪlɪtɪ] N Angemessenheit *f*; *(of person for job)* Eignung *f*; **they discussed his ~ as a husband for their daughter** sie diskutierten darüber, ob er sich als Ehemann für ihre Tochter eignete; **the ~ of a film for children** ob ein Film für Kinder geeignet ist

suitable ['suːtəbl] ADJ *(= convenient, practical, right for the purpose)* geeignet, passend; *(= socially, culturally appropriate to the occasion)* angemessen; **to be ~ for sb** *(date, place)* jdm passen; *(film, job)* für jdn geeignet sein; *(hairstyle, clothes)* das Richtige für jdn sein; **she's not ~ for him** sie passt nicht zu ihm; **to be ~ for sth** für etw geeignet sein, sich für etw eignen; *(socially)* einer Sache *(dat)* angemessen sein; **none of the dishes is ~ for freezing** keines der Rezepte eignet sich zum Einfrieren; **the most ~ man for the job** der am besten geeignete Mann für den Posten; **would 8 o'clock be a ~ time?** würde Ihnen *etc* 8 Uhr passen?; **Tuesday is the most ~ day** Dienstag ist der günstigste *or* beste Tag, Dienstag passt am besten; **quality machinery ~ to the task** Qualitätsmaschinen, die der Aufgabe gewachsen sind; **animals that are ~ as pets** Tiere, die als Haustiere geeignet sind; **you're not ~ to be parents** Sie eignen sich nicht als Eltern; **we couldn't find anything ~** wir konnten nichts Passendes *or* Geeignetes finden; **to be considered ~** als geeignet angesehen werden; **eminently ~** überaus passend; **to make sth ~ for sth** etw für etw passend machen

suitableness ['suːtəblnɪs] N = **suitability**

suitably ['suːtəblɪ] ADV angemessen; *behave also, apologize* geziemend *(geh)*, wie es sich gehört; **he was ~ impressed** er war gehörig beeindruckt; **I'm ~ impressed** ich bin ja auch beeindruckt; **~ refreshed** ausreichend erfrischt; **to look ~ embarrassed** überaus verlegen aussehen; **a ~ elegant room** ein Raum von angemessener Eleganz; **we camped ~ close to the hills** wir zelteten in günstiger Nähe der Berge

suitcase N Koffer *m*; **to live out of a ~** aus dem Koffer leben

suite [swiːt] N *(of retainers)* Gefolge *nt*; *(of furniture)* Garnitur *f*; *(= chairs and sofa)* Sitzgarnitur *f*; *(of rooms)* Suite *f*, Zimmerflucht *f*; *(Mus)* Suite *f*; **bedroom ~** Schlafzimmergarnitur *or* -einrichtung *f*; **3-piece ~** dreiteilige Sitzgarnitur

suiting ['suːtɪŋ] N *(= fabric)* Anzugstoff *m*

suitor ['suːtəʳ] N **a** *(old, of woman)* Freier *m (old)*, Verehrer *m* **b** *(Jur)* Kläger(in) *m(f)* **c** *(Econ)* Übernahmeinteressent *m*

sulfa *etc (US)* = **sulpha** *etc*

sulk [sʌlk] VI schmollen, eingeschnappt sein, beleidigt sein; *(photo model)* einen Schmollmund machen N Schmollen *nt*; **to have a ~** schmollen, den Eingeschnappten/die Eingeschnappte spielen; **she was in the ~s all day** sie schmollte den ganzen Tag; **to go into a ~** sich in den Schmollwinkel zurückziehen, einschnappen

sulkily ['sʌlkɪlɪ] ADV *say, look* beleidigt

sulkiness ['sʌlkɪnɪs] N Schmollen *nt*; **the ~ of his expression** sein beleidigt eingeschnappter *or* schmollender Gesichtsausdruck

sulky[1] ['sʌlkɪ] ADJ (+er) *answer* eingeschnappt, beleidigt; *person, expression also* schmollend; *silence* beleidigt; **to be/look ~ about sth** wegen etw beleidigt sein/aussehen; **~ mouth** Schmollmund *m*

sulky[2] N *(Sport)* Sulky *nt*

sullen ['sʌlən] ADJ **a** *(= morose)* mürrisch, missmutig, verdrießlich; *behaviour* unfreundlich, mürrisch; *silence* mürrisch **b** *(liter) landscape, sky etc* düster, finster

sullenly ['sʌlənlɪ] ADV mürrisch, missmutig

sullenness ['sʌlənnɪs] N **a** *(of person)* Missmutigkeit *f*, Verdrießlichkeit *f* **b** *(liter, of landscape, sky)* Düsterkeit *f*

sully ['sʌlɪ] VT *reputation* besudeln; **to ~ one's hands by doing sth** *(fig)* sich *(dat)* die Hände schmutzig machen, indem man etw tut

sulpha, *(US)* **sulfa** ['sʌlfə] ADJ **~ drug** Sulfonamid *nt*

sulphate, *(US)* **sulfate** ['sʌlfeɪt] N Sulfat *nt*, schwefelsaures Salz

sulphide, *(US)* **sulfide** ['sʌlfaɪd] N Sulfid *nt*

sulphite, *(US)* **sulfite** ['sʌlfaɪt] N Sulfit *nt*

sulphonamide, *(US)* **sulfonamide** [sʌl'fɒnəmaɪd] N Sulfonamid *nt*

sulphur, *(US)* **sulfur** ['sʌlfəʳ] N Schwefel *m*

sulphur dioxide, *(US)* **sulfur dioxide** N Schwefeldioxid *nt*

sulphuretted, *(US)* **sulfuretted** ['sʌlfjʊˌretɪd] ADJ geschwefelt; **~ hydrogen** Schwefelwasserstoff *m*

sulphuric, *(US)* **sulfuric** [sʌl'fjʊərɪk] ADJ Schwefel-

sulphuric acid, *(US)* **sulfuric acid** N Schwefelsäure *f*

sulphurize, *(US)* **sulfurize** ['sʌlfjʊˌraɪz] VT schwefeln

sulphurous, *(US)* **sulfurous** ['sʌlfərəs] ADJ schwefelig, schwefelhaltig; **~ acid** schwefelige Säure

sultan ['sʌltən] N Sultan *m*

sultana [sʌl'tɑːnə] N **a** *(= person)* Sultanin *f* **b** *(Brit: = fruit)* Sultanine *f*

sultanate ['sʌltənɪt] N Sultanat *nt*

sultriness ['sʌltrɪnɪs] N *(lit)* Schwüle *f*; *(fig)* Heißblütigkeit *f*; *(of look)* Glut *f*

sultry ['sʌltrɪ] ADJ *weather, atmosphere* schwül; *woman* heißblütig, temperamentvoll; *voice, beauty, look* glutvoll

sum [sʌm] N **a** *(= total)* Summe *f*; **that was the ~ (total) of his achievements** das war alles, was er geschafft hatte; **the ~ total of my ambitions** das Ziel meiner Wünsche **b** *(of money)* Betrag *m*, Summe *f* **c** *(esp Brit: = calculation)* Rechenaufgabe *f*; **to do ~s (in one's head)** (im Kopf) rechnen; **I was bad at ~s** ich war schlecht im Rechnen **d** *(form: = essence)* **in ~** mit einem Wort, zusammengefasst

▸ **sum up** VT sep **a** *(= review, summarize)* zusammenfassen **b** *(= evaluate rapidly)* ab- *or* einschätzen, taxieren; **she summed me up at a glance** sie taxierte mich mit einem Blick VI *(also Jur)* zusammenfassen, resümieren; **to sum up, we can say that ...** zusammenfassend *or* als Resümee können wir feststellen, dass ...; **the judge hasn't summed up yet** der Richter hat sein Resümee noch nicht gegeben

sumac(h) ['suːmæk] N *(= plant)* Sumach *m*, Gerberstrauch *m*; *(= preparation)* Schmack *m*

Sumatra [suː'mɑːtrə] N Sumatra *nt*

Sumatran [suː'mɑːtrən] ADJ von/aus Sumatra N Bewohner(in) *m(f)* von Sumatra

Sumerian [suː'mɪərɪən] ADJ sumerisch N **a** Sumerer(in) *m(f)* **b** *(Ling)* Sumerisch *nt*

summa cum laude [ˌsʊmɑːkʊm'laʊdeɪ] ADV *(US)* summa cum laude

summarily ['sʌmərɪlɪ] ADV *(= briefly)* knapp, kurz gefasst; *(= fast, without ceremony)* kurz und bündig, ohne viel Federlesen(s); *(Jur) punish, try* summarisch; *read* flüchtig, kursorisch *(geh)*; *execute* unverzüglich, auf der Stelle

summarize ['sʌməraɪz] VT zusammenfassen

summary ['sʌmərɪ] **N** Zusammenfassung *f; (Sci also)* Abriss *m;* **here is a ~ of the main points of the news** hier ein Überblick *m* über die wichtigsten Meldungen; **he gave us a short ~ of the film** er gab uns eine kurze Inhaltsangabe des Films; **~ of contents** Inhaltsangabe *f* **ADJ** **a** *(= brief) account* knapp, gedrängt, kurz gefasst; **in ~ form** in Zusammenfassung **b** *(= fast, without ceremony) treatment* kurz, knapp; *perusal* flüchtig; *(Jur) trial, punishment* summarisch; *dismissal* fristlos; **the court dealt out ~ justice** das Gericht sprach Recht im Schnellverfahren; **~ procedure** Schnellverfahren *nt*

summary execution N Hinrichtung *f* im Schnellverfahren

summary offence N *(Jur)* ≈ Übertretung *f*

summation [sʌ'meɪʃən] N *(= act)* Addition *f; (= total)* Summe *f; (= summary)* Zusammenfassung *f; (US Jur)* Plädoyers *pl;* **in ~** zusammenfassend

summer ['sʌmə^r] **N** Sommer *m;* **in (the) ~** im Sommer; **two ~s ago** im Sommer vor zwei Jahren; **a girl of seventeen ~s** *(liter)* ein Mädchen von siebzehn Lenzen *(liter);* **a ~'s day** ein Sommertag *m* **ADJ** *attr* Sommer-; **~ resort** Ferien- *or* Urlaubsort *m* (für die Sommersaison) **VI** den Sommer verbringen; *(birds also)* übersommern

summer: **summer camp** N Sommerlager *nt,* Ferienlager *nt;* **summer collection** N *(Fashion)* Sommerkollektion *f;* **summer fallow** N *(Agr)* Sommerbrache *f;* **summer holidays** PL *(esp Brit)* Sommerferien *pl,* Sommerurlaub *m;* **summerhouse** N Gartenhaus *nt,* (Garten)laube *f;* **summer house** N *(US)* Ferienhaus *nt*/-wohnung *f;* **summer lightning** N Wetterleuchten *nt;* **summer sales** PL Sommerschlussverkauf *m*

summersault N, VI = **somersault**

summer: **summer school** N Sommerkurs *m;* **summertime** N Sommer *m,* Sommer(s)zeit *f; (= daylight-saving time)* Sommerzeit *f;* **summerweight** ADJ sommerlich; **~ coat** Sommermantel *m*

summery ['sʌmərɪ] ADJ sommerlich

summing-up [ˌsʌmɪŋ'ʌp] N *(Jur)* Resümee *nt*

summit ['sʌmɪt] **N** *(lit)* Gipfel *m; (fig also)* Höhepunkt *m;* **to reach the ~** *(lit, fig)* den Gipfel *or* Höhepunkt erreichen; *(= summit conference)* Gipfelkonferenz *f,* Gipfel *m* **ADJ** *attr (Pol)* Gipfel-; **at ~ level** auf Gipfelebene

summiteer [ˌsʌmɪ'tɪə^r] N Gipfelteilnehmer(in) *m(f),* Teilnehmer(in) *m(f)* an der Gipfelkonferenz

summit meeting N Gipfeltreffen *nt*

summit talks PL Gipfelgespräche *pl*

summon ['sʌmən] VT **a** *servant etc* (herbei)rufen, kommen lassen, herbeizitieren; *police, fire brigade etc* (herbei)rufen; *help* holen; *members* zusammenrufen; *meeting, Parliament* einberufen; **to ~ sb to do sth** *(= order)* jdn auffordern, etw zu tun; **the King ~ed his ministers** der König rief seine Minister zusammen; **he was ~ed back** er wurde zurückgerufen; **to be ~ed into sb's presence** zu jdm befohlen *or* zitiert *(iro)* werden; **a bell ~ed them to their work** eine Glocke rief sie zur Arbeit
b *(Jur)* vorladen; **~ the next witness!** rufen Sie den nächsten Zeugen (auf)!
c to ~ the courage/strength to do sth den Mut/die Kraft aufbringen, etw zu tun

▶ **summon up** VT *sep courage* zusammennehmen, zusammenraffen; *strength* aufbieten; *enthusiasm, energy* aufbieten, aufbringen; *sympathy, image, memories* heraufbeschwören; **summoning up all his strength he lifted it up** unter Aufbietung aller Kräfte hob er es hoch

summons ['sʌmənz] **N** **a** *(Jur)* Vorladung *f;* **to take out a ~ against sb** jdn vorladen lassen, jdn vor Gericht laden **b** *(= order to appear etc)* Aufruf *m,* Aufforderung *f;* **he received a ~ to see the boss** er wurde zum Chef gerufen, er wurde aufgefordert, zum Chef zu kommen **VT** *(Jur)* vorladen

sumo ['suːməʊ] N Sumo *nt;* **~ wrestler** Sumoringer *m*

sump [sʌmp] N *(Brit Aut)* Ölwanne *f; (Min)* Sumpf *m*

sumptuary ['sʌmptjʊərɪ] ADJ den Aufwand betreffend

sumptuous ['sʌmptjʊəs] ADJ *(= splendid)* luxuriös; *(= costly)* aufwendig, kostspielig; *food etc* üppig, verschwenderisch

sumptuously ['sʌmptjʊəslɪ] ADV *(= splendidly)* luxuriös; *(= expensively)* aufwendig, kostspielig

sumptuousness ['sʌmptjʊəsnɪs] N *(= opulence)* Luxus *m; (= expensiveness)* Aufwand *m,* Kostspieligkeit *f; (of meal etc)* Üppigkeit *f*

Sun *abbr of* **Sunday** So.

sun [sʌn] **N** Sonne *f;* **I've got the ~ in my eyes** die Sonne scheint mir in die Augen, die Sonne blendet mich; **he was up with the ~** er stand in aller Frühe auf; **to have a touch of the ~** einen Sonnenstich haben *(also fig);* **you've caught the ~** dich hat die Sonne erwischt; **he's tried everything under the ~** er hat alles Menschenmögliche versucht; **a place in the ~** *(fig)* ein Platz an der Sonne; **there's nothing new under the ~** *(prov)* es ist alles schon einmal da gewesen *(Prov)* **VT** der Sonne aussetzen **VR** sich sonnen

sun: **sunbaked** ADJ ausgedörrt; **sun bath** N Sonnenbad *nt;* **sunbathe** VI in der Sonne liegen, sonnenbaden; **sunbather** N Sonnenanbeter(in) *m(f) (hum);* **all the ~s in the park** all die Leute, die sich im Park sonnen *or* die im Park in der Sonne liegen; **sunbathing** N Sonnenbaden *nt;* **sunbeam** N Sonnenstrahl *m;* **sun bed** N Sonnenbank *f*

> **SUNBELT**
>
> **Sunbelt** wird der südliche Teil der Vereinigten Staaten von North Carolina bis Kalifornien genannt, der diesen Namen wegen des ausgesprochen warmen und sonnigen Klimas bekommen hat. Mit diesem Begriff wird eine demografische, ökonomische und politische Verlagerung vom ehemals dominierenden Nordosten in die Staaten des Südens angesprochen: Aufgrund des wirtschaftlichen Aufstiegs ziehen immer mehr Menschen aus dem Norden in den Süden, was eine steigende politische Bedeutung dieser Staaten mit sich bringt. Über die nördlichen Staaten wird dagegen gesagt, dass sie im „Frostbelt" oder sogar im „Rustbelt" (nach den veralteten, vor sich hin rostenden Industrieanlagen) liegen.

sun: **sun blind** N *(= awning)* Markise *f; (= venetian blind)* Jalousie *f;* **sun block** N Sonnenschutzcreme *f,* Sunblockcreme *f;* **sun bonnet** N Sonnenhut *m;* **sunburn** N Bräune *f; (painful)* Sonnenbrand *m;* **sunburnt** ADJ sonnengebräunt, sonnenverbrannt; *(painfully)* von der Sonne verbrannt; **to get ~** braun werden; *(painfully)* (einen) Sonnenbrand bekommen; **sunburst** N **a** *(US)* plötzlicher Sonnenschein **b** *(= pattern)* Sonnenrad *nt*

sundae ['sʌndeɪ] N Eisbecher *m*

sun dance N Sonnenanbetungstanz *m*

Sunday ['sʌndɪ] **N** Sonntag *m;* **a month of ~s** *(inf)* ewig (lange), eine Ewigkeit; **not** *or* **never in a month of ~s** *(inf)* nie im Leben → *also* **Tuesday** **ADJ** *attr* Sonntags-; *trading* am Sonntag; **~ (news)paper** Sonntagszeitung *f*

Sunday: **Sunday best** N Sonntagskleider *pl,* Sonntagsstaat *m (old, hum);* **Sunday driver** N Sonntagsfahrer(in) *m(f);* **Sunday-go-to-meeting** ADJ *(US inf)* Sonntags-; **~ clothes** Sonntagskleider *pl,* Sonntagnachmittagsausgehkleider *pl (hum);* **Sunday painter** N Sonntagsmaler(in) *m(f)*

> **SUNDAY PAPERS**
>
> Zum klassischen britischen Sonntag gehört auf jeden Fall die Sonntagszeitung, wobei viele Haushalte sich mit mehreren **Sunday papers** eindecken. Einige Zeitungen veröffentlichen ausschließlich Sonntagsausgaben, darunter der „Observer", die älteste überregionale Sonntagszeitung der Welt, „News of the World" und „Sunday People". Andere Blätter veröffentlichen eine erweiterte Ausgabe, wie „Sunday Times", „Sunday Telegraph", „Independent on Sunday", „Sunday Express" etc. Die **Sunday papers** haben umfangreiche Kunst-, Reise-, Sport- und Wirtschaftsteile und legen meist ein farbiges Magazin bei. Die Artikel gehen mehr in die Tiefe als in der normalen Werktagsausgabe.
> In den USA, wo die Leute lieber Lokalblätter als nationale Tageszeitungen lesen, wird die größte überregionale Sonntagsausgabe von der „New York Times" veröffentlicht.

Sunday school N Sonntagsschule *f*

sun deck N Sonnendeck *nt*

sunder ['sʌndə^r] *(liter)* **VT** brechen; *chains* sprengen; *(fig) connection* abbrechen **VI** brechen; *(fig)* sich trennen

sun: **sundew** N *(Bot)* Sonnentau *m;* **sundial** N Sonnenuhr *f;* **sundown** N *(Brit)* Sonnenuntergang *m;* **at/before ~** bei/vor Sonnenuntergang; **sundowner** N **a** *(Austral inf: = tramp)* Penner *m (inf),* Vagabund *m* **b** *(= drink)* Abendtrunk *m;* **sun-drenched** ADJ *beaches* sonnenüberflutet, in Sonne getaucht; **sundress** N leichtes Sonnenkleid; **sun-dried** ADJ *fruit* an *or* in der Sonne getrocknet

sundry ['sʌndrɪ] **ADJ** verschiedene **PRON** **all and ~** jedermann **N** **sundries** **PL** Verschiedenes *(+sing vb)*

sun: **sunfast** ADJ *(esp US)* lichtecht; **sunflower** ['sʌnflaʊə^r] N Sonnenblume *f*

sung [sʌŋ] *ptp of* **sing**

sun: **sunglasses** PL Sonnenbrille *f;* **sun-god** N Sonnengott *m;* **sun-goddess** N Sonnengöttin *f;* **sunhat** N Sonnenhut *m;* **sun helmet** N Tropenhelm *m*

sunk [sʌŋk] *ptp of* **sink**[1]

sunken ['sʌŋkən] ADJ *wreck, ship* gesunken, versunken; *treasure* versunken; *garden* abgesenkt; *bath* eingelassen; *cheeks* eingefallen, hohl; *eyes* eingesunken

sun: **Sun King** N Sonnenkönig *m;* **sun-kissed** ADJ *(liter)* von der Sonne geküsst; **sun lamp** N Höhensonne *f;* **sunless** ADJ *garden* ohne Sonne; *room also* dunkel; *day also* trübe; **sunlight** N Sonnenlicht *nt;* **in the ~** in der Sonne, im Sonnenlicht; **sunlit** ADJ *room, day* sonnig; *fields etc also* sonnenbeschienen; **sun lounge** N Wintergarten *m,* Glasveranda *f;* **sun lounger** N Sonnenliege *f*

sunnily ['sʌnɪlɪ] ADV heiter; *smile also* sonnig

sunny ['sʌnɪ] ADJ *(+er) place, room, day etc* sonnig; *(fig) smile, disposition also, answer, face* heiter; *person* fröhlich; **~ intervals** *(Met)* Aufheiterungen *pl;* **on the ~ side of the house** auf der Sonnenseite (des Hauses); **~-side up** *(egg)* nur auf einer Seite gebraten; **the outlook is ~** *(Met)* die Wetteraussichten sind gut; *(fig)* die Aussichten sind rosig; **to look on the ~ side (of things)** die Dinge von der angenehmen Seite nehmen; **to be on the ~ side of forty** noch nicht vierzig sein, unter vierzig sein

sun: **sun parlor** N *(US)* Wintergarten *m,* Glasveranda *f;* **sun porch** N Veranda *f;* **sunray** **N** Sonnenstrahl *m* **ADJ** *attr* **~ lamp** Höhensonne *f;* **~ treatment** Ultraviolettbehandlung *f;* **sun-ripened** ADJ *fruit, vegetables* sonnengereift; **sunrise** N Sonnenaufgang *m;* **at ~** bei Sonnenaufgang; **sunrise industry** N Zukunftsindustrie *f;* **sunroof** N *(of car)* Schiebedach *nt; (of hotel etc)* Sonnenterrasse *f;* **sunscald** ['sʌnskɔːld] N *(Bot)* Sonnen- *or* Rindenbrand *m;* **sunscreen** N Sonnenschutzmittel *nt;* **sunseeker** N Sonnenhungrige(r) *mf;* **sunset** N Sonnenuntergang *m;* **at ~** bei Sonnenuntergang; **sunshade** N *(lady's, over table)* Sonnenschirm *m; (= awning)* Markise *f,* Sonnenblende *f;* **sunshine** N **a** Sonnenschein *m;* **hours of**

~ Sonnenstunden *pl*; **a daily average of 5 hours'** ~ durchschnittlich 5 Stunden Sonne täglich **b** *(inf, = person)* mein Lieber, meine Liebe; **sunshine roof** N *(Brit)* Schiebedach *nt*; **sunspot** N **a** Sonnenfleck *m* **b** *(inf, for holiday)* Ferienparadies *nt*; **sunstroke** N Sonnenstich *m*; **to get** ~ einen Sonnenstich bekommen; **sunstruck** ADJ **to be** ~ einen Sonnenstich haben; **sunsuit** N Spiel- *or* Sonnenanzug *m*; **suntan** N Sonnenbräune *f*; **to get a** ~ braun werden; ~ **lotion/oil** Sonnenöl *nt*; **suntanned** ADJ braun gebrannt; **suntrap** N sonniges Eckchen; **sunup** N *(US)* Sonnenaufgang *m*; **at** ~ bei Sonnenaufgang; **sun-worship** N *(lit, fig)* Sonnenanbetung *f*; **sun-worshipper** N *(lit, fig)* Sonnenanbeter(in) *m(f)*

sup [sʌp] VT *(esp N Engl, Scot)* trinken VI *(old: = dine)* zu Abend essen; **to ~ off** *or* **on sth** etw zu Abend essen; **he that ~s with the devil must have a long spoon** *(Prov)* wer den Teufel zum Freund hat, kommt leicht in die Hölle *(Prov)* N *(= drink)* Schluck *m*

▶ **sup up** *(esp N Engl, Scot)* VT *sep* austrinken VI austrinken

super¹ ['su:pəʳ] ADJ *(dated esp Brit inf)* fantastisch, phantastisch, sagenhaft, klasse *inv (inf)*; **~!** Klasse! *(inf)*; **we had a ~ time** es war große Klasse *(inf) or* fantastisch *or* phantastisch *or* sagenhaft

super² N **a** *(inf) abbr of* **superintendent** Aufseher(in) *m(f)*; *(of police)* ≈ Kommissar(in) *m(f)* **b** *(Theat, Film) abbr of* **supernumerary** Statist(in) *m(f)*

super- PREF super-, Super-

superable ['su:pərəbl] ADJ überwindbar, überwindlich

superabound [,su:pərə'baʊnd] VI **a** im Überfluss vorhanden sein **b** eine Überfülle haben *(in/with* an *+dat)*

superabundance [,su:pərə'bʌndəns] N *(of* an *+dat)* großer Reichtum; *(= excessive amount)* Überfluss *m*, Überschuss *m*; *(of enthusiasm)* Überschuss *m*

superabundant [,su:pərə'bʌndənt] ADJ überreichlich

superadd [,su:pər'æd] VT (noch) hinzufügen *(to* zu); **to be ~ed** noch dazukommen *(to* zu)

superannuate [,su:pə'rænjʊeɪt] VT *(esp Brit)* pensionieren, in den Ruhestand versetzen

superannuated [,su:pə'rænjʊeɪtɪd] ADJ *(esp Brit)* pensioniert, im Ruhestand; *(fig inf)* veraltet, überholt

superannuation [,su:pərænjʊ'eɪʃən] N *(esp Brit) (= act)* Pensionierung *f*, Versetzung *f* in den Ruhestand; *(= state)* Pension *f*, Ruhestand *m*; *(= pension)* Rente *f*; *(for civil servants, teachers)* Ruhegehalt *nt (form)*; ~ **contribution** Beitrag *m* zur Altersversicherung

superb [su:'pɜ:b] ADJ großartig; *design, painting also* meisterhaft; *quality, food also* vorzüglich, superb *(dated, geh)*

superblock ['su:pəblɒk] N *(US) durchgeplantes, meist autofreies Stadtviertel mit Geschäften, Sozial- und Freizeiteinrichtungen*

superbly [su:'pɜ:blɪ] ADV *play, perform* großartig; ~ **fit/self-confident** ungemein fit/selbstbewusst; ~ **well** großartig, hervorragend

superbness [su:'pɜ:bnɪs] N Großartigkeit *f*; *(of quality, food also)* Vorzüglichkeit *f*

Superbowl ['su:pə,bəʊl] N *(US)* Superbowl *m*, *jährlich ausgetragenes American-Football-Turnier zwischen den Spitzenreitern der beiden großen nationalen Ligen in den USA*

super: **superbug** N *(inf) gegen Antibiotika resistenter Krankheitserreger*, Superbazillus *m (inf)*; **supercargo** N *pl* **-es** Frachtaufseher *m*; **supercharged** ADJ *gas* vorverdichtet; *engine* aufgeladen; *(fig) atmosphere* gereizt; **supercharger** N Lader *m*

supercilious ADJ, **superciliously** ADV [,su:pə'sɪlɪəs, -lɪ] hochnäsig

superciliousness [,su:pə'sɪlɪəsnɪs] N Hochnäsigkeit *f*

super: **supercomputer** N Supercomputer *m*; **superconductor** N *(Phys, Tech)* Supraleiter *m*; **supercool** VT unterkühlen; **super-duper** [,su:pə'du:pəʳ] ADJ *(hum inf)* ganz toll *(inf)*; **super-duty** ADJ *(Tech)* Höchstleistungs-, für höchste Beanspruchung; **superego** N Über-ich *nt*

superelevation [,su:pərelɪ'veɪʃən] N *(of bend)* Überhöhung *f*

supererogation [,su:pərerə'geɪʃən] N *(form)* Mehrleistung *f*, Supererogation *(form) f*; *(Eccl)* freiwillige Gebete *pl*, gute Werke *pl*; **an act of** ~ eine Mehrleistung *or* Supererogation *(form)*

superficial [,su:pə'fɪʃəl] ADJ *person, behaviour, injury, treatment, knowledge* oberflächlich; *characteristics, resemblance* äußerlich

superficiality [,su:pəfɪʃɪ'ælɪtɪ] N *(of person, behaviour, injury, treatment, knowledge)* Oberflächlichkeit *f*; *(of characteristics, resemblance)* Äußerlichkeit *f*

superficially [,su:pə'fɪʃəlɪ] ADV *discuss, examine* oberflächlich; *similar, different* äußerlich; ~ **this may be true** oberflächlich gesehen mag das stimmen

superfine ['su:pəfaɪn] ADJ *clay, sugar* sehr fein; *distinction* übertrieben fein

superfluity [,su:pə'flʊɪtɪ] N Überfluss *m*; **his ~ of style, the ~ of his style** sein verschwenderischer Stil

superfluous [sʊ'pɜ:flʊəs] ADJ überflüssig; *style* verschwenderisch; **it is ~ to say ...** es ist überflüssig, zu sagen ...

superfluously [sʊ'pɜ:flʊəslɪ] ADV überflüssigerweise; **... he added ~** ... fügte er überflüssigerweise hinzu

super: **superglue** N Sekundenkleber *m*; **supergrass** N *(Brit inf: = informant)* Kronzeuge *m (inf)*, Kronzeugin *f (inf)*, Topinformant(in) *m(f)*; **supergroup** N *(Mus)* Supergruppe *f*; **superheat** VT überhitzen; **superheavyweight** *(Boxing)* N **a** *(= weight category)* Superschwergewicht *nt* **b** *(= boxer)* Superschwergewichtler(in) *m(f)* ADJ Superschwergewichts-; **superhero** N Superheld *m*; **superhighway** N *(US)* ≈ Autobahn *f*; **the information ~** die Datenautobahn; **superhuman** ADJ übermenschlich

superimpose [,su:pərɪm'pəʊz] VT **to ~ sth on sth** etw auf etw *(acc)* legen; *(Phot)* etw über etw *(acc)* fotografieren; *(Film)* etw über etw *(acc)* filmen; *(Geol)* etw über etw *(acc)* lagern; *(fig)* etw mit etw überlagern; **by superimposing one image on another** indem man zwei Bilder aufeinanderlegt; **the images were ~d** die Bilder hatten sich überlagert

superintend [,su:pərɪn'tend] VT beaufsichtigen, überwachen

superintendence [,su:pərɪn'tendəns] N (Ober)aufsicht *f*

superintendent [,su:pərɪn'tendənt] N Aufsicht *f*; *(US: in building)* Hausmeister(in) *m(f)*; *(in swimming pool)* Bademeister(in) *m(f)*; *(of hostel, Sunday school etc)* Leiter(in) *m(f)*; *(of police, Brit)* ≈ Kommissar(in) *m(f)*; *(US)* ≈ Polizeipräsident(in) *m(f)*

superior [sʊ'pɪərɪəʳ] ✪ 5.2 ADJ **a** *(= better) quality, equipment* besser *(to* als); *intellect, ability, skill, technique* überlegen *(to sb/sth* jdm/einer Sache); **he thinks he's so ~** er hält sich für so viel besser überlegen *or* für so viel besser **b** *(= excellent) work(manship), technique* großartig, hervorragend; *craftsman* ausgezeichnet; *intellect* überragend; **goods of ~ quality, ~ quality goods** Waren *pl* bester Qualität **c** *(= higher in rank etc)* höher; ~ **officer** Vorgesetzte(r) *mf*; ~ **court** höheres Gericht; **to be ~ to sb/sth** jdm/einer Sache übergeordnet sein, höherstehen als jd/etw **d** *(= greater) forces* stärker *(to* als); *strength* größer *(to* als); **they were ~ to us in number(s)** sie waren uns zahlenmäßig überlegen **e** *(= snobbish) person, manner* überheblich; *tone, smile* überlegen; *(= smart) restaurant, clientele* fein, vornehm **f** *(Typ) figure, letter* hochgestellt; ~ **number** Hochzahl *f* N **a** *(in rank)* Vorgesetzte(r) *mf* **b** *(in ability)* Überlegene(r) *mf*; **to be sb's ~** jdm überlegen sein; **he has no ~s when it comes to that** was das anbelangt, ist ihm keiner überlegen **c** *(Eccl)* **Father Superior** Vater Superior *m*; **Mother Superior** Mutter Superiorin *or* Oberin *f*

superiority [sʊ,pɪərɪ'ɒrɪtɪ] N **a** *(of cloth etc)* bessere Qualität; *(of technique, ability etc)* Überlegenheit *f*; **its ~ as a holiday resort** seine bessere Klasse als Ferienort **b** *(= excellence)* Großartigkeit *f*; *(of intellect)* überragende Eigenschaft **c** *(in rank)* höhere Stellung, höherer Rang **d** *(in numbers etc)* Überlegenheit *f* **e** *(= conceitedness)* Überheblichkeit *f*; *(of tone, smile)* Überlegenheit *f*; ~ **complex** Superioritätskomplex *m*

superlative [sʊ'pɜ:lətɪv] ADJ *(= excellent)* überragend, unübertrefflich; *happiness* größte(r, s), höchste(r, s); *indifference* höchste(r, s); *(Gram)* superlativisch, im Superlativ; *(= exaggerated) style* überschwänglich N Superlativ *m*; **to speak in ~s** zu Superlativen greifen

superlatively [sʊ'pɜ:lətɪvlɪ] ADV *(= excellently)* überragend, unübertrefflich; *happy, fit* höchst; ~ **well** überragend (gut)

superman ['su:pəmæn] N *pl* **-men** [-men] Übermensch *m*; **Superman** *(in comics)* Supermann *m*

supermarket ['su:pə,mɑ:kɪt] N Supermarkt *m*

supermarket trolley N Einkaufswagen *m*

supernatural [,su:pə'nætʃərəl] ADJ übernatürlich; **the ~ world** die Welt des Übernatürlichen N **the ~** das Übernatürliche

supernormal [,su:pə'nɔ:məl] ADJ übermenschlich

supernova [,su:pə'nəʊvə] N *pl* **-s** *or* **-e** [-'nəʊvi:] Supernova *f*

supernumerary [,su:pə'nju:mərərɪ] ADJ zusätzlich; *(= superfluous)* überzählig N Zusatzperson *f*, Supernumerar *m (form)*; *(Theat, Film)* Statist(in) *m(f)*

superpower ['su:pə,paʊəʳ] N *(Pol)* Supermacht *f*

supersaver ['su:pə,seɪvəʳ] N Supersparangebot *nt*, Superschnäppchen *nt (inf)*; *(Brit Rail, also* **supersaver ticket***)* Fahrkarte *f* zum Supersparpreis

superscribe [,su:pə'skraɪb] VT *one's name etc* obenan setzen; *document etc* beschriften, überschreiben

superscript ['su:pə,skrɪpt] *(Typ)* ADJ *character, number* hochgestellt N hochgestelltes Zeichen

supersede [,su:pə'si:d] VT ablösen; *person, belief also* an die Stelle treten von

supersize ['su:pəsaɪz] N Riesenformat *nt*, Übergröße *f* ADJ übergroß, riesig

supersonic [,su:pə'sɒnɪk] ADJ Überschall-; **at ~ speed** mit Überschallgeschwindigkeit; ~ **travel** Reisen *nt* mit Überschallgeschwindigkeit

superstar ['su:pəstɑ:ʳ] N (Super)star *m*

superstate ['su:pəsteɪt] N Superstaat *m*

superstition [,su:pə'stɪʃən] N Aberglaube *m no pl*; **this is a ~** das ist Aberglaube

superstitious [,su:pə'stɪʃəs] ADJ abergläubisch; ~ **belief** Aberglaube *m*; **to be ~ about sth** in Bezug auf etw *(acc)* abergläubisch sein

superstitiously [,su:pə'stɪʃəslɪ] ADV abergläubisch

superstitiousness [,su:pə'stɪʃəsnɪs] N Aberglaube *m*, Abergläubigkeit *f*

superstore ['su:pəstɔ:ʳ] N Großmarkt *m (für Endverbraucher)*

superstratum [,su:pə'strɑ:təm] N *pl* **-strata** [-'strɑ:tə] *(Geol)* obere Schicht; *(Ling)* Superstrat *nt*

superstructure ['su:pə,strʌktʃəʳ] N Überbau *m (also Sociol)*; *(of ship)* Aufbauten *pl*

supertanker ['su:pə,tæŋkəʳ] N Super- *or* Riesentanker *m*

supertax ['su:pətæks] N Höchststeuer *f*

Super Tuesday N *(US Pol) ein Dienstag im März eines Jahres in dem Präsidentenwahlen stattfinden, an dem in 20 Staaten Vorwahlen abgehalten werden*

supervene [ˌsuːpəˈviːn] VI dazwischenkommen, hinzukommen

supervise [ˈsuːpəvaɪz] VT beaufsichtigen; *work also* überwachen VI Aufsicht führen, die Aufsicht haben

supervision [ˌsuːpəˈvɪʒən] N Aufsicht *f*; *(= action)* Beaufsichtigung *f*; *(of work)* Überwachung *f*, Beaufsichtigung *f*; **under the ~ of** unter der Aufsicht von

supervision order N *(Brit Jur)* gerichtliche Verfügung der Aufsicht

supervisor [ˈsuːpəvaɪzəʳ] N *(of work)* Aufseher(in) *m(f)*, Aufsicht *f*; *(of research)* Leiter(in) *m(f)*; *(Brit Univ)* ≈ Tutor(in) *m(f)*; *(for PhD)* Doktorvater *m*/-mutter *f*

supervisory [ˈsuːpəvaɪzərɪ] ADJ *role* beaufsichtigend, überwachend; **in a ~ post** in einer Aufsichtsposition; **in his ~ capacity** in seiner Eigenschaft als Aufsichtsperson; **~ staff** Aufsichtspersonal *nt*; **~ powers** Kontrollbefugnis *f*

supervisory board N *(Comm, Ind)* Aufsichtsrat *m*

supervisory body N Aufsichtsgremium *nt*

superwaif [ˈsuːpəweɪf] N *(pej)* magersüchtig aussehendes Model

superwoman [ˈsuːpəˌwʊmən] *pl* **-women** [-wɪmɪn] N Superfrau *f*

supine [ˈsuːpaɪn] ADJ zurückliegend *attr*; *person (lit)* ausgestreckt; *(fig)* entspannt; *(fig liter) lethargy* träge, gleichgültig; **in a ~ position** auf dem Rücken liegend; **to be/lie ~** auf dem Rücken liegen N *(Gram)* Supinum *nt*

supper [ˈsʌpəʳ] N *(= evening meal)* Abendessen *nt*, Abendbrot *nt*, Abendmahl *nt (liter)*; *(= late evening snack)* (später) Imbiss; **they were at ~** sie waren beim Abendessen; **to have ~** zu Abend essen, Abendbrot essen

supper: **supper club** N *(US)* Luxusnachtklub *m*; **suppertime** [ˈsʌpətaɪm] N Abendessenszeit *f*, Abendbrotzeit *f*; **at ~** zur Abendbrotzeit; **when is ~?** wann wird zu Abend gegessen?

supplant [səˈplɑːnt] VT ablösen, ersetzen; *(forcibly)* verdrängen; *(by ruse) rival* ausstechen

supple [ˈsʌpl] ADJ *(+er) body, material etc* geschmeidig, elastisch; *person* beweglich; *shoes* weich; *mind, intellect* beweglich, flexibel; **to keep oneself/one's fingers ~** sich/seine Finger beweglich halten

supplement [ˈsʌplɪmənt] N **a** Ergänzung *f* *(to +gen)*; *(of book)* Ergänzungsband *m* *(to zu)*; *(= at end of book)* Anhang *m*, Nachtrag *m*; *(= food supplement)* Zusatz *m*; **a ~ to his pension** eine Aufbesserung seiner Rente; **family income ~s** Kindergeld *nt* **b** *(= colour supplement etc)* Beilage *f*, Magazin *nt* VT ergänzen; *income also* aufbessern

supplemental [ˌsʌplɪˈmentəl] ADJ *(esp US)* zusätzlich

supplementary [ˌsʌplɪˈmentərɪ] ADJ zusätzlich, ergänzend; *(Med) vitamins* ergänzend; **to be ~ to sth** etw ergänzen; **~ food** Zusatznahrung *f*; **~ volume** Ergänzungsband *m*

supplementary: **supplementary angle** N Supplement- *or* Ergänzungswinkel *m*; **supplementary benefit** N *(Brit)* ≈ Sozialhilfe *f*; **to be on ~** ≈ Sozialhilfe beziehen; **supplementary budget** N *(Pol)* Nachtragshaushalt *m*; **supplementary question** N *(Parl)* Zusatzfrage *f*

suppleness [ˈsʌplnɪs] N *(of body, material etc)* Geschmeidigkeit *f*, Elastizität *f*; *(of person)* Beweglichkeit *f*; *(of shoes)* Weichheit *f*; *(of mind, intellect)* Beweglichkeit *f*, Flexibilität *f*

suppliant [ˈsʌplɪənt], **supplicant** [ˈsʌplɪkənt] ADJ flehend *attr* N Flehende(r) *mf*, Bittsteller(in) *m(f)*

supplicate [ˈsʌplɪkeɪt] VT *(form)* flehen

supplication [ˌsʌplɪˈkeɪʃən] N Flehen *nt no pl*

supplier [səˈplaɪəʳ] N *(Comm)* Lieferant(in) *m(f)*

supply [səˈplaɪ] N **a** *(= supplying)* Versorgung *f*; *(Comm: = delivery)* Lieferung *f* *(to an +acc)*; *(Econ)* Angebot *nt*; **electricity ~** Stromversorgung *f*; **the ~ of blood to the brain** die Versorgung des Gehirns mit Blut; **~ and demand** Angebot und Nachfrage *(+pl vb)*

b *(= what is supplied)* Lieferung *f*; **to cut off the ~** *(of gas, water etc)* das Gas/Wasser abstellen; **our wholesaler has cut off our ~** unser Großhändler hat die Lieferungen eingestellt; **where does the badger get its food ~?** woher bekommt der Dachs seine Nahrung?

c *(= stock)* Vorrat *m*; **supplies** *pl (= food)* Vorräte *pl*; *(for expedition also, for journey)* Proviant *m*; **a good ~ of coal** ein guter Kohlenvorrat; **to get** *or* **lay in supplies** *or* **a ~ of sth** sich *(dat)* einen Vorrat an etw *(dat)* anlegen *or* zulegen; **a month's ~** ein Monatsbedarf *m*; **to be in short ~** knapp sein; **to be in good ~** reichlich vorhanden sein; **our supplies are running out** unser Vorrat geht *or* unsere Vorräte gehen zu Ende; **fresh supplies** *(Mil)* Nachschub *m*; **office supplies** Bürobedarf *m*, Büromaterial *nt*; **medical supplies** Arzneimittel *pl*; *(including bandages)* Ärztebedarf *m*; **electrical supplies** Elektrowaren *or* -artikel *pl*

d *(= supply teacher)* Aushilfslehrer(in) *m(f)*; **to be on ~** aushilfsweise *or* vertretungsweise unterrichten

e *(Parl)* (Militär- und Verwaltungs)etat *m*

VT **a** *material, food, tools etc* sorgen für; *(= deliver) goods, information, answer, details* liefern; *clue, evidence, gas, electricity* liefern; *(= put at sb's disposal)* stellen; **pens and paper are supplied by the firm** Schreibmaterial wird von der Firma gestellt

b *(with* mit*) person, army, city* versorgen; *(Comm)* beliefern; **she supplies the humour in the office** sie sorgt für (den) Humor im Büro; **this supplied me with the chance ...** das gab mir die Chance ...; **we were not supplied with a radio** wir hatten kein Radio

c *(= satisfy, make good) need* befriedigen; *want, deficiency* abhelfen *(+dat)*; *(Comm) demand* decken

supply: **supply base** N Vorratslager *nt*; **supply day** N *(Parl) Tag, an dem der Haushaltsplan vorgelegt wird*; **supply depot** N Versorgungslager *nt*; **supply industry** N Zulieferungsindustrie *f*; **supply lines, supply routes** PL *(Mil, fig)* Versorgungslinien *pl*; **supply ship** N Versorgungsschiff *nt*; **supply-side economics** N *sing or pl* Angebotswirtschaft *f*; **supply teacher** N *(Brit)* Aushilfslehrer(in) *m(f)*; **supply train** N Versorgungszug *m*

support [səˈpɔːt] ✪ 11.2, 12.2, 13, 26.3 N **a** *(lit)* Stütze *f*; **to give ~ to sb/sth** jdn/etw stützen; **the ceiling will need some kind of ~** die Decke muss irgendwie abgestützt werden; **the bridge ~s** die Stützpfeiler *pl* der Brücke; **to lean on sb for ~** sich auf jdn stützen

b *(fig, no pl: = moral, financial backing)* Unterstützung *f*; *(= person)* Stütze *f*; *(Comput etc)* Support *m*; **in ~ of** zur Unterstützung *(+gen)*; **in ~ of an allegation** zur Untermauerung *or* Stützung einer Behauptung; **to speak in ~ of sb/sth** etw/jdn unterstützen; **to depend on sb for financial ~** auf jds finanzielle Unterstützung angewiesen sein; **our ~ comes from the workers** wir stützen uns auf die Arbeiterschaft

ATTR *(Mil etc)* Hilfs-

VT **a** *(lit)* stützen; *(= bear the weight of)* tragen; **it is ~ed on 4 columns** es wird von 4 Säulen getragen *or* gestützt

b *(fig)* unterstützen *(also Comput)*; *plan, motion, sb's application* befürworten, unterstützen; *party, cause* eintreten für, unterstützen; *(= give moral support to)* beistehen *(+dat)*, Rückhalt geben *(+dat)*; *(= corroborate) claim, theory* erhärten, untermauern; *(financially) family* unterhalten; *party, orchestra* finanziell unterstützen; **he ~s Arsenal** er ist Arsenal-Anhänger *m*; **which team do you ~?** für welche Mannschaft bist du?; **without his family to ~ him** ohne die Unterstützung seiner Familie; **Burton and Taylor, ~ed by X and Y** Burton und Taylor, mit X und Y in den Nebenrollen; **his parents ~ed him through university** seine Eltern haben ihn während seines Studiums finanziell unterstützt

c *(= endure) bad behaviour, tantrums* dulden, ertragen

VR *(physically)* sich stützen *(on* auf *+acc)*; *(financially)* seinen Unterhalt (selbst) bestreiten

supportable [səˈpɔːtəbl] ADJ erträglich

support act N *(Mus)* Vorgruppe *f*

support band N Vorgruppe *f*

supporter [səˈpɔːtəʳ] N Anhänger(in) *m(f)*; *(of theory, cause, opinion also)* Befürworter(in) *m(f)*; *(Sport also)* Fan *m*; **~s' club** Fanklub *m*

support group N Selbsthilfegruppe *f*

supporting [səˈpɔːtɪŋ] ADJ **a** *documents* zur Unterstützung; **~ group** Vorgruppe *f*; **~ role** *(lit, fig)* Nebenrolle *f*; **with full ~ cast** mit vielen anderen (bedeutenden) Darstellern; **with full ~ programme** mit vollem Nebenprogramm **b** *(Tech: = load-bearing)* stützend, tragend; **~ wall** Stützwand *f*

supporting: **supporting actor** N *(Film, Theat)* Nebendarsteller *m*; **supporting actress** N *(Film, Theat)* Nebendarstellerin *f*; **supporting evidence** N Beweise *pl*; **supporting film** N Vorfilm *m*

supportive [səˈpɔːtɪv] ADJ stützend *attr*; *(fig)* unterstützend *attr*; **if his parents had been more ~** wenn seine Eltern ihn mehr unterstützt hätten; **try to be more ~ (of her/me)** du solltest versuchen, sie/mich mehr zu unterstützen; **to be ~ of sb/sth** jdn/etw unterstützen

supportiveness [səˈpɔːtɪvnɪs] N Unterstützung *f*

support tights PL Stützstrumpfhose *f*

support troops PL Hilfstruppen *pl*

suppose [səˈpəʊz] ✪ 1.1, 26.3 VT **a** *(= imagine)* sich *(dat)* vorstellen; *(= assume)* annehmen; **let us ~ we are living in the 8th century** stellen wir uns einmal vor, wir lebten im 8. Jahrhundert; **let us ~ that X equals 3** angenommen, X sei gleich 3; **even supposing it were** *or* **was true** (sogar) angenommen, dass es wahr ist, angenommen, es sei wahr; **always supposing he comes** immer vorausgesetzt, (dass) er kommt; **~ they could see us now!** wenn sie uns jetzt sehen könnten!

b *(= believe, think)* annehmen, denken; **I ~ he'll come** ich nehme an, (dass) er kommt, er wird wohl *or* vermutlich kommen; **I don't ~ he'll come** ich glaube kaum, dass er kommt; **I ~ he won't come** ich denke, er wird nicht kommen, er wird wohl nicht kommen; **I ~ that's the best thing, I ~** das ist *or* wäre vermutlich das Beste; **he's rich, I ~** er muss wohl reich sein; **you're coming, I ~?** ich nehme an, du kommst?; **I don't ~ you could lend me a pound?** Sie könnten mir nicht zufällig ein Pfund leihen?; **do you ~ we could have dinner some evening?** meinen Sie, wir könnten einmal abends zusammen essen gehen?; **will he be coming? – I ~ so** kommt er? – ich denke *or* glaube schon; **you ought to be leaving – I ~ so** du solltest jetzt gehen – stimmt wohl; **don't you agree with me? – I ~ so** bist du da nicht meiner Meinung? – na ja, schon; **I don't ~ so** ich glaube kaum; **isn't he coming? – I ~ not** kommt er nicht? – ich glaube kaum; **so you see, it can't be true – I ~ not** da siehst du selbst, es kann nicht stimmen – du wirst wohl recht haben; **he can't very well refuse, can he? – I ~ not** er kann wohl kaum ablehnen, oder? – eigentlich nicht; **I never ~d him (to be) a hero** ich habe ihn nie für einen Helden gehalten; **he is generally ~d to be rich** er gilt als reich; **he's ~d to be coming** er soll (angeblich) kommen; **and he's ~d to be an expert!** und der soll (angeblich) (ein) Experte sein!

c *(modal use in pass: = ought)* **to be ~d to do sth** etw tun sollen; **he's the one who's ~d to do it** er müsste es eigentlich tun; **you're ~d to be in bed** du solltest eigentlich im Bett sein, du

gehörst eigentlich ins Bett; **he isn't ~d to find out** er darf es nicht erfahren; **you're not ~d to (do that)** das darfst du nicht tun; **I am ~d to start work here today** ich soll hier heute anfangen; **you're ~d to report to the police** Sie müssen sich bei der Polizei melden
d *(in imper. = I suggest)* **~ we have a go?** warum versuchen wir es nicht einmal?; **~ we buy it?** wie wäre es, wenn wir es kauften?; **~ you have a wash?** wie wärs, wenn du dich mal wäschst?
e *(= presuppose)* voraussetzen; **that ~s unlimited resources** das setzt unbegrenzte Vorräte voraus

supposed [sə'pəʊzd] **ADJ** vermutet; *date of birth, site of temple, author also* mutmaßlich; *insult, glamour* angeblich

supposedly [sə'pəʊzɪdlɪ] **ADV** angeblich; **the atom was ~ indivisible** das Atom galt als unteilbar

supposing [sə'pəʊzɪŋ] **CONJ** angenommen; **but ~ …** aber wenn …; **~ he can't do it?** und wenn er es nicht schafft?; **even ~ that …** sogar wenn …; **always ~ …** immer unter der Annahme, dass …

supposition [ˌsʌpə'zɪʃən] **N** *(no pl: = hypothesizing)* Mutmaßung *f*, Spekulation *f*; *(= thing supposed)* Annahme *f*; **based on (a) pure ~** auf reiner Spekulation beruhend; **going on the ~ that you are right** vorausgesetzt, dass Sie recht haben

suppository [sə'pɒzɪtərɪ] **N** Zäpfchen *nt*, Suppositorium *nt (spec)*

suppress [sə'pres] **VT** **a** *feelings, smile, dissent, views, symptoms, protest* unterdrücken; *appetite* zügeln; *information, evidence* zurückhalten **b** *(Elec)* entstören

suppressant [sə'presnt] **N** *(Med) Medikament zur Unterdrückung bestimmter Körperfunktionen* **appetite ~** Appetitzügler *m*

suppression [sə'preʃən] **N** **a** *(of feelings, smile, dissent, views, symptoms, protest)* Unterdrückung *f*; *(of appetite)* Zügelung *f*; *(of information, evidence)* Zurückhalten *nt* **b** *(Elec)* Entstörung *f*

suppressive [sə'presɪv] **ADJ** Unterdrückungs-, repressiv

suppressor [sə'presə'] **N** *(Elec)* Entstörungselement *nt*

suppurate ['sʌpjʊəreɪt] **VI** eitern

suppuration [ˌsʌpjʊə'reɪʃən] **N** Eiterung *f*

supra- ['su:prə-] **PREF** über-; *(esp with foreign words)* supra-; **supranational** überstaatlich, supra- *or* übernational

supremacy [sʊ'preməsɪ] **N** Vormachtstellung *f*; *(Pol, Eccl, fig)* Supremat *nt or m*; **air/naval ~** Luft-/Seeherrschaft *f*

supreme [sʊ'pri:m] **ADJ** **a** *(= highest in authority)* höchste(r, s); *court, Soviet* oberste(r, s) **b** *(= very great) courage, indifference etc* äußerste(r, s), größte(r, s); **with ~ indifference** äußerst *or* völlig unbeteiligt **c** *(= ultimate)* **to make the ~ sacrifice** das höchste Opfer bringen; **the ~ moment of the opera** der Höhepunkt der Oper **ADV to rule** *or* **reign ~** *(monarch)* absolut herrschen; *(champion, justice)* unangefochten herrschen; *(silence)* überall herrschen

Supreme Being **N** höchstes Wesen

supreme commander **N** Oberbefehlshaber(in) *m(f)*

supremely [sʊ'pri:mlɪ] **ADV** *confident, self-satisfied, indifferent* zutiefst; *important, elegant* überaus; **~ gifted** hochbegabt, überaus begabt; **she does her job ~ well** sie macht ihre Arbeit außerordentlich gut

supremo [sʊ'pri:məʊ] **N** *(Brit inf)* Oberboss *m (inf)*

Supt *abbr of* **Superintendent**

surcharge ['sɜ:tʃɑ:dʒ] **N** Zuschlag *m*; *(postal)* Nachporto *nt*, Strafporto *nt (inf)*; **for a small ~** gegen einen geringen Aufschlag **VT** Zuschlag erheben auf *(+acc)*; **he was ~d** er musste Zuschlag bezahlen

surd [sɜ:d] **N** *(Math)* irrationaler Ausdruck

sure [ʃʊə'] ✪ 15.1, 16.1 **ADJ** *(+er)* **a** *(= reliable, steady, safe) hand, touch, marksman, footing, knowledge* sicher; *criterion, proof, facts* eindeutig; *method, remedy, friend* zuverlässig, verlässlich; *understanding* genau; **his aim was ~** er traf sicher ins Ziel; **in the ~ knowledge that …** in der Gewissheit, dass …
b *(= definite)* sicher; **it is ~ that he will come** es ist sicher, dass er kommt, er kommt ganz bestimmt; **it's ~ to rain** es regnet ganz bestimmt; **he was ~ to see her again** es war sicher, dass er sie wiedersehen würde; **be ~ to tell me** sag mir auf jeden Fall Bescheid; **be ~ to turn the gas off** vergiss nicht, das Gas abzudrehen; **be ~ to go and see her** du musst sie unbedingt besuchen; **you're ~ of a good meal/of success** ein gutes Essen/der Erfolg ist Ihnen sicher; **I want to be ~ of seeing him** ich möchte ihn auf jeden Fall sehen; **to make ~** *(= check)* nachsehen, kontrollieren; **to make ~ to do sth** nicht vergessen, etw zu tun; **make ~ you get the leads the right way round** achten Sie darauf, dass die Kabel richtig herum sind; **make ~ you take your keys** denk daran, deine Schlüssel mitzunehmen; **it's best to make ~** sicher ist sicher; **to make ~ of one's facts** sich der Fakten *(gen)* versichern; **to make ~ of a seat** sich *(dat)* einen Platz sichern; **I've made ~ that there's enough coffee for everyone** ich habe dafür gesorgt, dass genug Kaffee für alle da ist; **~ thing!** *(esp US inf)* klare Sache! *(inf)*; **he's a ~ thing for president** *(esp US inf)* er ist ein todsicherer Tipp für die Präsidentschaft; **he'll quit for ~** er kündigt ganz bestimmt; **I'll find out for ~** ich werde das genau herausfinden; **do you know for ~?** wissen Sie das ganz sicher?; **to be ~!** Mensch!, tatsächlich!; **and there he was, to be ~** *(esp Ir)* und da war er doch tatsächlich!
c *(= positive, convinced)* sicher; **I'm ~ she's right** ich bin sicher, sie hat recht; **do you want to see that film? – I'm not ~** willst du diesen Film sehen? – ich bin mir nicht sicher; **I'm perfectly ~** ich bin (mir da) ganz sicher; **to be ~ about sth** sich *(dat)* einer Sache *(gen)* sicher sein; **I'm not so ~ about that** da bin ich nicht so sicher; **to be ~ of one's facts** seiner Fakten sicher sein; **to be ~ about** *or* **of sb** *(= confident)* sich bei jdm *or* über jdn sicher sein; **to be ~ of oneself** sich *(dat)* seiner Sache sicher sein; *(= generally self-confident)* selbstsicher sein; **I'm ~ I don't know, I don't know, I'm ~** ich habe keine Ahnung; **I'm not ~ how/why …** ich bin (mir) nicht sicher *or* ich weiß nicht genau, wie/warum …
ADV **a** *(inf)* **will you do it? – ~!** machst du das? – klar! *(inf)*; **that meat was ~ tough** *or* **~ was tough** das Fleisch war vielleicht zäh!; **know what I mean? – ~ do** du weißt, was ich meine? – aber sicher *or* aber klar *(inf)*; **that's ~ pretty** *(US)* das ist doch schön, nicht?
b and ~ enough he did come und er ist tatsächlich gekommen; **he'll come ~ enough** er kommt ganz bestimmt, er kommt schon; **it's blood ~ enough** es ist tatsächlich Blut
c as ~ as ~ can be *(inf)* **as ~ as I'm standing here** *(inf)* garantiert, todsicher *(inf)*

sure: **sure-fire** **ADJ** *(inf)* todsicher *(inf)*, bombensicher *(inf)*; **sure-footed** **ADJ** (tritt)sicher; *(fig: = confident)* selbstsicher

surely ['ʃʊəlɪ] **ADV** **a** bestimmt, sicher; **~ you don't mean it?** das meinen Sie doch bestimmt *or* sicher nicht (so)?; **~ he's come(, hasn't he?)** er ist doch bestimmt gekommen(, oder?); **~ he hasn't come(, has he)?** er ist doch bestimmt *or* sicher nicht gekommen(, oder?); **~ not!** das kann doch nicht stimmen!; **~ someone must know the answer** irgendjemand muss doch die Antwort wissen; **there must ~ be something we can do** irgendetwas müssen wir doch (sicher) tun können; **I can't – oh, ~ you can** ich kann (es) nicht – aber sicher kannst du das!; **but ~ you can't expect us to believe that** Sie können doch wohl nicht erwarten, dass wir das glauben!; **~ if a equals b, then c must …** also, wenn a gleich b ist, dann muss c doch sicherlich …; **~ to God** *or* **goodness** *(inf)* sicherlich
b *(esp US: = gladly)* gern, mit Vergnügen
c *(= inevitably, with certainty)* zweifellos
d *(= undoubtedly)* **he is an artist, just as ~ as Rembrandt was** er ist ein Künstler, genauso wie Rembrandt einer war
e *(= confidently)* mit sicherer Hand; **slowly but ~** langsam aber sicher

sureness ['ʃʊənɪs] **N** **a** *(= positiveness, conviction)* Überzeugung *f*, Sicherheit *f* **b** *(= reliability, steadiness, sure-footedness)* Sicherheit *f*; *(of method, cure, sb's judgement)* Verlässlichkeit *f*, Zuverlässigkeit *f*; **~ of touch** *(Sport)* Treffsicherheit *f*; *(fig)* glückliche Hand

surety ['ʃʊərətɪ] **N** **a** *(= sum)* Bürgschaft *f*, Sicherheit *f*; *(= person)* Bürge *m*, Bürgin *f*; **to stand ~ for sb** für jdn bürgen; **he was granted bail with a ~ of £5,000** er wurde gegen Hinterlegung einer Kaution von £ 5.000 auf freien Fuß gesetzt **b** *(obs, = certainty)* Sicherheit *f*, Gewissheit *f*; **of a ~** gewiss, sicherlich

surf [sɜ:f] **N** Brandung *f* **VI** surfen **VT to ~ the waves** surfen, wellenreiten; **to ~ the Net** *(inf)* im Netz *or* (Inter)net surfen *(inf)*

surface ['sɜ:fɪs] **N** **a** *(lit, fig)* Oberfläche *f*; *(of road)* Decke *f*, Belag *m*; **on the ~ it seems that …** oberflächlich sieht es so aus, als ob …; **on the ~ he is friendly enough** nach außen hin ist er sehr freundlich **b** *(Math, of cube etc)* Fläche *f* **c** *(Min)* **at/on/up to the ~** über Tage **d** *(Aviat)* Tragfläche *f* **ADJ** *attr* **a** oberflächlich; **~ texture** Oberflächenstruktur *f* **b** *(= not by air) travel* auf dem Land-/Seeweg **c** *(Min) worker, job* über Tage **VT** **a** *road* mit einem Belag versehen; *wall* verblenden **b** *submarine* auftauchen lassen **VI** *(lit, fig)* auftauchen

surface: **surface area** **N** Fläche *f*; *(Math)* Flächeninhalt *m*; **surface dressing** **N** *(on roads, = method)* Straßenreparatur *f* mit Rollsplitt; *(= material)* Rollsplitt *m*; **surface grammar** **N** Oberflächengrammatik *f*; **surface mail** **N** Post *f* auf dem Land-/Seeweg; **by ~** auf dem Land-/Seeweg; **surface-mounted** **ADJ** oberflächenmontiert; **surface noise** **N** Rauschen *nt*; **surface structure** **N** *(Ling)* Oberflächenstruktur *f*; **surface tension** **N** Oberflächenspannung *f*; **surface-to-air** **ADJ** *attr* Boden-Luft-; **~ missile** Boden-Luft-Rakete *f*; **surface-to-surface** **ADJ** *attr* Boden-Boden-; **~ missile** Boden-Boden-Rakete *f*; **surface vessel** **N** Schiff *nt (im Gegensatz zu Unterseeboot)*

surfacing ['sɜ:fɪsɪŋ] **N** **what did they use as ~ for the roads/walls?** was für ein Material wurde für den Straßenbelag/als Wandbelag verwendet?

surfactant [sɜ:'fæktənt] **N** *(Chem)* Tensid *nt*

surfboard ['sɜ:fbɔ:d] **N** Surfbrett *nt*

surfeit ['sɜ:fɪt] **N** Übermaß *nt*, Zuviel *nt* (of an *+dat*) **VT** *sb, oneself* übersättigen, überfüttern (on, with mit)

surfer ['sɜ:fə'] **N** Surfer(in) *m(f)*, Wellenreiter(in) *m(f)*; *(on Internet)* (Net-)Surfer(in) *m(f)*

surfing ['sɜ:fɪŋ] **N** Surfen *nt*, Surfing *nt*, Wellenreiten *nt*; **a good ~ beach** ein guter Strand zum Surfen *or* Wellenreiten

surge [sɜ:dʒ] **N** *(of sea)* Wogen *nt*; *(of floodwater)* Schwall *m*; *(Elec)* Spannungsstoß *m*; **a ~ of people** eine wogende Menschenmenge; **there was a ~ of sympathy for him** es gab eine Sympathiewelle für ihn; **he felt a sudden ~ of rage** er fühlte, wie die Wut in ihm aufstieg; **a ~ in demand/exports** ein rascher Nachfrage-/Exportanstieg
VI *(sea)* branden; *(floods, river)* anschwellen; *(demand, exports)* rasch ansteigen; **blood ~d to her head** ihr schoss das Blut ins Gesicht; **they ~d toward(s)/(a)round him** sie drängten auf ihn zu/umdrängten ihn; **people ~d in/out** eine Menschenmenge flutete herein/heraus; **to ~ ahead/forward** vorpreschen

surgeon ['sɜ:dʒən] **N** Chirurg(in) *m(f)*; *(Mil)* Stabsarzt *m*/-ärztin *f*; *(Naut)* Marinearzt *m*/-ärztin *f* → **dental surgeon, veterinary surgeon**

surgeon general **N** *(Mil)* Sanitätsinspekteur(in) *m(f)*; *(US)* ≈ Gesundheitsminister(in) *m(f)*

surgery ['sɜːdʒərɪ] N **a** Chirurgie *f*; **to have ~** operiert werden; **to need (heart) ~** (am Herzen) operiert werden müssen; **to undergo major heart ~** sich einer größeren Herzoperation unterziehen; **~ is the only solution** Operieren ist die einzige Lösung; **a fine piece of ~** eine großartige chirurgische Leistung **b** *(Brit: = room)* Sprechzimmer *nt*; *(= consultation)* Sprechstunde *f*; **~ hours** Sprechstunden *pl*; **when is his ~?** wann hat er Sprechstunde?

surgical ['sɜːdʒɪkəl] ADJ *treatment, removal* operativ; *technique, instrument, training, skill, hospital* chirurgisch; **~ corset** Stützkorsett *nt*; **~ gloves** OP-Handschuhe *pl*, Chirurgenhandschuhe *pl*; **~ goods shop** orthopädisches Fachgeschäft; **~ intervention** chirurgischer Eingriff; **~ strike** *(Mil)* gezielter Angriff; **~ team** OP-Team *nt*, Chirurgenteam *nt*; **~ ward** chirurgische Station, Chirurgie *f (inf)*

surgical: **surgical appliance** N Stützapparat *m*; **surgical boot** N orthopädischer Schuh; **surgical gown** N OP-Kleidung *f*

surgically ['sɜːdʒɪkəlɪ] ADV *treat, remove* operativ; **~, we have advanced a long way** wir haben in der Chirurgie große Fortschritte gemacht

surgical mask N OP-Maske *f*

surgical spirit N *(Brit)* Wundbenzin *nt*

surgicenter ['sɜːdʒɪˌsentə'] N *(US Med)* Poliklinik *f*

surging ['sɜːdʒɪŋ] ADJ *water, corn, crowd* wogend; *price, power, demand, exports, imports* rasch ansteigend

Surinam, **Suriname** [ˌsʊərɪ'næm] N Suriname *nt*

surliness ['sɜːlɪnɪs] N Verdrießlichkeit *f*, Missmutigkeit *f*

surly ['sɜːlɪ] ADJ *(+er)* verdrießlich, mürrisch, missmutig

surmise ['sɜːmaɪz] N Vermutung *f*, Mutmaßung *f* VT [sɜː'maɪz] vermuten, mutmaßen; **I ~d as much** das hatte ich (schon) vermutet; **as one could ~ from his book** wie man nach seinem Buch vermuten *or* mutmaßen konnte

surmount [sɜː'maʊnt] VT **a** *difficulty, obstacle* überwinden **b** *(esp Archit, Her etc)* **~ed by sth** von *or* mit etw gekrönt

surmountable [sɜː'maʊntəbl] ADJ überwindlich, zu überwinden

surname ['sɜːneɪm] N Nachname *m*, Familienname *m*; **what is his ~?** wie heißt er mit Nachnamen?

surpass [sɜː'pɑːs] VT **a** *(= be better than)* übertreffen **b** *(= exceed) comprehension* hinausgehen über *(+acc)*; **to ~ all expectations** alle Erwartungen übertreffen VR sich selbst übertreffen

surpassing [sɜː'pɑːsɪŋ] ADJ *(liter) beauty* unvergleichlich

surplice ['sɜːpləs] N Chorrock *m*, Chorhemd *nt*

surplus ['sɜːpləs] N Überschuss *m (of an +dat)*; **a balance of trade ~** ein Überschuss *m* in der Handelsbilanz ADJ überschüssig; *(of countable objects)* überzählig; **~ value** Mehrwert *m*; **Army ~ boots** Stiefel *pl*; **sale of ~ stock** Verkauf *m* von Lagerbeständen; **have you any ~ sheets I could borrow?** hast du Laken übrig, die ich mir borgen könnte?; **it is ~ to (my) requirements** das benötige ich nicht; **~ store** *Geschäft, das billig Lagerbestände verkauft*

surprise [sə'praɪz] ✪ 15.2, 16.1, 16.2 N Überraschung *f*; **in ~** voller Überraschung, überrascht; **much to my ~, to my great ~** zu meiner großen Überraschung; **with a look of ~** mit überraschtem Gesicht; **it was a ~ (for** *or* **to me) to find that …** ich war überrascht, als ich entdeckte, dass …; **it came as a ~ to us** wir waren überrascht, es hat uns überrascht; **what a ~!** was für eine Überraschung!; **to give sb a ~** jdn überraschen; **to take sb by ~** jdn überraschen; **~, ~, it's me!** rate mal, wer hier ist?; **~, ~!** *(iro)* was du nicht sagst!

ATTR Überraschungs-, überraschend; **~ attack** Überraschungsangriff *m*; **~ success** Überraschungserfolg *m*; **~ winner** Überraschungssieger(in) *m(f)*

VT überraschen; *(= catch unawares also) army, sentry* überrumpeln; *thief* (auf frischer Tat) ertappen; **you ~ me!** *(also iro)* das überrascht mich!; **I was ~d to hear it** ich war überrascht, das zu hören; **I wouldn't be ~d if …** es würde mich nicht wundern, wenn …; **don't be ~d if he refuses** wundern Sie sich nicht, wenn er ablehnt; **it's nothing to be ~d at** das ist nicht weiter verwunderlich; **I'm ~d at** *or* **by his ignorance** ich bin überrascht über seine Unkenntnis; **I'm ~d you didn't think of that** es wundert mich, dass du nicht daran gedacht hast; **go on, ~ me!** ich lass mich überraschen!; **he ~d me into agreeing** er hat mich so verblüfft, dass ich zugestimmt habe

surprising [sə'praɪzɪŋ] ADJ überraschend, erstaunlich; **there's nothing ~ about that** das ist nicht weiter verwunderlich; **it's hardly ~ he said no** es ist kaum verwunderlich, dass er nein *or* Nein gesagt hat

surprisingly [sə'praɪzɪŋlɪ] ADV *big, successful* überraschend; **~ (enough), he was right** er hatte erstaunlicherweise recht; **and then ~ he left** und dann ist er überraschenderweise *or* zu unserer/ihrer *etc* Überraschung gegangen; **not ~ it didn't work** wie zu erwarten (war), hat es nicht geklappt

surreal [sə'rɪəl] ADJ unwirklich

surrealism [sə'rɪəlɪzəm] N Surrealismus *m*

surrealist [sə'rɪəlɪst] ADJ surrealistisch N Surrealist(in) *m(f)*

surrealistic [səˌrɪə'lɪstɪk] ADJ **a** surrealistisch **b** *(= surreal)* unwirklich

surrender [sə'rendə'] VI sich ergeben *(to +dat)*; *(to police)* sich stellen *(to +dat)*; **I ~!** ich ergebe mich!

VT *(Mil)* übergeben; *firearms also, control, power, title, lead* abgeben; *goods, suspect* ausliefern; *insurance policy* einlösen; *lease* kündigen; *claim, right, hope* aufgeben

VR **to ~ oneself to sth** sich einer Sache *(dat)* hingeben; *to fate* sich in etw *(acc)* ergeben

N **a** *(Mil: = capitulation)* Kapitulation *f (to* vor *+dat)*

b *(= handing over)* Übergabe *f (to* an *+acc)*; *(of control, power, title, lead)* Abgabe *f*; *(of suspect)* Auslieferung *f*, Aushändigung *f (to* an *+acc)*; *(of insurance policy)* Einlösen *nt*; *(of lease)* Kündigung *f*; *(of claim, right, hope)* Aufgabe *f*, Preisgabe *f*; **~ value** *(Insur)* Rückgabe- *or* Rückkaufswert *m*

surreptitious [ˌsʌrəp'tɪʃəs] ADJ heimlich; *whisper, glance, kiss also* verstohlen; **he made a few ~ changes** er machte heimlich ein paar Änderungen

surreptitiously [ˌsʌrəp'tɪʃəslɪ] ADV heimlich

surrey ['sʌrɪ] N *(US)* zweisitzige Kutsche

surrogacy ['sʌrəgəsɪ] N Leihmutterschaft *m*

surrogate ['sʌrəgɪt] N *(= substitute)* Ersatz *m*, Surrogat *nt (geh)* *(Brit, Eccl)* ≈ Weihbischof *m* ATTR Ersatz-; **~ bishop** ≈ Weihbischof *m*

surrogate: **surrogate family** N Ersatzfamilie *f*; **surrogate mother** N Leihmutter *f*; **surrogate motherhood** N Leihmutterschaft *f*

surround [sə'raʊnd] N *(esp Brit)* Umrandung *f*; *(= floor round carpet)* Ränder *pl*; **the ~s** die Umgebung VT umgeben; *(Mil)* umstellen, umzingeln; **she was ~ed by children/suitors** sie war von Kindern umgeben/von Verehrern umgeben *or* umschwärmt

surrounding [sə'raʊndɪŋ] ADJ umliegend; **in the ~ countryside** in der Umgebung *or* Umgegend; **in the ~ darkness** in der Dunkelheit, die mich/ihn *etc* umgab; **~ tissue** *(Med)* Bindegewebe *nt*

surroundings [sə'raʊndɪŋz] PL Umgebung *f*; **the ~ of Glasgow** die Umgebung von Glasgow

surround sound N *(TV, Radio)* Surround-Sound *m*; *(= sytem)* Surround-Sound-System *nt*

surtax ['sɜːtæks] N Steuerzuschlag *m*

surtitle ['sɜːˌtaɪtl] N *(in opera etc)* Übertitel *m*

surveillance [sɜː'veɪləns] N Überwachung *f*, Observation *f (form)*; **to be under ~** überwacht *or* observiert *(form)* werden; **to keep sb under ~** jdn überwachen *or* observieren *(form)*

survey ['sɜːveɪ] N **a** *(Surv, of land, coast)* Vermessung *f*; *(= report)* (Vermessungs)gutachten *nt*; *(of house)* Begutachtung *f*; *(= report)* Gutachten *nt*; **they are doing a ~ for a new motorway** sie führen Vermessungsarbeiten für eine neue Autobahn durch; **to have a ~ done on a house** ein Gutachten über ein Haus erstellen lassen

b *(= inquiry)* Untersuchung *f (of, on* über *+acc)*; *(by opinion poll, market research etc)* Umfrage *f (of, on* über *+acc)*

c *(= comprehensive look, review, of surroundings, countryside)* Musterung *f (of +gen)*, Überblick *m (of* über *+acc)*; *(of subject, recent development)* Überblick *m*

VT [sɜː'veɪ] **a** *(= look at) countryside, person, prospects, plans* betrachten, sich *(dat)* ansehen; *(esp appraisingly)* begutachten; *person, goods* mustern; **to ~ the situation** *(lit, fig)* die Lage peilen; **he is monarch of all he ~s** er beherrscht das Land, soweit er blicken kann

b *(= study) prospects, developments* untersuchen; *institutions* einer Prüfung *(gen)* unterziehen; *(= take general view of) events, trends* einen Überblick geben über *(+acc)*

c *(Surv) site, land* vermessen; *building* inspizieren

surveying [sɜː'veɪɪŋ] N **a** *(of site, land)* Vermessung *f*; *(of building)* Inspektion *f* **b** *(= profession)* Landvermessung *f*; *(of buildings)* Inspektion *f* von Gebäuden

surveyor [sə'veɪə'] N *(= land surveyor)* Landvermesser(in) *m(f)*; *(= building surveyor)* Bauinspektor(in) *m(f)*, Baugutachter(in) *m(f)*

survival [sə'vaɪvəl] N **a** Überleben *nt*; *(of customs, usages)* Weiterleben *nt*; **the ~ of the fittest** das Überleben der Stärkeren; **his ~ as prime minister seems unlikely** es ist unwahrscheinlich, dass er sich als Premierminister halten kann; **~ bag** Expeditionsschlafsack *m* **b** *(= relic)* Überbleibsel *nt (of, from* aus)

survival instinct N Überlebensinstinkt *m*

survivalist [sə'vaɪvəlɪst] N Überlebenskünstler(in) *m(f)*

survival kit N Überlebensausrüstung *f*

survive [sə'vaɪv] VI *(person, animal etc)* überleben, am Leben bleiben; *(in job)* sich halten (können); *(house, treasures, book, play)* erhalten bleiben; *(custom, religion)* weiterleben, fortbestehen; **only five copies ~** *or* **have ~d** nur fünf Exemplare sind erhalten; **will this play ~ despite the critics?** wird sich das Stück trotz der Kritiken halten?; **you'll ~** *(iro)* das wirst du schon überleben!; **he ~d to tell the tale** er hat als Zeuge überlebt; *(hum)* er hat es überlebt *(hum)*

VT überleben; *experience, accident also* (lebend) überstehen; *(house, objects) fire, flood* überstehen; *(inf) heat, boredom etc* aushalten; **to ~ the ages** die Jahrhunderte überdauern; **he was ~d by his wife** seine Frau überlebte ihn

surviving [sə'vaɪvɪŋ] ADJ **a** *(= still living)* noch lebend; **the oldest ~ member of the family** das älteste noch lebende Mitglied der Familie **b** *(= remaining)* noch existierend; **the largest ~ shipyard** die größte noch produzierende Werft

survivor [sə'vaɪvə'] N Überlebende(r) *mf*; *(Jur)* Hinterbliebene(r) *mf*; *(of abuse etc)* Opfer *nt*; **he's a ~** *(fig, in politics etc)* er ist ein Überlebenskünstler; **she is the sole ~ of the winning team** sie ist die einzige noch lebende Vertreterin der siegreichen Mannschaft

Susan ['suːzn] N Susanne *f*

susceptibility [səˌseptə'bɪlɪtɪ] N **a** *no pl* **~ to sth** *(to charms, flattery etc)* Empfänglichkeit *f* für etw; *to attack* Ausgesetztsein *nt (to sth* gegenüber etw); *to rheumatism, colds* Anfälligkeit *f* für etw; **~ to pain** Schmerzempfindlichkeit *f*; **~ to treatment** Behandelbarkeit *f*; **~ to unkind remarks** Empfindlichkeit *f* in Bezug auf unfreundliche Bemerkungen; **his ~ to her tears/pleas** dass er sich durch ihre Tränen/Bitten erweichen lässt/ließ **b** **susceptibilities** PL *(= sensibilities)* Feingefühl *nt*

susceptible [sə'septəbl] ADJ **a** *(= impressionable)* beeindruckbar, leicht zu beeindrucken *pred*; **~ to sth** *(to charms, flattery etc)* für etw empfänglich; *to kindness, suggestion, influence etc* einer Sache *(dat)* zugänglich; *to attack* einer Sache *(dat)* ausgesetzt; *to rheumatism, colds* für etw anfällig; **~ to pain** schmerzempfindlich; **~ to treatment** behandelbar; **he's very ~ to remarks about his big nose** er reagiert sehr empfindlich auf Anspielungen auf seine große Nase; **he was ~ to her tears/pleas** er ließ sich von ihren Tränen/Bitten erweichen
b *(form)* **to be ~ of proof** beweisbar sein; **to be ~ of interpretation** Interpretationssache sein

suspect ['sʌspekt] ADJ verdächtig, suspekt
N ['sʌspekt] Verdächtige(r) *mf*
VT [sə'spekt] **a** *person* verdächtigen *(of sth* einer Sache *gen)*, in Verdacht haben; *plot, swindle* vermuten, ahnen, argwöhnen *(geh)*; **I ~ her of having stolen it/written it** ich habe sie im Verdacht *or* ich verdächtige sie, es gestohlen/geschrieben zu haben; **he is ~ed of being a member of this sect, he is a ~ed member of this sect** er steht im Verdacht *or* man verdächtigt ihn, Mitglied dieser Sekte zu sein; **the ~ed bank robber/terrorist** *etc* der mutmaßliche Bankräuber/Terrorist *etc*; **he ~s nothing** er ahnt nichts; **does he ~ anything?** hat er Verdacht geschöpft?
b *(= doubt) truth* bezweifeln, anzweifeln; *motive* argwöhnisch sein gegenüber
c *(= think likely)* vermuten; **I ~ed as much** das habe ich doch vermutet *or* geahnt, das habe ich mir doch gedacht; **a ~ed case of measles** ein Fall, bei dem Verdacht auf Masern besteht; **he was taken to hospital with a ~ed heart attack** er wurde mit dem Verdacht auf Herzinfarkt ins Krankenhaus eingeliefert; **~ed cases of child abuse** mögliche Fälle von Kindesmissbrauch
VI [sə'spekt] einen Verdacht haben

suspend [sə'spend] VT **a** *(= hang)* (auf)hängen *(from* an *+dat)*; *(Chem)* suspendieren; **to be ~ed in sth** in etw *(dat)* hängen; *(Chem)* in etw *(dat)* suspendiert sein; **to hang ~ed from sth/in sth** von/in etw *(dat)* hängen
b *(= stop, defer) publication, payment* (zeitweilig) einstellen; *campaign, talks, judgement* aussetzen; *flights* aufschieben; **he was given a ~ed sentence** seine Strafe wurde zur Bewährung ausgesetzt; **to be in a state of ~ed animation** im Zustand vorübergehender Leblosigkeit sein; **to ~ one's disbelief** *(Theat)* sich verzaubern lassen; **~** *(Comput: command)* Standby-Modus *m*
c *person* suspendieren; *member, pupil, student* zeitweilig ausschließen; *(Sport)* sperren; *licence* zeitweilig einziehen; *law, privileges* aussetzen; *constitution* zeitweilig außer Kraft setzen; **to ~ sb from duty** jdn (vom Dienst) suspendieren

suspender [sə'spendə'] N *usu pl* **a** *(Brit, for stockings)* Strumpfhalter *m*, Straps *m*; *(for socks)* Sockenhalter *m*; **~ belt** Strumpf(halter)gürtel *m* **b** *(US)* **suspenders** PL Hosenträger *pl*

suspense [sə'spens] N *(in book, film etc)* Spannung *f*; **the ~ is killing me** ich bin gespannt wie ein Regenschirm *(hum inf)*; **to keep sb in ~** jdn in Spannung halten, jdn auf die Folter spannen *(inf)*; **to wait in ~** gespannt *or* voller Spannung warten

suspense account N Interimskonto *nt*

suspenseful [sə'spensfʊl] ADJ spannend

suspenser [sə'spensə'] N *(inf)* Thriller *m*, spannender Film

suspension [sə'spenʃən] N **a** *(of publication, payment)* zeitweilige Einstellung; *(of flights)* Aufschub *m*; *(of campaign, talks, judgement)* Aussetzung *f*; *(of prison sentence)* Aussetzung *f (zur Bewährung)* **b** *(of person)* Suspendierung *f*; *(of member, pupil, student)* zeitweiliger Ausschluss; *(Sport)* Sperrung *f*; *(of laws, privileges)* Aussetzen *nt*; **he got** *or* **received a five-match ~** er wurde für fünf Spiele gesperrt **c** *(Aut)* Federung *f*; *(of wheels)* Aufhängung *f* **d** *(Chem)* Suspension *f* **e** *(Mus)* **to be in ~** suspendiert sein, gehalten werden

suspension: **suspension bridge** N Hängebrücke *f*; **suspension file** N Hängemappe *f*; **suspension point** N *(Typ)* Auslassungspunkt *m*

suspensory [sə'spensərɪ] ADJ *(Anat)* Aufhänge-; **~ ligament** Aufhängeband *nt*

suspicion [sə'spɪʃən] N **a** Verdacht *m no pl*, Argwohn *m no pl (geh)*; **to arouse sb's ~s** jds Verdacht *or* Argwohn *(geh)* erregen; **I have a ~ that …** ich habe den Verdacht *or* das Gefühl, dass …; **to have one's ~s about sth/sb** seine Zweifel bezüglich einer Sache *(gen)*/bezüglich einer Person *(gen)* haben; **my ~s were right** mein Verdacht hat sich bestätigt; **to be above (all) ~** über jeden Verdacht erhaben sein; **to be under ~** unter Verdacht stehen; **to arrest sb on ~/on ~ of murder** jdn wegen Tatverdachts/Mordverdachts festnehmen; **to be open to ~** sich verdächtig machen; **~ fell on him** der Verdacht fiel auf ihn; **to view sb/sth with ~** jdn/etw argwöhnisch *or* misstrauisch betrachten
b *(= trace, touch)* Hauch *m*, Spur *f*

suspicious [sə'spɪʃəs] ADJ **a** *(= feeling suspicion)* argwöhnisch, misstrauisch (*of* gegenüber); **you have a ~ mind** Sie sind aber misstrauisch; **to be ~ about sth** etw mit Misstrauen *or* Argwohn *(geh)* betrachten **b** *(= causing suspicion)* verdächtig; **there were no ~ circumstances** es gab keine verdächtigen Umstände; **he died in ~ circumstances** er starb unter verdächtigen *or* zweifelhaften Umständen; **the police are treating her death as ~** die Polizei betrachtet ihren Tod als nicht natürlich

suspiciously [sə'spɪʃəslɪ] ADV **a** *(= with suspicion) examine, glance, ask* argwöhnisch, misstrauisch **b** *(= causing suspicion) behave, act* verdächtig **c** *(= probably)* verdächtig; **it looks ~ like measles to me** das sieht mir verdächtig nach Masern aus; **it sounds ~ as though …** es hört sich verdächtig danach an, als ob …

suspiciousness [sə'spɪʃəsnɪs] N **a** *(= feeling suspicion)* Verdacht *m*, Argwohn *m (geh)* **b** *(= causing suspicion)* Verdächtigkeit *f*

suss [sʌs] VT *(Brit inf)* **a** *(= suspect) plan* kommen hinter *(+acc) (inf)*; **to ~ it** dahinterkommen *(inf)*; **as soon as he ~ed what was going on** sobald er dahinterkam, was da gespielt wurde *(inf)* **b** **to ~ sb out** jdm auf den Zahn fühlen *(inf)*; **I can't ~ him out** bei ihm blicke ich nicht durch *(inf)*; **I've got him ~ed (out)** ich habe ihn durchschaut; **to ~ sth out** etw herausbekommen; **to ~ things out** die Lage peilen *(inf)*

sussed [sʌst] ADJ *(Brit inf: = knowledgeable)* bewandert; *(= clever)* clever

sustain [sə'steɪn] VT **a** *(= support) load, weight* aushalten, tragen; *life* erhalten; *family* unterhalten; *charity* unterstützen; *(= nourish) body* bei Kräften halten; **not enough to ~ life** nicht genug zum Leben; **that isn't enough food to ~ you** das wird Ihnen nicht reichen; **his love has ~ed her over the years** seine Liebe hat ihr über die Jahre hinweg viel Kraft gegeben
b *(= keep going, maintain) pretence, argument, theory, effort, veto, interest, support* aufrechterhalten; *growth, position* beibehalten; *(Mus) note* (aus)halten; *(Theat) accent, characterization* durchhalten; *(Jur) objection* stattgeben *(+dat)*; **objection ~ed** Einspruch stattgegeben → *also* **sustained**
c *(= receive) injury, damage, loss* erleiden; **to ~ an attack** angegriffen werden

sustainability [səs,teɪnə'bɪlɪtɪ] N *(of development, growth, recovery)* Nachhaltigkeit *f*; *(of argument)* Haltbarkeit *f*; *(of position)* Vertretbarkeit *f*

sustainable [sə'steɪnəbl] ADJ aufrechtzuerhalten *pred*, aufrechtzuerhaltend *attr*; *development, recovery, agriculture, forestry* nachhaltig; *resources* erneuerbar; *growth* nachhaltig, kontinuierlich; *level, situation, argument* haltbar; *position* vertretbar

sustained [sə'steɪnd] ADJ *effort etc* ausdauernd; *applause also, attack, pressure* anhaltend; *(Mus) note* (aus)gehalten; *(Econ) economic growth, recovery, recession* anhaltend

sustaining [sə'steɪnɪŋ] ADJ *food* nahrhaft, kräftig

sustaining pedal N *(Mus)* Fortepedal *nt*

sustaining program N *(US Rad, TV)* nichtkommerzielle *or* nicht kommerzielle Sendung

sustenance ['sʌstɪnəns] N *(= food and drink)* Nahrung *f*; *(= nutritive quality)* Nährwert *m*; **to get one's ~ from sth** sich von etw ernähren

susurration [,sju:sə'reɪʃən] N *(liter)* Säuseln *nt (liter)*

suture ['su:tʃə'] *(Med)* N Naht *f* VT (ver)nähen

SUV N *(esp US Aut) abbr of* **sport utility vehicle** Sport-utility-Fahrzeug *nt*, geländegängige Limousine

suzerainty ['su:zəreɪntɪ] N Suzeränität *f*

svelte [svelt] ADJ *(= slender)* grazil; *(= sophisticated)* vornehm, elegant

Svengali [sven'gɑ:lɪ] N *jd, der den Willen anderer, normalerweise mit finsteren Absichten, beherrscht*

SVGA *(Comput) abbr of* **super video graphics array** SVGA *nt*

SW *abbr* **a** *of* **south-west** SW **b** *of* **short wave** KW

swab [swɒb] N **a** *(Med)* Tupfer *m*; *(= specimen)* Abstrich *m*; **to take a ~** einen Abstrich machen **b** *(Naut)* Mop *m* VT **a** *(Med) wound etc* (ab)tupfen **b** *(Naut: also* **swab down***)* wischen

Swabia ['sweɪbɪə] N Schwaben *nt*

Swabian ['sweɪbɪən] ADJ schwäbisch N **a** Schwabe *m*, Schwäbin *f* **b** *(Ling)* Schwäbisch *nt*

swacked [swækt] ADJ *(esp US inf)* **a** *(from alcohol)* blau *(inf)* **b** *(from taking drugs)* high *(inf)*

swaddle ['swɒdl] VT *baby* wickeln *(in* in *+acc)*; **swaddling clothes** *(esp Bibl)* Windeln *pl*

swag [swæg] N *(inf)* Beute *f*

swagger ['swægə'] N **a** *(= gait)* Stolzieren *nt*; *(= behaviour)* Angeberei *f*, Großtuerei *f*; **to walk with a ~** stolzieren VI **a** *(= strut)* stolzieren; **he ~ed down the street/over to our table** er stolzierte die Straße hinunter/zu unserem Tisch herüber **b** *(= boast, act boastfully)* angeben

swaggerer [swægərə'] N Großtuer(in) *m(f)*

swaggering ['swægərɪŋ] ADJ **a** *gait, manner* forsch **b** *(= boastful)* großtuerisch, angeberisch N Großtuerei *f*, Angeberei *f*; **his ~ about** sein Herumstolzieren *nt*

swagger stick N Offiziersstöckchen *nt*

Swahili [swɑ'hi:lɪ] N *(= African language)* Suaheli *nt*

swain [sweɪn] N *(old, = suitor)* Freier *m*; *(= lad)* Bursch(e) *m*

SWALK [swɔ:lk] *abbr of* **sealed with a loving kiss** *(auf Briefumschlägen)*

swallow[1] ['swɒləʊ] N Schluck *m* VT *food, drink* (hinunter)schlucken; *(fig) story, evidence, insult* schlucken; **to ~ one's tongue** *(Med)* sich an seiner Zunge verschlucken; **to ~ one's pride** seinen Stolz schlucken; **to ~ sth whole** *(lit)* etw ganz schlucken; *(fig)* etw ohne weiteres schlucken; **that's a bit hard to ~** das glaubt ja kein Mensch *(inf)*; **to ~ one's words** *(= retract)* seine Worte zurücknehmen → **bait** VI schlucken; **to ~ hard** *(fig)* kräftig schlucken

▶ **swallow down** VT *sep* hinunterschlucken

▶ **swallow up** VT *sep (fig)* verschlingen; **the mist/darkness seemed to swallow them up** der Nebel/die Dunkelheit schien sie zu verschlucken; **I wished the ground would open and swallow me up** ich hätte vor Scham in den Boden versinken können

swallow² N *(= bird)* Schwalbe *f*; **one ~ doesn't make a summer** *(prov)* eine Schwalbe macht noch keinen Sommer *(Prov)*

swallow: **swallow dive** N Schwalbensprung *m*; **swallowtail** [ˈswɒləʊteɪl] N *(= butterfly)* Schwalbenschwanz *m*; **swallow-tailed coat** [ˈswɒləʊteɪldˈkəʊt] N Schwalbenschwanz *m*

swam [swæm] *pret of* **swim**

swamp [swɒmp] N Sumpf *m* VT unter Wasser setzen, überschwemmen; *(fig: = overwhelm)* überschwemmen; **to be ~ed with sth** mit etw überschwemmt werden

swamp: **swamp buggy** N Sumpffahrzeug *nt*; **swamp fever** N Sumpffieber *nt*; **swampland** [ˈswɒmplænd] N Sumpfland *nt*, Sumpf *m*

swampy [ˈswɒmpɪ] ADJ *(+er)* sumpfig; **to become ~** versumpfen

swan [swɒn] N Schwan *m* VI *(Brit inf)* **to ~ off** abziehen *(inf)*; **to ~ around New York** in New York herumziehen *(inf)*; **to ~ around (the house)** zu Hause herumschweben *(inf)*

swan dive N *(US)* Schwalbensprung *m*

swank [swæŋk] *(esp Brit inf)* N a *(= boastfulness)* Angabe *f*, Protzerei *f (inf)*; *(= ostentation)* Schau *f (inf)*; **it's just a lot of ~** das ist doch nur Angabe/Schau b *(= person)* Angeber(in) *m(f)* VI angeben *(about* mit); **to ~ around** protzen *(inf)*, große Töne spucken *(inf)*

swanky [ˈswæŋkɪ] ADJ *(+er) (esp Brit inf) manner, words, party* großspurig; *car, restaurant, house etc* protzig *(inf)*; *neighbourhood* hochnäsig

swannery [ˈswɒnərɪ] N Schwanenteich *m*

swan's-down [ˈswɒnzˌdaʊn] N *(= feathers)* Schwanendaunen *pl*; *(= fabric)* wolliges Material

swan: **swan song** N *(fig)* Schwanengesang *m*; **swan-upping** [ˌswɒnˈʌpɪŋ] N feierliche Zeichnung der jungen Schwäne

swap [swɒp] N Tausch *m*, Tauschhandel *m*; **~s** *(= stamps)* Tauschmarken *pl*; **it's a fair ~** das ist ein fairer Tausch; **to do a ~ (with sb)** (mit jdm) tauschen VT *stamps, cars, houses etc* tauschen; *stories, reminiscences, addresses, insults* austauschen; **to ~ sth for sth** etw für etw eintauschen; **to ~ places with sb** mit jdm tauschen; **to ~ sides** die Seiten wechseln; **I'll ~ you!** *(inf)* ich tausch mit dir *(inf)* VI tauschen

swap meet N *(US Comm)* Tauschbörse *f*

SWAPO [ˈswɑːpəʊ] *abbr of* **South-West Africa People's Organization** SWAPO *f*

swap shop N Tauschbörse *f*

sward [swɔːd] N *(obs, poet)* Rasen *m*

swarm [swɔːm] N *(of insects, birds)* Schwarm *m*; *(of people also)* Schar *f*; **the sightseeers came in ~s** die Touristen kamen scharenweise *or* in Scharen VI *(bees, flies, people)* schwärmen; **the place was ~ing with insects/people** es wimmelte von Insekten/Leuten; **the main street was ~ing (with people)** *(inf)* auf der Hauptstraße herrschte Hochbetrieb *(inf)*; **tourists were ~ing everywhere** es wimmelte überall von Touristen; **children ~ed all round the car** Kinder schwärmten um das Auto herum

▶ **swarm up** VI *+prep obj* hinauf- *or* hochklettern

swarthiness [ˈswɔːðɪnɪs] N *(of skin)* Dunkelheit *f*; *(of person also)* Dunkelhäutigkeit *f*, dunkle Farbe

swarthy [ˈswɔːðɪ] ADJ *(+er) skin* dunkel; *person also* dunkelhäutig

swashbuckler [ˈswɒʃˌbʌklə'] N verwegener Kerl

swashbuckling [ˈswɒʃˌbʌklɪŋ] ADJ *person, manner, performance* verwegen; **a ~ film** ein Mantel-und-Degen-Film *m*

swastika [ˈswɒstɪkə] N Hakenkreuz *nt*; *(= religious symbol also)* Swastika *f*

swat [swɒt] VT *fly* totschlagen; *table* schlagen auf *(+acc)* VI **to ~ at a fly** nach einer Fliege schlagen N a *(= blow)* Schlag *m* b *(= fly swat)* Fliegenklatsche *f*

swatch [swɒtʃ] N (Textil)muster *nt*; *(= collection of samples)* Musterbuch *nt*

swath [swɔːθ] N Schwade *f*; **to cut a ~ through sth** eine Bahn durch etw schneiden

swathe [sweɪð] N = **swath** VT wickeln *(in* in *+acc)*; *(in bandages also)* umwickeln *(in* mit); **to ~ oneself in sth** sich in etw *(acc)* einwickeln *or* einhüllen, etw um sich wickeln

swatter [ˈswɒtə'] N *(= fly swatter)* Fliegenklatsche *f*

sway [sweɪ] N a *(= movement, of trees)* Schwiegen *nt*; *(of hanging object)* Schwingen *nt*; *(of building, mast, bridge etc, unsteady person)* Schwanken *nt*; *(of train, boat)* Schaukeln *nt*; *(of hips)* Wackeln *nt*; *(fig)* Schwenken *nt*; **the graceful ~ of the dancer's body** das anmutige Wiegen der Tänzerin b *(= influence, rule)* Macht *f (over* über *+acc)*; **to bring a city/a people under one's ~** sich *(dat)* eine Stadt/ein Volk unterwerfen; **to hold ~ over sb/a nation** jdn/ein Volk beherrschen *or* in seiner Macht haben

VI *(trees)* sich wiegen; *(hanging object)* schwingen; *(building, mast, bridge etc, unsteady person)* schwanken; *(train, boat)* schaukeln; *(hips)* wackeln; *(fig)* schwenken; **she ~s as she walks** sie wiegt beim Gehen die Hüften; **the drunk ~ed up the road** der Betrunkene schwankte die Straße entlang; **to ~ between two alternatives** zwischen zwei Alternativen schwanken

VT a *hips* wiegen; *(wind)* hin und her bewegen b *(= influence)* beeinflussen; *(= change sb's mind)* umstimmen

sway bar N *(US Aut)* Stabilisator *m*

Swaziland [ˈswɑːzɪlænd] N Swasiland *nt*

swear [swɛə'] *vb: pret* **swore**, *ptp* **sworn** VT a *allegiance, love, revenge* schwören; *oath* leisten, schwören; **I ~ it!** ich kann das beschwören! b *(Jur) witness, jury* vereidigen; **to ~ sb to secrecy** jdn schwören lassen, dass er nichts verrät; **I've been sworn to secrecy** ich habe schwören müssen, dass ich nichts sage

VI a *(= use solemn oath)* schwören; **to ~ on the Bible** auf die Bibel schwören; **to ~ by all one holds dear** schwören bei allem, was einem lieb ist; **to ~ to sth** etw beschwören; **to ~ blind** *or (US)* **up and down that …** *(inf)* Stein und Bein schwören, dass … *(inf)* b *(= use swearwords)* fluchen *(about* über *+acc)*; **to ~ at sb/sth** jdn/etw beschimpfen

N **to have a (good) ~** (tüchtig) fluchen

▶ **swear by** VI *+prep obj (inf)* schwören auf *(+acc)*

▶ **swear in** VT *sep witness, jury, president* vereidigen

▶ **swear off** VI *+prep obj (inf)* abschwören *(+dat)*

swearing [ˈswɛərɪŋ] N Fluchen *nt*

swearing-in [ˌswɛərɪŋˈɪn] N Vereidigung *f*

swearword [ˈswɛəwɜːd] N Fluch *m*, Kraftausdruck *m*

sweat [swet] N a Schweiß *m no pl*; *(on walls)* (Kondens)wasser *nt*; **drops/beads of ~** Schweißtropfen *pl*/-perlen *pl*; **his face was running with ~** der Schweiß rann ihm von der Stirn; **by the ~ of one's brow** *(fig)* im Schweiße seines Angesichts *(liter)*; **to be in a ~** *(lit, fig)* schwitzen; **to get into a ~ about sth** *(fig)* wegen etw ins Schwitzen geraten *or* kommen; **no ~** *(inf)* kein Problem b *(inf: = work)* **what a ~ that was!** das war eine Heidenarbeit! *(inf)*; **that's too much ~ for me** das ist mir zu anstrengend

VI *(person, animal, wall)* schwitzen *(with* vor *+dat)*; *(fig inf: = work hard)* sich abrackern *(inf) (over* mit); *(= worry)* zittern, schwitzen *(inf) (with* vor *+dat)*; **to ~ like a pig** *(inf)* wie ein Affe schwitzen *(inf)*

VT *horse, athlete* schwitzen lassen; *(pej) worker* für einen Hungerlohn arbeiten lassen; *recruit* schleifen *(inf)*; **to ~ buckets** *(inf)* wie ein Affe schwitzen *(inf)*; **to ~ blood** *(with worry)* Blut und Wasser schwitzen; *(with effort, work)* sich abrackern *(inf)*; **don't ~ him** *(US inf)* mach dir wegen dem keinen Kopf *(inf)*

▶ **sweat out** VT *sep* a *illness, fever* herausschwitzen b **to sweat it out** *(fig inf)* durchhalten; *(= sit and wait)* abwarten

sweatband [ˈswetbænd] N Schweißband *nt*

sweated [ˈswetɪd] ADJ *worker* völlig unterbezahlt, ausgebeutet; *goods* für einen Hungerlohn hergestellt; **~ labour** billige Arbeitskräfte *pl*; **it was ~ labour!** *(inf)* das war Ausbeutung

sweater [ˈswetə'] N Pullover *m*

sweat gland N Schweißdrüse *f*

sweating system [ˈswetɪŋˌsɪstəm] N *(economy based on exploitation)* Ausbeutungssystem *nt*

sweat: **sweat lodge** N Schwitzhütte *f*; **sweat pants** PL *(esp US)* Jogginghose *f*; **sweatshirt** N Sweatshirt *nt*; *(Sport)* Trainingspullover *m*; **sweatshop** N *(pej, hum inf)* Ausbeuterbetrieb *m (pej)*; **sweatsuit** N *(Sport)* Trainingsanzug *m*

sweaty [ˈswetɪ] ADJ *(+er) hands* schweißig; *brow* schweißbedeckt; *body, person, socks* verschwitzt; *weather, day, work* zum Schwitzen; *place* heiß; **to get ~** ins Schwitzen geraten; **digging is ~ work** beim Graben kommt man leicht ins Schwitzen; **a hot and ~ job** eine heiße und schweißtreibende Arbeit; **to have a ~ smell** nach Schweiß riechen; **~ feet** Schweißfüße *pl*

Swede [swiːd] N Schwede *m*, Schwedin *f*

swede [swiːd] N *(esp Brit)* Kohlrübe *f*, Steckrübe *f*

Sweden [ˈswiːdn] N Schweden *nt*

Swedish [ˈswiːdɪʃ] ADJ schwedisch; **he is ~** er ist Schwede; **she is ~** sie ist Schwedin N a *(Ling)* Schwedisch *nt* b **the ~** die Schweden *pl*

Swedish mile N schwedische Meile *(10 km)*

Sweeney [ˈswiːnɪ] N *(Brit inf)* Überfallkommando *nt (inf)*

sweep [swiːp] *vb: pret, ptp* **swept** N a **to give the floor a ~** den Boden kehren *or* fegen; **the chimney needs a ~** der Schornstein muss gekehrt *or* gefegt werden b *(= chimney sweep)* Schornsteinfeger(in) *m(f)*, Kaminkehrer(in) *m(f)* c *(of arm, pendulum)* Schwung *m*; *(of sword)* Streich *m*; *(of oars)* Durchziehen *nt no pl*; *(of light, radar)* Strahl *m*; **in one ~** *(fig)* auf einen Schwung; **with a ~ of her skirts** mit rauschenden Gewändern; **to make a ~ for mines** nach Minen suchen; **the police made a ~ of the district** die Polizei hat die Gegend abgesucht; **to make a clean ~** *(fig)* gründlich aufräumen, gründlich Ordnung schaffen; **the Russians made a clean ~ of the athletic events** die Russen haben beim Leichtathletikkampf tüchtig abgeräumt *(inf) or* alle Preise eingesteckt d *(= range)* Bereich *m*; *(of gun)* Schussbereich *m* e *(= curve, line, of road, river)* Bogen *m*; *(of facade, contour, hair)* Schwung *m*; **a wide ~ of country** eine sich weit ausdehnende Landschaft; **a beautiful ~ of hills** herrliche Berge *pl* f = **sweepstake**

VT a *floor, street, chimney* kehren, fegen; *room* (aus)kehren, (aus)fegen; *dust, snow* wegfegen; **to ~ a path through the snow** einen Weg durch den Schnee bahnen; **to ~ sth under the carpet** *(fig)* etw unter den Teppich kehren b *(= scan, move searchingly over)* absuchen *(for* nach); *(bullets)* streichen über *(+acc)*; *minefield, sea* durchkämmen; *mines* räumen; **to ~ a channel clear of mines** einen Kanal von Minen säubern c *(= move quickly over, wind, skirt)* fegen über *(+acc)*; *(waves) deck, sand etc* überrollen, überschwemmen; *(glance)* gleiten über *(+acc)*; *(fig, wave of protest, violence, fashion)* überrollen; *(disease)* um sich greifen in *(+dat)* d *(= remove with sweeping movement, wave)* spülen, schwemmen; *(current)* reißen; *(wind)* fegen; *person* reißen; **to ~ sth off the table/onto the floor** etw vom Tisch/zu Boden fegen; **the crowd swept him into the square** er wurde von der Menge zum Platz hin mitgerissen; **he swept the obstacles from his path** er stieß die

Hindernisse aus dem Weg; **the army swept the enemy before them** die Armee jagte die feindlichen Truppen vor sich her
e *(= triumph)* große Triumphe feiern in *(+dat)*; **to ~ the polls** *(Pol)* die Wahlen haushoch gewinnen; **to ~ all before one** *(fig)* alle in die Tasche stecken *(inf)*; **to ~ the board** *(fig)* alle Preise/Medaillen gewinnen, abräumen *(inf)*
VI **a** *(with broom)* kehren, fegen → **broom**
b *(= move, person)* rauschen; *(vehicle, plane, quickly)* schießen; *(majestically)* gleiten; *(skier)* fegen; *(road, river)* in weitem Bogen führen; **panic/the disease swept through Europe** Panik/die Krankheit griff in Europa um sich *or* breitete sich in Europa aus; **the tornado swept across the fields** der Wirbelsturm fegte über die Felder

▶ **sweep along** **VI** dahin- *or* entlangrauschen; *(majestically)* dahin- *or* entlanggleiten **VT** *sep (lit, fig)* mitreißen

▶ **sweep aside** **VT** *sep (lit, fig)* wegfegen, beiseitefegen

▶ **sweep away** **VI** = **sweep off** **VT** *sep dust, leaves etc* wegfegen; *(storm also, avalanche)* wegreißen; *(flood etc)* wegspülen, wegschwemmen; *(fig) old laws* aufräumen mit; *work, accomplishments* zunichtemachen; *doubts* zerstreuen; *opposition* vernichten

▶ **sweep down** **VI** hinunterrauschen; *(car, plane)* hinunterschießen; *(majestically)* hinuntergleiten; *(road, hill)* in sanftem Bogen abfallen; **to sweep down on sb** sich auf jdn stürzen, über jdn herfallen **VT** *sep* abkehren, abfegen

▶ **sweep off** **VI** davonrauschen; *(car, plane)* davonschießen; *(majestically)* davongleiten; *(skier)* davonfegen **VT** *sep vase, clock* herunterfegen; **to sweep sb off somewhere** jdn irgendwohin entführen; **the children were swept off to bed** die Kinder wurden schleunigst ins Bett gesteckt *(inf)* *or* geschickt; **to sweep sb off his/her feet** *(lit)* jdn umreißen; *(fig) audience* jdn begeistern; **he swept her off her feet** *(fig)* sie hat sich Hals über Kopf in ihn verliebt *(inf)*

▶ **sweep out** **VI** hinausrauschen; *(car)* herausschießen; *(majestically)* hinausgleiten; **to sweep out of a room** aus einem Zimmer rauschen **VT** *sep room* auskehren, ausfegen; *dust* hinauskehren *or* -fegen

▶ **sweep up** **VI** **a** *(with broom)* zusammenkehren *or* -fegen; **to sweep up after sb** hinter jdm herfegen **b** *(= move)* **the car swept up to the house** der Wagen rollte aufs Haus zu; **she swept up in a Rolls Royce** sie rollte in einem Rolls Royce vor; **a broad driveway sweeps up to the manor** ein breiter Zufahrtsweg schwingt sich zum Herrenhaus hinauf **VT** *sep* zusammenkehren *or* -fegen; *(= collect up) objects* zusammenraffen; *person* hochreißen; *hair* hochbinden

sweepback ['swi:pbæk] **N** *(Aviat)* Pfeilform *f*

sweeper ['swi:pəʳ] **N** **a** *(= road sweeper)* Straßenkehrer(in) *m(f)* *or* -feger(in) *m(f)*; *(= machine)* Kehrmaschine *f*; *(= carpet sweeper)* Teppichkehrer *m* **b** *(Ftbl)* Ausputzer(in) *m(f)*

sweep hand **N** Sekundenzeiger *m*

sweeping ['swi:pɪŋ] **ADJ** **a** *gesture, stroke, curve* weit ausholend; *bow, curtsey, lines* schwungvoll; *glance* streifend; *staircase* geschwungen; *lawn* ausgedehnt; *view* weit **b** *(fig) change, reduction* radikal, drastisch; *statement* pauschal; *victory* überragend, glänzend; **to make a ~ condemnation of sth** etw in Bausch und Bogen verdammen **N** *(= cleaning)* Kehren *nt*, Fegen *nt*

sweepingly ['swi:pɪŋlɪ] **ADV** *gesture* schwungvoll; *speak* verallgemeinernd; *condemn* in Bausch und Bogen

sweepings ['swi:pɪŋz] **PL** Kehricht *m*, Dreck *m*; *(fig, of society etc)* Abschaum *m*

sweepstake ['swi:psteɪk] **N** *(= race) Rennen, in dem die Pferdebesitzer alle Einsätze machen,* Sweepstake *nt or m*; *(= prize) aus allen Einsätzen gebildeter Preis* *(= lottery)* *Wette, bei der die Preise aus den Einsätzen gebildet werden*

sweet [swi:t] **ADJ** *(+er)* **a** süß; **to like ~ things** gern Süßes essen; **to have a ~ tooth** gern Süßes essen, naschhaft sein
b *(= fresh) food, water* frisch; *air, breath* rein, frisch; *soil* nicht sauer; *(= fragrant) smell* süß; **the air was ~ with the scent of roses** die Luft war erfüllt vom Duft der Rosen
c *(fig)* süß; *(= kind)* lieb; **that's very ~ of you** das ist sehr lieb von dir; **that car/horse is a ~ little runner** das Auto/Pferd läuft prächtig; **to be ~ on sb** *(dated inf)* in jdn vernarrt sein; **to keep sb ~** *(inf)* jdn bei Laune halten; **the water tasted ~ to him** *(liter)* das Wasser schmeckte (ihm) so gut; **success was doubly ~ to him** er genoss den Erfolg doppelt; **once he caught the ~ smell of success** als erst der Erfolg lockte; **at his own ~ will** *(iro)* wie es ihm gerade passt *or* einfällt; **in his own ~ way** *(iro)* auf seine unübertroffene Art; **~ Fanny Adams** *or* **FA** *(Brit inf)* nix *(inf)*, nicht die Bohne *(inf)* → **dream, nothing**
N **a** *(Brit: = candy)* Bonbon *nt*
b *(Brit: = dessert)* Nachtisch *m*, Dessert *nt*; **for ~** zum *or* als Nachtisch *or* Dessert
c **yes, (my) ~** *(inf)* ja, (mein) Schätzchen *or* Liebling
d **sweets** **PL** *(fig: = pleasures)* Freuden *pl*; **once he had tasted the ~s of success** nachdem er einmal erfahren hatte, wie süß der Erfolg sein kann

sweet: **sweet-and-sour** **ADJ** süßsauer; **sweetbread** **N** Bries *nt*; **sweetbrier** **N** Weinrose *f*; **sweet chestnut** **N** Edelkastanie *f*; **sweetcorn** **N** Mais *m*

sweeten ['swi:tn] **VT** *coffee, sauce* süßen; *air, breath* reinigen; *(fig) temper* bessern; *task* versüßen; *deal, terms* schmackhaft machen; **to ~ sb** *(inf)* jdn gnädig stimmen; *(inf: = bribe)* jdn schmieren *(inf)*; **to ~ the pill** die bittere Pille versüßen **VI** *(temper)* sich bessern; *(person)* gute Laune bekommen

sweetener ['swi:tnəʳ] **N** *(Cook)* Süß(ungs)mittel *nt*; *(esp artificial)* Süßstoff *m*; *(inf, to make sth more acceptable)* Anreiz *m*; *(inf: = bribe)* Schmiergeld *nt*

sweetening ['swi:tnɪŋ] **N** *(Cook)* Süßungsmittel *nt*; *(artificial)* Süßstoff *m*

sweetheart ['swi:thɑ:t] **N** Schatz *m*, Liebste(r) *mf*; **~ swindler** *(esp US)* Heiratsschwindler(in) *m(f)*; **soon they were ~s** *(dated)* bald waren sie ein Pärchen; **Vera Lynn, the Forces' ~** Vera Lynn, der Liebling der Armee

sweet herbs **PL** Küchen- *or* Gewürzkräuter *pl*

sweetie ['swi:tɪ] **N** **a** *(inf: also* **sweetie-pie***)* **yes, ~** ja, Schatzi *(inf)* *or* Süße(r); **she's/he's a ~** sie/er ist ein Engel *or* ist süß *(inf)* **b** *(Brit baby-talk: = candy)* Bonbon *m*

sweetish ['swi:tɪʃ] **ADJ** *taste, smell* süßlich

sweetly ['swi:tlɪ] **ADV** **a** *sing, play* süß; *say* süßlich; *smile also, answer* lieb; **the engine was running ~** der Motor ist prächtig gelaufen; **he chipped the equalizer ~ into the net** er hat den Ausgleichstreffer wunderschön ins Netz gesetzt; **rather ~, he offered to drive me there** er bot an, mich hinzufahren, was wirklich süß *or* lieb von ihm war **b** *innocent* niedlich; *seductive* sanft, auf sanfte Art **c** *scented, fragrant* süßlich; **to smell ~ of sth** süßlich nach etw duften; **the ~ acid smell of peat smoke** der süßlich scharfe Geruch des Torfrauches

sweet: **sweetmeat** **N** *(old)* Leckerei *f*; **sweet-natured** [,swi:t'neɪtʃəd] **ADJ** lieb

sweetness ['swi:tnɪs] **N** *(lit)* Süßigkeit *f*, Süße *f*; *(fig)* Süße *f*; *(of smile, nature)* Liebenswürdigkeit *f*; *(of person)* liebe Art; *(= freshness, of food, water)* Frische *f*; *(of air, breath)* Reinheit *f*, Frische *f*; **now all is ~ and light** *(usu iro)* nun herrscht eitel Freude und Sonnenschein

sweet: **sweet pea** **N** Gartenwicke *f*; **sweet potato** **N** Süßkartoffel *f*, Batate *f*; **sweet-scented** **ADJ** süß duftend; **sweet shop** **N** *(Brit)* Süßwarenladen *m* *or* -geschäft *nt*; **sweet-smelling** **ADJ** süß riechend; **sweet talk** **N** *(inf)* süße Worte *pl*; **sweet-talk** **VT** *(inf)* **to ~ sb into doing sth** jdn mit süßen Worten dazu bringen, etw zu tun; **sweet-tempered** **ADJ** verträglich; **sweet tooth** **N** *(inf, fig)* Vorliebe *f* für Süßigkeiten; **she has a ~** sie isst gerne Süßigkeiten, sie ist eine Naschkatze *(inf)*; **sweet trolley** **N** *(Brit)* Dessertwagen *m*

sweetums ['swi:təmz] **N** *(inf: term of endearment)* Schatz(i) *m* *(inf)*

sweet william **N** Bartnelke *f*

swell [swel] *vb: pret* **swelled**, *ptp* **swollen** *or* **swelled** **N** **a** *(of sea)* Wogen *nt no pl*; *(= wave)* Woge *f*; **there was a heavy ~** es herrschte hoher Seegang *or* schwere See
b *(dated inf, = stylish person)* feine Dame, feiner Herr; *(= important person)* hohes Tier; *(of high society)* Größe *f*; **the ~s** *pl* die feinen Leute
c *(Mus, = sound)* Crescendo *nt*; *(= control, knob)* Schweller *m*; *(= mechanism)* Schwellwerk *nt*
ADJ **a** *(dated, = stylish)* fein, vornehm; *house, restaurant* nobel *(inf)*, vornehm
b *(esp US dated: = excellent)* klasse *(inf)*, prima *(inf)*
VT *ankle, river, sound etc* anschwellen lassen; *stomach* (auf)blähen; *wood* (auf)quellen; *sail* blähen; *numbers, population* anwachsen lassen; *sales* steigern; **to be swollen with pride** stolzgeschwellt sein; **your praise will only ~ her head** dein Lob wird ihr nur zu Kopf steigen
VI **a** *(ankle, arm, eye etc: also* **swell up***)* (an)schwellen; *(balloon, air bed, tyre)* sich füllen; **to ~ (up) with rage** vor Wut rot anlaufen; **to ~ (up) with pride** vor Stolz anschwellen; **the children's bellies had swollen with hunger** die Bäuche der Kinder waren vom Hunger (auf)gebläht
b *(river, lake, sound etc)* anschwellen; *(sails: also* **swell out***)* sich blähen; *(wood)* quellen; *(in size, number: population, debt etc)* anwachsen; **the crowd ~ed to 2000** die Menschenmenge wuchs auf 2000 an; **the cheers ~ed to a roar** der Jubel schwoll zu einem Begeisterungssturm an; **the debt had swollen to a massive sum** die Schuld war zu einer riesigen Summe angewachsen → *also* **swollen**

swell box **N** *(Mus)* Schwellwerk *nt*

swellhead ['swelhed] **N** *(dated esp US inf)* aufgeblasener Typ *(inf)*

swell-headed ['swel,hedɪd] **ADJ** *(inf)* aufgeblasen *(inf)*

swelling ['swelɪŋ] **N** **a** Verdickung *f*; *(Med)* Schwellung *f* **b** *(= act, of ankle, arm, eye, sound)* Anschwellen *nt*; *(of sails)* Blähen *nt*; *(of wood)* Quellen *nt*; *(of population, debt etc)* Anwachsen *nt* **ADJ** *attr ankle etc* (an)schwellend; *sails* gebläht; *sound* anschwellend; *numbers* steigend, anwachsend, zunehmend; *line, curve* geschwungen; **her ~ breasts** die Wölbung ihrer Brüste

swelter ['sweltəʳ] **VI** (vor Hitze) vergehen, verschmachten *(inf)*

sweltering ['sweltərɪŋ] **ADJ** *day, weather* glühend heiß; *heat* glühend; **it's ~ in here** *(inf)* hier verschmachtet man ja! *(inf)*

swept [swept] *pret, ptp of* **sweep**

swept: **sweptback** **ADJ** *wing* pfeilförmig; **swept volume** **N** *(Tech, Aut etc)* Hubraum *m*; **sweptwing** **ADJ** *aircraft* mit pfeilförmigen Flügeln

swerve [swɜ:v] **N** Bogen *m*; *(of road, coastline also)* Schwenkung *f*; *(of car etc also)* Schlenker *m* *(inf)*; *(= spin on ball)* Effet *m*; **with a ~ he avoided his opponent** er wich seinem Gegner mit einer geschickten Bewegung aus
VI einen Bogen machen; *(car, driver)* ausschwenken; *(boxer)* ausweichen; *(horse)* ausbrechen; *(ball)* im Bogen fliegen; *(fig, from truth)* abweichen; *(from chosen path)* abschwenken; **to ~ round sth** einen Bogen um etw machen; **the road ~s (round) to the right** die Straße schwenkt nach rechts; **he ~d in behind me** er schwenkte plötzlich hinter mir ein; **the car ~d in and out of the traffic** der Wagen schoss im

Slalom durch den Verkehrsstrom
VT *car etc* herumreißen; *ball* anschneiden

swift [swɪft] ADJ *(+er)* schnell; *movement, steps also* flink; *reaction, reply also, revenge* prompt; *runner also* flink, flott; *pace* flott, rasch; **to take ~ action** schnell handeln; **~ of foot** *(liter)* schnellfüßig; **to be ~ to anger** jähzornig sein; **to be ~ to do sth** etw schnell tun N *(= bird)* Mauersegler *m*

swift: **swift-flowing** [ˈswɪftˌfləʊɪŋ] ADJ schnell fließend; **swift-footed** ADJ *(liter)* schnellfüßig

swiftly [ˈswɪftlɪ] ADV schnell; *react* schnell, unverzüglich, prompt; **events have moved ~** die Ereignisse haben sich überstürzt; **time passes ~** die Zeit vergeht wie im Flug; **a ~ flowing river** ein schnell dahinfließender Fluss; **to act ~ to do sth** rasch handeln, um etw zu tun; **~ followed by …** rasch gefolgt von …

swiftness [ˈswɪftnɪs] N Schnelligkeit *f*; *(of movement, steps also)* Flinkheit *f*; *(of reaction, reply also)* Promptheit *f*; *(of pace)* Raschheit *f*; **the ~ of the current** die reißende Strömung

swig [swɪg] *(inf)* N Schluck *m*; **to have** *or* **take a ~ of beer** einen Schluck Bier trinken; **to have** *or* **take a ~ from a bottle** einen Schluck aus einer Flasche trinken; **have a ~ of this** trinken Sie mal einen Schluck (davon) *(inf)*; **to down a drink in one ~** das Glas in einem Zug leeren VT *(also* **swig down***)* herunterkippen *(inf)*

swill [swɪl] N a *(= animal food)* (Schweine)futter *nt*; (= *garbage, slops, solid)* Abfälle *pl*; *(liquid)* Schmutzwasser *nt*; *(fig pej)* (Schweine)fraß *m* *(inf)*; *(liquid)* Abwaschwasser *nt* b *(= cleaning)* **to give sth a ~ (out/down)** = **swill VT a** VT a *(esp Brit: also* **swill out***)* auswaschen; *cup, dish* ausschwenken; **to ~ sth down** etw abspülen; *floor* etw waschen b *(inf) beer etc* kippen *(inf)*; **he ~ed it down with beer** er hat es mit Bier runtergespült *(inf)* c **to ~ sth round** etw (herum)schwenken

swim [swɪm] *vb: pret* **swam**, *ptp* **swum** N a **after a 2 km ~** nach 2 km Schwimmen, nachdem ich/er *etc* 2 km geschwommen war; **it's a long ~** es ist weit (zu schwimmen); **that was a nice ~** das (Schwimmen) hat Spaß gemacht!; **I like** *or* **enjoy a ~** ich gehe gern (mal) schwimmen, ich schwimme gern (mal); **to have a ~** schwimmen
b *(inf)* **to be in the/out of the ~** up to date/nicht mehr up to date sein; *(= socially active)* mitmischen *(inf)*/den Anschluss verloren haben
VT schwimmen; *river, Channel* durchschwimmen
VI schwimmen; **to ~ back** zurückschwimmen; **we shall have to ~ for it** wir werden schwimmen müssen; **the room swam before my eyes** das Zimmer verschwamm vor meinen Augen; **my head is ~ming** mir dreht sich alles, mir ist ganz schwummrig *(inf)*

swim bladder [ˈswɪmˌblædəʳ] N Schwimmblase *f*

swimmer [ˈswɪməʳ] N Schwimmer(in) *m(f)*

swimming [ˈswɪmɪŋ] N Schwimmen *nt*; **do you like ~?** schwimmen Sie gern? ADJ *(= dizzy) feeling* schwummrig *(inf)*

swimming *in cpds* Schwimm-; **swimming bath** N *usu pl (Brit)* Schwimmbad *nt*; **swimming cap** N *(Brit)* Badekappe *f*, Bademütze *f*; **swimming costume** N *(Brit)* Badeanzug *m*; **swimming gala** N Schwimmfest *nt*; **swimming instructor** N Schwimmlehrer(in) *m(f)*

swimmingly [ˈswɪmɪŋlɪ] ADV *(inf)* glänzend; **to go ~** *(inf: = like clockwork)* wie geschmiert gehen *or* laufen *(inf)*; **they got along ~** sie verstanden sich glänzend

swimming: **swimming pool** N Schwimmbad *nt*; *(outdoor also)* Freibad *nt*; *(indoor also)* Hallenbad *nt*; **swimming ring** N Schwimmring *m*; **swimming things** PL Badesachen *pl*, Badezeug *nt*; **swimming trunks** PL *(Brit)* Badehose *f*

swim noodle N *(= swimming aid)* Schwimmnudel *f*, Aquanudel *f*

swimsuit [ˈswɪmsuːt] N Badeanzug *m*

swindle [ˈswɪndl] N Schwindel *m*, Betrug *m*; **it's a ~!** das ist (der reinste) Schwindel! VT *person* beschwindeln, betrügen; **to ~ sb out of sth** *(= take from)* jdm etw abschwindeln *or* abgaunern *(inf)*; *(= withhold from)* jdn um etw beschwindeln *or* betrügen

swindler [ˈswɪndləʳ] N Schwindler(in) *m(f)*, Gauner(in) *m(f)* *(inf)*

swine [swaɪn] N a *pl* - *(old, form)* Schwein *nt* → **pearl²** N b *pl* **-s** *(pej inf: = man)* (gemeiner) Hund *(inf)*; *(= woman)* gemeine Sau *(sl)*; **this translation is a ~** diese Übersetzung ist wirklich gemein *(inf)*

swine: **swine fever** N Schweinepest *f*; **swineherd** N *(old)* Schweinehirt(in) *m(f)*

swing [swɪŋ] *vb: pret, ptp* **swung** N a *(= movement)* Schwung *m*; *(to and fro)* Schwingen *nt*; *(of needle)* Ausschlag *m*; *(= distance)* Ausschlag *m*, Schwung(weite *f*) *m*; *(Boxing etc: = blow)* Schwinger *m*; *(Golf, Skiing etc)* Schwung *m*; *(fig, Pol)* (Meinungs)umschwung *m*; **to take a ~ at sb** nach jdm schlagen; **the golfer took a big ~ at the ball** der Golfer holte weit aus und schlug den Ball; **my ~ is too short** ich hole nicht weit genug aus; **a ~ in opinion** ein Meinungsumschwung *m*
b *(= rhythm)* Schwung *m*; *(= kind of music, dance)* Swing *m*; **to walk with a ~** schwungvoll gehen; **to go with a ~** *(fig)* ein voller Erfolg sein *(inf)*; **to be in full ~** voll im Gang sein; **to get into the ~ of sth** *(of new job, married life etc)* sich an etw *(acc)* gewöhnen; **to get into the ~ of things** *(inf)* reinkommen *(inf)*
c *(= seat for swinging)* Schaukel *f*; **to give sb a ~** jdn anstoßen *or* anschubsen *(inf)*; **to have a ~** schaukeln; **what you win** *or* **gain on the ~s (you lose on the roundabouts)** *(prov)* was man auf der einen Seite gewinnt, verliert man auf der anderen; **it's ~s and roundabouts** *(Brit inf)* es ist gehupft wie gesprungen
d *(esp US: = scope, freedom)* **he gave his imagination full ~** er ließ seiner Fantasie *or* Phantasie *(dat)* freien Lauf; **he was given full ~ to make decisions** man hat ihm bei allen Entscheidungen freie Hand gelassen
VT a *object* schwingen; *(to and fro)* hin und her schwingen; *(on swing, hammock)* schaukeln; *arms, legs (vigorously)* schwingen (mit); *(= dangle)* baumeln mit; *propeller* einen Schwung geben *(+dat)*; **to ~ a child** ein Kind schaukeln; **to ~ one's hips** sich in den Hüften wiegen; **to ~ the lead** *(Brit inf)* sich drücken *(inf)* → **cat**
b *(= move)* schwingen; **he swung his axe at the tree/at me** er schwang die Axt gegen den Baum/gegen mich; **he swung his racket at the ball** er holte mit dem Schläger aus; **to ~ a door open/shut** eine Tür aufstoßen/zustoßen; **he swung the case (up) onto his shoulder** er schwang sich *(dat)* die Kiste auf die Schulter; **he swung himself over the stream/wall/up into the saddle** er schwang sich über den Bach/über die Mauer/in den Sattel
c *(= influence) election, decision, voters* beeinflussen; *opinion* umschlagen lassen; *person* umstimmen, herumkriegen *(inf)*; **his speech swung the decision in our favour** seine Rede ließ die Entscheidung zu unseren Gunsten ausfallen; **what swung it for me was the fact that …** *(inf)* was dann letzten Endes den Ausschlag gegeben hat, war, dass …; **to ~ it (so that …)** *(inf)* es so drehen *or* deichseln *(inf)*(, dass …); **he managed to ~ it in our favour** es gelang ihm, es zu unseren Gunsten zu drehen; **he managed to ~ the deal** *(inf)* er hat das Geschäft gemacht *(inf)*
d *(turn: also* **swing round***) plane, car* herumschwenken
VI a *(object)* schwingen; *(to and fro)* (hin und her) schwingen; *(= pivot)* sich drehen; *(on swing)* schaukeln; *(arms, legs: = dangle)* baumeln; **he was left ~ing by his hands** er hing *or* *(dangerously)* baumelte nur noch an den Händen; **he swung at me with his axe** er schwang die Axt gegen mich; **the golfer swung at the ball** der Golfer holte aus; **to ~ both ways** *(inf: = be bisexual)* beide Ufer kennen *(inf)*
b *(= move: into saddle, along rope etc)* sich schwingen; **to ~ from tree to tree** sich von Baum zu Baum schwingen; **to ~ open** aufschwingen; **to ~ shut** zuschlagen; **to ~ into action** in Aktion treten; **the car swung into the square** der Wagen schwenkte auf den Platz ein; **opinion/the party has swung to the right** die Meinung/die Partei hat einen Rechtsschwenk gemacht
c *(music, tune)* Schwung haben; **the town/club began to ~** in der Stadt/im Klub kam Stimmung auf *(inf)*; **London really swung in the sixties** in den sechziger Jahren war in London schwer was los *(inf)*
d *(inf: = be hanged)* **he'll ~ for it** dafür wird er baumeln *(inf)*; **I'll ~ for him (yet)** ich bring ihn noch um *(inf)*; **he's not worth ~ing for** es lohnt sich nicht, sich an ihm die Hände schmutzig zu machen *(inf)*

▶ **swing across** VI hinüberschwingen; *(hand-over-hand)* sich hinüberhangeln; *(+prep obj)* schwingen über *(+acc)*; *(+prep obj, person, animal)* sich schwingen über *(+acc)*; *(hand-over-hand)* sich hangeln über *(+acc)*

▶ **swing (a)round** VI *(person)* sich umdrehen, herumfahren *(inf)*; *(car, ship, plane, crane)* herumschwenken; *(needle)* ausschlagen; *(fig: voters, opinion)* umschwenken VT *sep* herumschwenken; *voters* umstimmen; *opinion* umschlagen lassen

▶ **swing back** VI zurückschwingen; *(opinion)* zurückschlagen VT *sep* zurückschwingen; *opinion* zurückschlagen lassen

▶ **swing to** VI *(door)* zuschlagen

swing: **swingback** N *(fig)* Rückfall *m* *(to* in *+acc)*, Rückkehr *f* *(to* zu); **swingball** N *(Brit)* = **tetherball**; **swing band** N *(Mus)* Swingband *f*; **swing-bin** N Mülleimer *m* mit Schwingdeckel; **swingboat** N Schiffschaukel *f*; **swing bridge** N Drehbrücke *f*; **swing door** N *(Brit)* Pendeltür *f*

swingeing [ˈswɪndʒɪŋ] ADJ *(Brit) blow, penalty, punishment* hart; *attack* scharf; *defeat* vernichtend; *taxation, price increases, fee, charge* extrem hoch; *cuts* extrem

swinger [ˈswɪŋəʳ] N *(inf)* lockerer Typ *(inf)*

swinging [ˈswɪŋɪŋ] ADJ *step* schwungvoll; *movement* schaukelnd; *music* schwungvoll, swingend; *(fig inf) person* locker *(inf)*; **~ door** *(US)* Pendeltür *f*; **~ London** Swinging London *nt*; **London was a ~ place then** in London war damals wirklich was los *(inf)*; **the ~ sixties** die flotten sechziger Jahre, die „swinging sixties“ *(sl)*

swinging single N *(US)* flotter Single

swing: **swing seat** N Hollywoodschaukel *f*; **swing shift** N *(US Ind inf)* a *(= period)* Spätschicht *f* b *(= workers)* Spätschicht *f*; **swing vote** N *(esp US Pol)* Stimmenanteil *m* der Wechselwähler; **swing voter** N *(esp US Pol)* Wechselwähler(in) *m(f)*; **swing-wing** ADJ *aircraft* mit ausfahrbaren Tragflächenteilen

swinish [ˈswaɪnɪʃ] ADJ *(fig)* gemein

swipe [swaɪp] N *(= blow)* Schlag *m*; **to take** *or* **make a ~ at sb/sth** nach jdm/etw schlagen; *(fig: = criticize)* gegen jdn/etw ausholen VT a *person, ball etc* schlagen; **he ~d the wasp with the towel** er schlug mit dem Handtuch auf die Wespe b *(inf: = steal)* mopsen *(inf)*, klauen *(inf)* c *credit card* einlesen, durchziehen; *entry card* durchziehen VI **to ~ at sb/sth** nach jdm/etw schlagen

swipe card N Magnetstreifenkarte *f*

swirl [swɜːl] N Wirbel *m*; *(= whorl in pattern also)* Spirale *f*; **the ~ of the dancers' skirts** die wirbelnden Röcke der Tänzerinnen; **she put a ~ of cream on the cake** sie spritzte ein Sahnehäufchen auf den Kuchen VT *water, dust etc* wirbeln; **to ~ sth along** *(river)* etw wirbelnd mitreißen; **he ~ed his partner round the room** er wirbelte seine Partnerin durchs Zimmer VI wirbeln; **to ~ around** herumwirbeln

swish [swɪʃ] N *(of whip, cane)* Zischen *nt*, Sausen *nt*; *(of grass)* Rascheln *nt*; *(of skirts, water)*

Rauschen *nt*; *(of tyres)* Pfeifen *nt*, Zischen *nt*; *(of windscreen wipers)* Wischen *nt* ADJ *(+er)* *(esp Brit inf: = smart)* (tod)schick VT *cane* zischen *or* sausen lassen; *tail* schlagen mit; *skirt* rauschen mit; *water* schwenken; **she ~ed water round the bowl** sie schwenkte die Schüssel mit Wasser aus VI *(whip, cane)* zischen, sausen; *(grass)* rascheln; *(skirts)* rauschen, rascheln; *(water)* rauschen; *(tyres)* zischen, pfeifen; *(windscreen wipers)* wischen

Swiss [swɪs] ADJ Schweizer, schweizerisch; **he is ~** er ist Schweizer; **she is ~** sie ist Schweizerin; **the ~-German part of Switzerland** die deutsch(sprachig)e Schweiz; **the ~ Guard** die Schweizergarde; **a ~ Guard** ein Schweizer *m*; **~ steak** *(US, Cook)* *paniertes Steak mit Tomaten und Zwiebeln* N Schweizer(in) *m(f)*; **the ~** *pl* die Schweizer *pl*

Swiss: **Swiss army knife** N Schweizer Offiziersmesser *nt*, Schweizermesser *nt*; **Swiss cheese** N Schweizer Käse *m*; **her argument has more holes than ~** *(esp US)* ihre Argumentation hat mehr Löcher als ein Schweizer Käse; **~ plant** Fensterblatt *nt*, Philodendron *m or nt*; **Swiss franc** N Schweizer Franken *m*; **Swiss French** N **a** *(= person)* Welschschweizer(in) *m(f)* **b** *(Ling)* Schweizer Französisch *nt*; **Swiss German** N **a** *(= person)* Deutschschweizer(in) *m(f)* **b** *(Ling)* Schweizerdeutsch *nt*, Schwyzerdütsch *nt*; **Swiss roll** N *(Brit)* Biskuitrolle *f*

switch [swɪtʃ] N **a** *(Elec etc)* Schalter *m*

b *(US Rail)* Weiche *f*

c *(= change)* Wechsel *m*; *(in plans, policies)* Änderung *f*, Umstellung *f* *(in +gen)*; *(in opinion)* Änderung *f* *(in +gen)*; *(= exchange)* Tausch *m*; **to make a ~** tauschen

d *(= stick, cane)* Rute *f*, Gerte *f*; *(= riding whip)* Gerte *f*

e *(of hair)* falscher Zopf

VT **a** *(= change, alter)* wechseln; *direction, plans* ändern; *allegiance* übertragen *(to* auf *+acc)*; *attention, conversation* lenken *(to* auf *+acc)*; **to ~ schools** die Schule wechseln; **to ~ sides** die Seiten wechseln; **to ~ channels** auf einen anderen Kanal umschalten; **to ~ parties/jobs** zu einer anderen Partei/anderen Stelle überwechseln

b *(= move) production* verlegen; *object* umstellen

c *(= exchange)* tauschen; *(= transpose: also* **switch over, switch round***)* *objects, letters in word, figures in column* vertauschen; **I ~ed hats with him** ich tauschte meinen Hut mit ihm; **we ~ed hats** wir tauschten die Hüte; **to ~ A for B** A für *or* gegen B (ein)tauschen; **to ~ A and B (over)** A und B vertauschen

d *(Elec)* (um)schalten; **~ the radio to another programme** schalten Sie auf ein anderes Radioprogramm um

e *tail, cane* schlagen mit

f *(esp US, Rail)* rangieren

VI **a** *(= change: also* **switch over***)* (über)wechseln *(to* zu); *(Elec, TV, Rad)* umschalten *(to* auf *+acc)*; *(= exchange: also* **switch round, switch over***)* tauschen; **to ~ (over) from Y to Z** von Y auf Z *(acc)* (über)wechseln; **we've ~ed (over) to gas** wir haben auf Gas umgestellt; **the wind ~ed to the east** der Wind hat (sich) nach Osten gedreht; **he ~ed to another line of attack** er wechselte seine Angriffstaktik; **she ~ed to being in favour of it** sie änderte ihre Meinung und war auf einmal dafür

b *(Rail)* rangieren

▶ **switch (a)round** VT *sep (= swap round)* vertauschen; *(= rearrange)* umstellen VI = **switch VI a**

▶ **switch back** VI *(to original plan, product, allegiance etc)* zum Alten zurückkehren, auf das Alte zurückgreifen; *(Elec, Rad, TV)* zurückschalten (*to* zu) VT *sep heater, cooker* zurückschalten (*to* auf *+acc*); **to switch the light back on** das Licht wieder anschalten

▶ **switch off** VT *sep* **a** *light* ausschalten; *radio, TV* aus- *or* abschalten; *machine, engine* abschalten; *gas, water supply* abstellen; **the oven switches itself off** der Backofen schaltet sich selbsttätig ab *or* aus **b** *(inf)* **(can't somebody) switch him off for goodness' sake!** *(inf)* kann den denn niemand abstellen, um Himmels willen VI **a** *(light)* ausschalten; *(radio, TV also, machine, engine)* abschalten; *(gas, water supply)* abstellen **b** *(inf: person)* abschalten; **the TV won't switch off** der Fernseher lässt sich nicht aus- *or* abschalten

▶ **switch on** VT **a** *sep gas, water* anstellen; *machine* anschalten; *radio, TV, light* einschalten; *engine* anlassen; **please leave the TV switched on** lass den Fernseher bitte an

b *(inf) person (= interest)* munter machen, begeistern; *(emotionally, by drugs)* antörnen *(sl)*, high machen *(inf)*; *(sexually)* auf Touren bringen *(inf)*; **switched on** begeistert; *(emotionally, on drugs)* high *(inf)*; *(sexually)* auf Touren *(inf)*; *(= up-to-date)* in *(inf)*; **to be switched on to jazz** auf Jazz stehen *(inf)*

VI *(gas, water)* anstellen; *(machine)* anschalten; *(radio, TV, light)* einschalten; *(engine)* anlassen; **the cooker will switch on at 10 o'clock** der Herd schaltet sich um 10 Uhr an *or* ein

▶ **switch over** VI = **switch VI a** VT *sep* **a** = **switch VT c b** *(TV, Rad)* **to switch the programme over** auf ein anderes Programm umschalten

▶ **switch through** VT *sep (Telec)* durchstellen *(to* zu), verbinden *(to* mit)

switch: **switchback** N *(US)* Berg- und Talbahn *f*; *(Brit, = roller-coaster also)* Achterbahn *f*; **switchblade** N *(US)* Schnappmesser *nt*; **switchboard** N *(Telec: = exchange)* Vermittlung *f*; *(in office etc)* Zentrale *f*; *(= actual panel, Elec)* Schalttafel *f*; **switchboard operator** N *(in office)* Telefonist(in) *m(f)*; **switch box** N *(Elec)* Schaltkasten *m*; **switch clock** N *(Tech)* Schaltuhr *f*

switcheroo [ˌswɪtʃəˈruː] N *(esp US inf)* Kehrtwendung *f*; **to pull a ~** eine Kehrtwendung machen

switch: **switchgear** N *no pl (Elec)* Schaltgerät *nt*; **switch-hit** VI *(Baseball)* beidhändig schlagen; **switch-hitter** N *(Baseball)* beidhändiger Hitter; **switchman** N *(US Rail)* Weichensteller *m*; **switch-over** N Wechsel *m* *(to* auf *+acc*, zu), Umstellung *f* *(to* auf *+acc)*; *(= exchange)* Tausch *m*; *(of letters, figures etc)* Vertauschung *f*; **switch-round** N Tausch *m*; *(of letters, figures etc)* Vertauschung *f*; *(= rearrangement)* Umstellen *nt*; **switch yard** N *(US Rail)* Rangierbahnhof *m*

Switzerland [ˈswɪtsələnd] N die Schweiz; **to ~** in die Schweiz; **French-/German-/Italian-speaking ~** die französische/deutsche/italienische Schweiz, die französisch-/deutsch-/italienischsprachige Schweiz

swivel [ˈswɪvl] N Drehgelenk *nt* *attr* Dreh-; **~ base** *(of monitor etc)* Schwenksockel *m*; **~ chair** Drehstuhl *m* VT *(also* **swivel round***)* (herum)drehen VI *(also* **swivel round***)* sich drehen; *(person)* sich herumdrehen

swivel bridge N *(Tech)* Drehbrücke *f*

swivelling [ˈswɪvəlɪŋ] ADJ schwenkbar

swizz [swɪz], **swizzle** [ˈswɪzl] N *(Brit inf: = swindle)* Bauernfängerei *f* *(inf)*; *(= disappointment)* Gemeinheit *f* *(inf)*

swizzle stick N Sektquirl *m*

swollen [ˈswəʊlən] *ptp of* **swell** ADJ *ankle, face, glands etc* (an)geschwollen; *stomach* aufgedunsen, aufgebläht; *wood* verquollen, gequollen; *sails* gebläht; *river* angeschwollen, angestiegen; *numbers* (an)gestiegen, angewachsen; **her eyes were ~ with tears** ihre Augen waren verweint; **he has a ~ head** *(fig)* er ist so aufgeblasen

swollen-headed [ˌswəʊlənˈhedɪd] ADJ aufgeblasen *(inf)*

swollen-headedness [ˌswəʊlənˈhedɪdnɪs] N Aufgeblasenheit *f* *(inf)*

swoon [swuːn] N *(old)* Ohnmacht *f*; **to fall into a ~** in Ohnmacht fallen *or* sinken *(geh)*; **to be in a ~** ohnmächtig sein VI *(old: = faint)* in Ohnmacht fallen, ohnmächtig werden; *(fig: over pop star etc)* beinahe ohnmächtig werden *(over sb/sth* wegen jdm/einer Sache); **to ~ over sb/sth** vom jdm/etw schwärmen

swoop [swuːp] VI *(lit: also* **swoop down***, bird)* herabstoßen, niederstoßen *(on* auf *+acc)*; *(plane)* einen Sturzflug machen; *(fig, police)* einen Überraschungsangriff machen *(on* auf *+acc) or* landen *(inf)* *(on* bei); *(person)* sich stürzen *(on* auf *+acc)*; **the plane ~ed low over the village** das Flugzeug flog im Tiefflug über das Dorf hinweg; **the police ~ed on 8 suspects** die Polizei schlug überraschend bei 8 Verdächtigen zu; **they're just waiting to ~** die lauern nur darauf zuzuschlagen

N *(of bird, plane)* Sturzflug *m*; *(by police)* Razzia *f* *(on* in *+dat, on sb* bei jdm); **to make a ~** *(bird)* herabstoßen *(on* auf *+acc)*; **at** *or* **in one (fell) ~** auf einen Schlag

swoosh [swuːʃ] VI rauschen; *(tyres in rain etc)* pfeifen, sirren; *(air)* brausen; *(skirts, curtains)* rauschen N Rauschen *nt*; *(of air)* Brausen *nt*; *(of tyres in rain etc)* Pfeifen *nt*, Sirren *nt*; *(of skirts, curtains)* Rauschen *nt*

swop N, VTI = **swap**

sword [sɔːd] N Schwert *nt*; **to cross ~s with sb** *(lit, fig)* mit jdm die Klinge(n) kreuzen; **by fire and (the) ~** mit Feuer und Schwert; **those that live by the ~ die by the ~** *(prov)* wer das Schwert ergreift, der soll durchs Schwert umkommen

sword *in cpds* Schwert-; **sword and sorcery** N *(Liter)* *Sciencefiction mit mittelalterlichen Themen*; **swordbearer** N Schwertträger *m*; **sword cane** N Stockdegen *m*; **sword dance** N Schwert(er)tanz *m*; **swordfish** N Schwertfisch *m*; **swordplay** N (Schwert)fechten *nt*; **swordpoint** N **at ~** mit vorgehaltener Klinge

swordsman [ˈsɔːdzmən] N *pl* **-men** [-mən] Schwertkämpfer *m*; *(= fencer)* Fechter *m*

swordsmanship [ˈsɔːdzmənʃɪp] N Fechtkunst *f*

sword: **swordstick** N Stockdegen *m*; **sword swallower** [ˈsɔːdswɒləʊəʳ] N Schwertschlucker(in) *m(f)*

swore [swɔːʳ] *pret of* **swear**

sworn [swɔːn] *ptp of* **swear** ADJ *enemy* eingeschworen; **~ statement/testimony** *(Jur)* eidliche Aussage, Aussage *f* unter Eid

swot [swɒt] *(Brit inf)* VI büffeln *(inf)*, pauken *(inf)*; **to ~ up (on) one's maths** Mathe pauken *(inf)*; **to ~ at sth** etw pauken *(inf) or* büffeln *(inf)* VT büffeln *(inf)*, pauken *(inf)* N *(pej: = person)* Streber(in) *m(f)*

swotter [ˈswɒtəʳ] N *(Brit inf)* Büffler(in) *m(f)* *(inf)*, Streber(in) *m(f)* *(inf, pej)*

swotting [ˈswɒtɪŋ] N *(Brit inf)* Büffeln *(inf)*, Pauken *(inf) nt*; **to do some ~** büffeln *(inf)*, pauken *(inf)*

swum [swʌm] *ptp of* **swim**

swung [swʌŋ] *pret, ptp of* **swing** ADJ *(Typ)* **~ dash** Tilde *f*

sybarite [ˈsɪbəraɪt] N *(form)* Genussmensch *m*

sybaritic [ˌsɪbəˈrɪtɪk] ADJ *(form) person* genusssüchtig; *way of life* schwelgerisch

sycamore [ˈsɪkəmɔːʳ] N Bergahorn *m*; *(US: = plane tree)* nordamerikanische Platane; *(= wood)* Ahorn *m*

sycophancy [ˈsɪkəfənsɪ] N Kriecherei *f*, Speichelleckerei *f* *(inf)*

sycophant [ˈsɪkəfənt] N Kriecher(in) *m(f)*, Speichellecker(in) *m(f)* *(inf)*

sycophantic [ˌsɪkəˈfæntɪk] ADJ kriecherisch, unterwürfig

syllabary [ˈsɪləbərɪ] N Syllabar *nt*, Silbentabelle *f*

syllabic [sɪˈlæbɪk] ADJ silbisch

syllabification [sɪˌlæbɪfɪˈkeɪʃən] N Silbentrennung *f*

syllable [ˈsɪləbl] N Silbe *f*; **a two-~(d) word** ein zweisilbiges Wort; **in words of one ~** *(hum)* in einfachen Worten

syllabub [ˈsɪləbʌb] N *(= dessert)* *Obstspeise mit Sahne*

syllabus ['sɪləbəs] N *pl* **-es** *or* **syllabi** ['sɪləbaɪ] (*esp Brit: Sch, Univ*) Lehrplan *m*; (*of club etc*) Programm *nt*; **the Syllabus (of Errors)** (*Eccl*) der Syllabus (von Zeitirrtümern)

syllogism ['sɪlədʒɪzəm] N Syllogismus *m*

syllogistic [,sɪlə'dʒɪstɪk] ADJ syllogistisch

syllogize ['sɪlədʒaɪz] VI syllogistisch folgern

sylph [sɪlf] N (*Myth*) Sylphe *mf*; (*fig: = girl*) Sylphide *f*, Nymphe *f*

sylphid ['sɪlfɪd] N Sylphide *f*

sylphlike ['sɪlflaɪk] ADJ *figure etc* grazil, sylphidenhaft

sylvan, silvan ['sɪlvən] ADJ (*liter*) Wald-; *shade* des Waldes; *surroundings* waldig; **~ goddess** Waldgöttin *f*

symbiosis [,sɪmbɪ'əʊsɪs] N Symbiose *f*

symbiotic [,sɪmbɪ'ɒtɪk] ADJ symbiotisch

symbol ['sɪmbəl] N **a** Symbol *nt*, Zeichen *nt* (of für) **b** (*Comput*) Sonderzeichen *nt*; **"insert ~"** „Sonderzeichen einfügen"

symbolic(al) [sɪm'bɒlɪk(əl)] ADJ symbolisch (*of* für); **to be ~ of sth** etw symbolisieren, ein Symbol für etw sein; **symbolic logic** mathematische Logik

symbolically [sɪm'bɒlɪkəlɪ] ADV *represent* symbolisch; **~ important** von symbolischer Bedeutung

symbolism ['sɪmbəlɪzəm] N Symbolik *f*; (*Art, Liter, = movement*) Symbolismus *m*

symbolist ['sɪmbəlɪst] **N** Symbolist(in) *m(f)* **ADJ** symbolistisch

symbolization [,sɪmbəlaɪ'zeɪʃən] N Symbolisierung *f*

symbolize ['sɪmbəlaɪz] VT symbolisieren

symmetrical ADJ, **symmetrically** ADV [sɪ'metrɪkəl, -ɪ] symmetrisch

symmetry ['sɪmɪtrɪ] N Symmetrie *f*

sympathetic [,sɪmpə'θetɪk] ADJ **a** (*= showing pity*) mitfühlend, teilnahmsvoll; (*= understanding*) verständnisvoll; (*= well-disposed*) wohlwollend, wohlgesonnen (*geh*); *look, smile* verbindlich, freundlich; **to be** *or* **feel ~ to(wards) sb** (*= showing pity*) mit jdm mitfühlen; (*= understanding*) jdm Verständnis entgegenbringen, für jdn Verständnis haben; (*= being well-disposed*) mit jdm sympathisieren; **he was most ~ when I told him all my troubles** er zeigte sehr viel Mitgefühl für all meine Sorgen; **a ~ ear** ein offenes Ohr
b (*= likeable*) sympathisch
c (*Physiol, Phys*) sympathisch; **~ vibration** Mitschwingung *f*; **~ string** mitschwingende Saite, Bordunsaite *f*; **~ magic** Sympathiezauber *m*

sympathetically [,sɪmpə'θetɪkəlɪ] ADV (*= showing pity*) mitfühlend; (*= with understanding*) verständnisvoll; (*= well-disposed*) wohlwollend; **to be ~ inclined toward(s) sb/sth** jdm/einer Sache wohlwollend gegenüberstehen; **to respond/vibrate ~** (*Phys etc*) mitreagieren/-schwingen

sympathize ['sɪmpəθaɪz] VI (*= feel compassion*) mitfühlen, Mitleid haben (*with* mit); (*= understand*) Verständnis haben (*with* für); (*= agree*) sympathisieren (*with* mit) (*esp Pol*); (*= express sympathy*) sein Mitgefühl aussprechen; (*on bereavement*) sein Beileid aussprechen; **to ~ with sb over sth** (*= feel sorry*) mit jdm in einer Sache mitfühlen können; **to ~ with sb's views** jds Ansichten teilen; **to ~ with sb's problems** mit jdm mitfühlen; **I really do ~** (*= have pity*) das tut mir wirklich leid; (*= understand your feelings*) ich habe wirklich vollstes Verständnis; **I ~ with you** *or* **with what you say/feel, but …** ich teile Ihre Ansichten/Gefühle, aber …, ich kann Ihnen das nachfühlen, aber …; **to ~ with sb in his bereavement/grief** jds Verlust/Schmerz teilen; (*= express sympathy*) jdm sein Beileid/Mitgefühl aussprechen

sympathizer ['sɪmpəθaɪzə'] N Mitfühlende(r) *mf*; (*at death also*) Kondolierende(r) *mf*; (*with cause*) Sympathisant(in) *m(f)*

sympathy ['sɪmpəθɪ] ✪ 24.4 N **a** (*= pity, compassion*) Mitgefühl *nt*, Mitleid *nt* (*for* mit); (*at death*) Beileid *nt*; **to feel** *or* **have ~ for sb** Mitgefühl *or* Mitleid mit jdm haben; **a letter of ~** ein mitfühlender Brief, ein Beileidsbrief *m*; **you have our deepest** *or* **heartfelt ~** *or* **sympathies** wir fühlen mit Ihnen, (unser) aufrichtiges *or* herzliches Beileid; **you have my ~!** (*hum*) herzliches Beileid (*hum*); **my sympathies are with her family** mir tut ihre Familie leid; **to express one's ~** sein Mitgefühl aussprechen, sein Beileid aussprechen; **you won't get any ~ from me** erwarte kein Mitleid von mir
b (*= understanding*) Verständnis *nt*; (*= fellow-feeling, agreement*) Sympathie *f*; **to be in/out of ~ with sb/sth** mit jdm/etw einhergehen/nicht einhergehen; **the sympathies of the crowd were with him** (*in match, discussion*) die Zuschauer waren auf seiner Seite; **he has Democratic sympathies** er sympathisiert mit den Demokraten; **politically there was a lack of ~ between them** sie verstanden sich politisch nicht gut; **to come out** *or* **strike in ~** (*Ind*) in Sympathiestreik treten; **the dollar fell and the pound fell in ~** der Dollar fiel und das Pfund fiel mit; **to resonate/vibrate in ~** mitklingen/-schwingen

sympathy strike N Sympathiestreik *m*

symphonic [sɪm'fɒnɪk] ADJ sinfonisch, symphonisch

symphonic poem N sinfonische *or* symphonische Dichtung

symphony ['sɪmfənɪ] N Sinfonie *f*, Symphonie *f*; **a ~ of colours** (*liter*) eine Sinfonie von Farben, eine Farbensinfonie

symphony orchestra N Sinfonie- *or* Symphonieorchester *nt*; **the London Symphony Orchestra** die Londoner Symphoniker *pl*

symposium [sɪm'pəʊzɪəm] N *pl* **-s** *or* **symposia** [sɪm'pəʊzɪə] Symposium *nt*, Symposion *nt*

symptom ['sɪmptəm] N (*lit, fig*) Symptom *nt*

symptomatic [,sɪmptə'mætɪk] ADJ symptomatisch (*of* für)

symptomize ['sɪmptəmaɪz] VT symptomatisch sein für

synaesthesia, (*US*) **synesthesia** [,sɪnəs'θiːzɪə] N *no pl* Synästhesie *f*

synagogue ['sɪnəgɒg] N Synagoge *f*

synapse ['saɪnæps] N (*Physiol*) Synapse *f*

sync [sɪŋk] N (*Film, TV inf*) *abbr of* **synchronization**; **in ~** synchron; **out of ~** nicht synchron; **to be in ~ with the lights** (*Mot, inf*) grüne Welle haben (*inf*)

synchro ['sɪŋkrəʊ] (*Aut inf*) *abbr of* **synchromesh** **N** Synchrongetriebe *nt* **ATTR** **~ gearbox** Getriebe *nt* mit Synchroneinrichtung

synchromesh ['sɪŋkrəʊ,meʃ] N Synchrongetriebe *nt*

synchronic [sɪŋ'krɒnɪk] ADJ (*Ling*) synchronisch

synchronization [,sɪŋkrənaɪ'zeɪʃən] N Abstimmung *f*; (*Film*) Synchronisation *f*; (*of clocks*) Gleichstellung *f*; (*of actions*) Zusammenfall *m*, gleichzeitiger Ablauf; (*of movements*) Übereinstimmung *f*

synchronize ['sɪŋkrənaɪz] **VT** abstimmen (*with* auf *+acc*); *two actions, movements* aufeinander abstimmen; (*Film*) synchronisieren (*with* mit); *clocks* gleichstellen (*with* mit); **~ (your) watches!** Uhrenvergleich!; **~d swimming** Synchronschwimmen *nt* **VI** (*Film*) synchron sein (*with* mit); (*clocks*) gleich gehen; (*actions*) zusammenfallen, gleichzeitig ablaufen (*with* mit); (*movements*) in Übereinstimmung sein (*with* mit)

synchronous ['sɪŋkrənəs] ADJ gleichzeitig; (*Comput*) synchron

syncopate ['sɪŋkəpeɪt] VT (*Mus*) synkopieren; (*Ling also*) zusammenziehen

syncopation [,sɪŋkə'peɪʃən] N Synkope *f*; (*= act*) Synkopierung *f*

syncope ['sɪŋkəpɪ] N (*Ling, Med*) Synkope *f*

syncretism ['sɪŋkrɪtɪzəm] N (*Ling*) Synkretismus *m*

syndicalism ['sɪndɪkəlɪzəm] N Syndikalismus *m*

syndicate ['sɪndɪkɪt] **N** Interessengemeinschaft *f*; (*for gambling*) Wettgemeinschaft *f*; (*Comm*) Syndikat *nt*, Verband *m*; (*Press*) (Presse)zentrale *f*; (*= crime syndicate*) Ring *m* ['sɪndɪkeɪt] **VT** (*Press*) an mehrere Zeitungen verkaufen; **there are several ~d articles in this newspaper** mehrere Artikel dieser Zeitung stammen aus einer Pressezentrale

syndrome ['sɪndrəʊm] N (*Med*) Syndrom *nt*; (*fig, Sociol*) Phänomen *nt*

synecdoche [sɪ'nekdəkɪ] N Synekdoche *f*

synergistic ADJ, **synergistically** ADV [,sɪnə'dʒɪstɪk, -əlɪ] (*Med, Pharm, Physiol*) synergistisch, zusammenwirkend; **~ effect** (*Econ*) Synergieeffekt *m*

synergy ['sɪnədʒɪ] N Synergie *f*; **~ effect** Synergieeffekt *m*

synesthesia [,sɪnəs'θiːzɪə] N (*US*) = **synaesthesia**

synod ['sɪnəd] N Synode *f*

synodal ['sɪnədl], **synodic** [sɪ'nɒdɪk], **synodical** [sɪ'nɒdɪkl] ADJ **a** (*Rel*) synodal **b** (*Astron*) *month* synodisch

synonym ['sɪnənɪm] N Synonym *nt*

synonymous [sɪ'nɒnɪməs] ADJ synonym, synonymisch; **his name was ~ with sex** sein Name war gleichbedeutend mit Sex

synonymy [sɪ'nɒnəmɪ] N Synonymik *f*

synopsis [sɪ'nɒpsɪs] N *pl* **synopses** [sɪ'nɒpsiːz] Abriss *m* der Handlung; (*of article, book*) Zusammenfassung *f*

synoptic [sɪ'nɒptɪk] ADJ zusammenfassend; **~ view** Überblick *m*, Übersicht *f*; **Synoptic Gospels** die Evangelien des Markus, Matthäus und Lukas; **~ chart** (*Met*) synoptische Karte

syntactic(al) [sɪn'tæktɪk(əl)] ADJ syntaktisch

syntax ['sɪntæks] N Syntax *f*; (*of sentence also*) Satzbau *m*; **~ error** (*Comput*) Syntaxfehler *m*

synthesis ['sɪnθəsɪs] N *pl* **syntheses** ['sɪnθəsiːz] Synthese *f*; (*= artificial production also*) Synthetisieren *nt*

synthesize ['sɪnθəsaɪz] VT synthetisieren; *speech* synthetisch bilden; *theories etc* zusammenfassen

synthesizer ['sɪnθə,saɪzə'] N (*Mus*) Synthesizer *m*

synthetic [sɪn'θetɪk] **ADJ** **a** synthetisch; **~ fibre** Kunstfaser *f*; **~ smile** künstliches *or* gekünsteltes Lächeln **b** (*Ling, Philos*) synthetisch **N** Kunststoff *m*, synthetischer Stoff; **~s** Synthetik *f*

synthetically [sɪn'θetɪkəlɪ] ADV synthetisch, künstlich; (*fig*) *smile* gekünstelt

syphilis ['sɪfɪlɪs] N Syphilis *f*

syphilitic [,sɪfɪ'lɪtɪk] **ADJ** syphilitisch **N** Syphilitiker(in) *m(f)*

syphon N = **siphon**

Syracuse ['saɪərəkjuːz] N (*= town in Sicily*) Syrakus *nt*

Syria ['sɪrɪə] N Syrien *nt*

Syrian ['sɪrɪən] **ADJ** syrisch **N** Syr(i)er(in) *m(f)*

syringa [sɪ'rɪŋgə] N (*Bot*) Falscher Jasmin, Pfeifenstrauch *m*; (*= lilac*) Flieder *m*, Syringe *f*

syringe [sɪ'rɪndʒ] (*Med*) **N** Spritze *f* **VT** (aus)spülen

syrup, (*US also*) **sirup** ['sɪrəp] N Sirup *m* (*also Med*); (*= preservative also*) Saft *m*; **~ of figs** Feigensaft *m*; **fruit ~** Fruchtsirup *m*; **cough ~** (*Med*) Hustensaft *or* -sirup *m*

syrupy, (*US also*) **sirupy** ['sɪrəpɪ] ADJ sirupartig, sirupähnlich; (*pej*) *smile, voice* zucker- *or* honigsüß; (*= sentimental*) *voice, song* schmalzig

system ['sɪstəm] N **a** System *nt*; **new teaching ~s** neue Lehrmethoden *pl*; **the democratic ~ of government** das demokratische (Regierungs)system; **the Pitman ~ of shorthand** die Kurzschriftmethode nach Pitman; **~ of references** Bezugs- *or* Referenzsystem *nt*
b (*= working whole*) System *nt*; **digestive ~** Verdauungsapparat *m*; **respiratory ~** Atmungsapparat *m*; **it's good for the ~** das ist gesund; **to pass through the ~** den Körper auf natürlichem Wege verlassen; **to be absorbed into the ~** aufgenommen werden; **it was a shock to his ~** er hatte schwer damit zu schaffen; **to get sth**

out of one's ~ *(fig inf)* sich *(dat)* etw von der Seele schaffen, etw loswerden *(inf)*; **it's all ~s go!** *(inf)* jetzt heißt es: volle Kraft voraus!
c *(= established authority)* **the ~** das System; **you can't beat** *or* **buck the ~** gegen das System kommst du *or* kommt man einfach nicht an
d (*Comput*: *= machine, operating system*) System *nt*; **~ disk** Systemdiskette *f*; **~ software** Systemsoftware *f*

systematic [ˌsɪstəˈmætɪk] **ADJ** systematisch; *liar, cruelty* ständig; **he works in a ~ way** er arbeitet mit System; **on a ~ basis** systematisch

systematically [ˌsɪstəˈmætɪkəlɪ] **ADV** systematisch

systematization [ˌsɪstəmətaɪˈzeɪʃən] **N** Systematisierung *f*

systematize [ˈsɪstəmətaɪz] **VT** systematisieren

system: **system building** **N** *(Archit)* Systembauweise *f*; **system control** **N** *(Comput etc)* Systemsteuerung *f*; **system crash** **N** *(Comput)* Systemabsturz *m*; **system error** **N** *(Comput)* Systemfehler *m*; **system failure** **N** Systemausfall *m*; **system fault** **N** *(Comput)* Systemfehler *m*; **system file** **N** *(Comput)* Systemdatei *f*

systemic [sɪˈstemɪk] **ADJ** systemisch

system: **system information** **N** *(Comput)* Systeminformationen *pl*; **system menu** **N** *(Comput)* Systemmenü *nt*; **system policies** **N** *(Comput)* Systemrichtlinien *pl*; **system program** **N** *(Comput)* Systemprogramm *nt*; **system prompt** **N** *(Comput)* Eingabeaufforderung *f*

systems [ˈsɪstəmz]: **systems administrator** **N** *(Comput)* Systembetreuer(in) *m(f)*; **systems analysis** **N** Systemanalyse *f*; **systems analyst** **N** Systemanalytiker(in) *m(f)*; **systems disk** **N** *(Comput)* Systemdiskette *f*; **systems engineer** **N** Systemtechniker(in) *m(f)*; **systems manager** **N** Systemmanager(in) *m(f)*; **systems program** **N** *(Comput)* Systemprogramm *nt*; **systems software** **N** Systemsoftware *f*

system tools **N** *(Comput)* Systemprogramme *pl (in Windows®)*

systole [ˈsɪstəlɪ] **N** *(Physiol)* Systole *f*

systolic [sɪˈstɒlɪk] **ADJ** *(Physiol) blood pressure* systolisch

T

T, t [tiː] N T *nt*, t *nt*; **it suits him to a T** es ist genau das Richtige für ihn; **that's him to a T** das ist er, wie er leibt und lebt; **that's it to a T** genau so ist es; **he got him to a T** er hat ihn haargenau getroffen

TA *(Brit) abbr of* **Territorial Army** **a** *(US) abbr of* **teaching assistant**

ta [tɑː] INTERJ *(Brit inf)* danke

tab¹ [tæb] N **a** *(= loop on coat etc)* Aufhänger *m*; *(on back of boot, book)* Schlaufe *f*; *(= fastener on coat etc)* Riegel *m*; *(= name tab, of owner)* Namensschild *nt*; *(of maker)* Etikett *nt*; *(on collar)* Verschluss(riegel) *m*; *(Mil)* Spiegel *m*; *(on shoulder, pocket)* Klappe *f*, Patte *f*; *(on filing cards)* Tab *m*, Reiter *m*; **to keep ~s on sb/sth** *(inf)* jdn/etw genau im Auge behalten **b** *(Aviat)* Klappe *f* **c** *(esp US inf: = bill)* Rechnung *f*; **to pick up the ~** *(also Brit)* die Rechnung übernehmen **d** *(Drugs inf)* Pappe *f (sl)*, Paper *nt (sl)*, Ticket *nt (sl)*

tab² *(Comput etc)* **N** Tab(ulator) *m*; *(in dialog box)* Registerkarte *f*; *(on typewriter)* Tabulator *m*; **to set the ~s** tabulieren **VT** *columns* tabulieren

tabard [ˈtæbəd] N *(of knight, herald)* Heroldsrock *m*, Wappenrock *m*, Tappert *m*; *(Fashion) ärmelloser, an den Seiten offener Kasak*

Tabasco® [təˈbæskəʊ] N Tabasco® *m*, Tabascosoße *f*

tabbed [ˈtæbd] ADJ *(Comput) dialog box etc* im Registerformat

tabby [ˈtæbɪ] N **a** *(also* **tabby cat***)* getigerte Katze; *(= female cat)* (weibliche) Katze **b** *(inf, = old maid)* Tantchen *nt (inf)*

tabernacle [ˈtæbənækl] N *(= church)* Gotteshaus *nt*; *(= receptacle)* Tabernakel *m or nt*; **the Tabernacle** *(Bibl)* die Stiftshütte

tab key N Tabtaste *f*; *(on typewriter)* Tabulatortaste *f*

table [ˈteɪbl] **N** **a** Tisch *m*; *(= banquet table)* Tafel *f*; **at the ~** am Tisch; **at ~** bei Tisch; **to sit at ~** sich zu Tisch setzen; **to sit down at a ~** sich an einen Tisch setzen; **he was sitting at the Mayor's ~** er saß am Bürgermeistertisch; **who was on your ~?** wer saß an Ihrem Tisch *or* bei Ihnen am Tisch?; **to eat at sb's ~** seine Beine *or* Füße unter jds Tisch strecken *(inf)*; **to be under the ~** *(= drunk)* unter dem Tisch liegen; **to drink sb under the ~** jdn unter den Tisch trinken; **the motion is on the ~** *(Brit Parl)* der Antrag liegt vor; **on the ~** *(US: = postponed)* zurückgestellt, aufgeschoben; **to turn the ~s (on sb)** (gegenüber jdm) den Spieß umdrehen *or* umkehren

b *(= people at a table)* Tisch *m*, Tischrunde *f*; **the whole ~ laughed** der ganze Tisch *or* die ganze Runde lachte

c *(of figures, prices etc, Sport, Comput)* Tabelle *f*; *(= log table)* Logarithmentafel *f*; **(multiplication) ~s** Einmaleins *nt*; *(up to 10)* kleines Einmaleins; *(from 11 to 20)* großes Einmaleins; **to say one's three/five times ~** das Einmaldrei/Einmalfünf aufsagen; **~ of contents** Inhaltsverzeichnis *nt*

d *(Bibl: = tablet)* Tafel *f*

e *(Geog)* **water ~** Grundwasserspiegel *m*

f *(= tableland)* Tafelland *nt*, Plateau *nt*, Hochebene *f*

VT **a** *motion, amendment, resolution* einbringen

b *(US: = postpone) bill* zurückstellen

c *(= put in tabular form)* tabellarisieren *(form)*, in einer Tabelle zusammenstellen

tableau [ˈtæbləʊ] N *pl* **-s** *or* **-x** [ˈtæbləʊz] *(Art, Theat)* Tableau *nt*; *(fig)* Bild *nt*, Szene *f*

table: **table clamp** N Tisch(tuch)klammer *f*; **tablecloth** N Tischdecke *f or* -tuch *nt*; **table dancing** N *(on table)* Striptease *m* auf einem Tisch; **table d'hôte** [ˌtɑːblˈdəʊt] N Tagesmenü *or* -gedeck *nt*; **table d'hôte menu** N Tageskarte *f*; **table-hop** VI *(inf, in restaurant etc)* von einem Tisch zum andern gehen; **table lamp** N Tischlampe *f*; **tableland** N Tafelland *nt*, Plateau *nt*, Hochebene *f*; **table licence** N Schankerlaubnis *f* bei Abgabe von Speisen; **table-lifting** N Anheben *nt* von Tischen; **table lighter** N Tischfeuerzeug *nt*; **table linen** N *no pl* Tischwäsche *f*; **table manners** PL Tischmanieren *pl*; **table mat** N Untersetzer *m*; *(of cloth)* Set *nt*; **Table Mountain** N Tafelberg *m*; **table napkin** N Serviette *f*; **table-rapping** N Tischrücken *nt*; **table salt** N Tafelsalz *nt*; **table soccer** N Tischfußball *nt*; **tablespoon** N Esslöffel *m*; **tablespoonful** N Esslöffel *m* (voll)

tablet [ˈtæblɪt] N **a** *(Pharm)* Tablette *f* **b** *(of paper)* Block *m*; *(of wax, clay)* Täfelchen *nt*; *(of soap)* Stückchen *nt* **c** *(on wall etc)* Tafel *f*, Platte *f*

table: **table talk** N *no pl* Tischgespräch *nt*; **table tennis** N Tischtennis *nt*; **table top** N Tischplatte *f*; **table-turning** N Drehen *nt* von Tischen; **tableware** N *no pl* Tafelgeschirr *nt* und -besteck *nt*; **table water** N Tafelwasser *nt*; **table wine** N Tafelwein *m*

tabloid [ˈtæblɔɪd] N *(also* **tabloid newspaper***) bebilderte, kleinformatige Zeitung (pej)* Boulevardzeitung *f*, Revolverblatt *nt (inf)*; **~ journalism** Sensations- *or* Boulevardpresse *f*; **~ TV** Sensationsreportagen *pl* im Fernsehen

> **TABLOIDS, BROADSHEETS**
>
> In Großbritannien konnte man früher schon an der Größe einer Zeitung deren Ausrichtung erkennen. Die größeren Exemplare, **broadsheets** („Daily Telegraph", „Times", „Guardian" und „Independent"), konzentrierten sich auf ernsthafte Berichterstattung und fundierte Artikel, die kleinformatigen **tabloids** („Sun", „Daily Mirror", „Daily Express" und „Daily Star") dagegen zeichneten sich durch eine reißerische, prägnante Aufmachung aus: dicke Balkenüberschriften, kurze Artikel, viele Fotos, offen ausgesprochene Meinungen und eine Vorliebe für Liebes- und Skandalgeschichten. Inzwischen jedoch sind auch viele der seriöseren Zeitungen auf das handlichere **Tabloid**-Format, auch **Compact** genannt, umgestiegen.
> In den USA ist der übliche Begriff für seriöse Tageszeitungen „standard-sized newspaper". Die größte überregionale Zeitung dieser Prägung ist die landesweite Ausgabe der „New York Times". Zu den bekanntesten Boulevardblättern zählen „New York Daily News" und „Chicago Sun-Times".

taboo, tabu [təˈbuː] **N** Tabu *nt*; **to be a ~** tabu sein, unter einem Tabu stehen **ADJ** tabu; **~ words** Tabuwörter *pl* **VT** für tabu erklären, tabui(sier)eren

tabo(u)ret [ˈtæbʊreɪ] N *(Sew)* Stickrahmen *m*

tabo stop N *(Comput, typewriter)* Tabstopp *m*

tabu N, ADJ, VT = **taboo**

tabular [ˈtæbjʊləʳ] ADJ tabellenförmig, tabellarisch; **in ~ form** in Tabellenform, tabellarisch

tabulate [ˈtæbjʊleɪt] VT tabellarisch aufzeichnen *or* darstellen, tabellarisieren

tabulation [ˌtæbjʊˈleɪʃən] N tabellarische Aufstellung, Tabellarisierung *f*

tabulator [ˈtæbjʊleɪtəʳ] N *(on typewriter)* Tabulator *m*

tache [tæʃ] N *(Brit inf)* Schnurrbart *m*, Oberlippenbart *m*

tachograph [ˈtækəʊgrɑːf] N *(Brit)* Fahrtenschreiber *m*, Tachograf *m*

tachometer [tæˈkɒmɪtəʳ] N Drehzahlmesser *m*

tachycardia [ˌtækɪˈkɑːdɪə] N Herzjagen *nt*, Tachykardie *f (spec)*

tacit [ˈtæsɪt] ADJ stillschweigend

tacitly [ˈtæsɪtlɪ] ADV *accept, support, acknowledge, approve of* stillschweigend; **it was ~ understood that …** es bestand ein stillschweigendes Einvernehmen darüber, dass …

taciturn [ˈtæsɪtɜːn] ADJ schweigsam, wortkarg

taciturnity [ˌtæsɪˈtɜːnɪtɪ] N Schweigsamkeit *f*, Wortkargheit *f*

tack¹ [tæk] **N** **a** *(= nail)* kleiner Nagel; *(esp with small head)* Stift *m*; *(for shoes)* Tä(c)ks *m*; *(esp US: = drawing pin)* Reiß- *or* Heftzwecke *f*, Reißnagel *m*

b *(Brit, Sew)* Heftstich *m*

c *(Naut: = course)* Schlag *m*; *(fig)* Richtung *f*, Weg *m*; **to be on the port/starboard ~** auf Backbord-/Steuerbordbug segeln; **they are on a new/different ~** *(fig)* sie haben eine neue/andere Richtung eingeschlagen; **to be on the right/wrong ~** *(fig)* auf der richtigen/falschen Spur sein, richtig-/falschliegen *(inf)*; **to try another ~** *(fig)* es anders versuchen

d *(Naut: = zigzag)* Aufkreuzen *nt*; **to make a ~ toward(s) land** landwärts kreuzen

e *(for horse)* Sattel- und Zaumzeug *nt*

VT **a** *(with nail)* annageln *(to* an *+dat or acc)*; *(with clip, pin)* feststecken *(to* an *+dat)*

b *(Brit Sew)* heften

VI **a** *(Naut)* aufkreuzen; **to ~ to port** mit Backbordbug kreuzen

b *(Brit Sew)* heften

► **tack about** VI *(Naut)* wenden

► **tack down** VT *sep* festnageln; *(Brit Sew)* festheften

► **tack on** VT *sep* annageln *(-to* an *+acc or dat)*; *(with drawing pin)* anstecken *(-to* an *+acc or dat)*; *(with clips)* anheften, anstecken *(-to* an *+acc or dat)*; *(Sew)* anheften; *(fig)* anhängen *(-to +dat)*

► **tack together** VT *sep (with nails)* zusammennageln; *(with clips)* zusammenstecken *or* -heften; *(Sew)* zusammenheften

► **tack up** VT *sep* **a** *picture etc* anpinnen; *(with drawing pins)* mit Reißzwecken aufhängen; *(Brit) hem* heften **b** *horse* satteln

tack[2] N (*Naut: = biscuits*) Schiffszwieback *m*

tack[3] N (*inf*) = **tackiness**[2]

tackiness[1] ['tækɪnɪs] N (*of paint etc*) Klebrigkeit *f*

tackiness[2] N (*inf*) Billigkeit *f*; (*of area, bar*) heruntergekommener Zustand; (*of clothes, food, colour scheme*) Geschmacklosigkeit *f*

tacking ['tækɪŋ] N **a** (*Brit Sew*) Heften *nt* **b** (*Naut*) Aufkreuzen *nt*

tacking stitches PL (*Brit Sew*) Heftstiche *pl*

tacking thread N (*Brit Sew*) Heftfaden *m*

tackle ['tækl] **N** **a** (*= lifting gear*) Flaschenzug *m*; (*Naut*) Talje *f*, Takel *nt*, Zugwinde *f* **b** (*Naut, = rigging*) Tauwerk *nt* **c** (*= equipment*) Ausrüstung *f*, Zeug *nt* (*inf*); **fishing ~** Angelausrüstung *f* or -zeug *nt* (*inf*) **d** (*Sport*) Angriff *m*, Tackling *nt* **VT** **a** (*physically, Sport*) angreifen, angehen (*geh*); (*Rugby*) fassen; (*verbally*) zur Rede stellen (*about* wegen) **b** (*= undertake*) *job* in Angriff nehmen; *new challenge* sich versuchen an (*+dat*); *problem* angehen, anpacken (*inf*); (*= manage to cope with*) bewältigen, fertig werden mit; *blaze, fire* bekämpfen; **could you ~ another ice cream?** (*inf*) schaffst du noch ein Eis? (*inf*); **I don't know how to ~ it** ich weiß nicht, wie ich es anfangen soll **VI** angreifen

tack-weld VTI (*Tech*) heftschweißen

tacky[1] ['tækɪ] ADJ (*+er*) klebrig; **the paint is still ~** die Farbe klebt noch

tacky[2] ADJ (*+er*) (*inf*) billig; *area, bar* heruntergekommen; *clothes, food, colour scheme* geschmacklos; **Bill's outfit is totally ~** Bills Klamotten sind total out (*inf*)

tact [tækt] N *no pl* Takt *m*

tactful ['tæktfʊl] ADJ taktvoll; **to be ~ about sth** etw mit Feingefühl behandeln; **it was not the most ~ way to put it/of saying it** es war nicht besonders taktvoll, es so auszudrücken; **to be ~ with sb** taktvoll mit jdm umgehen

tactfully ['tæktfəlɪ] ADV taktvoll

tactfulness ['tæktfʊlnɪs] N Takt *m*; (*of person*) Feingefühl *nt*

tactic ['tæktɪk] N Taktik *f*

tactical ['tæktɪkəl] ADJ (*Mil, fig*) taktisch

tactically ['tæktɪkəlɪ] ADV (*Mil, fig*) taktisch

tactical voting N (*Brit Pol*) taktisches Wahlverhalten

tactician [tæk'tɪʃən] N (*Mil, fig*) Taktiker(in) *m(f)*

tactics ['tæktɪks] N *sing* (*= art, science, Mil*) Taktik *f*; (*fig also*) Taktiken *pl*

tactile ['tæktaɪl] ADJ **a** Tast-, taktil (*spec*); (*= tangible*) greifbar, fühlbar; (*form: = gained by touching*) *stimulation, experience* durch Berührung erfolgend; **~ sense** Tastsinn *m*; **~ organ** Tastorgan *nt*; **she is a very ~ person** sie ist ein Mensch, der gern Körperkontakt hat; **a more ~ society** eine Gesellschaft, in der Körperkontakte eine größere Rolle spielen **b** (*= interesting to touch*) **a ~ fabric** angenehm anzufühlende Stoffe

tactless ['tæktlɪs] ADJ taktlos; **it was ~ of me to ask** es war taktlos *or* eine Taktlosigkeit von mir, zu fragen

tactlessly ['tæktlɪslɪ] ADV taktlos

tactlessness ['tæktlɪsnɪs] N Taktlosigkeit *f*

tactual ['tæktjʊəl] ADJ taktil (*spec*); **~ pleasure** Berührungslust *f*

tactually ['tæktjʊəlɪ] ADV (*= by touch*) durch Berühren *or* Fühlen; **to be ~ pleasing** sich angenehm anfühlen; **~ oriented** berührungsorientiert

tad [tæd] N *no pl* (*inf*) **a ~** ein bisschen, etwas; **a ~ big/small** etwas *or* ein bisschen (zu) groß/klein

Tadjikistan [tɑː,dʒiːkɪ'stɑːn] N = **Tajikistan**

tadpole ['tædpəʊl] N Kaulquappe *f*

Tadzhikistan [tɑː,dʒɪkɪ'stɑːn] N = **Tajikistan**

taffeta ['tæfɪtə] N Taft *m*

taffrail ['tæfreɪl] N (*Naut*) Heckreling *f*

Taffy ['tæfɪ] N (*inf*) Waliser(in) *m(f)*

taffy ['tæfɪ] N (*US*) Toffee *nt*

tag [tæg] **N** **a** (*= label*) Schild(chen) *nt*; (*on clothes, with maker's name*) Etikett *nt*; (*with owner's name*) Namensschild(chen) *nt*; (*= loop*) Aufhänger *m*; (*= electronic tag*) elektronische Markierung; (*fig: = description*) Bezeichnung *f*; **the cattle had metal ~s in their ears** die Rinder hatten Blechmarken in den Ohren **b** = **electronic tag** **c** (*= hackneyed phrase*) stehende Redensart **d** (*Gram: = question tag*) Bestätigungsfrage *f* **e** (*= game*) Fangen *nt* **f** = **tag wrestling** **VT** **a** *specimen* mit Schildchen versehen; *cattle* (mit Blechmarke) zeichnen; *garment, goods* etikettieren; (*with price*) auszeichnen; (*with owner's name*) (mit Namensschildchen) zeichnen; *suitcase* mit einem Anhänger versehen; *offender* (*with electronic tag*) mit einer elektronischen Markierung versehen; (*fig: = describe*) bezeichnen **b** (*US Mot inf*) einen Strafzettel verpassen (*+dat*) **VI** **to ~ behind** *or* **after sb** hinter jdm hertrotten *or* -zockeln (*inf*)

▶ **tag along** VI (*unwillingly, unwanted*) mittrotten (*inf*) *or* -zockeln (*inf*); **to tag along behind sb** hinter jdm herzockeln (*inf*) *or* -trotten (*inf*); **why don't you tag along?** (*inf*) warum kommst/gehst du nicht mit?

▶ **tag on** **VI** sich anhängen (*to* an *+acc*) **VT** *sep* (*= attach*) anhängen (*to* an *+acc*), befestigen (*to* an *+dat*); (*= add as afterthought*) anhängen (*to* an *+acc*)

▶ **tag together** VT *sep* (*= fasten*) zusammenheften

Tagalog [tə'gɑːlɒg] N (*Ling*) Tagal *nt*

tag end N = **fag end**

tagliatelle [,tæljə'telɪ] N (*Cook*) Tagliatelle *pl*, Bandnudeln *pl*

tagmeme ['tægmiːm] N (*Ling*) Tagmem *nt*

tagmemics ['tægmemɪks] N (*Ling*) Tagmemik *f*

tag: **tag question** N Bestätigungsfrage *f*; **tag rope** N (*Sport*) Seil *nt* (*beim tag wrestling*); **tag sale** N (*US*) *privater Verkauf von Haushaltsgegenständen und Trödel*; **tag wrestler** N Ringer(in) *m(f)* (*beim tag wrestling*); **tag wrestling** N *Ringkampf zwischen 2 Ringerpaaren, wobei immer 2 auf der Matte sind, während die 2 Auswechselkämpfer an den Seilen warten*

tahini [tə'hiːnɪ] N *no pl* Tahina *f*, Sesampaste *f*

Tahiti [tɑː'hiːtɪ] N Tahiti *nt*

Tahitian [tɑː'hiːʃən] **ADJ** tahitisch **N** **a** Tahitianer(in) *m(f)* **b** (*Ling*) Tahitisch *nt*

t'ai chi [,taɪ'tʃiː] N Tai-Chi *nt*

taiga ['taɪgə] N Taiga *f*

tail [teɪl] **N** **a** (*of animal*) Schwanz *m*; (*hum inf, of person*) Hinterteil *nt* (*inf*), Allerwerteste(r) *m* (*hum inf*); **with his ~ between his legs** (*fig*) wie ein geprügelter Hund, mit eingezogenem Schwanz (*inf*); **to turn ~** ausreißen, die Flucht ergreifen; **he was right on my ~** er saß mir direkt im Nacken **b** (*of aeroplane, kite, procession, list*) Schwanz *m*; (*of comet*) Schweif *m*; (*of shirt*) Zipfel *m*; (*of jacket, coat*) Schoß *m*; (*of letter*) Schleife *f*; (*Mus, of note*) Notenhals *m* **c** (*inf: = person following sb*) Schatten *m* (*inf*), Beschatter(in) *m(f)* (*inf*); **to put a ~ on sb** jdn beschatten lassen **d** (*inf*) **they were out looking for ~** sie hielten nach Weibern (*inf*) *or* Bräuten (*sl*) Ausschau; **a nice piece of ~** ein geiler Arsch (*sl*) **e** **~s** **PL** (*on coin*) Rück- *or* Zahlseite *f*; **~s I win!** bei Zahl gewinne ich; **it came down ~s** die Zahl kam nach oben **f** **tails** **PL** (*= jacket*) Frack *m*, Schwalbenschwanz *m* (*inf*); **"tails (will be worn)"** „Frackzwang" *m* **VT** **a** *person, suspect* beschatten (*inf*); *car etc* folgen (*+dat*) **b** → **top**[1]

▶ **tail after** VI *+prep obj* hinterherzockeln (*+dat*) (*inf*)

▶ **tail away** VI = **tail off a**

▶ **tail back** VI (*Brit: traffic*) sich gestaut haben

▶ **tail off** VI **a** (*= diminish*) abnehmen, schrumpfen; (*interest*) abflauen, abnehmen, schwinden; (*sounds*) sich verlieren, schwächer werden; (*sentence*) mittendrin abbrechen; **his voice tailed off into silence** seine Stimme wurde immer schwächer, bis sie schließlich verstummte **b** (*= deteriorate*) sich verschlechtern, nachlassen; **the article tailed off into a jumble of figures** der Artikel war zum Schluss nur noch ein Gewirr von Zahlen

tail: **tailback** N (*Brit*) Rückstau *m*; **tailboard** N Ladeklappe *f*; **tail coat** N Frack *m*

-tailed [-teɪld] ADJ *suf* -schwänzig; **short-tailed** kurzschwänzig

tail: **tail end** N Ende *nt*; (*of procession also*) Schwanz *m* (*inf*); **to come in at** *or* **on the ~** (*of discussion etc*) erst am Ende dazukommen; (*of race*) den Schwanz bilden; **tail feather** N Schwanzfeder *f*; **tail fin** N (*Aut*) Heckflosse *f*; **tailgate** **N** (*of car*) Hecktür *f*; (*of lorry*) Ladeklappe *f* **VI** (*inf*) zu dicht auffahren, schieben (*inf*) **VT** (*inf*) **to ~ sb** dicht hinter jdm herfahren; **tail gun** N Heckkanone *f*; **tail gunner** N Heckschütze *m*/-schützin *f*; **tail-heavy** ADJ (*Aviat*) *plane* schwanzlastig; **tail-hopping** N (*Ski*) Sprungwedeln *nt*; **tailless** ADJ schwanzlos; **tail-light** N (*Aut*) Rücklicht *nt*; (*Aviat*) Hecklicht *nt*

tailor ['teɪlə'] **N** Schneider(in) *m(f)* **VT** **a** *dress etc* schneidern; **the dress was ~ed to show off her figure** das Kleid war so geschnitten, dass es ihre Figur betonte **b** (*fig*) *plans, insurance, holiday, message, policy, testimony* zuschneiden (*to* auf *+acc*); *products, salary structure* abstimmen (*to* auf *+acc*); **~ed to meet his needs** auf seine Bedürfnisse abgestimmt

tailored ['teɪləd] ADJ (*= classically styled*) klassisch; (*= made by tailor*) vom Schneider gemacht; **a well-~ suit** ein gut gearbeiteter Anzug; **his personally ~ clothes** seine für ihn persönlich gefertigten Kleider

tailoring ['teɪlərɪŋ] N Verarbeitung *f*; (*= profession*) Schneiderei *f*; **this is a nice piece of ~** das ist sehr gut gearbeitet

tailor-made [,teɪlə'meɪd] ADJ **a** maßgeschneidert, nach Maß gearbeitet; **~ suit** Maßanzug *m*; **~ costume** Schneiderkostüm *nt* **b** (*fig*) *role, holiday* maßgeschneidert (*for* für), zugeschnitten (*for* auf *+acc*); *car* nach Kundenwünschen ausgelegt; **the job was ~ for him** die Stelle war ihm wie auf den Leib geschnitten; **she seemed ~ for the part** sie schien für die Rolle wie geschaffen

tailor-make [,teɪlə'meɪk] VT **the company can ~ your entire trip** die Firma kann Ihre ganze Reise für Sie persönlich zusammenstellen; **you can ~ running to suit your needs** Sie können das Dauerlaufen auf Ihre eigenen Bedürfnisse zuschneiden; **the therapist will ~ the session for you** der Therapeut stimmt die Sitzung auf Ihre persönlichen Bedürfnisse ab

tailor's ['teɪləz]: **tailor's chalk** N Schneiderkreide *f*; **tailor's dummy** [,teɪləz'dʌmɪ] N (*lit*) Schneiderpuppe *f*; (*fig inf*) Ölgötze *m* (*inf*); **tailor's-tack**, **tailor-tack** N Schlinge *f* beim Durchschlagen eines Musters

tail: **tailpiece** N **a** Anhang *m*, Anhängsel *nt* (*inf*) **b** (*Aviat*) Heck *nt* **c** (*on violin*) Saitenhalter *m* **d** (*Typ*) Schlussvignette *f*; **tailpipe** N (*US*) Auspuffrohr *nt*; **tailplane** N (*Aviat*) Höhenleitwerk *nt*; **tail section** N (*Aviat*) hinterer Bereich; **tail side** N (*of coin*) Zahlseite *f*; **tail-skid** N **a** (*Aviat*) Schwanzsporn *m* **b** (*Aut*) Schleudern *nt no pl* der Hinterräder; **to go into a ~** mit den Hinterrädern herumrutschen *or* schleudern; **tailspin** N (*Aviat*) Trudeln *nt*; **tail unit** N (*Aviat*) Schwanzstück *nt*; **tail wheel** N

(Aviat) Spornrad *nt*; **tailwind** N Rückenwind *m*

taint [teɪnt] **N** **a** *(lit, of food etc)* Stich *m*; **meat free from ~** einwandfreies Fleisch **b** *(fig: = blemish)* Makel *m*; *(= trace)* Spur *f*; **a ~ of madness** eine Anlage zum Irrsinn; **the hereditary ~** die krankhafte Erbanlage; **the ~ of sin** der Makel der Sünde; **a nasty ~ of fascism** ein übler faschistischer Beigeschmack **VT** **a** *food* verderben **b** *air, atmosphere* verderben, verpesten **c** *(fig) reputation* beflecken, beschmutzen

tainted ['teɪntɪd] ADJ **a** *(fig) money* unsauber; *evidence* unsauber, manipuliert; *reputation* beschmutzt; **not ~ by prejudice** von Vorurteilen unbelastet; **to be ~ with sth** mit etw belastet *or* behaftet sein; **to become ~ with racism** den Ruch des Rassismus erhalten **b** *(= contaminated) food* verdorben; *blood* infiziert; *air* verpestet, verunreinigt; **to become ~** *(food)* schlecht werden, verderben

Taiwan [taɪ'wɑːn] N Taiwan *nt*

Taiwanese [ˌtaɪwɑː'niːz] **ADJ** taiwanisch **N** Taiwaner(in) *m(f)*

Tajikistan [tɑːˌdʒiːkɪ'stɑːn] N Tadschikistan *nt*

take [teɪk]

vb: pret **took**, *ptp* **taken**

1 TRANSITIVE VERB	3 NOUN
2 INTRANSITIVE VERB	4 PHRASAL VERBS

When *take* is part of a set combination, eg *to take sb by surprise, to take one's time, to take a bath*, look up the other word.

1 – TRANSITIVE VERB

a = remove, steal nehmen; *(= take away with one)* mitnehmen; *(= remove from its place)* wegnehmen; **to take sth from a drawer** etw aus einer Schublade nehmen; **to take sth from sb** jdm etw wegnehmen; **I took it by mistake** ich habe es aus Versehen mitgenommen; **the thieves took everything** die Einbrecher haben alles mitgenommen; **that man has taken my wallet** der Mann hat mir meine Brieftasche weggenommen *or* gestohlen; **how much did he take off you for that?** wie viel hat er dir dafür abverlangt *or* abgenommen?

b = accompany = carry, transport bringen; *(= take along with one) person, things* mitnehmen; **let me take your case** komm, ich nehme *or* trage deinen Koffer; **you can't take it with you when you die** wenn du tot bist, nützt es dir auch nichts mehr

♦ **to take sb somewhere** **I'll take you to the station** ich bringe Sie zum Bahnhof; **I'll take you (with me) to the party** ich nehme dich zur Party mit; **he took me a new way to the coast** er ist mit mir eine neue Strecke zur Küste gefahren; **to take sb to the cinema** jdn ins Kino mitnehmen; **I'll take you for a meal** *(Brit)* ich lade Sie zum Essen ein; **to take sb on a trip** mit jdm eine Reise machen; **this bus will take you to the town hall** der Bus fährt zum Rathaus; **this road will take you to Paris** diese Straße führt *or* geht nach Paris; **if it won't take you out of your way** wenn es kein Umweg für Sie ist; **what takes you to London this time?** was führt Sie diesmal nach London?; **his ability took him to the top of his profession** seine Begabung brachte ihn in seinem Beruf bis an die Spitze

c = get hold of nehmen; **to take sb's arm/hand** jds Arm/Hand nehmen; **to take sb by the throat** jdn am Kragen *(inf) or* an der Kehle packen; **to take a knife by the handle** ein Messer am Griff (an)fassen *or* beim Griff nehmen; **take three eggs** *(Cook)* man nehme drei Eier

♦ **to be taken ...** **to be taken sick** *or* **ill** krank werden; **she has been taken ill with pneumonia** sie hat eine Lungenentzündung bekommen

d = capture *person* fassen, fangen; *animal* fangen; *town, country etc* einnehmen, erobern; *ship* kapern; *(Chess etc)* schlagen, nehmen; *(Cards) trick* machen; **to take sb prisoner** jdn gefangen nehmen; **they took 200 prisoners** sie machten 200 Gefangene; **to be taken alive** lebend gefasst werden

e = accept, receive nehmen; *job, dye, perm* annehmen; *command, lead, second position, role* übernehmen; *phone call* entgegennehmen, annehmen; **take that!** da!; *(= hold that)* halt mal; **I won't take less than £200** ich verkaufe es nicht unter £ 200; **would you take an offer?** kann ich Ihnen ein Angebot machen?; **she took paying guests** sie vermietete Zimmer an Gäste; **to take things as they come** die Dinge nehmen, wie sie kommen; **to take a bet** eine Wette annehmen; **I wouldn't take a bet on it** darauf würde ich keine Wette eingehen; **take it from me!** das können Sie mir glauben; **take it from me, he'll never ...** eines können Sie mir glauben, er wird nie ...; **he took the blow on his left arm** der Schlag traf ihn am linken Arm; *(in defence)* er wehrte den Schlag mit dem linken Arm ab; **to take sb into partnership** jdn zu seinem Partner machen; **to take sb into the business** jdn ins Geschäft aufnehmen; **will it take a British plug?** passt da ein englischer Stecker (rein)?; **the school only takes boys/private pupils** die Schule nimmt nur Jungen/Privatschüler (auf); **he takes (private) pupils** er gibt (Privat)stunden

♦ **take it or leave it** **(you can) take it or leave it** ja oder nein(, ganz wie Sie wollen); **I can take it or leave it** ich mache mir nicht besonders viel daraus

f = occupy, possess sich *(dat)* nehmen; **take a seat/chair!** nehmen Sie Platz!, setzen Sie sich doch!; **take your seats!** nehmen Sie Ihre Plätze ein!; **this seat is taken** dieser Platz ist besetzt; **to take a wife** *(old)* sich *(dat)* eine Frau nehmen *(old)*; **he took her** *(sexually)* er nahm sie; **take your partners for a waltz** führen Sie Ihre Partnerinnen zum Walzer

g = buy, rent *esp Brit* nehmen; *(= buy regularly) newspaper etc* immer nehmen *or* kaufen; *(on subscription)* beziehen, bekommen; **I'll take a pound of apples** ich nehme ein Pfund Äpfel; **I think I'll take the steak** ich glaube, ich nehme das Steak

h = gain *prize, honours etc* bekommen; *game, match* gewinnen; **the shop takes £10,000 a week** *(Brit)* das Geschäft nimmt £ 10.000 pro Woche ein

i = sit exam machen, ablegen; *driving test* machen; **to take a PhD** promovieren, den Doktor machen *(inf)*; **he took his degree in 1995** er hat 1995 Examen gemacht *or* sein Examen abgelegt

j = teach *lesson* halten, geben; *subject* unterrichten, geben; *class* unterrichten, nehmen; **he takes 25 classes a week** er hat *or* gibt 25 Wochenstunden; **who takes you for Latin?** *(Brit)* **who are you taking for Latin?** *(US)* bei wem habt ihr Latein?, wer unterrichtet *or* gibt bei euch Latein?

k = study, learn *course, French* machen; *(as optional subject)* wählen; *lessons, private tuition* nehmen

l = organize *census, poll* durchführen; *church service* (ab)halten; **to take (the chair at) a meeting** den Vorsitz bei einer Versammlung führen; **he takes a scout troop in the evenings** abends hat er eine Pfadfindergruppe

m = go on *walk, stroll* machen; *trip* unternehmen

n = travel by *taxi, train* nehmen, fahren mit; *motorway, country roads* nehmen, fahren auf (+*dat*); **to take the plane** fliegen; **to take the next bus** den nächsten Bus nehmen; **we took a wrong turning** *(Brit) or* **turn** *(US)* wir sind falsch abgebogen

o = consume *drink, food* zu sich *(dat)* nehmen; *drugs, pill, medicine* nehmen; *(on directions for use)* einnehmen; **to take sugar in one's tea** den Tee mit Zucker trinken; **to take a sip/a drink** ein Schlückchen/einen Schluck trinken; **do you take sugar?** nehmen Sie Zucker?; **to take a meal** *(old)* (etwas) essen, speisen *(geh)*; **I took tea with her** *(dated form)* ich war bei ihr zum Tee; **they took tea together once a week** *(old)* sie trafen sich einmal wöchentlich zum Tee; **they took coffee on the veranda** sie tranken den Kaffee auf der Veranda; **will you take coffee or tea?** möchten Sie Kaffee oder Tee?; **not to be taken (internally)** *(Med)* nur zur äußerlichen Anwendung

p Film, Phot *photo* machen; *(= shoot)* drehen; **he took the whole group** er nahm die ganze Gruppe auf

q = write down *letter, dictation* aufnehmen; *address, details, particulars* (sich *dat*) aufschreiben, (sich *dat*) notieren; **to take notes** sich *(dat)* Notizen machen

r = measure *temperature, pulse* messen; **to take sb's measurements** bei jdm Maß nehmen; **to take the measurements of a room** ein Zimmer ausmessen; **to take sb's temperature/pulse** jds Temperatur *or* bei jdm Fieber/den Puls messen

s = tolerate sich *(dat)* gefallen lassen; *alcohol, climate* vertragen; *long journey* aushalten; *emotional experience, shock* fertig werden mit, verkraften; *(thing)* aushalten; **I can take it** ich kanns verkraften, ich werde damit fertig; **I just can't take any more** ich bin am Ende; **I just can't take it any more** das halte ich nicht mehr aus; **I won't take any nonsense!** ich dulde keinen Unsinn!

t = respond to *news, blow* aufnehmen, reagieren auf (+*acc*); *person* nehmen; **she never knows how to take him** sie weiß nie, woran sie bei ihm ist; **she took his death very badly** sein Tod hat sie sehr mitgenommen

u = understand auffassen, verstehen; **I would take that to mean ...** ich würde das so auffassen *or* verstehen ...; **how am I meant to take that?** wie soll ich das auffassen *or* verstehen?; **she took what he said as a compliment** sie hat das, was er sagte, als Kompliment aufgefasst; **do you take my meaning?** verstehen Sie mich?, verstehen Sie, was ich meine?

v = assume annehmen; **to take sb/sth for** *or* **to be ...** jdn/etw für ... halten; **how old do you take him to be?** für wie alt halten Sie ihn?, wie alt schätzen Sie ihn?; **what do you take me for?** wofür hältst du mich eigentlich?; **may I take it that ...?** darf ich annehmen, dass ...?; **I take it you don't want to come** ich nehme an, du willst nicht mitkommen, du willst wohl nicht mitkommen

w = consider *case, example* nehmen; **take (the case of) England in the 17th century** nehmen Sie zum Beispiel England im 17. Jahrhundert; **taking everything together, it's been a very successful day** alles in allem (genommen,) war es ein sehr erfolgreicher Tag; **taking one year with another** wenn man die Jahre zusammen betrachtet

x = extract entnehmen *(from +dat)*; **he takes his examples from real life** seine Beispiele sind aus dem Leben gegriffen; **to take a quotation from a text** eine Stelle aus einem Text zitieren

y = require brauchen; *clothes size* haben; **the journey takes 3 hours** die Fahrt dauert 3 Stunden; **the wound took five weeks to heal** es dauerte fünf Wochen, bis die Wunde verheilt war; **I took a long time over it** ich habe lange dazu gebraucht

♦ **it takes** **it takes five hours/men ...** man braucht *or* benötigt fünf Stunden/Leute ...; **it takes me five hours ...** ich brauche fünf Stunden ...; **it took ten men to complete the job** zehn Leute waren nötig *or* es wurden zehn Leute benötigt, um diese Arbeit zu erledigen; **it took him two hours to write a page, it took two hours for him to write a page** er brauchte zwei Stunden, um eine Seite zu schreiben; **it took a lot of courage/intelligence** dazu gehörte viel Mut/Intelligenz; **it takes more than that to make me angry** deswegen werde ich noch lange nicht wütend; **it takes time** es braucht (seine) Zeit, es dauert (eine Weile); **it took a long time** es hat lange gedauert; **it took me a long time** ich habe lange gebraucht; **it won't take long** das dauert nicht lange; **it won't take long to convince him** er ist schnell *or* leicht überzeugt; **that'll take some explaining** das wird schwer zu erklären sein; **it takes some believing** das kann man kaum glauben

♦ **what it takes she's got what it takes** *(inf)* sie ist nicht ohne *(inf)*, die bringts *(sl)*; *(= is capable also)* sie kann was *(inf)*; **it's a difficult job but he's got what it takes** *(inf)* es ist eine schwierige Arbeit, aber er hat das Zeug dazu

z = support *weight* aushalten; **the bridge can take 5 tons** die Brücke hat eine Höchstbelastung von 5 Tonnen

aa = have capacity or room for *people, books* Platz haben für; *gallons* fassen; **the road can take 3,500 cars an hour** die Straße bewältigt eine Verkehrsdichte von 3.500 Autos pro Stunde

bb = negotiate *obstacle* nehmen; *hurdle, fence* überspringen; *bend, corner (person)* nehmen; *(car)* fahren um; *hill* hinauffahren

cc = sing, dance, play etc **let's take it from the beginning of Act 2** fangen wir mit dem Anfang vom zweiten Akt an; **let's take that scene again** die Szene machen wir noch einmal; **the orchestra took that passage too quickly** das Orchester hat die Stelle zu schnell gespielt; **the director took her through her lines** der Regisseur ging die Rolle mit ihr durch

dd Math = *subtract* abziehen *(from* von)

ee Gram stehen mit; *(preposition) case* gebraucht werden mit, haben *(inf)*; **verbs that take "haben"** Verben, die mit „haben" konjugiert werden; **this word takes the accent on the first syllable** dieses Wort wird auf der ersten Silbe betont

ff illness *(old, dial)* bekommen; **to take a cold** sich erkälten

2 – INTRANSITIVE VERB

a = take hold *fire* angehen; *(dye, perm, graft)* angenommen werden; *(vaccination)* anschlagen; *(plant)* anwachsen; *(seeds)* kommen; *(fish: = bite)* anbeißen; *(fig, gimmick)* ankommen *(inf)*; *(novel, idea)* Anklang finden; **the ink won't take on this paper** dieses Papier nimmt die Druckfarbe nicht an

b = become **she took ill** *(inf)* sie wurde krank

c = detract **that doesn't take from his merit** das tut seinen Verdiensten keinen Abbruch, das schmälert seine Verdienste nicht; **that takes from its usefulness/attraction** das vermindert den Gebrauchswert/die Anziehungskraft

3 – NOUN

a Film Aufnahme *f*; **after several takes they ...** nachdem sie die Szene mehrmals gedreht hatten, ... sie ...

b = catch *(Hunt)* Beute *f*; *(Fishing)* Fang *m*

c = takings *US inf* Einnahmen *pl*

d = approach Einstellung *f (on* zu); **take on life** Lebenseinstellung *f*

4 – PHRASAL VERBS

▸ **take aback** VT *sep* überraschen; **I was completely taken aback** mir hatte es völlig den Atem verschlagen, ich war völlig perplex

▸ **take after** VI *+prep obj* nachschlagen *(+dat)*; *(in looks)* ähneln *(+dat)*, ähnlich sein *(+dat)*

▸ **take along** VT *sep* mitnehmen

▸ **take apart** VT *sep* auseinandernehmen; *(= dismantle also)* zerlegen; *(fig inf) person, team etc* auseinandernehmen

▸ **take (a)round** VT *sep* mitnehmen; *(= show around)* herumführen

▸ **take aside** VT *sep* beiseitenehmen

▸ **take away** VI **to take away from sth** etw schmälern; *from merit, reputation also* einer Sache *(dat)* Abbruch tun; *from worth* etw mindern *or* verringern; *from pleasure, fun etc* etw beeinträchtigen

VT *sep* **a** *(= subtract)* abziehen; **6 take away 2** 6 weniger 2

b *(= remove) child, thing, privilege* wegnehmen *(from sb* jdm); *(from school etc)* nehmen *(from* aus); *(= lead, transport, carry away)* weg- *or* fortbringen *(from* von); *prisoner* abführen *(to* in *+acc)*; **to take sb/sth away (with one)** jdn/etw mitnehmen; **to take away sb's pain/freedom** *etc* jdm die Schmerzen/Freiheit *etc* nehmen; **they've come to take him away** sie sind da, um ihn abzuholen; **"not to be taken away"** *(on library book)* „nicht für die Ausleihe"; **what takes you away so early?** warum müssen Sie denn schon so früh gehen?

c *food* mitnehmen; **pizza to take away** Pizza zum Mitnehmen

d from the 15th bar, take it away! noch mal von Takt 15, los!

▸ **take back** VT *sep* **a** *(= reclaim, get back)* sich *(dat)* zurückgeben lassen; *toy etc* wieder wegnehmen; *(fig: = retract) threat, statement* zurücknehmen

b *(= return)* zurückbringen; **he took us back (home)** er brachte uns (nach Hause) zurück, er brachte uns wieder heim

c *(= agree to receive again) thing* zurücknehmen; *employee* wieder einstellen; *husband* wieder aufnehmen; *boyfriend* wieder gehen mit; *tenant* wieder vermieten an *(+acc)*

d *(= remind)* **to take sb back to his childhood** jdn in seine Kindheit zurückversetzen; **this photograph/that takes me back** dieses Foto/das ruft Erinnerungen wach; **that takes me back fifteen years** das erinnert mich an die Zeit vor fünfzehn Jahren

▸ **take down** VT *sep* **a** *(lit, off high shelf etc)* herunternehmen; *curtains, decorations* abnehmen; *Christmas cards* wegräumen; *picture* abhängen; *flag* einholen; **to take one's trousers down** seine Hose herunterlassen

b *(= dismantle) scaffolding etc* abbauen; *tent* abbrechen, abbauen; *railing, gate* entfernen

c *(= write down)* (sich *dat*) notieren *or* aufschreiben; *notes* (sich *dat*) machen; *letter* aufnehmen; *speech, lecture* mitschreiben; **anything you say will be taken down and ...** alles, was Sie sagen, wird festgehalten und ...; **take this down please** notieren Sie bitte, bitte schreiben Sie

d *(= humble)* einen Dämpfer geben *(+dat)* → **peg**

▸ **take home** VT *sep £400 per week* netto verdienen *or* bekommen

▸ **take in** VT *sep* **a** *(= bring in) thing, person* hereinbringen *or* -nehmen; *harvest* einbringen; **I'll take the car in(to work) on Monday** ich fahre am Montag mit dem Auto (zur Arbeit); **when are you taking the car in (to the garage)?** wann bringen Sie das Auto in die Werkstatt?; **to take a lady in to dinner** eine Dame zu Tisch führen

b *(= receive in one's home) refugee* (bei sich) aufnehmen, beherbergen; *child, stray dog* zu sich nehmen, ins Haus nehmen; *(for payment) student* (Zimmer) vermieten an *(+acc)*; **she takes in lodgers** sie vermietet (Zimmer)

c *(= receive) money* einnehmen; **to take in laundry/sewing** Wasch-/Näharbeiten übernehmen

d *(= make narrower) dress* enger machen; **to take in sail** die Segel reffen

e *(usu insep: = include, cover)* einschließen; **the lecture took in all the more recent developments** der Vortrag berücksichtigte auch alle neueren Entwicklungen

f *(= note visually) surroundings, contents* wahrnehmen, registrieren *(inf)*; *area, room* überblicken; *(= grasp, understand) meaning, lecture* begreifen; *impressions, sights* aufnehmen; *situation* erfassen; **the children were taking it all in** die Kinder haben alles mitbekommen *or* mitgekriegt *(inf)*; **his death was so sudden that she couldn't take it in** sein Tod kam so plötzlich, dass sie es gar nicht fassen konnte

g *(= deceive)* hereinlegen; **to be taken in** hereingelegt werden; **to be taken in by sb/sth** auf jdn/etw hereinfallen; **to be taken in by appearances** sich vom äußeren Schein täuschen lassen

h *(= go to) film, party, town* (noch) mitnehmen *(inf)*

▸ **take off** VI **a** *(plane, passengers)* starten, abfliegen; *(plane: = leave the ground)* abheben; *(Sport)* abspringen; *(fig, project, sales)* anlaufen; *(film, product)* ankommen; *(career)* abheben

b *(inf: = leave)* sich absetzen, sich davonmachen *(inf)*

VT *sep* **a** *(= remove, cut off) beard, hat, lid* abnehmen *(prep obj* von); *tablecloth, bedspread* herunternehmen, entfernen *(prep obj* von); *pillowcases etc* abziehen *(prep obj* von); *coat, gloves etc* (sich *dat*) ausziehen; *leg, limb* abnehmen, amputieren; *(= withdraw) play* absetzen; *food from menu, train, bus* streichen *(prep obj* von); *service, tax* abschaffen; *(= remove from duty, job) detective, journalist etc* abziehen *(prep obj* von); *waitress, driver* ablösen; **to take sth off sb** jdm etw abnehmen; **double deckers have been taken off this route** Doppeldecker werden auf dieser Strecke nicht mehr eingesetzt; **to take the receiver off (the hook)** den Hörer abnehmen, den Hörer von der Gabel nehmen; **he took her dress off** er zog ihr das Kleid aus; **she took her dress off** sie zog ihr Kleid aus, sie zog (sich *dat*) das Kleid aus; **he took his/her clothes off** er zog sich/sie aus; **would you like to take your coat off?** möchten Sie ablegen?; **he had two inches taken off (his hair)** er hat sich *(dat)* die Haare 5 cm kürzer schneiden lassen; **please take a little off the top** bitte oben etwas kürzer; **the barber took too much off** der Friseur hat zu viel abgeschnitten; **the 5 o'clock train has been taken off today/for the summer** der 5-Uhr-Zug ist heute ausgefallen/wurde den Sommer über (vom Fahrplan) gestrichen

b *(= deduct)* abziehen *(prep obj* von); *(from price) 5%, 50p* nachlassen; **he took 50p off (the price)** er hat 50 Pence nachgelassen, er hat es 50 Pence billiger gemacht

c *(= lead away, go away with)* mitnehmen; *(under arrest etc)* abführen; **he was taken off to hospital** er wurde ins Krankenhaus gebracht; **to take oneself off** *(inf)* sich auf den Weg machen

d *(from ship, wreck)* von Bord holen; *(from island, mountain)* herunterholen *(prep obj* von)

e *(= have free) week, Monday* freinehmen; **to take time off (work)** sich *(dat)* freinehmen; **to take a day off (work)** einen Tag freinehmen

f *(Brit: = imitate)* nachmachen, nachahmen

g *+prep obj (in phrases)* **to take sb's mind off sth** jdn von etw ablenken; **to take the weight off one's feet** seine Beine ausruhen; **to take sb/sth off sb's hands** jdm jdn/etw abnehmen; **to take years/ten years off sb** jdn um Jahre/zehn Jahre verjüngen

▸ **take on** VI **a** *(inf: = become upset)* sich aufregen

b *(= become popular: song, fashion etc)* sich durchsetzen

VT *sep* **a** *(= undertake) job, work* an- *or* übernehmen; *responsibility* auf sich *(acc)* nehmen *or* laden, übernehmen; *sick person, backward child* sich annehmen *(+gen)*; *bet* annehmen; **when he married her he took on more than he bargained for** als er sie heiratete, hat er sich *(dat)* mehr aufgeladen *or* aufgebürdet, als er gedacht hatte; **he took on the fundraising** er hat es übernommen, das Geld aufzutreiben

b *(Sport etc: = accept as opponent)* antreten gegen; *union, shop steward* sich anlegen mit; **I could take on someone twice your size** ich könnte es mit einem aufnehmen, der zweimal so groß ist wie Sie; **I'll take you on at tennis** ich werde gegen Sie im Tennis antreten; **I bet you £50 – OK, I'll take you on** ich wette mit Ihnen um £ 50 – gut, die Wette gilt

c *(= employ)* einstellen, anstellen; *apprentice* annehmen

d *(= take aboard) passengers (coach, train etc)* aufnehmen; *(plane, ship)* an Bord nehmen, übernehmen; *cargo, stores* (über)nehmen, laden; *fuel* tanken

e *(= assume) colour, aspect, expression* bekommen, annehmen; **her face/eyes took on a doleful expression** ihr Gesicht nahm/ihre Augen nahmen einen traurigen Ausdruck an; **his face took on a greenish tinge** sein Gesicht verfärbte sich grün *or* bekam einen grünen Schimmer; **he took on an air of importance** er gab sich *(dat)* eine gewichtige Miene

▸ **take out** VT *sep* **a** *(= bring or carry out)* (hinaus)bringen *(of* aus); *(out of garage) car* herausfahren *(of* aus); *(for drive etc) car, boat* wegfah-

ren mit; **the current took the boat out to sea** die Strömung trieb das Boot aufs Meer hinaus
b *(to theatre etc)* ausgehen mit, ausführen; **to take the children/dog out (for a walk)** mit den Kindern/dem Hund spazieren gehen *or* einen Spaziergang machen, den Hund ausführen; **to take sb out for a drive** mit jdm eine Autofahrt machen; **to take sb out to** *or* **for dinner/to the opera** jdn zum Essen/in die Oper einladen *or* ausführen; **he has been taking her out for several months** er geht schon seit einigen Monaten mit ihr
c *(= pull out, extract)* herausnehmen; *tooth* ziehen; *appendix etc* herausnehmen, entfernen; *nail, screw* herausziehen *(of* aus); **to take sth out of sth** etw aus etw (heraus)nehmen; **take your hands out of your pockets** nimm die Hände aus der Tasche
d *(= cause to disappear) stain* entfernen *(from* aus); **cold water will take the stain out of the tablecloth** mit kaltem Wasser geht der Fleck aus dem Tischtuch heraus
e *(= withdraw from bank etc)* abheben
f *(= deduct)* **take it out of the housekeeping** nimm es vom Haushaltsgeld; **to take time out from sth** von etw (eine Zeit lang) Urlaub nehmen; **to take time out from doing sth** etw eine Zeit lang nicht tun
g *(= procure) insurance* abschließen; *mortgage* aufnehmen; **to take out a licence** eine Lizenz erwerben, sich *(dat)* eine Lizenz geben lassen → **patent, subscription, summons**
h to take sb out of himself jdn auf andere Gedanken bringen
i *(inf)* **to take sth out on sb** etw an jdm auslassen *(inf) or* abreagieren *(inf)*; **to take it out on sb** sich an jdm abreagieren
j *(= tire)* **to take it/a lot out of sb** jdn ziemlich/sehr schlauchen *(inf)*
k *(Mil, fig, Sport)* außer Gefecht setzen; *village* angreifen
l *(inf: = kill)* beseitigen
m *(US)* = **take away VT c**

► **take over** VI *(= assume government)* an die Macht kommen; *(military junta etc)* die Macht ergreifen; *(party)* an die Regierung kommen; *(new boss etc)* die Leitung übernehmen; *(in a place: tourists, guests etc)* sich breitmachen *(inf)*; **to take over (from sb)** jdn ablösen; **can you take over?** können Sie mich/ihn *etc* ablösen?; **he's ill so I have to take over** da er krank ist, muss ich (für ihn) einspringen; **his wife has taken over completely** seine Frau führt das Regiment; **the next shift takes over at 6 o'clock** die nächste Schicht übernimmt um 6 Uhr; **the Martians have taken over** die Marsmenschen haben die Erde/Stadt *etc* besetzt
VT sep **a** *(= take control or possession of)* übernehmen; **tourists take Edinburgh over in the summer** im Sommer machen sich die Touristen in Edinburgh breit *(inf)*; **she took over the whole show** *(inf)* sie riss das Regiment an sich
b *(= escort or carry across) person* hinüberbringen; *(+prep obj)* bringen über *(+acc)*; *(in boat)* übersetzen; *(to visit town, people etc)* mitnehmen (to nach, *to sb* zu jdm)
c to take sb over sth *(= show round)* jdn durch etw führen, jdm etw zeigen; *(= tell about) facts* etw mit jdm durchgehen

► **take round** VT *sep (esp Brit)* **a I'll take it round (to her place** *or* **to her)** ich bringe es zu ihr **b** *(= show round)* führen *(prep obj* durch)

► **take to** VI *+prep obj* **a** *(= form liking for) person* mögen, sympathisch finden; **sb takes to a game/subject/place** ein Spiel/Fach/Ort sagt jdm zu; **the children soon took to their new surroundings** den Kindern gefiel es bald in der neuen Umgebung; **I'll never take to it** dafür werde ich mich nie erwärmen *or* begeistern können; **I don't know how she'll take to him/it** ich weiß nicht, wie sie auf ihn/darauf reagieren wird; **I don't take kindly to that** ich kann das nicht leiden; **I don't take kindly to you doing that** ich kann es nicht leiden, wenn Sie das tun
b *(= form habit of)* **to take to doing sth** anfangen, etw zu tun; **to take to drink** zu trinken anfangen, sich *(dat)* das Trinken angewöhnen; **to take to drugs** anfangen, Drogen zu nehmen; **she took to telling everyone that ...** sie erzählte allen Leuten, dass ...
c *(= escape to) woods, hills* sich flüchten *or* zurückziehen in *(+acc)*, Zuflucht suchen in *(+dat)*; **to take to the boats** sich in die Boote retten; **to take to one's bed** sich ins Bett legen → **heel**[1]

► **take up** VI *(= continue) (person)* weitermachen; **chapter 3 takes up where chapter 1 left off** das dritte Kapitel schließt thematisch ans erste an
VT sep **a** *(= raise, lift)* aufnehmen; *carpet, floorboards* hochnehmen; *road* aufreißen; *dress* kürzer machen, kürzen; *pen* zur Hand nehmen, greifen zu; **take up your bed and walk** *(Bibl)* nimm dein Bett und wandle
b *(= lead or carry upstairs etc) invalid, child* hinaufbringen; *visitor* (mit) hinaufnehmen; *thing* hinauftragen
c *(vehicles) passengers* mitnehmen, einsteigen lassen
d *(= occupy) time, attention* in Anspruch nehmen, beanspruchen; *space* einnehmen
e *(= absorb)* (in sich *acc*) aufnehmen; *esp liquids* aufsaugen
f *matter, point (= raise)* besprechen, zur Sprache bringen; *(= go into)* eingehen auf *(+acc)*; **I'll take that up with the headmaster** das werde ich beim Rektor zur Sprache bringen *or* mit dem Rektor besprechen; **I'd like to take up the point you made earlier on** ich möchte auf das eingehen, was Sie vorhin sagten
g *(= start doing as hobby) photography, archaeology* zu seinem Hobby machen; *a hobby* sich *(dat)* zulegen; *a language* (anfangen zu) lernen; **to take up painting/pottery/the guitar** anfangen zu malen/zu töpfern/Gitarre zu spielen
h *(= adopt) cause* sich einsetzen für, verfechten; *idea* aufgreifen; *case* sich annehmen *(+gen)*; **to take up an attitude** eine Haltung einnehmen; **to take up a person** *(as protégé)* sich eines Menschen annehmen; **to take up a position** *(lit)* eine Stellung einnehmen; *(fig)* eine Haltung einnehmen
i *(= accept) challenge, invitation* annehmen; *suggestion* aufgreifen
j *(= start) job, employment* annehmen; *new job, post* antreten; *one's duties* übernehmen; *career* einschlagen; **he left to take up a job as a headmaster** er ist gegangen, um eine Stelle als Schulleiter zu übernehmen; **to take up residence** sich niederlassen *(at, in* in *+dat)*; *(in house)* einziehen *(in* in *+acc)*; *(sovereign etc)* Residenz beziehen *(in* in *+dat)*
k *(= continue) story* aufnehmen; *conversation* fortfahren mit, weiterführen; *(= join in) chorus, chant* einstimmen in *(+acc)*; **the crowd took up the cry** die Menge nahm den Schrei auf
l to take sb up on his/her invitation/offer von jds Einladung/Angebot Gebrauch machen; **to take sb up on his/her promise** jdn beim Wort nehmen; **I'll take you up on that** ich werde davon Gebrauch machen; *(on promise etc)* ich nehme Sie beim Wort
m *(= question, argue with)* **I would like to take you up on that** ich möchte gern etwas dazu sagen; **he took me up on that point** dagegen hatte er etwas einzuwenden; **I would like to take you up on what you said about strikes** zu ihrer Bemerkung über Streiks hätte ich noch etwas zu sagen
n *(Fin)* **to take up an option** Bezugsrecht ausüben; **to take up a bill** einen Wechsel einlösen; **to take up shares** Aktien beziehen
o *collection* durchführen
p to be taken up with sb/sth mit jdm/etw sehr beschäftigt sein

► **take upon** VT *+prep obj* **he took that job upon himself** er hat das völlig ungebeten getan; **he took it upon himself to answer for me** er meinte, er müsse für mich antworten

► **take up with** VI *+prep obj person* sich anfreunden mit; **to take up with bad company** in schlechte Gesellschaft geraten

take: **takeaway** *(esp Brit)* N **a** *(= meal)* Essen *nt* zum Mitnehmen; **let's get a ~** wir können uns ja etwas (zu essen) holen *or* mitnehmen **b** *(= restaurant)* Imbissstube *f* ADJ *attr food* zum Mitnehmen; **the ~ menu is quite different** für Gerichte zum Mitnehmen gibt es eine andere Speisekarte; **takedown** *(esp US)* ADJ *gun etc* zerlegbar, auseinandernehmbar N **a** *(= taking apart)* Zerlegen *nt* **b** *(= gadget)* (leicht) zerlegbares Gerät **c** *(Wrestling)* Niederwurf *m* **d** *(inf: = police raid or arrest)* Razzia *f*, Polizeiaktion *f*; **take-home pay** N Nettolohn *m*; **take-in** N *(inf)* Schwindel *m*

taken ['teɪkən] *ptp of* **take** ADJ **to be ~ with sb/sth** *(= attracted by)* von jdm/etw angetan sein; **she wasn't very ~ with him/it** sie war nicht sehr von ihm/davon angetan

take: **takeoff** N **a** *(Aviat)* Start *m*, Abflug *m*; *(= moment of leaving ground)* Abheben *nt*; *(Sport)* Absprung *m*; *(= place)* Absprungstelle *f or* -brett *nt*; **the plane was ready for ~** das Flugzeug war startbereit *or* flugklar; **at ~** beim Start *or* Abheben; **to be cleared for ~** Starterlaubnis haben/bekommen **b** *(Brit: = imitation)* Parodie *f*, Nachahmung *f*; **to do a ~ of sb** jdn nachahmen *or* nachmachen *(inf)*; **takeout** *(esp US)* ADJ *meal etc* zum Mitnehmen; *restaurant etc* mit Straßenverkauf N **a** *(= takeaway food)* Essen *nt* zum Mitnehmen; **should we get a ~?** holen wir uns Essen *or* was zum Mitnehmen? **b** *(= takeaway restaurant)* Restaurant *nt* mit Straßenverkauf; **takeover** N *(Comm)* Übernahme *f*; **takeover bid** N Übernahmeangebot *nt*

taker ['teɪkə'] N *(Betting)* Wettende(r) *mf*; *(at auction, fig)* Interessent(in) *m(f)*; **any ~s?** wer wettet?; *(at auction)* wer bietet?; *(fig)* wer ist daran interessiert?; **there were no ~s** *(Betting)* niemand wettete, niemand schloss eine Wette ab; *(at auction)* es wurden keine Angebote gemacht, niemand bot; *(fig)* niemand war daran interessiert

take-up ['teɪkʌp] N *(esp Brit)* **a** Inanspruchnahme *f*; **there is a very low ~ of housing benefit** nur wenige nehmen Wohngeld in Anspruch **b** *(Tech, of tape etc)* Aufwickeln *nt*, Aufspulen *nt*; **the rate of ~** die Aufwickel- *or* Aufspulgeschwindigkeit; **~ spool** Aufwickelspule *f*

taking ['teɪkɪŋ] N **a it's yours for the ~** das können Sie (umsonst) haben **b takings** PL *(Comm)* Einnahmen *pl* **c** *(Mil, of town)* Einnahme *f*, Eroberung *f* **d** *(old: = distress)* Aufregung *f*, Erregung *f*; **to be in a ~** aufgeregt *or* erregt sein ADJ *manners, ways* einnehmend, gewinnend; *person* sympathisch, anziehend

taking: **taking away** N Wegnahme *f*; **taking over** N Übernahme *f*

talc [tælk] N *(also* **talcum)** ['tælkəm] **a** Talk *m* **b** *(also* **talcum powder)** Talkumpuder *m*; *(esp perfumed)* (Körper)puder *m* VT pudern

tale [teɪl] N **a** Geschichte *f*; *(Liter)* Erzählung *f*; **Tales of King Arthur** Artussagen *pl*; **he had quite a ~ to tell** er hatte einiges zu erzählen, der hatte vielleicht was zu erzählen *(inf)*; **I bet he/that bed could tell a ~ or two** *(inf)* er/das Bett könnte bestimmt so einiges erzählen; **it tells its own ~** das spricht für sich; **at least he lived to tell the ~** zumindest hat er die Sache überlebt; **thereby hangs a ~** das ist eine lange Geschichte; **I've heard a fine ~ about you** *(iro)* von dir hört man ja schöne Geschichten!
b to tell ~s petzen *(inf)* (to *+dat*); *(dated: = fib)* flunkern; **to tell ~s out of school** *(inf)* aus der Schule plaudern; **to tell ~s about sb** jdn verpetzen *(inf)* (to bei)

tale-bearing ['teɪlbɛərɪŋ] N = **tale-telling**

talent ['tælənt] N **a** Begabung *f*, Talent *nt*; **to have a ~ for drawing/mathematics** Begabung *f* zum Zeichnen/für Mathematik haben; **a painter of great ~** ein hochbegabter *or* sehr talentierter Maler **b** *(= talented people)* Talente *pl* **c** *(inf: = girls)* Bräute *pl (sl)*; *(= boys)* Typen *pl (sl)*, Jungs *pl (inf)*; **they went to inspect the lo-**

cal ~ sie zogen los, um zu sehen, wie die Bräute dort waren *(sl)* **d** *(Hist)* Talent *nt*

talent competition, **talent contest** N Talentwettbewerb *m*

talented ['tæləntɪd] ADJ *person* begabt, talentiert

talent: **talent scout** N Talentsucher(in) *m(f)*; **talent show** N Talentwettbewerb *m*; **talent spotter** N Talentsucher(in) *m(f) (inf)*

talesman ['teɪlzmən] N *pl* **-men** [-mən] *(Jur)* Ersatzgeschworene(r) *mf*

tale: **tale-teller** N *(Sch)* Petzer(in) *m(f) (inf)*; **tale-telling** ['teɪltelɪŋ] N *(Sch)* Petzerei *f (inf)*

Taliban ['tælɪban] N Taliban *f*

talisman ['tælɪzmən] N *pl* **-s** Talisman *m*

talk [tɔːk] **N** **a** Gespräch *nt (also Pol)*; *(= conversation)* Gespräch *nt*, Unterhaltung *f*; *(esp heart-to-heart)* Aussprache *f*; **to have a ~** ein Gespräch führen/sich unterhalten/sich aussprechen *(with sb about sth* mit jdm über etw *acc)*; **could I have a ~ with you?** könnte ich Sie mal sprechen?; **to hold** *or* **have ~s** Gespräche führen; **to have a friendly ~ with sb** sich mit jdm nett unterhalten, mit jdm plaudern; *(giving advice, warning)* mit jdm (mal) in aller Freundschaft reden; **I have enjoyed our ~** ich habe mich gern mit Ihnen unterhalten; **to meet for ~s** sich zu Gesprächen treffen

b *no pl (= talking)* Reden *nt*, Rederei *f*; *(= rumour)* Gerede *nt*; **he's all ~** er ist ein fürchterlicher Schwätzer; *(and no action)* der führt bloß große Reden; **there is some ~ of his returning** es heißt, er kommt zurück; **there is too much ~ of going on strike in this factory** in dieser Fabrik wird zu viel vom Streiken geredet; **it's the ~ of the town** es ist Stadtgespräch; **she's the ~ of the town** sie ist zum Stadtgespräch geworden

c *(= lecture)* Vortrag *m*; **to give a ~** einen Vortrag halten *(on* über *+acc)*; **a series of ~s** eine Vortragsreihe; **her ~ on the dangers ...** ihre (kurze) Rede über die Gefahren ...

VI **a** *(= speak)* sprechen, reden *(of* von, *about* über *+acc)*; *(= have conversation)* reden, sich unterhalten *(of, about* über *+acc)*; *(bird, doll, child)* sprechen; **to ~ to** *or* **with sb** mit jdm sprechen *or* reden *(about* über *+acc)*; *(= converse also)* sich mit jdm unterhalten *(about* über *+acc)*; *(= reprimand also)* mit jdm ein ernstes Wort reden; **could I ~ to Mr Smith please?** kann ich bitte Herrn Smith sprechen?; **don't ~ silly!** *(inf)* red keinen Stuss! *(inf)*, red nicht so blöd (daher)! *(inf)*; **it's easy** *or* **all right for you to ~** *(inf)* du hast gut reden *(inf)*; **don't (you) ~ to me like that!** wie redest du denn mit mir?; **who do you think you're ~ing to?** was meinst du denn, wen du vor dir hast?; **that's no way to ~ to your parents** so redet man doch nicht mit seinen Eltern!; **hey, that's no way to ~** hör mal, sag doch so was nicht!; **he sat there without ~ing** er saß da und sagte kein Wort; **~ to me!** erzähl mir was!; **to get/be ~ing to sb** mit jdm ins Gespräch kommen/im Gespräch sein; **I'm not ~ing to you** *(= we're on bad terms)* mit dir spreche *or* rede ich nicht mehr; *(= I mean somebody else)* ich spreche nicht mit dir; **he knows/doesn't know what he's ~ing about** er weiß (schon)/weiß (doch) nicht, wovon er spricht, er hat (davon) ziemlich Ahnung *(inf)*/(doch) überhaupt keine Ahnung; **you can ~!** *(inf)* du kannst gerade reden!; **to keep sb ~ing** jdn (mit einem Gespräch) hinhalten; **to ~ to oneself** Selbstgespräche führen; **now you're ~ing!** das lässt sich schon eher hören!

b *(= mention)* sprechen, reden; **he's been ~ing of going abroad** er hat davon gesprochen *or* geredet, dass er ins Ausland fahren will; **~ing of salaries/films ...** da *or* wo *(inf)* wir gerade von Gehältern/Filmen sprechen ...; **~ about impertinence/rude/hot!** so was von Frechheit/unverschämt/heiß! *(inf)*

c *(= chatter)* reden, schwatzen; **stop ~ing!** sei/seid ruhig!

d *(= gossip)* reden, klatschen; **everyone was ~ing about them** sie waren in aller Munde; *(because of scandal also)* alle haben über sie geredet *or* geklatscht; **to get oneself ~ed about** von sich reden machen; *(because of scandal)* ins Gerede kommen

e *(= reveal secret)* reden; **the spy refused to ~** der Spion schwieg beharrlich *or* weigerte sich zu reden; **to make sb ~** jdn zum Reden bringen; **OK, Kowalski, ~!** O.K. *or* o.k., Kowalski, raus mit der Sprache! *(inf)*

f **we're ~ing about at least £2,000/3 months** es geht um mindestens £ 2.000/3 Monate, wir müssen mit mindestens £ 2.000/3 Monaten rechnen; **what sort of sum are we ~ing about?** um welche Summe geht es?

VT **a** *(= speak) a language, slang* sprechen; *nonsense* reden; **~ sense!** red keinen solchen Unsinn!; **he simply wasn't ~ing sense** er hat bloß Unsinn geredet *or* verzapft *(inf)*

b *(= discuss) politics, cricket, business* reden über *(+acc) or* von, sich unterhalten über *(+acc)*; **we're ~ing big money/serious crime** *etc* **here** *(inf)* heir gehts um große Geld/um schlimme Verbrechen *etc (inf)*; **we have to ~ business for a while** wir müssen mal kurz etwas Geschäftliches besprechen; **then they got down to ~ing business** dann sind sie zum geschäftlichen Teil übergegangen; **let's ~ business** kommen wir zur Sache; **now you're ~ing business** das lässt sich schon eher hören → **shop**

c *(= persuade)* **to ~ sb/oneself into doing sth** jdn überreden *or* jdn/sich dazu bringen, etw zu tun; *(against better judgement)* jdm/sich einreden, dass man etw tut; **he ~ed himself into believing she was unfaithful** er hat sich eingeredet, sie sei ihm nicht treu; **to ~ sb out of sth/doing sth** jdn von etw abbringen/davon abbringen, etw zu tun, jdm etw ausreden/jdm ausreden, etw zu tun

d *(= achieve by talking)* **he ~ed himself out of that job** durch sein Reden hat er sich *(dat)* diese Stelle verscherzt; **you won't be able to ~ your way out of this** jetzt können Sie sich nicht mehr herausreden; **he ~ed himself out of trouble** er redete sich (geschickt) heraus; **he ~ed himself into this situation** er hat sich selbst durch sein Reden in diese Lage gebracht; **to ~ sb into a better humour** jdn in eine bessere Laune bringen; **to ~ sb out of his bad temper** jdm die schlechte Laune vertreiben

e **to ~ oneself hoarse** sich heiser reden → **head**

▶ **talk at** VI *+prep obj person* einreden auf *(+acc)*

▶ **talk away** **VI** ununterbrochen reden, schwatzen; **we talked away for hours** wir haben stundenlang geschwatzt *or* uns stundenlang unterhalten **VT** *sep* **a** *(= spend talking)* im Gespräch verbringen; **we talked the evening away** wir haben den ganzen Abend lang geredet, wir haben den Abend im Gespräch verbracht **b** *debts, problems etc* wegdiskutieren

▶ **talk back** VI *(= be cheeky)* frech antworten *(to sb* jdm)

▶ **talk down** **VI** **to talk down to sb** mit jdm herablassend *or* von oben herab reden *or* sprechen **VT** *sep* **a** *(= reduce to silence)* über den Haufen reden *(inf)*, niederreden **b** *(Aviat) pilot, plane* zur Landung einweisen **c** *(esp Brit: in negotiations)* herunterhandeln **d** *(= play down)* herunterspielen

▶ **talk on** VI weiterreden; **they talked on and on** sie redeten und redeten

▶ **talk out** VT *sep* **a** *(= discuss) problems, differences* ausdiskutieren **b** *(Parl)* **to talk out a bill** die rechtzeitige Verabschiedung eines Gesetzes verschleppen

▶ **talk over** VT *sep* **a** *question, problem* bereden *(inf)*, besprechen; **let's talk it over quietly** wir wollen jetzt einmal in aller Ruhe darüber reden **b** *(= persuade)* = **talk round VT**

▶ **talk round** **VT** *always separate (Brit)* umstimmen; **I talked her round to my way of thinking** ich habe sie zu meiner Anschauung bekehrt **VI** *+prep obj (esp Brit) problem, subject* herumreden um

▶ **talk through** VT SEP **a** *(= discuss)* besprechen, durchsprechen **b** *(= explain)* besprechen; **to talk sb through sth** jdm etw erklären

▶ **talk up** VT SEP **a** *(in negotiations)* heraufreden **b** *(= play up)* heraufspielen

talkative ['tɔːkətɪv] ADJ *person* gesprächig, redselig

talkativeness ['tɔːkətɪvnɪs] N Gesprächigkeit *f*, Redseligkeit *f*

talkback ['tɔːkbæk] N *(= device)* Gegensprechanlage *f*; *(= talking)* Anweisungen *pl* im Hintergrund

talked-of ['tɔːktɒv] ADJ **much ~** berühmt; *plans also* viel besprochen; **his much ~ brilliance was apparent** seine viel gerühmte Brillanz wurde offensichtlich

talker ['tɔːkə'] N Redner(in) *m(f)*; **the parrot was a good ~** der Papagei konnte gut sprechen; **he's just a ~** er ist ein Schwätzer *m*

talkfest ['tɔːkfest] N *(US inf)* lange Diskussion, großes Palaver *(inf)*

talkie ['tɔːkɪ] N *(dated inf)* Tonfilm *m*

talking ['tɔːkɪŋ] N Reden *nt*, Sprechen *nt*; **no ~ please!** bitte Ruhe!, Sprechen verboten!; **I'll let you do the ~** ich überlasse das Reden Ihnen; **he did all the ~** er übernahm das Reden; **his constant ~ will drive me mad** sein dauerndes Gerede *or* Geschwätz macht mich noch verrückt; **that's enough ~!** Ruhe jetzt!, Schluss mit dem Reden!

talking: **talking bird** N sprechender Vogel; **talking book** N *(for the blind etc)* Hörbuch *nt*; **talking doll** N sprechende Puppe, Sprechpuppe *f*; **talking head** N *(TV)* Kopfaufnahme *f*, Brustbild *nt*; **talking picture** N *(old)* Tonfilm *m*; **talking point** N Gesprächsthema *nt*; **talking shop** N *(esp Brit pej inf)* Quasselbude *f (inf)*; **talking-to** N *(inf)* Standpauke *f (inf)*; **to give sb a good ~** jdm eine Standpauke halten *(inf)*

talk: **talk radio** N Talkradio *nt*; **talk show** N Talkshow *f*

tall [tɔːl] ADJ *(+er)* **a** *person* groß, lang *(inf)*; **~ and slim** groß und schlank; **how ~ are you?** wie groß sind Sie?; **he is 6 ft ~** er ist 1,80 m groß; **she's 5 cm ~er than me, she's ~er than me by 5 cm** sie ist 5 cm größer als ich; **to stand 6 ft ~** *(person)* 1,80 m groß sein; **a 6 ft ~ man** ein 1,80 m großer Mann; **to feel ten foot** *or* **feet ~** *(inf)* riesig stolz sein *(inf)*; *(after compliment also)* um einen halben Meter wachsen *(inf)*; **to stand ~** aufrecht dastehen; **to walk ~** stolz einhergehen

b *building, tree, grass, glass, window* hoch; *mast* lang, hoch

c *(inf)* **that's a ~ order** das ist ganz schön viel verlangt; *(indignant also)* das ist eine Zumutung; **a ~ story** *or* **tale** ein Märchen *nt (inf)*

tallboy ['tɔːlbɔɪ] N *(Brit)* hohe Schlafzimmerkommode

tallish ['tɔːlɪʃ] ADJ *person* ziemlich groß; *building* ziemlich hoch

tallness ['tɔːlnɪs] N **a** *(of person)* Größe *f*, Länge *f (inf)* **b** *(of building, tree, grass)* Höhe *f*; *(of mast also)* Länge *f*

tallow ['tæləʊ] N Talg *m*, Unschlitt *m (old)*; **~ candle** Talglicht *nt*

tallowy ['tæləʊɪ] ADJ talgig

tall ship N Klipper *m*; **~s race** Klipperregatta *f*

tally ['tælɪ] **N** **a** *(Hist, = stick)* Kerbholz *nt* **b** *(= count, account)* **to keep a ~ of** Buch führen über *(+acc)* **c** *(= result of counting, number)* (An)zahl *f*; **what's the ~?** wie viel ist/sind es?

VI übereinstimmen; *(reports etc also)* sich decken; **they don't ~** sie stimmen nicht (miteinander) überein **VT** *(also* **tally up**) zusammenrechnen *or* -zählen

tally clerk N Kontrolleur(in) *m(f)*

tally-ho [,tælɪ'həʊ] INTERJ halali **N** Halali *nt*

tally trade N *(Brit Comm)* Teilzahlungsgeschäft *nt*

Talmud ['tælmuːd] N Talmud *m*

talon ['tælən] N Kralle *f*, Klaue *f*; *(fig, of person)* Kralle *f*

talon-like ADJ krallemartig

tamable ADJ = **tameable**

tamarind ['tæmərɪnd] N *(= tree, fruit)* Tamarinde *f*

tamarisk ['tæmərɪsk] N Tamariske *f*

tambour ['tæm,bʊə'] N a *(old Mus)* Trommel *f* b *(on desk etc)* Rouleau *nt*, Rollo *nt*

tambourine [,tæmbə'ri:n] N Tamburin *nt*

tame [teɪm] ADJ *(+er)* a *animal* zahm; **the village has its own ~ novelist** *(hum)* der Ort hat seinen dorfeigenen Schriftsteller *(inf)*; **I'll get my ~ lawyer to do that** *(hum)* ich beauftrage meinen treuen Rechtsanwalt damit b *(= dull) person, life, adventure, answer, shot, tennis service etc* lahm *(inf)*; *story, criticism, joke* zahm, lahm *(inf)* VT *animal, person* zähmen, bändigen; *passion* (be)zähmen, zügeln; *garden, inflation, unions, deficit* unter Kontrolle bringen

tameable ['teɪməbl] ADJ zähmbar

tamely ['teɪmlɪ] ADV *(= meekly)* zahm; *agree, accept, surrender* lahm

tameness ['teɪmnɪs] N a *(of animal)* Zahmheit *f* b *(fig, of person, life, adventure etc)* Lahmheit *f (inf)*; *(of film, criticism, joke etc also)* Zahmheit *f*; *(of shot)* Lahmheit *f*, Zahmheit *f*

tamer ['teɪmə'] N *(of animals)* Bändiger(in) *m(f)*, Dompteur(in) *m(f)*

taming ['teɪmɪŋ] N Zähmung *f*, Bändigung *f*; **"The Taming of the Shrew"** „Der Widerspenstigen Zähmung"

tam-o'-shanter [,tæmə'ʃæntə'], **tammy** ['tæmɪ] N (schottische) Baskenmütze

tamp [tæmp] VT a *(= block up) drill hole etc* (ver)stopfen b *(= ram down) earth* (fest)stampfen; **to ~ (down) tobacco in a pipe** die Pfeife (fest) stopfen

Tampax® ['tæmpæks] N Tampon *m*

tamper ['tæmpə'] N *(for soil etc)* Stampfer *m*; *(for tobacco)* Stopfer *m*

▶ **tamper with** VI *+prep obj* herumhantieren an *(+dat)*; *(with evil intent)* sich *(dat)* zu schaffen machen an *(+dat)*; *plan, schedule, elections, system* herumpfuschen an *(+dat) (inf)*; *document, evidence* verfälschen; *(Jur) witness* beeinflussen; *(= bribe)* bestechen; **the car had been tampered with** jemand hatte sich am Auto zu schaffen gemacht

tamper-evident, **tamper-proof** ADJ *food* sicherheitsverpackt, mit Sicherheitsverpackung, gegen unbefugte Eingriffe gesichert, Sicherheits-

tampon ['tæmpən] N Tampon *m*

tan [tæn] N a *(= suntan)* Bräune *f*; **to get a ~** braun werden; **she's got a lovely ~** sie ist schön braun; **what a ~!** du bist/er ist *etc* aber schön braun! b *(= colour)* Hellbraun *nt* ADJ hellbraun VT a *skins* gerben; **to ~ sb's hide** *(fig inf)* jdm das Fell gerben b *(sun) face, body etc* bräunen, braun werden lassen VI braun werden; **she ~s easily** sie wird schnell braun

tandem ['tændəm] N *(= cycle)* Tandem *nt*; **the horses were in ~** die Pferde liefen hintereinander im Gespann; **in ~ (with)** *(fig)* zusammen (mit) ADV hintereinander im Gespann

tang [tæŋ] N *(= smell)* scharfer Geruch; *(= taste)* starker Geschmack; **the fish has a salty ~** der Fisch schmeckt salzig

tanga ['tæŋgə] N *(= bikini, briefs)* Tanga *m*

tangent ['tændʒənt] N *(Math)* Tangente *f*; **to go off at a ~** *(fig)* (plötzlich) vom Thema abkommen *or* abschweifen; **he went off at a ~ about flowers** er schweifte plötzlich ab und fing an, über Blumen zu reden

tangential [tæn'dʒenʃəl] ADJ *(Math)* tangential; **this is merely ~ to the problem** dies berührt das Problem nur am Rande

tangentially [tæn'dʒenʃəlɪ] ADV *(form: = indirectly)* indirekt; **the question was only touched on ~** die Frage wurde nur am Rande gestreift

tangerine [,tændʒə'ri:n] N *(also* **tangerine orange***)* Mandarine *f* ADJ *(colour)* stark orange, rötlich orange

tangibility [,tændʒɪ'bɪlɪtɪ] N Greifbarkeit *f*

tangible ['tændʒəbl] ADJ a *(lit)* greifbar, berührbar b *(fig) result* greifbar; *proof* handfest; *assets* handfest, real

tangibly ['tændʒəblɪ] ADV greifbar; **he would prefer to be rewarded more ~** ihm wäre etwas Handfesteres als Belohnung lieber; **the evidence ~ supports his claim** die Beweise unterstützen seine Behauptung nachhaltig

Tangier(s) [tæn'dʒɪə(z)] N Tanger *nt*

tangle ['tæŋgl] N a *(lit)* Gewirr *nt*; **the string was in a ~** die Schnur hatte sich verheddert; **the ~s in her hair** ihr verheddertes Haar; **to get into a ~** sich verheddern
b *(fig: = muddle)* Wirrwarr *m*, Durcheinander *nt*; **to get into a ~** sich verheddern; **I'm in such a ~ with my tax forms** ich komme bei meinen Steuerformularen überhaupt nicht klar; **she has got herself into an emotional ~** sie hat sich gefühlsmäßig verstrickt
c *(fig: = trouble)* Ärger *m*, Schwierigkeiten *pl*; **she's in a real ~ this time** diesmal hat sie sich aber böse hineingeritten; **he got into a ~ with the police** er ist mit der Polizei aneinandergeraten, er hat Schwierigkeiten mit der Polizei gehabt
VT *(lit, fig)* verwirren, durcheinanderbringen; *wool, string also* verheddern; *hair* durcheinanderbringen; **to get ~d** *(lit, fig)* sich verheddern; *(ropes)* sich verknoten; **a ~d web** ein Gespinst *nt*

▶ **tangle up** VT *sep (lit, fig)* verwirren, durcheinanderbringen; *wool, string also* verheddern; **to get tangled up** durcheinandergeraten; *(wool etc also)* sich verheddern; *(ropes)* sich verknoten; *(person, in talking, explaining etc)* sich verstricken *or* verheddern; *(= become involved)* verwickelt *or* verstrickt werden; **the string got all tangled up in the machine** die Schnur hat sich in der Maschine verheddert; **she got tangled up with a married man** sie hat sich mit einem verheirateten Mann eingelassen

▶ **tangle with** VI *+prep obj (inf)* aneinandergeraten mit; **I'm not tangling with him** mit ihm lass ich mich (doch) nicht ein

tangly ['tæŋlɪ] ADJ *(+er) (= confused)* verwickelt, verworren

tango ['tæŋgəʊ] N Tango *m* VI Tango tanzen; **they ~ed across the room** sie tanzten im Tangoschritt durch das Zimmer; **it takes two to ~** *(fig inf)* es gehören immer zwei dazu

tangy ['tæŋɪ] ADJ *(+er) taste* scharf, streng; *smell also* durchdringend

tank [tæŋk] N a *(= container)* Tank *m*; *(esp for water)* Wasserspeicher *m*; *(of boiler)* Kessel *m*; *(Naut, for water supply)* Kessel *m*; *(in submarines)* Tauchtank *m*; *(Rail, in engine)* Kessel *m*; *(for diver: = oxygen tank)* Flasche *f*; *(Phot)* Wanne *f*; **fill up the ~, please** *(Aut)* volltanken, bitte b *(Mil)* Panzer *m*, Tank *m* c *(US inf)* Kittchen *nt (inf)*, Knast *m (inf)*

▶ **tank along** VI *(inf: = move fast, car)* dahinbrettern *(inf)*; *(runner)* dahinsausen *(inf)*

▶ **tank up** VI a *(ship, plane)* auftanken; *(car, driver)* volltanken, auftanken b *(Brit inf, = get drunk)* sich volllaufen lassen *(inf)* VT *sep* a *ship, plane* auftanken; *car* volltanken, auftanken b *(Brit inf)* **to get tanked up** sich volllaufen lassen *(inf)* *(on* mit*)*; **to be tanked up** voll sein *(inf)*

tankage ['tæŋkɪdʒ] N a *(= storage capacity of tank)* Fassungsvermögen *nt* b *(= storage fee)* Gebühr *f* für Lagerung *(in einem Tank)*; *(= storage)* Lagerung *f (in einem Tank)* c *(Agr. = meat and bone meal)* Tierkörpermehl *nt (als Dünger oder Futtermittelzusatz)*

tankard ['tæŋkəd] N *(esp Brit)* Humpen *m*; *(for beer also)* Seidel *nt*

tank car N *(Rail)* Kesselwagen *m*

tanker ['tæŋkə'] N a *(= boat)* Tanker *m*, Tankschiff *nt* b *(= vehicle)* Tankwagen *m*

tank farm N *(US)* Tanklager *nt*

tank farming N Pflanzenanbau *m* in Hydrokultur

tankful ['tæŋkfʊl] N a Tank *m* (voll) b *(Brit inf: = drink)* **he's had a ~** der ist total voll *(inf)*

tankini [tæŋ'ki:nɪ] N Tankini *m (zweiteiliger Badeanzug)*

tank: **tank top** N Pullunder *m*; **tank town** N *(US)* Wasser(auffüll)station *f*; *(fig)* Kuhnest *nt (inf)*; **tank trap** N Panzersperre *f*; **tank truck** N *(esp US)* Tankwagen *m*; **tank wagon**, *(Brit)* **tank waggon** N *(Rail)* Kesselwagen *m*

tanned [tænd] ADJ a *person* braun (gebrannt) b *skins* gegerbt

tanner[1] ['tænə'] N Gerber(in) *m(f)*

tanner[2] N *(old Brit inf)* Sixpence *m*

tannery ['tænərɪ] N Gerberei *f*

tannic ['tænɪk] ADJ Gerb-

tannic acid N Tannin *nt*

tannin ['tænɪn] N Tannin *nt*

tanning ['tænɪŋ] N a *(of hides)* Gerben *nt*; *(= craft)* Gerberei *f* b *(= punishment)* Tracht *f* Prügel; **to give sb a ~** jdm das Fell gerben

Tannoy® ['tænɔɪ] N Lautsprecheranlage *f*; **over** *or* **on the ~** über den Lautsprecher

tansy ['tænzɪ] N Rainfarn *m*

tantalize ['tæntəlaɪz] VT reizen; *(= torment also)* quälen; **to be ~d** Tantalusqualen ausstehen

tantalizing ['tæntəlaɪzɪŋ] ADJ *smell, promise* verlockend, verführerisch; *behaviour, glimpse also* aufreizend; **he spoke with ~ slowness** er sprach aufreizend langsam; **it is ~ to think that ...** es ist zum Verrücktwerden, zu denken, dass ... *(inf)*

tantalizingly ['tæntəlaɪzɪŋlɪ] ADV verlockend, verführerisch; **success was ~ close** der Erfolg schien zum Greifen nahe

tantamount ['tæntəmaʊnt] ADJ **to be ~ to sth** einer Sache *(dat)* gleichkommen, auf etw *(acc)* hinauslaufen

tantrum ['tæntrəm] N Wutanfall *m*, Koller *m (inf)*; **to have** *or* **throw a ~** einen Koller *or* Wutanfall bekommen; **she drove off in a ~** sie fuhr wütend weg

Tanzania [,tænzə'nɪə] N Tansania *nt*

Tanzanian [,tænzə'nɪən] ADJ tansanisch N Tansanier(in) *m(f)*

Taoism ['taʊɪzəm] N Taoismus *m*

tap[1] [tæp] N a *(esp Brit)* Hahn *m*; **the hot/cold ~** der Kaltwasser-/Heißwasserhahn; **don't leave the ~s running** lass das Wasser nicht laufen!, dreh die Hähne zu!; **on ~** *(lit, beer etc)* vom Fass; *(fig)* zur Hand; **he has plenty of ideas on ~** er hat immer Ideen auf Lager *(inf)* b *(of phones)* Abhören *nt*, Abhöraktion *f*
VT a *tree* anzapfen; **to ~ a pine for resin** einer Kiefer *(dat)* Harz abzapfen
b *(fig) resources, market* erschließen; **to ~ an electric current** eine Stromleitung anzapfen; **to ~ telephone wires** Telefonleitungen anzapfen; **the wires are ~ped here** die Leitung hier wird abgehört; **to ~ sb for money/a loan** *(inf)* jdn anzapfen *(inf)*, jdn anpumpen *(inf)*; **he tried to ~ me for information** er wollte mich aushorchen

▶ **tap into** VI *+prep obj (= gain access to) system, network* anzapfen; *(= exploit) fear, enthusiasm* ausnutzen

tap[2] N a *(= light knock)* Klopfen *nt*
b *(= light touch)* Klaps *m*, leichter Schlag; **to give sb a ~ on the shoulder** jdn *or* jdm auf die Schulter klopfen
c **taps** SING OR PL *(Mil)* Zapfenstreich *m*
VT klopfen; **he ~ped me on the shoulder** er klopfte mir auf die Schulter; **to ~ in a nail** einen Nagel einschlagen; **he ~ped his foot impatiently** er klopfte ungeduldig mit dem Fuß auf den Boden; **he ~ped his fingers impatiently on the table** er trommelte ungeduldig (mit den Fingern) auf den Tisch
VI klopfen; **to ~ on** *or* **at the door** sachte an

die Tür klopfen *or* pochen *(geh)*, leise anklopfen; **she sat ~ping away at the typewriter** sie klapperte auf der Schreibmaschine herum; **he ~ped with his fingers on the table** er trommelte (mit den Fingern) auf den Tisch

▶ **tap out** VT *sep* **a** *pipe* ausklopfen **b** *rhythm* klopfen; **to tap out a message (in Morse)** eine Nachricht morsen

tap: **tap dance** N Stepptanz *m*; **tap-dance** VI steppen; **tap-dancer** N Stepptänzer(in) *m(f)*, Stepper(in) *m(f)*; **tap-dancing** N Steppen *nt*

tape [teɪp] N **a** Band *nt*; *(= sticky paper)* Klebeband *nt*; *(= Sellotape ® etc)* Kleb(e)streifen *m*, Tesafilm® *m*; *(= ticker-tape, computer tape etc)* Lochstreifen *m*; *(Sport)* Zielband *nt*; **to break** *or* **breast the ~** *(Sport)* durchs Ziel gehen **b** *(magnetic)* (Ton)band *nt*, Magnetband *nt*; **on ~** auf Band; **to put** *or* **get sth on ~** etw auf Band aufnehmen; **to make a ~ of sth** etw auf Band aufnehmen
VT **a** *parcel* (mit Kleb(e)streifen/Klebeband) verkleben *or* zukleben; **to ~ together two documents** zwei Dokumente mit Kleb(e)streifen/Klebeband zusammenkleben
b *(= tape-record) song, message* (auf Band) aufnehmen; *(= video-tape) show* (auf Video) aufnehmen
c *(inf)* **I've got the situation ~d** ich habe die Sache im Griff *(inf)*; **I've got him ~d** ich kenne mich mit ihm aus

▶ **tape back** VT *sep* (mit Kleb(e)streifen/Klebeband) zurückkleben

▶ **tape down** VT *sep* (mit Kleb(e)streifen/Klebeband) festkleben

▶ **tape on** VT *sep* (mit Kleb(e)streifen/Klebeband) ankleben *or* -heften; **to tape sth on(to) sth** etw auf etw *(acc)* kleben

▶ **tape over** *(Recording)* VI +*prep obj* überspielen VT SEP **to tape A over B** B mit A überspielen

▶ **tape up** VT *sep sth broken* mit Kleb(e)streifen/Klebeband zusammenkleben; *parcel* mit Kleb(e)streifen/Klebeband verkleben; *gap, windows, mouth* zukleben

tape: **tape cassette** N Tonbandkassette *f*; **tape deck** N Tapedeck *nt*; **tape head** N Tonkopf *m*; **tape measure** N Maßband *nt*, Bandmaß *nt*

taper [ˈteɪpəʳ] N *(= candle)* (dünne) Kerze VT *end of plank, stick etc* zuspitzen; *edge* abschrägen; *hair* spitz zuschneiden; *pair of trousers* (nach unten) verengen VI sich zuspitzen; *(vase)* sich verjüngen; *(trousers)* nach unten enger werden; *(hair)* (im Nacken) spitz zulaufen; **to ~ to a point** spitz zulaufen

▶ **taper off** VI **a** *(lit)* spitz zulaufen, sich zuspitzen; *(vase)* sich verjüngen; *(road, trousers)* sich verengen **b** *(fig: = decrease gradually)* langsam aufhören; *(numbers)* langsam zurückgehen; *(production)* langsam auslaufen VT *sep edge* abschrägen; *end of plank, stick etc* zuspitzen; *(fig) production* zurückschrauben; *(= bring to an end)* langsam auslaufen lassen

tape: **tape reader** N *(Comput)* Lochstreifenleser *m*; **tape-record** VT auf Band aufnehmen; **tape recorder** N Tonbandgerät *nt*; *(= cassette recorder)* Kassettenrekorder *m*; **tape recording** N Bandaufnahme *f*

tapered [ˈteɪpəd] ADJ spitz zulaufend; **~ trousers** Hosen, die unten enger werden

tapering [ˈteɪpərɪŋ] ADJ spitz zulaufend

tape streamer N *(Comput)* Streamer *m*

taper tap N *(Tech)* Gewindebohrer *m*

tapestry [ˈtæpɪstrɪ] N Wand- *or* Bildteppich *m*; *(= fabric)* Gobelin *m*; **~-making** Tapisserie *f*; **it's all part of life's rich ~** das gibt alles dem Leben mehr Würze

tapeworm [ˈteɪpwɜːm] N Bandwurm *m*

tapioca [ˌtæpɪˈəʊkə] N Tapioka *f*

tapir [ˈteɪpəʳ] N Tapir *m*

tappet [ˈtæpɪt] N *(Aut)* Stößel *m*

tapping [ˈtæpɪŋ] N **a** *(of barrel)* Anzapfen *nt*, Anstich *m*; *(of beer etc from barrel)* Abzapfen *nt* **b** *(of telephone etc)* Anzapfen *nt* **c** *(Med)* Punktieren *nt* **d** *(fig, of funds etc)* Erschließen *nt* **e** *(Tech)* Gewindebohren *nt or* -schneiden *nt*; **~ drill** Gewindebohrer *m*

tap: **taproom** [ˈtæpruːm] N Schankstube *f*, Schenke *f*, Schänke *f*; **taproot** N *(Bot)* Pfahlwurzel *f*

tapster [ˈtæpstəʳ] N *(old)* Schankkellner(in) *m(f)*, Zapfer(in) *m(f)*

tap water N Leitungswasser *nt*

tar¹ [tɑːʳ] N Teer *m* VT *road, fence* teeren; **they are all ~red with the same brush** *(fig)* sie sind alle vom gleichen Schlag; **to ~ and feather sb** jdn teeren und federn

tar² N *(old Naut sl)* Teerjacke *f (hum)*, Seemann *m*

tarantella [ˌtærənˈtelə] N Tarantella *f*

tarantula [təˈræntjʊlə] N Tarantel *f*

tarboard [ˈtɑːbɔːd] N Dach- *or* Teerpappe *f*

tarbrush [ˈtɑːbrʌʃ] N **a touch of the ~** *(pej inf)* schwarzes Blut

tardily [ˈtɑːdɪlɪ] ADV *arrive, offer, send* verspätet; *discover* zu spät

tardiness [ˈtɑːdɪnɪs] N **a** *(of person)* Säumigkeit *f (geh)* **b** *(US: = lateness)* Zuspätkommen *nt*; *(of train etc)* Verspätung *f*

tardy [ˈtɑːdɪ] ADJ *(+er)* **a** *(= belated) reply, arrival, offer to help* (reichlich) spät; *person* säumig *(geh)*; **to be ~ in doing sth** etw erst reichlich spät tun **b** *(US: = late)* **to be ~** *(person)* zu spät kommen; *(train etc)* Verspätung haben; **the train was ~ (in arriving at New York)** der Zug kam mit Verspätung (in New York) an

tare¹ [teəʳ] N *(Bot)* Wicke *f*

tare² N *(Comm)* Tara *f*; *(of vehicle)* Leergewicht *nt*

target [ˈtɑːgɪt] N **a** *(= person, object, Mil)* Ziel *nt*; *(Sport: = board)* Ziel- *or* Schießscheibe *f*; *(fig, of joke, criticism etc)* Zielscheibe *f*; **he was a ~ for racial abuse** er war Zielscheibe rassistischer Pöbeleien; **she was the ~ of a violent attack** sie war das Ziel eines brutalen Angriffs *or* Überfalls; **his shot was off/on ~** *(Mil)* sein Schuss ist danebengegangen/hat getroffen; *(Ftbl etc)* sein Schuss war ungenau/sehr genau; **the bombs were on/off ~** die Bomben haben getroffen/sind daneben niedergegangen; **Apollo III is on ~ for the moon** Apollo III ist auf direktem Kurs zum Mond; **they were at least 12 km off ~** sie hatten das Ziel um mindestens 12 km verfehlt
b *(= objective, goal)* Ziel *nt*; *(in production)* (Plan)soll *nt*; **production ~** Produktionssoll *nt no pl*; **production is above/on/below ~** das Produktionssoll ist überschritten/erfüllt/nicht erfüllt; **the government met its ~ for reducing unemployment** die Regierung hat mit der Abnahme der Arbeitslosigkeit ihren Plan erfüllt; **he set a ~ for spending** er setzte eine Höchstgrenze für die Ausgaben fest; **we set ourselves the ~ of £10,000** wir haben uns £ 10.000 zum Ziel gesetzt; **to be on ~** auf Kurs sein; **the project is on ~ for completion** das Projekt ist auf dem besten Weg, planmäßig fertig zu werden; **we're on ~ for £10,000** alles läuft nach Plan, um auf £ 10.000 zu kommen; **to stay on ~** den Kurs halten; **to be behind ~** hinter dem Soll zurückliegen
VT sich *(dat)* zum Ziel setzen; *group, audience* als Zielgruppe haben, abzielen auf *(+acc)*; *area, resources* abzielen auf *(+acc)*; **to ~ 500 tons per day** 500 Tonnen pro Tag anspielen

target: **targetable** [ˈtɑːgɪtəbl] ADJ *(Mil) warhead etc* aufs Ziel einstellbar *or* programmierbar; **target area** N Zielbereich *m*, Zielgebiet *nt*; **target cost** N Richtkosten *pl*, Plankosten *pl*; **target date** N angestrebter Termin; **target drive** N *(Comput)* Ziellaufwerk *nt*; **target figure** N Richtsumme *f*, Plansumme *f*; **we have a ~ of 100,000 visitors** wir haben uns *(dat)* 100.000 Besucher zum Ziel gesetzt; **target file** N *(Comput)* Zieldatei *f*; **target group** N Zielgruppe *f*; **target language** N Zielsprache *f*; **target market** N Zielmarkt *m*; **target practice** N *(Mil)* Zielschießen *nt*

targetting [ˈtɑːgɪtɪŋ] N *(= setting targets)* Zielsetzung *f*; **the ~ of teenagers as customers** das Ansteuern von Teenagern *or* das Abzielen auf Teenager als Kunden

tariff [ˈtærɪf] N **a** *(esp Brit)* (Gebühren)tarif *m*; *(in hotels)* Preisverzeichnis *nt*, Preisliste *f* **b** *(Econ: = tax)* Zoll *m*; *(= table)* Zolltarif *m*

tariff reform N *(Econ)* Zolltarifreform *f*; *(Hist)* Einführung *f* von Schutzzöllen

tariff walls PL *(Econ)* Zollschranken *pl*

tarmac [ˈtɑːmæk] N **a** **Tarmac®** Makadam *m*; *(generally)* Asphalt *m*, Makadam *m (spec)* **b** *(esp Brit Aviat)* Rollfeld *nt* VT *road (generally)* asphaltieren, makadamisieren *(spec)*

tarmacadam [ˌtɑːməˈkædəm] N Makadam *m*

tarn [tɑːn] N kleiner Berg- *or* Gebirgssee

tarnish [ˈtɑːnɪʃ] VT **a** *metal* stumpf werden lassen; **the silver was ~ed by exposure to air** das Silber war an der Luft angelaufen **b** *(fig) reputation, glory* beflecken; *ideals, image* trüben, den Glanz nehmen *(+dat)* VI *(metal)* anlaufen N Beschlag *m*; **to prevent ~** das Anlaufen verhindern

taro [ˈtɑːrəʊ] N Taro *m*

tarot [ˈtɑːrəʊ] N Tarot *nt or m*

tarot card N Tarotkarte *f*

tarp [tɑːp] N *(US inf)* = **tarpaulin**

tar paper N *(US)* Dachpappe *f*, Teerpappe *f*

tarpaulin [tɑːˈpɔːlɪn] N **a** *(= waterproof sheet)* Plane *f*; *(Naut)* Persenning *f* **b** **tarpaulins** PL *(= clothes)* Ölzeug *nt*

tarpon [ˈtɑːpɒn] N Atlantischer Tarpon, Silberkönig *m*

tarragon [ˈtærəgən] N Estragon *m*

tarry¹ [ˈtɑːrɪ] ADJ teerig

tarry² [tærɪ] VI *(old, liter)* **a** *(= remain)* verweilen *(old, liter)* **b** *(= delay)* säumen *(old, liter)*, zögern

tarsus [ˈtɑːsəs] N Tarsus *m*

tart¹ [tɑːt] ADJ *(+er)* **a** *flavour, wine* herb, sauer *(pej)*; *fruit* sauer **b** *(fig) remark, manner* scharf; *person* schroff

tart² N *(Cook)* Obstkuchen *m*, Obsttorte *f*; *(individual)* Obsttörtchen *nt*; **apple ~** Apfelkuchen *m*/-törtchen *nt*; **jam ~** Marmeladenkuchen *m*/-törtchen *nt*

tart³ N *(Brit inf: = prostitute)* Nutte *f (inf)*; *(= loose woman)* Flittchen *nt (pej inf)*; *(pej: = woman)* Schachtel *f (inf)*

▶ **tart up** VT *sep (esp Brit inf)* aufmachen *(inf)*; *oneself* auftakeln *(inf)*, aufdonnern *(inf)*; **there she was, all tarted up** da stand sie, aufgetakelt wie eine Fregatte *(inf)*

tartan [ˈtɑːtən] N *(= pattern)* Schottenkaro *nt*; *(= material)* Schottenstoff *m*; **what's your ~?** welches Clanmuster tragen Sie? ADJ *skirt etc* im Schottenkaro *or* -muster

Tartar [ˈtɑːtəʳ] N Tatar(in) *m(f)*; **to catch a ~** *(fig)* sich *(dat)* etwas Übles einhandeln

tartar¹ [ˈtɑːtəʳ] N *(fig)* Tyrann(in) *m(f)*

tartar² N *(on teeth)* Zahnstein *m*

tartare [tɑːˈtɑːʳ] ADJ → **steak**

tartaric acid [tɑːˌtærɪkˈæsɪd] N Weinsäure *f*

tartar(e) sauce N ≈ Remouladensoße *f*

Tartary [ˈtɑːtərɪ] N Tatarei *f*

tartlet [tɑːtlɪt] N *(Brit)* Törtchen *nt*

tartly [ˈtɑːtlɪ] ADV *speak* scharf; **a ~ flavoured tomato relish** ein scharf gewürztes Tomatenchutney

tartness [ˈtɑːtnɪs] N **a** *(of flavour, wine)* Herbheit *f*, Säure *f (pej)*; *(of fruit)* Säure *f* **b** *(fig, of remark, manner)* Schärfe *f*; *(of humour)* Beißende(s) *nt*; *(of person)* Schroffheit *f*

tash [tæʃ] N *(Brit inf)* = **tache**

task [tɑːsk] N Aufgabe *f*; **to set** *or* **give sb a ~** jdm eine Aufgabe stellen *or* geben; **it is the ~ of the politician to …** es ist Aufgabe des Politikers zu …; **to take sb to ~** jdn ins Gebet nehmen, sich *(dat)* jdn vornehmen *(inf)* (for, about wegen) VT = **tax VT b**

task: **task bar** N *(Comput)* Taskleiste *f*; **task force** N Sondereinheit *f*, Spezialeinheit *f*; **taskmaster** N (strenger) Arbeitgeber; **he's a hard ~** er ist ein strenger Meister; **task time** N *(US Econ)* Zeitnorm *f*

Tasmania [tæz'meɪnɪə] N Tasmanien *nt*

Tasmanian [tæz'meɪnɪən] ADJ tasmanisch N Tasmanier(in) *m(f)*

Tasman Sea [,tæzmən'siː] N Tasmansee *f*

tassel ['tæsəl] N Quaste *f*, Troddel *f*

tasselled ['tæsəld] ADJ mit Quasten *or* Troddeln verziert

taste [teɪst] N a *(= sense)* Geschmack(sinn) *m*; **to be sweet to the ~** süß schmecken, einen süßen Geschmack haben
b *(= flavour)* Geschmack *m*; **I don't like the ~** das schmeckt mir nicht; **her cooking has no ~** ihr Essen schmeckt nach nichts; **a ~ of onions** ein Zwiebelgeschmack; **to leave a bad ~ in the mouth** *(lit, fig)* einen üblen Nachgeschmack hinterlassen
c *(= small amount)* Kostprobe *f*, Versucherchen *nt (inf)*; *(fig, as an example)* Kostprobe *f*; *(of sth in the future)* Vorgeschmack *m*; **would you like some? – just a ~** möchten Sie etwas? – nur eine Idee; **to have a ~ (of sth)** *(lit)* (etw) probieren *or* kosten; *(fig)* eine Kostprobe (von etw) bekommen; *(of sth to come)* einen Vorgeschmack (von etw) haben; **two years in the army will give him a ~ of discipline** zwei Jahre bei der Armee werden ihm zeigen *or* werden ihn spüren lassen, was Disziplin ist; **to give sb a ~ of the whip** jdn die Peitsche *or* Knute spüren lassen; **he gave them a ~ of his bad temper** er gab ihnen eine (Kost)probe seiner schlechten Laune; **a ~ of what was to come** ein Vorgeschmack dessen, was noch kommen sollte
d *(= liking)* Geschmack *m no pl*; **to have a ~ for sth** eine Vorliebe für etw haben; **to acquire** *or* **develop a ~ for sth** Geschmack an etw *(dat)* finden; **it's an acquired ~** das ist etwas für Kenner; **she has expensive ~s in hats** was Hüte anbelangt, hat sie einen teuren Geschmack; **my ~ in music has changed over the years** mein musikalischer Geschmack hat sich mit der Zeit geändert; **to be to sb's ~** nach jds Geschmack sein; **it is a matter of ~** das ist Geschmack(s)sache; **there is no accounting for ~s** über Geschmack lässt sich (nicht) streiten; **~s differ** die Geschmäcker sind verschieden; **sweeten to ~** *(Cook)* nach Geschmack *or* Bedarf süßen; **her novels are too violent for my ~** ihre Romane enthalten für meinen Geschmack zu viel Gewalt
e *(= discernment)* Geschmack *m*; **she has very good ~ in furniture** was Möbel anbelangt, hat sie einen sehr guten Geschmack; **she has no ~ at all when it comes to choosing friends** sie ist nicht sehr wählerisch in der Auswahl ihrer Freunde; **a man of ~** ein Mann mit Geschmack; **in good ~** geschmackvoll; **in bad ~** geschmacklos; **to be in doubtful ~** von zweifelhaftem Geschmack zeugen; **that joke shows very poor ~** dieser Witz ist geschmacklos; **the house is furnished in impeccable ~** das Haus ist, was Geschmack betrifft, tadellos eingerichtet
VT a *(= perceive flavour of)* schmecken; *blood* lecken; **I can't ~ anything** ich schmecke überhaupt nichts; **I can't ~ anything wrong** ich kann nichts Besonderes schmecken; **once you've ~d real champagne** wenn Sie einmal echten Sekt getrunken haben; **I've never ~d caviar** ich habe noch nie Kaviar gekostet *(geh)* *or* gegessen; **wait till you ~ this** warten Sie mal, bis Sie das probiert haben; **he hadn't ~d food for a week** er hatte seit einer Woche nichts zu sich genommen
b *(= take a little)* versuchen, probieren, kosten
c *(= test) wine* verkosten; *food products* probieren; *(official)* prüfen; **~ the sauce before adding salt** schmecken Sie die Soße ab, bevor Sie Salz beigeben
d *(fig) power, freedom, success, victory* erfahren, erleben; **once the canary had ~d freedom ...** als der Kanarienvogel erst einmal Geschmack an der Freiheit gefunden hatte ...
VI a *(food, drink)* schmecken; **to ~ good** *or* **nice** (gut) schmecken; **it ~s all right to me** ich schmecke nichts; *(= I like it)* ich finde, das schmeckt nicht schlecht; **to ~ of sth** nach etw schmecken
b **to ~ of** *(liter)* erfahren; **those who have ~d of the knowledge of Zen** diejenigen, denen die Weisheit des Zen zuteilgeworden ist *(geh)*

taste bud N Geschmacksknospe *f*

tasteful ADJ, **tastefully** ADV ['teɪstfʊl, -fəlɪ] geschmackvoll

tastefulness ['teɪstfʊlnɪs] N guter Geschmack

tasteless ['teɪstlɪs] ADJ *(lit, fig)* geschmacklos; *food also* fade

tastelessly ['teɪstlɪslɪ] ADV geschmacklos; **~ inappropriate** geschmacklos und unangebracht; **~ extravagant** geschmacklos extravagant; **her ordeal was handled ~ in the press** ihre Tortur wurde in der Presse geschmacklos behandelt

tastelessness ['teɪstlɪsnɪs] N *(lit, fig)* Geschmacklosigkeit *f*; *(of food also)* Fadheit *f*

taster ['teɪstə'] N a *(of wine, tobacco)* Prüfer(in) *m(f)*, Probierer(in) *m(f)*; *(of tea)* Schmecker(in) *m(f)*; *(as bodyguard)* Vorkoster(in) *m(f)* b *(esp Brit fig)* Vorgeschmack *m*; **this is just a ~ of what's to come** dies ist nur ein kleiner Vorgeschmack von dem, was noch kommt

tastily ['teɪstɪlɪ] ADV schmackhaft

tastiness ['teɪstɪnɪs] N Schmackhaftigkeit *f*

tasty ['teɪstɪ] ADJ (+er) *dish* schmackhaft; **a ~ morsel** *(lit)* ein Leckerbissen *m*; **his new girlfriend is very ~** *(inf)* seine neue Freundin ist zum Anbeißen *(inf)*

tat¹ [tæt] VI Okkispitze *or* Schiffchenspitze machen VT in Okkispitze *or* Schiffchenspitze arbeiten; **she ~ted a strip of lace** sie stellte eine Spitze in Okkiarbeit her

tat² N → **tit²**

tat³ N *(US inf) abbr of* **tattoo** Tätowierung *f*; **prison ~s** Tätowierungen *pl* aus der Gefängniszeit

ta-ta [tæ'tɑː] INTERJ *(Brit inf)* tschüss *(inf)*, ata ata *(baby-talk)*

tattered ['tætəd] ADJ *clothes, person* zerlumpt; *book, sheet* zerfleddert, zerfetzt; *(fig) pride, reputation* angeschlagen; *nerves* zerrüttet

tatters ['tætəz] PL Lumpen *pl*, Fetzen *pl*; **to be in ~** in Fetzen sein *or* hängen; **his jacket hung in ~** sein Jackett war zerrissen *or* hing ihm in Fetzen vom Leib; **his reputation/confidence was in ~** sein Ruf/Selbstbewusstsein war sehr angeschlagen *or* hatte sehr gelitten

tattie, tatty ['tætɪ] N *(Scot inf)* Kartoffel *f*

tattily ['tætɪlɪ] ADV *(inf) dressed* schäbig; *produced, manufactured* schlampig *(inf)*

tattiness ['tætɪnɪs] N *(inf)* Schmuddeligkeit *f*; *(of clothes)* Schäbigkeit *f*

tatting ['tætɪŋ] N Okki- *or* Schiffchenspitze *f*, Frivolitätenarbeit *f*

tattle ['tætl] VI tratschen *(inf)*, klatschen N Geschwätz *nt*, Gerede *nt*; **office ~** Büroklatsch *m or* -tratsch *m (inf)*

tattler ['tætlə'] N Klatschmaul *nt (pej sl)*, Klatschbase *f (inf)*

tattoo¹ [tə'tuː] VT tätowieren N Tätowierung *f*

tattoo² N a *(Brit: = military pageant)* Musikparade *f* b *(Mil, on drum or bugle)* Zapfenstreich *m*; **to beat** *or* **sound the ~** den Zapfenstreich blasen; **to beat a ~ on the table** *(with one's fingers)* auf den Tisch trommeln

tattooer [tə'tuːə'], **tattooist** [tə'tuːɪst] N Tätowierer(in) *m(f)*

tatty¹ ['tætɪ] ADJ (+er) *(esp Brit inf)* schmuddelig; *clothes* schäbig

tatty² ['tætɪ] N *(Scot inf)* = **tattie**

taught [tɔːt] *pret, ptp of* **teach**

taunt [tɔːnt] N Spöttelei *f*, höhnische Bemerkung; **he paid no attention to their ~s of "traitor"** er kümmerte sich nicht darum, dass sie ihn als Verräter verhöhnten VT *person* verspotten, aufziehen *(inf) (about* wegen); **to ~ sb with racial abuse** jdn mit rassistischen Beschimpfungen verhöhnen

taunting ADJ, **tauntingly** ADV ['tɔːntɪŋ, -lɪ] höhnisch, spöttisch

Taurean [tɔː'rɪən] N *(Astrol)* Stier *m*

Taurus ['tɔːrəs] N *(Astron, Astrol)* Stier *m*; **he's (a) ~** er ist Stier

taut [tɔːt] ADJ (+er) a *rope* straff (gespannt); *skin* straff; *muscles* stramm, gestrafft; **to hold sth ~** etw straff halten; **to be stretched ~** straff gespannt sein; **to pull sth ~** etw stramm ziehen; **~ round thighs** pralle Oberschenkel *pl* b *(fig: = tense) nerves, situation* (an)gespannt; *person, voice* angespannt; *look* gespannt; **his face was ~ with anger** sein Gesicht war vor Wut verzogen
c *(fig: = precise, economical) style, prose* knapp
d *(= lean) person* schlank; *body* straff

tauten ['tɔːtn] VT *rope* spannen, straff anziehen, straffen; *sail* straffen; *muscle, body* anspannen VI sich spannen *or* straffen, straff werden

tautly ['tɔːtlɪ] ADV a *stretch* straff b *(fig: = precisely, economically)* knapp

tautness ['tɔːtnɪs] N *(of skin, rope)* Straffheit *f*; *(of muscles)* Strammheit *f*; *(fig, of atmosphere)* Gespanntheit *f*; *(of nerves)* Anspannung *f*; *(of style)* Knappheit *f*

tautological [,tɔːtə'lɒdʒɪkəl], **tautologous** [tɔː'tɒləgəs] ADJ tautologisch, doppelt gemoppelt *(inf)*

tautology [tɔː'tɒlədʒɪ] N Tautologie *f*, weißer Schimmel *(inf)*

tavern ['tævən] N *(old)* Taverne *f*, Schänke *f*, Schenke *f (old)*

tawdrily ['tɔːdrɪlɪ] ADV billig und geschmacklos; **~ dressed** aufgedonnert

tawdriness ['tɔːdrɪnɪs] N *(of jewellery, decorations etc)* ordinäre Protzigkeit; *(of story, idea)* Geschmacklosigkeit *f*; **the ~ of her appearance** ihre billige und geschmacklose Aufmachung

tawdry ['tɔːdrɪ] ADJ (+er) *clothes* billig und geschmacklos; *hat, splendour, decorations* ordinär; *person, appearance* aufgedonnert; *story, idea* geschmacklos; **all this cheap and ~ jewellery** all dieser billige Flitterkram

tawny ['tɔːnɪ] ADJ (+er) gelbbraun, goldbraun; **~ brown** gelbbraun; **~ port** bräunlicher Portwein, Tawny-Portwein *m*

tawny owl N Waldkauz *m*; **Tawny Owl** *(in Brownies)* Helferin *f* der Wichtelmutter

tax [tæks] N a *(Fin, Econ)* Steuer *f*; *(on a company's profit)* Abgabe *f*; *(= import tax)* Gebühr *f*; **before ~** brutto, vor Abzug der Steuern; **after ~** netto, nach Abzug der Steuern; **profits before/after ~** Brutto-/Nettoverdienst *m*; **that's done for ~ purposes** das wird aus steuerlichen Gründen getan; **free of ~** steuer-/abgaben-/gebührenfrei; **to put a ~ on sb/sth** jdn/etw besteuern, jdn/etw mit einer Steuer belegen; **the heavy ~ on the rich** die hohe Besteuerung der Reichen; **the ~ on alcohol/cars** *etc* die Getränke-/Kraftfahrzeugsteuer *etc*
b *(fig)* Belastung *f (on sth +gen, on sb* für jdn)
VT a *(Fin, Econ)* besteuern; *country* mit Steuern belegen; **this government is going to ~ us all out of existence** diese Regierung zieht uns den letzten Cent aus der Tasche *(inf)*
b *(fig) brain, imagination, nerves, patience etc* strapazieren; *strength* stark beanspruchen; *savings, resources* angreifen, schmälern
c *(liter, = accuse)* **to ~ sb with sth** jdn einer Sache *(gen)* beschuldigen *or* bezichtigen *or* zeihen *(liter)*

tax abatement N Steuernachlass *m*

taxability [,tæksə'bɪlɪtɪ] N *(subject to tax)* Steuerpflichtigkeit *f*; *(of income)* Besteuerungsfähigkeit *f*; *(Jur)* Gebührenpflichtigkeit *f*

taxable ['tæksəbl] ADJ *person* steuerpflichtig; *income also* (be)steuerbar *(form)*; *goods* besteuert, abgabenpflichtig

tax: **tax advantage** N Steuervorteil *m*; **tax adviser** N Steuerberater(in) *m(f)*; **tax allow-**

ance N Steuervergünstigung *f*; (= *tax-free income*) Steuerfreibetrag *m*

taxation [tæk'seɪʃən] N Besteuerung *f*; (= *taxes also*) Steuern *pl*; **money acquired from ~** Steuereinnahmen *or* -einkünfte *pl*; **exempt from ~** nicht besteuert; *goods, income also* steuerfrei; **subject to ~** steuerpflichtig

taxation system N Steuersystem *nt*

tax: **tax avoidance** N Steuerumgehung *f*; **tax bill** N (*Brit inf*) Steuerbescheid *m*; **tax bracket** N Steuergruppe *f or* -klasse *f*; **tax burden** N Steuernlast *f*; **tax code, tax coding** N Steuerkennziffer *f*; **tax collecting** N Steuereinziehung *f*; **tax collector** N Finanz- *or* Steuerbeamte(r) *m*/-beamtin *f*; (*Bibl, Hist*) Zöllner *m*; **tax competition** N Steuerwettbewerb *m*; **tax credit** N (auf Steuerschuld) anrechenbarer Betrag (*aus Verlusten bei Aktienverkauf etc*); **tax cut** N Steuersenkung *f*; **tax-deductible** ADJ (steuerlich *or* von der Steuer) absetzbar; *mortgage* steuerbegünstigt; **tax demand** N Steuerbescheid *m*; **tax disc** N (*Brit: on vehicle*) Steuermarke *f or* -plakette *f*; **tax dodge** N Trick *m* um Steuern zu umgehen; **tax dodger, tax evader** N Steuerhinterzieher(in) *m(f)*; (*who goes abroad*) Steuerflüchtling *m*; **tax evasion** N Steuerhinterziehung *f*; (*by going abroad*) Steuerflucht *f*; **tax-exempt** ADJ (*US*) *person* steuerbefreit; *business* abgabenfrei; *income, status* steuerfrei; **tax exile** N Steuerexil *nt*; (= *person*) Steuerflüchtling *m*; **tax fairness** N Steuergerechtigkeit *f*; **tax form** N Steuerformular *nt*; **tax-free** ADJ, ADV steuerfrei; **tax harmonization** N Steuerharmonisierung *f*; **tax haven** N Steuerparadies *nt*

taxi ['tæksɪ] **N** Taxi *nt*; **to go by ~** mit dem Taxi fahren **VI** (*Aviat*) rollen; **the plane ~ed to a halt** das Flugzeug rollte aus

taxi: **taxicab** ['tæksɪkæb] N (*esp US*) Taxi *nt*; **taxi dancer** N (*US*) Tanzdame *f*

taxidermist ['tæksɪdɜːmɪst] N Präparator(in) *m(f)*, Tierausstopfer(in) *m(f)*

taxidermy ['tæksɪdɜːmɪ] N Taxidermie *f*

taxi: **taxi driver** ['tæksɪdraɪvə'] N Taxifahrer(in) *m(f)*; **taximeter** N Fahrpreisanzeiger *m*, Taxameter *m* (*form*)

tax incentive N Steueranreiz *m*

tax increase N Steuererhöhung(en *pl*) *f*

taxing ['tæksɪŋ] ADJ *work etc* anstrengend, strapaziös

tax inspector N (*Brit*) Finanzbeamte(r) *mf*

taxi: **taxiplane** N (*US*) Lufttaxi *nt*; **taxi rank** (*Brit*), **taxi stand** (*esp US*) N Taxistand *m*; **taxiway** N (*Aviat*) Rollbahn *f*

tax: **tax loophole** N Steuerschlupfloch *nt*; **tax loss** N Steuerausfall *m*; **taxman** ['tæksmæn] N Steuer- *or* Finanzbeamte(r) *m*; **the ~ gets 35%** das Finanzamt bekommt 35%

taxonomy [tæk'sɒnəmɪ] N Taxonomie *f*

tax: **taxpayer** N Steuerzahler(in) *m(f)*; **tax policy** N Steuerpolitik *f*; **tax privilege** N Steuervorteil *m*; **tax rebate** N Steuervergütung *f or* -rückzahlung *f*; **tax receipts** PL Steuereinnahmen *pl*, Steueraufkommen *nt*; **tax reform** N Steuerreform *f*; **tax refund** N Steuer(rück)erstattung *f*; **tax regime** N Steuersystem *nt*; **tax relief** N Steuervergünstigung *f*, Steuererleichterung(en *pl*) *f*; **~ of 5%** ein Steuernachlass *m* von 5%; **it qualifies for ~** das ist steuerbegünstigt; **tax return** N Steuererklärung *f*; **tax revenue** N Steueraufkommen *nt*; **tax shelter** N **a** (= *tax avoidance*) steuersparende Maßnahme **b** (*minimalized tax*) Steuerbegünstigung *f*; **tax structure** N Steuersystem *nt*; **tax system** N Steuerwesen *nt*, Steuer- *or* Besteuerungssystem *nt*; **tax write-off** N Steuerabschreibung *f*; **tax year** N Steuerjahr *nt*

TB *abbr of* **tuberculosis** Tb *f*, Tbc *f*

tba *abbr of* **to be arranged, to be announced** Einzelheiten werden noch bekannt gegeben

T-bar ['tiːbɑː'] N Bügel *m*; (= *lift*) Schlepplift *m*; (*Tech*) T-Träger *m*

tbc *abbr of* **to be confirmed** noch zu bestätigen

T-bone steak ['tiːbəʊn'steɪk] N T-Bone-Steak *nt*

tbs(p) *abbr of* **tablespoonful(s)** *or* **tablespoon(s)** Essl.

TCP® N (*Brit*) *mildes Antiseptikum*

TD *abbr of* **touchdown**

T.D. (*US*) *abbr of* **Treasury Department**

tea [tiː] N **a** (= *substance, drink*) Tee *m*; **to make (the) ~** (den) Tee machen; **a cup of ~** eine Tasse Tee; **not for all the ~ in China** nicht um alles Gold der Welt **b** (*also* **tea plant**) Tee (-strauch) *m* **c** (*Brit*) (= *afternoon tea*) ≈ Kaffee und Kuchen; (= *meal*) Abendbrot *nt*; **we have ~ at five** wir essen um 5 Uhr Abendbrot *or* zu Abend

tea: **tea bag** N Teebeutel *m*; **tea ball** N (*esp US*) Tee-Ei *nt*, Teeei *nt*; **tea biscuit** N Butterkeks *m*; **~s** Teegebäck *nt*; **tea boy** N Stift *m*; **tea break** N (*esp Brit*) Pause *f*; **tea caddy** N (*esp Brit*) Teebüchse *f or* -dose *f*; (= *dispenser*) Teespender *m*; **teacake** N (*Brit*) Rosinenbrötchen *nt*; **teacart** N (*US*) Teewagen *m*, Servierwagen *m*

teach [tiːtʃ] *vb: pret, ptp* **taught** **VT** *subject, person* unterrichten, lehren (*geh*); *animal* abrichten; **to ~ sth to sb, to ~ sb sth** jdm etw beibringen; (*teacher*) jdn in etw (*dat*) unterrichten, jdm Unterricht in etw (*dat*) geben; **to ~ sb to do sth** jdm beibringen, etw zu tun; **the accident taught me to be careful** durch diesen Unfall habe ich gelernt, vorsichtiger zu sein; **to ~ sb how to do sth** jdm zeigen, wie man etw macht, jdm etw beibringen; **you can't ~ somebody how to be happy** man kann niemanden lehren, glücklich zu sein; **he ~es French** er unterrichtet *or* gibt (*inf*) *or* lehrt (*geh*) Französisch; **who taught you to drive?** bei wem haben Sie Fahren gelernt?; **to ~ school** (*US*) Lehrer(in) sein/werden; **to ~ oneself sth** sich (*dat*) etw beibringen; **I taught myself to ride a bike** ich habe mir das Radfahren (selbst) beigebracht; **let that ~ you not to …** lass dir das eine Lehre sein, nicht zu …; **that'll ~ him a thing or two!** da werden ihm die Augen aufgehen, da wird er erst mal sehen (*inf*); **it taught me a thing or two** es war sehr lehrreich, da habe ich einiges gelernt; **that'll ~ him!** das hat er nun davon!; **make her pay, that'll ~ her** lass sie bezahlen, das wird ihr eine Lehre sein; **that'll ~ you to break the speed limit/not to pay your insurance** das hast du (nun) davon, dass du die Geschwindigkeitsbegrenzung überschritten/die Versicherung nicht bezahlt hast; **I'll ~ you to speak to me like that!** ich werde dir schon austreiben (*inf*) *or* werde dich lehren, so mit mir zu sprechen!; **you can't ~ him anything about that** darüber können Sie ihm nichts Neues mehr erzählen

VI unterrichten, Unterricht geben; **he wants to ~** er möchte Lehrer werden; **he can't ~** **he can't ~** (= *not allowed*) er darf nicht unterrichten; (= *no ability*) er gibt keinen guten Unterricht

N (*esp US inf*: = *teacher: as address*) Herr *m*, Frau *f*

teachability [ˌtiːtʃə'bɪlɪtɪ] N (*of pupil*) Lernfähigkeit *f*; (*of subject*) Lehrbarkeit *f*

teachable ['tiːtʃəbl] ADJ *animal, child* lernfähig; **music is a very ~ subject** Musik ist ein Fach, das sich gut unterrichten *or* lehren (*geh*) lässt; **this is not a ~ skill** diese Fertigkeit kann man niemandem beibringen; **things in life which are not ~** Dinge, die man niemandem beibringen kann

teacher ['tiːtʃə'] N Lehrer(in) *m(f)*; **university ~s** Hochschullehrer *pl*, Lehrkräfte *pl* an (den) Universitäten (*form*); **~s of English, English ~s** Englischlehrer *pl*; **she is a German ~** sie ist Deutschlehrerin

teacher-training [ˌtiːtʃə'treɪnɪŋ] N Lehrer(aus)bildung *f*; (*for primary teachers*) Studium *nt or* Ausbildung *f* an einer pädagogischen Hochschule; (*for secondary teachers*) Referendarausbildung *f*; **~ course** Lehrerausbildung *f*; **~ college** (*for primary teachers*) pädagogische Hochschule; (*for secondary teachers*) Studienseminar *nt*

tea chest N (*Brit*) Kiste *f*

teach-in ['tiːtʃɪn] N Teach-in *nt*

teaching ['tiːtʃɪŋ] N **a** das Unterrichten *or* Lehren (*geh*); (*as profession*) der Lehrberuf; **to take up ~** den Lehrberuf ergreifen (*form*), Lehrer werden; **she enjoys ~** sie unterrichtet gern; **he is no good at ~** er ist kein guter Lehrer **b** (= *doctrine*: *also* **teachings**) Lehre *f*; **his ~ on this subject was somewhat vague** seine Ausführungen zu diesem Thema waren ziemlich vage

teaching: **teaching aid** N Lehr- *or* Unterrichtsmittel *nt*; **teaching diploma** N Lehrbefugnis *f*; **teaching hospital** N Ausbildungskrankenhaus *nt*; **teaching machine** N Lernmaschine *f*, Lehrmittel *nt* für den programmierten Unterricht; **teaching profession** N Lehrberuf *m*; (= *all teachers*) Lehrer *pl*; **teaching staff** N Lehrerkollegium *nt*, Lehrkörper *m* (*form*); **teaching time** N Unterrichtszeit *f*

tea: **tea cloth** N (*Brit*) Geschirrtuch *nt*; **tea cosy**, (*US*) **tea cozy** N Teewärmer *m*; **teacup** N **a** Teetasse *f* → **storm N a b** (*also* **teacupful**) Tasse *f* (voll); **tea dance** N Tanztee *m*; **tea garden** N Gartencafé *nt*; **teahouse** N Teehaus *nt*

teak [tiːk] N (= *wood*) Teak(holz) *nt*; (= *tree*) Teakbaum *m*

teakettle ['tiːketl] N Wasserkessel *m*

teal [tiːl] N *pl* - Krickente *f*

tea: **tea lady** N (*Brit*) *Frau, die in Büros etc für die Angestellten Tee zubereitet*; **tea leaf** N **a** Teeblatt *nt* → **read**[1] **VT b b** (*Brit inf*: = *thief*) Langfinger *m* (*inf*)

team [tiːm] **N** **a** Team *nt*; (*Sport*) Team *nt*, Mannschaft *f*; **football ~** Fußballmannschaft *f or* -elf *f*; **they work as a ~** sie arbeiten im *or* als Team; **they make a good ~** sie sind ein gutes Team *or* (*two also*) Gespann, sie arbeiten gut zusammen; **research ~** Forschungsgruppe *f or* -gemeinschaft *f or* -team *nt*;; **a ~ of scientists** eine Gruppe *or* ein Team *nt* von Wissenschaftlern; **she plays for both ~s** (*fig inf*: = *is bisexual*) sie kennt beide Ufer (*inf*) **b** (*of horses, oxen etc*) Gespann *nt* **VT** *horses, oxen* zusammenspannen; (*fig*) zusammentun

▶ **team up** **VI** (*people*) sich zusammentun (*with* mit); (= *join group*) sich anschließen (*with sb* jdm, an jdn); **I see that John and Mary have teamed up** John und Mary gehen jetzt (anscheinend) miteinander (*inf*) **VT** *sep* zusammenschließen

team: **team captain** N Mannschaftskapitän *m*; **team effort** N Teamarbeit *f*; **team game** N Mannschaftsspiel *nt*; **team leader** N Teamleiter(in) *m(f)*; **team-mate** N Mannschaftskamerad(in) *m(f)*; **team member** N Teammitglied *nt*; (*Sport also*) Mannschaftsmitglied *nt*; **team spirit** N Gemeinschaftsgeist *m*; (*Sport*) Mannschaftsgeist *m*

teamster ['tiːmstə'] N **a** (*US*: = *truck driver*) Lastwagenfahrer(in) *m(f)*, LKW-Fahrer(in) *m(f)* **b** (*old Agr*) Fuhrmann *m*

teamwork ['tiːmwɜːk] N Gemeinschaftsarbeit *f*, Teamarbeit *f*, Teamwork *nt*

tea: **tea party** N Teegesellschaft *f*; **teapot** N Teekanne *f*

tear[1] [tɛə'] *vb: pret* **tore**, *ptp* **torn** **VT** **a** *material, paper, dress* zerreißen; *flesh* verletzen, aufreißen; *hole* reißen; **I've torn a muscle** ich habe mir einen Muskel gezerrt; **the nail tore a gash in his arm** er hat sich (*dat*) an dem Nagel eine tiefe Wunde am Arm beigebracht; **to ~ sth in two** etw (in zwei Stücke *or* Hälften) zerreißen, etw in der Mitte durchreißen; **to ~ sth to pieces** etw in Stücke reißen; **the critics tore the play to pieces** die Kritiker haben das Stück total verrissen; **to ~ sth open** etw aufreißen; **that's torn it!** (*Brit fig inf*) das hat alles verdorben! **b** (= *pull away*) reißen; **the wind tore the tent from the pole** der Wind riss das Zelt von der Stange; **her child was torn from her/from her arms** das Kind wurde ihr entrissen/ihr aus den

Armen gerissen; **he tore it out of my hand** er riss es mir aus der Hand; **to ~ one's hair (out)** sich *(dat)* die Haare raufen
c *(fig, usu pass)* **a country torn by war** ein vom Krieg zerrissenes Land; **a heart torn with remorse** ein von Reue gequältes Herz; **to be torn between two things/people** zwischen zwei Dingen/Menschen hin und her gerissen sein; **she was completely torn** sie war innerlich zerrissen
VI a *(material etc)* (zer)reißen; **her coat tore on a nail** sie zerriss sich *(dat)* den Mantel an einem Nagel; **~ along the dotted line** an der gestrichelten Linie abtrennen
b *(= move quickly)* rasen; **to ~ past** vorbeirasen
N *(in material etc)* Riss *m*

▶ **tear along** VI entlangrasen; **he tore along the street** er raste die Straße entlang *or* hinunter

▶ **tear apart** VT *sep place, house* völlig durcheinanderbringen; *meat, flesh, country* zerreißen; **it tore me apart to leave you** es hat mir schier das Herz zerrissen, dich zu verlassen

▶ **tear at** VI *+prep obj* zerren an *(+dat)*; **he tore at the walls of his cell** er verkrallte sich in die Wände seiner Zelle; **the thorns tore at her hands** die Dornen zerkratzten ihr die Hände

▶ **tear away** VI davonrasen VT *sep wrapping* abreißen, wegreißen *(from* von); **to tear away sb's mask** jdm die Maske vom Gesicht reißen; **to tear sth away from sb** jdm etw wegreißen *or* entreißen *(geh)*; **if you can tear yourself away from the paper** wenn du dich von der Zeitung losreißen kannst; **if you can tear him away from the party** wenn du ihn von der Party wegkriegen *or* loseisen kannst *(inf)*

▶ **tear down** VI hinunterrasen *(prep obj +acc)* VT *sep poster* herunterreißen; *house* abreißen, abbrechen; *trade barriers* abbauen

▶ **tear into** VI *+prep obj* a *(shell, rocket)* ein Loch reißen in *(+acc)*; *(animals) deer etc* zerfleischen; *food* sich hermachen über *(+acc)*; *(saw) wood* sich fressen durch b *(= attack physically)* herfallen über *(+acc)* c *(= attack verbally)* abkanzeln, zur Schnecke machen *(inf)*; *(critic)* keinen guten Faden lassen an *(+dat)*

▶ **tear off** VI a *(= rush off)* wegrasen; **he tore off down the street** er raste die Straße hinunter b **the carbon tears off** die Durchschrift lässt sich abtrennen VT *sep label, wrapping, calendar leaf* abreißen; *cover* wegreißen; *clothes* herunterreißen; **please tear off this part and complete** bitte hier abtrennen und ausfüllen; **he tore a strip off me** *(Brit inf)* **he tore me off a strip** *(Brit inf)* er hat mich zur Minna *or* Schnecke gemacht *(inf)*

▶ **tear out** VI hinausrasen, wegrasen; **he tore out through the front door** er raste *or* rannte zur Vordertür hinaus VT *sep* (her)ausreißen *(of* aus); **the tree was torn out by the roots** der Baum wurde entwurzelt

▶ **tear up** VI angerast kommen; **he tore up the hill/road** er raste den Berg hinauf/die Straße entlang VT *sep* a *paper etc* zerreißen b *(fig: = cancel) contract, agreement* aufkündigen c *(= pull from ground) post, stake, plant* (her)ausreißen d *(= break surface of) ground* aufwühlen; *road* aufreißen

tear² [tɪəʳ] N Träne *f*; **in ~s** in Tränen aufgelöst; **wet with ~s** tränenfeucht; **there were ~s in her eyes** ihr standen Tränen in den Augen; **the news brought ~s to her eyes** als sie das hörte, stiegen ihr die Tränen in die Augen; **you are bringing ~s to my eyes** *(iro)* mir kommen die Tränen *(iro)*; **the ~s were running down her cheeks** ihr Gesicht war tränenüberströmt; **smiling bravely through her ~s** unter Tränen tapfer lächelnd; **to laugh till the ~s come** Tränen lachen; **to weep ~s of joy** Freudentränen weinen *or* vergießen → **shed¹**, **burst**

tearaway ['tɛərəweɪ] N *(Brit inf)* Rabauke *m (inf)*; **I used to be a bit of a ~** ich war ein ziemlicher Rabauke *(inf)*

tear drop N Träne *f*

tearful ['tɪəfʊl] ADJ *look* tränenfeucht; *face* tränenüberströmt; *farewell, reunion* tränenreich; **he looked at her with ~ eyes** er sah sie mit Tränen in den Augen an; **to become ~** zu weinen anfangen; **she is a ~ person** ihr kommen leicht die Tränen; **there were a few ~ moments** es gab ein paar tränenvolle Augenblicke; **..., she said in a ~ voice** ..., sagte sie unter Tränen

tearfully ['tɪəfəlɪ] ADV *look* mit Tränen in den Augen; *say* unter Tränen

tear gas N Tränengas *nt*

tearing ['tɛərɪŋ] ADJ *(dated)* **to be in a ~ hurry** es fürchterlich *or* schrecklich eilig haben

tear: **tear-jerker** N *(inf)* Schmachtfetzen *m (inf)*; **to be a ~** ein Schmachtfetzen sein *(inf)*, auf die Tränendrüsen drücken *(inf)*; **tear-jerking** ADJ *(inf)* **to be ~** *(film etc)* auf die Tränendrüsen drücken *(inf)*

tear-off ['tɛərɒf] ADJ *sheet, form* zum Abtrennen *or* Abreißen; **~ calendar** Abreißkalender *m*

tea: **tearoom** N *(Brit)* Teestube *f*, Café *nt*; **tea rose** N Teerose *f*

tear-stained ['tɪəsteɪnd] ADJ *face, person* verweint, verheult *(pej inf)*, tränenverschmiert; *pillow, handkerchief* nass geweint

tease [ti:z] VT a *person* necken; *animal* reizen; *(= torment)* quälen; *(= make fun of: because of stutter etc)* aufziehen, hänseln *(about* wegen); *(= pull leg, have on)* auf den Arm nehmen *(inf)*, veralbern *(inf)*
b = **tease out a**
c *(= raise nap on) cloth* kämmen
d *(= backcomb) hair* toupieren
e *(= ease gently)* **he ~d the red into the pocket/the rope through the crack** er manipulierte die rote Kugel ins Loch/schob das Seil geschickt durch den Spalt
VI a **give it back to her, don't ~** gib es ihr zurück und neck sie nicht
b *(= joke)* Spaß machen
N *(inf: = person)* Scherzbold *m (inf)*; **don't be a ~, give it back to her** neck sie nicht, gibs ihr zurück; **he's a real ~** ihm sitzt der Schalk im Nacken *(hum)*, er ist ein kleiner Schäker *(inf)*; **she's/he's just a ~** *(sexually)* sie/er geilt einen nur auf *(inf)*

▶ **tease out** VT *sep* a *fibres* kardieren, karden; *wool* krempeln, kämmen; *flax* hecheln; *tangles* auskämmen b *(fig) significant factors etc* herausdestillieren; *meaning* herauslesen; **to tease sth out of sth** etw aus etw herauspusseln *(inf)*; **he managed to tease the information out of her** er hat ihr die Auskunft abgelockt

teasel ['ti:zl] N a *(Bot)* Karde *f* b *(Tech)* Karde *f*, Krempel *f*

teaser ['ti:zəʳ] N a *(= difficult question)* harte Nuss *(inf)*; *(= riddle)* Denksportaufgabe *f* b *(= person)* Schelm *m*, Schäker(in) *m(f) (inf)*; **don't be such a ~, tell me** neck mich nicht so, sags schon; **he's a real ~** ihm sitzt der Schalk im Nacken *(hum)*; **she's/he's just a ~** *(sexually)* sie/er geilt einen nur auf *(inf)*

tea: **tea service**, **tea set** N Teeservice *nt*; **teashop** N Teestube *f*

teasing ['ti:zɪŋ] ADJ *voice, manner* neckend; *expression, smile* neckisch; *(= making fun)* hänselnd N *(of person)* Neckerei *f*; *(of animal)* Reizen *nt*; *(= tormenting)* Quälerei *f*; *(= mockery)* Hänselei *f*; *(= joking)* Veralbern *nt*

teasingly ['ti:zɪŋlɪ] ADV a *(= provocatively)* herausfordernd b *(= playfully)* neckend c *(sexually)* betörend, verführerisch

tea: **teaspoon** N a Teelöffel *m* b *(also* **teaspoonful**) Teelöffel *m* (voll); **tea strainer** N Teesieb *nt*

teat [ti:t] N *(of animal)* Zitze *f*; *(of woman)* Brustwarze *f*; *(Brit, on baby's bottle)* (Gummi)sauger *m*

tea: **tea table** N *(esp Brit)* **to lay the ~** den Tisch zum Tee/fürs Abendessen decken; **at the ~** beim Tee/Abendessen; **teatime** N *(Brit) (for afternoon tea)* Teestunde *f*; *(= mealtime)* Abendessen *nt*; **when is ~ in your house?** wann trinkt ihr Tee/esst ihr zu Abend?; **we'll talk about it at ~** wir werden uns beim Tee/beim Abendessen darüber unterhalten; **I'll meet you at ~** ich treffe Sie am späten Nachmittag; **tea towel** N *(Brit)* Geschirrtuch *nt*; **tea tray** N Tablett *nt*, Teebrett *nt*; **tea trolley** N Teewagen *m*, Servierwagen *m*; **tea urn** N Teebereiter *m*; **tea wagon** N *(US)* Teewagen *m*, Servierwagen *m*

teazel N = **teasel**

TEC N *(Brit) abbr of* **Training and Enterprise Council** *staatliche Einrichtung zur Förderung der Zusammenarbeit zwischen Berufsschulen und Unternehmen*

tech [tek] *(Brit) abbr of* **technical college**

techie ['tekɪ] N *(inf)* Technikfreak *m (inf)*

technical ['teknɪkəl] ADJ a *(= concerning technology and technique)* technisch; **~ hitch** technische Schwierigkeit, technisches Problem
b *(of particular branch)* fachlich, Fach-; *problems, vocabulary* fachspezifisch; *details* formal; **~ journal** Fachzeitschrift *f*; **~ dictionary** Fachwörterbuch *nt*; **~ term** Fachausdruck *m*, Terminus technicus *m (geh)*; **~ terminology** Fachsprache *f*; **~ question** *(Jur)* Verfahrensfrage *f*; **for ~ reasons** *(Jur)* aus verfahrenstechnischen Gründen; **the judgment was quashed on a ~ point** *(Jur)* das Urteil wurde aufgrund *or* auf Grund eines Verfahrensfehlers aufgehoben; **the book is a bit too ~ for me** in dem Buch sind mir zu viele Fachausdrücke; **he uses very ~ language** er benutzt sehr viele Fachausdrücke; **am I getting too ~ for you?** benutze ich zu viele Fachausdrücke?; **a 2L 54, if you want to be ~** ein 2L 54, um den Fachausdruck zu gebrauchen; **that's true, if you want to be ~** das stimmt schon, wenn mans genau nimmt

technical: **technical college** N *(esp Brit)* technische Fachschule; **technical defeat** N *(Mil)* rein formale Niederlage; **technical drawing** N technische Zeichnung; **technical institute** N technisches Institut

technicality [,teknɪ'kælɪtɪ] N a *no pl* **the ~ of the language** die Fülle von Fachausdrücken; **the ~ of his style** *(= complex style)* die formale Komplexität seines Stils; *(= technical terms)* sein Fachjargon *m (pej)*, seine Fachterminologie b *(= technical detail, difficulty)* technische Einzelheit; *(fig, Jur)* Formsache *f*; **because of a ~** aufgrund *or* auf Grund einer Formsache; **that's just a ~** das ist bloß ein Detail

technical knockout N *(Boxing)* technischer K.o.

technically ['teknɪkəlɪ] ADV a technisch; **~, Windows is a graphical user interface** technisch gesehen ist Windows eine grafische Benutzeroberfläche b *(= concerned with specialist field)* vom Fachlichen her gesehen; **he spoke very ~** er benutzte sehr viele Fachausdrücke; **~ speaking** *(= in technical language)* fachsprachlich c *(= strictly speaking)* **~ you're right** genau genommen haben Sie recht; **~ speaking** *(= strictly speaking)* streng genommen

technical: **technical offence** N Verstoß *m*; **technical school** N *(Brit)* Gewerbeschule *f*, Fachschule *f*; *(US: = technical college)* technische Fachschule; **technical sergeant** N *(US)* Oberfeldwebel *m*

technical support N *(Comput)* (technischer) Support

technician [tek'nɪʃən] N Techniker(in) *m(f)*; *(= skilled worker)* Facharbeiter(in) *m(f)*

Technicolor® ['teknɪ,kʌləʳ] N Technicolor® *nt*

technique [tek'ni:k] N Technik *f*; *(= method)* Methode *f*

techno ['teknəʊ] N *(Mus)* Techno *m*

technobabble ['teknəʊ,bæbl] N *(inf)* Fachchinesisch *nt (inf)*

technocracy [tek'nɒkrəsɪ] N Technokratie *f*

technocrat ['teknəʊkræt] N Technokrat(in) *m(f)*

technocratic [,teknəʊ'krætɪk] ADJ technokratisch

technofear ['teknəʊfɪə'] N Angst *f* vor allem Technischen

technological [ˌteknə'lɒdʒɪkəl] ADJ technologisch; *details, information* technisch; **the ~ age** das Technologiezeitalter

technologically [teknə'lɒdʒɪklɪ] ADV (= *technically*) *advanced, backward, oriented* technologisch; **~, these cars are nothing new** vom technologischen Standpunkt aus (gesehen) ist an diesen Autos nichts Neues

technologist [tek'nɒlədʒɪst] N Technologe *m*, Technologin *f*

technology [tek'nɒlədʒɪ] N Technologie *f*; **the ~ of printing** die Technik des Druckens, die Drucktechnik; **computer/communications ~** Computer-/Kommunikationstechnik *f*, Computer-/Kommunikationstechnologie *f*; **University/College of Technology** Technische Universität/Fachhochschule; **the age of ~** das technische Zeitalter, das Zeitalter der Technik; **~ transfer** Technologietransfer *m*

technology-dominated [tekˌnɒlədʒɪ'dɒmɪneɪtɪd] ADJ technologielastig

technology park N Technologiepark *m*

technophobe ['teknəʊfəʊb] N Technikfeind *m*

technophobia [ˌteknəʊ'fəʊbɪə] N Technikfeindlichkeit *f*, Technophobie *f*

technophobic [ˌteknəʊ'fəʊbɪk] ADJ technikfeindlich

tech stocks PL (*St Ex inf*) Technologiewerte *pl*

techy ADJ = **tetchy**

tectonics [tek'tɒnɪks] N *sing* (*Geol*) Tektonik *f*

Ted [ted] N *dim of* **Edward**

ted [ted] N (*dated Brit inf*) Halbstarke(r) *m*

tedder ['tedə'] N Heuwender *m*

Teddy ['tedɪ] N *dim of* **Edward**

teddy (bear) ['tedɪ(ˌbeə')] N Teddy(bär) *m*

teddy boy N Halbstarke(r) *m*; (*referring to style of dress*) Teddyboy *m*

tedious ['ti:dɪəs] ADJ langweilig, öde; *behaviour* ermüdend; **such lists are ~ to read** solche Listen lesen sich langweilig

tediously ['ti:dɪəslɪ] ADV langweilig; **a ~ long journey** eine lange und langweilige Reise; **~ repetitive** sich ewig wiederholend

tediousness ['ti:dɪəsnɪs] N Lang(e)weile *f*; **his ~** seine Langweiligkeit

tedium ['ti:dɪəm] N Lang(e)weile *f*

tee[1] [ti:] (*Golf*) **N** Tee *nt* **VT** *ball* auf das Tee legen

▸ **tee off** VI einen Ball vom (ersten) Abschlag spielen

▸ **tee up** **VI** den Ball auf das Tee legen, aufteen (*spec*) **VT** *sep* auf das Tee legen

tee[2] N = **T**

tee-hee ['ti:'hi:] INTERJ (*giggle*) hihi; (*snigger*) ätsch

teem [ti:m] VI **a** (*with people, insects etc*) wimmeln (*with* von); (*with mistakes, information etc*) strotzen (*with* vor); **his mind was ~ing with ideas** in seinem Kopf wimmelte es nur so von Ideen **b** (= *pour*) **it's ~ing with rain** es regnet *or* gießt (*inf*) in Strömen; **he watched the rain ~ing down** er sah zu, wie der Regen vom Himmel strömte

teeming ['ti:mɪŋ] ADJ **a** *streets* von Menschen wimmelnd; *crowd* wuselnd; **the world's ~ millions** die Millionen und Abermillionen von Menschen (auf der Erde) **b** (= *pouring*) *rain* strömend

teen [ti:n] ADJ (*esp US*) *movie, magazine* für Teenager; *boy, girl* im Teenageralter; *pregnancy* im Teenageralter; **~ crime** Jugendkriminalität *f*; **the ~ years** die Teenagerjahre *pl*; **~ idol** Teenie-Idol *nt* (*inf*)

teenage ['ti:neɪdʒ] ADJ Teenager-; *child, son, boy, girl* halbwüchsig, im Teenageralter; *pregnancy, suicide* unter Teenagern; **the ~ years** die Teenagerjahre *pl*; **~ idol** Teenie-Idol *nt* (*inf*)

teenaged ['ti:neɪdʒd] ADJ im Teenageralter; **she is the mother of two ~ daughters** sie ist Mutter zweier Töchter im Teenageralter; **~ boy/girl** Teenager *m*

teenager ['ti:nˌeɪdʒə'] N Teenager *m*

teener ['ti:nə'] N (*US*) = **teenager**

teens [ti:nz] PL **a** Teenageralter *nt*; **to be in one's ~** im Teenageralter sein; **to reach one's ~** ins Teenageralter kommen; **he is still in/barely out of his ~** er ist noch keine/knapp über zwanzig (Jahre alt) **b** (*inf:* = *teenagers*) Teenager *pl*

teensploitation [ˌti:nzplɔɪ'teɪʃən] N (*inf*) *kommerzielle Ausbeutung von Teenagern*; **~ movie** *billig produzierter Film mit für Teenager interessanten Themen*

teenybopper ['ti:nɪˌbɒpə'] N Teenager *m*, Teeny *m* (*inf*); (= *girl also*) Pipimädchen *nt* (*pej inf*)

teeny(weeny) ['ti:nɪ('wi:nɪ)] ADJ (*inf*) winzig (klein), klitzeklein (*inf*); **just a ~ drop** nur ein ganz klein wenig

tee shirt N = **T-shirt**

teeter ['ti:tə'] VI **a** (= *balance unsteadily*) taumeln, schwanken; **to ~ on the brink** *or* **edge of sth** (*lit*) am Rand von etw taumeln; (*fig*) am Rand von etw sein **b** (*US:* = *seesaw*) wippen, schaukeln

teeterboard ['ti:təˌbɔ:d], **teeter-totter** ['ti:təˌtɒtə'] N (*US*) Wippe *f*

teeth [ti:θ] *pl of* **tooth**

teethe [ti:ð] VI zahnen

teething ['ti:ðɪŋ] N Zahnen *nt*

teething: **teething ring** N Beißring *m*; **teething troubles** PL (*Brit fig*) Kinderkrankheiten *pl*

teetotal [ˌti:'təʊtl] ADJ *person* abstinent; *party etc* ohne Alkohol; **to be ~** abstinent sein, Antialkoholiker(in) *m(f)* sein

teetotaler N (*US*) = **teetotaller**

teetotalism [ˌti:'təʊtəlɪzəm] N Abstinenz *f*

teetotaller, (*US*) **teetotaler** [ˌti:'təʊtlə'] N Abstinenzler(in) *m(f)*, Nichttrinker(in) *m(f)*, Antialkoholiker(in) *m(f)*

TEFL *abbr of* **Teaching of English as a Foreign Language**

> **TEFL, TESL, TESOL, ELT**
>
> **TEFL (Teaching of English as a Foreign Language)** und **EFL (English as a Foreign Language)** sind Begriffe, die sich auf das Englisch beziehen, das Menschen aus nicht englischsprachigen Ländern gelehrt, bzw. von diesen gelernt wird.
>
> **TESL (Teaching of English as a Second Language)** und **ESL (English as a Second Language)** betreffen dagegen Englisch, das von Menschen gelernt wird, die in einem englischsprachigen Land leben, deren Muttersprache allerdings nicht Englisch ist, wie dies z. B. bei ethnischen Minderheiten der Fall ist. Im ESL-Unterricht wird versucht, den kulturellen Hintergrund und die Muttersprache der Schüler in den Lernprozess mit einzubeziehen.
>
> **TESOL (Teaching of English as a Second or Other Language)** ist der allgemeine amerikanische Begriff sowohl für **TEFL** als auch für **TESL**. **ESOL (English for Speakers of Other Languages)** ist das Äquivalent zu **EFL** und **ESL**.
>
> **ELT (English Language Teaching)** ist der allgemeine Begriff für das Unterrichten von Englisch als Fremd- oder zweite Sprache.

Teflon® ['teflɒn] N Teflon® *nt*

Tehran [teə'rɑ:n] N Teheran *nt*

tel *abbr of* **telephone (number)** Tel.

telebanking ['telɪˌbæŋkɪŋ] N Homebanking *nt*, Telebanking *nt*

telecamera ['telɪˌkæmərə] N Fernsehkamera *f*

telecast ['telɪkɑ:st] **N** Fernsehsendung *f* **VT** im Fernsehen übertragen *or* senden

telecaster ['telɪkɑ:stə'] N Fernsehjournalist(in) *m(f)*

telecommunications [ˌtelɪkəmju:nɪ'keɪʃənz] N **a** *pl* Fernmeldewesen *nt* **b** *sing* (= *science*) Fernmeldetechnik *f*

telecommute ['telɪkəmˌju:t] VI Telearbeit machen

telecommuter ['telɪkəmˌju:tə'] N jd, der Telearbeit macht

telecommuting ['telɪkəmˌju:tɪŋ] N Telearbeit *f*

teleconference ['telɪkɒnfərəns] N Telekonferenz *f*

teleconferencing ['telɪkɒnfərənsɪŋ] N Telekonferenzschaltung *f*

Telecopier® ['telɪˌkɒpɪə'] N Fernkopierer *m*, Telekopierer *m*

telecopy ['telɪˌkɒpɪ] N Fernkopie *f*, Telekopie *f*

telecottage ['telɪˌkɒtɪdʒ] N (*esp Brit*) (ländliches) Computerzentrum (*für jedermann*); (*for teleworking*) Telearbeit-Center *nt*

telediagnosis ['telɪˌdaɪəg'nəʊsɪs] N (*Med*) Ferndiagnose *f*

telegram ['telɪgræm] N Telegramm *nt*

telegrammatic [ˌtelɪgrə'mætɪk] ADJ im Telegrammstil

telegraph ['telɪgrɑ:f] **N** **a** (= *apparatus*) Telegraf *m* **b** (= *message*) Telegramm *nt* **VT** telegrafisch übermitteln; *message also* telegrafieren; *person* telegrafieren (+*dat*); (*fig*) *one's intentions, plans etc* offenlegen **VI** telegrafieren

telegraphese [ˌtelɪgrə'fi:z] N Telegrammstil *m*

telegraphic [ˌtelɪ'græfɪk] ADJ telegrafisch; *address, style, speech* Telegramm-; **by ~ transfer** per Telegramm

telegraphically [ˌtelɪ'græfɪkəlɪ] ADV (= *concisely*) knapp; **she writes almost ~** sie schreibt fast im Telegrammstil

telegraphist [tɪ'legrəfɪst] N Telegrafist(in) *m(f)*

telegraph: **telegraph pole** N (*Brit*) Telegrafenmast *m or* -stange *f*; **telegraph wire** N Telegrafendraht *m or* -leitung *f*; (*under ground*) Telegrafenkabel *nt*

telegraphy [tɪ'legrəfɪ] N Telegrafie *f*

telekinesis [ˌtelɪkɪ'ni:sɪs] N Telekinese *f*

telemark ['telɪmɑ:k] N (*Ski*) Telemark(schwung) *m*

telemarketing ['telɪmɑ:kɪtɪŋ] N Telemarketing *nt*, Telefonverkauf *m*

telemessage ['telɪmesɪdʒ] N (*Brit*) Telegramm *nt*

telemeter ['telɪmi:tə'] N Entfernungsmesser *m*, Telemeter *nt*

telemetry [te'lemɪtrɪ] N Telemetrie *f*, Fernmessung *f*

teleological [ˌtelɪə'lɒdʒɪkl] ADJ teleologisch

teleology [ˌtelɪ'ɒlədʒɪ] N Teleologie *f*

teleordering ['telɪˌɔ:dərɪŋ] N Teleordern *nt*

telepathic [ˌtelɪ'pæθɪk] ADJ telepathisch; **you must be ~!** du musst ja ein Hellseher sein!; **I'm not ~!** ich kann doch keine Gedanken lesen! (*inf*)

telepathically [ˌtelɪ'pæθɪkəlɪ] ADV telepathisch

telepathist [tɪ'lepəθɪst] N Telepath(in) *m(f)*; (= *believer in telepathy*) Telepathiegläubige(r) *mf*

telepathy [tɪ'lepəθɪ] N Telepathie *f*

telephone ['telɪfəʊn] **N** Telefon *nt*, Fernsprecher (*form*) *m*; **there's somebody on the ~ for you, you're wanted on the ~** Sie werden am Telefon verlangt; **are you on the ~?** (*Brit*) **have you got a ~?** haben Sie Telefon?; (= *can you be reached by telephone?*) sind Sie telefonisch zu erreichen?; **he's on the ~** (= *is using the telephone*) er telefoniert gerade; (= *wants to speak to you*) er ist am Telefon; **by ~** telefonisch; **I've just been on the ~ to him** ich habe eben mit ihm telefoniert; **I'll get on the ~ to her** ich werde sie anrufen; **we arranged it by ~** *or* **over the ~** wir haben es telefonisch vereinbart; **I heard a strange noise down the ~** ich hörte ein merkwürdiges Geräusch im Telefon; **to shout down the ~** ins

Telefon brüllen
VT anrufen; *message, reply* telefonisch mitteilen *or* übermitteln; **he ~d the news (through) to his mother** er rief seine Mutter an, um ihr die Nachricht mitzuteilen; **would you ~ the office to say …** würden Sie im Büro *or* das Büro anrufen und sagen …; **~ this number for further information** weitere Informationen unter folgender Telefonnummer, für weitere Informationen rufen Sie bitte diese Nummer an
VI anrufen, telefonieren; *(= make telephone call)* telefonieren; **to ~ for an ambulance/a taxi** einen Krankenwagen/ein Taxi rufen

▶ **telephone back** VTI *sep* = **phone back**

▶ **telephone in** VTI = **phone in**

telephone *in cpds* Telefon-, Fernsprech- *(form)*; **telephone answering machine** N Anrufbeantworter *m*; **telephone banking** N Telefonbanking *nt*; **telephone bill** N Telefonrechnung *f*; **telephone book** N Telefonbuch *nt*; **telephone box**, *(US)* **telephone booth** N Telefonzelle *f*; **telephone call** N Telefongespräch *nt*, Telefonanruf *m*; **telephone charges** PL Telefongebühren *pl*; **telephone directory** N Telefonbuch *nt*; **telephone exchange** N *(esp Brit)* Fernsprechamt *nt*, Vermittlungsstelle *f (form)*; **telephone kiosk** N Telefonzelle *f*, Sprechzelle *f (form)*; **telephone line** N Telefonleitung *f*; **telephone message** N telefonische Nachricht; **telephone network** N Telefonnetz *nt*; **telephone number** N Telefonnummer *f*, Rufnummer *f (form)*; **~s** *(fig inf: = large amount)* riesige Summen *pl*; **telephone operator** N *(esp US)* Telefonist(in) *m(f)*; **telephone sales** PL Telefonverkauf *m or* -verkäufe *pl*; **telephone sex** N Telefonsex *m*; **~ line** Telefonsexdienst *m*; **telephone subscriber** PL Fernsprechteilnehmer(in) *m(f)*

telephonic [ˌtelɪˈfɒnɪk] ADJ telefonisch; **~ technology** Telefontechnik *f*

telephonically [telɪˈfɒnɪkəlɪ] ADV fernsprechtechnisch; *(= by telephone)* telefonisch

telephonist [tɪˈlefənɪst] N *(Brit)* Telefonist(in) *m(f)*

telephony [tɪˈlefənɪ] **a** N Fernsprechwesen *nt* **b** *(Comput)* Telefonie *f*

telephotograph [ˌtelɪˈfəʊtəgrɑːf] N *(Telec)* durch Bildtelegrafie übertragenes Foto

telephoto (lens) [ˈtelɪˌfəʊtəʊ(ˈlenz)] N Teleobjektiv *nt*

teleport [ˈtelɪpɔːt] VT *(Sci-Fi)* teleportieren

teleprinter [ˈtelɪˌprɪntəʳ] N Fernschreiber *m*

Teleprompter® [ˈtelɪˌprɒmptəʳ] N *(esp US)* Teleprompter® *m*

telerecord [ˌtelɪrɪˈkɔːd] VT fürs Fernsehen aufzeichnen

telerecording [ˌtelɪrɪˈkɔːdɪŋ] N Fernsehaufzeichnung *f*

telesales [ˈtelɪseɪlz] N *sing or pl* Telefonverkauf *m or* -verkäufe, Verkauf *m* per Telefon

telescope [ˈtelɪskəʊp] **N** Teleskop *nt*, Fernrohr *nt* **VI** *(also* **telescope together***, train carriages)* sich ineinanderschieben; *(aerial, umbrella)* sich ineinanderschieben lassen **VT** *(also* **telescope together***)* ineinanderschieben; *umbrella, aerial* zusammenschieben; *(fig)* komprimieren

telescopic [ˌtelɪˈskɒpɪk] ADJ *aerial etc* ausziehbar, zusammenschiebbar; *view* teleskopisch; **~ arm** Teleskoparm *m*

telescopic: **telescopic lens** N Fernrohrlinse *f*; **telescopic sight** N Zielfernrohr *nt*; **telescopic umbrella** N Taschenschirm *m*, Knirps® *m*

teleshopping [ˈtelɪˌʃɒpɪŋ] N Teleshopping *nt*

Teletext® [ˈtelɪtekst] N ≈ Videotext *m*

telethon [ˈtelɪˌθɒn] N *sehr lange Fernsehsendung, in deren Verlauf Spenden für wohltätige Zwecke gesammelt werden*, Fernsehspendenaktion *f*

Teletype® [ˈtelɪtaɪp] N *(US: = apparatus)* Fernschreiber *m*; *(= message)* Fernschreiben *nt*, Telex *nt*

teletypewriter [ˌtelɪˈtaɪpraɪtəʳ] N *(US)* Fernschreiber *m*

televangelism [ˌtelɪˈvændʒəlɪzəm] N *no pl (esp US) Bekehrungssendungen im Fernsehen*

televangelist [ˌtelɪˈvændʒəlɪst] N *(esp US)* Fernsehevangelist(in) *m(f)*

televise [ˈtelɪvaɪz] VT (im Fernsehen) senden *or* übertragen; **~d debate** Fernsehdebatte *f*

television [ˈtelɪˌvɪʒən] N Fernsehen *nt*; *(= set)* Fernseher *m*, Fernsehapparat *m*; **to watch ~** fernsehen; **to be on ~** im Fernsehen kommen; **have you ever been on ~?** bist du schon einmal im Fernsehen gewesen?; **what's on ~ tonight?** was gibt es heute Abend im Fernsehen?; **jobs in ~** Stellen *pl* beim Fernsehen

television *in cpds* Fernseh-; **television camera** N Fernsehkamera *f*; **television licence** N *(Brit) Bescheinigung über die Entrichtung der Fernsehgebühren*; **to pay one's ~** die Fernsehgebühren bezahlen; **television personality** N bekannte Fernsehpersönlichkeit; **television rights** PL Übertragungsrechte *pl*, Fernsehrechte *pl*; **television screen** N Bildschirm *m*, Mattscheibe *f (inf)*; **television set** N Fernsehapparat *m*, Fernsehgerät *nt*, Fernseher *m*; **television studio** N Fernsehstudio *nt*; **television viewer** N Fernsehzuschauer(in) *m(f)*

televisual [ˌtelɪˈvɪʒjʊəl] ADJ Fernseh-, TV-; **to make ~ history** Fernsehgeschichte *or* TV-Geschichte machen

telework [ˈtelɪwɜːk] VI Telearbeit machen

teleworker [ˈtelɪwɜːkəʳ] N Telearbeiter(in) *m(f)*

teleworking [ˈtelɪwɜːkɪŋ] N *no pl* Telearbeit *f*

telex [ˈteleks] **N** Telex *nt*; *(= message also)* Fernschreiben *nt* **VT** *message* telexen, per Telex mitteilen; *person* ein Telex schicken *(+dat)*

tell [tel] *pret, ptp* **told** **VT** **a** *(= relate) story, experiences, adventures* erzählen *(sb sth, sth to sb* jdm etw *acc)*; *(= inform, say, announce)* sagen *(sb sth* jdm etw *acc)*; **to ~ lies** lügen; **to ~ tales** petzen *(inf)*; **to ~ fortunes** wahrsagen; **to ~ sb's fortune** jdm wahrsagen, jdm die Zukunft deuten; **to ~ the future** wahrsagen, die Zukunft deuten; **to ~ sb a secret** jdm ein Geheimnis anvertrauen *or (give away)* verraten; **to ~ sb about** *or* **of sth** jdm von etw erzählen; **I told my friend/boss about what had happened** ich erzählte meinem Freund/berichtete meinem Chef, was geschehen war; **… or so I've been told** … so hat man es mir jedenfalls gesagt *or* erzählt; **I can't ~ you how pleased I am** ich kann Ihnen gar nicht sagen, wie sehr ich mich freue; **you can't ~ her anything** *(= she can't keep a secret)* man kann ihr (aber auch) nichts sagen *or* anvertrauen; *(= she's a know-all)* sie lässt sich *(dat)* nichts sagen; **to ~ sb the way** jdm den Weg sagen; **could you ~ me the way to the station, please?** könn(t)en Sir mir bitte sagen, wie ich zum Bahnhof komme?; **don't let me have to ~ you that again** ich will dir das nicht noch einmal sagen müssen; **(I'll) ~ you what, let's go to the cinema** weißt du was, gehen wir doch ins Kino!; **don't ~ me you can't come!** sagen Sie bloß nicht, dass Sie nicht kommen können!; **I won't do it, I ~ you!** und ich sage dir, das mache ich nicht!; **let me ~ you that …** ich kann Ihnen sagen, dass …, lassen Sie sich von mir sagen, dass …; **it was cold, I can ~ you** ich kann dir sagen, das war vielleicht kalt!; **I told you so** ich habe es (dir) ja gesagt; **~ me another!** nicht möglich!, wers glaubt! *(inf)*; **that ~s me all I need to know** das sagt mir alles; **that ~s me a lot** das sagt mir allerlei
b *(= distinguish, discern)* erkennen; **to ~ the time** die Uhr kennen; **to ~ the time by the sun** die Zeit an der Sonne ablesen; **to ~ the difference** den Unterschied sehen/fühlen/schmecken *etc*; **you can ~ that he's clever/getting worried** man sieht *or* merkt, dass er intelligent ist/sich Sorgen macht; **we couldn't ~ much from his letter** wir konnten aus seinem Brief nicht viel entnehmen; **you can't ~ whether it's moving** man kann nicht sagen *or* sehen, ob es sich bewegt; **I couldn't ~ if he had been in a fight or had just fallen** ich hätte nicht sagen können, ob er in einem Kampf verwickelt oder nur hingefallen war; **it was impossible to ~ where the bullet had entered** es war unmöglich festzustellen, wo die Kugel eingetreten war; **to ~ sb/sth by sth** jdn/etw an etw *(dat)* erkennen; **I can't ~ butter from margarine** ich kann Butter nicht von Margarine unterscheiden; **to ~ right from wrong** wissen, was Recht und Unrecht ist, Recht von Unrecht unterscheiden → **apart**
c *(= know, be sure)* wissen; **how can I ~ that?** wie soll ich das wissen?; **how could I ~ that?** wie hätte ich das wissen können?; **how can I ~ that he will do it?** wie kann ich sicher sein, dass er es tut?
d *(= order)* sagen *(sb* jdm*)*; **we were told to bring sandwiches with us** es wurde uns gesagt, dass wir belegte Brote mitbringen sollten; **~ him to stop singing** sagen Sie ihm, er soll aufhören zu singen; **don't you ~ me what to do!** Sie haben mir nicht zu sagen, was ich tun soll!; **I told you not to do that** ich habe dir doch gesagt, du sollst das nicht tun!; **do as** *or* **what you are told!** tu, was man dir sagt!
e *(old: = count)* **to ~ one's beads** den Rosenkranz beten
VI *+indir obj* es sagen *(+dat)*; **I won't ~ you again** ich sage es dir nicht noch einmal; **you know what? – don't ~ me, let me guess** weißt du was? – sags mir nicht, lass mich raten; **she wouldn't be told** sie hat sich (ja) nichts sagen lassen; **you're ~ing me!** das kann man wohl sagen!, wem sagen Sie das!
VI **a** *(= discern, be sure)* wissen; **as** *or* **so far as one can ~** soweit man weiß; **who can ~?** wer weiß?; **how can I ~?** *(= how should I know)* woher soll ich das wissen?; **how will I be able to ~?** wie kann ich das erkennen *or* wissen?; **no-one can/could ~** niemand kann/konnte das sagen, das weiß/wusste keiner; **you never can ~, you can never ~** man kann nie wissen
b *(= talk, tell tales of)* sprechen; **his face told of his sorrow** aus seinem Gesicht sprach Kummer; **that would be ~ing!** das kann ich nicht verraten; **promise you won't ~** du musst versprechen, dass du nichts sagst
c *(= have effect)* sich bemerkbar machen; **his age told against him** *(in applying for job)* sein Alter war ein Nachteil für ihn; *(in competition)* sein Alter machte sich bemerkbar; **character always ~s in the end** zum Schluss schlägt doch die Veranlagung durch; **a boxer who makes every punch ~** ein Boxer, bei dem jeder Schlag sitzt

▶ **tell off** VT *sep* **a** *(inf: = scold)* ausschimpfen, schelten *(for* wegen*)*; **he told me off for being late** er schimpfte (mich aus), weil ich zu spät kam **b** *(Mil etc)* abkommandieren *(for* zu*)*

▶ **tell on** VI *+prep obj* **a** *(inf: = inform on)* verpetzen *(inf)* **b** *(= have a bad effect on)* sich bemerkbar machen bei; **the pressure is beginning to tell on her** der Druck, der auf ihr lastet, macht sich langsam bemerkbar

teller [ˈteləʳ] N **a** *(in bank)* Kassierer(in) *m(f)* **b** *(= vote counter)* Stimmenauszähler(in) *m(f)* **c** *(of story)* Erzähler(in) *m(f)* **d** *(esp US: = cash machine)* Geldautomat *m*

telling [ˈtelɪŋ] **ADJ** *(= effective)* wirkungsvoll; *argument also* schlagend; *blow (lit, fig)* empfindlich; *(= revealing)* aufschlussreich; *blush* verräterisch **N** **a** *(= narration)* Erzählen *nt*; **it loses a lot in the ~** das kann man gar nicht so schön erzählen **b** **there is no ~ what he may do** man kann nicht sagen *or* wissen, was er tut; **there's no ~** das lässt sich nicht sagen; **there's no ~ how long the talks could last** es lässt sich nicht absehen, wie lange die Gespräche dauern werden; **there's never any ~ with him** bei ihm lässt sich das nie sagen

telling-off [ˌtelɪŋˈɒf] N *(Brit inf)* Standpauke *f (inf)*; **to give sb a good ~** jdn kräftig ausschimpfen, jdm eine (kräftige) Standpauke halten *(inf)*; **to get a good ~** kräftig ausgeschimpft werden, eine Standpauke bekommen *(inf)*

telltale ['telteɪl] **N** **a** *(Brit)* Petzer *m*, Petze *f* **b** *(Tech)* Kontrolllicht *nt*, Kontrolllampe *f* **ADJ** *attr* verräterisch

tellurium [te'lʊərɪəm] **N** *(Chem)* Tellur *nt*

telly ['telɪ] **N** *(Brit inf)* Fernseher *m*, Glotze *f (inf)*; **on ~** im Fernsehen; **to watch ~** fernsehen → *also* **television**

temazepam [tɪ'mæzɪpæm] **N** *zu den Benzodiazepinen gehörendes Schlafmittel*

temerity [tɪ'merɪtɪ] **N** Kühnheit *f*, Unerhörtheit *f (pej)*

temp[1] **a** *abbr of* **temporary** **b** *abbr of* **temperature** Temp

temp[2] [temp] **N** Aushilfskraft *f*; Zeitarbeitskraft *f* **VI** als Aushilfskraft arbeiten

temp agency **N** Zeitarbeitsunternehmen *nt or* -firma *f*

temper ['tempə'] **N** **a** *(= disposition)* Wesen *nt*, Naturell *nt*; *(= angry mood)* Wut *f*; **~ tantrum** Wutanfall *m*; **to be in a ~** wütend sein; **to be in a good/bad ~** guter/schlechter Laune sein; **he was not in the best of ~s** er war nicht gerade bester Laune; **she's got a quick ~** sie kann sehr jähzornig sein; **she's got a terrible/foul/vicious ~** sie kann sehr unangenehm/ausfallend/tückisch werden; **what a ~ that child has!** was dieses Kind für Wutanfälle hat!; **to be in a (bad) ~ with sb/over** *or* **about sth** auf jdn/wegen einer Sache *(gen)* wütend sein; **to lose one's ~** die Beherrschung verlieren *(with sb* bei jdm); **to keep one's ~** sich beherrschen *(with sb* bei jdm); **~, ~!** aber, aber, wer wird denn gleich so zornig werden!; **to fly into a ~** einen Wutanfall bekommen, in die Luft gehen *(inf)*; **a fit of ~** ein Wutanfall *m*; **to put sb in a ~, to get sb's ~ up** jdn zur Weißglut bringen, jdn wütend machen; **he has quite a ~** er kann ziemlich aufbrausen; **to be out of ~** *(old)* verstimmt sein, übel gelaunt sein; **I hope he can control his ~** ich hoffe, er kann sich unter Kontrolle halten **b** *(of metal)* Härte *f*, Härtegrad *m*
VT **a** *metal* tempern
b *(old Mus)* temperieren *(old)*
c *(fig) action, passion* mäßigen; *criticism* mildern; *enthusiasm* zügeln; **to ~ justice with mercy** bei aller Gerechtigkeit Milde walten lassen; **to be ~ed by concern/realism** mit Fürsorge/Realismus vermischt sein

tempera ['tempərə] **N** Temperafarbe *f*; **to paint in ~** in Tempera malen

temperament ['tempərəmənt] **N** **a** *(= disposition)* Veranlagung *f*; *(of a people)* Temperament *nt*; **his ~ isn't suited to that job** er ist von seiner Veranlagung her nicht für diese Stelle geeignet; **he has an artistic ~** er ist eine Künstlernatur; **their ~s are quite different** sie sind völlig unterschiedlich veranlagt; **he has a happy ~** er hat ein fröhliches Wesen *or* Naturell **b** *no art (= temper, excitability)* Temperament *nt*; **she was given to fits of ~** sie war launisch

temperamental [,tempərə'mentl] **ADJ** **a** temperamentvoll, launenhaft *(pej)*; **~ outburst** Temperamentsausbruch *m* **b** *machine, car* launisch *(hum)*; **to be ~** Mucken haben *(inf)*, launisch sein *(hum)* **c** *(= caused by temperament) inability, unsuitability* veranlagungsmäßig; *laziness etc* angeboren

temperamentally [,temprə'mentəlɪ] **ADV** **a** *behave etc* temperamentvoll, launenhaft *(pej)* **b** *(of machine, car)* launisch *(hum)* **c** *(= as regards disposition)* charakterlich, veranlagungsmäßig; **to be ~ averse to sth** einer Sache *(dat)* vom Temperament her abgeneigt sein

temperance ['tempərəns] **N** **a** *(= moderation)* Mäßigung *f*; *(in speech etc)* Zurückhaltung *f*; *(in eating, drinking)* Maßhalten *nt*, Mäßigung *f* **b** *(= teetotalism)* Enthaltsamkeit *f*, Abstinenz *f*

temperance: **temperance hotel** **N** alkoholfreies Hotel; **temperance movement** **N** Temperenzler- *or* Temperenzbewegung *f*; **temperance society** **N** Temperenzverein *m or* -gesellschaft *f*

temperate ['tempərɪt] **ADJ** **a** *climate* gemäßigt; *forest* mit gemäßigtem Klima; *(Bot, Zool) plant, animal* in gemäßigten Klimazonen beheimatet; **the Temperate Zone** die gemäßigte Klimazone **b** *person, language* gemäßigt; *(in eating, demands)* maßvoll

temperature ['temprɪtʃə'] **N** Temperatur *f*; *(Med, above normal temperature also)* Fieber *nt*; **water boils at a ~ of 100° C** Wasser kocht bei einer Temperatur von 100° C; **to take sb's ~** jds Temperatur messen, bei jdm Fieber messen; **he has a ~** er hat Fieber; **he has a slight/high ~, he's running a slight/high ~** er hat erhöhte Temperatur/hohes Fieber; **he has a ~ of 39° C** er hat 39° Fieber

temperature: **temperature chart** **N** *(Med)* Fiebertabelle *f*; *(= curve of graph)* Fieberkurve *f*; **temperature gauge** **N** Temperaturanzeiger *m*; **temperature-sensitive** **ADJ** temperaturempfindlich

tempered ['tempəd] **ADJ** **a** *steel* gehärtet **b** *(Mus)* temperiert

-tempered **ADJ** *suf* … gelaunt; **good-tempered** gut gelaunt; **bad-tempered** schlecht gelaunt

tempest ['tempɪst] **N** *(liter)* Sturm *m (also fig)*, Unwetter *nt*; **it was a ~ in a teapot** *(US)* es war ein Sturm im Wasserglas

tempestuous [,tem'pestjʊəs] **ADJ** **a** *(lit liter) winds* stürmisch; *sea* tobend, stürmisch **b** *(fig)* stürmisch; *argument, rage* heftig; *speech* leidenschaftlich

tempestuously [,tem'pestjʊəslɪ] **ADV** *(lit liter, fig)* heftig

tempestuousness [,tem'pestjʊəsnɪs] **N** *(lit liter, fig)* Heftigkeit *f*; *(of sea)* Aufgewühltheit *f*

temping agency ['tempɪŋ,eɪdʒənsɪ] **N** Zeitarbeitsunternehmen *nt or* -firma *f*

Templar ['templə'] **N** *(also* **Knight Templar**) Tempelherr *m*, Templer *m*

template, templet ['templɪt] **N** Schablone *f*; *(fig)* Vorlage *f*; *(Comput)* Dokumentvorlage *f*

temple[1] ['templ] **N** *(Rel)* Tempel *m*

temple[2] **N** *(Anat)* Schläfe *f*

templet **N** = **template**

tempo ['tempəʊ] **N** *(Mus, fig)* Tempo *nt*

temporal ['tempərəl] **ADJ** **a** zeitlich; *(Gram)* Zeit-, temporal; **~ adverb** Zeitadverb *nt* **b** *(Rel)* weltlich

temporal bone **N** Schläfenbein *nt*

temporarily ['tempərərɪlɪ] **ADV** vorübergehend, für einige Zeit

temporariness ['tempərərɪnɪs] **N** vorübergehender Charakter

temporary ['tempərərɪ] **ADJ** vorübergehend; *job also* für kurze Zeit, befristet; *arrangement also, method, building, road surface* provisorisch; *powers* zeitweilig, befristet; *licence* zeitlich begrenzt; **our new secretary is only ~** unsere neue Sekretärin ist nur vorübergehend *or* für einige Zeit hier; **I'm only here for a ~ stay** ich bin nur für kurze Zeit hier; **she is a ~ resident here** sie wohnt hier nur vorübergehend; **~ worker** Zeitarbeiter(in) *m(f)*; **~ staff** Zeitpersonal *nt*; **~ refugee** *(Pol) Flüchtling mit zeitlich begrenzter Aufenthaltserlaubnis*; **~ injunction** *(Jur)* einstweilige Verfügung; **~ restraining order** *(Jur)* einstweilige (Verbots)verfügung
N Aushilfe *f*, Aushilfskraft *f*

temporize ['tempəraɪz] **VI** *(= delay)* ausweichen (um Zeit zu gewinnen), Verzögerungstaktiken anwenden; **to ~ with sb** jdn hinhalten

temporizer ['tempəraɪzə'] **N** Verzögerungstaktiker *m*

tempt [tempt] **VT** **a** *(= entice)* in Versuchung führen; *(successfully)* verführen, verleiten; **to ~ sb to do** *or* **into doing sth** jdn dazu verleiten *or* verführen, etw zu tun; **don't ~ me** bring *or* führ mich nicht in Versuchung!; **one is ~ed to believe that …** man möchte fast glauben, dass …; **I am very ~ed to accept** ich bin sehr versucht anzunehmen; **try and ~ her to eat a little** versuchen Sie, ob Sie sie nicht dazu bringen können, etwas zu essen; **may I ~ you to have a little more wine?** kann ich Sie noch zu etwas Wein überreden?; **are you sure you won't come? – no, I won't be ~ed!** willst du bestimmt nicht mitkommen? – nein, ich bleibe hart; **to ~ fate** *or* **providence** *(fig)* sein Schicksal herausfordern; *(in words)* den Teufel an die Wand malen
b *(Rel)* versuchen, in Versuchung führen; **the devil ~s us** der Teufel führt uns in Versuchung

temptation [temp'teɪʃən] **N** Versuchung *f (also Rel)*, Verlockung *f*; **to put ~ in sb's way** jdn in Versuchung führen; **lead us not into ~** *(Bibl)* führe uns nicht in Versuchung *(Bibl)*; **to yield to** *or* **to give way to ~** der Versuchung erliegen

tempter ['temptə'] **N** Versucher *m*, Verführer *m*; **the Tempter** *(Rel)* der Versucher

tempting ['temptɪŋ] **ADJ** verlockend, verführerisch; **it is ~ to say that …** es ist verlockend zu sagen, dass …

temptingly ['temptɪŋlɪ] **ADV** verlockend, verführerisch

temptress ['temptrɪs] **N** Verführerin *f*

ten [ten] **ADJ** zehn; **the Ten Commandments** die Zehn Gebote; **~ to one he won't come** (ich wette) zehn gegen *or* zu eins, dass er nicht kommt; **a packet of ~ (cigarettes)** eine Zehnerpackung (Zigaretten) **N** Zehn *f*; **~s** *(Math)* Zehner *pl*; **to count in ~s** in Zehnern zählen; **you can only buy them in ~s** man kann sie nur in Zehnerpackungen kaufen; **Lynn's a ~** *(inf: = very nice)* Lynn ist 'ne Nummer 10 *(inf)*, Lynn ist perfekt → *also* **six**

tenability [,tenə'bɪlɪtɪ] **N** *(Mil: of position)* Haltbarkeit *f*; *(fig, of opinion, theory also)* Vertretbarkeit *f*

tenable ['tenəbl] **ADJ** **a** *(Mil) position* haltbar; *(fig) opinion, theory* haltbar, vertretbar **b** *pred* **a post ~ for life** eine Lebensstellung, eine Stelle auf Lebenszeit; **a post ~ for two years** eine auf zwei Jahre befristete Stelle

tenacious [tɪ'neɪʃəs] **ADJ** zäh, hartnäckig; *character, person also* beharrlich; *memory* unschlagbar; **to be ~ in doing sth** etw hartnäckig *or* eisern tun; **the disease had a ~ hold on …** die Krankheit hielt … in eisernem Griff; **to be ~ of sth** *(form)* zäh an etw *(dat)* festhalten; **to be ~ of life** *(form)* **to have a ~ hold on life** zäh am Leben hängen

tenaciously [tɪ'neɪʃəslɪ] **ADV** zäh, hartnäckig; **she held ~ to her principles** sie hielt zäh an ihren Prinzipien fest; **the dog held on ~ to the bone** der Hund hielt den Knochen zäh fest; **he clung ~ to life** er hielt zäh am Leben fest

tenacity [tɪ'næsɪtɪ] **N** Zähigkeit *f*, Hartnäckigkeit *f*; *(of character, person also)* Beharrlichkeit *f*; **the ~ of his grip** sein eiserner Griff; **his ~ of purpose** seine zielstrebige Beharrlichkeit

tenancy ['tenənsɪ] **N** **right/conditions of ~** Mietrecht *nt*/-bedingungen *pl*; *(of farm)* Pachtrecht *nt*/-bedingungen *pl*; **during his ~** während er (dort) Mieter/Pächter ist/war; **period of ~** Dauer *f* des Miet-/Pachtverhältnisses

tenant ['tenənt] **N** Mieter(in) *m(f)*; *(of farm)* Pächter(in) *m(f)* **VT** *(form) house* zur Miete wohnen in *(+dat)*; *premises* gemietet haben; *farm* in Pacht haben

tenant farmer **N** Pächter(in) *m(f)*

tenantry ['tenəntrɪ] **N** *no pl (of estate)* Pächter *pl*; *(of building, premises)* Mieter *pl*; **the law of ~** das Mietrecht; *(of farm)* das Pachtrecht

tend[1] [tend] **VT** sich kümmern um; *sheep* hüten; *sick person* pflegen; *land* bestellen; *machine* bedienen

tend[2] **VI** **a** **to ~ to be/do sth** *(= have a habit of being/doing sth)* gewöhnlich *or* gern etw sein/tun, die Tendenz haben, etw zu sein/tun; *(person also)* dazu neigen *or* tendieren, etw zu sein/tun; **the lever ~s to stick** der Hebel bleibt oft hängen; **I ~ to believe him** ich neige *or* tendiere dazu, ihm zu glauben; **that would ~ to suggest**

that ... das würde gewissermaßen darauf hindeuten, dass ...
b **to ~ toward(s)** (*= be directed, lead, measures, actions etc*) führen zu, anstreben; (*= incline, person, views, designs etc*) neigen *or* tendieren *or* eine Tendenz haben zu; **his opinion is ~ing in our direction** seine Meinung tendiert in unsere Richtung

tendency ['tendənsɪ] N Tendenz *f* (*geh*); (*= physical predisposition*) Neigung *f*; **artistic tendencies** künstlerische Neigungen *pl*; **to have a ~ to be/do sth** gern *or* gewöhnlich etw sein/tun; (*person, style of writing also*) dazu neigen *or* tendieren, etw zu sein/zu tun; **he had an annoying ~ to forget things** er hatte die ärgerliche Angewohnheit, alles zu vergessen; **there is a ~ for prices to rise in autumn** gewöhnlich steigen die Preise im Herbst; **a strong upward ~** (*St Ex*) eine stark steigende Tendenz

tendentious ADJ, **tendentiously** ADV [ten'denʃəs, -lɪ] tendenziös

tendentiousness [ten'denʃəsnɪs] N tendenziöse Färbung

tender[1] ['tendəʳ] N **a** Hüter(in) *m(f)*; (*of sick person*) Pfleger(in) *m(f)*; **machine ~** Maschinenwart *m* **b** (*Naut, Rail*) Tender *m*

tender[2] VT *money, services, shares* (an)bieten, geben; *thanks, apology* aussprechen; *resignation* einreichen; **"please ~ exact fare"** „bitte Fahrgeld abgezählt bereithalten" VI (*Comm*) sich bewerben (*for* um) N (*Comm*) Angebot *nt*; **to invite ~s for a job** Angebote *pl* für eine Arbeit einholen; **to put work out to ~** Arbeiten *pl* ausschreiben; **to put in a ~ for sth** ein Angebot für etw machen *or* einreichen; **we won the ~** wir haben die Ausschreibung gewonnen; **~ documents** Ausschreibungsunterlagen *pl*; **~ price** Angebotspreis *m*; **call for ~** Ausschreibung *f*

tender[3] ADJ **a** (*= sore, easily hurt*) *spot, bruise* empfindlich; *skin, plant* zart, empfindlich; (*fig*) *subject* heikel; **of ~ years** im zarten Alter; **at the ~ age of 7** im zarten Alter von 7 Jahren; **she left home at a very ~ age** sie verließ sehr früh ihr Elternhaus; **my arm still feels ~** mein Arm ist noch sehr empfindlich; **~ to the touch** berührungsempfindlich; **she is a ~ plant** (*fig*) sie ist ein zartes Pflänzchen
b *meat* zart; **cook the carrots for about 10 minutes or until ~** die Möhren etwa 10 Minuten lang kochen oder bis sie weich sind
c (*= affectionate*) *person, voice, look* zärtlich, liebevoll; *memories* lieb, zärtlich; *heart* gut; *gesture* sanft; *kiss, embrace* zärtlich; **~ loving care** Liebe und Zuneigung *f*; **he gave her a ~ smile** er lächelte sie zärtlich an; **to bid sb a ~ farewell** liebevoll(en) *or* zärtlich(en) Abschied von jdm nehmen; **in sb's ~ care** in jds Obhut; **to leave sb to sb's ~ mercies** (*iro*) jdn jds liebevollen Händen anvertrauen

tender: **tenderfoot** N Neuling *m*; **tender-hearted** [ˌtendə'hɑːtɪd] ADJ gutherzig; **tender-heartedness** N Gutherzigkeit *f*

tendering ['tendərɪŋ] N *no pl* (*Comm*) Angebotsabgabe *f*

tenderize ['tendəraɪz] VT *meat* zart *or* weich machen; (*by beating*) klopfen

tenderizer ['tendəraɪzəʳ] N Mürbesalz *nt*; (*= hammer*) Fleischklopfer *m*

tenderloin ['tendəlɔɪn] N Lendenstück *nt*

tenderly ['tendəlɪ] ADV zärtlich, liebevoll

tenderness ['tendənɪs] N **a** (*= soreness*) Empfindlichkeit *f* **b** (*of meat*) Zartheit *f* **c** (*= affection, of person, voice, look*) Zärtlichkeit *f*; (*of heart*) Güte *f*

tendon ['tendən] N Sehne *f*

tendril ['tendrɪl] N Ranke *f*; (*of hair*) Ringellocke *f*

tenement ['tenɪmənt] N **a** (*also* **tenement house**) Mietshaus *nt*, Mietskaserne *f* (*pej*) **b** (*Jur*) Mietbesitz *m*; (*= farm*) Pachtbesitz *m*

Tenerife [ˌtenə'riːf] N Teneriffa *nt*

tenet ['tenət] N Lehrsatz *m*; (*Rel*) Glaubenssatz *m*

tenfold ['tenfəʊld] ADJ zehnfach ADV zehnfach, um das Zehnfache; **to increase ~** sich verzehnfachen

ten-gallon hat [ˌtengæln'hæt] N Cowboyhut *m*

tenish ['tenɪʃ] ADJ (so) um zehn herum (*inf*)

tenner ['tenəʳ] N (*Brit inf*) Zehner *m* (*inf*)

tennis ['tenɪs] N Tennis *nt*

tennis *in cpds* Tennis-; **tennis ball** N Tennisball *m*; **tennis club** N Tennisklub *m*, Tennisverein *m*; **tennis court** N Tennisplatz *m*; **tennis elbow** N (*Med*) Tennisarm *m*; **tennis player** N Tennisspieler(in) *m(f)*; **tennis racket**, **tennis racquet** N Tennisschläger *m*; **tennis shoe** N Tennisschuh *m*

tenon ['tenən] N Zapfen *m*; **~ joint** Zapfenverbindung *f*

tenon saw N Zapfenschneidsäge *f*

tenor ['tenəʳ] N **a** (*= voice, person*) Tenor *m*; **to sing ~** Tenor singen **b** (*= purport*) Tenor *m*; (*of theory*) Tendenz *f*; (*= general nature, of life*) Stil *m*; (*of events*) (Ver)lauf *m* ADJ (*Mus*) Tenor-; **~ voice** Tenorstimme *f*; **~ saxophone** Tenorsaxofon *nt*, Tenorsaxophon *nt*

tenor clef N (*Mus*) Tenorschlüssel *m*

ten: **tenpence** N zehn Pence; (*also* **tenpenny piece**) Zehnpencestück *nt*; **tenpin bowling**, (*US*) **tenpins** N Bowling *nt*

tense[1] [tens] N (*Gram*) Zeit *f*, Tempus *nt*; **present ~** Gegenwart *f*; **past ~** Vergangenheit *f*; **future ~** Zukunft *f*

tense[2] ADJ (+*er*) *rope* gespannt, straff; *muscles* (an)gespannt; *neck* verspannt; *person, expression, bearing* (*through stress, worry etc*) angespannt; (*through nervousness, fear etc*) verkrampft; *voice* nervös; *silence, atmosphere* gespannt; *situation* (an)gespannt; *time* gespannt, spannungsgeladen; *negotiations* spannungsgeladen; *relations* angespannt; (*= thrilling*) *scene* spannungsgeladen; **~ headache** Spannungskopfschmerz *m*; **to grow** *or* **become** *or* **get ~** (*person*) nervös werden; **to make sb ~** jdn in Anspannung versetzen; **I've been feeling rather ~ all day** ich bin schon den ganzen Tag so nervös; **in a voice with emotion** mit erregter Stimme; **things are getting rather ~** die Lage wird gespannter
VT anspannen; **to ~ oneself to do sth** sich darauf konzentrieren, etw zu tun
VI sich (an)spannen, sich straffen

▸ **tense up** VI (*person, muscle*) sich anspannen VT *sep muscle* anspannen

tensely ['tenslɪ] ADV (*lit*) *stretch* straff; (*fig*) *listen, sit* angespannt; *speak, wait* (*= nervously*) nervös; (*= excitedly*) gespannt

tenseness ['tensnɪs] N **a** (*= tautness, of rope*) Gespanntheit *f*, Straffheit *f*; (*of muscles*) (An)gespanntheit *f* **b** (*of person, expression, bearing, through stress, worry etc*) Angespanntheit *f*; (*through nervousness, fear etc*) Verkrampftheit *f*; (*of voice*) Nervosität *f*; (*of atmosphere, situation*) Gespanntheit *f*; (*of negotiations*) Spannungsgeladenheit *f*; (*of relations*) Angespanntheit *f* **c** (*= excitement: of scene*) Spannung(sgeladenheit) *f*

tensile ['tensaɪl] ADJ dehnbar, spannbar; **high ~ steel** Spannstahl *m*; **high ~ wire** besonders zugfester Draht

tensile: **tensile load** N Zugbelastung *f*; **tensile strength** N Zugfestigkeit *f*; **tensile stress** N Zugspannung *f*

tension ['tenʃən] N **a** (*lit*) Spannung *f*; (*of muscle*) Anspannung *f*; (*Knitting*) Festigkeit *f*; (*Sew*) Spannung *f*; **to check the ~** (*Knitting*) eine Maschenprobe machen **b** (*= nervous strain*) nervliche Belastung, Anspannung *f* **c** (*in relationship*) Spannungen *pl*

tensor (muscle) ['tensɔːʳ-] N Tensor *m*

tenspot ['tenspɒt] N (*US inf*) Zehner *m* (*inf*)

tent [tent] N Zelt *nt*

tentacle ['tentəkl] N (*Zool*) Tentakel *m or nt* (*spec*); (*of octopus etc also*) Fangarm *m*; (*of snail also*) Fühler *m*; (*fig*) Klaue *f*

tentative ['tentətɪv] ADJ (*= not definite, provisional*) vorläufig; *offer* unverbindlich; (*= hesitant*) *player, movement* vorsichtig; *conclusion, suggestion* vorsichtig, zögernd; *smile* zögernd; **this proposal** *or* **suggestion is only ~** das ist ja nur ein Vorschlag; **we've a ~ arrangement to play tennis tonight** wir haben halb abgemacht, heute Abend Tennis zu spielen

tentatively ['tentətɪvlɪ] ADV (*= hesitantly*) *smile* zögernd; (*= gingerly*) vorsichtig; (*= provisionally*) *agree* vorläufig; **he ~ suggested a weekend in Brighton** er machte den Vorschlag, eventuell ein Wochenende in Brighton zu verbringen

tent: **tent bed** N Feldbett *nt*; **tent city** N Zeltstadt *f*

tented ['tentɪd] ADJ *attr* **a** (*= with tents*) *field* mit Zelten (belegt); **~ camp** Zeltlager *nt* **b** (*= draped*) *room, ceiling* drapiert, verhangen

tenterhooks ['tentəhʊks] PL **to be on ~** wie auf glühenden Kohlen sitzen (*inf*); **to keep sb on ~** jdn zappeln lassen

tenth [tenθ] ADJ (*in series*) zehnte(r, s); **a ~ part** ein Zehntel *nt* N (*= fraction*) Zehntel *nt*; (*in series*) Zehnte(r, s); (*Mus*) Dezime *f* → *also* **sixth**

tenthly ['tenθlɪ] ADV zehntens

tent peg N Zeltpflock *m*, Hering *m*

tent pole N Zeltstange *f*

tenuity [te'njʊɪtɪ] N (*liter*) = **tenuousness**

tenuous ['tenjʊəs] ADJ **a** (*lit*) *thread* dünn, fein; *cobweb* zart, fein; *air* dünn; *gas* flüchtig **b** (*fig*) *connection, argument, relationship* schwach; (*= insecure*) *position* unsicher; *supply line* anfällig; **he kept a ~ hold on life** er hatte nur noch einen schwachen Lebenswillen; **to have a ~ grasp of sth** etw nur ansatzweise verstehen; **a ~ lead** eine mögliche Spur

tenuously ['tenjʊəslɪ] ADV (*= slightly*) schwach, leicht; **another world, connected to reality only ~** eine andere Welt, nur schwach mit der Realität verbunden

tenuousness ['tenjʊəsnɪs] N **a** (*lit, of thread*) Dünne *f*, Feinheit *f*; (*of cobweb*) Zartheit *f*, Feinheit *f*; (*of air*) Dünne *f*; (*of gas*) Flüchtigkeit *f* **b** (*fig, of connection, argument, relationship*) Schwäche *f*; (*= insecurity of position*) Unsicherheit *f*

tenure ['tenjʊəʳ] N **a** (*= holding of office*) Anstellung *f*; (*= period of office*) Amtszeit *f* **b** (*of property*) **during her ~ of the house/farm** während sie das Haus/die Farm innehatte; **laws governing land ~** Landpachtgesetze *pl*

TEOTWAWKI *abbr of* **the end of the world as we know it** das Ende der Welt, wie wir sie kennen

tepee ['tiːpiː] N Tipi *nt*

tepid ['tepɪd] ADJ (*lit, fig*) lau(warm)

tepidity [te'pɪdɪtɪ], **tepidness** ['tepɪdnɪs] N (*lit, fig*) Lauheit *f*

tequila [tɪ'kiːlə] N Tequila *m*

terabyte ['terəbaɪt] N (*Comput*) Terabyte *nt*

tercentenary [ˌtɜːsen'tiːnərɪ] N (*= anniversary*) dreihundertster Jahrestag; (*= celebration*) Dreihundertjahrfeier *f*, dreihundertjähriges Jubiläum ATTR für den dreihundertsten Jahrestag; **~ celebrations** Dreihundertjahrfeier *f*

tercet ['tɜːsɪt] N (*Poet*) Terzine *f*; (*Mus*) Triole *f*

tergiversate ['tɜːdʒɪvəseɪt] VI (*form, hum*) dauernd seine Gesinnung ändern

tergiversation [ˌtɜːdʒɪvə'seɪʃən] N *usu pl* (*form, hum*) (ständiger) Gesinnungswandel *no pl*

term [tɜːm] N **a** (*= period of time*) Dauer *f*, Zeitraum *m*; (*of contract*) Laufzeit *f*; (*= limit*) Frist *f*; **~ of government** Regierungszeit *f*; **~ of office** Amtsdauer *or* -zeit *f*; **~ of imprisonment** Gefängnisstrafe *f*; **~ of service** (*Mil*) Militärdienstzeit *f*; **to set a ~ (of three years) for sth** etw (auf drei Jahre) befristen; **elected for a three-year ~** auf *or* für drei Jahre gewählt; **the contract is nearing its ~** der Vertrag läuft bald ab; **in the long/short ~** auf lange/kurze Sicht;

at ~ *(Fin)* bei Fälligkeit; *(Med)* zur rechten Zeit; **to carry a baby to ~** ein Kind (voll) austragen
b *(Sch, three in one year)* Trimester *nt*; *(four in one year)* Vierteljahr *nt*, Quartal *nt*; *(two in one year)* Halbjahr *nt*; *(Univ)* Semester *nt*; **end-of-~ exam** Examen *nt* am Ende eines Trimesters *etc*; **during** *or* **in ~(-time)** während der Schulzeit; *(Univ)* während des Semesters; **out of ~(-time)** in den Ferien
c *(= expression)* Ausdruck *m*; **in simple ~s** in einfachen Worten; **a legal ~** ein juristischer (Fach)ausdruck *or* Terminus *(geh)*; **he spoke of her in the most flattering ~s** er äußerte sich sehr schmeichelhaft über sie; **a contradiction in ~s** ein Widerspruch in sich
d *(Math, Logic)* Term *m*; **~ in parentheses** Klammerausdruck *m*; **to express one thing in ~s of another** eine Sache mit einer anderen erklären; **in ~s of production we are doing well** was die Produktion betrifft, stehen wir gut da; **in ~s of money** geldlich, finanziell; **in ~s of time** zeitlich
e terms PL *(= conditions)* Bedingungen *pl*; **~s of surrender/service/sale/payment** Kapitulations-/Arbeits-/Verkaufs-/Zahlungsbedingungen *pl*; **~s of reference** *(of committee etc)* Aufgabenbereich *m*; *(of thesis etc)* Themenbereich *m*; **to buy sth on credit/easy ~s** etw auf Kredit/auf Raten kaufen; **the hotel offered reduced ~s in winter** das Hotel bot ermäßigte Winterpreise an; **on what ~s?** zu welchen Bedingungen?; **not on any ~s** unter gar keinen Umständen; **to accept sb on his/her own ~s** jdn nehmen, wie er/sie ist; **on equal ~s** auf gleicher Basis; **to come to ~s (with sb)** sich (mit jdm) einigen; **to come to ~s with sth** sich mit etw abfinden
f terms PL *(= relations)* **to be on good/bad ~s with sb** gut/nicht (gut) mit jdm auskommen; **to be on friendly ~s with sb** auf freundschaftlichem Fuß mit jdm stehen; **they are not on speaking ~s** sie reden nicht miteinander; **what sort of ~s are they on?** wie ist ihre Beziehung?
VT nennen, bezeichnen

termagant ['tɜːməgənt] N Furie *f*

terminal ['tɜːmɪnl] ADJ **a** *(= final)* End-; *(Med: = incurable) illness, patient* unheilbar; *(= for the dying) care* für Sterbende; *(= dire) problem* fatal; **~ stage** *(of illness etc)* Endstadium *nt*; **he's a ~ case** er ist unheilbar krank; **to be in ~ decline** sich in unaufhaltsamem Niedergang befinden
b *(inf: = utter) boredom* endlos; *stupidity* bodenlos; *adolescent* ewig; *workaholic* extrem
c *(Bot, Anat, = on extremity)* am Ende befindlich
N **a** *(Rail)* Endbahnhof *m*; *(for tramway, buses)* Endstation *f*; *(= container terminal)* Containerterminal *m*; **air** *or* **airport ~** (Flughafen)terminal *m*, Flughafengebäude *nt*; **cargo ~** Frachtterminal *m*; **ferry ~** Fährterminal *m*; **passenger ~** Passagierterminal *m*; **railway** *(Brit) or* **railroad** *(US)* **~** Zielbahnhof *m*; **sea ~** Seehafenanleger *m*
b *(Elec)* Pol *m*
c *(Comput)* Terminal *nt*

terminal bonus N *(Insur)* Zusatzdividende *f (fällig bei Vertragsablauf)*

terminal building N Terminal *m or nt*

terminally ['tɜːmɪnəlɪ] ADV **a ~ ill** unheilbar krank; **the ~ ill** die Todkranken *pl* **b** *(= utterly) boring* endlos; **~ stupid** *(inf)* saublöd *(inf)*; **~ unfashionable** heillos unmodern

terminal: **terminal station** N *(Rail)* Endbahnhof *m*; **terminal velocity** N *(Phys)* Endgeschwindigkeit *f*; **terminal voltage** N *(Elec)* Klemmenspannung *f*; **terminal ward** N Sterbestation *f*

terminate ['tɜːmɪneɪt] VT beenden, beschließen; *contract, lease etc* lösen; *pregnancy* unterbrechen; *employment* kündigen; *relationship, conversation, friendship, life* beenden VI enden; *(contract, lease)* ablaufen; **most plural nouns ~ in "s"** die meisten Substantive enden im Plural auf „s"

termination [ˌtɜːmɪ'neɪʃən] N **a** Ende *nt*; *(= bringing to an end)* Beendigung *f*; *(of contract, lease etc, = expiry)* Ablauf *m*, Erlöschen *nt*; *(= cancellation)* Lösung *f*; **~ of pregnancy** Schwangerschaftsabbruch *m* **b** *(Gram)* Endung *f*

terminological [ˌtɜːmɪnə'lɒdʒɪkəl] ADJ terminologisch

terminology [ˌtɜːmɪ'nɒlədʒɪ] N Terminologie *f*; **all the technical ~ in the article** all die Fachausdrücke in dem Artikel

term insurance N (zeitlich) befristete Versicherung

terminus ['tɜːmɪnəs] N *(Rail, bus)* Endstation *f*

termite ['tɜːmaɪt] N Termite *f*

term money N *(Fin)* Festgeld *nt*

tern [tɜːn] N *(Zool)* Seeschwalbe *f*

ternary ['tɜːnərɪ] ADJ ternär

Terpsichorean [ˌtɜːpsɪkə'rɪən] ADJ *(form, hum) skill etc* im Tanzen; **~ art** Tanzkunst *f*

terrace ['terəs] N **a** *(= patio)* Terrasse *f* **b** *(on hillside)* Terrasse *f*; **~ cultivation** Terrassenfeldbau *m* **c terraces** PL *(Brit Sport)* Ränge *pl* **d** *(Brit: = row of houses)* Häuserreihe *f*; *(as street name)* ≈ Weg *m* VT *garden, hill* in Terrassen anlegen, stufenförmig anlegen

terraced ['terəst] ADJ **a** *hillside etc* terrassenförmig *or* stufenförmig angelegt; *garden* in Terrassen angelegt **b** *(esp Brit) street* mit Reihenhäusern; **~ house** Reihenhaus *nt*

terracing ['terəsɪŋ] N *no pl* **a** *(on land)* Terrassen *pl* **b** *(Brit Sport)* Ränge *pl*

terracotta [ˌterə'kɒtə] N Terrakotta *f* ATTR Terrakotta-, aus Terrakotta; **~ floor** Terrakottaboden *m*

terra firma [ˌterə'fɜːmə] N fester Boden; **to be on ~ again** wieder festen Boden unter den Füßen haben

terrain [te'reɪn] N Terrain *nt (esp Mil)*, Gelände *nt*; *(fig)* Boden *m*

terrapin ['terəpɪn] N Sumpfschildkröte *f*

terrarium [tə'reərɪəm] N *(for plants)* Pflanzschale *f (in Kugelform)*; *(for animals)* Terrarium *nt*

terrazzo [te'rætsəʊ] N Terrazzo *m*

terrestrial [tɪ'restrɪəl] ADJ **a** *(= of land)* Land-; **~ animal** Landtier *nt*, auf dem Land lebendes Tier; **~ plant** Landpflanze *f* **b** *(= of the planet Earth)* terrestrisch, irdisch; *life* irdisch; *(Brit) TV channel, television, broadcasting* terrestrisch; **~ globe** Erdball *m*, Globus *m* **c** *(= worldly) problems* irdisch, weltlich N Erdbewohner(in) *m(f)*

terrible ['terəbl] ADJ **a** schrecklich, furchtbar; **he is ~ at golf** er spielt schrecklich *(inf) or* furchtbar schlecht Golf; **I feel ~** *(= feel ill)* mir ist fürchterlich schlecht; *(= feel guilty)* es ist mir furchtbar peinlich; **to sound ~** *(= ill)* sich schrecklich anhören; **I sound ~ on tape** auf Band klinge ich furchtbar **b** *(inf: = absolute) fool* furchtbar

terribleness ['terəblnɪs] N Schrecklichkeit *f*, Fürchterlichkeit *f*

terribly ['terəblɪ] ADV **a** *(= very) important, difficult* schrecklich *(inf)*; *disappointed, sorry* furchtbar; *(= very much) suffer* fürchterlich, furchtbar; **I'm not ~ good with money** ich kann nicht besonders gut mit Geld umgehen; **I miss him ~** ich vermisse ihn ganz furchtbar **b** *(= badly) behave* schrecklich, furchtbar; *play, sing* schrecklich, fürchterlich

terrier ['terɪəʳ] N Terrier *m*

terrific [tə'rɪfɪk] ADJ *shame, nuisance, shock* unheimlich *(inf)*; *person, success, idea, party also* sagenhaft *(inf)*, klasse *inv (inf)*; *speed, heat, strength, generosity* unwahrscheinlich *(inf)*; **that's ~ news** das sind tolle Nachrichten *(inf)*; **to look ~** *(person)* klasse aussehen *(inf)*; **to have a ~ time** viel Spaß haben; **~!** *(also iro)* prima! *(inf)*, toll! *(inf)*

terrifically [tə'rɪfɪkəlɪ] ADV *(inf: = very)* unheimlich *(inf)*; *(= very well)* unheimlich (gut) *(inf)*; **the party went ~** die Party war klasse *(inf)*

terrified ['terɪfaɪd] ADJ *person, animal* verängstigt; *look also* angstvoll; **to be ~ of sth** vor etw schreckliche Angst haben; **he was ~ when/in case ...** er hatte fürchterliche Angst, als .../davor, dass ...; **you look ~** du hast Angst, das sieht man!

terrify ['terɪfaɪ] VT *person* fürchterliche *or* schreckliche Angst machen *or* einjagen *(+dat)*, in Angst *or* Schrecken versetzen; **flying terrifies him** er hat schreckliche Angst vor dem Fliegen; **my driving terrifies her** wenn ich Auto fahre, bekommt sie es mit der Angst zu tun

terrifying ['terɪfaɪɪŋ] ADJ *film, story* grauenerregend; *thought, sight* entsetzlich; *speed* Angst erregend, furchterregend

terrifyingly ['terɪfaɪɪŋlɪ] ADV entsetzlich; **he came ~ close to disaster** er kam dem Unheil schrecklich nahe

terrine [te'riːn] N Pastete *f*

territorial [ˌterɪ'tɔːrɪəl] ADJ territorial; **~ sovereignty** Gebietshoheit *f*; **~ integrity** territoriale Unverletzlichkeit; **~ possessions** Territorialbesitz *m*; **~ rights** Hoheitsrechte *pl*; **~ behaviour** *(of animal)* Revierverhalten *nt*; **a strongly ~ bird** ein Vogel mit ausgeprägtem Territorial- *or* Revierverhalten N *(esp Brit)* **Territorial** Soldat *m* der Heimatschutztruppe; **the Territorials** *(Brit)* die Heimatschutztruppe

Territorial Army N *(Brit)* Territorialheer *nt*

> **TERRITORIAL ARMY**
>
> Die **Territorial Army** (abgekürzt auch **TA**) ist eine britische Organisation freiwilliger Armeereservisten. Die Mitglieder sind Zivilisten, die in ihrer Freizeit Militärübungen absolvieren und in Kriegs- oder Krisenzeiten zur Unterstützung der regulären Armee zur Verfügung stehen. Als Gegenleistung erhalten die Freiwilligen regelmäßige Bezüge.

territorial waters PL Territorialgewässer *pl*

territory ['terɪtərɪ] N (Staats)gebiet *nt*, Territorium *nt*; *(in US, Austral)* Territorium *nt*; *(of animals)* Revier *nt*, Territorium *nt*; *(Comm: of agent etc)* Bezirk *m*; *(fig)* Revier *nt*, Gebiet *nt*; **uncharted territories** *(lit)* unerforschte Gebiete *pl*; *(fig)* unerforschtes Terrain; **the occupied territories** die besetzen Gebiete; **that comes** *or* **goes with the ~** das gehört einfach dazu; **such problems have become familiar ~** solche Probleme sind allgegenwärtig geworden

terror ['terəʳ] N **a** *no pl (= great fear)* panische Angst *(of* vor *+dat)*; **in ~** in panischer Angst; **to be in ~ of one's life** um sein Leben bangen; **it held no ~ for him** er schreckte nicht davor zurück; **reign of ~** *(Hist, fig)* Terror- *or* Schreckensherrschaft *f*; **the IRA ~ campaign** die Terrorkampagne der IRA
b *(= cause of terror, terrible event)* Schrecken *m*; **he was the ~ of the other boys** er terrorisierte die anderen Jungen; **the headmaster was a ~ to boys who misbehaved** der Rektor war der Schrecken aller Jungen, die sich schlecht benahmen
c *(inf: = person)* Teufel *m*; *(= child)* Ungeheuer *nt*; **a ~ with the ladies** ein Weiberheld *m (inf)*

terror alert N Terrorwarnung *f*, Terroralarm *m*

terror bombing N Bombenterror *m*

terrorism ['terərɪzəm] N Terrorismus *m*; *(= acts of terrorism)* Terror *m*; **an act of ~** ein Terrorakt *m*

terrorist ['terərɪst] N Terrorist(in) *m(f)* ADJ *attr* terroristisch; **~ attack** Terroranschlag *m*; **~ plot** geplanter Terroranschlag; **~ threat** Terrorgefahr *or* -bedrohung *f*

terrorize ['terəraɪz] VT **a** terrorisieren **b** *(= intimidate)* einschüchtern; **to ~ sb into doing sth** jdn durch Einschüchterungen dazu bringen, etw zu tun

terrorization [ˌterəraɪ'zeɪʃən] N **a** Terrorisierung *f* **b** *(= intimidation)* Einschüchterung *f*

terror plot N geplanter Terroranschlag, Terrorplan *m*

terror-stricken ['terəˌstrɪkən] ADJ starr vor Schreck(en)

terry [ˈterɪ]: **terry cloth** N *(US)* Frottee *nt or m*; **terry towel** N *(Brit)* Frotteetuch *nt*, Frottier(-hand)tuch *nt*; **terry towelling** [ˌterɪˈtaʊəlɪŋ] N *(Brit)* Frottee *nt or m*

terse [tɜːs] ADJ *(+er)* knapp; **he was very ~** er war sehr kurz angebunden

tersely [ˈtɜːslɪ] ADV knapp, kurz; *say, answer* kurz (angebunden); **to dismiss sth ~** etw kurzerhand verwerfen

terseness [ˈtɜːsnɪs] N Knappheit *f*; *(of reply also, person)* Kürze *f*, Bündigkeit *f*

tertiary [ˈtɜːʃərɪ] ADJ tertiär; **~ education** *(Brit)* Universitätsausbildung *f*

tertiary: **tertiary burns** PL Verbrennungen *pl* dritten Grades; **tertiary colour** N Mischfarbe *f*; **Tertiary period** N *(Geol)* Tertiär *nt*

Terylene® [ˈterəliːn] N Terylen(e)® *nt*, ≈ Trevira® *nt*, ≈ Diolen® *nt*

TESL *abbr of* **Teaching of English as a Second Language**, → **TEFL**

TESOL *abbr of* **Teaching of English as a Second or Other Language**, → **TEFL**

tessellated [ˈtesɪleɪtɪd] ADJ Mosaik-; **~ floor** Mosaik(fuß)boden *m*

test [test] N **a** *(Sch)* Klassenarbeit *f*; *(Univ)* Klausur *f*; *(short)* Kurzarbeit *f*, Test *m*; *(= intelligence test, psychological test etc)* Test *m*; *(= driving test)* (Fahr)prüfung *f*; **he gave them a vocabulary ~** er ließ eine Vokabel- *or* Wörterarbeit schreiben; *(orally)* er hat sie Vokabeln abgefragt; **this is a ~ of public opinion** damit wird die öffentliche Meinung ausgelotet; **to put sb/sth to the ~** jdn/etw auf die Probe stellen; **to stand the ~** die Probe bestehen; **their marriage didn't stand up to the ~ of separation** ihre Ehe hat die Trennung nicht verkraftet; **to stand the ~ of time** die Zeit überdauern; **that was a real ~ of character/his endurance** das war eine wirkliche Charakterprüfung/Belastungsprobe für ihn; **to pass one's ~** *(Aut)* die (Fahr)prüfung bestehen; **to fail one's ~** *(Aut)* (durch die (Fahr)prüfung) durchfallen
b *(on vehicle, product, weapon etc)* Test *m*; *(= check)* Kontrolle *f*
c *(= chemical test)* Test *m*, Untersuchung *f*; **a skin ~** ein Hauttest; **to do a ~ for sugar** einen Zuckertest machen, eine Untersuchung auf Zucker machen; **the samples were sent for ~s** die Proben wurden zur Untersuchung geschickt
d *(Brit)* = **test match**
ADJ *attr* Test-; **~ model** Testmodell *nt*
VT **a** *(= examine, check)* testen, prüfen; *(Sch) pupil* prüfen; *(orally)* abfragen; *person, intelligence* testen; *(fig)* auf die Probe stellen; **the teacher ~ed them on that chapter** der Lehrer fragte sie das Kapitel ab; **to ~ sb for a job** jds Eignung für eine Stelle prüfen *or* testen; **to ~ sb/sth for accuracy** jdn/etw auf Genauigkeit prüfen; **I just wanted to ~ your reaction** ich wollte nur mal sehen, wie du reagierst; **have you been ~ed?** *(for AIDS etc)* hast du dich testen lasen?, hast du einen Test gemacht?
b *(chemically) gold* prüfen; *water, contents of stomach etc* untersuchen; **to ~ sth for sugar** etw auf seinen Zuckergehalt untersuchen; **the blood samples were sent for ~ing** *or* **to be ~ed** die Blutproben wurden zur Untersuchung geschickt
VI Tests/einen Test machen; *(chemically also)* untersuchen (*for* auf *+acc*); **~ing, ~ing one, two, three!** eins, zwei, drei; **we are ~ing for a gas leak/loose connection** wir überprüfen die Leitung auf eine undichte Stelle, wir überprüfen, ob irgendwo Gas austritt/ein Anschluss locker ist

▸ **test out** VT *sep* ausprobieren (*on* bei *or* an *+dat*)

testament [ˈtestəmənt] N **a** *(old)* Testament *nt*, letzter Wille **b** *(Bibl)* **Old/New Testament** Altes/Neues Testament

testamentary [ˌtestəˈmentərɪ] ADJ testamentarisch

testator [teˈsteɪtəʳ] N Erblasser(in) *m(f)* *(form)*

testatrix [teˈsteɪtrɪks] N Erblasserin *f* *(form)*

test: **test ban** N Versuchsverbot *nt*; **test ban treaty** N Teststoppabkommen *nt*; **test-bed** N Prüfstand *m*; **test card** N *(TV)* Testbild *nt*; **test case** N Musterfall *m*; **test cricket** N *(Brit: Cricket)* internationales Kricket, Testkricket *nt*; **test drive** N Probefahrt *f*; **test-drive** VT *car* probefahren

testee [teˈstiː] N **a** *(Psych etc)* Testperson *f* **b** *(Sch etc)* Prüfling *m*

tester [ˈtestəʳ] N *(of product etc)* Prüfer(in) *m(f)*; *(= machine)* Prüfgerät *nt*

testes [ˈtestiːz] PL Testikel *pl*, Hoden *pl*

test: **test flight** N Test- *or* Probeflug *m*; **test-fly** VT Test fliegen

testicle [ˈtestɪkl] N Testikel *m*, Hoden *m*

testify [ˈtestɪfaɪ] VT **to ~ that …** *(Jur)* bezeugen, dass … VI *(Jur)* eine Zeugenaussage machen, aussagen; **to ~ against/for sb** gegen/für jdn aussagen; **to ~ to sth** *(= speak for)* etw bezeugen *(also Jur)*; *(= be sign of) to sincerity, efforts etc* von etw zeugen, ein Zeichen für etw sein

testily [ˈtestɪlɪ] ADV *say* unwirsch, gereizt

testimonial [ˌtestɪˈməʊnɪəl] N **a** *(= character recommendation)* Referenz *f* **b** *(= gift)* Geschenk *nt* als Zeichen der Anerkennung *or* Wertschätzung *(geh)* **c** *(Sport)* Gedenkspiel *nt*

testimony [ˈtestɪmənɪ] N Aussage *f*; **he gave his ~** er machte seine Aussage; **to bear ~ to sth** etw bezeugen; **accept this gift as ~ of** *or* **to my friendship** nehmen Sie dieses Geschenk als Zeichen *or* Beweis meiner Freundschaft

testiness [ˈtestɪnɪs] N Gereiztheit *f*

testing [ˈtestɪŋ] ADJ hart; **I had a ~ time** es war hart (für mich)

testing ground N Test- *or* Versuchsgebiet *nt*; *(fig)* Versuchsfeld *nt*

test: **test-market** VT auf dem Markt testen; **test marketing** N Markttest *m*; **test match** N *(Brit)* Testmatch *nt*; *(Kricket also)* internationales Kricketmatch; *(Rugby also)* internationales Rugbymatch

testosterone [teˈstɒstərəʊn] N Testosteron *nt*

test: **test paper** N *(Sch)* Klassenarbeit *f*; *(Chem)* Reagenzpapier *nt*; **test pattern** N *(US)* = **test card**; **test piece** N *(of handwork)* Prüfungsstück *nt*; *(Mus)* Stück *nt* zum Vorspielen; **test pilot** N Testpilot(in) *m(f)*; **test print** N *(Phot)* Probeabzug *m*; **test results** PL *(Med etc)* Testwerte *pl*; **test stand** N *(Tech)* Prüfstand *m*; **test tube** N Reagenzglas *nt*; **test-tube baby** N Kind *nt* aus der Retorte, Retortenbaby *nt*

testy [ˈtestɪ] ADJ *(+er)* unwirsch, gereizt

tetanus [ˈtetənəs] N Wundstarrkrampf *m*, Tetanus *m*; **~ injection** Tetanusspritze *f*

tetchily [ˈtetʃɪlɪ] ADV *say* gereizt

tetchiness [ˈtetʃɪnɪs] N *(esp Brit inf)* *(on particular occasion)* Gereiztheit *f*; *(as general characteristic)* Reizbarkeit *f*

tetchy, **techy** [ˈtetʃɪ] ADJ *(+er)* *(esp Brit inf)* *(on particular occasion)* gereizt; *(as general characteristic)* reizbar

tête-à-tête [ˌteɪtɑːˈteɪt] ADJ, ADV unter vier Augen N Tete-a-tete *nt*, Tête-à-tête *nt*

tether [ˈteðəʳ] N *(lit)* Strick *m*; *(= chain)* Kette *f*; **he was at the end of his ~** *(Brit fig inf: = annoyed, impatient)* ihm hats gereicht *(inf)*; *(= desperate)* er war am Ende *(inf)* VT (*also* **tether up**) *animal* anbinden, festbinden

tetherball [ˈteðəbɔːl] N *(US) Spiel, bei dem ein Ball, der an einem an einer Stange befestigten Seil hängt, geschlagen wird, so dass sich das Seil um die Stange herumwickelt*

tetrachloride [ˌtetrəˈklɔːraɪd] N Tetrachlorid *nt*

tetrahedron [ˌtetrəˈhiːdrən] N Tetraeder *nt*

tetrameter [teˈtræmɪtəʳ] N *(Liter)* Tetrameter *m*

tetrapod [ˈtetrəpɒd] N Tetrapode *m* *(spec)*, Vierfüßer *m*

Teuton [ˈtjuːtɒn] N Teutone *m*, Teutonin *f*

Teutonic [tjʊˈtɒnɪk] ADJ *(Hist, hum)* teutonisch

Texan [ˈteksən] N Texaner(in) *m(f)* ADJ texanisch

Texas [ˈteksəs] N Texas *nt*

text [tekst] N **a** Text *m*; **to restore a ~** den Originaltext wiederherstellen **b** *(of sermon)* Text *m* VT **to ~ sb** *(on mobile phone)* jdm eine Textnachricht *or* SMS schicken

text: **textbook** [ˈtekstbʊk] N Lehrbuch *nt* ADJ **~ case** Paradefall *m*; **~ knowledge** (Lehr)buchwissen *nt*; **~ landing** Bilderbuchlandung *f*; **text box** N *(Comput)* Textfeld *nt*; **text editor** N *(Comput)* Texteditor *m*; **text frame** N *(Comput)* Textrahmen *m*

textile [ˈtekstaɪl] ADJ Textil-; **~ industry** Textilindustrie *f* N Stoff *m*; **~s** Textilien *pl*, Textilwaren *pl*

text *(Comput)*: **text input** N Texteingabe *f*; **text label** N Symbolunterschrift *f*; **text message** N Textnachricht *f*, SMS *f*; **text messaging** N *(Telec)* SMS-Messaging *nt*, SMS-Versand *m*; **text mode** N Textmodus *m*; **text processing** N Textverarbeitung *f*; **text processor** N Textverarbeitungssystem *nt*; *(= software also)* Textsystem *nt*

textual [ˈtekstjʊəl] ADJ Text-; **~ analysis** Textanalyse *f*

texture [ˈtekstʃəʳ] N (stoffliche) Beschaffenheit, Textur *f*; *(of dough also)* Konsistenz *f*; *(of food)* Substanz *f*, Textur *f*; *(of material, paper)* Griff *m* und Struktur, Textur *f*; *(fig, of music, poetry etc)* Gestalt *f*; **the ~ of velvet** wie sich Samt anfühlt; **the smooth ~ of silk makes it pleasant to wear** es ist angenehm, Seide zu tragen, weil sie so anschmiegsam ist; **a sculptor interested in ~** ein Bildhauer, der an der Materialgestalt *or* -beschaffenheit interessiert ist; **the ~ of one's life** seine Lebensqualität

textured [ˈtekstʃəd] ADJ strukturiert, texturiert *(form)*

TGIF *(hum) abbr of* **thank God it's Friday**

T-girder N *(Tech)* T-Träger *m*

TGWU *(Brit) abbr of* **Transport and General Workers' Union** *Transportarbeitergewerkschaft*

Thai [taɪ] ADJ thailändisch N **a** Thailänder(in) *m(f)*, Thai *mf* **b** *(= language)* Thai *nt*; *(= language family)* Tai *nt*

Thailand [ˈtaɪlænd] N Thailand *nt*

thalidomide [θəˈlɪdəʊmaɪd] N ≈ Contergan® *nt*, Thalidomid *nt*; **~ baby** Contergankind *nt*

thallium [ˈθælɪəm] N *(Chem)* Thallium *nt*

Thames [temz] N Themse *f*; **he'll never set the ~ on fire** *(prov)* er hat das Pulver auch nicht erfunden *(prov)*

than [ðæn, *(weak form)* ðən] ✪ 5.2, 5.3 CONJ als; **I'd rather do anything ~ that** das wäre das Letzte, was ich tun wollte; **no sooner had I sat down ~ he began to talk** kaum hatte ich mich hingesetzt, als er auch schon anfing zu reden; **who better to help us ~ he?** wer könnte uns besser helfen als er? → **more, other ADJ c, rather**

thank [θæŋk] ✪ 20.2, 20.4, 22 VT **a** danken *(+dat)*, sich bedanken bei; **I'll never be able to ~ him (enough) for what he has done** ich kann ihm nie genug dafür danken, was er für mich getan hat; **I don't know how to ~ you** ich weiß nicht, wie ich Ihnen danken soll
b *(phrases)* **he won't ~ you for it** er wird es Ihnen nicht danken; **I'll ~ you to mind your own business** ich wäre Ihnen dankbar, wenn Sie sich nicht einmischen würden; **he has his brother/he only has himself to ~ for this** das hat er seinem Bruder zu verdanken/sich selbst zuzuschreiben
c **~ you** danke (schön); **~ you very much** vielen Dank; **no ~ you** nein, danke; **yes, ~ you** ja, bitte *or* danke; **~ you for coming – not at all, ~ YOU!** vielen Dank, dass Sie gekommen sind – ich danke IHNEN *or* ICH habe zu danken; **~ you for the present** vielen Dank für Ihr Geschenk; **~ you for nothing** *(iro)* vielen Dank auch!; **to say ~ you** danke sagen (*to sb* jdm),

sich bedanken (*to* bei)
d ~ **goodness** *or* **heavens** *or* **God** *(inf)* Gott sei Dank! *(inf)*

thankee ['θæŋkiː] INTERJ *(dial)* = **thank you**, → **thank c**

thankful ['θæŋkfʊl] ADJ dankbar (*to sb* jdm); **to be ~ to sb for sth** jdm für etw dankbar sein; **to be ~ to sb for doing sth** jdm dankbar sein, dass er/sie etw getan hat; **we were ~ to be alive** wir waren dankbar, noch am Leben zu sein; **I'm only ~ that it didn't happen** ich bin bloß froh, dass es nicht passiert ist

thankfully ['θæŋkfəlɪ] ADV dankbar, voller Dankbarkeit; **~, no real harm has been done** zum Glück ist kein wirklicher Schaden entstanden; **~ for my family I wasn't hurt** zum Glück für meine Familie war ich unverletzt

thankfulness ['θæŋkfʊlnɪs] N Dankbarkeit *f*

thankless ['θæŋklɪs] ADJ undankbar; **a ~ task** eine undankbare Aufgabe

thank-offering ['θæŋk,ɒfərɪŋ] N *(lit)* Dankopfer *nt*; *(fig)* Dankesgabe *f*

thanks [θæŋks] ✪ 17.1, 22 PL **a** Dank *m*; **to accept sth with ~** etw dankend *or* mit Dank annehmen; **and that's all the ~ I get** und das ist jetzt der Dank dafür; **to give ~ to God** Gott danksagen *or* Dank sagen; **~ be to God** *(Eccl)* Dank sei Gott
b ~ to wegen *(+gen)*; *(with positive cause also)* dank *(+gen)*; **~ to his coming early ...** weil er so früh kam, ...; **it's all ~ to you that we're so late** bloß deinetwegen kommen wir so spät; **it was no ~ to him that ...** ich hatte/wir hatten *etc* es nicht ihm zu verdanken, dass ...; **you managed it then – yes, no ~ to you** du hast es also doch geschafft – ja, und das habe ich ganz bestimmt nicht dir zu verdanken
INTERJ *(inf)* danke (*for* für); **many ~** vielen *or* herzlichen Dank (*for* für); **~ a lot** *or* **a million** vielen *or* tausend Dank; *(iro)* (na,) vielen Dank *(inf)*; **~ for nothing!** *(iro)* vielen Dank auch!; **will you have some more? – no ~/yes, ~** etwas mehr? – nein/ja, danke

thanksgiving ['θæŋksgɪvɪŋ] N Dankbarkeit *f*

Thanksgiving (Day) ['θæŋksgɪvɪŋ(deɪ)] N *(US)* Thanksgiving Day *m*

> **THANKSGIVING**
>
> **Thanksgiving Day** oder auch einfach nur **Thanksgiving** ist ein Feiertag in den USA, der auf den vierten Donnerstag im November fällt. Er erinnert an das erste Erntedankfest der Pilgrim Fathers, als diese im Jahre 1621 ihre erste erfolgreiche Ernte auf amerikanischem Boden feierten. Deshalb darf bei keinem traditionellen Thanksgiving-Festessen der Truthahnbraten und der Kürbiskuchen fehlen. Bei einem solchen Essen versammelt sich häufig die gesamte Familie, wofür auch lange Anreisen in Kauf genommen werden.
> In Kanada gibt es am zweiten Montag im Oktober einen ähnlichen Feiertag (allerdings ohne den historischen Hintergrund der Pilgrim Fathers) → PILGRIM FATHERS

thank you N Dankeschön *nt*; **he grabbed the book without even a thank-you** er riss das Buch ohne ein Dankeschön *nt or* ohne ein Wort *nt* des Dankes an sich; **thank-you letter** Dankschreiben *nt*

that¹ [ðæt, *(weak form)* ðət] DEM PRON *pl* **those**
a das; **what is ~?** was ist das?; **they all say ~** das sagen alle; **~ is Joe (over there)** das (dort) ist Joe; **who is ~?** wer ist das?; **who is ~ speaking?** wer spricht (denn) da?; *(on phone)* wer ist am Apparat?; **~'s what I say** *or* **think too** das finde ich auch; **if she's as unhappy/stupid** *etc* **as (all) ~** wenn sie so *or* derart unglücklich/dumm *etc* ist; **she's not as stupid as all ~** so dumm ist sie nun auch (wieder) nicht; **I didn't think she'd get/be as angry as ~** ich hätte nicht gedacht, dass sie sich so ärgern würde; **... and all ~** ... und so *(inf)*; **like ~** so; **with luck/talent like ~ ...** bei solchem *or* so einem *(inf)* Glück/Talent ...; **just like ~** einfach so; **~'s got ~/him out of the way** so, das wäre geschafft/den wären wir los; **~'s what I'm here for** dafür bin ich ja hier, das ist meine Aufgabe; **~ is (to say)** das heißt; **oh well, ~'s ~** nun ja, damit ist der Fall erledigt; **there, ~'s ~** so, das wärs; **you can't go and ~'s ~** du darfst nicht gehen, und damit hat sichs *or* und damit basta *(inf)*; **well, ~'s ~ then** das wärs dann also; **so ~ was ~** damit hatte sichs; **~'s it!** das ist es!; *(= the right way)* gut so!, richtig!; *(= finished)* so, das wärs!; *(= the last straw)* jetzt reichts!; **will he come? – ~ he will** *(dial)* kommt er? – (der?) bestimmt
b *(after prep)* **after/before/below/over ~** danach/davor/darunter/darüber; **and ... at ~** und dabei ...; *(= on top of that)* und außerdem ...; **you can get it in any supermarket and quite cheaply at ~** man kann es in jedem Supermarkt, und zwar ganz billig, bekommen; **my watch is broken already and it was my good one at ~** meine Uhr ist schon kaputt und dabei war es meine gute; **what do you mean by ~?** *(not understanding)* was wollen Sie damit sagen?; *(amazed, annoyed)* was soll (denn) das heißen?; **as for ~** was das betrifft *or* angeht; **if things have** *or* **if it has come to ~** wenn es (schon) so weit gekommen ist; **with ~ she got up and left/burst into tears** damit stand sie auf und ging/brach sie in Tränen aus → **leave**
c *(opposed to "this" and "these")* das (da), jenes *(old, geh)*; **I prefer this to ~** dies ist mir lieber als das (da); **~'s the one I like, not this one** das (dort) mag ich, nicht dies (hier)
d *(followed by rel pron)* **this theory is different from ~ which ...** diese Theorie unterscheidet sich von derjenigen, die ...; **~ which we call ...** das, was wir ... nennen
DEM ADJ *pl* **those a** der/die/das, jene(r, s); **what was ~ noise?** was war das für ein Geräusch?; **~ child/dog!** dieses Kind/dieser Hund!; **~ poor girl!** das arme Mädchen!; **I only saw him on ~ one occasion** ich habe ihn nur bei dieser einen Gelegenheit gesehen; **~ morning I had put on my green dress** an jenem Morgen hatte ich mein grünes Kleid an(gezogen); **everyone agreed on ~ point** alle waren sich in dem Punkt einig; **I like ~ one** ich mag das da
b *(in opposition to this)* der/die/das; **I'd like ~ one, not this one** ich möchte das da, nicht dies hier; **she was rushing this way and ~** sie rannte hierhin und dorthin
c *(with poss)* **~ dog of yours!** Ihr Hund, dieser Hund von Ihnen *(inf)*; **what about ~ plan of yours now?** wie steht es denn jetzt mit Ihrem Plan?, was ist denn nun mit Ihrem Plan?
DEM ADV *(inf)* so; **he was at least ~ much taller than me** er war mindestens (um) so viel größer als ich; **it's not ~ good/cold** *etc* SO gut/kalt *etc* ist es auch wieder nicht; **it's not ~ good a film** SO ein guter Film ist es nun auch wieder nicht; **he was ~ angry** er hat sich DERart(ig) geärgert

that² REL PRON **a** der/die/das, die; **all/nothing/everything** *etc* **~ ...** alles/nichts/alles *etc*, was ...; **the best/cheapest** *etc* **~ ...** das Beste/Billigste *etc*, das *or* was ...; **fool ~ I am** ich Idiot; **the girl ~ I told you about** das Mädchen, von dem ich Ihnen erzählt habe; **no-one has come ~ I know of** meines Wissens *or* soviel ich weiß, ist niemand gekommen
b *(with expressions of time)* **the minute ~ he came the phone rang** genau in dem Augenblick, als er kam, klingelte das Telefon; **the day ~ we spent on the beach was one of the hottest** der Tag, den wir am Strand verbrachten, war einer der heißesten; **the day ~ ...** an dem Tag, als ...

that³ CONJ **a** dass; **she promised ~ she would come** sie versprach zu kommen; **he said ~ it was wrong** er sagte, es sei *or* wäre *(inf)* falsch, er sagte, dass es falsch sei *or* wäre *(inf)*; **not ~ I want to do it** nicht (etwa), dass ich das tun wollte → **so b** *(in exclamations)* **~ things** *or* **it should come to this!** dass es so weit kommen konnte!; **oh ~ I could only see you again** *(liter)* oh, dass ich dich doch wiedersehen könnte! *(liter)* **c** *(obs, liter, = in order that)* auf dass *(old)*

thatch [θætʃ] **N a** *(= straw)* Stroh *nt*; *(= reed)* Reet *nt*; *(= roof)* Stroh-/Reetdach *nt* **b** *(inf, = hair)* Mähne *f* VT *roof* mit Stroh/Reet decken

thatched [θætʃt] ADJ → **thatch N a** *cottage* mit Stroh-/Reetdach, stroh-/reetgedeckt; **~ roof** Stroh-/Reetdach *nt*; **to be ~** ein Stroh-/Reetdach haben, mit Stroh/Reet gedeckt sein

thatcher ['θætʃəʳ] N Dachdecker(in) *m(f)*

Thatcherism ['θætʃərɪzəm] N Thatcherismus *m*

Thatcherite ['θætʃəraɪt] N Thatcher-Anhänger(in) *m(f)*, Thatcherist(in) *m(f)* ADJ thatcheristisch

thatching ['θætʃɪŋ] N → **thatch N a** *(= act, skill)* Stroh-/Reetdachdecken *nt*; *(= roofing)* Stroh-/ /Reetdach *nt*

thaw [θɔː] VT auftauen (lassen); *ice, snow also* tauen lassen; *(= make warm) person, hands* aufwärmen; *(fig: = make friendly) person* auftauen *or* warm werden lassen; *relations* entspannen VI *(lit, fig)* auftauen; *(ice, snow)* tauen; *(person: = become warmer)* auftauen, sich aufwärmen; **it is ~ing** es taut N *(lit, fig)* Tauwetter *nt*; **before the ~/a ~ sets in** bevor das Tauwetter einsetzt; **there's been a ~ in relations between ...** die Beziehungen zwischen ... sind aufgetaut

▸ **thaw out** VI *(lit, fig)* auftauen VT *sep (lit) frozen food etc* auftauen (lassen); *person, hands* aufwärmen; *(fig) person* aus der Reserve locken; **it took several whiskies to thaw him out** *(inf)* er brauchte mehrere Whiskys, bis er auftaute *or* warm wurde

the [ðə, *(vor Vokalen auch, zur Betonung auch)* ðiː]
DEF ART **a** der/die/das; **in ~ room** im *or* in dem Zimmer; **on ~ edge** am *or* an dem Rand; **he went up on(to) ~ stage** er ging aufs *or* auf das Podium; **to play ~ piano/guitar** Klavier/Gitarre spielen; **all ~ windows** all die *or* alle Fenster; **have you invited ~ Browns?** haben Sie die Browns *or (with children)* die Familie Brown eingeladen?; **in ~ 20s** in den zwanziger Jahren *or* Zwanzigerjahren *pl*; **Henry ~ Eighth** Heinrich der Achte; **how's ~ leg/wife?** *(inf)* wie gehts dem Bein/Ihrer Frau? *(inf)*
b *(with adj used as n)* das, die; *(with comp or superl)* der/die/das; **~ Good** das Gute; **~ poor/rich** die Armen *pl*/Reichen *pl*; **translated from ~ German** aus dem Deutschen übersetzt; **she was ~ prettier/prettiest** sie war die Hübschere/Hübscheste
c *(denoting whole class)* der/die/das; **~ elephant is in danger of extinction** der Elefant ist vom Aussterben bedroht
d *(distributive use)* **80p ~ pound** 80 Pence das *or* pro Pfund; **by ~ hour** pro Stunde; **~ car does thirty miles to ~ gallon** das Auto braucht eine Gallone auf dreißig Meilen, das Auto verbraucht 11 Liter auf 100km
e [ðiː] *(stressed)* der/die/das; **it's THE restaurant in this part of town** das ist DAS Restaurant in diesem Stadtteil
ADV *(with comp adj or adv)* **all ~ more/better/harder** umso mehr/besser/schwieriger; **~ more he has ~ more he wants** je mehr er hat, desto mehr will er; **(all) ~ more so because ...** umso mehr, als ... → **better²**, **worse**

theatre, *(US)* **theater** ['θɪətəʳ] N **a** Theater *nt*; **to go to the ~** ins Theater gehen; **what's on at the ~?** was wird im Theater gegeben? **b** *no pl* *(= theatrical business, drama)* Theater *nt*; **he's always been keen on (the) ~** er war schon immer theaterbegeistert; **he has been in (the) ~ all his life** er war sein Leben lang beim Theater; **not all Shaw's plays are good ~** nicht alle Stücke von Shaw eignen sich für die Bühne **c** *(Brit: = operating theatre)* Operationssaal *m* **d** *(= scene of events)* Schauplatz *m*; **~ of war** Kriegsschauplatz *m*; **~ of operations** Schauplatz *m* der Handlungen

theatre, *(US)* **theater**: **theatre company** N Theaterensemble *nt*; *(touring)* Schauspiel- *or* Theatertruppe *f*; **theatre critic** N Theaterkritiker(in) *m(f)*; **theatregoer**, *(US)* **theatergoer** N Theaterbesucher(in) *m(f)*

theatreland [ˈθɪətəlænd] N *(Brit)* Theatergegend *f*; **in ~** in der Theatergegend

theatre nuclear weapon N *(Mil)* taktische Atomwaffe

theatre nurse N *(Brit Med)* Op-Schwester *f*

theatrical [θɪˈætrɪkəl] ADJ **a** Theater-; **~ production** Theaterproduktion *f* **b** *(pej) behaviour etc* theatralisch; **there was something very ~ about him** er hatte etwas sehr Theatralisches an sich N **theatricals** PL Theaterspielen *nt*; **most people have taken part in ~s** die meisten Menschen haben schon mal Theater gespielt

theatrical agent N Theateragent(in) *m(f)*

theatrical company N Theater- *or* Schauspieltruppe *f*

theatricality [θɪˌætrɪˈkælɪtɪ] N theatralische Art

theatrically [θɪˈætrɪkəlɪ] ADV **a** schauspielerisch; **~ it was a disaster** vom Theaterstandpunkt war das eine Katastrophe **b** *(pej) behave, speak* theatralisch

theatrical producer N Theaterproduzent(in) *m(f)*

thee [ðiː] PRON *(old, dial: objective case of thou, dir obj, with prep +acc)* Euch *(obs)*, dich *(also Eccl)*; *(indir obj, with prep +dat)* Euch *(obs)*, dir *(also Eccl)*; **God be with ~** Gott sei mit dir; **for ~ and thine** für dich und die deinen *or* Deinen

theft [θeft] N Diebstahl *m*

their [ðɛəʳ] POSS ADJ **a** ihr **b** *(inf: = belonging to him or her)* seine(r, s); **everyone knows ~ rights nowadays** jeder kennt heutzutage seine Rechte → *also* **my POSS ADJ**

theirs [ðɛəz] POSS PRON **a** ihre(r, s); **~ is not to reason why** es ist nicht an ihnen zu fragen; **~ is the Kingdom of Heaven** ihrer ist das Himmelreich **b** *(inf: = belonging to him or her)* seine(r, s) → *also* **mine[1] POSS PRON**

theism [ˈθiːɪzəm] N Theismus *m*

theist [ˈθiːɪst] N Theist(in) *m(f)*

theistic [θiːˈɪstɪk] ADJ theistisch

them [ðem, *(weak form)* ðəm] PERS PRON *pl* **a** *(dir obj, with prep +acc)* sie; *(indir obj, with prep +dat)* ihnen; **both of ~ saw me** beide haben mich gesehen; **neither of ~ saw me** keiner von beiden hat mich gesehen; **give me a few of ~** geben Sie mir ein paar davon; **none of ~** keiner/keinen (von ihnen); **he's one of ~** das ist einer von ihnen; *(= homosexual)* er ist andersrum *(inf)* **b** *(emph)* sie; **~ and us** *(inf)* sie *or* die *(inf)* und wir; **it's ~** sie sinds; **it's ~ who did it** SIE *or* DIE haben es gemacht **c** *(dial, incorrect)* **~ as wants to** die, die wollen ADJ *(incorrect)* diese

thematic ADJ, **thematically** ADV [θɪˈmætɪk, -əlɪ] thematisch

theme [θiːm] ✪ 26.2 N **a** *(= subject)* Thema *nt* **b** *(US Sch: = essay)* Aufsatz *m* **c** *(Mus)* Thema *nt*; *(Film, TV)* Thema *nt*, Melodie *f* *(from* aus)

themed [θiːmd] ADJ *(esp Brit) place* thematisch gestaltet; *event* thematisch ausgerichtet

theme: **theme evening** N *(TV etc)* Themenabend *m*; **theme music** N *(Film)* Titelmusik *f*; *(TV)* Erkennungsmelodie *f*; **theme park** N Themenpark *m*; **theme party** N Mottoparty *f* *(Party, die unter einem bestimmten Motto steht)*; **theme pub** N *(Brit) Lokal, das einem bestimmten Thema entsprechend ausgestattet ist*, Themenkneipe *f*; **theme restaurant** N erlebnisgastronomisches Restaurant, Themenrestaurant *nt*; **theme song** N *(Film)* Titelsong *m*; *(TV)* Erkennungssong *m*; *(of opera)* Leitmotiv *nt*; **theme tune** N = **theme music**

themselves [ðəmˈselvz] PERS PRON *pl* **a** *(reflexive)* sich **b** *(emph)* selbst; **the figures ~** die Zahlen selbst *or* an sich → *also* **myself**

then [ðen] ADV **a** *(= next, afterwards)* dann; **and ~ what happened?** und was geschah dann?

b *(= at this particular time)* da; *(= in those days)* damals; **it was ~ 8 o'clock** da war es 8 Uhr; **I was/will be in Paris ~** ich war da (gerade) in Paris/werde da in Paris sein; **he did it ~ and there** *or* **there and ~** er hat es auf der Stelle getan → **now**

c *(after prep)* **from ~ on(wards)** von da an; **before ~** vorher, zuvor; **but they had gone by ~** aber da waren sie schon weg; **we'll be ready by ~** bis dahin sind wir fertig; **since ~** seitdem, seit der Zeit; **between now and ~** bis dahin; **(up) until ~ I had never tried it** bis dahin hatte ich es nie versucht

d *(= in that case)* dann; **I don't want that – ~ what DO you want?** ich will das nicht – was willst du denn?; **what are you going to do, ~?** was wollen Sie dann tun?; **but ~ that means that ...** das bedeutet ja aber dann, dass ...; **all right, ~** also *or* dann meinetwegen; **so it's true ~** dann ist es (also) wahr, es ist also wahr; **(so) I was right ~** ich hatte also recht; **you don't want it ~?** Sie wollen es also nicht?, dann wollen Sie es (also) nicht?; **where is it ~?** wo ist es denn?

e *(= furthermore, and also)* dann, außerdem; **(and) ~ there's my aunt** und dann ist da noch meine Tante; **but ~ ...** aber ... auch; **but ~ he's my son** aber er ist (eben) auch mein Sohn; **but ~ again he is my friend** aber andererseits ist er mein Freund

f *(phrases)* **now ~, what's the matter?** na, was ist denn los?; **come on ~** nun komm doch

ADJ *attr* damalig; **the ~ Prime Minister** der damalige Premierminister

thence [ðens] ADV **a** *(old: = from that place)* von dannen *(old)*, von dort *or* da (weg) **b** *(old, = from that time)* **which dated from ~** was aus der (damaligen) Zeit stammt; **they met again a week ~** sie trafen eine Woche darauf wieder zusammen **c** *(form: = for that reason)* infolgedessen

thenceforth [ˌðensˈfɔːθ] ADV von da an, von der Zeit an

theocracy [θɪˈɒkrəsɪ] N Theokratie *f*

theocratic [ˌθɪəˈkrætɪk] ADJ theokratisch

theodolite [θɪˈɒdəlaɪt] N Theodolit *m*

theologian [ˌθɪəˈləʊdʒən] N Theologe *m*, Theologin *f*

theological [ˌθɪəˈlɒdʒɪkəl] ADJ theologisch; **~ college** Priesterseminar *nt*; **~ student** Theologiestudent(in) *m(f)*

theology [θɪˈɒlədʒɪ] N Theologie *f*

theorem [ˈθɪərəm] N Satz *m* *(also Math)*, Theorem *nt* *(geh, spec)*

theoretic(al) [θɪəˈretɪk(əl)] ADJ theoretisch

theoretically [θɪəˈretɪkəlɪ] ADV theoretisch

theoretician [ˌθɪərəˈtɪʃən], **theorist** [ˈθɪərɪst] N Theoretiker(in) *m(f)*

theorize [ˈθɪəraɪz] VI theoretisieren

theorizer [ˈθɪəraɪzəʳ] N Theoretiker(in) *m(f)*

theory [ˈθɪərɪ] N Theorie *f*; **in ~** theoretisch, in der Theorie; **~ of colour/evolution** Farben-/Evolutionslehre *or* -theorie *f*; **he has a ~ that ...** er hat die Theorie, dass ...; **well, it's a ~** das ist eine Möglichkeit; **he always goes on the ~ that ...** er geht immer davon aus, dass ...

theosophical [θɪəˈsɒfɪkəl] ADJ theosophisch

theosophist [θɪˈɒsəfɪst] N Theosoph(in) *m(f)*

theosophy [θɪˈɒsəfɪ] N Theosophie *f*

therapeutic(al) [ˌθerəˈpjuːtɪk(əl)] ADJ therapeutisch; **to be therapeutic** therapeutisch wirken

therapeutic community N Therapiegruppe *f*

therapeutics [ˌθerəˈpjuːtɪks] N *sing* Therapeutik *f*

therapeutic touch N Therapie *f* durch Handauflegen

therapist [ˈθerəpɪst] N Therapeut(in) *m(f)*

therapy [ˈθerəpɪ] N Therapie *f*

there [ðɛəʳ] ADV **a** dort, da; *(with movement)* dorthin, dahin; **look, ~'s Joe/~'s Joe coming** guck mal, da ist/kommt Joe; **it's under/over/in ~** es liegt dort *or* da drunter/drüben/drin; **put it under/over/in/on ~** stellen Sie es dort *or* da drunter/rüber *or* hinüber/rein *or* hinein/drauf *or* hinauf; **let's stop ~** hören wir doch da auf; *(travelling)* halten wir doch da *or* dort an; **~ and back** hin und zurück; **so ~ we were** da waren wir nun also; **is Gordon ~ please?** *(on telephone)* ist Gordon da?; **to be ~ for sb** *(inf: = supportive)* für jdn da sein

b *(fig: = on this point)* da; **~ you are wrong** da irren Sie sich; **you've got me ~** da bin ich überfragt; **I've got you ~** da *or* jetzt habe ich Sie

c *(in phrases)* **~ is/are** es *or* da ist/sind; *(= there exists/exist also)* es gibt; **~ were three of us** wir waren zu dritt; **~ is a mouse in the room** es ist eine Maus im Zimmer; **~ was once a castle here** hier war *or* stand einmal eine Burg; **~ is a chair in the corner** in der Ecke steht ein Stuhl; **~ is dancing afterwards** danach ist Tanz, danach wird getanzt; **is ~ any beer?** ist Bier da?; **~'s a book I want to read** da ist ein Buch, das ich lesen möchte; **afterwards ~ was coffee** anschließend gab es Kaffee; **is ~ any wine left? – well, ~ was** ist noch Wein da? – gerade war noch welcher da; **~ isn't any food/time/point, is ~? – yes ~ is** es gibt wohl nichts zu essen/dazu haben wir wohl keine Zeit/das hat wohl keinen Sinn, oder? – doch!; **~ seems to be no-one at home** es scheint keiner zu Hause zu sein; **~ appears to be a flaw in your argument** da scheint ein Fehler in Ihrer Beweisführung zu sein; **how many mistakes were ~?** wie viele Fehler waren es?; **~ is a page missing** es *or* da fehlt eine Seite; **~ comes a time when ...** es kommt eine Zeit, wo ...; **~ being no alternative solution** da es keine andere Lösung gibt; **~ will be an opportunity for shopping** es wird Gelegenheit zum Einkaufen geben; **God said: let ~ be light, and ~ was light** und Gott sprach: es werde Licht! und es ward Licht; **hi ~!** hallo!; **~ you go again** *(inf)* jetzt gehts schon wieder los; **now ~'s a real woman** das ist eine richtige Frau; **~'s gratitude for you!** *(iro)* da haben Sie Ihren Dank!; **now ~'s a good idea!** (das ist) eine gute Idee!; **so ~!** ätsch!; **~ you are** *(giving sb sth)* hier(, bitte)!; *(on finding sb)* da sind Sie ja!; **~ you** *or* **we are, you see, I knew he'd say that** na, sehen Sie, ich habe es ja gewusst, dass er das sagen würde; **wait, I'll help you ... ~ you are!** warten Sie, ich helfe Ihnen, ... so(, das wärs)!; **you press the switch and ~ you are!** Sie brauchen nur den Schalter zu drücken, das ist alles; **I can't dance, but ~ again, I never could** ich kann nicht tanzen, aber das habe ich eigentlich noch nie gekonnt

INTERJ **~! ~!** na, na!; **stop crying now, ~'s a good boy** hör auf zu weinen, na komm; **drop it, ~'s a good dog** lass das fallen, komm, sei brav; **now ~'s a good boy, don't tease your sister** komm, sei ein braver Junge und ärgere deine Schwester nicht; **hey, you ~!** *(inf)* he, Sie da!; **hurry up ~** *(inf)* Beeilung!, Tempo, Tempo! *(inf)*; **make way ~** Platz da!, machen Sie mal Platz!; **~, take this to your mother** da, bring das deiner Mutter; **but ~, what's the good of talking about it?** was solls, es hat doch keinen Zweck, darüber zu reden; **~! I knew it would break!** da! ich habs ja gewusst, dass es kaputtgehen würde!

thereabouts [ˌðɛərəˈbaʊts] ADV **a** *(place)* dort in der Nähe, dort irgendwo **b** *(quantity, degree)* **five pounds/fifteen or ~** so um die fünf Pfund/fünfzehn (herum); **four o'clock or ~** so um vier Uhr herum *(inf)*; **is it ten dollars I owe you? – ~** schulde ich dir nicht zehn Dollar? – so ungefähr

thereafter [ˌðɛərˈɑːftəʳ] ADV *(form)* danach, darauf *(geh)*

thereby [ˌðɛəˈbaɪ] ADV dadurch, damit; **and ~ hangs a tale** und da gibt es eine Geschichte dazu

therefore [ˈðɛəfɔːʳ] ✪ 17.1, 26.1, 26.3 ADV deshalb, daher; *(as logical consequence)* also; **so ~ I was wrong** ich hatte also unrecht; **we can deduce, ~, that ...** wir können also *or* daher folgern, dass ...

therein [ˌðɛərˈɪn] ADV *(form)* **a** *(= in that particular)* darin, in dieser Hinsicht; **~ lies the problem** darin liegt das Problem **b** *(= in that place)* darin, dort

thereof [ˌðɛər'ɒv] ADV *(form)* davon; **this town and the citizens ~** diese Stadt und deren Bürger; **a charge of ten pounds per hour or part ~** eine Gebühr von zehn Pfund pro angefangene Stunde

thereon [ˌðɛər'ɒn] ADV *(form: = on that)* darauf; *(= on that subject)* darüber

there's [ðɛəz] *contr of* **there is, there has**

thereto [ˌðɛə'tu:] ADV *(form)* damit; **official business and all expenses related ~** offizielle Geschäfte und alle damit verbundenen Ausgaben

thereunder [ˌðɛər'ʌndə'] ADV *(form)* darunter

thereupon [ˌðɛərə'pɒn] ADV **a** *(= then, at that point)* darauf(hin) **b** *(form: = on that subject)* darüber; *(= on that)* darauf

therewith [ˌðɛə'wɪθ] ADV *(form)* **a** *(= with that)* damit **b** *(= thereupon)* darauf

therm [θɜ:m] N *(Brit)* 100.000 Wärmeeinheiten (ca. 10^8 Joules)

thermal ['θɜ:məl] ADJ **a** *(Phys)* Wärme-; *neutron, reactor, equilibrium* thermisch; **~ expansion** Wärmeausdehnung *f*; **~ power station** Wärmekraftwerk *nt* **b** *clothing* Thermo-; **~ socks** Thermosocken *pl*; **~ blanket** Aluminiumdecke *f*; **~ underwear** Thermounterwäsche *f* N **a** *(Aviat, Met)* Thermik *f no pl* **b** **thermals** PL *(inf: = thermal underwear)* Thermounterwäsche *f*

thermal: **thermal barrier** N *(Phys, Aviat)* Temperatur- *or* Hitzebarriere *f*; **thermal baths** PL Thermalbäder *pl*; **thermal conductivity** N Wärmeleitfähigkeit *f*; **thermal imager** N Thermograf *m*; **thermal imaging** N Thermografie *f*; **thermal imaging system** N Thermografiesystem *nt*; **thermal paper** N Thermopapier *nt*; **thermal printer** N *(Comput)* Thermodrucker *m*; **thermal spa** N Thermalbad *nt*; **thermal spring** N Thermalquelle *f*; **thermal transfer** N Thermotransfer *m*; **thermal unit** N Wärmeeinheit *f*

thermic ['θɜ:mɪk] ADJ thermisch

thermionic [ˌθɜ:mɪ'ɒnɪk] ADJ thermionisch, glühelektrisch; **~ valve** *(Brit) or* **tube** *(US)* Glühelektronenröhre *f*

thermistor ['θɜ:mɪstə'] N *(Tech)* Heißleiter *m*, Thermistor *m*

thermo [θɜ:məʊ-]: **thermodynamic** ADJ thermodynamisch; **thermodynamics** PL Thermodynamik *f*; **thermoelectric** ADJ thermoelektrisch; **thermoelectricity** N Thermoelektrizität *f*

thermomat N Isomatte *f*

thermometer [θə'mɒmɪtə'] N Thermometer *nt*

thermo: **thermonuclear** ADJ thermonuklear; **~ war** Thermonuklearkrieg *m*; **~ strike** Thermonuklearschlag *m*; **~ weapon** Thermonuklearwaffe *f*; **thermopile** N Thermosäule *f*; **thermoplastic** ADJ thermoplastisch N Thermoplast *m*

Thermos® ['θɜ:məs] N *(also* **Thermos flask** *or (US)* **bottle***)* Thermosflasche® *f*

thermostat ['θɜ:məstæt] N Thermostat *m*

thermostatic [ˌθɜ:mə'stætɪk] ADJ thermostatisch; **~ regulator/switch** Temperaturregler *m*/-schalter *m*

thermostatically [ˌθɜ:mə'stætɪkəlɪ] ADV thermostatisch

thermotherapy [ˌθɜ:mə'θerəpɪ] N *(Med)* Thermotherapie *f (spec)*, Wärmebehandlung *f*

thesaurus [θɪ'sɔ:rəs] N Thesaurus *m*

these [ði:z] ADJ, PRON diese → **this**

thesis ['θi:sɪs] N *pl* **theses** ['θi:si:z] **a** *(= argument)* These *f* **b** *(Univ, for PhD)* Dissertation *f*, Doktorarbeit *f (inf)*; *(for diploma)* Diplomarbeit *f*

thespian ['θespɪən] *(liter, hum)* ADJ dramatisch; **~ art** Schauspielkunst *f* N Mime *m*, Mimin *f*

they [ðeɪ] PERS PRON *pl* **a** sie; **~ are very good people** es sind sehr gute Leute; **it is ~** *(form)* sie sind es; **~ who** diejenigen, die *or* welche, wer *(+sing vb)* **b** *(= people in general)* **~ say that ...** man sagt, dass ...; **~ are going to build a new road** man will *or* sie wollen eine neue Straße bauen; **~ are thinking of changing the law** es ist beabsichtigt, das Gesetz zu ändern **c** *(inf)* **if anyone looks at this closely, ~ will notice ...** wenn sich das jemand näher ansieht, wird er bemerken ...

they'd [ðeɪd] *contr of* **they had, they would**

they'd've ['ðeɪdəv] *contr of* **they would have**

they'll [ðeɪl] *contr of* **they will**

they're [ðɛə'] *contr of* **they are**

they've [ðeɪv] *contr of* **they have**

thiamine ['θaɪəmi:n] N Thiamin *nt*

thick [θɪk] ADJ *(+er)* **a** dick; *thread, legs, arms* dick, stark; *lips* dick, voll; **a wall three feet ~** eine drei Fuß dicke *or* starke Wand; **to give sb a ~ ear** *(Brit inf)* jdm ein paar hinter die Ohren hauen *(inf)*; **you'll get a ~ ear in a minute** *(Brit inf)* du kriegst gleich ein paar hinter die Ohren! *(inf)*; **the shelves were ~ with dust** auf den Regalen lag dick der Staub; **to have a ~ head** einen Brummschädel haben *(inf)*, einen dicken Kopf haben *(inf)*

b *hair, fog, smoke* dick, dicht; *forest, hedge, beard* dicht; *liquid, sauce, syrup etc* dick(flüssig); *mud* dick; *darkness* tief; *night* undurchdringlich; *crowd* dicht (gedrängt); *air* schlecht, dick *(inf)*; *(= airless) atmosphere* schwer; *(= unclear) voice* träge; *accent* stark, breit; **they are ~ on the ground** *(inf)* die gibt es wie Sand am Meer *(inf)*; **the hedgerows were ~ with wild flowers** die Hecken strotzten von wilden Blumen; **the streets are ~ with people/traffic** die Straßen sind voller Menschen/Verkehr; **his voice was ~ with a cold/emotion/fear/drink** er sprach mit belegter/bewegter/angstvoller Stimme/schwerer Zunge; **the air is pretty ~ in here** hier ist eine Luft zum Schneiden, hier ist sehr schlechte Luft; **the air is ~ with rumours** Gerüchte liegen in der Luft

c *(Brit inf: = stupid) person* dumm, doof *(inf)*; **to get sth into** *or* **through sb's ~ head** etw in jds dicken Schädel bekommen *(inf)*; **as ~ as a brick** *or* **as two (short) planks** dumm wie ein Brett *(inf)*, strohdoof *(inf)*

d *(inf: = intimate)* **they are very ~** sie sind dicke Freunde *(inf)*; **to be very ~ with sb** mit jdm eine dicke Freundschaft haben *(inf)*

e *(inf: = much)* **that's a bit ~!** das ist ein starkes Stück *(inf)*

N **a** **in the ~ of the crowd** mitten in der Menge; **to be in the ~ of the fighting** im dicksten Kampfgetümmel stecken; **in the ~ of it** mittendrin; **he likes to be in the ~ of things** er ist gern bei allem voll dabei; **to stick together through ~ and thin** zusammen durch dick und dünn gehen

b *(of finger, leg)* dickste Stelle; **the ~ of the calf** die Wade

ADV *(+er) spread, lie, cut* dick; *grow* dicht; **the snow lay ~** es lag eine dichte Schneedecke; **his blows fell ~ and fast** seine Schläge prasselten nieder; **offers of help poured in ~ and fast** es kam eine Flut von Hilfsangeboten; **they are falling ~ and fast** sie fallen um wie die Fliegen *(inf)*; **the jokes came ~ and fast** die Witze kamen Schlag auf Schlag; **to lay it on ~** *(inf)* (zu) dick auftragen *(inf)*; **that's laying it on a bit ~** *(inf)* das ist ja wohl etwas übertrieben

thicken ['θɪkən] VT *sauce etc* eindicken VI **a** *(fog, hair, crowd, forest)* dichter werden; *(smoke, darkness)* sich verdichten; *(sauce, mixture)* dick werden **b** *(fig: plot, mystery)* immer verwickelter *or* undurchsichtiger werden; **aha, the plot ~s!** aha, jetzt wirds interessant!

thickener ['θɪkənə'], **thickening** ['θɪkənɪŋ] N *(for sauces)* Bindemittel *nt*

thicket ['θɪkɪt] N Dickicht *nt*

thick: **thick-flowing** ADJ dickflüssig; **thickhead** ['θɪkhed] N *(inf)* Dummkopf *m*; **thickheaded** ADJ *(inf)* dumm, doof *(inf)*; **thickheadedness** N *(inf)* Dummheit *f*, Doofheit *f (inf)*

thickie ['θɪkɪ] N *(Brit inf)* Dummkopf *m*, Doofkopf *m (inf)*, Doofi *m (inf)*

thick-lipped ['θɪklɪpt] ADJ mit dicken *or* wulstigen Lippen, mit Wulstlippen

thickly ['θɪklɪ] ADV **a** *spread, paint, cut* dick; *populated, crowded, wooded* dicht **b** *(= deeply) lie* dick; **to be ~ covered with sth** dick mit etw bedeckt sein; **to be ~ carpeted** mit einem dicken Teppich ausgelegt sein; **snow was falling ~** dichter Schnee fiel; **the ~ falling snow** der dicht fallende Schnee **c** *speak (with a cold)* mit belegter Stimme; *(with drink)* mit schwerer Zunge; *(with emotion)* bewegt; *(with fear)* angstvoll

thickness ['θɪknɪs] N **a** Dicke *f*; *(of wall, thread, legs, arms also)* Stärke *f*; **the ~ of his lips** seine dicken *or* wulstigen Lippen; **it is sold in three different ~es** es wird in drei verschiedenen Dicken *or* Stärken verkauft **b** *(of hair, fog, smoke)* Dicke *f*; *(of forest, hedge, beard)* Dichte *f*; *(of liquid, sauce, syrup etc)* Dickflüssigkeit *f*; *(of accent)* Stärke *f*; **the ~ of his voice** *(through cold)* seine belegte Stimme; *(through drink)* seine schwere Zunge; *(through emotion)* seine bewegte Stimme; *(through fear)* seine bebende Stimme **c** *(= layer)* Lage *f*, Schicht *f*

thicko ['θɪkəʊ] N *(inf)* = **thickie**

thick: **thickset** ADJ gedrungen; *hedge* dicht; **thick-skinned** ADJ *(lit)* dickhäutig; *(fig)* dickfellig

thick-witted ADJ, **thick-wittedly** ADV dumm, begriffsstutzig

thicky ['θɪkɪ] N *(inf)* = **thickie**

thief [θi:f] N *pl* **thieves** [θi:vz] Dieb(in) *m(f)*; **to set a ~ to catch a ~** *(prov)* einen vom Fach benutzen; **to be as thick as thieves** *(Brit)* dicke Freunde sein *(inf)*

thieve [θi:v] VTI stehlen

thievery ['θi:vərɪ] N *(= theft)* Diebstahl *m*

thieving ['θi:vɪŋ] ADJ *magpie* diebisch; **keep your ~ hands off my cigarettes** lass die Finger weg von meinen Zigaretten *(inf)*; **this ~ lot** *(inf)* diese Räuberbande *(inf)* N *(= thefts)* Stehlen *nt*, Diebstähle *pl*

thievish ['θi:vɪʃ] ADJ diebisch *attr*

thievishness ['θi:vɪʃnɪs] N diebische Art

thigh [θaɪ] N (Ober)schenkel *m*

thigh: **thighbone** N Oberschenkelknochen *m*; **thigh-length** ADJ *boots* übers Knie reichend; *coat* kurz

thimble ['θɪmbl] N Fingerhut *m*

thimbleful ['θɪmblfʊl] N *(fig)* Fingerhut *m* (voll)

thimble printer N *(Comput)* Thimbledrucker *m*

thin [θɪn] ADJ *(+er)* **a** *(= not fat)* dünn; **as ~ as a rake** *(Brit) or* **rail** *(US)* dünn wie eine Bohnenstange

b *(= not thick) paper, slice, string, wall, blood, dress* dünn; *liquid* dünn(flüssig); *(= narrow) column* schmal

c *(= sparse) hair, grass* dünn, schütter; *eyebrows* schütter, licht; *vegetation* gering, spärlich, kümmerlich *(pej)*; *population, crowd* klein, kümmerlich *(pej)*; **his hair is getting quite ~** sein Haar lichtet sich; **he's a bit ~ on top** bei ihm lichtet es sich oben schon ein wenig; **to be ~ on the ground** *(fig)* dünn gesät sein

d *(= not dense) fog* leicht; *air* dünn; **to vanish into ~ air** *(fig)* sich in Luft auflösen; **the agent simply vanished into ~ air** der Agent schien sich einfach in Luft aufgelöst zu haben; **to appear out of ~ air** aus dem Nichts auftauchen

e *(fig: = weak, poor) voice, smile* schwach, dünn; *excuse* schwach, fadenscheinig; *disguise, story line, plot* schwach; *trading, profits* gering; **a ~ majority** eine knappe Mehrheit; **she had a ~ time of it** *(dated inf)* es war nicht gerade schön für sie; **to give sb a ~ time of it** *(dated inf)* jdm das Leben schwer machen

ADV *(+er) spread, cut* dünn; *lie* dünn, spärlich

VT *paint, sauce, ozone layer* verdünnen; *trees, ranks* lichten; *hair* ausdünnen; *blood* dünner werden lassen

VI *(fog, crowd)* sich lichten; *(hair also)* schütter werden; *(ozone layer)* dünner werden; *(population)* abnehmen

▸ **thin down** VI dünner werden; *(person also)* abnehmen, schlanker werden VT *sep paint, sauce* verdünnen

▸ **thin out** VI *(fog)* sich lichten, schwächer werden; *(crowd)* kleiner werden; *(audience)* sich lichten; *(hair)* sich lichten, schütter werden; **the trees started thinning out** die Bäume lichteten sich VT *sep hair* ausdünnen; *seedlings also* verziehen; *forest* lichten; *population* verkleinern

thine [ðaɪn] *(old, dial)* POSS PRON der/die/das deine *or* Deine; **for thee and ~** für dich und die deinen *or* Deinen → **mine**[1] POSS ADJ *(only before vowel)* Euer/Eure/Euer *(obs)*, dein/deine/dein *(also Eccl)*

thing [θɪŋ] N **a** *(= any material object)* Ding *nt*; **a ~ of beauty/great value** etwas Schönes/sehr Wertvolles; **she likes sweet ~s** sie mag Süßes *or* süße Sachen; **what's that ~?** was ist das?; **I don't have a ~ to wear** ich habe nichts zum Anziehen
b things PL *(= clothes, equipment, belongings)* Sachen *pl*; **have you got your swimming ~s?** hast du dein Badezeug *or* deine Badesachen dabei?; **they washed up the breakfast ~s** sie spülten das Frühstücksgeschirr **c** *(non material: = affair, subject)* Sache *f*; **you know, it's a funny ~** wissen Sie, es ist schon seltsam; **the odd/best ~ about it is ...** das Seltsame/Beste daran ist, ...; **it's a good ~ I came** nur gut, dass ich gekommen bin; **it's a bad/strange ~ but ...** es ist schlecht/seltsam, aber ...; **to make a big ~ of** *or* **about sth** viel Lärm um etw machen; **to make a big ~ of** *or* **about doing sth** eine große Sache daraus machen, dass man etw tut; **he's on to** *or* **onto a good ~** *(inf)* er hat da was Gutes aufgetan *(inf)*; **he's got a good ~ going there** *(inf)* der hat da was Gutes laufen *(inf)*; **what a (silly) ~ to do** wie kann man nur so was (Dummes) tun!; **you take the ~ too seriously** Sie nehmen die Sache *or* das zu ernst; **there is one/one other ~ I want to ask you** eines/und noch etwas möchte ich Sie fragen; **and there's another ~, why didn't you ...?** und noch etwas, warum haben Sie nicht ...?; **it's one ~ to talk about it, it's another to do it** es ist eine Sache, davon zu reden, eine völlig andere, es dann auch zu tun; **the ~s you do/say!** was du so machst/sagst!; **I must be hearing/seeing ~s!** ich glaube, ich höre/sehe nicht richtig, ich glaube, ich spinne! *(inf)*; **all the ~s I meant to say/do** alles, was ich sagen/tun wollte; **which ~s in life do you value most?** was *or* welche Dinge im Leben bewerten Sie am höchsten?; **to expect great ~s of sb/sth** Großes *or* große Dinge von jdm/etw erwarten; **I must think ~s over** ich muss mir die Sache *or* das überlegen; **~s are going from bad to worse** es wird immer schlimmer; **as ~s stand at the moment, as ~s are ...** so wie die Dinge im Moment liegen; **how are ~s (with you)?** wie gehts (bei) Ihnen?; **since that's how ~s are ...** wenn das so ist ..., in dem Fall ...; **it's bad enough as ~s are** es ist schon schlimm genug; **~s aren't what they used to be** es ist alles nicht mehr so wie früher; **to talk of one ~ and another** von diesem und jenem reden; **taking one ~ with another** im Großen und Ganzen, alles in allem; **it's been one ~ after the other (going wrong)** es kam eins zum anderen; **if it's not one ~ it's the other** es ist immer irgendetwas; **(what) with one ~ and another I haven't had time to do it yet** ich bin einfach noch nicht dazu gekommen; **it's neither one ~ nor the other** es ist weder das eine noch das andere; **one ~ led to another** eins führte zum anderen; **for one ~ it doesn't make sense** erst einmal ergibt das überhaupt keinen Sinn; **not to see/understand a ~** (absolut) nichts sehen/verstehen; **not to know a ~** (absolut) nichts wissen, keine Ahnung haben; **to tell sb a ~ or two** jdm einiges erzählen; **he knows a ~ or two** er hat etwas auf dem Kasten *(inf)*; **he knows a ~ or two about cars** er kennt sich mit Autos aus; **it's just one of those ~s** so was kommt eben vor *(inf)*; **in all ~s** in allem → **teach**
d *(= person, animal)* Ding *nt*; **poor little ~** das arme (kleine) Ding!; **you poor ~!** du Arme(r)!; **she's a funny old ~** sie ist ein komisches altes Haus *(inf)*; **I say, old ~** *(dated inf)* na, du altes Haus *(inf)*; **lucky ~!** der/die Glückliche/du Glückliche(r)!; **he looks quite the ~** er sieht (richtig) nach etwas aus
e *(= what is suitable, best)* **that's just the ~ for me** das ist genau das Richtige für mich; **that's not the ~ to do** so was macht *or* tut man nicht; **his behaviour isn't quite the ~** *(dated)* sein Benehmen ist nicht gerade berückend *(inf)*; **the latest ~ in ties** der letzte Schrei in der Krawattenmode; **the ~ to do now would be ...** was wir jetzt machen sollten, wäre ...; **that would be the honourable ~ to do** es wäre nur anständig, das zu tun
f *(in phrases)* **I'm not at my best first ~ in the morning** so früh am Morgen bin ich nicht gerade in Hochform; **I'll do that first ~ in the morning** ich werde das gleich *or* als Erstes morgen früh tun; **I'll do it first ~** ich werde das zuerst *or* als Erstes tun; **last ~ at night** vor dem Schlafengehen; **painting is his ~** das Malen liegt ihm *(inf)*; **the ~ is to know when ...** man muss wissen, wann ...; **yes, but the ~ is ...** ja, aber ...; **the ~ is we haven't got enough money** die Sache ist die, wir haben nicht genug Geld; **the ~ is, you see, he loves her** das Problem ist, dass er sie liebt; **yes but the ~ is it won't work** ja, aber das Dumme ist, es funktioniert nicht; **to do one's own ~** *(inf)* tun, was man will; **when Michael Jackson starts doing his ~** *(inf)* wenn Michael Jackson seine Schau abzieht *(inf)*; **she's got this ~ about Sartre/dogs** *(inf: = can't stand)* sie kann Sartre/Hunde einfach nicht ausstehen; *(= is fascinated by)* sie hat einen richtigen Sartre-/Hundefimmel *(inf)*; **she's got a ~ about spiders** *(inf)* bei Spinnen dreht sie durch *(inf)*; **he's got a ~ about her** *(inf: = can't stand)* er kann sie nicht ausstehen; *(= is infatuated with)* er ist verrückt nach ihr
g (all) ~s German/mystical/mechanical alles Deutsche/Geheimnisvolle/Mechanische
h *(inf, for forgotten name of person)* Dings(-bums) *mf (inf)*

thingummybob ['θɪŋəmɪ,bɒb], **thingamajig** ['θɪŋəmɪ,dʒɪg], **thingummy** ['θɪŋəmɪ] N Dings(-da) *nt or (for people) mf*, Dingsbums *nt or (for people) mf*

think [θɪŋk] ✪ 6.2, 16.1, 26.2 *vb: pret, ptp* **thought** VI denken; **to ~ to oneself** sich *(dat)* denken; **I was just sitting there ~ing to myself** ich saß so in Gedanken da; **~ before you speak/act** denk nach *or* überleg, bevor du sprichst/handelst; **do animals ~?** können Tiere denken?; **to act without ~ing** unüberlegt handeln; *(= stupidly also)* unbedacht handeln; **~ again!** denk noch mal nach; **so you ~ I'll give you the money? well, you'd better ~ again!** du denkst also, ich gebe dir das Geld? das hast du dir (wohl) gedacht!; **it makes you ~** es macht *or* stimmt einen nachdenklich; **I need time to ~** ich brauche Zeit zum Nachdenken; **it's so noisy you can't hear yourself ~** bei so einem Lärm kann doch kein Mensch denken; **now let me ~** lass (mich) mal überlegen *or* nachdenken; **stop and ~ before you make a big decision** denke in aller Ruhe nach, bevor du eine schwerwiegende *or* schwer wiegende Entscheidung triffst; **it's a good idea, don't you ~?** es ist eine gute Idee, findest *or* meinst du nicht auch?; **just ~** stellen Sie sich *(dat)* bloß mal vor; **just ~, you too could be rich** stell dir vor *or* denk dir nur, auch du könntest reich sein; **where was it? ~, man, ~!** wo war es?, denk doch mal nach!; **listen, I've been ~ing, ...** hör mal, ich habe mir überlegt ...; **sorry, I just wasn't ~ing** Entschuldigung, da habe ich geschlafen *(inf)*; **you just didn't ~, did you?** da hast du dir nichts gedacht, oder?; **you just don't ~, do you?** *(about other people)* du denkst auch immer nur an dich; *(about consequences)* was denkst du dir eigentlich? → **big**
VT **a** *(= believe)* denken; *(= be of opinion)* glauben, meinen, denken; **I ~ you'll find I'm right** ich glaube *or* denke, Sie werden zu der Überzeugung gelangen, dass ich recht habe; **I ~ it's too late** ich glaube, es ist zu spät; **I ~ I can do it** ich glaube *or* denke, dass ich es schaffen kann; **well, I THINK it was there!** nun, ich glaube zumindest, dass es da war!; **and what do you ~? asked the interviewer** und was meinen Sie *or* und was ist Ihre Meinung? fragte der Interviewer; **you never know what he's ~ing** ich weiß nie, was er (sich) denkt; **I ~ you'd better go/accept/be careful** ich denke, Sie gehen jetzt besser/Sie stimmen lieber zu/Sie wären besser vorsichtig; **well, I THINK he'll understand** na ja, ich nehme zumindest an, dass er das verstehen wird; **I ~ so** ich denke *or* glaube (schon); **I ~ so too** das meine *or* denke ich auch; **I don't ~ so, I shouldn't ~ so, I ~ not** ich denke *or* glaube nicht; **I'll take this one then – I ~ not, Mr Green** dann nehme ich dieses – das glaube ich kaum, Herr Green; **I should ~ so!** das will ich (aber) auch gemeint haben; **I should ~ not!** das will ich auch nicht hoffen; **I hardly ~/~ it likely that ...** ich glaube kaum/ich halte es nicht für wahrscheinlich, dass ...; **I wasn't even ~ing it** daran habe ich nicht einmal gedacht; **one would have thought there was an easier answer** man sollte eigentlich meinen, dass es da eine einfachere Lösung gäbe; **one would have thought you could have been more punctual** man könnte eigentlich erwarten, dass Sie etwas pünktlicher kommen; **one would have thought they'd have grasped it by now** man sollte eigentlich erwarten, dass sie das inzwischen begriffen haben; **what do you ~ I should do?** was glauben Sie, soll ich tun?, was soll ich Ihrer Meinung nach tun?; **well, what do you ~, shall we leave now?** nun, was meinst du, sollen wir jetzt gehen?; **I ~ I'll go for a walk** ich glaube, ich mache einen Spaziergang; **do you ~ you can manage?** glauben Sie, dass Sie es schaffen?
b *(= consider)* **you must ~ me very rude** Sie müssen mich für sehr unhöflich halten; **he ~s he's intelligent, he ~s himself intelligent** er hält sich für intelligent, er meint, er ist *or* sei intelligent; **they are thought to be rich** man hält sie für reich; **I wouldn't have thought it possible** das hätte ich nicht für möglich gehalten
c *(= imagine)* sich *(dat)* denken, sich *(dat)* vorstellen; **I don't know what to ~** ich weiß nicht, was ich davon halten soll; **that's what you ~!** denkste! *(inf)*; **that's what he ~s** hat der eine Ahnung! *(inf)*; **who do you ~ you are!** für wen hältst du dich eigentlich?, wofür hältst du dich eigentlich?; **you can't ~ how pleased I am to see you** Sie können sich *(dat)* (gar) nicht denken *or* vorstellen, wie froh ich bin, Sie zu sehen; **I can't ~ what he means!** ich kann mir (gar) nicht denken, was er meint; *(iro also)* was er damit bloß meinen kann *or* meint?; **anyone would ~ he was dying** man könnte beinahe glauben, er läge im Sterben; **one** *or* **you would ~ they'd already met** man könnte (geradezu) glauben *or* denken, sie seien alte Bekannte; **who would have thought it?** wer hätte das gedacht?; **to ~ that she's only ten!** wenn man bedenkt *or* sich *(dat)* vorstellt, dass sie erst zehn ist
d *(= reflect)* **to ~ how to do sth** sich *(dat)* überlegen, wie man etw macht; **I was ~ing (to myself) how ill he looked** ich dachte mir (im Stillen), dass er sehr krank aussah; **I never thought to ask you** ich habe gar nicht daran gedacht, Sie zu fragen
e *(= expect, intend: often neg or interrog)* **I didn't ~ to see you here** ich hätte nicht gedacht *or* erwartet, Sie hier zu treffen *or* dass ich Sie hier treffen würde; **I thought as much, I thought so** das habe ich mir schon gedacht
f to ~ one's way out of a difficulty sich *(dat)* einen Ausweg aus einer Schwierigkeit überlegen; **you'll ~ yourself into a rage again** du steigerst dich (nur) wieder in eine Wut hinein
N **have a ~ about it and let me know** denken Sie mal darüber nach *or* überlegen Sie es sich *(dat)* einmal, und geben Sie mir dann Bescheid; **to have a good ~** gründlich nachdenken; **you've got another ~ coming** *(Brit inf)* da

irrst du dich aber gewaltig *(inf)*, da bist du aber auf dem Holzweg *(inf)*

▶ **think about** ✪ 6.1, 6.3, 15.3 VI *+prep obj* **a** *(= reflect on) idea, suggestion* nachdenken über *(+acc)*; **OK, I'll think about it** okay, ich überlege es mir; **what are you thinking about?** woran denken Sie gerade?; **it's worth thinking about** das ist überlegenswert, das wäre zu überlegen; **to think twice about sth** sich *(dat)* etw zweimal überlegen; **that'll give him something to think about** das wird ihm zu denken geben
b *(in progressive tenses: = half intend to)* daran denken, vorhaben; **I was thinking about coming to see you** ich habe vorgehabt *or* daran gedacht, Sie zu besuchen; **we're thinking about a holiday in Spain** wir denken daran, in Spanien Urlaub zu machen
c → **think of a, b, f**

▶ **think ahead** VI vorausdenken; *(= anticipate: driver etc)* Voraussicht walten lassen

▶ **think back** VI sich zurückversetzen *(to* in *+acc)*

▶ **think of** ✪ 6.1, 12.2, 14, 25.2 VI *+prep obj* **a** *(= consider, give attention to)* denken an *(+acc)*; **I've too many things to think of just now** ich habe gerade zu viel um die Ohren *(inf)*; **I've enough things to think of as it is** ich habe sowieso schon den Kopf voll *or* schon genug um die Ohren *(inf)*; **he has his family to think of** er muss an seine Familie denken; **he thinks of nobody but himself** er denkt bloß an sich; **what was I thinking of!** *(inf)* was habe ich mir da(bei) bloß gedacht?; **come to think of it** wenn ich es mir recht überlege
b *(= remember)* denken an *(+acc)*; **will you think of me sometimes?** wirst du manchmal an mich denken?; **I can't think of her name** ich kann mich nicht an ihren Namen erinnern, ich komme nicht auf ihren Namen
c *(= imagine)* sich *(dat)* vorstellen, bedenken, sich *(dat)* denken; **and to think of her going there alone!** und wenn man bedenkt *or* sich *(dat)* vorstellt, dass sie ganz allein dorthin gehen will/geht/ging; **think of the cost of all that!** stell dir bloß vor *or* denk dir bloß, was das alles kostet; **just think of him in a kilt!** stellen Sie sich *(dat)* ihn mal in einem Schottenrock vor!
d *(= entertain possibility of)* **she'd never think of getting married** sie denkt gar nicht daran zu heiraten; **he'd never think of such a thing** so etwas würde ihm nicht im Traum einfallen; **would you think of lowering the price a little?** würden Sie unter Umständen den Preis etwas ermäßigen?
e *(= devise, suggest) solution, idea, scheme* sich *(dat)* ausdenken; **who thought of that idea?** wer ist auf diese Idee gekommen *or* verfallen?; **who thought of that plan?** wer hat sich diesen Plan ausgedacht?; **the best thing I can think of is to go home** ich halte es für das Beste, nach Hause zu gehen; **shoes for dogs! what will they think of next!** Schuhe für Hunde! was sie sich wohl (nächstens) noch alles einfallen lassen!
f *(= have opinion of)* halten von; **what do you think of it/him?** was halten Sie davon/von ihm?; **to think well** *or* **highly of sb/sth** eine gute *or* hohe Meinung von jdm/etw haben, viel von jdm/etw halten; **to think little** *or* **not to think much of sb/sth** wenig *or* nicht viel von jdm/etw halten; **I told him what I thought of him** ich habe ihm gründlich die *or* meine Meinung gesagt; **he is very well thought of in his own town** in seiner Heimatstadt hält man große Stücke auf ihn

▶ **think on** VI *+prep obj (old, dial)* = **think about a**

▶ **think out** VT *sep plan* durchdenken; *(= come up with) solution* sich *(dat)* ausdenken; **a person who likes to think things out for himself** ein Mensch, der sich *(dat)* seine eigene Meinung bildet

▶ **think over** VT *sep offer, suggestion* nachdenken über *(+acc)*, sich *(dat)* überlegen; **can I think it over?** darf ich darüber nachdenken?, kann ich es mir noch mal überlegen?

▶ **think through** VT *sep* (gründlich) durchdenken

▶ **think up** VT *sep* sich *(dat)* ausdenken; **who thought up that idea?** wer ist auf die Idee gekommen?

thinkable [ˈθɪŋkəbl] ADJ denkbar

thinker [ˈθɪŋkəʳ] N Denker(in) *m(f)*

thinking [ˈθɪŋkɪŋ] ADJ denkend; **he's not really a ~ man, he prefers action** er ist kein Denker, sondern ein Macher; **all ~ men will agree with me** alle vernünftigen Menschen werden mit mir übereinstimmen; **the ~ man's/woman's pin-up** das Pin-up für den gebildenten Mann/die gebildete Frau; **to put one's ~ cap on** scharf überlegen *or* nachdenken; **~ time** Bedenkzeit *f*; **~ process** Denkprozess *m or* -vorgang *m*; **~ patterns** Denkmuster *pl*
N **to do some hard ~ about a question** sich *(dat)* etwas gründlich überlegen, etwas genau durchdenken; **to my way of ~** meiner Meinung nach; **that might be his way of ~** das mag seine Meinung sein; **this calls for some quick ~** hier muss eine schnelle Lösung gefunden werden

think: **think-piece** N *(Press)* ausführlicher Kommentar; **think-tank** [ˈθɪŋktæŋk] N Expertenkommission *f*

thin-lipped [ˈθɪnlɪpt] ADJ dünnlippig; *smile* dünn

thinly [ˈθɪnlɪ] ADV **a** *(= in thin slices or layers)* dünn **b** *(= sparsely)* dünn; *wooded, attended* spärlich **c** *(= lightly) clad* leicht, dünn **d** *(fig) veiled, disguised* kaum, dürftig; *smile* schwach

thinner [ˈθɪnəʳ] N Verdünner *m*, Verdünnungsmittel *nt*

thinness [ˈθɪnnɪs] N **a** Dünnheit *f*, Dünnigkeit *f*; *(of dress, material)* Leichtheit *f*; *(of liquid)* Dünnflüssigkeit *f*; *(of paper, line, thread)* Feinheit *f*; *(of column of print)* geringe Breite **b** *(of person)* Magerkeit *f* **c** *(= sparseness)* **the ~ of his hair** sein schütterer *or* spärlicher Haarwuchs; **the ~ of the grass** das spärlich wachsende Gras **d** *(= lack of density: of air)* Dünnheit *f* **e** *(fig, of voice, smile)* Schwachheit *f*; *(of excuse, disguise, plot)* Dürftigkeit *f*; *(of trading)* Schlaffheit *f*; *(of profits)* geringe Höhe; *(of majority)* Knappheit *f* → **thin**

thin-skinned [ˈθɪnskɪnd] ADJ *(fig)* empfindlich, dünnhäutig

third [θɜːd] ADJ **a** *(in series)* dritte(r, s); **to be ~** Dritte(r, s) sein; **in ~ place** *(Sport etc)* an dritter Stelle; **in the ~ place** *(= thirdly)* drittens; **~ time around** beim dritten Mal; **she was** *or* **came ~ in her class** sie war die Drittbeste in der Klasse; **he was** *or* **came ~ in the race** er machte *or* belegte den dritten Platz beim Rennen; **~ time lucky** beim dritten Anlauf gelingts!; **the ~ finger** *(Anat)* der Ringfinger
b *(of fraction)* **a ~ part** ein Drittel *nt*
N **a** *(of series)* Dritte(r, s); *(= fraction)* Drittel *nt* → *also* **sixth**
b *(Mus)* Terz *f*
c *(Aut: = third gear)* dritter Gang; **to be in ~** im dritten Gang sein; **to change/go into ~** in den dritten Gang wechseln/gehen
d *(Brit Univ)* Drei *f*; **he got a ~** er bestand (sein Examen) mit „Befriedigend"

third: **third-class** ADV dritter Klasse ADJ **a** *(lit)* dritter Klasse; *(fig)* drittklassig; **~ degree** *(Brit Univ)* Abschluss *m* mit „Befriedigend" **b** *(US Post) mail, stamp* dritter Klasse; **third degree** N **to give sb the ~** *(lit)* (beim Verhör) Stufe drei einschalten; *(fig)* jdn in die Zange nehmen; **third-degree burn** N *(Med)* Verbrennung *f* dritten Grades; **third estate** N der dritte Stand, das Bürgertum

thirdly [ˈθɜːdlɪ] ✪ 26.2 ADV drittens

third: **third party** N Dritte(r) *mf*, dritte Person; **third-party** *(Brit)* ADJ *attr* Haftpflicht-; **~ insurance** Haftpflichtversicherung *f*; **~, fire and theft (insurance)** ≈ Teilkaskoversicherung *f* ADV **insured ~** in einer Haftpflichtversicherung, haftpflichtversichert; **third person** ADJ in der dritten Person N **the ~ singular/plural** *(Gram)* die dritte Person Singular/Plural; **third-rate** ADJ drittklassig, drittrangig; **third reading** N *(Parl)* dritte Lesung; **Third World** N Dritte Welt ATTR der Dritten Welt

thirst [θɜːst] N Durst *m*; **~ for knowledge** Wissensdurst *m*; **~ for adventure** Abenteuerlust *f*; **he's got a real ~ on him** *(inf)* er hat einen noblen Durst (am Leibe) *(inf)*; **to die of ~** verdursten VI **a** *(old)* **I ~** es dürstet *or* durstet mich **b** *(fig)* **to ~ for revenge/knowledge** *etc* nach Rache/Wissen *etc* dürsten; **the plants were ~ing for water** die Pflanzen dürsteten nach Wasser

thirstily [ˈθɜːstɪlɪ] ADV *(lit) drink* durstig; *(fig)* begierig

thirst-quenching [ˈθɜːstˌkwentʃɪŋ] ADJ durststillend

thirsty [ˈθɜːstɪ] ADJ *(+er)* **a** durstig; **to be/feel ~** Durst haben; **it made me ~** das machte mich durstig, das machte mir Durst; **to get ~** durstig werden, Durst bekommen; **~ for praise** begierig auf Lob; **~ for love/revenge/knowledge/blood** nach Liebe/Rache/Wissen/Blut dürstend *or* lechzend *(old, hum)*; **the land is ~ for rain** das Land dürstet nach Regen **b** *(fig inf) car* mit hohem Benzinverbrauch, durstig *(inf)* **c** *(= causing thirst)* **it's ~ work** diese Arbeit macht durstig

thirteen [ˈθɜːˈtiːn] ADJ dreizehn N Dreizehn *f*

thirteenth [ˈθɜːˈtiːnθ] ADJ *(in series)* dreizehnte(r, s); **a ~ part** ein Dreizehntel *nt* N *(in series)* Dreizehnte(r, s); *(= fraction)* Dreizehntel *nt* → *also* **sixth**

thirtieth [ˈθɜːtɪɪθ] ADJ *(in series)* dreißigste(r, s); **a ~ part** ein Dreißigstel *nt* N *(in series)* Dreißigste(r, s); *(= fraction)* Dreißigstel *nt* → *also* **sixth**

thirty [ˈθɜːtɪ] ADJ dreißig; **~-one/-two** ein-/zweiunddreißig; **a ~-second note** *(US Mus)* ein Zweiunddreißigstel *nt* N Dreißig *f*; **the thirties** *(= era)* die dreißiger Jahre *or* Dreißigerjahre; **one's thirties** *(= age)* die Dreißiger → *also* **sixty**

thirtyish [ˈθɜːtɪɪʃ] ADJ um die dreißig

this [ðɪs] DEM PRON *pl* **these** dies, das; **what is ~?** was ist das (hier)?; **who is ~?** wer ist das?; **~ is John** das *or* dies ist John; **these are my children** das *or* dies sind meine Kinder; **~ is where I live** hier wohne ich; **~ is what he showed me** dies *or* das (hier) hat er mir gezeigt; **do you like ~?** gefällt dir das?; **I prefer ~** ich mag das hier *or* dies(es) lieber; **~ is to certify that ...** hiermit wird bestätigt, dass ...; **under/in front of** *etc* **~** darunter/davor *etc*; **it ought to have been done before ~** es hätte schon vorher getan werden sollen; **with ~ he left us** damit *or* mit diesen Worten verließ er uns; **what's all ~?** was soll das?; **what's all ~ I hear about your new job?** was höre ich da so (alles) über deine neue Stelle?; **~ and that** mancherlei; **we were talking of ~ and that** wir haben von diesem und jenem *or* über dies und das geredet; **~, that and the other** alles Mögliche; **will you take ~ or that?** nehmen Sie dieses hier oder das da?; **it was like ~** es war so; **~ is Friday the 13th** heute ist Freitag der 13.; **but ~ is May** aber es ist doch Mai!; **and now ~!** und jetzt (auch noch) dies *or* das!; **~ is Mary (speaking)** hier (ist) Mary; **~ is what I mean!** das meine ich (ja)!; **~ is it!** *(= now)* jetzt!; *(showing sth)* das da!, das ist er/sie/es!; *(= exactly)* genau!
DEM ADJ *pl* **these** diese(r, s); **~ week** diese Woche; **~ month** diesen Monat; **~ year** dieses Jahr; **~ evening** heute Abend; **~ time last week** letzte Woche um diese Zeit; **~ coming week** jetzt die (kommende) Woche; **~ time** diesmal, dieses Mal; **these days** heutzutage; **all ~ talk** dieses ganze Gerede, all das *or* dies Gerede; **to run ~ way and that** hin und her rennen; **I have been waiting for you ~ past half-hour** ich habe bereits die letzte halbe Stunde auf dich gewartet; **~ boy of yours!** also, Ihr Junge!; **I met ~ guy who ...** *(inf)* ich habe (so) einen getroffen, der ...; **~ friend of hers** dieser Freund von ihr *(inf)*, ihr Freund

DEM ADV so; **it was ~ long** es war so lang; **~ far** *(time)* bis jetzt; *(place)* so weit, bis hierher; **~ much is certain** so viel ist sicher, eins steht fest

thistle ['θɪsl] N Distel *f*

thistledown ['θɪsldaʊn] N Distelwolle *f*; **as light as ~** federleicht

thither ['ðɪðəʳ] ADV *(old)* dorthin, dahin → **hither**

tho' [ðəʊ] *abbr of* **though**

thole [θəʊl] N *(Naut)* Dolle *f*, Riemenauflage *f*

Thomist ['təʊmɪst] N Thomist(in) *m(f)* ADJ thomistisch

thong [θɒŋ] N **a** *(of whip)* Peitschenschnur *f*, Peitschenriemen *m*; *(= fastening)* Lederriemen *m* **b** *(US: = flip-flop)* Badelatsche *f (inf)*, Gummilatsche *f (inf)* **c** *(= G-string)* Tangaslip *m*

thoracic [θɔː'ræsɪk] ADJ Brust-, thorakal *(spec)*; **~ vertebra** Brustwirbel *m*

thorax ['θɔːræks] N Brustkorb *m*, Brustkasten *m*, Thorax *m (spec)*

thorium ['θɔːrɪəm] N *(Chem)* Thorium *nt*

thorn [θɔːn] N Dorn *m*; *(= shrub)* Dornbusch *m*, Dornenstrauch *m*; **to be a ~ in sb's flesh** *or* **side** *(fig)* jdm ein Dorn im Auge sein

thorn apple N Stechapfel *m*

thornless ['θɔːnlɪs] ADJ ohne Dornen

thorny ['θɔːnɪ] ADJ *(+er)* *(lit)* dornig, dornenreich; *(fig)* haarig

thorough ['θʌrə] ADJ gründlich; *knowledge also* umfassend, solide; *contempt also* bodenlos; *success* voll, durchschlagend; *fool, rascal* ausgemacht; **to do a ~ job** gründliche Arbeit leisten; **to have/get a ~ grounding in sth** eine solide Basis in etw haben/bekommen; **to be ~ in doing sth** etw gründlich machen; **she's a ~ nuisance** sie ist wirklich eine Plage; **it's a ~ nuisance** das ist wirklich lästig

thorough: **thorough bass** N *(Mus)* Generalbass *m*; **thoroughbred** N reinrassiges Tier; *(= horse)* Vollblut(pferd) *nt*, Vollblüter *m* ADJ reinrassig; **~ horse** Vollblut(pferd) *nt*; **~ dog** Rassehund *m*; **thoroughfare** N Durchfahrts- *or* Durchgangsstraße *f*; **it's the most famous ~ of this town** es ist die berühmteste Straße dieser Stadt; **this isn't a public ~** das ist keine öffentliche Verkehrsstraße; **"no ~"** *(cul-de-sac)* „Sackgasse"; *(not open to public)* „Durchfahrt verboten"; **thoroughgoing** ADJ *changes* gründlich; *revision* grundlegend, tief greifend; *measure, reform* durchgreifend; *believer* eingefleischt; **to be a ~ professional** durch und durch Profi sein; **he is a ~ rascal** er ist ein Spitzbube durch und durch

thoroughly ['θʌrəlɪ] ADV **a** gründlich, von Grund auf **b** *(= extremely)* durch und durch, von Grund auf; *convinced* völlig, vollkommen; **we ~ enjoyed our meal** wir haben unser Essen von Herzen genossen; **I ~ enjoyed myself** es hat mir aufrichtig Spaß gemacht; **I ~ agree** ich stimme voll und ganz zu; **I'm ~ ashamed** ich schäme mich zutiefst, ich bin zutiefst beschämt; **a ~ nasty person** ein Scheusal durch und durch; **~ modern** durch und durch modern; **~ boring** ausgesprochen langweilig

thoroughness ['θʌrənɪs] N Gründlichkeit *f*; *(= carefulness)* Sorgfältigkeit *f*, Sorgfalt *f*; *(of knowledge)* Umfang *m*, Solidität *f*

Thos *abbr of* **Thomas**

those [ðəʊz] *pl of* **that** DEM PRON das (da) *sing*; **what are ~?** was ist das (denn) da?, was sind das für Dinger? *(inf)*; **whose are ~?** wem gehören diese da?; **~ are my suggestions** das *or* dies sind meine Vorschläge; **on top of ~** darauf; *(= moreover)* darüber hinaus; **above ~** darüber; **after ~** danach; *(place)* dahinter; **~ are the ones I want** ich möchte diese dort; **~ who want to go, may** wer möchte, kann gehen, diejenigen, die gehen möchten, können das tun *(form)*; **one of ~ who ...** einer/eine von denen *or* denjenigen, die ...; **there are ~ who say ...** einige sagen ...

DEM ADJ diese *or* die (da), jene *(old, liter)*; **what are ~ men doing?** was machen diese Männer da?; **on ~ two occasions** bei diesen beiden Gelegenheiten; **it was just one of ~ days/things** das war wieder so ein Tag/so eine Sache; **he is one of ~ people who ...** er ist einer von den Leuten *or* von denjenigen, die ...; **~ dogs!** also, diese Hunde!; **~ sons of yours!** also, deine Söhne!

thou [ðaʊ] PERS PRON *(old, to friend, servant etc)* Er/Sie *(obs)*; *(to stranger)* Ihr *(obs)*; *(Rel)* du; *(Brit: dial)* du

though [ðəʊ] ✪ 15.2 CONJ **a** *(= in spite of the fact that)* obwohl, obgleich, obschon; **even ~** obwohl *etc*; **~ poor she is generous** obwohl *etc* sie arm ist, ist sie großzügig; **strange ~ it may seem ...** so seltsam es auch scheinen mag ..., mag es auch noch so seltsam scheinen ... *(geh)*; **important ~ it may be/is ...** so wichtig es auch sein mag/ist, auch wenn es noch so wichtig ist ...; **~ I say it** *or* **so myself** auch wenn ich es selbst sage

b *(liter: = even if)* **I will go (even) ~ it may cost me my life** ich werde gehen und sollte es mich (auch) das Leben kosten *or* und koste es das Leben *(liter)*; **~ it take forever** *(liter)* und dauerte es auch ewig *(liter)*

c as ~ als ob

ADV **a** *(= nevertheless)* doch; **he didn't/did do it ~** er hat es aber (doch) nicht/aber doch gemacht; **I'm sure he didn't do it ~** ich bin aber sicher, dass er es nicht gemacht hat; **nice day – rather windy ~** schönes Wetter! – aber ziemlich windig!

b *(= really)* **but will he ~?** tatsächlich?, wirklich?

c *(inf)* **hot, isn't it? – isn't it ~!** warm, was? – allerdings!

thought [θɔːt] *pret, ptp of* **think** N **a** *no pl* *(= act or process of thinking)* Denken *nt*; **to spend hours in ~** stundenlang in Gedanken (vertieft) sein; **to be lost in ~** ganz in Gedanken sein, gedankenverloren sein *(geh)*; **to take ~** *(old)* denken; **logical ~** logisches Denken; **in ~** in Gedanken

b *(= idea, opinion)* Gedanke *m*; *(sudden)* Einfall *m*; **she hasn't a ~ in her head** sie hat nichts im Hirn *or* Kopf; **the ~s of Chairman Mao** die Gedanken des Vorsitzenden Mao; **he didn't express any ~s on the matter** er hat keine Ansichten zu diesem Thema geäußert; **that's a ~!** *(= amazing)* man stelle sich das mal vor!; *(= problem to be considered)* das ist wahr!; *(= good idea)* das ist eine (gute) Idee *or* ein guter Gedanke *or* Einfall; **what a ~!** was für ein Gedanke *or* eine Vorstellung!; **a ~ has just occurred to me, I've just had a ~** *(inf)* mir ist gerade ein Gedanke gekommen, mir ist gerade etwas eingefallen; **don't give it another ~** machen Sie sich *(dat)* keine Gedanken darüber; *(= forget it)* denken Sie nicht mehr daran; **his one ~ was ...** sein einziger Gedanke war ...; **to have no ~ of doing sth** gar nicht vorhaben *or* gar nicht daran denken, etw zu tun; **it's a shame it doesn't fit, but it's the ~ that counts** es ist ein Jammer, dass es nicht passt, aber es war gut gemeint; **it's the ~ that counts, not how much you spend** es kommt nur auf die Idee an, nicht auf den Preis; **to collect one's ~s** sich sammeln, seine Gedanken zusammennehmen; **her ~s were elsewhere** sie war in Gedanken woanders; **the mere** *or* **very ~ of it** der bloße Gedanke (daran), die bloße Vorstellung

c *no pl* *(= body of ideas)* Denken *nt*; **modern ~** das moderne Denken, das Denken der Moderne

d *no pl* *(= care, consideration)* Nachdenken *nt*, Überlegung *f*; **to give some ~ to sth** sich *(dat)* Gedanken über etw *(acc)* machen, etw bedenken *or* überlegen; **after much ~** nach langer Überlegung *or* langem Überlegen; **to act without ~** gedankenlos *or* ohne Überlegung handeln; **without ~ for sb/oneself/sth** ohne an jdn/sich selbst/etw zu denken, ohne Rücksicht auf jdn/sich selbst/etw; **he has no ~ for his parents' feelings** er nimmt keine Rücksicht auf die Gefühle seiner Eltern; **I never gave it a moment's ~** ich habe mir nie darüber Gedanken gemacht

e a ~ *(= a little)* eine Idee, ein Ideechen *nt (inf)*; **with a ~ more tact** mit einer Idee *or* einer Spur mehr Takt

thought: **thought blocking** N *(Psych)* Denkhemmung *f*; **thought experiment** N Gedankenexperiment *nt*

thoughtful ['θɔːtfʊl] ADJ **a** *(= full of thought) expression, person* nachdenklich, gedankenvoll, grüblerisch; *remark, analysis, book* gut durchdacht, wohlüberlegt; *present* gut ausgedacht; *silence* nachdenklich **b** *(= considerate)* rücksichtsvoll; *(= attentive, helpful)* aufmerksam; **to be ~ of sb's comfort/needs** an jds Wohlbefinden/Bedürfnisse denken; **to be ~ of/toward(s) sb** jdm gegenüber aufmerksam/rücksichtsvoll sein; **to be ~ of others** auf andere Rücksicht nehmen; **it was very ~ of you to ...** es war sehr aufmerksam von Ihnen, zu ...

thoughtfully ['θɔːtfəlɪ] ADV **a** *say, look* nachdenklich **b** *(= with much thought)* mit viel Überlegung; **a ~ written book** ein wohldurchdachtes Buch **c** *(= considerately)* rücksichtsvoll; *(= attentively, helpfully)* aufmerksam; **she ~ provided rugs** sie war so aufmerksam, Decken bereitzustellen, aufmerksamerweise hatte sie Decken bereitgestellt

thoughtfulness ['θɔːtfʊlnɪs] N **a** *(of expression, person)* Nachdenklichkeit *f*; *(of remark, analysis)* Tiefgang *m* **b** *(= consideration)* Rücksicht(nahme) *f*; *(= attentiveness, helpfulness)* Aufmerksamkeit *f*; **his ~ for his parents** seine Aufmerksamkeit/Rücksichtnahme seinen Eltern gegenüber

thoughtless ['θɔːtlɪs] ADJ **a** *(= inconsiderate) person* gedankenlos, rücksichtslos; *(= inattentive, unhelpful)* gedankenlos, unachtsam; **he's very ~ of** *or* **about/to(wards) other people** er ist sehr gedankenlos/rücksichtslos anderen gegenüber; **how ~ of you!** wie rücksichtslos von dir!; **it was ~ of her (to tell him)** es war gedankenlos von ihr(, es ihm zu erzählen) **b** *(= without reflection)* gedankenlos, unüberlegt, unbesonnen; **~ of the danger, he leapt** ungeachtet der Gefahr sprang er

thoughtlessly ['θɔːtlɪslɪ] ADV **a** *(= inconsiderately) act, behave* rücksichtslos **b** *(= unthinkingly)* gedankenlos, unüberlegt; **he had ~ taken it with him** er hatte es aus Gedankenlosigkeit mitgenommen

thoughtlessness ['θɔːtlɪsnɪs] N **a** *(= lack of consideration)* Gedankenlosigkeit *f*, Rücksichtslosigkeit *f*; *(= inattentiveness, unhelpfulness)* Unaufmerksamkeit *f* **b** *(= lack of reflection)* Gedankenlosigkeit *f*, Unüberlegtheit *f*

thought: **thought process** N Gedankengang *m*; **thought-provoking** ADJ *film, book, article, idea* zum Nachdenken anregend; **thought-reader** N Gedankenleser(in) *m(f)*; **thought-reading** N Gedankenlesen *nt*; **thought transference** N Gedankenübertragung *f*

thousand ['θaʊzənd] ADJ tausend; **a ~** (ein)tausend; **two ~** zweitausend; **a ~ times** tausendmal; **a ~ and one/two** tausend(und)eins/-zwei; **I died a ~ deaths** *(inf: = was embarrassed)* ich wäre fast in den Boden versunken; *(= was afraid)* ich habe tausend Ängste ausgestanden; **I have a ~ and one (different) things to do** *(inf)* ich habe tausenderlei *or* tausend Dinge zu tun; **Thousand Island dressing** Thousand-Islands-Dressing *nt*

N Tausend *nt*; **the ~s** *(Math)* die Tausender *pl*; **there were ~s of people present** es waren Tausende *or* tausende (von Menschen) anwesend; **the year three ~** das Jahr dreitausend; **people arrived in their ~s** die Menschen kamen zu tausenden *or* Tausenden

thousandfold ['θaʊzəndfəʊld] *(liter)* ADJ tausendfach ADV **a ~** tausendfach, tausendfältig

thousandth ['θaʊzəntθ] ADJ *(in series)* tausendste(r, s); **a** *or* **one ~ part** ein Tausendstel *nt* N *(in series)* Tausendste(r, s); *(= fraction)* Tausendstel *nt* → *also* **sixth**

thraldom, *(US)* **thralldom** ['θrɔːldəm] N *(liter)* Knechtschaft *f*; **he was held in ~ to her beauty**

(fig) ihre Schönheit hatte ihn in ihren Bann geschlagen

thrall [θrɔːl] N *(liter)* **a** *(= slave)* Leibeigene(r) *m*, Sklave *m (also fig)*, Knecht *m* **b** *(= condition)* **to be in ~ to sb/sth** in jds Bann *(dat)*/im Bann einer Sache *(gen)* stehen

thrash [θræʃ] VT **a** *(= beat)* verprügeln, verdreschen; *donkey etc* einschlagen auf *(+acc)*; **to ~ the (living) daylights out of sb** *(inf)* jdn grün und blau schlagen **b** *(Sport inf) opponent* (vernichtend) schlagen **c** *(= move wildly) arms* schlagen mit, fuchteln mit; *legs* strampeln mit; **he ~ed his arms (about) angrily** er schlug wütend (mit den Armen) um sich **d** *(Agr)* = **thresh** VI **to ~ about** *or* **around** um sich schlagen; *(in bed)* sich herumwerfen; *(fish)* zappeln; **the branches ~ed against the panes** die Zweige schlugen gegen die Fensterscheiben N *(dated Brit, inf, = party)* Party *f*

▶ **thrash out** VT *sep differences, deal, terms, details* ausdiskutieren; **to thrash things out** die Sache durchdiskutieren

thrashing [ˈθræʃɪŋ] N **a** *(= beating)* Prügel *pl*, Schläge *pl*, Dresche *f (inf)*; **to give sb a good ~** jdm eine ordentliche Tracht Prügel verpassen **b** *(Sport inf)* komplette Niederlage; **to give sb a ~** jdn vernichtend schlagen

thrash metal N *(Mus)* Thrash Metal *nt*

thread [θred] N **a** *(of cotton, wool etc)* Faden *m*; *(Sew)* Garn *nt*, Faden *m*; *(= strong thread)* Zwirn *m*; **to hang by a ~** *(fig)* an einem (seidenen *or* dünnen) Faden hängen
b *(fig, of story)* (roter) Faden; **to follow the ~ of a conversation** dem Gedankengang eines Gespräches folgen; **he lost the ~ of what he was saying** er hat den Faden verloren; **to pick up the ~s of one's story/a conversation** den (roten) Faden/den Gesprächsfaden wieder aufnehmen; **to gather up** *or* **pick up the ~s of one's career/life** alte Fäden wieder anknüpfen
c *(Tech, of screw)* Gewinde *nt*
d *(fig) (= thin line: of light)* Strahl *m*, Streifen *m*
e *(E-mail)* Subject *nt*
VT **a** *needle* einfädeln; *beads* aufreihen, auffädeln (*on* auf *+acc*); *necklace* aufziehen; **~ed with silver** von Silber(fäden) durchzogen, mit Silber(fäden) durchsetzt
b to ~ one's way through the crowd/trees *etc* sich durch die Menge/zwischen den Bäumen *etc* hindurchschlängeln; **he ~ed the ball through to Gascoigne** er spitzelte den Ball zu Gascoigne durch
c *(Tech) screw* mit einem Gewinde versehen
VI **he ~ed through the crowd** er schlängelte sich durch die Menge (hindurch)

threadbare [ˈθredbeəʳ] ADJ abgewetzt, fadenscheinig; *clothes also* abgetragen; *carpet also* abgelaufen; *(fig) argument* fadenscheinig; *joke* abgedroschen; *idea* veraltet

threaded [ˈθredɪd] ADJ *(Tech)* Gewinde-, mit Gewinde; **~ bolt** Gewindebolzen *m*

thread mark N Silberfaden *m (in Banknoten)*

threat [θret] N **a** Drohung *f*; **is that a ~?** soll das eine Drohung sein?; **to make a ~** drohen, eine Androhung machen *(against sb* jdm); **under ~ of sth** unter Androhung von etw; **he is under ~ of expulsion** ihm wurde der Ausschluss angedroht **b** *(= danger)* Bedrohung *(to +gen)*, Gefahr *f (to* für); **this war is a ~ to civilization** dieser Krieg stellt eine Gefahr für die Zivilisation *or* eine Bedrohung der Zivilisation dar; **~ management** *(Comput) Handling der Virenbedrohung durch Sicherheitssysteme*

threaten [ˈθretn] VT **a** *person* bedrohen, drohen *(+dat)*; *revenge, violence* androhen, drohen mit; **don't you ~ me!** von Ihnen lasse ich mir nicht drohen!; **to ~ to do sth** (an)drohen, etw zu tun; **to ~ sb with sth** jdm etw androhen, jdm mit etw drohen; **to ~ sb with a weapon** jdn mit der Waffe bedrohen; **to ~ legal action** mit rechtlichen Schritten drohen
b *(= put in danger)* bedrohen, gefährden; **the rain ~ed to spoil the harvest** der Regen drohte, die Ernte zu zerstören
c *(Met: = give warning of)* **the sky ~s rain** der Himmel sieht (bedrohlich) nach Regen aus; **it's ~ing to rain** es sieht (bedrohlich) nach Regen aus
VI *(danger, storm etc)* drohen, im Anzug sein

threatened [ˈθretnd] ADJ **a he felt ~** er fühlte sich bedroht **b** *(= endangered, under threat) species, jobs* gefährdet **c** *(= presaged)* angedroht

threatening [ˈθretnɪŋ] ADJ drohend; *weather, clouds also, situation* bedrohlich; **a ~ letter/phone call** ein Drohbrief *m*/-anruf *m*; **~ behaviour** Drohungen *pl*; **to find sb ~** sich von jdm bedroht fühlen

threateningly [ˈθretnɪŋlɪ] ADV drohend; **the sky darkened ~** der Himmel verfinsterte sich bedrohlich

three [θriː] ADJ drei N *(= figure, bus, Cards)* Drei *f*; **~'s a crowd** drei Leute sind schon zu viel, bei dreien ist einer zu viel → *also* **six**

three: **three-act play** N Dreiakter *m*; **three-colour**, *(US)* **three-color** ADJ *(Phot)* Dreifarben-; **~ printing** Dreifarbendruck *m*; **three-cornered** ADJ **~ contest** *or* **fight** Kampf *m* mit drei Beteiligten *or* Parteien, Dreieckskampf *m*; **~ hat** Dreispitz *m*; **three-D** N **to be in ~** dreidimensional *or* 3-D sein ADJ *(also* **three-dimensional**) dreidimensional, 3-D-; **~ movie** 3-D-Film *m*; **three-decker** N **a** *(Naut)* Dreidecker *m* **b** *(= sandwich)* Doppelsandwich *nt*; **three-dimensional** ADJ dreidimensional; *(= realistic) character* ausgereift; **threefold** ADJ, ADV dreifach; **three-fourths** N *(US)* = **three-quarters**; **three-legged** ADJ dreibeinig; **~ race** *(Sport) Wettlauf, bei dem zwei an einem Bein zusammengebunden werden*; **three-master** N Dreimaster *m*; **threepence** N *(Brit old)* Dreipennystück *nt*; **threepenny** N *(Brit old)* Dreipennystück *nt*; **threepenny bit** N *(Brit old)* Dreipennystück *nt*; **threepenny opera** N Dreigroschenoper *f*; **threepenny piece** N *(Brit old)* = **threepenny bit**; **three-phase** ADJ Dreistufen-; *(Elec)* Dreiphasen-; **~ circuit** Dreiphasenschaltung *f*; **~ plan/programme** Dreistufenplan *m*/-programm *nt*; **three-piece suit** N *(man's)* Anzug *m* mit Weste; *(lady's)* dreiteiliges Ensemble; **three-piece suite** N *(esp Brit)* dreiteilige Polster- *or* Sitzgarnitur; **three-pin plug** N Stecker *m* mit drei Kontakten; **three-ply** N *(= wool)* Dreifachwolle *f*; *(= wood)* dreischichtiges Spanholz ATTR *wood* dreischichtig; **~ wool** Dreifachwolle *f*; **three-point landing** N *(Aviat)* Dreipunktlandung *f*; **three-point turn** N *(Aut)* Wenden *nt* in drei Zügen; **three-quarter** N *(Sport)* Dreiviertelspieler(in) *m(f)* ATTR dreiviertel-; **~ length** dreiviertellang; **~ portrait** Halbbild *nt*; **three-quarters** N drei Viertel *pl*; **~ of an hour** eine Dreiviertelstunde ADV drei viertel, zu drei Vierteln; **three-ring circus** N *(US inf)* Affenzirkus *m*; **threescore** ADJ sechzig; **threesome** N Trio *nt*, Dreiergruppe *f*; *(inf = group sex)* flotter Dreier *(inf)*; **in a ~** zu dritt; **three-speed** ADJ *attr* **~ gears** Dreigangschaltung *f*; **three-way** ADJ *discussion* mit drei Parteien; **~ catalyst** Dreiwegkatalysator *m*; **a ~ split** eine Dreiteilung; **there's a ~ tie for the lead** es gibt drei punktgleiche Spitzenanwärter; **three-wheeler** N *(Aut)* dreirädriges Auto; *(= tricycle)* Dreirad *nt*

> **THREE Rs**
>
> Die **three Rs** sind „reading, writing and arithmetic" - Lesen, Schreiben, Rechnen - die allgemein wichtigsten Fähigkeiten, die man durch Erziehung und Bildung erlernen kann. Der Ausdruck kommt von der ironisch-falschen Schreibweise „reading, 'riting and 'rithmetic" und wird häufig in öffentlichen Diskussionen über den sich abzeichnenden Niedergang des Bildungsniveaus angeführt.

threnody [ˈθrenədɪ] N *(Liter)* Threnodie *f*

thresh [θreʃ] VTI dreschen

thresher [ˈθreʃəʳ] N **a** *(Agr: = machine)* Dreschmaschine *f*; *(= person)* Drescher(in) *m(f)* **b** *(= thresher shark)* Drescherhai *m*

threshing [ˈθreʃɪŋ] N Dreschen *nt*

threshing floor N Dreschboden *m*, Tenne *f*

threshing machine N Dreschmaschine *f*

threshold [ˈθreʃhəʊld] N *(lit, fig, Psych)* Schwelle *f*; *(of door also)* Türschwelle *f*; **on the ~** an der Schwelle; **we are on the ~ of a great discovery** wir stehen unmittelbar an der Schwelle zu einer großen Entdeckung; **to have a high/low pain ~** eine hohe/niedrige Schmerzschwelle haben

threw [θruː] *pret of* **throw**

thrice [θraɪs] ADV *(old)* dreimal; **he is ~ blessed** er ist dreifach *or* dreifältig gesegnet

thrift [θrɪft] N Sparsamkeit *f*

thriftily [ˈθrɪftɪlɪ] ADV **a** sparsam, wirtschaftlich, haushälterisch **b** *(US)* **his business is doing ~** sein Geschäft floriert

thriftiness [ˈθrɪftɪnɪs] N **a** Sparsamkeit *f*, Wirtschaftlichkeit *f* **b** *(US: = prosperity)* Gedeihen *nt*

thriftless [ˈθrɪftlɪs] ADJ verschwenderisch

thriftlessness [ˈθrɪftlɪsnɪs] N Verschwendung(ssucht) *f*

thrift shop, *(US)* **thrift store** N Secondhandladen *m (dessen Verkaufserlös wohltätigen Zwecken zukommt)*

thrifty [ˈθrɪftɪ] ADJ *(+er)* **a** *(= careful, economical)* sparsam, wirtschaftlich, haushälterisch **b** *(US: = thriving)* blühend

thrill [θrɪl] N Erregung *f*; **all the ~s and spills of the circus** all die Sensationen und der Nervenkitzel des Zirkus; **a ~ of joy** eine freudige Erregung; **a ~ of horror** ein Entsetzensschauder *m*; **she heard his voice with a ~ of excitement** sie hörte seine Stimme, und Erregung durchfuhr sie; **it gave me quite a ~, it was quite a ~ for me** es war ein richtiges Erlebnis; **what a ~!** wie aufregend!; **he gets a ~ out of hunting** Jagen hat für ihn einen ganz besonderen Reiz; **the real ~ comes at the end of the book** die eigentliche Sensation kommt erst am Ende des Buches; **that's how he gets his ~s** das erregt ihn; **this will give you the ~ of a lifetime** das wird DAS Erlebnis deines Lebens (sein); **go on, give us a ~!** *(inf)* nun lass uns mal was sehen *(inf)*
VT *person (story, crimes)* mitreißen, fesseln, packen; *(experience)* eine Sensation sein für; *(sb's touch, voice etc)* freudig erzittern lassen; *(sexually)* erregen; **I was quite ~ed by the sight of the Alps** ich war ganz hingerissen beim Anblick der Alpen; **I was ~ed to get your letter** ich habe mich riesig über deinen Brief gefreut; **the thought of going to America ~ed her** der Gedanke an eine Amerikareise versetzte sie in freudige Erregung; **to be ~ed to bits** *(inf)* sich freuen wie ein Kind; *(esp child)* ganz aus dem Häuschen sein vor Freude
VI **she ~ed at the sound of his voice/to his touch** ein freudiger Schauer durchlief sie, als sie seine Stimme hörte/bei seiner Berührung

thriller [ˈθrɪləʳ] N Reißer *m (inf)*; *(= whodunnit)* Krimi *m*, Thriller *m*

thrilling [ˈθrɪlɪŋ] ADJ aufregend; *book, film* spannend, fesselnd; *sensation* überwältigend, hinreißend; *music* hinreißend, mitreißend; *experience, victory* überwältigend, umwerfend *(inf)*; *(sexually)* erregend; **we had a ~ time** es war richtig aufregend

thrillingly [ˈθrɪlɪŋlɪ] ADV spannungsgeladen; **~ new** aufregend neu

thrive [θraɪv] VI *(= be in good health: animal, plant)* (gut) gedeihen; *(child also)* sich gut *or* prächtig entwickeln; *(= do well, business)* blühen, florieren; *(businessman)* erfolgreich sein

▶ **thrive on** VI *+prep obj* **the baby thrives on milk** mit Milch gedeiht das Baby prächtig; **this plant thrives on sun and light** bei Sonne und Licht gedeiht *or* entwickelt sich diese Pflanze prächtig; **he thrives on criticism/praise** Kritik/

Lob bringt ihn erst zur vollen Entfaltung; **like it? I thrive on it** ob mir das gefällt? ich brauche das

thriven [ˈθrɪvən] *(old) ptp of* **thrive**

thriving [ˈθraɪvɪŋ] ADJ **a** *plant* prächtig gedeihend, kräftig; *person, city, community* blühend; *child* gut gedeihend; **he's ~!** ihm gehts prächtig!; *(child)* er blüht und gedeiht! **b** *business, economy, night life* florierend, blühend; *businessman* erfolgreich

thro' [θruː] *abbr of* **through**

throat [θrəʊt] N *(external)* Kehle *f*; *(internal also)* Rachen *m*; **to grab sb by the ~** jdn bei *or* an der Kehle *or* Gurgel packen; **to cut sb's ~** jdm die Kehle *or* Gurgel durchschneiden; **to cut one's own ~** *(fig)* sich *(dat)* selbst das Wasser abgraben; **my ~ is really dry** ich habe einen völlig trockenen Hals *or* eine ganz trockene Kehle; **I've a fishbone stuck in my ~** mir ist eine Gräte im Hals stecken geblieben; **the doctor looked down her ~** der Arzt sah ihr in den Hals; **cancer of the ~** Kehlkopfkrebs *m*; **to clear one's ~** sich räuspern; **they've been pouring drink down my ~ all evening** *(inf)* sie haben den ganzen Abend lang Alkohol in mich hineingeschüttet *(inf)*; **to ram** *or* **force one's ideas down sb's ~** *(inf)* jdm seine eigenen Ideen aufzwingen; **the words stuck in my ~** die Worte blieben mir im Halse stecken; **it sticks in my ~** *(fig)* das geht mir gegen den Strich *(inf)*

throat microphone N Kehlkopfmikrofon *nt*

throaty ADJ *(+er)*, **throatily** ADV [ˈθrəʊtɪ, -lɪ] kehlig, rau

throb [θrɒb] VI *(engine)* klopfen, hämmern; *(drums, gunfire)* dröhnen; *(heart, pulse)* pochen, klopfen; *(painfully: wound)* pochen, pulsieren, klopfen; *(very strongly)* hämmern; *(fig: with life, activity)* pulsieren *(with* vor *+dat*, mit); **my head was still ~bing (with pain)** ich hatte immer noch dieses Pochen im Kopf; **my head is ~bing** ich habe rasende Kopfschmerzen; **a street ~bing with people** eine Straße, die von Menschen wimmelt
N *(of engine)* Klopfen *nt*, Hämmern *nt*; *(of drums, gunfire)* Dröhnen *nt*; *(of heart, pulse, wound)* Klopfen *nt*, Pochen *nt*, Hämmern *nt*; **the ~ of life** der Pulsschlag des Lebens

throbbing [ˈθrɒbɪŋ] N *(of engine)* Klopfen *nt*, Hämmern *nt*; *(of drums, gunfire)* Dröhnen *nt*; *(of heart, pulse)* Pochen *nt* ADJ **a** *pain* pulsierend; *headache, head* pochend **b** *music* hämmernd **c** *(fig: = pulsating) place, nightlife* pulsierend

throes [θrəʊz] PL **a the ~ of childbirth** die (Geburts)wehen *pl*; **in the ~ of death** im Todeskampf, in Todesqualen *pl*; **to be in the final ~ of sth** *(fig)* in den letzten Zügen einer Sache *(gen)* liegen **b** *(fig)* Wirren *pl*; **we are in the ~ of moving** wir stecken mitten im Umzug; **I was in the ~ of composition** ich war völlig vertieft in meine Kompositionen; **in the ~ of inspiration** in künstlerischer Versunkenheit

thrombosis [θrɒmˈbəʊsɪs] N Thrombose *f*

thrombus [ˈθrɒmbəs] N Thrombus *m (form)*, Blutpfropf *m*

throne [θrəʊn] N Thron *m*; *(Eccl)* Stuhl *m*; **to come to the ~** den Thron besteigen; **to swear allegiance to the ~** der Krone den Treueid leisten; **the power of the ~** die Macht der Krone VT **(he is) ~d in glory** *(Eccl)* er sitzet *or* thronet in Herrlichkeit

throne room N Thronsaal *m*; *(hum)* Klo *nt (inf)*

throng [θrɒŋ] N *(of people)* Scharen *pl*, Menschenmenge *f*; *(of angels)* Heerschar *f* VI sich drängen; **to ~ round sb/sth** sich um jdn/etw drängen *or* scharen; **to ~ toward(s) sb/sth** sich zu jdm/etw drängen, zu jdm/etw strömen VT belagern; **people ~ed the streets** die Menschen drängten sich in den Straßen; **to be ~ed with** wimmeln von *or* mit

throttle [ˈθrɒtl] VT **a** *(lit) person* erdrosseln, erwürgen **b** *(fig) feelings* ersticken, unterdrücken; *opposition* ersticken, unterbinden; *economy* drosseln; **to ~ the press** die Presse knebeln **c** *(Tech)* = **throttle back** N **a** *(on engine)* Drossel *f*; *(Aut etc: = lever)* Gashebel *m*; *(= valve)* Drosselklappe *f*; **at full ~** mit Vollgas; **to open/close the ~** die Drossel öffnen/schließen; *(Aut etc)* Gas geben/zurücknehmen **b** *(hum, = throat)* Kehle *f*

▸ **throttle back** *or* **down** VT *sep* drosseln VI Gas zurücknehmen, den Motor drosseln

through, *(US)* **thru** [θruː] PREP **a** *(place)* durch; **he couldn't get ~ the hedge** er konnte nicht durch die Hecke durchkommen *or* (hin)durchschlüpfen; **to listen ~ the door** durch die (geschlossene) Tür mithören, lauschen; **he was shot ~ the head** er bekam einen Kopfschuss; **he went right ~ the red light** er ist bei Rot einfach durchgefahren; **he has come ~ many hardships** er hat viel Schweres durchgemacht; **we're ~ that stage now** wir sind jetzt durch dieses Stadium hindurch; **to be halfway ~ a book** ein Buch halb *or* zur Hälfte durchhaben *(inf)*; **that happens halfway/three-quarters of the way ~ the book** das passiert in der Mitte/im letzten Viertel des Buches
b *(time)* **all ~ his life** sein ganzes Leben lang; **he won't live ~ the night** er wird die Nacht nicht überleben; **he worked ~ the night** er hat die Nacht durchgearbeitet; **he lives there ~ the week** er wohnt da während *or* unter *(dial)* der Woche *or* die Woche über; **he slept ~ the film** er hat den ganzen Film über *or* hindurch *or* lang geschlafen; **all ~ the autumn** den ganzen Herbst über *or* hindurch
c *(US: = up to and including)* bis (einschließlich); **Monday ~ Friday** von Montag bis (einschließlich) Freitag
d *(= means, agency)* durch; **~ the post** *(Brit) or* **mail** *(US)* mit der Post®, per Post®; **it happened ~ no fault of mine** *or* **my own** es geschah nicht durch meine Schuld; **absent ~ illness** abwesend wegen Krankheit; **~ neglect** durch Nachlässigkeit; **to act ~ fear** aus Angst handeln; **he spoke ~ an interpreter** er wurde gedolmetscht
ADV *(time, place)* durch; **he's a liar/gentleman ~ and ~** er ist durch und durch verlogen/ein Gentleman; **to sleep all night ~** die ganze Nacht durchschlafen; **did you stay right ~?** *(Brit)* sind Sie bis zum Schluss geblieben?; **they stayed ~ until Thursday** *(Brit)* sie blieben bis Donnerstag (da); **he knew all ~ what I was getting at** er wusste die ganze Zeit (über), worauf ich hinauswollte; **to let sb ~** jdn durchlassen; **to be wet ~** durch und durch *or* bis auf die Haut nass sein; **to read sth ~** etw durchlesen; **he's ~ in the other office** er ist (drüben) im anderen Büro; **the train goes ~ to Berlin** der Zug fährt bis nach Berlin durch
ADJ *pred* **a** *(= finished)* **to be ~ with sb/sth** mit jdm/etw fertig sein *(inf)*; **we're ~** *(= have finished relationship)* es ist (alles) aus zwischen uns; *(= have finished job)* wir sind fertig; **I'm ~ with him** der ist für mich gestorben *or* erledigt, ich bin fertig mit ihm *(all inf)*; **I'm ~ with that kind of work** ich habe genug von dieser Arbeit; **you're ~, Kowalski, fired** wir sind mit Ihnen fertig, Kowalski, Sie fliegen!; **are you ~?** sind Sie fertig?
b *(Brit Telec)* **to be ~ (to sb/London)** mit jdm/London verbunden sein; **to get ~ (to sb/London)** zu jdm/nach London durchkommen; **you're ~, caller** Ihre Verbindung!, Ihr Gespräch!

through: **through coach** N *(Rail)* Kurswagen *m* (for nach); *(= bus)* direkte Busverbindung; **through flight** N Direktflug *m*; **through freight** N Durchgangsfracht *f*; **through-hole** ADJ *(Comput)* durchkontaktiert

throughout [θrʊˈaʊt] PREP **a** *(place)* überall in *(+dat)*; **~ the country** im ganzen Land; **~ the world** in der ganzen Welt **b** *(time)* den ganzen/die/das ganze … hindurch *or* über; **~ his life** sein ganzes Leben lang ADV **a** *(= in every part)* **the house is carpeted ~** das Haus ist ganz *or* überall mit Teppichboden ausgelegt; **a house with electric light ~** ein Haus, das in jedem Raum elektrisches Licht hat; **a block of flats with water and gas ~** ein Wohnblock mit Wasser und Gas in allen Wohnungen; **the coat is lined ~** der Mantel ist ganz gefüttert **b** *(time)* die ganze Zeit hindurch *or* über

through: **throughput** N *(Ind, Comput)* Durchsatz *m*; **through ticket** N **can I get a ~ to London?** kann ich bis London durchlösen?; **through traffic** N Durchgangsverkehr *m*; **through train** N durchgehender Zug; **throughway** N *(US)* Schnellstraße *f*

throve [θrəʊv] *(old) pret of* **thrive**

throw [θrəʊ] *vb: pret* **threw**, *ptp* **thrown** N **a** *(of ball, javelin, dice)* Wurf *m*; **it's your ~** du bist dran; **have another ~** werfen Sie noch einmal; **to lose the ~** *(dice)* den Wurf verlieren; **a 30-metre ~** ein Wurf von 30 Metern; **the first ~ went to the German** *(Wrestling)* der Deutsche brachte seinen Gegner als erster zu Boden; **at 10 dollars a ~** zu 10 Dollar das Stück
b *(for covering furniture)* Überwurf *m*
VT **a** *ball, stone* werfen; *water* schütten; **to ~ the dice** würfeln; **to ~ a six** eine Sechs würfeln; **to ~ sth to sb** jdm etw zuwerfen; **~ me those keys** werfen Sie mir die Schlüssel herüber; **to ~ sth at sb** etw nach jdm werfen; *mud, paint etc* jdn mit etw bewerfen; **to ~ a ball 20 metres** einen Ball 20 Meter weit werfen; **to ~ sth across the room** etw (quer) durchs Zimmer werfen; **to ~ sb across the ring** jdn durch den Ring schleudern; **he threw himself to the floor** er warf sich auf den Boden *or* zu Boden; **to ~ oneself at sb** *(physically)* sich auf jdn werfen *or* stürzen; *(fig)* sich jdm an den Hals werfen *or* schmeißen *(inf)*; **to ~ oneself into the job** sich in die Arbeit stürzen; **to ~ one's voice** seine Stimme zum Tragen bringen; **to ~ money at sth** etw mit Geld überhäufen; **to ~ one's hat** *or* **cap into the ring** *(fig)* sich anbieten
b *(= send to ground) rider* abwerfen; *opponent* zu Boden werfen *or* bringen; **to be ~n from the saddle** aus dem Sattel geworfen werden
c *(= put hastily)* werfen; **to ~ a coat over sb** jdm einen Mantel überwerfen
d *(fig: = cast)* werfen; **to ~ a glance at sb/sth** einen Blick auf jdn/etw werfen; **to ~ an angry look at sb/sth** jdm/einer Sache einen wütenden Blick zuwerfen; **to ~ light** Licht geben; **to ~ sb off the scent** *or* **trail** jdn von der Spur abbringen; **to ~ sb into prison** jdn ins Gefängnis werfen; **to ~ the blame on sb** jdm die Schuld zuschieben *or* in die Schuhe schieben; **to ~ doubt on sth** etw in Zweifel ziehen; **he threw his troops into action** er warf seine Truppen ins Gefecht
e *switch, lever* betätigen
f *(inf: = disconcert)* aus dem Konzept bringen
g *party* geben, schmeißen *(inf)*
h *fit* bekommen, kriegen *(inf)*
i *(inf: = deliberately lose) match, game* absichtlich verlieren
j *vase* töpfern, drehen; *silk* zwirnen
k *(snake)* **to ~ its skin** sich häuten
l *(animal: = give birth to)* werfen
VI werfen; *(= throw dice)* würfeln

▸ **throw about** *(Brit) or* **around** VT *always separate* **a** *(= scatter)* verstreuen; *(fig) money, name, words* um sich werfen mit **b** *(= toss)* herumwerfen; *one's arms* fuchteln mit; *one's legs* strampeln mit; **to throw oneself around** *(in bed, on floor)* sich hin und her werfen, sich herumwerfen; **to throw a ball around** ein bisschen Ball spielen; **he was thrown around in the car/accident** er wurde im Auto hin und her geschleudert/bei dem Unfall herumgeschleudert

▸ **throw away** VT *sep* **a** *(= discard) rubbish* wegwerfen **b** *(= waste)* verschenken; *money* verschwenden (*on sth* auf *or* für etw, *on sb* an jdn), vergeuden (*on sth* für etw, *on sb* an jdn); **you are throwing yourself away on him** Sie sind zu schade für ihn, Sie verschwenden sich an ihn *(geh)*; **to throw one's life away** sein Leben wegwerfen **c** *(= say casually) remark* nebenbei machen, beiläufig sagen

▸ **throw back** VI *(Biol)* **a type which throws back to an earlier species** ein Typ, der Merk-

male einer früheren Art aufweist
VT *sep* **a** *(= send back) ball, enemy* zurückwerfen
b *(backwards) head, bedclothes* zurückwerfen; *curtains* aufreißen; **to throw oneself back** zurückweichen, zurückspringen
c *(fig)* **to be thrown back upon sth** auf etw *(acc)* wieder angewiesen sein, auf etw *(acc)* zurückgreifen müssen; **the crisis threw them back on their own resources** durch die Krise waren sie wieder auf sich selbst angewiesen
d **I don't want you throwing that back at me** ich möchte nicht, dass du mir meine eigenen Worte/Taten wieder vorhältst

▶ **throw down** VT *sep* **a** *(from a roof, the stairs etc)* herunterwerfen; **throw down your guns!** werfen Sie die Waffen weg!; **to throw oneself down on the floor** sich zu Boden werfen, sich auf den Boden fallen lassen; **to throw oneself down on the sofa** sich aufs Sofa fallen lassen; **it's throwing it down** *(inf: = raining)* es gießt (in Strömen) **b** *(fig)* **to throw down a challenge to sb** jdn herausfordern

▶ **throw in** VT *sep* **a** *extra* (gratis) dazugeben; **with a tour of London thrown in** mit einer Gratistour durch London extra **b** *(Sport) ball* einwerfen **c** *(fig)* **to throw in one's hand** aufgeben, sich geschlagen geben; **to throw in the sponge** *(Brit)* or **towel** das Handtuch werfen *(inf)* **d** *(= say casually) remark* einwerfen *(to* in *+acc)*

▶ **throw off** VT *sep* **a** *(= get rid of) clothes* abwerfen; *disguise, habits* ablegen; *pursuer* abschütteln; *cold* loswerden; **to throw off the yoke of tyranny** die Ketten der Tyrannei sprengen **b** *(= emit) sparks, smell* abgeben, von sich geben

▶ **throw on** VT *sep clothes* sich *(dat)* überwerfen

▶ **throw open** VT *sep* **a** *door, window* aufreißen; *arms* ausbreiten **b** *stately home etc* (öffentlich) zugänglich machen *(to* für*)*; **the doors were thrown open to the public** die breite Öffentlichkeit hatte Zutritt

▶ **throw out** VT *sep* **a** *(= discard) rubbish etc* wegwerfen
b *(= reject) suggestion, bill (Parl)* ablehnen, verwerfen *(geh)*; *case* verwerfen
c *person* hinauswerfen, rauswerfen *(inf)* (of aus); **to be thrown out of work** entlassen werden; **automation has thrown a lot of people out of work** die Automation hat viele Menschen arbeitslos gemacht *or* vielen Menschen ihren Arbeitsplatz genommen
d *(= utter) hint* machen; *idea* äußern; **to throw out a challenge to sb** jdn herausfordern
e *(plant) suckers, shoots* treiben; *(fire etc) heat* abgeben
f *one's chest* herausdrücken
g *(= make wrong) calculations etc* über den Haufen werfen *(inf)*, durcheinanderbringen; **to throw sb out in his calculations** jdn bei seinen Berechnungen durcheinanderbringen

▶ **throw over** VT *sep plan* über den Haufen werfen *(inf)*; *girlfriend* sitzen lassen *(for* wegen*)*

▶ **throw together** VT *sep* **a** *(= put hastily together) ingredients* zusammenwerfen; *clothes* zusammenpacken; *(= make quickly)* hinhauen; *essay* hinhauen *(inf)*, runterschreiben *(inf)* **b** *(= bring together) people (fate etc)* zusammenführen; *(friends etc)* zusammenbringen

▶ **throw up** VI *(inf)* sich übergeben, brechen; **it makes you want to throw up** da kann einem schlecht werden, da kommt einem das Kotzen *(sl)*
VT *sep* **a** *ball, hands* hochwerfen; *dust* aufwirbeln; *stones* aufspritzen lassen
b *(= abandon) job* aufgeben; *opportunity etc* verschenken; **I feel like throwing everything up** ich würde am liebsten alles hinwerfen *(inf)*
c *(= vomit up)* von sich *(dat)* geben, ausbrechen
d *(= produce)* hervorbringen; *problems, questions* aufwerfen; **the meeting threw up several good ideas** bei der Versammlung kamen ein paar gute Ideen zutage; **the new politicians thrown up by the war** die neuen Politiker, die der Krieg hervorgebracht hat
e *building etc* aus dem Boden stampfen

throw: **throwaway** ADJ **a** *(= casual) remark* achtlos gemacht; *style* unaufdringlich, leger; **a ~ line** eine hingeworfene Bemerkung **b** *(= disposable)* Wegwerf-, zum Wegwerfen; **~ wrapping** Wegwerf- *or* Einwegverpackung *f*; **~ society** Wegwerfgesellschaft *f*; **~ culture** Wegwerfkultur *f* **c** *(= cheap)* **~ prices** Schleuderpreise *pl* N **throwaways** PL Einwegprodukte *pl*; **throwback** N **a he's a ~ to his Irish ancestors** bei ihm kommen seine irischen Vorfahren wieder durch **b** *(fig: = return)* Rückkehr *f (to* zu*)*; *(= revival)* Neubelebung *f (to* gen*)*

throw-down [ˈθrəʊdaʊn] N *(Ftbl)* Schiedsrichterball *m*

thrower [ˈθrəʊəʳ] N Werfer(in) *m(f)*; **he's not a very good ~** er kann nicht sehr gut werfen

throw-in [ˈθrəʊɪn] N *(Sport)* Einwurf *m*

thrown [θrəʊn] *ptp of* **throw**

thru PREP, ADV, ADJ *(US)* = **through**

thrum [θrʌm] VT *guitar* klimpern auf *(+dat)*, schlagen; *tune* klimpern *(auf der Gitarre etc)*; **he ~med the desk with his fingers, he ~med his fingers on the desk** er trommelte mit seinen Fingern auf der Schreibtischplatte VI *(on guitar)* klimpern; *(air conditioning)* summen

thrupenny [ˈθrʌpnɪ] ADJ, N *(Brit inf)* = **threepenny**

thruppence [ˈθrʌpəns] N *(Brit inf)* = **threepence**

thrush¹ [θrʌʃ] N *(Orn)* Drossel *f*

thrush² N *(Med)* Soor *m (spec)*, Schwämmchen *nt*; *(of vagina)* Pilzkrankheit *f*; *(Vet, in horses)* Strahlfäule *f*

thrust [θrʌst] *vb: pret, ptp* **thrust** N **a** Stoß *m*; *(of knife)* Stich *m*, Stoß *m*; *(fig, of intellect)* Stoßkraft *f*
b *(Tech)* Druckkraft *f*; *(in rocket, turbine)* Schub *m*, Schubkraft *f*
c *(Mil: also* **thrust forward***)* Vorstoß *m*
d *(fig, of speech, article etc)* Tenor *m*; **I get the general ~ of what you're saying** ich weiß, worauf es Ihnen ankommt
VT **a** *(= push, drive)* stoßen; **the tree ~ its branches upward** der Baum streckte seine Äste in den Himmel; **to ~ one's hands into one's pockets** die Hände in die Tasche stecken *or* stopfen *(inf)*; **she ~ her books into the box** sie stopfte ihre Bücher in die Kiste; **she ~ the money into his hands** sie drückte ihm das Geld in die Hand
b *(fig)* **to ~ oneself upon sb** sich jdm aufdrängen; **I had the job ~ upon me** die Arbeit wurde mir aufgedrängt *or* aufgezwungen; **and some have greatness ~ upon them** und einigen wird Größe auferlegt *or* aufgebürdet; **to ~ one's way through a crowd** sich durch die Menge drängen *or* schieben; **to ~ one's way to the front** sich nach vorne vordrängeln, sich nach vorne kämpfen
VI stoßen *(at* nach*)*; *(with knife)* stechen *(at* nach*)*; *(Fencing)* einen Ausfall machen, ausfallen *(at* gegen*)*

▶ **thrust aside** VT *sep* beiseiteschieben; *person also* beiseitedrängen, zur Seite drängen; *(fig) objection also* zurückweisen

▶ **thrust forward** VT *sep* **to thrust sb forward** *(lit)* jdn vorschieben; *(fig)* sich für jdn starkmachen; **to thrust oneself forward** *(lit)* sich vorschieben, sich nach vorne durchdrängeln; *(fig)* sich einsetzen; *(pej)* sich in den Vordergrund drängen

▶ **thrust out** VT *sep leg* ausstrecken; *hand also* hinstrecken; *head, breasts* vorstrecken; *chest* herausdrücken, wölben; **she thrust her head out (of the window)** sie streckte den Kopf (zum Fenster) hinaus; **the goalie thrust out his legs** der Torwart streckte die Beine vor

▶ **thrust past** VI sich vorbeidrängen *(prep obj* an *+dat)*

thrust bearing N Drucklager *nt*

thruster [ˈθrʌstəʳ] N *(= directional rocket)* (Fein)steuerrakete *f*

thrustful [ˈθrʌstfʊl], **thrusting** ADJ *person, behaviour* energisch, zielstrebig, resolut; *(pej)* (etwas) zu zielstrebig

thrustfulness [ˈθrʌstfʊlnɪs] N energische Art, Zielstrebigkeit *f*, Resolutheit *f*; *(pej)* (etwas) zu große Zielstrebigkeit

thrusting [ˈθrʌstɪŋ] ADJ = **thrustful**

thrust: **thrust performance** N *(Aviat, Tech)* Schubleistung *f*; **thrust weapon** N Stich- *or* Stoßwaffe *f*

thruway [ˈθruːweɪ] N *(US)* Schnellstraße *f*

Thu *abbr of* **Thursday** Do.

thud [θʌd] N dumpfes Geräusch; **the ~ of his footsteps** seine dumpfen Schritte; **he fell to the ground with a ~** er fiel mit einem Plumps *(inf)* or einem dumpfen Aufschlag zu Boden; **the ~ of the waves against the hull** das dumpfe Schlagen der Wellen gegen den Schiffsrumpf
VI dumpf aufschlagen; *(= move heavily)* stampfen; **the blow ~ded against his chin** dumpf klatschte der Schlag gegen sein Kinn; **a ~ding noise** ein dumpfes Geräusch; **with ~ding heart** mit pochendem Herzen; **the heavy door ~ded shut** mit einem dumpfen Knall fiel die Tür zu

thug [θʌg] N Schlägertyp *m*

thuggish [ˈθʌgɪʃ] ADJ *person, behaviour* gewalttätig; **to be ~ in dealing with sb** mit jdm brutal umgehen

thulium [ˈθjuːlɪəm] N *(Chem)* Thulium *nt*

thumb [θʌm] N Daumen *m*; **to be under sb's ~** unter jds Pantoffel *(dat)* or Fuchtel *(dat)* stehen; **she has him under her ~** sie hat ihn unter ihrer Fuchtel; **to be all ~s** zwei linke Hände haben; **he gave me the ~s up/down** er gab mir zu verstehen, dass alles in Ordnung war/dass es nicht in Ordnung war; **the idea was given the ~s up/down** für den Vorschlag wurde grünes/rotes Licht gegeben; **it sticks out like a sore ~** das springt einem direkt ins Auge; **he sticks out like a sore ~** *(= doesn't fit in)* er ist auffallend anders
VT **a** *(inf)* **to ~ a ride** *or* **lift** per Anhalter fahren; **let's ~ a lift with this lorry** wir wollen versuchen, diesen Lastwagen anzuhalten
b **to ~ one's nose at sb/sth** jdm/einer Sache eine lange Nase machen; *(fig)* auf jdn/etw pfeifen
c **a well ~ed book** ein Buch mit abgegriffenen Seiten

▶ **thumb through** VI *+prep obj book* durchblättern; *card index* durchgehen, durchsehen

thumber [ˈθʌməʳ] N *(inf)* Anhalter(in) *m(f)*, Tramper(in) *m(f)*

thumb: **thumb index** N Daumenregister *nt*, Daumenindex *m*; **thumbnail** **a** N Daumennagel *m* **b** *(Comput)* Miniaturansicht *f*; **thumbnail sketch** N *(= drawing)* kleine Skizze; *(= description)* kurze Skizze, kurze Zusammenfassung; **thumbprint** N Daumenabdruck *m*; **thumbscrew** N *(Tech)* Flügelschraube *f*; *(torture)* Daumenschraube *f*; **to put the ~s on sb** *(fig)* jdm die Daumenschrauben anlegen

thumbs-down [ˌθʌmzˈdaʊn] N *(inf) (= rejection)* (totale) Ablehnung; *(= criticism)* vernichtende Kritik

thumbstall N Daumenkappe *f*, Daumenschützer *m*, Fingerling *m*

thumb-sucking N Daumenlutschen *nt*

thumbs-up [ˌθʌmzˈʌp] N *(inf) (= agreement)* Zustimmung *f*; *(= praise)* Lobeshymne *f (inf)*

thumbtack N *(US)* Reißnagel *m*, Reiß- *or* Heftzwecke *f*

thump [θʌmp] N *(= blow)* Schlag *m*; *(= noise)* (dumpfes) Krachen, Bums *m (inf)*
VT *table* klopfen *or* schlagen auf *(+acc)*; *door* klopfen *or* schlagen an *(+acc)*; *(esp Brit inf) person* verhauen *(inf)*; *(repeatedly)* trommeln auf/an *(+acc)*; *(accidentally) one's head* sich *(dat)* anschlagen *or* anhauen *(inf)*; *(dog) tail* klopfen mit; **he ~ed his fist on the desk** er donnerte die Faust auf den Tisch; **he ~ed his chest** er schlug sich *(dat)* auf die Brust; **he ~ed the box down on my desk** er knallte die Schachtel auf

meinen Tisch; **the prisoners started ~ing their stools on the floor** die Gefangenen schlugen mit ihren Hockern auf den Boden; **I ~ed him (one) on the nose** (*esp Brit inf*) ich habe ihm eins auf die Nase verpasst (*inf*); **I'll ~ you (one) if you don't shut up** (*esp Brit inf*) wenn du nicht gleich den Mund hältst, knallts (*inf*)
VI (*person*) schlagen; (*heart*) heftig schlagen *or* pochen; (*= move heavily*) stapfen; (*object: = fall loudly*) plumpsen (*inf*); **he ~ed on the door/table** er schlug gegen *or* an die Tür/auf den Tisch; **ask the people upstairs to stop ~ing around** sag den Leuten über uns, sie sollen aufhören herumzutrampeln

▶ **thump out** VT *sep tune* hämmern

thumping ['θʌmpɪŋ] ADJ (*inf: also* **thumping great**) kolossal, enorm

thunder ['θʌndəʳ] **N** **a** Donner *m*; **a long roll of ~** ein langer rollender Donner, ein langes Donnergrollen; **there is ~ in the air** es liegt ein Gewitter *nt* in der Luft **b** (*fig, of applause*) Sturm *m*; (*of cannons*) Donnern *nt*, Dröhnen *nt*; (*of waves*) Tosen *nt*; **a ~ of applause** ein Beifallssturm *m* → **steal** **VI** (*lit, fig*) donnern; (*guns, hooves also*) dröhnen; (*applause also*) brausen; (*waves, sea*) tosen, brausen; **the horses came ~ing up to the gate** die Pferde kamen aufs Tor zugeprescht; **the senator ~ed against them** der Senator wetterte gegen sie **VT** (*= shout*) brüllen, donnern, mit Donnerstimme brüllen

▶ **thunder out** **VT** *sep order* mit donnernder Stimme geben; *tune* donnern **VI** (*guns*) losdonnern; **his voice thundered out** er donnerte los

▶ **thunder past** VI (*train, traffic*) vorbeidonnern

thunder: **thunderbolt** N (*lit*) Blitz *m*, Blitz und Donner; **the news came like a ~** (*fig*) die Nachricht schlug wie der Blitz ein *or* kam wie ein Donnerschlag; **thunderclap** N Donnerschlag *m*; **thundercloud** N Gewitterwolke *f*

thunderer ['θʌndərəʳ] N **the Thunderer** (*Myth*) der Blitzeschleuderer

thunderhead ['θʌndəhed] N (*esp US Met*) Kumulonimbusspitze *f*

thundering ['θʌndərɪŋ] **ADJ** **a** (*= loud*) *applause, chords* donnernd; *waterfall* tosend **b** (*= forceful, direct*) *voice, question* donnernd **c** (*inf, = real*) verteufelt (*inf*), verflixt (*inf*); **a ~ success** ein Bombenerfolg *m* (*inf*); **to be in a ~ rage** vor Wut kochen *or* schäumen **ADV** (*inf: = really*) **a ~ great lorry** ein großer, donnernder Laster; **a ~ great nuisance** ein Riesenärgernis *nt* (*inf*); **~ good music** verdammt gute Musik (*inf*)

thunderous ['θʌndərəs] ADJ stürmisch; *voice, explosion, knock* donnernd; *volley, header* krachend

thunder: **thunderstorm** N Gewitter *nt*; **thunderstruck** ADJ (*fig*) wie vom Donner gerührt

thundery ['θʌndərɪ] ADJ *weather, showers* gewitterig

thurible ['θjʊərɪbl] N (*Eccl*) (Weih)rauchfass *nt*, Räucherfass *nt*

Thuringia [θjʊəˈrɪndʒɪə] N Thüringen *nt*

Thurs *abbr of* **Thursday** Do.

Thursday ['θɜːzdɪ] N Donnerstag *m* → *also* **Tuesday**

thus [ðʌs] ✪ 26.3 ADV **a** (*= in this way*) so, auf diese Art; **you must hold it ~** Sie müssen das so halten; **~ it was that ...** so kam es, dass ... **b** (*= consequently*) folglich, somit **c** (*+ptp or adj*) *reassured, encouraged etc* solchermaßen (*geh*), derart (*geh*); **~ far** so weit; **~ far and no further** so weit und keinen Schritt weiter

thwack [θwæk] **N** (*= blow*) Schlag *m*; (*= noise*) Klatschen *nt*, Bums *m* (*inf*) **VT** schlagen; (*waves*) klatschen gegen; **he ~ed his cane on the table** er ließ seinen Stock auf den Tisch heruntersausen **VI** schlagen (*against* gegen); (*waves, cane*) klatschen

thwart[1] [θwɔːt] VT vereiteln; *plan also* durchkreuzen; *robbery, attack also* verhindern; **he was ~ed** ihm wurde ein Strich durch die Rechnung gemacht; **to ~ sb in sth** jdm etw vereiteln; **to ~ the will of the people** gegen den Willen des Volkes handeln; **to be ~ed at every turn** überall auf Hindernisse stoßen; **~ed!** wieder nichts!

thwart[2] N (*Naut*) Ruderbank *f*, Ducht *f*

thx, **thxs** (*Internet etc*) *abbr of* **thanks**

thy [ðaɪ] POSS ADJ (*old, dial*) *before vowel* **thine** Euer/Eure/Euer (*obs*); (*dial, to God*) dein/deine/dein

thyme [taɪm] N Thymian *m*

thyroid ['θaɪrɔɪd] **N** (*also* **thyroid gland**) Schilddrüse *f* **ADJ** Schilddrüsen-; **~ hormone** Schilddrüsenhormon *nt*

thyself [ðaɪˈself] PERS PRON (*old, dial*) **a** (*reflexive dir obj with prep +acc*) Euch (*obs*); (*dial, to God*) dich; (*indir obj with prep +dat*) Euch (*obs*); (*dial, to God*) dir **b** (*emph*) Ihr selbst (*obs*), du selbst (*obs*); (*acc*) Euch selbst (*obs*), dich selbst; (*dat*) Ihnen selbst (*obs*), dir selbst

tiara [tɪˈɑːrə] N Diadem *nt*; (*of pope*) Tiara *f*

Tiber ['taɪbəʳ] N Tiber *m*

Tibet [tɪˈbet] N Tibet *nt*

Tibetan [tɪˈbetən] **ADJ** tibetanisch, tibetisch; **he is ~** er ist Tibeter **N** **a** Tibeter(in) *m(f)*, Tibetaner(in) *m(f)* **b** (*Ling*) Tibetisch *nt*

tibia ['tɪbɪə] N *pl* **-s** *or* **-e** ['tɪbɪiː] Schienbein *nt*, Tibia *f* (*spec*)

tic [tɪk] N (*Med*) Tick *m*, nervöses Zucken

tich, **titch** [tɪtʃ] N (*Brit inf*) Knirps *m*; **hey, ~!** he, Kleine(r)!

tichy, **titchy** ['tɪtʃɪ] ADJ (*+er*) (*Brit inf: also* **tichy little**) *person* winzig, knirpsig (*inf*); *things* klitzeklein (*inf*), winzig

tick[1] [tɪk] **N** **a** (*of clock etc*) Ticken *nt* **b** (*Brit inf: = moment*) Augenblick *m*, Sekunde *f*, Minütchen *nt* (*inf*); **half a ~** eine Sekunde; **are you ready yet? – half a ~** *or* **two ~s!** bist du schon fertig? – sofort; **I'll be ready in a ~** *or* **two ~s** bin sofort fertig (*inf*); **he did it in two ~s** er hat es in Sekundenschnelle *or* im Handumdrehen getan **c** (*esp Brit: = mark*) Häkchen *nt*, Haken *m*; **to put a ~ against a name/an answer** einen Namen/eine Antwort abhaken
VI **a** (*clock*) ticken; **the minutes ~ed by** *or* **past/away** die Minuten vergingen *or* verstrichen **b** (*inf*) **what makes him ~?** was geht in ihm vor?
VT (*Brit*) *name* abhaken; *box, answer* ankreuzen

▶ **tick off** VT *sep* (*Brit*) **a** *name etc* abhaken **b** (*inf: = scold*) ausschimpfen (*inf*), anpfeifen (*inf*); **he got ticked off for doing it** er wurde angepfiffen (*inf*) *or* er bekam einen Rüffel *or* Anpfiff (*inf*), weil er das getan hat **c** (*inf: = annoy*) total nerven (*inf*); **what really ticks me off ...** was mich absolut auf die Palme bringt ... (*inf*)

▶ **tick over** VI **a** (*= idle: engine*) im Leerlauf sein; **the engine is ticking over nicely** der Motor läuft ganz gut *or* ruhig **b** (*fig: business etc*) ganz ordentlich laufen; (*pej*) auf Sparflamme sein (*inf*); **to keep things ticking over** die Sache in Gang halten

tick[2] N (*Zool*) Zecke *f*

tick[3] N (*Brit inf*) **on ~** auf Pump (*inf*)

tick[4] N (*Tex: = cover, for mattress*) Matratzenbezug *m*; (*for pillow etc*) Inlett *nt*

ticker ['tɪkəʳ] N (*inf*) **a** (*= heart*) Pumpe *f* (*inf*) **b** (*= watch*) Zwiebel *f* (*dated hum inf*), Wecker *m* (*inf*)

ticker tape N Lochstreifen *m*; **~ welcome/parade** Konfettibegrüßung *f*/-parade *f*

ticket ['tɪkɪt] N **a** (*= rail ticket, bus ticket*) Fahrkarte *f*, Fahrschein *m*; (*= plane ticket*) Ticket *nt*, Flugkarte *f*, Flugschein *m*; (*Theat, for football match etc*) (Eintritts)karte *f*; (*= cloakroom ticket*) Garderobenmarke *f*; (*= library ticket*) ≈ Buchzettel *m*; (*for dry cleaner's, cobbler etc*) Abschnitt *m*, Zettel *m*; (*= luggage office ticket*) (Gepäck)schein *m*; (*= raffle ticket*) Los *nt*; (*= lottery ticket*) Lottoschein *m*; (*= price ticket*) Preisschild *nt*; (*for car park*) Parkschein *m*; **admission by ~ only** Einlass nur gegen Eintrittskarten **b** (*US Pol*) Wahlliste *f*; **he's running on the Democratic ~** er kandidiert für die Demokratische Partei → **split, straight** **c** (*Jur*) Strafzettel *m*; **to give sb a ~** jdm einen Strafzettel geben *or* verpassen (*inf*) **d** (*dated Brit, inf*) **that's just the ~!** das ist famos! (*dated inf*)

ticket: **ticket agency** N (*Theat*) Vorverkaufsstelle *f*; (*Rail etc*) Verkaufsstelle *f*; **ticket barrier** N (*Brit Rail*) Fahrkartensperre *f*; **ticket-cancelling machine**, (*US*) **ticket-canceling machine** ['tɪkɪtˌkænsəlɪŋməˌʃiːn] N (Fahrschein)entwerter *m*; **ticket collector** N (*Rail, on train*) Schaffner(in) *m(f)*; (*in station*) Bahnsteigschaffner(in) *m(f)*, Fahrkartenkontrolleur(in) *m(f)*; **ticketholder** N (*Theat etc*) *jd, der eine Eintrittskarte hat*; **~s only through this door** (*Theat etc*) Eingang nur für Besucher mit Eintrittskarten; **ticket inspector** N (Fahrkarten)kontrolleur(in) *m(f)*; **ticket machine** N (*public transport*) Fahrkartenautomat *m*; (*in car park*) Parkscheinautomat *m*; **ticket office** N (*Rail*) Fahrkartenschalter *m*, Fahrkartenausgabe *f*; (*Theat*) Kasse *f*; **ticket tout** N Kartenschwarzhändler(in) *m(f)*; **ticket window** N (*Rail*) (Fahrkarten)schalter *m*; (*Theat*) Kasse *f*

ticking ['tɪkɪŋ] N **a** (*for mattress*) Matratzendrell *m*; (*for pillows etc*) Inlett *nt* **b** (*of clock*) Ticken *nt*

ticking cover N Matratzenbezug *m*

ticking-off [ˌtɪkɪŋˈɒf] N (*Brit inf*) Rüffel *m*, Anpfiff *m* (*inf*); **he needs a good ~** dem muss man mal den Marsch blasen (*inf*)

tickle ['tɪkl] **VT** **a** (*lit*) kitzeln; **to ~ sb's ribs** jdn in der Seite kitzeln; **to ~ sb's toes** jdn an den Zehen kitzeln; **this wool ~s my skin** diese Wolle kratzt *or* juckt (auf der Haut) **b** (*fig inf*) *person* (*= please*) schmeicheln (*+dat*) und freuen; (*= amuse*) belustigen, amüsieren; **to be ~d** sich gebauchpinselt fühlen (*inf*); **here's a little story that might ~ your imagination** eine kleine Geschichte, die Sie wohl recht amüsant finden werden; **that story really ~d me** diese Geschichte fand ich wirklich köstlich; **to be ~d pink** *or* **to death** sich wie ein Schneekönig freuen (*inf*); **to ~ the ivories** (*inf*) auf den Tasten klimpern → **fancy**
VI kitzeln; (*wool*) kratzen, jucken; **stop it, that ~s** aufhören, das kitzelt; **my ear is tickling** mein Ohr juckt
N Kitzeln *nt*; **he gave the baby a little ~** er kitzelte das Baby ein bisschen; **to have a ~ in one's throat** einen Hustenreiz haben; **I didn't get a ~ all day** (*Fishing*) es hat den ganzen Tag keiner (an)gebissen

tickler ['tɪkləʳ] N (*inf*) kitz(e)lige Angelegenheit

ticklish ['tɪklɪʃ] ADJ (*lit*) kitz(e)lig; (*fig*) *situation also* heikel; (*= touchy*) empfindlich; **~ cough** Reizhusten *m*

tick: **tick-over** N (*Brit Aut*) Leerlauf *m*; **tick-tack** N Zeichensprache *f* der Buchmacher; **ticktack man** N Buchmachergehilfe *m*; **tick-tack-toe** N (*US*) Tic Tac Toe *nt*, *Kinderspiel mit Nullen und Kreuzen*; **ticktock** N (*= sound*) ticktack; (*baby-talk: = clock*) Ticktack *f*

ticky-tacky ['tɪkɪˌtækɪ] (*US inf*) **ADJ** *house, hotel* heruntergekommen **N** *no pl* (*= building material*) minderwertiges Baumaterial; (*= goods*) Schund *m*, Ramsch *m* (*inf*)

tidal ['taɪdl] ADJ Tide-, Gezeiten-; *waters* den Gezeiten unterworfen; **this river is not ~** in diesem Fluss gibt es keine Gezeiten, das ist kein Tidefluss

tidal: **tidal atlas** N Gezeitenatlas *m*; **tidal barrier**, **tidal barrage** N Staudamm *m*, Staumauer *f*; **tidal basin** N Tidebecken *nt*; **tidal current** N Gezeitenstrom *m*; **tidal harbour** N Tidehafen *m*; **tidal inlet** N Priel *m*; **tidal lift** N Tidenhub *m*; **tidal power plant**, **tidal power station** N Tide- *or* Gezeitenkraftwerk *nt*; **tidal wave** N (*lit*) Flutwelle *f*; **a great ~ of enthusiasm swept over the country** (*fig*) eine Welle der Begeisterung ging durch das Land

tidbit ['tɪdbɪt] N (*US*) = **titbit**

tiddler ['tɪdlǝ'] N (Brit) **a** (= fish) winziger Fisch **b** (inf: = child) Knirps m; **she teaches ~s** sie unterrichtet die ganz Kleinen

tiddly ['tɪdlɪ] ADJ (+er) (Brit inf) **a** (= tiny) winzig, klitzeklein (inf); **a ~ little scratch** ein klitzekleiner (inf) or winzig kleiner Kratzer **b** (= tipsy) angesäuselt (inf), beschwipst; **she gets ~ on half a glass of sherry** sie bekommt von einem halben Glas Sherry schon einen Schwips

tiddlywinks ['tɪdlɪwɪŋks] N Floh(hüpf)spiel nt; **to play ~** Flohhüpfen spielen

tide [taɪd] N **a** (lit) Gezeiten pl, Tide f (N Ger); **(at) high ~** (bei) Hochwasser nt or Flut f; **(at) low ~** (bei) Niedrigwasser nt or Ebbe f; **the rise and fall of the ~** Ebbe f und Flut f, der Tidenhub (spec); **we'll sail on the next ~** wir fahren mit der nächsten Flut; **the ~ is in/out** es ist Flut/Ebbe, es ist Hochwasser/Niedrigwasser (form); **the ~ comes in very fast** die Flut kommt sehr schnell; **the ~s are influenced by the moon** Ebbe und Flut or die Gezeiten werden vom Mond beeinflusst; **stranded by the ~** in der Ebbe/Flut gestrandet; **until the ~ turns** bis zum Gezeitenwechsel, bis die Flut/Ebbe einsetzt
b (fig: = trend) **the ~ of history** der Lauf der Geschichte; **the ~ of public opinion** der Trend der öffentlichen Meinung; **carried away by the ~ of events** vom Strom der Ereignisse mitgerissen; **to go** or **swim against/with the ~** gegen den/mit dem Strom schwimmen; **the ~ has turned** das Blatt hat sich gewendet; **the ~ of the battle turned** das Glück (der Schlacht) wendete sich → **turn, time**
c (old: = time) Zeit f

▶ **tide over** VT always separate **that will tide me over until tomorrow** damit werde ich bis morgen auskommen; **is that enough to tide you over?** reicht Ihnen das vorläufig?

tide: **tide-bound** ADJ boat etc von der Ebbe am Auslaufen gehindert; **tide gate** N Seeschleuse f; **tideland** N (US) Watt nt; **tidemark** N Flutmarke f; (man-made) Pegelstand m; (hum, on neck, in bath) schwarzer Rand; **tide race** N Gezeitenstrom m; **tidewater** N Flut f; (US: = lowlands) Watt nt; **tideway** N Priel m

tidily ['taɪdɪlɪ] ADV ordentlich

tidiness ['taɪdɪnɪs] N (of person) Ordentlichkeit f; (of appearance) Gepflegtheit f; (of room) Aufgeräumtheit f; (of desk) Ordnung f; (of handwriting, schoolwork) Sauberkeit f

tidings ['taɪdɪŋz] PL (old, liter) Kunde f (old, liter), Botschaft f (liter), Nachricht f

tidy ['taɪdɪ] ADJ (+er) **a** (= orderly) ordentlich; appearance gepflegt, ordentlich; room aufgeräumt; desk ordentlich; handwriting, schoolwork sauber; **to look ~** (person) ordentlich or gepflegt aussehen; (room) ordentlich aussehen; **she has very ~ habits** sie ist ein sehr ordentlicher or ordnungsliebender Mensch; **to teach sb ~ habits** jdn zur Ordnung erziehen; **to keep sth ~** etw in Ordnung halten; **to get a room ~** ein Zimmer aufräumen; **she's very ~ in her dress** sie ist immer sehr ordentlich gekleidet; **to make oneself ~** sich zurechtmachen; **to have a ~ mind** klar or logisch denken
b (inf: = considerable) ordentlich (inf), ganz schön (inf); **a ~ sum** eine ordentliche Stange Geld (inf)
VT hair in Ordnung bringen; room also aufräumen; (also **tidy up**) drawer, desk aufräumen
N Behälter m

▶ **tidy away** VT sep wegräumen, aufräumen

▶ **tidy out** VT sep entrümpeln, ausmisten (inf)

▶ **tidy up** VI **a** (= clear away) aufräumen, Ordnung machen **b** (= clean oneself) sich zurechtmachen VT sep books, room aufräumen, in Ordnung bringen; drawer, desk aufräumen; piece of work in Ordnung bringen; **to tidy oneself up** sich zurechtmachen; **to tidy up the loose ends** die Fäden vernähen

tidy: **tidy-out** N Entrümpelung f; **the cupboards could do with a ~** die Schränke müssten mal entrümpelt or ausgemistet (inf) werden; **tidy-up** N Aufräumen nt; **this room needs a ~** dieses Zimmer muss aufgeräumt werden; **go and give yourself a ~** mach dich ein bisschen zurecht

tie [taɪ] N **a** (esp US: also **neck tie**) Krawatte f, Schlips m (inf), Binder m (dated form)
b (Archit, Build, also **tie beam**) Binderbalken m, Bundbalken m; (= tie piece) Stichbalken m; (Mus) Haltebogen m; (US Rail) Schwelle f; (= cord) Schnur f
c (fig: = bond) Band nt (liter), Beziehung f, (Ver)bindung f; **~s of friendship** freundschaftliche Beziehungen or Bande (liter) pl; **the blood ~** Blutsbande pl; **business ~s** Geschäftsverbindungen pl; **he's investigating the ~s between Pasternak and Rilke** er untersucht die Beziehung zwischen Pasternak und Rilke; **family ~s** familiäre Bindungen pl
d (= hindrance) Belastung f (on für); **family ~s** familiäre Bindungen or Fesseln pl; **I don't want any ~s** ich will keine Bindung, ich will mich nicht gebunden fühlen
e (Sport etc: = result) Unentschieden nt; (= match etc ending in draw) unentschiedenes Spiel; **the match ended in a ~** das Spiel endete mit einem Unentschieden; **the result of the competition was a ~** der Wettkampf ging unentschieden aus; **there was a ~ for second place** es gab zwei zweite Plätze
f (Brit esp Ftbl: = match) Spiel nt
VT **a** (= fasten) binden (to an +acc), befestigen (to an +dat); **~ the string round the tree** binde die Schnur um den Baum; **my hands are ~d** (fig) mir sind die Hände gebunden
b (= knot) shoelace, tie, ribbon binden; **to ~ a knot in sth** einen Knoten in etw (acc) machen; **to ~ a bow in a ribbon** or **a ribbon in a bow** ein Band zu einer Schleife binden
c (fig: = unite, link) verbinden
d (= restrict) person binden (to an +acc)
e (Sport) **the match was ~d** das Spiel ging unentschieden aus
f **~d** (Mus, notes) gebunden
VI **a** (ribbon etc) **it won't ~ properly** es lässt sich nicht richtig binden; **it ~s at the back** es wird hinten (zu)gebunden
b (Sport) unentschieden spielen; (in competition, vote) gleichstehen; **they ~d for first place** (Sport, competition) sie teilten sich den ersten Platz; (Sch) sie waren (mit den gleichen Noten) die Klassenbesten

▶ **tie back** VT sep hair, roses, door zurückbinden

▶ **tie down** VT sep **a** (lit) festbinden (to an +dat); huts, tents verankern (to in +dat); horse fesseln **b** (fig: = restrict) binden (to an +acc); meaning genau bestimmen; **to tie sb/oneself down to sth** jdn/sich auf etw (acc) festlegen; **to tie oneself down to doing sth** sich verpflichten, etw zu tun; **marriage/owning property ties you down** durch die Ehe/durch Eigentum ist man gebunden; **she's tied down because of the children, the children tie her down** durch die Kinder ist sie sehr gebunden

▶ **tie in** VI dazu passen; **to tie in with sth** zu etw passen, dazu passen; **it all ties in** das passt alles zusammen; **the new evidence didn't tie in** das neue Beweismaterial passte nicht ins Bild VT sep plans verbinden, in Einklang bringen

▶ **tie on** VT sep anbinden, festbinden; **to tie sth on(to) sth** etw an etw (dat) anbinden

▶ **tie up** VI **a** **now it all ties up** jetzt passt alles zusammen; **it all ties up with his marital problems** das hängt alles mit seinen Eheproblemen zusammen
b (Naut) festmachen
VT sep **a** parcel verschnüren; shoelaces binden
b boat festmachen; animal festbinden, anbinden (to an +dat); prisoner, hands etc fesseln
c (= settle) deal, arrangements etc unter Dach und Fach bringen → **loose**
d (Fin) capital (fest) anlegen, festlegen
e (= link) **to be tied up with sth** mit etw zusammenhängen; **are you still tied up with that firm?** haben Sie noch Verbindungen zu der Firma?
f (= keep busy) beschäftigen; machines auslasten; **he's tied up all tomorrow** er ist morgen den ganzen Tag belegt or beschäftigt; **he's tied up with the manager at the moment** er hat momentan beim Betriebsleiter zu tun
g (= obstruct, hinder) production etc stilllegen

tie: **tie beam** N (Archit) Spannbalken m; **tie-break, tie-breaker** N (Tennis, in quiz etc) Tiebreak m, Tie-Break m; **tie clip** N Krawattennadel f

tied [taɪd]: **tied cottage** N (Brit) Gesindehaus nt; **tied house** N (Brit: = pub) Brauereigaststätte f, brauereieigene Gaststätte

tie: **tie-dye** VT nach dem Bindebatikverfahren färben; **tie-in** N **a** (= connection, relationship) Verbindung f, Beziehung f, Zusammenhang m **b** (US: = sale) Kopplungsgeschäft nt ATTR **~ edition** (of book) Begleitbuch nt, Buch nt zum Film/zur Serie; **~ sale** (US) Kopplungsgeschäft nt; **tie line** N (Telec) Direktverbindung f; **tie-on** ADJ attr cover, cushion zum Anbinden or Festbinden; **tiepin** N Krawattennadel f, Schlipsnadel f (inf)

tier [tɪǝ'] N (of cake) Etage f, Stufe f; (of amphitheatre) Reihe f; (Theat, of stadium) Rang m; (fig, in hierarchy etc) Stufe f, Rang m; **a cake with three ~s** ein dreistöckiger Kuchen; **a three-~ hierarchy** eine dreigestufte Hierarchie; **to arrange sth in ~s** etw stufenförmig aufbauen

tiered [tɪǝd] ADJ gestuft; **a three-~ cake** ein dreistöckiger Kuchen

tie: **tie rod** N (Aut) Lenkspurstange f; **tie-up** ['taɪʌp] N **a** (= connection) Verbindung f **b** (US: = stoppage) Stillstand m; **there is a ~ in transportation** der Verkehr steht still or ist lahmgelegt

tiff [tɪf] N (inf) Krach m (inf); **he's had a ~ with his girlfriend** er hat mit seiner Freundin Krach gehabt (inf)

tiger ['taɪgǝ'] N Tiger m

tiger: **tiger cat** N Tigerkatze f; (= striped domestic cat) getigerte (Haus)katze; **tiger economy** N schnell wachsende Wirtschaft f; (= tiger state) Tigerstaat m; **tiger lily** N Tigerlilie f; **tiger moth** N Bärenspinner m; **tiger shark** N Tigerhai m

tight [taɪt] ADJ (+er) **a** (= close-fitting) clothes eng; join dicht; **these jeans/shoes are too ~** diese Jeans/Schuhe sind zu eng
b (= stiff, difficult to move) screw, bolt festsitzend, unbeweglich; **the tap is (too) ~** der Hahn ist zu fest zu; **the cork/screw/bolt is (too) ~** der Korken/die Schraube/der Bolzen sitzt fest; **the drawer/window is a bit ~** die Schublade/das Fenster klemmt ein bisschen or geht schwer auf
c (= firm) screw fest angezogen; tap, window dicht; lid, embrace fest; control, discipline, security streng; organization straff; **to have/keep a ~ hold of sth** (lit) etw gut festhalten; **to keep a ~ hold on the reins** (fig) die Zügel fest in der Hand haben; **to keep a ~ lid on sth** (fig) etw streng unter Kontrolle halten; **to run a ~ ship** (lit, fig) ein strenges Regiment führen
d (= taut) rope, skin straff; knot fest (angezogen); **she wears her hair in a ~ bun** sie trägt ihr Haar in einem festen Knoten; **to be as ~ as a drum** straff sein; (inf: = drunk) sturzbetrunken sein (inf)
e (= leaving little space) eng; weave eng, dicht; **~ curls** kleine Locken; **things are getting rather ~ in this office** es wird ziemlich eng im Büro; **it's a ~ space for lorries** es ist eng hier für Lastwagen
f (= leaving little time) timing etc knapp; schedule knapp bemessen; **4 o'clock is a bit ~ for me** 4 Uhr ist ein bisschen knapp für mich
g (= difficult) situation schwierig; **in a ~ corner** or **spot** (fig) in der Klemme (inf); **things are getting a bit ~ for him round here** es wird langsam brenzlig für ihn (inf); **things were ~** die Lage war schwierig
h (= close) race, match knapp
i (= tense) voice fest; lips zusammengepresst; mouth verkniffen; smile verkrampft; throat zu-

sammengeschnürt; *muscle* verspannt **j** *(= constricted) chest, stomach* zusammengeschnürt; **a ~ feeling in the chest** ein beengtes Gefühl in der Brust **k** *(= close, close-knit)* eng; **the Common Market is a ~ federation of states** der gemeinsame Markt ist ein enger Staatenbund **l** *(= sharp) bend* eng **m** *(Fin) budget, money* knapp **n** *(inf: = miserly)* knick(e)rig *(inf)*, geizig; **to be ~ with one's money** geizig mit seinem Geld sein **o** *(inf: = drunk)* voll *(inf)*, blau *(inf)*; **to get ~** blau werden *(inf)*

ADV *(+er) hold, shut, screw, fasten* fest; *stretch* straff; **the suitcase/train was packed ~ with ...** der Koffer/Zug war vollgestopft mit ...; **he kept his mouth shut ~** er schwieg eisern; *(at dentist etc)* er hielt den Mund fest geschlossen; **to hold sb/sth ~** jdn/etw festhalten; **to do sth up ~** etw festmachen *or* gut befestigen; **to pull sth ~** etw festziehen *or* stramm ziehen; **to stretch sth ~** etw straff spannen; **to sit ~** sich nicht rühren; **sleep ~!** schlaf(t) gut!; **hold ~!** festhalten!; **she held ~ to her assertion** sie blieb felsenfest bei ihrer Behauptung

ADJ *suf* -dicht; **watertight** wasserdicht; **airtight** luftdicht

tightarsed ['taɪtɑːst] **ADJ** *(inf: = inhibited) person, behaviour* verklemmt *(inf)*, verbohrt *(inf)*, stur *(inf)*; *(= miserly)* knick(e)rig *(inf)*

tightass ['taɪtæs] **N** *(US inf: = inhibited person)* verklemmter Typ; **he's a ~** er ist total verklemmt *or* unentspannt *inf*

tightassed ['taɪtæst] **ADJ** *(US)* = **tightarsed**

tighten ['taɪtn] *(also* **tighten up)** **VT** **a** *knot* fester machen, anziehen; *screw* anziehen; *(= re--tighten)* nachziehen; *muscles* anspannen; *lips* verkneifen; *rope* straffen, anziehen; *(= stretch tighter)* straffer spannen; **to ~ one's grip** *(lit)* fester zugreifen; *(fig)* die Schraube fester ziehen; **to ~ one's grip on sth** *(lit)* etw fester halten; *(fig)* etw besser unter Kontrolle bringen; **to ~ the steering in a car** die Lenkung an einem Auto nachziehen **b** *(fig) rules, security, control, law, procedures, restrictions* verschärfen; **to ~ the screw on sth/a country** den Druck auf etw *(acc)*/ein Land verstärken → **belt**

VI *(rope)* sich spannen, sich straffen; *(knot)* sich zusammenziehen; **whenever he's angry his mouth ~s** immer wenn er wütend ist, wird sein Mund schmal und verkniffen

▶ **tighten up** **VI** **a** = **tighten VI** **b** *(in discipline)* strenger werden, härter durchgreifen; **they've tightened up on security** sie haben die Sicherheitsvorkehrungen verschärft **VT** *sep* **a** = **tighten VT a** **b** *organization, procedure* straffen; *discipline, controls* verschärfen

tight: **tightfisted** [,taɪt'fɪstɪd] **ADJ** knauserig, knickerig *(inf)*; **to be ~** die Hand auf der Tasche halten; **tight-fitting ADJ** eng anliegend; **tightknit ADJ** *community* eng (miteinander) verbunden *or* verwachsen; **tight-lipped ADJ** **a** *(lit)* mit schmalen Lippen; *(= silent)* verschwiegen, verschlossen; **he kept a ~ silence** er wahrte absolutes *or* eisernes Schweigen; **to be ~ about sth** sich nicht zu etw äußern **b** *(= angry) person* verbissen; *expression* abweisend; *smile* verkniffen; **~ disapproval** verbissene Ablehnung

tightly ['taɪtlɪ] **ADV** **a** *(= closely) hold* fest; **~ fitting** eng anliegend **b** *(= securely) closed, bound* fest; *wrapped* eng; **a ~ knit community** eine eng verbundene Gemeinschaft; **behind ~-closed doors** hinter fest verschlossenen Türen **c** *(= tautly) stretch* stramm, straff **d** *(= compactly)* dicht; **~ packed** dicht gedrängt; **a ~ packed crowd** eine dicht gedrängte Menge **e** *(= rigorously)* scharf, streng, rigoros; **~ controlled** streng kontrolliert; **a ~-guarded border** eine streng bewachte Grenze

tight-mouthed ['taɪtmaʊθt] **ADJ** *(fig: = silent)* verschwiegen, verschlossen

tightness ['taɪtnɪs] **N** **a** *(of clothes)* enges Anliegen; *(of join)* Dichtheit *f* **b** *(= stiffness: of screw, bolt)* Festsitzen *nt*, Unbeweglichkeit *f*; **the ~ of the drawer/window** das Klemmen der Schublade/des Fensters **c** *(= firmness, of screw, tap)* fester Sitz; *(of window)* Dichtheit *f*; *(of control, discipline, security)* Strenge *f*; *(of organization)* Straffheit *f*; **the ~ of his embrace** seine feste Umarmung **d** *(= tautness, of rope, skin)* Straffheit *f*; *(of knot)* Festigkeit *f* **e** *(= crowdedness)* Enge *f*; *(of weave also)* Dichte *f* **f** *(of schedule)* Knappheit *f* **g** *(= closeness: of race, match)* Knappheit *f* **h** *(= constriction: in chest, stomach)* Beengtheit *f* **i** *(inf, = miserliness)* Knick(e)rigkeit *f (inf)*, Geiz *m* **j** *(inf, = drunkenness)* Besoffenheit *f (inf)*

tightrope ['taɪtrəʊp] **N** Seil *nt*; **to walk a ~** *(fig)* einen Balanceakt vollführen

tightrope act **N** *(lit, fig)* Balanceakt *m*

tightrope walker **N** Seiltänzer(in) *m(f)*

tights [taɪts] **PL** *(Brit)* Strumpfhose *f*; **a pair of ~** ein Paar *nt* Strumpfhosen, eine Strumpfhose

tightwad ['taɪtwɒd] **N** *(US)* Geizhals *m*, Geizkragen *m (inf)*

tigress ['taɪgrɪs] **N** Tigerin *f*

tilapia [tɪ'læpɪə] **N** Tilapia *m*, Buntbarsch *m*

tilde ['tɪldə] **N** Tilde *f*

tile [taɪl] **N** *(on roof)* (Dach)ziegel *m*; *(= ceramic tile)* Fliese *f*; *(on wall)* Kachel *f*, Fliese *f*; *(= lino tile, cork tile, polystyrene tile etc)* Platte *f*, Fliese *f*; *(= carpet tile)* (Teppich)fliese *f*; **to have a night on the ~s** *(Brit inf)* einen draufmachen *(inf)* **VT** **a** *roof* (mit Ziegeln) decken; *floor* mit Fliesen/Platten auslegen; *wall* kacheln, mit Platten bedecken; *bathroom* kacheln, Fliesen anbringen in *(+dat)* **b** *(Comput) windows* nebeneinander anordnen; **~ horizontally** nebeneinander; **~ vertically** untereinander *or* übereinander

tiled [taɪld] **ADJ** *floor* gefliest; *path* mit Platten ausgelegt; *wall, room, fireplace* gekachelt; **~ roof** Ziegeldach *nt*

tiler ['taɪəʳ] **N** **a** *(for roof)* Dachdecker(in) *m(f)* **b** *(for floor)* Fliesen- *or* Plattenleger(in) *m(f)*

tiling ['taɪlɪŋ] **N** **a** *(= action, of roof)* (Dach)decken *nt*; *(of floor)* Fliesenlegen *nt*; *(of wall)* Kacheln *nt*, Belegen *nt* mit Platten; **the ~ of the floor ...** das Legen der Bodenfliesen ... **b** *(= tiled surface, on roof)* Ziegel *pl*; *(on floor)* Fliesen *pl*, Platten *pl*; *(on wall)* Kacheln *pl*, Fliesen *pl*, Platten *pl*

till[1] [tɪl] **PREP, CONJ** = **until**

till[2] **N** *(Brit: = cash register)* Kasse *f*; *(= drawer, in bank)* Geldkasse *f*, Geldkasten *m*; *(in shop)* Ladenkasse *f*; **pay at the ~** an der Kasse bezahlen; **to be caught with one's hand in the ~** *(fig)* beim Griff in die Kasse ertappt werden

till[3] **VT** *(Agr)* bestellen

tillable ['tɪləbl] **ADJ** *(= Agr) land* anbaufähig

tillage ['tɪlɪdʒ] **N** *(= act)* Bestellen *nt*; *(= land)* bestelltes Land

tiller[1] ['tɪləʳ] **N** *(Naut)* Ruderpinne *f*; **at the ~** am Ruder; **to take the ~** das Ruder übernehmen

tiller[2] **N** *(Agr)* Landmann *m (old)*; **~ of the soil** *(liter)* Ackersmann *m (old)*, Bebauer *m* der Scholle *(liter)*

tilt [tɪlt] **N** **a** *(= slope)* Neigung *f*; **the sideways ~ of his head** seine schräge Kopfhaltung; **if you increase the (angle of) ~ of the conveyor belt ...** wenn Sie das Fließband schräger stellen ...; *(sideways also)* wenn Sie das Fließband weiter kippen ...; **to have a ~** sich neigen; **the wall has developed rather a dangerous ~** die Wand neigt sich ziemlich gefährlich; **the bird's/plane's wings have a slight downward ~** die Flügel des Vogels/Flugzeugs neigen sich leicht nach unten **b** *(Hist, = tournament)* Turnier *nt*; *(= thrust)* Stoß *m*; **to have a ~ at sb/sth** *(fig)* jdn/etw aufs Korn nehmen → **full**

VT **a** kippen, schräg stellen; *head* (seitwärts) neigen **b** *(fig) argument* kippen; **to ~ the balance of power toward(s)/against sb** das Kräftegleichgewicht zugunsten/zuungunsten von jdm verschieben

VI **a** *(= slant)* sich neigen; **this part of the machine ~s** dieser Teil der Maschine lässt sich kippen **b** *(fig)* **to ~ at sb/sth** jdn/etw attackieren → **windmill**

▶ **tilt back** **VI** sich nach hinten neigen **VT** *sep* nach hinten neigen; *chair also, machine part* nach hinten kippen

▶ **tilt forward** **VI** sich nach vorne neigen; *(machine part)* nach vorn kippen **VT** *sep* nach vorne neigen; *chair also, machine part* nach vorne kippen

▶ **tilt over** **VI** *(= lean)* sich neigen; *(= fall)* (um)kippen **VT** *sep (= slant)* neigen, schräg stellen; *barrel, chair* kippen

▶ **tilt up** **VI** nach oben kippen; **the back of the truck tilts up** die Ladefläche des Lastwagens kippt **VT** *sep bottle* kippen; *kaleidoscope* schräg nach oben halten

tilth [tɪlθ] **N** **a** *(= topsoil)* (Acker)krume *f* **b** *(= cultivated land)* Ackerland *nt*

tilting ['tɪltɪŋ] **ADJ** schwenkbar, kippbar

tilting train [,tɪltɪŋ'treɪn] **N** Neigezug *m*

Tim [tɪm] **N** *abbr of* **Timothy** *(Brit Telec)* der Zeitservice

timber ['tɪmbəʳ] **N** **a** Holz *nt*; *(for building)* (Bau)holz *nt*; *(= land planted with trees)* (Nutz)wald *m*; **to put land under ~** Land mit Bäumen bepflanzen; **standing ~** Nutzwald *m*; **~!** Baum fällt! **b** *(= beam)* Balken *m*; *(esp Naut)* Spant *nt* **c** *(Hunt)* (Holz)zäune und -gatter *pl* **d** *(US: = character)* **a man of that ~** ein Mann dieses Kalibers; **a woman of presidential ~** eine Frau, die das Zeug zum Präsidenten hat **VT** *house* mit Fachwerk versehen; *gallery (in mine)* abstützen, verzimmern

timbered ['tɪmbəd] **ADJ** **a** **~ house** Fachwerkhaus *nt* **b** *(= wooded)* bewaldet

timber: **timber-framed ADJ** Fachwerk-; **~ house** Fachwerkhaus *nt*; **timber framing** **N** Fachwerk *nt*

timbering ['tɪmbərɪŋ] **N** *(inside house)* Gebälk *nt*, Balkenwerk *nt*; *(outside house)* Fachwerk *nt*; *(Naut)* Spanten *pl*; *(Min)* Stützbalken *pl*; *(= material)* (Bau)holz *nt*

timber: **timberland** **N** *(US)* Waldland *nt*; **timber line** **N** Baumgrenze *f*; **timberman** ['tɪmbəmən] **N** Holzfäller *m*; **timber mill** **N** Sägemühle *f*, Sägewerk *nt*; **timber tree** **N** Nutzholzbaum *m*; **timber wolf** **N** Timberwolf *m*; **timberwork** **N** *(= beams)* Gebälk *nt*, Balkenwerk *nt*; *(= timber framing)* Fachwerk *nt*; **timberyard** **N** *(Brit)* Holzlager *nt*

timbre, *(US)* **timber** ['tɪmbəʳ] **N** Timbre *nt*; *(Phon)* Tonqualität *f*

time [taɪm]

1 NOUN	2 TRANSITIVE VERB

1 – NOUN

a Zeit *f*; **how time flies!** wie die Zeit vergeht!; **only time will tell whether ...** es muss sich erst herausstellen, ob ...; **it takes time to do that** das erfordert *or* braucht (seine) Zeit; **to take (one's) time (over sth)** sich *(dat)* (bei etw) Zeit lassen; **it took me all my time to finish** ich bin gerade noch fertig geworden; **in (the course of) time** mit der Zeit; **in (next to** *or* **less than) no time** im Nu, im Handumdrehen; **at this (present) point** *or* **moment in time** zu diesem *or* zum gegenwärtigen Zeitpunkt; **to have a lot of/no time for sb/sth** viel/keine Zeit für jdn/etw haben; *(fig: = be for/against)* viel/nichts für jdn/etw übrighaben; **to find time (for sb/sth)** Zeit (für jdn/etw) finden; **to make time (for sb/sth)** sich *(dat)* Zeit (für jdn/etw) nehmen; **time is on our side** die Zeit arbeitet für uns;

he lost no time in telling her er verlor keine Zeit und sagte es ihr sofort; **there is no time to lose** es gibt keine Zeit (mehr) zu verlieren; **my time is my own** ich kann frei über meine Zeit verfügen; **in** *or* **given time** mit der Zeit; **in one's own/the company's time** in *or* während der Freizeit/Arbeitszeit; **don't rush, do it in your own time** nur keine Hast, tun Sie es, wie Sie es können; **time is money** *(prov)* Zeit ist Geld *(prov)*; **time and tide wait for no man** *(Prov)* das Rad der Zeit hält niemand auf *(Prov)*; **for some time past** seit einiger Zeit; **I don't know what she's saying half the time** *(inf)* meistens verstehe ich gar nicht, was sie sagt; **in two weeks' time** in zwei Wochen; **for a time** eine Zeit lang; **not before time** *(Brit)* das wurde auch (langsam) Zeit; **to do time** *(inf, in prison)* sitzen *(inf)*; **to make time with sb** *(dated esp US inf: = have sex with)* es mit jdm treiben *(inf)*

♦ **all the time** *(= always)* immer; *(= all along)* die ganze Zeit; **I get them mixed up all the time** ich verwechsle sie immer; **I knew that all the time** das wusste ich die ganze Zeit

♦ **in good time to be in good time** rechtzeitig dran sein; **let me know in good time** sagen Sie mir rechtzeitig Bescheid; **all in good time** alles zu seiner Zeit

♦ **in one's own good time he'll let you know in his own good time** er wird Ihnen Bescheid sagen, wenn er so weit ist; **he does everything in his own good time** er lässt sich bei nichts hetzen

♦ **a long time (for) a long time** lange; **I'm going away for a long time** ich fahre für *or* auf längere Zeit weg; **it's a long time (since ...)** es ist schon lange her(, seit ...); **what a (long) time you have been!** du hast (aber) lange gebraucht!

♦ **a short time (for) a short time** kurz; **a short time later** kurz darauf; **a short time ago** vor Kurzem; **in a short time they were all gone** nach kurzer Zeit waren alle gegangen

♦ **for the time being** *(= provisionally)* vorläufig; *(= temporarily)* vorübergehend

♦ **time on one's hands to have time on one's hands** viel freie Zeit haben; **too many people who have time on their hands** zu viele Leute, die zu viel freie Zeit haben; **having time on my hands I went into a café** da ich (noch) Zeit hatte, ging ich ins Café

b [by clock] **what time is it?, what's the time?** wie spät ist es?, wie viel Uhr ist es?; **what time do you make it?** wie spät haben Sies?; **my watch keeps good time** meine Uhr geht genau; **the time is 2.30** es ist 2.30 Uhr, die Zeit: 2.30 Uhr; **it's 2 o'clock local time** es ist 2.00 Uhr Ortszeit; **what was his time?** *(in race)* welche Zeit hatte er?; **the winning time was ...** die Zeit des Siegers war ...; **it's time (for me/us etc) to go, it's time I was/we were** *etc* **going, it's time I/we** *etc* **went** es wird Zeit, dass ich gehe/wir gehen *etc*; **it's time for tea** es ist Teezeit; **time gentlemen please!** Feierabend! *(inf)*, bitte, trinken Sie aus, wir schließen gleich

♦ **the time of day to pass the time of day (with sb)** (mit jdm) über Belanglosigkeiten reden; **I wouldn't even give him the time of day** ich würde ihm nicht einmal guten *or* Guten Tag sagen

♦ **to tell the time** *(person)* die Uhr kennen; *(instrument)* die Uhrzeit anzeigen; **can you tell the time?** kennst du die Uhr?

♦ **to make good time** gut *or* schnell vorankommen; **if we get to Birmingham by 3 we'll be making good time** wenn wir um 3 Uhr in Birmingham sind, sind wir ziemlich schnell

♦ **about time it's about time he was here** *(he has arrived)* es wird (aber) auch Zeit, dass er kommt; *(he has not arrived)* es wird langsam Zeit, dass er kommt; **(and) about time too!** das wird aber auch Zeit!

♦ **ahead of time** zu früh; **we are ahead of time** wir sind früh dran

♦ **behind time** zu spät; **we are behind time** wir sind spät dran

♦ **at + time at any time during the day** zu jeder Tageszeit; **not at this time of night!** nicht zu dieser nachtschlafenden Zeit *or* Stunde!; **at one time** früher, einmal; **at any time** jederzeit; **come (at) any time** du kannst jederzeit kommen; **at no time** niemals; **at the same time** *(lit)* gleichzeitig; **they arrived at the same time as us** sie kamen zur gleichen Zeit an wie wir; **but at the same time, you must admit that ...** aber andererseits müssen Sie zugeben, dass ...; **it was hard, but at the same time you could have tried** es war schwierig, aber Sie hätten es trotzdem versuchen können

♦ **in/on time** rechtzeitig; **to be in time for sth** rechtzeitig zu etw kommen; **on time** pünktlich; **the trains are on time** die Züge fahren pünktlich

♦ **to time the trains are running to time** die Züge fahren pünktlich

c [= moment, season] Zeit *f*; **there's a time and a place for everything** alles zu seiner Zeit; **this is hardly the time or the place to ...** dies ist wohl kaum die rechte Zeit oder der rechte Ort, um ...; **this is no time for quarrelling** *or* **to quarrel** jetzt ist nicht die Zeit, sich zu streiten; **well, this is a fine time to tell me that** *(iro)* Sie haben sich *(dat)* wahrhaftig eine gute Zeit ausgesucht, um mir das zu sagen; **there are times when ...** es gibt Augenblicke, wo *or* da *(geh)* ...; **at the** *or* **that time** damals, zu der Zeit, seinerzeit; **at this (particular) time, at the present time** zurzeit; **sometimes ..., (at) other times ...** (manch)mal ..., (manch)mal ...; **from that time on** von der Zeit an, von da an; **since that time** seit der Zeit; **this time last year/week** letztes Jahr/letzte Woche um diese Zeit; **to choose** *or* **pick one's time** sich *(dat)* einen günstigen Zeitpunkt aussuchen; **to die before one's time** zu früh sterben; **my time is (almost) up** meine *or* die Zeit ist (gleich) um

♦ **time + come the time has come (to do sth)** es ist an der Zeit(, etw zu tun); **the time has come for us to leave** es ist Zeit für uns zu gehen; **when the time comes** wenn es so weit ist; **when her time comes** *(of pregnant woman)* wenn es (mit dem Baby) so weit ist; **when my time comes** *(= when I die)* wenn meine Zeit gekommen ist; **when the time comes for you to be the leader** wenn Sie an der Reihe sind, die Führung zu übernehmen

♦ **at + times** manchmal; **at all times** jederzeit, immer; **at various times in the past** schon verschiedene Male *or* verschiedentlich

♦ **between times** *(inf)* zwischendurch

♦ **by the time by the time it had finished** als es zu Ende war; **by the time we arrive, there's not going to be anything left** bis wir ankommen, ist nichts mehr übrig

♦ **by that time by that time we knew** da *or* inzwischen wussten wir es; **by that time we'll know** dann *or* bis dahin wissen wir es

♦ **by this time** inzwischen; **by this time next year/tomorrow** nächstes Jahr/morgen um diese Zeit

♦ **from time to time, (US) time to time** dann und wann, von Zeit zu Zeit

♦ **such time until such time as ...** so lange bis ...; **until such time as you apologize** solange du dich nicht entschuldigst, bis du dich entschuldigst

♦ **time of this time of the day/year** diese Tages-/Jahreszeit; **at this time of the week/month** zu diesem Zeitpunkt der Woche/des Monats; **it's my** *or* **the time of the month** *(= period)* ich habe meine *or* die Tage *(inf)*

♦ **time to now's the time to do it** jetzt ist der richtige Zeitpunkt *or* die richtige Zeit, es zu tun; **now's my/your** *etc* **time to do it** jetzt habe ich/hast du *etc* Gelegenheit, es zu tun

d [= occasion] **this time** diesmal, dieses Mal; **every** *or* **each time ...** jedes Mal, wenn ...; **many a time, many times** viele Male; **many's the time I have heard him say ...** ich habe ihn schon oft sagen hören ...; **for the last time** zum letzten Mal; **and he's not very bright at the best of times** und er ist ohnehin *or* sowieso nicht sehr intelligent; **the time before** das letzte *or* vorige Mal; **the time before last** das vorletzte Mal; **time and (time) again, time after time** immer wieder, wieder und wieder *(geh)*; **I've told you a dozen times ...** ich habe dir schon x-mal gesagt ...; **nine times out of ten ...** neun von zehn Malen ...; **she comes three times a week** sie kommt dreimal pro Woche *or* in der Woche

♦ **at a time they came in one/three** *etc* **at a time** sie kamen einzeln/immer zu dritt *etc* herein; **four at a time** vier auf einmal; **for weeks at a time** wochenlang

♦ **a time** *(Brit)* **he pays me £10 a time** er zahlt mir jedes Mal £ 10; **rides on the roundabout cost £2 a time** eine Fahrt auf dem Karussell kostet £ 2

♦ **(the) next time** nächstes Mal, das nächste Mal; **(the) next time I see you** wenn ich dich nächstes Mal *or* das nächste Mal sehe

♦ **(the) last time** letztes Mal, das letzte Mal; **(the) last time he was here** letztes Mal *or* das letzte Mal, als er hier war

e [Math] **2 times 3 is 6** 2 mal 3 ist 6; **it was ten times as big as** *or* **ten times the size of ...** es war zehnmal so groß wie ...; **our profits are rising four times faster than our competitors'** unsere Gewinne steigen viermal so schnell wie die unserer Konkurrenten

f [= rate] **Sunday is (paid) double time/time and a half** sonntags gibt es 100%/50% Zuschlag

g [= era] Zeit *f*; **this is the greatest problem of our time** das ist das größte Problem unserer Zeit; **in my time** zu meiner Zeit; **it happened before my time** das war vor meiner Zeit; **of all time** aller Zeiten; **time was when ...** es gab Zeiten, da ...; **he is ahead of his time** *or* **before his time** er ist seiner Zeit (weit) voraus; **in Victorian times** im Viktorianischen Zeitalter; **in olden times** in alten Zeiten; **times are hard** die Zeiten sind hart *or* schwer; **when times are hard** in harten *or* schweren Zeiten; **times change** die Zeiten ändern sich; **times are changing** es kommen andere Zeiten; **times are changing for the better/worse** es kommen bessere/schlechtere Zeiten; **times have changed for the better/worse** die Zeiten haben sich gebessert/verschlechtert

♦ **the times to be behind the times** rückständig sein, hinter dem Mond leben *(inf)*; *(= be out of touch)* nicht auf dem Laufenden sein; **to keep up with the times** mit der Zeit gehen; *(= keep in touch)* auf dem Laufenden bleiben

h [= experience] **to have the time of one's life** eine herrliche Zeit verbringen, sich glänzend amüsieren; **what a time we had** *or* **that was!** das war eine Zeit!; **what times we had!, what times they were!** das waren (noch) Zeiten!; **to have an easy/a hard time** es leicht/schwer haben; **we had an easy/a hard time getting to the finals** es war leicht für uns/wir hatten Schwierigkeiten, in die Endrunde zu kommen; **was it difficult? – no, we had an easy time (of it)** war es schwierig? – nein, (es war) ganz leicht; **he didn't have an easy time of it in the operating theatre** er war im Operationssaal schlimm dran; **to have a bad/rough time** viel mitmachen; **to give sb a bad/rough** *etc* **time (of it)** jdm das Leben schwer machen; **we had such a bad time with the travel agency** wir hatten solches Pech mit dem Reisebüro; **the goalkeeper had a rough time** der Torwart hatte schwer zu kämpfen

♦ **a good time we had a good time** es war (sehr) schön, es hat uns *(dat)* gut gefallen; **he doesn't look as though he's having a good time** es scheint ihm hier nicht besonders gut zu gefallen; **have a good time!** viel Vergnügen *or* Spaß!; **to show sb a good time** jdn ausführen; **she'll give you a good time for £30** bei ihr kannst du dich für £ 30 amüsieren

i [= rhythm] Takt *m*; **(to be) in time (with)** im Takt (sein) (mit); **(to be) out of time** aus dem Takt (sein); **you're singing out of time (with the others)** du singst nicht im Takt (mit den anderen); **3/4 time** Dreivierteltakt *m*; **to keep time** *(= beat time)* den Takt angeben *or* schlagen; *(= keep in time)* (den) Takt halten

2 – TRANSITIVE VERB

a [= choose time of] **to time sth perfectly** genau den richtigen Zeitpunkt für etw wählen; **you must learn to time your requests a little more tactfully** du musst lernen, deine Forderungen zu einem geeigneteren Zeitpunkt vorzubringen; **he timed his arrival to coincide with …** er legte seine Ankunft so, dass sie mit … zusammenfiel; **you timed that well** du hast dir den richtigen Zeitpunkt (dafür) ausgesucht; **the bomb is timed to explode at …** die Bombe ist so eingestellt, dass sie um … explodiert

b [= measure time of] *with stopwatch* stoppen; *speed* messen; **to time sb (over 1000 metres)** jdn (auf 1000 Meter) stoppen, jds Zeit (auf *or* über 1000 Meter) nehmen; **time how long it takes you, time yourself** sieh auf die Uhr, wie lange du brauchst; *(with stopwatch)* stopp, wie lange du brauchst; **to time an egg** auf die Uhr sehen, wenn man ein Ei kocht; **a computer that times its operator** ein Computer, der die Zeit misst, die sein Operator braucht

time: **time and motion expert** N Fachmann *m*/Fachfrau *f* für Zeitstudien, ≈ REFA-Fachmann *m*/-Fachfrau *f*; **time and motion study** N Zeitstudie *f*, Bewegungsstudie *f*; **time bargain** N *(Brit St Ex)* Termingeschäft *nt*; **time bomb** N *(lit, fig)* Zeitbombe *f*; **time capsule** N Kassette *f* mit Zeitdokumentationen; **timecard** N *(for workers)* Stechkarte *f*; **time change** N Zeitumstellung *f*; **time check** N *(general)* Zeitkontrolle *f*; *(Rad, TV)* Zeitvergleich *m*; **time clock** N Stechuhr *f*; **time-consuming** ADJ zeitraubend; **time credit** N *(flex(i)time)* Zeitguthaben *f*; **time-critical** ADJ *(Comput) application* zeitkritisch; **time debit** N *(flex(i)time)* Fehlzeit *f*; **time delay** N *(gen, Telec)* Zeitverzögerung *f*; *(in bank)* Zeitschloss *nt*; **time-delay** ADJ *mechanism, safe* mit Zeitschloss; **time deposit** N *(Fin)* Festgeld *nt*, Termingeld *nt*; **time difference** N Zeitunterschied *m*; **time exposure** N Langzeitbelichtung *f*; *(= photograph)* Langzeitaufnahme *f*; **time fault** N *(Show-jumping)* Zeitfehler *m*; **timed-release** ADJ *(Pharm)* = **time-release**; **time frame, timeframe** N Zeitrahmen *m*, zeitlicher Rahmen; **to set a ~ for sth** den Zeitrahmen *or* zeitlichen Rahmen für etw festlegen; **time fuse**, *(US)* **time fuze** N Zeitzünder *m*; **time-honoured**, *(US)* **time-honored** ADJ althergebracht, altehrwürdig; **timekeeper** N *(Sport)* Zeitnehmer(in) *m(f)*; **to be a good/bad ~** *(watch)* richtig *or* genau/nicht richtig gehen; *(Brit: employee)* immer/nie das Zeitsoll erfüllen; **timekeeping** N *(in sports)* Zeitnahme *f*, Zeitmessung *f*; *(in factories etc)* Zeitkontrolle *f*; *(of worker)* Erfüllung *f* des Zeitsolls; **bad ~** *(Brit)* ständiges Zuspätkommen; **time-lag** N Zeitdifferenz *f*; *(= delay)* Zeitverschiebung *f*; **cultural/technical ~** Unterschied *m* in der kulturellen/technischen Entwicklung; **time-lapse** ADJ *camera* für Zeitrafferaufnahmen; **~ photography** Zeitraffertechnik *f*

timeless [ˈtaɪmlɪs] ADJ zeitlos; *(= everlasting)* immer während

timelessly [ˈtaɪmlɪslɪ] ADV zeitlos; *(= eternally)* immerfort

timelessness [ˈtaɪmlɪsnɪs] N Zeitlosigkeit *f*; *(= eternal nature)* Unvergänglichkeit *f*

time limit N zeitliche Begrenzung; *(for the completion of a job)* Frist *f*; **to put a ~ on sth** etw befristen

timeliness [ˈtaɪmlɪnɪs] N Rechtzeitigkeit *f*; **the ~ of his warning soon became apparent** man merkte bald, dass seine Warnung genau zum richtigen Zeitpunkt erfolgt war

time lock N Zeitschloss *nt*

timely [ˈtaɪmlɪ] ADJ rechtzeitig; **~ advice** ein Rat zur rechten Zeit; **that was very ~** das war genau zur rechten Zeit

time: **time machine** N Zeitmaschine *f*; **time management** N Zeitmanagement *nt*; **time money** N *(Fin)* Festgeld *nt*

timeous [ˈtaɪməs] ADJ rechtzeitig, zur rechten Zeit

time-out N *(US)* **a** *(Ftbl, Basketball)* Auszeit *f* **b** *(= break)* **to take ~** Pause machen

timepiece [ˈtaɪmpiːs] N Uhr *f*, Chronometer *nt (geh)*

timer [ˈtaɪməʳ] N Zeitmesser *m*; *(= switch)* Schaltuhr *f*; *(= person)* Zeitnehmer(in) *m(f)*

time-release ADJ *(Pharm)* mit Depotwirkung; **~ drug** Depotpräparat *nt*

times [taɪmz] *(Math)* ADV mal VT *(inf)* multiplizieren

time: **time-saver** N **to be a ~** Zeit sparen; **time-saving** ADJ zeitsparend; **timescale** N *(in novel, drama etc)* zeitlicher Rahmen; *(= perception of time)* Zeitmaßstab *m*; **to think on a different ~** einen anderen Zeitbegriff haben; **time-sensitive** ADJ *project, information, money transfers etc* zeitabhängig, zeitgebunden; **time-served** ADJ *apprentice* ausgelernt; **timeserver** N Opportunist *m*, Gesinnungslump *m (pej inf)*; **timeserving** N Opportunismus *m*, Gesinnungslumperei *f (pej inf)* ADJ opportunistisch; **timeshare** N Wohnung *f*/Haus *nt etc* auf Timesharingbasis ADJ *attr salesman, company, apartment, holiday* Timesharing-; *development, resort* für Timesharingurlauber; **a ~ home** eine Wohnung/ein Haus *nt* auf Timesharingbasis; **a ~ week** eine Woche auf Timesharingbasis; **timesharing** N Teilnehmerrechensystem *nt*, Timesharing *nt*; **time sheet** N Stundenzettel *m*, Arbeitszeitkontrollliste *f (form)*; **time signal** N *(Brit)* Zeitzeichen *nt*; **time signature** N Taktvorzeichnung *f*; **time span** N Zeitspanne *f*; **time switch** N Schaltuhr *f*, Zeitschalter *m*; **timetable** N *(Transport)* Fahrplan *m*; *(Brit Sch)* Stundenplan *m*; *(for work)* Zeitplan *m*; **to have a busy ~** ein volles Programm haben; **what's on the ~?** was steht auf dem Programm?; **time-tested** ADJ (alt)bewährt; **time travel** N Zeitreise *f*, Reise *f* durch die Zeit; **time traveller** N Zeitreisende(r) *mf*; **time trial** N Zeitrennen *nt*; **time unit** N *(Telec)* Zeiteinheit *f*; **time warp** N *(Sci-Fi, fig)* Zeitverzerrung *f*; **we're entering a ~** wir werden in eine andere Zeit versetzt; **time-waster** N *(pej)* **to be a ~** *(activity)* eine Zeitverschwendung sein; *(person)* seine Zeit verschwenden; **calls from ~s** nicht ernst gemeinte Anrufe *pl*; **"no ~s"** *(in ad)* „nur ernst gemeinte Angebote"; **time-wasting** N *(Sport)* Bummelei *f*; **timeworker** N nach Zeit bezahlter Arbeiter, nach Zeit bezahlte Arbeiterin; **timeworn** ADJ *stones* verwittert; *(through use)* abgetreten; *cliché, joke* abgedroschen; **time zone** N Zeitzone *f*

timid [ˈtɪmɪd] ADJ scheu, ängstlich; *person, behaviour, words also* schüchtern, zaghaft; *measure* zaghaft; **to be ~ about doing sth** etw nur zögernd tun

timidity [tɪˈmɪdɪtɪ] N Scheu *f*, Ängstlichkeit *f*; *(of person, behaviour, words also)* Schüchternheit *f*, Zaghaftigkeit *f*; *(of measure)* Zaghaftigkeit *f*

timidly [ˈtɪmɪdlɪ] ADV *say, ask* zaghaft; *enter, approach* schüchtern, ängstlich

timidness [ˈtɪmɪdnɪs] N = **timidity**

timing [ˈtaɪmɪŋ] N **a** *(= choice of time)* Wahl *f* des richtigen Zeitpunkts (of für), Timing *nt*; *(Tennis, Ftbl)* Timing *nt*; **it's all a question of ~** es ist eine Frage (der Wahl) des richtigen Zeitpunkts *or* des Timings; **perfect ~, I'd just opened a bottle** ihr kommt gerade richtig, ich habe eben eine Flasche aufgemacht; **the ~ of the statement was wrong/excellent** die Erklärung kam zum falschen/genau zum richtigen Zeitpunkt; **what's the ~ for the reform?** wie sieht der Zeitplan für die Reform aus?; **the actors' ~ was terrible** die Schauspieler zeigten eine erbärmliche Synchronisierung; **to improve one's ~** sein Timing verbessern; **the dancer showed a good sense of ~** der Tänzer bewies ein gutes Gefühl fürs Timing **b** *(Aut, = mechanism)* Steuerung *f*; *(= adjustment)* Einstellung *f*; **~ mechanism** Steuermechanismus *m*

c *(= measuring of time)* Zeitnahme *f*, Zeitmessung *f (of bei)*; *(of race, runners etc)* Stoppen *nt*

timorous [ˈtɪmərəs] ADJ furchtsam, ängstlich, scheu

Timothy [ˈtɪməθɪ] N Timotheus *m*

timpani [ˈtɪmpənɪ] PL *(Mus)* Timpani *pl*, Kesselpauken *pl*

timpanist [ˈtɪmpənɪst] N Timpanist(in) *m(f)*, Paukist(in) *m(f)*

tin [tɪn] N **a** Blech *nt*; *(Chem: = metal)* Zinn *nt* **b** *(esp Brit: = can)* Dose *f*, Büchse *f*; **a ~ of beans** eine Dose *or* Büchse Bohnen; **a ~ of biscuits** eine Dose Kekse VT **a** *(= coat with tin)* verzinnen **b** *(esp Brit: = can)* in Dosen *or* Büchsen konservieren

tin can N **a** (Blech)dose *f*, (Blech)büchse *f* **b** *(US, Naut inf, = destroyer)* Zerstörer *m*

tincture [ˈtɪŋktʃəʳ] N **a** *(Pharm, Her)* Tinktur *f*; **~ of iodine** Jodtinktur *f* **b** *(fig: = tinge)* Spur *f*, Andeutung *f* VT *views, opinions* einen Anstrich *or* Beigeschmack geben *(+dat)* (*with* von); **to be ~d with sth** einen Anstrich *or* Beigeschmack von etw haben

tinder [ˈtɪndəʳ] N Zunder *m*

tinderbox [ˈtɪndəbɒks] N Zunderbüchse *f*; **to be (like) a ~** wie Zunder brennen; *(country etc)* ein Pulverfass sein

tine [taɪn] N *(of fork)* Zinke *f*; *(of antlers)* Ende *nt*, Sprosse *f*

tinfoil [ˈtɪnfɔɪl] N *(= wrapping)* Stanniolpapier *nt*; *(= aluminium foil)* Aluminiumfolie *f*

ting [tɪŋ] VT *bell* läuten; **to ~ the bell** klingeln; **he ~ed his knife against the glass, he ~ed the glass with his knife** er schlug mit dem Messer an das Glas, dass es klirrte VI *(bell)* klingen N Klingen *nt*; **to give the bell a (quick) ~** (kurz) klingeln

ting-a-ling [ˌtɪŋəˈlɪŋ] N Kling(e)ling *nt* INTERJ kling(e)ling

tinge [tɪndʒ] N **a** *(of colour)* Hauch *m*, Spur *f*; **a ~ of red** ein (leichter) Rotstich, ein Hauch *m* von Rot **b** *(fig: = hint, trace)* Spur *f*; *(of sadness)* Anflug *m*, Spur *f* VT **a** *(= colour)* (leicht) tönen; **lavender water ~d with pink** Lavendelwasser, das leicht rosa getönt ist **b** *(fig)* **to ~ sth with sth** einer Sache *(dat)* eine Spur von etw geben; **~d with …** mit einer Spur von …; **our happiness was ~d with sorrow** unser Glück war getrübt

tingle [ˈtɪŋgl] VI prickeln, kribbeln *(inf)* (*with* vor *+dat*); *(with blows)* leicht brennen (*with* von); **to ~ with excitement** vor Aufregung beben, ganz kribbelig sein *(inf)* N Prickeln *nt*, Kribbeln *nt (inf)*; *(from blows)* leichtes Brennen; **she felt a ~ of excitement** sie war ganz kribbelig *(inf)*; **a ~ of excitement ran up her spine** ihr lief (vor Aufregung) ein Schauer über den Rücken

tingling [ˈtɪŋglɪŋ] N Prickeln *nt*, Kribbeln *nt (inf)*; *(from blows)* leichtes Brennen ADJ *(with cold, freshness, excitement)* prickelnd; *(with blows)* brennend

tingly [ˈtɪŋglɪ] ADJ prickelnd; **my arm feels (all) ~** ich habe ein prickelndes Gefühl im Arm, mein Arm kribbelt *(inf)*; **I feel ~ all over** es kribbelt mich überall *(inf)*; *(with excitement)* es prickelt mir unter der Haut, ich bin ganz kribbelig *(inf)*

tin: **tin god** N *(fig)* Bonze *m*; *(= idol)* Abgott *m*, Abgöttin *f*; **tin hat** N *(inf)* Stahlhelm *m*, steifer Hut *(inf)*; **tinhorn** N *(dated US sl)* Angeber(in) *m(f) (inf)*

tinker [ˈtɪŋkəʳ] N *(Brit pej)* Kesselflicker *m*; **you little ~!** *(inf)* du kleiner Stromer *or* Zigeuner! *(neg!)*; **not to give a ~'s curse** *or* **cuss** *or* **damn about sb/sth** *(inf)* sich einen feuchten Kehricht um jdn/etw scheren *(inf)*; **not to be worth a ~'s curse** *or* **cuss** *or* **damn** *(inf)* keinen Pfifferling wert sein *(inf)*; *(person)* keinen Schuss Pulver wert sein *(inf)* VI **a** (*also* **tinker about**) herumbasteln (*with, on* an *+dat*) **b** *(unskilfully)* **to ~ with sth** an etw *(dat)* herumpfuschen

tinkle [ˈtɪŋkl] VT zum Klingen bringen; **he ~d the bell** er klingelte (mit der Glocke) VI **a** *(bells etc)* klingen, bimmeln *(inf)*; *(on piano)* klimpern; *(breaking glass, ice cubes)* klirren **b** *(inf: = to urinate)* pinkeln *(inf)* N Klingen *nt no pl*, Bimmeln *nt no pl (inf)*; *(of breaking glass, ice cubes)* Klirren *nt no pl*; **to give sb a ~** *(Brit inf, on telephone)* jdn anbimmeln *(inf)*

tinkling [ˈtɪŋklɪŋ] N *(of bells etc)* Klingen *nt*, Bimmeln *nt (inf)*; *(of piano)* Klimpern *nt*; *(of broken glass, ice cubes)* Klirren *nt* ADJ *bells* klingend, bimmelnd *(inf)*; *piano* klimpernd; *broken glass, ice cubes* klirrend

tin: **tin lizzie** N *(inf: = car)* Klapperkiste *f*; **tin mine** N Zinnmine *f*, Zinnbergwerk *nt*

tinned [tɪnd] ADJ *(esp Brit) peas, fruit etc* aus der Dose; **~ food** Dosennahrung *f*; **~ meat** Dosen- *or* Büchsenfleisch *nt*

tinnery [ˈtɪnərɪ] N *(Brit)* Konservenfabrik *f*

tinnitus [ˈtɪnɪtəs] N *(Med)* Tinnitus *m*, Ohrenklingen *nt*, Ohrenpfeifen *nt*

tinny [ˈtɪnɪ] ADJ *(+er) sound* blechern; *instrument* blechern klingend; *taste* nach Blech; *(pej) typewriter etc* schäbig; **these cars are so ~** diese Autos bestehen fast nur aus Blech

tin: **tin-opener** N *(esp Brit)* Dosen- *or* Büchsenöffner *m*; **Tin Pan Alley** N die Schlagerindustrie; *(= district)* das Zentrum der Schlagerindustrie; **tin plate** N Zinnblech *nt*; **tin-plate** VT verzinnen; **tinpot** ADJ *(esp Brit inf)* mickrig *(inf)*; **~ dictator** Westentaschendiktator(in) *m(f) (inf)*

tinsel [ˈtɪnsəl] N **a** *(= foil)* Girlanden *pl* aus Rauschgold *etc*; *(on dress)* Lamé *nt* **b** *(pej)* Talmi *nt (pej)*, Tand *m (geh)*

Tinseltown [ˈtɪnsəltaʊn] N *(usu pej)* Hollywood *nt*

tin: **tinsmith** N Blechschmied(in) *m(f)*; **tin soldier** N Zinnsoldat *m*

tint [tɪnt] N Ton *m*; *(= product for hair)* Tönung(smittel *nt*) *f*; **~s of purple** Violetttöne *pl* VT *hair* tönen

tintack [ˈtɪntæk] N Tapeziernagel *m*

tinted [ˈtɪntɪd] ADJ *hair, spectacles, glass* getönt

tintinnabulation [ˌtɪntɪnæbjʊˈleɪʃən] N *(liter, form)* Klingeln *nt or* Geläut *nt* (von Glocken)

tin whistle N Blechflöte *f*

tiny [ˈtaɪnɪ] ADJ *(+er)* winzig, sehr klein; *baby, child* sehr *or* ganz klein; **~ little** winzig klein; **a ~ mind** *(pej)* ein winziger Verstand, ein Zwergenverstand *m*

tip[1] [tɪp] N Spitze *f*; *(of cigarette)* Filter *m*; **to stand on the ~s of one's toes** auf Zehenspitzen stehen; **it's on the ~ of my tongue** es liegt mir auf der Zunge; **it was on the ~ of my tongue to tell her what I thought of her** ich war fast so weit, ihr zu sagen, was ich von ihr hielt; **it's just the ~ of the iceberg** *(fig)* das ist nur die Spitze des Eisbergs → **fingertip, wing tip** VT *(= put tip on)* **to ~ sth with copper/steel** *etc* etw mit einer Kupfer-/Stahlspitze versehen; **copper/steel-~ped** mit Kupfer-/Stahlspitze; **~ped** *(cigarette)* mit Filter

tip[2] N **a** *(= gratuity)* Trinkgeld *nt*; **what do your ~s amount to?** wie viel Trinkgeld bekommen Sie (insgesamt)?; **£100 a week, plus ~s** £ 100 pro Woche, plus Trinkgeld(er); **50p is sufficient as a ~** 50 Pence Trinkgeld reichen
b *(= warning)* Wink *m*, Tipp *m*; *(= advice)* Tipp *m*, Hinweis *m*, Ratschlag *m*; *(Racing)* Tipp *m*; **if you take my ~** wenn Sie meinen Tipp *or* Wink beachten
c *(= tap)* **to give the ball a ~** den Ball nur antippen
VT **a** *(= give gratuity to)* Trinkgeld geben *(+dat)*; **to ~ sb £3** jdm £ 3 Trinkgeld geben
b *(Racing)* tippen auf *(+acc)*, setzen auf *(+acc)*; **he ~ped Golden Boy for the 3.30** er setzte *or* tippte im 3.30-Uhr-Rennen auf Golden Boy; **to be ~ped for success** *(Brit)* als sicherer Erfolgskandidat gelten; **they are ~ped to win the competition/election** *(Brit fig)* sie sind die Favoriten in dem Wettbewerb/in der Wahl; **you ~ped a winner** *(lit, fig)* da hast du auf das richtige Pferd gesetzt
c *(= tap, with fingers)* tippen *or* schnipsen an *(+acc)*; *(with bat, racket)* antippen; **to ~ one's hat (to sb)** an den Hut tippen
VI **Americans ~ better** Amerikaner geben mehr Trinkgeld

▶ **tip off** VT *sep* einen Tipp *or* Wink geben *+dat (about* über *+acc)*; **he tipped off the police as to her whereabouts** er verriet der Polizei, wo sie war *(inf)*; **they've been tipped off** man hat ihnen einen Tipp *or* Wink gegeben

tip[3] VT *(= tilt, incline)* kippen; *(= overturn)* umkippen; *(= pour) liquid* kippen, schütten; *(= empty) load, sand, rubbish* schütten; *books, clothes etc* schmeißen; **to ~ sth backwards/forwards** etw nach hinten/vorne kippen *or* neigen; **to ~ a load into a ship** eine Ladung in ein Schiff leeren *or* kippen; **he ~s the scales at 70kg** er bringt 70 kg auf die Waage; **it ~ped the scales in his favour** *(fig)* das hat für ihn den Ausschlag gegeben; **to ~ the balance** *(fig)* den Ausschlag geben; **~ the case upside down** dreh die Kiste um, stell die Kiste auf den Kopf; **to ~ sb off his chair** jdn vom Stuhl kippen; **to ~ one's hat over one's eyes** sich *(dat)* den Hut über die Augen ziehen/schieben
VI *(= incline)* kippen; *(= dump rubbish)* Schutt abladen; **the boat ~ped to and fro** das Boot schaukelte auf und ab; **"no ~ping", "tipping prohibited"** „Schutt abladen verboten"
N **a** *(Brit, for rubbish)* Müllkippe *f*; *(for coal)* Halde *f*; *(inf: = untidy place)* Saustall *m (inf)*
b **to give sth a ~** etw (um)kippen

▶ **tip back** VI *(chair, person, mirror)* nach hinten (weg)kippen VT *sep* nach hinten kippen; *head* nach hinten neigen; *person* nach hinten legen

▶ **tip out** VT *sep* auskippen; *liquid, sand also* ausschütten; *load, objects, rubbish* abladen, ausleeren; **they tipped him out of bed** sie kippten ihn aus dem Bett VI herauskippen; *(liquid)* herauslaufen; *(sand)* herausrutschen; *(load, objects, rubbish also)* herausfallen

▶ **tip over** VT *sep (= overturn)* umkippen VI *(= overturn)* umkippen

▶ **tip up** VT *sep (= tilt)* kippen; *(= overturn)* umkippen VI *(= tilt)* kippen; *(= overturn)* umkippen; *(folding seat)* hochklappen

tip-and-run raid [ˌtɪpənˈrʌnˌreɪd] N *(Mil)* Blitzangriff *m* mit sofortigem Rückzug

tip-off [ˈtɪpɒf] N *(inf)* Tipp *m*, Wink *m*

tipper [ˈtɪpəʳ] N **a** *(also* **tipper lorry** *(Brit),* **tipper truck***)* Kipplaster *m*, Kipper *m* **b** *(= person)* **he's a generous ~** er gibt großzügig Trinkgeld

tipper lorry, tipper truck *(US)* N *(Mot, Tech)* Kipper *m*, Kippfahrzeug *nt*

tippet [ˈtɪpɪt] N *(old, woman's)* Schultertuch *nt*; *(Eccl)* Stola *f*

Tipp-Ex® [ˈtɪpeks] N Tipp-Ex® *nt* VT **to ~ (out)** mit Tipp-Ex® löschen

tipple [ˈtɪpl] *(esp Brit inf)* N **he enjoys a ~** er trinkt ganz gerne mal einen; **gin is his ~** er trinkt am liebsten Gin VI (ganz schön) süffeln *(inf)*, picheln *(inf)*

tippler [ˈtɪpləʳ] N *(esp Brit inf)* Schluckspecht *m (inf)*

tippy-toe [ˈtɪpɪtəʊ] VI, N *(US inf)* = **tiptoe**

tipsily [ˈtɪpsɪlɪ] ADV beschwipst, angesäuselt *(inf)*

tipsiness [ˈtɪpsɪnɪs] N Beschwipstheit *f*

tipstaff [ˈtɪpstɑːf] N *(Brit Jur)* ≈ Ordnungsbeamte(r) *m*/-beamtin *f*

tipster [ˈtɪpstəʳ] N *jd, der bei Pferderennen Wetttipps verkauft*

tipsy [ˈtɪpsɪ] ADJ *(+er)* beschwipst, angesäuselt *(inf)*; **to be ~** beschwipst *or* angesäuselt *(inf)* sein, einen Schwips haben

tipsy cake N mit Alkohol getränkter Kuchen

tip: **tiptoe** VI auf Zehenspitzen gehen N **on ~** auf Zehenspitzen; **they stood on ~** sie standen auf Zehenspitzen; **they raised themselves on ~** sie stellten sich auf die Zehenspitzen; **tiptop** ADJ *(inf: = first-rate)* tipptopp *(inf) pred*, erstklassig; **tip-up lorry** *(Brit)*, **tip-up truck** N Kipplaster *m*, Kipper *m*; **tip-up seat** N Klappsitz *m*

tirade [taɪˈreɪd] N Tirade *f*, Schimpfkanonade *f*

tire[1] [taɪəʳ] VT ermüden, müde machen VI **a** *(= become fatigued)* ermüden, müde werden **b** *(= become bored)* **to ~ of sb/sth** jdn/etw satthaben, jds/einer Sache *(gen)* müde *(geh) or* überdrüssig *(geh)* werden; **she never ~s of talking about her son** sie wird es nie müde, über ihren Sohn zu sprechen

▶ **tire out** VT *sep* (völlig) erschöpfen

tire[2] N *(US)* = **tyre**

tired [ˈtaɪəd] ADJ **a** *(= fatigued)* müde; *cliché* abgegriffen; **~ out** völlig erschöpft; **~ and emotional** *(hum inf: = drunk)* nicht mehr ganz nüchtern
b **to be ~ of sb/sth** jds/einer Sache *(gen)* müde *or* überdrüssig sein *(geh)*, jdn/etw leid sein, jdn/etw satthaben; **to get ~ of sb/sth** jdn/etw sattbekommen; **I'm ~ of telling you** ich habe es satt, dir das zu sagen; **I'm ~ of people making money out of me** ich habe es satt, dass Leute mich finanziell ausnutzen; **to be ~ to death (of sth)** *(inf)* die Nase (von etw) gestrichen voll haben *(inf)*; **you make me ~!** du regst mich auf!
c *(= old)* müde; **a ~, worn-out organization** eine müde, verbrauchte Organisation; **a ~ lettuce leaf** ein schlaffes Salatblatt
d *(pej: = boring, stale)* langweilig; **another one of his ~ excuses** wieder eine seiner langweiligen Ausreden; **their advertising is getting rather ~** ihrer Werbung fehlt allmählich der Schwung *or* Pep *(inf)*

tiredly [ˈtaɪədlɪ] ADV müde; *say also* mit müder Stimme

tiredness [ˈtaɪədnɪs] N Müdigkeit *f*; **~ had got the better of him** (die) Müdigkeit hatte ihn übermannt; **the accident was a result of (his) ~** (seine) Übermüdung war die Unfallursache

tireless [ˈtaɪəlɪs] ADJ unermüdlich; *patience also* unerschöpflich; **to be ~ in sth** unermüdlich in etw *(dat)* sein

tirelessly [ˈtaɪəlɪslɪ] ADV *work, campaign* unermüdlich

tirelessness [ˈtaɪəlɪsnɪs] N Unermüdlichkeit *f*

tiresome [ˈtaɪəsəm] ADJ *(= irritating)* lästig; *(= boring)* langweilig

tiresomeness [ˈtaɪəsəmnɪs] N *(= irritating nature)* Lästigkeit *f*; *(= boringness)* Langweiligkeit *f*

tiring [ˈtaɪərɪŋ] ADJ anstrengend, ermüdend; **looking after 6 children under 5 is ~** es ist sehr anstrengend *or* es macht (einen) sehr müde, auf 6 Kinder unter 5 Jahren aufzupassen; **this is ~ work/a ~ job** diese Arbeit ist anstrengend

tiro N = **tyro**

Tirol N = **Tyrol**

'tis [tɪz] *(Poet, dial) contr of* **it is** es ist

tissue [ˈtɪʃuː] N **a** *(Anat, Bot, fig)* Gewebe *nt*; **a ~ of lies** ein Lügengewebe *nt*, ein Lügengespinst *nt* **b** *(= handkerchief)* Papier(taschen)tuch *nt* **c** *(also* **tissue paper***)* Seidenpapier *nt*

tissue: **tissue cell** N Gewebezelle *f*; **tissue culture** N Gewebekultur *f*

tit[1] [tɪt] N *(= bird)* Meise *f*

tit[2] N **~ for tat** wie du mir, so ich dir, Auge um Auge(, Zahn um Zahn); **it was ~ for tat** es ging Auge um Auge(, Zahn um Zahn)

tit[3] N *(sl)* **a** *(= breast)* Titte *f (sl)*; **~ and bum press** *(Brit hum)* Arsch-und-Titten-Presse *f (hum sl)*; **he/it gets on my ~s** er/das geht mir auf den Sack *(sl)* **b** *(esp Brit pej inf: = stupid person)* (blöde) Sau *(sl)*; **I felt a right ~** ich kam mir total bescheuert vor *(inf)*

Titan [ˈtaɪtən] N *(Myth)* Titan *m*

titan [ˈtaɪtən] N *(fig)* Titan(in) *m(f)*, Gigant(in) *m(f)*

titanic [taɪˈtænɪk] ADJ **a** *(= huge)* gigantisch **b** *(Chem)* Titan-; **~ oxide** Titandioxid *nt*

titanium [tɪ'teɪnɪəm] N *(Chem)* Titan *nt*

titbit ['tɪtbɪt], *(US)* **tidbit** ['tɪdbɪt] N **a** Leckerbissen *m* **b** *(= piece of information)* Pikanterie *f*

titch [tɪtʃ] N *(Brit inf)* = **tich**

titchy ['tɪtʃɪ] ADJ *(Brit inf)* = **tichy**

titfer ['tɪtfə'] N *(Brit inf: = hat)* Deckel *m (inf)*

tithe [taɪð] N *usu pl* Zehnte *m*; **to pay ~s** den Zehnten bezahlen *or* abgeben

titillate ['tɪtɪleɪt] VT *person, senses* anregen, angenehm erregen; *interest* erregen; **it ~s the palate** es kitzelt den Gaumen

titillation [,tɪtɪ'leɪʃən] N *(of person, senses)* Anregung *f*, angenehme Erregung; *(of interest)* Erregen *nt*; **such ~ is not for the serious-minded** solcher Kitzel ist nichts für ernsthaft gesinnte Menschen

titivate ['tɪtɪveɪt] *(old, hum)* **VI** sich fein machen **VT** *oneself, hair etc, restaurant* herausputzen, verschönern

titivation [tɪtɪ'veɪʃən] N *(old, hum)* Verschönerung *f*

title ['taɪtl] N **a** Titel *m (also Sport)*; *(of chapter)* Überschrift *f*; *(Film)* Untertitel *m*; *(= form of address)* Anrede *f*; **what ~ do you give a bishop?** wie redet *or* spricht man einen Bischof an? **b** *(Jur: = right)* (Rechts)anspruch *m (to* auf *+acc)*, Titel *m (spec)*; *(= document)* Eigentumsurkunde *f*

title bar N *(Comput)* Titelleiste *f*

title bout N *(Boxing)* Titelkampf *m*

titled ['taɪtld] N *person, classes* mit (Adels)titel; **is he ~?** hat er einen Titel?

title: title deed N Eigentumsurkunde *f*; **title fight** N Titelkampf *m*; **titleholder** N *(Sport)* Titelträger(in) *m(f)*, Titelinhaber(in) *m(f)*; **title page** N *(Typ)* Titelseite *f*; **title part**, **title role** N *(Theat, Film)* Titelrolle *f*

titmouse ['tɪtmaʊs] N Meise *f*

titrate ['taɪtreɪt] VT *(Chem)* titrieren

titter ['tɪtə'] **VTI** kichern **N** Kichern *nt*, Gekicher *nt*

tittie ['tɪtɪ] N *(inf)* = **titty**

tittle ['tɪtl] N → **jot**

tittle-tattle ['tɪtl,tætl] **N** Geschwätz *nt*; *(= gossip also)* Klatsch *m*, Tratsch *m (inf)* **VI** quatschen, schwatzen; *(= gossip also)* klatschen, tratschen *(inf)*

titty ['tɪtɪ] N **a** *(inf: = breast)* Brüstchen *nt (inf)* **b that's tough ~** *(inf)* das ist Pech *(inf)*; **that's tough ~ for you** *(inf)* da hast du wohl Pech gehabt *(inf)*, dumm gelaufen *(inf)*

titular ['tɪtjʊlə'] ADJ **a** *possessions* zum Titel gehörend **b** *(= without real authority)* nominell; *(Univ) degree* Ehren-; **~ bishop** Titularbischof *m*

TiVo® ['ti:vəʊ] N *(TV) digitaler Festplatten-Rekorder*

tizzy ['tɪzɪ], **tizwoz** ['tɪzwɒz] N *(inf)* **to be in a ~** höchst aufgeregt sein; **to get into a ~** sich schrecklich aufregen

T-junction ['ti:,dʒʌŋkʃən] N *(Brit)* T-Kreuzung *f*; **"T-junction ahead"** „Achtung Vorfahrtsstraße"

TLC *(inf) abbr of* **tender loving care**

TLS *(Brit) abbr of* **Times Literary Supplement** *von der Times herausgegebene Literaturbeilage*

TM *abbr of* **trademark** Wz

TNT *abbr of* **trinitrotoluene** TNT *nt*

to [tu:]

1 PREPOSITION 3 ADVERB
2 ADJECTIVE

1 – PREPOSITION

a [= in direction of, towards] zu; **to go to the station** zum Bahnhof gehen; **to go to the doctor('s)/greengrocer's** *etc* zum Arzt/Gemüsehändler *etc* gehen; **to go to the opera/concert** *etc* in die Oper/ins Konzert *etc* gehen; **to go to France/London** nach Frankreich/London fahren; **to go to Switzerland** in die Schweiz fahren; **to go to school** zur Schule *or* in die Schule gehen; **to go to bed** ins *or* zu Bett gehen; **to the left** nach links; **to the west** nach Westen; **he came up to where I was standing** er kam dahin *or* zu der Stelle, wo ich stand; **to fall to the ground** auf den Boden *or* zu Boden fallen; **to turn a picture/one's face to the wall** ein Bild/sich mit dem Gesicht zur Wand drehen; **hold it up to the light** halte es gegen das Licht

b [= as far as, until] bis; **to count (up) to 20** bis 20 zählen; **there were (from) 40 to 60 people** es waren 40 bis 60 Leute da; **it's 90 kms to Paris** nach Paris sind es 90 km; **it's correct to a millimetre** es stimmt bis auf den Millimeter; **8 years ago to the day** auf den Tag genau vor 8 Jahren; **to this day** bis auf den heutigen Tag; **they perished to a man** sie kamen alle bis auf den letzten Mann ums Leben

c [= in] in *(+dat)*; **I have never been to Brussels/India** ich war noch nie in Brüssel/Indien

d [= secure to] **he nailed it to the wall/floor** *etc* er nagelte es an die Wand/auf den Boden *etc*; **they tied him to the tree** sie banden ihn am Baum fest; **they held him to the ground** sie hielten ihn am Boden

e [with indirect object] **to give sth to sb** jdm etw geben; **a present from me to you** ein Geschenk für dich von mir *or* von mir an dich; **who did you give it to?** wem haben Sie es gegeben?; **I said to myself ...** ich habe mir gesagt ...; **he was muttering/singing to himself** er murmelte/sang vor sich hin; **what is it to you?** was geht dich das an?; **he is kind to everyone** er ist zu allen freundlich; **it's a great help to me** das ist eine große Hilfe für mich; **he has been a good friend to us** er war uns *(dat)* ein guter Freund; **"To ... "** *(on envelope etc)* „An *(+acc)* ..."; **to pray to God** zu Gott beten

f [in toasts] auf *(+acc)*; **to drink to sb** jdm zutrinken; **to drink to sb's health** auf jds Wohl *(acc)* trinken

g [= next to] *with position* **bumper to bumper** Stoßstange an Stoßstange; **close to sb/sth** nahe bei jdm/etw; **at right angles to the wall** im rechten Winkel zur Wand; **parallel to the wall** parallel zur Wand; **to the west (of)/the left (of)** westlich/links (von)

h [with expressions of time] vor; **20 (minutes) to 2** 20 (Minuten) vor 2; **at (a) quarter to 2** um Viertel vor 2; **25 to 3** 5 (Minuten) nach halb 3; **it was five to when we arrived** es war fünf vor, als wir ankamen

i [= in relation to] zu; **A is to B as C is to D** A verhält sich zu B wie C zu D; **by a majority of 10 to 7** mit einer Mehrheit von 10 zu 7; **they won by 4 goals to 2** sie haben mit 4:2 *(spoken:* vier zu zwei) Toren gewonnen

j [= per] pro; *(in recipes, when mixing)* auf *(+acc)*; **one person to a room** eine Person pro Zimmer

k [Math] **3 to the 4th, 3 to the power of 4** 3 hoch 4

l [= concerning] **what do you say to the idea?** was hältst du von der Idee?; **what would you say to a beer?** was hältst du von einem Bier?; **there's nothing to it** *(= it's very easy)* es ist nichts dabei; **that's all there is to it** das ist alles; **to repairing television £30** *(Comm)* (für) Reparatur eines Fernsehers £ 30

m [= according to] **to the best of my knowledge** nach bestem Wissen; **it's not to my taste** das ist nicht nach meinem Geschmack

n [= accompanied by] **to sing to the guitar** zur Gitarre singen; **to sing sth to the tune of ...** etw nach der Melodie von ... singen; **to dance to a tune/a band** zu einer Melodie/den Klängen *or* der Musik eines Orchesters tanzen

o [= of] **ambassador to America/the King of France** Botschafter in Amerika/am Hofe des Königs von Frankreich; **secretary to the director** Sekretärin des Direktors

p [= producing] **to everyone's surprise** zu jedermanns Überraschung

q [infinitive] **to begin to do sth** anfangen, etw zu tun; **he decided to come** er beschloss zu kommen; **I want to do it** ich will es tun; **I want him to do it** ich will, dass er es tut

r [conditional use of infinitive] **to see him now, one would never think ...** wenn man ihn jetzt sieht, würde man nicht glauben, ...

s [infinitive expressing purpose, result] **to eat/work to live** essen/arbeiten, um zu leben; **I did it to help you** ich tat es, um dir zu helfen; **to get to the point, ...** um zur Sache zu kommen, ...; **well, not to exaggerate ...** ohne zu übertreiben, ...; **I arrived to find she had gone** als ich ankam, war sie weg; **never to be found again** und wurde nie wiedergefunden

t [omitting verb] **I don't want to** ich will nicht; **I'll try to** ich werde es versuchen; **you have to** du musst; **I'd love to** sehr gerne; **we didn't want to but we were forced to** wir wollten nicht, aber wir waren dazu gezwungen; **I intended to (do it), but I forgot (to)** ich wollte es tun, aber ich habe es vergessen; **buy it, it would be silly not to** kaufe es, es wäre dumm, es nicht zu tun; **he often does things one doesn't expect him to** er macht oft Dinge, die man nicht von ihm erwartet

u [set structures]

♦ **noun/pronoun + to + infinitive** **he is not the sort to do that** er ist nicht der Typ, der das täte, er ist nicht der Typ dazu; **I have done nothing to deserve this** ich habe nichts getan, womit ich das verdient hätte; **there's no-one to help us** es ist niemand da, der uns helfen könnte; **who is he to order you around?** wer ist er denn, dass er dich so herumkommandiert?; **he was the first to arrive** er kam als Erster an, er war der Erste, der ankam; **who was the last to see her?** wer hat sie zuletzt gesehen?; **there is much to be done** es gibt viel zu tun; **what is there to do here?** was gibt es hier zu tun?; **now is the time to do it** jetzt ist die (beste) Zeit, es zu tun; **the book is still to be written** das Buch muss noch geschrieben werden

♦ **adjective + to + infinitive** **to be ready to do sth** *(= willing)* bereit sein, etw zu tun; **are you ready to go at last?** bist du endlich fertig?; **it's hard to understand** es ist schwer zu verstehen; **it's impossible to believe** das kann man einfach nicht glauben; **you are foolish to try it** du bist dumm, das überhaupt zu versuchen; **is it good to eat?** schmeckt es gut?; **it's too heavy to lift** es ist zu schwer zum Heben; **too young to marry** zu jung zum Heiraten; **he's too old to be still in short trousers** er ist schon so alt und trägt noch kurze Hosen

2 – ADJECTIVE

door (= ajar) angelehnt; *(= shut)* zu

3 – ADVERB

to and fro hin und her; *walk* auf und ab

---

toad [təʊd] N Kröte *f*; *(fig: = repulsive person)* Ekel *nt*

toad-in-the-hole [,təʊdɪnðə'həʊl] N *Teigspeise mit Würsten*

toadstool ['təʊdstu:l] N (nicht essbarer) Pilz; **poisonous ~** Giftpilz *m*

toady ['təʊdɪ] **N** *(pej)* Kriecher(in) *m(f)*, Speichellecker(in) *m(f)* **VI** Rad fahren *(pej inf)*; **to ~ to sb** vor jdm kriechen

to and fro ADV hin und her

toast[1] [təʊst] **N** Toast *m*; **a piece of ~** ein Toast *m*, eine Scheibe Toast; **on ~** auf Toast; **as warm as ~** *(fig)* mollig warm **VT** *bread* toasten; *(on open fire, in oven)* rösten; **to ~ one's feet by the fire** sich *(dat)* die Füße am Feuer wärmen **VI** *(bread etc)* sich toasten/rösten lassen; *(inf: person)* braten *(inf)*, rösten *(inf)*

toast[2] **N** **a** Toast *m*, Trinkspruch *m*; **to drink** *or* **raise a ~ to sb** auf jdn trinken, einen Toast auf jdn ausbringen; **to propose a ~** einen Toast *or* Trinkspruch ausbringen *(to* auf *+acc)*; **they raised their glasses in a ~ (to him)** sie hoben ihre Gläser (um auf ihn zu trinken) **b she was the ~ of the town** sie war der gefeierte Star der Stadt VT **to ~ sb/sth** auf jds Wohl *or* jdn/etw trinken; **we ~ed the victory in champagne** wir haben unseren Sieg mit Champagner gefeiert *or* begossen *(inf)*

toasted cheese [ˌtəʊstɪd'tʃiːz] N *(Brit)* überbackener Käsetoast

toasted teacakes [ˌtəʊstɪd'tiːkeɪks] PL *(Brit)* getoastete Rosinenbrötchen

toaster ['təʊstəʳ] N Toaster *m*

toastie ['təʊstɪ] N *(Brit)* Toastschnitte *f*, getoastetes Sandwich

toasting fork ['təʊstɪŋfɔːk] N Gabel *f* zum Brotrösten

toastmaster ['təʊstmɑːstəʳ] N *jd, der bei Diners Toasts ankündigt oder ausbringt und Tischreden ansagt*

toast rack N Toastständer *m*

toasty ['təʊstɪ] N = **toastie** ADJ *(inf: also* **toasty warm**) mollig warm *(inf)*

tobacco [tə'bækəʊ] N Tabak *m*

tobacco: **tobacco group** N Tabakkonzern *m*; **tobacco jar** N Tabak(s)dose *f*; **tobacco leaf** N Tabakblatt *nt*

tobacconist [tə'bækənɪst] N Tabak(waren)händler(in) *m(f)*; *(= shop)* Tabak(waren)laden *m*; **at the ~'s** im Tabak(waren)laden

tobacco: **tobacco plantation** N Tabakplantage *f*; **tobacco pouch** N Tabak(s)beutel *m*

to-be [tə'biː] ADJ zukünftig; **the bride-~** die zukünftige Braut; **the husband-~** der zukünftige Mann; **the mother-~** die werdende Mutter

toboggan [tə'bɒgən] N Schlitten *m*, Rodel (-schlitten) *m*; **~ run** Schlitten- *or* Rodelbahn *f* VI Schlitten fahren, rodeln; **to ~ down a slope** mit dem Schlitten einen Hang hinunterfahren; **to go ~ing** Schlitten fahren, rodeln

toby jug ['təʊbɪˌdʒʌg] N Figurkrug *m*

toccata [tə'kɑːtə] N Toccata *f*

tocsin ['tɒksɪn] N *(old)* Alarmglocke *f*, Alarm *m*

tod [tɒd] N *(Brit inf)* **on one's ~** ganz allein

today [tə'deɪ] ADV, N **a** heute; **a week/fortnight ~** heute in einer Woche/zwei Wochen; **he's been here a week ~** heute ist er eine Woche da; **a year ago ~** heute vor einem Jahr; **~ is Monday, it's Monday ~** heute ist Montag; **from ~** von heute an, vom heutigen Tag an, ab heute; **later ~** später (am Tag); **~'s paper/news** die heutige Zeitung/heutigen Nachrichten, die Zeitung/Nachrichten von heute; **what's ~'s date?** welches Datum ist heute?, der Wievielte ist heute?; **~'s rate** *(Fin)* der Tageskurs; **here ~ and gone tomorrow** *(fig)* heute hier und morgen da; **our yesterdays, our ~s and our tomorrows** unsere Vergangenheit, unsere Gegenwart und unsere Zukunft
b *(= these days)* heutzutage; **the cinema ~** das Kino (von) heute; **the world/youth/writers of ~** die Welt/Jugend/Schriftsteller von heute; **~'s world/youth** die heutige Welt/Jugend, die Welt/Jugend von heute; **live for ~ and let tomorrow take care of itself** lebe dem Heute und lass das Morgen morgen sein

toddle ['tɒdl] VI **a** *(child)* wackelnd laufen; **the little boy ~d into the room** der kleine Junge kam ins Zimmer gewackelt **b** *(inf: = walk)* gehen; *(= leave: also* **toddle off**) abzwitschern *(inf)*; **well, I'd better be toddling (off)** ich zwitschere wohl besser mal ab *(inf)*; **could you just ~ down to the shops and …** könntest du mal zu den Geschäften runtergehen und … N *(inf)* **to go for a ~** an die Luft gehen

toddler ['tɒdləʳ] N Kleinkind *nt*

toddy ['tɒdɪ] N Grog *m*

todger ['tɒdʒəʳ] N *(Brit sl)* Schniedel *m (inf)*

to-do [tə'duː] N *(inf)* Theater *nt (inf)*, Gedöns *nt (inf)*; **she made quite a ~ about it** sie machte viel Wind *or* vielleicht ein Theater *or* Gedöns darum *(inf)*; **what a ~!** so ein Theater! *(inf)*; **what's all the ~?** was soll denn das ganze Theater *or* Getue *or* Gedöns? *(inf)*

toe [təʊ] N Zehe *f*, Zeh *m*; *(of sock, shoe)* Spitze *f*; **to tread** *or* **step on sb's ~s** *(lit)* jdm auf die Zehen treten; *(fig)* jdm ins Handwerk pfuschen *(inf)*; **with so many of us we'll be treading on each other's ~s** wir sind so viele, dass wir uns gegenseitig ins Gehege kommen; **to be on one's ~s** *(fig)* auf Zack sein *(inf)*; **to keep sb on his ~s** *(fig)* jdn auf Zack halten *(inf)*; **to go** *or* **stand ~ to ~ with sb** *(esp US fig)* jdm offen gegenübertreten; **there are scenes in the film that make your ~s curl** in dem Film sind Szenen, da bekommt man das kalte Grausen *(inf)* VT *(fig)* **to ~ the line** sich einfügen, spuren *(inf)*; **to ~ the party line** *(Pol)* sich nach der Parteilinie richten

toe: **toecap** N (Schuh)kappe *f*; **toeclip** N *(on bicycle)* Rennbügel *m*

-toed [-təʊd] ADJ *suf* -zehig; **two-toed** zweizehig, mit zwei Zehen

toe-dance ['təʊdɑːns] VI *(US)* auf den Spitzen tanzen

TOEFL *abbr of* **Test of English as a Foreign Language** TOEFL-Test *m*, *englische Sprachprüfung für ausländische Studenten*

toe: **toehold** N Halt *m* für die Fußspitzen; *(fig)* Einstieg *m*; **toe-in** N Vorlauf *m*; **toenail** N Zehennagel *m*; **toe-piece** N *(on shoe, Ski)* Zehenteil *nt*; **toerag** N *(pej inf)* Arsch *m (vulg)*; **toe shoe** N *(US)* Spitzenschuh *m*

toey ADJ *(Austral inf: = nervous)* nervös

toff [tɒf] N *(Brit inf)* feiner Pinkel *(inf)*

toffee ['tɒfɪ] N *(Brit) (= substance)* (Sahne)karamell *m*; *(= sweet)* Toffee *nt*, (weiches) Karamellbonbon; **he can't sing for ~** *(inf)* er kann überhaupt nicht singen, er kann nicht die Bohne singen *(inf)*

toffee: **toffee apple** N kandierter Apfel; **toffee-nosed** ADJ *(Brit inf)* eingebildet, hochnäsig

tofu ['tɒfuː] N Tofu *m*

tog [tɒg] N *(Brit: = measure of insulation) Maß für die Wärmeableitung von Bettdecken etc*

toga ['təʊgə] N Toga *f*

together [tə'geðəʳ] ADV **a** zusammen; **to do sth ~** etw zusammen tun; *(= with one another) discuss, play, dance etc also* etw miteinander tun; *(= jointly) try, achieve, do research etc also* etw gemeinsam tun; **to sit/stand** *etc* **~** zusammensitzen/-stehen *etc*, beieinandersitzen/-stehen *etc*; **to be (all) ~** *(people)* (alle) zusammen *or* beieinander *or* beisammen sein; **to tie/fit/glue** *etc* **two things ~** zwei Dinge zusammenbinden/-setzen/-kleben *etc*; **we're in this ~** wir hängen da alle *or (two people)* beide zusammen drin *(inf)*; **they were both in it ~** sie waren beide zusammen *or* miteinander daran beteiligt; **just you and me ~** nur wir beide zusammen; **to go ~** *(= match)* zusammenpassen
b *(= at the same time)* zusammen; **all ~ now** jetzt alle zusammen; **you're not ~** *(Mus)* ihr seid im Takt auseinander
c *(= continuously)* **for hours ~** stundenlang; **can't you sit still for two minutes ~!** kannst du nicht mal zwei Minuten (lang) still sitzen?
d **~ with** (zusammen) mit
ADJ *(inf)* cool *(inf)*; **she's more ~ now** sie ist jetzt besser beieinander *(inf)*

togethering [tə'geðərɪŋ] N *(inf) gemeinsamer Urlaub mit Familie und Freunden*

togetherness [tə'geðənɪs] N *(physical)* Beisammensein *nt*; *(mental, emotional)* Zusammengehörigkeit *f*; **a feeling** *or* **sense of ~** ein Gefühl *nt* der Zusammengehörigkeit, ein Zusammengehörigkeitsgefühl *nt*

toggle ['tɒgl] N Knebel *m*; *(on clothes)* Knebelknopf *m*; *(on tent)* Seilzug *m* VI *(Comput)* hin- und herschalten, ein-/ausschalten

toggle: **toggle button** N *(Comput)* Umschaltfläche *f*; **toggle key** N *(Comput)* Umschalttaste *f*; **toggle switch** N Kipp(hebel)schalter *m*

Togo ['təʊgəʊ] N Togo *nt*

Togoland ['təʊgəʊlænd] N Togo *nt*

togs [tɒgz] PL *(inf)* Sachen *pl*, Klamotten *pl (inf)*, Zeug *nt*

▶ **tog up** VT *sep (inf)* **to tog oneself up, to get togged up** sich in Schale werfen *(inf)*; *(for tennis etc)* seine Kluft anlegen; **to be togged up in one's best clothes** seine besten Sachen anhaben *(inf)*

toil [tɔɪl] VI **a** *(liter: = work)* sich plagen, sich abmühen *(at, over* mit) **b** *(= move with effort)* sich schleppen; **to ~ up a hill** sich einen Berg hinaufschleppen N *(liter: = work)* Mühe *f*, Plage *f (geh)*; **after months of ~** nach monatelanger Mühe *or* Plage

toiler ['tɔɪləʳ] N Schwerarbeiter(in) *m(f)*

toilet ['tɔɪlɪt] N **a** *(= lavatory)* Toilette *f*, Klosett *nt (dated)*; **to go to the ~** *(esp Brit)* auf die Toilette gehen; **she's in the ~/~s** sie ist auf *or* in der Toilette; **to put sth down the ~** etw in die Toilette werfen; **the cat's done the ~ on the carpet** die Katze hat auf den Teppich gemacht *(inf)* **b** *(old)* Toilette *f (geh)*

toilet *in cpds* Toiletten-; **toilet bag** N *(Brit)* Kulturbeutel *m*, Toilettentasche *f*; **toilet bowl** N Toilettenbecken *nt*; **toilet brush** N Klobürste *f (inf)*; **toilet case** N = **toilet bag**; **toilet humour** N Gossenhumor *m*; **toilet paper** N Toilettenpapier *nt*; **toilet requisites** PL Toilettenartikel *pl*

toiletries ['tɔɪlɪtrɪz] PL Toilettenartikel *pl*

toilet: **toilet roll** N Rolle *f* Toilettenpapier; **toilet seat** N Toilettensitz *m*, Brille *f (inf)*; **toilet set** N *(= brush and comb)* Toilettengarnitur *f*; *(= bathroom set)* Badezimmergarnitur *f*; **toilet soap** N Toilettenseife *f*; **toilet tissue** N Toilettenpapier *nt*; **toilet training** N Erziehung *f* zur Sauberkeit; **has he started his ~ yet?** geht er schon auf den Topf?; **toilet water** N Duftwasser *nt*, Eau de Toilette *nt*

toils [tɔɪlz] PL *(old, lit)* Netze *pl*; *(fig)* Maschen *pl*, Schlingen *pl*

toilsome ['tɔɪlsəm] ADJ *(liter)* mühselig, mühsam

to-ing and fro-ing [ˌtuːɪŋən'frəʊɪŋ] N *(esp Brit)* Hin und Her *nt*

Tokay [tə'kaɪ] N *(= wine)* Tokaier *m*

token ['təʊkən] ✪ 22 N **a** *(= sign)* Zeichen *nt*; **as a ~ of, in ~ of** als *or* zum Zeichen *(+gen)*; **by the same ~** ebenso; *(with neg)* aber auch; **… then by the same ~ you can't object to** … dann können Sie aber auch nichts gegen … einwenden
b *(= chip: for gambling, jukebox etc)* Spielmarke *f*
c *(Brit: = voucher, gift token)* Gutschein *m*
ATTR Schein-, pro forma; **~ gesture** leere Geste; **it was just a ~ offer** das hat er/sie *etc* nur pro forma *or* nur so zum Schein angeboten; **~ payment** symbolische Bezahlung; **~ resistance** Scheinwiderstand *m*; **~ strike** Warnstreik *m*; **~ fine** symbolische Strafe; **~ female** Quotenfrau *f (inf)*; **the one ~ woman** die Alibifrau

Tokyo ['təʊkɪəʊ] N Tokio *nt*

told [təʊld] *pret, ptp of* **tell**; **there were 50 people there all ~** es waren insgesamt *or* alles in allem 50 Leute da

tolerable ['tɒlərəbl] ADJ *(lit) pain, noise level etc* erträglich; *(fig: = not too bad also)* annehmbar, leidlich, passabel *(inf)*; **to keep sth at a ~ level** etw im erträglichen Rahmen *or* im Rahmen des Erträglichen halten; **how are you? – ~** wie gehts dir? – ganz leidlich *or* passabel *(inf)*; **to be ~ to sb** für jdn annehmbar sein

tolerably ['tɒlərəblɪ] ADV ziemlich; **~ well** ganz leidlich *or* annehmbar, ziemlich gut; **they are ~ well-educated** sie sind leidlich gebildet *or (rather well)* ziemlich gebildet

tolerance ['tɒlərəns] N **a** Toleranz *f*, Duldsamkeit *f* *(of, for, towards* gegenüber); *(towards children, one's juniors)* Nachsicht *f* *(of* mit); **racial ~** Toleranz in Rassenfragen; **I have no ~ for such behaviour** für solch ein Benehmen habe ich kein Verständnis **b** *(Med, Tech)* Toleranz *f*; **to work to fine ~s** mit kleinen *or* engen Toleranzen arbeiten

tolerant ['tɒlərənt] ADJ **a** *(of, towards, with* gegenüber) tolerant, duldsam; *(towards children, one's juniors)* nachsichtig; **the Lord is ~ of our**

mistakes der Herr sieht uns unsere Schwächen nach; **to adopt a more ~ attitude to** *or* **toward(s) sth** einer Sache *(dat)* toleranter gegenüberstehen **b** *(Tech, Med)* **to be ~ of heat** hitzebeständig sein; **to be ~ to light** Licht vertragen können; **to be ~ to a drug** ein Medikament (gut) vertragen

tolerantly [ˈtɒlərəntlɪ] ADV *smile* nachsichtig; *wait, listen* geduldig

tolerate [ˈtɒləreɪt] ✪ 14 VT **a** *pain, noise, weather etc* ertragen; *drug* vertragen **b** *person* tolerieren; *behaviour, injustice etc* dulden, tolerieren, hinnehmen; *ideas* tolerieren; **he can ~ anything except intolerance** er kann alles tolerieren, nur keine Intoleranz; **it is not to be ~d** so etwas kann man nicht dulden *or* hinnehmen; **I won't ~ this disobedience!** ich dulde diesen Ungehorsam nicht!

toleration [ˌtɒləˈreɪʃən] N Duldung *f*, Tolerierung *f*

toll¹ [təʊl] VI läuten; **for whom the bell ~s** wem die Stunde schlägt VT *bell* läuten N Läuten *nt*; *(= single stroke)* Glockenschlag *m*

toll² N **a** *(= bridge toll, road toll)* Maut *f*, Zoll *m*, Benutzungsgebühr *f*; *(US Telec)* (Fernsprech)gebühr *f*; **~ charge** Maut *f*, Mautgebühr *f* **b** *(= deaths, loss etc)* **the ~ on the roads** die Zahl der Verkehrsopfer; **the ~ of the floods continues to rise** *(in terms of people)* die Zahl der Opfer der Flutkatastrophe steigt ständig weiter; *(in terms of property)* das Ausmaß der Flutschäden wird immer größer; **the earthquake took a heavy ~ of human life** das Erdbeben forderte *or* kostete viele Menschenleben; **the ~ of the war** der Blutzoll des Krieges

toll: **tollbar** N Zahlschranke *f*, Mautschranke *f*; **tollbooth** N Zahlstelle *f*, Mautstelle *f*; **toll bridge** N gebührenpflichtige Brücke, Mautbrücke *f*; **toll call** N *(US)* Ferngespräch *nt*; **toll-free** *(US Telec)* ADJ *number, call* gebührenfrei ADV *call* gebührenfrei; **tollgate** N Schlagbaum *m*, Mautschranke *f*; **tollhouse** N Mauthaus *nt*

tolling [ˈtəʊlɪŋ] N *no pl* Läuten *nt*

toll: **tollkeeper** N Mautner(in) *m(f)* *(esp Aus)*; **toll plaza** N *(US: Mot)* (Reihe *f* von) Mauthäuschen *pl*; **toll road** N Mautstraße *f*, gebührenpflichtige Straße

toluene [ˈtɒljʊiːn] N *(Chem)* Toluol *nt*

Tom [tɒm] N *dim of* **Thomas any ~, Dick or Harry** *(inf)* jeder x-Beliebige; **you don't have to invite every ~, Dick and Harry** *(inf)* du brauchst ja nicht gerade Hinz und Kunz einzuladen *(inf)*; **it's not every ~, Dick and Harry who can afford this** nicht jeder kann sich *(dat)* so was leisten

tom [tɒm] N *(= cat)* Kater *m*

tomahawk [ˈtɒməhɔːk] N Tomahawk *m*

tomato [təˈmɑːtəʊ, *(US)* təˈmeɪtəʊ] N *pl* **-es** Tomate *f*

tomato *in cpds* Tomaten-; **tomato juice** N Tomatensaft *m*; **tomato ketchup** N (Tomaten)ket(s)chup *m or nt*; **tomato puree** N Tomatenmark *nt*; **tomato sauce** N Tomatensoße *f*; *(= ketchup)* (Tomaten)ket(s)chup *m or nt*

tomb [tuːm] N *(= grave)* Grab *nt*; *(= building)* Grabmal *nt*

tomb chamber N Grabkammer *f*

tombola [tɒmˈbəʊlə] N Tombola *f*

tomboy [ˈtɒmbɔɪ] N Wildfang *m*; **she is a real ~** sie ist ein richtiger Junge *or* Wildfang

tomboyish [ˈtɒmbɔɪɪʃ] ADJ *girl* jungenhaft

tomboyishness [ˈtɒmbɔɪɪʃnɪs] N Jungenhaftigkeit *f*

tombstone [ˈtuːmstəʊn] N Grabstein *m*

tomcat [ˈtɒmkæt] N **a** Kater *m* **b** *(US fig inf: = woman-chaser)* Schürzenjäger *m (inf)*

tome [təʊm] N dickes Buch, Wälzer *m (inf)*

tomfool [ˈtɒmˈfuːl] N Blödian *m* ADJ *attr* blöd(sinnig)

tomfoolery [tɒmˈfuːlərɪ] N Blödsinn *m*, Unsinn *m*

Tommy [ˈtɒmɪ] N *dim of* **Thomas** *(Brit Mil sl)* Tommy *m (sl)*

tommy: **Tommy gun** [ˈtɒmɪɡʌn] N Maschinenpistole *f*; **tommyrot** N *(dated inf)* dummes Zeug, Mumpitz *m (dated)*

tomogram [ˈtɒməɡræm] N *(Med)* Tomogramm *nt*, Tomografie *f*

tomograph [ˈtɒməɡrɑːf] N *(Med)* Tomograf *m*

tomography [təˈmɒɡrəfɪ] N Tomografie *f*

tomorrow [təˈmɒrəʊ] ADV, N morgen; *(= future)* Morgen *nt*; **~ week, a week ~** morgen in einer Woche; **a fortnight ~** morgen in zwei Wochen; **he'll have been here a week ~** morgen ist er eine Woche da; **a year ago ~** morgen vor einem Jahr; **the day after ~** übermorgen; **~ morning/lunchtime/afternoon/evening** morgen früh/Mittag/Nachmittag/Abend; **late/early ~** morgen spät/früh; **~ is Monday, it's Monday ~** morgen ist Montag; **(as) from ~** ab morgen, von morgen an, vom morgigen Tag an; **see you ~!** bis morgen!; **~'s paper** die morgige Zeitung, die Zeitung von morgen; **the article will be in ~'s paper** der Artikel wird morgen in der Zeitung sein; **will ~ do?** *(early enough)* reicht es noch bis morgen?, hat es noch bis morgen Zeit?; *(convenient)* ist es morgen recht?; **~ is another day** *(prov)* morgen ist auch noch ein Tag *(prov)*; **~ may never come** wer weiß, was morgen ist; **~ never comes** *(prov)* es heißt immer „morgen, morgen, nur nicht heute"; **who knows what ~ will bring?** wer weiß, was das Morgen bringt?; **a brighter ~** eine bessere Zukunft; **the science of ~** die Wissenschaft von morgen; **the stars of ~** die Stars von morgen; **~'s problems** die Probleme von morgen; **like there was no ~** als wenn es kein morgen (mehr) gäbe; *eat, drink* was das Zeug hält *(inf)*

tom: **Tom Thumb** N der Däumling; **tomtit** N (Blau)meise *f*; **tom-tom** [ˈtɒmtɒm] N Tamtam *nt*

ton [tʌn] N **a** (britische) Tonne; **she/it weighs a ~** *(fig inf)* sie/das wiegt ja eine Tonne **b tons** PL *(inf: = lots)* jede Menge *(inf)*; **to have ~s of time/friends/money** *etc* jede Menge *(inf) or* massenhaft *(inf)* Zeit/Freunde/Geld *etc* haben **c** *(inf, of speed)* **to do a ~** mit hundertsechzig Sachen fahren *(inf)*

tonal [ˈtəʊnl] ADJ klanglich, Klang-; *(Mus: = regarding form)* tonal; *(Art)* farblich, Farb-; **~ variation** Klangvariation *f*; *(in colours)* Farbabstufung *f*; **~ effects** *(in music)* Klangeffekte *pl*; *(in painting)* Farbeffekte *pl*; **~ music** tonale Musik; **~ value** *(Phot)* Farbwert *m*

tonality [təʊˈnælɪtɪ] N *(Mus)* Tonalität *f*; *(of voice)* Klang *m*; *(of poem)* Tonart *f*; *(of painting)* Farbkomposition *f*

tone [təʊn] N **a** *(of sound, = tone of voice, Phon)* Ton *m*; *(= quality of sound)* Klang *m*; **the soft ~s of a flute** die sanften Töne einer Flöte; **the soft ~s of her voice** der sanfte Klang ihrer Stimme; **... he said in a friendly ~** ... sagte er in freundlichem Ton; **I don't like your ~ (of voice)** mir gefällt dein Ton nicht; **don't speak to me in that ~ (of voice)** in diesem Ton kannst du mit mir nicht reden

b *(of colour)* (Farb)ton *m*

c *(fig: = mood, character)* Ton *m*; **what was the ~ of his letter?** wie war denn der Ton seines Briefes?; **the new people have lowered/raised the ~ of the neighbourhood** die neuen Leute haben dem Ansehen *or* Ruf des Viertels geschadet/das Ansehen *or* den Ruf des Viertels verbessert; **of course, Trevor had to lower the ~ (of the conversation)** Trevor musste natürlich ausfallend werden

d *(Mus)* Ton *m*; *(US: = note)* Note *f*

e *(Physiol)* Tonus *m (spec)*

VT **a** *(Phot, = tint)* einfärben, tonen *(spec)*

b *body, muscles* in Form bringen

VI *(colours)* (im Farbton) harmonieren

▶ **tone down** VT *sep (lit, fig)* abmildern; *colour also* abschwächen; *criticism also, language, demands* mäßigen

▶ **tone in** VI (im Farbton) harmonieren

▶ **tone up** VT *sep muscles* kräftigen; *person, body* in Form bringen; **cycling keeps you toned up** Radfahren hält einen in Form

tone: **tone arm** N Tonarm *m*; **tone colour**, *(US)* **tone color** N *(Mus)* Klangfarbe *f*; **tone control** N Klangfarbeneinstellung *f*, Tonblende *f*

-toned [təʊnd] ADJ *suf* **sepia-toned** sepiafarben; **pastel-toned drawings** Zeichnungen *pl* in Pastelltönen; **high-toned philosophising** hochtrabendes Philosophieren; **a beautiful silver-toned voice** eine schöne, silbern klingende Stimme

tone: **tone-deaf** [təʊnˈdef] ADJ nicht in der Lage, Tonhöhen zu unterscheiden; **he's ~** er hat kein Gehör für Tonhöhen; **tone language** N Tonsprache *f*, Tonhöhensprache *f*

toneless [ˈtəʊnlɪs] ADJ tonlos; *music* eintönig; *colour* stumpf

tonelessly [ˈtəʊnlɪslɪ] ADV *reply* tonlos; *sing* eintönig

tone poem N Tongedicht *nt*

toner [ˈtəʊnəˈ] N **a** *(for printer, copier)* Toner *m* **b** *(= cosmetic)* Tönung *f*

toner cartridge N Tonerpatrone *f*

toner cassette N Tonerkassette *f*

tone row, tone series *(US)* N *(twelve-tone music)* Reihe *f*

tongs [tɒŋz] PL Zange *f*; *(= curling tongs, Hist)* Brennschere *f*; *(electric)* Lockenstab *m*; **a pair of ~** eine Zange

tongue [tʌŋ] N **a** Zunge *f*; **to put** *or* **stick one's ~ out at sb** jdm die Zunge herausstrecken; **to lose/find one's ~** *(fig)* die Sprache verlieren/wiederfinden; **to hold one's ~** den Mund halten; **to have a ready ~** schlagfertig sein, nicht auf den Mund gefallen sein; **to have a sharp ~** eine scharfe Zunge haben; **keep a civil ~ in your head!** werden Sie nicht ausfallend!; **I can't get my ~ round it** dabei breche ich mir fast die Zunge ab → **slip, tip, tongue-in-cheek**

b *(liter: = language)* Sprache *f*; *(old Bibl)* Zunge *f*; **the gift of ~s** *(Bibl)* die Gabe, in fremden Zungen zu reden

c *(of shoe)* Zunge *f*, Lasche *f*; *(of bell)* Klöppel *m*; *(of land)* (Land)zunge *f*; *(of wood)* Spund *m*, Zapfen *m*; **a ~ of fire licked the building** eine Flamme züngelte an dem Gebäude empor

VT *(Mus) note* (mit der Zunge) stoßen

tongue: **tongue-and-groove joint** N Anschlitzzunge *f*, Spundung *f*; **tongue-in-cheek** ADJ *attr*, **tongue in cheek¹** ADJ *pred humour, approach* ironisch; *remark* ironisch gemeint; **tongue in cheek²** ADV nicht ganz ernst gemeint; **tongue-lashing** N **to give sb a ~** jdm gehörig die Meinung sagen; **to get a ~** gehörig die Meinung gesagt bekommen; **tongue-tied** ADJ **to be ~** keinen Ton herausbringen; **she sat there ~** sie saß da und brachte keinen Ton heraus; **tongue twister** N Zungenbrecher *m*

tonguing [ˈtʌŋɪŋ] N *(Mus)* Zungenschlag *m*

tonic [ˈtɒnɪk] N **a** *(Med)* Tonikum *nt*; *(= hair tonic)* Haarwasser *nt*; *(= skin tonic)* Lotion *f*; **it was a real ~ to see him again** *(fig)* es hat richtig gutgetan, ihn wiederzusehen **b ~ (water)** Tonic(water) *nt*; **gin and ~** Gin *m* (mit) Tonic **c** *(Mus)* Tonika *f*, Grundton *m*; **~ sol-fa** Solmisation *f* ADJ **a** *(Med)* stärkend, kräftigend, tonisch *(spec)*; **~ wine** Stärkungswein *m* **b** *(Phon) syllable, stress* tontragend **c** *(Mus) note* tonisch

tonicity [təʊˈnɪsɪtɪ] N *(of muscles)* Tonus *m (spec)*, Spannungszustand *m*

tonight, *(US)* **tonite**: *(inf)* [təˈnaɪt] ADV *(= this evening)* heute Abend; *(= during the coming night)* heute Nacht; **see you ~!** bis heute Abend! N *(= this evening)* der heutige Abend; *(= the coming night)* die heutige Nacht; **~'s party** die Party heute Abend; **I'm looking forward to ~** ich freue mich auf heute Abend *or* auf den heutigen Abend; **~ is the night we've been looking forward to** heute ist der Abend, auf den wir uns gefreut haben; **~ is a night I'll re-**

member all my life an den heutigen Abend/an heute Nacht werde ich mich mein ganzes Leben lang erinnern; **~'s weather: ~ will be clear but cold** das Wetter heute Nacht: heute Nacht wird es klar, aber kalt sein; **~'s paper** die heutige Abendzeitung, die Abendzeitung von heute

tonnage ['tʌnɪdʒ] N Tonnage *f*

tonne [tʌn] N Tonne *f*

tonneau ['tɒnəʊ] N *(Aut)* **a** *(of car)* hinterer Teil *(mit Rücksitzen/Rückbank)* **b** *(also* **tonneau cover**) Verdeck *nt*

-tonner [-'tʌnə'] N *suf (inf)* -tonner *m*; **two-tonner** Zweitonner *m*

tonsil ['tɒnsl] N Mandel *f*; **to have one's ~s out** sich *(dat)* die Mandeln herausnehmen lassen; **~ action** *or* **hockey** *(inf)* Knutscherei *f*, Herumknutschen *nt*

tonsillectomy [,tɒnsɪ'lektəmɪ] N Mandeloperation *f*

tonsillitis [,tɒnsɪ'laɪtɪs] N Mandelentzündung *f*

tonsorial [tɒn'sɔːrɪəl] ADJ *(hum, rare form)* Barbier- *(hum)*; **~ artist** Barbier *m*

tonsure ['tɒnʃə'] **N** Tonsur *f* **VT** scheren, die Tonsur erteilen *(+dat) (spec)*

ton-up ['tʌnʌp] ADJ *(inf)* **~ kids** Motorradrocker *pl (inf)*

too [tuː] ADV **a** *(+adj or adv)* zu; **that's ~/not ~ difficult a question to answer** diese Frage ist zu/nicht zu schwer zu beantworten; **~ much** zu viel *inv*; **~ many** zu viele; **he's had ~ much to drink** er hat zu viel getrunken; **you can have ~ much of a good thing** allzu viel ist ungesund *(prov)*; **it's ~ much for her** es ist zu viel für sie; **don't worry ~ much** mach dir nicht zu viel Sorgen; **~ much!** *(inf)* geil! *(sl)*, Klasse! *(inf)*; **~ right!** *(inf)* das kannste laut sagen *(inf)*
b *(= very)* zu; **all ~ ...** allzu ...; **only ~ ...** nur zu ...; **none ~ ...** gar nicht ..., keineswegs ...; **not ~ ...** nicht zu ...; **not any ~ ...** nicht allzu ...; **he wasn't ~ interested** er war nicht allzu interessiert; **I'm not/none ~ sure** ich bin nicht ganz/gar nicht *or* keineswegs sicher; **(that's) ~ kind of you** *(iro)* (das ist) wirklich zu nett von Ihnen; **none ~ soon** keineswegs zu früh; **all ~ soon** allzu früh
c *(= also)* auch; **HE can swim ~, he ~ can swim** er kann AUCH schwimmen, auch ER kann schwimmen
d *(= moreover, into the bargain)* auch noch; **it was really cheap, and it works ~!** es war wirklich billig, und es funktioniert sogar *or* auch noch!; **they asked for a price reduction ~!** sie wollten auch noch einen Preisnachlass!

toodle-pip [,tuːdl'pɪp] INTERJ *(dated Brit, inf)* tschau *(inf)*

took [tʊk] *pret of* **take**

tool [tuːl] **N** **a** Werkzeug *nt*; *(= gardening tool)* (Garten)gerät *nt*; *(Comput)* Tool *nt*, Hilfsmittel *nt*, Dienstprogramm *nt*; **~s** Werkzeuge *pl*; *(= set)* Werkzeug *nt*; *(in Windows®)* Extras *pl*; **that's one of the ~s of the trade** das gehört zum Handwerkszeug; **to have the ~s for the job** das richtige *or* nötige Werkzeug haben **b** *(fig: = person)* Werkzeug *nt* **c** *(sl: = penis)* Ding *nt (inf)*, Apparat *m (sl)* **VT** *book, leather* punzen

▶ **tool along** VI *(inf)* dahinbrausen *(inf)*

▶ **tool up** **VT** *factory* (mit Maschinen) ausrüsten **VI** *(factory)* (mit Maschinen) ausgerüstet werden *(for* für)

tool: **toolbag** N Werkzeugtasche *f*; **toolbar** N *(Comput)* Symbolleiste *f*, Funktionsleiste *f*; **~ button** Symbolleistenschaltfläche *f*; **~ icon** Bildsymbol *nt* auf der Symbolleiste; **toolbox** N Werkzeugkasten *m*; *(Comput)* Toolbox *f*; **tool chest** N = **toolbox**

tooling ['tuːlɪŋ] N Punzarbeit *f*

tool: **toolkit** N Werkzeug(ausrüstung *f*) *nt*; **tool-maker** N Werkzeugmacher(in) *m(f)*; **tool-making** ADJ *attr* Werkzeugbau-; **~ firm** Werkzeughersteller *m*, Werkzeugbaufirma *f*; **tool shed** N Geräteschuppen *m*; **tooltip** N *(Comput)* Quickinfo *nt*

toot [tuːt] **VT** **to ~ a horn** auf dem Horn blasen *or (child's trumpet)* tuten; *(in car, on bicycle)* auf die Hupe drücken, hupen; **to ~ a whistle** pfeifen, auf der Pfeife blasen **VI** *(in car, on bicycle)* hupen; *(train)* pfeifen; *(ship)* tuten **N** *(in car, on bicycle)* Hupen *nt*; *(of train)* Pfiff *m*, Pfeifsignal *nt*; **give a quick ~** *(on car horn)* drück mal kurz auf die Hupe

tooth [tuːθ] N *pl* **teeth** **a** *(of person, animal)* Zahn *m*; **to have a ~ out/filled** sich *(dat)* einen Zahn ziehen/plombieren lassen; **to get one's teeth into sth** *(lit)* etw zwischen die Zähne bekommen; *(fig)* sich in etw *(dat)* festbeißen; **armed to the teeth** bis an die Zähne bewaffnet; **to show one's teeth** die Zähne zeigen *(also fig) or* fletschen; **to fight ~ and nail** bis aufs Blut kämpfen; **in the teeth of the wind** gegen den Wind; **in the teeth of all opposition** ungeachtet allen Widerstands; **to lie through** *or* **in one's teeth** das Blaue vom Himmel herunterlügen; **I'm fed up to the (back) teeth with that** *(inf) or* **sick to the (back) teeth of that** *(inf)* ich habe die Nase gestrichen voll davon *(inf)*, es hängt mir zum Hals heraus *(inf)*; **to give a law/an organization some teeth** *(fig)* einem Gesetz/einer Organisation Wirksamkeit verleihen; **selling a car these days is like pulling teeth** *(esp US)* ein Auto zu verkaufen ist heutzutage ein mühsames Geschäft
b *(of zip, wheel etc)* Zahn *m*; *(of comb, rake)* Zinke *f*, Zahn *m*

tooth *in cpds* Zahn-; **toothache** N Zahnweh *nt*, Zahnschmerzen *pl*; **toothbrush** N Zahnbürste *f*; **toothbrush moustache** N Bürste *f*; **tooth decay** N Karies *f*, Zahnverfall *m*

toothed [tuːθt] ADJ gezahnt, mit Zähnen; **~ wheel** Zahnrad *nt*

tooth: **tooth fairy** N *Fantasiefigur, die die Milchzähne der Kinder einsammelt und ihnen dafür eine Münze gibt*; **toothless** ADJ zahnlos; *(fig: = powerless) body* zahnlos, ohne Biss; *law, agreement* wirkungslos; **a ~ tiger** *(fig)* ein Papiertiger *m*; **toothpaste** N Zahnpasta *or* -creme *f*; **toothpick** N Zahnstocher *m*; **tooth powder** N Zahnpulver *nt*; **toothsome** ADJ schmackhaft, wohlschmeckend

toothy ['tuːθɪ] ADJ *(+er)* **she's a bit ~** sie hat ein ziemliches Pferdegebiss *(pej inf)*; **he gave me a ~ smile** er lachte mich an und zeigte dabei seine Zähne/Zahnlücken

toothypeg ['tuːθɪpeg] N *(baby-talk)* Beißerchen *nt (baby-talk)*

tootle ['tuːtl] *(esp Brit inf)* **VI** **a** *(on whistle etc: also* **tootle away**) vor sich hin dudeln *(inf)*
b *(= drive)* juckeln *(inf)*; *(= go)* trotten, zotteln; **I'll just ~ (down) to the shops** ich geh bloß mal eben (runter) einkaufen; **it's time I was tootling off** es wird Zeit, dass ich abzottele *(inf)* **N** **to give a ~ on the car horn** hupen; **to give a ~ on a whistle** auf einer Flöte herumdudeln *(inf)*

▶ **tootle along** VI *(dated inf)* dahinzuckeln *(inf)*; **I'd better tootle along now** ich zottele jetzt mal lieber ab *(inf)*; **I thought I'd tootle along to the party** *(inf)* ich dachte, ich zottel mal mit zu der Party *(inf)*

too-too ['tuː'tuː] **ADJ** *pred (dated inf: = marvellous)* pfundig *(inf)*; *(iro, = affected)* affig *(inf)* **ADV** *(= excessively)* zu

toots [tʊts] N *(inf)* Schätzchen *nt (inf)*

tootsy ['tʊtsɪ] N *(baby-talk)* Füßchen *nt*

top[1] [tɒp] **N** **a** *(= highest part)* oberer Teil; *(of spire, pyramid, cone etc, fig, of league, company etc)* Spitze *f*; *(of mountain)* Gipfel *m*; *(of tree)* Krone *f*, Spitze *f*; *(of pine tree)* Wipfel *m*, Spitze *f*; *(of branch)* oberes Ende; *(of wave)* Kamm *m*; *(of carrots, radishes)* Ende *nt*; *(= leafy part)* Kraut *nt*; *(= detachable part: of cupboard etc)* Aufsatz *m*; *(= head end: of table, bed, sheet)* Kopfende *nt*, oberes Ende; *(of road, beach)* oberes Ende; **which is the ~?** wo ist oben?; **the ~ of the tree/page/list/wall** *etc* **is ...** der Baum/die Seite/Liste/Wand *etc* ist oben ...; **the ~ of the milk** die Rahmschicht (auf der Milch); **at the ~** oben; **at the ~ of the page/list** oben auf der Seite/Liste; **at the ~ of the league/pile** oben in der Tabelle/im Stapel; **at the ~ of the stairs/wall/hill/tree** oben an der Treppe/Wand/am Berg/Baum; **at the ~ of the table/road** am oberen Ende des Tisches/der Straße; **to be (at the) ~ of the class** Klassenbeste(r) *or* -erste(r) sein, der/die Beste in der Klasse sein; **to come out at the ~ of the list** Erste(r) sein; **near the ~** (ziemlich) weit oben; **he's near the ~ in English** in Englisch gehört er zu den Besten; **the liquid was cloudy near the ~** die Flüssigkeit war oben wolkig; **she bashed the ~ of her head on the luggage rack** sie schlug sich *(dat)* den Kopf an der Gepäckablage an; **he looked over the ~ of his spectacles** er sah über den Brillenrand (hinweg); **he curled his fingers over the ~ of the window** er klammerte sich mit den Fingern an den oberen Fensterrand; **she fell from the ~ of the stairs to the bottom** sie fiel die ganze Treppe von oben bis unten hinunter; **five lines from the ~** in der fünften Zeile von oben; **from ~ to toe** von Kopf bis Fuß; **from ~ to bottom** von oben bis unten; **the system is rotten from ~ to bottom** das System ist von vorn bis hinten schlecht *(inf)*; **to scream at the ~ of one's voice** aus vollem Hals *or* aus Leibeskräften brüllen; **they were talking at the ~(s) of their voices** sie haben sich in voller Lautstärke unterhalten; **to be at the ~ of the ladder** *or* **the tree** *(fig)* auf dem Gipfel (des Erfolgs) sein; **go to the ~ of the class** *(inf)* du bist gar nicht so dumm!; **off the ~ of my head** *(fig)* grob gesagt; *(with figures)* über den Daumen gepeilt *(inf)*; **just a quick comment please, off the ~ of your head** bitte einen kurzen Kommentar, ganz spontan; **to talk off the ~ of one's head** *(inf)* nur so daherreden; **to go over the ~** *(in trenches)* aus dem Schützengraben klettern; *(= exaggerate)* zu viel des Guten tun; **that's a bit over the ~** das ist ein bisschen übertrieben, das geht ein bisschen zu weit; **I find him a bit over the ~** ich finde, er übertreibt es ein bisschen; **he's over the ~** *(= past his best)* er ist auf dem absteigenden Ast; **~ of the pops** *(record)* Spitzenreiter *m* (in der Hitparade); **the ~ of the morning to you!** *(Ir)* grüß Gott! *(S Ger, Aus)*, (schönen) guten Morgen! → **bill**[2]
b *(= upper surface)* Oberfläche *f*; *(Comput)* Vordergrund *m*; **to be on ~** oben sein *or* liegen; *(fig)* obenauf sein; **it was on ~ of/on the ~ of the cupboard/pile** *etc* es war auf/oben auf dem Schrank/Stapel *etc*; **put it on ~ of/the ~ of the cupboard** *etc* leg es oben auf den Schrank *etc*; **to go up on ~** *(on boat)* an Deck gehen; **seats on ~!** *(in bus)* oben sind noch Sitzplätze!; **to see London from the ~ of a bus** London vom Oberdeck eines Busses aus sehen; **on ~ of** *(in addition to)* zusätzlich zu; **things are getting on ~ of me** die Dinge wachsen mir über den Kopf; **then, on ~ of all that ...** und dann, um das Maß vollzumachen ...; **and, on ~ of that ...** und zusätzlich ..., und außerdem ...; **it's just one thing on ~ of another** es kommt eines zum anderen; **he didn't see it until he was right on ~ of it** er sah es erst, als er ganz nah dran war; **he felt he was on ~ of the situation** er hatte das Gefühl, die Situation im Griff *or* unter Kontrolle zu haben; **to come out on ~** sich durchsetzen; *(over rival)* die Oberhand gewinnen
c *(inf, of body)* Oberkörper *m*; **to blow one's ~** in die Luft *or* an die Decke gehen *(inf)*, aus der Haut fahren *(inf)*; **she's rather big round the ~** sie ist oben herum ganz schön füllig *(inf)*
d *(= working surface)* Arbeitsfläche *f*
e *(= bikini top)* Oberteil *nt*; *(= blouse)* Top *nt*
f *(= lid, of jar, suitcase)* Deckel *m*; *(of bottle)* Verschluss *m*; *(of pen)* Hülle *f*; *(of car)* Dach *nt*; **hard ~** *(Aut)* Hardtop *nt*; **soft ~** *(Aut)* Weichverdeck *nt*
g *(Aut: = top gear)* höchster Gang; **in ~** im vierten/fünften, im höchsten Gang
h *(inf: = big top)* Großzelt *nt*, Zirkuszelt *nt*
i *(inf)* **to be (the) ~s** klasse sein *(inf)*, spitze sein *(inf)*

j *(Naut)* Mars *m*

ADJ *(= upper)* obere(r, s); *(= highest)* oberste(r, s); *branches, note, honours, price* höchste(r, s); *(= best)* Spitzen-, Top-; *pupil, school, marks* beste(r, s); **~ athlete** Spitzenathlet(in) *m(f)*; **he was the ~ seed** er war an erste Stelle gesetzt; **~ job** Spitzenjob *m*; **~ prices** Höchstpreise *pl*; **today's ~ story** die wichtigste Meldung von heute; **on the ~ floor** im obersten Stockwerk; **a ~-floor flat** eine Dachgeschosswohnung; **he's out of the ~ drawer** *(fig)* er gehört zu den oberen zehntausend; **the ~ end of the market** das obere Marktsegment; **the car has a ~ speed of 120** das Auto hat eine Höchstgeschwindigkeit von 120; **at ~ speed** mit Höchstgeschwindigkeit; **in ~ form** in Höchstform; **to be ~** *(Sch)* Beste(r) *or* Erste(r) sein; **the ~ men in the party/government/firm** die Partei-/Regierungs-/Unternehmensspitze; **the newspaper for ~ people** die Zeitung für Führungskräfte; **the ~ people** *(in a company)* die Leute an der Spitze; *(in society)* die oberen zehntausend; **the Top Ten** *(Mus)* die Top Ten *pl*

ADV **a** **to come ~** *(Sch)* Beste(r) werden

b **~s** *(inf)* höchstens, maximal; **it'll take an hour ~s** das dauert höchstens *or* maximal eine Stunde

VT **a** *(= cover, cap)* bedecken; **~ped by a dome** gekrönt von einer Kuppel; **fruit ~ped with cream** Obst mit Sahne darauf

b *(= reach top of)* **just as the car/he ~ped the hill** gerade, als das Auto/er oben auf dem Berg angekommen war *or* den Gipfel des Berges erreicht hatte

c *(= be at top of)* **his name ~ped the list** sein Name stand ganz oben auf der Liste *or* an der Spitze der Liste → **bill**[2]

d *(= be higher than, fig: = surpass)* übersteigen; **that ~s the lot** *(inf)* das übertrifft alles; **and to ~ it all …** *(inf)* und um das Maß vollzumachen …

e **to ~ a tree/radish/carrot** die Spitze eines Baumes/das Ende eines Rettichs/einer Mohrrübe abschneiden; **to ~ and tail gooseberries** *(Brit)* Stachelbeeren putzen

f **to ~ oneself** *(inf)* sich umbringen

▶ **top off** VT *sep* **a** abrunden **b** *(US)* = **top up**

▶ **top out** VT *sep* **to top out a building** den letzten Stein legen; **topping out ceremony** ≈ Richtfest *nt*

▶ **top up** VT *sep (Brit) glass, battery, tank, account* auffüllen; *pension, income* ergänzen; **to top up the oil** Öl nachfüllen; **can I top you up?** *(inf)* darf ich dir nachschenken?

top[2] N Kreisel *m*; **to sleep like a ~** wie ein Murmeltier schlafen

topaz ['təʊpæz] N Topas *m*

top: **topcoat** N **a** *(= overcoat)* Mantel *m*; *(for men also)* Überzieher *m* **b** *(= coat of paint)* Deckanstrich *m*, letzter Anstrich; **top copy** N Original *nt*; **top dog** N *(fig)* **he always has to be ~** er muss immer das Sagen haben; **top dollar** N *(esp US inf)* Spitzenpreise *pl*; **to pay ~ for sth** Höchstpreise für etw bezahlen; **I'm paying ~** *(as wage/salary)* ich zahle einen Spitzenlohn/ein Spitzengehalt; **security earns ~** mit Sicherheit(sdiensten) lässt sich spitzenmäßig verdienen; **top-dollar** ADJ *(esp US inf)* spitzenmäßig *(inf)*; **~ prices** Spitzenpreise *pl*; **~ lyrics** spitzenmäßig gute Liedtexte; **top-down** ADJ *approach, view, analysis* von oben nach unten; **top-dress** VT *(Agr)* mit Kopfdünger düngen; **top dressing** N *(Agr)* Kopfdünger *m*

topee ['təʊpiː] N Tropenhelm *m*

top: **top-fermented** ADJ obergärig; **top-flight** ADJ Spitzen-, erstklassig; **~ football** Spitzenfußball *m*; **top-full** ADJ *glass etc* randvoll; **top gear** N höchster Gang; **to be in ~** *(lit)* im höchsten Gang sein; *(fig)* auf Hochtouren sein; **top hat** N Zylinder *m*; **top-hatted** [tɒp'hætɪd] ADJ mit Zylinder; **top-heavy** ADJ *(lit, fig)* kopflastig; **she's a bit ~** *(hum inf)* sie hat einen ziemlichen Vorbau *(inf)*; **the army is ~ with officers** die Armee hat zu viele hohe Offiziere; **top-hole** ADJ, INTERJ *(dated inf)* famos *(dated)*, erstklassig

topi ['təʊpiː] N = **topee**

topiary ['təʊpɪərɪ] N *(Hort)* Formschnitt *m*

topic ['tɒpɪk] N Thema *nt*; **~ of conversation** Gesprächsthema *nt*

topical ['tɒpɪkəl] ADJ **a** *problem, speech, event* aktuell; **he made a few ~ remarks/allusions** er ging kurz auf aktuelle Geschehnisse ein/spielte kurz auf aktuelle Geschehnisse an **b** *(= according to subject)* **~ index** Sachregister *nt*

topicality [ˌtɒpɪ'kælɪtɪ] N *(of problem, event)* Aktualität *f*

topically ['tɒpɪkəlɪ] ADV **a** aktuell **b** *(= according to subject)* nach Sachgebieten

topic sentence N *(US Gram)* Einleitungssatz *m*

top: **topknot** N Dutt *m*; **topless** ADJ oben ohne, Oben-ohne-; **pictures of ~ women** Bilder von Frauen oben ohne; **~ waitresses** Oben-ohne-Bedienung *f*; **~ model** Oben-ohne-Modell *nt*; **~ bar** Oben-ohne-Bar *f*, Toplessbar *f* ADV *sunbathe, pose, dance* oben ohne; **to go ~** oben ohne gehen; **top-level** ADJ Spitzen-; *inquiry, negotiations* auf höchster Ebene; **~ meeting** Spitzentreffen *nt*; **~ folder** *(Comput)* Hauptordner *m*; **top light** N *(Phot, Painting)* Oberlicht *nt*; **top-line** ADJ *actor etc* prominent; *news* wichtigste(r, s); *hotel etc* erstklassig, renommiert; **top loader** N *(= washing machine)* Toplader *m*; **top management** N Spitzenmanagement *nt*; **topmast** N *(Naut)* Toppmast *m*, Marsstenge *f*; **topmost** ADJ oberste(r, s); **on the ~ floor** im obersten Stockwerk; **top-notch** ADJ *(inf)* eins a *(inf)*, prächtig; **top-of-the-range, top-of-the-line** ADJ *attr* Spitzen-, der Spitzenklasse; **~ model** Spitzenmodell *nt*

topographer [tə'pɒgrəfə'] N Topograf(in) *m(f)*, Vermessungsingenieur(in) *m(f)*

topographic(al) [ˌtɒpə'græfɪk(əl)] ADJ topografisch

topography [tə'pɒgrəfɪ] N Topografie *f*

topological [ˌtɒpə'lɒdʒɪkəl] ADJ topologisch

topology [tə'pɒlədʒɪ] N Topologie *f*

toponym ['tɒpənɪm] N Ortsname *m*

topper ['tɒpə'] N *(inf, = hat)* Angströhre *f (inf)*

topping ['tɒpɪŋ] ADJ *(dated Brit, inf)* famos *(dated)* N *(Cook)* **with a ~ of cream/nuts** *etc* mit Sahne/Nüssen *etc* (oben) darauf; **recipes for various different ~s for ice cream** verschiedene Rezepte, wie man Eis überziehen kann; **artificial cream ~** Schlagschaum *m*

topping-out (ceremony) ['tɒpɪŋaʊt (-'serɪmənɪ)] N *(Build)* Richtfest *nt*

topple ['tɒpl] VI wackeln; *(= fall)* fallen; *(fig, from power)* gestürzt werden VT umwerfen; *(from a height)* hinunterkippen *or* -werfen; *(fig) government etc* stürzen; **to ~ sb from power** jdn stürzen *or* entmachten

▶ **topple down** VI umfallen; *(thing also)* umkippen; *(group of objects)* runterpurzeln; *(from chair, top of stairs etc)* herunterfallen; *(+prep obj)* hinunterfallen; **they all came toppling down** sie kamen alle runtergepurzelt

▶ **topple over** VI schwanken und fallen *(prep obj* über *+acc)*

top: **top quality** N Spitzenqualität *f*; **top-quality** ADJ Spitzen-; **top quality product** Spitzenprodukt *nt*; **top-ranked** ADJ *attr (Sport)* Spitzen-; **~ player** Spitzenspieler(in) *m(f)*; **~ Miami** das Spitzenteam Miami; **top-ranking** ADJ von hohem Rang; *civil servant, officer also* hohe(r); *personality* hochgestellt; *tennis player etc* der Spitzenklasse; **~ author** Spitzenautor(in) *m(f)*; **top-rated** ADJ *attr* führend

TOPS [tɒps] N *(Brit) abbr of* **Training Opportunities Scheme** *Umschulungsprogramm für Arbeitnehmer*

tops [tɒps] ADJ *(Brit sl)* **to be ~** cool sein *(sl)*

top: **topsail** N *(Naut)* Marssegel *nt*; **top-secret** ADJ streng geheim; **top-shelf** ADJ *(Brit) magazine* pornografisch; **topside** N *(Brit: of beef)* Oberschale *f* ADV *(Naut)* **to go ~** an Deck gehen; **topsoil** N *(Agr)* Ackerkrume *f*; **topspin** N Topspin *m*; **top station** N Bergstation *f*

topsy-turvy [ˌtɒpsɪ'tɜːvɪ] *(inf)* ADJ *(lit: = upside down)* umgedreht; *(= in disorder)* kunterbunt durcheinander *pred*; *(fig)* auf den Kopf gestellt; **it's a ~ world** es ist eine verkehrte Welt; **the room was all ~** alles im Zimmer war kunterbunt durcheinander ADV **to turn sth ~** *(lit, fig)* etw auf den Kopf stellen; *plans* etw über den Haufen werfen

top table N *Tisch mit den wichtigsten Leuten/Gästen etc*; **to be at the ~** *(fig)* ganz oben sein

top ten N Top Ten *pl*; **the ~ books** die zehn meistgekauften Bücher

top-up ['tɒpʌp] *(Brit)* N *(inf)* **the oil needs a ~** es muss Öl nachgefüllt werden; **would you like a ~?** darf man dir noch nachschenken? ADJ Zusatz-; **~ loan** Zusatzdarlehen *nt*

toque [təʊk] N Toque *f*

tor [tɔː'] N *(esp in names)* Berg *m*

Torah ['tɔːrə] N Thora *f*

torch [tɔːtʃ] N *(lit, fig)* Fackel *f*; *(Brit: = flashlight)* Taschenlampe *f*; *(= blowlamp)* Schweißbrenner *m*; **the ~ of learning** die Fackel der Wissenschaft; **to carry a ~ for sb** nach jdm schmachten; **to carry the ~ of** *or* **for sth** ein eifriger Verfechter einer Sache *(gen)* sein VT *(= to set fire to)* anstecken, anzünden

torch battery N *(Brit)* Taschenlampenbatterie *f*

torchbearer N *(lit, fig)* Fackelträger(in) *m(f)*

torchiere N *(also* **torchiere lamp***)* Deckenfluter *m*, Lampe *f* für indirekte Beleuchtung

torchlight N Licht *nt* der Fackel/Taschenlampe

torchlight procession N Fackelzug *m*

tore [tɔː'] *pret of* **tear**[1]

toreador ['tɒrɪədɔː'] N Torero *m*

torment ['tɔːment] N Qual *f*; *(inf: = person)* Quälgeist *m*; **to be in ~, to suffer ~(s)** Qualen leiden [tɔː'ment] VT quälen; *(= annoy, tease)* plagen; **~ed by remorse** von Reue gequält *or* geplagt

tormentor [tɔː'mentə'] N Peiniger(in) *m(f)*

torn [tɔːn] *ptp of* **tear**[1]

tornado [tɔː'neɪdəʊ] N *pl* **-es** Tornado *m*

torpedo [tɔː'piːdəʊ] N *pl* **-es** Torpedo *m* VT torpedieren

torpedo boat N Torpedoboot *nt*

torpedo tube N Torpedoausstoßrohr *nt*

torpid ['tɔːpɪd] ADJ *(= lethargic)* träge; *(= apathetic)* abgestumpft; *(Zool)* torpid

torpidity [tɔː'pɪdɪtɪ] N = **torpor**

torpor ['tɔːpə'] N *(= lethargy)* Trägheit *f*; *(= apathy)* Abgestumpftheit *f*; *(Zool)* Torpidität *f*

torque [tɔːk] N *(Mech)* Drehmoment *nt*

torque spanner N (signalgebender) Drehmomentenschlüssel

torrent ['tɒrənt] N *(= river)* reißender Strom; *(fig, of lava)* Strom *m*; *(of words, insults)* Sturzbach *m*, Schwall *m*, Flut *f*; **the rain came down in ~s** der Regen kam in wahren Sturzbächen herunter; **a ~ of abuse** ein Schwall *m* von Beschimpfungen

torrential [tɒ'renʃəl] ADJ *rain* sintflutartig

torrid ['tɒrɪd] ADJ *(lit, fig)* heiß; *heat, air, sun* sengend; **to have a ~ time** *(= stressful)* eine anstrengende Zeit durchmachen

torsion ['tɔːʃən] N Drehung *f*, Torsion *f (spec)*; **degree of ~** Drehbeanspruchung *f*, Torsionsschwingung *f (spec)*

torso ['tɔːsəʊ] N Körper *m*; *(Art)* Torso *m*

tort [tɔːt] N *(Jur)* Delikt *nt*

tortilla [tɔː'tiːə] N Tortilla *f*

tortilla chip N Tortilla Chip *m*

tortoise ['tɔːtəs] N Schildkröte *f*

tortoiseshell ['tɔːtəsʃel] N **a** Schildpatt *m;* *(esp for spectacle frames)* Horn *nt* **b** *(also* **tortoiseshell cat***)* Schildpattkatze *f*

tortuous ['tɔːtjʊəs] ADJ *(lit) path* gewunden; *(fig)* verwickelt; *methods also, person, journey* umständlich

torture ['tɔːtʃə'] **N** Folter *f; (fig)* Qual *f;* **instrument of ~** Folterwerkzeug *nt;* **it was sheer ~!** *(inf)* es war eine wahre Qual *or* Folter **VT** **a** *(lit)* foltern **b** *(fig: = torment)* quälen, peinigen *(geh)* **c** *(fig: = distort)* verzerren; *language* vergewaltigen; **~d language** verkrampfte Sprache; **~d steel** grotesk verbogener Stahl; **her hair had been ~d into elaborate curls** ihr Haar war mühsam in kunstvolle Locken gedreht

torture chamber N Folterkammer *f*

torturer ['tɔːtʃərə'] N *(lit)* Folterknecht *m;* *(fig: = tormentor)* Peiniger(in) *m(f)*

torturous ['tɔːtʃərəs] ADJ qualvoll

Tory ['tɔːrɪ] *(Brit Pol)* **N** Tory *m,* Konservative(r) *mf* **ADJ** konservativ, Tory-; **the ~ government** die Tory-Regierung, die konservative Regierung

Toryism ['tɔːrɪɪzəm] N *(Brit Pol)* Konservativismus *m*

tosh [tɒʃ] N *(dated Brit inf)* dummes Zeug

toss [tɒs] **N** **a** *(= throw)* Wurf *m;* **to take a ~** *(from horse)* abgeworfen werden; **with a proud ~ of her head** mit einer stolzen Kopfbewegung **b** *(of coin)* Münzwurf *m;* **to win/lose the ~** *(esp Sport)* die Seitenwahl gewinnen/verlieren; **there is no point in arguing the ~ (with me)** *(Brit)* es hat keinen Sinn, (mit mir) darüber zu streiten *or* (mit mir) herumzustreiten; **there'll always be somebody who'll want to argue the ~** *(Brit)* es gibt immer einen, der Einwände hat; **I don't give a ~ about ...** *(Brit inf)* ... ist mir völlig schnuppe *(inf)*
VT **a** *(= throw) ball* werfen; *salad* anmachen; *pancake* wenden *(durch Hochwerfen); rider* abwerfen; **to ~ sth to sb** jdm etw zuwerfen; **~ it** *(US, rubbish)* schmeiß *or* wirf es weg; **~ it over!** wirf es herüber, schmeiß mal her *(inf);* **to ~ sth aside** etw zur Seite werfen; **to ~ sb aside** jdn fallen lassen; **~ing the caber** Baumstammwerfen *nt;* **to be ~ed by a bull** auf die Hörner genommen werden; **to be ~ed by a horse** vom Pferd (ab)geworfen werden
b *(= move)* schütteln, zerren an *(+dat);* **the boat, ~ed by the wind ...** das Boot, vom Wind hin und her geworfen, ...; **to ~ one's head** den Kopf zurückwerfen *or* hochwerfen; **to ~ one's hair** das Haar nach hinten werfen
c **to ~ a coin** eine Münze (zum Losen) hochwerfen; **we settled it by ~ing a coin** wir haben eine Münze hochgeworfen und es ausgeknobelt; **to ~ sb for sth** mit jdm (durch Münzenwerfen) um etw knobeln; **I'll ~ you for it** lass uns darum knobeln
VI **a** *(ship)* rollen; *(corn)* wogen; *(plumes)* flattern; **to ~ and turn (in bed)** sich (im Bett) hin und her wälzen *or* hin und her werfen[2]
b *(with coin)* (durch Münzenwerfen) knobeln; **to ~ for sth** um etw knobeln

▶ **toss about** *(Brit) or* **around** **VI** sich heftig hin und her bewegen; *(person)* sich hin und her werfen **VT** *sep (= move)* hin und her schütteln, durchschütteln; *boat* schaukeln; *(= throw) ball* herumwerfen; *(fig) ideas* zur Debatte stellen

▶ **toss away** VT *sep* wegwerfen

▶ **toss back** VT *sep head* zurückwerfen, hochwerfen; *drink* hinunterstürzen, (runter)kippen *(inf)*

▶ **toss off** **VT** *sep* **a** *drink* hinunterstürzen, (runter)kippen *(inf)* **b** *clothes* abstreifen **c** *(inf: = produce quickly) essay* hinhauen *(inf); remark* hinwerfen **d** *(sl: = masturbate)* einen runterholen *(+dat) (inf)* **VI** *(sl)* sich *(dat)* einen runterholen *(inf)*

▶ **toss out** VT *sep rubbish* wegschmeißen *(inf),* wegwerfen; *person* hinauswerfen, rausschmeißen *(inf); comment, rules, idea* verwerfen

▶ **toss up** **VI** knobeln *(for* um) **VT** *sep* werfen; **to toss sth up (into the air)** etw hochwerfen, etw in die Luft werfen

tosser ['tɒsə'] N *(Brit sl)* Wichser *m (sl)*

tosspot ['tɒspɒt] N **a** *(sl)* = **tosser** **b** *(old inf, = drunkard)* Säufer(in) *m(f) (inf)*

toss-up ['tɒsʌp] N *(lit)* Knobeln *nt* durch Münzenwerfen; **it was a ~ whether ...** *(inf)* es war völlig offen, ob ...

tot [tɒt] N **a** *(= child: also* **tiny tot***)* Steppke *(inf),* Knirps *(inf) m* **b** *(esp Brit, of alcohol)* Schlückchen *nt*

▶ **tot up** VT *sep (esp Brit inf)* zusammenzählen, zusammenrechnen

total ['təʊtl] **ADJ** *(= complete)* völlig, absolut; *(= comprising the whole)* Gesamt-; *war, eclipse* total; *disaster* absolut, total; **~ sum/amount** Gesamtsumme *f;* **the ~ cost** die Gesamtkosten *pl;* **~ income** Gesamteinkommen *nt;* **what is the ~ number of rooms you have?** wie viele Zimmer haben Sie (insgesamt)?; **a ~ population of 650,000** eine Gesamtbevölkerung von 650.000; **the ~ effect of all this worry was ...** im Endeffekt haben seine Sorgen bewirkt, dass ...; **a ~ stranger** ein völlig Fremder; **to be in ~ disagreement** völlig verschiedener Meinung sein; **to be in ~ ignorance (of sth)** (von etw) überhaupt nichts wissen; **the silence was ~** es herrschte völlige *or* vollkommene *or* totale Stille; **my bewilderment was ~** meine Verwirrung war vollkommen *or* komplett
N Gesamtmenge *f;* *(= money, figures)* Endsumme *f;* **a ~ of 50 people** insgesamt 50 Leute; **this brings the ~ to £100** das bringt die Gesamtsumme auf £ 100; **the true jobless ~ was 4 million** die wahre Arbeitslosenzahl belief sich auf insgesamt 4 Millionen; **in ~** *(= in all)* insgesamt → **grand, sum**
VT **a** *(= amount to)* sich belaufen auf *(+acc);* **the visitors ~led 5000** insgesamt kamen 5000 Besucher; **prizes ~ling £3000** Preise im Gesamtwert von £ 3000
b *(= add: also* **total up***)* zusammenzählen, zusammenrechnen
c *(US inf: = wreck) car* zu Schrott fahren

total allergy syndrome N *no pl* multiallergisches Syndrom

totalitarian [,təʊtælɪ'teərɪən] ADJ totalitär

totalitarianism [,təʊtælɪ'teərɪənɪzəm] N Totalitarismus *m*

totality [təʊ'tælɪtɪ] N Gesamtheit *f,* Totalität *f* *(esp Philos); (Astron)* totale Finsternis

totalizator ['təʊtəlaɪ,zeɪtə'], **totalizer** ['təʊtəlaɪzə'] N *(Horse-racing)* Totalisator *m*

totally ['təʊtəlɪ] ADV völlig, total

total recall N *(Psych)* lückenlose Erinnerung

tote[1] [təʊt] N *(Brit inf)* **the ~** der Totalisator

tote[2] VT *(inf: = carry) sth heavy* schleppen; *gun* bei sich haben; **to ~ sth around** etw herumschleppen; **gun-/camera-toting people** Leute, die immer ein Gewehr/eine Kamera mit sich herumschleppen

tote bag N *(US)* (Einkaufs)tasche *f*

tote board N Totalisator *m*

totem ['təʊtəm] N Totem *nt*

totemism ['təʊtəmɪzəm] N Totemismus *m*

totem pole N Totempfahl *m*

totter ['tɒtə'] VI **a** *(= wobble before falling)* wanken, schwanken; *(= stagger)* taumeln, unsicher gehen; *(old man, baby)* tapsen; *(invalid)* schwanken, taumeln; **to ~ about** *or* **around** herumwanken/-taumeln/-tapsen **b** *(fig)* schwanken; *(economy)* kränkeln; **the country was ~ing on the brink of war** das Land befand sich am Rande eines Krieges

tottering ['tɒtərɪŋ] ADJ schwankend, wankend; *person also* taumelnd; *regime* bröckelig; *economy, government* wack(e)lig, kränklich; **a ~ monarch** ein Monarch auf einem wackeligen Thron

tottery ['tɒtərɪ] ADJ wack(e)lig; *person* tatterig; **a ~ old man** ein Tattergreis *m (inf)*

totty ['tɒtɪ] N *(Brit inf)* Weiber *pl (inf);* **a nice piece of ~** ein tolles Weib *(inf)*

toucan ['tuːkən] N Tukan *m,* Pfefferfresser *m*

touch [tʌtʃ] **N** **a** *(= sense of touch)* (Tast)gefühl *nt;* **to be cold/soft to the ~** sich kalt/weich anfühlen
b *(= act of touching)* Berühren *nt,* Berührung *f; (of pianist, typist, piano, typewriter)* Anschlag *m;* **she thrilled to his ~** es durchzuckte sie, als er sie berührte; **it opens at a ~** es öffnet sich auf Fingerdruck; **at the ~ of a button** auf Knopfdruck; **the wheel responds to the slightest ~** das Lenkrad reagiert sofort *or* reagiert auf jede Bewegung; **braille is read by ~** Blindenschrift wird durch Abtasten gelesen
c *(= skill)* Hand *f;* *(= style)* Stil *m;* **the ~ of a master** die Hand eines Meisters; **it has the ~ of genius/the professional ~** es hat etwas Geniales/Professionelles *or* einen genialen/professionellen Anstrich; **he's losing his ~** er wird langsam alt; **to have the right ~ with sb/sth** mit jdm/etw umgehen können; **a personal ~** eine persönliche Note
d *(= stroke, Art)* Strich *m;* *(fig)* Einfall *m;* **a book with humorous ~es** ein stellenweise humorvolles Buch; **a nice ~** eine hübsche Note; *(gesture)* eine nette Geste; **to put the final** *or* **finishing ~es to sth** letzte Hand an etw *(acc)* legen, einer Sache *(dat)* den letzten Schliff geben; **the house lacks a woman's ~** es fehlt eine Frau im Haus
e *(= small quantity)* Spur *f;* *(esp of irony, sadness etc)* Anflug *m;* **a ~ of flu** eine leichte Grippe; **a ~ of fever** leichtes Fieber; **a ~ of spring** ein Hauch *m* (von) Frühling; **he gave the horse a ~ of the whip** er ließ das Pferd die Peitsche fühlen *or* spüren; **it is a ~ expensive** *(esp Brit)* es ist eine Spur zu teuer → **sun**
f *(= communication)* **to be in (constant) ~ with sb** mit jdm in (ständiger) Verbindung stehen; **they were in ~ with us yesterday** sie haben sich gestern mit uns in Verbindung gesetzt; **to be/keep in ~ with (political) developments** (politisch) auf dem Laufenden sein/bleiben; **I'll be in ~!** ich lasse von mir hören!, ich melde mich!; **keep in ~!** lass wieder einmal von dir hören!; **to be out of ~ with sb** keine Verbindung mehr zu jdm haben; **to be completely out of ~ (with sth)** (in Bezug auf etw *acc*) überhaupt nicht auf dem Laufenden sein; **you can get in ~ with me at this number** Sie können mich unter dieser Nummer erreichen; **you ought to get in ~ with the police** Sie sollten sich mit der Polizei in Verbindung setzen; **to lose ~ (with sb)** den Kontakt (zu jdm) verlieren; **to lose ~ (with sth)** (in Bezug auf etw *acc*) nicht mehr auf dem Laufenden sein; **a husband and wife who have lost ~ with each other** ein Ehepaar, das sich fremd geworden ist *or* sich entfremdet hat; **I'll put you in ~ with Mr Brown** ich werde Sie mit Herrn Brown in Verbindung bringen
g *(Ftbl)* Aus *nt;* *(Rugby)* Aus *nt,* Mark *f;* **in ~** im Aus/in der Mark; **to kick for ~** *(Rugby)* ins Aus *or* in die Mark schlagen; **to kick sb/sth into ~** *(Brit fig)* etw zurückstellen, etw auf Eis legen
h *(inf)* **to make a ~** Geld schnorren *(inf);* **he's usually good for a ~** ihn kann man normalerweise gut anpumpen *(inf) or* anzapfen *(inf);* **to be an easy** *or* **soft ~** leicht anzupumpen *(inf) or* anzuzapfen *(inf)* sein
VT **a** *(= be in or make contact with)* berühren; *(= get hold of)* anfassen; *(= press lightly) piano keys* anschlagen, leicht drücken; *(= strike lightly) harp strings* streichen über *(+acc);* *(= brush against)* streifen; **she was so happy, her feet hardly ~ed the ground** *(fig)* sie war so glücklich, dass sie in den Wolken schwebte; **to ~ glasses** anstoßen; **don't ~ that!** fass das nicht an!; **he ~ed his hat to me** er tippte (zum Gruß) an den Hut; **the speedometer needle ~ed 100** die Tachonadel ging auf 100; **I was ~ing 100 most of the way** ich fuhr fast immer 100; **once I ~ed 100** einmal habe ich 100 geschafft
b *(= lay hands on)* anrühren, anfassen; **the po-**

lice/tax authorities can't ~ me die Polizei/das Finanzamt kann mir nichts anhaben; **the paintings weren't ~ed by the fire** die Gemälde blieben vom Feuer verschont
c *food, drink* anrühren; *capital* herankommen an *(+acc) (inf)*; *(= use)* antasten; **I haven't ~ed the piano for months** ich habe seit Monaten nicht mehr Klavier gespielt
d *(= equal)* herankommen an *(+acc)*, erreichen; **there's nothing to ~ hot lemon for a cold** bei einer Erkältung geht nichts über heiße Zitrone
e *(= deal with) problem etc* anrühren; **everything he ~es turns to gold** ihm gelingt einfach alles; **I wouldn't ~ those shares** ich würde meine Finger von den Aktien lassen; **an ordinary detergent won't ~ dirt like that** ein normales Reinigungsmittel wird mit diesem Schmutz nicht fertig; **I asked them not to ~ my desk** ich bat darum, nicht an meinen Schreibtisch zu gehen
f *(= concern)* berühren, betreffen
g *(= move emotionally)* rühren, bewegen; *(= affect)* berühren; *(= wound) pride* treffen; **deeply ~ed** tief gerührt *or* bewegt; **to ~ sb's heart** jds Herz (an)rühren
h *(Brit inf)* **to ~ sb for a loan** jdn um einen Kredit angehen; **he ~ed me for £10** er hat mich um £ 10 angepumpt *(inf)*
i **his hair was ~ed with grey** sein Haar war von Grau durchzogen
VI *(= come into contact)* sich berühren; *(estates etc: = be adjacent also)* aneinanderstoßen, aneinandergrenzen; **don't ~!** Finger weg!; **"please do not ~"** „bitte nicht berühren"

▶ **touch at** VI *+prep obj (Naut)* anlaufen

▶ **touch down** **VI** **a** *(Aviat, Space)* aufsetzen **b** *(Rugby, US Ftbl)* einen Versuch erzielen **VT** *sep ball* niederlegen

▶ **touch in** VT *sep details, shading etc* einfügen

▶ **touch off** VT *sep explosion, argument, fire, flood* auslösen

▶ **touch up** VT *sep* **a** *colour, make-up* auffrischen; *picture, paintwork* ausbessern; *photo* retuschieren; *essay, article* ausbessern **b** *(Brit inf) woman, man* betatschen *(inf)*, befummeln *(inf)*

▶ **touch (up)on** VI *+prep obj subject* kurz berühren, antippen; **he barely touched on the question** er hat die Frage kaum berührt

touch-and-go [ˌtʌtʃən'gəʊ] ADJ **to be ~** riskant *or* prekär sein; **it's ~ whether ...** es steht auf des Messers Schneide, ob ...; **he won eventually but it was ~ for a while** er gewann schließlich, aber es stand eine Zeit lang auf des Messers Schneide; **it's ~ if we'll make it** es ist noch vollkommen offen, ob wir es schaffen; **after his operation it was ~** nach der Operation hing sein Leben an einem Faden

touchdown ['tʌtʃdaʊn] N **a** *(Aviat, Space)* Aufsetzen *nt* **b** *(Rugby, US Ftbl)* Versuch *m, Niederlegen des Balles im Malfeld des Gegners*

touché [tu:'ʃeɪ] INTERJ *(Fencing)* Treffer; *(fig inf)* eins zu null für dich *(inf)*

touched [tʌtʃt] ADJ *pred* **a** *(= moved)* gerührt, bewegt **b** **to be a bit ~** *(inf: = mad)* einen leichten Stich haben *(inf)*

touch football N *(US) sanftere Art des Football, bei der der Gegner berührt wird, anstatt zu Fall gebracht zu werden*

touchiness ['tʌtʃɪnɪs] N Empfindlichkeit *f (on* in Bezug auf *+acc)*; *(= irritability also)* leichte Reizbarkeit; **because of the ~ of this subject** weil dieses Thema so heikel ist

touching ['tʌtʃɪŋ] **ADJ** rührend, bewegend **PREP** *(form)* bezüglich *(form)*

touchingly ['tʌtʃɪŋlɪ] ADV rührend, bewegend; **she is ~ naive** sie ist rührend naiv; **~, his daughter has supported him throughout** seine Tochter hat ihn in rührender Weise während der ganzen Zeit unterstützt

touch: **touch judge** N *(Rugby)* Seitenrichter(in) *m(f)*; **touchline** N *(esp Brit Sport)* Seitenlinie *f*, Auslinie *f*; **touchpaper** N Zündpapier *nt*; **to light the (blue) ~** *(fig)* für helle Aufregung sorgen; **touchscreen** ['tʌtʃskri:n] N *(Comput)* Touchscreen *m*, Berührungsbildschirm *m*; **touch-sensitive** ADJ berührungsempfindlich; **~ screen** Touchsccreen *m*; **~ switch** Kontaktschalter *m*; **touchstone** N *(fig)* Prüfstein *m*; **touch system** N *(Typing)* Zehnfingersystem *nt*; **touch-tone** ADJ *telephone* Tonwahl-; **touch-type** VI blindschreiben; **touch-typing** N Blindschreiben *nt*; **touch-up paint** N Tupflack *m*

touchy ['tʌtʃɪ] ADJ empfindlich *(about* in Bezug auf *+acc)*; *(= irritable also)* leicht reizbar; *subject* heikel, kitzlig *(inf)*

touchy-feely ['tʌtʃɪ'fi:lɪ] ADJ *(pej)* sentimental; **she is very ~** sie hat gern viel Körperkontakt; **a ~ song** eine zuckersüße Schnulze *(inf)*

tough [tʌf] **ADJ** *(+er)* **a** zäh; *(= resistant)* widerstandsfähig; *cloth* strapazierfähig; *membrane* widerstandsfähig; *skin* rau; *(towards others)* hart, knallhart *(inf)*; *bargaining, negotiator, opponent, fight, struggle, lesson* hart; *district, city* hart, rau; **as ~ as leather** zäh wie Leder *(inf)*; **(as) ~ as old boots** *(Brit hum inf) or* **shoe leather** *(US hum inf)* zäh wie Leder *(inf)*; **he'll get over it, he's pretty ~** er wird schon darüber hinwegkommen, er ist hart im Nehmen *(inf)*; **to get ~ (with sb)** *(physically)* grob werden (mit jdm *or* gegen jdn), handgreiflich werden (gegen jdn); *(fig)* hart durchgreifen (gegen jdn); **~ guy** *(inf)* (knall)harter Kerl *or* Bursche *(inf)*; **getting him to agree took some ~ talking** er musste ganz schon bearbeitet werden, damit er zustimmte
b *(= difficult) task, problem* hart; *journey* strapaziös, anstrengend; *choice* schwierig; *competition* hart, zäh; **it was ~ going** *(lit, fig)* es war eine Strapaze *or* ein Schlauch *m (inf)*; **to have a ~ time of it** nichts zu lachen haben; **I had a ~ time controlling my anger** es fiel mir schwer, meinen Zorn unter Kontrolle zu halten; **it's a ~ job being Prime Minister** Premierminister zu sein, ist eine schwierige Aufgabe *or* ein harter Job *(inf)*; **it's ~ when you have kids** es ist schwierig, wenn man Kinder hat; **it must have been ~ being** *or* **to be a child in the war** für ein Kind muss die Zeit während des Krieges sehr schwer gewesen sein; **she's a ~ customer** sie ist zäh wie Leder *(inf)*
c *(= strict) policy, controls* hart; **to take a ~ line with sb/on sth** bei jdm/einer Sache eine starre Haltung einnehmen
d *(inf: = unfortunate)* hart; **that's pretty ~!** das ist ganz schön hart!; **it was ~ on the others** das war hart für die andern; **~ (luck)!** Pech!; **~ luck on Taylor** Pech für Taylor; **~ shit** *(sl)* Scheißpech *nt (inf)*
N *(inf)* Schlägertyp *m (pej inf)*, (knall)harter Bursche *(inf)*
ADV *(+er) (inf)* **to treat sb ~** jdn hart rannehmen; **to talk ~** große Sprüche machen; **to act ~** hart durchgreifen; **to hang ~** unnachgiebig festhalten

▶ **tough out** VT *always separate* **to tough it out** hartnäckig auf seine Standpunkt beharren

toughbook ['tʌfbʊk] N Toughbook *m, besonders robuster Laptop*

toughen ['tʌfn] **VT** **a** *glass, metal* härten **b** *(fig) person* zäh *or* hart machen; *(esp physically)* abhärten; *laws, rules, terms, sentence, sanctions* verschärfen; **to ~ one's stance (on sth)** einen härteren Standpunkt beziehen (in Bezug auf etw *acc*); **they will have to ~ their policy** sie müssen einen härteren politischen Kurs einschlagen **VI** *(glass, metal)* aushärten, hart werden; *(meat)* zäh werden; *(attitude)* sich verhärten

▶ **toughen up** **VT** *sep person* hart *or* zäh machen, stählen *(geh)*; *muscles* trainieren; *sportsman also* fit machen; *regulations* verschärfen **VI** hart *or* zäh werden; *(attitude)* sich verhärten; **to toughen up on sth** härter gegen etw vorgehen

toughie ['tʌfɪ] N *(inf: = ruffian)* Raubein *nt (inf)*; *(= child)* Rabauke *m (inf)*; *(= problem, question)* harte Nuss; **she thinks she's a ~ and can take it** sie hält sich für hart genug, das auszuhalten

tough love N *(esp US inf)* liebevolle, aber strenge Haltung

toughly ['tʌflɪ] ADV *made* robust; *built also* stabil; *say* fest; **~ worded** geharnischt; **to behave ~** *(= like a tough guy)* den harten Mann spielen *or* markieren *(inf)*; *(= decisively)* hart auftreten

tough-minded [tʌf'maɪndɪd] ADJ störrisch

toughness ['tʌfnɪs] N **a** *(of meat etc)* Zähheit *f*; *(of person)* Zähigkeit *f*; *(= resistance)* Widerstandsfähigkeit *f*; *(of cloth)* Strapazierfähigkeit *f*; *(of skin)* Rauheit *f*; *(of bargaining, negotiator, opponent, fight, struggle, lesson)* Härte *f*; *(of district, city)* Rauheit *f* **b** *(= difficulty)* Schwierigkeit *f*; *(of journey)* Strapazen *pl* **c** *(= harshness: of policy, controls)* Härte *f*

toupee ['tu:peɪ] N Toupet *nt*

tour [tʊə'] **N** **a** *(= journey, walking tour etc)* Tour *f*; *(by bus, car etc also)* Fahrt *f*, Reise *f*, Tour *f*; *(of town, building, exhibition etc)* Rundgang *m (of* durch); *(also* **guided tour**) Führung *f (of* durch); *(by bus)* Rundfahrt *f (of* durch); **to go on a ~ of Scotland** auf eine Schottlandreise gehen; **to make a ~ of Germany** eine Deutschlandreise machen; **he took us on a ~ of the Highlands** er machte mit uns eine Reise durch die Highlands
b *(also* **tour of inspection**) Runde *f (of* durch); *(esp on foot)* Rundgang *m (of* durch); **he had a 3-year ~ (of duty) in Africa** er wurde für drei Jahre nach Afrika versetzt; **leave between ~s (of duty)** Urlaub *m* zwischen zwei Versetzungen; **to make a ~ of the site/house** einen Rundgang durch das Gelände/das Haus machen
c *(Theat)* Gastspielreise *f*, Tournee *f (of* durch); *(Sport)* Tournee *f*; **to go/be on ~** auf Gastspielreise *or* Tournee gehen/sein; **to take a company/play on ~** mit einer Truppe/einem Stück auf Gastspielreise *or* Tournee gehen
VT **a** *country, district etc* fahren durch; *(on foot)* ziehen durch *(inf)*; *(= travel around)* bereisen; **to ~ the world** um die Welt reisen, eine Weltreise machen
b *(= visit) town, building, exhibition* einen Rundgang machen durch, besichtigen; *(by bus etc)* eine Rundfahrt machen durch
c *(Theat, Sport)* eine Tournee machen durch
VI **a** *(on holiday)* eine Reise *or* Tour *or* Fahrt machen; **we're ~ing (around)** wir reisen herum; **to go ~ing** eine Tour machen
b *(Theat, Sport)* eine Tournee machen; **to go/be ~ing** auf Tournee gehen/sein

tour de force ['tʊədə'fɔ:s] N Glanzleistung *f*

tour director N *(US)* Reiseleiter(in) *m(f)*

Tourette('s) syndrome [tʊə'ret(s)ˌsɪndrəʊm] N Tourettesyndrom *nt*

tour guide N Reiseleiter(in) *m(f)*

touring ['tʊərɪŋ] N (Herum)reisen *nt*, (Herum)fahren *nt*

touring: **touring club** N Touring-Club *m*; **touring coach** N Reisebus *m*; **touring company** N *(Theat)* Tourneetheater *nt*; **touring holiday** N *(Brit)* Reiseurlaub *m*; **touring party** N Reisegruppe *f*; **touring team** N Gastmannschaft *f*

tourism ['tʊərɪzəm] N Fremdenverkehr *m*, Tourismus *m*

tourist ['tʊərɪst] **N** *(= person)* Tourist(in) *m(f)*, Fremde(r) *mf*; *(Sport)* Gast *m*; *(= tourist class)* Touristenklasse *f*; **to travel ~** in der Touristenklasse reisen **ATTR** Touristen-; **~ season** Reisesaison *or* -zeit *f*; **~ traffic** Reiseverkehr *m*

tourist: **tourist agency** N Reisebüro *nt*; **tourist association** N Fremdenverkehrsverband *m*; **tourist centre**, *(US)* **tourist center** N Touristenort *m*; **tourist class** **N** Touristenklasse *f* **ADV** *travel, fly* in der Touristenklasse; **tourist-class** ADJ *ticket, fare, passenger* der Touristenklasse; **tourist guide** N Fremdenführer(in) *m(f)*; **tourist information centre** N *(Brit)* Touristen-Informationsbüro *nt*, Touristen-Informationszentrum *nt*; **tourist office** N Fremdenverkehrsbüro *nt*; **tourist trade** N Fremdenverkehrsgewerbe *nt*

touristy ['tʊərɪstɪ] ADJ *(pej)* auf Tourismus getrimmt; *resorts, shops, souvenirs* für Touristen; **to do ~ things** das machen, was man so als Tourist tut

tour manager N *(Sport, Mus)* Tourmanager(in) *m(f)*, Tourneeleiter(in) *m(f)*

tournament ['tʊənəmənt] N *(Sport etc, also Hist)* Turnier *nt*

tournedos [tʊə'neɪdəʊ] N *(Cook)* Tournedos *nt*

tourney ['tʊənɪ] N *(Hist, US Sport)* Turnier *nt*

tourniquet ['tʊənɪkeɪ] N Aderpresse *f*, Tourniquet *nt (spec)*

tour operator N Reiseveranstalter *m*

tousle ['taʊzl] VT *hair* zerzausen; *(affectionately also)* zausen

tousled ['taʊzld] ADJ *hair* zerzaust, wuschelig *(inf)*; **~ head** Wuschelkopf *m (inf)*

tout [taʊt] *(inf)* **N** *(= tipster)* Wettberater(in) *m(f)*; *(esp Brit: = spy)* Schnüffler(in) *m(f) (inf)*, Spion(in) *m(f) (inf)*; *(= ticket tout)* (Karten)schwarzhändler(in) *m(f)*; *(for business)* Kundenfänger(in) *m(f)*
VT *(Racing) horse* als Favorit angeben, als heißen Tipp nennen; *(= spy) stables* ausspionieren *(inf)*; *horse* herumschnüffeln bei *(inf)*; *(= sell: also* **tout around**) *information* anbieten; *tickets* anbieten, schwarz verkaufen *(inf)*; *goods* (den Leuten) aufschwatzen *(inf)*; *ideas* propagieren
VI *(Racing, = offer tips)* Wetttipps (gegen Honorar) verteilen; *(= spy)* herumspionieren, herumschnüffeln *(inf)*; **to ~ for business** (aufdringlich) Reklame machen; **to ~ for customers** auf Kundenfang sein *(inf)*, Kunden schleppen *(inf)*

touter ['taʊtə'] N Kundenfänger(in) *m(f)*

tow[1] [təʊ] N Werg *nt*, Hede *f*

tow[2] **N to take a car in ~** ein Auto abschleppen; **to take a yacht in ~** eine Jacht schleppen *or* ins Schlepptau nehmen; **to give sb/a car a ~** *(in car)* jdn/ein Auto abschleppen; *(to start)* jdn/ein Auto anschleppen; **do you want a ~?** soll ich Sie abschleppen/anschleppen?; **to give a yacht a ~** eine Jacht schleppen *or* ins Schlepptau nehmen; **"on ~"** ≈ „Fahrzeug wird abgeschleppt"; **in ~** *(fig)* im Schlepptau **VT** *boat, glider* schleppen; *car also* abschleppen; *(to start)* anschleppen; *trailer, caravan* ziehen; **he was ~ing a huge dog behind him** er zog *or* schleifte einen riesigen Hund hinter sich *(dat)* her

▶ **tow away** VT *sep car* (gebührenpflichtig) abschleppen

towage ['təʊɪdʒ] N **a** *(of ships)* Bugsieren *nt*, Schleppen *nt*; *(of cars)* Abschleppen *nt* **b** *(= fee, for ships)* Schlepp- *or* Bugsiergebühr *f*; *(for cars)* Abschleppgebühr *f*; **~ charges** *(for ships)* Schlepp- *or* Bugsiergebühren *pl*; *(for cars)* Abschleppgebühren *pl*, Abschleppkosten *pl*

toward [tə'wɔːd] ADJ *(form: = favourable)* angemessen

toward(s) [tə'wɔːd(z)] PREP **a** *(= in direction of)* *(with verbs of motion)* auf *(+acc)* … zu; **they walked ~ the town** sie gingen auf die Stadt zu; **we sailed ~ China** wir segelten in Richtung China; **it's further north, ~ Dortmund** es liegt weiter im Norden, Richtung Dortmund; **~ the south** nach *or* gen *(liter)* Süden; **he turned ~ her** er wandte sich ihr zu; **with his back ~ the wall** mit dem Rücken zur Wand; **you should read with your back ~ the light** Sie sollten mit dem Rücken zum Licht lesen; **on the side (facing) ~ the sea** zum Meer hin; **a hotel facing ~ the sea** ein Hotel mit Blick aufs Meer; **they are working ~ a solution** sie arbeiten auf eine Lösung hin; **if it helps ~ finding a solution** wenn es dazu beiträgt, eine Lösung zu finden; **~ a better understanding of …** zum besseren Verständnis von …; **I gave him some money ~ a car** ich gab ihm etwas Geld als Beitrag zu seinem Auto
b *(= in relation to)* … *(dat)* gegenüber; **what are your feelings ~ him?** was empfinden Sie ihm gegenüber?, was empfinden Sie für ihn?
c ~ ten o'clock gegen zehn Uhr; **~ the end of the 60's/the year** gegen Ende der sechziger Jahre *or* Sechzigerjahre/des Jahres

tow: **towbar** ['təʊbɑː'] N Anhängerkupplung *f*; **towboat** N Schleppschiff *nt*, Schlepper *m*; **towcar** N *(esp US)* Abschleppwagen *m*

towel ['taʊəl] **N** Handtuch *nt* → **throw in VT** (mit einem Handtuch) (ab)trocknen

▶ **towel down** VT *sep* (ab)trocknen, trocken reiben

towel dispenser N Handtuchautomat *m*

towelette [taʊə'let] N Feuchtigkeits- *or* Erfrischungstuch *nt*

towelling ['taʊəlɪŋ] N Frottee(stoff) *m*

towel rail N Handtuchhalter *m*

tower ['taʊə'] **N a** Turm *m* **b** *(fig: = person)* **a ~ of strength** eine Stütze, ein starker (Rück)halt **c** *(Comput)* Tower *m* **VI** ragen

▶ **tower above** *or* **over** VI *+prep obj* **a** *(buildings etc)* emporragen über *(+acc)* **b** *(lit, fig: people)* überragen

▶ **tower up** VI hinaufragen, emporragen

tower block N *(Brit)* Hochhaus *nt*

towering ['taʊərɪŋ] ADJ **a** *building* hochragend, alles überragend; *mountain* (steil) aufragend; *tree* hochgewachsen; **the boy stood before the ~ figure of his father** der Schüler stand vor der hoch aufragenden Gestalt seines Vaters **b** *(fig: = magnificent) achievement, presence, talent* überragend; *performance* hervorragend; **a ~ rage** eine rasende *or* unbändige Wut; **one of the ~ giants of literature** eine der einsamen Größen der Literatur, ein Titan *m* der Literatur

tower system N *(Comput)* Towersystem *nt*

towheaded ['təʊhedɪd] ADJ flachsblond

towline ['təʊlaɪn] N *(Aut)* Abschleppseil *nt*; *(Naut, for glider)* Schleppseil *nt*

town [taʊn] N **a** Stadt *f*; **the ~ of Brighton** (die Stadt) Brighton; **to go into** *or* **down ~** in die Stadt gehen; **to live in ~** in der Stadt wohnen; **guess who's in ~?** raten Sie mal, wer zurzeit hier (in der Stadt) ist?; **he's out of ~** er ist nicht in der Stadt, er ist außerhalb; **~ and gown** *(Univ)* (die) Bevölkerung und (die) Studenten; **to have a night on the ~** *(inf)* die Nacht durchmachen; **you didn't know? but it's all over ~** du hattest keine Ahnung? das ist doch stadtbekannt; **it's all over ~ now that he has …** es hat sich herumgesprochen, dass er …; **to go to ~ on sth** *(fig inf: = go to great trouble with)* sich *(dat)* bei etw einen abbrechen *(inf)*; *(to please)* sich bei etw ins Zeug legen; *(= exaggerate)* etw übertreiben; **you've really gone to ~ on this essay** bei diesem Aufsatz sind Sie wirklich ins Detail gegangen; **John's really gone to ~ on his new house** John hat bei seinem neuen Haus wirklich keine Kosten gescheut
b *(Brit: = London)* London *nt*; **to go up to ~** nach London gehen *or* fahren; **he is out of ~** er ist nicht in London

town: **town centre**, *(US)* **town center** N Stadtmitte *f*, (Stadt)zentrum *nt*, Stadtinnere(s) *nt*; **town clerk** N Stadtdirektor(in) *m(f)*, Stadtschreiber(in) *m(f)* *(old, Sw)*; *(of bigger town)* Oberstadtdirektor(in) *m(f)*; **town council** N Stadtrat *m*; **town councillor**, *(US)* **town councilor** N Stadtrat *m*, Stadträtin *f*; **town crier** N *(Hist)* Ausrufer(in) *m(f)*; **town dweller** N *(Brit)* Städter(in) *m(f)*, Stadtbewohner(in) *m(f)*

townee [taʊ'niː] N *(pej)* Städter(in) *m(f)*, Stadtmensch *m*; *(Univ) Bewohner einer Universitätsstadt, der nicht der Universität angehört*

towner ['taʊnə'] N *(esp US)* Stadtbewohner(in) *m(f)*, Stadtmensch *m*

town: **town gas** N Stadtgas *nt*; **town hall** N Rathaus *nt*; **town house** N Stadthaus *nt*, Haus *nt* in der Stadt; *(= type of house)* Reihenhaus *nt*

townie ['taʊniː] N = **townee**

townish ['taʊnɪʃ] ADJ städtisch

townlet ['taʊnlət] N *(esp US)* Städtchen *nt*

town: **town life** N Stadtleben *nt*, Leben *nt* in der Stadt; **town meeting** N *(US Pol)* Gemeindeversammlung *f*; **town planner** N Stadt- *or* Städteplaner(in) *m(f)*; **town planning** N Stadtplanung *f*, Städteplanung *f*; **townscape** N Stadtbild *nt*, Stadtlandschaft *f*; *(Art)* Stadtansicht *f*

townsfolk ['taʊnzfəʊk] PL Städter *pl*, Stadtmenschen *pl*, Stadtbevölkerung *f*; *(= citizens)* Bürger *pl*

township ['taʊnʃɪp] N (Stadt)gemeinde *f*; *(US)* Verwaltungsbezirk *m*; *(US Surv)* 6 Meilen großes Gebiet; *(in South Africa)* Township *f*

towns: **townsman** N Städter *m*, Stadtmensch *m*; *(= citizen)* Bürger *m*; **my fellow townsmen** meine (lieben) Mitbürger; **townspeople** PL Städter *pl*, Stadtmenschen *pl*; *(= citizens)* Bürger *pl*; **townswoman** N Bürgerin *f*; **the townswomen of Paisley** die Bewohnerinnen *or* Bürgerinnen *pl* von Paisley; **townswomen's guild** *Frauenvereinigung mit gesellschaftlichen Aufgaben*

tow: **towpath** N Treidelpfad *m*; **towplane** N Schleppflugzeug *nt*; **towrope** N = **towline**; **tow start** N *(Aut)* Anschleppen *nt*; **to give sb a ~** jdn anschleppen; **tow truck** N *(US)* Abschleppwagen *m*

toxaemia, *(US)* **toxemia** [tɒk'siːmɪə] N Blutvergiftung *f*, Sepsis *f (spec)*

toxic ['tɒksɪk] ADJ giftig, Gift-, toxisch; *effects* schädlich; **to be ~ to sb/sth** für jdn/etw schädlich sein

toxicity [tɒk'sɪsɪtɪ] N Giftigkeit *f*, Giftgehalt *m*

toxicological [ˌtɒksɪkə'lɒdʒɪkəl] ADJ toxikologisch

toxicology [ˌtɒksɪ'kɒlədʒɪ] N Toxikologie *f*

toxic shock syndrome N toxisches Schocksyndrom

toxic waste N Giftmüll *m*

toxin ['tɒksɪn] N Giftstoff *m*, Toxin *nt*

toy [tɔɪ] ✪ 8.2 **N** Spielzeug *nt*; **~s** Spielsachen *pl*, Spielzeug *nt*; *(in shops also)* Spielwaren *pl*; **it's not a ~!** das ist kein (Kinder)spielzeug! **VI to ~ with an object/idea** *etc* mit einer Sache/Idee *etc* spielen; **to ~ with one's food** mit dem Essen (herum)spielen

toy *in cpds* Spielzeug-; **toy boy** N *(inf)* jugendlicher Liebhaber; **he looks like my ideal ~** so was Junges wie er wäre ideal zum Vernaschen *(inf)*; **toy car** N Spielzeugauto *nt*; **toy dog** N Zwerghund *m*; *(made of material)* Stoffhund *m*; **toy poodle** N Zwergpudel *m*; **toyshop** N Spielzeug- *or* Spielwarenladen *m*; **toytown** ADJ *(esp Brit pej) (= childish)* kindisch; *(= worthless)* wertlos; **~ money** Spielgeld *nt*; **~ revolutionary** Möchtegern-Revoluzzer(in) *m(f)*

trace[1] [treɪs] **N a** *(= sign)* Spur *f*; **I can't find any ~ of your file** Ihre Akte ist spurlos verschwunden; **there's no ~ of it** keine Spur davon; **to vanish without ~** spurlos verschwinden; **to sink without ~** spurlos *or* ohne Spur versinken *or* untergehen; *(fig also)* sang- und klanglos untergehen; **to lose all ~ of sb/sth** jdn/etw aus den Augen verlieren
b *(= small amount) (of poison, spice)* Spur *f*; *(of irony etc)* Hauch *m*, Spur *f*
VT a *(= draw)* zeichnen; *(= copy)* nachziehen, nachzeichnen; *(with tracing paper)* durchpausen, abpausen; **he ~d his name in the sand** er malte seinen Namen in den Sand
b *(= follow trail of) trail, progress, developments* verfolgen; *steps* folgen *(+dat)*; **to ~ a phone call** einen Anruf zurückverfolgen; **she was ~d to a house in Soho** ihre Spur führte zu einem Haus in Soho
c *(= find)* ausfindig machen, auffinden; **I can't ~ your file** ich kann Ihre Akte nicht finden

▶ **trace back** **VI** zurückgehen *(to* auf *+acc)*
VT *sep descent* zurückverfolgen; *rumour* auf seinen Ursprung zurückverfolgen; *neurosis, problem etc* zurückführen *(to* auf *+acc)*; **he can trace his family back to Henry VIII** seine Familie lässt sich bis zu Heinrich VIII. zurückverfolgen; **we traced the story back to one of the secretaries**

wir fanden heraus, dass die Geschichte von einer der Sekretärinnen in die Welt gesetzt worden war

▶ **trace out** VT *sep (= copy)* nachzeichnen; *(with tracing paper)* durchpausen (*onto* auf *+acc*); *(= draw)* zeichnen; **we traced out the route on the map** wir zeichneten die Route auf der Karte ein

trace² N *(of harness)* Zuggurt *m*, Zugriemen *m* → **kick over**

traceable ['treɪsəbl] ADJ **a** *(= can be found)* auffindbar **b to be ~ to sth** sich auf etw *(acc)* zurückführen lassen

trace element, **trace mineral** N Spurenelement *nt*

tracer ['treɪsəʳ] N **a** *(Mil: also* **tracer bullet***)* Leuchtspurgeschoss *nt* **b** *(Med)* Isotopenindikator *m* **c** *(= inquiry form)* Suchzettel *m*, Laufzettel *m*

tracery ['treɪsərɪ] N *(Archit)* Maßwerk *nt*; *(= pattern: of threads, branches etc)* Filigranmuster *nt*

trachea [trə'kɪə] N Luftröhre *f*; *(of insects)* Trachea *f*

tracheotomy [ˌtrækɪ'ɒtəmɪ] N Luftröhrenschnitt *m*

trachoma [trə'kəʊmə] N Körnerkrankheit *f*, (hartnäckige) Bindehautentzündung

tracing ['treɪsɪŋ] N *(= drawing)* Durchpausen *nt*, Durchzeichnen *nt*; *(= result)* Pause *f*

tracing: **tracing file** N Suchkartei *f*; **tracing paper** N Pauspapier *nt*; **tracing service** N Suchdienst *m*

track [træk] **N a** *(= trail)* Fährte *f*, Spur *f*; *(of tyres)* (Fahr)spur *f*; **to be on sb's ~** jdm auf der Spur sein; **you can't expect to keep ~ of your friends if you never write to them** du kannst nicht erwarten, Kontakt zu deinen Freunden zu behalten, wenn du nie schreibst; **to keep ~ of sb/sth** *(= watch, follow)* jdn/etw im Auge behalten; *(= keep up to date with)* über jdn/etw auf dem Laufenden bleiben; **I can't keep ~ of his movements** *or* **of him** ich weiß nie, wo er sich gerade aufhält; **how do you keep ~ of the time without a watch?** wie können Sie wissen, wie spät es ist, wenn Sie keine Uhr haben?; **I can't keep ~ of your girlfriends** du hast so viele Freundinnen, da komme ich nicht mit *(inf)*; **no-one can keep ~ of the situation** niemand hat mehr einen Überblick über die Lage; **to lose ~ of sb/sth** *(= lose count of, be confused about)* über Leute/etw den Überblick verlieren; *(= not be up to date with)* über jdn/etw nicht mehr auf dem Laufenden sein; **we lost ~ of time** wir haben die Zeit ganz vergessen, wir haben einfach nicht auf die Uhr *or* Zeit geachtet; **he lost ~ of what he was saying** er hat den Faden verloren; **I lost ~ of what he was saying** ich habe nicht (mehr) mitbekommen, was er gesagt hat

b *(fig)* **we must be making ~s** *(inf)* wir müssen uns auf die Socken *(inf) or* auf den Weg machen; **to make ~s for home** sich auf den Nachhauseweg machen; **he made ~s for London** er ging/fuhr nach London; **he stopped dead in his ~s** er blieb abrupt stehen; **to stop sth (dead) in its ~s** etw abrupt zum Stillstand bringen; **to stop sb (dead) in his/her ~s** jdn abrupt zum Stillstand bringen; **to cover (up) one's ~s** seine Spuren verwischen

c *(= path)* Weg *m*, Pfad *m*; **to throw sb off the ~** *(fig)* jdn aus der Bahn bringen *or* werfen; **to be on ~** *(fig)* auf Kurs sein; **to be on the right ~** *(fig)* auf der richtigen Spur sein; **to be on the wrong ~** *(fig)* auf dem falschen Weg sein, auf dem Holzweg sein *(inf)*; **to get the economy back on ~** die Wirtschaft wieder auf Kurs bringen

d *(= course, of hurricane)* Weg *m*; *(of comet)* (Lauf)bahn *f*; *(of rocket)* Bahn *f*, Kurs *m*

e *(Rail)* Gleise *pl*; *(US: = platform)* Bahnsteig *m*; **a new section of ~** eine neue (Gleis)strecke; **the ~ to Paisley** die (Bahn)strecke nach Paisley; **"keep off the ~"** „Betreten der Gleise verboten"; **two miles of new ~** zwei Meilen neuer Gleise *or* Schienen; **to leave the ~(s)** entgleisen; **double/single ~ line** zwei-/eingleisige Strecke; **to be born on the wrong side of the ~s** *(US fig)* aus niedrigem Milieu stammen

f *(Sport)* Rennbahn *f*; *(Athletics)* Bahn *f*; *(Motorsport)* Piste *f*, Bahn *f*; *(= circuit)* Rennstrecke *f*; *(Cycling)* Radrennbahn *f*

g *(on tape, diskette, CD)* Spur *f*; *(= song etc)* Stück *nt*

h *(also* **caterpillar track***)* Raupenkette *f*

i *(Aut, between wheels)* Spur(weite) *f*

VT a *(= follow) person, animal* verfolgen; *movements* folgen *(+dat)*; *(Comput)* nachverfolgen; *(Space) rocket* die Flugbahn *(+gen)* verfolgen; **~ changes** *(Comput: command)* Änderungen nachverfolgen

b *(US)* **the children ~ed dirt all over the carpet** die Kinder hinterließen überall auf dem Teppich Schmutzspuren

VI a *(= follow trail)* Fährten lesen

b *(Aut)* spurgenau laufen

c *(Film, TV)* fahren

d *(= move) (hurricane etc)* ziehen; *(stylus)* sich bewegen

▶ **track down** VT *sep* aufspüren (*to* in *+dat*); *thing* aufstöbern, auftreiben *(inf)*, finden; *reference, source of infection* ausfindig machen

▶ **track in** VI *(Film, TV)* heranfahren (*on* an *+acc*)

track: **track and field** N Leichtathletik *f*; **track-and-field** ADJ Leichtathletik-; **~ events** Leichtathletikwettbewerbe *pl*; **track athletics** N *sing* Laufdisziplinen *pl*; **trackball** N *(Comput, in laptop)* Trackball *m*; *(in mouse)* Rollkugel *f*

tracked [trækt] ADJ **~ vehicle** Ketten- *or* Raupenfahrzeug *nt*

tracker ['trækəʳ] N *(= American Indian etc)* Fährtenleser *m*; *(Hunt)* Tracker *m*

tracker dog N Spürhund *m*

track event N Laufwettbewerb *m*

tracking ['trækɪŋ] N Verfolgen *nt*

tracking station N Bodenstation *f*

tracklayer ['træk͵leɪəʳ] N **a** *(= caterpillar (vehicle))* Raupenfahrzeug *nt or* -schlepper *m* **b** *(US Rail)* Streckenarbeiter(in) *m(f)*

tracklaying vehicle [ˌtrækleɪɪŋ'viːɪkl] N Kettenfahrzeug *nt*

trackless ['træklɪs] ADJ **a** *vehicle* ohne Ketten **b** *forest* weglos

trackless surgery N Schlüssellochchirurgie *f*

track: **track maintenance** N *(Rail)* Streckenwartung *f*; **track meeting**, *(US)* **track meet** N Leichtathletikwettbewerb *or* -wettkampf *m*; **track race** N Rennen *nt*; *(Athletics also)* Lauf *m*; **track racing** N Laufwettbewerb *m*; *(Motorsport)* Rennen *nt*; *(Cycling)* Radrennen *nt*; **track record** N *(fig)* **what's his ~?** was hat er vorzuweisen?; **to have a good/poor ~** gute/schlechte Leistungen vorweisen können; **he's got a pretty good ~** er hat einiges vorzuweisen; **they've got an abysmal ~ for delivering on schedule** sie stehen nicht gerade im Ruf, pünktlich zu liefern; **track rod** N Spurstange *f*; **track shoe** N Rennschuh *m*; **tracksuit** N Trainingsanzug *m*; **~ trousers** Tracksuit- *or* Jogginghose *f*

tract¹ [trækt] N **a** *(of land)* Gebiet *nt*; **narrow ~** Streifen *m* **b** *(respiratory)* Wege *pl*; *(digestive)* Trakt *m*

tract² N Traktat *nt*, Schrift *f*

tractability [træktə'bɪlɪtɪ] N *(lit: of metal)* Formbarkeit *f*, Bearbeitbarkeit *f*; *(fig) (of child, animal, disposition)* Fügsamkeit *f*, Lenkbarkeit *f*; *(of problem)* (leichte) Lösbarkeit

tractable ['træktəbl] ADJ *(lit) metal etc* leicht zu bearbeiten, formbar; *(fig) child, animal, disposition* fügsam, lenkbar; *problem* leicht lösbar

traction ['trækʃən] N Zugkraft *f*, Ziehkraft *f*, Zugleistung *f*; *(Mot: = drive)* Antrieb *m*; *(of wheels)* Bodenhaftung *f*; *(Med)* Streckverband *m*; **in ~** im Streckverband; **diesel ~** Dieselantrieb *m*

traction engine N Zugmaschine *f*, Dampftraktor *m*

tractor ['træktəʳ] N **a** Traktor *m*, Trecker *m*, Zugmaschine *f* **b** *(of truck)* Sattelschlepper *m*

tractor: **tractor driver** N Traktorfahrer(in) *m(f)*, Traktorist(in) *m(f)*; **tractorfeed** ['træktəfiːd] N *(Comput)* Traktor *m*; **tractor-trailer** [ˌtræktə'treɪləʳ] N *(Aut)* Sattelzug *m*

trad [træd] *(inf)*, **trad jazz** N Traditional *m*, Oldtime *m*

trade [treɪd] **N a** *(= commerce)* Handel *m*, Gewerbe *nt*; *(= hotel trade, catering trade)* Gewerbe *nt*; (= *turnover: of shop, hotel etc)* die Geschäfte *pl*; **he used to be in ~** er war Geschäftsmann; **how's ~?** wie gehen die Geschäfte?; **to do ~ with sb** mit jdm Handel treiben; **to do a good ~** gute Geschäfte machen; **to do a brisk ~ in sth** einen reißenden Absatz an etw *(dat)* haben

b *(= line of business)* Branche *f*, Geschäftszweig *m*; **he's in the wool ~** er ist in der Wollbranche, er ist im Wollhandel tätig; **what ~ are you in?** in welcher Branche sind Sie (tätig)?; **he's in the ~** er ist in der Branche, er ist vom Fach; **as we call it in the ~** wie es in unserer Branche heißt

c *(= job)* Handwerk *nt*; **he's a bricklayer by ~** er ist Maurer von Beruf; **a lawyer by ~** *(hum)* ein gelernter Rechtsanwalt *(hum)*; **to put sb to a ~** *(old)* jdn ein Handwerk erlernen lassen

d *(= people)* Geschäftsleute *pl*, Branche *f*; **special terms for the ~** Vergünstigungen *pl* für Leute aus der Branche; **to sell to the ~** an Gewerbetreibende verkaufen

e *(= exchange)* Tauschgeschäft *nt*, Tauschhandel *m*

f the Trades PL *(Geog)* der Passat

VT tauschen; **to ~ sth for sth else** etw gegen etw anderes (ein)tauschen; **to ~ secrets** Geheimnisse austauschen; **to ~ places (with sb)** *(lit)* (mit jdm) die Plätze wechseln; *(fig)* (mit jdm) tauschen

VI a *(Comm)* Handel treiben, handeln; **to ~ in sth** mit etw handeln; **to ~ with sb** mit jdm Geschäfte machen *or* Handel treiben

b *(US inf)* einkaufen (*at* bei)

ADV to get sth ~ etw zum Großhandelspreis bekommen

▶ **trade in** VT *sep* in Zahlung geben (*for* für)

▶ **trade up** VI **to trade up to a bigger house** sich ein größeres Haus kaufen; **he traded up to a more powerful car** er kaufte sich ein Auto mit mehr Leistung

▶ **trade (up)on** VI *+prep obj* ausnützen

trade: **trade agreement** N Handelsabkommen *nt*; **trade balance** N Handelsbilanz *f*; **trade barrier** N Handelsschranke *f*; **trade cycle** N *(Brit)* Konjunkturzyklus *m*; **trade deficit** N Handelsdefizit *nt*; **Trade Descriptions Act** N *Gesetz über die korrekte Beschreibung von Waren*; **trade directory** N Branchenverzeichnis *nt*, Firmenverzeichnis *nt*; **trade discount** N Händlerrabatt *m*; **trade disputes** PL Arbeitsstreitigkeiten *pl*; **trade fair** N Handelsmesse *f*; **trade figures** PL Handelsziffern *pl*; **trade gap** N Außenhandelsdefizit *nt*; **trade-in** **N** Altgerät *nt*; *(= car)* in Zahlung gegebenes Auto; **we offer £50 as a ~ if you buy a new cooker** beim Kauf eines neuen Herds nehmen wir Ihren alten für £ 50 in Zahlung; **we will take your old car as a ~** wir nehmen Ihren alten Wagen in Zahlung **ATTR ~ value** Gebrauchtwert *m*; **they don't give very good ~ terms** sie bezahlen nicht sehr viel für Altgeräte/Gebrauchtwagen; **trade margin** N Handelsspanne *f*; **trademark** N *(lit)* Warenzeichen *nt*; **honesty was his ~** er war für seine Ehrlichkeit bekannt; **trade mission** N Handelsreise *f*; **trade name** N Handelsname *m*; **trade-off** N **there's always a ~** etwas geht immer verloren; **there's bound to be a ~ between speed and quality** es gibt entweder Einbußen bei der Schnelligkeit oder bei der Qualität; **trade paper** N Fachzeitschrift *f*, Fachblatt *nt*; **trade press** N Fachpresse *f*; **trade price** N Großhandelspreis *m*

trader ['treɪdəʳ] N **a** *(= person)* Händler(in) *m(f)* **b** *(= ship)* Handelsschiff *nt*

trade route N Handelsweg *m*, Handelsstraße *f*

tradescantia [ˌtrædə'skæntɪə] N *(Pflanze)* Tradeskantie *f*

trade: **trade school** N Gewerbe- *or* Berufsschule *f*; **trade secret** N *(lit, fig)* Betriebsgeheimnis *nt*

trades: **tradesman** N *(= delivery man)* Lieferant *m*; *(= shopkeeper)* Händler *m*, Ladenbesitzer *m*; *(= plumber, electrician etc)* Handwerker *m*; **~'s entrance** Lieferanteneingang *m*; **tradespeople** PL Geschäftsleute *pl*, Händler *pl*; **trades union** N *(Brit)* = **trade union**; **Trades Union Congress** (britischer) Gewerkschaftsbund; **tradeswoman** N *(= shopkeeper)* Händlerin *f*, Ladenbesitzerin *f*; *(= plumber, electrician etc)* Handwerkerin *f*

trade: **trade union** N *(Brit)* Gewerkschaft *f*; **trade unionism** N *(Brit)* Gewerkschaftsbewegung *f*; **trade unionist** N *(Brit)* Gewerkschaft(l)er(in) *m(f)*; **trade war** N Handelskrieg *m*; **trade wind** N Passat *m*

trading ['treɪdɪŋ] N Handel *m*, Handeln *nt* (*in* mit); **~ was brisk at the Stock Exchange today** der Handel an der Börse war heute lebhaft; **there was heavy ~ in …** … wurde(n) verstärkt gehandelt

trading *in cpds* Handels-; **trading account** N Geschäftskonto *nt*; **trading centre**, *(US)* **trading center** N Handelszentrum *nt*; **trading company** N Handelsgesellschaft *f*; **trading estate** N Industriegelände *nt*; **trading floor** N *(St Ex)* Börsenparkett *nt*; **trading licence**, *(US)* **trading license** N Gewerbeerlaubnis *f*, Gewerbeschein *m*; **trading loss** N Betriebsverlust *m*; **trading partner** N Handelspartner(in) *m(f)*; **trading post** N Laden *m*; **trading profits** PL Geschäfts- *or* Handelsgewinn *m*; **trading results** PL Betriebsergebnis *nt*; **trading stamp** N Rabattmarke *f*

tradition [trə'dɪʃən] N Tradition *f*; **village ~s** Dorfbräuche *pl or* -traditionen *pl or* -brauchtum *nt*; **it has become a ~ for the chairman to propose the first toast** es ist jetzt so üblich *or* ist zum festen Brauch geworden, dass der Vorsitzende den ersten Toast ausbringt; **according to ~ he …, ~ has it that he …** es ist überliefert, dass er …; **there is a ~ in the village that Queen Mary slept here** im Dorf erzählt man sich, dass Königin Mary dort übernachtet hat; **in the French ~** in der französischen Tradition; **in the best ~ (of …)** nach bester Tradition (*+gen* …)

traditional [trə'dɪʃənl] ADJ **a** traditionell; *story, custom also* alt; *virtues also* überkommen; **it's ~ for us to spend New Year's Day at my mother's** es ist bei uns so üblich *or* Brauch, dass wir den Neujahrstag bei meiner Mutter verbringen; **in the ~ way** auf traditionelle Weise; **the ~ way of doing sth** die traditionelle Weise, etw zu tun; **this custom is ~ to Somerset** dieser Brauch hat in Somerset Tradition **b** *(= conventional)* **to be ~ in one's outlook** eine konservative Auffassung haben

traditionalism [trə'dɪʃnəlɪzəm] N Festhalten *nt* am Alten, Traditionalismus *m*

traditionalist [trə'dɪʃnəlɪst] N Traditionalist(in) *m(f)* ADJ traditionsgebunden, an Traditionen hängend *or* festhaltend

traditional jazz N Traditional Jazz *m*, Oldtime-Jazz *m*

traditionally [trə'dɪʃnəlɪ] ADV traditionell; *(= customarily)* üblicherweise, normalerweise; **they have ~ voted Conservative** sie haben schon immer konservativ gewählt; **it's ~ a holiday** es ist schon immer ein Feiertag gewesen; **turkey is ~ eaten at Christmas** es ist Tradition *or* ein Brauch, Weihnachten Truthahn zu essen

traditional medicine N Schulmedizin *f*

trad jazz N = **trad**

traduce [trə'djuːs] VT *(liter)* verleumden

traducer [trə'djuːsəʳ] N *(liter)* Ehrabschneider(in) *m(f) (geh)*

traffic ['træfɪk] N **a** Verkehr *m*; *(Aviat)* Flug- *or* Luftverkehr *m*; **a policeman was directing ~** ein Polizist regelte den Verkehr; **~ coming into London is advised to avoid Putney Bridge** Fahrern in Richtung Innenstadt London wird empfohlen, Putney Bridge zu meiden **b** *(= business: of port, airport)* Umschlag *m*; **~ in steel** Stahlumschlag *m*; **freight ~** Frachtumschlag *m* **c** *(usu pej: = trading)* Handel *m* (*in* mit); *(in pornography)* Vertrieb *m* (*in* von); *(in illegal alcohol)* Schieberei *f* (*in* von) VI *(usu pej)* handeln (*in* mit); *(in drugs also)* dealen *(inf)* (*in* mit); *(in pornography)* vertreiben (*in +acc*); *(in illegal alcohol)* verschieben *(in acc)*

trafficability [ˌtræfɪkə'bɪlɪtɪ] N *(esp US)* **a** *(Econ)* Marktfähigkeit *f* **b** *(of road)* Passierbarkeit *f*

trafficator ['træfɪkeɪtəʳ] N *(dated Brit)* (Fahrt)richtungsanzeiger *m (form)*

traffic *in cpds* Verkehrs-; **traffic calming** N Verkehrsberuhigung *f*; **traffic circle** N *(US)* Kreisverkehr *m*; **traffic control tower** N *(Aviat)* Kontrollturm *m*, Tower *m*; **traffic cop** N *(US inf)* Verkehrspolizist(in) *m(f)*; **traffic court** N *(US Jur)* Verkehrsgericht *nt*; **traffic diversion** N Umleitung *f*; **traffic duty** N Verkehrsdienst *m*; **to be on ~** Verkehrsdienst haben; **traffic-guidance system** N Verkehrsleitsystem *nt*; **traffic hold-up** N = **traffic jam**; **traffic indicator** N *(Brit)* (Fahrt)richtungsanzeiger *m (form)*; *(flashing)* Blinker *m*; **traffic island** N Verkehrsinsel *f*; **traffic jam** N Verkehrsstockung *or* -stauung *f*

trafficker ['træfɪkəʳ] N *(usu pej)* Händler(in) *m(f)*, Schieber(in) *m(f) (pej)*; *(in drugs also)* Dealer(in) *m(f) (inf)*

trafficking ['træfɪkɪŋ] N Handel *m* (*in* mit); *(in illegal alcohol)* Schieberei *f* (*in* von); *(in pornography)* Vertrieb *m* (*in* von)

traffic: **traffic lights** PL, *(US)* **traffic light** N Verkehrsampel *f*; **traffic management** N Verkehrsmanagement *nt*; **traffic offender** N Verkehrssünder(in) *m(f)*; **traffic planning** N Verkehrsplanung *f*; **traffic police** PL Verkehrspolizei *f*; **traffic policeman** N Verkehrspolizist *m*; **traffic sign** N Verkehrszeichen *nt or* -schild *nt*; **traffic signals** PL = **traffic lights**; **traffic warden** N *(Brit)* ≈ Verkehrspolizist(in) *m(f)* ohne polizeiliche Befugnisse; *(woman)* ≈ Politesse *f*

tragedian [trə'dʒiːdɪən] N *(= writer)* Tragiker *m*, Tragödiendichter *m*; *(= actor)* Tragöde *m (geh)*, Darsteller *m* tragischer Rollen

tragedienne [trəˌdʒiːdɪ'en] N *(= writer)* Tragikerin *f*, Tragödiendichterin *f*; *(= actress)* Tragödin *f (geh)*, Darstellerin *f* tragischer Rollen

tragedy ['trædʒɪdɪ] N *(= tragic incident)* Tragödie *f*; *(Theat also)* Trauerspiel *nt*; *(no pl: = tragicness)* Tragische(s) *nt*; **he often acts in ~** er tritt oft in Tragödien auf; **six killed in bus crash ~** tragischer Busunfall forderte sechs Todesopfer; **the ~ of it is that …** das Tragische daran ist, dass …; **it is a ~ that …** es ist (wirklich) tragisch *or* ein Unglück, dass …

tragic ['trædʒɪk] ADJ tragisch; **the ~ and the comic** *(Theat)* das Tragische und das Komische; **~ actor** Tragöde *m*; **~ actress** Tragödin *f*

tragically ['trædʒɪkəlɪ] ADV **~, he was killed** tragischerweise kam er ums Leben; **she was ~ unaware of what had happened** tragischerweise wusste sie nicht, was geschehen war; **her career ended ~ at the age of 19** ihre Karriere endete tragisch, als sie 19 Jahre alt war; **her husband's ~ short life/early death** das tragisch kurze Leben/der tragisch frühe Tod ihres Mannes; **he died ~ young** es war tragisch, dass er so jung starb; **the operation went ~ wrong** die Operation nahm einen tragischen Verlauf; **don't take it too ~!** nehmen Sie es nicht zu tragisch!

tragicomedy ['trædʒɪ'kɒmɪdɪ] N Tragikomödie *f*

tragicomic ['trædʒɪ'kɒmɪk] ADJ tragikomisch

trail [treɪl] N **a** Spur *f*; *(of meteor)* Schwanz *m*, Schweif *m*; **~ of blood** Blutspur *f*; **~ of smoke** Rauchfahne *f*; **~ of dust** Staubwolke *f*; **the hurricane left a ~ of destruction** der Hurrikan hinterließ eine Spur der Verwüstung **b** *(= track)* Fährte *f*, Spur *f*; **hot on the ~** dicht auf den Fersen; **to be on the ~ of an animal** die Spur eines Tieres verfolgen; **the police are on his ~** die Polizei ist ihm auf der Spur **c** *(= path)* Weg *m*, Pfad *m*; *(= nature trail etc)* (Wander)weg *m* **d** *(Ski, cross-country)* Loipe *f* VT **a** *(esp Brit: = follow) person* folgen *(+dat)*, verfolgen; **to ~ an animal** ein Tier *or* die Spur eines Tieres verfolgen **b** *(= drag)* schleppen, schleifen; **the bird ~ed its broken wing** der Vogel zog seinen gebrochenen Flügel nach **c** *(US: = tow)* ziehen, schleppen **d** *team, rival* zurückliegen hinter *(+dat)*; **we are ~ing them by 4 points** wir liegen 4 Punkte hinter ihnen (zurück) VI **a** *(on floor)* schleifen **b** *(plant)* sich ranken; **a house with ivy ~ing round the windows** ein Haus mit efeuumrankten Fenstern **c** *(= walk)* zuckeln, trotten **d** *(= be behind) (in competition etc)* weit zurückliegen, hinterherhinken; *(Sport)* weit zurückgefallen sein; **our team is ~ing by 3 points** unsere Mannschaft ist mit 3 Punkten im Rückstand

▶ **trail along** VI entlangzuckeln; **the child trailed along behind his mother** das Kind trottete *or* zuckelte hinter der Mutter her VT entlangschleppen *or* -schleifen; **the child trailed his coat along behind him** das Kind schleifte *or* schleppte seinen Mantel hinter sich *(dat)* her

▶ **trail away** *or* **off** VI *(voice)* sich verlieren (*into* in *+dat*), verhallen; **his voice trailed off into silence** er verstummte

▶ **trail behind** VI hinterhertrotten *or* -zuckeln (*+prep obj* hinter *+dat*); *(in competition etc)* zurückgefallen sein (*+prep obj* hinter *+acc*) VT *sep* hinter sich *(dat)* herziehen

trailblazer ['treɪlbleɪzəʳ] N *(fig)* Wegbereiter(in) *m(f)*, Bahnbrecher(in) *m(f)*

trailblazing ['treɪlbleɪzɪŋ] ADJ *(fig)* bahnbrechend

trailer ['treɪləʳ] N **a** *(Aut)* Anhänger *m*; *(esp US, of lorry)* Sattelauflieger *m* **b** *(US)* Wohnwagen *m*, Caravan *m* **c** *(Bot)* Hängepflanze *f* **d** *(Film, TV)* Trailer *m*

trailer camp N Platz *m* für Wohnwagen *or* Caravans

trailing ['treɪlɪŋ] ADJ **a** *(Bot)* hängend; **~ plant** Hängepflanze *f* **b** *(Aviat)* **~ edge** Hinterkante *f*, Achterkante *f*

trail mix N *Trockenfrüchte und Nüsse*, ≈ Studentenfutter *nt*

train[1] [treɪn] N **a** *(Rail)* Zug *m*; **to go/travel by ~** mit dem Zug *or* der (Eisen)bahn fahren/reisen; **a ~ journey** eine Bahn- *or* Zugfahrt; **to take** *or* **catch** *or* **get the 11 o'clock ~** den Elfuhrzug nehmen; **to change ~s** umsteigen; **on the ~** im Zug **b** *(= line)* Kolonne *f*; *(of people)* Schlange *f*; *(of camels)* Karawane *f*; *(= retinue)* Gefolge *nt*; **in his ~** in seinem Gefolge; **the war brought famine in its ~** der Krieg brachte eine Hungersnot mit sich; **to set** *or* **put sth in ~** *(esp Brit form)* etw einleiten *or* in Gang setzen; **to be in ~** *(esp Brit form)* im Gang(e) sein **c** *(of events)* Folge *f*, Kette *f*; **he interrupted my ~ of thought** er unterbrach meinen Gedankengang **d** *(of dress)* Schleppe *f* **e** **~ of gunpowder** Pulverspur *f*

train[2] VT **a** *person* ausbilden; *staff* weiterbilden; *child* erziehen; *animal* abrichten, dressieren; *mind* schulen; *(Sport)* trainieren; **to ~ sb as sth** jdn als *or* zu etw ausbilden; **to ~ oneself to do sth** sich dazu erziehen, etw zu tun; **to ~ sb**

to be assertive jdm Bestimmtheit anerziehen; **to ~ an animal to do sth** ein Tier dazu abrichten, etw zu tun; **this dog has been ~ed to kill** dieser Hund ist aufs Töten abgerichtet; **a lion ~ed to do tricks** ein dressierter Löwe, der Kunststücke macht; **she has her husband well ~ed** *(hum)* sie hat ihren Mann gut dressiert *(hum)*
b *(= aim) gun, telescope* richten *(on* auf *+acc)*
c *plant* wachsen lassen *(over* über *+acc)*; **she ~ed her roses along/up the trellis** sie ließ ihre Rosen am Gitter entlang-/hochwachsen
VI a *(esp Sport)* trainieren *(for* für); **let's go ~** *(Brit)* komm, wir gehen trainieren
b *(= study)* ausgebildet werden; **he ~ed as a teacher** er hat eine Lehrerausbildung gemacht, er ist ausgebildeter Lehrer; **where did you ~?** wo haben Sie Ihre Ausbildung erhalten?, wo sind Sie ausgebildet worden?

▶ **train up** VT *sep (esp Brit)* heranbilden *(to* zu); *team* trainieren

train: **train accident** N Zugunglück *nt*, Zugsunglück *nt (Aus)*; **trainbearer** N Schleppenträger(in) *m(f)*; **train driver** N Zug- *or* Lokführer(in) *m(f)*

trained [treɪnd] ADJ *worker* gelernt; *nurse, teacher* ausgebildet; *animal* dressiert; *dog* abgerichtet, dressiert; *mind, ear* geschult; *eye* geübt, geschult; *voice* ausgebildet; **to be highly/specially ~** hoch qualifiziert/speziell ausgebildet sein; **to be ~ for sth** für etw ausgebildet sein; **a well--child** ein gut erzogenes Kind

trainee [treɪˈniː] N Auszubildende(r) *mf*; *(academic, technical)* Praktikant(in) *m(f)*; *(= nurse)* Krankenpflegeschüler(in) *m(f)*, Schwesternschülerin *f*; *(management)* Trainee *m*; **I am a ~** ich bin *or* ich befinde mich in der Ausbildung

trainee: **trainee manager** N Managementtrainee *m*; **trainee mechanic** N Schlosserlehrling *m*; **trainee nurse** N Krankenpflegeschüler(in) *m(f)*, Schwesternschülerin *f*; **trainee teacher** N *(in primary school)* ≈ Praktikant(in) *m(f)*; *(in secondary school)* ≈ Referendar(in) *m(f)*

trainer [ˈtreɪnəʳ] N **a** *(Sport, of racehorse)* Trainer(in) *m(f)*; *(of animals)* Dresseur(in) *m(f)*; *(in circus)* Dompteur *m*, Dompteuse *f* **b** *(Brit: = shoe)* Turnschuh *m*

trainer: **trainer pants** PL Windelslip *m*; **trainer plane** N *(Aviat)* Schulflugzeug *nt*; **trainer's bench** N *(Sport)* Trainerbank *f*

train ferry N Eisenbahnfähre *f*

training [ˈtreɪnɪŋ] N **a** Ausbildung *f (also Mil)*; *(of staff)* Schulung *f*; *(of animal)* Dressur *f*, Abrichten *nt*; **it's good ~ for the mind** es ist eine gute Denkschulung **b** *(Sport)* Training *nt*; **to be in ~** im Training stehen *or* sein, trainieren; *(= be fit)* gut in Form sein, fit *or* durchtrainiert sein; **to be out of ~** nicht in Form sein, aus dem Training sein; **to go into ~** das Training beginnen, anfangen zu trainieren

training: **Training and Enterprise Council** N *(Brit) staatliches Programm zur Förderung der Zusammenarbeit zwischen Berufsschulen und Unternehmen*; **training area** N *(Mil)* Truppenübungsplatz *m*; **training camp** N Trainingslager *nt*; **training centre**, *(US)* **training center** N Lehr- *or* Ausbildungszentrum *nt*; **training college** N *(for teachers)* pädagogische Hochschule; **training course** N Ausbildungskurs *m*; **training ground** N *(Sport, fig)* Trainingsgelände *nt*; **training injury** N *(Med, Sport)* Trainingsverletzung *f*; **training manual** N Lehrbuch *nt*; **Training Opportunities Scheme** N *(Brit) Umschulungsprogramm für Arbeitnehmer*; **training period** N Ausbildungsdauer *f*; **training plane** N Schulflugzeug *nt*; **training scheme** N Ausbildungsprogramm *nt*; **training session** N *(Sport)* Trainingseinheit *f*; **training ship** N Schulschiff *nt*; **training shoes** PL *(Brit)* Turnschuhe *pl*

train: **trainload** N *(of goods)* Zugladung *f*; **~s of holidaymakers** *(Brit) or* **vacationers** *(US)* ganze Züge voller Urlauber; **soldiers were sent there by the ~** ganze Zugladungen Soldaten wurden hingeschickt; **trainman** N *(US)* Eisenbahner *m*; *(= brakeman)* Bremser *m*; **train oil** N Tran *m*; **train service** N Zugverkehr *m*; *(between two places)* (Eisen)bahnverbindung *f*; **train set** N (Spielzeug)eisenbahn *f*; **trainsick** ADJ **he gets ~** ihm wird beim Zugfahren schlecht *or* übel; **trainsickness** N **I've never suffered from ~** mir ist beim Zugfahren noch nie schlecht *or* übel geworden; **train spotter** N Eisenbahnfan *m*; *(Brit pej inf: = nerd)* Schwachkopf *m (inf)*; **trainspotting** N *Hobby, bei dem Züge begutachtet und deren Nummern notiert werden*; **train surfing** N S-Bahn-Surfen *nt*

traipse [treɪps] *(inf)* VI latschen *(inf)*; **to ~ (a)round the shops** in den Geschäften rumlatschen *(inf)*; **to ~ (a)round the shops for sth** die Geschäfte nach etw abklappern *(inf)* N **it's a long ~** da muss man lange latschen *(inf)*

trait [treɪt, treɪ] N Eigenschaft *f*; *(of particular person also)* Charakter- *or* Wesenszug *m*

traitor [ˈtreɪtəʳ] N Verräter(in) *m(f)*; **to be a ~ to one's country** sein Vaterland verraten; **to turn ~** zum Verräter werden

traitorous [ˈtreɪtərəs] ADJ *behaviour, action* verräterisch; *coward also* treulos

traitorously [ˈtreɪtərəslɪ] ADV in verräterischer Weise

traitress [ˈtreɪtrɪs] N Verräterin *f*

trajectory [trəˈdʒektərɪ] N Flugbahn *f*

tram [træm] N **a** *(esp Brit)* Straßenbahn *f*, Tram(bahn) *f (S Ger, Sw, Aus)*; **Blackpool still has ~s** in Blackpool gibt es noch Straßenbahnen; **to go by ~** mit der Straßenbahn fahren; **I saw her on a ~** ich habe sie in einer Straßenbahn gesehen **b** *(Min)* Grubenbahn *f*

tram: **tramcar** N *(esp Brit)* Straßenbahn *f*; *(= single car)* Straßenbahnwagen *m*; **tram driver** N *(esp Brit)* Straßenbahnfahrer(in) *m(f)*; **tramline** N *(esp Brit) (= track)* Straßenbahnschiene *f*; *(= route)* Straßenbahnlinie *f*; **~s** *(Tennis)* Linien *pl* des Doppelspielfelds

trammel [ˈtræməl] VT einengen; **to feel ~led by sth** sich durch etw behindert *or* eingeengt fühlen N **trammels** PL Fesseln *pl*

tramp [træmp] VI **a** *(= walk heavily, trudge)* stapfen, mit schweren Schritten gehen, stampfen; **the soldiers ~ed along for hours** die Soldaten marschierten stundenlang (mit schweren Schritten); **I've been ~ing (a)round town all day** ich bin den ganzen Tag in der Stadt herumgestiefelt *(inf)*; **to ~ up and down the platform** auf dem Bahnsteig auf und ab marschieren
b *(= hike)* marschieren, wandern; *(vagabond)* umherziehen; **he ~ed all over Europe** er wanderte in ganz Europa umher
VT a *(= spread by walking)* herumtreten; **don't ~ that mud into the carpet** tritt den Dreck nicht in den Teppich
b *(= walk) streets* latschen durch *(inf)*
N a *(= vagabond)* Landstreicher(in) *m(f)*, Tramp *m*; *(in town)* Stadtstreicher(in) *m(f)*
b *(= sound)* Stapfen *nt*, schwere Schritte *pl*
c *(= walk)* Wanderung *f*; **it's a long ~** es ist ein weiter Weg
d *(Naut)* Trampdampfer *m*
e *(inf: = loose woman)* Flittchen *nt (pej)*

▶ **tramp down** VT *sep* feststampfen, festtreten; *corn, flowers etc* platt treten, niedertrampeln

▶ **tramp in** VT *sep* festtreten, in den Boden treten

trample [ˈtræmpl] VT niedertrampeln, niedertreten, zertrampeln; **to ~ sth underfoot** *(lit, fig)* auf etw *(dat)* herumtrampeln; **she ~s her husband underfoot** *(fig)* ihr Mann hat bei ihr nichts zu sagen *(inf)*; **he was ~d to death by a bull** er wurde von einem Bullen zu Tode getrampelt; **to ~ sth into the ground** etw in den Boden treten *or* trampeln VI stapfen, trampeln; **he lets his wife ~ all over him** *(fig)* er lässt sich *(dat)* von seiner Frau auf dem Kopf herumtanzen N Getrampel *nt*, Trampeln *nt*

▶ **trample about** *(Brit) or* **around** VI herumtrampeln

▶ **trample down** VT *sep* heruntertreten, niedertreten

▶ **trample on** VI *+prep obj* herumtreten auf *(+dat)*; **several children were trampled on** mehrere Kinder wurden getreten; **to trample on sb** *(fig)* jdn herumschikanieren; **to trample on sb's feelings** *(fig)* auf jds Gefühlen herumtrampeln, jds Gefühle mit Füßen treten

trampoline [ˈtræmpəlɪn] N Trampolin *nt*

tramp steamer N Trampdampfer *m*

tram: **tramride** N *(esp Brit)* Straßenbahnfahrt *f*; **tramway** N *(esp Brit)* Straßenbahn *f*; *(= route)* Straßenbahnstrecke *f*

trance [trɑːns] N Trance *f*; *(Med)* tiefe Bewusstlosigkeit; **to go into a ~** in Trance verfallen; **to put sb into a ~** jdn in Trance versetzen; **she's been going about in a ~ for the past few days** die letzten paar Tage ist sie wie in Trance *or* im Tran *(inf)* durch die Gegend gelaufen

tranche [trɑːnʃ] N *(of shares, cash)* Tranche *f*

tranny [ˈtrænɪ] N **a** *(Brit inf)* Transistor *m (inf)*, Kofferradio *nt* **b** *(inf: = transvestite)* Transvestit *m*

tranquil [ˈtræŋkwɪl] ADJ ruhig, friedlich, still; *life* friedlich, ohne Aufregung; *mind, appearance* ruhig, gelassen; *music* ruhig, sanft; *person* gelassen, ausgeglichen

tranquillity, *(US)* **tranquility** [træŋˈkwɪlɪtɪ] N Ruhe *f*, Friedlichkeit *f*, Stille *f*; *(of life)* Friede *m*; *(of mind)* Gelassenheit *f*; *(of music)* Sanftheit *f*; *(of person)* Gelassenheit *f*, Ausgeglichenheit *f*; **the ~ of the home** die friedliche Atmosphäre des Hauses; **he was soothed by the ~ of the music** die sanfte Musik beruhigte ihn

tranquillize, *(US)* **tranquilize** [ˈtræŋkwɪlaɪz] VT beruhigen

tranquillizer, *(US)* **tranquilizer** [ˈtræŋkwɪlaɪzəʳ] N Beruhigungstablette *f*, Beruhigungsmittel *nt*

tranquillizer dart, *(US)* **tranquilizer dart** Betäubungspfeil *m*

tranquillizing dart [ˈtræŋkwɪlaɪzɪŋˈdɑːt] N Betäubungspfeil *m*

tranquilly [ˈtræŋkwɪlɪ] ADV *say, gaze* gelassen; *rest, sleep* ruhig

trans- [trænz-] PREF trans-, Trans-

transact [trænˈzækt] VT abwickeln; *business also* abschließen, durchführen; *deal* abschließen

transaction [trænˈzækʃən] N **a** *(= act)* Abwicklung *f*; *(= deal)* Abschluss *m*; **~ of business** Geschäftsbetrieb *m*; **the bank will be closed for the ~ of business at 3 p.m.** die Bank hat *or* ist ab 15.00 Uhr geschlossen **b** *(= piece of business)* Geschäft *nt*; *(Fin, St Ex)* Transaktion *f* **c transactions** PL *(of society)* Sitzungsbericht *m*

transalpine [trænzˈælpaɪn] ADJ transalpin

transatlantic [ˈtrænsətˈlæntɪk] ADJ transatlantisch, Transatlantik-; *customs* auf der anderen Seite (des Atlantiks); *cousins, fashion, accent etc (= American)* amerikanisch; *(= British)* britisch; **~ flight** Transatlantikflug *m*; **a ~ phone call** ein Anruf *m* aus/nach Übersee

transceiver [trænˈsiːvəʳ] N Sender-Empfänger *m*, Sende-Empfangsgerät *nt*

transcend [trænˈsend] VT übersteigen, überschreiten, hinausgehen über *(+acc)*; *(Philos)* transzendieren

transcendence [trænˈsendəns], **transcendency** [trænˈsendənsɪ] N Erhabenheit *f*; *(Philos)* Transzendenz *f*

transcendent [trænˈsendənt] ADJ *(Philos)* transzendent; *(= supreme)* hervorragend, alles übersteigend, überragend

transcendental [ˌtrænsenˈdentl] ADJ überirdisch; *(Philos)* transzendental; *vision* transzendierend; **~ meditation** transzendentale Meditation; **~ number** *(Math)* transzendente Zahl, Transzendente *f*

transcendentalism [ˌtrænsenˈdentəlɪzəm] N transzendentale Philosophie, Transzendentalismus *m*

transcontinental [ˈtrænzˌkɒntɪˈnentl] ADJ transkontinental

transcribe [træn'skraɪb] VT *manuscripts* abschreiben, transkribieren; *(from shorthand)* (in Langschrift) übertragen; *speech, proceedings, interview etc* niederschreiben, mitschreiben; *(Mus)* transkribieren; **to ~ sth phonetically** etw in phonetische (Um)schrift übertragen

transcript ['trænskrɪpt] N **a** *(of court proceedings)* Protokoll *nt*; *(of tapes)* Niederschrift *f*; *(= copy)* Kopie *f*, Abschrift *f* **b** *(US: = academic record)* Abschrift *f (Studienunterlagen)*

transcription [træn'skrɪpʃən] N *(Mus, Phon)* Transkription *f*; *(= copy, of shorthand notes)* Abschrift *f*; *(= act)* Abschrift *f*, Abschreiben *nt*; *(of speech, proceedings)* Niederschrift *f*, Protokoll *nt*; *(Rad, TV: = recording)* Aufnahme *f*; **phonetic ~** Lautschrift *f*, phonetische (Um)schrift

transducer [ˌtrænz'djuːsəʳ] N Umformer *m*, Umwandler *m*

transept ['trænsept] N Querschiff *nt*, Transept *nt (spec)*

trans-European ['trænsˌjʊərə'piːən] ADJ transeuropäisch; *journey* quer durch Europa

transfer [træns'fɜːʳ] VT **a** *(= move)* übertragen (*to* auf *+acc*); *prisoner* überführen (*to* in *+acc*), verlegen (*to* nach); *premises, soldiers* verlegen (*to* in *+acc*, *to town* nach); *soldier, employee* versetzen (*to* in *+acc*, *to town, country* nach); *(Sport) player* transferieren (*to* zu), abgeben (*to* an *+acc*); *(Fin) funds, money* überweisen (*to* auf *+acc*), transferieren (*to* nach); *account* verlegen; *stocks* transferieren; *(Jur) property* übertragen, überschreiben (*to* über *+acc*); *right* übertragen (*to* auf *+acc*); **he ~red the bigger engine into his old car** er baute den größeren Motor in sein altes Auto ein; **to ~ one's concentration from one task to another** seine Konzentration von einer Aufgabe auf eine andere umstellen; **he ~red his capital into gold shares** er investierte sein Kapital in Goldaktien, er legte sein Kapital in Goldaktien an; **he ~red the money from the box to his pocket** er nahm das Geld aus der Schachtel und steckte es in die Tasche; **the magician had somehow ~red the rabbit from the hat to the box** der Zauberer hatte das Kaninchen irgendwie aus dem Hut in die Kiste praktiziert; **she ~red her affections to another man** sie schenkte ihre Zuneigung einem anderen; **~red charge call** *(Brit Telec)* R-Gespräch *nt*

VI **a** *(= move)* überwechseln (*to* zu); *(to new system, working conditions)* umstellen (*to* auf *+acc*); **he can easily ~ from one language to another** er kann leicht von einer Sprache auf eine andere überwechseln *or* umschalten

b *(Fin)* umsteigen (*into* auf *+acc*); **just before the crash he ~red into government bonds** gerade rechtzeitig vor dem Zusammenbruch stieg er auf Regierungsanleihen um

c *(in travelling)* umsteigen (*to* in *+acc*); *(Univ)* das Studienfach wechseln, umsatteln *(inf)* (*from* … *to* von … auf *+acc*)

N ['trænsfɜːʳ] **a** *(= act)* Übertragung *f*; *(of prisoner)* Überführung *f*; *(of premises, troops)* Verlegung *f*; *(of employee)* Versetzung *f*; *(Sport: of player)* Transfer *m*, Wechsel *m*; *(Fin: of funds, money)* Überweisung *f*; *(of account)* Verlegung *f*; *(of stocks)* Transfer *m*; *(Jur, of property)* Überschreibung *f*; *(of right)* Übertragung *f*; **he asked for a ~** *(soldier, employee)* er bat um Versetzung; *(footballer)* er bat, auf die Transferliste gesetzt zu werden

b *(= person transferred)* **he's a ~ from another regiment** er ist von einem anderen Regiment hierher versetzt *or* verlegt worden; **he's a ~ from Chelsea** er ist von Chelsea hierher gewechselt; **Chelsea's latest ~** Chelseas jüngste Neuerwerbung

c *(= picture)* Abziehbild *nt*

d *(in travelling)* Umsteigen *nt*

e *(= transfer ticket)* Umsteige(fahr)karte *f*

transferable [træns'fɜːrəbl] ADJ übertragbar; *money, stocks* transferierbar; **"not ~"** „nicht übertragbar"; **the ticket/prize is not ~** die Fahrkarte/der Preis ist nicht übertragbar

transfer desk N *(Aviat)* Transitschalter *m*

transference ['trænsfərəns] N **a** *(Psych)* Übertragung *f* **b** *(Jur: of holdings, real estate)* Übertragung *f*, Überschreibung *f* (*to sb* auf jdn); *(Fin: of money)* Transfer *m*

transfer: **transfer fee** N *(Ftbl)* Transfersumme *f*; **transfer list** N *(Ftbl)* Transferliste *f*; **transfer lounge** N *(Aviat)* Transitraum *m*; **transfer passenger** N *(esp Aviat)* Transitreisende(r) *mf*; **transfer payments** PL (staatliche) Unterstützungszahlungen *pl*; **transfer picture** N Abziehbild *nt*; **transfer rate, transfer speed** N *(Comput: of data)* Übertragungsgeschwindigkeit *f*; **transfer ticket** N Umsteige(fahr)karte *f*

transfiguration [ˌtrænsfɪgə'reɪʃən] N **a** Verklärtheit *f*; *(= transformation)* Wandel *m*, Wandlung *f* **b** *(Rel)* **Transfiguration** Verklärung *f* Jesu, Transfiguration *f*

transfigure [træns'fɪgəʳ] VT verklären; *(= transform)* verwandeln

transfix [træns'fɪks] VT **a** *(= fix)* annageln, feststecken (*to* an *+acc*); *butterflies* aufspießen **b** *(fig)* **to be** *or* **stand ~ed with horror** starr vor Entsetzen sein; **he stood as though ~ed (to the ground)** er stand da wie angewurzelt

transform [træns'fɔːm] VT umwandeln, umformen, umgestalten (*into* zu); *ideas, views* (von Grund auf) verändern; *person, life, country, caterpillar* verwandeln; *(Phys)* umwandeln, verwandeln (*into* in *+acc*); *(Elec)* (um)wandeln, umformen (*into* in *+acc*), transformieren (*into* in *+acc*); **the old house was ~ed into three luxury apartments** das alte Haus wurde in drei Luxuswohnungen umgebaut; **when she came out of the hairdresser's she was ~ed** als sie aus dem Friseursalon kam, sah sie wie umgewandelt aus; **a coat of paint ~ed the dull old room** ein Anstrich ließ den langweiligen alten Raum in neuem Glanz erstrahlen

transformation [ˌtrænsfə'meɪʃən] N Umwandlung *f*, Umformung *f*; *(of ideas, views etc)* (grundlegende) Veränderung; *(of person, caterpillar etc)* Verwandlung *f*; *(Phys, Elec)* Umwandlung *f*; *(Ling)* Umformung *f*, Transformation *f*; **~ scene** *(Theat)* Verwandlungsszene *f*

transformational [ˌtrænsfə'meɪʃənl] ADJ *(Ling)* Transformations-; **~ grammar** Transformationsgrammatik *f*

transformer [træns'fɔːməʳ] N *(Elec)* Transformator *m*

transfuse [træns'fjuːz] VT *(Med) blood* übertragen; *(fig)* erfüllen, durchdringen

transfusion [træns'fjuːʒən] N **a** (*also* **blood transfusion**) Blutübertragung *f*, (Blut)transfusion *f*; **to give sb a ~** jdm eine Blutübertragung *or* (Blut)transfusion geben; **(blood) ~ service** Blutspendedienst *m* **b** *(fig)* **a ~ of public money into …** eine Finanzspritze aus öffentlichen Geldern für …; **it was like a ~ of new life into their friendship** es war, als ob ihre Freundschaft von neuem Leben durchdrungen *or* erfüllt würde

transgress [træns'gres] VT *standards* verstoßen gegen, verletzen; *law also* überschreiten VI sündigen; **to ~ against the Lord** gegen Gottes Gebote sündigen *or* verstoßen

transgression [træns'greʃən] N **a** *(of law)* Verstoß *m*, Verletzung *f*, Überschreitung *f* **b** *(= sin)* Sünde *f*, Verstoß *m*

transgressor [træns'gresəʳ] N Übeltäter(in) *m(f)*, Missetäter(in) *m(f)*; *(= sinner)* Sünder(in) *m(f)*

tranship [træn'ʃɪp] VT umladen, umschlagen

transhipment [træn'ʃɪpmənt] N Umladung *f*

transhumance [træns'hjuːməns] N *(Agr)* Transhumanz *f*

transience ['trænzɪəns] N *(of life)* Kürze *f*, Vergänglichkeit *f*; *(of grief, joy)* Kurzlebigkeit *f*, Vergänglichkeit *f*; *(of interest)* Kurzlebigkeit *f*, Flüchtigkeit *f*

transient ['trænzɪənt] ADJ **a** *life* kurz; *grief, joy, pleasure* kurzlebig, vergänglich, vorübergehend; *interest* kurzlebig, flüchtig, vorübergehend; **the ~ nature of sth** die Kurzlebigkeit von etw **b** *(US)* **~ population** nichtansässiger *or* nicht ansässiger Teil der Bevölkerung eines Ortes N *(US)* Durchreisende(r) *mf*

transistor [træn'zɪstəʳ] N **a** *(Elec)* Transistor *m* **b** (*also* **transistor radio**) Transistorradio *nt*, Kofferradio *nt*, Transistor *m (inf)*

transistorize [træn'zɪstəraɪz] VT transistorisieren, transistorieren; **~d** transistorisiert

transit ['trænzɪt] N Durchfahrt *f*, Transit *m*; *(of goods)* Transport *m*; **the books were damaged in ~** die Bücher wurden auf dem Transport beschädigt; **passengers in ~ for New York** Transitreisende *pl* nach New York; **goods in ~ for New York** Güter *pl* für den Weitertransport nach New York; **they are stationed here in ~** sie sind hier zwischendurch stationiert

transit: **transit camp** N Durchgangslager *nt*; **transit desk** N Transitschalter *m*; **transit freight** N Transitfracht *f*

transition [træn'zɪʃən] N Übergang *m* (*from* … *to* von … zu); *(of weather)* Wechsel *m*, Umschwung *m*; *(Mus: = act)* Übergang *m*; *(= passage)* Überleitung *f*; **period of ~, ~ period** Übergangsperiode *or* -zeit *f*; **~ agreement** Übergangsregelung *f*; **~ stage** Übergangsstadium *nt*

transitional [træn'zɪʃənl] ADJ Übergangs-; *(= provisional) arrangements, costs* vorläufig; **~ government** Übergangsregierung *f*; **~ period** Übergangszeit *f*; **~ relief** vorübergehende Entlastung

transition element N *(Chem)* Übergangselement *nt*

transitive ['trænzɪtɪv] ADJ transitiv; **~ verb** transitives Verb, Handlungsverb *nt*, Transitiv(um) *nt*

transitively ['trænzɪtɪvlɪ] ADV transitiv

transitivity [ˌtrænzɪ'tɪvɪtɪ] N transitive Eigenschaft *or* Funktion

transit lounge N Warteraum *m*, Transitraum *m*

transitory ['trænzɪtərɪ] ADJ *life* kurz; *grief, joy* kurzlebig, vergänglich, vorübergehend; *interest* kurzlebig, flüchtig; **~ period** Übergangsperiode *f*; **the ~ nature of sth** die Kurzlebigkeit von etw

transit: **transit passenger** N Durchgangsreisende(r) *mf*, Transitreisende(r) *mf*; **Transit (van)®** N *(Brit)* Lieferwagen *m*, Transporter *m*; **transit visa** N Durchreisevisum *nt*, Transitvisum *nt*

translatable [trænz'leɪtəbl] ADJ übersetzbar

translate [trænz'leɪt] VT **a** *(lit) text, novel* übersetzen; **to ~ a text from German (in)to English** einen Text aus dem Deutschen ins Englische übersetzen; **it is ~d as …** es wird mit … übersetzt

b *(fig)* übertragen; **to ~ feelings into action** Gefühle in die Tat umsetzen; **to ~ a novel into a film** aus einem Roman einen Film machen; **could you ~ that into cash terms?** lässt sich das geldmäßig ausdrücken?

c *(Eccl) bishop* in eine andere Diözese berufen; *(Rel, to heaven)* aufnehmen

d *(rare, = transfer)* übertragen; *person* versetzen

VI **a** *(lit)* übersetzen; **it ~s well (into English)** es lässt sich gut (ins Englische) übersetzen *or* übertragen

b *(fig)* übertragbar sein; **the novel didn't ~ easily into screen terms** es war nicht einfach, aus dem Roman einen Film zu machen; **how does that ~ into cash?** was kommt geldmäßig dabei heraus?

translation [trænz'leɪʃən] N **a** *(= act, translated work)* Übersetzung *f* (*from* aus); *(of work of literature also, fig)* Übertragung *f*; **to do a ~ of sth** von etw eine Übersetzung machen *or* anfertigen; **errors in ~** Übersetzungsfehler *pl*; **it loses (something) in ~** es verliert (etwas) bei der Übersetzung; **a ~ problem** ein Übersetzungsproblem *nt*; **he is not good at ~** er kann nicht gut übersetzen; **~ program/software** *(Comput)* Übersetzungsprogramm *nt*/-software *f*; **~ table** *(Comput)* Umsetzungs- *or* Übersetzungstabelle *f* **b** *(Eccl)* Berufung *f* in eine andere Diözese; *(to heaven)* Himmelfahrt *f*

translator [trænzˈleɪtəʳ] N Übersetzer(in) *m(f)*

transliterate [trænzˈlɪtəreɪt] VT transliterieren

transliteration [ˌtrænzlɪtəˈreɪʃən] N Transliteration *f*

translucence [trænzˈluːsns], **translucency** [trænzˈluːsnsɪ] N Lichtdurchlässigkeit *f*, Durchsichtigkeit *f*

translucent [trænzˈluːsnt], **translucid** [trænzˈluːsɪd] ADJ *glass etc* lichtdurchlässig; *skin* durchsichtig; **~ glass** Milchglas *nt*; **a prose of ~ clarity** eine Prosa von brillanter Klarheit

transmigrate [ˌtrænzmaɪˈgreɪt] VI *(Rel)* wiedergeboren werden

transmigration [ˌtrænzmaɪˈgreɪʃən] N *(Rel)* (Seelen)wanderung *f*, Transmigration *f (spec)*; **the ~ of souls** die Seelenwanderung; **the ~ of a human soul into an animal body** die Wiedergeburt einer menschlichen Seele in einem Tierleib

transmissible [trænzˈmɪsəbl] ADJ übertragbar

transmission [trænzˈmɪʃən] N **a** *(= transmitting)* Übertragung *f*; *(through heredity)* Vererbung *f*; *(of news)* Übermittlung *f*; *(of heat)* Leitung *f*; *(= programme)* Sendung *f* **b** *(Aut)* Getriebe *nt*

transmission: **transmission belt** N *(Tech)* Treibriemen *f*; **transmission error** N *(Comput)* Übertragungsfehler *m*; **transmission gear** N *(Tech)* Wechselgetriebe *nt*; **transmission rate** N *(Telec, Comput)* Übertragungsrate *f or* -geschwindigkeit *f*; **transmission shaft** N Kardanwelle *f*

transmit [trænzˈmɪt] VT *(= convey) message* übermitteln; *sound waves* übertragen; *information, knowledge* vermitteln, übermitteln; *illness* übertragen; *(by heredity)* vererben; *heat etc* leiten; *radio/TV programme, picture* übertragen, senden VI senden, Programme *pl* ausstrahlen

transmitter [trænzˈmɪtəʳ] N *(Tech)* Sender *m*; *(in telephone)* Mikrofon *nt*, Mikrophon *nt*

transmitting [trænzˈmɪtɪŋ]: **transmitting set** N Sender *m*; **transmitting station** [trænzˈmɪtɪŋˌsteɪʃən] N *(of broadcasting company)* Sendestation *f*; *(general)* Sendestelle *f*

transmogrification [ˌtrænzmɒgrɪfɪˈkeɪʃən] N *(hum)* wunderbare Wandlung *(hum)*

transmogrify [trænzˈmɒgrɪfaɪ] VT *(hum)* auf wunderbare Weise verwandeln *or* umwandeln *(hum)*

transmutable [trænzˈmjuːtəbl] ADJ verwandelbar

transmutation [ˌtrænzmjuːˈteɪʃən] N Verwandlung *f*, Umwandlung *f*; *(Biol)* Umbildung *f*, Transmutation *f*

transmute [trænzˈmjuːt] VT umwandeln, verwandeln *(into* in *+acc)*; *metal* verwandeln *(into* in *+acc)*

transoceanic [ˌtrænzəʊʃɪˈænɪk] ADJ *travel* nach Übersee; *countries* überseeisch; *migration* über den Ozean

transom [ˈtrænsəm] N *(= transom window)* Oberlicht *nt*; *(= cross-piece)* Querbalken *m*

transpacific [ˌtrænzpəˈsɪfɪk] ADJ über den Pazifik; *countries* jenseits des Pazifik

transparency [trænsˈpærənsɪ] N **a** Transparenz *f*, Durchsichtigkeit *f* **b** *(of lies, excuses etc)* Durchschaubarkeit *f* **c** *(of system, institution)* Transparenz *f* **d** *(Phot)* Dia(positiv) *nt*; **colour** *(Brit) or* **color** *(US)* ~ Farbdia *nt* **e** *(for overhead projector)* Folie *f*

transparent [trænsˈpærənt] ADJ **a** durchsichtig, lichtdurchlässig, transparent; *blouse* durchsichtig; **to be ~ to light** lichtdurchlässig sein **b** *(fig: = obvious) lie, intentions* durchschaubar, durchsichtig; *personality* durchschaubar; *guilt, meaning* klar, eindeutig, offensichtlich; **it became ~ that ...** es wurde offensichtlich, dass ...; **you're so ~** du bist so leicht zu durchschauen; **to be ~ to sb** für jdn leicht durchschaubar sein **c** *(= open) system, institution* transparent

transparently [trænsˈpærəntlɪ] ADV **a** *(= blatantly) lie* durchschaubar, offensichtlich, offenkundig; **it was ~ obvious that ...** es war ganz offensichtlich *or* ganz klar zu erkennen, dass ...; **it had been organized, pretty ~, as a public relations exercise** es war ganz unverhohlen zu Werbezwecken veranstaltet worden **b** *(= unambiguously)* offensichtlich, offenkundig; **he had been ~ honest with her about his intentions** er hatte ihr seine Absichten ganz offen dargelegt

transpiration [ˌtrænspɪˈreɪʃən] N *(Anat)* Schweißabsonderung *f*, Transpiration *f*; *(Bot)* Transpiration *f*, Ausdunstung *f*

transpire [trænˈspaɪəʳ] VI **a** *(= become clear)* sich herausstellen; *(slowly)* durchsickern **b** *(= happen)* passieren *(inf)* **c** *(Anat)* schwitzen, transpirieren *(geh)*; *(Bot)* Feuchtigkeit abgeben *or* verdunsten, transpirieren *(spec)* VT *(Bot) moisture* verdunsten, abgeben

transplant [trænsˈplɑːnt] VT **a** *(Hort)* umpflanzen, umsetzen, verpflanzen **b** *(Med)* verpflanzen, transplantieren *(spec)* **c** *(fig) people* verpflanzen; **his wealth ~ed him into a new world** sein Reichtum versetzte ihn in eine neue Welt [ˈtrɑːnsplɑːnt] N *(= operation)* Verpflanzung *f*, Transplantation *f*; *(= organ)* Transplantat *nt*, transplantiertes *or* verpflanztes Organ; **to have a ~** sich einer Organverpflanzung unterziehen; **~ medicine** Transplantationsmedizin *f*

transplantation [ˌtrænsplɑːnˈteɪʃən] N *(Hort)* Umpflanzung *f*, Verpflanzung *f*; *(Med)* Transplantation *f*, Verpflanzung *f*; **~ medicine** Transplantationsmedizin *f*

transplantee [ˌtrænsplɑːnˈtiː] N *(Med)* Organempfänger(in) *m(f)*

transpolar [trænsˈpəʊləʳ] ADJ über den (Nord-/ /Süd)pol *or* das Polargebiet; **the ~ route** die Polroute

transponder [trænsˈpɒndəʳ] N *(Tech)* Transponder *m*, Antwortsender *m*

transport [ˈtrænspɔːt] N **a** *(of goods)* Transport *m*, Beförderung *f*; *(of troops)* Transport *m*; **road ~** Straßentransport *m*; **rail ~** Beförderung *f or* Transport *m* per Bahn, (Eisen)bahntransport *m*; **Ministry of Transport** *(Brit)* Verkehrsministerium *nt*
b *(= vehicle)* **have you got your own ~?** hast du einen fahrbaren Untersatz? *(inf)*, bist du motorisiert?; **public ~** öffentliche Verkehrsmittel *pl*; **what are we going to do about ~?** wie lösen wir die Transportfrage?; **~ will be provided** für An- und Abfahrt wird gesorgt
c *(Mil, = ship)* (Truppen)transporter *m*; *(= plane)* Transportflugzeug *nt*
d *(US: = shipment)* (Schiffs)fracht *f*, Ladung *f*
e *(liter)* **~(s) of delight** freudige Entzückung *or (Rel)* Entrückung *(liter)*; **it sent her into ~s of delight** es erfüllte sie mit freudigem Entzücken *(liter)*
VT [trænˈspɔːt] **a** *goods* befördern, transportieren; *people* befördern
b *(Hist) convict* deportieren
c *(liter)* **to be ~ed by joy** freudig entzückt sein *(liter)*

transportable [trænˈspɔːtəbl] ADJ transportabel, transportierbar

transportation [ˌtrænspɔːˈteɪʃən] N **a** Beförderung *f*, Transport *m*; *(= means)* Beförderungsmittel *nt*; *(public)* Verkehrsmittel *nt*; *(= cost)* Transport- *or* Beförderungskosten *pl*; **Department of Transportation** *(US)* Verkehrsministerium *nt*; **~ infrastructure** Verkehrsinfrastruktur *f* **b** *(Hist, of criminal)* Deportation *f*

transport café N *(Brit)* Fernfahrerlokal *nt*

transporter [trænˈspɔːtəʳ] N *(Brit: = car transporter)* Transporter *m*; *(= transporter crane)* Verladebrücke *f*; *(in factory)* Transportband *nt*

transport: **transport infrastructure** N Verkehrsinfrastruktur *f*; **transport line** N *(in factory)* Transportband *nt*; **transport plane** N Transportflugzeug *nt*; **transport ship** N (Truppen)transporter *m*; **transport system** N Verkehrswesen *nt*

transpose [trænsˈpəʊz] VT *(= move)* übertragen; *(= switch round)* vertauschen, umstellen; *(Mus)* transponieren

transposition [ˌtrænspəˈzɪʃən] N Umstellung *f*, Vertauschung *f*; *(Mus)* Transponierung *f*

transputer [trænsˈpjuːtəʳ] N *(Comput)* Transputer *m*

transsexual [trænzˈseksjʊəl] N Transsexuelle(r) *mf*

transship [trænzˈʃɪp] VT = **tranship**

transshipment [trænzˈʃɪpmənt] N = **transhipment**

transubstantiate [ˌtrænsəbˈstænʃɪeɪt] VT *(Rel)* verwandeln

transubstantiation [ˈtrænsəbˌstænʃɪˈeɪʃən] N *(Rel)* Wandlung *f*, Transsubstantiation *f (spec)*

transverse [ˈtrænzvɜːs] ADJ Quer-; *muscles* transversal; *position* horizontal; *engine* quer stehend; **~ beam** Querbalken *m*; **~ section** Querschnitt *m*

transversely [trænzˈvɜːslɪ] ADV quer; *divided* diagonal

transvestism [trænzˈvestɪzəm] N Transves(ti)tismus *m*

transvestite [trænzˈvestaɪt] N Transvestit(in) *m(f)*

trap [træp] N **a** *(for animal, fig)* Falle *f*; **to set** *or* **lay a ~ for an animal** eine Falle für ein Tier (auf)stellen; **to set a ~ for sb** *(fig)* jdm eine Falle stellen; **be careful of this question, there is a ~ in it** pass bei dieser Frage auf, da ist ein Haken dabei; **to be caught in a ~** *(lit, fig)* in der Falle sitzen; **the lawyer had caught him in a ~** er war dem Rechtsanwalt in die Falle gegangen; **to fall into a ~** in die Falle gehen; **to fall into the ~ of doing sth** den Fehler begehen, etw zu tun
b *(in greyhound racing)* Box *f*; *(Shooting)* Wurftaubenanlage *f*, Wurfmaschine *f*
c *(in drainpipe)* Siphon *m*, Geruchsverschluss *m*
d *(Brit: = vehicle)* zweirädriger Pferdewagen
e *(also* **trap door***)* Falltür *f*; *(Theat)* Versenkung *f*
f *(inf: = mouth)* Klappe *f (inf)*, Fresse *f (vulg)*, Schnauze *f (inf)*; **shut your ~!** (halt die) Klappe! *(inf)*, halt die Fresse *(vulg) or* Schnauze *(inf)*!; **keep your ~ shut about this** darüber hältst du aber die Klappe *(inf)*, halt ja die Schnauze! *(inf)*
VT **a** *animal* (mit einer Falle) fangen
b *(fig) person* in die Falle locken; **he realized he was ~ped** er merkte, dass er in der Falle saß; **to ~ sb into saying sth** jdn dazu bringen, etw zu sagen; **I was ~ped into saying I would organize the party** ich hatte mich darauf eingelassen, die Party zu organisieren; **she ~ped him into marriage** sie hat ihn geködert *(inf)*, sie hat ihn ins Netz gelockt
c *(= block off, leave no way of escape)* in die Enge treiben; **the miners are ~ped** die Bergleute sind eingeschlossen; **the ship was ~ped in the port by the storm** das Schiff saß wegen des Sturms im Hafen fest; **to be ~ped in the snow** im Schnee festsitzen; **the soldiers found themselves ~ped at the end of the gully** am Ende des Hohlweges stellten die Soldaten fest, dass sie in der Falle saßen; **he feels ~ped in his marriage** er fühlt sich in seiner Ehe als Gefangener; **I get this ~ped feeling** ich fühle mich wie gefangen *or* im Gefängnis *or* eingeschlossen; **my arm was ~ped behind my back** mein Arm war hinter meinem Rücken eingeklemmt
d *(= catch) ball* stoppen; **to ~ one's finger/ one's foot in the door** sich *(dat)* den Finger/ Fuß in der Tür einklemmen; **to ~ a nerve** sich *(dat)* einen Nerv (ein)klemmen
e *gas, liquid* stauen; **pools of water lay ~ped among the rocks as the tide receded** als die Flut zurückging, blieben Wasserpfützen zwischen den Felsen zurück
VI *(trapper)* Trapper sein

trap door N Falltür *f*; *(Theat)* Versenkung *f*

trapeze [trəˈpiːz] N *(in circus)* Trapez *nt*

trapeze artist N Trapezkünstler(in) *m(f)*

trapezium [trə'pi:zɪəm] N *(Brit)* Trapez *nt*; *(US)* Trapezoid *nt*

trapezoid ['træpɪzɔɪd] N *(Brit)* Trapezoid *nt*; *(US)* Trapez *nt*

trapper ['træpəʳ] N Fallensteller(in) *m(f)*, Trapper(in) *m(f)*

trappings ['træpɪŋz] PL **a** *(of admiral, chieftain etc)* Rangabzeichen *pl*; *(of horse)* Schmuck *m* **b** *(fig)* äußere Aufmachung, äußeres Drum und Dran *(inf)*; **~ of office** Amtsinsignien *pl*; **shorn of all its ~** aller Ausschmückungen entkleidet; **he surrounded himself with all the ~ of power** er umgab sich mit allen Insignien der Macht

Trappist ['træpɪst] N *(also* **Trappist monk***)* Trappist *m*

trappy ['træpɪ] ADJ *(+er) ground etc* tückisch

trapse VI = **traipse**

trapshooting ['træpʃu:tɪŋ] N Wurftaubenschießen *nt*

trash [træʃ] N **a** *(US: = refuse)* Abfall *m* **b** *(= goods)* Schund *m*, Ramsch *m (inf)*, billiges Zeug; *(= book, play etc)* Schund *m*; *(= pop group etc)* Mist *m (inf)*; **don't talk ~** red nicht so einen Quatsch *(inf)* **c** *(pej inf: = people)* Gesindel *nt*, Pack *nt*; **~ like her** Gesindel wie sie; **she/he is ~** sie/er taugt nichts → **white trash** VT **a** *(inf) place* verwüsten; *car (= crash)* zu Schrott fahren; *(= vandalize)* kaputt machen *(inf)* **b** *(esp US inf: = criticize)* verreißen, schlechtmachen

trash: **trash can** N *(US)* Abfalleimer *m*; **trashman** ['træʃmən] N *(US)* Müllmann *m*

trashy ['træʃɪ] ADJ *(+er) goods* minderwertig, wertlos; *play* minderwertig; *pop group* billig; *place* schäbig; **~ novel** Schundroman *m*; **clothes for teenagers are often ~** Teenagerkleidung ist oft Schund *or* billiges Zeug

trattoria [,trætə'ri:ə] N Trattoria *f*

trauma ['trɔ:mə] N *(Psych)* Trauma *nt*, seelischer Schock

traumatic [trɔ:'mætɪk] ADJ traumatisch; **it is ~ to lose one's job** seine Arbeit zu verlieren ist eine traumatische Erfahrung

traumatize ['trɔ:mətaɪz] VT *(Med, Psych)* traumatisieren

travail ['træveɪl] N **a** *usu pl (= toils)* Mühen *pl*; **after all the ~s of Watergate** nach den schweren Belastungen durch die Watergate-Affäre **b** *(old, liter: = exhausting labour)* Plackerei *f*, Mühsal *f* **c** *(old: = childbirth)* (Geburts)wehen *pl* VI **a** *(old, liter: = toil)* sich plagen *(old)*; **he ~ed in the depths of despair** er litt in tiefer Verzweiflung **b** *(old: in childbirth)* in den Wehen liegen, Wehen haben

travel ['trævl] VI **a** *(= make a journey)* reisen; **they have ~led** *(Brit) or* **~ed** *(US)* **a lot** sie sind viel gereist, sie haben viele Reisen gemacht; **he ~s to work by car** er fährt mit dem Auto zur Arbeit; **she is ~ling** *(Brit) or* **~ing** *(US)* **to London tomorrow** sie fährt morgen nach London; **the President is ~ling** *(Brit) or* **~ing** *(US)* **to Paris tomorrow** der Präsident reist morgen nach Paris; **they have ~led** *(Brit) or* **~ed** *(US)* **a long way** sie haben eine weite Reise *or* lange Fahrt hinter sich *(dat)*; *(fig)* sie haben es weit gebracht (im Leben); **they ~led** *(Brit) or* **~ed** *(US)* **for 6 hours/300 kms** sie fuhren 6 Stunden lang/300 km; **to ~ (a)round the world** eine Reise um die Welt machen; **to ~ around a country** ein Land durchreisen *or* bereisen **b** *(= go, move)* sich bewegen; *(sound, light)* sich fortpflanzen; **light ~s at ...** die Lichtgeschwindigkeit beträgt ...; **we were ~ling** *(Brit) or* **~ing** *(US)* **at 80 kph** wir fuhren 80 km/h; **the parts ~ along the conveyor belt** die Teile werden vom Förderband weiterbefördert; **the electricity ~s along the wire** der Strom fließt durch den Draht; **you were ~ling** *(Brit) or* **~ing** *(US)* **too fast** Sie sind zu schnell gefahren; **he was certainly ~ling** *(Brit) or* **~ing** *(US)*! *(inf)* er hatte vielleicht einen Zahn drauf! *(inf)*; **wow! that's ~ling** *(Brit) or* **~ing** *(US)*! *(inf)* Mann, das ist aber schnell! **c** *(Comm)* Vertreter(in) *m(f)* sein; **he ~s for a Berlin insurance firm** er ist Vertreter einer Berliner Versicherungsgesellschaft **d** *(wine etc)* **some wines do not ~ well** manche Weine vertragen den Transport nicht; **his humour** *(Brit) or* **humor** *(US)* **~s well** sein Humor kommt auch anderswo gut an **e** *(= pass)* **his eye ~led** *(Brit) or* **~ed** *(US)* **over the scene** seine Augen wanderten über die Szene **f** *(Tech)* sich hin- und herbewegen; **as the piston ~s from A to B** während sich der Kolben von A nach B bewegt; **it doesn't ~ freely** es bewegt sich schwer; **the sliding doors don't ~ freely** diese Schiebetüren gleiten nicht gut **g** *(Basketball)* einen Schrittfehler machen VT *area* bereisen; *distance* zurücklegen, fahren; *route* fahren N **a** *no pl (= travelling)* Reisen *nt*; **to be fond of ~** gerne reisen; **~ was difficult in the 18th century** im 18. Jahrhundert war das Reisen beschwerlich **b** **travels** PL *(in country)* Reisen *pl*; *(hum, in town, building)* Ausflüge *pl*, Gänge *pl*; **if you meet him on your ~s** wenn Sie ihm auf einer Ihrer Reisen begegnen; **he's off on his ~s again tomorrow** er verreist morgen wieder **c** *(Tech)* Weg *m*; *(of instrument's needle etc)* Ausschlag *m*; *(of piston)* Hub *m*

travel: **travel agency** N Reisebüro *nt*; **travel agent** N Reisebürokaufmann *m*/-kauffrau *f*; *(of package tours)* Reiseveranstalter(in) *m(f)*; **~('s)** *(= travel agency)* Reisebüro *nt*; **travel allowance** N Reisekostenzuschuss *m*

travelator ['trævəleɪtəʳ] N Rollband *nt*, Fahrband *nt*

travel: **travel brochure** N Reiseprospekt *m*; **travel bureau** N Reisebüro *nt*; **travel card** N *(Brit, for a week)* Wochenkarte *f*; *(for a month)* Monatskarte *f*; *(for a year)* Jahreskarte *f*; **travel companion** N Reisebegleiter(in) *m(f)*, Reisegefährte *m*/-gefährtin *f*; **travel expenses** PL *(esp US)* Reisekosten *pl or* -spesen *pl*; **travel insurance** N Reiseversicherung *f*

travelled, *(US)* **traveled** ['trævld] ADJ **well-~** *(person)* weit gereist; *route* viel befahren; **widely ~** weit gereist

traveller, *(US)* **traveler** ['trævləʳ] N **a** Reisende(r) *mf*; **I am a poor ~** ich vertrage das Reisen nicht **b** *(also* **commercial traveller***)* Vertreter(in) *m(f)*, Handelsreisende(r) *mf*

traveller's cheque, *(US)* **traveler's check** N Reisescheck *m*, Travellerscheck *m*

travelling, *(US)* **traveling** ['trævlɪŋ] N Reisen *nt*; **I hate ~** ich reise sehr ungern, ich hasse das Reisen

travelling, *(US)* **traveling**: **travelling bag** N Reisetasche *f*; **travelling circus** N Wanderzirkus *m*; **travelling clock** N Reisewecker *m*; **travelling crane** N Lauf- *or* Rollkran *m*; **travelling exhibition** N Wanderausstellung *f*; **travelling expenses** PL Reisekosten *pl*; *(on business)* Reisespesen *pl*; **travelling people** PL fahrendes Volk; **travelling rug** N Reisedecke *f*; **travelling salesman** N Vertreter *m*, Handelsreisende(r) *m*; **travelling scholarship** N Auslandsstipendium *nt*; **travelling theatre** N Wandertheater *nt*, Tourneetheater *nt*

travel: **travel literature** N Reisebeschreibung *f*; **travel novel** N Reisebeschreibung *f*

travelogue, *(US)* **travelog** ['trævəlɒg] N *(= film)* filmischer Reisebericht; *(= slides)* Lichtbildervortrag *m* (über eine Reise); *(= lecture)* Reisebericht *m*

travel: **travel-sick** ADJ reisekrank; **travel-sickness** N Reisekrankheit *f*; **travel-sickness pill** N Pille *f* gegen Reisekrankheit; **travel-weary**, **travel-worn** ADJ von der Reise ermüdet *or* erschöpft

traverse ['trævɜ:s] VT **a** *(= cross) land* durchqueren; *(bridge, person) water* überqueren; **to ~ the globe** den Erdball bereisen; **the searchlight ~d the sky from east to west** der Suchscheinwerfer leuchtete den Himmel von Osten nach Westen ab **b** *(= cross and recross)* **the searchlight ~d the sky** der Suchscheinwerfer leuchtete den Himmel ab **c** *(= extend over) period* überdauern **d** *(Mountaineering) ice, slope* queren, traversieren VI *(Mountaineering, Ski)* sich quer zum Hang bewegen, (den Hang) traversieren N *(on mountain, = movement)* Queren *nt*, Traversieren *nt*; *(= place)* Quergang *m*; *(Archit)* Querbalken *m*, Traverse *f*

travesty ['trævɪstɪ] N *(Liter)* Travestie *f*; **a ~ of justice** ein Hohn *m* auf die Gerechtigkeit; **the elections were a ~** die Wahlen waren ein Hohn *m or* eine Farce VT ins Lächerliche ziehen, travestieren *(esp Liter)*

trawl [trɔ:l] N *(also* **trawl net***)* Schleppnetz *nt*, Trawl *nt*; *(US: also* **trawl line***)* Grundleine *f* VI **a** **to ~ (for fish)** mit dem Schleppnetz fischen; *(US)* mit einer Grundleine fischen **b** *(esp Brit)* **to ~ for players/lawyers** Spieler/Rechtsanwälte fischen VT **a** *fish* mit dem Schleppnetz fangen; **they ~ed the sea-bottom** sie fischten mit Schleppnetzen auf dem Meeresboden; **they ~ed the net along the sea-bottom** sie schleppten das Netz über den Meeresboden **b** *(esp Brit) world, streets, bars, files, Internet* durchkämmen

trawler ['trɔ:ləʳ] N *(= boat)* Fischdampfer *m*, Trawler *m*

trawlerman ['trɔ:ləmən] N *pl* **-men** [-mən] Trawlerfischer *m*

trawling ['trɔ:lɪŋ] N Dampfer- *or* Trawlfischerei *f*

tray [treɪ] N Tablett *nt*; *(= tea tray)* Teebrett *nt*, Servierbrett *nt*; *(of cakes, small)* Platte *f*; *(big)* Brett *nt*; *(for display)* Auslagekästchen *nt*; *(= baking tray)* (Back)blech *nt*; *(for pencils etc)* (Feder)schale *f*; *(for papers, mail)* Ablage *f*; *(= drawer)* (Schub)fach *nt*; *(of printer)* Schacht *m*; *(of street vendor etc)* Bauchladen *m*; *(in suitcase, trunk)* Einsatz *m*; *(Phot: = ice tray)* Schale *f*; *(for ash)* Kasten *m*; *(in bird cage)* Schublade *f*

tray cloth N Deckchen *nt (für ein Tablett)*

treacherous ['tretʃərəs] ADJ **a** *person, action* verräterisch **b** *(= unreliable)* trügerisch, irreführend; *memory* trügerisch; **my memory is rather ~ now** mein Gedächtnis lässt mich neuerdings ziemlich im Stich **c** *(= dangerous)* tückisch; *corner* gefährlich; *weather conditions, ice* trügerisch; *journey* gefahrvoll

treacherously ['tretʃərəslɪ] ADV **a** *(= disloyally)* verräterisch, in verräterischer Weise **b** *(= unreliably)* trügerisch, irreführend; **at times he can be ~ convincing** er wirkt manchmal gefährlich überzeugend **c** *(= dangerously)* tückisch; **rocks hidden ~ beneath the surface** Felsen, die gefährlich dicht unter der Wasseroberfläche liegen; **in ~ bad conditions** unter gefährlich schlechten Bedingungen

treacherousness ['tretʃərəsnɪs] N **a** *(= disloyalty)* **the ~ of these generals** diese verräterischen Generäle **b** *(= unreliability: of memory etc)* Unzuverlässigkeit *f* **c** *(of road/weather conditions)* Tücke *f*, Gefährlichkeit *f*; **because of the ~ of the snow** wegen der trügerischen Schneeverhältnisse

treachery ['tretʃərɪ] N Verrat *m*; *(of weather)* Tücke *f*; **an act of ~** Verrat *m*, eine verräterische Tat

treacle ['tri:kl] N *(Brit)* Sirup *m*

treacle pudding N *im Dampfbad gekochter, mit Sirup angereicherter Teig*

treacle tart N *Kuchen mit Überzugmasse aus Sirup*

treacly ['tri:klɪ] ADJ *(+er) (lit)* sirupartig; *(fig) voice* honig- *or* zuckersüß; *song, sentiment* schmalzig

tread [tred] *vb: pret* **trod**, *ptp* **trodden** N **a** *(= act)* **over the years the ~ of feet has worn the steps away** über die Jahre sind die Stufen völlig ausgetreten worden

b *(= gait, noise)* Schritt *m*, Tritt *m*; **to walk with a heavy/springy ~** mit schweren/hüpfenden Schritten gehen, einen schweren/hüpfenden Gang haben; **I could hear his ~ on the stairs** ich konnte seine Schritte auf der Treppe hören
c *(of stair)* Stufe *f*
d *(of shoe, tyre)* Profil *nt*, Lauffläche *f*
VI a *(= walk)* gehen
b *(= bring foot down)* treten (*on* auf *+acc*); **mind you don't ~ on it!** passen Sie auf, dass Sie nicht darauf treten!; **will you ~ on that cigarette end?** könnten Sie den Zigarettenstummel austreten?; **he trod on my foot** er trat mir auf den Fuß; **to ~ on sb's heels** *(lit)* jdm auf die Fersen treten; *(fig)* an jds Fersen *(dat)* hängen; **to ~ softly** *or* **lightly** leise *or* leicht auftreten; **to ~ carefully** *(lit)* vorsichtig gehen; *(fig)* vorsichtig vorgehen; **to ~ in sb's footsteps** *(fig)* in jds Fuß(s)tapfen *(acc)* treten
VT *path (= make)* treten; *(= follow)* gehen; **he's ~ing the same path as his father** *(fig)* er hat den gleichen Weg wie sein Vater eingeschlagen; **to ~ a fine line between ...** sich vorsichtig zwischen ... bewegen; **it got trodden underfoot** es wurde zertreten; **to ~ grapes** Trauben stampfen; **he trod his cigarette into the sand** er trat seine Zigarette im Sand aus; **to ~ water** Wasser treten; *(fig)* auf der Stelle treten; **to ~ the boards** *(Theat)* auf der Bühne *or* den Brettern stehen; **don't ~ that earth into the carpet** treten Sie die Erde nicht in den Teppich

▸ **tread down** VT *sep* festtreten
▸ **tread in** VT *sep* festtreten
▸ **tread out** VT *sep fire, cigarette* austreten

treadle ['tredl] **N** *(of sewing machine)* Tretkurbel *f*, Pedal *nt*; *(of lathe also)* Fußhebel *m* **VI** treten

treadmill ['tredmɪl] **N** *(lit)* Tretwerk *nt*; *(fig)* Tretmühle *f*; *(in gym)* Laufband *nt*; **to work in the ~** auf dem Laufband trainieren

treas. *abbr of* **treasurer**

treason ['tri:zn] **N** Verrat *m* (*to* an *+dat*); **an act of ~** Verrat *m*

treasonable ['tri:zənəbl], **treasonous** ['tri:zənəs] **ADJ** verräterisch; **it was ~ to do such a thing** so etwas zu tun, war Verrat

treasure ['treʒəʳ] **N** *(lit)* Schatz *m*; *(fig also)* Kostbarkeit *f*; *(= dear person)* Schatz *m*; **many ~s of modern art** viele moderne Kunstschätze; **she's a real ~** sie ist eine Perle *or* ein Juwel *nt* **VT** (hoch) schätzen, zu schätzen wissen; **he really ~s his books** seine Bücher bedeuten ihm sehr viel; **I shall ~ this memory** ich werde das in lieber Erinnerung behalten

▸ **treasure up** VT *sep* horten, ansammeln, anhäufen; *(in memory)* aufbewahren

treasure: **treasure chest** **N** *(lit)* Schatztruhe *f*; *(fig)* Fundgrube *f*; **treasure house** **N** *(lit)* Schatzkammer *f*; **a ~ of knowledge** eine Fundgrube des Wissens; **treasure hunt** **N** Schatzsuche *f*

treasurer ['treʒərəʳ] **N** *(of club)* Kassenwart(in) *m(f)*, Kassenverwalter(in) *m(f)*; *(= city treasurer)* Stadtkämmerer *m*/-kämmerin *f*; *(of business)* Leiter(in) *m(f)* der Finanzabteilung; *(of king)* Schatzmeister(in) *m(f)*

treasure trove **N** Schatzfund *m*; *(= market)* Fundgrube *f*; *(= collection, source)* Schatzhöhle *f*

treasury ['treʒərɪ] **N a** *(Pol)* **the Treasury** *(Brit)* **the Treasury Department** *(US)* das Finanzministerium **b** *(of society)* Kasse *f* **c** *(= anthology)* Schatzkästlein *nt*, Schatzgrube *f*

> **TREASURY**
>
> **Her/His Majesty's Treasury**, allgemein bekannt als **the Treasury**, ist das britische Finanzministerium, das auch auf dem Gebiet der Wirtschaftsstrategie Kompetenzen besitzt. Seine Rechnungsbehörde ist das Schatzamt, **Exchequer**, das für Einnahme und Ausgabe der öffentlichen Finanzmittel verantwortlich ist. Der Schatzkanzler, das für die Finanzen zuständige Kabinettsmitglied (**Chancellor of the Exchequer**) hat seinen offiziellen Wohnsitz direkt neben dem des Premierministers, nämlich in 11 Downing Street.
> In den USA steht dem **Department of Treasury**, dem Finanzministerium, der **Secretary of the Treasury** vor, zu dessen Kompetenzbereich auch der Schutz des Präsidenten, der Zoll, die Finanzbehörde - **Internal Revenue Service (IRS)** - die Verschuldung der öffentlichen Hand und außerdem Alkohol, Tabakwaren und Feuerwaffen gehören → BUDGET

treasury: **Treasury Bench** **N** *(Brit)* Regierungsbank *f* (im Parlament); **Treasury bill** **N** kurzfristiger Schatzwechsel; **treasury bond** **N** *(US)* Schatzobligation *f*; **treasury note** **N** *(US)* Schatzanweisung *f or* -wechsel *m*

treat [tri:t] **VT a** *(= behave towards) person, animal* behandeln; *(= handle) books* behandeln, umgehen mit
b *(= consider)* betrachten (*as* als); **you should ~ your work more seriously** Sie sollten Ihre Arbeit ernster nehmen
c *(Med)* behandeln; **which doctor is ~ing you?** bei welchem Arzt sind Sie in Behandlung?, welcher Arzt behandelt Sie?; **the doctor is ~ing him for nervous exhaustion** er ist wegen Nervenüberlastung in Behandlung
d *(= process)* behandeln (*with* mit); *leather* bearbeiten, behandeln (*with* mit); *sewage* klären; *wastepaper* verarbeiten
e *subject* behandeln; *(esp scientifically, philosophically)* abhandeln
f *(= pay for, give)* einladen; **to ~ sb to sth** jdn zu etw einladen, jdm etw spendieren; *to drink, ice cream also* jdm etw ausgeben; **I'm ~ing you** ich lade Sie ein; **to ~ oneself to sth** sich *(dat)* etw gönnen; **he ~ed his wife to a weekend in Paris** er spendierte seiner Frau ein Wochenende in Paris; **he ~ed us to a preview of the exhibition** er machte uns *(dat)* eine Freude und zeigte uns die Ausstellung vorher; **for once she ~ed us to the sight of her knees** endlich einmal gönnte sie uns den Anblick ihrer Knie; **he ~ed us to a display of his temper** *(iro)* er gab uns *(dat)* eine Kostprobe seiner Launenhaftigkeit
VI *(= deal)* **to ~ with sb for sth** mit jdm über etw *(acc)* Verhandlungen führen, mit jdm um *or* über etw *(acc)* verhandeln; **the general decided to ~ for peace** der General entschloss sich, Friedensverhandlungen zu führen
N a *(= special outing, present)* besondere Freude; **tomorrow we're going on our Christmas ~** morgen machen wir unsere Weihnachtsfeier *(inf)*; **children's ~** Kinderfest *nt*, Kindernachmittag *m*; **I thought I'd give myself a ~** ich dachte, ich gönne mir mal etwas; **I'm taking them to the circus as** *or* **for a ~** ich mache ihnen eine Freude und lade sie in den Zirkus ein *or* nehme sie in den Zirkus mit; **it's my ~** das geht auf meine Kosten *or* Rechnung, ich lade Sie ein; **I want to give them a ~** ich möchte ihnen eine besondere Freude machen; **our uncle's ~ was to give us tickets for the opera** unser Onkel hat uns *(dat)* Opernkarten spendiert; **that was a ~!** das war ein Genuss!; **what a ~ to have a quiet afternoon** das ist ein Genuss *or* tut gut, mal einen ruhigen Nachmittag zu verbringen; **there's a ~ in store** es gibt etwas, worauf wir uns noch freuen können; **this time you can carry the bags as a ~!** *(iro)* dieses Mal darfst du ausnahmsweise die Taschen tragen; **it's a (real) ~ to see you again** was für eine Freude, Sie mal wiederzusehen!
b *(inf)* **it's coming on a ~** es macht sich prima *(inf)*; **it worked a ~** es klappte *or* lief wie am Schnürchen *(inf) or* wie eine Eins *(inf)*

▸ **treat of** VI *+prep obj (form)* handeln von, behandeln

treatise ['tri:tɪz] **N** Abhandlung *f* (*on* über *+acc*)

treatment ['tri:tmənt] **N a** Behandlung *f*; **their ~ of foreigners** ihre Art, Ausländer zu behandeln; **to give sb the ~** *(inf, violently, sexually)* es jdm ordentlich besorgen *(inf)*; **during his two-day interview, they gave him the full ~** *(inf)* bei seinem zweitägigen Einstellungsgespräch wurde er ganz schön in die Mangel genommen *(inf)*; **she went to the beauty parlour and they really gave her the ~** *(inf)* sie ging in den Schönheitssalon und wurde dort nach allen Regeln der Kunst bearbeitet *(inf)*; **when the foreign delegates visited the factory, they were given the full ~** *(inf)* als die ausländischen Delegierten die Firma besichtigten, wurde ein enormes Tamtam gemacht *(inf) or* eine große Schau abgezogen *(inf)*
b *(Med)* Behandlung *f*; **there are many ~s for ...** es gibt viele Behandlungsarten *or* Heilverfahren für ...; **to be having ~ for sth** wegen etw in Behandlung sein
c *(= processing)* Behandlung *f*; *(of sewage)* Klärung *f*; *(of wastepaper)* Verarbeitung *f*
d *(of subject)* Behandlung *f*, Bearbeitung *f*

treaty ['tri:tɪ] **N** Vertrag *m*

treaty port **N** Vertragshafen *m*

treble[1] ['trebl] **ADJ** dreifach; **it's in ~ figures** es ist eine dreistellige Summe; **~ chance (pools)** *eine Variante des Fußballtotos mit dreifacher Gewinnchance* **ADV** **they had ~ our numbers** sie waren dreimal so viele wie wir; **clothes are ~ the price** Kleider kosten dreimal so viel **VT** verdreifachen **VI** sich verdreifachen **N** *(on dartboard etc)* Dreifache(s) *nt*; *(Brit Sport: = three victories/trophies etc)* Hattrick *m*

treble[2] **N** *(Mus: = boy's voice)* (Knaben)sopran *m*; *(= highest part)* Oberstimme *f*; *(of piano)* Diskant *m*; *(= child's speaking voice)* Diskantstimme *f* **ADJ** **~ voice** (Knaben)sopranstimme *f*

treble clef **N** *(Mus)* Violinschlüssel *m*

treble recorder **N** Altblockflöte *f*

trebly ['treblɪ] **ADV** dreifach; **the child was ~ dear to him** er liebte das Kind dreimal mehr

tree [tri:] **N a** Baum *m*; **an oak ~** eine Eiche; **a cherry ~** ein Kirschbaum *m*; **rose ~** Rosenstämmchen *nt*; **~ of knowledge** Baum *m* der Erkenntnis; **~ of life** Baum *m* des Lebens; **money doesn't/good teachers don't grow on ~s** das Geld fällt/gute Lehrer fallen nicht vom Himmel; **to be up a ~** *(inf)* in der Patsche *or* Tinte *or* Klemme sitzen *(inf)*; **he's at the top of the ~** *(fig inf)* er ist ganz oben (an der Spitze); **he's out of his ~** *(inf) (= drunk)* er ist total zu *(inf)*; *(= crazy)* er tickt nicht richtig *(inf)*
b *(= family tree)* Stammbaum *m*
c *(= shoe tree)* Spanner *m*, Leisten *m*
d *(Rel, = cross)* Kreuz *nt*
VT auf einen Baum jagen *or* treiben

tree *in cpds* Baum-; **tree-covered** **ADJ** baumbestanden; **tree fern** **N** Baumfarn *m*; **tree frog** **N** Laub- *or* Baumfrosch *m*; **tree house** **N** Baumhaus *nt*; **tree hugger** **N** *(esp US hum inf)* Umweltapostel *m (hum inf)*, Umweltfreak *m (hum inf)*; **treeless** **ADJ** baumlos; **tree line** **N** Baumgrenze *f*; **above/below the ~** oberhalb/unterhalb der Baumgrenze; **tree-lined** **ADJ** baumbestanden, von Bäumen gesäumt *(geh)*; **tree ring** **N** *(Bot)* Jahresring *m*; **tree structure** **N** *(Comput)* Baumstruktur *f*; **tree surgeon** **N** Baumchirurg(in) *m(f)*; **treetop** **N** Baumkrone *f*, Wipfel *m*; **tree trunk** **N** Baumstamm *m*

trefoil ['trefɔɪl] **N** *(Bot)* Klee *m*; *(symbol of Girl Guide movement)* Kleeblatt *nt*; *(Archit)* Dreipass *m*

trek [trek] **VI** trecken; *(inf)* latschen *(inf)*; **they ~ked across the desert** sie zogen durch die Wüste; **I had to ~ up to the top floor** ich musste bis ins oberste Stockwerk latschen *(inf)* **N** Treck *m*, Zug *m*; *(inf)* anstrengender Weg *or* Marsch

Trekkie ['trekɪ] **N** *(inf)* Trekkie *m*, *Fan der Fernsehserie „Raumschiff Enterprise"*

trekking ['trekɪŋ] **N** Trekking *nt*, Trecking *nt*

trellis ['trelɪs] **N** Gitter *nt*; *(for plants also)* Spalier *nt* **VT** *(= furnish with trellis)* mit einem Gitter *or* Spalier versehen; *vines etc* am Spalier ziehen

trelliswork ['trelɪswɜ:k] **N** Rankspalier *nt*

tremble ['trembl] **VI** *(person, hand etc)* zittern (*with* vor); *(voice also)* beben (*with* vor); *(ground,* *building)* beben, zittern; **I ~ to think what might have happened** mir wird angst *or* ich zittere, wenn ich daran denke, was hätte geschehen können; **to ~ for sb/sth** um jdn/etw zittern *or* bangen **N** Zittern *nt*, Beben *nt*; **to be all of a ~** *(inf)* am ganzen Körper zittern, das große Zittern haben *(inf)*

trembling [ˈtremblɪŋ] **ADJ** *hands* zitternd; *voice, lip also* bebend **N** *(of person, hand)* Zittern *nt*; *(of voice, ground, building also)* Beben *nt*

trembling: **trembling grass** N Zittergras *nt*; **trembling poplar** N Zitterpappel *f*, Espe *f*

tremendous [trəˈmendəs] ADJ **a** gewaltig, enorm; *size, number, crowd* riesig, enorm; *storm, explosion* gewaltig, ungeheuer stark; **he's a ~ eater** er isst unglaublich viel; **a ~ success** ein Riesenerfolg *m* **b** *(= very good)* klasse, prima, toll *(all inf)*; **we had a ~ time** wir haben uns prima *or* ganz toll amüsiert *(inf)*; **he's a ~ person** er ist ein toller Mensch *(inf)*, er ist klasse *or* prima *(all inf)*; **she has done a ~ job** sie hat fantastische *or* phantastische Arbeit geleistet

tremendously [trəˈmendəslɪ] ADV sehr; *fat, tall, long etc also* enorm; *relieved, upset, grateful, dangerous also* ungeheuer, äußerst; *pretty also* äußerst; *intelligent, difficult also* enorm, äußerst; **it was ~ good** es war einfach prima *or* umwerfend gut *or* sagenhaft *(inf)*; **they enjoyed themselves ~** sie haben sich prächtig *or* prima *or* ausgezeichnet amüsiert *(inf)*

tremolo [ˈtreməbləʊ] N *(Mus)* Tremolo *nt*

tremor [ˈtremə'] N Zittern *nt*, Beben *nt*; *(Med)* Tremor *m*; *(of emotion)* Zittern *nt*, Zucken *nt*; *(= earth tremor)* Beben *nt*, Erschütterung *f*; **a ~ of fear** ein Schaudern *nt*; **without a ~** völlig ruhig, unbewegt

tremulous [ˈtremjʊləs] ADJ *(= trembling) voice* zitternd, bebend; *hand* zitternd; *handwriting* zittrig; *breath* bebend; *(= timid) smile, person* zaghaft, schüchtern; *request* zaghaft

tremulously [ˈtremjʊləslɪ] ADV *(= timidly)* zaghaft, ängstlich

trench [trentʃ] **N** Graben *m*; *(Mil)* Schützengraben *m*; **in the ~es** *(Mil)* im Schützengraben **VT** Gräben *pl* ziehen in *(+dat)*; *(Mil)* Schützengräben *pl* ausheben in *(+dat)*

trenchancy [ˈtrentʃənsɪ] N *(of language)* Treffsicherheit *f*; *(of style)* Prägnanz *f*; *(of satire, statement)* Bissigkeit *f*; *(of view, speech)* Pointiertheit *f*; *(of wit, criticism)* Schärfe *f*

trenchant [ˈtrentʃənt] ADJ *language* treffsicher; *style* prägnant; *satire* beißend; *view, speech* pointiert; *wit, criticism* scharf; *statement* bissig; **to be ~ on** *or* **about sth** in Bezug auf etw *(acc)* kein Blatt vor den Mund nehmen

trenchantly [ˈtrentʃəntlɪ] ADV *say, observe* scharf; **he made his point ~** er argumentierte sicher; **a ~ witty remark** eine scharfe, geistreiche Bemerkung

trench coat N Trenchcoat *m*, Regenmantel *m*

trencher [ˈtrentʃə'] N **a** *(Tech)* Grabenbagger *m* **b** *(old: = platter)* Tran(s)chierbrett *nt*

trencherman [ˈtrentʃəmən] N *pl* **-men** [-mən] **good/poor ~** guter/schlechter Esser

trench: **trench mortar** N *(Mil)* Granatwerfer *m*; **trench warfare** N Stellungskrieg *m*, Grabenkrieg *m*

trend [trend] **N** **a** *(= tendency)* Tendenz *f*, Richtung *f*, Trend *m*; **the ~ toward(s) violence** der Trend *or* die Tendenz zur Gewalttätigkeit; **upward ~** steigende Tendenz, Aufwärtstrend *m*; **the downward ~ in the birth rate** die Rückläufigkeit *or* der Abwärtstrend der Geburtenrate; **the ~ away from materialism** die zunehmende Abkehr vom Materialismus; **to set a ~** eine neue Richtung setzen, richtungweisend sein **b** *(= fashion)* Mode *f*, Trend *m*; **that is the ~/the latest ~ among young people** das ist bei jungen Leuten jetzt Mode/der letzte Schrei *(inf)*; **to follow a ~** einem Trend folgen; *(fashion)* eine Mode mitmachen **c** *(Geog)* Verlauf *m* **VI** verlaufen *(towards* nach); **prices are ~ing upwards** die Preise haben eine steigende Tendenz; **his views are ~ing toward(s) the anarchistic** seine Auffassungen neigen *or* tendieren zum Anarchismus

trendily [ˈtrendɪlɪ] ADV modern; **to dress ~** sich nach der neuesten Mode kleiden

trendiness [ˈtrendɪnɪs] N *(of person)* Modebewusstsein *nt*; *(of ideas etc)* Modernität *f*; **the ~ of her clothes** ihre modische Kleidung

trend: **trendsetter** N Trendsetter(in) *m(f)*; **trendsetting** **N** Entwicklung *f* neuer Trends **ADJ** trendsetzend; *(in fashion also)* Mode machend

trendy [ˈtrendɪ] **ADJ** (+er) modern, trendy *(inf)*, in *pred (inf)*; *image* modisch, schick; **to be ~** als schick gelten, große Mode sein; **it's no longer ~ to smoke** Rauchen ist nicht mehr in *(inf)*, Rauchen ist aus der Mode geraten; **a restaurant where all the ~ people go** ein Restaurant, in dem sich die Schickeria trifft; **this is a ~ club** dieser Klub ist zur Zeit in *(inf)*; **Elaine is totally ~** Elaine ist total trendy *(inf)* **N** *(inf)* Schickimicki *m (inf)*; **the trendies** die Schickeria *sing*; **he looks a real ~** der macht vielleicht auf modern!

trepan [trɪˈpæn] **VT** *(Med)* trepanieren **N** Trepan *m*

trepidation [ˌtrepɪˈdeɪʃən] N Bangigkeit *f*, Beklommenheit *f*, Ängstlichkeit *f*; **full of ~ he knocked on the door** voll ängstlicher Erwartung klopfte er an die Tür; **a look of ~** ein banger *or* beunruhigter *or* ängstlicher Blick; **a feeling of ~** ein beklommenes Gefühl, ein Gefühl der Bangigkeit *or* Verzagtheit; **I am writing, not without some ~, to tell you …** nicht ohne ein Gefühl der Beklommenheit teile ich Ihnen mit …

trespass [ˈtrespəs] **VI** **a** *(on property)* unbefugt betreten *(on sth* etw *acc)*; **"no ~ing"** „Betreten verboten"; **you're ~ing** Sie dürfen sich hier nicht aufhalten **b** **to ~ (up)on sb's rights/area of responsibility** in jds Rechte/Verantwortungsbereich *(acc)* eingreifen; **to ~ (up)on sb's privacy** jds Privatsphäre verletzen; **to ~ (up)on sb's kindness/time** jds Freundlichkeit/Zeit überbeanspruchen **c** *(Bibl)* **as we forgive them that ~ against us** wie wir vergeben unseren Schuldigern **N** **a** *(Jur)* unbefugtes Betreten **b** *(Bibl)* **forgive us our ~es** vergib uns unsere Schuld

trespasser [ˈtrespəsə'] N Unbefugte(r) *mf*; **"trespassers will be prosecuted"** „widerrechtliches Betreten wird strafrechtlich verfolgt"; **the farmer found a ~ on his land** der Bauer fand einen Eindringling auf seinem Land

tress [tres] N *(liter)* Locke *f (liter)*

tressed [trest] ADJ *hair (= plaited)* geflochten; *(= curly)* gelockt

trestle [ˈtresl] N (Auflage)bock *m*

trestle: **trestle bridge** N Bockbrücke *f*; **trestle table** N auf Böcken stehender Tisch; *(decorator's)* Tapeziertisch *m*

trews [truːz] PL *(Scot)* eng anliegende Hose im Schottenkaro; *(Brit inf: = trousers)* Hose *f*; **a pair of ~** eine Hose

Triad [ˈtraɪæd] N *(= Chinese secret society)* Triade *f*

triad [ˈtraɪæd] N Triade *f*, Trias *f*; *(Mus)* Dreiklang *m*; *(Chem)* dreiwertiges Element

trial [ˈtraɪəl] N **a** *(Jur)* (Gerichts)verfahren *nt*, Prozess *m*; *(= actual hearing)* (Gerichts)verhandlung *f*; **to be on ~** angeklagt sein, unter Anklage stehen; **he goes on ~ tomorrow** seine Verhandlung ist morgen; **to be on ~ for theft** des Diebstahls angeklagt sein, wegen Diebstahls unter Anklage stehen; **to be on ~ for one's life** wegen eines mit Todesstrafe bedrohten Verbrechens angeklagt sein; **to stand ~ (for sth)** (wegen etw) vor Gericht stehen; **at the ~** bei *or* während der Verhandlung; **to bring sb to ~** jdn vor Gericht stellen, jdm den Prozess machen; **the case comes up for ~ next month** der Fall wird nächsten Monat verhandelt; **~ by jury** Schwurgerichtsverfahren *nt*; **~ by television/the media** *(fig)* Vorverurteilung *f* durch das Fernsehen/die Medien **b** *(= test)* Versuch *m*, Probe *f*, Erprobung *f*; **~s** *(of machine, aeroplane)* Test(s) *m(pl)*, (Über)prüfung *f*; *(Sport)* Qualifikationsspiel *nt*; **horse ~s** Querfeldeinrennen *nt*; **to give sth a ~** etw ausprobieren; **the manager has promised to give me a ~ as a clerk** der Betriebsleiter hat versprochen, mir eine Chance als Büroangestellter zu geben; **to take sb/sth on ~** jdn/etw zur Probe nehmen, jdn/etw probeweise nehmen; **to put sb/sth to the ~** jdn/etw testen *or* auf die Probe stellen; **to be on ~** *(new product etc)* getestet werden; **the new clerk is on ~** der neue Büroangestellte ist auf Probe eingestellt; **~ of strength** Kraftprobe *f*; **by ~ and error** durch Ausprobieren; **a system of ~ and error** ein System der empirischen Lösung **c** *(= hardship)* Widrigkeit *f*, Unannehmlichkeit *f*; *(= nuisance)* Plage *f*, Problem *nt (to* für); **he's a ~ to his mother** er macht seiner Mutter sehr viel Kummer; **~s and tribulations** Aufregungen *pl*, Schwierigkeiten *pl*, Drangsale *pl (liter)*

trial: **trial-and-error method** N Trial-and-Error-Methode *f*, empirische Methode; **trial balance** N Saldenbilanz *f*, Probebilanz *f*; **trial basis** N **to employ sb on a ~** jdn auf Probe einstellen; **trial flight** N Testflug *m*; **trial judge** N Richter(in) *m(f)* der ersten Instanz, Hauptverhandlungsrichter(in) *m(f)*; **trial lawyer** N *(US Jur)* Prozessanwalt *m*, Prozessanwältin *f*; **trial marriage** N Ehe *f* auf Probe; **trial offer** N Einführungsangebot *nt*; **trial order** N Probeauftrag *m*; **trial package** N Probepackung *f*; **trial period** N *(for people)* Probezeit *f*; *(for goods) Zeit, die man etw zur Probe oder Prüfung hat*; **trial program** N *(Comput)* Evaluationsprogramm *nt*; **trial run** N Generalprobe *f*; *(with car etc)* Versuchsfahrt *f*, Probefahrt *f*; *(of machine)* Probelauf *m*; **give the new method a ~** probieren Sie diese neue Methode einmal aus *or* durch

triangle [ˈtraɪæŋgl] N Dreieck *nt*; *(= set square)* (Zeichen)dreieck *nt*; *(Mus)* Triangel *m*; *(fig: = relationship)* Dreiecksbeziehung *f*

triangular [traɪˈæŋgjʊlə'] ADJ **a** *(Math)* dreieckig **b** **~ relationship** Dreiecksverhältnis *nt*; **~ contest** Dreipersonenwettkampf *m*; *(between nations)* Dreinationenwettkampf *m*

triangulate [traɪˈæŋgʊlɪt] **ADJ** *(Math)* triangulär *(form)* [traɪˈæŋgʊleɪt] **VT** in Dreiecke einteilen; *(Surv)* triangulieren

triangulation station [traɪˌæŋgjʊˈleɪʃənˌsteɪʃən] N *(Surv)* Vermessungspunkt *m*

triathlete [traɪˈæθliːt] N Triathlet(in) *m(f)*

triathlon [traɪˈæθlən] N Triathlon *nt*

tribal [ˈtraɪbəl] ADJ Stammes-; **~ chief** Stammeshäuptling *m*; **~ region/settlement** Stammesgebiet *nt*/-siedlung *f*; **~ rituals** Stammesrituale *pl*; **~ loyalties** Stammestreue *f*; **Celtic society was basically ~** die Gesellschaftsordnung der Kelten war stammesgebunden; **to be divided on** *or* **along ~ lines** *(lit)* nach Stammeszugehörigkeit geteilt sein; *(fig)* in feindliche Lager gespalten sein

tribalism [ˈtraɪbəlɪzəm] N Stammesstruktur *f*

tribe [traɪb] N **a** Stamm *m*; *(Bot, Zool)* Gattung *f* **b** *(fig inf)* Korona *f*

tribesman [ˈtraɪbzmən] N *pl* **-men** [-mən] Stammesangehörige(r) *m*

tribeswoman [ˈtraɪbzwʊmən] N *pl* **-women** [-wɪmɪn] Stammesangehörige *f*

tribulation [ˌtrɪbjʊˈleɪʃən] N Kummer *m no pl*; **~s** Sorgen *pl*; *(less serious)* Kümmernisse *pl*; **to bear one's ~s bravely** sein Leid *nt* tapfer tragen → **trial**

tribunal [traɪˈbjuːnl] N Gericht *nt*; *(= inquiry)* Untersuchungsausschuss *m*; *(held by revolutionaries etc, fig)* Tribunal *nt*

tribune[1] [ˈtrɪbjuːn] N *(Hist)* (Volks)tribun *m*

tribune[2] N *(= platform)* Tribüne *f*

tributary [ˈtrɪbjʊtərɪ] **ADJ** **a** *state* tributpflichtig **b** **~ river** Nebenfluss *m*; **~ valley** Seitental *nt*

N a (= state) tributpflichtiger Staat b (= river) Nebenfluss m

tribute ['trɪbjuːt] N a (Hist, = payment) Tribut m b (= admiration) Tribut m; **to pay ~ to sb/sth** jdm/einer Sache (den schuldigen) Tribut zollen; **they stood in silent ~ to him** sie zollten ihm (stehend) ihren stillen Tribut; **after her performance ~s came flooding in** nach ihrer Vorstellung wurde sie mit Ehrungen überschüttet; **to be a ~ to one's parents/school** seinen Eltern/seiner Schule (alle) Ehre machen

trice[1] [traɪs] N (Brit) **in a ~** im Handumdrehen, im Nu

trice[2] VT (Naut: also **trice up**) sail aufholen

Tricel® ['traɪsel] N Tricel nt

triceps ['traɪseps] N pl **-(es)** Trizeps m

trichina [trɪ'kaɪnə] N pl **-e** [-iː] Trichine f

trichinosis [trɪkɪ'nəʊsɪs] N Trichinenkrankheit f, Trichinose f

trick [trɪk] N a (= ruse) Trick m; **be careful, it's a ~** pass auf, das ist eine Falle!; **be careful with this question, there's a ~ in it** sei vorsichtig bei dieser Frage, sie enthält eine Falle!; **he knows a ~ or two** (inf) der kennt sich aus, der weiß, wie der Hase läuft; **he never misses a ~** (inf) er lässt sich (dat) nichts entgehen; **he knows all the ~s of the trade** er ist ein alter Hase; (= is crafty) er ist mit allen Wassern gewaschen; **he is full of ~s** (child, footballer etc) er steckt voller Tricks; (salesman, politician etc) er hat es faustdick hinter den Ohren; **it's a ~ of the light** da täuscht das Licht → **book N a**

b (= mischief) Streich m; **to play a ~ on sb** jdm einen Streich spielen; **unless my eyes are playing ~s on me** wenn meine Augen mich nicht täuschen; **a dirty ~** ein ganz gemeiner Trick; **he's up to his (old) ~s again** jetzt macht er wieder seine (alten) Mätzchen (inf); **how's ~s?** (Brit inf) wie gehts?

c (= skilful act) Kunststück nt; **to teach a dog to do ~s** einem Hund Kunststücke beibringen; **once you get the ~ of adjusting it** wenn du einmal den Dreh or Trick heraushast, wie man das einstellt; **there's a special ~ to it** da ist ein Trick dabei; **that should do the ~** (inf) das müsste eigentlich hinhauen (inf) → **dog**

d (= habit) Eigenart f; **to have a ~ of doing sth** die Eigenart haben, etw zu tun; **he has a ~ of always arriving as I'm pouring out the tea** er hat eine merkwürdige Art, immer gerade dann zu erscheinen, wenn ich den Tee einschenke; **history has a ~ of repeating itself** die Geschichte hat die merkwürdige Eigenschaft, sich immer zu wiederholen

e (Cards) Stich m; **to take a ~** einen Stich machen

f (inf, of prostitute) Nummer f (inf); **to turn a ~** es einem Kunden machen or besorgen (sl)

ATTR cigar, spider, glass als Scherzartikel

VT mit einem Trick betrügen, hereinlegen (inf); **I've been ~ed!** ich bin hereingelegt or übers Ohr gehauen (inf) worden!; **to ~ sb into doing sth** jdn (mit einem Trick or mit List) dazu bringen, etw zu tun; **he ~ed the old lady into giving him her life savings** er hat die alte Dame mit einem Trick um all ihre Ersparnisse betrogen; **to ~ sb out of sth** jdn um etw prellen, jdm etw abtricksen (inf)

▸ **trick out** VT sep herausputzen; **tricked out in her Sunday best** in ihrem Sonntagsstaat; **tricked out in all one's finery** in vollem Staat

trick cyclist N Kunstradfahrer(in) m(f); (Brit fig inf) Klapsdoktor m (inf)

trickery ['trɪkərɪ] N Tricks pl (inf); **a piece of ~** ein Trick m; **financial ~** Finanztrickserei f (inf); **beware of verbal ~ in the contract** passen Sie auf, dass der Vertragstext nicht irgendwelche Fallen enthält!

trickiness ['trɪkɪnɪs] N a (= difficulty) Schwierigkeit f; (= fiddliness) Kniffligkeit f b (of situation) Schwierigkeit f, Kitzligkeit f (inf); **the ~ of the present industrial situation ...** die heikle or kitzlige (inf) augenblickliche Lage in der Industrie ... c (= slyness) Durchtriebenheit f, Gerissenheit f

trickle ['trɪkl] VI a (liquid) tröpfeln, tropfen; **tears ~d down her cheeks** Tränen kullerten ihr über die Wangen; **the rain ~d down his neck** der Regen tropfte ihm in den Kragen; **if you don't fix the leak the water will all ~ away/out** wenn Sie die undichte Stelle nicht abdichten, tropft das ganze Wasser heraus; **the sand ~d through his fingers** der Sand rieselte ihm durch die Finger

b (fig) **people/escapees began to ~ in/out/back** die Leute/Flüchtlinge begannen, vereinzelt herein-/hinaus-/zurückzukommen; **the ball ~d into the net** der Ball trudelte (langsam) ins Netz; **reports/donations are beginning to ~ in** so langsam trudeln die Berichte/Spenden ein (inf)

VT liquid tröpfeln, träufeln, tropfenweise gießen

N a (of liquid) Tröpfeln nt; (= stream) Rinnsal nt

b (fig) **a steady ~ of people gradually filled the lecture hall** der Hörsaal füllte sich langsam aber stetig mit Leuten; **news reports have dwindled to a mere ~** Berichte pl kommen or (secretively) sickern nur noch ganz selten durch; **arms deliveries have shrunk to a ~** die Waffenlieferungen sind spärlich geworden; **we cut their supplies to a ~** wir haben ihren Nachschub drastisch reduziert

trickle: **trickle charger** N (Elec) Kleinlader m; **trickle-down** ['trɪkldaʊn] N (Econ) *Wirtschaftstheorie, nach der sich der Reichtum einiger positiv auf die Gesamtgesellschaft auswirkt*

trick: **trick or treat** N *Spiel zu Halloween, bei dem Kinder von Tür zu Tür gehen und von den Bewohnern entweder Geld oder Geschenke erhalten oder ihnen einen Streich spielen*; **trick photography** N Trickfotografie f; **trick question** N Fangfrage f; **to ask sb a ~** jdm eine Falle stellen

trickster ['trɪkstə'] N Schwindler(in) m(f), Betrüger(in) m(f)

tricksy ['trɪksɪ] ADJ (+er) (inf) = **tricky c**

tricky ['trɪkɪ] ADJ (+er) a (= difficult) schwierig; (= fiddly) knifflig; **he is a very ~ person to get on with** es ist äußerst schwierig, mit ihm auszukommen; **warts can be ~ to get rid of** Warzen loszuwerden kann schwierig sein; **it is going to be ~ explaining** or **to explain his absence** es wird nicht einfach sein, seine Abwesenheit zu erklären; **it's ~ for me to give you an answer now** es ist nicht einfach für mich, Ihnen jetzt darauf zu antworten

b (= requiring tact) situation, problem heikel, kitzlig

c (= sly, crafty) person, plan durchtrieben, gerissen; question schwierig, knifflig (inf); **a ~ customer** ein schwieriger Typ

tricolour, (US) **tricolor** ['trɪkələ'] N Trikolore f

tricorn ['traɪkɔːn] N Dreispitz m

tricot ['triːkəʊ] N (Tex) Trikot m

tricuspid [traɪ'kʌspɪd] ADJ trikuspidal (spec)

tricycle ['traɪsɪkl] N Dreirad nt

trident ['traɪdənt] N Dreizack m

Tridentine [traɪ'dentaɪn] ADJ Tridentinisch

tried [traɪd] ADJ erprobt, bewährt

tried-and-tested ['traɪdənd'testɪd], **tried and tested** ADJ method erprobt, bewährt; recipe, technology bewährt, ausgereift; product getestet; system bewährt; **the airbag technology is tried and tested** die Airbagtechnologie hat sich vielfach bewährt

triennial [traɪ'enɪəl] ADJ (= lasting 3 years) dreijährig; (= every 3 years) dreijährlich, alle drei Jahre stattfindend

triennially [traɪ'enɪəlɪ] ADV alle drei Jahre, dreijährlich

triennium [traɪ'enɪəm] N Zeitraum m von drei Jahren

trier ['traɪə'] N **to be a ~** sich (dat) (ernsthaft) Mühe geben

trifle ['traɪfl] N a Kleinigkeit f; (= trivial matter) Lappalie f (inf), Kleinigkeit f; **the merest ~ upsets her** die geringste or kleinste Kleinigkeit regt sie auf; **I'm so sorry – a ~, don't let it worry you** es tut mir außerordentlich leid – das ist doch nicht der Rede wert, machen Sie sich deswegen keine Sorgen! b (= small amount) Kleinigkeit f; **have some more cake – just a ~, thank you** noch etwas Kuchen? – bloß ein ganz kleines Stückchen, bitte; **a ~ hot/small** etc ein bisschen heiß/klein etc; **a ~ too ...** ein wenig or eine Spur zu ... c (Brit Cook) Trifle nt

▸ **trifle away** VT sep vergeuden

▸ **trifle with** VI +prep obj person zu leicht nehmen; affections, food spielen mit; **he is not a person to be trifled with** mit ihm ist nicht zu spaßen

trifling ['traɪflɪŋ] ADJ unbedeutend, geringfügig

trifoliate [traɪ'fəʊlɪɪt] ADJ dreiblättrig

trigger ['trɪgə'] ✪ 17.2 N (of gun) Abzug(shahn) m, Drücker m (inf); (of bomb) Zünder m; (of cine camera, machine) Auslöser m; (Elec) Trigger m; **to pull the ~** abdrücken; **to be quick on the ~** schnell abdrücken VT (also **trigger off**) auslösen; bomb zünden

trigger: **trigger finger** N Zeigefinger m; **my ~'s itching** es juckt mich abzudrücken; **trigger grip** N Pistolengriff m; **trigger guard** N Abzugsbügel m; **trigger-happy** ADJ (inf) schießfreudig (inf), schießwütig (pej); (hum) photographer knipswütig (inf)

trigonometric(al) [ˌtrɪgənə'metrɪk(əl)] ADJ trigonometrisch

trigonometry [ˌtrɪgə'nɒmɪtrɪ] N Trigonometrie f

trihedron [ˌtraɪ'hiːdrən] N Dreiflächner m, Trieder nt

trike [traɪk] N (inf) abbr of **tricycle**

trilateral [ˌtraɪ'lætərəl] ADJ dreiseitig; conference, agreement also trilateral

trilby ['trɪlbɪ] N (also **trilby hat**) weicher Filzhut

trilingual [ˌtraɪ'lɪŋgwəl] ADJ dreisprachig

trill [trɪl] N a (of bird) Trillern nt; (of voice) Tremolo nt b (Mus) Triller m c (Phon) Rollen nt, rollende Aussprache VT a (person) trällern b (Mus) note trillern c (Phon) consonant rollen, rollend aussprechen VI a (bird) trillern, tirilieren (geh); (person) trällern b (Mus) trillern

trillion ['trɪljən] N Billion f; (dated Brit) Trillion f; **there were ~s of them there** (fig) es waren Millionen und Abermillionen da

trilogy ['trɪlədʒɪ] N Trilogie f

trim [trɪm] ADJ (+er) a sauber; appearance gepflegt, sauber; hair, haircut gepflegt; **he keeps his lawn/garden/house very ~** sein Rasen/Garten/Haus ist immer sehr gepflegt

b (= slim) person schlank; waist schmal; **to stay ~** in Form bleiben; **she has a ~ figure** sie hat eine schlanke Figur

N a (Brit: = condition) Zustand m, Verfassung f; (= fitness) Form f; **in good ~** (house, car etc) in gutem Zustand; (person) gut in Form; **to get in-to ~** sich trimmen, sich in Form bringen; **in fighting ~** kampfbereit

b **to give sth a ~** etw schneiden; tree, hedge, beard also etw stutzen; **your hair needs a ~** du musst dir die Haare etwas nachschneiden lassen; **just a ~, please** nur etwas kürzen or nachschneiden, bitte

c (Aut, outside) Zierleisten pl; (inside) Innenausstattung f

d (Naut) Trimm m, Gleichgewichtslage f; **in/out of ~** (ship) in/nicht in Trimm or Gleichgewichtslage

e (Aviat) Trimm m, Fluglage f

f (= edging) Rand m; (= decoration) Bordüre f

g (inf: of book) Format nt

VT a (= cut) hair nachschneiden; beard, hedge, branch stutzen; dog trimmen; wick, roses beschneiden; piece of wood (with knife/saw/plane) zurechtschneiden/-sägen/-hobeln; **to ~ the fat** *(lit)* das Fett weg- *or* abschneiden; *(fig)* sich bescheiden

b *(fig: = cut down) budget, essay* kürzen; *interest rates* (etwas) senken; *staff* reduzieren

c *(= decorate) dress* besetzen; *Christmas tree* schmücken

d *boat, plane* trimmen; *sails* richtig stellen

e *(US inf) (= defeat)* schlagen; *(= cheat)* übers Ohr hauen *(inf)*

▶ **trim away** VT *sep* weg- *or* abschneiden; *details etc* entfernen

▶ **trim back** VT *sep hedge, roses* zurückschneiden; *costs* senken; *staff* reduzieren

▶ **trim down** VT *sep wick, budget, essay* kürzen *(to* auf *+acc)*; *hedge* (zurecht)stutzen; *roses* zurückschneiden; **to trim down one's figure** etwas für seine Figur tun

▶ **trim off** VT *sep bits of beard, ends of branch* abschneiden; *rough edges (with knife/saw/plane/file)* abschneiden/-sägen/-hobeln/-feilen; *fat* ab- *or* wegschneiden; **they have trimmed 1p off income tax** sie haben den Einkommenssteuersatz um 1p gesenkt

trimaran [ˈtraɪmərən] N Dreirumpfboot *nt*, Trimaran *m*

trimester [trɪˈmestəʳ] N Trimester *nt*

trimming [ˈtrɪmɪŋ] N *(on clothes)* Besatz *m* → **trimmings**

trimmings [ˈtrɪmɪŋz] PL **a** *(on clothes)* Verzierungen *pl* **b** *(= accessories)* Zubehör *nt*; **roast beef with all the ~** Roastbeef mit allem Drum und Dran *(inf) or* mit allen Beilagen; **the car costs £20,000 with all the ~s** das Auto kostet £ 20.000 mit allen Extras *or* mit allem Zubehör **c** *(= cuttings)* Abfälle *pl*; *(of paper also)* (Papier)schnitzel *pl*, Schnipsel *(inf) pl*

trimness [ˈtrɪmnɪs] N *(of hair, lawn etc)* Gepflegtheit *f*, gepflegtes Aussehen; *(of figure)* Schlankheit *f*

trimonthly [ˈtraɪˈmʌnθlɪ] ADJ dreimonatlich, vierteljährig, Vierteljahres- N *periodical, journal* Vierteljahresschrift *f*

trim: **trim size** N *(of book)* Format *nt*; **trim trail** N Trim-dich-Pfad *m*

Trinidad [ˈtrɪnɪdæd] N Trinidad *nt*

trinitrotoluene [traɪˌnaɪtrəʊˈtɒljʊiːn] N Trinitrotoluol *nt*

Trinity [ˈtrɪnɪtɪ] N **a** Trinität *f*, Dreieinigkeit *f*, Dreifaltigkeit *f* **b** *(= Trinity term)* Sommertrimester *nt*

Trinity Sunday N Trinitatis(fest) *nt*, Dreieinigkeitsfest *nt*, Dreifaltigkeitsfest *nt*

trinket [ˈtrɪŋkɪt] N Schmuckstück *nt*; *(= ornament)* Schmuckgegenstand *m*; **the ~s hanging from her bracelet** die Anhänger an ihrem Armband

trinket box N Schmuckkästchen *nt*

trinketry [ˈtrɪŋkɪtrɪ] N billiger *or* wertloser Schmuck

trinomial [traɪˈnəʊmɪəl] ADJ trinomisch, dreigliedrig N Trinom *nt*

trio [ˈtrɪəʊ] N Trio *nt*

trip [trɪp] N **a** *(= journey)* Reise *f*; *(= excursion)* Ausflug *m*, Tour *f*; *(esp shorter)* Trip *m*; **let's go on a ~ to the seaside** machen wir doch einen Ausflug ans Meer!, fahren wir doch ans Meer!; **when was your last ~ to the dentist's?** wann waren Sie zuletzt beim Zahnarzt?; **that's his fifth ~ to the bathroom already!** er geht jetzt schon zum fünften Mal auf die Toilette! *(inf)*; **he is away on a ~** er ist verreist *or* auf Reisen; **she's away on a ~ to Canada** sie macht zur Zeit eine Reise nach Kanada; **to take a ~ (to)** eine Reise machen (nach), verreisen (nach)

b *(inf: on drugs)* Trip *m (inf)*; **to go on a ~** auf einen Trip *or* auf die Reise gehen *(inf)*

c *(= stumble)* Stolpern *nt*; **that was a nasty ~** da sind Sie aber übel gestolpert

d *(esp Sport)* Beinstellen *nt*; **he didn't fall, it was a ~** er ist nicht (von selbst) hingefallen, man hat ihm ein Bein gestellt

e *(= mistake)* Fehler *m*, Ausrutscher *m (inf)*

f *(Mech)* Auslösung *f*

VI **a** *(= stumble)* stolpern *(on, over* über *+acc)*

b *(fig)* → **trip up VI b**

c *(= skip)* trippeln; **to ~ in/out** hinein-/hinaustrippeln; **a phrase which ~s off the tongue** ein Ausdruck, der einem leicht von der Zunge geht; **the notes should come ~ping off the tongue** die Töne müssen richtig perlend kommen

VT **a** *(= make fall)* stolpern lassen; *(deliberately)* ein Bein stellen *(+dat)*; **I was ~ped** jemand hat mir ein Bein gestellt → *also* **trip up VT b**

b *(Mech) lever* betätigen; *mechanism* auslösen

c *(old: = dance)* tanzen; **to ~ the light fantastic** *(hum)* das Tanzbein schwingen *(inf)*

▶ **trip over** VI stolpern *(+prep obj* über *+acc)*

▶ **trip up** VI **a** *(lit)* stolpern **b** *(fig)* sich vertun VT *sep* **a** *(= make fall)* stolpern lassen; *(deliberately)* zu Fall bringen **b** *(fig: = cause to make a mistake etc)* eine Falle stellen *(+dat)*, aufs Glatteis führen; **he was trying to trip me up with his ad-libbing** er versuchte, mich mit seinem Improvisieren aus dem Konzept zu bringen; **question six managed to trip most of the candidates up** die meisten Prüflinge sind über die sechste Frage gestolpert

tripartite [ˌtraɪˈpɑːtaɪt] ADJ *agreement, talks* dreiseitig; **~ division** Dreiteilung *f*

tripe [traɪp] N **a** *(Cook)* Kaldaunen *pl*, Kutteln *pl (S Ger, Aus, Sw)* **b** *(fig inf)* Quatsch *m*, Stuss *m (inf)*

triphammer [ˈtrɪpˌhæməʳ] N Aufwerfhammer *m*

triplane [ˈtraɪpleɪn] N Dreidecker *m*

triple [ˈtrɪpl] ADJ dreifach ADV dreimal so viel; **it's ~ the distance** es ist dreimal so weit; **at ~ the speed** mit dreifacher Geschwindigkeit; **it costs ~ what it used to** es kostet dreimal so viel wie früher, es kostet das Dreifache von früher N Dreifache(s) *nt* VT verdreifachen VI sich verdreifachen

triple: **triple-digit** ADJ *(esp US) number* dreistellig; **triple glazing** N Dreifachverglasung *f*; **triple jump** N Dreisprung *m*

triplet [ˈtrɪplɪt] N **a** *(= baby)* Drilling *m* **b** *(Mus)* Triole *f*; *(Poet)* Dreireim *m*

triple time N *(Mus)* Dreiertakt *m*

Triplex® [ˈtrɪpleks] N Verbundglas *nt*

triplicate [ˈtrɪplɪkɪt] N **in ~** in dreifacher Ausfertigung ADJ in dreifacher Ausfertigung VT [ˈtrɪplɪkeɪt] *document* dreifach *or* in drei Exemplaren ausfertigen

triply [ˈtrɪplɪ] ADV dreimal; **~ expensive** dreimal so teuer

tripod [ˈtraɪpɒd] N *(Phot)* Stativ *nt*; *(Hist)* Dreifuß *m*

tripos [ˈtraɪpɒs] N Abschlussexamen *nt (an der Universität Cambridge)*

tripper [ˈtrɪpəʳ] N *(esp Brit inf)* Ausflügler(in) *m(f)* → **day-tripper**

tripping [ˈtrɪpɪŋ] ADJ *walk* trippelnd; *notes* perlend; *metre* fließend

tripping device N *(Mech)* Auslösemechanismus *m*

trippingly [ˈtrɪpɪŋlɪ] ADV *walk* trippelnd; **grand phrases roll ~ off his tongue** ihm kommen große Worte über die Lippen

trippy [ˈtrɪpɪ] ADJ *(inf)* ausgeflippt *(inf)*

trip: **trip recorder** N *(Aut)* Tageszähler *m*; **trip switch** N *(Elec)* Sicherheitsschalter *m*

triptych [ˈtrɪptɪk] N Triptychon *nt*

triptyche [trɪpˈtiːk] N *(Aut: = customs document)* Triptyk *nt*, Triptik *nt*

tripwire [ˈtrɪpwaɪəʳ] N Stolperdraht *m*

trireme [ˈtraɪriːm] N Triere *f*, Trireme *f*

trisect [traɪˈsekt] VT in drei Teile teilen, dreiteilen; *angle* in drei gleiche Teile teilen

trisection [traɪˈsekʃən] N Dreiteilung *f*; *(of angle)* Einteilung *f* in drei gleiche Teile

trisyllabic [ˈtraɪsɪˈlæbɪk] ADJ dreisilbig

trisyllable [ˌtraɪˈsɪləbl] N dreisilbiges Wort

trite [traɪt] ADJ *(+er) (= trivial, banal)* banal, nichtssagend; *(= hackneyed)* abgedroschen; **it would be ~ to say that ...** es wäre banal zu sagen, dass ...

tritely [ˈtraɪtlɪ] ADV **a ~ obvious remark** eine Binsenweisheit; **nobody is perfect, he said ~** er machte die banale Bemerkung: niemand ist vollkommen

triteness [ˈtraɪtnɪs] N *(= banality)* Banalität *f*; *(= hackneyed quality)* Abgedroschenheit *f*

tritium [ˈtrɪtɪəm] N Tritium *nt*

triumph [ˈtraɪʌmf] N **a** Triumph *m*; **in ~** triumphierend, im Triumph; **shouts of ~** Triumphgeschrei *nt*; **to score a ~ over sb/sth** einen Triumph über jdn/etw erzielen **b** *(Hist, = procession)* Triumphzug *m* VI den Sieg davontragen *(over* über *+acc)*; **to ~ over sb/sth** über jdn/etw triumphieren; **they ~ed over incredible odds** sie setzten sich gegen unglaubliche Widerstände durch; **we've made it! he ~ed** wir habens geschafft! triumphierte er

triumphal [traɪˈʌmfəl] ADJ triumphal

triumphal arch N Triumphbogen *m*

triumphant [traɪˈʌmfənt] ADJ *(= victorious)* siegreich; *(= rejoicing)* triumphierend; *moment* triumphal; **to be ~ (over sth)** triumphieren (über etw *acc*); **to emerge ~** triumphieren; **to be** *or* **prove a ~ success** ein triumphaler Erfolg sein; **he was ~ in his success** er jubelte triumphierend *or* triumphierte über seinen Erfolg; **in our ~ hour** in unserer Stunde des Triumphs

triumphantly [traɪˈʌmfəntlɪ] ADV triumphierend; **it was a ~ successful expedition** die Expedition war ein triumphaler Erfolg

triumvir [ˈtraɪəmviːr] N *(Hist)* Triumvir *m*

triumvirate [traɪˈʌmvɪrɪt] N *(Hist)* Triumvirat *nt*

triune [ˈtraɪjuːn] ADJ *(Rel)* dreieinig

trivalent [ˌtraɪˈveɪlənt] ADJ *(Chem)* dreiwertig

trivia [ˈtrɪvɪə] PL belangloses Zeug; **the ~ of daily life** die Trivialitäten des täglichen Lebens

trivial [ˈtrɪvɪəl] ADJ **a** trivial; *objection, loss, details, matters* geringfügig, belanglos, trivial; *mistake* belanglos; **look, your health is not something ~** hör mal, mit der Gesundheit ist nicht zu spaßen!; **the ~ round** das triviale Einerlei **b** *person* oberflächlich

triviality [ˌtrɪvɪˈælɪtɪ] N Trivialität *f*; *(of objection, loss, details, matters also)* Geringfügigkeit *f*, Belanglosigkeit *f*

trivialization [ˌtrɪvɪəlaɪˈzeɪʃən] N Trivialisierung *f*

trivialize [ˈtrɪvɪəlaɪz] VT trivialisieren

Trivial Pursuit® N Trivial Pursuit® *nt*

trochaic [trɒˈkeɪɪk] ADJ trochäisch

trochee [ˈtrəʊkiː] N Trochäus *m*

trod [trɒd] *pret of* **tread**

trodden [ˈtrɒdn] *ptp of* **tread**

troglodyte [ˈtrɒglədaɪt] N Höhlenmensch *m*, Troglodyt *m (liter)*; *(fig: = recluse)* Einsiedler(in) *m(f)*

troika [ˈtrɔɪkə] N Troika *f*

troilism [ˈtrɔɪlɪzəm] N, *no pl (form)* Troilismus *m*

Trojan [ˈtrəʊdʒən] N **a** *(Hist)* Trojaner(in) *m(f)*, Troer(in) *m(f)*; **to work like a ~** *(fig)* wie ein Pferd arbeiten; **he's a real ~** *(fig)* er ist wirklich eine treue Seele **b** *(Comput, Internet)* Trojaner *m (inf)* ADJ trojanisch; *(fig)* übermenschlich

Trojan Horse N *(lit, fig)* Trojanisches Pferd; *(Comput, Internet) (also* **Trojan horse***)* trojanisches Pferd, Trojaner *m (inf)*

Trojan War N Trojanischer Krieg

troll[1] [trəʊl] N *(Myth)* Troll *m*

troll[2] VI *(inf: = walk)* laufen

trolley [ˈtrɒlɪ] N **a** *(Brit: = cart, four wheels)* Handwagen *m*; *(in supermarket)* Einkaufswagen *m*; *(in station)* Gepäckwagen *m*, Ladekasten *m*; *(for passengers)* Kofferkuli *m*; *(two wheels, for golf clubs)* Caddy *m*; *(in station, factory etc)* Sackkarre *f*

b *(Brit: = tea trolley)* Teewagen *m*

c *(Brit Rail)* Lore *f*, Förderkarren *m*; *(hand-driven)* Draisine *f*, Dräsine *f*
d *(Elec, = trolley pole)* Kontaktarm *m*, Stromabnehmerstange *f*; *(= trolley-wheel)* Kontaktrolle *f*, Rollenstromabnehmer *m*
e *(= passenger vehicle)* = **trolleybus** *(US: = trolley car)* Straßenbahn *f*
f **to be off one's ~** *(Brit inf)* nicht mehr alle Tassen im Schrank haben *(inf)*

trolley: **trolleybus** N Obus *m*, Oberleitungsomnibus *m (form)*, Trolleybus *m (dated)*; **trolley car** N *(US)* Straßenbahn *f*; **trolley pole** N Kontaktarm *m*, Stromabnehmerstange *f*

trollop ['trɒləp] N *(dated: = prostitute)* leichtes Mädchen, Straßenmädchen *nt*; *(pej)* Schlampe *f*

trombone [trɒm'bəʊn] N *(Mus)* Posaune *f*

trombonist [trɒm'bəʊnɪst] N Posaunist(in) *m(f)*

troop [tru:p] N **a** *(Mil, of cavalry)* Trupp *m*; *(= unit)* Schwadron *f* **b** **troops** PL *(Mil)* Truppen *pl*; **a dozen of our best ~s** zwölf unserer besten Soldaten; **200 ~s** 200 Soldaten **c** *(of Scouts)* Stamm *m* **d** *(of people)* Horde *f (pej)*, Schar *f* VI **to ~ out/in** hinaus-/hineinströmen; **to ~ upstairs** nach oben strömen; **to ~ past sth** an etw *(dat)* vorbeiziehen; **to ~ away** *or* **off** abziehen *(inf)*; **to ~ up** herbeiströmen VT *(Brit Mil)* **to ~ the colours** die Fahnenparade abhalten; **the colours being ~ed today** die Fahnen bei der heutigen Parade; **the ~ing of the colours** die Fahnenparade

troop carrier ['tru:p,kærɪə'] N *(= vehicle)* Truppentransporter *m*

troop-carrying vehicle ['tru:p,kærɪɪŋ'vi:ɪkl] N *(Brit Mil)* Mannschaftswagen *m*

trooper ['tru:pə'] N *(Mil)* berittener Soldat, Kavallerist *m*; *(US: = state trooper)* Staatspolizist(in) *m(f)*; **to swear like a ~** *(Brit inf)* wie ein Kutscher fluchen

troop: **troop reduction** N Truppenabbau *m*; **troopship** N (Truppen)transportschiff *nt*; **trooptrain** N Truppentransportzug *m*; **troop withdrawal** N Truppenabzug *m*

trope [trəʊp] N *(Liter)* Trope *f*

trophy ['trəʊfɪ] N *(Hunt, Mil, Sport)* Trophäe *f*

trophy wife N *(pej inf)* junge, gut aussehende Gattin eines erfolgreichen Mannes; **she denies that she is a ~** sie streitet ab, dass ihr Mann sie nur wegen ihrer Jugend und ihres Aussehens geheiratet hat

tropic ['trɒpɪk] N **a** Wendekreis *m*; **Tropic of Cancer/Capricorn** Wendekreis *m* des Krebses/Steinbocks **b** **tropics** PL Tropen *pl*

tropical ['trɒpɪkəl] ADJ tropisch, Tropen-; **~ diseases** Tropenkrankheiten *pl*; **the heat was ~** es herrschte tropische Hitze

tropical forest N Tropenwald *m*

tropical medicine N Tropenmedizin *f*

tropical rainforest N tropischer Regenwald

tropism ['trəʊpɪzəm] N *(Biol)* Tropismus *m*

tropopause ['trɒpəpɔ:z] N *(Met)* Tropopause *f*

troposphere ['trɒpəsfɪə'] N *(Met)* Troposphäre *f*

trot [trɒt] N **a** *(= pace)* Trab *m*; **to go at a ~** traben; **to go for a ~** einen Ausritt machen; **I've been on the ~ all day** *(fig inf)* ich bin schon den ganzen Tag auf Trab **b** *(inf)* **for five days on the ~** fünf Tage lang in einer Tour; **he won three games on the ~** er gewann drei Spiele hintereinander **c** *(inf: = diarrhoea)* **the ~s** die Renneritis *(hum inf)* VI *(horse, person)* traben; *(pony)* zockeln; *(small child)* trippeln; **he ~ted obediently (a)round the shops after her** er zottelte folgsam hinter ihr her durch die Geschäfte VT *horse* traben lassen

▶ **trot along** VI *(horse, person)* traben; *(pony)* zockeln; *(small child)* trippeln; *(= go away)* abmarschieren; **to trot along behind sb** hinter jdm hertraben *etc*

▶ **trot away** *or* **off** VI → **trot VI** davon- *or* wegtraben/-zockeln/-trippeln

▶ **trot out** VI → **trot VI** hinaustraben/-zockeln/-trippeln VT sep *excuses, theories, names, list* aufwarten *or* kommen mit

▶ **trot round** VI *(esp Brit: = go quickly)* hinüberlaufen; **to trot round to the grocer's** zum Kaufmann laufen

troth [trəʊθ] N *(old)* → **plight**¹

trotter¹ ['trɒtə'] N *(= horse)* Traber *m*

trotter² N *(of animal)* Fuß *m*; **pigs' ~s** *(Cook)* Schweinsfüße *pl*

trotting race ['trɒtɪŋ,reɪs] N *(horse racing)* Trabrennen *nt*

troubadour ['tru:bədɔ:'] N Troubadour *m*

trouble ['trʌbl] ✪ 2.3, 17.2 N **a** Schwierigkeiten *pl*; *(bothersome)* Ärger *m*; **did you have any ~ (in) getting it?** hatten Sie Schwierigkeiten es zu bekommen?; **to be in ~** in Schwierigkeiten sein; **you'll be in ~ for this** da bekommen Sie Ärger *or* Schwierigkeiten; **to be in ~ with sb** mit jdm Schwierigkeiten *or* Ärger haben; **to get into ~** in Schwierigkeiten geraten; *(with authority)* Schwierigkeiten *or* Ärger bekommen *(with* mit*)*; **to get sb into ~** jdn in Schwierigkeiten bringen *(with* mit*)*; **to get a girl into ~** *(euph)* ein Mädchen ins Unglück bringen; **to get out of ~** aus den Schwierigkeiten herauskommen; **to get sb out of ~** jdm aus seinen Schwierigkeiten heraushelfen; **to keep** *or* **stay out of ~** nicht in Schwierigkeiten kommen, sauber bleiben *(inf)*; **now we're out of ~** jetzt sind wir aus den Schwierigkeiten heraus; **the children are never out of ~** die Kinder stellen dauernd etwas an; **to make ~** *(= cause a row etc)* Krach schlagen *(inf)*, Ärger machen; **to make ~ for sb/oneself** *(with authority)* jdn/sich selbst in Schwierigkeiten bringen; **that's/you're asking for ~** das kann ja nicht gut gehen; **are you looking for ~?** Sie wollen wohl Ärger?; **to look for ~, to go around looking for ~** sich *(dat)* Ärger einhandeln; **there'll be ~ if he finds out** wenn er das erfährt, gibts Ärger *or* Trouble *(inf)*; **here comes ~** *(inf)* jetzt geht es los! *(inf)*, jetzt gibt es Ärger *or* Trouble! *(inf)*; **what's the ~?** was ist los?; *(to sick person)* wo fehlts?; **the ~ is that ...** das Problem ist, dass ...; **that's the ~** das ist das Problem; **family/money ~s** Familien-/Geldsorgen *pl*; **his ~s are not yet over** seine Sorgen *or* Probleme sind noch nicht vorbei
b *(= bother, effort)* Mühe *f*; **it's no ~ (at all)!** das mache ich doch gern; **thank you – (it was) no ~** vielen Dank – (das ist) gern geschehen; **it's no ~ to do it properly** man kann es genauso gut ordentlich machen; **it's not worth the ~** das ist nicht der Mühe wert; **she's/it's more ~ than she's/it's worth** sie/es macht mehr Ärger *or* Umstände als sie/es wert ist; **nothing is too much ~ for her** nichts ist ihr zu viel; **to go to the ~ (of doing sth), to take the ~ (to do sth)** sich *(dat)* die Mühe machen(, etw zu tun); **to go to/to take a lot of ~ (over** *or* **with sth)** sich *(dat)* (mit etw) viel Mühe geben; **you have gone to a lot of ~ over the food** Sie haben sich *(dat)* solche Umstände mit dem Essen gemacht; **he went to enormous ~** er hat alles nur Erdenkliche getan; **to put sb to the ~ of doing sth** jdn bemühen, etw zu tun; **to put sb to a lot of ~** jdm viel Mühe machen
c *(= nuisance)* **to be a ~ (to sb)** (jdm) Mühe machen; *(dependent person also)* (jdm) zur Last fallen; **the child is nothing but ~ to his parents** das Kind macht seinen Eltern nur Sorgen; **he's been no ~ at all** *(of child)* er war ganz lieb
d *(Med: = illness)* Leiden *nt*; *(fig)* Schaden *m*; **heart/back ~** Herz-/Rückenleiden *nt*; **my back is giving me ~** mein Rücken macht mir zu schaffen; **engine ~** (ein) Motorschaden *m*
e *(= unrest, upheaval)* Unruhe *f*; **labour** *(Brit)* *or* **labor** *(US)* **~s** Arbeiterunruhen *pl*; **there's ~ at the factory/in Iran** in der Fabrik/im Iran herrscht Unruhe; **he caused/made ~ between them** er hat Unruhe zwischen ihnen gestiftet → **stir up**
VT **a** *(= worry)* beunruhigen; *(= disturb, grieve)* bekümmern; **to be ~d by sth** wegen etw besorgt *or* beunruhigt/bekümmert sein; **he's ~d with a bad back** er leidet an Rückenschmerzen
b *(= bother)* bemühen, belästigen; **I'm sorry to ~ you, but could you tell me if ...** entschuldigen Sie die Störung, aber könnten Sie mir sagen, ob ...; **may I ~ you for a light?** darf ich Sie um Feuer bitten?; **will it ~ you if I smoke?** stört es Sie, wenn ich rauche?; **I shan't ~ you with the details** ich werde Ihnen die Einzelheiten ersparen; **we are ~d with mice just now** wir werden zurzeit von Mäusen geplagt; **I'll ~ you to remember who you're speaking to!** *(iro)* würden Sie bitte daran denken, mit wem Sie sprechen!
c *(= take the trouble)* **to ~ to do sth** sich bemühen, etw zu tun; **please don't ~ yourself** bitte bemühen Sie sich nicht; **don't ~ to write until you've settled down** schreib erst, wenn du dich eingelebt hast; **if you had ~d to ask, you might have found out the truth** wenn du dir die Mühe gemacht und gefragt hättest, hättest du wahrscheinlich die Wahrheit erfahren; **oh, don't ~ to apologize!** *(iro)* bemüh dich nicht, dich zu entschuldigen
VI sich bemühen

troubled ['trʌbld] ADJ **a** *person, look, sleep* unruhig, beunruhigt; *(= grieved)* bekümmert; *mind, conscience* aufgewühlt; *water* aufgewühlt; *(= unsettled) relationship, marriage* gestört; *life* schwer; *times, area, country, region* unruhig; **the ~ waters of industrial relations** die gestörte Beziehung zwischen Arbeitgebern und Arbeitnehmern → **oil** **b** *(Ind, Fin)* in Schwierigkeiten *pred*; **financially ~** in finanziellen Nöten

trouble: **trouble-free** ADJ *period, process, car* problemlos; *relationship also* reibungslos; *area* ruhig; *machine* störungsfrei; **troublemaker** N Tunichtgut *m*; *(deliberate)* Unruhestifter(in) *m(f)*; **troubleproof** ADJ störungsfrei; **troubleshooter** N Störungssucher(in) *m(f)*; *(Pol, Ind: = mediator)* Vermittler(in) *m(f)*; **~s** *(Pol etc: = organization)* Krisenfeuerwehr *f*; **troubleshooting** N *(Comput etc)* Troubleshooting *nt*, Problembehandlung *f*; **troublesome** ADJ *(= bothersome)* lästig; *person, problem* schwierig; **the most ~ boy in the school** der schwierigste Junge in der Schule; *(= troublemaker)* der größte Störenfried in der Schule; **don't be ~!** sei nicht so schwierig!; **trouble spot** N Unruheherd *m*; *(in system)* Störung *f*

troublous ['trʌbləs] ADJ *(liter)* unruhig

trough [trɒf] N **a** *(= container)* Trog *m*; **drinking ~** Wassertrog *m* **b** *(= depression)* Furche *f*, Rille *f*; *(between waves, on graph)* Tal *nt*; *(Met)* Trog *m*; **~ of depression** Tiefdrucktrog *m*

trounce [traʊns] VT verprügeln; *(Sport)* vernichtend schlagen

trouncing ['traʊnsɪŋ] N Prügel *pl (also Sport)*; **to give sb a ~** jdm Prügel verpassen

troupe [tru:p] N *(Theat)* Truppe *f*

trouper ['tru:pə'] N *(Theat)* Mime *m*, Mimin *f (dated)*; **an old ~** *(fig)* ein alter Hase; **he/she is a real ~** er/sie packt immer mit an

trouser ['traʊzə'] *(esp Brit)*: **trouser clip** N Hosenklammer *f*; **trouser leg** N Hosenbein *nt*; **trouser press** N Hosenpresse *f*

trousers ['traʊzɪz] PL *(esp Brit)* *(also* **pair of trousers***)* Hose *f*; **she was wearing ~** sie hatte Hosen *or* eine Hose an; **to wear the ~** *(fig inf)* die Hosen anhaben *(inf)*; **to be caught with one's ~ down** *(inf, lit: sexually)* in flagranti erwischt werden *(inf)*; *(fig)* überrumpelt werden; *(= unprepared)* sich kalt erwischen lassen *(inf)*

trouser suit N *(Brit)* Hosenanzug *m*

trousseau ['tru:səʊ] N Aussteuer *f*

trout [traʊt] N Forelle *f*; **~ fishing** Forellenfang *m*, Forellenangeln *nt*; **silly old ~!** *(inf)* blöde alte (Zimt)ziege *(inf)*

trove [trəʊv] N = **treasure trove**

trowel ['traʊəl] N Kelle *f*; **to lay sth on with a ~** *(Brit inf)* bei etw dick auftragen

Troy [trɔɪ] N *(Hist)* Troja *nt* → **Helen**

troy [trɔɪ] N *(also* **troy weight***)* Troygewicht *nt*

truancy ['truənsɪ] N (Schule)schwänzen *nt*, unentschuldigtes Fehlen (in der Schule) *(form)*, (Schul)schwänzerei *f (inf)*

truancy officer N *Sozialarbeiter, der sich um Schulschwänzer kümmert*

truant ['truənt] N (Schul)schwänzer(in) *m(f)*; **to play ~ (from sth)** (bei etw) unentschuldigt fehlen, (etw) schwänzen *(inf)* VI schwänzen *(inf)*

truce [tru:s] N *(Mil, fig)* Waffenstillstand *m*; *(Mil, interrupting fighting)* Waffenruhe *f*; **~!** Friede!

truck[1] [trʌk] N a *(esp Brit Rail)* Güterwagen *m* b *(= barrow)* Karren *m*, Wagen *m*; *(for luggage)* Gepäckkarren *m*; *(motorized)* Elektrokarren *m* c *(= lorry)* Last(kraft)wagen *m*; *(= van, pick-up)* Lieferwagen *m* VT *(US)* transportieren, spedieren VI *(US)* Lastwagen fahren

truck[2] N a *(fig: = dealings)* **to have no ~ with sb/sth** mit jdm/etw nichts zu tun haben b *(Hist: = payment)* **~ (system)** Trucksystem *nt (spec)*; **they were paid in ~** sie wurden in Waren bezahlt c *(US: = garden produce)* Gemüse *nt (für den Verkauf angebaut)*

truckage ['trʌkɪdʒ] N *(US: = transport)* Transport *m*, Spedition *f*; *(= charge)* Transportkosten *pl*

truckage company N Spedition(sfirma) *f*, Transportunternehmen *nt*

truck driver N Lastwagenfahrer(in) *m(f)*

trucker ['trʌkəʳ] N a *(esp US: = truck driver)* Lastwagenfahrer(in) *m(f)*; *(= haulage contractor)* Spediteur(in) *m(f)* b *(US: = farmer)* Gemüsegärtner(in) *m(f)*

truck *(US)*: **truck farm** N Gemüsefarm *f*; **truck farmer** N Gemüsegärtner(in) *m(f)*; **truck garden** N Gemüsegärtnerei *f*

trucking ['trʌkɪŋ] N *(esp US)* Spedition *f*, Transport *m*

truckle ['trʌkl] VI klein beigeben *(to sb* jdm gegenüber)

truckle bed N niedriges Rollbett

truck: **truckload** N Wagenladung *f*; **they came by the ~** sie kamen in ganzen Wagenladungen; **truckman** N Lastwagenfahrer *m*; **truckstop** N *(US)* Fernfahrerlokal *nt*

truculence ['trʌkjʊləns] N Trotzigkeit *f*, Aufsässigkeit *f*

truculent ['trʌkjʊlənt] ADJ trotzig, aufsässig

trudge [trʌdʒ] VI **to ~ in/out/along** *etc* hinein-/hinaus-/entlangtrotten *etc*; **to ~ through the mud** durch den Matsch stapfen; **we ~d (a)round the shops** wir sind durch die Geschäfte getrottet *or* gelatscht *(inf)* VT *streets, town* trotten durch; *(looking for sth)* abklappern N mühseliger Marsch

true [tru:] ✪ 26.1, 26.3 ADJ a *(= not false) story, news, rumour, statement* wahr; **to come ~** *(dream, wishes)* Wirklichkeit werden, wahr werden; *(prophecy)* sich verwirklichen; *(fears)* sich bewahrheiten; **to make sth come ~** etw wahr werden lassen; **it is ~ that …** es stimmt, dass …, es ist wahr *or* richtig, dass …; **that's ~** das stimmt, das ist wahr; **can it be ~ (that he didn't know)?** kann es stimmen *or* sein(, dass er das nicht wusste)?; **it is ~ to say that …** es ist richtig, dass …; **~!** richtig!; **too ~!** (das ist nur) zu wahr!, wie wahr!; **it is only too ~ that …** es ist nur allzu wahr, dass …; **we mustn't generalize, (it's) ~, but …** wir sollten natürlich nicht verallgemeinern, aber …; **that's wrong! – ~, but …** das ist falsch! – stimmt *or* richtig, aber …; **is it ~ about Harry?** stimmt es, was man über Harry sagt?; **the reverse is ~** ganz im Gegenteil; **the reverse is ~ for …** für … trifft das Gegenteil zu; **he's got so much money it's not ~!** *(inf)* es ist unfassbar, wie viel Geld er hat!
b *(= accurate) description, report, account* wahrheitsgetreu; *likeness* (lebens)getreu; *copy* getreu; *aim* genau; **the ~ meaning of** die wahre Bedeutung *(+gen)*; **in the ~ sense (of the word)** im wahren Sinne (des Wortes)
c *(= real, genuine) feeling, friendship, friend, Christian, heir, opinion* wahr, echt; *reason* wirklich; *leather, antique* echt; **the frog is not a ~ reptile** der Frosch ist kein echtes Reptil; **spoken like a ~ football fan** so spricht ein wahrer Fußballfan; **in a ~ spirit of friendship/love** im wahren Geist der Freundschaft/Liebe; **~ love** die wahre Liebe; *(= person)* Schatz *m*, Herzallerliebste(r) *mf (old)*; **the path of ~ love ne'er did run smooth** *(prov)* die Pfade der Liebe sind gewunden; **what is the ~ situation?** wie verhält es sich wirklich?; **in ~ life** im wirklichen Leben; **the one ~ God** der einzige wahre Gott; **the True Cross** *(Rel)* das wahre Kreuz
d *(= faithful) friend, follower* treu; **to be ~ to sb** jdm treu sein/bleiben; **to be ~ to one's word/promise** (treu) zu seinem Wort/Versprechen stehen, seinem Wort treu bleiben; **to be ~ to oneself** sich selbst treu bleiben; **to thine own self be ~** *(liter)* bleibe dir selbst treu; **twelve good men and ~** zwölf ehrbare Männer; **~ to life** lebensnah; *(Art)* lebensecht; **the horse ran ~ to form** das Pferd lief erwartungsgemäß; **~ to type** erwartungsgemäß; *(Bot)* artgetreu
e *wall, surface* gerade; *join* genau; *circle* rund
f *(Phys)* tatsächlich; **~ north** der eigentliche *or* tatsächliche *or* geografische Norden
g *(= applicable)* **to be ~ for sb/sth** für jdn/etw wahr sein; **to be ~ of sb/sth** auf jdn/etw zutreffen; **the same is** *or* **holds ~ for …** dasselbe gilt auch für …, dasselbe trifft auch auf … *(acc)* zu
h *(Mus) note* richtig; *voice* rein
N **out of ~** *(upright, beam, wheels)* schief; *join* verschoben
ADV *aim* genau; *sing* richtig; **to breed ~** sich reinrassig fortpflanzen; **he speaks ~** *(old)* er spricht die Wahrheit; **they speak ~r than they know** *(old)* sie kommen der Wahrheit näher, als ihnen bewusst ist → **ring**[2]

▶ **true up** VT *sep machinery* genau einstellen; *beam* genau ausrichten; *wheel* einrichten; **to true up the edges of the planks** die Bretterkanten plan machen

true: **true blue** N *(Brit: = Tory)* echter Tory, waschechter Tory *(inf)*; **true-blue** ADJ waschecht *(inf)*, echt; **true-born** ADJ echt, gebürtig; *(= legitimate)* rechtmäßig; **true-bred** ADJ wahr, echt; *cattle* reinrassig; **true-hearted** ADJ getreu, aufrichtig; **true-life** ADJ *attr* aus dem Leben gegriffen; **true rib** N wahre Rippe

truffle ['trʌfl] N Trüffel *f or m*

trug [trʌg] N Korb *m*

truism ['tru:ɪzəm] N *(= obvious truth)* Binsenwahrheit *f*; *(= platitude)* Plattitüde *f*, Gemeinplatz *m*

truly ['tru:lɪ] ADV a *(= truthfully, genuinely)* wirklich, wahrhaftig; **(really and) ~?** wirklich und wahrhaftig?; **he did it, ~ he did!** er hat es wirklich und wahrhaftig getan!; **the only man she had ever ~ loved** der einzige Mann, den sie je wahrhaft geliebt hat; **I am ~ sorry** es tut mir aufrichtig leid; **it can ~ be said that …** es lässt sich wahrhaftig sagen, dass …; **~ amazing/terrible** wirklich erstaunlich/furchtbar → **well**[2]
b *(= faithfully) serve, love* treu; *reflect* wahrheitsgetreu

trump[1] [trʌmp] N *(Cards, fig)* Trumpf *m*; **spades are ~s** Pik ist Trumpf; **what's ~s?** was ist Trumpf?; **to hold all the ~s** *(fig)* alle Trümpfe in der Hand halten; **he's absolutely ~s** *(dated inf)* er ist große Klasse *(inf)*; **to come** *or* **turn up ~s** *(Brit inf)* sich als Sieger erweisen VT *(Cards)* stechen; *(fig)* übertrumpfen

▶ **trump up** VT *sep* erfinden

trump[2] N *(liter)* Trompete *f*; **at the Last Trump** wenn die Posaunen des Jüngsten Gerichts erklingen

trump card N *(Cards)* Trumpfkarte *f*; *(fig)* Trumpf *m*; **to play one's ~** *(lit, fig)* seinen Trumpf ausspielen

trumped-up ['trʌmptʌp] ADJ *charge* erfunden

trumpery ['trʌmpərɪ] N Plunder *m no pl*; *(= ornaments)* Kitsch *m*; *(= jewellery)* Flitterkram *m*; *(= nonsense)* Unsinn *m* ADJ billig; *ornaments also* kitschig

trumpet ['trʌmpɪt] N a *(Mus)* Trompete *f* → **blow**[2] b *(of elephant)* Trompeten *nt no pl* c *(of flower)* Trompete *f*; *(= hearing trumpet)* Hörrohr *m*; *(= speaking trumpet)* Sprachrohr *nt*, Megaphon *nt* VT *(rare: also* **trumpet forth**) hinaustrompeten VI *(elephant)* trompeten

trumpet call N Trompetensignal *nt*

trumpeter ['trʌmpɪtəʳ] N Trompeter(in) *m(f)*

trumpeting ['trʌmpɪtɪŋ] N *(of elephant)* Trompeten *nt*

trumpet major N Stabstrompeter *m*

truncate [trʌŋ'keɪt] VT kürzen, beschneiden; *(Comput) number* abschneiden; *process* abbrechen ADJ ['trʌŋkeɪt] *cone* stumpf; *leaf* abgestumpft

truncated [trʌŋ'keɪtɪd] ADJ *tree* gestutzt; *article, speech, version* gekürzt; *presidency* verkürzt; *cone* stumpf; *leaf* abgestumpft; *(Comput) text, file* abgeschnitten

truncation [trʌŋ'keɪʃən] N Kürzung *f*, Beschneidung *f*; *(Comput) (of number)* Abschneiden *nt*; *(of process)* Abbruch *m*

truncheon ['trʌntʃən] N (Gummi)knüppel *m*; *(esp of riot police)* Schlagstock *m*

trundle ['trʌndl] VT *(= push)* rollen; *(= pull)* ziehen VI **to ~ in/along/down** hinein-/entlang-/hinunterzockeln; *(= clatter)* hinein-/entlang-/hinunterrumpeln

trundle bed N *(US)* Rollbett *nt*

trunk [trʌŋk] N a *(of tree)* Stamm *m*; *(of body)* Rumpf *m* b *(of elephant)* Rüssel *m* c *(= case)* Schrankkoffer *m* d *(US Aut)* Kofferraum *m* e **trunks** PL *(for swimming)* Badehose *f*; *(for sport)* Shorts *pl*; **a pair of ~s** eine Badehose; *(for sport)* Shorts *pl*; (ein Paar *nt*) *(Brit: = underwear)* eine Unterhose

trunk: **trunk call** N *(Brit Telec)* Ferngespräch *nt*; **trunk hose** N *(Hist)* Pluderhose *f*; **trunk line** N *(Rail)* Hauptstrecke *f*; *(Telec)* Fernleitung *f*; **trunk road** N *(Brit)* Fernstraße *f*

truss [trʌs] N a *(Brit, = bundle)* Bündel *nt*, Garbe *f* b *(Build, of bridge)* Fachwerk *nt*; *(of roof)* Gespärre *nt*; *(= single beam)* Dachsparren *m*; *(vertical)* Dachbalken *m* c *(Med)* Bruchband *nt* VT a *(= tie) hay* bündeln; *person* fesseln b *(Cook) chicken etc* dressieren c *(Build)* (ab)stützen

▶ **truss up** VT *sep (Cook) chicken etc* dressieren; *(inf) person* fesseln

trust [trʌst] N a *(= confidence, reliance)* Vertrauen *nt (in* zu); **I have every ~ in him** ich habe volles Vertrauen zu ihm; **to put** *or* **place one's ~ in sb** Vertrauen in jdn setzen; **to take sth on ~** etw einfach glauben; **to give sb sth on ~** *(= without payment)* jdm etw auf sein ehrliches Gesicht hin *(inf) or* im guten Glauben geben; **position of ~** Vertrauensstellung *f*
b *(= charge)* Verantwortung *f*; **to commit sth to sb's ~** jdm etw anvertrauen
c *(Jur, Fin)* Treuhand(schaft) *f*; *(= property)* Treuhandeigentum *nt*; *(= charitable fund)* Fonds *m*, Stiftung *f*; **to hold sth in ~ for sb** etw für jdn treuhänderisch verwalten; **all his money was tied up in a ~** sein ganzes Geld wurde treuhänderisch verwaltet
d *(Comm: also* **trust company**) Trust *m*
e *(Brit: also* **trust hospital**) *finanziell eigenverantwortliches, vom staatlichen Gesundheitswesen getragenes Krankenhaus*
VT a *(= have confidence in)* trauen *(+dat)*; *person* (ver)trauen *(+dat)*; *words* glauben; **to ~ sb to do sth** *(= believe him honest etc)* jdm vertrauen, dass er etw tut; *(= believe him capable)* jdm zutrauen, dass er etw tut; **don't you ~ me?** vertraust du mir nicht?; **to ~ sb with sth, to ~ sth to sb** jdm etw anvertrauen; **I don't ~ her with my boyfriend** ich traue ihr mit meinem Freund nicht; **can he be ~ed not to lose it?** kann man sich darauf verlassen, dass er es nicht verliert?; **can we ~ him to go shopping alone?** können wir ihn allein einkaufen gehen lassen?; **you can't ~ a word he says** man kann ihm kein Wort glauben; **I wouldn't ~ him (any) farther than I can throw him** *(inf)* ich traue ihm nicht über den Weg *(inf)*

b *(iro inf)* ~ **you/him!** typisch!; ~ **him to break it!** er muss es natürlich kaputt machen
c *(= hope)* hoffen; **I ~ not** hoffentlich nicht, ich hoffe nicht; **you're going to help, I ~** du wirst doch hoffentlich mithelfen
VI a *(= have confidence)* vertrauen; **to ~ in sb** auf jdn vertrauen
b *(= rely on)* **to ~ to sth** sich auf etw *(acc)* verlassen, auf etw *(acc)* vertrauen; **to ~ to luck** *or* **chance** sich auf sein Glück verlassen; **I'll have to ~ to luck to find it** ich kann nur hoffen, dass ich es finde

trust: **trust account** N Treuhandkonto *nt*; **trust company** N *(Econ, Fin)* Treuhandgesellschaft *f*, Treuhandbank *f*

trusted ['trʌstɪd] ADJ *method* bewährt; *friend, servant* getreu

trustee [trʌs'tiː] N **a** *(of estate)* Treuhänder(in) *m(f)*, Vermögensverwalter(in) *m(f)* **b** *(of institution)* Kurator(in) *m(f)*, Verwalter(in) *m(f)*; **~s** Vorstand *m*; **Trustee Savings Bank** ≈ Sparkasse *f*

trusteeship [trʌs'tiːʃɪp] N **a** Treuhandschaft *f* **b** *(of a territory)* Treuhandschaft *f*, Mandat *nt* **c** *(also* **trusteeship territory***)* Treuhandgebiet *nt*, Mandat(sgebiet) *nt*

trustful ['trʌstfʊl] ADJ *look, expression* vertrauensvoll; *person also* gutgläubig, arglos

trustfully ['trʌstfəlɪ] ADV vertrauensvoll

trust fund N Treuhandvermögen *nt*, Stiftungsgelder *pl*

trusting ['trʌstɪŋ] ADJ *person, nature* arglos, gutgläubig; *relationship* vertrauensvoll; *face* arglos

trustingly ['trʌstɪŋlɪ] ADV vertrauensvoll; *look* arglos

trust territory N *(Pol)* Treuhandgebiet *nt*

trustworthiness ['trʌst,wɜːðɪnɪs] N *(of person)* Vertrauenswürdigkeit *f*; *(of statement, account)* Glaubhaftigkeit *f*, Glaubwürdigkeit *f*

trustworthy ['trʌst,wɜːðɪ] ADJ *person* vertrauenswürdig; *statement, account* glaubhaft, glaubwürdig

trusty ['trʌstɪ] ADJ *(+er) (liter, hum)* getreu *(liter)*; **~ steed** *(dated)* treues Ross N *(= prisoner)* vertrauenswürdiger Häftling

truth [truːθ] N *pl* **-s** [truːðz] **a** *no pl* Wahrheit *f*; **you must always tell the ~** du musst immer die Wahrheit sagen; **to tell the ~ …, ~ to tell …** um ehrlich zu sein …, um die Wahrheit zu sagen …; **the ~ of it** *or* **the matter is that …** die Wahrheit ist dass …, in Wahrheit …; **there's no ~** *or* **or not a word of ~ in what he says** es ist kein Wort wahr von dem, was er sagt; **there's some ~ in that** es ist etwas Wahres daran, da ist etwas Wahres dran *(inf)*; **the ~, the whole ~ and nothing but the ~** *(Jur)* die Wahrheit, die reine Wahrheit und nichts als die Wahrheit; **in ~** in Wahrheit, in Wirklichkeit; **~ will out** *(prov)* die Wahrheit wird ans Licht kommen, die Sonne wird es an den Tag bringen *(prov)*
b *(= belief, fact)* Wahrheit *f* → **home truth**

truth drug N Wahrheitsdroge *f*

truthful ['truːθfʊl] ADJ *person* ehrlich; *statement* ehrlich, wahrheitsgetreu; **to be ~ about it** ehrlich sein

truthfully ['truːθfəlɪ] ADV ehrlich; *answer, say also, explain* wahrheitsgemäß, der Wahrheit entsprechend

truthfulness ['truːθfʊlnɪs] N Ehrlichkeit *f*, Aufrichtigkeit *f*; *(of statement)* Wahrheit *f*

truth serum N Wahrheitsdroge *f*

truth-value N *(Logic)* Wahrheitswert *m*

try [traɪ] N **a** *(= attempt)* Versuch *m*; **to have a ~** es versuchen; **let me have a ~** lass mich mal versuchen!, lass mich mal! *(inf)*; **to have a ~ at doing sth** (sich daran) versuchen, etw zu tun, (es) probieren, etw zu tun; **have another ~ (at it)** versuchs noch mal; **I'll give it a ~** *(= will attempt it)* ich werde es mal versuchen; *(= will test it out)* ich werde es ausprobieren; **I'll give him a ~** ich werde ihm eine Chance geben; **it was a good ~** das war schon ganz gut; **it's worth a ~** es ist einen Versuch wert; **at the first ~** beim ersten Versuch, auf Anhieb; **can I have a ~ at your bicycle?** kann ich mal dein Rad ausprobieren?
b *(Rugby)* Versuch *m*; **to score a ~** einen Versuch erzielen
VT a *(= attempt)* versuchen; **you have only tried two questions** du hast dich nur an zwei Fragen versucht *(inf)*, du hast nur zwei Fragen zu beantworten versucht; **to ~ one's hardest** *or* **one's best** sein Bestes tun *or* versuchen; **do ~ to understand** bitte versuche doch zu verstehen!; **I've given up ~ing to help him** ich habe es aufgegeben, ihm helfen zu wollen; **it's ~ing to snow** *(inf)* es sieht aus, als würde es schneien; **the sun's ~ing to come out** es sieht so aus, als wollte die Sonne rauskommen; **to ~ one's hand at sth** etw probieren; **I'll ~ anything once** ich probiere alles einmal; **just you ~ it!** *(= you dare)* versuchs bloß!
b *(= try out) new detergent, bicycle etc* ausprobieren; *job applicant* eine Chance geben *(+dat)*, es versuchen mit *(inf)*; *glue, aspirin* es versuchen mit; *(= try to buy or get sth at) newsagent, next door* es versuchen (bei); *(= try to open) door, window* ausprobieren; **I can't shut this case – ~ sitting on it** ich kriege diesen Koffer nicht zu – setz dich doch mal drauf! *(inf)*; **you could ~ seeing whether John would help** Sie könnten doch John mal um Hilfe angehen; **I've tried everything** ich habe alles versucht *or* probiert; **~ whether …** probieren Sie, ob …; **~ this for size** probieren Sie mal, ob dieser/diese *etc* passt; *(fig inf)* wie wärs denn damit? *(inf)*; **to ~ one's strength** seine Kraft erproben
c *(= sample, taste) beer, olives* probieren
d *(= test) courage, patience* auf die Probe stellen; *(= strain) eyes* anstrengen; **he was tried and found wanting** *(liter)* er wurde gewogen und zu leicht befunden; **(just) ~ me!** *(inf)* wetten?, wetten dass?; **they have been sorely tried** sie sind schwer geprüft (worden); **these things are sent to ~ us** ja, ja, das Leben ist nicht so einfach → **tried-and-tested**
e *(Jur) person* vor Gericht stellen; *case* verhandeln; **he is being tried for theft** er steht wegen Diebstahls vor Gericht
VI versuchen; **~ and arrive on time** versuch mal, pünktlich zu sein; **~ as he might, he didn't succeed** sosehr er es auch versuchte *or* sosehr er sich auch bemühte, er schaffte es einfach nicht; **he didn't even ~** er hat sich *(dat)* überhaupt keine Mühe gegeben; *(= didn't attempt it)* er hat es überhaupt nicht versucht; **you can't say I didn't ~** du kannst nicht sagen, ich hätte es nicht versucht → **succeed**

▶ **try for** VI *+prep obj* sich bemühen um

▶ **try on** VT *sep* **a** *clothes* anprobieren; *hat* aufprobieren **b** *(fig inf)* **to try it on with sb** probieren, wie weit man bei jdm gehen kann, jdn provozieren; **the policeman warned the thief not to try anything on** der Polizist warnte den Dieb, keine Mätzchen *(inf) or* Dummheiten zu machen; **he's just trying it on** er probiert nur, wie weit er gehen *or* wie weit er es treiben kann; **don't you try it on with me, or I'll tell my husband** versuchs nicht bei *or* mit mir, sonst sag ichs meinem Mann

▶ **try out** VT *sep* ausprobieren (*on* bei, an *+dat*); *person* eine Chance geben *(+dat)*, einen Versuch machen mit VI **two of their players are trying out for Arsenal** zwei ihrer Spieler machen bei Arsenal ein Probetraining

▶ **try over** VT *sep (Mus) piece* proben

trying ['traɪɪŋ] ADJ schwierig, anstrengend; *work, day, time* anstrengend, aufreibend; *experience* schwer; **it has been a ~ time for them recently** sie haben es in letzter Zeit sehr schwer gehabt; **how ~!** wie ärgerlich!

try: **try-on** N *(inf)* **do you think he'll do what he threatened? – no, it was just a ~** glaubst du, er wird seine Drohung wahr machen? – nein, er wollte uns nur auf den Arm nehmen *(inf)*; **try-out** ['traɪaʊt] N *(of machine etc)* Erprobung *f*; *(of car)* Probefahrt *f*; *(Ftbl etc)* Probespiel *nt*; *(of applicant)* Probezeit *f*; *(of actor)* Probevortrag *m*; **to give sb a ~** jdm eine Chance geben; **to give sth a ~** etw ausprobieren

tryst [trɪst] N *(old)* Stelldichein *nt (dated)*

trysting place ['trɪstɪŋ,pleɪs] N *(old)* Stelldichein *nt (dated)*

tsar [zɑː'] N Zar *m*

tsarevitch ['zɑːrəvɪtʃ] N Zarewitsch *m*

tsarina [zɑː'riːnə] N Zarin *f*

tsarist ['zɑːrɪst] N Zarist(in) *m(f)* ADJ zaristisch

tsetse (fly) ['tsetsɪ('flaɪ)] N Tsetsefliege *f*

T-shirt ['tiːʃɜːt] N T-Shirt *nt*

tsp(s) *abbr of* **teaspoonful(s)** *or* **teaspoon(s)** Teel.

T-square ['tiːskwɛə'] N Reißschiene *f*

t-storm ['tiːstɔːm] N *(US: inf)* Gewitter *nt*

tsunami [tsʊ'nɑːmɪ] N *(= tidal wave)* Tsunami *m*

TT *abbr* **a** *of* **teetotal** **b** *of* **teetotaller** **c** *(Mot) of* **Tourist Trophy** *jährlich auf der Insel Man abgehaltenes Motorradrennen* **d** *(Agr) of* **tuberculin-tested** **e** *of* **telegraphic transfer** telegrafische Geldüberweisung

TU *(Brit) abbr of* **Trade Union** Gew.

tub [tʌb] N **a** Kübel *m*; *(for rainwater)* Tonne *f*, Traufe *f*; *(for washing)* Zuber *m*, Bottich *m*, Trog *m*; *(of ice cream, margarine)* Becher *m* **b** *(esp US inf: = bath tub)* Wanne *f* **c** *(inf: = boat)* Kahn *m*

tuba ['tjuːbə] N Tuba *f*

tubby ['tʌbɪ] ADJ *(+er) (inf)* dick; *woman* mollig, rundlich; *child* pummelig, kugelrund; *man* rundlich; **he is getting quite ~** er geht immer mehr in die Breite, er wird immer runder

tube [tjuːb] N **a** *(= pipe)* Rohr *nt*; *(of rubber, plastic)* Schlauch *m*; *(= speaking tube)* Sprachrohr *nt*; *(= torpedo tube)* (Torpedo)rohr *nt*; **to go down the ~s** *(fig inf)* den Bach runtergehen *(inf)* **b** *(= container, of toothpaste, paint, glue)* Tube *f*; *(of sweets)* Röhrchen *nt*, Rolle *f* **c** *(Brit: = London underground)* U-Bahn *f*; **to travel by ~** mit der U-Bahn fahren **d** *(Elec, TV, US Rad)* Röhre *f*; **the ~** *(US inf)* die Glotze *(inf)* **e** *(Anat)* Röhre *f*; *(= Fallopian tube)* Eileiter *m*; **the bronchial ~s** die Bronchien *pl*

tubeless ['tjuːblɪs] ADJ *tyre* schlauchlos

tuber ['tjuːbə'] N *(Bot)* Knolle *f*

tubercle ['tjuːbɜːkl] N *(Bot)* Knoten *m*, Knötchen *nt*; *(Med also)* Tuberkel *m*

tubercular [tjʊ'bɜːkjʊlə'] ADJ tuberkulös

tuberculin [tjʊ'bɜːkjʊlɪn] N Tuberkulin *nt*; **~-tested** tuberkulingetestet

tuberculosis [tjʊ,bɜːkjʊ'ləʊsɪs] N Tuberkulose *f*

tuberculous [tjʊ'bɜːkjʊləs] ADJ tuberkulös

tube station N *(Brit)* U-Bahnstation *f*

tube top N *(US Tex)* Bandeau-Top *nt*

tube train N *(Brit)* U-Bahnzug *m*

tubing ['tjuːbɪŋ] N Schlauch *m*

tub: **tub-thumper** N *(pej)* Demagoge *m*, Demagogin *f*, Volksredner(in) *m(f)*; **tub-thumping** ['tʌbθʌmpɪŋ] *(esp Brit)* N Demagogie *f* ADJ demagogisch

tubular ['tjuːbjʊlə'] ADJ röhrenförmig; **~ furniture/scaffolding** Stahlrohrmöbel *pl*/-gerüst *nt*

tubular bells N Glockenspiel *nt*

TUC *(Brit) abbr of* **Trades Union Congress** ≈ DGB *m*

tuck [tʌk] N **a** *(Sew)* Saum *m*; *(ornamental)* Biese *f*; **to put a ~ in sth** einen Saum in etw *(acc)* nähen
b *(Brit Sch inf: = food)* Süßigkeiten *pl*
VT a *(= put)* stecken; **he ~ed his umbrella under his arm** er steckte *or* klemmte *(inf)* sich *(dat)* den Regenschirm unter den Arm; **the bird's head was ~ed under its wing** der Vogel hatte den Kopf unter den Flügel gesteckt; **he ~ed his coat (a)round the shivering child** er legte seinen Mantel fest um das frierende Kind; **she sat with her feet ~ed under her** sie saß mit untergeschlagenen Beinen da
b *(Sew)* Biesen *pl* steppen in *(+acc)*; **a ~ed bodice** ein Oberteil mit Biesen

VI **your bag will ~ under the seat** du kannst deine Tasche unter dem Sitz verstauen

▸ **tuck away** VT sep **a** (= hide) wegstecken; **he tucked it away in his pocket** er steckte es in die Tasche; **the hut is tucked away among the trees** die Hütte liegt versteckt zwischen den Bäumen **b** (inf, = eat) **he can certainly tuck it away!** er kann ganz schön was wegputzen *(inf)*; **I can't think where he tucks it all away** ich weiß nicht, wo er das alles lässt *(inf)*

▸ **tuck in** **VI** (Brit inf) zulangen, reinhauen *(inf)*; **tuck in!** langt zu!, haut rein! *(inf)*; **to tuck into sth** sich *(dat)* etw schmecken lassen **VT** sep **a** flap etc hineinstecken, reinstecken *(inf)*; sheet also an den Seiten feststecken; **to tuck one's shirt in(to) one's trousers, to tuck one's shirt in** das Hemd in die Hose stecken; **tuck your tummy in!** zieh den Bauch ein! **b** **to tuck sb in** jdn zudecken; **to tuck sb into bed** jdn ins Bett stecken

▸ **tuck up** VT sep **a** skirt, hair hochnehmen; sleeve hochkrempeln; legs unterschlagen **b** (Brit) **to tuck sb up (in bed)** jdn zudecken

tuck box N (Brit) *Schachtel mit Süßigkeiten*

tucker[1] ['tʌkəʳ] VT (US inf) fertigmachen *(inf)*

tucker[2] N (esp Austral) Proviant *m*

tucker[3] ['tʌkəʳ] N (old: Fashion) Schultertuch *nt* → **bib**

tucker-bag ['tʌkəbæg] N (esp Austral) Provianttasche *f*

tuck-in ['tʌkɪn] N (inf) Essen *nt*; **to have a (good) ~** kräftig zulangen, ordentlich futtern *(inf)* or reinhauen *(inf)*

tuck shop N (Brit) Bonbonladen *m*

Tudor ['tju:dəʳ] **ADJ** Tudor-; **~ period** Tudorzeit *f* **N** Tudor *mf*

Tue(s) abbr of **Tuesday** Di.

Tuesday ['tju:zdɪ] N Dienstag *m*; **on ~** (am) Dienstag; **on ~s, on a ~** dienstags, an Dienstagen *(form)*; **I met her on a ~** ich habe sie an einem Dienstag kennengelernt; **on ~ morning/evening** am Dienstagmorgen/-abend; **on ~ mornings/evenings** dienstagmorgens/-abends or dienstags morgens/abends; **I'll never forget that ~ evening** diesen Dienstagabend werde ich nie vergessen; **last/next/this ~** Dienstag letzter/nächster/dieser Woche, letzten/nächsten/diesen Dienstag; **a year (ago) last/next ~** letzten/nächsten Dienstag vor einem Jahr; **~'s newspaper** die Zeitung vom Dienstag; **our ~ meeting** (this week) unser Treffen am Dienstag; (every week) unser dienstägliches Treffen, unser Dienstagstreffen; **~ December 5th** (in letter) Dienstag, den 5. Dezember

tuffet ['tʌfɪt] N (old) kleiner Hügel, Buckel *m*

tuft [tʌft] N Büschel *nt*; **a ~ of hair** ein Haarbüschel *nt*; **a ~ of feathers** ein Federbusch *m*

tufted ['tʌftɪd] ADJ (Orn) mit Federbusch; (Bot) büschelförmig

tufted duck N Reiherente *f*

tufty ['tʌftɪ] ADJ büschelig

tug [tʌg] **VT** zerren, ziehen; vessel (ab)schleppen; **she ~ged his sleeve** sie zog an seinem Ärmel; **she ~ged a tuft of his hair out by the roots** sie zog or riss ihm ein Büschel Haare aus **VI** ziehen, zerren (at an +dat) → **heartstrings** **N** **a** (= pull) **to give sth a ~** an etw *(dat)* ziehen; **I felt a ~ on my sleeve** ich spürte, wie mich jemand am Ärmel zog; **parting with it was quite a ~** es fiel mir etc sehr schwer, mich etc davon zu trennen **b** (also **tugboat**) Schlepper *m*, Schleppkahn *m*

tug: **tug-of-love** N Tauziehen um das Kind/die Kinder bei einer Ehescheidung; **tug-of-war** N (Sport, fig) Tauziehen *nt*

tuition [tju'ɪʃən] N Unterricht *m*; **extra ~** Nachhilfeunterricht *m*

tulip ['tju:lɪp] N Tulpe *f*; **~ tree** Tulpenbaum *m*

tulle [tju:l] N Tüll *m*

tumble ['tʌmbl] **N** **a** (= fall) Sturz *m*; **to take a ~** stürzen, straucheln; (fig) fallen **b** (= mess) Durcheinander *nt* **VI** **a** (= fall) straucheln, (hin)fallen; (= move quickly) stürzen; (fig: prices) fallen; **he ~d off his bicycle** er stürzte vom Fahrrad; **to ~ out of/into bed** aus dem Bett/ins Bett fallen; **to ~ over sth** über etw *(acc)* fallen or stolpern **b** (inf: = realize) **to ~ to sth** etw kapieren *(inf)* **c** (gymnast) Bodenakrobatik machen **VT** (= make fall) stoßen; (= make untidy) hair zerzausen, durcheinanderbringen

▸ **tumble about** (Brit) or **around** VI durcheinanderpurzeln; (children, kittens etc) herumpurzeln; **the clothes tumbled about in the drier** die Wäsche wurde im Trockenautomaten durcheinandergewirbelt

▸ **tumble down** VI **a** (= fall down, person) hinfallen, stürzen; (object) herunterfallen; (building) einstürzen; **to tumble down the stairs** die Treppe hinunterfallen **b** (= move quickly) **they came tumbling down the stairs** sie kamen die Treppe heruntergestürzt

▸ **tumble in** VI (= come in) hereinpurzeln

▸ **tumble out** VI (= go out) hinauspurzeln

▸ **tumble over** VI umfallen, umkippen

tumble: **tumbledown** ADJ verfallen, baufällig; **tumble drier, tumble dryer** N Trockenautomat *m*, Heißlufttrockner *m*, Trockner *m (inf)*

tumbler ['tʌmbləʳ] N **a** (= glass) (Becher)glas *nt*, Tumbler *m* **b** (in lock) Zuhaltung *f* **c** (= acrobat) Bodenakrobat(in) *m(f)* **d** (= toy) Stehaufmännchen *nt* **e** (= tumble drier) Trockenautomat *m*, Trockner *m (inf)* **f** (Orn) Tümmler *m*

tumbleweed ['tʌmbl,wi:d] N Steppenläufer *m* or -hexe *f*

tumbrel, tumbril ['tʌmbrəl] N (Hist) Karren *m*

tumescence [tu:'mesns] N (form) Schwellung *f*

tumescent [tju:'mesnt] ADJ (form) anschwellend

tumid ['tju:mɪd] ADJ (Med) geschwollen; (fig) style geschwollen; speech schwülstig

tummy ['tʌmɪ] N (inf) Bauch *m*, Bäuchlein *nt* *(baby-talk)*; **those green tomatoes will give you a sore ~** von diesen grünen Tomaten kriegst du Bauchschmerzen or Bauchweh

tummy tuck N (Med inf) Fettabsaugung *f* am Bauch

tumour, (US) **tumor** ['tju:məʳ] N Geschwulst *f*, Tumor *m*; **a ~ on the brain, a brain ~** ein Gehirntumor *m*

tumult ['tju:mʌlt] N **a** (= uproar) Tumult *m*; **the ~ of battle** das Schlachtgetümmel **b** (emotional) **his mind was in a ~** sein Inneres befand sich in Aufruhr; **a ~ of emotion/weeping** ein Gefühls-/Tränenausbruch *m*

tumultuous [tju:'mʌltjʊəs] ADJ applause, day, times, relationship stürmisch; **they gave him a ~ welcome** sie begrüßten ihn stürmisch; **a ~ sea** eine stürmische See

tumultuously [tju:'mʌltjʊəslɪ] ADV stürmisch

tumulus ['tju:mjʊləs] N Tumulus *m*, Grabhügel *m*

tun [tʌn] N (= cask) Fass *nt*

tuna (fish) ['tju:nə('fɪʃ)] N T(h)unfisch *m*

tundra ['tʌndrə] N Tundra *f*

tune [tju:n] **N** **a** (= melody) Melodie *f*; **sung to the ~ of ...** gesungen nach der Melodie (von) ...; **there's not much ~ to it** das ist or klingt nicht sehr melodisch; **give us a ~!** spiel uns was vor!; **to change one's ~** (fig) seine Meinung ändern; **to dance to sb's ~** (fig) nach jds Pfeife tanzen; **to call the ~** (fig) den Ton angeben; **to the ~ of £100** in Höhe von £ 100 **b** (= pitch) **to sing in ~/out of ~** richtig/falsch singen; **the piano is out of ~** das Klavier ist verstimmt; **to go out of ~** (instrument) sich verstimmen; (singer) anfangen, falsch zu singen; **the piano is not in ~ with the flute** das Klavier und die Flöte sind nicht gleich gestimmt; **to be in/out of ~ with sb/sth** (fig) mit jdm/etw harmonieren/nicht harmonieren, mit jdm/etw in Einklang/nicht in Einklang stehen; **he's a successful teacher because he's in ~ with young people** er ist ein erfolgreicher Lehrer, weil er auf der gleichen Wellenlänge mit den Jugendlichen ist *(inf)*; **he felt out of ~ with his new environment** er fühlte sich in seiner neuen Umgebung fehl am Platze **c** (Aut) **the carburettor is out of ~** der Vergaser ist falsch eingestellt **VT** **a** (Mus) instrument stimmen **b** (Rad, TV) einstellen; **you are ~d to the BBC World Service** Sie hören den or hier ist der BBC World Service **c** (Aut) engine, carburettor einstellen

▸ **tune down** VT (fig) enthusiasm etc dämpfen

▸ **tune in** **VI** **a** (Rad) einschalten; **to tune in to Radio London** Radio London einschalten or hören **b** **to tune in to sth** (to feelings etc) sich einstellen auf etw *(acc)* **VT** sep **a** radio einschalten (to +acc); **you are tuned in to Radio 2** Sie hören or hier ist Radio 2 **b** **to be tuned in to sth** (to feelings etc) auf etw *(acc)* eingestellt sein

▸ **tune up** **VI** (Mus) (sein Instrument) stimmen **VT** sep (Aut) engine tunen

tuneful ADJ, **tunefully** ADV ['tju:nfʊl, -fəlɪ] melodisch

tunefulness ['tju:nfʊlnɪs] N Melodik *f*

tuneless ADJ, **tunelessly** ADV ['tju:nlɪs, -lɪ] unmelodisch

tuner ['tju:nəʳ] N **a** (Mus) Stimmer(in) *m(f)* **b** (Rad etc: = part of set) Empfangsteil *nt*; (= separate set) Empfänger *m*, Tuner *m*

tuner-amp(lifier) [,tju:nər'æmp(lɪfaɪəʳ)] N (Rad etc) Steuergerät *nt*, Receiver *m*

tune-up ['tju:nʌp] N (Aut) **the car needs/has had a ~** das Auto muss getunt werden/ist getunt worden

tungsten ['tʌŋstən] N Wolfram *nt*

tungsten lamp N Wolframlampe *f*

tungsten steel N Wolframstahl *m*

tunic ['tju:nɪk] N Kasack *m*, Hemdbluse *f*; (of uniform) Uniformrock *m*; (of school uniform) Kittel *m*; (in ancient Greece) Chiton *m*; (in ancient Rome) Tunika *f*

tuning ['tju:nɪŋ] N **a** (Mus) Stimmen *nt* **b** (Rad) Einstellen *nt*; **it takes a lot of ~ to find the right station** man muss lange suchen, bis man den richtigen Sender gefunden hat **c** (Aut) Einstellen *nt*; **all the engine needed was a little ~** der Motor musste nur richtig eingestellt werden

tuning fork N (Mus) Stimmgabel *f*

tuning knob N (Rad) Stationswahlknopf *m*

Tunisia [tju:'nɪzɪə] N Tunesien *nt*

Tunisian [tju:'nɪzɪən] **N** Tunesier(in) *m(f)* **ADJ** tunesisch; **he is ~** er ist Tunesier

tunnel ['tʌnl] **N** Tunnel *m*; (under road, railway also) Unterführung *f*; (Min) Stollen *m*; **at last we can see the light at the end of the ~** (fig) endlich sehen wir wieder Licht; **that for me was always the light at the end of the ~** (fig) das war für mich immer ein Hoffnungsfunken **VI** (into in +acc) (through durch) einen Tunnel bauen; (rabbit) einen Bau graben; (mole) Gänge *pl* graben; **they ~led** (Brit) or **~ed** (US) **under the walls of the jail** sie gruben (sich *dat*) einen Tunnel unter den Mauern des Gefängnisses hindurch **VT** **they ~led** (Brit) or **~ed** (US) **a road through the mountain** sie bauten einen Straßentunnel durch den Berg; **the hillside had been ~led** (Brit) or **~ed** (US) **by rabbits** die Kaninchen hatten ihre Baue in den Hang gegraben; **to ~ one's way through sth** sich durch etw hindurchgraben

▸ **tunnel out** VI sich *(dat)* einen Fluchttunnel graben

tunnel vision N (Med) Gesichtsfeldeinengung *f*; (fig) Engstirnigkeit *f*, beschränkter Horizont

tunny (fish) ['tʌnɪ('fɪʃ)] N Thunfisch *m*

tuppence ['tʌpəns] N (Brit) zwei Pence; **I don't care ~** *(inf)* das interessiert mich nicht für fünf Pfennig *(inf)*, das ist mir doch so egal *(inf)*

tuppenny ['tʌpənɪ] ADJ *(Brit) sweets etc* für zwei Pence; **he doesn't give a ~ damn about you** *(inf)* er schert sich einen (feuchten) Dreck um dich *(inf)*

tuppenny bit, tuppenny piece N *(Brit)* Zweipencestück *nt*

tuppenny-ha'penny ['tʌpnɪ'heɪpnɪ] ADJ *(Brit inf)* lächerlich

turban ['tɜːbən] N Turban *m*

turbid ['tɜːbɪd] ADJ **a** *liquid* trübe, schmutzig **b** *(fig: = confused)* verworren

turbidity [tɜː'bɪdɪtɪ] N **a** *(of liquid)* Trübheit *f*, Schmutzigkeit *f* **b** *(fig: = confusion)* Verworrenheit *f*

turbine ['tɜːbaɪn] N Turbine *f*

turbocar ['tɜːbəʊkaː'] N Wagen *m* mit Turbomotor

turbo-charged ['tɜːbəʊˌtʃɑːdʒd] ADJ *car, engine* mit Turboaufladung; *(= exciting, powerful) gadget, person, performance* rasant

turbocharger ['tɜːbəʊˌtʃɑːdʒə'] N Turbolader *m*

turbojet ['tɜːbəʊ'dʒet] N *(= engine)* Turbotriebwerk *nt*; *(= aircraft)* Düsenflugzeug *nt*, Turbojet *m*

turboprop ['tɜːbəʊ'prɒp] N *(= engine)* Propellerturbine *f*, Turboprop *f*; *(= aircraft)* Turbo-Prop-Flugzeug *nt*

turbosupercharger [ˌtɜːbəʊ'suːpəˌtʃɑːdʒə'] N Turbolader *m*

turbot ['tɜːbət] N Steinbutt *m*

turbulence ['tɜːbjʊləns] N *(of person, crowd)* Ungestüm *nt*, Wildheit *f*; *(of emotions)* Aufgewühltheit *f*; *(of career, period)* Turbulenz *f*; **air ~** Turbulenzen *pl*; **the ~ of the water** das stürmische Wasser

turbulent ['tɜːbjʊlənt] ADJ stürmisch; *person, crowd* ungestüm, wild; *emotions* aufgewühlt; *career, period, world, politics* turbulent

turd [tɜːd] N *(sl)* **a** Kacke *f (vulg)*, Scheiße *f no pl (vulg)*; *(single)* Haufen *m (inf)* **b** *(pej: = person)* Scheißkerl *m (inf)*

tureen [tə'riːn] N (Suppen)terrine *f*

turf [tɜːf] N *pl* **-s** *or* **turves** **a** *(no pl: = lawn)* Rasen *m*; *(no pl: = squares of grass)* Soden *pl*; *(= square of grass)* Sode *f* **b** *(no pl, = peat)* Torf *m*; *(= square of peat)* Torfsode *f*; **to cut ~** Torf(soden) stechen **c** *(Sport)* **the Turf** die (Pferde)rennbahn; **all his life he was a devotee of the Turf** sein Leben galt dem Pferderennsport VT **a** **he ~ed the lawn** er verlegte (Gras)soden *or* Fertigrasen im Garten **b** *(inf)* **to ~ sb down the stairs** jdn die Treppe hinunterscheuchen *(inf)*; **to ~ sth into the corner** etw in die Ecke werfen

▶ **turf out** VT *sep (Brit inf) person* rauswerfen, rausschmeißen *(inf)*; *plan* umschmeißen *(inf)*, verwerfen; *suggestions* abtun; *(= throw away)* wegschmeißen *(inf)*

▶ **turf over** VT *sep* **a** *garden* mit (Gras)soden *or* Fertigrasen bedecken **b** *(inf, = throw over)* rüberwerfen *(inf) (to sb* jdm)

turf accountant N *(Brit)* Buchmacher(in) *m(f)*

turfman ['tɜːfmən] N *(esp US)* Pferderennsportliebhaber *m*

turgid ['tɜːdʒɪd] ADJ *(= swollen)* (an)geschwollen; *(fig) style* schwülstig, überladen

turgidity [tɜː'dʒɪdɪtɪ] N *(lit)* Schwellung *f*; *(fig, of style)* Schwülstigkeit *f*; **the ~ of this writer's style** der schwülstige Stil dieses Schriftstellers

Turk [tɜːk] N Türke *m*, Türkin *f*

Turkey ['tɜːkɪ] N die Türkei

turkey ['tɜːkɪ] N **a** Truthahn *m*/-henne *f*; *(esp Cook)* Puter *m*, Pute *f*; **it would be like ~s voting for Christmas** *(esp Brit)* das wäre ja, als wenn die Gänse für Weihnachten stimmten **b** **to talk ~** *(dated US inf)* Tacheles reden *(inf)* **c** *(esp US inf: Film, Theat: = flop)* Reinfall *m (inf)*

turkey: **turkey buzzard** N Truthahngeier *m*; **turkey cock** N Truthahn *m*; *(esp Cook)* Puter *m*; **turkey shoot** N *(esp US fig)* Abschlachten *nt*

Turkish ['tɜːkɪʃ] ADJ türkisch; **she is ~** sie ist Türkin N *(Ling)* Türkisch *nt*

Turkish: **Turkish bath** N türkisches Bad; **Turkish coffee** N türkischer Kaffee; **Turkish delight** N Lokum *nt*; **Turkish towel** N Frotteehandtuch *nt*

Turkmenistan ['tɜːkmenɪsˌtɑːn] N Turkmenistan *nt*, Turkmenien *nt*

turmeric ['tɜːmərɪk] N Kurkuma *f*, Gelbwurz *f*

turmoil ['tɜːmɔɪl] N Aufruhr *m*; *(= confusion)* Durcheinander *nt*; **he was glad to escape from the ~ of politics** er war froh, dass er sich aus der Hektik der Politik zurückziehen konnte; **everything is in a ~** alles ist in Aufruhr; **her mind was in a ~** sie war völlig verwirrt; **her mind was in a ~ of indecision** sie wusste überhaupt nicht mehr, wie sie sich entscheiden sollte

turn [tɜːn]

1 NOUN	3 INTRANSITIVE VERB
2 TRANSITIVE VERB	4 PHRASAL VERBS

1 – NOUN

a [= movement] Drehung *f*; **six turns of the wheel** sechs Umdrehungen des Rades; **to give sth a turn** etw drehen; **give the handle another turn** dreh den Griff noch einmal herum; **done to a turn** *(Cook)* genau richtig

b [= change of direction] *in road* Kurve *f*; *(Sport)* Wende *f*; **watch out for a sharp turn in the road** pass auf, wo die Straße eine scharfe Kurve macht; **take the left-hand turn** biegen Sie links ab; **"no left turn"** „Linksabbiegen verboten"; **to make a turn to the left** *(driver, car)* nach links abbiegen; *(road also)* eine Linkskurve machen; **to make a turn to port** *(Naut)* nach Backbord abdrehen; **the Canadian swimmer made the better turn** der kanadische Schwimmer wendete besser; **he gets his horse to make a very tight turn** er wendet sein Pferd sehr eng

♦ **on the turn** *(= changing)* **the leaves are on the turn** die Blätter werden gelb; **the tide is on the turn** *(lit)* die Ebbe/Flut setzt ein, die See ist im Stau *(spec)*; **their fortunes may be on the turn** ihr Glück könnte sich wandeln; **the economy is on the turn** die Wirtschaft steht vor einem Umschwung

♦ **to take a turn (for)** **things took a turn for the better/the worse** die Dinge wendeten sich zum Guten/zum Schlechten; **the patient took a turn for the worse/the better** das Befinden des Patienten wendete sich zum Schlechteren/zum Besseren; **things took a new turn** die Dinge nahmen eine neue Wendung; **events took a tragic turn** die Dinge nahmen einen tragischen *or* verhängnisvollen Verlauf

♦ **turn of + noun** **at the turn of the century** um die Jahrhundertwende; **at the turn of the 18th century** an der *or* um die Wende des 18. Jahrhunderts; **the turn of the year** die Jahreswende, der Jahreswechsel; **turn of events** Lauf *m* der Ereignisse; **the latest turn of events** der neueste Lauf der Ereignisse, die neueste Wendung; **I'm very upset by the turn of events** ich bin über den Verlauf der Dinge sehr beunruhigt; **turn of phrase** Ausdrucksweise *f*; **turn of mind** Hang *m*, Neigung *f*; **to have a mathematical turn of mind** mathematisch begabt sein; **an optimistic/a serious turn of mind** eine optimistische/ernsthafte Einstellung; **an imaginative turn of mind** ein Hang *m* zur Kreativität; **to have a good turn of speed** *(car)* sehr schnell fahren; *(horse, athlete)* sehr schnell sein; **the turn of the tide** der Gezeitenwechsel; **the children were trapped on the island by the turn of the tide** die Kinder wurden durch das Einsetzen der Flut auf der Insel festgehalten; **the government just seems to be sitting back waiting for the turn of the tide** *(fig)* die Regierung scheint einfach nur dazusitzen und auf einen Umschwung *or* eine Wende zu warten

♦ **at every turn** *(fig)* **he has pledged to fight at every turn** er hat geschworen, mit Zähnen und Klauen *or* mit aller Macht zu kämpfen; **at nearly every turn, their efforts have been criticized** bei beinahe jedem Schritt wurden ihre Bemühungen kritisiert; **he was thwarted at every turn** ihm wurde auf Schritt und Tritt ein Strich durch die Rechnung gemacht

c [in game, queue, series] **it's your turn** du bist an der Reihe, du bist dran; **it's your turn to wash the dishes** du bist mit (dem) Abwaschen an der Reihe *or* dran; **now it's his turn to be jealous** jetzt ist er zur Abwechslung eifersüchtig; **whose turn is it?** wer ist an der Reihe?, wer ist dran?; **it's my turn next** ich komme als Nächste(r) an die Reihe *or* dran; **wait your turn** warten Sie, bis Sie an der Reihe sind; **to miss a turn** eine Runde aussetzen; **your turn will come** du kommst auch noch mal dran; **to take a turn at the wheel** (für eine Weile) das Steuer übernehmen; **to take turns to do sth** *or* **at doing sth** etw abwechselnd tun; **to take turns at the wheel** sich am Steuer *or* beim Fahren abwechseln; **to take it in turn(s) to do sth** etw abwechselnd tun; **take it in turns!** wechselt euch ab!

♦ **in turn** **he told a colleague, who in turn told a reporter** er sagte es einem Kollegen, der es wiederum einem Reporter erzählte; **that in turn will increase the budget deficit** dies wiederum erhöht das Defizit im Etat; **and then Anne Boleyn too, in (her) turn, …** und dann kam die Reihe auch an Anne Boleyn …; **they answered in turn** sie antworteten der Reihe nach; *(2 people only)* sie antworteten abwechselnd

♦ **by turn(s)** abwechselnd; **she was confident then depressed by turn(s)** sie war abwechselnd zuversichtlich und deprimiert

♦ **out of turn** außer der Reihe; **my secretary was speaking out of turn** es stand meiner Sekretärin nicht zu, sich darüber zu äußern; **sorry, have I spoken out of turn?** Entschuldigung, habe ich etwas Falsches gesagt?

♦ **turn and turn about** abwechselnd; **the children will just have to take turn and turn about on the swing** die Kinder werden eben abwechselnd schaukeln müssen

d [= service]

♦ **a good/bad turn** **to do sb a good/bad turn** jdm einen guten/schlechten Dienst erweisen; **a boy scout has to do a good turn every day** ein Pfadfinder muss jeden Tag eine gute Tat tun; **one good turn deserves another** *(Prov)* eine Hand wäscht die andere *(prov)*, hilfst du mir, so helf ich dir

e [= attack] *Brit inf* **he had one of his (funny) turns last night** er hatte letzte Nacht wieder einen Anfall

f [= shock, fright] **to give sb a turn** jdm Angst *or* einen Schrecken einjagen; **you/it gave me quite a turn** du hast/es hat mir einen schönen Schrecken eingejagt

g [Theat etc] Nummer *f*; **they got him to do a turn at the party** sie brachten ihn dazu, auf der Party etwas zum Besten zu geben

h [= purpose] **it will serve my turn** das ist für meine Zwecke gerade richtig; **we'll throw these old carpets away once they've served their turn** wir werfen diese alten Teppiche weg, wenn sie ausgedient haben

i [= walk, stroll] Runde *f*; **to take a turn in the park** eine Runde durch den Park machen

2 – TRANSITIVE VERB

a [= rotate] *knob, key, screw, steering wheel* drehen; **to turn the key in the lock** den Schlüssel im Schloss herumdrehen; **what turns the wheel?** wie wird das Rad angetrieben?; **he turned the wheel sharply** er riss das Steuer herum; **he turned his head toward(s) me** er wandte mir den Kopf zu; **he turned his back to the wall** er kehrte den Rücken zur Wand; **as soon as his back is turned** sobald er den Rücken kehrt; **to turn one's eyes toward(s) sb** jdn anblicken

b [fig uses] **the sight of all that food quite turned my stomach** beim Anblick des vielen Essens drehte sich mir regelrecht der Magen um; **without turning a hair** ohne mit der Wimper zu zucken; **success has turned his head** der Erfolg ist ihm zu Kopf gestiegen; **she seems to have turned his head** sie scheint ihm den Kopf verdreht zu haben; **she can still turn a few heads** die Leute schauen sich immer noch nach ihr um; **to turn one's hand to sth** sich an etw *(dat)* versuchen; **she turned her hand to cooking** sie versuchte sich im Kochen; **he can turn his hand to anything** er kann alles, er ist sehr geschickt → **corner**

c [= turn over] *mattress, collar, hay* wenden; *soil* umgraben; *record* umdrehen; *page* umblättern

d [= change position of, turn round] *car, lorry* wenden; *chair, picture etc* umdrehen

e [= direct] **to turn one's thoughts/attention to sth** seine Gedanken/Aufmerksamkeit einer Sache *(dat)* zuwenden; **to turn one's steps homeward** seine Schritte heimwärts lenken *(liter, hum)*; **to turn a gun on sb** ein Gewehr auf jdn richten; **the police turned the hoses on the demonstrators** die Polizei richtete die Wasserwerfer auf die Demonstranten

f [= transform, make become] verwandeln *(in(to)* in *+acc)*; **the shock turned his hair white overnight** durch den Schock bekam er über Nacht weiße Haare; **his success turns me green with envy** sein Erfolg lässt mich vor Neid erblassen; **the smoke turned the walls black** der Rauch schwärzte die Wände; **to turn the lights down low** das Licht herunterdrehen; **this hot weather has turned the milk (sour)** bei dieser Hitze ist die Milch sauer geworden; **to turn a boat adrift** ein Boot losmachen und treiben lassen; **his goal turned the game** sein Tor gab dem Spiel eine andere Wendung; **to turn a profit** *(esp US)* einen Gewinn machen, einen Profit einfahren *(inf)*

♦ **to turn sth into … the play was turned into a film** das Stück wurde verfilmt; **to turn verse into prose** Lyrik in Prosa übertragen; **to turn English expressions into German** aus englischen Ausdrücken deutsche machen

♦ **to turn sb loose** jdn loslassen *or* laufen lassen

g [= deflect] abbringen; **measures to turn young people from criminal behaviour** Maßnahmen, um junge Leute or Jugendliche von kriminellem Verhalten abzubringen; **nothing will turn him from his purpose** nichts wird ihn von seinem Vorhaben ablenken *or* abbringen

h [= shape] *wood* drechseln; *metal, pot* drehen; **a well-turned sentence** ein gut formulierter Satz; **a well-turned leg** ein wohlgeformtes Bein

3 – INTRANSITIVE VERB

a [= rotate, move round] *key, screw, wheel* sich drehen; **the world turns on its axis** die Erde dreht sich um ihre Achse; **he turned to me and smiled** er drehte sich mir zu und lächelte; **this key won't turn** dieser Schlüssel lässt sich nicht drehen; **to turn upside down** umkippen; **his stomach turned at the sight** bei dem Anblick drehte sich ihm der Magen um → **tail N a, toss VI a, turtle**

b [= change direction] *to one side, person, car* abbiegen; *(plane, boat)* abdrehen; *(= turn around)* wenden; *(person, on the spot)* sich umdrehen; *(wind)* drehen; *(tide)* wechseln; **to turn and go back** umkehren; **to turn (to the) left** links abbiegen; **left turn!** *(Mil)* linksum!; **our luck turned** unser Glück wendete sich; **the game turned in the second half** das Spiel wendete sich in der zweiten Hälfte *or* Halbzeit

c [= go] **I don't know which way** *or* **where to turn for help/money** ich weiß nicht, an wen ich mich um Hilfe wenden kann/wen ich um Geld bitten kann; **I don't know which way to turn** ich weiß nicht, was ich machen soll; **to turn to sb** sich an jdn wenden; **our thoughts turn to those who …** wir gedenken derer, die …; **to turn to sth** sich einer Sache *(dat)* zuwenden; **turn to page 306** gehen *or* blättern Sie weiter bis Seite 306, schlagen Sie jetzt Seite 306 auf; **after her death, he turned to his books for comfort** nach ihrem Tod suchte er Trost bei seinen Büchern; **this job would make anyone turn to drink!** bei dieser Arbeit muss man ja zum Trinker werden!; **the conversation turned to the accident** das Gespräch kam auf den Unfall, man kam auf den Unfall zu sprechen

d [= change] *leaves* sich (ver)färben; *(milk)* sauer werden; *(meat)* schlecht werden; *(weather)* umschlagen; **to turn to stone** zu Stein werden; **his admiration turned to scorn** seine Bewunderung verwandelte sich in Verachtung

♦ **to turn into sth** sich in etw *(acc)* verwandeln; *(= develop into)* sich zu etw entwickeln; **their short stay turned into a three-month visit** aus ihrem Kurzaufenthalt wurde ein Aufenthalt von drei Monaten; **the prince turned into a frog** der Prinz verwandelte sich in einen Frosch; **the whole thing turned into a nightmare** die ganze Sache wurde zum Albtraum

e [= become] werden; **to turn traitor** zum Verräter werden; **Paul Crooks, an actor turned director, …** der Regisseur Paul Crooks, ein ehemaliger Schauspieler, …; **he began to turn awkward** er wurde unangenehm *or* ungemütlich; **to turn nasty/violent** unangenehm/gewalttätig werden; **to turn red** *(leaves etc)* sich rot färben; *(person: = blush)* rot werden; *(traffic lights)* auf Rot umspringen; **it has recently turned cold** es ist vor Kurzem kalt geworden; **he has just turned 18** er ist gerade 18 geworden; **it has turned 2 o'clock** es ist 2 Uhr vorbei

4 – PHRASAL VERBS

▶ **turn about** *(Brit)* **VI** *(person)* sich umdrehen; *(car, boat, driver etc)* wenden; **we had to turn about and go home** wir mussten umkehren (und nach Hause gehen) **VT** *sep car* wenden; **he turned himself about** er wandte sich um

▶ **turn against VI** *+prep obj* sich wenden gegen **VT** *sep +prep obj* **they turned him against his parents** sie brachten ihn gegen seine Eltern auf; **they turned his argument against him** sie verwendeten sein Argument gegen ihn

▶ **turn around VT** *sep* **a** = **turn about VT** **b** *(factory, docks) ship etc* abfertigen; *goods* fertigstellen **c** *argument* umdrehen; *game, fortune* wenden; *country, economy, company* aus der Krise führen; **she has turned my life around** sie hat mein Leben in Ordnung gebracht **VI** *+prep obj corner* biegen um **VI** = **turn about VI**; **the wheel turns around on its axis** das Rad dreht sich um seine Achse

▶ **turn aside VI** sich abwenden *(from* von) **VT** *sep* abwenden

▶ **turn away VI** sich abwenden **VT** *sep* **a** *(= move) head, eyes, gun* abwenden **b** *(= send away) person* wegschicken, abweisen; *business* zurückweisen, ablehnen

▶ **turn back VI** **a** *(traveller)* zurückgehen, umkehren; *(plane)* umkehren; *(= look back)* sich umdrehen; **we can't turn back now, there's no turning back now** *(fig)* jetzt gibt es kein Zurück mehr

b *(in book)* zurückblättern *(to* auf *+acc)*

VT *sep* **a** *(= fold) bedclothes* zurück- *or* aufschlagen; *corner* umknicken; *hem* umschlagen

b *(= send back) person* zurückschicken; **bad weather turned the plane back to Heathrow** schlechtes Wetter zwang das Flugzeug zur Rückkehr nach Heathrow; **they were turned back at the frontier** sie wurden an der Grenze zurückgewiesen

c *clock* zurückstellen; *(fig)* zurückdrehen; **to turn the clock back fifty years** *(fig)* die Uhr um fünfzig Jahre zurückdrehen

▶ **turn down VT** *sep* **a** *bedclothes* zurück- *or* aufschlagen; *collar, brim* herunterklappen; *corner of page* umknicken **b** *gas, heat* herunterdrehen, kleiner stellen; *volume, radio, television* leiser stellen; *lights* herunterdrehen **c** *(= refuse) candidate, novel, offer etc* ablehnen; *suitor* abweisen; *invitation* ablehnen, ausschlagen **d** *card* verdeckt hin- *or* ablegen **VI** *+prep obj* **he turned down a side street** er bog in eine Seitenstraße ab

▶ **turn in VI** **a** **her toes turn in when she walks** sie läuft nach innen, sie läuft über den großen Onkel *(inf)*

b *(= drive in)* **the car turned in at the top of the drive** das Auto bog in die Einfahrt ein

c *(inf: = go to bed)* sich hinhauen *(inf)*, in die Falle gehen *(inf)*

d to turn in on oneself sich in sich *(acc)* selbst zurückziehen

VT *sep* **a she turned in her toes as she walked** sie lief nach innen, sie lief über den großen Onkel *(inf)*; **to turn in the ends of sth** die Enden von etw umschlagen

b *(inf, to police)* **to turn sb in** jdn anzeigen *or* verpfeifen *(inf)*; **to turn oneself in** sich (der Polizei) stellen

c *(esp US inf: = give back) equipment* zurückgeben *or* -bringen; *weapons (to police)* abgeben *(to* bei)

d *(= exchange)* eintauschen *(for* gegen)

e *(Brit, inf)* **turn it in!** jetzt mach aber mal einen Punkt! *(inf)*

▶ **turn into** VTI *+prep obj* = **turn 2 f 3 d**

▶ **turn off VI** abbiegen *(for* nach, *prep obj* von)

VT *sep* **a** *light, radio* ausmachen, abschalten; *gas* abdrehen; *tap* zudrehen; *TV programme* abschalten; *water, electricity, engine, machine* abstellen **b** *(inf)* **to turn sb off** *(= disgust)* jdn anwidern; *(= put off)* jdm die Lust verderben *or* nehmen; **when they mentioned the price that turned me right off** als sie den Preis nannten, war für mich die Sache gegessen *(inf)*

▶ **turn on VI** *(Rad, TV)* **we turned on at 8 o'clock** wir haben um 8 Uhr eingeschaltet

VT *sep* **a** *gas, heat* anstellen, anmachen; *radio, television, the news* einschalten; *light* einschalten, anmachen; *tap, central heating* aufdrehen; *bath water* einlaufen lassen; *engine, machine* anstellen; **to turn on the charm** seinen (ganzen) Charme spielen lassen; **he can really turn on the charm** er kann wirklich sehr charmant sein

b *(sl: with drugs)* antörnen *(sl)*

c *(inf: = appeal to: music, novel etc)* **sth turns sb on** jd steht auf etw *(acc) (sl)*, jd findet etw spitze *(sl)*, jd fährt auf etw *(acc)* voll ab *(sl)*; **whatever turns you on** wenn du das gut findest *(inf)*; **he/it doesn't turn me on** er/das lässt mich kalt *(also sexually)*

d *(inf: sexually)* scharf machen *(inf)*, anmachen *(inf)*; **she really turns me on** auf sie kann ich voll abfahren *(inf)*; **you know how to turn me on** du kannst mich wirklich auf Touren bringen *(inf)*; **it turns me on when …** ich werde ganz scharf, wenn … *(inf)*

VI *+prep obj* **a** *(= turn against)* sich wenden gegen; *(= attack)* angreifen

b *(= depend on)* abhängen von, ankommen auf *(+acc)*

▶ **turn out VI** **a** *(= appear, attend)* erscheinen, kommen

b *(firemen, police)* ausrücken; *(doctor)* einen Krankenbesuch machen

c *(= point)* **his feet turn out** er läuft nach außen

d the car turned out of the drive das Auto bog aus der Einfahrt

e *(= transpire)* sich herausstellen; **he turned out to be the murderer** es stellte sich heraus, dass er der Mörder war

f *(= develop, progress)* sich entwickeln, sich machen *(inf)*; **how did it turn out?** *(= what happened?)* was ist daraus geworden?; *(cake etc)* wie ist er *etc* geworden?; **it all depends how things turn out** es kommt darauf an, wie sich die Dinge ergeben; **as it turned out** wie sich herausstellte; **everything will turn out all right** es wird sich schon alles ergeben; **it turned out nice in the afternoon** *(Brit)* am Nachmittag wurde es noch schön

VT *sep* **a** *light* ausmachen; *gas* abstellen

b he turns his feet out er läuft nach außen

c *(= produce)* produzieren; *novel etc* schreiben; **the college turns out good teachers** das College bringt gute Lehrer hervor

d *(= expel)* vertreiben *(of* aus), hinauswerfen *(inf) (of* aus); *tenant* kündigen *(+dat)*, auf die Straße setzen *(inf)*; **he was turned out of his job** er verlor seinen Arbeitsplatz

e (Cook: = tip out) cake stürzen; **he turned the photos out of the box** er kippte die Fotos aus der Schachtel
f (= empty) pockets (aus)leeren
g (= clean) room gründlich sauber machen
h guard antreten lassen
i (usu pass: = dress) **well turned-out** gut gekleidet or ausstaffiert; troops tadellos, geschniegelt und gestriegelt (inf)

▶ **turn over** VI **a** (person) sich umdrehen; (car, plane etc) sich überschlagen; (boat) umkippen, kentern; (stomach) sich umdrehen; **he turned over on(to) his back/stomach** er drehte sich auf den Rücken/Bauch
b **please turn over** (with pages) bitte wenden
c (Aut, engine) laufen; **with the engine turning over** mit laufendem Motor
d (TV, Rad) umschalten (to auf +acc)
VT sep **a** umdrehen; patient wenden; tape, card umdrehen, wenden; (= turn upside down) umkippen; page umblättern; soil umgraben; mattress, steak wenden; **he turned the car over** er überschlug sich (mit dem Auto); **the police turned the whole house over** (= searched) die Polizei durchsuchte das ganze Haus; **this doesn't make sense, I must have turned over two pages** das ergibt keinen Sinn, ich muss eine Seite überschlagen haben; **to turn an idea over in one's mind** eine Idee überdenken, sich (dat) eine Idee durch den Kopf gehen lassen → **leaf N a**
b (= hand over) übergeben (to dat)
c (Comm) goods umsetzen; **to turn over £500 a week** einen Umsatz von £ 500 in der Woche haben; **how much do you turn over per week?** welchen Umsatz haben Sie pro Woche?
d (Aut) engine laufen lassen

▶ **turn round** (esp Brit) VI **a** (= face other way) sich umdrehen; (= go back) umkehren; **to turn round and go back** umkehren; **to turn round and go back to camp** ins Lager zurückkehren; **he just turned round and hit him** er drehte sich einfach um und schlug ihn
b (inf) **one day she'll just turn round and leave you** eines Tages wird sie dich ganz einfach verlassen; **you can't just turn round and refuse** du kannst dich doch nicht einfach weigern!
VI +prep obj **we turned round the corner** wir bogen um die Ecke; **the earth turns round the sun** die Erde dreht sich um die Sonne
VT sep **a** head drehen; box umdrehen; **turn the picture round the other way** dreh das Bild andersherum
b (= process) job etc bearbeiten
c (factory, docks etc) ship abfertigen; goods fertigstellen
d = **turn around VT c**

▶ **turn to** VI (= get busy) sich an die Arbeit machen VI +prep obj **a** **to turn to sb/sth** → **turn 3 c** **b** (= get busy) **after a short rest, they turned to their work again** nach einer kurzen Pause machten sie sich wieder an die Arbeit

▶ **turn up** VI **a** (= arrive) erscheinen, auftauchen (inf); **I was afraid you wouldn't turn up** ich hatte Angst, du würdest nicht kommen; **two years later he turned up in London** zwei Jahre später tauchte er in London auf (inf); **the queen hasn't turned up yet** (Cards) die Dame ist noch im Spiel
b (= be found) sich (an)finden, (wieder)auftauchen (inf); (esp smaller things) zum Vorschein kommen
c (= happen) **something is sure to turn up** irgendetwas passiert schon; **things have a habit of turning up** irgendwie findet sich alles; **it's amazing the way things turn up** es ist manchmal erstaunlich, wie sich die Dinge finden
d (= point up) **his nose turns up, he has a turned-up nose** er hat eine Himmelfahrts- (inf) or Stupsnase; **to turn up at the ends** sich an den Enden hochbiegen
VT sep **a** (= fold) collar hochklappen; sleeve aufrollen, aufkrempeln (inf); hem umnähen; **to turn up one's nose at sth** (fig) die Nase über etw (acc) rümpfen
b heat, gas aufdrehen, höherdrehen; radio lauter drehen; volume aufdrehen; light heller machen; pressure verstärken, erhöhen
c (= find) finden, entdecken; **to turn up some information** Informationen auftreiben, an Informationen kommen
d soil umpflügen
e (Brit, inf) **turn it up!** Mensch, hör auf damit! (inf)

turnable [ˈtɜːnəbl] ADJ drehbar

turnaround [ˈtɜːnəraʊnd], **turnround** [ˈtɜːnraʊnd] N **a** (also **turnabout**: in position, fig: in opinion etc) Kehrtwendung f; **she has done a complete ~ on fiscal policy** sie hat in der Finanzpolitik eine totale Kehrtwendung gemacht or vollführt **b** (also **turnaround time**) Bearbeitungszeit f; (= production time) Fertigstellungszeit f **c** (of situation, company) Umschwung m, Wende f **d** (of ship, aircraft) Abfertigung f

turncoat [ˈtɜːnkəʊt] N Abtrünnige(r) mf, Überläufer(in) m(f)

turner [ˈtɜːnəʳ] N (of metal) Dreher(in) m(f); (of wood) Drechsler(in) m(f)

turning [ˈtɜːnɪŋ] N **a** (in road) Abzweigung f; **take the second ~ on the left** nimm die zweite Abfahrt links; **it's a long road that has no ~** (prov) nichts dauert ewig **b** (Tech, of metal) Drehen nt; (of wood) Drechseln nt

turning: **turning circle** N (Aut) Wendekreis m; **turning lane** N (Mot) Abbiegespur f; **turning lathe** N Drehbank f; **turning point** N Wendepunkt m

turnip [ˈtɜːnɪp] N Rübe f; (= swede) Steckrübe f; (hum inf, = pocket watch) Zwiebel f (hum inf)

turn: **turnkey** N (old) Kerkermeister m (old), Gefängniswärter(in) m(f); **turnkey project** N schlüsselfertiges Projekt; **turn-off** N **a** Abzweigung f; (on motorway) Abfahrt f, Ausfahrt f; **the Birmingham ~** die Abzweigung nach Birmingham, die Abfahrt or Ausfahrt Birmingham **b** (inf) **it was a real ~** das hat einem die Lust verdorben; **hairy armpits are the ultimate ~ for me** bei Haaren unter den Achseln hörts bei mir auf (inf); **turn-on** N (inf) **that's a real ~** das macht einen an (inf); **she finds him/his accent a real ~** sie fährt voll auf ihn/seinen Akzent ab (inf)

turnout [ˈtɜːnaʊt] N **a** (= attendance) Teilnahme f, Beteiligung f; **in spite of the rain there was a good ~** (for a match etc) trotz des Regens war das Spiel gut besucht; (in election) trotz des Regens war die Wahlbeteiligung gut or hoch; **there was a big ~ of friends to meet us at the station** eine Menge Freunde waren gekommen, um uns am Bahnhof zu begrüßen **b** (= clean-out) **she gave the room a thorough ~** sie machte den Raum gründlich sauber **c** (Comm: = output) Produktion f **d** (= dress) Aufmachung f **e** (US) (in town) Parkbucht f; (in country) Parkplatz m; (big) Rastplatz m

turnover [ˈtɜːnəʊvəʳ] N (= total business) Umsatz m; (Comm, Fin: of capital) Umlauf m; (Comm, of stock) (Lager)umschlag m; (of staff) Personalwechsel m, Fluktuation f

turnover tax N Umsatzsteuer f

turn: **turnpike** N (Brit Hist) Mautschranke f; (US) gebührenpflichtige Autobahn; **turnround** N = **turnaround**; **turnscrew** N Schraubendreher m or -zieher m; **turn signal** N (US Aut) Fahrtrichtungsanzeiger m; **turnstile** N Drehkreuz nt; **turntable** N Drehscheibe f; (on record player) Plattenteller m; **turntable ladder** N Drehleiter f; **turn-up** N (Brit) **a** (on trousers) Aufschlag m **b** (inf: = event) **that was a ~ for the books** das war eine (echte) Überraschung, das war (vielleicht) ein Ding (inf)

turpentine [ˈtɜːpəntaɪn] N Terpentin(öl) nt; **~ substitute** Terpentin(öl)ersatz m

turpitude [ˈtɜːpɪtjuːd] N Verderbtheit f

turps [tɜːps] N sing (Brit inf) abbr of **turpentine**

turquoise [ˈtɜːkwɔɪz] N **a** (= gem) Türkis m **b** (= colour) Türkis nt ADJ türkis(farben); **~ blue/green** türkisblau/-grün; **~ jewellery** (Brit) or **jewelry** (US) Türkisschmuck m

turret [ˈtʌrɪt] N (Archit) Mauer- or Eckturm m; (on tank) Turm m; (on ship) Gefechtsturm m

turreted [ˈtʌrɪtɪd] ADJ **a ~ castle** ein Schloss mit Mauer- or Ecktürmen

turret gun N Turmgeschütz nt

turtle [ˈtɜːtl] N (Wasser)schildkröte f; (US also) (Land)schildkröte f; **to turn ~** kentern

turtle: **turtledove** N (lit, fig inf) Turteltaube f; **turtleneck (pullover)** N Pullover m mit Stehkragen

turves [tɜːvz] PL of **turf**

Tuscan [ˈtʌskən] ADJ toskanisch N **a** Toskaner(in) m(f) **b** (Ling) Toskanisch nt

Tuscany [ˈtʌskənɪ] N die Toskana

tush [tʊʃ], **tushie, tushy** [tʊʃɪ] N (US sl) Arsch m (inf), Hintern m

tusk [tʌsk] N (of elephant) Stoßzahn m; (of walrus) Eckzahn m; (of boar) Hauer m

tusker [ˈtʌskəʳ] N (= elephant) Elefant m mit ausgebildeten Stoßzähnen; (= boar) Keiler m

tussle [ˈtʌsl] N (lit, fig) Gerangel nt VI sich rangeln (with sb for sth mit jdm um etw)

tussock [ˈtʌsək] N (Gras)büschel nt

tussock grass N Rispengras nt

tut [tʌt] INTERJ, VTI → **tut-tut**

tutelage [ˈtjuːtɪlɪdʒ] N (form) **a** (= teaching) Führung f, Anleitung f; **the students made good progress under his able ~** in seinem guten Unterricht machten die Schüler große Fortschritte **b** (= guardianship) Vormundschaft f

tutelary [ˈtjuːtɪlərɪ] ADJ (form, of guardian) vormundschaftlich; **~ deity** Schutzgott m, Schutzgöttin f

tutor [ˈtjuːtəʳ] N **a** (= private teacher) Privat- or Hauslehrer(in) m(f) **b** (Brit Univ) Tutor(in) m(f) VT **a** (as private teacher) privat unterrichten; (= give extra lessons to) Nachhilfe(unterricht) geben (+dat); **to ~ sb in Latin** jdm Privatunterricht/Nachhilfe in Latein geben **b** (liter, = discipline) emotions beherrschen

tutorial [tjuːˈtɔːrɪəl] N **a** (Brit Univ) Kolloquium nt **b** (Comput) Lernprogramm nt ADJ Tutoren-; **the ~ system** das Tutorensystem; **the ~ staff** die Tutoren pl; **~ group** Seminargruppe f; **~ work** Arbeit f im Seminar

tutorship [ˈtjuːtəʃɪp] N (private) Privat- or Hauslehrerstelle f; (Univ) Amt nt or Stelle f eines Tutors

tutti-frutti [ˈtuːtɪˈfruːtɪ] N (= ice cream) Tuttifrutti nt

tut-tut [ˈtʌtˈtʌt] INTERJ (in disapproval) na, na, aber, aber VI **she ~ted in disapproval** na, na! or aber, aber!, sagte sie missbilligend VT idea missbilligen

tutu [ˈtuːtuː] N Tutu nt, Ballettröckchen nt

tu-whit tu-whoo [tʊˈwɪttʊˈwuː] INTERJ (sch)uhu

tux [tʌks] (inf), **tuxedo** [tʌkˈsiːdəʊ] N (esp US) Smoking m

TV [tiːˈviː] N (inf) abbr of **television** Fernsehen nt; (= set) Fernseher m (inf); **on TV** im Fernsehen; **a TV programme** (Brit) or **program** (US) eine Fernsehsendung; **a TV personality** ein Fernsehstar m → also **television**

TVA abbr of **Tennessee Valley Authority**

TV [tiːˈviː]: **TV dinner** N Fertigmahlzeit f; **TV guide** N (esp US) Fernsehzeitung f; (Web-based) Fernsehprogramm-Website f; **TV listings** PL Fernsehprogramm m; (= magazine) Fernsehprogrammzeitschrift f

twaddle [ˈtwɒdl] N (inf) Geschwätz nt, dummes Zeug (inf); **to talk ~** dummes Zeug reden (inf)

twain [tweɪn] N (old) zwei; **in ~** entzwei (old); **and ne'er the ~ shall meet** sie werden nie zueinanderfinden

twang [twæŋ] N **a** (of wire, guitar string) Doing nt; (of rubber band, bowstring) scharfer Ton **b** (of voice) Näseln nt, näselnder Tonfall; **to speak**

with a ~ mit näselndem Tonfall *or* mit einem Näseln sprechen VT zupfen; *guitar, banjo also* klimpern auf *(+dat)* VI **a** *(guitar, string etc)* einen scharfen Ton von sich geben; *(rubber band)* pitschen *(inf)* **b to ~ on a guitar** *etc* auf einer Gitarre *etc* herumklimpern

twangy ['twæŋɪ] ADJ *(+er) voice* näselnd; *guitar etc* klimpernd

'twas [twɒz] *(old) contr of* **it was**

twat [twæt] N **a** *(vulg: = vagina)* Fotze *f (vulg)*, Möse *f (vulg)* **b** *(inf: = fool)* Blödmann *m (inf)*

tweak [twi:k] VT **a** *(= pull gently)* kneifen; **she ~ed (back) the curtain** sie schob den Vorhang etwas zur Seite; **to ~ sb's ear** jdn am Ohr ziehen; **to ~ sb's nose** *(lit)* jdn an der Nase ziehen; *(fig)* jdm eins auswischen *(inf)*; **to ~ sth off/out** etw abkneifen/auszupfen
b *(inf) engine* hochfrisieren *(inf)*
c *(inf: = alter slightly) system, rules, schedule, text* herumdoktern an *(+dat) (inf)*
N **a** *(= gentle pull)* **to give sth a ~** an etw *(dat)* (herum)zupfen; **to give sb's ear/nose a ~** jdn am Ohr/an der Nase ziehen
b *(inf: = slight alteration: to system, rules, schedule, text)* kleine Änderung; **to give sth a ~** *(system, rules, schedule, text)* an etw *(dat)* herumdoktern *(inf)*

twee [twi:] ADJ *(+er) (Brit inf)* niedlich, putzig *(inf)*; *manner* geziert; *clothes* niedlich; *description* verniedlichend; *expression* gekünstelt; *words* zuckersüß; **it sounds ~** es klingt geziert

tweed [twi:d] N **a** *(= cloth)* Tweed *m* **b tweeds** PL *(= clothes)* Tweedkleidung *f*, Tweedsachen *pl*; **his old ~s** sein alter Tweedanzug, seine alten Tweedsachen ADJ Tweed-; **~ jacket** Tweedjacke *f*

Tweedledum [,twi:dl'dʌm] N **the twins were as alike as ~ and Tweedledee** die Zwillinge glichen sich wie ein Ei dem anderen

tweedy ['twi:dɪ] ADJ *(+er) material* tweedartig; *clothes* aus Tweed; *(fig) person, shop* konservativ; **~ jacket** Tweedjacke *f*

'tween [twi:n] *(poet)* ADV, PREP = **between**

tweeny ['twi:nɪ] N *(old)* Hausmagd *f*

tweet [twi:t] N *(of birds)* Ziepen *nt*, Piepsen *nt no pl*; **~ ~** ziep, ziep, pieps, pieps VI ziepen, piepsen

tweeter ['twi:tə'] N Hochtonlautsprecher *m*

tweezers ['twi:zəz] PL *(also* **pair of tweezers***)* Pinzette *f*

twelfth [twelfθ] ADJ zwölfte(r, s); **a ~ part** ein Zwölftel *nt* N *(in series)* Zwölfte(r, s); *(= fraction)* Zwölftel *nt* → *also* **sixth**

twelfth man N *(Brit: Cricket)* Ersatzspieler *m*

Twelfth Night N Dreikönige; *(= evening)* Dreikönigsabend *m*

twelve [twelv] ADJ zwölf; **~ noon** zwölf Uhr (mittags) N Zwölf *f* → *also* **six**

twelve: **twelve-mile limit** [twelvmaɪl'lɪmɪt] N Zwölfmeilenzone *f*; **twelvemonth** N *(old)* zwölf Monate *pl*, ein Jahr *nt*; **twelve-tone** ADJ *(Mus)* Zwölfton-; **~ music** Zwölftonmusik *f*

twentieth ['twentɪɪθ] ADJ zwanzigste(r, s); **a ~ part** ein Zwanzigstel *nt* N *(in series)* Zwanzigste(r, s); *(= fraction)* Zwanzigstel *nt* → *also* **sixth**

twenty ['twentɪ] ADJ zwanzig N Zwanzig *f*; *(= banknote)* Zwanziger *m* → *also* **sixty**

twenty: **twentyfold** ['twentɪfəʊld] ADJ, ADV *(old)* zwanzigfach; **twenty-four seven** [,twentɪfɔ:'sevn] N *Geschäft, das sieben Tage die Woche und 24 Stunden am Tag geöffnet hat* ADJ rund um die Uhr; **~ service** Service, der rund um die Uhr zur Verfügung steht; **twenty-twenty vision** [,twentɪtwentɪ'vɪʒən] N 100-prozentige Sehschärfe

'twere [twɜ:'] *(old) contr of* **it were**

twerp [twɜ:p] N *(inf)* Einfaltspinsel *m (inf)*, Hohlkopf *m (inf)*

twice [twaɪs] ADV zweimal; **~ as much/many** doppelt *or* zweimal so viel/so viele; **~ as much bread** doppelt so viel *or* zweimal so viel Brot, die doppelte Menge Brot; **~ as long as ...** doppelt *or* zweimal so lange wie ...; **at ~ the speed of sound** mit doppelter Schallgeschwindigkeit; **she is ~ your age** sie ist doppelt so alt wie du; **~ 2 is 4** zweimal 2 ist 4; **~ weekly, ~ a week** zweimal wöchentlich, zweimal pro Woche; **a ~-weekly newspaper** eine Zeitung, die zweimal wöchentlich erscheint; **he didn't need to be asked ~** da brauchte man ihn nicht zweimal zu fragen; **he's ~ the man John is** er steckt John in die Tasche *(inf)*; **he's ~ the man he was** er ist ein ganz anderer Mensch geworden; **I'd think ~ before trusting him with it** ihm würde ich das nicht so ohne Weiteres anvertrauen

twiddle ['twɪdl] VT herumdrehen an *(+dat)*; **she ~d the pencil in her fingers** ihre Finger spielten mit dem Bleistift; **to ~ one's thumbs** *(lit, fig)* Däumchen drehen VI **to ~ with a knob** an einem Knopf herumdrehen N **he gave the knob a ~** er drehte den Knopf herum

twig[1] [twɪg] N *(= thin branch)* Zweig *m*

twig[2] *(Brit inf)* VT *(= realize)* mitkriegen *(inf)*, mitbekommen; **when she saw his face, she ~ged his secret** als sie sein Gesicht sah, erriet sie sein Geheimnis *(inf)*; **he's ~ged it** er hats kapiert *(inf)* VI schalten *(inf)*, es mitkriegen *(inf) or* mitbekommen

twiggy ['twɪgɪ] ADJ **a** *tree etc* voller Zweige **b** *(= very slim) girl (= gertenschlank)*

twilight ['twaɪlaɪt] N *(= time)* Dämmerung *f*; *(= semi-darkness also)* Dämmer- *or* Zwielicht *nt*; **at ~** in der Dämmerung; **the ~ of the gods** die Götterdämmerung; **the ~ of western civilization** der Herbst der westlichen Zivilisation *(liter)*; **the ~ of his life, his ~ years** sein Lebensabend *m*

twilight: **twilight sleep** N *(Med)* Dämmerschlaf *m*; **twilight world** N Welt *f* des Zwielichts; **twilight zone** N Zwielicht *nt*

twill [twɪl] N *(Tex)* Köper *m*

'twill [twɪl] *(old) contr of* **it will**

twin [twɪn] N Zwilling *m*; *(of vase, object)* Gegenstück *nt*, Pendant *nt*; **her ~** *(= sister)* ihre Zwillingsschwester; *(= brother)* ihr Zwillingsbruder *m*; **where's the ~ of this sock?** wo ist die andere Socke?; **the Twins** *(Astrol)* die Zwillinge *pl* ADJ *attr* **a** Zwillings-; *(fig)* genau gleiche(r, s); **~ boys/girls** Zwillingsjungen *pl*/-mädchen *pl*; **~ birth** Zwillingsgeburt *f*; **~ souls** *(fig)* verwandte Seelen *pl* **b** *(= double)* **~ towers** Zwillingstürme *pl*; **~ peaks** Doppelgipfel *pl* VT *(Brit) town* verschwistern; **Oxford was ~ned with Bonn** Oxford und Bonn wurden zu/waren Partnerstädten

twin: **twin-bedded** [,twɪn'bedɪd] ADJ Zweibett-; **~ room** Zweibettzimmer *nt*; **twin beds** PL zwei (gleiche) Einzelbetten *pl*; **twin bill** N *(US inf)* **a** *(Sport)* zwei hintereinander gesendete Spiele *pl* **b** *(Film)* Programm *nt* mit zwei Hauptfilmen; **twin brother** N Zwillingsbruder *m*; **twin carburettors** PL Doppelvergaser *m*; **twin-cylinder engine** N Zweizylinder(-motor) *m*

twine [twaɪn] N Schnur *f*, Bindfaden *m* VT winden; **to ~ one's arms (a)round sb** seine Arme um jdn schlingen VI *(around* um *+acc)* sich winden; *(plants also)* sich ranken

twin-engined [,twɪn'endʒɪnd] ADJ zweimotorig

twin engines PL zwei Motoren *pl*

twinge [twɪndʒ] N *(of pain)* Zucken *nt*, leichtes Stechen; **a ~ of pain** ein zuckender Schmerz; **my back still gives me the occasional ~** ich spüre gelegentlich noch ein Stechen im Rücken; **a ~ of rheumatism** rheumatisches Reißen; **a ~ of regret** leichtes Bedauern; **a ~ of conscience/remorse** Gewissensbisse *pl*

twining ['twaɪnɪŋ] ADJ *(Bot)* rankend, Kletter-; **~ plant** Kletterpflanze *f*

twinkle ['twɪŋkl] VI *(stars)* funkeln, flimmern, glitzern; *(eyes)* blitzen, funkeln; **her feet ~d across the stage** sie bewegte sich leichtfüßig über die Bühne N **a** *(of stars, lights)* Funkeln *nt*, Flimmern *nt*, Glitzern *nt*; **there was a (mischievous) ~ in her eye** man sah den Schalk in ihren Augen; **no, he said with a ~ (in his eye)** nein, sagte er augenzwinkernd **b** *(= instant)* **in a ~** sofort, im Handumdrehen

twinkletoes ['twɪŋkl,təʊz] N **here comes ~!** *(iro)* da kommt ja unser Trampeltier! *(inf)*

twinkling ['twɪŋklɪŋ] N **in the ~ of an eye** im Nu, im Handumdrehen

twinning ['twɪnɪŋ] N **a** *(Brit: of two towns)* Städtepartnerschaft *f* **b** *(= pregnancy)* Zwillingsschwangerschaft *f*

twin: **twin propellors** PL Doppelschiffsschraube *f*; **twinset** N *(Brit)* Twinset *nt*; **twin sister** N Zwillingsschwester *f*; **twin-tone horn** N Zweiklanghorn *nt*; **twin town** N *(Brit)* Partnerstadt *f*; **twin-track** ADJ *approach, process, strategy* zweigleisig; **twin-tub (washing machine)** N Waschmaschine *f* mit getrennter Schleuder

twirl [twɜ:l] VT (herum)wirbeln; *skirt* herumwirbeln; *glass* drehen; *moustache* zwirbeln; **he ~ed his partner (a)round the dance floor** er wirbelte seine Partnerin übers Parkett VI wirbeln; **the skater ~ed (a)round on the ice** der Eiskunstläufer wirbelte über das Eis N Wirbel *m*; *(in dance)* Drehung *f*; *(of moustache)* hoch stehende *or* hoch gezwirbelte Spitze; *(in writing)* Schnörkel *m*; **to give a knob a ~** einen Knopf herumdrehen; **he gave his partner a ~** er wirbelte seine Partnerin herum; **give us a ~** dreh dich doch mal

twirp [twɜ:p] N *(inf)* = **twerp**

twist [twɪst] N **a** *(= action)* **to give sth a ~** etw (herum)drehen; **to give sb's arm a ~** jdm den Arm verdrehen *or* umdrehen; **to give one's ankle a ~** sich *(dat)* den Fuß vertreten; **with a quick ~ of the hand** mit einer schnellen Handbewegung
b *(= bend)* Kurve *f*, Biegung *f*; *(fig: in story etc)* Wendung *f*; **the road is full of ~s and turns** die Straße hat viele Biegungen und Windungen; **by** *or* **in a cruel ~ of fate** durch eine grausame Laune des Schicksals
c *(= coiled shape)* **salt in little ~s of paper** in kleine Papierstückchen eingewickeltes Salz; **~s of thread** Garnknäuel *nt*; **a ~ of French bread** ein französisches Weißbrot *(in Zopfform)*
d *(= type of yarn)* Twist *m*, Stopfgarn *nt*
e *(Brit inf)* **to be/go round the ~** verrückt sein/werden; **it's/she's driving me round the ~!** das/sie macht mich wahnsinnig!
f *(= dance)* Twist *m*; **to do the ~** Twist tanzen, twisten
g *(on ball)* Drall *m*; *(esp Billiards)* Effet *m*; **to give a ~ to** *or* **put a ~ on a ball** einem Ball einen Drall geben
VT **a** *(= wind, turn)* drehen; *(= coil)* wickeln *(into* zu *+dat)*; **to ~ threads** *etc* **together** Fäden *etc* zusammendrehen *or* verflechten; **to ~ pieces of string into a rope** Bindfäden zu einem Seil drehen; **to ~ flowers into a garland** Blumen zu einer Girlande binden; **she ~ed her hair into a bun** sie drehte sich *(dat)* die Haare zu einem Knoten; **to ~ the top off a jar** den Deckel von einem Glas abdrehen; **to ~ sth (a)round sth** etw um etw *(acc)* wickeln → **finger**
b *(= bend, distort) rod, key* verbiegen; *part of body* verdrehen; *(fig) meaning, words, truth* verdrehen, entstellen; **to ~ sth out of shape** etw verbiegen; **to ~ sb's arm** *(lit)* jdm den Arm verdrehen; **she had to ~ my arm to get me to do it** *(fig)* sie musste mich sehr überreden, bis ich es tat; **to ~ one's ankle** sich *(dat)* den Fuß vertreten; **his face was ~ed with pain** sein Gesicht war verzerrt vor Schmerz *or* schmerzverzerrt
c *ball* einen Drall geben *(+dat)*; **she somehow managed to ~ the red around the black** sie hat es irgendwie geschafft, die rote an der schwarzen Kugel vorbeizumanövrieren
VI **a** *(= wind)* sich drehen; *(smoke)* sich kringeln *or* ringeln; *(plant)* sich winden *or* ranken; *(= wriggle: road, river, person)* sich schlängeln *or* winden; **the kite strings have ~ed (a)round the pole** die Drachenschnüre haben sich um den Pfahl verwickelt

b (= dance) Twist tanzen, twisten
c (Cards) aufnehmen und ablegen

▶ **twist about** (Brit) or **around** VI sich (her)umdrehen; (road, river, = wind its way) sich dahinschlängeln; (= be twisty) gewunden sein; **he twisted around in pain** er wand or krümmte sich vor Schmerzen VT sep = **twist round VT**

▶ **twist off** VI **the top twists off** der Deckel lässt sich abschrauben or ist abschraubbar VT sep abdrehen; lid abschrauben; flower heads abknipsen

▶ **twist out** VI **to twist out of sb's grasp** sich jds Griff (dat) entwinden VT sep herausdrehen

▶ **twist round** (esp Brit) VI sich umdrehen; (road etc) eine Biegung machen VT sep head, chair herumdrehen; **she twisted her handkerchief round in her fingers** sie drehte ihr Taschentuch zwischen den Fingern

▶ **twist up** VI (rope etc) sich verdrehen; (smoke) in Kringeln hochsteigen; (person: with pain etc) sich winden or krümmen VT sep ropes, wires verwickeln

twisted ['twɪstɪd] ADJ a wires, rope (zusammen)gedreht; (= bent) verbogen; (= tangled) strap verdreht; **~-pair cable** verdrilltes Kabel b ankle verrenkt c (fig pej: = warped) mind, logic verdreht; **bitter and ~** verbittert und verwirrt d (inf: = dishonest) unredlich e (= disfigured) limbs verwachsen f (= sneering) face, smile verzerrt

twister ['twɪstəʳ] N a (Brit, pej, = person) Gauner(in) *m(f)*, Halunke *m* b (Brit, = question) harte Nuss *(inf)*; (= problem) harter Brocken *(inf)* c (US inf: = tornado) Wirbelsturm *m*, Tornado *m* d (= dancer) Twisttänzer(in) *m(f)*

twisty ['twɪstɪ] ADJ (+er) road kurvenreich, gewunden; story, film kompliziert

twit [twɪt] VT **to ~ sb (about sth)** jdn (mit or wegen etw) aufziehen or hochnehmen N (esp Brit inf: = person) Trottel *m (inf)*

twitch [twɪtʃ] N a (= tic) Zucken *nt*; (= individual spasm) Zuckung *f*; **to give a ~** zucken b (= pull) Ruck *m* (of an *+dat*); **to give sth a ~** an etw *(dat)* rucken VI (face, muscles) zucken; **the cat's nose ~ed when I brought in the fish** die Katze schnupperte, als ich den Fisch hereinbrachte VT a tail, ears, nose, eyebrows zucken mit b (= pull) zupfen; **he ~ed the letter from her hands** er schnappte ihr den Brief aus den Händen

twitcher ['twɪtʃəʳ] N (Brit inf) Vogelliebhaber(in) *m(f)*, Vogelnarr *m*, Vogelnärrin *f (inf)*

twitch grass ['twɪtʃgrɑːs] N Quecke *f*

twitchy ['twɪtʃɪ] ADJ (inf) a (physically) person unruhig; legs zuckend b (= nervous, uneasy) person nervös; market unruhig; **to be ~ about sth** über etw *(acc)* beunruhigt sein c car wack(e)lig *(inf)*

Twitter® ['twɪtəʳ] N (Internet) Twitter® *no art*

twitter ['twɪtəʳ] VI (lit, fig) zwitschern VT zwitschern N a (of birds) Zwitschern *nt*, Gezwitscher *nt* b (inf) **to be all of a ~** ganz aufgeregt or aufgelöst sein

twittery ['twɪtərɪ] ADJ attr zwitschernd

twittish ['twɪtɪʃ] ADJ (Brit inf: = stupid) hirnlos *(inf)*

'twixt [twɪkst] PREP (old) = **betwixt**

two [tuː] ADJ zwei; **to break/cut sth in ~** etw in zwei Teile brechen/schneiden; **~ by ~, in ~s** zwei und zwei, zu zweit, zu zweien; **in ~s and threes** immer zwei oder drei (Leute) auf einmal; **~ minds with but a single thought** (prov) zwei Seelen - ein Gedanke; **to put ~ and ~ together** (fig) seine Schlüsse ziehen, zwei und zwei zusammenzählen; **to put ~ and ~ together and make five** einen Fehlschluss or einen falschen Schluss ziehen; **~'s company, three's a crowd** ein Dritter stört nur; **~ can play at that game** (inf) den Spieß kann man auch umdrehen → also **six**
N Zwei *f*; **just the ~ of us/them** nur wir beide/die beiden

two: **two-bit** ADJ (US inf) mies *(inf)*; **two-by-four** N (= wood) *Stück Holz mit den Maßen 2 x 4 Zoll* ADJ (esp US) (inf: = small) apartment winzig; (= petty) life, job nullachtfünfzehn *(inf)*

twoccing ['twɒkɪŋ] N (Brit inf) Autodiebstahl *m*

two: **two-chamber system** N Zweikammersystem *nt*; **two-cycle** ADJ (US) = **two-stroke**; **two-cylinder** ADJ Zweizylinder-; **~ engine** Zweizylindermotor *m*; **two-dimensional** ADJ zweidimensional; (fig: = superficial) performance flach; **two-door** ADJ zweitürig; **two-edged** ADJ a (lit) zweischneidig, doppelschneidig b (fig) zweideutig; argument zweischneidig; **a ~ sword** or **weapon** (fig) ein zweischneidiges Schwert; **two-faced** ADJ (lit) doppelgesichtig; (fig) falsch; **two-family house** N (US) Zweifamilienhaus *nt*; **two-fisted** ADJ a **a ~ boxer** ein Boxer, der mit beiden Fäusten gleich gut boxen kann b (dated US sl) knallhart; **two-fold** ADJ zweifach, doppelt; **a ~ increase** ein Anstieg um das Doppelte; **the advantages of this method are ~** diese Methode hat einen doppelten or zweifachen Vorteil ADV **to increase ~** um das Doppelte steigern; **two-four time** N (Mus) Zweivierteltakt *m*; **two-handed** ADJ grip, blow, catch beidhändig; **a ~ sword** ein Zweihänder *m*; **a ~ saw** eine Säge mit zwei Griffen; **a ~ backhand** *eine Rückhand, bei der der Schläger mit beiden Händen gehalten wird*; **a ~ game** ein Spiel *nt* für zwei Spieler ADV zweihändig; **she caught the ball ~** sie fing den Ball mit beiden Händen; **two-hander** [ˌtuːˈhændəʳ] N (Theat) Zweipersonenstück *nt*; **two-horse race** N (fig) *Wettstreit, bei dem nur zwei der Teilnehmer eine Chance haben zu gewinnen*; **two-income family** N Doppelverdiener *pl*; **two-legged** ADJ zweibeinig; **a ~ animal** ein Zweibeiner *m*; **two-man bobsleigh**, (US) **two-man bobsled** N (Sport) Zweierbob *m*; **two-part** ADJ a zweiteilig b (Mus) zweistimmig, für zwei Stimmen; **two-party system** N Zweiparteiensystem *nt*; **twopence** ['tʌpəns] N = **tuppence**; **two-pence piece** [ˌtuːpensˈpiːs] N Zweipencestück *nt*; **twopenny** ['tʌpənɪ] ADJ = **tuppenny**; **two-phase** ADJ (Elec) Zweiphasen-; **~ current** Zweiphasenstrom *m*; **two-piece** ADJ zweiteilig N (= suit) Zweiteiler *m*; (= swimming costume) zweiteiliger Badeanzug, Bikini *m*; **two-pin plug** N Stecker *m* mit zwei Kontakten; **two-ply** ADJ wool zweifädig; wood aus zwei Lagen or **Schichten bestehend**; tissue zweilagig; **~ sweater** aus zweifädiger Wolle gestrickter Pullover; **two-seater** ADJ zweisitzig N (= car, plane) Zweisitzer *m*; **twosome** N a (= people) Paar *nt*, Pärchen *nt*; **to go out in a ~** zu zweit ausgehen b (= game) **to have a ~ at golf** zu zweit Golf spielen; **two-star** ADJ Zweisterne-; **~ petrol** (Brit dated) Normalbenzin *nt*; **~ hotel** Zweisternehotel *nt*; **~ general** (US) Zweisternegeneral(in) *m(f)*; **two-step** N Twostepp *m*; **two-storey**, (US) **two-story** ADJ zweistöckig; **two-stroke** (Brit) ADJ Zweitakt-; **~ engine** Zweitaktmotor *m* N Zweitakter *m*; (= fuel) Zweitaktgemisch *nt*

two: **two-time** VT (inf) boyfriend, accomplice betrügen; **the crooks realized that he was two-timing them** die Ganoven merkten, dass er ein doppeltes Spiel spielte or trieb; **two-timer** N (inf) falscher Hund *(inf)*; **two-timing** ADJ (inf) falsch; **two-tone** ADJ (in colour) zweifarbig; (in sound) zweitönig

'twould [twʊd] (old) contr of **it would**

two: **two-up two-down** N (Brit inf) kleines Reihenhäuschen; **two-way** ADJ (= reciprocal) trade, exchange, relationship wechselseitig; **~ communications** (Telec) Sprechverkehr *m* in beide Richtungen; **~ fabric** von beiden Seiten zu tragender Stoff; **~ street** Straße *f* mit Gegenverkehr or mit Verkehr in beiden Richtungen; **~ traffic** Gegenverkehr *m*, Verkehr *m* in beiden Richtungen; **education is a ~ process** Erziehung ist ein wechselseitiger Prozess; **two-way adaptor** N Doppelstecker *m*; **two-way mirror** N Spion(spiegel) *m*; **two-way radio** N Funksprechgerät *nt*; **two-way switch** N Wechselschalter *m*; **two-wheeler (bike)** N Zweirad *nt*, Fahrrad *nt*

tycoon [taɪˈkuːn] N Magnat(in) *m(f)*; **business/oil ~** Industrie-/Ölmagnat(in) *m(f)*

tyke [taɪk] N a (= dog) Köter *m* b (inf: = child) Lausbub *m*

tympani PL = **timpani**

tympanic [tɪmˈpænɪk] ADJ (Anat) **~ bone** Mittelohrknochen *m*; **~ membrane** Trommelfell *nt*, Tympanum *nt (spec)*

tympanist ['tɪmpənɪst] N Pauker(in) *m(f)*

tympanum ['tɪmpənəm] N (Anat: = membrane) Trommelfell *nt*, Tympanum *nt (spec)*; (= middle ear) Mittelohr *nt*; (Archit) Tympanon *nt*

typal ['taɪpl] ADJ artspezifisch

type[1] [taɪp] N a (= kind) Art *f*; (of produce, plant) Sorte *f*, Art *f*; (esp of people: = character) Typ *m*, Typus *m*; **different ~s of aircraft** verschiedene Flugzeugtypen *pl*; **different ~s of roses** verschiedene Rosensorten or -arten *pl*; **what ~ of car is it?** was für ein Auto(typ) ist das?; **the very latest ~ of hi-fi** das allerneuste Hi-Fi-Gerät; **she has her own particular ~ of charm** sie hat ihren ganz besonderen Charme; **he has an English ~ of face** dem Gesicht nach könnte er Engländer sein; **Cheddar-~ cheese** eine Art Cheddar; **most of the characters are recognizable ~s** die meisten Charaktere lassen sich einem bestimmten Typ zuordnen; **they're totally different ~s of person** sie sind vom Typ her völlig verschieden, sie sind völlig verschiedene Typen; **a man of this ~** ein Mann dieser Art or dieses Schlages, diese Art or Sorte (von) Mann; **that ~ of behaviour** (Brit) or **behavior** (US) ein solches Benehmen; **it's not my ~ of film** diese Art Film gefällt mir nicht; **he's not my ~** er ist nicht mein Typ; **she's my ~ of girl** sie ist mein Typ; **he's not the ~ to hit a lady** er ist nicht der Typ or Mensch, der eine Frau schlägt
b (inf: = man) Typ *m*; **a strange ~** ein seltsamer Mensch, ein komischer Typ *(inf)*, eine Type *(inf)*
VT bestimmen

type[2] N (Typ) Type *f*; **large/small ~** große/kleine Schrift; **to set ~** setzen; **in ~** (= typed) maschinegeschrieben, getippt *(inf)*; (= set) gesetzt, gedruckt; **to set sth up in ~** etw setzen; **printed in italic ~** kursiv gedruckt VT tippen, (mit der Maschine) schreiben; **a badly ~d letter** ein schlecht geschriebener or getippter Brief VI Maschine schreiben, tippen *(inf)*

▶ **type in** VT SEP eintippen; (esp Comput) eingeben; (with typewriter) mit Schreibmaschine ausfüllen

▶ **type out** VT sep a letter etc schreiben, tippen *(inf)* b error ausixen

▶ **type up** VT sep auf der Maschine zusammenschreiben

type: **type area** N (Typ) Satzspiegel *m*; **typecast** VT irreg (Theat) (auf eine bestimmte Rolle) festlegen; **to be ~ as a villain** auf die Rolle des Schurken festgelegt werden/sein; **typeface** N Schrift *f*; **typeover mode** N (Comput) Überschreibmodus *m*; **typescript** N mit Maschine geschriebenes Manuskript, Typoskript *nt (geh)*; **to be in ~** mit Maschine geschrieben sein; **typeset** VT setzen; **typesetter** N (Schrift)setzer(in) *m(f)*; (= machine) Setzmaschine *f*; **typesetting** N Setzen *nt*, (Schrift)satz *m*; **new ~ methods** neue Satztechniken; **type size** N Schriftgrad *m*, Schriftgröße *f*

typewrite ['taɪpraɪt] irreg VI Maschine schreiben, tippen *(inf)* VT (mit der Maschine) schreiben, tippen *(inf)*

typewriter ['taɪpˌraɪtəʳ] N Schreibmaschine *f*

typewriter ribbon N Farbband *nt*

typewriting ['taɪpˌraɪtɪŋ] N Maschinenschreiben *nt*

typewritten ['taɪpˌrɪtn] ADJ maschinegeschrieben, getippt

typhoid ['taɪfɔɪd] N (*also* **typhoid fever**) Typhus *m*; ~ **injection** Impfung *f* gegen Typhus, Typhusimpfung *f*

typhoon [taɪ'fuːn] N Taifun *m*

typhus ['taɪfəs] N Fleckfieber *nt*, Flecktyphus *m*

typical ['tɪpɪkəl] ADJ typisch (*of* für); **a ~ English town** eine typisch englische Stadt; **that's ~ of him** das ist typisch für ihn; **isn't that ~!** ist das nicht wieder mal typisch!; ~ **male!** typisch Mann!

typically ['tɪpɪkəlɪ] ADV typisch; **~, he did nothing but complain about the food** bezeichnenderweise hat er sich ständig über das Essen beschwert; **~, he insisted on getting there early** er wollte natürlich unbedingt früh hingehen, typisch

typify ['tɪpɪfaɪ] VT bezeichnend sein für; **he typifies the reserved Englishman** er verkörpert (genau) den Typ des zurückhaltenden Engländers

typing ['taɪpɪŋ] N Tippen *nt* (*inf*); (*with typewriter*) Maschinenschreiben *nt*; **the noise of her ~ drove me mad** ihr Tippen machte mich wahnsinnig; **his ~ isn't very good** er kann nicht besonders gut tippen

typing: **typing error** N Tippfehler *m*; **typing pool** N Schreibzentrale *f*; **typing speed** N Schreibgeschwindigkeit *f*

typist ['taɪpɪst] N (*professional*) Schreibkraft *f*, Stenotypist(in) *m(f)*, Tippse *f* (*pej inf*); **he couldn't find a ~ for his thesis** er konnte niemanden finden, der ihm seine Doktorarbeit tippte

typo ['taɪpəʊ] N (*Typ inf*) Druckfehler *m*; (*on typewriter, computer*) Tippfehler *m*

typographer [taɪ'pɒgrəfə'] N Typograf(in) *m(f)*

typographic(al) [,taɪpə'græfɪk(əl)] ADJ typografisch; **typographical error** Druckfehler *m*

typography [taɪ'pɒgrəfɪ] N Typografie *f*; (*= subject also*) Buchdruckerkunst *f*

typological [,taɪpə'lɒdʒɪkəl] ADJ typologisch

typology [taɪ'pɒlədʒɪ] N Typologie *f*

tyrannic(al) ADJ, **tyrannically** ADV [tɪ'rænɪk(əl), tɪ'rænɪkəlɪ] tyrannisch

tyrannize ['tɪrənaɪz] VT (*lit, fig*) tyrannisieren

tyrannosaur [tɪ'rænəsɔː] N Tyrannosaurier *m*

tyrannosaurus (rex) [tɪ,rænə'sɔːrəs(reks)] N Tyrannosaurus rex *m*

tyrannous ['tɪrənəs] ADJ tyrannisch

tyranny ['tɪrənɪ] N (*lit, fig*) Tyrannei *f*, Tyrannenherrschaft *f*; **he ruled by ~** er führte eine Tyrannenherrschaft

tyrant ['taɪərənt] N (*lit, fig*) Tyrann(in) *m(f)*

tyre, (*US*) **tire** [taɪə'] N **a** (*Aut*) Reifen *m*; **a burst** (*Brit*) *or* **blown ~** ein geplatzter Reifen **b he has ~s** (*hum inf*) er hat Speckrollen am Bauch (*inf*)

tyre, (*US*) **tire**: **tyre gauge** N Reifendruckmesser *m*; **tyre lever** N Montiereisen *nt*; **tyre pressure** N Reifendruck *m*

tyro ['taɪərəʊ] N Anfänger(in) *m(f)*; **a ~ skier** *etc* ein Anfänger beim *or* im Skilaufen *etc*

Tyrol [tɪ'rəʊl] N **the ~** Tirol *nt*

Tyrolean ['tɪrəlɪən], **Tyrolese** [tɪrə'liːz] ADJ Tiroler; **~ hat** Tirolerhut *m* N Tiroler(in) *m(f)*

Tyrrhenian Sea [tɪ'riːnɪən'siː] N Tyrrhenisches Meer

tzar N = **tsar**

tzarina N = **tsarina**

tzarist ADJ, N = **tsarist**

tzatziki [t(s)æt'siːkɪ] N (*Cook*) Tsatsiki *nt or m*, Zaziki *nt or m*

tzetze (fly) N = **tsetse (fly)**

U

U, u [juː] N a U *nt*, u *nt* b (*Brit Film inf*) jugendfreier Film ADJ (*Brit*, = *upper class*) *charakteristisch für die Gewohnheiten, Sprechweise etc der Oberschicht*, vornehm

UAR *abbr of* **United Arab Republic**

UAW (*US*) *abbr of* **United Automobile Workers** *Gewerkschaft der Beschäftigten in der Kraftfahrzeugindustrie*

UB40 [juːbiːˈfɔːtɪ] N (*Brit*) a *Ausweis für Arbeitslose* b (= *unemployed person*) Arbeitslose(r) *mf*

U-bend [ˈjuːbend] N (*in pipe*) U-Bogen *m*; (*in road*) Haarnadelkurve *f*

ubiquitous [juːˈbɪkwɪtəs] ADJ allgegenwärtig; **sandstone is ~ in this district** Sandstein ist in dieser Gegend überall zu finden

ubiquity [juːˈbɪkwɪtɪ] N Allgegenwart *f*; (= *prevalence*) weite Verbreitung

U-boat [ˈjuːbəʊt] N U-Boot *nt*

UCAS [ˈjuːkæs] (*Brit*) *abbr of* **Universities and Colleges Admissions Service** ≈ ZVS *f*

UCCA [ˈʌkə] (*Brit dated*) *abbr of* **Universities Central Council on Admissions** ≈ ZVS *f*

UDA *abbr of* **Ulster Defence Association**

udder [ˈʌdəʳ] N Euter *nt*

UDF *abbr of* **Ulster Defence Force**

UDI *abbr of* **Unilateral Declaration of Independence**

UDP *abbr of* **Ulster Democratic Party**

UDR *abbr of* **Ulster Defence Regiment**

UEFA [juːˈeɪfə] *abbr of* **Union of European Football Associations** die UEFA

UFO [ˈjuːfəʊ] *abbr of* **unidentified flying object** Ufo *nt*, UFO *nt*

ufologist [juːˈfɒlədʒɪst] N Ufologe *m*, Ufologin *f*

ufology [juːˈfɒlədʒɪ] N Ufologie *f*

Uganda [juːˈgændə] N Uganda *nt*

Ugandan [jʊˈgændən] ADJ ugandisch; **he is ~** er ist Ugander N Ugander(in) *m(f)*

UGC (*Brit*) *abbr of* **University Grants Committee**

ugh [ɜːh] INTERJ i, igitt

Ugli (fruit)® [ˈʌglɪ(fruːt)] N *Kreuzung aus Grapefruit, Apfelsine und Mandarine*

uglify [ˈʌglɪfaɪ] VT hässlich machen, verunstalten

ugliness [ˈʌglɪnɪs] N Hässlichkeit *f*; (*of news*) Unerfreulichkeit *f*; (*of wound*) übler Zustand; (*of situation*) Ekelhaftigkeit *f*; (*of crime*) Gemeinheit *f*; (*of vice*) Hässlichkeit *f*, Garstigkeit *f*

ugly [ˈʌglɪ] ADJ (+*er*) a (= *not pretty*) hässlich; **as ~ as sin** hässlich wie die Sünde *or* Nacht b (= *unpleasant, nasty*) übel; *news, wound* schlimm, übel; *rumour, scenes, crime, clouds* hässlich; *crime* übel, gemein; *vice* hässlich, übel; *situation, sky* bedrohlich; **an ~ customer** ein übler Kunde; **to cut up** *or* **grow** *or* **turn ~** (*inf*) gemein *or* fies (*inf*) werden; **censorship is an ~ word these days** Zensur ist heutzutage ein hässliches Wort

ugly duckling N (*fig*) hässliches Entlein

UHF *abbr of* **ultra-high frequency** UHF

uh-huh INTERJ a [ˈʌˈhʌ] (*agreeing, understanding*) ja b [ˈʌˌʌ] (*disagreeing, forbidding*) nichts da (*inf*)

UHT *abbr of* **ultra heat treated** ultrahocherhitzt; **~ milk** H-Milch *f*

UK *abbr of* **United Kingdom** Vereinigtes Königreich

uke [juːk] (*inf*), **ukelele** N = **ukulele**

Ukraine [juːˈkreɪn] N **the ~** die Ukraine

Ukrainian [juːˈkreɪnɪən] ADJ ukrainisch; **he is ~** er ist Ukrainer N a Ukrainer(in) *m(f)* b (*Ling*) Ukrainisch *nt*

ukulele, ukelele [juːkəˈleɪlɪ] N Ukulele *f*

ulcer [ˈʌlsəʳ] N (*Med*) Geschwür *nt*; (= *stomach ulcer*) Magengeschwür *nt*; (*fig*) Übel *nt*

ulcerate [ˈʌlsəreɪt] VT *stomach* ein Geschwür *nt* verursachen in (+*dat*); *skin* Geschwüre verursachen auf (+*dat*); *wound* eitern lassen VI (*stomach*) ein Geschwür *nt* bilden *or* bekommen; (*skin*) geschwürig werden; (*wound*) eitern

ulcerated [ˈʌlsəreɪtɪd] ADJ geschwürig; *wound* vereitert; **an ~ stomach** ein Magengeschwür *nt*

ulceration [ˌʌlsəˈreɪʃən] N (= *process*) Geschwürbildung *f*; (*of wound*) Vereiterung *f*; (= *state*) Geschwüre *pl*, Vereiterung *f*

ulcerous [ˈʌlsərəs] ADJ geschwürig; *wound* vereitert; (= *causing ulcers*) geschwürbildend

ullage [ˈʌlɪdʒ] N Leckage *f*, Flüssigkeitsschwund *m*

'ullo [əˈləʊ] INTERJ (*Brit inf*) = **hello**

ulna [ˈʌlnə] N *pl* **-e** *or* **-s** [ˈʌlniː] (*Anat*) Elle *f*

Ulster [ˈʌlstəʳ] N Ulster *nt*

ulster [ˈʌlstəʳ] N (*dated*: = *coat*) Ulster *m*

Ulsterman [ˈʌlstəmæn] N *pl* **-men** [-men] Mann *m* aus Ulster, Einwohner *m* von Ulster

Ulsterwoman [ˈʌlstəwʊmən] N *pl* **-women** [-wɪmɪn] Frau *f* aus Ulster, Einwohnerin *f* von Ulster

ult [ʌlt] *abbr of* **ultimo**

ulterior [ʌlˈtɪərɪəʳ] ADJ a *purpose* verborgen; **~ motive** Hintergedanke *m*; **I have no ~ motive(s) for** *or* **in doing that** ich tue das ganz ohne Hintergedanken b (*rare*, = *lying beyond*) jenseitig

ultimata [ˌʌltɪˈmeɪtə] *pl of* **ultimatum**

ultimate [ˈʌltɪmɪt] ADJ a (= *final*) letzte(r, s); *destiny, solution, decision* endgültig; *control* oberste(r, s); *authority* höchste(r, s); *beneficiary* eigentlich; **~ goal** *or* **aim** Endziel *nt*; **~ result/outcome** Endergebnis *nt*; **he came to the ~ conclusion that …** er kam schließlich zu der Einsicht, dass …; **what is your ~ ambition in life?** was streben Sie letzten Endes *or* letztlich im Leben an?; **although they had no ~ hope of escape** obwohl letztlich *or* im Endeffekt keine Hoffnung auf Flucht bestand
b (= *that cannot be improved on*) vollendet, perfekt, ultimativ; **the ~ sports car** der Sportwagen in höchster Vollendung, der ultimative Sportwagen; **the ~ insult** der Gipfel der Beleidigung; **the ~ sin** die schlimmste Sünde; **the ~ disgrace** die größte Schande; **the ~ deterrent** (*Mil*) das endgültige Abschreckungsmittel; (*fig*) die äußerste Abschreckungsmaßnahme; **the ~ weapon** (*Mil*) die Superwaffe; (*fig*) das letzte und äußerste Mittel; **death is the ~ sacrifice** der Tod ist das allergrößte Opfer
c (= *basic*) *cause* eigentlich; *explanation* grundsätzlich; *truth* letzte(r, s); **~ principle/problem** Grundprinzip/-problem *nt*; **~ constituents** Grundbestandteile *pl*
d (= *furthest*) entfernteste(r, s); *boundary of universe, frontier* äußerste(r, s); *ancestors* früheste(r, s); **the ~ origins of man** die frühesten Ursprünge des Menschen
N Nonplusultra *nt*; **that is the ~ in comfort** das ist Superkomfort *or* das Höchste an Komfort

ultimately [ˈʌltɪmɪtlɪ] ADV (= *in the end*) letztlich, letzten Endes; (= *eventually*) schließlich; (= *fundamentally*) im Grunde genommen, letztlich; **it's ~ your decision** letztlich müssen Sie das entscheiden

ultimatum [ˌʌltɪˈmeɪtəm] N *pl* **-s** *or* **ultimata** (*Mil, fig*) Ultimatum *nt*; **to deliver** *or* **issue an ~ to sb** jdm ein Ultimatum stellen

ultimo [ˈʌltɪməʊ] ADV (*dated Comm*) des letzten *or* vorigen Monats

ultra- [ˈʌltrə-] PREF ultra-; **ultraconservative** ADJ erzkonservativ, ultrakonservativ; **ultrafashionable** ADJ ultramodern, supermodisch; **ultrahigh frequency** N Ultrahochfrequenz *f*; **ultra-left-wing** ADJ (*Pol*) ultralinke(r, s); **ultralight** ADJ *materials etc* ultraleicht N (*Aviat*) Ultraleichtflugzeug *nt*; **ultramarine** N Ultramarin *nt* ADJ ultramarin(blau); **ultramodern** ADJ ultra- *or* hypermodern; **ultramontane** ADJ (*Eccl*) ultramontan; **ultra-right-wing** ADJ (*Pol*) ultrarechte(r, s); **ultrashort wave** N Ultrakurzwelle *f*; **ultrasound** N Ultraschall *m*; (= *scan*) Ultraschalluntersuchung *f*; **ultrasound picture** N Ultraschallbild *nt* *or* -aufnahme *f*; **ultrasound scan** N Ultraschalluntersuchung *f*; **untrasound scanner** N Ultraschallgerät *nt*; **ultraviolet** ADJ ultraviolett; **~ treatment** Ultraviolettbestrahlung *f*

ululate [ˈjuːljʊleɪt] VI (*liter, mourning women*) (weh)klagen (*liter*); (*dog etc*) heulen

ululation [ˌjuːljʊˈleɪʃən] N (*liter, of mourning women*) (Weh)klagen *nt* (*liter*); (*of dog etc*) Heulen *nt*

Ulysses [juːˈlɪsiːz] N Odysseus, Ulixes (*rare*), Ulysses (*rare*) *m*

um [əm] INTERJ äh; (*in decision, answering*) hm VI **to um and err** herumdrucksen; **after a lot of umming and erring** nach vielen Ähs und Öhs

umbel [ˈʌmbəl] N Dolde *f*

umber [ˈʌmbəʳ] N (= *earth*) Umbraerde *f*; (= *pigment*: *also* **raw umber**) Umbra *f*, Umber *m*; **burned ~** gebrannte Umbra ADJ umbrabraun

umbilical [ʌmˈbɪlɪkəl] ADJ Nabel- N (*Space, Anat*: *also* **umbilical cord**) Nabelschnur *f*

umbilical cord N Nabelschnur *f*

umbilicus [ˌʌmbɪˈlaɪkəs] N Nabel *m*

umbra [ˈʌmbrə] N *pl* **-s** *or* **-e** [ˈʌmbriː] (*Astron*: = *shadow*) Kernschatten *m*; (*in sunspot*) Umbra *f*

umbrage [ˈʌmbrɪdʒ] N **to take ~ at sth** an etw (*dat*) Anstoß nehmen; **he took ~** er nahm daran Anstoß

umbrella [ʌmˈbrelə] N (Regen)schirm *m*; (= *sun umbrella*) (Sonnen)schirm *m*; (*Mil*: = *air umbrella, for ground troops*) Abschirmung *f*, Luftschirm *m*; (*for plane*) Jagdschutz *m*; **under the ~ of** (*fig*) unter der Kontrolle von; **to bring sth under one ~** etw zusammenfassen

umbrella: **umbrella organization** N Dachorganisation *f*; **umbrella stand** N Schirmständer *m*

umlaut [ˈʊmlaʊt] N *(= sign)* Umlautpunkte *pl*; *(= sound change)* Umlaut *m*; **a ~** ä

ump [ʌmp] N *(US inf)* = **umpire**

umpire [ˈʌmpaɪəˈ] **N** Schiedsrichter(in) *m(f)*; *(fig)* Unparteiische(r) *mf*; **to act as ~** *(lit)* als Schiedsrichter(in) fungieren, Schiedsrichter(in) sein; *(fig)* schlichten **VT** *(Sport)* als Schiedsrichter(in) fungieren bei, Schiedsrichter(in) sein bei, schiedsrichtern bei; *(fig)* schlichten **VI** *(in bei)* Schiedsrichter(in) sein, schiedsrichtern; *(fig)* schlichten

umpireship [ˈʌmpaɪəʃɪp] N *(Jur, Sport)* Schiedsrichteramt *nt*

umpteen [ˈʌmpˈtiːn] ADJ *(inf)* zig *(inf)*, x *(inf)*; **I've told you ~ times** ich habe dir zigmal *or* x-mal gesagt *(inf)*

umpteenth [ˈʌmpˈtiːnθ] ADJ *(inf)* x-te(r, s); **for the ~ time** zum x-ten Mal

UMTS *(Telec) abbr of* **universal mobile telecommunications system** UMTS *nt*

UN *abbr of* **United Nations** UNO *f*, UN *pl*; **UN soldier** UN-Soldat(in) *m(f)*, Blauhelm *m*; **UN troops** UNO-Truppen *pl*

'un [ən] PRON *(inf)* **he's a good ~** er ist 'n feiner Kerl; **a big ~** 'n großer; **the little ~s** die Kleinen *pl*

un- [ʌn-] PREF *(before adj, adv)* un-, nicht; *(before n)* Un-

unabashed [ˌʌnəˈbæʃt] ADJ *(= not ashamed, embarrassed)* dreist, unverfroren; *(= not overawed)* unbeeindruckt; **he is an ~ romantic** er ist ein schamloser Romantiker

unabated [ˌʌnəˈbeɪtɪd] ADJ unvermindert; **the rain/storm continued ~** der Regen/Sturm ließ nicht nach

unabbreviated [ˌʌnəˈbriːvɪeɪtɪd] ADJ unabgekürzt, nicht abgekürzt

unable [ʌnˈeɪbl] ✪ 16.3, 25.1 ADJ *pred* **to be ~ to do sth** etw nicht tun können, außerstande *or* außer Stande sein, etw zu tun; **we're still ~ to cure cancer** wir sind immer noch außerstande *or* außer Stande *or* immer noch nicht in der Lage, Krebs zu heilen

unabridged [ˌʌnəˈbrɪdʒd] ADJ ungekürzt

unacceptable [ˌʌnəkˈseptəbl] ADJ *plans, terms* unannehmbar; *excuse, offer, behaviour* nicht akzeptabel; *standard, unemployment level, working conditions* nicht tragbar, untragbar; **it's quite ~ that we should be expected to ...** es kann doch nicht von uns verlangt werden, dass ...; **it's quite ~ for young children to ...** es kann nicht zugelassen werden, dass kleine Kinder ...; **the ~ face of capitalism** die Kehrseite des Kapitalismus; **he behaved in an ~ way** er benahm sich unmöglich

unacceptably [ˌʌnəkˈseptɪblɪ] ADV untragbar; *high* unannehmbar; *poor, bad* unzumutbar; **these fuels are ~ dangerous** diese Brennstoffe sind in nicht mehr tragbarem Maße gefährlich; **he suggested, quite ~, that ...** er schlug vor, was völlig unakzeptabel war, dass ...

unaccommodating [ˌʌnəˈkɒmədeɪtɪŋ] ADJ ungefällig; *attitude* unnachgiebig

unaccompanied [ˌʌnəˈkʌmpənɪd] ADJ *person, child, singing* ohne Begleitung; *bag, suitcase (= abandoned)* herrenlos; *(= travelling separately)* aufgegeben; **~ violin** Solovioline *f*

unaccomplished [ˌʌnəˈkʌmplɪʃt] ADJ *(= unfinished)* unvollendet, unfertig; *(fig)* ungebildet; *(= untalented)* untalentiert

unaccountable [ˌʌnəˈkaʊntəbl] ADJ **a** *(= inexplicable)* unerklärlich; *phenomenon also* unerklärbar **b** *(= not answerable) person* niemandem unterstellt; **to be ~ to sb** sich jdm gegenüber nicht verantworten müssen

unaccountably [ˌʌnəˈkaʊntəblɪ] ADV unerklärlicherweise; *disappear* auf unerklärliche Weise; **an ~ long time** unerklärlich lange; **~ happy** ohne besonderen Grund glücklich

unaccounted for [ˌʌnəˈkaʊntɪdˈfɔːˈ] ADJ ungeklärt; **£30 is still ~** es ist noch ungeklärt, wo die £ 30 geblieben sind; **three of the passengers are still ~** drei Passagiere werden noch vermisst, der Verbleib von drei Passagieren ist noch nicht geklärt

unaccustomed [ˌʌnəˈkʌstəmd] ADJ **a** *(= unusual)* ungewohnt; **with ~ anger/zeal** mit untypischem Zorn/Eifer **b** *(of person: = unused)* **to be ~ to sth** etw nicht gewohnt sein, an etw *(acc)* nicht gewöhnt sein; **to be ~ to doing sth** es nicht gewohnt sein, etw zu tun, nicht daran gewöhnt sein, etw zu tun; **~ as I am to public speaking ...** ich bin kein großer Redner, aber ...

unachievable [ˌʌnəˈtʃiːvəbl] ADJ *task etc* unausführbar; *quality etc* unerreichbar

unacknowledged [ˌʌnəkˈnɒlɪdʒd] ADJ *letter* unbeantwortet; *mistake* uneingestanden; *champion* verkannt; **to leave a letter ~** den Empfang eines Briefes nicht bestätigen; **to go ~** *(person, achievement etc)* nicht anerkannt werden

unacquainted [ˌʌnəˈkweɪntɪd] ADJ *pred* **to be ~ with poverty** die Armut nicht kennen; **to be ~ with the facts** mit den Tatsachen nicht vertraut sein; **I'm not ~ with fame** Ruhm *or* Berühmtheit ist mir nicht gänzlich fremd; **they're ~ with each other** sie kennen sich nicht

unadaptable [ˌʌnəˈdæptəbl] ADJ nicht anpassungsfähig, nicht flexibel; **to be ~ to sth** sich an etw *(acc)* nicht anpassen können

unadapted [ˌʌnəˈdæptɪd] ADJ *version of novel etc* unadaptiert; **in the ~ version** in der Originalversion

unadopted [ˌʌnəˈdɒptɪd] ADJ **a** *(Brit)* **~ road** *öffentliche Straße, für deren Instandhaltung die Anlieger allein verantwortlich sind* **b** *child* nicht adoptiert; **many children remain ~** viele Kinder werden nicht adoptiert **c** *proposal* nicht aufgegriffen

unadorned [ˌʌnəˈdɔːnd] ADJ schlicht; *woman's beauty* natürlich; *truth* ungeschminkt; *prose* schmucklos

unadulterated [ˌʌnəˈdʌltəreɪtɪd] ADJ **a** unverfälscht, rein; *wine* rein, ungepan(t)scht; *(hum) whisky* unverdünnt; **~ by foreign influences** durch fremde Einflüsse nicht verfälscht **b** *(fig) nonsense* schier; *bliss* ungetrübt; **this is ~ filth** das ist der reinste Schmutz, das ist Schmutz in Reinkultur *(inf)*

unadventurous [ˌʌnədˈventʃərəs] ADJ *time, life* wenig abenteuerlich, ereignislos; *tastes* hausbacken, bieder; *style, theatrical production, football* einfallslos; *person* wenig unternehmungslustig; **where food is concerned he is very ~** in Bezug aufs Essen ist er nicht experimentierfreudig

unadventurously [ˌʌnədˈventʃərəslɪ] ADV *directed* einfallslos; *dressed, decorated* bieder, hausbacken; **rather ~ they chose Tenerife again** einfallslos *or* wenig abenteuerlich, wie sie sind, haben sie sich wieder für Teneriffa entschieden

unadvisable [ˌʌnədˈvaɪzəbl] ADJ unratsam, nicht ratsam

unaesthetic, *(US)* **unesthetic** [ˌʌniːsˈθetɪk] ADJ unästhetisch

unaffected [ˌʌnəˈfektɪd] ADJ **a** *(= sincere)* ungekünstelt, natürlich, unaffektiert; *pleasure, gratitude* echt **b** *(= not damaged)* nicht angegriffen *(also Med)*, nicht in Mitleidenschaft gezogen, nicht beeinträchtigt; *(= not influenced)* unbeeinflusst, nicht beeinflusst; *(= not involved)* nicht betroffen; *(= unmoved)* ungerührt, unbewegt; **she remained quite ~ by his tears** sie blieb beim Anblick seiner Tränen völlig ungerührt; **our exports were ~ by the strike** unsere Exporte wurden durch den Streik nicht beeinträchtigt; **he remained quite ~ by all the noise** der Lärm berührte *or* störte ihn überhaupt nicht

unaffectedly [ˌʌnəˈfektɪdlɪ] ADV *(= sincerely)* ungeziert, natürlich; *say* unaffektiert; **she was ~ pleased** ihre Freude war echt

unaffectedness [ˌʌnəˈfektɪdnɪs] N *(= sincerity)* Ungeziertheit *f*, Natürlichkeit *f*, Unaffektiertheit *f*; *(of joy etc)* Aufrichtigkeit *f*

unafraid [ˌʌnəˈfreɪd] ADJ unerschrocken, furchtlos; **to be ~ of sb/sth** vor jdm/etw keine Angst haben; **to be ~ to do sth** keine Angst haben, etw zu tun

unaided [ʌnˈeɪdɪd] **ADV** ohne fremde Hilfe; **to do sth ~** etw allein *or* ohne fremde Hilfe tun **ADJ** **his own ~ work** seine eigene Arbeit; **by my own ~ efforts** ganz ohne fremde Hilfe; **~ by sb** ohne jds Hilfe; **~ by sth** ohne Zuhilfenahme von etw; **with the ~ eye** mit dem bloßen Auge; **to be invisible to the ~ eye** mit dem bloßen Auge nicht sichtbar sein

unaired [ʌnˈɛəd] ADJ *room, bed, clothes* ungelüftet; *argument* nicht vorgebracht

unalike [ˌʌnəˈlaɪk] ADJ *pred* unähnlich, ungleich; **the two children are so ~** die beiden Kinder sind so verschieden *or* sind sich so unähnlich

unallocated [ʌnˈæləkeɪtɪd] ADJ *funds* nicht zugewiesen *or* zugeteilt; **~ tickets** Karten im freien Verkauf

unalloyed [ˌʌnəˈlɔɪd] ADJ *usu attr happiness, success* ungetrübt

unalterable [ʌnˈɒltərəbl] ADJ *intention, decision, fact* unabänderlich; *laws* unveränderlich

unalterably [ʌnˈɒltərəblɪ] ADV unveränderlich; **to be ~ opposed to sth** entschieden gegen etw sein

unaltered [ʌnˈɒltəd] ADJ unverändert

unambiguous ADJ, **unambiguously** ADV [ˌʌnæmˈbɪgjʊəs, -lɪ] eindeutig, unzweideutig

unambitious [ˌʌnæmˈbɪʃəs] ADJ *person, plan* nicht ehrgeizig (genug); *theatrical production* anspruchslos

unamenable [ˌʌnəˈmiːnəbl] ADJ unzugänglich *(to +dat)*; **he is ~ to persuasion** er lässt sich nicht überreden; **~ to medical treatment** auf ärztliche Behandlung nicht ansprechend

un-American [ˌʌnəˈmerɪkən] ADJ unamerikanisch; **~ activities** unamerikanische Umtriebe *pl*

unamiable [ʌnˈeɪmɪəbl] ADJ unliebenswürdig

unamused [ˌʌnəˈmjuːzd] ADJ *laugh* gezwungen, unfroh; **she was ~ (by this)** sie fand es *or* das überhaupt nicht lustig

unanimity [juːnəˈnɪmɪtɪ] N Einmütigkeit *f*; *(of decision also)* Einstimmigkeit *f*

unanimous [juːˈnænɪməs] ADJ einmütig; *decision also (Jur)* einstimmig; **we were ~ in thinking ...** wir waren einmütig der Ansicht ...; **they are ~ in wanting a change** sie sind sich (darin) einig, dass sie eine Veränderung wollen; **they were ~ in their condemnation of him** sie haben ihn einmütig verdammt; **by a ~ vote** einstimmig

unanimously [juːˈnænɪməslɪ] ADV einstimmig, einmütig; *agree* einmütig; *vote* einstimmig

unannounced [ˌʌnəˈnaʊnst] ADJ, ADV unangemeldet

unanswerable [ʌnˈɑːnsərəbl] ADJ *question* nicht zu beantworten *pred*, nicht zu beantwortend *attr*; *argument, case* zwingend, unwiderlegbar; **that question is ~** diese Frage lässt sich nicht beantworten

unanswered [ʌnˈɑːnsəd] ADJ unbeantwortet; **to be left ~** unbeantwortet bleiben

unapologetic [ˌʌnəˌpɒləˈdʒetɪk] ADJ unverfroren, dreist; **he was so ~ about it** es schien ihm überhaupt nicht leidzutun

unappealable [ˌʌnəˈpiːləbl] ADJ *(Jur)* nicht berufungsfähig; **the judgement is ~** gegen das Urteil kann keine Berufung eingelegt werden

unappealing [ˌʌnəˈpiːlɪŋ] ADJ nicht ansprechend, nicht reizvoll; *person also* unansehnlich; *prospect, sight* nicht verlockend; **to be ~ to sb** für jdn nicht verlockend sein

unappeased [ˌʌnəˈpiːzd] ADJ *appetite, lust* unbefriedigt; *hunger, thirst* ungestillt; *person* nicht besänftigt

unappetizing [ʌnˈæpɪtaɪzɪŋ] ADJ unappetitlich; *prospect, thought* wenig verlockend

unappreciated [ˌʌnəˈpriːʃɪeɪtɪd] ADJ nicht geschätzt *or* gewürdigt; **she felt she was ~ by him** sie hatte den Eindruck, dass er sie nicht zu schätzen wusste; **the ~ heroines of the war** die ungewürdigten *or* unbeachteten Heldinnen des Krieges

unappreciative [ˌʌnəˈpriːʃɪətɪv] ADJ undankbar; *audience* verständnislos; **to be ~ of sth** etw nicht zu würdigen wissen

unapprehensive [ˌʌnæprɪˈhensɪv] ADJ **a** *(= slow)* schwerfällig; *(= slow on the uptake)* schwer von Begriff **b** *(= unconcerned)* unbekümmert, furchtlos

unapproachable [ˌʌnəˈprəʊtʃəbl] ADJ *place* unzugänglich; *person also* unnahbar

unapt [ʌnˈæpt] ADJ *(= inappropriate)* unpassend, unangebracht

unarguable [ʌnˈɑːgjʊəbl] ADJ *theory etc* nicht vertretbar

unarguably [ʌnˈɑːgjʊəblɪ] ADV unbestreitbar, zweifellos

unargued [ʌnˈɑːgjuːd] ADJ *(= without argumentation)* unbegründet; *(= undisputed)* unangefochten, unbestritten; **the point was left ~** dieser Punkt wurde nicht begründet; *(= undiscussed)* dieser Punkt wurde nicht erörtert

unarm [ʌnˈɑːm] VT = **disarm**

unarmed [ʌnˈɑːmd] ADJ unbewaffnet ADV unbewaffnet

unarmed combat N Nahkampf *m* ohne Waffe

unashamed [ˌʌnəˈʃeɪmd] ADJ schamlos; *admirer, liberal, reactionary, populist* unverhohlen; **naked but ~** nackt aber ohne Scham; **his ~ conservatism** sein unverhohlener Konservatismus; **he was quite ~ about** *or* **of it** er schämte sich dessen überhaupt nicht, er war darüber kein bisschen beschämt; **to be ~ to do sth** keine Hemmungen haben, etw zu tun

unashamedly [ˌʌnəˈʃeɪmɪdlɪ] ADV unverschämt; *say, admit* ohne Scham; *romantic* unverhohlen; *cry* hemmungslos; *in favour of, partisan* ganz offen, unverhohlen; **he's ~ proud of ...** er zeigt unverhohlen, wie stolz er auf ... ist; **they are ~ in love** sie schämen sich ihrer Liebe nicht; **this book is ~ a love story** das Buch ist ganz unverhohlen eine Liebesgeschichte

unasked [ʌnˈɑːskt] ADJ *(= unrequested)* unaufgefordert, ungefragt, ungebeten; *(= uninvited)* un(ein)geladen, ungebeten; **the question went ~** die Frage wurde nicht gestellt ADV *(= voluntarily)* unaufgefordert

unasked-for [ʌnˈɑːsktfɔːˈ] ADJ ungewünscht, unwillkommen

unaspirated [ʌnˈæspɪreɪtɪd] ADJ unbehaucht

unaspiring ADJ, **unaspiringly** ADV [ˌʌnəˈspaɪərɪŋ, -lɪ] **a** *(= unambitious)* ohne Ehrgeiz **b** *(= undemanding)* anspruchslos; *(= unpretentious)* bescheiden

unassailable [ˌʌnəˈseɪləbl] ADJ unangreifbar; *fortress* uneinnehmbar, unbezwingbar; *position, reputation, record, majority* unantastbar, unanfechtbar; *conviction* unerschütterlich; *argument* unwiderlegbar, unanfechtbar, zwingend

unassisted [ˌʌnəˈsɪstɪd] ADJ, ADV = **unaided**

unassuming [ˌʌnəˈsjuːmɪŋ] ADJ bescheiden

unattached [ˌʌnəˈtætʃt] ADJ **a** *(= not fastened)* unbefestigt; *(Mil)* keinem Regiment/keiner Einheit *etc* zugeteilt; *(US) athlete* ohne Vereinszugehörigkeit; **~ vote** Wechselwähler *m* **b** *(emotionally)* ungebunden; **she's worried about still being ~** sie macht sich Sorgen, weil sie immer noch keinen Partner gefunden hat; **there aren't many ~ girls around** die meisten Mädchen hier sind nicht mehr zu haben *or* sind nicht mehr frei

unattainability [ˈʌnəˌteɪnəˈbɪlɪtɪ] N Unerreichbarkeit *f*

unattainable [ˌʌnəˈteɪnəbl] ADJ unerreichbar

unattended [ˌʌnəˈtendɪd] ADJ **a** *(= not looked after) children* unbeaufsichtigt; *car park, car, luggage* unbewacht; *patient* unbehandelt, nicht behandelt; *shop* ohne Bedienung; *customer* nicht bedient; *business* unerledigt; **to leave sb ~** *(= leave alone, child)* jdn unbeaufsichtigt lassen; **to leave sth ~** *(car, luggage)* etw unbewacht lassen; *shop* etw unbeaufsichtigt lassen; **to leave sb/sth ~ (to)** *(= not deal with, guests, problem)* sich nicht um jdn/etw kümmern; *work* etw liegen lassen, etw nicht erledigen; *patient* jdn nicht behandeln; *customer* jdn nicht bedienen; **to leave a wound ~** eine Wunde nicht versorgen; **to leave a car ~ to** ein Auto nicht reparieren lassen; **to be** *or* **go ~ to** *(wound, injury)* nicht behandelt werden; *(car, fault)* nicht repariert werden; *(customer)* nicht bedient werden; *(work)* nicht erledigt sein/werden **b** *(= not escorted)* ohne Begleitung *(by +gen)*, unbegleitet

unattested [ˌʌnəˈtestɪd] ADJ **a** *(= unconfirmed)* unbezeugt, unbestätigt **b** *(Brit: = not formally certified)* (behördlich) nicht überprüft

unattractive [ˌʌnəˈtræktɪv] ADJ *sight, place* unschön, wenig reizvoll; *offer* unattraktiv, uninteressant; *trait, scar* unschön; *character* unsympathisch; *woman* unattraktiv; **he's ~ to women** Frauen finden ihn nicht attraktiv *or* anziehend; **to be ~ to sb** *(fig: = unappealing)* für jdn nicht reizvoll sein

unattractiveness [ˌʌnəˈtræktɪvnɪs] N Unschönheit *f*; *(of woman)* geringe Attraktivität; **the ~ of the offer** das unattraktive *or* nicht verlockende Angebot

unattributed [ˌʌnəˈtrɪbuːtɪd] ADJ *quotation* ohne Quellenangabe; *remarks* anonym; *source* ungenannt

unauthenticated [ˌʌnɔːˈθentɪkeɪtɪd] ADJ unverbürgt; *document* unbeglaubigt

unauthorized [ʌnˈɔːθəraɪzd] ADJ unbefugt, unberechtigt; **no entry for ~ persons** Zutritt für Unbefugte verboten!

unavailable [ˌʌnəˈveɪləbl] ADJ nicht erhältlich; *person* nicht zu erreichen *pred*; *library book* nicht verfügbar; **the minister was ~ for comment** der Minister lehnte eine Stellungnahme ab

unavailing [ˌʌnəˈveɪlɪŋ] ADJ vergeblich, umsonst *pred*

unavailingly [ˌʌnəˈveɪlɪŋlɪ] ADV vergeblich

unavenged [ˌʌnəˈvendʒd] ADJ ungerächt

unavoidable [ˌʌnəˈvɔɪdəbl] ADJ unvermeidlich, unvermeidbar; *conclusion, consequence* zwangsläufig, unausweichlich

unavoidably [ˌʌnəˈvɔɪdəblɪ] ADV notgedrungen; **to be ~ detained** verhindert sein; **~, war films poured out of Hollywood in 1941** es war unvermeidlich, dass 1941 Unmengen von Kriegsfilmen in Hollywood produziert wurden

unaware [ˌʌnəˈwɛəˈ] ADJ *pred* **to be ~ of sth** sich *(dat)* einer Sache *(gen)* nicht bewusst sein; **I was ~ of his presence** ich hatte nicht bemerkt, dass er da war; **I was ~ that he was interested** es war mir nicht bewusst *or* ich war mir nicht bewusst, dass er interessiert war; **I was ~ that there was a meeting going on** ich wusste nicht, dass da gerade eine Besprechung stattfand; **not ~ of sth** sich *(dat)* einer Sache *(gen)* durchaus bewusst; **I was not ~ that ...** es war mir durchaus bewusst *or* klar, dass ...; **he's so ~** er weiß überhaupt nicht Bescheid; **politically ~** ohne politisches Bewusstsein

unawares [ˌʌnəˈwɛəz] ADV *(= by surprise)* unerwartet; *(= accidentally)* unbeabsichtigt, versehentlich; *(= without knowing)* unwissentlich; **to catch** *or* **take sb ~** jdn überraschen

unbalance [ʌnˈbæləns] VT *(physically, mentally)* aus dem Gleichgewicht bringen; *painting* das Gleichgewicht *(+gen)* stören; **to ~ sb's mind** jdn um den Verstand bringen

unbalanced [ʌnˈbælənst] ADJ **a** *painting, diet, economy* unausgewogen; *report, view of life* einseitig; *ship etc* nicht im Gleichgewicht; **the structure of the committee was ~** der Ausschuss war unausgewogen *or* sehr einseitig besetzt **b** *mind* unstet; *(also* **mentally unbalanced**, *= deranged, mad)* irre, verrückt; *(= slightly crazy)* nicht ganz normal **c** *account, budget* nicht saldiert *or* ausgeglichen

unban [ʌnˈbæn] VT wieder zulassen

unbandage [ʌnˈbændɪdʒ] VT den Verband abnehmen von

unbaptized [ˌʌnbæpˈtaɪzd] ADJ ungetauft

unbar [ʌnˈbɑːˈ] VT aufsperren

unbearable [ʌnˈbɛərəbl] ADJ unerträglich; **to make life ~ for sb** jdm das Leben unerträglich machen

unbearably [ʌnˈbɛərəblɪ] ADV *sad, painful, loud* unerträglich; **almost ~ beautiful** überwältigend *or* hinreißend schön, fast zu schön

unbeatable [ʌnˈbiːtəbl] ADJ unschlagbar; *army also* unbesiegbar; *record also* nicht zu überbieten *pred*, nicht zu überbietend *attr*; *offer, price also* unübertrefflich

unbeaten [ʌnˈbiːtn] ADJ ungeschlagen; *army also* unbesiegt; *record* ungebrochen, nicht überboten

unbecoming [ˌʌnbɪˈkʌmɪŋ] ADJ **a** *behaviour, language etc* unschicklich, unziemlich *(geh)*; **conduct ~ to a gentleman** ein Benehmen, das sich für einen Herrn nicht schickt **b** *(= unflattering) clothes* unvorteilhaft; *facial hair* unschön

unbeknown(st) [ˌʌnbɪˈnəʊn(st)] ADV ohne dass es jemand wusste; **~ to me** ohne mein Wissen; **~ to his father** ohne Wissen seines Vaters

unbelief [ˌʌnbɪˈliːf] N Ungläubigkeit *f*; **in ~** ungläubig

unbelievable [ˌʌnbɪˈliːvəbl] ADJ unglaublich; *(inf: = bad)* unglaublich; *(= good)* sagenhaft *(inf)*; **he has so much talent it's ~** es ist unglaublich *or* es ist nicht zu fassen, wie begabt er ist

unbelievably [ˌʌnbɪˈliːvəblɪ] ADV unglaublich; *good, pretty etc also* sagenhaft *(inf)*; **they had, ~, lost both games** es war unglaublich, aber sie hatten beide Spiele verloren

unbeliever [ˌʌnbɪˈliːvəˈ] N Ungläubige(r) *mf*

unbelieving ADJ, **unbelievingly** ADV [ˌʌnbɪˈliːvɪŋ, -lɪ] ungläubig

unbend [ʌnˈbend] *pret, ptp* **unbent** VT *(= straighten) metal etc* gerade biegen; *arms* strecken; **~ your body** richten Sie sich auf; *(lying down)* legen Sie sich ausgestreckt hin VI *(person, = relax)* aus sich herausgehen; *(= straighten body)* sich aufrichten, sich gerade hinlegen

unbending [ʌnˈbendɪŋ] ADJ *person, attitude* unnachgiebig; *determination* unbeugsam; *commitment* unerschütterlich

unbent [ʌnˈbent] *pret, ptp of* **unbend**

unbias(s)ed [ʌnˈbaɪəst] ADJ unvoreingenommen; *opinion, report also* unparteiisch

unbidden [ʌnˈbɪdn] ADV *(form)* ungebeten; *(= not ordered also)* unaufgefordert; *(= uninvited also)* ungeladen; **to do sth ~** etw unaufgefordert tun; **the phrase came ~ into her mind** der Satz kam ihr spontan in den Sinn

unbind [ʌnˈbaɪnd] *pret, ptp* **unbound** VT *(= free) prisoner* losbinden, befreien; *(= untie) hair* lösen; *(= unbandage)* den Verband ablösen von

unbleached [ʌnˈbliːtʃt] ADJ ungebleicht

unblemished [ʌnˈblemɪʃt] ADJ *(lit, fig)* makellos; *reputation also* unbescholten; *skin also* tadellos; **their relationship was ~ by arguments** kein Streit hatte je ihre Beziehung getrübt

unblinking [ʌnˈblɪŋkɪŋ] ADJ *look, attention* unverwandt; *eyes* starr

unblinkingly [ʌnˈblɪŋkɪŋlɪ] ADV *stare* starr, stoisch, unverwandt

unblock [ʌnˈblɒk] VT frei machen; *sink, pipe* die Verstopfung in *(+dat)* beseitigen; *chimney* ausputzen; *(fig) talks* wieder in Gang bringen; *obstacles* aus dem Weg räumen

unblushing [ʌnˈblʌʃɪŋ] ADJ schamlos; *liar also* unverschämt

unblushingly [ʌnˈblʌʃɪŋlɪ] ADV ohne sich zu schämen, frech

unbolt [ʌnˈbəʊlt] VT aufriegeln; **he left the door ~ed** er verriegelte die Tür nicht

unborn [ʌnˈbɔːn] ADJ ungeboren; **generations yet ~** kommende Generationen

unbosom [ʌnˈbʊzəm] VT *feelings* offenbaren, enthüllen (*to sb* jdm); **to ~ oneself to sb** jdm sein Herz ausschütten

unbound [ʌnˈbaʊnd] *pret, ptp of* **unbind** ADJ **a** *(= not tied) hair* gelöst, nicht zusammengehalten *or* zusammengebunden; *prisoner* losgekettet, von den Fesseln befreit; *(= loose) wheat* ungebündelt; **Prometheus ~** der befreite Prometheus **b** *book* ungebunden

unbounded [ʌnˈbaʊndɪd] ADJ grenzenlos; *(fig also)* unermesslich, unendlich

unbowed [ʌnˈbaʊd] ADJ *(fig)* ungebrochen; *pride* ungebeugt; **he was ~ by misfortune** sein Unglück hatte ihn nicht gebrochen *or* gebeugt; **the army was defeated but ~** das Heer war besiegt, sein Mut aber ungebrochen

unbreakable [ʌnˈbreɪkəbl] ADJ *glass, toy* unzerbrechlich; *record* nicht zu brechen *pred*; *rule, law* unumstößlich, feststehend *attr*; *promise, silence* unverbrüchlich; **an ~ habit** eine Angewohnheit, die man nicht loswerden *or* ablegen kann; **an ~ union** eine unlösbare Verbindung

unbribable [ʌnˈbraɪbəbl] ADJ unbestechlich

unbridgeable [ʌnˈbrɪdʒəbl] ADJ unüberbrückbar

unbridled [ʌnˈbraɪdld] ADJ *lust, passion* ungezügelt, zügellos; *anger* hemmungslos; *tongue* lose; *capitalism* ungehemmt

un-British [ʌnˈbrɪtɪʃ] ADJ unbritisch

unbroken [ʌnˈbrəʊkən] ADJ **a** *(= intact)* unbeschädigt; *seal* nicht erbrochen; *heart, promise* nicht gebrochen
b *(= continuous)* ununterbrochen; *(Mil) ranks* geschlossen, nicht durchbrochen; *line of descent* direkt; **an ~ night's sleep** eine ungestörte Nacht; **a whole morning of ~ sunshine** ein ganzer Vormittag mit strahlendem Sonnenschein; **she was in government for eleven ~ years** sie regierte elf Jahre ohne Unterbrechung
c *(= unbeaten) record* ungebrochen, unüberboten
d *horse* nicht zugeritten
e *pride* ungebeugt; **his spirit remained ~** er war ungebrochen
f *voice* nicht gebrochen; **boys with ~ voices** Jungen vor dem Stimmbruch

unbrotherly [ʌnˈbrʌðəlɪ] ADJ unbrüderlich

unbuckle [ʌnˈbʌkl] VT aufschnallen

unbudgeted [ʌnˈbʌdʒɪtɪd] ADJ *costs, items* außerplanmäßig

unbundle [ʌnˈbʌndl] VT **a** *(US: = itemize)* aufschlüsseln, aufgliedern **b** *(Comm: = asset-strip)* *finanziell gefährdete Firmen aufkaufen und anschließend deren Vermögenswerte veräußern*

unbundling [ʌnˈbʌndlɪŋ] N *(Comm)* *Aufkauf finanziell gefährdeter Firmen und anschließende Veräußerung ihrer Vermögenswerte*

unburden [ʌnˈbɜːdn] VT *(liter: = unload)* abladen; *(fig) conscience, heart* erleichtern; **to ~ oneself/one's heart/one's soul to sb** jdm sein Herz ausschütten; **to ~ oneself of sth** *(lit liter)* etw abladen, sich von etw befreien; *(fig)* sich *(dat)* etw von der Seele reden; *of anxiety, guilt* sich von etw befreien *or* losmachen; *of sins* etw offenbaren *or* gestehen

unbusinesslike [ʌnˈbɪznɪslaɪk] ADJ wenig geschäftsmäßig; **it's very ~ to keep all your correspondence in cardboard boxes** es ist äußerst unprofessionell, die ganze Korrespondenz in Kartons aufzubewahren; **the firm handled the transaction in such an ~ way** die Firma hat die Transaktion so ungeschäftsmäßig abgewickelt; **in spite of his ~ appearance ...** obwohl er gar nicht wie ein Geschäftsmann aussieht ...

unbutton [ʌnˈbʌtn] VT aufknöpfen

uncalled-for [ʌnˈkɔːldfɔːʳ] ADJ *(= unjustified) criticism* ungerechtfertigt; *(= unnecessary)* unnötig; *(= rude) remark* ungebührlich, deplatziert; **that was quite ~** das war nun wirklich nicht nötig *or* nett

uncannily [ʌnˈkænɪlɪ] ADV unheimlich; **his guesses are ~ accurate** es ist unheimlich *or* nicht ganz geheuer, wie genau er alles errät; **to look ~ like sb/sth** jdm/einer Sache auf unheimliche Weise ähnlich sehen

uncanny [ʌnˈkænɪ] ADJ unheimlich; **it's quite ~** das ist geradezu unheimlich; **to bear an ~ resemblance to sb** jdm auf unheimliche Weise ähnlich sehen

uncap [ʌnˈkæp] VT *bottle* aufmachen, öffnen; *tax* nicht mehr kappen

uncapped [ʌnˈkæpt] ADJ *(Brit Sport)* **~ player** Spieler, der/Spielerin, die noch nie in der Nationalmannschaft gespielt hat, Nationalmannschaftsneuling *m*; **he is ~** er hat noch nie in der Nationalmannschaft gespielt

uncared-for [ʌnˈkɛədfɔːʳ] ADJ *garden, hands* ungepflegt; *child* vernachlässigt, verwahrlost

uncaring [ʌnˈkɛərɪŋ] ADJ gleichgültig, teilnahmslos; *parents* lieblos; **the state as an impersonal and ~ machine** der Staat als unpersönliche und gefühllose Maschine

uncarpeted [ʌnˈkɑːpɪtɪd] ADJ ohne Teppich, nicht ausgelegt

uncatalogued [ʌnˈkætəlɒgd] ADJ nicht katalogisiert

unceasing ADJ, **unceasingly** ADV [ʌnˈsiːsɪŋ, -lɪ] unaufhörlich

uncensored [ʌnˈsensəd] ADJ *film, version* unzensiert; *(= unblamed) remark* ungetadelt, ungerügt

unceremonious [ˌʌnserɪˈməʊnɪəs] ADJ **a** *(= abrupt, rude) dismissal, manner* brüsk, barsch; *reply* unverbrämt, unverblümt; *behaviour* ungehobelt, ruppig; *exit, departure* überstürzt; *haste* unfein, unfeierlich; **the rather ~ treatment we got** so kurz, wie wir abgefertigt wurden **b** *(= informal, simple)* zwanglos, formlos

unceremoniously [ˌʌnserɪˈməʊnɪəslɪ] ADV **a** *(= abruptly, rudely)* ohne Umschweife, ohne viel Federlesen(s), kurzerhand **b** *(= informally, simply)* zwanglos, formlos

uncertain [ʌnˈsɜːtn] ADJ **a** *(= unsure, unsteady)* unsicher; *light* undeutlich, schwach; **I was ~ as to what to do** ich war unsicher, was ich tun sollte; **to be ~ whether ...** sich *(dat)* nicht sicher sein, ob ...; **to be ~ of** *or* **about sth** sich *(dat)* einer Sache *(gen)* nicht sicher sein; **he's still ~ of the contract** er ist noch im Ungewissen über den Vertrag
b *(= unknown) date, result* ungewiss; *origins* unbestimmt; **a woman of ~ age** *(hum)* eine Frau von unbestimmtem Alter
c *(= unreliable) weather, prices* unbeständig; *temper* unberechenbar; *judgement* unverlässlich, unzuverlässig
d *(= unclear)* vage; **in no ~ terms** klar und deutlich, unzweideutig

uncertainly [ʌnˈsɜːtnlɪ] ADV *say* unbestimmt; *look, move* unsicher; *smile* unsicher, zögernd

uncertainty [ʌnˈsɜːtntɪ] ✪ 16.1 N *(= state)* Ungewissheit *f*; *(= indefiniteness)* Unbestimmtheit *f*; *(= doubt)* Zweifel *m*, Unsicherheit *f*; **in order to remove any ~** um alle eventuellen Unklarheiten zu beseitigen; **there is still some ~ as to whether ...** es besteht noch Ungewissheit, ob ...

uncertainty principle N *(Phys)* Unbestimmtheits- *or* Ungenauigkeits- *or* Unschärferelation *f*

unchain [ʌnˈtʃeɪn] VT *dog, prisoner* losketten, losbinden; *door* die Sicherheitskette *(+gen)* lösen; *(fig liter: = free)* befreien, erlösen; *heart* freigeben

unchallengeable [ʌnˈtʃælɪndʒəbl] ADJ unanfechtbar; *proof also* unwiderlegbar; *confidence* unerschütterlich

unchallenged [ʌnˈtʃælɪndʒd] ADJ unbestritten, unangefochten; *(Jur) juryman* nicht abgelehnt; *evidence* nicht angefochten, unangefochten; **to leave sb/sth ~** *(= unopposed)* jdm/einer Sache nicht widersprechen; **to rule ~** uneingeschränkt regieren; **to go ~** *(Mil)* ohne Anruf passieren; **we passed the sentry ~** die Wache ließ uns ohne Anruf passieren; **the record was** *or* **went ~ for several years** der Rekord wurde jahrelang nicht überboten; **I cannot let that remark go** *or* **pass ~** diese Bemerkung kann ich nicht unwidersprochen hinnehmen

unchangeable ADJ, **unchangeably** ADV [ʌnˈtʃeɪndʒəbl, -ɪ] unveränderlich

unchanged [ʌnˈtʃeɪndʒd] ADJ unverändert

unchanging [ʌnˈtʃeɪndʒɪŋ] ADJ unveränderlich

unchaperoned [ʌnˈʃæpərəʊnd] ADJ unbegleitet

uncharacteristic [ˌʌnkærəktəˈrɪstɪk] ADJ uncharakteristisch, untypisch (*of* für); **such rudeness is ~ of him** es ist gar nicht seine Art, so unhöflich zu sein; **with ~ enthusiasm/modesty** mit (für ihn/sie *etc*) völlig untypischer Begeisterung/Bescheidenheit

uncharacteristically [ˌʌnkærəktəˈrɪstɪklɪ] ADV auf uncharakteristische *or* untypische Weise; **she was ~ silent** sie war ungewöhnlich still für ihre Verhältnisse

uncharged [ʌnˈtʃɑːdʒd] ADJ **a** *(Elec)* nicht (auf)geladen **b** *(Econ, Fin) account* unbelastet; *service etc* unberechnet

uncharitable [ʌnˈtʃærɪtəbl] ADJ *remark* unfreundlich, nicht nett, lieblos; *view, person* unbarmherzig, herzlos; *criticism* schonungslos, unbarmherzig; *attitude* hartherzig; **it was most ~ of you to ...** es war wirklich nicht nett, dass Sie ...

uncharted [ʌnˈtʃɑːtɪd] ADJ *(= not explored)* unerforscht, unergründet; *(= not on map)* nicht verzeichnet *or* eingezeichnet; **~ waters** *or* **territory** *(fig)* unbekanntes Terrain; **to enter ~ waters** *or* **territory** *(fig)* sich in unbekanntes Terrain begeben

unchaste [ʌnˈtʃeɪst] ADJ unzüchtig; *thoughts, actions* unkeusch; *life, wife* untugendhaft

uncheck [ʌnˈtʃek] VT *(Comput) control box* deaktivieren

unchecked [ʌnˈtʃekt] ADJ **a** *(= unrestrained)* ungehemmt, unkontrolliert; *advance* ungehindert; *anger* hemmungslos, ungezügelt; **to go ~** *(abuse)* geduldet werden; *(advance)* nicht gehindert werden; *(inflation)* nicht eingedämmt *or* aufgehalten werden; **if the epidemic goes ~** wenn der Epidemie nicht Einhalt geboten wird; **if left ~, the fungus can spread extensively** wenn der Pilzbefall nicht unter Kontrolle gebracht wird, kann er sich weit ausbreiten
b *(= not verified)* ungeprüft, nicht überprüft
c *(Comput) control box* deaktiviert

unchivalrous [ʌnˈʃɪvəlrəs] ADJ unritterlich; *remark* ungalant

unchristened [ʌnˈkrɪsnd] ADJ ungetauft

unchristian [ʌnˈkrɪstjən] ADJ unchristlich

uncial [ˈʌnsɪəl] ADJ Unzial-; **~ letter** Unzialbuchstabe *m* N *(= letter)* Unzialbuchstabe *m*; *(= script)* Unziale *f*, Unzialschrift *f*; *(= manuscript)* Schriftstück *or* Dokument *nt* in Unzialschrift

uncircumcised [ʌnˈsɜːkəmsaɪzd] ADJ unbeschnitten

uncivil [ʌnˈsɪvɪl] ADJ unhöflich

uncivilly [ʌnˈsɪvɪlɪ] ADV *ask* unhöflich

uncivilized [ʌnˈsɪvɪlaɪzd] ADJ *country, tribe, behaviour* unzivilisiert; *(inf) habit* barbarisch; **sorry to wake you at this ~ hour** *(inf: = early)* entschuldige, dass ich dich zu nachtschlafender *or* einer so unchristlichen Zeit wecke *(inf)*

unclad [ʌnˈklæd] ADJ *(euph, hum)* bar jeglicher Kleidung

unclaimed [ʌnˈkleɪmd] ADJ *prize* nicht abgeholt; *property also* herrenlos; *right, inheritance* nicht geltend gemacht; *social security etc* nicht beansprucht; **to go ~** *(prize)* nicht abgeholt werden; *(right, inheritance)* nicht geltend gemacht werden; *(social security etc)* nicht beansprucht werden

unclasp [ʌnˈklɑːsp] VT *necklace* lösen; *cloak* öffnen, aufhaken; *hands* voneinander lösen; **he ~ed her hand** er löste ihre Hand

unclassified [ʌnˈklæsɪfaɪd] ADJ **a** *(= not arranged)* nicht klassifiziert *or* eingeordnet **b** *(= not secret)* nicht geheim

unclassified degree N *(Brit Univ)* Hochschulabschluss *m* ohne Klassifikation

unclassified road N *(Brit)* schlecht ausgebaute Landstraße

uncle [ˈʌŋkl] N Onkel *m*; **Uncle Sam** Uncle *or* Onkel Sam; **to say** *or* **cry ~** *(US)* aufgeben

unclean [ʌnˈkliːn] ADJ unsauber *(also Bibl)*; *(Rel) animal* unrein; *thoughts* unkeusch; *(fig: = contaminated)* schmutzig

unclear [ʌnˈklɪəˈ] ADJ unklar; *essay etc* undurchsichtig; **to be ~ about sth** sich *(dat)* über etw *(acc)* im Unklaren *or* nicht im Klaren sein; **his motives are ~ to me** mir sind seine Motive nicht klar; **it is ~ to me why ...** es ist mir unklar *or* nicht klar, warum ...

unclimbable [ʌnˈklaɪməbl] ADJ unbesteigbar

unclimbed [ʌnˈklaɪmd] ADJ unbestiegen, unbezwungen

unclog [ʌnˈklɒg] VT *pipe, drain* die Verstopfung in *(+dat)* beseitigen; *artery* frei machen; *wheel* befreien

unclothed [ʌnˈkləʊðd] ADJ unbekleidet

unclouded [ʌnˈklaʊdɪd] ADJ *sky* unbewölkt; *(fig) happiness, vision, mind* ungetrübt; *mind* klar

unclubbable [ʌnˈklʌbəbl] ADJ ohne Gruppenzugehörigkeitsgefühl

uncluttered [ʌnˈklʌtəd] ADJ schlicht, einfach; *desk, room* nicht überfüllt *or* überladen; **a mind ~ by excess information** ein von überflüssigem Wissen freier *or* unbelasteter Kopf

unco [ˈʌŋkəʊ] ADV *(Scot: = very)* sehr

uncock [ʌnˈkɒk] VT *gun* sichern

uncoil [ʌnˈkɔɪl] **VT** abwickeln **VI/R** *(snake)* sich langsam strecken; *(person)* sich ausstrecken; *(wire etc)* sich abwickeln, sich abspulen; **to ~ (oneself) from an armchair** sich im Sessel strecken und aufstehen

uncollected [ˌʌnkəˈlektɪd] ADJ *rubbish* nicht abgeholt; *tax* nicht eingezogen *or* vereinnahmt; *fare* nicht kassiert, unkassiert

uncoloured, *(US)* **uncolored** [ʌnˈkʌləd] ADJ *(= colourless)* farblos; *(= white)* weiß; *(fig: = unprejudiced)* nicht gefärbt; *judgement* unparteiisch

uncombed [ʌnˈkəʊmd] ADJ ungekämmt

uncomfortable [ʌnˈkʌmfətəbl] ADJ **a** unbequem; *chair, position* ungemütlich, unbequem; **I feel ~ sitting like this** es ist unbequem so zu sitzen; **if the room is too hot it'll make you feel ~** wenn das Zimmer zu heiß ist, fühlt man sich nicht wohl; **I feel ~ in this jacket** in dieser Jacke fühle ich mich nicht wohl; **it feels ~** es ist unbequem
b *(= uneasy) feeling* unangenehm, ungut; *silence (= awkward)* peinlich; *(= nerve-racking)* beklemmend; **to feel ~** sich unbehaglich fühlen, sich nicht wohlfühlen; **I felt ~ about it/about doing it** ich hatte ein ungutes Gefühl dabei, mir war nicht wohl dabei; **he looked ~** er sah aus, als ob er sich unbehaglich fühlte; **he was ~ in that job** er fühlte sich in dieser Stelle nicht wohl; **they make me feel ~** in ihrer Gegenwart fühle ich mich unbehaglich; **to put sb in an ~ position** jdn in eine heikle Lage bringen; **he is ~ with the idea of having no control** ihm ist nicht wohl bei der Vorstellung, die Dinge nicht unter Kontrolle zu haben
c *(= unpleasant) truth, fact, time, position* unerfreulich; **we could make things ~ for you** *(euph)* wir können ungemütlich werden

uncomfortably [ʌnˈkʌmfətəblɪ] ADV **a** unbequem **b** *(= uneasily)* unbehaglich, unruhig **c** *(= unpleasantly)* unangenehm; **I became ~ aware of having insulted him** es wurde mir peinlich bewusst, dass ich ihn beleidigt hatte; **I feel ~ full** ich habe ein unangenehmes Völlegefühl

uncommissioned [ˌʌnkəˈmɪʃnd] ADJ *(= unauthorized)* nicht beauftragt *or* ermächtigt

uncommitted [ˌʌnkəˈmɪtɪd] ADJ **a** nicht engagiert; *party, country* neutral; **she is ~ on this issue** sie hat dazu keine Meinung; **we want to remain ~ till we get a full report** wir wollen uns nicht festlegen, bevor wir einen ausführlichen Bericht haben; **~ to** nicht festgelegt auf *(+acc)* **b** *(= half-hearted) attitude* gleichgültig; *performance* halbherzig

uncommon [ʌnˈkɒmən] ADJ **a** *(= unusual)* ungewöhnlich; **it is not ~ for her to be late** es ist nichts Ungewöhnliches, dass sie zu spät kommt; **a not ~ occurrence** eine häufige Erscheinung; **a not ~ problem/sight** ein nicht ganz ungewöhnliches Problem/ungewöhnlicher Anblick **b** *(= outstanding)* außergewöhnlich

uncommonly [ʌnˈkɒmənlɪ] ADV **a** *(= unusually)* ungewöhnlich **b** *(= exceptionally)* außergewöhnlich; **that's ~ civil of you** *(dated)* das ist äußerst freundlich von Ihnen

uncommunicative [ˌʌnkəˈmjuːnɪkətɪv] ADJ *(by nature)* verschlossen, wortkarg; *(temporarily)* schweigsam

uncompetitive [ˌʌnkɒmˈpetɪtɪv] ADJ *industry* nicht wettbewerbsfähig, wettbewerbsunfähig; *price* nicht konkurrenzfähig

uncomplaining [ˌʌnkəmˈpleɪnɪŋ] ADJ duldsam

uncomplainingly [ˌʌnkəmˈpleɪnɪŋlɪ] ADV geduldig, klaglos

uncompleted [ˌʌnkəmˈpliːtɪd] ADJ unbeendet, unvollendet

uncomplicated [ʌnˈkɒmplɪkeɪtɪd] ADJ unkompliziert; **his life was ~ by emotional problems** sein Leben wurde nicht durch emotionale Probleme kompliziert *or* erschwert

uncomplimentary [ˌʌnkɒmplɪˈmentərɪ] ADJ unschmeichelhaft; **to be ~ about sb/sth** sich nicht sehr schmeichelhaft über jdn/etw äußern

uncomprehending ADJ, **uncomprehendingly** ADV [ˌʌnkɒmprɪˈhendɪŋ, -lɪ] verständnislos

uncompress [ˌʌnkəmˈpres] VT *(Comput) data* dekomprimieren

uncompromising [ʌnˈkɒmprəmaɪzɪŋ] ADJ kompromisslos; *dedication, honesty* rückhaltlos; *commitment* hundertprozentig; **to be ~ in sth** sich bei etw auf keinen Kompromiss einlassen

uncompromisingly [ʌnˈkɒmprəmaɪzɪŋlɪ] ADV unerbittlich; *frank* rückhaltlos, völlig; *committed* hundertprozentig; **he is ~ opposed to ...** er ist ein kompromissloser Gegner *(+gen)* ...

unconcealed [ˌʌnkənˈsiːld] ADJ *joy, delight etc* offen, unverhüllt; *hatred, distaste, anger, satisfaction etc also* unverhohlen

unconcern [ˌʌnkənˈsɜːn] N *(= lack of worry)* Unbesorgtheit *f*, Unbekümmertheit *f*; *(= indifference)* Gleichgültigkeit *f*

unconcerned [ˌʌnkənˈsɜːnd] ADJ **a** *(= unworried)* unbekümmert; *(= indifferent)* gleichgültig; **to be ~ about sth** sich nicht um etw kümmern; **how could he be so ~ about her safety/the problem?** wie konnte ihm ihre Sicherheit/das Problem so egal *or* gleichgültig sein?; **I was not ~ about your safety** ich habe mir Sorgen um deine Sicherheit gemacht; **to be ~ by sth, to be ~ at sth** von etw unberührt sein **b** *(= not involved)* unbeteiligt *(in* an *+dat)*

unconcernedly [ˌʌnkənˈsɜːnɪdlɪ] ADV unbekümmert; *(= indifferently)* gleichgültig

unconditional [ˌʌnkənˈdɪʃənl] ADJ vorbehaltlos; *surrender, love* bedingungslos; *support* vorbehaltlos, uneingeschränkt; **he was remanded on ~ bail** *(Jur)* er wurde gegen Kaution freigelassen

unconditionally [ˌʌnkənˈdɪʃnəlɪ] ADV *offer, agree, give* vorbehaltlos; *support* vorbehaltlos, uneingeschränkt; *surrender, withdraw, release, love* bedingungslos

unconditioned [ˌʌnkənˈdɪʃənd] ADJ *(Psych)* nicht konditioniert

unconfined [ˌʌnkənˈfaɪnd] ADJ *(= unrestricted)* unbegrenzt, unbeschränkt

unconfirmed [ˌʌnkənˈfɜːmd] ADJ unbestätigt

unconformable [ˌʌnkənˈfɔːməbl] ADJ **a** *(= incompatible)* unvereinbar *(with* mit) **b** *(= inconsistent)* nicht übereinstimmend *(to, with* mit) **c** *(Geol) layer, stratum* diskordant, nicht gleichstrebend *or* gleich gelagert **d** *(Rel, Hist)* nonkonformistisch

uncongenial [ˌʌnkənˈdʒiːnɪəl] ADJ *person* unliebenswürdig, nicht einnehmend; *work, surroundings* unerfreulich; **he finds this place ~** dieser Ort entspricht ihm *or* seinem Wesen nicht; **to be ~ to sb** sich jdm gegenüber wenig liebenswürdig verhalten

unconnected [ˌʌnkəˈnektɪd] ADJ **a** *(= unrelated)* nicht miteinander in Beziehung stehend *attr*; *fact* losgelöst; *several facts* unzusammenhängend; **the two events are ~** es besteht keine Beziehung zwischen den beiden Ereignissen; **the two incidents were not ~** die beiden Zwischenfälle waren nicht ohne Zusammenhang; **to be ~ with** *or* **to sth** zu *or* mit etw nicht in Beziehung stehen **b** *(= incoherent)* zusammenhanglos, unzusammenhängend **c** *(Elec)* nicht angeschlossen

unconquerable [ʌnˈkɒŋkərəbl] ADJ *army* unbesiegbar; *peak* unbezwinglich, unerreichbar; *spirit* unbezwinglich, unbezwingbar; *courage* unbezähmbar

unconquered [ʌnˈkɒŋkəd] ADJ *army* unbesiegt; *mountain* unbezwungen; *courage, spirit* ungebrochen; **large parts of Britain remained ~** weite Teile Großbritanniens wurden nicht erobert

unconscionable [ʌnˈkɒnʃənəbl] ADJ unerhört; **an ~ time** eine unerhört lange Zeit, unerhört lange

unconscious [ʌnˈkɒnʃəs] **ADJ** **a** *(Med)* bewusstlos; **to fall ~** bewusstlos zu Boden fallen; **the blow knocked him ~** durch den Schlag wurde er bewusstlos; **to become ~** das Bewusstsein verlieren, bewusstlos werden; **to beat sb ~** jdn bewusstlos schlagen
b *pred (= unaware)* **to be ~ of sth** sich *(dat)* einer Sache *(gen)* nicht bewusst sein; **I was ~ of the fact that ...** ich war mir *or* es war mir nicht bewusst, dass ...
c *(= unintentional) insult, allusion etc* unbewusst, unbeabsichtigt; *blunder* ungewollt, unbeabsichtigt; *humour* unfreiwillig; **she was the ~ cause of his unhappiness** ohne es zu wissen, wurde sie zur Ursache seines Unglücks; **he was the ~ tool of ...** er wurde unwissentlich zum Werkzeug *(+gen)* ...
d *(Psych)* unbewusst; **the ~ mind** das Unbewusste; **at** *or* **on an ~ level** auf der Ebene des Unbewussten
N *(Psych)* **the ~** das Unbewusste; **he probed his ~** er erforschte das Unbewusste in sich *(dat)*

unconsciously [ʌnˈkɒnʃəslɪ] ADV unbewusst; **an ~ funny remark** eine ungewollt *or* unbeabsichtigt lustige Bemerkung; **consciously or ~** bewusst oder unbewusst

unconsciousness [ʌnˈkɒnʃəsnɪs] N **a** *(Med)* Bewusstlosigkeit *f* **b** *(= unawareness)* mangelndes Bewusstsein **c** *(of insult etc)* Ungewolltheit *f*; *(of humour)* Unfreiwilligkeit *f*

unconsecrated [ʌnˈkɒnsɪkreɪtɪd] ADJ *(Rel)* ungeweiht

unconsidered [ˌʌnkənˈsɪdəd] ADJ *fact etc* unberücksichtigt; *(= rash) action etc* unbedacht, unüberlegt; **he was an ~ outsider** er war ein Außenseiter, auf den niemand achtete

unconstitutional [ˌʌnkɒnstɪˈtjuːʃənl] ADJ nicht verfassungsgemäß, verfassungswidrig

unconstitutionally [ˌʌnkɒnstɪˈtjuːʃnəlɪ] ADV verfassungswidrig

unconstrained ADJ, **unconstrainedly** ADV [ˌʌnkənˈstreɪnd, -nɪdlɪ] ungezwungen, zwanglos

unconstructive [ˌʌnkənˈstrʌktɪv] ADJ nicht konstruktiv; **this is the most ~ suggestion I've ever heard** einen so wenig konstruktiven Vorschlag habe ich noch nie gehört

unconsummated [ʌnˈkɒnsjʊmeɪtɪd] ADJ unvollzogen

uncontaminated [ˌʌnkənˈtæmɪneɪtɪd] ADJ nicht verseucht; *people (by disease)* nicht angesteckt; *(fig)* unverdorben

uncontested [ˌʌnkənˈtestɪd] ADJ unbestritten; *divorce* unangefochten; *election, seat* ohne Gegenkandidat; **the seat/district was ~ by the Liberals** die Liberalen stellten für das Mandat/in dem Wahlkreis keinen Kandidaten auf; **the championship went ~ for many years** der Meisterschaftstitel wurde jahrelang nicht angefochten; **the chairmanship was ~** in der Wahl für den Vorsitz gab es keinen Gegenkandidaten

uncontrollable [ˌʌnkənˈtrəʊləbl] ADJ unkontrollierbar; *child* nicht zu bändigend *attr*, nicht zu bändigen *pred*; *car, boat, aeroplane, horse, dog* nicht unter Kontrolle zu bringend *attr*, nicht unter Kontrolle zu bringen *pred*; *rage, laughter, mirth* unbezähmbar; *desire, urge* unbezwinglich, unwiderstehlich; *(physical)* unkontrollierbar; *twitch* unkontrolliert; **the epidemic is now ~** die Epidemie ist nicht mehr unter Kontrolle zu bekommen; **to become ~** außer Kontrolle geraten; **to have an ~ temper** unbeherrscht sein

uncontrollably [ˌʌnkənˈtrəʊləblɪ] ADV unkontrollierbar; *weep* hemmungslos; *laugh* unkontrolliert

uncontrolled [ˌʌnkənˈtrəʊld] ADJ ungehindert; *dogs, children* unbeaufsichtigt; *behaviour* undiszipliniert; *laughter* unkontrolliert; *weeping* hemmungslos, haltlos; **if inflation is allowed to go ~** wenn die Inflation nicht unter Kontrolle gebracht wird

uncontroversial [ˌʌnkɒntrəˈvɜːʃəl] ADJ unverfänglich

unconventional [ˌʌnkənˈvenʃənl] ADJ unkonventionell; *weapons* nicht konventionell

unconventionality [ˌʌnkənvenʃəˈnælɪtɪ] N Unkonventionalität *f*

unconventionally [ˌʌnkənˈvenʃənəlɪ] ADV unkonventionell

unconversant [ˌʌnkənˈvɜːsnt] ADJ **to be ~ with sth** mit etw nicht vertraut sein

unconvinced [ˌʌnkənˈvɪnst] ADJ nicht überzeugt (*of* von); *look* wenig überzeugt; **his arguments leave me ~** seine Argumente überzeugen mich nicht; **I remain ~** ich bin noch immer nicht überzeugt; **to be ~ by sth** von etw nicht überzeugt sein

unconvincing [ˌʌnkənˈvɪnsɪŋ] ADJ nicht überzeugend; **rather ~** wenig überzeugend; **to become ~** an Überzeugungskraft verlieren; **to look/sound ~** nicht überzeugend aussehen/klingen

unconvincingly [ˌʌnkənˈvɪnsɪŋlɪ] ADV wenig überzeugend; **somewhat ~** ohne rechte Überzeugungskraft

uncooked [ʌnˈkʊkt] ADJ ungekocht, roh

uncool [ʌnˈkuːl] ADJ *(inf)* nicht (sehr) cool *(sl)*

uncooperative [ˌʌnkəʊˈɒpərətɪv] ADJ *attitude* stur, wenig entgegenkommend; *witness, colleague* wenig hilfreich, nicht hilfsbereit; **the government office remained ~** das Regierungsamt war auch weiterhin nicht zur Kooperation bereit; **if the prisoner is still ~** wenn sich der Gefangene weiterhin weigert, mit uns zusammenzuarbeiten; **why are you being so ~?** warum helfen Sie denn nicht mit?; **you're being rather ~** Sie sind nicht sehr hilfreich; **an ~ partner** ein Partner, der nicht mitmacht; **they didn't exactly go on strike, they just became ~** sie haben nicht gerade gestreikt, sie haben nur auf stur geschaltet

uncooperatively [ˌʌnkəʊˈɒpərətɪvlɪ] ADV wenig entgegenkommend; *say* wenig hilfreich

uncoordinated [ˌʌnkəʊˈɔːdɪneɪtɪd] ADJ unkoordiniert

uncork [ʌnˈkɔːk] VT *bottle* entkorken; *(fig)* herauslassen

uncorroborated [ˌʌnkəˈrɒbəreɪtɪd] ADJ unbestätigt; *evidence* nicht bekräftigt

uncorrupted [ˌʌnkəˈrʌptɪd] ADJ unverdorben, nicht korrumpiert; *person also* rechtschaffen

uncountable [ʌnˈkaʊntəbl] ADJ *(Gram)* unzählbar

uncounted [ʌnˈkaʊntɪd] ADJ *(= innumerable)* unzählig

uncouple [ʌnˈkʌpl] VT *train, trailer* abkuppeln, abkoppeln; **to ~ sth from sth** *(fig)* etw von etw loslösen

uncourteous ADJ, **uncourteously** ADV [ʌnkɜːtɪəs, -lɪ] unhöflich, grob

uncouth [ʌnˈkuːθ] ADJ *person* ungehobelt, ordinär; *behaviour* unflätig, ungehobelt; *manners* ungeschliffen, ungehobelt; *expression, word* unflätig, unfein; **it's very ~ to eat with your hands** es ist sehr unfein, mit den Fingern zu essen

uncover [ʌnˈkʌvəˈ] VT **a** *(= remove cover from)* aufdecken; *head* entblößen *(liter)*; **to ~ one's face** sein Gesicht frei machen; **the men ~ed their heads** die Männer nahmen ihre Kopfbedeckung ab **b** *scandal, plot, truth, evidence etc* aufdecken; *ancient ruins, cache of weapons etc* zum Vorschein bringen

uncritical [ʌnˈkrɪtɪkəl] ADJ unkritisch (*of, about* in Bezug auf *+acc*)

uncritically [ʌnˈkrɪtɪkəlɪ] ADV unkritisch

uncross [ʌnˈkrɒs] VT **he ~ed his legs** er nahm das Bein vom Knie; **she ~ed her arms** sie löste ihre verschränkten Arme

uncrossed [ʌnˈkrɒst] ADJ *legs* nicht übereinandergeschlagen *or* -gekreuzt; **~ cheque** *(dated Brit)* Barscheck *m*

uncrowded [ʌnˈkraʊdɪd] ADJ ziemlich leer, nicht überlaufen

uncrowned [ʌnˈkraʊnd] ADJ *(lit, fig)* ungekrönt

uncrushable [ʌnˈkrʌʃəbl] ADJ *dress* knitterfrei; *carton* hart, fest; *(fig) belief, spirit* unerschütterlich, durch nichts kleinzukriegen *(inf)*

unction [ˈʌŋkʃən] N **a** *(Rel: = anointing)* Salbung *f*, Ölung *f*; **extreme ~** Letzte Ölung **b** *(= insincere fervour)* hohles *or* unechtes Pathos

unctuous ADJ, **unctuously** ADV [ˈʌŋktjʊəs, -lɪ] salbungsvoll

unctuousness [ˈʌŋktjʊəsnɪs] N salbungsvolle Art; *(of speech)* falsches Pathos; **the ~ of his manner** seine salbungsvolle Art

uncultivated [ʌnˈkʌltɪveɪtɪd] ADJ *land* unkultiviert, unbebaut; *person, behaviour* unkultiviert; *mind* nicht ausgebildet; *talent* brachliegend

uncultured [ʌnˈkʌltʃəd] ADJ *person, mind* ungebildet; *behaviour* unkultiviert, unzivilisiert

uncurl [ʌnˈkɜːl] **VT** auseinanderrollen; **to ~ oneself** sich strecken; **she ~ed herself from the chair** sie streckte sich im Sessel und stand auf **VI** glatt werden; *(cat, snake)* sich langsam strecken; *(person)* sich ausstrecken

uncut [ʌnˈkʌt] ADJ **a** ungeschnitten; *ham, untrimmed pages* nicht aufgeschnitten; *stone, rock* unbehauen; *lawn* nicht gemäht; **~ diamond** Rohdiamant *m*; **an ~ rug** ein Schlingenteppich *m* **b** *(= unabridged) film, play, novel* ungekürzt; **to show a film ~** einen Film ungekürzt zeigen **c** *(= pure) drug* unverschnitten; **~ heroin** unverschnittenes Heroin **d** *(Med: = not circumcised)* nicht beschnitten

undamaged [ʌnˈdæmɪdʒd] ADJ unbeschädigt; *(fig) reputation* makellos; **to be ~ by sth** von etw nicht beschädigt worden sein

undated [ʌnˈdeɪtɪd] ADJ undatiert

undaunted [ʌnˈdɔːntɪd] ADJ *(= not discouraged)* nicht entmutigt, unverzagt; *(= fearless)* unerschrocken; *courage* unerschütterlich; **in spite of these failures he continued ~** trotz dieser Misserfolge machte er unverzagt weiter; **~ by these threats …** nicht eingeschüchtert von diesen Drohungen …

undead [ʌnˈded] N **the ~** *pl* die Untoten *pl*

undeceive [ˌʌndɪˈsiːv] VT aufklären

undecided [ˌʌndɪˈsaɪdɪd] ADJ **a** *person* unentschlossen; **he is ~ as to whether he should go or not** er ist (sich) noch unschlüssig, ob er gehen soll oder nicht; **to be ~ about sth** sich *(dat)* über etw *(acc)* im Unklaren sein **b** *question* unentschieden; **what are we going to do? – I don't know, it's ~** was sollen wir tun? – ich weiß nicht, das steht noch nicht fest *or* ist noch nicht entschieden

undecipherable [ˌʌndɪˈsaɪfərəbl] ADJ *handwriting* unleserlich, schwer zu entziffernd *attr*; *code, signs* nicht entzifferbar

undeclared [ˌʌndɪˈkleəd] ADJ *love, candidate* heimlich, unerklärt; *war* unerklärt; *interest* uneingestanden; *supporter* heimlich; *(Customs) goods* nicht deklariert; **~ income** nicht angegebenes Einkommen

undefeated [ˌʌndɪˈfiːtɪd] ADJ *army, team* unbesiegt; *champion, record* ungeschlagen; *spirit* ungebrochen

undefendable [ˌʌndɪˈfendəbl] ADJ *(Mil) coast, frontier* schwer zu verteidigend *attr*, schwer zu verteidigen *pred*

undefended [ˌʌndɪˈfendɪd] ADJ *town, goal* unverteidigt; **the case was ~** in dem Fall wurde auf Verteidigung verzichtet

undefiled [ˌʌndɪˈfaɪld] ADJ unbefleckt

undefinable ADJ, **undefinably** ADV [ˌʌndɪˈfaɪnəbl, -ɪ] undefinierbar, unbestimmbar

undefined [ˌʌndɪˈfaɪnd] ADJ undefiniert, nicht definiert; *(= vague)* undefinierbar

undelete [ˈʌndɪˈliːt] VT *(Comput)* wiederherstellen; **to ~ sth** das Löschen von etw rückgängig machen

undeliverable [ˌʌndɪˈlɪvərəbl] ADJ *mail* unzustellbar

undemanding [ˌʌndɪˈmɑːndɪŋ] ADJ anspruchslos, keine Anforderungen *or* Ansprüche stellend *attr*; *task* wenig fordernd, keine großen Anforderungen stellend *attr*; **this job is so ~** dieser Job fordert mich überhaupt nicht

undemocratic ADJ, **undemocratically** ADV [ˌʌndeməˈkrætɪk, -əlɪ] undemokratisch

undemonstrative [ˌʌndɪˈmɒnstrətɪv] ADJ reserviert, zurückhaltend; **a fairly ~ race** ein Volk, das seine Gefühle wenig zeigt

undeniable [ˌʌndɪˈnaɪəbl] ADJ unbestreitbar, unleugbar; **it is ~ that …** es lässt sich nicht bestreiten *or* leugnen, dass …

undeniably [ˌʌndɪˈnaɪəblɪ] ✪ 26.3 ADV zweifelsohne, zweifellos; *successful, proud* unbestreitbar

undenominational [ˌʌndɪnɒmɪˈneɪʃənl] ADJ interkonfessionell; **~ school** Gemeinschaftsschule *f*

undependable [ˌʌndɪˈpendəbl] ADJ unzuverlässig

under [ˈʌndəˈ] **PREP** **a** *(= beneath, place)* unter *(+dat)*; *(direction)* unter *(+acc)*; **~ it** darunter; **to come out from ~ the bed** unter dem Bett hervorkommen; **it's ~ there** es ist da drunter *(inf)*; **they held his head ~ the water** sie hielten seinen Kopf unter Wasser; **~ barley** mit Gerste bebaut

b *(= less than)* unter *(+dat)*; **it took ~ an hour** es dauerte weniger als eine Stunde; **there were ~ 50 of them** es waren weniger als 50, es waren unter 50

c *(= subordinate to, under influence of etc)* unter *(+dat)*; **he had 50 men ~ him** er hatte 50 Männer unter sich; **to study ~ sb** bei jdm studieren; **who were you ~?** *(Univ)* bei wem haben Sie studiert?; *(Mil)* unter wem haben Sie gedient?; **he was born ~ Virgo** *(Astrol)* er wurde im Zeichen der Jungfrau geboren; **he died ~ the anaesthetic** *(Brit) or* **anesthetic** *(US)* er starb in der Narkose; **you're ~ a misapprehension** Sie befinden sich im Irrtum; **~ construction** im Bau; **the matter ~ discussion** der Diskussionsgegenstand; **to be ~ treatment** *(Med)* in Behandlung sein; **to be ~ the doctor** in (ärztlicher) Behandlung sein; **which doctor are you ~?** bei welchem Arzt sind Sie?; **it's classified ~ history** es ist unter „Geschichte" eingeordnet; **you'll find the number ~ "garages"** Sie finden die Nummer unter „Werkstätten"; **~ sentence of death** zum Tode verurteilt; **~ penalty of death** unter Androhung der Todesstrafe; **~ an assumed name** unter falschem Namen; **the house is ~ threat of demolition** das Haus ist vom Abbruch bedroht

d *(= according to)* nach *(+dat)*, gemäß *(+dat)*,

laut (+dat); ~ his will in seinem Testament; ~ the terms of the contract nach or gemäß den Vertragsbedingungen
ADV a (= beneath) unten; (= unconscious) bewusstlos; he came to the fence and crawled ~ er kam zum Zaun und kroch darunter durch; to go ~ untergehen; to get out from ~ (fig inf) wieder Licht sehen (inf)
b (= less) darunter

under- PREF a (in rank) Unter-; for the ~twelves/-eighteens/-forties für Kinder unter zwölf/Jugendliche unter achtzehn/Leute unter vierzig b (= insufficiently) zu wenig, ungenügend

under: **underachieve** VI hinter den Erwartungen zurückbleiben; **underachievement** N schwache or enttäuschende Leistungen pl; **underachiever** N Johnny is an ~ Johnnys Leistungen bleiben hinter den Erwartungen zurück; **underact** VTI betont zurückhaltend spielen; (pej) schwach spielen; **underage** ADJ attr minderjährig; **underappreciation** N m Unterschätzung f, zu geringes Verständnis; **underarm** ADJ a Unterarm-; ~ hair Unterarmbehaarung f; ~ deodorant Achselhöhlen-Deodorant nt b throw von unten; ~ serve (Tennis) Aufschlag m von unten ADV throw, serve von unten; **underbelly** N (Zool, fig, of plane) Bauch m; the soft ~ of Europe/democracy die Achillesferse Europas/der Demokratie; **underbid** pret, ptp underbid VT (Comm) unterbieten VI (Cards) nicht hoch genug reizen; **underbody** N (of vehicle) Unterboden m; **underbrush** N = undergrowth; **underbuy** pret, ptp underbought VI zu wenig kaufen; **undercapitalized** ADJ (Fin) unterkapitalisiert; **undercarriage** N (Aviat) Fahrwerk nt, Fahrgestell nt; **undercharge** VI zu wenig berechnen VT to ~ sb jdm zu wenig berechnen; he ~d me by 50p er berechnete mir 50 Pence zu wenig; **underclass** N Unterklasse f; **underclothes** PL, **underclothing** N Unterwäsche f; **undercoat** N (= paint) Grundierfarbe f; (= coat) Grundierung f; (US Aut) Unterbodenschutz m; **undercook** VT nicht durchgaren; (accidentally also) nicht lange genug kochen; **undercover** ADJ geheim; ~ agent Geheimagent(in) m(f); (= investigator) verdeckter Ermittler, verdeckte Ermittlerin; he did ~ work for the police er arbeitete für die Polizei als verdeckter Ermittler ADV to work ~ undercover arbeiten; (with police) als verdeckter Ermittler/verdeckte Ermittlerin arbeiten; **undercroft** N (Archit) unterirdisches Gewölbe f, Gruft f; (of church) Krypta f; **undercurrent** N (lit, fig) Unterströmung f; (in speech, attitude) Unterton m; **undercut** pret, ptp undercut VT competitor, fare (im Preis) unterbieten; (fig) efforts etc untergraben; **underdeveloped** ADJ unterentwickelt; resources ungenutzt; **underdog** N (in society) Schwächere(r) mf, Benachteiligte(r) mf, Underdog m; (in game also) sicherer Verlierer, sichere Verliererin; **underdone** ADJ nicht gar; (deliberately) steak nicht durchgebraten; **underdressed** ADJ to be ~ (= too lightly) zu leicht angezogen sein; (= not formally enough) zu einfach angezogen sein; **underemphasize** VT nicht genügend or nicht ausreichend betonen; I don't want to ~ her role ich möchte ihre Rolle nicht herunterspielen; to deliberately ~ sth etw bewusst herunterspielen; **underemployed** ADJ nicht ausgelastet; person also unterbeschäftigt; plant, equipment also nicht voll (aus)genutzt; **underemployment** N Unterbeschäftigung f; (of person, plant also) mangelnde Auslastung; (of abilities, plant also) mangelnde Ausnutzung; **underestimate** [ˌʌndərˈestɪmeɪt] VT unterschätzen N [ˌʌndərˈestɪmɪt] Unterschätzung f; **underestimation** N Unterschätzung f; **underexpose** VT (Phot) unterbelichten; **underexposed** ADJ (Phot) unterbelichtet; **underexposure** N (Phot) Unterbelichtung f; (fig) Mangel m an Publizität; **underfed** ADJ unterernährt; **underfeed** pret, ptp underfed VT zu wenig zu essen geben (+dat); animals zu wenig füttern; **underfeeding** N (of animals) Unterernährung f; **underfelt** N Filzunterlage f; **underfinanced** ADJ unterfinanziert; **underfloor heating** N Fußbodenheizung f; **underfoot** ADV am Boden; it is wet ~ der Boden ist nass; to trample sb/sth ~ (lit, fig) auf jdm/etw herumtrampeln; **underfund** VT unterfinanzieren; **underfunded** ADJ unterfinanziert; **underfunding** N Unterfinanzierung f; **undergarment** N Unterkleid nt; ~s Unterkleidung f; **undergo** pret underwent, ptp undergone VT suffering durchmachen, mitmachen; process durchmachen, durchlaufen; training mitmachen; change also erleben; test, treatment, operation sich unterziehen (+dat); (machine) test unterzogen werden (+dat); to ~ repairs in Reparatur sein; **undergrad** (inf), **undergraduate** N Student(in) m(f) ATTR class, course für nichtgraduierte or nicht graduierte Studenten; ~uate student Student(in) m(f)

underground [ˈʌndəgraʊnd] ADJ a explosion, lake, cave, passage unterirdisch; ~ cable Erdkabel nt; ~ mining Untertagebau m; ~ railway (Brit) or railroad (US) Untergrundbahn f; ~ line U-Bahn-Linie f b (fig: = secret) Untergrund-; ~ movement Untergrundbewegung f; ~ activities Untergrundtätigkeit f c (= alternative) Underground-; ~ magazine Underground-Magazin nt ADV a unterirdisch; (Min) unter Tage; 3 m ~ 3 m unter der Erde b (fig) to go ~ untertauchen N a (Brit Rail) U-Bahn f, Untergrundbahn f b (= movement) Untergrundbewegung f; (= subculture) Underground m

underground (Brit Rail): **underground station** N U-Bahnhof m; **underground system** N U-Bahn-Netz nt; **underground train** N U-Bahn-Zug m

under: **undergrowth** N Gestrüpp nt, Gebüsch nt; (under trees) Unterholz nt; **underhand** ADJ a (= sly) hinterhältig b (Sport) = underarm; **underhanded** ADJ = underhand a; **underhandedly** ADV hinterhältigerweise; **underhung** ADJ jaw vorgeschoben; meat ungenügend or nicht genug abgehangen; **underinsured** ADJ unterversichert; **underinvestment** N mangelnde or unzureichende Investitionen pl; industry is suffering from ~ die Industrie leidet unter Investitionsmangel; **underlay** N (Brit) Unterlage f; **underlie** pret underlay, ptp underlain VT (lit) liegen unter (+dat); (fig: = be basis for or cause of) zugrunde or zu Grunde liegen (+dat); **underline** VT (lit, fig) unterstreichen N (Typ) Unterstrich m, tiefgestellter Bindestrich

underling [ˈʌndəlɪŋ] N (pej) Untergebene(r) mf, Befehlsempfänger(in) m(f) (pej)

under: **underlining** N Unterstreichung f; with red ~ rot unterstrichen; why all this ~? warum ist so viel unterstrichen?; **underlying** ADJ a soil, rocks tiefer liegend b cause eigentlich; (= deeper) tiefer; problem, message, theme zugrunde or zu Grunde liegend; honesty, strength grundlegend; tension unterschwellig; the ~ cause of all this was all dem zugrunde or zu Grunde liegt; a certain ~ sense of tragedy eine gewisse unterschwellige Tragik c (Econ) ~ rate of inflation Basis-Inflationsrate f; **undermanned** ADJ unterbesetzt; **undermanning** N Personalmangel m, Personalknappheit f; (deliberate) Unterbesetzung f; (Mil, of police force etc) Unterbemannung f; **undermentioned** ADJ unten genannt, unten erwähnt; **undermine** VT a (= tunnel under) unterhöhlen; (Mil) unterminieren; (= weaken) schwächen; (sea) cliffs unterspülen, unterhöhlen b (fig: = weaken) unterminieren, untergraben; health angreifen; **undermost** ADJ unterste(r, s)

underneath [ˌʌndəˈniːθ] PREP (place) unter (+dat); (direction) unter (+acc); ~ it darunter; the cat came out from ~ the table die Katze kam unter dem Tisch hervor; from ~ the trees we could only see ... unter den Bäumen stehend/sitzend konnten wir nur ... sehen ADV darunter; the ones ~ die darunter N Unterseite f

under: **undernourished** ADJ unterernährt; **undernourishment** N Unterernährung f; **underoccupied** ADJ hostel, hospital etc unterbelegt; **underpaid** ADJ unterbezahlt; **underpants** PL Unterhose(n) f(pl); a pair of ~ eine Unterhose, ein Paar nt Unterhosen; **underpart** N Unterteil nt; **underpass** N Unterführung f; **underpay** pret, ptp underpaid VT unterbezahlen; **underpayment** N zu geringe Bezahlung, Unterbezahlung f; because of ~ of tax ... weil zu wenig Steuer gezahlt wurde ...; there was an ~ of £5 in your salary Sie bekamen £ 5 zu wenig Gehalt ausbezahlt; **underpin** VT (Archit) wall, building untermauern; (fig) argument, claim untermauern; economy, market, shares etc (ab)stützen; **underpinning** N (Archit) Untermauerung f; **underplay** VT a (Cards) hand nicht voll ausspielen; to ~ one's hand (fig) nicht alle Trümpfe ausspielen b (Theat) role zurückhaltend spielen c significance, role, extent herunterspielen; **underplot** N (of novel etc) Nebenhandlung f; **underpopulated** ADJ unterbevölkert; **underprice** VT zu billig or unter Preis anbieten; to be ~d zu billig gehandelt werden; at £10 it is ~d mit £ 10 ist es zu billig; **underpricing** N Festlegung f zu niedriger Preise; **underprivileged** ADJ unterprivilegiert N the ~ pl die Unterprivilegierten pl; **underproduce** VI zu wenig produzieren; **underproduction** N Unterproduktion f; **underproof** ADJ spirits unterprozentig; **underqualified** ADJ unterqualifiziert; **underrate** VT (= underestimate) danger, chance, opponent, person unterschätzen; (= undervalue) qualities unterbewerten; **underrated** ADJ unterschätzt; he is probably the most ~ songwriter in the business er ist vielleicht der am meisten unterschätzte Songwriter der ganzen Branche; **underrepresented** ADJ unterrepräsentiert; **underripe** ADJ fruit unreif; slightly ~ (noch) nicht ganz reif; **underscore** VT, N = underline; **undersea** ADJ Unterwasser-; ~ explorer Unterwasserforscher(in) m(f); **underseal** (Brit Aut) N Unterbodenschutz m VT mit Unterbodenschutz versehen; is it ~ed? hat es Unterbodenschutz?; I must have my car ~ed ich muss Unterbodenschutz machen lassen; **underseas** ADJ Unterwasser-, untermeerisch; **undersecretary** (Brit) N a (also Parliamentary Undersecretary) (parlamentarischer) Staatssekretär b Permanent Undersecretary Ständiger Unterstaatssekretär; **undersell** pret, ptp undersold VT a competitor unterbieten; (= sell at lower price) goods unter Preis verkaufen, verschleudern b (= not publicize) nicht gut verkaufen; (as advertising technique) nicht anpreisen; he tends to ~ himself/his ideas er kann sich/seine Ideen normalerweise nicht verkaufen; **undersexed** ADJ to be ~ einen unterentwickelten Geschlechtstrieb haben (form), nicht viel für Sex übrighaben; he's not exactly ~ er ist der reinste Lustmolch (inf); **undershirt** N (US) Unterhemd nt; **undershoot** pret, ptp undershot VI (Aviat, missile) zu früh landen VT to ~ the runway vor der Landebahn aufsetzen; to ~ the target das Ziel nicht erreichen; **undershorts** PL (US) Unterhose(n) f(pl); **underside** N Unterseite f; **undersign** VTI unterschreiben, unterzeichnen; **undersigned** ADJ (form) unterzeichnet N we the ~ wir, die Unterzeichneten; **undersized** ADJ klein; (= less than proper size) zu klein; clothes in einer zu kleinen Größe; (pej) person also zu kurz geraten (hum); **underskirt** N Unterrock m; **undersold** pret, ptp of undersell; **underspend** pret, ptp underspent VI zu wenig ausgeben (on für); we have underspent by £1000 wir haben £ 1000 weniger ausgegeben als geplant; **understaffed** ADJ office unterbesetzt; prison, hospital mit zu wenig Personal; we are very ~ at the moment wir haben momentan zu wenig Leute

understand [ˌʌndəˈstænd] ✪ 12.1, 26.3 pret, ptp understood VT a language, painting, statement, speaker verstehen; action, event, person, difficulty also begreifen; I don't ~ Russian ich verstehe or kann kein Russisch; that's what I can't ~ das kann ich eben nicht verstehen or begreifen; I can't ~ his agreeing to do it ich kann

nicht verstehen *or* es ist mir unbegreiflich, warum er sich dazu bereit erklärt hat; **but ~ this!** aber eins sollte klar sein; **what do you ~ by "pragmatism"?** was verstehen Sie unter „Pragmatismus"?
b *(= comprehend sympathetically) children, people, animals, doubts, fears* verstehen; **to ~ one another** sich verstehen
c *(= believe)* **I ~ that you are going to Australia** ich höre, Sie gehen nach Australien; **I ~ that you've already met her** Sie haben sich, soviel ich weiß, schon kennengelernt; **I understood (that) he was abroad/we were to have been consulted** ich dachte, er sei im Ausland/wir sollten dazu befragt werden; **am I/are we to ~ that ...?** soll das etwa heißen, dass ...?; **as I ~ it, ...** soweit ich weiß, ...; **did I ~ him to say that ...?** habe ich richtig verstanden, dass er sagte, ...?; **but I understood her to say that she agreed** aber soweit ich sie verstanden habe, hat sie zugestimmt; **to give sb to ~ that ...** jdm zu verstehen geben, dass ...; **I was given to ~ that ...** man hat mir bedeutet, dass ...; **I understood from his speech that ...** ich schloss aus seiner Rede, dass ...; **what do you ~ from his remarks?** wie verstehen Sie seine Bemerkungen?
d *(Gram: = supply) word* sich *(dat)* denken, (im Stillen) ergänzen → *also* **understood**
VI **a** *(= comprehend)* verstehen; **(do you) ~?** (hast du/haben Sie das) verstanden?; **you don't ~!** du verstehst mich nicht!; **but you don't ~, I must have the money now** aber verstehen Sie doch, ich brauche das Geld jetzt!; **I quite ~** ich verstehe schon
b *(= believe)* **so I ~** es scheint so; **he was, I ~, a widower** wie ich hörte, war er Witwer

understandable [ˌʌndəˈstændəbl] **ADJ** **a** *(= intelligible)* verständlich **b** *(= reasonable, natural)* verständlich, begreiflich

understandably [ˌʌndəˈstændəblɪ] **ADV** **a** *(= intelligibly)* verständlich **b** *(= reasonably, naturally)* verständlicherweise, begreiflicherweise

understanding [ˌʌndəˈstændɪŋ] **ADJ** verständnisvoll; **he asked me to be ~** er bat mich um Verständnis
N **a** *(= intelligence)* Auffassungsgabe *f*; *(= knowledge)* Kenntnisse *pl*; *(= comprehension, sympathy)* Verständnis *nt*; **her ~ of children** ihr Verständnis *nt* für Kinder; **because of his complete lack of ~ for the problems** da ihm jedes Verständnis für die Probleme fehlte; **my ~ of the situation is that ...** ich verstehe die Situation so, dass ...; **his conduct is beyond human ~** sein Verhalten ist absolut unbegreiflich; **she's a woman of great ~** sie ist eine sehr verständnisvolle Frau; **it was my ~ that ...** ich nahm an *or* ich war der Meinung, dass ...; **he has a good ~ of the problem** er kennt sich mit dem Problem gut aus; **to promote international ~** um die internationale Verständigung zu fördern
b *(= agreement)* Abmachung *f*, Vereinbarung *f*, Verständigung *f*; **to come to** *or* **reach an ~ with sb** eine Abmachung *or* Vereinbarung mit jdm treffen; **Susie and I have an ~** Susie und ich haben unsere Abmachung; **a degree of ~** eine gewisse Übereinstimmung, ein gewisses Einvernehmen
c *(= assumption)* Voraussetzung *f*; **on the ~ that ...** unter der Voraussetzung, dass ...; **on this ~** unter dieser Voraussetzung

understandingly [ˌʌndəˈstændɪŋlɪ] **ADV** verständnisvoll

understate [ˌʌndəˈsteɪt] **VT** herunterspielen; **to ~ one's case** untertreiben

understated [ˌʌndəˈsteɪtɪd] **ADJ** *film etc* subtil; *picture, music, colours* gedämpft; *clothes* unaufdringlich; *performance, acting* zurückhaltend, untertrieben; *manner* zurückhaltend; *make-up* unaufdringlich

understatement [ˈʌndəˌsteɪtmənt] **N** Untertreibung *f*, Understatement *nt*

understeer [ˈʌndəˌstɪəˈ] *(Aut)* **N** Untersteuerung *f* **VI** [ˌʌndəˈstɪəˈ] untersteuern

understock [ˌʌndəˈstɒk] **VTI** (sich) ungenügend eindecken *(with* mit)

understood [ˌʌndəˈstʊd] *pret, ptp of* **understand**
ADJ **a** *(= clear)* klar; **to make oneself ~** sich verständlich machen; **do I make myself ~?** ist das klar?; **I wish it to be ~ that ...** ich möchte klarstellen, dass ...; **(is that) ~?** (ist das) klar?; **~!** gut!
b *(= agreed)* **it was ~ between them that ...** sie hatten eine Vereinbarung, dass ...; **I thought that was ~!** ich dachte, das sei klar; **certain things always have to be ~ in a relationship** einige Dinge sollten in einer Beziehung immer stillschweigend vorausgesetzt werden *or* immer von vornherein klar sein
c *(= believed)* angenommen, geglaubt; **he is ~ to have left** es heißt, dass er gegangen ist; **it is ~ that ...** es heißt *or* man hört, dass ...; **he let it be ~ that ...** er gab zu verstehen, dass ...
d *pred (Gram)* ausgelassen

understudy [ˈʌndəˌstʌdɪ] **N** *(Theat)* zweite Besetzung; *(fig)* Stellvertreter(in) *m(f)* **VT** *(Theat)* zweite Besetzung sein für

undersurface **N** [ˈʌndəˌsɜːfɪs] *(= underside)* Unterseite *f* **ADJ** [ˌʌndəˈsɜːfɪs] *(= undersea(s))* Unterwasser-; *(= subterranean)* unterirdisch

undertake [ˌʌndəˈteɪk] *pret* **undertook** [ˌʌndəˈtʊk] *ptp* **undertaken** [ˌʌndəˈteɪkn] **VT** **a** *job, duty, responsibility* übernehmen; *risk* eingehen, auf sich *(acc)* nehmen; *study, research, reform* durchführen; *tour* machen; **he undertook to be our guide** er übernahm es, unser Führer zu sein
b *(= agree, promise)* sich verpflichten; *(= guarantee)* garantieren

undertaker [ˈʌndəˌteɪkəˈ] **N** (Leichen)bestatter(in) *m(f)*; *(= company)* Bestattungs- *or* Beerdigungsinstitut *nt*

undertaking¹ [ˌʌndəˈteɪkɪŋ] **N** **a** *(= enterprise)* Vorhaben *nt*, Unternehmen *nt*; *(esp Comm: = project)* Projekt *nt* **b** *(= promise)* Zusicherung *f*, Wort *nt*; **I give you my solemn ~ that I will never do it again** ich verpflichte mich feierlich, es nie wieder zu tun; **I can give no such ~** das kann ich nicht versprechen **c** *(= funeral business)* Bestattungsgewerbe *nt*

undertaking² **N** *(Brit Aut inf)* Überholen *nt* auf der Innenseite

under: **undertax** [ˌʌndəˈtæks] **VT** unterbesteuern, zu niedrig besteuern; **undertenant** [ˈʌndəˌtenənt] **N** Untermieter(in) *m(f)*; *(of land)* Unterpächter(in) *m(f)*; **under-the-counter** **ADJ** → **counter**; **undertone** **N** **a** *(of voice)* **in an ~** mit gedämpfter Stimme **b** *(fig, of criticism, discontent)* Unterton *m*; *(of colour)* Tönung *f*; **an ~ of racism** ein rassistischer Unterton; **undertook** *pret of* **undertake**; **undertow** **N** *(lit, fig)* Unterströmung *f*; **there is a lot of ~** es gibt viele Unterströmungen; **underused** **ADJ** *land, muscles* nicht voll genutzt; *resources, facilities also* unausgeschöpft; **underutilization** **N** mangelnde *or* unzureichende Nutzung; **underutilized** **ADJ** unzureichend *or* nicht voll genutzt; **undervalue** **VT** *antique, artist* unterbewerten, unterschätzen; *(= price too low) company, assets, shares* zu niedrig schätzen *or* veranschlagen; *person* zu wenig schätzen; **underwater** **ADJ** Unterwasser-; **~ photography** Unterwasserfotografie *f* **ADV** unter Wasser; **underway** **ADJ** *(esp US)* unterwegs; *(= in progress)* im Gang → *also* **way**; **underwear** **N** Unterwäsche *f*; **underweight** **ADJ** untergewichtig; **to be (2 kg) ~** (2 kg) Untergewicht haben; **underwent** *pret of* **undergo**; **underwhelm** **VT** *(hum)* **the critics were ~ed by his second novel** sein zweiter Roman hat die Kritiker nicht gerade umgehauen *(inf)*; **underworld** **N** *(= criminals, Myth)* Unterwelt *f*; **underwrite** *pret* **underwrote**, *ptp* **underwritten** **VT** *(= finance) company, loss, project* tragen, garantieren; *(= guarantee) insurance policy* garantieren, bürgen für; *(= insure) shipping, risk* versichern; *(St Ex) shares, issue* zeichnen; *(fig: = agree to) policies etc* billigen; **underwriter** **N** *(Insur: = company)* Versicherer *m*, Versicherungsgeber *m*

undeserved [ˌʌndɪˈzɜːvd] **ADJ** unverdient

undeservedly [ˌʌndɪˈzɜːvɪdlɪ] **ADV** unverdient(ermaßen)

undeserving [ˌʌndɪˈzɜːvɪŋ] **ADJ** *person, cause* unwürdig; **the ~ poor** die Armen, die es nicht besser verdienen; **to be ~ of sth** *(form)* einer Sache *(gen)* unwürdig sein *(form)*

undesirability [ˌʌndɪzaɪərəˈbɪlɪtɪ] **N** **a** *(of policy, effect)* Unerwünschtheit *f*; **because of the general ~ of the site** da der Bauplatz durchweg nur Nachteile hat **b** *(of influence, characters, area)* Übelkeit *f*

undesirable [ˌʌndɪˈzaɪərəbl] **ADJ** **a** *policy, effect* unerwünscht; **~ alien** unerwünschter Ausländer, unerwünschte Ausländerin; **an ~ person to have as a manager** kein wünschenswerter Manager; **they consider her fiancé ~** sie glauben, dass ihr Verlobter keine wünschenswerte Partie ist; **it is ~ that ...** es wäre höchst unerwünscht, wenn ... **b** *influence, characters, area* übel; **~ elements** unerwünschte Elemente *pl*; **he's just generally ~** er ist ganz einfach ein übler Kerl **N** *(= person)* unerfreuliches Element; *(= foreigner)* unerwünschtes Element

undetachable [ˌʌndɪˈtætʃəbl] **ADJ** nicht (ab)trennbar *or* abnehmbar

undetected [ˌʌndɪˈtektɪd] **ADJ** unentdeckt; **to go ~** nicht entdeckt werden; **to remain ~** unentdeckt bleiben

undetermined [ˌʌndɪˈtɜːmɪnd] **ADJ** *(= indefinite)* unbestimmt; *(= unsure) person* unentschlossen, unschlüssig; **an ~ amount (of money)** eine (Geld)summe in unbestimmter Höhe

undeterred [ˌʌndɪˈtɜːd] **ADJ** keineswegs entmutigt; **to continue ~** unverzagt weitermachen; **the teams were ~ by the weather** das Wetter schreckte die Mannschaften nicht ab

undeveloped [ˌʌndɪˈveləpt] **ADJ** unentwickelt; *land, resources* ungenutzt

undeviating [ʌnˈdiːvɪeɪtɪŋ] **ADJ** *(= straight) line* gerade; *(fig: = unchanging) route, path* direkt; *fairness, determination* unbeirrbar; *accuracy* unfehlbar

undiagnosed [ˌʌndaɪəgˈnəʊzd] **ADJ** *disease* unerkannt

undid [ʌnˈdɪd] *pret of* **undo**

undies [ˈʌndɪz] **PL** *(inf)* (Unter)wäsche *f*

undifferentiated [ˌʌndɪfəˈrenʃɪeɪtɪd] **ADJ** undifferenziert

undigested [ˌʌndaɪˈdʒestɪd] **ADJ** *(lit, fig)* unverdaut

undignified [ʌnˈdɪgnɪfaɪd] **ADJ** *person, behaviour* würdelos; *(= inelegant) way of sitting etc* unelegant; **he was never afraid of appearing ~** er hatte keine Angst, seine Würde zu verlieren

undiluted [ˌʌndaɪˈluːtɪd] **ADJ** unverdünnt; *(fig) truth, version, accent* unverfälscht; *pleasure* rein, voll; *enthusiasm, praise* unvermindert

undiminished [ˌʌndɪˈmɪnɪʃt] **ADJ** *enthusiasm* unvermindert; *strength, courage also* unbeeinträchtigt

undiplomatic **ADJ**, **undiplomatically** **ADV** [ˌʌndɪpləˈmætɪk, -əlɪ] undiplomatisch

undipped [ʌnˈdɪpt] **ADJ** *(Brit Aut)* **~ headlights** Fernlicht *nt*

undiscerned **ADJ**, **undiscernedly** **ADV** [ˌʌndɪˈsɜːnd, -nɪdlɪ] *(form)* unbemerkt

undiscerning [ˌʌndɪˈsɜːnɪŋ] **ADJ** *reader, palate* anspruchslos, unkritisch; *critic* unbedarft

undischarged [ˌʌndɪsˈtʃɑːdʒd] **ADJ** **a** *(Fin) debt* unbezahlt, unbeglichen; *bankrupt* nicht entlastet **b** *cargo* nicht abgeladen; *gun* nicht abgefeuert

undisciplined [ʌnˈdɪsɪplɪnd] **ADJ** *mind, person* undiszipliniert; *imagination* zügellos; *hair* ungebändigt

undisclosed [ˌʌndɪsˈkləʊzd] **ADJ** *secret* (bisher) unaufgedeckt; *details, location, price etc also* geheim gehalten; *fee, reason, number* ungenannt, geheim gehalten; **an ~ sum** eine ungenannte *or* geheim gehaltene Summe

undiscovered [ˌʌndɪ'skʌvəd] **ADJ** unentdeckt; **to lie ~** unentdeckt *or* noch nicht entdeckt sein

undiscriminating [ˌʌndɪ'skrɪmɪneɪtɪŋ] **ADJ** = **undiscerning**

undisguised [ˌʌndɪs'gaɪzd] **ADJ** ungetarnt; *(fig) truth* unverhüllt; *dislike, affection* unverhohlen; **an ~ attempt to do sth** ein unverhüllter Versuch, etw zu tun

undismayed [ˌʌndɪs'meɪd] **ADJ** ungerührt, unbeeindruckt

undisposed [ˌʌndɪ'spəʊzd] **ADJ ~ of** *(Comm)* unverkauft

undisputed [ˌʌndɪ'spju:tɪd] **ADJ** unbestritten

undistinguished [ˌʌndɪ'stɪŋgwɪʃt] **ADJ** *performance* (mittel)mäßig; *appearance* durchschnittlich

undisturbed [ˌʌndɪ'stɜ:bd] **ADJ** **a** *(= untouched) papers, dust* unberührt; *(= uninterrupted) person, sleep, quiet etc* ungestört; *(= quiet) village* unberührt; **to be ~ by tourism** vom Tourismus unberührt sein **b** *(= unworried)* unberührt

undivided [ˌʌndɪ'vaɪdɪd] **ADJ** *country, opinion, attention* ungeteilt; *support* voll; *loyalty* absolut; *love* uneingeschränkt; **we must stand firm and ~** wir müssen fest und einig sein

undo [ʌn'du:] *pret* **undid**, *ptp* **undone** **VT** **a** *(= unfasten)* aufmachen; *button, dress, zip, parcel* aufmachen, öffnen; *knot* lösen; *knitting* aufziehen; *sewing* auftrennen; **will you ~ me?** *(inf)* kannst du mir den Reißverschluss/die Knöpfe *etc* aufmachen? **b** *(= reverse) mischief, wrong* ungeschehen machen; *work* zunichtemachen, ruinieren; *decision* rückgängig machen; (*Comput: command*) rückgängig machen; **we cannot ~ the past** wir können die Vergangenheit nicht ungeschehen machen **VI** aufgehen

undock [ʌn'dɒk] *(Space)* **VT** entkoppeln **VI** sich trennen

undoing [ʌn'du:ɪŋ] **N** Ruin *m*, Verderben *nt*

undomesticated [ˌʌndə'mestɪkeɪtɪd] **ADJ** *animal, pet* nicht ans Haus gewöhnt; *woman, husband* nicht häuslich; **men aren't as ~ as they used to be** Männer sind heute häuslicher als früher

undone [ʌn'dʌn] **PTP** *of* **undo** **ADJ** **a** *(= unfastened) button, shoelace, tie, hair* offen; **to come ~** aufgehen **b** *(= neglected) task, work* unerledigt; **to leave sth ~** etw ungetan lassen; **we have left ~ what we ought to have done** *(Rel)* wir haben unser Tagwerk nicht getan **c** *(= cancelled out)* **she has seen her life's work ~** sie musste zusehen, wie ihr Lebenswerk zerstört wurde **d** *(obs: = ruined)* **I am ~!** ich bin ruiniert; **to be ~** zu Fall gebracht werden

undoubted [ʌn'daʊtɪd] **ADJ** unbestritten; *success also* unzweifelhaft

undoubtedly [ʌn'daʊtɪdlɪ] ✪ 15.1 **ADV** zweifellos, ohne Zweifel

undoubting [ʌn'daʊtɪŋ] **ADJ** unerschütterlich

undramatic [ˌʌndrə'mætɪk] **ADJ** undramatisch

undreamt-of [ʌn'dremtɒv], *(US)* **undreamed-of** [ʌn'dri:mdɒv] **ADJ** ungeahnt; **in their time this was ~** zu ihrer Zeit hätte man sich das nie träumen lassen

undress [ʌn'dres] **VT** ausziehen; **to get ~ed** sich ausziehen **VI** sich ausziehen **N** **in a state of ~** halb bekleidet

undressed [ʌn'drest] **ADJ** **a** *person (still)* (noch) nicht angezogen; *(already)* (schon) ausgezogen; **I feel ~ without my watch** ohne Uhr komme ich mir nackt vor **b** *leather* ungegerbt; *wood* unbehandelt, frisch; *stone* ungeschliffen; *(Cook) salad* nicht angemacht; *wound* unverbunden

undrinkable [ʌn'drɪŋkəbl] **ADJ** ungenießbar

undue [ʌn'dju:] **ADJ** *(= excessive)* übertrieben, übermäßig; *(= improper)* ungebührlich

undulant ['ʌndjʊlənt] **ADJ** = **undulating**

undulate ['ʌndjʊleɪt] **VI** *(sea, corn)* wogen; *(river, snake)* sich schlängeln; *(hills)* sich in sanften Wellenlinien erstrecken; *(path)* auf und ab führen; *(hair)* wallen; **her hips ~d in time to the music** ihre Hüften wiegten sich im Takt mit der Musik

undulating ['ʌndjʊleɪtɪŋ] **ADJ** *movement, line* wellenförmig; *waves, sea* wogend; *hair* wallend; *countryside* hügelig; *hills* sanft; *path* auf und ab führend; *hips* wiegend

undulation [ˌʌndjʊ'leɪʃən] **N** *(of waves, countryside)* Auf und Ab *nt*; *(of snake, single movement)* Windung *f*, schlängelnde Bewegung; *(= curve)* Rundung *f*

undulatory ['ʌndjʊlətrɪ] **ADJ** *movement* wellenförmig

unduly [ʌn'dju:lɪ] **ADV** übermäßig, übertrieben; *optimistic, pessimistic, lenient* zu; *punish* unangemessen *or* übermäßig streng; **you're worrying ~** Sie machen sich *(dat)* unnötige Sorgen

undutiful [ʌn'dju:tɪfʊl] **ADJ** pflichtvergessen; *child* ungehorsam

undying [ʌn'daɪɪŋ] **ADJ** *love* unsterblich, ewig; *fame also* unvergänglich

unearned [ʌn'ɜ:nd] **ADJ** **a** *increment* unverdient **b** *(= undeserved)* unverdient

unearned income **N** Kapitalertrag *m*, arbeitsloses Einkommen

unearth [ʌn'ɜ:θ] **VT** ausgraben; *(fig) book etc* aufstöbern; *information, evidence, talent* zutage *or* zu Tage bringen, ausfindig machen

unearthly [ʌn'ɜ:θlɪ] **ADJ** *(= eerie) calm* gespenstisch, unheimlich; *scream* schauerlich, unheimlich; *beauty* überirdisch; (*inf: = awful*) *sound, noise, racket* schauerlich; **at the ~ hour of 5 o'clock** *(inf)* zu nachtschlafender Stunde um 5 Uhr

unease [ʌn'i:z] **N** Unbehagen *nt*, Beklommenheit *f*

uneasily [ʌn'i:zɪlɪ] **ADV** *sit* unbehaglich; *smile, listen, speak etc also* beklommen, unsicher; *sleep* unruhig; **to be ~ balanced** sehr prekär sein; **to be ~ poised** sehr wack(e)lig stehen; **to be ~ aware that …** sich *(dat)* mit Unbehagen bewusst sein, dass …; **to be ~ aware of sth** etw mit Unbehagen erkennen; **to sit ~ with sth** nur schlecht zu etw passen

uneasiness [ʌn'i:zɪnɪs] **N** (= *anxiety: of laugh, look, = awkwardness: of silence, atmosphere*) Unbehaglichkeit *f*, Beklommenheit *f*; *(of peace, balance)* Unsicherheit *f*, Wack(e)ligkeit *f (inf)*; *(of alliance, coalition, relationship)* Instabilität *f*, Wack(e)ligkeit *f (inf)*; *(of person) (= awkwardness)* Beklommenheit *f*; *(= anxiety)* Unruhe *f*

uneasy [ʌn'i:zɪ] **ADJ** *(= uncomfortable) sleep, night* unruhig; *conscience* schlecht; *(= worried) laugh, look* unbehaglich, beklommen; *(= awkward) silence, atmosphere* unbehaglich, beklommen; *behaviour* unsicher; *peace, balance* unsicher, prekär, wack(e)lig *(inf)*; *alliance, coalition, relationship* instabil, wack(e)lig *(inf)*; *(= worrying) suspicion, feeling* beunruhigend, beklemmend, unangenehm; **to be ~** *(person, = ill at ease)* beklommen sein; *(= worried)* beunruhigt sein; **I am** *or* **feel ~ about it** mir ist nicht wohl dabei; **to make sb ~** jdn beunruhigen, jdn unruhig machen; **I have an ~ feeling that …** ich habe das ungute *or* unangenehme Gefühl, dass …; **to become ~** unruhig werden; **to grow** *or* **become ~ about sth** sich über etw *(acc)* beunruhigen; **his conscience was ~** sein Gewissen plagte ihn, er hatte ein schlechtes Gewissen

uneatable [ʌn'i:təbl] **ADJ** ungenießbar

uneaten [ʌn'i:tn] **ADJ** nicht gegessen; **he left the frogs' legs ~** er rührte die Froschschenkel nicht an; **the ~ food** das übrig gebliebene Essen

uneconomic [ʌnˌi:kə'nɒmɪk] **ADJ** unwirtschaftlich, unökonomisch

uneconomical [ʌnˌi:kə'nɒmɪkəl] **ADJ** unwirtschaftlich, unökonomisch; *style of running* unökonomisch; *person* verschwenderisch

unedifying [ˌʌn'edɪfaɪɪŋ] **ADJ** unerbaulich; **rather ~** nicht gerade erbaulich

uneducated [ˌʌn'edjʊkeɪtɪd] **ADJ** *person* ungebildet; *speech, handwriting also* unkultiviert; *style also* ungeschliffen

unemotional [ˌʌnɪ'məʊʃənl] **ADJ** *person, character, approach, voice* nüchtern; *reaction, description also* unbewegt; *(= without passion)* leidenschaftslos, kühl *(pej)*; **try and stay ~** versuchen Sie, nüchtern und sachlich zu bleiben

unemotionally [ˌʌnɪ'məʊʃnəlɪ] **ADV** unbewegt, kühl *(pej)*; *say, describe also* nüchtern; **state your opinion ~** bringen Sie Ihre Meinung sachlich vor

unemployable [ˌʌnɪm'plɔɪəbl] **ADJ** *person* als Arbeitskraft nicht brauchbar; *(because of illness)* arbeitsunfähig

unemployed [ˌʌnɪm'plɔɪd] **ADJ** *person* arbeitslos, erwerbslos; *(= unused) machinery* ungenutzt; *(Fin) capital* tot, brachliegend **PL** **the ~** *pl* die Arbeitslosen *pl*, die Erwerbslosen *pl*

unemployment [ˌʌnɪm'plɔɪmənt] **N** Arbeitslosigkeit *f*, Erwerbslosigkeit *f*; **~ has risen this month** die Arbeitslosenziffer ist diesen Monat gestiegen

unemployment: **unemployment benefit**, *(US)* **unemployment compensation** **N** Arbeitslosenunterstützung *f*; **unemployment figures** **PL** Arbeitslosenziffer *f*; **unemployment insurance** **N** Arbeitslosenversicherung *f*; **unemployment line** **N** *(US)* **to be in the ~** arbeitslos sein, stempeln gehen *(inf)*; **many white-collar workers find themselves in the ~s** viele Schreibtischarbeiter finden sich auf dem Arbeitsamt wieder; **unemployment rate** **N** Arbeitslosenquote *f*

unencumbered [ˌʌnɪn'kʌmbəd] **ADJ** unbelastet; **~ property** unbelasteter Grundbesitz

unending [ʌn'endɪŋ] **ADJ** *(= everlasting)* ewig, nie endend *attr*; *stream* nicht enden wollend *attr*, endlos; *(= incessant)* endlos, unaufhörlich; **it seems ~** es scheint nicht enden zu wollen

unendurable [ˌʌnɪn'djʊərəbl] **ADJ** unerträglich

unenforceable [ˌʌnɪn'fɔ:sɪbl] **ADJ** *law* nicht durchsetzbar; *policy* undurchführbar

un-English [ʌn'ɪŋglɪʃ] **ADJ** unenglisch

unenlightened [ˌʌnɪn'laɪtnd] **ADJ** **a** *(= uninformed) reader, listener* uneingeweiht; **to leave sb ~** jdn im Dunkeln lassen **b** *age, country, person* rückständig; *(= prejudiced)* intolerant

unenterprising [ˌʌn'entəpraɪzɪŋ] **ADJ** *person, policy* ohne Unternehmungsgeist, hausbacken *(inf)*; **it was very ~ of them to turn it down** dass sie abgelehnt haben beweist, wie wenig Unternehmungsgeist sie haben

unenthusiastic [ˌʌnɪnθu:zɪ'æstɪk] **ADJ** kühl, wenig begeistert; **he was ~ about it** er war wenig begeistert davon; **don't be so ~** zeige doch ein bisschen Begeisterung!

unenthusiastically [ˌʌnɪnθu:zɪ'æstɪkəlɪ] **ADV** wenig begeistert, ohne Begeisterung

unenviable [ʌn'envɪəbl] **ADJ** wenig beneidenswert

unequal [ʌn'i:kwəl] **ADJ** ungleich; *standard, quality* unterschiedlich, ungleichförmig; *work* unausgeglichen; **~ in length** unterschiedlich *or* verschieden *or* ungleich lang; **to be ~ to a task** einer Aufgabe *(dat)* nicht gewachsen sein; **to be ~ to doing sth** unfähig *or* nicht fähig sein, etw zu tun

unequalled, *(US)* **unequaled** [ʌn'i:kwəld] **ADJ** unübertroffen; *skill, record, civilization also* unerreicht; *beauty also, stupidity, ignorance* beispiellos, ohnegleichen *(after noun)*; **he is ~ by any other player** kein anderer Spieler kommt ihm gleich

unequally [ʌn'i:kwəlɪ] **ADV** ungleichmäßig

unequivocal [ˌʌnɪ'kwɪvəkəl] **ADJ** **a** unmissverständlich, eindeutig; *answer also* unzweideutig; *evidence, proof* eindeutig, unzweifelhaft; **he was quite ~ about it** er sagte es ganz unmissverständlich *or* eindeutig *or* klar **b** *(= categorical) commitment, support* rückhaltlos; **to be ~ in one's support of sth** etw rückhaltlos *or* ohne Vorbehalte unterstützen

unequivocally [ˌʌnɪ'kwɪvəkəlɪ] **ADV** *state, answer* unmissverständlich, eindeutig; *reject* unmissverständlich, klipp und klar *(inf)*; *support* rückhaltlos, ohne Vorbehalte

unerring [ʌnˈɜːrɪŋ] ADJ *judgement, eye, accuracy, ability* unfehlbar; *instinct* untrüglich; *aim, blow* treffsicher

unerringly [ʌnˈɜːrɪŋlɪ] ADV *judge* unfehlbar; *aim* treffsicher

unescapable ADJ, **unescapably** ADV [ˌʌnɪˈskeɪpəbl, -ɪ] *fate etc* unentrinnbar

UNESCO [juːˈneskəʊ] *abbr of* **United Nations Educational, Scientific and Cultural Organization** UNESCO *f*

unesthetic ADJ *(US)* = **unaesthetic**

unethical [ʌnˈeθɪkəl] ADJ unmoralisch; *(in more serious matters)* unethisch; **it's ~ for a doctor to do that** es verstößt gegen das Berufsethos *or* die Berufsehre, wenn ein Arzt das macht

uneven [ʌnˈiːvən] ADJ **a** *(= not level) surface* uneben; *(= irregular) line* ungerade; *thickness* ungleich; *pulse, breathing, teeth* unregelmäßig; *voice* unsicher, schwankend; *pace, rate, colour, distribution* ungleichmäßig; *quality* unterschiedlich; *temper* unausgeglichen; *contest, competition* ungleich; **the engine sounds ~** der Motor läuft ungleichmäßig **b** *number* ungerade

unevenly [ʌnˈiːvənlɪ] ADV *(= irregularly) move, spread, develop* ungleichmäßig, unregelmäßig; *(= unequally) share, distribute* ungleichmäßig; **the teams were ~ matched** die Mannschaften waren sehr ungleich

unevenness [ʌnˈiːvənnɪs] N *(of surface)* Unebenheit *f*; *(= irregularity, of line)* Ungeradheit *f*; *(of thickness)* Ungleichheit *f*; *(of pulse, breathing, teeth)* Unregelmäßigkeit *f*; *(of voice)* Unsicherheit *f*; *(of pace, rate, colour, distribution)* Ungleichmäßigkeit *f*; *(= inconsistency: of quality)* Unterschiedlichkeit *f*; *(of contest, competition)* Ungleichheit *f*

uneventful [ˌʌnɪˈventfʊl] ADJ *day, meeting* ereignislos; *career* wenig bewegt; *life* ruhig, eintönig *(pej)*

uneventfully [ˌʌnɪˈventfəlɪ] ADV ereignislos

unexacting [ˌʌnɪɡˈzæktɪŋ] ADJ *standards etc* anspruchlos, keine hohen Anforderungen stellend; *work etc* leicht, nicht anstrengend

unexampled [ˌʌnɪkˈzɑːmpld] ADJ beispiellos, unvergleichlich

unexceptionable [ˌʌnɪkˈsepʃnəbl] ADJ einwandfrei; *person* solide

unexceptional [ˌʌnɪkˈsepʃənl] ADJ alltäglich, durchschnittlich

unexciting [ˌʌnɪkˈsaɪtɪŋ] ADJ nicht besonders aufregend; *(= boring)* langweilig; **not ~** nicht gerade eintönig

unexpected [ˌʌnɪkˈspektɪd] ADJ unerwartet; *arrival, result, development also* unvorhergesehen; **this is an ~ pleasure** *(also iro)* welch eine Überraschung!; **their success was not ~** ihr Erfolg kam nicht unerwartet *or* überraschend; **the role of the ~ in this novel** der Überraschungseffekt in diesem Roman

unexpectedly [ˌʌnɪkˈspektɪdlɪ] ADV unerwartet; *arrive, happen also* plötzlich, unvorhergesehen; **but then, ~** aber dann, wie aus heiterem Himmel, …

unexplainable [ˌʌnɪkˈspleɪnəbl] ADJ unerklärlich

unexplained [ˌʌnɪkˈspleɪnd] ADJ nicht geklärt, ungeklärt; *mystery* unaufgeklärt; *lateness, absence* unbegründet; **a few ~ technical terms** einige unerklärte Fachausdrücke; **to go ~** nicht erklärt werden; **his actions remain ~** für seine Handlungen gibt es immer noch keine Erklärung; **for some ~ reason** ohne ersichtlichen Grund, aus unerklärlichen Gründen

unexploded [ˌʌnɪkˈspləʊdɪd] ADJ nicht explodiert

unexploited [ˌʌnɪkˈsplɔɪtɪd] ADJ *resources* ungenutzt; *market* (noch) nicht erschlossen; *talent also* brachliegend *attr*; *minerals also* unausgebeutet

unexplored [ˌʌnɪkˈsplɔːd] ADJ *mystery* unerforscht; *territory also* unerschlossen

unexposed [ˌʌnɪkˈspəʊzd] ADJ **a** *(= hidden) villain* nicht entlarvt; *crime* unaufgedeckt **b** *(Phot) film* unbelichtet

unexpressed [ˌʌnɪkˈsprest] ADJ *sorrow, wish* unausgesprochen

unexpressive [ˌʌnɪkˈspresɪv] ADJ *style, eyes* ausdruckslos

unexpurgated [ʌnˈekspɜːɡeɪtɪd] ADJ *book, version* ungekürzt, unzensiert

unfading [ʌnˈfeɪdɪŋ] ADJ *(fig)* unvergänglich, nie verblassend

unfailing [ʌnˈfeɪlɪŋ] ADJ *zeal, interest, source* unerschöpflich; *optimism, humour also* unbezwinglich; *supply also* endlos; *remedy* unfehlbar; *friend* treu; *support, encouragement, generosity* unfehlbar, beständig; *regularity, accuracy* beständig

unfailingly [ʌnˈfeɪlɪŋlɪ] ADV immer, stets

unfair [ʌnˈfɛəʳ] ✪ 26.3 ADJ unfair; *decision, method, remark, criticism also* ungerecht; *(Comm) competition also* unlauter; **to be ~ to sb** jdm gegenüber unfair sein; **to have an ~ advantage over sb/sth** einen unfairen Vorteil gegenüber jdm/etw haben; **it is ~ to expect her to do that** es ist nicht fair, von ihr zu erwarten, dass sie das tut

unfair dismissal N ungerechtfertigte Entlassung

unfairly [ʌnˈfɛəlɪ] ADV unfair; *treat, criticize etc also* ungerecht; *accuse, punish* zu Unrecht; *dismissed* ungerechterweise, zu Unrecht; **to charge ~ high prices** ungerechtfertigt hohe Preise verlangen

unfairness [ʌnˈfɛənɪs] N Ungerechtigkeit *f*

unfaithful [ʌnˈfeɪθfʊl] ADJ **a** *wife, husband, lover* untreu; *friend, servant* treulos; **to be ~ to sb** jdm untreu sein **b** *(= inaccurate) translation, description* ungenau; **the translator was ~ to the original poem** der Übersetzer verfälschte das Gedicht

unfaithfulness [ʌnˈfeɪθfʊlnɪs] N **a** *(of wife, husband, lover)* Untreue *f*; *(of friend, servant)* Treulosigkeit *f* **b** *(of translation, description)* Ungenauigkeit *f*

unfaltering [ʌnˈfɔːltərɪŋ] ADJ *step, voice* fest; *courage* unerschütterlich

unfalteringly [ʌnˈfɔːltərɪŋlɪ] ADV *walk* mit festen Schritten; *say* mit fester Stimme

unfamiliar [ˌʌnfəˈmɪljəʳ] ADJ **a** *(= strange, unknown) experience, taste, sight, surroundings* ungewohnt; *subject, person* fremd, unbekannt; **~ territory** *(fig)* Neuland *nt*; **it is ~ to me** es ist ungewohnt für mich, es ist mir fremd *or* unbekannt **b** *(= unacquainted)* **to be ~ with sth** etw nicht kennen, mit etw nicht vertraut sein; *with machine etc* sich mit etw nicht auskennen; **I am not ~ with the situation** die Situation ist mir nicht gänzlich unbekannt

unfamiliarity [ˌʌnfəmɪlɪˈærɪtɪ] N **a** *(= strangeness, novelty, of experience, taste, sight, surroundings)* Ungewohntheit *f*; *(of subject, person)* Fremdheit *f*, Unbekanntheit *f* **b** *(= lack of acquaintance)* **his ~ with economics** sein Mangel *m* an ökonomischem Wissen; **because of my ~ with …** wegen meiner mangelnden Kenntnisse *(+gen)* … *or* Vertrautheit mit …

unfashionable [ʌnˈfæʃnəbl] ADJ unmodern; *district* wenig gefragt; *hotel, habit, subject* nicht in Mode; *image* überholt; **science became ~** Naturwissenschaft geriet aus der Mode

unfashionably [ʌnˈfæʃnəblɪ] ADV *dressed* unmodern; *strict etc* altmodisch

unfasten [ʌnˈfɑːsn] VT aufmachen; *string, belt also* losmachen; *(= detach) tag, dog, horse etc* losbinden; *hair, bonds* lösen VI aufgehen; **how does this dress ~?** wie macht man das Kleid auf?

unfathomable [ʌnˈfæðəməbl] ADJ unergründlich

unfathomed [ʌnˈfæðəmd] ADJ *(lit, fig)* unergründet

unfavourable, *(US)* **unfavorable** [ʌnˈfeɪvərəbl] ADJ *outlook, weather, moment, result* ungünstig; *conditions, circumstances also, wind* widrig; *opinion, reaction* negativ; *reply* ablehnend, negativ; *trade balance* passiv; **conditions ~ to** *or* **for trade** ungünstige Handelsbedingungen *pl*; **on ~ terms** zu ungünstigen Bedingungen; **to be ~ to sb** ungünstig für jdn sein; **to draw** *or* **make ~ comparisons** nachteilige Vergleiche ziehen; **to show sb/sth in an ~ light** jdn/etw in einem ungünstigen Licht darstellen

unfavourably, *(US)* **unfavorably** [ʌnˈfeɪvərəblɪ] ADV *contrast, compare* unvorteilhaft; *react, comment* ablehnend; *respond, review* negativ; *regard* ungünstig; **to compare ~ with sth** im Vergleich mit etw schlecht abschneiden; **to look ~ on sth** einer Sache *(dat)* ablehnend gegenüberstehen; **to report ~ on/speak ~ of sth** etw negativ *or* ablehnend *or* ungünstig beurteilen; **to be ~ impressed by sth** einen negativen Eindruck *or* keinen guten Eindruck von etw bekommen

unfeasible [ʌnˈfiːzəbl] ADJ nicht machbar; **the weather made it ~ to be outdoors** bei dem Wetter konnte man nicht draußen sein

unfeeling [ʌnˈfiːlɪŋ] ADJ gefühllos; *response, reply also* herzlos; *look* ungerührt; *(= without sensation also)* empfindungslos

unfeelingly [ʌnˈfiːlɪŋlɪ] ADV gefühllos, herzlos; *look, listen* ungerührt

unfeigned [ʌnˈfeɪnd] ADJ aufrichtig, echt, ungeheuchelt

unfeminine [ʌnˈfemɪnɪn] ADJ unweiblich

unfetter [ʌnˈfetəʳ] VT *(fig)* befreien *(from* von)

unfettered [ʌnˈfetəd] ADJ *(fig)* frei, unbehindert *(by* von); *right, power, freedom* uneingeschränkt

unfilial [ʌnˈfɪljəl] ADJ nicht pflichtbewusst; *(= impudent)* ungehörig, respektlos

unfilled [ʌnˈfɪld] ADJ ungefüllt; *job* offen, unbesetzt; *seat (= not taken)* leer; *(Pol)* unbesetzt; *order book* un(aus)gefüllt; **~ vacancies** offene Stellen *pl*

unfinished [ʌnˈfɪnɪʃt] ADJ **a** *(= incomplete)* unfertig; *work of art* unvollendet; **Schubert's Unfinished** Schuberts Unvollendete *f*; **~ business** unerledigte Geschäfte *pl*; **to leave sth ~** etw unvollendet lassen **b** *(Tech)* unbearbeitet; *wood* naturbelassen; **~ product** Rohprodukt *nt*

unfit [ʌnˈfɪt] ADJ **a** *(= unsuitable) person, thing* ungeeignet, untauglich; *(= incompetent)* unfähig; **to be ~ to do sth** *(physically)* nicht fähig sein, etw zu tun; *(mentally)* außerstande sein, etw zu tun; **~ to drive** fahruntüchtig, nicht in der Lage zu fahren; **he is ~ to be a lawyer/for teaching** er ist als Jurist/Lehrer untauglich; **to be ~ for (human) habitation** (für Menschen) unbewohnbar sein; **this is ~ for publication** das kann nicht veröffentlicht werden; **to be ~ for (human) consumption** nicht zum Verzehr geeignet sein; **~ to eat** ungenießbar; **road ~ for lorries** für Lastkraftwagen nicht geeignete Straße; **~ to live in** unbewohnbar; **~ to plead** *(Jur)* nicht zurechnungsfähig
b *(Sport: = injured)* nicht fit; *(in health)* schlecht in Form, nicht fit; **he is very ~** er ist in sehr schlechter Form; **~ (for military service)** (dienst)untauglich; **to be ~ for work** arbeitsunfähig sein
VT *(form)* **to ~ sb for sth** jdn für etw untauglich machen; **to ~ sb to do sth** jdn untauglich machen, etw zu tun

unfitness [ʌnˈfɪtnɪs] N **a** *(= unsuitableness)* mangelnde Eignung, Untauglichkeit *f*; *(= incompetence)* Unfähigkeit *f* **b** *(= unhealthiness)* mangelnde Fitness; *(for military service)* Untauglichkeit *f*

unfitted [ʌnˈfɪtɪd] ADJ ungeeignet, untauglich *(for, to* für)

unfitting [ʌnˈfɪtɪŋ] ADJ *language, behaviour* unpassend, unschicklich, unziemlich

unfittingly [ʌnˈfɪtɪŋlɪ] ADV *behave* unpassend, unschicklich, unziemlich; *dressed* unpassend

unfix [ʌnˈfɪks] VT losmachen; *bayonets* abmachen; **it came ~ed** es hat sich gelöst

unflagging [ʌnˈflægɪŋ] ADJ *person, zeal, patience* unermüdlich, unentwegt; *enthusiasm* unerschöpflich; *devotion, interest* unverändert stark; **he has an ~ devotion to the cause** er stellt sich unermüdlich in den Dienst der Sache; **to be ~ in one's support of sth** etw unermüdlich unterstützen; **to be ~ in doing sth** unermüdlich darin sein, etw zu tun

unflaggingly [ʌnˈflægɪŋlɪ] ADV unentwegt, unermüdlich

unflappability [ˌʌnflæpəˈbɪlɪtɪ] N *(inf)* Unerschütterlichkeit *f*

unflappable [ʌnˈflæpəbl] ADJ *(inf)* unerschütterlich, nicht aus der Ruhe zu bringend *attr*; **to be ~** die Ruhe selbst sein, die Ruhe weghaben *(inf)*

unflattering [ʌnˈflætərɪŋ] ADJ *portrait, comments* wenig schmeichelhaft; *dress, hairstyle, light also* unvorteilhaft; **to portray sb/sth in an ~ light** jdn/etw in einem wenig schmeichelhaften Licht erscheinen lassen

unfledged [ʌnˈfledʒd] ADJ *bird* (noch) nicht flügge; *(fig)* unerfahren

unflinching [ʌnˈflɪntʃɪŋ] ADJ unerschrocken; *determination, loyalty, support* unbeirrbar; *gaze* unbeirrt; **with ~ courage** unverzagt

unflinchingly [ʌnˈflɪntʃɪŋlɪ] ADV unerschrocken

unflyable [ʌnˈflaɪəbl] ADJ *plane* unfliegbar

unfocus(s)ed [ʌnˈfəʊkəst] ADJ *eyes* unkoordiniert; *debate* weitschweifig; *campaign* zu allgemein angelegt; **to be ~** *(person)* sich nicht aufs Wesentliche konzentrieren

unfold [ʌnˈfəʊld] VT **a** *paper, cloth* auseinanderfalten, entfalten; *(= spread out) wings* ausbreiten; *arms* lösen; *chair, table* aufklappen, auseinanderklappen **b** *(fig) story* entwickeln *(to* vor *+dat)*; *plans, ideas* entfalten, darlegen *(to +dat)*; *secret* enthüllen, eröffnen VI *(story, plot)* sich abwickeln; *(truth)* an den Tag kommen, sich herausstellen; *(view, personality, flower)* sich entfalten; *(countryside)* sich ausbreiten

unforced [ʌnˈfɔːst] ADJ ungezwungen, natürlich

unforeseeable [ˌʌnfɔːˈsiːəbl] ADJ unvorhersehbar

unforeseen [ˌʌnfɔːˈsiːn] ADJ unvorhergesehen, unerwartet; **due to ~ circumstances** aufgrund unvorhergesehener Umstände

unforgettable [ˌʌnfəˈgetəbl] ADJ unvergesslich

unforgettably [ˌʌnfəˈgetəblɪ] ADV auf unvergessliche Weise

unforgivable [ˌʌnfəˈgɪvəbl] ✪ 18.1 ADJ unverzeihlich

unforgivably [ˌʌnfəˈgɪvəblɪ] ADV unverzeihlich; **he said, quite ~, that ...** er sagte, und das war einfach unverzeihlich, dass ...

unforgiving [ˌʌnfəˈgɪvɪŋ] ADJ unversöhnlich

unforgotten [ˌʌnfəˈgɒtn] ADJ unvergessen

unformatted [ʌnˈfɔːmætɪd] ADJ *(Comput)* unformatiert

unformed [ʌnˈfɔːmd] ADJ *(= unshaped) clay, foetus* ungeformt; *(= undeveloped) character, idea* unfertig

unforthcoming [ˌʌnfɔːθˈkʌmɪŋ] ADJ *person* nicht sehr mitteilsam; *reply* wenig aufschlussreich; **to be ~ about sth** sich nicht zu etw äußern wollen

unfortified [ʌnˈfɔːtɪfaɪd] ADJ *(Mil)* unbefestigt; *(Tech)* nicht verstärkt; *food* nicht angereichert

unfortunate [ʌnˈfɔːtʃnɪt] ADJ unglücklich; *person* glücklos; *day, event, error* unglückselig; *turn of phrase* ungeschickt, unglücklich; *time* ungünstig; **to be ~** *(person)* Pech haben; **to be ~ in life/in love** kein Glück im Leben/in der Liebe haben; **it is most ~ that ...** es ist höchst bedauerlich, dass ...; **how very ~ (for you)** welch ein Pech; **it was ~ that he hadn't been informed** ihm ist bedauerlicherweise nicht Bescheid gesagt worden; **the ~ Mr Brown** der arme *or* bedauernswerte Herr Brown N Arme(r) *mf*, Unglückliche(r) *mf*

unfortunately [ʌnˈfɔːtʃnɪtlɪ] ✪ 9.3, 20.4, 26.3 ADV leider; *chosen* unglücklich; *worded* ungeschickt; **the ~-named ...** der unglücklich benannte ...; **~ for you** bedauerlicherweise für Sie; **~ not** leider nicht

unfounded [ʌnˈfaʊndɪd] ADJ unbegründet, nicht fundiert; *suspicion also* grundlos; *rumour also, allegations* aus der Luft gegriffen; **to prove (to be) ~** sich als unbegründet *or* grundlos erweisen

unframed [ʌnˈfreɪmd] ADJ *picture* ungerahmt

unfreeze [ʌnˈfriːz] *pret* **unfroze**, *ptp* **unfrozen** VT **a** *(= thaw) food etc* auftauen **b** *(Fin) wages, prices, assets* freigeben VI auftauen

unfrequented [ˌʌnfrɪˈkwentɪd] ADJ einsam; **the place is ~ except for ...** außer ... kommt niemand dahin

unfriend [ʌnˈfrend] VT *(Internet)* entfreunden

unfriendliness [ʌnˈfrendlɪnɪs] N Unfreundlichkeit *f*; *(of country, natives also)* Feindseligkeit *f*

unfriendly [ʌnˈfrendlɪ] ADJ unfreundlich *(to sb* zu jdm*)*; *(= hostile) natives, country, act* feindselig; *territory* unwirtlich; *(Fin) takeover* feindlich; *(= harmful)* schädlich

unfrock [ʌnˈfrɒk] VT laisieren *(spec)*, in den Laienstand zurückversetzen

unfroze [ʌnˈfrəʊz] *pret of* **unfreeze**

unfrozen [ʌnˈfrəʊzn] *ptp of* **unfreeze** ADJ **a** *lake* nicht zugefroren; *earth, food* ungefroren **b** *assets, prices* freigegeben; *(= not yet frozen)* frei

unfruitful [ʌnˈfruːtfʊl] ADJ *soil, woman, discussion* unfruchtbar; *attempt* fruchtlos

unfulfilled [ˌʌnfʊlˈfɪld] ADJ unerfüllt; *person, life* unausgefüllt; **their potential is ~** sie haben ihre Fähigkeiten nicht voll ausgenutzt; **to have an ~ desire** schon immer den Wunsch gehabt haben

unfunded [ʌnˈfʌndɪd] ADJ *(Fin)* unfundiert

unfunny [ʌnˈfʌnɪ] ADJ *(inf)* (gar) nicht komisch; **distinctly ~** alles andere als komisch

unfurl [ʌnˈfɜːl] VT *flag* aufrollen; *sail* losmachen; *(peacock) tail* entfalten VI sich entfalten; *(flag, sails also)* sich aufrollen

unfurnished [ʌnˈfɜːnɪʃt] ADJ unmöbliert

ungainly [ʌnˈgeɪnlɪ] ADJ *animal, movement* unbeholfen; *appearance* unelegant, unansehnlich, unschön; *posture* ungraziös, unschön

ungenerous [ʌnˈdʒenərəs] ADJ kleinlich

ungentlemanly [ʌnˈdʒentlmənlɪ], **ungentlemanlike** [ʌnˈdʒentlmənlaɪk] ADJ unfein; *(= impolite)* unhöflich; **it is ~ to do so** das gehört sich nicht für einen Gentleman; **it is ~ not to do so** ein Gentleman sollte das tun

un-get-at-able [ˌʌngetˈætəbl] ADJ *(inf)* unerreichbar; **he/the cottage is ~** man kommt an ihn/das Haus einfach nicht ran *(inf)*

ungifted [ʌnˈgɪftɪd] ADJ unbegabt

ungird [ʌnˈgɜːd] VT *sword* ablegen; *loins* entgürten

unglazed [ʌnˈgleɪzd] ADJ *window* unverglast; *pottery* unglasiert; *photograph* nicht satiniert

ungodliness [ʌnˈgɒdlɪnɪs] N Gottlosigkeit *f*

ungodly [ʌnˈgɒdlɪ] ADJ gottlos; *(inf) noise, hour* unchristlich *(inf)*; **an ~ noise** ein Heidenlärm *m (inf)* N **the ~** *pl* die Gottlosen *pl*

ungovernable [ʌnˈgʌvənəbl] ADJ **a** *desire, passion, rage* unbezähmbar; *temper* unbeherrscht **b** *country, people* unlenkbar, nicht zu regieren *pred*

ungraceful [ʌnˈgreɪsfʊl] ADJ nicht anmutig; *movement, build* plump, ungelenk; *behaviour* unfein

ungracefully [ʌnˈgreɪsfəlɪ] ADV plump; *behave* unfein; **to grow old ~** *(hum)* würdelos alt werden

ungracious [ʌnˈgreɪʃəs] ADJ unhöflich; *(= gruff) grunt, refusal* schroff; *answer* rüde

ungraciously [ʌnˈgreɪʃəslɪ] ADV *say* schroff; *react, respond* schroff, rüde

ungrammatical [ˌʌngrəˈmætɪkəl] ADJ ungrammatisch, grammatikalisch falsch; **she does tend to be ~ at times** sie drückt sich manchmal grammatikalisch falsch aus

ungrammatically [ˌʌngrəˈmætɪkəlɪ] ADV *speak, write* grammatisch falsch

ungrateful ADJ, **ungratefully** ADV [ʌnˈgreɪtfʊl, -fəlɪ] undankbar *(to* gegenüber*)*

ungrounded [ʌnˈgraʊndɪd] ADJ **a** *(= unfounded)* unfundiert; *accusations* grundlos, aus der Luft gegriffen; *fears* grundlos, unbegründet **b** *(US, Elec)* ungeerdet, ohne Erdung

ungrudging [ʌnˈgrʌdʒɪŋ] ADJ *help, support* bereitwillig; *admiration* neidlos; *(= generous) person, contribution* großzügig; *praise, gratitude* von ganzem Herzen kommend *attr*

ungrudgingly [ʌnˈgrʌdʒɪŋlɪ] ADV *help, support, consent, say* bereitwillig; *admire, praise* von ganzem Herzen; *give, contribute* großzügig

unguarded [ʌnˈgɑːdɪd] ADJ **a** *(= undefended)* unbewacht **b** *(fig: = careless)* unvorsichtig, unachtsam; **to have ~ conversations** sich sorglos unterhalten; **in an ~ moment he ...** als er einen Augenblick nicht aufpasste *or* sich einen Augenblick nicht vorsah, ... er ... **c** *(Tech: = unshielded) machine* ungeschützt, ohne Schutzvorrichtung

unguardedly [ˈʌnˈgɑːdɪdlɪ] ADV *(= carelessly)* unachtsam, unvorsichtig; **he spoke ~ about his job with the bank** er sprach unachtsam über seine Arbeit bei der Bank

unguent [ˈʌŋgwənt] N Salbe *f*, Unguentum *nt (spec)*

unguessable [ʌnˈgesəbl] ADJ nicht erratbar

ungulate [ˈʌŋgjʊleɪt] N Huftier *nt*, Ungulat *m (spec)* ADJ *mammal* mit Hufen

unhair [ʌnˈhɛəˈ] VT enthaaren

unhallowed [ʌnˈhæləʊd] ADJ *ground* ungeweiht

unhampered [ʌnˈhæmpəd] ADJ ungehindert; **~ by clothes** ohne hemmende Kleidung; **~ by regulations** ohne den Zwang von Bestimmungen

unhand [ʌnˈhænd] VT *(old, hum)* freigeben, loslassen

unhandy [ʌnˈhændɪ] ADJ unpraktisch

unhang [ʌnˈhæŋ] VT *painting etc* ab- *or* herunternehmen

unhappily [ʌnˈhæpɪlɪ] ADV *(= unfortunately)* leider, unglücklicherweise; *(= miserably)* unglücklich; **rather ~ expressed** ziemlich unglücklich ausgedrückt; **~ for you** bedauerlicherweise für Sie; **~ married** unglücklich verheiratet

unhappiness [ʌnˈhæpɪnɪs] N Traurigkeit *f*; *(= discontent)* Unzufriedenheit *f (with* mit*)*; **this is a source of much ~ to me** das macht mich ganz unglücklich

unhappy [ʌnˈhæpɪ] ADJ *(+er)* **a** *(= sad)* unglücklich; *look, voice* traurig; *state of affairs* bedauerlich, traurig **b** *(= not pleased)* unzufrieden *(about* mit*)*, nicht glücklich *(about* über *+acc)*; *(= uneasy)* unwohl; **to be ~ with sb/sth** mit jdm/etw unzufrieden sein; **to be ~ at work/school** unzufrieden mit der Arbeit/der Schule sein; **to be ~ about** *or* **at doing sth** nicht glücklich darüber sein, etw zu tun; **he was ~ about** *or* **at getting a decrease in his salary** er war nicht glücklich darüber, dass sein Gehalt gekürzt wurde; **if you feel ~ about it** wenn Sie darüber nicht glücklich sind; *(= worried)* wenn Ihnen dabei nicht wohl ist; **I feel ~ about letting him go** ich lasse ihn nur ungern gehen; **some were ~ to see him go** einige sahen ihn nur ungern gehen **c** *(= unfortunate) coincidence, day, match, phrasing* unglücklich; *person* glücklos; **an ~ choice/colour** *(Brit)* *or* **color** *(US)* **scheme** keine gute Wahl/Farbzusammenstellung

unharmed [ʌnˈhɑːmd] ADJ *person* unverletzt; *thing* unbeschädigt; *reputation* ungeschädigt; *beauty* nicht beeinträchtigt; **to be ~ by sth** durch etw nicht gelitten haben

unharness [ʌnˈhɑːnɪs] VT *horse* abschirren; *(from carriage)* abspannen; *(fig) energy* freisetzen

unhealthy [ʌnˈhelθɪ] ADJ **a** *person* nicht gesund; *climate, place, life, complexion* ungesund;

(inf) car nicht in Ordnung; *(Econ: = weak) economy, company, finances* kränkelnd **b** *curiosity, interest* krankhaft; *influence, magazine* schädlich, schlecht; **it's an ~ relationship** das ist eine verderbliche Beziehung **c** *(inf: = dangerous)* ungesund *(inf)*, gefährlich

unheard [ʌn'hɜːd] ADJ ungehört; *(fig) voice* unbeachtet; **to condemn sb ~** jdn verurteilen, ohne ihn angehört zu haben; **to go ~** *(lit)* ungehört bleiben; *(fig also)* unbeachtet bleiben

unheard-of [ʌn'hɜːdɒv] ADJ *(= unknown)* gänzlich unbekannt; *(= unprecedented)* einmalig, noch nicht da gewesen; *(= outrageous)* unerhört

unheeded [ʌn'hiːdɪd] ADJ unbeachtet; **to go ~** keine Beachtung finden, auf taube Ohren stoßen

unheedful [ʌn'hiːdfʊl] ADJ **~ of the danger** ohne von der Gefahr Notiz zu nehmen, ungeachtet der Gefahr *(gen)*

unheeding [ʌn'hiːdɪŋ] ADJ *(= not attending)* unbekümmert; *(= not caring also)* gleichgültig, achtlos

unhelpful [ʌn'helpfʊl] ADJ *person* nicht hilfreich; *advice, book* nutzlos, wenig hilfreich; **that was very ~ of you** das war wirklich keine Hilfe; **you are being very ~** du bist aber wirklich keine Hilfe; **it is ~ to pretend the problem does not exist** es hilft nichts, so zu tun, als ob das Problem nicht existiert; **to be ~ to sb/sth** keine Hilfe für jdn/etw sein

unhelpfully [ʌn'helpfəlɪ] ADV wenig hilfreich

unheralded [ʌn'herəldəd] ADJ **a** *(= unrecognized)* unentdeckt **b** *(= unexpected)* unangekündigt

unhesitating [ʌn'hezɪteɪtɪŋ] ADJ *(= immediate) answer, offer* prompt, unverzüglich; *help also, generosity* bereitwillig; *(= steady) steps, progress* stet; *(= undoubting) answer* fest; **he gave his ~ support** er half ohne zu zögern

unhesitatingly [ʌn'hezɪteɪtɪŋlɪ] ADV ohne Zögern, ohne zu zögern; *(= undoubtingly also)* ohne zu zweifeln

unhindered [ʌn'hɪndəd] ADJ *(by clothes, luggage etc)* unbehindert, nicht behindert; *(by regulations)* ungehindert, nicht gehindert; *(by distraction)* ungestört

unhinge [ʌn'hɪndʒ] VT **to ~ sb/sb's mind** jdn aus der Bahn werfen, jdn völlig verstören; **he/his mind was ~d** er hatte den Verstand verloren

unhip ['ʌn'hɪp] ADJ *(inf)* unmodern; **to be ~** nicht in sein *(inf)*

unhistorical [ˌʌnhɪs'tɒrɪkəl] ADJ *(= inaccurate)* unhistorisch, ungeschichtlich; *(= legendary)* legendär

unhitch [ʌn'hɪtʃ] VT *horse (from post)* losbinden; *(from wagon)* ausspannen; *caravan, engine* abkoppeln

unholy [ʌn'həʊlɪ] ADJ *(+er) (Rel) place* ungeweiht; *spirits* böse; *(= evil, = sinful) activities* übel; *(inf) (= reprehensible) delight* diebisch *(inf)*; *alliance* übel; *(= awful) mess* heillos; *noise, hour* unchristlich *(inf)*

unhook [ʌn'hʊk] **VT** *latch, gate* loshaken; *dress* aufhaken; *(= take from hook) picture* abhaken; *(= free)* losmachen; **the dress came ~ed** das Kleid ging auf **VI** sich aufhaken lassen

unhoped-for [ʌn'həʊptfɔː'] ADJ unverhofft

unhorse [ʌn'hɔːs] VT *rider* abwerfen

unhurried [ʌn'hʌrɪd] ADJ *pace, person* gelassen; *steps, movement* gemächlich; *meal, journey, life* gemütlich, geruhsam; **after a little ~ reflection I ...** nachdem ich mir das in Ruhe überlegt habe, ... ich ...; **we made our ~ way home** wir gingen gemächlich nach Hause

unhurriedly [ʌn'hʌrɪdlɪ] ADV gemächlich, in aller Ruhe

unhurt [ʌn'hɜːt] ADJ unverletzt

unhusk [ʌn'hʌsk] VT *beans* enthülsen, schälen

unhygienic [ˌʌnhaɪ'dʒiːnɪk] ADJ unhygienisch

uni- ['juːnɪ-] PREF ein-; **unicellular** einzellig

unibrow ['juːnɪbraʊ] N *(inf)* zusammengewachsene Augenbrauen *pl*

UNICEF ['juːnɪsef] *abbr of* **United Nations International Children's Emergency Fund** UNICEF *f*, Weltkinderhilfswerk *nt* der UNO

unicolour, *(US)* **unicolor** ['juːnɪˌkʌlə'], **unicoloured**, *(US)* **unicolored** [-ˌkʌləd] ADJ einfarbig; *clothes* uni

unicorn ['juːnɪkɔːn] N Einhorn *nt*

unicycle ['juːnɪsaɪkl] N Einrad *nt*

unidentifiable ['ʌnaɪ'dentɪˌfaɪəbl] ADJ *object, smell, sound* unidentifizierbar; *body* nicht identifizierbar; **all the bodies were ~** keine der Leichen konnte identifiziert werden

unidentified [ˌʌnaɪ'dentɪfaɪd] ADJ unbekannt; *body* nicht identifiziert; *belongings* herrenlos; **~ flying object** unbekanntes Flugobjekt

unidiomatic [ˌʌnɪdɪə'mætɪk] ADJ unidiomatisch

unification [juːnɪfɪ'keɪʃən] N *(of country)* Einigung *f*; *(of system)* Vereinheitlichung *f*; **~ process** Einigungsprozess *m*; **Unification Church** Vereinigungskirche *f (der Mun-Sekte)*

uniform ['juːnɪfɔːm] **ADJ** **a** *(= unvarying) length, colour, tax* einheitlich; *treatment* gleich, einheitlich; *temperature, pace* gleichmäßig, gleichbleibend; *(= lacking variation) life* gleichförmig, eintönig *(pej)*; *thinking* gleichartig, gleichförmig, uniform *(pej)*; *scenery* einförmig, eintönig *(pej)*; **these houses are so ~** die Häuser gleichen sich alle so; **~ in shape/size** von gleicher Form/Größe
b *(Mil, Sch etc)* Uniform-; **~ jacket** Uniformjacke *f*
N Uniform *f*; *(fig: inf)* uniformierter Polizist, uniformierte Polizistin; **in ~** in Uniform; **in full ~** in voller Uniform; **out of ~** in Zivil, ohne Uniform

uniformed ['juːnɪfɔːmd] ADJ uniformiert; *person also* in Uniform

uniformity [juːnɪ'fɔːmɪtɪ] N *(of length, colour, tax)* Einheitlichkeit *f*; *(of treatment also)* Gleichheit *f*; *(of temperature, pace)* Gleichmäßigkeit *f*; *(of life)* Gleichförmigkeit *f*, Eintönigkeit *f (pej)*; *(of thinking)* Gleichartigkeit *f*, Uniformität *f (pej)*; *(of scenery)* Einförmigkeit *f*, Eintönigkeit *f*

uniformly ['juːnɪfɔːmlɪ] ADV *measure, paint, tax* einheitlich; *heat* gleichmäßig; *treat* gleich; *(pej)* einförmig *(pej)*; *think* uniform *(pej)*

uniform resource locator N *(Comput)* URL-Adresse *f*

unify ['juːnɪfaɪ] VT einigen, einen *(geh)*; *theories, systems* vereinheitlichen

unifying ['juːnɪfaɪɪŋ] ADJ *factor, force, purpose* verbindend; **the struggle had a ~ effect on all blacks** der Kampf hatte eine einigende Wirkung auf alle Schwarzen

unilateral [juːnɪ'lætərəl] ADJ *(Jur)* einseitig; *(Pol also)* unilateral; **~ declaration of independence** einseitige Unabhängigkeitserklärung; **to take ~ action against sb** einseitig gegen jdn vorgehen; **~ (nuclear) disarmament** einseitige *or* unilaterale (atomare) Abrüstung

unilateralism [juːnɪ'lætərəlɪzəm] N einseitige Abrüstung

unilateralist [juːnɪ'lætərəlɪst] **N** Befürworter(in) *m(f)* einseitiger Abrüstung **ADJ** *policies etc* auf einseitige Abrüstung ausgerichtet

unilaterally [juːnɪ'lætərəlɪ] ADV einseitig; *(Pol also)* unilateral

unilingual ADJ

unilingually ADV [juːnɪ'lɪŋgwəl, -ɪ] einsprachig

unimaginable [ˌʌnɪ'mædʒɪnəbl] ADJ unvorstellbar; **this is ~ to me** das ist für mich unvorstellbar, das kann ich mir nicht vorstellen; **thrillers are ~ without violence** Thriller ohne Gewalt sind unvorstellbar *or* undenkbar

unimaginative [ˌʌnɪ'mædʒɪnətɪv] ADJ fantasielos, phantasielos, einfallslos; *remark, book* geistlos, fantasielos

unimaginatively [ˌʌnɪ'mædʒɪnətɪvlɪ] ADV fantasielos, phantasielos, einfallslos

unimpaired [ˌʌnɪm'peəd] ADJ *quality, prestige, relationship* unbeeinträchtigt; *health* unvermindert; *eyesight, mental powers* unbeeinträchtigt, unvermindert; *faith, belief* unerschüttert; **to be ~** nicht gelitten haben

unimpassioned [ˌʌnɪm'pæʃənd] ADJ leidenschaftslos

unimpeachable [ˌʌnɪm'piːtʃəbl] ADJ *reputation, conduct, character* untadelig; *proof, honesty, integrity* unanfechtbar; *source* absolut zuverlässig; *person* über jeden Zweifel erhaben

unimpeded [ˌʌnɪm'piːdɪd] ADJ ungehindert

unimportant [ˌʌnɪm'pɔːtənt] ADJ unwichtig, unbedeutend; *detail also* unwesentlich

unimposing [ˌʌnɪm'pəʊzɪŋ] ADJ unscheinbar; *building also* wenig imponierend *or* beeindruckend

unimpressed [ˌʌnɪm'prest] ADJ unbeeindruckt, nicht beeindruckt; **I was ~ by him/his story** er/seine Geschichte hat mich überhaupt nicht beeindruckt; **I remain ~** das beeindruckt mich überhaupt nicht

unimpressive [ˌʌnɪm'presɪv] ADJ wenig beeindruckend; *person also* unscheinbar; *argument, performance also, speaker* wenig überzeugend

unimproved [ˌʌnɪm'pruːvd] ADJ **a** (noch) nicht besser, unverändert schlecht; *method* nicht verbessert; **to leave sth ~** etw nicht verbessern **b** *land* unbebaut, nicht kultiviert; *house* nicht modernisiert *or* saniert

uninfluenced [ʌn'ɪnflʊənst] ADJ unbeeinflusst

uninfluential [ˌʌnɪnflʊ'enʃəl] ADJ ohne Einfluss

uninformative [ˌʌnɪn'fɔːmɪtɪv] ADJ *person* wenig mitteilsam; *document* ohne Informationsgehalt

uninformed [ˌʌnɪn'fɔːmd] ADJ *(= not knowing)* nicht informiert *or* unterrichtet *(about* über *+acc)*; *(= ignorant also)* unwissend; *criticism* blindwütig; *comment, rumour* unfundiert; **the ~ observer** der uninformierte Beobachter; **to be ~ about sth** über etw *(acc)* nicht Bescheid wissen; **to keep sb ~** jdn im Dunkeln lassen; **the ~** *pl* die schlecht Informierten *pl*

uninhabitable [ˌʌnɪn'hæbɪtəbl] ADJ unbewohnbar

uninhabited [ˌʌnɪn'hæbɪtɪd] ADJ unbewohnt

uninhibited [ˌʌnɪn'hɪbɪtɪd] ADJ *person* frei von Hemmungen, ohne Hemmungen; *greed, laughter* hemmungslos, ungezügelt; **to be ~** keine Hemmungen haben; **to be ~ by sth** sich von etw nicht einschüchtern lassen; **to be ~ in** *or* **about doing sth** keine Hemmungen haben, etw zu tun

uninitiated [ˌʌnɪ'nɪʃɪeɪtɪd] **ADJ** nicht eingeweiht; **~ listeners/viewers** Hörer/Zuschauer, die die näheren Zusammenhänge nicht kennen *or* die nicht Bescheid wissen **N** **the ~** *pl* Nichteingeweihte *pl*; **for the ~ that may seem strange** Nichteingeweihten mag das merkwürdig vorkommen

uninjured [ʌn'ɪndʒəd] ADJ *person* unverletzt; *arm etc also* heil

uninspired [ˌʌnɪn'spaɪəd] ADJ *teacher, performance* fantasielos, phantasielos, ideenlos, einfallslos; *lecture, book* einfallslos; *food* fantasielos, phantasielos, einfallslos; **to be ~ by a subject** von einem Thema nicht begeistert werden

uninspiring [ˌʌnɪn'spaɪərɪŋ] ADJ trocken; *suggestion, idea* nicht gerade aufregend

uninstall [ˌʌnɪn'stɔːl] VT *(Comput)* deinstallieren

uninsured [ˌʌnɪn'ʃʊəd] ADJ nicht versichert

unintelligent [ˌʌnɪn'telɪdʒənt] ADJ unintelligent; *approach, action* unklug, ungeschickt; **not ~** eigentlich ganz intelligent

unintelligibility ['ʌnɪnˌtelɪdʒɪ'bɪlɪtɪ] N Unverständlichkeit *f*

unintelligible [ˌʌnɪn'telɪdʒɪbl] ADJ *person* nicht zu verstehen; *speech, writing* unverständlich; *(TV) image, picture* nicht erkennbar; **this makes him almost ~** das macht es fast unmöglich, ihn zu verstehen

unintelligibly [ˌʌnɪn'telɪdʒɪblɪ] ADV unverständlich

unintended [ˌʌnɪn'tendɪd], **unintentional** [ˌʌnɪn'tenʃənl] ADJ unbeabsichtigt, unabsichtlich; *joke also* unfreiwillig

unintentionally [ˌʌnɪnˈtenʃnəlɪ] ADV unabsichtlich, unbeabsichtigt, ohne Absicht; *funny* unfreiwillig; **intentionally or ~** absichtlich oder unabsichtlich

uninterested [ʌnˈɪntrɪstɪd] ADJ desinteressiert, interesselos; **to be ~ in sth** an etw *(dat)* nicht interessiert sein

uninteresting [ʌnˈɪntrɪstɪŋ] ADJ uninteressant

uninterrupted [ˌʌnɪntəˈrʌptɪd] ADJ *(= continuous) line* ununterbrochen, kontinuierlich; *noise, rain also* anhaltend; *(= undisturbed) rest, view* ungestört; **to have an ~ view of sth** eine ungestörte Aussicht auf etw *(acc)* haben; **to continue ~** ungestört fortfahren; **~ by advertisements** nicht durch Werbung unterbrochen

uninterruptedly [ˌʌnɪntəˈrʌptɪdlɪ] ADV *speak, sleep, rule* ununterbrochen; *flow* kontinuierlich

uninvited [ˌʌnɪnˈvaɪtɪd] ADJ *guest* ungeladen, ungebeten; *criticism* unerwünscht, ungebeten; *question, sexual advances* unwillkommen, unerwünscht; **to arrive ~** unaufgefordert *or* uneingeladen eintreffen; **to do sth ~** etw ungebeten *or* unaufgefordert tun

uninviting [ˌʌnɪnˈvaɪtɪŋ] ADJ *appearance, atmosphere* nicht (gerade) einladend; *prospect* nicht (gerade) verlockend; *smell, food, sight* unappetitlich; **rather ~** wenig einladend/wenig verlockend/ziemlich unappetitlich

union [ˈjuːnjən] N **a** Vereinigung *f*, Verbindung *f*; *(Pol)* Union *f*, Vereinigung *f*; **the Union** *(US)* die Vereinigten Staaten; *(in civil war)* die Unionsstaaten *pl*; **State of the Union Address** *(US)* ≈ Bericht *m* zur Lage der Nation **b** *(= trade union)* Gewerkschaft *f* **c** *(= association)* Vereinigung *f*; *(= customs union)* Union *f*; *(= postal union)* Postverein *m*; *(= students' union)* Studentenklub *m* **d** *(= harmony)* Eintracht *f*, Harmonie *f* **e** *(form: = marriage)* Verbindung *f* **f** *(Tech)* Verbindung *f*; **~ joint** Anschlussstück *nt*, Verbindungsstück *nt* **g** *(Math)* Vereinigung(smenge) *f* ADJ *attr (= trade union)* Gewerkschafts-; **~ card** Gewerkschaftsausweis *m*

union bashing N *(inf)* Angriffe *pl* auf die Gewerkschaften, Herumhacken *nt* auf den Gewerkschaften

union dues PL Gewerkschaftsbeitrag *m*

unionism [ˈjuːnjənɪzəm] N **a** *(= trade unionism)* Gewerkschaftswesen *nt* **b** *(Pol)* Einigungsbewegung *f*; **Unionism** *(Brit)* Unionismus *m*, unionistische Bewegung

unionist [ˈjuːnjənɪst] N **a** *(= trade unionist)* Gewerkschaftler(in) *m(f)* **b** *(Pol)* Unionist(in) *m(f)*; **Ulster Unionist** Ulster Unionist *m* ADJ **a** *(= trade unionist)* gewerkschaftlich **b** *(Pol)* unionistisch

unionization [ˌjuːnjənaɪˈzeɪʃən] N (gewerkschaftliche) Organisierung

unionize [ˈjuːnjənaɪz] VT gewerkschaftlich organisieren VI sich gewerkschaftlich organisieren

union: **Union Jack** N Union Jack *m*; **Union of Soviet Socialist Republics** N *(Hist)* Union *f* der Sozialistischen Sowjetrepubliken; **union rates** PL *(= wages)* Tariflohn *m*; *(= salary)* Tarifgehalt *nt*; **union shop** N gewerkschaftspflichtiger Betrieb; **union suit** N *(US)* lange Hemdhose

unique [juːˈniːk] ADJ einzig *attr*; *(= outstanding)* einzigartig, einmalig *(inf)*; *(Math)* eindeutig; **you are not ~ in that** da bist du nicht der/die Einzige; **such cases are not ~ to Britain** solche Fälle sind nicht nur auf Großbritannien beschränkt; **~ among ...** einzigartig unter ... *(dat)*; **~ selling point** einzigartiger Verkaufsanreiz

uniquely [juːˈniːklɪ] ADV *(= solely)* einzig und allein, nur; *(= outstandingly)* einmalig *(inf)*, unübertrefflich; **~ suited** außergewöhnlich geeignet; **Mary is ~ qualified for the job** Mary hat einzigartige *or* außergewöhnliche Qualifikationen für die Stellung; **~ among ...** einzigartig unter ... *(+dat)*

uniqueness [juːˈniːknɪs] N Einmaligkeit *f*, Einzigartigkeit *f*

unisex [ˈjuːnɪseks] ADJ für Männer und Frauen; *(Fashion also)* Unisex-; **~ clothing** Unisexkleidung *f*; **~ salon** Unisexsalon *m*, Salon *m* für Damen und Herren

unisexual ADJ

unisexually ADV [juːnɪˈseksjʊəl, -ɪ] eingeschlechtig; *(Bot, Zool also)* getrenntgeschlechtig

unison [ˈjuːnɪzn] N *(Mus)* Gleichklang *m*, Einklang *m (also fig)*; **in ~** unisono *(geh)*, einstimmig; **~ singing** einstimmiger Gesang; **to be in ~ (with sth)** übereinstimmen (mit etw); **to act in ~ with sb** *(fig)* in Übereinstimmung mit jdm handeln

unisonous ADJ

unisonously ADV [juːˈnɪsənəs, -lɪ] **a** *(Mus)* unisono **b** *(fig)* übereinstimmend

unit [ˈjuːnɪt] N **a** *(= entity, Mil)* Einheit *f*; *(= set of equipment)* Anlage *f*, Einheit *f*; **camera ~** Kameraeinheit *f*; **X-ray ~** Röntgenanlage *f* **b** *(= section)* Einheit *f*; *(of furniture)* Element *nt*; *(of machine)* Element *nt*, Teil *nt*; *(of organization)* Abteilung *f*; *(of course book)* Lektion *f*; **power ~** Aggregat *nt*; *(of a rocket)* Triebwerk *nt*; **where did you get those ~s in your bedroom?** wo haben Sie die Anbauelemente in Ihrem Schlafzimmer her?; **the new research ~** die neue Forschungsabteilung *or* -gruppe; **the family as the basic ~** die Familie als Grundelement **c** *(= measure)* Einheit *f*; **~ of account/length** Rechnungs-/Längeneinheit *f* **d** *(Math)* Einer *m*; **tens and ~s** Zehner und Einer *pl*

Unitarian [juːnɪˈteərɪən] ADJ unitarisch N Unitarier(in) *m(f)*

Unitarianism [juːnɪˈteərɪənɪzəm] N Unitarismus *m*

unitary [ˈjuːnɪtərɪ] ADJ *(= unified)* einheitlich; *(Pol) state, system* unitaristisch, zentralistisch; **~ tax** einheitlicher Steuersatz

unit cost N *(Fin)* Stückkosten *pl*

unite [juːˈnaɪt] VT *(= join, also form: = marry)* vereinigen, verbinden; *party, country (treaty etc)* (ver)einigen, zusammenschließen; *(emotions, ties, loyalties)* (ver)einen; **the common interests which ~ us** die gemeinsamen Interessen, die uns verbinden VI sich zusammenschließen, sich vereinigen; **to ~ in doing sth** gemeinsam etw tun; **to ~ in grief/opposition to sth** gemeinsam trauern/gegen etw Opposition machen; **workers of the world, ~!** Proletarier aller Länder, vereinigt euch!

united [juːˈnaɪtɪd] ADJ verbunden; *group, nation, front* geschlossen; *(= unified) people, nation* einig; *efforts* vereint; **~ we stand, divided we fall** *(prov)* Einigkeit macht stark *(Prov)*; **a ~ Ireland** ein vereintes *or* vereinigtes Irland; **to be ~ in the** *or* **one's belief that ...** einig sein in seiner Überzeugung, dass ...; **to be ~ in opposing sth** etw vereint ablehnen; **to be ~ by a common interest** durch ein gemeinsames Interesse verbunden sein; **to form/maintain/present a ~ front** eine geschlossene Front bilden/aufrechterhalten/bieten

United: **United Arab Emirates** PL Vereinigte Arabische Emirate *pl*; **United Arab Republic** N Vereinigte Arabische Republik; **United Kingdom** N Vereinigtes Königreich *(Großbritannien und Nordirland)*; **United Nations (Organization)** N Vereinte Nationen *pl*; **United Service Organization** N *(US) Hilfsorganisation für die US-Armee, besonders für im Ausland stationierte Truppen*; **United States (of America)** PL Vereinigte Staaten *pl* (von Amerika)

unit: **unit furniture** N Anbaumöbel *pl*; **unit-linked** ADJ *(Insur)* fondsgebunden; **unit price** N *(= price per unit)* Preis *m* pro Einheit; *(= inclusive price)* Pauschalpreis *m*; **unit trust** N *(Brit Fin)* Unit Trust *m*, Investmentgesellschaft *f*; *(= share)* Unit-Trust-Papiere *pl*, Investmentpapiere *pl*

unity [ˈjuːnɪtɪ] N **a** *(= oneness, Liter)* Einheit *f*; *(= harmony)* Einmütigkeit *f*, Einigkeit *f*; *(of a novel, painting etc)* Einheitlichkeit *f*, Geschlossenheit *f*; **national ~** (nationale) Einheit; **this ~ of purpose** diese gemeinsamen Ziele; **to live in ~** in Eintracht leben; **~ is strength** Einigkeit macht stark *(Prov)* **b** *(Math)* Einheit *f*; *(= one)* Eins *f*; *(in set theory)* neutrales Element

Univ *abbr of* **University** Univ.

univalent [juːnɪˈveɪlənt] ADJ einwertig

univalve [ˈjuːnɪvælv] N Gastropod *m* ADJ einschalig

universal [juːnɪˈvɜːsəl] ADJ **a** *phenomenon, applicability, remedy* universal, universell; *(= prevailing everywhere) custom, game* allgemein *or* überall verbreitet; *(= applying to all) truth, rule* allgemeingültig, universell; *(= general) approval, peace* allgemein; **~ education** Allgemeinbildung *f*; **~ language** Weltsprache *f*; **~ peace** Weltfrieden *m*; **~ remedy** Allheilmittel *nt*; **to be a ~ favourite** überall beliebt sein; **to become ~** allgemein verbreitet werden **b** *(Logic)* universal, universell, allgemein N *(Philos)* Allgemeinbegriff *m*; *(Logic: = universal proposition)* Universalaussage *f*; **the ~** das Allgemeine; **the various ~s of human experience** die verschiedenen Grundelemente menschlicher Erfahrung

universal: **universal coupling** N = **universal joint**; **universal donor** N Universalspender(in) *m(f)*

universality [juːnɪvɜːˈsælɪtɪ] N Universalität *f*; *(of person also)* Vielseitigkeit *f*; *(= prevalence also)* allgemeine Verbreitung; *(= general applicability)* Allgemeingültigkeit *f*

universal joint N Universalgelenk *nt*

universally [juːnɪˈvɜːsəlɪ] ADV allgemein; **~ applicable** allgemeingültig; **he was ~ liked** er erfreute sich allgemeiner Beliebtheit; **tips are now almost ~ included in hotel bills** Trinkgelder sind heutzutage fast immer in Hotelrechnungen inbegriffen

universal: **Universal Postal Union** N Weltpostverein *m*; **universal product code** N *(US: = bar code)* Barkode *m*; **universal suffrage** N allgemeines Wahlrecht; **universal time** N Weltzeit *f*

universe [ˈjuːnɪvɜːs] N **a** *(= cosmos)* (Welt)all *nt*, Universum *nt*; *(= galaxy)* Sternsystem *nt*; *(= world)* Welt *f*; **he's the funniest writer in the ~** *(inf)* er schreibt die komischsten Sachen überhaupt **b** *(Logic)* **~ of discourse** Gesamtheit *f* aller Gegenstände der Abhandlung

Universities and Colleges Admissions Service N *(Brit)* ≈ Zentralstelle *f* für die Vergabe von Studienplätzen

university [juːnɪˈvɜːsɪtɪ] N Universität *f*; **the ~ of life** die Schule des Lebens; **which ~ does he go to?** wo studiert er?; **to be at/go to ~** studieren; **to be at/go to London University** in London studieren ADJ *attr* Universitäts-; *qualifications, education* akademisch; **~ library** Universitätsbibliothek *f*; **~ teacher** Hochschullehrer(in) *m(f)*

university: **university entrance (examination)** N Zulassungsprüfung *f* or Aufnahmeprüfung *f* zum Studium; **university hospital** N Universitätsklinik *f*; **university man** N Akademiker *m*; **university town** N Universitätsstadt *f*

unjaundiced [ʌnˈdʒɔːndɪst] ADJ *(geh)* unvoreingenommen

unjust [ʌnˈdʒʌst] ADJ ungerecht *(to* gegen); **you're being ~** das ist ungerecht

unjustifiable [ʌnˈdʒʌstɪfaɪəbl] ADJ nicht zu rechtfertigend *attr*, nicht zu rechtfertigen *pred*; **it was ~ of them not to ...** es war ihrerseits nicht zu rechtfertigen, nicht zu ...

unjustifiably [ʌnˈdʒʌstɪfaɪəblɪ] ADV *expensive, severe, critical* ungerechtfertigt; *rude* unnötig; *criticize, dismiss, praise* zu Unrecht; *act* ungerechtfertigt; **they have been ~ wronged by the media**

sie sind von den Medien zu Unrecht angegriffen worden

unjustified [ʌn'dʒʌstɪfaɪd] ADJ **a** ungerechtfertigt **b** *text* nicht bündig; **to set sth ~** etw im Flattersatz setzen

unjustly [ʌn'dʒʌstlɪ] ADV zu Unrecht; *judge, treat* ungerecht

unjustness [ʌn'dʒʌstnɪs] N Ungerechtigkeit *f*

unkempt [ʌn'kempt] ADJ *hair* ungekämmt; *appearance, garden etc* ungepflegt, vernachlässigt; *person, beard* ungepflegt

unkind [ʌn'kaɪnd] ADJ (+er) **a** *person, remark, action (= not nice)* unfreundlich, nicht nett; *(= cruel)* lieblos, gemein; *(= harsh) climate, country, action* schlecht (*to* für); **don't be (so) ~!** das ist aber gar nicht nett (von dir)!; **she was ~ enough to say that…** sie hatte die Unfreundlichkeit zu sagen, dass …; **she never has an ~ word to say about anyone** von ihr ist niemals ein unfreundliches *or* böses Wort über irgendjemanden zu hören; **to be ~ to animals** nicht gut zu Tieren sein; **~ to the skin** nicht hautfreundlich; **fate has been very ~ to him** das Schicksal hat ihn grausam behandelt; **the weather was ~ to us** das Wetter war uns nicht wohl gesonnen; **it would be ~ not to tell him the truth** es wäre gemein, ihm nicht die Wahrheit zu sagen **b** *(Sport) bounce* unglücklich

unkindly [ʌn'kaɪndlɪ] ADV unfreundlich, nicht nett; *(= cruelly)* lieblos, gemein; **how ~ fate had treated her** wie grausam das Schicksal ihr mitgespielt hatte; **don't take it ~ if …** nimm es nicht übel, wenn …; **to take ~ to sth** etw übel nehmen

unkindness [ʌn'kaɪndnɪs] N Unfreundlichkeit *f*; *(= cruelty)* Lieblosigkeit *f*, Gemeinheit *f*; **the ~ of the weather** das schlechte Wetter

unknot [ʌn'nɒt] VT aufknoten, entknoten

unknowable [ʌn'nəʊəbl] ADJ *truths* unbegreiflich, unfassbar; *person* verschlossen N **the Unknowable** das Unfassbare

unknowing [ʌn'nəʊɪŋ] ADJ *agent* unbewusst, ohne es zu wissen; **he was the ~ cause of …** er war unwissentlich *or* ohne es zu wissen die Ursache für …

unknowingly [ʌn'nəʊɪŋlɪ] ADV unwissentlich, ohne es zu wissen; **knowingly or ~** wissentlich oder unwissentlich

unknown [ʌn'nəʊn] ADJ unbekannt; **the ~ soldier** *or* **warrior** der Unbekannte Soldat; **~ territory** *(lit, fig)* Neuland *nt*; **some ~ person** irgendein Unbekannter; **to be ~ to sb** *(feeling, territory)* jdm fremd sein; **it's ~ for him to get up for breakfast** man ist es von ihm gar nicht gewohnt, dass er zum Frühstück aufsteht; **this substance is ~ to science** diese Substanz ist der Wissenschaft nicht bekannt → **person** N *(= person)* Unbekannte(r) *mf*; *(= factor, Math)* Unbekannte *f*; *(= territory)* unerforschtes Gebiet, Neuland *nt*; **the ~** das Unbekannte; **a journey into the ~** *(lit, fig)* eine Fahrt ins Ungewisse ADV **~ to me** *etc* ohne dass ich *etc* es wusste; **~ to me, the contents of my suitcase were inspected** ohne mein Wissen *or* ohne dass ich davon wusste, wurde der Inhalt meines Koffers untersucht

unknown quantity N *(= person)* unbekannte Größe; *(Math)* Unbekannte *f*

unlabelled, *(US)* **unlabeled** [ʌn'leɪbld] ADJ nicht etikettiert, ohne Etikett *or* Aufschrift, unbeschriftet

unlace [ʌn'leɪs] VT aufbinden, aufschnüren

unladylike [ʌn'leɪdɪlaɪk] ADJ undamenhaft, nicht damenhaft

unlamented [ˌʌnlə'mentɪd] ADJ *death, loss* unbeklagt, unbeweint; **he died ~** niemand trauerte um ihn

unlatch [ʌn'lætʃ] VT entriegeln

unlawful [ʌn'lɔːfʊl] ADJ gesetzwidrig; *means, sex, imprisonment, act* ungesetzlich, illegal; *wedding* ungültig

unlawful: **unlawful assembly** N *(Jur)* verbotene *or* illegale Versammlung; **unlawful entry** N *(Jur)* Einbruch *m*; **unlawful killing** N *(Jur: = offence)* Tötungsdelikt *nt*

unlawfully [ʌn'lɔːfəlɪ] ADV gesetzwidrig, illegal; *married* ungültig; *imprison* ungesetzlich

unleaded [ʌn'ledɪd] ADJ *petrol* unverbleit, bleifrei N unverbleites *or* bleifreies Benzin; **I use ~** ich fahre bleifrei

unlearn [ʌn'lɜːn] VT sich *(dat)* abgewöhnen; *habit also* ablegen

unleash [ʌn'liːʃ] VT *dog* von der Leine lassen; *(fig: = cause) anger, war* entfesseln, auslösen; **to ~ a storm of criticism** einen Sturm der Kritik entfesseln; **he ~ed his fury on his wife** er ließ seine Frau seinen Zorn spüren; **to ~ a war upon the whole world** die ganze Welt in einen Krieg stürzen

unleavened [ʌn'levnd] ADJ *bread* ungesäuert

unless [ən'les] CONJ es sei denn; *(at beginning of sentence)* wenn … nicht, sofern … nicht; **don't do it ~ I tell you to** mach das nicht, es sei denn, ich sage es dir; **~ I tell you to, don't do it** sofern *or* wenn ich es dir nicht sage, mach das nicht; **~ I am mistaken …** wenn *or* falls ich mich nicht irre …; **~ otherwise stated** sofern nicht anders angezeigt *or* angegeben; **~ there is an interruption** vorausgesetzt, alles läuft ohne Unterbrechung

unlettered [ʌn'letəd] ADJ ungebildet; *(= illiterate)* analphabetisch *attr*

unliberated [ʌn'lɪbəreɪtɪd] ADJ *women* unemanzipiert, nicht emanzipiert; *masses, countries* nicht befreit

unlicensed [ʌn'laɪsənst] ADJ *(= having no licence) car, dog, TV* nicht angemeldet; *premises* ohne Lizenz *or* (Schank)konzession; *software* nicht lizenziert; *(= unauthorized)* unbefugt, unberechtigt; **people with ~ TV sets** Schwarzseher *pl*

unlike [ʌn'laɪk] ADJ unähnlich, nicht ähnlich; *poles* ungleich, gegensätzlich PREP **a** im Gegensatz zu, anders als **b** *(= uncharacteristic of)* **to be quite ~ sb** jdm (gar) nicht ähnlichsehen; *(behaviour also)* überhaupt nicht zu jdm passen; **how ~ him not to have told us** das sieht ihm gar nicht ähnlich, dass er uns nichts gesagt hat **c** *(= not resembling)* **this photograph is quite ~ her** dieses Foto sieht ihr gar nicht ähnlich; **this house is ~ their former one** dieses Haus ist ganz anders als ihr früheres

unlikeable [ʌn'laɪkəbl] ADJ unsympathisch

unlikelihood [ʌn'laɪklɪhʊd] N Unwahrscheinlichkeit *f*; **despite the ~ of success** obwohl der Erfolg unwahrscheinlich war

unlikely [ʌn'laɪklɪ] ✪ 16.2 ADJ (+er) unwahrscheinlich; *explanation also* unglaubwürdig; *(= odd also) clothes* merkwürdig, komisch; *friendship* merkwürdig; *candidate* unpassend; **it is (most) ~/not ~ that …** es ist (höchst) unwahrscheinlich/es kann durchaus sein, dass …; **she is ~ to come** sie kommt höchstwahrscheinlich nicht; **it looks an ~ place for mushrooms** es sieht mir nicht nach der geeigneten Stelle für Pilze aus; **they are such an ~ couple** sie sind ein so merkwürdiges Paar; **he's an ~ choice** seine Wahl ist sehr unwahrscheinlich; **he's ~ to be chosen** es ist unwahrscheinlich, dass er gewählt wird; **in the ~ event that …** im unwahrscheinlichen Fall, dass …; **in the ~ event of war** im unwahrscheinlichen Fall eines Krieges

unlimited [ʌn'lɪmɪtɪd] ADJ *wealth, time* unbegrenzt; *power also* schrankenlos; *patience* unendlich; *access, use* uneingeschränkt

unlimited company N *(Fin)* Gesellschaft *f* mit unbeschränkter Haftung

unlimited liability N *(Comm, Jur)* unbeschränkte Haftung

unlined [ʌn'laɪnd] ADJ *paper* unliniert; *face* faltenlos; *(= without lining) dress* ungefüttert

unlisted [ʌn'lɪstɪd] ✪ 27.1 ADJ *company, items* nicht verzeichnet; *name* nicht aufgeführt; *bonds, stock* nicht notiert; **the number is ~** *(US Telec)* die Nummer steht nicht im Telefonbuch

unlisted securities market N Freiverkehr *m*

unlit [ˌʌn'lɪt] ADJ *road* unbeleuchtet; *lamp* nicht angezündet; *fire, cigarette* unangezündet

unload [ʌn'ləʊd] VT **a** *ship, gun* entladen; *boot, luggage* ausladen; *car* entladen, ausladen; *cargo* löschen; *passengers* absetzen; *bomb* abwerfen **b** *(inf: = get rid of) (Fin) shares* abstoßen; *furniture, children, problem* abladen (*on(to)* bei); *job, problem* abwälzen (*on(to)* auf *+acc*) VI *(ship)* löschen; *(truck)* abladen

unlock [ʌn'lɒk] VT *door etc* aufschließen; *(fig) heart, secret* offenbaren; **the door is ~ed** die Tür ist nicht abgeschlossen; **to leave a door ~ed** eine Tür nicht abschließen

unlooked-for [ʌn'lʊktfɔː] ADJ unerwartet, unvorhergesehen; *welcome also* unverhofft

unloose [ʌn'luːs] VT **a** *(also* **unloosen**) *knot, grasp, hair* lösen; *rope, chains* lösen, losmachen **b** *prisoner* losbinden; *dog* losmachen, loslassen

unlovable [ʌn'lʌvəbl] ADJ wenig liebenswert *or* liebenswürdig, unsympathisch

unloved [ʌn'lʌvd] ADJ ungeliebt

unlovely [ʌn'lʌvlɪ] ADJ *sight* unschön; *person (in appearance)* abstoßend; *(in character)* garstig, unliebenswert

unloving [ʌn'lʌvɪŋ] ADJ *person, home* lieblos, kalt

unluckily [ʌn'lʌkɪlɪ] ADV zum Pech, zum Unglück; **~ for him** zu seinem Pech

unlucky [ʌn'lʌkɪ] ADJ (+er) **a** *person* unglückselig; *defeat, loser, victim* unglücklich; **~ wretch** Unglücksrabe *m*, Pechvogel *m*; **he's always ~** er ist vom Pech verfolgt; **to be ~** Pech haben; *(= not succeed)* keinen Erfolg haben; **~ in love** unglücklich verliebt; **it was ~ for her that she was seen** Pech für sie, dass man sie gesehen hat; **how ~ for you!** was für ein Pech!, das ist wirklich dumm (für dich)!; **he was ~ enough to meet her** er hatte das Pech, sie zu treffen; **Smith was ~ not to score a second goal** Smith hatte Pech gehabt, dass er kein zweites Tor schoss **b** *object, action, place* unglückselig; *coincidence, event, choice* unglücklich; *moment* ungünstig, schlecht gewählt; **~ day** Unglückstag *m*; **to be ~** Unglück *or* Pech bringen; **London has been an ~ place for me** London hat mir nur Pech gebracht; **broken mirrors are ~** zerbrochene Spiegel bringen Unglück; **~ number** Unglückszahl *f*; **number 13: ~ for some** Nummer 13: für manche bedeutet das Unglück; **it's not through any fault of yours, it's just ~** es ist nicht dein Fehler, es ist nur Pech

unmade [ʌn'meɪd] ADJ *bed* ungemacht

unmade-up [ˌʌnmeɪd'ʌp] ADJ *face* ungeschminkt, ohne Make-up; *road* ungeteert

unmailable [ʌn'meɪləbl] ADJ *(esp US)* nicht postversandfähig

unman [ʌn'mæn] VT schwach werden lassen; *(= make lose courage)* entmutigen, verzagen lassen

unmanageable [ʌn'mænɪdʒəbl] ADJ *(= unwieldy) vehicle, boat* schwer zu handhaben *or* manövrieren; *parcel, size* unhandlich; *number* nicht zu bewältigen; *problem* unlösbar; *(= uncontrollable) animal, person, hair, child* widerspenstig, nicht zu bändigen; *situation* unkontrollierbar; **she finds the stairs ~** sie kann die Treppe nicht schaffen *(inf)* or bewältigen; **this company is ~** es ist unmöglich, dieses Unternehmen zu leiten; **the crowd had reached ~ proportions** die Menge hatte unkontrollierbare Ausmaße angenommen

unmanly [ʌn'mænlɪ] ADJ *tears, behaviour* unmännlich; *(= cowardly)* feige; *(= effeminate)* weibisch

unmanned [ʌn'mænd] ADJ *(= not requiring crew) lighthouse, aircraft, spacecraft, border post, level crossing* unbemannt; *vehicle* fahrerlos; *(= lacking crew) telephone exchange* unbesetzt, nicht besetzt

unmannerly [ʌn'mænəlɪ] ADJ ungesittet; *child also* ungezogen; *behaviour* ungehörig; *(at table al-*

so) unmanierlich; **it is ~ to ...** es gehört sich nicht, zu ...

unmarked [ʌnˈmɑːkt] **ADJ** **a** *(= unstained)* ohne Flecken *or* Spuren, fleckenlos; *(= without marking) face* ungezeichnet *(also fig)*; *banknotes* unmarkiert; *linen* nicht gezeichnet; *boxes, crates, suitcases etc* ohne Namen *or* Adresse; *police car* nicht gekennzeichnet; *(= anonymous) grave* anonym; **luckily the carpet was ~ by the wine** glücklicherweise blieben keine Weinspuren auf dem Teppich zurück; **to leave sb ~** spurlos an jdm vorübergehen **b** *(Sport) player* ungedeckt **c** *(Sch) papers* unkorrigiert **d** *(= unnoticed)* unbemerkt **e** *(Ling)* unmarkiert

unmarketable [ʌnˈmɑːkɪtəbl] **ADJ** unverkäuflich, schlecht *or* nicht zu verkaufen

unmarriageable [ʌnˈmærɪdʒəbl] **ADJ** nicht zu verheiraten *pred*, nicht unter die Haube zu kriegen *pred (inf)*

unmarried [ʌnˈmærɪd] **ADJ** unverheiratet; **~ mother** ledige Mutter

unmask [ʌnˈmɑːsk] **VT** *(lit)* demaskieren; *(fig)* entlarven **VI** die Maske abnehmen, sich demaskieren

unmasking [ʌnˈmɑːskɪŋ] **N** *(fig)* Entlarvung *f*

unmatched [ʌnˈmætʃt] **ADJ** unübertrefflich, einmalig, unübertroffen *(for* in Bezug auf *+acc)*; **~ by anyone** von niemandem übertroffen; **the scenery is ~ anywhere in the world** die Landschaft sucht (in der Welt) ihresgleichen; **to be ~ for beauty** alle anderen an Schönheit übertreffen

unmeasured **ADJ**, **unmeasuredly** **ADV** [ʌnˈmeʒəd, -lɪ] **a** *risk factors etc* nicht untersucht, unergründet **b** *(esp liter, poet)* unermesslich *(geh)*, grenzenlos, unbegrenzt **c** *(fig: = unrestrained)* unmäßig, maßlos

unmechanical [ˌʌnmɪˈkænɪkəl] **ADJ** *person* technisch unbegabt

unmentionable [ʌnˈmenʃnəbl] **ADJ** tabu *pred*; *word also* unaussprechlich; **to be ~** tabu sein; **to be an ~ subject** (als Thema) tabu sein; **an ~ disease** eine Krankheit, über die man nicht spricht **PL** **the ~s** *(Brit hum dated)* die Unterwäsche *f*

unmerciful **ADJ**, **unmercifully** **ADV** [ʌnˈmɜːsɪfʊl, -fəlɪ] unbarmherzig, erbarmungslos

unmerited [ʌnˈmerɪtɪd] **ADJ** unverdient

unmet [ˈʌnˈmet] **ADJ** *needs* unbefriedigt; *demands* unerfüllt; **to go ~** *(needs)* unbefriedigt bleiben; *(demands)* unerfüllt bleiben

unmetalled [ʌnˈmetld] **ADJ** *(Brit)* ungeteert

unmethodical [ˌʌnmɪˈθɒdɪkəl] **ADJ** unmethodisch

unmindful [ʌnˈmaɪndfʊl] **ADJ** **to be ~ of sth** nicht auf etw *(acc)* achten, etw nicht beachten; **I was not ~ of your needs** ich stand Ihren Bedürfnissen nicht gleichgültig gegenüber

unmingled [ʌnˈmɪŋgld] **ADJ** = **unmixed**

unmissable [ˈʌnˈmɪsəbl] **ADJ** *(Brit inf)* **to be ~** ein Muss sein; **this ~ conference** diese Konferenz, die man sich nicht entgehen lassen sollte

unmistak(e)able [ˌʌnmɪˈsteɪkəbl] **ADJ** unverkennbar; *(visually)* nicht zu verwechseln; **to send an ~ message to sb** *(fig)* jdm eine unmissverständliche Botschaft senden

unmistak(e)ably [ˌʌnmɪˈsteɪkəblɪ] **ADV** zweifelsohne *(geh)*, unverkennbar

unmitigated [ʌnˈmɪtɪgeɪtɪd] **ADJ** *(= not lessened) wrath, severity* ungemildert; *(inf: = complete) disaster* vollkommen, total; *success* total, absolut; *rubbish* komplett *(inf)*; *liar, rogue* Erz- *(inf)*

unmixed [ʌnˈmɪkst] **ADJ** *blood* unvermischt; *delight, pleasure* rein, ungetrübt; **to be an ~ blessing** der reine Segen sein

unmodified [ʌnˈmɒdɪfaɪd] **ADJ** unverändert, nicht (ab)geändert

unmolested [ˌʌnməˈlestɪd] **ADJ** *(= unattacked)* unbelästigt; *(= undisturbed)* in Frieden, in Ruhe

unmoor [ʌnˈmʊəʳ] **VTI** losmachen

unmotivated [ʌnˈməʊtɪveɪtɪd] **ADJ** unmotiviert; *attack also* grundlos

unmounted [ʌnˈmaʊntɪd] **ADJ** *horse* ohne Reiter; *gem* ungefasst; *gun* nicht fest montiert; *picture (= not on mount)* nicht aufgezogen; *(= not in album)* lose

unmourned [ʌnˈmɔːnd] **ADJ** unbeweint; *death also* unbeklagt; **an ~ tyrant** ein Tyrann *m*, dem niemand nachtrauert *or* nachweint; **they died largely ~** kaum einer trauerte um sie *or* trauerte ihnen nach ihrem Tod(e) nach

unmoved [ʌnˈmuːvd] **ADJ** *person* ungerührt; **they were ~ by his playing** sein Spiel(en) ergriff sie nicht; **it leaves me ~** das (be)rührt mich nicht; **he remained ~ by her pleas** ihr Flehen ließ ihn kalt, ihr Flehen rührte *or* erweichte ihn nicht

unmoving [ʌnˈmuːvɪŋ] **ADJ** regungslos

unmusical [ʌnˈmjuːzɪkəl] **ADJ** *person* unmusikalisch; *sound* unmelodisch

unnam(e)able [ʌnˈneɪməbl] **ADJ** unsagbar

unnamed [ʌnˈneɪmd] **ADJ** *(= nameless)* namenlos; *(= anonymous)* ungenannt

unnatural [ʌnˈnætʃrəl] **ADJ** unnatürlich; *(= abnormal also) relationship, crime* nicht normal *pred*, widernatürlich, wider die Natur *pred*; **~ death** widernatürlicher Tod; **to die an ~ death** keines natürlichen Todes sterben; **it is ~ for him to be so rude** normalerweise ist er nicht so grob, es ist ungewöhnlich, dass er so grob ist; **it's not ~ to be upset** es ist nur natürlich, da bestürzt zu sein

unnaturally [ʌnˈnætʃrəlɪ] **ADV** unnatürlich; *(= extraordinarily also) loud, anxious* ungewöhnlich; **not ~, we were worried** es war nur normal *or* natürlich, dass wir uns Sorgen machten

unnavigable [ʌnˈnævɪgəbl] **ADJ** nicht schiffbar, nicht befahrbar

unnecessarily [ʌnˈnesɪsərɪlɪ] **ADV** unnötigerweise; *strict, serious* unnötig, übertrieben

unnecessary [ʌnˈnesɪsərɪ] **ADJ** unnötig; *(= superfluous also)* überflüssig; *(= not requisite)* nicht notwendig *or* nötig; **no, you needn't bother thanks, that's quite ~** nein, machen Sie sich keine Umstände, das ist wirklich nicht nötig; **it was quite ~ to be so rude** es war wirklich nicht nötig, so grob zu werden; **it was ~ for you to do that** es war nicht nötig, dass du das getan hast; **really, that was quite ~ of you!** also, das war wirklich überflüssig!

unneighbourly, *(US)* **unneighborly** [ʌnˈneɪbəlɪ] **ADJ** *behaviour* nicht gutnachbarlich; **an ~ person** ein schlechter Nachbar, eine schlechte Nachbarin; **it's ~ to do that** als guter Nachbar tut man so etwas nicht

unnerve [ʌnˈnɜːv] **VT** entnerven; *(gradually)* zermürben; *(= discourage) speaker* entmutigen; **~d by their reaction** durch ihre Reaktion aus der Ruhe gebracht

unnerving [ʌnˈnɜːvɪŋ] **ADJ** *experience, sincerity* entnervend; *silence also* zermürbend; *(= discouraging also)* entmutigend; **an ~ habit** eine entnervende *or* irritierende Angewohnheit

unnoticed [ʌnˈnəʊtɪst] **ADJ** unbemerkt; **to go *or* pass ~** unbemerkt bleiben; **to be ~ by sb** von jdm nicht bemerkt werden

unnumbered [ʌnˈnʌmbəd] **ADJ** **a** *(= countless)* unzählig, zahllos **b** *(= not numbered)* nicht nummeriert; *house* ohne Hausnummer

UNO *abbr of* **United Nations Organization** UNO *f*

unobjectionable [ˌʌnəbˈdʒekʃnəbl] **ADJ** einwandfrei; **he is a pretty ~ person** gegen ihn lässt sich kaum etwas einwenden

unobliging **ADJ**, **unobligingly** **ADV** [ˌʌnəˈblaɪdʒɪŋ, lɪ] ungefällig

unobservant [ˌʌnəbˈzɜːvənt] **ADJ** unaufmerksam; **to be ~** ein schlechter Beobachter sein; **how ~ of me** wie unaufmerksam (von mir)

unobserved [ˌʌnəbˈzɜːvd] **ADJ** *(= not seen)* unbemerkt; *(= not celebrated)* nicht (mehr) eingehalten *or* beachtet

unobstructed [ˌʌnəbˈstrʌktɪd] **ADJ** *view* ungehindert; *pipe* frei, unverstopft; *path, road* frei, unversperrt

unobtainable [ˌʌnəbˈteɪnəbl] ✪ 27.7 **ADJ** **a** nicht erhältlich, nicht zu bekommen; *goal* unerreichbar; **number ~** *(Brit Telec)* kein Anschluss unter dieser Nummer; **your number was ~** deine Nummer war nicht zu bekommen **b** *(= out of bounds) person* unantastbar

unobtrusive **ADJ**, **unobtrusively** **ADV** [ˌʌnəbˈtruːsɪv, -lɪ] unauffällig

unoccupied [ʌnˈɒkjʊpaɪd] **ADJ** *person* unbeschäftigt; *house* leer stehend, unbewohnt; *seat, table* frei; *(Mil) zone* unbesetzt

unofficial [ˌʌnəˈfɪʃəl] **ADJ** inoffiziell; *(= unconfirmed also) information* nicht amtlich; **to take ~ action** *(Ind)* inoffiziell streiken; **~ strike** inoffizieller *or* wilder Streik; **in an ~ capacity** inoffiziell

unofficially [ˌʌnəˈfɪʃəlɪ] **ADV** inoffiziell

unopened [ʌnˈəʊpənd] **ADJ** ungeöffnet

unopposed [ˌʌnəˈpəʊzd] **ADJ** **they marched on ~** sie marschierten weiter, ohne auf Widerstand zu treffen; **~ by the committee** ohne Widerspruch *or* Beanstandung seitens des Ausschusses; **to be returned ~** *(Pol)* ohne Gegenstimmen gewählt werden; **an ~ second reading** *(Parl)* eine zweite Lesung ohne Gegenstimmen

unorganized [ʌnˈɔːgənaɪzd] **ADJ** unsystematisch; *person also* unmethodisch; *life* ungeregelt; *(Ind)* nicht (gewerkschaftlich) organisiert; **he is so ~** er hat überhaupt kein System

unoriginal [ˌʌnəˈrɪdʒɪnəl] **ADJ** wenig originell

unorthodox [ʌnˈɔːθədɒks] **ADJ** unkonventionell, unorthodox; **~ entrepreneur** *(iro) Bezeichnung für Bettler, Prostituierte, Drogenhändler etc*

unpack [ʌnˈpæk] **VTI** auspacken; *(Comput) file* dekomprimieren, entpacken

unpacking [ʌnˈpækɪŋ] **N** Auspacken *nt*; **to do one's ~** auspacken

unpaged [ʌnəˈpeɪdʒd] **ADJ** unpaginiert, ohne Seitenzahl(en)

unpaid [ʌnˈpeɪd] **ADJ** unbezahlt **ADV** **to work ~** unbezahlt *or* ohne Bezahlung arbeiten

unpalatable [ʌnˈpælɪtəbl] **ADJ** *food, drink* ungenießbar; *(fig) fact, truth, mixture* unverdaulich, schwer zu verdauen; **he finds the truth ~** die Wahrheit schmeckt ihm nicht; **to be ~ to sb** *(fig)* für jdn schwer zu akzeptieren *or* zu schlucken *(inf)* sein

unparalleled [ʌnˈpærəleld] **ADJ** einmalig, beispiellos; *(= unprecedented also)* noch nie da gewesen; **an ~ success** ein Erfolg ohnegleichen; **~ in the history of mankind** beispiellos *or* ohne Beispiel in der Geschichte der Menschheit

unpardonable [ʌnˈpɑːdnəbl] **ADJ** unverzeihlich

unparliamentary [ˌʌnpɑːləˈmentərɪ] **ADJ** *behaviour, language* nicht parlamentsfähig, der Würde des Parlamentes nicht entsprechend *attr*; *procedure* unparlamentarisch

unpatented [ʌnˈpeɪtntɪd] **ADJ** nicht patentiert

unpatriotic [ˌʌnpætrɪˈɒtɪk] **ADJ** unpatriotisch

unpaved [ʌnˈpeɪvd] **ADJ** *road, courtyard* nicht gepflastert

unpeeled [ʌnˈpiːld] **ADJ** *Obst* ungeschält

unpeg [ʌnˈpeg] **VT** *washing* abnehmen; *prices* freigeben

unperceived [ˌʌnpəˈsiːvd] **ADJ** unbemerkt

unperceptive [ˌʌnpəˈseptɪv] **ADJ** unaufmerksam

unperfumed [ʌnˈpɜːfjuːmd] **ADJ** nicht parfümiert

unperson [ˈʌnpɜːsən] **N** *(Pol)* Unperson *f*

unperturbable [ˌʌnpəˈtɜːbəbl] **ADJ** nicht aus der Ruhe zu bringen *pred or* bringend *attr*

unperturbed [ˌʌnpəˈtɜːbd] **ADJ** nicht beunruhigt *(by* von, durch), gelassen

unphilosophical [ˌʌnfɪləˈsɒfɪkəl] **ADJ** unphilosophisch

unpick [ʌnˈpɪk] **VT** auftrennen; *(Brit fig) plan, policy* auseinandernehmen

unpin [ʌn'pɪn] VT *dress, hair* die Nadeln entfernen aus; *notice* abnehmen

unplaced [ʌn'pleɪst] ADJ *(Sport)* nicht platziert; **to be ~** sich nicht platziert haben

unplanned [ʌn'plænd] ADJ ungeplant, nicht geplant

unplasticized ['ʌn'plæstɪsaɪzd] ADJ **~ polyvinyl chloride** weichmacherfreies Polyvinylchlorid

unplayable [ʌn'pleɪəbl] ADJ unspielbar; *pitch* unbespielbar; **the ball was in an ~ position** der Ball war nicht spielbar

unpleasant [ʌn'pleznt] ADJ unangenehm; *experience, situation also* unerfreulich; *person, smile, remark* unliebenswürdig, unfreundlich; **something ~** etwas Unangenehmes *or* Unerfreuliches; **to be ~ to sb** unfreundlich zu jdm sein

unpleasantly [ʌn'plezntlɪ] ADV *reply* unliebenswürdig, unfreundlich; *warm, smell* unangenehm; **he was getting ~ close to the truth** es war unangenehm, wie nah er an der Wahrheit war; **not ~ so** auf nicht unangenehme Weise

unpleasantness [ʌn'plezntnɪs] N **a** *(= quality)* Unangenehmheit *f*; *(of experience, situation also)* Unerfreulichkeit *f*; *(of person, smile, remark)* Unfreundlichkeit *f* **b** *(= bad feeling, quarrel)* Unstimmigkeit *f*

unplug [ʌn'plʌg] VT *radio, lamp* rausziehen; *plug* abziehen, rausziehen; **~ it first** zieh zuerst den Stecker heraus

unplugged ['ʌn'plʌgd] ADJ *(Mus)* (rein) akustisch, unplugged *pred (inf)*

unplumbed [ʌn'plʌmd] ADJ unergründet

unpoetic, unpoetical ADJ [ˌʌnpəʊ'etɪk, -əl], **unpoetically** [ˌʌnpəʊ'etɪkəlɪ] ADV unpoetisch, undichterisch

unpolished [ʌn'pɒlɪʃt] ADJ **a** unpoliert; *stone* ungeschliffen; *shoes* ungeputzt **b** *(fig) person, manners* ungeschliffen, ungehobelt; *performance* unausgefeilt; *style, language* holprig, unausgefeilt

unpolitical ADJ, **unpolitically** ADV [ˌʌnpə'lɪtɪkəl, -ɪ] unpolitisch

unpolled ADJ *(= not having voted)* nicht gewählt habend *attr*; **~ elector** Nichtwähler(in) *m(f)*

unpolluted [ˌʌnpə'lu:tɪd] ADJ sauber, unverschmutzt; **to be ~ by sth** *(lit)* nicht durch etw verschmutzt *or* verunreinigt sein; *(fig)* unverdorben von etw sein

unpopular [ʌn'pɒpjʊlə'] ADJ *person* unbeliebt *(with sb* bei jdm); *decision, move, measures, tax* unpopulär; **to make oneself ~ (with sb)** sich (bei jdm) unbeliebt machen; **I'm ~ with him just now** zur Zeit bin ich bei ihm nicht gut angeschrieben *(inf)*

unpopularity [ʌnˌpɒpjʊ'lærɪtɪ] N Unbeliebtheit *f*; *(of decision, move)* Unpopularität *f*, geringe Popularität

unpractical [ʌn'præktɪkəl] ADJ unpraktisch

unpractised, *(US)* **unpracticed** [ʌn'præktɪst] ADJ ungeübt

unprecedented [ʌn'presɪdəntɪd] ADJ noch nie da gewesen; *success also* beispiellos, ohnegleichen *(after noun)*; *profit, step* unerhört; **this event is ~** dieses Ereignis ist bisher einmalig; **an ~ success** ein beispielloser *or* noch nie da gewesener Erfolg, ein Erfolg ohnegleichen; **on an ~ scale** in einem noch nie da gewesenen Ausmaß; **you realize it's quite ~ for a president to …** es ist Ihnen wohl klar, dass es keinen Präzedenzfall dafür gibt, dass ein Präsident …

unpredictable [ˌʌnprɪ'dɪktəbl] ADJ unvorhersehbar; *result* nicht vorherzusagen *pred*, nicht vorherzusagend *attr*; *behaviour, person, weather, nature* unberechenbar

unpredictably [ˌʌnprɪ'dɪktəblɪ] ADV *violent, dangerous* unberechenbar; **many children behave ~** viele Kinder verhalten sich unberechenbar

unprejudiced [ʌn'predʒʊdɪst] ADJ *(= impartial)* objektiv, unparteiisch; *(= not having prejudices)* vorurteilslos

unpremeditated [ˌʌnprɪ'medɪteɪtɪd] ADJ unüberlegt; *crime* nicht vorsätzlich; *murder* nicht geplant

unprepared [ˌʌnprɪ'pɛəd] ADJ nicht vorbereitet, unvorbereitet; **to be ~ for sth** für etw nicht vorbereitet sein; *(= be surprised)* auf etw *(acc)* nicht vorbereitet *or* gefasst sein; **you've caught me ~** darauf bin ich nicht vorbereitet; **to be ~ to do sth** *(= not willing)* nicht bereit sein, etw zu tun

unprepossessing [ˌʌnpri:pə'zesɪŋ] ADJ wenig gewinnend, wenig einnehmend; *building, room* wenig ansprechend

unpresentable [ˌʌnprɪ'zentəbl] ADJ *(in appearance)* nicht präsentabel; *clothes also* unansehnlich; *(socially)* nicht gesellschaftsfähig; **most of his friends are ~** mit den meisten seiner Freunde kann man sich in der Öffentlichkeit nicht blicken lassen

unpretentious [ˌʌnprɪ'tenʃəs] ADJ schlicht, bescheiden; *person, manner also* natürlich; *house, meal etc also* einfach; *style, book* einfach, nicht schwülstig

unpretentiously [ˌʌnprɪ'tenʃəslɪ] ADV schlicht, bescheiden, einfach; *speak* natürlich; *write* in einfachen Worten

unpriced [ʌn'praɪst] ADJ ohne Preisschild, nicht ausgezeichnet

unprincipled [ʌn'prɪnsɪpld] ADJ skrupellos; *person also* charakterlos

unprintable [ʌn'prɪntəbl] ADJ nicht druckfähig; **his answer was ~** seine Antwort war nicht druckreif

unproductive [ˌʌnprə'dʌktɪv] ADJ *capital* nicht gewinnbringend, keinen Gewinn bringend *attr*; *soil* unfruchtbar, ertragsarm; *discussion, meeting* unproduktiv, unergiebig; *factory, worker* unproduktiv

unprofessional [ˌʌnprə'feʃənl] ADJ unprofessionell; *work also* unfachmännisch, laienhaft, stümperhaft; *conduct* berufswidrig

unprofitable [ʌn'prɒfɪtəbl] ADJ *(financially)* keinen Profit bringend *or* abwerfend, wenig einträglich; *mine, activities, business etc* unrentabel; *(fig)* nutzlos, sinnlos; **the company was ~** die Firma machte keinen Profit *or* warf keinen Profit ab; **we spent an ~ hour on it** wir haben eine Stunde damit verplempert; **it would be ~ to go on** es wäre sinnlos, noch weiterzumachen

unpromising [ʌn'prɒmɪsɪŋ] ADJ nicht sehr vielversprechend; *start also* nicht sehr erfolgversprechend, wenig erfolgversprechend; **to look ~** nicht sehr hoffnungsvoll *or* gut aussehen; *(weather)* nichts Gutes versprechen

unprompted [ʌn'prɒmptɪd] ADJ spontan; **~ by me** unaufgefordert; **his invitation was quite ~** seine Einladung kam ganz aus freien Stücken; **I'd rather he answered the questions ~** es wäre mir lieber, wenn er ohne Vorsagen antwortete

unpronounceable [ˌʌnprə'naʊnsɪbl] ADJ unaussprechbar; **that word is ~** das Wort ist nicht auszusprechen

unpropitious [ˌʌnprə'pɪʃəs] ADJ *omen, moment, circumstances* ungünstig

unproportional ADJ, **unproportionally** ADV [ˌʌnprə'pɔ:ʃənl, -ʃnəlɪ] unverhältnismäßig; *(also Math)* unproportional

unprotected [ˌʌnprə'tektɪd] ADJ ohne Schutz, schutzlos; *machine, skin, eyes* ungeschützt; *(by insurance)* ohne Versicherungsschutz; *(Mil) building etc* ungeschützt, ohne Deckung; **~ by** nicht geschützt durch; **to be ~ from the sun** nicht vor der Sonne geschützt sein

unprotected: **unprotected intercourse** N ungeschützter Geschlechtsverkehr; **unprotected sex** N ungeschützter Sex

unprovable [ʌn'pru:vəbl] ADJ nicht beweisbar

unproven [ʌn'pru:vən], **unproved** [ʌn'pru:vd] ADJ **a** *(= not proved) allegation, charge* nicht bewiesen, unbewiesen; **the charge remains ~** die Anschuldigung bleibt unbewiesen **b** *(= not tested) person, technology* (noch) nicht bewährt

unprovided [ˌʌnprə'vaɪdɪd] ADJ *person* unversorgt

unprovided-for [ˌʌnprə'vaɪdɪdfɔ:'] ADJ **a** *(= lacking)* unversorgt; **he died and left his children ~** er starb, ohne für seine Kinder gesorgt zu haben **b** *(= not anticipated)* **that eventuality was ~** auf dieses Ereignis war man nicht eingerichtet

unprovoked [ˌʌnprə'vəʊkt] ADJ ohne Anlass, grundlos

unpublished [ʌn'pʌblɪʃt] ADJ unveröffentlicht

unpunctual [ʌn'pʌŋktjʊəl] ADJ unpünktlich

unpunctuality [ˌʌnpʌŋktjʊ'ælɪtɪ] N Unpünktlichkeit *f*

unpunished [ʌn'pʌnɪʃt] ADJ unbestraft; **to go ~** ohne Strafe bleiben; **if this goes ~ …** wenn das nicht bestraft wird …

unputdownable [ˌʌnpʊt'daʊnəbl] ADJ *(inf)* **it's absolutely ~** *(book)* es lässt einen nicht los

unqualified [ʌn'kwɒlɪfaɪd] ADJ **a** unqualifiziert; **to be ~ (for a job)** (für eine Arbeit) nicht qualifiziert sein; **he is ~ to do it** er ist dafür nicht qualifiziert; **I was ~ to judge** ich konnte mir darüber kein Urteil erlauben **b** *(= absolute) delight, praise, acceptance* uneingeschränkt; *denial* vollständig; *success* voll(ständig); *(inf) idiot, liar* ausgesprochen; **the party was an ~ disaster** die Party war eine absolute Katastrophe; **an ~ yes/no** ein uneingeschränktes Ja/Nein **c** *(Gram)* nicht bestimmt

unquenchable [ʌn'kwentʃəbl] ADJ *fire* unlöschbar; *thirst, desire* unstillbar; *optimism* unerschütterlich; **she has an ~ spirit** sie lässt sich nicht unterkriegen *(inf)*

unquestionable [ʌn'kwestʃənəbl] ADJ *authority* unbestritten, unangefochten; *evidence, fact* unbezweifelbar; *sincerity, honesty* fraglos; **a man of ~ courage** ein zweifellos *or* fraglos mutiger Mann; **one's parents' authority used to be ~** früher konnte man die Autorität seiner Eltern nicht infrage *or* in Frage stellen; **his courage is ~** sein Mut steht außer Frage

unquestionably [ʌn'kwestʃənəblɪ] ADV fraglos, zweifellos

unquestioned [ʌn'kwestʃənd] ADJ unbestritten; *(= unquestioning) belief, acceptance* bedingungslos; **I can't let that statement pass ~** ich kann diese Behauptung nicht fraglos hinnehmen; **to be ~** *(honesty etc)* außer Frage stehen; *(social order etc)* nicht infrage *or* in Frage gestellt werden

unquestioning [ʌn'kwestʃənɪŋ] ADJ bedingungslos; *belief, faith also* blind

unquestioningly [ʌn'kwestʃənɪŋlɪ] ADV *accept* bedingungslos; *obey* widerspruchslos, blind; **he ~ accepts everything you say** er akzeptiert alles, was Sie sagen, ohne Widerrede

unquiet [ʌn'kwaɪət] ADJ *(liter)* unruhig; *(= restless)* ruhelos

unquote [ʌn'kwəʊt] VI *imper only* **quote … ~** Zitat (Anfang) … Zitat Ende *or* Ende des Zitats → *also* **quote VT a**

unratified [ʌn'rætɪfaɪd] ADJ *(Pol) treaty etc* nicht ratifiziert

unrationed [ʌn'ræʃənd, *(US)* ʌn'reɪʃənd] ADJ *food, petrol etc* nicht rationiert, frei erhältlich

unravel [ʌn'rævəl] **VT** *knitting* aufziehen; *(lit, fig: = untangle)* entwirren; *mystery* lösen **VI** *(knitting)* sich aufziehen; *(fig)* sich entwirren, sich auflösen; *(mystery)* sich lösen; *(plan, system)* aufdecken

unread [ʌn'red] ADJ *book* ungelesen; *person* wenig belesen

unreadable [ʌn'ri:dəbl] ADJ **a** *writing* unleserlich; *book* schwer zu lesen *pred*, schwer lesbar **b** *(Comput) data* nicht lesbar **c** *(liter: = impenetrable) face, eyes* undurchdringlich

unreadiness [ʌn'redɪnɪs] N Unvorbereitetheit *f*; *(of troops)* mangelnde Bereitschaft

unready [ʌn'redɪ] ADJ (noch) nicht fertig; **~ to do sth** nicht bereit, etw zu tun; **he was ~ for what happened next** er war nicht auf das eingestellt *or* vorbereitet, was dann kam; **he is ~ for such responsibility** er ist noch nicht reif genug, solch eine Verantwortung zu übernehmen

unreal [ʌnˈrɪəl] ADJ unwirklich; *(= fake)* unecht; **this is just ~!** *(inf: = unbelievable)* das darf doch nicht wahr sein!, das gibts doch nicht! *(inf)*; **he's ~** er ist unmöglich

unrealistic [ˌʌnrɪəˈlɪstɪk] ADJ unrealistisch; **it is ~ to expect her to do it** es ist unrealistisch von ihr zu erwarten, dass sie es tut

unrealistically [ˌʌnrɪəˈlɪstɪkəlɪ] ADV *high, low* unrealistisch; *optimistic* unangemessen

unreality [ˌʌnrɪˈælɪtɪ] N Unwirklichkeit *f*; **there is an air of ~ about it** es hat etwas Unwirkliches an sich; **extreme exhaustion gives a feeling of ~** extreme Erschöpfung lässt alles unwirklich erscheinen; **the ~ of the characters' emotions** die Unnatürlichkeit *or* Unechtheit der Gefühle der Personen

unrealized [ʌnˈrɪəlaɪzd] ADJ unverwirklicht; *(Fin) assets* unverwertet; *profit* nicht realisiert

unreasonable [ʌnˈriːznəbl] ADJ *demand, price etc* unzumutbar, übertrieben; *request* unzumutbar; *expectations* übertrieben; *person* uneinsichtig; *(= showing lack of sense)* unvernünftig; **to be ~ about sth** *(= not be understanding)* kein Verständnis für etw zeigen; *(= be overdemanding)* in Bezug auf etw *(acc)* zu viel verlangen; **it is ~ to …** es ist zu viel verlangt, zu …; **it is ~ to blame her** es ist nicht gerechtfertigt, ihr die Schuld zu geben; **it is ~ to expect children to keep quiet** man kann doch von Kindern nicht verlangen, ruhig zu sein; **that's not ~, is it?** das ist doch nicht zu viel verlangt, oder?; **you are being very ~!** das ist wirklich zu viel verlangt!; **look, don't be ~, it is 100 miles** nun mach mal einen Punkt *or* nun sei mal vernünftig, es sind immerhin 100 Meilen; **an ~ length of time** übermäßig *or* übertrieben lange; **at this ~ hour** zu dieser unzumutbaren Zeit

unreasonableness [ʌnˈriːznəblnɪs] N *(of demands etc)* Unzumutbarkeit *f*, Übermäßigkeit *f*; *(of person)* Uneinsichtigkeit *f*; **I hadn't reckoned with his ~** ich hatte nicht damit gerechnet, dass er so uneinsichtig sein würde; **I commented on his ~ in expecting 20%** ich bemerkte, dass 20% wohl zu viel verlangt wären

unreasonably [ʌnˈriːznəblɪ] ADV *long, slow, high, strict* übermäßig, übertrieben; **he remained ~ stubborn** er blieb unnötig stur; **he argued, quite ~ I think, that we should have known** er sagte, meiner Meinung nach ungerechtfertigterweise, dass wir das hätten wissen müssen; **you must prove that your employer acted ~** Sie müssen nachweisen, dass Ihr Arbeitgeber ungerechtfertigt gehandelt hat; **not ~** nicht ohne Grund

unreasoning [ʌnˈriːznɪŋ] ADJ *person* kopflos, unvernünftig; *action, fear, hatred* blind, unsinnig

unreceptive [ˌʌnrɪˈseptɪv] ADJ unempfänglich *(to* für*)*; *audience also* unaufgeschlossen

unrecognizable [ʌnˈrekəgnaɪzəbl] ADJ nicht wiederzuerkennen *pred*, nicht wiederzuerkennend *attr*; **he was ~ in his disguise** er war in seiner Verkleidung nicht zu erkennen; **they've made the old school ~** die alte Schule ist nicht wiederzuerkennen; **it was ~ as an aircraft** es war nicht als Flugzeug zu erkennen; **to be ~ to sb** für jdn nicht zu erkennen sein

unrecognized [ʌnˈrekəgnaɪzd] ADJ *(= not noticed) person, danger, value* unerkannt; *(= not acknowledged) government, record* nicht anerkannt; *genius, talent* ungewürdigt, unerkannt; **to go ~** *(person, talent, achievement)* nicht gewürdigt *or* anerkannt werden; **~ by the crowds** ohne von den Leuten erkannt zu werden

unreconciled [ʌnˈrekənsaɪld] ADJ unversöhnt *(to, with* mit*)*

unreconstructed [ˈʌnriːkənˈstrʌktɪd] ADJ *(pej) system, idea, policy* unverändert; **she's an ~ communist** sie ist eingefleischte Kommunistin

unrecorded [ˌʌnrɪˈkɔːdɪd] ADJ nicht aufgenommen; *(Rad, TV)* nicht aufgezeichnet; *(in documents)* nicht schriftlich erfasst *or* festgehalten; **to go ~** nicht aufgenommen/festgehalten werden

unredeemed [ˌʌnrɪˈdiːmd] ADJ **a** *sinner, world* unerlöst; **~ by** nicht ausgeglichen *or* wettgemacht durch **b** *bill, (from pawn) pledge* uneingelöst; *mortgage, debt* ungetilgt

unreel [ʌnˈriːl] VT abspulen, abwickeln VI sich abspulen, sich abwickeln, abrollen

unrefined [ˌʌnrɪˈfaɪnd] ADJ **a** *petroleum, sugar, metal* nicht raffiniert; *food* naturbelassen; *cereal* unbehandelt **b** *person* unkultiviert; *manners* unfein

unreflecting [ˌʌnrɪˈflektɪŋ] ADJ *person* gedankenlos, unbedacht; *act, haste* unbesonnen; *emotion* unreflektiert

unregarded [ˌʌnrɪˈgɑːdɪd] ADJ unbeachtet, nicht beachtet; **to go ~** unbeachtet bleiben; **to be ~** nicht beachtet werden

unregardful [ˌʌnrɪˈgɑːdfʊl] ADJ *(form)* ohne Rücksicht *(of* auf *+acc)*, rücksichtslos *(of* gegen*)*; **to be ~ of** keine Rücksicht nehmen auf *+acc*

unregenerate [ˌʌnrɪˈdʒenɪrɪt] ADJ *(= unrepentant)* reu(e)los, nicht reuig; *(= unreformed)* unbekehrbar; *(= stubborn) reactionary* hartnäckig; *(= wicked) life* sündig

unregistered [ʌnˈredʒɪstəd] ADJ *birth* nicht gemeldet; *car, firearm, worker* nicht angemeldet; *voter* nicht (im Wählerverzeichnis) eingetragen; *land* nicht (im Grundbuch) eingetragen; *trademark* nicht gesetzlich geschützt; *letter* nicht eingeschrieben; *lawyer, taxi, agent* nicht zugelassen; *doctor* nicht approbiert

unregretted [ˌʌnrɪˈgretɪd] ADJ *absence, death* nicht bedauert; *person* nicht vermisst; *words* nicht bereut

unregulated [ʌnˈregjʊleɪtɪd] ADJ unkontrolliert

unrehearsed [ˌʌnrɪˈhɜːst] ADJ *(Theat etc)* nicht geprobt; *cast* schlecht eingespielt; *(= spontaneous) incident* spontan

unrelated [ˌʌnrɪˈleɪtɪd] ADJ *(= unconnected)* ohne Beziehung *(to* zu*)*; *(by family)* nicht verwandt; **~ to reality** wirklichkeitsfremd; **the two events are ~/are not ~** die beiden Ereignisse stehen in keinem Zusammenhang miteinander/sind nicht gänzlich ohne Zusammenhang; **they are ~ (to each other)** *(people)* sie sind nicht (miteinander) verwandt

unrelenting [ˌʌnrɪˈlentɪŋ] ADJ *pressure* unablässig; *opposition* unerbittlich; *violence, criticism, pain* unvermindert, anhaltend; *determination* hartnäckig; *pace, severity* unvermindert; *attack, struggle* unerbittlich, unvermindert; *rain* anhaltend *attr*, nicht nachlassend *attr*; *(= not merciful) person, heat* unbarmherzig; **we must be ~ in our struggle** wir müssen unablässig weiterkämpfen; **they kept up an ~ attack** sie führten den Angriff mit unverminderter Stärke durch

unreliability [ˈʌnrɪˌlaɪəˈbɪlɪtɪ] N Unzuverlässigkeit *f*

unreliable [ˌʌnrɪˈlaɪəbl] ADJ unzuverlässig; **to prove (to be) ~** sich als unzuverlässig erweisen

unrelieved [ˌʌnrɪˈliːvd] ADJ *pain, stress, gloom, anguish* ungemindert; *mediocrity* unverändert, gleichbleibend; *grey* einheitlich, durch nichts aufgelockert; *monotony, boredom* tödlich; **a life of ~ misery** ein Leben, das ein einziges Elend ist; **to be ~ by** nicht aufgelockert sein durch *or* von

unremarkable [ˌʌnrɪˈmɑːkəbl] ADJ nicht sehr bemerkenswert, wenig bemerkenswert; **he would be ~ in a crowd** inmitten einer Menschenmenge würde ihn niemand bemerken *or* würde er nicht auffallen

unremarked [ˌʌnrɪˈmɑːkt] ADJ unbemerkt; **to go ~** unbemerkt bleiben

unremitting [ˌʌnrɪˈmɪtɪŋ] ADJ *efforts, toil* unaufhörlich, unablässig; *zeal* unermüdlich; *hatred* unversöhnlich

unremittingly [ˌʌnrɪˈmɪtɪŋlɪ] ADV unaufhörlich, ohne Unterlass; *strive* unermüdlich

unremunerative [ˌʌnrɪˈmjuːnərətɪv] ADJ nicht lohnend, nicht einträglich

unrepeatable [ˌʌnrɪˈpiːtəbl] ADJ **a** *words, views* nicht wiederholbar **b** *offer, chance, experience* einmalig

unrepentant [ˌʌnrɪˈpentənt] ADJ nicht reuig, nicht reumütig, reu(e)los; **he is ~ about it** er bereut es nicht

unreported [ˌʌnrɪˈpɔːtɪd] ADJ *events* nicht berichtet; *crime* nicht angezeigt; **to go ~** nicht berichtet werden; *(crime)* nicht angezeigt werden

unrepresentative [ˌʌnreprɪˈzentətɪv] ADJ *minority, sample etc* nicht repräsentativ; *(Pol) government* nicht frei gewählt; **~ of sth** nicht repräsentativ für etw; **the Party is ~ of the people** die Partei repräsentiert das Volk nicht

unrepresented [ˌʌnreprɪˈzentɪd] ADJ nicht vertreten; **to go ~** *(Jur)* nicht vertreten werden; *(Parl)* nicht vertreten sein

unrequited [ˌʌnrɪˈkwaɪtɪd] ADJ *love* unerwidert, unglücklich

unreserved [ˌʌnrɪˈzɜːvd] ADJ **a** *(= frank) person* nicht reserviert, offen; **he's quite ~ about his feelings** er zeigt seine Gefühle ganz offen **b** *(= complete) approval, apology, support* uneingeschränkt; *praise, admiration* uneingeschränkt, rückhaltlos **c** *(= not booked)* nicht reserviert

unreservedly [ˌʌnrɪˈzɜːvɪdlɪ] ADV *speak* freimütig, offen; *approve, trust, recommend* uneingeschränkt; *sob, condemn* rückhaltlos; **to apologize (to sb) ~ for sth** sich (bei jdm) uneingeschränkt für etw entschuldigen

unresisting [ˌʌnrɪˈzɪstɪŋ] ADJ widerstandslos, keinen Widerstand leistend *attr*; **I pushed open the ~ door** ich stieß die Tür auf, die ohne Weiteres nachgab

unresolved [ˌʌnrɪˈzɒlvd] ADJ **a** *difficulty, problem* ungelöst **b** *(= uncertain) person* unschlüssig; **he is still ~ as to what to do** er ist sich *(dat)* noch (darüber) unschlüssig, was er tun soll

unresponsive [ˌʌnrɪˈspɒnsɪv] ADJ *(physically)* nicht reagierend *attr*; *(emotionally, intellectually)* gleichgültig, unempfänglich; **to be ~** nicht reagieren *(to* auf *+acc)*; *(to advances, pleas, request also)* nicht empfänglich sein *(to* für*)*; **an ~ audience** ein Publikum, das nicht mitgeht *or* nicht reagiert; **I suggested it but he was fairly ~** ich habe es vorgeschlagen, aber er ist nicht groß darauf eingegangen *or* er zeigte sich nicht sehr interessiert; **still heavily sedated and totally ~** unter starkem Drogeneinfluss und völlig teilnahmslos

unrest [ʌnˈrest] N Unruhen *pl*; *(= discontent)* Unzufriedenheit *f*; **there was ~ among the workers** die Arbeiter waren unzufrieden

unrested [ʌnˈrestɪd] ADJ unausgeruht

unresting [ʌnˈrestɪŋ] ADJ *efforts* unermüdlich

unrestrained [ˌʌnrɪˈstreɪnd] ADJ **a** uneingeschränkt, unkontrolliert; *feelings* offen, ungehemmt; *joy, enthusiasm, atmosphere* ungezügelt; *language, behaviour* ausfallend, unbeherrscht; *laughter* hemmungslos, unkontrolliert; *violence* hemmungslos, ungezügelt; **to be ~ in one's views** in seinen Ansichten nicht zurückhaltend sein **b** *(physically)* ungehindert

unrestrainedly [ˌʌnrɪˈstreɪnɪdlɪ] ADV hemmungslos, rückhaltlos; **she wept ~** sie weinte hemmungslos

unrestricted [ˌʌnrɪˈstrɪktɪd] ADJ **a** *power, use, growth* unbeschränkt, uneingeschränkt; *right* uneingeschränkt; *travel, access* ungehindert **b** *(= unobstructed) view* ungehindert

unreturned [ˌʌnrɪˈtɜːnd] ADJ **a** nicht zurückgegeben **b** *love etc* unerwidert, unvergolten **c** *(Brit Parl)* nicht gewählt *(ins Parlament)*

unrevealed [ˌʌnrɪˈviːld] ADJ *facts, report* nicht veröffentlicht; *secret* ungelüftet

unrewarded [ˌʌnrɪˈwɔːdɪd] ADJ unbelohnt; **to go ~** unbelohnt bleiben; *(= not gain recognition)* keine Anerkennung finden; **his efforts were ~ by any success** seine Bemühungen waren nicht von Erfolg gekrönt

unrewarding [ˌʌnrɪˈwɔːdɪŋ] ADJ *work* undankbar; *(financially)* wenig einträglich; **further study**

of this book would be ~ es würde sich nicht lohnen, das Buch weiterzulesen

unrhymed [ʌnˈraɪmd] ADJ ungereimt

unrhythmical [ʌnˈrɪðmɪkəl] ADJ *tune, person* unrhythmisch

unrig [ʌnˈrɪg] VT *(Naut)* abtakeln

unrighteous [ʌnˈraɪtʃəs] **ADJ** *(Rel)* sündig **N the ~** *pl* die Sünder *pl*

unripe [ʌnˈraɪp] ADJ unreif

unrivalled, *(US)* **unrivaled** [ʌnˈraɪvəld] ADJ unerreicht, unübertroffen; **~ in** *or* **for quality** von unübertroffener Qualität; **to be ~ in sth** in etw *(dat)* unerreicht *or* unübertroffen sein

unroadworthiness [ʌnˈrəʊd,wɜːðɪnɪs] N mangelnde Verkehrssicherheit

unroadworthy [ʌnˈrəʊd,wɜːðɪ] ADJ nicht verkehrssicher

unrobe [ʌnˈrəʊb] **VI** *(form)* sich entkleiden *(geh)*; *(hum)* sich enthüllen *(hum)* **VT** *(form)* entkleiden *(geh)*; *(hum)* enthüllen *(hum)*

unroll [ʌnˈrəʊl] **VT** *carpet, map* aufrollen, auseinanderrollen; *(fig) story also* darlegen, schildern **VI** *(carpet etc)* sich aufrollen; *(fig, plot)* sich abwickeln; *(landscape)* sich ausbreiten

unromantic [,ʌnrəˈmæntɪk] ADJ unromantisch

unroot [ʌnˈruːt] VT *(esp US)* = **uproot**

unrope [ʌnˈrəʊp] **VT** *box* losbinden **VI** *(Mountaineering)* sich vom Seil losmachen

unrounded [ʌnˈraʊndɪd] ADJ *(Phon)* ungerundet

unruffled [ʌnˈrʌfld] ADJ *person* gelassen; *sea* ruhig, unbewegt; *hair* ordentlich, unzerzaust; *bedclothes, sheets* glatt gestrichen; *calm* unerschütterlich; **she was** *or* **remained quite ~** sie blieb ruhig und gelassen, sie bewahrte die Ruhe; **to be ~ by criticism** sich durch Kritik nicht aus der Ruhe bringen lassen

unruled [ʌnˈruːld] ADJ *paper* unliniert

unruliness [ʌnˈruːlɪnɪs] N Wildheit *f*, Ungebärdigkeit *f*

unruly [ʌnˈruːlɪ] ADJ *(+er) child, behaviour* wild, ungebärdig; *employee* schwer kontrollierbar, aufmüpfig *(hum inf)*; *elements, crowd, mob* wild, tobend; *hair* widerspenstig, nicht zu bändigend *attr*; **~ passenger** *(Aviat)* randalierender Passagier

unsaddle [ʌnˈsædl] VT *horse* absatteln; *rider* abwerfen

unsaddling enclosure [ʌnˈsædlɪŋɪnˈkləʊʒəˈ] N *(Horse-racing)* Absattelring *m*

unsafe [ʌnˈseɪf] ADJ **a** *ladder, machine, car, person* nicht sicher; *(= dangerous) journey, toy, wiring* gefährlich; *drug* gesundheitsschädigend; *street* gefährlich, unsicher; *activity* gefährlich, riskant; **this is ~ to eat/drink** das ist nicht genießbar/trinkbar; **the car is ~ to drive** das Auto ist nicht verkehrssicher; **it is ~ to walk there at night** es ist gefährlich, dort nachts spazieren zu gehen; **to be ~ for human consumption** nicht zum Verzehr geeignet sein; **to declare a house ~ for habitation** ein Haus für unbewohnbar erklären; **to feel ~** sich nicht sicher fühlen; **he looked ~ swaying about at the top of the ladder** es sah gefährlich aus, wie er oben auf der Leiter hin und her schaukelte **b** *(Jur. = unreliable) conviction, verdict* ungesichert; *evidence* ungesichert, unzuverlässig; **~ and unsatisfactory** ungesichert und unbefriedigend

unsafe sex N ungeschützter Sex

unsaid [ʌnˈsed] *pret, ptp of* **unsay** ADJ ungesagt, unausgesprochen; **to leave sth ~** etw unausgesprochen lassen; **it's best left ~** das bleibt besser ungesagt

unsalaried [ʌnˈsælərɪd] ADJ ehrenamtlich

unsaleable, *(US)* **unsalable** [ʌnˈseɪləbl] ADJ unverkäuflich; **to be ~** sich nicht verkaufen lassen; **bread becomes ~ after 2 days** Brot kann man nach 2 Tagen nicht mehr verkaufen

unsalted [ʌnˈsɔːltɪd] ADJ ungesalzen

unsanitary [ʌnˈsænɪtrɪ] ADJ unhygienisch

unsatisfactoriness [,ʌnsætɪsˈfæktərɪnɪs] N *(of service, hotel, work)* Unzulänglichkeit *f*; **the ~ of such a solution** eine so unbefriedigende Lösung; **because of his ~ he was not kept on** da er nicht den Erwartungen entsprach, behielt man ihn nicht

unsatisfactory [,ʌnsætɪsˈfæktərɪ] ADJ unbefriedigend; *result also* nicht zufriedenstellend; *profits, figures* nicht ausreichend; *service, hotel* unzulänglich, schlecht; *(Sch)* mangelhaft, ungenügend; **he was ~** er entsprach nicht den Erwartungen; **this is highly ~** das lässt sehr zu wünschen übrig

unsatisfied [ʌnˈsætɪsfaɪd] ADJ *person* nicht zufrieden, unzufrieden; *(= not fulfilled)* unbefriedigt, nicht zufrieden; *(= not convinced)* nicht überzeugt; *appetite, desire, need* unbefriedigt; *curiosity* unbefriedigt, ungestillt; **the meal left me ~** das Essen hat mich nicht gesättigt; **the book's ending left us ~** wir fanden den Schluss des Buches unbefriedigend; **a job that leaves him ~** eine Arbeit, die ihn nicht befriedigt; **to be ~ with sb/sth** mit jdm/etw unzufrieden sein

unsatisfying [ʌnˈsætɪsfaɪɪŋ] ADJ unbefriedigend; *meal* unzureichend, nicht sättigend

unsaturated [ʌnˈsætʃəreɪtɪd] ADJ *(Chem)* ungesättigt

unsavoury, *(US)* **unsavory** [ʌnˈseɪvərɪ] ADJ **a** *(= tasteless) food* fade, geschmacklos **b** *(= unpleasant) smell, sight* widerwärtig, widerlich; *appearance (= repulsive)* abstoßend, widerwärtig; *(= dishonest, shady etc)* fragwürdig; *subject, details, rumours* unerfreulich; *joke* unfein; *district* übel, fragwürdig; *characters* zwielichtig, übel; *reputation* zweifelhaft, schlecht; **an ~ business** eine unfeine Geschichte

unsay [ʌnˈseɪ] *pret, ptp* **unsaid** VT ungesagt machen

unscalable [ʌnˈskeɪləbl] ADJ unbezwingbar

unscaled [ʌnˈskeɪld] ADJ *heights, peak* unbezwungen

unscarred [ʌnˈskɑːd] ADJ *(fig)* nicht gezeichnet

unscathed [ʌnˈskeɪðd] ADJ *(lit)* unverletzt, unversehrt; *(by war etc)* unverwundet; *(fig)* unbeschadet; *relationship* heil; **to leave sb/sth ~** jdn/etw ungeschoren lassen; **to survive ~** unbeschadet *or* unversehrt überleben; **to emerge** *or* **escape ~** *(lit)* ohne einen Kratzer davonkommen; *(fig)* mit heiler Haut davonkommen, ungeschoren davonkommen

unscented [ʌnˈsentɪd] ADJ ohne Duftstoffe, geruchlos

unscheduled [ʌnˈʃedjuːld] ADJ *stop, flight etc* außerfahrplanmäßig; *meeting, visit* außerplanmäßig

unscholarly [ʌnˈskɒləlɪ] ADJ *work, approach* unwissenschaftlich; *person* unakademisch; *(= not learned)* ungelehrt

unschooled [ʌnˈskuːld] ADJ ungebildet, ohne Schulbildung; *talent* unausgebildet; **to be ~ in sth** nichts wissen über etw *(acc)*

unscientific [,ʌnsaɪənˈtɪfɪk] ADJ unwissenschaftlich

unscramble [ʌnˈskræmbl] VT entwirren, auseinanderklauben *(inf)*; *(Telec) message, signal* entschlüsseln

unscratched [ʌnˈskrætʃt] ADJ nicht zerkratzt; *record* ohne Kratzer; *(= unhurt)* heil, ungeschoren

unscreened [ʌnˈskriːnd] ADJ **a** *film* nicht gezeigt, unaufgeführt; **many films remain ~** viele Filme werden nie gezeigt *or* bleiben unaufgeführt **b** *(= not protected) door, window* offen, nicht abgeschirmt **c** *(= not inspected, by security)* nicht überprüft; *(for disease)* nicht untersucht

unscrew [ʌnˈskruː] **VT** *(= loosen)* losschrauben; *plate, lid also* abschrauben; **to come ~ed** sich lösen **VI** sich los- *or* abschrauben lassen; *(= become loose)* sich lösen

unscripted [ʌnˈskrɪptɪd] ADJ improvisiert

unscrupulous [ʌnˈskruːpjʊləs] ADJ *person, behaviour* skrupellos, gewissenlos; **he is ~ where money is concerned** er ist skrupellos *or* gewissenlos, wenn es um Geld geht

unscrupulously [ʌnˈskruːpjʊləslɪ] ADV *behave, exploit* skrupellos

unscrupulousness [ʌnˈskruːpjʊləsnɪs] N Skrupellosigkeit *f*, Gewissenlosigkeit *f*

unseal [ʌnˈsiːl] VT öffnen; *(= remove wax seal also)* entsiegeln

unsealed [ʌnˈsiːld] ADJ offen, unverschlossen; *(= without wax seal also)* unversiegelt

unseasonable [ʌnˈsiːznəbl] ADJ nicht der Jahreszeit entsprechend *attr*; **the weather is ~** das Wetter entspricht nicht der Jahreszeit

unseasonably [ʌnˈsiːznəblɪ] ADV (für die Jahreszeit) ungewöhnlich *or* außergewöhnlich; **we had an ~ warm/cold/mild winter** wir hatten einen (für die Jahreszeit) ungewöhnlich warmen/kalten/milden Winter

unseasoned [ʌnˈsiːznd] ADJ *timber* nicht abgelagert; *food* ungewürzt; *(fig, = inexperienced) troops* unerfahren, unerprobt

unseat [ʌnˈsiːt] VT *rider* abwerfen; *person (from office)* seines Amtes entheben

unseaworthiness [ʌnˈsiː,wɜːðɪnɪs] N Seeuntüchtigkeit *f*

unseaworthy [ʌnˈsiː,wɜːðɪ] ADJ seeuntüchtig, nicht seetüchtig

unsecured [,ʌnsɪˈkjʊəd] ADJ *(Fin) loan, bond* ohne Sicherheit(en)

unseeded [ʌnˈsiːdɪd] ADJ unplatziert

unseeing [ʌnˈsiːɪŋ] ADJ *(lit, fig)* blind; *gaze* leer; **to stare at sb/sth with ~ eyes** jdn/etw mit leerem Blick anstarren

unseemliness [ʌnˈsiːmlɪnɪs] N Unschicklichkeit *f*, Ungebührlichkeit *f*

unseemly [ʌnˈsiːmlɪ] ADJ unschicklich, ungebührlich

unseen [ʌnˈsiːn] **ADJ** ungesehen; *(= invisible)* unsichtbar; *(= unobserved) escape* unbemerkt; **~ by the public** der Öffentlichkeit nicht vorgestellt; **~ translation/examination paper** *(esp Brit Sch, Univ)* unvorbereitete Übersetzung/Prüfung **N** *(esp Brit)* unvorbereitete Herübersetzung

unselfconscious ADJ, **unselfconsciously** ADV [,ʌnselfˈkɒnʃəs, -lɪ] unbefangen

unselfconsciousness [,ʌnselfˈkɒnʃəsnɪs] N Unbefangenheit *f*

unselfish [ʌnˈselfɪʃ] ADJ uneigennützig, selbstlos; *(esp Ftbl) player* mit selbstlosem Einsatz spielend

unselfishly [ʌnˈselfɪʃlɪ] ADV uneigennützig, selbstlos; *(esp Ftbl)* mit selbstlosem Einsatz

unselfishness [ʌnˈselfɪʃnɪs] N Uneigennützigkeit *f*, Selbstlosigkeit *f*

unsensational [,ʌnsenˈseɪʃənl] ADJ wenig aufregend *or* sensationell

unsentimental [,ʌnsentɪˈmentl] ADJ unsentimental; **to be ~ about sth** von etw ungerührt sein

unserviceable [ʌnˈsɜːvɪsəbl] ADJ unbrauchbar

unsettle [ʌnˈsetl] VT **a** *(= throw off balance, confuse)* aus dem Gleichgewicht bringen; *(= agitate, upset)* aufregen; *(= disturb emotionally)* verstören; *person (news)* beunruhigen; *(defeat, failure, criticism)* verunsichern; *market* aus dem Gleichgewicht bringen, verunsichern; *faith* erschüttern **b** *foundations* erschüttern

unsettled [ʌnˈsetld] ADJ **a** *(= unpaid)* unbezahlt, unbeglichen; *(= undecided) question* ungeklärt, offen; *future* unbestimmt, ungewiss, in der Schwebe; **to be in an ~ state of mind** mit sich selbst nicht eins sein; **he was ~ in his mind about what to do** er war sich *(dat)* nicht schlüssig, was er tun sollte; **the question remains ~** die Frage bleibt ungelöst **b** *(= changeable) weather* unbeständig, veränderlich; *life, character* unstet, unruhig; *(Fin) market* unbeständig, veränderlich; *(Pol) conditions* unsicher; **to be ~** durcheinander sein; *(= thrown off balance)* aus dem Gleis geworfen sein; *(= emotionally disturbed)* verstört sein; **to feel ~** sich nicht wohlfühlen

c *(= unpopulated) territory* unbesiedelt **d** *(= itinerant) person* nomadenhaft

unsettling [ʌnˈsetlɪŋ] ADJ *change, pace of life* aufreibend; *time also* aufregend; *defeat, knowledge* verunsichernd; *question, thought, news, book, film, atmosphere* beunruhigend; *music* irritierend; **to have an ~ effect on sb** jdn aus dem Gleis werfen; *(defeat, failure also)* jdn verunsichern; *on children also* jdn verstören; **it is ~ to know he could be watching me** es beunruhigt mich zu wissen, dass er mich beobachten könnte

unsexy [ʌnˈseksɪ] ADJ *(inf)* nicht sexy *(inf)*

unshackle [ʌnˈʃækl] VT *prisoner* befreien; *(fig also)* von seinen Fesseln befreien

unshaded [ʌnˈʃeɪdɪd] ADJ *(from sun)* schattenlos; *eyes etc* ungeschützt; *part of drawing* nicht schattiert; **~ bulb** nackte Glühbirne

unshak(e)able ADJ, **unshak(e)ably** ADV [ʌnˈʃeɪkəbl, -ɪ] unerschütterlich; **Anna is unshakeably honest** Anna ist grundehrlich

unshaken [ʌnˈʃeɪkən] ADJ unerschüttert; **he was ~ by the accident** der Unfall erschütterte ihn nicht; **his nerve was ~** er behielt seine Kaltblütigkeit; **to be ~ in one's belief that …** unerschüttert in seinem Glauben sein, dass …

unshaven [ʌnˈʃeɪvn] ADJ unrasiert; *(= bearded)* bärtig

unsheathe [ʌnˈʃiːð] VT *sword* (aus der Scheide) ziehen

unshed [ʌnˈʃed] ADJ *tears* ungeweint, unvergossen

unship [ʌnˈʃɪp] VT *cargo* löschen, ausladen, entladen; *tiller, oars* abnehmen; *mast* abbauen

unshockable [ʌnˈʃɒkəbl] ADJ durch nichts zu schockieren

unshod [ʌnˈʃɒd] ADJ *horse* unbeschlagen; *person* barfuß, ohne Schuhe; **with ~ feet** barfuß, mit nackten Füßen

unshrinkable [ʌnˈʃrɪŋkəbl] ADJ *fabric* nicht einlaufend

unshrinking [ʌnˈʃrɪŋkɪŋ] ADJ unverzagt, furchtlos, fest

unsighted [ʌnˈsaɪtɪd] ADJ **to be ~** in der *or* seiner Sicht behindert sein

unsightliness [ʌnˈsaɪtlɪnɪs] N Unansehnlichkeit *f*; *(stronger)* Hässlichkeit *f*

unsightly [ʌnˈsaɪtlɪ] ADJ unansehnlich; *(stronger)* hässlich

unsigned [ʌnˈsaɪnd] ADJ **a** *painting* unsigniert; *letter* nicht unterzeichnet, nicht unterschrieben; *newspaper article* anonym **b** *pop band* nicht unter Vertrag stehend *attr*; **they are still ~** sie stehen noch nicht unter Vertrag

unsinkable [ʌnˈsɪŋkəbl] ADJ unsinkbar; *battleship* unversenkbar

unsisterly [ʌnˈsɪstəlɪ] ADJ nicht schwesterlich

unskilful, *(US)* **unskillful** [ʌnˈskɪlfʊl] ADJ *(= inexpert)* ungeschickt; *(= clumsy)* unbeholfen

unskilfully, *(US)* **unskillfully** [ʌnˈskɪlfəlɪ] ADV *(= inexpertly)* ungeschickt; *(= clumsily)* unbeholfen

unskilfulness, *(US)* **unskillfulness** [ʌnˈskɪlfʊlnɪs] N *(= lack of expertise)* Ungeschicklichkeit *f*, Mangel *m* an Geschick; *(= clumsiness)* Unbeholfenheit *f*

unskilled [ʌnˈskɪld] ADJ **a** *work, worker* ungelernt; **many people remained ~** viele Menschen erlernten keinen Beruf; **to be ~ in sth** ungeübt in etw *(dat)* sein; **to be ~ in doing sth** ungeübt darin sein, etw zu tun; **~ labour** *(Brit) or* **labor** *(US) (= workers)* Hilfsarbeiter *pl* **b** *(= inexperienced)* ungeübt, unerfahren N **the ~** *pl* die ungelernten Arbeiter *pl*, die Hilfsarbeiter *pl*

unskillful *etc (US)* = **unskilful** *etc*

unslept-in [ʌnˈsleptɪn] ADJ unberührt

unsmilingly [ʌnˈsmaɪlɪŋlɪ] ADV ohne zu lächeln; **she stared at him ~** sie starrte ihn ohne zu lächeln an

unsnubbable [ʌnˈsnʌbəbl] ADJ *(inf)* dickfellig *(inf)*

unsociability [ʌnˌsəʊʃəˈbɪlɪtɪ] N Ungeselligkeit *f*

unsociable [ʌnˈsəʊʃəbl] ADJ ungesellig

unsocial [ʌnˈsəʊʃəl] ADJ **to work ~ hours** außerhalb der normalen Arbeitszeiten arbeiten; **at this ~ hour** zu so nachtschlafender Zeit

unsold [ʌnˈsəʊld] ADJ unverkauft; **to go** *or* **be left** *or* **remain ~** nicht verkauft werden

unsoldierly [ʌnˈsəʊldʒəlɪ] ADJ unsoldatisch

unsolicited [ˌʌnsəˈlɪsɪtɪd] ADJ unerbeten; *manuscript* nicht angefordert, unangefordert

unsolvable [ʌnˈsɒlvəbl] ADJ **a** *(Chem)* unauflöslich **b** *(fig) problem etc* unlösbar

unsolved [ʌnˈsɒlvd] ADJ *crossword, problem etc* ungelöst; *mystery also, crime* unaufgeklärt

unsophisticated [ˌʌnsəˈfɪstɪkeɪtɪd] ADJ **a** *(= simple) person* einfach; *style also* natürlich, simpel *(pej)*; *tastes* schlicht; *film, machine also* unkompliziert; *technique also* simpel; *(= naïve)* naiv, simpel; *(= undiscriminating)* unkritisch **b** *(= crude) method* grob(schlächtig) N **the ~** *pl* das einfache Volk

unsought [ʌnˈsɔːt] ADJ unaufgefordert; *(= unwanted)* unerwünscht; **his help was ~** seine Hilfe kam unaufgefordert

unsound [ʌnˈsaʊnd] ADJ **a** *heart, teeth* krank; *health, gums* angegriffen; *floorboards, timber* morsch; *construction, design* unsolide; *foundations, finances* unsicher, schwach; **the ship was quite ~** das Schiff war überhaupt nicht seetüchtig; **structurally ~** *(building)* bautechnische Mängel aufweisend *attr*
b *argument* nicht stichhaltig, anfechtbar; *advice* unvernünftig; *judgement* unzuverlässig; *doctrine* unvertretbar; *policy, move* unklug; *(Jur) conviction* ungesichert; **of ~ mind** *(Jur)* unzurechnungsfähig; **politically ~** *(person)* politisch unzuverlässig; *policy* politisch unklug; **ideologically/ecologically ~** ideologisch/ökologisch nicht vertretbar; **environmentally ~** umweltschädlich; **~ banking procedures** heikle Bankgeschäfte *pl*; **the company is ~** die Firma steht auf schwachen Füßen; **our financial position is ~** unsere Finanzlage ist heikel; **I'm ~ on French grammar** ich bin unsicher in französischer Grammatik; **the book is ~ on some points** das Buch weist an einigen Stellen Schwächen auf; **his views on this are ~** seine Ansichten sind nicht vertretbar

unsoundness [ʌnˈsaʊndnɪs] N **a** *(of heart etc)* Krankheit *f*; *(of health)* Angegriffenheit *f*; *(of timber)* Morschheit *f*; *(of construction, design)* unsolide Bauweise; *(of foundations, finances)* Unsicherheit *f*, Schwäche *f* **b** *(of argument)* geringe Stichhaltigkeit, Anfechtbarkeit *f*; *(of advice)* Unvernünftigkeit *f*; *(of judgement)* Unzuverlässigkeit *f*; *(of doctrine)* Unvertretbarkeit *f*; *(of policy, move)* mangelnde Klugheit; *(Jur. of conviction)* Ungesichertheit *f*; **~ of mind** *(Jur)* Unzurechnungsfähigkeit *f*; **political ~** *(of person)* politische Unzuverlässigkeit; *(of policy)* politische Unklugheit

unsparing [ʌnˈspeərɪŋ] ADJ **a** *(= lavish)* großzügig, verschwenderisch, nicht kleinlich; **to be ~ with sth** mit etw nicht geizen; **to be ~ in one's efforts** keine Kosten und Mühen scheuen **b** *(= unmerciful) criticism* schonungslos; **the report was ~ in its criticism** der Bericht übte schonungslos Kritik

unsparingly [ʌnˈspeərɪŋlɪ] ADV **a** *(= generously)* großzügig, verschwenderisch; **to work ~ for sth** unermüdlich für etw arbeiten; **he gave ~ of his time** er opferte unendlich viel Zeit **b** *(= mercilessly) criticize* schonungslos

unspeakable [ʌnˈspiːkəbl] ADJ unbeschreiblich; **their ~ trade** ihr abscheuliches Geschäft; **to do/say ~ things to sb** jdm unaussprechliche Dinge antun/sagen

unspeakably [ʌnˈspiːkəblɪ] ADV unbeschreiblich, unsagbar

unspecified [ʌnˈspesɪfaɪd] ADJ *time, amount* nicht spezifiziert *or* genannt, nicht genau angegeben; *location* unbestimmt; **to be imprisoned on ~ charges** ohne nähere Angabe von Gründen inhaftiert werden/sein; **to seek/claim ~ damages** *(Jur)* Schadenersatz in unbestimmter Höhe verlangen/einklagen; **for ~ reasons** aus nicht näher ausgeführten Gründen

unspectacular [ˌʌnspekˈtækjʊləʳ] ADJ wenig eindrucksvoll; *career* wenig aufsehenerregend

unspent [ʌnˈspent] ADJ *money* nicht ausgegeben; *energy* nicht verbraucht

unspoiled [ʌnˈspɔɪld], **unspoilt** [ʌnˈspɔɪlt] ADJ **a** *person, fruit* unverdorben; *goods* unbeschädigt; *child* nicht verwöhnt **b** *(= unchanged: by tourism, civilization)* unberührt; **to remain unspoilt** unberührt bleiben

unspoken [ʌnˈspəʊkən] ADJ *words, thoughts* unausgesprochen; *agreement, consent* stillschweigend

unsporting [ʌnˈspɔːtɪŋ], **unsportsmanlike** [ʌnˈspɔːtsmənlaɪk] ADJ *conduct, person* unsportlich, unfair

unsprung [ʌnˈsprʌŋ] ADJ *seat* ungefedert; *trap* offen, nicht zugeschnappt

unstable [ʌnˈsteɪbl] ADJ **a** *structure* nicht *or* wenig stabil; *foundations also, area* unsicher; *vehicle, government, country* instabil; *weather* unbeständig; *economy* unsicher, schwankend; *prices* schwankend; *(Chem, Phys)* instabil; **the patient is in an ~ condition** der Zustand des Patienten ist labil *or* nicht stabil **b** *(Psych, mentally)* labil; **mentally/emotionally ~** geistig/emotional labil

unstamped [ʌnˈstæmpt] ADJ *letter* unfrankiert; *document, passport* ungestempelt

unstated [ʌnˈsteɪtɪd] ADJ *(= unsaid) assumption, aim* unausgesprochen; *reason* nicht angegeben; **to leave something ~** etw ungesagt lassen; **for reasons ~** aus nicht weiter angegebenen *or* ausgeführten Gründen

unstatesmanlike [ʌnˈsteɪtsmənlaɪk] ADJ unstaatsmännisch

unsteadily [ʌnˈstedɪlɪ] ADV *rise, walk* schwankend, unsicher; *say* mit schwankender *or* unsicherer Stimme

unsteadiness [ʌnˈstedɪnɪs] N *(of hand, legs, steps)* Unsicherheit *f*; *(of ladder)* Wack(e)ligkeit *f*; *(of flame)* Flackern *nt*; *(of voice, economy)* Schwanken *nt*; *(of progress)* Ungleichmäßigkeit *f*; *(of growth)* Unregelmäßigkeit *f*

unsteady [ʌnˈstedɪ] ADJ *hand* unsicher; *legs, steps* schwankend, unsicher; *ladder* wack(e)lig; *flame* unruhig, flackernd; *voice, economy* schwankend; *(= irregular) progress* schwankend, ungleichmäßig; *growth* unregelmäßig; **to be ~ on one's feet** unsicher *or* wackelig auf den Beinen sein; **the pound is still ~** das Pfund schwankt noch VT durcheinanderbringen; *(stronger)* aus dem Gleichgewicht bringen

unstick [ʌnˈstɪk] *pret, ptp* **unstuck** VT lösen, losmachen → *also* **unstuck**

unstinted [ʌnˈstɪntɪd] ADJ *praise* uneingeschränkt, vorbehaltlos; *generosity, devotion, efforts* unbegrenzt

unstinting [ʌnˈstɪntɪŋ] ADJ *person* großzügig; *kindness, generosity* uneingeschränkt, unbegrenzt; *support* uneingeschränkt, vorbehaltlos; *work* unermüdlich; **to be ~ in one's efforts** keine Kosten und Mühen scheuen; **to be ~ in one's praise of sth** etw uneingeschränkt *or* vorbehaltlos loben; **to be ~ of one's time** unendlich viel Zeit opfern

unstintingly [ʌnˈstɪntɪŋlɪ] ADV großzügig; *generous* unendlich; *work* unermüdlich; *donate, contribute* verschwenderisch

unstitch [ʌnˈstɪtʃ] VT *seam* auftrennen; *zip* heraustrennen; **to come ~ed** aufgehen; *(fig)* nicht klappen, danebengehen

unstop [ʌnˈstɒp] VT *drain* frei machen; *bottle* öffnen, aufmachen

unstoppable [ʌnˈstɒpəbl] ADJ nicht aufzuhalten; **the Labour candidate seems ~** der Labour-Kandidat scheint unaufhaltbar zu sein

unstrap [ʌnˈstræp] VT *case etc* aufschnallen; **to ~ sb/sth from sth** jdn/etw von etw los- *or* abschnallen

unstreamed [ʌnˈstriːmd] ADJ *(Brit Sch)* nicht in Leistungsgruppen eingeteilt

unstressed [ʌn'strest] **ADJ** *(Phon)* unbetont

unstring [ʌn'strɪŋ] *pret, ptp* **unstrung VT** *violin* die Saiten abnehmen *or* entfernen von; *beads* abfädeln

unstructured [ʌn'strʌktʃəd] **ADJ** unstrukturiert, nicht strukturiert

unstrung [ʌn'strʌŋ] *pret, ptp of* **unstring ADJ a** *person* demoralisiert, entnervt; *nerves* zerrüttet **b** *violin* unbesaitet

unstuck [ʌn'stʌk] **ADJ to come ~** *(stamp, notice)* sich lösen; *(inf, plan)* danebengehen *(inf)*, schiefgehen *(inf)*; *(speaker, actor)* stecken bleiben; *(pupil: in exam)* ins Schwimmen geraten; **the pay policy seems to have come ~** die Lohnpolitik scheint aus dem Gleis gekommen zu sein; **where they came ~ was …** sie sind daran gescheitert, dass …

unstudied [ʌn'stʌdɪd] **ADJ** *grace etc* ungekünstelt, natürlich

unstylish ADJ, unstylishly ADV [ʌn'staɪlɪʃ, -lɪ] unmodisch, unelegant

unsubdued [ˌʌnsəb'djuːd] **ADJ** unbezwungen, unbesiegt

unsubsidized [ʌn'sʌbsɪdaɪzd] **ADJ** unsubventioniert

unsubstantial [ˌʌnsəb'stænʃəl] **ADJ** *(= flimsy) structure* leicht, dürftig; *meal* leicht; *evidence, proof* nicht überzeugend, nicht schlagkräftig; *claim* ungerechtfertigt

unsubstantiated [ˌʌnsəb'stænʃɪeɪtɪd] **ADJ** *accusation, testimony, rumour* unbegründet; *gossip* unbestätigt; **these reports remain ~** diese Berichte sind weiterhin unbestätigt; **his claim was ~ by any evidence** seine Behauptung wurde durch keinerlei Indizien erhärtet

unsubtle [ʌn'sʌtl] **ADJ** plump; **how ~ can you get!** plumper gehts nicht!

unsuccessful [ˌʌnsək'sesfʊl] **ADJ** *negotiations, venture, visit, meeting, person etc* erfolglos, ergebnislos; *writer, painter* erfolglos, ohne Erfolg; *candidate* abgewiesen; *attempt* vergeblich; *marriage, outcome* unglücklich; **to prove ~** sich als erfolglos erweisen; **I tried to persuade him but was ~** ich habe versucht, ihn zu überreden, hatte aber keinen Erfolg; **to be ~ in doing sth** keinen Erfolg damit haben, etw zu tun; **to be ~ in one's efforts to do sth** erfolglos in seinem Bemühen sein, etw zu tun; **he is ~ in everything he does** nichts gelingt ihm; **he was ~ in his exam** er hat kein Glück in seinem Examen gehabt; **he is ~ with women** er hat kein Glück *or* keinen Erfolg bei Frauen; **unfortunately, your application has been ~** wir haben uns leider nicht zur Annahme Ihrer Bewerbung entschließen können

unsuccessfully [ˌʌnsək'sesfəlɪ] **ADV** erfolglos; *try* vergeblich; *apply* ohne Erfolg, vergebens; **I tried ~ to grow tomatoes** ich habe ohne Erfolg versucht, Tomaten zu ziehen

unsuitability [ˌʌnsuːtə'bɪlɪtɪ] **N** *(of moment, clothes, colour, candidate, land)* Ungeeignetsein *nt*; *(of language, attitude)* Unangebrachtheit *f*; **his ~ for the job** seine mangelnde Eignung für die Stelle; **I commented on the ~ of his clothes** ich machte eine Bemerkung über seine unpassende Kleidung; **their ~ as partners is clear** es ist klar, dass sie keine geeigneten Partner füreinander sind

unsuitable [ʌn'suːtəbl] **ADJ** unpassend; *language, attitude also* unangebracht; *moment, clothes, colour also, candidate, land, ground* ungeeignet; **it would be ~ at this moment to …** es wäre im Augenblick unangebracht, …; **this film is ~ for children** dieser Film ist für Kinder ungeeignet *or* nicht geeignet; **he's ~ for the position** er ist für die Stelle nicht geeignet; **she is ~ for him** sie ist nicht die Richtige für ihn; **we're ~ for each other** wir passen nicht zusammen; **she married a very ~ person** sie hat jemanden geheiratet, der gar nicht zu ihr passt

unsuitably [ʌn'suːtəblɪ] **ADV** *dressed (for weather conditions)* unzweckmäßig; *(for occasion)* unpassend; *designed* ungeeignet, schlecht; **they are ~ matched** sie passen nicht zusammen

unsuited [ʌn'suːtɪd] **ADJ to be ~ for** *or* **to sth** für etw ungeeignet *or* untauglich sein; **to be ~ to doing sth** sich nicht dazu eignen *or* nicht dazu taugen, etw zu tun; **to be ~ to sb** nicht zu jdm passen; **they are ~ (to each other)** sie passen nicht zusammen

unsullied [ʌn'sʌlɪd] **ADJ** *virtue, honour etc* makellos, unbefleckt *(liter)*; *snow* unberührt; **to be ~ by sth** *(by scandal, past)* von etw unberührt sein

unsung [ʌn'sʌŋ] **ADJ** *heroes, deeds* unbesungen

unsupportable ADJ, unsupportably ADV [ˌʌnsə'pɔːtəbl, -ɪ] unerträglich

unsupported [ˌʌnsə'pɔːtɪd] **ADJ** *roof, person* ungestützt, ohne Stütze; *troops* ohne Unterstützung; *mother* alleinstehend; *family* ohne Unterhalt; *claim, theory* ohne Beweise, nicht auf Fakten gestützt; *statement* unbestätigt, durch nichts gestützt; **if such families were ~ by the State** wenn solche Familien nicht vom Staat unterstützt würden; **should the bank leave us financially ~** sollte die Bank uns finanziell nicht absichern; **the candidate/motion was ~** der Kandidat/Antrag fand keine Unterstützung; **~ by evidence** nicht durch Beweise gestützt

unsuppressed [ˌʌnsə'prest] **ADJ** nicht unterdrückt

unsure [ʌn'ʃʊəʳ] **ADJ** *person* unsicher; *(= unreliable) method also* unzuverlässig; **to be ~ of oneself** unsicher sein; **to be ~ (of sth)** sich *(dat)* (einer Sache *gen*) nicht sicher sein; **I'm ~ of him** ich bin mir bei ihm nicht sicher; **I am ~ of my welcome** ich bin nicht sicher, ob ich willkommen bin

unsureness [ʌn'ʃʊənɪs] **N** Unsicherheit *f*

unsurmountable [ˌʌnsə'maʊntəbl] **ADJ** unübersteigbar; *(fig)* unüberwindlich

unsurpassable [ˌʌnsə'pɑːsəbl] **ADJ** unübertrefflich

unsurpassed [ˌʌnsə'pɑːst] **ADJ** unübertroffen; **to be ~ by anybody** von niemandem übertroffen werden

unsurprising [ˌʌnsə'praɪzɪŋ] **ADJ** wenig überraschend

unsurprisingly [ˌʌnsə'praɪzɪŋlɪ] **ADV** wenig *or* kaum überraschend

unsuspected [ˌʌnsə'spektɪd] **ADJ** *presence* nicht vermutet, unvermutet; *oilfields, coal deposits, causes* unvermutet; *wealth, skill, powers* ungeahnt; *consequences* unerwartet, ungeahnt; *problem* unerwartet; **to be ~** *(person)* nicht unter Verdacht stehen

unsuspecting ADJ, unsuspectingly ADV [ˌʌnsə'spektɪŋ, -lɪ] ahnungslos, nichts ahnend

unsuspicious [ˌʌnsə'spɪʃəs] **ADJ** *(= feeling no suspicion)* arglos; *(= causing no suspicion)* unverdächtig, harmlos

unsweetened [ʌn'swiːtnd] **ADJ** ungesüßt

unswerving [ʌn'swɜːvɪŋ] **ADJ** *resolve, loyalty* unerschütterlich, unbeirrbar; **the road followed its ~ course across the desert** die Straße führte schnurgerade durch die Wüste; **to be ~ in one's belief (in sth)** in seinem Glauben (an etw *acc*) unbeirrbar sein

unswervingly [ʌn'swɜːvɪŋlɪ] **ADV to be ~ loyal to sb** jdm unerschütterlich *or* unbeirrbar treu sein; **to hold ~ to one's course** unbeirrbar seinen Weg gehen

unsymmetrical [ˌʌnsɪ'metrɪkəl] **ADJ** unsymmetrisch

unsympathetic [ˌʌnsɪmpə'θetɪk] **ADJ a** *(= unfeeling)* gefühllos, wenig mitfühlend; *reaction, attitude, response* ablehnend, abweisend; **I am not ~ to your request** ich stehe Ihrer Bitte nicht ablehnend gegenüber **b** *(= unlikeable)* unsympathisch

unsympathetically [ˌʌnsɪmpə'θetɪkəlɪ] **ADV** ohne Mitgefühl; *say also* gefühllos, hart

unsystematic ADJ, unsystematically ADV [ˌʌnsɪstɪ'mætɪk, -əlɪ] planlos, unsystematisch, ohne System

untainted [ʌn'teɪntɪd] **ADJ** einwandfrei, tadellos; *food also, person, mind* unverdorben; *reputation* tadellos, makellos

untalented [ʌn'tælɪntɪd] **ADJ** unbegabt, untalentiert

untam(e)able [ʌn'teɪməbl] **ADJ** *animal* unzähmbar; *(fig)* unbezähmbar, nicht zu bändigen *pred*

untamed [ʌn'teɪmd] **ADJ** *animal* ungezähmt; *jungle* wild; *landscape, environment, beauty* ungezähmt, wild; *person, pride* ungebändigt; *temper* ungezügelt

untangle [ʌn'tæŋgl] **VT** *(lit, fig)* entwirren

untanned [ʌn'tænd] **ADJ** *hide* ungegerbt; *skin* nicht gebräunt

untapped [ʌn'tæpt] **ADJ** *barrel* unangezapft; *resources also, source of wealth, talent* ungenutzt; *market* unerschlossen

untarnished [ʌn'tɑːnɪʃt] **ADJ** makellos; *silver also* nicht angelaufen; *(fig) name* makellos, unbefleckt *(liter)*

untasted [ʌn'teɪstɪd] **ADJ** *(lit, fig)* ungekostet

untaught [ʌn'tɔːt] **ADJ** *(= not trained) person* nicht ausgebildet; *ability* angeboren; *behaviour* natürlich; **basic skills which remain ~ in our schools** Grundfähigkeiten, die in unseren Schulen weiterhin nicht vermittelt werden

untaxed [ʌn'tækst] **ADJ** *goods, income* steuerfrei, unbesteuert; *car* unversteuert

unteachable [ʌn'tiːtʃəbl] **ADJ** *person* unbelehrbar; *subject* nicht lehrbar; **it is ~ at this level** auf diesem Niveau kann man es nicht lehren

untearable [ʌn'tɛərəbl] **ADJ** unzerreißbar

untempered [ʌn'tempəd] **ADJ** *steel* ungehärtet, unvergütet; *rage* ungemildert; **justice ~ by mercy** Gerechtigkeit, die durch keinerlei Gnade gemildert wird

untenable [ʌn'tenəbl] **ADJ** *(lit, fig)* unhaltbar

untenanted [ʌn'tenəntɪd] **ADJ** *house* unbewohnt, leer

untended [ʌn'tendɪd] **ADJ** *patient* unbehütet, unbewacht; *garden* vernachlässigt, ungepflegt

untested [ʌn'testɪd] **ADJ** *person* unerprobt; *theory, product also* ungetestet, ungeprüft; **~ players** Spieler, die sich noch nicht bewährt haben

unthankful ADJ, unthankfully ADV [ʌn'θæŋkfʊl, -ɪ] undankbar

unthinkable [ʌn'θɪŋkəbl] **ADJ** undenkbar, unvorstellbar; *(Philos)* undenkbar; *(= too horrible)* unvorstellbar

unthinking [ʌn'θɪŋkɪŋ] **ADJ** *(= thoughtless, unintentional)* unbedacht, gedankenlos; *(= uncritical)* bedenkenlos, blind

unthinkingly [ʌn'θɪŋkɪŋlɪ] **ADV** *(= thoughtlessly, unintentionally)* unbedacht, gedankenlos; *assume, suppose* ohne nachzudenken

unthoughtful ADJ, unthoughtfully ADV [ʌn'θɔːtfʊl, -ɪ] gedankenlos; *(= careless)* unachtsam (of mit)

unthought-of [ʌn'θɔːtɒv] **ADJ** *(= inconceivable)* undenkbar, unvorstellbar; **these hitherto ~ objections** diese Einwände, auf die bis dahin niemand gekommen war

unthought-out [ˌʌnθɔːt'aʊt] **ADJ** nicht (gut) durchdacht, unausgegoren *(inf)*

unthread [ʌn'θred] **VT** *needle* ausfädeln; *pearls* abfädeln

untidily [ʌn'taɪdɪlɪ] **ADV** unordentlich

untidiness [ʌn'taɪdɪnɪs] **N** *(of room)* Unordnung *f*, Unaufgeräumtheit *f*; *(of person, dress)* Unordentlichkeit *f*; **the ~ of the kitchen** die Unordnung in der Küche

untidy [ʌn'taɪdɪ] **ADJ** *(+er)* unordentlich; **to lie in an ~ heap** *or* **pile** unordentlich übereinanderliegen

untie [ʌn'taɪ] **VT** *knot* lösen; *string, tie, shoelaces also* aufbinden; *shoes* aufmachen; *parcel* aufknoten; *person, animal, hands, apron* losbinden

until [ən'tɪl] **PREP a** bis; **from morning ~ night** von morgens bis abends, vom Morgen bis zum Abend; **~ now** bis jetzt; **~ then** bis dahin **b not ~** *(in future)* nicht vor *(+dat)*; *(in past)*

erst; **I didn't leave him ~ the following day** ich habe ihn erst am folgenden Tag verlassen, ich bin bis zum nächsten Tag bei ihm geblieben; **the work was not begun ~ 1990** die Arbeiten wurden erst 1990 begonnen; **I had heard nothing of it ~ five minutes ago** bis vor fünf Minuten wusste ich (noch) nichts davon, ich habe erst vor fünf Minuten davon gehört
CONJ **a** bis; **wait ~ I come** warten Sie, bis ich komme
b **not ~** *(in future)* nicht bevor, erst wenn; *(in past)* nicht bis, erst als; **he won't come ~ you invite him** er kommt erst, wenn Sie ihn einladen; **they did nothing ~ we came** bis wir kamen, taten sie nichts; **don't start ~ I come** fangen Sie nicht an, bevor ich da bin, fangen Sie erst an, wenn ich da bin; **they didn't start ~ we came** sie fingen erst an, als wir da waren, sie fingen nicht an, bevor wir da waren

untimeliness [ʌnˈtaɪmlɪnɪs] **N** *(of death)* Vorzeitigkeit *f*; *(of end also)* Verfrühtheit *f*; **because of the ~ of his arrival** weil er zur falschen Zeit kam

untimely [ʌnˈtaɪmlɪ] **ADJ** *(= premature) death* vorzeitig; *end also* verfrüht; *(= inopportune) moment* unpassend, ungelegen; *development, occurrence* unpassend, ungelegen, zur falschen Zeit; *shower, remark* zur falschen Zeit; *visit* ungelegen; **to come to** *or* **meet an ~ end** ein vorzeitiges Ende finden; **his arrival was most ~** seine Ankunft kam sehr ungelegen

untiring [ʌnˈtaɪərɪŋ] **ADJ** *campaigner, energy, enthusiasm, work, effort* unermüdlich; **to be ~ in one's efforts to do sth** unermüdliche Anstrengungen machen, etw zu tun

untiringly [ʌnˈtaɪərɪŋlɪ] **ADV** unermüdlich

untitled [ʌnˈtaɪtld] **ADJ** *painting* unbetitelt, ohne Titel; *person* ohne (Adels)titel

unto [ˈʌntʊ] **PREP** *(old, liter)* = **to**

untold [ʌnˈtəʊld] **ADJ** *story* nicht erzählt, nicht berichtet; *secret* ungelüftet; *wealth* unermesslich; *agony, delights* unsäglich; *damage, suffering* unsäglich, unermesslich; *stars etc* ungezählt, unzählig, zahllos; *losses, varieties* unzählig; **this story is better left ~** über diese Geschichte schweigt man besser; **he died with his secret still ~** er nahm sein Geheimnis mit ins Grab; **~ thousands** unzählig viele; **to remain ~** im Dunkeln bleiben

untouchable [ʌnˈtʌtʃəbl] **ADJ** **a** unberührbar **b** *(= immune) person, rights* unantastbar **c** *(= supreme)* unantastbar **N** Unberührbare(r) *mf*

untouched [ʌnˈtʌtʃt] **ADJ** **a** *(= unhandled, unused)* unberührt, unangetastet; *bottle, box of sweets etc* unberührt, nicht angebrochen; *(= unmentioned)* nicht erwähnt; **~ by human hand** nicht von Menschenhand berührt; **he left his meal ~** er ließ sein Essen unberührt stehen **b** *(= unharmed)* heil, unversehrt; *(= unaffected)* unberührt; *(= unmoved)* ungerührt, unbewegt, unbeeindruckt; **he was ~ by her tears** ihre Tränen ließen ihn kalt **c** *(= unequalled)* unerreicht; **he is ~ by anyone** niemand kommt ihm gleich

untoward [ˌʌntəˈwɔːd] **ADJ** *(= unfortunate) event* unglücklich, bedauerlich; *(= unseemly)* unpassend, ungehörig; **nothing ~ had happened** es war kein Unheil geschehen

untraceable [ʌnˈtreɪsəbl] **ADJ** *person* unauffindbar; *note, bill* unbekannter Herkunft

untrained [ʌnˈtreɪnd] **ADJ** *person, teacher* unausgebildet; *voice, mind* ungeschult; *animal* undressiert; **to the ~ ear/eye** dem ungeschulten Ohr/Auge; **to be ~ for sth** für etw nicht ausgebildet sein; **to be ~ in sth** in etw *(dat)* nicht ausgebildet sein

untrammelled, *(US)* **untrammeled** [ʌnˈtræməld] **ADJ** unbeschränkt; **to be ~ by sth** nicht von etw beschränkt werden

untranslatable [ˌʌntrænzˈleɪtəbl] **ADJ** unübersetzbar

untravelled, *(US)* **untraveled** [ʌnˈtrævld] **ADJ** *road* unbefahren; *person* nicht weit gereist, nicht weit herumgekommen

untreated [ʌnˈtriːtɪd] **ADJ** unbehandelt; **to be ~ with sth** mit etw nicht behandelt sein

untried [ʌnˈtraɪd] **ADJ** **a** *(= not tested) person* unerprobt; *product, method* ungetestet, unerprobt; *(= not attempted)* unversucht **b** *(Jur) case* nicht verhandelt; *person* nicht vor Gericht gestellt; **the case is still ~** der Fall ist noch nicht verhandelt worden; **the offender can remain ~ for months** der Rechtsbrecher wird zuweilen erst nach Monaten vor Gericht gestellt

untrodden [ʌnˈtrɒdn] **ADJ** *path* verlassen; *snow* unberührt; **~ ground** *(fig)* neuer Boden

untroubled [ʌnˈtrʌbld] **ADJ** **a** *(= serene) appearance* unbekümmert; *sleep* ungestört; *life* sorglos; *period, ghost, person* friedlich, ruhig; *smile* unbeschwert; **to be ~ by the news** eine Nachricht gleichmütig hinnehmen; **the children seemed ~ by the heat** die Hitze schien den Kindern nichts anzuhaben *or* auszumachen; **they were ~ by thoughts of the future** der Gedanke an die Zukunft belastete sie nicht **b** *(= free from)* **to be ~ by war/injury** vom Krieg/von Verletzungen verschont bleiben; **to be ~ by the authorities/police** von den Behörden/der Polizei nicht belästigt werden

untrue [ʌnˈtruː] **ADJ** **a** *(= false)* unwahr, falsch; *(Tech) reading, instrument* inkorrekt, ungenau **b** *(= unfaithful) person* untreu; **to be ~ to sb** jdm untreu sein; **to be ~ to one's principles/word** seinen Prinzipien/seinem Wort untreu sein

untrustworthy [ʌnˈtrʌstˌwɜːðɪ] **ADJ** *(= not reliable) source, book, person* unzuverlässig; *(= not worthy of confidence) person* nicht vertrauenswürdig

untruth [ʌnˈtruːθ] **N** Unwahrheit *f*

untruthful [ʌnˈtruːθfʊl] **ADJ** *statement* unwahr; *person* unaufrichtig; **you're being ~** da bist du unaufrichtig

untruthfully [ʌnˈtruːθfəlɪ] **ADV** fälschlich; **he said, quite ~, that …** er sagte, und das war nicht die Wahrheit, dass …

untruthfulness [ʌnˈtruːθfʊlnɪs] **N** *(of statement)* Unwahrheit *f*; *(of person)* Unaufrichtigkeit *f*

untuneful [ʌnˈtjuːnfʊl] **ADJ** unmelodisch

unturned [ʌnˈtɜːnd] **ADJ** → **stone**

untutored [ʌnˈtjuːtəd] **ADJ** *taste, person* ungeschult; **to the ~ eye/ear** für das ungeschulte Auge/Ohr; **to be ~ in sth** in etw *(dat)* nicht unterrichtet sein

untypical [ʌnˈtɪpɪkl] **ADJ** untypisch (*of* für)

unusable [ʌnˈjuːzəbl] **ADJ** unbrauchbar; *road* unbefahrbar

unused[1] [ʌnˈjuːzd] **ADJ** *(= new)* unbenutzt, ungebraucht; *clothes* ungetragen; *banknote* druckfrisch; *(= not made use of)* ungenutzt; *(= no longer used)* nicht mehr benutzt *or* gebraucht; *(= left over) food* übrig geblieben

unused[2] [ʌnˈjuːst] **ADJ** **to be ~ to sth** nicht an etw *(acc)* gewöhnt sein, etw *(acc)* nicht gewohnt sein; **to be ~ to doing sth** nicht daran gewöhnt sein *or* es nicht gewohnt sein, etw zu tun

unusual [ʌnˈjuːʒʊəl] **ADJ** *(= uncommon)* ungewöhnlich; *(= exceptional)* außergewöhnlich; **it's ~ for him to be late** er kommt normalerweise nicht zu spät; **that's ~ for him** das ist sonst nicht seine Art; **that's not ~ for him** das wundert mich überhaupt nicht; **it is ~ to see this** das ist ein ungewöhnlicher Anblick; **nothing ~** nichts Außergewöhnliches; **there is something ~ about this** es hat etwas Ungewöhnliches an sich; **how ~!** das kommt selten vor; *(iro)* welch Wunder!; **how do you like my new hat? – well, it's ~** wie gefällt Ihnen mein neuer Hut? – na, es ist mal was anderes

unusually [ʌnˈjuːʒʊəlɪ] **ADV** *large, quiet, cheerful* ungewöhnlich; **most ~, he was late** ganz gegen jede Gewohnheit kam er zu spät; **~ for her, she was late** ganz gegen ihre Gewohnheit kam sie zu spät; **~ for a big city, it has no cinema** obwohl das für eine Großstadt ungewöhnlich ist, gibt es hier/dort kein Kino

unutterable [ʌnˈʌtərəbl] **ADJ** *word* unaussprechlich; *joy, longing, sadness* unsäglich, unbeschreiblich; **he talks ~ rubbish** er redet völligen Unsinn

unutterably [ʌnˈʌtərəblɪ] *(liter)* **ADV** *sad* unbeschreiblich, unsagbar; *tired, boring* unbeschreiblich

unvaried [ʌnˈveərɪd] **ADJ** unverändert; *(pej)* eintönig

unvarnished [ʌnˈvɑːnɪʃt] **ADJ** *wood* ungefirnisst, unlackiert; *(fig) truth, language, report* ungeschminkt

unvarying [ʌnˈveərɪɪŋ] **ADJ** gleichbleibend, unveränderlich

unveil [ʌnˈveɪl] **VT** *statue, painting, plan* enthüllen; *results* bekannt geben; *(Comm) car* vorstellen; *face* entschleiern; **women mustn't go ~ed** Frauen dürfen nicht unverschleiert gehen **VI** sich entschleiern, den Schleier fallen lassen

unveiling [ʌnˈveɪlɪŋ] **N** *(lit, fig)* Enthüllung *f*; **~ ceremony** Enthüllung *f*

unventilated [ʌnˈventɪleɪtɪd] **ADJ** ungelüftet, nicht ventiliert

unverifiable [ʌnˈverɪfaɪəbl] **ADJ** nicht beweisbar, unverifizierbar *(geh)*

unverified [ʌnˈverɪfaɪd] **ADJ** unbewiesen

unversed [ʌnˈvɜːst] **ADJ** **~ in** nicht vertraut mit, unbewandert in *(+dat)*

unvisited [ʌnˈvɪzɪtɪd] **ADJ** nicht besucht; **we left Heidelberg with the castle ~** wir verließen Heidelberg, ohne das Schloss besucht zu haben

unvoiced [ʌnˈvɔɪst] **ADJ** **a** unausgesprochen **b** *(Phon)* stimmlos

unwaged [ʌnˈweɪdʒd] **ADJ** ohne Einkommen **N** **the ~** *pl* Personen *pl* ohne (festes) Einkommen

unwanted [ʌnˈwɒntɪd] **ADJ** **a** *(= unwelcome, unplanned)* unerwünscht; **sometimes you make me feel ~** manchmal komme ich mir (bei dir) richtig unerwünscht vor **b** *(= superfluous) food* überflüssig

unwarily [ʌnˈweərɪlɪ] **ADV** unvorsichtig, unbesonnen, unachtsam

unwariness [ʌnˈweərɪnɪs] **N** Unvorsichtigkeit *f*, Unbesonnenheit *f*, Unachtsamkeit *f*

unwarlike [ʌnˈwɔːlaɪk] **ADJ** friedliebend, friedlich

unwarrantable [ʌnˈwɒrəntəbl] **ADJ** nicht zu rechtfertigen *pred*, nicht zu rechtfertigend *attr*

unwarranted [ʌnˈwɒrəntɪd] **ADJ** ungerechtfertigt

unwary [ʌnˈweərɪ] **ADJ** unvorsichtig, unbesonnen, unachtsam

unwashed [ʌnˈwɒʃt] **ADJ** ungewaschen; *dishes* ungespült **N** **the great ~** *pl (hum)* der Pöbel

unwavering [ʌnˈweɪvərɪŋ] **ADJ** *faith, resolve* unerschütterlich; *gaze* fest, unbewegt; *course* beharrlich; *voice* fest; **to be ~ in one's opposition to sth** gegen etw beharrlich Widerstand leisten

unwaveringly [ʌnˈweɪvərɪŋlɪ] **ADV** *gaze, aim* fest; *support, oppose* beharrlich

unweaned [ʌnˈwiːnd] **ADJ** *baby* (noch) nicht entwöhnt

unwearable [ʌnˈweərəbl] **ADJ** **it's ~** das kann man nicht tragen

unwearied [ʌnˈwɪərɪd], **unwearying** [ʌnˈwɪərɪɪŋ] **ADJ** unermüdlich

unwed [ʌnˈwed] **ADJ** unverheiratet, unvermählt *(geh)*

unwelcome [ʌnˈwelkəm] **ADJ** *visitor* unwillkommen, unerwünscht; *news, memories* unerfreulich, unangenehm; *fact, thought, side effect, surprise* unangenehm; *reminder, change, publicity, advances* unwillkommen; **to make sb feel ~** sich jdm gegenüber abweisend verhalten; **the money was not ~** das Geld war höchst willkommen

unwelcoming [ʌnˈwelkəmɪŋ] **ADJ** *manner* abweisend, unfreundlich; *host also* ungastlich; *place* abweisend, ungastlich

unwell [ʌn'wel] ADJ *pred* unwohl, nicht wohl; **to be** *or* **feel (a little)** ~ sich nicht (recht) wohlfühlen; **I am afraid he's rather ~ today** es geht ihm heute leider gar nicht gut

unwholesome [ʌn'həʊlsəm] ADJ ungesund; *influence* ungut, verderblich; *appearance, character* schmierig; *food* minderwertig; *smell* faul; *desire, thoughts, story, jokes* schmutzig; **they are rather ~ company for her** sie sind nicht gerade ein guter Umgang für sie; **to have an ~ interest in sb/sth** ein perverses Interesse an jdm/etw haben

unwholesomeness [ʌn'həʊlsəmnɪs] N Ungesundheit *f*; *(of influence)* Verderblichkeit *f*; *(of appearance, character)* Schmierigkeit *f*; *(of food)* Minderwertigkeit *f*; *(of smell)* Verfaultheit *f*; *(of desire, thoughts, story, joke)* Schmutzigkeit *f*

unwieldy [ʌn'wi:ldɪ] ADJ **a** *tool* unhandlich; *object also* sperrig; *(= clumsy) body* schwerfällig, unbeholfen **b** *(= over-complex) system, bureaucracy* schwerfällig; *name* kompliziert

unwilling [ʌn'wɪlɪŋ] ADJ *helper, admiration, pupil* widerwillig; *accomplice* unfreiwillig; **to be ~ to do sth** nicht bereit *or* gewillt *or* willens *(geh)* sein, etw zu tun; **to be ~ for sb to do sth** nicht wollen, dass jd etw tut

unwillingly [ʌn'wɪlɪŋlɪ] ADV widerwillig

unwillingness [ʌn'wɪlɪŋnɪs] N Widerwillen *nt*, Weigerung *f*; **their ~ to compromise** ihre mangelnde Kompromissbereitschaft

unwind [ʌn'waɪnd] *pret, ptp* **unwound** VT *thread, film, tape* abwickeln; *(= untangle)* entwirren VI **a** *(lit)* sich abwickeln; *(fig: story, plot)* sich entwickeln, sich entfalten **b** *(inf: = relax)* abschalten *(inf)*, sich entspannen

unwise [ʌn'waɪz] ADJ unklug; **they were ~ enough to believe him** sie waren so töricht, ihm das zu glauben; **I thought it ~ to travel alone** ich hielt es für unklug *or* töricht, allein zu reisen

unwisely [ʌn'waɪzlɪ] ADV *act* unklug; **rather ~ the Government agreed** die Regierung hat unklugerweise zugestimmt

unwished-for [ʌn'wɪʃtfɔ:ʳ] ADJ unerwünscht

unwitting [ʌn'wɪtɪŋ] ADJ *accomplice* unbewusst, unwissentlich; *action also* unabsichtlich; *victim* ahnungslos; *involvement* unabsichtlich, unwissentlich; **he was the ~ cause of the argument** er war unbewusst die Ursache des Streits, er war, ohne es zu wissen, die Ursache des Streits

unwittingly [ʌn'wɪtɪŋlɪ] ADV unbewusst; **I had agreed, albeit ~, to take part** ich hatte mich völlig ahnungslos dazu bereit erklärt, mitzumachen

unwomanly [ʌn'wʊmənlɪ] ADJ unweiblich

unwonted [ʌn'wəʊntɪd] ADJ ungewohnt

unwontedly [ʌn'wəʊntɪdlɪ] ADV ungewöhnlich

unworkable [ʌn'wɜ:kəbl] ADJ *scheme, idea* undurchführbar; *law* nicht durchsetzbar; *land* nicht nutzbar; *(Min) mine* nicht abbaubar

unworkmanlike [ʌn'wɜ:kmənlaɪk] ADJ *job* unfachmännisch

unworldliness [ʌn'wɜ:ldlɪnɪs] N Weltabgewandtheit *f*; *(= naivety)* Weltfremdheit *f*

unworldly [ʌn'wɜ:ldlɪ] ADJ *life* weltabgewandt; *(= naive)* weltfremd

unworn [ʌn'wɔ:n] ADJ *(= new)* ungetragen

unworried [ʌn'wʌrɪd] ADJ unbekümmert, sorglos; **he was ~ by my criticism** meine Kritik (be)kümmerte ihn nicht

unworthily [ʌn'wɜ:ðɪlɪ] ADV *behave* unwürdig; **he said, rather ~, that …** er sagte, und das war eigentlich unter seiner Würde, dass …

unworthiness [ʌn'wɜ:ðɪnɪs] N Unwürdigkeit *f*

unworthy [ʌn'wɜ:ðɪ] ADJ *person* nicht wert *(of +gen)*; *conduct also* nicht würdig, unwürdig *(of +gen)*; **to be ~ to do sth** (es) nicht wert sein, etw zu tun; **to be ~ of an honour** *(Brit) or* **honor** *(US)* einer Ehre *(gen)* nicht wert sein *(geh)*; **this is ~ of you** das ist unter deiner Würde; **it is ~ of our attention** das verdient unsere Aufmerksamkeit nicht, das ist unserer Aufmerksamkeit *(gen)* nicht wert; **it was ~ of you not to accept their kind offer** es war nicht anständig von dir, ihren freundlichen Vorschlag nicht anzunehmen; **it would be ~ of me not to mention also …** es wäre nicht recht, wenn ich nicht auch … erwähnen würde; **it is ~ of comment** es verdient keinen Kommentar

unwound [ʌn'waʊnd] *pret, ptp of* **unwind**

unwounded [ʌn'wu:ndɪd] ADJ nicht verwundet, unverwundet

unwrap [ʌn'ræp] VT auspacken, auswickeln

unwritten [ʌn'rɪtn] ADJ *story, book, constitution* ungeschrieben; *agreement* stillschweigend

unwritten law N *(Jur, fig)* ungeschriebenes Gesetz

unyielding [ʌn'ji:ldɪŋ] ADJ *substance* unnachgiebig; *(fig) person, demand also, resistance* hart

unyoke [ʌn'jəʊk] VT ausspannen; **he ~d his oxen from the plough** er spannte seine Ochsen aus

unzip [ʌn'zɪp] VT **a** *zip* aufmachen; *dress, trousers, case* den Reißverschluss aufmachen an *(+dat)*; **would you please ~ me?** kannst du bitte mir den Reißverschluss aufmachen? **b** *file* auspacken, entzippen VI *(zip)* aufgehen, sich öffnen; **this dress won't ~** der Reißverschluss an dem Kleid geht nicht auf *or* lässt sich nicht öffnen; **my dress must have come ~ped** der Reißverschluss an meinem Kleid muss aufgegangen sein

up [ʌp]
⊙ 16.4

1 ADVERB	4 ADJECTIVE
2 PREPOSITION	5 TRANSITIVE VERB
3 NOUN	6 INTRANSITIVE VERB

1 – ADVERB

a [indicating position] *= in high or higher position* oben; *(= to higher position)* nach oben; **up there** dort oben, droben *(liter, S Ger)*; **up here on the roof** hier oben auf dem Dach; **on your way up (to see us/them)** auf dem Weg (zu uns/ihnen) hinauf; **he climbed all the way up (to us/them)** er ist den ganzen Weg (zu uns/ihnen) hochgeklettert; **to stop halfway up** auf halber Höhe anhalten; **we were 6,000 m up when …** wir waren 6.000 m hoch, als …; **5 floors up** 5 Stockwerke hoch; **3 floors up from me** 3 Stockwerke über mir; **they were up above** sie waren hoch oben; **I looked up (above)** ich schaute nach oben; **this side up** diese Seite oben!; **a little further up** ein bisschen weiter oben; **to go a little further up** ein bisschen höher (hinauf)gehen; **hang the picture a bit higher up** häng das Bild ein bisschen höher; **stick the notice up here** häng den Anschlag hier hin; **from up on the hill** vom Berg oben; **up on top (of the cupboard)** ganz oben (auf dem Schrank); **up in the mountains/sky** oben *or* droben *(liter, S Ger)* in den Bergen/am Himmel; **the temperature was up in the thirties** die Temperatur war über dreißig Grad; **the sun/moon is up** die Sonne/der Mond ist aufgegangen; **the tide is up** es ist Flut, die Flut ist da; **the wind is up** der Wind hat aufgefrischt; **with his collar up** mit hochgeschlagenem Kragen; **the road is up** *(Brit)* die Straße ist aufgegraben; **to be up with the leaders** vorn bei den Führenden sein; **to move up into the lead** nach vorn an die Spitze kommen; **Red Rum with Joe Smith up** Red Rum unter Joe Smith; **up and away the balloon sailed** der Ballon stieg auf und schwebte davon; **then up jumps Richard and says …** und dann springt Richard auf und sagt …; **the needle was up at 95** die Nadel stand auf 95; **come on, up, that's my chair!** komm, auf mit dir, das ist mein Stuhl!; **up! he shouted to his horse** spring! schrie er seinem Pferd zu; **up with the Liberals!** hoch die Liberalen!; **up with Spurs!** Spurs hoch!; **up yours!** *(sl)* leck mich *(inf)*, fick dich! *(vulg)*

b [= installed, built] **to be up** *(building)* stehen; *(tent also)* aufgeschlagen sein; *(scaffolding)* aufgestellt sein; *(notice)* hängen, angeschlagen sein; *(picture)* hängen, aufgehängt sein; *(shutters)* zu sein; *(shelves, wallpaper, curtains, pictures)* hängen; **the new houses went up very quickly** die neuen Häuser sind sehr schnell gebaut *or* hochgezogen *(inf)* worden

♦ **to be up and running** laufen; *(committee etc)* in Gang sein; *(business etc)* einwandfrei funktionieren; *(= be on the market)* auf dem Markt sein

♦ **to get sth up and running** etw zum Laufen bringen; *committee etc* etw in Gang setzen; **have you got your computer up and running yet?** läuft dein Computer schon?

c [= not in bed] auf; **up (with you)!** auf mit dir!, raus aus dem Bett *(inf)*; **to be up and about** auf sein; *(after illness also)* auf den Beinen sein; **she was up all night with him** *(= looking after him)* sie war seinetwegen die ganze Nacht auf

d [= north] oben; **up in Inverness** in Inverness oben, oben in Inverness; **we are going up to Aberdeen** wir fahren nach Aberdeen (hinauf); **to be/live up north** im Norden sein/wohnen; **to go up north** in den Norden fahren; **up from the country** vom Lande; **we're up for the day** wir sind (nur) für heute hier; **he was up at Susie's place** er war bei Susie zu Hause

e [= at university] *Brit* am Studienort; **the students are only up for half the year** die Studenten sind nur die Hälfte des Jahres am Studienort; **to go up to Cambridge** (zum Studium) nach Cambridge gehen; **he was up at Oxford in 1982** er hat 1982 in Oxford studiert

f [in price, value] gestiegen *(on* gegenüber); **my shares are up 70p** meine Aktien sind um 70 Pence gestiegen; **then up go prices again** und wieder steigen die Preise

g [in score] **to be 3 goals up** mit 3 Toren führen *or* vorn liegen *(on* gegenüber); **the score was 9 up** *(US)* es stand 9 beide; **I'll play you 100 up** ich spiele auf 100 (mit dir); **we were £100 up on the deal** wir haben bei dem Geschäft £ 100 gemacht; **to be one up on sb** jdm um einen Schritt voraus sein

h [= upwards] **from £10 up** von £ 10 (an) aufwärts, ab £ 10; **from the age of 13 up** ab (dem Alter von) 13 Jahren, von 13 Jahren aufwärts

i [= wrong] *inf* **what's up?** was ist los?; **what's up with him?** was ist mit dem los?, was ist los mit ihm?; **something is up** *(= wrong)* da stimmt irgendetwas nicht; *(= happening)* da ist irgendetwas im Gange; **there's something up with it** irgendetwas stimmt damit nicht *or* hier nicht

j [= knowledgeable] firm, beschlagen *(in, on in +dat)*; **he's well up on foreign affairs** in außenpolitischen Fragen kennt er sich aus *or* ist er firm; **I'm not very up on French history** in französischer Geschichte bin ich nicht sehr beschlagen

k [= finished] **time's up** die Zeit ist um, die Zeit ist zu Ende; **the weekend is nearly up** das Wochenende ist fast zu Ende *or* fast vorüber; **to eat/use sth up** etw aufessen/aufbrauchen; **it's all up with him** *(inf)* es ist aus mit ihm *(inf)*, es ist mit ihm zu Ende

l [set structures]

♦ **up against** **it was up against the wall** es war an die Wand gelehnt; **put it up against the wall** lehne es an die Wand; **to be up against a difficulty/an opponent** einem Problem/Gegner gegenüberstehen, es mit einem Problem/Gegner zu tun haben; **I fully realize what I'm up against** mir ist völlig klar, womit ich es hier zu tun habe; **they were really up against it** sie hatten wirklich schwer zu schaffen

♦ **up and down** auf und ab; **to walk up and down** auf und ab gehen; **to bounce up and down** hochfedern, auf und ab hüpfen; **he's been up and down all evening** *(from seat)* er hat den ganzen Abend keine Minute still gesessen; *(on stairs)* er ist den ganzen Abend die Treppe rauf- und runtergerannt; **she's still a bit up and down** *(after illness etc)* es geht ihr immer noch mal besser, mal schlechter

♦ **up before** **the matter is up before the committee** die Sache ist vor dem Ausschuss; **the boys were up before the head teacher** die Jungen sind vor den Direktor zitiert worden; **to be up before the Court/before Judge Smith** *(case)* verhandelt werden/von Richter Smith verhandelt werden; *(person)* vor Gericht/Richter Smith stehen

♦ **up for** **to be up for sale** zu verkaufen sein; **to be up for discussion** zur Diskussion stehen; **to be up for election** *(candidate)* zur Wahl aufgestellt sein; *(candidates)* zur Wahl stehen; **to be up for trial** vor Gericht stehen

♦ **up to**

= as far as bis; **up to now/here** bis jetzt/hier; **to count up to 100** bis 100 zählen; **up to £100** bis zu £ 100; **it holds up to 8** es fasst bis zu 8; **I'm up to here in work/debt** *(inf)* ich stecke bis hier in Arbeit/Schulden; **I'm full up to here** *(inf)* ich bin bis oben (hin) voll *(inf)*; **what page are you up to?** bis zu welcher Seite bist du gekommen?

= equal to **I don't feel up to it** ich fühle mich dem nicht gewachsen; *(= not well enough)* ich fühle mich nicht wohl genug dazu; **it isn't up to much** damit ist nicht viel los *(inf)*; **is he up to the heavier weights?** schafft er schwerere Gewichte?; **he isn't up to running the company by himself** er hat nicht das Zeug dazu, die Firma allein zu leiten; **it isn't up to his usual standard** das ist nicht sein sonstiges Niveau; **we're going up Ben Nevis – are you sure you're up to it?** wir wollen Ben Nevis besteigen – glaubst du, dass du das schaffst?

♦ **to be up to sb**

= depend on **it's up to us to help him** wir sollten ihm helfen; **if it were up to me** wenn es nach mir ginge; **the success of this project is up to you now** wie erfolgreich dieses Projekt wird, hängt jetzt nur noch von Ihnen (selbst) ab, es liegt jetzt ganz an Ihnen, ob dieses Projekt ein Erfolg wird; **it's up to you whether you go or not** es liegt an *or* bei dir *or* es bleibt dir überlassen, ob du gehst oder nicht; **I'd like to accept, but it isn't up to me** ich würde gerne annehmen, aber ich habe da nicht zu bestimmen *or* aber das hängt nicht von mir ab; **shall I take it? – that's entirely up to you** soll ich es nehmen? – das müssen Sie selbst wissen; **what colour shall I choose? – (it's) up to you** welche Farbe soll ich nehmen? – das ist deine Entscheidung

= be duty of **it's up to the government to put this right** es ist Sache der Regierung, das richtigzustellen; **it's not up to the government** das ist nicht Sache der Regierung

♦ **to be up to sth** *(inf)* **what's he up to?** *(= actually doing)* was macht er da?; *(= planning etc)* was hat er vor?; *(suspiciously)* was führt er im Schilde?; **what have you been up to?** was hast du angestellt?; **what are you up to with that?** was hast du damit vor?; **he's up to no good** er führt nichts Gutes im Schilde; **I'm sure he's up to something** ich bin sicher, er hat etwas vor *or (sth suspicious)* er führt irgendetwas im Schilde; *(child)* ich bin sicher, er stellt irgendetwas an; **hey you! what do you think you're up to!** he Sie, was machen Sie eigentlich da!; **what does he think he's up to?** was soll das eigentlich?, was hat er eigentlich vor?

2 – PREPOSITION

oben auf *(+dat)*; *(with movement)* hinauf *(+acc)*; **further up the page** weiter oben auf der Seite; **to live up the hill** am Berg wohnen; **to go up the hill** den Berg hinaufgehen; **they live further up the hill/street** sie wohnen weiter oben am Berg/weiter die Straße entlang; **he lives up a dark alley** er wohnt am Ende einer dunklen Gasse; **up the road from me** (von mir) die Straße entlang; **he went off up the road** er ging (weg) die Straße hinauf; **he hid it up the chimney** er versteckte es (oben) im Kamin; **the water goes up this pipe** das Wasser geht durch dieses Rohr; **up one's sleeve** *(position)* im Ärmel; *(motion)* in den Ärmel; **as I travel up and down the country** wenn ich so durchs Land reise; **I've been up and down the stairs all night** ich bin in der Nacht immer nur die Treppe rauf- und runtergerannt; **he was up the pub** *(Brit inf)* er war in der Kneipe *(inf)*; **let's go up the pub/up Johnny's place** *(inf)* gehen wir doch zur Kneipe/zu Johnny *(inf)*; **to go up to sb** auf jdn zugehen

3 – NOUN

♦ **ups and downs** gute und schlechte Zeiten *pl*; *(of life)* Höhen und Tiefen *pl*; **after many ups and downs** nach vielen Höhen und Tiefen; **they have their ups and downs** bei ihnen gibt es auch gute und schlechte Zeiten

♦ **to be on the up and up** *(inf: = improving)* auf dem aufsteigenden Ast sein *(inf)*; **he/his career is on the up and up** *(inf)* mit ihm/seiner Karriere geht es aufwärts

4 – ADJECTIVE

(= going up) escalator nach oben; *(Rail) train, line* zur nächsten größeren Stadt; **platform 14 is the up platform** auf Bahnsteig 14 fahren die Züge nach London *etc*

5 – TRANSITIVE VERB

(inf) price, offer hinaufsetzen; *production* ankurbeln; *bet* erhöhen *(to* auf *+acc)*

6 – INTRANSITIVE VERB

(inf) **she upped and left him** sie verließ ihn ganz plötzlich *or* Knall auf Fall *(inf)*; **he upped and ran** er rannte ganz plötzlich davon

---

up-and-coming ['ʌpən'kʌmɪŋ] ADJ *city* aufstrebend; **an ~ actor/star** ein Schauspieler/Star, der im Kommen ist

up-and-down ['ʌpən'daʊn] ADJ **a** *(lit)* **~ movement** Auf- und Abbewegung *f* **b** *(fig) career, fortunes, relationship, period* wechselhaft

up-and-under ['ʌpən'ʌndəʳ] N *(Rugby)* hohe Selbstvorlage

up arrow N *(Comput)* Aufwärtspfeil *m*

upbeat ['ʌpbiːt] N *(Mus)* Auftakt *m* ADJ *(inf) (= cheerful)* fröhlich; *(= optimistic)* optimistisch; **to be ~ about sth** über etw *(acc)* optimistisch gestimmt sein

up-bow ['ʌpbəʊ] N Aufstrich *m*

upbraid [ʌp'breɪd] VT rügen; **to ~ sb for doing sth** jdn dafür rügen, dass er etw getan hat

upbringing ['ʌpbrɪŋɪŋ] N Erziehung *f*; *(= manners also)* Kinderstube *f*; **to have a good ~** eine gute Kinderstube haben; **we had a strict ~** wir hatten (als Kinder) eine strenge Erziehung; **he hasn't got any ~** er hat keine Kinderstube

upchuck ['ʌptʃʌk] VI *(US inf: = vomit)* kotzen *(sl)*, reihern *(sl)*

upcoming [ʌp'kʌmɪŋ] ADJ *(= coming soon)* kommend, bevorstehend

upcountry ['ʌp'kʌntrɪ] ADV landeinwärts ADJ *town, village, person* im Landesinnern; *trip, tour* ins Landesinnere

up-current ['ʌpkʌrənt] N *(Aviat)* Aufwind *m*, Aufströmung *f*

update [ʌp'deɪt] VT aktualisieren; *file, book also, person* auf den neuesten Stand bringen; **to ~ sb on sth** jdn über etw *(acc)* auf den neuesten Stand bringen N ['ʌpdeɪt] Aktualisierung *f*; *(= updated version)* Neufassung *f*; *(of software package)* Update *nt*; *(= progress report)* Bericht *m*; **can you give me an ~ on ...?** können Sie mich bezüglich ... *(gen)* auf den neuesten Stand bringen?

updraught, *(US)* **updraft** ['ʌpdrɑːft] N Zug *m*; *(Aviat)* Aufwind *m*, Aufströmung *f*

upend [ʌp'end] VT *box, sofa* hochkant stellen; *person, animal* umdrehen

upfront [ʌp'frʌnt] ADJ **a** *person* offen; **to be ~ about sth** sich offen über etw *(acc)* äußern **b ~ money** Vorschuss *m*; **an ~ commission/fee** eine Kommission/Gebühr, die im Voraus zu entrichten ist ADV **a** *(= in advance) pay, charge* im Voraus; **we'd like 20% ~** wir hätten gern 20% (als) Vorschuss; **we need all the cash ~** wir benötigen die ganze Summe im Voraus **b** *(esp US: = openly)* offen

upgrade ['ʌpgreɪd] N **a** *(= improved version)* verbesserte Version; *(Comput)* Upgrade *nt* **b** *(US)* Steigung *f* **c** *(fig)* **to be on the ~** sich auf dem aufsteigenden Ast befinden *(inf)* VT [ʌp'greɪd] *employee* befördern; *job* anheben; *(= improve)* verbessern; *(= expand) computer system etc* ausbauen, nachrüsten

upgrad(e)ability [ˌʌpgreɪdə'bɪlɪtɪ] N *(of computer system etc)* Ausbaufähigkeit *f*, Nachrüstbarkeit *f*

upgrad(e)able [ʌp'greɪdəbl] ADJ *computer system etc* ausbaufähig *(to* auf *+acc)*, nachrüstbar *(to* auf *+acc)*

upheaval [ʌp'hiːvəl] N *(Geol)* Aufwölbung *f*, Erhebung *f*; *(fig)* Aufruhr *m*; **emotional ~** Aufruhr *m* der Gefühle; **social/political ~s** soziale/politische Umwälzungen *pl*

upheld [ʌp'held] *pret, ptp of* **uphold**

uphill ['ʌp'hɪl] ADV bergauf; **to go ~** bergauf gehen, steigen; *(road also)* bergauf führen; *(car)* den Berg hinauffahren ADJ *road* bergauf (führend); *(fig) work, struggle* mühsam, mühselig; **it's ~ all the way** *(lit)* es geht die ganze Strecke bergauf; *(fig)* es ist ein harter Kampf; **an ~ struggle** *or* **battle** ein mühsamer *or* mühseliger Kampf; **~ ski** Bergski *m*

uphold [ʌp'həʊld] *pret, ptp* **upheld** VT *(= sustain) tradition, principle, honour* wahren; *the law* hüten; *right, values* schützen; *(= support) person, decision, objection* (unter)stützen; *complaint* anerkennen; *(Jur) verdict, appeal* bestätigen

upholder [ʌp'həʊldəʳ] N Wahrer(in) *m(f)*; *(= supporter)* Verteidiger(in) *m(f)*

upholster [ʌp'həʊlstəʳ] VT *chair etc* polstern; *(= cover)* beziehen; **~ed furniture** Polstermöbel *pl*; **well-~ed** *(hum inf)* gut gepolstert *(hum inf)*

upholsterer [ʌp'həʊlstərəʳ] N Polsterer *m*, Polsterin *f*

upholstery [ʌp'həʊlstərɪ] N *(= padding and springs)* Polsterung *f*; *(= cover)* Bezug *m*; *(= trade)* Polsterei *f*; *(= skill)* das Polstern

upkeep ['ʌpkiːp] N *(= running)* Unterhalt *m*; *(= cost)* Unterhaltskosten *pl*; *(= maintenance)* Instandhaltung *f*, Instandhaltungskosten *pl*; *(of public gardens etc)* Pflege *f*

upland ['ʌplənd] N *(usu pl)* Hochland *nt no pl* ADJ Hochland-; **~ area** Hochlandgebiet *nt*

uplift ['ʌplɪft] N *(= exaltation)* Erhebung *f*; *(= moral inspiration)* Erbauung *f*; **his sermons were full of ~** seine Predigten waren voll erbaulicher Worte; **to give sb spiritual ~** jdn erbauen; **an ~ in the economy** ein Wirtschaftsaufschwung *m* VT [ʌp'lɪft] **a** *spirit, heart, voice* erheben; *person, mind* erbauen; **with ~ed arms** mit erhobenen Armen; **to feel ~ed** sich erbaut fühlen **b** *(Scot: = collect)* abholen

uplift bra N Stützbüstenhalter *m*

uplifting [ʌp'lɪftɪŋ] ADJ *experience* erhebend; *music, film, story* erhebend, erbaulich

uplighter ['ʌplaɪtəʳ] N *(= light)* Wandfluter *m*

upload ['ʌpləʊd] *(Comput)* VT (hoch)laden N Laden *nt*, Upload *m*

up-market ['ʌp'mɑːkɪt] ADJ *customer* anspruchsvoll; *person* vornehm; *image, version, hotel* exklusiv ADV *sell* an anspruchsvollere Kunden; **his shop has gone ~** in seinem Laden verkauft er jetzt Waren der höheren Preisklasse; **Japanese car-makers have gone ~** Japans Autohersteller produzieren jetzt für einen anspruchsvolleren Kundenkreis

upmost ['ʌpməʊst] ADJ, ADV = **uppermost**

upon [ə'pɒn] PREP = **on**

upper ['ʌpəʳ] ADJ **a** obere(r, s); *(Anat, Geog)* Ober-; **temperatures in the ~ thirties** Temperaturen hoch in den dreißig; **~ arm** Oberarm *m*; **~ lip** Oberlippe *f*; **~ body** Oberkörper *m*; **the ~ reaches of the Thames** der Oberlauf der Themse; **the ~ Loire** die obere Loire; **Upper Rhine** Oberrhein *m*

b *(in importance, rank)* höhere(r, s), obere(r, s); **the ~ ranks of the Civil Service** das gehobene Beamtentum; **in the ~ income bracket** in der oberen Einkommensklasse; **the ~ middle**

class(es) die gehobene Mittelschicht → **hand 1 j**

N a **uppers** PL (*of shoe*) Obermaterial *nt*; **to be on one's ~s** (*= destitute*) auf den Hund gekommen sein
b (*inf: = drug*) Aufputschmittel *nt*, Muntermacher *m* (*inf*)
c (*US Rail*) oberes Bett (*im Schlafwagen*)

upper: **upper brain** N (*Anat*) Großhirn *nt*; **upper case** N (*Typ: also* **upper-case letter**) Großbuchstabe *m*, Versal *m* (*spec*); **to set sth in ~** etw in Versalien setzen; **upper-case** ADJ groß; **an ~ T** ein großes T, ein Versal-T (*spec*); **upper circle** N (*Brit Theat*) zweiter Rang; **upper class** N obere Klasse, Oberschicht *f*; **the ~es** die Oberschicht; **upper-class** ADJ *accent, district, person* vornehm, fein; *sport, expression, attitude* der Oberschicht; **to be ~** (*person*) zur Oberschicht gehören; **upperclassman** N (*US*) *Mitglied einer High School oder eines College*; **upper crust** N (*inf*) obere zehntausend *pl* (*inf*); **upper-crust** ADJ (*inf*) (schrecklich) vornehm (*inf*); **uppercut** N Aufwärtshaken *m*, Uppercut *m*; **Upper Egypt** N Oberägypten *nt*; **upper hand** N **to gain** *or* **get the ~** die Oberhand gewinnen (*of, over* über *+acc*), Oberwasser bekommen; **Upper House** N (*Parl*) Oberhaus *nt*

uppermost [ˈʌpəˈməʊst] ADJ oberste(r, s); (*fig*) *ambition* größte(r, s), höchste(r, s); **safety should be ~ in your minds** Sicherheit sollte für Sie an erster Stelle stehen; **it's quite obvious what is ~ in your mind** es ist ziemlich klar, wo deine Prioritäten liegen ADV **face/the blue side ~** mit dem Gesicht/der blauen Seite nach oben

upper: **upper school** N Oberschule *f*; **upper sixth** N (*Brit Sch*) ≈ Oberprima *f*; **Upper Volta** [ˌʌpəˈvɒltə] N (*Hist*) Obervolta *nt* → **Burkina Faso**

uppish [ˈʌpɪʃ] ADJ = **uppity**

uppity [ˈʌpɪtɪ] ADJ (*inf: = arrogant*) hochnäsig (*inf*), hochmütig; *woman also* schnippisch; **to get ~ with sb** jdm gegenüber frech *or* anmaßend werden, jdm frech kommen

upraised [ʌpˈreɪzd] ADJ erhoben

upright [ˈʌpraɪt] ADJ a (*= erect*) aufrecht; (*= vertical*) *post* senkrecht; **~ chair** Stuhl *m*; **~ vacuum cleaner** Bürst(staub)sauger *m*; **~ freezer** Gefrierschrank *m* b (*fig: = honest*) *person, character* aufrecht, rechtschaffen ADV (*= erect*) aufrecht, gerade; (*vertical*) senkrecht; **to hold oneself ~** sich gerade halten; **to pull sb/oneself ~** jdn/sich aufrichten N a (*= post*) Pfosten *m* b (*= piano*) Klavier *nt*

uprightly [ˈʌpˌraɪtlɪ] ADV aufrecht, rechtschaffen

uprightness [ˈʌpˌraɪtnɪs] N Rechtschaffenheit *f*

upright piano N Klavier *nt*

uprising [ˈʌpraɪzɪŋ] N Aufstand *m*, Erhebung *f*

upriver [ˈʌpˈrɪvəˈ] ADV flussaufwärts; **2 miles ~ from Fen Ditton** 2 Meilen flussaufwärts von Fen Ditton ADJ *place* flussaufwärts gelegen; **an ~ journey** eine Reise flussaufwärts

uproar [ˈʌprɔːˈ] N Aufruhr *m*, Tumult *m*; **he tried to make himself heard above the ~** er versuchte, sich über den Lärm hinweg verständlich zu machen; **at this there was ~, this caused an ~** das verursachte einen (wahren) Aufruhr *or* Tumult; **the whole room/town was in ~** der ganze Saal/die ganze Stadt war in Aufruhr

uproarious [ʌpˈrɔːrɪəs] ADJ *meeting* tumultartig; *crowd* lärmend; *laughter* brüllend; *success, welcome* überwältigend, spektakulär; *personality* überschäumend; (*= very funny*) *joke* wahnsinnig komisch, zum Schreien *pred*; **in ~ spirits** in überschäumender Stimmung

uproariously [ʌpˈrɔːrɪəslɪ] ADV lärmend; *laugh* brüllend; **~ funny** wahnsinnig komisch, zum Schreien *or* Brüllen

uproot [ʌpˈruːt] VT *plant* entwurzeln; (*fig: = eradicate*) *evil* ausmerzen; **~ed by the war** durch den Krieg entwurzelt; **he ~ed his whole family (from their home) and moved to New York** er riss seine Familie aus ihrer gewohnten Umgebung und zog nach New York

UPS *abbr of* **uninterruptible power supply** USV

upsadaisy [ˈʌpsəˌdeɪzɪ] INTERJ (*inf*) hoppla

upscale [ˈʌpskeɪl] ADJ (*US*) anspruchsvoll; *goods, products* hochwertig; *restaurant, hotel* der gehobenen Preisklasse

upset [ʌpˈset] *vb: pret, ptp* **upset** VT a (*= knock over*) umstoßen, umwerfen; *boat* umkippen, zum Kentern bringen; **she ~ the milk all over the new carpet** sie stieß die Milch um und alles lief auf den neuen Teppich
b (*= make sad: news, death*) bestürzen, erschüttern, mitnehmen (*inf*); (*question, insolence etc*) aus der Fassung bringen; (*divorce, experience, accident etc*) mitnehmen (*inf*); (*= distress, excite*) *patient, parent etc* aufregen; (*= offend: unkind behaviour, words etc*) verletzen, wehtun (*+dat*); (*= annoy*) ärgern; **you shouldn't have said/done that, now you've ~ her** das hätten Sie nicht sagen/tun sollen, jetzt regt sie sich auf *or* (*offended*) jetzt ist sie beleidigt; **don't ~ yourself** regen Sie sich nicht auf; **there's no point in ~ting yourself** es hat doch keinen Zweck, das so tragisch zu nehmen; **I don't know what's ~ him** ich weiß nicht, was er hat
c (*= disorganize*) *calculations, balance, plan, timetable etc* durcheinanderbringen; **that's ~ my theory** das hat meine Theorie umgestoßen; **to ~ the odds** die Chancen verändern; **Henman ~ the top seed** Henman hat den auf Nummer eins gesetzten Spieler überraschend geschlagen
d (*= make ill*) **the rich food ~ his stomach** das schwere Essen ist ihm nicht bekommen; **onions ~ me** von Zwiebeln bekomme ich Magenbeschwerden
VI umkippen
ADJ a (*about divorce, accident, dismissal etc*) mitgenommen (*inf*) (*about* von); (*about death, bad news etc*) bestürzt (*about* über *+acc*); (*= sad*) betrübt, geknickt (*inf*) (*about* über *+acc*); (*= distressed, worried*) aufgeregt (*about* wegen); *baby, child* durcheinander *pred*; (*= annoyed*) ärgerlich, aufgebracht (*about* über *+acc*); (*= hurt*) gekränkt, verletzt (*about* über *+acc*); **she was pretty ~ about it** das ist ihr ziemlich nahegegangen, das hat sie ziemlich mitgenommen (*inf*); (*= distressed, worried*) sie hat sich deswegen ziemlich aufgeregt; (*= annoyed*) das hat sie ziemlich geärgert; (*= hurt*) das hat sie ziemlich gekränkt *or* verletzt; **she was ~ about something** irgendetwas hatte sie aus der Fassung gebracht; **she was ~ about the news/that he'd left her** es hat sie ziemlich mitgenommen, als sie das hörte/dass er sie verlassen hat (*inf*); **she was ~ about him leaving** sein Abschied war ihr sehr nahegegangen; **we were very ~ to hear about her illness** wir waren sehr bestürzt, als wir von ihrer Krankheit hörten; **don't look so ~, they'll come back** guck doch nicht so traurig, sie kommen ja zurück; **would you be ~ if I decided not to go after all?** wärst du traurig *or* würdest dus tragisch nehmen, wenn ich doch nicht ginge?; **I'd be very ~ if ...** ich wäre sehr traurig *or* betrübt wenn ...; **she'd be ~ if I used a word like that** sie wäre entsetzt, wenn ich so etwas sagen würde; **the house has been broken into so of course I'm ~** bei mir ist eingebrochen worden und natürlich rege ich mich auf; **to get ~** sich aufregen (*about* über *+acc*); (*= hurt*) gekränkt *or* verletzt werden; **don't get ~ about it, you'll find another** nimm das noch nicht so tragisch, du findest bestimmt einen anderen; **to feel ~** gekränkt sein; **to sound/look ~** verstört klingen/aussehen
b [ˈʌpset] *stomach* verstimmt, verdorben *attr*; **to have an ~ stomach** sich (*dat*) den Magen verdorben haben, eine Magenverstimmung haben
N [ˈʌpset] a (*= disturbance*) Störung *f*; (*emotional*) Aufregung *f*; (*inf: = quarrel*) Verstimmung *f*, Ärger *m*; (*= unexpected defeat etc*) unliebsame *or* böse Überraschung; **I don't want to cause any ~s in your work** ich möchte bei Ihrer Arbeit kein Durcheinander verursachen; **children don't like ~s in their routine** Kinder mögen es nicht, wenn man ihre Routine durcheinanderbringt; **it was an ~ to our plans** es hat unsere Pläne durcheinandergebracht; **it was an ~ for us** es war eine böse Überraschung für uns; **he's had a bit of an ~** er ist etwas mitgenommen (*inf*) *or* geknickt (*inf*)
b **stomach ~** Magenverstimmung *f*, verdorbener Magen

upset price N (*esp US Comm*) Mindestpreis *m*

upsetting [ʌpˈsetɪŋ] ADJ (*= saddening*) traurig; (*stronger*) bestürzend; (*= disturbing*) *changes* störend; *situation* unangenehm, schwierig; (*= offending*) beleidigend, verletzend; (*= annoying*) ärgerlich; **that must have been very ~ for you** das war bestimmt nicht einfach für Sie; (*= annoying*) das muss sehr ärgerlich für Sie gewesen sein; **it is ~ (for them) to see such terrible things** es ist schlimm (für sie), so schreckliche Dinge zu sehen; **she found this experience most ~** diese Erfahrung hat sie sehr mitgenommen (*inf*), diese Erfahrung ist ihr sehr nahegegangen; **the divorce/the change was very ~ for the child** das Kind hat unter der Scheidung/dem Wechsel sehr gelitten; **he mustn't have any more ~ experiences** es darf nichts mehr passieren, was ihn aufregt; **it's ~ to my routine** das bringt meine Routine durcheinander

upshot [ˈʌpʃɒt] N (*= result*) Ergebnis *nt*; **the ~ of it all was that ...** es lief darauf hinaus, dass ...; **what was the ~ of your meeting?** was kam bei Ihrem Treffen heraus?; **in the ~** letzten Endes

upside down [ˈʌpsaɪdˈdaʊn] ADV verkehrt herum; **the monkey was hanging ~** der Affe hing verkehrt herum *or* mit dem Kopf nach unten; **to turn sth ~** (*lit*) etw umdrehen; (*fig*) etw auf den Kopf stellen (*inf*); **when my daughter was born my world turned ~** als meine Tochter geboren wurde, wurde mein Leben auf den Kopf gestellt

upside-down [ˈʌpsaɪdˈdaʊn] ADJ a **in an ~ position** verkehrt herum; **to be ~** (*picture*) verkehrt herum hängen, auf dem Kopf stehen; (*world*) kopfstehen; **an ~ map of Britain** eine auf dem Kopf stehende Karte Großbritanniens; **a pineapple ~ cake** ein versunkener Ananaskuchen b (*fig, = bizarre*) **the weather is completely ~** das Wetter spielt völlig verrückt (*inf*)

upstage [ʌpˈsteɪdʒ] ADV (*Theat*) im Hintergrund der Bühne; (*with movement*) in den Bühnenhintergrund; **~ centre/left/right** im mittleren/linken/rechten Bühnenhintergrund; (*with movement*) in den mittleren/linken/rechten Bühnenhintergrund ADJ (*fig*) blasiert, hochnäsig (*with* gegenüber) VT **to ~ sb** (*Theat*) jdn zwingen, dem Publikum den Rücken zuzukehren; (*fig*) jdn ausstechen, jdm die Schau stehlen (*inf*)

upstairs [ʌpˈstɛəz] ADV oben; (*with movement*) nach oben; **the people/apartment ~** die Leute/die Wohnung über uns; **to kick sb ~** (*fig*) jdn wegloben; **may I go ~?** (*euph*) kann ich mal aufs Örtchen?; **he hasn't got much ~** (*inf*) er ist ein bisschen schwach im Oberstübchen (*inf*) ADJ *window* im oberen Stock(werk); *room also* obere(r, s) N oberes Stockwerk

upstanding [ʌpˈstændɪŋ] ADJ a (*= strong*) kräftig; (*= honourable*) rechtschaffen b (*form*) **to be ~** stehen; **gentlemen, please be ~ for the toast** (meine Herren,) bitte erheben Sie sich zum Toast; **the court will be ~** bitte erheben Sie sich

upstart [ˈʌpstɑːt] N Emporkömmling *m* ADJ *behaviour* eines Emporkömmlings; *rival, company* emporgekommen

upstate [ˈʌpsteɪt] (*US*) ADJ im Norden (des Bundesstaates); **to live in ~ New York** im Norden des Staates New York wohnen ADV im Norden (des Bundesstaates); (*with movement*) in den Norden (des Bundesstaates)

upstream [ˈʌpstriːm] ADV flussaufwärts; **3 kms ~ from Henley** 3 km flussaufwärts von Henley ADJ *place* flussaufwärts gelegen

upstretched [ʌpˈstretʃt] ADJ *arms* ausgestreckt; *neck* gereckt

upstroke [ˈʌpstrəʊk] N (*of pen*) Aufstrich *m*; (*of piston*) aufgehender Hub, Aufwärtsgang *m*

upsurge ['ʌpsɜːdʒ] N Zunahme *f*; *(of fighting)* Eskalation *f (pej)*; **she felt an ~ of hatred** sie fühlte Hass in sich *(dat)* aufwallen

upswept [ʌp'swept] ADJ *hair* hoch- *or* zurückgebürstet

upswing ['ʌpswɪŋ] N *(lit, fig)* Aufschwung *m*; *(Sport)* Ausholen *nt no pl*

upsy-daisy ['ʌpsə,deɪzɪ] INTERJ = **upsadaisy**

uptake ['ʌpteɪk] N **a** *(inf)* **to be quick on the ~** schnell verstehen; **to be slow on the ~** schwer von Begriff sein *(inf)*, eine lange Leitung haben *(inf)* **b** *(= intake)* Aufnahme *f*

up-tempo ['ʌptempəʊ] ADJ schnell

upthrust ['ʌpθrʌst] N *(= upward movement)* Aufwärtsdruck *m*; *(Geol)* Hebung *f*

uptight ['ʌp'taɪt] ADJ *(inf: = nervous)* nervös; *(= inhibited)* verklemmt *(inf)*; *(= angry)* sauer *(inf)*; *voice* gepresst; *expression* verkrampft, verkniffen; **to get ~ (about sth)** sich (wegen etw) aufregen; (auf etw *acc*) verklemmt reagieren *(inf)*; (wegen etw) sauer werden *(inf)*; **he's pretty ~ about these things** der sieht so was ziemlich eng *(inf)*; **no need to get ~ about it!** nun krieg dich mal wieder ein *(inf)*; **she's so ~ about sex** sie ist so verklemmt was Sex angeht

uptime ['ʌptaɪm] N *(of machine)* Betriebszeit *f*

up-to-date ['ʌptə'deɪt] ADJ *attr*, **up to date** ADJ *pred* auf dem neusten Stand; *fashion also, book, news, information* aktuell; *person, method, technique also* up to date *pred (inf)*; **to keep ~ with the fashions/news** mit der Mode/den Nachrichten auf dem Laufenden bleiben; **to keep sb/sth/oneself up to date** jdn/etw/sich auf dem Laufenden halten; **would you bring me up to date on developments?** würden Sie mich über den neusten Stand der Dinge informieren?; **to be ~ with one's payments** mit seinen Zahlungen auf dem Laufenden sein; **to bring sth ~** *(= modernize)* etw auf den neuesten Stand bringen

up-to-the-minute ['ʌptəðə'mɪnɪt] ADJ *news, reports* allerneuste(r, s), allerletzte(r, s); *style also* hochmodern; **her clothes are ~** ihre Kleider sind immer der allerletzte Schrei

uptown ['ʌptaʊn] *(US)* ADJ *(= in Northern part of town)* im Norden (der Stadt); *(= in residential area)* im Villenviertel; *person* anspruchsvoll; *bar, club, theatre, store* vornehm; **~ New York** der Norden von New York ADV im Norden der Stadt; im Villenviertel; *(with movement)* in den Norden der Stadt; ins Villenviertel N Villenviertel *nt*

uptrend ['ʌptrend] N *(Econ)* Aufwärtstrend *m*; **to be in** *or* **on an ~** eine steigende Tendenz zeigen

upturn [ʌp'tɜːn] VT umdrehen N ['ʌptɜːn] *(fig: = improvement)* Aufschwung *m*

upturned [ʌp'tɜːnd] ADJ *boat, bucket, table, box etc* umgedreht; *face* nach oben gewandt; *eyes* nach oben gerichtet; *collar* aufgeschlagen; **~ nose** Stupsnase *f*, Himmelfahrtsnase *f (inf)*

UPVC *abbr of* **unplasticized polyvinyl chloride** UPVC *nt*

upward ['ʌpwəd] ADJ Aufwärts-, nach oben; *glance* nach oben; **~ compatibility** Aufwärtskompatibilität *f*; **~ compatible** aufwärtskompatibel; **~ movement** Aufwärtsbewegung *f*; **~ slope** Steigung *f*; **~ (social) mobility** *(Sociol)* soziale Aufstiegsmöglichkeiten *pl* ADV *(esp US)* = **upwards**

upwardly ['ʌpwədlɪ] ADV aufwärts, nach oben

upwardly mobile ADJ **to be ~** ein Aufsteiger/eine Aufsteigerin sein

upwards ['ʌpwədz] ADV *(esp Brit)* **a** *move* aufwärts, nach oben; **to look ~** hochsehen, nach oben sehen; **face ~** mit dem Gesicht nach oben; **from the waist ~** von der Hüfte aufwärts; **onwards and ~** vorwärts und aufwärts **b** *(with numbers)* **prices from £4 ~** Preise von £ 4 an, Preise ab £ 4; **to be revised ~** *(figures)* nach oben korrigiert werden; **from childhood ~** von Kind auf *or* an, von Kindheit an; **and ~** und darüber; **~ of 3000** über 3000

upwind ['ʌpwɪnd] ADJ, ADV im Aufwind; **to be/stand ~ of sb** gegen den Wind zu jdm sein/stehen; **to sail ~** gegen den Wind segeln

Ural ['jʊːrəl] N **the ~** *(= river)* der Ural; **the ~ Mountains, the ~s** das Uralgebirge, der Ural

uranium [jʊə'reɪnɪəm] N Uran *nt*

Uranus [jʊə'reɪnəs] N *(Astron)* Uranus *m*

urban ['ɜːbən] ADJ städtisch; *life also* in der Stadt; **~ decay** Verfall *m* der Städte; **~ motorway** Stadtautobahn *f*; **~ America** das städtische Amerika; **~ clearway** Stadtautobahn *f*

urban: **urban centre**, *(US)* **urban center** N *(= town)* Ballungsgebiet *nt*; *(= town centre)* Stadtzentrum *nt*; **urban development** N Stadtentwicklung *f*; **urban dweller** N Stadtbewohner(in) *m(f)*

urbane [ɜː'beɪn] ADJ *person, manner* weltmännisch, gewandt, urban *(geh)*; *(= civil)* höflich; *manner, words* verbindlich

urbanely [ɜː'beɪnlɪ] ADV *say, smile* weltmännisch, gewandt

urban guerilla N Stadtguerilla *m*

urbanity [ɜː'bænɪtɪ] N *(of person, manner)* weltmännische Art, Gewandtheit *f*, Urbanität *f (geh)*; *(= civility)* Höflichkeit *f*; *(of manner, words)* Verbindlichkeit *f*

urbanization [,ɜːbənaɪ'zeɪʃən] N Urbanisierung *f*, Verstädterung *f (pej)*

urbanize ['ɜːbənaɪz] VT urbanisieren, verstädtern *(pej)*

urban: **urban planning** N Stadtplanung *f*; **urban renewal** N Stadterneuerung *f*; **urban warfare** N Stadtkampf *m*

urchin ['ɜːtʃɪn] N Gassenkind *nt*; *(mischievous)* Range *f*

Urdu ['ʊəduː] N Urdu *nt*

urea ['jʊərɪə] N Harnstoff *m*, Urea *f (spec)*

ureter [jʊə'riːtə'] N Harnleiter *m*, Ureter *m (spec)*

urethra [jʊə'riːθrə] N Harnröhre *f*, Urethra *f (spec)*

urge [ɜːdʒ] N *(= need)* Verlangen *nt*, Bedürfnis *nt*; *(= drive)* Drang *m no pl*; *(physical, sexual)* Trieb *m*; **to feel the ~ to do sth** das Bedürfnis verspüren, etw zu tun; **I resisted the ~ (to contradict him)** ich habe mich beherrscht (und ihm nicht widersprochen); **an ~ to steal it came over me** der Drang, es zu stehlen, überkam mich; **creative ~s** Schaffensdrang *m*, Kreativität *f*; **come and stay with us if you get the ~** *(inf)* komm uns besuchen, wenn du Lust hast

VT **a** *(= try to persuade) sb* eindringlich bitten; **to ~ sb to do sth** *(= plead with)* jdn eindringlich bitten, etw zu tun; *(= earnestly recommend)* darauf dringen, dass jd etw tut; **to ~ sb to accept/join in/come along** jdn drängen, anzunehmen/mitzumachen/mitzukommen; **he needed no urging** er ließ sich nicht lange bitten; **do it now! he ~d** tun Sies jetzt!, drängte er

b **to ~ sb onward/back** jdn vorwärtstreiben *or* weitertreiben/zurücktreiben

c *(= advocate) measure etc, acceptance* drängen auf *(+acc)*; **to ~ that sth should be done** darauf drängen, dass etw getan wird; **to ~ sth (up)on sb** jdm etw eindringlich nahelegen; **to ~ caution/restraint** zur Vorsicht/Zurückhaltung mahnen

d *(= press) claim* betonen; *argument* vorbringen, anführen

▶ **urge on** VT *sep (lit) horse, person, troops* antreiben, vorwärtstreiben; *(fig) team, workers* antreiben *(to* zu*)*; *team* anfeuern; **to urge sb on to do sth** jdn (dazu) antreiben, etw zu tun

urgency ['ɜːdʒənsɪ] N Dringlichkeit *f*; *(of tone of voice, pleas also)* Eindringlichkeit *f*; **it's a matter of ~** das ist dringend; **to treat sth as a matter of ~** etw als dringend behandeln; **there's no ~** es eilt nicht, das hat keine Eile; **there was a note of ~ in his voice** es klang sehr dringend; **the ~ of our needs** die dringende Notwendigkeit; **his statement lacked ~** seinen Worten fehlte der Nachdruck; **the ~ of his step** seine eiligen Schritte; **the sense of ~ in the music** das Drängen in der Musik

urgent ['ɜːdʒənt] ADJ **a** dringend; **is it ~?** *(= important)* ist es dringend?; *(= needing speed)* eilt es?; **to be in ~ need of medical attention** dringend ärztliche Hilfe benötigen; **~ letter** Eilbrief *m*; **the letter was marked "urgent"** der Brief trug einen Dringlichkeitsvermerk **b** *(= insistent) tone, plea* dringend, dringlich; *(= hurrying) steps* eilig; **he was very ~ about the need for swift action** er betonte nachdrücklich, wie notwendig schnelles Handeln sei

urgently ['ɜːdʒəntlɪ] ADV *required* dringend; *requested also* dringlich; *talk* eindringlich; **he is ~ in need of help** er braucht dringend Hilfe

uric ['jʊərɪk] ADJ Harn-, Urin-

uric acid N Harnsäure *f*

urinal ['jʊərɪnl] N *(= room)* Pissoir *nt*; *(= vessel)* Urinal *nt*; *(for patient)* Urinflasche *f*

urinary ['jʊərɪnərɪ] ADJ Harn-, Urin-; *infection* der Harnorgane

urinary tract N Harntrakt *m*

urinate ['jʊərɪneɪt] VI Wasser lassen, urinieren *(geh)*, harnen *(spec)*

urine ['jʊərɪn] N Urin *m*, Harn *m*

urine sample, **urine specimen** N *(Med)* Urinprobe *f*

URL *(Comput) abbr of* **uniform resource locator** URL-Adresse *f*

urn [ɜːn] N **a** Urne *f* **b** *(also* **tea urn, coffee urn)** Kessel *m*

urogenital [,jʊərəʊ'dʒenɪtl] ADJ urogenital

urological [,jʊərəʊ'lɒdʒɪkl] ADJ urologisch

urologist [jʊə'rɒlədʒɪst] N Urologe *m*, Urologin *f*

urology [jʊə'rɒlədʒɪ] N Urologie *f*

Ursa Major ['ɜːsə'meɪdʒə'] N Großer Bär *or* Wagen

Ursa Minor ['ɜːsə'maɪnə'] N Kleiner Bär *or* Wagen

Uruguay ['jʊərəgwaɪ] N Uruguay *nt*

Uruguayan [,jʊərə'gwaɪən] N *(= person)* Uruguayer(in) *m(f)* ADJ uruguayisch

US *abbr of* **United States** USA *pl*

us [ʌs] PERS PRON **a** *(dir and indir obj)* uns; **give it (to) us** gib es uns; **who, us?** wer, wir?; **younger than us** jünger als wir; **it's us** wir sinds; **he is one of us** er gehört zu uns, er ist einer von uns; **this table shows us the tides** auf dieser Tafel sieht man die Gezeiten; **us and them** wir und die **b** *(inf: = me, dir obj)* mich; *(indir obj)* mir; *(pl subj)* wir; **give us a look** lass mal sehen; **us English** wir Engländer; **as for us English** was uns Engländer betrifft

USA **a** *abbr of* **United States of America** USA *pl* **b** *abbr of* **United States Army**

usability [,juːzə'bɪlɪtɪ] N Verwendbarkeit *f*; *(of ideas, suggestions)* Brauchbarkeit *f*

usable ['juːzəbl] ADJ verwendbar; *suggestion, ideas* brauchbar; **to be no longer ~** nicht mehr zu gebrauchen sein; **in ~ condition** in brauchbarem Zustand; **to be ~ for sth** für etw verwendbar *or* brauchbar sein; **is this evidence ~ in court?** kann diese Aussage vor Gericht verwendet werden?

USAF *abbr of* **United States Air Force**

usage ['juːzɪdʒ] N **a** *(= treatment, handling)* Behandlung *f*; **it's had some rough ~** es ist ziemlich unsanft behandelt worden **b** *(= custom, practice)* Brauch *m*, Sitte *f*, Usus *m (geh)*; **it's common ~** es ist allgemein üblich *or* Sitte *or* Brauch **c** *(Ling: = use, way of using)* Gebrauch *m no pl*, Anwendung *f*; **words in common ~** allgemein gebräuchliche Wörter *pl*; **it's common in Northern ~** es ist im Norden allgemein gebräuchlich; **it's not correct ~** so darf das nicht gebraucht werden; **~ notes** *(in book)* Anwendungshinweise *pl*

USB *(Comput) abbr of* **universal serial bus**

USB flash drive N *(Comput)* USB-Stick *m*

USCG *(US) abbr of* **United States Coast Guard**

use¹ [juːz] VT **a** (= *utilize*) benutzen; *dictionary, means, tools, object, materials* verwenden, benutzen; *sb's suggestion, idea* verwenden; *word, literary style* gebrauchen, verwenden, benutzen; *swear words* gebrauchen, benutzen; *brains, intelligence* gebrauchen; *method, system, technique, therapy, force, trickery* anwenden; *one's abilities, powers of persuasion, one's strength* aufwenden, anwenden; *tact, care* walten lassen; *drugs* einnehmen; **~ only in emergencies** nur im Notfall gebrauchen *or* benutzen; **I have to ~ the toilet before I go** ich muss noch einmal zur Toilette, bevor ich gehe; **what's this ~d for?** wofür wird das benutzt *or* gebraucht?; **to ~ sth for sth** etw zu etw verwenden; **he ~d it as a spoon** er hat es als Löffel benutzt *or* verwendet; **the police ~d truncheons** die Polizei setzte Schlagstöcke ein, die Polizei benutzte *or* gebrauchte Schlagstöcke; **what did you ~ the money for?** wofür haben Sie das Geld benutzt *or* verwendet *or* gebraucht?; **the money is to be ~d to set up a trust** das Geld soll dazu verwendet werden, eine Stiftung einzurichten; **what toothpaste do you ~?** welche Zahnpasta benutzen *or* verwenden Sie?; **what sort of fuel do you ~?** welchen Treibstoff verwenden Sie?, mit welchem Treibstoff fahren Sie?; **what sort of fuel does this rocket ~?** welcher Treibstoff wird für diese Rakete verwendet?; **ointment to be ~d sparingly** Salbe nur sparsam verwenden *or* anwenden; **why don't you ~ a hammer?** warum nehmen Sie nicht einen Hammer dazu?, warum benutzen *or* verwenden Sie nicht einen Hammer dazu?; **to ~ sb's name** jds Namen verwenden *or* benutzen; *(as reference)* jds Namen angeben, sich auf jdn berufen; **~ your imagination!** zeig mal ein bisschen Fantasie *or* Phantasie!; **we can ~ the extra staff to do this** dafür können wir das übrige Personal einsetzen *or* verwenden; **I'll have to ~ some of your men** ich brauche ein paar Ihrer Leute
b (= *make use of, exploit*) *information, one's training, talents, resources, chances, opportunity* (aus)nutzen, (aus)nützen *(S Ger)*; *advantage* nutzen; *waste products* nutzen, verwerten; **not ~d to capacity** nicht voll genutzt; **you can ~ the leftovers to make a soup** Sie können die Reste zu einer Suppe verwerten; **you should ~ your free time for something creative** Sie sollten Ihre Freizeit für etwas Schöpferisches nutzen *or* gebrauchen
c *(inf)* **I could ~ a new pair of shoes** ich könnte ein neues Paar Schuhe (ge)brauchen; **I could ~ a drink** ich könnte etwas zu trinken (ge)brauchen *or* vertragen *(inf)*; **it could ~ a coat of paint** das könnte ein bisschen Farbe vertragen
d (= *use up, consume*) verbrauchen; **this car ~s too much petrol** dieses Auto verbraucht zu viel Benzin; **have you ~d all the ink?** haben Sie die Tinte aufgebraucht *(inf) or* die ganze Tinte verbraucht?
e *(obs, liter,* = *treat)* behandeln; **she was ill ~d** ihr ist übel mitgespielt worden; **how has the world been using you?** *(not obs, liter)* wie gehts, wie stehts?
f *(pej:* = *exploit)* ausnutzen; **I feel (I've just been) ~d** ich habe das Gefühl, man hat mich ausgenutzt; *(sexually)* ich komme mir missbraucht vor
N [juːs] **a** (= *employment*) Verwendung *f*; *(of materials, tools, means, dictionary)* Benutzung *f*, Verwendung *f*; (= *operation: of machines etc*) Benutzung *f*; (= *working with: of dictionary, calculator etc*) Gebrauch *m*; *(of word, style)* Gebrauch *m*, Verwendung *f*; *(of swearwords, arms, intelligence)* Gebrauch *m*; *(of method, system, technique, force, powers of persuasion)* Anwendung *f*; *(of personnel, truncheons etc)* Verwendung *f*, Einsatz *m*; *(of drugs)* Einnahme *f*; **once you've mastered the ~ of the clutch** wenn Sie erst einmal den Gebrauch der Kupplung beherrschen; **the ~ of a calculator to solve …** die Verwendung eines Rechners, um … zu lösen; **directions for ~** Gebrauchsanweisung *f*; **for the ~ of** für; **for ~ in case of emergency** für Notfälle; **for external ~** äußerlich anzuwenden, zur äußerlichen Anwendung; **it's for ~ not ornament** es ist ein Gebrauchsgegenstand und nicht zur Zierde; **ready for ~** gebrauchsfertig; *machine* einsatzbereit; **to improve with ~** sich mit der Zeit bessern; **worn with ~** abgenutzt; **to make ~ of sth** von etw Gebrauch machen, etw benutzen; **can you make ~ of that?** können Sie das brauchen?; **in ~/out of ~** in *or* im/außer Gebrauch; *machines also* in/außer Betrieb; **to be in daily ~/no longer in ~** täglich/nicht mehr benutzt *or* verwendet *or* gebraucht werden; **to come into ~** in Gebrauch kommen; **to go** *or* **fall out of ~** nicht mehr benutzt *or* verwendet *or* gebraucht werden
b (= *exploitation, making use of*) Nutzung *f*; *(of waste products, leftovers etc)* Verwertung *f*; **to make ~ of sth** etw nutzen; **to put sth to ~** etw benutzen; **to put sth to good ~** etw gut nutzen; **to make good/bad ~ of sth** etw gut/schlecht nutzen
c (= *way of using*) Verwendung *f*; **to learn the ~ of sth** lernen, wie etw verwendet *or* benutzt *or* gebraucht wird; **it has many ~s** es ist vielseitig verwendbar; **to find a ~ for sth** für etw Verwendung finden; **to have no ~ for** *(lit, fig)* nicht gebrauchen können, keine Verwendung haben für; **to have no further ~ for sb/sth** keine Verwendung mehr haben für jdn/etw, jdn/etw nicht mehr brauchen
d (= *usefulness*) Nutzen *m*; **to be of ~ to sb** für jdn von Nutzen sein *or* nützlich sein; **this is no ~ any more** das taugt nichts mehr, das ist zu nichts mehr zu gebrauchen; **does it have a ~ in our society?** ist es für unsere Gesellschaft von Nutzen?; **is this (of) any ~ to you?** können Sie das brauchen?, können Sie damit was anfangen?; **he/it has his/its ~s** er/das ist ganz nützlich; **you're no ~ to me if you can't spell** du nützt mir nichts, wenn du keine Rechtschreibung kannst; **he's no ~ as a goalkeeper** er taugt nicht als Torhüter, er ist als Torhüter nicht zu gebrauchen; **can I be of any ~?** kann ich irgendwie behilflich sein?; **a (fat) lot of ~ that will be to you!** *(iro inf)* da hast du aber was davon *(inf)*; **this is no ~, we must start work** so hat das keinen Zweck *or* Sinn, wir müssen etwas tun; **it's no ~ you** *or* **your protesting** es hat keinen Sinn *or* es nützt nichts, wenn du protestierst; **what's the ~ of telling him?** was nützt es, wenn man es ihm sagt?; **what's the ~ in trying/going?** wozu überhaupt versuchen/gehen?; **it's no ~** es hat keinen Zweck; **ah, what's the ~!** ach, was solls!
e (= *right*) Nutznießung *f (Jur)*; **to have the ~ of the gardens** die Gartenanlagen benutzen können; **to have the ~ of a car** ein Auto zur Verfügung haben; **to give sb the ~ of sth** jdn etw benutzen lassen; *of car also, of money* jdm etw zur Verfügung stellen; **to have lost the ~ of one's arm** seinen Arm nicht mehr gebrauchen *or* benutzen können; **to have the full ~ of one's faculties** im Vollbesitz seiner (geistigen und körperlichen) Kräfte sein; **have you lost the ~ of your legs?** *(hum)* hast du das Gehen verlernt?
f (= *custom*) Brauch *m*, Usus *m (geh)*
g *(Eccl)* Brauch *m*; **in the Roman ~** nach römisch-katholischem Brauch

▸ **use up** VT *sep food, objects, one's strength* verbrauchen; (= *finish also*) aufbrauchen; *scraps, leftovers etc* verwerten; **the butter is all used up** die Butter ist alle *(inf) or* aufgebraucht; **all his energy was used up** all seine Energie war verbraucht

use² [juːs] VB AUX **I didn't ~ to …** *etc* → **used²**

use-by date [ˈjuːzbaɪˌdeɪt] N (Mindest)haltbarkeitsdatum *nt*

used¹ [juːzd] ADJ (= *second-hand*) *clothes, car etc* gebraucht; (= *soiled*) *towel etc* benutzt; *stamp* gestempelt; *(Comput) memory space* belegt; **a ~-car salesman** ein Gebrauchtwagenhändler *m*; **would you buy a ~ car from this man?** *(fig hum)* würden Sie diesem Mann nicht über den Weg trauen?

used² [juːst] VB AUX *(only in past)* **I ~ to swim every day** ich bin früher täglich geschwommen, ich pflegte täglich zu schwimmen *(geh)*; **I ~ not to smoke, I didn't use to smoke** ich habe früher nicht geraucht, ich pflegte nicht zu rauchen *(geh)*; **what ~ he to do** *or* **what did he use to do on Sundays?** was hat er früher *or* sonst sonntags getan?; **he ~ to play golf, didn't he?** er hat doch früher Golf gespielt, nicht wahr?; **I didn't know you smoked – I ~ not to** ich habe nicht gewusst, dass Sie rauchen – habe ich früher auch nicht; **I don't now but I ~ to** früher schon, jetzt nicht mehr!; **he ~ to be a well-known singer** er war einmal ein bekannter Sänger; **there ~ to be a field here** hier war (früher) einmal ein Feld; **things aren't what they ~ to be** es ist alles nicht mehr (so) wie früher; **life is more hectic than it ~ to be** das Leben ist hektischer als früher

used³ [juːst] ADJ **to be ~ to sb** an jdn gewöhnt sein; **to be ~ to sth** an etw *(acc)* gewöhnt sein, etw gewohnt sein; **to be ~ to doing sth** daran gewöhnt sein *or* es gewohnt sein, etw zu tun; **to be ~ to sb** *or* **sb's doing sth** daran gewöhnt sein, dass jd etw tut; **I'm not ~ to it** ich bin das nicht gewohnt; **to get ~ to sb/sth** sich an jdn/etw gewöhnen; **to get ~ to doing sth** sich daran gewöhnen, etw zu tun; **she needed to get ~ to him** *or* **his being there** sie musste sich erst an seine Anwesenheit gewöhnen; **you might as well get ~ to it!** *(inf)* daran wirst du dich gewöhnen müssen!

useful [ˈjuːsfʊl] ADJ **a** nützlich; *person, citizen, contribution, addition* wertvoll, nützlich; (= *handy*) *tool, language* praktisch, nützlich; *size* zweckmäßig; *discussion* fruchtbar; *life, employment* nutzbringend; **it is ~ for him to be able to …** das ist günstig *or* praktisch, dass er … kann; **to make oneself ~** sich nützlich machen; **he likes to feel ~** er hat gern das Gefühl, nützlich zu sein; **he wants to be ~ to others** er möchte anderen nützen; **thank you, you've been very ~** vielen Dank, Sie haben mir/uns *etc* sehr geholfen; **is that ~ information?** nützt diese Information etwas?; **to come in ~** sich als nützlich erweisen; **we spent a ~ week in London** wir waren eine Woche in London, was sehr nützlich war; **that's ~!** *(iro)* das nützt uns was!; **he's a ~ man to know** es ist sehr nützlich ihn zu kennen; **that advice was most ~ to me** der Rat hat mir sehr genützt; **that's a ~ thing to know** es ist gut das zu wissen; **it has a ~ life of 10 years** es hat eine Nutzungsdauer von 10 Jahren; **the machine has reached the end of its ~ life** die Maschine hat das Ende ihrer Nutzungsdauer erreicht; **these drugs are ~ in treating cancer** diese Medikamente sind bei der Krebsbehandlung nützlich; **you may find it ~ to discuss the problem with your doctor** es könnte hilfreich sein, wenn Sie das Problem mit Ihrem Arzt besprechen würden; **to perform a ~ function** eine sinnvolle Funktion haben; **to prove ~** sich als nützlich erweisen; **they ought to be doing something ~ with their time** sie sollten etwas Sinnvolles mit ihrer Zeit anfangen
b *(inf)* (= *capable*) *player* brauchbar, fähig; (= *creditable*) *score* wertvoll; **to be ~ with one's hands** geschickt mit den Händen sein; **he's quite ~ with a gun/his fists** er kann ziemlich gut mit der Pistole/seinen Fäusten umgehen

usefully [ˈjuːsfəlɪ] ADV *employed, spend time* nutzbringend; **you could ~ come along** es wäre von Nutzen, wenn Sie kämen; **is there anything I can ~ do?** kann ich mich irgendwie nützlich machen?; **this book can ~ be given to first-year students** dieses Buch ist für Erstsemester nützlich

usefulness [ˈjuːsfʊlnɪs] N Nützlichkeit *f*; *(of person, contribution also)* Wert *m (of discussion)* Fruchtbarkeit *f* → **outlive**

useless [ˈjuːslɪs] ADJ **a** nutzlos; (= *unusable*) unbrauchbar; *advice, suggestion* nutzlos, unnütz; *person* nutzlos, zu nichts nütze; *teacher, manager, player* untauglich, unbrauchbar; *school* untauglich; *remedy* unwirksam, wirkungslos; **to render sth ~** etw unbrauchbar machen; **to be ~ to sb** für jdn nutzlos *or* ohne Nutzen sein; **to**

prove ~ sich als nutzlos erweisen; *(machine, object)* sich als unbrauchbar erweisen; **to be worse than ~** völlig nutzlos sein; **it is ~ (for you) to complain** es hat keinen Sinn, sich zu beschweren; **shouting is ~** Schreien nützt nichts; **it's ~ without a handle** ohne Griff nützt es nichts *or* ist es unbrauchbar; **he's full of ~ information** er steckt voller nutzloser Informationen; **he's ~ as a goalkeeper** er ist als Torwart nicht zu gebrauchen, er taugt nichts als Torwart; **you're just ~!** du bist auch zu nichts zu gebrauchen; **to be ~ at doing sth** unfähig dazu sein, etw zu tun; **I'm ~ at languages** Sprachen kann ich überhaupt nicht; **to feel ~** sich unnütz fühlen
b *(= pointless)* zwecklos, sinnlos

uselessly [ˈjuːslɪslɪ] ADV nutzlos

uselessness [ˈjuːslɪsnɪs] N **a** *(= worthlessness)* Nutzlosigkeit *f*; *(of sth unusable)* Unbrauchbarkeit *f*; *(of person)* Nutzlosigkeit *f*; *(of teacher, manager, player)* Unbrauchbarkeit *f*; *(of school)* Untauglichkeit *f*; *(of remedy)* Unwirksamkeit *f* **b** *(= pointlessness)* Zwecklosigkeit *f*, Sinnlosigkeit *f*

user [ˈjuːzəʳ] N Benutzer(in) *m(f)*; *(of machines also)* Anwender(in) *m(f)*; *(of Internet, software etc)* User(in) *m(f)*; **he's a ~ of heroin** *or* **a heroin ~** er nimmt Heroin; **my last boyfriend was just a ~** *(pej)* mein letzter Freund hat mich nur benutzt

user: **user-definable** ADJ *(Comput) keys* frei definierbar; **user-defined** ADJ *(Comput) keys* benutzerdefiniert, frei definiert; **user file** N *(Comput)* Benutzerdatei *f*; **user-friendliness** N Benutzer- *or* Anwenderfreundlichkeit *f*; **user-friendly** ADJ benutzer- *or* anwenderfreundlich; **user-generated** ADJ *(Comput, Internet) content* von den Benutzern eingebracht; **user group** N Nutzergruppe *f*; *(Comput)* Anwendergruppe *f*; **user ID**, **user identification** N *(Comput)* Benutzerkennung *f*; **user interface** N *(esp Comput)* Benutzerschnittstelle *f*, Benutzeroberfläche *f*; **user language** N *(Comput)* Benutzersprache *f*; **user name** N *(Comput)* Benutzername *m*; **user password** N *(Comput)* Benutzerkennwort *nt*; **user profile** N *(also Comput, Internet)* Benutzerprofil *nt*; **user software** N *(Comput)* Anwendersoftware *f*; **user support** N *(esp Comput)* Benutzerunterstützung *f*

U-shaped [ˈjuːʃeɪpt] ADJ U-förmig

usher [ˈʌʃəʳ] **N** *(Theat, at wedding etc)* Platzanweiser(in) *m(f)*; *(Jur)* Gerichtsdiener(in) *m(f)* **VT to ~ sb into a room/to his seat** jdn in ein Zimmer/zu seinem Sitz bringen *or* geleiten *(geh)*; **the drunk was discreetly ~ed out (of the hall)** der Betrunkene wurde unauffällig (aus dem Saal) hinauskomplimentiert

► **usher in** VT *sep people* hineinführen *or* -bringen *or* -geleiten *(geh)*; **to usher in a new era** ein neues Zeitalter einleiten

usherette [ˌʌʃəˈret] N Platzanweiserin *f*

USIA *(US) abbr of* **United States Information Agency** *US-Informationsdienst, der Informationen über die amerikanische Nation, Kultur und Politik in anderen Ländern verbreitet*

USM **a** *(US) abbr of* **United States Mail** *of* **United States Mint** **b** *abbr of* **unlisted securities market**

USMC *(US) abbr of* **United States Marine Corps**

USN *abbr of* **United States Navy**

USNG *abbr of* **United States National Guard**

USNR *abbr of* **United States Naval Reserve**

USO *(US) abbr of* **United Service Organization** *Hilfsorganisation für die amerikanische Armee, besonders für im Ausland stationierte Truppen*

USP *abbr of* **unique selling proposition** (einzigartiges) verkaufsförderndes Merkmal

USS *abbr* **a** *of* **United States Ship** **b** *of* **United States Senate**

USSR *abbr of* **Union of Soviet Socialist Republics** UdSSR *f*

usual [ˈjuːʒʊəl] **ADJ** *(= customary)* üblich; *(= normal)* gewöhnlich, normal, üblich; **beer is his ~ drink** er trinkt gewöhnlich *or* normalerweise Bier; **when shall I come? – oh, the ~ time** wann soll ich kommen? – oh, wie üblich *or* oh, zur üblichen Zeit; **as is ~ on these occasions** wie (es) bei derartigen Gelegenheiten üblich (ist); **as is ~ with second-hand cars** wie gewöhnlich bei Gebrauchtwagen; **it's the ~ thing nowadays** das ist heute so üblich; **small families are the ~ thing nowadays** kleine Familien sind heutzutage die Norm; **the journey took four hours instead of** *or* **rather than the ~ two** die Reise dauerte vier Stunden statt der üblichen zwei; **the ~ stuff** *(inf)* das Übliche; **with his ~ tact** *(iro)* taktvoll wie immer, mit dem ihm eigenen Takt; **it is ~ for soldiers to wear a uniform** es ist üblich *or* normal für Soldaten, eine Uniform zu tragen; **it wasn't ~ for him to arrive early** es war nicht normal *or* typisch für ihn, zu früh da zu sein; **it's ~ to ask first** normalerweise fragt man erst; **to do sth in the** *or* **one's ~ way** *or* **manner** etw auf die einem übliche Art und Weise tun; **as ~, as per ~** *(inf)* wie üblich, wie gewöhnlich; **business as ~** normaler Betrieb; *(in shop)* Verkauf geht weiter; **to carry on as ~** weitermachen wie immer *or* wie üblich; **later/less/more than ~** später/weniger/mehr als sonst; **it's hardly ~** es ist eigentlich nicht üblich
N *(inf)* der/die/das Übliche; **the ~ please!** *(= drink)* dasselbe wie immer, bitte!; **a pint of the ~** eine Halbe, wie immer; **what's his ~?** *(= drink)* was trinkt er gewöhnlich?; **what sort of mood was he in? – the ~** wie war er gelaunt? – wie üblich

usually [ˈjuːʒʊəlɪ] ADV gewöhnlich, normalerweise; **more than ~ careful/drunk** noch vorsichtiger/betrunkener als sonst; **do you drive to work/work overtime? – ~** fahren Sie mit dem Auto zur Arbeit/machen Sie Überstunden? – normalerweise *or* meistens; **is he ~ so rude?** ist er sonst auch so unhöflich?; **he's not ~ late** er kommt sonst *or* normalerweise nicht zu spät; **he's ~ early, but …** er kommt sonst *or* meist *or* normalerweise früh, aber …

usufruct [ˈjuːzjʊfrʌkt] N *(Jur)* Nutznießung *f*

usufructuary [ˌjuːzjʊˈfrʌktjʊərɪ] N *(Jur)* Nutznießer(in) *m(f)*

usurer [ˈjuːʒərəʳ] N Wucherer *m*, Wucherin *f*

usurious [juːˈzjʊərɪəs] ADJ wucherisch; *person* Wucher treibend *attr*; **~ price** Wucherpreis *m*

usurp [juːˈzɜːp] VT sich *(dat)* widerrechtlich aneignen, usurpieren *(geh)*; *power, title, inheritance also* an sich *(acc)* reißen; *throne* sich bemächtigen *(+gen)* *(geh)*; *role* sich *(dat)* anmaßen; *person* verdrängen; **he ~ed his father** er hat seinen Vater verdrängt; **she has ~ed his wife's place** sie hat seine Frau von ihrem Platz verdrängt

usurpation [ˌjuːzɜːˈpeɪʃən] N Usurpation *f* *(geh)*; *(of power also)* widerrechtliche Übernahme; *(of title, inheritance)* widerrechtliche Aneignung; **~ of the throne** Thronraub *m*, Usurpation *f* des Thrones *(geh)*

usurper [juːˈzɜːpəʳ] N unrechtmäßiger Machthaber, unrechtmäßige Machthaberin, Usurpator(in) *m(f)* *(geh)*; *(fig)* Eindringling *m*; **the ~ of the throne** der Thronräuber; **the ~ of his father's throne** der unrechtmäßige Nachfolger seines Vaters auf dem Thron

usury [ˈjuːʒʊrɪ] N Wucher *m*; **to practise** *(Brit)* *or* **practice** *(US)* **~** Wucher treiben; **32% interest is ~** 32% Zinsen sind *or* ist Wucher

UTC *abbr of* **universal time coordinated** UTC *f*, Weltzeit *f*

ute [juːt] N *(Austral Mot)* Kleintransporter *m*, kleiner Lieferwagen

utensil [juːˈtensl] N Gerät *nt*, Utensil *nt*

uterine [ˈjuːtəraɪn] ADJ *(Anat)* uterin; **~ brother** Halbbruder *m* mütterlicherseits

uterus [ˈjuːtərəs] N Gebärmutter *f*, Uterus *m* *(spec)*

utilitarian [ˌjuːtɪlɪˈteərɪən] **ADJ** auf Nützlichkeit ausgerichtet; *qualities* nützlich, praktisch; *(= functional) object* zweckmäßig, praktisch; *building, room* zweckmäßig; *(Philos)* utilitaristisch **N** *(Philos)* Utilitarist(in) *m(f)*, Utilitarier(in) *m(f)*

utilitarianism [ˌjuːtɪlɪˈteərɪənɪzəm] N *(Philos)* Utilitarismus *m*

utility [juːˈtɪlɪtɪ] **N** **a** *(= usefulness)* Nützlichkeit *f*, Nutzen *m* **b** **public ~** *(= company)* Versorgungsbetrieb *m*; *(= service)* Leistung *f* der Versorgungsbetriebe; **the utilities** versorgungswirtschaftliche Einrichtungen *pl* **c** *(Comput)* Utility *nt*, Hilfs- *or* Dienstprogramm *nt* **d** *(Austral: = utility vehicle)* Kleintransporter *m* **ATTR** **~ industry** Versorgungsindustrie *f*; **~ goods** Gebrauchsgüter *pl*; **~ furniture** *im 2. Weltkrieg in Großbritannien hergestellte Möbel, die einfach, aber zweckmäßig waren*

utility: **utility box** N *(for nails, screws etc)* Kleinteilemagazin *nt*; **utility company** N Versorgungsbetrieb *m*; **utility man** N *(US)* Mädchen *nt* für alles *(inf)*; **utility player** N *(Sport)* Spieler, der/ Spielerin, die auf mehreren Positionen spielen kann; **utility program** N *(Comput)* Hilfsprogramm *nt*, Dienstprogramm *nt*; **utility room** N Allzweckraum *m*; **utility software** N *(Comput)* Hilfssoftware *f*, Utility-Software *f*; **utility vehicle** N Kleintransporter *nt*, kleiner Lieferwagen

utilization [ˌjuːtɪlaɪˈzeɪʃən] N Verwendung *f*; *(of situation, time)* Ausnutzung *f*; *(of opportunity, talent)* Nutzung *f*; *(of materials, resources)* Verwertung *f*

utilize [ˈjuːtɪlaɪz] VT verwenden; *situation, time* (be)nutzen; *(= take advantage of) opportunity, talent* nutzen; *(= make sth new) wastepaper, old wool etc* verwerten

utmost [ˈʌtməʊst] **ADJ** **a** *(= greatest) ease, danger* größte(r, s), höchste(r, s); *caution, candour* äußerste(r, s), größte(r, s); **they used their ~ skill** sie taten ihr Äußerstes; **with the ~ speed/care** so schnell/sorgfältig wie nur möglich; **matters of the ~ importance** Angelegenheiten *pl* von äußerster Wichtigkeit; **it is of the ~ importance that …** es ist äußerst wichtig, dass …; **I have the ~ respect for him** ich habe den allergrößten Respekt vor ihm; **a matter of (the) ~ urgency** ein Fall von äußerster Dringlichkeit; **with the ~ reluctance** mit allergrößtem Widerwillen
b *(= furthest)* äußerste(r, s)
N to do/try one's ~ (to do sth) sein Möglichstes *or* Bestes tun/versuchen(, um etw zu tun); **we have done our ~ to help him** wir haben unser Bestmöglichstes *or* Äußerstes getan, um ihm zu helfen; **that is the ~ I can do** mehr kann ich wirklich nicht tun; **to the ~ of one's ability** so gut man nur kann; **he tried my patience to the ~** er strapazierte meine Geduld aufs äußerste *or* Äußerste; **he trusts them to the ~** er vertraut ihnen voll und ganz; **one should enjoy life/oneself to the ~** man sollte das Leben in vollen Zügen genießen/sich amüsieren, so gut man nur kann; **I can give you £50 at the ~** ich kann Ihnen allerhöchstens £ 50 geben

Utopia [juːˈtəʊpɪə] N Utopia *nt*

Utopian [juːˈtəʊpɪən] **ADJ** utopisch, utopistisch *(pej)* **N** Utopist(in) *m(f)*

Utopianism [juːˈtəʊpɪənɪzəm] N Utopismus *m*

utricle [ˈjuːtrɪkl] N *(Bot)* Fangbläschen *nt*, Schlauch *m*, Utrikel *m (spec)*; *(Anat)* Utriculus *m (spec)*

utter[1] [ˈʌtəʳ] ADJ total, vollkommen; *rogue, drunkard* unverbesserlich; *disgust, misery* grenzenlos; *disbelief* total; *despair* total, absolut; **a complete and ~ waste of time** eine totale Zeitverschwendung; **with ~ certainty/conviction** mit absoluter Sicherheit/Überzeugung; **an ~ stranger** ein Wildfremder *m*, eine Wildfremde; **what ~ nonsense!** so ein totaler Blödsinn! *(inf)*

utter[2] VT **a** *(= say)* von sich *(dat)* geben; *word* sagen; *word of complaint* äußern; *cry, sigh, threat* ausstoßen; *libel* verbreiten **b** *(form) forged money* in Umlauf bringen; *cheque* ausstellen

utterance [ˈʌtərəns] **N** **a** *(= sth said)* Äußerung *f*; **the child's first ~s** die ersten Worte des Kindes; **his last ~** seine letzten Worte; **his recent ~s in the press** seine jüngsten Presseäußerungen **b** *(= act of speaking)* Sprechen *nt*; **upon her dying father's ~ of her name** als ihr sterbender Vater ihren Namen nannte; **to give ~ to a feeling** einem Gefühl Ausdruck geben *or* verleihen *(geh)*, ein Gefühl zum Ausdruck bringen

utterly [ˈʌtəlɪ] **ADV** total, völlig; *depraved also, despise* zutiefst; **~ beautiful** ausgesprochen schön; **he's ~ under her thumb** sie hat ihn vollkommen *or* ganz und gar unterm Pantoffel *(inf)*

uttermost [ˈʌtəməʊst] **N, ADJ** = **utmost**

U-turn [ˈjuːtɜːn] **N** *(lit, fig)* Wende *f*; **no ~s** Wenden verboten!; **to do a ~** *(fig)* seine Meinung völlig ändern; **the government has done a ~ over pensions** die Rentenpolitik der Regierung hat sich um 180 Grad gedreht

UVF *abbr of* **Ulster Volunteer Force**

uvula [ˈjuːvjələ] **N** Zäpfchen *nt*, Uvula *f (spec)*

uvular [ˈjuːvjələʳ] **ADJ** uvular; **the ~ R** das Zäpfchen-R **N** Zäpfchenlaut *m*, Uvular *m*

uxorious [ʌkˈsɔːrɪəs] **ADJ** *husband* treu ergeben

uxoriousness [ʌkˈsɔːrɪəsnɪs] **N** Ergebenheit *f* seiner Frau gegenüber

Uzbek [ˈʊzbek] **ADJ** usbekisch; **he is ~** er ist Usbeke **N** **a** Usbeke *m*, Usbekin *f* **b** *(Ling)* Usbekisch *nt*

Uzbekistan [ˌʌzbekɪˈstɑːn] **N** Usbekistan *nt*

V, v [viː] N V *nt,* v *nt*

V, v *abbr of* **versus**; *abbr of* **vide** v

VA *(US) abbr of* **Veterans Administration**

Va *abbr of* **Virginia**

vac [væk] N *(Univ inf)* Semesterferien *pl*

vacancy [ˈveɪkənsɪ] N **a** *(= emptiness)* Leere *f; (of look)* Ausdruckslosigkeit *f,* Leere *f; (of post)* Unbesetztsein *nt,* Freisein *nt*
b *(in boarding house)* (freies) Zimmer; **have you any vacancies for August?** haben Sie im August noch Zimmer frei?; **"no vacancies"** „belegt"; **"vacancies"** „Zimmer frei"
c *(= job)* offene *or* freie Stelle; *(at university)* Vakanz *f,* unbesetzte Stelle; **we have a ~ in our personnel department** in unserer Personalabteilung ist eine Stelle zu vergeben; **we have a ~ for an editor** wir suchen einen Redakteur/eine Redakteurin; **to fill a ~** eine Stelle besetzen; **we are looking for somebody to fill a ~ in our personnel department** wir suchen einen Mitarbeiter für unsere Personalabteilung; **vacancies** Stellenangebote *pl,* offene Stellen *pl*

vacant [ˈveɪkənt] ADJ **a** *post* frei, offen; *(Univ)* unbesetzt, vakant; *WC, seat, hotel room, parking space* frei; *house, room* unbewohnt, leer stehend; *land* unbebaut; *table* frei, unbesetzt; *hospital bed* leer (stehend); **the house has been ~ for two months** das Haus steht seit zwei Monaten leer; **~ lot** unbebautes Grundstück; **with ~ possession** *(Jur)* bezugsfertig; **to become** *or* **fall ~** frei werden **b** *(= empty) days* unausgefüllt, lang; **the ~ future stretched before him** die Zukunft lag leer vor ihm **c** *mind, stare* leer

vacantly [ˈveɪkəntlɪ] ADV *(= stupidly)* blöde; *(= dreamily)* abwesend; **he gazed ~ at me** er sah mich mit leerem Blick an

vacate [vəˈkeɪt] VT *seat* frei machen; *post, throne* aufgeben; *presidency etc* niederlegen; *house, room, premises* räumen; **this post is going to be ~d** diese Stelle wird frei

vacation [vəˈkeɪʃən] N **a** *(Univ)* Semesterferien *pl; (Jur)* Gerichtsferien *pl* → **long vacation**
b *(US)* Ferien *pl,* Urlaub *m;* **on ~** im *or* auf Urlaub; **to take a ~** Urlaub machen; **where are you going for your ~?** wohin fahren Sie in Urlaub?, wo machen Sie Urlaub?; **to go on ~** auf Urlaub *or* in die Ferien gehen; **~ trip** (Ferien)reise *f* **c** *(of post)* Aufgabe *f; (of presidency etc)* Niederlegung *f; (of house)* Räumung *f* VI *(US)* Urlaub *or* Ferien machen

vacation course N *(US)* Ferienkurs *m*

vacationer [veɪˈkeɪʃənəˈ], **vacationist** [veɪˈkeɪʃənɪst] N *(US)* Urlauber(in) *m(f)*

vaccinate [ˈvæksɪneɪt] VT impfen

vaccination [ˌvæksɪˈneɪʃən] N (Schutz)impfung *f;* **have you had your ~ yet?** sind Sie schon geimpft?, haben Sie sich schon impfen lassen?

vaccine [ˈvæksiːn] N Impfstoff *m,* Vakzine *f (spec)*

vaccinee [ˌvæksɪˈniː] N *(US)* Impfling *m*

vacillate [ˈvæsɪleɪt] VI *(lit, fig)* schwanken; **she ~d for a long time about accepting** sie schwankte lange, ob sie annehmen sollte oder nicht

vacillating [ˈvæsɪleɪtɪŋ] ADJ *(fig)* schwankend, unschlüssig, unentschlossen

vacillation [ˌvæsɪˈleɪʃən] N Schwanken *nt; (fig also)* Unentschlossenheit *f,* Unschlüssigkeit *f*

vacua [ˈvækjʊə] *pl of* **vacuum**

vacuity [væˈkjuːɪtɪ] N *(liter: = lack of intelligence)* Geistlosigkeit *f; (= emptiness)* Leere *f;* **vacuities** *(= inane remarks)* Plattheiten *pl,* Plattitüden *pl*

vacuous [ˈvækjʊəs] ADJ *eyes, face, stare* ausdruckslos, leer; *film, play, book, remarks* nichtssagend

vacuum [ˈvækjʊəm] N *pl* **-s** *or* **vacua** *(form)* N **a** *(Phys, fig)* (luft)leerer Raum, Vakuum *nt;* **cultural ~** kulturelles Vakuum; **this left a ~ in my life** das hinterließ eine Lücke in meinem Leben **b** *(= vacuum cleaner)* Staubsauger *m* VT *carpet, living room* (staub)saugen

vacuum: vacuum bottle N *(US)* = **vacuum flask**; **vacuum brake** N Unterdruckbremse *f;* **vacuum cleaner** N Staubsauger *m;* **vacuum flask** N *(Brit)* Thermosflasche *f;* **vacuum pack** N Vakuumpackung *f;* **vacuum-packed** ADJ vakuumverpackt; **vacuum pump** N Vakuum- *or* Aussaugepumpe *f;* **vacuum-sealed** ADJ vakuumdicht, vakuumversiegelt; **vacuum tube** N Vakuumröhre *f*

vade mecum [ˈvɑːdɪˈmeɪkʊm] N *(liter)* Vademekum *nt (liter)*

vagabond [ˈvægəbɒnd] N Vagabund *m,* Landstreicher(in) *m(f)* ADJ vagabundenhaft; *person* vagabundierend, umherziehend; *thoughts* (ab)schweifend; **~ life** Vagabundenleben *nt*

vagary [ˈveɪgərɪ] N *usu pl* Laune *f; (= strange idea)* verrückter Einfall; **the vagaries of life** die Wechselfälle *pl* des Lebens

vagina [vəˈdʒaɪnə] N Scheide *f,* Vagina *f*

vaginal [vəˈdʒaɪnl] ADJ vaginal, Scheiden-; **~ intercourse** vaginaler Geschlechtsverkehr; **~ wall** Scheidenwand *f*

vaginismus [ˌvædʒɪˈnɪzməs] N *(Med)* Vaginismus *m*

vagrancy [ˈveɪgrənsɪ] N Land-/Stadtstreicherei *f (also Jur)*

vagrant [ˈveɪgrənt] N Landstreicher(in) *m(f); (in town)* Stadtstreicher(in) *m(f)* ADJ *person* umherziehend; *life* unstet, nomadenhaft

vague [veɪg] ADJ *(+er)* **a** *(= not clear) person, plan* vage, unbestimmt; *outline, shape* verschwommen; *photograph* unscharf, verschwommen; *report, question* vage, ungenau; *murmur* dumpf, undeutlich; **I haven't the ~st idea** ich habe nicht die leiseste Ahnung; **there's a ~ resemblance** es besteht eine entfernte Ähnlichkeit; **I had a ~ idea she would come** ich hatte so eine (dunkle) Ahnung, dass sie kommen würde; **I am still very ~ on this theory** die Theorie ist mir noch nicht sehr klar; **I am very ~ on Dutch politics** von holländischer Politik habe ich nicht viel Ahnung; **he was ~ about the time of his arrival** er äußerte sich nur vage *or* unbestimmt über seine Ankunftszeit; **a ~ sense of unease** ein leichtes Unbehagen
b *(= absent-minded)* geistesabwesend, zerstreut; **do you really understand, you look rather ~?** verstehst du das wirklich, du siehst so verwirrt aus?; **to have a ~ look in one's eyes** einen abwesenden *or (not having understood)* verständnislosen Gesichtsausdruck haben

vaguely [ˈveɪglɪ] ADV vage; *remember also* dunkel; *speak also* unbestimmt; *understand* ungefähr, in etwa; *(= uncertainly) look* flüchtig; *nod, wave* zögernd; *(= slightly) interested* flüchtig; *embarrassed, disappointed, surprised* leicht; **to look ~ at sb** jdn verständnislos ansehen; **to be ~ aware of sth** ein dunkles *or* vages Bewusstsein von etw haben; **to be ~ aware that ...** sich dunkel *or* vage bewusst sein, dass ...; **they're ~ similar** sie haben eine entfernte Ähnlichkeit; **it sounded ~ familiar** es kam einem irgendwie bekannt vor; **to be ~ reminiscent of sth** vage an etw erinnern; **it's only ~ like yours** es ist nur ungefähr wie deines; **it's ~ blue** es ist bläulich; **there's something ~ sinister about it** es hat so etwas Düsteres an sich; **a ~ worded agreement** eine vage formulierte Übereinkunft

vagueness [ˈveɪgnɪs] N **a** Unbestimmtheit *f,* Vagheit *f; (of outline, shape)* Verschwommenheit *f; (of report, question)* Vagheit *f,* Ungenauigkeit *f;* **the ~ of the resemblance** die entfernte Ähnlichkeit; **his ~ on Dutch politics** seine lückenhafte *or* wenig fundierte Kenntnis der holländischen Politik **b** *(= absent-mindedness)* Geistesabwesenheit *f,* Zerstreutheit *f;* **the ~ of her look** ihr abwesender *or (puzzled)* verwirrter Blick

vain [veɪn] ADJ **a** *(+er) (about looks)* eitel; *(about qualities)* eingebildet; **he's very ~ about his musical abilities** er bildet sich *(dat)* auf sein musikalisches Können viel ein; **he is ~ about his appearance** er ist eitel
b *(= useless, empty)* eitel *(liter); attempt also* vergeblich; *pleasures, promises, words also, threat* leer; *hope also* töricht; **he had ~ hopes of getting the job** er machte sich vergeblich Hoffnung auf den Posten; **in the ~ hope that ...** in der vergeblichen Hoffnung, dass ...; **in ~** umsonst, vergeblich, vergebens; **it was all in ~** das war alles umsonst *or* vergeblich *or* vergebens; **in a ~ attempt to do sth** in einem vergeblichen Versuch, etw zu tun
c to take God's name in ~ den Namen Gottes missbrauchen, Gott lästern; **was someone taking my name in ~?** *(hum)* hat da wieder jemand von mir geredet?
d *(liter, = worthless) display, ceremony* eitel *(liter)*

vainglorious [veɪnˈglɔːrɪəs] ADJ *(old) person* dünkelhaft; *talk* prahlerisch, ruhmredig *(old liter); spectacle* pompös

vainglory [veɪnˈglɔːrɪ] N *(old)* Prahlerei *f,* Selbstverherrlichung *f; (= characteristic)* Dünkel *m; (of appearance)* Pomp *m*

vainly [ˈveɪnlɪ] ADV **a** *(= to no effect)* vergeblich, vergebens **b** *(= conceitedly, about looks)* eitel; *(about qualities also)* eingebildet

valance [ˈvæləns] N *(round bed frame)* Volant *m; (on window)* Querbehang *m,* Schabracke *f; (wooden)* Blende *f; (US: = pelmet)* Zierleiste *f*

vale [veɪl] N *(liter)* Tal *nt;* **this ~ of tears** dies Jammertal

valediction [ˌvælɪˈdɪkʃən] N **a** *(form: = act)* Abschied *m; (= words)* Abschiedsworte *pl; (= speech)* Abschiedsrede *f* **b** *(US Sch)* Abschieds- *or* Entlassungsrede *f*

valedictorian [ˌvælɪdɪk'tɔːrɪən] N *(US Sch)* Abschiedsredner(in) *m(f) (bei der Schulentlassungsfeier)*

valedictory [ˌvælɪ'dɪktərɪ] ADJ *(form)* Abschieds-; ~ **speech** Abschiedsrede *f* N *(US Sch)* = **valediction b**

valence ['veɪləns], **valency** ['veɪlənsɪ] N *(Chem)* Wertigkeit *f*, Valenz *f*; *(Ling)* Valenz *f*

valentine ['væləntaɪn] N *(= person) Freund(in), dem/der man am Valentinstag einen Gruß schickt*; ~ **(card)** Valentinskarte *f*; **St Valentine's Day** Valentinstag *m*

valerian [və'lɪərɪən] N Baldrian *m*

valet ['væleɪ] N Kammerdiener *m*; ~ **service** Reinigungsdienst *m*

valet parking N Parkservice *m (für Hotelgäste etc)*

valetudinarian ['vælɪˌtjuːdɪ'nɛərɪən] *(form)* N kränkelnde Person; *(= health fiend)* Gesundheitsfanatiker(in) *m(f)* ADJ *(= sickly)* kränklich, kränkelnd; *person* sehr um seine Gesundheit besorgt; *habits, attitude* gesundheitsbewusst

Valhalla [væl'hælə] N Walhall *nt*, Walhalla *nt or f*

valiant ['væljənt] ADJ **a** *(liter) soldier, deed* tapfer, kühn *(geh)* **b** **he made a ~ effort to save her** er unternahm einen kühnen Versuch, sie zu retten; **she made a ~ effort to smile** sie versuchte tapfer zu lächeln; **never mind, it was a ~ attempt** machen Sie sich nichts draus, es war ein löblicher Versuch

valiantly ['væljəntlɪ] ADV **a** *(liter)* mutig, tapfer **b** **he ~ said he would help out** er sagte großzügig seine Hilfe zu

valid ['vælɪd] ADJ **a** *ticket, passport* gültig *(also Comput)*; *(Jur) document, marriage* (rechts)gültig; *contract* bindend, rechtsgültig; *claim* berechtigt, begründet; **no longer ~** *(ticket)* nicht mehr gültig; *passport also* abgelaufen **b** *argument, reasoning, interpretation* stichhaltig; *excuse, reason* triftig, einleuchtend; *objection* berechtigt, begründet; **this argument isn't ~** *(in itself)* dieses Argument ist nicht stichhaltig; *(= not relevant)* dieses Argument ist nicht zulässig *or* gilt nicht; **is it ~ to assume this?** ist es zulässig, das anzunehmen?; **that's a very ~ point** das ist ein sehr wertvoller Hinweis

validate ['vælɪdeɪt] VT *document (= check validity)* für gültig erklären; *(with stamp, signature)* (rechts)gültig machen; *claim* bestätigen; *theory* bestätigen, beweisen; *(Comput)* validieren, einer Gültigkeitsprüfung unterziehen; *password etc* bestätigen

validation [ˌvælɪ'deɪʃən] N *(of document)* Gültigkeitserklärung *f*; *(of claim)* Bestätigung *f*; *(of theory)* Beweis *m*, Nachweis *m*; *(Comput)* Validierung *f*, Gültigkeitsprüfung *f*; *(of password)* Bestätigung *f*

validity [və'lɪdɪtɪ] N **a** *(Jur etc: of document)* (Rechts)gültigkeit *f*; *(of ticket etc)* Gültigkeit *f*; *(of claim)* Berechtigung *f* **b** *(of argument)* Stichhaltigkeit *f*; *(of excuse etc)* Triftigkeit *f*; **the ~ of your objection** Ihr berechtigter *or* begründeter Einwand; **we discussed the ~ of merging these two cinematic styles** wir diskutierten, ob es zulässig ist, diese beiden Filmstile zu mischen

valise [və'liːz] N Reisetasche *f*

Valium® ['vælɪəm] N Valium® *nt*; **to be on ~** Valium® nehmen

Valkyrie ['vælkɪrɪ] N Walküre *f*

valley ['vælɪ] N Tal *nt*; *(big and flat)* Niederung *f*; **to go up/down the ~** talaufwärts/talabwärts gehen/fließen *etc*; **the Upper Rhine ~** die Oberrheinische Tiefebene

valor N *(US)* = **valour**

valorous ['vælərəs] ADJ *(liter)* heldenmütig *(liter)*, tapfer

valour, *(US)* **valor** ['vælə'] N *(liter)* Heldenmut *m (liter)*, Tapferkeit *f*

valuable ['væljʊəbl] ADJ **a** *jewel, possessions, resources* wertvoll; *time, oxygen* kostbar **b** *(= useful)* wertvoll; *help, advice* nützlich, wertvoll N

valuables PL Wertsachen *pl*, Wertgegenstände *pl*

valuation [ˌvæljʊ'eɪʃən] N *(= act)* Schätzung *f*; *(fig: of person's character)* Einschätzung *f*; *(= value decided upon)* Schätzwert *m*, Schätzung *f*; *(fig)* Beurteilung *f*; **what's your ~ of him?** wie schätzen Sie ihn ein?; **to have a ~ of a painting/house done** ein Gemälde/Haus schätzen lassen; **to make a correct ~ of sth** etw genau abschätzen; **we shouldn't take him at his own ~** wir sollten seine Selbsteinschätzung nicht einfach übernehmen

value ['væljuː] N **a** Wert *m*; *(= usefulness)* Nutzen *m*; **to be of ~** Wert/Nutzen haben, wertvoll/nützlich sein; **her education has been of no ~ to her** ihre Ausbildung hat ihr nichts genützt; **to put a ~ on sth** etw schätzen *or* bewerten; *on leisure etc* einer Sache *(dat)* (hohen) Wert beimessen; **what ~ do you put on this?** was für einen Wert hat das?; *(fig also)* wie bewerten Sie das?; **to put too high a ~ on sth** etw zu hoch schätzen *or* bewerten; *on leisure etc* etw überbewerten; **he places a high ~ on the education of his children** er misst der Ausbildung seiner Kinder großen Wert bei; **he attaches no ~/great ~ to it** er legt keinen Wert/großen Wert darauf, ihm liegt nicht viel/sehr viel daran; **of little ~** nicht sehr wertvoll/nützlich; **of no ~** wert-/nutzlos; **of great ~** sehr wertvoll **b** *(in money)* Wert *m*; **what's the ~ of your house?** wie viel ist Ihr Haus wert?; **what is its second-hand ~?** wie viel ist es gebraucht wert?; **to gain/lose (in) ~** im Wert steigen/fallen; **increase in ~** Wertzuwachs *m*; **loss of ~** Wertminderung *f*, Wertverlust *m*; **it's good ~** es ist preisgünstig; **in our restaurant you get ~ for money** in unserem Restaurant bekommen Sie etwas für Ihr Geld *(inf)*; **this TV was good ~** dieser Fernseher ist sein Geld wert; **lazy employees don't give you ~ for money** faule Angestellte sind ihr Geld nicht wert; **goods to the ~ of £500** Waren im Wert von £ 500; **they put a ~ of £200 on it** sie haben es auf £ 200 geschätzt; **propaganda/shock/novelty ~** Propaganda-/Schock-/Neuigkeitswert *m* **c** **values** PL *(= moral standards)* (sittliche) Werte *pl*, Wertwelt *f*; **he has no sense of ~s** er hat keine sittlichen Maßstäbe **d** *(Math)* (Zahlen)wert *m*; *(Mus)* (Zeit- *or* Noten)wert *m*, Dauer *f*; *(Phon)* (Laut)wert *m*; *(of colour)* Farbwert *m*; **what exactly is the ~ of this word in the poem?** welchen Ausdrucks- *or* Stellenwert hat dieses Wort innerhalb des Gedichtes?
VT **a** *house, jewels* schätzen; **the property was ~d at £100,000** das Grundstück wurde auf £ 100.000 geschätzt **b** *friendship, person* (wert)schätzen, (hoch) achten; *opinion, advice* schätzen; *comforts, liberty, independence* schätzen, Wert legen auf *(+acc)*; **I ~ it/her (highly)** ich weiß es/sie (sehr) zu schätzen; **if you ~ my opinion ...** wenn Sie Wert auf meine Meinung legen ...; **if you ~ your life, you'll stay away** bleiben Sie weg, wenn Ihnen Ihr Leben lieb ist

value-added tax [ˌvæljuː'ædɪdtæks] N *(Brit)* Mehrwertsteuer *f*

valued ['væljuːd] ADJ *friend* (hoch) geschätzt, lieb; *employee* (hoch) geschätzt; *contribution* geschätzt; **he is a ~ colleague** er ist als Kollege hoch geschätzt; **as a ~ customer** als (ein) geschätzter Kunde; **to be ~ for sth** für etw geschätzt werden

value: **value-creating activity** N *(Econ)* Wertschöpfung *f*; **value date** N *(esp Brit Fin)* Verbuchungsdatum *nt*; *(of a cheque)* Eingangsdatum *nt*; **value-free** ['væljuː'friː] ADJ wertfrei; **value judg(e)ment** N Werturteil *nt*; **valueless** ADJ wertlos; *(= useless also)* nutzlos, unnütz; *judgement* wertfrei

valuer ['væljʊə'] N *(Brit)* Schätzer(in) *m(f)*

value system N Wertsystem *nt*

valve [vælv] N *(Anat)* Klappe *f*; *(Tech, on musical instrument)* Ventil *nt*; *(in pipe system)* Absperrhahn *m*; *(Rad, TV)* Röhre *f*; **inlet/outlet ~** *(Aut)* Einlass-/Auslassventil *nt*

valvular ['vælvjʊlə'] ADJ *(= shaped like valve)* ventilartig; *(Med)* Herzklappen-; **~ inflammation** *(Med)* Herzklappenentzündung *f*

vamoose [və'muːs] VI *(US inf)* abhauen *(inf)*, abzischen *(inf)*

vamp¹ [væmp] N *(= woman)* Vamp *m* VT **she's been ~ing him all the time** sie hat die ganze Zeit ihre Reize bei ihm spielen lassen VI den Vamp spielen

vamp² N **a** *(of shoe: = upper)* Oberleder *nt* **b** *(Mus)* Improvisation *f* VT **a** *(= repair)* flicken **b** *(Mus) accompaniment* improvisieren, sich *(dat)* einfallen lassen VI *(Mus)* improvisieren, aus dem Stegreif spielen

▶ **vamp up** VT *sep* aufpolieren *(inf)*, aufmotzen *(inf)*

vampire ['væmpaɪə'] N *(lit, fig)* Vampir(in) *m(f)*, Blutsauger(in) *m(f)*

vampire bat N Vampir *m*, Blutsauger *m*

vampiric [væm'pɪrɪk] ADJ vampiristisch; *figure* vampirähnlich

vampirism ['væmpaɪərɪzəm] N Vampirismus *m*

van¹ [væn] N **a** *(Brit Aut)* Liefer- *or* Kastenwagen *m*, Transporter *m* **b** *(Brit Rail)* Wag(g)on *m*, Wagen *m* **c** *(inf: = caravan)* (Wohn)wagen *m*; **gipsy's ~** Zigeunerwagen *m (neg!)*

van² N *abbr of* **vanguard** *(lit, fig)* Vorhut *f*; *(fig also)* Spitze *f*, Führung *f*; **he was in the ~ of legal reform** er stand an der Spitze der Rechtsreformer

van³ N *abbr of* **advantage** *(Tennis inf)* Vorteil *m*

vanadium [və'neɪdɪəm] N Vanadin *nt*, Vanadium *nt*

vandal ['vændəl] N **a** *(fig)* Vandale *m*, Vandalin *f*; **it was damaged by ~s** es ist mutwillig beschädigt worden **b** **Vandal** *(Hist)* Vandale *m*, Vandalin *f*

vandalism ['vændəlɪzəm] N Vandalismus *m*, blinde Zerstörungswut; *(Jur)* mutwillige Beschädigung (fremden Eigentums); **destroyed by an act of ~** mutwillig zerstört; **these acts of ~** dieser Vandalismus, diese mutwilligen Beschädigungen

vandalize ['vændəlaɪz] VT *painting etc* mutwillig beschädigen; *building* verwüsten; *(= wreck)* demolieren

vane [veɪn] N *(also* **weather vane***)* Wetterfahne *f*, Wetterhahn *m*; *(of windmill)* Flügel *m*; *(of propeller)* Flügel *m*, Blatt *nt (of turbine)* (Leit)schaufel *f*

vanguard ['vængɑːd] N *(Mil, Naut)* Vorhut *f*; *(fig also)* Spitze *f*, Führung *f*; **in the ~ of reform** an der Spitze der Reformen

vanilla [və'nɪlə] N Vanille *f* ADJ Vanille-; **~ ice cream** Vanilleeis *nt*

vanilla essence N Vanilleextrakt *m*

vanish ['vænɪʃ] VI verschwinden, entschwinden *(liter)*; *(traces also)* sich verlieren; *(fears)* sich legen; *(hopes)* schwinden; *(= become extinct)* untergehen; **I've got to ~** *(inf)* ich muss weg *(inf)* → **thin d**

vanishing ['vænɪʃɪŋ]: **vanishing act** N = **vanishing trick**; **vanishing cream** N (Haut)pflegecreme *f*; **vanishing point** N *(Math)* Fluchtpunkt *m*; *(fig)* Nullpunkt *m*; **vanishing trick** N **to do a ~** *(magician)* etwas verschwinden lassen; **he did a ~ with the rabbit** er hat das Kaninchen weggezaubert; **every time he's needed he does a ~** *(inf)* jedes Mal, wenn man ihn braucht, verdrückt er sich *(inf)*

vanity ['vænɪtɪ] N **a** *(concerning looks)* Eitelkeit *f*; *(concerning own value)* Einbildung *f*, Eingebildetheit *f*; **~ made him think he was bound to succeed** er war so eingebildet *or* so von sich eingenommen, dass er einen Misserfolg für ausgeschlossen hielt **b** *(= worthlessness, of life, pleasures)* Nichtigkeit *f*, Hohlheit *f*; *(of words)* Hohlheit *f*; *(of efforts)* Vergeblichkeit *f*; **all is ~** alles ist vergebens **c** *(US: = dressing table)* Frisiertisch *m*

vanity: **vanity case** N Schmink- *or* Kosmetikkoffer *m*; **Vanity Fair** N Jahrmarkt *m* der Eitelkeiten; **vanity plates** PL *(US Aut)* *Nummernschild mit persönlicher Note*; **vanity press** N *(esp US)* Selbstkostenverlag *m*; **vanity publishing** N *Veröffentlichung, für die ein Autor selbst bezahlt, da es sonst nicht zur Veröffentlichung kommen würde*

> **VANITY PLATES**
>
> In Großbritannien und in den USA legen einige Kfz-Halter Wert darauf, dass die Nummernschilder ihres Wagens ihre Initialen tragen, die am besten zusätzlich noch ein Wort oder einen kurzen Satz ergeben sollten. Solche Schilder heißen **personalized number plates** (in Großbritannien) oder **vanity plates** (in den USA). Zuweilen werden erkleckliche Summen für solch ein Schild bezahlt. So könnte zum Beispiel jemand mit dem Namen James Allan Gordon sehr stolz auf folgendes Kennzeichen sein: „JAG 1".

vanquish ['væŋkwɪʃ] VT *(liter) enemy, fears* bezwingen *(geh)*

vantage ['vɑːntɪdʒ] N *(rare)* Vorteil *m*; *(Tennis)* Vorteil *m*

vantage: **vantage ground** N *(Mil)* günstige (Ausgangs)stellung; **vantage point** ['vɑːntɪdʒpɔɪnt] N *(Mil)* (günstiger) Aussichtspunkt; **our window is a good ~ for watching the procession** von unserem Fenster aus hat man einen guten Blick auf die Prozession; **from the ~ of the present** aus heutiger Sicht

vapid ['væpɪd] ADJ *(liter) conversation, remark* nichtssagend, geistlos; *person* geistlos; *book, song* nichtssagend; *smile (= insincere)* leer; *(= bored)* matt; *style* kraftlos; *beer, taste* schal

vapidity [væ'pɪdɪtɪ] N *(liter, of conversation, remark, person)* Geistlosigkeit *f*; *(of book, song)* Inhaltslosigkeit *f*; *(of smile) (= insincerity)* Ausdruckslosigkeit *f*; *(showing boredom)* Mattheit *f*; *(of style)* Kraftlosigkeit *f no pl*; *(of taste)* Schalheit *f*

vapor *etc (US)* = **vapour** *etc*

vaporization [ˌveɪpəraɪ'zeɪʃən] N *(by boiling etc)* Verdampfung *f*; *(natural)* Verdunstung *f*

vaporize ['veɪpəraɪz] VT *(by boiling etc)* verdampfen; *(naturally)* verdunsten lassen VI *(by boiling etc)* verdampfen; *(naturally)* verdunsten

vaporizer ['veɪpəraɪzə'] N Verdampfer *m*, Verdampfapparat *m*; *(Chem, for perfume)* Zerstäuber *m*; *(Med: for inhalation)* Inhalationsgerät *nt*

vaporous ['veɪpərəs] ADJ **a** *(= like vapour)* dampfförmig; *(= full of vapour)* dunstig; *(= of vapour)* Dunst-; **~ mists rising from the swamp** Dünste, die aus dem Sumpf aufsteigen; **~ gases round the planet** nebelartige Gase um den Planeten **b** *(liter. = fanciful)* nebulös, verblasen *(geh)*

vapour, *(US)* **vapor** ['veɪpə'] N Dunst *m*; *(Phys also)* Gas *nt*; *(steamy)* Dampf *m*; **the ~s** *(Med old)* Schwermut *f*; **thick ~s around the planet** eine dichte Dunsthülle um den Planeten

vapouring, *(US)* **vaporing** ['veɪpərɪŋ] N *(liter) (boastful)* Prahlerei *f*; *(empty)* Geschwafel *nt*

vapour trail, *(US)* **vapor trail** N Kondensstreifen *m*

variability [ˌvɛərɪə'bɪlɪtɪ] N *(Math)* Veränderlichkeit *f*; *(Biol)* Variabilität *f*; *(of weather, mood)* Unbeständigkeit *f*, Wechselhaftigkeit *f*; *(of costs)* Schwankung(en) *f(pl)*, Unbeständigkeit *f*; *(of work)* unterschiedliche Qualität

variable ['vɛərɪəbl] ADJ **a** *(= likely to vary) (Math)* veränderlich, variabel; *(Biol)* variabel; *weather, mood* unbeständig, wechselhaft; **infinitely ~** *(Tech)* stufenlos; **~ winds** wechselnde Winde *pl*; **his work is very ~** er arbeitet sehr unterschiedlich **b** *speed* regulierbar; *salary level* flexibel; **the height of the seat is ~** die Höhe des Sitzes kann reguliert werden N *(Chem, Math, Phys, Comput)* Variable *f*; *(fig also)* veränderliche Größe; **dependent/independent ~** *(Math)* abhängige/unabhängige Variable

variable cost N variable Kosten *pl*

variable rate N *(Fin)* variabler Zinssatz; **~ mortgage** Hypothek *f* mit variablem Zinssatz

variance ['vɛərɪəns] N **a** **to be at ~ with sb** anderer Meinung sein als jd *(about* hinsichtlich *+gen)*; **he is constantly at ~ with his parents** er hat ständig Meinungsverschiedenheiten mit seinen Eltern; **this is at ~ with what he said earlier** dies stimmt nicht mit dem überein, was er vorher gesagt hat **b** *(= difference)* Unterschied *m*; **a slight ~ of opinion** eine unterschiedliche Auffassung; **the predictable ~ between the two sets of figures** die vorhersehbare Abweichung der beiden Zahlenreihen (voneinander)

variant ['vɛərɪənt] N Variante *f*; **a spelling ~** eine Schreibvariante ADJ **a** *(= alternative)* andere(r, s); **there are two ~ spellings (of his name)** es gibt zwei verschiedene Schreibweisen *or* Schreibungen (für seinen Namen) **b** *(liter. = diverse)* verschieden, unterschiedlich

variation [ˌvɛərɪ'eɪʃən] N **a** *(= varying)* Veränderung *f*; *(Sci)* Variation *f*; *(Met)* Schwankung *f*, Wechsel *m*; *(of temperature)* Unterschiede *pl*, Schwankung(en) *f(pl)*; *(of prices)* Schwankung *f*; **an unexpected ~ in conditions** eine unerwartete Veränderung der Bedingungen; **there's been a lot of ~ in the prices recently** in letzter Zeit gab es viele Preisschwankungen; **these figures are subject to seasonal ~** diese Zahlen sind saisonbedingten Schwankungen unterworfen; **~ in opinions** unterschiedliche Ansichten *pl*; **he does it every day without ~** er macht es jeden Tag ohne Ausnahme **b** *(Mus)* Variation *f*; **~s on a theme** Thema mit Variationen, Variationen zu einem *or* über ein Thema **c** *(= different form)* Variation *f*, Variante *f*; *(Biol)* Variante *f*; **this is a ~ on that** das ist eine Variation *or* Abänderung dessen *or* davon; **a new ~ in the design** eine neue Variation des Musters; **regional ~s in pronunciation** regionale Aussprachevarianten *pl*; **several ~s on a basic idea** mehrere Variationsmöglichkeiten einer Grundidee

varicoloured, *(US)* **varicolored** ['værɪˈkʌləd] ADJ mehrfarbig

varicose veins [ˌværɪkəʊs'veɪnz] PL Krampfadern *pl*

varied ['vɛərɪd] ADJ unterschiedlich; *career, life* bewegt; *selection* reichhaltig; *interests* vielfältig; *diet, work* abwechslungsreich; **a ~ group of people** eine gemischte Gruppe; **a ~ collection of records** eine vielseitige *or* sehr gemischte Plattensammlung

variegated ['vɛərɪgeɪtɪd] ADJ buntscheckig; *(Bot)* geflammt, panaschiert

variegation [ˌvɛərɪ'geɪʃən] N Buntscheckigkeit *f*; *(Bot)* Panaschierung *f*

variety [və'raɪətɪ] N **a** *(= diversity)* Abwechslung *f*; **to add ~ to sth** Abwechslung in etw *(acc)* bringen; **a job with a lot of ~** eine sehr abwechslungsreiche Arbeit; **~ is the spice of life** *(prov)* öfter mal was Neues *(inf)* **b** *(= assortment)* Vielfalt *f*; *(Comm)* Auswahl *f* *(of* an *+dat)*; **that's quite a ~ for one company** das ist ein ziemlich breites Spektrum für eine (einzige) Firma; **I have seen him in a ~ of different moods** ich habe ihn in einer Vielzahl unterschiedlicher Stimmungen erlebt; **in a great ~ of ways** auf die verschiedensten Arten *pl*; **in a ~ of colours** *(Brit) or* **colors** *(US)* in den verschiedensten Farben *pl*; **for a ~ of reasons** aus verschiedenen *or* mehreren Gründen; **for a great ~ of reasons** aus vielen verschiedenen Gründen; **a wide ~ of birds** eine große Vielfalt an Vogelarten, viele verschiedene Vogelarten; **you meet a great ~ of people at this hotel** in diesem Hotel können Sie die verschiedensten Leute treffen **c** *(Biol, Bot: = species)* Art *f*, Varietät *f (spec)* **d** *(= type)* Art *f*; *(of cigarette, potato)* Sorte *f*; *(of chair)* Modell *nt*; **a new ~ of tulip/potato** eine neue Tulpen-/Kartoffelsorte **e** *(esp Brit Theat)* Varieté *nt*, Varietee *nt*

variety: **variety act** N Varieté- *or* Varieteenummer *f*; **variety artist** N Varieté- *or* Varieteekünstler(in) *m(f)*; **variety show** N *(Theat)* Varieté- *or* Varieteevorführung *f*; *(TV)* Fernsehshow *f*; *(Rad, TV)* Unterhaltungssendung *f*; **variety theatre**, *(US)* **variety theater** N Varieté- *or* Varieteetheater *nt*

varifocal [vɛərɪ'fəʊkl] ADJ Gleitsicht-; **~ lenses** Gleitsichtgläser *pl* **varifocals** PL Gleitsichtbrille *f*

variform ['vɛərɪfɔːm] ADJ vielgestaltig

variola [və'raɪələ] N *(Med)* Pocken *pl*

various ['vɛərɪəs] ADJ **a** *(= different)* verschieden; **his excuses are many and ~** seine Entschuldigungen sind zahlreich und vielfältig **b** *(= several)* mehrere, verschiedene

variously ['vɛərɪəslɪ] ADV **a** unterschiedlich; **the news was ~ reported in the papers** die Nachricht wurde in den Zeitungen unterschiedlich wiedergegeben **b** verschiedentlich; **he has been ~ described as a rogue and a charmer** er wurde verschiedentlich ein Schlitzohr und Charmeur genannt

varlet ['vɑːlɪt] N *(obs, = page)* Knappe *m*; *(= rascal)* Schurke *m*, Halunke *m*

varmint ['vɑːmɪnt] N **a** *(dial: esp US)* Schurke *m*, Schurkin *f*, Halunke *m* **b** *(= animal)* Schädling *m*

varnish ['vɑːnɪʃ] N *(lit)* Lack *m*; *(on pottery)* Glasur *f*; *(on furniture also, on painting)* Firnis *m*; *(fig)* Politur *f* VT lackieren; *floorboards also* versiegeln, einlassen *(S Ger, Aus)*; *painting* firnissen; *pottery* glasieren; *(fig) truth, facts* beschönigen

varnished ['vɑːnɪʃt] ADJ *table, chair, nails* lackiert; *floorboards also* versiegelt, eingelassen *(S Ger, Aus)*

varnisher ['vɑːnɪʃə'] N Lackierer(in) *m(f)*

varsity ['vɑːsɪtɪ] N *(Brit Univ inf)* Uni *f (inf)*; *(US: also* **varsity team***)* Schul-/Uniauswahl *f*

vary ['vɛərɪ] VI **a** *(= diverge, differ)* sich unterscheiden, abweichen *(from* von); **they ~ in price from the others** sie unterscheiden sich im Preis von den anderen; **opinions ~ on this point** in diesem Punkt gehen die Meinungen auseinander; **opinions ~ about the value** der Wert wird unterschiedlich eingeschätzt **b** *(= be different)* unterschiedlich sein; **the price varies from shop to shop** der Preis ist von Geschäft zu Geschäft verschieden; **his work varies** seine Arbeit ist sehr unterschiedlich; **it varies** es ist unterschiedlich, das ist verschieden **c** *(= change, fluctuate)* sich (ver)ändern; *(pressure, prices)* schwanken; **prices that ~ with the season** saisonbedingte Preise *pl*; **to ~ with the weather** sich nach dem Wetter richten VT *(= alter)* verändern, abwandeln; *(= give variety)* abwechslungsreich(er) gestalten, variieren; **they never ~ their diet** sie essen sehr eintönig; **try to ~ your approach to the problem** Sie sollten das Problem mal von einer anderen Seite angehen

varying ['vɛərɪɪŋ] ADJ *(= changing)* veränderlich; *(= different)* unterschiedlich; **our different results were due to ~ conditions** unsere verschiedenen Resultate beruhen auf unterschiedlichen Voraussetzungen; **the ~ weather conditions here** die veränderlichen Wetterverhältnisse hier; **with ~ degrees of success** mit unterschiedlichem Erfolg; **to ~ degrees** mehr oder weniger; **in ~ degrees** mehr oder minder; **of ~ degrees of complexity** unterschiedlich komplex, von unterschiedlicher Komplexität; **of ~ sizes/abilities/ages** unterschiedlich groß/begabt/alt

vascular ['væskjʊlə'] ADJ vaskulär

vasculitis [ˌvæskjʊ'laɪtɪs] N *(Med)* Vaskulitis *f (spec)*, Gefäßentzündung *f*

vas deferens ['væs'defərenz] N *pl* **vasa deferentia** ['veɪsəˌdefə'renʃɪə] Samenleiter *m*

vase [vɑːz, (*US*) veɪz] N Vase *f*

vasectomy [væˈsektəmɪ] N Vasektomie *f (spec)*, Sterilisation *f (des Mannes)*

Vaseline® [ˈvæsɪliːn] N Vaseline *f*

vasoconstriction [ˌveɪzəʊkənˈstrɪkʃən] N *(Med)* Vasokonstriktion *f (spec)*, Gefäßverengung *f*

vasoconstrictor [ˌveɪzəʊkənˈstrɪktəʳ] N *(Med)* Mittel *nt* zur Verengung der Blutgefäße

vasodilation [ˌveɪzəʊdaɪˈleɪʃən] N *(Med)* Vasodilatation *f (spec)*, Gefäßerweiterung *f*

vasodilator [ˌveɪzəʊdaɪˈleɪtəʳ] N *(Med)* Mittel *nt* zur Erweiterung der Blutgefäße

vassal [ˈvæsəl] **N** *(lit, fig)* Vasall *m* **ADJ** vasallisch, Vasallen-; **~ state** Vasallenstaat *m*

vassalage [ˈvæsəlɪdʒ] N *(Hist) (= condition)* Vasallentum *nt*, Vasallität *f*; *(= services due)* Vasallen- *or* Lehenspflicht *f*; *(= land)* Lehen *nt*; *(fig)* Unterworfenheit *f (geh)* (to unter *+acc*)

vast [vɑːst] ADJ *(+er)* gewaltig, riesig; *area also* weit, ausgedehnt; *bulk, difference also* riesengroß; *knowledge* enorm; *majority* überwältigend; *wealth, powers* riesig, unermesslich; **a ~ expanse** eine weite Ebene; **the ~ expanse of the ocean** die unermessliche Weite des Ozeans; **to a ~ extent** in sehr hohem Maße; **a ~ success** ein Riesenerfolg *m*; **at ~ expense** zu enormen Kosten; **to be a ~ improvement on sth** eine enorme Verbesserung gegenüber etw sein

vastly [ˈvɑːstlɪ] ADV erheblich, wesentlich, bedeutend; *grateful* überaus, äußerst; *experienced* äußerst, enorm; **I was ~ amused** ich habe mich köstlich amüsiert; **it is ~ different** da besteht ein erheblicher *or* wesentlicher Unterschied; **~ rich** steinreich; **he is ~ superior to her** er ist ihr haushoch überlegen

vastness [ˈvɑːstnɪs] N *(of size)* riesiges *or* gewaltiges Ausmaß, riesige Größe; *(of distance)* ungeheures Ausmaß; *(of ocean, plane, area)* riesige Weite; *(of sums of money)* ungeheure Höhe; *(of success)* Ausmaß *nt*; *(of difference)* Größe *f*; *(of knowledge, wealth)* gewaltiger Umfang

VAT [ˈviːeɪˈtiː, væt] *(Brit) abbr of* **value-added tax** Mehrwertsteuer *f*, MwSt.

vat [væt] N Fass *nt*; *(without lid)* Bottich *m*

vatic [ˈvætɪk] ADJ *(liter)* prophetisch

Vatican [ˈvætɪkən] N Vatikan *m*; **the ~ Council** das Vatikanische Konzil; **~ roulette** *(hum inf)* Knaus-Ogino(-Methode) *f*

Vatican City N Vatikanstadt *f*

VAT *(Brit)*: **VAT man** N Steuerprüfer *m* (für die Mehrwertsteuer); **VAT-registered** ADJ zur Mehrwertsteuer veranlagt; **VAT return** N Mehrwertsteuerausgleich *m*

vaudeville [ˈvəʊdəvɪl] N *(US)* Varieté *nt*, Varietee *nt*

vaudeville: **vaudeville show** N Varieté(-) *or* Varietee(vorführung *f*) *nt*; **vaudeville singer** N Varieté- *or* Varieteesänger(in) *m(f)*

vault¹ [vɔːlt] N **a** *(= cellar)* (Keller)gewölbe *nt*; *(= tomb)* Gruft *f*; *(in bank)* Tresor(raum) *m*; **in the ~s** im Gewölbe *etc* **b** *(Archit)* Gewölbe *nt*; **the ~ of heaven** *(liter)* das Himmelsgewölbe *(liter)*

vault² **N** Sprung *m*; *(= scissors jump)* Schersprung *m*; *(legs behind)* Flanke *f*; *(legs through arms)* Hocke *f*; *(legs apart)* Grätsche *f* → **pole vault** **VI** springen, einen Schersprung/eine Flanke/eine Hocke/eine Grätsche machen; **to ~ into the saddle** sich in den Sattel schwingen **VT** springen über *(+acc)*, überspringen, einen Schersprung/eine Flanke/eine Hocke/eine Grätsche machen über *(+acc)*

vaulted [ˈvɔːltɪd] ADJ *(Archit)* gewölbt

vaulting [ˈvɔːltɪŋ] N *(Archit)* Wölbung *f*

vaulting horse N *(in gym)* Pferd *nt*

vaunt [vɔːnt] **VT** rühmen, preisen *(geh)*; **much-~ed** viel gepriesen; **Cologne ~s a splendid cathedral** Köln kann sich eines herrlichen Doms rühmen **N** Loblied *nt*, Lobgesang *m*

VC *abbr of* **Victoria Cross**

V-chip [ˈviːtʃɪp] N V-Chip *m*

VCR *abbr of* **video cassette recorder** Videorekorder *m*

VD *abbr of* **venereal disease** Geschlechtskrankheit *f*; **VD clinic** *Klinik für Geschlechtskrankheiten*, ≈ Hautklinik *f*

VDT *abbr of* **visual display terminal**

VDU *abbr of* **visual display unit**

veal [viːl] N Kalbfleisch *nt*; **~ cutlet** Kalbsschnitzel *nt*

veal crate [ˈviːlkreɪt] N Kälberbox *f*

vector [ˈvektəʳ] N *(Math, Aviat)* Vektor *m*; *(Biol)* Träger *m*

vector *in cpds (Math)* Vektor(en)-; **vector graphics** PL Vektorgrafik *f*

vectorial [vekˈtɔːrɪəl] ADJ vektoriell

Veda [ˈveɪdə] N Weda *m*

> **V-E DAY**
>
> In Großbritannien und in den Vereinigten Staaten ist der achte Mai der **V-E Day (Victory in Europe Day)**, weil an diesen Tag der Sieg der Allierten im Zweiten Weltkrieg 1945 in Europa gefeiert wird. Der Sieg über Japan im selben Jahr wird am 15. August begangen, am **V-J Day (Victory over Japan Day)**.

veep [viːp] N *(US inf)* = **vice president**

veer [vɪəʳ] **VI** *(wind)* (sich) drehen *(im Uhrzeigersinn)* (to nach); *(ship)* abdrehen; *(car)* ausscheren; *(road)* scharf abbiegen, abknicken; **the ship ~ed round** das Schiff drehte ab; **the road ~ed to the left** die Straße machte eine scharfe Linkskurve; **the car ~ed to the left** das Auto scherte nach links aus; **the car ~ed off the road** das Auto kam von der Straße ab; **the driver was forced to ~ sharply** der Fahrer musste plötzlich das Steuer herumreißen; **to ~ off course** vom Kurs abkommen; **it ~s from one extreme to the other** es schwankt zwischen zwei Extremen; **he ~ed round to my point of view** er ist auf meine Richtung umgeschwenkt; **he ~ed away from the subject** er kam (völlig) vom Thema ab; **the country has ~ed to the right under Thatcher** das Land ist unter Thatcher nach rechts geschwenkt
N *(of wind)* Drehung *f*; *(of ship, fig: in policy)* Kurswechsel *m*; *(of car)* Ausscheren *nt*; *(of road)* Knick *m*; **a ~ to the left politically** ein politischer Ruck nach links

veg [vedʒ] *(esp Brit)* N *no pl abbr of* **vegetable**; **meat and two ~** Fleisch und zwei Sorten Gemüse; **he likes his meat and two ~** er liebt gutbürgerliche Kost

▶ **veg out** VI *(inf)* herumhängen *(inf)*; **I just want to veg out tonight** ich will heute Abend einfach zu Hause abhängen *(inf)*

vegan [ˈviːgən] **N** Veganer(in) *m(f)* **ADJ** vegan, veganisch; **~ cheese** Käse *m* für Veganer; **to be ~** Veganer(in) *m(f)* sein

Vegeburger® [ˈvedʒɪˌbɜːgəʳ] N *(Brit)* Gemüseburger *m*

vegetable [ˈvedʒɪtəbl] N **a** Gemüse *nt*; **with fresh ~s** mit frischem Gemüse; *(on menu)* mit frischen Gemüsen; **what ~s do you grow in your garden?** welche Gemüsesorten hast du in deinem Garten?; **cabbage is a ~** Kohl ist eine Gemüsepflanze **b** *(generic term: = plant)* Pflanze *f* **c** *(fig pej)* **she's become a ~** sie ist zum körperlichen und geistigen Krüppel geworden, sie vegetiert nur noch dahin

vegetable: **vegetable dish** N *(= food)* Gemüsegericht *nt*; *(= bowl)* Gemüseschüssel *f*; **vegetable garden** N Gemüsegarten *m*; **vegetable kingdom** N Pflanzenreich *nt*; **vegetable knife** N kleines Küchenmesser; **vegetable marrow** N Gartenkürbis *m*; **vegetable matter** N pflanzliche Stoffe *pl*; **vegetable oil** N pflanzliches Öl; *(Cook)* Pflanzenöl *nt*; **vegetable salad** N Gemüsesalat *m*; **vegetable soup** N Gemüsesuppe *f*

vegetarian [ˌvedʒɪˈteərɪən] **N** Vegetarier(in) *m(f)* **ADJ** vegetarisch; **~ cheese** Käse *m* für Vegetarier; **to go** *or* **become ~** Vegetarier(in) *m(f)* werden

vegetarianism [ˌvedʒɪˈteərɪənɪzəm] N Vegetarismus *m*

vegetate [ˈvedʒɪteɪt] VI **a** *(lit)* wachsen **b** *(fig)* dahinvegetieren

vegetation [ˌvedʒɪˈteɪʃən] N **a** Vegetation *f*; **could we live on the ~ here?** könnten wir uns von dem ernähren, was hier wächst? **b** *(= wasting away) (of sick people)* Dahinvegetieren *nt*; *(of mind)* Verödung *f*, Verarmung *f*; **the patients just lie there in a state of ~** die Patienten dämmern nur noch vor sich hin *or* vegetieren nur noch dahin

vegetative [ˈvedʒɪtətɪv] ADJ *(Bot)* vegetativ → **persistent**

veggie [ˈvedʒɪ] *(inf)* **N** **a** *(= vegetarian)* Vegetarier(in) *m(f)* **b** **~s** *pl (US)* = **veg** **ADJ** *(= vegetarian)* vegetarisch

veggieburger [ˈvedʒɪˌbɜːgəʳ] N Gemüseburger *m*

vehemence [ˈviːɪməns] N Vehemenz *f (geh)*; *(of actions, feelings also)* Heftigkeit *f*; *(of love, hatred also)* Leidenschaftlichkeit *f*; *(of protests also)* Schärfe *f*, Heftigkeit *f*

vehement [ˈviːɪmənt] ADJ vehement *(geh)*; *attack also* heftig, scharf; *critic, opponent, opposition, protest* scharf; *dislike, desire* heftig, stark; *ally, supporter, speech* leidenschaftlich; **to become** *or* **grow ~** heftig werden; **to be ~ in one's demands for sth** etw vehement fordern; **to be ~ in one's attack on sb/sth** jdn/etw scharf angreifen

vehemently [ˈviːɪməntlɪ] ADV vehement *(geh)*, heftig; *love, hate also* leidenschaftlich; *protest also* heftig, mit aller Schärfe; *attack* scharf; *deny* heftig

vehicle [ˈviːɪkl] N Fahrzeug *nt*; *(Pharm)* Vehikel *nt*, Trägersubstanz *f*; *(Art)* Lösungsmittel *nt*; *(fig: = medium)* Mittel *nt*, Vehikel *nt (geh)*; **this paper is a ~ of right-wing opinions** diese Zeitung ist ein Sprachrohr *nt* der Rechten; **language is the ~ of thought** die Sprache ist das Medium des Denkens

vehicular [vɪˈhɪkjʊləʳ] ADJ Fahrzeug-; **~ traffic** Fahrzeugverkehr *m*; **~ accident** Verkehrsunfall *m*; **there is no ~ access** die Zufahrt ist nicht möglich

veil [veɪl] **N** Schleier *m*; **to take the ~** den Schleier nehmen, ins Kloster gehen; **the valley lay in a ~ of mist** über dem Tal lag ein Nebelschleier; **to draw** *or* **throw a ~ over sth** den Schleier des Vergessens über etw *(acc)* breiten; **under a ~ of secrecy** unter dem Mantel der Verschwiegenheit; **the ~ of secrecy over all their activities** der Schleier des Geheimnisses, der all ihre Aktivitäten umgibt
VT **a** *(lit) person* verschleiern; *statue, painting* verhüllen
b *(fig) facts, truth* verschleiern; *feelings* verbergen; **the clouds ~ed the moon** die Wolken verhüllten *or* verdeckten den Mond; **the town was ~ed by mist** die Stadt lag in Nebel gehüllt

veiled [veɪld] ADJ **a** *reference, attack, criticism, threat, warning* versteckt **b** *(= covered) woman, face* verschleiert; **to be ~ in black** schwarz verschleiert sein **c** *(liter, = obscured)* verborgen; *mountains* umhüllt

veiling [ˈveɪlɪŋ] N Schleier *m*; *(fig: of facts, truth)* Verschleierung *f*

vein [veɪn] N **a** *(Anat, Bot, Min)* Ader *f*; **~s and arteries** Venen und Arterien *pl*; **a ~ of racism** ein Hauch *m* von Rassismus; **there is a ~ of truth in what he says** es ist eine Spur von Wahrheit in dem, was er sagt; **a creative ~** eine künstlerische Ader; **there's a ~ of spitefulness in his character** er hat einen gehässigen Zug in seinem Charakter; **the ~ of humour** *(Brit) or* **humor** *(US)* **which runs through the book** ein humorvoller Zug, der durch das ganze Buch geht **b** *(fig: = mood)* Stimmung *f*, Laune *f*; **in a humorous ~** in lustiger Stimmung; **in the same ~** in derselben Art

veined [veɪnd] ADJ geädert; *hand* mit hervortretenden Adern; **blue-~ cheese** Blauschimmelkäse *m*

velar ['viːlə'] ADJ velar N Velar(laut) *m*

Velcro® ['velkrəʊ] N Klettband *nt* ADJ **~® fastener** Klettverschluss® *m*

veld, veldt [velt] N *(in South Africa)* Steppe *f*

vellum ['veləm] N Pergament *nt*

vellum: vellum binding N Pergamenteinband *m*; **vellum paper** N Pergamentpapier *nt*

velocipede [və'lɒsɪpiːd] N *(form)* Fahrrad *nt*, Veloziped *nt (old)*

velocity [və'lɒsɪtɪ] N Geschwindigkeit *f*

velodrome ['velədrəʊm] N Velodrom *nt*, Radrennbahn *f*

velour(s) [və'lʊə'] N Velours *m*

velvet ['velvɪt] N Samt *m*; **like ~** wie Samt, samtig ADJ Samt-; *skin, feel* samtweich, samten *(geh)*; **~ dress** Samtkleid *nt*; **the ~ touch of his hand** seine sanften Hände

velveteen ['velvɪtiːn] N Veloursamt *m*

Velvet Revolution N **the ~** die sanfte *or* samtene Revolution

velvety ['velvɪtɪ] ADJ samtig

Ven. *abbr of* **Venerable**

venal ['viːnl] ADJ *(liter) person* käuflich, feil *(liter)*; *practices* korrupt

venality [viː'nælɪtɪ] N *(liter) (of person)* Käuflichkeit *f*; *(of practices)* Korruption *f*; **the ~ of his interests** seine eigennützigen Motive

vend [vend] VT verkaufen

vendee [ven'diː] N *(esp Jur)* Käufer(in) *m(f)*

vendetta [ven'detə] N Fehde *f*; *(in family)* Blutrache *f*; *(of gangsters)* Vendetta *f*; **to carry on a ~ against sb** sich mit jdm bekriegen, mit jdm in Fehde liegen; *against family member* an jdm Blutrache üben

vendible ['vendɪbl] ADJ *(Comm)* verkäuflich

vending: vending machine ['vendɪŋmə'ʃiːn] N Automat *m*; **vending pack** ['vendɪŋ,pæk] N Automatenpackung *f*

vendition [ven'dɪʃən] N *(Econ)* Verkauf *m*

vendor ['vendɔː'] N *(esp Jur)* Verkäufer(in) *m(f)*; **newspaper ~** Zeitungsverkäufer(in) *m(f)*; **street ~** Straßenhändler(in) *m(f)*

vendue [ven'djuː] N *(US Econ)* Auktion *f*, Versteigerung *f*

veneer [və'nɪə'] N *(lit)* Furnier *nt*; *(fig)* Politur *f*; **it's just a ~** es ist nur Politur *or* schöner Schein; **he had a ~ of respectability** nach außen hin machte er einen sehr ehrbaren Eindruck; **the cities with their thin ~ of civilization** die Städte mit ihrem dünnen Lack *or* Putz der Zivilisation VT *wood* furnieren

venerable ['venərəbl] ADJ ehrwürdig

venerate ['venəreɪt] VT verehren, hoch achten; *sb's memory* ehren; **his name was deeply ~d** sein Andenken wurde sehr in Ehren gehalten

veneration [,venə'reɪʃən] N Bewunderung *f*, Verehrung *f* (of für); *(of idols)* Verehrung *f*; *(of traditions)* Ehrfurcht *f* (of vor +*dat*); **to hold sb in ~** jdn hoch achten *or* verehren

venereal [vɪ'nɪərɪəl] ADJ venerisch

venereal disease [vɪ'nɪərɪəldɪ,ziːz] N Geschlechtskrankheit *f*, venerische Krankheit *(spec)*

Venetian [vɪ'niːʃən] ADJ venezianisch N Venezianer(in) *m(f)*

Venetian: Venetian blind N Jalousie *f*; **Venetian glass** N venezianisches Glas

Venezuela [,vene'zweɪlə] N Venezuela *nt*

Venezuelan [,vene'zweɪlən] ADJ venezolanisch N Venezolaner(in) *m(f)*

vengeance ['vendʒəns] N **a** Vergeltung *f*, Rache *f*; **to take ~ (up)on sb** Vergeltung an jdm üben **b** *(inf)* **with a ~** gewaltig *(inf)*; **then the brass section comes in with a ~** dann kommt der kraftvolle *or* gewaltige Einsatz der Bläser; **to work with a ~** hart *or* mächtig *(inf)* arbeiten

vengeful ['vendʒfʊl] ADJ rachsüchtig

venial ['viːnɪəl] ADJ verzeihlich, entschuldbar; **~ sin** lässliche Sünde

veniality [,viːnɪ'ælɪtɪ] N Entschuldbarkeit *f*; *(of sin)* Lässlichkeit *f*

Venice ['venɪs] N Venedig *nt*

venison ['venɪsən] N Reh(fleisch) *nt*

venom ['venəm] N *(lit)* Gift *nt*; *(fig)* Bosheit *f*, Gehässigkeit *f*; **he spoke with real ~ in his voice** er sprach mit hasserfüllter Stimme; **a book review full of ~** ein giftiger Verriss eines Buches; **she spat her ~ at him** sie giftete ihn wütend an; **his pen, dipped in ~** seine giftige Feder

venomous ['venəməs] ADJ *(lit, fig)* giftig; *tone also* gehässig; *tongue also* scharf, böse; *attack* scharf; *sarcasm* beißend; *hatred* vernichtend, tödlich; **~ snake** Giftschlange *f*

venomously ['venəməslɪ] ADV *(fig)* boshaft; *look, say* giftig; **~ racist** auf böse Weise rassistisch

venous ['viːnəs] ADJ *(form, Anat)* venös; *(Bot)* geädert

vent [vent] N *(for gas, liquid)* Öffnung *f*; *(in chimney)* Abzug *m*; *(in barrel)* Spundloch *nt*; *(in coat)* Schlitz *m*; *(for feelings)* Ventil *nt*; **jacket with a single/double ~** Jacke mit Rückenschlitz *m*/Seitenschlitzen *pl*; **to give ~ to sth** *(fig)* einer Sache *(dat)* Ausdruck verleihen; **to give ~ to one's feelings** seinen Gefühlen freien Lauf lassen; **to give ~ to one's anger** seinem Ärger Luft machen VT *feelings, anger* abreagieren (*on* an +*dat*); **to ~ one's spleen** sich *(dat)* Luft machen; **to ~ one's spleen on sb** seine Wut an jdm auslassen

ventilate ['ventɪleɪt] VT **a** *(= control air flow)* belüften; *(= let fresh air in)* lüften **b** *blood* Sauerstoff zuführen (+*dat*), mit Sauerstoff versorgen **c** *(fig) grievance* vorbringen **d** *(fig) question, issue* erörtern; *opinion, view* äußern, kundtun

ventilated ['ventɪleɪtɪd] ADJ *room, building* belüftet; **well/poorly ~** gut/schlecht belüftet

ventilation [,ventɪ'leɪʃən] N **a** *(= control of air flow)* Belüftung *f*, Ventilation *f*; *(= letting fresh air in)* Lüften *nt*; **there's very poor ~ in here** die Belüftung dieses Raumes ist schlecht **b** *(of blood)* Sauerstoffzufuhr *f* **c** *(of grievance)* Vorbringen *nt* **d** *(of question, issue)* Erörterung *f*; *(of opinion, view)* Äußerung *f*

ventilation shaft N Luftschacht *m*

ventilator ['ventɪleɪtə'] N **a** Ventilator *m* **b** *(Med)* Beatmungsgerät *nt*; **to be on a ~** künstlich beatmet werden

ventral ['ventrəl] ADJ *(form)* ventral *(form)*, Bauch-

ventral fin [,ventrəl'fɪn] N Bauchflosse *f*

ventricle ['ventrɪkəl] N Kammer *f*, Ventrikel *m (form)*

ventriloquism [ven'trɪləkwɪzəm] N Bauchredekunst *f*, Bauchreden *nt*

ventriloquist [ven'trɪləkwɪst] N Bauchredner(in) *m(f)*

ventriloquist's dummy N Bauchrednerpuppe *f*

ventriloquy [ven'trɪləkwɪ] N Bauchredekunst *f*, Bauchreden *nt*

venture ['ventʃə'] N Unternehmung *f*, Unternehmen *nt*, Unterfangen *nt*; **mountain-climbing is his latest ~** seit neuestem hat er sich aufs Bergsteigen verlegt; **a new ~ in publishing** ein neuer verlegerischer Versuch, ein neues verlegerisches Experiment; **this was a disastrous ~ for the company** dieses Projekt *or* dieser Versuch war für die Firma ein Fiasko; **his first ~ into novel-writing** sein erster Versuch, Romane zu schreiben; **he made a lot of money out of his ~s in the world of finance** er verdiente bei seinen Spekulationen in der Finanzwelt viel Geld; **his purchase of stocks was his first ~ into the world of finance** mit dem Erwerb von Aktien wagte er sich zum ersten Mal in die Finanzwelt; **his early ~s into music were successful** seine frühen musikalischen Versuche waren erfolgreich; **rowing the Atlantic alone was quite a ~** allein über den Atlantik zu rudern war ein ziemlich gewagtes Abenteuer; **the astronauts on their ~ into the unknown** die Astronauten auf ihrer abenteuerlichen Reise ins Unbekannte

VT **a** *life, reputation, money* aufs Spiel setzen, riskieren (*on* bei); **nothing ~d nothing gained** *(Prov)* wer nicht wagt, der nicht gewinnt *(prov)* **b** *guess, explanation, statement* wagen; *opinion* zu äußern wagen; **if I may ~ an opinion** wenn ich mir erlauben darf, meine Meinung zu sagen; **in his latest article he ~s an explanation of the phenomenon** in seinem letzten Artikel versucht er, eine Erklärung des Phänomens zu geben; **I would ~ to say that ...** ich wage sogar zu behaupten, dass ...

VI sich wagen; **no other man had dared to ~ so far** noch kein anderer Mensch hatte sich so weit vorgewagt; **to ~ out of doors** sich vor die Tür wagen; **they lost money when they ~d into book publishing** sie verloren Geld bei ihrem Versuch, Bücher zu verlegen; **the company ~d into a new field** die Firma wagte sich in ein neues Gebiet vor

▶ **venture forth** VI *(liter)* sich hinauswagen; **the soldiers ventured forth to find the enemy** die Soldaten wagten sich vor, um den Feind ausfindig zu machen; **the astronauts ventured forth into the unknown** die Astronauten wagten sich ins Unbekannte; **we ventured forth on this intellectual enterprise** wir wagten uns an dieses intellektuelle Unterfangen heran

▶ **venture on** VI +*prep obj* sich wagen an (+*acc*); **to venture on a voyage of exploration/scientific discovery** sich auf eine Entdeckungsreise/eine wissenschaftliche Forschungsreise wagen; **they ventured on a programme** *(Brit) or* **program** *(US)* **of reform** sie wagten sich an ein Reformprogramm heran

▶ **venture out** VI = **venture forth**

venture: venture capital N Beteiligungs- *or* Risikokapital *nt*; **venture capitalist** N Risikokapitalgeber(in) *m(f)*; **~s** Kapitalbeteiligungsgesellschaft *f*; **Venture Scout** N *(Brit)* Rover *m*

venturesome ['ventʃəsəm] ADJ *person, action* abenteuerlich

venue ['venjuː] N *(= meeting place)* Treffpunkt *m*; *(Sport)* Austragungsort *m*; *(Jur)* Verhandlungsort *m*

Venus ['viːnəs] N Venus *f*

Venus flytrap [,viːnəs'flaɪtræp] N Venusfliegenfalle *f*

Venusian [və'njuːʃən] N Venusbewohner(in) *m(f)* ADJ Venus-; **~ landscape** Venuslandschaft *f*

veracious [və'reɪʃəs] ADJ *person* ehrlich, aufrichtig; *report* wahrheitsgemäß

veracity [və'ræsɪtɪ] N *(of person)* Ehrlichkeit *f*, Aufrichtigkeit *f*; *(of report, evidence)* Wahrheit *f*, Richtigkeit *f*

veranda(h) [və'rændə] N Veranda *f*

verb [vɜːb] N Verb *nt*, Zeitwort *nt*, Verbum *nt*

verbal ['vɜːbəl] ADJ **a** *(= spoken) statement, agreement* mündlich; **~ abuse** Beschimpfung *f*; **~ attack** Verbalattacke *f*; **~ warning** mündliche Verwarnung **b** *(= of words) error, skills, distinction* sprachlich; **~ memory** Wortgedächtnis *nt*; **a ~ reasoning test** ein Test *m* des logischen Denkvermögens **c** *(= literal) translation* wörtlich **d** *(Gram)* verbal

verbalize ['vɜːbəlaɪz] VT **a** *(= put into words)* ausdrücken, in Worte fassen **b** *(Gram)* verbal ausdrücken

verbally ['vɜːbəlɪ] ADV **a** *(= spoken)* mündlich, verbal; *threaten* verbal; **to ~ abuse sb** jdn beschimpfen; **~ abusive** ausfällig **b** *(= as a verb)* verbal

verbal noun N Verbalsubstantiv *nt*

verbatim [vɜː'beɪtɪm] ADJ wörtlich ADV wortwörtlich

verbena [vɜː'biːnə] N Eisenkraut *nt*

verbiage ['vɜːbɪɪdʒ] N Wortwust *m*, Wortfülle *f*, Blabla *nt (inf)*; **you won't impress the examiners with a lot of ~** mit Geschwafel *nt or* Blabla *nt (inf)* kannst du die Prüfer nicht beeindrucken; **there's too much ~ in this report** dieser Bericht ist zu umständlich geschrieben

verbose [vɜː'bəʊs] ADJ wortreich, langatmig, weitschweifig

verbosely [vɜː'bəʊslɪ] ADV langatmig

verbosity [vɜː'bɒsɪtɪ] N Langatmigkeit *f*; **it sounds impressive but it's sheer ~** es klingt beeindruckend, ist aber nichts als Geschwafel

verdant ['vɜːdənt] ADJ *(liter)* grün

verdict ['vɜːdɪkt] N **a** *(Jur)* Urteil *nt*; **a ~ of guilty/not guilty** ein Schuldspruch *m*/Freispruch *m*; **what's the ~?** wie lautet das Urteil? → **bring in, return b** *(of doctor, critic etc)* Urteil *nt*; *(of electors)* Entscheidung *f*, Votum *nt*; **what's your ~ on this wine?** wie beurteilst du diesen Wein?; **to give one's ~ about** *or* **on sth** sein Urteil über etw *(acc)* abgeben

verdigris ['vɜːdɪgriːs] N Grünspan *m* ADJ *metal, copper, bronze* mit Grünspan bedeckt; *finish, effect* grünspanig

verdure ['vɜːdjʊə'] N *(liter)* *(= colour)* sattes Grün; *(= vegetation)* reiche Flora *(geh)*

verge [vɜːdʒ] N **a** *(Brit lit)* Rand *m*; **"keep off the ~"** „Bankette *or* Seitenstreifen nicht befahrbar" **b** *(fig)* **to be on the ~ of ruin/war** am Rande des Ruins/eines Krieges stehen; **to be on the ~ of a nervous breakdown** am Rande eines Nervenzusammenbruchs sein; **to be on the ~ of a discovery** kurz vor einer Entdeckung stehen; **to be on the ~ of tears** den Tränen nahe sein; **to be on the ~ of doing sth** im Begriff sein, etw zu tun; **I was on the ~ of giving away the secret** *(accidentally)* ich hätte das Geheimnis um ein Haar ausgeplaudert

▶ **verge on** VI +prep obj *(ideas, actions)* grenzen an *(+acc)*; **the plot verges on the ridiculous** die Handlung grenzt ans Lächerliche; **he's verging on bankruptcy** er steht kurz vor dem Bankrott; **she is verging on fifty** sie geht auf die fünfzig zu; **she was verging on madness** sie stand am Rande des Wahnsinns

verger ['vɜːdʒə'] N *(Eccl)* Küster(in) *m(f)*

Vergil ['vɜːdʒɪl] N Virgil *m*, Vergil *m*

veridical [və'rɪdɪkl] ADJ *(form)* wahrheitsgetreu, wahrheitsgemäß

verifiability [,verɪfaɪə'bɪlɪtɪ] N Nachweisbarkeit *f*, Nachprüfbarkeit *f*, Verifizierbarkeit *f (geh)*

verifiable ['verɪfaɪəbl] ADJ nachweisbar, nachprüfbar, verifizierbar *(geh)*

verification [,verɪfɪ'keɪʃən] N *(= check)* Überprüfung *f*; *(= confirmation)* Bestätigung *f*, Verifikation *f (geh)*; *(= proof)* Nachweis *m*; **these claims are open to empirical ~** diese Behauptungen lassen sich empirisch nachweisen

verify ['verɪfaɪ] VT **a** *(= check up)* (über)prüfen; *(= confirm)* bestätigen, beglaubigen; *theory* beweisen, verifizieren *(geh)* **b** *suspicions, fears* bestätigen

verily ['verɪlɪ] ADV *(obs)* wahrlich *(obs)*, fürwahr *(obs)*; **~ I say unto you** wahrlich, ich sage euch

verisimilitude [,verɪsɪ'mɪlɪtjuːd] N *(form)* Wahrhaftigkeit *f (liter)*, Echtheit *f*; *(of theory)* Plausibilität *f*, Evidenz *f (liter)*

veritable ['verɪtəbl] ADJ *genius* wahr; **a ~ disaster** die reinste Katastrophe; **a ~ miracle** das reinste Wunder

veritably ['verɪtəblɪ] ADV *(liter)* in der Tat, fürwahr *(obs)*

verity ['verɪtɪ] N *(liter)* Wahrheit *f*

vermicelli [,vɜːmɪ'selɪ] N Fadennudeln *pl*, Vermicelli *pl*

vermicide ['vɜːmɪsaɪd] N Wurmmittel *nt*, Vermizid *nt (spec)*

vermifuge ['vɜːmɪfjuːdʒ] N Wurmmittel *nt*, Vermifugum *nt (spec)*

vermilion [və'mɪljən] N Zinnoberrot *nt* ADJ zinnoberrot

vermin ['vɜːmɪn] N *no pl* **a** *(= animal)* Schädling *m* **b** *(= insects)* Ungeziefer *nt* **c** *(pej: = people)* Pack *nt*, Ungeziefer *nt*

vermination [,vɜːmɪ'neɪʃən] N Verseuchung *f* mit Ungeziefer

verminous ['vɜːmɪnəs] ADJ *people, clothes* voller Ungeziefer; *place* mit Ungeziefer verseucht

vermouth ['vɜːməθ] N Wermut *m*

vernacular [və'nækjʊlə'] N **a** *(= dialect)* Mundart *f*; *(= not Latin, not official language)* Landessprache *f*; **this word has now come into the ~** dieses Wort ist jetzt in die Alltagssprache eingegangen **b** *(= jargon)* Fachsprache *f or* -jargon *m* **c** *(hum: = strong language)* deftige Sprache; **please excuse the ~** entschuldigen Sie bitte, dass ich mich so drastisch ausdrücke **d** *(Archit)* traditioneller Baustil ADJ **a ~ newspaper** Zeitung *f* in der regionalen Landessprache; **~ language** mundartliche Sprache; **~ poet** Mundartdichter(in) *m(f)* **b** *(Archit)* traditionell **c** *(= indigenous) style* traditionell; *crafts, furniture* einheimisch

vernal ['vɜːnl] ADJ Frühlings-; **~ equinox** Frühlingsäquinoktium *nt*; **~ flowers** *(liter)* Frühlingsblumen *pl*

veronica [və'rɒnɪkə] N *(Bot)* Ehrenpreis *m or nt*, Veronika *f*

verruca [ve'ruːkə] N Warze *f*

versatile ['vɜːsətaɪl] ADJ vielseitig; **he has a very ~ mind** er ist geistig sehr flexibel

versatility [,vɜːsə'tɪlɪtɪ] N Vielseitigkeit *f*; *(of sb's mind)* Flexibilität *f*

verse [vɜːs] N **a** *(= stanza)* Strophe *f*; **a ~ from "The Tempest"** ein Vers *m* aus dem „Sturm" **b** *no pl (= poetry)* Poesie *f*, Dichtung *f*; **in ~** in Versform; **~ drama** Versdrama *nt* **c** *(of Bible, Koran)* Vers *m*

versed [vɜːst] ADJ *(also* **well versed***)* bewandert, beschlagen *(in* in *+dat)*; **he's well ~ in the art of judo** er beherrscht die Kunst des Judos; **I'm not very well ~ in ...** ich verstehe nicht viel *or* ich habe wenig Ahnung von ...

versemonger ['vɜːs,mʌŋgə'] N *(pej)* Verseschmied(in) *m(f) (pej)*

versification [,vɜːsɪfɪ'keɪʃən] N *(= act)* Versbildung *f*; *(= style)* Versform *f*; *(= rules)* Verskunst *f*

versifier ['vɜːsɪfaɪə'] N *(pej)* Verseschmied(in) *m(f)*, Dichterling *m*

versify ['vɜːsɪfaɪ] VT in Versform bringen VI Verse schmieden *(pej)*, dichten

version ['vɜːʃən] N **a** *(= account: of event, facts)* Version *f*, Darstellung *f* **b** *(= variant)* Version *f*; *(of text)* Fassung *f*; *(of car)* Modell *nt*, Typ *m* **c** *(= translation)* Übersetzung *f*

verso ['vɜːsəʊ] N Rückseite *f*; *(of book also)* Verso *nt (spec)*; *(of coin also)* Revers *m (spec)*

versus ['vɜːsəs] PREP gegen *(+acc)*

vertebra ['vɜːtɪbrə] N *pl* **-e** ['vɜːtɪbriː] Rückenwirbel *m*

vertebral ['vɜːtɪbrəl] ADJ *(form)* Wirbel-

vertebral column [,vɜːtɪbrəl'kɒləm] N Wirbelsäule *f*

vertebrate ['vɜːtɪbrət] N Wirbeltier *nt*; **the ~s** die Wirbeltiere *or* Vertebraten *(spec)* ADJ *brain, eye etc* von Wirbeltieren

vertex ['vɜːteks] N *pl* **vertices** Scheitel(punkt) *m*

vertical ['vɜːtɪkəl] ADJ **a** *line, surface* senkrecht, vertikal; *pillar* senkrecht; *(Comm, Econ)* vertikal; **~ cliffs** senkrecht abfallende Klippen; **~ axis** y-Achse *f*, Ordinatenachse *f*; **~ take-off aircraft** Senkrechtstarter *m*; **~ stripes** Längsstreifen *pl* **b** *(= steep)* **there is a ~ drop from the cliffs into the sea below** die Klippen fallen steil *or* senkrecht ins Meer ab **c** *(fig: = hierarchical)* vertikal N *(= line)* Vertikale *f*, Senkrechte *f*; **to be off the** *or* **out of the ~** nicht im Lot stehen

vertically ['vɜːtɪkəlɪ] ADV senkrecht, vertikal; **stand it ~ or it'll fall over** stell es aufrecht hin, sonst fällt es um; **~ integrated** *(Comm)* vertikal integriert

vertices ['vɜːtɪsiːz] *pl of* **vertex**

vertiginous [vɜː'tɪdʒɪnəs] ADJ *(liter) cliffs, descent, drop* schwindelerregend; *heights also* schwindelnd *(geh)*; *sensation* atemberaubend

vertigo ['vɜːtɪgəʊ] N Schwindel *m*; *(Med)* Gleichgewichtsstörung *f*; **he suffers from ~** ihm wird leicht schwindlig; *(Med)* er leidet an Gleichgewichtsstörungen *pl*

verve [vɜːv] N Schwung *m*; *(of person, team also)* Elan *m*; *(of play, performance also)* Ausdruckskraft *f*, Verve *f (geh)*

Very® ['vɪərɪ] ADJ *(Mil)* **~ light** Leuchtkugel *f*

very ['verɪ] ADV **a** *(= extremely)* sehr; **it's ~ well written** es ist sehr gut geschrieben; **I'm ~ sorry** es tut mir sehr leid; **that's not ~ funny** das ist überhaupt nicht lustig; **I'm not ~ good at maths** ich bin in Mathe nicht besonders gut; **it's ~ possible** es ist durchaus *or* (sehr) gut möglich; **~ probably** höchstwahrscheinlich; **he is so ~ lazy** er ist SO faul; **how ~ odd** wie eigenartig; **Very Important Person** prominente Persönlichkeit; **~ little** sehr wenig; **~ little milk** ganz *or* sehr wenig Milch; **how well do you know her? – not ~** wie gut kennst du sie? – nicht besonders gut **b** *(= absolutely)* aller-; **~ best quality** allerbeste Qualität; **~ last** allerletzte(r, s); **~ first** allererste(r, s); **she is the ~ cleverest in the class** sie ist die Klassenbeste; **at the ~ latest** allerspätestens; **this is the ~ last time I'll warn you** ich warne dich jetzt zum allerletzten Mal; **to do one's ~ best** sein Äußerstes tun; **this is the ~ best** das ist das Allerbeste; **this is the ~ most I can offer** das ist mein äußerstes Angebot; **at the ~ most** allerhöchstens; **at the ~ least** allerwenigstens; **to be in the ~ best of health** sich bester Gesundheit erfreuen; **they are the ~ best of friends** sie sind die dicksten Freunde **c ~ much** sehr; **thank you ~ much** vielen Dank; **I liked it ~ much** es hat mir sehr gut gefallen; **~ much bigger** sehr viel größer; **~ much respected** sehr angesehen; **he is ~ much the more intelligent** er ist bei Weitem der Intelligentere; **he doesn't work ~ much** er arbeitet nicht sehr viel; **~ much so** sehr (sogar) **d** *(for emphasis)* **he fell ill and died the ~ same day** er wurde krank und starb noch am selben Tag; **he died the ~ same day as Kennedy** er starb genau am selben Tag wie Kennedy; **the ~ same hat** genau der gleiche Hut; **we met again the ~ next day** wir trafen uns am nächsten *or* folgenden Tag schon wieder; **the ~ next day he was tragically killed** schon einen Tag später kam er unter tragischen Umständen ums Leben; **what he predicted happened the ~ next week** was er vorhersagte, trat in der Woche darauf tatsächlich ein; **my ~ own car** mein eigenes Auto; **a house of your ~ own** ein eigenes Häuschen **e ~ well, if that's what you want** nun gut, wenn du das willst; **~ good, sir** geht in Ordnung, mein Herr, sehr wohl, mein Herr *(dated)*; **if you want that, ~ well, but ...** wenn du das willst, in Ordnung *or* bitte, aber ...; **I couldn't ~ well say no** ich konnte schlecht Nein sagen

ADJ **a** *(= precise, exact)* genau; **that ~ day/moment** genau an diesem Tag/in diesem Augenblick; **in the ~ middle of the picture** genau in der Mitte des Bildes; **this laboratory is the ~ heart of our factory** dieses Labor ist der Kern unseres Werkes; **at the ~ heart of the organization** direkt im Zentrum der Organisation; **on the ~ spot where ...** genau an der Stelle, wo ...; **those were his ~ words** genau das waren seine Worte; **before my ~ eyes** direkt vor meinen Augen; **you are the ~ person I want to speak to** mit IHNEN wollte ich sprechen; **the ~ thing/man I need** genau das, was/genau der Mann, den ich brauche; **the ~ thing!** genau das Richtige!; **to catch sb in the ~ act** jdn auf frischer Tat ertappen **b** *(= extreme)* äußerste(r, s); **in the ~ beginning** ganz am Anfang; **at the ~ end** ganz am Ende; **at the ~ back/front** ganz hinten/vorn(e); **go to the ~ end of the road** gehen Sie die Straße ganz entlang *or* durch; **to the ~ end of his life** bis an sein Lebensende; **in the ~ depths of his soul** im Tiefsten seines Herzens **c** *(= mere)* **the ~ thought of it** allein schon der Gedanke daran, der bloße Gedanke daran; **the ~ idea!** nein, so etwas!

very high frequency N Ultrakurzwelle *f*

vesicle [ˈvesɪkl] N Bläschen *nt; (Med also)* Vesicula *f (form)*

vespers [ˈvespəz] PL Vesper *f*

vessel [ˈvesl] N **a** *(Naut)* Schiff *nt* **b** *(form: = receptacle)* Gefäß *nt*; **drinking ~** Trinkgefäß *nt* **c** *(Anat, Bot)* Gefäß *nt*

vest¹ [vest] N **a** *(Brit)* Unterhemd *nt* **b** *(US)* Weste *f*

vest² VT *(form)* **to ~ sb with sth, to ~ sth in sb** jdm etw verleihen; **the rights ~ed in the Crown** die der Krone zustehenden Rechte; **Congress is ~ed with the power to declare war** der Kongress verfügt über das Recht, den Krieg zu erklären; **the authority ~ed in me** die mir verliehene Macht; **he has ~ed interests in the oil business** er ist (finanziell) am Ölgeschäft beteiligt; **the ~ed interests in the oil business** *(people)* die am Ölgeschäft Beteiligten *pl*; **he has a ~ed interest in the play** *(fig)* er hat ein persönliches Interesse an dem Stück

vestal [ˈvestl] ADJ vestalisch; **~ virgin** Vestalin *f*, vestalische Jungfrau N Vestalin *f*

vestibule [ˈvestɪbjuːl] N **a** *(of house)* Vorhalle *f*, Vestibül *nt (dated)*; *(of hotel)* Halle *f*, Foyer *nt*; *(of church)* Vorhalle *f* **b** *(Anat)* Vorhof *m*, Vestibulum *nt (spec)*

vestige [ˈvestɪdʒ] N **a** Spur *f*; **the ~ of a moustache** *(Brit) or* **mustache** *(US)* der Anflug eines Schnurrbarts; **there is not a ~ of truth in what he says** es ist kein Körnchen Wahrheit an dem, was er sagt **b** *(Anat)* Rudiment *nt*

vestigial [veˈstɪdʒɪəl] ADJ spurenhaft; *moustache, growth* spärlich; *(Anat)* rudimentär; **the ~ remains of the old city walls** die Spuren *or* die rudimentären Reste der alten Stadtmauer; **the ~ remains of a custom** die letzten Reste eines Brauches; **the ~ remains of my interest in art** die kümmerlichen Reste meines Interesses für Kunst

vestment [ˈvestmənt] N **a** *(of priest)* Ornat *m*, Gewand *nt* **b** *(= ceremonial robe)* Robe *f*, Ornat *m*

vest-pocket [ˌvestˈpɒkɪt] ADJ *(US)* im Westentaschenformat

vestry [ˈvestrɪ] N Sakristei *f*

Vesuvius [vɪˈsuːvɪəs] N der Vesuv

vet [vet] N *abbr of* **veterinary surgeon, veterinarian** Tierarzt *m*/-ärztin *f* VT überprüfen

vetch [vetʃ] N Wicke *f*

veteran [ˈvetərən] N *(Mil, fig)* Veteran(in) *m(f)*; **a ~ teacher/golfer** ein (alt)erfahrener Lehrer/Golfspieler; **a ~ actor** ein Veteran *m* der Schauspielkunst, ein altgedienter Schauspieler; **she's a ~ campaigner for women's rights** sie ist eine Veteranin der Frauenbewegung

veteran car N Oldtimer *m*, Schnauferl *nt (inf)*

veterinarian [ˌvetərɪˈneərɪən] N *(US)* Tierarzt *m*/-ärztin *f*

veterinary [ˈvetərɪnərɪ] ADJ Veterinär-; *training* tierärztlich; *school, college* für Tierärzte; **~ hospital** Tierklinik *f*

veterinary: **veterinary medicine** N Veterinärmedizin *f*; **veterinary practice** N Tierarztpraxis *f*; **veterinary surgeon** N Tierarzt *m*/-ärztin *f*

veto [ˈviːtəʊ] N *pl* **-es** Veto *nt*; **power of ~** Vetorecht *nt*; **to have a ~** das Vetorecht haben; **to use one's ~** von seinem Vetorecht Gebrauch machen VT sein Veto einlegen gegen; **if they ~ it** wenn sie ihr Veto einlegen

vetting [ˈvetɪŋ] N Überprüfung *f*; **~ process** Überprüfungsverfahren *nt or* -prozess *m*

vex [veks] VT **a** *(= annoy)* ärgern, irritieren; *animals* quälen; **a problem which has been ~ing me** ein Problem, das mich quält *or* das mir keine Ruhe lässt **b** *(= afflict)* plagen, bedrücken

vexation [vekˈseɪʃən] N **a** *(= state)* Ärger *m*; *(= act)* Verärgerung *f*, Ärgern *nt*; *(of animal)* Quälen *nt*, Quälerei *f* **b** *(= affliction)* Bedrückung *f*; *(= cause)* Plage *f* **c** *(= thing)* Ärgernis *nt*; **the little ~s of life** die kleinen Sorgen und Nöte des Lebens

vexatious [vekˈseɪʃəs] ADJ **a** ärgerlich; *regulations, headache* lästig; *child* unausstehlich **b** *(Jur)* schikanös

vexed [vekst] ADJ **a** *(= annoyed)* verärgert; **to be ~ with sb** mit jdm böse sein, auf jdn ärgerlich sein; **to be ~ about sth** sich über etw *(acc)* ärgern; **to be/get ~** ärgerlich *or* wütend sein/werden **b** *question* viel diskutiert, schwierig

vexing [ˈveksɪŋ] ADJ ärgerlich, irritierend; *problem* verzwickt

vg *abbr of* **very good**

VGA *abbr of* **video graphics array** VGA

vgc *abbr of* **very good condition** in sehr gutem Zustand

VHF *(Rad) abbr of* **very high frequency** UKW

via [ˈvaɪə] PREP über *(+acc)*; *(with town names also)* via; **they got in ~ the window** sie kamen durchs Fenster herein

viability [ˌvaɪəˈbɪlɪtɪ] N **a** *(of life forms)* Lebensfähigkeit *f* **b** *(of plan, project)* Durchführbarkeit *f*, Realisierbarkeit *f*; *(of firm)* Rentabilität *f*; **the ~ of the EC** die Lebens- *or* Existenzfähigkeit der EG

viable [ˈvaɪəbl] ADJ **a** *plant, foetus* lebensfähig **b** *company* rentabel; *economy* lebensfähig; *suggestion, proposition* brauchbar; *plan, project* machbar; *alternative, solution* gangbar; *option* realisierbar; **in order to secure a ~ future for the car industry** um der Autoindustrie eine Überlebenschance zu geben; **the company is not economically ~** die Firma ist unrentabel; **is this newly created state ~?** ist dieser neu entstandene Staat lebens- *or* existenzfähig?; **a ~ form of government** eine funktionsfähige Regierungsform

viaduct [ˈvaɪədʌkt] N Viadukt *m*

Viagra® [vaɪˈægrə] N Viagra® *nt*

vial [ˈvaɪəl] N Fläschchen *nt*, Gefäß *nt*

via media [ˌvaɪəˈmiːdɪə, ˌviːə-] N *(fig form)* Mittelweg *m*

viands [ˈvaɪəndz] PL *(form)* Lebensmittel *pl*; *(for journey)* Proviant *m*

vibes [vaɪbz] PL *(inf)* **a** Vibrafon *nt*, Vibraphon *nt* **b** **what sort of ~ do you get from him?** wie wirkt er auf dich?; **I get good ~ from this music** diese Musik bringt mich auf Touren; **this town is giving me bad ~** diese Stadt macht mich ganz fertig *(inf)*

vibrancy [ˈvaɪbrənsɪ] N *(of personality)* Dynamik *f*; *(of voice)* voller Klang, Sonorität *f*

vibrant [ˈvaɪbrənt] ADJ **a** *personality etc* dynamisch; *voice* volltönend, sonor; *city, community, culture* lebendig, voller Leben; *discussion* lebhaft, angeregt; *economy* boomend; *performance* mitreißend; **the shipyard was ~ with activity** auf der Werft herrschte emsiges Treiben; **the ~ life of the city** das pulsierende Leben der Großstadt **b** *(= brilliant) colour* leuchtend

vibraphone [ˈvaɪbrəfəʊn] N Vibrafon *nt*, Vibraphon *nt*

vibrate [vaɪˈbreɪt] VI *(lit, fig)* zittern, beben *(with* vor *+dat)*; *(machine, string, air)* vibrieren; *(notes)* schwingen; **the painting ~s with life** das Bild bebt *or* sprüht vor Leben; **Glasgow's West End ~s with activity** im Glasgower West End pulsiert das Leben; **the town was vibrating with excitement** Aufregung hatte die Stadt ergriffen VT zum Vibrieren bringen; *string* zum Schwingen bringen; **they study the way the machine ~s the body** sie studieren, wie die Maschine den Körper erschüttert

vibration [vaɪˈbreɪʃən] N **a** *(of string, sound waves)* Schwingung *f*; *(of machine)* Vibrieren *nt*; *(of voice, ground)* Beben *nt*; *(of body)* Zittern *nt*, Beben *nt* **b** *(inf, usu pl)* = **vibes b**

vibrato [vɪˈbrɑːtəʊ] N Vibrato *nt* ADV vibrato

vibrator [vaɪˈbreɪtəʳ] N Vibrator *m*

vibratory [ˈvaɪbrətərɪ] ADJ vibrierend, Vibrations-

vic [vɪk] N *(inf)* = **victim**

vicar [ˈvɪkəʳ] N Pfarrer(in) *m(f)*; **good evening, ~** guten Abend, Herr Pfarrer/Frau Pfarrerin

vicar apostolic N apostolischer Vikar

vicar general N Generalvikar(in) *m(f)*

vicarage [ˈvɪkərɪdʒ] N Pfarrhaus *nt*

vicarious [vɪˈkeərɪəs] ADJ **a** *pleasure, enjoyment* indirekt, mittelbar, nachempfunden; *experience* ersatzweise; **~ sexual thrill** Ersatzbefriedigung *f*; **he can't walk himself but he gets enormous ~ pleasure from watching athletics** er kann nicht gehen, aber das Zuschauen bei sportlichen Wettkämpfen vermittelt ihm einen großen Genuss; **to get a ~ thrill from** *or* **out of sth** sich an etw *(dat)* aufgeilen *(sl)*; **to get ~ satisfaction (from sth)** (bei etw) eine Ersatzbefriedigung empfinden **b** *authority, suffering* stellvertretend **c** *(form) liability, responsibility* für fremdes Verschulden

vicariously [vɪˈkeərɪəslɪ] ADV indirekt, mittelbar; **I can appreciate the island's beauty ~ through your writing** Ihre Beschreibung vermittelt mir die Schönheit der Insel *or* lässt mich die Schönheit der Insel nachempfinden

vicariousness [vɪˈkeərɪəsnɪs] N Indirektheit *f*, Mittelbarkeit *f*; **the appreciation of art always involves a degree of ~** Kunstgenuss setzt immer eine bestimmte Fähigkeit des Nachempfindens voraus

vice¹ [vaɪs] N Laster *nt*; *(of horse)* Unart *f*, Untugend *f*, Mucken *pl (inf)*; **his main ~ is laziness** sein größter Fehler ist die Faulheit; **you don't smoke or drink, don't you have any ~s?** *(hum)* Sie rauchen nicht, Sie trinken nicht, haben Sie denn gar kein Laster? *(hum)*; **a life of ~** ein Lasterleben *nt*

vice², *(US)* **vise** N Schraubstock *m*; **to have/hold sth in a ~-like grip** etw fest umklammern; *(between legs, under arm)* etw fest einklemmen

vice- PREF Vize-; **vice admiral** N Vizeadmiral(in) *m(f)*; **vice-chairman** N stellvertretender Vorsitzender; **vice-chairmanship** N stellvertretender Vorsitz; **vice-chairwoman** N stellvertretende Vorsitzende; **vice chancellor** N *(Brit Univ)* ≈ Rektor(in) *m(f)*; **vice-consul** N Vizekonsul(in) *m(f)*; **vice-presidency** N Vizepräsidentschaft *f*; **vice president** N Vizepräsident(in) *m(f)*

viceroy [ˈvaɪsrɔɪ] N Vizekönig *m*

vice squad N Sittenpolizei *f*, Sittendezernat *nt*, Sitte *f (sl)*

vice versa [ˈvaɪsɪˈvɜːsə] ADV umgekehrt; **economics determine politics, rather than ~** die Volkswirtschaft bestimmt die Politik und nicht umgekehrt

vicinity [vɪˈsɪnɪtɪ] N **a** Umgebung *f*; **in the ~** in der Nähe *(of* von, *gen)*; **in the immediate ~** in unmittelbarer Umgebung; **in the ~ of £500** um die £ 500 (herum) **b** *(= closeness)* Nähe *f*

vicious [ˈvɪʃəs] ADJ **a** *animal* bösartig; *dog* bissig; *blow, kick, gang, attack, crime, criminal* brutal; *murder* grauenhaft, brutal; *campaign* bösartig, gemein; **that animal can be ~** das Tier kann heimtückisch sein; **to have a ~ temper** jähzornig sein **b** *(= nasty)* gemein, boshaft; *remark* boshaft, gehässig; *look* boshaft, böse; **to have a ~ tongue** eine böse *or* spitze Zunge haben **c** *habit* lasterhaft **d** *(inf: = strong, nasty) headache* fies *(inf)*, gemein *(inf)*

vicious circle N Teufelskreis *m*, Circulus vitiosus *m (geh)*; **to be caught in a ~** sich in einem Teufelskreis befinden

vicious cycle N Teufelskreis *m*

viciously [ˈvɪʃəslɪ] ADV **a** *(= violently)* bösartig; *hit, kick* brutal; *murder* auf grauenhafte Art; **the dog ~ attacked him** der Hund fiel wütend über ihn her **b** (= nastily) gemein, boshaft; *remark* gemein, gehässig; *look* böse; *think* boshaft

viciousness [ˈvɪʃəsnɪs] N **a** (of animal) Bösartigkeit *f*; (of dog) Bissigkeit *f*; (of blow, kick) Brutalität *f*; (of murder) Grauenhaftigkeit *f* **b** (= nastiness) Gemeinheit *f*; (of remark) Gemeinheit *f*, Gehässigkeit *f*; (of look) Boshaftigkeit *f*

vicissitude [vɪˈsɪsɪtjuːd] N usu pl Wandel *m*; **the ~s of life** die Launen des Schicksals, die Wechselfälle des Lebens; **the ~s of war** die Wirren des Krieges

victim [ˈvɪktɪm] N Opfer *nt*; **he was the ~ of a practical joke** ihm wurde ein Streich gespielt; **to be the ~ of sb's sarcasm** eine Zielscheibe für jds Sarkasmus sein; **the hawk flew off with its ~ in its claws** der Falke flog mit seiner Beute in den Klauen davon; **to fall (a) ~ to sth** einer Sache *(dat)* zum Opfer fallen; **I fell ~ to the flu** mich hatte die Grippe erwischt *(inf)*; **to fall ~ to sb's charms** jds Charme *(dat)* erliegen; **the whole of the region fell ~ to the drought** die ganze Gegend wurde ein Opfer der Dürre

victimization [ˌvɪktɪmaɪˈzeɪʃən] N ungerechte Behandlung; (= harassment) Schikanierung *f*

victimize [ˈvɪktɪmaɪz] VT ungerecht behandeln; (= pick on) schikanieren; **she feels ~d** sie fühlt sich ungerecht behandelt; **this ~s the public** darunter hat die Öffentlichkeit zu leiden

victimless [ˈvɪktɪmlɪs] ADJ *crime* ohne Opfer

victimology [ˌvɪktɪˈmɒlədʒɪ] N (branch of criminology) Viktimologie *f*

victor [ˈvɪktəʳ] N Sieger(in) *m(f)*

Victoria Cross [vɪkˈtɔːrɪəˈkrɒs] N (Brit) Viktoriakreuz *nt (höchste britische Tapferkeitsauszeichnung)*

Victoria Falls [vɪkˈtɔːrɪəˈfɔːlz] PL Viktoriafälle *f*

Victorian [vɪkˈtɔːrɪən] **N** Viktorianer(in) *m(f)* **ADJ** viktorianisch; *(fig)* (sitten)streng

> **VICTORIAN**
>
> Das Adjektiv **Victorian**, viktorianisch, wird für das Großbritannien, seine Bevölkerung und Kultur unter der Regentschaft von Königin Viktoria (1837 - 1901) verwendet: „a Victorian house", „the great Victorian Prime Minister, Gladstone". Als Substantiv kann es auch auf eine Person bezogen werden, die zur damaligen Zeit lebte.
>
> Mit **Victorian** kann man aber auch die vorherrschenden Meinungen und gesellschaftlichen Vorstellungen jener Epoche in ihrem negativen wie positiven Sinn bezeichnen. Unangenehme viktorianische Eigenschaften sind das äußerste Bedachtsein auf den gesellschaftlichen Ruf, repressiv strenge Moralvorstellungen, Humorlosigkeit, Bigotterie und Heuchelei.
>
> Dagegen lieben es britische Politiker, die viktorianischen Tugenden hervorzuheben, wie das Streben nach Weiterbildung und gesellschaftlichem Aufstieg, Anstand, Respekt vor der Autorität und Familiensinn, Eigenschaften, die in der gegenwärtigen Gesellschaft vermisst werden.

Victoriana [vɪkˌtɔːrɪˈɑːnə] N viktorianische Antiquitäten *pl*

victorious [vɪkˈtɔːrɪəs] ADJ *army, allies* siegreich; *smile* triumphierend, siegesbewusst; *battle, war, campaign* erfolgreich; **to be ~ over sb/sth** jdn/etw besiegen; **to be ~ in the struggle against …** siegen *or* den Sieg davontragen im Kampf gegen …; **to emerge ~ from sth** als Sieger(in) *m(f)* aus etw hervorgehen; **to be ~ in an election** eine Wahl gewinnen

victoriously [vɪkˈtɔːrɪəslɪ] ADV siegreich, als Sieger(in)

victory [ˈvɪktərɪ] N Sieg *m*; **to gain** *or* **win a ~ over sb/sth** einen Sieg über jdn/etw erringen, jdn/etw besiegen; **his final ~ over his fear** die endgültige Überwindung seiner Angst

victory roll N (Aviat) Siegesrolle *f*

victual [ˈvɪtl] (form) **VT** *army, troop* verpflegen, verproviantieren **VI** sich verpflegen *or* verproviantieren

victualler [ˈvɪtləʳ] N → **licensed**

victuals [ˈvɪtlz] PL Lebensmittel *pl*; (for journey) Proviant *m*, Verpflegung *f*

vicuña [vɪˈkuːnjə] N (= animal, wool) Vicunja *nt*

vide [ˈvɪdeɪ] IMPER (form, Jur) siehe, vide *(liter)*

videlicet [vɪˈdiːlɪset] ADV (abbr **viz**) nämlich

video [ˈvɪdɪəʊ] **N** **a** (= film) Video *nt* **b** (= recorder) Videorekorder *m* **c** (US) Fernsehen *nt*; **on ~** im Fernsehen **VT** (auf Video) aufnehmen

video: **video arcade** N Spielhalle *f*; **video camera** N Videokamera *f*; **video cassette** N Videokassette *f*; **video clip** N Videoclip *m*; **video conference** N Videokonferenz *f*; **video conferencing** N Videokonferenzschaltung *f*; **video diary** N (TV) Videotagebuch *nt*; **video disc** N Bildplatte *f*; **video disc player** N Bildplattenspieler *m*; **video game** N Telespiel *nt*; **video library** N Videothek *f*; **video nasty** N (Brit) Horrorvideo *nt*; **videophone** N Fernsehtelefon *nt*; **video recorder** N Videorekorder *m*; **video-recording** N Videoaufnahme *f*; **video rental** N Videoverleih *m*; **~ shop** (esp Brit) *or* **store** Videothek *f*; **video screen** N Videoschirm *m*; **video shop** N Videothek *f*; **video tape** N Videoband *nt*; **video-tape** VT (auf Video) aufzeichnen; **video wall** N Videowand *f*

vidkid [ˈvɪdkɪd] N (US inf) fernseh- *or* videosüchtiges Kind, fernseh- *or* videosüchtiger Jugendlicher

vie [vaɪ] VI wetteifern; (Comm) konkurrieren; **to ~ with sb for sth** mit jdm um etw wetteifern; **to ~ with sb to do sth** mit jdm darum wetteifern, etw zu tun; **they are vying for the championship** sie kämpfen um die Meisterschaft

Vienna [vɪˈenə] **N** Wien *nt* **ADJ** Wiener

Viennese [ˌvɪəˈniːz] **ADJ** wienerisch **N** Wiener(in) *m(f)*

Vietcong [vjetˈkɒŋ] N Vietcong *m*

Vietnam [ˌvjetˈnæm] N Vietnam *nt*

Vietnamese [ˌvjetnəˈmiːz] **ADJ** vietnamesisch **N** **a** Vietnamese *m*, Vietnamesin *f* **b** (Ling) Vietnamesisch *nt*

Viet Vet [ˈviːetˈvet] N (dated US) Vietnam(kriegs)veteran(in) *m(f)*

view [vjuː] ✪ 17.1, 26.2, 26.3 **N** **a** (= range of vision) Sicht *f*; **in full ~ of thousands of people** vor den Augen von tausenden *or* Tausenden von Menschen; **the magician placed the box in full ~ of the audience** der Zauberer stellte die Kiste so auf, dass das ganze Publikum sie sehen konnte; **the ship came into ~** das Schiff kam in Sicht; **I came into ~ of the lake** der See kam in Sicht *or* lag vor mir; **to keep sth in ~** etw im Auge behalten; **the cameraman had a job keeping the plane in ~** der Kameramann fand es schwierig, das Flugzeug zu verfolgen; **to go out of ~** außer Sicht kommen, verschwinden; **the house is within ~ of the sea** vom Haus aus ist das Meer zu sehen; **the house is exposed to ~ from passing trains** das Haus kann von vorbeifahrenden Zügen aus eingesehen werden; **hidden from ~** verborgen, versteckt; **the horses were hidden from ~ behind the trees** die Pferde waren von den Bäumen verdeckt; **she keeps the old china hidden from ~** sie bewahrt das alte Porzellan im Verborgenen auf; **the house is hidden from ~ from the main road** das Haus ist von der Hauptstraße aus nicht zu sehen; **on ~** (for purchasing) zur Ansicht; (of exhibits) ausgestellt; **the painting will be on ~ tomorrow** das Bild kann morgen besichtigt werden

b (= prospect, sight) Aussicht *f*; **there is a splendid ~ from here/from the top** von hier/von der Spitze hat man einen herrlichen Blick *or* eine wunderschöne Aussicht; **a ~ over …** ein Blick *m* über … *(acc)*; **a good ~ of the sea** ein schöner Blick auf das Meer; **a room with a ~** ein Zimmer mit schöner Aussicht; **I only got a side ~ of his head** ich habe seinen Kopf nur im Profil gesehen; **he stood up to get a better ~** er stand auf, um besser sehen zu können

c (= photograph etc) Ansicht *f (also Comput)*; **I want to take a ~ of the forest** ich möchte eine Aufnahme vom Wald machen; **~s of London** Ansichten *pl or* Stadtbilder *pl* von London; **~s of the Alps** Alpenbilder *pl*; **quick ~** (Comput) Schnellansicht *f*

d (= opinion) Ansicht *f*, Meinung *f*; **in my ~** meiner Ansicht *or* Meinung nach; **to have** *or* **hold ~s on sth** Ansichten über etw *(acc)* haben; **what are his ~s on this problem?** was meint er zu diesem Problem?; **do you have any special ~s on the matter?** haben Sie eine besondere Meinung zu dieser Sache?; **I have no ~s on that** ich habe keine Meinung dazu; **to take the ~ that …** die Ansicht vertreten, dass …; **to take a dim** *(inf) or* **poor ~ of sb's conduct** jds Verhalten missbilligen → **point**

e (= mental survey) **an idealistic ~ of the world** eine idealistische Welt(an)sicht; **a general** *or* **overall ~ of a problem** ein allgemeiner *or* umfassender Überblick über ein Problem; **a clear ~ of the facts** eine klare Übersicht über die Fakten; **in ~ of** wegen *(+gen)*, angesichts *(+gen)*; **at first ~** auf den ersten Blick; **we must not lose from ~ the fact that …** wir dürfen die Tatsache nicht aus dem Auge verlieren, dass …; **I'll keep it in ~** ich werde es im Auge behalten

f (= intention, plan) Absicht *f*; **to have sth in ~** etw beabsichtigen; **with a ~ to doing sth** mit der Absicht, etw zu tun; **with this in ~** im Hinblick darauf; **he has the weekend in ~ when he says …** er denkt an das Wochenende, wenn er sagt …

VT **a** (= see) betrachten

b (= examine) *house* besichtigen

c (= consider) *problem etc* sehen; **he ~s the prospect with dismay** er sieht dieser Sache mit Schrecken entgegen

d (Comput: *command*) anzeigen

VI (= watch television) fernsehen

viewable [ˈvjuːəbl] ADJ (= visible) zu sehen(d), sichtbar; *film etc* sehenswert; (Comput) lesbar

Viewdata® [ˈvjuːdeɪtə] N Bildschirmtext *m*, Btx *m*

viewer [ˈvjuːəʳ] N **a** (TV) Zuschauer(in) *m(f)* **b** (for slides) Dia- *or* Bildbetrachter *m*

viewership [ˈvjuːəʃɪp] N Fernsehpublikum *nt*

viewfinder [ˈvjuːˌfaɪndəʳ] N Sucher *m*

viewing [ˈvjuːɪŋ] N **a** (of house, at auction etc) Besichtigung *f*; **~ time** Besichtigungszeiten *pl* **b** (TV) Fernsehen *nt*; **tennis makes compulsive ~** Tennis macht die Fernsehzuschauer süchtig; **9 o'clock is peak ~ time** neun Uhr ist (die) Haupteinschaltzeit; **this programme will be given another ~ next week** dieses Programm wird nächste Woche wiederholt; **I don't do much ~** ich sehe nicht viel fern

viewing figures PL (TV) Zuschauerzahlen *pl*

viewing public N (TV) Zuschauer *pl*

viewpoint [ˈvjuːpɔɪnt] N **a** Standpunkt *m*; **from the ~ of economic growth** unter dem Gesichtspunkt des Wirtschaftswachstums; **to see sth from sb's ~** etw aus jds Sicht sehen **b** (for scenic view) Aussichtspunkt *m*

vigil [ˈvɪdʒɪl] N **a** (Nacht)wache *f*; **to keep ~ over sb** bei jdm wachen; **the dog kept ~ over his injured master** der Hund hielt bei seinem verletzten Herrn Wache; **her long ~s at his bedside** ihr langes Wachen an seinem Krankenbett **b** (Rel) Vigil *f*, Nachtwache *f*

vigilance [ˈvɪdʒɪləns] N Wachsamkeit *f*; **no move escaped their ~** keine Bewegung entging ihrem wachsamen Auge

vigilance committee N Bürgerwehr *f*, Selbstschutzkomitee *nt*

vigilant [ˈvɪdʒɪlənt] ADJ wachsam; **to be ~ about sth** auf etw *(acc)* achten; **to be ~ about over-exposing oneself to the sun** darauf achten, sich nicht zu sehr der Sonne auszusetzen; **to be ~ against sth** sich vor etw *(dat)* hüten;

to keep a ~ eye on sb/sth ein wachsames Auge auf jdn/etw haben; **to be under sb's ~ eye** von jdm genau beobachtet werden; **the customs officers are ever ~ for drug traffickers** die Zollbeamten haben stets ein wachsames Auge auf Drogenhändler

vigilante [ˌvɪdʒɪˈlæntɪ] N *Mitglied einer Selbstschutzorganisation*; **the ~s** die Bürgerwehr, der Selbstschutz ADJ *attr* Selbstschutz-; **~ group** Selbstschutzgruppe *f*

vigilantism [ˌvɪdʒɪˈlæntɪzəm] N Bürgerwehraktionen *pl*

vigilantly [ˈvɪdʒɪləntlɪ] ADV aufmerksam; *patrol* wachsam

vignette [vɪˈnjet] N Vignette *f*; *(= character sketch)* Skizze *f*, kurze und prägnante Darstellung

vigor N *(US)* = **vigour**

vigorous [ˈvɪgərəs] ADJ **a** *(= powerful)* kräftig; *prose, tune* kraftvoll; *protest, denial, measures, exercises, training* energisch; *walk* forsch, flott; *nod* eifrig, heftig; *match, player, activity* dynamisch; *speech* feurig; *debater* leidenschaftlich **b** *(= active) defence, campaign* energisch; *opponent, advocate* engagiert

vigorously [ˈvɪgərəslɪ] ADV **a** *(= energetically) shake one's head* energisch; *shake hands* kräftig **b** *(= strongly) deny, protest* energisch; *defend, campaign* engagiert; *oppose* heftig

vigour, *(US)* **vigor** [ˈvɪgəʳ] N Kraft *f*, Energie *f*; *(of protest, denial)* Heftigkeit *f*; *(of exercises)* Energie *f*; *(of player)* Dynamik *f*; *(of speech, debater)* Leidenschaftlichkeit *f*; *(of prose)* Ausdruckskraft *f*; **sexual/youthful ~** sexuelle/jugendliche Spannkraft; **all the ~ has gone out of the undertaking** das Unternehmen hat jeglichen Schwung verloren

Viking [ˈvaɪkɪŋ] N Wikinger(in) *m(f)* ADJ Wikinger-; **~ ship** Wikingerschiff *nt*

vile [vaɪl] ADJ abscheulich; *mood, smell, habit also, regime, conditions* übel; *thoughts* niedrig, gemein; *language* unflätig; *weather, food* scheußlich, widerlich; **that was a ~ thing to say** es war eine Gemeinheit, so etwas zu sagen; **he was ~ to his wife** er benahm sich scheußlich gegenüber seiner Frau; **to be in a ~ temper** *or* **mood** ganz übel gelaunt sein

vilely [ˈvaɪllɪ] ADV abscheulich, scheußlich; *(= shamefully) exploit* übel

vileness [ˈvaɪlnɪs] N Abscheulichkeit *f*; *(of thoughts)* Niederträchtigkeit *f*; *(of smell)* Widerwärtigkeit *f*; *(of language)* Unflätigkeit *f*; *(of weather)* Scheußlichkeit *f*; **the ~ of his mood** seine Übellaunigkeit

vilification [ˌvɪlɪfɪˈkeɪʃən] N Diffamierung *f*, Verleumdung *f*

vilify [ˈvɪlɪfaɪ] VT diffamieren, verleumden

villa [ˈvɪlə] N Villa *f*

village [ˈvɪlɪdʒ] N Dorf *nt*

village *in cpds* Dorf-; **village green** N Dorfwiese *f or* -anger *m*; **village hall** N Gemeindesaal *m*; **village idiot** N Dorftrottel *m (inf)*

villager [ˈvɪlɪdʒəʳ] N Dörfler(in) *m(f)*, Dorfbewohner(in) *m(f) (also Admin)*

villain [ˈvɪlən] N **a** *(= scoundrel)* Schurke *m*, Schurkin *f*; *(inf: = criminal)* Verbrecher(in) *m(f)*, Ganove *m (inf)* **b** *(in drama, novel)* Bösewicht *m* **c** *(inf: = rascal)* Bengel *m*; **he's the ~ of the piece** er ist der Übeltäter

villainous [ˈvɪlənəs] ADJ **a** böse; *deed* niederträchtig, gemein; **a ~ face** ein Verbrechergesicht *nt* **b** *(inf: = bad)* scheußlich

villainously [ˈvɪlənəslɪ] ADV *smile* hämisch; **he ~ murdered his brothers** in seiner Niedertracht ermordete er seine Brüder

villainy [ˈvɪlənɪ] N Gemeinheit *f*, Niederträchtigkeit *f*

villein [ˈvɪlɪn] N *(Hist)* Leibeigene(r) *mf*

vim [vɪm] N *(inf)* Schwung *m*; **he writes with great ~** er schreibt sehr schwungvoll; **full of ~ and vigour** *(Brit) or* **vigor** *(US)* voller Schwung und Elan

vinaigrette [ˌvɪnɪˈgret] N Vinaigrette *f (Cook)*; *(for salad)* Salatsoße *f*

vindaloo [ˌvɪndəˈluː] N *sehr scharf gewürztes indisches Currygericht*

vindicate [ˈvɪndɪkeɪt] VT **a** *opinion, action, decision* rechtfertigen **b** *(= exonerate)* rehabilitieren

vindication [ˌvɪndɪˈkeɪʃən] N **a** *(of opinion, action, decision)* Rechtfertigung *f*; **in ~ of** zur Rechtfertigung *(+gen)* **b** *(= exoneration)* Rehabilitation *f*

vindictive [vɪnˈdɪktɪv] ADJ *speech, person* rachsüchtig; *mood* nachtragend, unversöhnlich; **he is not a ~ person** er ist nicht nachtragend; **these measures are likely to make the unions feel ~** diese Maßnahmen könnten bei den Gewerkschaften auf Unwillen *or* Ressentiments stoßen; **I hope you won't feel ~ because of my rather harsh criticism** ich hoffe, Sie tragen mir meine etwas harte Kritik nicht nach *or* Sie nehmen mir meine etwas harte Kritik nicht übel; **corporal punishment can make pupils feel ~ toward(s) the teacher** die Prügelstrafe kann die Schüler gegen den Lehrer aufbringen; **to feel a moment's ~ pleasure** einen Moment der Schadenfreude verspüren

vindictively [vɪnˈdɪktɪvlɪ] ADV *say, behave* gemein

vindictiveness [vɪnˈdɪktɪvnɪs] N Rachsucht *f*; *(of mood)* Unversöhnlichkeit *f*; **the ~ of his speech** seine rachsüchtige Rede

vine [vaɪn] N **a** *(= grapevine)* Rebe *f*, Weinrebe *f* **b** *(= similar plant)* Rebengewächs *nt*

vinedresser [ˈvaɪndresəʳ] N Winzer(in) *m(f)*

vinegar [ˈvɪnɪgəʳ] N Essig *m*

vinegary [ˈvɪnɪgərɪ] ADJ *(lit, fig)* säuerlich; **~ smell** Essiggeruch *m*

vine: **vine grower** N Weinbauer *m*/-bäuerin *f*; **vine-growing district** N Weingegend *f*, Weinbaugebiet *nt*; **vine harvest** N Weinlese *f*, Weinernte *f*; **vine leaf** N Rebenblatt *nt*; **vineyard** [ˈvɪnjəd] N Weinberg *m*

viniculture [ˈvɪnɪˌkʌltʃəʳ] N Weinbau *m*

vino [ˈviːnəʊ] N *(inf: = wine)* Vino *m (inf)*

vintage [ˈvɪntɪdʒ] N **a** *(= given year) (of wine, fig)* Jahrgang *m*; *(of car)* Baujahr *nt* **b** *(= wine of particular year)* **the 1984 ~** der Jahrgang 1984, der 84er **c** *(= harvesting, season)* Weinlese *f*, Weinernte *f* ADJ *attr (= old)* uralt; *(= high quality)* glänzend, hervorragend; **this typewriter is a ~ model** diese Schreibmaschine hat Museumswert; **a ~ performance from Humphrey Bogart** eine einmalige künstlerische Leistung Humphrey Bogarts

vintage: **vintage car** N Vorkriegsmodell *nt*, Vintage-Car *nt*; **vintage port** N Vintage-Port *m*, *schwerer Port eines besonderen Jahrgangs*; **vintage shop** N *(US)* Secondhandladen *m*; **vintage wine** N edler Wein; **vintage year** N **a ~ for wine** ein besonders gutes Weinjahr; **a ~ for Burgundy** ein besonders gutes Jahr für Burgunder; **it was a ~ for investment** es war ein ausgezeichnetes Jahr für Investitionen

vintner [ˈvɪntnəʳ] N Weinhändler(in) *m(f)*

vinyl [ˈvaɪnɪl] N Vinyl *nt*

viol [ˈvaɪəl] N Viola *f*

viola[1] [vɪˈəʊlə] N *(Mus)* Bratsche *f*

viola[2] [ˈvaɪəʊlə] N *(Bot)* Veilchen *nt*

viola da gamba [vɪˈəʊlədəˈgæmbə] N Gambe *f*

violate [ˈvaɪəleɪt] VT **a** *treaty, promise* brechen; *(partially)* verletzen; *law, rule, moral code* verletzen, verstoßen gegen; *rights, airspace* verletzen; *truth* vergewaltigen **b** *(= disturb) holy place* entweihen, schänden; *peacefulness* stören; **to ~ sb's privacy** in jds Privatsphäre eindringen; **it's violating a person's privacy to …** es ist ein Eingriff in jemandes Privatsphäre, wenn man …; **the shriek of the jets now ~s that once peaceful spot** durch das Heulen der Düsenflugzeuge ist die Idylle dieses Fleckchens zerstört worden **c** *(= rape)* vergewaltigen, schänden

violation [ˌvaɪəˈleɪʃən] N **a** *(of law)* Übertretung (of +*gen*), Verletzung *f* (of +*gen*), Verstoß *m* (of gegen); *(of rule)* Verstoß *m* (of gegen); *(of rights)* Verletzung *f*; *(of truth)* Vergewaltigung *f*; **a ~ of a treaty** ein Vertragsbruch *m*; *(partial)* eine Vertragsverletzung; **traffic ~** Verkehrsvergehen *nt*; **he did this in ~ of the conditions agreed** er verstieß damit gegen die Vereinbarungen **b** *(of holy place)* Entweihung *f*, Schändung *f*; *(of peacefulness)* Störung *f*; *(of privacy)* Eingriff *m* (of in +*acc*) **c** *(= rape)* Vergewaltigung *f*, Schändung *f*

violator [ˈvaɪəleɪtəʳ] N *(of treaty)* Vertragsbrüchige(r) *mf*; *(of laws)* Gesetzesverletzer(in) *m(f)*; *(of holy place)* Schänder(in) *m(f)*; *(of woman)* Schänder *m*; **the ~ of these rules …** wer gegen diese Regeln verstößt, …

violence [ˈvaɪələns] N **a** *(= forcefulness, strength)* Heftigkeit *f*; *(of protest)* Schärfe *f*, Heftigkeit *f*; *(of speech also)* Leidenschaftlichkeit *f*; **the ~ of the contrast** der krasse Gegensatz; **the ~ of his temper** sein jähzorniges Temperament, seine Jähzornigkeit

b *(= brutality)* Gewalt *f*; *(of people)* Gewalttätigkeit *f*; *(of actions)* Brutalität *f*; **the ~ of his nature** seine gewalttätige Art; **crime of ~** Gewaltverbrechen *nt*; **act of ~** Gewalttat *f*; **robbery with ~** Raubüberfall *m*; **an increase in ~** eine Zunahme der Gewalttätigkeit; **to use ~ against sb** Gewalt gegen jdn anwenden; **was there any ~?** kam es zu Gewalttätigkeiten?; **outbreak of ~** Ausbruch *m* von Gewalttätigkeiten

c *(fig)* **to do ~ to sth** etw entstellen; **it does ~ to the human spirit** das vergewaltigt den gesunden Menschenverstand

violent [ˈvaɪələnt] ADJ **a** *(= brutal) person, nature, action* brutal, gewalttätig; *crime* Gewalt-; *times, period, age* voller Gewalt; *attack, blow* heftig; *death* gewaltsam; *sport, game* brutal; *film, programme, book* gewalttätig; **to have a ~ temper** jähzornig sein; **to be in a ~ temper** toben; **to turn ~** gewalttätig werden; **to meet a ~ end** eines gewaltsamen Todes sterben; **the beginning of the second movement is rather ~** der zweite Satz beginnt sehr leidenschaftlich; **to get** *or* **become ~** gewalttätig werden; **by ~ means** *(open sth)* mit Gewalt(anwendung); *(persuade)* unter Gewaltanwendung

b *(= forceful) demonstration, protest* heftig; *expulsion, impact* gewaltig; *wind, storm, earthquake* heftig, stark, gewaltig; **don't be so ~, open it gently** sei nicht so stürmisch, öffne es vorsichtig

c *(= dramatic) contrast* krass; *change* tief greifend

d *(= vehement) argument, row, opposition* heftig

e *(= intense) blush* heftig, tief; *feeling, affair, speech* leidenschaftlich; *pain, dislike* heftig, stark; *colour* grell

violently [ˈvaɪələntlɪ] ADV **a** *(= brutally) kick, beat, attack, react, act* brutal; **to die ~** eines gewaltsamen Todes sterben

b *(= forcefully) push, fling, hurl* kräftig; *tremble, shake, shudder* heftig; *swerve, brake* abrupt

c *(= dramatically)* **red and pink clash ~** Rot und Rosa beißen sich; **they have quite ~ opposed temperaments** sie haben völlig unvereinbare Temperamente

d *(= vehemently) speak* heftig, leidenschaftlich; *disagree* scharf; **they are ~ anti-communist** sie sind militante Antikommunisten; **to be ~ against sth** *or* **opposed to sth** ein scharfer Gegner/eine scharfe Gegnerin einer Sache *(gen)* sein; **he expresses himself rather ~** er drückt sich sehr krass aus

e *(= intensely) blush* tief, heftig; *fall in love* unsterblich; **to be ~ ill** *or* **sick** sich furchtbar übergeben; **he was ~ angry** er war außer sich *(dat)* vor Wut; **to retch/cough ~** gewaltig würgen/husten

violet [ˈvaɪəlɪt] N *(Bot)* Veilchen *nt*; *(= colour)* Violett *nt* ADJ violett

violin [ˌvaɪəˈlɪn] N Geige *f*, Violine *f*

violin case N Geigenkasten *m*

violin concerto N Violinkonzert *nt*

violinist [ˌvaɪəˈlɪnɪst] N Geiger(in) *m(f)*, Violinist(in) *m(f)*

violin player N Geiger(in) *m(f)*, Geigenspieler(in) *m(f)*

violin sonata N Violinsonate *f*

violist [vɪˈəʊlɪst] N *(US)* Bratschist(in) *m(f)*

violoncello [ˌvaɪələnˈtʃeləʊ] N *(form)* Violoncello *nt*

VIP N prominente Persönlichkeit, VIP *m*, Promi *m (hum inf)*; **he got/we gave him ~ treatment** er wurde/wir haben ihn als Ehrengast behandelt; **~ lounge** Prominentensuite *f*, VIP-Lounge *f*

viper [ˈvaɪpəʳ] N *(Zool)* Viper *f*; *(fig)* Schlange *f*

viperish [ˈvaɪpərɪʃ] ADJ *(fig)* giftig

virago [vɪˈrɑːgəʊ] N Xanthippe *f*

viral [ˈvaɪərəl] ADJ Virus-; **~ infection** Virusinfektion *f*

Virgil [ˈvɜːdʒɪl] N Vergil(ius) *m*, Virgil *m*

virgin [ˈvɜːdʒɪn] N Jungfrau *f*; **the (Blessed) Virgin** *(Rel)* die (Heilige) Jungfrau Maria; **the Virgin Mary** die Jungfrau Maria; **the Black Virgin** die Schwarze Madonna; **he's still a ~** er ist noch unschuldig; **she's a political ~** sie ist in der Politik noch unbeleckt ADJ *girl, woman* jungfräulich, unberührt; *(fig) forest, land* unberührt; *freshness* rein; *snow* jungfräulich, unberührt; **~ olive oil** natives Olivenöl; **the Virgin Queen** *Königin Elisabeth I.*; **to be ~ territory (for sb)** Neuland *nt* (für jdn) sein

virginal [ˈvɜːdʒɪnl] ADJ **a** jungfräulich; **dressed in ~ white** in jungfräuliches Weiß gekleidet **b** *(form, = unused)* jungfräulich PL *(Mus)* Tafelklavier *nt*

virgin birth N jungfräuliche Geburt; *(Biol)* Jungfernzeugung *f*

Virginia [vəˈdʒɪnjə] N *(= state)* Virginia *nt*; *(= tobacco)* Virginia *m*; **he smokes ~s** er raucht Virginiazigaretten

Virginia creeper N wilder Wein, Jungfernrebe *f*

Virginian [vəˈdʒɪnjən] N Einwohner(in) *m(f)* von Virginia, Virginier(in) *m(f)* ADJ von/aus Virginia

Virginia tobacco N Virginiatabak *m*

Virgin Isles N **the ~** die Jungferninseln *pl*

virginity [vɜːˈdʒɪnɪtɪ] N Unschuld *f*; *(of girls also)* Jungfräulichkeit *f*; **to take sb's ~** jds Unschuld rauben

Virgo [ˈvɜːgəʊ] N Jungfrau *f*; **he's (a) ~** er ist Jungfrau

Virgoan [vɜːˈgəʊən] *(Astrol)* N Jungfrau *f*; **he's a ~** er ist (eine) Jungfrau ADJ **he's ~** er ist (eine) Jungfrau

virgule [ˈvɜːgjuːl] N *(US Typ: = oblique)* Schrägstrich *m*, Virgel *f (spec)*

virile [ˈvɪraɪl] ADJ *(lit)* männlich; *(fig)* ausdrucksvoll, kraftvoll

virility [vɪˈrɪlɪtɪ] N *(lit)* Männlichkeit *f*; *(= sexual power)* Potenz *f*; *(fig)* Ausdruckskraft *f*; **political ~** politische Potenz

virologist [ˌvaɪəˈrɒlədʒɪst] N Virologe *m*, Virologin *f*, Virusforscher(in) *m(f)*

virology [ˌvaɪəˈrɒlədʒɪ] N Virologie *f*, Virusforschung *f*

virtual [ˈvɜːtjʊəl] ADJ *attr* **a** *certainty, impossibility* fast völlig; **it led to the ~ collapse of the economy** es führte dazu, dass die Wirtschaft so gut wie zusammenbrach; **they have a ~ monopoly** sie haben so gut wie das Monopol; **to come to a ~ halt** *or* **standstill** so gut wie zum Erliegen kommen; **she was a ~ prisoner/recluse/stranger** sie war so gut wie eine Gefangene/Einsiedlerin/Fremde; **he is the ~ leader** er ist quasi der Führer, praktisch ist er der Führer; **it was a ~ admission of guilt** es war praktisch ein Schuldgeständnis; **it was a ~ disaster** es war geradezu eine Katastrophe; **it was a ~ failure** es war praktisch ein Misserfolg *m*
b *(Phys)* virtuell
c *(Comput)* virtuell; **~ address** *(Comput)* virtuelle Adresse; **~ sex** virtueller Sex

virtuality [vɜːtjʊˈælɪtɪ] N Virtualität *f*

virtually [ˈvɜːtjʊəlɪ] ADV **a** praktisch; *blind, lost also* fast, nahezu, mehr oder weniger; **yes, ~** ja, fast, ja so gut wie; **he is ~ the boss** er ist praktisch *or* quasi der Chef; **to be ~ certain** sich *(dat)* so gut wie sicher sein **b** *(Comput)* virtuell

virtual memory N *(Comput)* virtueller Speicher

virtual reality N *(Comput)* virtuelle Realität; **~ computer** virtueller Computer; **~ helmet** Datenhelm *m*

virtue [ˈvɜːtjuː] N **a** *(= moral quality)* Tugend *f*; **to make a ~ of necessity** aus der Not eine Tugend machen; **a life of ~** ein tugendhaftes Leben **b** *(= chastity)* Keuschheit *f*, Tugendhaftigkeit *f*; **a woman of easy ~** *(euph)* ein leichtes Mädchen **c** *(= advantage, point)* Vorteil *m*; **what's the ~ of that?** welchen Vorteil hat das?, wozu ist das gut?; **there is no ~ in doing that** es scheint nicht sehr zweckmäßig, das zu tun **d** *(= healing power)* Heilkraft *f*; **in** *or* **by ~ of** aufgrund *or* auf Grund *(+gen)*; **in** *or* **by ~ of the authority/power** *etc* **vested in me** kraft meiner Autorität/Macht *etc (form)*

virtuosity [ˌvɜːtjʊˈɒsɪtɪ] N Virtuosität *f*

virtuoso [ˌvɜːtjʊˈəʊzəʊ] N *(esp Mus)* Virtuose *m*, Virtuosin *f* ADJ *performance* meisterhaft, virtuos

virtuous [ˈvɜːtjʊəs] ADJ **a** tugendhaft, tugendsam **b** *(pej: = self-satisfied, righteous) person, attitude* selbstgerecht

virtuous circle N positiver Kreislauf *m*, Circulus virtuosus *m*; **the ~ of investment and growth** die positive Auswirkung von Investitionen auf das Wachstum und umgekehrt

virtuously [ˈvɜːtjʊəslɪ] ADV *(pej: = righteously) say* selbstgerecht

virulence [ˈvɪrʊləns] N **a** *(Med)* Heftigkeit *f*, Bösartigkeit *f*; *(of poison)* Stärke *f* **b** *(fig)* Schärfe *f*, Virulenz *f (geh)*

virulent [ˈvɪrʊlənt] ADJ **a** *(Med)* bösartig; *poison* stark, tödlich **b** *(fig: = vicious) attack, speech, critic, opponent* scharf; *hatred* unversöhnlich; *colour* grell

virulently [ˈvɪrʊləntlɪ] ADV **a** *(Med)* virulent **b** *(fig)* scharf; **~ racist** virulent rassistisch

virus [ˈvaɪərəs] N **a** *(Med)* Virus *nt or m*, Erreger *m*; **polio ~** Polioerreger *m*; **the AIDS ~** das Aidsvirus; **~ disease** Viruskrankheit *f*; **she's got** *or* **caught a ~** *(inf: = flu etc)* sie hat sich *(dat)* was geholt *or* eingefangen *(inf)* **b** *(fig)* Geschwür *nt* **c** *(Comput)* Virus *nt or m*; **~-infected** virenbefallen; **~ detection** Viruserkennung *f*

virus checker N *(Comput inf)* Virensuchprogramm *nt*

virus-fighting program N *(Comput)* Antivirenprogramm *nt*

visa [ˈviːzə] N Visum *nt*; *(= stamp also)* Sichtvermerk *m* VT ein Visum ausstellen *(+dat)*; **to get a passport ~ed** einen Sichtvermerk in den Pass bekommen

visage [ˈvɪzɪdʒ] N *(liter)* Antlitz *nt (liter)*

visagiste [ˌvizɑːˈʒiːst, ˈvɪzədʒɪst] N Visagist(in) *m(f)*

vis-à-vis [ˈviːzəviː] PREP in Anbetracht *(+gen)* ADV gegenüber

viscera [ˈvɪsərə] PL innere Organe *pl*; *(in abdomen)* Eingeweide *pl*

visceral [ˈvɪsərəl] ADJ viszeral *(spec)*; *(of intestines also)* der Eingeweide; *(fig) hatred, dislike* tief sitzend; **on a ~ level** auf einer emotionalen Ebene; **a ~ feeling** *(fig liter)* ein inneres Gefühl

viscid [ˈvɪsɪd] ADJ *(form)* zähflüssig; *(Bot)* klebrig

viscose [ˈvɪskəʊs] N Viskose *f*

viscosity [vɪsˈkɒsɪtɪ] N Zähflüssigkeit *f*; *(Phys)* Viskosität *f*

viscount [ˈvaɪkaʊnt] N Viscount *m*

viscountcy [ˈvaɪkaʊntsɪ] N Rang *m* des Viscounts

viscountess [ˈvaɪkaʊntɪs] N Viscountess *f*

viscounty [ˈvaɪkaʊntɪ] N = **viscountcy**

viscous [ˈvɪskəs] ADJ *(form)* zähflüssig; *(Phys)* viskos

vise [vaɪs] N *(US)* = **vice²**

visibility [ˌvɪzɪˈbɪlɪtɪ] N **a** Sichtbarkeit *f* **b** *(Met)* Sichtweite *f*; **poor/good ~** schlechte/gute Sicht; **low ~** geringe Sichtweite; **~ is down to 100 metres** die Sichtweite beträgt nur 100 Meter

visible [ˈvɪzəbl] ADJ **a** sichtbar; **~ to the naked eye** mit dem bloßen Auge zu erkennen; **it wasn't ~ in the fog** es war im Nebel nicht zu erkennen; **the Englishman prefers his emotions not to be ~** der Engländer zeigt nicht gern seine Gefühle; **the house is ~ from the road** das Haus ist von der Straße aus zu sehen; **there is no ~ difference** man kann keinen Unterschied erkennen; **with a ~ effort** mit sichtlicher Mühe **b** *(= obvious)* sichtlich; *(= prominent) person* eminent, herausragend; **at management level women are becoming increasing ~** auf Führungsebene treten Frauen immer deutlicher in Erscheinung; **with no ~ means of support** *(Jur)* ohne bekannte Einkommensquellen *pl*

visible: **visible exports** PL *(Econ)* sichtbare Ausfuhr; **visible light** N *(Phys)* sichtbares Licht; **visible panty line** N *(inf)* sichtbare Slipkontur

visibly [ˈvɪzəblɪ] ADV sichtbar, sichtlich; *deteriorate, decay* zusehends

Visigoth [ˈvɪzɪgɒθ] N Westgote *m*

vision [ˈvɪʒən] N **a** *(= power of sight)* Sehvermögen *nt*; **within/beyond the range of ~** in/außer Sichtweite; **he has good ~** er sieht gut → **field g** **b** *(= foresight)* Weitblick *m*; **a man of ~** ein Mann mit Weitblick **c** *(in dream, trance)* Vision *f*, Gesicht *nt (liter)*; **it came to me in a ~** ich hatte eine Vision **d** *(= image)* Vorstellung *f*; **Orwell's ~ of the future** Orwells Zukunftsvision *f* **e** **to have ~s of wealth** von Reichtum träumen, sich *(dat)* Reichtum vorgaukeln; **I had ~s of having to walk all the way home** *(inf)* ich sah mich im Geiste schon den ganzen Weg nach Hause laufen

visionary [ˈvɪʒənərɪ] ADJ **a** *(= impractical)* unrealistisch; *(= of visions)* vorhersehend, visionär *(geh)*; *(= unreal)* eingebildet **b** *(= with a vision) idea, book, writer, artist* visionär N Visionär(in) *m(f)*, Seher(in) *m(f) (geh)*; *(pej)* Fantast(in) *m(f)*, Phantast(in) *m(f)*

vision mixer N *(TV) (= person)* Bildmischer(in) *m(f)*; *(= equipment)* Bildmischpult *nt*

visit [ˈvɪzɪt] N **a** *(= call, to museum etc)* Besuch *m*; *(of doctor)* Hausbesuch *m*; *(of inspector)* Kontrolle *f*; **I felt better after a ~ to the doctor's/solicitor's** nachdem ich beim Arzt/Anwalt gewesen war, ging es mir besser; **to pay sb/sth a ~** jdm/einer Sache einen Besuch abstatten *(form)*, jdn/etw besuchen; **to pay a ~** *(euph)* mal verschwinden (müssen); **to have a ~ from sb** von jdm besucht werden; **give us a ~ some time** besuchen Sie uns (doch) mal; **he went on a two-day ~ to Paris** er fuhr für zwei Tage nach Paris; **I'm going on a ~ to Glasgow next week** ich fahre nächste Woche (zu einem Besuch) nach Glasgow; **we're expecting a ~ from the police any day** wir rechnen jeden Tag mit dem Besuch der Polizei
b *(= stay)* Aufenthalt *m*, Besuch *m*; **to be on a ~ to London** zu einem Besuch in London sein; **to be on a private/official ~** inoffiziell/offiziell da sein
VT **a** *person, the sick, museum* besuchen; *doctor, solicitor* aufsuchen; **you never ~ us these days** Sie kommen uns ja gar nicht mehr besuchen; **the prime minister will ~ Germany next week** der Premierminister wird nächste Woche Deutschland besuchen
b *(= go and stay with)* besuchen, aufsuchen *(geh)*
c *(= inspect)* inspizieren, besichtigen, besuchen; **to ~ the scene of the crime** *(Jur)* den Tatort besichtigen
d *(Bibl) sins* heimsuchen *(upon* an *+dat*, über *+acc)*
VI **a** *(= call in)* einen Besuch machen; **come**

and ~ some time komm mich mal besuchen; **I'm only ~ing here** ich bin nur auf Besuch hier **b** (*US inf:* = *chat*) schwatzen, ein Schwätzchen halten

▶ **visit with** VI +*prep obj* (*US*) schwatzen mit

visitation [ˌvɪzɪˈteɪʃən] N **a** (*form:* = *visit, by official*) Besichtigung *f*, Besuch *m*; (*by ghost*) Erscheinung *f*; **after another ~ from the mother-in-law** (*hum*) nachdem uns die Schwiegermutter wieder einmal heimgesucht hatte **b** (*Rel*) **the Visitation** Mariä Heimsuchung *f* **c** (*Rel,* = *affliction*) Heimsuchung *f*; **a ~ for their sins** die Strafe für ihre Sünden; **the ~ of the sins of the fathers on succeeding generations** die Bestrafung der folgenden Generationen für die Sünden ihrer Väter

visiting [ˈvɪzɪtɪŋ] **N** Besuche *pl* **ADJ** *scholar, expert* Gast-; *dignitary, monarch, royalty, queen* der/die zu Besuch ist

visiting: **visiting card** N Visitenkarte *f*; **visiting hours** PL Besuchszeiten *pl*; **visiting nurse** N (*US*) ≈ Bezirkskrankenschwester *f*; **visiting professor** N Gastprofessor(in) *m(f)*; **visiting rights** PL Besuchsrecht *nt*; **visiting team** N **the ~** die Gäste *pl*; **visiting terms** PL **I'm not on ~ with him** ich kenne ihn nicht so gut, dass ich ihn besuchen gehen würde; **visiting time** N Besuchszeit *f*

visitor [ˈvɪzɪtəʳ] N Besucher(in) *m(f)*; (*in hotel*) Gast *m*; **to have ~s/a ~** Besuch haben; **the great tit is a rare ~ in these parts** die Kohlmeise hält sich selten in diesen Breiten auf; **~s' book** Gästebuch *nt*

visor [ˈvaɪzəʳ] N (*on helmet*) Visier *nt*; (*on cap*) Schirm *m*; (*Aut*) Blende *f*; **sun ~** Schild *m*, Schirm *m*; (*Aut*) Sonnenblende *f*

VISTA (*US*) *abbr of* **Volunteers in Service to America** *US-Hilfsorganisation, die Freiwillige zur Hilfe Einkommensschwacher abstellt*

vista [ˈvɪstə] N **a** (= *view*) Aussicht *f*, Blick *m* **b** (*of past*) Bild *nt*; (*of future*) Aussicht (*of* auf +*acc*), Perspektive (*of* von) *f*

visual [ˈvɪzjʊəl] **ADJ** Seh-; *image, memory, impression, depiction, joke* visuell; **~ cortex** Sehzentrum *nt*; **~ disorder** Sehstörung *f*; **he is a very ~ songwriter** er schreibt sehr bildliche Liedertexte **N** (grafischer) Entwurf

visual: **visual aids** PL Anschauungsmaterial *nt*; **visual arts** N **the ~** die darstellenden Künste *pl*; **visual display terminal** N Bildschirmterminal *nt*; **visual display unit** N Sichtgerät *nt*; **visual field** N Sehfeld *nt*, Gesichtsfeld *nt*

visualize [ˈvɪzjʊəlaɪz] VT **a** (= *see in mind*) sich (*dat*) vorstellen **b** (= *foresee*) erwarten; **we do not ~ many changes** wir rechnen nicht mit großen Veränderungen; **he ~s some changes** (= *intends*) er hat einige Veränderungen im Auge; **that's not how I'd ~d things** so hatte ich mir das nicht vorgestellt

visually [ˈvɪzjʊəlɪ] ADV visuell; **~ stunning/exciting/attractive** umwerfend/aufregend/attraktiv anzusehen; **~, the film is good entertainment** von der Aufmachung her ist der Film sehr unterhaltend; **I remember things ~** ich habe ein visuelles Gedächtnis

visually handicapped, **visually impaired** ADJ sehbehindert

vital [ˈvaɪtl] **ADJ** **a** (= *of life*) vital, Lebens-; (= *necessary for life*) lebenswichtig; **~ organs** lebenswichtige Organe *pl*; **~ spark** (*fig*) zündender Funke
b (= *essential*) unerlässlich; **of ~ importance** von größter Wichtigkeit; **this is ~** das ist unbedingt notwendig; **your support is ~ to us** wir brauchen unbedingt Ihre Unterstützung; **is it ~ for you to go?, is it ~ that you go?** müssen Sie denn unbedingt gehen?; **it's ~ that this is finished by Tuesday** das muss bis Dienstag unbedingt fertig sein; **how ~ is this?** wie wichtig ist das?; **such skills are ~ for survival** derartige Fähigkeiten sind überlebenswichtig
c (= *critical*) *argument, issue* entscheidend; *error* schwerwiegend, schwer wiegend; **at the ~ moment** im kritischen *or* entscheidenden Moment; **the ~ problem** das Kernproblem
d (= *lively*) *person* vital; *artistic style* lebendig
N **the ~s** die lebenswichtigen Organe; (*hum:* = *genitals*) die edlen Teile (*hum*)

vital force N Lebenskraft *f*

vitality [vaɪˈtælɪtɪ] N (= *energy*) Energie *f*, Leben *nt*, Vitalität *f*; (*of prose, language*) Lebendigkeit *f*, Vitalität *f*; (*of companies, new state*) Dynamik *f*; (= *durability*) Beständigkeit *f*

vitalization [ˌvaɪtəlaɪˈzeɪʃən] N Belebung *f*, Aktivierung *f*

vitalize [ˈvaɪtəlaɪz] VT beleben

vitally [ˈvaɪtəlɪ] ADV **a** *important* äußerst, ungeheuer; *necessary, needed* dringend; (*emph:* = *greatly*) *interested, concerned* äußerst **b** (= *intensely*) **~ alive** quicklebendig; **~ alert** hellwach; **he writes freshly and ~** er schreibt einen frischen und lebendigen *or* kraftvollen Stil

vital: **vital parts** PL wichtige Teile *pl*; **vital signs** PL (*Med*) Lebenszeichen *pl*; **vital statistics** PL Bevölkerungsstatistik *f*; (*inf, of woman*) Maße *pl*

vitamin [ˈvɪtəmɪn] N Vitamin *nt*; **~ A** Vitamin A; **with added ~s** mit Vitaminen angereichert

vitamin: **vitamin deficiency** N Vitaminmangel *m*; **vitamin-deficiency disease** N Vitaminmangelkrankheit *f*; **vitamin pill** N Vitamintablette *f*

vitiate [ˈvɪʃɪeɪt] VT **a** (= *spoil*) *air, blood* verunreinigen **b** (*Jur etc:* = *invalidate*) ungültig machen; *thesis* widerlegen; *meeting, decision, agreement* aufheben

viticulture [ˈvɪtɪkʌltʃəʳ] N Weinbau *m*

vitreous [ˈvɪtrɪəs] ADJ Glas-; **~ china** Porzellanemail *nt*; **~ enamel** Glasemail *nt*

vitrifaction [ˌvɪtrɪˈfækʃən], **vitrification** [ˌvɪtrɪfɪˈkeɪʃən] N Verglasung *f*, Frittung *f*

vitrify [ˈvɪtrɪfaɪ] **VT** zu Glas schmelzen, verglasen **VI** verglasen

vitriol [ˈvɪtrɪəl] N (*Chem*) (= *salt*) Sulfat *nt*, Vitriol *nt*; (= *acid*) Schwefelsäure *f*; (*fig*) Bissigkeit *f*, Bosheit *f*

vitriolic [ˌvɪtrɪˈɒlɪk] ADJ **a** (*fig*) *remark* beißend, hasserfüllt; *criticism* ätzend, beißend; *attack, speech* hasserfüllt **b** (*Chem*) vitriolhaltig; (= *vitriolic acid*) Vitriolsäure *f*

vitro [ˈviːtrəʊ] ADJ, ADV → **in vitro**

vituperate [vɪˈtjuːpəreɪt] VI schmähen (*geh*) (*against* +*acc*), verunglimpfen (*against* +*acc*)

vituperation [vɪˌtjuːpəˈreɪʃən] N (*form*) Schmähungen *pl* (*geh*)

vituperative [vɪˈtjuːpərətɪv] ADJ (*form*) *language* schmähend (*geh*); *criticism, remark, attack, abuse* beißend; *person* scharfzüngig; **~ speech** Schmährede *f*

viva [ˈvaɪvə] N (*Brit*) = **viva voce**

vivacious [vɪˈveɪʃəs] ADJ lebhaft; *character, person also* temperamentvoll; *colour, clothes also* leuchtend bunt; *smile, laugh* munter, aufgeweckt

vivaciously [vɪˈveɪʃəslɪ] ADV *say, laugh* munter

vivaciousness [vɪˈveɪʃəsnɪs] N Lebhaftigkeit *f*; (*of smile, laugh*) Munterkeit *f*, Aufgewecktheit *f*

vivacity [vɪˈvæsɪtɪ] N Lebhaftigkeit *f*; (*of style*) Lebendigkeit *f*; (*of smile, laugh*) Munterkeit *f*, Aufgewecktheit *f*

vivarium [vɪˈvɛərɪəm] N Vivarium *nt*

viva voce [ˈvaɪvəˈvəʊtʃɪ] **ADJ, ADV** mündlich **N** (*Brit*) mündliche Prüfung

vivid [ˈvɪvɪd] ADJ **a** *light* hell; *colour* kräftig, leuchtend, lebhaft; **the ~ feathers of the bird** das bunte *or* auffallende Gefieder des Vogels; **a ~ blue dress** ein leuchtend blaues Kleid; **a ~ tie** eine auffällige Krawatte
b (= *lively*) *imagination, recollection* lebhaft; *description, metaphor, image* lebendig, anschaulich; *emotions* stark; **in ~ detail** in allen plastischen Einzelheiten; **the memory of that day is still quite ~** der Tag ist mir noch in lebhafter Erinnerung
c (= *powerful*) *example, contrast* deutlich; **to give a ~ demonstration of one's power** seine Macht klar und deutlich unter Beweis stellen; **to be a ~ reminder of sth** lebhaft an etw (*acc*) erinnern

vividly [ˈvɪvɪdlɪ] ADV **a** *coloured* lebhaft; *shine* hell, leuchtend; **the red stands out ~ against its background** das Rot hebt sich stark vom Hintergrund ab; **a ~ coloured** (*Brit*) *or* **colored** (*US*) **bird** ein bunt gefiederter *or* auffällig gefiederter Vogel **b** *remember, recall* lebhaft; *describe, illustrate* anschaulich, lebendig; *demonstrate* klar und deutlich; *portray, bring to life* anschaulich, plastisch

vividness [ˈvɪvɪdnɪs] N **a** (*of colour*) Lebhaftigkeit *f*; (*of light*) Helligkeit *f* **b** (*of style*) Lebendigkeit *f*; (*of description, metaphor, image*) Anschaulichkeit *f*; (*of imagination, memory*) Lebhaftigkeit *f*

vivify [ˈvɪvɪfaɪ] VT beleben

viviparous [vɪˈvɪpərəs] ADJ (*Zool*) lebend gebärend

vivisect [ˌvɪvɪˈsekt] VT vivisezieren

vivisection [ˌvɪvɪˈsekʃən] N Vivisektion *f*

vivisectionist [ˌvɪvɪˈsekʃənɪst] N *jd, der Eingriffe am lebenden Tier vornimmt/befürwortet*

vixen [ˈvɪksn] N (*Zool*) Füchsin *f*; (*fig*) zänkisches Weib, Drachen *m* (*inf*)

viz [vɪz] ADV nämlich

vizier [vɪˈzɪəʳ] N Wesir *m*

V-J Day N *Tag des Sieges gegen Japan im 2. Weltkrieg*

VLSI *abbr of* **very large scale integration** Höchst- *or* Größtintegration *f*, VLSI *f*

V: **V-neck** N V-Ausschnitt *m*; **V-necked** ADJ mit V-Ausschnitt

VoA (*US*) *abbr of* **Voice of America**; **the ~** die Stimme Amerikas

vocabulary [vəʊˈkæbjʊlərɪ] N Wortschatz *m*, Vokabular *nt* (*geh*); (*in textbook*) Wörterverzeichnis *f*; **he has a limited ~** er hat einen beschränkten Wortschatz; **the ~ of the legal profession** das Vokabular der Juristen; **~ book** Vokabelheft *nt*; (*printed*) Vokabelbuch *nt*; **~ test** (*Sch*) Vokabelarbeit *f*

vocal [ˈvəʊkəl] **ADJ** **a** (= *using voice*) Stimm-; *talent* stimmlich; **~ style** Singstil *m*; **~ range/training** Stimmumfang *m*/-bildung *f*; **~ performance** gesangliche Leistung; **best male ~ performer** bester Vokalsänger; **~ music** Vokalmusik *f*; **~ group** Gesangsgruppe *f*
b *communication* mündlich
c (= *voicing one's opinions*) *group, person* lautstark; **to be/become ~** sich zu Wort melden; **to be ~ in sth** etw deutlich zum Ausdruck bringen; **to be ~ in demanding sth** etw laut fordern; **to become increasingly ~ in one's opposition to sth** seinen Widerstand gegen etw immer deutlicher *or* lauter zum Ausdruck bringen
N (*of pop song*) (gesungener) Schlager; (*in jazz*) Vocal *nt*; **who's doing** *or* **singing the ~s for your group now?** wen habt ihr denn jetzt als Sänger?; **~s: Van Morrison** Gesang: Van Morrison; **featuring Madonna on ~s** mit Madonna als Sängerin; **backing ~s** Hintergrundgesang *m*; **lead ~s ...** Leadsänger(in) *m(f)* ...

vocal cords PL Stimmbänder *pl*

vocalic [vəʊˈkælɪk] ADJ vokalisch

vocalist [ˈvəʊkəlɪst] N Sänger(in) *m(f)*

vocalize [ˈvəʊkəlaɪz] VT **a** *thoughts* aussprechen, Ausdruck verleihen (+*dat*); *feelings* zum Ausdruck bringen **b** (*Phon*) *consonant* vokalisieren

vocally [ˈvəʊkəlɪ] ADV **a** mündlich; **the tune has now been done ~ by ...** die Melodie wurde jetzt auch gesungen von ... **b** (= *outspokenly*) *support, oppose* klar und deutlich

vocation [vəʊˈkeɪʃən] N **a** (*Rel etc*) Berufung *f*; (*form:* = *profession*) Beruf *m*; **to have a ~ for teaching** zum Lehrer berufen sein **b** (= *aptitude*) Begabung *f*, Talent *nt*

vocational [vəʊˈkeɪʃənl] ADJ Berufs-; *qualifications* beruflich; **~ course** Weiterbildungskurs *m*; **~ training** Berufsausbildung *f*; **~ retraining** berufliche Umschulung

vocational guidance N Berufsberatung *f*

vocationally [vəʊˈkeɪʃənlɪ] ADV *train* beruflich; **~ oriented** berufsorientiert

vocational school N *(US)* ≈ Berufsschule *f*

vocative [ˈvɒkətɪv] N Anredeform *f*, Vokativ *m*; **~ case** Anredefall *m*, Vokativ *m*

vociferate [vəʊˈsɪfəreɪt] VT schreien; **he ~d his grievances** er machte seinem Unmut Luft VI *(fig)* seinem Unmut Luft machen *(about* über *+acc)*

vociferation [vəʊˌsɪfəˈreɪʃən] N Geschrei *nt*; **their ~ of their discontent** ihr lautstarker Protest

vociferous [vəʊˈsɪfərəs] ADJ *class, audience* laut; *demands, protest, critic, minority, opponent* lautstark; **to be ~ in one's opposition to sth** lautstark gegen etw opponieren; **to be ~ in demanding one's rights** lautstark seine Rechte einfordern

vociferously [vəʊˈsɪfərəslɪ] ADV lautstark

vodka [ˈvɒdkə] N Wodka *m*

vogue [vəʊg] N Mode *f*; **the ~ for jeans** die Jeansmode; **to be the ~** *or* **in ~** (in) Mode *or* en vogue sein; **to come into ~** *(clothes)* in Mode kommen, modern werden; *(writers)* populär werden, in Mode kommen; **to go out of ~** *(clothes)* aus der Mode kommen, unmodern werden; *(writers)* aus der Mode kommen; **to enjoy a great ~ with** sehr beliebt sein unter *(+dat)*, große Mode sein unter *(+dat)*

vogue expression, vogue word N Modewort *nt*

voice [vɔɪs] N **a** (= *faculty of speech, Mus, fig)* Stimme *f*; **to lose one's ~** die Stimme verlieren; **I've lost my ~** ich habe keine Stimme mehr; **to find one's ~** sich *(dat)* Gehör verschaffen; **she hasn't got much of a ~** sie hat keine besonders gute Stimme; **to be in good/poor ~** gut/nicht gut bei Stimme sein; **in a deep ~** mit tiefer Stimme; **in a low ~** leise, mit leiser Stimme; **to like the sound of one's own ~** sich gern(e) reden hören; **his ~ has broken** er hat den Stimmbruch hinter sich; **tenor ~** Tenor *m*; **bass ~** Bass *m*; **a piece for ~ and piano** ein Gesangsstück *nt* mit Klavierbegleitung; **with one ~** einstimmig; **to give ~ to sth** etw aussprechen, einer Sache *(dat)* Ausdruck verleihen; **the Voice of America** *(Rad)* die Stimme Amerikas
b *(fig: = say)* **we have a/no ~ in the matter** wir haben in dieser Angelegenheit ein/kein Mitspracherecht
c *(Gram)* Aktionsart *f*, Genus (verbi) *nt*; **the active/passive ~** das Aktiv/Passiv
d *(Phon)* Stimmhaftigkeit *f*; **plus ~** stimmhaft
VT **a** (= *express) feelings, opinion* zum Ausdruck bringen
b *(Phon)* stimmhaft aussprechen

voice-activated ADJ *(Comput)* sprachgesteuert

voice box N Kehlkopf *m*

voiced [vɔɪst] ADJ *(Phon)* stimmhaft

-voiced ADJ *suf* mit ... Stimme; **soft-voiced** mit sanfter Stimme

voice: voiceless ADJ **a** stumm; **in a ~ whisper** mit lautlosem Flüstern **b** (= *having no say)* ohne Mitspracherecht **c** *(Phon) consonant* stimmlos; **voice mail** N Voicemail *f*, Voice-Mail *f*; **voice-operated** ADJ sprachgesteuert; **voice-over** N Filmkommentar *m*; **voice part** N **the ~s** *(Mus)* die Singstimmen *pl*; **voice production** N Stimmbildung *f*; **voice projection** N Stimmresonanz *f*; **voice range** N Stimmumfang *m*; **voice recognition** N Spracherkennung *f*; **voice synthesizer** N Sprachsynthesizer *m*

void [vɔɪd] N *(lit, fig)* Leere *f*; **the dead astronaut floated off into the ~** der tote Astronaut schwebte in das All ADJ **a** (= *empty)* leer; **~ of any sense of decency** bar jeglichen Gefühls *(geh) or* ohne jegliches Gefühl für Anstand; **~ of humour** *(Brit) or* **humor** *(US)* ohne jeglichen Humor **b** *(Jur)* ungültig, nichtig **c** (= *useless)* nichtig *(geh)*; **you've made all my efforts totally ~** du hast all meine Bemühungen völlig zunichtegemacht VT **a** *(Jur)* ungültig machen, aufheben **b** *(form, = empty) bowels* entleeren

voile [vɔɪl] N Voile *m*, Schleierstoff *m*

VoIP *abbr of* **voice over Internet protocol** Voive over IP *nt (Transport von Sprachdaten mittels Internetprotokoll)*

vol *abbr of* **volume** Bd; *(Measure)* V(ol.)

volatile [ˈvɒlətaɪl] ADJ **a** *(Chem)* flüchtig **b** *person (in moods)* impulsiv; *(in interests)* sprunghaft; *(Psych: = unpredictable)* sprunghaft; *relationship* wechselhaft; *political situation* brisant; *(St Ex)* unbeständig; **a person with a ~ temper** ein sehr unberechenbarer Mensch **c** *(Comput)* **~ memory** flüchtiger Speicher

volatile oils PL ätherische Öle *pl*

volatility [ˌvɒləˈtɪlɪtɪ] N **a** *(Chem)* Flüchtigkeit *f* **b** *(of person, in moods)* Impulsivität *f*; *(of relationship)* Wechselhaftigkeit *f*; *(of political situation)* Brisanz *f*; *(of stock market)* Unbeständigkeit *f*; *(of share price)* Volatilität *f*

volatilize [vɒˈlætəlaɪz] VT verflüchtigen VI sich verflüchtigen

vol-au-vent [ˈvɒləʊvɑː] N (Königin)pastetchen *nt*

volcanic [vɒlˈkænɪk] ADJ *(lit)* Vulkan-; *rock, dust, activity* vulkanisch; *(fig)* heftig; **~ activity** Vulkantätigkeit *f*; **~ eruption** Vulkanausbruch *m*; **~ island** Vulkaninsel *f*

volcano [vɒlˈkeɪnəʊ] N Vulkan *m*

volcanologist [ˌvɒlkəˈnɒlədʒɪst] N Vulkanologe *m*, Vulkanologin *f*

volcanology [ˌvɒlkəˈnɒlədʒɪ] N Vulkanologie *f*

vole [vəʊl] N Wühlmaus *f*; (= *common vole)* Feldmaus *f*

Volga [ˈvɒlgə] N Wolga *f*

volition [vəˈlɪʃən] N Wille *m*; **simply by the exercise of your ~** mit dem Willen allein; **of one's own ~** aus freiem Willen

volitional [vəˈlɪʃənl] ADJ Willens-, willentlich; *control* des Willens; **~ act** Willensakt *m*

volley [ˈvɒlɪ] N **a** *(of shots)* Salve *f*; *(of arrows, stones)* Hagel *m*; *(fig) (of insults)* Flut *f*, Hagel *m*; *(of applause)* Sturm *m* **b** *(Tennis)* Volley *m*, Flugball *m* VT **to ~ a ball** *(Tennis)* einen Ball im Volley spielen, einen Volley spielen *or* schlagen VI **a** *(Mil)* eine Salve abfeuern; *(guns, shots)* (in einer Salve) abgefeuert werden **b** *(Tennis)* einen Volley schlagen

volleyball [ˈvɒlɪˌbɔːl] N Volleyball *m*

volleyer [ˈvɒlɪəˈ] N **he's a superb ~** er schlägt tolle Volleys

Vols *abbr of* **Volumes** Bde

volt [vəʊlt] N Volt *nt*

voltage [ˈvəʊltɪdʒ] N Spannung *f*; **what ~ is this cable?** wie viel Volt hat dieses Kabel?

voltaic [vɒlˈteɪɪk] ADJ voltaisch, galvanisch; **~ cell** galvanisches Element

volte-face [ˈvɒltˈfɑːs] N *(fig)* Kehrtwendung *f*; **to perform a ~** sich um 180 Grad drehen

voltmeter [ˈvəʊltmiːtəˈ] N Voltmeter *nt*

volubility [ˌvɒljʊˈbɪlɪtɪ] N Redseligkeit *f*

voluble [ˈvɒljʊbl] ADJ *speaker* redegewandt, redselig *(pej)*; *protest* wortreich

volubly [ˈvɒljʊblɪ] ADV wortreich; **to talk ~** sehr redselig sein

volume [ˈvɒljuːm] N **a** Band *m*; **in six ~s** in sechs Bänden; **a six-~ dictionary** ein sechsbändiges Wörterbuch; **to write ~s** ganze Bände *pl* schreiben; **that speaks ~s** *(fig)* das spricht Bände *(for* für); **it speaks ~s for him** das spricht sehr für ihn
b (= *space occupied by sth)* Volumen *nt*, Rauminhalt *m*
c (= *size, amount)* Umfang *m*, Ausmaß *nt (of* an *+dat)*; **a large ~ of sales/business** ein großer Umsatz; **the ~ of traffic** das Verkehrsaufkommen; **trade has increased in ~** das Handelsvolumen hat sich vergrößert
d (= *large amount)* **~s of smoke** Rauchschwaden *pl*; **~s of white silk** Massen *pl* von weißer Seide; **we've ~s of work to get through** wir haben noch Berge von Arbeit
e (= *sound)* Lautstärke *f*; **is the ~ right up?** ist das volle Lautstärke?; **turn the ~ up/down** *(Rad, TV)* stell (das Gerät) lauter/leiser
f *(Comput)* Datenträger *m*
ATTR **~ discount** Mengenrabatt *m*; **~ sales** Mengenabsatz *m*

volume control N *(Rad, TV etc)* Lautstärkeregler *m*

volume label N *(Comput)* Datenträgerbezeichnung *f*

volumetric [ˌvɒljʊˈmetrɪk] ADJ volumetrisch

voluminous [vəˈluːmɪnəs] ADJ voluminös *(geh)*; *figure also* üppig; *writings* umfangreich; *skirts, shirt, pockets* wallend

voluntarily [ˈvɒləntərɪlɪ] ADV freiwillig, von sich aus; (= *unpaid) work* ehrenamtlich

voluntarism [ˈvɒləntərɪzəm] N *no pl* Voluntarismus *m*

voluntary [ˈvɒləntərɪ] ADJ **a** (= *not obligatory)* freiwillig; **to go into ~ liquidation** in die freiwillige Liquidation gehen
b (= *unpaid) help, service, work* freiwillig; **~ worker** freiwilliger Helfer, freiwillige Helferin; *(overseas)* Entwicklungshelfer(in) *m(f)*; **on a ~ basis** auf freiwilliger Basis, freiwillig
c (= *supported by charity, charitable) body, agency* karitativ; **a ~ organization for social work** ein freiwilliger Wohlfahrtsverband
d (= *having will) movements* willkürlich, willentlich; *crime* vorsätzlich; **man is a ~ agent** der Mensch handelt aus freiem Willen
e *(Physiol)* **~ muscles** willkürliche Muskeln *pl*
N *(Eccl, Mus)* Solo *nt*

voluntary: voluntary euthanasia N aktive Sterbehilfe; **voluntary manslaughter** N *(US Jur)* vorsätzliche Tötung; **voluntary redundancy** N freiwilliges Ausscheiden; **to take ~** sich abfinden lassen

volunteer [ˌvɒlənˈtɪəˈ] N *(also Mil)* Freiwillige(r) *mf*; **~ army** Freiwilligenheer *nt*; **any ~s?** wer meldet sich freiwillig?; **Volunteers in Service to America** *(US) US-Hilfsorganisation, die Freiwillige zur Hilfe Einkommensschwacher abstellt*
VT *help, services* anbieten; *suggestion* machen; *information* geben, herausrücken mit *(inf)*; **we didn't ask you to ~ any advice** wir haben Sie nicht um Rat gebeten; **he ~ed his brother** *(hum)* er hat seinen Bruder (als Freiwilligen) gemeldet
VI **a** (= *offer one's services)* sich freiwillig melden; **to ~ for sth** sich freiwillig für etw zur Verfügung stellen; **to ~ to do sth** sich anbieten, etw zu tun; **who will ~ to clean the windows?** wer meldet sich freiwillig zum Fensterputzen?
b *(Mil)* sich freiwillig melden *(for* zu, *for places* nach)

voluptuary [vəˈlʌptjʊərɪ] N Lüstling *m*

voluptuous [vəˈlʌptjʊəs] ADJ **a** *mouth, woman, movement* sinnlich; *curves* üppig; *body* verlockend; *life* ausschweifend; *kiss* hingebungsvoll; *photograph, painting* erotisch **b** (= *pleasing)* stimulierend; **~ to touch** angenehm zu berühren

voluptuously [vəˈlʌptjʊəslɪ] ADV *move* aufreizend, sinnlich; *kiss* hingebungsvoll; *live* ausschweifend; **her ~ curved body** ihr üppig geformter Körper; **her lips were ~ full** sie hatte einen sinnlichen Mund

voluptuousness [vəˈlʌptjʊəsnɪs] N *(of woman, movement)* Sinnlichkeit *f*; *(of curves)* Üppigkeit *f*; *(of body)* verlockende Formen *pl*; *(of kiss)* Hingabe *f*

volute [vəˈluːt] N *(Archit)* Volute *f*

voluted [vəˈluːtɪd] ADJ *(Archit)* mit Voluten (versehen)

vomit [ˈvɒmɪt] N Erbrochene(s) *nt*; (= *act)* Erbrechen *nt* VT *(lit, fig)* spucken, speien *(geh)*; *food* erbrechen VI sich erbrechen, sich übergeben

▶ **vomit out** VT *sep (lit)* erbrechen; *(fig) smoke, flames* speien; *words, secret* ausspucken *(inf)* VI *(fig)* **the flames were still vomiting out of the volcano** der Vulkan spie immer noch Feuer

▶**vomit up** VT *sep food* (wieder) erbrechen

voodoo ['vu:du:] N Voodoo *m*, Wodu *m*

voodooism ['vu:du:ɪzəm] N Voodoo- *or* Wodukult *m*

voracious [və'reɪʃəs] ADJ *person* gefräßig; *collector* besessen; **she is a ~ reader** sie verschlingt die Bücher geradezu; **to be a ~ eater** Unmengen vertilgen; **to have a ~ appetite** einen Riesenappetit haben

voraciously [və'reɪʃəslɪ] ADV *eat* gierig; **to read ~** die Bücher nur so verschlingen

voracity [vɒ'ræsɪtɪ] N Gefräßigkeit *f*; *(fig)* Gier *f* *(for* nach)

vortex ['vɔ:teks] N *pl* **-es** *or* **vortices** ['vɔ:tɪsi:z] *(lit)* Wirbel *m*, Strudel *m (also fig)*

vorticism ['vɔ:tɪˌsɪzəm] N *(Art)* Vortizismus *m*

votary ['vəʊtərɪ] N *(Rel)* Geweihte(r) *mf*; *(fig)* Jünger(in) *m(f)*

vote [vəʊt] **N** **a** *(= expression of opinion)* Stimme *f*; *(= act of voting)* Abstimmung *f*, Wahl *f*; *(= result)* Abstimmungs- *or* Wahlergebnis *nt*; **to put sth to the ~** über etw *(acc)* abstimmen lassen; **to take a ~ on sth** über etw *(acc)* abstimmen; **elected by popular ~** vom Volk gewählt; **the ~ for/against the change surprised him** dass für/gegen den Wechsel gestimmt wurde, erstaunte ihn; **the ~ was 150 to 95** das Abstimmungsergebnis war 150 zu 95; **we would like to offer a ~ of thanks to Mr Smith** wir möchten Herrn Smith unseren aufrichtigen Dank aussprechen → **censure, confidence**

b *(= vote cast)* Stimme *f*; **to give one's ~ to a party/person** einer Partei/jdm seine Stimme geben; **single-~ majority** Mehrheit *f* von einer Stimme; **one man one ~** eine Stimme pro Wähler, ein Mann *or* Bürger, eine Stimme; **a photo of the Prime Minister casting his ~** ein Foto des Premierministers bei der Stimmabgabe; **what's your ~?** *(in panel game, competition)* wie lautet Ihr Urteil?; **he won by 22 ~s** er gewann mit einer Mehrheit von 22 Stimmen; **10% of the ~rs invalidated their ~s** 10% der Wähler machten ihren Stimmzettel ungültig

c *(Pol, collective)* **the Labour ~** die Labourstimmen *pl*; **the Labour ~ has increased** der Stimmenanteil von Labour hat sich erhöht

d *(= franchise)* Wahlrecht *nt*; **~s for women!** Wahlrecht für die Frauen!

e *(= money allotted)* Bewilligung *f*

VT **a** *(= elect)* wählen; **he was ~d chairman** er wurde zum Vorsitzenden gewählt; **to ~ Labour** Labour wählen

b *(inf: = judge)* wählen zu; **the group ~d her the best cook** die Gruppe wählte sie zur besten Köchin; **the panel ~d the record a miss** die Jury erklärte die Platte für einen Misserfolg; **I ~ we go back** ich schlage vor, dass wir umkehren

c *(= approve)* bewilligen

VI *(= cast one's vote)* wählen; **to ~ for/against sth** für/gegen etw stimmen; **~ for Clark!** wählen Sie Clark!; **to ~ with one's feet** mit den Füßen abstimmen

▶**vote down** VT *sep proposal* niederstimmen

▶**vote in** VT *sep law* beschließen; *person* wählen

▶**vote on** VI *+prep obj* abstimmen über *(+acc)*

▶**vote out** VT *sep* abwählen; *amendment* ablehnen

vote-loser ['vəʊtˌlu:zə'] N *unpopuläre Politik, durch die Wählerstimmen verloren gehen können*

voter ['vəʊtə'] N Wähler(in) *m(f)*

voting ['vəʊtɪŋ] N Wahl *f*; **which way is the ~ going?** welchen Verlauf nimmt die Wahl?; **a system of ~** ein Wahlsystem *nt*; **to analyze the ~** das Wahlergebnis analysieren; **~ was heavy** die Wahlbeteiligung war hoch; **light ~** geringe Wahlbeteiligung

voting: **voting age** N Wahlalter *nt*; **voting booth** N Wahlkabine *f*; **voting machine** N *(US)* Wahlmaschine *f*; **voting paper** N Stimmzettel *m*; **voting power** N *(= right to vote)* Stimmberechtigung *f*, Stimmrecht *nt*; *(power of a certain group)* Wahlstärke *f*; **voting precinct** N *(US Pol)* Wahlbezirk *m*; **voting right** N Stimmrecht *nt*

votive ['vəʊtɪv] ADJ Votiv-; **~ candle** Votivkerze *f*; **~ painting** Votivbild *nt*

vouch [vaʊtʃ] VI **to ~ for sb/sth** sich für jdn/etw verbürgen; *(legally)* für jdn/etw bürgen; **to ~ for the truth of sth** sich für die Richtigkeit einer Sache verbürgen

voucher ['vaʊtʃə'] N **a** *(for cash, petrol, meals etc)* Gutschein *m* **b** *(= receipt)* Beleg *m*; *(for debt)* Schuldschein *m*

vouchsafe [vaʊtʃ'seɪf] VT *(form)* gewähren *(sb* jdm); **to ~ to do sth** geruhen *(geh)* *or* die Güte haben, etw zu tun

vow [vaʊ] **N** Versprechen *nt*, Gelöbnis *nt*; *(Rel)* Gelübde *nt*; **to make a ~ to do sth** geloben, etw zu tun; **to take one's ~s** sein Gelübde ablegen; **to take a ~ of chastity** ein Keuschheitsgelübde *nt* ablegen; **to take a ~ of silence** Schweigen *nt* geloben **VT** *obedience* geloben; **to ~ vengeance on sb** jdm Rache schwören; **he is ~ed to silence** er hat Schweigen gelobt

vowel ['vaʊəl] N Vokal *m*, Selbstlaut *m*; **~ system** Vokalismus *m*; **~ sound** Vokal(laut) *m*

vox pop [ˌvɒks'pɒp] N *(Rad, TV)* Befragungen *pl* auf der Straße

voyage ['vɔɪɪdʒ] **N** **a** Reise *f*, Fahrt *f*; *(esp by sea)* Seereise *f*; *(Aviat)* Flug *m*, Reise *f*; *(Space)* Flug *m*; **to go on a ~** auf eine Reise *etc* gehen; **to make a ~** eine Reise *etc* machen; **the ~ out** die Hinreise; *(Aviat)* der Hinflug; **the ~ back** *or* **home** die Rück- *or* Heimreise; *(Aviat)* der Rückflug **b** *(fig)* **~ of discovery** Entdeckungsreise *f* **VI** eine Seereise machen; *(spaceship)* fliegen; **to ~ across an ocean** einen Ozean überqueren

voyager ['vɔɪədʒə'] N Passagier(in) *m(f)*; *(Space)* Raumfahrer(in) *m(f)*

voyeur [vwɑ:'jɜ:'] N Voyeur(in) *m(f)*

voyeurism [vwɑ:'jɜ:rɪzəm] N Voyeurismus *m*, Voyeurtum *nt*

voyeuristic [vwɑ:jɜ:'rɪstɪk] ADJ voyeuristisch

VP *abbr of* **vice president**

VPL *(inf) abbr of* **visible panty line**

VR *abbr of* **virtual reality**

vroom [vru:m] INTERJ brumm

vs *abbr of* **versus**

V: **V-shaped** ADJ pfeilförmig, V-förmig; **V-sign** ['vi:saɪn] N *(Brit)* *(victory)* Victoryzeichen *nt*; *(rude)* ≈ Stinkefinger *m (inf)*; **he gave me the ~** ≈ er zeigte mir den Stinkefinger *(inf)*

VSO *(Brit) abbr of* **Voluntary Service Overseas** ≈ Entwicklungsdienst *m*

VSOP *abbr of* **Very Special Old Pale** *(brandy, port)* VSOP

VTR *abbr of* **video tape recorder** Videorekorder *m*

Vulcan ['vʌlkən] N Vulcanus *m*

vulcanite ['vʌlkənaɪt] N Hartgummi *m*, Ebonit *nt*

vulcanization [ˌvʌlkənaɪ'zeɪʃən] N Vulkanisierung *f*

vulcanize ['vʌlkənaɪz] VT vulkanisieren

vulcanologist [ˌvɒlkə'nɒlədʒɪst] N = **volcanologist**

vulcanology [ˌvɒlkə'nɒlədʒɪ] N = **volcanology**

vulgar ['vʌlgə'] ADJ **a** *(pej)* *(= unrefined)* ordinär, vulgär; *clothes, joke* ordinär; *(= tasteless)* geschmacklos; **it is ~ to talk about money** es ist unfein, über Geld zu reden **b** *(old, = of the common people)* gemein *(old)*; **~ beliefs** volkstümliche Auffassungen *pl*; **in the ~ tongue** in der Sprache des Volkes

vulgar fraction N *(Math)* gemeiner Bruch

vulgarism ['vʌlgərɪzəm] N Gassenausdruck *m*, primitiver Ausdruck; *(= swearword)* vulgärer Ausdruck

vulgarity [vʌl'gærɪtɪ] N Vulgarität *f*; *(of gesture, joke also)* Anstößigkeit *f*; *(of colour, tie etc)* Geschmacklosigkeit *f*; **the ~ of his conduct** sein ordinäres *or* pöbelhaftes Benehmen

vulgarize ['vʌlgəraɪz] VT **a** *(= make coarse)* vulgarisieren **b** *(= popularize)* popularisieren, allgemein verständlich machen

Vulgar Latin N Vulgärlatein *nt*

vulgarly ['vʌlgəlɪ] ADV **a** *(= coarsely)* vulgär; *dressed* geschmacklos **b** *(= commonly)* allgemein, gemeinhin; **~ called ...** gemeinhin auch genannt ...

Vulgate ['vʌlgɪt] N Vulgata *f*

vulnerability [ˌvʌlnərə'bɪlɪtɪ] N Verwundbarkeit *f*; *(= susceptibility)* Verletzlichkeit *f*; *(fig)* Verletzbarkeit *f*; *(of police, troops, fortress)* Ungeschütztheit *f*; **the ~ of the young fish to predators** die Wehrlosigkeit der jungen Fische gegen Raubtiere; **such is their ~ only 2% survive** sie sind so wehrlos, dass nur 2% überleben; **his emotional ~** seine Empfindsamkeit *or* Verletzbarkeit

vulnerable ['vʌlnərəbl] ADJ **a** verwundbar; *(= exposed)* verletzlich; *(fig)* verletzbar; *police, troops, fortress* ungeschützt; *(Mil) target, country* verwundbar; **to feel ~** sich verwundbar fühlen; **she is at a very ~ age** sie ist in einem sehr schwierigen Alter; **to be ~ to disease** anfällig für Krankheiten sein; **the skin is ~ to radiation** die Haut hat keinen Schutz gegen Radioaktivität; **the turtle on its back is completely ~** auf dem Rücken liegend ist die Schildkröte völlig wehrlos; **to be ~ to the cold** kälteanfällig sein; **to be ~ to attack** Angriffen schutzlos ausgesetzt sein; **to be ~ to temptation** für Versuchungen anfällig sein; **to be ~ to criticism** *(= exposed)* der Kritik ausgesetzt sein; *(= sensitive)* keine Kritik vertragen; **I felt extremely ~ in the discussion** ich kam mir in der Diskussion völlig wehrlos vor; **the one ~ spot in his armour** *(Brit)* *or* **armor** *(US)* die einzige ungeschützte Stelle in seiner Rüstung; **a ~ point in our argument** ein schwacher *or* wunder Punkt unseres Arguments; **economically ~** wirtschaftlich wehrlos; **hotels are acutely ~ to recession** Hotels sind äußerst rezessionsanfällig

b *(Bridge)* in Gefahr; **not ~, non-vulnerable** in Nichtgefahr

vulpine ['vʌlpaɪn] ADJ schlau, listig

vulture ['vʌltʃə'] N *(lit, fig)* Geier *m*

vulva ['vʌlvə] N (weibliche) Scham, Vulva *f* *(geh)*

vv *abbr of* **verses**

V wings ['vi:wɪŋz] PL pfeilförmige Tragflügel *pl*

vying ['vaɪɪŋ] N (Konkurrenz)kampf *m* *(for* um)

W, w ['dʌblju:] N W *nt*, w *nt*

W *abbr of* **west** W

W *abbr of* **watt(s)** W

W/ *abbr of* **with** m.

WAAF *abbr of* **Women's Auxiliary Air Force**

Waaf [wæf] N *(Brit)* Mitglied *nt* der weiblichen Luftwaffe

WAC *(US) abbr of* **Women's Army Corps**

wack [wæk] N *(Brit inf: as address)* Kumpel *m (inf)*

wacko ['wækəʊ] ADJ *(inf)* durchgedreht *(inf)*

wacky ['wækɪ] ADJ *(+er) (inf)* verrückt *(inf)*

wacky baccy N *(hum inf)* Gras(s) *nt (inf)*

wad [wɒd] N **a** *(= compact mass)* Knäuel *m or nt*; *(in gun, cartridge)* Pfropfen *m*; *(of cotton wool etc)* Bausch *m*; **to use sth as a ~** etw zum Ausstopfen *or* als Polster benutzen **b** *(of papers, banknotes)* Bündel *nt*; **he's got ~s of money** *(inf)* er hat Geld wie Heu *(inf)* VT *(= secure, stuff)* stopfen; *(= squeeze)* zusammenknüllen; *(Sew)* wattieren

wadding ['wɒdɪŋ] N *(for packing)* Material *nt* zum Ausstopfen; *(Sew)* Wattierung *f*; *(Med, on plaster)* (Mull)tupfer *m*

waddle ['wɒdl] N Watscheln *nt*; **to walk with a ~** einen watschelnden Gang haben VI watscheln

wade [weɪd] VT durchwaten VI waten

▸ **wade in** VI **a** *(lit)* hineinwaten **b** *(fig inf) (= join in a fight, controversy)* sich einmischen *(inf)*; *(= tackle problem etc)* sich voll reinstürzen *or* -werfen *(inf)*, sich hineinknien *(inf)*; **the new boss waded in with a few staff changes** der neue Chef hat sich gleich mächtig ins Zeug gelegt und ein paar Umbesetzungen vorgenommen *(inf)*

▸ **wade into** VI *+prep obj (fig inf: = attack)* **to wade into sb** auf jdn losgehen; **to wade into sth** etw in Angriff nehmen

▸ **wade through** VI *+prep obj* **a** *(lit)* waten durch **b** *(fig)* sich (durch)kämpfen durch

wader ['weɪdə'] N **a** *(Orn)* Watvogel *m* **b** **waders** PL *(= boots)* Watstiefel *pl*

wadi ['wɒdɪ] N Wadi *nt*

wading: **wading bird** ['weɪdɪŋ,bɜ:d] N = **wader a**; **wading pool** ['weɪdɪŋpu:l] N *(US)* Plan(t)schbecken *nt*

wafer ['weɪfə'] N **a** *(= biscuit)* Waffel *f*; **a vanilla ~** eine Vanilleeiswaffel **b** *(Eccl)* Hostie *f* **c** *(= silicon wafer)* Wafer *f*

wafer-thin ['weɪfə'θɪn] ADJ hauchdünn

waffle[1] ['wɒfl] N *(Cook)* Waffel *f*

waffle[2] *(Brit inf)* N Geschwafel *nt (inf)* VI *(also* **waffle on***)* schwafeln *(inf)*; **I managed to ~ on somehow** irgendwie habe ich was (daher)geschwafelt *(inf)*

waffle iron N Waffeleisen *nt*

waffler ['wɒflə'] N *(Brit inf)* Schwätzer(in) *m(f)*

waft [wɑ:ft] N Hauch *m*; **a ~ of smoke** eine dünne Rauchschwade; **a ~ of cool air** ein kühler Lufthauch VT tragen, wehen VI wehen; **a delicious smell ~ed up from the kitchen** ein köstlicher Geruch zog aus der Küche herauf

wag[1] [wæg] N **he admonished me with a ~ of his finger** tadelnd drohte er mir mit dem Finger; **with a ~ of its tail** mit einem Schwanzwedeln VT *tail* wedeln mit; *(bird)* wippen mit; **to ~ one's finger at sb** jdm mit dem Finger drohen VI *(tail)* wedeln; *(of bird)* wippen; **as soon as he left the tongues started ~ging** *(inf)* sobald er gegangen war, fing das Gerede an; **to stop the tongues ~ging** *(inf)* um dem Gerede ein Ende zu machen; **that'll set the tongues ~ging** *(inf)* dann geht das Gerede los

wag[2] N *(= wit, clown)* Witzbold *m (inf)*; **a bit of a ~** ein alter Witzbold

wage[1] [weɪdʒ] N *usu pl* Lohn *m*

wage[2] VT *war, campaign* führen; **to ~ war against sth** *(fig)* gegen etw einen Feldzug führen

wage *in cpds* Lohn-; **wage agreement** N Lohnabkommen *nt*, Tarifvertrag *m*; **wage bargaining** N *no pl* Tarifverhandlung *f*, Lohnverhandlung *f*; **wage check** N *(US)* Lohnscheck *m*; **wage claim** N Lohnforderung *f*; **wage-cost inflation** N Lohnkosteninflation *f*

waged [weɪdʒd] ADJ erwerbstätig

wage: **wage demand** N Lohnforderung *f*; **wage determination** N Lohnfestsetzung *f*; **wage dispute** N Lohnkonflikt *m*, Lohnkampf *m*; **wage earner** N *(esp Brit)* Lohnempfänger(in) *m(f)*; **wage freeze** N Lohnstopp *m*; **wage incidentals** PL Lohnnebenkosten *pl*; **wage increase** N Lohnerhöhung *f*; **wage-intensive** ADJ lohnintensiv; **wage level** N Lohnniveau *nt*; **wage packet** N *(esp Brit)* Lohntüte *f*; **wage payment** N Lohnzahlung *f*; **wage-price spiral** N Lohn-Preis-Spirale *f*

wager ['weɪdʒə'] N Wette *f (on* auf *+acc)*; **to make a ~** eine Wette eingehen *or* abschließen VT wetten *(on* auf *+acc)*; *one's honour, life* verpfänden; **I'll ~ you £2 my horse wins** ich wette mit Ihnen um £ 2, dass mein Pferd gewinnt; **he won't do it, I ~!** *(dated)* ich wette, dass er es nicht tut! VI wetten *(on* auf *+acc)*

wage rates PL Lohnsatz *m*, Tarifsatz *m*

wages ['weɪdʒɪz] PL Lohn *m*; **the ~ of sin** die gerechte Strafe, der Sünde Lohn *(old)*

wages bill N *(Brit)* Lohnkosten *pl*

wage scale N Lohnskala *f*

wages clerk N *(Brit)* Lohnbuchhalter(in) *m(f)*

wage: **wage settlement** N Lohnabkommen *nt*, Tarifabschluss *m*; **wage slave** N *(hum inf)* Lohnsklave *m (hum inf)*, Lohnsklavin *f (hum inf)*; **wage slip** N Lohnstreifen *m*, Lohnzettel *m*; **wage worker** N *(US)* Lohnempfänger(in) *m(f)*

waggish ['wægɪʃ] ADJ schalkhaft, schelmisch; **he has a ~ sense of humour** ihm sitzt der Schalk im Nacken

waggishly ['wægɪʃlɪ] ADV schalkhaft

waggle ['wægl] VT wackeln mit; *tail* wedeln mit; *(bird)* wippen mit; **he ~d his loose tooth** er wackelte an dem lockeren Zahn VI wackeln; *(tail)* wedeln; *(of bird)* wippen N **with a ~ of her hips she left the stage** mit den Hüften wackelnd ging sie von der Bühne

waggly ['wæglɪ] ADJ *(= loose)* wackelig; *hips* wackelnd; *tail* wedelnd

waggon N ['wægən] *(Brit)* = **wagon**

Wagnerian [vɑ:g'nɪərɪən] N Wagnerianer(in) *m(f)* ADJ Wagner-; *(= like Wagner)* wagner(i)sch; **a ~ opera** eine Wagneroper

wagon ['wægən] N **a** *(horse-drawn)* Fuhrwerk *nt*, Wagen *m*; *(= covered wagon)* Planwagen *m*; *(US: = delivery truck)* Lieferwagen *m*; *(= child's toy cart)* Leiterwagen *m*; *(= tea wagon etc)* Wagen *m*; *(US inf) (= police car)* Streifenwagen *m*; *(for transporting prisoners)* grüne Minna *(inf)*; *(Brit inf) (= car)* Karre *f (inf)*; *(= lorry)* Laster *m (inf)* **b** *(Brit Rail)* Wag(g)on *m* **c** *(inf)* **I'm on the ~** ich trinke nichts; **to go on the ~** unter die Abstinenzler gehen *(inf)*

wagoner ['wægənə'] N Fuhrmann *m*

wagon: **wagonload** ['wægənləʊd] N Wagenladung *f*; **books/prisoners arrived by the ~** ganze Wagenladungen von Büchern/Gefangenen kamen an; **wagon train** N Zug *m* von Planwagen

wagtail ['wægteɪl] N *(Orn)* Bachstelze *f*

wah-wah pedal ['wɑ:wɑ:,pedl] N *(Mus)* Wah-Wah-Pedal *nt*

waif [weɪf] N obdachloses *or* heimatloses Kind; *(= animal)* herrenloses Tier; **the poor little ~ …** das arme kleine Ding, hat kein Zuhause, …; **~s and strays** *(= children)* obdachlose *or* heimatlose Kinder *pl*; *(= animals)* herrenlose Tiere *pl*

wail [weɪl] N *(of baby)* Geschrei *nt*; *(of mourner, music)* Klagen *nt*; *(of sirens, wind)* Heulen *nt*; *(inf: = complaint)* Gejammer *nt (inf)*; **a great ~/a ~ of protest went up** es erhob sich lautes Wehklagen/Protestgeheul VI *(baby, cat)* schreien; *(mourner, music)* klagen; *(siren, wind)* heulen; *(inf: = complain)* jammern *(over* über *+acc)*

Wailing Wall ['weɪlɪŋ'wɔ:l] N Klagemauer *f*

wain [weɪn] N *(old)* Wagen *m*; **the Wain** *(Astron)* der Große Wagen

wainscot ['weɪnskət] N *no pl* Täfelung *f*

wainscot(t)ed ['weɪnskətɪd] ADJ holzgetäfelt, paneeliert

wainscot(t)ing ['weɪnskətɪŋ] N Täfelung *f*

waist [weɪst] N Taille *f*; *(of violin)* Mittelbügel *m*; *(Naut)* Mittelteil *m*; **stripped to the ~** mit nacktem *or* bloßem Oberkörper; **too tight round the ~** zu eng in der Taille

waist: **waistband** N Rock-/Hosenbund *m*; **waistcoat** N *(Brit)* Weste *f*; **waist-deep** ADJ hüfthoch, bis zur Taille reichend; **the water was ~** das Wasser reichte bis zur Taille; **we stood ~ in …** wir standen bis zur Hüfte in …

waisted ['weɪstɪd] ADJ *clothes* tailliert

-waisted [-'weɪstɪd] ADJ *suf* mit einer … Taille; **narrow-waisted** mit schmaler Taille

waist: **waist-high** ADJ hüfthoch, bis zur Taille reichend; **we picnicked in a field of ~ grass** wir picknickten in einem Feld, wo uns das Gras bis zur Hüfte reichte; **waistline** N Taille *f*

wait [weɪt] VI **a** warten *(for* auf *+acc)*; **to ~ for sb to do sth** darauf warten, dass jd etw tut; **it was definitely worth ~ing for** es hat sich wirklich gelohnt, darauf zu warten; **that'll be worth ~ing for** *(iro)* da bin ich aber gespannt *(inf)*; **well, what are you ~ing for?** worauf wartest du denn (noch)?; **~ for it, now he's going to get mad** warts ab, gleich wird er wild *(inf)*; **this stamp is worth, ~ for it, £10,000** diese Brief-

marke kostet sage und schreibe £ 10.000; **let him ~!, he can ~!** lass ihn warten!, soll er warten!, der kann warten!; **can't it ~?** kann das nicht warten?, hat das nicht Zeit?; **this work will have to ~ till later** diese Arbeit muss bis später warten *or* liegen bleiben; **this work is still ~ing to be done** diese Arbeit muss noch gemacht *or* erledigt werden; **~ a minute** *or* **moment** *or* **second** (einen) Augenblick *or* Moment (mal); **(just) you ~!** warte nur ab!; *(threatening)* warte nur!; **Mummy, I can't ~** Mami, ich muss dringend mal!; **I can't ~** ich kanns kaum erwarten; *(out of curiosity)* ich bin gespannt; **I can't ~ to see his face** da bin ich (aber) auf sein Gesicht gespannt; **I can't ~ to try out my new boat** ich kann es kaum noch erwarten, bis ich mein neues Boot ausprobiere; **I can hardly ~** *(usu iro)* ich kann es kaum erwarten!; **"repairs while you ~"** „Sofortreparaturen", „Reparaturschnelldienst"; **~ and see!** warten Sie (es) ab!, abwarten und Tee trinken! *(inf)*; **we'll have to ~ and see how …** wir müssen abwarten, wie …
b **to ~ at table** *(Brit)* servieren, bedienen; **she used to ~ at the …** sie bediente früher im …
VT **a** **to ~ one's turn** (ab)warten, bis man an der Reihe ist; **to ~ one's moment** *or* **chance** auf eine günstige Gelegenheit warten, eine günstige Gelegenheit abwarten; **don't ~ supper for me** warte mit dem Abendessen nicht auf mich
b *(US)* **to ~ a table** servieren, bedienen
N **a** Wartezeit *f*; **did you have a long ~?** mussten Sie lange warten?
b **to lie in ~ for sb/sth** jdm/einer Sache auflauern
c **waits** **PL** ≈ Sternsinger *pl*

▸**wait about** *(Brit) or* **around** VI warten *(for* auf *+acc)*

▸**wait behind** VI zurückbleiben; **to wait behind for sb** zurückbleiben und auf jdn warten

▸**wait in** VI zu Hause bleiben *(for* wegen*)*

▸**wait on** **VI** *(= continue to wait)* noch (weiter) warten **VI** *+prep obj* **a** *(also* **wait upon***: = serve)* bedienen **b** *(US)* **to wait on table** servieren, bei Tisch bedienen **c** *(= wait for)* warten auf *(+acc)*; **I'm waiting on him finishing** ich warte, bis er fertig ist

▸**wait out** VT *sep* das Ende *(+gen)* abwarten; **to wait it out** abwarten

▸**wait up** VI **a** aufbleiben *(for* wegen, für*)* **b** *(esp US inf)* **wait up!** langsam!

wait-and-see policy [ˌweɪtənˈsiːpɒlɪsɪ] N Politik *f* des Abwartens

waiter [ˈweɪtəʳ] N Kellner *m*, Ober *m*; **~!** (Herr) Ober!

waiting [ˈweɪtɪŋ] N **a** Warten *nt*; **all this ~ (around)** dieses ewige Warten, diese ewige Warterei *(inf)*; **no ~** Halteverbot *nt* **b** *(= royal service)* **those in ~ at the court …** wer bei Hof dient … **c** *(by waiter etc)* Servieren *nt*, Bedienen *nt*

waiting: **waiting game** N Wartespiel *nt*; **to play a ~** ein Wartespiel spielen; **the siege/negotiations developed into a ~** die Belagerung entwickelte sich/die Verhandlungen entwickelten sich zu einer Geduldsprobe; **waiting list** N Warteliste *f*; **waiting room** N Warteraum *m*; *(at doctor's)* Wartezimmer *nt*; *(in railway station)* Wartesaal *m*

waitlist [ˈweɪtlɪst] *(US)* **N** Warteliste *f* **VT** **to be ~ed** auf der Warteliste stehen

waitress [ˈweɪtrɪs] **N** Kellnerin *f*, Serviererin *f*; **~!** Fräulein! **VI** kellnern

waitressing [ˈweɪtrɪsɪŋ] N Kellnern *nt*

wait state N *(Comput)* Wartezyklus *m*; **with zero ~s** ohne Wartezyklen

waive [weɪv] VT **a** *(= not insist on) rights, claim, fee* verzichten auf *(+acc)*; *principles, rules, age limit etc* außer Acht lassen **b** *(= put aside, dismiss) question, objection* abtun

waiver [ˈweɪvəʳ] N *(Jur)* Verzicht *m* *(of* auf *+acc)*; *(= document)* Verzichterklärung *f*; *(of law, contract, clause)* Außerkraftsetzung *f*

wake¹ [weɪk] N *(Naut)* Kielwasser *nt*; **in the ~ of** *(fig)* im Gefolge *(+gen)*; **to follow in sb's ~** in jds Kielwasser segeln; **X follows in the ~ of Y** Y bringt X mit sich; **X brings Y in its ~** X bringt Y mit sich; **X leaves Y in its ~** X hinterlässt Y; **with ten children in her ~** *(inf)* mit zehn Kindern im Schlepptau *(inf)*

wake² N *(esp Ir: over corpse)* Totenwache *f*

wake³ *pret* **woke**, *ptp* **woken** *or* **waked** **VT** (auf)wecken; *(fig)* wecken, erwecken *(geh)* **VI** aufwachen, erwachen *(geh)*; **he woke to find himself in prison** als er aufwachte *or* erwachte, fand er sich im Gefängnis wieder; **he woke to the sound of birds singing** als er aufwachte, sangen die Vögel; **he woke one day to find himself a rich man** als er eines Tages erwachte *or* aufwachte, war er ein reicher Mann; **they woke to their danger too late** *(fig)* sie haben die Gefahr zu spät erkannt

▸**wake up** **VI** *(lit, fig)* aufwachen; **to wake up to sth** *(fig)* sich *(dat)* einer Sache *(gen)* bewusst werden; **I wish he'd wake up to what's happening** ich wünschte, ihm würde endlich bewusst *or* aufgehen *or* klar, was (hier) vor sich geht; **he woke up to a new life** ein neues Leben brach für ihn an; **wake up and smell the coffee!** *(esp US inf)* wach endlich auf! **VT** *sep (lit)* aufwecken; *(fig: = rouse from sloth)* wach- *or* aufrütteln; **to wake sb up to sth** *(fig)* jdm etw klarmachen *or* bewusst machen *or* vor Augen führen; **to wake one's ideas up** sich zusammenreißen

wakeboarding [ˈweɪkˌbɔːdɪŋ] N *(Sport)* Wakeboarding *nt*, Wakeboarden *nt*

wakeful [ˈweɪkfʊl] ADJ *(= sleepless)* schlaflos; *(= alert)* wachsam

wakefulness [ˈweɪkfʊlnɪs] N *(= sleeplessness)* Schlaflosigkeit *f*; *(= alertness)* Wachsamkeit *f*

waken [ˈweɪkən] **VT** (auf)wecken **VI** *(liter, Scot)* erwachen *(geh)*, aufwachen; **he ~ed to see …** beim Erwachen sah er …; **he ~ed to another dreary day** ein neuer, trostloser Tag brach für ihn an

waker [ˈweɪkəʳ] N **to be an early ~** früh aufwachen

wake-up call [ˈweɪkʌpˌkɔːl] N **a** *(Telec)* Weckruf *m* **b** *(esp US: = warning)* Warnsignal *nt*

wakey wakey [ˌweɪkɪˈweɪkɪ] INTERJ aufwachen!

waking [ˈweɪkɪŋ] ADJ **one's ~ hours** von früh bis spät; **thoughts of her filled all his ~ hours** der Gedanke an sie beschäftigte ihn von früh bis spät; **his ~ hours were spent …** von früh bis spät beschäftigte er sich mit …; **~ dream** Wachtraum *m*

Wales [weɪlz] N Wales *nt*; **Prince/Princess of ~** Prinz *m*/Prinzessin *f* von Wales

walk [wɔːk] **N** **a** *(= stroll)* Spaziergang *m*; *(= hike)* Wanderung *f*; *(Sport)* Gehen *nt*; *(= competition)* Geher-Wettkampf *m*; *(= charity walk)* Marsch *m* *(für Wohltätigkeitszwecke)*; **a 20-mile ~ along the roads** ein 20-Meilen-Marsch die Straße entlang; **it's only 10 minutes' ~** es sind nur 10 Minuten zu Fuß; **it's a long/short ~ to the shops** zu den Läden ist es weit/nicht weit zu Fuß *or* zu gehen *or* zu laufen *(inf)*; **it's a long ~ but a short drive** zu Fuß ist es weit, aber mit dem Auto ganz nah; **that's quite a ~** das ist eine ganz schöne Strecke, das ist ganz schön weit zu laufen *(inf)*; **he thinks nothing of a 10-mile ~** 10 Meilen zu Fuß sind für ihn gar nichts; **to go for a ~, to have** *or* **take a ~** einen Spaziergang machen, spazieren gehen; **to take sb/the dog for a ~** mit jdm/dem Hund spazieren gehen *or* einen Spaziergang machen, den Hund ausführen *or* spazieren führen; **a ~ in the park** *(fig inf: = easy)* ein Kinderspiel *nt*
b *(= gait)* Gang *m*; *(of horse)* Gangart *f*; **he went at a brisk ~** er ging schnellen Schrittes *(geh) or* schnell; **the horse went at a ~** das Pferd ging im Schritt; **he slowed his horse to a ~** er brachte sein Pferd in den Schritt; **he ran for a bit, then slowed to a ~** er rannte ein Stück und ging dann im Schritttempo weiter
c *(= path) (in garden etc)* (Park)weg *m*; *(in hills etc)* Weg *m*
d *(= route)* Weg *m*; *(signposted etc)* Wander-/ /Spazierweg *m*; **he knows some good ~s in the Lake District** er kennt ein paar gute Wandermöglichkeiten *or* Wanderungen im Lake District
e **~ of life** Milieu *nt*; **people from all ~s of life** Leute aus allen Schichten und Berufen
f *(US Baseball)* Walk *m*, Freibase *nt*
VT **a** *(= lead) person, horse* (spazieren) führen; *dog* ausführen; *(= ride at a walk)* im Schritt gehen lassen; **to ~ sb home/to the bus** jdn nach Hause/zum Bus bringen; **she ~ed her baby up to the table** das Kind lief, von der Mutter gehalten *or* mit Hilfe der Mutter, zum Tisch; **to ~ sb off his feet** *or* **legs** *(inf)* jdn total erschöpfen; **if we go hiking, I'll ~ the legs off you** *(inf)* wenn wir zusammen wandern gehen, dann wirst du (bald) nicht mehr mithalten können
b *distance* laufen, gehen; **I've ~ed this road many times** ich bin diese Straße oft gegangen
c **to ~ the streets** *(prostitute)* auf den Strich gehen *(inf)*; *(in search of sth)* durch die Straßen irren; *(aimlessly)* durch die Straßen streichen; **to ~ the boards** *(Theat)* auf den Brettern stehen; **he learned his trade by ~ing the boards before turning to films** er hat sein Handwerk auf den Brettern gelernt, bevor er zum Film ging; **to ~ the plank** *mit verbundenen Augen über eine Schiffsplanke ins Wasser getrieben werden*; **to ~ the wards** *(Med)* famulieren
d *(US Baseball)* einen Walk *or* ein Freibase geben *(+dat)*
VI **a** gehen, laufen; **~ a little with me** gehen Sie ein Stück mit mir; **to learn to ~** laufen lernen; **you must learn to ~ before you can run** *(prov)* man sollte den ersten Schritt vor dem zweiten tun; **to ~ in one's sleep** schlaf- *or* nachtwandeln; **to ~ with a stick** am Stock gehen
b *(= not ride)* zu Fuß gehen, laufen *(inf)*; *(= stroll)* spazieren gehen; *(= hike)* wandern; **you can ~ there in 5 minutes** da ist man in *or* bis dahin sind es 5 Minuten zu Fuß; **to ~ home** nach Hause laufen *(inf)*, zu Fuß nach Hause gehen; **we were out ~ing when the telegram arrived** wir waren gerade spazieren *or* auf einem Spaziergang, als das Telegramm kam
c *(ghost)* umgehen, spuken
d *(inf: = disappear)* Beine bekommen *(inf)*
e *(US inf) (= quit one's job)* kündigen; *(= go on strike)* in den Ausstand treten

▸**walk about** *(Brit) or* **around** **VI** herumlaufen *(inf)* **VT** *sep (= lead) person, horse* auf und ab führen; *(= ride at a walk)* im Schritt gehen lassen

▸**walk away** VI weg- *or* davongehen; **he walked away from the crash unhurt** er ist bei dem Unfall ohne Verletzungen davongekommen; **you can't just walk away from ten years of marriage** du kannst doch zehn Jahre Ehe nicht einfach so abschreiben; **to walk away with a prize** *etc* einen Preis *etc* kassieren *or* einstecken *(inf)*

▸**walk in** VI hereinkommen; *(casually)* hereinspazieren *(inf)*; **"please walk in"** „bitte eintreten"

▸**walk in on** VI *+prep obj* hereinplatzen bei *(inf)*

▸**walk into** VI *+prep obj room* hereinkommen in *(+acc)*; *person* anrempeln; *wall* laufen gegen; **to walk into sb** *(= meet unexpectedly)* jdm in die Arme laufen, jdn zufällig treffen; **to walk into a trap** in eine Falle gehen; **to walk into a job** eine Stelle ohne Schwierigkeiten bekommen; **he just walked into the first job he applied for** er hat gleich die erste Stelle bekommen, um die er sich beworben hat; **to walk right into sth** *(lit)* mit voller Wucht gegen etw rennen; **I didn't know I was going to walk into an argument** ich wusste nicht, dass ich hier mitten in einen Streit hineingeraten würde; **you walked right into that one, didn't you?** da bist du aber ganz schön reingefallen *(inf)*

▸**walk off** **VT** *sep pounds* ablaufen *(inf)*; **I'm going out to try and walk off this headache/hang-**

over ich gehe jetzt an die Luft, um meine Kopfschmerzen/meinen Kater loszuwerden; **we walked off our lunch with a stroll in the park** nach dem Mittagessen haben wir einen Verdauungsspaziergang im Park gemacht VI weggehen; **he walked off in the opposite direction** er ging in die andere Richtung davon

▶ **walk off with** VI *+prep obj (inf)* **a** *(= take) (unintentionally)* abziehen mit *(inf)*; *(intentionally)* abhauen mit *(inf)* **b** *(= win easily) prize* kassieren, einstecken *(inf)*

▶ **walk on** VI *+prep obj grass etc* betreten VI **a** *(= continue walking)* weitergehen; **she hesitated, then walked on by** sie zögerte und ging dann weiter **b** *(Theat)* auftreten; *(in walk-on part)* auf die Bühne gehen; **to walk on(to) the stage** auf die Bühne treten, auf der Bühne erscheinen

▶ **walk out** VI **a** *(= quit)* gehen; **to walk out of a meeting/room** eine Versammlung/einen Saal verlassen; **to walk out on sb** jdn verlassen; *(= let down)* jdn im Stich lassen; *(= abandon) girlfriend etc* jdn sitzen lassen *(inf)*; **to walk out on sth** aus etw aussteigen *(inf)* **b** *(= strike)* streiken, in Streik treten **c to walk out with sb** *(dated)* mit jdm gehen VT *sep (dated, = court)* gehen mit

▶ **walk over** VI *+prep obj* **a** *(= defeat)* in die Tasche stecken *(inf)* **b to walk all over sb** *(inf) (= dominate)* jdn unterbuttern *(inf)*; *(= treat harshly)* jdn fertigmachen *(inf)*; **she lets her husband walk all over her** sie lässt sich von ihrem Mann herumschikanieren *(inf)* or völlig unterbuttern *(inf)*

▶ **walk through** VI *+prep obj* **a** *(inf: = do easily) exam etc* spielend schaffen *(inf)* **b** *(Theat) part* durchgehen

▶ **walk up** VI **a** *(= go up, ascend)* hinaufgehen; **the escalator is broken so you'll have to walk up** die Rolltreppe ist außer Betrieb, Sie müssen zu Fuß hinaufgehen **b** *(= approach)* zugehen *(to* auf *+acc)*; **a man walked up (to me/her)** ein Mann kam auf mich zu/ging auf sie zu; **walk up!, walk up!** treten Sie näher!

walkable ['wɔːkəbl] ADJ **to be ~** sich zu Fuß machen lassen

walk: **walkabout** N *(esp Brit: by king etc)* Rundgang *m*; **the Queen went (on a) ~** die Königin nahm ein Bad in der Menge; **walkaway** N *(US)* = **walkover**

walker ['wɔːkəʳ] N **a** *(= stroller)* Spaziergänger(in) *m(f)*; *(= hiker)* Wanderer *m*, Wanderin *f*; *(Sport)* Geher(in) *m(f)*; **to be a fast/slow ~** schnell/langsam gehen **b** *(for baby, invalid)* Gehhilfe *f*; *(US: = Zimmer®)* Gehwagen *m*

walker-on ['wɔːkər'ɒn] N Statist(in) *m(f)*

walkies ['wɔːkɪz] PL Gassi *nt*; **to go ~** *(Brit inf)* Gassi gehen *(inf)*

walkie-talkie ['wɔːkɪ'tɔːkɪ] N Sprechfunkgerät *nt*, Walkie-Talkie *nt*

walk-in ['wɔːkɪn] ADJ **a ~ cupboard** ein begehbarer Einbau- or Wandschrank N *(US) (= cupboard)* begehbarer Einbau- or Wandschrank; *(= victory)* spielender Sieg

walking ['wɔːkɪŋ] N Gehen *nt*; *(as recreation)* Spazierengehen *nt*; *(= hiking)* Wandern *nt*; **there's some good ~ in these hills** in diesen Bergen gibt es ein paar gute Wandermöglichkeiten; **we did a lot of ~ while we were in Wales** als wir in Wales waren, sind wir viel gewandert or gelaufen ADJ *attr encyclopaedia, miracle etc* wandelnd; **at (a) ~ pace** im Schrittempo; **the ~ wounded** die Leichtverwundeten *pl*, die leicht Verwundeten *pl*; **it's within ~ distance** dahin kann man laufen or zu Fuß gehen

walking: **walking bass** N *(Mus) einfache Kontrabassbegleitung*, Walking-Bass *m*; **walking boots** PL Wanderstiefel *pl*; **walking frame** N Gehhilfe *f*, Gehwagen *m*, Gehbock *m*; **walking holiday** N *(Brit)* Wanderferien *pl*; **walking papers** N *(US)* **he got his ~** er ist gegangen worden; **she gave him his ~** sie hat ihm den Laufpass gegeben; **walking shoes** PL Wanderschuhe *pl*; **walking stick** N Spazierstock *m*; **walking tour** N Wanderung *f*

Walkman® ['wɔːkmən] N Walkman® *m*

walk: **walk-on** ADJ **~ part/role** *(Theat)* Statistenrolle *f* N Statistenrolle *f*; **walkout** N *(= strike)* Streik *m*; **to stage a ~** *(from conference etc)* demonstrativ den Saal verlassen; **walkover** N *(Sport)* Walkover *m*, Walk-over *m*; *(= easy victory)* spielender Sieg; *(fig)* Kinderspiel *nt*; **the government had a ~ in the debate** die Regierung hatte leichtes Spiel in der Debatte ADJ *attr* **~ victory** spielender Sieg; **walk-up** N *(US inf)* **a** Haus *nt* ohne Fahrstuhl or Lift **b** Wohnung *f* in einem Haus ohne Fahrstuhl or Lift ADJ *house, apartment* ohne Fahrstuhl or Lift; **a ~ hotel** ein Hotel ohne Fahrstuhl or Lift; **walkway** N Fußweg *m*; **a pedestrian ~** ein Fuß(gänger)weg *m*

wall [wɔːl] N **a** *(outside)* Mauer *f*; *(inside, of mountain)* Wand *f*; **the Great Wall of China** die Chinesische Mauer; **the north ~ of the Eiger** die Eigernordwand; **a ~ of fire** eine Feuerwand; **a ~ of policemen/troops** eine Mauer von Polizisten/Soldaten; **~s have ears** die Wände haben Ohren; **to come up against a ~ of silence** auf eine Mauer des Schweigens stoßen; **to go up the ~** *(inf)* die Wände rauf- or hochgehen *(inf)*; **I'm climbing the ~s** *(inf)* ich könnte die Wände hochgehen *(inf)*; **he/his questions drive me up the ~** *(inf)* er/seine Fragerei bringt mich auf die Palme *(inf)*; **this constant noise is driving me up the ~** *(inf)* bei diesem ständigen Lärm könnte ich die Wände rauf- or hochgehen *(inf)*; **to go to the ~** *(inf: firm etc)* kaputtgehen *(inf)* → **brick wall, back b** *(Anat)* Wand *f*; **abdominal ~** Bauchdecke *f* VT mit einer Mauer umgeben

▶ **wall about** VT *sep (esp Brit old, liter)* ummauern

▶ **wall in** VT *sep* mit einer Mauer/von Mauern umgeben; **walled in on all sides by bodyguards** auf allen Seiten von Leibwächtern abgeriegelt or eingeschlossen

▶ **wall off** VT *sep (= cut off)* durch eine Mauer (ab)trennen; *(= separate into different parts)* unterteilen; **the monks walled themselves off from the outside world** die Mönche riegelten sich hinter ihren Mauern von der Welt ab

▶ **wall round** VT *sep (esp Brit)* ummauern

▶ **wall up** VT *sep* zumauern

wallaby ['wɒləbɪ] N Wallaby *nt*

wallah ['wɒlə] N *(dated sl)* Typ *m (inf)*

wall: **wall anchor** N *(US)* Dübel *m*; **wall bars** PL Sprossenwand *f*; **wallboard** N *(US)* Sperrholz *nt*; **wall cabinet** N Wandschrank *m*; **wall chart** N Plantafel *f*; **wall clock** N Wanduhr *f*; **wall covering** N Wandbekleidung *f*; **wall cupboard** N Wandschrank *m*

walled [wɔːld] ADJ von Mauern umgeben

wallet ['wɒlɪt] N Brieftasche *f*

wall: **wallflower** N *(Bot)* Goldlack *m*; *(fig inf)* Mauerblümchen *nt (inf)*; **wall hanging** N Wandbehang *m*, Wandteppich *m*; **wall lamp** N Wandleuchte *f*; **wall map** N Wandkarte *f*; **wall of death** N Todeswand *f*

Walloon [wɒ'luːn] N **a** Wallone *m*, Wallonin *f* **b** *(dialect)* Wallonisch *nt* ADJ wallonisch

wallop ['wɒləp] N **a** *(inf: = blow)* Schlag *m*; **he fell flat on his face with a ~** mit einem Plumps fiel er auf die Nase *(inf)*; **to give sb/sth a ~** jdm/einer Sache einen Schlag versetzen **b at a fair old ~** *(dated inf)* mit Karacho *(inf)* **c** *(Brit, inf, = beer)* Bölkstoff *m (sl)* VT *(esp Brit inf) (= hit)* schlagen; *(= punish)* verdreschen *(inf)*, versohlen *(inf)*; *(= defeat)* fertigmachen *(inf)*; **to ~ sb one/over the head** jdm eins reinhauen *(inf)*/eins überziehen

walloping ['wɒləpɪŋ] *(inf)* N Prügel *pl (inf)*, Abreibung *f (inf)*; *(= defeat)* Schlappe *f (inf)*; **to give sb a ~** jdm eine Tracht Prügel geben *(inf)*; *(= defeat)* jdn fertigmachen *(inf)*; **to get a ~** *(= defeat)* eine Schlappe erleiden *(inf)* ADJ *(also* **walloping great***)* riesig; *price* gesalzen *(inf)*, saftig *(inf)*; *loss, defeat* gewaltig *(inf)*; *lie* faustdick *(inf)*

wallow ['wɒləʊ] N *(= act)* Bad *nt*; *(= place)* Suhle *f* VI **a** *(lit) (animal)* sich wälzen, sich suhlen; *(boat)* rollen **b** *(fig)* **to ~ in luxury/self-pity** *etc* im Luxus/Selbstmitleid *etc* schwelgen; **to ~ in money** *(inf)* im Geld schwimmen *(inf)*

▶ **wallow about** *(Brit)* or **around** VI sich herumwälzen

wall: **wall painting** N Wandmalerei *f*; **wallpaper** N Tapete *f*; *(Comput)* Hintergrundbild *nt* VT tapezieren; **wall pass** N *(Ftbl)* Doppelpass *m*; **wall safe** N Wandsafe *m*; **wall socket** N Steckdose *f*; **Wall Street** N Wall Street *f*; **wall-to-wall** ADJ **~ carpeting** Teppichboden *m*; **his apartment is just about ~ stereo equipment** seine Wohnung ist fast eine einzige Stereoanlage; **what a bar! ~ punks** was für eine Bar! randvoll mit Punks; **the event got ~ coverage (in the media)** über das Ereignis wurde (in den Medien) umfassend berichtet

wally ['wɒlɪ] N *(Brit inf: = fool)* Trottel *m (inf)*

walnut ['wɔːlnʌt] N *(= nut)* Walnuss *f*; *(= walnut tree)* (Wal)nussbaum *m*; *(= wood)* Nussbaumholz *nt*, Nussbaum *m*

walrus ['wɔːlrəs] N Walross *nt*

walrus moustache, *(US)* **walrus mustache** N Walrossbart *m*

Walter Mitty [ˌwɔːltə'mɪtɪ] N **a ~ (character)** ein Schwärmer *m*

waltz [wɔːls] N Walzer *m* VI **a** *(= dance waltz)* Walzer tanzen; **would you care to ~?** möchten Sie einen Walzer tanzen?; **they ~ed expertly** sie tanzten ausgezeichnet Walzer; **they ~ed across the ballroom** sie walzten durch den Ballsaal **b** *(inf: = move, come etc)* walzen *(inf)*; **he came ~ing up** er kam angetanzt *(inf)* VT Walzer tanzen mit; **he ~ed her out onto the balcony** er walzte mit ihr auf den Balkon hinaus

▶ **waltz about** *(Brit)* or **around** VI *(inf)* herumtanzen or -tänzeln

▶ **waltz in** VI *(inf)* hereintanzen *(inf)*; **to come waltzing in** angetanzt kommen *(inf)*

▶ **waltz off** VI *(inf)* abtanzen *(inf)*

▶ **waltz off with** VI *+prep obj (inf) prizes* abziehen mit

▶ **waltz through** VI *+prep obj (fig inf) match, game* spielend bewältigen; **she waltzed through the first round** die erste Runde war ein Spaziergang für sie *(inf)*

waltzer ['wɔːlsəʳ] N **a** *(= dancer)* Walzertänzer(in) *m(f)* **b** *(at fairground)* Krake *f*

waltz: **waltz music** N Walzermusik *f*; **waltz time** N Walzertakt *m*

wan [wɒn] ADJ bleich; *light, smile, look* matt

wand [wɒnd] N *(= magic wand)* Zauberstab *m*; *(of office)* Amtsstab *m*; *(Comput, for bar codes)* Lesestift *m*

wander ['wɒndəʳ] N Spaziergang *m*; *(through town, park also)* Bummel *m*; **I'm going for a ~ (a)round the shops** ich mache einen Ladenbummel

VT *hills, world* durchstreifen *(geh)*; **to ~ the streets** durch die Straßen wandern or *(looking for sb/sth also)* irren

VI **a** *(= walk around casually)* herumlaufen; *(more aimlessly)* umherwandern *(through, about* in *+dat)*; *(leisurely)* schlendern; *(to see the shops)* bummeln; **he ~ed past me in a dream** er ging wie im Traum an mir vorbei; **he ~ed over to speak to me** er kam zu mir herüber, um mit mir zu reden; **his hands ~ed over the keys** seine Hände wanderten über die Tasten; **the bus ~ed along the lanes for a couple of hours** der Bus zuckelte ein paar Stunden durch die Sträßchen; **the river ~ed through the valley** der Fluss zog sich durch das Tal; **I enjoy just ~ing around** ich bummele gerne einfach nur herum; **if his hands start ~ing ...** *(hum)* wenn er seine Finger nicht bei sich *(dat)* behalten kann ...

b *(= go off, stray)* **to ~ from the path** vom Wege or Pfad abkommen; **the cattle must not be allowed to ~** das Vieh darf nicht einfach so herumlaufen; **he ~ed too near the edge of the**

cliff er geriet zu nahe an den Rand des Abhangs; **I accidentally ~ed into Squire Thomas' property** ich bin aus Versehen in das Gelände von Squire Thomas geraten; **the children had ~ed out onto the street** die Kinder waren auf die Straße gelaufen; **the needle tends to ~ a bit** der Zeiger schwankt ein bisschen
c *(fig: thoughts, eye)* schweifen, wandern; **to let one's mind ~** seine Gedanken schweifen lassen; **during the lecture his mind ~ed a bit** während der Vorlesung wanderten seine Gedanken umher *or* schweiften seine Gedanken ab; **the old man's mind is beginning to ~ a bit** der alte Mann wird ein wenig wirr; **to ~ from the straight and narrow** vom Pfad der Tugend abirren *or* abkommen; **to ~ off a point/the subject** von einem Punkt/vom Thema abschweifen *or* abkommen

▶ **wander about** *(Brit) or* **around** VI umherziehen, umherwandern

▶ **wander back** VI *(cows, strays)* zurückkommen *or* -wandern; **shall we start wandering back to the car?** *(inf)* wollen wir langsam *or* allmählich zum Auto zurückgehen?; **after two years she wandered back to her husband** nach zwei Jahren fand *or* ging sie zu ihrem Mann zurück

▶ **wander in** VI ankommen *(inf)*, anspazieren *(inf)*; **he wandered in to see me this morning** *(inf)* er ist heute Morgen bei mir vorbeigekommen

▶ **wander off** VI **a** *(= go off)* weggehen, davonziehen *(geh)*; **to wander off course** vom Kurs abkommen; **he wandered off into one of his fantasies** er geriet wieder ins Fantasieren *or* Phantasieren; **he must have wandered off somewhere** er muss (doch) irgendwohin verschwunden sein **b** *(inf: = leave)* allmählich *or* langsam gehen

wanderer ['wɒndərəʳ] N Wandervogel *m*; **the Masai are ~s** die Massai sind ein Wanderstamm *m*; **that child is a real ~** das Kind treibt sich überall herum

wandering ['wɒndərɪŋ] ADJ *tribesman, refugees* umherziehend; *minstrel* fahrend; *thoughts* (ab)schweifend; *gaze* schweifend; *path* gewunden; **the old man's ~ mind** die wirren Gedanken des Alten; **to have ~ hands** *(hum)* seine Finger nicht bei sich *(dat)* behalten können; **the Wandering Jew** der Ewige Jude

wanderings ['wɒndərɪŋz] PL Streifzüge *pl*, Fahrten *pl*; *(verbal)* wirres Gerede; **it's time he stopped his ~ and settled down** es wird Zeit, dass er mit dem Herumstromern aufhört und sesshaft wird

wanderlust ['wɒndəlʌst] N Fernweh *nt*

wane [weɪn] **N** **to be on the ~** *(fig)* im Schwinden sein **VI** *(moon)* abnehmen; *(daylight)* nachlassen; *(fig) (influence, strength, life, power)* schwinden; *(reputation)* verblassen

wangle ['wæŋgl] *(inf)* **N** Schiebung *f (inf)*, Mauschelei *f (inf)*; **it's a ~** das ist Schiebung; **I think we can arrange some sort of ~** ich glaube, wir können es so hinbiegen *(inf)* *or* hindrehen *(inf)* **VT** *job, ticket etc* organisieren *(inf)*, verschaffen; **to ~ oneself** *or* **one's way in** sich hineinlavieren *or* -mogeln *(inf)*; **to ~ sb in** jdn reinschleusen *(inf)*; **he'll ~ it for you** er wird das schon für dich drehen *(inf) or* deichseln *(inf)*; **to ~ money out of sb** jdm Geld abluchsen *(inf)*; **we ~d an extra day off** wir haben noch einen zusätzlichen freien Tag rausgeschlagen *(inf)*

wangler ['wæŋgləʳ] N *(inf)* Schlawiner *m (inf)*

wangling ['wæŋglɪŋ] N *(inf)* Schiebung *f (inf)*; **there's a lot of ~ goes on** da gibts ziemlich viel Schiebung *(inf) or* Mauschelei *(inf)*

wank [wæŋk] *(Brit vulg)* **VI** *(also* **wank off)** wichsen *(sl)* **VT to ~ sb (off)** jdm einen abwichsen *(sl) or* runterholen *(inf)* **N to have a ~** sich *(dat)* einen runterholen *(inf)*

wanker ['wæŋkəʳ] N *(Brit vulg)* Wichser *m (sl)*, Arsch *m (vulg)*; *(= idiot)* Schwachkopf *m (inf)*

wankered ['wæŋkəd] ADJ *(Brit vulg: = drunk)* rotzbesoffen *(sl)*

wanky ['wæŋkɪ] ADJ *(sl)* beschissen *(inf)*

wanly ['wɒnlɪ] ADV matt

wannabe ['wɒnə,bi:] *(inf)* **N** Möchtegern *m (inf)* **ADJ** Möchtegern- *(inf)*; **a ~ film star** ein Möchtegern-Filmstar *m (inf)*

wanness ['wɒnnɪs] N *(= paleness)* Blässe *f*; *(of light)* Mattheit *f*

want [wɒnt] ✪ 8.1, 8.2, 9.5, 12.2, 18.4, 21.3 **N** **a** *(= lack)* Mangel *m (of* an *+dat)*; **~ of judgement** mangelndes Urteilsvermögen, Mangel *m* an Urteilsvermögen; **for ~ of** aus Mangel an *(+dat)*; **for ~ of anything better** mangels Besserem, in Ermangelung von etwas Besserem *or* eines Besseren; **for ~ of something to do I joined a sports club** weil ich nichts zu tun hatte, bin ich einem Sportverein beigetreten; **though it wasn't for ~ of trying** nicht, dass er sich/ich mich *etc* nicht bemüht hätte; **to feel the ~ of sth** etw vermissen
b *(= poverty)* Not *f*; **to be in ~** Not leiden
c *(= need)* Bedürfnis *nt*; *(= wish)* Wunsch *m*; **my ~s are few** meine Ansprüche *or* Bedürfnisse sind gering, meine Ansprüche sind bescheiden; **the farm supplied all their ~s** der Bauernhof versorgte sie mit allem Nötigen *or* Notwendigen; **to be in ~ of sth** einer Sache *(gen)* bedürfen *(geh)*, etw brauchen *or* benötigen; **to be in ~ of help** Hilfe brauchen; **to be in ~ of repair** reparaturbedürftig sein; **to attend to sb's ~s** sich um jdn kümmern
VT **a** *(= wish, desire)* wollen; *(more polite)* mögen; **to ~ to do sth** etw tun wollen; **I ~ you to come here** ich will *or* möchte, dass du herkommst; **I ~ it done now** ich will *or* möchte das sofort erledigt haben; **I was ~ing to leave the job next month** ich hätte gerne nächsten Monat mit der Arbeit aufgehört; **what does he ~ with me?** was will er von mir?; **darling, I ~ you** Liebling, ich will dich; **I ~ my mummy** ich will meine Mami, ich will zu meiner Mami; **you don't ~ much** *(iro)* sonst willst du nichts? *(iro)*; **I don't ~ strangers coming in** ich wünsche *or* möchte nicht, dass Fremde (hier) hereinkommen
b *(= need, require)* brauchen; **you ~ to see a doctor/lawyer** Sie sollten zum Arzt/Rechtsanwalt gehen; **you ~ to be careful!** *(inf)* du musst aufpassen; **you ~ to stop doing that** *(inf)* du musst damit aufhören; **he ~s to be more careful** *(inf)* er sollte etwas vorsichtiger sein; **that's the last thing I ~** *(inf)* alles, bloß das nicht *(inf)*; **that's all we ~ed!** *(iro inf)* das hat uns gerade noch gefehlt!; **it only ~ed the police to turn up ...** das hätte gerade noch gefehlt, dass auch noch die Polizei anrückt ...; **does my hair ~ cutting?** muss mein Haar geschnitten werden?; **"wanted"** „gesucht"; **he's a ~ed man** er wird (polizeilich) gesucht; **to feel ~ed** das Gefühl haben, gebraucht zu werden; **you're ~ed on the phone** Sie werden am Telefon verlangt *or* gewünscht
c *(= lack)* **he ~s talent/confidence** *etc* es mangelt *(geh) or* fehlt ihm an Talent/Selbstvertrauen *etc*; **all the soup ~s is a little salt** das Einzige, was an der Suppe fehlt, ist etwas Salz
VI **a** *(= wish, desire)* wollen; *(more polite)* mögen; **you can go if you ~ (to)** wenn du willst *or* möchtest, kannst du gehen; **I don't ~ to** ich will *or* möchte nicht; **without ~ing to sound rude, ...** ich will ja nicht unhöflich sein, aber ...; **do as you ~** tu, was du willst; **he said he'd do it, but does he really ~ to?** er sagte, er würde es machen, aber will er es wirklich?
b **he does not ~ for friends** es fehlt *or* mangelt *(geh)* ihm nicht an Freunden; **they ~ for nothing** es fehlt *or* mangelt *(geh)* ihnen an nichts; **he doesn't ~ for a pound or two** er ist nicht gerade arm *(inf)*, ihm fehlt es nicht an Kleingeld *(inf)*
c *(liter, = live in poverty)* darben *(liter)*

▶ **want in** VI *(inf)* reinwollen

▶ **want out** VI *(inf)* rauswollen

want ad N Kaufgesuch *nt*

wantage ['wɒntɪdʒ] N *(US Econ)* Fehlbetrag *m*, Defizit *nt*

wanted list ['wɒntɪd,lɪst] N Fahndungsliste *f*

wanting ['wɒntɪŋ] ADJ **a** *(= lacking, missing)* fehlend; **romance is ~ in the novel** diesem Roman fehlt es an Romantik; **it's a good novel, but there is something ~** der Roman ist gut, aber irgendetwas fehlt
b *(= deficient, inadequate)* **he is ~ in confidence/enterprise** *etc* es fehlt *or* mangelt *(geh)* ihm an Selbstvertrauen/Unternehmungslust *etc*; **his courage was found ~** sein Mut war nicht groß genug; **the new engine was found ~** der neue Motor hat sich als unzulänglich erwiesen; **he was (weighed in the balance and) found ~** *(liter)* er wurde (gewogen und) (für) zu leicht befunden; **he was not found ~** *(liter)* er hat sich bewährt
c *(inf: = mentally deficient)* **he's a bit ~ (up top)** er ist ein bisschen unterbelichtet *(inf)*

wanton ['wɒntən] **ADJ** **a** *(= licentious) life* liederlich; *behaviour, woman, pleasures* schamlos; *looks, thoughts* lüstern; **Cupid, that ~ boy** *(liter)* Amor, dieser kleine Lüstling **b** *(= wilful) cruelty, destruction* mutwillig; *disregard, negligence* sträflich, völlig unverantwortlich; *waste* sträflich, kriminell *(inf)*; **to spend money with ~ extravagance** Geld mit sträflichem Leichtsinn ausgeben; **decorated with ~ extravagance** üppig und verschwenderisch eingerichtet **c** *(poet: = capricious) persons* übermütig, mutwillig *(poet)* **N** *(old: = immoral woman)* Dirne *f*

wantonly ['wɒntənlɪ] ADV **a** *(= immorally)* liederlich, schamlos; *look* lüstern **b** *(= wilfully)* mutwillig; *neglect, waste* sträflich; **he was ~ extravagant with his wife's money** er gab das Geld seiner Frau mit sträflichem Leichtsinn aus

wantonness ['wɒntənnɪs] N **a** *(= immorality) (of sb's life)* Liederlichkeit *f*; *(of behaviour, woman)* Schamlosigkeit *f*; *(of look, thought)* Lüsternheit *f* **b** *(= wilfulness) (of cruelty)* Mutwilligkeit *f*; *(of disregard, negligence)* Sträflichkeit *f*

WAP N *(Comput, Telec) abbr of* **wireless application protocol** WAP *nt*

war [wɔ:ʳ] **N** Krieg *m*; **the art of ~** die Kriegskunst; **this is ~!** *(fig)* das bedeutet Krieg!; **the ~ against poverty/disease** der Kampf gegen die Armut/Krankheit; **~ of nerves** Nervenkrieg *m*; **~ of words** Wortgefecht *nt*; **to be at ~** sich im Krieg(szustand) befinden; **to declare ~** den Krieg erklären *(on +dat)*; *(fig also)* den Kampf ansagen *(on +dat)*; **to go to ~** *(= start)* (einen) Krieg anfangen *(against* mit); *(= declare)* den Krieg erklären *(against +dat)*; *(person)* in den Krieg ziehen; **to make** *or* **wage ~** Krieg führen *(on, against* gegen); **he/this car has been in the ~s a bit** *(inf)* er/dieses Auto sieht ziemlich ramponiert *(inf) or* mitgenommen aus; **I hear you've been in the ~s recently** *(inf)* ich höre, dass du zur Zeit ganz schön angeschlagen bist *(inf)*
VI sich bekriegen; *(fig)* ringen *(geh) (for* um)

war baby N Kriegskind *nt*

warble ['wɔ:bl] **N** Trällern *nt* **VI** trällern; **he ~d away as he stood in the shower** *(inf)* er trällerte fröhlich vor sich hin, während er unter der Dusche stand **VT** trällern

warbler ['wɔ:bləʳ] N *(Orn)* Grasmücke *f*; *(= wood warbler)* Waldsänger *m*

war: war bond N Kriegsanleihe *f*; **war bride** N Kriegsbraut *f*; **war cabinet** N *(Pol)* Kriegskabinett *nt*

warchalking ['wɔ,tʃɔ:kɪŋ] N *(Comput, Telec)* Warchalking *nt*

war: war clouds PL **the ~ are gathering** Kriegsgefahr droht; **war correspondent** N Kriegsberichterstatter(in) *m(f)*, Kriegskorrespondent(in) *m(f)*; **war crime** N Kriegsverbrechen *nt*; **war criminal** N Kriegsverbrecher(in) *m(f)*; **war cry** N Kriegsruf *m*; *(fig)* Schlachtruf *m*; **the war cries of the Red Indians** das Kriegsgeheul *or* Kriegsgeschrei der Indianer

ward [wɔ:d] N **a** *(part of hospital)* Station *f*; *(= room) (small)* (Kranken)zimmer *nt*; *(large)*

(Kranken)saal *m* **b** (*Jur: = person*) Mündel *nt*; **~ of court** Mündel *nt* unter Amtsvormundschaft; **to make sb a ~ of court** jdn unter Amtsvormundschaft stellen **c** (*Jur: state*) **(to be) in ~** unter Vormundschaft (stehen) **d** (*Admin*) Stadtbezirk *m*; (*= election ward*) Wahlbezirk *m* **e** (*of key*) Einschnitt *m* (im Schlüsselbart); (*of lock*) Aussparung *f*, Angriff *m*

▶ **ward off** VT *sep attack, blow, person, evil spirits* abwehren; *danger also, recession* abwenden; *depression* nicht aufkommen lassen

war dance N Kriegstanz *m*

warden ['wɔːdn] N (*of youth hostel*) Herbergsvater *m*, Herbergsmutter *f*; (*= game warden*) Jagdaufseher(in) *m(f)*; (*= traffic warden*) ≈ Verkehrspolizist *m*, ≈ Politesse *f*; (*= air-raid warden*) Luftschutzwart *m*; (*= fire warden*) Feuerwart(in) *m(f)*; (*of castle, museum etc*) Aufseher(in) *m(f)*; (*= head warden*) Kustos *m*; (*of port*) (Hafen)aufseher(in) *m(f)*; (*of mint*) Münzwardein *m*; (*Univ*) Heimleiter(in) *m(f)*; (*of Oxbridge college*) Rektor(in) *m(f)*; (*of prison*) (*Brit*) Wärter(in) *m(f)*, Aufseher(in) *m(f)*; (*US*) Gefängnisdirektor(in) *m(f)*

War Department N (*old US*) Kriegsministerium *nt (old)*

warder ['wɔːdəʳ] N (*Brit*) Wärter(in) *m(f)*, Aufseher(in) *m(f)*

war-disabled ['wɔːdɪs'eɪbld] PL **the ~** die Kriegsversehrten *pl*

ward heeler ['wɔːdhiːləʳ] N (*US Pol sl*) Handlanger(in) *m(f)* (*inf*)

wardress ['wɔːdrɪs] N (*Brit*) Wärterin *f*, Aufsehe-
…n *f*

…**ving** ['wɔːˌdraɪvɪŋ] N (*Comput, Telec*) War-
…g *nt*

…**obe** ['wɔːdrəʊb] N **a** (*esp Brit: = cupboard*)
…der)schrank *m* **b** (*= clothes*) Garderobe *f*
(*Theat*) (*= clothes*) Kostüme *pl*; (*= room*)
…eiderkammer *f*, Kostümfundus *m*

…**drobe**: **wardrobe mistress** N (*Theat*) Ge-
…andmeisterin *f*; **wardrobe trunk** N Kleider-
…koffer *m*

…**ard**: **wardroom** N (*Naut*) Offiziersmesse *f*; **ward round** N (*Med*) Visite *f*

-ward(s) [-wəd(z)] ADV *suf* -wärts; **southward(s)** südwärts; **town-/parkward(s)** in Richtung Stadt/Park; **in a homeward(s) direction** Richtung Heimat

wardship ['wɔːdʃɪp] N (*Jur*) Vormundschaft *f*

ward sister N (*Brit Med*) Stationsschwester *f*

ware [wɛəʳ] N **Delft/Derby ~** Delfter/Derby Porzellan *nt*

-ware N *suf* -waren *pl*; **glassware** Glaswaren *pl*; **kitchenware** Küchenutensilien *pl*

war effort N Kriegsanstrengungen *pl*

warehouse ['wɛəhaʊs] N Lager(haus) *nt* VT einlagern

warehouse club N (*esp US Comm*) *Geschäft, in dem Waren zu Großhandelspreisen an Mitglieder verkauft werden*

warehouseman ['wɛəhaʊsmən] N *pl* **-men** [-mən] Lagerarbeiter *m*

warehousing ['wɛəhaʊzɪŋ] N Lagerung *f*; **what sort of ~ is available?** welche Lagerungsmöglichkeiten gibt es?

wares [wɛəz] PL Waren *pl*; **to cry one's ~** (*dated*) seine Waren anpreisen

warfare ['wɔːfɛəʳ] N Krieg *m*; (*= techniques*) Kriegskunst *f*

war: **war fever** N Kriegsbegeisterung *f*; **war game** N Kriegsspiel *nt*; **war grave** N Kriegsgrab *nt*; **warhead** N Sprengkopf *m*; **war hero** N Kriegsheld *m*; **warhorse** N (*lit, fig*) Schlachtross *nt*

warily ['wɛərɪlɪ] ADV vorsichtig; (*= suspiciously*) misstrauisch, argwöhnisch; **to tread ~** (*lit, fig*) sich vorsehen

wariness ['wɛərɪnɪs] N Vorsicht *f*; (*= mistrust*) Misstrauen *nt*, Argwohn *m*; **the ~ of his reply** die Zurückhaltung, mit der er antwortete; **she had a great ~ of strangers** sie hegte starkes Misstrauen *or* großen Argwohn gegen Fremde

Warks (*Brit*) *abbr of* **Warwickshire**

war: **warlike** ADJ kriegerisch; *tone, speech* militant; **warlock** N Hexer *m*; **warlord** N Kriegsherr *m*

warm [wɔːm] ADJ (+*er*) **a** warm; **I am** *or* **feel ~** mir ist warm; **come to the fire and get ~** komm ans Feuer und wärm dich; **it's ~ work moving furniture about** beim Möbelumstellen wird einem ganz schön warm; **to make things ~ for sb** (*inf*) es jdm ungemütlich machen (*inf*); **~ start** (*Comput*) Warmstart *m*
b (*in party games*) **am I ~?** ist es (hier) warm?; **you're getting ~** es wird schon wärmer; **you're very ~!** heiß!
c (*= hearty, warm-hearted*) *person, welcome, smile* herzlich, warm
d (*= heated*) *dispute, words* hitzig, heftig
N **we were glad to get into the ~** wir waren froh, dass wir ins Warme kamen; **come and have a ~ at the fire** komm und wärm dich am Feuer; **to give sth a ~** etw wärmen
VT wärmen; **it ~s my heart to …** mir wird (es) ganz warm ums Herz, wenn …; **his kind gesture ~ed my heart** bei seiner freundlichen Geste wurde mir ganz warm ums Herz
VI **the milk was ~ing on the stove** die Milch wurde auf dem Herd angewärmt; **my heart ~ed** mir wurde warm ums Herz; **I ~ed to him** er wurde mir sympathischer; **his voice ~ed as he spoke of his family** seine Stimme bekam einen warmen Ton, als er von seiner Familie sprach; **he spoke rather hesitantly at first but soon ~ed to his subject** anfangs sprach er noch sehr zögernd, doch dann fand er sich in sein Thema hinein; **to ~ to one's work** sich mit seiner Arbeit anfreunden, Gefallen an seiner Arbeit finden

▶ **warm over** VT *sep* (*esp US*) **a** *food* aufwärmen **b** (*inf*) *idea* (wieder) aufwärmen

▶ **warm through** VT *food* aufwärmen

▶ **warm up** VI (*lit, fig*) warm werden; (*party, game, speaker*) in Schwung kommen; (*Sport*) sich aufwärmen; **things are warming up** es kommt Schwung in die Sache; (*= becoming dangerous*) es wird allmählich brenzlig *or* ungemütlich (*inf*) VT *sep engine* warm werden lassen, warm laufen lassen; *food etc* aufwärmen; (*fig*) *party* in Schwung bringen; *audience* in Stimmung bringen

warm-blooded ['wɔːm'blʌdɪd] ADJ warmblütig; (*fig*) heißblütig; **~ animal** Warmblüter *m*

warm boot N (*Comput*) Warmstart *m*

warmer ['wɔːməʳ] N **foot/bottle ~** Fuß-/Flaschenwärmer *m*

warm-hearted ['wɔːm'hɑːtɪd] ADJ *person* warmherzig; *action, gesture* großzügig

warm-heartedness ['wɔːm'hɑːtɪdnɪs] N Warmherzigkeit *f*, Herzlichkeit *f*; (*of action, gesture*) Großherzigkeit *f*

warming pan ['wɔːmɪŋ,pæn] N Wärmepfanne *f*

warmish ['wɔːmɪʃ] ADJ ein bisschen warm; **~ weather** ziemlich warmes Wetter

warmly ['wɔːmlɪ] ADV warm; *welcome* herzlich; *recommend* wärmstens; **we ~ welcome it** wir begrüßen es sehr

warmness ['wɔːmnɪs] N = **warmth**

war: **warmonger** ['wɔːˌmʌŋgəʳ] N Kriegshetzer(in) *m(f)*; **warmongering** ['wɔːˌmʌŋgərɪŋ] ADJ kriegshetzerisch N Kriegshetze *f*

warm start N (*Comput*) Warmstart *m*

warmth [wɔːmθ] N **a** (*lit*) Wärme *f* **b** (*fig*) (*= friendliness: of voice, welcome etc*) Wärme *f*, Herzlichkeit *f*; (*= heatedness*) Heftigkeit *f*, Hitzigkeit *f*

warm-up ['wɔːmʌp] N (*Sport*) Aufwärmen *nt*; (*Mus*) Einspielen *nt*; **the teams had a ~ before the game** die Mannschaften wärmten sich vor dem Spiel auf; **the audience was entertained with a ~ before the TV transmission began** das Publikum wurde vor der Fernsehübertragung in Stimmung gebracht

warm-ups ['wɔːmʌps] PL (*US*) Trainingsanzug *m*

warn [wɔːn] VT **a** (*= give warning*) warnen (*of, about, against* vor +*dat*); (*police, judge etc*) verwarnen; **to ~ sb not to do sth** jdn davor warnen, etw zu tun; **be ~ed** sei gewarnt!, lass dich warnen!; **I'm ~ing you** ich warne dich!; **you have been ~ed!** sag nicht, ich hätte dich nicht gewarnt *or* es hätte dich niemand gewarnt!; **she just won't be ~ed** sie hört auf keine Warnung(en)
b (*= inform*) **to ~ sb that …** jdn darauf aufmerksam machen *or* darauf hinweisen, dass …; **her expression ~ed me that she was not enjoying the conversation** ich merkte schon an ihrem Gesichtsausdruck, dass ihr die Unterhaltung nicht gefiel; **you might have ~ed us that you were coming** du hättest uns ruhig vorher Bescheid sagen können, dass du kommst
VI warnen (*of* vor +*dat*)

▶ **warn off** VT *sep* warnen; **to warn sb off doing sth** jdn (davor) warnen, etw zu tun; **he warned me off** er hat mich davor gewarnt; **I warned him off my property** ich habe ihn von meinem Grundstück verwiesen; **to warn sb off a subject** jdm von einem Thema abraten; **he sat there shaking his head, obviously trying to warn me off** er saß da und schüttelte den Kopf, offensichtlich um mich davon abzubringen; **he warns everybody off who tries to get friendly with her** er lässt nicht zu, dass sich jemand um sie bemüht

warning ['wɔːnɪŋ] ✪ 2.3 N Warnung *f*; (*from police, judge etc*) Verwarnung *f*; **without ~** unerwartet, ohne Vorwarnung; **they had no ~ of the enemy attack** der Feind griff sie ohne Vorwarnung an; **he had plenty of ~** er ist oft *or* häufig genug gewarnt worden; (*early enough*) er wusste früh genug Bescheid; **to give sb a ~** jdn warnen; (*police, judge etc*) jdm eine Verwarnung geben; **let this be a ~ to you** lassen Sie sich (*dat*) das eine Warnung sein!, das soll Ihnen eine Warnung sein; **let this be a ~ to all those who …** allen denjenigen, die …, soll das eine Warnung sein; **to take ~ from sth** sich (*dat*) etw eine Warnung sein lassen; **the bell gives ~** *or* **is a ~ that …** die Klingel zeigt an, dass …; **they gave us no ~ of their arrival** sie kamen unangekündigt *or* ohne Vorankündigung; **please give me a few days' ~** bitte sagen *or* geben Sie mir ein paar Tage vorher Bescheid; **to give sb due ~** (*= inform*) jdm rechtzeitig Bescheid sagen
ADJ Warn-; *look, tone* warnend; **a ~ sign** (*lit: = signboard etc*) ein Warnschild *nt*; (*fig*) ein Warnzeichen *nt*; **to fire ~ shots** Warnschüsse abgeben

warning: **warning flasher** N (*Aut*) Warnblinkanlage *f*; **warning light** N Warnleuchte *f*

warningly ['wɔːnɪŋlɪ] ADV warnend

warning: **warning message** N (*Comput*) Warnmeldung *f*; **warning shot** N Warnschuss *m*; **warning signal** N Warnsignal *nt*; **warning strike** N (*Econ*) Warnstreik *m*; **warning triangle** N Warndreieck *m*

war: **War Office** N (*old Brit*) Kriegsministerium *nt (old)*; **war orphan** N Kriegswaise *f*

warp [wɔːp] N **a** (*in weaving*) Kette *f*
b (*in wood etc*) Welle *f*; **the ~ makes it impossible to use this wood** das Holz ist zu verzogen *or* wellig, als dass man es noch verwenden könnte
c (*= towing cable*) Schleppleine *f*
d (*of mind*) **hatred of his mother had given his mind an evil ~** der Hass, den er gegen seine Mutter hegte, hatte seinen ganzen Charakter entstellt *or* verbogen; **the ~ in his personality** das Abartige in seinem Wesen
VT *wood* wellig werden lassen, wellen; *character* verbiegen, entstellen; *judgement* verzerren; (*Aviat*) verwinden
VI (*wood*) sich wellen, sich verziehen, sich werfen

war: **war paint** N (*lit, fig inf*) Kriegsbemalung *f*; **warpath** N Kriegspfad *m*; **on the ~** auf dem Kriegspfad

warped [wɔːpt] ADJ **a** (*lit*) verzogen, wellig **b** (*fig: = twisted*) *sense of humour, character* abartig; *judgement* verzerrt; **he has a ~ mind** er hat eine abartige Fantasie *or* Phantasie

warping ['wɔːpɪŋ] N Krümmung *f*

warplane N Kampfflugzeug *nt*

warrant ['wɒrənt] **N** **a** *(Comm)* Garantie *f*; *(Mil)* Patent *nt*; *(= search warrant)* Durchsuchungsbefehl *m*; *(= death warrant)* Hinrichtungsbefehl *m*; **a ~ of arrest** ein Haftbefehl *m*; **there is a ~ out for his arrest** gegen ihn ist Haftbefehl erlassen worden *(Jur)*, er wird steckbrieflich gesucht
b *(rare) (= justification)* Berechtigung *f*; *(= authority)* Befugnis *f*, Ermächtigung *f*
VT **a** *(= justify) action etc* rechtfertigen; **to ~ sb doing sth** jdn dazu berechtigen, etw zu tun
b *(= merit)* verdienen
c *(dated inf: = assure)* wetten; **I('ll) ~ (you)** ich wette
d *(= guarantee)* gewährleisten; **these goods are ~ed for three months by the manufacturers** für diese Waren übernimmt der Hersteller eine Garantie von drei Monaten; **a pill ~ed to cure influenza** eine Pille, die garantiert Grippe heilt

warrant card N *(Brit Police)* Dienstmarke *f*

warranted ['wɒrəntɪd] ADJ *(= justifiable) fears* berechtigt

warrantee [,wɒrən'tiː] N Garantieinhaber(in) *m(f)*

warrant officer N *Rang zwischen Offizier und Unteroffizier*

warrantor ['wɒrəntɔː'] N Garantiegeber(in) *m(f)*

warranty ['wɒrəntɪ] N *(Comm)* Garantie *f*; **it's still under ~** darauf ist noch Garantie

warren ['wɒrən] N *(= rabbit warren)* Kaninchenbau *m*; *(fig)* Labyrinth *nt*

warring ['wɔːrɪŋ] ADJ **a** *(lit) parties, sides* gegnerisch; *nations* Krieg führend; *interests, ideologies* gegensätzlich; *factions* sich bekriegend **b** *(fig) parents, couple* sich bekriegend

warrior ['wɒrɪə'] N Krieger(in) *m(f)*

Warsaw ['wɔːsɔː] N Warschau *nt*; **~ Pact** Warschauer Pakt *m*

warship ['wɔːʃɪp] N Kriegsschiff *nt*

wart [wɔːt] N Warze *f*; **~s and all** *(hum inf)* mit allen seinen/ihren *etc* Fehlern

warthog ['wɔːthɒg] N Warzenschwein *nt*

wartime ['wɔːtaɪm] **N** Kriegszeit *f*; **in ~** in Kriegszeiten **ADJ** Kriegs-; **~ atrocities** Kriegsgräuel *pl*; **in ~ England** in England im Krieg *or* während des Krieges; **~ regulations/rationing** *etc* Vorschriften *pl*/Rationierungen *pl etc* in Kriegszeiten, Kriegsvorschriften *pl*/-rationierungen *pl etc*

wartorn ['wɔːtɔːn] ADJ vom Krieg erschüttert

war: war toy N Kriegsspielzeug *nt*; **war-weary** ADJ kriegsmüde; **war widow** N Kriegswitwe *f*; **war-wounded** PL **the ~** die Kriegsversehrten *pl*

wary ['wɛərɪ] ADJ *(+er)* vorsichtig; *(= looking and planning ahead)* umsichtig, klug, wachsam; *look* misstrauisch, argwöhnisch; **to be ~ of** *or* **about sb/sth** sich vor jdm/einer Sache in Acht nehmen, vor jdm/einer Sache auf der Hut sein; **to be ~ of** *or* **about doing sth** seine Zweifel *or* Bedenken haben, ob man etw tun soll; **be ~ of talking to strangers** hüte dich davor, mit Fremden zu sprechen; **to keep a ~ eye on sb/sth** ein wachsames Auge auf jdn/etw haben

war zone N Kriegsgebiet *nt*

was [wɒz] *pret of* **be**

wash [wɒʃ] **N** **a** *(= act of washing)* **sb/sth needs a ~** jd/etw muss gewaschen werden; **to give sb/sth a (good) ~** jdn/etw (gründlich) waschen; **to give one's hands/face a ~** sich *(dat)* die Hände/das Gesicht waschen; **to have a ~** sich waschen
b *(= laundry)* Wäsche *f*; **to be in the ~** in der Wäsche sein; **it will all come out in the ~** *(fig inf)* es wird schon alles rauskommen, es wird sich schon noch alles zeigen *(inf)*
c *(of ship)* Kielwasser *nt*; *(Aviat)* Luftstrudel *m*
d *(= lapping) (gentle sound)* Geplätscher *nt*; *(of ocean)* sanftes Klatschen der Wellen
e *(= mouthwash)* Mundwasser *nt*; *(= liquid remains, also pej)* Spülwasser *nt*; *(for walls etc)* Tünche *f*
f *(in painting)* **a ~ of brown ink** eine leichte *or* schwache Tönung mit brauner Tünche
VT **a** *car, hair, clothes etc* waschen; *dishes* spülen, abwaschen; *floor* aufwaschen, aufwischen; *parts of body* sich *(dat)* waschen; **to ~ one's hands** *(euph)* sich *(dat)* die Hände waschen *(euph)*; **to ~ one's hands of sb/sth** mit jdm/etw nichts mehr zu tun haben wollen; **I ~ my hands of it** ich wasche meine Hände in Unschuld; **to ~ sth clean** etw rein waschen; **the sea ~ed it clean of oil** das Öl wurde vom Meer weggewaschen; **to ~ one's dirty linen** *(Brit) or* **laundry** *(US)* **in public** *(fig)* seine schmutzige Wäsche in der Öffentlichkeit waschen
b *(sea etc)* umspülen; *wall, cliffs etc* schlagen gegen
c *(river, sea: = carry)* spülen; **the body was ~ed downstream** die Leiche wurde flussabwärts getrieben; **to ~ ashore** an Land spülen *or* schwemmen, anschwemmen
d **the water had ~ed a channel in the rocks** das Wasser hatte eine Rinne in die Felsen gefressen
e *(= paint) walls* tünchen; *paper* kolorieren
VI **a** *(= have a wash)* sich waschen
b *(= do the laundry etc)* waschen; *(Brit: = wash up)* abwaschen
c **a material that ~es well/doesn't ~ well** ein Stoff, der sich gut wäscht/den man nicht waschen kann *or* der sich nicht waschen lässt; **that excuse won't ~** *(Brit fig inf)* diese Entschuldigung nimmt *or* kauft dir keiner ab! *(inf)*
d *(sea etc)* schlagen; **the sea ~ed over the promenade** das Meer überspülte die Strandpromenade

▶ **wash away** VT *sep* **a** *(lit)* (hin)wegspülen **b** *(fig)* **to wash away sb's sins** jdn von seinen Sünden reinwaschen

▶ **wash down** VT *sep* **a** *(= clean) car, walls, deck* abwaschen **b** *meal, food* hinunterspülen, runterspülen *(inf)*

▶ **wash off** **VI** *(stain, dirt)* sich rauswaschen lassen; **most of the pattern has washed off** das Muster ist fast ganz verwaschen **VT** *sep* abwaschen; **wash that grease off your hands** wasch dir die Schmiere von den Händen (ab)!

▶ **wash out** **VI** sich (r)auswaschen lassen **VT** *sep* **a** *(= clean)* auswaschen; *mouth* ausspülen **b** *(= stop, cancel) game etc* ins Wasser fallen lassen *(inf)*; **the game was washed out** das Spiel fiel buchstäblich ins Wasser *(inf)*

▶ **wash over** VI *+prep obj* **the criticism just seemed to wash over him** die Kritik schien an ihm abzuprallen; **he lets everything just wash over him** er lässt alles einfach ruhig über sich ergehen; **waves of panic washed over her** Panik überkam sie

▶ **wash up** **VI** **a** *(Brit: = clean dishes)* abwaschen, (ab)spülen **b** *(US: = have a wash)* sich waschen **VT** *sep* **a** *(Brit) dishes* abwaschen, (ab)spülen **b** *(sea etc)* anschwemmen, anspülen **c** **that's/we're all washed up** *(fig inf: = finished)* das ist gelaufen *(inf)*

washable ['wɒʃəbl] ADJ waschbar; *wallpaper* abwaschbar

wash: wash-and-wear ADJ *clothing, fabric* bügelfrei; **washbag** N *(US)* Kulturbeutel *m*; **washbasin** N Waschbecken *nt*; **washboard** N Waschbrett *nt*; **~ belly** *or* **stomach** *(inf)* Waschbrettbauch *m (inf)*; **washbowl** N Waschschüssel *f*; *(in unit)* Waschbecken *nt*; **washcloth** N *(US)* Waschlappen *m*; **washday** N Waschtag *m*; **wash drawing** N Tuschezeichnung *f*

washed out ADJ *pred*, **washed-out** ADJ *attr* [,wɒʃt'aʊt] *(inf)* erledigt *(inf)*, schlapp *(inf)*; **to feel ~** sich wie ausgelaugt fühlen *(inf)*; **to look ~** mitgenommen aussehen

washer ['wɒʃə'] N **a** *(Tech)* Dichtungsring *m* **b** *(= washing machine)* Waschmaschine *f (= dishwasher)* (Geschirr)spülmaschine *f*

washerwoman ['wɒʃə,wʊmən] N *pl* **-women** [-,wɪmɪn] Waschfrau *f*, Wäscherin *f*

wash: wash-hand basin N Handwaschbecken *nt*; **wash house** N Waschhaus *nt*

washing ['wɒʃɪŋ] N Waschen *nt*; *(= clothes)* Wäsche *f*; **many boys dislike ~** viele Jungen waschen sich nicht gerne; **to do the ~** Wäsche waschen; **to take in ~** (für Kunden) waschen; **if we don't get a pay increase, I'll have to take in ~!** *(hum)* wenn wir keine Gehaltserhöhung bekommen, muss ich noch putzen gehen *(inf)*

washing: washing day N = **washday**; **washing line** N Wäscheleine *f*; **washing machine** N Waschmaschine *f*; **washing powder** N Waschpulver *nt*; **washing soda** N Bleichsoda *nt*; **washing-up** N *(Brit)* Abwasch *m*; **to do the ~** spülen, den Abwasch machen; **washing-up basin**, **washing-up bowl** N *(Brit)* Spülschüssel *f*; **washing-up cloth** N *(Brit)* Spültuch *nt*, Spüllappen *m*; **washing-up liquid** N *(Brit)* Spülmittel *nt*

wash: wash leather N Waschleder *nt*; **wash load** N Waschmaschinenladung *f*; **washout** N *(inf)* Reinfall *m (inf)*; *(= person)* Flasche *f (inf)*, Niete *f (inf)*; **washrag** N *(US)* = **washcloth**; **washroom** N Waschraum *m*; **washstand** N **a** Waschbecken *nt* **b** *(old)* Waschgestell *nt*; **washtub** N (Wasch)zuber *m*; **wash-wipe** [,wɒʃ'waɪp] N *(Aut) (on window)* Scheibenwischer *m*; *(on headlamp)* Scheinwerferwischer *m*

washy ['wɒʃɪ] ADJ wässerig → **wishy-washy**

wasn't ['wɒznt] *contr of* **was not**

WASP [wɒsp] *(US) abbr of* **White Anglo-Saxon Protestant** weißer angelsächsischer Protestant

wasp [wɒsp] N Wespe *f*

waspish ADJ, **waspishly** ADV ['wɒspɪʃ, -lɪ] giftig

wasp sting N Wespenstich *m*

wasp waist N Wespentaille *f*

wassail ['wɒseɪl] *(Brit, old)* **N** **a** *(= toast)* Trinkspruch *m*; **~ cup** Kelch *m* **b** *(= revelry)* Gelage *nt* **VI** **a** *(= revel)* zechen, ein Gelage abhalten **b** **to go ~ing** *(= carol-singing)* ≈ als Sternsinger gehen

wastage ['weɪstɪdʒ] N Schwund *m*; *(= action)* Verschwendung *f*; *(= amount also)* Materialverlust *m*; *(from container also)* Verlust *m*; *(unusable products etc also)* Abfall *m*; **a ~ rate of 10%** eine Verlustquote von 10% → **natural wastage**

waste [weɪst] **ADJ** *(= superfluous)* überschüssig, überflüssig; *(= left over)* ungenutzt; *land* brachliegend, ungenutzt; **~ food** Abfall *m*; **~ material/matter** Abfallstoffe *pl*; **to lay sth ~, to lay ~ to sth** *(liter: = annihilate)* etw verwüsten
N **a** Verschwendung *f*; *(= unusable materials)* Abfall *m*; **it's a ~ of time/money** es ist Zeit-/ /Geldverschwendung; **it's a ~ of your time and mine** das ist nur (eine) Zeitverschwendung für uns beide; **it's a ~ of effort** das ist nicht der Mühe *(gen)* wert; **he's/it's a ~ of space** *(inf)* er/ das taugt nichts; **to go to ~** *(food)* umkommen; *(training, money, land)* ungenutzt sein/bleiben, brachliegen; *(talent etc)* verkümmern
b *(= waste material)* Abfallstoffe *pl*; *(in factory)* Schwund *m*; *(= rubbish)* Abfall *m*; **metal ~** Metallabfall *m*
c *(= land, expanse)* Wildnis *f no pl*, Einöde *f*; **the snowy ~s of Siberia** die Schneewüsten *pl* Sibiriens
VT **a** *(= use badly or wrongly)* verschwenden, vergeuden *(on* an *+acc,* für); *food* verschwenden; *life, time* vergeuden, vertun; *opportunity* vertun; **you're wasting your time** das ist reine Zeitverschwendung, damit vertust du nur deine Zeit; **don't ~ my time** stiehl mir nicht meine Zeit; **you didn't ~ much time getting here!** *(inf)* da bist du ja schon, du hast ja nicht gerade getrödelt! *(inf)*; **all our efforts were ~d** all unsere Bemühungen waren umsonst *or* vergeblich; **nothing is ~d** es wird nichts verschwendet; **your work won't be ~d** deine Arbeit ist nicht vergeblich *or* umsonst getan; **he didn't ~ any words in telling me …** ohne viel(e) Worte zu machen *or* zu verlieren, sagte er mir …; **to ~**

oneself on sb sich an jdn verschwenden; **I wouldn't ~ my breath talking to him** ich würde doch nicht für den meine Spucke vergeuden! *(inf)*; **don't ~ your efforts on him** vergeuden Sie keine Mühe mit ihm!; **Beethoven/your joke is ~d on him** Beethoven/dein Witz ist an den verschwendet *or* vergeudet; **you're ~d in this job** Sie sind zu schade für diese Arbeit
b *(= weaken)* auszehren; *strength* aufzehren
c *(= lay waste)* verwüsten
d *(inf: = kill)* kaltmachen *(inf)*
VI *(food)* umkommen; *(skills)* verkümmern; *(body)* verfallen; *(strength, assets)* schwinden; **~ not, want not** *(Prov)* spare in der Zeit, so hast du in der Not *(Prov)*

▶**waste away** VI *(physically)* dahinschwinden *(geh)*, immer weniger werden

wastebasket [ˈweɪstbɑːskɪt], **wastebin** [ˈweɪstbɪn] N *(esp US)* Papierkorb *m*

wasted [ˈweɪstɪd] ADJ **a** **I've had a ~ journey** ich bin umsonst hingefahren; **a vote for him is a ~ vote** ihn zu wählen heißt eine Stimme verschenken **b** *(= emaciated) organs, muscles* geschwächt; *(inf: = worn out)* verbraucht, ausgelaugt *(inf)* **c** *(sl: = drunk, high)* dicht *(sl)*, platt *(sl)*, breit *(sl)*

waste: **waste disposal** N Müllbeseitigung *f*, Abfallentsorgung *f*; **waste disposal unit** N Müllschlucker *m*

wasteful [ˈweɪstfʊl] ADJ verschwenderisch; *method, process* aufwendig, aufwändig, unwirtschaftlich; *expenditure* unnütz; **leaving all the lights on is a ~ habit** es ist Verschwendung, überall Licht brennen zu lassen; **to be ~ with sth** verschwenderisch mit etw umgehen; **it is ~ of effort** es ist unnötiger Aufwand; **this project is ~ of our resources** dieses Projekt ist eine unnütze Vergeudung unserer Ressourcen

wastefully [ˈweɪstfəlɪ] ADV verschwenderisch; *organized* unwirtschaftlich

wastefulness [ˈweɪstfʊlnɪs] N *(of person)* verschwenderische Art; *(in method, organization, of process etc)* Unwirtschaftlichkeit *f*, Aufwendigkeit *f*, Aufwändigkeit *f*; **throwing it away is sheer ~** es ist reine Verschwendung, das wegzuwerfen; **sb's ~ with sth/in doing sth** jds verschwenderische Art, mit etw umzugehen/etw zu machen; **the ~ of the government's expenditure in the field of education** die Verschwendung, die die Regierung auf dem Gebiet des Bildungswesens betreibt

waste: **waste gas** N *(Tech)* Abgas *nt*; **waste heat** N *(from engine etc)* Abwärme *f*; **waste heat recovery** N Abwärmerückgewinnung *f*; **wasteland** N Ödland *nt*; *(fig)* Einöde *f*; **waste management** N Abfallentsorgung *f*; **waste oil** N Altöl *nt*; **wastepaper** N Papierabfall *m*; *(fig)* Makulatur *f*; **wastepaper basket** N Papierkorb *m*; **they go straight into the ~** die wandern sofort in den Papierkorb; **wastepaper collection** N Altpapiersammlung *f*; **waste pipe** N Abflussrohr *nt*; **waste product** N Abfallprodukt *nt*

waster [ˈweɪstəʳ] N **a** Verschwender(in) *m(f)*; **it's a real time-/money-~** das ist wirklich Zeit-/Geldverschwendung; **she's a terrible ~ of electricity** sie verschwendet schrecklich viel Strom **b** *(= good-for-nothing)* Taugenichts *m*

waste: **waste recovery** N Abfallaufbereitung *f*, Müllaufbereitung *f*; **waste recycling** N Abfallverwertung *f*, Müllverwertung *f*; **waste reprocessing plant** N Abfallwiederaufbereitungsanlage *f*, Müllverwertungswerk *nt*; **waste separation** N Abfalltrennung *f*, Mülltrennung *f*; **waste water** N Abwasser *nt*

wasting [ˈweɪstɪŋ] ADJ *attr* **~ disease** Auszehrung *f*; **this is a ~ disease** das ist eine Krankheit, bei der der Körper allmählich verfällt

wastrel [ˈweɪstrəl] N *(liter)* Prasser *m (liter)*

watch¹ [wɒtʃ] N (Armband)uhr *f*

watch² **N** **a** *(= vigilance)* Wache *f*; **to be on the ~** aufpassen; **to be on the ~ for sb/sth** nach jdm/etw Ausschau halten; **to keep ~** Wache halten; **to keep a close ~ on sb/sth** jdn/etw scharf bewachen; **to keep a close ~ on the time** genau auf die Zeit achten; **to keep ~ over sb/sth** bei jdm/etw wachen *or* Wache halten; **to set a ~ on sb/sth** jdn/etw überwachen lassen
b *(= period of duty, people)* Wache *f*; **to be on ~** Wache haben, auf Wacht sein *(geh)*; **officer of the ~** wachhabender Offizier; **in the still ~es of the night** *(old, liter)* in den stillen Stunden der Nacht
c *(Hist, to protect public)* Wache *f*
VT **a** *(= guard)* aufpassen auf *(+acc)*; *(police etc)* überwachen
b *(= observe)* beobachten; *match* zusehen *or* zuschauen bei; *film, play, programme on TV* sich *(dat)* ansehen; **to ~ TV** fernsehen; **to ~ sb doing sth** jdm bei etw zusehen *or* zuschauen, sich *(dat)* ansehen, wie jd etw macht; **I'll come and ~ you play** ich komme und sehe dir beim Spielen zu; **he just stood there and ~ed her drown** er stand einfach da und sah zu, wie sie ertrank; **I ~ed her coming down the street** ich habe sie beobachtet, wie *or* als sie die Straße entlang kam; **she has a habit of ~ing my mouth when I speak** sie hat die Angewohnheit, mir auf den Mund zu sehen *or* schauen, wenn ich rede; **let's go and ~ the tennis** gehen wir uns (das) Tennis ansehen; **are you ~ing the blackboard!** du guckst *or* siehst zur Tafel!; **don't ~ the camera** sehen Sie nicht zur Kamera!; **~ this young actor, he'll be a star** beachten Sie diesen jungen Schauspieler, der wird mal ein Star; **~ the road in front of you** pass auf die Straße auf!, guck *or* achte auf die Straße!; **to ~ a case/negotiations for sb** für jdn als Beobachter bei einem Prozess/einer Verhandlung auftreten; **now ~ this closely** sehen *or* schauen Sie jetzt gut zu!, passen Sie mal genau auf!; **~ this!** pass auf!; **~ this space** warten Sies ab, demnächst mehr; **I want everyone to ~ me** ich möchte, dass mir alle zusehen *or* zuschauen!, alle mal hersehen *or* herschauen!; **just ~ me!** guck *or* schau mal, wie ich das mache!; **just ~ me go and make a mess of it!** da siehst du mal, was für einen Mist ich mache *(inf)*; **we are being ~ed** wir werden beobachtet; **I can't stand being ~ed** ich kann es nicht ausstehen, wenn mir ständig einer zusieht; **a new talent to be ~ed** ein neues Talent, das man im Auge behalten muss; **it's about as exciting as ~ing grass grow** *or* **~ing paint dry** es ist sterbenslangweilig, das ist so spannend, dass einem das Gähnen kommt; **a ~ed pot never boils** *(Prov)* wenn man daneben steht, kocht das Wasser nie
c *(= be careful of)* achtgeben *or* aufpassen auf *(+acc)*; *expenses* achten auf *(+acc)*; *time* achten auf *(+acc)*, aufpassen auf *(+acc)*; **(you'd better) ~ it!** *(inf)* pass (bloß) auf! *(inf)*; **~ yourself** sieh dich vor!, sei vorsichtig!; *(well-wishing)* machs gut!; **~ your manners!** bitte benimm dich!; **~ your language!** drück dich bitte etwas gepflegter aus!; **~ him, he's crafty** sieh dich vor *or* pass auf, er ist raffiniert; **~ where you put your feet** pass auf, wo du hintrittst; **~ how you talk to him, he's very touchy** sei vorsichtig, wenn du mit ihm sprichst, er ist sehr empfindlich; **~ how you drive, the roads are icy** fahr vorsichtig *or* pass beim Fahren auf, die Straßen sind vereist!; **~ how you go!** machs gut!; *(on icy surface etc)* pass beim Laufen/Fahren auf! → **step**
d *chance* abpassen, abwarten; **to ~ one's chance/time** eine günstige Gelegenheit/einen günstigen Zeitpunkt abwarten
VI **a** *(= observe)* zusehen, zuschauen; **to ~ for sb/sth** nach jdm/etw Ausschau halten *or* ausschauen; **they ~ed for a signal from the soldiers** sie warteten auf ein Signal von den Soldaten; **to ~ for sth to happen** darauf warten, dass etw geschieht; **to be ~ing for signs of …** nach Anzeichen von … Ausschau halten; **you should ~ for symptoms of …** du solltest auf …symptome achten
b *(= keep watch)* Wache halten; **there are policemen ~ing all (a)round the house** das Haus wird rundherum von Polizisten bewacht

▶**watch out** VI **a** *(= look carefully)* Ausschau halten, ausschauen *(for sb/sth* nach jdm/etw); **a newcomer to watch out for** ein Neuling, auf den man achten sollte **b** *(= be careful)* aufpassen, achtgeben *(for* auf *+acc)*; **there were hundreds of policemen watching out for trouble at the match** bei dem Spiel waren hunderte *or* Hunderte von Polizisten, die aufpassten, dass es nicht zu Zwischenfällen kam; **watch out!** Achtung!, Vorsicht!; **you'd better watch out!** *(threat)* pass bloß auf!, nimm dich in Acht!, sieh dich ja vor!; **watch out for him** nimm dich vor ihm in Acht

▶**watch over** VI *+prep obj* wachen über *(+acc)*

watchable [ˈwɒtʃəbl] ADJ sehenswert

watch: **watchband** N *(US)* Uhrarmband *nt*; **watchcase** N Uhrengehäuse *nt*; **watch chain** N Uhrkette *f*; **Watch Committee** N *(Brit)* Aufsichtskommission *f*; **watchdog** N *(lit)* Wachhund *m*; *(fig)* Aufpasser *m (inf)*, Überwachungsbeauftragte(r) *m*; **government ~** Regierungsbeauftragter *m* mit Überwachungsaufgaben; **~ body** Überwachungsgremium *nt*

watcher [ˈwɒtʃəʳ] N Schaulustige(r) *mf*; *(= observer)* Beobachter(in) *m(f)*; **the ~s by the dying man's bedside** die am Bett des Sterbenden Wachenden

watchful [ˈwɒtʃfʊl] ADJ wachsam; **to keep a ~ eye on sb/sth** ein wachsames Auge auf jdn/etw werfen; **to be ~ for** wachsam Ausschau halten nach

watchfully [ˈwɒtʃfəlɪ] ADV wachsam; **policemen sat ~ at the back of the hall** ganz hinten im Saal saßen Polizisten, die aufpassten; **the opposition waited ~ for the Government's next move** die Opposition beobachtete aufmerksam, welchen Schritt die Regierung als nächstes unternehmen würde

watchfulness [ˈwɒtʃfʊlnɪs] N Wachsamkeit *f*

watch-glass [ˈwɒtʃglɑːs] N Uhrenglas *nt*

watching brief [ˈwɒtʃɪŋˈbriːf] N **to hold** *or* **keep a ~** eine Kontrollfunktion ausüben; **he holds a ~ for the Government over all aspects of industrial development** er ist der Regierungsbeauftragte zur Überwachung der gesamten industriellen Entwicklung

watch: **watchmaker** N Uhrmacher(in) *m(f)*; **watchman** N *(in bank, factory etc)* Wächter(in) *m(f)*; (*also* **night watchman**) Nachtwächter(in) *m(f)*; **watch-night service** N Jahresschlussmette *f*; **watchstrap** N Uhrarmband *nt*; **watchtower** N Wachtturm *m*; **watchword** N *(= password, motto)* Parole *f*, Losung *f*

water [ˈwɔːtəʳ] **N** **a** Wasser *nt*; **the field is under (two feet of) ~** das Feld steht (zwei Fuß) unter Wasser; **to take in** *or* **make ~** *(ship)* lecken; **to hold ~** wasserdicht sein; **that excuse/argument** *etc* **won't hold ~** *(inf)* diese Entschuldigung/dieses Argument *etc* ist nicht hieb- und stichfest *(inf)*
b *(of sea, of lake etc)* **by ~** auf dem Wasserweg, zu Wasser *(geh)*; **on land and ~** zu Land und zu Wasser; **we spent an afternoon on the ~** wir verbrachten einen Nachmittag auf dem Wasser; **~s** Gewässer *pl*; **the ~s** *(Bibl, liter)* die Wasser *pl*; **the ~s of the Rhine** die Wasser des Rheins *(liter)*
c *(= urine)* Wasser *nt*; **to pass ~** Wasser lassen
d *(at spa)* **the ~s** die Heilquelle; **to drink** *or* **take the ~s** eine Kur machen; *(drinking only)* eine Trinkkur machen
e *(Med)* **~ on the brain** Wasserkopf *m*; **~ on the knee** Kniegelenkerguss *m*; **her ~s broke at midnight** die Fruchtblase ist um Mitternacht geplatzt
f *(= toilet water)* **rose** *etc* **~** Rosenwasser *nt etc*
g *(fig phrases)* **to keep one's head above ~** sich über Wasser halten; **to pour cold ~ on sb's idea** jds Idee etw miesmachen *(inf)*; **to get (oneself) into deep ~(s)** ins Schwimmen kommen; **of the first ~** *(dated Brit liter)* erster Güte; **that's all ~ under the bridge now** das ist aller längst vorbei; **a lot of ~ has flowed under the bridge since then** seitdem ist so viel Wasser den Berg *or* den Bach hinuntergeflossen; **to be**

in/get into hot ~ *(inf)* in Schwierigkeiten *or* in (des) Teufels Küche *(inf)* sein/geraten *(over* wegen *+gen)*; **he's in hot ~ with his father** *(inf)* er hat Zoff mit seinem Vater *(inf)*; **to spend money like ~** *(inf)* mit dem Geld nur so um sich werfen *(inf)*

VT **a** *garden, lawn, roads* sprengen; *land, field* bewässern; *plant* (be)gießen
b *horses, cattle* tränken
c *wine* verwässern, verdünnen
d to ~ capital *(Fin)* Aktienkapital verwässern
VI **a** *(mouth)* wässern; *(eye)* tränen; **the smoke made his eyes ~** ihm tränten die Augen vom Rauch; **my mouth ~ed** mir lief das Wasser im Mund zusammen; **to make sb's mouth ~** jdm den Mund wässerig machen
b *(animals)* trinken

▶ **water down** VT *sep (lit, fig)* verwässern; *(fig also)* abmildern, abschwächen; *liquids* (mit Wasser) verdünnen

water: water bed N Wasserbett *nt*; **water beetle** N Wasserkäfer *m*; **water bird** N Wasservogel *m*; **water biscuit** N *(Brit)* ≈ Kräcker *m*; **water blister** N Wasserblase *f*; **water boatman** N *(Zool: = aquatic bug)* Rückenschwimmer *m*; **water bomb** N Wasserbombe *f*; **waterborne** ADJ **to be ~** *(ship)* auf dem *or* im Wasser sein; **~ goods/troops** Güter/Truppen, die auf dem Wasserweg *or* zu Wasser befördert werden; **a ~ disease** eine Krankheit, die durch das Wasser übertragen wird; **water bottle** N Wasserflasche *f*; *(for troops, travellers etc)* Feldflasche *f*; **water brash** N *(Med)* Sodbrennen *nt*; **waterbuck** N Wasserbock *m*; **water buffalo** N Wasserbüffel *m*; **water butt** N Regentonne *f*; **water cannon** N Wasserwerfer *m*; **water carrier** N Wasserträger(in) *m(f)*; **the Water Carrier** *(Astrol)* der Wassermann; **water cart** N Wasserwagen *m*; *(for roads)* Sprengwagen *m*; **water chestnut** N Wasserkastanie *f*; **water closet** N *(abbr* **WC**) *(esp Brit)* Wasserklosett *nt*; **watercolour**, *(US)* **watercolor** N Wasserfarbe *f*, Aquarellfarbe *f*; *(= picture)* Aquarell *nt* ATTR Aquarell-; **~ painter** Aquarellmaler(in) *m(f)*; **a ~ painting** ein Aquarell *nt*; **watercolourist**, *(US)* **watercolorist** N Aquarellmaler(in) *m(f)*; **water-cooled** ADJ wassergekühlt; **water cooler** N Wasserspender *m*; **watercourse** N *(= stream)* Wasserlauf *m*; *(= bed)* Flussbett *nt*; *(artificial)* Kanal *m*; **water cracker** N *(US)* = **water biscuit**; **watercress** N (Brunnen)kresse *f*; **water cure** N Wasserkur *f*; **water diviner** N (Wünschel)rutengänger(in) *m(f)*; **watered-down** [ˌwɔːtəd'daʊn] ADJ *(lit, fig)* verwässert; **waterfall** N Wasserfall *m*; **waterfast** ADJ *(colour)* wasserecht; **water filter** N Wasserfilter *m*; **waterfowl** N Wasservogel *m*; *(pl)* Wassergeflügel *nt*; **waterfront** N Hafenviertel *nt*; **we drove along the ~/down to the ~** wir fuhren am Wasser entlang/hinunter zum Wasser ATTR am Wasser; **a ~ restaurant** ein Restaurant direkt am Hafen *or* am Wasser; **they live on the Mississippi ~** sie wohnen direkt am Mississippi

Watergate ['wɔtəgeɪt] N Watergate *no art*, die Watergate-Affäre

water: water gauge N *(in tank)* Wasserstandsmesser *or* -anzeiger *m*; *(in rivers, lakes etc also)* Pegel *m*; **water gun** N *(esp US)* = **water pistol**; **water heater** N Heißwassergerät *nt*; **water hole** N Wasserloch *nt*; **water hose** N Wasserschlauch *m*; **water ice** N Fruchteis *nt*

wateriness ['wɔːtərɪnɪs] N *(= weakness)* Wässerigkeit *f*, Wässrigkeit *f*; *(of colour)* Blässe *f*

watering ['wɔːtərɪŋ] N *(of land, field)* Bewässern *nt*; *(of garden, lawn)* Sprengen *nt*; *(of plant)* (Be)gießen *nt*

watering: watering can N Gießkanne *f*; **watering hole** N *(for animals)* Wasserstelle *f*; *(fig hum: = pub)* Pinte *f (inf)*, Kneipe *f (inf)*; **watering place** N *(= spa)* Kurort *m*; *(= seaside resort)* Badeort *m*, Seebad *nt*; *(for animals)* Tränke *f*, Wasserstelle *f*; **watering pot** N *(US)* Gießkanne *f*

water: water jacket N Kühlmantel *m*, Kühlwassermantel *m*; **water jet** N **a** *(= jet of water)* Wasserstrahl *m* **b** *(for cleaning teeth)* Mundddusche *f*; **water jump** N Wassergraben *m*; **waterless** ADJ trocken; *desert* arid *(spec)*; **a ~ planet** ein Planet *m* ohne Wasser; **water level** N Wasserstand *m*; *(= measured level: of river, reservoir etc also)* Pegelstand *m*; *(= surface of water)* Wasserspiegel *m*; **water lily** N Seerose *f*; **water line** N Wasserlinie *f*; **waterlogged** ADJ **the fields are ~** die Felder stehen unter Wasser; **the ship was completely ~** das Schiff war voll Wasser gelaufen; **to get ~** sich voll Wasser saugen; *(ship)* voll Wasser laufen

Waterloo [ˌwɔːtə'luː] N **to meet one's ~** *(hum)* Schiffbruch erleiden; **with that woman he has finally met his ~** bei dieser Frau hat er sein Waterloo erlebt *(hum)*

water: water main N Haupt(wasser)leitung *f*; *(= pipe)* Hauptwasserrohr *nt*; **waterman** N Fährmann *m*; **watermark** N **a** *(on wall)* Wasserstandsmarke *f* **b** *(on paper)* Wasserzeichen *nt*; **water meadow** N *(Agr)* Feuchtwiese *f*; **watermelon** N Wassermelone *f*; **water meter** N Wasseruhr *f*; **water metering** N Berechnen *nt* von Wasserverbrauch; **water mill** N Wassermühle *f*; **water noodle** N *(= swimming aid)* Wassernudel *f*, Schwimmnudel *f*; **water nymph** N (Wasser)nixe *f*; **waterpick®** N Mundddusche *f*; **water pipe** N Wasserrohr *nt*; *(for smoking)* Wasserpfeife *f*; **water pistol** N Wasserpistole *f*; **water plant** N *(Bot)* Wasserpflanze *f*; **water pollution** N Wasserverschmutzung *f*; **water polo** N Wasserball *m*; **water power** N Wasserkraft *f*; **waterproof** ADJ *(= unaffected by water) watch* wasserdicht; *clothes* wasserundurchlässig; *window* (wasser)dicht; *roof* (wasser)dicht, wasserundurchlässig; *mascara, make-up, paint* wasserfest N **~s** *(esp Brit)* Regenhaut® *f*; **remember to put your ~s on** zieh was Wasserdichtes an VT wasserundurchlässig machen; *material also* wasserdicht machen; *clothes also* imprägnieren; **waterproofer** N = **waterproofing b**; **waterproofing** N **a** *(= process)* Wasserdichtmachen *nt*; *(of clothes)* Imprägnieren *nt* **b** *(= material)* Dichtungsmittel *nt*; *(for clothes)* Imprägniermaterial *nt*; **water pump** N *(Tech)* Wasserpumpe *f*; **waterquake** N *(Geol)* Seebeben *nt*; **water rat** N Wasserratte *f*; **water rate** N *(Brit)* Wassergeld *nt*; **water-repellent** ADJ wasserabstoßend; **water-resistant** ADJ **a** *tent* wasserdicht **b** *(= unaffected by water)* wasserbeständig; *sunscreen* wasserfest; **to be ~ to 50 m** bis zu 50 m wasserdicht sein; **watershed** N *(Geol)* Wasserscheide *f*; *(fig)* Wendepunkt *m*; **the 9 o'clock ~** *(Brit TV) Regelung, dass vor 9 Uhr nur jugendfreie Progamme gesendet werden dürfen*; **waterside** N Ufer *nt*; *(at sea)* Strand *m* ATTR *plant* am Wasser wachsend; *house, restaurant* am Wasser; **water-ski** N Wasserski *m* VI Wasserski laufen; **water-skiing** N Wasserskilaufen *nt*; **water slide** N Wasserrutsche *f*; **water snake** N Wasserschlange *f*; *(in lake)* Seeschlange *f*; **water softener** N Wasserenthärter *m*; **water-soluble** ADJ wasserlöslich; **water spaniel** N Wasserspaniel *m*; **water sports** PL Wassersport *m*; **water spout** N **a** *(Met)* Wasserhose *f*, Trombe *f* **b** *(= pipe)* Regenrinne *f*; **water spray** N Wassernebel *m or* -staub *m*; **water supply** N Wasserversorgung *f*; *(= reserves)* Wasserreserven *pl*; **water table** N Grundwasserspiegel *m*; **water tank** N Wassertank *m*; **watertight** ADJ *(lit)* wasserdicht; *(fig) agreement, argument, alibi, contract also* hieb- und stichfest; **water tower** N Wasserturm *m*; **water vapour**, *(US)* **water vapor** N Wasserdampf *m*; **waterway** N Wasserstraße *f*; *(= channel)* Fahrrinne *f*; **water wheel** N *(Mech)* Wasserrad *nt*; *(Agr)* Wasserschöpfrad *nt*; **water wings** PL Schwimmflügel *pl*, Schwimmarme *pl (inf)*; **waterworks** N SING OR PL Wasserwerk *nt*; **to have trouble with one's ~** *(Brit hum inf)* Probleme mit der Blase haben

watery ['wɔːtərɪ] ADJ *(= weak) soup, beer, colour etc* wäss(e)rig; *eye* tränend; *(= pale) sky, sun* blass; **all the sailors went to a ~ grave** alle Seeleute fanden ihr Grab in den Wellen

watt [wɒt] N Watt *nt*

wattage ['wɒtɪdʒ] N Wattleistung *f*; **what ~ is that bulb?** wie viel Watt hat diese Birne?

wattle ['wɒtl] N **a** *(= material)* Flechtwerk *nt*; **a ~ fence** ein Zaun *m* aus Flechtwerk **b** *(Bot)* australische Akazie **c** *(Orn)* Kehllappen *m*

wave [weɪv] N **a** *(of water, Phys, Rad, in hair, fig)* Welle *f*; *(of hatred, enthusiasm)* Welle *f*, Woge *f (liter)*; **who rules the ~s?** wer beherrscht die Meere?; **a ~ of strikes** eine Streikwelle; **a ~ of enthusiasm** eine Welle der Begeisterung; **during the first ~ of the attack** beim ersten Ansturm *or* in der ersten Angriffswelle; **the attacks/attackers came in ~s** die Angriffe/Angreifer kamen in Wellen *or* wellenweise; **from the 5th century onwards England was attacked by ~s of invaders** vom 5. Jahrhundert an wurde England immer wieder von Eroberungswellen heimgesucht; **to make ~s** *(fig inf)* Unruhe stiften; **I don't want to make ~s but ...** *(fig inf)* ich will ja keinen Staub aufwirbeln, aber ...
b *(= movement of hand)* **to give sb a ~** jdm (zu)winken; **he gave us a ~ to show that he was ready** er winkte uns zu, um zu zeigen, dass er bereit war; **with a ~ he was gone** er winkte kurz und verschwand; **with a ~ of his hand** mit einer Handbewegung

VT **a** *(in order to give a sign or greeting)* winken mit *(at, to sb* jdm); *(= to wave about)* schwenken; *(gesticulating, in a dangerous manner)* herumfuchteln mit; **to ~ one's hand to sb** jdm winken; **he ~d a greeting to the crowd** er winkte grüßend der Menge zu; **to ~ sb goodbye, to ~ goodbye to sb** jdm zum Abschied winken; **he ~d his hat** er schwenkte seinen Hut; **he ~d the ticket under my nose** er fuchtelte mir mit der Karte vor der Nase herum; **he ~d his stick at the children who were stealing the apples** er drohte den Kindern, die die Äpfel stahlen, mit dem Stock; **he ~d his fist at the intruders** er drohte den Eindringlingen mit der Faust
b *(to indicate sb should move)* **he ~d the children across the road** er winkte die Kinder über die Straße; **he ~d me over to his table** er winkte mich zu sich an den Tisch; **he ~d me over** er winkte mich zu sich herüber
c *hair* wellen

VI **a** *(person)* winken; **to ~ at** *or* **to sb** jdm (zu)winken; **there's daddy, ~!** da ist der Papi, wink mal!; **don't just ~ at the ball, aim to hit it** nicht nur in Richtung Ball fuchteln, du sollst ihn auch treffen!
b *(flag)* wehen; *(branches)* sich hin und her bewegen; *(corn)* wogen
c *(hair)* sich wellen

▶ **wave aside** VT *sep* **a** *(lit) person* auf die Seite *or* zur Seite winken **b** *(fig) person, objection, suggestions etc* ab- *or* zurückweisen; *help* ausschlagen, zurückweisen

▶ **wave away** VT *sep* abwinken *(+dat)*

▶ **wave down** VT *sep* anhalten, stoppen

▶ **wave on** VT *sep* **the policeman waved us on** der Polizist winkte uns weiter

wave: waveband N *(Rad)* Wellenband *nt*; **wavelength** ['weɪvleŋθ] N *(Rad)* Wellenlänge *f*; **we're not on the same ~** *(fig)* wir haben nicht dieselbe Wellenlänge

wavelet ['weɪvlɪt] N *(poet)* kleine Welle

wave power N Wellenkraft *f*

waver ['weɪvə'] VI **a** *(= quiver) (light, flame, eyes)* flackern; *(voice)* zittern **b** *(= weaken) (courage, self-assurance)* wanken, ins Wanken geraten; *(support)* nachlassen **c** *(= hesitate)* schwanken *(between* zwischen *+dat)*; **if he begins to ~** wenn er ins Schwanken *or* Wanken gerät; **he's ~ing between accepting and ...** er ist sich *(dat)* darüber unschlüssig, ob er annehmen soll oder ...

waverer ['weɪvərə'] N Zauderer *m*, Zauderin *f*

wavering ['weɪvərɪŋ] ADJ **a** *(= shaky) voice* bebend; *shadow* tanzend **b** *(= uncertain) loyalty* unsicher; *courage, determination* wankend; *support (= hesitating)* wechselhaft; *(= decreasing)* nachlassend **N** *(= hesitation)* Schwanken *nt*; **there will be no ~ from the course of reform** der Reformkurs wird strikt eingehalten

wavy [ˈweɪvɪ] **ADJ** *(+er) hair, surface* wellig, gewellt; **~ line** Schlangenlinie *f*

wax¹ [wæks] **N** Wachs *nt*; *(= ear wax)* Ohrenschmalz *nt*; *(= sealing wax)* Siegellack *m* **ADJ** Wachs-; **~ crayon** Wachsmalstift *m* **VT** *car, furniture* wachsen; *floor* bohnern; *moustache* wichsen; *legs* mit Wachs behandeln

wax² **VI** **a** *(moon)* zunehmen; **to ~ and wane** *(fig)* schwanken, kommen und gehen **b** *(liter: = become)* werden; **to ~ enthusiastic** in Begeisterung geraten → **lyrical**

wax: **wax bean** **N** *(US)* Wachsbohne *f*; **wax candle** **N** Wachskerze *f*; **wax doll** **N** Wachspuppe *f*

waxed [wækst] **ADJ** gewachst; *moustache* gewichst; **~ cotton** gewachster Baumwollstoff; **~ paper** Wachspapier *nt*; **~ jacket** Wachsjacke *f*

waxen [ˈwæksən] **ADJ** **a** *(old)* wächsern **b** *(fig: = pale)* wachsbleich, wächsern

waxing¹ [ˈwæksɪŋ] **ADJ** *moon* zunehmend; *enthusiasm etc also* wachsend **N** Zunehmen *nt*, Wachsen *nt*

waxing² **N** *(= wax treatment)* Epilation *f*, Entfernung *f* von Körperhaaren

wax: **wax museum** **N** *(esp US)* Wachsfigurenkabinett *nt*; **wax paper** **N** Wachspapier *nt*; **waxwork** **N** Wachsfigur *f*; **waxworks** **N** *sing or pl* Wachsfigurenkabinett *nt*

waxy [ˈwæksɪ] **ADJ** *(+er)* wächsern

way [weɪ]
⊙ 8.3, 16.3

1 NOUN	3 ADVERB
2 PLURAL NOUN	

1 – NOUN

a [= road] Weg *m*; **across** *or* **over the way** gegenüber, vis-à-vis; *(motion)* rüber; **Way of the Cross** Kreuzweg *m*; **to fall by the way** *(fig)* auf der Strecke bleiben

b [= route] Weg *m*; **to ask the way** nach dem Weg fragen; **you'll learn new skills along the way** Sie werden nebenbei auch neue Fertigkeiten erlernen; **to go the wrong way** sich verlaufen; *(in car)* sich verfahren; **to go down the wrong way** *(food, drink)* in die falsche Kehle kommen; **there's no way out** *(fig)* es gibt keinen Ausweg; **to find a way in** hineinfinden; **the way up/down** der Weg nach oben/unten; *(climbing)* der Auf-/Abstieg; **the way there/back** der Hin-/Rückweg; **prices are on the way up/down** die Preise steigen/fallen; **the way forward** der Weg vorwärts *or* in die Zukunft

♦ **by way of** *(= via)* über *(+acc)*; **by way of an answer/excuse** als Antwort/Entschuldigung; **by way of illustration** zur Illustration; **he's by way of being a painter** *(inf)* er ist eine Art Maler *(inf)*

♦ **the way to** **the way to the station** der Weg zum Bahnhof; **can you tell me the way to the town hall, please?** können Sie mir bitte sagen, wie ich zum Rathaus komme?

♦ **on the/one's way (to)** **is it on the way?** *(place)* liegt das auf dem Weg?; *(parcel etc)* ist es unterwegs?; **the shop is on the/your way** der Laden liegt auf dem/deinem Weg; **to stop on the way** unterwegs anhalten; **on the way (here)** auf dem Weg (hierher); **on the way to London** auf dem Weg nach London; **you pass it on your way home** du kommst auf deinem Nachhauseweg *or* Heimweg daran vorbei; **they're on their way now** sie sind jetzt auf dem Weg *or* unterwegs; **to go on one's way** sich auf den Weg machen; **there's another baby on the way** da ist wieder ein Kind unterwegs; **he's on the way to becoming an alcoholic** er ist dabei *or* auf dem besten Weg, Alkoholiker zu werden; **she's well on the way to being a first-rate singer** sie ist auf dem besten Weg, eine erstklassige Sängerin zu werden; **I haven't finished it yet but it's on the way** ich bin noch nicht damit fertig, aber es ist im Werden *(inf)*

♦ **out of the/sb's way** **if it is out of your way** wenn es ein Umweg für Sie ist; **it took us out of our way** es war ein Umweg für uns; **to go out of one's way to do sth** *(fig)* sich besonders anstrengen, um etw zu tun; **please, don't go out of your way for us** *(fig)* machen Sie sich *(dat)* bitte unsertwegen keine Umstände

♦ **under way** **to get under way** in Gang kommen, losgehen *(inf)*; *(Naut)* Fahrt aufnehmen *or* machen; **to be (well) under way** im Gang/in vollem Gang sein; *(Naut)* in (voller) Fahrt sein; *(with indication of place)* unterwegs sein

♦ **the/one's way in** **the way in** der Eingang; **on the way in** beim Hereingehen; *(in car)* beim Hineinfahren; **to be on the way in** *(fig inf)* im Kommen sein

♦ **the/one's way out** **the way out** der Ausgang; **please show me the way out** bitte zeigen Sie mir, wo es hinausgeht *(inf)* *or* wie ich hinauskomme; **can you find your own way out?** finden Sie selbst hinaus?; **on the way out** beim Hinausgehen; *(in car)* beim Hinausfahren; **to be on the way out** *(fig inf)* am Verschwinden *or* Aussterben sein → **easy**

♦ *verb* + **the/one's way** **I know my way around the town** ich finde mich in der Stadt zurecht, ich kenne mich in der Stadt aus; **she knows her way around the system** *(fig inf)* sie kennt sich im System aus; **can you find your way home?** finden Sie nach Hause?; **to lose/gather way** *(Naut)* Fahrt verlieren/aufnehmen; **to make one's way to somewhere** sich an einen Ort *or* irgendwohin bewegen *or* begeben; **can you make your own way to the restaurant?** kannst du allein zu dem Restaurant kommen?; **to make one's way home** nach Hause gehen; *(= start)* sich auf den Heimweg begeben; **to make/fight/push one's way through the crowd** sich einen Weg durch die Menge bahnen, sich durch die Menge (durch)drängen/-kämpfen/-schieben; **to make one's way in the world** seinen Weg machen, sich durchsetzen; **to go one's own way** *(fig)* eigene Wege gehen; **they went their separate ways** *(lit, fig)* ihre Wege trennten sich; **to pay one's way** für sich selbst bezahlen; *(company, project, machine)* sich rentieren; **can the nation pay its way?** kann das Volk *or* Land für sich selber aufkommen?; **to prepare the way** *(fig)* den Weg bereiten *(for sb/sth* jdm/einer Sache) → **feel, lose**

c [= path] Weg *m*; **to bar** *or* **block the way** den Weg ab- *or* versperren; **to leave the way open** *(fig)* die Möglichkeit offenlassen, einen Weg frei lassen *(for sth* für etw)

♦ **in the/sb's way** **to be in sb's way** jdm im Weg stehen *or* sein; *(fig also)* jdn stören; **to get in the way** in den Weg kommen; *(fig)* stören; **her job gets in the way of her leisure interests** ihr Beruf stört sie nur bei ihren Freizeitvergnügungen; **to put difficulties in sb's way** jdm Hindernisse in den Weg stellen; **to stand in sb's way** *(lit, fig)* jdm im Weg stehen *or* sein; **don't let me stand in your way** ich will dir nicht im Weg stehen; **he lets nothing stand in his way** er lässt sich durch nichts aufhalten *or* beirren; **now nothing stands in our way** jetzt steht uns *(dat)* nichts mehr im Weg, jetzt haben wir freie Bahn; **to stand in the way of progress** den Fortschritt aufhalten *or* hemmen; **to put sb in the way of sth** *(inf)* jdm zu etw verhelfen

♦ **out of the/sb's way** **get out of the/my way!** (geh) aus dem Weg!, weg da!; **to get sb out of the way** *(= get rid of)* jdn loswerden *(inf)*; *(= remove: lit, fig)* jdn aus dem Wege räumen; **to want sb out of the way** jdn aus dem Weg haben wollen; **to get sth out of the way** *(work)* etw hinter sich *(acc)* bringen; *difficulties, problems etc* etw loswerden *(inf)*, etw aus dem Weg räumen, etw beseitigen; **to get sth out of the way of sb** jdm etw aus dem Weg räumen; **they got the children out of the way of the firemen** sie sorgten dafür, dass die Kinder den Feuerwehrleuten nicht im Weg waren; **get those people out of the way of the trucks** sieh zu, dass die Leute vor den Lastwagen Platz machen *or* aus der Bahn gehen; **to keep** *or* **stay out of sb's/the way** *(= not get in the way)* jdm nicht in den Weg kommen, (jdm) aus dem Weg bleiben; *(= avoid)* (jdm) aus dem Weg gehen; **keep** *or* **stay out of the way!** weg da!, zurück!; **keep** *or* **stay out of my way!** komm mir nicht mehr über den Weg!; **to keep sb/sth out of the way of sb** jdn/etw nicht in jds Nähe *or* Reichweite *(acc)* kommen lassen

♦ **to make way for sb/sth** *(lit, fig)* für jdn/etw Platz machen; *(fig also)* für jdn/etw den Platz räumen; **make way!** mach Platz!, Platz machen!, Platz da!

d [= direction] Richtung *f*; **which way are you going?** in welche Richtung *or* wohin gehen Sie?; **down our way** *(inf)* bei uns (in der Nähe), in unserer Gegend *or* Ecke *(inf)*; **it's out Windsor way** es ist *or* liegt in Richtung Windsor; **look both ways** schau nach beiden Seiten; **to look the other way** *(fig)* wegschauen, wegsehen; **if the chance comes your way** wenn Sie (dazu) die Gelegenheit haben; **if a good job comes my way** wenn ein guter Job für mich auftaucht; **each way, both ways** *(Racing)* auf Sieg und Platz; **we'll split it three/ten ways** wir werden es dritteln/in zehn Teile (auf)teilen *or* durch zehn teilen; **she didn't know which way to look** *(fig)* sie wusste nicht, wo sie hinschauen *or* hinsehen sollte

♦ **this way** **this way, please** hier(her) *or* hier entlang, bitte; **look this way** schau hierher!; **"this way for the lions"** „zu den Löwen"

♦ **that way** **he went that way** er ging dorthin *or* in diese Richtung

♦ **this way and that** hierhin und dorthin

♦ **every which way** ungeordnet, durcheinander; **cars parked every which way** ungeordnet *or* durcheinander geparkte Autos

e [= side] **it's the wrong way up** es steht verkehrt herum *or* auf dem Kopf *(inf)*; **"this way up"** „hier oben"; **it's the other way (a)round** es ist (genau) umgekehrt; **put it the right way up/the other way (a)round** stellen Sie es richtig (herum) hin/andersherum *or* andersrum *(inf)* hin

f [= distance] Weg *m*, Strecke *f*; **five miles? that's quite a way!** *(inf)* fünf Meilen? das ist eine ganz schöne Strecke! *(inf)*; **a little/good way away** *or* **off** nicht/sehr weit weg *or* entfernt, ein kleines/ganzes *or* gutes Stück weit weg *or* entfernt; **it's only a little way to the next stop** es ist nur ein kleines Stück bis zur nächsten Haltestelle

♦ **all the way** **it rained all the way there** es hat auf der ganzen Strecke geregnet; **I'm behind you all the way** *(fig)* ich stehe voll (und ganz) hinter Ihnen; **I haven't read it all the way through yet** ich habe es noch nicht ganz gelesen

♦ **a long way** **that's a long way away** bis dahin ist es weit *or* *(time)* noch lange; **a long way out of town** weit von der Stadt weg; *(live also)* weit draußen *or* außerhalb; **that's a long way back** das war schon vor einer ganzen Weile; **a long way back, in 1942, when ...** vor langer Zeit, im Jahre 1942, als ...; **he's come a long way since then** *(fig)* er hat sich seitdem sehr gebessert; **he'll go a long way** *(fig)* er wird es weit bringen; **to have a long way to go** *(lit, fit)* weit vom Ziel entfernt sein; *(with work)* bei Weitem nicht fertig sein; **it should go a long way toward(s) solving the problem** das sollte *or* müsste bei dem Problem schon ein gutes Stück weiterhelfen; **a little goes a long way** ein kleines bisschen reicht sehr lange; **a little kindness goes a long way** ein bisschen Freundlichkeit hilft viel; **that's a long way from the truth** das ist weit von der Wahrheit entfernt; **better by a long way** bei Weitem *or* um vieles besser; **not by a long way** bei Weitem nicht

g [= manner] Art *f*, Weise *f*; **I'd rather do it my way** ich möchte es lieber auf meine (eigene) Art *or* Weise machen; **that's his way of saying thank you** das ist seine Art, sich zu bedanken;

the French way of doing it (die Art,) wie man es in Frankreich macht; **a funny way of talking** eine komische Art zu reden; **to learn the hard way** aus dem eigenen Schaden lernen; **way of thinking** Denk(ungs)art *f*, Denkweise *f*; **to my way of thinking** meiner Meinung *or* Auffassung *or* Anschauung nach; **to go on in the same old way** wie vorher weitermachen, auf die alte Tour weitermachen *(inf)*; **in a general way this is true** ganz allgemein ist das richtig; **what a way to talk!** so etwas sagt man nicht!; **what a way to live/die!** *(= unpleasant)* so möchte ich nicht leben/sterben

♦ **in a big/small way** **in a big way** im großen Stil; *(= on a large scale)* in großem Ausmaß; **in a small way** in kleinem Ausmaß, im Kleinen

♦ **one way or another/the other** so oder so; **it does not matter (to me) one way or the other** es macht (mir) so oder so nichts aus, es ist mir gleich

♦ **either way** so oder so; **either way, we're bound to lose** (so oder so,) wir verlieren auf jeden Fall *or* auf alle Fälle

♦ **no way** *(inf)* **no way!** nichts drin! *(inf)*, was? *(inf)*, ausgeschlossen!; **there's no way I'm going to agree/you'll persuade him** auf keinen Fall werde ich zustimmen/werden Sie ihn überreden können; **there's no way that's a Porsche** ausgeschlossen, dass das ein Porsche ist; **that's no way to speak to your mother** so spricht man nicht mit seiner Mutter

♦ **have/want it both ways** **you can't have it both ways** du kannst nicht beides haben, beides (zugleich) geht nicht *(inf)*; **he wants it both ways** er will das eine haben und das andere nicht lassen

♦ **no two ways about it** **this one is better, there are no two ways about it** *(inf)* dieses hier ist besser, da gibt es gar keinen Zweifel *or* das steht fest

♦ **this way** *(= like this)* so, auf diese (Art und) Weise; **do it this way** machen Sie es so *or* auf diese (Art und) Weise; **it was this way ...** es war so *or* folgendermaßen ...; **this way he need never know** auf diese Weise muss er es nie erfahren

♦ **that way** *(= like that)* in dieser Hinsicht; **I've always had a job, I've been lucky that way** ich hatte immer einen Job, in dieser Hinsicht habe ich Glück gehabt

♦ **that's the way!** ja(, so geht das)!, ja, genau!

♦ **the way (that) ...**

= how wie; **the way she walks/talks** (so) wie sie geht/spricht; **I don't like the way (that) he's looking at you** ich mag nicht, wie er dich ansieht, ich mag die Art nicht, wie er dich ansieht; **do you understand the way things are developing?** verstehst du, wie sich die Dinge entwickeln?; **do you remember the way it was/we were?** erinnerst du dich noch (daran), wie es war/wie wir damals waren?; **that's not the way we do things here** so *or* auf die Art machen wir das hier nicht; **you could tell by the way he was dressed** das merkte man schon an seiner Kleidung; **it's just the way you said it** es ist die Art, wie du es gesagt hast; **do it any way you like** machen Sie es, wie Sie wollen; **that's the way it goes!** so ist das eben, so ist das nun mal!; **the way things are** so, wie es ist *or* wie die Dinge liegen; **the way things are going** so, wie die Dinge sich entwickeln; **that's the way the money goes** so geht das Geld weg; **it's not what you do, it's the way (that) you do it** es kommt nicht darauf an, was man macht, sondern wie man es macht

= exactly as so, wie; **leave everything the way it is** lass alles so, wie es ist; **it was all the way you said it would be** es war alles so, wie du (es) gesagt hattest; **do it the way I do (it)** machen Sie es so *or* auf dieselbe Art und Weise wie ich (es mache)

♦ **the way to do sth** **to show sb the way to do sth** jdm zeigen, wie *or* auf welche Art und Weise etw gemacht wird; **show me the way to do it** zeig mir, wie (ich es machen soll); **that's not the right way to do it** so geht das nicht, so kann man das nicht machen; **what's the best way to do it?** wie macht man das am besten?; **there is only one way to speak to him** man kann mit ihm nur auf (die) eine Art und Weise reden

♦ **ways and means** Mittel und Wege *pl*; **Ways and Means Committee** *(US)* Steuerausschuss *m*

h = means Weg *m*; **we'll find a way** wir werden (schon) einen Weg finden; **love will find a way** die Liebe überwindet jedes Hindernis *or* alle Schwierigkeiten

i = method, technique Art *f*; **he has a way of knowing what I'm thinking** er hat eine Art zu wissen, was ich denke; **we have ways of making you talk** wir haben gewisse Mittel, um Sie zum Reden zu bringen; **there are many ways of solving the problem** es gibt viele Wege *or* Möglichkeiten, das Problem zu lösen; **ha, that's one way of solving it!** ja, so kann man das auch machen!; **the best way is to put it in the freezer for ten minutes** am besten legt man es für zehn Minuten ins Gefrierfach; **he has a way with children** er versteht es, mit Kindern umzugehen, er hat eine geschickte Art (im Umgang) mit Kindern; **he has a way with him** er hat so eine (gewisse) Art

j = habit Art *f*; **it is not/only his way to ...** es ist nicht/eben seine Art, zu ...; **to get out of/into the way of doing sth** sich *(dat)* ab-/angewöhnen, etw zu tun; **the ways of the Spaniards** die spanische Lebensweise; **the ways of Providence/God** die Wege der Vorsehung/Gottes; **the way of the world** der Lauf der Welt *or* der Dinge; **that is our way with traitors** so machen wir das mit Verrätern; **he has his little ways** er hat so seine Eigenheiten *or* Marotten *(inf)*; **as is the way with ...** wie das mit ... so ist; **way of life** Lebensstil *m*; *(of nation)* Lebensart *f*

k = respect Hinsicht *f*; **in a way** in gewisser Hinsicht *or* Weise; **in no way** in keiner Weise; **in many/some ways** in vieler/gewisser Hinsicht; **in every possible way** in jeder Hinsicht; **to be better in every possible way** in jeder Hinsicht besser sein; **in more ways than one** in mehr als nur einer Hinsicht

♦ **in the way of** **what have you got in the way of drink/food?** was haben Sie an Getränken *or* zu trinken/an Lebensmitteln *or* zu essen?

l = desire **to get** *or* **have one's (own) way** seinen Willen durchsetzen *or* bekommen; **our team had it all their own way in the second half** in der zweiten Halbzeit ging für unsere Mannschaft alles nach Wunsch; **have it your own way!** wie du willst!

m = state Zustand *m*; **he's in a bad way** er ist in schlechter Verfassung; **things are in a bad way** die Dinge stehen schlecht; **to want sth in the worst way** *(US: = desperately)* etw unbedingt brauchen *or* benötigen

2 – ways PLURAL NOUN

(Naut, = slipway) Helling *f*, Ablaufbahn *f*

3 – ADVERB

(inf) **way over/up** weit drüben/oben; **it's way too big** das ist viel zu groß; **way hip** *(US)* total hip *(inf)*

♦ **way back** **way back when** vor langer Zeit, als; **since way back** seit Urzeiten; **that was way back** das ist schon lange her, das war schon vor langer Zeit

♦ **way out** **he was way out with his guess** er hatte weit daneben- *or* vorbeigeraten, er hatte weit gefehlt *or* er lag weit daneben *(inf)* mit seiner Annahme; **his guess was way out** seine Annahme war weit gefehlt; **you're way out if you think ...** da liegst du aber schief *(inf) or* da hast du dich aber gewaltig geirrt, wenn du glaubst, ...

---

way: **waybill** N Frachtbrief *m*; **wayfarer** [ˈweɪˌfɛərəʳ] N *(liter)* Wanderer *m*, Wanderin *f*, Wandersmann *m (liter)*; **wayfaring** ADJ *(liter)* wandernd, reisend; **~ man** Wandervogel *m*; **waylay** *pret, ptp* **waylaid** VT *(= ambush)* überfallen; *(= stop)* abfangen; **I was waylaid by the manager** der Manager hat mich abgefangen; **way-out** ADJ *(inf)* irr(e) *(dated inf)*, extrem *(dated sl)*; **wayside** N *(of path, track)* Wegrand *m*; *(of road)* Straßenrand *m*; **by the ~** am Weg(es)-/Straßenrand; **to fall** *or* **go by the ~** *(fig)* auf der Strecke bleiben ADJ *café, inn* am Weg/an der Straße gelegen; **~ flowers** Blumen, die am Weg-/Straßenrand blühen; **way station** N *(US)* Zwischenstation *f*, Kleinbahnhof *m*; **way train** N *(US)* Personenzug *m*

wayward [ˈweɪwəd] ADJ *(= self-willed) child, horse, disposition* eigenwillig, eigensinnig; *(= capricious) fancy, request, passion* abwegig; *(liter) stream, breeze* unberechenbar, launisch *(liter)*; **their ~ son** ihr ungeratener Sohn

waywardness [ˈweɪwədnɪs] N *(= stubbornness: of child, horse, disposition)* Eigenwilligkeit *f*, Eigensinn *m*; *(= capriciousness: of imagination, request, passion)* Abwegigkeit *f*; *(liter, of stream, breeze)* Unberechenbarkeit *f*, Launenhaftigkeit *f (liter)*

WBA N *abbr of* **World Boxing Association**

WC *(esp Brit) abbr of* **water closet** WC *nt*

we [wiː] PRON wir; **the royal we** der Pluralis Majestatis, der Majestätsplural; **the editorial we** der Autorenplural; *(in narrative)* das Wir des Erzählers; **how are we this morning?** *(inf)* wie geht es uns (denn) heute Morgen? *(inf)*

w/e **a** *abbr of* **weekend** **b** *abbr of* **week ending**

weak [wiːk] ADJ (+er) schwach; *character* labil; *tea, solution etc* dünn; *stomach* empfindlich; **he was ~ from hunger** ihm war schwach vor Hunger; **to go/feel ~ at the knees** *(after illness)* sich wackelig fühlen, wackelig *or* schwach auf den Beinen sein *(inf)*; *(with fear, excitement etc)* weiche Knie haben/bekommen; **the ~er sex** das schwache Geschlecht; **he must be a bit ~ in the head** *(inf)* er ist wohl nicht ganz bei Trost *(inf)*; **her maths is ~, she is ~ at** *or* **in maths** sie ist schwach in Mathe; **the dollar is ~ against the pound** der Dollar steht schwach zum Pfund; **what are his ~ points?** wo liegen seine Schwächen?; **the ~ link (in the chain)** das schwache Glied in der Kette
N **the ~** *pl (= needy, vulnerable)* die Schwachen *pl*

weaken [ˈwiːkən] VT *(lit, fig)* schwächen; *influence also, control, suspicion etc* verringern; *argument also* entkräften; *walls, foundations* angreifen; *hold* lockern; **he ~ed his grip on my arm** er hielt meinen Arm nicht mehr ganz so fest VI *(lit, fig)* schwächer werden, nachlassen; *(person)* schwach *or* weich werden; *(foundations)* nachgeben; *(defence, strength)* erlahmen; *(dollar)* nachlassen; **his grip on my arm ~ed** er hielt meinen Arm nicht mehr ganz so fest

weak-kneed [ˈwiːkˈniːd] ADJ *(after illness)* wackelig auf den Beinen *(inf)*; *(with fear, excitement)* mit weichen Knien; *(fig inf)* schwach, feige

weakling [ˈwiːklɪŋ] N Schwächling *m*; *(of litter etc)* Schwächste(s) *nt*

weakly [ˈwiːklɪ] ADJ *(dated)* schwächlich ADV schwach; **he ~ gave in to their demands** schwach wie er war, ging er gleich auf ihre Forderungen ein

weak-minded [ˈwiːkˈmaɪndɪd] ADJ **a** *(= feeble-minded)* schwachsinnig **b** *(= weak-willed)* willensschwach

weakness [ˈwiːknɪs] ✪ 7.2 N *(all senses)* Schwäche *f*; *(= weak point)* schwacher Punkt; **the opposition criticized the ~ of the party's manifesto** die Opposition kritisierte, wie schwach das Wahlprogramm der Partei sei; **to have a ~ for sth** für etw eine Schwäche *or* Vorliebe haben

weak-willed [ˈwiːkˈwɪld] ADJ willensschwach

weal[1] [wiːl] N *(liter)* Wohl *nt*; **the common/public ~** das allgemeine/öffentliche Wohl, das Allgemeinwohl; **~ and woe** Wohl und Wehe *nt*

weal[2] N *(= welt)* Striemen *m*

wealth [welθ] N **a** Reichtum *m*; *(= private fortune)* Vermögen *nt* **b** *(fig: = abundance)* Fülle *f*

wealth-creating [ˈwelθkrɪˈeɪtɪŋ] ADJ vermögensbildend

wealthily [ˈwelθɪlɪ] ADV wohlhabend

wealthiness ['welθɪnɪs] N Wohlhabenheit *f*

wealth tax N Vermögenssteuer *f*

wealthy ['welθɪ] ADJ (+er) wohlhabend, reich; *(= having a private fortune also)* vermögend N **the ~** *pl* die Reichen *pl*

wean [wiːn] VT *baby* entwöhnen; **to ~ sb from** *or* **off sb/sth** jdn jdm/einer Sache entwöhnen *(geh)*

weaning ['wiːnɪŋ] N *(of baby)* Entwöhnung *f*

weapon ['wepən] N *(lit, fig)* Waffe *f*; **~s of mass destruction** Massenvernichtungswaffen *pl*

weaponry ['wepənrɪ] N Waffen *pl*

weapons-grade ['wepənzˌgreɪd] ADJ **~ plutonium/uranium** waffenfähiges Plutonium/Uran

wear [wɛəʳ] *vb: pret* **wore**, *ptp* **worn** N a *(= use)* **I've had a lot of/I haven't had much ~ out of** *or* **from this jacket** *(= worn it often/not often)* ich habe diese Jacke viel/wenig getragen; *(= it wore well/badly)* ich habe diese Jacke lange/nur kurz getragen; **he got four years' ~ out of these trousers/that carpet** diese Hose/dieser Teppich hat vier Jahre lang gehalten; **there isn't much ~/there is still a lot of ~ left in this coat/carpet** dieser Mantel/Teppich hält nicht mehr lange/hält noch lange; **this coat will stand any amount of hard ~** dieser Mantel ist sehr strapazierfähig; **for casual/evening/everyday ~** für die Freizeit/den Abend/jeden Tag

b *(= clothing)* Kleidung *f*

c *(= damage through use)* Abnutzung *f*, Verschleiß *m*; **~ and tear** Abnutzung *f*, Verschleiß *m*; **fair ~ and tear** normale Abnutzungs- *or* Verschleißerscheinungen; **to show signs of ~** *(lit)* anfangen, alt auszusehen; *(fig)* angegriffen aussehen; **to look the worse for ~** *(lit) (curtains, carpets etc)* verschlissen aussehen; *(shoes, clothes)* abgetragen aussehen; *(furniture etc)* abgenutzt aussehen; *(fig)* verbraucht aussehen; **I felt a bit the worse for ~** *(inf)* ich fühlte mich etwas angeknackst *(inf) or* angegriffen

VT a *clothing, jewellery, spectacles, beard etc* tragen; **what shall I ~?** was soll ich anziehen?; **I haven't a thing to ~!** ich habe nichts zum Anziehen *or* nichts anzuziehen; **I haven't worn that for ages** das habe ich schon seit Ewigkeiten nicht mehr angezogen *or* angehabt *(inf) or* getragen; **to ~ white/rags** *etc* Weiß/Lumpen *etc* tragen, in Weiß/Lumpen *etc* gehen; **he wore an air of triumph** er trug eine triumphierende Miene zur Schau; **he wore a big smile** er strahlte über das ganze Gesicht

b *(= reduce to a worn condition)* abnutzen; *clothes* abtragen; *sleeve, knee etc* durchwetzen; *velvet etc* blank wetzen; *leather articles* abwetzen; *steps* austreten; *tyres* abfahren; *engine* kaputt machen; **to ~ holes in sth** etw durchwetzen; *in shoes* etw durchlaufen; **the carpet has been worn threadbare** der Teppich ist abgewetzt *or* ganz abgelaufen; **to ~ smooth** *(by handling)* abgreifen; *(by walking)* austreten; *pattern* angreifen; *sharp edges* glatt machen; **centuries of storms had worn the inscription smooth** die Inschrift war durch die Stürme im Laufe der Jahrhunderte verwittert; **the sea had worn the rocks smooth** die See hatte die Felsen glatt gewaschen; **you'll ~ a track in the carpet** *(hum)* du machst noch mal eine richtige Bahn *or* einen Trampelpfad *(inf)* in den Teppich → *also* **worn**

c *(Brit inf: = accept, tolerate)* schlucken *(inf)*

VI a *(= last)* halten; **she has worn well** *(inf)* sie hat sich gut gehalten *(inf)*; **the theory has worn well** die Theorie hat sich bewährt

b *(= become worn)* kaputtgehen; *(engine, material)* sich abnutzen; **to ~ smooth** *(by water)* glatt gewaschen sein; *(by weather)* verwittern; *(pattern)* abgegriffen sein; **the sharp edges will ~ smooth in time/with use** die scharfen Kanten werden sich mit der Zeit/im Gebrauch abschleifen; **to ~ thin** *(lit)* dünn werden, durchgehen *(inf)*; **my patience is ~ing thin** meine Geduld ist langsam erschöpft *or* geht langsam zu Ende; **that excuse/joke is ~ing thin** diese Ausrede/dieser Witz ist (doch) schon etwas alt

c *(= proceed gradually)* **the party** *etc* **is ~ing to a close** die Party *etc* geht dem Ende zu

▸ **wear away** VT *sep (= erode) steps* austreten; *rock* abschleifen, abtragen; *(from underneath)* aushöhlen; *pattern, inscription* tilgen *(geh)*, verwischen; *(fig) determination* untergraben; *sb's patience* zehren an *(+dat)* VI *(= disappear) (rocks, rough edges etc)* sich abschleifen; *(inscription)* verwittern; *(pattern)* verwischen; *(fig: patience, determination)* schwinden

▸ **wear down** VT *sep* a *(= reduce by friction)* abnutzen; *heel* ablaufen, abtreten; *tyre tread* abfahren; *lipstick* verbrauchen; *pencil* verschreiben b *(fig) opposition, strength etc* zermürben; *person (= make more amenable)* mürbe- *or* weichmachen *(inf)*; *(= tire out, depress)* fix und fertig machen *(inf)* VI sich abnutzen; *(heels)* sich ablaufen *or* abtreten; *(tyre tread)* sich abfahren; *(lipstick etc)* sich verbrauchen; *(pencil)* sich verschreiben

▸ **wear off** VI a *(= diminish)* nachlassen, sich verlieren; **don't worry, it'll wear off!** keine Sorge, das gibt sich → **novelty** b *(= disappear) (paint)* abgehen; *(plating, gilt)* sich abwetzen

▸ **wear on** VI sich hinziehen, sich (da)hinschleppen; *(year)* voranschreiten; **as the evening/year** *etc* **wore on** im Laufe des Abends/Jahres *etc*

▸ **wear out** VT *sep* a *(lit)* kaputt machen; *carpet* abtreten; *clothes, shoes* kaputt tragen; *record, machinery* abnutzen b *(fig: = exhaust) (physically)* erschöpfen, erledigen *(inf)*; *(mentally)* fertigmachen *(inf)*; **to be worn out** erschöpft *or* erledigt sein; *(mentally)* am Ende sein *(inf)*; **to wear oneself out** sich überanstrengen, sich kaputtmachen *(inf)* VI kaputtgehen; *(clothes, curtains, carpets)* verschleißen; **his patience has worn out/is rapidly wearing out** seine Geduld ist erschöpft/ist am Ende/erschöpft sich zusehends

▸ **wear through** VT *sep* durchwetzen; *elbows, trousers also* durchscheuern; *soles of shoes* durchlaufen VI sich durchwetzen; *(elbows, trousers also)* sich durchscheuern; *(soles of shoes)* sich durchlaufen; **his sweater has worn through at the elbows** sein Pullover ist an den Ellenbogen durchgewetzt

wearable ['wɛərəbl] ADJ *(= not worn out etc)* tragbar; **fashionable clothes which are also very ~** modische Kleidung, die sich auch gut trägt

wearer ['wɛərəʳ] N Träger(in) *m(f)*; **~ of spectacles, spectacle ~** Brillenträger(in) *m(f)*

wearily ['wɪərɪlɪ] ADV *say* müde; *smile, gaze, nod, sigh* matt

weariness ['wɪərɪnɪs] N *(physical)* Müdigkeit *f*; *(mental)* Lustlosigkeit *f*; *(of smile, gaze)* Mattheit *f*; **he felt a great ~ of life** er empfand großen Lebensüberdruss *or* große Lebensmüdigkeit

wearing ['wɛərɪŋ] ADJ a **~ apparel** *(form)* (Be)kleidung *f* b *(= exhausting)* anstrengend; *(= boring)* ermüdend

wearisome ['wɪərɪsəm] ADJ ermüdend; *climb etc* beschwerlich; *(= bothersome) questions* lästig; *(= tedious) discussion* langweilig

weary ['wɪərɪ] ADJ (+er) a *(= tired, dispirited)* müde; *(= fed up)* lustlos; *smile, groan* matt; **to feel** *or* **be ~** müde sein; **to be/grow ~ of sth** etw leid sein/werden, einer Sache *(gen)* überdrüssig *or* müde sein/werden *(geh)* b *(= tiring) wait, routine etc* ermüdend; **for three ~ hours** drei endlose Stunden (lang); **five ~ miles** fünf lange *or* beschwerliche Meilen VT ermüden VI **to ~ of sth** einer Sache *(gen)* müde *or* überdrüssig werden *(geh)*; **she wearied of being alone** sie wurde es leid *or* müde *(geh) or* überdrüssig *(geh)*, allein zu sein

weasel ['wiːzl] N a Wiesel *nt* b *(inf: = person)* Heimtücker *m* VI *(esp US inf: = be evasive)* schwafeln *(inf)*

▸ **weasel out** VI *(= wriggle out)* sich rauslavieren *(inf)* (of aus)

weaselly ['wiːzəlɪ] ADJ *appearance, face* fuchsartig; *(inf: = shifty) character* aalglatt

weasel words PL *(inf)* Ausweichmanöver *pl*

weather ['weðəʳ] N Wetter *nt*; *(in weather reports)* Wetterlage *f*; *(= climate)* Witterung *f*; **in cold/wet/this ~** bei kaltem/nassem/diesem Wetter; **what's the ~ like?** wie ist das Wetter?; **lovely ~ for ducks!** bei dem Wetter schwimmt man ja fast weg!; **in all ~s** bei jedem Wetter, bei jeder Witterung *(geh)*; **to be** *or* **feel under the ~** *(inf)* angeschlagen sein *(inf)*; **to make heavy ~ of sth** *(Brit inf)* sich mit etw fürchterlich anstellen *(inf)*; **to keep a ~ eye open** *(inf)* Ausschau halten (for nach)

VT a *(storms, winds etc)* angreifen; *skin* gerben; **the rock had been ~ed** der Fels war verwittert

b *(= expose to weather) wood* ablagern

c *(= survive: also* **weather out)** *crisis, awkward situation* überstehen; **to ~ (out) the storm** *(lit, fig)* den Sturm überstehen

VI *(rock etc)* verwittern; *(paint etc)* verblassen; *(= resist exposure to weather)* wetterfest sein; *(= become seasoned: wood)* ablagern

weather: **weather balloon** N *(Met)* Wetterballon *m*, Versuchsballon *m*; **weather-beaten** ADJ *face* vom Wetter gegerbt; *house, wood, stone* verwittert; *skin* wettergegerbt; **weatherboarding** N, **weatherboards** PL Schindeln *pl*; **weather-bound** ADJ *boat* aufgrund *or* auf Grund der schlechten Wetterverhältnisse manövrierunfähig; **weather bureau** N Wetteramt *nt*; **weathercast** N *(US)* Wettervorhersage *f*; **weathercaster** N *(US)* Wetteransager(in) *m(f)*; **weather chart** N Wetterkarte *f*; **weathercock** N Wetterhahn *m*; **weather conditions** PL Wetterverhältnisse *pl*, Witterungsverhältnisse *pl*

weathered ['weðəd] ADJ verwittert; *skin* wettergegerbt

weather: **weather eye** N **to keep a ~ on sth** *(fig)* etw scharf im Auge behalten; **to keep one's ~ open** *(fig)* gut aufpassen; **weather forecast** N Wettervorhersage *f*; **weather girl** N Wetterfrau *f (inf)*, Wetterfee *f (inf)*; **weatherglass** N Wetterglas *nt*, Barometer *nt*

weathering ['weðərɪŋ] N *(Geol)* Verwitterung *f*

weather: **weatherman** N Wettermann *m (inf)*; **weather map** N Wetterkarte *f*; **weather outlook** N Wetteraussichten *pl*; **weatherproof** ADJ wetterfest VT wetterfest machen; **weather report** N Wetterbericht *m*; **weather service** N Wetterdienst *m*; **weather ship** N Wetterschiff *nt*; **weather station** N Wetterwarte *f*; **weatherstrip** N *(on door, window)* Dichtungsstreifen *m or* -leiste *f*; **weathertight** ADJ wetterfest; **weather vane** N Wetterfahne *f*; **weatherwise** ADV wettermäßig

weave [wiːv] *vb: pret* **wove**, *ptp* **woven** N *(= patterns of threads)* Webart *f*; *(= loosely/tightly etc woven fabric)* Gewebe *nt*; **material in a loose ~** Stoff *m* in einer lockeren Webart; **you need a tighter ~ for a skirt** für einen Rock braucht man ein festeres Gewebe

VT a *thread, cloth etc* weben (*into* zu); *cane, flowers, garland* flechten (*into* zu); *web* spinnen; **he wove the threads together** er verwob die Fäden miteinander

b *(fig) plot, story* ersinnen, erfinden; *(= add into story etc) details, episode* einflechten (*into* in *+acc*); **he wove a romantic tale (a)round his experiences abroad** er spann seine Erlebnisse im Ausland zu einer romantischen Geschichte aus

c *pret also* **weaved** *(= wind)* **to ~ one's way through the traffic/to the front** sich durch den Verkehr fädeln *or* schlängeln/nach vorne (durch)schlängeln; **the drunk ~d his way down the street** der Betrunkene torkelte die Straße hinunter

VI a *(lit)* weben

b *pret also* **weaved** *(= twist and turn)* sich schlängeln; *(drunk)* torkeln

c *(inf)* **to get weaving** sich ranhalten *(inf)*; **to get weaving with sth** sich hinter etw *(acc)* klemmen *(inf)*

weaver ['wiːvəʳ] N Weber(in) *m(f)*

weaverbird ['wiːvəbɜːd] N Webervogel *m*

weaving ['wi:vɪŋ] N Weberei *f*; *(as craft)* Webkunst *f*

web [web] N **a** *(lit, fig)* Netz *nt*; *(of lies)* Gewebe *nt*, Netz *nt*; **a ~ of snow-covered branches** ein Geflecht *nt* von schneebedeckten Ästen; **a ~ of little streets** ein Gewirr *nt* von kleinen Gassen **b** *(of duck etc)* Schwimmhaut *f* **c** *(Comput)* **the Web** das (World Wide) Web; **to be on the ~** im Internet sein

webbed [webd] ADJ **a** *animal* mit Schwimmfüßen; **~ feet** Schwimmfüße *pl* **b** *seats* gurtbespannt

webbing ['webɪŋ] N Gurte *pl*; *(= material)* Gurtband *nt*

web: **web browser** N *(Comput)* Browser *m*; **webcam** ['webkæm] N Webcam *f*; **web-footed** ADJ schwimmfüßig, mit Schwimmfüßen

webinar ['webɪnɑ:'] N *(Internet)* Webinar *nt*

web: **webmail** N *(Comput)* Webmail *f*; **webmaster** N *(Comput)* Webmaster(in) *m(f)*; **web-offset** N Rollenrotations-Offsetdruck *m*; **web page** *(Comput)* N Webseite *f*, Homepage *f*; **website** *(Comput)* N Website *f*; **webspace** N *(Comput)* Webspace *m*; **web-toed** ADJ = **web-footed**; **webzine** N *(Comput)* Onlinemagazin *nt*, Internetmagazin *nt*

Wed *abbr of* **Wednesday** Mittw.

wed [wed] *(old) pret, ptp* **wed** *or* **wedded** VI sich vermählen *(form)*, heiraten VT **a** *(bride, bridegroom)* ehelichen *(form)*, sich vermählen mit *(form)*; *(priest)* vermählen *(form)*, trauen **b** *(fig: = combine)* paaren; **his ability ~ded to her money should make the business a success** mit seinen Fähigkeiten und ihrem Geld müsste das Geschäft eigentlich ein Erfolg werden **c** *(fig)* **to be ~ded to sth** *(= devoted)* mit etw verheiratet sein; **he's ~ded to the view that ...** er ist felsenfest der Ansicht, dass ...

we'd [wi:d] *contr of* **we would, we had**

wedded ['wedɪd] ADJ Ehe-; **~ bliss** Eheglück *nt*; **~ life** Eheleben *nt* → **lawful**

wedding ['wedɪŋ] N **a** *(= ceremony)* Trauung *f*; *(= ceremony and festivities)* Hochzeit *f*, Vermählung *f (form)*; *(= silver, golden wedding etc)* Hochzeit *f*; **to have a registry office** *(Brit)***/church ~** sich standesamtlich/kirchlich trauen lassen, standesamtlich/kirchlich heiraten; **when's the ~?** wann ist die Hochzeit?, wann wird geheiratet?; **to have a quiet ~** in aller Stille heiraten; **to go to a ~** zu einer *or* auf eine Hochzeit gehen **b** *(fig)* Verbindung *f*

wedding *in cpds* Hochzeits-; **wedding anniversary** N Hochzeitstag *m*; **wedding band** N Ehering *m*; **wedding breakfast** N Hochzeitsessen *nt*; **wedding cake** N Hochzeitskuchen *m*; **wedding card** N Hochzeitskarte *f*; **wedding day** N Hochzeitstag *m*; **wedding dress** N Brautkleid *nt*, Hochzeitskleid *nt*; **wedding guest** N Hochzeitsgast *m*; **wedding march** N Hochzeitsmarsch *m*; **wedding night** N Hochzeitsnacht *f*; **wedding present** N Hochzeitsgeschenk *nt*; **wedding reception** N Hochzeitsempfang *m*; **wedding ring** N Trauring *m*, Ehering *m*; **wedding vows** PL Ehegelübde *nt*, Eheversprechen *nt*

wedge [wedʒ] N **a** *(of wood etc, fig)* Keil *m*; **rubber ~** Gummibolzen *m*; **it's the thin end of the ~** so fängts immer an; **that would be the thin end of the ~** das wäre der Anfang vom Ende; **she is driving a ~ between us** sie treibt einen Keil zwischen uns **b** *(= triangular shape) (of cake etc)* Stück *nt*; *(of cheese)* Ecke *f*; **a ~ of land** ein keilförmiges Stück Land; **the seats were arranged in a ~** die Sitzreihen waren keilförmig angeordnet **c** *(= shoe)* Schuh *m* mit Keilabsatz; *(also* **wedge heel***)* Keilabsatz *m*

VT **a** *(= fix with a wedge)* verkeilen, (mit einem Keil) festklemmen; **to ~ a door/window open/shut** eine Tür/ein Fenster festklemmen *or* verkeilen **b** *(fig: = pack tightly)* **to ~ oneself/sth** sich/etw zwängen *(in* in *+acc)*; **to be ~d between two things/people** zwischen zwei Dingen/Personen eingekeilt *or* eingezwängt sein; **the fat man sat ~d in his chair** der dicke Mann saß in seinen Stuhl gezwängt; **we were all ~d together in the back of the car** wir saßen alle zusammengepfercht *or* eingezwängt im Fond des Wagens; **try wedging the cracks with newspaper** versuchen Sie, die Spalten mit Zeitungspapier zuzustopfen

▶**wedge in** VT *sep (lit) post* festkeilen; **to be wedged in** *(car, house, person etc)* eingekeilt *or* eingezwängt sein; **if you park there, you'll wedge me/my car in** wenn du da parkst, keilst du mich ein/wird mein Auto eingekeilt; **he wedged himself in between them** er zwängte sich zwischen sie

wedge-shaped ['wedʒʃeɪpt] ADJ keilförmig

Wedgwood® ['wedʒwʊd] N Wedgwood *nt*; **~ blue** wedgwoodblau

wedlock ['wedlɒk] N *(form)* Ehe *f*; **to be born out of/in ~** unehelich/ehelich geboren sein

Wednesday ['wenzdɪ] N Mittwoch *m*; **~ draw** *(in lottery)* Mittwochsziehung f → *also* **Tuesday**

Weds *abbr of* **Wednesday** Mittw.

wee[1] [wi:] ADJ *(+er) (inf)* winzig; *(Scot)* klein; **a ~ bit** ein kleines bisschen; **the ~ (small) hours** *(Brit)* die frühen Morgenstunden

wee[2] *(Brit inf)* N **to have** *or* **do/need a ~** Pipi machen/machen müssen *(inf)* VI Pipi machen *(inf)*

weed [wi:d] N **a** Unkraut *nt no pl* **b** *(dated inf, = tobacco)* Kraut *nt (inf)* **c** *(inf: = marijuana)* Gras(s) *nt (inf)* **d** *(inf: = person)* Schwächling *m*, Kümmerling *m (inf)* VT **a** *(lit)* jäten **b** *(fig)* = **weed out b** VI jäten

▶**weed out** VT *sep* **a** *plant* ausreißen; *flowerbed* Unkraut *nt* jäten in *(+dat)* **b** *(fig)* aussondern

▶**weed through** VT *sep* durchsortieren

weeding ['wi:dɪŋ] N Unkrautjäten *nt*; **to do some ~** Unkraut *nt* jäten

weedkiller ['wi:dkɪlə'] N Unkrautvernichter *m*, Unkrautbekämpfungsmittel *nt*

weeds [wi:dz] PL *(= mourning clothes)* Trauerkleider *pl*

weedy ['wi:dɪ] ADJ *(+er)* **a** *ground* unkrautbewachsen, voll(er) Unkraut **b** *(inf) person* schmächtig; *(in character)* blutarm

week [wi:k] N Woche *f*; **it'll be ready in a ~** in einer Woche *or* in acht Tagen ist es fertig; **my husband works away during the ~** mein Mann arbeitet die Woche über auswärts; **~ in, ~ out** Woche für Woche; **twice/£15 a ~** zweimal/£ 15 in der Woche *or* pro Woche *or* die Woche *(inf)*; **a ~ today, today** *or* **this day ~** *(Brit dial)* heute in einer Woche *or* in acht Tagen; **a ~ tomorrow/on Tuesday, tomorrow/Tuesday ~** *(esp Brit)* morgen/Dienstag in einer Woche *or* in acht Tagen; **a ~ (ago) last Monday** letzten Montag vor einer Woche; **for ~s** wochenlang; **a ~'s/a two-~ holiday** *(Brit) or* **vacation** *(US)* ein einwöchiger/zweiwöchiger Urlaub; **he works a 40-hour ~** er hat eine Vierzigstundenwoche *or* 40-Stunden-woche; **two ~s' holiday** *(Brit) or* **vacation** *(US)* zwei Wochen Ferien; **that is a ~'s work** das ist eine Woche Arbeit; **to knock sb into the middle of next ~** *(inf)* jdn windelweich schlagen *(inf)*

week: **weekday** N Wochentag *m* ATTR *morning, afternoon* eines Werktages; *routine* an Werktagen *or* Wochentagen; **weekend** N Wochenende *nt*; **to go/be away for the ~** übers *or* am Wochenende verreisen/nicht da sein; **at** *(Brit) or* **on** *(esp US)* **the ~** am Wochenende; **to take a long ~** ein langes Wochenende machen ATTR Wochenend-; **~ trip** Wochenendreise *f*; **~ bag** Reisetasche *f* VI **he ~s in the country** er verbringt seine Wochenenden auf dem Land; **weekender** [ˌwi:k'endə'] N *(= person)* Wochenendler(in) *m(f)*

weekly ['wi:klɪ] ADJ Wochen-; *wage, salary, income also, meeting* wöchentlich; *visit* allwöchentlich; **~ newspaper** Wochenzeitung *f*; **the ~ shopping expedition** der (all)wöchentliche Großeinkauf ADV wöchentlich; **twice/three times ~** zwei/drei Mal die Woche; **he is paid ~** er wird wöchentlich *or* pro Woche bezahlt N Wochenzeitschrift *f*

weeknight ['wi:knaɪt] N Abend *nt* unter der Woche; **she's not allowed out on ~s** sie darf unter der Woche abends nicht weg

weenie ['wi:nɪ] N *(US inf)* (Wiener) Würstchen *nt*

weeny ['wi:nɪ] ADJ *(+er) (inf)* klitzeklein *(inf)*, winzig

weeny-bopper ['wi:nɪˌbɒpə'] N popbesessenes Kind, Pipimädchen *nt (pej inf)*

weep [wi:p] *vb: pret, ptp* **wept** VI **a** *(person)* weinen *(over* über *+acc)*; **to ~ for sb/sth** *(because sb/sth is missed)* um jdn/etw weinen; *(out of sympathy)* für jdn/etw weinen; **the child was ~ing for his mother** das Kind weinte nach seiner Mutter; **to ~ with** *or* **for joy/with rage** vor *or* aus Freude/Wut weinen; **I wept to hear the news** mir kamen die Tränen, als ich die Nachricht hörte **b** *(wound, cut etc)* tränen, nässen VT *tears* weinen N **to have a good/little ~** tüchtig/ein bisschen weinen

weepie N *(inf)* = **weepy N**

weeping ['wi:pɪŋ] N Weinen *nt* ADJ weinend; *wound* nässend

weeping willow N Trauerweide *f*

weepy ['wi:pɪ] *(inf)* ADJ *(+er) person* weinerlich; *(inf) film* rührselig; **that was a very ~ film** *(inf)* der Film hat schwer auf die Tränendrüsen gedrückt *(inf)* N *(inf: = film etc)* Schmachtfetzen *m (inf)*

weevil ['wi:vl] N Rüsselkäfer *m*

wee-wee ['wi:wi:] N, VI *(baby-talk)* = **wee**[2]

weft [weft] N Einschlagfaden *m*, Schussfaden *m*

weigh [weɪ] VT **a** *(lit) goods, person, oneself etc* wiegen; **could you ~ these bananas/this piece of cheese for me?** könnten Sie mir diese Bananen/dieses Stück Käse abwiegen *or* auswiegen?

b *(fig) words, problem, merits etc* abwägen; **to ~ sth in one's mind** etw erwägen; **to ~ A against B** A gegen B abwägen, A und B gegeneinander abwägen

c *(Naut)* **to ~ anchor** den Anker lichten

VI **a** *(lit)* wiegen; **to ~ heavy/light** *(scales)* zu viel/zu wenig anzeigen; *(inf: material)* schwer/leicht wiegen

b *(fig: = be a burden)* lasten *(on* auf *+dat)*

c *(fig: = be important)* gelten; **to ~ with sb** Gewicht bei jdm haben, jdm etwas gelten; **his age ~ed against him** sein Alter wurde gegen ihn in die Waagschale geworfen

▶**weigh down** VT *sep* **a** *(= bear down with weight)* niederbeugen; **the heavy snow weighed the branches down** die schwere Schneelast drückte *or* bog die Zweige nieder; **a branch weighed down with fruit** ein Ast, der sich unter der Last des Obstes biegt; **she was weighed down with packages** sie war mit Paketen überladen; **she was weighed down with a heavy suitcase** der schwere Koffer zog sie fast zu Boden **b** *(fig)* niederdrücken; **to be weighed down with** *or* **by worry** von Sorgen niedergedrückt werden, mit Sorgen beladen sein

▶**weigh in** VI **a** *(Sport)* sich (vor dem Kampf/Rennen) wiegen lassen; **he weighed in at 70 kilos** er brachte 70 Kilo auf die Waage **b** *(at airport)* das Gepäck (ab)wiegen lassen **c** *(fig inf) (= join in)* zu Hilfe kommen *(with* mit*)*; *(= interfere)* sich einschalten VT *sep luggage* wiegen lassen

▶**weigh out** VT *sep* abwiegen

▶**weigh up** VT *sep* abwägen; *person* einschätzen

weigh: **weighbridge** N Brückenwaage *f*; **weigh-in** N *(Sport)* Wiegen *nt*

weighing machine ['weɪɪŋmə'ʃi:n] N *(for people)* Personenwaage *f*; *(coin-operated)* Münzwaage *f*, Wiegeautomat *m*; *(for goods)* Waage *f*

weighing scales PL Waage *f*

weight [weɪt] N **a** *(= heaviness, also Phys)* Gewicht *nt*; *(Sport, esp Boxing)* Gewichtsklasse *f*,

Gewicht *nt (inf)*; *(of cloth)* Schwere *f*; *(of blow)* Wucht *f*, Heftigkeit *f*; **3 kilos in ~** 3 Kilo Gewicht, ein Gewicht von 3 Kilo; **the grocer gave me short ~** der Kaufmann hat (mir) schlecht *or* knapp gewogen; **a suit in a heavier ~ for winter** ein Anzug in einer schwereren Qualität für den Winter; **a blow without much ~ behind it** ein Schlag mit wenig *or* ohne viel Wucht *or* Kraft dahinter; **to feel/test the ~ of sth** sehen/probieren, wie schwer etw ist; **the branches broke under the ~ of the snow** die Zweige brachen unter der Schneelast; **to gain** *or* **put on ~** zunehmen; **to lose ~** abnehmen; **he carries his ~ well** man sieht ihm sein Gewicht nicht an; **I hope the chair takes my ~** ich hoffe, der Stuhl hält mein Gewicht aus; **he's/it's worth his/its ~ in gold** er/das ist Gold(es) wert

b *(= metal weight, unit of weight, heavy object)* Gewicht *nt*; **~s and measures** Maße und Gewichte *(+pl vb)*; **to lift ~s** Gewichte heben; **will he manage to lift the 90kg ~?** wird er die 90 Kilo heben können?; **the doctor warned him not to lift heavy ~s** der Arzt warnte ihn davor, schwere Lasten zu heben; **she's quite a ~** sie ist ganz schön schwer

c *(fig: = load, burden)* Last *f*; **the ~ of evidence** die Beweislast; **they won by ~ of numbers** sie gewannen durch die zahlenmäßige Überlegenheit; **that's a ~ off my mind** mir fällt ein Stein vom Herzen

d *(fig: = importance)* Bedeutung *f*, Gewicht *nt*; **he/his opinion carries no ~** seine Stimme/Meinung hat kein Gewicht *or* fällt nicht ins Gewicht; **those arguments carry ~ with the minister/carry great ~** diesen Argumenten misst der Minister Gewicht bei/wird großes Gewicht beigemessen; **to give due ~ to an argument** einem Argument das entsprechende Gewicht geben *or* beimessen; **to add ~ to sth** einer Sache *(dat)* zusätzliches Gewicht geben *or* verleihen; **to pull one's ~** seinen Teil dazutun, seinen Beitrag leisten; **to put** *or* **throw one's full ~ behind sb/sth** sich mit seinem ganzen Gewicht *or* mit dem ganzen Gewicht seiner Persönlichkeit für jdn/etw einsetzen; **to throw** *or* **chuck** *(inf)* **one's ~ about** *(Brit)* *or* **around** seinen Einfluss geltend machen

VT a *(= make heavier, put weights on)* beschweren

b *(fig: = bias) results* verfälschen; **to ~ sth in favour** *(Brit)* *or* **favor** *(US)* **of/against sb** etw zu jds Gunsten/gegen jdn beeinflussen; **to ~ sth in favour** *(Brit)* *or* **favor** *(US)* **of/against sth** etw zugunsten *or* zu Gunsten einer Sache/gegen etw beeinflussen; **to be ~ed in favour** *(Brit)* *or* **favor** *(US)* **of sb/sth** so angelegt sein, dass es zugunsten *or* zu Gunsten einer Person/Sache ist; **to be ~ed against sb/sth** jdn/etw benachteiligen

▶ **weight down** VT *sep person (with parcels etc)* überladen; *corpse* beschweren; *(fig)* belasten, niederdrücken

weight: **weight advantage** N *(Sport)* Gewichtsvorteil *m*; **weight category** N *(Sport)* Gewichtsklasse *f*; **weight-conscious** ADJ gewichtsbewusst

weighted ['weɪtɪd] ADJ *(Econ)* gewogen, gewichtet

weighted average N gewogener Durchschnitt

weightily ['weɪtɪlɪ] ADV gewichtig

weightiness ['weɪtɪnɪs] N *(lit)* Gewicht *nt*; *(fig)* Gewichtigkeit *f*; *(of responsibility)* Schwere *f*

weighting ['weɪtɪŋ] N *(Brit: = supplement)* Zulage *f*

weight: **weightless** ADJ schwerelos; **weightlessness** N Schwerelosigkeit *f*; **weightlifter** N Gewichtheber(in) *m(f)*; **weightlifting** N Gewichtheben *nt*; **weight loss** N *no pl* Gewichtsverlust *m*; **weight reduction** N Gewichtsreduzierung *f*; **weight-train** ['weɪttreɪn] VI Kraft- *or* Gewichtstraining machen; **weight training** N Kraft- *or* Gewichtstraining *nt*; **weight watcher** N Figurbewusste(r) *mf*

weighty ['weɪtɪ] ADJ *(+er)* **a** *(lit)* schwer **b** *(fig)* gewichtig; *(= influential) argument* schwerwiegend; *(= burdensome) responsibility* schwerwiegend, schwer

weir [wɪəʳ] N **a** *(= barrier)* Wehr *nt* **b** *(= fish trap)* Fischreuse *f*

weird [wɪəd] ADJ *(+er)* *(= uncanny)* unheimlich; *(inf: = odd)* seltsam

weirdie ['wɪədɪ] N *(inf)* verrückter Typ *(inf)*

weirdly ['wɪədlɪ] ADV *(= eerily)* unheimlich; *(inf: = oddly) behave, dress* seltsam; **~ enough** seltsamerweise, merkwürdigerweise

weirdness ['wɪədnɪs] N *(inf: = oddness)* Seltsamkeit *f*

weirdo ['wɪədəʊ] *(inf)* **N** verrückter Typ *(inf)* **ADJ** *hairstyle etc* verrückt, ausgefallen

welch VI = **welsh**

welcome ['welkəm] ✪ 13, 19.3 **N** Willkommen *nt*; **to give sb a hearty** *or* **warm ~** jdm einen herzlichen Empfang bereiten; **to receive a cold/warm ~** kühl/herzlich empfangen werden, einen kühlen/herzlichen Empfang bekommen; **to bid sb ~** *(form)* jdm ein Willkommen entbieten *(geh)*; **what sort of a ~ will this product get from the public?** wie wird das Produkt von der Öffentlichkeit aufgenommen werden?

ADJ a *(= received with pleasure, pleasing)* willkommen; *visitor* gern gesehen *attr*, willkommen; *news* angenehm, willkommen; **the money is very ~ just now** das Geld kommt gerade jetzt sehr gelegen; **to make sb ~** jdn sehr freundlich aufnehmen *or* empfangen; **to make sb feel ~** jdm das Gefühl geben, ein willkommener *or* gern gesehener Gast zu sein; **you will always be ~ here** Sie sind uns *(dat)* jederzeit willkommen; **I didn't feel very ~ there** ich habe mich dort nicht sehr wohlgefühlt; **a ~ addition to ...** eine willkommene Bereicherung ... *(gen)*

b you're ~! nichts zu danken!, keine Ursache!, bitte sehr!, aber gerne!; *(iro)* von mir aus gerne!, wenns Ihnen Spaß macht!; **you're ~ to use my room** Sie können gerne mein Zimmer benutzen; **you're ~ to try** *(iro)* Sie können es gerne versuchen; **you're ~ to it/her!** *(iro)* von mir aus herzlich gerne, das/die kannst du gerne haben!

VT *(lit, fig)* begrüßen, willkommen heißen *(geh)*; **to ~ sb to one's house** jdn bei sich zu Hause *or* in seinem Haus begrüßen *or* willkommen heißen *(geh)*; **they ~d him home with a big party** sie veranstalteten zu seiner Heimkehr ein großes Fest

INTERJ ~ home/to Scotland/on board! herzlich willkommen!, willkommen daheim/in Schottland/an Bord!; **~ back!** willkommen zurück!

welcome-home ['welkəm'həʊm] ADJ *attr* Begrüßungs-, Willkommens-; **~ party** Begrüßungs- *or* Willkommensparty *f*; **~ present** Begrüßungs- *or* Willkommensgeschenk *nt*

welcoming ['welkəmɪŋ] ADJ zur Begrüßung; *smile, gesture, house, room, pub* einladend; **~ ceremony** Begrüßungszeremonie *f*; **~ speech** Begrüßungsrede *f*; **to be ~ to sb** *(person)* jdn freundlich empfangen; **a ~ cup of tea was on the table for her** eine Tasse Tee stand zu ihrer Begrüßung auf dem Tisch; **a ~ fire blazed in the hearth when he arrived** ein warmes Feuer begrüßte ihn bei seiner Ankunft; **the crowds raised a ~ cheer for him** die Menge jubelte ihm zur Begrüßung zu

welcoming committee, **welcoming party** N *(lit, fig)* Begrüßungskomitee *nt*

weld [weld] **VT a** *(Tech)* schweißen; **to ~ parts together** Teile zusammenschweißen *or* verschweißen; **to ~ sth on** etw anschweißen *(to an +acc)*; **~ed joint** Schweißnaht *f* **b** *(fig: also* **weld together***)* zusammenschmieden *(into* zu*)* **VI** schweißen **N** Schweißnaht *f*, Schweißstelle *f*

welder ['weldəʳ] N *(= person)* Schweißer(in) *m(f)*; *(= machine)* Schweißapparat *m*, Schweißgerät *nt*

welding ['weldɪŋ] N Schweißen *nt*

welding torch N Schweißbrenner *m*

welfare ['welfɛəʳ] N **a** *(= wellbeing)* Wohl *nt*, Wohlergehen *nt* **b** *(= welfare work)* Fürsorge *f*, Wohlfahrt *f (dated)*; **child ~** Kinderfürsorge *f*; **social ~** soziale Fürsorge **c** *(US: = social security)* Sozialhilfe *f*; **to be on ~** Sozialhilfeempfänger(in) *m(f)* sein

welfare: **welfare benefits** PL Sozialleistungen *pl*; **welfare case** N Sozialfall *m*; **welfare check** N *(US)* Sozialhilfeüberweisung *f*; **welfare hotel** N *(US) Hotel zur vorübergehenden Unterbringung von Sozialhilfeempfängern*; **welfare officer** N Sozialarbeiter(in) *m(f)*, Mitarbeiter(in) *m(f)* des Sozialamts; **welfare recipient** N *(US)* Sozialhilfeempfänger(in) *m(f)*; **welfare services** PL soziale Einrichtungen *pl*; **welfare state** N Wohlfahrtsstaat *m*; **welfare system** N Sozialsystem *nt*; **welfare work** N Fürsorgearbeit *f*, Wohlfahrtsarbeit *f (dated)*; **welfare worker** N Fürsorger(in) *m(f)*

well[1] [wel] **N a** *(= water well)* Brunnen *m*; *(= oil well)* Ölquelle *f*; *(drilled)* Bohrloch *nt*; *(fig: = source)* Quelle *f*; **to sink a ~** einen Brunnen bohren *or* anlegen *or* graben; *(for oil)* ein Bohrloch *nt* anlegen *or* vorantreiben

b *(= shaft) (for lift)* Schacht *m*; *(for stairs)* Treppenschacht *m*; *(down centre of staircase)* Treppenhaus *nt*

c *(of theatre)* Parkett *nt*; *(of auditorium) ebenerdiger Teil des Zuschauer-/Konferenz-/Versammlungsraums* *(Brit: of court) Teil des Gerichtssaals, in dem die Rechtsanwälte und Protokollschreiber sitzen*

d *(= ink well)* Tintenfass *nt*

VI quellen; **tears ~ed in her eyes** Tränen stiegen *or* schossen ihr in die Augen

▶ **well up** VI *(water, liquid)* emporsteigen, emporquellen; *(fig)* aufsteigen; *(noise)* anschwellen; **tears welled up in her eyes** Tränen stiegen *or* schossen ihr in die Augen

well[2] ✪ 11.2, 13, 23.6, 26.3 *comp* **better**, *superl* **best ADV a** *(= in a good or satisfactory manner)* gut; **the child speaks ~** *(= is well-spoken)* das Kind spricht ordentlich Deutsch/Englisch *etc* *or* gutes Deutsch/Englisch *etc*; **it is ~ painted** *(portrait)* es ist gut gemalt; *(house, fence)* es ist sauber *or* ordentlich angestrichen; **he did it as ~ as he could/as I could have done** er machte es so gut er konnte/ebenso gut, wie ich es hätte machen können; **he's doing ~ at school/in history** er ist gut *or* er kommt gut voran in der Schule/in Geschichte; **he did ~ in the history exam** er hat in der Geschichtsprüfung gut abgeschnitten; **for an eight-year-old he did very ~** für einen Achtjährigen hat er seine Sache sehr gut gemacht; **his business is doing ~** sein Geschäft geht gut; **mother and child are/the patient is doing ~** Mutter und Kind/dem Patienten geht es gut, Mutter und Kind sind/der Patient ist wohlauf; **he did quite ~ at improving sales** er war recht erfolgreich in der Erhöhung des Absatzes; **if you do ~ you'll be promoted** wenn Sie sich bewähren, werden Sie befördert; **you did ~ to help** du tatest gut daran zu helfen, es war gut, dass du geholfen hast; **~ done!** gut gemacht!, bravo!, sehr gut!; **~ played!** gut gespielt!; **to do oneself ~** *(inf)* es sich *(dat)* gut gehen lassen; **to do ~ by sb** *(inf)* jdm gegenüber *or* zu jdm großzügig sein; **everything went ~/quite ~** es ging alles gut *or* glatt *(inf)*/recht *or* ganz gut

b *(= favourably, fortunately)* gut; **to speak/think ~ of sb** über jdn Gutes sagen/Positives denken, von jdm positiv sprechen/denken; **to be ~ spoken of in certain circles/by one's colleagues** einen guten Ruf in gewissen Kreisen/bei seinen Kollegen haben; **to stand ~ with sb** bei jdm angesehen sein; **to be ~ in with sb** *(inf)* auf gutem Fuß mit jdm stehen; **to marry ~** eine gute Partie machen; **to do ~ out of sth** von etw ganz schön *or* ordentlich profitieren, bei etw gut wegkommen *(inf)*; **you would do ~ to arrive early** Sie täten gut daran, früh zu kommen; **you might as ~ go** du könntest eigentlich geradeso gut *or* ebenso gut (auch) gehen; **are you coming? – I might as ~** kommst du? – ach, könnte ich eigentlich (auch) *(inf)* *or* ach, warum nicht

c *(= thoroughly, considerably, to a great degree)* gut, gründlich; **shake the bottle ~** *(on medicine)* Flasche kräftig *or* gut schütteln; **he loved her too ~ to leave her** *(liter)* er liebte sie zu sehr, als dass er sie verlassen hätte; **we were ~ beaten** wir sind gründlich geschlagen worden; **he could ~ afford it** er konnte es sich *(dat)* sehr wohl leisten; **I'm ~ content with my lot** ich bin wohl zufrieden mit meinem Schicksal; **all** *or* **only too ~** nur (all)zu gut; **~ and truly** (ganz) gründlich; *married, settled in* ganz richtig; *(iro also)* fest; *westernized, conditioned* durch und durch; **he was ~ away** *(inf)* er war in Fahrt *or* Schwung *(inf)*; *(= drunk)* er hatte einen sitzen *(inf)*; **he sat ~ forward in his seat** er saß weit vorne auf seinem Sitz; **it was ~ worth the trouble** das hat sich wohl *or* sehr gelohnt; **~ out of sight** weit außer Sichtweite; **~ within ...** durchaus in ... *(dat)*; **~ past midnight** lange nach Mitternacht; **it continued ~ into 1996/the night** es zog sich bis weit ins Jahr 1996/in die Nacht hin; **he's ~ over fifty** er ist weit über fünfzig

d *(= probably, reasonably)* ohne Weiteres, gut, wohl; **I may ~ be late** es kann leicht *or* wohl *or* ohne Weiteres sein, dass ich spät komme; **it may ~ be that ...** es ist gut *or* wohl *or* ohne Weiteres möglich, dass ...; **you may ~ be right** Sie mögen wohl recht haben; **she cried, as ~ she might** sie weinte, und das (auch) mit Grund *or* wozu sie auch allen Grund hatte; **you may ~ ask!** *(iro)* das kann man wohl fragen; **I couldn't very ~ stay** ich konnte schlecht bleiben, ich konnte wohl nicht mehr gut bleiben

e *(= in addition)* **as ~** auch; **if he comes as ~** wenn er auch kommt; **x as ~ as y** x sowohl als auch y, x und auch y; **she sings as ~ as dances** sie singt und tanzt auch noch

f *(Brit inf: = very)* **~ happy** total glücklich *(inf)*; **~ annoyed** ganz schön verärgert *(inf)*

ADJ **a** *(= in good health)* gesund; **get ~ soon!** gute Besserung; **are you ~?** geht es Ihnen gut?; **I'm very ~, thanks** danke, es geht mir sehr gut; **he's not a ~ man** er ist gar nicht gesund; **she's not been ~ lately** ihr ging es in letzter Zeit (gesundheitlich) gar nicht gut; **I don't feel at all ~** ich fühle mich gar nicht gut *or* wohl

b *(= satisfactory, desirable, advantageous)* gut; **all is not ~ with him/in the world** mit ihm/mit *or* in der Welt steht es nicht zum Besten; **that's all very ~, but ...** das ist ja alles schön und gut, aber ...; **if that's the case, (all) ~ and good** wenn das der Fall ist, dann soll es mir recht sein; **it's all very ~ for you to suggest ...** Sie können leicht vorschlagen ...; **it's all very ~ for you, you don't have to ...** Sie haben gut reden *or* Sie können leicht reden, Sie müssen ja nicht ...; **it was ~ for him that no-one found out** es war sein Glück, dass es niemand entdeckt hat; **it would be as ~ to ask first** es wäre wohl besser *or* gescheiter *(inf)*, sich erst mal zu erkundigen; **it's just as ~ he came** es ist (nur *or* schon) gut, dass er gekommen ist; **you're ~ out of that** seien Sie froh, dass Sie damit nichts mehr zu tun haben; **all's ~ that ends ~** Ende gut, alles gut

INTERJ also; *(expectantly also)* na; *(doubtfully)* na ja; **~, ~!, ~ I never (did)!** also, so was!, na so was!; **~ now** also; **~, it was like this** also, es war so *or* folgendermaßen; **~ there you are, that proves it!** na bitte *or* also bitte, das beweist es doch; **~, as I was saying** also, wie (bereits) gesagt; **~ then?** also (gut); *(in question)* na?, nun?, also?; **very ~ then!** na gut, also gut!; *(indignantly)* also bitte (sehr)!; **oh ~, never mind** macht nichts; **~, that's a relief!** na (also), das ist ja eine Erleichterung!

N Gute(s) *nt*; **to wish sb ~** *(in general)* jdm alles Gute wünschen; *(in an attempt, also iro)* jdm Glück wünschen *(in* bei); **I wish him ~, but ...** ich wünsche ihm nichts Böses, aber ...

we'll [wi:l] *contr of* **we shall, we will**

well *in cpds* gut; **well-adjusted** ADJ *attr,* **well adjusted** ADJ *pred (Psych)* gut angepasst; **well-advised** ADJ *attr,* **well advised** ADJ *pred plan, move* klug; **to be well advised to ...** wohl *or* gut beraten sein zu ..., gut daran tun, zu ...; **well-aimed** ADJ *attr,* **well aimed** ADJ *pred shot, blow, sarcasm* gut gezielt, wohlgezielt; **well-appointed** ADJ *attr,* **well appointed** ADJ *pred* gut ausgestattet; **well-argued** ADJ *attr,* **well argued** ADJ *pred* wohlbegründet, gut begründet; **well-assorted** ADJ *attr,* **well assorted** ADJ *pred* gut zusammenpassend; **they're a ~ pair** sie passen gut zusammen *or* zueinander; **well-attended** ADJ *attr,* **well attended** ADJ *pred* gut besucht; **well-baby clinic** N Neugeborenenklinik *f*; **well-balanced** ADJ *attr,* **well balanced** ADJ *pred* **a** *person, mind* ausgeglichen **b** *budget, diet* (gut) ausgewogen; **well-behaved** ADJ *attr,* **well behaved** ADJ *pred child* artig, wohlerzogen; *animal* gut erzogen; **wellbeing** N Wohl *nt*, Wohlergehen *nt*; **to have a sense of ~** (ein Gefühl *nt* der) Behaglichkeit *or* Wohligkeit empfinden; **well-born** ADJ *attr,* **well born** ADJ *pred* aus vornehmer Familie, aus vornehmem Haus; **well-bred** ADJ *attr,* **well bred** ADJ *pred* **a** *(= polite) person* wohlerzogen; *manners* vornehm, gepflegt; *accent* distinguiert **b** *(= of good stock) animal* aus guter Zucht; *(iro) person* aus gutem Stall; **well-built** ADJ *attr,* **well built** ADJ *pred house* gut *or* solide gebaut; *person* stämmig, kräftig; **well-chosen** ADJ *attr,* **well chosen** ADJ *pred remarks, words* gut *or* glücklich gewählt; **in a few ~ words** in wenigen wohlgesetzten Worten; **well-connected** ADJ *attr,* **well connected** ADJ *pred* **to be well connected** Beziehungen zu *or* in höheren Kreisen haben; **well-cooked** ADJ *attr,* **well cooked** ADJ *pred* gut zubereitet; *(= well-done) meat* gut durchgebraten; **well-defined** [ˌweldɪˈfaɪnd] ADJ *attr,* **well defined** ADJ *pred* **a** *problem* klar umrissen; *goals* klar **b** *eyebrows, cheekbones* markant; *muscles* ausgeprägt; **well-deserved** ADJ *attr,* **well deserved** ADJ *pred* wohlverdient; **well-developed** ADJ *attr,* **well developed** ADJ *pred muscle* gut entwickelt; *sense* (gut) ausgeprägt; *system* ausgereift; *market, industry* gut entwickelt; **well-disposed** ADJ *attr,* **well disposed** ADJ *pred* **to be well disposed toward(s) sb/sth** jdm/einer Sache gewogen sein *or* freundlich gesonnen sein; **well-done** ADJ *attr,* **well done** ADJ *pred steak* durchgebraten, durch *inv*; **well-dressed** ADJ *attr,* **well dressed** ADJ *pred* gut angezogen *or* gekleidet; **well-earned** ADJ *attr,* **well earned** ADJ *pred* wohlverdient; **well-educated** ADJ *attr,* **well educated** ADJ *pred person* gebildet; *voice* (gut) ausgebildet; **well-endowed** [ˌwelɪnˈdaʊd] ADJ *attr,* **well endowed** ADJ *pred (euph)* **to be well endowed** von Natur aus gut *or* reichlich ausgestattet sein; **well-equipped** ADJ *attr,* **well equipped** ADJ *pred office, studio* gut ausgestattet; *expedition, army* gut ausgerüstet; **well-established** ADJ *attr,* **well established** ADJ *pred practice, custom* fest; *pattern also* klar; *tradition* alt; *family* alteingesessen; *reputation* gut; *company, player, writer, artist* bekannt; **it's a ~ fact that ...** es ist eine bekannte Tatsache, dass ...; **well-favoured** ADJ *attr,* **well favoured** ADJ *pred (old) girl, family* ansehnlich *(old)*; **well-fed** ADJ *attr,* **well fed** ADJ *pred* wohlgenährt, gut genährt; **well-founded** ADJ *attr,* **well founded** ADJ *pred* wohlbegründet; **the warnings proved (to be) well founded** die Warnungen erwiesen sich als begründet; **well-groomed** ADJ *attr,* **well groomed** ADJ *pred* gepflegt; **well-grown** ADJ *attr,* **well grown** ADJ *pred animal, child* groß (gewachsen)

wellhead [ˈwelhed] N **a** *(of spring etc)* Quelle *f*; *(fig)* Ursprung *m* **b** *(= head of oil well)* Bohrturm *m*

well: **well-heeled** ADJ *attr,* **well heeled** ADJ *pred (Brit inf)* betucht *(inf)*; **well-hung** ADJ *attr,* **well hung** ADJ *pred meat* abgehangen; *(inf) man* gut ausgestattet; **he's ~** er hat ein großes Gehänge *(inf)* *or* eine Mördergurke *(sl)*; **well-informed** ADJ *attr,* **well informed** ADJ *pred* gut informiert; *sources also* wohlunterrichtet; **to be well informed about sb/sth** über jdn/etw gut informiert *or* gut unterrichtet sein

wellington (boot) [ˈwelɪŋtən(ˈbu:t)] N *(Brit)* Gummistiefel *m*

well: **well-intentioned** ADJ *attr,* **well intentioned** ADJ *pred* wohlmeinend; **well-kept** ADJ *attr,* **well kept** ADJ *pred garden, hair etc* gepflegt; *secret* streng gehütet, gut gewahrt; **well-knit** ADJ *attr,* **well knit** ADJ *pred body* drahtig, straff; *(fig)* gut durchdacht *or* aufgebaut; **well-known** ADJ *attr,* **well known** ADJ *pred place, singer* bekannt; *fact also* wohlbekannt, altbekannt; **it's well known that ...** es ist allgemein bekannt, dass ...; **to be well known for sth** für etw bekannt sein; **to be well known to sb** jdm bekannt sein; **well-loved** ADJ *attr,* **well loved** ADJ *pred* viel geliebt; **well-made** ADJ *attr,* **well made** ADJ *pred* **a** *piece of furniture etc* gut gearbeitet **b** *person* gut gebaut; **well-man clinic** N Männerklinik *f*; **well-mannered** ADJ *attr,* **well mannered** ADJ *pred* mit guten Manieren; **to be well mannered** gute Manieren haben; **well-matched** ADJ *attr,* **well matched** ADJ *pred teams* gleich stark; **they're a ~ pair** sie passen gut zusammen; **well-meaning** ADJ *attr,* **well meaning** ADJ *pred* wohlmeinend; **well-meant** ADJ *attr,* **well meant** ADJ *pred action, lie* gut gemeint; **well-nigh** ADV *(form)* nahezu, beinahe, nachgerade *(geh)*; **this is ~ impossible** das ist nahezu *or* beinahe unmöglich; **well-off** **ADJ** *attr,* **well off** **ADJ** *pred (= affluent)* reich, begütert, gut d(a)ran *(inf)*; **to be well off** *(= fortunate)* gut daran sein; **you don't know when you're well off** *(inf)* du weißt (ja) nicht, wenn es dir gut geht **N** **the ~** *pl* die Begüterten *pl*;; **well-oiled** ADJ *attr,* **well oiled** ADJ *pred (inf: = drunk)* beduselt *(inf)*; **well-padded** ADJ *attr,* **well padded** ADJ *pred (inf: = not thin)* gut gepolstert *(inf)*; **well-paid** ADJ *attr,* **well paid** ADJ *pred* gut bezahlt; **well-preserved** ADJ *attr,* **well preserved** ADJ *pred* gut erhalten; *person also* wohlerhalten; **well-read** ADJ *attr,* **well read** ADJ *pred* belesen; **well-respected** ADJ *attr,* **well respected** ADJ *pred* hoch angesehen; **well-spent** ADJ *attr,* **well spent** ADJ *pred time* gut genützt *or* verbracht; *money* sinnvoll *or* vernünftig ausgegeben *or* verwendet; **well-spoken** ADJ *attr,* **well spoken** ADJ *pred* mit gutem Deutsch/Englisch *etc*; **to be well spoken** gutes Deutsch/Englisch *etc* sprechen; **well-stacked** ADJ *attr,* **well stacked** ADJ *pred (inf) woman* **to be well stacked** Holz vor der Hütte haben *(inf)*; **well-stocked** ADJ *attr,* **well stocked** ADJ *pred* gut bestückt; *(Comm also)* mit gutem Sortiment; *larder, shelves also* gut gefüllt, reichlich gefüllt; *library also* reichhaltig, umfangreich; **well-thought-of** ADJ angesehen; **well-thumbed** [ˌwelˈθʌmd] ADJ *book* zerlesen, zerfleddert *(inf)*; **well-timed** ADJ *attr,* **well timed** ADJ *pred* (zeitlich) gut abgepasst, zeitlich günstig; **that was a ~ interruption** die Unterbrechung kam im richtigen Augenblick; **well-to-do** **ADJ** wohlhabend, reich; *district also* vornehm **N** **the ~** *pl* die Begüterten *pl*; **well-tried** ADJ *attr,* **well tried** ADJ *pred method etc* erprobt; **well-trodden** ADJ *attr,* **well trodden** ADJ *pred (lit)* viel begangen; **a ~ path** *(fig)* eine beliebte Methode; **well water** N Brunnenwasser *nt*; **well-wisher** N **cards from ~s** Karten von Leuten, die ihm/ihr *etc* alles Gute wünschten; **our cause has many ~s** unsere Sache hat viele Sympathisanten; **"from a ~"** „jemand, der es gut mit Ihnen meint"; **well-woman clinic** N Frauenklinik *f*; **well-worn** ADJ *attr,* **well worn** ADJ *pred garment* abgetragen; *carpet etc* abgelaufen; *book* abgenützt, abgegriffen; *path* ausgetreten; *saying, subject etc* abgedroschen

welly [ˈwelɪ] N *(Brit inf)* Gummistiefel *m*

Welsh [welʃ] **ADJ** walisisch; **the ~ National Party** *walisische Partei, die sich für die Unabhängigkeit des Landes einsetzt* **N** **a** *(Ling)* Walisisch *nt* **b** **the Welsh** **PL** die Waliser *pl*

welsh, welch [welʃ] VI *(inf)* sich drücken *(on sth* vor etw *dat)* *(inf)*; *(bookmaker etc: = avoid payment)* die Gewinne nicht ausbezahlen *(on sb* jdm); *(by disappearing)* mit dem Geld durchgehen *(inf)*

Welsh: **Welsh Assembly** N **the ~** die walisische Versammlung; **Welsh dresser** N *(Brit)* Anrichte *f* mit Tellerbord; **Welshman** N Waliser *m*; **Welsh Nationalism** N walisischer Nationalismus; **Welsh rabbit**, **Welsh rarebit** N überbackene Käseschnitte; **Welshwoman** N Waliserin *f*

welt [welt] N **a** *(of shoe)* Rahmen *m*; *(of pullover)* Bündchen *nt* **b** *(= weal)* Striemen *m*

welted ['weltɪd] ADJ *shoe* randgenäht

welter ['weltəʳ] N Unzahl *f*; *(of blood, cheers)* Meer *nt*; *(of emotions)* Sturm *m*, Tumult *m*; *(of verbiage)* Flut *f*

welterweight ['weltəweɪt] N Weltergewicht *nt*

wench [wentʃ] N *(old)* Maid *f (old)*; *(= serving wench)* Magd *f*; *(hum)* Frauenzimmer *nt* VI sich mit Mädchen herumtreiben

wend [wend] VT **to ~ one's way home/to the bar** *etc* sich auf den Heimweg/zur Bar *etc* begeben

Wendy house ['wendɪ,haʊs] N Spielhaus *nt*

went [went] *pret of* **go**

wept [wept] *pret, ptp of* **weep**

were [wɜː] *2nd pers sing, 1st, 2nd, 3rd pers pl pret of* **be**

we're [wɪəʳ] *contr of* **we are**

weren't [wɜːnt] *contr of* **were not**

werewolf ['wɪəwʊlf] N Werwolf *m*

wert [wɜːt] *(old) 2nd pers sing pret of* **be**

Wesleyan ['wezlɪən] *(Eccl)* ADJ wesleyanisch N Wesleyaner(in) *m(f)*

west [west] N **a** **the ~**, **the West** *(also Pol)* der Westen; **in the ~** im Westen; **to the ~** nach *or* gen *(liter)* Westen; **to the ~ of** westlich von, im Westen von; **he comes from the ~ (of Ireland)** er kommt aus dem Westen (von Irland); **the wind is coming from the ~** der Wind kommt von West(en) *or* aus (dem) Westen; **the south and ~ of the square** die Südseite und die Westseite des Platzes **b** *(= western world)* **the ~** *or* **West** der Westen ADJ West-; **the ~ coast** die Westküste; **~ wind** Westwind *m*; **Salford West** Salford West ADV **a** nach Westen, westwärts; **it faces ~** es geht nach Westen; **~ of** westlich von **b** **to go ~** *(fig inf)* flöten gehen *(inf)*; *(= to die)* vor die Hunde gehen *(inf)*

west *in cpds* West-; **West Africa** N Westafrika *nt*; **West Bank** N *(in Middle East)* Westjordanland *nt*, West Bank *f*; **West Berlin** N Westberlin *nt*; **westbound** ['westbaʊnd] ADJ *traffic, carriageway* (in) Richtung Westen; **the ~ carriageway of the M4** *(Brit)* die M4 in Richtung Westen; **to be ~** nach Westen unterwegs sein, westwärts reisen *or* fahren ADV nach Westen, (in) Richtung Westen; **West Country** N *(Brit)* Südwestengland *nt (esp Cornwall, Devon und Somerset)*; **West End** N **the ~** *(in London)* der (Londoner) Westen, das Westend; **West Ender** N Bewohner(in) *m(f)* des Londoner Westens *or* des Westend

westerly ['westəlɪ] ADJ westlich; **~ wind** Westwind *m*, Wind *m* aus westlicher Richtung; **in a ~ direction** in westlicher Richtung N *(= wind)* Westwind *m*, West *m (poet)* ADV nach Westen

western ['westən] ADJ westlich; **on the Western front** an der Westfront; **Western Europe** Westeuropa *nt*; **the Western Sahara** die westliche Sahara N Western *m*

Western Australia N Westaustralien *nt*

westerner ['westənəʳ] N **a** *(Pol)* Abendländer(in) *m(f)* **b** *(US)* Weststaatler(in) *m(f)*

Western Isles PL **the ~** die Hebriden *pl*

westernization [ˌwestənaɪ'zeɪʃən] N *(= westernizing)* Einführung *f* der westlichen Kultur *or* Zivilisation; *(= western character)* westliche Zivilisation *f*; *(pej)* Verwestlichung *f*

westernize ['westənaɪz] VT die westliche Zivilisation/Kultur einführen in *(+dat)*; *(pej)* verwestlichen

westernized ['westənaɪzd] ADJ *person, culture* vom Westen beeinflusst, westlich ausgerichtet; *(pej)* verwestlicht

westernmost ['westənməʊst] ADJ westlichste(r, s), am weitesten westlich (gelegen)

Western Samoa [ˌwestənsə'məʊə] N Westsamoa *nt*

west: **West Europe** N *(esp US)* Westeuropa *nt*; **West European** ADJ westeuropäisch N Westeuropäer(in) *m(f)*; **West Germany** N Westdeutschland *nt*, Bundesrepublik *f* (Deutschland); **West Indian** ADJ westindisch N Westindier(in) *m(f)*; **West Indies** PL Westindische Inseln *pl*; **west-northwest** N Westnordwest *no art* ADV nach Westnordwesten; **~ of X/the lake** westnordwestlich von X/des Sees

Westphalia [west'feɪlɪə] N Westfalen *nt*

Westphalian [west'feɪlɪən] ADJ westfälisch N Westfale *m*, Westfälin *f*

west: **West Side** N **the ~**, **the Upper ~** die West Side, *der Westen von Manhattan*; **west-southwest** [ˌwestsaʊθ'west] N Westsüdwest *no art* ADV nach Westsüdwesten; **~ of X/the lake** westsüdwestlich von X/des Sees

westward ['westwəd] ADJ *direction* westlich; *route* nach Westen, (in) Richtung Westen ADV *(also* **westwards**) westwärts, nach Westen, (in) Richtung Westen

westwardly ['westwədlɪ] ADJ ADV = **westward**

wet [wet] *vb: pret, ptp* **wet** *or* **wetted** ADJ *(+er)* **a** nass; **to be ~** *(paint, varnish, ink)* nass *or* feucht sein; **to be ~ through** durch und durch nass sein, völlig durchnässt sein; **~ with tears** tränenfeucht; **her eyes were ~ with tears** sie hatte feuchte Augen, sie hatte Tränen in den Augen; **"wet paint"** *(esp Brit)* „Vorsicht, frisch gestrichen"; **to get one's feet ~** nasse Füße bekommen, sich *(dat)* nasse Füße holen *(inf)*; **to be ~ behind the ears** *(inf)* noch feucht *or* noch nicht trocken hinter den Ohren sein *(inf)* **b** *(= rainy)* nass, feucht; *climate, country* feucht; **the ~ season** die Regenzeit; **in ~ weather** bei nassem Wetter, bei Regenwetter; **it's been ~ all week** es war die ganze Woche (über) regnerisch **c** *(= allowing alcohol) state, city* wo kein Alkoholverbot besteht, nicht prohibitionistisch **d** *(Brit inf) (= weak, spiritless)* weichlich, lasch; *(Pol pej)* gemäßigt; **don't be so ~!** sei nicht so ein Waschlappen! *(inf)* **e** *(with urine) child, nappy* nass **f** *(US inf: = wrong)* **you're all ~** da liegst du völlig falsch *(inf)* **g** *(Brit Pol)* liberal-konservativ N **a** *(= moisture)* Feuchtigkeit *f* **b** *(= rain)* Nässe *f*; **it's out in the ~** es ist draußen im Nassen **c** *(inf: = wet season)* Regenzeit *f* **d** *(US, inf: = anti-prohibitionist)* Antiprohibitionist(in) *m(f)* **e** *(Brit) (inf: = person)* Waschlappen *m (inf)*, Weichei *nt (sl)*; *(Pol pej inf)* Gemäßigte(r) *mf* VT nass machen; *lips, washing* befeuchten; **to ~ the baby's head** *(inf)* den Sohn/die Tochter begießen *(inf)*; **to ~ one's whistle** *(inf)* sich *(dat)* die Kehle anfeuchten *(inf)*; **to ~ the bed/one's pants/oneself** das Bett/seine Hosen/sich nass machen, ins Bett/in die Hose(n) machen; **I nearly ~ myself** *(inf)* ich habe mir fast in die Hose gemacht *(inf)*

wet: **wet-and-dry** N Schmirgelpapier *nt* VT (nass) schmirgeln; **wet bar** N *(US)* Bartresen *m* mit Wasseranschluss; **wet blanket** N *(inf)* Miesmacher(in) *m(f) (inf)*, Spielverderber(in) *m(f)*; **wet cell** N Nasselement *nt*; **wet dock** N Dock *nt*, Flutbecken *nt*; **wet dream** N feuchter Traum

wether ['weðəʳ] N Hammel *m*, Schöps *m (dial)*

wet-look ADJ *material* (hoch)glänzend; *hair* (vor Gel) glänzend; **~ leather** Knautschlackleder *nt*

wetly ['wetlɪ] ADV **a** nass **b** *(Brit inf)* weich, lasch

wetness ['wetnɪs] N **a** Nässe *f*; *(of climate, paint, ink)* Feuchtigkeit *f* **b** *(Brit, inf)* Weichlichkeit *f*

wet: **wet nurse** N Amme *f*; **wet pack** N Kulturbeutel *m*; *(Med)* feuchte Packung, feuchter Umschlag; **wet rot** N Nassfäule *f*; **wet suit** N Neoprenanzug *m*, Taucheranzug *m*

wetting ['wetɪŋ] N unfreiwillige Dusche *(inf)*; *(= falling into water)* unfreiwilliges Bad; **to get a ~** klatschnass werden, eine Dusche abbekommen *(inf)*, ein unfreiwilliges Bad nehmen; **to give sb a ~** jdm eine Dusche/ein Bad verabreichen *(inf)* ADJ *(Chem)* **~ agent** Netzmittel *nt*; **~ solution** *(for contact lenses)* Benetzungsflüssigkeit *f*

wettish ['wetɪʃ] ADJ feucht

wet-weather tyre, *(US)* **wet-weather tire** N *(Mot)* Regenreifen *m*

we've [wiːv] *contr of* **we have**

whack [wæk] N **a** *(inf: = blow)* (knallender) Schlag; **to give sb a ~** jdm einen Schlag versetzen; **to give sth a ~** auf etw *(acc)* schlagen **b** *(esp Brit inf: = attempt)* Versuch *m*; **to have a ~ at sth/at doing sth** etw probieren *or* versuchen, sich an etw *(dat)* versuchen; **I'll have a ~ at it** ich will mich mal (d)ranwagen **c** *(esp Brit inf: = share)* (An)teil *m*; **we're offering £50,000, top ~** wir bieten höchstens *or* maximal £ 50.000; **he's earning the top ~** er bekommt das Spitzengehalt VT **a** *(inf: = hit)* schlagen, hauen *(inf)* **b** *(inf: = defeat)* (haushoch) schlagen **c** *(inf: = exhaust)* erschlagen *(inf)*

▶ **whack off** VI *(sl: = masturbate)* wichsen *(sl)*, sich *(dat)* einen runterholen *(inf)*

whacked [wækt] ADJ *(Brit inf: = exhausted)* kaputt *(inf)*

whacking ['wækɪŋ] ADJ *(Brit inf)* Mords- *(inf)*; **a ~ lie** eine Mordslüge *(inf)*; **~ great** riesengroß; **a ~ big book** *(also US)* ein Monstrum *nt* von (einem) Buch *(inf)*; **he earns a ~ £100,000 a year** *(also US)* er verdient mordsmäßige £ 100.000 pro Jahr *(inf)* N **a** *(= beating)* Keile *f (inf)*; **to give sb a ~** jdm Keile *or* eine Tracht Prügel verpassen *(inf)* **b** *(inf: = defeat)* **we got a real ~** sie haben uns richtig in die Pfanne gehauen *(inf)*

whacko ['wæ,kəʊ] INTERJ *(dated)* trefflich *(dated)*, tipp-topp, eins a *(inf)*

whacky ADJ *(+er) (inf)* = **wacky**

whale [weɪl] N **a** Wal *m* **b** *(inf)* **a ~ of** *(= exceedingly great, good etc)* ein(e) riesige(r, s); **a ~ of a difference** ein himmelweiter Unterschied; **a ~ of a party** eine Wahnsinnsparty *(inf)*; **to have a ~ of a time** sich prima amüsieren

whale: **whalebone** N Fischbein *nt*; **whale fishing** N Wal(fisch)fang *m*; **whaleman** N *(US)* Walfänger *m*; **whale oil** N Walöl *nt*, Tran *m*

whaler ['weɪləʳ] N *(= ship)* Walfänger *m*, Walfangschiff *nt*; *(= person)* Walfänger(in) *m(f)*

whaling ['weɪlɪŋ] N Wal(fisch)fang *m*; **to go ~** auf Walfang gehen; **~ ship** Walfänger *m*, Walfangschiff *nt*; **~ station** Walfangstation *f*

wham [wæm], **whang** [wæŋ] INTERJ wumm N *(= blow)* Schlag *m*; *(= bang, thump)* Knall *m* VT *(= hit)* schlagen; *(= bang, thump)* knallen VI knallen; **to ~ into sth** auf etw *(acc)* krachen *(inf)*

whammy ['wæmɪ] N **a double/triple ~** ein doppelter/dreifacher Schlag

wharf [wɔːf] N *pl* **-s** *or* **wharves** [wɔːvz] Kai *m*

what [wɒt] PRON **a** *(interrog)* was; **~ is this called?** wie heißt das?, wie nennt man das?; **~'s the weather like?** wie ist das Wetter?; **~ do 4 and 3 make?** wie viel ist *or* macht 4 und *or* plus 3?; **you need (a) ~?** WAS brauchen Sie?; **~ is it now?**, **~ do you want now?** was ist denn?; **~?** *(= pardon?)* was?; **~'s that (you/he** *etc* **said)?** WAS hast du/hat er *etc* da gerade gesagt?, wie *or* was war das noch mal? *(inf)*; **~'s that to you?** was geht dich das an?; **~ for?** wozu?, wofür?, für was? *(inf)*; **~'s that tool for?**

wofür ist das Werkzeug?; **~ are you looking at me like that for?** warum *or* was *(inf)* siehst du mich denn so an?; **~ did you do that for?** warum hast du denn das gemacht?; **~ about ...?** wie wärs mit ...?; **well, ~ about it? are we going?** na, wie ists, gehen wir?; **you know that restaurant? – ~ about it?** kennst du das Restaurant? – was ist damit?; **~ of** *or* **about it?** na und? *(inf)*; **~ if ...?** was ist, wenn ...?; **so ~?** *(inf)* ja *or* na und?; **~ does it matter?** was macht das schon?; **you ~?** *(inf)* wie bitte?; **~-d'you(-ma)-call-him/-her/-it** *(inf)* wie heißt er/sie/es gleich *or* schnell

b *(rel)* was; **he knows ~ it is to suffer** er weiß, was leiden heißt *or* ist; **that is not ~ I asked for** danach habe ich nicht gefragt; **that's exactly ~ I want/said** genau das möchte ich/habe ich gesagt; **do you know ~ you are looking for?** weißt du, wonach du suchst?; **come ~ may** komme was wolle; **~ I'd like is a cup of tea** was ich jetzt gerne hätte, (das) wäre ein Tee; **~ with work and the new baby, life's been very hectic** die ganze Arbeit, das Baby ist da - es ist alles sehr hektisch; **~ with one thing and the other** und wie es sich dann so ergab/ergibt, wie das so ist *or* geht; **and ~'s more** und außerdem, und noch dazu; **he knows ~'s ~** *(inf)* er kennt sich aus, der weiß Bescheid *(inf)*; **(I'll) tell you ~** *(inf)* weißt du was?; **and ~ have you** *(inf)* und was sonst noch (alles), und was weiß ich; **to give sb ~ for** *(inf)* es jdm ordentlich geben *(inf)* → **whatnot**

c *(with vb +prep see also there)* **~ did he agree to?** wozu hat er zugestimmt?; **~ did he object to?** wogegen *or* gegen was hat er Einwände erhoben?; **he agreed/objected to ~ we suggested** er stimmte unseren Vorschlägen zu/lehnte unsere Vorschläge ab, er lehnte ab, was wir vorschlugen; **he didn't know ~ he was agreeing/objecting to** er wusste nicht, wozu er zustimmte/was er ablehnte; **she fell in with ~ everyone else wanted** sie schloss sich den Wünschen der Allgemeinheit an; **he didn't go into ~ he meant** er erläuterte nicht im Einzelnen, was er meinte

ADJ **a** *(interrog)* welche(r, s), was für (ein/eine) *(inf)*; **~ age is he?** wie alt ist er?; **~ good would that be?** *(inf)* wozu sollte das gut sein?; **~ book do you want?** was für ein Buch wollen Sie?

b *(rel)* der/die/das; **~ little I had** das wenige, das ich hatte; **buy ~ food you like** kauf das Essen, das du willst

c *(in set constructions)* **~ sort of** was für ein/eine; **~ else** was noch; **~ more could a girl ask for?** was könnte sich ein Mädchen sonst noch wünschen

d *(in interj, also iro)* was für (ein/eine); **~ a man!** was für ein *or* welch ein *(geh)* Mann!; **~ luck!** welch(es) Glück, was für ein Glück, so ein Glück; **~ a fool I've been/I am!** ich Idiot!; **~ terrible weather** was für ein scheußliches Wetter

INTERJ was; *(dated: = isn't it/he etc also)* wie; **is he good-looking, or ~?** sieht der aber gut aus! *(inf)*

whatchamacallit ['wɔtʃəmə͵kɔːlɪt] **N** *(inf)* Dingsbums *nt (inf)*, Dingsda *nt (inf)*

whate'er [wɒt'ɛəʳ] **PRON, ADJ** *(poet)* = **whatever**

whatever [wɒt'evəʳ] **PRON** **a** was (auch) (immer); *(= no matter what)* egal was, ganz gleich was; **~ you like** was (immer) du (auch) möchtest; **shall we go home now? – ~ you like** *or* **say** gehen wir jetzt nach Hause? – ganz wie du willst; **~ it's called** egal wie es heißt, soll es heißen, wie es will; **... or ~ they're called** ... oder wie sie sonst heißen; **or ~** oder sonst (so) etwas

b *(interrog)* was ... wohl; *(impatiently)* was zum Kuckuck *(inf)*; **~ does he want?** was will er wohl?, was er wohl will?; *(impatiently)* was, zum Kuckuck, will er denn?; **~ do you mean?** was meinst du denn bloß?

ADJ **a** egal welche(r, s), welche(r, s) (auch) (immer); **~ book you choose** welches Buch Sie auch wählen; **~ else you do** was immer du *or* egal was du auch sonst machst; **for ~ reasons** aus welchen Gründen auch immer

b *(with neg)* überhaupt, absolut; **nothing ~** überhaupt *or* absolut gar nichts; **it's of no use ~** es hat überhaupt *or* absolut keinen Zweck

c *(interrog)* **~ good can come of it?** was kann daraus nur Gutes werden?; **~ reason can he have?** was für einen Grund kann er nur *or* bloß *or* wohl haben?; **~ else will he do?** was wird er nur *or* bloß *or* wohl noch alles machen?

whatnot ['wɒtnɒt] **N** *(inf)* **a** **and ~** *(inf)* und was sonst noch (alles), und was weiß ich **b** *(= thingummyjig)* Dingsbums *nt (inf)*, Dingsda *nt (inf)*

what's [wɒts] *contr of* **what is, what has**

whatshername ['wɒtsənem] **N** *(inf)* Soundso *f*

whatshisname ['wɒtsɪznem] **N** *(inf)* Soundso *m*

whatsit ['wɒtsɪt] **N** *(inf)* Dingsbums *nt (inf)*, Dingsda *nt (inf)*, Dingens *nt (dial inf)*

whatsitsname ['wɒtsɪtsnem] **N** *(inf)* Soundso *nt*

whatsoever [͵wɒtsəʊ'evəʳ], **whatsoe'er** [͵wɒtsəʊ'ɛəʳ] *(poet)* **PRON, ADJ** = **whatever PRON a ADJ a, b**

wheat [wiːt] **N** Weizen *m*; **to separate the ~ from the chaff** *(fig)* die Spreu vom Weizen trennen

wheaten ['wiːtn] **ADJ** Weizen-; **~ bread** Weizenbrot *nt*

wheat germ **N** Weizenkeim *m*

wheedle ['wiːdl] **VT** **to ~ sb into doing sth** jdn überreden *or* herumkriegen *(inf)*, etw zu tun; **to ~ sth out of sb** jdm etw abschmeicheln

wheedler **N** Schmeichler(in) *m(f)*

wheedling ['wiːdlɪŋ] **ADJ** *tone, voice* schmeichelnd, schmeichlerisch **N** Schmeicheln *nt*

wheel [wiːl] **N** **a** Rad *nt*; *(= steering wheel)* Lenkrad *nt*; *(Naut)* Steuer(rad) *nt*; *(= roulette wheel)* Drehscheibe *f*; *(= paddle wheel)* Schaufelrad *nt*; *(= potter's wheel)* (Töpfer)scheibe *f*; **at the ~** *(lit)* am Steuer; *(fig also)* am Ruder; **~ (of fortune)** Glücksrad *nt*; **the ~s of progress** der Fortschritt; *(in history)* die Weiterentwicklung; **the ~s of government/justice** die Mühlen der Regierung/der Gerechtigkeit; **~s within ~s** gewisse Verbindungen *or* Beziehungen

b *(Mil)* Schwenkung *f*; **a ~ to the right, a right ~** eine Schwenkung nach rechts, eine Rechtsschwenkung

c **wheels** **PL** *(inf: = car)* fahrbare(r) Untersatz *(hum inf)*; **do you have ~s?** bist du motorisiert? *(inf)*

VT **a** *(= push) bicycle, pram, child* schieben; *(= pull)* ziehen; *(invalid) wheelchair* fahren; **the cripple ~ed himself into the room/along** der Krüppel fuhr mit seinem Rollstuhl ins Zimmer/fuhr in seinem Rollstuhl

b *(= cause to turn)* drehen

VI *(= turn)* drehen; *(birds, planes)* kreisen; *(Mil)* schwenken; **to ~ left** nach links schwenken; **left ~!** links schwenkt!

▶ **wheel (a)round** **VI** sich (rasch) umdrehen; *(troops)* (ab)schwenken

▶ **wheel in** **VT** *sep* **a** *trolley, invalid* hereinrollen **b** *(inf: = bring into room)* vorführen *(inf)*

▶ **wheel out** **VT SEP** **a** *trolley, invalid* hinausrollen, hinausschieben **b** *(fig)* hervorkramen

wheel: **wheelbarrow** **N** Schubkarre *f*, Schubkarren *m*; **wheelbarrow race** **N** Schubkarrenrennen *nt*; **wheelbase** **N** Rad(ab)stand *m*; **wheel brace** **N** Kreuzschlüssel *m*; **wheel button** **N** *(of computer mouse)* Radtaste *f*; **wheelchair** **N** Rollstuhl *m*; **he spent six months in a ~** er saß sechs Monate im Rollstuhl; **wheelchair-bound** **ADJ** an den Rollstuhl gefesselt *or* gebunden; **wheelchair user** **N** Rollstuhlfahrer(in) *m(f)*; **wheel clamp** **N** *(Brit)* (Park)kralle *f* **VT** krallen

wheeled [wiːld] **ADJ** *traffic, transport* auf Rädern; *vehicle* mit Rädern

-wheeled **ADJ** *suf* -räd(e)rig; **four-wheeled** vierräd(e)rig

wheeler-dealer ['wiːlə'diːləʳ] **N** *(inf)* Schlitzohr *nt (inf)*, gerissener Typ *(inf)*; *(in finance also)* Geschäftemacher(in) *m(f)*

wheelhouse ['wiːlhaʊs] **N** Ruderhaus *nt*

wheelie ['wiːlɪ] **N** *(inf)* **to do a ~** nur auf dem Hinterrad fahren

wheelie bin ['wiːlɪ͵bɪn] **N** *(Brit inf)* Mülltonne *f* auf Rollen

wheeling and dealing ['wiːlɪŋən'diːlɪŋ] **N** Machenschaften *pl*, Gemauschel *nt (inf)*; *(in business)* Geschäftemacherei *f*

wheelwork ['wiːlwɜːk] **N** *(Tech)* Räderwerk *nt*

wheelwright ['wiːlraɪt] **N** Stellmacher(in) *m(f)*

wheeze [wiːz] **N** **a** *(of person)* pfeifender Atem *no pl*; *(of machine)* Fauchen *nt no pl* **b** *(dated inf)* Jokus *m (dated)*, Scherz *m*; **to think up a ~** sich *(dat)* etwas einfallen lassen **VT** keuchen; **to ~ out a tune** eine Melodie herauspressen **VI** pfeifend atmen; *(machines, asthmatic)* keuchen; **if he smokes too much he starts to ~** wenn er zu stark raucht, bekommt er einen pfeifenden Atem

wheezily ['wiːzɪlɪ] **ADV** pfeifend, keuchend

wheeziness ['wiːzɪnɪs] **N** Keuchen *nt*; *(of breath)* Pfeifen *nt*

wheezy ['wiːzɪ] **ADJ** (+er) *old man* mit pfeifendem Atem; *breath* pfeifend; *voice, cough* keuchend; *car* keuchend, schnaufend; **to have a ~ chest** keuchend atmen

whelk [welk] **N** Wellhornschnecke *f*

whelp [welp] **N** Welpe *m*; *(pej: = boy)* Lauser *m (inf)*, Lausbub *m (inf)* **VI** werfen, jungen

when [wen] **ADV** **a** *(= at what time)* wann; **since ~ have you been here?** seit wann sind Sie hier?; **... since ~ he has been here** ... und seitdem ist er hier; **say ~!** *(inf)* sag *or* schrei *(inf)* halt!

b *(rel)* **on the day ~** an dem Tag, an dem *or* als *or* da *(liter)* *or* wo *(inf)*; **at the time ~** zu der Zeit, zu der *or* als *or* da *(liter)* *or* wo *(inf)*; **he wrote last week, up till ~ I had heard nothing from him** er schrieb letzte Woche und bis dahin hatte ich nichts von ihm gehört; **in 1960, up till ~ he ...** im Jahre 1960, bis zu welchem Zeitpunkt er ...; **during the time ~ he was in Germany** während der Zeit, als *or* wo *or* die *(inf)* er in Deutschland war

CONJ **a** wenn; *(with past reference)* als; **you can go ~ I have finished** du kannst gehen, sobald *or* wenn ich fertig bin; **he did it ~ young** er tat es in seiner Jugend

b *(+gerund)* beim; *(= at or during which time)* wobei; **~ operating the machine** beim Benutzen *or* bei Benutzung der Maschine; **be careful ~ crossing the road** seien Sie beim Überqueren der Straße vorsichtig, seien Sie vorsichtig, wenn Sie über die Straße gehen; **the PM is coming here in May, ~ he will ...** der Premier kommt im Mai hierher und wird dann ...

c *(= although, whereas)* wo ... doch; **why do you do it that way ~ it would be much easier like this?** warum machst du es denn auf die Art, wo es doch so viel einfacher wäre?

whence [wens] **ADV** **a** *(old, form)* woher, von wannen *(old, liter)* **b** *(form)* **~ I conclude ...** woraus ich schließe, ...

whenever [wen'evəʳ] **ADV** **a** *(= each time)* jedes Mal wenn **b** *(= at whatever time)* wann (auch) immer, ganz egal *or* gleich *or* einerlei wann; *(= as soon as)* sobald; **I'll visit you ~ you like** ich werde dich besuchen, wann immer du willst; **~ you like!** wann du willst!; **we'll leave ~ he's ready** wir brechen auf, sobald er fertig ist **c** *(emph)* **~ can he have done it?** wann kann er das nur *or* wohl getan haben?; **~ do I have the time for such things?** wann habe ich schon *or* je Zeit für so was?; **tomorrow, or ~** *(inf)* morgen, oder wann auch immer

where [wɛəʳ] **ADV** wo; **~ (to)** wohin, wo ... hin; **~ ... from** woher, wo ... her; **~ are you going (to)?** wohin gehst du?, wo gehst du hin?; **~ to, sir?** wohin (wollen Sie) bitte?; **~ are you from?** woher kommen Sie?, wo kommen Sie her?; **from ~ I'm sitting I can see the church** von mei-

nem Platz aus kann ich die Kirche sehen; **~ should we be if …?** was wäre nur, wenn …?
CONJ wo; *(= in the place where)* da, wo …, an der Stelle, wo …; **go ~ you like** geh, wohin du willst, geh hin, wo du willst; **the bag is ~ you left it** die Tasche ist an der Stelle *or* da, wo du sie liegen gelassen hast; **this is ~ we got out** hier sind wir ausgestiegen; **that's ~ I used to live** hier *or* da habe ich (früher) gewohnt; **that's ~ we differ** in diesem Punkt haben wir unterschiedliche Ansichten; **we carried on from ~ we left off** wir haben da weitergemacht, wo wir vorher aufgehört haben; **I've read up to ~ the king …** ich habe bis dahin *or* bis an die Stelle gelesen, wo der König …; **this is ~ we got to** soweit *or* bis hierhin *or* bis dahin sind wir gekommen; **we succeeded ~ we expected to fail** wir hatten da Erfolg, wo wir ihn nicht erwartet hatten; **you can trust him ~ money is concerned** in Geldsachen können Sie ihm trauen, Sie können ihm trauen, wo es ums Geld geht; **that's ~ da; that's ~ his strong point is** da liegt seine Stärke

whereabouts [ˌweərəˈbaʊts] ADV wo, in welcher Gegend; **I wonder ~ Martin put it** ich frage mich, wohin Martin es wohl gelegt hat [ˈweərəbaʊts] N *sing or pl* Verbleib *m*; *(of people also)* Aufenthaltsort *m*

whereafter [ˌweərˈɑːftəʳ] CONJ *(form)* woraufhin

whereas [weərˈæz] ✪ 5.1, 26.3 CONJ **a** *(= whilst)* während; *(= while on the other hand)* wohingegen **b** *(esp Jur: = considering that)* da, in Anbetracht der Tatsache, dass …

whereat [weərˈæt] ADV *(old)* wobei

whereby [weəˈbaɪ] ADV *(form)* **the sign ~ you will recognize him** das Zeichen, an dem *or* woran Sie ihn erkennen; **the rule ~ it is not allowed** die Vorschrift, wonach es verboten ist; **a plan ~ the country can be saved** ein Plan, durch den *or* wodurch das Land gerettet werden kann

where'er [weərˈeəʳ] CONJ, ADV *(poet) contr of* **wherever**

wherefore [ˈweəfɔːʳ] ADV *(obs)* warum, weswegen CONJ *(obs)* weswegen N → **why N**

wherein [weərˈɪn] ADV *(form)* worin

whereof [weərˈɒv] ADV *(obs) (= about which)* worüber; *(= out of which)* woraus; *(Jur)* dessen; **in witness ~ …** zu Urkund *or* Zeugnis dessen … *(old)*

whereon [weərˈɒn] ADV *(obs)* worauf; *(= whereupon)* woraufhin

wheresoever [ˌweəsəʊˈevəʳ] ADV *(obs)*, **where-soe'er** [ˌweəsəʊˈeəʳ] ADV *(obs, poet)* = **wherever**

wherever [weərˈevəʳ] CONJ **a** *(= no matter where)* egal *or* einerlei wo, wo (auch) immer; **~ it came from** egal *or* einerlei *or* ganz gleich, woher es kommt, woher es auch kommt
b *(= anywhere, in or to whatever place)* wohin; **we'll go ~ you like** wir gehen, wohin Sie wollen; **he comes from Bishopbriggs, ~ that is** *or* **may be** er kommt aus Bishopbriggs, wo auch immer das sein mag
c *(= everywhere)* überall wo; **~ you see this sign** überall, wo Sie dieses Zeichen sehen
ADV wo nur, wo bloß; **~ have I seen that before?** wo habe ich das nur *or* bloß schon gesehen?; **~ did you get that hat?** wo haben Sie nur *or* bloß diesen Hut her?; **in London or Liverpool or ~** in London oder Liverpool oder sonstwo

wherewith [weəˈwɪθ] ADV *(obs)* womit, mit dem/der

wherewithal [ˈweəwɪðɔːl] N nötiges Kleingeld; *(= implements)* Utensilien *pl*

wherry [ˈwerɪ] N *(= light rowing boat)* Ruderkahn *m*; *(Brit: = barge)* (Fluss)kahn *m*; *(US: = scull)* Einer *m*, Skiff *nt*

whet [wet] VT *knife, scythe* wetzen; *axe* schleifen, schärfen; *appetite, curiosity* anregen

whether [ˈweðəʳ] ✪ 5.4, 6.3 CONJ ob; *(= no matter whether)* egal *or* ganz gleich *or* einerlei, ob; **I am not certain ~ they're coming or not** *or* **~ or not they're coming** ich bin nicht sicher, ob sie kommen oder nicht; **~ they come or not, we'll go ahead** egal *or* ganz gleich *or* einerlei, ob sie kommen oder nicht (kommen), wir fangen (schon mal) an; **he's not sure ~ to go or stay** er weiß nicht, ob er gehen oder bleiben soll

whetstone [ˈwetstəʊn] N Wetzstein *m*

whew [hwjuː] INTERJ puh, uff

whey [weɪ] N Molke *f*

wheyfaced [ˌweɪˈfeɪst] ADJ *(liter)* bleichgesichtig *(geh)*

which [wɪtʃ] ADJ **a** *(interrog)* welche(r, s); **~ one?** welche(r, s)?; *(of people also)* wer?; **I can't tell ~ key is ~** ich kann die Schlüssel nicht auseinanderhalten
b *(rel)* welche(r, s); **… by ~ time I was asleep** … und zu dieser Zeit schlief ich (bereits); **look at it ~ way you will …** man kann es betrachten *or* sehen, wie man will …; **… he said, ~ remark made me very angry** … sagte er, was mich sehr ärgerte
PRON **a** *(interrog)* welche(r, s); **~ of the children/books** welches Kind/Buch; **~ is ~?** *(of people)* wer ist wer?, welche(r) ist welche(r)?; *(of things)* welche(r, s) ist welche(r, s)?, welche(r, s) ist der/die/das eine und welche(r, s) der/die/das andere?; **~ is for ~?** was ist wofür?
b *(rel) (with n antecedent)* der/die/das, welche(r, s) *(geh)*; *(with clause antecedent)* was; **the bear ~ I saw** der Bär, den ich sah; **at ~ he remarked …** woraufhin er bemerkte, …; **it rained hard, ~ upset her plans** es regnete stark, was ihre Pläne durcheinanderbrachte; **~ reminds me …** dabei fällt mir ein, …; **from ~ we deduce that …** woraus wir ableiten, dass …; **after ~ we went to bed** worauf *or* wonach wir zu Bett gingen; **the day before/after ~ he left her** an dem Tag, bevor er sie verließ/nachdem er sie verlassen hatte; **the shelf on ~ I put it** das Brett, auf das *or* worauf ich es gelegt habe

whichever [wɪtʃˈevəʳ] ADJ welche(r, s) auch immer; *(= no matter which)* ganz gleich *or* egal *or* einerlei welche(r, s) PRON welche(r, s) auch immer; **~ (of you) has the most money** wer immer (von euch) das meiste Geld hat

whichsoever [ˌwɪtʃsəʊˈevəʳ] ADJ, PRON *(form)* = **whichever**

whiff [wɪf] N **a** *(= puff)* Zug *m*; *(= wisp)* kleine Fahne, Wolke *f*; *(= smell)* Hauch *m*; *(pleasant)* Duft *m*, Hauch *m*; *(fig: = trace)* Spur *f*; *(of spring)* Hauch *m*, Ahnung *f*; **to catch a ~ of sth** den Geruch von etw wahrnehmen **b** *(= small cigar)* kleiner Zigarillo

whiffle [ˈwɪfl] VI *(wind)* böig wehen; *(flame)* flackern; *(flag etc)* flattern; *(fig: = be unsteady)* schwanken, flatterhaft sein

whiffy [ˈwɪfɪ] ADJ *(+er) (inf)* **to be ~** streng riechen; **it's a bit ~ here** hier müffelt es etwas *(inf)*

Whig [wɪg] *(Brit Hist)* N *frühere Bezeichnung für ein Mitglied der liberalen Partei*, Whig *m* ADJ *attr* Whig-; **~ government** Whig-Regierung *f*

while [waɪl] ✪ 26.1, 26.3 N **a** Weile *f*, Weilchen *nt (inf)*; **for a ~** (für) eine Weile, eine Zeit lang; *(= a short moment)* (für) einen Augenblick *or* Moment; **a good** *or* **long ~** eine ganze *or* lange Weile, eine ganze Zeit lang; **for/after quite a ~** ziemlich *or* recht lange, (für) eine geraume/nach einer geraumen Weile *(geh)*; **a little** *or* **short ~** ein Weilchen *(inf)*, kurze Zeit; **it'll be ready in a short ~** es wird bald fertig sein; **a little ~ ago** vor Kurzem; **a long ~ ago** vor einer ganzen Weile, vor längerer *or* langer Zeit; **some ~ ago** vor einiger Zeit; **all the ~** die ganze Zeit (über)
b the ~ *(liter)* derweil, unterdessen
c to be worth (one's) ~ to … sich (für jdn) lohnen, zu …; **we'll make it worth your ~** es soll ihr Schaden nicht sein
CONJ **a** während; *(= as long as)* solange; **she fell asleep ~ reading** sie schlief beim Lesen ein; **he became famous ~ still young** er wurde berühmt, als er noch jung war; **you must not drink ~ on duty** Sie dürfen im Dienst nicht trinken
b *(= although)* **~ one must admit there are difficulties …** man muss zwar zugeben, dass es Schwierigkeiten gibt, trotzdem …; **~ the text is not absolutely perfect, nevertheless …** obwohl (zwar) der Text nicht einwandfrei ist, … trotzdem; **it is difficult to be fair ~ at the same time being honest** es ist schwierig, fair und gleichzeitig auch gerecht zu sein
c *(= whereas)* während

▶ **while away** VT *sep time* sich *(dat)* vertreiben

whilst [waɪlst] CONJ = **while CONJ**

whim [wɪm] N Laune *f*; **her every ~** jede ihrer Launen; **at** *or* **on ~, at** *or* **on a ~** aus Jux und Tollerei *(inf)*; **as the ~ takes me** *etc* ganz nach Lust und Laune

whimper [ˈwɪmpəʳ] N *(of dog)* Winseln *nt no pl*; *(of person)* Wimmern *nt no pl*; **a ~ of pain** ein schmerzliches Wimmern; **without a ~** ohne einen (Klage)laut VI *(dog)* winseln; *(person)* wimmern VT *person* wimmern

whimsical [ˈwɪmzɪkəl] ADJ wunderlich; *look, remark* neckisch; *smile* verschmitzt; *idea, tale* schnurrig; *decision* seltsam, spinnig *(inf)*; *notion* grillenhaft; *ornament* verrückt; **to be in a ~ mood** in einer neckischen Laune sein

whimsicality [ˌwɪmzɪˈkælɪtɪ] N Wunderlichkeit *f*; *(of behaviour)* Launenhaftigkeit *f*, Grillenhaftigkeit *f*; *(of decision)* Seltsamkeit *f*; *(of architecture)* Verrücktheit *f*, Manierismus *m*

whimsically [ˈwɪmzɪkəlɪ] ADV *look, say* neckisch; *smile* verschmitzt

whimsy [ˈwɪmzɪ] N **a** *(= caprice, fancy)* Spleen *m*, Grille *f (dated)* **b** = **whimsicality**

whin [wɪn] N *(esp Brit)* Ginster *m*

whine [waɪn] N *(of dog)* Jaulen *nt no pl*, Heulen *nt no pl*; *(= complaining cry)* Jammern *nt no pl*, Gejammer *nt no pl*; *(of child)* Quengelei *f no pl*; *(of siren, jet engine)* Heulen *nt no pl*; *(of bullet)* Pfeifen *nt no pl* VI *(dog)* jaulen; *(person: = speak, complain)* jammern, klagen; *(child)* quengeln; *(siren, jet engine)* heulen; *(bullet)* pfeifen; **the dog was whining to be let in** der Hund jaulte, um hereingelassen zu werden; **don't come whining to me about it** du brauchst nicht anzukommen und mir was vorzujammern

whiner [ˈwaɪnəʳ] N *(= complainer)* Jammerer *m*

whinge [wɪndʒ] *(Brit inf)* VI *(= complain)* jammern, meckern *(inf)*; *(baby)* plärren; **~ing Pom** *(Austral)* ewig meckernder Engländer *(inf)*, ewig meckernde Engländerin *(inf)* N **to have a ~** meckern *(inf)*, jammern

whingey [ˈwɪndʒɪ] ADJ *(Brit inf)* **to be ~** dauernd jammern *or* meckern *(inf)*; *(baby)* dauernd plärren; **the kid's starting to get ~** das Kind fängt an zu plärren; **don't be so ~** mecker doch nicht so! *(inf)*

whining [ˈwaɪnɪŋ] N *(of dog)* Gejaule *nt*; *(= complaining)* Gejammer *nt* ADJ **a** *(= complaining) voice* weinerlich; *person* jammernd, meckernd *(inf)* **b** *sound* wimmernd; *(of machine)* schrillend; *dog* jaulend

whinny [ˈwɪnɪ] N Wiehern *nt no pl*, Gewieher *nt no pl* VI wiehern

whip [wɪp] N **a** Peitsche *f*; *(= riding whip)* Reitgerte *f*; **to give sb a fair crack of the ~** *(inf)* jdm eine faire Chance geben
b *(Parl) (= person)* Fraktions- *or* Geschäftsführer(in) *m(f)*; *(Brit: = call)* Anordnung *f* des Fraktionsführers; **three-line ~** *(Brit)* Fraktionszwang *m*; **they have put a three-line ~ on the vote** *(Brit)* bei der Abstimmung besteht Fraktionszwang
c *(Cook)* Creme *f*, Speise *f*
VT **a** *(with whip) people* auspeitschen; *horse* peitschen; *(with stick etc)* schlagen; **the conductor ~ped the orchestra into a frenzy** der Dirigent brachte das Orchester in Ekstase; **to ~ sb/sth into shape** *(fig)* jdn/etw zurechtschleifen
b *(Cook) cream, eggs* schlagen
c *(= bind) seam* umnähen; *stick, rope* umwickeln
d *(inf: = defeat)* vernichtend schlagen

c *(fig: = move quickly)* **he ~ped the book off the desk** er schnappte sich *(dat)* das Buch vom Schreibtisch; **he ~ped his hand out of the way** er zog blitzschnell seine Hand weg; **the thief ~ped the jewel into his pocket** der Dieb ließ den Edelstein schnell in seiner Tasche verschwinden; **to ~ sb into hospital** jdn in Windeseile ins Krankenhaus bringen; *(doctor)* jdn schnell ins Krankenhaus einweisen
f *(inf: = steal)* mitgehen lassen *(inf)*
VI a branches ~ped against the window Äste schlugen gegen das Fenster
b *(= move quickly) (person)* schnell (mal) laufen; **the car ~ped past** das Auto brauste *or* sauste *or* fegte *(inf)* vorbei

▶ **whip away** VT *sep* wegreißen, wegziehen *(from sb* jdm)

▶ **whip back** VI **a** *(spring, plank)* zurückschnellen, zurückfedern **b** *(inf: = go back quickly)* schnell (mal) zurücklaufen

▶ **whip off** VT *sep clothes* herunterreißen, vom Leib reißen; *tablecloth* wegziehen; **the wind whipped my hat off** der Wind riss mir den Hut vom Kopf; **a car whipped him off to the airport** ein Auto brachte ihn in Windeseile zum Flugplatz

▶ **whip on** VT *sep* **a** *(= urge on) horse* anpeitschen, antreiben; *(fig)* antreiben **b** *(= put on quickly) clothes* sich *(dat)* überwerfen; *lid* schnell drauftun

▶ **whip out** VT *sep gun, pencil, camera etc* zücken; **he whipped a gun/pencil** *etc* **out of his pocket** er zog rasch eine Pistole/einen Bleistift *etc* aus der Tasche; **they whipped out his tonsils** *(inf)* sie haben ihm schnell die Mandeln entfernt VI *(inf: = go out quickly)* schnell (mal) rausgehen *(inf)*

▶ **whip round** VI *(esp Brit)* **a** *(= move quickly)* **I'll just whip round to the shops** ich geh nur mal schnell einkaufen *(inf)*; **he whipped round when he heard …** er fuhr herum, als er hörte …; **the car whipped round the corner** das Auto brauste *or* sauste *or* fegte *(inf)* um die Ecke **b** *(= collect money)* zusammenlegen, den Hut herumgehen lassen

▶ **whip up** VT *sep* **a** *(= pick up)* schnappen **b** *(= set in motion) horses* antreiben; *(Cook) cream* schlagen; *mixture* verrühren; *eggs* verquirlen; *(inf: = prepare quickly) meal* hinzaubern; *(fig: = stir up) interest, feeling* anheizen, entfachen; *support* finden, auftreiben *(inf)*; *audience, crowd* mitreißen; **I'll just whip up something to eat** *(inf)* ich mach nur schnell was zu essen; **the sea, whipped up by the wind** das Meer, vom Wind aufgepeitscht

whip: **whipcord** N *(= rope)* Peitschenschnur *f*; *(= fabric)* Whipkord *m*; **whip hand** N **to have the ~ (over sb)** (über jdn) die Oberhand haben; **whiplash** N (Peitschen)riemen *m*; *(Med: also* **whiplash injury**) Peitschenschlagverletzung *f*

whipped cream [wɪpt'kriːm] N Schlagsahne *f*, Schlagrahm *m*

whipper-in [ˌwɪpər'ɪn] N Pikör(in) *m(f)*, Vorreiter(in) *m(f) (bei der Parforcejagd)*

whippersnapper ['wɪpəˌsnæpəʳ] N *(dated inf)* junger Spund

whippet ['wɪpɪt] N Whippet *m*

whipping ['wɪpɪŋ] N *(= beating)* Tracht *f* Prügel; *(inf: = defeat)* Niederlage *f*; *(fig: in debate etc)* Pleite *f*; **to give sb a ~** *(lit)* jdm eine Tracht Prügel versetzen; *(with whip)* jdn auspeitschen; *(fig inf)* jdn in die Pfanne hauen *(inf)*; **the government got a ~** die Regierung erlebte eine Pleite *(inf)*

whipping: **whipping boy** N Prügelknabe *m*; **to use sb as a ~** jdn zum Prügelknaben machen; **whipping cream** N Schlagsahne *f*; **whipping top** N Kreisel *m*

whippoorwill ['wɪpˌpʊəˌwɪl] N *(Zool)* schreiender Ziegenmelker

whippy ['wɪpɪ] ADJ *cane, fishing rod* biegsam, elastisch

whip-round ['wɪpraʊnd] N *(esp Brit inf)* **to have a ~** den Hut herumgehen lassen

whir [wɜːʳ] N, VI = **whirr**

whirl [wɜːl] N **a** *(= spin)* Wirbeln *nt no pl*; *(of dust, water etc, also fig)* Wirbel *m*; *(of cream etc)* Tupfer *m*; **to give sth a ~** *(lit)* etw herumwirbeln; *(fig inf: = try out)* etw ausprobieren; **the social ~** der Trubel des gesellschaftlichen Lebens; **my head is in a ~** mir schwirrt der Kopf
VT a *(= make turn)* wirbeln; **to ~ sb/sth round** jdn/etw herumwirbeln; **he ~ed his hat round his head** er schwenkte seinen Hut; **he ~ed the water around with his stick** er rührte mit seinem Stock im Wasser herum
b *(transport)* eilends wegbringen; *(person)* mit sich nehmen, entführen *(inf)*
VI *(= spin)* wirbeln; *(water)* strudeln; **to ~ (a)round** herumwirbeln; *(water)* strudeln; *(person: = turn round quickly)* herumfahren; **my head is ~ing** mir schwirrt der Kopf; **after a few drinks the room started ~ing** nach ein paar Gläsern fing der Raum an, sich zu drehen; **they/the countryside ~ed past us** sie wirbelten/die Landschaft flog an uns vorbei

whirligig ['wɜːlɪgɪg] N *(= top)* Kreisel *m*; *(= roundabout)* Karussell *nt*, Ringelspiel *nt*; *(fig)* (ewiges) Wechselspiel *nt*

whirlpool ['wɜːlpuːl] N **a** *(in water)* Strudel *m*; *(fig: = turbulence also)* Durcheinander *nt* **b** *(pool with water jets)* Whirlpool *m*

whirlwind ['wɜːlwɪnd] N Wirbelwind *m*; *(fig)* Trubel *m*, Wirbel *m*; **like a ~** wie der Wirbelwind; **to reap the ~** *(prov)* Sturm ernten; **he did some very stupid things, and now he's reaping the ~** er hat einige sehr große Dummheiten gemacht und jetzt muss er dafür büßen; **a ~ romance** eine stürmische Romanze

whirlybird ['wɜːlɪˌbɜːd] N *(esp US inf)* Hubschrauber *m*

whirr, whir [wɜːʳ] N *(of wings)* Schwirren *nt*; *(of wheels, camera, machine, quiet)* Surren *nt*; *(louder)* Brummen *nt*, Dröhnen *nt* VI *(wings)* schwirren; *(wheels, camera, machine, quietly)* surren; *(louder)* brummen, dröhnen

whish [wɪʃ] N Schwirren *nt*, Sausen *nt*, Zischen *nt*; *(of silk etc)* Rascheln *nt* VI schwirren, sausen, zischen; *(silk etc)* rascheln

whisk [wɪsk] N **a** *(= fly whisk)* Wedel *m*; *(Cook)* Schneebesen *m*; *(electric)* Rührbesen *m*, Rührstab *m*, Rührgerät *nt*; **give the eggs a good ~** schlagen Sie die Eier gut durch **b** *(= movement)* Wischen *nt*; *(of skirts)* Schwingen *nt*; **with a ~ of its tail** mit einem Schwanzschlag **VT a** *(Cook)* schlagen; *eggs* verquirlen; **to ~ the eggs into the mixture** die Eier unter die Masse einrühren **b the horse ~ed its tail** das Pferd schlug mit dem Schwanz **c** *(= move quickly)* **she ~ed the book out of my hand** sie riss mir das Buch aus der Hand VI *(= move quickly)* fegen *(inf)*, stieben

▶ **whisk away** VT *sep* **a** *fly, wasp etc* wegscheuchen **b** *(= take away suddenly)* **the magician whisked away the tablecloth** der Zauberer zog das Tischtuch schnell weg; **her mother whisked the bottle away from her just in time** ihre Mutter schnappte *(inf) or* zog ihr die Flasche gerade noch rechtzeitig weg; **he whisked her away to the Bahamas** er entführte sie auf die Bahamas; **a big black car turned up and whisked him away** ein großes schwarzes Auto erschien und sauste *or* brauste mit ihm davon

▶ **whisk off** VT *sep* = **whisk away b**

▶ **whisk up** VT *sep eggs, mixture etc* schaumig schlagen

whisker ['wɪskəʳ] N Schnurrhaar *nt*; *(of person)* Barthaar *nt*; **~s** *(= moustache)* Schnurrbart *m*; *(= side whiskers)* Backenbart *m*; *(Zool)* Schnurrbart *m*; **to win sth by a ~** etw fast gewinnen; **to miss sth by a ~** etw um Haaresbreite verpassen

whiskered ['wɪskəd] ADJ schnurrbärtig

whiskery ['wɪskərɪ] ADJ *man* schnurrbärtig; *face* bärtig, stoppelig; *kiss* kratzend

whisky, *(US, Ir)* **whiskey** ['wɪskɪ] N Whisky *m*; **~ and soda** Whisky (mit) Soda *m*; **two whiskies, please** zwei Whisky, bitte

whisper ['wɪspəʳ] N **a** *(= low tone)* Geflüster *nt no pl*, Flüstern *nt no pl*; *(of wind, leaves)* Wispern *nt no pl*; *(mysterious)* Raunen *nt no pl*; **to speak in a ~** im Flüsterton sprechen; **to say sth in a ~** etw im Flüsterton sagen; **they were talking in ~s** sie sprachen flüsternd *or* im Flüsterton
b *(= rumour)* Gerücht *nt*; **there are ~s (going round) that …** es geht das Gerücht *or* es gehen Gerüchte um, dass …; **have you heard any ~s about who might be promoted?** haben Sie irgendwelche Andeutungen gehört *or* haben Sie etwas läuten hören *(inf)*, wer befördert werden soll?
VT a *(= say quietly)* flüstern, wispern; **to ~ sth to sb** jdm etw zuflüstern *or* zuwispern; *(secretively)* jdm etw zuraunen; **to ~ a word in(to) sb's ear** *(fig)* jdm einen leisen Tipp geben, jdm etw andeuten
b *(= rumour)* **it's (being) ~ed that …** es geht das Gerücht *or* es gehen Gerüchte um, dass …, man munkelt *or* es wird gemunkelt, dass …
VI flüstern, wispern *(also fig)*; *(secretively)* raunen; *(schoolchildren)* tuscheln; *(poet: wind)* säuseln; **to ~ to sb** jdm zuflüstern/zuwispern/zuraunen, mit jdm tuscheln; **just ~ to me** sags mir flüsternd; **stop ~ing!** hör/hört auf zu flüstern!; *(schoolchildren)* hört auf zu tuscheln, lasst das Getuschel!

whispering ['wɪspərɪŋ] N Geflüster *nt no pl*, Flüstern *nt no pl*; *(poet: of wind)* Säuseln *nt no pl*; *(of schoolchildren)* Tuscheln *nt no pl*, Getuschel *nt no pl*; *(fig)* Gemunkel *nt no pl*, Getuschel *nt no pl*

whispering: **whispering campaign** N Verleumdungskampagne *f*; **whispering gallery** N Flüstergewölbe *nt or* -galerie *f*

whist [wɪst] N Whist *nt*

whist drive N Whistrunde *f* mit wechselnden Parteien

whistle ['wɪsl] N **a** *(= sound)* Pfiff *m*; *(of wind)* Pfeifen *nt*; *(of kettle)* Pfeifton *m*; **the ~ of the escaping steam** das Pfeifen des ausströmenden Dampfes; **to give a ~** einen Pfiff ausstoßen
b *(= instrument)* Pfeife *f*; **to blow a/one's ~** pfeifen; **to blow the ~ on sb/sth** *(fig inf)* über jdn/etw auspacken *(inf)*; **to be as clean as a ~** *(= clean)* blitzsauber sein; *(fig also)* eine schneeweiße Weste haben → **wet VT**
VT pfeifen; **to ~ (to) sb to stop** jdn durch einen Pfiff stoppen; **to ~ sb back/over** *etc* jdn zurück-/herüberpfeifen *etc*
VI pfeifen; **the boys ~d at her** die Jungen pfiffen ihr nach; **the crowd ~d at the referee** die Menge pfiff den Schiedsrichter aus; **he ~d for a taxi** er pfiff ein Taxi heran, er pfiff nach einem Taxi; **the referee ~d for a foul** der Schiedsrichter pfiff ein Foul; **the referee ~d for play to stop** der Schiedsrichter pfiff eine Spielunterbrechung; *(at the end)* der Schiedsrichter pfiff das Spiel ab; **he can ~ for it** *(inf)* da kann er lange warten, da kann er warten, bis er schwarz wird *(inf)*

whistle-blowing ['wɪslˌbləʊɪŋ] N *(fig)* Verrat *m*

whistle-blower ['wɪslbləʊəʳ] N **he was the ~ in this affair** er hat über diese Affäre ausgepackt *(inf)*

whistle stop *(US)* N **a** *(dated: = small town)* Kleinstadt *f*, Nest *nt (pej inf)* **b** *(= stop)* kurzer Aufenthalt an einem kleinen Ort; *(fig)* Stippvisite *f*

whistle-stop ['wɪslˌstɒp] ATTR **~ tour** *(Pol)* Wahlreise *f*; *(fig) Reise mit Kurzaufenthalten an allen Orten* VI auf die Dörfer gehen

whistling ['wɪslɪŋ] N Pfeifen *nt*

whistling kettle ['wɪslɪŋ'ketl] N Pfeifkessel *m*

whit [wɪt] N **not a** *or* **one ~** keine *or* nicht eine Spur; *(of humour)* kein *or* nicht ein Funke(n); *(of truth, common sense)* kein *or* nicht ein Gramm *or* Körnchen; **every ~ as good** genauso gut, (um) keinen Deut schlechter

white [waɪt] ADJ (+er) **a** weiß; *(with fear, anger, exhaustion etc also)* blass, kreidebleich; **to go** *or* **turn ~** *(thing)* weiß werden; *(person also)* bleich *or* blass werden; **as ~ as a sheet** *or* **ghost** leichenblass; **~r than ~** *(lit, fig)* weißer als weiß **b** *(= refined: Cook) flour* Weiß-; *rice* weiß
N **a** *(= colour)* Weiß *nt*; *(= person)* Weiße(r) *mf*; *(of egg)* Eiweiß *nt*, Klar *nt (Aus)*; *(of eye)* Weiße(s) *nt*; **shoot when you see the ~s of their eyes** schießt, wenn ihr das Weiße im Auge des Feinds erkennen könnt; **~s** *(Brit) (household)* Weißwäsche *f*; *(Sport)* weiße Kleidung; **the tennis players were wearing ~s** *(Brit)* die Tennisspieler trugen Weiß; **I've forgotten my ~s** ich habe mein Zeug vergessen
b *(also* **white wine***)* Weißwein *m*

white: white ant N Termite *f*, weiße Ameise; **whitebait** N *pl* **-bait** Breitling *m*; **whitebeam** N Mehlbeere *f*; **white bear** N Eisbär *m*; **white blood cell** N weißes Blutkörperchen; **whiteboard** N Weißwandtafel *f*; *(Comput)* weiße Tafel; **white book** N *(US Pol)* Weißbuch *nt*; **white bread** N Weißbrot *nt*; **whitecap** N Welle *f* mit Schaumkronen; **white Christmas** N **a ~** weiße Weihnacht(en); **white coal** N weiße Kohle; **white coffee** N *(Brit)* Kaffee *m* mit Milch, Milchkaffee *m*; **white-collar** ADJ **~ worker** Schreibtischarbeiter(in) *m(f)*; **~ job** Angestelltenstelle *f*, Schreibtisch- *or* Büroposten *m*; **~ criminal** Wirtschaftskriminelle(r) *mf*; **~ crime** Wirtschaftskriminalität *f*; **a ~ crime** ein Wirtschaftsverbrechen *nt*; **~ union** Angestelltengewerkschaft *f*; **white corpuscle** N weißes Blutkörperchen

whited sepulchre ['waɪtɪd'seplkəʳ] N *(liter)* Pharisäer *m*

white: white dwarf N *(Astron)* weißer Zwerg(-stern); **white elephant** N nutzloser Gegenstand; *(= waste of money)* Fehlinvestition *f*; **white elephant stall** N Stand *m* mit allerlei Krimskrams; **White Ensign** N *Fahne der Royal Navy*; **white feather** N weiße Feder *(Zeichen der Feigheit)*; **to show the ~** den Schwanz einziehen; **whitefish** N Weißfisch *m*; **white flag** N *(Mil, fig)* weiße Fahne; **to raise** *or* **wave the ~** *(lit)* die weiße Fahne schwenken; *(fig)* sich geschlagen geben; **white food** N *(= flour, rice, white sugar etc)* weiße Lebensmittel *pl*, weißes Essen; **white fox** N Polarfuchs *m*; **white frost** N Raureif *m*; **white gold** N Weißgold *nt*; **white goods** PL *(Comm: = electrical appliances)* Haushaltsgeräte *pl (Kühlschrank, Waschmaschine, Herd etc)*; **white-haired** ADJ **a** weißhaarig; *(= blond)* weißblond, semmelblond **b** *(US inf: = favourite)* **the boss's ~ boy** der Liebling des Chefs; **Whitehall** N *(= British government)* Whitehall *no art*; **if ~ decides …** wenn London beschließt …; **white-headed** ADJ **a** = **white-haired b** *gull, duck* weißköpfig; **white heat** N Weißglut *f*; *(fig)* Hitze *f*; *(with enthusiasm)* Feuereifer *m*; **to work at ~** *(under pressure)* fieberhaft arbeiten; **in the ~ of his rage/passion** in seiner besinnungslosen Wut/Leidenschaft; **his rage reached ~** seine Wut erreichte den Siedepunkt; **white hope** N große *or* **einzige Hoffnung**; **white horse** N **a** Schimmel *m* **b** *(= wave)* Welle *f* mit einer Schaumkrone; **now there are ~s** jetzt haben die Wellen Reiter; **white-hot** ADJ weiß glühend; *(fig)* brennend, glühend; **White House** N **the ~** das Weiße Haus; **white knight** N *(St Ex)* weißer Ritter; **white lead** N Bleiweiß *nt*; **white lie** N kleine Unwahrheit, Notlüge *f*; **we all tell a ~ from time to time** wir alle sagen nicht immer ganz die Wahrheit; **white light** N weißes Licht; **white-lipped** ADJ mit bleichen Lippen, angstbleich; **white list** N *(Internet)* White List *f*, *Liste spam- und virenfreier Websites, Absender und Programme*; **whitelist** VT *(Internet) website, address, program* auf die White List setzen; **white magic** N weiße Magie; **white man** N Weiße(r) *m*; **white man's burden** N **the ~** die Bürde des weißen Mannes; **white meat** N helles Fleisch

whiten ['waɪtn] VT weiß machen VI weiß werden

whitener N **a** *(= bleach)* Weißmacher *m* **b** *(also* **coffee whitener***)* Kaffeeweißer *m*

whiteness ['waɪtnɪs] N Weiße *f*; *(of skin)* Helligkeit *f*; *(due to illness etc)* Blässe *f*; **the dazzling ~ of …** das strahlende Weiß des/der …

white night N **a** *(= sleepless night)* schlaflose Nacht **b** *(= bright night)* weiße Nacht, *helle Nacht im Mittsommer*

White Nile N **the ~** der Weiße Nil

whitening ['waɪtnɪŋ] N weiße Farbe, Schlämmkreide *f*

white: white noise N weißes Rauschen; **White-Out®** N *(US: = correction fluid)* Korrekturflüssigkeit *f*, ≈ Tipp-Ex® *nt*; **whiteout** N **a** heftiger Schneesturm; **in ~ conditions** bei starkem Schneegestöber **b** *(= snow blindness)* Whiteout *m*; **white paper** N *(Pol)* Weißbuch *nt* (on zu); **white pepper** N *(Cook)* weißer Pfeffer; **white rhino, white rhinoceros** N weißes Nashorn; **White Russia** N Weißrussland *nt*; **White Russian** N Weißrusse *m*, Weißrussin *f*; **white sale** N weiße Woche, Ausverkauf *m* von Haus- und Tischwäsche; **white sauce** N Mehlsoße *f*, helle Soße; **White Sea** N **the ~** das Weiße Meer; **white settler** N weißer Siedler, weiße Siedlerin; **white shark** N weißer Hai; **white sidewall haircut** N *(inf)* Bürstenschnitt *m (mit seitlich rasierten oder sehr kurzen Haaren)*; **white slave** N weiße Sklavin; **white slaver** N Mädchenhändler(in) *m(f)*; **white slavery, white slave trade** N Mädchenhandel *m*; **white spirit** N *(Brit)* Terpentinersatz *m*; **white stick** N Blindenstock *m*; **white supremacy** N Vorherrschaft *f* der weißen Rasse; **whitethorn** N Weißdorn *m*; **whitethroat** N Grasmücke *f*; **white tie** N *(= tie)* weiße Fliege; *(= evening dress)* Frack *m*; **a ~ occasion/dinner** eine Veranstaltung/ein Essen mit Frackzwang; **white trash** N *(US pej inf)* weißes Pack *(pej inf)*

> **WHITE TRASH**
>
> **White trash** ist ein abfälliger amerikanischer Ausdruck für arme, ungebildete Weiße, vor allem für die in den Südstaaten. Sie werden als die unterste gesellschaftliche Schicht von Weißen angesehen, gelten als dumm, schmutzig und faul und haben einen ebenso schweren Stand wie ihre gleichfalls armen schwarzen, hispanischen oder indianischen Mitbürger. Der Begriff wurde bereits in der Mitte des neunzehnten Jahrhunderts von Schwarzen der Südstaaten verwendet, die damit im Elend lebende Weiße bezeichneten, die sich nichtsdestoweniger den Schwarzen immer noch aufgrund ihrer Hautfarbe überlegen fühlten.

white: whitewall (tyre) N Weißwandreifen *m*; **whitewash** N Tünche *f*; *(fig)* Augenwischerei *f* VT *walls* tünchen; *(fig)* schönfärben, beschönigen; *(inf) person* reinwaschen; *opponent* zu null schlagen; **white water** N Wildwasser *nt*; **white-water rafting** N Rafting *nt*, Wildwasserfahren *nt*; **white wedding** N Hochzeit *f* in Weiß; **white whale** N Weißwal *m*, Beluga *m*; **white wine** N Weißwein *m*; **white witch** N weiße Hexe *(die weiße Magie praktiziert)*; **white woman** N Weiße *f*; **whitewood** ADJ **~ furniture** Möbel *pl* aus hellem Weichholz

whitey ['waɪtɪ] N *(pej inf)* Weiße(r) *mf*

whither ['wɪðəʳ] ADV **a** *(old)* wohin **b** *(journalese)* **~ America/socialism?** Amerika/Sozialismus, wohin? *or* was nun?

whiting[1] ['waɪtɪŋ] N *no pl* = **whitening**

whiting[2] N *pl* - Weißling *m*, Weißfisch *m*

whitish ['waɪtɪʃ] ADJ *colour* weißlich; **~-yellow/ /blue** weißlich-gelb/blau

whitlow ['wɪtləʊ] N Nagelbettentzündung *f*, Umlauf *m*

Whit Monday [ˌwɪt'mʌndɪ] N *(Brit)* Pfingstmontag *m*

Whitsun ['wɪtsən] *(Brit)* N Pfingsten *nt*; *(Eccl also)* Pfingstfest *nt* ATTR Pfingst-; **~ weekend** Pfingstwochenende *nt*

Whit Sunday [ˌwɪt'sʌndɪ] N *(Brit)* Pfingstsonntag *m*

Whitsuntide ['wɪtsəntaɪd] N *(Brit)* Pfingstzeit *f*; **around ~** um Pfingsten (herum)

whittle ['wɪtl] VT schnitzen VI **to ~ (away) at sth** an etw *(dat)* (herum)schnippeln *or* -schnitzen *or* -schneiden

► **whittle away** VT *sep* **a** *bark etc* wegschneiden, wegschnitzen **b** *(= gradually reduce)* allmählich abbauen, nach und nach abbauen; *rights, power etc* allmählich *or* nach und nach beschneiden *or* stutzen; **the benefit/pay increase has been whittled away by inflation** der Gewinn/die Gehaltserhöhung ist durch die Inflation langsam zunichtegemacht worden

► **whittle down** VT *sep* **a** *piece of wood* herunterschneiden; **to whittle down to size** zurechtschneiden, zurechtstutzen **b** *(= reduce)* kürzen, reduzieren, stutzen (*to* auf *+acc*); *gap, difference* verringern

whiz(z) [wɪz] N **a** *(of arrow)* Schwirren *nt*, Sausen *nt* **b** *(inf)* Kanone *f (inf)*; **a computer/ financial ~** ein Computer-/Finanzgenie *nt (inf)* VI *(arrow)* schwirren, sausen

whiz(z) kid N *(inf, in career)* Senkrechtstarter(in) *m(f)*; **financial/publishing ~** Finanz-/Verlagsgenie *nt or* -größe *f*; **a ~ like him will soon find a solution** ein solcher Intelligenzbolzen wird bald auf eine Lösung kommen *(inf)*

whizz [wɪz] N *(sl)* **a** *(Brit Drugs)* Speed *nt* **b to got for** *(Brit) or* **take a ~** *(= urinate)* strullern *(sl)*, pissen gehen *(vulg)*

WHO *abbr of* **World Health Organization** WHO *f*, Weltgesundheitsorganisation *f*

who [huː] PRON **a** *(interrog)* wer; *(acc)* wen; *(dat)* wem; **and ~ should it be but Jeremy?** und wer wars? natürlich Jeremy!; **~ do you think you are?** was glaubst du *or* bildest du dir ein, wer du bist?, für wen hältst du dich eigentlich?; **"Who's Who"** „Wer ist Wer"; **you'll soon find out ~'s ~ in the office** Sie werden bald im Büro alle kennenlernen; **~ are you looking for?** wen suchen Sie?; **~ did you stay with?** bei wem haben Sie gewohnt? **b** *(rel)* der/die/das, welche(r, s); **any man ~ …** jeder (Mensch), der …; **anyone ~ wishes** *or* **those ~ wish to go …** wer gehen will …; **deny it ~ may** *(form)* bestreite das, wer will

whoa [wəʊ] INTERJ brr

who'd [huːd] *contr of* **who had, who would**

whodun(n)it [huː'dʌnɪt] N *(inf)* Krimi *m (inf, bei dem der Täter bis zum Schluss unbekannt ist)*

whoever [huː'evəʳ] PRON wer (auch immer); *(acc)* wen (auch immer); *(dat)* wem (auch immer); *(= no matter who)* einerlei *or* ganz gleich *or* egal *(inf)* wer/wen/wem; **~ told you that?** wer hat dir das denn (bloß) gesagt?

whole [həʊl] ADJ *(= entire, unbroken, undivided)* ganz; *truth* voll; *(Bibl: = well)* heil; **but the ~ purpose was to …** aber der ganze Sinn der Sache *or* aber der Zweck der Übung *(inf)* war, dass …; **three ~ weeks** drei volle *or* ganze Wochen; **the ~ lot** das Ganze; *(of people)* alle, der ganze Verein *(inf)*; **a ~ lot of people** eine ganze Menge Leute; **a ~ lot better** *(inf)* ein ganzes Stück besser *(inf)*, sehr viel besser; **she is a ~ lot of woman** *(esp US inf)* sie ist eine richtige *or* echte Frau; **let's forget the ~ thing** vergessen wir das Ganze; **the figures don't tell the ~ story/the ~ truth** die Zahlen sagen nicht alles/nicht die ganze Wahrheit; **a ~ new wardrobe** eine völlig neue Garderobe; **out of ~ cloth** *(US)* von Anfang bis Ende erdichtet; **not a cup was left ~** nicht eine Tasse blieb ganz *or* heil; **she swallowed it ~** sie schluckte es ganz *or* unzerkaut (hinunter); **a pig roasted ~** ein ganzes Schwein im *or* am Stück gebraten
N Ganze(s) *nt*; **the ~ of the month** der ganze *or* gesamte Monat; **we spent the ~ of the morning at the airport** wir waren den ganzen Mor-

gen (lang) auf dem Flughafen; **the ~ of the time** die ganze Zeit; **the ~ of his savings** seine gesamten *or* sämtlichen Ersparnisse; **the ~ of London** ganz London; **nearly the ~ of our production** fast unsere gesamte Produktion; **as a ~** als Ganzes; **these people, as a ~, are ...** diese Leute sind in ihrer Gesamtheit ...; **on the ~** im Großen und Ganzen, im Ganzen gesehen, alles in allem

whole: **wholefood** N *(also* **wholefoods***)* Vollwertkost *f* ADJ *attr (esp Brit)* Vollwert(-kost)-; **~ diet** Vollwert(kost)diät *f*; **~ shop** Bioladen *m*; **wholehearted** ADJ völlig, uneingeschränkt; **~ congratulations/thanks to X** X *(dat)* gratulieren/danken wir von ganzem Herzen; **to be ~ in one's cooperation** sich rückhaltlos mit einsetzen; **wholeheartedly** ✪ 11.1, 26.3 ADV voll und ganz; **wholeheartedness** N Rückhaltlosigkeit *f*; **whole hog** N **to go the ~** *(inf)* aufs Ganze gehen; **wholemeal** *(Brit)* ADJ Vollkorn-; **~ bread** Vollkornbrot *nt*; **~ pasta** Vollkornnudeln *pl* N feiner Vollkornschrot; **whole milk** N Vollmilch *f*

wholeness [ˈhəʊlnɪs] N Gesamtheit *f*, Ganzheit *f*

whole: **whole note** N *(esp US Mus)* ganze Note; **whole number** N ganze Zahl

wholesale [ˈhəʊlseɪl] N Großhandel *m* ADJ *attr* **a** *(Comm)* Großhandels-; **~ price** Großhandelspreis *m*; **~ dealer** Großhändler(in) *m(f)*, Grossist(in) *m(f)*; **~ purchase** Groß- *or* Engroseinkauf *m* **b** *(fig) (= widespread)* umfassend, massiv; *(= indiscriminate)* wild, generell; **~ redundancies** Massenentlassungen *pl*; **the ~ slaughter of the infected animals** die Abschlachtung aller infizierten Tiere ADV **a** im Großhandel **b** *(fig)* in Bausch und Bogen; *(= in great numbers)* massenweise, massenhaft; *(= without modification)* (so) ohne Weiteres VT *goods* einen Großhandel betreiben mit VI *(item)* einen Großhandelspreis haben (*at* von)

wholesale business N Großhandel *m*

wholesale price index N Großhandelspreisindex *m*

wholesaler [ˈhəʊlseɪləʳ] N Großhändler(in) *m(f)*, Grossist(in) *m(f)*

wholesale trade N Großhandel *m*

wholesaling [ˈhəʊlseɪlɪŋ] N Großhandel *m*

wholesome [ˈhəʊlsəm] ADJ **a** gesund; *food* gesund, bekömmlich **b** *(= moral) entertainment, film* erbaulich; *person* mustergültig

wholesomeness [ˈhəʊlsəmnɪs] N *(of food)* Bekömmlichkeit *f*; *(of appearance)* Gesundheit *f*

whole-wheat [ˈhəʊlwiːt] N Voll(korn)weizen *m*

who'll [huːl] *contr of* **who will, who shall**

wholly [ˈhəʊlɪ] ADV völlig, gänzlich; **the project was ~ successful** das Projekt war gänzlich erfolgreich *or* war ein voller Erfolg; **I'm not ~ convinced that ...** ich bin nicht völlig *or* gänzlich überzeugt, dass ...; **this is ~ but ~ ...** das ist völlig und ganz ...

whom [huːm] PRON **a** *(interrog) (acc)* wen; *(dat)* wem **b** *(rel) (acc)* den/die/das; *(dat)* dem/der/dem; **..., all/both of ~ were drunk** ..., die alle/beide betrunken waren; **none/all of ~** von denen keine(r, s)/alle

whomp [wɒmp] *(US inf)* VT *(= hit)* einschlagen auf *(+acc)*; *(= defeat)* schlagen N Schlag *m*

whom(so)ever [ˌhuːm(səʊ)ˈevəʳ] PRON *(form)* wen/wem auch immer; *(= no matter who)* ganz gleich *or* egal wen/wem

whoop [huːp] N Ruf *m*, Schrei *m*; *(= war cry also)* Geschrei *nt no pl*, Geheul *nt no pl*; **with a ~ of joy** unter Freudengeschrei VT **to ~ it up** *(inf)* auf die Pauke hauen *(inf)* VI rufen, schreien; *(with whooping cough)* pfeifen; *(with joy)* jauchzen

whoop-de-doo [ˌhuːpdɪˈduː, ˌwuːp-] N *(US inf)* ausgelassene Fröhlichkeit, Ausgelassenheit *f*

whoopee [ˈwʊpiː] N **to make ~** *(dated inf)* Rabatz machen *(dated inf)* INTERJ [wʊˈpiː] hurra, juchhe(i)

whooping cough [ˈhuːpɪŋˌkɒf] N Keuchhusten *m*

whoops [wuːps] INTERJ hoppla, huch, hups

whoosh [wuːʃ] N *(of water)* Rauschen *nt*; *(of air)* Zischen *nt* VI rauschen; *(air)* zischen; **a train ~ed past** ein Zug schoss *or* brauste vorbei

whop [wɒp] VT *(inf)* schlagen; **he ~ped me on the chin** er hat mir eine ans Kinn gegeben *(inf)*

whopper [ˈwɒpəʳ] N *(inf) (= sth big)* Brocken *m (inf)*, Apparat *m (inf)*; *(= lie)* faustdicke Lüge

whopping [ˈwɒpɪŋ] ADJ *(inf)* Mords- *(inf)*, Riesen-; **a ~ amount** ein Riesenbetrag *m*, ein Mordsbetrag *m (inf)*; **a ~ big fish** ein mordsgroßer Fisch *(inf)*, ein Monstrum *nt* von einem Fisch *(inf)*

whore [hɔːʳ] N Hure *f* VI *(also* **to go whoring***)* herumhuren *(inf)*

whore: **whorehouse** [ˈhɔːhaʊs] N *(inf)* Bordell *nt*, Freudenhaus *nt*; **whoremonger** N *(old)* Hurenbock *m*

whorl [wɜːl] N Kringel *m*; *(of shell)* (Spiral)windung *f*; *(Bot)* Quirl *m*, Wirtel *m*; *(of fingerprint)* Wirbel *m*

whortleberry [ˈwɜːtlbərɪ] N Heidelbeere *f*, Blaubeere *f (dial)*

who's [huːz] *contr of* **who has, who is**

whose [huːz] POSS PRON **a** *(interrog)* wessen; **~ is this?** wem gehört das?; **~ car did you go in?** in wessen Auto sind Sie gefahren? **b** *(rel)* dessen; *(after f and pl)* deren

whosoever [ˌhuːsəʊˈevəʳ] PRON *(old)* = **whoever**

wh-question N **a** *Frage, die mit einem wh--Wort beginnt* **b** *(Ling)* Ergänzungsfrage *f*

whunk [wʌŋk] INTERJ knall!, bumm!, peng! VT *head* (sich *dat*) anstoßen VI knallen *(against* gegen), bumsen *(inf) (against* gegen)

why [waɪ] ✪ 1.1, 17.2, 26.3 ADV warum, weshalb; *(asking for the purpose)* wozu; *(= how come that ...)* wieso; **~ not ask him?** warum fragst du/fragen wir *etc* ihn nicht?; **~ wait?** warum *or* wozu (noch) warten?; **~ do it this way?** warum denn so?; **that's ~** darum, deshalb, deswegen; **that's exactly ~ ...** genau deshalb *or* deswegen ...

INTERJ **~, of course, that's right!** ja doch *or* aber sicher, das stimmt so!; **are you sure? – ~ yes (of course/I think so)** sind Sie sicher? – aber ja doch; **~ that's easy!** na, das ist doch einfach!; **take the bus! ~, it's only a short walk** den Bus nehmen? ach was, das ist doch nur ein Katzensprung; **~, if it isn't Charles!** na so was, das ist doch (der) Charles!; **who did it? ~ it's obvious** wer das war? na *or* also, das ist doch klar N **the ~s and (the) wherefores** das Warum und Weshalb

WI **a** *abbr of* **Women's Institute** **b** *abbr of* **West Indies**

wick [wɪk] N Docht *m*; **to get on sb's ~** *(Brit inf)* jdm auf den Wecker gehen *(inf) or* fallen *(inf)*

wicked [ˈwɪkɪd] ADJ **a** *(= evil) person etc* böse; *(= immoral)* schlecht, gottlos; *(= indulging in vices)* lasterhaft; **that was a ~ thing to do** das war aber gemein *or* böse *or* niederträchtig (von dir/ihm *etc*); **it's ~ to tease animals** Tiere zu quälen ist gemein; **it's ~ to tell lies/swear** Lügen/Fluchen ist hässlich **b** *(= vicious)* böse; *weapon* gemein *(inf)*, niederträchtig, heimtückisch; *satire* boshaft; *blow, frost, wind, weather* gemein *(inf)*, böse; **he has a ~ temper** er ist unbeherrscht *or* aufbrausend *or* jähzornig; **the dog has a ~ temper** der Hund ist bösartig **c** *(= mischievous) smile, look, grin* frech, boshaft; **you ~ girl, you** du schlimmes Mädchen *or* du freches Stück *(inf)* (du)!; **I've just had a ~ idea** mir fällt (gerade) was Tolles *(inf) or (practical joke)* ein guter Streich ein **d** *(inf: = scandalous) price etc* hanebüchen *(inf)*, unverschämt; **it's a ~ shame** es ist jammerschade; **it's ~ what they charge** es ist hanebüchen *(inf) or* unverschämt *or* nicht mehr feierlich *(inf)*, was sie verlangen **e** *(sl: = very good)* geil *(sl)*

wickedly [ˈwɪkɪdlɪ] ADV **a** *(= with evil intentions)* böse; *(= immorally)* schlecht, gottlos; *(= dissolutely)* lasterhaft **b** *cold* gemein; **a ~ accurate satire** eine scharf treffende Satire **c** *(= mischievously) smile, look, grin* frech **d** *(inf) expensive* unverschämt

wickedness [ˈwɪkɪdnɪs] N **a** *(of person)* Schlechtigkeit *f*; *(= immorality)* Verderbtheit *f*; *(= indulgence in vices)* Lasterhaftigkeit *f* **b** *(= viciousness)* Bösartigkeit *f*; *(of satire)* Boshaftigkeit *f*; *(of frost, wind, weather)* Gemeinheit *f*; **the ~ of his temper** seine aufbrausende *or* unbeherrschte Art **c** *(= mischievousness)* Boshaftigkeit *f*, Bosheit *f* **d** *(inf, of prices etc)* Unverschämtheit *f*

wicker [ˈwɪkəʳ] N Korbgeflecht *nt* ADJ *attr* Korb-; **~ furniture** Korbmöbel *pl*

wicker: **wicker (arm)chair** N Korbsessel *m*; **wicker basket** N (Weiden)korb *m*; **wicker fence** N Weidenzaun *m*; **wickerwork** N *(= activity)* Korbflechten *nt*; *(= material)* Korbgeflecht *nt*; *(= articles)* Korbwaren *pl* ADJ Korb-; **~ chair** Korbsessel *m*; **~ basket** Weidenkorb *m*

wicket [ˈwɪkɪt] N **a** Gatter *nt*; *(for selling tickets)* Fenster *nt* **b** *(Cricket) (= stumps: also* **wickets***)* Wicket *nt*, Pfostentor *nt*; *(= pitch)* Spielbahn *f*; **three ~s fell before lunch** es gab drei Wicketwürfe vor der Mittagspause; **we won by four ~s** wir gewannen und hatten vier Schlagmänner noch nicht in Einsatz gehabt; **to keep ~** Torwächter sein → **sticky** **c** *(US: = croquet hoop)* Tor *nt*

wicketkeeper [ˈwɪkɪtˈkiːpəʳ] N *(Cricket)* Torwächter(in) *m(f)*

widdle [ˈwɪdl] *(inf)* VI pinkeln *(inf)* N **to go for a ~** *(hum)* pinkeln gehen *(inf)*

wide [waɪd] ADJ (+er) **a** *road, smile, feet, gap* breit; *skirt, trousers, plain* weit; *eyes* groß; **it is three feet ~** es ist drei Fuß breit; *(material)* es liegt drei Fuß breit; *(room)* es ist drei Fuß in der Breite; **the big ~ world** die (große) weite Welt; **her eyes were ~ with amazement** sie machte große Augen vor Erstaunen **b** *(= considerable, comprehensive) difference, variety* groß; *experience, choice* reich, umfangreich; *public, knowledge, range* breit; *interests* vielfältig, breit gefächert; *coverage of report* umfassend; *network* weitverzweigt; *circulation* weit, groß; *question* weitreichend, weit reichend; **~ reading is the best education** viel zu lesen ist die beste Art der Erziehung *or* Bildung; **his ~ reading** seine große Belesenheit **c** *(missing the target)* daneben *pred*, gefehlt; **you're a bit ~ there** da liegst du etwas daneben; **~ of the truth** nicht ganz wahrheitsgetreu; **a ~ ball** *(Cricket)* ein Ball, der nicht in Reichweite des Schlagmanns aufspringt; **it was ~ of the target** es verpasste das Ziel, es ging daneben

ADV **a** *(= extending far)* weit; **they are set ~ apart** sie liegen weit auseinander → **far** **b** *(= fully)* weit; **open ~!** bitte weit öffnen; **the general/writer left himself ~ open to attack** der General/Verfasser hat sich (überhaupt) nicht gegen Angriffe abgesichert; **the law is ~ open to criticism/abuse** das Gesetz bietet viele Ansatzpunkte für Kritik/öffnet dem Missbrauch Tür und Tor **c** *(= far from the target)* daneben; **to go ~ of sth** über etw *(acc)* hinausgehen, an etw *(dat)* vorbeigehen

-wide [-waɪd] ADJ *suf* in dem/der gesamten; *(country-wide etc)* -weit; **Europe-wide** europaweit; **a company-wide pay increase** eine Gehaltserhöhung für die ganze Firma

wide: **wide-angle (lens)** N *(Phot)* Weitwinkel(-objektiv *nt*) *m*; **wide area network** N *(Comput)* Weitverkehrsnetz *nt*; **wide-awake** ADJ *attr*, **wide awake** ADJ *pred (= fully awake)* hellwach; *(= alert)* wach; **you can't fool her, she's much too wide awake** du kannst ihr nichts vormachen, dazu passt sie viel zu genau auf *or* dazu ist sie viel zu helle *(inf)*; **wide-awake hat** N Schlapphut *m*; **wide-band** ADJ *(Rad)* Breitband-; **~ transmission** Breitbandübertragung *f*;

wide-bodied ['waɪd,bɒdiːd] ADJ *(Aviat)* *Großraum-* ~ **jet** Großraumflugzeug *nt*; **wide-body** ['waɪd,bɒdɪ-] *(Aviat)* ADJ = **wide-bodied** N *(also* **wide-body aircraft***)* Großraumflugzeug *nt*; **wide boy** N *(Brit inf)* Fuchs *m (inf)*, Gauner *m*; **wide-eyed** ADJ mit großen Augen; **she gazed at him with ~ innocence** sie starrte ihn mit großen, unschuldigen Kinderaugen an; **in ~ amazement** mit großen, erstaunten Augen

widely ['waɪdlɪ] ADV weit; *(= by or to many people)* weit und breit, überall, allgemein; *(= greatly) vary* stark; *differing* völlig; *(= extensively) available* fast überall; **his remarks were ~ publicized** seine Bemerkungen fanden weite Verbreitung; **the opinion is ~ held ...** es herrscht in weiten Kreisen die Ansicht ...; **it is not ~ understood why ...** es wird nicht überall *or* von allen verstanden, warum ...; **he became ~ known as ...** er wurde überall *or* in weiten Kreisen bekannt als ...; **a ~ read student** ein sehr belesener Student

widen ['waɪdn] VT *road* verbreitern; *passage, scope* erweitern; *circle of friends* vergrößern; *appeal* erhöhen; *knowledge etc* erweitern VI breiter werden; *(interests etc)* sich ausweiten

▸ **widen out** VI **a** *(river, valley etc)* sich erweitern *(into* zu) **b** *(interests etc)* sich ausweiten

wideness ['waɪdnɪs] N **a** *(of road, gap)* Breite *f*; *(of skirt)* Weite *f* **b** *(of knowledge, coverage, interests)* Breite *f*; *(of variety, choice)* Reichtum *m*

wide: **wide-open** ADJ *attr*, **wide open** ADJ *pred* **a** *(= fully open) door, window* ganz *or* weit *or* sperrangelweit *(inf)* offen; *beak* weit aufgerissen *or* aufgesperrt; *eyes* weit aufgerissen **b** *(= not decided) match etc* völlig offen; **the game is still wide open** der Spielausgang ist noch völlig offen **c** *(US inf) wo liberale Gesetze bezüglich Prostitution, Glückspiele etc herrschen*; **wide-ranging** ADJ weitreichend, weit reichend; **wide-screen** ADJ *(Film)* Breitwand-; **in ~ format** im Breitwandformat; **~ television set** Breitbildfernseher *m*; **widespread** ADJ weitverbreitet *attr*; **to become ~** weite Verbreitung erlangen

widgeon ['wɪdʒən] N Pfeifente *f*

widget ['wɪdʒɪt] N *(inf)* **a** *(= manufactured product)* Produkt *nt*, Ding *nt (inf)*; **10,000 ~s per month** 10.000 Produkte *or* Dinger *(inf)* pro Monat **b** *(Brit: in beer can)* Widget *nt*, *in eine Bierdose eingebaute zweite Kammer, die das Bier beim Öffnen zum Aufschäumen bringt*

widish ['waɪdɪʃ] ADJ ziemlich breit

widow ['wɪdəʊ] N **a** Witwe *f*; **to be left a ~** als Witwe zurückbleiben; **golf ~** *(hum)* Golfwitwe *f* → *also* **grass widow** **b** *(Typ)* Hurenkind *nt* VT zur Witwe/zum Witwer machen; **she was twice ~ed** sie ist zweimal verwitwet

widowed ['wɪdəʊd] ADJ verwitwet; **a ~ mother of four** eine Witwe mit vier Kindern

widower ['wɪdəʊəʳ] N Witwer *m*

widowhood ['wɪdəʊhʊd] N *(of woman) (= period)* Witwenschaft *f*; *(= state also)* Witwentum *nt*; *(rare, of man)* Witwerschaft *f*

widow's ['wɪdəʊz]: **widow's allowance** N *(Brit)* (zeitweilige) Witwenbeihilfe *f*; **widow's annuity** N Witwenrente *f*; **widow's benefits** PL *(Brit)* Sozialversicherungsleistungen *pl* an Witwen; **widow's mite** N *(fig)* Scherflein *nt* (der armen Witwe); **widow's peak** N spitzer Haaransatz; **widow's pension** N Witwenrente *f*

width [wɪdθ] N **a** Breite *f*; *(of trouser legs, skirts etc)* Weite *f*; **six feet in ~** sechs Fuß breit; **what is the ~ of the material?** wie breit liegt dieser Stoff? **b** *(= piece of material)* Breite *f*; **three ~s of cloth** drei mal die Breite

widthways ['wɪdθweɪz] ADV der Breite nach

wield [wiːld] VT *pen, sword* führen; *axe* schwingen; *power, influence* ausüben, haben; **~ing his sword above his head** das Schwert über seinem Haupte schwingend; **to ~ power over sth** über etw *(acc)* Macht ausüben

wiener ['wiːnəʳ] N *(US: = frankfurter)* Wiener Würstchen *nt*

wiener dog N *(US hum)* Dackel *m*

wife [waɪf] N *pl* **wives** Frau *f*, Gattin *f (form)*, Gemahlin *f (liter, form)*; **the ~** *(inf)* die Frau; **a woman whom he would never make his ~** eine Person, die er niemals zu seiner Frau machen würde; **businessmen who take their wives with them on their trips** Geschäftsleute, die ihre (Ehe)frauen *or* Damen mit auf Geschäftsreise nehmen; **to take a ~** *(old)* sich *(dat)* eine Frau *or* ein Weib *(old)* nehmen; **to take sb to ~** *(old)* jdn zum Weibe nehmen *(old)*

wife-batterer ['waɪf,bætərəʳ], **wife-beater** ['waɪf,biːtəʳ] N prügelnder Eheman

wifeless ['waɪflɪs] ADJ *man* unverheiratet

wifely ['waɪflɪ] ADJ **~ duties** Pflichten *pl* als Ehefrau; **~ devotion** Hingabe *f* einer Ehefrau

wife-swapping ['waɪf,swɒpɪŋ] N Partnertausch *m*; **~ party** Party *f* mit Partnertausch

wifey ['waɪfɪ] N *(inf pej)* Ehefrauchen *nt*

wi-fi ['waɪ,faɪ] N *abbr of* **wireless fidelity** Wi-Fi *nt*

wig [wɪg] N Perücke *f*

wigeon N = **widgeon**

wigged [wɪgd] ADJ eine Perücke tragend; **the judges were ceremonially ~ and robed** die Richter waren zeremoniell in Roben gekleidet und trugen Perücken

wigging ['wɪgɪŋ] N *(dated inf)* Standpauke *f*, Gardinenpredigt *f*; **to give sb a ~** jdm eine Standpauke *or* Gardinenpredigt halten, jdm die Leviten lesen *(dated)*

wiggle ['wɪgl] N Wackeln *nt no pl*; **give it a ~ and it might come free** wackeln Sie mal daran, dann geht es vielleicht raus; **to get a ~ on** *(inf)* Dampf dahintermachen *(inf)* VT wackeln mit; *eyebrows* zucken mit VI wackeln; *(eyebrows)* zucken

wiggly ['wɪglɪ] ADJ wackelnd; *amateur film etc* wackelig, verwackelt; **~ line** Schlangenlinie *f*; *(drawn)* Wellenlinie *f*

wight [waɪt] N *(old)* Wicht *m*

wigmaker ['wɪgmeɪkəʳ] N Perückenmacher(in) *m(f)*

wigwam ['wɪgwæm] N Wigwam *m*

wilco ['wɪlkəʊ] INTERJ *(Mil etc)* wird gemacht, zu Befehl

wild [waɪld] ADJ (+er) **a** *(= not domesticated, not civilized)* wild; *people* unzivilisiert; *garden, wood* verwildert; *flowers* wild wachsend; **~ animals** Tiere *pl* in freier Wildbahn; **the ~ animals of Northern Europe** Tiere *pl* Nordeuropas, die Tierwelt Nordeuropas; **a lion is a ~ animal** der Löwe lebt in freier Wildbahn; **the plant in its ~ state** die Pflanze im Naturzustand **b** *(= stormy) weather, wind, sea* rau, stürmisch **c** *(= excited, frantic, unruly, riotous)* wild *(with* vor *+dat)*; *(= disordered) hair* wirr, unordentlich; *joy, desire* unbändig **d** *(inf: = angry)* wütend *(with, at* mit, auf *+acc)*, rasend; **it drives** *or* **makes me ~** das macht mich ganz wild *or* rasend; **to get ~** wild werden *(inf)* **e** *(inf: = very keen)* **to be ~ about sb/sth** auf jdn/etw wild *or* scharf *(inf)* *or* versessen sein; **to be ~ to do sth** *(esp US)* wild *or* scharf *(inf)* *or* versessen darauf sein, etw zu tun **f** *(= rash, extravagant)* verrückt; *promise* unüberlegt; *exaggeration* maßlos, wild; *allegation* wild; *fluctuations* stark; *expectations, imagination, fancies* kühn; **never in my ~est dreams** auch in meinen kühnsten Träumen nicht **g** *(= wide of the mark, erratic)* Fehl-; *spelling* unsicher; **~ throw** Fehlwurf *m*; **~ shot** Fehlschuss *m*; **it was just/he took a ~ guess** es war/er hatte nur so (wild) drauflosgeraten **h** *(Cards)* beliebig verwendbar **i** *(inf: = fantastic, great) film, concert etc* toll *(inf)*
ADV **a** *(= in the natural state) grow* wild; *run* frei; **to let one's imagination run ~** seiner Fantasie *or* Phantasie *(dat)* freien Lauf lassen; **the roses/the children have run ~** die Rosen/die Kinder sind verwildert; **he lets his kids run ~** *(pej)* er lässt seine Kinder auf der Straße aufwachsen; **in the country the kids can run ~** auf dem Land kann man die Kinder einfach laufen *or* herumspringen lassen **b** *(= without aim) shoot* ins Blaue, drauflos; *(= off the mark) go, throw* daneben
N Wildnis *f*; **in the ~** in der Wildnis, in freier Wildbahn; **the call of the ~** der Ruf der Wildnis; **the ~s** die Wildnis; **out in the ~s** *(hum: = not in the city)* auf dem platten Lande *(inf)*, jwd *(inf)*; **out in the ~s of Berkshire** im hintersten Berkshire

wild: **wild boar** N Wildschwein *nt*; **wildcard** ADJ *attr (Comput)* **~ character** Jokerzeichen *nt*, Platzhalter *m*; **wild card** N *(Comput)* Wildcard *f*, Platzhalter *m*; **wildcat** N **a** *(Zool)* Wildkatze *f* **b** *(inf: = woman)* Wildkatze *f* **c** *(US inf) (Comm: = risky venture)* gewagte *or* riskante Sache; *(= trial oil well)* Probe- *or* Versuchsbohrung *f* ADJ *attr (= risky)* riskant, gewagt; **~ company** Schwindelfirma *f*; **wildcat strike** N wilder Streik; **wild child** N *(Brit)* Wildfang *m*; **wild duck** N Wildente *f*

wildebeest ['wɪldəbiːst] N Gnu *nt*

wilderness ['wɪldənɪs] N Wildnis *f*; *(fig)* Wüste *f*; **a voice crying in the ~** die Stimme eines Rufenden in der Wüste

wild: **wild-eyed** ADJ *person* wild dreinblickend *attr*; *look* wild; **wildfire** N **to spread like ~** sich wie ein Lauffeuer ausbreiten; **wildfowl** N *no pl* Wildgeflügel *nt*; **wild garlic** N *(Bot)* Bärlauch *m*; **wild goose** N Wildgans *f*; **wild-goose chase** N fruchtloses Unterfangen, Wolpertingerjagd *f (S Ger)*; **to send sb out on a ~** jdn für nichts und wieder nichts losschicken; **wildlife** N die Tierwelt; **~ sanctuary** *or* **park** Wildschutzgebiet *nt*, Wildreservat *nt*; **wildlifer** ['waɪldlaɪfəʳ] N Naturschützer(in) *m(f)*

wildly ['waɪldlɪ] ADV **a** *(= violently)* wild, heftig **b** *(= in disorder)* wirr; **his hair fell ~ over his forehead** sein Haar fiel ihm wirr in die Stirn **c** *(= without aim)* wild; **to hit out ~** wild um sich schlagen; **to shoot ~** wild drauflosschießen **d** *(= extravagantly) guess* drauflos, ins Blaue hinein; *talk* unausgegoren; *happy* rasend; *exaggerated* stark, maßlos; *wrong, different* total, völlig; **I think she is being ~ optimistic** ich denke, dass sie maßlos *or* übertrieben optimistisch ist **e** *(= excitedly, distractedly)* wild, aufgeregt **f** *(= riotously)* wild

wildness ['waɪldnɪs] N **a** *(= rough, uncivilized state)* Wildheit *f* **b** *(of storm etc)* Wildheit *f*, Stärke *f*, Heftigkeit *f*; **the ~ of the weather** das rauhe *or* stürmische Wetter **c** *(= frenzy, unruliness)* Wildheit *f* **d** *(= extravagance) (of promise)* Unüberlegtheit *f*; *(of exaggeration)* Maßlosigkeit *f*; *(of fluctuations)* Stärke *f*; *(of expectations, imagination)* Kühnheit *f* **e** *(= lack of aim)* Unkontrolliertheit *f*; *(= erratic nature: of spelling)* Unsicherheit *f*

wild: **wild oat** N Windhafer *m* → **oat**; **wild silk** N Wildseide *f*; **wildwater** ['waɪld,wɔːtəʳ] N Wildwasser *nt*; **Wild West** N **the ~** der Wilde Westen

wile [waɪl] N *usu pl* List *f*, Schliche *pl*; **she used all her ~s to persuade him** sie ließ ihren ganzen Charme spielen, um ihn zu überreden

wilful, *(US)* **willful** ['wɪlfʊl] ADJ **a** *(= self-willed)* eigensinnig, eigenwillig **b** *(= deliberate) neglect, damage, waste* mutwillig; *murder* vorsätzlich; *disobedience* wissentlich

wilfully, *(US)* **willfully** ['wɪlfəlɪ] ADV **a** *(= stubbornly)* eigensinnig **b** *(= deliberately) destroy, damage, waste* mutwillig; *ignore, neglect, disobey* vorsätzlich

wilfulness, *(US)* **willfulness** ['wɪlfʊlnɪs] N **a** *(of person)* Eigensinn *m*, Eigenwilligkeit *f* **b** *(of action)* Mutwilligkeit *f*, Vorsätzlichkeit *f*

wiliness ['waɪlɪnɪs] N Listigkeit *f*, Schläue *f*, Hinterlist *f (pej)*

will[1] [wɪl] ✪ 20.5 *pret* **would** MODAL AUX VB **a** *(future)* werden; **I'm sure that he ~ come** ich bin sicher, dass er kommt; **you ~ come to see us,**

won't you? Sie kommen uns doch besuchen, ja?; I'll be right there komme sofort!, bin gleich da!; I ~ have finished by Tuesday bis Dienstag bin ich fertig; you won't lose it, ~ you? du wirst es doch nicht verlieren, oder?; you won't insist on that, ~ you? – oh yes, I ~ Sie bestehen doch nicht darauf, oder? – o doch! *or* o ja! *or* doch, doch!

b *(emphatic, expressing determination, compulsion etc)* I ~ not have it! das dulde ich nicht, das kommt mir nicht infrage *or* in Frage *(inf)*; ~ you be quiet! willst du jetzt wohl ruhig sein!, bist du *or* sei jetzt endlich ruhig!; you ~ not talk to me like that! so lasse ich nicht mit mir reden!; he says he ~ go and I say he won't er sagt, er geht, und ich sage, er geht nicht

c *(expressing willingness, consent etc)* wollen; he won't sign er unterschreibt nicht, er will nicht unterschreiben; if she won't say yes wenn sie nicht ja sagt; he wouldn't help me er wollte *or* mochte mir nicht helfen; wait a moment, ~ you? warten Sie einen Moment, ja bitte?; *(impatiently)* jetzt warte doch mal einen Moment!; ~ she, won't she? ob sie wohl …?

d *(in questions)* ~ you have some more tea? möchten Sie noch Tee?; ~ you accept these conditions? akzeptieren Sie diese Bedingungen?; won't you take a seat? wollen *or* möchten Sie sich nicht setzen?; won't you please come home? komm doch bitte nach Hause!; there isn't any tea, ~ coffee do? es ist kein Tee da, darf es auch Kaffee sein? *or* tut es Kaffee auch? *(inf)*

e *(insistence)* well, if he ~ drive so fast also, wenn er (eben) unbedingt so schnell fahren muss; well, if you won't take advice wenn du (eben) keinen Rat annimmst, na bitte; he ~ interrupt all the time er muss ständig dazwischenreden

f *(assumption)* he'll be there by now jetzt ist er schon da, jetzt dürfte er schon da sein; was that the doorbell? that ~ be for you hats geklingelt? – das ist bestimmt für dich *or* das wird *or* dürfte für dich sein; this ~ be our bus das wird *or* dürfte unser Bus sein; this ~ be the one you want das dürfte (es) wohl sein, was Sie wünschen

g *(tendency)* the solution ~ turn red if … die Lösung färbt sich rot, wenn …; sometimes he ~ sit in his room for hours manchmal sitzt er auch stundenlang in seinem Zimmer

h *(capability)* ~ the engine start now? springt der Motor jetzt an?; the car won't start das Auto springt nicht an *or* will nicht anspringen; the door won't open die Tür lässt sich nicht öffnen *or* geht nicht auf *(inf)*; the cut won't heal die Schnittwunde will nicht (ver)heilen; the car ~ do up to 120 mph das Auto fährt bis zu 120 Meilen pro Stunde

VI wollen; say what you ~ du kannst sagen, was du willst; as you ~! wie du willst!; it is, if you ~, a kind of mystery das ist, wenn du so willst, eine Art Rätsel

will[2] ✪ 9.3 N **a** Wille *m*; to have a ~ of one's own einen eigenen Willen haben; *(hum)* so seine Mucken haben *(inf)*; the ~ to win/live der Wille *or* das Bestreben, zu gewinnen/zu leben, der Sieges-/Lebenswille; (to go) against one's/sb's ~ gegen seinen/jds Willen (handeln); if that's your ~ wenn das dein Wunsch ist; at ~ nach Belieben, nach Lust und Laune, beliebig; fire at ~! ohne Befehl schießen; of one's own free ~ aus freien Stücken, aus freiem Willen; with the best ~ in the world beim *or* mit (dem) (aller)besten Willen; where there is a ~ there is a way *(Prov)* wo ein Wille ist, ist auch ein Weg *(Prov)*; to do sb's ~ *(dated)* jdm seinen Willen tun; to have one's ~ *(dated)* seinen Kopf durchsetzen; Thy ~ be done Dein Wille geschehe; to work with a ~ mit (Feuer)eifer arbeiten → goodwill, ill ADJ b

b *(= testament)* Letzter Wille, Testament *nt*; the last ~ and testament of … der Letzte Wille *or* das Testament des/der …; to make one's ~ sein Testament machen

VT **a** *(old: = ordain)* wollen, bestimmen, verfügen *(geh)*; God has so ~ed Gott hat es so gewollt *or* gefügt *or* bestimmt

b *(= urge by willpower)* (durch Willenskraft) erzwingen; to ~ sb to do sth jdn durch die eigene Willensanstrengung dazu bringen, dass er etw tut; he ~ed himself to stay awake er hat sich (dazu) gezwungen, wach zu bleiben; she ~ed herself to get better sie hat ihre Genesung durch ihre Willenskraft erzwungen; he ~ed the ball into the net er hat den Ball ins Netz hypnotisiert *(inf)*

c *(by testament)* (testamentarisch) vermachen, vererben *(sth to sb* jdm etw)

VI wollen; if God ~s so Gott will

will-call [ˈwɪlkɔːl] N **a** *(= purchase) Kauf, bei dem eine Anzahlung gemacht und die Ware zurückgelegt wird* **b** *(= goods)* angezahlte und zurückgelegte Ware

willful *etc (US)* = wilful *etc*

William [ˈwɪljəm] N Wilhelm *m*

Williams pear [ˈwɪljəmzˌpeəˈ] N *(Bot)* Williams Christbirne *f*

willie [ˈwɪlɪ] N *(Brit inf: = penis)* Pimmel *m (inf)*

willies [ˈwɪlɪz] PL *(inf)* to get the ~ Zustände kriegen *(inf)*; it/he gives me the ~ da/bei dem wird mir ganz anders *(inf)*

willing [ˈwɪlɪŋ] ADJ **a** *(= prepared)* to be ~ to do sth bereit *or* gewillt *(geh) or* willens *(liter, old)* sein, etw zu tun; God ~ so Gott will; he was ~ for me to take it es war ihm recht, dass ich es nahm; he was not ~ for us to go/for this to be done er war nicht gewillt, uns gehen zu lassen/das geschehen zu lassen; ~ to compromise kompromissbereit; ~ to help hilfsbereit; ~ to make concessions konzessionsbereit; ~ to negotiate verhandlungsbereit; ~ to pay zahlungswillig *or* -bereit; ~ to work arbeitswillig

b *(= ready to help, cheerfully ready) workers, helpers* bereitwillig; prepared to lend a ~ hand gerne dazu bereit zu helfen

c *(= voluntary) sacrifice* willentlich

willingly [ˈwɪlɪŋlɪ] ADV bereitwillig, gerne; will you help? – yes, ~ wollen Sie helfen? – (ja,) gerne

willingness [ˈwɪlɪŋnɪs] N **a** *(= readiness)* Bereitschaft *f*; ~ to compromise Kompromissbereitschaft *f*; ~ to help Hilfsbereitschaft *f*; ~ to make concessions Konzessionsbereitschaft *f*; ~ to negotiate Verhandlungsbereitschaft *f*; ~ to work Arbeitswilligkeit *f* **b** *(= enthusiasm)* Bereitwilligkeit *f*

will-o'-the-wisp [ˈwɪləðəˈwɪsp] N Irrlicht *nt*; *(fig)* Trugbild *nt*

willow [ˈwɪləʊ] N *(also* **willow tree***)* Weide *f*, Weidenbaum *m*; *(= wood)* Weidenholz *nt*; *(= twigs)* Weidenruten *or* -gerten *pl*

willowherb [ˈwɪləʊˌhɜːb] N Weidenröschen *nt*

willow pattern N chinesisches Weidenmotiv *(auf Porzellan)* ADJ *attr* mit chinesischem Weidenmotiv

willowy [ˈwɪləʊɪ] ADJ gertenschlank

willpower [ˈwɪlˌpaʊəˈ] N Willenskraft *f*

willy [ˈwɪlɪ] N *(Brit inf)* = **willie**

willy-nilly [ˈwɪlɪˈnɪlɪ] ADV **a** *(= at random) choose, allocate* aufs Geratewohl; *accept* wahllos, ohne Weiteres **b** *(= willingly or not)* wohl oder übel, nolens volens

wilt[1] [wɪlt] *(old) 2nd pers sing of* **will**[1]

wilt[2] [wɪlt] VI **a** *(flowers)* welken, verwelken, welk werden **b** *(person)* matt werden; *(after physical exercise)* schlapp werden; *(enthusiasm, energy)* abflauen VT ausdörren

Wilts [wɪlts] *abbr of* **Wiltshire**

wily [ˈwaɪlɪ] ADJ *(+er)* listig, schlau, hinterlistig *(pej)*

wimp [wɪmp] N *(inf)* Schwächling *m*, Waschlappen *m (inf)*

▶ **wimp out** VI *(inf)* kneifen *(inf)*; to wimp out of sth bei etw kneifen *(inf)*

wimpish [ˈwɪmpɪʃ] ADJ *(inf)* weichlich, schlapp *(inf)*

wimpishly [ˈwɪmpɪʃlɪ] ADV *(inf)* schlapp *(inf)*; he ~ agreed to sell Schwächling *or* Waschlappen *(inf)*, der er ist, stimmte er dem Verkauf zu

wimpishness [ˈwɪmpɪʃnɪs] N *(inf)* Weichlichkeit *f*, Schlappheit *f (inf)*

wimple [ˈwɪmpl] N Rise *f (spec)*, Schleier *m*; *(worn by nuns)* (Nonnen)schleier *m*

win [wɪn] *vb: pret, ptp* **won** N Sieg *m*; to back a horse for a ~ auf den Sieg eines Pferdes setzen; to have a ~ *(money)* einen Gewinn machen; *(victory)* einen Sieg erzielen; to play for a ~ auf Sieg spielen

VT **a** *race, prize, battle, election, money, bet, sympathy, support, friends, glory* gewinnen; *reputation* erwerben; *scholarship, contract* bekommen; *victory* erringen; to ~ sb's heart/love/hand jds Herz/Liebe/Hand gewinnen; he tried to ~ her er versuchte, sie für sich zu gewinnen; it won him the first prize es brachte ihm den ersten Preis ein; to ~ sth from *or* off *(inf)* sb jdm etw abgewinnen

b *(= obtain, extract)* gewinnen; the oil won from the North Sea das aus der Nordsee gewonnene Öl; land won from the sea dem Meer abgewonnenes Land

c *(liter: = reach with effort) shore, summit* erreichen

VI **a** *(in race, election, argument etc)* gewinnen, siegen; if ~ning becomes too important wenn das Siegen *or* das Gewinnen zu wichtig wird; OK, you ~, I was wrong okay, du hast gewonnen, ich habe mich geirrt; whatever I do, I just can't ~ egal, was ich mache, ich machs immer falsch

b *(liter)* to ~ free sich freikämpfen, sich befreien

▶ **win back** VT *sep* zurück- *or* wiedergewinnen

▶ **win out** VI letztlich siegen *(over sb* über jdn), sich durchsetzen *(over sb* jdm gegenüber)

▶ **win over** VT *sep* für sich gewinnen; it is hard to win him over *or* round es ist schwer, ihn für uns *or* für unsere Seite zu gewinnen; his speech won over *or* round all the government's critics mit seiner Rede hat er alle Kritiker der Regierung für sich gewonnen; to win sb over to Catholicism/one's own way of thinking jdn zum Katholizismus/zur eigenen Denkungsart bekehren; to win sb over to a plan jdn für einen Plan gewinnen

▶ **win round** VT *sep (esp Brit)* = **win over**

▶ **win through** VI *(patient)* durchkommen; to win through to the finals das Finale schaffen; we'll win through in the end wir werden es schon schaffen *(inf)*

wince [wɪns] N (Zusammen)zucken *nt*; ouch, he said with a ~ autsch, sagte er und zuckte zusammen; to give a ~ (of pain) (vor Schmerz) zusammenzucken VI zusammenzucken

winceyette [ˌwɪnsɪˈet] N Flanellette *nt*

winch [wɪntʃ] N Winde *f*, Winsch *f* VT winschen

▶ **winch up** VT *sep* hochwinschen

Winchester rifle® [ˈwɪntʃestəˈraɪfl] N Winchesterbüchse *f*

wind[1] [wɪnd] N **a** Wind *m*; the ~ is from the east der Wind kommt aus dem Osten *or* von Osten; before the ~ *(Naut)* vor dem Wind; into the ~ *(Naut)* in den Wind; to sail close to the ~ *(fig)* sich hart an der Grenze des Erlaubten bewegen; *(Naut)* hart am Wind segeln; (to run) like the ~ (rennen) wie der Wind; a ~ of change *(fig)* ein frischer(er) Wind; there's change in the ~ (irgend)etwas bahnt sich an *or* liegt in der Luft; to get/have the ~ up *(Brit inf: = be nervous)* Angst *or* Schiss *(sl)* kriegen/haben; to put the ~ up sb *(Brit inf)* jdm Angst machen, jdn ins Bockshorn jagen; to raise the ~ *(dated Brit inf)* das nötige Kleingeld auftreiben *(inf)*; to see which way the ~ blows *(fig)* sehen, woher der Wind weht; to take the ~ out of sb's sails *(fig)* jdm den Wind aus den Segeln nehmen; he's full of ~ *(fig)* er ist ein Schaumschläger *(inf)*, er macht viel Wind *(inf)*

b *(= scent)* to get ~ of sth *(lit, fig)* von etw

Wind bekommen
c *(compass point)* **to the four ~s** in alle (vier) Winde; **to throw caution to the ~s** Bedenken in den Wind schlagen
d *(from bowel, stomach)* Wind *m*, Blähung *f*; **to break ~** einen Wind streichen lassen; **to bring up ~** aufstoßen; *(baby also)* ein Bäuerchen machen; **to have a touch of ~** leichte Blähungen haben
e *(= breath)* Atem *m*, Luft *f (inf)*; **to get one's ~ back** wieder Luft bekommen *or* zu Atem kommen; **to get one's second ~** den toten Punkt überwunden haben; **he's losing his ~** ihm geht der Atem aus; **sound in ~ and limb** kerngesund
f *(Mus: = wind instruments)* Bläser *pl*, Blasinstrumente *pl*; **music for ~** Blasmusik *f*
VT a *(Brit: = knock breathless)* den Atem nehmen *(+dat)*; **he was ~ed by the ball** der Ball nahm ihm den Atem
b *(= scent)* wittern
c *horses* verschnaufen lassen
d *baby* ein Bäuerchen machen lassen

wind² [waɪnd] *vb: pret, ptp* **wound VT a** *(= twist, wrap) wool, bandage* wickeln; *turban etc* winden; *(on to a reel)* spulen
b *(= turn, wind up) handle* kurbeln, drehen; *clock, watch, clockwork toy* aufziehen
c *(= proceed by twisting)* **to ~ one's way** sich schlängeln
VI a *(river etc)* sich winden *or* schlängeln
b how does it ~? *(watch)* wie herum zieht man es auf?; *(handle)* wie dreht *or* kurbelt man es?; **it won't ~** er/es lässt sich nicht aufziehen; *(handle)* er/es lässt sich nicht drehen *or* kurbeln
N a I'll give the clock a ~ ich werde die Uhr aufziehen; **give it one more ~** zieh es noch eine Umdrehung weiter auf; *(handle)* kurbele *or* drehe es noch einmal weiter
b *(= bend)* Kehre *f*, Windung *f*

▶ **wind around VT** *sep +prep obj* wickeln um; **wind it once/twice around the post** winde *or* wickele es einmal/zweimal um den Pfosten; **to wind one's arms around sb** seine Arme um jdn schlingen *or* winden *(geh)*; **to wind itself around sth** sich um etw schlingen **VI** *(road)* sich winden **VI** *+prep obj (road)* sich schlängeln durch; *(procession)* sich winden durch

▶ **wind back VT** *sep film, tape* zurückspulen

▶ **wind down VT** *sep* **a** *car windows etc* herunterdrehen *or* -kurbeln **b** *(= reduce) operations* reduzieren; *production* zurückschrauben **VI a** *(= lose speed: clock)* ablaufen **b** *(path etc)* sich hinunterwinden *or* -schlängeln **c** *(inf: = relax)* abspannen, entspannen

▶ **wind forward VT** *sep film* weiterspulen

▶ **wind in VT** *sep fish* einziehen *or* -holen; *rope also* aufspulen

▶ **wind on VT** *sep film* weiterspulen

▶ **wind out VT** *sep cable* abwickeln, ab- *or* runterspulen

▶ **wind round VTI** *sep (esp Brit)* = **wind around**

▶ **wind up VT** *sep* **a** *bucket* herauf- *or* hochholen; *car window* hinaufkurbeln *or* -drehen
b *clock, mechanism* aufziehen
c *(Brit fig inf) person* aufziehen; **to be wound up about sth** *(fig)* über etw *(acc) or* wegen einer Sache *(gen)* erregt sein
d *(= close, end) meeting, debate, speech* beschließen, zu Ende bringen; **he wound up the arguments for the government** er fasste die Argumente der Regierung(sseite) zusammen
e *company* auflösen; *service, series* auslaufen lassen; **to wind up one's affairs** seine Angelegenheiten abwickeln
VI a *(inf: = end up)* enden; **to wind up in hospital/Munich** im Krankenhaus/in München landen; **to wind up doing sth** am Ende etw tun; **to wind up with nothing** am Ende ohne etwas dastehen; **he'll wind up as director** er wird es noch bis zum Direktor bringen
b *(= conclude)* **to wind up for the government** die abschließende Rede für die Regierung halten; **we sang a song to wind up** abschließend *or* zum Schluss sangen wir noch ein Lied
c *(= proceed by twisting)* sich hinaufwinden; *(road)* sich hinaufschlängeln

wind ['wɪnd-]: **windbag N** *(inf)* Schwätzer(in) *m(f)*, Schaumschläger(in) *m(f)*; **windblown ADJ** *(= windswept) hair, tree, person* windzerzaust; **windborne ADJ** vom Wind getrieben; **windbreak N** Windschutz *m*; **Windbreaker® N** *(US)* = **windcheater**; **windburn N** Rötung *f* der Haut aufgrund *or* auf Grund von Wind; **windcheater N** *(Brit)* Windjacke *or* -bluse *f*; **wind-chill factor N** Wind-Kälte-Faktor *m*; **wind cone N** *(Aviat)* Wind- *or* Luftsack *m*

winded ['wɪndɪd] **ADJ** atemlos, außer Atem

wind energy N Windenergie *f*

winder ['waɪndəʳ] **N** *(of watch)* Krone *f*, (Aufzieh)rädchen *nt*; *(of alarm clock, toy etc)* Aufziehschraube *f*

windfall ['wɪndfɔːl] **N** Fallobst *nt*; *(fig)* unerwartetes Geschenk, unverhoffter Glücksfall

windfall: **windfall profit N** *(Econ)* Marktlagengewinn *m*, Q-Gewinn *m*; **windfall tax N** *(Econ)* Spekulationssteuer *f*, Steuer *f* auf Aktiengewinne

wind: **wind farm N** Windfarm *f*; **wind force N** *(Met)* Windstärke *f*; **wind gauge N** Wind(stärke)messer *m*; **wind generator N** Windgenerator *m*

windiness ['wɪndɪnɪs] **N** Wind *m*; **because of the ~ of the area** wegen des starken Windes in dieser Gegend

winding ['waɪndɪŋ] **ADJ** *river, staircase* gewunden; *road also* kurvenreich **N a** *(of road, river)* Windung *f*, Kehre *f*; *(fig)* Verwicklung *f* **b** *(Elec) (= coil)* Wicklung *f*; *(= simple twist)* Windung *f*

winding: **winding sheet N** *(old)* Leichentuch *nt*; **winding staircase N** Wendeltreppe *f*; **winding-up N** *(of project)* Abschluss *m*; *(of company, society)* Auflösung *f*; **winding-up sale N** Räumungsverkauf *m*

wind instrument N Blasinstrument *nt*

windjammer ['wɪnddʒæməʳ] **N** Windjammer *m*

windlass ['wɪndləs] **N** *(= winch)* Winde *f*; *(Naut)* Ankerwinde *f*

windless ['wɪndlɪs] **ADJ** windfrei, ohne Wind, windstill

wind machine N Windmaschine *f*

windmill ['wɪndmɪl] **N** Windmühle *f*; *(Brit: = toy)* Windrädchen *nt*; **to tilt at ~s** *(fig)* gegen Windmühlen(flügel) kämpfen

window ['wɪndəʊ] **N** *(also Comput)* Fenster *nt*; *(= shop window)* (Schau)fenster *nt*; *(of booking office, bank)* Schalter *m*; *(Comm inf: = opportunity)* Gelegenheit *f*; **a ~ on the world** *(fig)* ein Fenster zur Welt; **~ of opportunity** Chance *f*, (Fenster *nt* der) Gelegenheit *f*

window: **window background N** *(Comput)* Fensterhintergrund *m*; **window border N** *(Comput)* Fensterrand *m*; **window box N** Blumenkasten *m*; **windowcleaner N** Fensterputzer(in) *m(f)*; **window display N** (Schaufenster)auslage *f*; **window-dresser N** (Schaufenster)dekorateur(in) *m(f)*; **window-dressing N** Auslagen- *or* Schaufensterdekoration *f*; *(fig)* Mache *f*, Schau *f (inf)*, Augen(aus)wischerei *f (pej)*; **that's just ~** das ist alles nur Mache *or* alles, um nach Außen hin zu wirken; **window envelope N** Fensterbriefumschlag *m*; **window frame N** *(also Comput)* Fensterrahmen *m*; **window glass N** Fensterglas *nt*

windowing ['wɪndəʊɪŋ] **N** *(Comput)* Fenstertechnik *f*

window: **window ledge N** = **windowsill**; **windowpane N** Fensterscheibe *f*; *(Comput)* Fensterausschnitt *m*; **window seat N** *(in house)* Fensterbank *f or* -sitz *m*; *(Rail etc)* Fensterplatz *m*; **window shade N** *(esp US)* Springrollo *nt*; **window-shopper N** jd, der einen Schaufensterbummel macht; **window-shopping N** Schaufensterbummel *m*; **to go ~** einen Schaufensterbummel machen; **windowsill N** Fensterbank *f or* -brett *nt*; *(outside also)* Fenstersims *m*; **window size N** *(Comput)* Fenstergröße *f*

wind: **wind park N** *(Tech)* Wind(energie)park *m*; **windpipe N** Luftröhre *f*; **wind power N** Windkraft *f*, Windenergie *f*; **wind power plant N** Windkraftanlage *f*; **windproof ADJ** luftdicht, windundurchlässig; **wind quartet N** *(Mus)* Bläserquartett *nt*; **wind rose N** *(Met)* Windrose *f*; **wind scale N** Windstärkenskala *f*; **windscreen**, *(US)* **windshield N** Windschutzscheibe *f*; **windscreen washer**, *(US)* **windshield washer N** Scheibenwaschanlage *f*; **windscreen wiper**, *(US)* **windshield wiper N** Scheibenwischer *m*; **wind section N** *(Mus)* Bläser *pl*; **wind sleeve**, **windsock N** Luft- *or* Windsack *m*; **windsurf VI** windsurfen; **windsurfer N** *(= person)* Windsurfer(in) *m(f)*; *(= board)* Windsurfbrett *nt*; **windsurfing N** Windsurfen *nt*; **windswept ADJ** *beach, field* über den/die/das der Wind fegt; *person, hair* (vom Wind) zerzaust; **wind tunnel N** Windkanal *m*; **wind turbine N** Windturbine *f*

wind-up ['waɪndʌp] **N a** *(US)* = **winding-up**
b *(Brit inf: = joke)* Witz *m*

windward ['wɪndwəd] **ADJ** Wind-, dem Wind zugekehrt; *direction* zum Wind; **~ side** dem Wind zugekehrte Seite, Windseite *f* **N** Windseite *f*; **to steer to ~ of an island** auf die Windseite einer Insel zusteuern

Windward Islands PL the Windward islands die Inseln *pl* über dem Winde *(von Dominica bis Grenada)*

windy ['wɪndɪ] **ADJ** *(+er)* **a** *day, weather, place* windig **b** *(inf: = verbose) speech, style* langatmig **c** *(esp Brit inf: = frightened)* **to be/get ~** Angst *or* Schiss *(sl)* haben/bekommen

Windy City N the ~ *(US inf)* Chicago

wine [waɪn] **N** Wein *m*; **cheese and ~ party** *Party, bei der Wein und Käse gereicht wird*; **to put new ~ in old bottles** *(fig)* jungen Wein in alte Schläuche füllen **VT to ~ and dine sb** jdn zu einem guten Abendessen einladen; **the businessmen were ~d and dined in every city they visited** die Geschäftsleute wurden in jeder Stadt, die sie besuchten, ausgezeichnet bewirtet; **he ~d and dined her for months** er hat sie monatelang zum Abendessen ausgeführt **ADJ** *(colour)* burgunderrot

wine: **wine bar N** Weinlokal *nt*; **wine bottle N** Weinflasche *f*; **wine box N** Zapfpack *m*; **wine bucket N** Sektkühler *m*; **wine cask N** Weinfass *nt*; **wine cellar N** Weinkeller *m*; **wine cooler N** Weinkühler *m*; **wineglass N** Weinglas *nt*; **wine grower N** Winzer(in) *m(f)*, Weinbauer(in) *m(f)*; **wine growing ADJ** Wein(an)bau-; **~ region** Wein(an)baugebiet *nt* **N** Wein(an)bau *m*; **wine gum N** Weingummi *nt*; **wine list N** Weinkarte *f*; **wine-making N** Weinherstellung *f*; **wine merchant N** Weinhändler(in) *m(f)*; **winepress N** Weinpresse *f*, Kelter *f*; **wine rack N** Flaschenregal *nt* (für Weinflaschen)

winery ['waɪnərɪ] **N** *(US)* (Wein)kellerei *f*

wine: **wine shop N** Weinhandlung *f*; **wineskin N** Weinschlauch *m*; **wine taster N** Weinverkoster(in) *or* -prüfer(in) *m(f)*; **wine tasting N** Weinprobe *f*; **wine waiter N** *(Brit)* Weinkellner *m*, Getränkekellner *m*

wing [wɪŋ] **N a** *(of bird, plane, building, Mil, Pol, Sport)* Flügel *m*; *(of chair)* Backe *f*; *(Brit Aut)* Kotflügel *m*; **on the ~** im Flug(e); **to take sb under one's ~** *(fig)* jdn unter seine Fittiche nehmen; **to spread one's ~s** *(fig: children)* flügge werden; **to take ~** *(lit)* davonfliegen; *(project etc)* Auftrieb bekommen; **on the ~s of fantasy** *(liter)* auf den Flügeln *or* Schwingen der Fantasie *or* Phantasie; **on the ~s of song** *(liter)* auf (des) Gesanges Flügeln *(liter)*; **on a ~ and a prayer** auf gut Glück; **do you expect me to grow *or* sprout ~s?** *(inf)* du glaubst wohl, ich kann fliegen? *(inf)*; **to play on the (left/right) ~** *(Sport)* auf dem (linken/rechten) Flügel spielen
b *(Aviat: = section of air force)* Geschwader *nt*; **~s** *pl (= pilot's badge)* Pilotenabzeichen *nt*; **to get one's ~s** *(fig)* sich *(dat)* seine Sporen verdienen
c wings PL *(Theat)* Kulisse *f*; **to wait in the**

~s *(lit, fig)* in den Kulissen warten
VT a to ~ one's way *(= fly)* fliegen
b *(fig: liter, = give wings to)* beflügeln
c *(= graze) person, bird* (mit einem Schuss) streifen; **you only ~ed it** das war nur ein Streifschuss, du hast es nur gestreift
VI fliegen

wing: **wingback** ['wɪŋ,bæk] N *(Ftbl) (Brit)* offensiver Außenverteidiger, offensive Außenverteidigerin; *(US)* Flügelverteidiger(in) *m(f)*; **wing beat** N Flügelschlag *m*; **wing-case** N Deckflügel *pl*, Flügeldecken *pl*; **wing chair** N Ohren- *or* Backensessel *m*; **wing collar** N Eckenkragen *m*; **wing commander** N *(Brit)* Oberstleutnant *m* (der Luftwaffe)

wingding ['wɪŋ,dɪŋ] N *(dated US inf)* tolle Party *(inf)*

winge [wɪndʒ] VI = **whinge**

winged [wɪŋd] ADJ a *(Zool, Bot)* mit Flügeln; **the Winged Victory (of Samothrace)** die Nike von Samothrake; **the Winged Horse** (der) Pegasus b *(liter) sentiments, words* geflügelt

-winged ADJ *suf* mit … Flügeln; *bird also* -flügelig; **red-winged** mit roten Flügeln; *bird also* rotflügelig

winger ['wɪŋə'] N *(Sport)* Flügelspieler(in) *m(f)*, Außenstürmer(in) *m(f)*

wingey ['wɪndʒɪ] ADJ = **whingey**

wing: **wing feather** N Flügelfeder *f*; **wing-forward** N *(Rugby)* Flügelstürmer(in) *m(f)*; **wingless** ADJ flügellos; **wing nut** N Flügelmutter *f*; **wingspan** N Flügelspannweite *f*; **wingspread** N Spannweite *f*; **wing-three-quarter** N *(Rugby)* Dreiviertelspieler(in) *m(f)* auf dem Flügel; **wing tip** N Flügelspitze *f*

wink [wɪŋk] N a *(with eye)* Zwinkern *nt*, Blinzeln *nt*; **to give sb a ~** jdm zuzwinkern *or* zublinzeln; **to tip sb the ~** *(Brit inf)* jdm einen Wink geben → **nod**
b *(= instant)* **I didn't get a ~ of sleep, I didn't sleep a ~** *(inf)* ich habe kein Auge zugetan
VT *eye* blinzeln, zwinkern mit *(+dat)*
VI *(meaningfully)* zwinkern, blinzeln; *(light, star etc)* blinken, funkeln; **to ~ at sb** jdm zuzwinkern *or* zublinzeln; **to ~ at sth** *(inf)* etw geflissentlich übersehen, bei etw einfach wegsehen *or* -schauen; **it's as easy as ~ing** *(dated inf)* das ist ein Kinderspiel; **~ing lights** *(Aut)* Blinklichter *pl*, Blinker *pl*

winker ['wɪŋkə'] N *(Brit Aut inf)* Blinker *m*

winkle ['wɪŋkl] N *(Brit)* Strandschnecke *f*

▶ **winkle out** VT *sep (Brit inf)* **to winkle sth/sb out** etw herausklauben *or (behind sth)* hervorklauben *(inf)*/jdn loseisen *(inf)*; **to winkle sth out of sb** etw aus jdm herauskriegen *(inf)*

winkle-pickers ['wɪŋklpɪkəz] PL *(Brit hum inf)* spitze Schuhe *pl*

winnable ['wɪnəbl] ADJ zu gewinnen *pred*

winner ['wɪnə'] N *(in race, competition)* Sieger(in) *m(f)*; *(of bet, pools etc)* Gewinner(in) *m(f)*; *(= card)* Gewinnkarte *f*; *(Tennis etc: = shot)* Treffer *m*; *(inf: = sth successful)* Renner *m (inf)*, (Verkaufs)schlager *m*; **to be onto a ~** *(inf)* das große Los gezogen haben *(inf)*

winning ['wɪnɪŋ] ADJ a *(= successful) person, entry* der/die gewinnt; *horse, team* siegreich; *goal* Sieges-; *point, stroke* (das Spiel) entscheidend; **the ~ time** die beste Zeit; **~ score** Spielergebnis *nt* b *(= charming) smile, ways* gewinnend, einnehmend N **winnings** PL Gewinn *m*

winningly ['wɪnɪŋlɪ] ADV *smile* gewinnend, einnehmend

winning post N Zielpfosten *m*, Zielstange *f*

winnow ['wɪnəʊ] VT a *(fig liter)* sichten b *(also* **winnow out)** *(= remove)* aussortieren; *(= identify, find out)* herausfinden

winnower ['wɪnəʊə'], **winnowing machine** ['wɪnəʊɪŋmə'ʃi:n] N Worfschaufel *f*, Worfelmaschine *f*

wino ['waɪnəʊ] N *(inf)* Penner *m (inf)*, Saufbruder *m (inf)*

winsome ['wɪnsəm] ADJ *child, lass* reizend, sympathisch; *ways, smile* gewinnend, einnehmend

winter ['wɪntə'] N *(lit, fig)* Winter *m* ADJ *attr* Winter- VI überwintern, den Winter verbringen VT *cattle, horses* durch den Winter bringen

winter collection N *(Fashion)* Winterkollektion *f*

wintergreen ['wɪntə,gri:n] N *(= plant)* Teebeere *f*; *(= flavouring)* Wintergrünöl *nt*

winterize ['wɪntəraɪz] VT *(US)* winterfest machen

winter jasmine N gelber Jasmin

winterly ADJ winterlich

winter: **Winter Olympics** PL Winterolympiade *f*; **winter quarters** PL Winterquartier *nt*; **winter resort** N Winterkurort *m*, Winterurlaubsort *m*; **winter sales** PL Winterschlussverkauf *m*; **winter solstice** N Wintersonnenwende *f*; **winter sports** PL Wintersport *m*; **winter term** N *(Univ)* Wintersemester *nt*; **wintertime** N Winter *m*; *(for clocks)* Winterzeit *f*; **winter-weight** ADJ *clothes* Winter-; **winter wheat** N *(Agr)* Winterweizen *m*

wintery ['wɪntərɪ], **wintry** ['wɪntrɪ] ADJ winterlich; *(fig) look* eisig; *smile* frostig, kühl

wintriness ['wɪntrɪnɪs] N Winterlichkeit *f*

wintry ['wɪntrɪ] ADJ = **wintery**

win-win situation [,wɪn'wɪnsɪtjʊ,eɪʃən] N beidseitige Gewinnsituation, Win-Win-Situation *f*

wipe [waɪp] N Wischen *nt*; **to give sth a ~** etw abwischen
VT wischen; *floor* aufwischen; *window* überwischen; *hands, feet* abwischen, abputzen *(rare)*; **to ~ sb/sth dry** jdn/etw abtrocknen *or* trocken reiben; **to ~ sb/sth clean** jdn/etw sauber wischen *or* säubern; **to ~ sth with/on a cloth** etw mit/an einem Tuch abwischen; **to ~ one's brow** sich *(dat)* die Stirn abwischen; **to ~ one's eyes** sich *(dat)* die Augen wischen; **to ~ one's nose** sich *(dat)* die Nase putzen; **to ~ one's feet** sich *(dat)* die Füße *or* Schuhe abstreifen *or* -wischen *or* -treten; **to ~ the tears from one's eyes** sich *(dat)* die Tränen aus den Augen wischen; **to ~ one's bottom** sich *(dat)* den Hintern abputzen, sich abputzen; **to ~ the floor with sb** *(fig inf)* jdn fertigmachen *(inf)*

▶ **wipe at** VI *+prep obj* abwischen

▶ **wipe away** VT *sep (lit, fig)* wegwischen; *tears also* abwischen

▶ **wipe down** VT *sep* abwaschen; *(with dry cloth)* abreiben; *window* überwischen

▶ **wipe off** VT *sep* a *mark* weg- *or* abwischen; *(from blackboard also)* ab- *or* auslöschen; **wipe that smile off your face** *(inf)* hör auf zu grinsen *(inf)*; **I'll soon wipe that smile off his face** *(inf)* dem wird bald das Lachen vergehen; **to be wiped off the map** *or* **the face of the earth** von der Landkarte *or* Erdoberfläche getilgt werden b *(Fin)* **millions were wiped off share values yesterday** gestern kam es zu Aktienverlusten in Millionenhöhe VI sich weg- *or* abwischen lassen

▶ **wipe out** VT *sep* a *(= clean) bath, bowl* auswischen b *(= erase) memory, part of brain, sth on blackboard* (aus)löschen; *guilty feelings* verschwinden lassen c *(= cancel) debt* bereinigen; *gain, benefit* zunichtemachen d *(= destroy) disease, village, race* ausrotten; *enemy, battalion* aufreiben

▶ **wipe up** VT *sep liquid* aufwischen, aufputzen *(Sw)*; *dishes* abtrocknen VI abtrocknen

wipe: **wipe-down** N Abreibung *f*; **wipe-over** N **to give sth a ~** etw über- *or* abwischen

wiper ['waɪpə'] N (Scheiben)wischer *m*

wiper blade N *(Aut)* Wischblatt *nt*, Wischerblatt *nt*

wiping-up ['waɪpɪŋ'ʌp] N **to do the ~** abtrocknen

wire [waɪə'] N a Draht *m*; *(for electricity supply)* Leitung *f*; *(= insulated flex)* *(for home appliance etc)* Schnur *f*; *(for television)* Fernsehanschluss *m or* -kabel *nt*; *(in circus: = high wire)* (Hoch)seil *nt*; **to get in under the ~** *(US inf)* etwas gerade (eben) noch rechtzeitig *or* mit Hängen und Würgen *(inf)* schaffen; **to pull ~s** *(esp US inf)* seinen Einfluss geltend machen, seine Beziehungen spielen lassen; **he's pulling your ~** *(Brit inf)* er nimmt dich auf den Arm *(inf)*; **you've got your ~s crossed there** *(inf)* Sie verwechseln da etwas; *(said to two people)* Sie reden aneinander vorbei
b *(Telec)* Telegramm *nt*, Kabel *nt (old)*
c *(= microphone)* Wanze *f (inf)*
VT a *(= put in wiring) plug* anschließen; *house* die (elektrischen) Leitungen verlegen in *(+dat)*; *(= connect to electricity)* (an das Stromnetz) anschließen; **it's all ~d (up) for television** die Verkabelung für das Fernsehen ist vorhanden
b *(Telec)* telegrafieren, kabeln *(old)*
c *(= fix on wire) beads* auf Draht auffädeln; *(= fix with wire)* mit Draht zusammen- *or* verbinden; **to ~ the parts together** die Teile mit Draht zusammen- *or* verbinden
VI telegrafieren, drahten, kabeln *(old)*

▶ **wire up** VT *sep lights, battery, speakers* anschließen; *house* elektrische Leitungen *or* den Strom verlegen in *(+dat)*; **we wired the room up as a recording studio** wir haben den Raum als Aufnahmestudio eingerichtet

wire: **wire brush** N Drahtbürste *f*; **wire cutters** PL Drahtschere *f*; **wire gauze** N Drahtgaze *f or* -netz *nt*; **wire-haired** ADJ drahthaarig, Drahthaar-; **~ terrier** Drahthaarterrier *m*

wireless ['waɪəlɪs] *(esp Brit dated)* N a *(also* **wireless set)** Radio *nt*, Rundfunkgerät *nt*, Radioapparat *m* b *(= radio)* Rundfunk *m*; *(also* **wireless telegraphy)** drahtlose Telegrafie; *(also* **wireless telephony)** drahtlose Übertragung, drahtloses Telefon; **~ operator** *(on ship, plane)* Funker(in) *m(f)*; **to send a message by ~** eine Botschaft über Funk schicken *or* senden
VT funken; *base etc* anfunken VI funken

wireless: **wireless card** N *(Comput)* kabellose Netzwerkkarte; **wireless phone** N schnurloses Telefon

wire: **wireman** N *(esp US)* a *(= electrician)* Elektroinstallateur(in) *m(f)*, Elektriker(in) *m(f)* b *(inf, for wiretapping etc)* Abhörspezialist(in) *m(f)* c *(= journalist) Journalist, der für eine Nachrichtenagentur arbeitet*; **wire mesh** N Maschendraht *m*; **wire netting** N Maschendraht *m*; **wirephoto** N *(= method)* Bildtelegrafie *f*; *(= picture)* Bildtelegramm *nt*; **wirepuller** ['waɪə,pʊlə'] N *(esp US inf)* Drahtzieher(in) *m(f)*; **wire-pulling** ['waɪə,pʊlɪŋ] N *(esp US inf)* Drahtziehen *nt*, Drahtzieherei *f*; **wire rope** N Drahtseil *nt*; **wire service** N *(US)* Nachrichtendienst *m*, Nachrichtenagentur *f*; **wiretap** ['waɪətæp] N *(= device)* Abhörgerät *nt*, Wanze *f*; *(= activity)* Abhören *nt* VT *phone, conversation* abhören, anzapfen; *building* abhören in *(+dat)*; **wiretapper** ['waɪətæpə'] N Abhörer(in) *m(f)*; **wiretapping** ['waɪətæpɪŋ] N Abhören *nt*, Anzapfen *nt* von Leitungen; **wire wheel** N Rad *nt* mit Sportfelgen; **wire wool** N Stahlwolle *f*; **wireworm** N Drahtwurm *m*

wiring ['waɪərɪŋ] N elektrische Leitungen *pl*, Stromkabel *pl*

wiring diagram N Schaltplan *m or* -schema *nt*

wiry ['waɪərɪ] ADJ *(+er)* a *(= coarse)* drahtig; *hair also* borstig b *(= thin) frame* drahtig

Wis N *(dated US) abbr of* **Wisconsin**

wisdom ['wɪzdəm] N Weisheit *f*; *(= prudence)* Einsicht *f*; **to show great ~** große Klugheit *or* Einsicht zeigen; **to doubt the ~ of sth** bezweifeln, ob etw klug *or* sinnvoll ist; **the conventional ~** die herkömmliche Überzeugung

wisdom tooth N Weisheitszahn *m*

wise[1] [waɪz] ADJ *(+er)* weise; *(= prudent, sensible) move, step etc* klug, gescheit, vernünftig; *(inf: = smart)* klug, schlau; **a ~ choice** eine kluge *or* gute Wahl; **the Three Wise Men** die drei Weisen; **to be ~ in the ways of the world** Lebenserfahrung haben, das Leben kennen; **to be ~ after the event** hinterher den Schlauen spielen *or* gut reden haben; **I'm none the ~r** *(inf)* ich bin nicht klüger als zuvor *or* vorher; **nobody will be any the ~r** *(inf)* niemand wird etwas (davon) merken *or* das spitzkriegen *(inf)*; **you'd be ~ to …** du tätest gut daran, …; **it would be ~ to accept the offer** es wäre klug, das Angebot anzunehmen; **you'd better get ~** *(US inf)* nimm endlich Vernunft an; **to get ~ to sb/sth** *(inf)* jd/etw spitzkriegen *(inf)*, dahinterkommen, wie jd/etw ist; **to be ~ to sb/sth** *(inf)* jdn/etw kennen; **he fooled her twice, then she got ~ to him** zweimal hat er sie hereingelegt, dann ist sie ihm auf die Schliche gekommen; **to put sb ~ to sb/sth** *(inf)* jdn über jdn/etw aufklären *(inf)*

▸ **wise up** *(inf)* VI **if he doesn't wise up soon to what's going on …** wenn er nicht bald dahinterkommt *or* wenn ihm nicht bald ein Licht aufgeht *(inf)*, was da gespielt wird …; **if he doesn't wise up soon to the need for …** wenn er nicht bald hinter die Notwendigkeit zu … kommt; **he's never going to wise up** der lernts nie!, der wird auch nie klüger; **wise up, man!** Mann, wach auf *or* nimm Vernunft an! VT *sep* aufklären *(inf)* (*to* über *+acc*)

wise² N, *no pl (old)* Weise *f*; **in this ~** auf diese Weise, so; **in no ~** in keiner Weise, keineswegs

-wise ADV *suf* -mäßig, in puncto, in Bezug auf *(+acc)*; **money-wise** geldmäßig, in puncto Geld, in Bezug auf Geld

wise: **wiseacre** N Besserwisser(in) *m(f)*, Neunmalkluge(r) *mf*; **wisecrack** N Witzelei *f*; *(pej)* Stichelei *f*; **to make a ~ (about sb/sth)** witzeln (über jdn/etw) VTI witzeln; **wise guy** N *(inf)* Klugscheißer *m (inf)*

wisely ['waɪzlɪ] ADV weise; *(= sensibly)* klugerweise

wish [wɪʃ] ✪ 8.4, 18.3, 20.6, 21.2, 23.1, 23.3, 24.2, 24.3 N **a** Wunsch *m* (*for* nach); **your ~ is my command** dein Wunsch ist *or* sei mir Befehl; **I have no great ~ to see him** ich habe kein Bedürfnis *or* keine große Lust, ihn zu sehen; **to make a ~** sich *(dat)* etwas wünschen; **you can make three ~es** du hast drei Wünsche; **the ~ is father to the thought** *(prov)* der Wunsch ist Vater des Gedankens *(prov)*; **well, you got your ~** jetzt hast du ja, was du wolltest; **you shall have your ~** dein Wunsch soll (dir) erfüllt werden *or* soll in Erfüllung gehen
b wishes PL *(in greetings)* **with best ~es** mit den besten Wünschen *or* Grüßen, alles Gute; **please give him my good ~es** bitte grüßen Sie ihn (vielmals) von mir, bitte richten Sie ihm meine besten Wünsche aus; **he sends his best ~es** er lässt (vielmals) grüßen; **a message of good ~es** eine Gruß- *or* Glückwunschbotschaft; **best ~es for a speedy recovery** alles Gute für eine baldige Genesung
VT **a** *(= want)* wünschen; **I do not ~ it** ich möchte *or* wünsche *(form)* es nicht; **he ~es to be alone/to see you immediately** er möchte allein sein/dich sofort sehen; **I ~ you to be present** ich wünsche, dass Sie anwesend sind; **what do you ~ me to do?** was soll ich (bitte) tun?; **do you ~ more coffee, sir?** *(Scot form)* hätten Sie gern *or* wünschen Sie noch Kaffee?
b *(= desire, hope, desire sth unlikely)* wünschen, wollen; **I ~ the play would begin** ich wünschte *or* wollte, das Stück finge an; **I ~ you'd be quiet** ich wünschte *or* wollte, du wärest ruhig; **how he ~ed that his wife was** *or* **were there** wie sehr er sich *(dat)* wünschte, dass seine Frau hier wäre; **~ you were here** ich wünschte *or* wollte, du wärest hier
c *(= entertain wishes towards sb)* wünschen; **to ~ sb well/ill** jdm Glück *or* alles Gute/Schlechtes *or* Böses wünschen; **I don't ~ her any harm** ich wünsche ihr nichts Böses; **to ~ sb good luck/happiness** jdm viel Glück *or* alles Gute/Glück (und Zufriedenheit) wünschen
d *(= bid, express wish)* wünschen; **to ~ sb a pleasant journey/good morning/merry Christmas** jdm eine gute Reise/guten Morgen/frohe Weihnachten wünschen; **to ~ sb goodbye** jdm Auf *or* auf Wiedersehen sagen
e to ~ a ~ sich *(dat)* etwas wünschen; **he ~ed himself anywhere but there** er wünschte sich nur möglichst weit weg; **if I could ~ myself into the castle** wenn ich mich nur in das Schloss wünschen könnte
VI *(= make a wish)* sich *(dat)* etwas wünschen; **~ing won't solve the problem** der Wunsch allein wird das Problem nicht lösen; **to ~ upon a star** *(liter)* sich *(dat)* bei einer Sternschnuppe etwas wünschen

▸ **wish away** VT *sep difficulty* weg- *or* fortwünschen *(inf)*

▸ **wish for** VI *+prep obj* **to wish for sth** sich *(dat)* etw wünschen; **what more could you wish for?** etwas Besseres kann man sich doch gar nicht wünschen, was kann sich der Mensch noch mehr wünschen? *(inf)*; **it was everything we had wished for** es war genauso, wie wir es uns gewünscht hatten; **she had everything she could wish for** sie hatte alles, was man sich nur wünschen kann

▸ **wish on** *or* **upon** VT *sep +prep obj* (*inf*: *= foist*) **to wish sb/sth on** *or* **upon sb** jdn jdm/jdm etw aufhängen *(inf)*; **I would not wish that/that job on** *or* **upon my worst enemy!** das/diese Arbeit würde ich meinem ärgsten Feind nicht wünschen

wishbone ['wɪʃbəʊn] N Gabelbein *nt*

wishful ['wɪʃfʊl] ADJ **that's just ~ thinking** das ist reines Wunschdenken, das ist nur ein frommer Wunsch

wish fulfilment, *(US)* **wish fulfillment** ['wɪʃfʊl'fɪlmənt] N Wunscherfüllung *f*

wishing well ['wɪʃɪŋ'wel] N Wunschbrunnen *m*

wishwash ['wɪʃwɒʃ] N (*inf*: *drink*) labb(e)riges Zeug; (*fig*: *= talk*) seichtes Geschwätz *(pej)*

wishy-washiness ['wɪʃɪ,wɒʃɪnɪs] N *(of coffee, soup)* Labberigkeit *f*, Wässrigkeit *f*; *(of person, character)* saft- und kraftlose Art, Farblosigkeit *f*, Laschheit *f*; *(of colour)* Verwaschenheit *f*; *(of argument)* Schwachheit *f*; **the ~ of this report** das allgemeine Geschwätz *(inf)* in diesem Bericht

wishy-washy ['wɪʃɪ,wɒʃɪ] ADJ *coffee, soup* labberig, wässrig; *person, character* saft- und kraftlos, farblos, lasch; *colour* verwaschen; *argument* schwach *(inf)*; *report, story* ungenau, wachsweich, wischiwaschi *(inf)*

wisp [wɪsp] N **a** *(of straw, hair etc)* kleines Büschel; *(of cloud)* Fetzen *m*; *(of smoke)* Fahne *f*, Wölkchen *nt* **b** *(= person)* elfenhaftes *or* zartes *or* zerbrechliches Geschöpf **c** *(= trace)* zarte Spur *or* Andeutung; *(= fragment)* Hauch *m*

wispy ['wɪspɪ] ADJ *(+er) grass* dürr, fein; *girl* zerbrechlich, zart; **~ clouds** Wolkenfetzen *pl*; **~ hair** dünne Haarbüschel

wisteria [wɪs'tɪərɪə] N Glyzinie *f*, Wistarie *f*

wistful ['wɪstfʊl] ADJ *smile, thoughts, mood, eyes* wehmütig; *song also* schwermütig

wistfully ['wɪstfəlɪ] ADV *smile, think, look, sigh* wehmütig

wistfulness ['wɪstfʊlnɪs] N *(of smile, thoughts, look)* Wehmut *f*; *(of song)* Schwermut *f*

wit¹ [wɪt] VI *(old Jur)* **to ~** nämlich, und zwar

wit² [wɪt] N **a** *(= understanding)* Verstand *m*; **beyond the ~ of man** über den menschlichen Verstand *or* Horizont hinaus; **a battle of ~s** ein geistiges Kräftemessen; **to be at one's ~s' end** am Ende seiner Weisheit sein, mit seinem Latein am Ende sein *(hum inf)*; **I was at my ~s' end (to find a solution)** ich wusste mir keinen Rat *or* Ausweg mehr(, wie ich eine Lösung finden könnte); **to drive sb out of his ~s** jdn um seinen Verstand bringen; **to lose one's ~s** den *or* seinen Verstand verlieren; **to collect one's ~s** seine fünf Sinne (wieder) zusammennehmen; **to frighten** *or* **scare sb out of his ~s** jdn zu Tode erschrecken; **to be frightened** *or* **scared out of one's ~s** zu Tode erschreckt sein; **to have** *or* **keep one's ~s about one** seine (fünf) Sinne zusammen- *or* beisammenhaben, einen klaren Kopf haben; **to sharpen one's ~s** seinen Verstand schärfen; **to use one's ~s** seinen Verstand gebrauchen, sein Köpfchen *or* seinen Grips anstrengen *(inf)*; **to live by** *or* **on one's ~s** sich schlau *or* klug durchs Leben schlagen
b *(= humour, wittiness)* Geist *m*, Witz *m*; **full of ~** geistreich; **the book is full of ~** es ist sehr viel Geistreiches in dem Buch
c *(= person)* geistreicher Kopf

witch [wɪtʃ] N *(lit, fig)* Hexe *f*

witch: **witchcraft** N Hexerei *f*, Zauberei *f*; **a book on ~** ein Buch über (die) Hexenkunst; **witch doctor** N Medizinmann *m*

witch-elm ['wɪtʃelm] N Bergulme *f*

witchery ['wɪtʃərɪ] N *(= witchcraft)* Hexerei *f*; *(= fascination)* Zauber *m*

witches' ['wɪtʃɪz]: **witches' brew** N Zaubertrank *m*; *(fig)* Teufelszeug *nt (inf)*; **witches' Sabbath** N Hexensabbat *m*

witch hazel N *(Bot)* Zaubernuss *f*; *(Med)* Hamamelis *f*

witch-hunt ['wɪtʃhʌnt] N *(lit, fig)* Hexenjagd *f*

witching ['wɪtʃɪŋ] ADJ **the ~ hour** die Geisterstunde

with [wɪð, wɪθ] PREP **a** mit; **are you pleased ~ it?** bist du damit zufrieden?; **bring a book ~ you** bring ein Buch mit; **~ no …** ohne …; **(together) ~ the Victory, it's the biggest ship of its class** neben der Victory ist es das größte Schiff in seiner Klasse; **to walk ~ a stick** am *or* mit einem Stock gehen; **put it ~ the rest** leg es zu den anderen; **the wind was ~ us** wir hatten den Wind im Rücken, wir fuhren *etc* mit dem Wind; **how are things ~ you?** wie gehts?, wie stehts? *(inf)* → **with it**
b *(= at house of, in company of etc)* bei; **I'll be ~ you in a moment** einen Augenblick bitte, ich bin gleich da; **10 years ~ the company** 10 Jahre bei *or* in der Firma; **the problem is still ~ us** wir haben immer noch das alte Problem
c *(on person, in bag etc)* bei; **I haven't got my cheque book ~ me** ich habe mein Scheckbuch nicht bei mir
d *(cause)* vor *(+dat)*; **to shiver ~ cold** vor Kälte zittern; **the hills are white ~ snow** die Berge sind weiß vom Schnee; **to be ill ~ measles** die Masern haben, an Masern erkrankt sein
e *(= in the case of)* bei, mit; **it's always the same ~ you** es ist (doch) immer dasselbe mit dir; **the trouble ~ him is that he …** die Schwierigkeit bei *or* mit ihm ist (die), dass er …; **it's a habit ~ him** das ist bei ihm Gewohnheit; **~ God, all things are possible** bei *or* für Gott ist kein Ding unmöglich
f *(= while sb/sth is)* wo; **you can't go ~ your mother ill in bed** wo deine Mutter krank im Bett liegt, kannst du nicht gehen; **~ all this noise going on** bei diesem Lärm; **to quit ~ the job half-finished** von der halb fertigen Arbeit weglaufen; **~ the window open** bei offenem Fenster
g *(= in proportion)* mit; **it varies ~ the temperature** es verändert sich je nach Temperatur; **wine improves ~ age** Wein wird mit zunehmendem Alter immer besser; **it gets bigger ~ the heat** in der Wärme wird es immer größer
h *(= in spite of)* trotz, bei; **~ all his faults** bei allen seinen Fehlern, trotz aller seiner Fehler
i *(= in agreement, on side of)* **I'm ~ you there** *(inf)* da stimme ich dir zu; **is he ~ us or against us?** ist er für oder gegen uns?
j *(inf, expressing comprehension)* **are you ~ me?** kapierst du? *(inf)*, hast dus? *(inf)*, kommst du mit? *(inf)*; **I'm not ~ you** da komm ich nicht mit *(inf)*; **are you still ~ me?** kommst du (da) noch mit? *(inf)*, ist das noch klar?

withdraw [wɪθ'drɔː] *pret* **withdrew**, *ptp* **withdrawn** VT *object, motion, charge, offer* zurückziehen; *troops, team also* abziehen; *ambassador* zurückrufen *or* -beordern; *coins, stamps* einziehen, aus dem Verkehr ziehen; *(from bank) money* abheben; *words, comment* zurücknehmen, widerrufen; *privileges* entziehen; **the workers withdrew their labour** *(Brit) or* **labor** *(US)* die Arbeiter haben ihre Arbeit niedergelegt; **she withdrew her hand from his** sie entzog ihm ihre Hand
VI sich zurückziehen; *(Sport also)* zurücktreten (*from* von), nicht antreten (*from* von/bei); *(= move away)* zurücktreten *or* -gehen; **to ~ in favour** *(Brit) or* **favor** *(US)* **of sb else** zugunsten *or*

zu Gunsten eines anderen zurücktreten; **to ~ into oneself** sich in sich *(acc)* selber zurückziehen; **to ~ to one's room** sich in sein Zimmer zurückziehen; **you can't ~ now** *(from agreement)* du kannst jetzt nicht zurücktreten *or* abspringen *(inf)*

withdrawal [wɪθ'drɔːəl] N *(of objects, charge)* Zurückziehen *nt*; *(of ambassador)* Abziehen *nt*; *(of coins, stamps)* Einziehen *nt*; *(of money)* Abheben *nt*; *(of words)* Zurücknehmen *nt*, Zurücknahme *f*; *(of troops)* Rückzug *m*; *(= withdrawing)* Abziehen *nt*; *(in sport)* Abzug *m*; *(from drugs)* Entzug *m*; **to make a ~ from a bank** von einer Bank Geld abheben

withdrawal: **withdrawal slip** N Rückzahlungsschein *m*; **withdrawal symptoms** PL Entzugserscheinungen *pl*

withdrawn [wɪθ'drɔːn] *ptp of* **withdraw** ADJ *person* verschlossen; *manner also* reserviert, zurückhaltend; *life* zurückgezogen

withdrew [wɪθ'druː] *pret of* **withdraw**

withe [wɪθ] N *(old)* (dünne) Weidenrute

wither ['wɪðəʳ] VT *plants etc* verdörren, austrocknen; *(fig)* zum Schwinden bringen; **to ~ sb with a look** jdm einen vernichtenden Blick zuwerfen VI **a** *(lit)* verdorren, ausdorren; *(limb)* verkümmern **b** *(fig)* welken; *(religion)* dahinschwinden

▶ **wither away** VI = **wither VI**

▶ **wither up** VI = **wither VI a**

withered ['wɪðəd] ADJ *plant, grass* verdorrt, vertrocknet; *skin* verhutzelt, hutzelig; *limb* verkümmert; **a ~ old man** ein verschrumpfter *or* hutzeliger Alter

withering ['wɪðərɪŋ] ADJ *heat* ausdörrend; *criticism, look, tone* vernichtend

witheringly ['wɪðərɪŋlɪ] ADV *say, look* vernichtend

withers ['wɪðəz] PL Widerrist *m*

withhold [wɪθ'həʊld] *pret, ptp* **withheld** [wɪθ'held] VT vorenthalten; *truth also* verschweigen; *(= refuse) consent, help* verweigern, versagen *(geh)*; **the members threatened to ~ their payments** die Mitglieder drohten, die Zahlung der Beiträge zu verweigern; **to ~ sth from sb** jdm etw vorenthalten/verweigern; **name withheld** *(in newspaper, report etc)* Name der Redaktion bekannt

withholding tax [wɪθ'həʊldɪŋtæks] *(US)* (vom Arbeitgeber) einbehaltene Steuer

within [wɪð'ɪn] PREP innerhalb *(+gen)*; *(temporal also)* binnen *(+dat or (geh) +gen)*, innert *(+gen) (Aus, S Ger)*; **a voice ~ me said ...** eine Stimme in meinem Inneren *or* in mir sagte ...; **we were ~ 100 feet of the finish** wir waren auf den letzten 100 Fuß vor dem Ziel; **we came ~ 50 feet of the summit** wir kamen bis auf 50 Fuß an den Gipfel heran; **~ his power** in seiner Macht; **to keep ~ the law** sich im Rahmen des Gesetzes bewegen; **to live ~ one's means** *or* **income** im Rahmen seiner finanziellen Möglichkeiten leben
ADV *(old, liter)* innen; **from ~** von drinnen; *(= on the inside)* von innen; **let us go ~** wollen wir hineingehen; **but he's rotten ~** aber innerlich ist er verderbt

with-it ['wɪðɪt] ADJ *attr*, **with it** ADJ *pred (inf)* **a** *(= up-to-date, trendy)* up to date **b** *pred (= awake, alert)* **to be with it** da sein *(inf)*

without [wɪð'aʊt] PREP ohne; **~ a tie/passport** ohne Krawatte/(einen) Pass; **~ a friend in the world** ohne einen einzigen Freund; **~ speaking** ohne zu sprechen, wortlos; **~ my noticing it** ohne dass ich es bemerkte; **times ~ number** unzählige Male *pl* ADV *(old, liter)* außen; **from ~** von draußen; *(= on the outside)* von außen ADJ *pred* ohne; **to be ~ sth** etw nicht haben, einer Sache *(gen)* entbehren *(form)*; **those who are ~** *(= needy)* die Bedürftigen *pl*

without-profits [wɪð'aʊtˌprɒfɪts] ADJ *policy etc* ohne Gewinnbeteiligung

with-profits ['wɪðˌprɒfɪts] ADJ *policy etc* mit Gewinnbeteiligung

withstand [wɪθ'stænd] *pret, ptp* **withstood** [wɪθ'stʊd] VT *cold, scrutiny, pressure* standhalten *(+dat)*; *enemy, climate, attack, temptation also* trotzen *(+dat)*; *persuasion etc* widerstehen *(+dat)*; *loss* verkraften

withy ['wɪðɪ] N *(= willow)* Korbweide *f*; *(= twig)* Weide(nrute) *f*

witless ['wɪtlɪs] ADJ *(= mentally defective)* schwachsinnig; *(= stupid, silly)* dumm, blöd(e) *(inf)*; *(= lacking wit) prose* geistlos; **to be scared ~** zu Tode erschreckt sein; **to be bored ~** sich zu Tode langweilen

witlessness ['wɪtlɪsnɪs] N *(= stupidity)* Dummheit *f*, Blödheit *f (inf)*

witness ['wɪtnɪs] N **a** *(= person: Jur, fig)* Zeuge *m*, Zeugin *f*; **~ for the defence** *(Brit) or* **defense** *(US)* Zeuge *m*/Zeugin *f* der Verteidigung; **~ for the prosecution** Zeuge *m*/Zeugin *f* der Anklage; **as God is my ~** Gott sei *or* ist mein Zeuge; **to call sb as a ~** jdn als Zeugen/Zeugin vorladen; **I was then ~ to a scene ...** ich wurde Zeuge einer Szene ...
b *(= evidence)* Zeugnis *nt*; **in ~ whereof** *(form)* zu Urkund *or* zum Zeugnis dessen; **to bear ~ to sth** *(lit, fig)* Zeugnis über etw *(acc)* ablegen; *(actions, events also)* von etw zeugen
VT **a** *(= see) accident* Zeuge/Zeugin sein bei *or (+gen)*; *scenes* (mit)erleben, mit ansehen; *changes* erleben; **the year 1945 ~ed great changes** das Jahr 1945 sah einen großen Wandel
b *(= testify)* bezeugen; **to call sb to ~ that ...** jdn zum Zeugen dafür rufen, dass ...
c *(= consider as evidence)* denken an *(+acc)*, zum Beispiel nehmen; **~ the case of X** denken Sie nur an den Fall X, nehmen Sie nur den Fall X zum Beispiel
d *(= attest by signature) signature, will* bestätigen
VI *(= testify)* bestätigen, bezeugen; **to ~ to sth** etw bestätigen *or* bezeugen; **to ~ against sb** gegen jdn aussagen

witness box, *(US)* **witness stand** N Zeugenbank *f*, Zeugenstand *m*

witness protection program N *(US Jur)* Zeugenschutzprogramm *nt*

witness statement N Zeugenaussage *f*

-witted [-'wɪtɪd] ADJ *suf* **dull-witted** geistig träge; **quick-witted** geistig rege

witter ['wɪtəʳ] VI *(Brit inf: also* **witter on***)* labern *(inf)*

witticism ['wɪtɪsɪzəm] N geistreiche Bemerkung

wittily ['wɪtɪlɪ] ADV *(= humorously)* witzig, geistreich

wittiness ['wɪtɪnɪs] N Witzigkeit *f*

wittingly ['wɪtɪŋlɪ] ADV bewusst, absichtlich, wissentlich *(form)*; **~ or unwittingly** bewusst oder unbewusst

witty ['wɪtɪ] ADJ *(+er)* witzig, geistreich

wives [waɪvz] *pl of* **wife**

wizard ['wɪzəd] N **a** Zauberer *m*, Hexenmeister *m* **b** *(inf)* Genie *nt*, Leuchte *f (inf)*; **a financial ~** ein Finanzgenie *nt*; **a ~ with the ball** ein Zauberer *m* am *or* mit dem Ball; **a ~ at computing** ein Computergenie *nt (inf)* **c** *(Comput)* Assistent *m* ADJ *(dated Brit inf)* famos, prima *(inf)*

wizardry ['wɪzədrɪ] N *(= magic)* Hexerei *f*, Zauberei *f*; *(= great skill)* Zauberkünste *pl*; **his ~ with the ball** seine Zauberkunststücke *pl* mit dem Ball

wizened ['wɪznd] ADJ verhutzelt, verschrumpelt

wk *abbr of* **week** Wo.

wkly *abbr of* **weekly** wö.

WLTM *(inf) abbr of* **would like to meet**

Wm *abbr of* **William**

WMD *(Mil) abbr of* **weapons of mass destruction** Massenvernichtungswaffen *pl*

WNW *abbr of* **west-north-west** WNW

w/o *abbr of* **without** o.

woad [wəʊd] N *(= dye)* Waid *m*; *(= plant)* (Färber)waid *m*

wobble ['wɒbl] N Wackeln *nt*; **the chair has a ~** der Stuhl wackelt VI wackeln; *(tightrope walker, dancer also, cyclist)* schwanken; *(voice, hand, compass needle)* zittern; *(wheel)* eiern *(inf)*, einen Schlag haben; *(chin, jelly etc)* schwabbeln; **he ~d about on his new bike** er wackelte auf seinem neuen Fahrrad durch die Gegend; **his massive stomach was wobbling like a jelly** *(Brit)* sein rieseger Bauch wabbelte wie ein Wackelpudding *(inf)* VT rütteln an *(+dat)*, ruckeln an *(+dat)*, wackeln an *(+dat)*

wobbly ['wɒblɪ] ADJ *(+er)* wackelig; *voice, notes also, hand* zitterig, zitternd; *jelly* (sch)wabbelig; *wheel* eiernd; **to be ~** *(inf, after illness)* wackelig auf den Beinen sein *(inf)*; **to feel ~** sich schwach fühlen, wackelig auf den Beinen sein *(inf)* N *(inf: = fit of rage)* **to throw a ~** ausrasten *(inf)*, einen Wutanfall bekommen

wodge [wɒdʒ] N *(Brit inf) (of cake, plaster etc)* Brocken *m*; *(of paper)* Knäuel *nt or m*; *(of cotton wool)* Bausch *m*; *(of documents, papers)* Stoß *m*

woe [wəʊ] N **a** *(liter, hum, sorrow)* Jammer *m*; **~ (is me)!** weh mir!; **~ betide him who ...!** wehe dem, der ...!; **a tale of ~** eine Geschichte des Jammers **b** *(esp pl: = trouble, affliction)* Kummer *m*; **to pour out one's ~s to sb** sich *(dat)* seinen Kummer bei jdm von der Seele reden

woebegone ['wəʊbɪˌgɒn] ADJ kläglich, jämmerlich; *expression also* jammervoll; *voice* (weh)klagend, jammernd

woeful ['wəʊfʊl] ADJ *(= sad)* traurig; *(= deplorable) neglect also, ignorance, lack* bedauerlich, beklagenswert

woefully ['wəʊfəlɪ] ADV kläglich, jämmerlich; *(= very)* bedauerlich; **he is ~ ignorant of ...** es ist bestürzend, wie wenig er über ... weiß; **he discovered they were ~ ignorant of ...** er stellte zu seiner Bestürzung fest, wie wenig sie über ... wussten; **sb/sth is ~ short of** *or* **lacking in sth** jdm/einer Sache *(dat)* fehlt es bedauerlicherweise an etw *(dat)*

wog [wɒg] N *(Brit pej sl) (= non-white foreigner)* Kanake *m (pej sl)*; *(= Arab)* Ali *m (pej sl)*

wok [wɒk] N *(Cook)* Wok *m*

woke [wəʊk] *pret of* **wake**

woken ['wəʊkn] *ptp of* **wake**

wolf [wʊlf] N *pl* **wolves** **a** Wolf *m* **b** *(fig inf: = womanizer)* Don Juan *m* **c** *(phrases)* **a ~ in sheep's clothing** ein Wolf im Schafspelz; **to cry ~** blinden Alarm schlagen; **to keep the ~ from the door** sich über Wasser halten; **to throw sb to the wolves** jdn den Wölfen zum Fraß vorwerfen → **lone** VT *(inf: also* **wolf down***) food* hinunterschlingen

wolf: **wolf cub** N *(lit)* Wolfsjunge(s) *nt*; *(Brit: = boy scout)* Wölfling *m*; **wolfhound** N Wolfshund *m*

wolfish ['wʊlfɪʃ] ADJ *grin, look* anzüglich

wolfishly ['wʊlfɪʃlɪ] ADV *grin* anzüglich

wolf pack N Rudel *nt* Wölfe; *(of submarines)* Geschwader *nt*

wolfram ['wʊlfrəm] N Wolfram *nt*

wolfsbane ['wʊlfsbeɪn] N *(Bot)* Eisenhut *m*

wolf whistle *(inf)* N bewundernder Pfiff; **they gave her a ~** sie pfiffen ihr nach VI nachpfeifen

wolverine ['wʊlvəriːn] N Vielfraß *m*

wolves [wʊlvz] *pl of* **wolf**

woman ['wʊmən] N *pl* **women** Frau *f*, Frauenzimmer *nt (pej hum)*; *(= domestic help)* (Haushalts)hilfe *f*; *(inf) (= girlfriend)* Mädchen *nt*; *(= mistress)* Geliebte *f*, Weib *nt (pej)*; **a ~'s work is never done** *(prov)* Frauenhände ruhen nie *(Prov)*; **man that is made of ~** *(Rel)* der Mensch, vom Weib geboren; **how like a ~!** typisch Frau!; **cleaning ~** Putzfrau *f*, Reinmachefrau *f*; **~ is a mysterious creature** Frauen sind geheimnisvolle Wesen; **where's my supper, ~!** Weib, wo ist das Essen!; **the little ~** *(inf: = wife)* die *or* meine Frau; **to run after women** den Frauen nachrennen; **that's ~'s work** das ist Frauenarbeit; **women's talk** Gespräche *pl* von Frau zu

Frau → **old woman**
ADJ *attr* ~ **doctor** Ärztin *f*; ~ **lawyer** Anwältin *f*; ~ **teacher** Lehrerin *f*; ~ **driver** Frau *f* am Steuer

woman: **woman-hater** N Frauenhasser(in) *m(f)*; **womanhood** N *(= women in general)* alle Frauen, die Frauen *pl*; **to reach** ~ (zur) Frau werden

womanish [ˈwʊmənɪʃ] ADJ *(= womanly) woman* fraulich; *(pej: = effeminate) man* weibisch

womanize [ˈwʊmənaɪz] VI hinter den Frauen her sein; **this womanizing will have to stop** die Frauengeschichten müssen aufhören; **young men out for an evening's womanizing** junge Männer, die ausziehen, um sich mit Mädchen zu amüsieren

womanizer [ˈwʊmənaɪzəʳ] N Frauenheld *m*, Aufreißer(typ) *m (inf)*

womankind [ˈwʊmənˌkaɪnd] N das weibliche Geschlecht

womanliness [ˈwʊmənlɪnɪs] N Weiblichkeit *f*

womanly [ˈwʊmənlɪ] ADJ *figure, person* fraulich; *qualities, virtues* weiblich

womb [wuːm] N Mutterleib *m*, Gebärmutter *f (Med)*; *(fig)* Schoß *m*; **the foetus in the** ~ der Embryo im Mutterleib; **it's just a yearning to return to the** ~ das ist nur die Sehnsucht nach der Geborgenheit des Mutterschoßes

wombat [ˈwɒmbæt] N Wombat *m*

women [ˈwɪmɪn] *pl of* **woman**

womenfolk [ˈwɪmɪnfəʊk] PL Frauen *pl*

women-only ADJ nur für Frauen

women's [ˈwɪmɪnz]: **women's department** N *(in department store)* Frauenabteilung *f*; **women's lib** N *(inf)* Frauen(rechts)bewegung *f*; **women's libber** [ˈwɪmɪnzˈlɪbəʳ] N *(inf)* Frauenrechtlerin *f*, Emanze *f*; **women's magazine** N Frauenzeitschrift *f*; **Women's Movement** N Frauenbewegung *f*; **women's page** N Frauenseite *f*; **women's prison** N Frauengefängnis *nt*; **women's refuge** N Frauenhaus *nt*; **women's rights** PL Frauenrechte *pl*, die Rechte *pl* der Frau; **women's room** N *(US)* Damentoilette *f*; **women's studies** PL *(Univ)* Frauenforschung *f*

won [wʌn] *pret, ptp of* **win**

wonder [ˈwʌndəʳ] ✪ 16.1, 19.1, 26.1 N **a** *(= feeling)* Staunen *nt*, Verwunderung *f*; **in** ~ voller Staunen; **the birth of a baby never loses its** ~ eine Geburt bleibt immer etwas Wunderbares; **it fills one with a sense of** ~ es erfüllt einen mit Erstaunen; **he has never lost that almost childlike sense of** ~ er hat nie dieses kindliche Staunen verlernt
b *(= object or cause of wonder)* Wunder *nt*; **the** ~ **of electricity** das Wunder der Elektrizität; **the seven ~s of the world** die sieben Weltwunder; **the** ~ **of it was that ...** das Erstaunliche *or* Verblüffende daran war, dass ...; **it is a** ~ **that ...** es ist ein Wunder, dass ...; **it is no** *or* **little** *or* **small** ~ (es ist) kein Wunder, es ist nicht zu verwundern; **no** ~ **(he refused)!** kein Wunder(, dass er abgelehnt hat)!; **to do** *or* **work ~s** wahre Wunder vollbringen, Wunder wirken; **~s will never cease!** es geschehen noch Zeichen und Wunder! → **nine**
VT **I** ~ **what he'll do now** ich bin gespannt, was er jetzt tun wird *(inf)*; **I** ~ **why he did it** ich möchte (zu gern) wissen *or* ich wüsste (zu) gern, warum er das getan hat; **I** ~ **why!** *(iro)* ich frag mich warum?; **I was ~ing if you'd like to come too** möchten Sie nicht vielleicht auch kommen?; **I was ~ing when you'd realize that** ich habe mich (schon) gefragt, wann du das merkst; **I was ~ing if you could ...** könnten Sie nicht vielleicht ...
VI **a** *(= ask oneself, speculate)* **it set me ~ing** *or* **made me** ~ es gab mir zu denken; **why do you ask? – oh, I was just ~ing** warum fragst du? – ach, nur so; **what will happen next, I ~?** ich frage mich *or* ich bin gespannt, was als Nächstes kommt; **what's going to happen next? – I ~!** was kommt als Nächstes? – das frage ich mich auch!; **I was ~ing about that** ich habe mir darüber schon Gedanken gemacht, ich habe mich das auch schon gefragt; **I've been ~ing about him** ich habe mir auch schon über ihn Gedanken gemacht; **I've been ~ing about him as a possibility** ich hatte ihn auch schon als eine Möglichkeit ins Auge gefasst; **I expect that will be the end of the matter – I ~!** ich denke, damit ist die Angelegenheit erledigt – da habe ich meine Zweifel *or* da bin ich gespannt; **I'm ~ing about going to the party** ich habe daran gedacht, vielleicht auf die Party zu gehen; **John, I've been ~ing, is there really any point?** John, ich frage mich, ob es wirklich (einen) Zweck hat; **could you possibly help me, I** ~ könnten Sie mir vielleicht helfen
b *(= be surprised)* sich wundern; **I** ~ **(that) he didn't tell me** es wundert mich, dass er es mir nicht gesagt hat; **to** ~ **at sth** sich über etw *(acc)* wundern, über etw *(acc)* erstaunt sein; **that's hardly to be ~ed at** das ist kaum verwunderlich; **she'll be married by now, I shouldn't** ~ es würde mich nicht wundern, wenn sie inzwischen verheiratet wäre

wonder *in cpds* Wunder-; **wonder boy** N Wunderknabe *m*; **wonder drug** N Wunderheilmittel *nt*

wonderful [ˈwʌndəfʊl] ADJ wunderbar

wonderfully [ˈwʌndəfəlɪ] ADV wunderbar; **he looks** ~ **well** er sieht wunderbar aus

wondering [ˈwʌndərɪŋ] ADJ *(= astonished) tone, look* verwundert, erstaunt; *(= doubtful)* fragend

wonderingly [ˈwʌndərɪŋlɪ] ADV *(= with astonishment)* verwundert, erstaunt; *(= thoughtfully)* nachdenklich

wonderland [ˈwʌndəˌlænd] N *(= fairyland)* Wunderland *nt*; *(= wonderful place)* Paradies *nt*; **the** ~ **of the Alps** die Wunderwelt der Alpen

wonderment [ˈwʌndəmənt] N = **wonder N a**

wonder-worker [ˈwʌndəˌwɜːkəʳ] N Wundertäter(in) *m(f)*

wondrous [ˈwʌndrəs] *(old, liter)* ADJ wunderbar; *ways also* wundersam ADV *wise, fair* wunderbar

wondrously [ˈwʌndrəslɪ] ADV *(old, liter)* wunderbar; ~ **beautiful** wunderschön

wonga [ˈwɒŋə] N *(dated inf)* Moos *nt (dated sl)*, Knete *f (dated sl)*

wonk [wɒŋk] N *(US inf)* Streber(in) *m(f) (inf)*; **she's a policy** ~ sie kennt die (Politik)richtlinien bis zum letzten Komma

wonky [ˈwɒŋkɪ] ADJ *(+er) (Brit inf) chair, marriage, grammar* wackelig; *nose* krumm, schief; *machine* nicht (ganz) in Ordnung; *sense of judgement etc* nicht ganz richtig, aus dem Lot; **your hat's a bit/your collar's all** ~ dein Hut/dein Kragen sitzt ganz schief

wont [wəʊnt] ADJ gewohnt; **to be** ~ **to do sth** gewöhnlich etw tun, etw zu tun pflegen N (An)gewohnheit *f*; **as is/was his** ~ wie er zu tun pflegt/pflegte

won't [wəʊnt] *contr of* **will not**

wonted [ˈwəʊntɪd] ADJ *(liter)* gewohnt

woo [wuː] VT **a** *(dated, = court) woman* den Hof machen *(+dat)*, umwerben **b** *person* umwerben; *(fig) stardom, sleep etc* suchen; *audience etc* für sich zu gewinnen versuchen

▶ **woo away** VT *sep employee, executive, voter, customer* abwerben

wood [wʊd] N **a** *(= material)* Holz *nt*; **touch ~!** *(esp Brit)* **knock on ~!** *(esp US)* dreimal auf Holz geklopft!
b *(= small forest)* Wald *m*; **~s** Wald *m*; **we're not out of the ~s yet** *(fig)* wir sind noch nicht über den Berg *or* aus dem Schneider *(inf)*; **he can't see the** ~ **for the trees** *(Brit, prov)* er sieht den Wald vor (lauter) Bäumen nicht *(prov)*
c *(= cask)* Holzfass *nt*; *(Bowls)* Kugel *f*; *(Golf)* Holz *nt*; **whisky matured in the** ~ im Holzfass gereifter Whisky; **that was off the** ~ *(Tennis)* das war Holz, das war vom Rahmen
d *(Mus)* **the woods** PL die Holzblasinstrumente *pl*, die Holzbläser *pl*
ADJ *attr (= made of wood)* Holz-; ~ **floor** Holzboden *m*

wood: **wood alcohol** N Holzgeist *m*; **wood anemone** N Buschwindröschen *nt*

woodbine [ˈwʊdbaɪn] N *(= honeysuckle)* Geißblatt *nt*; *(US: = Virginia creeper)* wilder Wein, Jungfernrebe *f*

wood: **wood block** N *(Art)* Holzschnitt *m*; **wood carver** N (Holz)schnitzer(in) *m(f)*; **wood carving** N (Holz)schnitzerei *f*; **woodchip** N *(Brit: = wallpaper)* Raufaser *f*; **woodchuck** N Waldmurmeltier *nt*; **woodcock** N *no pl* Waldschnepfe *f*; **woodcraft** N **a** *(= skill at living in forest)* Waldläufertum *nt* **b** *(= skill at woodwork)* Geschick *nt* im Arbeiten mit Holz;; **woodcut** N Holzschnitt *m*; **woodcutter** N **a** Holzfäller(in) *m(f)*; *(of logs)* Holzhacker(in) *m(f)* **b** *(Art)* Holzschnitzer(in) *m(f)*;; **woodcutting** N **a** Holzfällen *nt*; *(of logs)* Holzhacken *nt* **b** *(Art)* Holzschnitzen *nt*; *(= item)* Holzplastik *f*, Holzschnitzerei *f*

wooded [ˈwʊdɪd] ADJ bewaldet

wooden [ˈwʊdn] ADJ **a** Holz-; ~ **chair** Holzstuhl *m*; **the** ~ **horse** das hölzerne Pferd **b** *(fig) expression, smile, manner, performance, acting* hölzern; *(pej: = dull) personality* steif

woodenheaded [ˈwʊdnˈhedɪd] ADJ dumm

wooden leg N Holzbein *nt*

woodenly [ˈwʊdnlɪ] ADV *(fig) smile, act, bow* gekünstelt, steif; *stand* wie ein Klotz; *look, stare* mit unbeweglicher Miene

wooden: **wooden spoon** N *(lit)* Holzlöffel *m*, hölzerner Löffel; *(fig)* Trostpreis *m*; **woodenware** N Holzwaren *pl*

wood: **woodfree** ADJ *paper* holzfrei; **woodland** N Waldland *nt*, Waldung *f*; **woodlark** N Heidelerche *f*; **woodlouse** N Bohrassel *f*; **woodman** N = **woodsman**; **wood nymph** N Waldnymphe *f*; **woodpecker** N Specht *m*; **wood pigeon** N Ringeltaube *f*; **woodpile** N Holzhaufen *m*; **wood pulp** N Holzschliff *m*; **woodshed** N Holzschuppen *m*

woodsman [ˈwʊdzmən] N *pl* **-men** [-mən] Waldarbeiter *m*

wood sorrel N Waldsauerklee *m*

woodsy [ˈwʊdzɪ] ADJ *(+er) (US inf)* waldig; ~ **smell** Waldgeruch *m*, Geruch *m* von Wald

wood: **wood-turning** N Drechslerei *f*; **wood wasp** N Holzwespe *f*; **woodwind** N Holzblasinstrument *nt*; **the ~(s), the** ~ **section** die Holzbläser *pl*; **wood wool** N Holzwolle *f*; **woodwork** N **a** Holzarbeit *f*; *(= craft)* Tischlerei *f*; **the boys do** ~ **on Tuesday afternoons** dienstags nachmittags beschäftigen sich die Jungen mit Tischlern **b** *(= wooden parts)* Holzteile *pl*; **to hit the** ~ *(Ftbl inf)* den Pfosten/die Latte treffen; **to come out of the** ~ *(fig)* aus dem Unterholz *or* der Versenkung hervorkommen; **woodworking** [ˈwʊdˌwɜːkɪŋ] N Holzbearbeitung *f* ADJ Holz bearbeitend, Holzbearbeitungs-; **woodworm** N Holzwurm *m*; **it's got** ~ da ist der Holzwurm drin

woody [ˈwʊdɪ] ADJ *(+er)* **a** *(= wooded)* waldig, bewaldet **b** *(= like wood in texture) tissue* holzig; ~ **paper** holzhaltiges Papier

wooer [ˈwuːəʳ] N *(dated)* Werber *m*; *(fig)* Buhler(in) *m(f) (of sth* um etw); **a** ~ **of the unions** ein Buhler um die Gunst der Gewerkschaften

woof[1] [wʊf] N *(Tex)* Schuss *m*

woof[2] N *(of dog)* Wuff *nt* VI kläffen; **~, ~!** wau, wau!, wuff, wuff!

woofer [ˈwʊfəʳ] N Tieftöner *m*

woofter [ˈwʊftəʳ], **wooftah** [ˈwʊftə] N *(Brit sl)* Warme(r) *m (dated inf)*, Schwule(r) *m (inf)*

wool [wʊl] N **a** Wolle *f*; *(= cloth)* Wollstoff *m*; **all ~, pure** ~ reine Wolle; **to pull the** ~ **over sb's eyes** *(inf)* jdm Sand in die Augen streuen *(inf)* **b** *(= glass wool, wire wool)* Wolle *f* ADJ Woll-; *(= made of wool also)* aus Wolle; ~ **coat** Wollmantel *m*

woolen *etc (US)* = **woollen** *etc*

wool: **woolgathering** [ˈwʊlˌgæðərɪŋ] N Träumen *nt*; **to be** ~ vor sich *(acc)* hin träumen; **woolgrower** [ˈwʊlˌgrəʊəʳ] N Schafzüchter(in) *m(f) (für Wolle)*

woollen, *(US)* **woolen** ['wʊlən] ADJ Woll-; *(= made of wool also)* wollen, aus Wolle; **~ blanket** Wolldecke *f* N **woollens** PL *(= garments)* Wollsachen *pl*, Stricksachen *pl*; *(= fabrics, blankets)* Wollwaren *pl*

woolliness, *(US)* **wooliness** ['wʊlɪnɪs] N Wolligkeit *f*; *(= softness also)* Flauschigkeit *f*; *(fig: of outline)* Verschwommenheit *f*; *(pej, of mind, idea)* Verworrenheit *f*, Wirrheit *f*

woolly, *(US)* **wooly** ['wʊlɪ] ADJ *(+er)* **a** wollig; *(= soft also)* flauschig; **~ mammoth** *(Zool)* Kältesteppenmammut *m* **b** *(fig) outline* verschwommen; *(pej) mind, thinking, idea* verworren, wirr; **~ thoughts** wirre Gedanken *pl*; **a ~ liberal** ein sentimentaler Liberaler, eine sentimentale Liberale N *(inf: = sweater etc)* Pulli *m (inf)*; **winter woollies** *(esp Brit: = sweaters etc)* dicke Wollsachen *pl (inf)*; *(esp US: = underwear)* Wollene *pl (inf)*

wool: **woolmark** ['wʊlmɑːk] N Wollsiegel *nt*; **woolsack** ['wʊlsæk] N *(= seat)* Wollsack *m (Sitz des Lordkanzlers im britischen Oberhaus)*; *(= office)* Amt *nt* des Lordkanzlers

wooziness ['wuːzɪnɪs] N *(inf)* Benommenheit *f*

woozy ['wuːzɪ] ADJ *(+er) (inf)* benommen, duselig *(inf)*

wop [wɒp] N *(pej sl)* Spag(h)ettifresser(in) *m(f) (pej sl)*

Worcs *abbr of* **Worcestershire**

word [wɜːd] N **a** *(= unit of language)* Wort *nt*; **~s** Wörter *pl*; *(in meaningful sequence)* Worte *pl*; **~ division** Silbentrennung *f*; **foreign ~s** Fremdwörter *pl*; **~ for ~** Wort für Wort; *(= exactly also)* wortwörtlich; **cold isn't the ~ for it** kalt ist gar kein Ausdruck (dafür); **"irresponsible" would be a better ~ for it** „unverantwortlich" wäre wohl das treffendere Wort dafür; **~s cannot describe it** so etwas kann man mit Worten gar nicht beschreiben; **beyond ~s** unbeschreiblich; **too funny for ~s** unbeschreiblich komisch; **to put one's thoughts into ~s** seine Gedanken in Worte fassen *or* kleiden; **in a ~** mit einem Wort, kurz gesagt; **(not) in so many ~s** (nicht) direkt *or* ausdrücklich; **in other ~s** mit anderen Worten, anders gesagt *or* ausgedrückt; **in one's own ~s** mit eigenen Worten; **the last ~** *(fig)* der letzte Schrei (*in* an *+dat*); **he had the last ~** er hatte das letzte Wort; **that's not the ~ I would have chosen** ich hätte es nicht so ausgedrückt; **in the ~s of Goethe** mit Goethe gesprochen, um mit Goethe zu sprechen

b *(= remark)* Wort *nt*; **~s** Worte *pl*; **a ~ of advice** ein Rat(schlag) *m*; **a ~ of encouragement/warning** eine Ermunterung/Warnung; **fine ~s** schöne Worte *pl*; **a man of few ~s** ein Mann, der nicht viele Worte macht; **I can't get a ~ out of him** ich kann kein Wort aus ihm herausbekommen; **by ~ of mouth** durch mündliche Überlieferung; **to say a few ~s** ein paar Worte sprechen; **to be lost** *or* **at a loss for ~s** nicht wissen, was man sagen soll; **to take sb at his ~** jdn beim Wort nehmen; **to have a ~ with sb (about sth)** *(= talk to)* mit jdm (über etw) sprechen; **to have a ~ with sb** *(= reprimand, discipline)* jdn ins Gebet nehmen; **John, could I have a ~?** John, kann ich dich mal sprechen?; **(could I have) a ~ in your ear?** kann ich Sie bitte allein *or* unter vier Augen sprechen?; **a ~ to the wise** ein guter Rat; **you took the ~s out of my mouth** du hast mir das Wort aus dem Mund genommen; **I wish you wouldn't put ~s into my mouth** ich wünschte, Sie würden mir nicht das Wort im Munde herumdrehen; **to put in** *or* **say a (good) ~ for sb** für jdn ein gutes Wort einlegen; **nobody had a good ~ to say for him** niemand wusste etwas Gutes über ihn zu sagen; **without a ~** ohne ein Wort; **don't say** *or* **breathe a ~ about it** sag aber bitte keinen Ton *or* kein Sterbenswörtchen *(inf)* davon; **remember, not a ~ to anyone** vergiss nicht, kein Sterbenswörtchen *(inf)*

c **words** PL *(= quarrel)* **to have ~s with sb** mit jdm eine Auseinandersetzung haben

d **words** PL *(= text, lyrics)* Text *m*

e *no pl (= message, news)* Nachricht *f*; **~ went round that …** es ging die Nachricht um, dass …; **to leave ~ (with sb/for sb) that …** (bei jdm/für jdn) (die Nachricht) hinterlassen, dass …; **is there any ~ from John yet?** schon von John gehört?, schon Nachrichten von John?; **to send ~** Nachricht geben; **to send ~ to sb** jdn benachrichtigen; **to send sb ~ of sth** jdn von etw benachrichtigen; **to spread the ~ (around)** *(inf)* es allen sagen *(inf)*; **what's the ~ on Charlie?** *(inf)* was gibts Neues von Charlie?

f *(= promise, assurance)* Wort *nt*; **~ of honour** *(Brit) or* **honor** *(US)* Ehrenwort *nt*; **a man of his ~** ein Mann, der zu seinem Wort steht; **to be true to** *or* **as good as one's ~, to keep one's ~** sein Wort halten; **I give you my ~** ich gebe dir mein (Ehren)wort; **to go back on one's ~** sein Wort nicht halten; **to break one's ~** sein Wort brechen; **I only have his ~ for it** ich habe nur sein Wort dafür; **take my ~ for it** verlass dich drauf, das kannst du mir glauben; **you don't have to take my ~ for it** du kannst das ruhig nachprüfen; **it's his ~ against mine** Aussage steht gegen Aussage; **upon my ~!** *(old)* **my ~!** meine Güte!

g *(= order)* Wort *nt*; (*also* **word of command**) Kommando *nt*, Befehl *m*; **to give the ~ (to do sth)** *(Mil)* das Kommando geben(, etw zu tun); **just say the ~** sag nur ein Wort; **his ~ is law here** sein Wort ist hier Gesetz

h *(Rel)* Wort *nt*; **the Word of God** das Wort Gottes; **to preach the Word** das Wort Gottes *or* das Evangelium verkünden

VT (in Worten) ausdrücken, formulieren, in Worte fassen *(geh)*; *letter* formulieren; *speech* abfassen

word: **word association** N Wortassoziation *f*; **word-blind** ADJ wortblind; **word blindness** N Wortblindheit *f*; **wordbook** N Wörterbuch *nt*; *(Mus)* Textbuch *nt*, Libretto *nt*; **word break** ['wɜːdbreɪk] N *(of a word)* (Silben)trennung *f*; **word class** N Wortklasse *f*; **word-count** N *(Comput)* Wortzählung *f*; **word-crunch** VT *(Comput inf) text* (nach Wörtern) analysieren; **word deafness** N *(Med, Psych)* Worttaubheit *f*; **word ending** N *(Ling)* Wortendung *f*; **word formation** N Wortbildung *f*; **word game** N Buchstabenspiel *nt*

wordily ['wɜːdɪlɪ] ADV wortreich, langatmig *(pej)*

wordiness ['wɜːdɪnɪs] N Wortreichtum *m*, Langatmigkeit *f (pej)*

wording ['wɜːdɪŋ] N Formulierung *f*

word: **wordless** ADJ wortlos; *grief* stumm; **word list** N Wortliste *f*; **word order** N Satzstellung *f*, Wortstellung *f*; **word-perfect** ADJ sicher im Text; **to be ~** den Text perfekt beherrschen, den Text bis aufs Wort beherrschen; **word picture** N Bild *nt* (in Worten); **to paint a vivid ~ of sth** etw in lebhaften Farben beschreiben; **wordplay** N Wortspiel *nt*; **word-process** VT mit Textverarbeitung schreiben *or* erstellen; **word processing** N Textverarbeitung *f*; **word-processing** ADJ ATTR Textverarbeitungs-; **~ software** Textverarbeitungssoftware *f*; **word processor** N *(= machine)* Textverarbeitungssystem *nt*, Textverarbeitungsanlage *f*; *(= software)* Textverarbeitungsprogramm *nt*; **word split** N Worttrennung *f*; **word square** N magisches Quadrat; **word wrap** N *(Comput)* (automatischer) Zeilenumbruch

wordy ['wɜːdɪ] ADJ *(+er)* wortreich, langatmig *(pej)*

wore [wɔː'] *pret of* **wear**

work [wɜːk] ✪ 19.1, 19.2 N **a** *(= toil, labour, task)* Arbeit *f*; **have you got any ~ for me?** haben Sie was für mich zu tun?; *(= employment)* haben Sie Arbeit für mich?; **he doesn't like ~** er arbeitet nicht gern; **that's a good piece of ~** das ist gute Arbeit; **is this all your own ~?** haben Sie das alles selbst gemacht?; **closed for ~ on the roof** wegen (Reparatur)arbeiten am Dach geschlossen; **when ~ begins on the new bridge** wenn die Arbeiten an der neuen Brücke anfangen; **to be at ~ (on sth)** (an etw *dat*) arbeiten; **there are forces at ~ which …** es sind Kräfte am Werk, die …; **it's the ~ of the devil** das ist Teufelswerk *or* ein Machwerk des Teufels; **to do a good day's ~** ein schönes Stück Arbeit leisten; **nice** *or* **good ~!** gut *or* super *(inf)* gemacht!; **we've a lot of ~ to do before this choir can give a concert** wir haben noch viel zu tun, ehe dieser Chor ein Konzert geben kann; **you need to do some more ~ on your accent/your technique** Sie müssen noch an Ihrem Akzent/an Ihrer Technik arbeiten; **to get** *or* **set to ~ on sth** sich an etw *(acc)* machen; **I've been trying to get some ~ done** ich habe versucht zu arbeiten; **to put a lot of ~ into sth** eine Menge Arbeit in etw *(acc)* stecken; **it's in the ~s** *(inf)* es ist in der Mache *(inf)*; **to get on with one's ~** sich (wieder) an die Arbeit machen; **to make short** *or* **quick ~ of sb/sth** mit jdm/etw kurzen Prozess machen; **to make ~ for sb** jdm Arbeit machen; **time/the medicine had done its ~** die Zeit/Arznei hatte ihr Werk vollbracht/ihre Wirkung getan; **the ~ of a moment** eine Angelegenheit von Sekunden; **it was hard ~ for the old car to get up the hill** das alte Auto hatte beim Anstieg schwer zu schaffen

b *(= employment, job)* Arbeit *f*; **to be (out) at ~** arbeiten sein; **to go out to ~** arbeiten gehen; **to be out of ~** arbeitslos sein; **to be in ~** eine Stelle haben; **he travels to ~ by car** er fährt mit dem Auto zur Arbeit; **do you live close to your ~?** hast du es weit zur Arbeit?; **how long does it take you to get to ~?** wie lange brauchst du, um zu deiner Arbeitsstelle zu kommen?; **at ~** an der Arbeitsstelle, am Arbeitsplatz; **what is your ~?** was tun Sie (beruflich)?; **to put** *or* **throw sb out of ~** jdn arbeitslos machen; **to be off ~** (am Arbeitsplatz) fehlen

c *(= product) Arbeit f*; *(Art, Liter)* Werk *nt*; **a ~ of art** ein Kunstwerk *nt*; **a ~ of reference** ein Nachschlagewerk *nt*; **a ~ of literature** ein literarisches Werk; **a fine piece of ~** eine schöne Arbeit; **good ~s** gute Werke *pl*; **a chance for artists to show their ~** eine Gelegenheit für Künstler, ihre Arbeiten *or* Werke zu zeigen

d **works** PL *(Mil)* Befestigungen *pl*

e **works** PL *(Mech)* Getriebe, Innere(s) *nt*; *(of watch, clock)* Uhrwerk *nt*

f **works** SING OR PL *(Brit: = factory)* Betrieb *m*, Fabrik *f*; **gas/steel ~s** Gas-/Stahlwerk *nt*; **~s gate** Fabrik- *or* Werkstor *nt*; **~s outing** Betriebsausflug *m*

g *(inf)* **the works** PL alles Drum und Dran; **to give sb the ~s** *(= treat harshly)* jdn gehörig in die Mangel nehmen *(inf)*; *(= treat generously)* jdn nach allen Regeln der Kunst *or* nach Strich und Faden verwöhnen *(inf)*; **to get the ~s** *(= be treated harshly)* gehörig in die Mangel genommen werden *(inf)*; *(= be treated generously)* nach allen Regeln der Kunst *or* nach Strich und Faden verwöhnt werden *(inf)*; **we had fantastic food, wine, brandy, the ~s** es gab tolles Essen, Wein, Kognak, alle Schikanen *(inf)*; **he was giving his opponent the ~s** er machte seinen Gegner nach allen Regeln der Kunst fertig *(inf)*

VI **a** *person* arbeiten (*at* an *+dat*); **to ~ toward(s)/for sth** auf etw *(acc)* hin/für etw arbeiten; **to ~ for better conditions** *etc* sich für bessere Bedingungen *etc* einsetzen; **to ~ against a reform** gegen eine Reform kämpfen; **these factors which ~ against us/in our favour** *(Brit) or* **favor** *(US)* diese Faktoren, die gegen uns/zu unseren Gunsten arbeiten

b *(= function, operate)* funktionieren; *(plan)* funktionieren, klappen *(inf)*; *(medicine, spell)* wirken; *(= be successful)* klappen *(inf)*; **it won't ~** das klappt nicht; **"not ~ing"** *(lift etc)* „außer Betrieb"; **to get sth ~ing** etw in Gang bringen; **it ~s by** *or* **on electricity** es läuft auf Strom; **it ~s both ways** es trifft auch andersherum zu; **but this arrangement will have to ~ both ways** aber diese Abmachung muss für beide Seiten gelten

c *(yeast)* arbeiten, treiben

d *(mouth, face)* zucken; *(jaws)* mahlen

e *(= move gradually)* **to ~ loose** sich lockern; **to ~ along** sich entlangarbeiten; **to ~ round**

(wind, object) sich langsam drehen (*to* nach); **he ~ed (a)round to asking her** er hat sich aufgerafft, sie zu fragen; **OK, I'm ~ing (a)round to it** okay, das mache ich schon noch

VT **a** *(= make work) staff, employees, students* arbeiten lassen, herannehmen *(inf)*, schinden *(pej)*; **to ~ oneself/sb hard** sich/jdn nicht schonen; **he ~s himself too hard** er übernimmt sich; **to ~ oneself to death** sich zu Tode arbeiten

b *(= operate) machine* bedienen; *lever, brake* betätigen; **to ~ sth by electricity/hand** etw elektrisch/mit Hand betreiben; **can we ~ that trick again?** können wir den Trick noch einmal anbringen *or* anwenden?

c *(= bring about) change, cure* bewirken, herbeiführen; **to ~ mischief** Unheil anrichten; **to ~ it (so that ...)** *(inf)* es so deichseln(, dass ...) *(inf)*; **to ~ one's passage** seine Überfahrt abarbeiten; **you don't have to ~ your notice** Sie brauchen Ihre Kündigungsfrist nicht einzuhalten → **work up**

d *(Sew)* arbeiten; *design etc* sticken

e *(= shape) wood, metal* bearbeiten; *dough, clay also* kneten, bearbeiten; **he ~ed the clay into a human shape** er formte den Ton zu einer menschlichen Gestalt; **~ the flour in gradually/the ingredients together** mischen Sie das Mehl allmählich unter/die Zutaten (zusammen)

f *(= exploit) mine* ausbeuten, abbauen; *land* bearbeiten; *smallholding* bewirtschaften; *(salesman) area* bereisen

g *muscles* trainieren

h *(= move gradually)* **to ~ one's hands free** seine Hände freibekommen; **to ~ sth loose** etw losbekommen; **to ~ one's way through a book** sich durch ein Buch arbeiten; **to ~ one's way to the top** sich nach oben arbeiten *or* kämpfen; **to ~ one's way up from nothing** sich von ganz unten hocharbeiten; **to ~ one's way through college** sein Studium selbst *or* durch eigene Arbeit finanzieren; **he ~ed his way across the rock face/through the tunnel** er überquerte die Felswand/kroch durch den Tunnel; **to ~ oneself into sb's confidence** sich in jds Vertrauen *(acc)* einschleichen

▶ **work away** VI vor sich hin arbeiten

▶ **work down** VI *(stockings)* (herunter)rutschen *(inf)*

▶ **work in** **VT** *sep* **a** *(= rub in)* einarbeiten; *lotion* einmassieren; **it had worked its way right in** es war (tief) eingedrungen **b** *(= insert) bolt etc* (vorsichtig) einführen **c** *(in book, speech) reference* einbauen, einarbeiten; *jokes* einbauen; **to work sth into sth** etw in etw *(acc)* einbauen **d** *(in schedule etc)* einschieben; **to work sb into a plan** jdn in einen Plan miteinbeziehen **VI** **a** *(= fit in)* passen (*with* in *+acc*); **that'll work in quite well** das passt ganz gut **b** *(Ind)* den Arbeitsplatz besetzen

▶ **work off** **VI** sich losmachen *or* lockern **VT** *sep debts, fat* abarbeiten; *energy* loswerden; *feelings* auslassen, abreagieren (*on* an *+dat*)

▶ **work on** **VI** weiterarbeiten

VT *sep lid, washer* daraufbringen

VI *+prep obj* **a** *car, book, subject, accent* arbeiten an *(+dat)*; **who's working on this case?** wer bearbeitet diesen Fall?

b *evidence, assumption* ausgehen von; *principle (person)* ausgehen von; *(machine)* arbeiten nach; **there are not many clues to work on** es gibt nicht viele Hinweise, auf die man zurückgreifen könnte; **I'm working on this one lead** ich habe alles an diesem einen Anhaltspunkt aufgehängt

c **we haven't solved it yet but we're still working on it** wir haben es noch nicht gelöst, aber wir sind dabei; **if we work on him a little longer we might persuade him** wenn wir ihn noch ein Weilchen bearbeiten, können wir ihn vielleicht überreden; **obviously the other side have been working on him** ihn hat offensichtlich die Gegenseite in der Mache gehabt *(inf)*

▶ **work out** **VI** **a** *(= allow solution: puzzle, sum etc)* aufgehen

b *(= amount to)* **that works out at £105** das gibt *or* macht £ 105; **it works out more expensive in the end** am Ende kommt *or* ist es teurer; **how much does that work out at?** was macht das?

c *(= succeed: plan, marriage, idea)* funktionieren, klappen *(inf)*; **things didn't work out at all well for him** es ist ihm alles schiefgegangen; **how's your new job working out?** was macht die neue Arbeit?; **I hope it all works out for you** ich hoffe, dass alles klappt *(inf) or* dass dir alles gelingt; **things didn't work out that way** es kam ganz anders

d *(in gym etc)* Fitnesssport machen, trainieren

VT *sep* **a** *(= solve, calculate)* herausbringen; *code* entschlüsseln, knacken *(inf)*; *mathematical problem* lösen; *problem* fertig werden mit; *sum* ausrechnen; **you can work that out for yourself** das kannst du dir (doch) selbst denken; **surely he can manage to work things out for himself** *(in life)* er kann doch bestimmt allein zurechtkommen; **things will always work themselves out** Probleme lösen sich stets von selbst

b *(= devise) scheme* (sich *dat*) ausdenken; *(in detail)* ausarbeiten

c *(= understand) person* schlau werden aus *(+dat)*; **can you work out where we are on the map?** kannst du herausfinden *or* -bringen, wo wir auf der Karte sind?; **I can't work out why it went wrong** ich kann nicht verstehen, wieso es nicht geklappt hat

d *(= complete) prison sentence* absitzen; **to work out one's notice** seine Kündigungsfrist einhalten

e *(= exhaust) mine* ausbeuten, erschöpfen; *minerals* abbauen; **to work sth out of one's system** *(fig)* etw überwinden, mit etw fertig werden

f *(= remove) nail, tooth etc* (allmählich) herausbringen

▶ **work over** VT *sep (inf)* zusammenschlagen *(inf)*

▶ **work through** **VI** *+prep obj* **a** *(blade etc)* sich arbeiten durch; *(water)* sickern durch **b** *(= read through)* sich (durch)arbeiten *or* (durch)ackern durch **c** *(Psych) problem* aufarbeiten **VT SEP** *+prep obj* **he worked the rope through the crack** er führte das Seil durch die Spalte **VI** *(= come through: benefit, pay rise etc)* durchsickern

▶ **work up** **VT** *sep* **a** *(= develop) business* zu etwas bringen, entwickeln; *enthusiasm (in oneself)* aufbringen; *appetite* sich *(dat)* holen; *courage* sich *(dat)* machen; **to work one's way up (through the ranks)** von der Pike auf dienen; **to work up a sweat** richtig ins Schwitzen kommen **b** *lecture, theme, notes* ausarbeiten **c** *(= stimulate) audience* aufstacheln; **to work up feeling against sb** gegen jdn Stimmung machen; **to be worked up** aufgeregt sein; **to get worked up** sich aufregen; **to work oneself up** sich erhitzen → **frenzy** **VI** *(skirt etc)* sich hochschieben

▶ **work up to** VI *+prep obj question, proposal etc* zusteuern auf *(+acc)*; **I know what you're working up to** ich weiß, worauf Sie hinauswollen; **the music works up to a tremendous climax** die Musik steigert sich zu einem gewaltigen Höhepunkt

workability [ˌwɜːkəˈbɪlɪtɪ] N **a** *(Tech, of material)* Bearbeitungsfähigkeit *f* **b** *(Tech, of machine)* Betriebsfähigkeit *f* **c** *(of a plan etc)* Durchführbarkeit *f*

workable [ˈwɜːkəbl] ADJ **a** *mine* abbaufähig; *land* bebaubar; *plan, system, agreement* durchführbar; *solution, alternative* machbar; *relationship* funktionierend **b** *(= malleable) clay, metal* formbar

workaday [ˈwɜːkədeɪ] ADJ Alltags-; **~ life** Alltagsleben *nt*

workaholic [ˌwɜːkəˈhɒlɪk] N *(inf)* Arbeitswütige(r) *mf*, Arbeitssüchtige(r) *mf*, Arbeitstier *nt*

workaholism [ˈwɜːkəhɒlɪzəm] N Workaholismus *m (spec)*, Arbeitssucht *f*

work: **work area** N Arbeitsplatz *or* -bereich *m*; **work associate** N Arbeitskollege *m*/-kollegin *f*; **workbag** N *(Sew)* Näh- *or* Handarbeitsbeutel *m*; **work basket** N *(Sew)* Näh- *or* Handarbeitskorb *m*; **workbench** N Werkbank *f*; **workbook** N Arbeitsheft *nt*; **work camp** N Arbeitslager *nt*; **work coat** N *(US)* Arbeitsmantel *m*, Arbeitskittel *m*; **workday** N *(esp US)* Arbeitstag *m*; *(= weekday)* Werktag *m*

worker [ˈwɜːkəʳ] N **a** Arbeiter(in) *m(f)*; **~s' education** Arbeiterbildung *f* → **fast¹** ADJ **a** **b** *(also* **worker ant/bee***)* Arbeiterin *f*

worker: **worker bee** N Arbeiterbiene *f*, Arbeitsbiene *f*; **worker director** N *Arbeitnehmer, der gleichzeitig dem Unternehmensvorstand angehört*; **worker participation** N Mitbestimmung *f*; **worker-priest** N Arbeiterpriester *m*

work: **work ethic** N Arbeitsmoral *f*; **workfare** [ˈwɜːkfɛəʳ] N *Programm, das Arbeitslose verpflichtet, eine Tätigkeit oder Ausbildung zu absolvieren, um weiterhin Zahlungen zu empfangen*; **work file** N *(Comput)* Arbeitsdatei *f*; **workflow** N Arbeitsablauf *m*; **workflow schedule** N Arbeitsablaufplan *m*; **workforce** N Arbeitskräfte *pl*; **work glove** N Arbeitshandschuh *m*; **workhorse** N *(lit, fig)* Arbeitspferd *nt*; **work hour** N = **working hour**; **workhouse** N *(Brit Hist)* Armenhaus *nt*; **work-in** N Work-in *nt*

working [ˈwɜːkɪŋ] **ADJ** **a** *(= engaged in work) population* arbeitend, berufstätig; *(Comm) partner* aktiv; **~ man** Arbeiter *m*; **I'm a ~ man, I need my rest** ich arbeite den ganzen Tag, ich brauche meine Ruhe; **~ wives** berufstätige Ehefrauen *pl*; **~ woman** berufstätige Frau

b *(= spent in or used for working)* Arbeits-; **~ conditions** Arbeitsbedingungen *pl*; **~ hours** Arbeitszeit *f*; **during ~ hours** während der Arbeitszeit; **your order will be sent within three ~ days** ihre Bestellung wird innerhalb von drei Werktagen geschickt

c *(= provisional)* Arbeits-; *(= sufficient) majority* arbeitsfähig; **to have a ~ majority** eine arbeitsfähige Mehrheit haben; **~ hypothesis** Arbeitshypothese *f*; **in ~ order** funktionsfähig; **in good/perfect ~ order** voll funktionsfähig; **~ knowledge** Grundkenntnisse *pl*

d *farm, mill, sailing ship, steam train* in Betrieb

N **a** *(= work)* Arbeiten *nt*, Arbeit *f*

b **workings** **PL** *(= way sth works)* Arbeitsweise *f*, Funktionsweise *f*; **~s of fate** Wege *pl* des Schicksal; **~s of the mind** Gedankengänge *pl*; **in order to understand the ~s of this machine/system** um zu verstehen, wie die Maschine/das System funktioniert

c **workings** **PL** *(Min)* Schächte *pl*, Gänge *pl*; *(of quarry)* Grube *f*

working: **working assets** PL *(Econ)* Betriebsvermögen *nt*; **working capital** N Betriebskapital *nt*; **working class** N *(also* **working classes***)* Arbeiterklasse *f*; **working-class** ADJ der Arbeiterklasse; *(pej)* ordinär, proletenhaft; **to be ~** zur Arbeiterklasse gehören; **~ culture** Arbeiterkultur *f*; **working companion** N Arbeitskamerad(in) *m(f)*; **working condition** N **a** *(Tech)* Betriebszustand *m* **b** **~s** *pl* Arbeitsbedingungen *pl*; **working copy** N Arbeitsexemplar *nt*; **working dinner** N = **working lunch**; **working directory** N *(Comput)* Arbeitsverzeichnis *nt*; **working dog** N Arbeitshund *m*, *Hund, der für bestimmte Aufgaben abgerichtet ist*; **working expenses** PL *(Econ)* Betriebskosten *pl*; **working girl** N *(euph)* Prostituierte *f*; **working group** N Arbeitsgruppe *f*, Arbeitskreis *m*; **working holiday** N *(Brit) Urlaub, in dem eine bezahlte Tätigkeit ausgeübt wird*; **working hour** N Arbeitsstunde *f*; **~s** *pl* Arbeitszeit *f*; **reduction in** *or* **of ~s** Arbeitszeitverkürzung *f*; **working life** N *(of machine part)* Lebensdauer *f*; *(of animal)* Nutzungsdauer *f*; *(of person)* Berufsleben *nt*; **working lunch** N Arbeitsessen *nt*; **working materials** PL Arbeitsmittel *pl*; **working memory** N *(Comput)* Arbeitsspeicher *m*; **working men's club** N *(Brit)* Arbeiterklub *m*; **working morale** N Arbeitsmoral *f*; **working-out** N *(of a plan etc)* Ausarbeitung *f*; *(of a question etc)* Lösung *f*; **working-over** N *(inf)* Abreibung *f* *(inf)*; **to give sb a good ~** jdm eine tüchtige Abreibung verpassen *(inf)*; **working papers** PL *(Econ)* Arbeitspapiere *pl*; **working party** N (Arbeits)ausschuss *m*; **working pool** N Arbeitsgemeinschaft *f*; **working power** N Arbeitskraft *f*; **working relationship** N Zusammenarbeit *f*; **to have a good ~ with sb** mit jdm gut zusammenarbeiten; **working title** N Arbeitstitel *m*; **working vacation** N *(US)* = **working holiday**; **working visa** N *(US)* Arbeitserlaubnis *f*; **working week** N Arbeitswoche *f*

work: work-in-progress N *(Fin)* laufende Arbeiten *pl*; **workless** [ˈwɜːklɪs] ADJ arbeitslos; **work-life balance** N Work-Life-Balance *f*, Vereinbarkeit *f* von Beruf und Privatleben; **workload** [ˈwɜːkləʊd] N Arbeit(slast) *f*; **workman** N Handwerker *m*; **a bad ~ always blames his tools** *(prov)* ein schlechter Arbeiter gibt immer seinem Werkzeug die Schuld; **workmanlike** [ˈwɜːkmənˈlaɪk] ADJ *attitude, job* fachmännisch; *product* fachmännisch gearbeitet; **workmanship** [ˈwɜːkmənʃɪp] N Arbeit(squalität) *f*; **workmate** N *(inf)* (Arbeits)kollege *m*, (Arbeits)kollegin *f*; **workmen's comp** N *(inf)*, **workmen's compensation** N *(US, in case of occupational disease etc)* Entschädigung *f*; **work-out** N *(Sport)* Training *nt*; **to have a ~** Übungen machen; *(boxer)* Sparring machen; **work permit** N Arbeitserlaubnis *f*; **workpiece** N Werkstück *nt*; **workplace** N Arbeitsplatz *m*; **in** *or* **at the ~** am Arbeitsplatz; **workplace bullying** [-ˈbʊlɪŋ] N Mobbing *nt* (am Arbeitsplatz); **work programme**, *(US)* **work program** N Arbeitsprogramm *nt*; **workroom** N Arbeitszimmer *nt*

works [wɜːks] PL = **work N d-f**

works council, **works committee** N *(esp Brit)* Betriebsrat *m*

work: work-sharing [ˈwɜːkʃeərɪŋ] N Arbeitsteilung *f*; **workshop** N Werkstatt *f*; **a music ~** ein Musikkurs *m*, ein Musik-Workshop *m*; **work-shy** ADJ arbeitsscheu; **work space** N **a** = **work area b** *(Comput)* Workspace *m*; **workstation** N Arbeitsplatz *m*, Arbeitsbereich *m*; *(Comput)* Workstation *f*; **work stoppage** N Arbeitsniederlegung *f*; **work-study** [ˈwɜːkstʌdɪ] N REFA- *or* Arbeitsstudie *f*; **work surface** N Arbeitsfläche *f*; **worktable** N Arbeitstisch *m*; **work ticket** N Arbeitszettel *m*; **worktop** N *(Brit)* Arbeitsfläche *f*; **work-to-rule** N Dienst *m* nach Vorschrift; **work visa** N *(US)* Arbeitserlaubnis *f*; **workwear** [ˈwɜːkweəˈ] N Arbeitskleidung *f*; **workweek** [ˈwɜːkwiːk] N *(esp US)* Arbeitswoche *f*

world [wɜːld] N **a** Welt *f*; **in the ~** auf der Welt; **all over the ~** auf der ganzen Welt; **he jets/sails all over the ~** er jettet/segelt in der Weltgeschichte herum; **it's the same the whole ~ over** es ist (doch) überall das Gleiche; **to go (a)round the ~** eine Weltreise machen; **to sail (a)round the ~** rund um die Welt segeln; **to feel** *or* **be on top of the ~** munter und fidel sein; **it's not the end of the ~!** *(inf)* deshalb *or* davon geht die Welt nicht unter! *(inf)*; **it's a small ~** wie klein doch die Welt ist; **to live in a ~ of one's own** in seiner eigenen (kleinen) Welt leben; **love makes the ~ go round** es dreht sich alles um die Liebe; **money makes the ~ go round** es dreht sich alles um das Geld, Geld regiert die Welt; **in an ideal** *or* **a perfect ~** in einer idealen Welt

b the New/Old/Third World die Neue/Alte/Dritte Welt; **the business ~** die Geschäftswelt; **the sporting ~** die Welt des Sports; **the literary ~** die literarische Welt; **the animal/vegetable ~** die Tier-/Pflanzenwelt; **in the Roman ~** zur Zeit der Römer

c *(= society)* Welt *f*; **man/woman of the ~** Mann *m*/Frau *f* von Welt; **to come** *or* **go down in the ~** herunterkommen; **to go up** *or* **to rise in the ~** es (in der Welt) zu etwas bringen; **he had the ~ at his feet** die ganze Welt lag ihm zu Füßen; **to lead the ~ in sth** in etw *(dat)* in der Welt führend sein; **how goes the ~ with you?** wie gehts?, wie stehts?; **all the ~ knows ...** alle Welt *or* jeder weiß ...; **all the ~ and his wife were there** Gott und die Welt waren da *(inf)*; **in the eyes of the ~** vor der Welt

d *(= this life)* Welt *f*; **to come into the ~** zur Welt kommen, auf die Welt kommen; **~ without end** *(Eccl)* von Ewigkeit zu Ewigkeit; **to renounce the ~** *(Rel)* der Welt *(dat)* entsagen; **to have the best of both ~s** das eine tun und das andere nicht lassen; **out of this ~** *(inf)* fantastisch, phantastisch; **he is not long for this ~** er steht schon mit einem Fuß im Jenseits; **to bring sb into the ~** jdn zur Welt bringen; **to bring sth into the ~** etw in die Welt setzen; **to go to a better ~** in eine bessere Welt eingehen; **to be (all) alone in the ~** allein auf der Welt sein

e *(emph)* Welt *f*; **not for (all) the ~** nicht um alles in der Welt; **nothing in the ~** nichts auf der Welt; **what/who in the ~** was/wer in aller Welt; **it did him a ~ of good** es hat ihm (unwahrscheinlich) gutgetan; **a ~ of difference** ein himmelweiter Unterschied; **they're ~s apart** sie sind total verschieden; **for all the ~ like ...** beinahe wie ...; **he looked for all the ~ as if nothing had happened** er sah aus, als wäre überhaupt nichts geschehen; **to mean the ~ to sb** jdm alles bedeuten; **to think the ~ of sb** große Stücke auf jdn halten

world *in cpds* Welt-; **World Bank** N Weltbank *f*; **world-beater** N *(Brit inf)* **to be a ~** unschlagbar sein; **world champion** N Weltmeister(in) *m(f)*; **world championship** N Weltmeisterschaft *f*; **world class** N *(Sport etc)* Weltklasse *f*; **world-class** [ˌwɜːldˈklɑːs] ADJ Weltklasse-, der Weltklasse; **~ player** Weltklassespieler(in) *m(f)*; **world clock** N Weltzeituhr *f*; **World Court** N Weltgerichtshof *m*; **World Cup** N Fußballweltmeisterschaft *f*; *(= cup)* Weltpokal *m*; **world economy** N Weltwirtschaft *f*; **World Fair** N Weltausstellung *f*; **world-famous** ADJ weltberühmt; **World Health Organization** N Weltgesundheitsorganisation *f*; **World Heritage Site** N Weltkulturerbe *nt or* -denkmal *nt*; **world language** N Weltsprache *f*; **world leader** N **a** *(Pol)* **the ~s** die führenden Regierungschefs der Welt **b** *(Comm: = country, company)* weltweiter Marktführer, Weltführer *m*

world league N *(Sport)* Weltliga *f*

worldliness [ˈwɜːldlɪnɪs] N Weltlichkeit *f*; *(of person)* weltliche Gesinnung

world literature N Weltliteratur *f*

worldly [ˈwɜːldlɪ] ADJ *(+er)* **a** *(= material) success, ambition, wealth* materiell; **~ things** weltliche Dinge **b** weltlich; *person* weltlich gesinnt; *(= sophisticated) manner* weltmännisch; **~ innocence** Weltfremdheit *f*; **~ wisdom** Weltklugheit *f*

worldly-wise [ˈwɜːldlɪˈwaɪz] ADJ weltklug

world: world market N *(Econ)* Weltmarkt *m*; **world music** N Weltmusik *f*; **world peace** N Weltfrieden *m*; **world picture** N = **world-view**; **world power** N Weltmacht *f*; **world rankings** PL Weltrangliste *f*; **world record** N Weltrekord *m*; **world record holder** N Weltrekordinhaber(in) *m(f)*; **world's champion** N *(US)* Weltmeister(in) *m(f)*; **World Service** N **the ~** *(Brit Rad) internationaler Rundfunksender der BBC*; **World's Fair** N *(US)* Weltausstellung *f*; **world-shattering** ADJ welterschütternd, weltbewegend; **world's record** N *(US)* Weltrekord *m*; **world trade** N *(Econ)* Welthandel *m*; **World Trade Organization** N Welthandelsorganisation *f*; **world-view** N Weltbild *nt*; **world war** N Weltkrieg *m*; **World War One, World War I** N Erster Weltkrieg; **World War Two, World War II** N Zweiter Weltkrieg; **world-weariness** N Lebensmüdigkeit *f*, Lebensüberdruss *m*; **world-weary** ADJ lebensmüde, lebensüberdrüssig; **worldwide** ADJ, ADV weltweit; **on a ~ scale** weltweit; **World Wide Web** N World Wide Web *nt*

worm [wɜːm] N **a** *(lit, fig inf)* Wurm *m*; *(= wood worm)* Holzwurm *m*; **~s** *(Med)* Würmer *pl*; **the ~ has turned** *(prov)* das Blatt hat sich gewendet; **to get a ~'s eye view of sth** etw aus der Froschperspektive sehen; **to open a can of ~s** in ein Wespennest stechen; **this has opened a whole new can of ~s** das wirft ganz neue Probleme auf

b *(= screw)* Schnecke *f*; *(= thread)* Schneckengewinde *nt*

c *(Comput, Internet)* Wurm *m*

VT **a** *(= wriggle)* zwängen; **to ~ one's way along/through/into sth** sich an etw *(dat)* entlangdrücken/durch etw *(acc)* durchschlängeln/in etw *(acc)* hineinzwängen; **to ~ one's way forward** *(= creep)* sich nach vorne schleichen; **to ~ one's way into a position/into a group** sich in eine Stellung/eine Gruppe einschleichen; **to ~ one's way into sb's affection** sich bei jdm einschmeicheln; **to ~ one's way out of a difficulty** sich aus einer schwierigen Lage herauswinden

b *(= extract)* **to ~ sth out of sb** jdm etw entlocken; **you have to ~ everything out of him** ihm muss man die Würmer aus der Nase ziehen

c *dog* eine Wurmkur machen mit *(+dat)*

worm: wormcast [ˈwɜːmkɑːst] N *vom Regenwurm aufgeworfenes Erdhäufchen*; **worm-eaten** ADJ *wood* wurmstichig; *(fig inf)* wurmzerfressen; **worm gear** N Schneckengetriebe *nt*; **wormhole** N Wurmloch *nt*

worming tablet [ˈwɜːmɪŋˌtæblɪt] N Entwurmungstablette *f*

worm powder N Wurmmittel *nt*

worm's-eye view [wɜːmzaɪvjuː] N Froschperspektive *f*; **to have a ~ of sth** etw aus der Froschperspektive betrachten

worm wheel N Schneckenrad *nt*

wormwood [ˈwɜːmwʊd] N Wermut *m*; *(fig)* Wermutstropfen *m*

wormy [ˈwɜːmɪ] ADJ *apple* wurmig; *wood* wurmstichig; *soil* wurmreich

worn [wɔːn] *ptp of* **wear** ADJ **a** *(= worn-out) coat* abgetragen; *book* zerlesen; *carpet* abgetreten; *tyre* abgefahren **b** *(= weary) smile* müde; *person* angegriffen; **to look ~ (with care)** verhärmt aussehen

worn-out [ˈwɔːnˌaʊt] ADJ *attr*, **worn out** ADJ *pred* **a** *coat* abgetragen; *carpet* abgetreten; *(fig) phrase* abgedroschen **b** *(= exhausted) person* erschöpft; *horse* ausgemergelt

worried [ˈwʌrɪd] ADJ besorgt *(about, by* wegen); *(= anxious also)* beunruhigt; **to be ~ sick** krank vor Sorge(n) sein *(inf)*

worriedly [ˈwʌrɪdlɪ] ADV besorgt; *(= anxiously also)* beunruhigt

worrier [ˈwʌrɪəˈ] N **she's a great ~** sie macht sich *(dat)* immerzu Sorgen

worriment [ˈwʌrɪmənt] N *(esp US inf)* **a** *(= vexation)* Plage *f*, Quälerei *f* **b** *(= anxiety)* Angst *f*, Sorge *f*

worrisome [ˈwʌrɪsəm] ADJ *(esp US)* beunruhigend, besorgniserregend; *(= annoying)* lästig

worry [ˈwʌrɪ] N Sorge *f*; **the ~ of bringing up a family** die Sorgen, die eine Familie mit sich bringt; **it's a great ~ to us all** wir machen uns alle große Sorgen darüber; **I know it's a ~ for you** ich weiß, es macht dir Sorgen; **what's your main ~?** was drückt dich?; **that's the least of my worries** das macht mir noch am wenigsten Sorgen; **no worries!** *(inf)* kein Problem!

VT **a** *(= cause concern)* beunruhigen, Sorgen machen *(+dat)*; **it worries me** es macht mir Sorgen; **you ~ me sometimes** manchmal machst du mir wirklich Sorgen; **it's no use just ~ing, do something** es hat keinen Zweck, sich nur den Kopf zu zerbrechen, tu endlich was; **to ~ oneself sick** *or* **silly/to death (about** *or* **over sth)** *(inf)* sich krank machen/sich umbringen vor Sorge (um *or* wegen etw) *(inf)*

b *(= bother)* stören; **to ~ sb with sth** jdn mit etw stören; **don't ~ me with trivialities** komm mir nicht mit Kleinigkeiten; **to ~ sb to do sth** jdn plagen, etw zu tun

c *(dog etc) sheep* nachstellen *(+dat)*; *(= bite)* reißen; *bone* (herum)nagen an *(+dat)*

VI sich sorgen, sich *(dat)* Sorgen *or* Gedanken machen *(about, over* um, wegen); **he worries a lot** er macht sich immer so viel Sorgen; **don't**

~!, not to ~! keine Angst *or* Sorge!; **don't ~, I'll do it** lass mal, das mach ich schon; **he said not to ~** er sagte, wir sollten uns keine Sorgen machen; **don't ~ about letting me know** es macht nichts, wenn du mich nicht benachrichtigen kannst; **don't you ~ about that, I'll do it** mach dir darum keine Sorgen, das mach ich; **you should ~!** *(inf)* du hast (vielleicht) Sorgen!

worry beads PL Betperlen *pl*

worrying ['wʌrɪɪŋ] ADJ *problem* beunruhigend, besorgniserregend; **it's very ~** es macht mir große Sorge; **I know it's ~ for you** ich weiß, es macht dir Sorgen; **it is a ~ time for us** wir haben zurzeit viel Sorgen N **~ won't help** sich nur Sorgen machen, nützt nichts

worry: **worry line** N *(on face)* Sorgenfalte *f*; **worrywart** ['wʌrɪwɔːt] N *(inf) jd, der sich ständig unnötige Sorgen macht*

worse [wɜːs] ✪ 5.3, 26.2 ADJ *comp of* **bad** schlechter; *(morally, with bad consequences)* schlimmer, ärger; **it gets ~ and ~** es wird immer schlimmer; **the patient is ~ than he was yesterday** dem Patienten geht es schlechter als gestern; **the patient is getting ~** der Zustand des Patienten verschlechtert sich *or* wird schlechter; **and to make matters ~** und zu allem Übel; **his "corrections" only made it ~** er hat alles nur verschlimmbessert; **it could have been ~** es hätte schlimmer kommen können; **~ luck!** (so ein) Pech!; **it will be the ~ for you** das wird für dich unangenehme Folgen haben; **so much the ~ for him** umso schlimmer; **to be the ~ for drink** betrunken sein; **he's none the ~ for it** er hat sich nichts dabei getan, es ist ihm nichts dabei passiert; **you'll be none the ~ for some work** etwas Arbeit wird dir nicht schaden; **I don't think any the ~ of you for it** ich halte deswegen aber nicht weniger von dir; **~ things happen at sea** *(inf)* es könnte schlimmer sein

ADV *comp of* **badly** schlechter; **it hurts ~** es tut mehr weh; **to be ~ off than ...** schlechter dran sein als ... *(inf)*, in einer schlechteren Lage sein als ...; **I could do a lot ~ than accept their offer** es wäre bestimmt kein Fehler, wenn ich das Angebot annähme

N Schlechtere(s) *nt*; *(morally, with regard to consequences)* Schlimmere(s) *nt*; **there is ~ to come** es kommt noch schlimmer; **it's changed for the ~** es hat sich zum Schlechteren gewendet

worsen ['wɜːsn] VT verschlechtern, schlechter machen VI sich verschlechtern, schlechter werden

worship ['wɜːʃɪp] N **a** *(of God, person etc)* Verehrung *f*; **public ~** Gottesdienst *m*; **place of ~** Andachtsstätte *f*; *(non-Christian)* Kultstätte *f*

b *(Brit: in titles)* **Your Worship** *(to judge)* Euer Ehren/Gnaden; *(to mayor)* (verehrter *or* sehr geehrter) Herr Bürgermeister; **His Worship the Mayor of ...** der verehrte Bürgermeister von ...; **if your Worship wishes** wenn Euer Ehren *or* Gnaden wünschen

VT anbeten; **he ~ped the ground she walked on** er betete den Boden unter ihren Füßen an

VI *(Rel)* den Gottesdienst abhalten; *(RC)* die Messe feiern; **the church where we used to ~** die Kirche, die wir besuchten

worshipful ['wɜːʃɪpfʊl] ADJ **a** *look, gaze* verehrend **b** *(Brit: in titles)* sehr verehrt *or* geehrt

worshipper ['wɜːʃɪpəʳ] N Kirchgänger(in) *m(f)*; **~ of Baal** Baalsverehrer(in) *m(f)*; **sun ~** Sonnenanbeter(in) *m(f)*; **he was a lifelong ~ at this church** er ist sein Leben lang hier zur Kirche gegangen; **to be a ~ of wealth** das Geld anbeten

worst [wɜːst] ADJ *superl of* **bad** schlechteste(r, s); *(morally, with regard to consequences)* schlimmste(r, s); **the ~ possible time** die ungünstigste Zeit

ADV *superl of* **badly** am schlechtesten

N **the ~ is over** das Schlimmste *or* Ärgste ist vorbei; **in the ~ of the storm** im ärgsten Sturm; **when the crisis/storm was at its ~** als die Krise/der Sturm ihren/seinen Höhepunkt erreicht hatte; **at (the) ~** schlimmstenfalls; **you've never seen him at his ~** er kann noch (viel) schlimmer (sein); **the ~ of it is ...** das Schlimmste daran ist, ...; **if the ~ comes to the ~, if ~ comes to ~** *(US)* wenn alle Stricke reißen *(inf)*; **do your ~!** *(liter)* mach zu!; **to get the ~ of it** den Kürzeren ziehen

VT *enemy, opponent* besiegen, schlagen

worst case ['wɜːstkeɪs] N Schlimmstfall *m*, ungünstigster Fall

worst-case scenario ['wɜːstkeɪssɪ'nɑːrɪəʊ] N Schlimmstfall *m*

worsted ['wʊstɪd] N *(= yarn)* Kammgarn *nt*; *(= cloth also)* Kammgarnstoff *m* ADJ Kammgarn-; **~ suit** Kammgarnanzug *m*; **~ wool** Kammgarn *nt*

wort [wɜːt] N Bierwürze *f*

worth [wɜːθ] ADJ **a** wert; **it's ~ £5** es ist £ 5 wert; **it's not ~ £5** es ist keine £ 5 wert; **what's this ~?** was *or* wie viel ist das wert?; **it can't be ~ that!** so viel kann es unmöglich wert sein; **it's ~ a great deal to me** es ist mir viel wert; *(sentimentally)* es bedeutet mir sehr viel; **what's it ~ to me to do that?** *(in money)* was springt für mich dabei heraus? *(inf)*; *(in advantages)* was bringt es mir, wenn ich das tue?; **will you do this for me? – what's it ~ to you?** tust du das für mich? – was ist es dir wert?; **he was ~ a million** er besaß eine Million; **he's ~ all his brothers put together** er ist so viel wert wie all seine Brüder zusammen; **for all one is ~** so sehr man nur kann; **to sing for all one is ~** aus voller Kehle *or* vollem Halse singen; **you need to exploit the idea for all it's ~** du musst aus der Idee machen, was du nur kannst; **for what it's ~, I personally don't think ...** wenn mich einer fragt, ich persönlich glaube nicht, dass ...; **I'll tell you this for what it's ~** ich sage dir das, ich weiß nicht, ob was dran ist; **that's my opinion for what it's ~** das ist meine bescheidene Meinung; **it's more than my life/job is ~ to tell you** ich sage es dir nicht, dazu ist mir mein Leben zu lieb/dazu liegt mir zu viel an meiner Stelle

b *(= deserving, meriting)* wert; **to be ~ it** sich lohnen; **to be ~ sth** etw wert sein; **it's not ~ it** es lohnt sich nicht; **it's not ~ the trouble** es ist der Mühe nicht wert; **the museum is ~ a visit** das Museum ist einen Besuch wert; **the book is ~ reading** das Buch ist lesenswert; **life isn't ~ living** das Leben ist nicht lebenswert; **is there anything ~ seeing in this town?** gibt es in dieser Stadt etwas Sehenswertes?; **it's a film ~ seeing** es lohnt sich, diesen Film anzusehen; **hardly ~ mentioning** kaum der Rede wert; **an experience ~ having** eine lohnenswerte Erfahrung; **it's not ~ having** es ist nichts; **if a thing's ~ doing, it's ~ doing well** wennschon, dennschon → **salt N a, while N c**

N Wert *m*; **hundreds of pounds' ~ of books** Bücher im Werte von hunderten von Pfund; **a man of great ~** ein sehr wertvoller Mensch; **to show one's true ~** zeigen, was man wirklich wert ist, seinen wahren Wert zeigen; **to increase in ~** im Wert steigen; **what's the current ~ of this?** wie viel ist das momentan wert? → **money**

worthily ['wɜːðɪlɪ] ADV löblich, lobenswert

worthiness ['wɜːðɪnɪs] N *(of charity, cause etc)* Wert *m*; *(of person)* Ehrenhaftigkeit *f*

worthless ['wɜːθlɪs] ADJ wertlos; *person also* nichtsnutzig

worthlessness ['wɜːθlɪsnɪs] N Wertlosigkeit *f*; *(of person also)* Nichtsnutzigkeit *f*

worthwhile ['wɜːθ'waɪl] ADJ lohnend *attr*; **to be ~** sich lohnen; *(= worth the trouble also)* der Mühe *(gen)* wert sein; **it's a thoroughly ~ film/book** es lohnt sich wirklich, den Film zu sehen/das Buch zu lesen; **it's hardly ~ (asking him)** es lohnt sich wohl kaum(, ihn zu fragen) → *also* **while N c**

worthy ['wɜːðɪ] ✪ 26.3 ADJ *(+er)* **a** ehrenwert, achtbar; *opponent* würdig; *motive, cause* lobenswert, löblich; **my ~ friend** mein werter Freund

b *pred* wert, würdig; **~ of remark** bemerkenswert; **~ of mention** erwähnenswert; **to be ~ of sb/sth** jds/einer Sache würdig sein *(geh)*; **any journalist ~ of the name** jeder Journalist, der diese Bezeichnung verdient; **this makes him ~ of (our) respect** dafür verdient er unseren Respekt; **he is ~ to be ranked among ...** er ist es wert, zu ... gezählt zu werden N *(hum)* **the local worthies** die Ortsgrößen *pl (hum)*

would [wʊd] ✪ 3.3, 4, 8.3, 9.1, 12.3 *pret of* **will**[1] MODAL AUX VB **a** *(conditional)* **if you asked him he ~ do it** wenn du ihn fragtest, würde er es tun; **if you had asked him he ~ have done it** wenn du ihn gefragt hättest, hätte er es getan; **I thought you ~ want to know** ich dachte, du wüsstest es gerne *or* du würdest es gerne wissen; **if I were you, I ~ ...** wenn ich du wäre, würde ich ...; **who ~ have thought it?** wer hätte das gedacht?; **you ~ think ...** man sollte meinen ...; **you ~ never know he was fifty** die Fünfzig sieht man ihm wirklich nicht an

b *(in indirect speech)* **she said she ~ come** sie sagte, sie würde kommen *or* sie käme; **I said I ~, so I will** ich habe gesagt, ich würde es tun und ich werde es auch tun

c *(emph)* **you ~ be the one to get hit** typisch, dass ausgerechnet du getroffen worden bist; **you ~ be the one to forget** typisch, dass du das vergessen hast, das sieht dir ähnlich, dass du es vergessen hast; **I ~n't know** keine Ahnung; **you ~!** das sieht dir ähnlich!; **he ~ have to come right now** ausgerechnet jetzt muss er kommen; **you ~ think of that/say that, ~n't you!** von dir kann man ja nichts anderes erwarten; **it ~ have to rain** es muss auch ausgerechnet regnen!

d *(insistence)* **I warned him, but he ~ do it** ich habe ihn gewarnt, aber er musste es ja unbedingt *or* um jeden Preis tun; **he ~n't listen/behave** er wollte partout nicht zuhören/sich partout nicht benehmen; **he ~n't be told** er wollte sich *(dat)* einfach nichts sagen lassen

e *(conjecture)* **it ~ seem so** es sieht wohl so aus; **it ~ have been about 8 o'clock** es war (wohl) so ungefähr 8 Uhr; **what ~ this be?** was ist das wohl?; **you ~n't have a cigarette, ~ you?** Sie hätten nicht zufällig eine Zigarette?

f *(= wish)* möchten; **what ~ you have me do?** was soll ich tun?; **try as he ~** sosehr er es auch versuchte; **the place where I ~ be** *(old, liter)* der Ort, an dem ich sein möchte; **~ (that) it were not so!** *(old, liter)* wenn das doch nur nicht wahr wäre!; **~ to God he ~ come** gebe Gott, dass er kommt; **~ to God he hadn't come** ich wünsche zu Gott, er wäre nicht gekommen

g *(in questions)* **~ he come?** würde er vielleicht kommen?; **~ he have come?** wäre er gekommen?; **~ you mind closing the window?** würden Sie bitte das Fenster schließen?; **~ you care for some tea?** hätten Sie gerne etwas Tee?

h *(habit)* **he ~ paint it each year** er strich es jedes Jahr, er pflegte es jedes Jahr zu streichen *(geh)*; **50 years ago the streets ~ be empty on a Sunday** vor 50 Jahren waren sonntags die Straßen immer leer

would-be ['wʊdbiː] ADJ *attr* **~ poet/politician** jemand, der gerne (ein) Dichter/(ein) Politiker würde; *(pej)* Möchtegerndichter(in) *m(f)*/-politiker(in) *m(f)*

wouldn't ['wʊdnt] *contr of* **would not**

wound[1] [wuːnd] N *(lit)* Wunde *f*; *(fig also)* Kränkung *f*; **my old war ~** meine alte Kriegsverletzung; **to receive** *or* **sustain a serious ~** schwer verwundet werden; **to open** *or* **re-open old ~s** *(fig)* alte Wunden öffnen; **the ~ to his pride** sein verletzter Stolz → **lick** VT *(lit)* verwunden, verletzen; *(fig)* verletzen; **~ed pride** verletzter Stolz; **~ed veteran** Kriegsversehrte(r) *m(f)* N **the ~ed** *pl* die Verwundeten *pl*

wound[2] [waʊnd] *pret, ptp of* **wind**[2]

wounding ['wuːndɪŋ] ADJ *remark, tone* verletzend

wound sepsis N *(Med)* Wundsepsis *f*

wove [wəʊv] *pret of* **weave**

woven ['wəʊvən] *ptp of* **weave**

wow¹ [waʊ] INTERJ hui *(inf)*, Mann *(inf)*, Mensch *(inf)* **N** *(inf)* **it's a ~** das ist spitze *(inf)* or 'ne Wucht *(inf)*

wow² N *(on recording)* Jaulen *nt*

wowser ['waʊzə] N *(Austral inf)* **a** *(= killjoy)* Miesmacher(in) *m(f) (inf)* **b** *(= teetotaller)* Abstinenzler(in) *m(f)*

WP **a** *abbr of* **word processor** **b** *(inf) abbr of* **weather permitting** bei gutem Wetter

WPC *(Brit)* N *abbr of* **Woman Police Constable** Polizistin *f*

wpm *abbr of* **words per minute** WpM, wpm

WRAC [ræk] *(Brit) abbr of* **Women's Royal Army Corps**

wrack¹ [ræk] N *(Bot)* Tang *m*

wrack² N, VT = **rack¹**, **rack²**

WRAF [ræf] *(Brit) abbr of* **Women's Royal Air Force**

wraith [reɪθ] N Gespenst *nt*, Geist *m*

wraithlike ['reɪθlaɪk] ADJ durchgeistigt, ätherisch

wrangle ['ræŋgl] **N** Gerangel *nt no pl*, Hin und Her *nt no pl* **VI** streiten, rangeln *(about* um); *(in bargaining)* feilschen

wrangler ['ræŋglə'] N *(US: = cowboy)* Cowboy *m*; *(Univ) Mathematikstudent in Cambridge, der mit Auszeichnung bestanden hat*

wrap [ræp] **N** **a** *(= garment)* Umhangtuch *nt*; *(for child)* Wickeltuch *nt*; *(= stole)* Stola *f*; *(= cape)* Cape *nt*; *(= coat)* Mantel *m*
b **under ~s** *(lit)* verhüllt; *car, weapon* getarnt; *(fig)* geheim; **they took the ~s off the new project** sie haben, was das neue Projekt betrifft, die Katze aus dem Sack gelassen *(inf)*
c **it's a ~** *(inf: = completed)* das wärs
VT **a** *(lit)* einwickeln; *parcel, present* verpacken, einwickeln; *person (for warmth)* einpacken *(inf)*; **shall I ~ it for you?** soll ich es Ihnen einpacken or einwickeln?; **~ the joint in foil** den Braten in Folie einschlagen; **~ped bread** abgepacktes Brot; **to ~ sth (a)round sth** etw um etw wickeln; **he ~ped the car (a)round a lamppost** *(inf)* er hat das Auto um eine Laterne gewickelt *(inf)*; **to ~ one's arms (a)round sb** jdn in die Arme schließen
b *(fig)* **to be ~ped in sth** in etw gehüllt sein; **she lay ~ped in his arms** sie lag in seinen Armen; **~ped in secrecy** vom Schleier des Geheimnisses umhüllt
c *(Comput) line, text etc* umbrechen
VI **a** *(Comput)* **the lines ~ automatically** der Zeilenumbruch erfolgt automatisch
b *(Comput, when searching)* (am Dateianfang) weitersuchen

▶ **wrap up** **VT** *sep* **a** *(lit, fig)* einpacken, einwickeln, verpacken **b** *(inf: = finalize) deal* festmachen, unter Dach und Fach bringen; **that just about wraps things up for today** das wärs (dann wohl) für heute **c** **to be wrapped up in sb/sth** in jdm/etw aufgehen **VI** **a** *(= dress warmly)* sich warm einpacken *(inf)* **b** *(inf, = be quiet)* den Mund halten *(inf)*

wraparound ['ræpəraʊnd], **wrapover** ['ræpəʊvə'] ADJ *attr* Wickel-; **~ skirt** Wickelrock *m*

wrappage ['ræpɪdʒ] N Umschlag *m*, Hülle *f*; *(= wrapping)* Verpackung *f*

wrapper ['ræpə'] N **a** Verpackung *f*; *(of sweets)* Papier(chen) *nt*; *(of cigar)* Deckblatt *nt*; *(of book)* (Schutz)umschlag *m*; *(postal)* Streifband *nt* **b** *(= garment)* leichter Morgenmantel **c** *(= person: in factory etc)* Packer(in) *m(f)*

wrapping ['ræpɪŋ] N Verpackung *f (round +gen,* von)

wrapping paper N Packpapier *nt*; *(decorative)* Geschenkpapier *nt*

wrapround ['ræpraʊnd] ADJ *attr* = **wraparound**

wrath [rɒθ] N Zorn *m*; *(liter, of storm)* Wut *f*

wrathful ADJ, **wrathfully** ADV ['rɒθfʊl, -fəlɪ] wutentbrannt, zornentbrannt

wreak [ri:k] VT *destruction* anrichten; *chaos also* stiften; *(liter) vengeance* üben *(on* an *+dat)*; *punishment* auferlegen *(on +dat)*; *anger* auslassen *(on* an *+dat)* → **havoc**

wreath [ri:θ] N *pl* **-s** [ri:ðz] Kranz *m*; **~ of laurel** Lorbeerkranz *m*

wreathe [ri:ð] **VT** *(= encircle)* (um)winden; *(clouds, mist)* umhüllen; *(= entwine)* flechten; **a garland ~d the victor's head** ein Kranz (um)krönte das Haupt des Siegers; **his face was ~d in smiles** er strahlte über das ganze Gesicht **VI** **the smoke ~d upwards** der Rauch stieg in Kringeln auf; **to ~ round sth** *(ivy etc)* sich um etw ranken; *(snake)* sich um etw schlängeln or ringeln; *(smoke)* sich um etw kringeln or kräuseln; *(mist)* um etw wallen

wreck [rek] **N** **a** *(Naut)* Schiffbruch *m*; *(= wrecked ship, car, train)* Wrack *nt*; **lost in the ~** beim Schiffbruch verloren; **he was killed in a car ~** *(US)* er kam bei einem Autounfall ums Leben
b *(fig inf) (= old bicycle, furniture etc)* Trümmerhaufen *m*; *(= person)* Wrack *nt*; *(of hopes, life, marriage etc)* Trümmer *pl*, Ruinen *pl*; **I'm a ~, I feel a ~** ich bin ein (völliges) Wrack; *(= exhausted)* ich bin vollkommen fertig or erledigt; *(in appearance)* ich sehe verheerend or unmöglich aus → **nervous wreck**
VT **a** *ship, train, plane* zum Wrack machen, einen Totalschaden verursachen an *(+dat)*; *car* kaputt fahren *(inf)*, zu Schrott fahren *(inf)*; *machine, mechanism* zerstören, kaputt machen *(inf)*; *furniture, house* zerstören; *(person)* zertrümmern, kurz und klein schlagen *(inf)*; **to be ~ed** *(Naut)* Schiffbruch erleiden; *(sl: = drunk)* zu *(inf)* or dicht *(sl)* sein; **~ed ship** wrackes or havariertes Schiff; **~ed car** zu Schrott gefahrenes Auto
b *(fig) hopes, plans, chances* zunichtemachen; *marriage* zerrütten; *career, health, sb's life* zerstören, ruinieren; *person* kaputtmachen *(inf)*; *party, holiday* verderben

wreckage ['rekɪdʒ] N *(lit, fig: = remains)* Trümmer *pl*; *(of ship also)* Wrackteile *pl*; *(washed ashore)* Strandgut *nt*; *(of house, town)* Ruinen *pl*

wrecker ['rekə'] N **a** *(= ship wrecker)* Strandräuber *m (der Schiffe durch falsche Lichtsignale zum Stranden bringt)* **b** *(Naut, = salvager)* Bergungsarbeiter(in) *m(f)*; *(= vessel)* Bergungsschiff *nt* **c** *(US) (= breaker, salvager)* Schrotthändler(in) *m(f)*; *(for buildings)* Abbrucharbeiter(in) *m(f)* **d** *(US: = breakdown van)* Abschleppwagen *m*

wrecking ['rekɪŋ]: **wrecking ball** N Abrissbirne *f*; **wrecking bar** N *(US)* Brechstange *f*; **wrecking service** N *(US Aut)* Abschleppdienst *m*

Wren [ren] N *(Brit) weibliches Mitglied der britischen Marine*

wren [ren] N Zaunkönig *m*

wrench [rentʃ] **N** **a** *(= tug)* Ruck *m*; *(Med)* Verrenkung *f*; **to give sth a ~** einer Sache *(dat)* einen Ruck geben; **he gave his shoulder a nasty ~** er hat sich *(dat)* die Schulter schlimm verrenkt
b *(= tool)* Schraubenschlüssel *m*
c *(fig)* **to be a ~** wehtun; **the ~ of parting** der Trennungsschmerz
VT **a** *(= tug)* winden; **to ~ sth (away) from sb** jdm etw entwinden; **to ~ a door open** eine Tür aufzwingen; **to ~ a door off its hinges** eine Tür aus den Angeln reißen; **he ~ed the steering wheel round** er riss das Lenkrad herum; **to ~ sb's arm out of its socket** jdm den Arm ausrenken
b *(Med)* **to ~ one's ankle/shoulder** sich *(dat)* den Fuß/die Schulter verrenken
c *(fig)* reißen; **if you could ~ yourself away from the TV** wenn du dich vom Fernseher losreißen könntest

wrest [rest] VT **to ~ sth from sb/sth** jdm/einer Sache etw abringen; *leadership, title* jdm etw entreißen; **to ~ sth from sb's grasp** jdm etw entreißen; **to ~ oneself free** sich losreißen

wrestle ['resl] **N** Ringkampf *m* **VT** ringen mit; *(Sport also)* einen Ringkampf bestreiten gegen; **he ~d the thief to the ground** er brachte or zwang den Dieb zu Boden **VI** **a** *(lit)* ringen *(for sth* um etw) **b** *(fig: with problem, conscience etc)* ringen, kämpfen *(with* mit); **the pilot ~d with the controls** der Pilot kämpfte mit den Instrumenten

wrestler ['reslə'] N Ringkämpfer *m*; *(modern)* Ringer(in) *m(f)*

wrestling ['reslɪŋ] N Ringen *nt*

wrestling match N Ringkampf *m*

wretch [retʃ] N **a** *(miserable)* armer Teufel or Schlucker *(inf)* **b** *(contemptible)* Wicht *m*, Schuft *m*; *(= nuisance)* Blödmann *m (inf)*; *(= child)* Schlingel *m*

wretched ['retʃɪd] ADJ **a** elend; *conditions, life* elend, erbärmlich; *clothing* erbärmlich; *(= unhappy, depressed)* (tod)unglücklich; **I feel ~** *(= ill)* mir geht es miserabel *(inf)*, ich fühle mich elend; **I feel ~ about having to say no** es tut mir in der Seele weh, dass ich Nein or nein sagen muss **b** *(= very bad) housing conditions, weather, novel, player* erbärmlich, miserabel *(inf)*; *(inf: = damned)* verflixt, elend, Mist- *(all inf)*; **what a ~ thing to do!** so etwas Schäbiges!; **what ~ luck!** was für ein verflixtes or elendes Pech *(inf)*

wretchedly ['retʃɪdlɪ] ADV **a** *(= in misery)* erbärmlich; *weep, apologize, look* kläglich **b** *(inf: = extremely)* verflixt *(inf)*, verdammt *(inf)*

wretchedness ['retʃɪdnɪs] N Erbärmlichkeit *f*; *(of person: = misery)* Elend *nt*

wrick [rɪk] **VT** **to ~ one's neck/shoulder** sich *(dat)* den Hals/die Schulter ausrenken **N** **to have a ~ in one's neck** sich *(dat)* den Hals ausgerenkt haben; **to get a ~ in one's neck** sich *(dat)* den Hals ausrenken

wriggle ['rɪgl] **N** Schlängeln *nt no pl*; *(of child, fish)* Zappeln *nt no pl*; **to give a ~** *(worm, snake, eel)* sich schlängeln; *(fish)* sich winden, zappeln
VT *toes, ears* wackeln mit; **to ~ one's way through sth** sich durch etw (hin)durchwinden or -schlängeln
VI *(also* **wriggle about** or **around**) *(worm, snake, eel)* sich schlängeln; *(fish)* sich winden, zappeln; *(person) (restlessly, excitedly)* zappeln; *(in embarrassment)* sich winden; **to ~ along/down** sich vorwärtsschlängeln/nach unten schlängeln; **the fish ~d off the hook** der Fisch wand sich vom Haken; **she managed to ~ free** es gelang ihr, sich loszuwinden; **he ~d through the hole in the hedge** er wand or schlängelte sich durch das Loch in der Hecke; **do stop wriggling about** hör endlich mit der Zappelei auf

▶ **wriggle out** VI *(lit)* sich herauswinden *(of* aus); *(fig also)* sich herausmanövrieren *(of* aus); **he's wriggled (his way) out of it** er hat sich gedrückt

wriggly ['rɪglɪ] ADJ *(+er)* sich windend *attr*, sich krümmend *attr*; *fish, child* zappelnd *attr*

wring [rɪŋ] *vb: pret, ptp* **wrung** **VT** **a** *(also* **wring out**) *clothes, wet rag etc* auswringen, auswinden; **to ~ water out of clothes** (nasse) Kleider auswringen or auswinden; **"do not ~"** *(on washing instructions)* nicht wringen
b *hands (in distress)* ringen; **to ~ a duck's neck** einer Ente *(dat)* den Hals umdrehen; **I could have wrung his neck** ich hätte ihm den Hals or den Kragen *(inf)* umdrehen können; **he wrung my hand** er schüttelte mir (kräftig) die Hand; **to ~ sb's heart** jdm in der Seele wehtun
c *(= extract)* **to ~ sth out of** or **from sb** etw aus jdm herausquetschen, jdm etw abringen
N **to give clothes a ~** Kleider auswringen or auswinden

wringer ['rɪŋə'] N (Wäsche)mangel *f*; **to go** or **be put through the ~** *(fig inf)* durch die Mangel gedreht werden

wringing ['rɪŋɪŋ] ADJ *(also* **wringing wet**) tropfnass; *person also* patschnass *(inf)*

wrinkle ['rɪŋkl] **N** **a** *(in clothes, paper)* Knitter *m*; *(on face, skin)* Runzel *f*, Falte *f*; *(in stocking)* Falte *f* **b** *(inf, = dodge, scheme)* Kniff *m (inf)*
VT *fabric, paper, surface, sheet* verknittern, verkrumpeln *(inf)*; *skin* runzlig or faltig machen; **to ~ one's nose** die Nase rümpfen; **to ~ one's**

brow die Stirne runzeln **VI** *(sheet, material)* (ver)knittern; *(stockings)* Falten schlagen; *(skin etc)* runzlig *or* faltig werden

▶ **wrinkle up** VT *sep nose* rümpfen

wrinkled [ˈrɪŋkld] ADJ *sheet, skirt, paper* zerknittert; *skin* runzlig, faltig; *brow* gerunzelt; *apple, old lady* schrumpelig, verschrumpelt; **~ stockings** Ziehharmonikastrümpfe *pl (inf)*

wrinkly [ˈrɪŋklɪ] **ADJ** *(+er)* schrumpelig; *fabric* zerknittert **N** *(Brit inf: = old person)* Opa *m (inf)*, Oma *f (inf)*

wrist [rɪst] N Handgelenk *nt*; **to slash one's ~s** sich *(dat)* die Pulsadern aufschneiden

wrist: **wristband** [ˈrɪstˌbænd] N Armband *nt*; *(on dress, shirt)* Ärmelbündchen *nt*; *(Sport)* Schweißband *nt*; **wristlet** [ˈrɪstlɪt] N Armband *nt*; **~s** *pl (sl: = handcuffs)* Manschetten *pl (inf)*

wrist: **wristlock** [ˈrɪstlɒk] N Polizeigriff *m*; **to put a ~ on sb** jdn im Polizeigriff halten; **wrist rest** N *(Comput)* Handballenauflage *f*; **wristwatch** N Armbanduhr *f*

writ [rɪt] N **a** *(Jur)* Verfügung *f*; **~ of attachment** Haft- *or* Verhaftungsbefehl *m*; **~ of execution** Vollstreckungsbefehl *m*; **to issue a ~** eine Verfügung herausgeben; **to issue a ~ against sb** jdn vorladen *(for* wegen) **b** **the Holy Writ** *(old, form)* die Heilige Schrift

write [raɪt] ✪ 21.1, 21.2 *pret* **wrote** *or (obs)* **writ** [rɪt] *ptp* **written** *or (obs)* **writ** [rɪt] **VT** **a** *(also Comput)* schreiben; *cheque, copy* ausstellen; *notes* sich *(dat)* aufschreiben, sich *(dat)* machen; *application form* ausfüllen; **he wrote me a letter** er schrieb mir einen Brief; **he wrote himself a note so that he wouldn't forget** er machte sich *(dat)* eine Notiz, um sich zu erinnern; **he wrote five pages** er schrieb fünf Seiten voll; **print your name, don't ~ it** schreiben Sie Ihren Namen in Druckschrift, nicht in Schreibschrift; **how is that written?** wie schreibt man das?; **to ~ sth to disk** etw auf Diskette schreiben; **it is written that …** *(old)* es steht geschrieben, dass …; **writ(ten) large** *(fig)* verdeutlicht; *(= on a larger scale)* im Großen; **it was written all over his face** es stand ihm im *or* auf dem Gesicht geschrieben; **he had "policeman" written all over him** man sah ihm den Polizisten schon von Weitem an → **shorthand**

b *(Insur) policy* abschließen

c *CD, DVD* brennen

VI schreiben; **as I ~ …** während ich dies schreibe, …; **to ~ to sb** jdm schreiben; **we ~ to each other** wir schreiben uns; **I wrote to him to come** ich habe ihm geschrieben, er solle kommen *or* dass er kommen solle; **that's nothing to ~ home about** *(inf)* das ist nichts Weltbewegendes; **I'll ~ for it at once** ich bestelle es sofort, ich fordere es gleich an; **he has always wanted to ~** er wollte immer (ein) Schriftsteller werden

▶ **write away** VI schreiben; **to write away for sth** etw anfordern; **he wrote away asking for further information** er forderte weitere Information an

▶ **write back** VI zurückschreiben, antworten; **he wrote back saying …** er schrieb zurück, um zu sagen, …

▶ **write down** VT *sep (= make a note of)* aufschreiben; *(= record, put in writing)* niederschreiben

▶ **write in** **VT** *sep* **a** *word, correction etc* hineinschreiben, einfügen *(prep obj* in *+acc)* **b** *(US Pol)* **to write sb in** seine Stimme für jdn abgeben, der nicht in der Liste aufgeführt ist **c** *(= build in) condition, provision* aufnehmen; **is there anything written in about that?** steht was dazu drin? **VI** schreiben *(to* an *+acc)*; **someone has written in (to us) requesting this record** jemand hat uns *(dat)* geschrieben und um diese Platte gebeten; **to write in for sth** etw anfordern, um etw schreiben

▶ **write off** **VI** = **write away** **VT** *sep* **a** *(= write quickly)* (schnell) hinschreiben; *essay, poem* herunterschreiben **b** *debt, losses* abschreiben; *(fig: = regard as failure)* abschreiben; **don't write him off just yet** schreib ihn noch nicht ganz ab **c** *car etc (driver)* zu Schrott fahren *(inf)*; *(insurance company)* als Totalschaden abschreiben

▶ **write out** VT *sep* **a** *(in full) notes* ausarbeiten; *name etc* ausschreiben **b** *cheque, prescription* ausstellen **c** *actor, character* einen Abgang schaffen *(+dat)*; **he's been written out** ihm wurde ein Abgang aus der Serie geschaffen

▶ **write up** VT *sep notes* ausarbeiten; *report, diary* schreiben; *event* schreiben über *(+acc)*; *(= review) play, film* eine Kritik schreiben über *(+acc)*

write: **write-in** N *(US)* Stimmabgabe *f* für einen nicht in der Liste aufgeführten Kandidaten; **write-off** N **a** *(= car etc)* Totalschaden *m*; *(inf: = holiday, picnic etc)* Katastrophe *f (inf)* **b** *(Comm)* Abschreibung *f*

write-only [ˈraɪtˌəʊnlɪ] ADJ *(Comput)* lesegeschützt

write-protected [ˈraɪtprəˌtektɪd] ADJ *(Comput)* schreibgeschützt

write protection N *(Comput)* Schreibschutz *m*, Schreibsperre *f*

writer [ˈraɪtəʳ] N Schreiber(in) *m(f)*; *(of scenario, report etc also)* Autor(in) *m(f)*; *(of TV commercials, subtitles)* Texter(in) *m(f)*; *(of music)* Komponist(in) *m(f)*; *(as profession)* Schriftsteller(in) *m(f)*; **the (present) ~** der Schreiber (dieser Zeilen/dieses Artikels etc); **he's a very poor ~** er schreibt sehr schlecht; *(= correspondent)* er ist kein großer Briefschreiber

writer's cramp [ˈraɪtəzˈkræmp] N Schreibkrampf *m*

write-up [ˈraɪtʌp] N Pressebericht *m*; *(of play, film)* Kritik *f*

writhe [raɪð] VI sich krümmen, sich winden *(with, in* vor *+dat)*; **to ~ in ecstasy** sich vor Lust wälzen; **to make sb ~** *(painfully)* jdn vor Schmerzen zusammenzucken lassen; *(with disgust)* jdm kalte Schauer über den Rücken jagen, jdn erschauern lassen; *(with embarrassment)* jdn in peinliche Verlegenheit bringen

writing [ˈraɪtɪŋ] N Schrift *f*; *(= act, profession)* Schreiben *nt*; *(= inscription)* Inschrift *f*; **at the time of ~** als dies geschrieben wurde; *(in present)* während ich dies schreibe; **in ~** schriftlich; **permission in ~** schriftliche Genehmigung; **to commit sth to ~** etw schriftlich festhalten; **this is a fantastic piece of ~** das ist fantastisch geschrieben; **his ~s** seine Werke *or* Schriften; **in sb's own ~** *(= not typed)* handgeschrieben; *(= not written by sb else)* in jds eigener (Hand)schrift *(dat)*; **he earns a bit from his ~** er verdient sich ein bisschen (Geld) mit Schreiben; **the ~ is on the wall for them** ihre Stunde hat geschlagen; **he had seen the ~ on the wall** er hat die Zeichen erkannt

writing *in cpds* Schreib-; **writing book** N Schreibheft *nt*; **writing case** N Schreibmappe *f*; **writing desk** N Schreibtisch *m*, Schreibpult *nt*; **writing materials** PL Schreibmaterial *nt*, Schreibmaterialien *pl*; **writing pad** N Schreib- *or* Notizblock *m*; **writing paper** N Schreibpapier *nt*; **writing stand** N Stehpult *nt*; **writing table** N Schreibtisch *m*

written [ˈrɪtn] *ptp of* **write** ADJ *examination, statement, evidence* schriftlich; *language* Schrift-; *word* geschrieben; *constitution* schriftlich niedergelegt

WRNS [renz] *(Brit) abbr of* **Women's Royal Naval Service**

wrong [rɒŋ] ✪ 12.1, 14, 18.3, 26.3 **ADJ** **a** falsch; **to be ~** nicht stimmen; *(answer also)* falsch sein; *(person)* unrecht haben; *(watch)* falsch gehen; **it's all ~** das ist völlig verkehrt *or* falsch; *(= not true)* das stimmt alles nicht; **it's all ~ that I should have to …** das ist doch nicht richtig, dass ich … muss; **I was ~ about him** ich habe mich in ihm getäuscht *or* geirrt; **you were ~ in thinking he did it** du hast unrecht gehabt, als du dachtest, er sei es gewesen; **how ~ can you get!** falscher gehts (wohl) nicht!; **I took a ~ turning** ich habe eine verkehrte *or* falsche Abzweigung genommen; **he went in the ~ direction** er ging in die verkehrte *or* falsche Richtung; **this is the ~ train for Bournemouth** dies ist der falsche Zug, wenn Sie nach Bournemouth wollen; **to say/do the ~ thing** das Falsche sagen/tun; **the ~ side of the fabric** die linke Seite des Stoffes; **you live in the ~ part of town** du wohnst nicht im richtigen Stadtteil; **he's got the ~ kind of friends** er hat die falschen Freunde; **you've come to the ~ man** *or* **person/place** da sind Sie an den Falschen/an die Falsche/an die falsche Adresse geraten; **brown is definitely the ~ colour to be wearing this season** Braun ist diese Saison absolut nicht modern; **it feels all ~ not working** es ist ganz komisch nicht zu arbeiten; **it's the ~ time for jokes** es ist nicht die richtige Zeit für Witze; **it's the ~ time and the ~ place for that** das ist weder die Zeit noch der Ort dafür; **to do sth the ~ way** etw falsch *or* verkehrt machen → **number N c**, **side N e**

b *(morally)* schlecht, unrecht; *(= unfair)* ungerecht, unfair; **it's ~ to steal** es ist unrecht zu stehlen, Stehlen ist unrecht; **that was very ~ of you** das war absolut nicht richtig von dir; **you were ~ to do that** es war falsch *or* unrecht *or* nicht richtig von dir, das zu tun; **it's ~ of you to laugh** Sie sollten nicht lachen; **it's ~ that he should have to ask** es ist unrecht *or* falsch, dass er überhaupt fragen muss; **what's ~ with a drink now and again?** was ist schon (Schlimmes) dabei, wenn man ab und zu einen trinkt?; **what's ~ with working on Sundays?** was ist denn schon dabei, wenn man sonntags arbeitet?; **I don't see anything ~ in** *or* **with that** ich kann nichts Falsches daran finden, ich finde nichts daran auszusetzen

c *pred (= amiss)* **something is ~** (irgend)etwas stimmt nicht *or* ist nicht in Ordnung *(with* mit); *(suspiciously)* irgendetwas stimmt da nicht *or* ist da faul *(inf)*; **is anything** *or* **something ~?** ist was? *(inf)*; **there's nothing ~** (es ist) alles in Ordnung; **what's ~?** was ist los?; **what's ~ with you?** was fehlt Ihnen?; **there's nothing medically ~ with her** medizinisch (gesehen) fehlt ihr nichts; **I hope there's nothing ~ at home** ich hoffe, dass zu Hause alles in Ordnung ist

ADV falsch; **you do him ~** du tust ihm unrecht; **you did ~ to do it** es war falsch *or* unrecht *or* nicht richtig von dir, das zu tun; **to get sth ~** sich mit etw vertun; **he got the answer ~** er hat die falsche Antwort gegeben; *(Math)* er hat sich verrechnet; **I think you got things a bit ~** ich glaube, Sie sehen die Sache *or* das nicht ganz richtig; **to get one's sums ~** sich verrechnen; **you've got him (all) ~** *(= misunderstood him)* Sie haben ihn falsch verstanden; *(= he's not like that)* Sie haben sich in ihm getäuscht; **you thought ~** Sie haben sich geirrt; **to go ~** *(on route)* falsch gehen/fahren; *(in calculation)* einen Fehler machen; *(morally)* auf Abwege geraten; *(plan etc)* schiefgehen; *(affair etc)* schieflaufen; **my washing machine has gone ~** meine Waschmaschine ist nicht in Ordnung; **I hope the television doesn't go ~** hoffentlich bleibt der Fernseher in Ordnung; **you can't go ~** du kannst gar nichts verkehrt machen; **you can't go ~ if you buy him a bottle of whisky** mit einer Flasche Whisky liegst du bei ihm immer richtig

N Unrecht *nt no pl*; **(social) ~s** (soziale) Ungerechtigkeiten *pl*; **to be in the ~** im Unrecht sein; **two ~s don't make a right** Unrecht und Unrecht ergibt noch kein Recht; **to do sb a great ~** jdm ein großes Unrecht antun; **he can do no ~** er macht natürlich immer alles richtig; **all the little ~s he'd done her** all die kleinen Kränkungen, die er ihr zugefügt hatte

VT **to ~ sb** jdm unrecht tun; **to be ~ed** ungerecht behandelt werden

wrongdoer [ˈrɒŋˌduːəʳ] N Missetäter(in) *m(f)*, Übeltäter(in) *m(f)*

wrongdoing [ˈrɒŋˌduːɪŋ] N Missetaten *pl*; *(single act)* Missetat *f*, Übeltat *f*; **financial ~** finanzielle Manipulationen *pl or* Unregelmäßigkeiten *pl*

wrong-foot [ˌrɒŋˈfʊt] VT *(Sport, fig)* auf dem falschen Fuß erwischen; **to ~ sb** *(fig)* jdn aus dem

Gleichgewicht bringen; *(= embarrass)* jdn in Verlegenheit bringen

wrongful ['rɒŋfʊl] **ADJ** ungerechtfertigt

wrongfully ['rɒŋfəlɪ] **ADV** zu Unrecht

wrong-headed ['rɒŋ'hedɪd] **ADJ** querköpfig, verbohrt (*about sth* in etw *acc or dat*)

wrong-headedness ['rɒŋ'hedɪdnɪs] **N** Verbohrtheit *f*

wrongly ['rɒŋlɪ] **ADV** **a** *(= unjustly, improperly)* unrecht; *punished, accused* zu Unrecht **b** *(= incorrectly)* falsch, verkehrt; *maintain* zu Unrecht; *believe* fälschlicherweise

wrongness ['rɒŋnɪs] **N** *(= incorrectness)* Unrichtigkeit *f*; *(= unfairness)* Ungerechtigkeit *f*; **the ~ of your behaviour** dein falsches Benehmen

wrote [rəʊt] *pret of* **write**

wrought [rɔːt] **VT** **a** *(obs, liter) pret, ptp of* **work** **b** **great changes have been ~** große Veränderungen wurden errungen *or* herbeigeführt; **the accident ~ havoc with his plans** der Unfall durchkreuzte alle seine Pläne; **the storm ~ great destruction** der Sturm richtete große Verheerungen an **ADJ** *silver* getrieben, gehämmert

wrought: **wrought iron** **N** Schmiedeeisen *nt*; **wrought-iron** **ADJ** schmiedeeisern *attr*, aus Schmiedeeisen; **~ gate** schmiedeeisernes Tor; **wrought ironwork** **N** Kunstschmiedearbeit *f*; **wrought-up** **ADJ** **to be ~** aufgelöst sein, außer sich *(dat)* sein

wrung [rʌŋ] *pret, ptp of* **wring**

WRVS *(Brit) abbr of* **Women's Royal Voluntary Service**

wry [raɪ] **ADJ** *(= ironical)* ironisch; *joke, sense of humour etc* trocken; **to make** *or* **pull a ~ face** das Gesicht verziehen

wryly ['raɪlɪ] **ADV** ironisch

WSW *abbr of* **west-southwest** WSW

wt *abbr of* **weight** Gew.

wunderkind ['wʌndəˌkɪnt, 'vʊndəˌkɪnt] **N** *pl* **-kinds** *or* **-kinder** [-ˌkɪndz, -ˌkɪndəˈ] Wunderkind *nt*

wuss [wʌs] **N** *(esp US inf)* Weichei *nt (inf)*, Schlappschwanz *m (inf)*

WWI *abbr of* **World War One**

WWII *abbr of* **World War Two**

WWW *(Comput) abbr of* **World Wide Web** WWW

WX *abbr of* **women's extra-large size**

wych-elm ['wɪtʃelm] **N** = **witch-elm**

wych-hazel ['wɪtʃheɪzl] **N** = **witch hazel**

WYSIWYG ['wɪzɪwɪg] **N** *(Comput) abbr of* **what you see is what you get** WYSIWYG *nt*

X, **x** [eks] N **a** X *nt*, x *nt* **b** (*Math, fig*) x; **Mr X** Herr X; **X pounds** x Pfund; **X marks the spot** die Stelle ist mit einem Kreuzchen gekennzeichnet **c** (*dated Brit*) **X-certificate film** für Jugendliche nicht geeigneter Film, für Jugendliche ab 18 Jahren freigegebener Film

X (*esp US sl*) *abbr of* **ecstasy** Ecstasy *nt*

x-axis ['eksæksɪs] N X-Achse *f*

X-chromosome ['ekskrəʊməsəʊm] N X-Chromosom *nt*

xenophobe ['zenəfəʊb] N Fremdenhasser(in) *m(f)*

xenophobia [ˌzenə'fəʊbɪə] N Fremdenfeindlichkeit *f*, Fremdenhass *m*, Xenophobie *f* (*geh*)

xenophobic [ˌzenə'fəʊbɪk] ADJ fremdenfeindlich, xenophob (*geh*)

Xerox® ['zɪərɒks] **N** (*= copy*) Xerokopie *f*; (*= process*) Xeroxverfahren *nt* **VT** xerokopieren

Xing ['eksɪŋ, 'krɒsɪŋ] N = **crossing**

XL *abbr of* **extra large**

Xmas ['eksməs, 'krɪsməs] N = **Christmas** Weihnachten *nt*

X-rated, **x-rated** ['eksˌreɪtɪd] ADJ *magazine etc* pornografisch; *humour* unflätig

X-ray ['eks'reɪ] **N** Röntgenstrahl *m*; (*also* **X-ray photograph**) Röntgenaufnahme *f or* -bild *nt*; **to take an ~ of sth** etw röntgen, eine Röntgenaufnahme von etw machen; **to have an ~** geröntgt werden; **she has gone for an ~** sie ist zum Röntgen gegangen; **~ depiction** Röntgendarstellung *f*; **~ machine** *or* **hnit** Röntgengerät *nt* **VT** *person, heart* röntgen, durchleuchten (*dated*); *envelope, baggage* durchleuchten

X-ray *in cpds* Röntgen-; **X-ray examination** N Röntgenuntersuchung *f*, röntgenologische Untersuchung; **X-ray eyes** PL (*fig*) Röntgenaugen *pl*

xylograph ['zaɪləgrɑːf] N Holzschnitt *m*

xylography [zaɪ'lɒgrəfɪ] N Holzschneidekunst *f*, Xylografie *f*

xylophone ['zaɪləfəʊn] N Xylofon *nt*

Y

Y, y [waɪ] N Y *nt*, y *nt*

yacht [jɒt] **N** Jacht *f*, Yacht *f*; **~ club** Jacht- *or* Segelklub *m*; **~ race** (Segel)regatta *f* **VI** segeln; **to go ~ing** segeln gehen; *(on cruise)* eine Segeltour *or* einen Törn machen

yachting [ˈjɒtɪŋ] N Segeln *nt*

yachting: **yachting cap** N Seglermütze *f*; **yachting circles** PL Segelkreise *pl*; **yachting cruise** N (Segel)kreuzfahrt *f*, Segelreise *f*; **yachting holiday** N *(Brit)* Segelurlaub *m*; **yachting jacket** N Segeljacke *f*

yachtsman [ˈjɒtsmən] N *pl* **-men** [-mən] Segler *m*

yachtsmanship [ˈjɒtsmənʃɪp] N Segelkunst *f*

yachtswoman [ˈjɒtswʊmən] N *pl* **-women** [-wɪmɪn] Seglerin *f*

yackety-yak [ˈjækɪtɪˈjæk] *(inf)* **VI** schnattern *(inf)*, quasseln *(inf)* **N** Blabla *nt (pej inf)*, Gequassel *nt (pej inf)*; **listen to those two, ~** hör dir mal die beiden Schnattergänse an *(inf)*; **it was ~ all evening** den ganzen Abend nichts als Gequatsche *(inf) or* Geschnatter *(inf)*

yah [jɑː] INTERJ *(expressing disgust)* uh, igitt(igitt); *(expressing derision)* ätsch, hähä

yahoo [jɑːˈhuː] N Schwein *nt (inf)*

yak¹ [jæk] N *(Zool)* Jak *m*, Yak *m*, Grunzochse *m*

yak² VI *(inf)* schnattern *(inf)*, quasseln *(inf)*; **to ~ away on sth** über etw *(acc)* quasseln

Yakuza [jəˈkuːzə] PL Yakuza *pl*, *Mitglieder einer geheimen japanischen Verbrecherorganisation*

Yale lock® [ˈjeɪlˌlɒk] N Sicherheitsschloss *nt*

y'all [jɔːl] PRON *(US inf)* = **you-all**

yam [jæm] N **a** *(= plant)* Yamswurzel *f*, Jamswurzel *f* **b** *(= sweet potato)* Süßkartoffel *f*, Batate *f*

yammer [ˈjæməʳ] VI *(inf: = moan)* jammern

Yank [jæŋk] *(inf)* **N** Ami *m (inf)* **ADJ** *attr* Ami- *(inf)*

yank [jæŋk] **N** Ruck *m*; **give it a good ~** zieh mal kräftig dran **VT** **to ~ sth** mit einem Ruck an etw *(dat)* ziehen, einer Sache *(dat)* einen Ruck geben; **he ~ed the rope free** er riss das Seil los

▶ **yank off** VT *sep* abreißen

▶ **yank out** VT *sep* ausreißen; *tooth* ziehen

Yankee [ˈjæŋkɪ] *(inf)* **N** Yankee *m (inf)*; *(Hist also)* Nordstaatler(in) *m(f)* **ADJ** *attr* Yankee- *(inf)*

> **YANKEE**
>
> Auch wenn in Europa mit **Yankee** jeder Amerikaner bezeichnet wird, meint man in den USA damit stets einen Nordstaatler. Im Norden wiederum gelten nur die Einwohner New Englands als die wahren Yankees. Der Name entstand für das Lied „Yankee Doodle", mit dem sich ein Engländer über die Amerikaner lustig machte. Während der amerikanischen Revolution machten die Soldaten von General Washington aus diesem Spottlied ein patriotisches Kampflied, weshalb Yankee heutzutage ein durchaus positiver Begriff ist. Die Abkürzung **Yank** wird allerdings in den USA weniger benutzt, es handelt sich dabei um einen eher abfälligen Ausdruck der Briten.

yap [jæp] **VI** *(dog)* kläffen; *(= talk noisily)* quatschen *(inf)*, labern *(inf)*; **it's been ~, ~, ~ all day** von morgens bis abends nur Gequatsche *(inf)* **N** *(of dog)* Kläffen *nt*, Gekläff *nt*; *(inf, of person)* Gequatsche *nt (inf)*, Gelaber *nt (inf)*; **she spoke in a high-pitched ~** sie schnatterte mit schriller Stimme *(inf)*

yapping [ˈjæpɪŋ] **ADJ** kläffend; *(inf) women* quatschend *(inf)* **N** = **yap N**

yappy [ˈjæpɪ] ADJ *dog* kläffend; *(inf)* **a ~ little dog** ein kleiner Kläffer

yard¹ [jɑːd] N **a** *(Measure)* Yard *nt (0.91 m)*; **he can't see a ~ in front of him** er kann keinen Meter weit sehen; **to buy cloth by the ~** ≈ Stoff meterweise *or* im Meter kaufen; **he pulled out ~s of handkerchief** *(inf)* er zog ein riesiges Taschentuch hervor *(inf)*; **to have a list a ~ long of things to do** *(inf)* eine ellenlange Liste von Dingen haben, die man noch tun muss *(inf)*; **his guess was ~s out** *(inf)* er lag mit seiner Schätzung völlig schief; **he wrote poetry by the ~** er produzierte Gedichte am Fließband *or* am laufenden Meter; **to go the whole nine ~s** *(US inf)* es ganz gründlich machen **b** *(Naut)* Rah *f*

yard² N **a** *(of farm, hospital, prison, school, house etc)* Hof *m*; **in the ~** auf dem Hof **b** *(= worksite)* Werksgelände *nt*; *(for storage)* Lagerplatz *m*; **builder's ~** Bauhof *m*; **shipbuilding ~** Werft *f*; **naval (dock)yard, navy ~** *(US)* Marinewerft *f*; **railway ~** *(Brit)* Rangierbahnhof *m*, Verschiebebahnhof *m*; **goods ~, freight ~** *(US)* Güterbahnhof *m* **c** *(Brit inf)* **the Yard, Scotland Yard** Scotland Yard *m* **d** *(US: = garden)* Garten *m*

yardage [ˈjɑːdɪdʒ] N Anzahl *f* von Yards, ≈ Meterzahl *f*

yardarm [ˈjɑːdɑːm] N *(Naut)* Nock *f*; **to hang sb from the ~** jdn am Mast aufknüpfen; **when the sun is over the ~** *(dated inf)* wenn es (endlich) soweit ist, dass man sich einen genehmigen darf *(inf)*

Yardie [ˈjɑːdɪ] N *(Brit) Mitglied einer geheimen Verbrecherorganisation in Jamaika*

yardstick [ˈjɑːdstɪk] N **a** *(= measuring rod)* Elle *f* **b** *(fig)* Maßstab *m*

yarmulke [ˈjɑːmʊlkə] N Jarmulke *f*, Gebetskäppchen *nt*

yarn [jɑːn] **N** **a** *(Tex)* Garn *nt* **b** *(= tale)* Seemannsgarn *nt*; **to spin a ~** Seemannsgarn spinnen; **to spin sb a ~ about sth** jdm eine Lügengeschichte über etw *(acc)* erzählen **VI** Seemannsgarn spinnen, Geschichten erzählen

yarrow [ˈjærəʊ] N *(Bot)* (gemeine) Schafgarbe

yashmak [ˈjæʃmæk] N Schleier *m (von Moslemfrauen)*

yaw [jɔː] **VI** *(Naut)* gieren, vom Kurs abkommen; *(Aviat, Space) (off course)* vom Kurs abkommen *or* abweichen; *(about axis)* gieren; **it ~ed 20 degrees to port** es gierte um 20 Grad nach Backbord **N** Kursabweichung *f*; *(about axis)* Gieren *nt*

yawl [jɔːl] N *(Naut) (= rowing boat)* Beiboot *nt*; *(= sailing boat)* (Segel)jolle *f*

yawn [jɔːn] **VI** **a** *(person)* gähnen; **to ~ with boredom** vor Langeweile gähnen **b** *(chasm etc)* gähnen **VT** gähnen; **to ~ one's head off** *(inf)* fürchterlich gähnen *(inf)* **N** **a** *(of person)* Gähnen *nt*; **I could tell by your ~s ...** an deinem Gähnen konnte ich sehen ...; **to give a ~** gähnen **b** *(inf: = bore)* **the film was a ~** der Film war zum Gähnen (langweilig); **what a ~!** wie langweilig!; **life is just one big ~** das Leben ist vielleicht langweilig

yawning [ˈjɔːnɪŋ] **ADJ** *chasm etc* gähnend **N** Gähnen *nt*

yawp [jɔːp] *(US)* **N** **a** *(inf: = yelp)* Aufschrei *m*; **to give a ~** aufschreien, kreischen **b** *(inf: = chatter)* Geschwätz *nt*; **to have a ~** schwatzen **VI** **a** *(inf: = yelp)* aufschreien, kreischen **b** *(inf: = chatter)* schwatzen

yaws [jɔːz] N *sing* Frambösie *f*

y-axis [ˈwaɪæksɪs] N Y-Achse *f*

Y-chromosome [ˈwaɪkrəʊməsəʊm] N Y-Chromosom *nt*

yd *abbr of* **yard(s)**

ye [jiː] *(obs)* **PERS PRON** *(nominative)* Ihr *(obs)*; *(objective)* Euch *(obs)*; **ye gods!** *(not obs)* allmächtiger Gott! **DEF ART** = **the**

yea [jeɪ] **ADV** *(obs)* **a** *(= yes)* ja; **~ or nay** ja oder nein **b** *(= indeed)* fürwahr *(old)* **N** **the ~s and the nays** die Jastimmen und die Neinstimmen

yeah [jɛə] ADV *(inf)* ja

year [jɪəʳ] N **a** Jahr *nt*; **this/last ~** dieses/letztes Jahr; **every other ~** jedes zweite Jahr; **three times a ~** dreimal pro *or* im Jahr; **in the ~ 1989** im Jahr(e) 1989; **in the ~ of Our Lord 1997** *(form)* im Jahr(e) des Herrn 1997 *(geh)*; **~ after ~** Jahr für Jahr; **~ by ~, from ~ to ~** von Jahr zu Jahr; **~ in, ~ out** jahrein, jahraus; **all (the) ~ round** das ganze Jahr über *or* hindurch; **as (the) ~s go by** mit den Jahren; **~s (and ~s) ago** vor (langen) Jahren; **to pay by the ~** jährlich zahlen; **a ~ last January** (im) Januar vor einem Jahr; **it'll be a ~ in** *or* **next January** *(duration)* es wird nächsten Januar ein Jahr sein; *(point in time)* es wird nächsten Januar ein Jahr her sein; **a ~ from now** nächstes Jahr um diese Zeit; **a hundred-~-old tree** ein hundert Jahre alter Baum, ein hundertjähriger Baum; **a hundred-year-old tree** ein hundert Jahre alter Baum, ein hundertjähriger Baum; **he is six ~s old** *or* **six ~s of age** er ist sechs Jahre (alt); **he is in his fortieth ~** er steht *(geh) or* ist im vierzigsten Lebensjahr; **he gets £23,000 a ~** er bekommt £ 23.000 jährlich *or* pro Jahr *or* im Jahr; **I haven't laughed so much in ~s** ich habe schon lange nicht mehr so gelacht; **that new hairdo has taken ~s off you** *(inf)* diese neue Frisur macht dich um Jahre jünger; **it's taken ~s off my life** es hat mich Jahre meines Lebens gekostet; **it has put ~s on me** es hat mich (um) Jahre älter gemacht **b** *(Univ, Sch, of coin, stamp, wine)* Jahrgang *m*; **the 2001/02 academic ~** das akademische Jahr 2001/02; **he is bottom in his ~** *(Univ, Sch)* er ist der Schlechteste seines Jahrgangs *or* in seinem Jahrgang; **first-~ student, first ~** Student(in) *m(f)* im ersten Jahr; *(= first term student)* Student(in) *m(f)* im ersten Semester, Erstsemester *nt*; **she was in my ~ at school** sie war im selben Schuljahrgang wie ich **c** **from his earliest ~s** von frühester Kindheit an, seit seiner frühesten Kindheit; **he looks old for his ~s** er sieht älter aus als er ist; **young for his ~s** jung für sein Alter; **well advanced** *or* **well on in ~s** im vorgerückten Alter; **to get on in ~s** in die Jahre kommen; **difference in ~s** Altersunterschied *m*

yearbook [ˈjɪəbʊk] N Jahrbuch *nt*

year-end [ˌjɪəˈrend] N Jahresende *nt*; **~ report** Jahresbericht *m*, Geschäftsbericht *m*

yearling [ˈjɪəlɪŋ] N *(= animal)* Jährling *m*; *(= racehorse also)* Einjährige(r) *mf* ADJ einjährig

yearlong [ˈjɪəˈlɒŋ] ADJ einjährig; **she had a ~ battle against cancer** ihr Kampf gegen den Krebs dauerte ein Jahr

yearly [ˈjɪəlɪ] ADJ jährlich ADV jährlich, einmal im Jahr; *(= per year)* jährlich; **twice ~** zweimal jährlich *or* im Jahr

yearn [jɜːn] VI sich sehnen *(after, for* nach); **to ~ to do sth** sich danach sehnen, etw zu tun; **to ~ for home** sich nach Hause sehnen; **to ~ for sb** sich nach jdm sehnen, nach jdm verlangen

yearning [ˈjɜːnɪŋ] N Sehnsucht *f*, Verlangen *nt* *(to do sth* etw zu tun, *for* nach); **a look full of ~** ein sehnsuchtsvoller Blick; **a ~ for the past** die Sehnsucht nach der Vergangenheit ADJ *desire* sehnsüchtig; *look also* sehnsuchtsvoll, verlangend

yearningly [ˈjɜːnɪŋlɪ] ADV sehnsuchtsvoll, voller Sehnsucht; *gaze also* sehnsüchtig

year-round [ˈjɪəˈraʊnd] ADJ ADV das ganze Jahr über

yeast [jiːst] N *no pl* Hefe *f*

yeast: **yeast cake** N **a** *(= cake)* Hefekuchen *m* **b** *(= cube)* Hefewürfel *m*; **yeast extract** N Hefeextrakt *m*

yeasty [ˈjiːstɪ] ADJ *taste* hefig; *smell* nach Hefe; *bread* nach Hefe schmeckend; **the beer's very ~** das Bier schmeckt stark nach Hefe

yeh [jɛə] ADV *(Brit inf)* ja; **~, whatever** mal sehen, passt schon *(inf)*

yell [jel] N Schrei *m*; **to let out** *or* **give a ~** einen Schrei ausstoßen, schreien; **could you give me a ~ when we get there?** könnten Sie mich rufen, wenn wir da sind?; **college ~** *(US)* Schlachtruf *m* eines College

VI *(also* **yell out)** schreien, brüllen *(with* vor *+dat)*; **he ~ed at her** er schrie *or* brüllte sie an; **just ~ if you need help** ruf, wenn du Hilfe brauchst; **to ~ with laughter** vor Lachen brüllen

VT *(also* **yell out)** schreien, brüllen; *name* brüllen; **he ~ed abuse at the teacher** er beschimpfte den Lehrer wüst; **she ~ed up the stairs that dinner was ready** sie rief die Treppe hinauf, dass das Essen fertig sei

yellow [ˈjeləʊ] ADJ *(+er)* **a** gelb; **~ hair** strohblondes *or* gelbblondes Haar; **to go** *or* **turn ~** gelb werden; *(paper)* vergilben **b** *(inf: = cowardly)* feige **c** *(pej, by race)* gelb N *(= colour)* Gelb *nt*; *(of egg)* Eigelb; *(inf, = cowardice)* Feigheit *f* VT gelb färben; **the sunlight had ~ed the pages** die Sonne hatte die Seiten vergilben lassen; **paper ~ed with age** vor Alter vergilbtes Papier VI gelb werden, sich gelb färben; *(corn also)* reifen; *(pages)* vergilben; **the leaves were ~ing** die Blätter färbten sich gelb

yellow: **yellow-bellied** ADJ *(sl)* feige; **yellow-belly** N *(inf)* Angsthase *m (inf)*, Waschlappen *m (inf)*; **yellow brick road** N *(fig)* Straße *f* des Erfolgs; **yellow card** N *(Ftbl)* Gelbe Karte; **yellow fever** N Gelbfieber *nt*; **yellow flag** N *(Naut)* gelbe Flagge, Quarantäneflagge *f*; **yellowhammer** N *(Orn)* Goldammer *f*

yellowish [ˈjeləʊɪʃ] ADJ gelblich; **~-brown/-green** gelblich braun/grün

yellow: **yellow jack** N *(Naut)* gelbe Flagge, Quarantäneflagge *f*; **yellow jersey** N *(Cycling)* gelbes Trikot; **yellow journalism** N Regenbogenjournalismus *m*; **yellow Labrador** N Gelber Labrador; **yellow legal pad** N Notizblock *m*; **yellow line** N *(Brit)* Halteverbot *nt*; **double ~** absolutes Halteverbot; **to be parked on a (double) ~** im (absoluten) Halteverbot stehen; **yellow metal** N Münzmetall *nt*

yellowness [ˈjeləʊnɪs] N **a** *no pl* Gelb *nt*; *(of skin)* gelbliche Färbung **b** *(inf, = cowardice)* Feigheit *f*

yellow: **yellow ochre** ADJ ockergelb; **Yellow Pages®** N SING **the ~** das Branchenverzeichnis, die Gelben Seiten® *pl*; **yellow peril** N gelbe Gefahr; **yellow press** N *(dated Press)* Regenbogenpresse *f*; **Yellow River** N Gelber Fluss; **Yellow Sea** N Gelbes Meer; **yellow wagtail** N Gelbe Bachstelze *f*

yellowy [ˈjeləʊɪ] ADJ gelblich

yelp [jelp] N *(of animal)* Jaulen *nt no pl*; *(of person)* Aufschrei *m*; **to give a ~** (auf)jaulen; *(person)* aufschreien VI *(animal)* (auf)jaulen; *(person)* aufschreien

yelping [ˈjelpɪŋ] N *(of animal)* Jaulen *nt*; *(of person)* Aufschreien *nt*

Yemen [ˈjemən] N **the ~** der Jemen

Yemeni [ˈjemənɪ] N Jemenit(in) *m(f)* ADJ jemenitisch

yen¹ [jen] N *(Fin)* Yen *m*

yen² N *(inf)* Lust *f (for* auf *+acc)*; **I've always had a ~ to go to Pasadena** es hat mich schon immer nach Pasadena gezogen; **I had a ~ to do that/for oysters** ich hatte plötzlich Lust, das zu machen/auf Austern

yeoman [ˈjəʊmən] N *pl* **-men** [-mən] **a** *(Hist: = small landowner)* Freibauer *m*; **~ farmer** *(Hist)* Freibauer *m* **b** **Yeoman of the Guard** königlicher Leibgardist; **to do ~ service** treue Dienste leisten *(for sb* jdm)

yeomanry [ˈjəʊmənrɪ] N **a** *(Hist)* Freibauernschaft *f*, Freibauernstand *m* **b** *(Mil) freiwillige Kavallerietruppe*

yep [jep] ADV *(inf)* ja; **is he sure? – ~!** ist er sicher? – klar!

yer [jɜːʳ] PRON *(sl)* = **your**

yes [jes] ADV ja; *(answering neg question)* doch; **to say ~** Ja *or* ja sagen; **to say ~ to a proposal** einer Forderung *(dat)* nachkommen; **he said ~ to all my questions** er hat alle meine Fragen bejaht *or* mit Ja beantwortet; **if they say ~ to an increase** wenn sie eine Lohnerhöhung bewilligen; **I'd say ~ to 35%, no to 32%** ich würde 35% akzeptieren, 32% nicht; **she says ~ to everything** sie kann nicht Nein *or* nein sagen; **~ sir!** *(Mil)* jawohl, Herr General/Leutnant *etc*; *(general)* jawohl, mein Herr!; **waiter! – ~ sir?** Herr Ober! – ja, bitte?; **~ indeed** o ja, allerdings; **I didn't say that – oh ~, you did** das habe ich nicht gesagt – o doch *or* o ja, das hast du; **~ and no** ja und nein, jein *(inf)*; **~ ~, I know!** jaja, ich weiß doch

N Ja *nt*; **he just answered with ~es and noes** er hat einfach mit Ja oder Nein geantwortet

yes: **yes man** N Jasager *m*; **yes/no question** N Ja-Nein-Frage *f*

yesterday [ˈjestədeɪ] N Gestern *nt*; **the fashions of ~** die Mode von gestern; **all our ~s** unsere ganze Vergangenheit ADV *(lit, fig)* gestern; **~ morning/afternoon/evening** gestern Morgen/Nachmittag/Abend; **he was at home all (day) ~** er war gestern den ganzen Tag zu Hause; **the day before ~** vorgestern; **a week ago ~** gestern vor einer Woche → **born**

yesteryear [ˈjestəˈjɪəʳ] N *(poet)* **of ~** vergangener Jahre *(gen)*

yes woman N Jasagerin *f*

yet [jet] ✪ 20.5 ADV **a** *(= still)* noch; *(= thus far)* bis jetzt, bisher; **they haven't ~ returned** *or* **returned ~** sie sind noch nicht zurückgekommen; **this is his best book ~** das ist bis jetzt sein bestes Buch, das ist sein bisher bestes Buch; **as ~** *(with present tenses)* bis jetzt, bisher; *(with past)* bis dahin; **no, not ~** nein, noch nicht; **I've hardly begun ~** ich habe noch gar nicht richtig angefangen; **not just ~** jetzt noch nicht; **don't come in (just) ~** komm (jetzt) noch nicht herein; **you ain't seen nothing ~** *(inf)* du hast noch gar nichts gesehen

b *(with interrog: = so far, already)* schon; **has he arrived ~?** ist er schon angekommen?, ist er schon da?; **do you have to go just ~?** müssen Sie jetzt schon gehen?

c *(with affirmative: = still, remaining)* noch; **they have a few days ~** sie haben noch ein paar Tage; **we've got ages ~** wir haben noch viel Zeit; **not for some time ~** noch nicht so schnell *or* bald; **a ~ to be decided question** eine noch unentschiedene Frage, eine Frage, die noch entschieden werden muss; **I've ~ to learn how to do it** ich muss erst noch lernen, wie man es macht; **and they are doubtless waiting ~** und sie warten zweifellos noch immer; **he is ~ alive** er lebt noch

d *(with comp: = still, even)* noch; **this is ~ more difficult** dies ist (sogar) noch schwieriger; **~ more money** noch mehr Geld

e *(= in addition)* **(and) ~ again** und wieder, und noch einmal; **and ~ again they rode off** und sie ritten wieder weg; **another arrived and ~ another** es kam noch einer und noch einer

f *(with future and conditional: = before all is over)* noch; **he may come ~** *or* **~ come** er kann noch kommen; **he could come ~** er könnte noch kommen; **I may ~ go to Italy** ich fahre vielleicht noch nach Italien; **I'll do it ~** ich schaffe es schon noch

g *(liter)* **nor ~** noch; **they didn't come nor ~ write** sie sind weder gekommen, noch haben sie geschrieben

CONJ doch, dennoch, trotzdem; **and ~** und doch *or* trotzdem *or* dennoch; **it's strange ~ true** es ist seltsam, aber wahr

yeti [ˈjetɪ] N Yeti *m*, Schneemensch *m*

yew [juː] N *(also* **yew tree)** Eibe *f*; *(= wood)* Eibe(nholz *nt*) *f*

Y-fronts® [ˈwaɪfrʌnts] PL *(esp Brit)* (Herren-)Slip *m*

YHA *abbr of* **Youth Hostels Association** ≈ DJH *nt*

Yid [jɪd] N *(pej)* Jud *m (pej)*

Yiddish [ˈjɪdɪʃ] ADJ jiddisch N *(Ling)* Jiddisch *nt*

yield [jiːld] VT **a** *(land) fruit, crop* hervorbringen; *(tree) fruit* tragen; *(mine, oil well)* bringen; *(shares, money) interest, profit* (ein)bringen, abwerfen; *result* (hervor)bringen; *opportunity, clue* ergeben; **the information ~ed by the poll** die Information, die die Meinungsumfrage ergeben hat; **this ~ed a weekly increase of 20%** das brachte eine wöchentliche Steigerung von 20%

b *(= surrender, concede)* aufgeben; **to ~ sth to sb** etw an jdn abtreten; **to ~ ground to sb** vor jdm zurückstecken; **to ~ the floor to sb** *(fig)* jdm das Feld überlassen; **to ~ a point to sb** jdm einen Punkt zukommen lassen; *(in competition)* einen Punkt an jdn abgeben; **to ~ concessions** Zugeständnisse machen; **to ~ right of way to sb** *(Mot)* jdm die Vorfahrt gewähren *or* lassen

VI **a** *(tree, land)* tragen; *(mine, oil well)* Ertrag bringen; *(shares, money)* sich verzinsen, Zinsen *or* Profit einbringen *or* abwerfen; **land that ~s well** Land, das ertragreich ist

b *(= surrender, give way)* **they ~ed to us** *(Mil)* sie haben sich uns *(dat)* ergeben; *(general)* sie haben nachgegeben; **at last she ~ed to him/to his charm** schließlich erlag sie ihm/seinem Charme doch; **to ~ to force/superior forces** *(Mil)* der Gewalt/Übermacht weichen *or* nachgeben; **to ~ to sb's threats** sich jds Drohungen *(dat)* beugen; **he ~ed to her requests** er gab ihren Bitten nach; **the disease ~ed to treatment** die Krankheit sprach auf die Behandlung an; **to ~ to temptation** der Versuchung erliegen; **to ~ to one's emotions** seinen Gefühlen nachgeben; **I'll have to ~ to you on that point** in diesem Punkt muss ich Ihnen recht geben

c *(= give way: branch, beam, rope, floor, ground)* nachgeben; **to ~ under pressure** unter Druck nachgeben; *(fig)* dem Druck weichen

d *(Mot)* **to ~ to oncoming traffic** den Gegenverkehr vorbeilassen; **"yield"** *(US, Ir)* „Vorfahrt beachten!"

N *(of land, tree)* Ertrag *m*; *(of work also)* Ergebnis *nt*; *(of mine, well)* Ausbeute *f*; *(of industry)* (=

goods) Produktion *f*; (= profit) Gewinne *pl*, Erträge *pl*; (Fin, of shares, business) Ertrag *m*, Gewinn *m*; ~ **of tax** Steueraufkommen *nt*

▸**yield up** VT *sep rights, privileges* abtreten, verzichten auf (+acc); *secret* enthüllen; **to yield sth up to sb** etw an jdn abtreten; **he yielded himself up to his fate** er ergab sich in sein Schicksal

yielding ['ji:ldɪŋ] ADJ *person* nachgiebig; *surface, material* nachgebend; **the ground is ~** der Boden gibt nach

yike(s) [jaɪk(s)] INTERJ (dated esp US inf) ach du Schande (inf)

yip [jɪp] N, VI (US) = **yelp**

yipe(s) [jaɪp(s)] INTERJ (dated esp US inf) = **yike(s)**

yippee [jɪ'pi:] INTERJ juchhu, hurra

YMCA abbr of **Young Men's Christian Association** CVJM *m*

yob [jɒb] N (Brit inf) Halbstarke(r) *m*, Rowdy *m*

Y.O.B., **YOB** abbr of **year of birth**

yobbish ['jɒbɪʃ] ADJ (Brit inf) *behaviour, person* rowdyhaft; ~ **mentality** Halbstarken- or Rowdymentalität *f*

yobbo ['jɒbəʊ] N (Brit inf) Halbstarke(r) *m*, Rowdy *m*

yodel ['jəʊdl] VTI jodeln

yodeller, (US) **yodeler** ['jəʊdlə'] N Jodler(in) *m(f)*

yodelling, (US) **yodeling** ['jəʊdlɪŋ] N Jodeln *nt*

yoga ['jəʊgə] N Joga *m or nt*, Yoga *m or nt*

yoghourt, **yog(h)urt** ['jɒgət] N Jog(h)urt *m or nt*

yogi ['jəʊgɪ] N Jogi *m*, Yogi *m*

yogic flying [jəʊgɪk'flaɪɪŋ] N yogisches Fliegen

yo-heave-ho ['jəʊ'hi:v'həʊ] INTERJ hau ruck

yoke [jəʊk] **N** **a** (for oxen) Joch *nt*; (for carrying pails) (Trag)joch *nt*, Schultertrage *f* **b** *pl* - (= pair of oxen) Joch *nt*, Gespann *nt* **c** (fig: = oppression) Joch *nt*; **to throw off the ~** das Joch abschütteln **d** (on dress, blouse etc) Passe *f* **VT** **a** (also **yoke up**) *oxen* (ins Joch) einspannen; **to ~ oxen to the plough** Ochsen vor den Pflug spannen **b** *pieces of machinery* zusammenschließen; **to ~ sth to sth** etw an etw (acc) anschließen **c** (fig: = join together) zusammenschließen, vereinen

yokel ['jəʊkəl] N (pej) Bauerntölpel *m*, Bauerntrampel *m*

yolk [jəʊk] N (of egg) Eigelb *nt*

yomp [jɒmp] VI (Mil sl) sich schleppen

yon [jɒn] ADV, ADJ (poet, dial) = **yonder**

yonder ['jɒndə'] (poet, dial) **ADV** **(over)** ~ dort drüben **ADJ** **from ~ house** von dem Haus (dort) drüben

yonks [jɒŋks] N (Brit inf: = ages) eine (halbe) Ewigkeit (inf); **that was ~ ago** das war vor einer (halben) Ewigkeit (inf); **I haven't seen her for ~** ich habe sie schon ewig nicht mehr gesehen (inf)

yoo-hoo [ju:'hu:] INTERJ huhu, hallo

yore [jɔ:'] N (obs, liter) **in days of ~** in alten Zeiten; **men of ~** die Menschen in alten Zeiten; **in the Britain of ~** im Großbritannien längst vergangener Zeiten

Yorkshire pudding [jɔ:kʃə'pʊdɪŋ] N Yorkshire Pudding *m (Beilage zu Rinderbraten)*

Yorkshire terrier [jɔ:kʃə'terɪə'] N Yorkshireterrier *m*

you [ju:] PRON **a** (German familiar form) (sing) (nom) du; (acc) dich; (dat) dir; (pl) (nom) ihr; (acc, dat) euch; (German polite form: sing, pl) (nom, acc) Sie; (dat) Ihnen; **all of ~** (pl) ihr alle/Sie alle; **I want all of ~** (sing) ich will dich ganz; **if I were ~** wenn ich du/Sie wäre, an deiner/Ihrer Stelle; **~ Germans** ihr Deutschen; **~ two/three wait here!** ihr beide/drei wartet hier; **silly old ~** du Dussel (inf), du Dumm(er)chen (inf); **~ darling** du bist ein Schatz or Engel; **is that ~?** bist dus/seid ihrs/sind Sies?; **it's ~** du bist es/ihr seids/Sie sinds; **what's the matter? – it's ~ or ~ are** was ist los? – es liegt an dir/euch/Ihnen; **there's a fine house for ~!** das ist mal ein schönes Haus!; **now there's a woman for ~!** das ist mal eine (tolle) Frau!; **now ~ say something** sag du/sagt ihr/sagen Sie (auch) mal was; **just ~ dare!** trau dich bloß!, untersteh dich!; **sit ~ down** (hum) setz dich/setzt euch/setzen Sie sich; **that hat just isn't ~** (inf) der Hut passt einfach nicht zu dir/zu Ihnen **b** (indef) (nom) man; (acc) einen; (dat) einem; **~ never know, ~ never can tell** man kann nie wissen, man weiß nie; **it's not good for ~** es ist nicht gut

you-all ['ju:ɔ:l] PRON (US inf) ihr

you'd [ju:d] contr of **you would**; of **you had**

you'd've ['ju:dəv] contr of **you would have**

you'll [ju:l] contr of **you will, you shall**

young [jʌŋ] **ADJ** (+er) jung; *wine, grass also* neu; **the ~ moon** der Mond im ersten Viertel; **~ people** junge Leute *pl*; **a ~ people's magazine** eine Jugendzeitschrift; **~ people's fashions** Jugendmoden *pl*; **~ lady** junge Dame; **~ man** junger Mann; **they have a ~ family** sie haben kleine Kinder; **he is ~ at heart** er ist innerlich jung geblieben; **you are only ~ once** man ist or du bist nur einmal jung; **at a ~ age** in frühen Jahren; **if I were ten years ~er** wenn ich zehn Jahre jünger wäre; **I'm not getting any ~er** ich werde auch nicht jünger; **he is ~ for his age** er ist noch sehr jung; **that dress is too ~ for her** sie ist zu alt für dieses Kleid; **you ~ rascal!** (inf) du kleiner Schlingel!; **~ Mr Brown** der junge Herr Brown; **Pitt the Younger** Pitt der Jüngere; **the night is ~** die Nacht ist (noch) jung; **Young America** die Jugend in Amerika, die amerikanische Jugend; **he's a very ~ forty** er ist ein sehr jugendlicher or sehr jung gebliebener Vierziger **ADV** *marry, have children* jung; **live fast, die ~** leb jetzt und stirb jung **PL** **a** (= people) **the ~** die Jugend, die jungen Leute; **~ and old** jung und alt; **books for the ~** Jugendbücher *pl* **b** (= animals) Junge *pl*; **with ~** trächtig

Young Conservative N (Brit Pol) Mitglied *nt* der Jungen Konservativen; **the ~s** die Jungen Konservativen

youngest ['jʌŋgɪst] **ADJ** attr superl of **young** jüngste(r, s) **N** **the ~** der/die/das Jüngste; (pl) die Jüngsten *pl*; **the ~ of four children** das jüngste von vier Kindern; **my ~** (inf) (= son) mein Jüngster; (= daughter) meine Jüngste

youngish ['jʌŋɪʃ] ADJ ziemlich jung

young offender N jugendlicher Straftäter; **home for ~s** Jugendstrafanstalt *f*

young offenders' institution N Einrichtung *f* für jugendliche Straftäter

youngster ['jʌŋstə'] N (= boy) Junge *m*; (= child) Kind *nt*; **he's just a ~** er ist eben noch jung or ein Kind

your [jɔ:', jə'] POSS ADJ **a** (German familiar form) (sing) dein/deine/dein; (pl) euer/eure/euer; (German polite form: sing, pl) Ihr/Ihre/Ihr; **~ mother and father** deine/Ihre Mutter und dein/Ihr Vater; **one of ~ friends** einer deiner/Ihrer Freunde, einer von deinen/Ihren Freunden; **the climate here is bad for ~ health** das Klima hier ist ungesund or ist nicht gut für die Gesundheit → **majesty, worship** etc **b** (= typical) der/die/das; **~ average Englishman** der durchschnittliche Engländer

you're [jʊə', jɔ:'] contr of **you are**

yours [jɔ:z] POSS PRON (German familiar form, sing) deiner/deine/deins; (pl) eurer/eure/euers; (German polite form: sing, pl) Ihrer/Ihre/Ihr(e)s; **this is my book and that is ~** dies ist mein Buch und das (ist) deins/Ihres; **the idea was ~** es war deine/Ihre Idee, die Idee stammt von dir/Ihnen; **she is a cousin of ~** sie ist deine Cousine, sie ist eine Cousine von dir; **that is no business of ~** das geht dich/Sie nichts an; **that dog of ~!** dein/Ihr blöder Hund!; **you and ~** du und deine Familie/Sie und Ihre Familie, du und die deinen or Deinen/Sie und die Ihren (geh); **~** (in letter-writing) Ihr/Ihre; **~ faithfully, ~ truly** (Brit: on letter) mit freundlichem Gruß, mit freundlichen Grüßen, hochachtungsvoll (form); **in reply to ~ of the 15th May** (Comm, form) in Antwort auf Ihr Schreiben vom 15. Mai; **what's ~?** (to drink) was möchtest du/was möchten Sie?, was trinkst du/was trinken Sie?; **guess who had to do all the dirty work? ~ truly** (inf) und wer musste die Dreckarbeit machen? ich natürlich; **and then ~ truly got up and said ...** und dann stand ich höchstpersönlich auf und sagte ... → **affectionately, up**

yourself [jɔ:'self, jə'self] PRON *pl* **yourselves** [jɔ:'selvz, jə'selvz] **a** (reflexive) (German familiar form) (sing) (acc) dich; (dat) dir; (pl) euch; (German polite form: sing, pl) sich; **have you hurt ~?** hast du dir/haben Sie sich wehgetan?; **you never speak about ~** du redest nie über dich (selbst)/Sie reden nie über sich (selbst) **b** (emph) selbst; **you ~ told me, you told me ~** du hast/Sie haben mir selbst gesagt; **you are not quite ~ today** du bist heute gar nicht du selbst, du bist/Sie sind heute irgendwie verändert or anders; **how's ~?** (inf) und wie gehts dir/Ihnen?; **you will see for ~** du wirst/Sie werden selbst sehen; **did you do it by ~?** hast du/haben Sie das allein gemacht?

yous [ju:z] PRON (PL) (dial) ihr; (acc, dat) euch

youth [ju:θ] N **a** no pl Jugend *f*; **in (the days of) my ~** in meiner Jugend(zeit); **the town of my ~** die Stadt or Stätte (hum) meiner Jugend; **in early ~** in früher Jugend; **she has kept her ~** sie ist jung geblieben **b** pl **-s** [ju:ðz] (= young man) junger Mann, Jugendliche(r) *m*; **when he was a ~** als er ein junger Mann war; **pimply ~** pickliger Jüngling **c** **youth** PL (= young men and women) Jugend *f*; **she likes working with (the) ~** sie arbeitet gerne mit Jugendlichen; **the ~ of today** die Jugend von heute; **the Hitler Youth Movement** die Hitlerjugend

youth: **youth centre**, (US) **youth center** N Jugendzentrum *nt*; **youth club** N Jugendklub *m*; **youth custody** N (Brit Jur) Jugendarrest *m*; **Youth Employment Scheme** N (Brit) Programm *nt* or Aktionsplan *m* für jugendliche Arbeitslose

youthful ['ju:θfʊl] ADJ jugendlich; **he's a ~ 65** er ist ein jugendlicher Fünfundsechziger; **a ~ mistake** eine Jugendsünde

youthfully ['ju:θfʊlɪ] ADV jugendlich; **she leapt up ~** sie sprang jugendlich frisch auf

youthfulness ['ju:θfʊlnɪs] N Jugendlichkeit *f*

youth: **youth hostel®** N Jugendherberge® *f*; **youth hosteller, youth hosteler** N *jd, der in Jugendherbergen übernachtet*, Jugendherbergsgast *m*; **Youth Training Scheme** N (Brit) Ausbildungsprogramm *nt* für Jugendliche; **youth worker** N Jugendarbeiter(in) *m(f)*

you've [ju:v] contr of **you have**

yowl [jaʊl] **N** (of person, wolf) Heulen *nt no pl*; (of dog) Jaulen *nt no pl*; (of cat) Maunzen *nt*; **to give a ~** heulen; jaulen; maunzen **VI** (person) heulen; (dog) jaulen; (cat) kläglich miauen

yo-yo ['jəʊjəʊ] N Jo-Jo *nt*, Yo-Yo *nt*; **I've been going up- and downstairs like a ~ all morning** ich bin den ganzen Morgen wie irre die Treppe rauf- und runtergerannt (inf); **~ diet/effect** (hum) Jo-Jo-Diät *f*/-Effekt *m*; **~ dieting** *unmittelbarer Wechsel von Abnehmen und erneutem Zunehmen*

yr **a** abbr of **year(s)** **b** abbr of **your**

yrs **a** abbr of **years** **b** abbr of **yours**

Y-shaped ['waɪʃeɪpt] ADJ Y-förmig

YTS (Brit) N **a** abbr of **Youth Training Scheme** **b** (= person) Auszubildende(r) *mf*

ytterbium [ɪ'tɜ:bɪəm] N (Chem) Ytterbium *nt*

yttrium ['ɪtrɪəm] N (Chem) Yttrium *nt*

yucca ['jʌkə] N Yucca *f*, Palmlilie *f*

yuck [jʌk] INTERJ (inf) = **yuk**

yuck factor N (inf) Igitt-Faktor *m* (inf)

Yugoslav ['ju:gəʊ'slɑ:v] ADJ *(Hist)* jugoslawisch *(Hist)* N *(Hist)* Jugoslawe *m (Hist)*, Jugoslawin *f (Hist)*

Yugoslavia ['ju:gəʊ'slɑ:vɪə] N *(Hist)* Jugoslawien *nt (Hist)*; **the former ~** das ehemalige Jugoslawien, Ex-Jugoslawien *nt* (*Press sl*)

Yugoslavian ['ju:gəʊ'slɑ:vɪən] ADJ *(Hist)* jugoslawisch *(Hist)*

yuk [jʌk] INTERJ *(inf)* i, igitt, igittigitt

yukky ['jʌkɪ] ADJ *(+er) (inf)* eklig, widerlich, fies *(inf)*

yule [ju:l] N *(old)* Weihnachten *nt*, Julfest *nt*; **~ log** Julblock *m*

Yuletide N ['ju:ltaɪd] Weihnachtszeit *f*, Julzeit *f*

yummy ['jʌmɪ] *(inf)* ADJ *(+er) food* lecker; *man* toll INTERJ **~!, ~ ~!** lecker!, jamjam! *(inf)*

yum yum ['jʌm'jʌm] INTERJ lecker, jamjam *(inf)*

yup [jʌp] ADV (*US inf: = yes*) ja, jawoll *(inf)*

yuppie, yuppy ['jʌpɪ] N Yuppie *m* ADJ yuppiehaft; **~ car** Yuppieauto *nt*; **~ job** Yuppiejob *m*

yuppie flu N *krankhafter Energiemangel*

yuppiedom ['jʌpɪdəm] N *(inf)* **the rise of ~ in the eighties** der Aufstieg der Yuppies in den 80er Jahren

yuppy N ADJ = **yuppie**

YWCA *abbr of* **Young Women's Christian Association** CVJF *m*

Z

Z, z [(*Brit*) zed] [(*US*) ziː] N Z *nt*, z *nt*; **to catch some Zs** (*US inf*: = *take a nap*) sich aufs Ohr hauen *(inf)*

Zaire [zɑːˈɪəˈ] N *(Hist)* Zaire *nt*

Zambesi, Zambezi [zæmˈbiːzɪ] N Sambesi *m*

Zambia [ˈzæmbɪə] N Sambia *nt*

zany [ˈzeɪnɪ] ADJ *(+er)* (= *crazy, funny*) verrückt; *person also* irrsinnig komisch N *(Theat Hist)* Narr *m*, Hanswurst *m*

Zanzibar [ˈzænzɪbɑːˈ] N Sansibar *nt*

zap [zæp] *(inf)* N (= *energy, pep*) Schwung *m*, Pep *m (inf)* INTERJ zack VT **a** (= *hit*) **to ~ sb** jdm eine pfeffern *(inf)* or kleben *(inf)* **b** (*Comput*: = *delete*) löschen **c** *(inf)* (= *kill*) abknallen *(inf)*; (= *destroy*) kaputt machen *(inf)* **d** (*inf*, = *send quickly*) **he ~ped us back down to London in his Porsche** er hat uns in seinem Porsche im Düsentempo nach London zurückgebracht *(inf)* VI *(inf)* **a** (= *move fast*) düsen *(inf)* **b** (= *change channel*) umschalten; **to ~ through the channels** zappen *(inf)*

▶ **zap along** VI (*inf*: = *move fast*) düsen *(inf)*; **the project's zapping along** das Projekt geht mit Volldampf voran *(inf)*

zapped [zæpt] ADJ (*inf*: = *tired, exhausted*) total geschafft *(inf)*

zapper [ˈzæpəˈ] N (*US inf*) **a** *(TV)* Fernbedienung *f* **b** (*for insects*) Insektenkiller *m (inf)* *(elektrisch betrieben)*

zappiness [ˈzæpɪnɪs] N (*of pace, car*) Fetzigkeit *f (inf)*; (*of prose, style*) Spritzigkeit *f*; (*of management style*) Dynamik *f*

zappy [ˈzæpɪ] ADJ *pace, car* fetzig *(inf)*; (= *lively*) *prose, style* spritzig; *management style* dynamisch

zeal [ziːl] N *no pl* Eifer *m*; **to work with great ~** mit Feuereifer arbeiten; **he is full of ~ for the cause** er ist mit Feuereifer bei der Sache

zealot [ˈzelət] N Fanatiker(in) *m(f)*; (*religious also*) (Glaubens)eiferer(in) *m(f)*; **Zealot** *(Hist)* Zelot *m*

zealotry [ˈzelətrɪ] N Fanatismus *m*, blinder Eifer

zealous [ˈzeləs] ADJ *student, worker* eifrig, emsig; *official, officer* eifrig; **~ for sth** eifrig um etw bemüht; **to be ~ to begin/help** erpicht darauf sein, anzufangen/zu helfen; **~ for the cause** für die Sache begeistert; **~ for a change** auf einen Wechsel erpicht

zealously [ˈzeləslɪ] ADV *pursue, guard, support* eifrig

zebra [ˈzebrə] N Zebra *nt*

zebra: **zebra crossing** N *(Brit)* Zebrastreifen *m*; **zebra finch** N *(Orn)* Zebrafink *m*

Zeitgeist [ˈzaɪtgaɪst] N Zeitgeist *m*

Zen [zen] N Zen *nt*; **~ Buddhism** Zen-Buddhismus *m*

zenith [ˈzenɪθ] N *(Astron, fig)* Zenit *m*

zephyr [ˈzefəˈ] N *(poet)* Zephir *m (poet)*, Zephyr *m (poet)*

zeppelin [ˈzeplɪn] N Zeppelin *m*

zero [ˈzɪərəʊ] N *pl* **-(e)s** **a** (= *figure*) Null *f*; (= *point on scale*) Nullpunkt *m*; *(Roulette)* Zero *f*; **15 degrees below ~** 15 Grad unter null; **the needle is at** *or* **on ~** der Zeiger steht auf null; **his chances were put at ~** man meinte, seine Aussichten seien gleich null; **snow reduced visibility to near ~** es schneite so stark, dass die Sicht fast gleich null war
b (*fig*: = *nonentity*) Null *f (inf)*
ADJ **at ~ altitude** *(Aviat)* im Tiefflug; **~ altitude flying** Tiefflug *m*; **~ degrees** null Grad; **~ growth** Nullwachstum *nt*; **he's getting absolutely ~ satisfaction from it** *(inf)* das bringt ihm überhaupt nichts *(inf)*; **she showed ~ interest in him** *(inf)* sie zeigte nicht im Geringsten an ihm interessiert

▶ **zero in** VI *(Mil)* sich einschießen (*on* auf *+acc*); **to zero in on sb/sth** (*fig, on gang leader, core of problem*) jdn/etw einkreisen; *on difficulty* sich *(dat)* etw herausgreifen; *on opportunity* sich auf etw *(acc)* stürzen

▶ **zero out** VT (= *eliminate*) eliminieren; *data, e-mails* löschen VI (*US Telec*) *die Taste 0 drücken, um von einem Anrufbeantworter zu einem direkten Gesprächspartner durchgestellt zu werden*

> **ZERO**
>
> Null, „0", wird je nach Kontext verschieden gesprochen. Dabei ist **zero** der gebräuchlichste Ausdruck in fast allen amerikanischen Kontexten, im britischen Englisch wird **zero** in Mathematik und Naturwissenschaften verwendet, auch bei Temperaturen und anderen Skalen.
>
> **Nought** ist ein britischer Ausdruck, den man beim Aussprechen von Dezimalzahlen heranzieht: „nought point nought seven" ist 0.07. Auch bei der Benotung greift man darauf zurück, z. B. „nought out of ten". „Oh" wird „0" dagegen sowohl im britischen wie auch amerikanischen Englisch gesprochen, wenn man Zahlenreihen, wie bei einer Telefonnummer oder Kreditkarte, vorlesen muss: „oh one four one" (0141).
>
> **Nil** wird häufig im britischen Sport für den Punktestand verwendet: „Liverpool won five nil/by five goals to nil". Die amerikanische Entsprechung ist **nothing**, was in Großbritannien, allerdings in der Umgangssprache, ebenfalls verwendet wird. Beim Tennis und Squash heißt es dagegen **love**: „Fifteen - love". In der amerikanischen Umgangssprache gibt es auch noch **zip**: „We won seven-zip".

zero: **zero-emission** ADJ emissionsfrei; **~ car** Null-Emissions-Auto *nt*; **zero gravity** N Schwerelosigkeit *f*; **at ~** unter Schwerelosigkeit; **zero hour** N *(Mil, fig)* die Stunde X; **zero option** N *(Pol)* Nulllösung *f*; **zero-rated** ADJ (*for VAT*) mehrwertsteuerfrei; **zero rating** N (*for VAT*) Befreiung *f* von der Mehrwertsteuer; **zero-sum game** N Nullsummenspiel *nt*; **zero tolerance** N Nulltoleranz *f*; **zero-tolerance** ADJ kompromisslos; **~ policing** Polizeiarbeit *f* nach dem Nulltoleranzprinzip

zest [zest] N **a** (= *enthusiasm*) Begeisterung *f*; **~ for life** Lebensfreude *f*; **he hasn't got much ~** er hat keinen Schwung **b** (*in style, of food etc*) Pfiff *m (inf)*, Schwung *m*; **a story full of ~** eine Geschichte mit Schwung; **add ~ to your meals with ...!** geben Sie Ihren Gerichten Pfiff mit ...! *(inf)* **c** (= *lemon etc peel*) Zitronen-/Orangenschale *f*

zestful ADJ, **zestfully** ADV [ˈzestfʊl, -fəlɪ] schwungvoll

zesty [ˈzestɪ] ADJ *wine* pikant

zeugma [ˈzjuːgmə] N Zeugma *nt*

Zeus [zjuːs] N *(Myth)* Zeus *m*

ziggurat [ˈzɪgəræt] N Zikkur(r)at *f*

zigzag [ˈzɪgzæg] N Zickzack *m or nt*; **in a ~** im Zickzack; **the river cuts a ~ through the rocks** der Fluss bahnt sich im Zickzack einen Weg durch die Felsen; **we had to make a long ~ across the ice** wir mussten uns lange im Zickzack über das Eis bewegen; **a pattern of straight lines and ~s** ein Muster aus Geraden und Zickzacklinien ADJ Zickzack-; *road, path* zickzackförmig; **~ line** Zickzacklinie *f*; **to steer a ~ course** *(Naut)* Zickzack(kurs) fahren ADV zickzackförmig, im Zickzack VI im Zickzack laufen/fahren *etc*; *(Naut)* Zickzack(kurs) fahren; **to ~ along** im Zickzack laufen/fahren *etc*

zilch [zɪltʃ] N (*inf*: = *nothing*) nix *(inf)*

zillion [ˈzɪljən] (*US inf*) N **~s of dollars** zig Milliarden Dollar *(inf)* ADJ **I've told you a ~ times ...** ich hab dir hunderttausendmal *or* zigmal gesagt ... *(inf)*

Zimbabwe [zɪmˈbɑːbwɪ] N Simbabwe *nt*, Zimbabwe *nt*

Zimbabwean [zɪmˈbɑːbwɪən] ADJ zimbabwisch, simbabwisch N Zimbabwer(in) *m(f)*, Simbabwer(in) *m(f)*

Zimmer® [ˈzɪməˈ] N (*Brit*: *also* **Zimmer frame®**) Gehgerät *nt*

zinc [zɪŋk] N Zink *nt*

zinc ointment N Zinksalbe *f*

zinc oxide N Zinkoxid *nt*

zine, 'zine [ziːn] *(inf)* N *kleine, amateurhaft produzierte Zeitschrift*, Magazin *nt*, Heftchen *nt*

Zinfandel [ˈzɪnfən,del] N Zinfandel *m*, *kalifornischer trockener Rotwein*

zing [zɪŋ] *(inf)* N **a** (*noise of bullet etc*) Pfeifen *nt*, Zischen *nt* **b** (= *zest*) Pfiff *m (inf)* VI (*bullets*) pfeifen, zischen

zinger [ˈzɪŋəˈ] N **to be a real ~** *(inf)* wie eine Bombe einschlagen

zinnia [ˈzɪnɪə] N Zinnie *f*

Zion [ˈzaɪən] N Zion *nt*

Zionism [ˈzaɪənɪzəm] N Zionismus *m*

Zionist [ˈzaɪənɪst] ADJ zionistisch N Zionist(in) *m(f)*

ZIP [zɪp] *(US) abbr of* **zone improvement plan** PLZ

zip [zɪp] N **a** (*Brit*: = *fastener*) Reißverschluss *m*
b (*sound of bullet*) Pfeifen *nt*, Zischen *nt*
c (*inf*: = *energy*) Schwung *m*; **we need a bit more ~ in these translations** wir müssen etwas mehr Schwung in diese Übersetzungen kriegen *(inf)*
d (*inf*: = *nothing*) nichts, nix *(inf)*
VT **to ~ sth shut/open** etw mit einem Reißverschluss schließen/öffnen; **it ~s shut/open** es lässt sich mit einem Reißverschluss schließen/öffnen; **to ~ a dress/bag** den Reißverschluss eines Kleides/einer Tasche zumachen *or* zuziehen; **to ~ a file** eine Datei zippen
VI (*inf, car*) flitzen *(inf)*; (*person also*) wetzen

(inf); **to ~ past/along** *etc* vorbei-/daherflitzen *etc (inf)*; **he ~ped through the book in no time** er hatte das Buch in null Komma nichts durch *(inf)*

▶ **zip on** VT *sep* **he zipped on his special gloves** er zog die Reißverschlüsse seiner Spezialhandschuhe zu VI **the hood zips onto the jacket** die Kapuze wird mit einem Reißverschluss an der Jacke befestigt

▶ **zip up** VT *sep* **to zip up a dress** den Reißverschluss eines Kleides zumachen; **will you zip me up please?** kannst du mir bitte den Reißverschluss zumachen?; **to zip up a file** eine Datei zippen VI **it zips up** es hat einen Reißverschluss; **it zips up at the back** der Reißverschluss ist hinten

zip: **zip code** N *(US)* Postleitzahl *f*; **zip fastener** N *(Brit)* Reißverschluss *m*; **zip file** N Zipdatei *f*; **zip gun** N *(US)* selbst gebastelte Pistole

ZIP CODE

In den USA ist die Postleitzahl ein **zip code** aus normalerweise fünf oder neun Ziffern, wobei sich die ersten drei Ziffern auf eine bestimmte Gegend des Landes beziehen, die anderen dagegen auf ein örtliches Postamt oder einen lokalen Zustellbereich: z. B. Portland, OR 97201.

zipped [zɪpt] ADJ mit Reißverschluss, Reißverschluss-; *file* gezippt

zipper [ˈzɪpəˈ] N *(US)* Reißverschluss *m*

zipping [ˈzɪpɪŋ] N *(Comput, of file)* Zippen *nt*, Packen *nt*

zippy [ˈzɪpɪ] ADJ *(+er) (inf) car* flott; *person also* flink

zircon [ˈzɜːkən] N Zirkon *m*

zirconium [zɜːˈkəʊnɪəm] N *(Chem)* Zirkonium *nt*

zit [zɪt] N *(inf: = spot)* Pickel *m*

zither [ˈzɪðəˈ] N Zither *f*

zloty [ˈzlɒtɪ] N *pl* **zlotys** *or* **zloty** Zloty *m*

zodiac [ˈzəʊdɪæk] N Tierkreis *m*; **signs of the ~** Tierkreiszeichen *pl*

zombie [ˈzɒmbɪ] N **a** *(lit: = revived corpse)* Zombie *m* **b** *(fig)* Idiot(in) *m(f) (inf)*, Schwachkopf *m (inf)*; **like ~s/a ~** wie im Tran; **that new hairstyle makes her look a complete ~** mit der neuen Frisur sieht sie total bescheuert *or* bekloppt aus *(inf)*

zonal [ˈzəʊnl] ADJ Zonen-, zonal; **~ boundary** Zonengrenze *f*

zone [ˈzəʊn] N **a** *(Geog, fig)* Zone *f*; *(US: = postal zone)* Post(zustell)bezirk *m*; **no-parking ~** Parkverbot *nt*; **time ~** Zeitzone *f*; **~s of the body** Körperzonen *pl*; **to be in the ~** in einer Sache völlig aufgehen; *athlete* in Topform sein VT **a** *town, area* in Zonen aufteilen **b** **to ~ a district for industry** einen Bezirk zur Industriezone ernennen

zone marking N *(Sport)* Raumdeckung *f*

zone therapy N *(Med)* Reflexzonenmassage *f*

zoning [ˈzəʊnɪŋ] N **a** Zoneneinteilung *f* **b** **the ~ of this area as …** die Erklärung dieses Gebietes zum …

zonked [zɒŋkt] ADJ *(inf) (= drunk, high)* breit *(sl)*, zu *(inf)*; *(= exhausted)* total geschafft *(inf)*

zoo [zuː] N Zoo *m*, Tierpark *m*, Tiergarten *m*

zoo keeper N Tierpfleger(in) *m(f)*, Wärter(in) *m(f)*

zoological [ˌzʊəˈlɒdʒɪkəl] ADJ zoologisch; **~ gardens** zoologischer Garten

zoologist [zʊˈɒlədʒɪst] N Zoologe *m*, Zoologin *f*

zoology [zʊˈɒlədʒɪ] N Zoologie *f*

zoom [zuːm] N **a** *(= sound of engine)* Surren *nt* **b** *(Aviat, = upward flight)* Steilanstieg *m* **c** *(Phot: also* **zoom lens***)* Zoom(objektiv) *nt*

VI **a** *(engine)* surren **b** *(inf)* sausen *(inf)*; **the car ~ed past us** der Wagen sauste an uns vorbei *(inf)*; **we were ~ing along at 90** wir sausten mit 90 daher *(inf)*; **he ~ed through it so quickly he can't possibly have read it properly** er war in null Komma nichts damit fertig, er kann das unmöglich gründlich gelesen haben *(inf)* **c** *(Aviat, plane, rocket)* steil (auf)steigen; **the rocket ~ed up into the sky** die Rakete schoss in den Himmel; **prices have ~ed up to a new high** die Preise sind in unerreichte Höhen geschnellt

VT *plane* steil hochziehen *or* hochreißen; *engine* auf Hochtouren laufen lassen

▶ **zoom in** VI **a** *(Phot)* hinzoomen, nah herangehen; **to zoom in on sth** etw heranholen; **zoom in!** näher fahren!; **he zoomed in on the problem** *(inf)* er kam direkt auf das Problem zu sprechen **b** *(inf, = come or go in)* hereinsausen *(inf)*

▶ **zoom out** VI **a** *(Phot)* wegzoomen **b** *(inf: = go or come out)* hinaussausen *(inf)*

zoomorphic [ˌzəʊəʊˈmɔːfɪk] ADJ zoomorph

zoot suit [ˈzuːtsuːt] N *(US inf) Anzug mit wattierten Schultern und eng zulaufender Hose*

Zoroaster [ˌzɒrəʊˈæstəˈ] N Zoroaster *m*, Zarathustra *m*

Zoroastrian [ˌzɒrəʊˈæstrɪən] ADJ zoroastrisch

zouk [zuːk] N *(Mus)* Zouk *m*

zucchini [zuːˈkiːnɪ] N *(esp US)* Zucchini *pl*

Zulu [ˈzuːluː] ADJ Zulu-, der Zulus; **~ chief** Zuluhäuptling *m*; **the ~ people** die Zulus *pl* N **a** Zulu *mf* **b** *(Ling)* Zulu *nt*

Zululand [ˈzuːluːlænd] N Zululand *nt (old)*, Kwazulu *nt*

zwieback [ˈzwiːbæk] N *(US)* Zwieback *m*

zygote [ˈzaɪgəʊt] N *(Biol)* Zygote *f*

Language In Use

Sprache Aktiv

First Edition
by
Ulrike Seeberger and Roswitha Morris

New Edition
by
Elspeth Anderson Horst Kopleck Christine Bahr

Language in Use

Contents

German-English

Sprache Aktiv

Inhalt

Deutsch-Englisch

Corpus Acknowledgements

We would like to acknowledge the assistance of the many hundreds of individuals and companies who have kindly given permission for copyright material to be used in the Collins Corpus. The written sources include many national and regional newspapers in Britain and overseas; magazine and periodical publishers in Britain, the United States and Australia. Extensive spoken data has been provided by radio and television broadcasting companies; research workers at many universities and other institutions; and numerous individual contributors. We are grateful to them all.

Korpusmaterial

Für ihre Unterstützung danken wir den vielen Einzelpersonen und Firmen, die freundlicherweise urheberrechtlich geschütztes Textmaterial zur Verwendung in unseren deutschen Korpora bereitgestellt haben. Dazu zählen eine Vielzahl von Zeitungs-, Zeitschriften- und Buchverlagen in Deutschland, Österreich und der Schweiz. Ihnen allen gilt unser Dank.

Introduction to Language in Use – New Edition

Our aim in writing Language in Use has been to help non-native speakers find fluent, natural ways of expressing themselves in the foreign language, without risk of the native-language distortion that sometimes results from literal translation. To achieve this, we have identified a number of essential language functions, such as *agreement*, *suggestions* and *apologies*, and provided a wealth of examples to show typical ways of expressing them. Users can select phrases to meet their needs using either their knowledge of the foreign language alone or by looking at the translations of the key elements.

In this revised edition of Language in Use, the authentic examples are taken from Collins' vast computerized language databases of modern English and German. These databases consist of around 700 million English and German words from a variety of modern written and spoken sources: literature, magazines, newspapers, letters, radio and television. The user-friendly layout is designed to make consultation even easier. Clear headings and subdivisions enable you to find the topic of your choice at a glance. We have given guidance, where appropriate, so that you can be confident that the phrase you have chosen is as assertive, tentative, direct or indirect as you want it to be.

The linking of the main dictionary text to the Language in Use section is particularly helpful. Certain words, *suggestion*, for example, have been marked in the main dictionary to show that additional material is given in Language in Use. In these cases the Language in Use symbol ✪ appears after the relevant headword and phonetics. Numbers (**suggestion** 1.1, 1.2) tell you which Language in Use section(s) to go to – in this case, sections 1.1 and 1.2 for examples relating to *suggestion*. As all cross-referred words are underlined in the relevant Language in Use section, you will quickly be able to locate them there.

Since German forms of address corresponding to the English *you* vary according to the formality of the relationship, we have tried to reflect this in a consistent manner. As a general rule, the *Sie* form has been used, with the exception of such idioms and translations which are either spoken or by their nature demand the use of the *du* form.

Sprache aktiv – Einleitung zur Neubearbeitung

Bei der Zusammenstellung von "Sprache aktiv" ging es darum, Nichtmuttersprachlern eine Hilfestellung zur idiomatischen Ausdrucksweise in der Fremdsprache zu geben, sodass Verzerrungen, wie sie manchmal bei wörtlichen Übersetzungen auftreten, vermieden werden können.

Um dies zu erreichen, wurde eine Reihe grundlegender sprachlicher Funktionen, wie *Zustimmung*, *Ablehnung* und *Entschuldigungen*, identifiziert und eine Vielzahl von Beispielen zusammengestellt, die typische Ausdrucksweisen für die jeweilige Situation zeigen. Der Wörterbuchbenutzer hat die Möglichkeit, Wendungen auszuwählen und dabei entweder nur auf die fremdsprachlichen Muster zurückzugreifen, also seine eigenen Sprachkenntnisse anzuwenden, oder die Übersetzungen der Schlüsselelemente in den Beispielsätzen heranzuziehen.

Die vorliegende Bearbeitung von "Sprache aktiv" basiert auf authentischen Beispielen aus den von Collins unterhaltenen, umfassenden Datenbanken des heutigen Englisch und Deutsch, in denen etwa 700 Millionen Wörter beider Sprachen aus einer Vielzahl von modernen schriftlichen und mündlichen Quellen gespeichert sind: Bücher, Zeitschriften, Zeitungen, Briefe, Rundfunk- und Fernsehsendungen.

Durch das sehr übersichtlich gestaltete grafische Erscheinungsbild soll die Benutzung von "Sprache aktiv" noch leichter gemacht werden. Klare Überschriften und Unterteilungen ermöglichen das schnelle Auffinden eines gesuchten Abschnitts. Wo es sich als angebracht erwies, wurden stilistische Angaben hinzugefügt, mit deren Hilfe man feststellen kann, ob die gewählte Wendung auch genauso direkt, indirekt, bestimmt oder zögernd ist wie der entsprechende Ausgangstext.

Besonders hilfreich ist die Verknüpfung von "Sprache aktiv" mit dem Wörterbuchtext. Bestimmte Wörter, zum Beispiel *Vorschlag*, wurden im Wörterbuchtext gekennzeichnet, um darauf hinzuweisen, dass "Sprache aktiv" hierzu weiteres Material enthält. Dabei folgt auf das jeweilige Stichwort und seine Lautschrift das Symbol ✪ für "Sprache aktiv". Die Ziffern zeigen, in welchem Abschnitt nachgeschlagen werden kann. Im Fall von **Vorschlag** ✪ 28.1, 28.2 zum Beispiel finden sich in den Abschnitten 28.1 und 28.2 Beispielsätze, die sich auf das Stichwort **Vorschlag** beziehen. Da alle Wörter, die so kenntlich gemacht wurden, in "Sprache aktiv" unterstrichen sind, können die Querverweise dort schnell aufgefunden werden. Bezüglich der deutschen Anrede mit *du* oder *Sie* wurde generell die *Sie*-Form verwendet, mit Ausnahme solcher Wendungen und Übersetzungen, deren situatives Umfeld und sprachliche Ebene das *Du* verlangen.

1 SUGGESTIONS

1.1 Making suggestions

Tentatively

- **Wenn ich vielleicht einen Vorschlag machen dürfte**: Wir sollten den Altbau besser abreißen
  = *if I might make a suggestion*
- **Wir möchten Ihnen gerne einige Vorschläge** zu Ihrer Altersversorgung **unterbreiten**
  = *we would be pleased to suggest a few ideas*
- **Ich würde vorschlagen**, Sie sprechen persönlich mit Ihrem Chef
  = *I would suggest*
- **Angenommen**, Sie würden mit ihr noch einmal über alles sprechen. Vielleicht ändert sie dann ihre Meinung
  = *suppose*
- **Sie sollten** sich für eine solche Einladung **vielleicht besser** schriftlich bedanken
  = *perhaps you ought to*

More assertively

- **An Ihrer Stelle würde ich** dieses Angebot zurückweisen
  = *if I were you, I would*
- **Ich schlage vor**, die Sitzung auf morgen zu vertagen
  = *I suggest*
- **Ich denke**, wir sollten für heute Schluss machen
  = *I think*
- **Am besten sollten wir** wohl einen Spezialisten zurate ziehen
  = *the best thing would be to*
- **Wenn Sie** nächste Woche in Bonn sind, **könnten Sie doch** mal bei uns vorbeischauen
  = *if you ..., you could*
- **Wenn Sie meine Meinung hören wollen**: Sagen Sie zu
  = *if you want my opinion*
- **Eigentlich brauchten Sie** Ihren Abfall **nur** ein bisschen vorzusortieren
  = *you only need to*
- **In diesem Falle bleibt uns wohl nichts anderes übrig, als** unser gutes Recht über das Gericht ein**zu**klagen
  = *in that case, we have no choice but to*

Using direct questions

- **Was würden Sie von** einer neuen Büroausstattung **halten?**
  = *how about*
- **Was würden Sie sagen, wenn** wir Ihnen weitere 10 Prozent Rabatt bieten?
  = *what would you say if*
- **Warum** sprechen Sie **nicht** einfach mit Ihrem Chef über diese Angelegenheit?
  = *why don't you*
- **Haben Sie schon einmal daran gedacht**, sich um den Posten der Kulturreferentin **zu** bewerben?
  = *have you ever thought of*
- **Was hältst du von** einer kleinen Spritztour mit dem neuen Auto?
  = *how about*

In an impersonal way

Tentatively

- **Vielleicht wäre es angebracht**, in dieser heiklen Angelegenheit etwas mehr Diskretion **zu** üben
  = *perhaps it would be appropriate*
- **Vielleicht wäre es besser**, die Polizei **zu** benachrichtigen
  = *it might be better*
- **Es wäre ja immerhin möglich, dass** wir das Programm noch einmal ändern
  = *we could always*
- **Wäre es nicht eine mögliche Lösung**, einerseits die Selbstbeschränkung **zu** lockern und andererseits Sozialklauseln durch**zu**setzen?
  = *one possible solution might be*

More assertively

- **Es wäre eine gute Idee**, am Wochenende aufs Land **zu** fahren
  = *I think it would be a good idea*
- **Es wäre ratsam**, eine Sicherheitskopie an**zu**legen
  = *you would certainly be advised to*
- **Man sollte** diesen Versuch noch einmal bei einer anderen Temperatur durchführen
  = *... should be*
- **Wie wäre es mit** einer Tasse Kaffee?
  = *how about*
- **Noch** ein Bier **gefällig?**
  = *would you like another*

1.2 Asking for suggestions

- **Haben Sie vielleicht eine Idee, wie** wir die Außenfassade gestalten könnten?
  = *do you have any suggestions about how*
- **Hat vielleicht noch jemand einen besseren Vorschlag?**
  = *does anyone have a better suggestion*
- **Was würden Sie an meiner Stelle tun?**
  = *what would you do if you were me*
- **Was könnten wir** am Wochenende **unternehmen?**
  = *what could we do*
- **Was würden Sie vorschlagen?**
  = *what would you suggest*

2 ADVICE

2.1 Asking for advice

- **Was würden Sie mir** in dieser Sache **raten?**
  = *what would you advise*
- **Was würden Sie an meiner Stelle tun?**
  = *what would you do if you were me*
- Welchen Zahnarzt **würden Sie mir empfehlen?**
  = *would you recommend*
- **Meinen Sie, ich sollte lieber nicht** nach Hongkong fliegen?
  = *do you think it would be better if I didn't*
- **Meinen Sie, ich sollte** mich in dieser Sache mit meinem Anwalt absprechen?
  = *do you think I should*
- **Ich hätte** in dieser Sache **gern Ihren Rat**
  = *I'd like your advice*
- **Ich wäre Ihnen wirklich sehr dankbar, wenn Sie mir** in dieser delikaten Angelegenheit **mit Ihrem Rat zur Seite stehen könnten**
  = *I should be very grateful if you would help me out with some advice*
- **Ich möchte mich** in diesem schwierigen Fall **von Ihnen in Ihrer Eigenschaft als** Rechtsanwalt **beraten lassen**
  = *I'd like your opinion as ... on*

2.2 Giving advice

- **Ich würde Ihnen raten**, so schnell wie möglich einen Arzt auf**zu**suchen
  = *I would advise you to*
- **Ich würde Ihnen dringend anraten**, sich in dieser Sache mit Ihrem Anwalt ab**zu**sprechen
  = *I would strongly advise you to*

- **An Ihrer Stelle würde ich** mich beschweren
  = *if I were you, I would*
- **Sie wären gut beraten**, die Kondition des Vertrages vorerst geheim **zu** halten
  = *you would be well advised to*
- **Sie wären schlecht beraten**, jetzt klein bei**zu**geben
  = *you would be ill-advised to*
- **Sie sollten unbedingt** die Packungsbeilage lesen
  = *you really ought to*
- **Es liegt ganz in Ihrem Interesse**, wenn die Konkurrenz ein wenig eingeschüchtert wird
  = *it is entirely in your interest*
- **Es empfiehlt sich nicht**, bei der Ersatzteilsuche auf ältere Fahrzeugtypen zurück**zu**greifen
  = *it is inadvisable to*

More tentatively

- **Wenn ich dir raten darf**, lass sie besser in Ruhe
  = *can I give you some advice*
- **Wenn ich Ihnen einen Hinweis geben darf**: Meiden Sie lawinengefährdete Skigebiete
  = *can I give you some advice*
- **Es scheint mir ratsam**, den Vertrag genaustens unter die Lupe **zu** nehmen
  = *I think it would be advisable to*
- **Am besten sollten Sie vielleicht** mit der Bahn fahren
  = *you might be best to*
- **Haben Sie schon einmal über** eine Gehaltserhöhung **nachgedacht?**
  = *have you ever thought of*
- **Könntest du** mir das **vielleicht** selbst erklären?
  = *could you maybe*

2.3 Giving warnings

- **Ich kann Sie nur warnen**, am langen Samstag ist in der Stadt die Hölle los
  = *a word of warning*
- **Ich rate Ihnen dringend davon ab**, diese Vereinbarung **zu** unterschreiben
  = *I strongly advise you not to*
- **Ich würde mich vor** übereilten Schlussfolgerungen **hüten**
  = *beware of*
- **Sie sollten** noch einmal alle Einzelheiten überprüfen, **sonst** geht am Ende noch etwas schief
  = *you'd better ..., otherwise*
- **Sie laufen Gefahr**, in diesen undurchsichtigen Geschäften viel Geld **zu** verlieren
  = *you run the risk of*
- **Versuchen Sie bloß nicht**, mit ihm über seine letzten Geschäfte **zu** reden
  = *do not try to*
- **Es wäre reiner Wahnsinn**, ausgerechnet jetzt nach Berlin **zu** fahren
  = *it would be sheer madness to*
- **Du wirst noch in ernstliche Schwierigkeiten geraten, wenn** du den Umgang mit Geld nicht bald lernst
  = *you'll get yourself into serious trouble if*
- **Du riskierst Kopf und Kragen, wenn** du diesen holprigen Feldweg benutzt
  = *you're risking life and limb if*
- **Pass auf, dass** du nicht ins Wasser fällst
  = *be careful (that)*

3 OFFERS

3.1 Direct offers

- **Wir möchten** unsere Mitarbeit in diesem Projekt **anbieten**
  = *we should like to offer*
- **Ich könnte** Ihnen eine zuverlässige Bürokraft vermitteln, **wenn Sie das möchten**
  = *I could ..., if you like*
- **Lassen Sie mich zumindest** die Getränke bezahlen, **bitte**
  = *please allow me to*
- **Ich kümmere mich gerne um** die Sache, **wenn** sich sonst niemand dafür findet
  = *I would be glad to take care of ... if*
- **Ich bin gerne bereit**, Sie zum Flughafen **zu** fahren
  = *I'd be happy to*
- **Wenden Sie sich bitte jederzeit an mich**, wenn Sie noch zusätzliche Informationen benötigen
  = *please feel free to contact me at any time*

3.2 Indirect offers

- **Es würde mir sehr viel Freude machen**, Ihnen die Stadt **zu** zeigen
  = *it would be a great pleasure to*
- **Es wäre uns ein Vergnügen**, Sie in unserem Sommerhaus begrüßen **zu** können
  = *we would be delighted to*
- **Ich würde wirklich gerne** mit Ihnen nach Weimar fahren
  = *I would be more than happy to*

3.3 Using direct questions

- **Möchten Sie** mit uns in die Oper gehen?
  = *would you like to*
- **Kann ich** Ihnen behilflich sein?
  = *can I*
- **Soll ich** für Sie bei der Zimmervermittlung anrufen?
  = *shall I*
- **Darf ich** Ihnen etwas zu trinken **anbieten?**
  = *may I offer*
- **Was würden Sie zu** einem kleinen Wochenendausflug **sagen?**
  = *what would you say to*
- **Wie wäre es**, wenn **ich** nächste Woche mal vorbeikommen **würde?**
  = *what if I were to*
- **Und wenn** ich dir einfach ein bisschen im Haushalt helfe?
  = *what if*

 REQUESTS

Tentatively

- **Würde es Ihnen etwas ausmachen**, mir Ihr Programmheft **zu** leihen?
  = *would you mind*
- **Mir wäre sehr geholfen, wenn** Sie mir einen Teil meiner Auslagen vorstrecken könnten
  = *it would be very helpful if*
- **Ich wäre Ihnen sehr dankbar, wenn** Sie mein Anliegen noch in dieser Woche klären könnten
  = *I would be very grateful if*
- **Dürfte ich Sie vielleicht bitten**, sich um die Zimmerreservierung **zu** kümmern
  = *could I ask you to*
- **Wenn Sie vielleicht** etwas zur Seite rücken **würden?**
  = *could you maybe*
- **Es wäre schön, wenn** Sie am Freitag zum Abendessen zu uns kommen würden
  = *it would be nice if*

More assertively

- **Ich möchte Sie bitten**, das Telefon nicht für Privatgespräche **zu** benutzen
  = *I must ask you*
- **Könnten Sie** mir während meines Aufenthaltes einen Wagen mit Fahrer zur Verfügung stellen?
  = *could you*

- **Würden Sie bitte** in diesem Zimmer nicht rauchen?
  = *please*
- **Wären Sie bitte so freundlich**, mir die Tür auf**zu**halten?
  = *would you be so kind as to*

More formally

- **Ich wäre Ihnen sehr zu Dank verpflichtet, wenn** Sie in dieser sehr persönlichen Sache äußerste Diskretion walten lassen könnten
  = *I would be obliged if*
- **Ich wäre Ihnen sehr verbunden, wenn** Sie mich baldmöglichst persönlich empfangen könnten
  = *I would be most obliged if*
- **Wir möchten Sie dringend auffordern**, die ausgeliehenen Bücher so schnell wie möglich zurück**zu**bringen
  = *you are urgently requested*
- **Wir danken im Voraus für** Ihre sofortige Antwort
  = *we would be grateful for*

5 COMPARISONS

5.1 Objective comparisons

- **Im Vergleich zu** anderen Mittelgebirgen ist die Rhön arm an Bodenschätzen
  = *compared to/with*
- Singapur hat, **verglichen mit** ähnlich großen Städten in den USA, eine niedrige Kriminalitätsrate
  = *if you compare it to/with*
- **Wenn man** Hans **und** Paul **vergleicht**, ist Paul doch der angenehmere Charakter
  = *if you compare ... and*
- Der Anteil stark geschädigter Bäume ist in Nordwestdeutschland mit 16 Prozent **vergleichsweise** gering
  = *comparatively*
- **Im Gegensatz zu** den drückenden Außentemperaturen ist es in deiner Wohnung angenehm kühl
  = *in contrast with*
- Es wird **immer schwieriger**, Museen zu Leihgaben zu überreden, weil die alten Kunstwerke Ortsveränderungen nicht ohne Schaden überstehen
  = *increasingly difficult*
- Die Mitgliedsstaaten zeigen **immer weniger** Neigung, die Weltorganisation mit der Lösung neuer Konflikte zu beauftragen
  = *less and less*
- Die neue Wohnung ist **so** groß **wie** die alte, **allerdings** etwas besser gelegen
  = *as ... as ..., but*
- Es **sieht so aus wie** ein U-Boot, **nur** etwas kleiner
  = *is like ... but*
- Das Design dieser Lampe **erinnert in gewisser Weise an** die Automodelle der 50er-Jahre
  = *is reminiscent of*
- Das neue Haus hat einen großen Garten, **während** unsere alte Wohnung nur einen kleinen Balkon hatte
  = *whereas*
- **Was** ihn **von** vielen anderen Schriftstellern **unterscheidet**, ist sein Sprachwitz und seine positive Lebenshaltung
  = *what differentiates ... from*

5.2 Making favourable comparisons

- Die Mitbewerber sind ihm aufgrund ihrer Qualifikation **weit überlegen**
  = *far superior*
- Das Gulasch, das seine Mutter kocht, **ist eine Klasse für sich**
  = *is in a class of its own*
- Ein Pianist **ist um mehrere Klassen besser** für den Ruf eines Restaurants in Wien **als** eine Zigeunerkapelle
  = *is very much better ... than*
- Was das Klima angeht, **ist mir** Südfrankreich natürlich **lieber als** die Bretagne
  = *I prefer ... to*
- Das **ist** noch **gar nichts im Vergleich zu** den Scherereien, die die FDP mit ihrer Figaro-Affäre hat
  = *is nothing in comparison to*

5.3 Making unfavourable comparisons

- Die Filmversion des Stoffes ist **bei Weitem nicht so** interessant **wie** das Buch
  = *far less ... than*
- Die Tonqualität ist **viel schlechter als** bei einem CD-Player
  = *much worse than*
- Die heutigen Essgewohnheiten **ähneln kaum mehr** denen vor 100 Jahren
  = *bear little resemblance to*
- **Man kann** seinen ersten Roman **nicht mit** seinen Kurzgeschichten **vergleichen**
  = *does not compare with*
- Seine Gedichte **können sich nicht mit** seiner Prosa **messen**
  = *cannot compare with*
- Auf fachlichem Niveau **können** die Aushilfskräfte **nicht mit** den Facharbeitern **mithalten**
  = *cannot match*
- Er **kann** seinem Bruder **nicht das Wasser reichen**
  = *can't hold a candle to*
- Die Verteidigung **war** dem Ansturm der gegnerischen Mannschaft **in keiner Hinsicht gewachsen**
  = *were no match for*

5.4 Great similarity

- Vieles in dem Roman **entspricht** der Wirklichkeit
  = *corresponds to*
- Er behandelt Frauen **genauso** schlecht **wie** Männer
  = *just as ... as*
- Ich **kann keinen Unterschied zwischen** diesen beiden Methoden **feststellen**
  = *I can see no difference between*
- Mit seinem Sieg hat er bewiesen, **dass** sein Leistungsvermögen **an** das der Spitzenspieler **heranreicht**
  = *that ... match(es)*
- Die Steuern dürfen nicht mehr erhöht werden, **das Gleiche gilt für** die Staatsverschuldung
  = *the same goes for*
- Rein äußerlich **sehen sich** die beiden Herren **sehr ähnlich**
  = *are very alike*
- **Das nimmt sich** zeitlich **nichts, ob** wir über die Autobahn oder über die Landstraße fahren
  = *it makes no difference ... whether*

5.5 Great difference

- Sie **sind** in ihrer Lebenseinstellung **nicht miteinander zu vergleichen**
  = *there is no comparison between*
- Unsere Ansichten zu diesem Thema sind **grundverschieden**
  = *totally different*
- Auf den ersten Blick **haben** die beiden **gar nichts gemein**
  = *have absolutely nothing in common*
- Er **hat mit** dem normalen Bürger **nichts gemein**
  = *has nothing in common with*
- Beide haben rote Haare, **aber da hört die Ähnlichkeit auch schon auf**
  = *but there the likeness ends*

6 OPINION

6.1 Asking for opinions

- **Was halten Sie (persönlich) von** einer Anhebung der Benzinpreise?
  = *what do you (personally) think of*
- **Wie denken Sie über** eine Reform des Schulwesens?
  = *what do you think about*
- **Wie sehen Sie** die weitere Entwicklung?
  = *how do you see*
- **Wie schätzen Sie** den Erfolg unserer Maßnahmen **ein?**
  = *how do you see*
- **Wie stehen Sie zu** einer möglichen Mehrwertsteuererhöhung?
  = *what is your attitude to*
- **Mir wäre sehr an Ihrer** fachlichen **Meinung zu** diesem Problem **gelegen**
  = *I would be very interested in your ... opinion on*
- **Es würde mich interessieren, was Ihre persönliche Meinung zu** dieser Erbschaftsangelegenheit **ist**
  = *I would be interested to know your opinion on*

6.2 Expressing opinions

- **Ich meine**, es ist höchste Zeit für Reformen
  = *I think*
- **Ich nehme (stark) an, dass** wir alle mehr Steuern zahlen müssen
  = *I (fully) expect that*
- **Ich fürchte**, wir haben keine andere Wahl
  = *I'm afraid*
- **Ich finde**, der Bundeskanzler muss in der Hauptstadt präsent sein
  = *I feel*
- **Mir scheint**, besser und knapper kann man sich über dieses Thema gar nicht auslassen
  = *it seems to me that*
- **Ich bin (fest) davon überzeugt, dass** der Forschungsbedarf langfristig steigen wird
  = *I am convinced that*
- **Ich kann nicht umhin**, darin einen weiteren Beweis für die geschwächte Stellung des Staates **zu** sehen
  = *I can't help*
- **Meiner Meinung nach** ist die Wiederverwertung von Metallen nach wie vor sinnvoll
  = *in my opinion*
- **Ich bin der Meinung, dass** es sich hierbei um ein Missverständnis handelt
  = *I'm of the opinion that*
- **Ich kann mir (gut) vorstellen, dass** unser Vorschlag die Zustimmung des Aufsichtsrates findet
  = *I have a (good) idea that*
- **Wenn Sie meine Meinung hören wollen:** Ich rechne fest mit einer Umsatzsteigerung
  = *if you want my opinion*
- **Wenn ich mich auch einmal zu diesem Problem äußern darf:** Ich halte Ihren Vorschlag für keine gute Lösung
  = *if I could just say one thing about this problem*
- **Ich werde den Eindruck nicht los, dass** mir hier etwas angehängt werden soll
  = *I can't help feeling that*
- **Ich habe den Eindruck, dass** der Feminismus sich vor allem auf die weibliche Opferrolle konzentriert
  = *I get the impression that*
- **So wie ich die Sache sehe**, ist der Streit noch lange nicht beigelegt
  = *as I see it*
- **Wenn du mich fragst**, geht es mit ihr bergab
  = *if you ask me*

6.3 Avoiding expressing one's opinion

- **Ich habe eigentlich keine besondere Meinung zu** diesem Thema
  = *I have no particular opinion about*
- **Ich möchte mich zu** dieser Angelegenheit **nicht äußern**
  = *I would rather not comment on*
- **Ich möchte mir darüber besser kein Urteil erlauben**
  = *I'd rather not express an opinion on that*
- **Es ist schwer zu sagen**, wie sich die Situation entwickeln wird
  = *it is hard to say*
- **Es scheint mir schwierig**, die Lage objektiv **zu beurteilen**
  = *I find it hard to judge*
- **Darüber habe ich mir ehrlich gesagt noch keine Gedanken gemacht**
  = *I've honestly never thought about it*
- **Ich habe keine Ahnung, ob** sich der ganze Aufwand lohnt
  = *I have no idea whether*
- **Das kommt darauf an, was Sie unter** Kunst **verstehen**
  = *it depends on what you mean by*

7 LIKES, DISLIKES AND PREFERENCES

7.1 Asking what someone likes

- **Würden Sie gerne** zu den Salzburger Festspielen fahren?
  = *would you like to*
- **Würde es Ihnen Freude machen**, am Sonntag mit in ein Konzert **zu** kommen?
  = *how would you like to*
- **Hätten Sie Lust auf** eine Partie Schach?
  = *do you feel like*
- **Was würden Sie bevorzugen** - ein neues Auto oder das Geld?
  = *which would you prefer*
- **Was mögen Sie lieber** - Pop oder Klassik?
  = *which do you prefer*
- **Ich wüsste gern, was Ihre Lieblings**beschäftigung **ist?**
  = *I would like to know what your favourite ... is*
- **Was machst du** in den Ferien **am liebsten?**
  = *what do you like doing best*

7.2 Saying what you like

- **Ich gehe gern** ins Kino
  = *I like going*
- Die Führung durch den Dom **hat mir sehr gut gefallen**
  = *I really enjoyed*
- Kreuzworträtsel **machen mir sehr viel Spaß**
  = *I really enjoy ... a lot*
- **Ich schätze es sehr, wenn** Leute ihre Versprechungen halten
  = *I really appreciate it when*
- **Es geht doch nichts über** ein gemütliches Frühstück am Sonntagmorgen
  = *there's nothing like*
- **Nichts mag ich lieber, als** eine heiße Tasse Kakao in der Dämmerung am Kamin zu trinken
  = *there's nothing I like better than*
- **Ich habe eine Schwäche für** Schokoladenkuchen
  = *I have a weakness for*
- Kasslerbraten **ist mein Leib- und Magengericht**
  = *is my absolute favourite dish*

7.3 Saying what you dislike

- **Mir gefällt** seine ganze Art **nicht**
  = *I don't like*
- **Ich mag keine** langen Abendkleider
  = *I don't like*
- **Ich finde es schrecklich**, immer auf der Flucht sein zu müssen
  = *I think it's dreadful*

- **Ich kann** rechthaberische Leute **nicht ausstehen**
  = *I can't stand*
- **Ich habe** die ewigen Tennisübertragungen **satt**
  = *I'm fed up with*
- Die Schauspielerei **ist nichts für mich**
  = *isn't my cup of tea*
- Die heutige Mode **ist nicht mein Fall**
  = *isn't my cup of tea*
- Abwaschen **ist nicht gerade meine Lieblings**beschäftigung
  = *isn't exactly my favourite*
- **Mir graust vor** dem eklig süßen Tee, den sie uns immer vorsetzt
  = *... makes me sick*
- **Ich bin nicht gerade begeistert von** deinen Kommentaren
  = *I'm not wildly enthusiastic about*
- Der neueste Hormonskandal **hat mir den Appetit auf** Rindfleisch **gründlich verleidet**
  = *has put me off ... completely*
- **Am meisten hasse ich** seine ewigen Nörgeleien
  = *the thing I hate most is*
- **Nichts hasse ich mehr, als** stundenlang im Regen auf den Bus **zu** warten
  = *there's nothing I hate more than*

7.4 Saying what you prefer

- Die roten Vorhänge **gefallen mir besser als** die blauen
  = *I like ... better than*
- **Ich mag** Pfirsiche **lieber als** Aprikosen
  = *I prefer ... to*
- **Ich würde lieber** ins Kino gehen, **als** zu Hause vor der Glotze **zu** hocken
  = *I would rather ... than*
- **Es wäre mir lieber, wenn** ihr jetzt gehen würdet
  = *I'd rather*
- **Ich halte es für besser, wenn** wir vorerst Stillschweigen bewahren
  = *I think it would be better if*
- Lesen **ist eine meiner Lieblings**beschäftigungen
  = *is one of my favourite*
- **Sie hat eine ausgeprägte Vorliebe für** Goldschmuck
  = *she has a marked preference for*
- 14 Uhr **würde mir besser passen**
  = *would suit me better*

7.5 Expressing indifference

- **Ich habe keine spezielle Vorliebe**
  = *I don't have any particular preference*
- Diese Art von Filmen **interessiert mich überhaupt nicht**
  = *doesn't interest me in the slightest*
- Die Frage, ob die Romanfiguren wirklich existiert haben, **ist** dabei **völlig belanglos**
  = *of no importance whatsoever*
- Dem Kunden **ist es völlig gleichgültig**, welche Technik im Hintergrund arbeitet
  = *doesn't really care*
- Die Bilder blutiger Massaker **lassen ihn kalt**
  = *leave him cold*
- **Es ist mir egal**, was die Leute von mir denken
  = *I don't care*
- Ganz wie du willst, **mir ist alles recht**
  = *I'm not bothered*
- Wofür er sein Geld zum Fenster rausschmeißt, **ist mir doch schnuppe**
  = *I couldn't care less*

8 INTENTIONS AND DESIRES

8.1 Asking what someone intends to do

- **Was beabsichtigen Sie zu tun?**
  = *what do you intend to do*
- **Was haben Sie** am Wochenende **vor?**
  = *what plans do you have for*
- **Wie hatten Sie sich** Ihr weiteres Vorgehen in dieser Sache **vorgestellt?**
  = *how had you envisaged*
- **Was versprechen Sie sich von** derlei drastischen Maßnahmen?
  = *what do you expect to achieve by*
- **Welche Vorsätze haben Sie** für das neue Jahr?
  = *what resolutions have you made*
- **Was bezwecken Sie damit?**
  = *what do you expect to gain by that*
- **Ich wüsste gerne, was Sie** nächste Woche **machen wollen**
  = *I would like to know what you want to do*
- **Haben Sie schon** einen bestimmten Bewerber **ins Auge gefasst?**
  = *have you already got your eye on*
- Wir wären Ihnen dankbar, wenn Sie uns bis zum Monatsende mitteilen könnten, **was Sie** in dieser Sache **zu unternehmen gedenken**
  = *what you propose to do*
- **Habt ihr schon Pläne** für die Ferien **geschmiedet?**
  = *have you made any plans*
- **Was führst du wieder im Schilde?**
  = *what are you up to this time*

8.2 Saying what someone intends or wants to do

Tentatively

- **Er spielt mit dem Gedanken**, noch dieses Jahr zurück**zu**treten
  = *he's toying with the idea of*
- **Eines Tages kaufe ich mir doch noch** ein Ferienhaus in Südfrankreich
  = *one day I'm going to buy*
- **Sie hatte eigentlich nur vor**, kurz bei euch vorbei**zu**schauen
  = *she just wanted to*
- **Ich wollte** schon vorhin mit Ihnen darüber sprechen
  = *I meant to*

More assertively

- Der Aufsichtsrat **hat die Absicht**, in der Innenstadt ein neues Hotel bauen **zu** lassen
  = *intends to*
- **Unsere Absicht besteht darin**, das gesamte Gewerbegebiet neu **zu** erschließen
  = *it is our intention to*
- **Wir haben uns fest vorgenommen**, den Titel erfolgreich **zu** verteidigen
  = *we have every intention of*
- **Sie hat den Entschluss gefasst**, das Rauchen auf**zu**geben
  = *she has made up her mind to*
- **Ich habe beschlossen**, schon morgen ab**zu**reisen
  = *I have decided to*
- Ich gehe **ganz bestimmt** morgen zum Zahnarzt
  = *definitely*
- **Ich möchte wirklich** ein paar Kilo abnehmen
  = *I'd really like to*
- **Ich plane** eine Reise nach Ungarn
  = *I'm planning*
- **Er ist (wild) entschlossen**, sein ganzes Leben auf den Kopf **zu** stellen
  = *he is (really) determined to*

8.3 Saying what someone does not intend or want to do

- **Ich möchte** mich **nicht** zu diesem Thema äußern
  = *I would rather not*
- **Ich hatte eigentlich nicht vor**, an diesem Seminar teil**zu**nehmen
  = *I didn't really intend to*
- **Ich habe nicht die (geringste) Absicht**, den ganzen Abend Buchungsberichte durch**zu**sehen
  = *I have no (not the slightest) intention of*
- **Ich habe nicht das Verlangen nach** neuen Abenteuern
  = *I have no desire for*
- **Ich gedenke nicht**, mich noch einmal auf so ein Unternehmen ein**zu**lassen
  = *I don't propose to*
- **Ich bin nicht geneigt,** mit Ihnen auch noch das Hotelzimmer **zu** teilen
  = *I have no intention of*
- **Ich bin nicht darauf erpicht**, am Ende wieder als einziger den Kopf hinhalten **zu** müssen
  = *I'm not keen on the idea of*
- **Es kommt überhaupt nicht infrage, dass** ich morgen schon wieder die Spätschicht übernehme
  = *there's absolutely no question of*
- Spätabends noch Gruselfilme angucken wollen, **kommt gar nicht in die Tüte**
  = *no way!*

8.4 Saying what you would like to do

- **Ich hätte jetzt Lust auf** eine Partie Schach
  = *I feel like*
- **Ich möchte gerne** die Kunstsammlung besuchen
  = *I would like to*
- **Ich hätte** ihm **gerne** selbst zu seinem Erfolg gratuliert
  = *I would have liked to*
- **Wenn ich bloß** mehr Zeit hätte!
  = *if only I*
- **Es wäre wünschenswert, dass** die Bahn ihr Güterzentrum neben unserem Frachtpostamt baut
  = *it is to be hoped that*
- **Mein innigster Wunsch ist es**, vor dem Ende meiner Tage noch einmal nach Paris **zu** fahren
  = *my dearest wish is to*
- **Ich würde** jetzt **wahnsinnig gerne** eine Riesenportion Eis verschlingen
  = *what I'd really love*

9 PERMISSION

9.1 Asking for permission

- **Könnte ich (vielleicht)** in eine andere Arbeitsgruppe wechseln?
  = *could I*
- **Wäre es möglich, dass** ich der Gerichtsverhandlung beiwohne?
  = *would it be possible to*
- **Darf ich** mich zu Ihnen setzen?
  = *may I*
- **Macht es Ihnen etwas aus, wenn** ich rauche?
  = *do you mind if*
- **Hätten Sie etwas dagegen, wenn** ich das Fenster öffne?
  = *would you mind if*
- **Mit Ihrer Erlaubnis würde ich gern** einige Änderungen am Grundriss vornehmen
  = *with your permission I'd like to*
- **Wenn es geht**, möchte ich morgen freinehmen
  = *if possible*
- **Ist** hier Rauchen **gestattet?**
  = *is ... permitted*
- **Sind** Ballspiele in diesem Park **erlaubt?**
  = *are ... permitted*

9.2 Giving permission

- **Ich habe nichts dagegen, wenn** mein Name unter dem Artikel erscheint
  = *I don't object to*
- **Selbstverständlich können Sie** die Arbeitsgruppe wechseln
  = *of course you can*
- **Gerne gestatten wir Ihnen** Einsicht in unsere Steuerunterlagen
  = *we are pleased to allow you*
- Rauchen **ist** hier ausdrücklich **gestattet**
  = *is permitted*
- **Sie dürfen** ihm **gerne** berichten, was wir besprochen haben
  = *you can... if you wish*
- **Ich erlaube Ihnen gerne**, morgen einen Tag frei**zu**nehmen
  = *I'll happily give you permission to*

9.3 Refusing permission

- **Ich möchte nicht, dass** mein Foto in diesem Zusammenhang veröffentlicht wird
  = *I do not want*
- **Sie können** sich für dieses Seminar **nicht** mehr einschreiben
  = *you can't*
- **Sie sind nicht zu** einer Hausdurchsuchung **befugt**
  = *you do not have the authorization for*
- **Ich untersage Ihnen (in aller Form)** die Teilnahme an dieser Verstanstaltung
  = *I (absolutely) forbid you to*
- **Ich verbiete Ihnen**, mein Grundstück **zu** betreten
  = *I forbid you to*
- **Leider muss ich** diesem Plan **meine Zustimmung verweigern**
  = *unfortunately I cannot consent to*
- **Ich weigere mich**, diesem waghalsigen Projekt zu**zu**stimmen
  = *I refuse to*
- **Ich kann dir beim besten Willen nicht erlauben**, bei diesem Wetter mit dem Fahrrad in die Stadt **zu** fahren
  = *with the best will in the world I can't let you*

9.4 Saying that permission has been granted

- **Wir brauchen** unseren Bericht **erst** nächste Woche ab**zu**geben
  = *we don't need to ... until*
- **Ich bin bevollmächtigt**, während der Abwesenheit des Chefs Anweisungen **zu** erteilen
  = *I am authorized to*
- **Ich darf** morgen freinehmen
  = *I can*
- In dieser Prüfung **ist** die Benutzung von Wörterbüchern **gestattet**
  = *is permitted*

9.5 Saying that permission has been refused

- Mein Arzt **hat mir** das Rauchen strengstens **untersagt**
  = *has forbidden me to*
- **Ich darf** zurzeit **nicht** arbeiten
  = *I mustn't*
- **Es ist nicht gestattet**, Gefahrenstoffe einfach in den Hausmüll **zu** geben
  = *it is forbidden to*
- **Es ist** gesetzlich **verboten**, rassistische Äußerungen **zu** publizieren
  = *... is prohibited*
- **Ich bin nicht berechtigt**, Ihnen Auskünfte über unsere Klienten **zu** erteilen
  = *I am not authorized to*
- Mein Chef **ist dagegen, dass** ich nächste Woche Urlaub nehme
  = *does not want*

10 OBLIGATION

10.1 Saying what someone must do

- **Sie müssen** sie **unbedingt** um Erlaubnis fragen, ehe Sie renovieren
  = *you really must*
- **Ich bin verpflichtet**, Sie auf Ihre Rechte aus diesem Kaufvertrag hin**zu**weisen
  = *it is my duty to*
- **Ich kann nicht umhin**, der Behörde die Einzelheiten mit**zu**teilen
  = *I cannot avoid*
- Die Zulieferfirmen **sehen sich zu** weiteren Umstrukturierungen **gezwungen**
  = *find themselves forced into*
- Die Neuregelung der Tierschutzverordnung **ist ein unbedingtes Erfordernis**
  = *is absolutely essential*
- **Es ist gesetzlich vorgeschrieben**, alle Inhaltsstoffe auf der Verpackung an**zu**geben
  = *the law demands*
- Alle Einwohner **sind aufgefordert**, den Anweisungen der Rettungsdienste Folge **zu** leisten
  = *are requested to*
- **Der Mieter hat** pünktlich am 1. des Monats den fälligen Betrag **zu** überweisen
  = *must*
- **Ohne** Hits **kann man** im Musikgeschäft **nicht** überleben
  = *no-one can ... without*
- **Es bleibt mir wohl nichts anderes übrig, als** die unangenehme Aufgabe selbst **zu** übernehmen
  = *the only thing left for me to do is*
- **Ich habe keine andere Wahl, als** gute Miene zum bösen Spiel **zu** machen
  = *I have no choice but to*

10.2 Enquiring if one is obliged to do something

- **Muss ich (wirklich)** zu Hause bleiben?
  = *do I (really) have to*
- **Brauche ich** eine Einladung?
  = *do I need*
- **Ist es (wirklich) nötig**, noch heute Abend ab**zu**reisen?
  = *do I/we really have to*
- **Erwartet man wirklich allen Ernstes von mir, dass** ich diesen Unsinn gutheiße?
  = *am I really expected to*

10.3 Saying what someone is not obliged to do

- **Es ist nicht nötig,** vorher noch einmal an**zu**rufen
  = *you don't have to*
- **Es ist Ihnen freigestellt, ob** Sie den gesamten Betrag sofort oder in Raten zahlen
  = *you can choose whether*
- **Es zwingt Sie niemand**, an diesem Treffen teil**zu**nehmen
  = *no-one is forcing you to*
- **Ich kann Sie nicht zu** einem Geständnis **zwingen,** aber früher oder später finde ich doch die Wahrheit heraus
  = *I can't force you into*
- **Sie sind nicht verpflichtet**, den Unfall **zu** melden
  = *it is not compulsory to*
- **Sie müssen ja nicht** in der Kantine essen, **wenn** es Ihnen dort nicht schmeckt
  = *you don't have to ... if*

10.4 Saying what someone must not do

- Unbefugten Betreten **verboten!**
  = *prohibited*
- **Es ist nicht gestattet**, hier **zu** parken
  = *it is forbidden to*
- **Sie können nicht einfach** die Mittagspause für private Erledigungen nutzen
  = *you can't simply*
- **Sie dürfen nicht von vornherein** mit einer Gehaltserhöhung rechnen
  = *you can't automatically*
- **Auf gar keinen Fall dürfen Sie** einer Verfassungsänderung zustimmen
  = *whatever you do, don't*
- **Ich verbiete Ihnen**, mein Büro je wieder **zu** betreten
  = *I forbid you to*
- **Wir können nicht zulassen, dass** die Sozialausgaben noch weiter gekürzt werden
  = *we cannot allow ... to*

11 AGREEMENT

11.1 Agreeing with a statement

- **Ich bin ganz Ihrer Meinung**
  = *I entirely agree*
- Das Museum ist ein Ort der Inspiration – **Ich kann Ihnen da nur beipflichten**
  = *I entirely agree (with you)*
- **Ich teile Ihre Meinung zum** Verhältniswahlrecht **uneingeschränkt**
  = *I agree wholeheartedly with your opinion on*
- **Ich schließe mich** den Worten des Vorredners **an**
  = *I entirely endorse*
- **Ich stehe voll hinter** dieser Erklärung
  = *I entirely agree with*
- **Ich muss gestehen, dass er recht hat**
  = *I must admit he's right*
- **Sie haben natürlich recht, wenn** Sie ihn einen Verbrecher nennen, aber sagen Sie das lieber nicht laut
  = *you are quite right to*
- **Wie Sie schon richtig bemerkt haben,** muss die Produktivität des neuen Standortes noch deutlich gesteigert werden
  = *as you so rightly say*
- **Im Großen und Ganzen stimme ich Ihnen zu, wenn** Sie gegen diese unseriösen Praktiken protestieren
  = *broadly speaking, I agree with you*
- **Ich neige sehr zu Ihrer Ansicht, dass** die Anklage eine unverhältnismäßig hohe Haftstrafe gefordert hat
  = *I am very much inclined to agree with you*
- Der Baum hinter dem Haus muss weg – **Meine Rede!**
  = *hear, hear!*

11.2 Agreeing to a proposal

- **Ich bin mit** Ihrem Vorschlag **(voll und ganz) einverstanden**
  = *I am in (complete) agreement with*
- **Ich gehe auf Ihren Vorschlag ein** und werde mich um alles Weitere kümmern
  = *I agree with your proposal*
- **Wir schließen uns** Ihrem Vorschlag **gerne an**
  = *we are happy to agree to/with*
- **Er hat** Ihrem Vorschlag **zugestimmt, ich bin auch dafür**
  = *he agrees with ... and I am in favour (of it) as well*
- Er ist in diesem Falle zwar nicht sachkundig, **geht** aber **mit unserer Entscheidung konform**
  = *agrees with our decision*
- **Ich werde** dieses interessante Projekt **nach Kräften unterstützen**
  = *I will give my full support to*
- **Ich gebe gern meine Einwilligung zu** den neuen Vorhaben
  = *I am happy to agree to*

- **Hiermit gebe ich mein Einverständnis zur** gewerblichen Nutzung der Räume im Erdgeschoss des Hauses Augustusplatz 9
  = *I hereby give my consent to*
- Wir könnten ins Kino gehen – **Gute Idee!**
  = *good idea!*

11.3 Agreeing to a request

- **Ich nehme** Ihre freundliche Einladung **mit großem Vergnügen an**
  = *I have much pleasure in accepting*
- **Gerne komme ich Ihrer Bitte nach** und begleiche die offenstehenden Rechnungen noch diese Woche
  = *I am happy to comply with your request*
- **Ich werde mich selbstverständlich an** Ihre Anweisungen **halten**
  = *I will, of course, follow*
- **Ich werde mich bei** der Auswahl der Stoffe **ganz nach Ihren Wünschen richten**
  = *I will respect your wishes completely in the matter of*
- **Es wird mir ein besonderes Vergnügen sein**, Sie persönlich vom Bahnhof ab**zu**holen
  = *I shall be delighted to*
- Der vorgeschlagene Termin **passt mir sehr gut**
  = *suits me perfectly*
- Die Verschiebung der Sitzung **kommt mir sehr gelegen**
  = *suits me perfectly*

12 DISAGREEMENT

12.1 Disagreeing with a statement

- **Ich bin nicht damit einverstanden, dass** wir ihm allein die Schuld geben
  = *I don't agree that*
- **Ich teile Ihre Meinung zu** dieser Frage **nicht**
  = *I don't share your views on*
- **Ich kann Ihren Standpunkt unmöglich akzeptieren**
  = *I really cannot accept your point of view*
- **Ich muss Ihnen widersprechen:** Sein Kunstbegriff ist sehr vage gefasst
  = *I disagree*
- **Ich kann mich Ihrer Interpretation** von Goethes Spätwerk **nicht anschließen**
  = *I cannot subscribe to your interpretation*
- **Ich möchte bestreiten, dass** dies das Ende seiner Karriere ist
  = *I don't agree that*
- **Ihren Schlussfolgerungen kann ich nicht zustimmen**
  = *I disagree with your conclusions*
- **Ich verstehe nicht, wie** Sie zu dieser Schlussfolgerung kommen
  = *I don't understand how*
- Das mag ja Ihre Ansicht sein, **ich sehe die Sache anders**
  = *I see things differently*
- **Sie gehen fehl in der Annahme**, der Roman habe keinen Bezug zur Wirklichkeit
  = *your assumption that ... is mistaken*
- **Sie liegen falsch, wenn Sie** behaupten, die Verkehrsprobleme ließen sich durch höhere Benzinpreise lösen
  = *you are wrong to*
- **Sie irren sich, wenn** Sie meinen, man könne diese Affäre so einfach unter den Teppich kehren
  = *you are mistaken if*
- **Sie täuschen sich in ihr**: Sie ist gar nicht so unschuldig, wie sie uns glauben machen will
  = *you are wrong about her*
- **Wie können Sie behaupten, dass** ausgerechnet die Rentner die Gewinner der Einheit sind?
  = *how can you say that*
- **Ich verwahre mich gegen** solche Vorwürfe
  = *I object to*
- **Ich bin völlig gegen** diese hinterhältigen Machenschaften
  = *I am completely opposed to*

12.2 Disagreeing with a proposal

- **Ich kann Ihren Vorschlag nicht gutheißen**
  = *I cannot agree to your proposal*
- **Ich kann** Ihren Vorschlag **nicht uneingeschränkt billigen**
  = *I can't give ... my unqualified support*
- **Ich halte nicht viel von** dieser Variante
  = *I don't think much of*
- **Vielen Dank für Ihr freundliches Angebot, aber** ich komme allein zurecht
  = *thank you very much for your kind offer, but*
- **Es tut mir leid, aber ich kann** Ihren Vorschlag **nicht annehmen**
  = *I am sorry but I cannot accept*
- **Sie können** Ihr Programm jetzt **wirklich nicht** mehr ändern
  = *you really cannot*
- **Wir protestieren in aller Schärfe gegen** den geplanten Autobahnneubau
  = *we wish to protest in the strongest possible terms against*
- **Von** solchen Tagträumen **will ich nichts mehr hören**
  = *I don't want to hear any more about*
- **Du glaubst doch nicht im Ernst, dass** ich mich auf solchen Unsinn einlasse
  = *you don't seriously think that*
- **Ich weigere mich**, damit meine kostbare Zeit **zu** vertun
  = *I refuse to*

12.3 Refusing a request

- **Leider kann ich Ihrer Bitte nicht nachkommen**
  = *I am afraid I cannot fulfil your request*
- **Ich kann** Ihre Wünsche **leider nicht erfüllen**
  = *I am afraid I cannot comply with*
- **Es ist mir leider nicht möglich**, Sie am Dienstag in meinem Büro **zu** empfangen
  = *I am afraid I will not be able to*
- **Ich bin nicht in der Lage**, Ihnen Auskünfte **zu** erteilen
  = *I am not in a position to*
- **Ich kann das unmöglich** bis Freitag **schaffen**
  = *I can't possibly manage it*
- **Sie können unmöglich von mir verlangen, dass** ich die ganze Woche Überstunden mache
  = *you cannot expect me to*
- **Es kommt überhaupt nicht infrage, dass** Sie meine Sekretärin für Ihre Schreibarbeiten in Anspruch nehmen
  = *it is out of the question for ... to*
- **Es fällt mir nicht im Traum ein**, Ihrer Bitte um Gehaltserhöhung nach**zu**kommen
  = *I wouldn't dream of*

In writing

- Ich danke Ihnen vielmals für Ihre freundliche Einladung, **muss aber leider ablehnen**, da ich schon eine Verabredung habe
  = *but I am afraid I must decline*
- **Leider müssen wir Ihnen mitteilen, dass** die bestellten Artikel zurzeit nicht auf Lager sind
  = *we regret to have to inform you that*

13 APPROVAL

- **Wirklich eine gute** *or* **tolle Idee!**
  = *what a great idea!*
- **Gut, dass** Sie uns so bald Bescheid gegeben haben
  = *(this context): thank you for*

- **Sie haben recht, wenn** Sie sich über diese Arbeitsbedingungen beschweren
  = *you are right to ...*
- **Wir sind mit Ihrer Entscheidung**, heute nicht mehr nach Paris abzureisen, **einverstanden**
  = *we agree with your decision*
- **Ich schätze** Ihre Offenheit in dieser Frage **sehr**
  = *I greatly appreciate*
- **Ich finde es gut, dass Sie** sich auf die wesentlichen Punkte beschränkt haben
  = *I think you were right to ...*
- **Es hat mir gut gefallen, dass** die Diskussion sachlich verlaufen ist
  = *I liked the way*
- **Es spricht sehr für ihn, dass** er sich erst jetzt mit dieser Bitte an Sie gewandt hat
  = *it says a lot for him that*
- Dieser neue Vorschlag **verdient unsere Aufmerksamkeit**
  = *deserves our attention*
- Der Entwurf des Bühnenbildes **ist** ihm **sehr gelungen**
  = *turned out really well*
- **Ich hätte es selbst nicht besser machen können**
  = *I couldn't have made a better job of it myself*

More formally

- **Wir stimmen im Großen und Ganzen** Ihren Vorschlägen **zu**, würden aber gern einige Details verändern
  = *we are in broad agreement with*
- Der Autor **betont** diesen Aspekt **(völlig) zu Recht**
  = *(quite) rightly emphasizes*
- **Man kann** ihren klaren Stil und ihre Eleganz **nur bewundern**
  = *one can only admire*
- **Wir sind von** ihrer Arbeitsweise **sehr beeindruckt**
  = *we are very impressed with*
- **Wir begrüßen** Ihre Eigeninitiative auf diesem Gebiet
  = *we welcome*
- **Wir sind hocherfreut über** diese positive Entwicklung
  = *we are delighted about*
- Sein Vortrag **hat auf uns einen hervorragenden Eindruck gemacht**
  = *we were enormously impressed by*
- **Ich möchte meine Unterstützung für** diese gute Sache **betonen**
  = *I would like to express my complete support for*
- **Ich habe eine hohe Meinung von** seiner Forschungsarbeit
  = *I have a high opinion of*
- Der Vorschlag, die Gewerbesteuer abzuschaffen, **wurde mit Wohlwollen zur Kenntnis genommen**
  = *was given a favourable reception*

14 DISAPPROVAL

- **Ich bin mit** Ihrem Umgangston **gar nicht einverstanden**
  = *I really don't approve of*
- **Ich bin gar nicht glücklich über** seine Wahl zum Parteivorsitzenden
  = *I am far from happy about*
- **Ich halte nicht viel von** seiner Interpretation des Mephisto
  = *I don't think much of*
- **Ich bin von** den Leistungen dieses Schülers **sehr enttäuscht**
  = *I am very disappointed with*
- **Ich muss energisch gegen** diese Vorwürfe **protestieren**
  = *I must protest in the strongest possible terms against*
- Die Kunden **sind nicht gerade begeistert von** unserer neuen Marketingstrategie
  = *are not particularly enthusiastic about*
- **Wir sind gegen** eine totale Preiskontrolle
  = *we are opposed to*
- **Das hätte** Ihnen **wirklich nicht** passieren **dürfen**
  = *that really should not have*
- **Er hätte besser** die Polizei verständigt
  = *he would have been wiser to ...*
- **Ich finde, es war falsch**, gleich so ausfällig **zu** werden
  = *I think it was wrong to*
- **Es gefällt mir überhaupt nicht, dass** ausgerechnet diese Firma mit dem Bau beauftragt wurde
  = *I'm not at all happy that*
- **Es ist wirklich schade, dass** die Stadt diese Truppe nicht mehr finanziell unterstützt
  = *it is a real shame that*
- **Es ist zu bedauern, dass** dieses verantwortungslose Vorgehen wieder zu Gewaltausbrüchen geführt hat
  = *it is regrettable that*
- **Es passt mir gar nicht, dass** wir morgen schon wieder Besuch bekommen
  = *it is really inconvenient that*
- Alle Parteien **verurteilten** diesen Anschlag **einstimmig**
  = *were united in their condemnation of*
- **Man darf** diese undemokratischen Umtriebe **nicht tolerieren**
  = *we must not tolerate*
- **Ich bin eine erklärte Gegnerin** jeglicher Tierversuche
  = *I am an avowed opponent of*
- **Was fällt dir ein**, mich so an**zu**schreien
  = *how dare you*

15 CERTAINTY, PROBABILITY, POSSIBILITY AND CAPABILITY

15.1 Expressing certainty

In an impersonal way

- **Es gibt nicht den geringsten Zweifel, dass** dieses Gesetz morgen verabschiedet wird
  = *there is absolutely no doubt that*
- **Es lässt sich kaum bestreiten, dass** die Arbeitslosenzahlen in dieser Region sehr hoch sind
  = *no-one can deny that*
- **Es steht völlig außer Frage, dass** die Flüchtlinge in ihre Heimat zurückgeschickt werden
  = *there is no doubt that*
- **Es versteht sich von selbst, dass** alle Abgeordneten zur ersten Sitzung erscheinen
  = *it goes without saying that*
- **Es hat sich deutlich gezeigt, dass** man auf dem glatten Parkett der Börse auch ausrutschen kann
  = *it has been clearly established that*
- **Es lässt sich nicht leugnen, dass** das Waldsterben weiter um sich greift
  = *no-one can deny that*
- **Man muss sich darüber im Klaren sein, dass** diese Friedensmission erhebliche Risiken birgt
  = *it must be realized that*
- **Zweifellos** wird sich die wirtschaftliche Lage noch weiter verschlechtern
  = *undoubtedly*
- **Tatsache ist, dass** sich das ökonomische Klima deutlich verbessert hat
  = *the fact is that*
- Eine Neuregelung **lässt sich nicht vermeiden**
  = *is inevitable*

More directly

- **Wir können mit Sicherheit sagen, dass** wichtige Informationen ohne unsere Zustimmung weitergegeben wurden
  = *we know for certain that*

- **Ich versichere Ihnen, dass** wir das Problem bis morgen gelöst haben
  = *I can assure you that*
- **Ich bin mir sicher, dass** ich den Brief gestern abgeschickt habe
  = *I am sure that*
- **Er ist davon überzeugt, dass** er die Goldmedaille gewinnen wird
  = *he is convinced that*
- Sie hören von meinem Anwalt. **Verlassen Sie sich darauf!**
  = *you can be sure of that*

15.2 Expressing probability

- **Höchstwahrscheinlich** ist dieses Verfahren rechtswidrig
  = *it is highly probable that*
- **Wahrscheinlich** wird die Sitzung vertagt
  = *probably*
- **Aller Wahrscheinlichkeit nach** schlägt die Therapie an
  = *in all probability*
- **Anscheinend** kann er nie genug kriegen
  = *it looks as if*
- **Es besteht Grund zu der Annahme, dass** er von seinen Zielen abgerückt ist
  = *there are grounds for believing that*
- **Es deutet alles darauf hin, dass** er zu schnell gefahren ist
  = *everything points to the fact that*
- **Es sieht fast so aus, als** hätten die Spieler alles verlernt
  = *it looks as though*
- **Es könnte gut sein, dass** ich heute Abend kurz vorbeischaue
  = *... might well*
- **Es dürfte zu spät für** eine Sanierung der maroden Finanzen **sein**
  = *it may well be too late for*
- **Es muss** ihm etwas passiert sein
  = *must have happened*
- Das Päckchen **müsste** morgen bei Ihnen ankommen
  = *should*
- **Es sollte mich nicht überraschen, wenn** er jeden Moment wie ein Unschuldslamm hier hereinspaziert kommt
  = *it wouldn't surprise me if*
- **Es würde mich überhaupt nicht wundern, wenn** er wieder zu spät kommt
  = *I wouldn't be at all surprised if*
- **Ich werde wohl** nächste Woche nicht da sein
  = *I probably*
- **Ich sehe es schon kommen, dass** ich noch einmal von ganz vorne anfangen muss
  = *I can see it coming*

15.3 Expressing possibility

- **Vielleicht** ist das der neue Deutschlehrer
  = *perhaps*
- **Es könnte unter Umständen schon zu spät sein**, um sich noch einzuschreiben
  = *it might already be too late*
- Die Lage **kann sich** von einem Tag zum anderen schlagartig **ändern**
  = *could change*
- **Es ist immerhin möglich, dass** man Ihnen nicht die Wahrheit gesagt hat
  = *after all, it is possible that*
- **Es besteht die Möglichkeit, dass** uns die Konkurrenz zuvorgekommen ist
  = *there is a possibility that*
- **Es sieht so aus, als könnten wir** den Bericht doch noch bis morgen fertigstellen
  = *it looks as though we should be able to ...*
- Sehen Sie sich das Haus gut an: **Es käme eventuell als** Bürogebäude **für uns infrage**
  = *we might think about it for our*
- **Es ist durchaus im Rahmen des Möglichen, dass** das Parlament einer Verfassungsänderung zustimmt
  = *it is quite within the bounds of possibility that*
- Vier Fünftel aller Maschinenbaubetriebe sind **potenziell** bankrott
  = *potentially*

15.4 Expressing capability

- **Können Sie** mit einem Computer umgehen?
  = *do you know how*
- **Er kann** hervorragend Gitarre spielen
  = *he can*
- Alle Bewerber sollten **in der Lage sein**, einfache technische Texte zu übersetzen
  = *be able to*
- **Wissen Sie, wie** diese neue Maschine bedient wird?
  = *do you know how*

16 DOUBT, IMPROBABILITY, IMPOSSIBILITY AND INCAPABILITY

16.1 Expressing doubt

In an impersonal way

- **Es ist zweifelhaft, ob** der Außenminister dem Druck der Verhandlungspartner gewachsen ist
  = *it is doubtful whether*
- **Es besteht immer noch Ungewissheit über** die Zahl der Todesopfer
  = *there is still some uncertainty about*
- **Es ist immer noch nicht sicher, ob** er krank ist oder nur simuliert
  = *it is still not certain whether*
- **Es lässt sich noch nicht mit Sicherheit sagen, ob** das Opfer den Anschlag überleben wird
  = *it is still impossible to say with any certainty whether*
- **Es gibt keinen Grund zu der Annahme, dass** diese Methode umweltfreundlicher ist
  = *there is no reason to assume that*
- **Das muss nicht unbedingt bedeuten, dass** sich die wirtschaftliche Lage schlagartig verbessern wird
  = *that does not necessarily mean that*

More directly

- **Ich bezweifle, dass** ich das Pensum bis heute Abend schaffe
  = *I doubt if*
- **Ich glaube nicht, dass wir je** einen derart waghalsigen Plan hatten
  = *I don't think we ever*
- **Ich bin nicht sicher, ob** ich Ihnen die richtige Zahl genannt habe
  = *I'm not sure whether*
- **Ich bin nicht überzeugt, dass** diese Methode funktioniert
  = *I'm not sure whether*
- **Ich frage mich, ob** es sich überhaupt lohnt, sich so viel Mühe zu machen
  = *I wonder if*
- **Es würde mich sehr wundern, wenn** er noch einmal wiederkäme
  = *I would be very surprised if*
- **Wir wissen noch immer nicht genau, wie** wir das Wohnzimmer streichen wollen
  = *we still don't know exactly how*
- **Sie tappen immer noch im Dunkeln, was** das Motiv für die Tat **angeht**
  = *they are still in the dark about*

16.2 Expressing improbability

- Einen Sieger wird es am Sonntag **wahrscheinlich nicht** geben
  = *probably not*

- **Es ist höchst unwahrscheinlich, dass** die Regierung auf Atomenergie verzichtet
  = *it is highly unlikely that*
- **Es besteht die Gefahr, dass** Sie Ihren Pass nicht mehr rechtzeitig bekommen
  = *there is a risk that*
- **Es ist fraglich, ob** der Verein sich in der Bundesliga halten kann
  = *it is doubtful whether*
- **Es würde mich wirklich überraschen, wenn** er diese Prüfung besteht
  = *I would be very surprised if*
- **Allem Anschein nach ist** sie **nicht** wirklich krank
  = *to all appearances ... is not*
- **Die Chancen**, diesen Winter ohne Grippe **zu** überstehen, **sind äußerst gering**
  = *the chances of ... are very slim*
- **Ich fürchte, dass es uns nicht gelingen wird**, ihn **zu** überzeugen
  = *I am afraid that we will not succeed in*
- **Sollte wider Erwarten doch** etwas Passendes dabei sein, gebe ich Ihnen Bescheid
  = *in the unlikely event that*
- Ein Umschwung der öffentlichen Meinung **steht nicht zu erwarten**
  = *is not to be expected*

16.3 Expressing impossibility

- **Es ist unmöglich, dass** diese Schäden beim Verladen entstanden sind
  = *... cannot possibly*
- **Es ist ausgeschlossen, dass** wir Ihnen schon nächste Woche fertige Skizzen zeigen können
  = *there is no way we can*
- **Es kann sich einfach nicht um** ein und dieselbe Person **handeln**
  = *it can't possibly be*
- **Ich kann mir unmöglich** nächste Woche schon wieder freinehmen
  = *I can't possibly*
- **Auf gar keinen Fall** wird diese Übersetzung noch vor Weihnachten fertig
  = *there is no way that*
- Leider **ist es mir nicht möglich**, diese Einladung an**zu**nehmen
  = *I am unable to*
- Eine Zusammenarbeit mit dieser Firma **kommt nicht infrage**
  = *is out of the question*
- Der Staatsstreich **macht** jede Verhandlung fürs Erste **unmöglich**
  = *has ruled out*
- **Es besteht nicht die geringste Möglichkeit** einer friedlichen Lösung
  = *there is not the remotest chance of*

16.4 Expressing incapability

- **Ich kann nicht** schwimmen
  = *I can't*
- **Ich kann kein** Französisch
  = *I don't speak*
- **Er ist nicht in der Lage** *or* **imstande**, selbstständig Entscheidungen **zu** fällen
  = *he is totally incapable of*
- **Ich weiß nicht, wie** man Topfkuchen bäckt
  = *I don't know how*
- **Er hat einfach kein Talent für** Sprachen
  = *he has simply no gift for*
- **Er ist zu** einer solchen Tat **nicht fähig**
  = *he is incapable of*
- **Ich bin nicht sehr gut** in Mathematik
  = *I am not very good at*
- **Sie waren** dieser schweren Aufgabe **nicht gewachsen**
  = *they were not up to*

17 EXPLANATIONS

17.1 Emphasizing the reason for something

- **Angesichts** der schwierigen Finanzlage müssen wir das Projekt vorerst auf Eis legen
  = *in view of*
- **In Anbetracht der Tatsache, dass** die Wahlen über die Macht entscheiden, ist es logisch, dass die Siegerparteien Einfluss auf die Medien gewinnen
  = *in view of the fact that*
- **Dank** steigender Auftragszahlen wird sich der Umsatz erhöhen
  = *thanks to*
- Die U-Bahn-Station wurde **aus** Sicherheits**gründen** geschlossen
  = *for ... reasons*
- Er wurde **aus Mangel an** Beweisen freigesprochen
  = *for lack of*
- Kurzsichtigkeit läßt sich **mittels** Lasertherapie behandeln
  = *by means of*
- **Bei** solchen Windverhältnissen sollte man sich besser nicht aufs offene Meer wagen
  = *in*
- **Durch** seine Popularität hat er einen gewissen Einfluss auf die Medien
  = *through*
- **Aufgrund** der schlechten Sichtverhältnisse verschiebt sich der Abflug auf unbestimmte Zeit
  = *owing to*
- **Wegen** des erhöhten Koffeingehaltes sollte dieses Produkt nur in geringen Mengen verzehrt werden
  = *because of*
- **Infolge** des Konsums berauschender Mittel war der Angeklagte nicht zurechnungsfähig
  = *as a result of*
- Mehrere Bauarbeiter fanden den Tod, **weil** die Gerüste nur unzureichend gesichert waren
  = *because*
- Wir haben Ihren Roman nicht lesen können, **denn** wir sind ein Verlag und kein Lektürezirkel
  = *because*
- Fruchtsäfte sollten nicht eiskalt getrunken werden, **da** sonst leicht eine Magenreizung entstehen kann
  = *as*
- Er ist ohnmächtig geworden und **deswegen** erinnert er sich an nichts mehr
  = *therefore*
- Sie hat die Angestellten **nur aus dem einen Grund** zusammengerufen, **um** mit ihnen ein Machtwort **zu** reden
  = *simply (in order) to*
- Der Präsident verurteilte den Bericht **mit der Begründung**, er enthalte nicht zu rechtfertigende Schlussfolgerungen
  = *claiming*
- **Wenn** ihm keine überzeugende Erklärung für sein Handeln einfällt, wird er sich schon bald vor dem Militärgericht wiederfinden
  = *if*
- **Solange** keine Besserung eintritt, dürfen Sie das Haus nicht verlassen
  = *as long as*

17.2 Other useful vocabulary

- **Die** Unfall**ursache war** überhöhte Geschwindigkeit bei schlechter Sicht
  = *the ... was caused by*
- **Das war so**: Ich stand auf der Leiter, als es an der Tür klingelte ...
  = *it was like this:*
- **Es geht um Folgendes**: Ich möchte gerne meine Wohnung renovieren
  = *it's like this:*

- **Das Problem ist**, dass wir ziemlich weit weg vom Bahnhof wohnen
  = *the trouble is,*
- **Die Sache ist die**: Ich habe ihm den Kredit schon versprochen
  = *the thing is,*
- **Es lässt sich alles auf** diese Versorgungsprobleme **zurückführen**
  = *it is all due/down to*
- Das **lässt sich alles aus** seiner Weltanschauung **herleiten**
  = *all stems from*
- Der Börsenkrach **hat** diese Katastrophe **ausgelöst**
  = *triggered off*
- Das **lässt sich** alles **durch** die Zerstörung der Regenwälder **erklären**
  = *can be attributed to*
- **Woran liegt es, dass** der Neubau nicht vorankommt?
  = *why is it that*
- Das **hat** natürlich wieder **mit** dem Treibhauseffekt **zu tun**
  = *is connected with*
- **Es hat sich** dann **herausgestellt, dass** er gar kein Kapital hatte
  = *it emerged that*
- **Ich schreibe das alles** seinem krankhaften Ehrgeiz **zu**
  = *I put it all down to*
- **Und aus genau diesem Grund** möchte ich nicht, dass Sie mir helfen
  = *that is exactly why*
- **Der Grund für** ihren kometenhaften Aufstieg ist wohl nicht nur in ihrer unbestrittenen Begabung, sondern auch in ihrem Fleiß zu suchen
  = *the reason for*
- Sein plötzliches Verschwinden **gab Anlass zu** wüsten Spekulationen
  = *gave rise to*

18 APOLOGIES

18.1 Apologizing for one's actions

- **Entschuldigen Sie bitte**, ich habe mich verwählt
  = *I'm sorry*
- **Bitte verzeihen Sie, dass ich nicht** früher angerufen habe
  = *please forgive me for not*
- **Es tut mir schrecklich leid, dass** ich gestern nicht kommen konnte
  = *I'm terribly sorry that*
- **Ich möchte Sie wirklich wegen** dieses Missverständnisses **um Entschuldigung bitten**
  = *I really must apologize for*
- **Können Sie mir** noch einmal **verzeihen, dass ich** die Karten nicht besorgt habe?
  = *can you forgive me for*
- **Es ist einfach unverzeihlich, dass ich** ihren Geburtstag vergessen **habe**
  = *it was unforgivable of me to ...*
- **Ich bitte tausendmal um Entschuldigung!** Ich wollte Ihnen nicht zu nahe treten
  = *I really am most terribly sorry*
- **Wir möchten Sie wegen** des bedauerlichen Zwischenfalls **in aller Form um Verzeihung bitten**
  = *we should like to offer our most sincere apologies for*
- **Dürfen wir Sie wegen** der gestrigen Störung **um Nachsicht bitten**
  = *we hope that you will forgive us for*
- **Ich bedaure zutiefst, dass** Sie sich durch meine Ausführungen in Ihrer persönlichen Ehre gekränkt sehen
  = *I greatly regret that*

18.2 Apologizing for being unable to do something

- **Es ist wirklich schade, aber** wir können euch nicht begleiten
  = *it is a real shame, but*
- **Bedauerlicherweise** können wir Ihren Artikel in der Märzausgabe nicht mehr veröffentlichen
  = *regrettably*
- **Zu unserem größten Bedauern** können wir Ihrer Einladung nicht nachkommen
  = *much to our regret*
- **Ich bin untröstlich darüber, dass** ich Ihren Vortrag versäumen muss
  = *I am deeply sorry that*
- **Wir müssen Ihnen leider mitteilen, dass** Ihr Antrag abgelehnt wurde
  = *we regret to inform you that*
- **Ich kann es mir nicht verzeihen, dass** ich Ihnen in dieser für Sie so schweren Zeit nicht beistehen konnte
  = *I cannot forgive myself for*

18.3 Admitting responsibility

- **Es ist ganz allein meine Schuld, ich hätte** sie **nicht** alleinlassen **dürfen**
  = *it's entirely my fault: I shouldn't have*
- **Ich übernehme die volle Verantwortung für** diesen Irrtum
  = *I take full responsibility for*
- **Wir hatten keine andere Wahl, als** die Polizei zu informieren
  = *we had no choice but to*
- **Wir waren der irrigen Meinung, dass** wir Ihnen damit helfen würden
  = *we mistakenly believed that*
- **Es war ein Fehler unserer Buchhaltung, dass** Sie zwei Rechnungen über den gleichen Betrag bekommen haben
  = *because of an error in our Accounts Department*
- Das **hätte ich nie** sagen sollen
  = *I should never have*
- **Ich weiß, dass es nicht richtig war**, ihm das Auto **zu** leihen, aber ...
  = *I know I was wrong to*
- **Ich gebe zu, dass** ich vielleicht nicht gut vorbereitet war, **aber** ...
  = *I admit that ... but*
- **Hätte ich doch nie** ein Sterbenswörtchen gesagt!
  = *I wish I had never*
- **Dummerweise** habe ich dann gleich bei ihnen angerufen
  = *foolishly*

18.4 Disclaiming responsibility

- **Ich hoffe, dass Sie Verständnis für** diese Verzögerung **haben**, die sich ohne unsere Schuld ergeben hat
  = *I hope that you will pardon*
- **Sicher können Sie verstehen, dass** wir in dieser Situation gar nicht anders reagieren konnten
  = *I am sure that you will appreciate that*
- **Ich habe** diese Vase **ganz bestimmt nicht mit Absicht** fallen lassen, sie ist mir aus der Hand gerutscht
  = *I certainly didn't ... deliberately*
- **Es war doch nur meine Absicht, Sie nicht** mit solchen Kleinigkeiten **zu belästigen**
  = *I simply wanted to avoid bothering you*
- **Ich weiß (auch) nicht, wie das passieren konnte**
  = *I don't know how it happened (either)*

19 JOB APPLICATIONS

19.1 Opening the letter

- **Ich beziehe mich auf** Ihre Stellenanzeige in der heutigen Ausgabe der „Süddeutschen Zeitung“ **und möchte Sie bitten, mir nähere Angaben über** die Stelle **zuzusenden**
  = *in reply to ... I should be grateful if you would please send me further details of*
- **Ich möchte mich um die Stelle** einer Reiseleiterin **bewerben, die Sie** im „Globus“ vom Mai **ausgeschrieben haben**
  = *I wish to apply for the post of ... which you advertised*

19 Job Applications

LEBENSLAUF

Persönliche Daten:	Müller, Dorothea Hinter dem Stausee 25 60388 Frankfurt/Main Tel.: 069/324 754 E-Mail: dormu@web.de geb. am 21.04.1978 in Nürnberg ledig
Schulausbildung:[1]	
1984 - 1988	Grundschule Nürnberg
1988 - 1997	Humboldt-Gymnasium Nürnberg
Hochschulausbildung:[2]	
10/1997 - 4/2003	Goethe-Universität Frankfurt/Main Studium der Psychologie Schwerpunkte: Betriebs- und Arbeitspsychologie
Praktika:	
1999	Personalabteilung Volkswagen, Wolfsburg
2001	Marketingabteilung Siemens, München
Berufspraxis:	
6/03 - 6/05	Wissenschaftliche Assistentin Lehrstuhl für Arbeitspsychologie Goethe-Universität Frankfurt/Main
7/05 - 6/08	Tutor für Organisationspsychologie Universität Birmingham/Großbritannien
seit 7/08	Referentin für Arbeitspsychologie bei der IHK Frankfurt/Main
Besondere Kenntnisse:	
EDV	Textverarbeitung (Word für Windows) Tabellenkalkulation (Excel) Präsentationsprogramme (PowerPoint)
Fremdsprachen	Englisch sehr gut Russisch Grundkenntnisse

Frankfurt/Main,
31. Juli 2013

[1] People with British or American etc qualifications applying for jobs in a German-speaking country might use some form of wording like "entspricht Abitur (3 A-levels)", "entspricht Staatsprüfung (MA Hons)" etc.

[2] Note that when applying for a job in Germany you must send photocopies of certificates for all qualifications gained as well as your CV.

[3] This address is appropriate when writing to a firm or institution. However, when writing to the holder of a particular post, you should put:

An den
Personaldirektor
„Mensch und Maschine" GmbH etc.

In this case, you should begin your letter with "Sehr geehrter Herr Personaldirektor" and end with "mit freundlichen Grüßen".

If you know the name of the person you should write:

An Herrn
Josef Schmidthuber
Personaldirektor
„Mensch und Maschine" GmbH

OR

An Frau
Dr. Christine Meier
Leiterin der Personalabteilung
„Mensch und Maschine" GmbH

Your letter should then begin "Sehr geehrter Herr Schmidthuber" or "Sehr geehrte Frau Dr. Meier".

Dorothea Müller
Hinter dem Sausee 25
60388 Frankfurt/Main
Tel.: 069/324 754
Fax: 069/324 755

Frankfurt, 31. Juli 2013

Infocomp International AG[3]
Personalabteilung
Postfach 70
40489 Düsseldorf

Ihre Anzeige vom 21.6.13 in der „Frankfurter Allgemeinen Zeitung"

Sehr geehrte Damen und Herren,

Für die von Ihnen ausgeschriebene Stelle als Personalreferentin im Bereich Personalentwicklung erfülle ich alle Voraussetzungen.

Ich bin Diplompsychologin und arbeite als Referentin bei der IHK Frankfurt. Mein Tätigkeitsbereich umfasst dabei die Konzeption, Organisation und Durchführung von Weiterbildungsseminaren für Fach- und Führungskräfte in Handel und Management sowie die psychologische Beratertätigkeit in Fragen der beruflichen Weiterbildung.

Für die Stelle bringe ich eine breite fächerübergreifende Ausbildung und eine umfassende Allgemeinbildung mit. Hinzu kommen Spezialkenntnisse der Arbeits- und Betriebspsychologie. Ich verfüge über mehrjährige Erfahrung im Umgang mit der EDV und bin selbstständiges Arbeiten gewöhnt.

Ich möchte mein Können gerne in Ihrem Unternehmen beweisen. Über eine persönliche Vorstellung würde ich mich sehr freuen.

Mit freundlichen Grüßen

Anlagen
Lebenslauf mit Foto
Zeugniskopien

- **Ich bewerbe mich auf Ihr Stellenangebot** in der heutigen Ausgabe der „Sächsischen Zeitung“, **weil ich sicher bin**, Ihren Anforderungen an einen Betriebswirt zu entsprechen
  = *I refer to your advertisement ... I am sure*
- **Auf das von Ihnen ausgeschriebene Stellenangebot bewerbe ich mich gern, weil** es meiner beruflichen Qualifikation und meinen Erwartungen entspricht
  = *I have pleasure in applying for the advertised position, as*
- **Ich möchte sehr gern während meiner Sommersemesterferien** in Österreich **arbeiten** (möglichst im Hotelbereich) **und würde mich freuen, wenn Sie eine entsprechende Arbeit für mich hätten**
  = *I am anxious to find a job in ... during my summer vacation from University ..., and wonder whether you are able to offer me work in any capacity*

19.2 Detailing your experience and giving your reasons for applying

- Englisch **ist meine Muttersprache. Ich verfüge über sehr gute** Deutsch**kenntnisse** in Wort und Schrift. **Außerdem besitze ich solide Grundkenntnisse** des Russischen
  = *my first language is ... I have an excellent command of ... I also have a working knowledge of*
- **Ich habe** drei Jahre Büro**erfahrung**
  = *I have ... experience of*
- **Ich arbeite seit** 3 Jahren in der Maschinenbaufirma Komplex in Hannover. **Meine Aufgabe besteht im** Anfertigen von technischen Zeichnungen aller Art sowie von elektronischen Schaltplänen
  = *I have been working for ... My duties consist of*
- **Ich besitze gute Kenntnisse** im Umgang mit Tabellenkalkulationen und Textverarbeitungen
  = *I am an experienced user of*
- **Ich habe zwar keine Erfahrung auf** diesem speziellen Arbeitsgebiet, **habe aber** verschiedene Ferienjobs ausgeübt
  = *although I have no previous experience ..., I have had*
- **Auf Verlangen kann ich Ihnen** jederzeit **Zeugnisse** meiner früheren Arbeitgeber **vorlegen**
  = *I can supply references from ..., if you would like them*
- **Zurzeit verdiene ich** ... im Jahr **und habe einen jährlichen Anspruch auf** 25 Tage bezahlten **Urlaub**
  = *my present salary is ..., and I have ... holiday per year*
- **Ich interessiere mich ganz besonders für diese Stelle, weil** ich sehr gerne im Verlagswesen arbeiten möchte
  = *I am particularly interested in this job, as*
- **Ich möchte** in der Schweiz arbeiten, **um meine Sprachkenntnisse zu verbessern und Erfahrungen** in der Hotelbranche **zu sammeln**
  = *I would like to ... in order to improve my languages and to gain experience*

19.3 Closing the letter

- **Ich bin seit 5 Jahren in ungekündigter Stellung** als Leiterin der Fertigung in einem Spitzenunternehmen der Halbleiterbranche **tätig und möchte mich verändern**
  = *for the past five years I have been working ... but I would welcome a change*
- **Ich könnte Ihnen ab** April 2008 **zur Verfügung stehen**
  = *I shall be available from*
- **Die Tätigkeit könnte ich zum** frühestmöglichen Termin **aufnehmen**
  = *I am available to commence duties at*
- **Ich würde mich freuen**, in Ihrem Unternehmen **meine Fähigkeiten beweisen zu können**
  = *I would be pleased to use my skills for*
- **Über eine persönliche Vorstellung würde ich mich sehr freuen**
  = *I would be happy to attend for interview*
- Wenn Sie an meiner Bewerbung interessiert sind, **sende ich Ihnen gerne meine vollständigen Bewerbungsunterlagen zu**
  = *I shall be pleased to forward my full application pack*

19.4 Asking for and giving references

- Ich habe mich um eine Stelle als Privatsekretärin beworben und bin in die engere Wahl gezogen worden. Man hat mich nun gebeten, Zeugnisse meiner früheren Arbeitgeber vorzulegen. **Ich wäre Ihnen sehr dankbar, wenn Sie mir so bald wie möglich ein Zeugnis über meine Tätigkeit in Ihrer Kanzlei zuschicken könnten**
  = *I should be very grateful if you would send me a reference relating to my time in your office as soon as possible*
- **Wir wären Ihnen sehr dankbar, wenn Sie uns mitteilen könnten, ob** er Ihrer Meinung nach **für diesen Posten geeignet ist**
  = *I should be grateful if you would kindly let me know whether ... is suitable for this post*
- **Ihre Antwort wird selbstverständlich streng vertraulich behandelt**
  = *your answer will be treated in strict confidence*
- **Könnten Sie uns bitte in Ihrer Antwort mitteilen** wie lange und in welcher Eigenschaft Sie Frau Heinisch kennen und **ob Sie sie für diese Tätigkeit empfehlen können**
  = *would you be kind enough to mention in your reply ... whether you can recommend her for this type of employment*

19.5 Accepting and refusing

- **Ich komme gern** am Donnerstag, dem 24. März, um 10.30 Uhr **zu einem Vorstellungsgespräch** in Ihr Büro
  = *I shall be delighted to attend for interview*
- **Ich nehme das Angebot**, in Ihrer Klinik als Krankengymnastin arbeiten zu können, **gerne an und werde den Dienst am vorgesehenen Eintrittsdatum antreten**
  = *I am pleased to accept your offer of ... and will take up my duties on the stated date*
- Es hat mich sehr gefreut, dass Sie an meiner Mitarbeit interessiert sind, **ich habe mich jedoch zwischenzeitlich für ein anderes Angebot entschieden**
  = *however, in the interim, I have accepted another offer*

20 COMMERCIAL CORRESPONDENCE

20.1 Making an enquiry

- **Ihrer Anzeige in der Mai-Ausgabe von** „Sport und Freizeit“ **entnehmen wir, dass** Sie eine neue Sportartikelserie anbieten
  = *we see from your advertisement in the May edition of ... that*
- **Wir bitten Sie, uns nähere Angaben über** das neue Sortiment **zukommen zu lassen und uns auch über** Preise, Rabatte und Lieferzeiten **zu informieren**
  = *we should be grateful if you would send us full details of ..., including*

20.2 Replying to an enquiry

- **Wir beziehen uns auf Ihre Anfrage vom** 3. März **und senden Ihnen in der Anlage Einzelheiten zu** unserem derzeitigen Warenangebot **sowie** unsere Preisliste
  = *in response to your enquiry of ..., we enclose details of ... and*
- **Wir danken Ihnen für Ihre Anfrage vom** 6. Juni **und erlauben uns, Ihnen folgendes Angebot zu machen**:
  = *we thank you for your enquiry of ..., and are pleased to submit the following offer:*
- **Dieses Angebot gilt bei** verbindlicher **Bestellung** vor dem 31. Januar des nächsten Jahres
  = *this offer is subject to acceptance*

20.3 Placing an order

- **Bitte senden Sie uns umgehend die folgenden Posten** in den angegebenen Größen und Stückzahlen zu: ...
  = *please send us the following items by return*

20 Commercial correspondence

Architekturbüro Mittermayer & Partner

Bürogebäude, Hotels, Villen

Eschenallee 67

52078 Aachen

Tel.: 0241 / 453 2376 Durchwahl: 0241 / 453 23

Fax: 0241 / 453 2312 E-Mail: mittermayer@aachen.co.de

City Datenservice GmbH
Alexanderstr. 43
52062 Aachen

Ihr Zeichen	Unser Zeichen	Ihr Schreiben vom	Datum
	EDV 25/08	23. Mai 2013	31. Mai 2013

Sehr geehrte Frau Ackermann,

Bezug nehmend auf Ihr Schreiben vom 23. Mai 2013 bestätigen wir den von Ihnen vorgeschlagenen Termin für eine Vorführung Ihres Programmes „Draw Help". Für die notwendigen Absprachen wenden Sie sich bitte an Frau Dembinski (Apparat 51).

Des Weiteren möchten wir Sie bitten, uns einen Kostenvoranschlag für eine Schulung unserer Mitarbeiter an diesem System zu unterbreiten. Wir sind auch an einem Programm zur statischen Berechnung von Dachkonstruktionen interessiert und bitten um ein diesbezügliches Angebot.

Mit freundlichen Grüßen

Jürgen Schneider

Jürgen Schneider
Leiter Datenverarbeitung

Eduard Papenbrock & Sohn

Glas und Porzellan

Genthiner Str. 20

39114 Magdeburg

Tel.: 0391/857 902 Fax: 0391/857 903

Eschebach Porzellan
Verkaufsabteilung
z. Hd. Frau Klein
Erfurter Str. 105
98693 Ilmenau/Thüringen

Magdeburg, 24. Juni 2013

Sehr geehrte Frau Klein,

vielen Dank für die Zusendung Ihres neuesten Kataloges.

Hiermit bestellen wir 100 Exemplare des Speiseservice „Thüringen" sowie 75 Exemplare des Kaffeegedeckes „Junior".

Mehrere Kunden möchten von Ihrer Nachkaufgarantie Gebrauch machen. Daher bitten wir zusätzlich um die Lieferung folgender Posten:

2 Speiseteller aus der Serie „Inselberg"
1 Untertasse aus der Serie „Oberhof"
1 Sauciere aus der Serie „Schmalkalden"

Wir erwarten Ihre Lieferung fristgerecht innerhalb der nächsten 14 Tage und verbleiben

mit freundlichen Grüßen

Herbert Papenbrock

Herbert Papenbrock
Inhaber

- **Diese Bestellung bezieht sich auf** Ihre aktuelle Preisliste, und **wir gehen von Ihrem normalen Mengenrabatt** von 10% **aus**
  = this order is based on ..., assuming your usual discount of ... on bulk orders
- **Anbei unsere Bestellung Nr.** 12-566 **über** 3000 Paar feuerfeste Handschuhe
  = please find enclosed our order No. ... for

20.4 Replying to an order

- **Wir danken Ihnen für Ihre Bestellung vom** 9. Mai und werden sie so bald wie möglich ausführen
  = we thank you for your order of
- **Wir brauchen** etwa drei Wochen, **um Ihren Auftrag auszuführen**
  = we shall require ... to complete this order
- **Leider wird sich wegen** eines Engpasses in der Versorgung mit Rohmaterialien **der Beginn der Produktion** bis zum 1. April **verzögern**
  = unfortunately, because of ..., we cannot start manufacture

20.5 Delivery

- **Unsere Lieferzeit beträgt** 2 Monate, vom Eingang einer verbindlichen Bestellung aus gerechnet
  = our delivery time is
- **Wir erwarten ihre Lieferanweisungen**
  = we await your instructions with regard to delivery
- **Diese Waren sind am** 4. Juli per Bahn an Sie **abgegangen**
  = these goods were sent ... on
- Die bestellte Ware **ist bei uns noch nicht eingegangen**
  = we have not yet received
- Sollten wir die bestellten Waren nicht bis zum Ende des Monats erhalten, **sehen wir uns gezwungen, unsere Bestellung zu stornieren**
  = the order will be formally cancelled
- **Wir bestätigen den Erhalt** der beiden von Ihnen am 3. März versandten Lieferungen
  = we acknowledge receipt of

20.6 Complaining and replying to a complaint

- **Wir möchten Sie auf einen Fehler in** der hier am 3. Februar eingegangenen Lieferung **hinweisen**
  = we wish to draw your attention to an error in
- **Wir bedauern sehr, dass die Lieferung nicht einwandfrei war,** und sind bereit, die entsprechenden Waren zu ersetzen
  = we regret that the consignment was unsatisfactory
- **Für** diesen Schaden **können wir keine Haftung übernehmen**
  = we cannot accept responsibility for

20.7 Payment

- **Anbei unsere Rechnung Nr.** 64321
  = please find enclosed our invoice No.
- **Der zu zahlende Gesamtbetrag ist ...**
  = the total amount payable is ...
- Wir wären Ihnen dankbar, **wenn Sie diese Rechnung umgehend begleichen könnten**
  = if you would attend to this account immediately
- **In der Anlage übersenden wir Ihnen einen Scheck über ... zur Begleichung Ihrer Rechnung** Nr. 67813/31
  = we have pleasure in enclosing our cheque for ... in settlement of your invoice
- **Wir müssen Sie leider auf einen Fehler in** Ihrer Rechnung Nr. 12-556 **aufmerksam machen.** Wir wären Ihnen dankbar, wenn Sie die Rechnung entsprechend berichtigen könnten
  = we must point out an error in
- **In der Anlage erhalten Sie eine Gutschrift über** diesen Betrag
  = we enclose a credit note for

21 GENERAL CORRESPONDENCE

21.1 Starting a letter

To a friend or acquaintance

- **Vielen Dank für deinen Brief**, der hier gestern angekommen ist
  = thank you for your letter
- **Ich habe micht gefreut, wieder von dir zu hören**
  = it was good to hear from you again
- **Es tut mir sehr leid, dass ich so lange nicht geschrieben habe.** Hoffentlich bist du mir nicht böse, aber ich hatte in letzter Zeit viel zu tun und ...
  = I am very sorry I haven't written for so long
- **Wir haben so lange nichts voneinander gehört.** Da dachte ich, ich muss einfach schnell ein paar Zeilen schreiben ...
  = it's such a long time since we had any contact

In formal correspondence

- **Ich möchte Sie bitten mir mitzuteilen, ob** Sie ein Buch mit dem Titel ... vorrätig haben
  = I am writing to ask whether
- **Schicken Sie mir bitte ... In der Anlage sende ich** Ihnen einen Scheck über DM 129,95
  = would you please send me ... I enclose
- **Ich habe** nähere Angaben über Ihre Sommerkurse **erhalten und möchte mich erkundigen, ob** Sie für ... noch Plätze frei haben
  = I have seen the details of ... and wish to know whether

21.2 Ending a letter (before the closing formulae)

- **Viele herzliche Grüße an** Euch alle, **auch von Peter**
  = Peter joins me in sending very best wishes to
- **Viele liebe Grüße an Matthias**
  = give my love to Matthias
- Barbara **lässt ganz herzlich grüßen**
  = ... sends her kindest regards (oder her love)
- Catherine **lässt auch grüßen**
  = ... asks me to give you ... best wishes
- **Bitte grüße auch** Deine Mutter **von mir**. Ich hoffe, es geht ihr gut
  = please remember me to
- **Ganz liebe Grüße an** Miriam und Tom, **sage ihnen, wie sehr sie mir fehlen**
  = give my love to ... and tell them how much I miss them
- **Mary lässt** Euch beide **recht herzlich grüßen**
  = Mary sends her love to
- **Und grüße** David **schön von mir**
  = say hello to ... for me
- **Ich würde mich sehr freuen, bald von Ihnen zu hören**
  = I look forward to hearing from you soon
- **Ich hoffe, dass ich recht bald eine Antwort** von Dir **bekomme**
  = I hope ... will write back very soon
- **Schreib mal wieder, wenn** Du Zeit hast
  = do write when
- **Lasst** ab und zu **wieder von Euch hören**
  = send me (oder us) your news

21.3 Enquiring about and booking accommodation

- **Bitte schicken Sie mir nähere Informationen zu** Ihren Preisen
  = please give me details of
- **Ich möchte** bei Ihnen Übernachtungen mit Frühstück **buchen**
  = I would like to book
- **Ich würde gerne** ein Doppelzimmer für meine Frau und mich **sowie** ein Zweibettzimmer für unsere beiden Söhne (beide unter 12 Jahren) **reservieren**
  = I wish to book ... and

21 General correspondence

Hamburg, 22. Mai 2013

Liebe Thekla und Andreas,

vielen Dank für Euren Brief, der schon vor einiger Zeit hier ankam. Es tut mir leid, dass ich so lange nicht geantwortet habe, aber seit meinem Umzug hierher bleibt mir kaum ein ruhiger Augenblick, um ein paar Briefe zu beantworten. Das soll aber nicht heißen, dass ich Euch vergessen habe. Im Gegenteil, ich denke oft an die gemeinsame Zeit in Berlin zurück.

Mittlerweile habe ich mich hier schon recht gut eingelebt. Meine Wohnung muss noch ein bisschen renoviert werden, aber ich hoffe, damit bald fertig zu sein. Die neue Arbeitsstelle gefällt mir sehr gut, so dass ich den Wechsel hierher keinesfalls bedaure.

Wenn Ihr im Sommer etwas Zeit habt, seid Ihr natürlich ganz herzlich eingeladen, ein paar Tage bei mir in Hamburg zu verbringen. Ich hoffe, es lässt sich einrichten, denn ich würde mich über ein Wiedersehen mit Euch sehr freuen.

Viele liebe Grüße, auch an Beate und Jens
von Eurer

Christine

Elke Linke
Hertzstr. 10
13158 Berlin

Berlin, 13. Juli 2013

Edition Peters
Versandabteilung
Nürnberger Str. 35
04103 Leipzig

Sehr geehrte Damen und Herren,

einem bereits 23 Jahre alten Katalog Ihres Verlages entnahm ich, dass Sie damals verschiedene Nachdrucke der Erstausgaben von Wagners Sopranarien angeboten hatten.

Ich möchte nachfragen, ob noch Exemplare der damaligen Ausgabe der Arien in „Tannhäuser" und „Rienzi" vorhanden sind und zu welchem Preis und Versandkosten diese bei Ihnen bestellt werden können.

Ich danke Ihnen im Voraus für Ihre Bemühungen.

Mit freundlichen Grüßen

Elke Linke

Elke Linke
Kammersängerin

Standard opening and closing formulae

OPENING FORMULAE	CLOSING FORMULAE
Used when you do not know the person's name	
Sehr geehrte Damen und Herren, Sehr geehrte gnädige Frau	Mit freundlichen Grüßen
Used if you know the person's name	
Sehr geehrter Herr Wagner, Sehr geehrte Frau Professor Müller, Sehr geehrte Frau Kühn, Sehr geehrter Herr Kühn,	*As above, plus:* Ich verbleibe, sehr geehrte Frau Professor, mit vorzüglicher Hochachtung Ihr/Ihre

To acquaintances and friends

OPENING FORMULA	CLOSING FORMULAE	
More formal		
Sehr geehrter Herr Dr. Braun,	Mit freundlichen Grüßen	*If the letter is fairly formal, "Sie" should be used*
Liebe Freunde,	Mit besten Grüßen	
Fairly informal: 'Du' or 'Sie' forms could be used		
Lieber Peter,	Es grüßt Sie	
Liebe Ingrid,	Herzliche Grüße von Ihrem	
Liebe Ingrid, lieber Peter,	Viele Grüße an Euch beide	

To close friends and family

OPENING FORMULAE	CLOSING FORMULAE
	'du' and 'Ihr' are used in all these expressions
Lieber Frank, Lieber Onkel Hans, Liebe Oma, lieber Opa, Liebe Mutti, Lieber Vati,	Liebe Grüße von Bis bald. Viele liebe Grüße Viele Grüße und Küsse von Eurem Viele liebe Grüße und Küsse

Writing to a firm or an institution (see also 20)

OPENING FORMULAE	CLOSING FORMULAE	
Sehr geehrte Damen und Herren	Mit freundlichen Grüßen[1] *or* Mit besten Empfehlungen (*in business letters*)	[1] *The first is more common and should generally be used*
To someone in the same profession		
Sehr geehrter Herr Kollege, Lieber Kollege, Liebe Kollegin,	Mit freundlichen kollegialen Grüßen	

To a person in an important position

OPENING FORMULAE	CLOSING FORMULAE
Very formal	
Sehr geehrter Herr Bundesminister, Sehr geehrte Frau Präsidentin, Sehr verehrter, lieber Herr Professor,	Hochachtungsvoll

- **Bitte teilen Sie mir umgehend mit, ob** Sie für die Woche nach dem 24. Juni noch ein Einzelzimmer mit Dusche und Vollpension haben
  = *please let me know by return of post if*
- **Ich möchte für** Frau Klein ein Einzelzimmer mit Bad für die Woche nach dem 8. Juni **buchen.** Frau Klein **bezahlt ihre Rechnung selbst**
  = *I want to reserve ... in the name of ... will settle the bill herself*
- **Bitte senden Sie die Rechnung an** die obige Adresse
  = *please send the bill to*

21.4 Confirming and cancelling a booking

- **Bitte betrachten Sie diese Reservierung als verbindlich** und halten Sie mir das Zimmer frei, auch wenn ich sehr spät am Abend ankommen sollte
  = *please consider this a firm booking*
- **Wir wollen gegen Abend eintreffen, falls** nichts dazwischenkommt
  = *we expect to arrive in the early evening, unless*
- **Leider muss ich Sie bitten, meine Reservierung vom** 24. August **auf den** 3. September **umzubuchen**
  = *I am afraid I must ask you to alter my booking from ... to*
- **Ich muss Ihnen leider mitteilen, dass ich aufgrund** unvorhersehbarer Umstände **meine Zimmerreservierung** für die Woche ab dem 5. September **stornieren muss**
  = *owing to ..., I am afraid that I must cancel my booking*

22 THANKS

- **Herzlichen Dank für** das schöne Geschenk und Deinen lieben Brief
  = *many thanks for*
- **Ich möchte Ihnen, auch im Namen meines Mannes, unseren Dank für** den schönen Abend **übermitteln**
  = *I would like to thank you on behalf of my husband and myself for*
- **Ich weiß gar nicht, wie ich Ihnen für** Ihre Hilfe **danken soll**
  = *I really don't know how to thank you for*
- **Als kleines Dankeschön für** Deine Hilfe möchten wir Dich nächste Woche einmal zum Abendessen einladen
  = *as a small token of our gratitude for*
- **Für** die vielen Glückwünsche und Geschenke zu unserer Verlobung **möchten wir uns bei** allen Freunden und Bekannten **herzlich bedanken**
  = *we would like to extend our warmest thanks to ... for*
- **Bitte leiten Sie unseren aufrichtigen Dank auch an** Ihre Mitarbeiterin, Frau Wagner, **weiter**
  = *please pass on our sincere thanks to*
- **Keine Ursache. Ganz im Gegenteil: wir haben Ihnen zu danken**
  = *don't mention it. On the contrary: we must thank you*
- **Wir sind Ihnen für** diesen Beitrag **äußerst dankbar**
  = *we are very grateful to you for*
- Der Vorsitzende **hat mir die ehrenvolle Aufgabe übertragen, Ihnen im Namen** des Forschungskomitees **unseren herzlichen Dank für** die bereitgestellten Spendenmittel **auszusprechen**
  = *I have the honour of conveying, on behalf of ..., our sincere thanks for*

23 BEST WISHES

General expressions (*used on special occasions only*)

- **Mit den besten Wünschen** [...] **von** (+ *signature* [...] *will be expressions like "für Ihren Ruhestand", "für die neue Stelle", "für Glück im neuen Heim", "für eine baldige Genesung" etc*
  = *with best wishes for/on ... from*
- **Erlauben Sie mir, dass ich Ihnen meine besten Wünsche [...] übermittle**
  = *please accept my best wishes for*
- **Bitte richten Sie** Edgar **meine besten Wünsche aus**
  = *please give ... my best wishes*
- **Viele herzliche Grüße und Wünsche**
  = *best wishes*

- **Alle Liebe**
  = *love*
- **Unsere besten Wünsche [...]**
  = *best wishes from both/all of us*
- **Alles Gute [...]!**
  = *all the best*

23.2 Season's greetings

- **Fröhliche Weihnachten und ein glückliches neues Jahr** wünscht Ihnen/Euch (+ *signature*)
  = *Merry Christmas and a Happy New Year from*
- **Mit den besten Wünschen für ein gesegnetes Weihnachtsfest und ein glückliches und erfolgreiches neues Jahr**
  = *(often on company Christmas card sent to clients, suppliers etc.)*
- **Frohe Weihnachten und einen guten Rutsch!**
  = *(more informal, only to friends)*

23.3 Birthday greetings

- **Alles Gute zum Geburtstag!**
  = *happy birthday!*
- **Herzlichen Glückwunsch zum Geburtstag** von (+ *signature*)
  = *many happy returns of the day from*
- **Herzlichen Glückwunsch zum Namenstag** von (+ *signature*)
  = *best wishes on your saint's day*
- **Zu Ihrem Geburtstag unsere herzlichen Glückwünsche** und alles Gute für das neue Lebensjahr
  = *(more formal) many happy returns of the day and best wishes for the year ahead*

23.4 Get well wishes

- **Gute Besserung!**
  = *(on cards) get well soon*

23.5 Wishing someone luck

- **Ich möchte Ihnen für** Ihre Unternehmungen **viel Glück und Erfolg wünschen**
  = *I wish you the best of luck and every success in ...*
- **Viel Erfolg an** Ihrer neuen Arbeitsstätte
  = *I wish you every success in ...*
- **Wir möchten Dir viel Erfolg beim** Examen **wünschen**
  = *we'd like to wish you every success in*
- **Wir drücken Dir** am Freitag alle **die Daumen**
  = *we're keeping our fingers crossed*
- **Viel Glück für** die Fahrprüfung!
  = *good luck in*

23.6 Congratulations

- **Herzlichen Glückwunsche zum** bestandenen Examen
  = *congratulations on*
- **Zu** Ihrer Beförderung **möchten wir Ihnen unsere herzlichsten Glückwünsche aussprechen**
  = *(more formal) we would like to send you our congratulations on*
- **Ich gratuliere zur** bestandenen Fahrprüfung. **Gut gemacht!**
  = *congratulations on ... Well done!*

24 ANNOUNCEMENTS

24.1 Announcing a birth and responding

- **Wir freuen uns über die Geburt** unserer Tochter Julia am 15. Juli. Katharina und Hans Graf, Schönberg
  = *are happy to announce the birth of*
- Unsere Annika **hat ein Brüderchen bekommen. Am** 7. September **wurde** unser Sohn Christoph-Johannes **geboren. Es freuen sich** Katja und Uwe Braun
  = *are happy to announce the birth of ... on ... A brother for ...*
- Karin und Rainer **haben** am 7. September **eine kleine Tochter** Sabine **bekommen.** Karin **geht es schon wieder ganz gut. Die beiden sind natürlich überglücklich**
  = *I'm happy to tell you that ... now have a little daughter ... is fully recovered. They are both delighted, of course*
- **Herzlichen Glückwunsch zum freudigen Ereignis**
  = *congratulations on the happy event*
- **Herzlichen Glückwunsch zur Geburt** Ihrer/Eurer Tochter
  = *congratulations on the birth of*
- Andreas und ich **freuen uns mit Euch über die Geburt** Eures Sohnes. **Wir gratulieren von ganzem Herzen und wünschen Euch und ihm alles Gute**
  = *were delighted to hear of the birth of ... Many congratulations. We wish all three of you all the best*

24.2 Announcing an engagement and responding

- **Wir haben uns verlobt**. Judith Winter und Christian Schütte
  = *are engaged*
- Professor Wolfgang Schwarz und Frau Gabriele **beehren sich, die Verlobung** ihrer Tochter Erika mit Herrn Ulrich von Schlieffenberg **anzuzeigen**
  = *are happy to announce the engagement of*
- **Herzlichen Glückwunsch zur Verlobung und alles Gute für** die gemeinsame Zukunft
  = *congratulations on your engagement and best wishes for*
- **Wir freuen uns mit Euch über die Verlobung** Eures Sohnes und wünschen dem jungen Paar viel Glück für die Zukunft
  = *we were very happy to hear of the engagement*

24.3 Announcing a marriage and responding

- **Wir heiraten am 27. April**. Heinz Müller und Jutta Müller geb. Heinisch. **Die kirkliche Trauung findet** um 10 Uhr in der Dorfkirche **statt**. Tagesadresse: Hotel Weißer Schwan, Oberammergau
  = *...are getting married on 27 April. The ceremony will take place*
- **Mit großer Freude geben wir die Vermählung** unserer Kinder **bekannt** (+ *names of both sets of parents*)
  = *we are happy to announce the wedding/marriage of*
- **Wir haben geheiratet**. Fred Heine und Maria Heine-Obermann
  = *... have got married*
- **Zur Vermählung** Ihrer Tochter mit Herrn Dr Friedhelm Klöbner **möchten wir Ihnen unsere herzlichen Glückwünsche aussprechen**
  = *may we offer our congratulations on the marriage of*
- **Zu Eurer Hochzeit unseren herzlichen Glückwunsch** und alles Gute für Eure gemeinsame Zukunft
  = *congratulations on your marriage*
- **Wir freuen uns mit Euch über die Heirat** von Anne und Stefan **und möchten dem jungen Paar alles Gute wünschen**
  = *we are delighted to hear of ...'s wedding. Best wishes to the newly-weds*
- **Für die vielen Glückwünsche und Geschenke** von Familie, Freunden und Bekannten **anlässlich unserer Hochzeit möchten wir uns herzlich bedanken**
  = *we would like to thank all our ... for the many gifts and good wishes on the occasion of our marriage*

24.4 Announcing a death and responding

- **Plötzlich und unerwartet ist** mein geliebter Mann, unser lieber Vater, Onkel und Großvater Hans Meier **aus unserer Mitte gerissen worden. In tiefer Trauer:** Susanne Meier geb. Blume und die Kinder und Enkel
  = *it is with deep sorrow that I must announce the sudden and unexpected departure from this life of*
- **Nach schwerer Krankheit verstarb** am 15. März unsere liebe Schwester, Tante und Schwägerin Hanna Pietsch geb. Lehmann im Alter von 85 Jahren
  = *after a long and painful illness*

- **In tiefer Trauer muss ich Ihnen mitteilen, dass** mein Vater vergangene Woche nach kurzer schwerer Krankheit verstorben ist *or* für immer von uns gegangen ist
  = *it is with deep sorrow that I have to inform you that*
- **Mit tiefer Bestürzung haben wir die Nachricht vom Tod** Ihres Gatten **erhalten. Wir möchten Ihnen unser tief empfundenes Beileid aussprechen**
  = *it is with great sorrow that we learnt of the death of ... we would like to offer our deepest sympathy*
- **Wir sind alle sehr bestürzt über den plötzlichen Tod** Deines Bruders **und möchten Dir unser aufrichtiges Beileid aussprechen**. Wir sind in Gedanken bei Dir und wünschen Dir in dieser schweren Zeit viel Kraft und Liebe
  = *we are all deeply shocked to hear of the sudden death of ... and we would like to offer our deepest sympathy*
- **Für die zahlreichen Beweise und Mitgefühls** und der aufrichtigen Anteilnahme sowie für das ehrende Geleit zur letzten Ruhestätte unseres lieben Verstorbenen **danken wir allen herzlich**
  = *we would like to express our deep gratitude for the numerous expressions of sympathy*

24.5 Announcing a change of address

- **Wir sind umgezogen!** *or* **Wir ziehen um!** Ab 1. April ist unsere Adresse:
  = *we have moved! we're moving!*

25 INVITATIONS

25.1 Formal invitations

- **Wir würden uns freuen, Sie beim** Sektfrühstück im Anschluss an die Trauung im Hotel Goldener Schwan **als unseren Gast begrüßen zu dürfen**
  = *we would be delighted if you would join us*
- Der Verlag „Mensch und Technik" **gibt sich die Ehre, Sie** am 12. Oktober um 11 Uhr **zu** einem Sektfrühstück an Stand 15 **einzuladen** u.A.w.g.
  = *will be pleased to welcome you at*
- Karl und Greta Dauderstädt **geben sich die Ehre**, Herrn Günther Henrich **aus Anlass** ihrer silbernen Hochzeit am 14. Mai **zu einem festlichen Abendessen** im Hotel „Zum Goldenen Hirsch" **einzuladen**
  = *request the pleasure of your company at a dinner to celebrate*

...and responding

- Meine Frau und ich **möchten Ihnen unseren Dank für die freundliche Einladung zum Abendessen anlässlich** Ihrer Silberhochzeit **aussprechen, die wir mit Freuden annehmen/die wir leider nicht wahrnehmen kön nen, da ...**
  = *would like to thank you for your kind invitation to dinner on the occasion of ... which we have pleasure in accepting/but we regret that we cannot attend, because ...*
- **Ich möchte mich herzlich für Ihre Einladung zum** Abendessen am 12. Oktober **bedanken, die ich mit größtem Vergnügen annehme/der ich aber leider nicht nachkommen kann**
  = *I would like to thank you very much for your invitation to ... which I have much pleasure in accepting/I am unfortunately unable to accept*

25.2 Informal invitations

- Unsere Verlobung **möchten wir** am 15. März um 19 Uhr im kleinen Saal des Restaurants „Stadtkrone" **mit Freunden feiern. Wir würden uns freuen, wenn Ihr** zu unserem Fest **kommen könntet**
  = *we are having a party amongst friends to celebrate ... and we would be very glad if you could come*
- Nächsten Sonntag **möchten wir** für Ruth und Daniel Torberg, die zur Zeit bei uns zu Gast sind, **ein kleines Abendessen geben, zu dem wir auch Sie herzlich einladen möchten**
  = *we are giving a small dinner for ... and we would very much like you to come*
- **Hätten Sie Lust**, am Donnerstag mit mir in die Oper zu gehen?
  = *would you like*
- Könntest Du Dir, wenn Du nächste Woche in Bonn bist, einen Abend freihalten? **Wir würden Dich gerne einmal zum Abendessen einladen**
  = *we would very much like you to come to dinner*
- **Wir** wollen den ganzen Mai in unserem Ferienhaus auf Amrum verbringen und **würden uns freuen, wenn Ihr uns einmal dort besuchen könntet**
  = *we would be very happy if you could come and visit us there*

Accepting

- **Vielen Dank für** die freundliche Einladung. **Ich komme gerne**
  = *thanks very much for ... I will be pleased to come*
- **Ich habe mich über Ihre freundliche Einladung** zur Konfirmationsfeier Ihrer Tochter **sehr gefreut und nehme gerne an**
  = *thank you very much for ... I shall be happy to accept*
- **Ich hatte vor**, am nächsten Montag in Bonn anzukommen, und **werde mich dann telefonisch bei Euch melden**
  = *I was planning to ... and I will phone you when I arrive*
- **Wir haben uns riesig über Eure Einladung** nach Amrum **gefreut und würden gerne** das Wochenende nach Himmelfahrt **kommen**
  = *thank you so much for your invitation ... we would love to come*
- **Natürlich gehe ich gerne mit Ihnen** in die „Zauberflöte". **Es hat mich sehr gefreut, dass Sie an mich gedacht haben**
  = *I would love to go with you to ... it was very kind of you to think of me*

Declining

- **Vielen Dank für Ihre Einladung** zum Abendessen mit den Torbergs. **Ich wäre wirklich gerne gekommen, habe aber leider schon eine andere Verabredung**, die ich nicht mehr rückgängig machen kann
  = *many thanks for your invitation ... I would very much have liked to come, but I'm afraid I have a previous engagement*
- **Wir würden wirklich gern einmal** für ein Wochenende zu Euch zu Besuch kommen, aber **leider passt uns keiner der vorgeschlagenen Termine**
  = *we would very much like to ... but I'm afraid we can't make any of the dates you suggest*
- **Leider kann ich mich** am kommenden Dienstag **nicht freimachen. Könnten wir vielleicht** schon jetzt **etwas für** Oktober **ausmachen?**
  = *I'm afraid I'm not free ... perhaps we can arrange something for ...*

26 ESSAY WRITING

26.1 The broad outline of the essay

Introductory remarks

- Welche Auswirkungen die neue Kommunikations- und Medientechnik auf die Zukunft des Menschen hat, **darüber wird sehr viel geschrieben und gesprochen**
  = *a great deal is being written and said about*
- **Die Frage, ob** bakterielle Sporen auf geeigneten Himmelskörpern Fuß fassen können, **beschäftigt die Experten schon seit Längerem**
  = *the question whether ... has been preoccupying the experts for some time*
- **Es ist allgemein bekannt, dass** bestimmte Grundsätze sich immer durchsetzen
  = *it is a well-known fact that*
- **Heute gilt allgemein als bewiesen, dass** Kernkraftwerke eine Gefahr für den Menschen darstellen. **Trotzdem fragt sich**, wie man im Falle einer Schließung die Energieversorgung sichern kann. **Das lässt sich vermuten, dass** die Lösung des Problems so einfach nicht sein kann

= it is generally agreed today that ... however, one wonders ... this leads one to assume that

- **Man muss sich verstärkt fragen, ob** Fernsehen nicht eine echte Gefahr für unsere Kinder darstellt
  = one must seriously ask oneself whether
- **Beinahe täglich** hört man neue Katastrophenmeldungen zum Wärmehaushalt der Erde. **Manche** Experten sagen den Hitzetod unseres Planeten voraus, **während andere** die gleichen Daten dazu benutzen, das Nahen der nächsten Eiszeit anzukündigen
  = almost every day ... some ... while others
- **Man würde zu Recht** jeden auslachen, der die Aussagen der Politiker im Wahlkampf für bare Münzen nähme. Aber ...
  = one would be justified in
- **Es ist wohl kaum übertrieben, wenn man sagt, dass** sich die Rolle der Gewerkschaften grundlegend gewandelt hat
  = it would hardly be an exaggeration to say
- **Heutzutage kann man keine Zeitung mehr aufschlagen, ohne dass** einem alarmierende Meldungen über Mafiamethoden ins Auge springen
  = nowadays it is scarcely possible to open a newspaper without
- **Es gibt in der Geschichte unzählige Beispiele für** kluge Frauen, die im Schatten ihrer berühmten Männer standen. Ein Beispiel dafür ist ...
  = history offers us numerous examples of

Explaining the aim of the essay

- „Arbeitslose sind in Wirklichkeit nur zu faul zum Arbeiten." **Bemerkungen dieser Art hört man oft**, auch in sogenannten gebildeten Kreisen. **Deshalb sollen** hier die Statistiken der Bundesagentur für Arbeit einmal genauer **untersucht werden**
  = such remarks are often heard ... we will therefore examine
- „Stress macht krank". Diese Feststellung veranschaulicht eines der drängendsten Probleme unserer Gesellschaft. **Es scheint deshalb angebracht, sich einmal näher mit** dem Phänomen Stress unter seinen medizinischen und sozialen Aspekten zu **befassen**
  = it therefore seems appropriate to look more closely into
- Diese Einstellung **verdient es, genauer untersucht zu werden** und soll hier in einen größeren Gesamtzusammenhang eingeordnet werden
  = deserves closer attention
- Kafka hat einmal geschrieben: „Wirkliche Realität ist immer unrealistisch". **Aus dieser Aussage ergibt sich eine grundlegende Fragestellung**: Was ist Wirklichkeit, was ist Vorstellung?
  = this assertion raises a fundamental question
- **Heute werden wir immer wieder mit dem Problem** der zunehmenden Umweltverschmutzung **konfrontiert**
  = today we are repeatedly confronted with the problem of

Developing the argument

- **Ich möchte mit** einer kurzen Erläuterung einiger grundlegender physikalischer Prinzipien **beginnen**
  = I should like to begin by
- **Ich möchte zu Anfang** versuchen, die medizinische Definition von Stress einzugrenzen
  = I should like to begin by
- **Zunächst einmal muss man darauf aufmerksam machen, dass** der Autor selber lange Jahre im Exil verbracht hat
  = the first thing to point out is that
- **Betrachten wir zunächst** die Software als Arbeitsmittel
  = firstly let us look at
- **Bevor** ich näher auf die Frage des Bewusstseins bei Primaten eingehe, **möchte ich zunächst** verschiedene Meinungen über die Hirnstruktur von Menschenaffen zusammenfassen
  = before ... I should like to
- **Es wäre** an dieser Stelle **angebracht, einen Blick auf** die Familienverhältnisse des Komponisten **zu werfen**
  = it would be appropriate to consider
- **Als Erstes sollte man sich** ein wenig **mit** der Geschichte der Gewerkschaftsbewegung **beschäftigen**
  = let us start by considering
- **Ehe wir das** Umfrageergebnis **analysieren, müssen wir uns darüber klar werden, dass** nur Langzeitarbeitslose befragt wurden
  = before analysing the ... it must be made clear that
- **Als ersten überzeugenden Beweis für diese Behauptung kann man anführen, dass** die Orientierungslosigkeit heute eines der größten Probleme der Jugendlichen ist
  = the first convincing argument to support this statement is that
- **Es stellt sich zunächst die Frage nach** dem Motiv, das die Hauptfigur des Romans bewegt, ihre Familie so plötzlich zu verlassen
  = let us first consider
- **Wenn wir uns erinnern**: Im Vorjahr hatte sich Goethe gerade als Student der Rechte an der Universität von Straßburg aufgehalten
  = let us cast our minds back:
- **Es ergibt sich die Frage, ob** unsere Interpretation der spätantiken Prosa in dieser Form noch haltbar ist
  = this raises the question whether

Connecting elements

- **Wir kommen nun zur Analyse** der einzelnen Charaktere
  = let us now analyse
- Nachdem wir uns eingehend mit dem Verlauf der Handlung befasst haben, **wollen wir uns nun** dem Sprachstil **zuwenden**
  = let us now turn to
- **Wir** haben gesehen, dass Strahlenbelastung eine Ursache für diese Krankheit sein kann, und **wollen nun andere Faktoren untersuchen**, die für ihre Verbreitung von Bedeutung sein könnten
  = let us now examine other factors
- **Es ist nun klar, dass** es eine Lösung im Bereich der Schulmedizin allein nicht geben kann, und **wir wollen** nun Lösungsansätze aus den sogenannten Grenzbereichen **betrachten**
  = it is now clear that ... let us turn our attention to
- **Es wäre jetzt interessant, auch** die soziologischen Aspekte näher **zu** beleuchten
  = it would also be interesting to ...
- **Es drängt sich hier allerdings auch ein Gegenargument auf**: nämlich wie und vor allem von wem soll diese Zensur ausgeübt werden
  = moreover, one argument against this cannot be ignored:
- **Man kann das Problem aber auch von** der rein praktischen Seite **her betrachten**
  the problem can also be looked at from

The other side of the argument

- **Aber sind** diese traumatischen Jugenderlebnisse **wirklich der einzige Grund für** ihr Scheitern?
  = but are ... really the only explanation for
- **Wären diese Argumente schon ein ausreichender Grund für** die Wiedereinführung der Todesstrafe, **oder** sprechen nicht weitaus mehr und scherwiegendere Argumente dagegen?
  = do these arguments give sufficient grounds for ... or
- **Der Autor argumentiert, dass** die Form wichtiger sei als der Inhalt, **es ließe sich aber mit gleichem Recht auch das Gegenteil behaupten**
  = the author argues that ... but the opposite may be equally true
- **Es kann freilich nicht darum gehen**, die ganze Branche zu akademisieren
  = there is certainly no question of
- **Mit gleichem Recht lässt sich das Problem** natürlich auch dem Bereich der Psychoanalyse **zuordnen**
  = this problem belongs equally in

The balanced view

- **Nach eingehender Betrachtung muss man zu dem Ergebnis kommen, dass** eine verantwortliche Kontrollinstanz dringend nötig wäre
  = *on reflection, one is forced to conclude that*
- **Man sollte sich allerdings immer darüber im Klaren sein, dass** absolute Aussagen zwar eingängig, aber im Prinzip äußerst zweifelhaft sind
  = *one should always remember that*
- **Man sollte auch** den psychologischen Aspekt einer Währungsunion **nicht außer Acht lassen**
  = *... should also be taken into consideration*
- **Auch wenn** der Einfluss des Fernsehens auf die jugendliche Psyche unbestritten ist, **sollte man** ihn doch **nicht überschätzen**
  = *even if ... one must not overestimate*
- **Trotzdem sollte man auch einen weiteren Faktor nicht vergessen**
  = *there is however another factor which should not be ignored*
- **Schließlich müsste man sich fragen, ob** eine berufliche Karriere wirklich der einzig mögliche Lebensinhalt ist
  = *finally, we must ask ourselves whether*
- **Vielleicht sollte man noch einen Schritt weitergehen und sich fragen, ob** Städte kategorisch für Autos gesperrt werden sollten
  = *we should perhaps go further and ask ourselves whether*

In conclusion

- **Welche Schlussfolgerungen lassen sich aus** der Analyse **ziehen**?
  = *what conclusions may be drawn from*
- **Die aufgeführten Argumente beweisen, dass** der naturwissenschaftliche Unterricht an unseren Schulen in vielen Punkten mangelhaft ist
  = *the arguments given above prove that*
- **Wir sehen also, dass** dem Autor in seiner Erzählung wenig an stimmigen Handlungsabläufen und glaubhaften Personenbeschreibungen liegt. **Vielmehr** konzentriert er sich ganz auf Sprachartistik
  = *we can see then, that ... rather*
- **Es spricht also alles dafür, dass** Frauen heute wie früher mit anderen Leistungsmaßstäben gemessen werden als Männer
  = *all of this points to the fact that*
- **Aus all dem lässt sich nur folgern, dass** sich hinter Argumenten für die Kernkraft erhebliche wirtschaftliche Interessen verbergen
  = *from this one must conclude that*
- **Alles in allem** ist der Drogenmissbrauch eines der schwierigsten und wohl dringendsten Probleme unserer Zeit
  = *all in all*
- **Jedenfalls** verdienen gerade die sogenannten Randgruppen unserer ruppigen Leistungsgesellschaft mehr Einfühlsamkeit und Hilfe
  = *in any case*
- Sein Lebenslauf **lässt den Schluss zu, dass** der Dichter durchaus in das Gemeinschaftsleben des Dorfes eingebunden war
  = *leads us to the conclusion that*

26.2 Constructing a paragraph

Assessing an idea

- **Hier lassen sich** verschiedene Argumente **anführen**
  = *at this point, ... may be given/cited*
- **Ehe ich** mich einer ausführlichen Stilanalyse zuwende, **möchte ich noch kurz auf** die Verwendung des Tiroler Dialektes **zu sprechen kommen**
  = *before I ... I would just like to say a few words about*
- **Wie ich im Folgenden noch zeigen werde**, kann von einer genauen psychoanalytischen Bewertung hier keine Rede sein
  = *as I will show later*
- **Und hiermit greifen wir einen Gedanken auf**, der schon einleitend erwähnt wurde
  = *here we pick up an idea*
- **Um aber wieder auf unser Hauptthema zurückzukommen**, die Vollwertküche muss keineswegs langweilig und bieder sein
  = *but to return to our main theme*
- **Von** dieser Reise **wird später noch ausführlich die Rede sein**, es soll hier nur kurz erwähnt werden, dass sie einen tiefen Eindruck bei ihr hinterließ
  = *we will return to a more detailed discussion of ... later*
- **Zum Thema** Schwefelausstoß der Kohlekraftwerke **lässt sich sagen, dass** die neuen Filteranlagen ihn um mehr als 60% reduzieren
  = *on the subject of ... it must be said that*

Establishing parallels

- **Sowohl** im Inntal **als auch** in Trostberg lag die Kohlenmonoxidkonzentration bei 0,5 Milligramm
  = *both ... and*
- **In diesem Zusammenhang muss auch** die sogenannte Technologiefeindlichkeit der deutschen Gesellschaft **erwähnt werden**
  = *in this context we should also mention*
- **In gleicher Weise** sorgt das Programm selbstständig für die notwendigen Datei- und Satzsperren
  = *equally*
- Die Bodenversiegelung führt **einerseits** zu Hochwasser, **andererseits** zu Grundwasserabsenkungen und damit zu Wassernotstand im Sommer
  = *on (the) one hand ... and on the other (hand)*
- Eine Zeitung gewinnt Glanz durch exzentrische Schreiber, leben aber tut sie von guten Redakteuren. **Erstere** kommen und gehen, **Letztere** aber sind da und halten die Maschine am Laufen
  = *the former ... the latter*
- Das Strafrecht untersagt es den Fernsehanstalten, Filme auszustrahlen, die bei der Jugend Aggressionsbereitschaft fördern, und **das Gleiche gilt für** Sendungen, die offensichtlich die Menschenwürde verletzen
  = *and the same goes for*
- **In dem Maße wie** die Privatisierung fortschreitet, werden auch immer mehr Investitions- und Finanzierungsmöglichkeiten gefunden
  = *as*
- **Untrennbar hiermit verbunden ist die Tatsache, dass** Chopin bereits schwer erkrankt war, als er seine Schottlandreise antrat
  = *this cannot be dissociated from the fact that*
- **Von** den Kommunisten **bis zu** den extremen rechten Gruppen sind sich **alle** in der Verurteilung des Terrorismus einig
  = *everyone, from ... to*
- **Gleichermaßen** sollte ein Zeitungsartikel den Leser nicht wie einen unmündigen Ignoranten von oben herab belehren
  = *equally*

Adding

- **In diesem Zusammenhang** muss man auch ein merkliches Nachlassen der schulischen Leistungen erwähnen
  = *in this context*
- **Nebenbei bemerkt** hielt der junge Friedrich II. Luther und Calvin für recht triste Figuren
  = *incidentally*
- **Außerdem** muss man die ökologischen Folgen bedenken
  = *furthermore*
- **Man sollte auch nicht vergessen, dass** durch das Spülen von Mehrwegflaschen die Gewässer erheblich belastet werden
  = *one must also remember that*
- **Hinzu kommt noch** seine liebevolle Schilderung der englischen Landschaft
  = *in addition to this there is*

Detailing

- Hiervon sind verschiedene Berufsgruppen betroffen, **besonders** Berufe, die viel Bildschirmarbeit erfordern
  = *in particular*
- Es treten hier **vorzugsweise** Probleme mit den Augen, der Wirbelsäule und im Bereich des Unterarms und Handgelenks auf, **die noch** durch schlechte Sitzhaltung **verstärkt werden**
  = *chiefly ... which may be made still worse*
- **Was** nun die Bürgerinitiativen **betrifft,** so sind sie ihrerseits keineswegs einer Meinung zum heißen Eisen Müllverbrennung
  = *as far as ... are concerned*
- **Was** die Zigarettenwerbung **angeht**, ist der Zuschauer heute bedeutend kritischer
  = *as far as ... is concerned*

Enumerating

- Zum Erfolg dieser Fernsehserie tragen verschiedene Faktoren bei. **Erstens** *or* **Zum Ersten** spielt die Hauptrolle ein beliebter Star, **zweitens** liegt das Thema in der Luft und **schließlich** wurde ein erstklassiger Drehbuchautor gefunden
  = *first(ly) ... secondly ... finally*
- Das hat drei Hauptgründe: **erstens ..., zweitens ..., drittens**
  = *first(ly) ... secondly ... thirdly*
- Es werden dem Kunden mehrere Möglichkeiten angeboten: er kann **entweder** bar **oder** mit Scheck- oder Kreditkarte bezahlen **oder schließlich** ein Kundenkonto einrichten
  = *either ... or ... or alternatively/finally*
- Sollte man in diese Statistik alle Erkrankten aufnehmen? **Oder etwa** nur die chronisch Kranken? **Oder sollte man am Ende** sogar nach Art der Erkrankung getrennt analysieren?
  = *or else ... or should one simply*

Opposing

- **Entgegen** einem landläufigen Vorurteil hatten wohl auch die schrecklichen Wikinger Angst vor anderen Völkern
  = *contrary to*
- **Ungeachtet** ihrer Gräueltaten werden die Helden zu Märtyren erhoben
  = *in spite of*
- **Trotz** harter Arbeit konnten die Eltern die Kinder kaum ernähren
  = *in spite of*
- **Obwohl** es einen umfangreichen zivilen Apparat zur Verfolgung von Menschenrechtsverletzungen gibt, werden die Verantwortlichen nur selten bestraft
  = *although*
- **Wenngleich** die Schwierigkeiten des Balanceakts zwischen menschlicher Tragödie und politischem Verbrechen nicht immer zu übersehen sind, löst der Autor das Problem mit viel Mut und Geschick
  = *although*
- Schwellungen und Rötungen werden fast bei jedem Fall beobachtet, **trotzdem** stehen diese Nebenwirkungen in keinem Verhältnis zu den Folgen einer Infektion
  = *nevertheless*

Introducing one's own point of view

- **Meiner Meinung nach** ist dies sein bei Weitem bestes Buch
  = *in my opinion*
- **Ich für mein(en) Teil** bedaure diese Entwicklung im Schulwesen sehr
  = *I for my part*
- **Was ich hier am interessantesten finde**, ist die großartige Verflechtung der verschiedenen Charaktere
  = *what I find most interesting here*
- **Nach meinem Dafürhalten scheint** die Autorin sich hier auf das gewagte Terrain der Vermutung zu begeben
  = *it seems to me that*
- **Ich bin hingegen der Ansicht, dass** man Statistik nicht auf diese Weise zu seinem eigenen Zwecken umlügen darf
  = *my own point of view is that*
- Wie der Verfasser, **für meine Begriffe übrigens völlig zu Recht**, bemerkt, geht es hier um mehr als nur unsere Schulen
  = *quite rightly in my opinion*

Introducing somebody else's point of view

- **Laut Verfasser** *or* **Dem Verfasser zufolge** ist der Neid eine der Haupttriebfedern unseres Handelns
  = *in the author's view*
- **Nach Meinung einiger Experten** lassen sich diese Abweichungen durch unterschiedliche Ernährungsgewohnheiten erklären
  = *according to some experts*
- Die Ausgaben für den Umweltschutz bewegen sich **seiner Aussage zufolge** im Rahmen des Vertretbaren
  = *in his opinion*
- Er **glaubt/meint/erklärt dagegen**, dass dieses System unzählige Vorteile besitzt
  = *on the other hand, he thinks/believes/declares*
- Der Autor **lenkt nun unsere Aufmerksamkeit wieder auf** die verschiedenen vorangegangenen Krisensituationen
  = *once again draws our attention to*
- Er **weist** nun **auf** die unterschiedlichen Persönlichkeiten der Hauptakteure **hin**
  = *points out*
- Sie **behauptet, dass** die Mehrheit aller Jugendlichen sich heute nicht mehr für Bücher interessiert
  = *maintains that*
- **Die offizielle Lesart ist, dass** die Probleme für die Bevölkerung bei Weitem durch die Vorteile aufgewogen werden
  = *the official version is that*
- Hier **möchte uns** ein sogenannter Experte **glauben machen** *or* **davon überzeugen, dass** dieses Problem überhaupt nicht existiert
  = *would have us believe/would like to convince us that*

Introducing an example, quotation or source

- **Nehmen wir zum Beispiel** *or* **Da wäre zum Beispiel** Gretchen im „Faust"
  = *take for example*
- **Eines der interessantesten Beispiele findet sich** gleich im ersten Kapitel des Buches
  = *one of the most interesting examples occurs*
- **Als Beispiel braucht man nur** die problematische Lage der kleinen landwirtschaftlichen Betriebe **anzuführen**
  = *to illustrate this, one need only refer to*
- **Die Verfasser meinen dagegen, dass** „die zentrale Bedeutung der Hehlerei für die organisierte Kriminalität lange Zeit nicht deutlich genug gesehen worden ist"
  = *however, the authors are of the opinion that*
- In seinen „Xenien" **sagte/bemerkte** schon Goethe: „Amerika, du hast es besser"
  = *said/observed*
- **Was** der Minister **bereits sagte** *or* **gesagt hat, sei hier zitiert**: „Es hängt jetzt alles von der Einsatzbereitschaft und Toleranz unserer Mitbürger ab." **Zitat Ende**
  = *as ... said, and I quote ... end of quote*
- Schlegel **hat** in einem historischen Aufsatz **das Wort von** der „Revolution von oben" **geprägt, das später von** vielen kritischen Historikern **aufgenommen wurde**
  = *coined the phrase ... which was later taken up by*
- **Nach den Worten von** Börne fallen „Minister wie Butterbrote: gewöhnlich auf die gute Seite"
  = *in the words of*
- **In ihrer eindrucksvollen Studie zum** Leben der Insekten **weist** Maria Sybilla Merian bereits im 17. Jahrhundert **darauf hin, dass ...**
  = *in her remarkable study of ... (she) points out that*

- **In einem kürzlich erschienenen Artikel in** der Zeitschrift „Der Kreis" **finden wir folgende** treffende **Bemerkung von** Hans Meier:
  = *in a recent article in ... there is the following remark by*
- "Das größer gewordene Deutschland wird nicht regiert, Machterhalt ist alles." **So steht es in** der „Zeit" **aus der Feder von** Nina Grunenberg
  = *writes ... in*
- **Zitat Raddatz**: „Ähnlich einer Steinberg-Kontur setzt dieser Künstler sich selber aus Kunststücken zusammen." **Zitat Ende**
  = *to quote Raddatz ... end of quote*

26.3 The mechanics of the argument

Stating facts

- **Es ist richtig, dass** so manches Substitut eines Umweltgiftes sich im Nachhinein nicht als die erhoffte ökologische Alternative entpuppt
  = *it is true that*
- **Hierbei wäre zu bemerken, dass** die Experten zu diesem Thema gespaltener Auffassung sind
  = *one should note here that*
- **Es handelt sich um** den Versuch, durch Fiktionen etwas Realität zu erfahren
  = *this is a*
- Dieses Bauprogramm **zog die heftige Kritik** der Opposition **auf sich**
  = *attracted strong criticism from*
- **Erinnern wir uns**: Nach jahrzehntelangen Rangeleien war endlich eine Entscheidung gefallen. Das Steuerrecht würde grundlegend reformiert werden
  = *let us not forget:*
- **Beim Weiterlesen ergeben sich völlig neue Perspektiven**: ...
  = *as one reads on, entirely new perspectives open up*
- **Es sollte erwähnt werden, dass** Tschaikowski nicht der einzige Komponist ist, der in dieser Zeit historische Ereignisse in seinen Werken umsetzt
  = *mention should be made of the fact that*

Indicating a supposition

- **Es ist anzunehmen, dass** der wirtschaftliche Kurs sich zunehmend nach der liberalen Mitte hin einordnen wird
  = *it is to be expected that*
- **Es lässt sich hier vermuten, dass** ein Teil der Befragten den Begriff „Heimat" völlig anders verstanden hat
  = *one may suppose that*
- **Es kann gut sein, dass** Schiller dieses Gedicht im Konzept schon sehr viel früher verfasst hat
  = *... may well (have ...)*
- **Man spricht in diesem Zusammenhang von der Möglichkeit, dass** die Visumpflicht bereits in den nächsten Monaten entfallen könnte
  = *in this context, the possibility that ... has been mentioned*
- **Hierfür könnte es allerdings auch** eine andere Erklärung **geben**
  = *there could well be*
- **Es ist durchaus möglich, dass** er mit dieser Kandidatur politisches Kapital aus seiner Beliebtheit als Schauspieler schlagen wollte
  = *it is very possible that*
- **Es steht zu vermuten, dass** auch die Produktmanager in Japan in ihrem Sortiment nicht mehr so ganz durchblicken
  = *it must be supposed that*

Expressing a certainty

- Die wenigen Akten, die die Regierung bisher herausgerückt hat, **lassen nur den einen Schluss zu**: Bonn hat über das kriminelle Imperium Schalk fast alles gewusst
  = *leave us with only one conclusion*
- **Es steht fest, dass** Albrecht seinen späteren Mörder selbst eingelassen hat
  = *it is clear that*
- Aber **es ist sicher, dass** nicht alle Sprachen, die in Europa anerkannt sind, eine Ausgabe des EU-Amtsblattes haben werden
  = *it is certain that*
- Seine zweite Behauptung ist dagegen **unbestritten** *or* **unzweifelhaft** *or* **ohne Zweifel** den Argumenten seiner Gegner vorzuziehen
  = *indisputably/undeniably*
- **Unbestritten ist, dass** die Bundesrepublik im internationalen Umweltschutz eine Vorreiterrolle einnimmt
  = *what cannot be denied is that*
- Eine Limousine mit Chauffeur ist **zweifellos** besser gegen Diebstahl geschützt als ein Drahtesel
  = *doubtless*
- **Es deutet alles darauf hin, dass** es dem SC Freiburg so ergeht wie vielen seiner Vorgänger als Aufsteiger: am Ende steht der Neuanfang in der zweiten Liga
  = *all the indications are that*
- **Wie man weiß**, kann man auch in Bayern durchaus in den Genuss fiskalischer Milde gelangen
  = *as everyone knows*
- **Es ist völlig klar, dass** solchen innovativen Produkten die Märkte der Zukunft gehören
  = *it is very clear that*
- **Es lässt sich nicht leugnen, dass** die demografische Entwicklung das Zahlenverhältnis zwischen Beitragszahlern und Rentnern verschlechtern wird
  = *it cannot be denied that*

Indicating doubt or uncertainty

- **Es scheint wohl, dass** die Liebe zu antiken Modellen der Uhrmacherkunst wieder auflebt
  = *it would seem that*
- **Es könnte immerhin sein, dass** die Dauer der Studie zu kurz war
  = *all the same, it is possible that*
- **Vielleicht wäre es besser**, wenn die Städtebauer einen Teil ihrer Großgrundstücke nachträglich wieder parzellieren
  = *perhaps it would be better*
- **Es könnte sich** bei dem Streit **um** eine juristische Posse **handeln**
  = *we might be dealing with*
- **Dies könnte unter Umständen erklären, warum** man so lange auf den zweiten Band warten musste
  = *this might explain why*
- **Es fällt schwer**, in diesem Zusammenhang **an** die Objektivität der Wissenschaft **zu glauben**
  = *it is difficult to believe in*
- Diese Ergebnisse **stellen** erneut **die allgemeine Gültigkeit** statistischer Aussagen **infrage**
  = *cast doubt upon the general validity of*

Conceding a point

- In Berlin hat die Oper heute weniger Abonnenten als noch vor 10 Jahren, **trotzdem** sind sehr viele Aufführungen ausverkauft
  = *nonetheless*
- **Obwohl** seine Studien sehr sorgfältig waren, muss man ihm vorwerfen, dass er die Ergebnisse der sowjetischen Gruppe außer Acht ließ
  = *although*
- Ihr Stil ist sehr ausgefeilt, **allerdings** manchmal etwas langatmig
  = *although*
- **Bis zu einem gewissen Punkt** muss man ihm recht geben, wenn man sich auch nicht mit allen Rückschlüssen einverstanden erklären kann
  = *up to a point*
- **Ich stimme mit** der Verfasserin im Prinzip **überein, möchte aber zu bedenken geben, dass** manche Folgerungen sehr extrem sind
  = *I agree with ... but I would like to raise the point that*
- **Im Grunde bin ich mit** dem Autor **einer Meinung, möchte aber** einwenden, dass einige wichtige Punkte nicht berücksichtigt wurden
  = *basically, I agree with ... but I would like to*

- Fischer hält die Untersuchungen für abgeschlossen. **Es bleibt aber nach wie vor die Tatsache bestehen**, dass viele Versuche noch laufen
  = *but the fact remains that*
- **Gewiss** hat der Regisseur Talent und Mut. **Es stellt sich trotzdem die Frage, ob** man wirklich den „Ring" an einem Abend aufführen kann
  = *certainly ... but I would still question whether*
- Mit der Entwicklung des Laser-TV hat die Forschungsgruppe **zwar** Beachtliches geleistet, **ob es aber** wirklich ein Meilenstein in der Fernsehtechnik ist, bleibt umstritten
  = *certainly ... but whether it*
- **Ohne** den ästhetischen Reiz der Darstellung **schmälern zu wollen, hätte ich es doch begrüßt**, wenn ihre Quellen offengelegt worden wären
  = *without wishing to belittle ... I would have preferred*
- **Man muss zwar zugeben, dass** die Verbesserung des Lebensstandards ein vorrangiges Ziel ihrer Politik ist, **muss aber gleichzeitig sagen, dass** sie noch sehr weit von diesem Ziel entfernt ist
  = *one must admit that ... but one must also say that*
- **Zweifellos** ist ein hoher gesellschaftlicher Bedarf an Nervenkitzel vorhanden, **aber** das normale Leben ist keineswegs so langweilig, wie es scheint
  = *doubtless ... but*
- **Zumindest kann man sagen, dass** das Thema durch die Untersuchung einmal ins Bewusstsein der Öffentlichkeit gekommen ist
  = *at least one can say that*

Emphasizing particular points

- **Um** die Problematik **zu unterstreichen**, hat der Verfasser uns eine Reihe der häufigsten Nebenwirkungen genannt
  = *in order to emphasize*
- Die Verfasserin **betont wiederholt, dass** sie neutrale Zurückhaltung nicht für eine angemessene Reaktion auf dieses Problem hält
  = *repeatedly stresses that*
- **Wir müssen klarstellen, dass** wir es hier nicht mit einem Schüleraufsatz, sondern mit einem wissenschaftlichen Thesenpapier zu tun haben
  = *let us make it clear that*
- Diese Untersuchung **wirft ein bezeichnendes Licht auf** die gegenwärtige Situation am Arbeitsmarkt
  = *highlights*
- **Man sollte auf keinen Fall vergessen, dass** zu diesem Zeitpunkt niemand etwas von dem Unfall in Tschernobyl wusste
  = *let us not forget that*
- **Besonders** an den Universitäten lassen sich diese politischen Strömungen erkennen
  = *it is particularly ... that*
- Wenn er sich bisher noch nicht zu diesem Thema geäußert hat, **so liegt das an** politischen Erwägungen **und nicht an** mangelndem Interesse
  = *it is ... and not ... that have prevented him*
- Er spricht sich **nicht nur** gegen die Etaterhöhung aus, **sondern** fordert **auch** strenge Sparmaßnahmen in allen Ministerien
  = *not only ... but also*
- Er ist kein Dummkopf - **genau das** unterscheidet ihn von den meisten Argans der Theatergeschichte
  = *that is what*
- **Er** fällt **nicht** auf die Artistik stürmischer Läufe herein, **im Gegenteil**, er konzentriert sich auf die leisen, lyrischen Passagen
  = *he doesn't ..., on the contrary*
- Es wird wirtschaftlich weiter bergab gehen, **umso mehr, als** im Winter die Arbeitslosenzahlen ohnehin zunehmen
  = *all the more so because*
- **Ich möchte sogar behaupten, dass** Albrecht Schwarz eine lästige Person ist, die vielleicht früher einmal einen Zweck erfüllt haben mochte
  = *I would even go so far as to say that*
- Tritium kann die Transmutation von Thymin zu Cytosin bewirken, **und dazu kommt noch, dass** Schaden an der DNS verursacht wird
  = *and, furthermore*
- Die Inselbewohner brauchen keine Berührungsängste zu haben, **umso weniger, als** das Fischereiabkommen weit günstiger ausgefallen ist als angenommen
  = *even less so now that*

Moderating a statement

- **Ohne den Verfasser kritisieren zu wollen**, scheint es doch, dass er mit einer anderen Methode bessere Messergebnisse erzielt hätte
  = *without wishing to criticize the author*
- **Das soll nicht heißen, dass** Exportgeschäfte groß- und Menschenrechte kleingeschrieben werden, **sondern vielmehr, dass** eine wertorientierte Außenpolitik der Wirtschaft den Weg ebnen muss
  = *this does not mean that ..., but rather that*
- Dieses Verfahren ist **keineswegs** altruistischen Überlegungen des britischen Staates zu verdanken, **sondern vielmehr** als Instrument zur Sicherung des sozialen Friedens gedacht
  = *in no way ... but rather*
- An sich hat die Autorin **im Großen und Ganzen** recht, es ließe sich jedoch einwenden, dass sich inzwischen einige Details geändert haben
  = *by and large*
- **Ohne Kleinigkeiten zu viel Gewicht beimessen zu wollen**, muss man doch sagen, dass ihre Zeitangaben sehr unpräzise sind
  = *without laying too much emphasis on details*
- **Es wäre ungerecht** *or* **unfair**, von einem solchen Kompendium eine Art konzeptionelle Geschlossenheit zu erwarten
  = *it would be unfair to*

Indicating agreement

- **Man muss zugeben, dass** gerade dieser Aspekt faszinierend ist
  = *one must admit that*
- Seine Beschreibung der Situation **trifft in allen Punkten genau (zu)** *or* **ist bis ins Detail präzise**
  = *is correct in every detail*
- Dieses Argument **ist völlig überzeugend** *or* **überzeugt völlig**
  = *is completely convincing*
- **Wir können uns** diesen Schlussfolgerungen **nicht verschließen**
  = *we cannot ignore*
- **Wie** die Verfasserin **so richtig sagt**, kommt es auch auf Details an
  = *as ... so rightly says*
- **Es ist klar, dass** hier Geschichte geschrieben wurde
  = *it is clear that*
- Ich **kann mich der Meinung** des Verfassers nur **uneingeschränkt anschließen**
  = *support (his) view wholeheartedly*

Indicating disagreement

- Diese Sichtweise **kann man unmöglich** unwidersprochen **akzeptieren**
  = *one cannot possibly accept*
- Dieses Argument **ist keiner Beachtung wert** *or* **verdient keine Beachtung**
  = *is not worthy of our attention*
- Diesen Standpunkt **kann man** heute **nicht mehr vertreten**
  = *is no longer tenable*
- Die Äußerungen des Innenministers **stehen in völligem Widerspruch zur** Haltung des Verteidigungsministers
  = *completely contradict*
- Ich muss hier jedoch einige schwerwiegende **Bedenken gegen** diese Beweisführung **anmelden**
  = *express misgivings about*
- Die Untersuchung von Professor Sommerfeld **widerlegt** klar diese Behauptung
  = *disproves*

- Gegen alle diese Kritikpunkte **kann man** allerdings **einwenden** *or* **zu bedenken geben**, dass es hier um eine neue Kunstform geht
  = *one can object/one can argue*
- Diese Behauptung **scheint mir sehr zweifelhaft** *or* **fragwürdig**
  = *seems to me to be questionable*
- **Der Autor irrt sich, wenn er uns zu verstehen gibt, dass** das Ergebnis schon vor Beginn der Verhandlungen feststand
  = *the author is wrong to imply that*
- Die Beweisführung ist bestechend, **trotzdem kann ich die Meinung** *or* **den Standpunkt der Verfasser nicht teilen**
  = *however I cannot share the author's view*
- **Ich kann** seine pessimistische Weltsicht **nicht gutheißen**
  = *I cannot embrace*

Indicating approval

- **Es ist leicht zu verstehen, dass** er mit dieser Meinung gut ankommt
  = *it is easy to understand how*
- **Gewiss wäre die beste Lösung**, einen lockeren Staatenbund zu bilden
  = *the best solution would certainly be*
- Die Bundesbank **hat gut daran getan**, an der Zielvorgabe für die Geldmenge festzuhalten
  = *did well to*
- Der Student kritisiert **völlig zu Recht** die verbeamtete Mittelmäßigkeit der Professoren
  = *very rightly*
- **Es war wirklich an der Zeit, dass** man sich wieder an gewisse Grundwerte der Gesellschaft erinnert
  = *it was high time that*
- **Endlich einmal** ein Artikel, in dem ich mich als Lehrer wiederfinden kann
  = *at last*
- Dieses Buch **ist besonders willkommen, weil** alle bisherigen Biografien Clara Schumanns romantisch verklärt oder feministisch überzogen waren
  = *it is especially welcome, because*

Indicating disapproval

- **Es ist schade, dass** diese Poesie heute weitgehend verloren ist
  = *it is a pity that*
- **Leider** hat sich die Autorin mit der Zeichnung der Personen keine große Mühe gegeben
  = *unfortunately*
- **Es ist schwer einzusehen**, wie das Aktionsprogramm zusätzliche Arbeitsplätze schaffen soll
  = *it is hard to see*
- Ich möchte diese zynische Sichtweise aufs Schärfste **verurteilen**
  = *condemn*
- Man muss seine Haltung zur Geburtenkontrolle **scharf kritisieren**
  = *criticize ... very strongly*
- **Man kann** dem Bürgermeister **vorwerfen, dass** er zu sehr auf die nächsten Wahlen und zu wenig auf das Wohl der Bürger bedacht war
  = *one may reproach ... for*

Making a correction

- Möglicherweise habe ich mich missverständlich ausgedrückt, deshalb **möchte ich** das Gesagte **an dieser Stelle richtigstellen**
  = *I would like to put ... right here*
- **Tatsächlich** *or* **In Wirklichkeit** geht es um ganz etwas anderes
  = *in (actual) fact/in reality*
- **Es geht** hier **nicht um** Prinzipien, **sondern um** Menschenleben
  = *it is not a question of ... but of*
- Diese Schilderung **entspricht nicht den Tatsachen: in Wahrheit** ...
  = *is not in accordance with the facts: the truth is that*
- Diese Befürchtungen **sind völlig grundlos**
  = *are completely groundless*
- **Es wäre eine kleine Korrektur zu** dieser Behauptung **anzubringen**
  = *I would point out one small error in*

- Die Äußerungen des Pressesprechers **muss ich energisch dementieren**
  = *I emphatically deny*

Indicating the reason for something

- Die hohe Konzentration des Hormons **lässt sich auf** eine intravenöse Behandlung **zurückführen**
  = *arises from*
- Dieses Haus ist die Mühen und Ausgaben wert, **es handelt sich nämlich um** eines der wenigen erhaltenen gotischen Privathäuser
  = *for you see it is/because it is actually*
- **Angesichts der Tatsache, dass** die Berechnungen nur Richtwerte geben, muss man den weiteren Ergebnissen wirklich misstrauen
  = *in view of the fact that*
- **Das lässt sich sicher durch** die persönliche Vergangenheit des Autors **erklären**
  = *the reason for this doubtless lies in*

Setting out the consequences of something

- Diese Entscheidung sollte **unangenehme Folgen** haben
  = *unpleasant consequences*
- Das Verhandlungsergebnis wird langfristig **positive Auswirkungen** für die gesamte Region haben
  = *beneficial effects*
- Er war offensichtlich mit den angebotenen Bedingungen nicht zufrieden, **weshalb** er auch dem Ruf an die Universität Ulm nicht folgte
  = *which is why*
- **Und deshalb** spielt die Familie in allen seinen Romanen eine herausragende Rolle
  = *and that is why*
- Die Schließung der Fabrik **wird dazu führen, dass** ein großer Teil der Einwohner in andere Industriestädte abwandert
  = *will cause ... to*
- Die Flugpreise sind stark angestiegen, **was** zunächst eine rapide abnehmende Passagierzahl **zur Folge haben wird**
  = *and that will cause*
- Bei der heutigen Lebensweise kommen die evolutionär ausgebildeten Grundfähigkeiten des Menschen zu kurz, **folglich** sind seine Krankheiten biopsychosozialer Natur
  = *and consequently*
- Die Persönlichkeit der Anna ist **also doch** viel komplexer, als es auf den ersten Blick scheint
  = *thus/therefore*

Contrasting or comparing

- **Einerseits** sollen die Produktionsmengen erhöht werden, **andererseits** jedoch wird die damit verbundene Zunahme der Abfallmenge nicht einkalkuliert
  = *on (the) one hand ... on the other (hand)*
- **Einige** Kritiker **halten dies für** seine beste Inszenierung, **andere sind der Meinung, dass** er zu große Zugeständnisse an den Publikumsgeschmack gemacht hat
  = *some... consider this ... while others believe*
- **Manche** Experten reden heute vom Versagen der Schule. **Andere dagegen** bejubeln den Fortschritt im Bildungswesen
  = *some ... whereas others*
- Die Hirnfunktionen von Alkoholikern regenerieren sich **weitaus besser als** angenommen
  = *far better than (is)*
- **Mit** den Recherchewerkzeugen der spezialisierten Systeme **kann sich** eine einfache Textverarbeitung **nicht messen**
  = *is no match for*
- **Verglichen mit** seinen früheren Werken ist dieses Buch nur ein schwacher Abglanz
  = *compared to*
- Diese beiden Inszenierungen **lassen sich einfach nicht vergleichen**
  = *there is simply no comparison between*

27 TELEFONIEREN

27.1 Getting a number

Können Sie mich bitte mit Köln 465786 verbinden? *(vier-sechs-fünf-sieben-acht-sechs)*

Können Sie mich bitte mit der Auskunft verbinden?

Ich hätte gern eine Nummer in Köln, Firma Europost, Breite Straße 54

Ich kann die Nummer nicht finden

Das ist eine Geheimnummer

Wie lautet die Vorwahl von Leipzig?

Kann ich nach Peru durchwählen?

Wie bekomme ich das Amtszeichen?

Wie lautet die Nummer der Zeitansage?

Sie müssen die Nummer im Telefonbuch nachschlagen

Sie können die Nummer bei der internationalen Auskunft erfragen

Wenn Sie von Deutschland nach England anrufen, lassen Sie die Null weg

27.2 Different types of call

Es ist ein Ortsgespräch

Es ist ein Ferngespräch aus Hamburg

Ich möchte ins Ausland anrufen

Ich möchte ein R-Gespräch nach London anmelden

Ich möchte auf Kreditkarte nach Berlin anrufen

Ich hätte gern einen Weckruf für morgen früh 7.30 Uhr

27.3 The operator speaks

Welche Nummer möchten Sie?

Welche Nummer wünschen Sie?

Woher rufen Sie an?

Können Sie die Nummer bitte wiederholen?

Sie können durchwählen

Legen Sie auf und wählen Sie noch einmal

Ich habe Herrn Campbell mit einem R-Gespräch aus Canberra für Sie. Nehmen Sie das Gespräch an?

Ich verbinde

Ich habe keine Eintragung unter diesem Namen

Der Teilnehmer 45 77 57 84 antwortet nicht

Ich versuche es noch einmal

Bitte bleiben Sie am Apparat

Alle Leitungen nach Bonn sind besetzt, bitte rufen Sie später noch einmal an

Ich versuche Sie jetzt zu verbinden

Wir haben ein Rufzeichen

Die Leitung ist besetzt

27.4 When your number answers

Können Sie mich bitte mit Apparat 516 verbinden?

Bin ich mit dem Apparat von Herrn Lambert verbunden?

Kann ich bitte mit Herrn Schmiedel sprechen?

27 THE TELEPHONE

27.1 Nach einer Nummer fragen

Could you get me Newhaven 465786, please? *(four-six-five-seven-eight-six)*

Could you give me directory enquiries *(Brit) oder* directory assistance *(US)*, please?

Can you give me the number of Europost of 54 Broad Street, Newham?

It's not in the book

They're ex-directory *(Brit) oder* They're unlisted *(US)*

What is the code for Exeter?

Can I dial direct to Peru?

How do I make an outside call? *oder* What do I dial for an outside line?

What do I dial to get the speaking clock?

You'll have to look up the number in the directory

You should get the number from International Directory Enquiries

You omit the '0' when dialling England from Germany

27.2 Verschiedene Arten von Anrufen

It's a local call

It's a long-distance call from Worthing

I want to make an international call

I want to make a reverse charge call to a London number *(Brit) oder* I want to call a London number collect *(US)*

I'd like to make a credit card call to Berlin

I'd like an alarm call for 7.30 tomorrow morning

27.3 Vermittlung

Number, please

What number do you want? *oder* What number are you calling?

Where are you calling from?

Would you repeat the number, please?

You can dial the number direct

Replace the receiver and dial again

There's a Mr Campbell calling you from Canberra and wishes you to pay for the call. Will you accept it?

Go ahead, caller

There's no listing under that name

There's no reply from 45 77 57 84

I'll try to reconnect you

Hold the line, caller

All lines to Bristol are engaged - please try later

I'm trying it for you now

It's ringing *oder* Ringing for you now

The line is engaged *(Brit) oder* busy *(US)*

27.4 Der Teilnehmer antwortet

Could I have extension 516? *oder* Can you give me extension 516?

Is that Mr Lambert's phone?

Could I speak to Mr Swinton, please? *oder* I'd like to speak to Mr Swinton, please *oder* Is Mr Swinton there, please?

Können Sie mich bitte zu Herrn Dr. Graupner durchstellen?

Wer ist am Apparat?

Ich versuche es später noch einmal

Ich rufe in einer halben Stunde zurück

Könnte ich bitte meine Nummer hinterlassen, damit sie mich zurückrufen kann?

Ich rufe aus einer Telefonzelle an

Ich rufe aus England an

Könnten Sie ihn bitten mich zurückzurufen, wenn er wiederkommt?

27.5 The switchboard operator speaks

Hotel Maritim, guten Tag

Wer ist am Apparat, bitte?

Wen darf ich melden?

Wissen Sie, welchen Apparat er hat?

Ich verbinde Sie

Ein Gespräch aus Tokio für Frau Böhme

Frau Fehrmann für Sie

Frau Neubert aus Paris für Sie

Herr Dr. Schwendt spricht gerade auf der anderen Leitung

Bitte bleiben Sie am Apparat

Es meldet sich niemand

Sie sind mit unserer Verkaufsabteilung verbunden

27.6 Answering the telephone

Hallo, Anne hier

(Kann ich mit Anne sprechen?) Am Apparat

Möchten Sie eine Nachricht hinterlassen?

Kann ich ihm etwas ausrichten?

Bitte bleiben Sie am Apparat

Legen Sie bitte auf, ich rufe Sie zurück

Hier spricht der automatische Anrufbeantworter

Bitte sprechen Sie nach dem Tonzeichen

27.7 In case of difficulty

Ich komme nicht durch

Ich bekomme kein Rufzeichen

Ich bekomme immer nur „Kein Anschluss unter dieser Nummer“

Das Telefon ist gestört

Wir sind unterbrochen worden

Ich muss mich verwählt haben

Da ist noch jemand in der Leitung

Ich habe mehrmals angerufen, aber es hat sich niemand gemeldet

Sie haben mir die falsche Nummer gegeben

Ich bin mit dem falschen Apparat verbunden worden

Die Verbindung ist sehr schlecht

Could you put me through to Dr Henderson, please?

Who's speaking?

I'll try again later

I'll call back in half an hour

Could I leave my number for her to call me back?

I'm ringing from a phone box *(Brit)* *oder* I'm calling from a pay phone *(US)*

I'm phoning from England

Would you ask him to ring me when he gets back?

27.5 Die Zentrale antwortet

Queen's Hotel, can I help you?

Who is calling, please?

Who shall I say is calling?

Do you know his extension number?

I am connecting you now *oder* I'm putting you through now

I have a call from Tokyo for Mrs Thomas

I've got Miss Trotter on the line for you

Miss Paxton is calling you from Paris

Dr Craig is talking on the other line

Sorry to keep you waiting

There's no reply

You're through to our Sales Department

27.6 Sich am Telefon melden

Hello, this is Anne speaking

(Is that Anne?) Speaking

Would you like to leave a message?

Can I take a message for him?

Don't hang up yet

Put the phone down and I'll call you back

This is a recorded message

Please speak after the tone

27.7 Bei Schwierigkeiten

I can't get through

The number is not ringing

I'm getting "number unobtainable" *oder* I'm getting the "number unobtainable" signal

Their phone is out of order

We were cut off

I must have dialled the wrong number

We've got a crossed line

I've called them several times with no reply

You gave me a wrong number

I got the wrong extension

This is a very bad line

28 VORSCHLÄGE

28.1 Vorschläge machen

- **You might like to** think it over before giving me your decision
  = *vielleicht möchten Sie*
- **If you were to** give me the negative, **I could** get copies made
  = *wenn Sie ..., könnte ich*
- **You could** help me clear out my office, **if you don't mind**
  = *Sie könnten ..., wenn es Ihnen nichts ausmacht*
- **We could** stop off in Venice for a day or two, **if you like**
  = *wir könnten..., wenn Sie möchten*
- I've got an idea - **let's organize** a surprise birthday party for Hannah!
  = *lasst uns doch ... organisieren*
- **If you've no objection(s), I'll** speak to them personally
  = *wenn Sie keine Einwände haben, werde ich*
- **If I were you, I'd** go
  = *an Ihrer Stelle würde ich*
- **If you ask me, you'd better** take some extra cash
  = *wenn Sie mich fragen, Sie sollten besser*
- **I'd be very careful not to** commit myself at this stage
  = *ich würde mich hüten*
- **I would recommend (that) you** discuss it with him before making a decision
  = *ich würde vorschlagen, (dass) Sie*
- **It could be in your interest to** have a word with the owner first
  = *es könnte in Ihrem Interesse sein*
- **There's a lot to be said for** living alone
  = *es spricht vieles dafür*
- Go and see Pompeii - **it's a must!**
  = *das muss man gesehen haben*

Unschlüssiger

- **I suggest that you** go to bed and try to sleep
  = *ich schlage vor, dass Sie*
- **I'd like to suggest that you** seriously consider taking a long holiday
  = *ich würde vorschlagen, dass Sie*
- **We propose that** half the fee be paid in advance, and half on completion
  = *wir schlagen vor, dass*
- **It is very important that** you take an interest in what he is trying to do
  = *es ist sehr wichtig, dass*
- **I am convinced that** this would be a dangerous step to take
  = *ich bin überzeugt, dass*
- I cannot put it too strongly: **you really must** see a doctor
  = *Sie müssen wirklich*

Weniger direkt

- **Say you were to** approach the problem from a different angle
  = *wenn Sie nun*
- In these circumstances, **it might be better to** wait
  = *es wäre vielleicht besser*
- **Perhaps it would be as well to** change the locks
  = *vielleicht wäre es besser*
- **It might be a good thing** *oder* **a good idea to** warn her about this
  = *es wäre vielleicht gut*
- **Perhaps you should** take up sport
  = *vielleicht sollten Sie*
- **If I may make a suggestion**, a longer hemline might suit you better
  = *wenn ich einen Vorschlag machen dürfte*
- **If I might be permitted to suggest something**, installing bigger windows would make the office much brighter
  = *wenn ich vielleicht einen Vorschlag machen dürfte*
- **Might I be allowed to offer a little advice?** - talk it over with a solicitor before you go any further
  = *dürfte ich Ihnen einen Rat geben*

Als Frage

- **How do you fancy** a holiday in Australia?
  = *was hältst du von*
- **How would you feel about** taking calcium supplements?
  = *was halten Sie von*
- I was thinking of going for a drink later. **How about it?**
  = *wie wäre das*
- **What would you say to** a trip up to town next week?
  = *was würden Sie zu ... sagen*
- **Would you like to** stay in Paris for a couple of nights?
  = *möchten Sie*
- **Would you care to** have lunch with me?
  = *möchten Sie*
- **What if** you try ignoring her and see if that stops her complaining?
  = *und wenn*
- What you need is a change of scene. **Why not** go on a cruise?
  = *warum nicht*
- **Suppose** *oder* **Supposing** you left the kids with your mother for a few days?
  = *angenommen*
- **Have you ever thought of** starting up a magazine of your own?
  = *haben Sie schon mal daran gedacht*

28.2 Vorschläge erbitten

- **What would you do if you were me?**
  = *was würden Sie an meiner Stelle tun*
- **Have you any idea how I should** go about it to get the best results?
  = *haben Sie vielleicht eine Vorstellung, wie ich ... könnte*
- I've no idea what to call our new puppy: **have you any suggestions?**
  = *haben Sie vielleicht einen Vorschlag*
- **I wonder if you could suggest** where we might go for a few days?
  = *haben Sie vielleicht einen Vorschlag*
- I can only afford to buy one of them: **which do you suggest?**
  = *welchen würden Sie vorschlagen*
- **I'm a bit doubtful about** where to start
  = *ich weiß nicht genau*

29 RATSCHLÄGE

29.1 Ratschläge erbitten

- What would you do **if you were me?**
  = *an meiner Stelle*
- Would a pear tree grow in this spot? If not, **what would you recommend?**
  = *was würden Sie empfehlen*
- **Do you think I ought to** tell the truth if he asks me where I've been?
  = *denken Sie, ich sollte*
- **Would you advise me to** seek promotion within this firm or apply for another job?
  = *meinen Sie, ich sollte*
- **What would you advise me to do** in the circumstances?
  = *was würden Sie mir raten*
- **I'd like** *oder* **I'd appreciate your advice on** personal pensions
  = *ich würde Sie gern um Rat fragen*
- **I'd be grateful if you could advise me on** how to treat this problem
  = *ich wäre Ihnen sehr dankbar wenn Sie mir raten könnten*

29.2 Rat geben

- **It might be wise** *oder* **sensible to** consult a specialist
  = *es wäre vielleicht das Vernünftigste*

- **It might be a good idea to** seek professional advice
  = *es wäre vielleicht gut*
- **It might be better to** think the whole thing over before taking any decisions
  = *es wäre vielleicht besser*
- **It would certainly be advisable to** book a table
  = *es wäre sicherlich besser*
- **You'd be as well to** state your position at the outset, so there is no mistake
  = *am besten sollten Sie vielleicht*
- **You would be well-advised to** invest in a pair of sunglasses if you're going to Spain
  = *Sie wären gut beraten, wenn Sie*
- **You'd be ill-advised to** have any dealings with this firm
  = *Sie wären schlecht beraten, wenn Sie*
- **It is in your interest** *oder* **your best interests to** keep your dog under control if you don't want it to be reported
  = *es wäre ganz in Ihrem Interesse*
- **Do be sure to** read the small print before you sign anything
  = *auf jeden Fall sollten Sie*
- **Try to avoid** upsetting her; she'll only make your life a misery
  = *vermeiden Sie*
- **Whatever you do, don't** drink the local schnapps
  = *was auch immer Sie vorhaben, Sie sollten nie*
- **If you ask me, you'd better** take some extra cash
  = *wenn Sie mich fragen, Sie sollten besser*
- **If you want my advice, you should** steer well clear of them
  = *wenn Sie mich um Rat fragen, Sie sollten*
- **If you want my opinion, I'd** go by air to save time
  = *meiner Meinung nach sollten Sie*
- **In your shoes** *oder* **If I were you, I'd** be thinking about moving on
  = *an Ihrer Stelle würde ich*
- **Might I be allowed to offer a little advice?** - talk it over with a solicitor before going any further
  = *dürfte ich Ihnen einen Rat geben*
- **Take my advice** and don't rush into anything
  = *nehmen Sie meinen Ratschlag an*
- **I'd be very careful not to** commit myself at this stage
  = *ich würde mich davor hüten*
- **I think you ought to** *oder* **should** seek professional advice
  = *ich denke, Sie sollten*
- **My advice would be to** have nothing to do with them
  = *ich würde Ihnen raten*
- **I would advise you to** pay up promptly before they take you to court
  = *ich würde Ihnen raten*
- **I would advise against** calling in the police unless he threatens you
  = *ich würde Ihnen davon abraten, zu*
- **I would strongly advise you to** reconsider this decision
  = *ich würde Ihnen dringend anraten*
- **I would urge you to** reconsider selling the property
  = *Sie sollten unbedingt*

29.3 Warnende Hinweise

- It's really none of my business but **I don't think you should** get involved
  = *ich denke, Sie sollten nicht*
- **A word of caution**: watch what you say to him if you want it to remain a secret
  = *ein warnender Hinweis*
- **I should warn you that** he's not an easy customer to deal with
  = *ich sollte Sie vielleicht warnen, dass*
- **Take care not to** lose the vaccination certificate
  = *achten Sie darauf, dass Sie nicht*
- **Watch you don't** trip over your shoelaces
  = *pass auf, dass du nicht*
- **Make sure that** *oder* **Mind that** *oder* **See that you don't** say anything they might find offensive
  = *auf keinen Fall sollten Sie*
- **I'd think twice about** sharing a flat with him
  = *ich würde es mir gut überlegen, ob*
- **It would be sheer madness to** attempt to drive without your glasses
  = *es wäre reiner Wahnsinn*
- **You risk** a long delay in Amsterdam **if** you come back by that route
  = *Sie riskieren ..., wenn*

30 ANGEBOTE

- **I would be delighted to** help out, if I may
  = *ich würde sehr gerne*
- **It would give me great pleasure to** show you round the city
  = *ich würde sehr gerne*
- **We would like to offer you** the post of Sales Director
  = *wir möchten Ihnen ... anbieten*
- **I hope you will not be offended if I offer** a contribution towards your expenses
  = *ich hoffe, Sie nehmen es mir nicht übel, wenn ich*
- **Do let me know if I can** help in any way
  = *lassen Sie es mich wissen, wenn ich ... kann*
- **If we can** be of any further assistance, **please do not hesitate to** contact us
  = *falls wir ... können, zögern Sie bitte nicht*
- **Say we were to** offer you a 5% rise, **how would that sound?**
  = *und wenn wir ... wie wäre das*
- **What if I were to** call for you in the car?
  = *was halten Sie davon, wenn ich*
- **Could I** give you a hand with your luggage?
  = *kann ich vielleicht*
- **Shall I** do the photocopies for you?
  = *soll ich*
- **Would you like me to** find out more about it for you?
  = *soll ich*
- **Is there anything I can do to** help you find suitable accommodation?
  = *kann ich irgendetwas tun, um*
- **May** *oder* **Can I offer you** a drink?
  = *darf ich Ihnen ... anbieten*
- **Would you allow me to** pay for dinner, at least?
  = *würden Sie mir gestatten*
- **You will let me** show you around Glasgow, **won't you**?
  = *Sie werden es mir doch nicht abschlagen*

31 BITTEN

- **Please would you** drop by on your way home and pick up the papers you left here?
  = *würden Sie bitte*
- **Could you please** try to keep the noise down while I'm studying?
  = *könnten Sie bitte*
- **Could I ask you to** watch out for anything suspicious in my absence?
  = *könnte ich Sie bitten*
- **Would you mind** looking after Hannah for a couple of hours tomorrow?
  = *würde es Ihnen etwas ausmachen*

Förmlicher

- **I should be grateful if you could** confirm whether it would be possible to increase my credit limit to £5000
  = *ich wäre Ihnen dankbar, wenn Sie ... könnten*

- **We would ask you not to** use the telephone for long-distance calls
  = *wir möchten Sie darum bitten*
- **You are requested to** park at the rear of the building
  = *wir möchten Sie bitten*
- **We look forward to** receiving confirmation of your order within 14 days
  = *wir freuen uns darauf*
- **Kindly inform us if** you require alternative arrangements to be made
  = *bitte teilen Sie uns mit, wenn*

Weniger direkt

- **I would rather you didn't** breathe a word to anyone about this
  = *es wäre mir lieber, wenn Sie nicht*
- **I would appreciate it if you could** let me have copies of the best photos
  = *es wäre schön, wenn Sie ... könnten*
- **I was hoping that you might** have time to visit your grandmother
  = *ich hatte gehofft, du würdest vielleicht*
- **I wonder whether you could** spare a few pounds till I get to the bank?
  = *könntest du vielleicht*
- **I hope you don't mind if I** borrow your exercise bike for half an hour
  = *hoffentlich macht es dir nichts aus, wenn ich*
- **It would be very helpful** *oder* **useful if you could** have everything ready beforehand
  = *es wäre sehr zu begrüßen, wenn Sie ... könnten*
- **If it's not too much trouble, would you** pop my suit into the dry cleaner's on your way past?
  = *wenn es nicht zu viel Umstände macht, würden Sie*
- **You won't forget** to lock up before you leave, **will you?**
  = *vergiss nicht ..., ja*

32 VERGLEICHE

32.1 Objektive Vergleiche

- The streets, though wide for China, are narrow **compared with** English ones
  = *verglichen mit*
- The bomb used to blow the car up was small **in** oder **by comparison with** those often used nowadays
  = *im Vergleich zu*
- The quality of the paintings is disappointing **beside** that of the sculpture section
  = *im Vergleich zu*
- **If you compare** the facilities we have here **with** those in other towns, you soon realize how lucky we are
  = *wenn man ... mit ... vergleicht*
- It is interesting to note **the similarities and the differences between** the two approaches
  = *die Gemeinsamkeiten und Unterschiede zwischen*
- **In contrast to** the opulence of the Kirov, the Northern Ballet is a modest company
  = *im Gegensatz zu*
- Only 30% of the females died **as opposed to** 57% of the males
  = *im Gegensatz zu*
- **Unlike** other loan repayments, those to the IMF cannot simply be rescheduled
  = *im Gegensatz zu*
- **Whereas** burglars often used to make off only with video recorders, they now also tend to empty the fridge
  = *während*
- **What differentiates** these wines **from** a good champagne is their price
  = *was ... von ... unterscheidet*

32.2 Positive Vergleiche

- Orwell was, indeed, **far superior to** him intellectually
  = *wesentlich besser als*
- Personally I think high-speed trains **have the edge over** both cars and aircraft for sheer convenience
  = *sind ... überlegen*
- Emma was astute beyond her years and altogether **in a class of her own**
  = *einzigartig*

32.3 Negative Vergleiche

- Andrew's piano playing **is not a patch on** his sister's
  = *ist gar nichts verglichen mit*
- My old chair **was nowhere near as** comfortable **as** my new one
  = *war in keiner Hinsicht so .. wie*
- The parliamentary opposition **is no match for** the government, which has a massive majority
  = *ist .. nicht gewachsen*
- Commercially-made ice-cream **is far inferior to** the home-made variety
  = *ist viel schlechter als*
- The sad truth was that **he was never in the same class as** his friend
  = *er war einfach nicht mit ... zu vergleichen*
- Ella doesn't rate anything **that doesn't measure up to** Shakespeare
  = *das nicht an ... heranreicht*
- Her brash charms **don't bear comparison with** Marlene's sultry sex appeal
  = *halten einem Vergleich mit ... nicht stand*
- The Australians are far bigger and stronger than us - **we can't compete with** their robot-like style of play
  = *wir können mit ... nicht mithalten*

32.4 Vergleichbar

- The new computerized system costs **much the same as** a more conventional one
  = *fast dasselbe*
- When it comes to performance, **there's not much to choose between** them
  = *gibt es kaum Unterschiede zwischen*
- The impact **was equivalent to** 250 hydrogen bombs exploding
  = *entsprach*
- In Kleinian analysis, the psychoanalyst's role **corresponds to** that of mother
  = *entspricht*
- English literature written by people of the ex-colonies **is on a par with** the writings of native-born British people
  = *ist genauso gut wie*
- The immune system **can be likened to** *oder* **compared to** a complicated electronic network
  = *kann mit ... verglichen werden*
- **There was a close resemblance between** her **and** her son
  = *... und ... waren sich sehr ähnlich*
- **It's swings and roundabouts** - what you win in one round, you lose in another
  = *das ist gehupft wie gesprungen*

32.5 Nicht vergleichbar

- **You cannot compare** a small local library **with** a large city one
  = *man kann .. nicht mit ... vergleichen*
- **There's no comparison between** the sort of photos I take **and** those a professional could give you
  = *... und ... kann man einfach nicht miteinander vergleichen*
- Home-made clothes **just cannot compare with** bought ones
  = *sind eben nicht mit ... vergleichbar*
- His books **have little in common with** those approved by the Party
  = *haben wenig mit ... gemein*

- We might be twins, but **we have nothing in common**
  = *wir haben nichts gemein*
- The modern army **bears little resemblance to** the army of 1940
  = *hat kaum mehr Ähnlichkeit mit*

33 MEINUNGEN

33.1 Meinungen erfragen

- **What do you think of** the new Managing Director?
  = *was halten Sie von*
- **What is your opinion on** women's rights?
  = *wie denken Sie über*
- **What are your thoughts on** the way forward?
  = *wie ist Ihre Meinung zu*
- **What is your attitude to** people who say there is no such thing as sexual inequality?
  = *wie stehen Sie zu*
- **What are your own feelings about** the way the case was handled?
  = *was halten Sie persönlich von*
- **How do you see** the next stage developing?
  = *wie sehen Sie*
- **How do you view** an event like the Birmingham show in terms of the cultural life of the city?
  = *wie schätzen Sie ... ein*
- **I would value your opinion on** how to set this all up
  = *mir wäre sehr an Ihrer Meinung über ... gelegen*
- **I'd be interested to know what your reaction is to** the latest report on food additives
  = *ich wüsste gern, was Sie von ... halten*

33.2 Seine Meinung sagen

- **In my opinion**, eight years as President is quite enough for anyone
  = *meiner Meinung nach*
- We're prepared to prosecute the company, which **to my mind** has committed a criminal offence
  = *meiner Meinung nach*
- **From my point of view** activities like these should not be illegal
  = *aus meiner Sicht*
- **I am of the opinion that** the rules should be looked at and refined
  = *ich bin der Meinung, dass*
- **As I see it**, everything depended on Karlov being permitted to go to Finland
  = *so wie ich die Sache sehe*
- **I feel that** there is an epidemic of fear about cancer which is not helped by all the publicity about the people who die of it
  = *ich persönlich denke, dass*
- **Personally, I believe** the best way to change a government is through the electoral process
  = *persönlich glaube ich*
- **It seems to me that** the successful designer leads the public
  = *mir scheint, (dass)*
- **I am under the impression that** he is essentially a man of peace
  = *ich habe den Eindruck, dass*
- **I have an idea that** you are going to be very successful
  = *ich kann mir vorstellen, dass*
- **I'm convinced that** we all need a new vision of the future
  = *ich bin überzeugt, dass*
- **I daresay** there are so many names that you get them mixed up once in a while
  = *ich würde sagen*
- **As far as I'm concerned**, Barnes had it coming to him
  = *was mich betrifft*
- It's a matter of common sense, nothing more. **That's my view of the matter**
  = *so sehe ich die Sache*
- **It is our belief that** to be proactive is more positive than being reactive
  = *wir glauben, dass*
- **If you ask me**, there's something a bit strange going on
  = *wenn Sie mich fragen*
- **If you want my opinion**, if you don't do it soon you'll lose the opportunity altogether
  = *wenn Sie meine Meinung hören wollen*

33.3 Keine Meinung zum Ausdruck bringen

- Would I say she had been a help? **It depends what you mean by** help
  = *das hängt davon ab, was Sie unter ... verstehen*
- It could be seen as a triumph for capitalism but **it depends on your point of view**
  = *das hängt von Ihrer Meinung ab*
- **It's hard** *oder* **difficult to say whether** she has benefited from the treatment or not
  = *es ist schwer zu sagen, ob*
- **I'm not in a position to comment on whether** the director's accusations are well-founded
  = *ich kann mich nicht dazu äußern, ob*
- **I'd prefer not to comment on** operational decisions taken by the service in the past
  = *ich möchte mich lieber nicht zu ... äußern*
- **I'd rather not commit myself** at this stage
  = *ich möchte mich lieber nicht festlegen*
- **I don't have any strong feelings about** which of the two companies we decide to use for the job
  = *ich habe eigentlich keine besondere Meinung über*
- **This isn't something I've given much thought to**
  = *damit habe ich mich noch nicht eingehend beschäftigt*
- **I know nothing about** fine wine
  = *ich habe keine Ahnung von*

34 VORLIEBEN UND ABNEIGUNGEN

34.1 Vorlieben erfragen

- **Would you like to** visit the castle while you are here?
  = *möchten Sie*
- **How would you feel about** Simon join**ing** us?
  = *was halten Sie davon, wenn*
- **What do you like doing best** when you're on holiday?
  = *was machen Sie am liebsten*
- **What's your favourite** film?
  = *was ist Ihr Lieblings ...*
- **Which of the two** proposed options **do you prefer?**
  = *welche der beiden ... ist Ihnen lieber*
- We could either go to Rome or stay in Florence - **which would you rather do?**
  = *was würden Sie lieber tun*

34.2 Vorlieben ausdrücken

- **I'm very keen on** garden**ing**
  = *ich ... sehr gerne*
- **I'm very fond of** white geraniums and blue petunias
  = *ich mag ... sehr*
- **I really enjoy** a good game of squash after work
  = *... macht mir sehr viel Spaß*
- **There's nothing I like more than** a quiet night in with a good book
  = *nichts mag ich lieber als*
- **I have a weakness for** rich chocolate gateaux
  = *ich habe eine Schwäche für*
- **I've always had a soft spot for** the Dutch
  = *ich habe schon immer eine Schwäche für ... gehabt*

34.3 Abneigung ausdrücken

- Acting **isn't really my thing** - I'm better at singing
  = *ist nichts für mich*

- I enjoy playing golf, although this type of course **is not my cup of tea**
  = *ist nicht mein Fall*
- Watching football on television **isn't exactly my favourite** pastime
  = *ist nicht gerade meine Lieblings...*
- Some people might find it funny but **it's not my kind of** humour
  = *ist nicht meine Art von*
- Sitting for hours on motorways **is not my idea of** fun
  = *ist nicht gerade das, was ich mir unter ... vorstelle*
- The idea of walking home at 10 or 11 o'clock at night **doesn't appeal to me**
  = *gefällt mir nicht*
- **I've gone off the idea of** cycling round Holland
  = *ich habe das Interesse daran verloren*
- **I can't stand** *oder* **can't bear** the thought of seeing him
  = *ich kann ... nicht ertragen*
- **I'm not enthusiastic about** shopping in large supermarkets
  = *ich bin nicht gerade begeistert von*
- **I'm not keen on** seafood
  = *ich mag ... nicht*
- **I dislike** laziness since I'm such an energetic person myself
  = *ich mag ... nicht*
- **I don't like the fact that** he always gets away with not helping out in the kitchen
  = *mir gefällt nicht, dass*
- **What I hate most is** waiting in queues for buses
  = *am meisten hasse ich*
- **There's nothing I dislike more than** having to go to work in the dark
  = *nichts hasse ich mehr als*
- **I have a particular aversion to** the religious indoctrination of schoolchildren
  = *besonders abstoßend finde ich*
- **I find it intolerable that** people like him should have so much power
  = *ich finde es unerträglich, dass*

34.4 Ausdrücken, was man bevorzugt

- **I'd prefer to** *oder* **I'd rather** wait until I have enough money to go by air
  = *ich würde lieber*
- **I'd prefer not to** *oder* **I'd rather not** talk about it just now
  = *ich würde lieber nicht*
- **I'd prefer you to** give *oder* **I'd rather you** gave me your comments in writing
  = *es wäre mir lieber, wenn Sie*
- **I'd prefer you not to** *oder* **I'd rather you didn't** invite him
  = *es wäre mir lieber, wenn Sie nicht*
- **I like** the blue curtains **better than** the red ones
  = *... gefallen mir besser als*
- **I prefer** red wine **to** white wine
  = *ich mag lieber ... als ...*

34.5 Keine Vorliebe ausdrücken

- **It makes no odds whether** you have a million pounds or nothing, we won't judge you on your wealth
  = *es ist ganz egal, ob*
- **It doesn't matter which** method you choose to use
  = *es ist egal, welche*
- **It's all the same to me whether** he comes **or** not
  = *es ist mir vollkommen egal, ob ... oder*
- **I really don't care what** you tell her as long as you tell her something
  = *es kümmert mich wirklich nicht, was*
- **I don't mind at all** - let's do whatever is easiest
  = *das macht mir gar nichts aus*
- **I don't feel strongly about** the issue of privatization
  = *ich habe keine besondere Meinung über*
- **I have no particular preference**
  = *ich habe keine spezielle Vorliebe*

35 ABSICHTEN UND VORHABEN

35.1 Nach Absichten fragen

- **Will you** take the job?
  = *haben Sie vor*
- **What do you intend to do?**
  = *was beabsichtigen Sie zu tun*
- **Did you mean to** *oder* **intend to** tell him about it, or did it just slip out?
  = *hatten Sie die Absicht*
- **What do you propose to do** with the money?
  = *was wollen Sie ... machen*
- **What did you have in mind for** the rest of the programme?
  = *wie hatten Sie sich ...vorgestellt*
- **Have you anyone in mind for** the job?
  = *haben Sie jemanden Bestimmten für ... ins Auge gefasst*

35.2 Absichten ausdrücken

- **We're toying with the idea of** releasing a compilation album
  = *wir spielen mit dem Gedanken*
- **I'm thinking of** retiring next year
  = *ich trage mich mit dem Gedanken*
- **I'm hoping to** go and see her when I'm in Paris
  = *ich habe eigentlich vor*
- I studied history, **with a view to** becoming a politician
  = *mit der Absicht*
- We bought the land **in order to** farm it
  = *um zu*
- We do not penetrate foreign companies **for the purpose of** collecting business information
  = *um zu*
- **We plan to** move *oder* **We are planning on** moving next year
  = *wir planen*
- **Our aim** *oder* **Our object in** buying the company **is to** provide work for the villagers
  = *unsere Absicht bei ... besteht darin*
- **I aim to** reach Africa in three months
  = *ich habe mir vorgenommen*

Bestimmter

- **I am going to** sell the car as soon as possible
  = *ich habe vor*
- **I intend to** put the house on the market
  = *ich beabsichtige*
- I went to Rome **with the intention of** visiting her, but she had gone away
  = *mit der Absicht*
- **I have made up my mind to** *oder* **I have decided to** go to Japan
  = *ich habe mich entschieden*
- **We have every intention of** winning a sixth successive championship
  = *wir sind fest entschlossen*
- **I have set my sights on** recapturing the title
  = *ich habe mir das Ziel gesteckt*
- **My overriding ambition is to** get into politics
  = *mein allergrößter Ehrgeiz ist es*
- **I resolve to** do everything in my power to help you
  = *ich habe beschlossen*

35.3 Ausdrücken, was man nicht beabsichtigt

- **I don't mean to** offend you, but I think you're wrong
  = *ich möchte nicht*
- **I don't intend to** pay unless he completes the job
  = *ich habe nicht vor*
- **We are not thinking of** taking on more staff
  = *wir haben nicht vor*
- **I have no intention of** accepting the post
  = *ich habe nicht die Absicht*
- **We do not envisage** making changes at this late stage
  = *wir gedenken nicht*

35.4 Wünsche ausdrücken

- **I'd like to** see the Sistine Chapel some day
  = *ich würde gerne*
- **I want to** work abroad when I leave college
  = *ich möchte*
- **We want her to** be an architect when she grows up
  = *wir möchten, dass sie*
- **I'm keen to** develop the business
  = *ich möchte gerne*

Enthusiastisch

- **I'm dying to** leave home
  = *ich kann es kaum erwarten*
- **I long to** go to Australia but I can't afford it
  = *ich würde wahnsinnig gerne*
- **My ambition is to** become an opera singer
  = *mein Ehrgeiz geht dahin*
- **I insist on** speaking to the manager
  = *ich bestehe darauf*

35.5 Ausdrücken, was man nicht wünscht

- **I would prefer not to** *oder* **I would rather not** have to speak to her about this
  = *ich würde lieber nicht*
- **I wouldn't want to** have to change my plans just because of her
  = *ich möchte nicht*
- **I don't want to** take the credit for something I didn't do
  = *ich möchte nicht*
- **I have no wish** *oder* **desire to** become rich and famous
  = *ich habe nicht das Verlangen*
- **I refuse to** be patronized by the likes of her
  = *ich lehne es ab*

36 ERLAUBNIS

36.1 Um Erlaubnis bitten

- **Can I** *oder* **Could I** borrow your car this afternoon?
  = *kann ich vielleicht*
- **Can I** use the telephone, please?
  = *könnte ich*
- **Are we allowed to** say what we're up to or is it top secret at the moment?
  = *dürfen wir*
- **Would it be all right if** I arrived on Monday instead of Tuesday?
  = *wäre es in Ordnung, wenn*
- **Would it be possible for us to** leave the car in your garage for a week?
  = *wäre es möglich, dass wir*
- We leave tomorrow. **Is that all right by you?**
  = *ist das in Ordnung*
- **Do you mind if** I come to the meeting next week?
  = *haben Sie etwas dagegen, wenn*
- **Would it bother you if** I invited him?
  = *würde es Sie stören, wenn*
- **Would you let me** come into partnership with you?
  = *würden Sie mir gestatten*
- **Would you have any objection to** sailing at once?
  = *haben Sie irgendwelche Einwände dagegen*
- **With your permission, I'd like to** ask some questions
  = *mit Ihrer Erlaubnis würde ich gerne*
- **Can I have the go-ahead to** order the supplies?
  = *kann ich grünes Licht bekommen*

Zögernder

- **Is there any chance of** borrowing your boat while we're at the lake?
  = *wäre es vielleicht möglich*
- **I wonder if I could possibly** use your telephone?
  = *könnte ich vielleicht*
- **Might I be permitted to** suggest the following ideas?
  = *dürfte ich vielleicht*
- **May I be allowed to** set the record straight?
  = *dürfte ich vielleicht*

36.2 Erlaubnis erteilen

- **You can** have anything you want
  = *Sie können*
- **You are allowed to** visit the museum, as long as you apply in writing to the Curator first
  = *Sie haben die Erlaubnis*
- **You have my permission to** be absent for that week
  = *Sie haben meine Erlaubnis*
- **It's all right by me if** you want to skip the Cathedral visit
  = *es ist mir recht, wenn*
- **I've nothing against her** going there with us
  = *ich habe nichts dagegen, wenn sie*
- The Crown **was agreeable to** having the case called on March 23
  = *hat zugestimmt*
- **I do not mind if** my letter is forwarded to the lady concerned
  = *ich habe nichts dagegen, wenn*
- **You have been authorized to** use all necessary force to protect relief supply routes
  = *Sie sind bevollmächtigt*
- **We should be happy to allow you to** inspect the papers here
  = *gerne gestatten wir Ihnen*
- If you need to keep your secret, **of course you must** keep it
  = *müssen Sie selbstverständlich*
- **By all means** charge a reasonable consultation fee
  = *auf jeden Fall*
- **I have no objection at all to your** quoting me in your article
  = *ich erhebe keinerlei Einwände dagegen, dass Sie*
- **We would be delighted to** have you
  = *wir würden sehr gerne*

36.3 Erlaubnis verweigern

- **You can't** *oder* **you mustn't** go anywhere near the research lab
  = *Sie dürfen nicht*
- **You're not allowed to** leave the ship until relieved
  = *Sie dürfen nicht*
- **You must not** enter the premises without the owners' authority
  = *Sie dürfen auf keinen Fall*
- **I don't want you to** see that man again
  = *ich möchte nicht, dass Sie*
- **I'd rather you didn't** give them my name
  = *es wäre mir lieber, wenn Sie nicht*
- **I've been forbidden to** swim for the moment
  = *ich darf nicht*

- **I've been forbidden** alcohol **by** my doctor
  = *... hat mir verboten*
- **I couldn't possibly allow you to** pay for all this
  = *ich kann Ihnen beim besten Willen nicht erlauben*
- **We cannot allow** the marriage **to** take place
  = *wir können nicht zulassen, dass*

Bestimmter

- **You are forbidden to** contact my children
  = *ich verbiete es Ihnen*
- **I absolutely forbid you to** take part in any further search
  = *ich verbiete Ihnen strengstens*
- Smoking **is strictly forbidden** at all times
  = *ist streng verboten*
- **It is strictly forbidden to** carry weapons in this country
  = *es ist streng verboten*
- **We regret that it is not possible for you to** visit the castle at the moment, owing to the building works
  = *leider können Sie nicht*

37 VERPFLICHTUNG

37.1 Verpflichtung ausdrücken

- **You've got to** *oder* **You have to** be back before midnight
  = *du musst*
- **You must** have an address in Prague before you can apply for the job
  = *Sie müssen*
- **You need to** have a valid passport if you want to leave the country
  = *Sie müssen*
- I have no choice: this is how **I must** live and I cannot do otherwise
  = *ich muss*
- **He was forced to** ask his family for a loan
  = *er war gezwungen*
- Jews **are obliged to** accept the divine origin of the Law
  = *sind verpflichtet*
- A degree **is indispensable** for future entrants to the profession
  = *ist unentbehrlich*
- Party membership **is an essential prerequisite of** a successful career
  = *ist eine unbedingte Voraussetzung für*
- **It is essential to** know what the career options are before choosing a course of study
  = *man muss unbedingt*
- Wearing the kilt **is compulsory** for all those taking part
  = *ist obligatorisch*
- One cannot admit defeat, **one is driven to** keep on trying
  = *man wird dazu gezwungen*
- **We have no alternative but to** fight
  = *es bleibt uns nichts anderes übrig als zu*
- Three passport photos **are required**
  = *werden benötigt*
- Club members **must not fail to** observe the regulations about proper behaviour
  = *müssen unbedingt*
- **You will** go directly to the headmaster's office and wait for me there
  = *du wirst*

37.2 Erfragen, ob man etwas tun muss

- **Do I have to** *oder* **Have I got to** be home by midnight?
  = *muss ich*
- **Does one have to** *oder* **need to** book in advance?
  = *muss man*
- **Is it necessary to** go into so much detail?
  = *ist es nötig*
- **Ought I to** tell my colleagues?
  = *sollte ich*
- **Should I** call the police?
  = *soll ich*
- **Am I meant to** *oder* **Am I expected to** *oder* **Am I supposed to** fill in this bit of the form?
  = *soll ich*

37.3 Ausdrücken, was keine Verpflichtung ist

- **I don't have to** *oder* **I haven't got to** be home so early now the nights are lighter
  = *ich muss nicht unbedingt*
- **You don't have to** *oder* **You needn't** go there if you don't want to
  = *Sie müssen nicht*
- **You are not obliged to** *oder* **You are under no obligation to** invite him
  = *Sie sind nicht verpflichtet*
- **It is not compulsory** *oder* **obligatory to** have a letter of acceptance but it does help
  = *es ist nicht unbedingt notwendig*
- The Council **does not expect you to** pay all of your bill at once
  = *erwartet nicht von Ihnen, dass*

37.4 Verbote ausdrücken

- **On no account must you** be persuaded to give up the cause
  = *auf gar keinen Fall dürfen Sie*
- **You are not allowed to** sit the exam more than three times
  = *Sie dürfen nicht*
- **You mustn't** show this document to any unauthorized person
  = *Sie dürfen nicht*
- **You're not supposed to** *oder* **meant to** use this room unless you are a club member
  = *Sie dürfen nicht*
- Smoking **is not allowed** in the dining room
  = *ist nicht gestattet*
- These are tasks **you cannot** ignore, delegate or bungle
  = *Sie können nicht*
- **I forbid you to** return there
  = *ich verbiete Ihnen*
- **It is forbidden to** bring cameras into the gallery
  = *es ist nicht gestattet*
- **You are forbidden to** talk to anyone while the case is being heard
  = *es ist Ihnen nicht gestattet*
- Smoking **is prohibited** *oder* **is not permitted** in the dining room
  = *ist nicht gestattet*

38 ZUSTIMMUNG

38.1 Zustimmung zu Aussagen

- **I fully agree with you** *oder* **I totally agree with you** on this point
  = *ich bin ganz Ihrer Meinung*
- **We are in complete agreement** on this
  = *wir sind uns völlig einig*
- **I entirely take your point about** the extra vehicles needed
  = *ich akzeptiere Ihre Meinung vollkommen, was ... betrifft*
- I think **we see completely eye to eye** on this issue
  = *wir sind uns einig*
- I talked it over with the chairman and **we are both of the same mind**
  = *wir sind beide der gleichen Meinung*
- **You're quite right in** pointing at distribution as the main problem
  = *Sie haben recht, wenn Sie*
- **We share your views** on the proposed expansion of the site
  = *wir teilen Ihre Ansichten*

- **My own experience** certainly **bears out** *oder* **confirms** what you say
  = *meine eigene Erfahrung bestätigt*
- **It's true that** you had the original idea but many other people worked on it
  = *es stimmt, dass*
- **As you have quite rightly pointed out**, this will not be easy
  = *wie Sie bereits richtig bemerkten*
- **I have to concede that** the results are quite eye-catching
  = *ich muss gestehen, dass*
- **I have no objection to** this being done
  = *ich habe keine Einwände gegen*
- **I agree in theory**, but in practice it's never quite that simple
  = *theoretisch stimme ich zu*
- **I agree up to a point**
  = *bis zu einem gewissen Punkt stimme ich zu*
- Go for a drink instead of working late? **Sounds good to me!**
  = *klingt gut*
- **That's a lovely idea**
  = *das ist eine sehr gute Idee*
- **I'm all for** encourag**ing** a youth section in video clubs such as ours
  = *ich bin ganz dafür*
- **I couldn't agree with you more**
  = *ich bin völlig Ihrer Meinung*
- **I am delighted to wholeheartedly endorse** your campaign
  = *es ist mir eine Freude, ... von ganzem Herzen zu unterstützen*
- **Our conclusions are entirely consistent with** your findings
  = *unsere Schlussfolgerungen entsprechen vollkommen*
- Independent statistics **corroborate** those of your researcher
  = *bestätigen*
- **We applaud** the group's decision to stand firm on this point
  = *wir begrüßen*

38.2 Zustimmung zu Vorschlägen

- This certainly **seems the right way to go about it**
  = *scheint der richtige Verfahrensweg*
- **I will certainly give my backing to** such a scheme
  = *ich werde ... selbstverständlich unterstützen*
- **It makes sense to** enlist helping hands for the final stages
  = *es macht Sinn*
- **We certainly welcome** this development
  = *selbstverständlich begrüßen wir*
- **It's a great idea**
  = *das ist eine großartige Idee*
- Cruise control? **I like the sound of that**
  = *klingt wirklich gut*
- **I'll go along with** Ted's proposal that we open the club up to women
  = *ich schließe mich ... an*

Weniger direkt

- This solution **is most acceptable** to us
  = *ist sehr annehmbar*
- The proposed scheme **meets with our approval**
  = *trifft auf unsere Zustimmung*
- This is a proposal which **deserves our wholehearted support**
  = *verdient unsere uneingeschränkte Unterstützung*

38.3 Zustimmung zu Forderungen

- Of course **I'll be happy to** organize it for you
  = *werde ich gerne*
- **I'll do as you suggest** and send him the documents
  = *ich befolge Ihren Rat*
- **There's no problem about** getting tickets for him
  = *es ist kein Problem*

Weniger direkt

- Reputable builders **will not object to** this reasonable request
  = *werden ... nicht ablehnen*
- **We should be delighted to** cooperate with you in this enterprise
  = *wir würden uns freuen*
- An army statement said it **would comply with** the ceasefire
  = *sich an ... halten*
- **I consent to** the performance of such procedures as are considered necessary
  = *ich stimme ... zu*

39 WIDERSPRUCH

39.1 Widerspruch zu Gesagtem

- There must be some mistake - **it can't possibly** cost as much as that
  = *es kann auf gar keinen Fall*
- I'm afraid he **is quite wrong** if he has told you that
  = *irrt sich*
- **You're wrong in thinking that** I haven't understood
  = *Sie irren sich, wenn Sie denken*
- The article **is mistaken in** claim**ing** that debating the subject is a waste of public money
  = *geht falsch in der Annahme*
- Surveys **do not bear out** Mrs Fraser's assumption that these people will return to church at a later date
  = *bestätigen nicht*
- **I cannot agree with you** on this point
  = *ich kann Ihnen nicht zustimmen*
- **We cannot accept the view that** the lack of research and development explains the decline of Britain
  = *wir können die Ansicht, dass ..., nicht akzeptieren*
- To say we should forget about it, no, **I cannot go along with that**
  = *ich kann mich dem nicht anschließen*
- **We must agree to differ on this one**
  = *darüber sind wir wohl unterschiedlicher Meinung*

Bestimmter

- **This is most emphatically not the case**
  = *das ist auf gar keinen Fall so*
- **I entirely reject** his contentions
  = *ich lehne ... vollständig ab*
- **I totally disagree with** the previous two callers
  = *ich bin völlig anderer Meinung als*
- This is your view of the events: **it is certainly not mine**
  = *meine Ansicht ist das nicht*
- **I cannot support you** on this matter
  = *ich kann Sie ... nicht unterstützen*
- **Surely you can't believe that** he'd do such a thing?
  = *du kannst doch nicht wirklich glauben, dass*

39.2 Ablehnung von Vorschlägen

Bestimmt

- **I'm dead against** this idea
  = *ich bin völlig dagegen*
- **Right idea, wrong approach**
  = *ein guter Gedanke, aber er geht in die falsche Richtung*
- **I will not hear of** such a thing
  = *ich will von ... nichts hören*
- **It is not feasible to** change the schedule at this late stage
  = *es ist nicht möglich*
- This **is not a viable alternative**
  = *keine praktisch durchführbare Möglichkeit*

- Trade sanctions will have an immediate effect but it **is the wrong approach**
  = *ist die falsche Herangehensweise*

Weniger direkt

- **I'm not too keen on** this idea
  = *ich halte nicht viel von*
- **I don't think much of** this idea
  = *ich halte nicht viel von*
- **This doesn't seem to be the right way of** dealing with the problem
  = *dies scheint mir die falsche Methode zu sein*
- While we are grateful for the suggestion, **we are unfortunately unable to** implement this change
  = *leider ist es uns unmöglich*
- **I regret that I am not in a position to** accept your kind offer
  = *ich bedaure, dass ich nicht in der Lage bin*

39.3 Ablehnung von Forderungen

- **I wouldn't dream of** doing a thing like that
  = *es würde mir nicht im Traum einfallen*
- I'm sorry but **I just can't** do it
  = *ich kann das einfach nicht*
- **I cannot in all conscience** leave those kids in that atmosphere
  = *ich kann nicht guten Gewissens*

Bestimmt

- **This is quite out of the question** for the time being
  = *das steht ja wohl außer Frage*
- **I won't agree to** any plan that involves your brother
  = *ich werde ... nicht zustimmen*
- **I refuse point blank to** have anything to do with this affair
  = *ich weigere mich kategorisch*

Weniger direkt

- **I am afraid I must refuse**
  = *es tut mir leid, ich muss das ablehnen*
- **I cannot possibly comply with** this request
  = *ich kann ... wirklich nicht nachkommen*
- **It is unfortunately impracticable for us to** commit ourselves at this stage
  = *leider ist es uns unmöglich*
- In view of the proposed timescale, **I must reluctantly decline to** take part
  = *muss ich leider ablehnen*

40 ÜBEREINSTIMMUNG

40.1 Übereinstimmung mit Gesagtem

- **I couldn't agree** (with you) **more**
  = *ich stimme vollkommen zu*
- **I couldn't have put it better myself**
  = *ich hätte es selbst nicht besser sagen können*
- We must oppose terrorism, whatever its source - **Hear, hear!**
  = *ganz meine Meinung*
- **I endorse** his feelings regarding the condition of the Simpson memorial
  = *ich befürworte*

40.2 Übereinstimmung mit Vorschlägen

- **It's just the job!**
  = *das ist genau das Richtige*
- **This is just the sort of thing I wanted**
  = *das ist genau das, was ich wollte*
- **This is exactly what I had in mind**
  = *das ist genau das, was ich wollte*
- Thank you for sending the draft agenda: **I like the look of it very much**
  = *es gefällt mir sehr gut*
- **We are all very enthusiastic about** *oder* **very keen on** his latest set of proposals
  = *wir sind alle sehr begeistert von*
- **I shall certainly give it my backing**
  = *ich werde es auf jeden Fall befürworten*
- Any game which is as clearly enjoyable as this **meets with my approval**
  = *findet meine Zustimmung*
- Skinner's plan **deserves our total support** *oder* **our wholehearted approval**
  = *verdient unsere uneingeschränkte Zustimmung*
- **There are considerable advantages in** the alternative method you propose
  = *bietet entscheidende Vorteile*
- **We recognize the merits** of this scheme
  = *wir sehen die Vorzüge*
- **We view** your proposal to extend the site **favourably**
  = *wir betrachten ... mit Wohlwollen*
- This project **is worthy of our attention**
  = *verdient unsere Aufmerksamkeit*

40.3 Übereinstimmung mit einer Idee

- **You're quite right to** wait before making such an important decision
  = *Sie haben ganz recht, wenn Sie*
- **I entirely approve of** the idea
  = *ich finde ... sehr gut*
- **I'd certainly go along with that!**
  = *ich stimme dem auf jeden Fall zu*
- **I'm very much in favour of** that sort of thing
  = *ich bin sehr für*
- **What an excellent idea!**
  = *was für eine ausgezeichnete Idee*

40.4 Übereinstimmung mit einer Handlung

- **I applaud** Noble's perceptive analysis of the problems
  = *ich muss ... loben*
- **I have a very high opinion of** their new teaching methods
  = *ich habe eine sehr hohe Meinung von*
- **I think very highly of** the people who have been leading thus far
  = *ich habe eine sehr hohe Meinung von*
- **I have a very high regard for** the work of the Crown Prosecution Service
  = *ich habe großen Respekt vor*
- **I certainly admire** his courage in telling her what he thought of her
  = *ich bin voller Bewunderung für*
- **I must congratulate you on** the professional way you handled the situation
  = *ich muss Ihnen zu ... gratulieren*
- **I greatly appreciate** the enormous risk that they had all taken
  = *ich schätze ... sehr*
- **I can thoroughly recommend** the event to field sports enthusiasts
  = *ich kann ... von ganzem Herzen empfehlen*

41 ABLEHNUNG

- **This doesn't seem to be the right way of** going about it
  = *dies scheint nicht der richtige Weg zu sein*
- **I don't think much of** what this government has done so far
  = *ich halte nicht viel von*

- The police **took a dim view of** her attempt to help her son break out of jail
  = *hielt nicht viel von*
- **I can't say I'm pleased about** what has happened
  = *ich bin nicht gerade begeistert von*
- **We have a low** *oder* **poor opinion of** opportunists like him
  = *wir haben keine sehr hohe Meinung von*
- They **should not have refused to** give her the money
  = *hätten es nicht ablehnen sollen*

Bestimmter

- **I'm fed up with** having to wait so long for payments to be made
  = *ich habe es satt*
- **I've had (just) about enough of** this whole supermodel thing
  = *langsam reicht es mir mit*
- **I can't bear** *oder* **stand** people who smoke in restaurants
  = *ich kann ... nicht ausstehen*
- **How dare he** say that!
  = *was fällt ihm ein*
- **He was quite wrong to** repeat what I said about her
  = *es war nicht richtig von ihm*
- **I cannot approve of** *oder* **support** any sort of testing on live animals
  = *ich kann ... nicht zustimmen*
- **We are opposed to** all forms of professional malpractice
  = *wir sind gegen*
- **We condemn** any intervention which could damage race relations
  = *wir verurteilen*
- **I must object to** the tag "soft porn actress"
  = *ich muss ... zurückweisen*
- **I'm very unhappy about** your (idea of) going off to Turkey on your own
  = *ich bin gar nicht glücklich über*
- **I strongly disapprove of** such behaviour
  = *ich bin mit ... überhaupt nicht einverstanden*

42 GEWISSHEIT, WAHRSCHEINLICHKEIT, MÖGLICHKEIT UND FÄHIGKEIT

42.1 Gewissheit

- **She was bound to** discover that you and I had talked
  = *sie musste einfach*
- **It is inevitable that they** will get to know of our meeting
  = *es lässt sich nicht vermeiden, dass sie*
- **I'm sure** *oder* **certain (that)** he'll keep his word
  = *ich bin sicher, (dass)*
- **I'm positive** *oder* **convinced (that)** it was your mother I saw
  = *ich bin überzeugt, (dass)*
- **We now know for certain** *oder* **for sure that** the exam papers were seen by several students before the day of the exam
  = *wir können jetzt mit Sicherheit sagen, dass*
- **I made sure** *oder* **certain that** no one was listening to our conversation
  = *ich habe darauf geachtet, dass*
- From all the evidence **it is clear that** they were planning to sell up
  = *es ist klar, dass*
- **What is indisputable is that** a diet of fruit and vegetables is healthier
  = *es ist unbestreitbar, dass*
- **It is undeniable that** racial tensions in Britain have been increasing
  = *es lässt sich nicht leugnen, dass*
- **There is no doubt that** the talks will be long and difficult
  = *es steht außer Zweifel, dass*
- **There can be no doubt about** the objective of the animal liberationists
  = *... steht außer Zweifel*
- This crisis has demonstrated **beyond all (possible) doubt** that effective political control must be in place before the creation of such structures
  = *ohne (jeglichen) Zweifel*
- Her pedigree is **beyond dispute** *oder* **question**
  = *steht außer Frage*
- **You have my absolute assurance that** this is the case
  = *ich versichere Ihnen, dass*
- **I can assure you that** I have had nothing to do with any dishonest trading
  = *ich kann Ihnen versichern, dass*
- **Make no mistake about it** - I will return when I have proof of your involvement
  = *verlassen Sie sich darauf*

42.2 Wahrscheinlichkeit

- **It is quite likely that** you will get withdrawal symptoms at first
  = *wahrscheinlich*
- **There is a good** *oder* **strong chance that** they will agree to the deal
  = *höchstwahrscheinlich*
- **It seems highly likely that** it was Bert who told Peter what had happened
  = *höchstwahrscheinlich*
- You will **very probably** be met at the airport by one of our men
  = *höchstwahrscheinlich*
- **It is highly probable that** American companies will face retaliation abroad
  = *höchstwahrscheinlich*
- **The probability is that** your investment will be worth more in two years' time
  = *aller Wahrscheinlichkeit nach*
- The child's hearing will, **in all probability**, be severely affected
  = *aller Wahrscheinlichkeit nach*
- The person indicated is, **in all likelihood**, going to be guilty as charged
  = *aller Wahrscheinlichkeit nach*
- **The likelihood is that** the mood of mistrust and recrimination will intensify
  = *aller Wahrscheinlichkeit nach*
- **The chances** *oder* **the odds are that** he will play safe in the short term
  = *es könnte sehr wohl sein, dass*
- **There is reason to believe that** the books were stolen from the library
  = *es besteht Grund zu der Annahme, dass*
- **He must** know of the painting's existence
  = *er muss*
- The talks **could very well** spill over into tomorrow
  = *können gut und gerne*
- The cheque **should** reach you by Saturday
  = *müsste*
- **It wouldn't surprise me** *oder* **I wouldn't be surprised if** he was working for the Americans
  = *es sollte mich nicht überraschen, wenn*

42.3 Möglichkeit

- The situation **could** change from day to day
  = *kann*
- Britain **could perhaps** play a more positive role in developing policy
  = *könnte vielleicht*
- **It may be (the case) that** they got your name from the voters' roll
  = *möglicherweise*
- **It is possible that** psychological factors play some unknown role in the healing process
  = *es könnte sein, dass*
- **It may be that** the whole battle will have to be fought over again
  = *es könnte sein, dass*

- **It is conceivable that** the economy is already in recession
  = *es ist denkbar, dass*
- **It is well within the bounds of possibility that** England could be beaten
  = *es ist durchaus im Rahmen des Möglichen, dass*
- **I venture to suggest (that)** a lot of it is to do with his political ambitions
  = *ich wage zu behaupten, (dass)*
- **There is an outside chance that** the locomotive may appear in the Gala
  = *es könnte eventuell möglich sein, dass*
- **There is a small chance that** your body could reject the implants
  = *es besteht eine geringe Möglichkeit, dass*

42.4 Ausdruck von Fähigkeiten

- Our Design and Print Service **can** supply envelopes and package your existing literature
  = *kann*
- Applicants **must be able to** use a word processor
  = *müssen in der Lage sein*
- He **is qualified** to teach physics
  = *ist qualifiziert*

43 ZWEIFEL, UNWAHRSCHEINLICHKEIT, UNMÖGLICHKEIT UND UNFÄHIGKEIT

43.1 Zweifel

- **I doubt if** *oder* **It is doubtful whether** he knows where it came from
  = *ich bezweifle, dass*
- **There is still some doubt surrounding** his exact whereabouts
  = *man weiß immer noch nichts Genaues über*
- **I have my doubts about** replacing private donations with taxpayers' cash
  = *ich habe da so meine Zweifel an*
- **It isn't known for sure** *oder* **It isn't certain** where she is
  = *man weiß nicht genau*
- **No-one can say for sure** how any child will develop
  = *niemand kann mit Sicherheit sagen*
- It's still all up in the air - **we won't know for certain** until next week
  = *wir werden keine Gewissheit haben*
- You're asking why I should do such an extraordinary thing and **I'm not sure** *oder* **certain that** I really know the answer
  = *ich bin mir nicht sicher, dass*
- **I'm not convinced that** you can really teach people who don't want to learn
  = *ich bin nicht überzeugt, dass*
- **We are still in the dark about** where the letter came from
  = *wir tappen immer noch im Dunkeln über*
- How long this muddle can last **is anyone's guess**
  = *weiß niemand so recht*
- Sterling is going to come under further pressure. **It is touch and go whether** base rates will have to go up
  = *es steht auf des Messers Schneide, ob*
- **I'm wondering if** I should offer to help?
  = *vielleicht sollte ich*

43.2 Unwahrscheinlichkeit

- You have **probably not** yet seen the document I'm referring to
  = *wahrscheinlich nicht*
- **It is highly improbable that** there will be a challenge for the party leadership in the near future
  = *es ist höchst unwahrscheinlich, dass*
- **It is very doubtful whether** the expedition will reach the summit
  = *es bestehen starke Zweifel, ob*
- **In the unlikely event that** the room was bugged, the music would drown out their conversation
  = *sollte ... wider Erwarten doch*
- **It was hardly to be expected that** democratization would be easy
  = *es stand kaum zu erwarten, dass*

43.3 Unmöglichkeit

- **There can be no** changes in the schedule
  = *... sind nicht möglich*
- Nowadays Carnival **cannot** happen **without** the police tell**ing** us where to walk and what direction to walk in
  = *kann unmöglich ..., ohne dass*
- People said prices would inevitably rise; **this cannot be the case**
  = *das kann nicht sein*
- **I couldn't possibly** invite George and not his wife
  = *ich kann unmöglich*
- The report **rules out any possibility of** exceptions, and amounts to little more than a statement of the obvious
  = *schließt jede Möglichkeit ... aus*
- **There is no question of** us gett**ing** this finished on time
  = *es gibt keine Chance, dass*
- A West German spokesman said **it was out of the question that** these weapons would be based in Germany
  = *es steht außer Frage, dass*
- **There is not (even) the remotest chance that** *oder* **There is absolutely no chance that** he will succeed
  = *es besteht nicht die geringste Möglichkeit, dass*
- The idea of trying to govern twelve nations from one centre **is unthinkable**
  = *ist unvorstellbar*
- Since we had over 500 applicants, **it would be quite impossible to** interview them all
  = *wir können unmöglich*

43.4 Unfähigkeit

- **I can't** drive, I'm afraid
  = *ich kann nicht*
- **I don't know how to** use a word processor
  = *ich weiß nicht, wie*
- The army **has been unable to** suppress the political violence in the area
  = *war nicht in der Lage*
- The congress had shown itself **incapable of** real reform
  = *unfähig zu*
- His fellow-directors **were not up to** runn**ing** the business without him
  = *waren nicht imstande zu*
- We hoped the sales team would be able to think up new marketing strategies, but they **were** unfortunately **not equal to the task**
  = *waren der Aufgabe nicht gewachsen*
- **He simply couldn't cope with** the stresses of family life
  = *er war ... einfach nicht gewachsen*
- I'm afraid the task **proved** (to be) **beyond his capabilities**
  = *ging über seine Kräfte*
- I'd like to leave him but sometimes I feel that such a step **is beyond me**
  = *geht über meine Kräfte*
- Far too many women accept that they are **hopeless at** *oder* **no good at** manag**ing** money
  = *sind unfähig zu*
- **I'm not in a position to** say now how much substance there is in the reports
  = *ich bin nicht in der Lage*
- **It's quite impossible for me to** describe the confusion and horror of the scene
  = *ich kann unmöglich*

44 ERKLÄRUNGEN

44.1 Präpositionen und Konjunktionen

- He was sacked **for the simple reason that** he just wasn't up to it any more
  = *aus dem einfachen Grunde, dass*
- **The reason that** we admire him is that he knows what he is doing
  = *der Grund dafür, dass*
- He said he could not be more specific **for** security **reasons**
  = *aus ...gründen*
- I am absolutely in favour of civil disobedience **on** moral **grounds**
  = *aus ... Gründen*
- The court had ordered his release, **on the grounds that** he had already been acquitted of most of the charges against him
  = *mit der Begründung, dass*
- The students were arrested **because of** suspected dissident activities
  = *wegen*
- Teachers in the eastern part of Germany are assailed by fears of mass unemployment **on account of** their communist past
  = *wegen*
- They are facing higher costs **owing to** rising inflation
  = *wegen*
- Parliament has prevaricated, **largely because of** the unwillingness of the main opposition party to support the changes
  = *hauptsächlich wegen*
- Morocco has announced details of the austerity package it is adopting **as a result of** pressure from the International Monetary Fund
  = *infolge*
- The full effects will be delayed **due to** factors beyond our control
  = *aufgrund*
- What also had to go was the notion that some people were born superior to others **by virtue of** their skin colour
  = *aufgrund*
- He shot to fame **on the strength of** a letter he had written to the papers
  = *aufgrund*
- **Thanks to** their generosity, the charity can afford to buy new equipment
  = *dank*
- Both companies became profitable again **by means of** severe cost-cutting
  = *mittels*
- The King and Queen's defence of old-fashioned family values has acquired a poignancy **in view of** their inability to have children
  = *in Anbetracht*
- **In the face of** this continued disagreement, the parties have asked for the polling to be postponed
  = *in Anbetracht*
- It is unclear why they initiated this week's attack, **given that** negotiations were underway
  = *in Anbetracht der Tatsache, dass*
- The police have put considerable pressure on the Government to toughen its stance **in the light of** recent events
  = *mit Blick auf*
- His soldiers had been restraining themselves **for fear of** harming civilians
  = *aus Furcht davor*
- A survey by the World Health Organization says that two out of every five people are dying prematurely **for lack of** food or health care
  = *aus Mangel an*
- Babies have died **for want of** *oder* **for lack of** proper medical attention
  = *aus Mangel an*
- I refused her a divorce, **out of** spite, I suppose
  = *aus*
- **Seeing that** he had a police escort, the only time he could have switched containers was on the way to the airport
  = *angesichts der Tatsache, dass*
- **As** he had been up since 4am, he was doubtless very tired
  = *da*
- International intervention was appropriate **since** tensions had reached the point where there was talk of war
  = *da*
- She could not have been deaf, **for** she started at the sound of a bell
  = *weil*
- I cannot accept this decision. **So** I confirm it is my intention to appeal to a higher authority
  = *daher*
- What the Party said was taken to be right, **therefore** anyone who disagreed must be wrong
  = *daher*
- **The thing is that** once you've retired there's no going back
  = *das Problem ist, dass*

44.2 Andere nützliche Ausdrücke

- The serious dangers to your health **caused by** *oder* **brought about by** cigarettes are now better understood
  = *hervorgerufen durch*
- When the picture was published recently, **it gave rise to** *oder* **led to** speculation that the three were still alive and being held captive
  = *gab Anlass zu*
- The army argues that security concerns **necessitated** the demolitions
  = *erforderten*
- This lack of recognition **was at the root of** the dispute
  = *war der eigentliche Grund für*
- **I attribute** all this mismanagement **to** the fact that the General Staff in London is practically non-existent
  = *ich führe ... auf ... zurück*
- This unrest **dates from** colonial times
  = *geht zurück auf*
- The custom **goes back to** pre-Christian days
  = *geht zurück auf*

45 ENTSCHULDIGUNGEN

45.1 Entschuldigungen

- **I'm really sorry**, Steve, **but** we won't be able to come on Saturday
  = *es tut mir wirklich leid, aber*
- **I'm sorry that** your time had been wasted
  = *es tut mir leid, dass*
- **I am sorry to have to** say this to you but you're no good
  = *es tut mir leid, ... zu müssen*
- **Apologies if** I wasn't very good company last night
  = *Entschuldigung, wenn*
- **I must apologize for** what happened. Quite unforgivable, and the man responsible has been disciplined
  = *ich muss mich für ... entschuldigen*
- **I owe you an apology**. I didn't think you knew what you were talking about
  = *ich muss mich bei Ihnen entschuldigen*
- The general back-pedalled, saying that **he had not meant to** offend the German government
  = *es lag nicht in seiner Absicht*
- **Do forgive me for** being a little abrupt
  = *verzeihen Sie mir, wenn ich*
- **Please forgive me for** behaving so badly
  = *bitte entschuldigen Sie, dass ich*
- **Please accept our apologies** if this has caused you any inconvenience
  = *bitte entschuldigen Sie vielmals*

45.2 Verantwortung eingestehen

- **I admit** I overreacted, but someone needed to speak out against her
  = *ich gebe zu*
- **I have no excuse for** what happened
  = *ich kann keine Entschuldigung für ... vorbringen*
- **It is my fault that** our marriage is on the rocks
  = *es ist mein Fehler, dass*
- The Government **is not entirely to blame for** the crisis
  = *trägt nicht die alleinige Schuld an*
- **I should never have** let him rush out of the house in anger
  = *ich hätte nie ... dürfen*
- Oh, but **if only I hadn't** lost the keys
  = *wenn ich nur nicht ... hätte*
- I hate to admit that the old man was right, but **I made a stupid mistake**
  = *ich habe einen dummen Fehler gemacht*
- **My mistake was in** failing to push my concerns and convictions as hard as I could have done
  = *mein Fehler war, dass*
- **My mistake was to** arrive wearing a jacket and polo-neck jumper
  = *mein Fehler war*
- In December and January the markets raced ahead, and I missed out on that. **That was my mistake**
  = *das war mein Fehler*

45.3 Mit Bedauern

- **I'm very upset about** her decision but I accept she needs to move on to new challenges
  = *ich bin sehr mitgenommen von*
- **It's a shame that** the press gives so little coverage to these events
  = *schade, dass*
- **I feel awful about** saying this but you really ought to spend more time with your children
  = *es tut mir sehr leid, dass*
- **I'm afraid I can't** help you very much
  = *ich kann leider nicht*
- **It's a pity that** my profession can make a lot of money out of the misfortunes of others
  = *schade, dass*
- **It is unfortunate that** the matter should have come to a head just now
  = *es ist etwas unglücklich, dass*
- David and I **very much regret that** we have been unable to reach an agreement
  = *bedauern sehr, dass*
- The accused **bitterly regrets** this incident and it won't happen again
  = *bedauert zutiefst*
- **We regret to inform you that** the post of Editor has now been filled
  = *zu unserem Bedauern müssen wir Ihnen mitteilen, dass*

45.4 Zur Erklärung

- **I didn't do it on purpose**, it just happened
  = *ich habe es nicht absichtlich getan*
- Sorry, Nanna. **I didn't mean to** upset you
  = *ich hatte nicht die Absicht*
- Sorry about not coming to the meeting. **I was under the impression that** it was just for managers
  = *ich hatte den Eindruck, dass*
- **We are simply trying to** protect the interests of local householders
  = *wir versuchen nur*
- I know this hurt you but **I had no choice**. I had to put David's life above all else
  = *ich hatte keine Wahl*
- We are unhappy with 1.5%, but under the circumstances **we have no alternative but to** accept
  = *wir haben keine andere Wahl als*
- **We were obliged to** accept their conditions
  = *wir sahen uns gezwungen*
- **I had nothing to do with** the placing of any advertisement
  = *ich hatte nichts mit ... zu tun*
- A spokesman for the club assured supporters that **it was a genuine error** and **there was no intention to** mislead them
  = *es war ein reines Versehen ... es war nicht beabsichtigt*

46 BEWERBUNGEN

46.1 Nützliche Redewendungen

- **In reply to your advertisement** for a Trainee Manager in today's *Guardian*, **I would be grateful if you would send me further details of** the post
  = *mit Bezug auf Ihre Anzeige ... möchte ich Sie bitten, mir nähere Informationen über ... zuzusenden*
- **I wish to apply for the post of** bilingual correspondent, as advertised in this week's *Euronews*
  = *ich möchte mich um die Stelle ... bewerben*
- **I am writing to ask if** there is any possibility of work in your company
  = *ich möchte nachfragen, ob*
- **I am writing to enquire about the possibility of joining your company on work placement** for a period of 3 months
  = *ich möchte mich erkundigen, ob die Möglichkeit besteht, in IhremUnternehmen ein Praktikum zu absolvieren*

46.2 Berufserfahrung

- **I have** three years' **experience of** office work
  = *ich verfüge über ... Erfahrung*
- **I am familiar with** word processors
  = *ich bin mit ... vertraut*
- **As well as speaking fluent** English, **I have a working knowledge of** German
  = *ich spreche fließend ... und habe ausreichende ...kenntnisse*
- **As you will see from my CV**, I have worked in Belgium before
  = *wie Sie meinem Lebenslauf entnehmen können*
- **Although I have no experience of this type of work** I have had other holiday jobs and can supply references from my employers, if you wish
  = *ich habe zwar keine Erfahrung auf diesem Arbeitsgebiet*
- **My current salary is** ... per annum and I have four weeks' paid leave
  = *zurzeit verdiene ich*

46.3 Motivationen ausdrücken

- **I would like to make better use of** my languages
  = *ich möchte meine ...kenntnisse besser einsetzen*
- **I am keen to work in** public relations
  = *ich möchte gerne auf dem Gebiet ... arbeiten*

46.4 Briefschluss

- **I will be available from** the end of April
  = *ich stehe ab ... zur Verfügung*
- **I am available for interview** at any time
  = *über ein Vorstellungsgespräch würde ich mich freuen*
- **Please do not hesitate to contact me for further information**
  = *für weitere Informationen stehe ich Ihnen gerne jederzeit zur Verfügung*
- **Please do not contact** my current employers
  = *ich möchte Sie bitten, sich nicht mit ... in Verbindung zu setzen*
- **I enclose** a stamped addressed envelope for your reply
  = *ich lege ... bei*

Garrion Orchard
Middletown
MD8 1NP

18th August 2013

The Managing Director
Messrs. J.M. Thomson Ltd,
Leeside Works
Barnton, MC45 6RB

Dear Sir or Madam,[1]

With reference to your advertisement in today's *Guardian*, I wish to apply for the post of Human Resources Manager.

I enclose my curriculum vitae. Please do not hesitate to contact me if you require any further details.

Yours faithfully,

CURRICULUM VITAE

NAME:	Andrew Iain FERRIER
ADDRESS:	Garrion Orchard, Middletown
TELEPHONE:	(01234) 861483
DATE OF BIRTH:	6.5.1987
MARITAL STATUS:	Married (no children)
NATIONALITY:	British
QUALIFICATIONS:[2]	M.A. First class Honours Degree in German with French, University of Texas, USA (June 2008) Masters Diploma in Human Resources, Glasgow University (June 2009) A-levels (2005): German (A), French (A), English (B) O-levels: 9 subjects
PRESENT POST:	Assistant Human Resources Manager, Abbots Art Metal Company plc., Middletown (since July 2010)
PREVIOUS EMPLOYMENT:	Sept. 2009 - June 2010: Human resources trainee, Abbots Art Metal Company plc. Oct. 2008 - June 2009: Student, Glasgow University

SKILLS, INTERESTS AND EXPERIENCE: fluent German & French; adequate Italian; some Russian; car owner and driver (clean licence); riding and sailing.

The following have agreed to provide references:

Ms Jocelyn Meiklejohn
Human Resources Manager
Abbots Art Metal Company plc
Middletown MD1 4CU

Dr. Garth Tritt
Department of German
University of Texas
Arizona, USA

[1] Diese Form der Adresse wird verwendet, wenn der Name des Empfängers nicht bekannt ist. Wenn der Name bekannt ist, wird folgende Schreibung benutzt:

Mr Eric Swanson

ODER

Mrs. Anna Carter,
Personnel Director,
Messrs. J.M. Kenyon Ltd, usw.

Als Anrede benutzen Sie „Dear Sir" bzw. „Dear Madam".
Alle Briefe, die mit dieser Anrede beginnen, werden mit der Grußformel „Yours faithfully" und Unterschrift beendet. Eine ausführlichere Darstellung finden Sie auf den Seiten 1047 und 1049.

[2] Wenn Sie sich um eine Stelle im Ausland bewerben, sollten Sie auf die Entsprechungen Ihrer Qualifikationen im englischen Sprachraum hinweisen. Etwa „Abitur – German equivalent of A-levels" usw.

46.5 Referenzen erbitten und erteilen

- In my application for the position of lecturer, I have been asked to provide the names of two referees and **I wondered whether you would mind if I gave your name** as one of them
  = *ich möchte Sie um Ihr Einverständnis bitten, Ihren Namen angeben zu dürfen*
- Ms Lee has applied for the post of Marketing Executive with our company and has given us your name as a reference. **We would be grateful if you would let us know whether you would recommend her for this position**
  = *wir wären Ihnen sehr dankbar, wenn Sie uns mitteilen könnten, ob Sie sie für diesen Posten empfehlen können*
- **Your reply will be treated in the strictest confidence**
  = *Ihre Antwort wird selbstverständlich streng vertraulich behandelt*
- I have known Mr Chambers for four years in his capacity as Sales Manager and **can warmly recommend him for the position**
  = *ich kann ihn für die Stelle wärmstens empfehlen*

46.6 Ein Angebot annehmen oder ablehnen

- Thank you for your letter of 20 March. **I will be pleased to attend for interview** at your Manchester offices on Thursday 7 April at 10am
  = *ich finde mich gern ... zu einem Vorstellungsgespräch ein*
- **I would like to confirm my acceptance of** the post of Marketing Executive
  = *ich nehme Ihr Angebot an*
- **I would be delighted to accept this post. However, would it be possible** to postpone my starting date until 8 May?
  = *ich würde das Angebot sehr gerne annehmen. Wäre es jedoch möglich*
- **I would be glad to accept your offer; however**, the salary stated is somewhat lower than what I had hoped for
  = *ich würde Ihr Angebot gerne annehmen, ich hatte jedoch*
- Having given your offer careful thought, **I regret that I am unable to accept**
  = *bedauerlicherweise ist es mir nicht möglich, Ihr Angebot anzunehmen*

47 GESCHÄFTSBRIEFE

47.1 Informationen erbitten

- **We** see from your advertisement in the Healthy Holiday Guide that you are offering cut-price holidays in Scotland, and **would be grateful if you would send us** details
  = *wir ... wären Ihnen dankbar, wenn Sie uns nähere Informationen zusenden könnten*
- I read about the Happy Pet Society in the NCT newsletter and would be very interested to learn more about it. **Please send me details of** membership
  = *bitte senden Sie mir Einzelheiten über ... zu*

... und darauf antworten

- **In response to your enquiry of** 8 March, **we have pleasure in enclosing** full details on our activity holidays in Cumbria, **together with** our price list, valid until May 2015
  = *wir beziehen uns auf Ihre Anfrage vom ... und senden Ihnen gerne ... sowie ... zu*
- **Thank you for enquiry about** the Society for Wildlife Protection. **I enclose** a leaflet explaining our beliefs and the issues we campaign on. **Should you wish** to join, a membership application form is also enclosed
  = *ich danke für Ihre Anfrage bezüglich ... Ich lege ... bei ... Sollten Sie Interesse an ...haben*

47.2 Bestellungen und Antwort auf Bestellungen

- **We would like to place an order for** the following items, in the sizes and quantities specified below
  = *wir möchten eine Bestellung über ... aufgeben*
- **Please find enclosed our order no.** 3011 for ...
  = *anbei unsere Bestellung Nr.*
- **The enclosed order is based on** your current price list, assuming our usual discount
  = *der beigefügten Bestellung liegt ... zugrunde*
- **I wish to order** a can of "Buzz off!" wasp repellent, as advertised in the July issue of Gardeners' Monthly, **and enclose a cheque for** £19.50
  = *ich möchte ... bestellen. Ich füge einen Scheck über ... bei*
- **Thank you for your order of** 3 May, which will be dispatched within 30 days
  = *wir danken Ihnen für Ihre Bestellung vom*
- **We acknowledge receipt of your order no.** 3570 and advise that the goods will be dispatched within 7 working days
  = *wir bestätigen den Eingang Ihrer Bestellung Nr.*
- **We regret that the goods you ordered are temporarily out of stock**
  = *leider sind die von Ihnen bestellten Waren zurzeit nicht auf Lager*
- **Please allow** 28 days **for delivery**
  = *die Lieferung erfolgt innerhalb von*

47.3 Lieferungen

- **Our delivery time is** 60 days from receipt of order
  = *unsere Lieferzeit beträgt*
- **We await confirmation of your order**
  = *wir erwarten Ihre verbindliche Bestellung*
- **We confirm that the goods were dispatched on** 4 September
  = *wir bestätigen den Abgang der Waren am*
- **We cannot accept responsibility for** goods damaged in transit
  = *wir übernehmen keine Haftung für*

47.4 Sich beschweren

- **We have not yet received** the items ordered on 6 May (ref. order no. 541)
  = *... sind noch nicht bei uns eingegangen*
- **Unfortunately the goods were damaged** in transit
  = *leider wurden die Waren ... beschädigt*
- **The goods received differ significantly from** the description in your catalogue
  = *die eingegangenen Waren weichen wesentlich von ... ab*
- If the goods are not received by 20 October, **we shall have to cancel our order**
  = *sehen wir uns leider gezwungen, unsere Bestellung zu stornieren*

47.5 Bezahlung

- **The total amount outstanding is ...**
  = *der zu zahlende Gesamtbetrag beläuft sich auf ...*
- **We would be grateful if you would attend to this account** immediately
  = *wir wären Ihnen dankbar, wenn Sie diese Rechnung ... begleichen würden*
- **Please remit payment by return**
  = *bitte überweisen Sie den Betrag unverzüglich*
- Full payment **is due within** 14 working days from receipt of goods
  = *ist fällig innerhalb von*
- **We enclose** a cheque for ... **in settlement of your invoice no.** 2003L/58
  = *anbei übersenden wir Ihnen ... zur Begleichung Ihrer Rechnung Nr.*
- **We** must point out an error in your account and **would be grateful if you would adjust your invoice** accordingly
  = *wir ... wären Ihnen dankbar, wenn Sie die Rechnung berichtigen würden*
- The mistake was due to an accounting error, and **we enclose a credit note for** the sum involved
  = *in der Anlage erhalten Sie eine Gutschrift über*
- **Thank you for your cheque for** ... in settlement of our invoice
  = *wir bedanken uns für Ihren Scheck über ...*
- **We look forward to doing further business with you in the near future**
  = *wir würden uns freuen, schon bald wieder mit Ihnen zusammenarbeiten zu können*

Crosby Stills

PHOTOGRAPHIC LIBRARY
141 Academy Street
Glossop
Derby K9 4JP

22nd May 2013

Mr David Cooper
18 Crossdyke Road
Overdale
Lancs
LB3 WOD

Dear Mr Cooper,

Thank you for your recent enquiry about our limited edition photographs of classic cars. We have pleasure in enclosing our latest catalogue and current price list and would draw your attention to our free postage and packing on orders over £30. We are prepared to hold last year's prices on our range of frames and look forward to receiving your order.

Yours faithfully,

JAMES NASH
Managing Director

FABBY FABRICS LTD

Greenknowe Industrial Estate
Barbridge, Denholm
DT4 8HF

Our ref: WED/35/40 9th October, 2013
Your ref: HDF/JL

Moonshine Inn
3 Main Street
Newtown, NW1 4BB

For the attention of Ms H Boyle

Dear Madam,

Thank you for your letter of 21st September. We do stock a wide range of materials which are suitable for seating and would be delighted to send one of our representatives round at your earliest convenience. Please note that we also provide a made-to-measure service at very competitive prices and will be happy to supply you with a free quotation.

Yours faithfully,

Garry Scott
Sales Manager

48 ALLGEMEINE KORRESPONDENZ

48.1 Briefanfänge

An Bekannte

- **Thank you** *oder* **Thanks for your letter** which arrived yesterday
  = *vielen Dank für Deinen Brief*
- **It was good** *oder* **nice** *oder* **lovely to hear from you**
  = *ich habe mich sehr gefreut, von Dir zu hören*
- It's such a long time since we were last in touch that **I felt I must write a few lines** just to say hello
  = *und da dachte ich, ich muss einfach ein paar Zeilen schreiben*
- **I'm sorry I haven't written for so long**, and hope you'll forgive me; I've had a lot of work recently and ...
  = *es tut mir sehr leid, dass ich so lange nicht geschrieben habe*

An eine Firma oder Organisation

- **I am writing to ask whether** you have in stock a book entitled ...
  = *ich möchte mich erkundigen, ob*
- **Please send me** ... I enclose a cheque for ...
  = *würden Sie mir bitte ... schicken*
- When I left your hotel last week, I think I may have left a red coat in my room. **Would you be so kind as to** let me know whether it has been found?
  = *würden Sie mir bitte so freundlich sein und*
- I have seen the details of your summer courses, and **wish to know whether** you still have any vacancies on the beginners' Swedish course
  = *ich möchte nachfragen, ob*

48.2 Briefschlüsse

An Bekannte

- **Gerald joins me in sending very best wishes to you all**
  = *viele herzliche Grüße an Euch alle, auch von Gerald*
- **Please remember me to** your wife - I hope she is well
  = *bitte grüßen Sie auch ... von mir*
- **I look forward to hearing from you**
  = *ich würde mich sehr freuen, bald von Ihnen zu hören*

An Freunde

- **Say hello to Martin for me**
  = *grüß Martin von mir*
- **Give my love to** Daniel and Laura, and tell them how much I miss them
  = *grüß ... von mir*
- **Give my warmest regards to Vincent**
  = *grüße bitte Vincent ganz herzlich von mir*
- **Do write** when you have a minute
  = *schreib mal wieder*
- **Hoping to hear from you before too long**
  = *ich hoffe, dass ich schon bald von Dir höre*

An enge Freunde

- Rhona **sends her love**/Ray **sends his love**
  = *lässt herzlich grüssen*
- Jodie and Carla **send you a big hug**
  = *umarmen Dich*

48.3 Reiseplanung

Zimmerreservierung

- **Please send me details of** your prices
  = *bitte schicken Sie mir nähere Informationen über ... zu*
- **Please let me know by return of post if** you have one single room with bath, half board, for the week commencing 3 October
  = *bitte teilen Sie mir umgehend mit, ob*
- **I would like to book** bed-and-breakfast accommodation with you
  = *ich möchte ... buchen*

Eine Buchung bestätigen oder stornieren

- **Please consider this a firm booking** and hold the room until I arrive, however late in the evening
  = *bitte betrachten Sie diese Reservierung als verbindlich*
- **Please confirm the following by fax**: one single room with shower for the nights of 20-23 April 2013
  = *bitte bestätigen Sie Folgendes per Fax*
- **We expect to arrive** in the early evening, unless something unforeseen happens
  = *wir werden ... eintreffen*
- **I am afraid I must ask you to alter my booking from** 25 August **to** 3 September. I hope this will not cause too much inconvenience
  = *leider muss ich Sie bitten, meine Reservierung vom ... auf den ... umzubuchen*
- Owing to unforeseen circumstances, **I am afraid (that) I must cancel the booking** made with you for the week beginning 5 September
  = *muss ich meine Reservierung leider stornieren*

Der Empfänger (die Empfängerin) ist Ihnen persönlich bekannt

Dear Mr Brown, Dear Mrs Hughes, Dear Mr and Mrs Boyle, Dear Miss Roberts, Dear Ms Jones, Dear Dr Armstrong, Dear Professor Ferrier, Dear Sir John, Dear Lady McLeod, Dear Andrew, Dear Jenny,	Yours sincerely	
	With all good wishes, Yours sincerely With kindest regards, Yours sincerely	*persönlicher*

Der Empfänger (die Empfängerin) ist verwandt oder befreundet

Dear Grace, My dear Andrew, Dear Aunt Hazel, Dear Granny and Grandad, Dear Mum and Dad, My dear Caroline, Dearest Stephen, My dearest Mother, My dearest Heather, My darling Garry,	With love from Love from	
	Love to all Love from us all Yours All the best	*vertrauter*
	With much love from Lots of love from Much love as always, All my love	*herzlicher*

8. South Farmway
BARCOME
BN7 2BT

9th May, 2013

Dear Jenny,

I'm so sorry that I haven't written sooner, things were pretty hectic leading up to the wedding. I've never been so busy! Happily everything ran like clockwork and we all had a perfect day. The house is very quiet now with David away but I must admit I am enjoying it! Eric and I finally have the chance to take a short break at our cottage in the Lake District. Why don't you and James join us? There's plenty of room and I know how you love the lakes. We will be there on Saturday of the week beginning 16th of July for ten days. Give me a call soon if you're coming and we'll meet you at the station. Do say you'll come!

With love,

Kerry

11 South Street
BARCOME
BN7 2BT

5th June 2013

Mr. J. Sharpe
Sharpe Knives Ltd.,
Cromwell Place
ADDENBOROUGH
AG3 9LL

Dear Mr Sharpe,

Some years ago I bought a HANDYMAN penknife from you, and, as you suggested, it has been invaluable to me. Unfortunately, however, I have now lost it, and wonder if you still stock this range? If so, I should be grateful if you would let me have details of the various types of penknife you make, and of their prices.

Yours sincerely,

Thomas Thomson

In der unten stehenden Tabelle sind die üblichen Anreden und Schlussformeln für Privat- und Geschäftsbriefe aufgeführt.

Geschäftsbriefe (siehe auch 47)

Dear Sirs,[1]	Yours faithfully	1 *Wenn Sie an eine Firma oder Behörde schreiben*
Dear Sir,[2]		2 *Empfänger ist ein Mann*
Dear Madam,[3]		3 *Empfänger ist eine Frau*
Dear Sir or Madam,[4]		4 *Sie wissen nicht, ob der Empfänger ein Mann oder eine Frau ist*

An Bekannte und Freunde

Formeln, die Sie immer verwenden können		
Dear Alison, Dear Ann and Bob, Dear Uncle Alex, Dear Mrs Andrews, Dear Mr and Mrs Hope,	Yours sincerely	
	With best wishes, Yours sincerely	*persönlicher*
	With kindest regards,	
	Yours sincerely	
	All good wishes, Yours sincerely	
	With best wishes, Yours ever	*vertrauter*
	Kindest regards, Best wishes	
	With best wishes, As always	

49 DANKSAGUNGEN

- **Just a line to say thanks for** the lovely book which arrived today
  = *danke für*
- **I can't thank you enough for** finding my watch
  = *ich weiß gar nicht, wie ich Ihnen für ... danken kann*
- **(Would you) please thank him from me**
  = *Richten Sie ihm bitte meinen Dank aus*
- **We greatly appreciated** your support during our recent difficulties
  = *wir sind Ihnen wirklich sehr dankbar für*
- **Please accept our sincere thanks for** all your help and support
  = *wir möchten uns herzlich bei Ihnen für ... bedanken*
- **A big thank you to everyone** involved in the show this year
  = *ein herzliches Dankeschön an alle*
- **We would like to express our appreciation to** the University of Durham Research Committee for providing a grant
  = *wir möchten unserer Dankbarkeit gegenüber ... Ausdruck verleihen*

Im Namen einer Gruppe

- **Thank you on behalf of** the Manx Operatic Society **for** all your support
  = *wir danken Ihnen im Namen ... für*
- **I am instructed by** our committee **to convey our sincere thanks for** your assistance at our recent Valentine Social
  = *... hat mir die Aufgabe übertragen, unseren herzlichen Dank für ... zu übermitteln*

50 GLÜCKWÜNSCHE

50.1 Spezielle Anlässe

- **I hope you have** a lovely holiday
  = *hoffentlich hast Du*
- **With love and best wishes for** your wedding anniversary
  = *mit den besten Wünschen für*
- **(Do) give my best wishes to** your mother **for** a happy and healthy retirement
  = *grüße ... von mir und wünsche ... alles Gute für*
- Len **joins me in sending you our very best wishes for** your future career
  = *... schließt sich meinen besten Wünschen für ... an*

50.2 Zu Weihnachten und Neujahr

- **Merry Christmas and a Happy New Year**
  = *frohe Weihnachten und ein glückliches neues Jahr*
- **With Season's Greetings and very best wishes from**
  = *mit den besten Wünschen für ein gesegnetes Weihnachtsfest und ein glückliches neues Jahr*
- **May I send you all our very best wishes for** 2014
  = *ich sende Euch allen die besten Wünsche für*

50.3 Zum Geburtstag

- **All our love and best wishes on your** 21st **birthday**, from Simon, Liz, Kerry and the cats
  = *alles Liebe und Gute zu Deinem ... Geburtstag*
- I am writing to wish you **many happy returns (of the day)**. Hope your birthday brings you everything you wished for
  = *alles Gute zum Geburtstag*

50.4 Gute Besserung

- Sorry (to hear) you're ill - **get well soon!**
  = *gute Besserung*
- I was very sorry to learn that you were ill, and send you **my best wishes for a speedy recovery**
  = *meine besten Wünsche für eine baldige Genesung*

50.5 Erfolg wünschen

- **Good luck in** your driving test. I hope things go well for you on Friday
  = *viel Glück bei*
- Sorry to hear you didn't get the job - **better luck next time!**
  = *vielleicht klappt es beim nächsten Mal*
- **We all wish you the best of luck in** your new job
  = *wir alle wünschen Dir viel Glück in*

50.6 Gratulationen

- You're expecting a baby? **Congratulations!** When is the baby due?
  = *herzlichen Glückwunsch*
- You've finished the job already? **Well done!**
  = *gut gemacht*
- **We all send you our love and congratulations on** such an excellent result
  = *wir gratulieren alle zu*
- **This is to send you our warmest congratulations and best wishes on** your engagement
  = *herzlichen Glückwunsch und die besten Wünsche anlässlich*

51 ANZEIGEN

51.1 Geburtsanzeigen

- Julia Archer **gave birth to** a 6lb 5oz **baby daughter**, Amy, last Monday. **Mother and baby are doing well**
  = *hat ... eine Tochter bekommen. Mutter und Kind sind wohlauf*
- Ian and Zoë Pitt **are delighted to announce the birth of a son**, Garry, on 9th May, 2013, at Minehead Hospital
  = *freuen sich, die Geburt ihres Sohnes ... anzuzeigen*
- At the Southern General Hospital, on 1st December, 2012, **to Paul and Diane Kelly (née Smith) a son, John Alexander**, a brother for Helen
  = *Paul and Diane Kelly, geb. Smith, freuen sich, die Geburt ihres Sohnes John Alexander ... anzuzeigen*

... und darauf antworten

- **Congratulations on the birth of** your son
  = *herzliche Glückwünsche zur Geburt*
- **We were delighted to hear about the birth of** Stephanie, and send our very best wishes to all of you
  = *wir freuen uns mit Euch über die Geburt von*

51.2 Verlobungsanzeigen

- I'm sure you'll be pleased to hear that Jim and I **got engaged** yesterday
  = *haben uns verlobt*
- **It is with much pleasure that the engagement is announced between** Michael, younger son of Professor and Mrs Perkins, York, **and** Jennifer, only daugher of Dr and Mrs Campbell, Hucknall
  = *... freuen sich, die Verlobung zwischen ... und ... bekannt zu geben*

... und darauf antworten

- **Congratulations to you both on your engagement**, and very best wishes for a long and happy life together
  = *herzliche Glückwünsche anlässlich Eurer Verlobung Für Euch beide*
- **I was delighted to hear of your engagement** and wish you both all the best for your future together
  = *ich freue mich mit Euch über Eure Verlobung*

51.3 Heiratsanzeigen

- **I'm getting married** in June, to a wonderful man named Lester Thompson
  = *ich werde heiraten*

- **At Jurby Church, on 1st June, 2013, Eve, daughter of Ian and Mary Jones, Jurby, to John, son of Ray and Myra Watt, Ayr**
  = *die Vermählung wird bekannt gegeben zwischen Eve, Tochter von Ian und Mary Jones, Jurby, und John, Sohn von Ray und Myra Watt, Ayr, am 1. Juni 2008 in der Kirche von Jurby*

... und darauf antworten

- **Congratulations on your marriage, and best wishes to you both for your future happiness**
  = *zu Eurer Hochzeit herzliche Glückwünsche und alles Gute für Eure gemeinsame Zukunft*
- **We were delighted to hear about your daughter's marriage to** Iain, and wish them both all the best for their future life together
  = *mit großer Freude haben wir die Nachricht von der Vermählung Eurer Tochter mit ... zur Kenntnis genommen*

51.4 Todesanzeigen

- My husband **died suddenly** in March
  = *plötzlich und unerwartet verstarb*
- **It is with great sadness that I have to tell you that** Joe's father **passed away** three weeks ago
  = *in tiefer Trauer muss ich Ihnen mitteilen, dass ... für immer von uns gegangen ist*
- **Suddenly**, at home, in Newcastle-upon-Tyne, on Saturday 3rd July, 2013, Alan, aged 77 years, **the beloved husband of** Helen and **loving father of** Matthew and Chris
  = *plötzlich und unerwartet verstarb mein geliebter Mann, unser lieber Vater*

... und darauf antworten

- My husband and I **were greatly saddened to learn of the passing of** Dr Smith, and send (*oder* offer) you and your family our most sincere condolences
  = *mit tiefem Bedauern haben wir die Nachricht vom Tode ... erhalten*
- **We wish to extend our deepest sympathy for your sad loss to you and your wife**
  = *wir möchten Ihnen zum Tode ... unser tief empfundenes Beileid aussprechen*

51.5 Umzugsanzeigen

- We are moving house next week. **Our new address** as of 4 May 2013 **will be** ...
  = *unsere neue Adresse ... ist*

52 EINLADUNGEN

52.1 Offizielle Einladungen

- Mr and Mrs James Waller **request the pleasure of your company at the marriage of** their daughter Mary Elizabeth to Mr Richard Hanbury at St Mary's Church, Frampton on Saturday, 24th August, 2013 at 2 o'clock and afterwards at Moor House, Frampton
  = *geben sich die Ehre, Sie zur Hochzeit ... einzuladen*
- The Chairman and Governors of Hertford College, Oxford, **request the pleasure of the company of** Miss Charlotte Young and partner **at a dinner to mark** the anniversary of the founding of the College
  = *geben sich die Ehre, ... anlässlich ... zu einem festlichen Abendessen einzuladen*

... und darauf antworten

- **We thank you for your kind invitation to** the marriage of your daughter Annabel on 20th November, **and have much pleasure in accepting**
  = *wir möchten uns sehr herzlich für die freundliche Einladung zu ... bedanken, die wir mit großem Vergnügen annehmen*
- Mr and Mrs Ian Low **thank** Dr and Mrs Green for **their kind invitation to** the marriage of their daughter Ann on 21st July **and are delighted to accept**
  = *möchten uns herzlich bei Ihnen für die freundliche Einladung zu ... bedanken, die wir mit großem Vergnügen annehmen*
- **We regret that we are unable to accept your invitation to** the marriage of your daughter on 6th May
  = *zu unserem Bedauern können wir Ihre Einladung zu ... nicht annehmen*

52.2 Einladungen zu Feierlichkeiten

- **We are celebrating Rosemary's engagement to David** by holding a dinner dance at the Central Hotel on Friday 14th February, 2014, **and very much hope that you will be able to join us**
  = *wir würden uns sehr freuen, wenn wir Sie anlässlich der Verlobung von Rosemary und David ... begrüßen dürften*
- **We are giving a dinner party** next Saturday, **and would be delighted if you and your wife could come**
  = *wir möchten ... ein Abendessen geben und laden Sie und Ihre Frau herzlich dazu ein*
- **I'm having a party** next week for my 18th - **come along, and bring a friend**
  = *ich gebe eine Party ... komm doch vorbei und bring noch jemanden mit*
- **Would you and Gordon like to come** to dinner next Saturday?
  = *wollt Gordon und Du ... kommen*
- **Would you be free for** lunch next Tuesday?
  = *können wir uns zum ... treffen*
- **Perhaps we could** meet for coffee some time next week?
  = *vielleicht könnten wir*

52.3 Eine Einladung annehmen

- **Yes, I'd love to meet up with you** tomorrow
  = *ja, ich würde mich gern mit Dir treffen*
- **It was good of you to invite me**, I've been longing to do something like this for ages
  = *es war sehr freundlich von Dir, mich einzuladen*
- **Thank you for your invitation to** dinner - **I look forward to it very much**
  = *herzlichen Dank für Ihre Einladung zu ... ich freue mich sehr darauf*

52.4 Eine Einladung ablehnen

- **I'd love to come, but I'm afraid** I'm already going out that night
  = *ich würde gern kommen, aber leider*
- **I wish I could come, but unfortunately** I have something else on
  = *ich wünschte, ich könnte kommen, aber leider*
- It was very kind of you to invite me to your dinner party next Saturday. **Unfortunately I will not be able to accept**
  = *zu meinem Bedauern kann ich nicht zusagen*
- **Much to our regret, we are unable to accept**
  = *zu unserem größten Bedauern können wir nicht zusagen*

52.5 Keine feste Zusage geben

- **I'm not sure** what I'm doing that night, but I'll let you know later
  = *ich weiß nicht genau*
- **It all depends on whether** I can get a sitter for Rosie at short notice
  = *es hängt alles davon ab, ob*
- **I'm afraid I can't really make any definite plans** until I know when Alex will be able to take her holidays
  = *leider kann ich nichts Festes planen*

53 ERÖRTERUNGEN

53.1 Beweisführung

Ein Thema einführen

- **It is often said** *oder* **claimed that** teenagers get pregnant in order to get council accommodation
  = *es wird oft behauptet, dass*

- **It is a truism** *oder* **a commonplace (to say) that** American accents are infinitely more glamorous than their British counterparts
  = *es ist eine Binsenweisheit, dass*
- **It is undeniably true that** Gormley helped to turn his union members into far more sophisticated workers
  = *es steht außer Zweifel, dass*
- **It is a well-known fact that** in this age of technology, it is computer screens which are responsible for many illnesses
  = *es ist allgemein bekannt, dass*
- **It is sometimes forgotten that** much Christian doctrine comes from Judaism
  = *es gerät manchmal in Vergessenheit, dass*
- **It would be naïve to suppose that** in a radically changing world these 50-year-old arrangements can survive
  = *es wäre naiv anzunehmen, dass*
- **It would hardly be an exaggeration to say that** the friendship of both of them with Britten was among the most creative in the composer's life
  = *man kann ohne große Übertreibung sagen, dass*
- **It is hard to open a newspaper nowadays without reading that** electronic technology has made the written word obsolete
  = *man kann heutzutage schon keine Zeitung mehr aufschlagen, ohne zu lesen, dass*
- **First of all, it is important to try to understand** some of the systems and processes involved in order to create a healthier body
  = *zunächst einmal ist es wichtig, ... zu verstehen*
- **It is in the nature of** sociological theory **to** make broad generalizations about such things as the evolution of society
  = *es liegt in der Natur der ..., zu*
- **It is often the case that** early interests lead on to a career
  = *oftmals ist*
- **By way of introduction, let me** summarize the background to this question
  = *zur Einführung möchte ich*
- **I would like to start with** a very sweeping statement which can easily be challenged
  = *ich möchte mit ... beginnen*
- **Before going specifically into the issue of** criminal law, **I wish first to summarize** how Gewirth derives his principles of morality and justice
  = *bevor ich die Frage des ... näher erörtere, möchte ich zunächst zusammenfassen*
- **Let us look at** what self-respect in your job actually means
  = *betrachten wir*
- **We commonly think of** people **as** isolated individuals but, in fact, few of us ever spend more than an hour or two of our waking hours alone
  = *wir betrachten ... im Allgemeinen als*
- **What we are mainly concerned with here is** the conflict between what the hero says and what he actually does
  = *es geht uns hier hauptsächlich um*
- **We live in a world in which** the word "equality" is liberally bandied about
  = *in unserer Welt*

Vorstellungen und Probleme einführen

- **The concept of** controll**ing** harmful insects by genetic means isn't new
  = *die Vorstellung, zu*
- **The idea of** gett**ing** rich without too much effort has universal appeal
  = *die Idee, zu*
- **The question of whether** Hamlet was really insane has long occupied critics
  = *die Frage, ob*
- Why they were successful where their predecessors had failed **is a question that has been much debated**
  = *über die Frage ... ist schon viel debattiert worden*
- **One of the most striking aspects of this issue is** the way (in which) it arouses strong emotions
  = *einer der interessantesten Aspekte dieses Problems ist*
- **There are a number of issues** on which China and Britain openly disagree
  = *es gibt einige Fragen*

Verallgemeinerungen

- **People who** work outside the home **tend to believe that** parenting is an easy option
  = *diejenigen, die ..., nehmen oft an, dass*
- **There's** always **a tendency for people** to exaggerate their place in the world
  = *der Mensch neigt immer dazu*
- Many gardeners **have a tendency to** treat plants like humans
  = *neigen dazu*
- Viewed psychologically, it would seem that **we all have the propensity for** such traits
  = *wir alle neigen zu*
- **For the (vast) majority of people**, literature is a subject which is studied at school but which has no relevance to life as they know it
  = *für die (aller)meisten Menschen*
- **For most of us** housework is a necessary but boring task
  = *für die meisten von uns*
- History **provides numerous examples** *oder* **instances of** misguided national heroes who did more harm than good in the long run
  = *bietet zahllose Beispiele für*

Genauere Angaben machen

- The impact of these theories on the social sciences, and economics **in particular**, was extremely significant
  = *im Besonderen*
- **One particular issue** raised by Butt was, suppose Hughes at the time of his conviction had been old enough to be hanged, what would have happened?
  = *eine spezielle Frage*
- **A more specific point** relates to using this insight as a way of challenging our hidden assumptions about reality
  = *eine genauere Aussage*
- **More specifically**, he accuses Western governments of continuing to supply weapons and training to the rebels
  = *genauer gesagt*

53.2 Die These

Einführung

- **First of all, let us consider** the advantages of urban life
  = *zunächst sollen ... betrachtet werden*
- **Let us begin with an examination of** the social aspects of this question
  = *beginnen wir mit einer Untersuchung*
- **The first thing that needs to be said is that** the author is presenting a one-sided view
  = *zunächst muss erwähnt werden, dass*
- **What should be established at the very outset is that** we are dealing here with a practical issue rather than a philosophical one
  = *gleich zu Anfang sollte klargestellt werden, dass*

Die Diskussion eingrenzen

- **In the next section, I will pursue the question of whether** the expansion of the Dutch prison system can be explained by Box's theory
  = *im nächsten Abschnitt werde ich auf die Frage eingehen, ob*
- **I will then deal with the question of** whether or not the requirements for practical discourse are compatible with criminal procedure
  = *danach werde ich das Problem ... behandeln*
- We must distinguish between the psychic and the spiritual, and **we shall see how** the subtle level of consciousness is the basis for the spiritual level
  = *wir werden sehen, wie*
- **I will confine myself to** giving an account of certain decisive facts in my militant career with Sartre
  = *ich möchte mich darauf beschränken*
- In this chapter, **I shall largely confine myself to** a consideration of those therapeutic methods that use visualization as a part of their procedures
  = *ich werde mich im Großen und Ganzen auf ... beschränken*
- **We will not concern ourselves here with** the Christian legend of St James
  = *an dieser Stelle soll nicht auf ... eingegangen werden*
- **Let us now consider** to what extent the present municipal tribunals differ from the former popular tribunals in the above-mentioned points
  = *betrachten wir nun*
- **Let us now look at** the ideal types of corporatism that neo-corporatist theorists developed to clarify the concept
  = *betrachten wir nun*

Einzelaspekte umreißen

- **The main issue under discussion is** how the party should re-define itself if it is to play any future role in Hungarian politics
  = *die Hauptfrage ist*
- **A second, related problem is** that business ethics has mostly concerned itself with grand theorizing
  = *ein weiteres Problem in diesem Zusammenhang ist*
- **The basic issue at stake is this**: is research to be judged by its value in generating new ideas?
  = *das zur Debatte stehende Grundproblem ist*
- **An important aspect of** Milton's imagery **is** the play of light and shade
  = *ein wichtiger Aspekt von ... ist*
- **It is worth mentioning here that** when this was first translated, the opening reference to Heidegger was entirely deleted
  = *an dieser Stelle sollte man erwähnen, dass*
- **Finally, there is the argument that** watching too much television may stunt a child's imagination
  = *und schließlich wäre da noch die These, dass*

Ein Argument in Frage stellen

- World leaders appear to be taking a tough stand, but **is there any real substance in** what has been agreed?
  = *hat ... Substanz*
- This is a question which **merits close(r) examination**
  = *verdient nähere Betrachtung*
- The unity of the two separate German states **has raised fundamental questions** for Germany's neighbours
  = *hat grundlegende Fragen ... aufgeworfen*
- The failure to protect our fellow Europeans in Bosnia **raises fundamental questions on** the role of the armed forces
  = *wirft grundlegende Fragen über ... auf*
- **This raises once again the question of** whether a government's right to secrecy should override the public's right to know
  = *dies wirft erneut die Frage ... auf*
- **This poses the question of** whether these measures are really helping the people they were intended to help
  = *dies wirft die Frage auf*

Analyse anbieten

- **It is interesting to consider why** this scheme has been so successful
  = *es ist interessant zu betrachten, warum*
- **On the question of** whether civil disobedience is likely to help end the war, Chomsky is deliberately diffident
  = *was die Frage nach ... betrifft*
- **We are often faced with the choice between** our sense of duty **and** our own personal inclinations
  = *man steht oft vor der Wahl zwischen ... und ...*
- **When we speak of** realism in music, **we do not at all have in mind** the illustrative bases of music
  = *wenn wir von ... sprechen, meinen wir damit ganz bestimmt nicht*
- **It is reasonable to assume that** most people living in industrialized societies are to some extent contaminated by environmental poisons
  = *es hat seine Gründe anzunehmen, dass*

Ein Argument unterstützen

- **An argument in support of** this approach **is that** it produces ...
  = *ein Argument zur Bestätigung ... ist, dass*
- **In support of his theory**, Dr Gold notes that most oil contains higher-than-atmospheric concentrations of helium-3
  = *um seine Theorie zu bestätigen*
- **This is the most telling argument in favour of** an extension of the right to vote
  = *dies ist das wichtigste Argument, dass für ... spricht*
- **The second reason for advocating** this course of action **is that** it benefits the community at large
  = *ein weiterer Grund, ... zu unterstützen, besteht darin, dass*
- **The third, more fundamental, reason for** looking to the future **is that** even the angriest investors realize they need a successful market
  = *ein dritter, noch wichtigerer Grund für ... ist, dass*
- Despite communism's demise, confidence in capitalism seems to be at an all-time low. **The fundamental reason for** this contradiction seems to me quite simple
  = *der wesentliche Grund für*

53.3 Ein Gegenargument vorstellen

Etwas kritisieren oder ablehnen

- **In actual fact, the idea of** there being a rupture between a so-called old criminology and an emergent new criminology **is somewhat misleading**
  = *tatsächlich ist die Vorstellung davon, dass ..., etwas irreführend*
- In order to argue this, **I will show that** Wyeth's **position is**, in actual fact, **untenable**
  = *ich werde zeigen, dass ... Position unhaltbar ist*
- **It is claimed, however**, that the strict Leboyer method is not essential for a less traumatic birth experience
  = *es wird jedoch behauptet*
- **This need not mean that** we are destined to suffer for ever. **Indeed, the opposite may be true**
  = *das muss nicht unbedingt bedeuten, dass ... Es könnte auch das genaue Gegenteil zutreffen*

- Many observers, though, **find it difficult to share his opinion that** it could mean the end of the Tamil Tigers
  = *tun sich schwer damit, seine Meinung zu teilen, dass*
- **On the other hand**, there are more important factors that should be taken into consideration
  = *andererseits*
- The judgement made **may well be true but** the evidence given to sustain it is unlikely to convince the sceptical
  = *kann zwar zutreffen, aber*
- Reform **is all very well, but** it is pointless if the rules are not enforced
  = *ist ja schön und gut, aber*
- The case against the use of drugs in sport rests primarily on the argument that ... . **This argument is weak**, for two reasons
  = *dieses Argument ist schwach*
- According to one theory, the ancestors of vampire bats were fruit-eating bats. But **this idea does not hold water**
  = *diese Vorstellung ist nicht stichhaltig*
- Their claim to be a separate race **does not stand up to** historical scrutiny
  = *hält ... nicht stand*
- **This view does not stand up** if we examine the known facts about John
  = *diese Ansicht ist nicht haltbar*
- **The trouble with this idea is not that** it is wrong, **but rather that** it is uninformative
  = *das Problem mit dieser Idee ist nicht so sehr ..., sondern vielmehr*
- **The difficulty with this view is that** he bases the principle on a false premise
  = *die Schwierigkeit bei dieser Betrachtungsweise liegt, darin, dass*
- **The snag with** such speculations **is that** too much turns on one man or event
  = *der Nachteil von ... ist, dass*
- But removing healthy ovaries **is entirely unjustified in my opinion**
  = *ist meiner Meinung nach völlig ungerechtfertigt*

Eine Alternative vorschlagen

- **Another approach may be to** develop substances capable of blocking the effects of the insect's immune system
  = *eine andere Herangehensweise könnte sein*
- **Another way to** reduce failure is to improve vocational education
  = *ein anderer Weg, um*
- **However, the other side of the coin is** the fact that an improved self-image really can lead to prosperity
  = *die Kehrseite der Medaille ist jedoch*
- **It is more accurate to speak of** a plurality of new criminologies rather than of a single new criminology
  = *es ist präziser, von ... zu sprechen*
- **Paradoxical as it may seem**, computer models of mind can be positively humanizing
  = *so paradox wie es auch erscheinen mag*

53.4 Die Synthese der Beweisführung

- **How can we reconcile** these two apparently contradictory viewpoints?
  = *wie lassen sich ... vereinbaren*
- **On balance**, making money honestly is more profitable than making it dishonestly
  = *alles in allem*
- Since such vitamins are more expensive, **one has to weigh up the pros and cons**
  = *man muss das Für und Wider abwägen*
- **We need to look at the pros and cons of** normative theory as employed by Gewirth and Phillips
  = *wir müssen die Vor- und Nachteile der ... betrachten*
- **The benefits of** partnership in a giant trading market **will** almost certainly **outweigh the disadvantages**
  = *die Vorteile der ... werden ... die Nachteile überwiegen*
- **The two perspectives are not mutually exclusive**
  = *die beiden Betrachtungsweisen schließen sich nicht gegenseitig aus*

Eines von mehreren Argumenten unterstützen

- Dr Meaden's theory **is the most convincing explanation**
  = *ist die einleuchtendste Erklärung*
- **The truth** *oder* **fact of the matter is that** in a free society you can't turn every home into a fortress
  = *die Wahrheit ist, dass*
- But **the truth is that** Father Christmas has a rather mixed origin
  = *die Wahrheit ist, dass*
- Although this operation sounds extremely dangerous, **in actual fact** it is extremely safe
  = *in Wirklichkeit*
- **When all is said and done, it must be acknowledged that** a purely theoretical approach to social issues is sterile
  = *letzten Endes muss man erkennen, dass*

Zusammenfassen

- In this chapter, **I have demonstrated** *oder* **shown that** the Cuban alternative has been undergoing considerable transformations
  = *habe ich nachgewiesen, dass*
- **This shows how**, in the final analysis, adhering to a particular theory on crime is at best a matter of reasoned choice
  = *dies beweist, wie*
- **The overall picture shows that** prison sentences were relatively frequent, but not particularly severe
  = *der Gesamteindruck zeigt, dass*
- **To recap** *oder* **To sum up, then, (we may conclude that)** there are in effect two possible solutions to this problem
  = *zusammenfassend (können wir schlussfolgern, dass)*
- **To sum up this chapter** I will offer two examples ...
  = *um dieses Kapitel zusammenzufassen*
- **To summarize**, we have seen that the old staple industries in Britain had been hit after the First World War by a deteriorating international competitive position
  = *um noch einmal zusammenzufassen*
- Habermas's argument, **in a nutshell**, is as follows
  = *kurz gesagt*
- But **the key to the whole argument is** a single extraordinary paragraph
  = *der Schlüssel zur gesamten Beweisführung liegt in*
- **To round off this section on** slugs, gardeners may be interested to hear that there are three species of predatory slugs in the British Isles
  = *um diesen Abschnitt über ... abzurunden*

Schlussfolgerungen ziehen

- **From all this, it follows that** it is impossible to extend those kinds of security measures to all potential targets of terrorism
  = *aus alledem geht hervor, dass*
- This, of course, **leads to the logical conclusion that** those who actually produce do have a claim to the results of their efforts
  = *führt zu der logischen Schlussfolgerung, dass*

- **There is only one logical conclusion we can reach** which is that we ask our customers what is the Strategic Reality that they perceive in our marketing programme
  = *wir können hier nur zu einer logischen Schlussfolgerung gelangen*
- **The inescapable conclusion is that** the criminal justice system does not simply reflect the reality of crime; it helps create it
  = *die unweigerliche Schlussfolgerung ist, dass*
- **We must conclude that** there is no solution to the problem of defining crime
  = *wir müssen schlussfolgern, dass*
- **In conclusion**, because interpersonal relationships are so complex, there can be no easy way of preventing conflict
  = *die Schlussfolgerung ist, dass*
- **The upshot of all this is that** treatment is unlikely to be available
  = *all das läuft darauf hinaus, dass*
- **So it would appear that** butter is not significantly associated with heart disease after all
  = *es scheint also, dass*
- **This only goes to show that** a good man is hard to find
  = *all dies zeigt nur, dass*
- **The lesson to be learned** from this **is that** you cannot hope to please everyone all of the time
  = *aus ... kann man die Lehre ziehen, dass*
- **At the end of the day**, the only way the drug problem will be beaten is when people are encouraged not to take them
  = *letzten Endes*
- **Ultimately, then**, while we may have some sympathy for these young criminals, we must do our utmost to protect society from them
  = *letzten Endes*

Aufbau eines Absatzes

- **In addition**, the author does not really empathize with his hero
  = *darüber hinaus*
- **Also**, there is the question of language
  = *des Weiteren*
- This award-winning writer, **in addition to** being a critic, biographer and poet, has written 26 crime novels
  = *... ist nicht nur ..., sondern*
- But this is only part of the picture. **Added to this are** fears that a major price increase would cause riots
  = *hinzu kommen noch*
- **An added** complication **is** that the characters are not aware of their relationship to one another
  = *eine zusätzliche ... ist*
- But, **over and above that**, each list contains fictitious names and addresses
  = *darüber hinaus*
- **Furthermore**, ozone is, like carbon dioxide, a greenhouse gas
  = *des Weiteren*
- **The question also arises as to** how this idea can be put into practice
  = *es stellt sich auch die Frage*
- Politicians, **as well as** academics and educationalists, tend to feel strongly abut the way history is taught
  = *sowie*

Vergleiche

- **Compared with** the heroine, Alison is an insipid character
  = *verglichen mit*
- **In comparison with** the Czech Republic, the culture of Bulgaria is less westernized
  = *im Vergleich zu*
- This is a high percentage for the English Midlands but low **by comparison with** some other parts of Britain
  = *im Vergleich zu*
- **On the one hand**, there is no longer a Warsaw Pact threat. **On the other (hand)**, the positive changes could have negative side-effects.
  = *einerseits ... andererseits*
- **Similarly**, a good historian is not obsessed by dates
  = *in ähnlicher Weise*
- There can only be one total at the bottom of a column of figures and **likewise** only one solution to any problem
  = *in ähnlicher Weise*
- What others say of us will translate into reality. **Equally**, what we affirm as true of ourselves will likewise come true
  = *gleichermaßen*
- There will now be a change in the way we are regarded by our partners, and, **by the same token**, the way we regard them
  = *gleichermaßen*
- **There is a fundamental difference between** adequate nutrient intake **and** optimum nutrient intake
  = *es gibt einen wesentlichen Unterschied zwischen ... und*

Synthese der einzelnen Elemente

- **First of all** *oder* **Firstly**, I would like to outline the benefits of the system
  = *zunächst*
- In music we are concerned **first and foremost** with the practical application of controlled sounds relating to the human psyche
  = *in erster Linie*
- **In order to understand** the conflict between the two nations, **it is first of all necessary to** know something of the history of the area
  = *um ... zu verstehen, ist es zunächst notwendig*
- **Secondly**, it might be simpler to develop chemical or even nuclear warheads for a large shell than for a missile
  = *zweitens*
- **In the first/second/third place**, the objectives of privatization were contradictory
  = *erstens/zweitens/drittens*
- **Finally**, there is the argument that watching too much television may stunt a child's imagination
  = *schließlich*

Eine persönliche Meinung ausdrücken

- **In my opinion**, the government is underestimating the scale of the epidemic
  = *meiner Meinung nach*
- **My personal opinion is that** the argument lacks depth
  = *ich persönlich bin der Meinung, dass*
- This is a popular viewpoint, but **speaking personally** I cannot understand it
  = *persönlich*
- **Personally, I think that** no one can appreciate ethnicity more than black or African people themselves
  = *ich persönlich glaube, dass*
- **My own view is that** what largely determines the use of non-national workers are economic factors rather than political ones
  = *ich persönlich bin der Ansicht, dass*
- **In my view**, it only perpetuates the very problem that it sets out to address
  = *meiner Ansicht nach*
- **For my part**, I cannot agree with the leadership on this question
  = *was mich angeht*
- Although the author argues the case for patriotism, **I feel that** he does not do it with any great personal conviction
  = *ich denke, dass*

- **I believe that** people do understand that there can be no quick fix for Britain's economic problems
  = *ich glaube, dass*
- **It seems to me that** what we have is a political problem that needs to be solved at a political level
  = *es scheint mir, dass*
- **I would maintain that** we have made a significant effort to ensure that the results are made public
  = *ich möchte behaupten, dass*

Die Meinung anderer ausdrücken

- **He claims** *oder* **maintains that** intelligence is conditioned by upbringing
  = *er behauptet, dass*
- Bukharin **asserts that** all great revolutions are accompanied by destructive internal conflict
  = *stellt fest, dass*
- The communiqué **states that** some form of nuclear deterrent will continue to be needed for the foreseeable future
  = *stellt fest, dass*
- **What he is saying is that** the time of the old, highly structured political party is over
  = *er will damit sagen, dass*
- His admirers **would have us believe that** watching this film is more like attending a church service than having a night at the pictures
  = *wollen uns glauben machen, dass*
- **According to** the report, poverty creates a climate favourable to violence
  = *laut*

Beispiele geben

- **To take another example**: many thousands of people have been condemned to a life of sickness and pain because ...
  = *um noch ein weiteres Beispiel anzuführen:*
- Let us consider, **for example** *oder* **for instance**, the problems faced by immigrants arriving in a strange country
  = *zum Beispiel*
- His meteoric rise **is the most striking example yet of** voters' disillusionment with the record of the previous government
  = *ist das bisher beste Beispiel*
- The case of Henry Howey Robson **serves to illustrate** the courage exhibited by young men in the face of battle
  = *veranschaulicht*
- Just consider, **by way of illustration**, the difference in amounts accumulated if interest is paid gross, rather than having tax deducted
  = *um dies einmal zu veranschaulichen*
- **A case in point is** the decision to lift the ban on contacts with the republic
  = *ein positives Beispiel ist*
- **Take the case of** the soldier returning from war
  = *nehmen wir zum Beispiel*
- **As** the Prime Minister **remarked** recently, the Channel Tunnel will greatly benefit the whole of the European Community
  = *wie ... sagte*

53.6 Die Diskussion

Eine Annahme darlegen

- They have telephoned the president to put pressure on him. And **that could be interpreted as** trying to gain an unconstitutional political advantage
  = *dies könnte man als ... interpretieren*
- Retail sales rose sharply last month. This was higher than expected and **could be taken to mean that** inflationary pressures remain strong
  = *könnte als Zeichen dafür aufgefasst werden, dass*
- In such circumstances, **it might well be prudent** to diversify your investments
  = *könnte es weise sein*
- These substances do not remain effective for very long. **This is possibly because** they work against the insects' natural instinct to feed
  = *dies rührt wahrscheinlich daher, dass*
- His wife had become an embarrassment to him and therefore **it is not beyond the bounds of possibility that** he may have contemplated murdering her
  = *es kann nicht ausgeschlossen werden, dass*
- Mr Fraser's assertion **leads one to suppose that** he is in full agreement with Catholic teaching as regards marriage
  = *lässt vermuten, dass*
- **It is probably the case that** all long heavy ships are vulnerable
  = *wahrscheinlich*
- After hearing nothing from the taxman for so long, most people **might reasonably assume that** their tax affairs were in order
  = *könnten durchaus annehmen, dass*
- **One could be forgiven for thinking that** because the substances are chemicals they'd be easy to study
  = *man könnte fast annehmen, dass*
- **I venture to suggest that** very often when people like him talk about love, they actually mean lust
  = *ich wage zu behaupten, dass*

Gewissheit ausdrücken

- **It is clear that** any risk to the human foetus is very low
  = *es ist klar, dass*
- Benn is **indisputably** a fine orator, one of the most compelling speakers in politics today
  = *zweifelsohne*
- British universities are **undeniably** good, but they are not turning out enough top scientists
  = *unbestreitbar*
- **There can be no doubt that** the Earth underwent a dramatic cooling which destroyed the environment and lifestyle of these creatures
  = *es lässt sich nicht bezweifeln, dass*
- **It is undoubtedly true that** over the years there has been a much greater emphasis on safer sex
  = *es ist unbestreitbar, dass*
- **As we all know** adultery is far from uncommon, particularly in springtime
  = *wie wir alle wissen*
- **One thing is certain**: the party is far from united
  = *eins ist sicher*
- **It is (quite) certain that** unless peace can be brought to this troubled land no amount of aid will solve the long-term problems of the people
  = *es ist sicher, dass*

Zweifel ausdrücken

- **It is doubtful whether** in this present regressive climate, anyone would be brave or foolish enough to demonstrate publicly
  = *es ist fraglich, ob*
- **It remains to be seen whether** the security forces will try to intervene
  = *es bleibt abzuwarten, ob*
- **I have a few reservations about** the book
  = *ich habe einige Vorbehalte gegen*

- The judges are expected to endorse the recommendation, but **it is by no means certain that** they will make up their minds today
  = *es ist keineswegs sicher, dass*
- **It is questionable whether** media coverage of terrorist organizations actually affects terrorism
  = *es ist fraglich, ob*
- **This raises the whole question of** exactly when men and women should retire
  = *dies wirft die Frage nach ... auf*
- The crisis **puts a question mark against** the Prime Minister's stated commitment to intervention
  = *stellt ... infrage*
- **Both these claims are true up to a point** and they need to be made. But they are limited in their significance
  = *beide Behauptungen sind bis zu einem gewissen Punkt richtig*

Zustimmung ausdrücken

- **I agree wholeheartedly with** the opinion that smacking should be outlawed
  = *ich stimme ... voll und ganz zu*
- **One must acknowledge that** their history will make change more painful
  = *man muss eingestehen, dass*
- **It cannot be denied that** there are similarities between the two approaches
  = *es lässt sich nicht verleugnen, dass*
- Courtney - **rightly in my view** - is strongly critical of the snobbery and élitism that is all too evident in these circles
  = *für meine Begriffe zu Recht*
- Preaching was considered an important activity, **and rightly so** in a country with a high illiteracy rate
  = *und das zu Recht*
- You may dispute the Pope's right to tell people how to live their lives, **but it is hard to disagree with** his picture of modern society
  = *aber man kann ... nur schwer widersprechen*

Widerspruch ausdrücken

- **I must disagree with** Gordon's article on criminality: it is dangerous to suggest that to be a criminal one must look like a criminal
  = *ich kann ... nicht zustimmen*
- As a former teacher **I find it hard to believe that** there is no link at all between screen violence and violence on the streets
  = *ich kann nur schwer glauben, dass*
- The strength of their feelings **is scarcely credible**
  = *ist kaum glaubhaft*
- Her claim to have been the first to discover the phenomenon **lacks credibility**
  = *ist unglaubwürdig*
- Nevertheless, **I remain unconvinced by** Milton
  = *... überzeugt mich nicht*
- Many do not believe that water contains anything remotely dangerous. Sadly, **this is far from the truth**
  = *dies entspricht ganz und gar nicht der Wahrheit*
- To say that everyone requires the same amount of a vitamin is as stupid as saying we all have blonde hair and blue eyes. **It simply isn't true**
  = *es ist einfach nicht wahr*
- His remarks **were** not only highly offensive to black and other ethnic minorities but **totally inaccurate**
  = *waren vollkommen falsch*
- Stomach ulcers are often associated with good living and a fast-moving lifestyle. **(But) in reality** there is no evidence to support this theory
  = *in Wirklichkeit (jedoch)*
- This version of a political economy **does not stand up to close scrutiny**
  = *hält einer genaueren Untersuchung nicht stand*

Ein Argument betonen

- **Nowadays, there is clearly** less stigma attached to unmarried mothers
  = *heutzutage ist ganz offensichtlich*
- Evidence shows that ..., so once again **the facts speak for themselves**
  = *die Fakten sprechen für sich*
- **Few will argue with the principle that** such a fund should be set up
  = *der Ansicht, dass ..., stimmen im Prinzip fast alle zu*
- Hyams **supports this claim** by looking at sentences produced by young children learning German
  = *unterstützt diese Behauptung*
- **The most important thing is to** reach agreement from all sides
  = *am wichtigsten ist es*
- Perhaps **the most important aspect of** cognition is the ability to manipulate symbols
  = *der wichtigste Aspekt*
- **It would be impossible to exaggerate the importance of** these two volumes for anyone with a serious interest in the development of black gospel music
  = *man kann die Wichtigkeit ... gar nicht genug betonen*
- The symbolic importance of Jerusalem for both Palestinians and Jews **is almost impossible to overemphasize**
  = *kann gar nicht genug betont werden*
- **It is important to be clear that** Jesus did not identify himself with Yahweh
  = *vor allem muss man sich klarmachen, dass*
- **It is significant that** Mandalay seems to have become the central focus in this debate
  = *es ist bezeichnend, dass*
- **It should not be forgotten that** many of those now in exile were close to the centre of power until only one year ago
  = *man sollte nicht vergessen, dass*
- **It should be stressed that** the only way pet owners could possibly contract such a condition from their pets is by eating them
  = *es sollte betont werden, dass*
- **There is a very important point here and that is that** the accused claims that he was with Ms Martins all evening on the night of the crime
  = *hierbei ist es äußerst wichtig festzustellen, dass*
- At the beginning of the book Mr Stone **makes a telling point**. The Balkan peoples, he notes, are for the first time ...
  = *gibt ein aufschlussreiches Argument*
- Suspicion is **the chief feature of** Britain's attitude to European theatre
  = *das Hauptmerkmal*
- **In order to focus attention on** Hobson's distinctive contributions to macroeconomics, these wider issues are neglected here
  = *um die Aufmerksamkeit auf ... zu lenken*
- **These statements are interesting in that** they illustrate different views
  = *diese Äußerungen sind dahin gehend interessant, dass*

Language in Use

Contents

German-English

Sprache Aktiv

Inhalt

Deutsch-Englisch

Wörterbuch Deutsch ~ Englisch

German ~ English Dictionary

A, a [aː] NT **-, -** *or (inf)* **-s, -s** A, a; **das A und (das) O** *(fig)* the essential thing(s), the be-all and end-all; *(eines Wissensgebietes)* the basics *pl*; **von A bis Z** *(fig inf)* from beginning to end, from A to Z; **sie/ihr alle, von A bis Z** them/you, the whole lot *(Brit)* or all of them/you; **wer A sagt, muss auch B sagen** *(prov)* in for a penny, in for a pound *(esp Brit prov)*; *(moralisch)* if you start something, you should see it through

Ä, ä [ɛː] NT **-, -** *or (inf)* **-s, -s** Ae, ae, A/a umlaut

à [a] PREP *(esp Comm)* at

Aa [aˈla] NT **-,** *no pl (baby-talk)* **Aa machen** to do big jobs *(Brit baby-talk)*, to do a number two *or* a poo *(baby-talk)*

AA [aːˈlaː] NT **-s,** *no pl abbr von* **Auswärtiges Amt** FO *(Brit)*, State Department *(US)*

AA [aːˈlaː] M **-s, -s** *abbr von* **Anonyme Alkoholiker** AA

Aal [aːl] M **-(e)s, -e** eel; **sich (drehen und) winden wie ein ~** *(aus Verlegenheit)* to wriggle like an eel; *(aus Unaufrichtigkeit)* to try and wriggle (one's way) out of it; **glatt wie ein ~** *(fig)* (as) slippery as an eel

aa|len [ˈaːlən] VR *(inf)* to stretch out; **sich in der Sonne ~** to bask in the sun

Aal-: **aal|glatt** *(pej)* ADJ slippery (as an eel), slick ADV slickly; **sich ~ herauswinden** to worm one's way out of it; **Aal|sup|pe** F eel soup

a. a. O. *abbr von* **am angegebenen** *or* **angeführten Ort** loc. cit.

Aar [aːɐ] M **-(e)s, -e** *(obs liter)* eagle, lord of the skies *(liter)*

Aar|gau [ˈaːɐgau] M **-s der ~** Aargau

Aas [aːs] NT **-es, -e** [-zə] **a** *(= Tierleiche)* carrion, rotting carcass **b** *pl* **Äser** [ˈɛːzɐ] *(inf: = Luder)* bugger *(Brit inf)*, sod *(Brit inf)*, jerk *(sl)*, devil *(inf)*; **kein ~** not a single bloody person *(Brit inf)*, not a single soul

aa|sen [ˈaːzn] VI *(inf)* to be wasteful; **mit etw ~** to waste sth; *mit Geld, Gütern auch* to squander sth, to be extravagant *or* wasteful with sth

Aas-: **Aas|flie|ge** F *(Zool)* carrion fly; **Aas|fres|ser** M scavenger, carrion eater; **Aas|gei|er** M *(lit, fig)* vulture; **Aas|ge|ruch** M putrid *or* fetid stench, odour *(Brit)* or odor *(US)* of decomposition

aa|sig [ˈaːzɪç] ADJ *attr Geruch* horrible, disgusting; *(inf) Lächeln* mean ADV *(dated inf: = sehr)* horribly

Aas|kä|fer M burying *or* sexton beetle

ab [ap] ADV off, away; *(Theat)* exit *sing*, exeunt *pl*; **die nächste Straße rechts ab** the next street (off) to *or* on the right; **ab Zoologischer Garten** from Zoological Gardens; **ab Hamburg** after Hamburg; **München ab 12.20 Uhr** *(Rail)* leaving Munich 12.20; **ab wann?** from when?, as of when?; **ab nach Hause** go home, off you go home *(Brit)*; **ab ins Bett mit euch!** off to bed with you *or* you go *(Brit)*, time for bed; **Mütze/Helm ab!** caps/hats off; **Tell ab** *(Theat)* exit Tell; **N und M ab** *(Theat)* exeunt N and M; **ab durch die Mitte** *(inf)* beat it! *(inf)*, hop it! *(inf)*; **kommt jetzt, ab durch die Mitte!** come on, let's beat *(inf)* or hop *(Brit inf)* it!; **ab und zu** *or* *(N Ger)* **an** from time to time, now and again, now and then → **von**
PREP +*dat* **a** *(räumlich)* from; *(zeitlich)* from, as of, as from; **Kinder ab 14 Jahren** children from (the age of) 14 up; **alle ab Gehaltsstufe 4** everybody from grade 4 up; **ab Werk** *(Comm)* ex works; **ab sofort** as of now
b *(Sw: in Zeitangaben)* past; **Viertel ab 7** a quarter past *or* after *(US)* 7

Aba|kus [ˈaːbakʊs] M **-, -** abacus

ab|än|der|bar, ab|än|der|lich [ˈaplɛndɐlɪç] *(old)* ADJ alterable; *Urteil* revisable

ab+än|dern VT *sep* to alter *(in +acc* to); *(= überarbeiten auch)* to revise; *Gesetzentwurf* to amend *(in +acc* to); *Strafe, Urteil* to revise *(in +acc* to)

Ab|än|de|rung F alteration (+*gen* to); *(= Überarbeitung)* revision; *(von Strafe, Urteil)* revision; *(von Gesetzentwurf)* amendment; **in ~** *(Parl, Jur)* in amendment

Ab|än|de|rungs-: **Ab|än|de|rungs|an|trag** M *(Parl)* proposed amendment; **einen ~ einbringen** to submit an amendment; **Ab|än|de|rungs|vor|schlag** M proposed amendment; **einen ~ machen** to propose an amendment; **Abänderungsvorschläge machen** to propose amendments *or* modifications

ab+ar|bei|ten *sep* VT **a** *Schuld* to work off; *Überfahrt* to work; *(= hinter sich bringen) Vertragszeit* to work **b** *(Comput) Programm* to run; *Befehl* to execute VR to slave (away), to work like a slave → *auch* **abgearbeitet**

Ab|art F variety *(auch Biol)*; *(= Variation)* variation (+*gen* on)

ab|ar|tig ADJ **a** abnormal, deviant, unnatural **b** *(= widersinnig)* perverse; **ich halte das Ganze für ziemlich ~** I think the whole thing is really crazy *(inf)* ADV *(inf: = widerlich)* abnormally; **das tut ~ weh** that hurts like hell *(inf)*; **mir ist ~ schlecht** I feel terribly sick; **~ lang** a hell of a long time *(inf)*

Ab|ar|tig|keit F abnormality, deviancy

ab+äsen VT *sep (Wild) Blätter etc* to feed on; *Gras* to crop

Ab|bau M, *no pl* **a** *(= Förderung) (über Tage)* quarrying; *(unter Tage)* mining
b *(lit, fig: = Demontage)* dismantling
c *(Chem)* decomposition; *(im Körper)* breakdown
d *(fig: = Verfall)* decline; *(der Persönlichkeit)* disintegration
e *(= Verringerung) (von Personal, Produktion etc)* reduction (+*gen* in, of), cutback (+*gen* in); *(von überflüssigen Vorräten)* gradual elimination (+*gen* of); *(von Preisen)* cut (+*gen* in), reduction (+*gen* in, of); *(von Privilegien)* reduction (+*gen* of), stripping away (+*gen* of); *(von Vorurteilen)* breaking down (+*gen* of); **der ~ von Beamtenstellen** the reduction in the number of civil service positions

ab|bau|bar ADJ *(Chem)* degradable; **schwer ~e Chemikalien** chemicals that are difficult to break down; **biologisch ~** biodegradable

ab+bau|en *sep* VT **a** *(= fördern) (über Tage)* to quarry; *(unter Tage)* to mine
b *(= demontieren)* to dismantle; *Maschine* to strip down, to dismantle; *Gerüst* to take down, to dismantle; *Kulissen* to take down, to strike; *Zelt* to strike; *Lager* to break, to strike; **ein System allmählich ~** to phase out a system
c *(Chem)* to break down, to decompose; *(im Körper)* to break down
d *(= verringern) Produktion, Personal, Bürokratie* to cut back, to reduce, to cut down on; *Arbeitsplätze, Arbeitskräfte* to reduce the number of; *Privilegien* to cut back, to strip away
VI *(Sportler etc)* to go downhill; *(Patient)* to deteriorate, to weaken; *(= erlahmen)* to flag, to wilt; *(= abschalten)* to switch off

Ab|bau|pro|dukt NT *(Chem)* by-product

ab+bei|ßen *sep irreg* VT to bite off; **eine Zigarre ~** to bite the end off a cigar; **sich** *(dat)* **die Zunge ~** to bite one's tongue off VI to take a bite; **kann ich mal ~?** can I have a bite?; **nun beiß doch mal richtig ab!** now bite it off properly!

ab+bei|zen VT *sep* to strip

Ab|beiz|mit|tel NT paint stripper

ab+be|kom|men *ptp* **abbekommen** VT *sep irreg*
a *(= erhalten)* to get; **etwas ~** to get some (of it); *(= beschädigt werden)* to get damaged; *(= verletzt werden)* to get hurt; *(= Prügel abbekommen)* to catch *or* cop it *(Brit inf)*, to get yours *(US inf)*; **das Auto/er hat dabei ganz schön was ~** *(inf)* the car/he really copped it *(Brit inf)* or got it *(inf)*; **nichts ~** not to get any (of it); *(= nicht beschädigt werden)* not to get damaged; *(= nicht verletzt werden)* to come off unscathed; **sein(en) Teil ~** *(lit, fig)* to get one's fair share **b** *(= abmachen können)* to get off *(von etw* sth)

ab+be|ru|fen *ptp* **abberufen** VT *sep irreg Diplomaten, Minister* to recall; **(von Gott) ~ werden** *(euph)* to be called home *(US)* or to one's maker

Ab|be|ru|fung F **a** recall; **seine ~ nach England** his recall to England **b** *(euph: = Tod)* departure from this life

ab+be|stel|len *ptp* **abbestellt** VT *sep* to cancel; *jdn auch* to tell not to call *or* come; *Telefon* to have disconnected

Ab|be|stel|lung F cancellation; *(von Telefon)* disconnection

ab+bet|teln VT *sep* **jdm etw ~** to scrounge sth off *or* from sb *(inf)*

ab+be|zah|len *ptp* **abbezahlt** *sep* VT *Raten, Auto etc* to pay off VI *(auf Raten)* to pay in instalments *(Brit)* or installments *(US)*

Ab|be|zah|lung F repayment

ab+bie|gen *sep irreg* VT **a** *Ellbogen, Knie* to bend; *(= abbrechen)* to bend off **b** *(inf: = verhindern) Thema, Verfahren* to head off, to avoid; *Frage* to deflect; **das Gespräch ~** to change the subject; **zum Glück konnte ich das ~** luckily I managed to stop that; **diesen Vorschlag hat die Gewerkschaft abgebogen** the union put a stop to this proposal VI *aux sein* to turn off *(in +acc* into); *(bei Gabelungen auch)* to fork off; *(Straße)* to bend, to veer; **nach rechts ~** to turn (off to the) right; to fork right; to veer (to the) right

Ab|bie|ger [ˈapbiːgɐ] M **-s, -, Ab|bie|ge|rin** [-gərɪn] F **-, -nen** *(Mot)* car *etc* turning off

Ab|bie|ge-: **Ab|bie|ge|spur** F *(Mot)* filter *(Brit)* or turning *(US)* lane; **Ab|bie|ge|ver|bot** NT *(Mot)* turn ban; *(Schild)* no turning; **Ab|bie|ge|ver|kehr** M *(Mot)* turning traffic

Ab|bild NT *(= Nachahmung, Kopie)* copy, reproduction; *(= Spiegelbild)* reflection; *(= Wiedergabe)* picture, portrayal, representation; *(von Mensch)* image, likeness; **er ist das genaue ~ seines Vaters** he's the spitting image of his father

ab+bil|den VT *sep (lit, fig)* to depict, to portray, to show; *Verhältnisse etc auch* to reflect; *(= wiedergeben)* to reproduce; **auf der Titelseite ist ein Teddybär abgebildet** there's a picture of a teddy bear on the front page; **auf dem Foto ist eine Schulklasse abgebildet** there's a school class (shown) in the photo

Ab|bil|dung F **a** *(= das Abbilden)* depiction, portrayal; *(= Wiedergabe)* reproduction **b** *(= Illustration)* illustration; *(= Schaubild)* diagram;; *(Comput)* mapping **siehe ~ S.12** see the illustration on p12; **das Buch ist mit zahlreichen ~en versehen** the book is copiously illustrated *or* has numerous illustrations

ab+bin|den *sep irreg* VT **a** *(= abmachen)* to undo, to untie; **sich** *(dat)* **die Schürze ~** to take off one's apron **b** *(Med) Arm, Bein etc* to ligature **c** *(Cook)* to bind VI *(Beton, Mörtel)* to set; *(Cook)* to bind

Ab|bit|te F apology; **(bei jdm wegen etw) ~ tun** *or* **leisten** to make *or* offer one's apologies (to sb for sth)

ab+bit|ten VT *sep irreg (liter)* **jdm etw ~** to beg sb's pardon for sth, to make *or* offer one's apologies to sb for sth

ab+bla|sen *sep irreg* VT *(inf) Veranstaltung, Feier, Streik* to call off; **ein Treffen/ein Konzert/einen Besuch ~** to call off a meeting/concert/visit; **die Abendvorstellung musste abgeblasen werden** the evening performance had to be cancelled **a** *Staub, Schmutz* to blow off *(von etw* sth); *Tisch, Buch* to blow the dust *etc* off, to blow clean; *Gas* to release, to let off; **eine Hauswand mit Sandstrahl ~** to sandblast a house wall **b** *(Tech) Hochofen* to let burn down **c** *(inf) Veranstaltung, Feier, Streik* to call off VI *(Tech: Hochofen)* to burn down

ab+blät|tern VI *sep aux sein (Putz, Farbe)* to flake *or* peel (off)

ab+blei|ben VI *sep irreg aux sein (N Ger inf)* to get to *(inf)*; **wo ist er abgeblieben?** where has he got *(Brit) or* gone to?; **irgendwo muss er/es abgeblieben sein** he/it must be somewhere

ab|blend|bar ADJ *Rückspiegel* antidazzle *(Brit)*, antiglare *(US)*

Ab|blen|de F *(Film)* fade(-out)

ab+blen|den *sep* VT *Lampe* to shade, to screen; *(Aut) Scheinwerfer* to dip *(Brit)*, to dim *(esp US)* VI *(Phot)* to stop down; *(Film)* to fade out; *(Aut)* to dip *(Brit) or* dim *(esp US)* one's headlights; **abgeblendet** *(Comput) Schaltfläche etc* grayed (out); **es wurde abgeblendet** the scene (was) faded out

Ab|blend|licht NT *(Aut)* dipped *(Brit) or* dimmed *(esp US)* headlights *pl*; **mit ~ fahren** to drive on dipped *(Brit) or* dimmed *(esp US)* headlights

ab+blit|zen VI *sep aux sein (inf)* to be sent packing *(bei* by) *(inf)*; **jdn ~ lassen** to send sb packing *(inf)*, to give sb a knock-back *(Brit inf)*, to give sb the brush-off *(inf)*

ab+blo|cken *sep* VT *(Sport, fig)* to block; *Gegner* to stall VI to stall

ab+blü|hen VI *sep aux sein (rare)* = **verblühen**

Ab|brand M **a** *(= Verbrennen)* combustion **b** *(Kernenergie)* burn-up

ab+brau|sen *sep* VT to give a shower; *Körperteil* to wash under the shower; **sich ~** to have *or* take a shower, to shower VI *aux sein (inf)* to roar off *or* away

ab+bre|chen *sep irreg* VT **a** *(= beenden)* to break off; *Raumflug, Rennstart, Experiment* to abort; *(Comput) Vorgang* to abort; *(als Befehl auf Schaltfläche)* to cancel; *Veranstaltung, Verfahren, Verhandlung, Therapie, Start* to stop; *Streik, Suche, Mission* to call off; *Schwangerschaft* to terminate; **die diplomatischen Beziehungen ~** to break off diplomatic relations; **die Schule ~** to stop going to school → *auch* **abgebrochen**

b *Ast, Außenspiegel, Antenne, Fingernagel, Spitze* to break off; *Bleistift* to break, to snap; **etw von etw ~** to break sth off sth; **(nun) brich dir keinen ab!** *(inf)* don't make such a palaver *or* song and dance *(Brit inf)*, don't make such a fuss; **sich** *(dat)* **einen ~** *(inf) (= Umstände machen)* to make heavy weather of it *(Brit inf)*, to make a fuss about it; *(= sich sehr anstrengen)* to go to a lot of bother, to bust one's butt *(US sl)*; **abgebrochen** *(Stück, Bleistiftspitze)* broken off

c *(= abbauen) Zelt* to strike; *Lager* to break; *(= niederreißen)* to demolish; *Gebäude* to demolish, to pull *or* tear down → **Zelt, Brücke**

VI **a** *aux sein (Ast, Halterung, Griff)* to break (off); *(Bleistift, Fingernagel, Lippenstift)* to break; *(Eisscholle)* to break off

b *(= aufhören) (Kontakt)* to break off; *(Student)* to break off one's studies; **mitten im Satz ~** to break off in the middle of a sentence; **wir müssen jetzt leider ~** we have to stop now

c *(Comput)* to abort

d *(= abtreiben)* to abort; **es ist zu spät, um abzubrechen** it's too late for a termination *or* an abortion

Ab|bre|cher(in) M(F) *(= Student)* dropout

Ab|bre|cher|quo|te F dropout rate

ab+brem|sen *sep* VT *Motor* to brake; *(fig)* to curb VI to brake; **auf 30 ~** to brake down to 30

ab+bren|nen *sep irreg* VT *Wiesen* to burn off *or* away the stubble in; *Böschung* to burn off *or* away the scrub on; *Gehöft, Dorf* to burn down; *Feuerwerk, Rakete* to let off; *Kerze etc* to burn; *(= wegbrennen) Lack* to burn off; *(Tech: = abbeizen)* to pickle, to scour; **ein Feuerwerk ~** to have fireworks, to have a firework display; **abgebrannt** *(Gebäude)* burnt down

VI *aux sein* to burn down; **unser Gehöft ist abgebrannt** our farm was burned down; **wir sind abgebrannt** our house/farm *etc* was burned down; **dreimal umgezogen ist einmal abgebrannt** *(prov)* by the time you've moved house three times, you've lost as much as if the place had been burned out → *auch* **abgebrannt**

Ab|bre|vi|a|tur [abrevia'tu:ɐ] F **-, -en** *(Typ, Mus)* abbreviation

ab+brin|gen VT *sep irreg* **a jdn davon ~, etw zu tun** to stop sb (from) doing sth; *(= abraten auch)* to persuade sb not to do sth, to dissuade sb from doing sth; **jdn von etw ~** to make sb change his/her mind about sth; **sich von etw ~ lassen** to allow oneself to be put off sth *(Brit)*, to be dissuaded from sth; **ich lasse mich von meiner Meinung nicht ~** you won't get me to change my mind, nothing will make me change my mind; **jdn vom Thema ~** to get sb off the subject; **jdn/einen Hund von der Spur ~** to throw *or* put sb/a dog off the scent; **jdn/etw vom Kurs ~** to throw *or* put sb/sth off course **b** *(esp S Ger inf) Deckel etc* to get off

ab+brö|ckeln VI *sep aux sein* to crumble away; *(fig)* to fall off *(auch St Ex)*, to drop off; **die Aktienkurse sind am Abbröckeln** the share prices are falling (off); **die Familie/der Ruf der Firma ist am Abbröckeln** the family/firm's reputation is gradually declining

Ab|bruch M **a** *no pl (= das Niederreißen)* demolition; *(von Gebäuden)* pulling down, demolition; **auf ~ verkaufen** to sell for demolition; **auf ~ stehen** to be scheduled *or* due for demolition, to be condemned; **warmer ~** *(inf: = Brandstiftung)* torch job *(inf)*

b *no pl (= Beendigung) (von Schwangerschaft)* termination; *(von Beziehungen, Verhandlungen, Reise)* breaking off; *(von Raumflug etc)* abortion, aborting; *(Comput)* break; *(von Veranstaltung)* stopping; **einem Land mit ~ der diplomatischen Beziehungen drohen** to threaten to break off diplomatic relations with a country; **es kam zum ~ des Kampfes** the fight had to be stopped

c *no pl (= Schaden)* harm, damage; **einer Sache** *(dat)* **~ tun** to harm *or* damage sth, to do (some) harm *or* damage to sth; **das tut der Liebe keinen ~** it doesn't harm *or* hurt their/our relationship; **das tut unseren Interessen ~** that is detrimental to our interests

d *(= Schwangerschaftsabbruch)* termination

Ab|bruch-: **Ab|bruch|ar|bei|ten** PL demolition work; **Ab|bruch|bir|ne** F wrecking ball; **Ab|bruch|fir|ma** F demolition firm; **Ab|bruch|haus** NT condemned building; **Ab|bruch|lis|te** F = **Abrissliste**; **ab|bruch|reif** ADJ only fit for demolition; *(= zum Abbruch freigegeben)* condemned; **Ab|bruch|rei|fe** F **das Gebäude ist bis zur ~ geschädigt** the building is so badly damaged it will have to be demolished

ab+brü|hen VT *sep* to scald; *Mandeln* to blanch → *auch* **abgebrüht**

ab+brum|men *sep* VT *(inf) Zeit* to do *(inf)*; **eine Strafe ~** to do time *(inf)* VI *aux sein (inf)* to roar off *or* away

ab+bu|chen VT *sep (im Einzelfall)* to debit *(von* to, against); *(durch Dauerauftrag)* to pay by standing order *(von* from); *(fig: = abschreiben)* to write off; **für das Abbuchen erhebt die Bank Gebühren** the bank makes a charge for each debit/for a standing order

Ab|bu|chung F *(einzeln)* debit; *(durch Dauerauftrag)* (payment by) standing order; *(durch Einzugsermächtigung)* (payment by) direct debit; **etw durch ~ erledigen** to settle sth by standing order/direct debit

Ab|bu|chungs-: **Ab|bu|chungs|auf|trag** M *(Fin)* (direct) debit order; *(= Dauerauftrag)* standing order; **Ab|bu|chungs|kar|te** F *(TV)* pay--per-view card; **Ab|bu|chungs|kon|to** NT *(Fin)* debiting *or* charge *(US)* account; **Ab|bu|chungs|ver|fah|ren** NT *(Fin)* direct debiting (service), automatic payment system *(US)*

ab+bü|geln VT *sep (inf: = heruntermachen)* to pooh-pooh *(inf)*

ab+bum|meln VT *sep (inf) Stunden* to take off; **Überstunden ~** to take time off for overtime worked

ab+bürs|ten VT *sep* **a** *Staub* to brush off *(von etw* sth); *Kleid, Mantel, Jacke* to brush (down); *Schuhe* to brush **b** *(inf: = heruntermachen)* **jdn ~** to give sb the brushoff, to brush sb aside

ab+bus|seln VT *sep (Aus inf)* = **abküssen**

ab+bü|ßen VT *sep Strafe* to serve

Ab|bü|ßung F **-, -en** serving; **nach ~ der Strafe** after serving *or* having served the sentence

Abc [abe'tse:, a:be:'tse:] NT **-, -** *(lit, fig)* ABC; **Wörter/Namen nach dem ~ ordnen** to arrange words/names in alphabetical order *or* alphabetically

ABC- *in cpds (Mil)* atomic, biological and chemical, Abc

ab+che|cken ['aptʃɛkn] VT *sep* to check; *(= abhaken)* to tick off *(US)*, to tick off *(Brit)*

Abc-Schüt|ze M, **Abc-Schüt|zin** F *(hum)* school-beginner; **dies Bild zeigt mich als ~** this picture shows me when I was starting school

ABC-Waf|fen PL atomic, biological and chemical weapons *pl*

Ab|da|chung ['apdaxʊŋ] F **-, -en a** *(Geog)* declivity, downward slope **b** *(Build)* camber, cambering

ab+däm|men VT *sep See, Fluss* to dam (up)

Ab|däm|mung F *(von Fluss etc)* dam, damming (up); *(von tief liegendem Land)* dam, damming off; *(fig)* curb, check

Ab|dampf M exhaust steam

ab+damp|fen *sep* VI *aux sein* **a** *(Speisen)* to dry off **b** *(Chem: = verdunsten)* to evaporate **c** *(Zug)* to steam off; *(fig inf: = losgehen, -fahren)* to hit the trail *(esp Brit inf) or* road *(inf)*, to push off *(inf)* VT *(Chem: = verdunsten lassen)* to evaporate

ab+dämp|fen VT *sep* = **dämpfen a**

ab+dan|ken VI *sep* to resign; *(König etc)* to abdicate; **abgedankt** *(Soldat, Offizier, Dienstbote)* discharged

Ab|dan|kung F -, -en **a** *(= Thronverzicht)* abdication; *(= Rücktritt)* resignation; **jdn zur ~ zwingen** to force sb to abdicate/resign **b** *(old: = Dienstentlassung)* retirement **c** *(Sw: = Trauerfeier)* funeral service

Ab|deck|cre|me F *(= Stift)* concealer, cover-up or blemish stick

ab+de|cken VT *sep* **a** *(= decken) Bedarf, Kosten, Markt* to cover **b** *(= umfassen, einschließen) Thema, Spektrum, Umfang, Aspekt* to cover **c** *(= zudecken) Fläche, Grab, Loch, Möbel* to cover (over); *Boden* to cover **d** *(Ftbl)* to mark, to cover **e** *(= freilegen) Dach* to take off; *Haus* to take the roof off; *Tisch* to clear **f** *(old: = Fell abziehen von) Tierkadaver* to flay, to skin

Ab|de|cker ['apdɛkɐ] M -s, -, **Ab|de|cke|rin** [-ərɪn] F -, -nen knacker *(Brit inf)*, slaughterman

Ab|de|cke|rei [apdɛkə'rai] F -, -en slaughterhouse, knacker's yard *(Brit inf)*

Ab|deck-: **Ab|deck|fo|lie** F dust cover; *(für Möbel, Boden etc)* dustsheet; **Ab|deck|hau|be** F (dust) cover; **Ab|deck|pla|ne** F tarpaulin; **Ab|deck|stift** M *(Kosmetik)* concealer, cover-up or blemish stick

Ab|de|ckung F **a** cover **b** *no pl (= Vorgang)* covering

ab+dich|ten VT *sep (= isolieren)* to insulate; *(= verschließen) Loch, Leck, Rohr* to seal (up); *Ritzen* to fill, to stop up; **gegen Luft/Wasser ~** to make airtight/watertight; **gegen Feuchtigkeit ~** to damp-proof; **gegen Zugluft ~** to (make) draught-proof *(Brit)* or draft-proof *(US)*; **gegen Lärm/Geräusch/Schall ~** to soundproof

Ab|dich|tung F *(= Isolierung)* insulation; *(= Verschluss, Dichtung)* seal; *(= das Verschließen)* sealing; *(von Ritzen)* filling, stopping up; **~ gegen Zugluft** draught-proofing *(Brit)*, draft-proofing *(US)*; **~ gegen Feuchtigkeit** damp-proofing; **~ gegen Wasser** waterproofing; **~ gegen Lärm/Geräusch/Schall** soundproofing

ab+die|nen VT *sep (dated: = abarbeiten)* to work off; *(Mil: = ableisten)* to serve

Ab|di|ka|ti|on [apdika'tsio:n] F -, -en *(old)* abdication

ab|ding|bar ADJ *(Jur)* alterable subject to mutual agreement

ab+din|gen ['apdɪŋən] *pret* **dingte ab**, *ptp* **abgedungen** ['apgədʊŋən] VT *sep (rare)* **jdm etw ~** *(Zugeständnis)* to strike a deal with sb for sth; **diese Rechte lassen wir uns nicht ~** we shall not cede these rights

ab|di|zie|ren [apdi'tsi:rən] *ptp* **abdiziert** VI *insep (old)* to resign; *(König etc)* to abdicate

Ab|do|men [ap'do:mən] NT -s, - or **Abdomina** *(Med, Zool)* abdomen

ab+don|nern VI *sep aux sein (inf)* to roar off, to zoom off *(inf)*

ab+dor|ren VI *sep aux sein (Zweig)* to dry up, to wither

ab+drän|gen VT *sep* to push away (*von* from), to push out of the way (*von* of); *Menschenmenge* to force back; *(fig) Verfolger etc* to shake off; **ein Auto von der Straße ~** to force a car off the road; **jdn in eine bestimmte Richtung ~** to push sb in a certain direction; **einen Spieler vom Ball ~** to push or barge a player off the ball; **vom Wind abgedrängt werden** to be blown off course (by the wind); **jdn an den Rand der Gesellschaft ~** to marginalize sb to the fringes of society

ab+dre|hen *sep* VT **a** *Gas, Wasser, Hahn* to turn off **b** *Film* to shoot, to film; **abgedreht** *(Szene)* completed **c** *Hals* to wring; **er drehte dem Huhn den Kopf ab** he wrung the chicken's neck; **er drehte der Blume den Kopf ab** he twisted the head off the flower → *auch* **abgedreht** VI *aux sein or haben (= Richtung ändern)* to change course; *(zur Seite auch)* to veer off or away; **nach Osten ~** to turn east

Ab|drift F *(Naut, Aviat)* drift

ab+drif|ten VI *sep aux sein (Naut, Aviat, fig)* to drift off

ab+dros|seln VT *sep Motor* to throttle back or *(gänzlich auch)* down; *(fig) Produktion* to cut back, to cut down on

Ab|dros|se|lung F, **Ab|dross|lung** F throttling back or *(gänzlich auch)* down; *(fig)* cutback (*+gen* in)

Ab|druck M *pl* **-drücke** imprint, impression; *(= Stempelabdruck)* stamp; *(von Schlüssel)* impression, mould *(Brit)*, mold *(US)*; *(= Fingerabdruck, Fußabdruck)* print; *(= Gebissabdruck)* mould *(Brit)*, mold *(US)*, cast, impression; *(= Gesteinsabdruck)* imprint, impression, cast; **einen ~ abnehmen** or **machen** *(inf)* to take or make an impression

Ab|druck M *pl* **-drucke** *(= das Nachdrucken)* reprinting; *(= das Kopieren)* copying; *(= Kopie)* copy; *(= Nachdruck)* reprint; **der ~ dieses Romans wurde verboten** it was forbidden to reprint this novel; **ich habe den ~ des Interviews im „Spiegel" gelesen** I read the text or the printed version of the interview in "Der Spiegel"; **dieser Roman erschien auch als ~ in ...** this novel was also printed in ...

ab+dru|cken VT *sep* to print; **wieder ~** to reprint

ab+drü|cken *sep* VT **a** *Gewehr* to fire **b** *(inf) jdn* to squeeze, to hug **c** *(= nachbilden)* to make an impression of **d** *Vene* to constrict; **jdm fast die Finger/Hand ~** to almost squeeze sb's fingers/hand off; **jdm die Luft ~** *(inf) (lit)* to squeeze all the breath out of sb; *(fig)* to force sb into bankruptcy, to squeeze the life(blood) out of sb VI to pull or squeeze the trigger VR to leave an imprint or impression; **sich (durch etw) ~** to show through (sth)

ab+du|cken VI *sep (Boxen)* to duck

ab+dun|keln VT *sep Lampe* to dim; *Zimmer auch* to darken; *Farbe* to darken, to make darker

ab+du|schen VT *sep* to give a shower; *Körperteil* to wash under the shower; **sich ~** to have or take a shower

ab+eb|ben ['aplɛbn] VI *sep aux sein* to die or fade away; *(Zorn, Lärm auch)* to abate

abend △ ['a:bnt] ADV → **Abend**

Abend ['a:bnt] M -s, -e [-də] **a** evening; **am ~** in the evening; *(= jeden Abend)* in the evening(s); **am ~ des 4. April** on the evening or night of April 4th; **heute/gestern/morgen ~** this/yesterday/tomorrow evening, tonight/last night/tomorrow night; **Mittwochabend** Wednesday evening, Wednesday night; **die Vorstellung wird zweimal pro ~ gegeben** there are two performances every night or evening; **jeden ~** every evening or night; **gegen ~** toward(s) (the) evening; **~ für** or **um** *(geh)* **~** every evening or night, night after night; **am nächsten ~, den nächsten ~** the next evening; **eines ~s** one evening; **den ganzen ~ über** the whole evening; **es wird ~** it's getting late, evening is drawing on *(Brit)*; **es wurde ~** evening came; **jdm guten** or **Guten ~ sagen** to say good evening to sb, to bid sb good evening *(form)*; **guten ~** good evening; **'n ~** *(inf)* evening *(inf)*; **der ~ kommt** *(geh)* or **naht** *(liter)* evening is drawing nigh *(liter)* or on *(Brit)*, it's getting late; **des ~s** *(geh)* in the evening(s), of an evening; **du kannst mich am ~ besuchen!** *(euph inf)* you can take a running jump *(Brit inf)*, you can take a hike *(US inf)*; **zu ~ essen** to have supper or dinner; **je später der ~, desto schöner** or **netter die Gäste** *(prov)* the best guests always come late; **es ist noch nicht aller Tage ~** it's early days still or yet; **man soll den Tag nicht vor dem ~ loben** *(Prov)* don't count your chickens before they're hatched *(Prov)*
b *(= Vorabend)* eve; **am ~ vor der Schlacht** on the eve of the battle
c *(liter: = Ende)* close; **am ~ des Lebens** in the twilight or evening of one's life *(liter)*, in one's twilight years *(liter)*; **am ~ des Jahrhunderts** toward(s) the close or end of the century

-abend M *suf* **der Mittwochabend** Wednesday evening or night

Abend- *in cpds* evening; **Abend|an|dacht** F evening service; **Abend|an|zug** M dinner jacket or suit, DJ *(Brit inf)*, tuxedo *(US)*; **im ~ erscheinen** to come in a dinner jacket/dinner jackets *etc*; **Abend|aus|ga|be** F evening edition; **Abend|blatt** NT evening (news)paper; **Abend|brot** NT supper, tea *(Scot, N Engl)*; **~ essen** to have (one's) supper or tea; **Abend|däm|me|rung** F dusk, twilight

aben|de|lang ADJ *attr* night after night; **unsere ~en Diskussionen** our discussions night after night, our nightly discussions ADV night after night

Abend-: **Abend|es|sen** NT supper, evening meal, dinner; **mit dem ~ auf jdn warten** to wait with supper or dinner or one's evening meal for sb; **Abend|frie|de(n)** M *(liter)* still or quiet of the evening; **abend|fül|lend** ADJ taking up the whole evening; *Film, Stück* full-length; **~ sein** to take up or fill the whole evening; **Abend|gar|de|ro|be** F evening dress; **Abend|ge|bet** NT evening prayers *pl*; *(= Abendandacht)* evensong, vespers; *(baby-talk)* bedtime prayers *pl*; **Abend|ge|sell|schaft** F soirée; **Abend|gym|na|si|um** NT night school *(where one can study for the Abitur)*; **Abend|him|mel** M evening sky, (sky at) sunset; **Abend|kas|se** F *(Theat)* box office; **Abend|kleid** NT evening dress or gown; **Abend|kurs** M, **Abend|kur|sus** M evening course, evening classes *pl* (*für* in); **Abend|land** NT, *no pl (geh)* West, western world, Occident *(liter)*; **das christliche ~** the Christian West; **abend|län|disch** ['a:bntlɛndɪʃ] *(geh)* ADJ western, occidental *(liter)* ADV in a western way or fashion

abend|lich ['a:bntlɪç] ADJ *no pred* evening *attr*; **die ~e Stille** the quiet or still of the evening; **die ~e Kühle** the cool of the evening ADV **~ stattfindende Veranstaltungen** evening events, events taking place in the evening; **es war schon um drei Uhr ~ kühl** at three it was already as cool as (in the) evening; **~ gekleidet** dressed in evening clothes

Abend|mahl NT **a** *(Eccl)* Communion, Lord's Supper; **das ~ nehmen** or **empfangen** to take or receive Communion, to communicate *(form)*; **das ~ spenden** or **reichen** or **erteilen** to administer (Holy) Communion, to communicate *(form)*; **zum ~ gehen** to go to (Holy) Communion **b das (Letzte) ~** the Last Supper

Abend|mahls-: **Abend|mahls|got|tes|dienst** M (Holy) Communion, Communion service; **Abend|mahls|kelch** M Communion cup or chalice; **Abend|mahls|wein** M Communion wine

Abend-: **Abend|mahl|zeit** F evening meal; **Abend|nach|rich|ten** PL evening news *sing*; **Abend|pro|gramm** NT *(Rad, TV)* evening('s) programmes *pl (Brit)* or programs *pl (US)*; **damit ist unser heutiges ~ beendet** and that ends our programmes *(Brit)* or programs *(US)* for this evening; **Abend|rot** NT, **Abend|rö|te** F *(liter)* sunset; **die Felder lagen im ~** the fields lay bathed in the glow of the sunset or in the light of the setting sun

abends ['a:bnts] ADV in the evening; *(= jeden Abend)* in the evening(s); **spät ~** late in the evening; **~ um neun** at nine in the evening

Abend-: **Abend|schu|le** F night school; **Abend|schü|ler(in)** M(F) night-school student; **Abend|son|ne** F evening or late afternoon sun; **Abend|spa|zier|gang** M evening walk or stroll; **Abend|stern** M evening star; **Abend|stil|le** F still or quiet of the evening; **Abend|stim|mung** F evening mood or atmosphere, twilight mood; **Abend|stun|de** F evening (hour); **zu dieser späten ~** at this late hour of the evening; **die frühen ~n** the early hours of the evening; **die schönen ~n** the beautiful evening hours; **sich bis in die ~n hinziehen** to go on (late) into the evening; **Abend|toi|let|te** F (= *Kleidung*) evening dress; **Abend|ver|an|stal|tung** F evening event *or* do *(inf)*; **Abend|ver|kauf** M late-night shopping; **Abend|vor|stel|lung** F evening performance; *(Film auch)* evening showing; **Abend|wind** M evening breeze; **Abend|zeit** F **zur ~** in the evening; **Abend|zei|tung** F evening paper

Aben|teu|er ['a:bntɔyɐ] NT **-s, -** adventure; (= *Liebesabenteuer auch*) affair; **ein militärisches/politisches/verbrecherisches ~** a military/political/criminal venture; **auf ~ ausgehen** to go out in search of adventure; **auf ~ aus sein** to be looking for adventure; **die ~ des Geistes** *(liter)* intellectual adventure

Aben|teu|er- *in cpds* adventure; **Aben|teu|er|buch** NT adventure story *or* book *or* novel; **Aben|teu|er|durst** M thirst *or* longing for adventure; **Aben|teu|er|fe|ri|en** PL adventure holiday *(esp Brit) or* vacation *(US)*; **Aben|teu|er|film** M adventure film, action movie *(US)*; **Aben|teu|er|geist** M adventurous spirit, spirit of adventure; **Aben|teu|er|ge|schich|te** F adventure story

Aben|teu|e|rin ['a:bntɔyərɪn] F **-, -nen** adventuress *(auch pej)*

aben|teu|er|lich ['a:bntɔyɐlɪç] ADJ **a** *Reise, Unternehmung, Politik, Mensch* adventurous; (= *erlebnishungrig*) adventuresome **b** (= *fantastisch*) bizarre; *Gestalten, Verkleidung* eccentric, bizarre; *Erzählung* fantastic; *(inf) Preis* outrageous; *Argument* ludicrous ADV *klingen, sich anhören* bizarre, fantastic; *gekleidet* bizarrely, fantastically, eccentrically

Aben|teu|er|lich|keit F **-, -en** *(von Reise, Unternehmung, Politik, Mensch)* adventurousness; (= *Unwahrscheinlichkeit*) improbability, unlikeliness

Aben|teu|er-: **Aben|teu|er|lust** F thirst for adventure; **von der ~ gepackt werden** to be seized with a thirst for adventure; **aben|teu|er|lus|tig** ADJ adventurous, venturesome; **Aben|teu|er|ro|man** M adventure story; **Aben|teu|er|spiel|platz** M adventure playground; **Aben|teu|er|ur|laub** M adventure holiday *(esp Brit) or* vacation *(US)*

Aben|teu|rer ['a:bntɔyrɐ] M **-s, -** adventurer *(auch pej)*

A|ben|teu|rer- *in cpds* = **Abenteuer-**

Aben|teu|re|rin ['a:bntɔyrərɪn] F **-, -nen** adventuress

Aben|teu|rer-: **Aben|teu|rer|le|ben** NT adventurer's life, life of an adventurer; **ein ~ führen** to lead an adventurous life; **Aben|teu|rer|na|tur** F adventurous person, adventurer

aber ['a:bɐ] CONJ **a** but; **~ dennoch** *or* **trotzdem** but still; **es regnete, ~ dennoch haben wir uns köstlich amüsiert** it was raining, but we still had a great time *or* but we had a great time though *or* but we had a great time all the same; **schönes Wetter heute, was? – ja, ~ etwas kalt** nice weather, eh? – yes, a bit cold though *or* yes but it's a bit cold; **..., ~ ich wünschte, sie hätte es mir gesagt** ..., (al)though *or* but I wished she had told me; **komm doch mit! – ~ ich habe keine Zeit** *or* **ich habe ~ keine Zeit!** come with us! – but I haven't got the time!; **da er ~ nicht wusste ...** but since he didn't know ..., since, however, he didn't know ..., however, since he didn't know ...; **oder ~** or else

b *(zur Verstärkung)* **~ ja!** oh, yes!; (= *sicher*) but of course; **~ selbstverständlich** *or* **gewiss (doch)!** but of course; **~ nein!** oh, no!; (= *selbstverständlich nicht*) of course not!; **~ Renate!** but Renate!; **~, ~!** now, now!, tut, tut!, come, come!; **~ ich kann nichts dafür!** but I can't help it!; **~ das wollte ich doch gar nicht!** but I didn't want that!; **das ist ~ schrecklich!** but that's awful!; **das mach ich ~ nicht!** I will NOT do that!; **dann ist er ~ wütend geworden** then he really got mad, (God), did he get mad!; **das ist ~ heiß/schön!** that's really hot/nice; **du hast ~ einen schönen Ball** you have *or* you've got *(Brit)* a nice ball, haven't you?; **bist du ~ braun!** aren't you brown!; **das geht ~ zu weit!** that's just *or* really going too far!; **schreib das noch mal ab, ~ sauber!** write it out again, and do it neatly!

ADV *(liter)* **~ und ~mals** again and again, time and again → *auch* **abertausend**

Aber ['a:bɐ] NT **-s, -** *or (inf)* **-s** but; **kein ~!** no buts (about it); **die Sache hat ein ~** there's just one problem *or* snag

Aber|glau|be(n) M superstition; *(fig auch)* myth; **zum Aberglauben neigen** to be superstitious

aber|gläu|bisch ['a:bɐglɔybɪʃ] ADJ superstitious ADV **er hängt ~ an ...** he has a superstitious attachment to ...; **er fürchtet sich ~ vor ...** he has a superstitious fear of ...

ab+er|ken|nen *ptp* **aberkannt** VT *sep or (rare) insep irreg* **jdm etw ~** to deprive *or* strip sb of sth; **jdm den Sieg ~** *(Sport)* to disallow sb's victory

Ab|er|ken|nung F deprivation, stripping; *(von Sieg)* disallowing

aber-: **aber|ma|lig** ['a:bɐma:lɪç] ADJ *attr (geh)* repeated; **aber|mals** ['a:bɐma:ls] ADV *(geh)* once again *or* more

ab+ern|ten VTI *sep* to harvest

Ab|er|ra|ti|on [aplɛra'tsio:n] F **-, -en** *(Astron)* aberration

aber|tau|send ADJ thousands upon thousands of; **tausend und ~, Tausend und Abertausend** thousands and *or* upon thousands; **~e** *pl*, **Abertausende** *pl* thousands upon thousands *pl*

Aber|witz M, *no pl (liter)* utter *or* sheer foolishness

aber|wit|zig *(liter)* ADJ mad, crazy, lunatic *attr*; *Summe* crazy ADV terribly, awfully

ab+es|sen *sep irreg* VT **a** (= *herunteressen*) to eat; **sie aß nur die Erdbeeren von der Torte ab** she just ate the strawberries off the cake **b** (= *leer essen*) to eat *or* finish up; *Teller* to finish VI to eat up

Abes|si|ni|en [abɛ'si:niən] NT **-s** Abyssinia

Abes|si|ni|er [abɛ'si:niɐ] M **-s, -**, **Abes|si|ni|e|rin** [-iərɪn] F **-, -nen** Abyssinian

abes|si|nisch [abɛ'si:nɪʃ] ADJ Abyssinian

Abf. *abbr von* **Abfahrt** departure, dep.

ab+fa|ckeln VT **a** (= *verbrennen*) *Gas* to burn off; *Dschungel, Wald* to burn **b** (= *in Brand stecken*) *Gebäude, Auto* to torch

ab|fahr|be|reit ADJ ready to leave

ab+fah|ren *sep irreg aux sein* VI **a** *(Bus, Zug, Auto, Reisende)* to leave, to depart *(form)*; *(Ski: = zu Tal fahren)* to ski down; **~!** *(Rail) order given to a train driver to pull out*; **der Zug fährt um 8 Uhr in** *or* **von Bremen ab** the train leaves Bremen *or* departs from Bremen at 8 o'clock; **der Zug fährt in Kürze ab** the train will be leaving *or* will depart shortly; **„Ihr Zug fährt jetzt ab"** "your train is departing now"; **der Zug ist abgefahren** *(lit)* the train has left *or* gone; *(fig)* we've/you've *etc* missed the boat; **wir müssen schon um 7 Uhr ~** we must set off *or* start (out) *or* leave at 7 o'clock

b *(inf: = abgewiesen werden)* **jdn ~ lassen** to tell sb to push off *(Brit inf) or* to get lost *(inf)*; **er ist bei ihr abgefahren** she told him to push off *(Brit inf) or* to get lost *(inf)*

c *(inf)* **auf jdn/etw ~** to go for sb/sth *(inf)*, to be into sb/sth *(inf)*; **sie fährt voll auf ihn ab** she's into him *(Brit) or* she's fallen for him in a big way *(inf)*

VT **a** (= *abholen*) *Waren* to take away, to remove, to cart off *(inf)*; *Müll* to collect

b (= *abtrennen*) *Körperteil* to cut off, to sever; *Stück von Mauer etc* to knock off; **der Trecker hat ihm ein Bein abgefahren** the tractor cut off *or* severed his leg

c *aux sein or haben Strecke* (= *bereisen*) to cover, to do *(inf)*; (= *überprüfen, ausprobieren*) to go over; **er hat ganz Belgien abgefahren** he travelled *or* went all over Belgium; **wir mussten die ganze Strecke noch einmal ~, um ... zu suchen** we had to go over the whole stretch again to look for ...

d (= *abnutzen*) *Schienen* to wear out; *Reifen* to wear down *or* out; (= *benutzen*) *Fahrkarte* to use; (= *ausnutzen*) *Zeitkarte, Fahrkarte* to get one's money's worth for; **abgefahrene Reifen/Schienen** worn tyres *(Brit) or* tires *(US)*/rails; **das Geld fährst du doch allemal ab** you'll certainly get your money's worth

VR *(Reifen etc)* to wear out *or* down

Ab|fahrt F **a** *(von Zug, Bus etc)* departure; **bis zur ~ sind es noch fünf Minuten** there's still five minutes before the train/bus *etc* leaves *or* goes; **Vorsicht bei der ~ des Zuges!** stand clear, the train is about to leave! **b** *(Ski)* (= *Talfahrt*) descent; (= *Abfahrtsstrecke*) (ski) run **c** *(inf: = Autobahnabfahrt)* exit; **die ~ Gießen** the Gießen exit, the exit for Gießen

ab|fahrt|be|reit ADJ ready to leave

Ab|fahrts-: **Ab|fahrts|lauf** M *(Ski)* downhill; **Ab|fahrts|läu|fer(in)** M(F) *(Ski)* downhill racer *or* skier, downhiller; **Ab|fahrts|ren|nen** NT *(Ski)* downhill (racing); *(einzelnes Rennen)* downhill (race); **Ab|fahrts|zeit** F departure time

Ab|fall M **a** (= *Müll*) refuse; (= *Hausabfall*) rubbish *(Brit)*, garbage *(US)*, trash *(US)*; (= *Straßenabfall*) litter; **in den ~ kommen** to be thrown away *or* out, to go into the dustbin *(Brit) or* trash can *(US)*; **Fleisch-/Stoffabfälle** scraps of meat/material

b (= *Rückstand*) waste *no pl*

c *no pl* (= *Lossagung*) break *(von* with); *(von Partei)* breaking away *(von* from); **seit ihrem ~ von der Kirche ...** since they broke with *or* since their break with the Church ...; **seit ihrem ~ von der Partei ...** since they broke away from the party ...; **seit dem ~ der Niederlande von Spanien** since the Netherlands broke with Spain

d *no pl* (= *Rückgang*) drop (+*gen* in), fall (+*gen* in), falling off; (= *Verschlechterung*) deterioration

Ab|fall-: **Ab|fall|be|sei|ti|gung** F refuse *or* garbage *(US) or* trash *(US)* disposal; **Ab|fall|ei|mer** M rubbish bin *(Brit)*, waste bin, garbage can *(US)*, trash can *(US)*; *(auf öffentlichen Plätzen)* litter bin *(Brit)*, trash can *(US)*

ab+fal|len VI *sep irreg aux sein* **a** (= *herunterfallen*) to fall *or* drop off; *(Blätter, Blüten etc)* to fall; **von etw ~** to fall *or* drop off (from) sth

b (= *sich senken*: *Gelände*) to fall *or* drop away; (= *sich vermindern*: *Druck, Temperatur*) to fall, to drop; **der Weg talwärts verläuft sacht ~d** the path down to the valley slopes gently

c *(fig: = übrig bleiben)* to be left (over); **das, was in der Küche abfällt** the kitchen leftovers; **der Stoff, der beim Schneidern abfällt** the leftover scraps of material

d (= *schlechter werden*) to fall *or* drop off, to go downhill; *(Sport: = zurückbleiben)* to drop back; **gegen etw ~** to compare badly with sth

e *(fig: = sich lösen)* to melt away; **alle Unsicherheit/Furcht fiel von ihm ab** all his uncertainty/fear left him, all his uncertainty/fear melted away (from him) *or* dissolved

f *(von einer Partei)* to break *(von* with), to drop out *(von* of); *(Fraktion)* to break away *(von* from); **vom Glauben ~** to break with *or* leave the faith

g *(inf: = herausspringen)* **wie viel fällt bei dem Geschäft für mich ab?** how much do I get out of the deal?; **es fällt immer ziemlich viel Trinkgeld ab** you/they *etc* always get quite a lot of tips (out of it)

Ab|fall-: **Ab|fall|er|zeug|nis** NT waste product; **Ab|fall|gru|be** F rubbish *(Brit) or* garbage *(US)* pit; **Ab|fall|hau|fen** M rubbish *or* refuse dump *or* tip *(Brit)*, garbage dump *(US)*

ab|fäl|lig ADJ *Bemerkung, Kritik* disparaging, derisive; *Lächeln* derisive; *Urteil* adverse ADV **über jdn ~ reden** *or* **sprechen** to be disparaging of *or* about sb, to speak disparagingly of *or* about sb; **darüber wurde ~ geurteilt** a very dim view was taken of this; **über jdn/etw ~ urteilen** to be disparaging about sb/sth; **etw ~ beurteilen** to be disparaging about sth

Ab|fäl|lig|keit F derision

Ab|fall-: **Ab|fall|pro|dukt** NT waste product; *(von Forschung)* by-product, spin-off; **Ab|fall|schacht** M waste *or* garbage *(US)* disposal chute; **Ab|fall|tou|ris|mus** M international trade in (hazardous) waste; **Ab|fall|ver|wer|tung** F waste utilization

Ab|fall|wirt|schaft F *(= Industriezweig)* waste industry; *(als Umweltschutzmaßnahme)* waste management

ab+fäl|schen VTI *sep (Sport)* to deflect

ab+fan|gen VT *sep irreg* **a** *Flugzeug, Funkspruch, Brief, Ball* to intercept; *Menschen* to catch *(inf)*; *Schlag* to block **b** *(= abstützen) Gebäude* to prop up, to support **c** *(= bremsen) Fahrzeug* to bring under control; *Aufprall* to absorb; *Trend* to check

Ab|fang|jä|ger M *(Mil)* interceptor

ab+fär|ben VI *sep* **a** *(Wäsche)* to run; **pass auf, die Wand färbt ab!** be careful, the paint rubs off the wall; **das rote Handtuch hat auf die weißen Tischdecken abgefärbt** the colour *(Brit) or* color *(US)* has come out of the red towel onto the white tablecloths **b** *(fig)* **auf jdn ~** to rub off on sb

ab+fas|sen VT *sep* **a** *(= verfassen)* to write; *Erstentwurf* to draft **b** *(inf: = abtasten)* to touch up *(inf)*

Ab|fas|sung F writing; *(von Erstentwurf)* drafting

ab+fau|len VI *sep aux sein* to rot away *or* off

ab+fe|dern *sep* VT *Sprung, Stoß* to cushion; *(fig) Krise, Verluste* to cushion the impact of; **die sozialen Auswirkungen der Rationalisierung ~** to reduce *or* lessen the social consequences of rationalization VI to absorb the shock; *(Sport) (beim Abspringen)* to push off; *(beim Aufkommen)* to bend at the knees; **er ist** *or* **hat schlecht abgefedert** he landed stiffly

ab+fe|gen VT *sep Schmutz* to sweep away *or* off; *Balkon, Hof* to sweep; **den Schnee vom Dach ~** to sweep the snow off the roof

ab+fei|ern VT *sep (inf)* **Überstunden ~** to take time off in lieu (of overtime) *(Brit)*, to use up overtime without pay(ment) *(US)*

ab+fei|len VT *sep* to file off *or (glättend)* down

ab+fer|keln VI *sep* to have a litter

ab+fer|ti|gen *sep* VT **a** *(= versandfertig machen) Pakete, Waren* to prepare for dispatch, to make ready *or* get ready for dispatch, to process *(form)*; *Gepäck* to check (in); *(= be- und entladen) Flugzeug* to service, to make ready for takeoff; *Schiff* to make ready to sail; **die Schauerleute fertigen keine Schiffe aus Chile mehr ab** the dockers won't handle any more ships from Chile

b *(= bedienen) Kunden, Antragsteller, Patienten* to attend to, to deal with; *(inf: Sport) Gegner* to deal with; **jdn kurz** *or* **schroff ~** *(inf)* to snub sb; **ich lasse mich doch nicht mit 10 Euro ~** I'm not going to be fobbed off *(esp Brit)* with 10 euros

c *(= kontrollieren) Waren, Reisende* to clear; **beim Zoll/an der Grenze abgefertigt werden** to be cleared by customs/at the border; **die Zöllner fertigten (die Reisenden) sehr zügig ab** the customs officers dealt with the travellers *(Brit) or* travelers *(US)* very quickly; **die Zollbeamten hatten den Zug fast abgefertigt, als ...** the customs officials had almost finished checking the train when ...

Ab|fer|ti|gung F **a** *(zum Versand) (von Paketen, Waren)* getting ready for dispatch, processing *(form)*; *(von Gepäck)* checking; *(von Flugzeug)* servicing, getting ready for takeoff; *(von Schiff)* making ready to sail

b *(= Bedienung) (von Kunden)* service; *(von Antragstellern)* dealing with; *(fig: = Abweisung)* rebuff, snub; **die geschickte ~ des Gegners** *(Sport)* the skilful *(Brit) or* skillful *(US)* way of dealing with one's opponent

c *(von Waren, Reisenden)* clearance; **die ~ an der Grenze** customs clearance; **zollamtliche ~** customs clearance

d *(= Abfertigungsstelle) (für Waren)* dispatch office; *(im Flughafen)* check-in

Ab|fer|ti|gungs-: **Ab|fer|ti|gungs|hal|le** F *(Aviat)* terminal building; **Ab|fer|ti|gungs|schal|ter** M dispatch counter; *(von Zollamt)* customs clearance; *(im Flughafen)* check-in desk

ab+feu|ern VT *sep* to fire; *(Ftbl inf)* to let fire with

ab+fin|den *sep irreg* VT to pay off; *Gläubiger auch* to settle with; *(= entschädigen)* to compensate; **er wurde von der Versicherung mit 20.000 EUR abgefunden** he was paid 20,000 EUR (in) compensation by the insurance company; **einen Fürst/König mit einer Apanage ~** to endow a prince/king with an appanage; **jdn mit leeren Versprechungen ~** to fob sb off *(esp Brit)* with empty promises

VR **sich mit jdm/etw ~** to come to terms with sb/sth; **sich mit jdm/etw nicht ~ können** to be unable to accept sb/sth, to be unable to come to terms with sb/sth; **er konnte sich nie damit ~, dass ...** he could never accept the fact that ...; **sich mit jdm/etw schwer ~** to find it hard to accept sb/sth; **mit allem kann ich mich ~, aber nicht ...** I can put up with most things, but not ...

Ab|fin|dung ['apfɪndʊŋ] F **-, -en a** *(von Gläubigern)* paying off; *(= Entschädigung)* compensation **b** *(= Summe)* payment, (sum in) settlement; *(= Entschädigung)* compensation *no pl*, indemnity; *(bei Entlassung)* severance pay; *(wegen Rationalisierung)* redundancy payment *(Brit)*, buyout *(US)*

Ab|fin|dungs|sum|me F payment, (sum in) settlement; *(= Entschädigung)* compensation *no pl*, indemnity; **eine/keine ~ für einen Unfall bekommen** to receive an indemnity *or* a sum in compensation/no indemnity *or* no compensation for an accident

ab+fi|schen VT *sep* to fish dry

ab+fla|chen ['apflaxn] *sep* VT to level (off), to flatten (out) VR *(Land)* to flatten out, to grow *or* get flatter; *(fig: = sinken)* to drop *or* fall (off) VI *aux sein (fig: = sinken)* to drop *or* fall (off), to decline

Ab|fla|chung F **-, -en** flattening out; *(fig)* dropping off, falling off

ab+flau|en ['apflauən] VI *sep aux sein* **a** *(Wind)* to drop, to die away *or* down, to abate; **nach (dem) Abflauen des Windes** when the wind had dropped *or* died down *or* abated **b** *(fig) (Empörung, Erregung)* to fade, to die away; *(Interesse)* to flag, to wane, to fade; *(Börsenkurse)* to fall, to drop; *(Geschäfte)* to fall *or* drop off

ab+flie|gen *sep irreg* VI *aux sein (Aviat)* to take off *(nach* for); *(Zugvögel)* to migrate, to fly off *or* away; *(inf: = sich lösen)* to fly off; **sie sind gestern nach München/von Hamburg abgeflogen** they flew to Munich/from Hamburg yesterday VT *Gelände* to fly over; *Verwundete* to fly out *(aus* of)

ab+flie|ßen VI *sep irreg aux sein (= wegfließen)* to drain *or* run *or* flow away; *(durch ein Leck)* to leak away; *(Verkehr)* to flow away; **ins Ausland ~** *(Geld)* to flow out of the country; **der Ausguss/die Wanne fließt nicht ab** the water isn't running *or* draining out of the sink/bath (at all)

Ab|flug M takeoff; *(von Zugvögeln)* migration; *(inf: = Abflugstelle)* departure point; **~ Glasgow 8.00 Uhr** departure Glasgow 8.00 a.m.

Ab|flug-: **ab|flug|be|reit** ADJ ready for takeoff; **Ab|flug|ha|fen** M departure airport; **Ab|flug|hal|le** F departure lounge; **Ab|flug|schal|ter** M check-in desk; **Ab|flug|tag** M day of departure, departure date

Ab|fluss M **a** *(= Abfließen)* draining away; *(durch ein Leck)* leaking away; *(fig: von Geld)* draining away; **den ~ des Wassers verhindern** to prevent the water (from) draining *or* running *or* flowing away; **dem ~ von Kapital ins Ausland Schranken setzen** to impose limits on the (out)flow of capital out of the country **b** *(= Abflussstelle)* drain; *(von Teich etc)* outlet **c** *(= Abflussrohr)* drainpipe; *(von sanitären Anlagen)* waste pipe

Ab|fluss-: **Ab|fluss|gra|ben** M drainage ditch; **Ab|fluss|hahn** M tap, drain cock; **Ab|fluss|rei|ni|ger** M drain cleaner; **Ab|fluss|rin|ne** F gutter; **Ab|fluss|rohr** NT outlet; *(im Gebäude)* waste pipe; *(außen am Gebäude)* drainpipe; *(unterirdisch)* drain, sewer

ab+foh|len VI *sep (Zool)* to foal

Ab|fol|ge F *(geh)* sequence, succession

ab+for|dern VT *sep* **jdm etw ~** to demand sth from sb; **jdm den Ausweis ~** to ask to see sb's papers

ab+fo|to|gra|fie|ren *ptp* **abfotografiert** VT *sep* to photograph

Ab|fra|ge F *(Comput)* query; **eine ~ eingeben** to key in a query

ab+fra|gen VT *sep* **a** *(Comput) Information* to call up; *Datenbank* to query **b** *(esp Sch)* **jdn** *or* **jdm etw ~** to question sb on sth; *(Lehrer)* to test sb orally on sth; **eine Lektion ~** to give an oral test on a lesson

ab+fres|sen VT *sep irreg Blätter, Gras* to eat; *Metall, Schicht* to eat away, to corrode; **das Aas bis auf die Knochen ~** to strip the carcass to the bones; **die Giraffe frisst die Blätter von den Bäumen ab** the giraffe strips the leaves off the trees

ab+fret|ten ['apfrɛtn] VR *sep (Aus inf)* to struggle along

ab+frie|ren *sep irreg* VI *aux sein* to get frostbitten VT **sich** *(dat)* **etw ~** to get frostbite in sth; **ihm sind die Zehen abgefroren** he got frostbite in his toes; **abgefroren sein** *(Körperteil)* to be frostbitten; **sich** *(dat)* **einen ~** *(sl)* to freeze to death *(inf)*

ab+frot|tie|ren *ptp* **abfrottiert** VT *sep* to towel down *or* dry

Ab|fuhr ['apfu:ɐ] F **-, -en a** *no pl (= Abtransport)* removal **b** *(inf: = Zurückweisung)* snub, rebuff; **jdm eine ~ erteilen** to snub *or* rebuff sb, to give sb a snub *or* rebuff; *(Sport)* to thrash sb *(inf)*, to give sb a thrashing *(inf)*; **sich** *(dat)* **eine ~ holen** to meet with a snub *or* a rebuff, to be snubbed; **sich** *(dat)* **(gegen jdn) eine ~ holen** *(Sport)* to be given a thrashing (by sb) *(inf)*, to be thrashed (by sb) *(inf)*

ab+füh|ren *sep* VT **a** *(= wegführen)* to lead *or* take away; *Gefangenen* to take away; **~!** away with him/her *etc*, take him/her *etc* away!; **das führt uns vom Thema ab** that will take us away *or* divert us from our subject **b** *(= abgeben) Betrag* to pay *(an +acc* to) VI **a** *(= wegführen)* **der Weg führt hier (von der Straße) ab** the path leaves the road here; **das würde vom Thema ~** that would take us off the subject **b** *(= den Darm anregen)* to have a laxative effect **c** *(= Stuhlgang haben)* to move *or* evacuate one's bowels, to have a bowel movement

ab|füh|rend ADJ **a** *Mittel* laxative *no adv*, aperient *no adv (form)* **b** *Bergpfade* descending; *Blutgefäße* leading away from the heart ADV **~ wirken** to have a laxative effect

Ab|führ-: **Ab|führ|mit|tel** NT laxative, aperient *(form)*; **Ab|führ|tee** M (herbal) laxative tea

Ab|füll-: **Ab|füll|an|la|ge** F bottling plant; **Ab|füll|be|trieb** M bottling factory; **Ab|füll|da|tum** NT bottling date

ab+fül|len VT *sep* **a** *(= abziehen) Wein etc* to draw off *(in +acc* into); *(in Flaschen)* to bottle; *Flasche* to fill; **Wein in Flaschen ~** to bottle wine **b jdn ~** *(inf)* to get sb sloshed *(inf)*

Ab|fül|lung F filling, bottling; **aus eigener ~** *(Wein etc)* bottled by the grower, bottled on site; *(auf Etikett)* estate-bottled

ab+füt|tern VT *sep Vieh* to feed; *(hum) Menschen* to feed

ab+füt|tern VT *sep (Sew)* to line

Ab|füt|te|rung F feeding *no pl*; *(hum: = Mahlzeit)* meal *(inf)*

Ab|ga|be F **a** *no pl (= Abliefern)* handing *or* giving in; *(von Gepäck)* depositing; *(= Übergabe: von Brief etc)* delivery, handing over; **zur ~ von etw aufgefordert werden** to be told to hand sth in
b *no pl (= Verkauf)* sale; **~ von Prospekten kostenlos** leaflets given away free
c *no pl (von Wärme etc)* giving off, emission
d *no pl (von Schuss, Salve)* firing; **nach ~ von vier Schüssen** after firing four shots
e *(= Steuer)* tax; *(= soziale Abgabe)* contribution
f *no pl (von Erklärung, Urteil, Meinungsäußerung etc)* giving; *(von Gutachten)* submission, submitting; *(von Stimme)* casting
g *(Sport) (= Abspiel)* pass; **nach ~ von zwei Punkten …** after conceding two points …

Ab|ga|be(n)-: **ab|ga|be(n)|frei** ADJ *(= steuerfrei, beitragsfrei) Person, Unternehmen, Einkommen* not liable for tax/for social security contributions *(Brit)*, exempt from tax/welfare contributions *(US)*; **Ab|ga|be(n)|ord|nung** F *(Jur)* tax law; **Ab|ga|be(n)|pflicht** F *(von Person, Unternehmen, Einkommen)* liability for tax/for social security contributions *(Brit) or* welfare contributions *(US)*; **ab|ga|be(n)|pflich|tig** [-pflɪçtɪç] ADJ *Person, Unternehmen, Einkommen* liable for tax/for social security contributions *(Brit) or* welfare contributions *(US)*

Ab|ga|ben|sys|tem NT taxation system

Ab|ga|be|ter|min M closing date; *(für Dissertation etc)* submission date

Ab|gang M *pl* **-gänge a** *no pl (= Absendung)* dispatch; **vor ~ der Post** before the post *(Brit) or* mail goes
b *no pl (= Abfahrt)* departure
c *no pl (= Ausscheiden) (aus einem Amt)* leaving, departure; *(= Schulabgang)* leaving; **seit seinem ~ von der Schule** since he left school; **einen ~ machen** *(sl: = verschwinden)* to split *(sl)*
d *no pl (Theat, fig)* exit; **sich** *(dat)* **einen guten/glänzenden ~ verschaffen** to make a grand exit
e *(Sport)* dismount; **einen guten/schwierigen ~ turnen** to do a good/difficult dismount from the apparatus
f *(Med: = Ausscheidung)* passing; *(von Eiter)* discharging; *(= Fehlgeburt)* miscarriage, abortion *(form)*; *(= Fötus)* aborted foetus *(Brit) or* fetus *(esp US)*
g *(= Person) (Sch)* leaver *(Brit)*, high school graduate *(US)*; *(Med, Mil)* death
h *(sl: = Ejakulation)* ejaculation
i *(Comm)* waste; *(Aus: = Fehlbetrag)* missing amount

Ab|gän|ger [ˈapgɛŋɐ] M **-s, -**, **Ab|gän|ge|rin** [-ərɪn] F **-, -nen** *(Sch)* (school) leaver *(Brit)*, graduate *(US)*

ab|gän|gig ADJ *(Aus Admin)* missing *(aus* from); **ein Abgängiger** a missing person

Ab|gän|gig|keits|an|zei|ge F *(Aus Admin) notification to the authorities that a person is missing*; **~ erstatten** to report a person missing

Ab|gangs-: **Ab|gangs|al|ter** NT *(Sch)* school-leaving age; **Ab|gangs|prü|fung** F leaving examination *(Brit)*, final examination *(US)*; **Ab|gangs|zeug|nis** NT leaving certificate *(Brit)*, high school diploma *(US)*

Ab|gas NT exhaust *no pl*, exhaust fumes *pl*, waste gas *(esp Tech)*; **Luftverschmutzung durch ~e** exhaust gas pollution

Ab|gas-: **ab|gas|arm** ADJ *Fahrzeug* low-pollution; **das Auto ist ~** the car has a low level of exhaust emissions; **ab|gas|frei** ADJ *Motor, Fahrzeug* exhaust-free; **~e Produktionsverfahren** production methods which produce no waste gases ADV **~ verbrennen** to burn without producing exhaust fumes; **Ab|gas|norm** F exhaust emission standard; **Ab|gas|rei|ni|gung** F *(Aut)* purification of exhaust gases; **Ab|gas|rei|ni|gungs|an|la|ge** F exhaust emission purification system; **Ab|gas|rück|füh|rung** F *(Aut)* exhaust gas recirculation, EGR; **Ab|gas|(son|der)|un|ter|su|chung** F *(Aut)* emissions test; **Ab|gas|wol|ke** F cloud of exhaust

ab+gau|nern VT *sep (inf)* **jdm etw ~** to con *or* trick sb out of sth *(inf)*

ABGB [a:be:ge:ˈbe:] NT **-** *(Aus) abbr von* **Allgemeines Bürgerliches Gesetzbuch**

ab|ge|ar|bei|tet ADJ *(= verbraucht)* work-worn; *(= erschöpft)* worn out, exhausted; *(Comput) Programm* that has/had been run → *auch* **abarbeiten**

ab+ge|ben *sep irreg* VT **a** *(= abliefern)* to hand *or* give in; *(= hinterlassen)* to leave; *Gepäck, Koffer* to leave, to deposit; *(= übergeben)* to hand over, to deliver
b *(= weggeben)* to give away; *(= verkaufen)* to sell; *(an einen anderen Inhaber)* to hand over; **Matratze preisgünstig abzugeben** mattress for sale at (a) bargain price
c *(= verschenken)* to give away; **jdm etw ~** to give sth to sb; **jdm etwas von seinem Kuchen ~** to give sb some of one's cake
d *(= überlassen) Auftrag* to hand *or* pass on *(an +acc* to); *(= abtreten) Posten* to relinquish, to hand over *(an +acc* to)
e *(Sport) Punkte, Rang* to concede; *(= abspielen)* to pass
f *(= ausströmen) Wärme, Sauerstoff* to give off, to emit
g *(= abfeuern) Schuss, Salve* to fire
h *(= äußern) Erklärung* to give; *Gutachten* to submit; *Meinung* to express, to give; *Stimme* to cast
i *(= darstellen) Rahmen, Hintergrund* to give, to provide; *(= liefern) Stoff, Material etc* to give, to provide, to furnish; **den Vermittler ~** *(inf)* to act as mediator
j *(= verkörpern)* to make; **er würde einen guten Schauspieler ~** he would make a good actor
VR **sich mit jdm/etw ~** *(= sich beschäftigen)* to bother *or* concern oneself with sb/sth; *(= sich einlassen)* to associate with sb/sth
VI *(Sport)* to pass

ab|ge|brannt ADJ *pred (inf: = pleite)* broke *(inf)*; **völlig ~ sein** to be flat *or* stony *(Brit)* broke *(inf)* → *auch* **abbrennen**

ab|ge|bro|chen ADJ *(= nicht beendet) Studium* uncompleted; *Worte* disjointed; **mit einem ~en Studium kommt man nicht sehr weit** you don't get very far if you haven't finished university *or* your university course; **er ist ~er Mediziner** *(inf)* he broke off his medical studies → *auch* **abbrechen**

ab|ge|brüht [ˈapgəbry:t] ADJ *(inf: = skrupellos)* callous; *(= frech)* cool → *auch* **abbrühen**

Ab|ge|brüht|heit F **-**, *no pl (inf)* callousness

ab|ge|dreht [ˈapgədre:t] ADJ *(inf: = verrückt)* crazy *(inf)*; *(Aus inf: = skrupellos)* unscrupulous → *auch* **abdrehen**

ab|ge|dro|schen [ˈapgədrɔʃn] ADJ *(inf)* hackneyed *(Brit)*, well-worn; *Witz auch* corny *(inf)*; **eine ~e Phrase** a cliché; **eine ~e Redensart** a hackneyed *(Brit) or* trite saying

ab|ge|feimt [ˈapgəfaimt] ADJ cunning, wily

Ab|ge|feimt|heit F **-, -en** cunning, wiliness

ab|ge|fuckt [ˈapgəfakt] ADJ *(sl: = heruntergekommen) Gegenstand* knackered *(Brit sl)*, clapped-out *(Brit inf)*, on its last legs *(inf)*; *Mensch auch* fucked-up *(vulg)*

ab|ge|grif|fen [ˈapgəgrɪfn] ADJ *Buch* (well-)worn; *Leder* worn; *(fig) Klischees, Phrasen etc* well-worn, hackneyed *(Brit)*

ab|ge|hackt [ˈapgəhakt] ADJ *Sprechweise* clipped; *Schluchzen* broken ADV **~ schluchzen** to sob brokenly; **~ sprechen** to speak in a clipped manner → *auch* **abhacken**

ab|ge|half|tert [ˈapgəhalftɐt] ADJ haggard; **ein ~er Politiker** a political has-been

ab|ge|han|gen [ˈapgəhaŋən] ADJ **(gut) ~** *(fig: = etabliert)* well-established → *auch* **abhängen**

ab|ge|härmt [ˈapgəhɛrmt] ADJ careworn ADV **~ aussehen** to look careworn

ab|ge|här|tet [ˈapgəhɛrtət] ADJ tough, hardy; *(fig)* hardened; **gegen Erkältungen ~ sein** to be immune to colds → *auch* **abhärten**

ab+ge|hen *sep irreg aux sein* VI **a** *(= abfahren)* to leave, to depart *(nach* for); **der Zug ging in** *or* **von Frankfurt ab** the train left from Frankfurt; **der Zug ging in** *or* **von Frankfurt pünktlich ab** the train left Frankfurt on time
b *(Sport: = abspringen)* to jump down; **er ging mit einem Doppelsalto vom Barren ab** he did a double somersault down from *or* off the bars
c *(Theat: = abtreten)* to exit, to make one's exit; **Othello geht ab** exit Othello
d *(= ausscheiden) (von der Schule, old: aus einem Amt)* to leave; **von der Schule ~** to leave school; **mit dem Tode** *or* **mit Tod ~** *(old form)* to die in office
e *(Med sl: = sterben)* to die
f *(= sich lösen)* to come off; *(= herausgehen: Farbe etc)* to come out *or* off; **an meiner Jacke ist ein Knopf abgegangen** a button has come off my jacket
g *(= abgesondert werden)* to pass out; *(Eiter etc)* to be discharged; *(Fötus)* to be aborted; **ihm ist einer abgegangen** *(sl)* he shot *or* came off *(sl)*
h *(= losgehen: Schuss)* to be fired, to be loosed off
i *(= abgesandt werden)* to be sent *or* dispatched; *(Funkspruch)* to be sent; **etw ~ lassen** to send *or* dispatch sth
j *(inf: = fehlen)* **jdm geht Verständnis/Taktgefühl ab** sb lacks understanding/tact
k *(= abgezogen werden) (vom Preis)* to be taken off; *(von Verdienst)* to be taken off, to be deducted; *(vom Gewicht)* to come off; **(von etw) ~** *(von Preis)* to be taken off (sth); *(von Verdienst auch)* to be deducted (from sth); *(von Gewicht)* to be taken off (sth); **davon gehen 5% ab** 5% is taken off that
l *(= abzweigen)* to branch off; *(esp bei Gabelung)* to fork off
m *(= abweichen)* **von einem Plan/einer Forderung ~** to give up *or* drop a plan/demand; **von seiner Meinung ~** to change *or* alter one's opinion; **von einem Thema ~** to digress (from a subject); **davon kann ich nicht ~** I must insist on that; *(bei Versprechungen etc)* I can't go back on that
n *(= verlaufen)* to go; **gut/glatt/friedlich ~** to go well/smoothly/peacefully; **es ging nicht ohne Streit ab** there was an argument
o *(sl)* **das geht gut ab** it's really great; **da geht aber was ab** it's a really happening place *(inf)*; **gestern ging nichts ab** there was nothing doing yesterday *(inf)*; **was geht ab?** what's doing? *(inf)*
VT **a** *(= entlanggehen)* to go *or* walk along; *(hin und zurück)* to walk *or* go up and down; *(Mil) Gebäudekomplex, Gelände* to patrol; *(= inspizieren)* to inspect
b *(= messen)* to pace out
c *(Sch inf: = verweisen)* **abgegangen werden** to be thrown *or* chucked *(inf)* out

ab|ge|hend ADJ *Post, Anruf, Daten* outgoing; *Zug, Schiff* departing; **die ~en Pferde** *(Sport)* the starters; **die morgen ~e Post** the post *(Brit) or* mail which will go out tomorrow

ab|ge|hetzt [ˈapgəhɛtst] ADJ out of breath → *auch* **abhetzen**

ab|ge|ho|ben ADJ *(inf: = wirklichkeitsfremd) Mensch, Politik* divorced from reality, out of touch with the real world → *auch* **abheben**

ab|ge|kämpft [ˈapgəkɛmpft] ADJ exhausted, shattered *(Brit inf)*, worn-out → *auch* **abkämpfen**

ab|ge|kar|tet [ˈapgəkartət] ADJ fixed *(inf)*, rigged *(inf)*; **eine ~e Sache, ein ~es Spiel** a fix *(inf)*, a put-up job *(Brit inf)*, a frame-up *(US inf)*; **die Sache war von vornherein ~** the whole thing was a put-up job *(Brit inf) or* a frame-up *(US inf)* → *auch* **abkarten**

ab|ge|klärt [ˈapgəklɛ:ɐt] ADJ *Mensch* worldly-wise; *Urteil* well-considered; *Sicht* detached; **~ sein** to stand above things ADV *betrachten, beurteilen* with a certain detachment → *auch* **abklären**

Ab|ge|klärt|heit F -, *no pl* detachment

ab|ge|latscht ['apgəla:tʃt] ADJ *(sl) Schuhe, Teppich* worn-out

ab|ge|lebt ['apgəle:pt] ADJ **a** *(= verbraucht) Person* decrepit; *Badeort etc* run-down **b** *(= altmodisch) Tradition, Vorstellung* antiquated

ab|ge|le|gen ADJ *(= entfernt) Dorf, Land* remote; *(= einsam)* isolated → *auch* **abliegen**

Ab|ge|le|gen|heit F remoteness; *(= Einsamkeit)* isolation

ab|ge|lei|ert ['apgəlaiɐt] ADJ *(pej) Melodie etc* banal, trite; *Redensart etc* banal, trite, hackneyed *(Brit)*; *Schallplatte* worn out, crackly

ab+gel|ten VT *sep irreg (= bezahlen) Ansprüche* to satisfy; *(= sich revanchieren für) Gefallen* to return; **Umweltschäden mit Geldzahlungen ~** to provide financial compensation for environmental damage; **sein Urlaub wurde durch Bezahlung abgegolten** he was given payment in lieu of holiday *(Brit)* or instead of vacation *(US)*

ab|ge|macht ['apgəmaxt] INTERJ OK, that's settled; *(bei Kauf)* it's a deal, done ADJ **eine ~e Sache** a fix *(inf)*; **das war doch schon vorher eine ~e Sache** it was all fixed up *or* arranged beforehand → *auch* **abmachen**

ab|ge|ma|gert ['apgəma:gɐt] ADJ *(= sehr dünn)* thin; *(= ausgemergelt)* emaciated; *(fig: = reduziert)* scaled down → *auch* **abmagern**

ab|ge|mer|gelt ['apgəmɛrglt] ADJ emaciated → *auch* **abmergeln**

ab|ge|mes|sen ADJ *(lit, fig)* measured ADV **~ gehen** to walk with measured steps; **~ sprechen** to speak in measured tones → *auch* **abmessen**

ab|ge|neigt ADJ averse *pred* (*+dat* to); **ich wäre gar nicht ~** *(inf)* actually I wouldn't mind; **einer Sache nicht ~ sein** not to be averse to sth; **jdm ~ sein** to dislike sb

Ab|ge|neigt|heit F aversion *(gegenüber* to)

ab|ge|nutzt ['apgənʊtst] ADJ *Möbel, Teppich* worn, shabby; *Bürste, Besen* worn-out; *Reifen* worn-down; *(fig) Klischees, Phrasen* hackneyed *(Brit)*, well-worn → *auch* **abnutzen**

Ab|ge|ord|ne|ten-: **Ab|ge|ord|ne|ten|bank** F *pl* **-bänke** bench; **Ab|ge|ord|ne|ten|haus** NT parliament; *(in Berlin)* House of Representatives

Ab|ge|ord|ne|te(r) ['apgəlɔrdnətə] MF *decl as adj* (elected) representative; *(von Nationalversammlung)* member of parliament; **Herr ~r!** sir; **Frau ~!** madam

ab|ge|ris|sen ['apgərɪsn] ADJ **a** *(= zerlumpt) Kleidung, Eindruck* ragged, tattered; *Mensch* scruffy **b** *(= unzusammenhängend) Worte, Gedanken* disjointed, incoherent → *auch* **abreißen**

Ab|ge|sand|te(r) ['apgəzantə] MF *decl as adj* envoy

Ab|ge|sang M *(Poet)* abgesang *(concluding section of the final strophe of the minnesang)*; *(fig liter)* swan song, farewell

ab|ge|schabt ['apgəʃa:pt] ADJ *(= abgewetzt) Kleider* threadbare → *auch* **abschaben**

ab|ge|schie|den ['apgəʃi:dn] ADJ **a** *(geh: = einsam)* secluded **b** *(liter: = tot)* departed; **der Abgeschiedene/die Abgeschiedenen** the departed ADV **~ leben** to live a secluded life; **~ wohnen** to live in seclusion → *auch* **abscheiden**

Ab|ge|schie|den|heit F -, *no pl* seclusion

ab|ge|schlafft ['apgəʃlaft] ADJ **a** *Muskeln* flabby **b** *(inf: = erschöpft)* whacked *(Brit inf)*, exhausted; **~e Typen** lazy bums *(inf)* → *auch* **abschlaffen**

ab|ge|schla|gen ['apgəʃla:gn] ADJ **a** *(= erschöpft)* washed out *(inf)*, shattered *(Brit inf)* **b** *(= zurück)* behind; *(= besiegt)* well beaten; **auf einem ~en 8. Platz** in a poor 8th place ADV **weit ~ liegen** to be way behind; **er landete ~ auf dem 8. Platz** he finished up way down in 8th place → *auch* **abschlagen**

Ab|ge|schla|gen|heit F -, *no pl* (feeling of) exhaustion

ab|ge|schlos|sen ADJ *(= einsam)* isolated; *(attr: = geschlossen) Wohnung* self-contained; *Grundstück, Hof* enclosed ADV **~ leben** to live in isolation → *auch* **abschließen**

Ab|ge|schlos|sen|heit F isolation

ab|ge|schmackt ['apgəʃmakt] ADJ outrageous; *Bemerkung auch* crude; *Witz* corny, fatuous ADV outrageously

Ab|ge|schmackt|heit F -, -en **a** *no pl* tastelessness **b** *(= Bemerkung)* platitude; **alberne Witze und ähnliche ~en** stupid jokes and similar corny things

ab|ge|schrägt ['apgəʃrɛ:kt] ADJ *Brett, Wand* bevelled *(Brit)*, beveled *(US)*

ab|ge|se|hen ['apgəze:ən] *ptp* **es auf jdn ~ haben** to have it in for sb *(inf)*; **es auf jdn/etw ~ haben** *(= interessiert sein)* to have one's eye on sb/sth; **du hast es nur darauf ~, mich zu ärgern** you're only trying to annoy me ADV **~ von jdm/etw** apart from sb/sth; **~ davon, dass ...** apart from the fact that ... → *auch* **absehen**

ab|ge|son|dert ['apgəzɔndɐt] ADJ *(= isoliert)* isolated → *auch* **absondern**

ab|ge|spannt ADJ weary, tired → *auch* **abspannen**

Ab|ge|spannt|heit F weariness, tiredness

ab|ge|spielt ['apgəʃpi:lt] ADJ *(= abgenutzt) Schallplatte* worn → *auch* **abspielen**

ab|ge|stan|den ADJ *Luft, Wasser* stale; *Bier, Limonade etc* flat; *(fig) Witz, Redensart* hackneyed *(Brit)*, stale ADV **~ schmecken** to taste flat; *(Wasser)* to taste stale → *auch* **abstehen**

ab|ge|stor|ben ['apgəʃtɔrbn] ADJ *Glieder* numb; *Pflanze, Ast, Gewebe* dead; *(fig)* defunct; *Gefühle* that have/had died; **von der Kälte war mein Arm wie ~** my arm was numb with cold → *auch* **absterben**

ab|ge|straft ['apgəʃtra:ft] ADJ *(Aus)* = **vorbestraft**

ab|ge|stumpft ['apgəʃtʊmpft] ADJ **a** *(= gefühllos) Mensch* insensitive; *Gefühle, Gewissen* dulled, blunted; **sie war in ihren Gefühlen so ~, dass ...** her feelings had been dulled *or* blunted so much that ... **b** *(lit)* blunt; *Kegel* truncated → *auch* **abstumpfen**

Ab|ge|stumpft|heit F -, *no pl (von Mensch)* insensitivity; *(von Gefühlen)* dullness

ab|ge|ta|kelt ['apgəta:klt] ADJ *(pej inf)* past one's best, past it *pred (inf)*

ab|ge|tan ADJ *pred (= erledigt)* finished *or* done with; **damit ist die Sache ~** that settles the matter, that's the matter done with *(Brit)*; **damit ist es (noch) nicht ~** that's not the end of the matter → *auch* **abtun**

ab|ge|tra|gen ADJ worn; **~e Kleider** old clothes → *auch* **abtragen**

ab+ge|win|nen VT *sep irreg* **a** *(lit)* **jdm etw ~** to win sth from sb **b** *(fig)* **einer Sache etwas/nichts ~ können** to be able to see some/no attraction in sth; **jdm/einer Sache keinen Reiz ~ können** to be unable to see anything attractive in sb/sth; **einer Sache** *(dat)* **Geschmack ~** to acquire a taste for sth; **jdm Achtung ~** to win respect from sb, to win sb's respect; **jdm ein Lächeln ~** to persuade sb to smile; **dem Meer Land ~** to reclaim land from the sea

ab|ge|wirt|schaf|tet ['apgəvɪrtʃaftət] ADJ *(pej)* rotten; *Firma auch* run-down; **einen total ~en Eindruck machen** to be on its last legs → *auch* **abwirtschaften**

ab|ge|wo|gen ADJ *Urteil, Worte* balanced → *auch* **abwägen**

Ab|ge|wo|gen|heit F balance

ab+ge|wöh|nen VT *sep* **jdm etw ~** *(Gewohnheiten, schlechte Manieren)* to cure sb of sth; *das Rauchen, Trinken* to get sb to give up *or* stop sth; **sich** *(dat)* **etw ~** to give sth up; **sich** *(dat)* **das Trinken ~** to give up *or* stop drinking; **noch eins/einen zum Abgewöhnen** *(hum)* one last one; *(Alkohol auch)* one for the road; **das/die ist ja zum Abgewöhnen** *(inf)* that/she is enough to put anyone off

ab|ge|wrackt ['apgəvrakt] ADJ *(pej)* rotten; *(= abgetakelt) Mensch* washed-up → *auch* **abwracken**

ab|ge|zehrt ['apgətse:ɐt] ADJ emaciated

ab+gie|ßen VT *sep irreg* **a** *Flüssigkeit* to pour off *or* away; *Kartoffeln, Gemüse* to strain; **du musst den Eimer etwas ~** you must pour some of the water *etc* out of the bucket; **er goss einen Schluck in mein Glas ab** he poured a drop into my glass **b** *(Art, Metal)* to cast

Ab|glanz M reflection *(auch fig)*; **nur ein schwacher** *or* **matter ~** *(fig)* a pale reflection

Ab|gleich ['apglaiç] M **-s**, *no pl (von Dateien, Einträgen)* comparison

ab+glei|chen VT *sep irreg* **a** *(Build)* to level out **b** *(Elec)* to tune; *(fig) Termine, Vorgehensweise* to coordinate; *Dateien, Einträge* to compare

ab+glei|ten VI *sep irreg aux sein (geh)* **a** *(= abrutschen)* to slip; *(Gedanken)* to wander; *(Fin, Kurs)* to drop, to fall; **von etw ~** to slip off sth; **in Nebensächlichkeiten ~** to wander off *or* go off into side issues; **in Anarchie ~** to descend into anarchy; **er gleitet in Gedanken immer ab** his thoughts always wander; **von der rechten Bahn** *or* **dem rechten Weg ~** to wander *or* stray from the straight and narrow **b** *(fig: = abprallen)* **an** *or* **von jdm ~** to bounce off sb

ab+glit|schen VI *sep aux sein (inf)* to slip; **er glitschte mit den Händen ab** his hands slipped

Ab|gott M, **Ab|göt|tin** F idol; **Abgöttern dienen** to worship false gods; **jdn zum ~ machen** to idolize sb

ab|göt|tisch ['apgœtɪʃ] ADJ idolatrous; **~e Liebe** blind adoration ADV **jdn ~ lieben** to idolize sb; *Eltern, Sohn, Tochter auch* to dote on sb; **sie lieben sich ~** they are madly in love with one another, they love one another to pieces; **jdn ~ verehren** to idolize sb, to worship sb (like a god)

ab+gra|ben VT *sep irreg Erdreich* to dig away; **jdm das Wasser ~** *(fig inf)* to take the bread from sb's mouth *(esp Brit)*, to take away sb's livelihood

ab+gra|sen VT *sep Feld* to graze; *(fig inf) Ort, Geschäfte* to scour, to comb; *Gebiet, Thema* to do to death *(inf)*

ab+grät|schen VI *sep aux sein (Sport)* to straddle off

ab+grei|fen *sep irreg* VT **a** *Strecke, Entfernung* to measure off **b** *Buch, Heft* to wear → *auch* **abgegriffen c** *(= abtasten)* to feel; *(bei Durchsuchung)* to frisk **d** *(inf: = sich verschaffen) Geld* to get one's hands on VR to wear, to become worn

ab+gren|zen *sep* VT *Grundstück, Gelände* to fence off; *(fig) Rechte, Pflichten, Einflussbereich, Befugnisse, Begriff* to delimit *(gegen, von* from); **etw durch einen Zaun/ein Seil/eine Mauer/eine Hecke ~** to fence/rope/wall/hedge sth off; **diese Begriffe lassen sich nur schwer (gegeneinander) ~** it is hard to distinguish (between) these two concepts VR to dis(as)sociate oneself *(gegen* from)

Ab|gren|zung F -, -en **a** *no pl (von Gelände)* fencing off; *(fig)* delimitation **b** *(= Distanzierung)* dis(as)sociation *(gegen* from); **Politik der ~** politics of separation **c** *(= Umzäunung, Zaun)* fencing *no pl*

Ab|grund M precipice; *(= Schlucht, fig)* abyss, chasm; **sich am Rande eines ~es befinden** *(fig)* to be on the brink (of disaster); **diese Politik bedeutet ein Wandeln am Rande des ~es** this policy is an exercise in brinkmanship; **in einen ~ von Verrat/Gemeinheit blicken** *(fig)* to stare into a bottomless pit of treason/baseness; **die menschlichen Abgründe, der ~ der menschlichen Seele** the darkest depths of the human soul

ab|grund|häss|lich ADJ loathsome, incredibly hideous

ab|grün|dig ['apgrʏndɪç] ADJ *Humor, Ironie* cryptic ADV *lächeln* cryptically

Ab|grün|dig|keit F -, *no pl (von Humor etc)* subtlety

ab|grund|tief ADJ *Verachtung* profound; **~er Hass** all-consuming hatred ADV *verachten* profoundly; **jdn ~ hassen** to hate sb beyond words

ab+gu|cken VTI *sep* to copy; **jdm etw ~** to copy sth from sb; **bei jdm (etw) ~** *(Sch)* to copy (sth) from *or* off *(inf)* sb; **ich guck dir nichts ab!** *(inf)* don't worry, I've seen it all before

Ab|gunst F *(old)* resentment, enviousness *(gegenüber* of)

Ab|guss M **a** *(Art, Metal) (= Vorgang)* casting; *(= Form)* cast **b** *(dial: = Ausguss)* sink

ab+ha|ben VT *sep irreg (inf)* **a** *(= abgenommen haben) Brille, Hut* to have off; *(= abgemacht haben)* to have got off; *(= abgerissen haben)* to have off **b** *(= abbekommen)* to have; **willst du ein Stück/etwas (davon) ~?** do you want a bit/some (of it)?

ab+ha|cken VT *sep* to chop off, to hack off → **Rübe b**, → *auch* **abgehackt**

ab+ha|ken VT *sep* **a** *(= markieren)* to tick *(Brit) or* check *(esp US)* off; *(fig)* to cross off **b** *(= abnehmen)* to unhook

ab+half|tern VT *sep Pferd* to take the halter off → *auch* **abgehalftert**

ab+hal|ten VT *sep irreg* **a** *(= hindern)* to stop, to prevent; **jdn von etw/vom Trinken/von der Arbeit ~** to keep sb from sth/drinking/working; **jdn davon ~, etw zu tun** to stop sb (from) doing sth, to prevent sb (from) doing sth; **lass dich nicht ~!** don't let me/us *etc* stop you **b** *(= fernhalten) Kälte, Hitze* to keep off; *Mücken, Fliegen* to keep off *or* away; *(= draußenhalten)* to keep out **c** *(= veranstalten) Versammlung, Wahlen, Gottesdienst* to hold **d** **ein Kind auf der Toilette/Straße ~** to hold a child over the toilet/on the street *(while it goes to the toilet)*

Ab|hal|tung F, *no pl (= Durchführung)* holding; **nach ~ der Wahlen** after the elections (were held)

ab+han|deln VT *sep* **a** *Thema* to treat, to deal with **b** *(= abkaufen)* **jdm etw ~** to do *or* strike a deal with sb for sth; **sie wollte sich** *(dat)* **das Armband nicht ~ lassen** she didn't want to let her bracelet go **c** *(= vom Preis abhandeln)* **jdm 8 Euro/etwas ~** to beat sb down 8 euros/a bit *(Brit)*, to get sb to knock 8 euros/a bit off (the price); **er ließ sich von seinen Bedingungen nichts ~** he wouldn't give up any of his conditions

ab|han|den+kom|men [ap'handn-] VI *sep irreg aux sein* to get lost; **jdm ist etw abhandengekommen** sb has lost sth

Ab|han|den|kom|men NT loss

Ab|hand|lung F **a** treatise, discourse *(über +acc* (up)on); **~en** *(einer Akademie etc)* transactions **b** *(= das Abhandeln)* treatment

Ab|hang M slope, incline

ab+hän|gen *sep* ✪ 33.3 VT **a** *(= herunternehmen) Bild* to take down; *(= abkuppeln) Schlafwagen, Kurswagen* to uncouple; *Wohnwagen, Anhänger* to unhitch; **(gut) abgehangen** *(Fleisch)* well-hung → *auch* **abgehangen** **b** *(inf: = hinter sich lassen) jdn* to shake off *(inf)* VI **a** *irreg (Fleisch etc)* to hang **b** *irreg aux haben or (S Ger, Aus) sein* **von etw ~** to depend (up)on sth, to be dependent (up)on sth; **das hängt ganz davon ab** it all depends; **davon hängt viel/zu viel ab** a lot/too much depends on it; **von jdm (finanziell) ~** to be (financially) dependent on sb **c** *(inf: = Telefon auflegen)* to hang up *(inf)*

ab|hän|gig ['aphɛŋɪç] ADJ **a** *(= bedingt durch)* dependent *(auch Math)*; **etw von etw ~ machen** *(= Bedingungen stellen)* to make sth conditional (up)on sth **b** *(= angewiesen auf, euph: = süchtig)* dependent *(von* on); **gegenseitig** *or* **voneinander ~ sein** to be dependent on each other, to be mutually dependent, to be interdependent; **~ Beschäftigte(r)** employee **c** *(Gram) Satz* subordinate; *Rede* indirect; *Kasus* oblique; **von etw ~ sein** to be governed by sth

Ab|hän|gi|ge(r) ['aphɛŋɪgə] MF *decl as adj* dependent, dependant → **Unzucht**

-ab|hän|gi|ge(r) MF *decl as adj suf (= -süchtiger)* addict; **ein Heroinabhängiger** a heroin addict

Ab|hän|gig|keit F **-, -en** **a** *no pl (= Bedingtheit)* dependency *no pl (von* on); *(Gram: von Sätzen)* subordination *(von* to) **b** *(= Angewiesensein, euph: = Sucht)* dependence *(von* on); **gegenseitige ~** mutual dependence, interdependence

Ab|hän|gig|keits|ver|hält|nis NT dependent relationship; *(gegenseitig)* interdependence; **in einem ~ mit jdm stehen** to be dependent on sb

ab+här|men VR *sep* to pine away *(um* for) → *auch* **abgehärmt**

ab+här|ten *sep* VT to toughen up VI **das härtet (gegen Erkältung) ab** that toughens you up (and stops you catching cold) VR to toughen oneself up; **sich gegen etw ~** to toughen oneself against sth; *(fig)* to harden oneself to sth → *auch* **abgehärtet**

Ab|här|tung F toughening up; *(fig)* hardening

ab+hau|en *sep ptp* **abgehauen** VI *aux sein (inf)* to clear out; *(= verschwinden auch)* to push off; *(aus einem Land auch)* to get away; **hau ab!** beat it! *(inf)*, get lost! *(inf)* VT **a** *pret* **hieb** *or (inf)* **haute ab**, *ptp* **abgehauen** *Kopf* to chop *or* cut off; *Baum* to chop *or* cut down **b** *pret* **haute ab**, *ptp* **abgehauen** *(= wegschlagen) Verputz, Schicht* to knock off

ab+häu|ten VT *sep* to skin

ab+he|ben *sep irreg* VT **a** *(= anheben)* to lift (up), to raise; *(= abnehmen)* to take off; *Telefonhörer* to pick up, to lift (up); *Telefon* to answer; *(beim Stricken) Masche* to slip **b** *(Cards)* to take, to pick up **c** *Geld* to withdraw
VI **a** *(Flugzeug)* to take off; *(Rakete)* to lift off **b** *(= ans Telefon gehen)* to answer; *(beim Stricken)* to slip; **lass es doch klingeln, du brauchst nicht abzuheben** let it ring, you don't have to answer (it)
c *(= Geld abheben)* to withdraw money; **du kannst nicht dauernd ~!** you can't keep on withdrawing money *or* drawing money out; **wenn Sie ~ wollen** if you wish to make a withdrawal
d **auf etw** *(acc)* **~** *(form, Jur)* to emphasize sth
e *(Cards) (vor Spielbeginn etc)* to cut; *(= Karte nehmen)* to take a card
f *(inf: vor Freude)* to take off → *auch* **abgehoben**
VR **sich von jdm/etw ~** to stand out from sb/sth; **sich gegen jdn/etw ~** to stand out against sb/sth; **nur um sich von anderen** *or* **gegen andere abzuheben** just to be different (from other people), just to make oneself stand out; **sich wohltuend gegen etw ~** to make a pleasant contrast with sth, to contrast pleasantly with sth

ab+hef|ten VT *sep* **a** *Rechnungen, Schriftverkehr* to file away **b** *(Sew)* to tack, to baste

ab+hei|len VI *sep aux sein* to heal (up)

ab+hel|fen VI *sep irreg +dat* to remedy; *einem Fehler auch* to rectify, to correct; **dem ist leicht abzuhelfen** that can be *or* is easily remedied *etc*

ab+het|zen *sep* VT *Tiere* to exhaust, to tire out; **hetz mich nicht so ab!** *(inf)* stop rushing me like that! *(inf)* VR to wear *or* tire oneself out → *auch* **abgehetzt**

ab+heu|ern *sep (Naut)* VI to be paid off VT to pay off

Ab|hil|fe F, *no pl* remedy, cure; **~ schaffen** to take remedial action; **in einer Angelegenheit ~ schaffen** to remedy a matter

ab|hin [ap'hɪn] ADV *(Sw)* **vom 18.9.90 ~** from 18.9.90 onwards

Ab|hit|ze F waste heat

ab+ho|beln VT *sep Holz* to plane down; **wir müssen noch 2 cm ~** we need to plane another 2 cm off

ab|hold ['aphɔlt] ADJ *+dat (geh)* **jdm ~ sein** to be averse *or* ill-disposed to(wards) sb; **einer Sache** *(dat)* **~ sein** to be averse to sth; **jdm/einer Sache nicht ~ sein** *(iro)* not to be averse to sb/sth

ab+ho|len VT *sep* to collect *(bei* from); *Bestelltes auch* to call for *(bei* at); *Fundsache* to claim *(bei* from); *jdn* to call for; *(euph: = verhaften)* to take away; **jdn am Bahnhof/Flughafen ~** to collect sb from *or* to meet sb at the station/airport; *(mit dem Auto auch)* to pick sb up from the station/airport; **ich hole dich heute Abend ab** I'll call for you *or* I'll pick you up this evening; **er kam und wollte mich zu einem Spaziergang ~** he called and asked me to go for a walk; **etw ~ lassen** to have sth collected; **„Geldbörse gefunden, abzuholen bei …"** "purse found, claim from …"

Ab|ho|ler ['aphoːlɐ] M **-s, -**, **Ab|ho|le|rin** [-ərɪn] F **-, -nen** **a** **sie wartete auf ihren ~** she was waiting to be collected **b** *(Comm)* **~ sein** *to collect one's mail from the post office/parcels from the station etc*

Ab|hol|markt M warehouse *(selling furniture/drinks etc)*

Ab|ho|lung F **-, -en** collection; **zur ~ bereit** ready for *or* awaiting collection

ab+hol|zen VT *sep Wald* to clear, to deforest; *Baumreihe* to fell, to cut down

Ab|hol|zung F **-, -en** *(von Wald)* clearing, deforesting; *(von Baumreihe)* felling, cutting down

Ab|hör-: **Ab|hör|ak|ti|on** F bugging operation; **Ab|hör|an|la|ge** F bugging system

ab+hor|chen *sep* VT to sound, to listen to; *Brust auch, Patienten* to auscultate *(form)* VI to auscultate *(form)*

Ab|hör-: **Ab|hör|dienst** M monitoring service; **Ab|hör|ein|rich|tung** F bugging device; *(= System)* bugging system

ab+hö|ren VT *sep* **a** *auch vi (= überwachen) Raum, Gespräch* to bug; *(= mithören)* to listen in on; *Telefon* to tap; **abgehört werden** *(inf)* to be bugged; **der Geheimdienst darf (Telefone) ~** the Secret Service are allowed to tap telephones **b** *(= zuhören) Sender, Schallplatte etc* to listen to **c** *(Med)* to sound, to listen to; **jdm das Herz ~** to listen to *or* sound sb's heart **d** *(Sch: = abfragen)* **einen** *or* **einem Schüler etw ~** to test a pupil orally on sth; **kannst du mir mal Vokabeln ~?** can you test my vocabulary?; **einen** *or* **einem Schüler ein Gedicht ~** to hear a pupil recite a poem

Ab|hör-: **Ab|hör|ge|rät** NT bugging device; **Ab|hör|pro|to|koll** NT transcript *(of monitored conversations)*; **ab|hör|si|cher** ADJ *Raum* bug-proof; *Telefon* tap-proof; **Ab|hör|si|cher|heit** F **sich von der ~ des Zimmers/des Telefons überzeugen** to ensure the room is bug-proof/the phone is tap-proof; **hier muss absolute ~ gewährleistet sein** there must be no possibility of bugging/tapping conversations here

ab+hun|gern VT *sep* **er musste sich** *(dat)* **sein Studium ~** he had to starve himself to pay for his studies, he had to starve his way through college *etc*; **sich** *(dat)* **Gewicht/10 Kilo ~** to lose weight/10 kilos by going on a starvation diet; **abgehungerte Gestalten** emaciated figures

ab+hus|ten VI *sep* to have a good cough

abi ['abi] ADV, PREP *(Aus inf)* = **hinunter**

Abi ['abi] NT **-s, -s** *(Sch inf) abbr von* **Abitur**

ab+ir|ren VI *sep aux sein (geh)* to lose one's way; *(fig: = abschweifen) (Gedanken)* to wander; **vom Weg(e) ~** to wander off the path, to stray from the path; **vom rechten Weg ~** *(fig)* to stray *or* wander *or* err from the straight and narrow

Ab|ir|rung F *(geh)* **a** *(= Verirrung)* lapse, aberration **b** *(Astron)* aberration

Abi|tur [abi'tuːɐ] NT **-s,** *(rare)* **-e** *school-leaving exam and university entrance qualification*, ≈ A levels *pl (Brit)*, ≈ Highers *pl (Scot)*, ≈ high-school diploma *(US)*; **(sein** *or* **das) ~ machen** to do (one's) school-leaving exam *(Brit)*, ≈ to do one's A levels *(Brit) or* Highers *(Scot)*, ≈ to take one's high-school diploma *(US)*; **sein** *or* **das ~ ablegen** *(form)* to sit one's school-leaving exam *(Brit)*, ≈ to sit one's A levels *(Brit) or* Highers *(Scot)*, ≈ to take one's high-school diploma *(US)*

ABITUR

In Germany the **Abitur** examination is taken at the end of the **Gymnasium** when students

are 18 or 19. It consists of written and oral tests in four core subjects. The overall mark also takes account of students' performance throughout their **Kollegstufe**. The **Abitur** is also known as the **allgemeine Hochschulreife**, since it is a required for acceptance onto a university course.
The Austrian equivalent is the **Matura**, and in Switzerland it is the **Maturität**. → GYMNASIUM, KOLLEGSTUFE

Abi|tur|fei|er F school-leavers' *(Brit) or* graduation *(US)* party

Abi|tu|ri|ent [abituˈriɛnt] M **-en, -en, Abi|tu|ri|en|tin** [-ˈriɛntɪn] F **-, -nen** *person who is doing/has done the Abitur*

Abi|tur-: **Abi|tur|klas|se** F *final-year class at school which will take the Abitur,* ≈ sixth form *(Brit),* ≈ twelfth grade *(US);* **Abi|tur|prü|fung** F school-leaving exam; **Abi|tur|re|de** F school-leaving speech; **Abi|tur|zei|tung** F *humorous magazine compiled by school-leavers;* **Abi|tur|zeug|nis** NT certificate of having passed the Abitur, ≈ A level *(Brit) or* Highers *(Scot)* certificate, ≈ high-school diploma *(US)*

ab+ja|gen *sep* VT **jdm etw ~** to get sth off sb VR *(inf)* to wear oneself out

Abk. *abbr von* **Abkürzung** abbreviation, abbr

ab+kal|ben VI *sep (Agr)* to calve

ab+käm|men VT *sep (fig)* to comb, to scour

ab+kämp|fen *sep* VT *(geh)* **jdm etw ~** to wring sth out of sb VR to fight hard → *auch* **abgekämpft**

ab+kan|zeln [ˈapkantsln] VT *sep (inf)* **jdn ~** to give sb a dressing-down

Ab|kan|ze|lung F **-, -en, Ab|kanz|lung** [ˈapkantslʊŋ] F **-, -en** dressing-down

ab+kap|seln [ˈapkapsln] VR *sep (lit)* to become encapsulated; *(fig)* to shut *or* cut oneself off, to isolate oneself

Ab|kap|se|lung F **-, -en, Ab|kaps|lung** [ˈapkapslʊŋ] F **-, -en** *(lit)* encapsulation; *(fig)* isolation

ab+kar|ren VT *sep* to cart away; *(fig) Menschen* to cart off

ab+kar|ten [ˈapkartn] VT *sep* to rig *(inf),* to fix → *auch* **abgekartet**

ab+kas|sie|ren *ptp* **abkassiert** *sep* VT *Fahrgäste* to collect money from; *Geldsumme, Schutzgelder, Maut* to collect; *(= ausnehmen)* to clean out *(inf)* VI *(= großes Geld machen)* to make a killing *(inf);* **darf ich mal (bei Ihnen) ~?** could I ask you to pay now?

ab+kau|en VT *sep Nägel* to bite; *Bleistift* to chew; **er hat abgekaute Fingernägel** his nails are bitten right down

ab+kau|fen VT *sep* **jdm etw ~** to buy sth from *or* off *(inf)* sb; *(inf: = glauben)* to buy sth *(inf);* **diese Geschichte kauft uns keiner ab!** nobody will buy that story *(inf)*

Ab|kehr [ˈapkeːɐ] F **-,** *no pl* turning away (*von* from); *(von Glauben, von der Welt etc)* renunciation (*von* of); *(von der Familie)* estrangement (*von* from); **die ~ vom Materialismus** turning away from materialism, rejecting materialism

ab+keh|ren VT *sep (= abfegen) Schmutz* to sweep away *or* off; *Hof, Dach* to sweep

ab+keh|ren *sep* VT *(geh: = abwenden) Blick, Gesicht* to avert, to turn away; **sie musste den Blick (davon) ~** she had to look away (from it) VR *(fig)* to turn away (*von* from); *(von einer Politik)* to give up; **sich von Gott ~** to renounce God; **die von uns abgekehrte Seite des Mondes** the side of the moon away from us, the far side of the moon

ab+kip|pen *sep* VT *(= abladen) Abfälle, Baustoffe* to tip; *(= herunterklappen)* to let down VI *aux sein* to tilt; *(Flugzeug)* to nose-dive

ab+klap|pern VT *sep (inf) Läden, Gegend, Straße* to scour, to comb (*nach* for); *Kunden, Museen* to do *(inf)*

ab+klä|ren *sep* VT **a** *(= sich setzen lassen) Flüssigkeit* to clarify **b** *(= klarstellen) Angelegenheit* to clear up, to clarify VR **a** *(= sich setzen)* to clarify **b** *(= sich beruhigen)* to calm down → *auch* **abgeklärt**

Ab|klä|rung F **a** *(von Flüssigkeit)* clarification, clarifying **b** *(von Angelegenheit)* clearing up

Ab|klatsch M *(Art)* cast, casting; *(fig pej)* poor imitation *or* copy

ab+klat|schen VT *sep* **a** *(Sport) Ball* to palm away **b** *(mit Handflächen: zur Aufmunterung, Begrüßung etc)* **jdn ~** to high-five sb *(inf),* to give sb a high-five *(inf)* **c** *(inf: = kopieren)* **etw ~** to make a poor *or* lousy *(inf)* copy of sth

Ab|klat|scher M *(Ftbl sl)* rebound

ab+klem|men VT *sep Nabelschnur, Leitung, Adern* to clamp; **er hat sich** *(dat)* **in der Maschine den Finger abgeklemmt** he lost his finger in the machine

Ab|kling|be|cken NT *(in Atomkraftwerk)* spent fuel storage bay

ab+klin|gen VI *sep irreg aux sein* **a** *(= leiser werden)* to die *or* fade away **b** *(= nachlassen)* to wear off, to abate; *(Erregung, Fieber)* to subside, to abate; *(radioaktives Material)* to decay

ab+klop|fen *sep* VT **a** *(= herunterklopfen)* to knock off; *(= klopfend säubern)* to brush down; *Staub etc* to brush off; *Teppich, Polstermöbel* to beat; **er klopfte die Asche von der Zigarre ab** he tapped *or* knocked the ash off his cigar; **sich** *(dat)* **die Schuhe ~** to knock the mud *etc* off one's shoes; **den Staub nicht abbürsten, sondern ~** do not brush the dust off, pat it off **b** *(= beklopfen)* to tap; *(Med)* to sound, to percuss *(spec)* **c** *(fig inf: = untersuchen)* to look into; **etw auf etw** *(acc)* **~** to trace sth (back) to sth VI *(Mus)* **der Dirigent klopfte ab** the conductor stopped the orchestra *(by rapping his baton)*

ab+knab|bern VT *sep (inf)* to nibble off; *Knochen* to gnaw at

ab+kna|cken VI *sep (sl: = schlafen)* to crash (out) *(inf)*

ab+knal|len VT *sep (inf)* to shoot down *(inf)*

ab+knap|pen [ˈapknapn], **ab+knap|sen** VT *sep (inf)* **sich** *(dat)* **etw ~** to scrape together sth; **sich** *(dat)* **jeden Cent ~ müssen** to have to scrimp and save; **er hat mir 20 Euro abgeknapst** he got 20 euros off me

ab+knei|fen VT *sep irreg* to nip off; *(mit Zange auch)* to clip off

ab+kni|cken *sep* VT *(= abbrechen)* to break *or* snap off; *(= einknicken)* to break VI *aux sein (= abzweigen)* to fork *or* branch off; **~de Vorfahrt** traffic turning left/right has priority; **in den Knien ~** to bend at the knees

ab+knip|sen VT *sep (inf)* **a** *(mit Zange) Kabel* to snip off **b** *(= fotografieren)* to take snaps of *(inf)*

ab+knöp|fen VT *sep* **a** *(= abnehmen)* to unbutton **b** *(inf: = ablisten)* **jdm etw ~** to get sth off sb; **jdm Geld ~** to get money out of sb

ab+knut|schen VT *sep (inf)* to canoodle *(Brit inf) or* cuddle with; **sich ~** to canoodle *(Brit inf),* to cuddle

ab+ko|chen *sep* VT to boil; *(= durch Kochen keimfrei machen)* to sterilize (by boiling) VI to cook a meal in the open air, to have a cookout *(US)*

ab+kom|man|die|ren *ptp* **abkommandiert** VT *sep (Mil) (zu anderer Einheit)* to post; *(zu bestimmtem Dienst)* to detail (*zu* for); **jdn ins Ausland ~** to post sb abroad

Ab|kom|me [ˈapkɔmə] M **-n, -n** *(liter: Nachkomme)* descendant

ab+kom|men VI *sep irreg aux sein* **a von etw ~** *(= abweichen)* to leave sth; *(= abirren)* to wander off sth, to stray from sth; **vom Kurs ~** to deviate from one's course, to leave one's course; **(vom Thema) ~** to get off the subject, to digress; **vom rechten Weg ~** *(fig)* to stray *or* wander from the straight and narrow **b** *(= aufgeben)* **von etw ~** to drop sth, to give sth up; *von Angewohnheit* to give sth up; *von Idee, Plan* to abandon *or* drop sth; **von einer Meinung ~** to revise one's opinion, to change one's mind; **von diesem alten Brauch kommt man immer mehr ab** this old custom is dying out more and more **c** *(Sport: = wegkommen)* to get away; **schlecht/gut ~** *(= wegkommen)* to get away to a bad/good start, to make a bad/good start **d** *(beim Schießen)* to aim; **wie ist sie abgekommen?** how well did she shoot?, how was her shot?

Ab|kom|men [ˈapkɔmən] NT **-s, -** agreement *(auch Pol)*

Ab|kom|men|schaft [ˈapkɔmənʃaft] F **-,** *no pl (liter)* descendants *pl*

ab|kömm|lich [ˈapkœmlɪç] ADJ available; **nicht ~ sein** to be unavailable

Ab|kömm|ling [ˈapkœmlɪŋ] M **-s, -e a** *(= Nachkomme)* descendant; *(fig)* adherent; **er war (der) ~ einer Bankiersfamilie** he came from a banking family **b** *(Chem)* derivative **c Abkömmlinge** PL *(Jur)* issue *no pl*

ab+kön|nen VT *sep irreg (inf)* **a** *(= trinken)* **der kann ganz schön was ab** he can knock it back *(Brit inf),* he can put it away *(inf);* **er kann nicht viel ab** he can't take much (alcohol) **b** *(= vertragen)* to bear, to stand; **er kann nichts ab** he can't take it **c** *(= mögen)* **das kann ich überhaupt nicht ab** I can't stand *or* abide it; **ich kann ihn einfach nicht ab** I just can't stand *or* abide him

ab+kop|peln *sep* VT *(Rail)* to uncouple; *Pferd* to untie; *Degen, Pistole* to unbuckle, to take off; *Raumfähre* to undock; *Anhänger* to unhitch VR *(inf: = sich lösen)* to sever one's ties (*von* with)

Ab|kopp|lung F *(Rail)* uncoupling; *(von Raumfähre)* undocking; *(von Anhänger)* unhitching

ab+krat|zen *sep* VT *Schmutz etc* to scratch off; *(mit einem Werkzeug)* to scrape off; *Wand, Gegenstand* to scratch, to scrape; **die Schuhe ~** to scrape the mud/snow *etc* off one's shoes VI *aux sein (inf: = sterben)* to kick the bucket *(inf),* to croak *(inf)*

Ab|krat|zer M shoe scraper

ab+krie|gen VT *sep (inf)* = **abbekommen**

ab+ku|cken VTI = **abgucken**

ab+küh|len *sep* VT to cool; *Speise auch* to cool down; *(fig) Freundschaft, Zuneigung* to cool; *Zorn, Leidenschaft* to cool, to calm VI *aux sein* to cool down; *(fig) (Freundschaft etc)* to cool off; *(Begeisterung)* to cool VR to cool down *or* off; *(Wetter)* to become cool(er); *(fig)* to cool; *(Beziehungen)* to become cool(er), to cool

Ab|küh|lung F cooling

Ab|kunft [ˈapkʊnft] F **-,** *no pl (liter)* descent, origin; *(= Nationalität auch)* extraction; **französischer ~ sein** to be of French descent *etc*

ab+kup|fern [ˈapkʊpfɐn] VT *sep (inf)* to crib *(inf),* to copy

ab+kup|peln VT *sep* = **abkoppeln**

ab+kür|zen *sep* VT **a den Weg ~** to take a short cut **b** *(= verkürzen)* to cut short; *Verfahren* to shorten; *Aufenthalt, Urlaub* to cut short, to curtail **c** *(= verkürzt schreiben) Namen* to abbreviate; **Kilohertz wird kHz abgekürzt** kilohertz is abbreviated to kHz, kHz is the abbreviation for kilohertz VI **a** *(= eine Abkürzung nehmen)* to take a short cut; *(Weg)* to be a short cut **b** *(= verkürzt schreiben)* to abbreviate, to use abbreviations

Ab|kür|zung F **a** *(Weg)* short cut; **eine ~ nehmen** to take a short cut; **durch die ~ haben wir eine Stunde gespart** we've saved an hour by taking the short cut, taking the short cut has saved us an hour **b** *(von Aufenthalt)* curtailment, cutting short; *(von Verfahren)* shortening; *(von Vortrag)* shortening, cutting short; **gibt es keine ~ dieses Verfahrens?** isn't there any way of shortening this process? **c** *(von Wort)* abbreviation

Ab|kür|zungs|tas|te F *(Comput)* hotkey

Ab|kür|zungs|ver|zeich|nis NT list of abbreviations

ab+küs|sen VT *sep* to smother with kisses; **sie küssten sich stundenlang ab** they kissed away for hours

Abl. *abbr von* **Ablöse b**

ab+la|den *sep irreg* **VT** *Last, Wagen* to unload; *Schutt* to dump; *(esp Comm) Passagiere, Ware* to off-load; *(fig inf) Kummer, Ärger* to vent *(bei jdm* on sb); *Verantwortung* to off-load, to shove *(inf)* *(auf +acc* onto); **seine Kinder/Arbeit auf jdn ~** *(fig inf)* to unload *or* dump *(inf)* one's children/work on sb; **sie lud ihren ganzen Kummer bei ihrem Mann ab** *(inf)* she unburdened herself *or* all her worries on her husband **VI** *(= entladen)* to unload; **bei jdm ~** *(fig inf: = Sorgen loswerden)* to offload on sb

Ab|la|de|platz M unloading area; *(für Schrott, Müll etc)* dump, dumping ground

Ab|la|ge F **a** *(= Gestell)* place to put sth; *(zur Aufbewahrung)* place to keep sth; *(= Ablagekorb)* filing tray; *(= Gepäckablage)* luggage *(Brit) or* baggage *(US)* rack; **wir brauchen eine ~ für die Akten** we need somewhere for our files, we need somewhere where we can keep our files; **der Tisch dient als ~ für ihre Bücher** her books are kept on the table; **etw als ~ benutzen** *(für Akten, Bücher etc)* to use sth for storage; **sie haben das Bett als ~ benutzt** they put everything on the bed; **gibt es hier irgendeine ~ für Taschen und Schirme?** is there anywhere here for bags and umbrellas *or* where bags and umbrellas can be left?
b *(= Aktenordnung)* filing
c *(Sw)* = **Annahmestelle, Zweigstelle**

Ab|la|ge|korb M filing tray

ab+la|gern *sep* **VT** **a** *(= anhäufen)* to deposit
b *(= deponieren)* to leave, to store **VI** *aux sein or haben (= ausreifen)* to mature; *(Holz auch)* to season; **~ lassen** to allow to mature; *Holz auch* to (allow to) season; **abgelagert** *(Wein)* mature; *Holz, Tabak* seasoned **VR** to be deposited; **in einem Wasserkessel lagert sich Kalk ab** a chalk deposit builds up *or* forms in a kettle

Ab|la|ge|rung F *(= Vorgang)* depositing, deposition; *(von Wein)* maturing, maturation; *(von Holz)* maturing, seasoning; *(= abgelagerter Stoff)* deposit

ab|lan|dig ['aplandıç] ADJ *(Naut) Wind* offshore

Ab|lass ['aplas] M **-es, Ablässe** ['aplɛsə] **a** *(Eccl)* indulgence **b** *no pl (= das Ablassen)* letting out; *(von Dampf)* letting off; *(= Entleerung)* drainage, draining **c** *(= Vorrichtung)* outlet

Ab|lass|brief M *(Eccl)* letter of indulgence

ab+las|sen *sep irreg* **VT** **a** *(= herauslaufen lassen) Wasser, Luft* to let out; *Motoröl* to drain off; *Dampf* to let off; *(Zug, Kessel)* to give *or* let off; **die Luft aus den Reifen ~** to let the air out of the tyres *(Brit) or* tires *(US)*, to let the tyres *(Brit) or* tires *(US)* down
b *(= leerlaufen lassen) Teich, Schwimmbecken* to drain, to empty
c *(= verkaufen, geben)* **jdm etw ~** to let sb have sth
d *(= ermäßigen)* to knock off *(inf)*; **er hat mir 20 Euro (vom Preis) abgelassen** he knocked 20 euros off (the price) for me *(inf)*, he reduced the price by 20 euros for me
e *(inf) (= äußern) blöde Sprüche* to make; *(= abreagieren) Frust, Ärger, Aggressionen* to work off, to get rid off
f *(inf: = nicht befestigen, anziehen)* to leave off
VI **a** *(= mit etw aufhören)* to desist; **von einem Vorhaben** *etc* **~** to abandon a plan *etc*
b von jdm ~ *(= jdn in Ruhe lassen)* to leave sb alone

Ab|lass|han|del M *(Eccl)* selling of indulgences

Ab|lass|ven|til NT outlet valve

Ab|la|tiv ['ablatiːf, 'ap-] M **-s, -e** [-və] ablative (case)

Ab|lauf M **a** *(= Abfluss)* drain; *(= Ablaufstelle)* outlet; *(= Ablaufrohr)* drain(pipe); *(im Haus)* waste pipe; *(= Rinne)* drainage channel
b *(= Ablaufen)* draining *or* running away
c *(= Verlauf)* course; *(von Empfang, Staatsbesuch)* order of events (*+gen* in); *(von Verbrechen)* sequence of events (*+gen* in); *(von Handlung im Buch etc)* development; **er sprach mit uns den ~ der Prüfung durch** he took us through the exam; **er hat den ~ des Unglücks geschildert** he described the way the accident happened; **der ~ der Ereignisse vollzog sich wie geplant** the course of events was as planned; **nach ~ der Vorstellung ...** after the performance (was over) ...; **es gab keinerlei Störungen im ~ des Programms** the programme *(Brit) or* program *(US)* went off without any disturbances
d *(von Frist etc)* expiry; **nach ~ der Frist** after the deadline had passed *or* expired
e *(von Zeitraum)* passing; **nach ~ von 4 Stunden** after 4 hours (have/had gone by *or* passed); **nach ~ des Jahres/dieser Zeit** at the end of the year/this time

Ab|lauf|brett NT *(an Spüle)* draining board, drain board *(US)*

ab+lau|fen *sep irreg* **VT** **a** *(= abnützen) Schuhsohlen, Schuhe* to wear out; *Absätze* to wear down; **sich** *(dat)* **die Beine** *or* **Hacken** *or* **Absätze** *or* **Schuhsohlen nach etw ~** *(inf)* to walk one's legs off looking for sth → **Horn a**
b *aux sein or haben (= entlanglaufen) Strecke* to go *or* walk over; *(hin und zurück)* to go *or* walk up and down; *Stadt, Straßen, Geschäfte* to comb, to scour (round)
VI *aux sein* **a** *(= abfließen: Flüssigkeit)* to drain *or* run away *or* off; *(= sich leeren: Behälter)* to drain (off), to empty (itself); **aus der Badewanne ~** to run *or* drain out of the bath; **bei ~dem Wasser** *(Naut)* with an outgoing tide; **an ihm läuft alles ab** *(fig)* he just shrugs everything off; **jede Kritik läuft an ihm ab** *(fig)* with him criticism is just like water off a duck's back
b *(= vonstattengehen)* to go off; **wie ist das bei der Prüfung abgelaufen?** how did the exam go (off)?; **zuerst sah es sehr gefährlich aus, aber dann ist die Sache doch glimpflich abgelaufen** at first things looked pretty dangerous but it was all right in the end
c *(= sich abwickeln: Seil, Kabel)* to wind out, to unwind; *(= sich abspulen: Film, Tonband)* to run; *(Schallplatte)* to play; **einen Film ~ lassen** to run *or* show a film; **ein Tonband ~ lassen** to run *or* play a tape; **ein Programm ~ lassen** *(Comput)* to run a program; **abgelaufen sein** *(Film etc)* to have finished, to have come to an end
d *(= ungültig werden: Pass, Visum etc)* to expire, to run out; *(= enden: Frist, Vertrag etc)* to run out, to expire, to be up; **die Frist ist abgelaufen** the period has run out, the period is up
e *(= vergehen: Zeitraum)* to pass, to go by
f *(Sport: = starten)* to start

Ab|lauf|steu|e|rung M *(Comput)* sequencer

ab+lau|schen VT *sep (geh)* to learn (*+dat* from); **dem Leben abgelauscht** *(fig liter)* taken *or* culled *(liter)* from life

Ab|laut M *(Gram)* ablaut

ab+lau|ten VI *sep (Gram)* to undergo ablaut, to change by ablaut

Ab|le|ben NT, *no pl (form)* demise *(form)*, decease *(form)*

ab+le|cken VT *sep* to lick; *Teller, Löffel, Finger* to lick (clean); *Blut, Marmelade* to lick off; **sich** *(dat)* **etw von der Hand ~** to lick sth off one's hand

ab+le|dern ['apleːdɐn] VT *sep Fenster, Auto* to leather (off), to polish with a leather

ab+le|gen *sep* **VT** **a** *(= niederlegen)* to put down; *Last, Waffen* to lay *or* put down; *(Zool) Eier* to lay
b *(= abheften) Schriftwechsel, Dokumente* to file (away); *(Comput) Daten* to store; *(bei Drag & Drop)* to drop; *(in Zwischenablage)* to put
c *(= ausziehen) Hut, Mantel, Kleider* to take off, to remove *(form)*
d *(= nicht mehr tragen) Anzug, Kleid* to discard, to cast off; *Trauerkleidung, Ehering* to take off; *Orden, Auszeichnungen* to renounce; **abgelegte Kleider** cast-off *or* discarded clothes
e *(= aufgeben) Misstrauen, Scheu, Stolz* to lose, to shed, to cast off *(liter)*; *schlechte Gewohnheit* to give up, to get rid of; *kindische Angewohnheit* to put aside; *Namen* to give up
f *(= ableisten, machen) Schwur, Eid* to swear; *Gelübde* to make; *Zeugnis* to give; *Bekenntnis, Beichte, Geständnis* to make; *Prüfung* to take, to sit; *(erfolgreich)* to pass
g *(Cards)* to discard, to throw down
VI **a** *(= abfahren) (Schiff)* to cast off; *(Space)* to separate
b *(Schriftwechsel ablegen)* to file
c *(Garderobe ablegen)* to take one's things off; **wenn Sie ~ möchten ...** if you would like to take your things *or* your hats and coats off ...
d *(Cards)* to discard
VT *impers (geh: = absehen)* **es auf etw** *(acc)* **~** to be out for sth

Ab|le|ger ['apleːgɐ] M **-s, -** *(Bot)* layer; *(fig: = Zweigunternehmen)* branch, subsidiary; *(iro: = Sohn)* son, offspring *no pl*; **durch ~** by layering

ab+leh|nen *sep* ✪ 35.5, 38.3, 39.3, 41 **VT** **a** *(= zurückweisen, nein sagen)* to decline, to refuse; *Antrag, Angebot, Vorschlag, Bewerber, Stelle* to turn down, to reject; *(Parl) Gesetzentwurf* to throw out; **es ~, etw zu tun** to decline *or* refuse to do sth **b** *(= missbilligen)* to disapprove of; **jede Form von Gewalt ~** to be against any form of violence **VI** to decline, to refuse; **drei der erfolgreichen Bewerber haben abgelehnt** three of the successful applicants have declined the job offer; **eine ~de Antwort** a negative answer; **ein ~der Bescheid** a rejection; **dankend ~** to decline with thanks

Ab|leh|nung F **-, -en** **a** *(= Zurückweisung)* refusal; *(von Antrag, Bewerber etc)* rejection; **auf ~ stoßen** to be refused/rejected, to meet with a refusal/a rejection **b** *(= Missbilligung)* disapproval; **auf ~ stoßen** to meet with disapproval

Ab|leh|nungs-: **Ab|leh|nungs|an|trag** M petition *or* motion for rejection; **Ab|leh|nungs|be|scheid** M notice of rejection

ab+leis|ten VT *sep (form) Zeit* to complete

ab|leit|bar ADJ **a** *(= herleitbar)* derivable, deducible; *Wort* derivable *(aus* from) **b** *(= umleitbar) Fluss* able to be diverted; *Rauch, Dampf, Flüssigkeit* able to be drawn off *or* out

ab+lei|ten *sep* **VT** **a** *(= herleiten)* to derive; *(= logisch folgern)* to deduce *(aus* from); *(Math) Gleichung* to differentiate **b** *(= umleiten) Bach, Fluss* to divert; *(= herausleiten) Rauch, Dampf, Flüssigkeit* to draw off *or* out; *(= ablenken) Blitz* to conduct **VR** *(= sich herleiten)* to be derived *(aus* from); *(= logisch folgen)* to be deduced *(aus* from)

Ab|lei|tung F **a** *no pl (= das Herleiten)* derivation; *(= Folgerung)* deduction; *(Math: von Gleichung)* differentiation; *(= Umleitung: von Rauch, Dampf, Flüssigkeit)* drawing off *or* out **b** *(= Wort, Math)* derivative

Ab|lei|tungs|sil|be F derivative affix

ab|lenk|bar ADJ **leicht ~ sein** to be easily distracted

ab+len|ken *sep* **VT** **a** *(= ab-, wegleiten)* to deflect *(auch Phys)*, to turn aside *or* away; *Wellen, Licht* to refract; *Schlag* to parry; *Katastrophe* to avert
b *(= zerstreuen)* to distract; **er ließ sich durch nichts ~** he wouldn't let anything distract him; **wir mussten die Kinder ~** we had to find something to take the children's minds off things; **jdn von seinem Schmerz/seinen Sorgen ~** to make sb forget his/her pain/worries, to take sb's mind off his/her pain/worries
c *(= abbringen)* to divert; *Verdacht* to avert; **jdn von der Arbeit ~** to distract sb from his/her work
VI **a** *(= ausweichen)* **(vom Thema) ~** to change the subject; *(bei einem Gespräch auch)* to turn the conversation
b *(= zerstreuen)* to create a distraction; **sie**

geht jede Woche Schwimmen, das lenkt ab she goes swimming every week, which takes her mind off things
VR to take one's mind off things

Ab|len|kung F **a** *(= Ab-, Wegleitung)* deflection *(auch Phys)*; *(von Wellen, Licht)* refraction **b** *(= Zerstreuung)* diversion, distraction; **~ brauchen** to need something to take one's mind off things; **sich** *(dat)* **~ verschaffen** to provide oneself with a distraction, to provide oneself with something to take one's mind off things; **zur ~ einen Spaziergang machen** to take one's mind off things by going for a walk **c** *(= Störung)* distraction **d** *(von Plan, jds Interesse)* diversion; *(von Verdacht)* aversion, averting

Ab|len|kungs-: **Ab|len|kungs|kam|pag|ne** F diversion campaign; **Ab|len|kungs|ma|nö|ver** NT diversionary tactic; *(Ablenkung von Thema, Problem)* red herring

ab|les|bar ADJ *Rede, Messgerät* readable; **die Erregung war von seinem Gesicht noch deutlich ~** excitement was still written all over his face; **daraus ist ohne Weiteres ~, dass ...** it can be clearly seen from this that ...; **daran ist ~, ob ...** you can tell from that whether ...

Ab|les|bar|keit [ˈapleːsbaːɐ̯kait] F -, *no pl* readability

ab+le|sen VT *sep irreg* **a** *auch vi (vom Blatt)* to read; **er muss alles/seine Rede ~** he has to read everything/his speech (from notes *etc*); **(jdm) etw von den Lippen ~** to lip-read sth (that sb says)
b *auch vi (= registrieren) Messgeräte, Barometer, Strom* to read; *Barometerstand* to take; **nächste Woche wird abgelesen** the meter(s) will be read next week
c *(= herausfinden, erkennen, folgern)* to see; **jdm etw vom Gesicht** *or* **von der Stirn ~** to see *or* tell sth from sb's face, to read sth in sb's face; **das konnte man ihr vom Gesicht ~** it was written all over her face; **aus der Reaktion der Presse war die Stimmung im Volke deutlich abzulesen** the mood of the people could be clearly gauged *or* read from the press reaction; **jdm jeden Wunsch an** *or* **von den Augen ~** to anticipate sb's every wish
d *(= wegnehmen) Beeren, Raupen etc* to pick off *(von etw* sth); *(= leer machen) Acker, Strauch etc* to pick clean

Ab|le|ser(in) M(F) meter-reader

ab+leuch|ten *sep* VT **etw ~** to search sth with a lamp *or* torch *or* flashlight *(US)*; *(Scheinwerfer)* to sweep

ab+leug|nen *sep* **VT** *Schuld, Tat* to deny; *Glauben* to renounce **VI er hat weiter abgeleugnet** he continued to deny it

Ab|leug|nung F denial; *(von Glauben)* renunciation

ab+lich|ten VT *sep (form)* to photocopy; *(= fotografieren)* to photograph

Ab|lich|tung F *(form) (= Fotokopie)* photocopy; *(= Fotografie)* photograph

ab+lie|fern VT *sep (bei einer Person)* to hand over *(bei* to); *Examensarbeit auch* to hand in; *(bei einer Dienststelle)* to hand in *(bei* to); *(= liefern)* to deliver *(bei* to); *(inf) Kinder, Freundin* to deposit *(inf)*; *(= nach Hause bringen)* to take home

Ab|lie|fe|rung F *(bei einer Person)* handing-over *no pl*; *(bei einer Dienststelle)* handing-in *no pl*; *(= Lieferung)* delivery

Ab|lie|fe|rungs|ter|min M delivery date

ab+lie|gen VI *sep irreg (= entfernt sein)* to be at a distance; *(fig)* to be removed; **das Haus liegt weit ab** the house is a long way off *or* away *or* is quite a distance away; **das liegt sehr weit ab von unserem Thema** that is very far removed from *or* is a long way from the topic we are dealing with → *auch* **abgelegen**

ab+lis|ten [ˈaplɪstn] VT *sep* **jdm etw ~** to trick sb out of sth; **jdm die Erlaubnis ~, etw zu tun** to trick sb into giving one permission to do sth

ab+lo|cken VT *sep* **jdm etw ~** to get sth out of sb; **diese Äußerung lockte ihm nur ein müdes Lächeln ab** this statement only drew a tired smile from him *or* got a tired smile out of him; **er lockte seiner Geige süße Töne ab** he coaxed sweet sounds from his violin

ab|lös|bar ADJ **a** *(= abtrennbar)* removable, detachable; **die Etiketten sind nur schwer ~** the labels are difficult to remove **b** *(= ersetzbar)* replaceable **c** *(= tilgbar)* redeemable

ab+lö|schen VT *sep* **a** *(mit dem Löschblatt)* to blot **b** *(Cook)* to add water to

Ab|lö|se [ˈaplø:zə] F -, -n **a** *(Sport: = Ablösungssumme)* transfer fee **b** *(für Möbel etc) money paid to the previous tenant for furnishings and fittings*; **„Abl."** *(in Anzeige)* "furnishings (and fittings)" **c** *(generell bei Wohnungsübernahme)* key money

ab+lö|sen *sep* **VT** **a** *(= abmachen)* to take off, to remove; *Etikett* to detach, to take off
b *(Fin) (= kapitalisieren) Rente* to get paid in a lump sum; *(= auszahlen)* to pay (off) in a lump sum; *(= tilgen) Schuld, Hypothek* to pay off, to redeem
c *(= ersetzen) Wache* to relieve; *Kollegen* to take over from; **drei Minister wurden abgelöst** *(euph)* three ministers were relieved of their duties
d *(fig: = an Stelle treten von)* to take the place of; *Methode, System* to supersede; **Regen hat jetzt das schöne Wetter abgelöst** the fine weather has now given way to rain
VR **a** *(= abgehen)* to come off; *(Lack etc auch)* to peel off; *(Netzhaut)* to become detached
b *(auch* **einander ablösen***)* to take turns; *(Wachen)* to relieve each other; **wir lösen uns alle drei Stunden beim Babysitten ab** we each do three-hour shifts of babysitting, we take turns at babysitting, doing three hours each
c *(auch* **einander ablösen**: *= alternieren)* to alternate; **bei ihr lösen sich Fröhlichkeit und Trauer ständig ab** she constantly alternates between being happy and being miserable

Ab|lö|se|sum|me F *(Sport)* transfer fee

Ab|lö|sung F **a** *(Fin) (von Rente)* lump payment; *(von Hypothek, Schuld)* paying off, redemption **b** *(= Wachwechsel)* relieving; *(= Wache)* relief; *(= Entlassung)* replacement; **wann findet die ~ der Wache statt?** when will the guard be relieved?; **er kam als ~** he came as a replacement; **bei dieser Arbeit braucht man alle zwei Stunden eine ~** you need relieving every two hours in this work **c** *(= das Ablösen)* removal, detachment; *(= das Sichablösen)* separation; *(von Lack etc)* peeling off; *(von Netzhaut)* detachment

Ab|lö|sungs|sum|me F *(Sport)* transfer fee

ab+lot|sen, **ab+luch|sen** VT *sep (inf)* **jdm etw ~** to get *or* wangle *(inf)* sth out of sb

Ab|luft F, *no pl (Tech)* used air

Ab|luft-: **Ab|luft|rohr** NT air outlet; **Ab|luft|schacht** M *(von Brauerei etc)* ventilation shaft

ab+lut|schen VT *sep* to lick; **das Blut/den Honig (von etw) ~** to lick the blood/honey off (sth); **sich** *(dat)* **die Finger ~** to lick one's fingers (clean)

ABM [a:be:ˈlɛm] *abbr* **a** *von* **Antiballistic Missile** ABM **b** *von* **Arbeitsbeschaffungsmaßnahme**

> **ABM** [a:be:ˈlɛm]
>
> **ABM** is short for **Arbeitsbeschaffungsmaßnahme. ABM-Stellen** are jobs provided by an employment creation scheme to help groups such as the over-55s, the severely disabled and the long-term unemployed in areas of high unemployment. An **ABM** normally lasts for one year and must involve work that benefits the community. It must be a genuinely new job, so that no existing posts are filled.

ab+ma|chen VT *sep* **a** *(inf: = entfernen)* to take off; *Schnur, Kette etc* to undo, to take off; *(= herunternehmen)* to take down; **er machte dem Hund die Leine ab** he took the dog's lead *(Brit) or leash off* **b** *(= vereinbaren)* to agree (on); **wir haben abgemacht, dass wir das tun werden** we've agreed to do it, we've agreed on doing it; **es ist noch nichts abgemacht worden** nothing's been agreed (on) yet → *auch* **abgemacht**
c *(= besprechen)* to sort out, to settle; **etw mit sich allein ~** to sort sth out for oneself; **etw mit seinem Gewissen ~** to square sth with one's conscience

Ab|ma|chung [ˈapmaxʊŋ] F -, -en agreement

ab+ma|gern [ˈapma:gɐn] VI *sep aux sein* to get thinner, to lose weight; **sehr ~** to lose a lot of weight; **er war bis zum Skelett abgemagert** he was nothing but skin and bone(s), he was a walking skeleton → *auch* **abgemagert**

Ab|ma|ge|rung F -, *no pl (= Auszehrung)* emaciation; *(= Gewichtsverlust)* slimming

Ab|ma|ge|rungs|kur F diet; **eine ~ machen** to be on a diet, to be dieting; *(anfangen)* to go on a diet, to diet

ab+mä|hen VT *sep* to mow

ab+mah|nen VT *sep (form)* to caution

Ab|mah|nung F *(form)* caution

Ab|mah|nungs|schrei|ben NT *(form)* formal letter of caution

ab+ma|len VT *sep (= abzeichnen)* to paint

ab+mark|ten [ˈapmarktn] VT *sep* **davon lassen wir uns** *(dat)* **nichts ~** we will cede nothing on this point; **er ließ sich** *(dat)* **seine Rechte nicht ~** he would not bargain away his rights

Ab|marsch M departure; *(von Soldaten auch)* march-off; *(von Demonstranten etc auch)* moving off; **ich sah dem ~ der Bergsteiger zu** I watched the climbers setting out *or* off; **zum ~ antreten** *(Mil)* to fall in (ready) for the march-off

ab|marsch|be|reit ADJ ready to set out *or* off *or* move off; *(Mil)* ready to move off *or* march

ab+mar|schie|ren *ptp* **abmarschiert** VI *sep aux sein* to set out *or* off, to move off; *(Mil)* to march *or* move off

Ab|mel|de-: **Ab|mel|de|be|stä|ti|gung** F *document confirming that one has cancelled one's registration with the local authorities*; **Ab|mel|de|for|mu|lar** NT *form to be filled in when one cancels one's registration with the local authorities*

ab+mel|den *sep* **VT** **a** *Zeitungen etc* to cancel; *Telefon* to have disconnected; *(bei Verein)* jdn to cancel the membership of; **sein Auto ~** to take one's car off the road; **seinen Fernsehapparat ~** to cancel one's television licence *(Brit)*; **ein Kind von einer Schule ~** to take a child away from a school, to remove a child from a school; **seine Familie polizeilich ~** to inform *or* notify the police that one's family is moving away
b *(inf)* **abgemeldet sein** *(Sport)* to be outclassed; **jd/etw ist bei jdm abgemeldet** sb has lost interest in sb/sth; **er/sie ist bei mir abgemeldet** I don't want anything to do with him/her
VR **a** to ask for permission to be absent; *(vor Abreise)* to say one is leaving, to announce one's departure; *(im Hotel)* to check out; **sich bei jdm ~** to tell sb that one is leaving; **sich polizeilich** *or* **bei der Polizei ~** to inform *or* notify the police that one is moving away, to cancel one's registration with the police; **sich bei einem Verein ~** to cancel one's membership of a club
b *(Comput)* to log off

Ab|mel|dung F *(von Zeitungen etc)* cancellation; *(von Telefon)* disconnection; *(beim Einwohnermeldeamt)* cancellation of one's registration; *(Comput)* logoff, logout; *(inf: = Formular) form to be filled in so that one's registration with the local authorities is cancelled*; **seit der ~ meines Autos** since I took my car off the road; **die ~ meines Fernsehapparats** the cancellation of my television licence *(Brit)*; **die ~ eines Kindes von einer Schule** the removal of a child from a school; **nach seiner ~ bei dem Verein** after he had cancelled *(Brit) or* canceled *(US)* his membership of the club

ab+mer|geln ['apmɛrgln] VR *sep* to slave away → *auch* **abgemergelt**

ab+mes|sen VT *sep irreg* **a** *(= ausmessen)* to measure; *(= genaue Maße feststellen von)* to measure up; *(= abschätzen) Verlust, Schaden* to measure; **er maß seine Schritte genau ab** *(fig)* he walked with great deliberation *or* very deliberately *or* with measured tread *(liter)* → *auch* **abgemessen** **b** *(= abteilen)* to measure off

Ab|mes|sung F *usu pl* measurement; *(= Ausmaß)* dimension

ab+mil|dern VT *sep Geschmack* to tone down; *Äußerung auch* to moderate; *Aufprall* to cushion, to soften; *Schock* to lessen

ab+mi|schen VT *sep (TV, Rad)* to mix

ABM-Kraft [a:be:'ɛm-] F worker employed through a job creation scheme *or* program *(US)*

ab+mon|tie|ren *ptp* **abmontiert** VT *sep Räder, Teile* to take off *(von etw* sth); *Maschine* to dismantle

ABM-Stel|le [a:be:'ɛm-] F temporary position (through job creation scheme)

ab+mü|hen VR *sep* to struggle (away); **sich mit jdm/etw ~** to struggle *or* slave away with sb/sth

ab+murk|sen VT *sep (inf) jdn* to bump off *(inf)*, to do in *(inf)*; *(= schlachten)* to kill

ab+mus|tern *sep (Naut)* VT *Besatzung* to pay off VI to sign off, to leave the ship

ABM-Ver|trag [a:be:'ɛm-] M *(Pol)* ABM treaty

ab+na|beln ['apna:bln] *sep* VT **ein Kind ~** to cut a baby's umbilical cord VR to cut oneself loose, to make the break; **sich vom Elternhaus ~** to leave the parental home, to leave the nest *(inf)*; **abgenabelt vom Chef** independent of the boss

Ab|na|be|lung F **-, -en** *(lit)* cutting the cord; *(fig)* leaving the nest, flying the coop *(inf)*

ab+na|gen VT *sep* to gnaw off; *Knochen* to gnaw; **Fleisch vom Knochen ~** to gnaw meat off a bone

ab+nä|hen VT *sep* to take in

Ab|nä|her ['apnɛːɐ] M **-s, -** dart

Ab|nah|me ['apna:mə] F **-, -n** **a** *(= Wegnahme)* removal; *(= Herunternahme)* taking down; *(= Amputation)* amputation; **die ~ vom Kreuz(e)** the Descent from the Cross, the Deposition *(form)* **b** *(= Verringerung)* decrease (+*gen* in); *(bei Anzahl, Menge)* drop, decrease (+*gen* in); *(von Niveau, Kräften, Energie)* decline (+*gen* in); *(von Interesse, Nachfrage)* falling off, decline; *(von Aufmerksamkeit)* falling off, flagging, waning; *(= Verlust)* loss **c** *(von Prüfung)* holding; *(von Neubau, Fahrzeug etc)* inspection; *(von TÜV)* carrying out; *(von Eid)* administering; **die ~ der Parade** the taking of the parade, the review of the troops; **die ~ der Prüfung kann erst erfolgen, wenn ...** the exam can only be held if ... **d** *(Comm)* purchase; **bei ~ von 50 Kisten** if you/we *etc* purchase *or* take 50 crates; **keine ~ finden** to find no market; **gute ~ finden** to sell well

Ab|nah|me-: **Ab|nah|me|ga|ran|tie** F *(Econ)* guaranteed purchase, firm order; **Ab|nah|me|pro|to|koll** NT *(Tech)* acceptance *or* test certificate

ab|nehm|bar ADJ removable, detachable

ab+neh|men *sep irreg* VT **a** *(= herunternehmen)* to take off, to remove; *Hörer* to lift, to pick up; *(= lüften) Hut* to raise; *Vorhang, Bild, Wäsche* to take down; *Maschen* to decrease; *(= abrasieren) Bart* to take *or* shave off; *(= amputieren)* to amputate; *(Cards) Karte* to take from the pile; **das Telefon ~** to answer the telephone **b** *(= an sich nehmen)* **jdm etw ~** to take sth from sb, to relieve sb of sth *(form)*; *(fig) Arbeit, Sorgen* to take sth off sb's shoulders, to relieve sb of sth; **darf ich Ihnen den Mantel/die Tasche ~?** can I take your coat/bag?; **kann ich dir etwas ~?** *(= tragen)* can I take something for you?; *(= helfen)* can I do anything for you?; **jdm die Beichte ~** to hear confession from sb; **jdm einen Eid ~** to administer an oath to sb; **jdm ein Versprechen ~** to make sb promise something; **jdm einen Weg ~** to save sb a journey; **jdm eine Besorgung ~** to do some shopping for sb **c** *(= wegnehmen)* to take away *(jdm* from sb); *(= rauben, abgewinnen)* to take *(jdm* off sb); *(inf: = abverlangen)* to take *(jdm* off sb); **jdm den Ball ~** *(Sport)* to steal the ball from sb; **diese Schweine haben mir alles abgenommen** *(inf)* the bastards have taken everything (I had) *(sl)* **d** *(= begutachten) Gebäude, Wohnung, Auto* to inspect; *(= abhalten) Prüfung* to hold; *TÜV* to carry out **e** *(= abkaufen)* to take (+*dat* off), to buy (+*dat* from, off) **f** *Fingerabdrücke* to take; *Totenmaske* to make (+*dat* of) **g** *(fig inf: = glauben)* to buy *(inf)*; **dieses Märchen nimmt dir keiner ab!** *(inf)* nobody will buy that tale! *(inf)*
VI **a** *(= sich verringern)* to decrease; *(Vorräte)* to go down, to decrease; *(zahlenmäßig, mengenmäßig)* to drop, to decrease; *(Unfälle, Diebstähle etc)* to decrease (in number); *(Niveau)* to go down, to decline; *(Kräfte, Energie)* to fail, to decline; *(Fieber)* to lessen, to go down; *(Interesse, Nachfrage)* to fall off, to decline; *(Aufmerksamkeit)* to fall off, to flag, to wane; *(Mond)* to wane; *(Tage)* to grow *or* get shorter; *(beim Stricken)* to decrease; **(an Gewicht) ~** to lose weight; **in letzter Zeit hast du im Gesicht abgenommen** your face has got thinner recently **b** *(Telec)* to answer; **es hat keiner abgenommen** no-one answered

Ab|neh|mer(in) M(F) *(Comm)* buyer, purchaser, customer; **keine ~ finden** not to sell; **viele/wenige ~ finden** to sell well/badly

Ab|neh|mer|kreis M buyers *pl*, customers *pl*, market

Ab|nei|gung F dislike *(gegen* of); *(= Widerstreben)* aversion *(gegen* to)

ab+nib|beln ['apnɪbln] VI *sep aux sein (N Ger inf: = sterben)* to croak *(inf)*, to kick the bucket *(inf)*, to snuff it *(inf)*

ab+ni|cken VT *sep (inf)* **etw ~** to nod sth through *(inf)*

ab|norm [ap'nɔrm], **ab|nor|mal** ['apnɔrma:l, apnɔr'ma:l] ADJ abnormal ADV abnormally

Ab|nor|ma|li|tät F abnormality

Ab|nor|mi|tät [apnɔrmi'tɛːt] F **-, -en** abnormality; *(= Monstrum)* freak

ab+nö|ti|gen VT *sep (geh)* **jdm etw ~** to wring *or* force sth from sb; **jdm Bewunderung ~** to win *or* gain sb's admiration; **jdm Respekt ~** to gain sb's respect; **jdm ein Versprechen ~** to exact a promise from sb

ab+nut|zen, *(esp S Ger, Aus, Sw)* **ab+nüt|zen** *sep* VT to wear out; **dieser Begriff ist schon sehr abgenutzt worden** this idea is pretty well-worn, this idea has become hackneyed *(Brit)* → *auch* **abgenutzt** VR to wear out, to get worn out

Ab|nut|zung F, *(esp S Ger, Aus, Sw)* **Ab|nüt|zung** F **-, -en** wear (and tear); **die jahrelange ~ der Teppiche** the years of wear (and tear) on the carpets; **die normale ~ ist im Mietpreis berücksichtigt** general wear and tear is included in the rent

Ab|nut|zungs|er|schei|nung F sign of wear (and tear)

Ab|nut|zungs|krieg M war of attrition

Abo ['abo] NT **-s, -s** *(inf) abbr von* **Abonnement**

Abokün|di|gung F *(inf)* cancellation of subscription

Abon|ne|ment [abɔnə'mã, *(Sw)* abɔnə'mɛnt, abɔn'mã:] NT **-s, -s** *or* **-e** **a** *(von Zeitung, Fernsehsender)* subscription; **eine Zeitung im ~ beziehen** to subscribe to a newspaper, to have a subscription for a newspaper **b** *(= Theaterabonnement)* season ticket, subscription; **ein ~ im Theater haben** to have a season ticket *or* subscription for the theatre *(Brit) or* theater *(US)*, to have a theatre *(Brit) or* theater *(US)* season ticket

Abon|ne|ment|fern|se|hen [abɔnə'mã-] NT subscription television, pay TV *(inf)*

Abon|nent [abɔ'nɛnt] M **-en, -en**, **Abon|nen|tin** [-'nɛntɪn] F **-, -nen** *(von Zeitung, Fernsehsender)* subscriber; *(= Theaterabonnent)* season-ticket holder

Abon|nen|ten-Fern|se|hen NT subscription television, pay TV *(inf)*

abon|nie|ren [abɔ'ni:rən] *ptp* **abonniert** VT *Zeitung, Fernsehsender* to subscribe to, to have a subscription to; *Konzertreihe, Theater* to have a season ticket *or* subscription for VI **auf eine Zeitung/einen Fernsehsender abonniert sein** to subscribe to *or* to have a subscription to a newspaper/a TV channel; **auf eine Konzertreihe abonniert sein** to have a season ticket *or* subscription for a concert series

ab+ord|nen VT *sep* to delegate; **jdn zu einer Versammlung ~** to send sb as a delegate to a meeting

Ab|ord|nung F delegation; *(= Delegation auch)* deputation

Abort [a'bɔrt, 'aplɔrt] M **-s, -e** *(dated)* lavatory, toilet

Abort [a'bɔrt] M **-s, -e**, **Abor|tus** [a'bɔrtʊs] M **-, -** *(= Fehlgeburt)* miscarriage, abortion *(form)*; *(= Abtreibung)* abortion

Abo|wer|bung F *(inf)* subscription promotion

ab+pa|cken VT *sep* to pack; **ein abgepacktes Brot** a wrapped loaf

ab+pas|sen VT *sep* **a** *(= abwarten) Gelegenheit, Zeitpunkt* to wait for; *(= ergreifen)* to seize; **den richtigen Augenblick** *or* **Zeitpunkt ~** *(= abwarten)* to bide one's time, to wait for the right time; *(= ergreifen)* to move at the right time; **ich habe den Zeitpunkt nicht richtig abgepasst** I mistimed it; **etw gut ~** to manage *or* arrange sth well; *(zeitlich auch)* to time sth well **b** *(= auf jdn warten)* to catch; *(= jdm auflauern)* to waylay

ab+pau|sen VT *sep* to trace, to make a tracing of

ab+per|len VI *sep aux sein* to drip off *(von etw* sth); *(Tautropfen)* to fall

ab+pfei|fen *sep irreg (Sport)* VI *(Schiedsrichter)* to blow one's whistle VT **das Spiel/die erste Halbzeit ~** to blow the whistle for the end of the game/for half-time

Ab|pfiff M *(Sport)* final whistle; **~ zur Halbzeit** half-time whistle, whistle for half-time

ab+pflü|cken VT *sep* to pick

ab+pho|to|gra|phie|ren *ptp* **abphotographiert** VT *sep* = **abfotografieren**

ab+pla|cken *(inf)*, **ab+pla|gen** VR *sep* to struggle (away); **sich sein ganzes Leben lang (mit etw) ~** to slave away one's whole life (at sth)

ab+plat|ten ['applatn] VT *sep* to flatten (out)

ab+prä|gen VR *sep (Muster)* to leave an imprint *or* mark

Ab|prall M *(von Ball)* rebound; *(von Geschoss, Kugel)* ricochet *(von* off)

ab+pral|len VI *sep aux sein (Ball)* to bounce off; *(Kugel)* to ricochet (off); **von** *or* **an etw** *(dat)* **~** to bounce/ricochet off sth; **an jdm ~** *(fig)* to make no impression on sb; *(Beleidigungen)* to bounce off sb

Ab|pral|ler ['appralɐ] M **-s, -** *(Sport)* rebound; **er hat den ~ eingeköpft** he headed it in on the rebound

ab+pres|sen VT *sep* **jdm etw ~** to wring sth from sb; *Geld* to extort sth from sb **die Angst presste ihm den Atem ab** he could scarcely breathe for fear;; **die Angst presste ihm das Herz ab** fear ate into his heart

ab+pum|pen VT *sep Teich, Schwimmbecken* to pump dry, to pump the water out of; *Wasser, Öl* to pump off; *Muttermilch* to express

ab+put|zen *sep* VT to clean; *Schmutz* to clean off *or* up; **sich** *(dat)* **die Nase/den Mund/die Hände ~** to wipe one's nose/mouth/hands; **sich** *(dat)* **den Hintern ~** to wipe *or* clean one's bottom; **putz dir die Schuhe ab, bevor du ins Haus kommst** wipe your feet before you come into the house VR *(S Ger, Aus, Sw)* to clean oneself

ab+quä|len *sep* VR to struggle (away); **er quält sich immer noch mit seiner Doktorarbeit ab** he's still struggling with *or* sweating away over *(inf)* his PhD VT **sich** *(dat)* **ein Lächeln ~** to force (out) a smile; **sich** *(dat)* **eine Erklärung/Antwort ~** to finally manage to produce an explanation/answer

ab+qua|li|fi|zie|ren *ptp* **abqualifiziert** VT *sep* to dismiss, to write off

ab+quet|schen VT *sep* to crush; **sich** *(dat)* **den Arm ~** to get one's arm crushed; **sich** *(dat)* **ein paar Tränen ~** to force *or* squeeze out a couple of tears; **sich** *(dat)* **ein Gedicht/eine Rede ~** to deliver oneself of a poem/speech *(iro)*

ab+ra|ckern VR *sep (inf)* to struggle; **sich für jdn ~** to slave away for sb; **warum sollen wir uns hier ~?** why should we break our backs here? *(inf)*; **sich im Garten ~** to sweat away in the garden *(inf)*

Ab|ra|ham ['a:braham] M **-s** Abraham; **in ~s Schoß** in the bosom of Abraham; **sicher wie in ~s Schoß** safe and secure

ab+rah|men VT *sep Milch* to skim

Ab|ra|ka|da|bra [a:braka'da:bra, 'a:braka'da:bra] NT **-s**, *no pl (= Zauberwort)* abracadabra

ab+ra|sie|ren *ptp* **abrasiert** VT *sep* to shave off

ab+ra|ten ✪ 29.2 VTI *sep irreg* **jdm (von) etw ~** to advise sb against sth; **jdm davon ~, etw zu tun** to warn *or* advise sb against doing sth

Ab|raum M *(Min)* overburden, overlay shelf

ab+räu|men *sep* VT **a** *Geschirr, Frühstück* to clear up *or* away; **den Tisch ~** to clear the table **b** *(= entfernen) Sitzblockierer* to remove **c** *(= abkassieren) Konten* to clean out; *Preise, Medaillen* to walk off with **d** *(inf: = stehlen)* to pinch *(inf)* **e** *(esp Min) Flöz, Tonnen, Deich* to clear VI **a** *(= den Tisch abräumen)* to clear up **b** *(= sich bereichern)* to clean up **c** *(= großer Verkaufserfolg sein) (CD etc)* to hit the (record) stores with a bang *(inf)*, to clean up at the record stores *(inf)*; *(film)* to clean up at the box office *(inf)*

Ab|raum|hal|de F *(Min)* slag heap

ab+rau|schen VI *sep aux sein (inf)* to roar away *or* off; *(Aufmerksamkeit erregend)* to sweep away; *(aus Zimmer)* to sweep out

ab+re|a|gie|ren *ptp* **abreagiert** *sep* VT *Spannung, Wut* to work off, to get rid of, to abreact *(Psych)*; **seinen Ärger an anderen ~** to take it out on others VR to work it off; **er war ganz wütend, aber jetzt hat er sich abreagiert** he was furious, but he's simmered down *or* cooled down now; **sich an der Katze ~** to take it out on the cat

ab+rech|nen *sep* VI **a** *(= Kasse machen)* to cash up; **der Kellner wollte ~** the waiter was wanting us/them to pay our/their bill; **darf ich ~?** would you like to settle your bill now? **b mit jdm ~** to settle up with sb; *(fig)* to settle (the score with) sb, to get even with sb VT **a** *(= abziehen)* to deduct, to take off; *(= berücksichtigen)* to allow for, to make allowance(s) for **b die Kasse ~** to cash up

Ab|rech|nung F **a** *(= Aufstellung)* statement *(über +acc* for); *(= Rechnung)* bill, invoice; *(= das Kassemachen)* cashing up; *(fig: = Rache)* revenge; **wie viel mussten Sie ausgeben? – ich bin gerade dabei, die ~ zu machen** *or* **ich bin gerade bei der ~** how much did you have to spend? – I'm just working it out now; **bei der ~ der Konten** when the accounts are/were being balanced; **er muss noch die ganzen ~en machen** he still has to do all the accounts *or* the bookwork; **ich habe die ~ gemacht** I've been doing the books; **der Tag der ~** *(fig)* the day of reckoning **b** *(= Abzug)* deduction; **nach ~ von** after the deduction of; **in ~ bringen** *or* **stellen** *(form)* to deduct; **folgende Beträge kommen in ~** *(form)* the following sums are to be deducted

Ab|rech|nungs-: **Ab|rech|nungs|be|leg** M *(Econ)* voucher; **Ab|rech|nungs|kurs** M settlement price; **Ab|rech|nungs|tag** M accounting date; **Ab|rech|nungs|takt** M *(Telec)* billing unit; **Ab|rech|nungs|ter|min** M accounting date; **Ab|rech|nungs|ver|fah|ren** NT clearing procedure; **Ab|rech|nungs|ver|kehr** M clearing business; **Ab|rech|nungs|zeit|raum** M accounting period

Ab|re|de F *(form)* agreement; **etw in ~ stellen** to deny *or* dispute sth

ab+re|gen VR *sep (inf)* to calm *or* cool *or* simmer down; **reg dich ab!** relax!, cool it! *(inf)*

ab+rei|ben VT *sep irreg Schmutz, Rost* to clean *or* rub off; *(= säubern) Fenster, Schuhe* to wipe; *(= trocknen)* to rub down, to give a rubdown; *(Cook)* to grate

Ab|rei|bung F *(Med)* rubdown; *(inf: = Prügel)* hiding, beating, thrashing

ab+rei|chern ['apraiçɐn] VT *sep* to deplete; **abgereichertes Uran** depleted uranium

Ab|rei|se F departure *(nach* for); **bei der** *or* **meiner ~** when I left/leave, on my departure

ab+rei|sen VI *sep aux sein* to leave *(nach* for); **wann reisen Sie ab?** when will you be leaving?

Ab|rei|se-: **Ab|rei|se|tag** M day of departure, departure day; **Ab|rei|se|ter|min** M departure date

ab+rei|ßen *sep irreg* VT **a** *(= abtrennen)* to tear *or* rip off; *Tapete* to strip off; *Plakat* to tear *or* rip down; *Pflanzen* to tear out; **er hat sich** *(dat)* **den Knopf abgerissen** he's torn his button off; **den Kontakt nicht ~ lassen** to stay in touch; **er wird dir nicht (gleich) den Kopf ~** *(inf)* he won't bite your head off *(inf)* **b** *(= niederreißen) Gebäude* to pull down, to demolish; **das Abreißen von Gebäuden** the demolition of buildings; **ein abgerissenes Gebäude** a demolished building **c** *(sl: = absitzen) Haftstrafe* to do VI *aux sein (= sich lösen)* to tear *or* come off; *(Schnürsenkel)* to break (off); *(fig: = unterbrochen werden)* to break off; **das reißt nicht ab** *(fig)* there is no end to it → *auch* **abgerissen**

Ab|reiß-: **Ab|reiß|block** M *pl* **-blöcke** *or* **-blocks** tear-off pad; **Ab|reiß|ka|len|der** M tear-off calendar

ab+rei|ten *sep irreg* VI *aux sein* to ride off *or* away VT *aux sein or haben (= inspizieren) Front* to ride along; *(hin und zurück)* to ride up and down; *Strecke* to ride over; *Gelände* to patrol (on horseback)

ab+ren|nen *sep irreg* VT **a** *aux sein or haben Stadt, Geschäfte* to scour (around), to run around *(nach* looking for) **b sich** *(dat)* **die Hacken** *or* **Beine (nach etw) ~** to run one's legs off (looking for sth) VR to run oneself off one's feet

ab+rich|ten VT *sep* **a** *(= dressieren) Tier, Menschen* to train; **der Hund ist nur auf Einbrecher abgerichtet** the dog is trained to go only for burglars; **darauf abgerichtet sein, etw zu tun** to be trained to do sth **b** *(Tech) Werkstück, Brett* to true off *or* up

Ab|rich|ter(in) M(F) trainer

Ab|rich|tung F **a** *(von Tier)* training **b** *(Tech)* truing

ab+rie|geln ['apri:gln] VT *sep (= verschließen) Tür* to bolt; *(= absperren) Straße, Gebiet* to seal *or* cordon *or* block off

Ab|rie|ge|lung F **-, -en**, **Ab|rieg|lung** ['apri:glʊŋ] F **-, -en** *(von Tür)* bolting; *(von Straße, Gebiet)* sealing *or* cordoning *or* blocking off

ab+rin|gen VT *sep irreg* **jdm etw ~** to wring *or* force sth from *or* out of sb, to wrest sth from sb *(liter)*; **sich** *(dat)* **ein Lächeln ~** to force a smile; **sich** *(dat)* **eine Entscheidung ~** to force oneself into (making) a decision; **sich** *(dat)* **ein paar Worte ~** to manage to produce a few words; **dem Meer Land ~** *(liter)* to wrest land away from the sea *(liter)*

Ab|riss M **a** *(= Abbruch)* demolition **b** *(= Übersicht)* outline, summary **c** *(von Eintrittskarte etc)* tear-off part

Ab|riss-: **Ab|riss|ar|bei|ten** PL demolition work; **Ab|riss|bir|ne** F wrecking ball; **Ab|riss|lis|te** F *(inf)* demolition list; **auf der ~ stehen** to be condemned; **ab|riss|reif** ADJ only fit for demolition; *(= zum Abriss freigegeben)* condemned

ab+rol|len *sep* VT *Papier, Stoff* to unroll; *Film, Bindfaden* to unwind, to unreel; *Kabel, Tau* to uncoil, to unwind VI *aux sein* **a** *(Papier, Stoff)* to unroll, to come unrolled; *(Film, Bindfaden)* to unwind, to come unwound; *(Kabel, Tau)* to uncoil, to come uncoiled **b** *(Sport)* to roll **c** *(= abfahren) (Züge, Waggons)* to roll off *or* away; *(Flugzeug)* to taxi off **d** *(inf) (= vonstattengehen) (Programm)* to run; *(Veranstaltung)* to go off; *(Ereignisse)* to unfold; **etw rollt vor jds Augen ab** sth unfolds *or* unfurls before sb's (very) eyes; **mein ganzes Leben rollte noch einmal vor meinen Augen ab** my whole life passed before me again VR *(Papier, Stoff)* to unroll itself, to come unrolled; *(Film, Bindfaden)* to unwind itself, to come unwound; *(Kabel, Tau)* to uncoil itself, to come uncoiled

ab+rub|beln ['aprʊbln] *sep* VT **a** *(= entfernen)* to rub off; *Rubbelkarte* to scratch off; **etw von etw ~** to rub sth off sth **b** *(= frottieren)* to rub down VR to rub oneself down

ab+rü|cken *sep* VT *(= wegschieben)* to move away; **etw von der Wand ~** to move sth away from *or* out from the wall VI *aux sein* **a** *(= wegrücken)* to move away; *(fig: = sich distanzieren)* to dissociate oneself *(von* from) **b** *(= abmarschieren)* to move out

Ab|ruf M **a sich auf ~ bereithalten** to be ready to be called (for); **Ihr Wagen steht jederzeit auf ~ bereit** your car will be ready at any time; **auf ~ zur Verfügung stehen** to be available on call **b** *(Comm)* **etw auf ~ bestellen/kaufen** to order/buy sth (to be delivered) on call **c** *(Comput)* retrieval; **auf ~ bereit** readily retrievable; **der Computer hat diese Daten auf ~ bereit** this data is readily retrievable *or* can readily be called up from the computer

Ab|ruf-: **ab|ruf|bar** ADJ **a** *(Comput) Daten* retrievable **b** *(Fin)* ready on call **c** *(fig)* accessible; **Ab|ruf|bar|keit** ['apru:fba:ɐkait] F **-**, *no pl* retrievability; **ab|ruf|be|reit** ADJ **a** *Mensch* ready to be called (for); *(= einsatzbereit)* ready (and waiting); *(= abholbereit)* ready to be called for **b** *(Comm, Fin)* ready on call **c** *(Comput) Daten* ready to be called up *or* retrieved

ab+ru|fen VT *sep irreg* **a** *(= wegrufen)* to call away; **jdn aus dem Leben ~** *(euph)* to gather sb to his fathers *(euph)* **b** *(Comm)* to request delivery of; *(Fin: = abheben)* to withdraw; *staatliche Zuschüsse* to call **c** *Daten, Informationen* to call up, to retrieve

Ab|ruf|zah|len PL *(Internet, von Website)* hits *pl*

ab+run|den VT *sep (lit, fig)* to round off; **eine Zahl nach oben/unten ~** to round a number up/down; **wir haben die Summe abgerundet** we made it a round sum, we rounded it up/down; **EUR 13,12, also abgerundet EUR 13,10** 13 euros 12, so call it 13 euros 10; **die abgerundete, endgültige Form einer Sonate/eines Gedichts** the final polished *or* rounded form of a sonata/poem

Ab|run|dung F *(lit, fig)* rounding off; **zur ~ von etw** to round sth off

ab+rup|fen VT *sep Gras, Blumen* to rip *or* pull up; *Laub* to strip off; *Blätter* to pull *or* strip off

ab|rupt [ap'rʊpt, a'brʊpt] ADJ abrupt ADV abruptly

Ab|rupt|heit F **-**, *no pl* abruptness

ab+rüs|ten *sep* VI **a** *(Mil, Pol)* to disarm **b** *(Build)* to take down *or* remove the scaffolding

VT **a** *(Mil, Pol)* to disarm **b** *Gebäude* to take down *or* remove the scaffolding from *or* on

Ab|rüs|tung F, *no pl* **a** *(Mil, Pol)* disarmament **b** *(Build)* removal of the scaffolding

Ab|rüs|tungs-: **Ab|rüs|tungs|ab|kom|men** NT disarmament treaty; **Ab|rüs|tungs|ge|sprä|che** PL disarmament talks *pl*; **Ab|rüs|tungs|kon|fe|renz** F disarmament conference

ab+rut|schen VI *sep aux sein (= abgleiten)* to slip; *(nach unten)* to slip down; *(Wagen)* to skid; *(Aviat)* to sideslip; *(fig) (Mannschaft, Schüler)* to drop (down) (*auf +acc* to); *(Leistungen)* to drop off, to go downhill; *(moralisch)* to let oneself go, to go downhill

ABS [a:be:'ɛs] NT -, *no pl (Aut) abbr von* **Antiblockiersystem** ABS

Abs. *abbr von* **Absatz, Absender**

ab+sä|beln VT *sep (inf)* to hack *or* chop off

ab+sa|cken VI *sep aux sein (= sinken)* to sink; *(Boden, Gebäude auch)* to subside; *(Flugzeug, Blutdruck)* to drop, to fall; *(fig inf: = nachlassen)* to fall *or* drop off; *(Schüler)* to go down; *(= verkommen)* to go to pot *(inf)*; **sie ist in ihren Leistungen sehr abgesackt** her performance has dropped off a lot

Ab|sa|ge F refusal; *(auf Einladung auch)* negative reply; **das ist eine ~ an die Demokratie** that's a denial of democracy; **jdm/einer Sache eine ~ erteilen** to reject sb/sth

ab+sa|gen *sep* **VT** *(= rückgängig machen) Veranstaltung, Besuch* to cancel, to call off; *(= ablehnen) Einladung* to decline, to turn down, to refuse; **er hat seine Teilnahme abgesagt** he decided to withdraw his participation **VI** to cry off *(Brit)*, to cancel; **jdm ~** to tell sb that one can't come; **wenn ich ihn einlade, sagt er jedes Mal ab** whenever I invite him he says no

ab+sä|gen VT *sep* **a** *(= abtrennen)* to saw off **b** *(fig inf)* to chuck *or* sling out *(inf)*; *Minister, Beamten* to oust; *Schüler* to make fail

Ab|sah|ne ['apza:nə] F -, *no pl (inf)* bonanza

ab+sah|nen ['apza:nən] *sep* **VT** *Milch* to skim; *(fig inf) Geld* to rake in; *(= sich verschaffen)* to cream off; *das Beste* to take; **den Markt ~** to take the cream, to take the pick of the bunch **VI** to skim milk; *(fig inf)* to take the best; *(in Bezug auf Menschen)* to take the cream *or* the best; *(in Bezug auf Geld)* to clean up *(inf)*

ab+sat|teln VTI *sep* to unsaddle

Ab|satz M **a** *(= Abschnitt)* paragraph *(auch Comput)*; *(Typ)* indention; *(Jur)* section; **einen ~ machen** to start a new paragraph/to indent **b** *(= Treppenabsatz)* half landing; *(= Mauerabsatz)* overhang; *(herausragend)* ledge **c** *(= Schuhabsatz)* heel; **spitze Absätze** stilettos, stiletto heels; **sich auf dem ~ (her)umdrehen, auf dem ~ kehrtmachen** to turn on one's heel **d** *(= Verkauf)* sales *pl*; **um den/unseren ~ zu steigern** to increase sales/our sales; **~ finden** *or* **haben** to sell; **guten/begeisterten** *or* **starken** *or* **reißenden ~ finden** to sell well/like hot cakes

Ab|satz-: **Ab|satz|chan|ce** F sales potential *no pl*; **ab|satz|fä|hig** ADJ marketable, saleable; **Ab|satz|flau|te** F slump in sales, slump in the market; **Ab|satz|för|de|rung** F sales promotion; **Ab|satz|for|schung** F sales research; **Ab|satz|ga|ran|tie** F guaranteed sales *pl*; **Ab|satz|ge|biet** NT sales area; **Ab|satz|ge|nos|sen|schaft** F marketing cooperative; **Ab|satz|kri|se** F sales crisis; **Ab|satz|la|ge** F sales situation; **Ab|satz|land** NT customer, buyer; **Ab|satz|mar|ke** F *(Comput)* hard return, paragraph mark; **Ab|satz|markt** M market; **Ab|satz|pla|nung** F sales planning; **Ab|satz|rück|gang** M decline *or* decrease in sales; **Ab|satz|schwie|rig|kei|ten** PL sales problems *pl*; **auf ~ stoßen** to meet with sales resistance; **Ab|satz|stei|ge|rung** F increase in sales, sales increase; **Ab|satz|stra|te|gie** F sales strategy

ab|satz|wei|se **ADJ** in paragraphs **ADV** paragraph by paragraph

ab+sau|fen VI *sep irreg aux sein (sl: = ertrinken)* to drown; *(inf: Motor, Min: Grube)* to flood; *(sl: Schiff etc)* to go down

ab+sau|gen VT *sep Flüssigkeit, Gas, Staub* to suck out *or* off; *(mit Staubsauger)* to hoover® *(Brit)* *or* vacuum up; *Teppich, Sofa* to hoover® *(Brit)*, to vacuum

ABS-: **ABS-Brem|se** F ABS brakes *pl*; **ABS-Brems|sys|tem** NT ABS braking system

ab+scha|ben VT *sep* to scrape off; *(= säubern)* to scrape (clean); *Stoff* to wear thin

ab+schaf|fen *sep* **VT** **a** *(= außer Kraft setzen) Gesetz, Regelung* to abolish, to do away with **b** *(= nicht länger halten)* to get rid of; *Auto etc* to give up **VR** *(S Ger inf: = sich abarbeiten)* to slave away *(inf)*, to work like a slave

Ab|schaf|fung F **a** *(von Gesetz, Regelung)* abolition **b** *(= Loswerden)* getting rid of; *(von Auto etc)* giving up

ab+schä|len *sep* **VT** *Haut, Rinde* to peel off; *Baumstamm* to strip; **die Rinde eines Baumes ~** to strip *or* peel the bark off a tree **VR** to peel off

Ab|schalt|au|to|ma|tik F automatic shutoff

ab+schal|ten *sep* **VT** to switch off; *Kontakt* to break **VI** *(fig)* to unwind **VR** to switch itself off

Ab|schal|tung F switching off; *(von Kontakt)* breaking

ab+schat|ten ['apʃatn], **ab+schat|tie|ren** *ptp* **abschattiert** VT *sep (lit)* to shade; *(fig)* to give a slight nuance to

Ab|schat|tung F -, -en, **Ab|schat|tie|rung** F *(lit)* shading; *(fig)* nuance

ab+schät|zen VT *sep* to estimate, to assess; *Menschen, Fähigkeiten* to assess, to appraise; **seine Lage ~** to take stock of one's position, to assess one's position; **ein ~der Blick** an appraising look; **jdn mit einer ~den Miene betrachten** to look at sb appraisingly

ab|schät|zig ['apʃɛtsɪç] **ADJ** disparaging; *Bemerkung auch* derogatory **ADV** disparagingly; **sich ~ über jdn äußern** to make disparaging *or* derogatory remarks about sb

Ab|schaum M, *no pl* scum; **der ~ der Menschheit, der ~ der menschlichen Gesellschaft** the scum of the earth

ab+schei|den *sep irreg* **VT** *(= ausscheiden)* to give off, to produce; *(Biol)* to secrete; *(Chem)* to precipitate **VR** *(Flüssigkeit etc)* to be given off, to be produced; *(Biol auch)* to be secreted; *(Chem)* to be precipitated **VI** *aux sein (euph liter: = sterben)* to depart this life *(liter)*, to pass away; **sein Abscheiden** his passing → *auch* **abgeschieden**

Ab|schei|der ['apʃaidɐ] M -s, - *(für Öl, Metall)* separator

ab+sche|ren VT *sep Haare, Wolle* to shear off; *Bart* to shave off; *Kopf, Kinn* to shave

Ab|scheu M -(e)s *or f* -, *no pl* repugnance, repulsion, abhorrence (*vor +dat* at); **vor jdm/etw ~ haben** *or* **empfinden** to loathe *or* detest *or* abhor sb/sth; **~ in jdm erregen** to repulse sb; **~ erregend** → **abscheuerregend**

ab+scheu|ern *sep* **VT** **a** *(= reinigen) Fußboden, Wand* to scrub (down) **b** *(= abschürfen) Haut* to rub *or* scrape off **c** *(= abwetzen) Kleidung, Stoff* to rub *or* wear thin; **ein abgescheuerter Kragen** a worn collar **VR** *(Stoff)* to wear thin; *(Tierfell)* to get rubbed *or* scraped off

ab|scheu|er|re|gend ADJ repulsive, loathsome, abhorrent

ab|scheu|lich [ap'ʃɔylɪç] **ADJ** abominable, atrocious, loathsome; *Verbrechen auch* heinous; *Anblick auch* repulsive; *(inf)* awful, terrible *(inf)*; **wie ~!** how ghastly *or* awful *or* terrible! **ADV** *behandeln, zurichten* atrociously, abominably; *sich anziehen* terribly, awfully; **es ist ~ kalt** it's hideously cold; **~ riechen/schmecken** to smell/taste horrible; **das tut ~ weh** it hurts terribly

Ab|scheu|lich|keit F -, -en **a** *(= Untat)* atrocity, abomination **b** *no pl* heinousness; *(von Geschmack, Anblick)* repulsiveness; **die ~ des Kantinenessens** the awful *or* terrible food in the canteen; **ein Verbrechen von besonderer ~** a particularly heinous crime

ab+schi|cken VT *sep* to send; *Paket, Brief* to send off, to dispatch; *(mit der Post®)* to send, to post *(Brit)*, to mail *(esp US)*

Ab|schie|be|ge|wahr|sam M, **Ab|schie|be|haft** F *(Jur)* remand pending deportation, custody prior to deportation; **jdn in Abschiebegewahrsam nehmen** to put sb on remand pending deportation

ab+schie|ben *sep irreg* **VT** **a** *(= ausweisen) Ausländer, Häftling* to deport **b** *(inf: = loswerden)* to get rid of; **jdn in eine andere Abteilung ~** to shunt sb off to another department **c** *(= wegschieben) Schrank etc* to push out *or* away (*von* from); *(fig) Verantwortung, Schuld* to push *or* shift (*auf +acc* onto); **er versucht immer, die Verantwortung auf andere abzuschieben** he always tries to pass the buck

Ab|schie|bung F *(= Ausweisung)* deportation

Ab|schied ['apʃi:t] M -(e)s, *(rare)* -e [-də] **a** *(= Trennung)* farewell, parting; **von jdm/etw ~ nehmen** to say goodbye to sb/sth, to take one's leave of sb/sth; **ein Kuss zum ~** a farewell *or* goodbye kiss; **jdn zum ~ küssen** to kiss sb goodbye; **zum ~ überreichte er ihr einen Blumenstrauß** on parting, he presented her with a bunch of flowers; **ein trauriger ~** a sad farewell; **es war für beide ein schwerer ~** parting was hard for both of them; **ich hasse ~e** I hate farewells *or* goodbyes; **es war ein ~ für immer** *or* **fürs Leben** it was goodbye for ever; **beim ~ meinte er, ...** as he was leaving he said ...; **beim ~ auf Bahnhöfen ...** saying goodbye at stations ...; **der ~ von der Heimat fiel ihm schwer** it was hard for him to say goodbye to the land of his birth; **ihr ~ von der Bühne/vom Film** her farewell to the stage/to films; *(= letzte Vorstellung)* her farewell performance; **ihre Heirat bedeutete für sie den ~ von der Kindheit** her marriage marked the end of her childhood; **der ~ von der Vergangenheit** breaking *or* the break with the past **b** *(= Rücktritt) (von Beamten)* resignation; *(von Offizieren)* discharge; **seinen ~ nehmen** *or* **einreichen** to hand in *or* tender one's resignation; *(Offizier)* to apply for a discharge; **seinen ~ erhalten** *or* **bekommen** to be dismissed; *(Offizier)* to be discharged

Ab|schieds- *in cpds* farewell; **Ab|schieds|be|such** M farewell *or* goodbye visit; **Ab|schieds|brief** M letter of farewell, farewell letter; **Ab|schieds|fei|er** F farewell *or* going-away *or* leaving party; **Ab|schieds|fe|te** F *(inf)* leaving do *(inf)*; **Ab|schieds|ge|schenk** NT *(für Kollegen etc)* leaving present; *(für Freund)* going-away present; **Ab|schieds|ge|such** NT *(Pol)* letter of resignation; **sein ~ einreichen** to tender one's resignation; **Ab|schieds|gruß** M farewell; *(= Wort zum Abschied)* word of farewell; **Ab|schieds|kon|zert** NT farewell concert; **Ab|schieds|kuss** M farewell *or* parting *or* goodbye kiss; **Ab|schieds|re|de** F farewell speech, valedictory (speech) *(form)*; **Ab|schieds|schmerz** M pain of parting; **Ab|schieds|spiel** NT *(Sport)* testimonial (match); **Ab|schieds|stim|mung** F mood of parting *or* farewell; **Ab|schieds|stun|de** F time *or* hour of parting, time to say goodbye; **Ab|schieds|sze|ne** F farewell scene; **Ab|schieds|trä|ne** F tear at parting; **Ab|schieds|vor|stel|lung** F *(Theat)* farewell *or* final performance

ab+schie|ßen *sep irreg* **VT** **a** *(= losschießen) Geschoss, Gewehr, Kanone* to fire; *Pfeil* to shoot (off), to loose off; *Rakete* to launch; *(auf ein Ziel)* to fire; *(fig) Fragen, Befehle, Bemerkung* to fire (*auf +acc* at) **b** *(= außer Gefecht setzen) Flugzeug, Pilot* to shoot down; *(= wegschießen) Bein etc* to shoot off **c** *(= totschießen) Wild* to shoot; *(inf) Menschen* to shoot down → **Vogel** **d** *(fig inf: = loswerden)* to get rid of **VI** *(Sport)* to kick off

ab+schil|fern ['apʃɪlfɐn] VI *sep aux sein* to peel off

ab+schin|den VR *sep irreg (inf)* to knacker oneself (*Brit inf*), to tire oneself out; *(= schwer arbeiten)* to work one's fingers to the bone; **sich mit Gartenarbeit/einem schweren Koffer ~** to knacker oneself (*Brit sl*) *or* to tire oneself out gardening/carrying a heavy suitcase

Ab|schirm|dienst M *(Mil)* counterespionage service

ab+schir|men ['apʃɪrmən] *sep* VT to shield; *(= schützen auch)* to protect; *(vor Licht auch)* to screen; *Lampe* to cover; **jdn vor etw** *(dat)* **~** to shield *or* protect sb from sth; **etw gegen die Sonne ~** to screen *or* shield sth from the sun VR to shield oneself (*gegen* from); *(= sich schützen)* to protect oneself (*gegen* from *or* against); *(= sich isolieren)* to isolate oneself, to cut oneself off (*gegen* from)

Ab|schir|mung F -, -en **a** *(= das Abschirmen)* shielding; *(= Schutz)* protection; *(vor Licht)* screening; *(von Lampe)* covering **b** *(fig)* *(= Selbstschutz, auch Pol)* protection; *(= Isolierung)* isolation

ab+schir|ren ['apʃɪrən] VT *sep* to unharness; *Ochsen* to unyoke

ab+schlach|ten VT *sep* to slaughter; *Menschen auch* to butcher

Ab|schlach|tung F slaughter; *(von Menschen auch)* butchering *no pl*

ab+schlaf|fen ['apʃlafn] *sep* VI *aux sein (inf)* to flag → *auch* **abgeschlafft** VT to whack *(inf)*

Ab|schlag M **a** *(= Preisnachlass)* reduction; *(= Abzug)* deduction **b** *(= Zahlung)* part payment (*auf +acc* of) **c** *(Ftbl)* kickout, punt; *(Hockey)* bully(-off); *(Golf)* tee-off; *(= Abschlagfläche)* tee **d** *(= Abholzung)* felling

ab+schla|gen ✪ 30 VT *sep irreg* **a** *(mit Hammer etc)* to knock off; *(mit Schwert etc) Fuß, Kopf, Hand* to cut off; *(mit Beil)* to cut *or* chop off; *(= herunterschlagen)* to knock down **b** *Gerüst etc* to take down **c** *(= ablehnen)* to refuse; *Einladung, Bitte* to refuse, to turn down; **jdm etw ~** to refuse sb sth; **sie/er kann niemandem etwas ~** she/he can never refuse anybody anything **d** *auch vi (Ftbl)* to punt; *(Hockey)* to bully off; *(Golf)* to tee off **e** **sein Wasser ~** *(dated inf)* to relieve oneself → **abgeschlagen**

ab|schlä|gig ['apʃlɛːgɪç] ADJ negative; **~er Bescheid** rejection; *(bei Sozialamt, Kredit etc)* refusal ADV **jdn/etw ~ bescheiden** *(form)* to reject sb/sth, to turn sb/sth down

Ab|schlag(s)|zah|lung F part payment

ab+schle|cken VT *sep (S Ger, Aus)* = **ablecken**

ab+schlei|fen *sep irreg* VT *Kanten, Ecken, Unebenheiten* to grind down; *Rost* to polish off; *Messer* to grind; *Holz, Holzboden* to sand (down) VR to get worn off, to wear down; *(fig) (Angewohnheit etc)* to wear off; **das schleift sich (noch) ab** *(fig)* that'll wear off

Ab|schlepp|dienst M breakdown service, (vehicle) recovery service

ab+schlep|pen *sep* VT **a** *(= wegziehen)* to drag *or* haul off *or* away; *Fahrzeug, Schiff* to tow, to take in tow; *(Behörde)* to tow away **b** *(inf) Menschen* to drag along; *(= sich aneignen)* to get one's hands on *(inf)*; *(= aufgabeln)* to pick up *(inf)* VR **sich mit etw ~** *(inf)* to struggle with sth

Ab|schlepp-: **Ab|schlepp|fahr|zeug** NT breakdown *or* recovery vehicle; **Ab|schlepp|kos|ten** PL recovery costs *pl*; **Ab|schlepp|öse** F tow loop; **Ab|schlepp|seil** NT towrope; **Ab|schlepp|stan|ge** F towbar; **Ab|schlepp|wa|gen** M breakdown truck *or* lorry *(Brit)*, tow truck *(US)*, wrecker *(US)*

ab|schließ|bar ADJ *(= verschließbar)* lockable

ab+schlie|ßen *sep irreg* VT **a** *(= zuschließen)* to lock; *Auto, Raum, Schrank* to lock (up); **etw luftdicht ~** to put an airtight seal on sth **b** *(= beenden) Sitzung, Vortrag etc* to conclude, to bring to a close; *(mit Verzierung)* to finish off; *Kursus* to complete; **sein Studium ~** to take one's degree, to graduate; **mit abgeschlossenem Studium** with a degree **c** *(= vereinbaren) Geschäft* to conclude, to transact; *Versicherung* to take out; *Wette* to place; **einen Vertrag ~** *(Pol)* to conclude a treaty; *(Jur, Comm)* to conclude a contract **d** *(Comm: = abrechnen) Bücher* to balance; *Konto* to settle, to balance; *Geschäftsjahr* to close; *Inventur* to complete; *Rechnung* to make up VR *(= sich isolieren)* to cut oneself off, to shut oneself away; **sich von der Außenwelt ~** to cut *or* shut oneself off from the outside world → *auch* **abgeschlossen** VI **a** *(= zuschließen)* to lock up; **sieh mal nach, ob auch abgeschlossen ist** will you see if everything's locked? **b** *(= enden)* to close, to come to a close, to conclude; *(mit Verzierung)* to be finished off **c** *(Comm) (= Vertrag schließen)* to conclude the deal; *(= Endabrechnung machen)* to do the books **d** *(= Schluss machen)* to finish, to end; **mit allem/dem Leben ~** to finish with everything/life; **mit der Vergangenheit ~** to break with the past

ab|schlie|ßend ADJ concluding ADV in conclusion, finally

Ab|schluss M **a** *(= Beendigung)* end; *(von Untersuchung)* conclusion; *(inf: = Abschlussprüfung)* final examination; *(Univ)* degree; **zum ~ von etw** at the close *or* end of sth; **zum ~ möchte ich ...** finally *or* to conclude I would like ...; **seinen ~ finden** *(geh)* **zum ~ kommen** to come to an end; **etw zum ~ bringen** to finish sth; **ein Wort zum ~** a final word; **kurz vor dem ~ stehen** to be in the final stages; **seinen ~ machen** *(Univ)* to do one's final exams; **nach ~ des Studiums/der Lehre** after finishing university/one's apprenticeship; **sie hat die Universität ohne ~ verlassen** she left the university without taking her degree → **krönen** **b** *no pl (= Vereinbarung)* conclusion; *(von Wette)* placing; *(von Versicherung)* taking out; **bei ~ des Vertrages** on conclusion of the contract **c** *(Comm: = Geschäft)* business deal; **zum ~ kommen** to make a deal **d** *no pl (Comm) (der Bücher)* balancing; *(von Konto)* settlement; *(von Geschäftsjahr)* close; *(von Inventur)* completion **e** *(= Rand, abschließender Teil)* border

Ab|schluss-: **Ab|schluss|ball** M *(von Tanzkurs)* final ball; **Ab|schluss|bi|lanz** F *(Econ)* final *or* closing balance (sheet); **Ab|schluss|fei|er** F *(Sch)* speech *or* prize-giving day; **Ab|schluss|klas|se** F *(Sch)* final class *or* year; **Ab|schluss|kom|mu|ni|qué** NT, **Ab|schluss|kom|mu|ni|kee** NT final communiqué; **Ab|schluss|prü|fung** F **a** *(Sch)* final examination; *(Univ)* finals *pl (Brit)*, final exam **b** *(Comm)* audit; **Ab|schluss|rech|nung** F final account; **Ab|schluss|zeug|nis** NT *(Sch)* leaving certificate *(Brit)*, diploma *(US)*

ab+schmäl|zen ['apʃmɛltsn], *(Aus)* **ab+schmal|zen** VT *sep* to gratinate

ab+schmat|zen VT *sep (inf)* to slobber over *(inf)*

ab+schme|cken *sep* VT *(= kosten)* to taste, to sample; *(= würzen)* to season; **abgeschmeckt mit** flavoured *(Brit) or* flavored *(US)* with VI *(= kosten)* to taste; *(= nachwürzen)* to add some seasoning

ab+schmei|cheln VT *sep* **jdm etw ~** to wheedle *or* coax sth out of sb

ab+schmel|zen *sep* VT *Eis* to melt; *(Tech)* to melt down; *(fig: = reduzieren) Zulagen, Stellen, Kapital* to reduce VI *aux sein (Polkappe, Eis, Eisberg)* to melt; *(fig: Überschuss, Umsatz, Gewinne etc)* to melt away

ab+schmet|tern VT *sep (inf) (Sport)* to smash; *(fig: = zurückweisen)* to throw out; **mit seinem Antrag wurde er abgeschmettert** his application was thrown *or* flung out; **er wurde abgeschmettert** he was shot down *(inf)*

ab+schmie|ren *sep* VT **a** *(Tech) Auto* to grease, to lubricate **b** *(inf: = abschreiben)* to copy, to crib *(Brit inf)* VI *aux sein (Aviat)* to go down

Ab|schmier|pres|se F grease gun

ab+schmin|ken *sep* VT **a** *Gesicht, Haut* to remove the make-up from **b** *(inf: = aufgeben)* **sich** *(dat)* **etw ~** to get sth out of one's head VR to take off *or* remove one's make-up

ab+schmir|geln VT *sep* to sand down

ab+schmü|cken VT *sep* **den Weihnachtsbaum ~** to take the decorations down from the Christmas tree

Abschn. *abbr von* **Abschnitt** para

ab+schna|cken VT *sep (N Ger inf)* **jdm etw ~** to wheedle *or* coax sth out of sb

ab+schnal|len *sep* VT to unfasten, to undo VR to unfasten one's seat belt VI *(sl: = nicht mehr folgen können)* to give up

ab+schnei|den *sep irreg* VT *(lit, fig)* to cut off; *Flucht auch* to block off; *Blumen, Scheibe* to cut (off); *Zigarre* to cut the end off; *Haar* to cut; *Rock, Kleid* to cut the seam off; **jdm die Rede** *or* **das Wort ~** to cut sb short; **abgeschnitten** *(Comput) Datei, Text* truncated → **Scheibe b** VI **bei etw gut/schlecht ~** *(inf)* to come off well/badly in sth

ab+schnip|peln VT *sep (inf)* **etw von etw ~** to cut a bit off sth; *(mit Schere auch)* to snip sth off sth

Ab|schnitt M **a** section; *(Math)* segment; *(Mil)* sector, zone; *(= Geschichtsabschnitt, Zeitabschnitt)* period **b** *(= Kontrollabschnitt) (von Scheck etc)* counterfoil; *(von Karte)* section; *(von Papier)* slip

ab|schnitt(s)|wei|se ADV in sections; **der Lehrer nahm das Buch ~ durch** the teacher went through the book section by section ADJ sectionalized

ab+schnü|ren VT *sep* to cut off (*von* from); *(Med) Glied* to put a tourniquet on; **jdm das Blut ~** to cut off sb's circulation; **jdm die Luft ~** *(lit)* to stop sb breathing; *(fig)* to bankrupt *or* ruin sb; **die Angst schnürte ihr das Herz ab** *(liter)* she was paralyzed by fear

ab+schöp|fen VT *sep* to skim off; *(fig) Dank, Ruhm* to reap; *Kaufkraft* to absorb; *(= für sich gewinnen)* to cream off; **den Rahm** *or* **das Fett ~** *(fig)* to cream off the best part; **den Gewinn ~** to siphon off the profits

Ab|schöp|fung F *(Fin: von Kaufkraft)* absorption; **sparen Sie durch ~** save by automatic transfer

ab+schot|ten ['apʃɔtn] VT *sep (Naut)* to separate with a bulkhead, to bulkhead off; **sich gegen etw ~** *(fig)* to cut oneself off from sth; **etw ~** to shield *or* screen sth

ab+schrä|gen VT *sep* to slope; *Holz, Brett* to bevel; **ein abgeschrägtes Dach** a sloping roof; **er schrägte das Brett an den Kanten ab** he bevelled *(Brit) or* beveled *(US)* the edges of the board

Ab|schrä|gung F -, -en slope; *(von Brett)* bevel

ab+schrau|ben VT *sep* to unscrew

ab+schre|cken *sep* VT **a** *(= fernhalten)* to deter, to put off; *(= verjagen: Hund, Vogelscheuche)* to scare off; **jdn von etw ~** to deter sb from sth, to put sb off sth; **ich lasse mich dadurch nicht ~** that won't deter me, I won't be deterred by that **b** *(= abkühlen) Stahl* to quench; *(Cook)* to rinse with cold water VI *(Strafe)* to act as a deterrent

ab|schre|ckend ADJ **a** *(= warnend)* deterrent; **ein ~es Beispiel** a warning; **eine ~e Wirkung haben, ~ wirken** to act as a deterrent **b** *(= abstoßend) Hässlichkeit* repulsive

Ab|schre|ckung ['apʃrɛkʊŋ] F -, -en **a** *(= das Fernhalten, Mil)* deterrence; *(= das Verjagen)* scaring off; *(= Abschreckungsmittel)* deterrent **b** *(= Abkühlung) (von Stahl)* quenching; *(Cook)* rinsing with cold water

Ab|schre|ckungs-: **Ab|schre|ckungs|maß|nah|me** F deterrent; **Ab|schre|ckungs|mit|tel** NT deterrent; **Ab|schre|ckungs|po|li|tik** F *(Mil)* policy of deterrence; **Ab|schre|ckungs|stra|te|gie** F *(Mil)* strategy of deterrence; **Ab|schre|ckungs|the|o|rie** F *(Jur)* theory of deterrence; **Ab|schre|ckungs|waf|fe** F deterrent weapon

ab+schrei|ben *sep irreg* VT **a** *(= kopieren)* to copy out; *(Sch: = abgucken)* to copy, to crib *(Brit inf)*; *(= plagiieren)* to copy *(bei, von* from) **b** *(= schreibend abnutzen)* to use up → **Finger** **c** *(Comm) (= absetzen, abziehen)* to deduct; *(= im Wert mindern)* to depreciate **d** *(= verloren geben)* to write off; **er ist bei mir abgeschrieben** I'm through *or* finished with him VI **a** *(Sch)* to copy, to crib *(Brit inf)* **b jdm ~** to write to sb to tell him that one cannot come *etc* VR *(Bleistift, Farbband)* to get used up

Ab|schrei|ber(in) M(F) *(pej)* plagiarist; *(Sch)* cribber *(Brit inf)*, cheat

Ab|schrei|bung F *(= Steuerabschreibung)* tax write-off; *(Comm)* deduction; *(= Wertverminderung)* depreciation

Ab|schrei|bungs-: **Ab|schrei|bungs|be|trag** M *(Econ)* depreciation (allowance); **Ab|schrei|bungs|be|trug** M tax deduction fraud; **Ab|schrei|bungs|fonds** M depreciation fund; **Ab|schrei|bungs|ob|jekt** NT tax-deductible item; **Ab|schrei|bungs|pro|jekt** NT tax avoidance scheme

ab+schrei|ten VT *sep irreg* **a** *(= entlanggehen)* to walk along; *(hin und zurück)* to walk up and down; *Gelände* to patrol; *(= inspizieren) Front* to inspect **b** *(= messen)* to pace out

Ab|schrift F copy

ab+schröp|fen VT *sep* **jdm etw ~** *(inf)* to wangle sth out of sb *(inf)*

ab+schrub|ben VT *sep (inf) Schmutz* to scrub off *or* away; *Rücken, Kleid, Fußboden* to scrub (down); **schrubbt euch richtig ab!** give yourselves a good scrub!

ab+schuf|ten VR *sep (inf)* to slog one's guts out *(inf)*

ab+schup|pen *sep* VT *Fisch* to scale VR to flake off

ab+schür|fen VT *sep* to graze

Ab|schür|fung F -, -en *(= Wunde)* graze

Ab|schuss M **a** *(= das Abfeuern)* firing, shooting; *(von Pfeil)* shooting, loosing off; *(von Rakete)* launch(ing); *(auf ein Ziel)* firing **b** *(= das Außer-Gefecht-Setzen)* shooting down; *(von Panzer)* knocking out; **die Luftwaffe erzielte zwölf Abschüsse** the air force shot *or* brought down twelve planes **c** *(von Wild)* shooting; **Fasanen sind jetzt zum ~ freigegeben** pheasant-shooting is now permitted; **jdn zum ~ freigeben** *(fig)* to throw sb to the wolves; **die Zahl der Abschüsse** the number of kills; **durch ~ des Ministers** *(fig inf)* by getting rid of the minister **d** *(Sport)* (goal) kick

Ab|schuss|ba|sis F launching base

ab|schüs|sig ['apʃʏsɪç] ADJ sloping; **eine sehr ~e Straße** a steep road, a steeply sloping road; **auf einer ~en Bahn sein** *(fig)* to be going rapidly downhill

Ab|schüs|sig|keit F -, *no pl* slope

Ab|schuss-: **Ab|schuss|lis|te** F *(inf)* **er steht auf der ~** his days are numbered; **jdn auf die ~ setzen** to put sb on the hit list *(inf)*; **auf jds ~ stehen** to be on sb's hit list *(inf)*; **Ab|schuss|quo|te** F *(Hunt)* kill quota; **Ab|schuss|ram|pe** F launching pad

ab+schüt|teln VT *sep Staub, Schnee* to shake off; *Decke, Tuch* to shake (out); *(fig) lästige Menschen, Verfolger* to shake off, to lose *(inf)*; *Gedanken, Ärger etc* to get rid of; **das Joch der Knechtschaft ~** *(liter)* to throw off the yoke of slavery

ab+schüt|ten VT *sep Flüssigkeit, Mehl, Sand etc* to pour off; *(Cook) Flüssigkeit* to drain off; *Kartoffeln etc* to drain; *Eimer* to empty

ab+schwä|chen *sep* VT to weaken; *Wirkung, Einfluss auch* to lessen; *Behauptung, Formulierung, Kontrast* to tone down; *Schock, Aufprall* to lessen; *Stoß, Eindruck* to soften VR to drop *or* fall off, to diminish; *(Lärm)* to decrease; *(Met: Hoch, Tief)* to disperse; *(Preisauftrieb, Andrang)* to ease off; *(St Ex: Kurse)* to weaken

Ab|schwä|chung F weakening; *(von Behauptung, Formulierung)* toning down; *(von Schock, Aufprall)* lessening; *(von Eindruck)* softening; *(= Rückgang: von Lärm)* decrease; *(Met: von Hoch, Tief)* dispersal; *(von Andrang, Preisauftrieb)* easing off

ab+schwat|zen, *(S Ger)* **ab+schwät|zen** VT *sep (inf)* **jdm etw ~** to talk sb into giving one sth; **das habe ich mir von meinem Bruder ~ lassen** I let my brother talk me into giving it to him

ab+schwei|fen VI *sep aux sein (lit, fig)* to stray, to wander (off *or* away); *(Redner auch)* to digress; **er schweifte vom Thema ab** he deviated from the subject

Ab|schwei|fung F digression; *(vom Thema)* deviation

ab+schwel|len VI *sep irreg aux sein (Entzündung, Fluss)* to go down; *(Lärm)* to die *or* fade *or* ebb away; **der geschwollene Fuß ist wieder abgeschwollen** the swelling in his foot has gone down

ab+schwem|men VT *sep* to wash away

ab+schwen|ken VI *sep aux sein* to turn away; *(Kamera)* to swing round, to pan; **(von der Straße) ~** to turn off (the road); **er ist nach links abgeschwenkt** *(lit)* he turned off to the left; *(fig)* he swung (over) to the left; **(nach rechts) ~** *(Mil)* to wheel (right); **er schwenkte zur Medizin ab** he changed over to medicine

ab+schwim|men *sep irreg* VI *aux sein (= losschwimmen)* to swim off *or* away VT **a** *aux sein or haben Strecke* to swim; *Gewässer* to swim along **b** *(= verlieren)* **sich** *(dat)* **überflüssige Pfunde ~** to swim off those extra pounds

ab+schwin|deln VT *sep* **jdm etw ~** to swindle sb out of sth

ab+schwin|gen VI *sep irreg (Ski)* to do a downhill turn

ab+schwir|ren VI *sep aux sein* to whirr off; *(fig inf: = weggehen)* to buzz off *(inf)*; **die Vögel schwirrten plötzlich ab** with a flutter of wings the birds suddenly flew off

ab+schwit|zen VT *sep* to sweat off; **sich** *(dat)* **einen ~** *(sl)* to sweat like mad *(inf)* or crazy *(inf)*

ab+schwö|ren *sep irreg* VI **einer Sache** *(dat)* **~** to renounce sth; **dem Terrorismus/Glauben/Teufel ~** to renounce terrorism/one's faith/the devil; **seinen Ketzereien ~** to recant one's heresies; **dem Alkohol ~** *(inf)* to give up drinking VT *(old: = ableugnen) Schuld, Mittäterschaft* to deny, to repudiate; *Glauben* to renounce

Ab|schwung M *(Sport)* dismount; *(Ski)* downhill turn; *(Comm)* downward trend, recession

ab+se|geln *sep* VI **a** *aux sein (= lossegeln)* to sail off *or* away, to set sail; *(inf: = weggehen)* to sail off; **der Schoner segelte von Bremen ab** the schooner sailed from Bremen *or* set sail from Bremen **b** *(Sport: = die Saison beenden)* to have one's last sail VT *Strecke* to sail; *Küste* to sail along

ab+seg|nen VT *sep (inf) Vorschlag, Plan* to give one's blessing to; **von jdm abgesegnet sein** to have sb's blessing

ab|seh|bar ADJ foreseeable; **in ~er/auf ~e Zeit** in/for the foreseeable future; **das Ende seines Studiums ist noch nicht ~** the end of his studies is not yet in sight; **die Folgen sind noch gar nicht ~** there's no telling what the consequences will be

ab+se|hen *sep irreg* VT **a** *(= abgucken)* **(bei) jdm etw ~** to pick sth up from sb; *(= abschreiben)* to copy sth from sb
b *(= voraussehen)* to foresee; **es ist noch gar nicht abzusehen, wie lange die Arbeit dauern wird** there's no telling yet how long the work will take; **es ist ganz klar abzusehen, dass ...** it's easy to see that ...; **das Ende lässt sich noch nicht ~** the end is not yet in sight
VI **von etw ~** *(= verzichten)* to refrain from sth; *(= nicht berücksichtigen)* to disregard sth, to leave sth out of account *or* consideration; **davon ~, etw zu tun** to dispense with doing sth, to refrain from doing sth → *auch* **abgesehen**

ab+sei|fen VT *sep* to soap down; *Gegenstand auch* to wash down; **jdm den Rücken ~** to soap sb's back

ab+sei|hen VT *sep* to strain

ab+sei|len ['apzailən] *sep* VT to let *or* lower down on a rope VR to let *or* lower oneself down on a rope; *(Bergsteiger)* to abseil (down) *(Brit)*, to rappel *(US)*; *(fig inf)* to skedaddle *(inf)*

Ab|seil|ge|schirr NT abseil ropes *pl*

ab sein VI *irreg aux sein (inf)* **a** *(= weg sein)* to be off; **die Farbe/der Knopf ist ab** the paint/button has come off **b** *(= abgelegen sein)* to be far away

ab|sei|tig ['apzaitɪç] ADJ **a** *(geh: = abseits liegend)* remote **b** *Theorie, Thema* esoteric

ab|seits ['apzaits] ADV to one side; *(= abgelegen)* out of the way, remote; *(Sport)* offside; **~ vom Wege** off the beaten track; **~ von der Straße** away from the road; **nicht ~** *(Sport)* onside, not offside; **sich ~ halten** *(fig)* to hold or keep to oneself → **abseitsbleiben, abseitsliegen, abseitsstehen** PREP *+gen* away from; **~ des Weges** off the beaten track

Ab|seits ['apzaits] NT -, - *(Sport)* offside; **im ~ stehen** to be offside; **ein Leben im ~ führen** *(fig)* to live in the shadows; **ins politische ~ geraten** to end up on the political scrapheap

Ab|seits-: **ab|seits+blei|ben** VI *sep irreg aux sein (fig)* to hold *or* keep to oneself; **Ab|seits|fal|le** F *(Sport)* offside trap; **ab|seits+lie|gen** VI *sep irreg (S Ger, Aus, Sw: aux sein)* to be out of the way, to be remote; **Ab|seits|po|si|ti|on** F *(Sport)* offside position; **Ab|seits|re|gel** F *(Sport)* offside rule; **ab|seits+ste|hen** VI *sep irreg (S Ger, Aus, Sw: aux sein) (fig)* to be on the outside; *(Sport)* to be offside; **Ab|seits|stel|lung** F *(Sport)* offside position; **Ab|seits|tor** NT *(Sport)* offside goal

ab+sen|den VT *sep* to send; *Brief, Paket* to send off, to dispatch; *(mit der Post®)* to send, to post *(Brit)*, to mail *(esp US)*

Ab|sen|der M *(= Adresse)* (sender's) address

Ab|sen|der(in) M(F) sender

Ab|sen|der|ken|nung F sender's reference

ab+sen|gen VT *sep* to singe off

ab+sen|ken *sep* VT **a** *(Build) Grundwasserstand* to lower; *Fundamente* to sink **b** *(Agr) Weinstöcke etc* to layer VR to subside; **das Gelände senkt sich zum Seeufer ab** the terrain slopes down toward(s) the shore

Ab|sen|ker ['apzɛŋkɐ] M -s, - *(Hort: = Ableger)* layer

ab|sen|tie|ren [apzɛn'tiːrən] *ptp* **absentiert** VR *insep (old, hum)* to absent oneself

Ab|sen|tis|mus [apzɛn'tɪsmʊs] M -, *no pl (Ind, Sociol)* absenteeism

Ab|senz [ap'zɛnts] F -, -en *(Sch: Aus, Sw)* absence

ab+ser|vie|ren *ptp* **abserviert** *sep* VI to clear the table VT **a** *Geschirr, Tisch* to clear **b** *(inf: = entlassen, kaltstellen)* **jdn ~** to get rid of sb **c** *(Sport sl: = besiegen)* to thrash *(inf)*

ab|setz|bar ADJ *Ware* saleable; *Betrag* deductible; **steuerlich ~** tax-deductible

Ab|setz|bar|keit ['apzɛtsbaːɐkait] F *(von Steuern etc)* deductibility

ab+set|zen *sep* VT **a** *(= abnehmen) Hut, Brille* to take off, to remove; *(= hinstellen) Gepäck, Glas* to set *or* put down; *Geigenbogen, Feder* to lift; *Gewehr* to unshoulder
b *(= aussteigen lassen) Mitfahrer, Fahrgast* to set down, to drop; *Fallschirmjäger* to drop; **wo kann ich dich ~?** where can I drop you?
c *(Naut)* to push off
d *Theaterstück, Oper* to take off; *Fußballspiel, Turnier, Versammlung, Termin* to cancel; **etw vom Spielplan ~** to take sth off the programme *(Brit) or* program *(US)*
e *(= entlassen)* to dismiss; *Minister, Vorsitzenden* to dismiss, to remove from office; *König, Kaiser* to depose; *(sl) Freund, Freundin* to chuck *(inf)*

f (= entwöhnen) Jungtier to wean; (Med) Medikament, Tabletten to come off, to stop taking; Behandlung to break off, to discontinue; (Mil) Rationen etc to stop; **die Tabletten mussten abgesetzt werden** I/she etc had to stop taking the tablets or had to come off the tablets **g** (Comm: = verkaufen) Waren to sell; **sich gut ~ lassen** to sell well **h** (= abziehen) Betrag, Summe to deduct; **das kann man (von der Steuer) ~** that is tax-deductible **i** (= ablagern) Geröll to deposit **j** (Sew) to trim **k** (= kontrastieren) to contrast; **etw gegen etw ~** to set sth off against sth **l** (Typ) Manuskript to (type)set, to compose; **(eine Zeile) ~** to start a new line
VR **a** (Chem, Geol) to be deposited; (Feuchtigkeit, Staub etc) to collect **b** (inf: = weggehen) to get or clear out (aus of) (inf); (Sport: = Abstand vergrößern) to pull ahead; **sich nach Brasilien ~** to clear off to Brazil (inf) **c sich gegen jdn/etw ~** to stand out against sb/sth; **sich vorteilhaft gegen jdn/etw ~** to contrast favourably (Brit) or favorably (US) with sb/sth; **das macht er, nur um sich gegen die anderen abzusetzen** he only does that to be different from the others or to make himself stand out from the crowd
VI to put one's glass down; **er trank das Glas aus ohne abzusetzen** he emptied his glass in one

Ab|set|zung F -, -en **a** (= Entlassung) (von Beamten) dismissal; (von Minister, Vorsitzendem) dismissal, removal from office; (von König) deposing, deposition **b** (Fin: = Abschreibung) deduction **c** (von Theaterstück etc) withdrawal; (von Fußballspiel, Termin etc) cancellation **d** (von Jungtier) weaning; (Med) discontinuation

ab+si|chern sep VT to safeguard; (= garantieren) to cover; Bauplatz, Gefahrenstelle to make safe; Dach to support; (Comput) Daten to store; (= schützen) to protect; **jdn über die Landesliste ~** (Pol) ≈ to give sb a safe seat VR (= sich schützen) to protect oneself; (= sich versichern) to cover oneself

Ab|si|che|rung F protection; (von Gefahrenstelle) making safe; (von Ergebnissen) validation; **zur rechtlichen ~ von etw** to protect sth legally

Ab|sicht ✪ 35, 45.1, 45.4 F -, -en (= Vorsatz) intention; (= Zweck) purpose; (Jur) intent; **in der besten ~, in bester ~** with the best of intentions; **in der ~, etw zu tun** with the idea or object of doing sth, with a view to doing sth, with the intention of doing sth; **die ~ haben, etw zu tun** to intend to do sth; **eine ~ mit etw verfolgen** to have something in mind with sth; **etw mit/ohne ~ tun** to do/not to do sth on purpose or deliberately; **ernste ~en haben** (inf) to have serious intentions; **das war nicht meine ~!** I didn't intend that; **das war doch keine ~!** (inf) it wasn't deliberate or intentional; **das ist ~** (inf) that's deliberate or intentional

ab|sicht|lich ✪ 45.4 ADJ deliberate, intentional ADV deliberately, intentionally

Ab|sicht|lich|keit F -, no pl deliberateness

Ab|sichts-: **Ab|sichts|er|klä|rung** F declaration of intent; **ab|sichts|los** ADJ unintentional ADV unintentionally; **Ab|sichts|satz** M (Gram) final clause; **ab|sichts|voll** ADJ = **absichtlich**

ab+sie|deln VT sep **a** (Admin) Bürger to resettle **b** (Med) Tochtergeschwulst to form

Ab|sied|lung F **a** (Admin) resettlement **b** (Med) metastasis

ab+sin|gen VT sep irreg **a** (vom Blatt) to sight-read **b** (bis zu Ende) to sing (right) through; **unter Absingen der Nationalhymne/Internationale** with the singing of the national anthem/the Internationale

ab+sin|ken VI sep irreg aux sein to fall, to drop; (Boden) to subside, to sink; (Temperatur, Wasserspiegel, Kurs) to fall, to go down; (Interesse, Leistungen) to fall or drop off; (fig: = moralisch absinken) to go downhill; **auf 10%/ein niedriges Niveau ~** to fall or drop to 10%/a low level

Ab|sinth [ap'zɪnt] M -(e)s, -e absinth(e)

ab+sit|zen sep irreg VT (= verbringen) Zeit to sit out; (= verbüßen) Strafe to serve VI aux sein (vom Pferd) ~ to dismount (from a horse); **abgesessen!** dismount!

ab|so|lut [apzo'lu:t] ADJ (alle Bedeutungen) absolute; (= völlig auch) complete, total ADV absolutely; **das ist ~ unmöglich** that's quite or absolutely impossible; **~ genommen** or **betrachtet** considered in the absolute; **ich sehe ~ nicht ein, warum ...** I just don't understand why ...

Ab|so|lu|te(s) [apzo'lu:tə] NT decl as adj (Philos) Absolute, absolute

Ab|so|lut|heit F -, no pl absoluteness

Ab|so|lut|heits|an|spruch M claim to absolute right; **einen ~ vertreten** to claim absoluteness

Ab|so|lu|ti|on [apzolu'tsio:n] F -, -en (Eccl) absolution; **jdm die ~ erteilen** to grant or give sb absolution

Ab|so|lu|tis|mus [apzolu'tɪsmʊs] M -, no pl absolutism

ab|so|lu|tis|tisch [apzolu'tɪstɪʃ] ADJ absolutist ADV **~ herrschen** or **regieren** to be an absolute monarch

Ab|sol|vent [apzɔl'vɛnt] M -en, -en, **Ab|sol|ven|tin** [-'vɛntɪn] F -, -nen (Univ) graduate; **die ~en eines Lehrgangs** the students who have completed a course

ab|sol|vie|ren [apzɔl'vi:rən] ptp **absolviert** VT insep **a** (= durchlaufen) Studium, Probezeit to complete; Schule to finish, to graduate from (US); Prüfung to pass; **er hat die technische Fachschule absolviert** he completed a course at technical college **b** (= ableisten) to complete **c** (Eccl) to absolve

Ab|sol|vie|rung F -, -en (von Studium, Probezeit) completion; (von Schule) finishing, graduation (+gen from) (US); (von Prüfung) passing

ab|son|der|lich ADJ peculiar, strange ADV peculiarly, strangely

Ab|son|der|lich|keit F -, -en **a** no pl strangeness **b** (= Eigenart) peculiarity

ab+son|dern sep VT **a** (= trennen) to separate; (= isolieren) to isolate **b** (= ausscheiden) to secrete **c** (inf: = von sich geben) to come out with (inf), to utter VR **a** (Mensch) to cut oneself off; **sie sondert sich immer sehr ab** she always keeps herself very much to herself → auch **abgesondert** **b** (= ausgeschieden werden) to be secreted

Ab|son|de|rung F -, -en **a** (= das Trennen) separation; (= Isolierung) isolation; (= Ausscheidung) secretion **b** (von Menschen) segregation **c** (= abgeschiedener Stoff) secretion

Ab|sor|ber [ap'zɔrbɐ] M -s, - (Tech) absorber

ab|sor|bie|ren [apzɔr'bi:rən] ptp **absorbiert** VT insep (lit, fig) to absorb

Ab|sorp|ti|on [apzɔrp'tsio:n] F -, -en absorption

ab+spal|ten VTR sep to split off; (Chem) to separate (off)

Ab|spann ['apʃpan] M -s, -e (TV, Film) final credits pl

ab+span|nen sep VT **a** (= ausspannen) Pferd, Wagen to unhitch; Ochsen to unyoke **b** (Build) to anchor VI **a** (= Pferde, Wagen abspannen) to unhitch (the) horses etc; (= Ochsen abspannen) to unyoke (the) oxen **b** (fig: = entspannen) to relax → auch **abgespannt**

Ab|span|nung F **a** (= Erschöpfung) weariness, tiredness **b** (Build) anchoring; (= Spannseil) anchor (cable)

ab+spa|ren VT sep **sich** (dat) **Geld von etw ~** to save money from sth; **sich** (dat) **ein Auto vom Lohn ~** to save up for a car from one's wages; **sich** (dat) **etw vom** or **am Munde** or **am eigenen Leib ~** to scrimp and save for sth

ab+spe|cken ['apʃpɛkn] sep (inf) VT to shed; (fig: = verkleinern) to slim down, to trim VI to lose weight

ab+spei|chern VT sep Daten to store (away), to save (auf +dat onto)

ab+spei|sen VT sep **a** (= beköstigen) to feed **b** (fig inf: = abfertigen) **jdn mit etw ~** to fob sb off with sth (esp Brit)

ab|spens|tig ['apʃpɛnstɪç] ADJ **jdm jdn/etw ~ machen** to lure sb/sth away from sb; **jdm die Freundin ~ machen** to pinch (Brit) or steal sb's girlfriend (inf); **jdm die Kunden ~ machen** to lure or draw sb's customers away from him/her

ab+sper|ren sep VT **a** (= abriegeln) to block or close off **b** (= abdrehen) Wasser, Strom, Gas etc to turn or shut off **c** (= verschließen) to lock VI to lock up

Ab|sperr-: **Ab|sperr|git|ter** NT barrier; **Ab|sperr|hahn** M stopcock; **Ab|sperr|ket|te** F chain

Ab|sper|rung F **a** (= Abriegelung) blocking or closing off **b** (= Sperre) barrier; (= Kordon) cordon

Ab|sperr|ven|til NT stop or check or shut-off valve

Ab|spiel NT (= das Abspielen) passing; (= Schuss) pass

ab+spie|len sep VT **a** Schallplatte, Tonband to play (through); Nationalhymne to play; (vom Blatt) Musik to sight-read **b** (Sport) Ball to pass; (beim Billard) to play VR (= sich ereignen) to happen; (= stattfinden) to take place; **wie mein Leben sich abspielt** what my life is like; **da spielt sich (bei mir) nichts ab!** (inf) nothing doing! (inf)

ab+split|tern sep VI aux sein (Farbe) to drip off; (fig: Gruppe) to break away VR (fig: Gruppe) to break away

Ab|split|te|rung F -, -en (= das Absplittern) chipping off; (von Holz auch) splintering off

Ab|spra|che F arrangement; **eine ~ treffen** to make or come to an arrangement; **ohne vorherige ~** without prior consultation

ab|spra|che|ge|mäß ADV as arranged

ab|spra|che|wid|rig ADV contrary to (previous) agreement

ab+spre|chen sep irreg VT **a jdm etw ~** (= verweigern, Recht) to deny or refuse sb sth; (= in Abrede stellen) Begabung to deny or dispute sb's sth **b** (= verabreden) Termin to arrange; **die Zeugen hatten ihre Aussagen vorher abgesprochen** the witnesses had agreed on what to say in advance VR **sich mit jdm ~** to make an arrangement with sb; **die beiden hatten sich vorher abgesprochen** they had agreed on what to do/say etc in advance; **ich werde mich mit ihr ~** I'll arrange or fix things with her

ab+sprei|zen VT sep to extend; (Build) to brace

ab+sprin|gen VI sep irreg aux sein **a** (= herunterspringen) to jump down (von from); (= herausspringen) to jump out (von of); (Aviat) to jump (von from); (bei Gefahr) to bale out; (Sport) to dismount; (= losspringen) to take off; **mit dem rechten Bein ~** to take off on the right leg **b** (= sich lösen) to come off; (esp Farbe, Lack) to flake or peel off; (= abprallen) to bounce off (von etw sth) **c** (fig inf: = sich zurückziehen) to get out; (von Partei, Kurs etc) to back out; **von etw ~** to get or back out of sth

ab+sprit|zen sep VT **a etw/jdn/sich ~** to spray sth/sb/oneself down; Schmutz to spray off (von etw sth); (Cook) to sprinkle **b** (NS euph sl: = töten) to give a lethal injection to VI **a** aux sein to spray off **b** aux haben (sl: = ejakulieren) to spunk (vulg)

Ab|sprung M jump (auch Aviat), leap; (Sport) takeoff; (= Abgang) dismount; **den ~ schaffen** (fig) to make the break (inf), to make it (inf); **er hat den ~ gewagt** (fig) he took the jump; **den ~ verpassen** (fig: ins Berufsleben etc) to miss the boat

Ab|sprung-: **Ab|sprung|bal|ken** M (Sport) takeoff board; **Ab|sprung|hö|he** F (Sport)

drop altitude; **Ab|sprung|stel|le** F *(Sport)* jumping-off point

ab+spu|len VT *sep Kabel, Garn* to unwind; *(inf) (= filmen)* to shoot; *(= vorführen)* to show; *(fig)* to reel off

ab+spü|len *sep* VT *Hände, Geschirr* to rinse; *Fett etc* to rinse off VI to wash up *(Brit)*, to do the washing-up *(Brit)*, to wash the dishes

ab+stam|men VI *sep no ptp* to be descended *(von* from); *(Ling)* to be derived *(von* from)

Ab|stam|mung F -, -en descent; *(= Abkunft auch)* origin, extraction; *(Ling)* origin, derivation; **ehelicher/unehelicher ~** *(Jur)* of legitimate/illegitimate birth; **französischer ~** of French extraction *or* descent

Ab|stam|mungs|leh|re F, **Ab|stam|mungs|the|o|rie** F theory of evolution

Ab|stand M **a** *(= Zwischenraum)* distance; *(= kürzerer Abstand)* gap, space; *(= Zeitabstand)* interval; *(= Punkteabstand)* gap; *(fig) (= Distanz)* distance; *(= Unterschied)* difference; **mit ~** by far, far and away; **~ von etw gewinnen** *(fig)* to distance oneself from sth; **in regelmäßigen Abständen/Abständen von 10 Minuten** at regular/10 minute intervals; **in unregelmäßigen Abständen** at irregular intervals; **~ halten** to keep one's distance; **mit großem ~ führen/gewinnen** to lead/win by a wide margin; **automatischer ~** *(Comput)* automatic pair kerning
b *(form: = Verzicht)* **von etw ~ nehmen** to dispense with sth; *von Meinung, Absicht, Forderung* to abandon sth; **davon ~ nehmen, etw zu tun** to refrain from doing sth
c *(= Abfindung)* indemnity

Ab|stands|sum|me F *(form)* indemnity

ab+stat|ten ['apʃtatn] VT *sep (form)* **jdm einen Besuch ~** to pay sb a visit; **jdm seinen Dank ~** to give thanks to sb

ab+stau|ben VTI *sep* **a** *Möbel etc* to dust **b** *(inf) (= wegnehmen)* to pick up; *(= schnorren)* to cadge *(von, bei, +dat* off, from); **er will immer nur ~** he's always on the scrounge **c** *(Ftbl inf)* **(ein Tor** *or* **den Ball) ~** to put the ball into the net, to tuck the ball away

Ab|stau|ber ['apʃtaubɐ] M -s, - *(Ftbl inf: auch* **Abstaubertor)** easy goal

Ab|stau|ber ['apʃtaubɐ] M -s, -, **Ab|stau|be|rin** [-ərɪn] F -, -nen *(inf)* **a** *(Ftbl)* goal-hanger *(inf)* **b** *(= Schnorrer)* scrounger *(inf)*, sponger *(inf)*

ab+ste|chen *sep irreg* VT **a** **ein Tier ~** to cut an animal's throat; **jdn ~** *(inf)* to knife sb *(inf)* **b** *(= abtrennen) Torf* to cut; *Rasen* to trim (the edges of) **c** *(= ablaufen lassen) Hochofen, Metall* to tap VI **gegen jdn/etw ~, von jdm/etw ~** to stand out against sb/sth

Ab|ste|cher ['apʃtɛçɐ] M -s, - *(= Ausflug)* excursion, trip; *(= Umweg)* detour; *(fig)* sortie

ab+ste|cken VT *sep* **a** *Gelände, Grenze, Trasse* to mark out; *(mit Pflöcken)* to peg *or* stake out; *(fig) Verhandlungsposition, Programm* to work out **b** *Kleid, Naht* to pin

ab+ste|hen *sep irreg* VI *(= entfernt stehen)* to stand away; *(= nicht anliegen)* to stick out; **~de Ohren** ears that stick out → *auch* **abgestanden** VT *(inf)* **sich** *(dat)* **die Beine ~** to stand for hours and hours

ab+stei|fen VT *sep (Build)* to shore up

Ab|stei|ge F *(inf)* dosshouse *(Brit inf)*, flophouse *(dated US inf)*, cheap hotel

ab+stei|gen VI *sep irreg aux sein* **a** *(= heruntersteigen)* to get off *(von etw* sth); **von einem Pferd/Rad** *etc* **~** to dismount, to get off a horse/bicycle *etc*; **„Radfahrer ~!"** "cyclists dismount" **b** *(= abwärtsgehen)* to make one's way down; *(esp Bergsteiger)* to climb down; **in ~der Linie, in der ~den Linie** in the line of descent; **auf dem ~den Ast sein** *(inf)* **sich auf dem ~den Ast befinden** *(inf)* to be going downhill, to be on the decline **c** *(dated: = einkehren)* to stay **d** *(Sport: Mannschaft)* to go down, to be relegated; **aus der ersten Liga ~** to be relegated from the first division

Ab|stei|ge|quar|tier NT = **Absteige**

Ab|stei|ger(in) M(F) *(Sport)* relegated team; **gesellschaftlicher ~** *(fig)* someone who has come down in the world

Ab|stell|bahn|hof M railway yard

ab+stel|len *sep* VT **a** *(= hinstellen)* to put down **b** *(= unterbringen)* to put; *(Aut: = parken)* to park
c *(= abrücken, entfernt stellen)* to put away from; **das Klavier von der Wand ~** to leave the piano out from *or* away from the wall
d *(= abkommandieren)* to order off, to detail; *Offizier* to second, to detail; *(fig: = abordnen)* to assign; *(Sport) Spieler* to release
e *(= ausrichten auf)* **etw auf jdn/etw ~** to gear sth to sb/sth
f *(= abdrehen)* to turn off; *Geräte, Licht* to switch *or* turn off; *(= Zufuhr unterbrechen) Gas, Strom* to cut off; *Telefon* to disconnect; **den Haupthahn für das Gas ~** to turn the gas off at the mains
g *(= sich abgewöhnen)* to give up, to stop
h *(= unterbinden) Mangel, Unsitte etc* to bring to an end; **das lässt sich nicht/lässt sich ~** nothing/something can be done about that; **lässt sich das nicht ~?** couldn't that be changed?
VI **auf etw** *(acc)* **~** to be geared to sth; *(= etw berücksichtigen)* to take sth into account

Ab|stell-: **Ab|stell|flä|che** F storage surface; *(für Auto)* parking space *or* area; **Ab|stell|gleis** NT siding; **jdn aufs ~ schieben** *(fig)* to push *or* cast sb aside; **auf dem ~ sein** *or* **stehen** *(fig)* to have been pushed *or* cast aside; **Ab|stell|hahn** M stopcock; **Ab|stell|he|bel** M *(Tech)* (start-)stop lever; **Ab|stell|kam|mer** F boxroom; **Ab|stell|platz** M **a** *(für Auto)* parking space; **ein ~ für Fahrräder** a place for leaving bicycles **b** *(fig inf: = beruflich ungünstiger Posten)* inferior position; **Ab|stell|raum** M storeroom; **Ab|stell|tisch** M *(für Speisen und Getränke)* dumb waiter; *(bei der Arbeit)* stand

ab+stem|peln VT *sep* to stamp; *Post* to postmark; *(fig)* to stamp, to brand *(zu, als* as)

Ab|stem|pe|lung F -, -en, **Ab|stemp|lung** ['apʃtɛmplʊŋ] F -, -en stamping; *(von Post)* postmarking; *(fig)* branding

ab+step|pen VT *sep* to stitch, to sew; *Wattiertes, Daunendecke* to quilt; *Kragen etc* to topstitch

ab+ster|ben VI *sep irreg aux sein (= eingehen, auch Med)* to die; *(= gefühllos werden: Glieder)* to go *or* grow numb; *(fig) (Gefühle)* to die; *(= untergehen: Industriezweig, Sprachgruppe)* to die out; **mir sind die Zehen abgestorben** my toes have gone *or* grown numb → *auch* **abgestorben**

Ab|stich M *(von Wein)* racking; *(von Metall, Hochofen)* tapping; *(= Öffnung des Hochofens)* taphole

Ab|stieg M *(= das Absteigen)* way down, descent; *(= Weg)* descent; *(= Niedergang)* decline; *(Sport)* relegation; **einen alten Pfad als ~ benutzen** to come down (on) an old path; **vom ~ bedroht** *(Sport)* threatened by relegation, in danger of being relegated

Ab|stiegs-: **Ab|stiegs|ge|fahr** F *(Sport)* threat of relegation; **ab|stiegs|ge|fähr|det** ADJ *(Sport)* threatened by *or* in danger of relegation; **Ab|stiegs|kampf** M *(Sport)* relegation battle; **Ab|stiegs|kan|di|dat(in)** M(F) *(Sport)* relegation candidate, candidate for relegation

ab+stil|len *sep* VT *Kind* to wean, to stop breastfeeding VI to stop breastfeeding

ab+stim|men *sep* VI to take a vote; **über etw** *(acc)* **~** to vote *or* take a vote on sth; **über etw** *(acc)* **~ lassen** to put sth to the vote; **geheim ~** to have a secret ballot
VT *(= harmonisieren) Instrumente* to tune *(auf +acc* to); *Radio* to tune (in) *(auf +acc* to); *(= in Einklang bringen) Farben, Kleidung* to match *(auf +acc* with); *Termine* to coordinate *(auf +acc* with); *(= anpassen)* to suit *(auf +acc* to); *(Comm) Bücher* to balance; **gut auf etw** *(acc)***/aufeinander abgestimmt sein** *(Instrumente)* to be in tune with sth/with each other; *(Farben, Speisen etc)* to go well with sth/with each other *or* together; *(Termine)* to fit in well with sth/with each other; *(= einander angepasst sein)* to be well-suited to sth/(to each other); **etw miteinander ~** *(= vereinbaren)* to settle sth amongst ourselves/themselves *etc*; **abgestimmt** *(= vereinbart, Politik, Aktionen etc)* agreed; **(aufeinander) abgestimmt** *(Pläne, Strategien)* mutually agreed
VR **sich (mit jdm/miteinander) ~** to come to an agreement (with sb/amongst ourselves/themselves *etc*)

Ab|stim|mung F **a** *(= Stimmabgabe)* vote; *(= geheime Abstimmung)* ballot; *(= das Abstimmen)* voting; **eine ~ durchführen** *or* **vornehmen** to take a vote; to hold a ballot; **zur ~ bringen** *(form)* to put to the vote → **schreiten** **b** *(von Instrumenten)* tuning; *(von Farben, Kleidung)* matching; *(von Terminen)* coordination; *(= das Anpassen)* suiting; *(von Büchern)* balancing **c** *(= Vereinbarung)* agreement

Ab|stim|mungs-: **ab|stim|mungs|be|rech|tigt** ADJ = **stimmberechtigt**; **Ab|stim|mungs|be|rech|tig|te(r)** MF *decl as adj* person entitled to vote; **Ab|stim|mungs|er|geb|nis** NT result of the vote; **Ab|stim|mungs|nie|der|la|ge** F **eine ~ erleiden** to be defeated in a/the vote; **Ab|stim|mungs|sieg** M **einen ~ erringen** to win a/the vote

abs|ti|nent [apsti'nɛnt] ADJ teetotal; *(geschlechtlich)* abstinent, continent, not indulging in sex; *(fig)* unforthcoming; **sie sind politisch ~** they don't engage in politics ADV **~ leben** to live a life of abstinence

Abs|ti|nenz [apsti'nɛnts] F -, *no pl* teetotalism, abstinence; *(geschlechtlich)* abstinence

Abs|ti|nenz-: **Abs|ti|nenz|er|schei|nung** F *(Med)* withdrawal symptom; **Abs|ti|nenz|ge|bot** NT *(Eccl)* requirement of abstinence

Abs|ti|nenz|ler [apsti'nɛntslɐ] M -s, -, **Abs|ti|nenz|le|rin** [-ərɪn] F -, -nen teetotaller *(Brit)*, teetotaler *(US)*

Abs|ti|nenz|tag M *(Eccl)* day of abstinence

ab+stin|ken VI *sep irreg (sl: = einpacken)* **damit kannst du ~** you can forget it *(inf)*

ab+stop|pen *sep* VT **a** *Auto, Maschine, Verkehr* to stop, to bring to a standstill *or* halt; *(= drosseln)* to halt **b** *(Sport) Ball* to stop; *(mit Stoppuhr)* to time; **jds Zeit ~** to time sb VI to stop, to come to a halt

Ab|stoß M **a** *(Ftbl)* goal kick; *(nach Fangen des Balls)* clearance **b** **der ~ vom Ufer war so kräftig, dass ...** the boat was pushed away from *or* out from the shore so forcefully that ...

ab+sto|ßen *sep irreg* VT **a** *(= wegstoßen) Boot* to push off *or* away *or* out; *(= abschlagen) Ecken* to knock off; *Möbel* to batter; *(= abschaben) Ärmel* to wear thin; **sich** *(dat)* **die Ecken und Kanten ~** *(fig)* to have the rough edges knocked off one → **Horn a**
b *(= zurückstoßen)* to repel; *(Comm) Ware, Aktien* to get rid of, to sell off; *(Med) Organ* to reject; *(fig: = anwidern)* to repulse, to repel; **dieser Stoff stößt Wasser ab** this material is water-repellent
c *(Ftbl)* **den Ball ~** to take the goal kick; *(nach Fangen)* to clear (the ball)
VR **a** *(= abgeschlagen werden)* to get broken; *(Möbel)* to get battered
b *(esp Sport: Mensch)* to push oneself off; **sich mit den Füßen vom Boden ~** to push oneself off
c *(Phys)* to repel; **die beiden Pole stoßen sich ab** the two poles repel each other
VI **a** *aux sein or haben (= weggestoßen werden)* to push off
b *(= anwidern)* to be repulsive; **sich von etw abgestoßen fühlen** to be repelled by sth, to find sth repulsive
c *(Ftbl)* to take a goal kick; *(nach Fangen)* to clear (the ball)

ab|sto|ßend ADJ *Aussehen, Äußeres* repulsive; **sein Wesen hat etwas Abstoßendes** there's something repulsive about him ADV repulsively; **~ aussehen/riechen** to look/smell repulsive

Ab|sto|ßung F **-, -en** *(Phys)* repulsion; *(Med: von Organ)* rejection

Ab|sto|ßungs|re|ak|ti|on F *(Med)* rejection

ab+stot|tern VT *sep (inf)* to pay off

ab+stra|fen VT *sep* = **bestrafen**

abs|tra|hie|ren [apstra'hi:rən] *ptp* **abstrahiert** VTI *insep* to abstract (*aus* from)

ab+strah|len VT *sep* **a** *Wärme, Energie, Programm etc* to emit **b** *Fassade (mit Sandstrahlgebläse)* to sandblast

abs|trakt [ap'strakt] ADJ abstract; **~e Kunst** abstract art ADV abstractly; **etw zu ~ ausdrücken** to express sth too abstractly *or* too much in the abstract

Abs|trakt|heit F **-,** *(rare)* **-en** abstractness

Abs|trak|ti|on [apstrak'tsio:n] F **-, -en** abstraction

Abs|trak|ti|ons|ver|mö|gen NT ability to abstract

Abs|trak|tum [ap'straktʊm] NT **-s, Abstrakta** [-ta] *(= Begriff)* abstract (concept); *(Ling: = Substantiv)* abstract noun

ab+stram|peln VR *sep (inf)* to kick the bedclothes *(Brit) or* covers off; *(fig)* to sweat (away) *(inf)*, to bust a gut *(inf)*

ab+strei|chen *sep irreg* VT **a** *(= wegstreichen)* to wipe off *or* away; *(= säubern)* to wipe; **den Hals/die Zunge ~** *(Med)* to take a throat/tongue swab **b** *(= abziehen) Betrag* to knock off, to deduct; *(fig)* to discount; **davon kann** *or* **muss man die Hälfte ~** *(fig)* you have to take it with a pinch *(Brit) or* grain *(US)* of salt **c** *(Hunt) Feld* to beat; *(Mil) Gebiet, Himmel* to sweep VI *aux sein (Hunt)* to fly off *or* away

ab+strei|fen VT *sep* **a** *(= abtreten) Schuhe, Füße* to wipe; *Schmutz* to wipe off **b** *(= abziehen) Kleidung, Schmuck* to take off, to remove, to slip off; *(= entfernen) Haut* to cast, to shed; *(fig) Gewohnheit, Fehler* to get rid of

ab+strei|ten VT *sep irreg (= streitig machen)* to dispute; *(= leugnen)* to deny; **das kann man ihm nicht ~** you can't deny it

Ab|strich M **a** *(= Kürzung)* cutback; **~e machen** to cut back (*an +dat* on), to make cuts (*an +dat* in); *(= weniger erwarten etc)* to lower one's sights **b** *(Med)* swab; *(= Gebärmutterabstrich)* smear; **einen ~ machen** to take a swab/smear **c** *(Mus: beim Schreiben)* downstroke; **zu dicke ~e machen** to make one's downstrokes too thick

ab+strö|men VI *sep aux sein* to flow away *or* off; *(Wasser auch)* to run away *or* off; *(Menschenmassen)* to stream out

abs|trus [ap'stru:s] *(geh)* ADJ abstruse ADV abstrusely; **das ~ anmutende Drehbuch** the abstruse (film) script

Abs|tru|si|tät [apstruzi'tɛ:t] F **-, -en** *(geh)* **a** *no pl* abstruseness **b** *(= Bemerkung)* abstruse remark

ab+stu|fen *sep* VT *Gelände* to terrace; *Haare* to layer; *Farben* to shade; *Gehälter, Steuern, Preise* to grade VR to be terraced; **der Weinberg stuft sich zum Fluss hin ab** the vineyard goes down in terraces to the river

Ab|stu|fung F **-, -en** *(von Gelände)* terracing; *(= Nuancierung)* shading; *(= Nuance)* shade; *(= Staffelung)* grading; *(= Stufe)* grade

ab+stump|fen ['apʃtʊmpfn] *sep* VI *aux sein (fig: Geschmack etc)* to become dulled; **wenn man ewig dasselbe machen muss, stumpft man nach und nach ab** always having to do the same thing dulls the mind; **er ist als Kritiker abgestumpft** his critical sensibilities have become blunted; **gegen etw ~** to become inured to sth VT **a** *Menschen, Sinne* to deaden; *Gerechtigkeitssinn, Gewissen, Urteilsvermögen* to dull → *auch* **abgestumpft b** *(lit) Ecken, Kanten* to blunt; *Messer, Schneide* to take the edge off, to blunt

Ab|stump|fung F **-,** *no pl (von Menschen, Sinnen)* deadening; *(von Gewissen, Gerechtigkeitssinn)* dulling

Ab|sturz M crash; *(von Börse, Unternehmen auch)* fall; *(sozial)* disaster, ruin; *(von Politiker etc)* downfall; *(= Depression)* breakdown; *(Comput)* crash; **ein Flugzeug zum ~ bringen** to bring a plane down

ab+stür|zen VI *sep aux sein* **a** *(Flugzeug)* to crash; *(Bergsteiger)* to fall **b** *(inf: sozial)* to go to ruin **c** *(inf: psychisch)* to come a cropper *(Brit inf)*, to fall flat on one's face **d** *(sl: = betrunken werden)* to go on a bender *(Brit inf)*, to go on a binge *(inf)* **e** *(Comput)* to crash **f** *(sl)* **mit jdm ~** *(sich sexuell betätigen)* to have a fumble with sb *(inf)*

Ab|sturz|stel|le F location of a/the crash; *(beim Bergsteigen)* location of a/the fall; **die Rettungsarbeiten an der ~** the rescue work at the scene of the crash

ab+stüt|zen *sep* VT to support *(auch fig)*, to prop up; *Haus, Mauer auch* to shore up VR to support oneself, to prop oneself up; *(bei Bewegung)* to support oneself

ab+su|chen VT *sep* **a** *Unfallstelle, Gelände, Gebiet, Umgebung, Ort, Internet, Daten* to search; *(Med, Sci) Körper, Flüssigkeit* to scan; **jdn/etw nach etw ~** to search sb/sth for sth; **wir haben den ganzen Garten abgesucht** we searched all over the garden **b** *(= suchend absammeln) Raupen etc* to pick off; *Strauch etc* to pick clean

Ab|sud ['apzu:t, ap'zu:t] M **-(e)s, -e** [-də] *(old)* decoction

ab|surd [ap'zʊrt] ADJ absurd, preposterous; **~es Drama** *or* **Theater** theatre *(Brit) or* theater *(US)* of the absurd; **das Absurde** the absurd

Ab|sur|di|tät [apzʊrdi'tɛ:t] F **-, -en** absurdity *(auch Philos)*, preposterousness

Abs|zess [aps'tsɛs] M **-es, -e** abscess

Abs|zis|se [aps'tsɪsə] F **-, -n** abscissa

Abt [apt] M **-(e)s, ⸚e** ['ɛptə] abbot

Abt. *abbr von* **Abteilung** dept

ab+ta|keln VT *sep Schiff* to unrig; *(= außer Dienst stellen)* to lay up → *auch* **abgetakelt**

Ab|ta|ke|lung F **-, -en, Ab|tak|lung** ['apta:klʊŋ] F **-, -en** *(von Schiff)* unrigging; *(= Außerdienststellung)* laying up

ab+tan|zen VI *sep (inf)* **a** *aux haben (= austoben)* to really hit the dance floor *(Brit sl)*, to really cut up the floor *(US inf)* **b** *aux sein (= weggehen)* to push off *(inf)*

ab+tas|ten VT *sep* to feel; *(Med auch)* to palpate; *(Elec)* to scan; *(bei Durchsuchung)* to frisk (*auf +acc* for); *(fig: = erproben) jdn* to sound out, to suss out *(Brit inf)*; *(Sport)* to get the measure of, to size up, to suss out *(Brit inf)*

Ab|tas|tung F **-, -en** *(Elec, TV)* scanning

Ab|tau|au|to|ma|tik F *(von Kühlschrank)* auto (-matic) defroster

ab+tau|chen VI *sep aux sein* **a** *(U-Boot)* to dive **b** *(inf)* to go underground

ab+tau|en *sep* VT to thaw out; *Kühlschrank* to defrost VI *aux sein* to thaw; **der Schnee ist vom Dach abgetaut** the snow has thawed from the roof

Ab|tausch M *(Chess, Sw: = Tausch)* exchange

ab+tau|schen VT *sep (Chess, Sw: = tauschen)* to exchange

Ab|tei [ap'tai] F **-, -en** abbey

Ab|tei|kir|che F abbey (church)

Ab|teil [ap'tail, 'ap-] NT compartment; **~ erster Klasse, Erste-Klasse-~** first-class compartment; **~ für Mutter und Kind, Mutter-(-und-)Kind-~** *compartment reserved for mothers with young children*; **~ für Raucher** smoker, smoking compartment; **~ für Nichtraucher** nonsmoker, no-smoking compartment

ab+tei|len VT *sep* **a** *(= einteilen)* to divide up; **fünf Stücke ~** to cut off five pieces **b** *(= abtrennen)* to divide off; *(mit Wand)* to divide *or* partition off

Ab|tei|lung ['aptailʊŋ] F *(= das Einteilen)* dividing up; *(= das Abschneiden)* cutting off; *(= das Abtrennen)* dividing off; *(mit Wand)* partitioning off

Ab|tei|lung [ap'tailʊŋ] F **a** *(in Firma, Kaufhaus, Hochschule)* department; *(in Krankenhaus, Jur)* section; *(Mil)* unit, section **b** *(old: = Abschnitt)* section

Ab|tei|lungs|lei|ter(in) M(F) head of department; *(in Kaufhaus)* department manager/manageress

ab+te|le|fo|nie|ren *ptp* **abtelefoniert** *sep* VI to telephone *or* ring *or* call to say one can't make it *or* come VT *Prepaidkarte, Telefonguthaben* to use up

ab+teu|fen ['aptɔyfn] VT *sep Schacht* to sink

ab+tip|pen VT *sep (inf)* to type out

Äb|tis|sin [ɛp'tɪsɪn] F **-, -nen** abbess

ab+tö|nen VT *sep Farbe* to tone down; **zwei Farben gegeneinander ~** to tone two colours *(Brit) or* colors *(US)* in with each other

Ab|tö|nung F *(von Farbe)* toning down; *(= Farbton)* tone, shade

ab+tö|ten VT *sep (lit, fig)* to destroy, to kill (off); *Nerv* to deaden; *sinnliche Begierde* to mortify; **in mir ist jedes Gefühl abgetötet** I am dead to all feeling

Ab|tö|tung F *(lit, fig)* destruction, killing (off); *(von Nerv)* deadening; *(von Begierden)* mortification

Ab|trag ['aptra:k] M **-(e)s** [-gəs], *no pl (old)* harm; **einer Sache** *(dat)* **~ tun** to harm sth

ab+tra|gen VT *sep irreg* **a** *auch vi (= abräumen) Geschirr, Speisen* to clear away **b** *(= einebnen) Boden, Gelände* to level **c** *(= entfernen) Gebäude, Mauer* to take down; *Erdschicht, Straßenbelag* to remove; *(Wellen) Strand, Sand* to erode, to wear away **d** *(= abbezahlen) Schulden* to pay off; *Schuld* to pay; **einen Schuldenberg ~** to clear all one's debts **e** *(= abnutzen) Kleider, Schuhe* to wear out → *auch* **abgetragen**

ab|träg|lich ['aptrɛ:klɪç], *(Sw)* **ab|trä|gig** ['aptrɛ:gɪç] ADJ detrimental, harmful; *Bemerkung, Kritik etc* adverse, unfavourable *(Brit)*, unfavorable *(US)*; **einer Sache** *(dat)* **~ sein** to be detrimental *or* harmful to sth

Ab|tra|gung F **-, -en a** *(Geol)* erosion **b** *(= Abbau)* dismantling, taking down **c** *(= Tilgung)* paying off

Ab|trans|port M transportation; *(aus Katastrophengebiet)* evacuation; **beim ~ der Gefangenen** when the prisoners were being taken away

ab+trans|por|tie|ren *ptp* **abtransportiert** VT *sep Waren* to transport; *Personen auch* to take off *or* away; *(aus Katastrophengebiet)* to evacuate

ab+trei|ben *sep irreg* VT **a** **vom Kurs ~** *(Flugzeug)* to send *or* drive off course; *Boot auch, Schwimmer* to carry off course **b** *(= zu Tal treiben) Vieh* to bring down **c** *Kind, Leibesfrucht* to abort; **sie hat das Kind abgetrieben** *or* **~ lassen** she had an abortion **d** *(Aus, S Ger: Cook)* to whisk VI **a** *aux sein* **(vom Kurs) ~** *(Flugzeug)* to be sent *or* driven off course; *(Boot auch, Schwimmer)* to be carried off course **b** *(= Abort vornehmen)* to carry out an abortion; *(generell)* to carry out *or* do abortions; *(= Abort vornehmen lassen)* to have an abortion

Ab|trei|bung ['aptraibʊŋ] F **-, -en** abortion; **eine ~ vornehmen lassen** to have an abortion; **eine ~ vornehmen** to carry out an abortion

Ab|trei|bungs-: **Ab|trei|bungs|be|für|wor|ter(in)** M(F) pro-abortionist; **Ab|trei|bungs|geg|ner(in)** M(F) anti-abortionist, pro-lifer *(inf)*; **Ab|trei|bungs|ge|setz** NT abortion law(s *pl*); **Ab|trei|bungs|kli|nik** F abortion clinic; **Ab|trei|bungs|pa|ra|graf** △, **Ab|trei|bungs|pa|ra|graph** M abortion laws *pl*; **Ab|trei|bungs|pil|le** F abortion pill; **Ab|trei|bungs|pra|xis** F *(= Klinik)* abortion clinic; **Ab|trei|bungs|tou|ris|mus** M *(inf) going to another country/state to have an abortion*; **Ab|trei|bungs|ver|bot** NT abortion ban, ban on abortions; **Ab|trei|bungs|ver|such** M attempt at an abortion; **einen ~ vornehmen** to try to give oneself an abortion, to attempt an abortion

ab|trenn|bar ADJ *(= lostrennbar)* detachable; *Knöpfe, Besatz etc auch* removable; *(= abteilbar)* separable; *Verfahren* severable *(form)*

ab+tren|nen VT *sep* **a** *(= lostrennen)* to detach; *Knöpfe, Besatz etc* to remove, to take off; *(= abschneiden)* to cut off; *Bein, Finger etc (durch Unfall)* to sever, to cut off; **„hier ~"** "detach here" **b** *(= abteilen)* to separate off; *(mit Trennwand etc)* to divide *or* partition off; **diese Zeit lässt sich nicht einfach von der Geschichte des Landes ~** this period cannot simply be set aside from the history of the country

Ab|tren|nung F *(= das Abteilen)* separation; *(mit Trennwand etc)* partitioning

ab|tret|bar ADJ *(Jur) Ansprüche* transferable, cedable *(form)*

ab+tre|ten *sep irreg* VT **a** *(= überlassen) (jdm or an jdn* to sb) to hand over; *Gebiet, Land auch* to cede *(form)*; *Rechte, Ansprüche* to transfer, to cede *(form)*; *Haus, Geldsumme* to transfer, to assign *(form)*
b *Teppich* to wear; *(völlig)* to wear out; *Schnee, Schmutz* to stamp off; **sich** *(dat)* **die Füße** *or* **Schuhe ~** to wipe one's feet
VI *aux sein (Theat)* to go off (stage), to make one's exit; *(Mil)* to dismiss; *(inf: = zurücktreten) (Politiker)* to step down *(inf)*, to resign; *(Monarch)* to abdicate, to step down *(inf)*; *(euph: = sterben)* to make one's last exit; **~!** *(Mil)* dismiss!; **aus dem Leben ~** *(euph)* to quit this life
VR *(Teppich etc)* to wear, to get worn; *(völlig)* to wear out

Ab|tre|ter ['aptre:tɐ] M **-s, -** *(= Fußabtreter)* doormat

Ab|tre|tung F **-, -en** *(an +acc* to) transfer; *(von Rechten, Ansprüchen auch, von Gebiet)* ceding *(form)*, cession *(form)*; *(von Haus, Geldsumme auch)* assignment *(form)*; **durch ~ aller Ansprüche an seinen Teilhaber** by transferring all rights to his partner

Ab|tre|tungs|ur|kun|de F transfer deed; *(für Grundstück)* (deed of) conveyance; *(bei Konkurs)* (deed of) assignment

Ab|trieb M **a** *(= Viehabtrieb)* **im Herbst beginnt der ~ des Viehs von den Bergweiden** in autumn *(esp Brit)* or fall *(US)* they start to bring the cattle down from the mountain pastures **b** *(Tech)* output **c** *(Aus)* mixture

Ab|trift ['aptrɪft] F **-, -en** *(Naut, Aviat)* drift

ab+trin|ken VT *sep irreg* to drink; **einen Schluck ~** to have *or* take a sip

Ab|tritt M **a** *(Theat)* exit; *(= Rücktritt) (von Minister)* resignation; *(von Monarch)* abdication **b** *(old: = Klosett)* privy *(old)*

Ab|tro|cken|tuch NT *pl* **-tücher** tea towel *(Brit)*, dishtowel *(US)*

ab+trock|nen *sep* VT to dry (off); *Geschirr* to dry, to wipe VI to dry up, to do the drying-up

ab+trop|fen VI *sep aux sein* to drip; *(Geschirr)* to drain; **etw ~ lassen** *(Wäsche etc)* to let sth drip; *Salat* to drain sth; *Geschirr* to let sth drain

ab+trot|ten VI *sep aux sein (inf)* to creep off *(inf)*, to slink off *(inf)*

ab+trot|zen VT *sep* **jdm etw ~** *(geh)* to wring sth out of sb

ab+tru|deln VI *sep aux sein* **a** *(Aviat)* to go down in a spin **b** *(inf: = weggehen)* to push off *(inf)*

ab|trün|nig ['aptrʏnɪç] ADJ renegade, apostate *(form, esp Eccl)*; *(= rebellisch)* rebel; **jdm/einer Gruppe** *etc* **~ werden** to desert sb/a group; *(= sich erheben gegen)* to rebel against sb/a group; **er ist dem Glauben ~ geworden** he has left *or* deserted the faith, he has apostatized *(form)*

Ab|trün|nig|keit F **-,** *no pl* apostasy *(form)*; *(= rebellische Gesinnung)* rebelliousness; **die ~ einer der Mitverschwörer** the desertion *or* apostasy *(form)* of one of the plotters

ab+tun VT *sep irreg* **a** *(fig: = beiseiteschieben)* to dismiss; **etw mit einem Achselzucken/einem Lachen ~** to shrug/laugh sth off; **etw kurz ~** to brush sth aside → *auch* **abgetan** **b** *(dial: = ablegen)* to take off

ab+tup|fen VT *sep Tränen, Blut* to dab away; *Gesicht, Mundwinkel* to dab; *Wunde* to swab, to dab

ab+ur|tei|len VT *sep* to pass sentence *or* judgement on; *(fig: = verdammen)* to condemn; **Verbrecher, die noch nicht abgeurteilt worden sind** criminals upon whom sentence has not yet been passed

Ab|ur|tei|lung F **-, -en** sentencing; *(fig)* condemnation; **bei der ~ des Täters** when sentence was/is being passed on the accused

Ab|ver|kauf M *(Aus: = Ausverkauf)* sale

ab+ver|lan|gen *ptp* **abverlangt** VT *sep* = **abfordern**

ab+wä|gen VT *sep irreg* to weigh up; *Worte* to weigh; **er wog beide Möglichkeiten gegeneinander ab** he weighed up the two possibilities → *auch* **abgewogen**

Ab|wä|gung F **-, -en** weighing up; *(von Worten)* weighing

Ab|wahl F voting out; **es kam zur ~ des gesamten Vorstands** the whole committee was voted out

ab|wähl|bar ADJ **der Präsident ist nicht ~** the president cannot be voted out (of office)

ab+wäh|len VT *sep* to vote out (of office); *(Sch) Fach* to give up

ab+wäl|zen VT *sep Schuld, Verantwortung* to shift *(auf +acc* onto); *Arbeit* to unload *(auf +acc* onto); *Kosten* to pass on *(auf +acc* to); **die Schuld von sich ~** to shift the blame onto somebody else

ab|wan|del|bar ADJ *Melodie* adaptable; *Thema auch* modifiable

ab+wan|deln VT *sep Melodie* to adapt; *Thema auch* to modify

Ab|wan|de|lung F **-, -en** = **Abwandlung**

ab+wan|dern VI *sep aux sein* to move (away) *(aus* from); *(Bevölkerung: zu einem anderen Ort auch)* to migrate *(aus* from); *(Kapital)* to be transferred *(aus* out of); *(inf: aus einer Veranstaltung etc)* to wander away *or* off *(inf)*; **viele Spieler/Abonnenten** *etc* **wandern ab** a lot of players/subscribers *etc* are transferring

Ab|wan|de|rung F moving away; *(von Bevölkerung)* migration; *(von Kapital)* transference

Ab|wan|de|rungs|ver|lust M *(Sociol)* population drain

Ab|wand|lung F adaptation, variation; *(von Thema etc auch)* modification

Ab|wär|me F waste heat

Ab|wart ['apvart] M **-(e)s, -e, Ab|war|tin** [-tɪn] F **-, -nen** *(Sw)* concierge, caretaker

ab+war|ten *sep* ✪ 53.6 VT to wait for; **das Gewitter ~** to wait till the storm is over, to wait the storm out; **er kann es nicht mehr ~** he can't wait any longer; **das bleibt abzuwarten** that remains to be seen VI to wait; **warten Sie ab!** just wait a bit!; **~ und Tee trinken** *(inf)* to wait and see; **im Moment können wir gar nichts tun, wir müssen ~** we can't do anything at the moment, we'll have to bide our time; **eine ~de Haltung einnehmen** to play a waiting game, to adopt a policy of wait-and-see

ab|wärts ['apvɛrts] ADV down; *(= nach unten auch)* downwards; **den Fluss/Berg ~** down the river/mountain; **„abwärts!"** *(im Fahrstuhl)* "going down!"; **vom Abteilungsleiter ~** from the head of department down(wards)

Ab|wärts-: **Ab|wärts|ent|wick|lung** F downwards *or* downhill trend; **Ab|wärts|fahrt** F journey down; **ab|wärts+ge|hen** *sep impers irreg aux sein*, **ab|wärts ge|hen** △ *impers irreg aux sein* VI *(fig)* **mit ihm/dem Land geht es abwärts** he/the country is going downhill; **ab|wärts|kom|pa|ti|bel** ADJ *(Comput)* downward *or* backward compatible; **Ab|wärts|kom|pa|ti|bi|li|tät** F *(Comput)* downward *or* backward compatibility; **Ab|wärts|pfeil** M *(Comput)* down arrow; **Ab|wärts|trend** M downwards *or* downhill trend

Ab|wasch ['apvaʃ] M **-s,** *no pl* washing-up *(Brit)*, dirty dishes *pl*; **den ~ machen** to do the washing-up *(Brit)*, to wash up *(Brit)*, to wash the dishes; **... dann kannst du das auch machen, das ist (dann) ein ~** *(inf)* ... then you could do that as well and kill two birds with one stone

Ab|wasch F **-, -en** *(Aus: = Spülbecken)* sink

ab|wasch|bar ADJ *Tapete* washable; *Kleidung* wipeable; *Tinte* non-permanent

Ab|wasch|be|cken NT sink

ab+wa|schen *sep irreg* VT *Gesicht* to wash; *Geschirr* to wash, to wash up *(Brit)*; *Farbe, Schmutz* to wash off; *Pferd, Auto* to wash down; *(fig liter) Schande, Schmach* to wipe out; **den Schmutz (vom Gesicht) ~** to wash the dirt off (one's face) VI to wash up *(Brit)*, to do the washing-up *(Brit)*, to wash the dishes

Ab|wasch|lap|pen M dishcloth, washing-up cloth *(Brit)*

Ab|wasch|was|ser NT *pl* **-wässer** washing-up water *(Brit)*, dishwater; *(fig inf)* dishwater *(inf)*

Ab|was|ser NT *pl* **-wässer** sewage *no pl*; **industrielle Abwässer** industrial effluents *pl or* waste *sing*

Ab|was|ser-: **Ab|was|ser|auf|be|rei|tung** F reprocessing of sewage; *(von Industrieabwässern)* reprocessing of effluents; **Ab|was|ser|auf|be|rei|tungs|an|la|ge** F sewage treatment plant; **Ab|was|ser|ka|nal** M sewer; **Ab|was|ser|rei|ni|gung** F purification of sewage; *(von Industrieabwässern)* purification of effluents

ab+wech|seln VIR *sep* to alternate; **sich** *or* **einander ~** to alternate; *(Menschen auch)* to take turns; **sich mit jdm ~** to take turns with sb; **(sich) miteinander ~** to alternate (with each other *or* one another), to take turns; **Regen und Schnee wechselten (sich) miteinander ab** it rained and snowed alternately; **ihre Launen wechseln oft blitzschnell miteinander ab** her moods often change *or* vary from one minute to the next

ab|wech|selnd ADV alternately; **wir haben ~ Klavier gespielt** we took turns playing the piano; **er war ~ fröhlich und traurig** he alternated between being happy and sad, he was by turns happy and sad ADJ alternate

Ab|wechs|lung ['apvɛksluŋ] F **-, -en** change; *(= Zerstreuung)* diversion; **eine angenehme/schöne ~** a pleasant/nice change; **zur ~** for a change; **für ~ sorgen** to provide entertainment; **dort ist reichlich für ~ gesorgt** there's quite a variety of things going on there; **hier haben wir wenig ~** there's not much variety in life here; **da gibt es mehr ~** there's more going on there

ab|wechs|lungs-: **ab|wechs|lungs|hal|ber** ADV for a change, to make a change; **ab|wechs|lungs|los** ADJ monotonous; **ab|wechs|lungs|reich** ADJ varied ADV **den Unterricht ~ gestalten** to teach the class in an interesting and varied fashion; **Informationen ~ präsentieren** to present information in an interesting and varied way

Ab|weg ['apve:k] M *(fig)* mistake, error; **jdn auf ~e führen** to mislead sb, to lead sb astray *(auch moralisch)*; **auf ~e geraten** *or* **kommen** to go astray; *(moralisch auch)* to stray from the straight and narrow

ab|we|gig ['apve:gɪç] ADJ absurd; *Verdacht* unfounded, groundless

Ab|we|gig|keit F **-,** *no pl* absurdity; *(von Verdacht)* groundlessness

Ab|wehr F, *no pl* **a** *(Biol, Psych, Med)* defence *(Brit)*, defense *(US)* (*+gen* against); *(= Schutz)* protection (*+gen* against); **Mechanismen der ~** defence *(Brit)* or defense *(US)* mechanisms; **der ~ von etw dienen** to provide *or* give protection against sth
b *(= Zurückweisung)* repulse; *(= Abweisung)* rejection; *(= Spionageabwehr)* counterintelligence (service); **die ~ des Feindes** the repulsing *or* repelling of the enemy; **bei der ~ sein** to be with *or* in counterintelligence; **auf ~ stoßen** to be repulsed, to meet with a repulse
c *(Sport)* defence *(Brit)*, defense *(US)*; *(= Abwehraktion)* piece of defence *(Brit)* or defense *(US)* (work); **er ist besser in der ~** he's better in *or* at defence *(Brit)* or defense *(US)*

Ab|wehr-: **ab|wehr|be|reit** ADJ *(Mil, fig)* ~ **sein** to be ready to take defensive action; **Ab|wehr|be|reit|schaft** F *(Mil)* readiness to take defensive action; **die ~ des Körpers** the body's defences *pl (Brit) or* defenses *pl (US)*; **Ab|wehr|dienst** M counterintelligence service

ab+weh|ren *sep* VT **a** *Gegner* to fend *or* ward off; *Angriff, Feind* to repulse, to repel *(form)*; *Flugzeug, Rakete* to repel; *Ball* to clear; *Schlag* to parry, to ward off; **hervorragend, wie der Torwart den Ball abwehrte** that was a really good save the goalkeeper made (there) **b** *(= fernhalten)* to keep away; *Krankheitserreger* to protect against; *Gefahr, üble Folgen, Krise* to avert; *Inflation* to fight against **c** *(= abweisen)* **eine ~de Geste** a dismissive wave of the hand
VI **a** *(Sport)* to clear; *(Torwart)* to save; **mit dem Kopf ~** to head clear; **zur Ecke ~** to clear the ball *(so that a corner is given away)* **b** *(= ablehnen)* to refuse; **nein, wehrte sie ab** no, she said in refusal

Ab|wehr-: **Ab|wehr|feh|ler** M *(Sport)* defensive error; **Ab|wehr|hal|tung** F *(Sport, Psych) (= Einstellung)* defensiveness; *(= Körperhaltung)* defensive posture; **sich in ~ befinden** to be on the defensive; **Ab|wehr|hand|lung** F defence *(Brit) or* defense *(US)* reaction; **Ab|wehr|kampf** M *(Mil, Sport)* defence *(Brit)*, defense *(US)*; **ein ~** a defensive action; **Ab|wehr|kräf|te** PL *(Physiol)* (the body's) defences *pl (Brit) or* defenses *pl (US)*; **Ab|wehr|me|cha|nis|mus** M *(Psych)* defence *(Brit) or* defense *(US)* mechanism; **Ab|wehr|ra|ke|te** F anti-aircraft missile; **Ab|wehr|re|ak|ti|on** F *(Psych)* defence *(Brit) or* defense *(US)* reaction; **ab|wehr|schwach** ADJ **a** *(Sport)* weak in defence *(Brit) or* defense *(US)*, with a poor defence *(Brit) or* defense *(US)*; **das ist eine ~e Mannschaft** that's a team with a poor defence *(Brit) or* defense *(US)* **b** *(Med)* immunosuppressed; **Ab|wehr|spe|zi|a|list(in)** M(F) *(in Geheimdienst)* counterespionage expert; *(Mil)* defence *(Brit) or* defense *(US)* expert; *(Sport)* defensive expert; **Ab|wehr|spiel** NT *(Sport)* defensive play; **Ab|wehr|spie|ler(in)** M(F) defender; **ab|wehr|stark** ADJ *(Sport)* strong in defence *(Brit) or* defense *(US)*; **das ist eine ~e Mannschaft** they're a good defensive team

ab+wei|chen VI *sep irreg aux sein (= sich entfernen)* to deviate; *(= sich unterscheiden)* to differ; *(zwei Theorien, Auffassungen etc)* to differ, to diverge; **vom Kurs ~** to deviate *or* depart from one's course; **vom Thema ~** to digress, to go off the point; **vom rechten Weg ~** *(fig)* to wander *or* err from the straight and narrow; **ich weiche erheblich von seiner Meinung ab** I hold quite a different view from him; **~des Verhalten** *(Psych, Sociol)* deviant behaviour *(Brit) or* behavior *(US)*

ab+wei|chen VT *sep Briefmarke etc* to soak off

Ab|weich|ler [ˈapvaiçlɐ] M **-s, -**, **Ab|weich|le|rin** [-ərɪn] F **-, -nen** deviant

ab|weich|le|risch [ˈapvaiçlərɪʃ] ADJ deviant

Ab|weich|ler|tum [ˈapvaiçlɐtuːm] NT **-s**, *no pl (Pol)* deviancy

Ab|wei|chung [ˈapvaiçʊŋ] F **-, -en** *(von Kurs etc)* deviation; *(= Unterschied)* difference; *(von zwei Theorien, Auffassungen etc)* divergence; *(von Magnetnadel)* declination; **~ von der Norm/Wahrheit** departure from the norm/truth; **~ von der Parteilinie** failure to toe the party line, deviation from the party line; **zulässige ~** *(Tech)* tolerance; *(zeitlich, zahlenmäßig)* allowance

ab+wei|den VT *sep (rare) Wiese* to graze

ab+wei|sen VT *sep irreg* to turn down, to reject; *Bitte auch* to refuse; *(= wegschicken)* to turn away; *(Jur) Klage* to dismiss; **er lässt sich nicht ~** he won't take no for an answer

ab|wei|send ADJ *Ton, Blick* cold, chilly; *Mensch* cold ADV negatively; **er steht diesem Vorhaben nicht ~ gegenüber** he is not entirely opposed to the idea

Ab|wei|sung F rejection; *(= das Wegschicken)* turning away; *(von Bitte)* refusal; *(von Klage)* dismissal

ab|wend|bar ADJ avoidable

ab+wen|den *sep reg or irreg* VT **a** *(= verhindern) Unheil, Folgen* to avert **b** *(= zur Seite wenden)* to turn away; *Blick* to avert; *Kopf* to turn; **er wandte das Gesicht ab** he looked away VR to turn away

ab+wer|ben VT *sep irreg* to woo away *(+dat* from)

Ab|wer|be|ver|such *(Ind)* head-hunting *no pl*

Ab|wer|bung F wooing away

ab+wer|fen *sep irreg* VT to throw off; *Reiter* to throw; *Bomben, Flugblätter etc* to drop; *Ballast* to jettison; *Geweih* to shed, to cast; *Blätter, Nadeln* to shed; *(Cards)* to discard, to throw away; *(Sport) Ball, Speer* to throw; *Latte* to knock off *or* down; *(Comm) Gewinn* to yield, to return, to show; *Zinsen* to bear, to yield; *(fig liter) Joch, Fesseln* to cast *or* throw off VI *(Ftbl)* to throw

ab+wer|ten *sep* VT **a** *Währung* to devalue **b** *(fig) Ideale, Sprache, Kultur* to debase, to cheapen; *jds Leistung* to devalue VI *(Fin)* to devalue; **diese Tugend ist heute vollkommen abgewertet** this virtue is no longer valued today; **er muss immer alles ~** he always has to run everything down

ab|wer|tend ADJ derogatory, pejorative; *Blick* dismissive ADV derogatorily, pejoratively

Ab|wer|tung F **a** *(von Währung)* devaluation; **eine ~ vornehmen** to devalue (the currency) **b** *(fig)* debasement, cheapening; **solche Ideale erfahren eine immer stärkere ~** such ideals are valued less and less *or* are constantly losing their value

ab|we|send [ˈapveːznt] ADJ absent; *(von zu Hause auch)* away *pred*; *(iro: = zerstreut auch)* far away; *Blick* absent-minded; **die Abwesenden** the absentees

Ab|we|sen|heit [ˈapveːznhait] F **-, -en** absence; *(fig: = Geistesabwesenheit)* abstraction; **in ~** *(Jur)* in absence, in absentia; **durch ~ glänzen** *(iro)* to be conspicuous by one's absence

Ab|wet|ter PL *(Min)* used air

ab+wet|zen *sep* VT *(= abschaben)* to wear smooth VI *aux sein (inf)* to hare off *(Brit inf)*, to bolt *(Brit inf)*

ab+wi|ckeln *sep* VT **a** *(= abspulen)* to unwind; *Verband* to take off, to remove **b** *(fig: = erledigen)* to deal with; *Geschäft* to complete, to conclude; *Kontrolle* to carry out; *Veranstaltung* to run; *(Comm: = liquidieren)* to wind up; **die Versammlung wurde in aller Ruhe abgewickelt** the meeting went off peacefully VR to unwind; *(= vonstattengehen)* to go *or* pass off

Ab|wick|lung [ˈapvɪklʊŋ] F **-, -en** **a** *(= Erledigung)* completion, conclusion; *(von Kontrolle)* carrying out; *(von Veranstaltung)* running; *(Comm: = Liquidation)* winding up; **die Polizei sorgte für eine reibungslose ~ der Veranstaltung** the police made sure that the event went *or* passed off smoothly **b** *(= das Abspulen)* unwinding

ab+wie|geln [ˈapviːgln] *sep* VT to appease; *wütende Menge etc auch* to calm down VI to calm things down; **das Abwiegeln** appeasement

ab+wie|gen VT *sep irreg* to weigh out

Ab|wieg|ler [ˈapviːglɐ] M **-s, -**, **Ab|wieg|le|rin** [-ərɪn] F **-, -nen** appeaser, conciliator

ab+wim|meln VT *sep (inf) jdn* to get rid of *(inf)*; *Auftrag* to get out of *(inf)*; **die Sekretärin hat mich abgewimmelt** his secretary turned me away; **lass dich nicht ~** don't let them get rid of you *(inf)*

Ab|wind M *(Aviat)* downwash; *(Met)* down current

ab+win|keln [ˈapvɪŋkln] VT *sep Arm* to bend; **mit abgewinkelten Armen** *(in den Hüften)* with arms akimbo

ab+win|ken *sep* VI *(inf) (abwehrend)* to wave it/him *etc* aside; *(resignierend)* to groan; *(fig: = ablehnen)* to say no; **als er merkte, wovon ich reden wollte, winkte er gleich ab** when he realized what I wanted to talk about he immediately put me off *or* stopped me; **der Chef winkt bei so einem Vorschlag bestimmt gleich ab** the boss is bound to say no to *or* to turn down a suggestion like that; **wenn Bonn abwinkt ...** if the (German) government turns us/them *etc* down *or* says no ... → **müde**
VTI *(bei Zug)* to give the "go" signal; **ein Rennen ~** to wave the chequered *(Brit) or* checkered *(US)* flag; *(nach Unfall etc)* to stop the race; **einen Rennfahrer ~** to wave a driver down; **trinken/tanzen bis zum Abwinken** *(inf)* to drink/dance till one drops *(inf)*; **es gab Champagner bis zum Abwinken** *(inf)* there was loads and loads of champagne *(inf)*

ab+wirt|schaf|ten VI *sep (inf)* to go downhill; **abgewirtschaftet haben** to have reached rock bottom → *auch* **abgewirtschaftet**

ab+wi|schen VT *sep Staub, Schmutz etc* to wipe off *or* away; *Hände, Nase etc* to wipe; *Augen, Tränen* to dry; **er wischte sich** *(dat)* **den Schweiß von der Stirn ab** he mopped (the sweat from) his brow

ab+woh|nen VT *sep* **a** *Möbel* to wear out; *Haus, Zimmer* to make shabby **b** *Baukostenzuschuss* to pay off with the rent; **die Miete voll ~** to stay for the time for which rent has been paid

ab+wra|cken [ˈapvrakn] VT *sep Schiff, Auto, technische Anlage* to break (up) → *auch* **abgewrackt**

Ab|wurf M throwing off; *(von Reiter)* throw; *(von Bomben etc)* dropping; *(von Ballast)* jettisoning; *(von Geweih)* casting; (*Comm: von Zinsen, Gewinn*) yield; *(Sport) (der Latte)* knocking down *or* off; *(des Speers etc)* throwing; **ein ~ vom Tor** a goal throw, a throw-out

ab+wür|gen VT *sep (inf)* to scotch; *Motor* to stall; **etw von vornherein ~** to nip sth in the bud

ab+zah|len VT *sep* to pay off

ab+zäh|len *sep* VT to count; **er zählte zwanzig Hunderteuroscheine ab** he counted out twenty hundred-euro notes; **bitte das Fahrgeld abgezählt bereithalten** please tender exact *or* correct fare *(form)* → **Finger** VI to number off

Ab|zähl|reim M counting-out rhyme *(such as "eeny meeny miney mo", for choosing a person)*

Ab|zah|lung F **a** *(= Rückzahlung)* repayment, paying off **b** *(= Ratenzahlung)* hire purchase *(Brit)*, HP *(Brit)*, installment plan *(US)*; *(= Rate)* (re)payment, instalment *(Brit)*, installment *(US)*; **etw auf ~ kaufen** to buy sth on HP *(Brit) or* on hire purchase *(Brit) or* on the installment plan *(US)*

Ab|zah|lungs|ge|schäft NT hire purchase *(Brit)*, HP *(Brit)*, installment plan *(US)*

Ab|zähl|vers M = **Abzählreim**

ab+zap|fen VT *sep* to draw off; **jdm Blut ~** *(inf)* to take blood from sb; **jdm Geld ~** to get some money out of sb

ab+zäu|men VT *sep Pferd etc* to unbridle

ab+zäu|nen [ˈaptsɔynən] VT *sep* to fence off

Ab|zäu|nung F **-, -en** fencing

ab+zeh|ren *sep (liter)* VT to emaciate → *auch* **abgezehrt** VR to waste *or* pine away

Ab|zeh|rung F emaciation

Ab|zei|chen NT badge; *(Mil)* insignia *pl*; *(= Orden, Auszeichnung)* decoration

ab+zeich|nen *sep* VT **a** *(= abmalen)* to draw **b** *(= signieren)* to initial VR *(= sichtbar sein)* to stand out; *(Unterwäsche)* to show; *(fig) (= deutlich werden)* to emerge, to become apparent; *(= drohend bevorstehen)* to loom (on the horizon); **sich gegen etw ~** *(= kontrastieren)* to stand out against sth

abzgl. *abbr von* **abzüglich**

Ab|zieh|bild NT transfer

ab+zie|hen *sep irreg* VT **a** *Tier* to skin; *Fell, Haut* to remove, to take off; *grüne Bohnen* to string **b** *Bett* to strip; *Bettzeug* to strip off **c** *(Sw: = ausziehen) Mantel, Schürze, Ring etc* to

take off; *Hut* to raise
d *Schlüssel* to take out, to remove; *Abzugshahn* to press, to squeeze; *Pistole* to fire
e *(= zurückziehen) Truppen, Kapital* to withdraw
f *(= subtrahieren) Zahlen* to take away, to subtract; *Steuern* to deduct; **EUR 20 vom Preis ~** to take EUR 20 off the price; **man hatte mir zu viel abgezogen** they'd taken off *or* deducted too much, I'd had too much deducted
g *(= abfüllen) Wein* to bottle; **Wein auf Flaschen ~** to bottle wine
h *(Typ: = vervielfältigen)* to run off; *(Phot) Bilder* to make prints of, to print; **etw zwanzigmal ~** to run off twenty copies of sth
i *(= schleifen)* to sharpen; *Rasiermesser auch* to strop; *Parkett* to sand (down)
j *(Cook) Suppe, Sauce* to thicken; **die Suppe mit einem Ei ~** to beat an egg into the soup **b** → **Nummer, Schau b**
VI **a** *aux sein (= sich verflüchtigen) (Rauch, Dampf)* to escape, to go away; *(Sturmtief etc)* to move away
b *aux sein (Soldaten)* to pull out (*aus* of), to withdraw (*aus* from); (*inf*: = *weggehen*) to go off *or* away; **zieh ab!** *(inf)* clear off! *(Brit inf)*, beat it! *(inf)*
c *(= abdrücken)* to pull *or* squeeze the trigger, to fire
d (*sl*: = *schnell fahren*) **das Auto zieht ganz schön ab** that car can really move *(inf)*
VR (*Sw*: = *sich ausziehen*) to undress, to take off one's clothes

Ab|zie|her ['aptsiːɐ] **M -s, -**, **Ab|zie|he|rin** [-ərɪn] **F -, -nen** *(Typ)* proof puller

Ab|zieh|pres|se **F** proof press

ab+zie|len **VI** *sep* **auf etw** *(acc)* **~** *(Mensch)* to aim at sth; *(in Rede)* to get at sth; *(Bemerkung, Maßnahme etc)* to be aimed *or* directed at sth; **ich merkte sofort, worauf sie mit dieser Anspielung abzielte** I saw immediately what she was driving *or* getting at with that allusion

ab+zin|sen **VT** *sep (Fin)* to discount; **abgezinste Sparbriefe** savings certificates sold at discounted interest

Ab|zin|sung **F -, -en** *(Fin)* discounting

ab+zir|keln **VT** *sep* (*rare*: = *mit Zirkel abmessen*) to measure (off) with compasses; (*fig*: = *vorausplanen*) to calculate very carefully; *Worte, Bewegungen* to measure

ab+zi|schen **VI** *sep* (*inf*: = *abhauen*) to beat it *(inf)*; **zisch ab!** beat it! *(inf)*

ab+zo|cken **VT** *sep (inf)* **jdn ~** to rip sb off *(inf)*; **hier wird man nur abgezockt** they just rip you off here *(inf)*; **die haben mich wirklich abgezockt** they really screwed me *(inf)*; **sie wollen nur ~** they only want to cash in (*mit* on)

Ab|zo|cker(in) **M**, **Ab|zo|cke|rin** **F** *(pej)* con man/woman *(inf)*, swindler

Ab|zo|cke|rei **F** *(inf)* rip-off *(inf)*; **die Parkgebühren sind die reinste ~** the parking fees are a complete *or* total rip-off *(inf)*

ab+zot|teln **VI** *sep aux sein (inf)* to toddle off *(inf)*

Ab|zug ['aptsuːk] **M** **a** *no pl (= Weggang)* departure; (*Met*: *von Tief*) moving away; (*= Wegnahme*: *von Truppen, Kapital etc*) withdrawal; **jdm freien ~ gewähren** to give *or* grant sb a safe conduct
b *(usu pl: vom Lohn etc)* deduction; *(= Rabatt)* discount; **ohne ~** *(Comm)* net terms only; **er verdient ohne Abzüge ...** before deductions *or* stoppages he earns ...; **etw in ~ bringen** *(form)* to deduct sth
c *(Typ)* copy; *(= Korrekturfahne)* proof; *(Phot)* print
d *(= Öffnung für Rauch, Gas)* flue; **es muss für hinreichenden ~ gesorgt werden** there must be sufficient means for the gas/smoke to escape *or* to be drawn off
e *(am Gewehr)* trigger

ab|züg|lich ['aptsyːklɪç] **PREP** *+gen (Comm)* minus, less

Ab|zugs-: **ab|zugs|fä|hig** **ADJ** *(Fin)* (tax-)deductible; **ab|zugs|frei** **ADJ** *(Fin)* tax-free; **Ab|zugs|hau|be** **F** extractor hood; **Ab|zugs|rohr** **NT** flue (pipe)

ab+zup|fen **VT** *sep* to pull *or* pluck off (*von etw* sth); (*S Ger*: = *pflücken*) to pick

ab+zwa|cken ['aptsvakn] **VT** *sep (dial)* **a** *(= abkneifen)* to pinch off **b** = **abknapsen**

ab+zwe|cken ['aptsvɛkn] **VI** *sep* **auf etw** *(acc)* **~** to be aimed at sth

Ab|zweig **M** *(form)* junction; **der ~ nach Saarbrücken** the turn-off to *or* for Saarbrücken

Ab|zweig|do|se **F** junction box

ab+zwei|gen ['aptsvaign] *sep* **VI** *aux sein* to branch off **VT** *(inf)* to set *or* put on one side

Ab|zwei|gung **F -, -en** junction, turn-off; *(= Nebenstrecke)* turn-off; *(= Gabelung)* fork; (*Rail*: = *Nebenlinie*) branch line; *(Elec)* junction

ab+zwi|cken **VT** *sep* to pinch *or* nip off

ab+zwin|gen **VT** *sep irreg* **jdm Respekt** *etc* **~** to gain sb's respect *etc*; **er zwang sich** *(dat)* **ein Lächeln ab** he forced a smile

ab+zwit|schern **VI** *sep aux sein (inf)* to go off, to take oneself off

a cap|pel|la [a ka'pɛla] **ADV** *(Mus)* a cappella

Ac|ces|soires [aksɛ'soaːɐ(s)] **PL** accessories *pl*

Ace|tat [atse'taːt] **NT -s, -e** acetate

Ace|ton [atse'toːn] **NT -s, -e** acetone

Ace|ty|len [atsety'leːn] **NT -s**, *no pl* acetylene

Ace|ty|len(sau|er|stoff)|bren|ner **M** oxy-acetylene burner

ach [ax] **INTERJ** oh; *(poet auch)* O; *(bedauernd auch)* alas *(old, liter)*; **~ nein!** oh no!; *(überrascht)* no!, really!; *(ablehnend)* no, no!; **~ nein, ausgerechnet der!** well, well, him of all people; **~ so!** I see!, aha!; *(= ja richtig)* of course!; **~ was** *or* **wo, das ist doch nicht so schlimm!** come on now, it's not that bad; **~ was** *or* **wo, das ist nicht nötig!** no, no that's not necessary; **~ wirklich?** oh really?, do you/does he *etc* really?; **~ je!** oh dear!, oh dear(ie) me! **ADV** *(geh)* **~ so schnell/schön** *etc* oh so quickly/lovely *etc*

Ach [ax] **NT** **mit ~ und Krach** *(inf)* by the skin of one's teeth *(inf)*; **eine Prüfung mit ~ und Krach bestehen** to scrape through an exam (by the skin of one's teeth); **ich habe die Behandlung überstanden, aber nur mit ~ und Weh** I had the treatment but I screamed blue murder *(Brit inf) or* bloody murder *(inf)*

Achä|er [a'xɛːɐ] **M -s, -**, **Achä|e|rin** [-ərɪn] **F -, -nen** *(Hist)* Achaean

Achat [a'xaːt] **M -(e)s, -e** agate

acha|ten [a'xaːtn] **ADJ** *attr* agate

Achill [a'xɪl] **M -s**, **Achil|les** [a'xɪlɛs] **M -'** Achilles

Achil|les|fer|se **F** Achilles heel

Ach|laut **M** voiceless velar fricative *(the sound "ch" in the Scottish "loch")*

Achs-: **Achs|ab|stand** **M** wheelbase; **Achs|an|trieb** **M** *(Aut)* final drive; **Achs|auf|hän|gung** **F** *(Aut)* axle suspension; **Achs|bruch** **M** broken axle; **Achs|druck** **M** *pl* **-drücke** axle weight

Ach|se ['aksə] **F -, -n** **a** axis; **die ~ (Rom-Berlin)** *(Hist)* the (Rome-Berlin) Axis **b** *(Tech)* axle; *(= Propellerachse)* shaft; **auf (der) ~ sein** *(inf)* to be out (and about); *(Kraftfahrer, Vertreter etc)* to be on the road

Ach|sel ['aksl] **F -, -n** **a** shoulder; **die ~n** *or* **mit den ~n zucken** to shrug (one's shoulders) **b** *(= Achselhöhle)* armpit

Ach|sel-: **Ach|sel|griff** **M** underarm grip; **Ach|sel|haa|re** **PL** **die ~** underarm hair, the hair under one's arms; **Ach|sel|höh|le** **F** armpit; **Ach|sel|klap|pe** **F**, **Ach|sel|stück** **NT** *(Mil)* epaulette, epaulet *(US)*; **Ach|sel|zu|cken** **NT -s**, *no pl* shrug; **mit einem ~** with a shrug (of one's shoulders); **ach|sel|zu|ckend** **ADJ** shrugging **ADV** with a shrug of one's shoulders; **er stand ~ da** he stood there shrugging his shoulders

Ach|sen-: **Ach|sen|bruch** **M** broken axle; **Ach|sen|kreuz** **NT** *(Math)* coordinate system; **Ach|sen|mäch|te** **PL** *(Hist)* Axis powers *pl*

Achs-: **Achs|la|ger** **NT** axle bearing; **Achs|last** **F** axle weight; **Achs|schen|kel** **M** stub axle, steering knuckle *(US)*; **Achs|stand** **M** wheelbase; **Achs|wel|le** **F** axle shaft

acht [axt] **NUM** eight; **für** *or* **auf ~ Tage** for a week; **in ~ Tagen** in a week, in a week's time; **heute/morgen in ~ Tagen** a week today/tomorrow, today/tomorrow week; **heute vor ~ Tagen war ich ...** a week ago today I was ...; **vor ~ Tagen werden sie wohl nicht fertig sein** they won't be ready for a week at least → *auch* **vier**

Acht [axt] **F -, -en** eight; *(bei Fahrrad)* buckled wheel; *(beim Eislaufen etc)* figure (of) eight → *auch* **Vier**

Acht **F** **sich in ~ nehmen** to be careful, to take care, to watch *or* look out; **etw außer ~ lassen** to leave sth out of consideration, to disregard sth; **etw außer aller ~ lassen** *(geh)* to pay no attention *or* heed whatsoever to sth, not to heed sth; **~ geben** = **achtgeben**; **~ haben** = **achthaben**

Acht **F -**, *no pl (Hist)* outlawry, proscription; **jdn in ~ und Bann tun** to outlaw *or* proscribe sb; *(Eccl)* to place sb under the ban; *(fig)* to ostracize sb

acht|bar **ADJ** *(geh) Gesinnung, Person* worthy; *Platzierung* creditable, respectable

Acht|bar|keit ['axtbaːɐkait] **F -**, *no pl (von Gesinnung, Person)* worthiness

Acht|eck **NT** octagon

acht|eckig **ADJ** octagonal, eight-sided

ach|tel ['axtl] **ADJ** eighth → *auch* **viertel**

Ach|tel ['axtl] **NT -s, -** eighth → *auch* **Viertel** **a**

Ach|tel-: **Ach|tel|fi|na|le** **NT** *round before the quarterfinal*, 2nd/3rd *etc* round; **ein Platz im ~** a place in the last sixteen; **Ach|tel|no|te** **F** quaver, eighth note *(US)*; **Ach|tel|pau|se** **F** quaver rest *(Brit)*, eighth note rest *(US)*

ach|ten ['axtn] ✪ 29.3, 42.1 **VT** **a** *(= schätzen)* to respect, to think highly of, to hold in high regard; **geachtete Leute** respected people **b** *(= respektieren) Gesetze, Bräuche, jds Gesinnung* to respect **c** (*geh*: = *betrachten*) to regard; **etw (für) gering ~** to have scant regard for sth **VI** **auf etw** *(acc)* **~** to pay attention to sth; **auf die Kinder ~** to keep an eye on the children; **darauf ~, dass ...** to be careful *or* to see *or* to take care that ...

äch|ten ['ɛçtn] **VT** *(Hist)* to outlaw, to proscribe; *(fig)* to ostracize

ach|tens ['axtns] **ADV** eighthly, in the eighth place

ach|tens|wert ['axtnsveːɐt] **ADJ** *Person* worthy; *Motiv, Bemühungen, Handlung auch* commendable

Ach|te(r) ['axtə] **MF** *decl as adj* eighth → *auch* **Vierte(r)**

Ach|ter ['axtɐ] **M -s, -** *(Rudern)* eight; *(Eislauf etc)* figure (of) eight → *auch* **Vierer**

ach|te(r, s) ['axtə] **ADJ** eighth → *auch* **vierte(r, s)**

Ach|ter- ['axtɐ-]: **ach|ter|aus** [-laus] **ADV** *(Naut)* astern; **Ach|ter|bahn** **F** big dipper *(Brit)*, roller coaster, switchback; **Ach|ter|deck** **NT** *(Naut)* afterdeck; **ach|ter|las|tig** [-lastɪç] **ADJ** *(Naut) Schiff* stern-heavy

ach|tern ['axtɐn] **ADV** *(Naut)* aft, astern; **nach ~ gehen** to go aft; **nach ~ abdrehen** to turn astern; **von ~** from astern

Acht-: **acht|fach** [-fax] **ADJ** eightfold; **in ~er Ausfertigung** with seven copies → *auch* **vierfach** **ADV** eightfold, eight times; **Acht|fü|ßer** [-fyːsɐ] **M -s, -** *(Zool)* octopod

acht+ge|ben **VI** *sep irreg* to take care, to be careful (*auf +acc* of); *(= aufmerksam sein)* to pay attention (*auf +acc* to); **auf jdn/etw ~** *(= beaufsichtigen)* to keep an eye on sb/sth, to look after sb/sth; **wenn man im Straßenverkehr nur einen Augenblick nicht achtgibt, ...** if your attention wanders for just a second in traffic ...; **„O Mensch, gib acht!"** "O man, take heed"

acht+ha|ben **VI** *sep irreg (geh)* to take care, to be careful (*auf +acc* of); *(= aufmerksam sein)* to pay attention (*auf +acc* to)

Acht-: **acht|hun|dert** ['axt'hʊndɐt] NUM eight hundred; **Acht|kampf** M *a gymnastic competition with eight events*; **acht|kan|tig** ADJ (lit) eight-sided ADV ~ **rausfliegen** (inf) to be flung out on one's ear (inf)

acht|los ADJ careless, thoughtless ADV *durchblättern* casually; *wegwerfen* thoughtlessly; *sich verhalten* carelessly; **viele gehen ~ daran vorbei** many people just pass by without noticing it

Acht|lo|sig|keit F -, no pl carelessness, thoughtlessness

acht|mal ['axtma:l] ADV eight times

acht|sam ['axtza:m] (geh) ADJ attentive; (= *sorgfältig*) careful ADV carefully; **mit etw ~ umgehen** to be careful with sth; **sich ~ benehmen** to be careful

Acht|sam|keit F -, no pl (geh) attentiveness; (= *Sorgfalt*) care

Acht-: **Acht|stun|den|tag** M eight-hour day; **acht|tä|gig** ADJ lasting a week, week-long; **mit ~er Verspätung** a week late; **der ~e Streik ist ...** the week-old or week-long strike is ...; **acht|täg|lich** ADJ weekly; **acht|tau|send** ['axt'tauznt] NUM eight thousand; **ein Achttausender** *a mountain eight thousand metres in height* → auch **viertausend**; **Acht|und|sech|zi|ger(in)** [axtlʊnt'zɛçtsɪgɐ, -ərɪn] M(F), **68er (-in)** M(F) member of the '68 generation; **die ~** the '68 generation

Ach|tung ['axtʊŋ] F -, no pl **a** ~! watch or look out!; (Mil: *Befehl*) attention!; **~, ~!** (your) attention please!; **„Achtung Hochspannung!"** "danger, high voltage"; **„Achtung Lebensgefahr!"** "danger"; **„Achtung Stufe!"** "mind the step"; **~, fertig, los!** ready, steady or get set, go! **b** (= *Wertschätzung*) respect (vor +dat for); **die ~ vor sich selbst** one's self-respect or self-esteem; **bei aller ~ vor jdm/etw** with all due respect to sb/sth; **in hoher ~ bei jdm stehen** to be held in high esteem by sb, to be highly esteemed by sb; **jdm ~ einflößen** to command or gain sb's respect; **~ gebietend** (geh) awe-inspiring; **sich** (dat) **~ verschaffen** to make oneself respected, to gain respect for oneself; **jdm die nötige ~ entgegenbringen** to give sb the respect due to him/her etc; **alle ~!** good for you/him etc!

Äch|tung ['ɛçtʊŋ] F -, -en (Hist) proscription, outlawing; (fig: *gesellschaftlich*) ostracism

ach|tung|ge|bie|tend ADJ → **Achtung b**

Ach|tungs-: **Ach|tungs|ap|plaus** M polite applause; **Ach|tungs|er|folg** M succès d'estime; **ach|tungs|voll** ADJ (rare) respectful

acht|zehn ['axtse:n] NUM eighteen → auch **vierzehn**

acht|zig ['axtsɪç] NUM eighty; **auf ~ sein** (inf) to be livid, to be hopping mad (inf); **da war er gleich auf ~** (inf) then he got livid → auch **vierzig**

Acht|zi|ger ['axtsɪgɐ] M -s, -, **Acht|zi|ge|rin** [-ərɪn] F -, -nen eighty-year-old, octogenarian → auch **Vierziger**

äch|zen ['ɛçtsn] VI to groan (vor +dat with); (*Brücke, Baum etc auch*) to creak; **~ und stöhnen** to moan and groan

Äch|zer ['ɛçtsɐ] M -s, - groan

Acker ['akɐ] M -s, = ['ɛkɐ] **a** (= *Feld*) field; **den ~ bestellen** to till the soil; **die Äcker bestellen** to plough (Brit) or plow (US) the fields; **einen ~ bebauen** or **bewirtschaften** to work the land; **sich vom ~ machen** (sl: = *verschwinden*) to split (sl) **b** (old: *Feldmaß*) ≈ acre

Acker-: **Acker|bau** M, no pl agriculture, arable farming; **~ betreiben** to farm the land; **~ treibend** farming; **~ und Viehzucht** farming; **Acker|bau|er** M pl **-bauern**, **Acker|bäu|e|rin** F farmer; **acker|bau|trei|bend** ADJ attr → **Ackerbau**; **Acker|bür|ger** M (Hist) *townsman who farms a smallholding*; **Acker|flä|che** F area of arable land; **Acker|fur|che** F furrow; **Acker|gaul** M (pej) farm horse, old nag (pej) → **Rennpferd**; **Acker|ge|rät** NT farm or agricultural implement; **Acker|kru|me** F topsoil; **Acker|land** NT arable land; **Acker|mann** M pl **-leute** or **-männer** (old, liter) husbandman (old, liter)

ackern ['akɐn] VI **a** (inf) to slog away (inf) **b** (old) to till the soil VT (old: = *pflügen*) to till

Acker-: **Acker|sa|lat** M (S Ger) lamb's lettuce (Brit), corn salad; **Acker|schol|le** F (liter) soil

Ackers|mann M pl **-leute** or **-männer** (old, liter) husbandman (old, liter)

Acker-: **Acker|wal|ze** F (land) roller; **Acker|win|de** F (Bot) field bindweed

a con|to [a 'kɔnto] ADV (Comm) on account

Ac|ryl [a'kry:l] NT -s, no pl acrylic

Ac|ryl|amid NT (Chem) acrylamide

Ac|ryl- in cpds acrylic; **Ac|ryl|far|be** F acrylic paint; **Ac|ryl|glas** NT acrylic glass; **Ac|ryl|plat|te** F acrylic tile

Ac|tion ['ɛkʃən] F -, no pl (sl) action

Ac|tion|film ['ɛkʃən-] M action film

Ac|tive|wear F -, no pl (= *Sportbekleidung*) active wear, activewear

a. D. [a:'de:] abbr von **außer Dienst** ret(d)

A. D. [a:'de:] abbr von **Anno Domini** AD

Ada|bei ['a:dabai] M -s, -s (Aus inf) limelighter (inf)

ad ab|sur|dum [at ap'zʊrdʊm] ADV **~ führen** to make a nonsense of; *Argument etc* to reduce to absurdity or absurdum

ADAC [a:de:la:'tse:] -, no pl abbr von **Allgemeiner Deutscher Automobil-Club** ≈ AA (Brit), ≈ RAC (Brit), ≈ AAA (US)

ad ac|ta [at 'akta] ADV **etw ~ legen** (fig) to consider sth finished; *Frage, Problem* to consider sth closed

Adam ['a:dam] M -s Adam; **seit ~s Zeiten** (inf) since the year dot (inf); **das stammt noch von ~ und Eva** (inf) it's out of the ark (inf); **bei ~ und Eva anfangen** (inf) to start right from scratch (inf) or from square one (inf) → **Riese**

Adams|ap|fel M (inf) Adam's apple

Adams|kos|tüm NT (dated hum) birthday suit; **im ~** in one's birthday suit, as nature made one

Adap|ta|ti|on [adapta'tsio:n] F -, -en adaptation

A|dap|ter [a'daptɐ] M -s, - adapter, adaptor

Adap|ter|kar|te F (Comput) adapter card

adap|tie|ren [adap'ti:rən] ptp **adaptiert** VT **a** (= *anpassen*) to adapt **b** (Aus: = *herrichten*) to fix up

Adap|tie|rung F -, -en, **Adap|ti|on** [adap'tsio:n] F -, -en adaptation

adap|tiv [adap'ti:f] ADJ adaptive

adä|quat [adɛ'kva:t, atlɛ'kva:t] ADJ *Bemühung, Belohnung, Übersetzung* adequate; *Stellung, Verhalten* suitable; *Kritik* valid; **einer Sache** (dat) **~ sein** to be adequate to sth ADV adequately

Adä|quat|heit F -, no pl (geh) adequacy; (von *Stellung, Verhalten*) suitability; (von *Kritik*) validity

ad|die|ren [a'di:rən] ptp **addiert** VT to add (up) VI to add

Ad|dier|ma|schi|ne F adding machine

Ad|dis A|be|ba ['adɪs 'a(:)beba, - a'be:ba] NT - -s Addis Ababa

Ad|di|ti|on [adi'tsio:n] F -, -en addition; (fig) agglomeration

Ad|di|ti|ons|ma|schi|ne F adding machine

Ad|di|tiv [adi'ti:f] NT -s, -e [-və] additive

ade [a'de:] INTERJ (old, S Ger) farewell (old, liter), adieu (old, liter); **jdm ~ sagen** to bid sb farewell; **einer Sache** (dat) **~ sagen** to say farewell to sth

Ade|bar ['a:dəbar] M -s, -e (N Ger) stork

Adel ['a:dl] M -s, no pl **a** (= *Adelsgeschlecht, Adelsstand*) nobility; (esp Brit) peerage; (esp *hoher Adel*) aristocracy; **von ~ sein** to be a member of the nobility, to be of noble birth; **eine Familie von ~** an aristocratic family; **er stammt aus altem ~** he comes from an old aristocratic family; **der niedere ~** the lesser nobility, the gentry; **der hohe ~** the higher nobility, the aristocracy; **das ist verarmter ~** they are impoverished nobility; **~ verpflichtet** noblesse oblige **b** (= *Adelstitel*) title; (esp Brit) peerage; **erblicher ~** hereditary title/peerage **c** (liter: = *edle Gesinnung*) nobility; **~ der Seele/des Herzens/des Geistes** nobility of the soul/of the heart/of mind

ade|lig ['a:dəlɪç] ADJ = **adlig**

Ade|li|ge ['a:dəlɪgə] F decl as adj = **Adlige**

Ade|li|ge(r) ['a:dəlɪgə] M = **Adlige(r)**

adeln ['a:dln] VT to bestow a peerage on, to make a (life) peer (Brit), to ennoble; (= *den Titel „Sir" verleihen*) to knight; (= *niedrigen Adel verleihen*) to bestow a title on; (fig geh: = *auszeichnen*) to ennoble VI **etw adelt** (geh) sth ennobles the soul

Adels-: **Adels|be|zeich|nung** F title; **Adels|brief** M patent of nobility; **Adels|prä|di|kat** NT mark of nobility (*in a name*); **Adels|stand** M nobility; (Brit auch) peerage; (hoher auch) aristocracy; **in den ~ erheben** = **adeln VT**; **Adels|stolz** M pride in one's noble birth; **Adels|ti|tel** M title

Ade|lung ['a:dəlʊŋ] F -, -en raising to the peerage, ennoblement; (= *Verleihung des Titels „Sir"*) knighting; (= *Verleihung von niedrigem Adel*) bestowing a title (+gen on)

Adept [a'dɛpt] M -en, -en, **Adep|tin** [a'dɛptɪn] F -, -nen (old: *der Geheimwissenschaften*) initiate; (iro geh) disciple

Ader ['a:dɐ] F -, -n (Bot, Geol) vein; (Physiol) blood vessel; (Elec: = *Leitungsdraht*) core; (fig: = *Veranlagung*) bent; **das spricht seine künstlerische/musikalische ~ an** that appeals to the artist/musician in him; **eine/keine ~ für etw haben** to have feeling/no feeling for sth; **eine poetische/musikalische ~ haben** to have a poetical/musical streak; **sich** (dat) **die ~n öffnen** (geh) to slash one's wrists; **jdn zur ~ lassen** (old, fig inf) to bleed sb

Äder|chen ['ɛ:dɐçən] NT -s, - dim von **Ader**

Ader|lass [-las] M -es, **Aderlässe** [-lɛsə] (old Med) blood-letting (auch fig), bleeding; **bei jdm einen ~ machen** to bleed sb; **die Abwanderung der Akademiker ist ein ~, den sich das Land nicht länger leisten kann** the country can no longer afford the bleeding of its resources through the exodus of its academics

ädern ['ɛ:dɐn] VT → **geädert**

Äde|rung F -, -en veining

Ad|hä|si|on [athɛ'zio:n] F -, -en (Phys) adhesion

Ad|hä|si|ons-: **Ad|hä|si|ons|kraft** F adhesive power, power of adhesion; **Ad|hä|si|ons|ver|schluss** M adhesive seal

ad hoc [at 'hɔk, at 'ho:k] ADV (geh) ad hoc; **~ wurde ein Komitee gebildet** an ad hoc committee was set up

Ad-hoc- in cpds ad hoc; **Ad-hoc-Maß|nah|me** F ad hoc measure

adi|eu [a'diø:] INTERJ (old, dial) adieu (obs), farewell (old); **jdm ~ sagen** to bid sb farewell (old), to say farewell or adieu to sb

adi|pös [adi'pø:s] ADJ (Med: = *fettleibig*) obese, corpulent (liter)

Ad|jek|tiv ['atjɛkti:f] NT -s, -e [-və] adjective

ad|jek|ti|visch ['atjɛkti:vɪʃ, atjɛk'ti:vɪʃ] ADJ adjectival ADV adjectivally

Ad|jek|ti|vum ['atjɛkti:vʊm, atjɛk'ti:vʊm] NT -s, **Adjektiva** [-va] adjective

Ad|junkt [at'jʊŋkt] M -en, -en, **Ad|junk|tin** [at'jʊŋktɪn] F -, -nen (Aus, Sw) junior civil servant

ad|jus|tie|ren [atjʊs'ti:rən] ptp **adjustiert** VT **a** (Tech) *Werkstück* to adjust; *Messgerät* to set **b** (Aus) to issue with uniforms/a uniform

Ad|jus|tie|rung F -, -en **a** (Tech) (von *Werkstück*) adjustment; (von *Messgerät*) setting **b** (Aus: = *Uniform*) uniform

Ad|ju|tant [atju'tant] M -en, -en, **Ad|ju|tan|tin** [-'tantɪn] F -, -nen adjutant; (von *General*) aide (-de-camp)

Ad|la|tus [at'la:tʊs] M -, **Adlaten** or **Adlati** [-tn, -ti] (old, iro) assistant

Ad|ler ['a:dlɐ] M -s, - eagle

Ad|ler-: **Ad|ler|au|ge** NT (fig) eagle eye; **~n haben** to have eyes like a hawk, to be eagle-eyed; **Ad|ler|blick** M (fig) eagle eye; **Ad|ler|farn**

M bracken; **Ad|ler|horst** M (eagle's) eyrie; **Ad|ler|na|se** F aquiline nose
ad|lig ['a:dlɪç] ADJ *(lit, fig)* noble; **~ sein** to be of noble birth
Ad|li|ge ['a:dlɪgə] F *decl as adj* member of the nobility, noblewoman; *(Brit auch)* peeress; *(hohe auch)* aristocrat
Ad|li|ge(r) ['a:dlɪgə] M *decl as adj* member of the nobility, nobleman; *(Brit auch)* peer; *(hoher auch)* aristocrat
Ad|mi|nist|ra|ti|on [atmɪnɪstra'tsio:n] F **-, -en** administration
ad|mi|nist|ra|tiv [atmɪnɪstra'ti:f] ADJ administrative ADV administratively
Ad|mi|nist|ra|tor [atmɪnɪs'tra:to:ɐ] M **-s, Administratoren** [-'to:rən], **Ad|mi|nist|ra|to|rin** [-'to:rɪn] F **-, -nen** administrator
ad|mi|nist|rie|ren [atmɪnɪs'tri:rən] *ptp* **administriert** VI *(geh, auch Comput: = verwalten)* to administrate
Ad|mi|ral [atmi'ra:l] M **-s, -e** *(Zool)* red admiral
Ad|mi|ral [atmi'ra:l] M **-s, -e** *or* **Admiräle** [-'rɛ:lə], **Ad|mi|ra|lin** [-'ra:lɪn] F **-, -nen** admiral
Ad|mi|ra|li|tät [atmirali'tɛ:t] F **-, -en** **a** *(= die Admirale)* admirals *pl* **b** *(= Marineleitung)* admiralty
Ad|mi|rals|rang M rank of admiral
Ado|les|zenz [adolɛs'tsɛnts] F **-,** *no pl (form)* adolescence
Ado|nis [a'do:nɪs] M **-, -se** *(geh)* Adonis
Ado|nis|rös|chen [-rø:sçən] NT pheasant's eye
adop|tie|ren [adɔp'ti:rən] *ptp* **adoptiert** VT to adopt
Adop|ti|on [adɔp'tsio:n] F **-, -en** adoption
Adop|tiv-: **Adop|tiv|el|tern** PL adoptive parents *pl*; **Adop|tiv|kind** NT adopted child; **Adop|tiv|sohn** M adopted son; **Adop|tiv|toch|ter** F adopted daughter
Adr. *abbr von* **Adresse**
Ad|re|na|lin [adrena'li:n] NT **-s,** *no pl* adrenalin
Ad|re|na|lin-: **Ad|re|na|lin|jun|kie** M *(inf)* adrenalin junkie *(inf)*; **Ad|re|na|lin|kick** M *(inf)* adrenalin kick *(inf)*, buzz of adrenalin *(inf)*; **Ad|re|na|lin|schub** M surge of adrenalin; **Ad|re|na|lin|spie|gel** M, *no pl* adrenalin level; **Ad|re|na|lin|stoß** M surge of adrenalin
Ad|res|sant [adrɛ'sant] M **-en, -en**, **Ad|res|san|tin** [-'santɪn] F **-, -nen** *(geh)* sender; *(Comm auch)* consignor *(form)*
Ad|res|sat [adrɛ'sa:t] M **-en, -en**, **Ad|res|sa|tin** [-'sa:tɪn] F **-, -nen** *(geh)* addressee; *(Comm auch)* consignee *(form)*; **~en** *(fig)* target group
Ad|res|sa|ten|grup|pe F target group
Ad|ress|auf|kle|ber M address label
Ad|ress|buch NT directory; *(privat)* address book
Ad|res|se [a'drɛsə] F **-, -n** **a** *(= Anschrift, Comput)* address; **eine Warnung an jds ~** *(acc)* **richten** *(fig)* to address a warning to sb; **dieser Vorwurf geht an Ihre eigene ~** this reproach is directed at *or* addressed to you (personally); **sich an die richtige ~ wenden** *(inf)* to go/come to the right place *or* person; **da sind Sie bei mir an der richtigen/falschen** *or* **verkehrten ~** *(inf)* you've come to the right/wrong person; **eine erste/feine ~** *(inf: = Organisation)* a top-class/ /prominent establishment **b** *(form: = Botschaft)* address
Ad|res|sen-: **Ad|res|sen|än|de|rung** F change of address; **Ad|res|sen|auf|kle|ber** M address label; **Ad|res|sen|han|del** M mailing list trade *or* business; **Ad|res|sen|lis|te** F address list, list of addresses; *(für Werbung etc)* mailing list; **Ad|res|sen|ver|wal|tung** F *(Comput)* address filing system; **Ad|res|sen|ver|zeich|nis** NT directory of addresses
ad|res|sie|ren [adrɛ'si:rən] *ptp* **adressiert** VT to address *(an +acc* to)
Ad|res|sier|ma|schi|ne F Addressograph® *(Brit)*, addressing machine
ad|rett [a'drɛt] *(dated)* ADJ smart ADV smartly
Ad|ria ['a:dria] F **-** Adriatic (Sea)
Ad|ri|a|ti|sches Meer [adri'a:tɪʃəs] NT *(form)* Adriatic Sea
Ad|strin|gens [at'strɪŋgɛns] NT **-, Adstringenzien** [-tsiən] astringent
Ad|van|tage [əd'va:ntɪdʒ] M **-s, -s** *(Sport)* advantage
Ad|vent [at'vɛnt] M **-s, -e** Advent; **im ~** in Advent; **erster/vierter ~** first/fourth Sunday in Advent
Ad|ven|tist [atvɛn'tɪst] M **-en, -en**, **Ad|ven|tis|tin** [-'tɪstɪn] F **-, -nen** *(Rel)* (Second) Adventist
Ad|vents-: **Ad|vents|ka|len|der** M Advent calendar; **Ad|vents|kranz** M Advent wreath; **Ad|vents|sonn|tag** M Sunday in Advent; **Ad|vents|zeit** F (season of) Advent
Ad|verb [at'vɛrp] NT **-s, Adverbien** [-biən] adverb
ad|ver|bi|al [atvɛr'bia:l] ADJ adverbial ADV adverbially
Ad|ver|bi|al-: **Ad|ver|bi|al|be|stim|mung** F adverbial qualification; **mit ~** qualified adverbially; **Ad|ver|bi|al|satz** M adverbial clause
ad|ver|sa|tiv [atvɛrza'ti:f] ADJ *(Gram)* adversative
Ad|ver|sa|tiv|satz M adversative clause
Ad|vo|ca|tus Di|a|bo|li [atvo'ka:tʊs di'a:boli] M **- -, Advocati -** [-ti] *(geh)* devil's advocate
Ad|vo|kat [atvo'ka:t] M **-en, -en**, **Ad|vo|ka|tin** [-'ka:tɪn] F **-, -nen** *(old Jur, fig)* advocate; *(Aus, Sw auch pej)* lawyer
Ad|vo|ka|tur [atvoka'tu:ɐ] F **-, -en** **a** legal profession **b** *(= Büro)* lawyer's office
Ad|vo|ka|tur|bü|ro NT *(Sw)*, **Ad|vo|ka|turs|kanz|lei** F *(Aus)* lawyer's office
Ae|ro- [a'e:ro, 'ɛ:ro] *in cpds* aero
Ae|ro|bic [ɛ'ro:bɪk] NT **-(s),** *no pl* aerobics *sing*
Ae|ro-: **Ae|ro|dy|na|mik** [aerody'na:mɪk] F aerodynamics *sing or (bei Flugzeug etc) pl*; **ae|ro|dy|na|misch** [aerody'na:mɪʃ] ADJ aerodynamic ADV aerodynamically; **Ae|ro|gramm** [aero'gram] NT *pl* **-gramme** air letter, aerogram(me); **Ae|ro|nau|tik** [aero'nautɪk] F **-,** *no pl* aeronautics *sing*; **ae|ro|nau|tisch** [aero'nautɪʃ] ADJ aeronautic(al); **Ae|ro|sol** [aero'zo:l, ɛro-] NT **-s, -e** aerosol
Af|fä|re [a'fɛ:rə] F **-, -n** **a** *(= Angelegenheit)* affair, business *no pl*; *(= Liebesabenteuer)* affair; **in eine ~ verwickelt sein** to be mixed up *or* involved in an affair; **sich aus der ~ ziehen** *(inf)* to get (oneself) out of it *(inf)* **b** *(= Zwischenfall)* incident, episode
Äff|chen ['ɛfçən] NT **-s, -** *dim von* **Affe**
Af|fe ['afə] M **-n, -n** **a** monkey; *(= Menschenaffe)* ape; **der Mensch stammt vom ~n ab** man is descended from the apes; **der nackte ~** the naked ape; **klettern wie ein ~** to climb like a monkey; **an jdm einen ~n gefressen haben** *(inf)* to have been really taken by sb; **du bist wohl vom (wilden) ~n gebissen!** *(inf)* you must be out of your tiny mind! *(inf)*, you must be off your rocker! *(inf)* → **lausen, Schleifstein** **b** *(sl: = Kerl)* **ein eingebildeter ~** a conceited ass *(inf)* **c** *(Mil inf)* knapsack, backpack
Af|fekt [a'fɛkt] M **-(e)s, -e** emotion, affect *(form)*; **ein im ~ begangenes Verbrechen** a crime committed under the influence of emotion, a crime committed in the heat of the moment; **im ~ handeln** to act in the heat of the moment
Af|fekt-: **af|fekt|ge|la|den** ADJ *(geh)* impassioned; **Af|fekt|hand|lung** F act committed under the influence of emotion
af|fek|tiert [afɛk'ti:ɐt] *(pej)* ADJ affected ADV affectedly; **sich ~ benehmen** to be affected, to behave affectedly
Af|fek|tiert|heit F **-, -en** affectation
af|fek|tiv [afɛk'ti:f] ADJ *(Psych)* affective
Af|fekt|stau M *(Psych)* emotional block
Af|fen-: **af|fen|ar|tig** ADJ like a monkey; *(= menschenaffenartig)* apelike; **mit ~er Geschwindigkeit** *(inf)* like greased lightning *(inf)*, like *or* in a flash *(inf)*; **~e Hitze** *(inf)* sweltering heat ADV **~ klettern** to climb like a monkey; **Af|fen|brot|baum** M monkey bread (tree), baobab; **af|fen|geil** *(dated sl)* ADJ *(= super)* wicked *(inf)*, right on *pred (inf)*; *(= scharf)* horny *(inf)* ADV really bad *(inf)*; **Af|fen|ge|schwin|dig|keit** F *(inf)* = **Affentempo**; **Af|fen|haus** NT ape house; **Af|fen|hit|ze** F *(inf)* sweltering heat *(inf)*; **gestern war eine ~** yesterday was a scorcher *(inf)*, yesterday it was sweltering *(inf)*; **Af|fen|jäck|chen** NT, **Af|fen|ja|cke** F *(Mil inf)* monkey jacket; **Af|fen|kä|fig** M → **Affe a** a monkey's/ape's cage; **Af|fen|lie|be** F blind adoration *(zu* of); **Af|fen|mensch** M *(inf)* apeman; **Af|fen|pin|scher** M griffon (terrier); **Af|fen|schan|de** F *(inf)* crying shame *(inf)*; **Af|fen|schau|kel** F *(inf) (Mil)* fourragère; *(usu pl: Frisur)* looped plait *(Brit) or* braid *(US)*; **Af|fen|spek|ta|kel** NT *(inf)* hullabaloo *(Brit inf)*, uproar; **Af|fen|tanz** M *(inf)* = **Affentheater**; **Af|fen|tem|po** NT *(inf)* breakneck *(Brit) or* neck-breaking *(US)* speed *(inf)*; **in** *or* **mit einem ~** at breakneck *(Brit) or* neck-breaking *(US)* speed *(inf)*; *laufen auch* like the clappers *(Brit inf)*; **Af|fen|the|a|ter** NT *(inf)* to-do *(inf)*, carry-on *(inf)*, fuss; **ein ~ aufführen** to make a fuss; **Af|fen|weib|chen** NT → **Affe a** female monkey/ape; **Af|fen|zahn** M *(inf)* = **Affentempo**
af|fig ['afɪç] *(inf)* ADJ *(= eitel)* stuck-up *(inf)*, conceited; *(= geziert)* affected; *(= lächerlich)* ridiculous, ludicrous ADV **sich ~ anstellen** *or* **haben** to be stuck-up *(inf)*/affected/ridiculous *or* ludicrous; **~ wirken** to seem ludicrous *or* ridiculous
Af|fig|keit F **-, -en** *(inf) (= Geziertheit)* affectation; *(= Lächerlichkeit)* ridiculousness, ludicrousness
Äf|fin ['ɛfɪn] F **-, -nen** female monkey; *(= Menschenäffin)* female ape
Af|fi|ni|tät [afini'tɛ:t] F **-, -en** affinity
Af|fir|ma|ti|on [afɪrma'tsio:n] F **-, -en** *(geh)* affirmation
af|fir|ma|tiv [afɪrma'ti:f] ADJ *(geh)* affirmative
Af|fix [a'fɪks, 'afɪks] NT **-es, -e** *(Ling)* affix
Af|fri|ka|ta [afri'ka:ta] F **-, Affrikaten** [-tn] *(Ling)* affricate
Af|front [a'frõ:] M **-s, -s** *(geh)* affront, insult *(gegen* to)
Af|gha|ne [af'ga:nə] M **-n, -n**, **Af|gha|nin** [-'ga:nɪn] F **-, -nen** Afghan
af|gha|nisch [af'ga:nɪʃ] ADJ Afghan; **Afghanischer Windhund** Afghan (hound)
Af|gha|nis|tan [af'ga:nɪsta:n, -tan] NT **-s** Afghanistan
A|fi|ci|o|na|do [afitsio'na:do] M **-s, -s** aficionado
Af|ri|ka ['a:frika, 'afrika] NT **-s** Africa
Af|ri|kaans [afri'ka:ns] NT **-** Afrikaans
Af|ri|ka|ner [afri'ka:nɐ] M **-s, -**, **Af|ri|ka|ne|rin** [-ərɪn] F **-, -nen** African
af|ri|ka|nisch [afri'ka:nɪʃ] ADJ African
Af|ri|ka|nis|tik [afrika'nɪstɪk] F **-,** *no pl* African studies *pl*
Af|ro-: **Af|ro|ame|ri|ka|ner(in)** M(F) Afro-American; **Af|ro|asi|at(in)** M(F) Afro-Asian; **af|ro|asi|a|tisch** ADJ Afro-Asian; **af|ro|deutsch** ADJ Afro-German; **Af|ro|deut|sche(r)** MF Afro-German; **Af|ro|look** M Afro-look
Af|ter ['aftɐ] M **-s, -** *(form)* anus
Af|ter|shave ['a:ftɐʃe:v] NT **-(s), -s** aftershave
AG [a:'ge:] F **-, -s** *abbr von* **Aktiengesellschaft** ≈ plc *(Brit)*, ≈ corp. *(US)*, ≈ inc. *(US)*
Ägä|is [ɛ'gɛ:ɪs] F **-** Aegean (Sea)
ägä|isch [ɛ'gɛ:ɪʃ] ADJ Aegean; **Ägäisches Meer** Aegean Sea
Aga|ve [a'ga:və] F **-, -n** agave
Agen|da [a'gɛnda] F **-, Agenden** [-dn] **a** *(= Notizbuch)* notebook; *(= Terminkalender)* diary **b** *(= Tagesordnung)* agenda; *(= Aktionsplan)* agenda, plan of action
Agen|de [a'gɛndə] F **-, -n** *(Eccl)* liturgy
Agens ['a:gɛns] NT **-, Agenzien** [a'gɛntsiən] *(Philos, Med, Ling)* agent

Agent [a'gɛnt] M **-en, -en**, **Agen|tin** [a'gɛntɪn] F **-, -nen** agent; *(= Spion)* secret *or* foreign agent

Agen|ten-: **Agen|ten|aus|tausch** M spy swap; **Agen|ten|film** M spy film *or* movie *(US)*; **Agen|ten|füh|rer(in)** M(F) spymaster; **Agen|ten|netz** NT spy network; **Agen|ten|ring** M spy ring; **Agen|ten|tä|tig|keit** F espionage; **ihre ~** her activity as a secret *or* foreign agent; **Agen|ten|thril|ler** M spy thriller

Agen|tin [a'gɛntɪn] F **-, -nen** → **Agent**

Agent pro|vo|ca|teur [a'ʒã: provoka'tø:ɐ] M **-, -s -s** agent provocateur

Agen|tur [agɛn'tu:ɐ] F **-, -en** agency; **~ für Arbeit** *Ger* job centre *(Brit)*, unemployment office *(US)*

Agen|tur|be|richt M (news) agency report

Ag|glo|me|rat [aglome'ra:t] NT **-(e)s, -e** *(Tech, Geol)* agglomerate; *(fig geh auch)* agglomeration, conglomeration

Ag|glu|ti|na|ti|on [aglutina'tsio:n] F **-, -en** *(Ling)* agglutination

ag|glu|ti|nie|ren [agluti'ni:rən] *ptp* **agglutiniert** VI *(Ling)* to agglutinate; **~d** agglutinative; *Sprache auch* agglutinating

Ag|gre|gat [agre'ga:t] NT **-(e)s, -e** *(Geol)* aggregate; *(Tech)* unit, set of machines; *(Aut: = Motor)* engine

Ag|gre|gat|zu|stand M state; **die drei Aggregatzustände** the three states of matter

Ag|gres|si|on [agrɛ'sio:n] F **-, -en** aggression *(gegen* towards); **~en gegen jdn empfinden** to feel aggressive *or* aggression toward(s) sb

Ag|gres|si|ons-: **ag|gres|si|ons|ge|la|den** ADJ full of aggression; **Ag|gres|si|ons|hem|mung** F, *no pl* inhibition of aggression; **Ag|gres|si|ons|krieg** M war of aggression; **Ag|gres|si|ons|lust** F, *no pl* belligerence; **ag|gres|si|ons|lüs|tern** ADJ *(pej)* belligerent, bellicose; **Ag|gres|si|ons|po|li|tik** F policy of aggression; **Ag|gres|si|ons|stau** M *(Psych)* build-up of aggression; **Ag|gres|si|ons|trieb** M *(Psych)* aggressive impulse

ag|gres|siv [agre'si:f] ADJ aggressive ADV aggressively

Ag|gres|si|vi|tät [agrɛsivi'tɛ:t] F **-, -en** aggressivity

ag|gres|si|vi|täts|ge|la|den ADJ full of aggression

Ag|gres|sor [a'grɛso:ɐ] M **-s, Aggressoren** [-'so:rən], **Ag|gres|so|rin** [-'so:rɪn] F **-, -nen** aggressor

Ägi|de [ɛ'gi:də] F **-,** *no pl (liter)* **unter jds ~** *(dat) (= Schutz)* under the aegis of sb; *(= Schirmherrschaft auch)* under sb's patronage

agie|ren [a'gi:rən] *ptp* **agiert** VI to operate, to act; *(Theat)* to act; **als jd ~** *(Theat)* to act *or* play the part of sb

agil [a'gi:l] ADJ *(körperlich)* agile, nimble; **(geistig) ~** sharp, nimble-minded, mentally agile

Agi|li|tät [agili'tɛ:t] F **-,** *no pl (von Körper)* agility, nimbleness; *(von Geist)* sharpness

Agio ['a:dʒo, 'a:ʒio] NT **-, Agien** ['a:dʒən, 'a:ʒiən] *(Fin) (von Wertpapier)* premium; *(von Geldsorte)* agio

Agio|pa|pie|re PL *(Fin)* securities *pl* redeemable at a premium

Agi|ta|ti|on [agita'tsio:n] F **-, -en** *(Pol)* agitation; **~ treiben** to agitate

Agi|ta|tor [agi'ta:to:ɐ] M **-s, Agitatoren** [-'to:rən], **Agi|ta|to|rin** [-'to:rɪn] F **-, -nen** *(Pol)* agitator

agi|ta|to|risch [agita'to:rɪʃ] *(Pol)* ADJ agitational; *Rede, Inhalt* inflammatory ADV **~ argumentieren** to argue in an inflammatory style; **sich ~ betätigen** to be an agitator

agi|tie|ren [agi'ti:rən] *ptp* **agitiert** VI to agitate

Agit|prop [agɪt'prɔp] F **-,** *no pl* agitprop

Ag|nos|ti|ker [a'gnɔstikɐ] M **-s, -**, **Ag|nos|ti|ke|rin** [-ərɪn] F **-, -nen** agnostic

ag|nos|tisch [a'gnɔstɪʃ] ADJ agnostic

Ag|nos|ti|zis|mus [agnɔsti'tsɪsmʊs] M **-,** *no pl* agnosticism

Ago|nie [ago'ni:] F **-, -n** [-'ni:ən] *(lit, fig geh)* death throes *pl*, death pangs *pl*; **in (der) ~ liegen** to be in one's/its death throes

Ag|rar- *in cpds* agrarian; **Ag|rar|aus|ga|ben** PL *(von EU, Staat)* agricultural spending *sing*; **Ag|rar|fab|rik** F factory farm; **Ag|rar|ge|sell|schaft** F agrarian society

Ag|ra|ri|er [a'gra:riɐ] M **-s, -**, **Ag|ra|ri|e|rin** [-iərɪn] F **-, -nen** landowner

ag|ra|risch [a'gra:rɪʃ] ADJ agrarian; *Rohstoffe* agricultural

Ag|rar-: **Ag|rar|kri|se** F agricultural crisis, farm *or* farming crisis; **Ag|rar|land** NT agrarian country; **Ag|rar|markt** M agricultural commodities market; **Ag|rar|po|li|tik** F agricultural policy; **Ag|rar|prei|se** PL farm prices *pl*; **Ag|rar|pro|dukt** NT agricultural *or* farm product; **Ag|rar|re|form** F agricultural reform; **Ag|rar|staat** M agrarian state; **Ag|rar|sub|ven|tio|nen** PL farm subsidies *pl*; **Ag|rar|über|schuss** M agricultural surplus; **Ag|rar|wirt|schaft** F farming; **Ag|rar|wis|sen|schaft** F agronomy, agronomics; **Ag|rar|zoll** M import tariff *(on produce)*

Ag|ré|ment [agre'mã:] NT **-s, -s** *(Pol)* agrément

Ag|ri|kul|tur [agrikʊl'tu:ɐ] F *(form)* agriculture

Ag|ri|kul|tur|che|mie F, **Ag|ro|che|mie** ['a:gro-] F agricultural chemistry

Ag|ro|nom [agro'no:m] M **-en, -en**, **Ag|ro|no|min** [-'no:mɪn] F **-, -nen** agronomist

Ag|ro|no|mie [agrono'mi:] F **-,** *no pl* agronomy

Ag|ro|tech|nik ['a:gro-] F agricultural technology

Ägyp|ten [ɛ'gʏptn] NT **-s** Egypt

Ägyp|ter [ɛ'gʏptɐ] M **-s, -**, **Ägyp|te|rin** [-ərɪn] F **-, -nen** Egyptian

ägyp|tisch [ɛ'gʏptɪʃ] ADJ Egyptian; **~e Finsternis** *(liter)* Stygian darkness *(liter)*

Ägyp|to|lo|gie [ɛgʏptolo'gi:] F **-,** *no pl* Egyptology

ah [a:, a] INTERJ *(genießerisch)* ooh, ah, mmm; *(überrascht, bewundernd, verstehend)* ah, oh

Ah [a:, a] NT **-s, -s** oh, ah

äh [ɛ:] INTERJ *(beim Sprechen)* er, um; *(Ausdruck des Ekels)* ugh

aha [a'ha:, a'ha] INTERJ aha; *(verstehend auch)* I see

Aha-: **Aha-Ef|fekt** [a'ha:-, a'ha-] M aha effect, now I get it effect; **Aha-Er|leb|nis** [a'ha:-, a'ha-] NT sudden insight, aha-experience *(Psych)*

Ah|le ['a:lə] F **-, -n** awl; *(Typ)* bodkin

Ahn [a:n] M **-(e)s** *or* **-en, -en** *(geh)* ancestor, forefather *(liter)*; *(fig)* for(e)bear *(liter)*

ahn|den ['a:ndn] VT *(liter) Freveltat, Verbrechen* to avenge; *(form) Übertretung, Verstoß* to punish

Ahn|dung F **-, -en** *(liter: von Freveltat, Verbrechen)* avengement; *(form: von Übertretung, Verstoß)* punishment

Ah|ne ['a:nə] M **-n, -n** *(liter)* ancestor, forefather *(liter)*; *(fig)* for(e)bear *(liter)*

Ah|ne F **-, -n** *(geh) (= weiblicher Vorfahr)* ancestress; *(fig)* for(e)bear *(liter)*

äh|neln ['ɛ:nln] VI *+dat* to be like, to be similar to, to resemble; **sich** *or* **einander** *(geh)* **~** to be alike, to be similar, to resemble one another; **in diesem Punkt ähnelt sie sehr ihrem Vater** she's very like her father *or* very similar to her father in this respect, she greatly resembles her father in this respect; **diese Erklärung ähnelt seiner früheren Aussage überhaupt nicht mehr** this explanation bears no resemblance whatsoever to his earlier statement; **die beiden Systeme ~ einander nicht sehr/~ sich wenig** the two systems are not very similar *or* alike/have little in common

ah|nen ['a:nən] VT *(= voraussehen)* to foresee, to know; *Gefahr, Tod etc* to have a presentiment *or* premonition *or* foreboding of; *(= vermuten)* to suspect; *(= erraten)* to guess; **das kann ich doch nicht ~!** I couldn't be expected to know that!; **nichts Böses ~** to have no sense of foreboding, to be unsuspecting; **nichts Böses ~d** unsuspectingly; **da sitzt man friedlich an seinem Schreibtisch, nichts Böses ~d ...** *(hum)* there I was sitting peacefully at my desk minding my own business ... *(hum)*; **ohne zu ~, dass ...** without dreaming *or* suspecting (for one minute) that ...; **ohne es zu ~** without suspecting, without having the slightest idea; **davon habe ich nichts geahnt** I didn't have the slightest inkling of it, I didn't suspect it for one moment; **so etwas habe ich doch geahnt** I did suspect something like that; **(ach), du ahnst es nicht!** *(inf)* would you believe it! *(inf)*; **du ahnst es nicht, wen ich gestern getroffen habe!** you'll never guess *or* believe who I met yesterday!; **die Umrisse waren nur zu ~** the contours could only be guessed at

VI *(geh)* **mir ahnt etwas Schreckliches** I have a dreadful foreboding; **mir ahnt nichts Gutes** I have a premonition that all is not well

Ah|nen-: **Ah|nen|bild** NT ancestral portrait; *(auch* **Ahnenfigur***)* ancestral figure; **Ah|nen|for|schung** F genealogy; **Ah|nen|ga|le|rie** F ancestral portrait gallery; **Ah|nen|kult** M ancestor worship *or* cult; **Ah|nen|pass** M *(im Dritten Reich)* proof of ancestry, pedigree; **Ah|nen|rei|he** F ancestral line; **Ah|nen|ta|fel** F genealogical tree *or* table, genealogy, pedigree; **Ah|nen|ver|eh|rung** F ancestor worship

Ahn-: **Ahn|frau** F *(liter)* ancestress; *(= Stammmutter)* progenitrix *(form, liter)*; **Ahn|herr** M *(liter)* ancestor; *(= Stammvater)* progenitor *(form, liter)*

ähn|lich ['ɛ:nlɪç] ✪ 32.4, 53.5 ADJ similar *(+dat* to); **ein dem Rokoko ~er Stil** a style similar to rococo, a similar style to rococo; **das dem Vater ~e Kind** the child that resembles his father, the child that is like his father; **~ wie er/sie** like him/her; **~ wie damals** as then; **~ wie vor 10 Jahren** as 10 years ago; **sie sind sich ~** they are similar *or* alike; **(etwas) Ähnliches** something similar, something like it/that

ADV **ein ~ aussehender Gegenstand** a similar-looking object; **~ kompliziert/intelligent** just as complicated/intelligent; **eine ~ komplizierte Sachlage** a similarly complicated state of affairs; **ich denke ~** I feel the same way (about it); **er hat sie ~ hintergegangen wie seine frühere Freundin** he cheated on her just as he did with his former girlfriend; **jdm ~ sehen** to be like sb, to resemble sb → **ähnlichsehen**

PREP *+dat* similar to, like

Ähn|lich|keit F **-, -en** *(mit* to) *(= Vergleichbarkeit)* similarity; *(= ähnliches Aussehen)* similarity, resemblance; **mit jdm/etw ~ haben** to resemble sb/sth, to be like sb/sth

ähn|lich+se|hen VI *sep irreg* **das sieht ihm (ganz) ähnlich!** *(inf, fig)* that's just like him!, that's him all over! *(inf)*

Ah|nung ['a:nʊŋ] F **-, -en** **a** *(= Vorgefühl)* hunch, presentiment; *(düster)* foreboding, premonition

b *(= Vorstellung, Wissen)* idea; *(= Vermutung)* suspicion, hunch; **eine ~ von etw vermitteln** to give an idea of sth; **keine ~ (davon) haben, dass/wie/was** *etc* to have no idea that/how/what *etc*; **keine ~!** *(inf)* no idea! *(inf)*, I haven't a clue! *(inf)*; **er hat keine blasse** *or* **nicht die geringste ~** he hasn't a clue *or* the foggiest *(inf)*, he hasn't the faintest idea *(inf)*; **hast du eine ~, wo er sein könnte?** have you any *or* an idea where he could be?; **hast du eine ~!** *(iro inf)* a (fat) lot you know (about it)! *(inf)*, that's what YOU know (about it)!

Ah|nungs-: **ah|nungs|los** ADJ *(= nichts ahnend)* unsuspecting; *(= unwissend)* clueless *(inf)* ADV unsuspectingly, innocently; **Ah|nungs|lo|sig|keit** F **-,** *no pl (= Unwissenheit)* cluelessness *(inf)*; **er bewies seine völlige ~ darüber, dass ...** he showed how totally unsuspecting he was of the fact that ...; **ah|nungs|voll** ADJ *(geh)* full of presentiment *or (Böses ahnend)* foreboding

ahoi [a'hɔy] INTERJ *(Naut)* **Schiff ~!** ship ahoy!

Ahorn ['a:hɔrn] M **-s, -e** maple

Ahorn-: **Ahorn|blatt** NT maple leaf; **Ahorn|si|rup** M maple syrup

Äh|re ['ɛ:rə] F -, -n (= *Getreideähre*) ear; (*allgemeiner*, = *Grasähre*) head; **~n lesen** to glean (corn)

Äh|ren-: **Äh|ren|kranz** M garland of corn; **Äh|ren|le|se** F gleaning; **Äh|ren|le|ser(in)** M(F) gleaner

AHV [a:ha:'fau] (*Sw*) *abbr von* **Alters- und Hinderungsversicherung** age and disability insurance

Aide-Mé|moire [ɛ:tme'moa:ɐ] NT -, - aide-mémoire

Aids [e:ds] NT -, *no pl* Aids

Aids- *in cpds* Aids; **Aids-Er|re|ger** M Aids virus; **Aids|fall** M Aids case; **2000 neue Aidsfälle wurden registriert** 2000 new Aids cases were registered *or* reported; **Aids|hil|fe** F Aids support; **die Münchener ~** the Munich Aids support group; **aids|in|fi|ziert** [-ınfitsi:ɐt] ADJ infected with Aids; **~es Blut** Aids-infected blood; **Aids|in|fi|zier|te(r)** [-ınfitsi:ɐtə] MF *decl as adj* person infected with Aids, PWA (*US*); **aids|krank** ADJ suffering from Aids; **Aids|kran|ke(r)** MF *decl as adj* Aids sufferer; **Aids|op|fer** NT Aids victim; **Aids|test** M Aids test; **Aids|the|ra|pie** F Aids therapy; **Aids|to|te(r)** MF *decl as adj* person/man/woman who died of Aids; **2000 ~ pro Jahr** 2000 Aids deaths *or* deaths from Aids per year; **Aids|vi|rus** NT Aids virus

Ai|ki|do [ai'ki:do] NT -(s), *no pl* aikido

Air [ɛ:ɐ] NT -(s), -s (*geh*) air, aura

Air-: **Air|bag** ['ɛ:ɐbɛg] M -s, -s (*Aut*) airbag; **Air|bus®** M (*Aviat*) airbus®; **Air|surf|ing** ['ɛ:ɐ-] NT -s, *no pl* air surfing

ais, Ais ['a:ıs] NT -, - A sharp

Ai|schy|los ['aısçylɔs] M -' Aeschylus

AIZ [a:li:'tsɛt] F *abbr von* **Antiimperialistische Zelle**

Aja|tol|lah [aja'tɔla] M -(s), -s ayatollah

Aka|de|mie [akade'mi:] F -, -n [-'mi:ən] academy; (= *Fachschule*) college, school

Aka|de|mi|ker [aka'de:mikɐ] M -s, -, **Aka|de|mi|ke|rin** [-ərın] F -, -nen person with a university education; (= *Student*) (university) student; (= *Hochschulabsolvent*) (university) graduate; (= *Universitätslehrkraft*) academic; (*rare*: = *Akademiemitglied*) academician

a|ka|de|misch [aka'de:mıʃ] ADJ (*lit, fig*) academic; **die ~e Jugend** (the) students *pl*; **das ~e Proletariat** (the) jobless graduates *pl*; **der ~e Senat** (*Univ*) the senate; **das ~e Viertel** (*Univ*) *the quarter of an hour allowed between the announced start of a lecture etc and the actual start* ADV **~ gebildet sein** to have (had) a university education, to be a graduate

Aka|de|mi|sie|rung [akademi'zi:rʊŋ] F -, -en **die ~ des öffentlichen Dienstes** turning the Civil Service into a graduate profession

Akan|thus [a'kantʊs] M -, - acanthus

Akan|thus|blatt NT acanthus leaf

Aka|zie [a'ka:tsiə] F -, -n acacia

Ake|lei [akə'lai, 'a:kəlai] F -, -en aquilegia, columbine

Ak|kla|ma|ti|on [aklama'tsio:n] F -, -en (*form*) acclaim, acclamation; **Wahl per** *or* **durch ~** election by acclamation

ak|kla|mie|ren [akla'mi:rən] *ptp* **akklamiert** (*form, Aus*) VI to applaud (*jdm* sb) VT *Schauspieler, Szene* to acclaim, to applaud; (= *wählen*) to elect by acclamation

Ak|kli|ma|ti|sa|ti|on [aklimatiza'tsio:n] F -, -en (*form*) acclimatization

ak|kli|ma|ti|sie|ren [aklimati'zi:rən] *ptp* **akklimatisiert** VR (*lit, fig*) (*in +dat* to) to become acclimatized, to acclimatize oneself VT to acclimatize

Ak|kli|ma|ti|sie|rung F -, -en acclimatization

Ak|ko|la|de [ako'la:də] F -, -n **a** (*Typ*) brace; (*Mus*) accolade **b** (*Hist*) accolade

Ak|kord [a'kɔrt] M -(e)s, -e [-də] **a** (*Mus*) chord **b** (= *Stücklohn*) piece rate; **im** *or* **in** *or* **auf ~ arbeiten** to do piecework **c** (*Jur*) settlement

Ak|kord-: **Ak|kord|ar|beit** F piecework; **Ak|kord|ar|bei|ter(in)** M(F) pieceworker

Ak|kor|de|on [a'kɔrdeɔn] NT -s, -s accordion

Ak|kor|de|o|nist [akɔrdeo'nıst] M -en, -en, **Ak|kor|de|o|nis|tin** [-'nıstın] F -, -nen, **Ak|kor|de|on|spie|ler(in)** M(F) accordionist

Ak|kord-: **Ak|kord|lohn** M piece wages *pl*, piece rate; **Ak|kord|satz** M piece rate; **Ak|kord|zu|schlag** M piece rate bonus

ak|kre|di|tie|ren [akredi'ti:rən] *ptp* **akkreditiert** VT **a** *Botschafter, Journalisten* to accredit (*bei* to, at) **b** (*Fin*) **jdn ~** to give sb credit facilities; **akkreditiert sein** to have credit facilities; **jdn für einen Betrag ~** to credit an amount to sb *or* sb's account, to credit sb *or* sb's account with an amount

Ak|kre|di|tie|rung F -, -en **a** (*von Botschafter, Journalist*) accreditation (*bei* to, at) **b** (*Fin*) provision of credit facilities (*+gen* to); (*von Betrag*) crediting

Ak|kre|di|tiv [akredi'ti:f] NT -s, -e [-və] **a** (*Pol*) credentials *pl* **b** (*Fin*) letter of credit; **jdm ein ~ eröffnen** to open a credit in favour (*Brit*) *or* favor (*US*) of sb

Ak|ku ['aku] M -s, -s (*inf*) *abbr von* **Akkumulator** accumulator

Ak|ku|boh|rer M battery-operated *or* cordless drill

Ak|ku|la|de|ge|rät ['aku-] NT battery charger

Ak|ku|mu|la|ti|on [akumula'tsio:n] F -, -en accumulation

Ak|ku|mu|la|tor [akumu'la:to:ɐ] M -s, **Akkumulatoren** [-'to:rən] accumulator

ak|ku|mu|lie|ren [akumu'li:rən] *ptp* **akkumuliert** VTIR to accumulate

ak|ku|rat [aku'ra:t] ADJ precise; (= *sorgfältig auch*) meticulous ADV precisely, exactly; (= *tatsächlich*) naturally, of course

Ak|ku|ra|tes|se [akura'tɛsə] F -, *no pl* (*dated*) precision; (= *Sorgfalt*) meticulousness

Ak|ku|sa|tiv ['akuzati:f] M -s, -e [-və] accusative; **im ~ stehen** to be in the accusative

Ak|ku|sa|tiv|ob|jekt NT accusative object

Ak|ne ['aknə] F -, -n acne

Ako|luth [ako'lu:t] M -en, -en, **Ako|lyth** [ako'ly:t] M -en, -en (*Eccl*) acolyte

Akon|to|zah|lung [a'kɔnto-] F payment on account

AKP [a:ka'pe:] F *abbr von* **Afrika, Karibik und pazifischer Raum** ACP; **die ~-Staaten** the ACP countries; **~-Bananen** bananas from the ACP countries

ak|qui|rie|ren [akvi'ri:rən] *ptp* **akquiriert** VT **a** *Spenden* to collect; **Inserate ~** to sell advertising space; **Kunden ~** to canvass for customers **b** (*old*: = *erwerben*) to acquire VI (*Comm*) to canvass for custom

Ak|qui|si|teur [akvizi'tø:ɐ] M -s, -e, **Ak|qui|si|teu|rin** [-'tø:rın] F -, -nen agent, canvasser

Ak|qui|si|ti|on [akvizi'tsio:n] F -, -en (*old*) acquisition; (*Comm*) (customer) canvassing

Ak|ri|bie [akri'bi:] F -, *no pl* (*geh*) meticulousness, (meticulous) precision

ak|ri|bisch [a'kri:bıʃ] (*geh*) ADJ meticulous, precise ADV meticulously

Ak|ro|bat [akro'ba:t] M -en, -en, **Ak|ro|ba|tin** [-'ba:tın] F -, -nen acrobat

Ak|ro|ba|tik [akro'ba:tık] F -, *no pl* acrobatics *pl*; (= *Geschicklichkeit*) acrobatic abilities *pl* or skill

ak|ro|ba|tisch [akro'ba:tıʃ] ADJ acrobatic

Ak|ro|nym [akro'ny:m] NT -s, -e acronym

Akt [akt] M -(e)s, -e **a** (= *Tat*) act; (= *Zeremonie*) ceremony, ceremonial act **b** (*Theat*: = *Zirkusakt*) act **c** (*Art*: = *Aktbild*) nude **d** (= *Geschlechtsakt*) sexual act, coitus *no art* (*form*)

Akt M -(e)s, -en (*Aus*) = **Akte**

Akt-: **Akt|auf|nah|me** F nude (photograph); **Akt|bild** NT nude (picture *or* portrait)

Ak|te ['aktə] F -, -n file, record; **die ~ Schmidt** the Schmidt file; **das kommt in die ~n** this goes on file *or* record; **etw zu den ~n legen** to file sth away, to put sth on file; (*fig*) *Fall etc* to drop sth

Ak|ten-: **Ak|ten|berg** M (*inf*) mountain of files *or* records (*inf*); **Ak|ten|de|ckel** M folder; **Ak|ten|ein|sicht** F (*form*) inspection of records *or* files; **Ak|ten|kof|fer** M attaché case, executive case; **ak|ten|kun|dig** ADJ on record; **~ werden** to be put on record; **Ak|ten|la|ge** F **nach** *or* **laut ~** according to the files; **die ~ prüfen** to examine the files; **Ak|ten|map|pe** F **a** (= *Tasche*) briefcase, portfolio **b** (= *Umschlag*) folder, file; **Ak|ten|no|tiz** F memo(randum); **Ak|ten|ord|ner** M file; **Ak|ten|schrank** M filing cabinet; **Ak|ten|ta|sche** F briefcase, portfolio; **Ak|ten|ver|merk** M memo(randum); **Ak|ten|ver|nich|ter** [-fɛɐnıçtɐ] M -s, - document (*Brit*) *or* paper shredder; **Ak|ten|wolf** M shredder, shredding machine; **Ak|ten|zei|chen** NT reference

Ak|teur [ak'tø:ɐ] M -s, -e, **Ak|teu|rin** [-'tø:rın] F -, -nen (*geh*) participant, protagonist

Akt-: **Akt|fo|to** NT nude (photograph); **Akt|fo|to|gra|fie**, **Akt|pho|to|gra|phie** F nude photography; (= *Bild*) nude photograph

Ak|tie ['aktsiə] F -, -n share; (= *Aktienschein*) share certificate; **in ~n anlegen** to invest in (stocks and) shares; **die ~n fallen/steigen** share prices are falling/rising; **die ~n stehen gut/schlecht** (*lit*) share prices are looking good/bad; (*fig*) things *or* the prospects are looking good/bad; **wie stehen die ~n?** (*hum inf*) how are things?; (= *wie sind die Aussichten*) what are the prospects?

Ak|ti|en-: **Ak|ti|en|be|sitz** M shareholdings *pl*, shares *pl* held; **Ak|ti|en|be|sit|zer(in)** M(F) shareholder, stockholder (*esp US*); **Ak|ti|en|bör|se** F stock exchange; **Ak|ti|en|fonds** M share *or* stock (*US*) fund; **Ak|ti|en|ge|sell|schaft** F ≈ public limited company (*Brit*), ≈ corporation (*US*); **Ak|ti|en|in|dex** M (*Fin*) share index; **Ak|ti|en|ka|pi|tal** NT share capital; (*von Gesellschaft auch*) (capital) stock; **Ak|ti|en|kurs** M share price; **Ak|ti|en|markt** M stock market; **Ak|ti|en|mehr|heit** F majority holding; **Ak|ti|en|no|tie|rung** F share *or* stock (*US*) quotation *or* listing; **Ak|ti|en|op|ti|on** F stock option; **Ak|ti|en|pa|ket** NT block of shares; **ein ~ von 20 Prozent** a shareholding of 20 per cent (*Brit*) *or* percent (*US*); **Ak|ti|en|spe|ku|lant(in)** M(F) stock market speculator; **Ak|ti|en|spe|ku|la|tion** F speculation on the stock market; **Ak|ti|en|tausch** M share exchange

Ak|ti|ni|um [ak'ti:nium] NT -s, *no pl* (*abbr* **Ac**) actinium

Ak|ti|on [ak'tsio:n] F -, -en (= *Handlung*) action (*auch Mil*); (= *Kampagne*) campaign; (= *Werbeaktion*) promotion; (= *geplantes Unternehmen, Einsatz*) operation (*auch Mil*); (*Art*) action painting; **in ~** in action; **sie muss ständig in ~ sein** she always has to be active *or* on the go (*inf*); **in ~ treten** to go into action

Ak|ti|o|när [aktsio'nɛ:ɐ] M -s, -e, **Ak|ti|o|nä|rin** [-'nɛ:rın] F -, -nen shareholder, stockholder (*esp US*)

Ak|ti|o|närs|ver|samm|lung F shareholders' *or* stockholders' (*esp US*) meeting

Ak|ti|o|nis|mus [aktsio'nısmʊs] M -, *no pl* (*Pol*) actionism

ak|ti|o|nis|tisch [aktsio'nıstıʃ] ADJ (*Pol*) actionist(ic)

Ak|ti|ons-: **Ak|ti|ons|art** F (*Gram*) aspect; **Ak|ti|ons|aus|schuss** M action committee; **Ak|ti|ons|ein|heit** F (*Pol*) unity of action, working unity; **ak|ti|ons|fä|hig** ADJ capable of action; **Ak|ti|ons|ko|mi|tee** NT action committee; **Ak|ti|ons|ma|ler(in)** M(F) action painter; **Ak|ti|ons|ma|le|rei** F action painting; **Ak|ti|ons|preis** M special-offer price; **Ak|ti|ons|pro|gramm** NT programme (*Brit*) *or* program (*US*) of action; **Ak|ti|ons|ra|di|us** M (*Aviat, Naut*) range, radius; (*fig*: = *Wirkungsbereich*) scope (for action); **ak|ti|ons|un|fä|hig**

ADJ incapable of action; **Ak|ti|ons|wo|che** F (special) campaign week

ak|tiv [ak'ti:f, 'akti:f] ADJ active, *(Comput auch)* running; *(Econ) Bilanz* positive, favourable *(Brit)*, favorable *(US)*; *(Mil) Soldat etc* on active service *or* duty; **~ sein** *(Univ)* to be a full member of a/the students' association → **Wahlrecht** ADV actively; **sich ~ an etw** *(dat)* **beteiligen** to take an active part in sth; **~ dienen** *(Mil)* to be on active duty *or* service

Ak|tiv ['akti:f] NT **-s,** *(rare)* **-e** [-və] *(Gram)* active

Ak|tiv [ak'ti:f] NT **-s, -s** *or* **-e** [-və] *(DDR)* work team

Ak|ti|va [ak'ti:va] PL assets *pl*; **~ und Passiva** assets and liabilities

Ak|tiv-: **Ak|tiv|be|stand** M *(Fin)* assets *pl*; *(Mil)* present strength; **Ak|tiv|bi|lanz** F *(Fin)* credit balance

Ak|tiv|box F *(= Lautsprecherbox)* active speaker

Ak|ti|ven|spre|cher(in) M(F) *(Sport)* participants' spokesperson

Ak|ti|ve(r) [ak'ti:və] MF *decl as adj (Sport)* active participant; *(Univ)* full member (of a/the students' association)

Ak|tiv|fe|ri|en PL activity holiday *(esp Brit) or* vacation *(US)*

Ak|tiv|ge|schäft NT *(Fin)* lending business

ak|ti|vie|ren [akti'vi:rən] *ptp* **aktiviert** VT *(Sci)* to activate; *(fig) Arbeit, Kampagne* to step up; *Mitarbeiter* to get moving; *(Comput) Gerät, System* to enable, *Kontrollkästchen* to check; *(Comm)* to enter on the assets side

ak|ti|visch [ak'ti:vɪʃ, 'akti:vɪʃ] ADJ *(Gram)* active

Ak|ti|vis|mus [akti'vɪsmʊs] M **-,** *no pl* activism

Ak|ti|vist [akti'vɪst] M **-en, -en, Ak|ti|vis|tin** [-'vɪstɪn] F **-, -nen** activist

Ak|ti|vi|tät [aktivi'tɛ:t] F **-, -en** activity

Ak|tiv-: **Ak|tiv|koh|le** F *(Chem)* activated carbon; **Ak|tiv|koh|le|fil|ter** F activated carbon filter; **Ak|tiv|pos|ten** M *(lit, fig)* asset; **Ak|tiv|sal|do** M credit balance; **Ak|tiv|sei|te** F assets side; **Ak|tiv|ur|laub** M activity holiday *(esp Brit) or* vacation *(US)*; **Ak|tiv|ver|mö|gen** NT realizable assets *pl*; **Ak|tiv|zin|sen** PL interest receivable *sing*

Akt|ma|le|rei F nude painting

Akt|mo|dell NT nude model

Ak|tri|ce [ak'tri:sə] F **-, -n** *(dated)* actress

Akt|stu|die F nude study

ak|tu|a|li|sie|ren [aktuali'zi:rən] *ptp* **aktualisiert** VT to make topical; *Datei, Nachschlagewerk* to update; *Bildschirmanzeige* to refresh

Ak|tu|a|li|sie|rung F **-, -en** updating

Ak|tu|a|li|tät [aktuali'tɛ:t] F **-, -en** **a** relevance (to the present *or* current situation), topicality **b** **Aktualitäten** PL *(geh: = neueste Ereignisse)* current events *pl*

Ak|tu|ar [ak'tua:ɐ] M **-s, -e, Ak|tu|a|rin** [-'tua:rɪn] F **-, -nen** **a** *(old: = Gerichtsschreiber)* clerk of the court **b** *(Sw: = Schriftführer)* secretary

ak|tu|ell [ak'tuɛl] ADJ relevant (to the current situation); *Frage auch* of topical interest; *Thema* topical; *(= gegenwärtig) Problem, Theorie, Thema* current; *(= modern) Mode* latest *attr*, current; *Stil* latest *attr*, fashionable; *(Comput) Programmversion etc* current; *(Econ) Bedarf, Kaufkraft* actual; **von ~em Interesse** of topical interest; **von ~er Bedeutung** of relevance to the present situation; **dieses Problem ist nicht mehr ~** this is no longer a (current) problem; **das Buch ist wieder ~ geworden** the book has become relevant again, the book has regained topicality; **eine ~e Sendung** *(Rad, TV)* a current affairs programme *(Brit) or* program *(US)*; **Aktuelle Stunde** *(Parl)* ≈ question time *no art (Brit)*

Akt|zeich|nung F nude (drawing), drawing of a nude

Aku|pres|sur [akuprɛ'su:ɐ] F **-, -en** acupressure

Aku|punk|teur [akupʊŋk'tø:ɐ] M **-s, -e, Aku|punk|teu|rin** [-'tø:rɪn] F **-, -nen** acupuncturist

aku|punk|tie|ren [akupʊŋk'ti:rən] *ptp* **akupunktiert** VT to acupuncture VI to perform acupuncture

Aku|punk|tur [akupʊŋk'tu:ɐ] F **-, -en** acupuncture

Akus|tik [a'kʊstɪk] F **-,** *no pl (von Gebäude etc)* acoustics *pl*; *(Phys: = Lehre)* acoustics *sing*

Akus|tik|kopp|ler [-kɔplɐ] M **-s, -** *(Comput)* acoustic coupler

akus|tisch [a'kʊstɪʃ] ADJ acoustic; **~e Signale** *(Comput)* sounds ADV acoustically; **rein ~ ist die Stereoanlage prima** the acoustics of that stereo are fantastic; **etw ~ verbessern** to improve the acoustics of sth; **ich habe dich rein ~ nicht verstanden** I simply didn't catch what you said (properly)

akut [a'ku:t] ADJ *(Med, fig)* acute; *Frage auch* pressing, urgent ADV acutely; **~ auftretende Krankheiten** acute illnesses; **ihr Zustand ist ~ lebensgefährlich** her condition is listed as critical

Akut [a'ku:t] M **-(e)s, -e** acute (accent)

Akut|kran|ken|haus NT acute hospital

AKW [a:ka:'ve:] NT **-s, -s** *abbr von* **Atomkraftwerk**

Ak|zent [ak'tsɛnt] M **-(e)s, -e** *(= Zeichen, Aussprache)* accent; *(= Betonung auch)* stress; *(fig auch)* emphasis, stress; **mit ~/französischem ~ sprechen** to speak with an accent/a French accent; **den ~ auf etw** *(acc)* **legen** *(lit)* to stress sth, to put the stress *or* accent on sth; *(fig auch)* to emphasize sth; **dieses Jahr liegen die (modischen) ~e bei …** this year the accent *or* emphasis is on …; **~e setzen** *(fig) (= Wichtiges hervorheben)* to bring out *or* emphasize the main points *or* features; *(= Hinweise geben)* to give the main points; **dieses Jahr hat neue ~e gesetzt** this year has seen the introduction of new trends

Ak|zent-: **Ak|zent|buch|sta|be** M accented letter; **ak|zent|frei** ADJ, ADV without any *or* an accent

ak|zen|tu|ie|ren [aktsɛntu'i:rən] *ptp* **akzentuiert** VT to articulate, to enunciate; *(= betonen)* to stress; *(fig: = hervorheben)* to accentuate

Ak|zent|ver|schie|bung F *(Ling)* stress shift; *(fig)* shift of emphasis

Ak|zept [ak'tsɛpt] NT **-(e)s, -e** *(Comm)* acceptance

ak|zep|ta|bel [aktsɛp'ta:bl] ADJ acceptable

Ak|zep|tanz [aktsɛp'tants] F **-,** *no pl* acceptance; **unsere Produkte haben keine ~ auf dem deutschen Markt** our products have not been accepted by the German market; **um die ~ unserer Produkte zu erhöhen** to make our products more acceptable

ak|zep|tier|bar ADJ acceptable

ak|zep|tie|ren [aktsɛp'ti:rən] ✪ 38.1, 39.1 *ptp* **akzeptiert** VT to accept

Ak|zep|tie|rung F **-, -en** acceptance

Ak|zi|dens ['aktsidɛns] NT **-, Akzidenzien** [-'dɛntsiən] *(Philos)* accident; *(Mus)* accidental

ak|zi|den|tell [aktsidɛn'tɛl], **ak|zi|den|ti|ell** [aktsidɛn'tsiɛl] ADJ accidental

Ak|zi|denz [aktsi'dɛnts] F **-, -en** *(Typ)* job; **~en** job printing

Ak|zi|denz-: **Ak|zi|denz|druck** M *pl* **-drucke** job printing; **Ak|zi|denz|dru|cke|rei** F jobbing printer's

AL [a:'lɛl] F **-, -s** *abbr von* **Alternative Liste**

à la [a la] ADV à la

alaaf [a'la:f] INTERJ *(dial)* **Kölle ~!** up Cologne! *(used in carnival procession)*

Ala|bas|ter [ala'bastɐ] M **-s, -** **a** alabaster **b** *(dial: = Murmel)* marble

Alarm [a'larm] M **-(e)s, -e** *(= Warnung)* alarm; *(= Fliegeralarm)* air-raid warning; *(= Zustand)* alert; **bei ~** following an alarm/air-raid warning; *(während Alarm)* during an alert; **~!** fire!/air raid! *etc*; **~ schlagen** to give *or* raise *or* sound the alarm

Alarm-: **Alarm|an|la|ge** F alarm system; **alarm|be|reit** ADJ on the alert; *Feuerwehr, Polizei auch* standing by; **sich ~ halten** to be on the alert/standing by; **Alarm|be|reit|schaft** F alert; **erhöhte ~** high alert; **in ~ sein** *or* **stehen** to be on the alert; *(Feuerwehr, Polizei auch)* to be standing by; **in ~ versetzen** to put on the alert; **Alarm|glo|cke** F alarm bell

alar|mie|ren [alar'mi:rən] *ptp* **alarmiert** VT *Polizei etc* to alert; *(fig: = beunruhigen)* to alarm; **~d** *(fig)* alarming; **aufs höchste** *or* **Höchste alarmiert** *(fig)* highly alarmed

Alarm-: **Alarm|ruf** M, **Alarm|schrei** M warning cry; **Alarm|sig|nal** NT alarm signal; **Alarm|stu|fe** F alert stage; **Alarm|übung** F practice exercise *or* drill; **Alarm|vor|rich|tung** F alarm; **Alarm|zu|stand** M alert; **im ~ sein** to be on the alert

Alas|ka [a'laska] NT **-s** Alaska

Alaun [a'laun] M **-s, -e** alum

Alaun|stein M, **Alaun|stift** M styptic pencil

Alb [alp] F **-,** *no pl (Geog)* mountain region

Alb M **-(e)s, -e** [-bə] *(old: = Nachtmahr) demon believed to cause nightmares (fig geh: = Bedrückung)* nightmare; **ihn drückte der ~** *(old)* he had a nightmare; **jdm wie ein ~ auf der Brust liegen** *(fig geh)* **wie ein ~ auf jdm lasten** *(fig geh)* to lie *or* weigh heavily (up)on sb

Alb M **-(e)s, -en** [-bn] *(Myth)* elf

Al|ba|ner [al'ba:nɐ] M **-s, -, Al|ba|ne|rin** [-ərɪn] F **-, -nen** Albanian

Al|ba|ni|en [al'ba:niən] NT **-s** Albania

al|ba|nisch [al'ba:nɪʃ] ADJ Albanian

Al|bat|ros ['albatrɔs] M **-, -se** albatross

Alb|druck M *pl* **-drücke** *(lit, fig)* nightmare; **wie ein ~ auf jdm lasten** to weigh sb down

Al|be ['albə] F **-, -n** *(Eccl)* alb

Al|ben *pl von* **Album**

Al|be|rei [albə'rai] F **-, -en** silliness; *(= das Spaßmachen)* fooling about *(Brit) or* around; *(= Tat)* silly prank; *(= Bemerkung)* inanity

al|bern ['albɐn] ADJ silly, stupid, foolish; *(inf: = lächerlich)* stupid, silly, ridiculous; **~es Zeug** (silly) nonsense ADV *klingen* silly; **sich ~ benehmen** to act silly; *(= Quatsch machen)* to fool about *(Brit) or* around; **~ fragen** to ask a silly question VI to fool about *(Brit) or* around; **ich weiß, ich bin unwiderstehlich, alberte er** I know I'm irresistible, he said jokingly

Al|bern|heit F **-, -en** **a** *no pl (= albernes Wesen)* silliness, foolishness; *(= Lächerlichkeit)* ridiculousness **b** *(= Tat)* silly prank; *(= Bemerkung)* inanity

Al|bi|nis|mus [albi'nɪsmʊs] M **-,** *no pl* albinism, albinoism

Al|bi|no [al'bi:no] M **-s, -s** albino

Al|bi|on ['albiɔn] NT **-s** *(liter)* Albion *(poet)*

Alb|traum M *(lit, fig)* nightmare

alb|traum|ar|tig ADJ nightmarish

Al|bum ['album] NT **-s, Alben** ['albn] album

Al|bu|min [albu'mi:n] NT **-s, -e** albumen

Al|che|mie [alçe'mi:] F *(esp Aus)*, **Al|chi|mie** [alçi'mi:] F **-,** *no pl* alchemy

Al|che|mist [alçe'mɪst] M **-en, -en, Al|che|mis|tin** [-'mɪstɪn] F **-, -nen** *(esp Aus)*, **Al|chi|mist** [alçi'mɪst] M **-en, -en, Al|chi|mis|tin** [-'mɪstɪn] F **-, -nen** alchemist

al|che|mis|tisch [alçe'mɪstɪʃ] *(esp Aus)*, **al|chi|mis|tisch** [alçi'mɪstɪʃ] ADJ alchemic(al)

Al|co|mat® M **-, -** ≈ Breathalyzer®

al den|te [al 'dɛntə] ADJ al dente

Ale|man|ne [alə'manə] M **-n, -n, Ale|man|nin** [-'manɪn] F **-, -nen** Alemannic

ale|man|nisch [alə'manɪʃ] ADJ Alemannic

alert [a'lɛrt] ADJ *(geh)* vivacious, lively

Ale|u|ten [ale'u:tn] PL *(Geog)* **die ~** the Aleutians

Ale|xand|ria [alɛ'ksandria, alɛksan'dri:a] F **-, Ale|xand|ri|en** [alɛ'ksandriən] NT **-s** Alexandria

Ale|xand|ri|ner [alɛksan'dri:nɐ] M **-s, -** *(Poet)* alexandrine

Ale|xand|rit [alɛksan'dri:t] M **-s, -e** alexandrite

Al|ge ['algə] F **-, -n** alga

Al|geb|ra ['algebra] F **-,** *no pl* algebra

al|geb|ra|isch [alge'bra:ɪʃ] ADJ algebraic(al)

Al|gen-: **Al|gen|blü|te** F algae *or* algal bloom; **Al|gen|pest** F algae plague; **Al|gen|tep|pich** M algae slick

Al|ge|ri|en [al'ge:riən] NT **-s** Algeria

Al|ge|ri|er [al'ge:riɐ] M **-s, -**, **Al|ge|ri|e|rin** [-iərɪn] F **-, -nen** Algerian

al|ge|risch [al'ge:rɪʃ] ADJ Algerian

Al|gier ['alʒi:ɐ] NT **-s** Algiers

AL|GOL [al'go:l, 'algo:l] NT **-(s)**, *no pl (Comput)* Algol

al|go|rith|misch [algo'rɪtmɪʃ] ADJ algorithmic

Al|go|rith|mus [algo'rɪtmʊs] M **-, Algorithmen** [-mən] algorithm

Ali ['a:li] M **-s, -s** *(pej sl: = Araber)* wog *(Brit pej sl)*, Arab

ali|as ['a:lias] ADV alias, also *or* otherwise known as

Ali|bi ['a:libi] NT **-s, -s** *(Jur, fig)* alibi

Ali|bi-: **Ali|bi|be|weis** M evidence to support one's alibi; **Ali|bi|frau** F token woman; **Ali|bi|funk|ti|on** F *(fig)* **~ haben** to be used as an alibi

Ali|men|te [ali'mɛntə] PL maintenance *sing*

ali|men|tie|ren [alimɛn'ti:rən] *ptp* **alimentiert** VT *(geh)* to maintain, to support

Alk [alk] M **-(e)s, -en** *(Orn)* auk

Alk M **-(e)s**, *no pl (sl: = Alkohol)* booze *(inf)*

Al|ka|li [al'ka:li, 'alkali] NT **-s, Alkalien** [-'ka:liən] alkali; **mit ~ düngen** to fertilize with an alkali

al|ka|lisch [al'ka:lɪʃ] ADJ alkaline

Al|ka|lo|id [alkalo'i:t] NT **-(e)s, -e** [-də] alkaloid

Al|ki ['alki] M **-s, -s**, **Al|kie** M **-s, -s** *(sl: = Alkoholiker)* alky *(inf)*, alkie *(inf)*

Al|ko|hol ['alkoho:l, alko'ho:l] M **-s, -e** alcohol; *(= alkoholische Getränke auch)* drink; **seinen Kummer im ~ ertränken** to drown one's sorrows; **unter ~ stehen** to be under the influence (of alcohol *or* drink)

Al|ko|hol-: **al|ko|hol|ab|hän|gig** ADJ alcohol-dependent; **~ sein** to be an alcoholic; **al|ko|hol|arm** ADJ low in alcohol (content); **~es Bier** low-alcohol beer; **Al|ko|hol|aus|schank** M sale of alcohol(ic drinks); **Al|ko|hol|ein|fluss** M, **Al|ko|hol|ein|wir|kung** F influence of alcohol *or* drink; **unter ~** under the influence of alcohol *or* drink; **Al|ko|hol|fah|ne** F *(inf)* smell of alcohol; **eine ~ haben** to smell of alcohol *or* drink; **al|ko|hol|frei** ADJ *Bier* alcohol-free, nonalcoholic; *Getränk auch* soft; *Gegend, Stadt* dry; **~es Bier** nonalcoholic *or* alcohol-free beer; **ein ~er Tag** a day without drink *or* alcohol; **Al|ko|hol|geg|ner(in)** M(F) opponent of alcohol; *(selbst abstinent)* teetotaller *(Brit)*, teetotaler *(US)*; *(= Befürworter des Alkoholverbots)* prohibitionist; **Al|ko|hol|ge|halt** M alcohol(ic) content; **Al|ko|hol|ge|nuss** M consumption of alcohol; **al|ko|hol|hal|tig** ADJ alcoholic, containing alcohol

Al|ko|ho|li|ka [alko'ho:lika] PL alcoholic drinks *pl*, liquor *sing*

Al|ko|ho|li|ker [alko'ho:likɐ] M **-s, -**, **Al|ko|ho|li|ke|rin** [-ərɪn] F **-, -nen** alcoholic

al|ko|ho|lisch [alko'ho:lɪʃ] ADJ alcoholic

al|ko|ho|li|siert [alkoholi'zi:ɐt] ADJ *(= betrunken)* inebriated; **in ~em Zustand** in a state of inebriation; **leicht/stark ~** slightly/extremely inebriated

Al|ko|ho|lis|mus [alkoho'lɪsmʊs] M **-**, *no pl* alcoholism

Al|ko|hol-: **Al|ko|hol|kon|sum** [-kɔnzu:m] M consumption of alcohol; **Al|ko|hol|kon|trol|le** F roadside breath test; **al|ko|hol|krank** ADJ alcoholic; **Al|ko|hol|miss|brauch** M alcohol abuse; **Al|ko|hol|pe|gel** M *(hum)*, **Al|ko|hol|spie|gel** M **jds ~** *or* **Alkoholspiegel** the level of alcohol in sb's blood; **Al|ko|hol|steu|er** F duty *or* tax on alcohol; **Al|ko|hol|sucht** F alcohol addiction, alcoholism; **al|ko|hol|süch|tig** ADJ addicted to alcohol, suffering from alcoholism; **Al|ko|hol|süch|ti|ge(r)** MF *decl as adj* alcoholic; **Al|ko|hol|sün|der(in)** M(F) *(inf)* drunk(en) driver; **Al|ko|hol|test** M breath test; **Al|ko|hol|test|ge|rät** NT Breathalyzer®, drunkometer *(US hum)*; **Al|ko|hol|ver|bot** NT ban on alcohol; **der Arzt hat ihm ~ verordnet** the doctor told him not to touch alcohol; **Al|ko|hol|ver|gif|tung** F alcohol(ic) poisoning

Al|ko|ven [al'ko:vn, 'alko:vn] M **-s, -** alcove

all [al] INDEF PRON **~ das/mein ...** *etc* all the/my *etc* → **alle(r, s)**

All [al] NT **-s**, *no pl (Sci, Space)* space *no art*; *(außerhalb unseres Sternsystems)* outer space; *(liter, geh)* universe; **Spaziergang im ~** space walk, walk in space; **das weite ~** the immense universe

all-: **all|abend|lich** ADJ (which takes place) every evening; **der ~e Spaziergang** the regular evening walk ADV every evening; **all|be|kannt** ADJ known to all *or* everybody, universally known; **all|dem** [al'de:m] PRON = **alledem**; **all|die|weil** [aldi:'vail] *(old, hum)* ADV *(= währenddessen)* all the while CONJ *(= weil)* because

al|le ['alə] PRON → **alle(r, s)** ADV *(inf)* all gone; **die Milch ist ~** the milk's all gone, there's no milk left; **etw/jdn ~ machen** *(inf)* to finish sth/sb off; **ich bin ganz ~** I'm all in; **~ werden** to be finished; *(Vorräte auch)* to run out

al|le|dem [alə'de:m] PRON **bei/trotz** *etc* **~** with/in spite of *etc* all that; **von ~ stimmt kein Wort** there's no truth in any of that *or* it; **zu ~** moreover

Al|lee [a'le:] F **-, -n** [-'le:ən] avenue

Al|le|go|rie [alego'ri:] F **-, -n** [-'ri:ən] allegory

Al|le|go|rik [ale'go:rɪk] F **-**, *no pl* allegory; **in der griechischen ~** in Greek allegory

al|le|go|risch [ale'go:rɪʃ] ADJ allegorical ADV allegorically

Al|leg|ret|to [ale'grɛto] NT **-s, -s** *or* **Allegretti** [-ti] allegretto

Al|leg|ro [a'le:gro] NT **-s, -s** *or* **Allegri** [-gri] allegro

al|lein [a'lain] ADJ *pred (esp inf: auch* **alleine***)* alone; *(= Gegenstand, Wort auch* by itself, on its own; *(= ohne Gesellschaft, Begleitung, Hilfe auch)* by oneself, on one's own; *(= einsam)* lonely, lonesome; **für sich ~** by oneself, on one's own, alone; **sie waren endlich ~** they were alone (together) at last, they were on their own at last; **von ~** by oneself/itself; **ich tue es schon von ~e** I'll do that in any case; **das weiß ich von ~(e)** you don't have to tell me (that); **ganz ~** *(= einsam)* quite *or* all alone; *(= ohne Begleitung, Hilfe)* all by oneself, all on one's own; **jdm ganz ~ gehören** to belong to sb alone, to belong completely to sb; **auf sich** *(acc)* **~ angewiesen sein** to be left to cope on one's own, to be left to one's own devices

ADV *(= nur)* alone; **das ist ~ seine Verantwortung** that is his responsibility alone, that is exclusively *or* solely his responsibility; **nicht ~, ... sondern auch** not only ... but also; **~ schon der Gedanke, (schon) der Gedanke ~ ...** the very *or* mere thought ..., the thought alone ...; **das Porto ~ kostet ...** the postage alone costs ..., just the postage is ...; **~ erziehend** = **alleinerziehend**; **~ Erziehende(r)** = **Alleinerziehende(r)**; **die ~ selig machende Kirche** the one *or* only true church; **der ~ selig machende Glauben** the one *or* only true faith; **er betrachtet seine Lehre als die ~ selig machende** he considers his doctrine to be the only true one; **~ stehend** → **alleinstehend**; **~ Stehende(r)** → **Alleinstehende(r)**

CONJ *(old: = jedoch)* however, but

Al|lein-: **Al|lein|er|be** M, **Al|lein|er|bin** F sole *or* only heir; **al|lein|er|zie|hend** ADJ *(Mutter, Vater)* single, unmarried ADV; **Al|lein|er|zie|hen|de(r)** [-lɛɐtsi:əndə] MF *decl as adj* single parent; **Al|lein|flug** M solo flight; **im ~** solo; **Al|lein|gang** M *pl* **-gänge** *(inf) (Sport)* solo run; *(von Bergsteiger)* solo climb; *(fig: = Tat)* solo effort; **etw im ~ machen** *(fig)* to do sth on one's own; **die Möglichkeit eines ~s** the possibility of going it alone

Al|lein|heit F **-**, *no pl (Philos)* (universal) unity *or* oneness

Al|lein-: **Al|lein|herr|schaft** F autocratic rule, absolute dictatorship; *(fig)* monopoly; **Al|lein|herr|scher(in)** M(F) autocrat, absolute dictator; **der ~ in der Familie sein** *(fig)* to reign supreme in the family

al|lei|nig [a'lainɪç] ADJ *attr* sole, only; *(Aus, S Ger) (= allein stehend)* single; *(= ohne Begleitung)* unaccompanied; **die ~e Führung übernehmen** to go alone into the lead

Al|lein-: **Al|lein|sein** NT being on one's own *no def art*, solitude; *(= Einsamkeit)* loneliness; **al|lein|se|lig|ma|chend** △ ADJ → **allein** ADV; **al|lein|ste|hend** ADJ living on one's own, living alone; **Al|lein|ste|hen|de(r)** [-ʃte:əndə] MF *decl as adj* single person; **Al|lein|un|ter|hal|ter(in)** M(F) solo entertainer; **Al|lein|un|ter|mie|te** F *(Aus)* subletting *(where main tenant lives elsewhere)*; **in ~ wohnen** ≈ to live in a furnished flat *(Brit) or* apartment; **Al|lein|ver|die|ner(in)** M(F) sole (wage) earner; **Al|lein|ver|kauf** M sole *or* exclusive right of sale (*+gen, von* for); **Al|lein|ver|tre|ter(in)** M(F) *(Comm)* sole agent; **Al|lein|ver|tre|tung** F *(Comm)* sole agency; *(Pol)* sole representation; **Al|lein|ver|tre|tungs|an|spruch** M *(Pol)* claim to sole representation; **Al|lein|ver|trieb** M sole *or* exclusive marketing *or* distribution rights *pl*

al|le|lu|ja [ale'lu:ja] INTERJ halleluja(h)

al|le|mal ['alə'ma:l] ADV every *or* each time; *(= ohne Schwierigkeit)* without any problem *or* trouble; **was er kann, kann ich noch ~** anything he can do I can do too; **~!** no problem *or* trouble! *(inf)* → **Mal**

al|len|falls ['alən'fals, 'alənfals] ADV *(= nötigenfalls)* if need be, should the need arise; *(= höchstens)* at most, at the outside; *(= bestenfalls)* at best; **es waren ~ 40 Leute da** there were at most 40 people there, there were 40 people there at the outside; **das schaffen wir ~ in 3 Stunden/bis übermorgen** we'll do it in 3 hours/by the day after tomorrow at best

al|lent|hal|ben ['alənt'halbn] ADV *(liter)* everywhere, on all sides

al|ler- ['alɐ] *in cpds with superl (zur Verstärkung)* by far; **das Allergrößte** by far the biggest, the biggest by far; **die Allerhübscheste** by far the prettiest, the prettiest by far

al|le(r, s) ['alə] ✪ 50.1, 50.3, 51.3, 53.4 INDEF PRON **a** *attr* all; *(bestimmte Menge, Anzahl)* all the; *(auf eine Person bezüglich: = all sein) Geld, Liebe, Freunde, Erfahrungen* all one's; **~ Kinder unter 10 Jahren** all children under 10; **~ Kinder dieser Stadt** all the children in this town; **die Eltern fuhren mit ~n Kindern weg** the parents went off with all their children; **~s Brot wird gebacken** all bread is baked; **im Geschäft war ~s Brot ausverkauft** all the bread in the shop was sold out; **~ meine Kinder** all (of) my children; **wir haben ~n Hass vergessen** we have forgotten all (our *or* the) hatred; **~ Anwesenden/Beteiligten/Betroffenen** all those present/taking part/affected; **~s erforderliche Material** all the required material; **mit ~m Nachdruck** with every emphasis; **trotz ~r Mühe** in spite of every effort; **ohne ~n Grund** without any reason, with no reason at all; **mit ~r Deutlichkeit** quite distinctly; **ohne ~n Zweifel** without any doubt → *auch* **all**

b alles SING *(substantivisch)* everything; *(inf: = alle Menschen)* everybody, everyone; **~s, was ...** all *or* everything that ...; everybody *or* everyone who ...; **das ~s** all that; **~s Schöne** everything beautiful, all that is beautiful; **„alles für das Baby/den Heimwerker"** "everything for (the) baby/the handyman"; **(ich wünsche dir) ~s Gute** (I wish you) all the best; **~s und jedes** anything and everything; **in ~m** *(= in jeder Beziehung)* in everything; **~s in ~m** all in all; **trotz ~m** in spite of everything; **über ~s** above all else; *(= mehr als alles andere)* more than anything else; **vor**

~m above all; **das ist ~s, das wäre ~s** that's all, that's it *(inf)*; **das ist ~s andere als ...** that's anything but ...; **er ist ~s, nur kein Vertreter** he's anything but a salesman; **das ist mir ~s gleich** it's all the same to me; **was soll das ~s?** what's all this supposed to mean?; **~s schon mal da gewesen!** *(inf)* it's all been done before!; **es hat ~s keinen Sinn mehr** nothing makes sense any more, it has all become meaningless; **was habt ihr ~s gemacht?** what did you get up to?; **wer war ~s da?** who was there?; **was er (nicht) ~s weiß/kann!** the things he knows/can do!; **was es nicht ~s gibt!** well (now) I've seen everything!, well I never *(inf)*

c alle PL *(substantivisch)* all; *(= alle Menschen auch)* everybody, everyone; **sie sind ~ alt** they're all old; **die haben mir ~ nicht gefallen** I didn't like any of them; **ich habe (sie) ~ verschenkt** I've given them all away, I've given all of them away; **~ beide** both of them; **~ drei** all three of them; **~ drei/diejenigen, die ...** all three/(those) who ...; **diese ~** all (of) these; **der Kampf ~r gegen ~** the free-for-all; **~ für einen und einer für ~!** all for one and one for all; **sie kamen ~** they all came, all of them came; **sie haben ~ kein Geld mehr** none of them has any money left; **redet nicht ~ auf einmal!** don't all talk at once! *(mit Zeit-, Maßangaben) usu pl* every; **~ fünf Minuten/halbe Stunde/fünf Meilen** every five minutes/half-hour/five miles; **~ Jahre wieder** year after year

ADV → **alle**

al|ler|al|ler- ['alɐ'alɐ] *in cpds with superl (inf: zur Verstärkung)* far and away; **das Allerallergrößte** far and away the biggest; **die Allerallerhübscheste** far and away the prettiest

al|ler-: **al|ler|art** ['alɐ'la:ɐt] ADJ *attr inv (dated)* all sorts *or* kinds of; **al|ler|bes|te(r, s)** ['alɐ'bɛstə] ADJ very best, best of all, best ... of all; *(= exquisit) Waren, Qualität* very best; **ich wünsche Dir das Allerbeste** (I wish you) all the best; **der/die/das Allerbeste** the very best, the best of all; **es ist das ~** *or* **am ~n, zu .../wenn ...** the best thing would be to .../if ...; **al|ler|dings** ['alɐ'dɪŋs] ADV **a** *(einschränkend)* though, mind you; **ich komme mit, ich muss ~ erst zur Bank** I'm coming but I must go to the bank first though, I'm coming though I must go to the bank first; **das ist ~ wahr, aber ...** that may be true, but ..., (al)though that's true ... **b** *(bekräftigend)* certainly; **~!** (most) certainly!; **al|ler|ers|te(r, s)** ['alɐ'le:ɐstə] ADJ very first; **al|ler|frü|hes|tens** ['alɐ'fry:əstns] ADV at the very earliest

Al|ler|gen [alɛr'ge:n] NT **-s, -e** *(Med)* allergen

Al|ler|gie [alɛr'gi:] F **-, -n** [-'gi:ən] *(Med)* allergy; *(fig)* aversion *(gegen* to); **eine ~ gegen etw haben** to be allergic to sth *(auch fig hum)*; *(fig auch)* to have an aversion to sth

Al|ler|gie-: **al|ler|gie|an|fäl|lig** ADJ allergy-prone; **al|ler|gie|ge|prüft, al|ler|gie|ge|tes|tet** ADJ allergy-tested; **Al|ler|gie|pass** M *(Med)* allergy ID; **Al|ler|gie|schock** M *(Med)* anaphylactic shock; **Al|ler|gie|symp|tom** NT allergy symptom; **Al|ler|gie|test** M *(Med)* allergy test

Al|ler|gi|ker [a'lɛrgikɐ] M **-s, -, Al|ler|gi|ke|rin** [-ərɪn] F **-, -nen** person suffering from an allergy

al|ler|gisch [a'lɛrgɪʃ] ADJ *(Med, fig)* allergic *(gegen* to) ADV **auf etw** *(acc)* **~ reagieren** to have an allergic reaction to sth; *(fig)* to react oversensitively to sth; **~ bedingt sein** to be caused by an allergy

Al|ler|go|lo|ge [alɛrgo'lo:gə] M **-n, -n, Al|ler|go|lo|gin** [-'lo:gɪn] F **-, -nen** allergist

Al|ler|go|lo|gie [alɛrgolo'gi:] F **-,** *no pl (Med)* allergology

Al|ler-: **al|ler|hand** ['alɐ'hant] ADJ *inv (substantivisch) (= allerlei)* all kinds of things; *(= ziemlich viel)* rather a lot; *(attributiv)* all kinds *or* sorts of, rather a lot of; **das ist ~!** *(zustimmend)* that's quite something!, not bad at all! *(inf)*; **das ist ja** *or* **doch ~!** *(empört)* that's too much!, that's the limit!; **Al|ler|hei|li|gen** ['alɐ'hailɪgn] NT **-s** All Saints' Day, All Hallows (Day) *(Brit)*

> **ALLERHEILIGEN**
>
> **Allerheiligen** (All Saints' Day, celebrated on November 1st) is a holiday in Catholic areas of Germany and in Austria. The following day, November 2nd, is **Allerseelen** (All Souls' Day) when the dead are commemorated. On these days people traditionally visit cemeteries and place flowers, wreaths and lighted candles on the graves of loved ones. In Alpine regions children go from house to house asking for **Seelenwecken** (bread rolls). In the Protestant Church **Totensonntag** falls on the last Sunday before Advent and is devoted to the remembrance of the dead.

Al|ler-: **Al|ler|hei|ligs|te(s)** ['alɐ'hailɪgstə] NT *decl as adj (Rel: = Raum)* inner sanctum; *(jüdisch, fig)* Holy of Holies; *(katholisch)* Blessed Sacrament; **al|ler|höchs|tens** ['alɐ'hø:çstns] ADV at the very most; **al|ler|höchs|te(r, s)** ['alɐ'hø:çstə] ADJ *Berg etc* highest of all, highest ... of all, very highest; *Betrag, Belastung, Geschwindigkeit* maximum; *Funktionäre* highest, top *attr*; *Instanz, Kreise* very highest; **es wird ~ Zeit, dass ...** it's really high time that ...; **al|ler|lei** ['alɐ'lai] ADJ *inv (substantivisch)* all sorts *or* kinds of things; *(attributiv)* all sorts *or* kinds of; **Al|ler|lei** ['alɐ'lai] NT **-s,** *no pl (= Durcheinander)* farrago, potpourri, welter; **Leipziger ~** *(Cook)* Leipzig mixed vegetables *pl*; **al|ler|letz|te(r, s)** ['alɐ'lɛtstə] ADJ very last; *(= allerneueste)* very latest; *(inf: = unmöglich)* most awful *attr (inf)*; **in ~r Zeit** very recently; **der/die/das Allerletzte** the very last (person)/thing; **der/das ist (ja) das Allerletzte** *(inf)* he's/it's the absolute end! *(inf)*; **al|ler|liebst** ['alɐ'li:pst] ADJ *(old: = reizend)* enchanting, delightful; **al|ler|liebs|te(r, s)** ['alɐ'li:pstə] ADJ *(= Lieblings-)* most favourite *attr (Brit) or* favorite *attr (US)*; **sie ist mir die Allerliebste** she's my absolute favourite *(Brit) or* favorite *(US)*; **es wäre mir das Allerliebste** *or* **am ~n, wenn ...** I would much prefer it if ...; **am ~n geh ich ins Kino** I like going to the cinema most *or* best of all; **Al|ler|liebs|te(r)** ['alɐ'li:pstə] MF *decl as adj (old, hum)* beloved, love of one's life; *(Frau auch)* ladylove; **al|ler|meis|te(r, s)** ['alɐ'maistə] ADJ most of all, most ... of all; *(= weitaus beste)* by far the most; **am ~n** most of all; **die Allermeisten** the vast majority; **al|ler|nächs|te(r, s)** ['alɐ'nɛ:çstə] ADJ *(in Folge)* very next; *(räumlich)* nearest of all; *Verwandte* very closest; *Route* very shortest; **in ~r Nähe** right nearby, right close by; **in ~r Zeit** *or* **Zukunft** in the very near future; **al|ler|neu|es|te(r, s)** ['alɐ'nɔyəstə], **al|ler|neus|te(r, s)** ['alɐ'nɔystə] ADJ very latest; **al|ler|or|ten** ['alɐ'lɔrtn], **al|ler|orts** ['alɐ'lɔrts] ADV *(old)* everywhere; **Al|ler|see|len** [alɐ'ze:lən] NT **-s** All Souls' Day; **al|ler|seits** ['alɐ'zaits] ADV on all sides, on every side; **guten Abend ~!** good evening everybody *or* everyone *or* all; **vielen Dank ~** thank you all *or* everybody *or* everyone; **al|ler|spä|tes|tens** ['alɐ'ʃpɛ:təstns] ADV at the very latest

Al|ler|welts- *in cpds (= Durchschnitts-)* ordinary; *(= nichtssagend)* commonplace, general; **Al|ler|welts|kerl** M jack of all trades; **Al|ler|welts|the|ma** NT general subject; **Al|ler|welts|typ** M *(= Mann)* ordinary *or* average guy *(inf)*; *(= Frau)* ordinary *or* average woman

Al|ler-: **al|ler|we|nigs|tens** ['alɐ've:nɪçstns] ADV at the very least; **al|ler|we|nigs|te(r, s)** ['alɐ've:nɪçstə] ADJ least of all, least ... of all; *(pl)* fewest of all, fewest ... of all; *(= äußerst wenig)* very little; *(pl)* very few; *(= geringste) Mühe* least possible; **die ~n Menschen wissen das** very (very) few people know that; **das ist noch das Allerwenigste!** that's the very least of it; **das ist doch das Allerwenigste, was man erwarten könnte** but that's the very least one could expect; **er hat von uns allen das ~** *or* **am ~n Geld** he has the least money of any of us; **sie hat von uns allen die ~n** *or* **am ~n Sorgen** she has the fewest worries of any of us; **das am ~n!** least of all that!; **Al|ler|wer|tes|te(r)** ['alɐ've:ɐtəstə] M *decl as adj (hum)* posterior *(hum)*

al|les ['aləs] INDEF PRON → **alle(r, s) b**

al|le|samt ['alə'zamt] ADV all (of them/us *etc*), to a man; **ihr seid ~ Betrüger!** you're all cheats!, you're cheats, all of you *or* the lot of you!

Al|les-: **Al|les|fres|ser** M omnivore; **Al|les|kle|ber** M all-purpose adhesive *or* glue; **Al|les|schnei|der** M food-slicer; **Al|les|wis|ser** [-vɪsɐ] M **-s, -, Al|les|wis|se|rin** [-ərɪn] F **-, -nen** *(iro)* know-all *(Brit inf)*, know-it-all *(US inf)*

al|le|we|ge ['alə've:gə] ADV *(old)* everywhere

al|le|zeit ['alə'tsait] ADV *(liter)* = **allzeit**

All-: **all|fäl|lig** ['alfɛlɪç, al'fɛlɪç] *(Aus, Sw)* ADJ possible ADV *(= eventuell)* possibly; **All|ge|gen|wart** [al'ge:gnvart] F omnipresence, ubiquity; **all|ge|gen|wär|tig** [al'ge:gnvɛrtɪç] ADJ omnipresent, ubiquitous; **All|ge|gen|wär|tig|keit** F omnipresence, ubiquity

all|ge|mein ['algə'main] ADJ general; *Ablehnung, Zustimmung auch* common; *Feiertag* public; *Regelungen, Wahlrecht* universal; *Wehrpflicht* compulsory; *(= öffentlich)* public, general; **im Allgemeinen** in general, generally; **im ~en Interesse** in the common interest, in the public interest; **von ~em Interesse** of general interest; **~e Redensarten** *(= idiomatische Ausdrücke)* set expressions; *(= Phrasen)* commonplaces; **auf ~en Wunsch** by popular *or* general request; **die ~e Meinung** the general opinion, the generally held opinion, public opinion; **das ~e Wohl** the common good, (the) public welfare, the public good; **~es Aufsehen erregen** to cause *or* create a sensation; **die Diskussion darüber wurde ~** a general discussion developed; **wir sind ganz ~ geblieben** *(inf)* we stayed on a general level; **das Allgemeine und das Besondere** the general and the particular

ADV *(= überall, bei allen, von allen)* generally; *(= ausnahmslos von allen)* universally; *(= generell)* generally, in the main, for the most part; *(= nicht spezifisch)* in general terms; **seine Thesen sind so ~ abgefasst, dass ...** his theses are worded in such general terms that ...; **du kannst doch nicht so ~ behaupten, dass ...** you can't make such a generalization and say that ..., you can't generalize like that and say that ...; **seine Thesen sind so ~ abgefasst, dass ...** his theses are worded in such general terms that ...; **du kannst doch nicht so ~ behaupten, dass ...** you can't make such a generalization and say that ..., you can't generalize like that and say that ...; **es ist ~ bekannt** it's common knowledge; **~ bildend = allgemeinbildend**; **~ gültig = allgemeingültig**; **es ist ~ üblich, etw zu tun** it's the general rule that we/they *etc* do sth, it's commonly *or* generally the practice to do sth; **~ verbindlich** generally binding; **~ verständlich** *(adjektivisch)* generally intelligible, intelligible to all; *(adverbial)* in a way intelligible to all; **etw ~ verständlich ausdrücken** to express sth in a way which everyone can understand; **~ verbreitet** widespread; **~ zugänglich** open to all, open to the general public

All|ge|mein-: **All|ge|mein|arzt** M, **All|ge|mein|ärz|tin** F *(Med)* ≈ general practitioner, ≈ GP, ≈ family practitioner *(US)*; **All|ge|mein|be|fin|den** NT general condition, general state of being; **all|ge|mein|bil|dend** ADJ providing (a) general *or* (an) all-round *(Brit)* education; *Studium auch* with general educational value; **All|ge|mein|bil|dung** F general *or* all-round *(Brit)* education; **all|ge|mein|gül|tig** ADJ *attr* general, universal, universally *or* generally applicable *or* valid; **All|ge|mein|gül|tig|keit** F universal *or* general validity, universality; **All|ge|mein|gut** NT, *no pl (fig)* common property; **All|ge|mein|heit** F -, -en a *no pl (= Öffentlichkeit)* general public, public at large; *(= alle)* everyone, everybody b *(= Unbestimmtheit)* generality; **~en** generalities; **All|ge|mein|kran|ken|haus** NT *(Med)* general hospital; **All|ge|mein|me|di|zin** F general medicine; **Arzt für ~** general practitioner, GP; **All|ge|mein|me|di|zi|ner(in)** M(F) *(Med)* ≈ general practitioner, ≈ GP, ≈ family practitioner *(US)*; **All|ge|mein|platz** M *(pej)* commonplace, platitude; **all|ge|mein|ver|bind|lich** ADJ → **allgemein** ADV; **all|ge|mein|ver|ständ|lich** ADJ ADV → **allgemein** ADV; **All|ge|mein|ver|ständ|lich|keit** F general intelligibility; **All|ge|mein|wis|sen** NT general knowledge; **All|ge|mein|wohl** NT public good *or* welfare; **All|ge|mein|zu|stand** M general condition; *(= Lage)* general situation; *(= Gesundheit)* general wellbeing *or* health

All-: **All|ge|walt** ['algəvalt] F *(liter)* omnipotence; **all|ge|wal|tig** ['algəvaltɪç] ADJ omnipotent, all-powerful; **All|heil|mit|tel** [al'hailmɪtl] NT universal remedy, cure-all, panacea *(esp fig)*; **all|hier** [al'hiːɐ] ADV *(obs, liter)* here

Al|li|anz [a'liants] F -, -en a alliance b *(= NATO)* Alliance

Al|li|anz|part|ner(in) M(F) partner in the alliance; *(bei NATO)* partner in NATO, NATO partner

Al|li|ga|tor [ali'gaːtoːɐ] M -s, **Alligatoren** [-'toːrən] alligator

al|li|ie|ren [ali'iːrən] *ptp* **alliiert** VR *(geh)* to form an alliance; **sich mit jdm ~** to ally (oneself) with sb

al|li|iert [ali'iːɐt] ADJ *attr* allied; *(im 2. Weltkrieg)* Allied

Al|li|ier|te(r) [ali'iːɐtə] MF *decl as adj* ally; **die ~n** *(im 2. Weltkrieg)* the Allies

Al|li|te|ra|ti|on [alɪtera'tsioːn] F -, -en *(Poet)* alliteration

al|li|te|rie|rend [alɪte'riːrənt] ADJ *(Poet)* alliterative

allj. *abbr von* **alljährlich**

All-: **all|jähr|lich** [al'jɛːɐlɪç] ADJ annual, yearly ADV annually, yearly, every year; **All|macht** ['almaxt] F *(esp von Gott)* omnipotence; *(von Konzern etc)* all-pervading power; **all|mäch|tig** [al'mɛçtɪç] ADJ all-powerful, omnipotent; *Gott auch* almighty; **All|mäch|ti|ge(r)** [al'mɛçtɪgə] M *decl as adj (= Gott)* **der ~** Almighty God, God (the) Almighty, the Almighty; **~r!** good Lord!, heavens above!

all|mäh|lich [al'mɛːlɪç] ADJ *attr* gradual ADV gradually; *(= schrittweise auch)* bit by bit, step by step; *(inf: = endlich)* at last; **es wird ~ Zeit** *(inf)* it's about time; **~ verstand er, dass ...** it gradually dawned on him that ..., he realized gradually that ...; **ich werde (ganz) ~ müde** *(inf)* I'm beginning to get tired; **wir sollten ~ gehen** *(inf)* shall we think about going?

All|men|de [al'mɛndə] F -, -n common land

All-: **all|mo|nat|lich** [al'moːnatlɪç] ADJ monthly ADV every month, monthly; **all|mor|gend|lich** [al'mɔrgntlɪç] ADJ which takes place every morning; **die ~e Eile** the regular morning rush ADV every morning; **All|mut|ter** ['almʊtɐ] F, *no pl (liter)* Mother of all; **die ~ Natur** Mother Nature; **all|nächt|lich** [al'nɛçtlɪç] ADJ nightly ADV nightly, every night

Al|lo|fon NT = **Allophon**

Al|lo|path [alo'paːt] M -en, -en, **Al|lo|pa|thin** [-tɪn] F -, -nen allopath

Al|lo|pa|thie [alopa'tiː] F -, *no pl* allopathy

Al|lo|phon [alo'foːn] NT -s, -e *(Ling)* allophone

Al|lot|ria [a'loːtria] NT -(s), *no pl (inf) (= Unfug)* monkey business *(inf) no indef art*; *(ausgelassen, freudig)* skylarking *(inf) no indef art*, fooling about *(Brit) or* around *no indef art*; *(= Lärm)* racket *(inf)*, din; **~ treiben** *(inf)* to lark about *(inf)*, to fool about *(Brit) or* around

All|par|tei|en|ge|sprä|che ['alpar'taiən-] PL *(Pol)* all-party talks *pl*

All|par|tei|en|re|gie|rung F *(Pol)* all-party government

All|rad|an|trieb ['alraːt-] M *(Aut)* four-wheel drive; **Auto mit ~** four-by-four

All|rad|len|kung F *(Aut)* four-wheel steering

All|round- ['ɔːl'raund] *in cpds* all-round *(Brit)*, all-around *(US)*

All|roun|der[1] ['ɔːlraundɐ] M -s, - *(= Gerät)* all-rounder *(Brit)*, versatile device

All|roun|der[2] ['ɔːlraundɐ] M, **All|roun|de|rin** [-ərɪn] F -, -nen all-rounder *(Brit)*, multi-talent *(US)*

All|round-: **All|round|ge|nie** NT *(iro)* all-round *(Brit) or* all-around *(US)* genius; **All|round|sport|ler(in)** M(F) all-rounder *(Brit)*, multi-talent *(US)*

all|sei|tig ['alzaitɪç] ADJ *(= allgemein)* general; *(= ausnahmslos)* universal; *(= vielseitig)* all-round *attr (Brit)*, all-around *attr (US)*; **zur ~en Zufriedenheit** to the satisfaction of all *or* everyone ADV **~ begabt sein** to have all-round *(Brit) or* all-around *(US)* talents, to be an all-rounder *(Brit) or* a multi-talent *(US)*; **jdn ~ ausbilden** to provide sb with a general *or* an all-round *(Brit)* education; **er wurde ~ informiert** he was informed about every (possible) area; **~ interessiert sein** to be interested in everything

all|seits ['alzaits] ADV *(= überall)* everywhere, on all sides; *(= in jeder Beziehung)* in every respect; **~ beliebt/unbeliebt** popular/unpopular with everyone, universally popular/unpopular

All|strom-: **All|strom|emp|fän|ger** M *(Rad)* all-mains *(esp Brit) or* AC-DC receiver; **All|strom|ge|rät** NT *(Rad)* all-mains *(esp Brit) or* AC-DC appliance

All|tag ['altaːk] M a *(= Werktag)* weekday; **am ~, an ~en** on weekdays; **Kleidung, die man am ~ trägt** clothes for everyday wear; **mitten im ~** in the middle of the week b *(fig)* everyday life; **im ~** in everyday life; **der ~ der Ehe** the mundane side of married life

all|täg|lich [al'tɛːklɪç, 'altɛːklɪç, al'tɛːklɪç] ADJ a *(= tagtäglich)* daily b *(= üblich)* everyday *attr*, ordinary, mundane *(pej)*; *Gesicht, Mensch* ordinary; *Bemerkung* commonplace; **es ist ganz ~** it's nothing unusual, it's nothing out of the ordinary; **das ist nichts Alltägliches, dass/wenn ...** it doesn't happen every day that ..., it's not every day that ...; **was ich suche, ist nicht das Alltägliche** I'm looking for something a bit out of the ordinary

All|täg|lich|keit F -, -en a *no pl* ordinariness b *(= Gemeinplatz)* commonplace

all|tags ['altaːks] ADV on weekdays; **etw ~ tragen** to wear sth for every day

All|tags- *in cpds* everyday; **All|tags|ehe** F mundane marriage; **All|tags|klei|dung** F everyday clothes *pl*, everday wear *no pl*; **All|tags|kram** M *(inf)* everyday *or* day-to-day stuff *(inf)*; **All|tags|le|ben** NT everyday life; **danach begann wieder das ~** after that life got back to normal again; **All|tags|mensch** M ordinary person; **All|tags|rhyth|mus** M daily rhythm; **All|tags|sor|gen** PL everyday *or* day-to-day worries *pl or* cares *pl*; **All|tags|trott** M *(inf)* daily round, treadmill of everyday life

all|über|all ['ally:bɐ'lal] ADV *(old, poet)* everywhere

all|um|fas|send ['allʊm'fasnt] ADJ all-embracing

Al|lü|ren [a'lyːrən] PL behaviour *(Brit)*, behavior *(US)*; *(= geziertes Verhalten)* affectations *pl*; *(eines Stars etc)* airs and graces *pl*

Al|lu|vi|um [a'luːviʊm] NT -s, *no pl* diluvial *or* Holocene epoch

All-: **all|wis|send** ['alvɪsnt] ADJ omniscient; **(Gott,) der Allwissende** God the Omniscient; **ich bin nicht ~!** I don't know everything!, I'm not omniscient!; **All|wis|sen|heit** ['alvɪsnhait] F -, *no pl* omniscience; **all|wö|chent|lich** [al'vœçntlɪç] ADJ weekly ADV every week; **all|zeit** ['altsait] ADV *(geh)* always; **~ bereit!** be prepared!

all|zu ['altsuː] ADV all too; *(+neg)* too; **~ viele Fehler** far too many mistakes; **nur ~** only *or* all too; **~ früh** far too early; *(+neg)* too early; **~ gern** *(mögen)* only too much; *(= bereitwillig)* only too willingly; *(+neg)* all that much, too much; all that willingly, too willingly; **etw (nur) ~ gern machen** to like doing sth only too much; **etw nicht ~ gern machen** not to like doing sth all that much *or* too much *or* overmuch; **er isst Muscheln nur ~ gern** he's only too fond of mussels; **~ sehr** too much; *mögen* all too much; *(+neg)* too much, all that much, overmuch; *sich freuen, erfreut sein* only too; *(+neg)* too; *versuchen* too hard; *sich ärgern, enttäuscht sein* too; **sie war ~ sehr/nicht ~ sehr in ihn verliebt** she was too much in love with him/wasn't in love with him all that much; **~ viel** too much; **~ viel ist ungesund** *(Prov)* you can have too much of a good thing *(prov)*

All|zweck- *in cpds* general purpose; **All|zweck|hal|le** F multipurpose hall; **All|zweck|rei|ni|ger** M all-purpose cleaner

Alm [alm] F -, -en alpine pasture

Alm|ab|trieb M *driving cattle down from the alpine pastures*

Al|ma Ma|ter ['alma 'maːtɐ] F - -, *no pl* alma mater

Al|ma|nach ['almanax] M -s, -e almanac

Alm-: **Alm|auf|trieb** M *driving cattle up to the alpine pastures*; **Alm|hüt|te** F alpine hut

Al|mo|sen ['almoːzn] NT -s, - a *(geh: = Spende)* alms *pl (old)* b *(= geringer Lohn)* pittance c **Almosen** PL *(fig)* charity

Alm|rausch M, **Alm|ro|se** F Alpine rose *or* rhododendron

Aloe ['aːloe] F -, -n ['aːloən] aloe

alo|gisch ['aloːgɪʃ, a'loːgɪʃ] ADJ *(geh)* illogical

Alp[1] [alp] F -, -en *(= Alm)* alpine pasture

Alp[2] △ M -(e)s, -e *(old: = Nachtmahr)* → **Alb**

Al|pa|ka [al'paka] NT -s, -s a *(= Lamaart)* alpaca b *no pl (auch* **Alpakawolle***)* alpaca (wool) c *no pl (= Neusilber)* German *or* nickel silver

Alp|druck M *pl* **-drücke** *(lit, fig)* nightmare; **wie ein ~ auf jdm lasten** to weigh sb down

Al|pen ['alpn] PL Alps *pl*

Al|pen- *in cpds* alpine; **Al|pen|dol|lar** M *(Hist: hum)* Austrian schilling; **Al|pen|glü|hen** NT -s, - alpenglow; **Al|pen|jä|ger(in)** M(F) *(Mil)* mountain infantryman/-woman PL mountain troops *pl or* infantry; **Al|pen|ket|te** F alpine chain; **Al|pen|land** NT alpine country; **al|pen|län|disch** [-lɛndɪʃ] ADJ *Literatur, Kulturgut etc* of the alpine region; *Mensch* from the alpine region; **Al|pen|pass** M alpine pass; **Al|pen|re|pub|lik** F **die ~** *(hum)* Austria; **Al|pen|ro|se** F Alpine rose *or* rhododendron; **Al|pen|rot** NT, *no pl* red snow; **Al|pen|veil|chen** NT cyclamen; **Al|pen|vor|land** NT foothills *pl* of the Alps

alph. *abbr von* **alphabetisch**

Al|pha ['alfa] NT -(s), -s alpha

Al|pha|bet[1] [alfa'beːt] NT -(e)s, -e alphabet; **nach dem ~** alphabetically, in alphabetical order; **das ~ lernen/aufsagen** to learn/say the *or* one's alphabet

Al|pha|bet[2] [alfa'beːt] M -en, -en, **Al|pha|be|tin** [-'beːtɪn] F -, -nen literate person

al|pha|be|tisch [alfa'beːtɪʃ] ADJ alphabetical ADV alphabetically, in alphabetical order

al|pha|be|ti|sie|ren [alfabeti'ziːrən] *ptp* **alphabetisiert** VT to make literate

Al|pha|be|ti|sie|rung F -, -en **ein Programm zur ~ Indiens** a programme *(Brit) or* program *(US)* against illiteracy in India; **die ~ Kubas ist abgeschlossen** the population of Cuba is now largely literate

Al|pha-: **al|pha|nu|me|risch** [alfanu'meːrɪʃ] ADJ alphanumeric ADV alphanumerically; **Al|pha|strah|len** PL alpha rays *pl*; **Al|pha|teil|chen** NT alpha particle

Alp-: **Alp|horn** NT alp(en)horn; **Alp|hüt|te** F alpine hut

al|pin [al'pi:n] ADJ alpine *(auch Ski)*

Al|pi|nis|mus [alpi'nɪsmʊs] M -, *no pl* alpinism

Al|pi|nist [alpi'nɪst] M **-en, -en, Al|pi|nis|tin** [-'nɪstɪn] F **-, -nen** alpinist

Al|pi|nis|tik [alpi'nɪstɪk] F -, *no pl* alpinism

Älp|ler ['ɛlplɐ] M **-s, -, Älp|le|rin** [-ərɪn] F **-, -nen** inhabitant of the Alps

älp|le|risch ['ɛlplərɪʃ] ADJ *Kleidung, Dialekt* of the alpine region

Alp-: **Alp|traum** M *(lit, fig)* nightmare; **alp|traum|ar|tig** ADJ nightmarish

Al|raun [al'raun] M **-(e)s, -e, Al|rau|ne** [al'raunə] F **-, -n** mandrake

als [als] CONJ **a** *(nach comp)* than; **ich kam später ~ er** I came later than he (did) *or* him; **Hans ist größer ~ sein Bruder** Hans is taller than his brother; **mehr ~ arbeiten kann ich nicht** I can't do more than work
b *(bei Vergleichen)* **so … ~ …** as … as …; **so viel/so weit ~ möglich** as much/far as possible; **~ wie** as; **nichts/niemand/nirgend anders ~** nothing/nobody/nowhere but; **eher** *or* **lieber … ~** rather … than; **ich würde eher sterben ~ das zu tun** I would rather die than do that, I would die rather than do that; **anders sein ~** to be different from; **das machen wir anders ~ ihr** we do it differently to you; **alles andere ~** anything but
c *(in Modalsätzen)* as if *or* though; **es sieht aus, ~ würde es bald schneien** it looks as if *or* though it will snow soon; **sie sah aus, ~ ob** *or* **wenn sie schliefe** she looked as if *or* though she were asleep; **~ ob ich das nicht wüsste!** as if I didn't know! → *auch* **ob**
d *(in Aufzählung)* **~ (da sind) …** that is to say …, to wit … *(old, form)*
e *(in Konsekutivsätzen)* **sie ist zu alt, ~ dass sie das noch verstehen könnte** she is too old to understand that; **die Zeit war zu knapp, ~ dass wir …** the time was too short for us to …; **das ist umso trauriger, ~ es nicht das erste Mal war** that's all the sadder in that it wasn't the first time
f *(in Temporalsätzen)* when; *(= gleichzeitig)* as; **gleich, ~** as soon as; **damals, ~** (in the days) when; **gerade, ~** just as
g *(= in der Eigenschaft)* as; **~ Beweis** as proof; **~ Antwort/Warnung** as an answer/a warning; **sich ~ wahr/falsch erweisen** to prove to be true/false; **~ Held/Revolutionär** as a hero/revolutionary; **~ Kind/Mädchen** *etc* as a child/girl *etc*; **~ Rentner will er ein Buch schreiben** when he retires he is going to write a book → **sowohl, insofern**
ADV *(dial inf) (= immer)* **etw ~ (noch mal) tun** to keep on (and on) doing sth; **gehen Sie ~ geradeaus** keep going straight ahead

als-: **als|bald** [als'balt] ADV *(old, liter)* directly, straightway *(old)*; **als|bal|dig** [als'baldɪç] ADJ *(form)* immediate; **„zum ~en Verbrauch bestimmt"** "do not keep", "for immediate use only"; **als|dann** [als'dan] ADV **a** *(old liter. = dann)* then **b** *(dial)* well then, well … then

al|so ['alzo] CONJ **a** *(= folglich)* so, therefore; **er war Künstler, ein hochsensibler Mensch ~** he was an artist, (and) therefore a highly sensitive person
b *(old: = so, folgendermaßen)* thus
ADV so; *(nach Unterbrechung anknüpfend)* well; *(zusammenfassend, erklärend)* that is; **~ doch** so … after all; **du machst es ~?** so you'll do it then?; **~ wie ich schon sagte** well (then), as I said before
INTERJ *(verwundert, entrüstet, auffordernd)* well; *(drohend)* just; **~, dass du dich ordentlich benimmst!** (you) just see that you behave yourself!; **~ doch!** so he/they *etc* did!; **na ~!** there you are!, you see?; **~, ich habs doch gewusst!** I knew it!; **~ nein!** (oh) no!; **~ nein, dass sie sich das gefallen lässt** my God, she can't put up with that!; **~ gut** *or* **schön** well all right then; **~ dann!** right then!; **~ so was!** well (I never)!; **~ so eine Frechheit!** what impudence!

Als|ter|was|ser ['alstɐ-] NT *pl* **-wässer** *(N Ger)* shandy *(Brit)*, radler *(US)*, beer and lemonade

alt [alt] ADJ *comp* **=er** ['ɛltɐ], *superl* **=este(r, s)** ['ɛltəstə] **a** old; *(= sehr alt) Mythos, Sage, Aberglaube, Griechen, Geschichte* ancient; *Sprachen* classical; **das ~e Rom** ancient Rome; **das Alte Testament** the Old Testament; **die Alte Welt** the Old World; **mein ~er Herr** *(inf: = Vater)* the *or* one's old man *(inf)*; **~er Junge** *or* **Freund** old boy *(dated) or* fellow *(dated)*; **Alt und Jung** (everybody) old and young; **ein drei Jahre ~es Kind** a three-year-old child, a child of three years of age; **wie ~ bist du?** how old are you?; **etw ~ kaufen** to buy sth second-hand; **man ist so ~, wie man sich fühlt** you're only as old as you feel; **~ und grau werden** to grow old and grey *(Brit) or* gray *(US)*; **ich werde heute nicht ~ (werden)** *(inf)* I won't last long tonight *(inf)*; **hier werde ich nicht ~** *(inf)* this isn't my scene *(inf)*; **aus Alt mach Neu** *(inf)* make do and mend *(Prov)* → **Eisen, Hase**
b *(= dieselbe, gewohnt)* same old; **sie ist ganz die ~e Ingrid** *or* **die Alte** she's the same old Ingrid, she hasn't changed a bit; **jetzt ist sie wieder ganz die ~e lustige Veronika** she's the old happy Veronika again; **wir bleiben die Alten, auch wenn sich alle andern verändern** we stay the same even when everybody else changes; **er ist nicht mehr der Alte** he's not what he was, he's not the man he was; **es ist nicht mehr das ~e Glasgow** it's not the (same old) Glasgow I/we *etc* knew; **alles bleibt beim Alten** everything stays as it was; **alles beim Alten lassen** to leave everything as it was
c *(= lange bestehend)* old; **in ~er Freundschaft, dein …** yours as ever …
d ~ aussehen *(inf: = dumm dastehen)* to look stupid

Alt [alt] M **-s, -e** *(Mus)* alto; *(von Frau auch)* contralto; *(Gesamtheit der Stimmen)* altos *pl*, contraltos *pl*

Alt NT **-s, -** *(= Bier) top-fermented German dark beer*

Al|tan [al'ta:n] M **-(e)s, -e** balcony

alt-: **alt|an|ge|se|hen** ADJ *Familie* old and respected; *Firma* old-established; **alt|an|ge|ses|sen** ['alt'langəzesn], **alt|an|säs|sig** ADJ old-established

Al|tar [al'ta:ɐ] M **-s, Altäre** [-'tɛ:rə] altar; **eine Frau zum ~ führen** to lead a woman to the altar

Al|tar- *in cpds* altar; **Al|tar|bild** NT altarpiece, reredos; **Al|tar|ge|mäl|de** NT altarpiece; **Al|tar|ge|rät** NT altar furniture; **Al|tar|raum** M chancel; **Al|tar|schmuck** M altar decoration(s *pl*); **Al|tar|stu|fen** PL altar steps *pl*; **Al|tar|tuch** NT altar cloth, vesperal; **Al|tar|wein** M Communion wine

Alt-: **Alt|au|to** NT old car *(ready to be scrapped or recycled)*; **~-Recycling** recycling of old cars; **alt|ba|cken** [-bakn] ADJ **a** stale **b** *(fig) Mensch, Kleidung* old-fashioned; *Ansichten* outdated, old-fashioned; **Alt|bat|te|rie** F used battery; **Alt|bau** M *pl* **-bauten** old building; **Alt|bau|mo|der|ni|sie|rung** F modernization of an old building; **Alt|bau|sa|nie|rung** F refurbishment (of old buildings); **Alt|bau|woh|nung** F flat *(Brit) or* apartment in an old building; **alt|be|kannt** ADJ well-known; **alt|be|währt** ADJ *Mittel, Methode etc* well-tried; *Sitte, Tradition, Freundschaft etc* long-standing *usu attr*, of long standing; **Alt|bier** NT *top-fermented German dark beer*; **Alt|bun|des|kanz|ler(in)** M(F) former German/Austrian Chancellor; **Alt|bun|des|land** NT **die Altbundesländer** the former West German states, the states which formed the old West Germany; **Alt|bür|ger(in)** M(F) senior citizen; **alt|christ|lich** ADJ early Christian; **alt|deutsch** ADJ old German; *Möbel, Stil* German Renaissance

Al|te ['altə] F *decl as adj (= alte Frau, inf: = Ehefrau, Mutter)* old woman; *(inf: = Vorgesetzte)* boss → *auch* **Alte(r)**

Alt-: **alt|ehr|wür|dig** ADJ venerable; *Bräuche* time-honoured *(Brit)*, time-honored *(US)*; **Alt|ei|gen|tü|mer(in)** M(F) *(von Land, Gebäude)* original owner; **alt|ein|ge|führt** ['alt'laingəfy:ɐt] ADJ *Brauch, Firma, Arzneimittel* old-established; **alt|ein|ge|ses|sen** ['alt'laingəzesn] ADJ = **altangesessen**; **Alt|ei|sen** NT scrap metal; **alt|eng|lisch** ADJ old English; **Alt|eng|lisch(e)** NT Old English, Anglo-Saxon

Al|ten-: **al|ten|ge|recht** ADJ suitable for old *or* older people; **Al|ten|heim** NT old people's home; **Al|ten|herr|schaft** F gerontocracy; **Al|ten|hil|fe** F old people's welfare; **Al|ten|nach|mit|tag** M senior citizens' afternoon *or* club; **Al|ten|pfle|ge** F care *(for the elderly)*; **Al|ten|pfle|ge|heim** NT nursing home for the elderly; **Al|ten|pfle|ger(in)** M(F) old people's nurse; **Al|ten|ta|ges|stät|te** F old people's day centre *(Brit) or* center *(US)*; **Al|ten|teil** NT *cottage or part of a farm reserved for the farmer when he hands the estate over to his son* **sich aufs ~ setzen** *or* **zurückziehen** *(fig)* to retire *or* withdraw from public life; **Al|ten|treff** M senior citizens' club; **Al|ten|wohn|heim** NT sheltered housing complex (for the elderly); **sie lebt in einem ~** she lives in sheltered housing

Al|te(r) ['altə] M *decl as adj (= alter Mann, inf: = Ehemann, Vater)* old man; *(inf: = Vorgesetzter)* boss; **die ~n** *(= Eltern)* the folk(s) *pl (inf)*; *(= Tiereltern)* the parents *pl*; *(= ältere Generation)* the old people *pl or* folk *pl*; *(aus klassischer Zeit)* the ancients *pl*; **wie die ~n sungen, so zwitschern auch die Jungen** *(prov)* like father like son *(prov)*; **komischer ~r** *(Theat)* comic old man

äl|ter ['ɛltɐ] ADJ **a** *comp von* **alt** older; *Bruder, Tochter etc auch* elder; **werden Frauen ~ als Männer?** do women live longer than men? **b** *attr (= nicht ganz jung)* elderly; **die ~en Herrschaften** the older members of the party

Al|ter ['altɐ] NT **-s, -** age; *(= letzter Lebensabschnitt, hohes Alter)* old age; **im ~** in one's old age; **im ~ wird man weiser** one grows wiser with age; **in deinem ~** at your age; **er ist in deinem ~** he's your age; **im ~ von 18 Jahren** at the age of 18; **von mittlerem ~, mittleren ~s** middle-aged; **57 ist doch kein ~, um in Rente zu gehen** 57 is no age to retire; **er hat keinen Respekt vor dem ~** he has no respect for his elders; **~ schützt vor Torheit nicht** *(Prov)* there's no fool like an old fool *(Prov)*

Al|ter|chen ['altɐçən] NT **-s, -** *(inf)* Grandad *(inf)*

Al|ter Ego ['altɐ 'e:go, - 'ɛgo] NT **-**, *no pl (esp Psych)* alter ego

Äl|te|re(r) ['ɛltərə] MF *decl as adj* **a** *(= älterer Mensch)* older man/woman *etc*; **die ~n** the older ones **b** *(bei Namen)* Elder; **Holbein der ~** Holbein the Elder

al|ter|fah|ren ADJ very experienced, of long experience

al|tern ['altɐn] VI *aux sein or (rare) haben* to age; *(Mensch auch)* to get older; *(Wein)* to mature; **vorzeitig ~** to grow old before one's time; **~d** ageing VT to age; *Wein* to mature; *Metall* to age-harden

al|ter|na|tiv [altɛrna'ti:f] ADJ alternative; **Alternative Liste** *(Pol) electoral pact of alternative political groupings* ADV **~ leben** to live an alternative lifestyle; **~ vorgehen** to find an alternative; **~ eingestellt sein** to have alternative political views

Al|ter|na|tiv- *in cpds* alternative; **Al|ter|na|tiv|be|we|gung** F alternative *or* fringe movement

Al|ter|na|ti|ve [altɛrna'ti:və] F **-n, -n** alternative *(etw zu tun* of doing sth)

Al|ter|na|tiv|ener|gie F alternative energy

Al|ter|na|ti|ve(r) [altɛrna'ti:və] MF *decl as adj (Pol) person with alternative views (= alternativ lebender Mensch)* proponent of the alternative society; **die ~n** those who favour *(Brit)* or favor *(US)* the alternative society

Al|ter|na|tiv-: **Al|ter|na|tiv|kost** F biological foods *pl*; *(= Diät)* alternative diet; **Al|ter|na|tiv|kul|tur** F counter-culture, alternative culture; **al|ter|na|tiv|los** ADV with no alternative; **~ sein** to be the only alternative; **diese Politik ist nicht ~** there are alternatives to this policy; **Al|ter|na|tiv|me|di|zin** F alternative medicine; **Al|ter|na|tiv|pro|gramm** NT alternative programme *(Brit)* or program *(US)*; **Al|ter|na|tiv|sze|ne** F **die ~** alternative society, the fringe

al|ter|nie|ren [altɛr'niːrən] *ptp* **alterniert** VI to alternate

al|ter|nie|rend ADJ alternate; *Strom, Verse* alternating; *Fieber* intermittent

Al|terns|for|scher(in) ['altɐns-] M(F) gerontologist

Al|terns|for|schung F gerontology

alt|er|probt ['altlɛɐ'proːpt] ADJ well-tried

al|ters ['altɐs] ADV *(geh)* **von** or **seit ~ (her)** from time immemorial; **vor ~** in olden days or times, in days of yore *(old, liter)*

Al|ters-: **Al|ters|ab|stand** M age difference; **Al|ters|ar|mut** F poverty among old people; **Al|ters|asyl** NT *(Sw)* old people's home; **Al|ters|auf|bau** M *(Sociol)* age structure; **al|ters|be|dingt** ADJ age-related; **Al|ters|be|gren|zung** F age limit; **ohne ~** without age limit; **Al|ters|be|schwer|den** PL complaints *pl* of old age, geriatric complaints *pl*; **Al|ters|dis|kri|mi|nie|rung** F ageism; **Al|ters|durch|schnitt** M average age; **Al|ters|er|schei|nung** F sign of old age; **Al|ters|fleck** M age mark, blotch; **Al|ters|for|scher(in)** M(F) gerontologist; **Al|ters|for|schung** F gerontology; **Al|ters|für|sor|ge** F care of the elderly; **al|ters|ge|mäß** ADJ *Benehmen, Entwicklung* appropriate to one's/its age; **Al|ters|ge|nos|se** M, **Al|ters|ge|nos|sin** F contemporary; *(Kind)* child of the same age; *(Psych, Sociol)* peer; **wir sind ja ~n** we are the same age; **al|ters|ge|recht** ADJ suitable for one's/its age; **Al|ters|glie|de|rung** F age structure; **Al|ters|gren|ze** F age limit; *(= Rentenalter)* retirement age; **flexible ~** flexible retirement age; **Al|ters|grün|de** PL **aus ~n** for reasons of age; **Al|ters|grup|pe** F age group; **al|ters|hal|ber** ADV because of or on account of one's age; **Al|ters|heil|kun|de** F *(Med)* geriatrics *sing*; **Al|ters|heim** NT old people's home; **Al|ters|klas|se** F *(Sport)* age group; **Al|ters|krank|heit** F geriatric illness; **Al|ters|lei|den** NT complaint or infirmity of old age; **al|ters|los** ADJ ageless; **Al|ters|prä|si|dent(in)** M(F) president by seniority; **Al|ters|pro|zess** M ageing process; **Al|ters|py|ra|mi|de** F age pyramid or diagram; **Al|ters|ren|te** F old age pension; **Al|ters|ru|he|geld** NT retirement benefit; **al|ters|schwach** ADJ *Mensch* old and infirm; *Tier* old and weak; *Auto, Möbel etc* decrepit; **Al|ters|schwä|che** F *(von Mensch)* infirmity *(due to advancing years)*; *(von Tier)* weakness *(due to old age)*; *(hum: von Auto, Möbel etc)* decrepitude; **Al|ters|schwach|sinn** M senility; **al|ters|sich|tig** [-zɪçtɪç] ADJ presbyopic *(spec)*; **Al|ters|sich|tig|keit** F presbyopia *(spec)*; **Al|ters|sitz** M **sein ~ war München** he spent his retirement in Munich; **Al|ters|so|zio|lo|gie** F sociology of old age; **al|ters|spe|zi|fisch** ADJ age-specific; **Al|ters|sport** M sport for the elderly; **Al|ters|starr|sinn** M senile stubbornness; **Al|ters|struk|tur** F *(Sociol)* age structure; **Al|ters|stu|fe** F age group; *(= Lebensabschnitt)* age, stage in life; **Al|ters|teil|zeit** F semi-retirement, partial retirement; **in ~ gehen** to go into semi-retirement or partial retirement, to switch to part-time working *(when approaching retirement)*; **Al|ters|un|ter|schied** M age difference, difference in age; **Al|ters|ver|si|che|rung** F retirement insurance; **Al|ters|ver|sor|gung** F provision for (one's) old age; **betriebliche ~** ≈ company pension scheme; **Al|ters|vor|sor|ge** F old-age provision; **Al|ters|werk** NT later works *pl*; **Al|ters|weit|sich|tig|keit** F presbyopia *(spec)*; **Al|ters|zu|la|ge** F increment for age

Al|ter|tum ['altɐtuːm] NT **-s**, *no pl* antiquity *no art*; **das deutsche ~** early German history

Al|ter|tü|me|lei [altɐtyːmə'lai] F **-, -en** antiquarianism

al|ter|tü|meln ['altɐtyːmln] VI to antiquarianize

Al|ter|tü|mer ['altɐtyːmɐ] PL antiquities *pl*

al|ter|tüm|lich ['altɐtyːmlɪç] ADJ *(= aus dem Altertum)* ancient; *(= veraltet)* antiquated

Al|ter|tums-: **Al|ter|tums|for|scher(in)** M(F) archeologist; **Al|ter|tums|for|schung** F archeology, archeological research; **Al|ter|tums|kun|de** F archeology; **Al|ter|tums|wert** M **das hat schon ~** *(hum)* it has antique value *(hum)*

Al|te|rung ['altərʊŋ] F **-**, *no pl (= das Altern)* ageing; *(von Wein)* maturation; *(von Metall)* age hardening

Al|te|rungs|pro|zess M ageing process

Al|te(s) ['altə] NT *decl as adj* **das ~** *(= das Gewohnte, Traditionelle)* the old; *(= alte Dinge)* old things *pl*; **er hängt sehr am ~n** he clings to the past; **das ~ und das Neue** the old and the new, old and new; **sie hat Freude an allem ~n** she gets a lot of pleasure from anything old

Äl|tes|ten|rat M council of elders; *(Ger Pol)* parliamentary advisory committee, ≈ think--tank *(Brit)*

Äl|tes|te(r) ['ɛltəstə] MF *decl as adj* oldest; *(Sohn, Tochter auch)* eldest; *(Eccl)* elder

äl|tes|te(r, s) ['ɛltəstə] ADJ *superl von* **alt** oldest; *Sohn, Bruder etc auch* eldest

Alt-: **Alt|flö|te** F treble recorder; *(= Querflöte)* bass or alto flute; **alt|frän|kisch** ADJ quaint; *Stadt etc auch* olde-worlde *(inf)*; **Alt|fran|zö|sisch(e)** NT Old French; **Alt|ge|rät** NT old appliance; **ein ~ in Zahlung nehmen** to take an old appliance in part-exchange; **Alt|glas** NT, *no pl* waste glass; **Alt|glas|be|häl|ter** M, **Alt|glas|con|tai|ner** M bottle bank; **Alt|gold** NT old gold; *(= Goldart)* artificially darkened gold; **alt|grie|chisch** ADJ ancient Greek; *(Ling auch)* classical Greek; **Alt|grie|chisch(e)** NT ancient or classical Greek; **alt|her|ge|bracht**, **alt|her|kömm|lich** ADJ traditional; *Tradition* long-established; **Alt|her|ren|fuß|ball** [alt'hɛrən-] M veterans' football; **Alt|her|ren|mann|schaft** F *(Sport) team of players over thirty*; **alt|hoch|deutsch** ADJ Old High German; **Alt|hoch|deutsch(e)** NT Old High German

Al|tist [al'tɪst] M **-en, -en**, **Al|tis|tin** [-'tɪstɪn] F **-, -nen** *(Mus)* alto

Alt|jahr(s)-: **Alt|jahr(s)|abend** M *(dial)* New Year's Eve, Hogmanay *(esp Scot)*; **Alt|jahr(s)|tag** M *(dial)* New Year's Eve, Hogmanay *(esp Scot)*

Alt-: **alt|jüng|fer|lich** [alt'jʏŋfɐlɪç] ADJ old-maidish, spinsterish; **Alt|kanz|ler(in)** M(F) former chancellor; **Alt|ka|tho|lik(in)** M(F) Old Catholic; **alt|ka|tho|lisch** ADJ Old Catholic; **Alt|klei|der|händ|ler(in)** M(F) second--hand clothes dealer; **Alt|klei|der|samm|lung** F collection of old clothes; **alt|klug** ADJ precocious ADV precociously; **Alt|la|ge** F *(Mus)* alto range; **Alt|last** F *usu pl (Ökologie)* dangerous waste *(accumulated over the years)*

ält|lich ['ɛltlɪç] ADJ oldish

alt+ma|chen VTI *sep* → **machen VT g, VI b**

Alt-: **Alt|ma|te|ri|al** NT scrap; **Alt|meis|ter** M doyen; *(Sport)* ex-champion; **Alt|meis|te|rin** F doyenne; *(Sport)* ex-champion; **Alt|me|tall** NT scrap metal; **alt|mo|disch** ADJ old-fashioned; *(= rückständig)* outmoded ADV **sie kleidet sich sehr ~** the way she dresses is very old-fashioned; **ihr Haus ist ~ eingerichtet** the furnishings of her house are old-fashioned; **~ klingen** to sound old-fashioned; **sie denken ~** their ideas are old-fashioned; **Alt|neu|bau** M prewar building; **Alt|öl** NT used oil; **Alt|pa|pier** NT wastepaper; **Alt|pa|pier|con|tai|ner** M (waste)paper bank; **Alt|pa|pier|samm|lung** F wastepaper collection; **Alt|pa|pier|ton|ne** F paper bank; **Alt|pa|pier|ver|wer|tung** F (waste)paper recycling; **Alt|par|tie** F *(Mus)* alto part; **Alt|phi|lo|lo|ge** M, **Alt|phi|lo|lo|gin** F classical philologist; **Alt|phi|lo|lo|gie** F classical philology; **alt|phi|lo|lo|gisch** ADJ *Abteilung* of classical philology; *Bücher, Artikel* on classical philology; **alt|re|nom|miert** ADJ old-established; **alt|ro|sa** ADJ *inv* old rose

Alt|ru|is|mus [altru'ɪsmʊs] M **-**, *no pl (geh)* altruism

Alt|ru|ist [altru'ɪst] M **-en, -en**, **Alt|ru|is|tin** [-'ɪstɪn] F **-, -nen** *(geh)* altruist

alt|ru|is|tisch [altru'ɪstɪʃ] *(geh)* ADJ altruistic ADV altruistically

Alt-: **alt|säch|sisch** ADJ old Saxon; **Alt|sän|ge|rin** F contralto (singer); **Alt|schlüs|sel** M *(Mus)* alto clef; **Alt|schnee** M old snow; **Alt|sein** NT being old *no art*; **Alt|sil|ber** NT old silver; *(= Silberart)* artificially darkened silver; **Alt|sprach|ler** [-ʃpraːxlɐ] M **-s, -**, **Alt|sprach|le|rin** [-ərɪn] F **-, -nen** classicist; *(= Sprachwissenschaftler)* classical philologist; **alt|sprach|lich** ADJ *Zweig, Abteilung* classics *attr*; **~es Gymnasium** ≈ grammar school *(Brit)* or high school *(US)* teaching classical languages; **Alt|stadt** F old (part of a/the) town; **die Ulmer ~** the old part of Ulm; **Alt|stadt|sa|nie|rung** F renovation of the old part of a/the town; **Alt|stein|zeit** F Palaeolithic *(Brit)* or Paleolithic *(US)* Age, Old Stone Age; **alt|stein|zeit|lich** ADJ Palaeolithic *(Brit)*, Paleolithic *(US)*; **Alt|stim|me** F *(Mus)* alto; *(von Frau auch)* contralto, contralto voice; *(Partie)* alto/contralto part; **Alt|stoff** M *usu pl* waste material; **~e sammeln** to collect (recyclable) waste; **gefährliche ~e** dangerous waste

Alt-Tas|te F *(Comput)* Alt key

Alt-: **alt|tes|ta|men|ta|risch**, **alt|tes|ta|ment|lich** [-tɛstamɛntlɪç] ADJ Old Testament *attr*; **alt|über|kom|men**, **alt|über|lie|fert** ['altlyːbɐ'liːfɐt] ADJ traditional; **Alt|vä|ter|art** F **nach ~** in the old-fashioned way; **alt|vä|te|risch** [-fɛːtərɪʃ], **alt|vä|ter|lich** ADJ *Bräuche, Geister* ancestral; *(= altmodisch)* old-fashioned *no adv*; *Erscheinung etc* patriarchal; **Alt|vä|ter|sit|te** F **nach ~** in the old-fashioned way; **Alt|wäh|ler(in)** M(F) hardened voter; **Alt|wa|ren** PL second-hand goods *pl*; **Alt|wa|ren|händ|ler(in)** M(F) second-hand dealer

Alt|wei|ber-: **Alt|wei|ber|ge|schwätz** NT old woman's talk; **Alt|wei|ber|som|mer** M **a** *(= Nachsommer)* Indian summer **b** *(= Spinnfäden)* gossamer

Alu ['aːlu] NT **-s**, *no pl (inf: = Aluminium)* aluminium *(Brit)*, aluminum *(US)*

Alu ['aːlu] F **-**, *no pl (inf) abbr von* **Arbeitslosenunterstützung**

Alu-: **Alu|do|se** F aluminium *(Brit)* or aluminum *(US)* can, tin can; **Alu|fel|ge** F alloy wheel, alloy *(inf)*; **Alu|fo|lie** F tinfoil, kitchen foil, aluminium *(Brit)* or aluminum *(US)* foil; **in ~ verpackt** tinfoil-wrapped; **Alu|kof|fer** M aluminium *(Brit)* or aluminum *(US)* case

Alu|mi|ni|um [alu'miːniʊm] NT **-s**, *no pl (abbr* **Al**) aluminium *(Brit)*, aluminum *(US)*

Alu|mi|ni|um-: **Alu|mi|ni|um|fo|lie** F tin foil, aluminium *(Brit)* or aluminum *(US)* foil; **Alu|mi|ni|um|(staub)|lun|ge** F *(Med)* aluminosis *(form)*

Al|ve|o|lar [alveo'laːɐ] M **-s, -e** *(Phon)* alveolar (sound)

Alz|hei|mer|kran|ke(r) ['altshaimɐ-] MF *decl as adj* person/man/woman suffering from Alzheimer's (disease); *(= Patient)* Alzheimer's patient

Alz|hei|mer|krank|heit F Alzheimer's (disease)

am [am] PREP **a** *contr von* **an dem**
b *(zur Bildung des Superlativs)* **er war am tapfersten** he was (the) bravest; **sie hat es am besten/schönsten gemalt** she painted it best/(the) most beautifully; **am besten machen wir das morgen** we'd do best to do it tomorrow, the best thing would be for us to do it tomorrow; **am seltsamsten war ...** the strangest thing was ...
c *(als Zeitangabe)* on; **am letzten Sonntag** last Sunday; **am 8. Mai** on the eighth of May, on May (the *(Brit)*) eighth; *(geschrieben)* on May 8th; **am Morgen/Abend** in the morning/evening; **am Tag darauf/zuvor** (on) the following/previous day
d *(als Ortsangabe)* on the; *(bei Gebirgen)* at the foot of the → *auch* **an PREP** *+dat* **a**
e *(inf: als Verlaufsform)* **ich war gerade am Weggehen** I was just leaving
f *(Aus: = auf dem)* on the
g *(Comm)* **am Lager** in stock

Amal|gam [amal'ga:m] NT **-s, -e** amalgam

Amal|gam|fül|lung F *(Zahnmedizin)* amalgam filling

amal|ga|mie|ren [amalga'mi:rən] *ptp* **amalgamiert** VTR *(lit, fig)* to amalgamate

Ama|ryl|lis [ama'rʏlɪs] F **-, Amaryllen** [-lən] amaryllis

Ama|teur [ama'tø:ɐ] M **-s, -e, Ama|teu|rin** [ama'tø:rɪn] [-'tø:rɪn] F **-, -nen** amateur

Ama|teur- *in cpds* amateur; **Ama|teur|fil|mer(in)** M(F) amateur film-maker; **Ama|teur|funk** M amateur radio; **Ama|teur|fun|ker(in)** M(F) radio amateur *or* ham *(inf)*; **Ama|teur|sport|ler(in)** M(F) amateur sportsperson, amateur sportsman/-woman; *(bestimmte Sportart)* amateur athlete/player/runner *etc*

ama|teur|haft [ama'tø:ɐ-] ADJ amateurish ADV amateurishly

Ama|teu|rin [ama'tø:rɪn] [-'tø:rɪn] F **-, -nen** amateur

Ama|teur|li|ga [ama'tø:ɐ-] F *(Sport)* amateur league

Ama|zo|nas [ama'tso:nas] M **-** Amazon

Ama|zo|ne [ama'tso:nə] F **-, -n** **a** *(Myth)* Amazon; *(fig)* amazon **b** *(Sport)* woman showjumper

Ama|zo|ni|en [ama'tso:niən] NT **-s** Amazonia

Am|ber ['ambɐ] M **-s, -(n)** ambergris

Am|bi|en|te [am'biɛntə] NT **-,** *no pl (geh)* ambience

Am|bi|ti|on [ambi'tsio:n] F **-, -en** ambition; **~en auf etw** *(acc)* **haben** to have ambitions of getting sth

am|bi|va|lent [ambiva'lɛnt] ADJ ambivalent

Am|bi|va|lenz [ambiva'lɛnts] F **-, -en** ambivalence

Am|boss ['ambɔs] M **-es, -e** anvil; *(Anat auch)* incus

Amb|ra ['ambra] F **-, Ambren** [-brən] ambergris

Amb|ro|sia [am'bro:zia] F **-,** *no pl* ambrosia

am|bu|lant [ambu'lant] ADJ **a** *(Med: in Arztpraxis, Krankenhaus) Versorgung, Behandlung, Operation* outpatient *attr*; **~e Patienten** outpatients **b** *(= wandernd)* itinerant ADV **~ behandelt werden** *(Patient: in Praxis, Krankenhaus)* to receive outpatient treatment, to be treated as an outpatient; *(Fall)* to be treated in the outpatient department; **jdn ~ behandeln** to treat sb as an outpatient; **~ operieren/arbeiten** *or* **tätig sein** to operate on/treat outpatients

Am|bu|lanz [ambu'lants] F **-, -en** **a** *(= Klinikstation)* outpatient department, outpatients *sing (inf)* **b** *(= Ambulanzwagen)* ambulance

Am|bu|lanz-: **Am|bu|lanz|kli|nik** F outpatients clinic; **Am|bu|lanz|wa|gen** M ambulance

Amei|se ['a:maizə] F **-, -n** ant

Amei|sen-: **Amei|sen|bär** M anteater; *(größer)* ant bear, great anteater; **amei|sen|haft** ADJ antlike; *Getriebe, Fleiß etc* beaverlike; **Amei|sen|hau|fen** M anthill; **Amei|sen|säu|re** F formic acid; **Amei|sen|staat** M ant colony

amen ['a:mən] INTERJ amen → **ja a**

Amen ['a:mən] NT **-s, -** amen; **sein ~ zu etw geben** to give one's blessing to sth; **das ist so sicher wie das ~ in der Kirche** *(prov)* you can bet your bottom dollar on that *(inf)*

Ame|ri|ci|um [ame'ri:tsiʊm] NT **-s,** *no pl (abbr* **Am**) americium

Ame|ri|ka|ner [ameri'ka:nɐ] M **-s, -** *(Gebäck)* flat iced cookie

Ame|ri|ka|ner [ameri'ka:nɐ] M **-s, -, Ame|ri|ka|ne|rin** [-ərɪn] F **-, -nen** American

a|me|ri|ka|nisch [ameri'ka:nɪʃ] ADJ American

ame|ri|ka|ni|sie|ren [amerikani'zi:rən] *ptp* **amerikanisiert** VT to Americanize

Ame|ri|ka|ni|sie|rung F **-, -en** Americanization

Ame|ri|ka|nis|mus [amerika'nɪsmʊs] M **-, Amerikanismen** [-mən] Americanism

Ame|ri|ka|nist [amerika'nɪst] M **-en, -en, Ame|ri|ka|nis|tin** [-'nɪstɪn] F **-, -nen** specialist in American studies

Ame|ri|ka|nis|tik [amerika'nɪstɪk] F **-,** *no pl* American studies *pl*

Ame|thyst [ame'tʏst] M **-s, -e** amethyst

Ami ['ami] M **-s, -s** *(inf)* Yank *(inf)*; *(= Soldat)* GI *(inf)*

Ami|no|säu|re [a'mi:no-] F amino acid

Am|mann ['aman] M *pl* **-männer** *(Sw)* **a** mayor **b** *(Jur)* local magistrate

Am|me ['amə] F **-, -n** *(old)* foster mother; *(= Nährmutter)* wet nurse

Am|men|mär|chen NT fairy tale *or* story

Am|mer ['amɐ] F **-, -n** *(Orn)* bunting

Am|mo|ni|ak [amo'niak, 'amoniak] NT **-s,** *no pl* ammonia

Am|mo|nit [amo'ni:t] M **-en, -en** *(Geol)* ammonite

Am|mons|horn ['amɔns-] NT **a** *(Anat)* hippocampus major *(spec)* **b** *(Geol)* ammonite

Am|ne|sie [amne'zi:] F **-, -n** [-'zi:ən] *(Med)* amnesia

Am|nes|tie [amnɛs'ti:] F **-, -n** [-'ti:ən] amnesty

am|nes|tie|ren [amnɛs'ti:rən] *ptp* **amnestiert** VT to grant an amnesty to

Am|nio|zen|te|se [amniotsen'te:zə] F **-, -n** *(Med)* amniocentesis

Amö|be [a'mø:bə] F **-, -n** *(Biol)* amoeba

Amö|ben|ruhr F *(Med)* amoebic dysentery

Amok ['a:mɔk, a'mɔk] M **~ laufen** to run amok *(esp Brit) or* amuck; **~ fahren** to drive like a madman *or* lunatic

Amok-: **Amok|fah|rer(in)** M(F) mad *or* lunatic driver; **Amok|fahrt** F mad *or* crazy ride; **Amok|lauf** M **einen ~ aufführen** to run amok *(esp Brit) or* amuck; **Amok|läu|fer** M madman; **Amok|läu|fe|rin** F madwoman; **Amok|schüt|ze** M crazed gunman; **Amok|schüt|zin** F crazed gunwoman

Amor ['a:mo:ɐ] M **-s** Cupid

amo|ra|lisch ['amora:lɪʃ] ADJ amoral; *(= unmoralisch)* immoral

Amo|ra|li|tät [amorali'tɛ:t] F amorality; *(= Unmoral)* immorality

Amo|ret|te [amo'rɛtə] F **-, -n** little cupid, amoretto

amorph [a'mɔrf] ADJ *(geh)* amorphous

Amor|ti|sa|ti|on [amɔrtiza'tsio:n] F **-, -en** amortization

Amor|ti|sa|ti|ons|dau|er F length of amortization period

amor|ti|sie|ren [amɔrti'zi:rən] *ptp* **amortisiert** VT *(Econ)* **eine Investition ~** to ensure that an investment pays for itself VR to pay for itself

Amou|ren [a'mu:rən] PL *(old, hum)* amours *pl (old, hum)*

amou|rös [amu'rø:s] ADJ *(geh)* amorous

Am|pel ['ampl] F **-, -n** **a** *(= Verkehrsampel)* (traffic) lights *pl*; **er hat eine ~ umgefahren** he crashed into a traffic light and knocked it over; **halte an der nächsten ~** stop at the next (set of) (traffic) lights **b** *(geh)* *(= Hängelampe)* hanging lamp; *(= Hängeblumentopf)* hanging flowerpot

Am|pel-: **Am|pel|an|la|ge** F (set of) traffic lights *pl*; **Am|pel|ko|a|li|ti|on** F *(Pol inf)* coalition formed by SPD, FDP and Green Party; **Am|pel|kreu|zung** F *(inf)* junction controlled by traffic lights; **Am|pel|pha|se** F traffic light sequence; **die langen ~n an dieser Kreuzung** the length of time the lights take to change at this junction

Am|pere [am'pe:ɐ, am'pɛ:ɐ] NT **-(s), -** amp, ampere *(form)*

Am|pere-: **Am|pere|me|ter** NT ammeter; **Am|pere|se|kun|de** F ampere-second; **Am|pere|stun|de** F ampere-hour

Amp|fer ['ampfɐ] M **-s, -** *(Bot)* dock; *(= Sauerampfer)* sorrel

Am|phe|ta|min [amfeta'mi:n] NT **-s, -e** amphetamine

Am|phi|bie [am'fi:biə] F **-, -n** *(Zool)* amphibian

Am|phi|bi|en|fahr|zeug NT amphibious vehicle

am|phi|bisch [am'fi:bɪʃ] ADJ amphibious

Am|phi|the|a|ter [am'fi:-] NT amphitheatre *(Brit)*, amphitheater *(US)*

Am|pho|ra [am'fo:ra] F **-, Amphoren** [-rən] amphora

Amp|li|tu|de [ampli'tu:də] F **-, -n** *(Phys)* amplitude

Am|pul|le [am'pʊlə] F **-, -n** **a** *(= Behälter)* ampoule **b** *(Anat)* ampulla

Am|pu|ta|ti|on [amputa'tsio:n] F **-, -en** amputation

am|pu|tie|ren [ampu'ti:rən] *ptp* **amputiert** VT to amputate; **jdm den Arm ~** to amputate sb's arm; **amputiert werden** *(Mensch)* to have an amputation

am|pu|tiert ADJ *Körperteil* amputated; *(fig)* truncated

Am|pu|tier|te(r) [ampu'ti:ɐtə] MF *decl as adj* amputee

Am|sel ['amzl] F **-, -n** blackbird

Ams|ter|dam [amstɐ'dam, 'amstɐdam] NT **-s** Amsterdam

Ams|ter|da|mer [amstɐ'damɐ, 'amstɐdamɐ] ADJ *attr* Amsterdam

Ams|ter|da|mer [amstɐ'damɐ, 'amstɐdamɐ] M **-s, -, Ams|ter|da|me|rin** [-ərɪn] F **-, -nen** native of Amsterdam; *(= Einwohner)* inhabitant of Amsterdam

Amt [amt] NT **-(e)s, ¨er** ['ɛmtɐ] **a** post *(Brit)*, position; *(öffentlich)* office; **im ~ sein** to be in *or* hold office; **jdn aus einem ~ entfernen** to remove sb from office; **in ~ und Würden** in an exalted position; **von ~s wegen** *(= aufgrund von jds Beruf)* because of one's job; **kraft seines ~es** *(geh)* by virtue of one's office
b *(= Aufgabe)* duty, task; **seines ~es walten** *(geh)* to carry out *or* discharge *(form)* one's duties
c *(= Behörde) (= Fürsorgeamt)* welfare department; *(= Sozialamt)* department of social security; *(= Einwohnermeldeamt)* registration office; *(= Passamt)* passport office; *(= Finanzamt)* tax office; *(= Stadtverwaltung)* council offices *pl*; **zum zuständigen ~ gehen** to go to the relevant authority; **die Ämter der Stadt** the town authorities; **von ~s wegen** *(= auf behördliche Anordnung hin)* officially
d *(= Telefonamt)* operator; *(= Zentrale)* exchange; **geben Sie mir bitte ein ~** could you give me a line, please?

Äm|ter-: **Äm|ter|häu|fung** F accumulation of offices; **sie warfen ihm ~ vor** they accused him of holding too many offices at once; **Äm|ter|jagd** F position-hunting; **Äm|ter|kauf** M buying one's way into office; **Äm|ter|pat|ro|na|ge** F autocratic distribution of offices

am|tie|ren [am'ti:rən] *ptp* **amtiert** VI **a** *(= Amt innehaben)* to be in office; **~d** incumbent; **der ~de Bürgermeister** the (present) mayor; **der ~de Weltmeister** the reigning world champion; **als Minister/Bürgermeister ~** to hold the post *(Brit) or* position of minister/the office of mayor **b** *(= Amt vorübergehend wahrnehmen)* to act;

er amtiert als Bürgermeister he is acting mayor **c** *(= fungieren)* **als …** ~ to act as …

amtl. *abbr von* **amtlich**

amt|lich ['amtlɪç] ADJ official; *(= wichtig) Miene, Gebaren* officious; *(inf: = sicher)* certain; **~es Kennzeichen** registration (number), license number *(US)* ADV officially; **etw ~ haben** to have official confirmation of sth

amt|li|cher|seits ['amtlɪçɐzaits] ADV officially

Amt|lich|keit F -, *no pl* officialdom *no pl*

Amt|mann M *pl* **-männer** *or* **-leute, Amt|män|nin** [-mɛnɪn] F -, **-nen a** *(Admin)* senior civil servant **b** *(Jur)* local magistrate

Amts-: **Amts|adel** M *(Hist) non-hereditary nobility who were created peers because of their office*; **Amts|an|ma|ßung** F unauthorized assumption of authority; *(= Ausübung eines Amtes)* fraudulent exercise of a public office; **Amts|an|tritt** M → **Amt a** assumption of office/one's post *(Brit)* or position; **Amts|an|walt** M, **Amts|an|wäl|tin** F *prosecuting counsel in relatively minor cases*; **Amts|ap|pa|rat** M official machinery; **Amts|arzt** M, **Amts|ärz|tin** F medical officer; **amts|ärzt|lich** ADJ *Zeugnis* from the medical officer; *Untersuchung* by the medical officer ADV **~ untersucht werden** to have an official medical examination; **sich etw ~ bescheinigen lassen** to get a medical certificate for sth; **Amts|be|fug|nis** F, **Amts|be|reich** M area of competence; **Amts|be|zirk** M area of jurisdiction; **Amts|blatt** NT gazette; **Amts|bo|te** M, **Amts|bo|tin** F official messenger; **Amts|bru|der** M *(Eccl)* fellow clergyman; **Amts|dau|er** F term of office; **Amts|deutsch(e)** NT officialese; **Amts|die|ner(in)** M(F) clerk; *(= Bote)* messenger; **Amts|eid** M oath of office; **den ~ ablegen** to be sworn in, to take the oath of office; **Amts|ein|füh|rung** F, **Amts|ein|set|zung** F installation, inauguration; **Amts|ent|he|bung** [-lɛnthe:bʊŋ] F -, **-en**, *(Sw, Aus)* **Amts|ent|set|zung** [-lɛntzɛtsʊŋ] F -, **-en** dismissal *or* removal from office; **Amts|ent|he|bungs|ver|fah|ren** NT *(Jur)* impeachment trial; **Amts|er|schlei|chung** [-lɛɐʃlaiçʊŋ] F -, **-en** obtaining office by devious means; **Amts|ge|heim|nis** NT **a** *(= geheime Sache)* official secret **b** *(= Schweigepflicht)* official secrecy; **Amts|ge|richt** NT ≈ county *(Brit)* or district *(US)* court; **Amts|ge|richts|rat** M, **Amts|ge|richts|rä|tin** F ≈ county *(Brit)* or district *(US)* court judge; **Amts|ge|schäf|te** PL official duties *pl*; **Amts|ge|walt** F authority; **Amts|hal|te|tas|te** F *(am Telefon)* recall button; **amts|han|deln** VI *insep (Aus)* to take official action, to act officially; **Amts|hand|lung** F official duty; **seine erste ~ bestand darin, …** the first thing he did in office was …; **Amts|hil|fe** F cooperation between authorities; **Amts|kanz|lei** F *(Aus)* office; **Amts|ket|te** F chain of office; **Amts|kir|che** F church hierarchy; **Amts|klei|dung** F robes *pl* of office; **Amts|kol|le|ge** M, **Amts|kol|le|gin** F opposite number; **Amts|lei|tung** F *(Telec)* exchange line; **Amts|mie|ne** F official air; **seine ~ aufsetzen** to get *or* go all official *(inf)*; **Amts|miss|brauch** M abuse of one's position; **Amts|nach|fol|ger(in)** M(F) successor (in office); **Amts|nie|der|le|gung** F resignation; **Amts|pe|ri|o|de** F term of office; **Amts|per|son** F official; **Amts|pflicht** F official duty; **Amts|rich|ter(in)** M(F) ≈ county *(Brit)* or district *(US)* court judge; **Amts|schim|mel** M *(hum)* officialdom; **den ~ reiten** to do everything by the book; **der ~ wiehert** officialdom rears its ugly head; **Amts|schwes|ter** F *(Eccl)* fellow clergywoman; **Amts|spra|che** F official language; **Amts|stu|be** F *(dated)* office; **Amts|stun|den** PL hours *pl* open to the public; **Amts|tracht** F robes *pl* of office; *(Eccl)* vestments *pl*; **Amts|trä|ger(in)** M(F) office bearer; **Amts|über|ga|be** F handing-over of office; **bei der ~ an seinen Nachfolger** when handing over his office to his successor; **Amts|über|nah|me** F → **Amt a** assumption of office/a post *(Brit)* or position; **Amts|ver|ge|hen** NT malfeasance *(form)*; **Amts|ver|mitt|lung** F *(Telec)* connection by the operator; **Amts|ver|wal|ter(in)** M(F) deputy; **Amts|ver|we|ser(in)** M(F) *(old)* deputy; **Amts|vor|gän|ger(in)** M(F) predecessor (in office); **Amts|vor|mund** M *(Jur)* public guardian; **Amts|vor|mund|schaft** F *(Jur)* public guardianship; **Amts|vor|stand** M, **Amts|vor|ste|her(in)** M(F) → **Amt c** head *or* chief of a/the department *etc*; **Amts|wech|sel** M change in office; *(in Behörde)* rotation (in office); **Amts|weg** M official channels *pl*; **den ~ beschreiten** to go through the official channels; **Amts|zei|chen** NT *(Telec)* dialling tone *(Brit)*, dial tone *(US)*; **Amts|zeit** F period of office; **Amts|zim|mer** NT office

Amu|lett [amu'lɛt] NT **-(e)s, -e** amulet, charm, talisman

amü|sant [amy'zant] ADJ amusing; *Film, Geschichte auch* funny ADV amusingly; **er hat ~ geplaudert** he talked in an amusing way; **wir haben ~ geplaudert** we had an amusing conversation

Amü|se|ment [amyzə'mã:] NT **-s, -s** *(geh)* amusement, entertainment

Amü|sier|be|trieb M *(inf)* nightclub; *(= Spielhalle etc)* amusement arcade; **der ~ in Las Vegas** the pleasure industry in Las Vegas

amü|sie|ren [amy'zi:rən] *ptp* **amüsiert** VT to amuse; **was amüsiert dich denn so?** what do you find so amusing *or* funny?; **lassen Sie sich ein bisschen ~** have some fun; **amüsiert zuschauen** to look on amused *or* with amusement

VR *(= sich vergnügen)* to enjoy oneself, to have a good time, to have fun; **sich mit etw ~** to amuse oneself with sth; *(iro)* to keep oneself amused with sth; **sich über etw** *(acc)* **~** to find sth funny; *(= über etw lachen)* to laugh at sth; *(unfreundlich)* to make fun of sth; **sich darüber ~, dass …** to find it funny that …; **sich mit jdm ~** to have a good time with sb; **amüsiert euch gut** have fun, enjoy yourselves

Amü|sier-: **Amü|sier|lo|kal** NT nightclub; **Amü|sier|vier|tel** NT nightclub district

amu|sisch ['amu:zɪʃ] ADJ unartistic

an [an] PREP +*dat* **a** *(räumlich: wo?)* at; *(= an etw dran)* on; **am Haus/Bahnhof** at the house/station; **an dieser Schule** at this school; **an der Wand stehen** to stand by the wall; **am Fenster sitzen** to sit at *or* by the window; **am Tatort** at the scene of the crime; **an der Tür/Wand** on the door/wall; **an der Donau/Autobahn/am Ufer/am Rhein** by *or (direkt an gelegen)* on the Danube/motorway/bank/Rhine; **Frankfurt an der Oder** Frankfurt on (the) Oder; **an etw hängen** *(lit)* to hang from *or* on sth; **zu nahe an etw stehen** to be too near to sth; **etw an etw festmachen** to fasten sth to sth; **jdn an der Hand nehmen** to take sb by the hand; **oben am Berg** up the mountain; **unten am Fluss** down by the river; **sie wohnen Tür an Tür** they live next door to one another, they are next-door neighbours *(Brit)* or neighbors *(US)*; **Haus an Haus** one house after the other; **Laden an Laden** one shop after the other; **an etw vorbeigehen** to go past sth, to pass sth → **am, Bord, Land** *etc*

b *(zeitlich)* on; **an diesem Abend** (on) that evening; **am Tag zuvor** the day before, the previous day; **an dem Abend, als ich …** the evening I …; **an Ostern/Weihnachten** *(dial)* at Easter/Christmas → **am**

c *(fig) siehe auch Substantive, Adjektive, Verben* **jung an Jahren sein** to be young in years; **fünf an der Zahl** five in number; **jdn an etw erkennen** to recognize sb by sth; **der Mangel/das Angebot an Waren** the lack/choice of goods; **an etw arbeiten/schreiben/kauen** to be working on/writing/chewing sth; **an etw sterben/leiden** to die of/suffer from sth; **was haben Sie an Weinen da?** what wines do you have?; **unübertroffen an Qualität** unsurpassed in quality; **an etw schuld sein** to be to blame for sth; **an der ganzen Sache ist nichts** there is nothing in it; **es an der Leber** *etc* **haben** *(inf)* to have trouble with one's liver *etc*, to have liver *etc* trouble; **was findet sie an dem Mann?** what does she see in that man?; **es ist an dem** *(= es stimmt)* that's right; **sie hat etwas an sich, das …** there is something about her that …; **es ist an ihm, etwas zu tun** *(geh)* it's up to him to do something

PREP +*acc* **a** *(räumlich: wohin?)* to; *(= gegen)* on, against; **etw an die Wand/Tafel schreiben** to write sth on the wall/blackboard; **die Zweige reichten (bis) an den Boden/mein Fenster** the branches reached down to the ground/up to my window; **etw an etw hängen** to hang sth on sth; **er ging ans Fenster** he went (over) to the window; **An den Vorsitzenden …** *(bei Anschrift)* The Chairman …; **ans Telefon gehen** to answer the phone → **bis, Bord, Land**

b *(zeitlich: woran?)* **an die Zukunft/Vergangenheit denken** to think of the future/past; **bis an mein Lebensende** to the end of my days

c *(fig) siehe auch Substantive, Adjektive, Verben* **an die Arbeit gehen** to get down to work; **an jdn/etw glauben** to believe in sb/sth; **ich habe eine Bitte/Frage an Sie** I have a request to make of you/question to ask you; **an (und für) sich** actually; **eine an (und für) sich gute Idee** actually quite a good idea, as such quite a good idea; **wie war es? – an (und für) sich ganz schön** how was it? – on the whole it was quite nice → **ab**

ADV **a** *(= ungefähr)* about; **an (die) hundert** about a hundred

b *(Ankunftszeit)* **Frankfurt an: 18.30 Uhr** arriving Frankfurt 18.30

c von diesem Ort an from here onwards; **von diesem Tag an** from this day on(wards); **von heute an** from today onwards

d *(inf: = angeschaltet, angezogen)* on; **Licht an!** lights on!; **ohne etwas an** with nothing on, without anything on → **an sein**

Ana|bap|tis|mus [anabap'tɪsmʊs] M -, *no pl* anabaptism

Ana|bap|tist(in) [anabap'tɪst(ɪn)] M(F) Anabaptist

ana|bol [ana'bo:l] ADJ anabolic; **~e Steroide** anabolic steroids

Ana|bo|li|kum [ana'bo:likʊm] NT **-s, Anabolika** [-ka] anabolic steroid

Ana|chro|nis|mus [anakro'nɪsmʊs] M -, **Anachronismen** [-mən] *(geh)* anachronism

ana|chro|nis|tisch [anakro'nɪstɪʃ] ADJ *(geh)* anachronistic

an|ae|rob [anlae'ro:p] ADJ *attr* anaerobic

Ana|gramm [ana'gram] NT *pl* **-gramme** *(Liter)* anagram

Ana|ko|luth [anako'lu:t] NT **-s, -e** anacoluthon

Ana|kon|da [ana'kɔnda] F **-, -s** anaconda

ana|kre|on|tisch [anakre'ɔntɪʃ] ADJ Anacreontic

anal [a'na:l] ADJ *(Psych, Anat)* anal ADV *Fieber messen* anally; *einführen* into the anus; **~ untersucht werden** to undergo an anal examination; **~ fixiert sein** to have an anal fixation

Anal-: **Anal|ero|tik** F anal eroticism; **anal|fi|xiert** ADJ anally retentive; **Anal|öff|nung** F *(form)* anal orifice *(form)*

ana|log [ana'lo:k] ADJ **a** analogous (+*dat*, *zu* to) **b** *(Telec)* analogue *(Brit)*, analog *(US)* **c** *(Comput)* analog ADV **a** analogously **b** *(Telec, Comput)* in analogue *(Brit)* or analog format

Ana|log|an|schluss M *(Telec)* analogue *(Brit)* or analog *(US)* connection

Ana|lo|gie [analo'gi:] F **-, -n** [-'gi:ən] analogy

Ana|lo|gie-: **Ana|lo|gie|bil|dung** F *(Ling)* analogy; **Ana|lo|gie|schluss** M *(Philos, Jur)* argument by analogy

ana|lo|gisch [ana'lo:gɪʃ] ADJ analogous

Ana|log-: **Ana|log|mo|dem** NT *(Comput)* analogue *(Brit)* or analog *(US)* modem; **Ana|log|-**

rech|ner M analog computer; **Ana|log|uhr** F analogue *(Brit) or* analog *(US)* clock

An|al|pha|bet [anlalfa'be:t, 'an-] M **-en, -en,** **An|al|pha|be|tin** [-'be:tın] F **-, -nen** **a** illiterate (person) **b** *(pej: = Unwissender)* ignoramus, dunce

An|al|pha|be|ten|tum [anlalfa'be:tntu:m] NT **-s,** *no pl,* **An|al|pha|be|tis|mus** [anlalfabe'tısmʊs] M **-,** *no pl* illiteracy

an|al|pha|be|tisch [anlalfa'be:tıʃ, 'an-] ADJ illiterate

Anal|ver|kehr M anal intercourse

Ana|ly|se [ana'ly:zə] F **-, -n** analysis *(auch Psych)*

ana|ly|sie|ren [analy'zi:rən] *ptp* **analysiert** VT to analyze

Ana|ly|sis [a'na:lyzıs] F **-,** *no pl (Math)* analysis

Ana|lyst [ana'lʏst] M **-en, -en,** **Ana|lys|tin** [-'lʏstın] F **-, -nen** *(St Ex)* investment analyst

Ana|ly|ti|ker [ana'ly:tikɐ] M **-s, -,** **Ana|ly|ti|ke|rin** [-ərın] F **-, -nen** analyst; *(= analytisch Denkender)* analytical thinker

ana|ly|tisch [ana'ly:tıʃ] ADJ analytical ADV analytically; **~ begabt sein** to have a talent for analytical thinking

Anä|mie [anɛ'mi:] F **-, -n** [-'mi:ən] anaemia *(Brit),* anemia *(US)*

anä|misch [a'nɛ:mıʃ] ADJ anaemic *(Brit),* anemic *(US)*

Anam|ne|se [anam'ne:zə] F **-, -n** case history

Ana|nas ['ananas] F **-, -** *or* **-se** pineapple

Ana|nas|saft M pineapple juice

Ana|päst [ana'pɛst] M **-(e)s, -e** *(Poet)* anap(a)est

Anar|chie [anar'çi:] F **-, -n** [-'çi:ən] anarchy

anar|chisch [a'narçıʃ] ADJ anarchic ADV **~ leben** to live an anarchic life

Anar|chis|mus [anar'çısmʊs] M **-,** *no pl* anarchism

Anar|chist [anar'çıst] M **-en, -en,** **Anar|chis|tin** [-'çıstın] F **-, -nen** anarchist

anar|chis|tisch [anar'çıstıʃ] ADJ anarchistic; *(= den Anarchismus vertretend auch)* anarchist *attr*

Anar|cho [a'narço] M **-s, -s** *(pej)* anarchist

Anar|cho- *in cpds* anarchist; **Anar|cho|sze|ne** F anarchist scene

An|äs|the|sie [anlɛste'zi:] F **-, -n** [-'zi:ən] anaesthesia *(Brit),* anesthesia *(US)*

an|äs|the|sie|ren [anlɛste'zi:rən] *ptp* **anästhesiert** VT to anaesthetize *(Brit),* to anesthetize *(US)*

An|äs|the|sist [anlɛste'zıst] M **-en, -en,** **An|äs|the|sis|tin** [-'zıstın] F **-, -nen** anaesthetist *(Brit),* anesthesiologist *(US)*

An|äs|the|ti|kum [anlɛs'te:tikʊm] NT **-s, Anästhetika** [-ka] anaesthetic *(Brit),* anesthetic *(US)*

an|äs|the|tisch [anlɛs'te:tıʃ] ADJ anaesthetic *(Brit),* anesthetic *(US)*

Ana|to|li|en [ana'to:liən] NT **-s** Anatolia

Ana|to|li|er [ana'to:liɐ] M **-s, -,** **Ana|to|li|e|rin** [-iərın] F **-, -nen** Anatolian

ana|to|lisch [ana'to:lıʃ] ADJ Anatolian

Ana|tom [ana'to:m] M **-en, -en,** **Ana|to|min** [-'to:mın] F **-, -nen** anatomist

Ana|to|mie [anato'mi:] F **-, -n** [-'mi:ən] **a** *(= Wissenschaft, Körperbau)* anatomy **b** *(= Institut)* anatomical institute

Ana|to|mie|saal M anatomical *or* anatomy lecture theatre *(Brit) or* theater *(US)*

ana|to|misch [ana'to:mıʃ] ADJ anatomical ADV anatomically; **~ begründet sein** to have anatomical causes

an+ba|cken *sep* VT *(Cook)* to start baking VI *aux sein* **a** *(= kurz gebacken werden)* to bake for a short time **b** *(= sich festsetzen)* to bake on *(an +dat* -to); *(dial: Lehm, Schnee etc)* to stick *(an +dat* to)

an+bag|gern VT *sep (inf)* to chat up *(inf)*

an+bah|nen *sep* VT to initiate VR *(= sich andeuten)* to be in the offing; *(Unangenehmes)* to be looming; *(Möglichkeiten, Zukunft etc)* to be opening up; **zwischen den beiden bahnt sich etwas an** *(Liebesverhältnis)* there is something going on between those two

An|bah|nung ['anba:nʊŋ] F **-, -en** initiation *(von, +gen* of)

an+ban|deln ['anbandln] *(S Ger, Aus),* **an+bän|deln** ['anbɛndln] VI *sep* **a** *(= Bekanntschaft schließen)* to take up *(mit* with) **b** *(= Streit anfangen)* to start an argument *(mit* with)

An|bau M, *no pl* **a** *(= Anpflanzung)* cultivation, growing **b** *(von Gebäuden)* building; **den ~ einer Garage planen** to plan to build on a garage

An|bau M *pl* **-bauten** *(= Nebengebäude)* extension; *(frei stehend)* annexe; *(= Stallungen etc)* outhouse, outbuilding

an+bau|en *sep* VT **a** *Kartoffeln, Weizen, Hanf etc* to cultivate, to grow; *(= anpflanzen)* to plant; *(= säen)* to sow **b** *(Build)* to add, to build on; **etw ans Haus ~** to build sth onto the house VI to build an extension; **Möbel zum Anbauen** unit furniture

An|bau-: **an|bau|fä|hig** ADJ **a** *Boden* cultivable; *Gemüse* growable **b** *(Build)* extendible; **An|bau|flä|che** F (area of) cultivable land; *(= bebaute Ackerfläche)* area under cultivation; **An|bau|ge|biet** NT cultivable area, area of cultivation; **ein gutes ~ für etw** a good area for cultivating sth; **An|bau|gren|ze** F limit of cultivation; **An|bau|mö|bel** PL unit furniture; **An|bau|schrank** M cupboard unit; **An|bau|tech|nik** F, **An|bau|ver|fah|ren** NT *(Agr)* growing methods *pl*

an+be|feh|len *ptp* **anbefohlen** VT *sep irreg (liter)* **a** *(= befehlen)* to urge *(jdm etw* sth on sb) **b** *(= anvertrauen)* to commend *(jdm etw* sth to sb)

An|be|ginn M *(geh)* beginning; **von ~ (an)** from the (very) beginning; **seit ~ der Welt** since the world began

an+be|hal|ten *ptp* **anbehalten** VT *sep irreg* to keep on

an|bei [an'bai, 'anbai] ADV *(form)* enclosed; **~ schicken wir Ihnen ...** please find enclosed ...

an+bei|ßen *sep irreg* VI *(Fisch)* to bite; *(fig)* to take the bait VT *Apfel etc* to bite into; **ein angebissener Apfel** a half-eaten apple; **sie sieht zum Anbeißen aus** *(inf)* she looks good enough to eat

an+be|kom|men *ptp* **anbekommen** VT *sep irreg (inf)* to (manage to) get on; *Feuer* to (manage to) get going

an+be|lan|gen *ptp* **anbelangt** VT *sep* to concern; **was das/mich anbelangt ...** as far as that is/I am concerned ...

an+bel|len VT *sep* to bark at

an+be|que|men *ptp* **anbequemt** VR *sep (geh)* **sich einer Sache** *(dat)* **~** to adapt (oneself) to sth

an+be|rau|men ['anbəraumən] *ptp* **anberaumt** VT *sep or (rare) insep (form)* to arrange, to fix; *Termin, Tag auch* to set; *Treffen auch* to call

an+be|ten VT *sep* to worship; *Menschen auch* to adore

An|be|ter ['anbe:tɐ] M **-s, -,** **An|be|te|rin** [-ərın] F **-, -nen** *(= Verehrer)* admirer

An|be|tracht ✪ 44.1 M **in ~** *(+gen)* in consideration *or* view of; **in ~ dessen, dass ...** in consideration *or* view of the fact that ...

an+be|tref|fen *ptp* **anbetroffen** VT *sep irreg* to concern; **was das/mich anbetrifft ...** as far as that is/I am concerned ...

an+bet|teln VT *sep* **jdn ~** to beg from sb; **jdn um etw ~** to beg sth from sb

An|be|tung ['anbe:tʊŋ] F **-,** *(rare)* **-en** worship; *(von Menschen auch)* adoration

an|be|tungs|wür|dig ADJ admirable; *Schönheit* adorable

an+be|zah|len *ptp* **anbezahlt** VT *sep* = **anzahlen**

an+bie|dern ['anbi:dɐn] VR *sep (pej)* **sich (bei jdm) ~** to try to get pally (with sb) *(inf)*

An|bie|de|rung F **-, -en** currying favour *(Brit) or* favor *(US)* *(+gen* with)

An|bie|de|rungs|ver|such M **einen ~ bei jdm unternehmen** to attempt to curry favour *(Brit) or* favor *(US)* with sb

an+bie|ten *sep irreg* ✪ 30 VT to offer *(jdm etw* sb sth); *(Comm) Waren* to offer for sale; *seinen Rücktritt* to tender; **haben wir etwas zum Anbieten da?** have we anything to offer our guests?; **jdm das Du ~** *to suggest sb uses the familiar form of address*

VR **a** *(Mensch)* to offer one's services; *(Ftbl)* to be in position; **sich für die Arbeit ~, sich ~, die Arbeit zu tun** to offer to do the work; **sich zur Unzucht ~** to solicit; **der Ort bietet sich für die Konferenz an** that is the obvious place for the conference; **das Fahrrad bietet sich geradezu zum Mitnehmen an** that bicycle is just asking to be taken

b *(= in Betracht kommen: Gelegenheit)* to present itself; **das bietet sich als Lösung an** that would provide a solution; **es bieten sich mehrere Lösungsmöglichkeiten an** there are several possible solutions, several possible solutions present themselves; **es bietet sich an, das Museum zu besuchen** the thing to do would be to visit the museum

An|bie|ter(in) M(F) supplier, tenderer; *(Internet)* provider

an+bin|den VT *sep irreg (an +acc or dat* to) **a** *(= festbinden)* to tie (up); *Pferd* to tie up, to tether; *Boot* to tie up, to moor; **jdn ~** *(fig)* to tie sb down → *auch* **angebunden** **b** *(= verbinden)* to connect; *(= verketten)* to link

An|bin|dung F *(= Verbindung)* connection; *(= Verkettung)* linkage, linking

an+blaf|fen VT *sep (inf) (lit, fig)* to bark at

an+bla|sen VT *sep irreg* **a** *(= blasen gegen)* to blow at; *(= anfachen)* to blow on; **jdn mit Rauch ~** to blow smoke at sb **b** *(Mus) Instrument* to blow; *Ton* to sound **c** *(= durch Blassignal ankündigen)* **die Jagd ~** to sound the horn for the start of the hunt

an+ble|cken VT *sep (lit, fig)* to bare one's teeth at

an+blen|den VT *sep* to flash at; *(fig: = kurz erwähnen)* to touch on

An|blick M sight; **beim ersten ~** at first sight; **beim ~ des Hundes** when he *etc* saw the dog; **in den ~ von etw versunken sein** to be absorbed in looking at sth

an+bli|cken VT *sep* to look at; **jdn lange/feindselig ~** to gaze/glare at sb

an+blin|ken VT *sep* **jdn ~** *(Fahrer, Fahrzeug)* to flash (at) sb; *(Lampe)* to flash in sb's eyes; *(Gold)* to shine before sb's very eyes

an+blin|zeln VT *sep* **a** *(= blinzelnd ansehen)* to squint at **b** *(= zublinzeln)* to wink at

an+boh|ren VT *sep* **a** *(= teilweise durchbohren)* to bore into; *(mit Bohrmaschine)* to drill into **b** *(= zugänglich machen) Quellen etc* to open up (by boring/drilling)

an+bor|gen VT *sep (dated)* **jdn (um etw) ~** to borrow (sth) from sb

An|bot ['anbo:t] NT **-(e)s, -e** *(Aus)* = **Angebot**

an+bran|den VI *sep aux sein* to surge

an+bra|ten VT *sep irreg* to brown; *Steak etc* to sear; **etw zu scharf ~** to brown sth too much

an+brau|chen VT *sep* to start using; **eine angebrauchte Schachtel/Flasche** an opened box/bottle; **das ist schon angebraucht** that has already been used/opened

an+bräu|nen VT *sep (Cook)* to brown (lightly)

an+brau|sen VI *sep aux sein* to roar up; **angebraust kommen** to come roaring up

an+bre|chen *sep irreg* VT **a** *Packung, Flasche etc* to open; *Vorrat* to broach; *Ersparnisse, Geldsumme, Geldschein* to break into **b** *(= teilweise brechen) Brett, Gefäß, Knochen etc* to crack; **angebrochen sein** to be cracked → *auch* **angebrochen**

VI *aux sein (Epoche etc)* to dawn; *(Tag auch)* to break; *(Nacht)* to fall; *(Jahreszeit)* to begin; *(Winter)* to close in

an+brem|sen VTI *sep* **(den Wagen) ~** to brake, to apply the brakes

an+bren|nen *sep irreg* VI *aux sein* to start burning, to catch fire; *(Holz, Kohle etc)* to catch light; *(Essen)* to burn, to get burned; *(Stoff)* to scorch, to get scorched; **mir ist das Essen angebrannt** I burned the food, I let the food get burned;

nichts ~ lassen (*inf*: = *keine Zeit verschwenden*) to be quick, to be quick off the mark (*Brit inf*); (= *sich nichts entgehen lassen*) not to miss out on anything → *auch* **angebrannt** VT to light

an+brin|gen VT *sep irreg* **a** (= *befestigen*) to fix, to fasten (*an +dat* (on)to); (= *aufstellen, aufhängen*) to put up; *Telefon, Feuermelder etc* to put in, to install; *Stiel an Besen* to put on; *Beschläge, Hufeisen* to mount; *Komma* to insert
b (= *äußern*) *Bemerkung, Bitte, Gesuch, Beschwerde* to make (*bei* to); *Kenntnisse, Wissen* to display; *Argument* to use; **er konnte seine Kritik nicht mehr ~** he couldn't get his criticism in → *auch* **angebracht**
c (= *hierherbringen*) to bring (with one); (*nach Hause*) to bring home (with one)
d (*inf*: = *loswerden*) *Ware* to get rid of (*inf*)
e (*inf*: = *anbekommen*) to (manage to) get on; *Feuer* to (manage to) get going

An|brin|gung F -, *no pl* (= *das Befestigen*) fixing, fastening; (= *das Aufstellen, Aufhängen*) putting up; (*von Telefon, Feuermelder etc*) putting in, installing

An|bruch M, *no pl* **a** (*geh*: = *Anfang*) beginning; (*von Zeitalter, Epoche*) dawn(ing); **bei ~ des Tages** *or* **Morgens** at daybreak, at break of day; **bei ~ der Nacht** *or* **Dunkelheit** at nightfall **b** (*Min*) seam **c** (*Hunt*) rotting game **d** (*Forest*) decayed *or* rotten wood

an+brül|len *sep* VT (*Löwe etc*) to roar at; (*Kuh, Stier*) to bellow at; (*inf*: *Mensch*) to shout *or* bellow at VI **gegen etw ~** to shout above (the noise of) sth

an+brum|men *sep* VT to growl at; (*fig*) to grumble at VI *aux sein* **angebrummt kommen** to come roaring along *or* (*auf einen zu*) up

an+brü|ten VT *sep* to begin to sit on

An|chor|man ['ɛŋkərmən] M **-s, Anchormen** ['ɛŋkərmən] (*TV*) anchorman

An|cho|vis [an'ɡoːvɪs, an'ʃoːvɪs] F **-, -** anchovy

An|dacht ['andaxt] F **-, -en** **a** *no pl* (= *das Beten*) (silent) prayer *or* worship; **~ halten** to be at one's devotions; **in tiefer ~ versunken sein** to be sunk in deep devotion **b** (= *Gottesdienst*) prayers *pl* **c** (= *Versenkung*) rapt interest; (= *Ehrfurcht*) reverence; **in tiefe(r) ~ versunken sein** to be completely absorbed; **er trank den Wein mit ~** (*hum*) he drank the wine reverently; **etw voller ~ tun** to do sth reverently

an|däch|tig ['andɛçtɪç] ADJ **a** (= *im Gebet versunken*) in prayer; **die ~en Gläubigen** the worshippers at their devotions *or* prayers **b** (= *versunken*) rapt; (= *ehrfürchtig*) reverent ADV **a** (= *inbrünstig*) raptly **b** (*hum*: = *ehrfürchtig*) reverently

An|dachts-: **An|dachts|bild** NT devotional picture; **an|dachts|voll** ADJ, ADV = **andächtig b**

An|da|lu|si|en [anda'luːziən] NT **-s** Andalusia

An|da|lu|si|er [anda'luːziɐ] M **-s, -**, **An|da|lu|si|e|rin** [-iərɪn] F **-, -nen** Andalusian

an+dau|en VT *sep* to begin to digest; **angedaute Speisen** partially digested food

An|dau|er F, *no pl* **bei langer ~ des Fiebers** if the fever continues for a long time

an+dau|ern VI *sep* to continue; (= *anhalten*) to last; **das dauert noch an** that is still going on, that is continuing; **der Regen dauert noch an** the rain hasn't stopped; **das schöne Wetter wird nicht ~** the fine weather won't last; **die bis in den frühen Morgen ~den Verhandlungen** the negotiations which went on *or* continued till early morning

an|dau|ernd ADJ (= *ständig*) continuous; (= *anhaltend*) continual ADV constantly, continuously, continually; **wenn du mich ~ unterbrichst ...** if you keep on interrupting me ...

An|den ['andn] PL Andes *pl*

an+den|ken VT *sep irreg* **etw ~** to give a little thought to sth; **das sollten wir zumindest mal ~** we should at least start thinking about it

An|den|ken ['andɛŋkn] NT **-s, -** **a** *no pl* memory; **das ~ von etw feiern** to commemorate sth; **jdn in freundlichem ~ behalten** to have fond memories of sb; **im ~ an jdn/etw** in memory of sb/sth; **zum ~ an jdn** (*an Verstorbenen etc*) in memory *or* remembrance of sb; **zum ~ an etw** (*an Urlaub etc*) to remind you/us *etc* of sth **b** (= *Reiseandenken*) souvenir (*an +acc* of); (= *Erinnerungsstück*) memento, keepsake (*an +acc* from)

än|der|bar ADJ alterable, changeable; **eine nicht mehr ~e Entscheidung** a decision which can no longer be changed; **der Entwurf ist jederzeit ~** the draft can be altered *or* changed at any time

Än|der|bar|keit ['ɛndɐbaːɐkait] F **-**, *no pl* **die ~ von Vertragsbestimmungen** (the fact) that a contract's terms can be altered *or* changed

an|de|ren-: **an|de|ren|falls** ADV otherwise; **an|de|ren|orts** ADV (*geh*) elsewhere; **an|de|ren|tags** ADV (*geh*) (on) the next *or* following day; **an|de|ren|teils** ADV (*geh*) = **andererseits**

an|de|re(r, s) ['andərə] INDEF PRON (*adjektivisch*) **a** different; (= *weiterer*) other; **ein ~r Mann/~s Auto** a different man/car; (= *ein weiterer etc*) another man/car; **eine ~ Frau** a different woman; (= *eine weitere*) another woman; **jede ~ Frau hätte ...** any other woman would have ...; **haben Sie noch ~ Fragen?** do you have any more questions?; **ich habe eine ~ Auffassung als sie** my view is different from hers, I take a different view from her; **das machen wir ein ~s Mal** we'll do that another time; **das ~ Geschlecht** the other sex; **er ist ein ~r Mensch geworden** he is a changed *or* different man; **~ Länder, ~ Sitten** (*prov*) different countries have different customs
b (= *folgend*) next, following; **am ~n Tag, ~n Tags** (*liter*) (on) the next *or* following day
INDEF PRON (*substantivisch*) **a** (= *Ding*) **ein ~r** a different one; (= *noch einer*) another one; **etwas ~s** something *or* (*jedes, in Fragen*) anything else; **alle ~n** all the others; **er hat noch drei ~** he has three others *or* (*von demselben*) more; **ja, das ist etwas ~s** yes, that's a different matter; **das ist etwas ganz ~s** that's something quite different; **hast du etwas ~s gedacht?** did you think otherwise?; **ich muss mir etwas ~s anziehen** I must put on something else *or* different; **einen Tag um den ~n** every single day; **ein Mal ums ~** every single time; **ich habe ~s gehört** I heard differently; **nichts ~s** nothing else; **nichts ~s als ...** nothing but ...; **es blieb mir nichts ~s übrig, als selbst hinzugehen** I had no alternative but to go myself; **und ~s mehr** and more besides; **und vieles ~ mehr** and much more besides; **alles ~** (= *alle anderen Dinge*) everything else; **alles ~ als zufrieden** anything but pleased, far from pleased; **bist du müde? – nein, alles ~ als das** are you tired? – no, far from it *or* anything but; **unter ~m** among other things; **es kam eins zum ~n** one thing led to another; **... man kann doch eines tun, ohne das ~ zu lassen** ... but you can have the best of both worlds; **sie hat sich eines ~n besonnen** she changed her mind; **von einem Tag zum ~n** overnight; **von etwas ~m sprechen** to change the subject; **eines besser als das ~** each one better than the next
b (= *Person*) **ein ~r/eine ~** a different person; (= *noch einer*) another person; **er/sie und ~** he/she and others; **jeder ~/kein ~r** anyone/no-one else; **es war kein ~r als ...** it was none other than ...; **niemand ~s** no-one else; **jemand ~s** somebody else; **das haben mir ~ auch schon gesagt** other people *or* others have told me that too; **die ~n** the others; **alle ~n** all the others, everyone else; **jemand ~s** *or* (*S Ger*) **~r** somebody *or* (*jeder, in Fragen*) anybody else; **wer ~s?** who else?; **wir/ihr ~n** the rest of us/you; **sie hat einen ~n** she has someone else; **der eine oder der ~ von unseren Kollegen** one or other of our colleagues; **es gibt immer den einen oder den ~n, der faulenzt** there is always someone who is lazy; **der eine ..., der ~ ...** this person ..., that person...; **einer nach dem ~n** one after the other; **eine schöner als die ~** each one more beautiful than the next; **der eine kommt, der ~ geht** as one person comes another goes; (= *man geht ein und aus*) people are coming and going; **das kannst du ~n erzählen!** (*inf*) who are you kidding! (*inf*)

an|de|rer|seits ✪ 53.3, 53.5 ADV on the other hand

An|der|kon|to ['andɐ-] NT (*Fin*) nominee account

an|der|lei ['andɐlai] ADJ *inv* (*geh*) other

an|der|mal ['andɐ'maːl] ADV **ein ~** some other time

an|dern- *in cpds* = **anderen-**

än|dern ['ɛndɐn] VT (= *anders werden*) to change, to alter; *Meinung, Richtung* to change; *Kleidungsstück* to alter; (*Comput*) to change, to modify; **das ändert die Sache** that changes things, that puts a different complexion on things; **ich kann es nicht ~** I can't do anything about it; **das ist nicht zu ~, das lässt sich nicht (mehr) ~** nothing can be done about it; **das ändert nichts an der Tatsache, dass ...** that doesn't alter the fact that ...
VR **a** to change, to alter; (*Meinung, Richtung*) to change; **hier ändert sich das Wetter oft** the weather here is very changeable; **es hat sich nichts/viel geändert** nothing/a lot has changed **b** (*Mensch*) to change; (= *sich bessern*) to change for the better; **wenn sich das nicht ändert ...** if things don't improve ...

an|ders ['andɐs] ADV **a** (= *sonst*) else; **jemand/niemand ~** somebody *or* anybody/nobody else; **wer/wo ~?** who/where else?; **irgendwo ~** somewhere else; **wie ~ hätte ich es machen sollen?** how else should I have done it?
b (= *verschieden, besser, schöner*) differently; (= *andersartig*) *sein, aussehen, klingen, schmecken* different (*als* to); **~ als jd denken/reagieren** to think/react differently from sb; **~ denkend** = **andersdenkend**; **~ Denkende(r)** = **Andersdenkende(r)**; **~ als jd aussehen** to look different from sb; **~ als jd** (*geh*: = *im Gegensatz zu*) unlike sb; **es** *or* **die Sache verhält sich ganz ~** things *or* matters are quite different; **~ geartet** = **andersgeartet**; **~ gesinnt** of a different opinion; **~ gesinnt sein** to have a different opinion, to disagree (*in +dat* on); **~ ausgedrückt** to put it another way, in other words; **das machen wir so und nicht ~** we'll do it this way and no other; **das hat sie nicht ~ erwartet** she expected nothing else; **wie nicht ~ zu erwarten** as was to be expected; **sie ist ~ geworden** she has changed; **wie könnte es ~ sein?** how could it be otherwise?; **es geht nicht ~** there's no other way; **ich kann nicht ~** (= *kann es nicht lassen*) I can't help it; (= *muss leider*) I have no choice; **~ lautend** = **anderslautend**; **es sich** (*dat*) **~ überlegen** to change one's mind; **da wird mir ganz ~** I start to feel funny *or* (*übel auch*) peculiar; **ich kann auch ~** (*inf*) you'd/he'd *etc* better watch it (*inf*); **das klingt schon ~** (*inf*) now that's more like it
c (*inf*: = *anderenfalls*) otherwise, or else

An|ders-: **an|ders|ar|tig** ADJ *no comp* different; **An|ders|ar|tig|keit** F, *no pl* (*des Lebens*) different quality; **jdn wegen seiner ~ nicht verstehen** not to understand sb because he/she is different; **an|ders|den|kend** ADJ *attr* dissident, dissenting, of a different opinion; **An|ders|den|ken|de(r)** [-dɛŋkndə] MF *decl as adj* person of a different opinion; (= *Dissident*) dissident, dissenter; **die Freiheit des ~n** the freedom to have one's own opinion; **an|der|seits** ['andɐ'zaits] ADV = **andererseits**; **an|ders|far|big** ADJ of a different colour (*Brit*) *or* color (*US*); **an|ders|ge|ar|tet** ADJ **~ sein als jd** to be different from *or* to sb; **an|ders|ge|schlecht|lich** ADJ of the other *or* opposite sex; **an|ders|ge|sinnt** △ ADJ → **anders b**; **An|-**

ders|ge|sinn|te(r) [-gəzɪntə] MF *decl as adj* person of a different opinion; **an|ders|gläu|big** ADJ of a different faith *or* religion *or* creed; **~ sein** to be of *or* have a different faith *etc*; **An|ders|gläu|bi|ge(r)** MF *decl as adj* person of a different faith *or* religion *or* creed; **an|ders|he|rum** ADV the other way (a)round; **~ gehen** to go the other way (a)round; **dreh die Schraube mal ~** turn the screw the other way ADJ (*inf*: = *homosexuell*) **~ sein** to be bent (*inf*); **an|ders|lau|tend** ADJ *attr (form)* contrary; **~e Berichte** contrary reports, reports to the contrary; **entgegen ~en Berichten** despite reports to the contrary; **an|ders|rum** (*inf*) ADV ADJ = **andersherum**; **an|ders|spra|chig** ADJ *Literatur* foreign(-language); **die ~e Minderheit** the minority who speak a different language; **an|ders|wie** ADV (*inf*) (= *auf andere Weise*) some other way; (= *unterschiedlich*) differently; **an|ders|wo** ADV elsewhere; **das gibt es nicht ~** you don't get that anywhere else; **an|ders|wo|her** ADV from elsewhere; **an|ders|wo|hin** ADV elsewhere; **ich gehe nicht gerne ~** I don't like going anywhere else

an|dert|halb ['andɐt'halp] NUM one and a half; **~ Pfund Kaffee** a pound and a half of coffee; **~ Stunden** an hour and a half; **das Kind ist ~ Jahre alt** the child is eighteen months old, the child is one and a half

an|dert|halb-: **an|dert|halb|fach** ADJ one and a half times; **nimm die ~e Menge/das Anderthalbfache** use half as much again → *auch* **vierfach**; **an|dert|halb|mal** ADV one and a half times; **~ so viel/so viele** half as much/many again

Än|de|rung ['ɛndərʊŋ] F **-, -en** change, alteration (*an +dat, gen* in, to); (*in jdm*) change (*in +dat* in); (*an Kleidungsstück, Gebäude*) alteration (*an +dat* to); (*der Gesellschaft, der Politik etc*) change (*+gen* in); **~en speichern** (*Comput*) to save changes

Än|de|rungs-: **Än|de|rungs|an|trag** M (*Parl*) amendment; **Än|de|rungs|kün|di|gung** F (*Econ, Jur*) notification of a change (in the terms of employment); **Än|de|rungs|schnei|der(in)** M(F) tailor (who does alterations); **Än|de|rungs|vor|schlag** M suggested change *or* alteration; **einen ~ machen** to suggest a change *or* an alteration; **Än|de|rungs|wunsch** M wish to make changes *or* alterations; **haben Sie Änderungswünsche?** are there any changes *or* alterations you would like made?

an|der-: **an|der|wär|tig** ['andɐ'vɛrtɪç] ADJ *attr (geh)* = **anderweitig ADJ**; **an|der|wärts** ['andɐ'vɛrts] ADV elsewhere, somewhere else; **an|der|weit** ['andɐ'vait] ADV (*geh*) = **anderweitig ADV**; **an|der|wei|tig** ['andɐ'vaitɪç] ADJ *attr* (= *andere, weitere*) other; **~e Ölvorkommen** (= *an anderer Stelle*) other oil strikes, oil strikes elsewhere ADV (= *anders*) otherwise; (= *an anderer Stelle*) elsewhere; **~ vergeben/besetzt werden** to be given to/filled by someone else; **etw ~ verwenden** to use sth for a different purpose

an+deu|ten *sep* VT (= *zu verstehen geben*) to hint, to intimate (*jdm etw* sth to sb); (= *kurz erwähnen*) *Problem* to mention briefly; (*Art, Mus*) to suggest; (= *erkennen lassen*) to indicate; **der Wald war nur mit ein paar Strichen angedeutet** a few strokes gave a suggestion of the wood VR to be indicated; (*Melodie etc*) to be suggested; (*Gewitter*) to be in the offing

An|deu|tung F (= *Anspielung, Anzeichen*) hint; (= *flüchtiger Hinweis*) short *or* brief mention; (*Art, Mus*) suggestion *no pl*; (= *Spur*) sign, trace; (= *Anflug eines Lächelns etc*) faint suggestion, hint; **eine ~ machen** to hint (*über +acc* at), to drop a hint (*über +acc* about); **versteckte ~en machen** to drop veiled hints; **eine Besserung zeichnet sich in ~en ab** there are vague signs of an improvement

an|deu|tungs|wei|se ADV (= *als Anspielung, Anzeichen*) by way of a hint; (= *als flüchtiger Hinweis*) in passing; **jdm ~ zu verstehen geben, dass ...** to hint to sb that ...; **man kann die Mauern noch ~ erkennen** you can still see traces of the walls ADJ *attr (rare)* faint

an+dich|ten VT *sep* **a** **jdm etw ~** (*inf*) to impute sth to sb; *Fähigkeiten* to credit sb with sth; **alles kann man ihm ~, aber ...** you can say what you like about him but ... **b** **jdn ~** to write a poem/poems to sb; **jdn in Sonetten ~** to write sonnets to sb

an+di|cken ['andɪkn] VT *sep Suppe, Soße* to thicken

an+die|nen *sep (pej)* VT **jdm etw ~** to press sth on sb; **man diente ihm einen hohen Posten im Ausland an, um ihn loszuwerden** they tried to get rid of him by palming him off with a high position abroad VR **sich jdm ~** to offer sb one's services (*als* as)

An|die|nungs|stra|ße F (*Mot*) service road

an+dis|ku|tie|ren *ptp* **andiskutiert** VT *sep* to discuss briefly, to touch on

an+do|cken *sep* VI **a** (*Schiff*) to dock (*an +dat* at); (*Raumfähre*) to dock (*an +dat* with) **b** (*Physiol, Chem*) to link up (*an +dat* to) VT **a** *Raumfähre* to dock (*an +dat or acc* at) **b** (*Computer*) to connect up (*an +dat or acc* to)

An|dor|ra [an'dɔra] NT **-s** Andorra

An|dor|ra|ner [andɔ'ra:nɐ] M **-s, -**, **An|dor|ra|ne|rin** [-ərɪn] F **-, -nen** Andorran

an|dor|ra|nisch [andɔ'ra:nɪʃ] ADJ Andorran

An|drang M, *no pl* **a** (= *Zustrom, Gedränge*) crowd, crush; **es herrschte großer ~** there was a great crowd *or* crush **b** (*von Blut*) rush; (*von Wassermassen*) onrush

an+drän|gen VI *sep aux sein* to push forward; (*Menschenmenge auch*) to surge forward; (*Wassermassen*) to surge; **die ~de Menschenmenge** the surging crowd

And|re|as [an'dre:as] M **-'** Andrew

An|dre|as|kreuz NT diagonal cross; (*Rel*) St Andrew's cross

an+dre|hen VT *sep* **a** (= *anstellen*) to turn on **b** (= *festdrehen*) to screw on **c** **jdm etw ~** (*inf*) to palm sth off on sb

and|ren- ['andrən] *in cpds* = **anderen-**

and|re(r, s) ['andrə] ADJ = **andere(r, s)**

and|rer|seits ['andrɐ'zaits] ADV = **andererseits**

an+drin|gen VI *sep irreg aux sein* (*geh*) (*Menschen etc*) to push forward, to press (*gegen* towards); (*Wasser*) to press, to push (*gegen* against)

And|ro|gen [andro'ge:n] NT **-s, -e** androgen

an|dro|gyn [andro'gy:n] ADJ androgynous

And|ro|gyn [andro'gy:n] M **-s, -e** androgyne

And|ro|gy|ni|tät [androgyni'tɛ:t] F **-**, *no pl* androgyny

an+dro|hen VT *sep* to threaten (*jdm etw* sb with sth)

An|dro|hung F threat; **unter ~ der** *or* **von Gewalt** with the threat of violence; **unter der ~, etw zu tun** with the threat of doing sth; **unter ~** (*Jur*) under penalty (*von, +gen* of)

And|ro|id [andro'i:t] M **-en, -en** [-dn], **And|ro|i|de** [andro'i:də] M **-n, -n** android

An|druck M *pl* **-drucke** **a** (*Typ*) proof **b** *no pl* (*Space*) G-force, gravitational force

an+dru|cken *sep (Typ)* VT to pull a proof of VI to pull proofs; (= *mit dem Druck beginnen*) to start *or* begin printing

an+drü|cken VT *sep* **a** *Pflaster* to press on (*an +acc* to); **als ich kräftiger andrückte** when I pressed *or* pushed harder **b** (= *beschädigen*) *Obst etc* to bruise **c** (= *durch Druck einschalten*) *Licht etc* to switch on (by pressing a button)

An|druck|ex|emp|lar NT (*Typ*) proof copy

an+du|deln VT *sep* **sich** (*dat*) **einen ~** (*dated inf*) to get merry *or* tipsy (*inf*)

an+düns|ten VT *sep* (*Cook*) to braise lightly

Äne|as [ɛ'ne:as] M **-'** Aeneas

an+ecken ['anlɛkn] VI *sep aux sein* (*inf*) (**bei jdm/allen**) **~** to rub sb/everyone up the wrong way; **mit seinen** *or* **wegen seiner Bemerkungen ist er schon oft angeeckt** his remarks have often rubbed people up the wrong way

an+ei|fern VT *sep* (*S Ger, Aus*) = **anspornen**

an+eig|nen VT *sep* **sich** (*dat*) **etw ~** (= *etw erwerben*) to acquire sth; (= *etw wegnehmen*) to appropriate sth; (= *sich mit etw vertraut machen*) to learn sth; (= *sich etw angewöhnen*) to pick sth up

An|eig|nung F (= *Erwerb*) acquisition; (= *Wegnahme*) appropriation; (= *Lernen*) learning; **widerrechtliche ~** (*Jur*) misappropriation

an|ei|nan|der [anlai'nandɐ] ADV **a** (= *gegenseitig, an sich*) **~ denken** to think of each other; **~ hängen** (*fig: Menschen*) to be attached to each other; **sich ~ gewöhnen** to get used to each other; **sich ~ festhalten** to hold on to each other; **sich ~ stoßen** (*lit*) to knock into each other; **Freude ~ haben** to enjoy each other's company **b** (*mit Richtungsangabe*) **~ vorübergehen** *or* **vorbeigehen** to go past each other; **~ vorbeireden** to talk *or* be at cross-purposes **c** (= *einer am anderen, zusammen*) *befestigen* together

an|ei|nan|der-: **an|ei|nan|der+bau|en** *sep*, **an|ei|nan|der bau|en** △ VT to build together; **die Häuser waren ganz dicht aneinandergebaut** the houses were built very close together; **an|ei|nan|der+fü|gen** *sep*, **an|ei|nan|der fü|gen** △ VT to put together VR to join together; **an|ei|nan|der+ge|ra|ten** *sep irreg aux sein*, **an|ei|nan|der ge|ra|ten** △ *irreg aux sein* VI to come to blows (*mit* with); (= *streiten*) to have words (*mit* with); **an|ei|nan|der+gren|zen** *sep*, **an|ei|nan|der gren|zen** △ VI to border on each other; **in Istanbul grenzen Orient und Okzident aneinander** in Istanbul East and West meet; **an|ei|nan|der+hal|ten** *sep irreg*, **an|ei|nan|der hal|ten** △ *irreg* VT to hold against each other; **an|ei|nan|der+hän|gen** *sep irreg*, **an|ei|nan|der hän|gen** △ *irreg* VI (= *zusammenhängen*) to be linked (together) VT to link together; **an|ei|nan|der+kle|ben** *sep*, **an|ei|nan|der kle|ben** △ VT to stick together VI to be stuck together; (*inf*: = *unzertrennlich sein*) to be glued together (*inf*); **an|ei|nan|der+kop|peln** *sep*, **an|ei|nan|der kop|peln** △ VT to couple; *Raumschiffe* to link up; **an|ei|nan|der+leh|nen** *sep*, **an|ei|nan|der leh|nen** △ VR to lean on *or* against each other; **an|ei|nan|der+lie|gen** *sep irreg* (*S Ger, Aus, Sw: aux sein*), **an|ei|nan|der lie|gen** △ *irreg* (*S Ger, Aus, Sw: aux sein*) VI to be adjacent (to each other), to be next to each other; **an|ei|nan|der+pral|len** *sep aux sein*, **an|ei|nan|der pral|len** △ *aux sein* VI to collide; (*fig*) to clash; **an|ei|nan|der+rei|hen** *sep*, **an|ei|nan|der rei|hen** △ VT to string together VR to be strung together; (*zeitlich: Tage etc*) to run together

An|ei|nan|der|rei|hung F **-, -en** stringing together

an|ei|nan|der-: **an|ei|nan|der+schmie|gen** *sep*, **an|ei|nan|der schmie|gen** △ VR to snuggle up; **an|ei|nan|der+set|zen** *sep*, **an|ei|nan|der set|zen** △ VT to put together; **an|ei|nan|der+ste|hen** *sep irreg* (*S Ger, Aus, Sw: aux sein*), **an|ei|nan|der ste|hen** △*irreg* (*S Ger, Aus, Sw: aux sein*) VI to stand (very) close together; **die Häuser stehen zu dicht aneinander** the houses are built too close together; **an|ei|nan|der+stel|len** *sep*, **an|ei|nan|der stel|len** △ VT to put together; **an|ei|nan|der+sto|ßen** *sep irreg*, **an|ei|nan|der sto|ßen** △ *irreg* VT to bang together VI *aux sein* to collide; (*Fahrzeuge, Köpfe auch, Menschen*) to bump into each other; (= *aneinandergrenzen*) to meet

Äne|is [ɛ'ne:ɪs] F **-** Aeneid

Anek|döt|chen [anɛk'dø:tçən] NT **-s, -** (*hum*) little story *or* anecdote

Anek|do|te [anɛk'do:tə] F **-, -n** anecdote

anek|do|ten|haft ADJ anecdotal

anek|do|tisch [anɛk'do:tɪʃ] (*Liter*) ADJ anecdotic ADV **sein Vortrag war ~ aufgelockert** his lecture was lightened by anecdotes; **er erzählte ~ aus seinem Leben** he told anecdotes about his life; **~ über etw** (*acc*) **reden** to talk about sth in anecdotes; **~ überliefert** retold in the form of an anecdote

an+ekeln VT *sep* **a** *(= anwidern)* to disgust, to nauseate; **die beiden ekeln sich nur noch an** they just find each other nauseating, they just make each other sick → *auch* **angeekelt** **b** *(inf: = beleidigen)* to be offensive to; **..., ekelte er mich an** ..., he spat at me

Ane|mo|ne [ane'mo:nə] F **-, -n** anemone

an+emp|feh|len *ptp* **anempfohlen** VT *sep or insep irreg (geh)* to recommend

an|emp|fun|den ['anlɛmpfʊndn] ADJ *(geh)* artificial, spurious, false; **nicht echt, sondern nur ~** not genuine

An|er|be M *(old)* heir to a/the farm

an+er|bie|ten *ptp* **anerboten** VR *sep irreg (geh)* to offer one's services; **sich ~, etw zu tun** to offer to do sth

An|er|bie|ten ['anlɛɐbi:tn] NT **-s, -** *(geh)* offer

An|er|bin F *(old)* heiress to a/the farm

an|er|kannt ['anlɛɐkant] ADJ recognized; *Tatsache auch* established; *Werk* standard; *Bedeutung* accepted; *Experte* acknowledged → *auch* **anerkennen**

an|er|kann|ter|ma|ßen ['anlɛɐkantɐ'ma:sn] ADV **diese Mannschaft ist ~ besser** it is generally recognized *or* accepted *or* acknowledged that this team is better, this team is generally recognized *etc* to be better

an+er|ken|nen *ptp* **anerkannt** VT *sep or insep irreg Staat, König, Rekord* to recognize; *Forderung auch, Rechnung* to accept; *Vaterschaft* to accept, to acknowledge; *(= würdigen) Leistung, Bemühung* to appreciate; *Meinung* to respect; *(= loben)* to praise; **..., das muss man ~** *(= zugeben)* admittedly, ...; *(= würdigen)* ..., one has to appreciate that; **als gleichwertiger Partner anerkannt sein** to be accepted as an equal partner; **ihr ~der Blick** her appreciative look → *auch* **anerkannt**

an|er|ken|nens|wert ADJ commendable

An|er|kennt|nis NT *(Jur)* acknowledgement

An|er|ken|nung F recognition; *(von Forderung auch, von Rechnung)* acceptance; *(von Vaterschaft)* acknowledgement; *(= Würdigung)* appreciation; *(von Meinung)* respect; *(= Lob)* praise

An|er|ken|nungs|schrei|ben NT letter of appreciation *or* commendation

an|er|zie|hen *ptp* **anerzogen** VT *insep irreg* **jdm etw ~** *(Kindern)* to instil *(Brit) or* instill *(US)* sth into sb; *neuem Angestellten etc auch* to drum sth into sb; **sich** *(dat)* **etw ~** to train oneself to do sth

an|er|zo|gen ['anlɛɐtso:gn] ADJ *Eigenschaft, Verhalten* acquired; **das ist alles ~** he/she *etc* has been trained to be like that

Anf. *abbr von* **Anfang**

an+fa|chen ['anfaxn] VT *sep (geh)* **a** *Glut, Feuer* to fan **b** *(fig)* to arouse; *Leidenschaft* to inflame, to arouse

an+fah|ren *sep irreg* VI *aux sein* **a** *(= losfahren)* to start (up); **angefahren kommen** *(= herbeifahren) (Wagen, Fahrer)* to drive up; *(Fahrrad)* to ride up; *(Zug)* to pull up; *(= ankommen)* to arrive; **beim Anfahren** when starting (up); **das Anfahren am Berg üben** to practise *(Brit) or* practice *(US)* a hill start
b *(inf)* **lass mal noch eine Runde ~** let's have another round
VT **a** *(= liefern)* to deliver
b *(inf: = spendieren)* to lay on
c *(= ansteuern) Ort, Hafen* to stop *or* call at; *(Aut) Kurve* to approach; **die Insel wird zweimal wöchentlich von der Fähre angefahren** the ferry calls twice a week at the island
d *(= anstoßen) Passanten, Baum etc* to run into, to hit; *(fig: ausschelten)* to shout at
e *(= in Betrieb setzen) Reaktor, Anlage* to start up

An|fahrt F *(= Anfahrtsweg, Anfahrtszeit)* journey; *(= Zufahrt)* approach; *(= Einfahrt)* drive; **„nur ~ zum Krankenhaus"** "access to hospital only"

An|fall M **a** attack; *(= Wutanfall, epileptischer Anfall)* fit; **einen ~ haben/bekommen** *(lit)* to have an attack *or* fit; *(fig inf)* to have *or* throw a fit *(inf)*; **da könnte man Anfälle kriegen** *(inf)* it's enough to send *or* drive you round *(Brit) or* around *(US)* the bend *(inf)*; **in einem ~ von** *(fig)* in a fit of **b** *(= Ertrag, Nebenprodukte)* yield *(an +dat* of); *(von Zinsen)* accrual, yield **c** *(von Reparaturen, Kosten)* amount *(an +dat* of); *(form: = Anhäufung)* accumulation; **bei ~ von Reparaturen** if repairs are necessary

an+fal|len *sep irreg* VT **a** *(= überfallen)* to attack; *(Sittenstrolch etc)* to assault **b** *(liter)* **Heimweh/Sehnsucht fiel ihn an** he was assailed by homesickness/filled with longing VI *aux sein (= sich ergeben)* to arise; *(Zinsen)* to accrue; *(Nebenprodukte)* to be obtained; *(= sich anhäufen)* to accumulate; **die ~den Kosten/Reparaturen/Probleme** the costs/repairs/problems incurred; **die ~de Arbeit** the work which comes up

an|fäl|lig ADJ *(= nicht widerstandsfähig)* delicate; *Motor, Maschine* temperamental; **für etw ~ sein** to be susceptible to sth; **für eine Krankheit ~ sein** to be prone to an illness

An|fäl|lig|keit F delicate health; *(von Motor, Maschine etc)* temperamental nature

An|fang ['anfaŋ] M **-(e)s, Anfänge** [-fɛŋə] *(= Beginn)* beginning, start; *(= erster Teil)* beginning; *(= Ursprung)* beginnings *pl*, origin; **zu** *or* **am ~** to start with; *(= anfänglich)* at first; **gleich zu ~ darauf hinweisen, dass ...** to mention right at the beginning *or* outset that ...; **am ~ schuf Gott Himmel und Erde** *(Bibl)* in the beginning God created the heaven(s) and the earth; **im ~ war das Wort** *(Bibl)* in the beginning was the Word; **~ fünfzig** in one's early fifties; **~ Juni/1998** *etc* at the beginning of June/1998 *etc*; **von ~ an** (right) from the beginning *or* start; **von ~ bis Ende** from start to finish; **den ~ machen** to start *or* begin; *(= den ersten Schritt tun)* to make the first move; **wer macht den ~?** *(bei Spiel etc)* who's going to start?; **einen neuen ~ machen** to make a new start; *(im Leben)* to turn over a new leaf; **ein ~ ist gemacht** it's a start; **seinen ~ nehmen** *(geh)* to commence; **aller ~ ist schwer** *(Prov)* the first step is always the most difficult; **aus kleinen/bescheidenen Anfängen** from small/humble beginnings; **der ~ vom Ende** the beginning of the end

an+fan|gen *sep irreg* VT **a** *(= beginnen) Arbeit, Brief, Gespräch* to start, to begin; *(inf: = anbrauchen) neue Tube etc* to start, to begin; *Streit, Verhältnis, Fabrik* to start
b *(= anstellen, machen)* to do; **das musst du anders ~** you'll have to go about it differently; **was soll ich damit ~?** what am I supposed to do with that?; *(= was nützt mir das?)* what's the use of that?; **damit kann ich nichts ~** *(= nützt mir nichts)* that's no good to me; *(= verstehe ich nicht)* it doesn't mean a thing to me; **nichts mit sich/jdm anzufangen wissen** not to know what to do with oneself/sb; **mit dir ist heute (aber) gar nichts anzufangen!** you're no fun at all today!
VI to begin, to start; **wer fängt an?** who's going to start *or* begin?; **fang (du) an!** (you) begin *or* start!; **ich habe schon angefangen** I've already started; **du hast angefangen!** you started!; *(bei Streit)* you started it!; **es fing zu regnen an** *or* **an zu regnen** it started raining *or* to rain; **das fängt ja schön** *or* **heiter an!** *(iro)* that's a good start!; **jetzt fängt das Leben erst an** life is only just beginning; **fang nicht wieder davon** *or* **damit an!** don't start all that again!, don't bring all that up again!; **mit etw ~** to start sth; **klein/unten ~** to start small/at the bottom; **er hat als kleiner Handwerker angefangen** he started out as a small-time tradesman; **bei einer Firma ~** to start with a firm, to start working for a firm

An|fän|ger(in) M(F) beginner; *(= Neuling)* novice; *(Aut)* learner; *(inf: = Nichtskönner)* amateur *(pej)*; **du ~!** *(inf)* you amateur; **sie ist keine ~in mehr** *(hum)* she's certainly no beginner

An|fän|ger-: **An|fän|ger|kurs** M, **An|fän|ger|kur|sus** M beginners' course; **An|fän|ger|übung** F *(Univ)* introductory course

an|fäng|lich ['anfɛŋlɪç] ADJ *attr* initial ADV at first, initially

an|fangs ['anfaŋs] ADV at first, initially; **wie ich schon ~ erwähnte** as I mentioned at the beginning; **gleich ~ auf etw** *(acc)* **hinweisen** to mention sth right at the beginning *or* outset PREP *+gen* **~ der zwanziger Jahre** *or* **Zwanzigerjahre** in the early twenties; **~ des Monats** at the beginning of the month

An|fangs- *in cpds* initial; **An|fangs|buch|sta|be** M first letter; **kleine/große ~n** small/large *or* capital initials; **An|fangs|ge|halt** NT initial *or* starting salary; **An|fangs|ge|schwin|dig|keit** F starting speed; *(esp Phys)* initial velocity; **An|fangs|grün|de** PL rudiments *pl*, elements *pl*; **An|fangs|ka|pi|tal** NT starting capital; **An|fangs|kurs** M *(Fin)* opening price; **An|fangs|sil|be** F first *or* initial syllable; **An|fangs|sta|di|um** NT initial stage; **im ~ dieser Krankheit/dieses Projekts** in the initial stages of this illness/project; **meine Versuche sind schon im ~ stecken geblieben** my attempts never really got off the ground; **An|fangs|un|ter|richt** M first lessons *pl*; **An|fangs|zeit** F starting time

an+fas|sen *sep* VT **a** *(= berühren)* to touch; **fass mal meinen Kopf an** just feel my head
b *(= bei der Hand nehmen)* **jdn ~** to take sb's hand, to take sb by the hand; **sich** *or* **einander** *(geh)* **~** to take each other by the hand; **fasst euch an!** hold hands!; **angefasst gehen** to walk holding hands
c *(fig) (= anpacken) Problem* to tackle, to go about; *(= behandeln) Menschen* to treat
d *(geh: = befallen)* to seize
VI **a** *(= berühren)* to feel; **nicht ~!** don't touch!
b *(= mithelfen)* **mit ~** to give a hand
c *(fig)* **zum Anfassen** *(Sache)* accessible; *Mensch auch* approachable; **Politik zum Anfassen** grass-roots politics
VR *(= sich anfühlen)* to feel; **es fasst sich weich an** it feels *or* is soft (to the touch)

an+fau|chen VT *sep (Katze)* to spit at; *(fig inf)* to snap at

an+fau|len VI *sep aux sein* to begin to go bad; *(Holz)* to start rotting; **angefault** half-rotten

an|fecht|bar ADJ contestable; *(moralisch)* questionable *(form)*

An|fecht|bar|keit ['anfɛçtba:ɐkait] F **-,** *no pl* **wegen der ~ seiner Argumentation/des Urteils** because his argument/the judgement is/was contestable

an+fech|ten VT *sep irreg* **a** *(= nicht anerkennen)* to contest; *Meinung, Aussage* to challenge, to contest; *Urteil, Entscheidung* to appeal against; *Vertrag* to dispute; *Ehe* to contest the validity of **b** *(= beunruhigen)* to trouble; *(= in Versuchung bringen)* to tempt, to lead into temptation; **das ficht mich gar nicht an** that doesn't concern me in the slightest **c** *(obs: = einfallen, überkommen)* **was ficht/focht dich an, das zu tun?** what possessed you to do that?

An|fech|tung ['anfɛçtʊŋ] F **-, -en** **a** *(= das Nichtanerkennen)* contesting; *(von Meinung, Aussage)* challenging; *(von Urteil, Entscheidung)* appeal *(+gen* against); *(von Vertrag)* disputing; *(von Ehe)* action for nullification *or* annulment **b** *(= Versuchung)* temptation; *(= Selbstzweifel)* doubt

An|fech|tungs|kla|ge F *(Jur) (zu Ehescheidung)* action for nullification *or* annulment; *(zu Testament)* action to set aside a/the will; *(zu Patent)* opposition proceedings *pl*

an+fe|gen VI *sep aux sein (inf)* **angefegt kommen** to come belting *(Brit) or* racing along *or (auf einen zu)* up *(inf)*

an+fein|den ['anfaindn] VT *sep* to treat with hostility

An|fein|dung F **-, -en** hostility; **trotz aller ~en** although he/she *etc* had aroused so much animosity

an+fer|ti|gen VT *sep* to make; *Arznei* to make up; *Schriftstück* to draw up; *Hausaufgaben, Protokoll* to do; **jdm etw ~** to make sth for sb; **sich**

(dat) **einen Anzug** *etc* **~ lassen** to have a suit *etc* made

An|fer|ti|gung F making; *(von Arznei)* making up; *(von Schriftstück)* drawing up; *(von Protokoll, Hausaufgaben)* doing; **die ~ dieser Übersetzung/der Arznei hat eine halbe Stunde gedauert** it took half an hour to do the translation/to make up the prescription

an+feuch|ten ['anfɔyçtn] VT *sep* to moisten; *Schwamm, Lippen auch* to wet; *Bügelwäsche auch* to dampen

an+feu|ern VT *sep Ofen* to light; *(Ind)* to fire; *(fig: = ermutigen)* to spur on

An|feu|e|rung F *(fig)* spurring on

An|feu|e|rungs|ruf M cheer; *(esp Pol)* chant; *(= Anfeuerungswort)* shout of encouragement

an+fin|den VR *sep irreg* to be found, to turn up (again)

an+fi|xen VT *sep (sl)* **jdn ~** to give sb his/her first fix *(inf)*; *(= abhängig machen)* to get sb hooked (on drugs) *(inf)*

an+flach|sen ['anflaksn] VT *sep (inf: = veralbern)* **jdn ~** to make fun of sb, to tease sb, to take the piss out of sb *(Brit inf)*

an+flan|schen ['anflanʃn] VT *sep (Tech)* to fix on with a flange *(an +dat* to); *(fig, inf: = verbinden)* to link up *(an +dat* with)

an+flat|tern VI *sep aux sein Schmetterling, Vogel* to flutter along, to come fluttering up *or* along

an+fle|geln VT *sep (inf)* to speak rudely to; **ich lasse mich doch nicht von dir ~!** I'm not prepared to have you swearing at me!

an+fle|hen VT *sep* to beseech, to implore *(um* for); **ich flehe dich an, tu das nicht!** I beg you, don't!

an+flet|schen VT *sep* to bare one's teeth at

an+flie|gen *sep irreg* **VI** *aux sein (auch* **angeflogen kommen**) *(Flugzeug)* to come in to land; *(Vogel, Geschoss, fig geh: Pferd, Fuhrwerk, Reiter)* to come flying up **VT** **a** *(Flugzeug) Flughafen, Piste* to approach; *(Mil) Stellung* to approach; *(= landen)* to land *(in +dat* in, *auf +dat* on); **diese Fluggesellschaft fliegt Bali an** this airline flies to Bali *or* operates a service to Bali **b** *(geh: = befallen)* to overcome

an+flit|zen VI *sep aux sein (inf)* **angeflitzt kommen** to come racing along *or (auf einen zu)* up *(inf)*

An|flug M **a** *(= Flugweg)* flight; *(= das Heranfliegen)* approach; **wir befinden uns im ~ auf Paris** we are now approaching Paris **b** *(= Spur)* trace; *(fig: = Hauch)* hint, trace

An|flug-: **An|flug|hö|he** F approach altitude; **An|flug|weg** M landing path; **An|flug|zeit** F *(= Zeitraum)* descent; *(= Zeitpunkt)* time of starting a/the descent

an+flun|kern VT *sep (inf)* to tell fibs/a fib to

an+for|dern VT *sep* to request, to ask for

An|for|de|rung F **a** *(= Anspruch)* requirement; *(= Belastung)* demand; **große ~en an jdn/etw stellen** to make great demands on sb/sth; **hohe/zu hohe ~en stellen** to demand a lot/too much *(an +acc* of); **den ~en im Beruf/in der Schule gewachsen sein** to be able to meet the demands of one's job/of school **b Anforderungen** PL *(= Niveau)* standards *pl* **c** *no pl (= das Anfordern)* request *(+gen, von* for); **auf ~** on request; **bei der ~ von Ersatzteilen** when requesting spare parts

An|for|de|rungs|pro|fil NT *(für Personen)* job description; *(für Software etc)* product profile; **dem ~ entsprechen** to fit the job description/product profile

An|fra|ge ✪ 47.1 F *(auch Comput)* inquiry; *(Parl)* question; **Kleine ~** *Parliamentary question dealt with in writing;* **Große ~** *Parliamentary question dealt with at a meeting of the Lower House*

an+fra|gen VI *sep* to inquire *(bei jdm* of sb), to ask *(bei jdm* sb); **um Erlaubnis/Genehmigung ~** to ask for permission/approval

an+fres|sen VT *sep irreg* **a** *(Maus)* to nibble at; *(Vogel)* to peck (at); **sich** *(dat)* **einen Bauch ~** *(inf)* to get a potbelly through overeating **b** *(= zersetzen)* to eat away, to erode

an+freun|den ['anfrɔyndn] VR *sep* to make *or* become friends; **sich mit etw ~** *(fig)* to get to like sth; *mit Popmusik etc* to acquire a taste for sth

an+frie|ren VI *sep irreg aux sein (= leicht gefrieren)* to start to freeze; *(Pflanze)* to get a touch of frost; *(= haften bleiben)* to freeze on *(an +acc* -to); *(fig: Mensch)* to freeze stiff

an+fü|gen VT *sep* to add

An|fü|gung F addition; *(zu einem Buch)* addendum

an+füh|len *sep* **VT** to feel **VR** to feel; **sich glatt/weich** *etc* **~** to feel smooth/soft *etc*, to be smooth/soft *etc* to the touch

An|fuhr ['anfuːɐ] F **-, -en** transport(ation)

an|führ|bar ADJ quotable

an+füh|ren VT *sep* **a** *(= vorangehen, befehligen)* to lead **b** *(= zitieren)* to quote, to cite; *Tatsachen, Beispiel* to quote, to cite, to give; *Einzelheiten* to give; *Umstand* to cite, to refer to; *Grund, Beweis* to give, to offer; *(= benennen) jdn* to name, to cite **c** *(Typ)* to indicate *or* mark with quotation marks *or* inverted commas **d** **jdn ~** *(inf)* to have sb on *(inf)*, to take sb for a ride *(inf)*; **der lässt sich leicht ~** he's easily taken in

An|füh|rer(in) M(F) *(= Führer)* leader; *(pej: = Anstifter)* ringleader

An|füh|rung F **a** *(= das Vorangehen)* leadership; *(= Befehligung)* command; **unter ~ von ...** under the leadership of ..., led by ... **b** *(= das Zitieren)* quotation; *(von Tatsachen, Beispiel)* citation; *(von Umstand)* citing, referring to; *(von Grund, Beweis)* giving, offering; *(= Benennung)* naming, citing; *(= Zitat)* quotation; **die ~ von Zitaten/Einzelheiten** giving quotations/details

An|füh|rungs|strich M, **An|füh|rungs|zei|chen** NT quotation mark, inverted comma; **in ~en** *or* **Anführungszeichen** in inverted commas, in quotation marks, in quotes; **das habe ich in Anführungszeichen gesagt** I was saying that in inverted commas; **einfache/doppelte Anführungszeichen** *(pl) or* **~e** *(pl)* single/double quotation marks *pl or* quotes *pl*; **typografische Anführungszeichen** *(pl) (Comput)* smart quotes *pl*; **Anführungszeichen Anfang/Ende** *(beim Diktieren)* quote/unquote; *(beim Zitieren)* (I) quote/end of quote

an+fül|len VT *sep* to fill (up); **mit etw angefüllt sein** to be full of sth, to be filled with sth

an+fun|keln VT *sep* to flash at

an+fun|ken VT *sep* to radio

an+fut|tern VT *sep (inf)* **sich** *(dat)* **einen Bauch ~** to acquire *or* develop a potbelly

An|ga|be ['angaː-] F **a** *usu pl (= Aussage)* statement; *(= Anweisung)* instruction; *(= Zahl, Detail)* detail; **~n über etw** *(acc)* **machen** to give details about sth; **laut ~n** *(+gen)* according to; **nach Ihren eigenen ~n** by your own account; **nach ~n des Zeugen** according to (the testimony of) the witness; **~n zur Person** *(form)* personal details *or* particulars; **~n zur Sache machen** *(Jur)* to give details of the case **b** *(= Nennung)* giving; **wir bitten um ~ der Einzelheiten/Preise** please give *or* quote details/prices; **er ist ohne ~ seiner neuen Adresse verzogen** he moved without informing anyone of his new address *or* without telling anyone his new address; **ohne ~ von Gründen** without giving any reasons; **vergessen Sie nicht die ~ des Datums auf dem Brief** don't forget to give *or* put the date on the letter **c** *no pl (inf: = Prahlerei)* showing off; *(esp durch Reden)* bragging, boasting **d** *(Sport: = Aufschlag)* service, serve; **wer hat ~?** whose service *or* serve is it?, whose turn is it to serve?

an+gaf|fen ['anga-] VT *sep (pej)* to gape at

an+gäh|nen ['angɛː-] VT *sep* to yawn at

an+ga|lop|pie|ren ['anga-] *ptp* **angaloppiert** VI *sep aux sein* to gallop up; **angaloppiert kommen** to come galloping up

an|gän|gig ['angɛ-] ADJ *(form) (= erlaubt)* permissible; *(= möglich)* feasible

an+ge|ben ['angeː-] *sep irreg* **VT** **a** *(= nennen)* to give; *(als Zeugen)* to name, to cite; *(schriftlich)* to indicate; *(= erklären)* to explain; *(beim Zoll)* to declare; *(= anzeigen) Preis, Temperatur etc* to indicate; *(= aussagen)* to state; *(= behaupten)* to maintain → *auch* **angegeben** **b** *(= bestimmen) Tempo, Kurs* to set; *(Comput)* to specify; *(Mus) Tempo, Note* to give; **den Takt ~** *(= klopfen)* to beat time → **Ton** **a** **c** *(dated: = anzeigen)* to report *(bei* to) **VI** **a** *(= prahlen)* to show off, to pose *(inf)*; *(esp durch Reden)* to boast, to brag *(mit* about) **b** *(Tennis etc)* to serve **c** *(Cards)* to deal

An|ge|ber(in) ['angeː-] M(F) *(= Prahler)* show-off, poser *(inf)*; *(esp durch Reden)* boaster

An|ge|be|rei [angeːbəˈrai] F **-, -en** *(inf)* **a** *no pl (= Prahlerei)* showing off, posing *(inf) (mit* about); *(esp verbal)* boasting, bragging *(mit* about) **b** *usu pl (= Äußerung)* boast

an|ge|be|risch ['angeːbərɪʃ] **ADJ** *Reden* boastful; *Aussehen, Benehmen, Tonfall* pretentious, posy *(inf)* **ADV** pretentiously; **sich ~ benehmen** to be pretentious

An|ge|ber|tum ['angeːbɐtuːm] NT **-s**, *no pl (in äußerer Erscheinung)* ostentation; *(durch Reden)* boastfulness; *(in Benehmen)* pretension

An|ge|be|te|te(r) ['angəbeːtətə] MF *decl as adj (hum, geh) (= verehrter Mensch)* idol; *(= Geliebte(r))* beloved

An|ge|bin|de ['angə-] NT *(dated geh)* gift, present

an|geb|lich ['angeːplɪç] **ADJ** *attr* so-called, alleged **ADV** supposedly, allegedly; **er ist ~ Musiker** he says he's a musician

an|ge|bo|ren ['angə-] ADJ innate, inherent; *(Med, fig inf)* congenital *(bei* to); **an seine Faulheit musst du dich gewöhnen, die ist ~** *(inf)* you'll have to get used to his laziness, he was born that way

An|ge|bot ['angə-] ✪ 46.6 NT **a** *(= Anerbieten, angebotener Preis)* offer; *(bei Auktion)* bid; *(Comm: = Offerte)* offer, tender *(über +acc, für* for); *(Comm: = Kostenvoranschlag)* offer, quote; **im ~** *(preisgünstig)* on special offer **b** *no pl (Comm, Fin)* supply *(an +dat, von* of); *(inf: = Sonderangebot)* special offer; **~ und Nachfrage** supply and demand; **~ des Monats** this month's special offer

An|ge|bots-: **An|ge|bots|la|ge** F supply situation; **An|ge|bots|lü|cke** F gap in the market; **An|ge|bots|preis** M asking price; **An|ge|bots|über|hang** M surplus supply

an|ge|bracht ['angəbraxt] ADJ appropriate; *(= sinnvoll)* reasonable; **schlecht ~** uncalled-for → *auch* **anbringen**

an|ge|brannt ['angə-] **ADJ** burned **ADV** **~ riechen/schmecken** to smell/taste burned; **es riecht hier so ~** there's a smell of burning here → *auch* **anbrennen**

an|ge|bro|chen ['angə-] ADJ **a** *Packung, Flasche* open(ed); **wie viel ist von den ~en hundert Euro übrig?** how much is left from the 100 euros we'd started using?; **ein ~er Abend/Nachmittag/Urlaub** *(hum)* the rest of an evening/afternoon/a holiday *(esp Brit) or* vacation *(US)*; **er wusste mit dem ~en Tag nichts anzufangen** he didn't know what to do for the rest of the day; **das Parken kostet für jede ~e Stunde einen Euro** parking costs one euro for every hour or part of an hour **b** *Knochen* cracked → *auch* **anbrechen**

an|ge|bun|den ['angə-] ADJ *(= beschäftigt)* tied (down); **kurz ~ sein** *(inf)* to be abrupt *or* curt *or* brusque → *auch* **anbinden**

an+ge|dei|hen ['angə-] *ptp* **angediehen** VT *sep irreg* **jdm etw ~ lassen** *(geh)* to provide sb with sth

An|ge|den|ken ['angə-] NT, *no pl (geh)* remembrance; **mein Großvater seligen ~s** my late lamented grandfather

an|ge|du|selt ['angədu:zlt] ADJ *(inf)* tipsy, merry *(Brit inf)*

an|ge|ekelt ['angəle:klt] ADV in disgust ADJ disgusted → *auch* **anekeln**

an|ge|gam|melt ['angəgamlt] ADJ *(inf)* **~e Lebensmittel** food that is going off *(Brit) or* bad

an|ge|gan|gen ['angəgaŋən] ADJ *(inf)* **~ sein** to have gone off *(Brit) or* bad; **~e Lebensmittel** food which has gone off *(Brit) or* bad → *auch* **angehen**

an|ge|ge|ben ['angəge:bn] ADJ *Ziel* declared, stated; *Zeitraum* given, stated; **die ~e Telefonnummer** the phone number given; **am ~en Ort** loco citato → *auch* **angeben**

an|ge|gilbt ['angəgılpt] ADJ yellowed

an|ge|gos|sen ['angəgɔsn] ADV **wie ~ sitzen** *or* **passen** to fit like a glove

an|ge|graut ['angəgraut] ADJ grey *(Brit)*, gray *(US)*; *Schläfen, Haar auch* greying *(Brit)*, graying *(US)*

an|ge|grif|fen ['angəgrıfn] ADJ *Gesundheit* weakened; *Mensch, Aussehen* frail; *(= erschöpft)* exhausted; *(nervlich)* strained; **sie ist nervlich immer noch ~** her nerves are still strained; **sie ist gesundheitlich immer noch ~** she is still weak *or* frail → *auch* **angreifen**

an|ge|hal|ten ['angəhaltn] ADJ **~ sein, etw zu tun** to be required *or* obliged to do sth; **~ sein, etw zu unterlassen** to be required *or* obliged to refrain from doing sth; **zu Pünktlichkeit ~ sein** to be required to be punctual → *auch* **Atem, anhalten**

an|ge|haucht ['angəhauxt] ADJ **links/rechts ~ sein** to have *or* show left-wing/right-wing tendencies *or* leanings → *auch* **anhauchen**

an|ge|hei|ra|tet ['angəhairatət] ADJ related by marriage; **ein ~er Cousin** a cousin by marriage

an|ge|hei|tert ['angəhaitɐt] ADJ tipsy, merry *(Brit inf)*

an+ge|hen ['ange:-] *sep irreg* VI *aux sein* **a** *(inf: = beginnen) (Schule, Theater etc)* to start; *(Feuer)* to start burning, to catch; *(Radio)* to come on; *(Licht)* to come *or* go on; **es langsam ~ lassen** *(fig)* to take it slowly

b *(= entgegentreten)* **gegen jdn ~** to fight sb, to tackle sb; **gegen etw ~** to fight sth; *gegen Flammen, Hochwasser* to fight sth back, to combat sth; *gegen Missstände, Zustände* to take measures against sth; **dagegen muss man ~** something must be done about it

c → **angegangen**

VT **a** *aux haben or (S Ger) sein (= anpacken) Aufgabe, Schwierigkeiten, Hindernis* to tackle; *Gegner* to attack; *Kurve* to take

b *aux haben or (S Ger) sein (= bitten)* to ask *(jdn um etw* sb for sth)

c *aux sein (= betreffen)* to concern; **was mich angeht** for my part; **was geht das ihn an?** *(inf)* what's that got to do with him?; **das geht ihn gar nichts** *or* **einen Dreck** *or* **einen feuchten Staub an** *(inf)* that's none of his business, that's got nothing *or* damn all *(inf)* to do with him

VI *impers aux sein* **das geht nicht/keinesfalls an** that won't do, that's not on, that's quite out of the question

an|ge|hend ADJ *Musiker, Künstler, Manager etc* budding; *Lehrer, Ehemann, Vater* prospective; **mit 16 ist sie jetzt schon eine ~e junge Dame** at 16 she's rapidly becoming *or* is almost a young lady; **er ist ein ~er Sechziger** he's approaching sixty

an+ge|hö|ren ['angə-] *ptp* **angehört** VI *sep +dat* to belong to; *(einer Partei, einer Familie auch)* to be a member of; **jdm/einander ~** *(liter)* to belong to sb/one another *or* each other

an|ge|hö|rig ['angə-] ADJ belonging *(+dat* to); **keiner Partei ~e Bürger** citizens who do not belong to any party

An|ge|hö|ri|ge(r) ['angəhø:rıgə] MF *decl as adj* **a** *(= Mitglied)* member **b** *(= Familienangehörige)* relative, relation; **der nächste ~** the next of kin

An|ge|hö|rig|keit F *(zu einer Partei etc)* membership *(zu* of)

an|ge|jahrt ['angəja:ɐt] ADJ *(inf) Mensch* ageing; **dieser Film ist reichlich ~** this film is really dated

An|ge|klag|te(r) ['angəkla:ktə] MF *decl as adj* accused, defendant

an|ge|knackst ['angəknakst] ADJ *Wirbel, Bandscheibe* damaged; *(inf) Mensch (seelisch)* uptight *(inf)*; *Selbstvertrauen, Selbstbewusstsein* weakened; *Mythos* tarnished; **er/seine Gesundheit ist ~** he is in bad shape *or* a bad way; **sie ist noch immer etwas ~** she still hasn't got over it yet; **der Aufwärtstrend scheint ~ zu sein** the upward trend seems to be slowing → *auch* **anknacksen**

an|ge|krän|kelt ['angəkrɛŋklt] ADJ *(geh)* sickly, frail, ailing; **von keinem Zweifel ~ sein** not to have the slightest doubt; **von des Gedankens Blässe ~** *(liter)* plagued by *or* with misgivings

an|ge|kratzt ['angəkratst] ADJ *(inf) Person* the worse for wear; *Image, Mythos* dented → *auch* **ankratzen**

An|gel ['aŋl] F **-, -n** **a** *(= Türangel, Fensterangel)* hinge; **etw aus den ~n heben** *(lit)* to lift sth off its hinges; *(fig)* to revolutionize sth completely; **die Welt aus den ~n heben** *(fig)* to turn the world upside down **b** *(= Fischfanggerät)* (fishing) rod and line *(Brit)*, fishing pole *(US)*; *(zum Schwimmenlernen)* swimming harness; **die ~ auswerfen** to cast (the line); **jdm an die ~ gehen** *(fig)* to fall for *or* swallow sb's line

an|ge|le|gen ['angə-] ADJ **sich** *(dat)* **etw ~ sein lassen** *(form)* to concern oneself with sth

An|ge|le|gen|heit ['angə-] F matter; *(politisch, persönlich)* affair; *(= Aufgabe)* concern; **das ist meine/nicht meine ~** that's my/not my concern *or* business; **sich um seine eigenen ~en kümmern** to mind one's own business; **in einer dienstlichen ~** on official business; **in eigener ~** on a private *or* personal matter

an|ge|le|gent|lich ['angə-] *(geh)* ADJ *Bitte, Frage* pressing, insistent; *(= dringend)* pressing, urgent; *Bemühung* enthusiastic; *Empfehlung* warm, eager ADV in particular; **sich ~ nach jdm erkundigen** to ask particularly about sb

an|ge|legt ['angəle:kt] ADJ **a** *(= gerichtet)* calculated *(auf +acc* for) **b** **künstlich ~** *(Hügel, Landschaft)* artificial, man-made; **breit ~** *(Wissenschaft, Strategie)* wide-ranging → *auch* **anlegen**

an|ge|lernt ['angə-] ADJ **a** *Arbeiter* semiskilled; **der Lohn für Angelernte** the wage for semiskilled workers **b** *Verhalten* acquired; *Wissen* superficially acquired → *auch* **anlernen**

An|gel-: **An|gel|fi|sche|rei** F angling; **An|gel|ge|rät** NT fishing tackle *no pl*; **An|gel|ha|ken** M fish-hook; **An|gel|kar|te** F fishing *or* angler's licence *(Brit) or* license *(US)*; **An|gel|lei|ne** F fishing line

an|geln ['aŋln] VI **a** *(= fischen)* to angle *(esp Brit)*, to fish; **~ gehen** to go angling *(esp Brit) or* fishing; **nach etw** *or* **auf** *(form)* **etw** *(acc)* **~** *(lit)* to fish for sth; **nach Komplimenten/Lob** *etc* **~** to fish *or* angle *(esp Brit)* for compliments/praise *etc* **b** *(= zu greifen versuchen, hervorziehen)* to fish; **nach etw ~** to fish (around) for sth VT *Fisch* to fish for; *(= fangen)* to catch; **sich** *(dat)* **einen Mann ~** *(inf)* to catch (oneself) a man; **den werde ich mir ~** *(inf: = vornehmen)* I'll give him a piece of my mind

An|geln ['aŋln] PL *(Hist)* Angles *pl*

an+ge|lo|ben ['angə-] *ptp* **angelobt** VT *sep* **a** *(liter)* **jdm etw ~** to swear sth to sb **b** *(Aus: = vereidigen)* to swear in

An|gel-: **An|gel|platz** M fishing ground; **An|gel|punkt** M crucial *or* central point; *(= Frage)* key *or* central issue; **An|gel|ru|te** F fishing rod

An|gel|sach|se ['aŋl-] M, **An|gel|säch|sin** F Anglo-Saxon

an|gel|säch|sisch ADJ Anglo-Saxon

An|gel-: **An|gel|schein** M fishing permit; **An|gel|schnur** F fishing line; **An|gel|sport** M angling *(esp Brit)*, fishing; **an|gel|weit** ADV = **sperrangelweit**

an|ge|mes|sen ['angə-] ADJ *(= passend, entsprechend)* appropriate *(+dat* to, for); *(= adäquat)* adequate *(+dat* for); *Preis* reasonable, fair; **eine der Leistung ~e Bezahlung** payment commensurate with performance ADV appropriately; **jds Einsatz ~ würdigen** to give sb enough credit for their efforts

An|ge|mes|sen|heit F appropriateness; *(= Adäquatheit)* adequacy; *(von Preis)* fairness, reasonableness

an|ge|nehm ['angə-] ADJ pleasant, agreeable; **das wäre mir sehr ~** I should be very *or* most grateful, I should greatly appreciate it; **es ist mir gar nicht ~, wenn ich früh aufstehen muss** I don't like getting up early; **es ist mir gar nicht ~, dass er mich besuchen will** I don't like the idea of him wanting to visit me; **ist es Ihnen so ~?** is that all right for you?, is it all right like that for you?; **wenn Ihnen das ~er ist** if you prefer; **~e Ruhe/Reise!** *etc* have a good *or* pleasant rest/journey *etc*; **(sehr) ~!** *(form)* delighted (to meet you); **das Angenehme mit dem Nützlichen verbinden** to combine business with pleasure

ADV pleasantly, agreeably

an|ge|nom|men ['angənɔmən] ✪ 28.1 ADJ assumed; *Name auch, Kind* adopted CONJ assuming → *auch* **annehmen**

an|ge|passt ['angəpast] ADJ *Mensch* conformist; *(= modifiziert) Version* adapted *(dat* to); **gesellschaftlich ~** conformist ADV **sich ~ verhalten** to conform, to fit in; **sich ~ zeigen** to try to conform *or* to fit in → *auch* **anpassen**

An|ge|passt|heit F **-,** *no pl (von Mensch)* conformism

An|ger ['aŋɐ] M **-s, -** *(dial)* **a** *(= Dorfanger)* village green; *(old: = Wiese)* pasture, meadow **b** *(= Schindanger)* knacker's yard *(Brit)*, slaughterhouse

An|ger|dorf NT village built around a village green

an|ge|regt ['angəre:kt] ADJ lively, animated ADV **sie diskutierten ~** their discussion was lively *or* animated; **sie unterhielten sich ~** they had a lively *or* animated conversation → *auch* **anregen**

An|ge|regt|heit F **-,** *no pl* liveliness, animation

an|ge|säu|selt ['angəzɔyzlt] ADJ *(inf)* tipsy, merry *(Brit inf)* → *auch* **ansäuseln**

an|ge|schla|gen ['angəʃla:gn] ADJ *(inf) Mensch, Aussehen, Nerven* shattered *(inf)*; *Gesundheit* poor *(inf)*; *Ruf* tarnished; *Ehe, Unternehmen, Volkswirtschaft* failing, on the rocks *pred (inf)*; *(= betrunken)* sloshed *(inf)*; **von etw ~ sein** to be shattered by sth *(inf)* → *auch* **anschlagen**

an|ge|schmiert ['angəʃmi:ɐt] ADJ *pred (inf)* in trouble, in dead shtuck *(Brit inf)*; **mit dem/der Waschmaschine bist du ganz schön ~** he/the washing machine is not all he/it is cracked up to be *(inf)*; **der/die Angeschmierte sein** to have been had *(inf)* → *auch* **anschmieren**

an|ge|schmutzt ['angəʃmʊtst] ADJ soiled; *(Comm)* shopsoiled *(Brit)*, damaged

an|ge|schrie|ben ['angəʃri:bn] ADJ *(inf)* **bei jdm gut/schlecht ~ sein** to be in sb's good/bad books, to be well in/not very well in with sb *(inf)* → *auch* **anschreiben**

An|ge|schul|dig|te(r) ['angəʃʊldıçtə] MF *decl as adj* suspect

an|ge|se|hen ['angəze:ən] ADJ respected → *auch* **ansehen**

an|ge|ses|sen ['angəzɛsn] ADJ = **eingesessen**

An|ge|sicht ['angə-] NT **-(e)s, -er** *or Aus* **-e** *(geh)* face, countenance *(liter)*; **von ~ zu ~** face to face; **jdn von ~ sehen** to see sb face to face; **jdn von ~ kennen** to know sb by sight; **im ~** *+gen (fig)* in the face of

an|ge|sichts ['angəzıçts] PREP *+gen* in the face of; *(= im Hinblick auf)* in view of; **~ des Todes** in the face of death; **~ des Sternenhimmels kommt sich der Mensch winzig und nichtig vor** in contrast to the starry sky man seems minute and insignificant

an|ge|spannt ['angəʃpant] ADJ **a** (= *angestrengt*) *Nerven* tense, strained; *Aufmerksamkeit* close, keen; **aufs höchste** *or* **Höchste ~ sein** to be very *or* highly tense **b** (= *bedrohlich*) *politische Lage* tense, strained; *(Comm) Markt, Lage* tight, overstretched ADV *dasitzen, verfolgen* tensely; *zuhören* attentively, closely; **~ wirken** to seem tense → *auch* **anspannen**

An|ge|spannt|heit F **a** (*von Nerven*) tenseness **b** (= *Bedrohlichkeit: von Lage*) tension; *(Comm: von Marktlage)* tightness

Angest. *abbr von* **Angestellte(r)**

an|ge|stammt ['angəʃtamt] ADJ (= *überkommen*) traditional; (= *ererbt*) *Rechte* hereditary, ancestral; *Besitz* inherited

an|ge|stellt ['angəʃtɛlt] ADJ *pred* **~ sein** to be an employee (*bei* of), to be on the staff (*bei* of); **er ist bei Collins ~** he works for Collins; **fest ~ sein** to be on the permanent staff; **ich bin nicht beamtet, sondern nur ~** I don't have permanent tenure in my job → *auch* **anstellen**

An|ge|stell|ten-: **An|ge|stell|ten|ge|werk|schaft** F white-collar union; **An|ge|stell|ten|ver|hält|nis** NT employment (without permanent tenure); **im ~** in non-tenured employment; **An|ge|stell|ten|ver|si|che|rung** F (salaried) employees' insurance

An|ge|stell|te(r) ['angəʃtɛltə] MF *decl as adj* (salaried) employee; (= *Büroangestellte*) office worker, white-collar worker; (= *Behördenangestellte*) public employee (without tenure)

an|ge|sto|chen ['angəʃtɔxn] ADJ *(inf)* **wie ~** like a stuck pig *(inf)* → *auch* **anstechen**

an|ge|strengt ['angəʃtrɛŋt] ADJ *Gesicht* strained; *Arbeiten, Denken* hard ADV *diskutieren, nachdenken* carefully → *auch* **anstrengen**

an|ge|tan ['angəta:n] ADJ *pred* **a** **von jdm/etw ~ sein** to be taken with sb/sth; **es jdm ~ haben** to have made quite an impression on sb; **das Mädchen hat es ihm ~** he has fallen for that girl **b** **danach** *or* **dazu ~ sein, etw zu tun** *(geh)* to be suitable for doing sth; *(Wesen, Atmosphäre, Benehmen etc)* to be apt *or* calculated to do sth **c** (= *bekleidet*) **mit etw ~ sein** to be dressed in sth → *auch* **antun**

An|ge|trau|te(r) ['angətrautə] MF *decl as adj (hum)* spouse, better half *(hum)*

an|ge|trun|ken ['angətrʊŋkn] ADJ *Mensch, Zustand* inebriated, intoxicated; **in ~em Zustand Auto fahren** to drive under the influence (of alcohol) → *auch* **antrinken**

an|ge|wandt ['angə-] ADJ *attr Wissenschaft etc* applied → *auch* **anwenden**

an|ge|wie|sen ['angəvi:zn] ADJ **auf jdn/etw ~ sein** to have to rely on sb/sth, to be dependent on sb/sth; **auf sich selbst ~ sein** to have to fend for oneself; *(Kind)* to be left to one's own devices; **in dieser Arbeit war er auf sich selbst und sein eigenes Wissen ~** in this work he had to rely on himself and his own knowledge; **darauf bin ich nicht ~** I can get along without it, I don't need it; **ich bin selbst auf jeden Euro ~** I need every euro myself → *auch* **anweisen**

an+ge|wöh|nen ['angə-] *ptp* **angewöhnt** VT *sep* **jdm etw ~** to get sb used to sth, to accustom sb to sth; **sich** *(dat)* **etw ~** to get into the habit of sth; **es sich** *(dat)* **~, etw zu tun** to get into the habit of doing sth

An|ge|wohn|heit ['angə-] F habit

an|ge|zeigt ['angətsaikt] ADJ *(form)* advisable; (= *angebracht*) appropriate; **etw für ~ halten** to consider sth advisable/appropriate → *auch* **anzeigen**

an+gif|ten ['angɪ-] VT *sep (pej inf)* to snap at, to let fly at

An|gi|na [aŋ'gi:na] F **-, Anginen** [-nən] *(Med)* tonsillitis, sore throat; **~ Pectoris** angina (pectoris)

An|gio|gra|fie, **An|gio|gra|phie** [aŋgiogra'fi:] F **-, -n** [-'fi:ən] *(Med)* angiography

An|gio|plas|tie [aŋgioplas'ti:] F **-**, *no pl (Med)* angioplasty

an+glei|chen ['angl-] *sep irreg* VT to bring into line, to align (*+dat, an +acc* with) VR (*gegenseitig: Kulturen, Geschlechter, Methoden*) to grow closer together; **sich jdm/einer Sache ~** (*einseitig*) to become like sb/sth; **die beiden haben sich (aneinander) angeglichen** the two of them have become more alike

An|glei|chung F **a** (= *das Angleichen*) alignment (*an +acc* with) **b** (= *das Gleicherwerden*) **die zunehmende ~ der Kulturen** the increasing similarity between the cultures; **die ~ Deutschlands an Amerika** Germany's growing similarity with America

Ang|ler ['aŋlɐ] M **-s, -**, **Ang|le|rin** [-ərɪn] F **-, -nen** angler *(esp Brit)*, fisherman

an+glie|dern ['angl-] VT *sep Verein, Partei* to affiliate (*+dat, an +acc* to *(Brit) or* with *(US)*); *Land* to annexe *(Brit) or* annex *(US)* (*+dat, an +acc* to)

An|glie|de|rung F affiliation; (*von Land*) annexation

ang|li|ka|nisch [aŋgli'ka:nɪʃ] ADJ Anglican; **die ~e Kirche** the Anglican Church, the Church of England

Ang|li|ka|nis|mus [aŋglika'nɪsmʊs] M **-**, *no pl* Anglicanism

ang|li|sie|ren [aŋgli'zi:rən] *ptp* **anglisiert** VT to anglicize

Ang|li|sie|rung F **-**, *no pl* anglicizing

Ang|list [aŋ'glɪst] M **-en, -en**, **Ang|lis|tin** [-'glɪstɪn] F **-, -nen** English specialist, Anglicist; (= *Student*) student of English

Ang|lis|tik [aŋ'glɪstɪk] F **-**, *no pl* English (language and literature)

Ang|li|zis|mus [aŋgli'tsɪsmʊs] M **-, Anglizismen** [-mən] anglicism

Ang|lo- *in cpds* Anglo; **Ang|lo|ame|ri|ka|ner(in)** M(F) (= *aus England stammender Amerikaner*) Anglo-American; **die ~** (= *Briten und Amerikaner*) the Anglo-Saxons; **ang|lo|phil** [aŋglo'fi:l] ADJ anglophile; **ang|lo|phob** [aŋglo'fo:p] ADJ anglophobe, anglophobic

an+glot|zen ['angl-] VT *sep (inf)* to gawp *or* gape at *(inf)*

an+glü|hen ['angl-] VT *sep (lit)* to heat red-hot; *(fig)* to glow at

An|go|la [aŋ'go:la] NT **-s** Angola

An|go|la|ner [aŋgo'la:nɐ] M **-s, -**, **An|go|la|ne|rin** [-ərɪn] F **-, -nen** Angolan

an|go|la|nisch [aŋgo'la:nɪʃ] ADJ Angolan

An|go|ra- *in cpds* Angora; **An|go|ra|ka|nin|chen** NT Angora rabbit; **An|go|ra|kat|ze** F Angora cat; **An|go|ra|wol|le** F Angora (wool); **An|go|ra|zie|ge** F Angora goat

An|gos|tu|ra [aŋgɔs'tu:ra] M **-s, -s** Angostura (bitters® *pl*)

an|greif|bar ADJ *Behauptung, Politiker* open to attack

an+grei|fen ['angr-] *sep irreg* VT **a** (= *überfallen, kritisieren, Sport*) to attack **b** (= *schwächen*) *Organismus, Organ, Nerven* to weaken; *Gesundheit, Pflanzen* to affect; (= *ermüden, anstrengen*) to strain; (= *schädlich sein für, zersetzen*) *Lack, Farbe* to attack; **seine Krankheit hat ihn sehr angegriffen** his illness weakened him greatly; **das hat ihn sehr angegriffen** that affected him greatly → *auch* **angegriffen** **c** (= *anbrechen*) *Vorräte, Geld* to break into, to draw on **d** (*dial:* = *anfassen*) to touch **e** (*fig:* = *unternehmen, anpacken*) to attack, to tackle VI **a** (*Mil, Sport, fig*) to attack **b** (*geh:* = *ansetzen*) to proceed, to start (*an +dat* from) **c** (*dial:* = *anfassen*) to touch VR (*dial:* = *sich anfühlen*) to feel

An|grei|fer ['angraifɐ] M **-s, -**, **An|grei|fe|rin** [-ərɪn] F **-, -nen** attacker (*auch Sport, fig*)

an+gren|zen ['angr-] VI *sep* **an etw** *(acc)* **~** to border on sth, to adjoin sth

an|gren|zend ADJ *attr* adjacent (*an +acc* to), adjoining (*an etw acc* sth)

An|griff ['angr-] M (*Mil, Sport, fig*) attack (*gegen, auf +acc* on); (= *Luftangriff*) (air) raid; **~ ist die beste Verteidigung** *(prov)* attack is the best means of defence *(Brit) or* defense *(US)*; **zum ~ übergehen** to go over to the attack, to take the offensive; **zum ~ blasen** (*Mil, fig*) to sound the charge; **etw in ~ nehmen** to tackle sth, to set about sth

an|grif|fig ['angr-] ADJ *(Sw)* aggressive

An|griffs-: **An|griffs|flä|che** F target; **jdm/einer Sache eine ~ bieten** (*lit, fig*) to provide sb/sth with a target; **eine ~ bieten** to present a target; **An|griffs|fuß|ball** M attacking football; **An|griffs|krieg** M war of aggression; **An|griffs|li|nie** F (*Ballspiel*) attack line; **An|griffs|lust** F aggressiveness; **an|griffs|lus|tig** ADJ aggressive; **An|griffs|punkt** M target; **An|griffs|rei|he** F (*Sport*) forwards *pl*; **An|griffs|spiel** NT (*Sport*) aggressive *or* attacking game; **An|griffs|spie|ler(in)** M(F) (*Sport*) attacking player; (*Ftbl*) forward; **An|griffs|spit|ze** F (*Mil*) spearhead; **An|griffs|tak|tik** F attacking tactics *pl*; **An|griffs|waf|fe** F offensive weapon

an+grin|sen ['angr-] VT *sep* to grin at

angst [aŋst] ADJ *pred* afraid; **ihr wurde ~ (und bange)** she became worried *or* anxious; **mir ist um deine Gesundheit ~** I'm worried about your health → *auch* **Angst**

Angst [aŋst] F **-, ¨-e** ['ɛŋstə] (= *innere Unruhe, Psych*) anxiety (*um* about); (= *Sorge*) worry (*um* about); (= *Befürchtung*) fear (*um* for, *vor +dat* of); (*stärker:* = *Furcht, Grauen*) fear, dread (*vor +dat* of); (= *Existenzangst*) angst; **~ haben** to be afraid *or* scared; **~ vor Spinnen/vorm Fliegen haben** to be afraid *or* scared of spiders/flying; **~ um jdn/etw haben** to be anxious *or* worried about sb/sth; **~ bekommen** *or* **kriegen** to get *or* become afraid *or* scared; (= *erschrecken*) to take fright; **das machte ihm ~ (und Bange)** that worried him, that made him anxious; **aus ~, etw zu tun** for fear of doing sth; **keine ~!** don't be afraid; **keine ~, ich sage es ihm schon** don't you worry, I'll tell him; **jdm ~ machen** to scare sb; **jdm ~ einflößen** *or* **einjagen** to frighten sb; **jdn in ~ und Schrecken versetzen** to terrify sb; **in tausend Ängsten schweben** to be terribly worried *or* anxious

Angst-: **angst|er|füllt** [-ləɛfʏlt] ADJ *Gesicht, Stimme* frightened ADV fearfully, with fear; **angst|frei** ADJ free from fear, anxiety-free ADV without fear; **Angst|ge|fühl** NT feeling of anxiety; **Angst|geg|ner(in)** M(F) most feared opponent; **Bayern München ist unser ~** Bayern Munich is the team we fear (the) most; **Angst|ha|se** M *(inf)* scaredy-cat *(inf)*

ängs|ti|gen ['ɛŋstɪgn] VT to frighten; (= *unruhig machen*) to worry VR to be afraid; (= *sich sorgen*) to worry; **sich vor etw** *(dat)* **~** to be afraid of sth; **sich wegen etw ~** to worry about sth

Angst-: **Angst|kauf** M panic buying *no pl*; **Angst|laut** M alarm cry

ängst|lich ['ɛŋstlɪç] ADJ **a** (= *verängstigt*) anxious, apprehensive; (= *schüchtern*) timid, timorous **b** (= *übertrieben genau*) particular, fastidious ADV **~ darauf bedacht sein, etw zu tun** to be at pains to do sth; **ein ~ gehütetes Geheimnis** a closely guarded secret; **etw ~ verbergen** to conceal sth scrupulously

Ängst|lich|keit F **-**, *no pl* (= *das Verängstigtsein*) anxiety, apprehension; (= *Schüchternheit*) timidity, timorousness

Angst-: **Angst|lust** F *(Psych)* *enjoyment and excitement combined with fear*; **Angst|ma|che** F, *no pl (inf)* scaremongering *no pl (Brit)*, inciting *no pl* fear; **Angst|ma|cher(in)** M(F) *(inf)* scaremonger *(Brit)*, sb who incites fear; **Angst|neu|ro|se** F anxiety neurosis; **Angst|neu|ro|ti|ker(in)** M(F) neurotic; **Angst|pa|ro|le** F *(inf)* scaremongering *no pl (Brit)*, inciting *no pl* fear; **~n verbreiten** to incite fear, to scaremonger *(Brit)*; **Angst|par|tie** F *(inf)* nerve-racking affair; **Angst|psy|cho|se** F anxiety psychosis

Angst|röm ['aŋstrø:m, 'ɔŋstrø:m] NT **-(s), -** *(Phys)* angstrom

Angst-: **angst|schlot|ternd** [-ʃlɔtɐnd] ADJ *(inf)* trembling *or* shaking with fear; **Angst|schrei** M cry of fear; **Angst|schweiß** M cold sweat; **mir brach der ~ aus** I broke out in a cold sweat; **Angst|traum** M nightmare; **angst|ver|zerrt** [-fɛɐtsɛrt] ADJ *Gesicht* petrified, terror-struck; **angst|voll** ADJ *Stille, Schweigen* apprehensive; *Hast* fearful; **Angst|zu|stand** M state of panic; **Angstzustände bekommen** to get into a state of panic

an+gu|cken ['angʊ-] VT *sep (inf)* to look at

an+gur|ten ['angʊrtn] VT *sep* = **anschnallen VT b**

an+ha|ben VT *sep irreg* **a** *(= angezogen haben)* to have on, to wear **b** *(= zuleide tun)* to do harm; **jdm etwas ~ wollen** to want to harm sb; **die Kälte kann mir nichts ~** the cold doesn't worry *or* bother me **c** *(= am Zeuge flicken)* **Sie können/die Polizei kann mir nichts ~!** *(inf)* you/the police can't touch me

an+haf|ten VI *sep* **a** *(lit)* to stick *(an +dat* to), to cling *(an +dat* to); **~de Farbreste** bits of paint left sticking on **b** *(fig) +dat* to stick to, to stay with; *(= zugehören: Risiko etc)* to be attached to

An|halt M *(= Hinweis)* clue *(für* about); *(für Verdacht)* grounds *pl (für* for); *(= Hilfe)* hint, indication *(für* of, about)

an+hal|ten *sep irreg* VI **a** *(= stehen bleiben)* to stop; **mit dem Sprechen ~** to stop talking **b** *(= fortdauern)* to last **c** *(= werben)* **(bei jdm) um ein Mädchen** *or* **um die Hand eines Mädchens ~** to ask (sb) for a girl's hand in marriage VT **a** *(= stoppen)* to stop → **Atem a, Luft b b** *(= anlegen) Lineal* to use; **sie hielt mir/sich das Kleid an** she held the dress up against me/herself **c** *(= anleiten)* to urge, to encourage → *auch* **angehalten**

an|hal|tend ADJ continuous, incessant ADV continuously, constantly

An|hal|ter(in) M(F) hitchhiker, hitcher *(esp Brit inf)*; **per ~ fahren** to hitchhike, to hitch *(esp Brit inf)*

An|halts|punkt M *(= Vermutung)* clue *(für* about); *(für Verdacht)* grounds *pl*; **ich habe keinerlei ~e** I haven't a clue *(inf)*, I have no idea

an|hand [an'hant], **an Hand** PREP *+gen* **~ eines Beispiels** with an example; **~ dieses Berichts/dieser Unterlagen** from this report/these documents

An|hang M **a** *(= Nachtrag)* appendix; *(von Testament)* codicil; *(von E-Mail)* attachment; **im/als ~ finden Sie ...** *(E-Mail)* please find attached ... **b** *no pl (= Gefolgschaft)* following; *(= Angehörige)* family; **Witwe, 62, ohne ~** widow, 62, no family; **an ~ gewinnen/verlieren** to gain/lose support

an+hän|gen *sep* VT **a** *(= ankuppeln)* to attach *(an +acc* to); *(Rail)* to couple on *(an +acc* to); *Anhänger* to hitch up *(an +acc* to); *(fig: = anfügen)* to add *(+dat, an +acc* to); *(Comput)* to append; *Datei an E-Mail* to attach **b** *(inf)* **jdm etw ~** *(= verkaufen)* to palm sth off on sb; *(= andrehen)* to foist sth on sb; *Krankheit* to pass sth on to sb; *(= nachsagen, anlasten)* to blame sb for sth, to blame sth on sb; *schlechten Ruf, Spitznamen* to give sb sth; *Verdacht, Schuld* to pin sth on sb; **ich weiß nicht, warum er mir unbedingt etwas ~ will** I don't know why he always wants to give me a bad name VR *(lit)* to hang on *(+dat, an +acc* to); *(fig)* to tag along *(+dat, an +acc* with); *(= jdm hinterherfahren)* to follow *(+dat, an +acc* sth) VI *irreg (fig)* **a** *(= anhaften)* **jdm ~** to stay with sb; *(schlechter Ruf, Gefängnisstrafe auch)* to stick with sb **b** *(= sich zugehörig fühlen) +dat* to adhere to, to subscribe to

An|hän|ger M **a** *(= Wagen)* trailer; *(= Straßenbahnanhänger)* second car; **die Straßenbahn hatte zwei ~** the tram *(esp Brit) or* streetcar *(US)* had two extra cars **b** *(= Schmuckstück)* pendant **c** *(= Kofferanhänger etc)* tag, label

An|hän|ger(in) M(F) supporter; *(von Sportart auch)* fan; *(von Partei auch)* follower; *(von Verein)* member

An|hän|ger|kupp|lung F *(Aut)* trailer coupling

An|hän|ger|schaft ['anhɛŋɐʃaft] F **-,** *no pl* → **Anhänger(in)** supporters *pl*; fans *pl*; following, followers *pl*; membership, members *pl*

An|hän|ger|zahl F → **Anhänger(in)** number of supporters/fans/followers/members

An|hän|ge-: **An|hän|ge|schild** NT *pl* **-schilder** tag, label; **An|hän|ge|vor|rich|tung** F coupling device; *(an Auto etc)* towbar

an|hän|gig ['anhɛŋɪç] ADJ *(Jur)* sub judice; *Zivilverfahren* pending; **etw ~ machen** to start legal proceedings over sth

an|häng|lich ['anhɛŋlɪç] ADJ **mein Sohn/Hund ist sehr ~** my son/dog is very attached to me

An|häng|lich|keit F **-,** *no pl* **die ~ an etw** *(acc)* one's attachment to sth; **die ~ meiner Nichte/Katze** my niece's/cat's fondness for me *or* attachment to me; **aus ~** out of attachment to it/him *etc*

An|häng|sel ['anhɛŋzl] NT **-s, - a** *(= Überflüssiges, Mensch)* appendage *(an +dat* to); *(von Gruppe, Partei)* hanger-on; **das ist ein ~ am Wort** that is added onto the word **b** *(= Schildchen)* tag; *(rare: = Schmuckstück)* pendant; *(an Armband)* charm; *(an Uhrenkette)* fob; **die ~ am Weihnachtsbaum** the things hanging on the Christmas tree **c** *(= Zusatz)* addition; *(= Nachtrag)* appendix

An|hauch M *(geh)* aura; *(in Stimme)* trace, tinge

an+hau|chen VT *sep* to breathe on → *auch* **angehaucht**

an+hau|en VT *sep* **a** *(inf: = ansprechen)* to accost *(um* for); **jdn um etw ~** to be on the scrounge for sth from sb *(inf)*; *um Geld auch* to touch sb for sth *(Brit inf)*, to hit sb up for sth *(US inf)* **b** *(auch irreg) Baum* to cut a notch in

an+häu|fen *sep* VT to accumulate, to amass; *Vorräte, Geld* to hoard VR to pile up, to accumulate; *(Zinsen)* to accumulate, to accrue

An|häu|fung F accumulation, amassing; *(von Geld)* hoarding

an+he|ben *sep irreg* VT **a** *(= hochheben)* to lift (up); *Glas* to raise **b** *(= erhöhen)* to raise VI to lift

an+he|ben *pret* **hob** *or (obs)* **hub an**, *ptp* **angehoben** VI *sep irreg (old)* to commence, to begin; **zu singen ~** to begin singing; **..., hub er an** *(obs)* ..., quoth he *(old)*

An|he|bung F increase *(+gen, von* in); *(= das Anheben auch)* raising *(+gen, von* of); *(von Betrag, Größe auch)* rise *(+gen, von* in); **eine ~ der Gehälter um 5%** an increase *or* a rise *(Brit) or* raise *(US)* of 5% in salaries

an+hef|ten VT *sep (an +acc or dat* to) to fasten (on), to attach; **jdm einen Orden ~** to pin a medal on sb; **etw mit Reißzwecken/Heftklammern/Büroklammern/Stichen ~** to pin/staple/paperclip/tack sth on *(an +acc or dat* to)

an+hei|len VI *sep aux sein* to heal (up); *(Knochen)* to set, to mend

an|hei|melnd ['anhaimlnt] ADJ *(geh)* homely; *Klänge* familiar

an|heim-: **an|heim+fal|len** *sep irreg aux sein +dat*, **an|heim fal|len** △ *irreg aux sein +dat* VI *(liter)* to pass *or* fall to; *einer Krankheit* to fall prey to; *einem Betrug* to fall victim to; **der Vergessenheit ~** to sink into oblivion; **an|heim+ge|ben** *sep irreg +dat*, **an|heim ge|ben** △ *irreg +dat* VT *(liter)* to commit *or* entrust to; **etw den Flammen ~** to consign sth to the flames; **etw der Entscheidung eines anderen ~** to entrust the decision about sth to somebody else; **an|heim+stel|len** *sep +dat*, **an|heim stel|len** △ *+dat* VT *(geh)* **jdm etw ~** to leave sth to sb's discretion

an|hei|schig ['anhaiʃɪç] ADV *(form)* **sich ~ machen, etw zu tun** to take it upon oneself to do sth

an+hei|zen VT *sep* **a** *Ofen* to light **b** *(fig inf) (= ankurbeln) Wirtschaft, Wachstum* to stimulate; *(= verschlimmern) Krise* to aggravate; *Inflation* to fuel

an+herr|schen VT *sep* to bark at

an+het|zen VI *sep aux sein* **angehetzt kommen** to come rushing along *or (auf einen zu)* up

an+heu|ern VTI *sep (Naut, fig)* to sign on *or* up

An|hieb M **auf (den ersten) ~** *(inf)* straight *or* right away, straight off *(inf)*, first go *(inf)*; **das kann ich nicht auf ~ sagen** I can't say offhand

An|him|me|lei [anhɪmə'lai] F **-, -en** *(inf)* adulation, idolization; *(= schwärmerische Blicke)* adoring gaze

an+him|meln ['anhɪmln] VT *sep (inf)* to idolize, to worship; *(= schwärmerisch ansehen)* to gaze adoringly at

an|hin ['anhɪn] ADV **bis ~** *(Sw: = bisher)* until now

An|hö|he F hill

an+hö|ren *sep* VT **a** *(= Gehör schenken)* to hear; *Schallplatten, Konzert* to listen to; **jdn ganz ~** to hear sb out; **sich** *(dat)* **etw ~** to listen to sth; **das höre ich mir nicht mehr länger mit an** I'm not going to listen to that any longer; **können Sie sich mal einen Moment ~, was ich zu sagen habe?** can you just listen for a moment to what I have to say? **b** *(= zufällig mithören)* to overhear; **ich kann das nicht mehr mit ~** I can't listen to that any longer **c** *(= anmerken)* **man konnte ihr** *or* **ihrer Stimme die Verzweiflung ~** one could hear the despair in her voice; **das hört man ihm aber nicht an!** you can't tell that from his accent *or* from hearing him speak; **man hört ihm sofort den Ausländer an** you can hear at once that he's a foreigner VR *(= klingen)* to sound; **das hört sich ja gut an** *(inf)* that sounds good

An|hör|ter|min M date for a hearing

An|hö|rung ['anhø:rʊŋ] F **-, -en** hearing

An|hö|rungs|ver|fah|ren NT hearing

an+hu|pen VT *sep* to hoot at, to sound one's horn at

an+hus|ten VT *sep* to cough at; **jdn ~** to cough in sb's face

Änig|ma [ɛ'nɪgma] NT **-s, -ta** *or* **Änigmen** [-ta, -mən] *(liter)* enigma

Ani|lin [ani'li:n] NT **-s,** *no pl* aniline

Ani|lin|far|be F aniline dye

Ani|ma ['a:nima] F **-, -s** *(Psych)* anima

ani|ma|lisch [ani'ma:lɪʃ] ADJ animal; *(pej auch)* bestial, brutish

Ani|ma|teur [anima'tø:ɐ] M **-s, -e** host, entertainment officer

Ani|ma|teu|rin [anima'tø:rɪn] F **-, -nen** hostess, entertainment officer

Ani|ma|ti|on [anima'tsio:n] F **-, -en** *(Film)* animation

Ani|ma|ti|ons|film M (animated) cartoon (film)

Ani|ma|tor [ani'ma:to:ɐ] M **-s, Animatoren** [-'to:rən], **Ani|ma|to|rin** [-'to:rɪn] F **-, -nen** *(Film)* animator

Ani|mier|da|me F nightclub *or* bar hostess

ani|mie|ren [ani'mi:rən] *ptp* **animiert** VT **a** *(= anregen)* to encourage; **jdn zu einem Streich ~** to put sb up to a trick; **sich animiert fühlen, etw zu tun** to feel prompted to do sth; **durch das schöne Wetter animiert** encouraged *or* prompted by the good weather **b** *(Film)* to animate

ani|mie|rend *(geh)* ADJ stimulating ADV **~ wirken** to have a stimulating effect

Ani|mier-: **Ani|mier|lo|kal** NT hostess bar, clip joint *(pej)*; **Ani|mier|mäd|chen** NT nightclub *or* bar hostess

Ani|mo ['a:nimo] **NT -s,** *no pl (Aus)* **a** *(= Vorliebe)* liking **b** *(= Schwung)* **mit ~ mitmachen** to join in with gusto

Ani|mo|si|tät [animozi'tɛ:t] **F -, -en** *(geh) (gegen* towards) *(= Feindseligkeit)* animosity, hostility; *(= Abneigung)* hostility; *(= Äußerung)* hostile remark

Ani|mus ['a:nimʊs] **M -,** *no pl* **a** *(Psych)* animus **b** *(inf)* hunch *(inf)*, feeling

An|ion ['anio:n] **NT** *(Chem)* anion

Anis [a'ni:s, *(S Ger, Aus)* 'a:nɪs] **M -(es), -e** *(= Gewürz)* aniseed; *(= Schnaps)* aniseed brandy; *(= Pflanze)* anise

Ani|sett [ani'zɛt] **M -s, -s, Anis|li|kör M** anisette, aniseed liqueur

Anis-: Anis|plätz|chen NT aniseed biscuit *(Brit)* or cookie *(US)*; **Anis|schnaps M** aniseed brandy

Ank. *abbr von* **Ankunft** arr.

an+kämp|fen ['ankɛ-] **VI** *sep* **gegen etw ~** *(gegen die Elemente, Strömung)* to battle with sth; *gegen Gefühle, Neigungen, Versuchungen, Müdigkeit* to fight sth; *gegen Inflation, Missbrauch, Korruption, Ideen* to fight (against) sth; **gegen jdn ~** to fight (against) sb, to (do) battle with sb; **gegen die Tränen ~** to fight back one's tears

an+kar|ren ['anka-] **VT** *sep (inf)* to cart along

An|kauf ['ankauf] **M** purchase, purchasing; **durch den ~ einer Sache** *(gen)* through the purchase of sth, by purchasing sth; **An- und Verkauf von ...** we buy and sell ...; **An- und Verkauf(s-Geschäft)** ≈ second-hand shop

an+kau|fen ['ankau-] *sep* **VTI** to purchase, to buy **VR sich (an einem Ort) ~** to buy oneself a place (somewhere)

An|käu|fer(in) ['ankɔy-] **M(F)** purchaser, buyer

An|kaufs|recht NT *(Jur)* option, right of purchase

an+kei|fen ['ankai-] **VT** *sep (inf)* to scream *or* holler *(inf)* at

An|ker ['aŋkɐ] **M -s, -** *(Naut, Archit, fig)* anchor; *(Elec)* armature; *(von Uhr)* anchor; **~ werfen** to drop anchor; **vor ~ gehen** to drop anchor; *(fig) (hum: = heiraten)* to settle down *(bei* with); *(inf: = Rast machen)* to stop over; **sich vor ~ legen** to drop anchor; **vor ~ liegen** *or* **treiben** to lie *or* ride *or* be at anchor; **ein Schiff vor ~ legen** to bring a ship to anchor; **den/die ~ hieven** *or* **lichten** to weigh anchor

An|ker-: An|ker|bo|je F anchor buoy; **An|ker|grund M** anchorage; **An|ker|ket|te F** anchor cable; **An|ker|klü|se F** *(Naut)* hawsehole; **An|ker|mann M** *pl* **-männer** *(TV)* anchorman

an|kern ['aŋkɐn] **VI** *(= Anker werfen)* to anchor; *(= vor Anker liegen)* to be anchored

An|ker-: An|ker|platz M anchorage; **An|ker|tau NT** anchor hawser *or* rope; **An|ker|win|de F** capstan

an+ket|ten ['ankɛ-] **VT** *sep* to chain up *(an +acc or dat* to); **angekettet sein** *(fig)* to be tied up

an+keu|chen ['ankɔy-] **VI** *sep aux sein (inf)* **angekeucht kommen** to come panting along *or (auf einen zu)* up

an+kie|ken ['anki:-] **VT** *sep (N Ger inf)* to look at

an+kit|ten ['ankɪ-] **VT** *sep* to stick on (with putty) *(an +acc* -to)

an+kläf|fen ['ankl-] **VT** *sep (pej)* to bark at; *(kleiner Hund)* to yap at

An|kla|ge ['ankl-] **F a** *(Jur)* charge; *(= Anklagevertretung)* prosecution; **gegen jdn ~ erheben** to bring *or* prefer charges against sb; **jdn unter ~ stellen** to charge sb *(wegen* with); **(wegen etw) unter ~ stehen** to have been charged (with sth); **als Vertreter der ~ fragte Herr Stein ...** acting for the prosecution Mr Stein asked ..., Mr Stein, prosecuting *or* for the prosecution, asked ... **b** *(fig) (= Verurteilung)* condemnation *(gegen +gen* of); *(= Beschuldigung)* accusation; *(= Anprangerung)* indictment *(an +acc* of); **ihr Blick war voller ~** her eyes were full of reproach

An|kla|ge-: An|kla|ge|bank F *pl* **-bänke** dock; **auf der ~ (sitzen)** *(lit, fig)* (to be) in the dock; **jdn auf die ~ bringen** to put sb in the dock; **An|kla|ge|be|hör|de F** prosecution; **An|kla|ge|er|he|bung F** preferral of charges

an+kla|gen ['ankl-] *sep* **VT a** *(Jur)* to charge, to accuse; **jdn einer Sache** *(gen)* *or* **wegen etw ~** to charge sb with sth, to accuse sb of sth **b** *(fig) (= verurteilen)* to condemn; *(Buch, Rede)* to be a condemnation of; *(= anprangern)* to be an indictment of; **jdn einer Sache** *(gen)* **~** *(= beschuldigen)* to accuse sb of sth; **jdn ~, etw getan zu haben** to accuse sb of having done sth **VI** to cry out in protest *or* accusation; *(Buch, Bilder etc)* to cry out in condemnation

an|kla|gend ADJ *Ton* accusing, accusatory; *Blick* reproachful; *Buch, Bild etc* that cries out in condemnation **ADV** reproachfully

An|kla|ge|punkt M charge

An|klä|ger(in) ['ankl-] **M(F)** *(Jur)* prosecutor

an|klä|ge|risch ['anklɛ:gərɪʃ] **ADJ** = **anklagend**

An|kla|ge-: An|kla|ge|schrift F indictment; **An|kla|ge|ver|le|sung F** arraignment; **An|kla|ge|ver|tre|ter(in) M(F)** (public) prosecutor, counsel for the prosecution

an+klam|mern ['ankl-] *sep* **VT** *(mit Büroklammer)* to clip *(an +acc or dat* (on)to); *(mit Heftmaschine)* to staple *(an +acc or dat* on(to), to); *Wäsche* to peg *(an +acc or dat* on) **VR sich an etw** *(acc or dat)* **~** to cling (on)to sth, to hang onto sth

An|klang ['ankl-] **M a** *no pl (= Beifall)* approval; **~ (bei jdm) finden** to meet with (sb's) approval, to be well received (by sb); **großen/wenig/keinen ~ finden** to be very well/poorly/badly received **b** *(= Reminiszenz)* **Anklänge an etw** *(acc)* **enthalten** to be reminiscent of sth; **die Anklänge an Mozart sind unverkennbar** the echoes of Mozart are unmistakable; **ich konnte in seinem Buch einen deutlichen ~ an Thomas Mann erkennen** I found his book (to be) distinctly reminiscent of Thomas Mann

an|klat|schen ['ankl-] *sep (inf)* **VT** *Plakat etc* to slap *or* bung up *(inf)* **VI** *aux sein* **seine Kleider klatschen an** *or* **sind angeklatscht** his clothes are clinging to him; **seine Haare klatschen an** *or* **sind angeklatscht** his hair is plastered down

an+kle|ben ['ankl-] *sep* **VT** to stick up *(an +acc or dat* on) **VI** *aux sein* to stick

an+kle|ckern ['ankl-] **VI** *sep aux sein (inf)* **angekleckert kommen** to come drifting along *or (auf einen zu)* up; *(= nach und nach eintreffen)* to come in dribs and drabs *(inf)*

An|klei|de|ka|bi|ne F changing cubicle

an+klei|den ['ankl-] **VTR** *sep (geh)* to dress

An|klei|de|pup|pe F *(= Schaufensterpuppe)* display dummy, mannequin *(dated)*; *(= Anziehpuppe)* dress-up doll

An|klei|der ['anklaidɐ] **M -s, -, An|klei|de|rin** [-ərɪn] **F -, -nen** *(Theat)* dresser

An|klei|de|raum M, An|klei|de|zim|mer NT dressing room; *(im Schwimmbad, Geschäft)* changing room

an+kli|cken ['ankl-] **VT** *(Comput)* to click (on)

an+klin|geln ['ankl-] **VTI** *sep (inf)* to ring *or* phone (up) *(esp Brit)*, to call (up) *(esp US)*; **jdn** *or* **bei jdm ~** to give sb a ring *(esp Brit)* *or* a buzz *(inf)*, to ring *or* phone sb (up) *(esp Brit)*, to call sb (up) *(esp US)*

an+klin|gen ['ankl-] **VI** *sep aux sein (= erinnern)* to be reminiscent *(an +acc* of); *(= angeschnitten werden)* to be touched (up)on; *(= spürbar werden)* to be discernible; **in diesem Lied klingt etwas von Sehnsucht an** there is a suggestion *or* hint *or* note of longing (discernible) in this song

an+klop|fen ['ankl-] **VI** *sep* to knock *(an +acc or dat* at on); **bei jdm wegen etw ~** *(fig inf)* to go knocking on sb's door for sth; **Anklopfen** *(Telec)* call waiting (service)

an+knab|bern ['ankn-] **VT** *sep (inf) (= annagen)* to gnaw *or* nibble (at); *(fig) Ersparnisse etc* to gnaw away at, to nibble away at; **zum Anknabbern (aussehen)** *(fig)* (to look) good enough to eat

an+knack|sen ['anknaksn] **VT** *sep (inf)* **a** *Knochen* to crack; *Fuß, Gelenk etc* to crack a bone in **b** *(fig) Gesundheit* to affect; *Stolz* to injure, to deal a blow to; **sein Selbstvertrauen/Stolz wurde dadurch angeknackst** that was a blow to his self-confidence/pride → *auch* **angeknackst**

an+knat|tern ['ankn-] **VI** *sep aux sein (inf)* **angeknattert kommen** to come roaring along *or (auf einen zu)* up

an+knip|sen ['ankn-] **VT** *sep* to switch *or* put on; **ein Lächeln ~** *(inf)* to put on a smile

an+knöp|fen ['ankn-] **VT** *sep* to button on *(an +acc or dat* -to)

an+kno|ten ['ankn-] **VT** *sep* to tie on *(an +acc or dat* -to)

an+knüp|fen ['ankn-] *sep* **VT** to tie on *(an +acc or dat* -to); *Beziehungen* to establish; *Verhältnis* to form, to start up; *Gespräch* to start up, to enter into **VI an etw** *(acc)* **~** to take sth up

An|knüp|fung F -, -en *(von Beziehungen)* establishing; *(von Verhältnis)* forming, starting up; *(von Gespräch)* starting up; **in ~ an etw** *(acc)* following on from sth

An|knüp|fungs|punkt M link

an+knur|ren ['ankn-] **VT** *sep (lit, fig)* to growl at

an+ko|chen VT *sep (= kurz kochen)* to parboil; *(= blanchieren) Gemüse* to blanch

An|koch|stu|fe F *(bei Kochplatte)* full heat *or* high (setting)

an+koh|len ['anko-] **VT** *sep* **a** *(= ansengen) Baum, Einrichtung* to char **b** *(inf: = belügen)* to have on *(inf)*

an+kom|men ['anko-] *sep irreg aux sein* **VI a** *(= eintreffen)* to arrive; *(Zug, Bus etc)* to get in, to arrive; **bist du gut angekommen?** did you arrive safely?, did you get there all right?; **bei etw angekommen sein** to have reached sth, to have got to sth; **wir sind schon beim Dessert angekommen** we've already reached the dessert stage; **das Kind soll in 6 Wochen ~** the baby is due (to arrive) in 6 weeks

b *(= Anklang, Resonanz finden) (bei* with) to go down well; *(Mode, Neuerungen)* to catch on; **dieser Witz kam gut an** the joke went down very well; **mit deinem dummen Gerede kommst du bei ihm nicht an!** you won't get anywhere with him with your stupid talk!; **ein Lehrer, der bei seinen Schülern ausgezeichnet ankommt** a teacher who is a great success with his pupils, a teacher who hits it off marvellously *(Brit)* or marvelously *(US)* with his pupils

c *(inf) (= auftreten, erscheinen)* to come along; *(= wiederholt erwähnen)* to come up *(mit* with); **jdm mit etw ~** to come to sb with sth; **komm mir nachher nicht an und verlange, dass ich ...** don't come running to me afterwards wanting me to ...; **komm mir nur nicht wieder damit an, dass du Astronaut werden willst** don't start up again with this business about (your) wanting to be an astronaut

d *(= sich durchsetzen)* **gegen etw ~** *(gegen Gewohnheit, Sucht etc)* to be able to fight sth; **gegen jdn ~** to be able to cope with sb; **gegen diese Konkurrenz kommen wir nicht an** we can't fight this competition; **er ist zu stark, ich komme gegen ihn nicht an** he's too strong, I'm no match for him

VI *impers* **a** *(= wichtig sein)* **es kommt auf etw** *(acc)* **an** sth matters; **darauf kommt es (uns) an** that is what matters (to us); **es kommt darauf an, dass wir ...** what matters is that we ...; **auf eine halbe Stunde kommt es jetzt nicht mehr an** it doesn't matter about the odd half-hour, an extra half-hour is neither here nor there *(inf)*; **darauf soll es mir nicht ~** that's not the problem

b *(= abhängig sein)* to depend *(auf +acc* on); **es kommt darauf an** it (all) depends; **es käme auf einen Versuch an** we'd have to give it a try; **es kommt (ganz) darauf an, in welcher Laune er ist** it (all) depends (on) what mood he's in

c *(inf)* **es darauf ~ lassen** to take a chance, to chance it; **lass es nicht drauf ~!** don't push your luck! *(inf)*; **lassen wirs darauf ~** let's chance it; **er ließ es in der Prüfung darauf ~** he

took a chance in the exam; **er ließ es auf einen Streit/einen Versuch ~** he was prepared to argue about it/to give it a try; **lass es doch nicht deswegen auf einen Prozess ~** for goodness' sake don't let it get as far as the courts
VI (= *sein, erscheinen*) **etw kommt jdn schwer/hart an** sth is difficult/hard for sb; **das Rauchen aufzugeben, kommt ihn sauer an** he's finding it difficult to give up smoking

An|kömm|ling ['ankœmlɪŋ] M **-s, -e** (new) arrival

an+kop|peln ['ankɔ-] VT *sep* to hitch up (*an +acc* to) *or* on (*an +acc* -to); (*Rail*) to couple up (*an +acc* to) *or* on (*an +acc* -to); (*Space*) to link up (*an +acc* with, to)

an+kot|zen ['ankɔ-] VT *sep* (*sl:* = *anwidern*) to make sick (*inf*)

an+kral|len ['ankr-] VR *sep* to clutch (*an +dat* at)

an+krat|zen ['ankr-] VT *sep* to scratch; (*fig*) *jds Ruf etc* to damage

an+krau|sen ['ankr-] VT *sep* (*Sew*) to gather

an+krei|den ['ankraidn] VT *sep* **a** (*obs:* = *Schulden aufschreiben*) to chalk up **b** (*fig*) **jdm etw (dick** *or* **übel) ~** to hold sth against sb; **jdm sein Benehmen als Frechheit/Schwäche ~** to regard sb's behaviour (*Brit*) *or* behavior (*US*) as an impertinence/as weakness

An|kreis ['ankr-] M (*Math*) escribed circle

an+kreu|zen ['ankr-] *sep* VT *Stelle, Fehler, Antwort* to mark with a cross, to put a cross beside VI *aux sein or haben* (*Naut*) **gegen den Wind ~** to sail against *or* into the wind

an+kün|den ['ankʏ-] VTR *sep* (*old*) = **ankündigen**

an+kün|di|gen ['ankʏ-] *sep* VT **a** (= *ansagen, anmelden*) to announce; (*auf Plakat, in Zeitung etc*) to advertise; **heute kam endlich der angekündigte Brief** today the letter I/we had been expecting finally arrived **b** (= *auf etw hindeuten*) to be a sign of VR (*fig*) to be heralded (*durch* by); **der Frühling kündigt sich an** spring is in the air; **diese Krankheit kündigt sich durch … an** this illness is preceded by …; **er besucht uns nie, ohne sich (nicht) vorher anzukündigen** he never visits us without letting us know in advance *or* without giving us advance notice

An|kün|di|gung F announcement; (= *vorherige Benachrichtigung*) advance notice; **Preisänderungen nur nach vorheriger ~** price changes will be announced in advance, advance notice will be given of price changes

An|kunft ['ankʊnft] F **-, Ankünfte** [-kʏnftə] arrival; **bei** *or* **nach ~** on arrival; **„Ankunft"** (*Aviat*) "arrivals"

An|kunfts-: **An|kunfts|bahn|steig** M (*Rail*) arrival platform (*esp Brit*) *or* track (*US*); **An|kunfts|flug|ha|fen** M arrival *or* destination airport; **An|kunfts|hal|le** F arrivals lounge; **An|kunfts|ort** M *pl* **-orte** place of arrival; **An|kunfts|ta|fel** F arrivals (indicator) board; **An|kunfts|zeit** F time of arrival

an+kup|peln ['ankʊ-] VT *sep* = **ankoppeln**

an+kur|beln ['ankʊ-] VT *sep Maschine* to wind up; (*Aut*) to crank; (*fig*) *Wirtschaft, Konjunktur* to boost, to reflate

An|kur|be|lung F **-, -en** (*fig*) reflation

an+ku|scheln ['ankʊ-] VR *sep* **sich bei jdm** *or* **an jdn ~** to snuggle up to sb

Anl. *abbr von* **Anlage** encl.

an+la|bern VT *sep* (*sl*) to speak to; (*aufreißen wollen*) *Mädchen* to chat up (*Brit inf*), to put the moves on (*US inf*)

an+lä|cheln VT *sep* to smile at; (*fig: Schicksal, Glück etc*) to smile (up)on; **jdn ~** to smile at sb, to give sb a smile; **der Kuchen lächelte mich förmlich an** (*hum*) the cake sat there just asking to be eaten

an+la|chen VT *sep* to smile at; (*fig: Himmel, Sonne*) to smile (up)on; **sich** (*dat*) **jdn ~** (*inf*) to pick sb up (*inf*)

An|la|ge ✪ 47.5 F **a** (= *Fabrikanlage*) plant **b** (= *Grünanlage, Parkanlage*) (public) park; (*um ein Gebäude herum*) grounds *pl* **c** (= *Einrichtung*) (*Mil, Elec*) installation(s *pl*); (= *sanitäre Anlagen*) bathroom *or* sanitary (*form*) installations *pl*; (= *Sportanlage etc*) facilities *pl* **d** (*inf:* = *Stereoanlage*) (stereo) system *or* equipment; (= *EDV-Anlage*) system **e** (= *Plan, Grundidee*) conception; (*eines Dramas etc*) structure **f** *usu pl* (= *Veranlagung*) aptitude, gift, talent (*zu* for); (= *Neigung*) predisposition, tendency (*zu* to) **g** (= *das Anlegen*) (*von Park*) laying out; (*von Stausee etc*) construction, building; **die ~ einer Kartei veranlassen** to start a file; **die Stadt hat die ~ von weiteren Grünflächen beschlossen** the town has decided to provide more parks **h** (= *Kapitalanlage*) investment **i** (= *Beilage zu einem Schreiben*) enclosure; (*von E-Mail*) attachment; **als ~** *or* **in der ~ erhalten Sie …** please find enclosed …

an|la|ge|be|dingt ADJ inherent; **Krampfadern sind ~** some people have an inherent tendency *or* a predisposition to varicose veins

An|la|ge-: **An|la|ge|be|ra|ter(in)** M(F) investment advisor; **An|la|ge|be|ra|tung** F investment management *or* counselling (*Brit*) *or* counseling (*US*), investment consultancy, portfolio management; **An|la|ge|be|trag** M amount *or* sum (to be) invested; **An|la|ge|dau|er** F investment period; **An|la|ge|ka|pi|tal** NT investment capital; **An|la|ge|mög|lich|keit** F investment opportunity

An|la|gen|streu|ung F diversification of (capital) investment

An|la|ge|pa|pier NT long-term investment bond

an+la|gern *sep* VT to take up VR (*Chem*) to be taken up (*an +acc* by)

An|la|ge|ver|mö|gen NT fixed assets *pl*

an+lan|den *sep* VI **a** *aux sein* (*Naut*) to land **b** *aux sein or haben* (*Geol*) to accrete VT to land

an+lan|gen *sep* VI *aux sein* (*an einem Ort*) to arrive; **in der Stadt/am Gipfel angelangt sein** to have reached the town/summit, to have arrived in *or* at the town/at the summit VT **a** (= *betreffen*) to concern **b** (*S Ger:* = *anfassen*) to touch

An|lass ['anlas] ✪ 44.2 M **-es, Anlässe a** [-lɛsə] (= *Veranlassung*) (immediate) cause (*zu* for); **zum ~ von etw werden** to bring sth about, to trigger sth off; **das war zwar nicht der Grund aber der ~** that wasn't the real reason but that's what finally brought it about *or* triggered it off; **welchen ~ hatte er, das zu tun?** what prompted him to do that?; **er hat keinen ~ zur Freude** he has no cause *or* reason *or* grounds for rejoicing; **es besteht kein ~ …** there is no reason …; **es besteht ~ zur Hoffnung** there is reason for hope; **das ist kein ~ zu feiern** that's no reason to celebrate; **etw zum ~ nehmen, zu …** to use sth as an opportunity to …; **beim geringsten ~** for the slightest reason; **bei jedem ~** at every opportunity; **jdm ~ zu Beschwerden geben, jdm ~ geben, sich zu beschweren** to give sb reason *or* cause *or* grounds for complaint *or* for complaining **b** (= *Gelegenheit*) occasion; **aus ~** (*+gen*) on the occasion of; **aus gegebenem ~** in view of the occasion; **aus diesem ~** on this occasion; **dem ~ entsprechend** as befits the occasion, as is befitting to the occasion **c** (*Sw:* = *Lustbarkeit*) social

An|lass|bat|te|rie F (*Aut*) starter battery

an+las|sen *sep irreg* VT **a** (= *in Gang setzen*) *Motor, Wagen* to start (up) **b** (*inf*) *Schuhe, Mantel* to keep on **c** (*inf*) *Wasserhahn, Motor* to leave running *or* on; *Licht, Radio* to leave on; *Kerze* to leave burning; *Feuer* to leave in *or* burning VR **sich gut/schlecht ~** to get off to a good/bad start; (*Lehrling, Student, Geschäft etc auch*) to make a good/bad start *or* beginning; **das Wetter lässt sich gut an** the weather looks promising; **wie lässt er sich in der Sache denn an?** what sort of start has he made on it?

An|las|ser ['anlasɐ] M **-s, -** (*Aut*) starter

an|läss|lich ['anlɛslɪç] ✪ 50.6, 51.2, 52.1, 52.2 PREP *+gen* on the occasion of

an+las|ten VT *sep* **a** **jdm etw ~** to blame sb for sth, to lay the blame for sth on sb; **jdm die Schuld für etw ~** to lay the blame for sth at sb's door *or* on sb; **jdm etw als Schwäche ~** to regard *or* see sth as a weakness on sb's part **b** (*dated*) *Kosten* to charge (*jdm* to sb)

an+lat|schen VI *sep aux sein* **angelatscht kommen** (*inf*) to come slouching along *or* (*auf einen zu*) up

An|lauf M **a** (*Sport*) run-up; (*Ski*) approach run; (*Mil:* = *Ansturm*) onset, attack; **mit ~** with a run-up; **ohne ~** from standing; **Sprung mit/ohne ~** running/standing jump; **~ nehmen** to take a run-up; **~ zu etw nehmen** (*fig*) to pluck up courage to do sth **b** (*fig:* = *Versuch*) attempt, try; **beim ersten/zweiten ~** at the first/second attempt, first/second go (*inf*); **noch einen ~ nehmen** *or* **machen** to have another go (*inf*) *or* try, to make another attempt **c** (= *Beginn*) start

an+lau|fen *sep irreg* VI *aux sein* **a** (= *beginnen*) to begin, to start; (*Film*) to open; (*Motor*) to start **b** **angelaufen kommen** to come running along *or* (*auf einen zu*) up **c** (= *beschlagen*) (*Brille, Spiegel etc*) to steam *or* mist up; (*Metall*) to tarnish; **rot/blau ~** to turn *or* go red/blue **d** (*Sport*) (= *zu laufen beginnen*) to start off; (= *Anlauf nehmen*) to take a run-up **e** **gegen etw ~** (*fig*) to stand up to sth; **er kann kaum gegen so einen starken Wind ~** he can hardly walk against such a strong wind VT (*Naut*) *Hafen etc* to put into, to call at

An|lauf-: **An|lauf|ha|fen** M (*Naut*) port of call; **An|lauf|kos|ten** PL (*Econ*) initial *or* startup cost(s *pl*); **An|lauf|pha|se** F initial stage; **in der ~** in the initial stages; **An|lauf|stel|le** F shelter, refuge; **An|lauf|zeit** F (*Aut*) warming-up time *or* period; (*fig*) time to get going *or* started; (*Film, Theat*) (time of the) first few performances *pl*; **ein paar Wochen ~** a few weeks to get going *or* started

An|laut M (*Phon*) initial sound; **im ~ stehen** to be in initial position

an+lau|ten VI *sep* to begin

an+läu|ten VTI *sep* (*dial:* = *anrufen*) **jdn** *or* **bei jdm ~** to ring *or* phone sb (up) (*esp Brit*), to call sb

an|lau|tend ADJ *attr Vokal* initial

an+le|cken VT *sep* to lick

An|le|ge|brü|cke F landing stage, jetty

an+le|gen *sep* VT **a** *Leiter* to put up (*an +acc* against); *Brett, Karte, Dominostein* to lay (down) (*an +acc* next to, beside); *Lineal* to position, to set; **das Gewehr ~** to raise the gun to one's shoulder; **das Gewehr auf jdn/etw ~** to aim the gun at sb/sth; **den Säugling ~** to put the baby to one's breast; **strengere Maßstäbe ~** to lay down *or* impose stricter standards (*bei* in)
b (*geh:* = *anziehen*) to don (*form*)
c (= *anbringen*) **jdm etw ~** to put sth on sb → **Zügel**
d *Kartei, Akte* to start; *Datei* to create; *Vorräte* to lay in; *Garten, Gelände, Aufsatz, Bericht, Schaubild* to lay out; *Liste, Plan, Statistiken* to draw up; *Roman, Drama* to structure
e (= *investieren*) *Geld, Kapital* to invest; (= *ausgeben*) to spend (*für* on)
f **es darauf ~, dass …** to be determined that …; **du legst es wohl auf einen Streit mit mir an** you're determined to have a fight with me, aren't you? → *auch* **angelegt**
VI **a** (*Naut*) to berth, to dock
b (*Cards*) to lay down cards/a card (*bei jdm* on sb's hand)
c (= *Gewehr anlegen*) to aim (*auf +acc* at)
VR **sich mit jdm ~** to pick an argument *or* a quarrel *or* a fight with sb

An|le|ge|platz M berth

An|le|ger ['anle:gɐ] M **-s, -, An|le|ge|rin** [-ərın] F **-, -nen** *(Fin)* investor

An|le|ge-: **An|le|ge|steg** M jetty, landing stage; **An|le|ge|stel|le** F mooring

an+leh|nen *sep* VT to lean *or* rest *(an +acc* against); *Tür, Fenster* to leave ajar, to leave slightly open; **angelehnt sein** *(Tür, Fenster)* to be ajar, to be slightly open VR *(lit)* to lean *(an +acc* against); **sich an etw** *(acc)* ~ *(fig)* to follow sth

An|leh|nung F **-, -en** a *(= Stütze)* support *(an +acc* of); *(= Anschluss)* dependence *(an +acc* on); ~ **an jdn suchen** to seek sb's support b *(= Imitation)* following *(an jdn/etw* sb/sth); **in ~ an jdn/etw** following sb/sth

An|leh|nungs-: **An|leh|nungs|be|dürf|nis** NT need of loving care; **an|leh|nungs|be|dürf|tig** ADJ in need of loving care

an+lei|ern VT *sep (inf: = in die Wege leiten)* to get going

An|lei|he F, *(Sw)* **An|lei|hen** ['anlaiən] NT **-s, -** a *(Fin) (= Geldaufnahme)* loan; *(= Wertpapier)* bond; **eine ~ aufnehmen** to take out a loan; **bei jdm eine ~ machen** to borrow (money) from sb b *(von geistigem Eigentum)* borrowing; **bei jdm eine ~ machen** *(hum inf)* to borrow from sb

An|lei|he-: **An|lei|he|ka|pi|tal** NT *(Fin)* loan capital; **An|lei|he|pa|pier** NT *(Fin)* bond; **An|lei|he|schuld** F *(Fin)* bonded debt

an+lei|men VT *sep* to stick on *(an +acc or dat* -to); **jdn ~** *(inf) (= foppen)* to pull sb's leg; *(= betrügen)* to do sb *(inf)*

an+lei|nen ['anlainən] VT *sep (= festmachen)* to tie up; *(fig)* to keep tied to one's apron strings; **den Hund ~** to put the dog's lead *(esp Brit) or* leash on, to put the dog on the lead *(esp Brit) or* leash; **den Hund an etw** *(acc or dat)* ~ to tie the dog to sth

an+lei|ten VT *sep* a *(= unterweisen)* to show, to teach, to instruct; **jdn bei einer Arbeit ~** to teach sb a job, to show sb how to do a job b *(= erziehen)* **jdn zu etw ~** to teach sb sth; **jdn zu selbstständigem Denken ~** to teach sb to think for himself/herself

An|lei|tung F *(= Erklärung, Hilfe)* instructions *pl*; **unter der ~ seines Vaters** under his father's guidance *or* direction

An|lern|be|ruf M semiskilled job

an+ler|nen VT *sep* a *(= ausbilden)* to train b *(= oberflächlich lernen)* **sich** *(dat)* **etw ~** to learn sth up → *auch* **angelernt**

An|lern|ling ['anlɛrnlıŋ] M **-s, -e** trainee

an+le|sen VT *sep irreg* a *Buch, Aufsatz* to begin *or* start reading; **das angelesene Buch** the book I have/she has *etc* started reading b *(= aneignen)* **sich** *(dat)* **etw ~** to learn sth by reading; **angelesenes Wissen** knowledge which comes straight out of books

an+leuch|ten VT *sep* **jdn ~** to shine a light/lamp *etc* at sb; **jdn mit etw ~** to shine sth at sb

an+lie|fern VT *sep* to deliver

An|lie|fe|rung F delivery

an+lie|gen VI *sep irreg* a *(= anstehen, vorliegen)* to be on b *(Kleidung)* to fit closely *or* tightly *(an etw (dat)* sth); *(Haar)* to lie flat *(an +dat* against, on) c *(Naut)* **an den richtigen Kurs ~** to be (headed) on the right course

An|lie|gen ['anli:gn] NT **-s, -** a *(= Bitte)* request b *(= wichtige Angelegenheit)* matter of concern

an|lie|gend ADJ a *Ohren* flat; **(eng) ~** *(Kleidung)* tight-fitting, close-fitting b *(in Briefen)* enclosed c *Grundstück* adjacent

An|lie|ger ['anli:gɐ] M **-s, -, An|lie|ge|rin** [-ərın] F **-, -nen** neighbour *(Brit)*, neighbor *(US)*; *(= Anwohner)* (local) resident; **die ~ der Nordsee** the countries bordering (on) the North Sea; **~ frei, frei für ~** residents only

An|lie|ger-: **An|lie|ger|staat** M **die ~en des Schwarzen Meers** the countries bordering (on) the Black Sea; **An|lie|ger|ver|kehr** M access traffic, (local) residents' vehicles *pl*; **„Anliegerverkehr frei"** "residents only"

an+lin|sen ['anlınzn] VT *sep (inf)* to take a sly look at; **jdn aus den Augenwinkeln ~** to look at sb out of the corner of one's eye

an+lo|cken VT *sep Touristen* to attract; *Vögel, Tiere auch* to lure

An|lo|ckung F attraction

an+lö|ten VT *sep* to solder on *(an +acc or dat* -to)

an+lü|gen VT *sep irreg* to lie to, to tell lies to

an+lu|ven VT *sep (Naut)* to luff

Anm. *abbr von* **Anmerkung**

An|ma|che F *(sl)* chatting-up *(inf)*; *(= Spruch)* chat-up line *(inf)*; **sexuelle ~** advances *pl*

an+ma|chen VT *sep* a *(inf: = befestigen)* to put up *(an +acc or dat* on) b *(= zubereiten)* to mix; *Salat* to dress c *(= anstellen) Radio, Licht, Heizung etc* to put *or* turn on; *Feuer* to light d *(inf) (= ansprechen)* to chat up *(Brit inf)*, to put the moves on *(US inf)*; *(= scharfmachen)* to turn on *(inf)*; *(sl: = belästigen)* to harass; **mach mich nicht an** leave me alone e *(sl: sexuell)* to turn on *(inf)*; **der Typ macht mich total an** that guy really turns me on *(inf)* f *(sl: = kritisieren)* to slam *(inf)*

an+mah|nen VT *sep* to send a reminder about

An|mah|nung F *(Econ)* notice, reminder

an|mai|len ['anme:ln] VT *sep* to e-mail

an+ma|len *sep* VT a *(= bemalen) Wand, Gegenstand* to paint; *(= ausmalen)* to colour *(Brit) or* color *(US)* in b *(= anzeichnen)* to paint *(an +acc* on) c *(= schminken)* **sich** *(dat)* **die Lippen/Lider** *etc* ~ to paint one's lips/eyelids *etc*; **sich** *(dat)* **einen Schnurrbart/Sommersprossen ~** to paint a moustache *(Brit) or* mustache *(US)*/freckles on one's face *or* on oneself VR *(pej: = schminken)* to paint one's face *or* oneself

An|marsch M, *no pl (= Weg)* walk (there); *(Mil)* advance; **im ~ sein** to be advancing *(auf +acc* on); *(hum inf)* to be on the way

an+mar|schie|ren *ptp* **anmarschiert** VI *sep aux sein (Mil)* to advance; **anmarschiert kommen** to come marching along *or (auf einen zu)* up

An|marsch|weg M walk

an+ma|ßen ['anma:sn] VT *sep* **sich** *(dat)* **etw ~** *(Befugnis, Recht)* to claim sth (for oneself); *Kritik* to take sth upon oneself; *Titel, Macht, Autorität* to assume sth; **sich** *(dat)* **ein Urteil/eine Meinung über etw** *(acc)* ~ to presume to pass judgement on/have an opinion about sth; **sich** *(dat)* **~, etw zu tun** to presume to do sth

an|ma|ßend ADJ presumptuous

An|ma|ßung F **-, -en** presumption, presumptuousness; **mit seinen ständigen ~en machte er sich viele Feinde** his presumptuousness made him many enemies; **es ist eine ~ zu meinen, ...** it is presumptuous to maintain that ...

an+me|ckern VT *sep (inf)* to keep on at *(inf)*

An|mel|de-: **An|mel|de|be|schei|ni|gung** F, **An|mel|de|be|stä|ti|gung** F (resident's) registration document; **An|mel|de|for|mu|lar** NT application form; **An|mel|de|frist** F registration period; **An|mel|de|ge|bühr** F registration fee

an+mel|den *sep* VT a *(= ankündigen) Besuch* to announce; **einen Freund bei jdm ~** to let sb know that a friend is coming to visit

b *(bei Schule, Kurs etc)* to enrol *(Brit)*, to enroll *(US) (bei* at, *zu* for)

c *(= eintragen lassen) Patent* to apply for; *neuen Wohnsitz, Auto, Untermieter* to register *(bei* at); *Fernseher* to get a licence *(Brit) or* license *(US)* for; *Waffe* to register; **Konkurs ~** to declare oneself bankrupt

d *(= vormerken lassen)* to make an appointment for

e *(Telec)* **ein Gespräch nach Deutschland ~** to book a call to Germany

f *(= geltend machen) Recht, Ansprüche* to declare; *(zu Steuerzwecken, bei Zoll)* to declare; *Bedenken, Zweifel, Protest* to register; *Wünsche, Bedürfnisse* to make known; **ich melde starke Bedenken an** I have serious doubts about that, I'm very doubtful *or* dubious about that

VR a *(= ankündigen) (Besucher)* to announce one's arrival; *(im Hotel)* to book (in); *(fig) (Baby)* to be on the way; *(Probleme, Zweifel etc)* to appear on the horizon; *(Comput: in Netz)* to log on (in *+dat* to); **sich bei jdm ~** to tell sb one is coming

b *(an Schule, zu Kurs etc)* to enrol *(Brit) or* enroll *(US)* (oneself) *(an +dat* at, *zu* for); **sich polizeilich ~** to register with the police

c *(= sich einen Termin geben lassen)* to make an appointment; **sich beim Arzt** *etc* ~ to make an appointment at the doctor's *etc or* with the doctor *etc*

An|mel|de-: **An|mel|de|pflicht** F *(für Fernsehgerät, Hund)* compulsory licensing; *(für Auto, Untermieter, Ausländer, Waffe)* compulsory registration; *(für Einfuhr)* compulsory notification; **an|mel|de|pflich|tig** [-pflıçtıç] ADJ **~ sein** *(Fernsehgerät, Hund)* to have to be licensed; *(Auto, Untermieter, Ausländer, Waffe)* to have to be registered; *(Einfuhr)* to be notifiable; **An|mel|de|schein** M registration form; **An|mel|de|schluss** M deadline *or* closing date for registration(s); **An|mel|de|stel|le** F registration office; **An|mel|de|ter|min** M deadline for registration(s); **An|mel|de|ver|fah|ren** NT registration procedure

An|mel|dung F a *(von Besuch)* announcement; *(im Hotel)* booking; *(an Schule, zu Kurs etc)* enrolment *(Brit)*, enrollment *(US) (an +dat* at, *zu* for); *(bei Polizei)* registration; *(beim Arzt etc)* making an appointment; **die ~ eines Gespräches** booking a call; **nur nach vorheriger ~** by appointment only b *(von Patent)* application *(von, +gen* for); *(von Auto)* registration; *(von Fernseher)* licensing c *(= Anmelderaum)* reception

An|mel|dungs|for|mu|lar NT, **An|mel|dungs|vor|druck** M registration form

an+mer|ken VT *sep (= sagen)* to say; *(= anstreichen)* to mark; *(als Fußnote)* to note; **sich** *(dat)* **etw ~** to make a note of sth, to note sth down; **jdm seine Verlegenheit** *etc* ~ to notice sb's embarrassment *etc or* that sb is embarrassed *etc*; **sich** *(dat)* **etw ~ lassen** to let sth show; **man merkt ihm nicht an, dass ...** you wouldn't know *or* you can't tell that he ...

An|mer|kung ['anmɛrkʊŋ] F **-, -en** *(= Erläuterung)* note; *(= Fußnote)* (foot)note; *(iro: = Kommentar)* remark, comment

an+mes|sen VT *sep irreg* **jdm etw ~** *(geh)* to measure sb for sth

an+mie|ten VT *sep* to rent; *Auto etc auch* to hire

an|mit ['anmıt] ADV *(Sw)* herewith

an+mon|tie|ren *ptp* **anmontiert** VT *sep* to fix on *(an +acc or dat* -to)

an+mo|sern VT *sep (inf)* to have a (real) go at *(esp Brit inf)*, to tear *or* lay into

an+mot|zen VT *sep (inf)* to have a (real) go at *(esp Brit inf)*, to tear *or* lay into, to yell at

an+mus|tern VTI *(Naut)* to sign on

An|mut ['anmu:t] F **-,** *no pl* grace; *(= Grazie auch)* gracefulness; *(= Schönheit)* beauty, loveliness; *(von Landschaft, Gegenständen)* charm, beauty

an+mu|ten *sep* VT *(geh)* to appear, to seem *(jdn* to sb); **jdn seltsam ~** to appear *or* seem odd to sb; **es mutete ihn wie ein Traum an** it seemed like a dream to him VI **es mutet sonderbar an** it is *or* seems curious; **eine eigenartig ~de Geschichte** a story that strikes one as odd

an|mu|tig ADJ *(geh) (= geschmeidig, behende) Bewegung* graceful; *(= hübsch anzusehen)* lovely, charming

an|mut(s)- *(geh)*: **an|mut(s)|los** ADJ graceless, lacking grace; *(= nicht hübsch)* lacking charm; **an|mut(s)|voll** ADJ *Lächeln* lovely, charming; *(= geschmeidig, behände)* graceful

an+na|geln VT *sep* to nail on *(an +acc or dat* -to); **er stand wie angenagelt da** he stood there rooted to the spot

an+na|gen VT *sep* to gnaw (at); *(fig) Ersparnisse etc* to gnaw away at, to nibble away at

an+nä|hen VT *sep* to sew on *(an +acc or dat* -to)

an+nä|hern *sep* VT to bring closer (*+dat, an +acc* to); (*= in größere Übereinstimmung bringen auch*) to bring more into line (*+dat, an +acc* with); **zwei Standpunkte so weit als möglich ~** to bring two points of view as much into line (with each other) as possible VR **a** (*lit, fig: = sich nähern*) to approach (*einer Sache (dat)* sth) **b** (*= sich angleichen, näherkommen*) to come closer (*+dat, an +acc* to)

an|nä|hernd ADJ (*= ungefähr*) approximate, rough ADV (*= etwa*) roughly; (*= fast*) almost; **können Sie mir den Betrag ~ nennen?** can you give me an approximate *or* a rough idea of the amount?; **nicht ~** not nearly, nothing like; **nicht ~ so viel** not nearly as much, nothing like as much

An|nä|he|rung F (*lit: = das Näherkommen, fig: = Angleichung*) approach (*an +acc* towards); (*von Standpunkten*) convergence (*+dat, an +acc* with); **eine ~ an die Wirklichkeit** an approximation of reality; **die ~ zwischen Ost und West** the rapprochement of East and West; **die ~ von zwei Menschen** two people coming closer together; **die ~ an den Partner** coming closer to one's partner

An|nä|he|rungs-: **An|nä|he|rungs|po|li|tik** F policy of rapprochement; **An|nä|he|rungs|ver|such** M overtures *pl* → **plump**; **an|nä|he|rungs|wei|se** ADV approximately; **An|nä|he|rungs|wert** M (*Math*) approximate value

An|nah|me [ˈannaːmə] ✪ 39.1, 42.2 F **-, -n** **a** (*= Vermutung, Voraussetzung*) assumption; **in der ~, dass …** on the assumption that …; **gehe ich recht in der ~, dass …?** am I right in assuming *or* in the assumption that …?; **der ~ sein, dass …** to assume that …; **von einer ~ ausgehen** to work on *or* from an assumption **b** (*= das Annehmen*) acceptance; (*von Geld*) acceptance, taking; (*von Rat, Telegramm, Gespräch, Reparaturen*) taking; (*von Arbeit, Auftrag, Bewerber*) acceptance, taking on; (*von Herausforderung, Angebot*) taking up; (*= Billigung*) approval; (*von Gesetz*) passing; (*von Resolution, Staatsangehörigkeit*) adoption; (*von Antrag*) acceptance; (*von Gewohnheit*) picking up; (*von Akzent, Tonfall*) acquisition; (*von Gestalt, Name*) assuming; **~ an Kindes statt** (child) adoption **c** = **Annahmestelle**

An|nah|me-: **An|nah|me|be|stä|ti|gung** F acknowledgement of receipt; **An|nah|me|er|klä|rung** F (*Econ*) notice *or* declaration of acceptance; **An|nah|me|frist** F **~ bis zum 17. Juli** closing date 17th July; **die ~ für die Bewerbung ist schon vorbei** applications can no longer be accepted; **An|nah|me|schluss** M closing date; **An|nah|me|stel|le** F (*für Pakete, Telegramme*) counter; (*für Wetten, Lotto, Toto etc*) place where bets *etc* are accepted; (*für Reparaturen*) reception; (*für Material*) delivery point; **die ~ für Autobatterien ist …** please bring your old car batteries to …, old car batteries will be taken at …; **An|nah|me|ver|wei|ge|rung** F refusal; **bei ~** when delivery is refused

An|na|len [aˈnaːlən] PL annals *pl*; **in die ~ eingehen** (*fig*) to go down in the annals *or* in history

an|nehm|bar ADJ acceptable; (*= nicht schlecht*) reasonable, not bad; **sein altes Auto hat noch einen ~en Preis erzielt** he didn't get a bad price *or* he got a reasonable price for his old car ADV reasonably well

An|nehm|bar|keit [ˈanneːmbaːɐkait] F **-, -en** acceptability

an+neh|men *sep irreg* ✪ 27.3, 29.2, 46.6, 52.1, 53.1, 53.2, 53.6 VT **a** (*= entgegennehmen, akzeptieren*) to accept; *Geld* to accept, to take; *Nahrung, einen Rat, Telegramm, Gespräch, Telefonat, Lottoschein, Reparaturen* to take; *Arbeit, Auftrag* to accept, to take on; *Herausforderung, Angebot* to take up, to accept → **Vernunft** **b** (*= billigen*) to approve; *Gesetz* to pass; *Resolution* to adopt; *Antrag* to accept **c** (*= sich aneignen*) to adopt; *Gewohnheit etc* to pick up, to adopt; *Staatsangehörigkeit* to take on, to adopt; *Akzent, Tonfall* to acquire, to take on; *Gestalt, Namen* to assume, to take on; **ein angenommener Name** an assumed name **d** (*= zulassen*) *Patienten, Bewerber* to accept, to take on **e** (*= adoptieren*) to adopt; **jdn an Kindes statt ~** to adopt sb **f** (*= aufnehmen*) *Farbe* to take; **dieser Stoff/das Gefieder nimmt kein Wasser an** this material is/the feathers are water-repellent **g** (*= vermuten*) to presume, to assume; **von jdm etw ~** (*= erwarten*) to expect sth of sb; (*= glauben*) to believe sth of sb; **er ist nicht so dumm, wie man es von ihm ~ könnte** he's not as stupid as you might think *or* suppose **h** (*= voraussetzen*) to assume; **wir wollen ~, dass …** let us assume that …; **etw als gegeben** *or* **Tatsache ~** to take sth as read *or* for granted; **das kann man wohl ~** you can take that as read → *auch* **angenommen** **i** (*Sport*) to take VR **sich jds ~** to look after sb; **sich einer Sache** (*gen*) **~** to see to *or* look after a matter

an|nehm|lich [ˈanneːmlɪç] ADJ agreeable; *Bedingungen* acceptable

An|nehm|lich|keit F **-, -en** **a** (*= Bequemlichkeit*) convenience; (*= Vorteil*) advantage **b** **Annehmlichkeiten** PL comforts *pl*

an|nek|tie|ren [anɛkˈtiːrən] *ptp* **annektiert** VT to annex

An|nek|tie|rung F **-, -en** annexation

An|nex [aˈnɛks] M **-es, -e** (*Archit*) annexe (*Brit*), annex (*US*); (*Jur*) annex, appendix

An|ne|xi|on [anɛˈksioːn] F **-, -en** annexation

an+nie|sen VT *sep* to sneeze over *or* on

an+nie|ten VT *sep* to rivet on (*an +acc or dat* -to)

an|no [ˈano] ADV in (the year); **der härteste Winter seit ~ zwölf** the coldest winter since 1912; **ein harter Winter, wie ~ 81** a cold winter, like the winter of '81; **von ~ dazumal** *or* **dunnemals** *or* **Tobak** (*all inf*) from the year dot (*Brit inf*), forever; **das war im Deutschland von ~ dazumal so üblich** that was the custom in Germany in olden days; **ein Überbleibsel von ~ dazumal** *or* **dunnemals** *or* **Tobak** (*all inf*) a hangover from the olden days; **~ dazumal** *or* **dunnemals war alles viel billiger** in those days everything was much cheaper

An|no Do|mi|ni [ˈano ˈdoːmini] ADV in the year of Our Lord

An|non|ce [aˈnõːsə] F **-, -n** advertisement, advert (*Brit inf*), ad (*inf*)

An|non|cen|teil [aˈnõːsn-] M classified (advertisement) section

an|non|cie|ren [anõˈsiːrən, anɔŋˈsiːrən] *ptp* **annonciert** VI to advertise VT to advertise; (*geh: = ankündigen*) *Veröffentlichung, Heirat etc* to announce

an|nul|lie|ren [anʊˈliːrən] *ptp* **annulliert** VT (*Jur*) to annul

An|nul|lie|rung F **-, -en** annulment

An|o|de [aˈnoːdə] F **-, -n** anode

an+öden [ˈanløːdn] VT *sep* (*inf: = langweilen*) to bore stiff (*inf*) *or* to tears (*inf*)

ano|mal [anoˈmaːl, ˈanomaːl] ADJ (*= regelwidrig*) unusual, abnormal; (*= nicht normal*) strange, odd

Ano|ma|lie [anomaˈliː] F **-, -n** [-ˈliːən] anomaly; (*Med: = Missbildung*) abnormality

ano|nym [anoˈnyːm] ADJ anonymous; **Anonyme Alkoholiker** Alcoholics Anonymous ADV anonymously; **~ angerufen werden** to get anonymous phone calls

ano|ny|mi|sie|ren [anonymiˈziːrən] *ptp* **anonymisiert** VT (*Admin*) *Daten, Fragebögen* to make anonymous

Ano|ny|mi|sie|rung F **-, -en** (*Admin*) **die ~ der Daten ist erforderlich** data must be made anonymous

Ano|ny|mi|tät [anonymiˈtɛːt] F **-,** *no pl* anonymity; **er wollte die ~ wahren** he wanted to preserve his anonymity

Ano|ny|mus [aˈnoːnymʊs] M **-, Anonymi** *or* **Anonymen** [-mi, -mən] anonym (*rare*), anonymous artist/author *etc*

Ano|rak [ˈanorak] M **-s, -s** anorak

an+ord|nen VT *sep* **a** (*= befehlen, festsetzen*) to order **b** (*= nach Plan ordnen, aufstellen*) to arrange; (*systematisch*) to order

An|ord|nung F **a** (*= Befehl*) order; **laut (polizeilicher) ~** by order (of the police); **auf ~ des Arztes** on doctor's orders; **~en treffen** to give orders **b** (*= Aufstellung*) arrangement; (*= systematische Anordnung*) order; (*= Formation*) formation; **in welcher ~ wollen Sie die Tische für die Konferenz?** how do you want the tables arranged for the conference?

Ano|re|xie [anloreˈksiː] F **-, -n** [-ˈksiːən] anorexia (nervosa)

an|or|ga|nisch [ˈanlɔrgaːnɪʃ, anlɔrˈgaːnɪʃ] ADJ **a** (*Chem*) inorganic **b** (*rare*) haphazard; *Wachstum* random *attr* ADV **die Stadt ist ~ gewachsen** the town has grown in a haphazard way

anor|mal [ˈanɔrmaːl] ADJ (*inf*) = **anomal**

an+pa|cken *sep* (*inf*) VT **a** (*= anfassen*) to take hold of, to grab **b** (*= handhaben, beginnen*) *Problem, Thema* to tackle, to set about **c** (*= umgehen mit jdn*) to treat VI (*= helfen: auch* **mit anpacken**) to lend a hand

an+pap|pen *sep* (*inf*) VT to stick on (*an +dat* -to) VI *aux sein* to stick (*an +dat* to)

an+pas|sen *sep* VT **a** *Kleidung* to fit (*+dat* on); *Bauelemente* to fit (*+dat* to) **b** (*= abstimmen*) **etw einer Sache** (*dat*) **~** to suit sth to sth **c** (*= angleichen*) **etw einer Sache** (*dat*) **~** to bring sth into line with sth VR to adapt (oneself) (*+dat* to); (*gesellschaftlich*) to conform; **Kinder passen sich leichter an als Erwachsene** children adapt (themselves) more easily *or* are more adaptable than adults; **wir mussten uns ihren Wünschen ~** we had to fit in with their wishes *or* with them → *auch* **angepasst**

An|pas|sung F **-, -en** (*an +acc* to) adaptation; (*von Gehalt etc*) adjustment; (*an Gesellschaft, Normen etc*) conformity

An|pas|sungs-: **an|pas|sungs|fä|hig** ADJ adaptable; **An|pas|sungs|fä|hig|keit** F adaptability; **An|pas|sungs|me|cha|nis|mus** M (*Sociol*) adaptation mechanism; **An|pas|sungs|schwie|rig|kei|ten** PL difficulties *pl* in adapting; **An|pas|sungs|ver|mö|gen** NT (*Sociol*) adaptability; **An|pas|sungs|zeit|raum** M adjustment period

an+pei|len VT *sep* (*= ansteuern*) to steer *or* head for; (*mit Radar, Funk etc*) to take a bearing on; **etw ~** (*fig inf*) to set *or* have one's sights on sth; **jdn ~** (*inf*) to eye sb

an+peit|schen VT *sep* to push (hard); **von der Menge angepeitscht** driven *or* pushed on by the crowd

An|peit|scher [ˈanpaitʃɐ] M **-s, -**, **An|peit|sche|rin** [-ərɪn] F **-, -nen** slave-driver; (*fig*) rabble-rouser

an+pe|sen VI *sep aux sein* (*inf*) **angepest kommen** to come belting along *or* (*auf einen zu*) up (*inf*)

an+pfei|fen *sep irreg* VI (*Sport*) to blow the whistle VT **a** (*Sport*) **das Spiel ~** to start the game (by blowing one's whistle) **b** (*inf*) to bawl out (*inf*)

An|pfiff M **a** (*Sport*) (starting) whistle; (*= Spielbeginn*) (*Ftbl*) kickoff; (*Eishockey*) face-off **b** (*inf*) bawling out (*inf*)

an+pflan|zen VT *sep* (*= bepflanzen*) to plant; (*= anbauen*) to grow

An|pflan|zung F **a** *no pl* (*= das Bepflanzen*) planting; (*= Anbau*) growing **b** (*Fläche*) cultivated area; **eine ~ anlegen** to lay out an area for cultivation

an+pflau|men [ˈanpflaumən] VT *sep* (*inf*) to poke fun at; (*aggressiv*) to have a go at (*inf*)

an+pflo|cken ['anpflɔkn] VT *sep* to tie up; *Tier auch* to tether
an+piep|sen VT *sep* (*Telec inf*) to page, to bleep (*Brit*), to beep (*US*)
an+pin|keln VT *sep* (*inf*) to pee on (*inf*); (*fig:* = *kritisieren*) to put down
an+pin|nen ['anpɪnən] VT *sep* (*N Ger inf*) to pin up (*an +acc or dat* on)
an+pin|seln VT *sep* to paint; *Parolen etc* to paint (up)
an+pir|schen *sep* VT to stalk VR to creep up (*an +acc* on)
An|pö|be|lei F (*inf*) rudeness *no pl*
an+pö|beln VT *sep* (*inf*) to be rude to
an+po|chen VI *sep* to knock (*an +acc* on, at); **bei jdm ~, ob ...** (*inf*) to sound sb out (as to) whether ...
An|prall M impact; **beim ~ gegen** on impact with
an+pral|len VI *sep aux sein* to crash (*an or gegen jdn/etw* into sb/against sth)
an+pran|gern ['anpraŋɐn] VT *sep* to denounce; **jdn als Betrüger/etw als Korruption ~** to denounce sb as a fraud/sth as corrupt
An|pran|ge|rung F **-, -en** denunciation
an+prei|sen VT *sep irreg* to extol (*jdm etw* sth to sb); **sich (als etw) ~** to sell oneself (as sth)
an+pre|schen VI *sep aux sein* **angeprescht kommen** to come hurrying along *or* (*auf einen zu*) up
an+pres|sen VT *sep* to press on (*an +acc* -to); **das Ohr an die Tür ~** to press *or* put one's ear to the door
An|pro|be F **a** fitting **b** (= *Raum*) (*im Kaufhaus*) changing room; (*beim Schneider*) fitting room
an+pro|bie|ren *ptp* **anprobiert** *sep* VT to try on; **jdm etw ~** (*inf*) to try sth on sb VI (*beim Schneider*) to have a fitting; **kann ich mal ~?** can I try this/it *etc* on?; **ich muss noch ~** I'll have to try it on
an+pum|pen VT *sep* (*inf*) to borrow from; **jdn um 50 Euro ~** to touch sb for 50 euros (*Brit inf*), to hit sb up for 50 euros (*US inf*), to borrow 50 euros from sb
an+pus|ten VT *sep* (*inf*) to blow at; *Feuer* to blow on
an+quas|seln VT *sep* (*inf*) to speak to
an+quat|schen ['ankvatʃn] VT *sep* (*inf*) to speak to; *Mädchen* to chat up (*Brit inf*), to put the moves on (*US inf*)
An|rai|ner ['anrainɐ] M **-s, -**, **An|rai|ne|rin** [-ərɪn] F **-, -nen** **a** neighbour (*Brit*), neighbor (*US*); **die ~ der Nordsee** the countries bordering (on) the North Sea **b** (*esp Aus:* = *Anwohner*) (local) resident
An|rai|ner-: **An|rai|ner|grund|stück** NT neighbouring (*Brit*) *or* neighboring (*US*) property; **An|rai|ner|staat** M **die ~en des Mittelmeers/der Donau** the countries bordering (on) the Mediterranean/the Danube
an+ran|zen ['anrantsn] VT *sep* (*inf*) to bawl out (*inf*)
An|ran|zer ['anrantsɐ] M **-s, -** (*inf*) bawling out (*inf*)
an+ra|sen VI *sep aux sein* **angerast kommen** to come tearing *or* rushing along *or* (*auf einen zu*) up
an+ra|ten ✪ 29.2 VT *sep irreg* **jdm etw ~** to recommend sth to sb; **auf Anraten des Arztes** *etc* on the doctor's *etc* advice *or* recommendation
an+rat|tern VI *sep aux sein* **angerattert kommen** to come clattering *or* rattling along *or* (*auf einen zu*) up
an+rau|chen VT *sep* *Zigarre etc* to light (up); **eine angerauchte Zigarette** a partly *or* half-smoked cigarette
an+räu|chern VT *sep* to smoke lightly
an|rau|en, **an+rau|hen** △ VT *sep* to roughen; **angeraut sein** to be rough
an+raun|zen VT *sep* (*inf*) to tell off, to tick off (*Brit inf*)
An|raun|zer ['anrauntsɐ] M **-s, -** (*inf*) telling off, ticking off (*Brit inf*)
an+rau|schen VI *sep aux sein* **angerauscht kommen** to come rushing *or* hurrying along *or* (*auf einen zu*) up
an|re|chen|bar ADJ countable; **auf etw** (*acc*) **~ sein** to count toward(s) sth
an+rech|nen VT *sep* **a** (= *in Rechnung stellen*) to charge for (*jdm* sb); **das wird Ihnen später angerechnet** you'll be charged for that later, that will be charged to you later **b** (= *gutschreiben*) to count, to take into account (*jdm* for sb); **das alte Auto rechnen wir (Ihnen) mit EUR 500 an** we'll allow (you) EUR 500 for the old car; **den alten Fernseher ~** to allow something on the old television **c** (= *bewerten*) **dem Schüler wird die schlechte Arbeit nicht angerechnet** the pupil's bad piece of work is not being taken into account; **jdm etw hoch ~** to think highly of sb for sth; **jdm etw als Fehler ~** (*Lehrer*) to count sth as a mistake for sb; (*fig*) to consider sth as a fault on sb's part; **ich rechne es ihm als Verdienst an, dass ...** I think it is greatly to his credit that ..., I think it says a lot for him that ...; **ich rechne es mir zur Ehre an** (*form*) I consider it an honour (*Brit*) *or* an honor (*US*), I consider myself honoured (*Brit*) *or* honored (*US*)
An|rech|nung F allowance; (*fig:* = *Berücksichtigung*) counting, taking into account (*auf +acc* towards); **jdm etw in ~ bringen** *or* **stellen** (*form*) to charge sb for sth
an|rech|nungs|fä|hig ADJ = **anrechenbar**
An|recht NT **a** (= *Anspruch*) right, entitlement (*auf +acc* to); **ein ~ auf etw** (*acc*) **haben** *or* **besitzen** (*auf Respekt, Ruhe etc*) to be entitled to sth; *auf Geld, Land etc auch* to have a right to sth; **sein ~ (auf etw) geltend machen** to enforce one's right (to sth) **b** (= *Abonnement*) subscription
An|re|de F form of address; (= *Briefanrede auch*) salutation (*form*)
An|re|de|fall M, **An|re|de|ka|sus** M (*Gram*) vocative (case)
an+re|den *sep* VT to address; **jdn mit „du" ~** to address sb as "du", to use the "du" form (of address) to sb; **jdn mit seinem Titel ~** to address sb by his title VI **gegen jdn ~** to argue against sb; **gegen etw ~** to make oneself heard against sth
an+re|gen VT *sep* **a** (= *ermuntern*) to prompt (*zu* to); **jdn zum Denken ~** to make sb think **b** (*geh:* = *vorschlagen*) *Verbesserung* to propose, to suggest **c** (= *beleben*) to stimulate; *Appetit* to whet, to sharpen; **Kaffee** *etc* **regt an** coffee *etc* is a stimulant, coffee *etc* has a stimulating effect → *auch* **angeregt** **d** (*Phys*) to activate
an|re|gend ADJ stimulating; **ein ~es Mittel** a stimulant; **die Verdauung/den Kreislauf ~e Mittel** stimulants to the digestion/circulation ADV **~ wirken** to have a stimulating effect
An|re|gung F **a** (= *Antrieb, Impuls*) stimulus; **jdm eine ~ zum Denken geben** to make sb think **b** (= *Vorschlag*) idea; **auf ~ von** *or* *+gen* at *or* on the suggestion of **c** (= *Belebung*) stimulation
An|re|gungs|mit|tel NT stimulant
an+rei|chen VT *sep* to pass, to hand
an+rei|chern ['anraiçɐn] *sep* VT (= *gehaltvoller machen*) to enrich; (= *vergrößern*) *Sammlung* to enlarge, to increase; **hoch/niedrig** *or* **schwach angereichertes Uran** high/low enriched uranium; **das Gemisch mit Sauerstoff ~** (= *zufügen*) to add oxygen to the mixture; **angereichert werden** (*Chem:* = *gespeichert werden*) to be accumulated; **mit Rauch angereicherte Luft** smoky air VR (*Chem*) to accumulate
An|rei|che|rung F **-, -en** (= *Bereicherung*) enrichment; (= *Vergrößerung*) enlargement; (= *Speicherung*) accumulation; (*von Uran*) enriching
an+rei|hen *sep* VT **a** (= *einer Reihe anfügen*) to add (*an +acc* to) **b** (= *anheften*) to tack on; *Saum* to tack (up) VR to follow (*einer Sache* (*dat*) sth); **reihen Sie sich bitte hinten an!** join the end of the queue (*Brit*) *or* line (*US*), please
An|rei|se F **a** (= *Anfahrt*) journey there/here; **die ~ zu diesem abgelegenen Ort ist sehr mühsam** it is very difficult to get to this remote place **b** (= *Ankunft*) arrival; **Tag der ~ war Sonntag** the day of arrival was Sunday
an+rei|sen VI *sep aux sein* **a** (= *ein Ziel anfahren*) to make a/the journey *or* trip (there/here); **über welche Strecke wollen Sie ~?** which route do you want to take (there/here)? **b** (= *eintreffen: auch* **angereist kommen**) to come
An|rei|se|tag M day of arrival
an+rei|ßen VT *sep irreg* **a** (= *einreißen*) to tear, to rip **b** (*inf:* = *anbrechen*) to start, to open **c** *Außenbordmotor etc* to start (up) **d** (*Tech*) to mark (out) **e** (= *kurz zur Sprache bringen*) to touch on **f** (*pej inf*) *Kunden* to draw, to attract **g** *Streichholz* to strike
An|rei|ßer ['anraisɐ] M **-s, -** bait
An|rei|ßer ['anraisɐ] M **-s, -**, **An|rei|ße|rin** [-ərɪn] F **-, -nen** (*pej inf:* = *Kundenfänger*) tout
an|rei|ße|risch ADJ (*pej inf*) attention-grabbing *attr*
An|reiß|schab|lo|ne F (*Tech*) template
an+rei|ten *sep irreg* VI *aux sein* **angeritten kommen** to come riding along *or* (*auf einen zu*) up VT **a** *Ziel etc* to ride toward(s) **b** **gegen etw ~** (*Mil*) to charge sth
An|reiz M incentive; **ein ~ zum Lernen** *etc* an incentive to learn *etc* *or* for learning *etc*; **jdm den ~ nehmen, etw zu tun** to take away sb's incentive for doing sth
an+rei|zen *sep* VT **a** (= *anspornen*) to encourage; **jdn zum Kauf ~** to encourage sb to buy; **jdn zu großen Leistungen ~** to encourage sb to perform great feats **b** (= *erregen*) to stimulate, to excite VI to act as an incentive (*zu* to); **dazu ~, dass jd etw tut** to act as an incentive for sb to do sth
an+rem|peln VT *sep* **a** (= *anstoßen*) to bump into; (*absichtlich*) *Menschen* to jostle **b** (*fig:* = *beschimpfen*) to insult
an+ren|nen VI *sep irreg aux sein* **a** **gegen etw ~** (*gegen Wind etc*) to run against sth; (*Mil*) to storm sth; (*Sport*) to attack sth; (= *sich stoßen*) to run into sth; (*fig:* = *bekämpfen*) to fight against sth **b** **angerannt kommen** (*inf*) to come running
An|rich|te ['anrɪçtə] F **-, -n** **a** (= *Schrank*) dresser; (= *Büfett*) sideboard **b** (= *Raum*) pantry
an+rich|ten VT *sep* **a** (= *zubereiten*) *Speisen* to prepare; (= *servieren*) to serve; *Salat* to dress; **es ist angerichtet** (*form*) dinner *etc* is served (*form*) **b** (*fig:* = *verursachen*) *Schaden, Unheil* to cause, to bring about; **etwas ~** (*inf:* = *anstellen*) to get up to something (*inf*); **da hast du aber etwas angerichtet!** (*inf*) (= *verursachen*) you've started something there all right; (= *anstellen*) you've really made a mess there
an+rie|chen VT *sep irreg* to sniff at; **jdm/einer Sache etw ~** to be able to tell sth by smelling sb/sth; **ich rieche dir doch an, dass du geraucht hast** I can smell that you've been smoking
An|riss M (*Tech*) scribing, marking
An|ritt M (*old*) approach (on horseback) (*auf +acc* towards); (= *Angriff*) charge (*gegen* on, against)
an+rit|zen VT *sep* to slit (slightly)
an+rol|len *sep* VI *aux sein* (= *zu rollen beginnen*) to start to roll; (= *heranrollen*) to roll up; (*Aviat*) to taxi; **gegen etw/jdn ~** (*fig: in feindlicher Absicht*) to move against sth/sb; **angerollt kommen** to roll along *or* (*auf einen zu*) up VT to roll; (= *heranrollen*) to roll up
an+ros|ten VI *sep aux sein* to get (a bit) rusty
an+rös|ten VT *sep* to brown lightly
an|rü|chig ['anryçɪç] ADJ **a** (= *von üblem Ruf*) *Geschäfte* disreputable; (= *berüchtigt*) *Lokal etc* notorious, disreputable **b** (= *anstößig*) offensive; (= *unanständig*) indecent
An|rü|chig|keit F **-,** *no pl* (*von Lokal etc*) notoriety; (= *Anstößigkeit*) offensiveness; (= *Unanstän-*

digkeit) indecency; **einer Sache** *(dat)* **die ~ nehmen** to give sth an air of greater respectability; **dieser Branche haftet eine gewisse ~ an** this line of business is considered somewhat disreputable

an+rü|cken *sep* VI *aux sein* **a** *(Truppen)* to advance; *(Polizei etc)* to move in; *(hum: Essen, Besuch)* to turn up; **die Verwandten kamen angerückt** the relations turned up **b** *(= weiter heranrücken)* to move up *or* closer VT to move up; **etw an etw** *(acc)* **~** to push sth against sth

An|ruf M **a** *(Telec)* call; **einen ~ entgegennehmen** to take a (phone) call **b** *(Mil: eines Wachtpostens)* challenge; **etw auf ~ tun** to do sth when called; **ohne ~ schießen** to shoot without warning

An|ruf|be|ant|wor|ter [-bəlantvɔrtɐ] ✪ 27.6 M **-s, -** (telephone) answering machine, answerphone *(Brit)*

an+ru|fen *sep irreg* ✪ 27 VT **a** *(= zurufen)* to shout to; *(Telec)* to ring *(esp Brit)*, to phone, to call; *(Mil: Posten)* to challenge; **darf ich dich ~?** can I give you a ring? *(esp Brit)*, can I call you?; **kann man Sie ~?** *(= haben Sie Telefon?)* are you on the phone? **b** *(fig: = appellieren an)* *(um* for) to appeal to; *Gott* to call on VI *(inf: = telefonieren)* to phone, to make a (phone) call/phone calls; **bei jdm ~** to phone sb; **kann man hier bei Ihnen ~?** can I make a (phone) call from here?; **ins Ausland/nach Amerika ~** to phone abroad/America

An|ru|fer(in) M(F) caller

An|ruf|um|lei|tung F *(Telec)* call diversion

An|ru|fung F **-, -en** *(Gottes, der Heiligen etc)* invocation; *(Jur)* appeal *(+gen* to); **nach ~ des Gerichts** after an appeal to the court

An|ruf|wei|ter|lei|tung F call diversion *or* transfer

an+rüh|ren VT *sep* **a** *(= berühren, sich befassen mit)* to touch; *(fig) Thema* to touch upon; **er rührt kein Fleisch/keinen Alkohol an** he doesn't touch meat/alcohol **b** *(fig liter: = rühren)* to move, to touch **c** *(= mischen) Farben* to mix; *Sauce* to blend; *(= verrühren)* to stir

an|rüh|rend ADJ touching

an+ru|ßen VT *sep* to blacken

ans [ans] *contr von* **an das**; **sich ~ Arbeiten machen** *or (geh)* **begeben** to set to work; **wenn es ~ Sterben geht** when it comes to dying

an+sä|en VT *sep* to sow

An|sa|ge F announcement; *(= Diktat)* dictation; *(Cards)* bid; **er übernimmt bei diesem Programm die ~** he is doing the announcements for this programme *(Brit) or* program *(US)*; **einen Brief nach ~ schreiben** to take a letter down (on dictation); **er hat die ~** *(Cards)* it's his bid

an+sa|gen *sep* VT **a** *(= ankündigen)* to announce; **jdm den Kampf ~** to declare war on sb → **Bankrott**
b *(Cards) (Bridge)* to bid; *(Skat)* to declare
c *(inf)* **angesagt sein** *(= modisch sein)* to be in; *(= erforderlich sein)* to be called for; *(= auf dem Programm stehen)* to be the order of the day; **Spannung ist angesagt** we are in for a bit of excitement
VR *(= Besuch ankündigen)* to say that one is coming; *(= Termin vereinbaren)* to make an appointment; *(Zeit, Frühling)* to announce itself *(liter)*
VI **a** *(old, liter)* **sag an, Fremdling ...** pray tell, stranger *(old, liter)* ...
b sie sagt im Radio an she's an announcer on the radio

an+sä|gen VT *sep* to saw into

An|sa|ger ['anza:gɐ] M **-s, -**, **An|sa|ge|rin** [-ərɪn] F **-, -nen** *(Rad etc)* announcer; *(im Kabarett)* compère *(Brit)*, emcee *(US)*

an+sam|meln *sep* VT **a** *(= anhäufen)* to accumulate; *Reichtümer, Erfahrung* to amass; *Vorräte* to build up; *Zinsen* to build up, to accrue *(form)* **b** *(= zusammenkommen lassen)* to gather together VR **a** *(= sich versammeln)* to gather, to collect **b** *(= aufspeichern, aufhäufen)* to accumulate; *(Staub)* to collect, to accumulate; *(Flüssigkeit, Schadstoffe, Fragen)* to collect; *(fig: Wut, Frust, Misstrauen)* to build up; *(Zinsen)* to build up, to accrue *(form)*

An|samm|lung F **a** *(= Anhäufung)* accumulation; *(= Sammlung)* collection; *(von Druck, Stau, Wut)* build-up; *(= Haufen)* pile **b** *(= Auflauf)* gathering, crowd; *(von Truppen)* concentration

an|säs|sig ['anzɛsɪç] ADJ *(form)* resident; **eine in München ~e Firma** a firm based in Munich; **sich in London ~ machen** to settle *or* to take up residence *(form)* in London; **alle in diesem Ort Ansässigen** all local residents

An|satz M **a** *(von Hals, Arm, Henkel etc)* base; *(an Stirn)* hairline; *(= Haarwurzeln)* roots *pl*
b *(Tech) (= Zusatzstück)* attachment; *(zur Verlängerung)* extension; *(= Naht)* join
c *(= das Ansetzen: von Rost, Kalk etc)* formation, deposition; *(= Schicht)* coating, layer
d *(= erstes Anzeichen, Beginn)* first sign(s *pl*), beginning(s *pl*); *(= Versuch)* attempt *(zu etw* at sth); *(= Ausgangspunkt)* starting point; **den ~ zu etw zeigen** to show the first signs *or* the beginnings of sth; **einen neuen ~ zu etw machen** to make a fresh attempt at sth; **Ansätze zeigen, etw zu tun** to show signs of doing sth; **sie zeigte Ansätze von Senilität** she showed signs of senility; **die ersten Ansätze** the initial stages; **im ~** basically
e *(esp Philos, Liter etc)* approach
f *(Sport)* takeoff; *(= Anlauf)* run-up
g *(Math)* formulation
h *(Mus)* intonation; *(= Lippenstellung)* embouchure
i *(Econ form)* estimate; *(= Fonds für Sonderzwecke)* appropriation; **außer ~ bleiben** to be excluded, to be left out of account; **etw für etw in ~ bringen** to appropriate sth for sth

An|satz-: **An|satz|punkt** M starting point; **An|satz|stück** NT *(Tech)* attachment; *(zur Verlängerung)* extension; **an|satz|wei|se** ADV **~ zeigen/enthalten** to show/to have the beginnings of

an+säu|ern *sep* VT to make sour; *Brotteig* to leaven; *(Chem)* to acidify VI *aux sein* to start to go sour

an+sau|fen VT *sep irreg (inf)* **sich** *(dat)* **einen (Rausch) ~** to get plastered *or* sloshed *(inf)*; **sich** *(dat)* **einen Bauch ~** to get a beer belly

an+sau|gen *sep* VT to suck *or* draw in; *(= anfangen zu saugen)* to start to suck VR to attach itself *(by suction)*

An|saug-: **An|saug|ge|blä|se** NT *(Tech)* suction fan; **An|saug|lei|tung** F *(Chem)* inlet; **An|saug|rohr** NT induction pipe; *(Auto)* intake pipe

an+säu|seln VT *sep* **sich** *(dat)* **einen ~** *(hum inf)* to have a tipple *(inf)* → *auch* **angesäuselt**

an+schaf|fen *sep* VT **(sich** *dat)* **etw ~** to get oneself sth; *(= kaufen)* to buy sth; **sich** *(dat)* **Kinder ~** *(inf)* to have children VI **a** *(Aus, S Ger)* to give orders; **jdm ~** to order sb about, to give sb orders **b** *(sl: durch Prostitution)* **~ gehen** to be on the game *(inf)*; **für jdn ~ gehen** to go on the game for sb *(inf)*; **jdn ~** *or* **zum Anschaffen schicken** to send sb out on the game *(inf)*

An|schaf|fung F **a** *no pl* acquisition; **ich habe mich zur ~ eines Autos entschlossen** I have decided to get *or* buy a new car **b** *(= Gegenstand)* acquisition; *(gekauft)* purchase, buy; **~en machen** to acquire things; *(= kaufen)* to make purchases

An|schaf|fungs-: **An|schaf|fungs|kos|ten** PL cost *sing* of purchase, acquisition cost(s *pl*) *sing*, initial cost *sing*; **An|schaf|fungs|kre|dit** [-kredi:t] M loan; **An|schaf|fungs|preis** M purchase price; **An|schaf|fungs|wert** M value at the time of purchase

an+schal|ten VT *sep* to switch on

an+schau|en VT *sep (esp dial)* to look at; *(prüfend)* to examine; **sich** *(dat)* **etw ~** to have a look at sth; **(da) schau einer an!** *(inf)* well I never! *(inf)*

an|schau|lich ['anʃaulɪç] ADJ clear; *(= lebendig, bildhaft)* vivid; *Beschreibung* graphic; *Beispiel* concrete; **etw ~ machen** to illustrate sth; **den Unterricht sehr ~ machen** to make teaching come alive ADV clearly; *(= lebendig)* vividly

An|schau|lich|keit F **-,** *no pl* clearness; *(= Bildhaftigkeit)* vividness; *(von Beschreibung)* graphicness

An|schau|ung ['anʃauʊŋ] F **-, -en** *(= Ansicht, Auffassung)* view; *(= Meinung)* opinion; *(= Vorstellung)* idea, notion; *(= innere Versenkung)* contemplation; *(= Anschauungsvermögen)* ability to visualize things; **nach neuerer ~** according to the current way of thinking; **in ~** *+gen (geh)* in view of; **aus eigener ~** from one's own experience

An|schau|ungs-: **An|schau|ungs|ma|te|ri|al** NT illustrative material, visual aids *pl*; **An|schau|ungs|un|ter|richt** M visual instruction; **An|schau|ungs|ver|mö|gen** NT ability to visualize things; **An|schau|ungs|wei|se** F *(geh)* view

An|schein M appearance; *(= Eindruck)* impression; **dem ~ nach** apparently; **allem ~ nach** to all appearances, apparently; **den ~ erwecken, als ...** to give the impression that ...; **sich** *(dat)* **den ~ geben, als ob man informiert sei** to pretend to be informed; **es hat den ~, als ob ...** it appears that ..., it seems as if ...

an+schei|nen VT *sep irreg* to shine (up)on

an|schei|nend ADV apparently ADJ apparent

an+schei|ßen VT *sep irreg* **a** *(inf: = beschimpfen)* **jdn ~** to give sb a bollocking *(Brit sl)*, to kick sb's ass *(US sl)* **b** *(sl: = anöden)* to piss off *(sl)*

an+sche|sen VI *sep aux sein* **angeschest kommen** *(N Ger inf)* to come tearing along *or (auf einen zu)* up *(inf)*

an+schi|cken VR *sep* **sich ~, etw zu tun** *(geh)* *(= sich bereit machen)* to get ready to do sth, to prepare to do sth; *(= im Begriff sein)* to be on the point of doing sth, to be about to do sth

an+schie|ben VT *sep irreg* **a** *Fahrzeug* to push; **können Sie mich mal ~?** can you give me a push? **b** *(fig) Wirtschaft, Konjunktur* to kick-start

an+schie|ßen *sep irreg* VT **a** *(= verletzen)* to shoot (and wound); *Vogel (in Flügel)* to wing; **angeschossen** *(Mensch, Tier)* shot and wounded; **wie ein Angeschossener** *(inf)* like a scalded cat *(inf)* **b** *(Sport) Rennen* to start **c** *Tor* to shoot at; *Spieler* to hit; *(= treffen) Schiff, Billardkugel* to hit **d** *(inf: = kritisieren)* to hit out at *(inf)* VI *aux sein (inf) (= heranrasen)* to shoot up; **angeschossen kommen** to come shooting along *or (auf einen zu)* up

an+schim|meln VI *sep aux sein* to (start to) go mouldy *(Brit) or* moldy *(US)*

an+schir|ren ['anʃɪrən] VT *sep* to harness

An|schiss M **-es, -e** *(inf)* bollocking *(Brit sl)*, ass-kicking *(US sl)*

An|schlag M **a** *(= Plakat)* poster, bill, placard; *(= Bekanntmachung)* notice; **einen ~ machen** to put up a poster/notice
b *(= Überfall)* attack *(auf +acc* on); *(= Attentat)* attempt on sb's life; *(= Verschwörung)* plot *(auf +acc* against); **einen ~ auf jdn verüben** to make an attempt on sb's life; **einem ~ zum Opfer fallen** to be assassinated; **einen ~ auf jdn vorhaben** *(hum: = etwas von jdm wollen)* to have a favour *(Brit) or* favor *(US)* to ask of sb
c *(= Kostenanschlag)* estimate; **etw in ~ bringen** *(form)* to take sth into account; **eine Summe in ~ bringen** *(form)* to calculate an amount
d *(= Aufprall)* impact
e *(Sport) (beim Schwimmen)* touch; *(beim Versteckspiel)* home
f *(von Klavier(spieler), Schreibmaschine)* touch; **200 Anschläge in der Minute** ≈ 40 words per minute
g *(in Strickanleitung)* **~ von 20 Maschen** cast on 20 stitches
h *(von Hund)* bark
i *(bei Hebel, Knopf etc)* stop; **etw bis zum ~ durchdrücken** to push sth right down; **etw bis**

zum ~ drehen to turn sth as far as it will go
j *(Mil)* aiming *or* firing position; **ein Gewehr im ~ haben** to have a rifle at the ready

An|schlag|brett NT notice board *(esp Brit)*, bulletin board *(US)*

an+schla|gen *sep irreg* VT a *(= befestigen)* to fix on *(an +acc* to); *(mit Nägeln)* to nail on *(an +acc* to); *(= aushängen) Plakat* to put up, to post *(an +acc* on)
b *Stunde, Taste, Akkord* to strike; *(= anstimmen) Melodie* to strike up; *(Mus)* to play; **eine schnellere Gangart ~** *(fig)* to strike up a faster pace, to speed up; **ein anderes Thema/einen anderen Ton ~** *(fig)* to change the subject/one's tune; **einen weinerlichen/frechen Ton ~** to adopt a tearful tone/cheeky *(Brit) or* fresh *(US)* attitude
c *(= beschädigen, verletzen) Geschirr* to chip; **sich** *(dat)* **den Kopf** *etc* **~** to knock one's head *etc* → *auch* **angeschlagen**
d *(Sport) Ball* to hit; **den Ball seitlich ~** to chip the ball
e *(Aus: = anzapfen) Fass* to tap
f *(= vormarkieren) Baum* to mark (for felling)
g *(= aufnehmen) Maschen* to cast on
h *(Naut)* to fasten; *Segel, Tau* to bend
i *(geh) Kosten etc* to estimate
VI a *(Welle)* to beat *(an +acc* against); **mit etw gegen/an etw** *(acc)* **~** to strike *or* knock sth against/on sth
b *(Sport) (Tennis etc)* to serve; *(beim Schwimmen)* to touch
c *(Glocke)* to ring
d *(= Taste betätigen)* to strike the keys
e *(= Laut geben) (Hund)* to give a bark; *(Vogel)* to give a screech
f *(= wirken: Arznei etc)* to work, to take effect
g *(inf: = dick machen)* **bei jdm ~** to make sb put on weight

An|schlag-: **an|schlag|frei** ADJ *Drucker* non-impact; **An|schlag|säu|le** F advertising pillar; **An|schlag|ta|fel** F notice board *(esp Brit)*, bulletin board *(US)*; **An|schlag|zet|tel** M notice

an+schlei|chen *sep irreg* VI *aux sein* to creep along *or (auf einen zu)* up; **angeschlichen kommen** *(inf)* to come creeping along/up VR **sich an jdn/etw ~** to creep up on sb/sth; *(= sich anpirschen)* to stalk sb/sth

an+schlei|fen VT *sep (inf: = herbeischleppen)* to drag along; **was schleifst du denn da für einen Plunder an?** what's that junk you're carting up? *(inf)*

an+schlen|dern VI *sep aux sein* to stroll *or* saunter along *or (auf einen zu)* up

an+schlep|pen VT *sep* a *Auto* to tow-start b *(inf) (= unerwünscht mitbringen)* to bring along; *(nach Hause)* to bring home; *(= mühsam herbeibringen)* to drag along *(inf)*; *(hum: = hervorholen, anbieten)* to bring out

an+schlie|ßen *sep irreg* ✪ 38.2, 39.1, 50.1 VT a *(an +acc* to) *(Tech, Elec, Telec etc: = verbinden)* to connect; *(in Steckdose)* to plug in; **angeschlossen** connected(-up)
b *(an +acc* to) to lock; *(mit Schnappschloss)* to padlock; *(= anketten)* to chain (up)
c *(fig: = hinzufügen)* to add; **angeschlossen** *(Organisation etc)* affiliated *(dat* to *or (US)* with), associated *(dat* with)
VR **sich jdm** *or* **an jdn ~** *(= folgen)* to follow sb; *(= zugesellen)* to join sb; *(= beipflichten)* to side with sb; **sich einer Sache** *(dat) or* **an etw** *(acc)* **~** *(= folgen)* to follow sth; *(= beitreten, sich beteiligen)* to join sth; *(= beipflichten)* to endorse sth; *(= angrenzen)* to adjoin sth; **dem Vortrag** *or* **an den Vortrag schloss sich ein Film an** the lecture was followed by a film
VI **an etw** *(acc)* **~** to follow sth

an|schlie|ßend ADV afterwards ADJ following; *Ereignis, Diskussion auch* ensuing; **Essen mit ~em Tanz** dinner dance; **an einen Kurs ~e Prüfung** exam at the end of a course

An|schluss ✪ 27.7 M a *(= Verbindung)* connection; *(= Beitritt)* entry *(an +acc* into); *(an Klub)* joining *(an +acc* of); *(Hist euph)* Anschluss; **~ haben nach** *(Rail)* to have a connection to; **den ~ verpassen** *(Rail etc)* to miss one's connection; *(fig)* to miss the boat or bus; *(alte Jungfer)* to be left on the shelf *(inf)*; **ihm gelang der ~ an die Spitze** *(Sport)* he managed to catch up with the leaders
b *(Telec, Comput)* connection; *(= Anlage)* telephone (connection); *(= weiterer Apparat)* extension; *(= Wasseranschluss)* supply point; *(für Waschmaschine)* point; **elektrischer ~** power point; **einen ~ beantragen** *(Telec)* to apply for a telephone to be connected; **~ bekommen** *(Telec)* to get through; **der ~ ist besetzt** *(Telec)* the line is engaged *(Brit) or* busy *(esp US)*; **kein ~ unter dieser Nummer** *(Telec)* number unobtainable *(Brit)*, this number is not in service *(US)*
c **im ~ an** *(+acc) (= nach)* subsequent to, following; *(= mit Bezug auf)* in connection with, further to; *(= in Anlehnung an)* following, after
d *(fig) (= Kontakt)* contact *(an +acc* with); *(= Bekanntschaft)* friendship, companionship; *(= Aufnahme)* integration; **~ finden** to make friends *(an +acc* with); **er sucht ~** he wants to make friends

An|schluss-: **An|schluss|do|se** F a *(Elec)* junction box; *(= Steckdose)* socket b *(Telec)* connection box; **an|schluss|fer|tig** ADJ fully wired; **An|schluss|fi|nan|zie|rung** F follow-up financing; **An|schluss|flug** M connecting flight; **den ~ erreichen/verpassen** to catch/miss one's connecting flight; **An|schluss|num|mer** F extension; **An|schluss|rohr** NT connecting pipe; **An|schluss|schnur** F extension lead; **An|schluss|stel|le** F *(Mot)* junction; **An|schluss|zug** M *(Rail)* connecting train, connection

an+schmach|ten VT *sep* **jdn ~** to gaze lovingly at sb

an+schmei|ßen VT *sep irreg (inf: = in Gang setzen)* to turn on

an|schmie|den VT *sep* to forge on *(an +acc* -to); *(= anketten)* to chain *(an +acc* to); *(fig inf: = fesseln)* to rivet *(an +acc* to)

an+schmie|gen *sep* VT to nestle *(an +acc* against) VR **sich an jdn/etw ~** *(Kind, Hund)* to snuggle *or* nestle up to sb/sth; *(Kleidung)* to cling to sb/sth; *(geh: Dorf an Berg etc)* to nestle against sth

an|schmieg|sam [ˈanʃmiːkzaːm] ADJ *Wesen* affectionate; *Material* smooth

an+schmie|ren *sep* VT a *(= bemalen)* to smear b **jdn/sich mit etw ~** *(inf) (= beschmutzen)* to get sth all over sb/oneself; *(pej: = schminken)* to smear sth over sb's/one's lips/face *etc* c *(inf) (= betrügen)* to con *(inf)*, to take for a ride *(inf)*; *(= Streiche spielen)* to play tricks on → *auch* **angeschmiert** VR **sich bei jdm ~** *(inf)* to make up to sb *(Brit inf)*, to be all over sb *(inf)*

an+schmo|ren VT *sep (Cook)* to braise lightly

an+schnal|len *sep* VR *(Aut, Aviat)* to fasten one's seat belt; **bitte ~!** fasten your seat belts, please!; **hast du dich angeschnallt?, bist du angeschnallt?** have you fastened your seat belt?, are you strapped in? VT a *Skier* to clip on b *Person, Kind* to strap up; *(in etw)* to strap in; **jdn ~** *(Aviat, Aut)* to fasten sb's seat belt

An|schnall-: **An|schnall|gurt** M *(Aviat, Mot)* seatbelt; **An|schnall|pflicht** F, *no pl* mandatory wearing of seat belts; **für Kinder besteht ~** children must wear seat belts

an+schnau|ben *sep* VT to snort at; *(fig inf: = anschnauzen)* to bawl out *(inf)* VI *aux sein* **angeschnaubt kommen** *(inf)* to come along huffing and puffing

an+schnau|fen VI *sep aux sein* **angeschnauft kommen** to come panting along *or (auf einen zu)* up

an+schnau|zen VT *sep (inf)* to yell at

An|schnau|zer M *(inf)* **sich** *(dat)* **einen ~ holen, einen ~ kriegen** to get yelled at *(inf)*

an+schnei|den VT *sep irreg* a *Brot etc* to (start to) cut b *(fig) Frage, Thema* to touch on c *(Aut) Kurve* to cut; *(Sport) Ball* to cut d *(Archeol)* to come across

An|schnitt M *(= Schnittfläche)* cut part; *(= erstes Stück)* first slice; *(= Ende)* cut end

an+schnor|ren VT *sep (pej inf)* to (try to) tap *(Brit inf) or* bum *(US inf)*; **jdn um etw ~** to cadge sth from sb *(Brit)*, to tap sb for sth *(Brit inf)*, to bum sth from sb *(US inf)*

An|scho|vis [anˈʃoːvɪs] F **-, -** anchovy

an+schrau|ben VT *sep* to screw on *(an +acc* -to); *(= festschrauben)* to screw tight *or* up

an+schrei|ben *sep irreg* VT a *Behörde, Versandhaus etc* to write to; **es antworteten nur 20% der Angeschriebenen** only 20% of the people written to replied b *(= aufschreiben)* to write up *(an +acc* on); **etw mit Kreide ~** to chalk sth up; **angeschrieben stehen** to be written up → *auch* **angeschrieben** c *(inf: = in Rechnung stellen)* to chalk up *(inf)* VI *(inf)* **unser Kaufmann schreibt nicht an** our grocer doesn't give anything on tick *(Brit inf) or* on credit; **sie lässt immer ~** she always buys on tick *(Brit inf) or* on credit

An|schrei|ben NT **-s, -** *(= Brief)* cover note, covering letter

An|schrei|be|ta|fel F scoreboard; *(Billard)* billiard marker

an+schrei|en VT *sep irreg* to shout *or* yell at

An|schrift F address; **ein Brief ohne ~** an unaddressed letter

An|schub|fi|nan|zie|rung [ˈanʃuːp-] F *(Econ)* start-up funds *pl*

an+schul|di|gen [ˈanʃʊldɪgn] VT *sep* to accuse *(+gen* of)

An|schul|di|gung F **-, -en** accusation

an+schwär|men *sep* VT *(inf: = verehren)* to idolize, to have a crush on *(inf)* VI *aux sein (auch* **angeschwärmt kommen)** to come in swarms

an+schwär|zen VT *sep* a *(fig inf)* **jdn ~** to blacken sb's name *(bei* with); *(= denunzieren)* to run sb down *(bei* to) b *(lit)* to blacken; *(= beschmutzen)* to get dirty

an+schwe|ben VI *sep aux sein* a *(Aviat)* to come in to land b *(fig)* **sie kam angeschwebt** she came floating along *or (auf einen zu)* up

an+schwei|gen VT *sep irreg* to say nothing to; *(demonstrativ)* to refuse to speak to; **sich gegenseitig ~** to say nothing to each other

an+schwei|ßen VT *sep* a *(Tech)* to weld on *(an +acc* -to) b *(Hunt)* to wound, to draw blood from

an+schwel|len VI *sep irreg aux sein* to swell (up); *(Wasser auch, Lärm)* to rise; **dick angeschwollen** very swollen

an+schwem|men *sep* VT to wash up *or* ashore; **angeschwemmtes Land** alluvial land VI *aux sein* to be washed up *or* ashore

An|schwem|mung F **-, -en** *(in Fluss, Hafen)* silting up

an+schwim|men *sep irreg* VT *Ziel* to swim toward(s) VI a *aux sein* **angeschwommen kommen** *(Schwimmer, Wasservogel)* to come swimming along *or (auf einen zu)* up; *(Leiche, Brett)* to come drifting along *or (auf einen zu)* up; *(Flasche)* to come floating along *or (auf einen zu)* up b *aux sein* **gegen etw ~** to swim against sth

an+schwin|deln VT *sep (inf)* **jdn ~** to tell sb fibs *(inf)*

an+se|geln *sep* VT *(= zusegeln auf)* to sail for *or* toward(s), to make for; *(= anlegen in) Hafen* to put into VI *aux sein* **angesegelt kommen** *(inf: lit, fig)* to come sailing along *or (auf einen zu)* up

an+se|hen VT *sep irreg* a *(= betrachten)* to look at; **er sah mich ganz verwundert an** he looked at me with great surprise; **er sah mich ganz groß an** he stared at me; **er sah mich ganz böse an** he gave me an angry look; **hübsch/schrecklich** *etc* **anzusehen** pretty/terrible *etc* to look at; **jdn nicht mehr ~** *(fig inf)* not to want to know sb any more; **sieh mal einer an!** *(inf)* well, I never! *(inf)*

b *(fig)* to regard, to look upon *(als, für* as); **ich sehe es als meine Pflicht an** I consider it to be my duty; **sie sieht ihn nicht für voll an** she doesn't take him seriously → *auch* **angesehen**
c **(sich** *dat)* **etw ~** (= *besichtigen)* to (have a) look at sth; *Fernsehsendung* to watch sth; *Film, Stück, Sportveranstaltung* to see sth; **sich** *(dat)* **jdn/etw gründlich ~** *(lit, fig)* to take a close look at sb/sth; **sich** *(dat)* **die Welt ~** to see something of the world
d **das sieht man ihm an** he looks it; **das sieht man ihm nicht an** he doesn't look it; **das sieht man ihm an der Gesichtsfarbe an** you can tell (that) by the colour *(Brit) or* color *(US)* of his face; **man kann ihm die Strapazen der letzten Woche ~** he's showing the strain of the last week; **man sieht ihm sein Alter nicht an** he doesn't look his age; **jdm etw (an den Augen** *or* **an der Nasenspitze** *(hum))* **~** to tell *or* guess sth by looking at sb; **jeder konnte ihm sein Glück ~** everyone could see that he was happy
e **etw (mit) ~** to watch sth, to see sth happening; **das kann man doch nicht mit ~** you can't stand by and watch that; **ich kann das nicht länger mit ~** I can't stand it any more; **das habe ich (mir) lange genug (mit) angesehen!** I've had enough of that!

An|se|hen NT **-s,** *no pl* **a** (= *guter Ruf)* (good) reputation, standing; (= *Prestige)* prestige; **jdn zu ~ bringen** to bring sb standing, to bring sb a good reputation; **großes ~ genießen** to enjoy a good reputation, to have a lot of standing; **zu ~ kommen** to acquire standing, to acquire a good reputation; **(bei jdm) in hohem ~ stehen** to be held in high regard *or* esteem (by sb); **an ~ verlieren** to lose credit *or* standing **b** (= *Aussehen)* appearance; **ein anderes ~ gewinnen** to take on a different appearance *or (fig)* aspect; **jdn vom ~ kennen** to know sb by sight **c** *(Jur)* **ohne ~ der Person** without respect of person

an|sehn|lich [ˈanzeːnlɪç] ADJ **a** (= *beträchtlich)* considerable; *Leistung* impressive; **ein ~es Sümmchen** *(hum)* a pretty *or* tidy little sum; **ein ~er Bauch** *(hum)* quite a stomach **b** *(dated:* = *gut aussehend, stattlich)* handsome

An|sehn|lich|keit F **-,** *no pl* **a** *(von Leistung)* impressiveness; **die ~ seines Bankkontos** his considerable bank balance **b** *(dated:* = *respektables Äußeres)* handsome appearance

An|se|hung [ˈanzeːʊŋ] F **in ~** *+gen (form)* in view of

an+sei|len [ˈanzailən] VT *sep* **jdn/sich ~** to rope sb/oneself up; **etw ~ und herunterlassen** to fasten sth with a rope and let it down

an sein VI *irreg aux sein (inf)* to be on

an+sen|gen VT *sep* to singe; **es riecht angesengt** there's a smell of singeing

an+set|zen *sep* VT **a** (= *anfügen)* to attach *(an +acc* to), to add *(an +acc* to), to put on *(an +acc* -to); (= *annähen)* to sew on
b (= *in Ausgangsstellung bringen)* to place in position; **eine Leiter an etw** *(acc)* **~** to put a ladder up against sth; **den Bleistift/die Feder ~** to put pencil/pen to paper; **die Flöte/Trompete** *etc* **~** to raise the flute/trumpet to one's mouth; **das Glas ~** to raise the glass to one's lips; **an welcher Stelle muss man den Wagenheber ~?** where should the jack be put *or* placed?
c *(mit, auf +acc* at) (= *festlegen) Kosten, Termin* to fix; (= *veranschlagen) Kosten, Zeitspanne* to estimate, to calculate; **für 9 Uhr angesetzt sein** *(Besprechung etc)* to be scheduled for 9 o'clock
d (= *einsetzen)* **jdn auf jdn/etw ~** to put sb on (-to) sb/sth; **Hunde (auf jdn/jds Spur) ~** to put dogs on sb/sb's trail
e (= *entstehen lassen) Blätter etc* to put out; *Frucht* to form, to produce; **Fett ~** *(Mensch)* to put on weight; *(Tier)* to get fatter; **Rost ~** to get rusty
f *(Cook)* (= *vorbereiten)* to prepare; *Bowle* to start
g *(Math)* to formulate
VR *(Rost)* to form; *(Kalk etc)* to be deposited; *(Gekochtes)* to stick
VI **a** (= *beginnen)* to start, to begin; **zur Landung ~** *(Aviat)* to come in to land; **zum Sprung/Start ~** to get ready *or* prepare to jump/start; **er setzte immer wieder an, aber ...** *(zum Sprechen)* he kept opening his mouth to say something but ...
b (= *hervorkommen) (Knospen)* to come forth; *(Früchte)* to set; *(Bäume)* to sprout
c *(Cook:* = *sich festsetzen)* to stick

An|sicht ✪ 38.1, 39.1, 53.3, 53.5, 53.6 F **-, -en** **a** view; **~ von hinten/vorn** rear/front view; **~ von oben/unten** view from above/below, top/bottom view *(Tech)*
b (= *das Betrachten, Prüfen)* inspection; **bei ~ (von unten** *etc*) on inspection (from below *etc*); **zur ~** *(Comm)* for (your/our *etc*) inspection; **jdm Waren zur ~ schicken** *(Comm)* to send sb goods on approval
c *(Comput)* view; *(vor dem Drucken)* preview
d (= *Meinung)* opinion, view; **nach ~** *+gen* in the opinion of; **meiner ~ nach** in my opinion *or* view; **ich bin der ~, dass ...** I am of the opinion that ...; **anderer/der gleichen ~ sein** to be of a different/the same opinion, to disagree/agree; **über etw** *(acc)* **anderer ~ sein** to take a different view of sth, to have a different opinion about sth; **ich bin ganz Ihrer ~** I entirely agree with you; **die ~en sind geteilt** *or* **verschieden** opinions differ, opinion is divided

an|sich|tig [ˈanzɪçtɪç] ADJ **jds/einer Sache ~ werden** *(dated, geh)* to set eyes on sb/sth

An|sichts-: **An|sichts|ex|emp|lar** NT specimen *or* inspection copy; **An|sichts|(post)|kar|te** F picture postcard; **An|sichts|sa|che** F **das ist ~** that is a matter of opinion; **An|sichts|sen|dung** F article(s *pl*) sent on approval; **jdm eine ~ schicken** to send sb articles/an article on approval

ANSI-Code [ˈansiːkoːt] M ANSI code

an+sie|deln *sep* VT to settle; *Tierart* to introduce; *Vogelkolonie, Industrie* to establish; **dieser Begriff ist in der Literaturkritik angesiedelt** this term belongs to the field of literary criticism VR to settle; *(Industrie etc)* to get established; *(Bakterien etc)* to establish themselves

An|sied|ler(in) M(F) settler

An|sied|lung F **a** settlement **b** (= *das Ansiedeln)* settling; (= *Kolonisierung von Tieren)* colonization; *(von Betrieben)* establishing

An|sin|nen [ˈanzɪnən] NT **-s, -** *(dated, geh)* (= *Gedanke)* notion, idea; (= *Vorschlag)* suggestion; **ein seltsames ~ an jdn stellen** to make an unreasonable suggestion to sb

An|sitz M **a** *(Hunt)* raised hide **b** *(Aus)* residence; **„Ansitz Claudia"** "Claudia House"

an|sons|ten [anˈzɔnstn] ADV (= *im anderen Fall, inf:* = *im Übrigen)* otherwise; **~ gibts nichts Neues** *(inf)* there's nothing new apart from that; **~ hast du nichts auszusetzen?** *(iro)* have you any more complaints?

an+span|nen *sep* VT **a** (= *straffer spannen)* to tauten, to tighten; *Muskeln* to tense **b** (= *anstrengen)* to strain, to tax; **jdn zu sehr ~** to overtax sb; **alle seine Kräfte ~** to strain every nerve, to exert all one's energy → *auch* **angespannt** **c** *Wagen* to hitch up; *Pferd* to harness; *Ochsen* to yoke up *(zu* for); **jdn (zu einer Arbeit) ~** *(inf)* to get sb to do a job VI (= *Pferde/Wagen anspannen)* to hitch up; **~ lassen** to get a/the carriage ready; **es ist angespannt!** the carriage is ready

An|span|nung F *(fig)* strain; (= *körperliche Anstrengung auch)* effort; **unter ~ aller Kräfte** by exerting all one's energies

an+spa|ren VT *sep* to save

An|spar|pha|se F *(bei Bausparvertrag)* saving period

an+spa|zie|ren *ptp* **anspaziert** VI *sep aux sein* **anspaziert kommen** to come strolling along *or (auf einen zu)* up

an+spei|en VT *sep irreg* to spit at

An|spiel NT *(Sport)* start of play; *(Cards)* lead; *(Chess)* first move

an+spie|len *sep* VT **a** *(Sport)* to play the ball *etc* to; *Spieler* to pass to **b** *(Mus) Stück* to play part of; *Instrument* to try out (for the first time); **ein paar Takte ~** to play a few bars VI **a** (= *Spiel beginnen)* to start; *(Ftbl)* to kick off; *(Cards)* to lead, to open; *(Chess)* to open **b** **auf jdn/etw ~** to allude to sb/sth; **worauf wollen Sie ~?** what are you driving at?, what are you insinuating?; **spielst du damit auf mich an?** are you getting at me?

An|spie|lung [ˈanʃpiːlʊŋ] F **-, -en** allusion *(auf +acc* to); *(böse)* insinuation, innuendo *(auf +acc* regarding)

an+spin|nen *sep irreg* VT *Faden* to join; *(fig) Verhältnis, Thema* to develop, to enter into VR *(fig)* to develop, to start up; **da spinnt sich doch etwas an!** *(inf)* something is going on there!

an+spit|zen VT *sep* **a** *Bleistift etc* to sharpen **b** *(inf:* = *antreiben)* to have a go at; **jdn ~, dass er etw tut** to have a go at sb to do sth

An|sporn M, *no pl* incentive; **ihm fehlt der innere ~** he has no motivation

an+spor|nen VT *sep Pferd* to spur (on); *(fig auch)* to encourage *(zu* to); *Mannschaft* to cheer on; **Kinder zum Lernen ~** to encourage children to learn

An|spra|che F **a** (= *Rede)* address, speech; **eine ~ halten** to give an address, to make a speech **b** (= *Beachtung)* attention

an|sprech|bar ADJ (= *bereit, jdn anzuhören)* approachable; (= *gut gelaunt)* amenable; *Patient* responsive; **er ist beschäftigt/wütend und zurzeit nicht ~** he's so busy/angry that no-one can talk to him just now; **er ist jederzeit für seine Studenten ~** his students can speak to him at any time; **auf etw** *(acc)* **~ sein** to respond to sth

an+spre|chen *sep irreg* VT **a** (= *anreden)* to speak to; (= *das Wort an jdn richten, mit Titel, Vornamen etc)* to address; *(belästigend)* to accost; **jdn auf etw** *(acc)***/um etw ~** to ask *or* approach sb about/for sth; **es kommt darauf an, wie man die Leute anspricht** it depends on how you talk to people; **damit sind Sie alle angesprochen** this is directed at all of you
b (= *gefallen)* to appeal to; (= *Eindruck machen auf)* to make an impression on
c *(fig geh)* **etw als ... ~** (= *ansehen)* to declare sth to be ...; (= *beschreiben)* to describe sth as ...
d (= *erwähnen)* to mention
VI **a** *(auf +acc* to) (= *reagieren) (Patient, Gaspedal etc)* to respond; *(Messgerät)* to react, to respond; **diese Tabletten sprechen bei ihr nicht an** these tablets don't have any effect on her; **leicht ~de Bremsen** very responsive brakes
b (= *Anklang finden)* to go down well, to meet with a good response

an|spre|chend ADJ (= *reizvoll) Äußeres, Verpackung etc* attractive, appealing; (= *angenehm) Umgebung etc* pleasant ADV attractively; **~ wirken** to be attractive

An|sprech-: **An|sprech|part|ner(in)** M(F) *(form)* contact; **An|sprech|zeit** F *(Aut, Tech)* response *or* operating time

an+sprin|gen *sep irreg* VT **a** (= *anfallen)* to jump; *(Raubtier)* to pounce (up)on; *(Hund:* = *hochspringen)* to jump up at **b** *(Sport) Gerät, Latte* to jump at; *Rolle, Überschlag* to dive into VI *aux sein* **a** *(Motor)* to start; *(fig:* = *in Gang kommen)* to get going **b** **angesprungen kommen** to come bounding along *or (auf einen zu)* up; **auf etw** *(acc)* **~** *(fig inf)* to jump at sth *(inf)*; **gegen etw ~** to jump against sth **c** *(Sport)* to jump

an|sprit|zen *sep* VT (= *bespritzen)* to splash; *(mit Spritzpistole, -düse etc)* to spray VI *aux sein* **angespritzt kommen** *(inf)* to come tearing *(inf)* along *or (auf einen zu)* up

An|spruch M **a** *(esp Jur)* claim; (= *Recht)* right *(auf +acc* to); **~ auf etw** *(acc)* **haben** to be entitled to sth, to have a right to sth; **~ auf Schadenersatz erheben** to make a claim for damages; **~ auf Schadenersatz haben** to be entitled to damages

b *(= Anforderung)* demand; *(= Standard)* standard, requirement; **an jdn dauernd Ansprüche stellen** to make constant demands on sb; **große** *or* **hohe Ansprüche stellen** to be very demanding; *(= hohes Niveau verlangen)* to demand high standards; **den erforderlichen Ansprüchen gerecht werden** to meet the necessary requirements
c *(= Behauptung)* claim, pretension; **diese Theorie erhebt keinen ~ auf Unwiderlegbarkeit** this theory does not claim to be irrefutable, this theory lays no claim to irrefutability
d etw in ~ nehmen *(Recht)* to claim sth; *jds Hilfe, Dienste* to enlist sth; *Möglichkeiten, Kantine etc* to take advantage of sth; *Zeit, Aufmerksamkeit, Kräfte* to take up sth; **jdn völlig in ~ nehmen** to take up all of sb's time; *(jds Aufmerksamkeit, Gedanken)* to engross *or* preoccupy sb completely; **sehr in ~ genommen** very busy/preoccupied; **darf ich Ihre Aufmerksamkeit in ~ nehmen?** may I have your attention?

An|spruchs-: **an|spruchs|be|rech|tigt** ADJ ~ **sein** to be entitled to claim; **An|spruchs|be|rech|tig|te(r)** [-bərɛçtɪçtə] MF *decl as adj* person entitled to claim; **alle ~n** all those entitled to claim; **An|spruchs|den|ken** NT high expectations *pl* (of one's entitlements); **an|spruchs|los** ADJ *(= ohne große Ansprüche)* undemanding; *(= geistig nicht hochstehend)* lowbrow; *(= minderwertig) Produkte* down-market; *(= wenig Pflege, Geschick etc erfordernd)* undemanding ADV simply; **~ leben** to lead a modest life; **An|spruchs|lo|sig|keit** F -, *no pl (= anspruchslose Art)* undemanding nature; *(geistig)* lowbrow nature; *(wenig Pflege, Geschick etc erfordernd)* undemanding nature; **die stilistische ~ dieser Technokraten** the lack of stylistic sophistication of these technocrats; **er lehrte Disziplin und ~** he taught discipline and modesty in one's demands; **an|spruchs|voll** ADJ *(= viel verlangend)* demanding; *(= übertrieben anspruchsvoll)* hard to please, fastidious; *(= wählerisch)* discriminating; *(= kritisch)* critical; *(= hohe Ansprüche stellend) Stil, Buch* ambitious; *Geschmack, Musik* highbrow; *(= kultiviert)* sophisticated; *(= hochwertig)* high-quality, superior, up-market; **eine Zeitung für Anspruchsvolle** a newspaper for the discriminating reader; **der Füllhalter für Anspruchsvolle** the pen for people who are hard to please ADV *(= kultiviert)* in a sophisticated manner

an+spu|cken VT *sep* to spit at *or* on

an+spü|len VT *sep* to wash up *or* ashore

an+sta|cheln VT *sep* to spur (on); *(= antreiben)* to drive *or* goad on

An|stalt [ˈanʃtalt] F -, -en **a** institution *(auch euph)*; *(= Institut)* institute; **eine ~ öffentlichen Rechts** a public institution **b Anstalten** PL *(= Maßnahmen)* measures *pl*; *(= Vorbereitungen)* preparations *pl*; **für** *or* **zu etw ~en treffen** to take measures/make preparations for sth; **~en/keine ~en machen, etw zu tun** to make a/no move to do sth

An|stalts-: **An|stalts|arzt** M, **An|stalts|ärz|tin** F resident physician; **An|stalts|geist|li|che(r)** MF *decl as adj* resident chaplain; **An|stalts|klei|dung** F institutional clothing; *(in Gefängnis)* prison clothing; **An|stalts|lei|ter(in)** M(F) director of an/the institution; **An|stalts|zög|ling** M *(in Erziehungsanstalt)* child from an institution; *(in Internat)* boarding school pupil; *(in Fürsorgeheim)* child from a home

An|stand M **a** *no pl (= Schicklichkeit)* decency, propriety; *(= Manieren)* (good) manners *pl*; **keinen ~ haben** to have no sense of decency/no manners; **den ~ verletzen** to offend against decency; **das kann man mit ~ tun** it's quite in order to do that; **das kann man nicht mit ~ tun** you can't in all decency do that; **sich mit ~ zurückziehen** to withdraw with good grace
b *(geh: = Einwand)* **ohne ~** without demur *(form)* or hesitation; **~/keinen ~ an etw** *(dat)* **nehmen** to object/not to object to sth, to demur/not to demur at sth *(form)*; **keinen ~ nehmen, etw zu tun** not to hesitate to do sth
c *(esp S Ger: = Ärger)* trouble *no pl*

An|stand M *(Hunt)* raised hide; **auf den ~ gehen** to sit in the raised hide

an|stän|dig ADJ decent; *Witz auch* clean; *(= ehrbar)* respectable; *(inf: = beträchtlich)* sizeable, large; **das war nicht ~ von ihm** that was pretty bad of him; **bleib ~!** behave yourself!; **eine ~e Tracht Prügel** *(inf)* a good hiding ADV decently; **sich ~ benehmen** to behave oneself; **sich ~ hinsetzen** to sit properly; **jdn ~ bezahlen** *(inf)* to pay sb well; **~ essen/ausschlafen** *(inf)* to have a decent meal/sleep; **es regnet ganz ~** *(inf)* it's raining pretty hard; **sie hat sich ~ gestoßen** *(inf)* she really took a knock *(inf)*

an|stän|di|ger|wei|se ADV out of decency; **du könntest ihm die zerbrochene Vase ~ bezahlen** you could in all decency pay him for the broken vase

An|stän|dig|keit F -, *no pl* decency; *(= Ehrbarkeit)* respectability

An|stands-: **An|stands|be|such** M formal call; *(aus Pflichtgefühl)* duty visit; **An|stands|da|me** F chaperon(e); **An|stands|for|men** PL manners *pl*; **an|stands|hal|ber** ADV out of politeness; **An|stands|hap|pen** M *(inf)* **einen ~ übrig lassen** to leave something out of good manners; **an|stands|los** ADV without difficulty; **An|stands|un|ter|richt** M lessons *pl* in deportment; **An|stands|wau|wau** M *(hum inf)* chaperon(e); **den ~ spielen** to play gooseberry *(Brit)*, to be the third wheel *(US)*

an+star|ren VT *sep* to stare at

an|statt [anˈʃtat] PREP *+gen* instead of CONJ ~ **zu arbeiten** instead of working; **~, dass er das tut, ...** instead of doing that, he ...

an+stau|ben VI *sep aux sein* to become *or* get dusty

an+stau|en *sep* VT *Wasser* to dam up; *Gefühle* to bottle up VR to accumulate; *(Blut in Adern etc)* to congest; *(fig: Gefühle)* to build up, to accumulate; **angestaute Wut** pent-up rage

an+stau|nen VT *sep* to gaze *or* stare at in wonder, to marvel at; *(= bewundern)* to admire; **was staunst du mich so an?** what are you staring at me like that for?, why are you staring at me like that?

An|stau|ung F *(von Wasser)* accumulation; *(von Blut)* congestion; *(fig: von Gefühlen)* build-up

an+ste|chen VT *sep irreg* to make a hole in, to pierce; *Kartoffeln, Fleisch* to prick; *Reifen* to puncture; *Blase* to lance, to pierce; *Fass* to tap, to broach; *(Archeol)* to open up → *auch* **angestochen**

an+ste|cken *sep* VT **a** *(= befestigen)* to pin on; *Ring* to put *or* slip on **b** *(= anzünden)* to light; *(= in Brand stecken)* to set fire to, to set alight **c** *(Med, fig)* to infect; **ich will dich nicht ~** I don't want to give it to you VR **sich (mit etw) ~** to catch sth *(bei* from) VI *(Med, fig)* to be infectious *or* catching; *(durch Berührung, fig)* to be contagious

an|ste|ckend ADJ *(Med, fig)* infectious, catching *pred (inf)*; *(durch Berührung, fig)* contagious

An|ste|cker M *(inf) (= Button)* badge; *(= Schmuck)* small brooch

An|steck|na|del F *(= Button)* badge; *(= Schmuck)* small brooch

An|ste|ckung [ˈanʃtɛkʊŋ] F -, -en *(Med)* infection; *(durch Berührung)* contagion

An|ste|ckungs-: **An|ste|ckungs|ge|fahr** F risk of infection; **An|ste|ckungs|herd** M centre *(Brit)* or center *(US)* of infection

an+ste|hen VI *sep irreg aux haben or (S Ger, Aus, Sw also) sein* **a** *(in Schlange)* to queue (up) *(Brit)*, to stand in line *(nach* for)
b *(= auf Erledigung warten)* to be due to be dealt with; *(Verhandlungspunkt)* to be on the agenda; **zum Verkauf ~** *(Waren)* to be up for sale; **~de Probleme** problems facing us/them *etc*; **etw ~ lassen** to put off *or* delay *or* defer sth; **eine Schuld ~ lassen** to put off paying a debt, to defer payment of a debt *(form)*
c *(Jur: Termin etc)* to be fixed *or* set *(für* for)
d *(geh: = zögern)* **nicht ~, etw zu tun** not to hesitate to do sth
e *(geh: = geziemen)* **jdm ~** to become *or* befit sb *(form, old)*; **das steht ihm schlecht an** that ill becomes *or* befits him *(form, old)*
f *(Geol)* to be exposed, to crop out *(Geol)*; **~des Gestein** outcrop

an+stei|gen VI *sep irreg aux sein* to rise; *(Weg auch, Mensch)* to ascend; *(Temperatur, Preis, Zahl auch)* to go up, to increase

an|stel|le, an Stel|le [anˈʃtɛlə] PREP *+gen* instead of, in place of → *auch* **Stelle f**

an+stel|len *sep* VT **a** *(= danebenstellen)* to place; *(= anlehnen)* to lean *(an +acc* against)
b *(= dazustellen)* to add *(an +acc* to)
c *(= beschäftigen)* to employ, to take on; **jdn zu etw ~** *(inf)* to get sb to do sth → *auch* **angestellt**
d *(= anmachen, andrehen)* to turn on; *(= in Gang setzen)* to start
e *Betrachtung, Vermutung etc* to make; *Vergleich* to draw, to make; *Experiment* to conduct; **(neue) Überlegungen ~(, wie ...)** to (re)consider (how ...)
f *(= machen, unternehmen)* to do; *(= fertigbringen)* to manage; **ich weiß nicht, wie ich es ~ soll** *or* **kann** I don't know how to do *or* manage it
g *(inf: = Unfug treiben)* to get up to, to do; **etwas ~** to get up to mischief; **was hast du da wieder angestellt?** what have you done now?, what have you been up to now?
VR **a** *(= Schlange stehen)* to queue (up) *(Brit)*, to stand in line
b *(inf: = sich verhalten)* to act, to behave; **sich dumm/ungeschickt ~** to act stupid/clumsily, to be stupid/clumsy; **sich geschickt ~** to go about sth well
c *(inf: = sich zieren)* to make a fuss, to act up *(inf)*; **stell dich nicht so an!** don't make such a fuss!; *(= sich dumm anstellen)* don't act so stupid!

An|stel|le|rei [anʃtɛləˈrai] F -, -en *(inf)* **a** *(= Zierere)* fuss; **lass diese ~!** don't make such a fuss! **b** *(= Schlangestehen)* queueing *(Brit)*, standing in line

an|stel|lig [ˈanʃtɛlɪç] ADJ *(dated)* clever, quick to learn

An|stel|lung F employment; *(= Stelle)* position, employment

An|stel|lungs-: **An|stel|lungs|ver|hält|nis** NT contractual relationship between employer and employee; *(= Vertrag)* contract; **im** *or* **mit ~** under *or* with a contract (of employment); **im ~ sein** to have a contract, to be under contract; **An|stel|lungs|ver|trag** M employment contract

an|steu|ern VT *sep* to make *or* steer *or* head *(auch hum)* for; *(lit, fig) Kurs* to head on, to follow; *(fig) Thema* to steer onwards

An|stich M *(von Fass)* tapping, broaching; *(= erstes Glas)* first draught *(Brit)* or draft *(US)*; *(= erster Spatenstich)* digging the first sod; *(Archeol)* opening

an+stie|feln VI *sep aux sein* **angestiefelt kommen** *(inf)* to come marching along *or (auf einen zu)* up

An|stieg M -(e)s, -e **a** *(= Aufstieg)* climb, ascent; *(= Weg)* ascent **b** *(von Straße)* incline; *(von Temperatur, Kosten, Preisen etc)* rise, increase (*+gen* in)

an+stie|ren VT *sep (pej)* to stare at

an+stif|ten VT *sep (= anzetteln)* to instigate; *(= verursachen)* to bring about, to cause; **jdn zu etw ~** to incite sb to (do) sth, to put sb up to sth *(inf)*; **jdn zu einem Verbrechen ~** to incite sb to commit a crime

An|stif|ter(in) M(F) instigator (*+gen, zu* of); *(= Anführer)* ringleader

An|stif|tung F *(von Mensch)* incitement *(zu* to); *(von Tat)* instigation

an+stim|men *sep* VT **a** *(singen)* to begin singing; *(Chorleiter) Grundton* to give; *(spielen)* to start playing; *(Kapelle)* to strike up, to start playing **b** *(fig)* **ein Geheul/Geschrei/Proteste** *etc* ~ to start whining/crying/protesting *etc*; **ein Gelächter** ~ to burst out laughing VI to give the keynote

an+stin|ken *sep irreg (fig inf)* VT **das stinkt mich an** I'm sick of that VI **dagegen/gegen ihn kannst du nicht** ~ you can't do anything about it/him

an+stol|zie|ren *ptp* **anstolziert** VI *sep aux sein* **anstolziert kommen** to come strutting *or* swaggering along *or (auf einen zu)* up; *(Pfau etc)* to come strutting along/up

an|stöp|seln VT *Kopfhörer, Telefon* to plug in

An|stoß M **a den (ersten)** ~ **zu etw geben** to initiate sth, to get sth going; **den** ~ **zu weiteren Forschungen geben** to give the impetus to further research, to stimulate further research; **jdm den** ~ **geben, etw zu tun** to give sb the inducement to do sth, to induce sb to do sth; **der** ~ **zu diesem Plan/der** ~ **ging von ihr aus** she originally got this plan/things going; **den** ~ **zu etw bekommen, den** ~ **bekommen, etw zu tun** to be prompted *or* encouraged to do sth; **es bedurfte eines neuen ~es** new impetus *or* a new impulse was needed **b** *(Sport)* kickoff; *(Hockey)* bully-off **c** *(= Ärgernis)* annoyance *(für* to); ~ **erregen** to cause offence *(Brit) or* offense *(US) (bei* to); **ein Stein des ~es** *(= umstrittene Sache)* a bone of contention; **die ungenaue Formulierung des Vertrags war ein ständiger Stein des ~es** the inexact formulation of the contract was a constant obstacle *or* a constant stumbling block; **das ist mir ein Stein des ~es** *or* **ein Stein des ~es für mich** that really annoys me **d** *(= Hindernis)* difficulty; **ohne jeden** ~ without a hitch, without any difficulty

an+sto|ßen *sep irreg* VI **a** *aux sein* **an etw** *(acc)* ~ to bump into sth; **pass auf, dass du nicht anstößt** take care that you don't bump into anything; **mit dem Kopf an etw** *(acc)* ~ to bump *or* knock one's head on sth; **mit der Zunge** ~ to lisp **b (mit den Gläsern)** ~ to touch *or* clink glasses; **auf jdn/etw** ~ to drink to sb/sth **c** *(Sport)* to kick off; *(Hockey)* to bully off **d** *aux sein (= Anstoß erregen)* to cause offence *(Brit) or* offense *(US)*; **bei jdm** ~ to offend sb **e** *(= angrenzen)* **an etw** *(acc)* ~ to adjoin sth; *(Land auch)* to border on sth VT *jdn* to knock (into); *(mit dem Fuß)* to kick; *(= in Bewegung setzen)* to give a push; *Kugel, Ball* to hit; **sich** *(dat)* **den Kopf/Fuß** *etc* ~ to bang *or* knock one's head/foot

an|sto|ßend ADJ **a** *(= aneckend)* offensive **b** = **angrenzend**

An|stö|ßer ['anʃtøːsɐ] M **-s, -**, **An|stö|ße|rin** [-ərɪn] F **-, -nen** *(Sw: = Anwohner)* (local) resident

an|stö|ßig ['anʃtøːsɪç] ADJ offensive; *Kleidung* indecent ADV offensively; *gekleidet, aufgemacht* shockingly

An|stö|ßig|keit F **-, -en a** *no pl* offensiveness; *(von Kleidung)* indecency **b** *(= Bemerkung)* offensive remark; *(= Stelle)* offensive passage

an+strah|len VT *sep* to floodlight; *(im Theater)* to spotlight; *(= strahlend ansehen)* to beam at; **das Gebäude wird rot/von Scheinwerfern angestrahlt** the building is lit with a red light/is floodlit; **sie strahlte** *or* **ihre Augen strahlten mich an** she beamed at me

an+stre|ben VT *sep* to strive for

an|stre|bens|wert ADJ worth striving for

an+strei|chen VT *sep irreg* **a** *(mit Farbe etc)* to paint **b** *(= markieren)* to mark; **(jdm) etw als Fehler** ~ to mark sth wrong (for sb); **er hat das angestrichen** *(als Fehler)* he marked it wrong; **er hat nichts angestrichen** he didn't mark anything wrong

An|strei|cher ['anʃtraiçɐ] M **-s, -**, **An|strei|che|rin** [-ərɪn] F **-, -nen** (house) painter

an+stren|gen ['anʃtrɛŋən] *sep* VT **a** *Augen* to strain; *Muskel, Gehirn, Geist* to exert; *(= strapazieren) jdn* to tire out; *esp Patienten* to fatigue; **das viele Lesen strengt meine Augen/mich an** all this reading is *or* puts a strain on my eyes/is a strain (for me); **alle Kräfte** ~ to use all one's strength *or (geistig)* faculties; **sein Gedächtnis** ~ to rack one's brains; **streng doch mal deinen Verstand ein bisschen an** think hard → *auch* **angestrengt b** *(Jur)* **eine Klage/einen Prozess** ~ to initiate *or* institute proceedings *(gegen* against) VR to make an effort; *(körperlich auch)* to exert oneself; **sich mehr/sehr** ~ to make more of an effort/a big effort; **sich übermäßig** ~ to make too much of an effort; *(körperlich auch)* to overexert oneself; **sich ~, etw zu tun** to make an effort to do sth, to try hard to do sth; **unsere Gastgeberin hatte sich sehr angestrengt** our hostess had gone to *or* had taken a lot of trouble

an|stren|gend ADJ *(körperlich)* strenuous; *(geistig)* demanding, taxing; *Zeit* taxing, exhausting; *(= erschöpfend)* exhausting, tiring; **das ist** ~ **für die Augen** it's a strain on the eyes

An|stren|gung F **-, -en** effort; *(= Strapaze)* strain; **große ~en machen** to make every effort; **~en machen, etw zu tun** to make an effort to do sth; **mit äußerster/letzter** ~ with very great/one last effort

An|strich M **a** *(= das Anmalen, Tünchen)* painting; *(= Farbüberzug)* paint; *(fig) (= Anflug)* touch; *(von Wissenschaftlichkeit etc)* veneer; *(= Anschein)* air; **ein zweiter** ~ a second coat of paint **b** *(Mus)* first touch **c** *(beim Schreiben)* upstroke

an+stri|cken VT *sep* to knit on *(an +acc* -to); *Strumpf* to knit a piece onto

an+strö|men VI *sep aux sein (Menschenmassen)* to stream along; *(Wasser)* to flow in; **angeströmt kommen** to come streaming *or* rushing along *or (auf einen zu)* up; **~de Kaltluft** a stream of cold air

an+stü|ckeln, an+stü|cken VT *sep Stück* to attach *(an +acc* to); **etw (an etw** *acc)* ~ to add sth (onto sth)

An|sturm M onslaught; *(= Andrang) (auf Kaufhaus etc)* rush; *(auf Bank)* run; *(= Menschenmenge)* crowd

an+stür|men VI *sep aux sein* **gegen etw** ~ *(Mil)* to attack *or* storm sth; *(Wellen, Wind)* to pound sth; *(fig: = ankämpfen)* to attack sth; **angestürmt kommen** to come storming along *or (auf einen zu)* up

an+stür|zen VI *sep aux sein* **angestürzt kommen** to charge along *or (auf einen zu)* up

an+su|chen VI *sep (dated, Aus)* **bei jdm um etw** ~ *(= bitten um)* to ask sb for sth; *(= beantragen)* to apply to sb for sth

An|su|chen ['anzuːxn] NT **-s, -** *(dated, Aus)* request; *(= Gesuch)* application; **auf jds** ~ *(acc)* at sb's request

An|ta|go|nis|mus [antagoˈnɪsmʊs] M **-, Antagonismen** [-mən] antagonism

An|ta|go|nist [antagoˈnɪst] M **-en, -en**, **An|ta|go|nis|tin** [-ˈnɪstɪn] F **-, -nen** antagonist

an|ta|go|nis|tisch [antagoˈnɪstɪʃ] ADJ antagonistic

an+tan|zen VI *sep aux sein* **a** *(fig inf)* to turn *or* show up *(inf)*; **er kommt jeden Tag angetanzt** *(inf)* he turns up here every day **b** *(lit)* to come dancing along

Ant|ark|ti|ka [antˈlarktika] F **-**, *no pl* Antarctica

Ant|ark|tis [antˈlarktɪs] F, *no pl* Antarctic

ant|ark|tisch [antˈlarktɪʃ] ADJ antarctic

an+tas|ten VT *sep* **a** *(= verletzen) Ehre, Würde* to offend; *Rechte* to infringe, to encroach upon; *(= anbrechen) Vorräte, Ersparnisse etc* to break into **b** *(= berühren)* to touch; *(fig) Thema, Frage* to touch on, to mention

an+tau|en VTI *sep (vi: aux sein)* to begin to defrost

an+täu|schen VI *sep* to feint; *(Ftbl etc auch)* to dummy; *(Tennis)* to disguise one's shot; **links** ~ to feint/dummy to the left

An|teil M **a** share; *(Fin)* share, interest; **er hat bei dem Unternehmen ~e von 30%** he has a 30% interest *or* share in the company **b** *(= Beteiligung)* ~ **an etw** *(dat)* **haben** *(= beitragen)* to contribute to sth, to make a contribution to sth; *(= teilnehmen)* to take part in sth; **an dieser Sache will ich keinen** ~ **haben** I want no part in this **c** *(= Teilnahme: an Leid etc)* sympathy *(an +dat* with); **an etw** *(dat)* ~ **nehmen** *(an Leid etc)* to be deeply sympathetic over sth; *an Freude etc* to share in sth; **sie nahmen alle an dem Tod seiner Frau** ~ they all felt deeply for him when his wife died; **sie nahmen alle an seinem Leid** ~ they all felt for him in his sorrow **d** *(= Interesse)* interest *(an +dat* in), concern *(an +dat* about); **regen** ~ **an etw** *(dat)* **nehmen/zeigen** *or* **bekunden** *(geh)* to take/show a lively interest in sth

an|tei|lig, an|teil|mä|ßig ADJ proportionate, proportional ADV proportionately, proportionally

An|teil|nah|me [-naːmə] F **-**, *no pl* **a** *(= Beileid)* sympathy *(an +dat* with); **mit** ~ **zuhören** to listen sympathetically **b** *(= Beteiligung)* participation *(an +dat* in)

An|teil|schein M *(Fin: = Aktie)* share certificate

An|teils|eig|ner(in) M(F) *(Fin: = Aktionär)* shareholder, stockholder *(esp US)*

an|teils|mä|ßig ADJ ADV = **anteilig**

an+te|le|fo|nie|ren *ptp* **antelefoniert** VTI *sep (inf)* to phone; **jdn** *or* **bei jdm** ~ to phone sb up

An|ten|ne [anˈtɛnə] F **-, -n** *(Rad)* aerial, antenna *(esp US)*; *(Zool)* feeler, antenna; **eine/keine** ~ **für etw haben** *(fig inf)* to have a/no feeling for sth

An|ten|nen-: **An|ten|nen|ka|bel** NT aerial *or* antenna *(esp US)* cable *or* lead; **An|ten|nen|mast** M radio mast; **An|ten|nen|steck|do|se** F aerial *or* antenna *(esp US)* socket; **An|ten|nen|ste|cker** M aerial *or* antenna *(esp US)* plug *or* jack; **An|ten|nen|wald** M forest of aerials *or* antennas *(esp US)*

An|tho|lo|gie [antoloˈgiː] F **-, -n** [-ˈgiːən] anthology

Anth|rax [ˈantraks] NT **-**, *no pl (Biol)* anthrax

Anth|rax-: **Anth|rax|brief** M anthrax(-laced) letter; **Anth|rax|pul|ver** NT anthrax powder, powdered anthrax

Anth|ra|zit [antraˈtsiːt] M **-s**, *(rare)* **-e** anthracite

anth|ra|zit(far|ben) [antraˈtsiːt(farbn)], **anth|ra|zit|far|big** ADJ charcoal-grey *(Brit)*, charcoal-gray *(US)*, charcoal

Anth|ro|po|lo|ge [antropoˈloːgə] M **-n, -n**, **Anth|ro|po|lo|gin** [-ˈloːgɪn] F **-, -nen** anthropologist

Anth|ro|po|lo|gie [antropoloˈgiː] F **-**, *no pl* anthropology

anth|ro|po|lo|gisch [antropoˈloːgɪʃ] ADJ anthropological ADV anthropologically

anth|ro|po|morph [antropoˈmɔrf] ADJ anthropomorphous

Anth|ro|po|soph [antropoˈzoːf] M **-en, -en**, **Anth|ro|po|so|phin** [-ˈzoːfɪn] F **-, -nen** anthroposophist

Anth|ro|po|so|phie [antropozoˈfiː] F **-**, *no pl* anthroposophy

anth|ro|po|so|phisch [antropoˈzoːfɪʃ] ADJ anthroposophic ADV **jdn** ~ **erziehen** to raise sb according to anthroposophic ideals; ~ **angehaucht** influenced by anthroposophy

anth|ro|po|zent|risch [antropoˈtsɛntrɪʃ] ADJ anthropocentric

An|ti- PREF anti; **An|ti|a|ging** NT **-**, *no pl* anti-ageing; **An|ti|al|ko|ho|li|ker(in)** M(F) teetota(l)ler; **An|ti|ame|ri|ka|nis|mus** M, *no pl* anti-Americanism; **an|ti|au|to|ri|tär** ADJ anti-authoritarian ADV ~ **eingestellt sein** to be anti-authoritarian; **jdn** ~ **erziehen** to raise sb using anti-authoritarian methods *or* principles; **An|**

ti|ba|by|pil|le F *(inf)* contraceptive pill; **an|ti|bak|te|ri|ell** ADJ antibacterial ADV antibacterially; **~ wirken** to work as an antibacterial agent; **An|ti|be|schlag|tuch** NT *pl* **-tücher** *(Aut)* anti-mist cloth; **An|ti|bio|ti|kum** [anti'bio:tikʊm] NT **-s, Antibiotika** [-ka] antibiotic; **An|ti|blo|ckier|(brems)|sys|tem** [antiblɔ'ki:ɐ-] NT *(Aut)* antilock braking system; **an|ti|chamb|rie|ren** [antiʃam'bri:rən] *ptp* **antichambriert** VI *(pej)* **(bei jdm) ~** to bow and scrape (to sb), to kowtow (to sb); **An|ti|christ** ['anti-] M **-(s)** Antichrist; **An|ti|christ** ['anti-] M **-en, -en**, **An|ti|chris|tin** F **-, -en** opponent of Christianity, Antichristian; **an|ti|christ|lich** ADJ Antichristian ADV **~ eingestellt sein** to be Antichristian; **an|ti|de|mo|kra|tisch** ADJ antidemocratic; **An|ti|de|pres|si|vum** [antidepre'si:vʊm] NT **-s, Antidepressiva** [-va] antidepressant

An|ti|fa ['antifa] F *abbr von* **Antifaschismus** antifascism

> **ANTIFA**
>
> **Antifa** is an abbreviation of **Antifaschismus**. It became a slogan of the Communists and the New Left, who broadened the term to encompass the "struggle against Western colonialism and imperialism". **Antifa** demonstrations are organized to protest against the violence of right-wing extremist groups.

An|ti|fa F **-,** *no pl* *(inf: = autonome Bewegung)* antifascist movement; **~-Gruppe** antifascist group

An|ti-: **An|ti|fa|schis|mus** M antifascism; **An|ti|fa|schist(in)** M(F) antifascist; **an|ti|fa|schis|tisch** ADJ antifascist ADV **~ erzogen werden** to be raised to be antifascist; **~ orientiert sein** to be antifascist; **sich ~ geben** to pose as an antifascist

An|ti|gen [anti'ge:n] NT **-s, -e** *(Med, Biol)* antigen

An|ti-: **An|ti|haft|be|schich|tung** F nonstick surface *or* coating; **mit ~** *(Pfanne, Topf)* nonstick *attr*; **An|ti|held** M antihero; **An|ti|hel|din** F antiheroine; **An|ti|his|ta|min** NT antihistamine; **an|ti|im|pe|ri|a|lis|tisch** ADJ anti-imperialistic

an|tik [an'ti:k] ADJ **a** *(Hist)* ancient; **der ~e Mensch** man in the ancient world **b** *(Comm, inf)* antique

An|ti|ke [an'ti:kə] F **-, -n** **a** *no pl* antiquity; **die Kunst der ~** the art of the ancient world **b** *(= Kunstwerk)* antiquity

An|ti|kern|kraft|be|we|gung F antinuclear movement

an|ti|kisch ADJ in the ancient style

An|ti-: **an|ti|kle|ri|kal** ADJ anticlerical ADV **~ eingestellt** *or* **gesinnt sein** to be anticlerical; **An|ti|kle|ri|ka|lis|mus** M anticlericalism; **An|ti|klopf|mit|tel** [anti'klɔpf-] NT *(Tech)* antiknock (mixture); **An|ti|kom|mu|nis|mus** M anti-Communism; **An|ti|kom|mu|nist(in)** M(F) anti-Communist; **an|ti|kom|mu|nis|tisch** ADJ anti-Communist ADV **~ eingestellt** *or* **gesinnt sein** to be anti-Communist; **An|ti|kör|per** M *(Med)* antibody

An|ti|lo|pe [anti'lo:pə] F **-, -n** antelope

An|ti-: **An|ti-Ma|fia-Ge|setz** NT anti-Mafia law; **An|ti|ma|te|rie** F *(Phys)* antimatter; **An|ti|mi|li|ta|ris|mus** M antimilitarism; **An|ti|mi|li|ta|rist(in)** M(F) antimilitarist; **an|ti|mi|li|ta|ris|tisch** ADJ antimilitaristic

An|ti|mon [anti'mo:n] NT **-s,** *no pl* *(abbr* **Sb**) antimony

An|ti-: **an|ti|mo|nar|chisch** ADJ antimonarchist; **An|ti|oxi|dans** [anti'ɔksidans] NT **-, Antioxidanzien** [-ɔksi'dantsiən], **An|ti|oxi|da|ti|ons|mit|tel** NT *(Chem)* antioxidant; **An|ti|pa|thie** [antipa'ti:] F **-, -n** [-'ti:ən] antipathy *(gegen* to); **An|ti|per|so|nen|mi|ne** F antipersonnel mine

An|ti|po|de [anti'po:də] M **-n, -n** *(lit)* antipodean; *(fig)* adversary; **die Engländer sind die ~n Australiens** the English live on the opposite side of the world from Australia

an+tip|pen VT *sep* to tap; *Pedal, Bremse* to touch; *(fig) Thema* to touch on; **jdn ~** to tab sb on the shoulder/arm *etc*; **bei jdm ~(, ob …)** *(inf)* to sound sb out (as to whether …)

An|ti|qua [an'ti:kva] F **-,** *no pl* *(Typ)* roman (type)

An|ti|quar [anti'kva:ɐ] M **-s, -e**, **An|ti|qua|rin** [-'kva:rɪn] F **-, -nen** antiquarian *or (von moderneren Büchern)* second-hand bookseller

An|ti|qua|ri|at [antikva'ria:t] NT **-(e)s, -e** *(= Laden)* antiquarian *or (modernerer Bücher)* second-hand bookshop; *(= Abteilung)* antiquarian/second-hand department; *(= Handel)* antiquarian/second-hand book trade; **modernes ~** remainder bookshop/department

an|ti|qua|risch [anti'kva:rɪʃ] ADJ antiquarian; *(von moderneren Büchern)* second-hand ADV second-hand; **ein Buch ~ kaufen** to buy a book second-hand

an|ti|quiert [anti'kvi:ɐt] ADJ *(pej)* antiquated

An|ti|qui|tät [antikvi'tɛ:t] F **-, -en** *usu pl* antique

An|ti|qui|tä|ten-: **An|ti|qui|tä|ten|ge|schäft** NT antique shop; **An|ti|qui|tä|ten|han|del** M antique business *or* trade; **An|ti|qui|tä|ten|händ|ler(in)** M(F) antique dealer; **An|ti|qui|tä|ten|la|den** M antique shop; **An|ti|qui|tä|ten|samm|ler(in)** M(F) antique collector

An|ti-: **An|ti|ra|ke|te** F, **An|ti|ra|ke|ten|ra|ke|te** F anti(missile) missile; **An|ti|sa|tel|li|ten|waf|fe** F antisatellite weapon; **An|ti|se|mit(in)** M(F) antisemite; **an|ti|se|mi|tisch** ADJ anti-Semitic ADV anti-Semitically; **~ eingestellt sein** to be anti-Semitic; **sich ~ äußern** to make anti-Semitic remarks; **An|ti|se|mi|tis|mus** [antizemi'tɪsmʊs] M **-,** *no pl* antisemitism; **An|ti|sep|ti|kum** NT **-s, Antiseptika** *(Med, Pharm)* antiseptic; **an|ti|sep|tisch** ADJ antiseptic ADV antiseptically; **An|ti|sta|tik|tuch** NT antistatic cloth; **an|ti|sta|tisch** ADJ antistatic ADV **etw ~ behandeln** to treat sth with an antistatic agent; **An|ti|teil|chen** NT *(Phys)* antiparticle

An|ti|ter|ror- *in cpds* antiterrorist; **An|ti|ter|ror|ein|heit** F antiterrorist unit; **An|ti|ter|ror|kampf** M fight *or* struggle against terrorism, fighting terrorism; **An|ti|ter|ror|koa|li|ti|on** F anti-terror coalition

An|ti|the|se F antithesis

an|ti|the|tisch [-'te:tɪʃ] ADJ antithetical

An|ti-: **An|ti|trans|pi|rant** [-transpi'rant] NT **-s, -e** *or* **-s** *(form)* antiperspirant; **An|ti|typ** M **ein ~ zu jdm sein, jds ~ sein** to be the complete opposite of sb; **An|ti|vi|ren|pro|gramm** [anti'vi:rən-] NT *(Comput)* anti-virus program, virus checker; **An|ti-Vi|ren-Soft|ware** [anti'vi:rən-] F *(Comput)* anti-virus software

An|ti|zi|pa|ti|on [antitsipa'tsio:n] F **-, -en** *(geh)* anticipation *no pl*

an|ti|zi|pie|ren [antitsi'pi:rən] *ptp* **antizipiert** VT *insep (geh)* to anticipate

an|ti|zyk|lisch ADJ anticyclical ADV **~ verlaufen** to be anticyclical

Ant|litz ['antlɪts] NT **-es, -e** *(poet)* countenance *(liter)*, face

an+to|ben VI *sep* **a** **gegen jdn/etw ~** to rail at sb/sth **b** **angetobt kommen** to come storming along *or (auf einen zu)* up

An|to|nym [anto'ny:m] NT **-s, -e** antonym

an+tör|nen ['antœrnən] *sep (sl)* VT *(Drogen, Musik)* to turn on *(inf)* VI **das törnt an** it turns you on *(inf)*

an+tra|ben VI *sep aux sein* to start trotting, to go into a trot; **angetrabt kommen** to come trotting along *or (auf einen zu)* up

An|trag ['antra:k] M **-(e)s, Anträge** [-trɛ:gə] **a** *(auf +acc* for) application; *(= Gesuch)* request; *(= Formular)* application form; **einen ~ auf etw** *(acc)* **stellen** to make an application for sth; **auf ~** *+gen* at the request of **b** *(Jur)* petition; *(= Forderung bei Gericht)* claim; **einen ~ auf etw** *(acc)* **stellen** to file a petition/claim for sth **c** *(Parl)* motion; **einen ~ auf etw** *(acc)* **stellen** to propose a motion for sth **d** *(dated: = Angebot)* proposal; **jdm unzüchtige Anträge machen** to make improper suggestions to sb **e** *(= Heiratsantrag)* proposal; **jdm einen ~ machen** to propose (marriage) to sb

an+tra|gen VT *sep irreg (geh)* to offer *(jdm etw* sb sth)

An|trags-: **An|trags|for|mu|lar** NT application form; **An|trags|frist** F application period

An|trag|stel|ler [-ʃtɛlɐ] M **-s, -**, **An|trag|stel|le|rin** [-ərɪn] F **-, -nen** claimant; *(für Kredit etc)* applicant

an+trai|nie|ren *ptp* **antrainiert** VT *sep* **jdm/sich schnelle Reaktion/Tricks/gute Manieren ~** to train sb/oneself to have fast reactions/to do tricks/to be well-mannered

an+trau|en VT *sep (old)* **jdn jdm ~** to marry sb to sb; **mein angetrauter Ehemann** my lawful wedded husband

an+tref|fen VT *sep irreg* to find; *Situation auch* to meet; *(zufällig auch)* to come across; **er ist schwer anzutreffen** it's difficult to catch him in; **ich habe ihn in guter Laune angetroffen** I found him in a good mood

an+trei|ben *sep irreg* VT **a** *(= vorwärtstreiben) Tiere, Gefangene, Kolonne* to drive; *(fig)* to urge; *(= veranlassen: Neugier, Liebe, Wunsch etc)* to drive on; **jdn zur Eile/Arbeit ~** to urge sb to hurry up/to work; **jdn zu größerer Leistung ~** to urge sb to achieve more; **ich lasse mich nicht ~** I won't be pushed **b** *(= bewegen) Rad, Fahrzeug etc* to drive; *(mit Motor)* to power, to drive **c** *(= anschwemmen)* to wash up; *(an Strand)* to wash up *or* ashore; **etw ans Ufer ~** to wash sth (up) on to the bank VI *aux sein* to wash up; *(an Strand auch)* to wash ashore

An|trei|ber(in) M(F) *(pej)* slave-driver *(pej)*

an+tre|ten *sep irreg* VT **a** *Reise, Strafe* to begin; *Stellung* to take up; *Amt* to take up, to assume; *Erbe, Erbschaft* to come into; **den Beweis ~** to offer proof; **den Beweis ~, dass …** to prove that …; **seine Lehrzeit ~** to start one's apprenticeship; **seine Amtszeit ~** to take office; **die Regierung ~** to come to power

b *Motorrad* to kick-start

c *(= festtreten) Erde* to press *or* tread down firmly

VI *aux sein* **a** *(= sich aufstellen)* to line up; *(Mil)* to fall in

b *(= erscheinen)* to assemble; *(bei einer Stellung)* to start; *(zum Dienst)* to report

c *(zum Wettkampf)* to compete; *(= spurten)* to put on a spurt; *(Radfahrer)* to sprint

An|trieb M **a** impetus *no pl*; *(innerer)* drive; **jdm ~/neuen ~ geben, etw zu tun** to give sb the impetus/a new impetus to do sth; **aus eigenem ~** on one's own initiative, off one's own bat *(Brit inf)* **b** *(= Triebkraft)* drive; **Auto mit elektrischem ~** electrically driven *or* powered car; **welchen ~ hat das Auto?** how is the car driven *or* powered?

An|triebs-: **An|triebs|ach|se** F *(Aut)* propeller shaft; **An|triebs|ag|gre|gat** NT *(Tech)* drive unit; **an|triebs|arm** ADJ = **antriebsschwach**; **An|triebs|kraft** F *(Tech)* power; **An|triebs|leis|tung** F drive *or* driving power; **an|triebs|los** ADJ *(= träge)* (completely) lacking in drive *or* motivation; **An|triebs|ma|schi|ne** F *(Tech)* engine; **An|triebs|rad** NT drive wheel; **An|triebs|rie|men** M drive belt; **An|triebs|schei|be** F drive *or* driving pulley; **an|triebs|schwach** ADJ *(Psych)* lacking in drive; **An|triebs|schwä|che** F *(Med)* lack of drive *or* motivation; **an|triebs|stark** ADJ *(Psych)* full of drive; **An|triebs|stu|fe** F *(von Rakete)* propulsion stage; **An|triebs|wel|le** F drive shaft, half-shaft

an+trin|ken VT *sep irreg (inf)* to start drinking; **sie hat ihren Kaffee nur angetrunken** she only drank some of her coffee; **sich** *(dat)* **einen** *or* **einen Rausch/Schwips ~** to get (oneself) drunk/tipsy; **sich** *(dat)* **Mut ~** to give oneself Dutch courage; **eine angetrunkene Flasche** an opened bottle → *auch* **angetrunken**

An|tritt M, *no pl* **a** *(= Beginn)* beginning, commencement *(form)*; **bei ~ der Reise** when beginning one's journey; **nach ~ der Stellung/des Amtes/der Erbschaft/der Regierung** after taking up the position/taking up *or* assuming office/coming into the inheritance/coming to power **b** *(Sport: = Spurt)* acceleration *no indef art*

An|tritts-: **An|tritts|be|such** M *(esp Pol)* (formal) first visit; **An|tritts|re|de** F inaugural speech; *(Parl)* maiden speech; **An|tritts|vor|le|sung** F inaugural lecture

an+trock|nen VI *sep aux sein* to dry on *(an, in +dat* -to); *(= trocken werden)* to begin *or* start to dry

an+tu|ckern VI *sep aux sein (inf)* **angetuckert kommen** to chug along *or (auf einen zu)* up

an+tun VT *sep irreg* **a** *(= erweisen)* **jdm etw ~** to do sth for sb; **jdm etwas Gutes ~** to do sb a good turn; **tun Sie mir die Ehre an, und speisen Sie mit mir** *(geh)* do me the honour *(Brit) or* honor *(US)* of dining with me **b** *(= zufügen)* **jdm etw ~** to do sth to sb; **das könnte ich ihr nicht ~** I couldn't do that to her; **sich** *(dat)* **etwas ~** *(euph)* to do away with oneself; **jdm Schaden/Unrecht ~** to do sb an injury/injustice; **tu mir keine Schande an!** don't bring shame upon me; **tu mir das nicht an!** don't do this to me!; **tun Sie sich** *(dat)* **keinen Zwang an!** *(inf)* don't stand on ceremony; **darf ich rauchen? – tu dir keinen Zwang an!** may I smoke? – feel free *or* please yourself **c** *(= Sympathie erregen)* **es jdm ~** to appeal to sb **d** *(Aus)* **sich** *(dat)* **etwas ~** *(= sich aufregen)* to get het up *(esp Brit inf) or* excited; *(= sich Mühe geben)* to take a lot of trouble **e** *Kleid etc* to put on → *auch* **angetan**

an+tur|nen [ˈanturnən] VI *sep (Sport) to open the season with a gymnastic event*

an+tur|nen [ˈantœrnən] *sep* = **antörnen**

Antw. *abbr von* **Antwort**

Ant|wort [ˈantvɔrt] ✪ 46.5 F -, -en **a** answer, reply; *(= Lösung, bei Examen, auf Fragebogen)* answer; **sie gab mir keine ~** she didn't reply (to me), she didn't answer (me); **sie gab mir keine ~ auf die Frage** she didn't reply to *or* answer my question; **das ist doch keine ~** that's no answer; **in ~ auf etw** *(acc) (form)* in reply to sth; **etw zur ~ bekommen** to receive sth as a response; **jdm etw zur ~ geben** to give sb sth as a response; **um umgehende ~ wird gebeten** please reply by return; **um ~ wird gebeten** *(auf Einladungen)* RSVP; **keine ~ ist auch eine ~** *(Prov)* your silence is answer enough → **Rede b** *(= Reaktion)* response; **als ~ auf etw** *(acc)* in response to sth; **die deutsche ~ auf Hollywood** *(= Entsprechung)* Germany's answer to Hollywood

Ant|wort|brief M reply, answer

ant|wor|ten [ˈantvɔrtn] ✪ 27.3 VI **a** *(= Antwort geben)* to answer, to reply; **jdm ~** to answer sb, to reply to sb; **auf etw** *(acc)* **~** to answer sth, to reply to sth; **was soll ich ihm ~?** what answer should I give him?, what should I tell him?; **jdm auf eine Frage ~** to reply to *or* answer sb's question; **mit Ja/Nein ~** to answer yes/no, to answer in the affirmative/negative **b** *(= reagieren)* to respond *(auf +acc* to, *mit* with)

Ant|wort-: **Ant|wort|kar|te** F reply card; **Ant|wort|schein** M (international) reply coupon; **Ant|wort|schrei|ben** NT reply, answer

an+ver|trau|en *ptp* **anvertraut** *sep* VT **a** *(= übergeben, anheimstellen)* **jdm etw ~** to entrust sth to sb *or* sb with sth **b** *(= vertraulich erzählen)* **jdm etw ~** to confide sth to sb; **etw seinem Tagebuch ~** to confide sth to one's diary VR **sich jdm ~** *(= sich mitteilen)* to confide in sb; *(= sich in jds Schutz begeben)* to entrust oneself to sb; **sich jds Führung** *(dat)***/Schutz** *(dat)* **~** to entrust oneself to sb's leadership/protection

an|ver|wandt ADJ *(geh)* related

An|ver|wand|te(r) MF *decl as adj (geh)* relative, relation

an+vi|sie|ren [ˈanviziːrən] *ptp* **anvisiert** VT *sep (lit)* to sight; *(fig)* to set one's sights on; *Entwicklung, Zukunft etc* to envisage

an+wach|sen VI *sep irreg aux sein* **a** *(= festwachsen)* to grow on; *(Haut)* to take; *(Nagel)* to grow; *(Pflanze etc)* to take root; **auf etw** *(dat)* **~** to grow onto sth; **bei ihr sind die Ohrläppchen angewachsen** her ear lobes are attached to the side of her head **b** *(= zunehmen)* to increase *(auf +acc* to)

An|wach|sen NT -s, *no pl* **a** *(= das Festwachsen)* growing on; *(von Haut)* taking; *(von Nagel)* growing; *(von Pflanze)* taking root **b** *(= Zunahme)* increase; *(von Lärm)* growth; **im ~ (begriffen) sein** to be on the increase, to be growing

an+wa|ckeln VI *sep aux sein* **angewackelt kommen** to come waddling along *or (auf einen zu)* up; *(fig inf)* to come wandering up

an+wäh|len VT *sep* to dial; *jdn* to call; *(Comput) Funktion, Befehl* to call up

An|walt [ˈanvalt] M -(e)s, Anwälte [-vɛltə], **An|wäl|tin** [-vɛltɪn] F -, -nen **a** → **Rechtsanwalt b** *(fig: = Fürsprecher)* advocate

An|walts|bü|ro NT **a** lawyer's office **b** *(= Firma)* firm of solicitors *(Brit) or* lawyers

An|walt|schaft [ˈanvaltʃaft] F -, -en **a** *(= Vertretung)* **eine ~ übernehmen** to take over a case; **die ~ für jdn übernehmen** to accept sb's brief, to take over sb's case **b** *(= Gesamtheit der Anwälte)* solicitors *pl (Brit)*, lawyers *pl*, legal profession

An|walts-: **An|walts|ge|bühr** F lawyer's fees *pl*; **An|walts|kam|mer** F *professional association of lawyers*, ≈ Law Society *(Brit)*; **An|walts|kanz|lei** F *(S Ger)* → **Anwaltsbüro**; **An|walts|kos|ten** PL legal expenses *pl*; **An|walts|pra|xis** F legal practice; *(= Räume)* lawyer's office; **An|walts|zwang** M *obligation to be represented in court*

an+wal|zen VI *sep aux sein* **angewalzt kommen** to come rolling along *or (auf einen zu)* up

an+wan|deln VT *sep (geh)* to come over; **jdn wandelt die Lust an, etw zu tun** sb feels the desire to do sth

An|wand|lung F *(von Furcht etc)* feeling; *(= Laune)* mood; *(= Drang)* impulse; **aus einer ~ heraus** on (an) impulse; **in einer ~ von Freigebigkeit** *etc* in a fit of generosity *etc*; **dann bekam er wieder seine ~en** *(inf)* then he had one of his fits again

an+wär|men VT *sep* to warm up

An|wär|ter(in) M(F) *(= Kandidat)* candidate *(auf +acc* for); *(Sport)* contender *(auf +acc* for); *(= Thronanwärter)* heir *(auf +acc* to); **der ~ auf den Thron** the pretender *or (= Thronerbe)* heir to the throne

An|wart|schaft [ˈanvartʃaft] F -, *no pl* candidature; *(Sport)* contention; **seine ~ auf die Titel anmelden** to say one is in contention for the title; **~ auf den Thron** claim to the throne

An|wart|schafts|zeit F *(Admin) minimum period between registering as unemployed and receiving unemployment benefit*, waiting days *pl*

an+wat|scheln VI *sep aux sein (inf)* **angewatschelt kommen** to come waddling along *or (auf einen zu)* up

an+we|hen *sep* VT *Sand* to blow; *Schnee* to drift; *jdn (fig geh: Gefühl)* to come over; **warme Luft wehte ihn/sein Gesicht an** warm air blew over him/his face VI *aux sein* to drift

an+wei|sen VT *sep irreg* **a** *(= anleiten) Schüler, Lehrling etc* to instruct; *(= beauftragen, befehlen)* to order, to instruct **b** *(= zuweisen) (jdm etw* sb sth) to allocate; *Zimmer auch* to give; **jdm einen Platz ~** to show sb to a seat **c** *Geld* to transfer → *auch* **angewiesen**

An|wei|sung F **a** *(Fin)* payment; *(auf Konto etc)* transfer; *(= Formular)* payment slip; *(= Postanweisung)* postal order **b** *(= Anordnung)* instruction, order; **eine ~ befolgen** to follow an instruction, to obey an order; **~ haben, etw zu tun** to have instructions to do sth; **auf ~ der Schulbehörde** on the instructions of *or* on instruction from the school authorities **c** *(= Zuweisung)* allocation **d** *(= Anleitung)* instructions *pl*

an|wend|bar ADJ *Produkt* usable; *Theorie, Regel* applicable *(auf +acc* to); **die Methode ist auch hier ~** the method can also be applied *or* used here; **das ist in der Praxis nicht ~** that is not practicable

An|wend|bar|keit [ˈanvɛntbaːɐkait] F -, -en *(von Theorie, Regel)* applicability *(auf +acc* to)

an+wen|den VT *sep auch irreg* **a** *(= gebrauchen) Methode, Mittel, Technik, Gewalt* to use *(auf +acc* on); *Sorgfalt, Mühe* to take *(auf +acc* over); **etw gut** *or* **nützlich ~** to make good use of sth **b** *Theorie, Prinzipien, Regel* to apply *(auf +acc* to); *Erfahrung, Einfluss* to use *(auf +acc* on), to bring to bear *(auf +acc* on); **sich auf etw** *(acc)* **~ lassen** to be applicable to sth → *auch* **angewandt**

An|wen|der [ˈanvɛndɐ] M -s, -, **An|wen|de|rin** [-ərɪn] F -, -nen *(Comput)* user

An|wen|der-: **An|wen|der|grup|pe** F user group; **An|wen|der|pro|gramm** NT user *or* application program; **An|wen|der|soft|ware** F user *or* applications software

An|wen|dung F **a** *(= Gebrauch)* use *(auf +acc* on); *(von Sorgfalt, Mühe)* taking; **etw in ~** *(acc) or* **zur ~ bringen** *(form)* to apply sth; **zur ~ gelangen** *or* **kommen** *(form)* **~ finden** *(form)* to be applied **b** *(von Theorie, Prinzipien, Regel)* application *(auf +acc* to); *(von Erfahrung, Einfluss)* bringing to bear *(auf +acc* on) **c** *(Comput)* application

An|wen|dungs-: **An|wen|dungs|bei|spiel** NT example of use, usage example; **An|wen|dungs|be|reich** M, **An|wen|dungs|ge|biet** NT area of application; **An|wen|dungs|mög|lich|keit** F possible application; **An|wen|dungs|vor|schrift** F instructions *pl* for use

an+wer|ben VT *sep irreg* to recruit *(für* to); *(Mil auch)* to enlist *(für* in); **sich ~ lassen** to enlist

An|wer|bung F recruitment *(für* to); *(Mil auch)* enlistment *(für* in)

an+wer|fen *sep irreg* VT *(Tech)* to start up; *Propeller* to swing; *(inf) Gerät* to switch on VI *(Sport)* to take the first throw

An|we|sen NT *(geh)* estate

an|we|send [ˈanveːznt] ADJ present; **die nicht ~en Mitglieder** the members who are not present; **~ sein** to be present *(bei, auf +dat* at); **ich war nicht ganz ~** *(hum inf)* my thoughts were elsewhere, I was thinking of something else

An|we|sen|de(r) [ˈanveːzndə] MF *decl as adj* person present; **die ~n** those present; **jeder ~** everyone present; **alle ~n** all those present; **~ ausgenommen** present company excepted

An|we|sen|heit [ˈanveːznhait] F -, *no pl* presence; **in ~** *+gen or* **von** in the presence of

An|we|sen|heits-: **An|we|sen|heits|kon|trol|le** F roll call; **An|we|sen|heits|lis|te** F attendance list; **An|we|sen|heits|pflicht** F compulsory attendance, obligation to attend; **es herrscht** *or* **gilt** *or* **besteht ~** it is compulsory *or* obligatory to attend

an+wi|dern [ˈanviːdɐn] VT *sep* **jdn ~** *(Essen, Anblick)* to make sb feel sick; **es/er widert mich an** I can't stand it/him, I detest it/him; **er wandte sich angewidert ab** he turned away in disgust

an+win|keln [ˈanvɪŋkln] VT *sep* to bend

An|woh|ner [ˈanvoːnɐ] M -s, -, **An|woh|ne|rin** [-ərɪn] F -, -nen resident; **die ~ des Rheins** the people who live on the Rhine

An|woh|ner|schaft [ˈanvoːnɐʃaft] F -, *no pl* residents *pl*

An|wurf M **a** *(Sport)* first throw **b** *(dated Build)* roughcast

an+wur|zeln VI *sep aux sein* to take root; **wie angewurzelt dastehen/stehen bleiben** to stand rooted to the spot

An|zahl F, *no pl* number; **die Parteien waren in ungleicher ~ vertreten** the parties were not represented in equal numbers; **eine ganze ~** quite a number

an+zah|len VT *sep Ware* to pay a deposit on, to make a down payment on; **einen Betrag/100 Euro ~** to pay an amount/100 euros as a deposit

an+zäh|len VT *sep (Sport)* **jdn ~** to start giving sb the count

An|zah|lung F deposit, down payment *(für, auf +acc* on); *(= erste Rate)* first instalment *(Brit) or* installment *(US)*; **eine ~ machen** *or* **leisten** *(form)* to pay a deposit

an+zap|fen VT *sep Fass* to broach; *Fluss* to breach; *Baum, Telefon, elektrische Leitung* to tap; **jdn (um Geld) ~** *(inf)* to touch sb *(Brit) or* hit sb up *(US)* (for money); **jdn ~** *(inf) (= ausfragen)* to pump sb; *(Telec)* to tap sb's phone

An|zei|chen NT sign; *(Med auch)* symptom; **alle ~ deuten darauf hin, dass ...** all the signs are that ...; **es gibt ~ dafür, dass ...** signs are emerging that ...; **wenn nicht alle ~ trügen** if all the signs are to be believed

an+zeich|nen VT *sep* to mark; *(= zeichnen)* to draw *(an +acc* on)

An|zei|ge ['antsaigə] ✪ 46.1 F -, -n **a** *(bei Behörde)* report *(wegen* of); *(bei Gericht)* legal proceedings *pl*; **gegen jdn ~ erstatten** to report sb to the authorities; **wegen etw (eine) ~ bei der Polizei erstatten** *or* **machen** to report sth to the police; **wegen etw (eine) ~ bei Gericht erstatten** *or* **machen** to institute legal proceedings over sth; **jdn/etw zur ~ bringen** *(form) (bei Polizei)* to report sb/sth to the police; *(bei Gericht)* to take sb/bring sth to court
b *(= Bekanntgabe) (auf Karte, Brief)* announcement; *(in Zeitung)* notice; *(= Inserat, Reklame)* advertisement
c *(= das Anzeigen: von Temperatur, Geschwindigkeit etc)* indication; *(= Messwerte)* reading; *(auf Informationstafel)* information; **auf die ~ des Spielstands warten** to wait for the score to be shown *or* indicated
d *(= Anzeigetafel, Comput)* display
e *(= Instrument)* indicator, gauge

an+zei|gen *sep* VT ✪ 51.1 **a** *(= angeben) Spielstand, Temperatur, Zeit, Wetterlage, Geschwindigkeit, Messwert* to show, to indicate; *Datum* to show; *(fig: = deuten auf)* to indicate, to show
b *(= bekannt geben) Heirat, Verlobung etc* to announce; *(= Reklame machen für)* to advertise
c *(= mitteilen)* to announce; *Richtung* to indicate; **jdm etw ~** *(durch Zeichen)* to signal sth to sb
d *(Comput)* to display
e jdn ~ *(bei der Polizei)* to report sb (to the police); *(bei Gericht)* to institute legal proceedings against sb; **sich selbst ~** to give oneself up
f → **angezeigt**
VI *(Zeiger, Kompassnadel etc)* to register; *(Messgerät, Instrument)* to show, to indicate

An|zei|gen-: **An|zei|gen|ab|tei|lung** F advertising department; **An|zei|gen|an|nah|me** F **a** *no pl (= das Annehmen)* acceptance *or* taking of advertisements *or* ads *(inf)* **b** *(= Anzeigenstelle)* advertising office; **An|zei|gen|blatt** NT advertiser, freesheet; **An|zei|gen|kam|pag|ne** F advertising campaign; **An|zei|gen|kun|de** M, **An|zei|gen|kun|din** F advertiser, advertising customer; **An|zei|gen|lei|ter(in)** M(F) *(bei Zeitung, Verlag)* head of advertising; **An|zei|gen|prei|se** PL advertising rates *pl*; **An|zei|gen|schluss** M deadline (for advertisements); *(Tag)* closing date (for advertisements); **An|zei|gen|teil** M advertisement section; **An|zei|gen|wer|bung** F newspaper and magazine advertising

An|zei|ge|pflicht F, *no pl obligation to notify or report an event, illness etc*; **der ~ unterliegen** *(form: Krankheit)* to be notifiable

an|zei|ge|pflich|tig [-pflıçtıç] ADJ notifiable

An|zei|ger M **a** *(Tech)* indicator **b** *(= Zeitung)* advertiser, gazette

An|zei|ger(in) M(F) *(bei Polizei) person reporting crime etc to the police*

An|zei|ge|ta|fel F indicator board; *(Sport)* scoreboard

an+zet|teln ['antsɛtln] VT *sep* to instigate; *Unsinn* to cause

an+zie|hen *sep irreg* VT **a** *Kleidung* to put on; **sich** *(dat)* **etw ~** to put sth on; *(fig inf)* to take sth personally; **angezogen** dressed
b *(= straffen)* to pull (tight); *Bremse (= betätigen)* to apply, to put on; *(= härter einstellen)* to adjust; *Zügel* to pull; *Saite, Schraube* to tighten; *(dial) Tür* to pull to
c *(= an den Körper ziehen)* to draw up
d *(lit) Geruch, Feuchtigkeit* to absorb; *(Magnet, fig)* to attract; *Besucher* to attract, to draw; **sich von etw angezogen fühlen** to feel attracted to *or* drawn by sth
e *(obs: = zitieren)* to quote, to cite
VI **a** *(= sich in Bewegung setzen) (Pferde)* to start pulling *or* moving; *(Zug, Auto)* to start moving; *(= beschleunigen)* to accelerate
b *(Chess etc)* to make the first move
c *(Fin: Preise, Aktien)* to rise
d *aux sein (= heranziehen)* to approach; **aus vielen Ländern angezogen kommen** to come from far and near
VR **a** *(= sich kleiden)* to get dressed
b *(fig) (Menschen)* to be attracted to each other; *(Gegensätze)* to attract

an|zie|hend ADJ *(= ansprechend)* attractive; *(= sympathisch)* pleasant

An|zieh|pup|pe F dress-up doll

An|zie|hung F, *no pl* attraction; **die Stadt hat eine große ~ für sie** she is very attracted to the town

An|zie|hungs|kraft F *(Phys)* force of attraction; *(fig)* attraction, appeal; **eine große ~ auf jdn ausüben** to attract sb strongly

an+zi|schen *sep* VT *(lit, fig inf)* to hiss at VI *aux sein* **angezischt kommen** to come whizzing along *or (auf einen zu)* up

An|zug M **a** *(= Herrenanzug)* suit; **aus dem ~ kippen** *(inf)* to be bowled over *(inf)*, to be flabbergasted *(inf)*; *(= ohnmächtig werden)* to pass out → **hauen VT e b** *(Sw: = Bezug)* cover **c** *(= das Heranrücken)* approach; **im ~ sein** to be coming; *(Mil)* to be advancing; *(fig) (Gewitter, Gefahr)* to be in the offing; *(Krankheit)* to be coming on **d** *(Chess etc)* opening move; **Weiß ist als erster im ~** white has first move **e** *(von Auto etc)* acceleration

an|züg|lich ['antsy:klıç] ADJ suggestive; **~ werden** to start making suggestive remarks; **er ist mir gegenüber immer so ~** he always makes suggestive remarks to me ADV suggestively

An|züg|lich|keit F -, -en suggestiveness; **~en** suggestive remarks

An|zugs|kraft F, **An|zugs|ver|mö|gen** NT acceleration

an+zün|den VT *sep Feuer* to light; **das Haus** *etc* **~** to set fire to the house *etc*, to set the house *etc* on fire

An|zün|der M lighter

an+zwei|feln VT *sep* to question, to doubt

an+zwin|kern VT *sep* to wink at

an+zwit|schern *sep (inf)* VT **sich** *(dat)* **einen ~** to get tipsy VI *aux sein* **angezwitschert kommen** to come strolling along *or (auf einen zu)* up

AOK [a:lo:'ka:] F -, -s *abbr von* **Allgemeine Ortskrankenkasse**

> **AOK**
>
> The **AOK** – short for **Allgemeine Ortskrankenkasse** – is the largest state health insurance scheme in Germany. Almost half of all employees are insured by it. In every large town there is an independently run **AOK** office. Foreigners may also receive help from these offices if they fall ill while in Germany.

Äols|har|fe ['ɛ:ɔls-] F aeolian harp

Äon [ɛ'o:n, 'ɛ:ɔn] M -s, -en *usu pl (geh)* aeon *(Brit)*, eon *(US)*

Aor|ta [a'ɔrta] F -, **Aorten** [-tn] aorta

Apal|li|ker [a'palikɐ] M -s, -, **Apal|li|ke|rin** [-ərın] F -, -nen *(Med) person suffering from PVS*

Apa|na|ge [apa'na:ʒə] F -, -n appanage *(obs)*, (large) allowance *(auch fig)*

apart [a'part] ADJ distinctive, unusual; *Mensch, Aussehen, Kleidungsstück auch* striking ADV **a** *(= schick)* chicly **b** *(old: = separat)* separately, individually

Apart|heid [a'pa:ɐthait] F -, *no pl* apartheid

Apart|heid|po|li|tik F policy of apartheid, apartheid policy

A|part|ment [a'partmənt] NT -s, -s flat *(Brit)*, apartment

Apart|ment-: **Apart|ment|haus** NT block of flats *(Brit)*, apartment house *(esp US)*, condominium *(US)*, condo *(US inf)*; **Apart|ment|woh|nung** F flat *(Brit)*, apartment

Apa|thie [apa'ti:] F -, -n [-'ti:ən] apathy; *(von Patienten)* listlessness

apa|thisch [a'pa:tıʃ] ADJ apathetic; *Patient* listless ADV apathetically; *(= matt)* listlessly

aper ['a:pɐ] ADJ *(Sw, Aus, S Ger)* snowless

Aper|çu [apɛr'sy:] NT -s, -s *(geh)* witty remark, bon mot

Ape|ri|tif [aperi'ti:f] M -s, -s *or* -e aperitif

apern ['a:pɐn] VI *(Sw, Aus, S Ger)* **es apert** the snow is going; **die Hänge ~** the snow on the slopes is going

Apex ['a:pɛks,] M -, **Apizes** ['a:pitse:s] **a** *(Astron)* apex **b** *(Phon) (= Längezeichen)* length mark; *(= Akzentzeichen)* stress mark

Ap|fel ['apfl] M -s, ⸗ ['ɛpfl] apple; **in den sauren ~ beißen** *(fig inf)* to bite the bullet, to swallow the bitter pill; **etw für einen ~ (und ein Ei) kaufen** *(inf)* to buy sth dirt cheap *(inf)*, to buy sth for a song *(inf)*; **der ~ fällt nicht weit vom Stamm** *(Prov)* it's in the blood, an apple doesn't fall far from the tree *(US)*, like father like son *(prov)*

Ap|fel- *in cpds* apple; **Ap|fel|aus|ste|cher** [-lausʃtɛçɐ] M -s, - *(Gerät)* apple corer; **Ap|fel|baum** M apple tree; **Ap|fel|blü|te** F **a** apple blossom **b** *(= das Blühen)* blossoming of the apple trees; **zur Zeit der ~ geboren** born when the apple trees were in blossom

Äp|fel|chen ['ɛpflçən] NT -s, - *dim von* **Apfel**

Ap|fel-: **Ap|fel|es|sig** M apple cider vinegar; **Ap|fel|ge|lee** M OR NT apple jelly; **Ap|fel|griebs** [-gri:ps] M -(es), -e *(dial)* apple core; **ap|fel|grün** ADJ apple-green *attr*, apple green *pred*; **Ap|fel|kern** M (apple) pip, appleseed *(US)*; **Ap|fel|kla|re(r)** M *decl as adj* clear apple schnapps; **Ap|fel|kom|pott** NT stewed apple, apple compote; **Ap|fel|ku|chen** M apple cake; **Ap|fel|küch|le** NT -s, - *(S Ger)* ≈ apple fritter; **Ap|fel|most** M apple juice; **Ap|fel|mus** NT apple purée *or (als Beilage)* sauce; **jdn zu ~ hauen** *(inf)* to beat sb to a pulp; **Ap|fel|saft** M apple juice; **Ap|fel|saft|schor|le** F *apple juice and sparkling mineral water*; **Ap|fel|säu|re** F malic acid; **Ap|fel|scha|le** F apple skin *or* peel; **Ap|fel|schim|mel** M dapple-grey *(Brit) or* dapple-gray *(US)* (horse); **Ap|fel|schor|le** F = **Apfelsaftschorle**

Ap|fel|si|ne [apfl'zi:nə] F -, -n **a** orange **b** *(= Baum)* orange tree

Ap|fel-: **Ap|fel|stru|del** M apple strudel; **Ap|fel|ta|sche** F apple turnover; **Ap|fel|wein** M cider

Ap|fel|wick|ler [-vıklɐ] M -s, - *(Zool)* codlin moth

Apha|sie [afa'zi:] F -, -n [-'zi:ən] *(Psych)* aphasia

Apho|ris|mus [afo'rısmʊs] M -, **Aphorismen** [-mən] aphorism

apho|ris|tisch [afo'rɪstɪʃ] ADJ aphoristic

Aphro|di|si|a|kum [afrodi'zi:akʊm] NT -s, **Aphrodisiaka** [-ka] aphrodisiac

Ap|lomb [a'plõ:] M -s, *no pl (geh)* **mit ~** with aplomb *(form)*

Apo, APO ['a:po] F -, *no pl abbr von* **außerparlamentarische Opposition**

apo|dik|tisch [apo'dɪktɪʃ] *(geh)* ADJ apodictic ADV apodictically

Apo|ka|lyp|se [apoka'lʏpsə] F -, -n apocalypse

apo|ka|lyp|tisch [apoka'lʏptɪʃ] ADJ apocalyptic; **die ~en Reiter** the Four Horsemen of the Apocalypse

apo|li|tisch ['apoli:tɪʃ, apo'li:tɪʃ] ADJ nonpolitical, apolitical

Apoll [a'pɔl] M -s, *(rare)* -s **a** *(Myth)* Apollo **b** *(fig geh: = schöner Mann)* **er ist nicht gerade ein ~** he doesn't exactly look like a Greek god

apol|li|nisch [apɔ'li:nɪʃ] ADJ *(geh)* Apollonian

Apol|lo [a'pɔlo] M -s Apollo

Apo|lo|get [apolo'ge:t] M -en, -en, **Apo|lo|ge|tin** [-'ge:tɪn] F -, -nen *(geh)* apologist

Apo|lo|ge|tik [apolo'ge:tɪk] F -, -en *(geh)* **a** *(= Apologie)* apologia **b** *(Theologie)* apologetics *sing*

Apo|lo|gie [apolo'gi:] F -, -n [-'gi:ən] apologia

Apo|rie [apo'ri:] F -, -n [-'ri:ən] *(geh)* aporia *(rare)*, problem

Apos|tel [a'pɔstl] M -s, - apostle

Apos|tel-: **Apos|tel|brief** M epistle; **Apos|tel|ge|schich|te** F Acts of the Apostles *pl*

apos|te|ri|o|risch [apɔste'rio:rɪʃ] ADJ *(Philos)* a posteriori

apos|to|lisch [apɔs'to:lɪʃ] ADJ apostolic; **der Apostolische Stuhl** the Holy See; **das Apostolische Glaubensbekenntnis** the Apostles' Creed; **Apostolischer Nuntius** Apostolic Nuncio

Apo|stroph [apo'stro:f] M -s, -e apostrophe

apo|stro|phie|ren [apostro'fi:rən] *ptp* **apostrophiert** VT **a** *(Gram)* to apostrophize **b** *(= bezeichnen)* **jdn als etw** *(acc)* **~** to call sb sth, to refer to sb as sth

Apo|the|ke [apo'te:kə] F -, -n **a** (dispensing) chemist's *(Brit)*, pharmacy **b** *(= Hausapotheke)* medicine chest *or* cupboard; *(= Reiseapotheke, Autoapotheke)* first-aid box

Apo|the|ken|hel|fer(in) M(F) chemist's *(Brit) or* pharmacist's assistant, assistant pharmacist

apo|the|ken|pflich|tig [-pflɪçtɪç] ADJ available only at a chemist's shop *(Brit) or* pharmacy

Apo|the|ker [apo'te:kɐ] M -s, -, **Apo|the|ke|rin** [-ərɪn] F -, -nen pharmacist, (dispensing) chemist *(Brit)*

Apo|the|ker|ge|wicht NT apothecaries' weight

Apo|the|ker|waa|ge F (set of) precision scales *pl*

Apo|the|o|se [apote'o:zə] F -, -n apotheosis

App [ap] F -, -s *(Comput inf)* app *(inf)*

Ap|pa|la|chen [apa'laxn] PL *(Geog)* Appalachian Mountains *pl*, Appalachians *pl*

Ap|pa|rat [apa'ra:t] ✪ 27 M -(e)s, -e **a** apparatus *no pl*, appliance; *(= esp kleineres, technisches, mechanisches Gerät)* gadget; *(= Röntgenapparat etc)* machine **b** *(= Radio)* radio; *(= Fernseher)* set; *(= Rasierapparat)* razor; *(= Fotoapparat)* camera **c** *(= Telefon)* (tele)phone; *(= Anschluss)* extension; **am ~** on the phone; *(als Antwort)* speaking; **wer war am ~?** who did you speak to?; **jdn am ~ verlangen** to ask to speak to sb; **bleiben Sie am ~!** hold the line **d** *(inf) (= unbestimmter Gegenstand)* thing; *(= großer Gegenstand)* whopper *(inf)* **e** *(sl: = Penis)* tool *(sl)*; **einen geilen ~ haben** to be hung like a horse *(inf)*, to be well-hung *(inf)* **f** *(= Personen und Hilfsmittel)* setup; *(= Verwaltungsapparat, Parteiapparat)* machinery, apparatus; *(technischer etc)* equipment, apparatus **g** *(= Zusammenstellung von Büchern)* collection of books to be used in conjunction with a particular course **h** *(Liter)* **(text)kritischer ~** critical apparatus

Ap|pa|ra|te-: **Ap|pa|ra|te|bau** M, *no pl* instrument-making, machine-making; **Ap|pa|ra|te|me|di|zin** F *(pej)* hi-tech medicine

ap|pa|ra|tiv [apara'ti:f] ADJ **~e Einrichtungen** (technical) appliances *or* equipment; **~e Neuerungen** new ideas in technical equipment; **~er Aufwand** expenditure on equipment; **~e Untersuchung** examination using technical equipment; **~er Versuch** experiment using technical equipment; **~e Lernhilfen** technical teaching aids

Ap|pa|rat|schik [apa'ratʃɪk] M -s, -s *(pej)* apparatchik

Ap|pa|ra|tur [apara'tu:ɐ] F -, -en **a** equipment *no pl*, apparatus *no pl*; **~en** pieces of equipment; **eine ~** a piece of equipment **b** *(fig Pol)* machinery, apparatus

Ap|pa|ril|lo [apa'rɪlo] M -s, -s *(hum inf)* contraption

Ap|par|te|ment [apartə'mã:] NT -s, -s **a** *(= Wohnung)* flat *(Brit)*, apartment **b** *(= Zimmerflucht)* suite

Ap|pel ['apl] M -s, = ['ɛpl] *(N Ger: = Apfel)* apple; **für 'n ~ und 'n Ei** *(inf)* for peanuts *(inf)*

Ap|pell [a'pɛl] M -s, -e **a** *(= Aufruf)* appeal *(an +acc* to, *zu* for); **einen ~ an jdn richten** to (make an) appeal to sb **b** *(Mil)* roll call; **zum ~ antreten** to line up for roll call

Ap|pel|la|ti|on [apɛla'tsio:n] F -, -en *(Jur: obs, Sw)* appeal

Ap|pel|la|tiv ['apɛlati:f] NT -s, -a [-va], **Ap|pel|la|ti|vum** [apɛla'ti:vʊm] NT -s, **Appellativa** [-va] *(Ling)* appellative

ap|pel|lie|ren [apɛ'li:rən] *ptp* **appelliert** VI to appeal *(an +acc* to)

Ap|pen|dix [a'pɛndɪks] M -, **Appendizes** [-dise:s] appendix; *(fig: = Anhängsel)* appendage

Ap|pen|zell [apn'tsɛl, 'apntsɛl] NT -s Appenzell

Ap|pe|tit [ape'ti:t] M -(e)s, *no pl (lit, fig)* appetite; **~ auf etw** *(acc)* **haben** *(lit, fig)* to feel like sth; **jdm ~ auf etw** *(acc)* **machen** to whet sb's appetite for sth; **das kann man mit ~ essen** that's something you can really tuck into *(inf) or* enjoy; **guten ~!** enjoy your meal; **den ~ anregen** to sharpen the appetite; **jdm den ~ verderben** to spoil sb's appetite; *(inf: Witz etc)* to make sb feel sick; **jdm den ~ an etw** *(dat)* **verderben** *(fig)* to put sb off sth; **der ~ kommt beim** *or* **mit dem Essen** *(prov)* appetite grows with the eating *(prov)*

Ap|pe|tit-: **ap|pe|tit|an|re|gend** ADJ *Speise etc* appetizing; **~es Mittel** appetite stimulant ADV **~ wirken** to stimulate the appetite; **Ap|pe|tit|bis|sen** M, **Ap|pe|tit|hap|pen** M canapé; **ap|pe|tit|hem|mend** ADJ appetite-suppressing; **~es Mittel** appetite suppressant ADV **~ wirken** to curb the appetite; **Ap|pe|tit|hem|mer** [-hɛmɐ] M -s, - appetite suppressant; **ap|pe|tit|lich** [ape'ti:tlɪç] ADJ *(= lecker)* appetizing; *(= verlockend aussehend, riechend)* tempting; *(= hygienisch)* hygienic, savoury *(Brit)*, savory *(US)*; *(fig) Mädchen, Anblick* attractive ADV appetizingly; **ap|pe|tit|los** ADJ without any appetite; **~ sein** to have lost one's appetite; **Ap|pe|tit|lo|sig|keit** F -, *no pl* lack of appetite; **Ap|pe|tit|züg|ler** [-tsy:glɐ] M -s, - appetite suppressant

Ap|pe|ti|zer ['ɛpitaizɐ] M -s, -s *(Pharm)* appetite stimulant

ap|plau|die|ren [aplau'di:rən] *ptp* **applaudiert** VTI to applaud; **jdm/einer Sache ~** to applaud sb/sth

Ap|plaus [a'plaus] M -es [-zəs], *no pl* applause

App|let ['ɛplet] NT -s, -s *(Comput)* applet

ap|pli|ka|bel [apli'ka:bl] ADJ *(geh)* applicable

Ap|pli|ka|ti|on [aplika'tsio:n] F -, -en **a** *(Comput)* application **b** *(geh, Med) (= Anwendung)* application; *(von Heilmethode)* administering **c** *(Sew)* appliqué

Ap|pli|ka|tor [apli'ka:to:ɐ] M -s, **Applikatoren** [-'to:rən] *(für Salbe, Makeup)* applicator

ap|pli|zie|ren [apli'tsi:rən] *ptp* **appliziert** VT **a** *(geh: = anwenden)* to apply; *(Med) Heilmethode* to administer **b** *(Sew) (= aufbügeln)* to apply; *(= aufnähen)* to appliqué

ap|port [a'pɔrt] INTERJ *(Hunt)* fetch

Ap|port [a'pɔrt] M -s, -e **a** *(Hunt)* retrieving, fetching **b** *(Parapsychologie)* apport

ap|por|tie|ren [apɔr'ti:rən] *ptp* **apportiert** VTI to retrieve, to fetch

Ap|por|tier|hund M retriever

Ap|po|si|ti|on [apozi'tsio:n] F apposition

ap|pre|tie|ren [apre'ti:rən] *ptp* **appretiert** VT *(Tex)* to starch; *(= imprägnieren)* to waterproof; *Holz* to dress, to finish; *Papier* to glaze

Ap|pre|tur [apre'tu:ɐ] F -, -en *(= Mittel)* finish; *(Tex)* starch; *(= Wasserundurchlässigkeit)* waterproofing; *(für Papier)* glaze, finish

Ap|pro|ba|ti|on [aproba'tsio:n] F -, -en *(von Arzt, Apotheker)* certificate *(enabling a doctor etc to practise)*; **einem Arzt die ~ entziehen** to take away a doctor's licence to practise *(Brit) or* license to practice *(US)*, to strike a doctor off (the register) *(Brit)*

ap|pro|bie|ren [apro'bi:rən] *ptp* **approbiert** VT *(old: = genehmigen)* to approve

ap|pro|biert [apro'bi:ɐt] ADJ *Arzt, Apotheker* registered, certified

Ap|pro|xi|ma|ti|on [aprɔksima'tsio:n] F -, -en *(Math)* approximation, approximate value

Ap|rès-Ski [apre'ʃi:] NT -, -s après-ski; *(= Kleidung)* après-ski clothes *pl*

Ap|ri|ko|se [apri'ko:zə] F -, -n apricot; **Wangen wie ~n** soft rosy cheeks

Ap|ri|ko|sen-: **Ap|ri|ko|sen|li|kör** M apricot brandy; **Ap|ri|ko|sen|mar|me|la|de** F apricot jam

Ap|ril [a'prɪl] M -(s), -e April; **~, ~!** April fool!; **jdn in den ~ schicken** to make an April fool of sb → *auch* **März**

Ap|ril-: **Ap|ril|scherz** M April fool's trick; **das ist doch wohl ein ~** *(fig)* you/they *etc* must be joking; **Ap|ril|wet|ter** NT April weather

a pri|o|ri [a pri'o:ri] ADV *(Philos, geh)* a priori

a|pri|o|risch [apri'o:rɪʃ] ADJ *(Philos)* a priori

A-Pro|be F *(bei Dopingkontrolle)* A test

ap|ro|pos [apro'po:] ADV by the way, that reminds me; **~ Afrika** talking about Africa

Ap|si|de [a'psi:də] F -, -n *(Astron)* apsis

Ap|sis ['apsɪs] F -, **Apsiden** [a'psi:dn] **a** *(Archit)* apse **b** *(von Zelt)* bell

Aqua|drom [akva'dro:m] NT -s, -e aquadrome

Aquä|dukt [akvɛ'dʊkt] NT -(e)s, -e aqueduct

Aqua-: **Aqua|ma|rin** [akvama'ri:n] NT -s, -e aquamarine; **aqua|ma|rin|blau** ADJ aquamarine; **Aqua|naut** [akva'naut] M -en, -en, **Aqua|nau|tin** [-'nautɪn] F -, -nen aquanaut; **Aqua|nu|del** ['a:kvanu:dl] F -, -n *(Sport)* aqua *or* swim *or* water noodle; **Aqua|pla|ning** [akva'pla:nɪŋ] NT -s, *no pl (Aut)* aquaplaning

Aqua|rell [akva'rɛl] NT -s, -e watercolour *(Brit) or* watercolor *(US)* (painting); **~ malen** to paint in watercolours *(Brit) or* watercolors *(US)*

Aqua|rell-: **Aqua|rell|far|be** F watercolour *(Brit)*, watercolor *(US)*; **Aqua|rell|ma|ler(in)** M(F) watercolourist *(Brit)*, watercolorist *(US)*; **Aqua|rell|ma|le|rei** F **a** *(Bild)* watercolour *(Brit) or* watercolor *(US)* (painting) **b** *(= Vorgang)* painting in watercolours *(Brit) or* watercolors *(US)*, watercolour *(Brit) or* watercolor *(US)* painting

Aqua|ri|en- *in cpds* aquarium; **Aqua|ri|en|fisch** M aquarium fish

Aqua|ri|um [a'kva:riʊm] NT -s, **Aquarien** [-riən] aquarium

Aqua|tin|ta [akva'tɪnta] F -, **Aquatinten** [-tn] aquatint

Äqua|tor [ɛ'kva:to:ɐ] M -s, *no pl* equator

äqua|to|ri|al [ɛkvato'ria:l] ADJ equatorial

Äqua|tor|tau|fe F *(Naut)* crossing-the-line ceremony

Aqua|vit [akva'vi:t] M -s, -e aquavit

Äqui|lib|rist [ɛkvili'brɪst] M **-en, -en, Äqui|lib|ris|tin** [-'brɪstɪn] F **-, -nen** juggler; *(= Seiltänzer)* tightrope walker

Äqui|nok|ti|um [ɛkvi'nɔktsiʊm] NT **-s, Äqui|noktien** [-tsiən] equinox

Aqui|ta|ni|en [akvi'ta:niən] NT **-s** Aquitaine

äqui|va|lent [ɛkviva'lɛnt] ADJ equivalent

Äqui|va|lent [ɛkviva'lɛnt] NT **-s, -e** equivalent; *(= Ausgleich)* compensation

Äqui|va|lenz [ɛkviva'lɛnts] F equivalence

Ar [a:ɐ] NT OR M **-s, -e** *(Measure)* are *(100 m²)*

Ära ['ɛ:ra] F **-, Ären** ['ɛ:rən] era; **die ~ Adenauer** the Adenauer era

Ara|ber ['arabɐ, 'a:rabɐ, a'ra:bɐ] M **-s, -** *(= Pferd)* Arab

Ara|ber ['arabɐ, 'a:rabɐ, a'ra:bɐ] M **-s, -, Ara|be|rin** [-ərɪn] F **-, -nen** Arab

Ara|bes|ke [ara'bɛskə] F **-, -n** arabesque; *(= Verzierung)* flourish

Ara|bi|en [a'ra:biən] NT **-s** Arabia

ara|bisch [a'ra:bɪʃ] ADJ Arab; *Ziffer, Sprache, Schrift etc* Arabic; **die Arabische Halbinsel** *(Geog)* the Arabian Peninsula, Arabia

Ara|bisch(e) [a'ra:bɪʃ] NT Arabic → *auch* **Deutsch(e)**

Ara|bist [ara'bɪst] M **-en, -en, Ara|bis|tin** [-'bɪstɪn] F **-, -nen** specialist in Arabic studies

Ara|bis|tik [ara'bɪstɪk] F **-,** *no pl* Arabic studies *pl*

Ara|gón [ara'gɔn] NT **-s** = **Aragonien**

Ara|go|ni|en [ara'go:niən] NT **-s** Aragon

ara|go|nisch [ara'go:nɪʃ] ADJ Aragonese

Aral|see ['a:ra(:)l-] M Aral Sea, Lake Aral

ara|mä|isch [ara'mɛ:ɪʃ] ADJ Aramaic

Ara|mid|fa|ser [ara'mi:t-] F aramid fibre *(Brit)* or fiber *(US)*

Ar|beit ['arbait] F **-, -en** **a** (= *Tätigkeit, Phys, Sport*) work; *(Pol, Econ)* labour *(Brit)*, labor *(US)*; **~ und Kapital** capital and labour *(Brit)* or labor *(US)*; **Tag der ~** Labour *(Brit)* or Labor *(US)* Day; **die ~en am Stadium** the work on the stadium; **es kann mit den ~en begonnen werden** work can begin; **bei der ~ mit Kindern** when working with children; **~ sparend** labour-saving *(Brit)*, labor-saving *(US)*; **viel ~ machen** to be a lot of work (*jdm* for sb); **das ist/kostet viel ~** it's a lot of work, it's a big job; **an** *or* **bei der ~ sein** to be working; **sich an die ~ machen, an die ~ gehen** to get down to work, to start working; **an die ~!** to work!; **jdm bei der ~ zusehen** to watch sb working; **etw ist in ~** work on sth has started, work on sth is in progress; **Ihr Bier ist in ~** *(inf)* your beer is on its way; **etw in ~ haben** to be working on sth; **etw in ~ nehmen** to undertake to do *or (manuelle Arbeit)* make sth; **etw in ~ geben** to have sth done/made; **jdm etw in ~ geben** to get sb to do/make sth; **die ~ läuft dir nicht davon** *(hum)* the work will still be there when you get back; **erst die ~, dann das Vergnügen** *(prov)* business before pleasure *(prov)*; **~ schändet nicht** *(Prov)* work is no disgrace
b *no pl (= Ausführung)* work; **gute** *or* **ganze** *or* **gründliche ~ leisten** *(lit, fig iro)* to do a good job
c *no pl (= Mühe)* trouble, bother; **jdm ~ machen** to put sb to trouble; **machen Sie sich keine ~!** don't go to any trouble *or* bother; **das war vielleicht eine ~!** what hard work that was!, what a job that was!; **die ~ zahlt sich aus** it's worth the trouble *or* effort
d (= *Berufstätigkeit, inf: = Arbeitsplatz, Arbeitsstelle, Arbeitszeit*) work *no indef art*; *(= Arbeitsverhältnis)* employment; *(= Position)* job; **eine ~ als etw** work *or* a job as sth; **(eine) ~ suchen/finden** to look for/find work *or* a job; **~ suchend** looking for work *or* a job, seeking employment; **~ Suchende(r)** = **Arbeitsuchende(r)**; **einer (geregelten) ~ nachgehen** to have a (steady) job; **ohne ~ sein** to be out of work, to be unemployed; **zur** *or* **auf** *(inf)* **~ gehen** to go to work; **auf ~ sein** *(inf)* to be at work; **von der ~ kommen** to come back from work
e *(= Aufgabe)* job; **seine ~ besteht darin, zu ...** his job is to ...
f *(= Produkt)* work; *(handwerkliche)* piece of work; *(= Prüfungsarbeit)* (examination) paper; *(wissenschaftliche)* paper; *(= Buch, Kunstwerk)* work
g *(Sch)* test; **~en korrigieren** to mark test papers; **eine ~ schreiben/schreiben lassen** to do/set a test

ar|bei|ten ['arbaitn] ✪ 46.3 VI **a** *(= sich betätigen)* to work (*an +dat* on); **der Sänger hat viel an sich** *(dat)* **gearbeitet** the singer has worked hard *or* has done a lot of work; **~ wie ein Pferd/Wilder** *(inf)* to work like a Trojan *or* horse/like mad *(inf)*; **die Zeit arbeitet für uns** we have time on our side, time is on our side; **die Zeit arbeitet gegen uns** time is against us; **er arbeitet für zwei** *(inf)* he does the work of two, he does enough work for two; **er arbeitet über Schiller** he's working on Schiller; **er arbeitet mit Ölfarben** he works in *or* uses oils
b *(= funktionieren) (Organ, Maschine)* to function, to work; **die Anlage arbeitet automatisch** the plant is automatic; **die Anlage arbeitet elektrisch/mit Kohle** the plant runs *or* operates on electricity/coal
c *(= berufstätig sein)* to work; **~ gehen** *(= zur Arbeit gehen)* to go to work; *(= einen Arbeitsplatz haben)* to have a job; **seine Frau arbeitet auch** his wife works too, his wife goes out to work too; **für eine** *or* **bei einer Firma/Zeitung ~** to work for a firm/newspaper; **die ~de Bevölkerung** the working population
d *(= in Bewegung sein)* to work; *(Most etc)* to ferment; *(Holz)* to warp; **in meinem Magen arbeitet es** my stomach's rumbling; **in seinem Kopf arbeitet es** his mind is at work; **in ihm begann es zu ~** he started to react, it began to work on him
VR **a** **sich krank/müde ~** to make oneself ill/tire oneself out with work; **sich krüpplig ~** *(inf)* to work oneself silly *(inf)*; **sich zu Tode ~** to work oneself to death; **sich** *(dat)* **die Hände wund ~** to work one's fingers to the bone
b *(= sich fortbewegen)* to work oneself (*in +acc* into, *durch* through, *zu* to); **sich in die Höhe** *or* **nach oben/an die Spitze ~** *(fig)* to work one's way up/(up) to the top
c *impers* **es arbeitet sich gut/schlecht** you can/can't work well; **es arbeitet sich hier auch nicht besser** it's no better working here either; **mit ihr arbeitet es sich angenehm** it's nice working with her
VT **a** *(= herstellen)* to make; **bei jdm ~ lassen** *(= schneidern)* to have *or* get one's clothes made by sb
b *(= tun)* to do; **was arbeitest du dort?** what are you doing there?; *(beruflich)* what do you do there?; **ich habe heute noch nichts gearbeitet** I haven't done any work *or* anything today; **du kannst auch ruhig mal was ~!** *(inf)* it wouldn't hurt you to do some work either!

Ar|bei|ter ['arbaitɐ] M **-s, -, Ar|bei|te|rin** [-ərɪn] F **-, -nen** worker; *(im Gegensatz zum Angestellten)* blue-collar worker; *(auf Bau, Bauernhof)* labourer *(Brit)*, laborer *(US)*; *(bei Straßenbau, im Haus)* workman; **der 22-jährige ~ Horst Kuhn** the 22-year-old factory worker/labourer *(Brit)* or laborer *(US)*/workman Horst Kuhn; **die ~** *(= Proletariat, Arbeitskräfte)* the workers; **~ und ~innen** male and female workers; **er ist ein guter/langsamer ~** he is a good/slow worker

Ar|bei|ter-: **Ar|bei|ter|amei|se** F worker (ant); **Ar|bei|ter|auf|stand** M workers' revolt; **Ar|bei|ter|be|we|gung** F labour *(Brit)* or labor *(US)* movement; **Ar|bei|ter|bie|ne** F worker (bee); **Ar|bei|ter|de|monst|ra|ti|on** F workers' demonstration; **Ar|bei|ter|denk|mal** NT **a** *(lit)* monument erected to the labouring *(Brit)* or laboring *(US)* or working classes **b** *(hum)* monument to inactivity *(hum)*; **Ar|bei|ter|dich|ter(in)** M(F) poet of the working class; **Ar|bei|ter|dich|tung** F working-class literature; **Ar|bei|ter|fa|mi|lie** F working-class family; **ar|bei|ter|feind|lich** ADJ anti-working-class; **ar|bei|ter|freund|lich** ADJ pro-working-class; **Ar|bei|ter|füh|rer(in)** M(F) *(Pol)* leader of the working classes; **Ar|bei|ter|ge|werk|schaft** F blue-collar (trade) union, labor union *(US)*

Ar|bei|te|rin [-ərɪn] F **-, -nen** **a** → **Arbeiter** **b** *(Zool)* worker

Ar|bei|ter-: **Ar|bei|ter|ju|gend** F young workers *pl*; **Ar|bei|ter|kam|mer** F *(Aus)* ≈ workers' and employees' professional association; **Ar|bei|ter|kampf|gruß** M clenched-fist salute; **Ar|bei|ter|kampf|lied** NT socialist workers' song; **Ar|bei|ter|kind** NT child from a working-class family *or* background; **Ar|bei|ter|klas|se** F working class(es *pl*); **Ar|bei|ter|knei|pe** F workers' pub *(Brit)*, bar frequented by workers; **Ar|bei|ter|lied** NT workers' song; **Ar|bei|ter|li|te|ra|tur** F working-class literature; **Ar|bei|ter|mas|sen** PL working masses *pl*; **Ar|bei|ter|mi|li|eu** NT working-class environment; **im ~** in a working-class environment; **Ar|bei|ter|or|ga|ni|sa|ti|on** F association of workers, labour *(Brit)* or labor *(US)* organization; **Ar|bei|ter|par|tei** F workers' party; **Ar|bei|ter|pries|ter** M worker-priest; **Ar|bei|ter|rat** M workers' council; **Ar|bei|ter|schaft** ['arbaitɐʃaft] F **-, -en** workforce; **Ar|bei|ter|schrift|stel|ler(in)** M(F) working-class writer; **Ar|bei|ter|selbst|ver|wal|tung** F workers' control; **Ar|bei|ter|sied|lung** F workers' housing estate *(Brit)* or development *(US)*; **Ar|bei|ter|sohn** M son of a working-class family; **Ar|bei|ter|stadt** F working-class town; **Ar|bei|ter|toch|ter** F daughter of a working-class family; **Ar|bei|ter-und-Bau|ern-Staat** M *(DDR Hist)* workers' and peasants' state; **Ar|bei|ter-und-Sol|da|ten-Rat** M *(Hist)* workers' and soldiers' council; **Ar|bei|ter|un|ru|hen** PL worker unrest, unrest among the workers; **Ar|bei|ter|vier|tel** NT working-class area; **Ar|bei|ter|wohl|fahrt** F workers' welfare association; **Ar|bei|ter|zei|tung** F paper of the labour *(Brit)* or labor *(US)* movement

Ar|beit|ge|ber(in) M(F) employer

Ar|beit|ge|ber-: **Ar|beit|ge|ber|an|teil** M employer's contribution; **Ar|beit|ge|ber|sei|te** F employers' side; **Ar|beit|ge|ber|ver|band** M employers' federation

Ar|beit|neh|mer(in) M(F) employee

Ar|beit|neh|mer-: **Ar|beit|neh|mer|an|teil** M employee's contribution; **Ar|beit|neh|mer|frei|be|trag** M, **Ar|beit|neh|mer|pau|scha|le** F *(Fin)* personal *or* income tax allowance; **Ar|beit|neh|mer|schaft** ['arbaitne:mɐʃaft] F **-, -en** employees *pl*; **Ar|beit|neh|mer|sei|te** F employees' side; **Ar|beit|neh|mer|ver|tre|tung** F *(= Organ)* employee representation; *(= Vertreter)* employee representatives *pl*

Ar|beits-: **Ar|beits|ab|lauf** M work routine; *(von Fabrik)* production *no art*; **Ar|beits|agen|tur** F **-, -en** *Ger* job centre *(Brit)*, unemployment office *(US)*

ar|beit|sam ['arbaitza:m] ADJ industrious, hard-working

Ar|beits|amei|se F worker (ant)

Ar|beit|sam|keit F **-,** *no pl* industriousness

Ar|beits-: **Ar|beits|amt** NT *(old)* employment exchange *(Brit old)*, job centre *(Brit)*, unemployment office *(US)*; **Ar|beits|an|fall** M workload; **Ar|beits|an|ge|bot** NT (job) vacancies *pl*; **Ar|beits|an|lei|tung** F instructions *pl*; **Ar|beits|an|tritt** M commencement of work *(form)*; **beim ~** when starting work; **Ar|beits|an|wei|sung** F working instructions *pl*; **Ar|beits|an|zug** M working suit; **Ar|beits|at|mos|phä|re** F work(ing) atmosphere, work climate; **Ar|beits|auf|fas|sung** F attitude to work; **Ar|beits|auf|trag** M job order, commission; **Ar|beits|auf|wand** M labour *(Brit)*, labor *(US)*; **mit geringem/großem ~** with little/a lot of work; **ar|beits|auf|wän|**

dig ADJ = **arbeitsaufwendig**; **ar|beits|auf|wen|dig** ADJ labour-intensive *(Brit)*, labor-intensive *(US)*; **~/nicht sehr ~ sein** to involve a lot of/not much work; **Ar|beits|aus|fall** M loss of working hours; **Ar|beits|aus|schuss** M working party; **Ar|beits|be|din|gun|gen** PL working conditions *pl*; **Ar|beits|be|ginn** M start of work; **bei ~** when one starts work; **Ar|beits|be|las|tung** F workload; **Ar|beits|be|reich** M **a** *(= Arbeitsgebiet)* field of work; *(= Aufgabenbereich)* area of work; **das gehört nicht in meinen ~** that's not my job **b** *(= Umkreis)* field of operations; *(von Kran etc)* operating radius; **Ar|beits|be|richt** M work report; **Ar|beits|be|schaf|fung** F **a** *(= Arbeitsplatzbeschaffung)* job creation **b** *(= Auftragsbeschaffung)* getting *or* bringing work in *no art*; **Ar|beits|be|schaf|fungs|maß|nah|me** F *(Admin)* job creation scheme; **Ar|beits|be|schaf|fungs|pro|gramm** NT job creation scheme *or* program *(US)*; **Ar|beits|be|schei|ni|gung** F certificate of employment; **Ar|beits|be|such** M working visit; **Ar|beits|bie|ne** F worker (bee); *(fig)* busy bee; **Ar|beits|blatt** NT *(Comput)* worksheet, spreadsheet; **Ar|beits|dienst** M *(NS)* labour *(Brit) or* labor *(US)* service; **Ar|beits|di|rek|tor(in)** M(F) personnel manager; **Ar|beits|dis|zip|lin** F discipline at work *no art*; **Ar|beits|ei|fer** M enthusiasm for one's work; **Ar|beits|ein|heit** F **a** *(Ind)* work group **b** *(Phys)* unit of work **c** *(Comput)* work unit **d** *(DDR: = Maßeinheit)* unit of work; **Ar|beits|ein|kom|men** NT earned income; **Ar|beits|ein|stel|lung** F **a** *(= Arbeitsauffassung)* attitude to work **b** *(= Arbeitsniederlegung)* walkout; **die Belegschaft reagierte mit ~** the workforce reacted by downing tools *or* by walking out; **Ar|beits|emig|rant(in)** M(F) immigrant worker; **Ar|beits|en|de** NT = **Arbeitsschluss**; **Ar|beits|ent|gelt** NT remuneration; **einmalig gezahltes ~** one-off payment; **Ar|beits|er|laub|nis** F *(= Recht)* permission to work; *(= Bescheinigung)* work permit; **Ar|beits|er|leich|te|rung** F **das bedeutet eine große ~** that makes the work much easier; **Ar|beits|er|spar|nis** F labour-saving *no pl (Brit)*, labor-saving *no pl (US)*; **die neuen Maschinen bedeuten eine große ~** the new machines are very labour-saving *(Brit) or* labor-saving *(US)*; **Ar|beits|es|sen** NT *(mittags)* working lunch; *(abends)* working dinner; **Ar|beits|ethos** NT work ethic; **Ar|beits|ex|emp|lar** NT desk copy; **ar|beits|fä|hig** ADJ *Person* able to work; *(= gesund)* fit for *or* to work; *Regierung etc* viable; **im ~en Alter sein** to be of working age; **Ar|beits|fä|hig|keit** F *(von Person)* ability to work; *(= Gesundheit)* fitness for work; *(von Regierung)* viability; **Ar|beits|feld** NT *(geh)* field of work; **Ar|beits|fie|ber** NT work mania; **Ar|beits|flä|che** F work surface, worktop; **Ar|beits|för|de|rung** F job creation *or* promotion; **Ar|beits|för|de|rungs|ge|setz** NT *law for the promotion of employment measures*; **ar|beits|frei** ADJ **~er Tag** day off; *(Feiertag)* public *or* legal *(US)* holiday; **~er Vormittag/Nachmittag** morning/afternoon off; **Ar|beits|freu|de** F willingness to work; **ar|beits|freu|dig** ADJ keen to work, willing to work; *(bei der Arbeit)* enthusiastic about work; **Ar|beits|frie|de(n)** M peaceful labour *(Brit) or* labor *(US)* relations *pl, no art*; **Ar|beits|gang** M *pl* **-gänge a** *(= Abschnitt)* operation **b** *(= Arbeitsablauf)* work routine; *(von Fabrik)* production *no art*; **Ar|beits|ge|biet** NT field of work; **Ar|beits|ge|mein|schaft** F team; *(Sch, Univ)* study group; *(in Namen)* association; **Ar|beits|ge|neh|mi|gung** F *(= Recht)* permission to work; *(= Bescheinigung)* work permit; **Ar|beits|ge|rät** NT **a** tool **b** *no pl* tools *pl*, equipment *no pl*; **Ar|beits|ge|richt** NT industrial tribunal *(Brit)*, labor court *(US)*; **Ar|beits|ge|setz** NT labour *(Brit) or* labor *(US)* law; **Ar|beits|ge|spräch** NT discussion about work; **Ar|beits|grup|pe** F team; **Ar|beits|hal|tung** F attitude to work; **Ar|beits|haus** NT *(old)* workhouse; **Ar|beits|heft** NT *(Sch)* workbook; **Ar|beits|hil|fe** F aid; **Ar|beits|hy|gi|e|ne** F work hygiene; **Ar|beits|hy|po|the|se** F working hypothesis; **Ar|beits|in|spek|ti|on** F *(Aus, Sw)* factory supervision; **ar|beits|in|ten|siv** ADJ labour-intensive *(Brit)*, labor-intensive *(US)*; **Ar|beits|kampf** M industrial action; **Ar|beits|kampf|maß|nah|men** PL industrial action *sing*; **Ar|beits|kit|tel** M overall *(Brit)*, overalls *pl (US)*; **Ar|beits|klei|dung** F working clothes *pl*; **Ar|beits|kli|ma** NT work climate, work(ing) atmosphere; **Ar|beits|kol|le|ge** M, **Ar|beits|kol|le|gin** F *(bei Angestellten etc)* colleague; *(bei Arbeitern auch)* workmate; **Ar|beits|kol|lek|tiv** NT *(DDR)* team; **Ar|beits|kon|flikt** M industrial dispute; **Ar|beits|kos|ten** PL labour *(Brit) or* labor *(US)* costs *pl*; **hohe/niedrige/steigende/sinkende ~** high/low/rising/falling labour *(Brit) or* labor *(US)* costs; **die ~ senken** to cut down on labour *(Brit) or* labor *(US)* costs

Ar|beits|kraft F **a** *no pl* capacity for work; **die menschliche ~ ersetzen** to replace human labour *(Brit) or* labor *(US)*; **seine ~ verkaufen** to sell one's labour *(Brit) or* labor *(US)* **b** *(= Arbeiter)* worker

Ar|beits|kräf|te PL workforce

Ar|beits|kräf|te-: **Ar|beits|kräf|te|ab|bau** M reduction *or* cuts *pl* in manpower, downsizing; **Ar|beits|kräf|te|man|gel** M labour *(Brit) or* labor *(US)* shortage; **Ar|beits|kräf|te|über|hang** M labour *(Brit) or* labor *(US)* surplus

Ar|beits-: **Ar|beits|kreis** M team; *(Sch, Univ)* study group; *(in Namen)* association; **Ar|beits|la|ger** NT labour *(Brit) or* labor *(US)* camp, work camp; **Ar|beits|lärm** M industrial noise; **Ar|beits|last** F burden of work; **Ar|beits|le|ben** NT working life; **Ar|beits|leis|tung** F *(quantitativ)* output, performance; *(qualitativ)* performance; **Ar|beits|lohn** M wages *pl*, earnings *pl*

ar|beits|los ADJ **a** *Mensch* unemployed, out of work **b** *Einkommen* unearned

Ar|beits|lo|sen-: **Ar|beits|lo|sen|geld** NT earnings-related unemployment benefit, jobseeker's allowance *(Brit)*; **Ar|beits|lo|sen|heer** NT army of unemployed; **Ar|beits|lo|sen|hil|fe** F unemployment benefit; **Ar|beits|lo|sen|quo|te** F rate of unemployment; **Ar|beits|lo|sen|un|ter|stüt|zung** F *(dated)* unemployment benefit, dole (money) *(Brit inf)*; **Ar|beits|lo|sen|ver|si|che|rung** F **a** ≈ National Insurance *(Brit)*, ≈ social insurance *(US)* **b** *(Amt)* ≈ Department of Social Security *(Brit)*, ≈ social insurance office *(US)*; **Ar|beits|lo|sen|zah|len** PL, **Ar|beits|lo|sen|zif|fer** F unemployment figures *pl*

> **ARBEITSLOSENVERSICHERUNG**
>
> All German workers have insurance against unemployment, i. e. **Arbeitslosenversicherung**, since they have to contribute to the **Bundesanstalt für Arbeit**, which is responsible among other things for running job centres. If someone loses their job they can claim **Arbeitslosengeld. Arbeitslosengeld I** is initially about two-thirds of previous net earnings. After a period from six months to one year, depending on the length of previous employment, if someone is still unemployed, the payment is reduced (and called **Arbeitslosengeld II**). From the age of 55, **Arbeitslosengeld I** is granted for between 15 and 18 months, again depending on the length of previous employment. The amount received as **Arbeitslosengeld II** will depend on whether the claimant's spouse or even their parents or children have an income. Unemployed people must report at regular intervals to the job centre, and prove that they are actively seeking work.

Ar|beits|lo|se(r) ['arbaitslo:zə] MF *decl as adj* unemployed person/man/woman *etc*; **die ~n** the unemployed; **die Zahl der ~n** the number of unemployed, the number of people out of work

Ar|beits|lo|sig|keit F -, *no pl* unemployment; **saisonbedingte ~** seasonal unemployment

Ar|beits-: **Ar|beits|lust** F enthusiasm for work; **Ar|beits|man|gel** M lack of work; **Ar|beits|markt** M labour *(Brit) or* labor *(US)* market; **ar|beits|mä|ßig** ADJ with respect to work ADV professionally; **er ist ~ stark engagiert** he's very involved in his work; **~ ist der Job okay** the work I do is okay; **Ar|beits|ma|te|ri|al** NT material for one's work; *(Sch)* teaching aids *pl*; **Ar|beits|me|di|zin** F industrial medicine; **Ar|beits|me|di|zi|ner(in)** M(F) occupational health specialist *or* practitioner; **Ar|beits|mensch** M (hard) worker; **Ar|beits|merk|ma|le** PL job characteristics *pl*; **Ar|beits|me|tho|de** F method of working; **Ar|beits|mi|nis|ter(in)** M(F) Employment Secretary *(Brit)*, Secretary of Labor *(US)*; **Ar|beits|mit|tel** NT material for one's work; *(Sch)* teaching aid; **Ar|beits|mo|dell** NT working model; **Ar|beits|mög|lich|keit** F **a** *(= Gelegenheit)* job opportunity **b** *(= freie Stelle)* vacancy; **Ar|beits|mo|ral** F work ethic; **Ar|beits|mo|ti|va|ti|on** F motivation *or* incentive to work, work incentive; **Ar|beits|nach|weis** M **a** employment agency; *(amtlich)* employment exchange *(Brit old)* **b** *(= Bescheinigung)* certificate of employment; **Ar|beits|nie|der|le|gung** F walkout; **Ar|beits|norm** F average work rate; **Ar|beits|ord|nung** F work regulations *pl*, work rules *pl (US)*; **Ar|beits|or|ga|ni|sa|ti|on** F organization of the/one's work; **Ar|beits|ort** M *pl* **-orte** place of work; **Ar|beits|pa|pier** NT **a** working paper **b** **Arbeitspapiere** PL cards *pl*, employment papers *pl (form)*

ar|beit|spa|rend ADJ → **Arbeit a**

Ar|beits-: **Ar|beits|pau|se** F break; **Ar|beits|pen|sum** NT quota of work; **Ar|beits|pferd** NT *(lit)* workhorse; *(fig)* slogger *(Brit inf)*, hard worker; **Ar|beits|pflicht** F requirement to work; **Ar|beits|plan** M work schedule; *(in Fabrik)* production schedule; **Ar|beits|plat|te** F worktop

Ar|beits|platz M **a** *(= Arbeitsstätte)* place of work, workplace; **am ~** at work; *(in Büro auch)* in the office; *(in Fabrik auch)* on the shop floor; **Demokratie am ~** industrial democracy **b** *(in Fabrik)* work station; *(in Büro)* workspace; *(= Computerarbeitsplatz)* workstation; **die Bibliothek hat 75 Arbeitsplätze** the library has room for 75 people to work *or* has working space for 75 people **c** *(= Stelle)* job; **freie Arbeitsplätze** vacancies

Ar|beits|platz-: **Ar|beits|platz|ab|bau** M job cuts *pl*; **Ar|beits|platz|an|ge|bot** NT job offer; *(mehrere)* job vacancies *pl*; **Ar|beits|platz|be|schaf|fung** F job creation; **Ar|beits|platz|be|schrei|bung** F job description; **Ar|beits|platz|com|pu|ter** M personal computer; **Ar|beits|platz|ga|ran|tie** F guaranteed job; **eine ~ aussprechen** to offer guaranteed employment, to offer a job guarantee; **Ar|beits|platz|ge|stal|tung** F workplace design; **Ar|beits|platz|rech|ner** M *(Comput)* workstation; **Ar|beits|platz|si|che|rung** F safeguarding of jobs; **Ar|beits|platz|stu|die** F workplace study; **Ar|beits|platz|tei|lung** F job sharing; **Ar|beits|platz|ver|lust** M loss of a job; *(insgesamt)* job losses *pl*; **Ar|beits|platz|ver|nich|tung** F destruction of jobs *or* workplaces; **Ar|beits|platz|wech|sel** M change of jobs *or* employment *(form)*

Ar|beits-: **Ar|beits|pro|be** F sample of one's work; **Ar|beits|pro|duk|ti|vi|tät** F productivity per man-hour worked; **Ar|beits|pro|-**

gramm NT work programme *(Brit) or* program *(US)*; **Ar|beits|pro|zess** M work process; **Ar|beits|psy|cho|lo|gie** F industrial psychology; **Ar|beits|raum** M workroom; *(für geistige Arbeit)* study; **Ar|beits|recht** NT industrial law; **Ar|beits|recht|ler** [-rɛçtlɐ] M **-s, -**, **Ar|beits|recht|le|rin** [-ərɪn] F **-, -nen** industrial *or* labor *(US)* lawyer; **ar|beits|recht|lich** ADJ *Streitfall, Angelegenheit* concerning industrial law; *Verbot* in accordance with industrial law; **~e Konsequenzen/Literatur** consequences in terms of/literature in industrial law; **ar|beits|reich** ADJ *Leben, Wochen etc* full of work, filled with work, busy; **es ist ~, das zu tun** it requires a lot of work to do that; **Ar|beits|re|ser|ven** PL labour *(Brit) or* labor *(US)* reserves *pl*; **Ar|beits|rhyth|mus** M work rhythm; **Ar|beits|rich|ter(in)** M(F) judge in an industrial tribunal; **Ar|beits|ru|he** F *(kurze Zeit)* break from work; **gestern herrschte ~** the factories and offices were closed yesterday; **Ar|beits|sa|chen** PL *(inf)* working clothes *pl or* things *pl (inf)*; **ar|beits|scheu** ADJ workshy; **Ar|beits|scheu** F workshyness; **Ar|beits|scheue(r)** MF *decl as adj* workshy person; **Ar|beits|schicht** F (work)shift; **Ar|beits|schluss** M end of work; **~ ist um 17.00 Uhr** work finishes at 5 pm; **nach ~** after work

Ar|beits|schutz M maintenance of industrial health and safety standards

Ar|beits|schutz-: **Ar|beits|schutz|be|stim|mung** F health and safety regulation; **Ar|beits|schutz|ge|setz|ge|bung** F legislation concerning health and safety at work; **Ar|beits|schutz|vor|schrif|ten** PL health and safety regulations *pl*

Ar|beits-: **Ar|beits|sit|zung** F working session; *(Comput)* session; **Ar|beits|skla|ve** M, **Ar|beits|skla|vin** F slave labourer *(Brit) or* laborer *(US)*; **~n** *pl* slave labour *(Brit) or* labor *(US) sing*; **Ar|beits|so|zio|lo|gie** F industrial sociology; **ar|beits|spa|rend** ADJ labour-saving; **Ar|beits|spei|cher** M *(Comput)* random access memory, main memory; **Ar|beits|spra|che** F *(bei Konferenz etc)* working language; **Ar|beits|stab** M planning staff; **Ar|beits|stät|te** F place of work; **Goethes ~** the place where Goethe worked; **Ar|beits|stel|le** F **a** place of work **b** *(= Stellung)* job **c** *(= Abteilung)* section; **Ar|beits|stil** M work style, style of working; **Ar|beits|stim|mung** F **in der richtigen ~ sein** to be in the (right) mood for work; **Ar|beits|stu|die** F time and motion study; **Ar|beits|stun|de** F man-hour; **~n werden extra berechnet** labour *(Brit) or* labor *(US)* will be charged separately; **Ar|beits|su|che** F search for work *or* employment *or* a job; **auf ~ sein** to be looking for a job, to be job hunting; **Ar|beits|su|chen|de(r)** MF *decl as adj* job-seeker; **Ar|beits|sucht** F addiction to work, workaholism *(inf)*; **ar|beits|süch|tig** ADJ addicted to work(ing), workaholic *(inf)*; **~ sein/werden** to be/become a workaholic *(inf)*; **Ar|beits|tag** M working day; **ein harter ~** a hard day; **Ar|beits|ta|gung** F conference, symposium; **Ar|beits|takt** M *(Tech)* **a** *(von Motor)* power stroke **b** *(bei Fließbandarbeit)* time for an/the operation, phase time; **Ar|beits|tä|tig|keit** F work; **Ar|beits|team** NT team; **Ar|beits|tech|nik** F technique of working; **ar|beits|tei|lig** ADJ based on the division of labour *(Brit) or* labor *(US)* ADV on the principle of the division of labour *(Brit) or* labor *(US)*; **Ar|beits|tei|lung** F division of labour *(Brit) or* labor *(US)*; **Ar|beits|tem|po** NT rate of work; **Ar|beits|the|ra|pie** F work therapy; **Ar|beits|tier** NT **a** *(lit)* working animal **b** *(fig inf)* workaholic *(inf)*; **Ar|beits|tisch** M worktable; *(für geistige Arbeit)* desk; *(für handwerkliche Arbeit)* workbench; **Ar|beits|ti|tel** M provisional *or* draft title; **Ar|beits|über|las|tung** F *(von Mensch)* overworking; *(von Maschine)* overloading; **wegen ~ ist es uns nicht möglich, ...** pressure of work makes it impossible for us to ...

Ar|beit-: **Ar|beit|su|che** F = **Arbeitssuche**; **ar|beit|su|chend** ADJ *attr* → **Arbeit d**; **Ar|beit|su|chen|de(r)** [-zu:xndə] MF *decl as adj* person/man/woman looking for work *or* a job

Ar|beits-: **ar|beits|un|fä|hig** ADJ unable to work; *(= krank)* unfit for *or* to work; *Regierung etc* non-viable; **Ar|beits|un|fä|hig|keit** F inability to work; *(wegen Krankheit)* unfitness for work; *(von Regierung etc)* non-viability; **dauernde ~** permanent disability; **Ar|beits|un|fä|hig|keits|be|schei|ni|gung** F certificate of unfitness for work; **Ar|beits|un|fall** M industrial accident, accident at work; **Ar|beits|un|lust** F disinclination to work; **Ar|beits|un|ter|la|ge** F work paper; *(Buch etc)* source for one's work; **ar|beits|un|wil|lig** ADJ reluctant *or* unwilling to work; **Ar|beits|un|wil|li|ge(r)** MF *decl as adj* person/man/woman reluctant *or* unwilling to work; **Ar|beits|ur|laub** M working holiday, combined business trip and vacation *(US)*; *(Mil)* *leave from the forces to carry on one's usual employment*; **Ar|beits|ver|bot** NT prohibition from employment; **er wurde mit ~ belegt** he has been banned from working; **Ar|beits|ver|dienst** M earned income; **Ar|beits|ver|ein|fa|chung** F simplification of the/one's work; **Ar|beits|ver|fah|ren** NT process; **Ar|beits|ver|hält|nis** NT **a** employee-employer relationship; **ein ~ eingehen** to enter employment **b Arbeitsverhältnisse** PL working conditions *pl*; **Ar|beits|ver|lust** M loss of working hours; **Ar|beits|ver|mitt|ler(in)** M(F) **privater ~** job placement officer, employment officer; **Ar|beits|ver|mitt|lung** F **a** *(= Vorgang)* arranging employment **b** *(= Amt)* employment exchange; *(privat)* employment agency; **Ar|beits|ver|trag** M contract of employment; **Ar|beits|ver|wei|ge|rung** F refusal to work; **Ar|beits|ver|zeich|nis** NT *(Comput)* working directory; **Ar|beits|vor|be|rei|tung** F **a** preparation for the/one's work **b** *(Ind)* production planning; **Ar|beits|vor|gang** M work process; **Ar|beits|vor|ha|ben** NT project; **Ar|beits|vor|la|ge** F sketch *or (= Modell)* model to work from; *(= Schablone)* template; **Ar|beits|weg** M way to (one's) work; *(von Pendler)* commute; **Ar|beits|wei|se** F *(= Praxis)* way *or* method of working, working method; *(von Maschine)* mode of operation; **die ~ dieser Maschine** the way this machine works; **Ar|beits|welt** F working world; **die industrielle ~** the world of industry; **Ar|beits|wil|le** M **ihm fehlt der ~** he has no desire to work; **ar|beits|wil|lig** ADJ willing to work; **Ar|beits|wil|li|ge(r)** [-vɪlɪgə] MF *decl as adj* person/man/woman *etc* willing to work; **Ar|beits|wis|sen|schaft** F industrial science, manpower studies *sing (US)*; **Ar|beits|wo|che** F working week; **Ar|beits|wut** F work mania; **ihn hat die ~ gepackt** he's turned into a workaholic *(inf)*; **ar|beits|wü|tig** ADJ work-happy *(inf)*

Ar|beits|zeit F **a** working hours *pl*; **während der ~** in *or* during working hours; **eine wöchentliche ~ von 35 Stunden** a working week of 35 hours; **flexible ~** flexible working hours **b** *(= benötigte Zeit)* **die ~ für etw** the time spent on sth; *(in Fabrik)* the production time for sth; **er ließ sich die ~ bezahlen** he wanted to be paid for his time

Ar|beits|zeit-: **Ar|beits|zeit|kon|to** NT record of hours worked; **Überstunden auf dem ~ gutschreiben** to record hours worked as overtime; **Ar|beits|zeit|mo|dell** NT working hours model *or* scheme; **Ar|beits|zeit|ord|nung** F working-time regulations *pl*; **Ar|beits|zeit|re|ge|lung** F *(= Regulierung)* regulation of working hours; *(= Vorschrift)* regulation on working hours; **Ar|beits|zeit|ver|kür|zung** F reduction in working hours

Ar|beits-: **Ar|beits|zeug** NT *pl* **-zeuge** *(inf)* **a** *(= Arbeitskleidung)* working clothes *pl* **b** *(= Werkzeug)* tools *pl*; **Ar|beits|zeug|nis** NT reference from one's employer; **Ar|beits|zim|mer** NT study; **Ar|beits|zwang** M requirement to work

Ar|bit|ra|ge [arbi'tra:ʒə] F **-, -n** *(St Ex)* arbitrage no *art*; *(= Arbitragegeschäft)* arbitrage business

ar|bit|rär [arbi'trɛ:ɐ] ADJ *(geh)* arbitrary

Ar|bo|re|tum [arbo're:tʊm] NT **-s, Arboreten** [-tn] arboretum

Ar|cha|i|kum [ar'ça:ikʊm] NT **-s,** *no pl*, **Ar|chä|i|kum** [ar'çɛ:ikʊm] NT **-s,** *no pl (Geol)* Archaean *(Brit) or* Archean *(US)* period

ar|cha|isch [ar'ça:ɪʃ] ADJ archaic

Ar|cha|is|mus [arça'ɪsmʊs] M **-, Archaismen** [-mən] archaism

Ar|chäo|lo|ge [arçɛo'lo:gə] M **-n, -n**, **Ar|chäo|lo|gin** [-'lo:gɪn] F **-, -nen** archaeologist *(Brit)*, archeologist *(US)*

Ar|chäo|lo|gie [arçɛolo'gi:] F **-,** *no pl* archaeology *(Brit)*, archeology *(US)*

ar|chäo|lo|gisch [arçɛo'lo:gɪʃ] ADJ archaeological *(Brit)*, archeological *(US)* ADV archaeologically *(Brit)*, archeologically *(US)*; **~ interessiert** interested in archaeology *(Brit) or* archeology *(US)*; **~ vorgebildet sein** to have a basic background in archaeology *(Brit) or* archeology *(US)*

Ar|che ['arçə] F **-, -n die ~ Noah** Noah's Ark

Ar|che|typ [arçe'ty:p, 'arçe-] M archetype

ar|che|ty|pisch [arçe'ty:pɪʃ] ADJ archetypal

Ar|che|ty|pus [arçe'ty:pʊs] M archetype

Ar|chi|me|des [arçi'me:dɛs] M **-'** Archimedes

ar|chi|me|disch [arçi'me:dɪʃ] ADJ Archimedean; **~es Axiom** *(Math)* Archimedes' theorem; **~e Schraube** *(Tech)* Archimedes' screw; **~er Punkt** *(fig)* crucial *or* central point

Ar|chi|pel [arçi'pe:l] M **-s, -e** archipelago

Ar|chi|tekt [arçi'tɛkt] M **-en, -en**, **Ar|chi|tek|tin** [-'tɛktɪn] F **-, -nen** *(lit, fig)* architect

Ar|chi|tek|ten-: **Ar|chi|tek|ten|bü|ro** NT architect's office; **Ar|chi|tek|ten|kol|lek|tiv** NT team of architects

Ar|chi|tek|to|nik [arçitɛk'to:nɪk] F **-, -en** architecture; *(geh: = Aufbau von Kunstwerk)* structure, architectonics *sing (form)*

ar|chi|tek|to|nisch [arçitɛk'to:nɪʃ] ADJ architectural; *(geh) Aufbau (von Kunstwerk)* structural, architectonic *(form)* ADV architecturally

Ar|chi|tek|tur [arçitɛk'tu:ɐ] F **-, -en** architecture *(auch Comput)*; *(= Bau)* piece of architecture

Ar|chi|tek|tur|bü|ro NT architect's *or* architects office

Ar|chit|rav [arçi'tra:f] M **-s, -e** [-və] architrave

Ar|chiv [ar'çi:f] NT **-s, -e** [-və] archives *pl*; *(Comput: Dateiattribut)* archive

Ar|chi|va|li|en [arçi'va:liən] PL records *pl*

Ar|chi|var [arçi'va:ɐ] M **-s, -e**, **Ar|chi|va|rin** [-'va:rɪn] F **-, -nen** archivist

Ar|chiv-: **Ar|chiv|bild** NT library photo, photo from the archives; **Ar|chiv|ex|emp|lar** NT file copy

ar|chi|vie|ren [arçi'vi:rən] *ptp* **archiviert** VT to archive *(auch Comput)*

Ar|chi|vie|rung F **-, -en** archiving *(auch Computer)*

Ar|chiv|ma|te|ri|al NT records *pl*

Ar|cus ['arkʊs] M **-, -** ['arku:s] *(Math)* arc

ARD [a:lɛr'de:] F **-,** *no pl abbr von* **Arbeitsgemeinschaft der öffentlich-rechtlichen Rundfunkanstalten der Bundesrepublik Deutschland**

ARD

ARD is an amalgamation of the broadcasting stations of the **Länder**. It runs **das Erste**, the first German national TV channel. The individual stations produce programmes for the network and for the regional channels, which concentrate on local interest and educational programming. They also control up to five regional radio stations each. **ARD** is financed through licence fees and strictly controlled advertising. It concentrates on information, news and educational programmes.

Are ['a:rə] F -, -n (*Sw:* = *Ar*) are (*100 m*)

Are|al [are'a:l] NT -s, -e area

are|li|gi|ös ['areligiø:s] ADJ areligious

Ären *pl von* **Ära**

Are|na [a're:na] F -, **Arenen** [-nən] (*lit, fig*) arena; (*= Zirkusarena, Stierkampfarena*) ring

Are|o|pag [areo'pa:k] M -s, *no pl* (*Hist*) Areopagus

arg [ark] ADJ *comp* **≃er** ['ɛrgɐ], *superl* **≃ste(r, s)** ['ɛrkstə] (*esp S Ger*) **a** (*old:* = *böse*) evil, wicked; ~ **denken** to think evil thoughts **b** (*= schlimm*) bad; *Gestank, Katastrophe, Verlust, Blamage, Verlegenheit, Schicksal* terrible; *Enttäuschung, Feind* bitter; *Säufer, Raucher* confirmed, inveterate; **sein ärgster Feind** his worst enemy; **etw noch ärger machen** to make sth worse; **das Ärgste befürchten** to fear the worst; **ich habe an nichts Arges gedacht** I didn't think anything of it; **etw liegt im Argen** sth is at sixes and sevens; **das ist mir** ~ (*dial*) I'm very sorry about that **c** *attr* (*= stark, groß*) terrible; (*dial*) *Freude, Liebenswürdigkeit etc* tremendous

ADV *comp* **≃er**, *superl* **am ≃sten** (*= schlimm*) badly; (*dial inf:* = *sehr*) terribly (*inf*); **es geht ihr ~ schlecht** (*inf*) she's in a really bad way; **er hat sich ~ vertan** (*inf*) he's made a bad mistake; **sie ist ~ verliebt** (*inf*) she is very much in love, she is terribly in love; **es zu ~ treiben** to go too far, to take things too far

Arg [ark] NT -s, *no pl* (*old*) malice

Ar|gen|ti|ni|en [argɛn'ti:niən] NT -s Argentina, the Argentine

Ar|gen|ti|ni|er [argɛn'ti:niɐ] M -s, -, **Ar|gen|ti|ni|e|rin** [-iərɪn] F -, -nen Argentine, Argentinian

ar|gen|ti|nisch [argɛn'ti:nɪʃ] ADJ Argentine, Argentinian

Ar|ge(r) ['argə] M *decl as adj no pl* (*old*) **der** ~ Satan, the devil

är|ger *comp von* **arg**

Är|ger ['ɛrgɐ] M -s, *no pl* **a** annoyance; (*stärker*) anger; **wenn ihn der ~ packt** when he gets annoyed/angry; ~ **über etw** (*acc*) **empfinden** to feel annoyed about sth; **zu jds ~, jdm zum ~** to sb's annoyance **b** (*= Unannehmlichkeiten, Streitigkeiten*) trouble; (*= ärgerliche Erlebnisse*) bother, trouble; (*= Sorgen*) worry; **jdm ~ machen** *or* **bereiten** to cause sb a lot of trouble *or* bother; **der tägliche ~ im Büro** the hassle in the office every day (*inf*); **~ bekommen** *or* **kriegen** (*inf*) to get into trouble; **~ mit jdm haben** to be having trouble with sb; **mach keinen ~!** (*inf*) don't make *or* cause any trouble!, cool it! (*inf*); **mach mir keinen ~** (*inf*) don't make any trouble for me; **so ein ~!** (*inf*) how annoying!, what a nuisance!; **es gibt ~** (*inf*) there'll be trouble

är|ger|lich ['ɛrgɐlɪç] ADJ **a** (*= verärgert*) annoyed, cross; *Tonfall, Handbewegung* angry; ~ **über** *or* **auf jdn/über etw sein** to be annoyed *or* cross with sb/about sth, to be angry *or* infuriated with sb/about sth, to be mad at sb/about sth (*inf*) **b** (*= unangenehm*) annoying; (*stärker*) maddening, infuriating; **eine ~e Tatsache** an unpleasant fact ADV crossly; (*= böse*) angrily; **~ klingen** to sound cross/angry; **jdn ~ ansehen** to give sb an angry look

Är|ger|lich|keit F -, -en **a** *no pl* (*= das Verärgertsein*) annoyance, crossness; **die ~ seines Tons** the annoyance in his voice **b** (*= ärgerlicher Vorfall*) nuisance, annoyance

är|gern ['ɛrgɐn] VT **a** (*= ärgerlich machen*) to annoy, to irritate; (*stärker*) to make angry; **jdn krank** *or* **zu Tode ~** to drive sb mad; **das ärgert einen doch!** but it's so annoying! **b** (*= necken*) to torment VR (*= ärgerlich sein/werden*) to be/get annoyed; (*stärker*) to be/get angry *or* infuriated (*über jdn/etw* with sb/about sth); **sich krank** *or* **zu Tode ~** to drive oneself to distraction; **über so etwas könnte ich mich krank** *or* **zu Tode ~** that sort of thing drives me mad (*inf*); **du darfst dich darüber nicht so ~** you shouldn't let it annoy you so much; **nicht ~, nur wundern!** (*inf*) that's life

Är|ger|nis ['ɛrgɐnɪs] NT -ses, -se **a** *no pl* (*= Anstoß*) offence (*Brit*), offense (*US*), outrage; **~ erregen** to cause offence (*Brit*) *or* offense (*US*); **~ an etw** (*dat*) **nehmen** (*old*) to be offended by sth; **bei jdm ~ erregen** to offend sb; **wegen Erregung öffentlichen ~ses angeklagt werden** to be charged with offending public decency **b** (*= etwas Anstößiges*) outrage; (*= etwas Ärgerliches*) terrible nuisance; **es ist ein ~ für sie, wenn ...** it annoys her (terribly) when ...; **um ~se zu vermeiden** to avoid upsetting anybody **c** (*= Ärgerlichkeit, Unannehmlichkeit*) trouble *no pl*

Arg|list ['arklɪst] F, *no pl* (*= Hinterlist*) cunning, guile, craftiness; (*= Boshaftigkeit*) malice; (*Jur*) fraud

arg|lis|tig ['arklɪstɪç] ADJ cunning, crafty; (*= böswillig*) malicious; **~e Täuschung** fraud ADV cunningly, craftily; (*= böswillig*) maliciously

Arg|lis|tig|keit F -, *no pl* cunning, craftiness; (*= Böswilligkeit*) maliciousness

arg|los ADJ innocent; (*= ohne Täuschungsabsicht*) guileless ADV innocently

Arg|lo|sig|keit F -, *no pl* innocence

Ar|gon ['argɔn] NT -s, *no pl* (*abbr* **Ar**) argon

Ar|go|naut [argo'naut] M -en, -en (*Myth*) Argonaut

Ar|got [ar'go:] M OR NT -s, -s argot

ärgs|te(r, s) *superl von* **arg**

Ar|gu|ment [argu'mɛnt] ✪ 53.2, 53.3, 53.6 NT -(e)s, -e argument; **das ist kein ~** that's no argument; (*= wäre unsinnig*) that's no way to go about things; (*= keine Entschuldigung*) that's no excuse

Ar|gu|men|ta|ti|on [argumɛnta'tsio:n] F -, -en **a** argument; (*= Darlegung*) argumentation *no pl* **b** (*Sch:* = *Aufsatz*) critical analysis

Ar|gu|men|ta|ti|ons|hil|fe F (*form*) advice on how to present one's case

ar|gu|men|ta|tiv [argumɛnta'ti:f] (*geh*), **ar|gu|men|ta|to|risch** [argumɛnta'to:rɪʃ] (*rare*) ADJ **~e Werbung betreiben** to use persuasive advertising; **einen ~en Wahlkampf führen** to run an election campaign that concentrates on issues; **~e Funktion** (*Ling*) argumentative function ADV **die Beweisführung war ~ überzeugend/schwach** the arguments presented were very convincing/weak; **eine Aussage ~ widerlegen** to refute an argument; **~ ist er sehr schwach** his argumentation is very weak; **etw ~ erreichen** to achieve sth by (force of) argument; **etw ~ bekämpfen** to fight sth with arguments

ar|gu|men|tie|ren [argumɛn'ti:rən] *ptp* **argumentiert** VI to argue; **mit etw ~** to use sth as an argument

Ar|gus ['argʊs] M -, -se Argus

Ar|gus|au|ge NT (*geh*) Argus eye; **mit ~n** Argus-eyed

Arg|wohn ['arkvo:n] M -s, *no pl* suspicion; **jds ~ erregen/zerstreuen** to arouse/allay sb's suspicions; **~ gegen jdn hegen/schöpfen** (*geh*) to have/form doubts about sb, to be/become suspicious of sb; **mit** *or* **voller ~** suspiciously

arg|wöh|nen ['arkvø:nən] VT *insep* (*geh*) to suspect

arg|wöh|nisch ['arkvø:nɪʃ] ADJ suspicious ADV suspiciously

arid [a'ri:t] ADJ (*Geog*) arid

Ari|di|tät [aridi'tɛ:t] F -, *no pl* (*Geog*) aridity

Arie ['a:riə] F -, -n (*Mus*) aria

Ari|er ['a:riɐ] M -s, -, **Ari|e|rin** [-iərɪn] F -, -nen Aryan

Ari|er|pa|ra|graf, **Ari|er|pa|ra|graph** M (*NS*) *law precluding non-Aryans from becoming public servants*

Ari|es ['a:riɛs] M - (*Astron*) Aries

arisch ['a:rɪʃ] ADJ **a** (*Ling*) Indo-European, Indo-Germanic **b** (*NS*) Aryan

ari|sie|ren [ari'zi:rən] *ptp* **arisiert** VT (*NS sl*) to Aryanize

Aris|to|krat [arɪsto'kra:t] M -en, -en, **Aris|to|kra|tin** [-'kra:tɪn] F -, -nen aristocrat

Aris|to|kra|tie [arɪstokra'ti:] F -, -n [-'ti:ən] aristocracy

aris|to|kra|tisch [arɪsto'kra:tɪʃ] ADJ aristocratic

Aris|to|te|les [arɪs'to:telɛs] M -' Aristotle

Aris|to|te|li|ker [arɪsto'te:likɐ] M -s, -, **Aris|to|te|li|ke|rin** [-ərɪn] F -, -nen Aristotelian

aris|to|te|lisch [arɪsto'te:lɪʃ] ADJ Aristotelian

Arith|me|tik [arɪt'me:tɪk] F -, *no pl* arithmetic

Arith|me|ti|ker [arɪt'me:tikɐ] M -s, -, **Arith|me|ti|ke|rin** [-ərɪn] F -, -nen arithmetician

arith|me|tisch [arɪt'me:tɪʃ] ADJ arithmetic(al); (*Comput*) arithmetic

Ar|ka|de [ar'ka:də] F -, -n **a** (*= Bogen*) arch (-way) **b** **Arkaden** PL (*= Bogengang*) arcade

Ar|ka|di|en [ar'ka:diən] NT -s Arcadia

ar|ka|disch [ar'ka:dɪʃ] ADJ (*geh*) Arcadian

Ark|tis ['arktɪs] F -, *no pl* Arctic

ark|tisch ['arktɪʃ] ADJ arctic ADV ~ **kalt** cold as the arctic

Ar|kus ['arkʊs] M -, - ['arku:s] (*Math*) arc

arm [arm] ADJ *comp* **≃er** ['ɛrmɐ], *superl* **≃ste(r, s)** ['ɛrmstə] (*lit, fig*) poor; (*= gering*) *Vegetation, Wachstum* sparse; **Arm und Reich** rich and poor; **die Armen** the poor *pl*; **du machst mich noch mal ~** (*inf*) you'll ruin me yet; **~ an etw** (*dat*) **sein** to be somewhat lacking in sth; **der Boden ist ~ an Nährstoffen** the soil is poor in nutrients; **~ an Vitaminen** low in vitamins; **um jdn/etw ärmer werden** to lose sb/sth; **um jdn/etw ärmer sein** to have lost sb/sth; **um 55 Euro ärmer sein** to be 55 euros poorer *or* worse off; **ach, du/Sie Armer!** (*auch iro*) you poor thing!, poor you!; **ich Armer!** poor me!, woe is me! (*poet*); **~e Seelen** (*Rel*) holy souls; **~es Schwein** (*inf*) poor so-and-so (*inf*); **~er Irrer** (*inf*) mad fool (*inf*); (*= bedauernswert*) poor fool

ADV *comp* **≃er**, *superl* **am ≃sten jdn ~ plündern** to take everything sb has; **jdn ~ rauben** to rob sb of everything they have; **du isst mich noch mal ~!** (*inf*) you'll eat me out of house and home!; **~ dran sein** (*inf*) to have a hard time of it

Arm [arm] M -(e)s, -e (*Anat, Tech, fig*) arm; (*von Fluss, Baum*) branch; (*von Waage*) beam; (*= Ärmel*) sleeve; **~ in ~** arm in arm; **über/unter den ~** over/under one's arm; **~ voll = Armvoll**; **die ~e voll haben** to have one's arms full; **jds ~ nehmen** to take sb's arm, to take sb by the arm; **jdm den ~ bieten** (*geh*) *or* **reichen** to offer sb one's arm; **jdn im ~** *or* **in den ~en halten** to hold sb in one's arms; **jdn am ~ führen** to lead sb by the arm; **jdn in die ~e nehmen** to take sb in one's arms; **jdn in die ~e schließen** to take *or* clasp sb in an embrace; **sich in den ~en liegen** to lie in each other's arms; **jdm/sich in die ~e fallen** *or* **sinken** to fall into sb's/each other's arms; **sich aus jds ~en lösen** (*geh*) to free oneself from sb's embrace; **jdn auf den ~ nehmen** to take sb onto one's arm; (*fig inf*) to pull sb's leg (*inf*); **jdm unter die ~e greifen** (*fig*) to help sb out; **jdm in die ~e laufen** (*fig inf*) to run *or* bump (*inf*) into sb; **jdn mit offenen ~en empfangen** (*fig*) to welcome sb with open arms; **jdm in den ~ fallen** (*fig*) to put a spoke in sb's wheel (*Brit*), to spike sb's guns (*Brit*), to throw sb a curve ball (*US*); **sich jdm/einer Sache in die ~e werfen** (*fig*) to throw oneself at sb/into sth; **jdn jdm/einer Sache in die ~e treiben** (*fig*) to drive sb into sb's arms/to sth; **jdn am steifen ~ verhungern lassen** (*lit hum*) to get sb in an armlock; (*fig*) to put the screws on sb (*inf*); **der ~ des Gesetzes** the long arm of the law; **der ~ der Gerechtigkeit** (*fig*) justice; **einen langen/den längeren ~ haben** (*fig*) to have a lot of/more pull (*inf*) *or* influence; **jds verlängerter ~** an extension of sb

-arm ADJ *suf* **a** (*= wenig enthaltend*) low in; **vitaminarm** low in vitamins; **salzarm** low in salt **b** (*= gering an*) lacking in; **emotionsarm** lacking in emotion; **fantasiearm** lacking in imagination, unimaginative **c** *(Elec, Phys etc)* low-; **rauscharm** low-noise; **strahlungsarm** low-radiation

Ar|ma|da [arˈmaːda] F -, -s *or* **Armaden** [-dn] *(lit, fig)* armada

Ar|ma|ged|don [armaˈgɛdɔn] NT -(s) Armageddon

Arm- *in cpds* arm; **arm|am|pu|tiert** [-amputiːɐt] ADJ with an arm amputated; ~ **sein** to have had an arm amputated; **Arm|ar|beit** F *(Boxen)* fist work

Ar|ma|tur [armaˈtuːɐ] F -, -en *usu pl (Tech) (= Hahn, Leitung etc)* fitting; *(= Instrument)* instrument

Ar|ma|tu|ren-: **Ar|ma|tu|ren|be|leuch|tung** F *(Aut)* dash light; **Ar|ma|tu|ren|brett** NT instrument panel; *(Aut)* dashboard

Arm-: **Arm|band** [-bant] NT *pl* **-bänder** bracelet; *(von Uhr)* (watch)strap; **Arm|band|uhr** F wristwatch; **Arm|beu|ge** F **a** inside of one's elbow **b** *(Sport)* arm bend; **Arm|bin|de** F armband; *(Med)* sling; **Arm|bruch** M *(Med)* broken *or* fractured arm; **Arm|brust** F crossbow

Ärm|chen [ˈɛrmçən] NT -s, - *dim von* **Arm**

arm|dick ADJ as thick as one's arm

Ar|mee [arˈmeː] F -, -n [-ˈmeːən] *(Mil, fig)* army; *(= Gesamtheit der Streitkräfte)* (armed) forces *pl*; **bei der** ~ in the army/forces

Ar|mee- *in cpds* army; **Ar|mee|be|fehl** M army order

Är|mel [ˈɛrml] M -s, - sleeve; **sich** *(dat)* **die ~ hochkrempeln** *or* **aufkrempeln** *(lit, fig)* to roll up one's sleeves; **etw aus dem ~ schütteln** to produce sth just like that

Är|mel|auf|schlag M cuff

Är|me|leu|te-: **Är|me|leu|te|es|sen** NT poor man's food; **Är|me|leu|te|ge|ruch** M smell of poverty

Är|mel|hal|ter M sleeve band

-är|me|lig [ɛrməlɪç] ADJ *suf* -sleeved; **kurzärmelig** short-sleeved

Är|mel|ka|nal M (English) Channel

Är|mel|ka|nal|tun|nel M Channel tunnel, Chunnel *(inf)*

är|mel|los ADJ sleeveless

Är|mel|scho|ner M oversleeve

Ar|men|haus NT *(old, fig)* poorhouse

Ar|me|ni|en [arˈmeːniən] NT -s Armenia

Ar|me|ni|er [arˈmeːniɐ] M -s, -, **Ar|me|ni|e|rin** [-iərɪn] F -, -nen Armenian

ar|me|nisch [arˈmeːnɪʃ] ADJ Armenian

Ar|men-: **Ar|men|kas|se** F *(Hist)* poor box; **Ar|men|kü|che** F soup kitchen; **Ar|men|recht** NT *(dated Jur)* legal aid

Ar|men|sün|der- [armənˈzʏndɐ] *in cpds (Aus)* = **Armsünder-**

Ar|men|vier|tel NT poor district *or* quarter

är|mer *comp von* **arm**

Ar|mes|län|ge F arm's length; **um zwei ~n** by two arms' length

Ar|me|sün|der [arməˈzʏndɐ] M **Armensünders, Armensünder** *(obs)* condemned man

Ar|me|sün|der- *in cpds* = **Armsünder-**

Arm-: **Arm|flor** M black armband; **Arm|ge|lenk** NT elbow joint; **Arm|he|bel** M *(Sport)* arm lever

ar|mie|ren [arˈmiːrən] *ptp* **armiert** VT **a** *(old Mil)* to arm **b** *(Tech) Kabel* to sheathe; *Beton* to reinforce

-ar|mig [armɪç] ADJ *suf* -armed; **einarmig** one-armed; **ein siebenarmiger Leuchter** a seven-branched candelabra

Arm-: **arm|lang** ADJ arm-length; **Arm|län|ge** F arm length; **Arm|leh|ne** F armrest; *(von Stuhl etc auch)* arm; **Arm|leuch|ter** M **a** chandelier **b** *(pej inf: = Mensch)* twit *(inf)*, fool, twerp *(inf)*

ärm|lich [ˈɛrmlɪç] ADJ *(lit, fig)* poor; *Kleidung, Wohnung* shabby; *Essen* meagre *(Brit)*, meager *(US)*; *Verhältnisse* humble; **einen ~en Eindruck machen** to look poor/shabby; **aus ~en Verhältnissen** from a poor family ADV poorly, shabbily; ~ **leben** to live in poor conditions

Ärm|lich|keit F -, *no pl (von Kleidung, Wohnung)* shabbiness; *(von Essen)* meagreness *(Brit)*, meagerness *(US)*; **die ~ der Verhältnisse** the poor conditions

-ärm|lig [ɛrmlɪç] ADJ *suf* = **-ärmelig**

Ärm|ling [ˈɛrmlɪŋ] M -s, -e oversleeve

Arm-: **Arm|loch** NT **a** armhole **b** *(euph: = Arschloch)* bum *(inf)*; **Arm|mus|kel** M biceps; **Arm|pols|ter** NT **a** *(an Kleidung)* shoulder padding **b** *(= Armlehne)* padded armrest; **Arm|pro|the|se** F artificial arm; **Arm|reif** M, **Arm|rei|fen** M bangle; **Arm|schlüs|sel** M *(Sport)* armlock, hammerlock *(US)*; **Arm|schutz** M *(Sport)* arm guard

arm|se|lig ADJ *(= dürftig)* miserable; *(= jämmerlich)* pathetic, pitiful, piteous; *Feigling, Lügner* miserable, wretched; *Summe, Ausrede* paltry; **für ~e zwei Euro** for a paltry two euros, for two paltry euros; **das ist wirklich ~!** it's really pathetic!

Arm|se|lig|keit F *(= Jämmerlichkeit)* piteousness; *(von Feigling)* wretchedness; **die ~ ihrer Hütten** the miserable condition of their huts; **die ~ dieser Männer!** these pathetic men!; **die ~ dieser Ausrede** this paltry excuse; **die ~ dieses Lügners** such a wretched liar

Arm|ses|sel M, **Arm|stuhl** *(old)* M armchair

ärms|te(r, s) *superl von* **arm**

Arm-: **Arm|stum|mel** M *(inf)*, **Arm|stumpf** M stump of one's arm; **Arm|stüt|ze** F armrest

Arm|sün|der-: **Arm|sün|der|bank** F *pl* **-bänke**, **Arm|sün|der|bänk|chen** NT *(hum) (beim Essen) small table at which children sit (bei Prüfung, Quiz etc)* hot seat; **dasitzen wie auf dem Armsünderbänkchen** to be sitting there looking as though the world were about to end; **Arm|sün|der|glo|cke** F *knell tolled during an execution*; **Arm|sün|der|mie|ne** F *(hum)* hangdog expression

Ar|mut [ˈarmuːt] F -, *no pl (lit, fig)* poverty; **charakterliche ~** lack of character; **geistige ~** intellectual poverty; *(von Mensch)* lack of intellect; **neue ~** new poverty

-ar|mut F *suf in cpds* lack of

Ar|muts-: **Ar|muts|gren|ze** F, *no pl* poverty line; **Ar|muts|zeug|nis** NT *(fig)* **jdm/sich (selbst) ein ~ ausstellen** to show *or* prove sb's/one's (own) shortcomings; **das ist ein ~ für ihn** that shows him up

Arm|voll M -, - armful; **zwei ~ Holz** two armfuls of wood

Ar|ni|ka [ˈarnika] F -, -s arnica

Arom [aˈroːm] NT -s, -e *(poet)* fragrance, scent

Aro|ma [aˈroːma] NT -s, **Aromen** *or* -s *or (dated)* **-ta** **a** *(= Geruch)* aroma **b** *(= Geschmack)* flavour *(Brit)*, flavor *(US)*, taste **c** *no pl* flavouring *(Brit)*, flavoring *(US)*

Aro|ma|the|ra|pie F *(Med)* aromatherapy

aro|ma|tisch [aroˈmaːtɪʃ] ADJ **a** *(= wohlriechend)* aromatic **b** *(= wohlschmeckend)* savoury *(Brit)*, savory *(US)* **c** *(Chem)* aromatic ADV ~ **riechen** to smell fragrant *or* aromatic; ~ **schmecken** to taste aromatic

aro|ma|ti|sie|ren [aromatiˈziːrən] *ptp* **aromatisiert** VT to give aroma to; **aromatisiert** aromatic; **zu stark aromatisiert sein** to have too strong an aroma

Arons|stab [ˈaːrɔns-] M arum

Ar|rak [ˈarak] M -s, -s *or* -e arrack

Ar|ran|ge|ment [arãʒəˈmãː] NT -s, -s *(alle Bedeutungen)* arrangement

Ar|ran|geur [arãˈʒøːɐ] M -s, -e, **Ar|ran|geu|rin** [-ˈʒøːrɪn] F -, -nen *(geh)* organizer; *(Mus)* arranger; **er war der ~ dieses Abkommens** he arranged this agreement

ar|ran|gie|ren [arãˈʒiːrən] *ptp* **arrangiert** VTI *(alle Bedeutungen)* to arrange *(jdm* for sb) VR **sich mit jdm ~** to come to an arrangement with sb; **sich mit etw ~** to come to terms with sth

Ar|rest [aˈrɛst] M -(e)s, -s **a** *(Sch, Mil, Jur: = Jugendarrest)* detention; **seine Eltern bestraften ihn mit ~** his parents punished him by grounding him **b** *(Econ, Jur) (auch* **persönlicher Arrest)** attachment; *(auch* **dinglicher Arrest)** distress *(form)*, distraint; ~ **in jds Vermögen** distress *(form)* upon sb's property

Ar|res|tant [arɛsˈtant] M -en, -en, **Ar|res|tan|tin** [-ˈtantɪn] F -, -nen *(dated Jur)* detainee

Ar|rest-: **Ar|rest|lo|kal** NT *(dated)* detention room; *(Mil)* guardroom; **Ar|rest|zel|le** F detention cell

ar|re|tie|ren [areˈtiːrən] *ptp* **arretiert** VT **a** *(dated) jdn* to take into custody **b** *(Tech)* to lock (in place)

Ar|re|tie|rung F -, -en **a** *(dated: = Verhaftung)* taking into custody **b** *(Tech)* locking; *(= Vorrichtung)* locking mechanism

Ar|rhyth|mie [arʏtˈmiː] F -, -n [-ˈmiːən] *(Med)* arrhythmia

ar|ri|vie|ren [ariˈviːrən] **arriviert** VI *aux sein* to make it *(inf)*, to become a success; **zu etw ~** to rise to become sth

ar|ri|viert [ariˈviːɐt] ADJ successful; *(pej)* upstart; **er ist jetzt ~** he has arrived, he has made it *(inf)*

Ar|ri|vier|te(r) [ariˈviːɐtə] MF *decl as adj* arrivé, parvenu *(pej)*

ar|ro|gant [aroˈgant] ADJ arrogant ADV arrogantly

Ar|ro|ganz [aroˈgants] F -, *no pl* arrogance

ar|ron|die|ren [arɔnˈdiːrən, arõ-] *ptp* **arrondiert** VT *(geh)* **a** *Grenze* to realign, to adjust; *Grundstück* to realign *or* adjust the boundaries of **b** *Kanten etc* to round off

Arsch [arʃ, aːɐʃ] M -(e)s, ⸚e [ˈɛrʃə, ˈɛːɐʃə] **a** *(vulg)* arse *(Brit sl)*, ass *(US sl)*, bum *(Brit inf)*, fanny *(US sl)*, butt *(US inf)*; **jdm** *or* **jdn in den ~ treten** to give sb a kick up the arse *(Brit sl) or* ass *(US sl)*; **den ~ vollkriegen** to get a bloody good hiding *(Brit inf)*, to get an ass-kicking *(US sl)*; **leck mich am ~!** *(= lass mich in Ruhe)* get stuffed! *(inf)*, fuck off! *(vulg)*; *(= verdammt noch mal)* bugger! *(Brit sl)*, fuck it! *(vulg)*; *(sl: überrascht)* bugger me! *(Brit sl)*, fuck me! *(vulg)*; **er kann mich (mal) am ~ lecken** he can get stuffed *(Brit inf)*, he can fuck off *(vulg)*; **ich könnte mich** *or* **mir in den ~ beißen** *(sl)* I could kick myself; **jdm in den ~ kriechen** *(inf)* to lick sb's arse *(Brit sl) or* ass *(US sl)*; **du hast wohl den ~ offen!** *(sl)* you're out of your tiny mind *(inf)*; **er kriegt wieder den ~ nicht hoch** *(inf)* he won't get his arse *(Brit) or* ass *(US)* in gear *(sl)*; **~ mit Ohren** *(dated sl)* silly bugger *(Brit sl)*; **am ~ der Welt** *(inf)* in the back of beyond; **im** *or* **am ~ sein** *(sl)* to be fucked up *(vulg)*; **fürn ~ sein** *(sl)* to be crap *(inf)*; **einen kalten ~ kriegen** *(sl: = Angst kriegen)* to shit oneself *(sl)*; **den ~ zukneifen** *(sl)* to kick the bucket *(inf)*; **jdm den ~ aufreißen** *(sl, esp Mil)* to work the shit out of sb *(sl)*; **sich** *(dat)* **den ~ aufreißen** *(sl)* to bust a gut *(inf)*; **ihm geht der ~ mit** *or* **auf Grundeis** *(dated sl)* he's scared shitless *(sl)*, he's shit-scared *(Brit sl)*; **das geht mir am ~ vorbei** *(sl: = ist mir egal)* I don't give a shit (about it) *(sl)*; **Schütze ~** *(Mil)* simple private; **sich auf den** *or* **seinen ~ setzen** *(lit)* to park one's arse *(Brit sl) or* ass *(US sl)*; *(fig dated sl: = sich Mühe geben)* to get one's arse *(Brit) or* ass *(US)* in gear *(sl)*, to get one's finger out *(inf)*; **sich** *(dat)* **den ~ abfrieren** *(sl)* to freeze one's arse *(Brit) or* ass *(US)* off *(sl)*; **seinen ~ in Bewegung setzen** *(sl)* to get one's arse *(Brit) or* ass *(US)* in gear *(sl)*; **schwing deinen ~ weg** *(sl)* move your fat arse *(Brit sl) or* ass *(US sl)*
b *(sl: = Mensch)* bastard *(sl)*, bugger *(Brit sl)*, sod *(sl)*; *(= Dummkopf)* stupid bastard *etc (sl)*; **kein ~ war da** nobody fucking turned up *(vulg)*

Arsch-: **Arsch|ba|cke** F *(sl)* buttock, cheek; **Arsch|fi|cker** [-fɪkɐ] M -s, - **a** *(lit vulg)* bum-fucker *(Brit vulg)*, butt-fucker *(US vulg)* **b** *(fig vulg)* slimy bastard *(sl)*; **Arsch|gei|ge** F *(dated sl)* = **Arsch b**; **arsch|kalt** ADJ *(inf)* bloody *(Brit inf) or* damn *(inf)* cold; **Arsch|krie|cher(in)** M(F) *(sl)* ass-kisser *(sl)*; **Arsch|krie|che|rei** F *(sl)* ass-kissing *(sl)*

ärsch|lings [ˈɛrʃlɪŋs, ˈɛːɐʃ-] ADV *(old)* backwards, arse *(Brit)* or ass *(US)* first *(sl)*

Arsch-: **Arsch|loch** NT *(vulg)* **a** *(lit)* arsehole *(Brit sl)*, asshole *(US sl)* **b** = Arsch b; **Arsch|tritt** M *(sl)* kick up the arse *(Brit sl)* or ass *(US sl)*; **Arsch-und-Tit|ten-Pres|se** F *(sl)* tit-and-bum press *(Brit inf)*, tit-and-ass media *pl (US inf)*

Ar|sen [arˈzeːn] NT **-s**, *no pl (abbr* **As***)* arsenic

Ar|se|nal [arzeˈnaːl] NT **-s, -e** *(lit, fig)* arsenal

ar|sen|hal|tig ADJ containing arsenic

Ar|se|nik [arˈzeːnɪk] NT **-s**, *no pl* arsenic, arsenic trioxide *(form)*

Ar|sen|ver|gif|tung F arsenic poisoning

Art [aːɐt] F **-, -en** **a** kind, sort, type; **diese ~ Leute/Buch** people/books like that, that kind or sort of person/book; **jede ~ (von) Buch/Terror** any kind *etc* of book/terrorism, a book of any kind *etc*/terrorism in any form; **alle möglichen ~en von Büchern, Bücher aller ~** all kinds or sorts of books, books of all kinds or sorts; **einzig in seiner ~ sein** to be the only one of its kind, to be unique; **aus der ~ schlagen** not to take after anyone in the family

b *(Biol)* species

c *(= Methode)* way; **auf die ~** in that way or manner; **auf die ~ geht es am schnellsten** that is the quickest way; **auf merkwürdige/grausame** *etc* **~** in a strange/cruel *etc* way; **die einfachste ~, etw zu tun** the simplest way to do sth or of doing sth; **auf diese ~ und Weise** in this way

d *(= Wesen)* nature; *(= übliche Verhaltensweise)* way; **es entspricht nicht meiner ~** it's not my nature; **das ist eigentlich nicht seine ~** it's not like him; **von lebhafter ~ sein** to have a lively nature; to have a lively way (with one)

e *(= Stil)* style; **nach bayrischer ~** Bavarian style; **Schnitzel nach ~ des Hauses** schnitzel à la maison

f *(= Benehmen)* behaviour *(Brit)*, behavior *(US)*; **das ist doch keine ~!** that's no way to behave!; **was ist das (denn) für eine ~?** what sort of a way to behave is that?; **ist das vielleicht** or **etwa eine ~!** that's no way to behave!

Art. *abbr von* **Artikel**

Art-: **Art|an|ga|be** F *(Gram)* adverb of manner; *(= Adverbialbestimmung)* adverbial phrase of manner; **Art|bil|dung** F speciation *(form)*

Ar|te|fakt [arteˈfakt] NT **-(e)s, -e** *(geh)* artefact

art|ei|gen ADJ *(Biol)* species-specific

ar|ten [ˈaːɐtn] VI *aux sein (geh)* **nach jdm ~** to take after sb → *auch* **geartet**

Ar|ten-: **ar|ten|reich** ADJ *Lebensraum, Wald etc* species-rich; **diese Tierklasse ist sehr ~** this class of animal contains a large number of species; **Ar|ten|reich|tum** M *(Biol)* diversity of species; **Ar|ten|schutz** M protection of species

Ar|ten|schutz-: **Ar|ten|schutz|ab|kom|men** NT agreement on the protection of endangered species, biodiversity treaty; **Ar|ten|schutz|kon|fe|renz** F conference on the protection of endangered species

Ar|ten|schwund M extinction of species

Ar|ten|ster|ben NT extinction of species

Ar|ten|tod M extinction as a species; **vom ~ bedroht sein** to be threatened with extinction as a species; **den ~ sterben** to become extinct or die out as a species

Art-: **art|er|hal|tend** ADJ survival *attr* ADV **das wirkte sich ~ aus** that contributed to the survival of the species; **Art|er|hal|tung** F survival of the species

Ar|te|rie [arˈteːriə] F **-, -n** artery

ar|te|ri|ell [arteˈriɛl] ADJ arterial

Ar|te|ri|en|ver|kal|kung F *(inf)* hardening of the arteries; **~ haben** *(fig)* to be senile

Ar|te|rio|skle|ro|se [arterioskleˈroːzə] F arteriosclerosis

ar|te|sisch [arˈteːzɪʃ] ADJ **~er Brunnen** artesian well

Art-: **art|fremd** ADJ *(Biol)* foreign (to the species); **Art|ge|nos|se** M, **Art|ge|nos|sin** F *(= Tier/Pflanze)* animal/plant of the same species; *(= Mensch)* person of the same type; **art|ge|recht** ADJ appropriate to the species; **eine ~e Tierhaltung** livestock farming methods which are appropriate for each species; **art|gleich** ADJ *(Biol)* of the same species; *Mensch* of the same type

Arth|ri|tis [arˈtriːtɪs] F **-, Arthritiden** [artriˈtiːdn] arthritis

arth|ri|tisch [arˈtriːtɪʃ] ADJ arthritic

Arth|ro|se [arˈtroːzə] F **-, -n** arthrosis

ar|ti|fi|zi|ell [artifiˈtsiɛl] ADJ *(geh)* artificial

ar|tig [ˈaːɐtɪç] ADJ **a** *Kind, Hund etc* good, well-behaved *no adv*; **sei schön ~** be a good boy/dog *etc*!, be good! **b** *(old: = galant)* courteous **c** *(old: = anmutig)* charming

-ar|tig ADJ *suf* -like; **gummiartig** rubberlike, rubbery

Ar|tig|keit F **-, -en** **a** *(= Wohlerzogenheit)* good behaviour *(Brit)* or behavior *(US)*; *(old) (= Galanterie)* courtesy, courteousness; *(= Anmut)* charm **b** *(old) (= Kompliment)* compliment; *(= höfliche Bemerkung)* pleasantry; **jdm einige ~en sagen** to make a few courteous remarks to sb

Ar|ti|kel [arˈtiːkl, -ˈtɪkl] M **-s, -** *(alle Bedeutungen)* article; *(= Lexikonartikel auch)* entry; *(Comm auch)* item

Ar|ti|kel-: **Ar|ti|kel|rei|he** F, **Ar|ti|kel|se|rie** F series of articles; **Ar|ti|kel|über|schrift** F *(= Schlagzeile)* headline

Ar|ti|ku|la|ti|on [artikulaˈtsioːn] F **-, -en** articulation; *(= deutliche Aussprache auch)* enunciation; *(Mus)* phrasing

Ar|ti|ku|la|ti|ons-: **ar|ti|ku|la|ti|ons|fä|hig** ADJ articulate; *(Phon)* able to articulate; **Ar|ti|ku|la|ti|ons|fä|hig|keit** F articulateness; *(Phon)* ability to articulate; **Ar|ti|ku|la|ti|ons|or|ga|ne** PL organs *pl* of speech; **Ar|ti|ku|la|ti|ons|ver|mö|gen** NT = **Artikulationsfähigkeit**

ar|ti|ku|la|to|risch [artikulaˈtoːrɪʃ] ADJ *(Phon)* articulatory

ar|ti|ku|lie|ren [artikuˈliːrən] *ptp* **artikuliert** VTI to articulate; *(= deutlich aussprechen auch)* to enunciate; *(Mus)* to phrase; **sich artikuliert ausdrücken** to be articulate VR *(fig geh)* to express oneself

Ar|ti|ku|lie|rung F **-, -en** articulation; *(= deutliche Aussprache auch)* enunciation; *(Mus)* phrasing

Ar|til|le|rie [ˈartɪləriː, artɪləˈriː] F **-, -n** [-ˈriːən] artillery

Ar|til|le|rie- *in cpds* artillery; **Ar|til|le|rie|be|schuss** M artillery fire; **Ar|til|le|rie|ge|fecht** NT artillery fighting or engagement

Ar|til|le|rist [ˈartɪlərɪst, artɪləˈrɪst] M **-en, -en** artilleryman

Ar|ti|scho|cke [artiˈʃɔkə] F **-, -n** (globe) artichoke

Ar|ti|scho|cken|bo|den M *usu pl* artichoke bottom

Ar|ti|scho|cken|herz NT artichoke heart

Ar|tist [arˈtɪst] M **-en, -en**, **Ar|tis|tin** [-ˈtɪstɪn] F **-, -nen** **a** (circus or *(im Varietee)* variety) artiste or performer **b** *(obs, geh: = Meister)* artist (+*gen* at) **c** *(inf: = spielerisch handelnder Mensch)* joker *(inf)*

Ar|tis|ten|fa|kul|tät F *(Hist)* Faculty of Arts

Ar|tis|tik [arˈtɪstɪk] F **-**, *no pl* artistry; *(= Zirkus/Varieteekunst)* circus/variety performing

ar|tis|tisch [arˈtɪstɪʃ] ADJ **a** **sein ~es Können** his ability as a performer; **eine ~e Glanzleistung/~ einmalige Leistung** *(in Zirkus/Varietee)* a miraculous/unique feat of circus/variety artistry; **eine ~e Sensation** a sensational performance **b** *(= geschickt)* masterly *no adv* **c** *(= formalkünstlerisch)* artistic

Ar|to|thek [artoˈteːk] F **-, -en** picture (lending) library

Ar|tur [ˈartʊr] M **-s** Arthur

Ar|tus [ˈartʊs] M **-'** *(Hist, Myth)* (King) Arthur

Art-: **art|ver|schie|den** ADJ of different species; **art|ver|wandt** ADJ of the same type; *(Biol)* species-related; **Art|ver|wandt|schaft** F *(Biol)* species relationship; **Art|wort** NT *pl* **-wörter** *(Gram)* adjective

Arz|nei [aːɐtsˈnai, artsˈnai] F **-, -en** *(lit, fig)* medicine; **das war für ihn eine bittere/heilsame ~** *(fig)* that was a painful/useful lesson for him

Arz|nei-: **Arz|nei|buch** NT pharmacopoeia; **Arz|nei|fläsch|chen** NT medicine bottle; **Arz|nei|kun|de** F, **Arz|nei|leh|re** F pharmacology

Arz|nei|mit|tel NT drug

Arz|nei|mit|tel-: **Arz|nei|mit|tel|for|schung** F pharmacological research; **Arz|nei|mit|tel|ge|setz** NT law governing the manufacture and prescription of drugs; **Arz|nei|mit|tel|her|stel|ler(in)** M(F) drug manufacturer or company; **Arz|nei|mit|tel|leh|re** F pharmacology; **Arz|nei|mit|tel|miss|brauch** M drug abuse; **Arz|nei|mit|tel|sucht** F addiction to medicines, dependency on medication, pharmacomania *(spec)*; **Arz|nei|mit|tel|ver|sor|gung** F provision of drugs (+*gen* to)

Arz|nei-: **Arz|nei|pflan|ze** F medicinal plant; **Arz|nei|schränk|chen** NT medicine cupboard

Arzt [aːɐtst, artst] M **-es, =e** [ˈɛːɐtstə, ˈɛrtstə], **Ärz|tin** [ˈɛːɐtstɪn, ˈɛrtstɪn] F **-, -nen** doctor, physician *(old, form)*, medical practitioner *(form)*; *(= Facharzt)* specialist; *(= Chirurg)* surgeon; **praktischer ~, praktische Ärztin** general practitioner, GP; **eine Ärztin** a (woman or female) doctor

Arzt|be|ruf M medical profession

Ärz|te-: **Ärz|te|be|steck** NT set of surgical instruments; **Ärz|te|haus** NT health clinic, medical centre *(Brit)*, medical building *(US)*; **Ärz|te|kam|mer** F ≈ General Medical Council *(Brit)*, ≈ State Medical Board of Registration *(US)*; **Ärz|te|kol|le|gi|um** NT, **Ärz|te|kom|mis|si|on** F medical advisory board; **Ärz|te|kon|gress** M medical or doctors' congress; **Ärz|te|man|gel** M shortage of doctors

Ärz|te|schaft [ˈɛːɐtstəʃaft, ˈɛrtstə-] F **-, -en** medical profession

Ärz|te|ver|tre|ter(in) M(F) *(von Arzneimittelfirma)* medical representative

Arzt-: **Arzt|feh|ler** M doctor's professional error; **Arzt|frau** F doctor's wife; **Arzt|hel|fer(in)** M(F), **Arzt|hil|fe** F doctor's assistant

Ärz|tin [ˈɛːɐtstɪn, ˈɛrtstɪn] F → **Arzt**

Arzt-: **Arzt|kit|tel** M (doctor's) white coat; **Arzt|kos|ten** PL doctor's or medical fees *pl*

ärzt|lich [ˈɛːɐtstlɪç, ˈɛrtst-] ADJ medical ADV *beraten, untersuchen* medically; **er ließ sich ~ behandeln** he went to a doctor for treatment; **~ empfohlen** recommended by doctors; **bei uns sind Sie bestens ~ aufgehoben** you get the best medical treatment here

Arzt-: **Arzt|pra|xis** F doctor's practice; **Arzt|rech|nung** F doctor's bill; **Arzt|ro|man** M hospital romance; **Arzt|ter|min** M doctor's or medical appointment; **Arzt|wahl** F choice of doctor

As △ [as] NT **-es, -e** → **Ass**

As NT **-, -** *(Mus)* A flat

As|best [asˈbɛst] NT **-(e)s**, *no pl* asbestos

As|best- *in cpds* asbestos; **As|best|be|ton** M asbestos cement; **as|best|frei** ADJ free from or of asbestos, asbestos-free; **as|best|hal|tig** ADJ containing asbestos *pred*, asbestos-containing *attr*

As|bes|to|se [asbɛsˈtoːzə] F **-, -n** asbestosis

As|best-: **As|best|plat|te** F *(für Topf)* asbestos mat; *(für Bügeleisen)* asbestos stand; **As|best|sa|nie|rung** F asbestos abatement; **As|best|staub** M asbestos particles *pl*, asbestos dust; **as|best|ver|seucht** ADJ contaminated with asbestos *pred*

Aschan|ti|nuss [aˈʃanti-] F *(Aus)* peanut, groundnut

Asch-: **Asch|be|cher** M ashtray; **asch|blond** ADJ ash blond

Asche ['aʃə] F -, -n ash(es *pl*); *(von Zigarette, Vulkan)* ash; *(fig) (= sterbliche Überreste)* ashes *pl*; *(= Trümmer)* ruins *pl*; *(nach Feuer)* ashes *pl*; **zu ~ werden** to turn to dust; **sich** *(dat)* **~ aufs Haupt streuen** *(fig geh)* to wear sackcloth and ashes

Äsche ['ɛʃə] F -, -n grayling

Asch|ei|mer ['aʃ-] M *(dial)* ash can *(esp US)*, ash bin

Aschen-: **Aschen|bahn** F cinder track; **Aschen|be|cher** M ashtray; **Aschen|brö|del** [-brøːdl] NT -s, - *(Liter, fig)* Cinderella, Cinders *(Brit inf)*; **Aschen|brö|del|da|sein** NT Cinderella existence; **Aschen|ei|mer** M ash can *(esp US)*, ash bin; **Aschen|kas|ten** M ash pan; **Aschen|platz** M *(Ftbl)* cinder pitch; *(Tennis)* clay court; **Aschen|put|tel** [-pʊtl] NT -s, - *(Liter, fig)* Cinderella, Cinders *(Brit inf)*; **Aschen|re|gen** M shower of ash

Ascher ['aʃɐ] M -s, - *(inf)* ashtray

Asche|re|gen M ashfall, shower of ash

Ascher|mitt|woch [aʃɐ'mɪtvɔx] M Ash Wednesday

> **ASCHERMITTWOCH**
>
> **Aschermittwoch** (Ash Wednesday) marks the end of **Karneval** and is the first day of Lent. Devout Catholics go to church and have a cross of ashes smeared on their foreheads as a reminder of the transience of human life.
> In Bavaria there is also **politischer Aschermittwoch**. Political parties hold rallies at which they review their own policies and those of their rivals. National party leaders are often among the speakers. For this reason **politischer Aschermittwoch** is a focus of attention for the whole of Germany. → KARNEVAL

Asch-: **asch|fahl** ADJ ashen; **asch|far|ben** [-farbn], **asch|far|big** ADJ ash-coloured *(Brit)*, ash-colored *(US)*; **asch|grau** ADJ ash-grey *(Brit)*, ash-gray *(US)*; **Asch|kas|ten** M ash pan

Asch|ram ['aːʃram] M -s, -s ashram

ASCII- ['askiː-] *(Comput)*: **ASCII-Code** M ASCII code; **ASCII-Da|tei** F ASCII file

As|cor|bin|säu|re [askɔr'biːn-] F ascorbic acid

ASEAN ['eːsiɛn] F OR M - *abbr von* **Association of South East Asian Nations** ASEAN; **~-Staat** ASEAN country *or* state

A-Sei|te ['aː-] F *(von Schallplatte)* A-side

Asen ['aːzn] PL *(Myth)* Aesir *pl*

äsen ['ɛːzn] *(Hunt)* VI/R to graze, to browse VT to graze on

asep|tisch [a'zɛptɪʃ] ADJ aseptic ADV aseptically

Äser ['ɛːzɐ] M -s, - *(Hunt)* mouth

Äser ['ɛːzɐ] *pl von* **Aas**

Aser|baid|schan [azɛrbai'dʒaːn] NT -s Azerbaijan

Aser|baid|scha|ner [azɛrbai'dʒaːnɐ] M -s, -, **Aser|baid|scha|ne|rin** [-ərɪn] F -, -nen Azerbaijani

aser|baid|scha|nisch [azɛrbai'dʒaːnɪʃ] ADJ Azerbaijani

Aser|beid|schan *etc* [azɛrbai'dʒaːn] NT = **Aserbaidschan** *etc*

ase|xu|ell ['azɛksuɛl, azɛ'ksuɛl] ADJ asexual

Ash|ram ['aːʃram] M -s, -s ashram

Asi|at [a'ziaːt] M -en, -en, **Asi|a|tin** [a'ziaːtɪn] F -, -nen Asian

Asi|a|ti|ka [a'ziaːtika] PL Orientalia *pl*

asi|a|tisch [a'ziaːtɪʃ] ADJ Asian, Asiatic; **~e Grippe** Asian *or* Asiatic *(US)* flu; **der ~-pazifische Raum** the Pacific Rim

Asi|en ['aːziən] NT -s Asia

As|ke|se [as'keːzə] F -, *no pl* asceticism

As|ket [as'keːt] M -en, -en, **As|ke|tin** [-'keːtɪn] F -, -nen ascetic

as|ke|tisch [as'keːtɪʃ] ADJ ascetic ADV ascetically

As|kor|bin|säu|re [askɔr'biːn-] F ascorbic acid

Äs|ku|lap-: **Äs|ku|lap|schlan|ge** F snake of Aesculapius; **Äs|ku|lap|stab** M staff of Aesculapius

Äsop [ɛ'zoːp] M -s Aesop

äso|pisch [ɛ'zoːpɪʃ] ADJ Aesopic; **eine ~e Fabel** one of Aesop's Fables

aso|zi|al ['azotsiaːl, azo'tsiaːl] ADJ asocial ADV asocially

Aso|zi|a|le(r) ['azotsiaːlə] MF *decl as adj (pej)* antisocial person/man/woman *etc*; **~** *pl* antisocial elements

Aso|zi|a|li|tät [azotsiali'tɛːt] F -, *no pl (von Mensch)* antisocial nature; *(= Verhalten)* antisocial behaviour *(Brit) or* behavior *(US)*

As|par|tam® [aspar'taːm] NT -s, -e aspartame

As|pekt [as'pɛkt] M -(e)s, -e aspect; **unter diesem ~ betrachtet** looking at it from this aspect *or* from this point of view; **einen neuen ~ bekommen** to take on a different complexion

As|phalt [as'falt, 'asfalt] M -(e)s, -e asphalt

As|phalt-: **As|phalt|be|ton** M asphalt; **As|phalt|blatt** NT *(pej inf)* scandal sheet; *(= Boulevardzeitung)* tabloid (newspaper); **As|phalt|de|cke** F asphalt surface; **As|phalt|dschun|gel** M *(pej inf: = Großstadt)* asphalt jungle

as|phal|tie|ren [asfal'tiːrən] *ptp* **asphaltiert** VT to asphalt, to tarmac

as|phal|tiert [asfal'tiːɐt] ADJ asphalt

As|phalt-: **As|phalt|ma|le|rei** F pavement *(Brit) or* sidewalk *(US)* art; **As|phalt|stra|ße** F asphalt road

As|pik [as'piːk, as'pɪk] M OR (AUS) NT -s, -e aspic

As|pi|rant [aspi'rant] M -en, -en, **As|pi|ran|tin** [-'rantɪn] F -, -nen **a** *(geh)* candidate *(für, auf +acc* for) **b** *(DDR Univ)* research assistant

As|pi|ran|tur [aspiran'tuːɐ] F -, -en *(DDR)* research assistantship

As|pi|ra|ta [aspi'raːta] F -, **Aspiraten** [-tn] *(Phon)* aspirate

As|pi|ra|ti|on [aspira'tsioːn] F -, -en **a** *usu pl (geh)* aspiration; **~en auf etw** *(acc) or* **nach etw haben** to have aspirations toward(s) sth, to aspire to sth **b** *(Phon)* aspiration

as|pi|rie|ren [aspi'riːrən] *ptp* **aspiriert** VI *(geh)* to aspire *(auf +acc* to); *(Aus)* to apply *(auf +acc* for) VT *(Phon)* to aspirate

aß *pret von* **essen**

Ass [as] NT -es, -e *(lit, fig)* ace; **alle vier ~e** *(lit)* all the aces

As|se|ku|ranz [aseku'rants] F -, -en *(old)* assurance; *(= Gesellschaft)* assurance company

As|sel ['asl] F -, -n isopod *(spec)*; *(= Rollassel, Kellerassel, Landassel auch)* woodlouse

As|semb|ler [ə'sɛmblɐ] M -s, - *(Comput)* assembler

As|semb|ler|spra|che F *(Comput)* assembly language

As|ser|vat [asɛr'vaːt] NT -(e)s, -e (court) exhibit

As|ser|va|ten|kam|mer F, **As|ser|va|ten|raum** M *room where court exhibits are kept*

As|ses|sor [a'sɛsoːɐ] M -s, **Assessoren** [-'soːrən], **As|ses|so|rin** [-'soːrɪn] F -, -nen *graduate civil servant who has completed his/her traineeship*

As|si|mi|la|ti|on [asimila'tsioːn] F -, -en assimilation; *(= Anpassung)* adjustment *(an +acc* to)

as|si|mi|la|to|risch [asimila'toːrɪʃ] ADJ assimilatory, assimilative

as|si|mi|lie|ren [asimi'liːrən] *ptp* **assimiliert** VT to assimilate VR to become assimilated; **sich an etw** *(acc)* **~** *(Mensch)* to adjust to sth

As|sis|tent [asɪs'tɛnt] M -en, -en, **As|sis|ten|tin** [-'tɛntɪn] F -, -nen assistant

As|sis|tenz [asɪs'tɛnts] F -, *(rare)* -en assistance; **unter ~ von ...** with the assistance of ...

As|sis|tenz-: **As|sis|tenz|arzt** M, **As|sis|tenz|ärz|tin** F junior doctor *(Brit)*, intern *(US)*; **As|sis|tenz|pro|fes|sor(in)** M(F) assistant professor

as|sis|tie|ren [asɪs'tiːrən] *ptp* **assistiert** VI to assist *(jdm* sb)

As|so|nanz [aso'nants] F -, -en *(Poet)* assonance

As|so|zi|a|ti|on [asotsia'tsioːn] F -, -en association

As|so|zi|a|ti|ons-: **As|so|zi|a|ti|ons|frei|heit** F freedom of association; **As|so|zi|a|ti|ons|ket|te** F chain of associations; **As|so|zi|a|ti|ons|test** M *(Psych)* (free) association test

as|so|zi|a|tiv [asotsia'tiːf] *(Psych, geh)* ADJ associative ADV *verbunden* through association; **Erinnerungen ~ hervorrufen** to evoke memories through association; **etw ~ mit etw verbinden** to associate sth with sth

as|so|zi|ie|ren [asotsi'iːrən] *ptp* **assoziiert** *(geh)* VT to associate; **mit etw assoziiert werden** to be associated with sth; **mit Grün assoziiere ich Ruhe** I associate green with peace; **die Musik assoziierte bei mir Unangenehmes** the music suggested something unpleasant to me VI to make associations; **frei ~** to make free associations VR **a** *(Vorstellungen etc)* to have associations *(in +dat, bei* for); **beim Anblick des Hauses ~ sich in** *or* **bei mir Kindheitserinnerungen** when I see the house I think of my childhood **b** *(= an-, zusammenschließen)* **sich mit jdm ~** to join with sb; **sich an jdn/etw ~** to become associated to sb/sth

as|so|zi|iert [asotsi'iːɐt] ADJ associated; *Mitgliedschaft* associate; **mit der EU ~ sein** to be an associate member of the EU

As|su|an|(stau)|damm [a'suaːn-] M Aswan (High) Dam

As|sy|rer [a'syːrɐ] M -s, -, **As|sy|re|rin** [-ərɪn] F -, -nen Assyrian

As|sy|ri|en [a'syːriən] NT -s Assyria

As|sy|ri|er [a'syːriɐ] M -s, -, **As|sy|ri|e|rin** [-iərɪn] F -, -nen Assyrian

as|sy|risch [a'syːrɪʃ] ADJ Assyrian

Ast [ast] M -(e)s, =e ['ɛstə] **a** branch, bough; *(fig: von Nerv)* branch; **sich in Äste teilen** to branch; **den ~ absägen, auf dem man sitzt** *(fig)* to dig one's own grave; **einen ~ durchsägen** *(hum)* to snore like a grampus *(inf)*, to saw wood *(US inf)* → **absteigen b b** *(im Holz)* knot **c** *(inf) (= Rücken)* back; *(= Buckel)* hump(back), hunchback; **sich** *(dat)* **einen ~ lachen** *(inf)* to double up (with laughter)

AStA ['asta] M -s, **Asten** ['astn] *(Univ) abbr von* **Allgemeiner Studentenausschuss**

As|tat [as'taːt, as'taːt] NT -s, *no pl*, **As|ta|tin** [asta'tiːn] NT -s, *no pl (abbr* **At**) astatine

Äst|chen ['ɛstçən] NT -s, - *dim von* **Ast**

as|ten ['astn] *(inf)* VI **a** *(= sich anstrengen)* to slog *(inf)* **b** *(= büffeln)* to swot *(Brit)*, to cram **c** *aux sein (= sich fortbewegen)* to drag oneself VT to hump *(inf)*, to lug *(Brit inf)*

As|ter ['astɐ] F -, -n aster, Michaelmas daisy

As|te|ro|id [astero'iːt] M -en, -en [-dn] *(Astron)* asteroid

Ast|ga|bel F fork (of a branch); **eine ~** a fork of a branch

As|the|ni|ker [a'steːnikɐ, as'teː-] M -s, -, **As|the|ni|ke|rin** [-ərɪn] F -, -nen asthenic

Äs|thet [ɛs'teːt] M -en, -en, **Äs|the|tin** [-'teːtɪn] F -, -nen aesthete

Äs|the|tik [ɛs'teːtɪk] F -, *no pl* **a** *(= Wissenschaft)* aesthetics *sing* **b** *(= Schönheit)* aesthetics *pl* **c** *(= Schönheitssinn)* aesthetic sense

Äs|the|ti|ker [ɛs'teːtikɐ] M -s, -, **Äs|the|ti|ke|rin** [-ərɪn] F -, -nen aesthetician

äs|the|tisch [ɛs'teːtɪʃ] ADJ aesthetic

äs|the|ti|sie|ren [ɛsteti'ziːrən] *ptp* **ästhetisiert** *(geh: usu pej)* VT to aestheticize VI to talk about aesthetics

Äs|the|ti|zis|mus [ɛsteti'tsɪsmʊs] M -, *no pl (pej geh)* aestheticism

Äs|the|ti|zist [ɛsteti'tsɪst] M -en, -en, **Äs|the|ti|zis|tin** [-'tsɪstɪn] F -, -nen aestheticist

Asth|ma ['astma] NT -s, *no pl* asthma

Asth|ma-: **Asth|ma|an|fall** M asthma attack; **asth|ma|krank** ADJ astmatic, suffering from asthma *pred*

Asth|ma|ti|ker [ast'ma:tikɐ] M -s, -, **Asth|ma|ti|ke|rin** [-ərɪn] F -, -nen asthmatic

asth|ma|tisch [ast'ma:tɪʃ] ADJ asthmatic

as|tig ['astɪç] ADJ *Holz* knotty, gnarled

As|tig|ma|tis|mus [astɪgma'tɪsmʊs] M -, *no pl* *(Med)* astigmatism, astigmia

Ast|loch NT knothole

ast|ral [as'tra:l] ADJ astral

Ast|ral-: **Ast|ral|kör|per** M, **Ast|ral|leib** M *(Philos)* astral body; *(iro inf)* beautiful *or* heavenly body; **Ast|ral|rei|se** F astral journey

ast|rein ADJ **a** *Holz, Brett* free of knots **b** *(fig inf: = moralisch einwandfrei)* straight *(inf)*, above board, on the level *(inf)* **c** *(fig inf: = echt)* genuine **d** *(dated sl: = prima)* fantastic ADV *(dated sl: = prima)* fantastically

Ast|ro-: **Ast|ro|lo|ge** [astro'lo:gə] M -n, -n, **Ast|ro|lo|gin** [-'lo:gɪn] F -, -nen astrologer; **Ast|ro|lo|gie** [astrolo'gi:] F -, *no pl* astrology; **ast|ro|lo|gisch** [astro'lo:gɪʃ] ADJ astrological ADV ~ **interessiert sein** to be interested in astrology; **Ast|ro|me|di|zin** F astro-medicine; **Ast|ro|naut** [astro'naut] M -en, -en, **Ast|ro|nau|tin** [-'nautɪn] F -, -nen astronaut; **Ast|ro|nau|tik** [astro'nautɪk] F astronautics *sing*; **ast|ro|nau|tisch** [astro'nautɪʃ] ADJ astronautic(al); **Ast|ro|nom** [astro'no:m] M -en, -en, **Ast|ro|no|min** [-'no:mɪn] F -, -nen astronomer; **Ast|ro|no|mie** [astrono'mi:] F -, *no pl* astronomy; **ast|ro|no|misch** [astro'no:mɪʃ] ADJ *(lit)* astronomical; *(fig auch)* astronomic; **~e Navigation** astronavigation

ast|ro|phisch ['astro:fɪʃ, a'stro:-] ADJ *(Poet)* not divided into strophes

Ast|ro-: **Ast|ro|phy|sik** F astrophysics *sing*; **ast|ro|phy|si|ka|lisch** ADJ astrophysical; **Ast|ro|phy|si|ker(in)** M(F) astrophysicist

Ast|werk NT branches *pl*

ASU ['a:zu] F -, *no pl abbr von* **Abgassonderuntersuchung**

Äsung ['ɛ:zʊŋ] F -, -en *(Hunt)* grazing

ASW [a:lɛs've:] *no art* -, *no pl abbr von* **außersinnliche Wahrnehmung** ESP

Asyl [a'zy:l] NT -s, -e **a** *(= Schutz)* sanctuary *no art (liter)*; *(= politisches Asyl)* (political) asylum *no art*; **jdm ~ gewähren** to grant sb sanctuary *(liter)*/(political) asylum; **um ~ bitten** *or* **nachsuchen** *(form)* to ask *or* apply *(form)* for (political) asylum **b** *(old: = Heim)* home, asylum

Asy|lant [azy'lant] M -en, -en *(oft neg!)*, **Asy|lan|tin** [-'lantɪn] F -, -nen *(oft neg!)* asylum seeker

Asy|lan|ten|wohn|heim NT *(oft neg!)* hostel for asylum seekers

Asyl-: **Asyl|an|trag** M application for (political) asylum; **asyl|be|rech|tigt** ADJ entitled to (political) asylum; **Asyl|be|rech|tig|te(r)** MF *decl as adj* person entitled to (political) asylum; **Asyl|be|wer|ber(in)** M(F) asylum seeker; **Asyl|po|li|tik** F policy on asylum; **Asyl|recht** NT **a** *sing (Pol)* right of (political) asylum **b** *(Jur)* asylum laws *pl*; **Asyl|su|chen|de(r)** [-zu:xndə] MF *decl as adj* asylum seeker; **Asyl|ver|fah|ren** NT **a** procedure for seeking asylum **b** *(Jur: = Verhandlung)* court hearing to determine a person's right to political asylum; **Asyl|wer|ber(in)** M(F) *(Aus)* asylum seeker

Asym|met|rie [azyme'tri:] F lack of symmetry, asymmetry

asym|met|risch ['azyme:trɪʃ, azy'me:trɪʃ] ADJ asymmetric(al); *(Comput)* asymmetric; *(fig) Gespräch* one-sided ADV asymmetrically

Asymp|to|te [azym'pto:tə] F -, -n asymptote

asymp|to|tisch [azym'pto:tɪʃ] ADJ asymptotic

asyn|chron ['azynkro:n, azyn'kro:n] ADJ asynchronous *(form, Comput)*, out of synchronism ADV *(Comput)* out of synchronism

Asyn|chron|mo|tor [azyn'kro:n-] M *(Tech)* asynchronous motor

asyn|de|tisch ['azynde:tɪʃ, azyn'de:tɪʃ] ADJ *(Ling)* asyndetic

Asyn|de|ton [a'zyndetɔn] NT -s, **Asyndeta** [-ta] *(Ling)* parataxis

As|zen|dent [astsɛn'dɛnt] M -en, -en **a** *(Astrol)* ascendant **b** *(= Vorfahr)* ancestor, ascendant *(form)*

as|zen|die|ren [astsɛn'di:rən] *ptp* **aszendiert** VI **a** *aux sein (Astrol)* to be in the ascendant **b** *aux sein or haben (obs)* to be promoted *(zu* to)

As|ze|se [as'tse:zə] F -, *no pl* asceticism

at [a:'te:] *abbr von* **Atmosphäre** *(Phys)*

A. T. *abbr von* **Altes Testament** OT

ata ['ata] ADV *(baby-talk)* ~ (~) **gehen** to go walkies *(baby-talk)*

atak|tisch [a'taktɪʃ, 'ataktɪʃ] ADJ uncoordinated

Ata|vis|mus [ata'vɪsmʊs] M -, **Atavismen** [-mən] atavism

ata|vis|tisch [ata'vɪstɪʃ] ADJ atavistic ADV atavistically

Ate|li|er [ate'lie:, atə'lie:] NT -s, -s studio; **das Filmprojekt ging letzte Woche ins ~** shooting (on the film) started last week

Ate|li|er-: **Ate|li|er|auf|nah|me** F **a** *(= Produkt)* studio shot **b** *usu pl (= Vorgang)* studio work *no pl*; **Ate|li|er|fens|ter** NT studio window; **Ate|li|er|fest** NT studio party; **Ate|li|er|woh|nung** F studio apartment

Atem ['a:təm] M -s, *no pl* **a** *(= das Atmen)* breathing; **den ~ anhalten** *(lit, fig)* to hold one's breath; **mit angehaltenem ~** *(lit)* holding one's breath; *(fig)* with bated breath; **einen kurzen ~ haben** to be short-winded; **außer ~ sein** to be out of breath; **wieder zu ~ kommen** to get one's breath back; **einen langen/den längeren ~ haben** *(fig)* to have a lot of/more staying power; **jdn in ~ halten** to keep sb in suspense *or* on tenterhooks; **das verschlug mir den ~** that took my breath away → **ausgehen VI j**

b *(lit, fig: = Atemluft)* breath; **~ holen** *or* **schöpfen** *(lit)* to take *or* draw a breath; *(fig)* to get one's breath back

c *(fig geh: = Augenblick)* **in einem/im selben ~** in one/the same breath

Atem-: **Atem|be|klem|mung** F difficulty in breathing; **atem|be|rau|bend** ADJ breathtaking ADV breathtakingly; **Atem|be|schwer|den** PL trouble *sing* in breathing; **Atem|ge|rät** NT breathing apparatus; *(Med)* respirator; **Atem|ge|räusch** NT respiratory sounds *pl*; **Atem|gift** NT respiratory poison; **Atem|gym|nas|tik** F breathing exercises *pl*; **Atem|ho|len** NT -s, *no pl* breathing; **man kommt nicht mehr zum ~** *(fig)* you hardly have time to breathe; **zum ~ auftauchen** to come up for air; **Atem|läh|mung** F respiratory paralysis; **atem|los** ADJ *(lit, fig)* breathless ADV breathlessly; **Atem|lo|sig|keit** F -, *no pl* breathlessness; **Atem|luft** F **unsere ~** the air we breathe; **Atem|mas|ke** F breathing mask; **Atem|not** F difficulty in breathing; **Atem|pau|se** F *(fig)* breathing time *no art*, breathing space; **eine ~ einlegen/brauchen** to take/need a breather; **Atem|schutz|ge|rät** NT breathing apparatus; **Atem|schutz|mas|ke** F breathing mask; **Atem|still|stand** M respiratory standstill, apnoea *(Brit)*, apnea *(US)*; **Atem|tech|nik** F breathing technique; **Atem|übung** F *(Med)* breathing exercise; **Atem|we|ge** PL *(Anat)* respiratory tracts *pl*; **Atem|wegs|er|kran|kung** F respiratory disease; **Atem|zent|rum** NT *(Anat)* respiratory centre *(Brit) or* center *(US)*; **Atem|zug** M breath; **in einem/im selben ~** *(fig)* in one/the same breath

a ter|go [a 'tɛrgo] ADV on top

Athe|is|mus [ate'ɪsmʊs] M -, *no pl* atheism

Athe|ist [ate'ɪst] M -en, -en, **Athe|is|tin** [-'ɪstɪn] F -, -nen atheist

athe|is|tisch [ate'ɪstɪʃ] ADJ atheist(ic)

Athen [a'te:n] NT -s Athens

Athe|ner [a'te:nɐ] ADJ Athenian

Athe|ner [a'te:nɐ] M -s, -, **Athe|ne|rin** [-ərɪn] F -, -nen Athenian

athe|nisch [a'te:nɪʃ] ADJ Athenian

Äther ['ɛ:tɐ] M -s, *no pl* **a** ether **b** *(poet)* (a)ether *(poet)*; *(Rad)* air; **etw in den ~ schicken** to put sth on the air; **über den ~** over the air

äthe|risch [ɛ'te:rɪʃ] ADJ *(Liter)* ethereal; *(Chem)* essential

äthe|ri|sie|ren [ɛteri'zi:rən] *ptp* **ätherisiert** VT to etherize

Äther-: **Äther|nar|ko|se** F etherization; **Äther|wel|len** PL *(Rad)* radio waves *pl*

Äthi|o|pi|en [ɛ'tio:piən] NT -s Ethiopia

Äthi|o|pi|er [ɛ'tio:piɐ] M -s, -, **Äthi|o|pi|e|rin** [-iərɪn] F -, -nen Ethiopian

äthi|o|pisch [ɛ'tio:pɪʃ] ADJ Ethiopian

Ath|let [at'le:t] M -en, -en, **Ath|le|tin** [-'le:tɪn] F -, -nen athlete

Ath|le|tik [at'le:tɪk] F -, *no pl* athletics *sing*

Ath|le|ti|ker [at'le:tikɐ] M -s, -, **Ath|le|ti|ke|rin** [-ərɪn] F -, -nen athletic type

ath|le|tisch [at'le:tɪʃ] ADJ athletic ADV athletically; **~ aussehen** to look athletic

Äthyl|al|ko|hol [ɛ'ty:l-] M ethyl alcohol

Äthyl|äther M ethyl ether

At|lant [at'lant] M -en, -en atlas

At|lan|ten *pl von* **Atlas, Atlant**

At|lan|tik [at'lantɪk] M -s Atlantic

At|lan|tik|wall M *(Mil Hist)* Atlantic Wall

at|lan|tisch [at'lantɪʃ] ADJ Atlantic; **ein ~es Hoch** a high-pressure area over the Atlantic; *(vom Atlantik kommend)* a high-pressure area from the Atlantic; **der Atlantische Ozean** the Atlantic Ocean; **das Atlantische Bündnis** the Atlantic Alliance

At|las ['atlas] M - *or* **-ses, -se** *or* **Atlanten** [at'lantn] atlas

At|las M -', *no pl (Myth)* Atlas

At|las M **-ses, -se** *(= Seidenatlas)* satin; *(mit Baumwolle)* sateen

At|las M - *(Geog)* Atlas Mountains *pl*

At|las|sei|de F satin

at|men ['a:tmən] VT *(lit, fig geh)* to breathe VI to breathe, to respire *(form)*; **frei ~** *(fig)* to breathe freely

At|mo|sphä|re [atmo'sfɛ:rə] F *(Phys, fig)* atmosphere

At|mo|sphä|ren-: **At|mo|sphä|ren|druck** M *pl* **-drücke** atmospheric pressure; *(= Maßeinheit)* atmosphere; **At|mo|sphä|ren|über|druck** M **a** atmospheric excess pressure **b** *(= Maßeinheit)* atmosphere (of pressure) above atmospheric pressure

at|mo|sphä|risch [atmo'sfɛ:rɪʃ] ADJ atmospheric; **~e Störungen** atmospherics *pl* ADV **~ dichte Musik** very atmospheric music; **ein ~ reiches Bild/Bühnenbild** a picture/scene full of atmosphere; **die Beziehungen zwischen den beiden Ländern haben sich ~ verbessert** the atmosphere between the two countries has improved

At|mung ['a:tmʊŋ] F -, *no pl* breathing; *(Eccl, Med)* respiration

At|mungs-: **at|mungs|ak|tiv** ADJ *Material, Kleidung* breathable; **At|mungs|ap|pa|rat** M breathing apparatus; *(Med)* respirator; **At|mungs|or|ga|ne** PL respiratory organs *pl*; **At|mungs|zent|rum** NT respiratory centre *(Brit) or* center *(US)*

Atoll [a'tɔl] NT -s, -e atoll

Atom [a'to:m] NT -s, -e atom

Atom- *in cpds* atomic → *auch* **Kern-**; **Atom|ab|fall** M nuclear *or* radioactive *or* atomic waste; **Atom|an|griff** M nuclear attack; **Atom|an|la|ge** F atomic plant; **Atom|an|trieb** M nuclear *or* atomic propulsion; **ein U-Boot mit ~** a nuclear-powered submarine

ato|mar [ato'ma:ɐ] ADJ atomic, nuclear; *Struktur* atomic; *Drohung* nuclear; **~e Abfälle** nuclear waste ADV *bedrohen, vernichten* with a nuclear attack; **~ bestückt** armed with nuclear warheads; **~ angetrieben** nuclear-powered

Atom-: **Atom|aus|stieg** M, *no pl* abandonment of nuclear energy; **Atom|ba|sis** F nuclear base; **Atom|be|hör|de** F Atomic Energy Authority *(Brit) or* Commission *(US)*; **atom|be|trie|ben** [-bətri:bn] ADJ nuclear-powered;

Atom|bom|be F atomic *or* atom *(esp Brit)* bomb; **Atom|bom|ben|ex|plo|si|on** F atomic *or* nuclear explosion; **atom|bom|ben|si|cher** ADJ atomic *or* nuclear blast-proof ADV **~ gebaut** capable of withstanding a nuclear attack; **~ untergebracht** protected against nuclear attack; **Atom|bom|ben|ver|such** M atomic *or* nuclear test; **Atom|bom|ber** M nuclear bomber; **Atom|bun|ker** M atomic *or* nuclear blast-proof bunker; **Atom|bu|sen** M *(dated inf)* big bust *or* boobs *pl (inf)*; **Atom|club** M *(Press sl)* = **Atomklub**; **Atom|ener|gie** F nuclear energy; **Atom|ener|gie|be|hör|de** F **die (Internationale) ~** the (International) Atomic Energy Agency; **Atom|ex|plo|si|on** F atomic *or* nuclear explosion; **Atom|for|scher(in)** M(F) nuclear scientist; **Atom|for|schung** F atomic *or* nuclear research; **Atom|for|schungs|zent|rum** NT atomic *or* nuclear research centre *(Brit) or* center *(US)*; **Atom|geg|ner(in)** M(F) **~ sein** to be antinuclear; **aktiver ~** antinuclear activist; **Atom|ge|mein|de** F pronuclear lobby; **atom|ge|trie|ben** [-gətri:bn] ADJ nuclear-powered; **Atom|ge|wicht** NT atomic weight; **Atom|in|dust|rie** F nuclear industry

ato|misch [a'to:mɪʃ] ADJ *(Sw)* = **atomar**

ato|mi|sie|ren [atomi'zi:rən] *ptp* **atomisiert** VT to atomize; *(fig)* to smash to pieces *or* smithereens

Ato|mis|mus [ato'mɪsmʊs] M -, *no pl* atomism

Atom-: **Atom|ka|ta|stro|phe** F nuclear disaster; **Atom|kern** M atomic nucleus; **Atom|klub** M *(Press sl)* nuclear club; **Atom|kraft** F atomic *or* nuclear power *or* energy; **Atom|kraft|geg|ner(in)** M(F) anti-nuclear (power) protester; **Atom|kraft|werk** NT atomic *or* nuclear power station; **Atom|krieg** M atomic *or* nuclear war; **Atom|lob|by** F nuclear power lobby; **Atom|macht** F nuclear power; **Atom|mas|se** F *(Chem, Phys)* atomic mass; **Atom|me|di|zin** F, *no pl* nuclear medicine; **Atom|mei|ler** M nuclear reactor; **Atom|mo|dell** NT model of the atom

Atom|müll M atomic *or* nuclear *or* radioactive waste

Atom|müll-: **Atom|müll|de|po|nie** F nuclear waste disposal site; **Atom|müll|end|la|ger** NT (final) disposal *or* dumping *(pej)* site for nuclear *or* radioactive waste; **Atom|müll|trans|port** M transport of nuclear *or* radioactive waste

Atom-: **Atom|phy|sik** F atomic *or* nuclear physics *sing*; **Atom|phy|si|ker(in)** M(F) nuclear physicist; **Atom|pilz** M mushroom cloud; **Atom|po|li|tik** F nuclear policy; **Atom|ra|ke|te** F nuclear-powered rocket; *(= Waffe)* nuclear missile; **Atom|re|ak|tor** M nuclear reactor; **Atom|rüs|tung** F nuclear armament; **Atom|schwel|le** F nuclear threshold; **Atom|spal|tung** F nuclear fission; **die erste ~** the first splitting of the atom; **Atom|sperr|ver|trag** M nuclear *or* atomic weapons non-proliferation treaty; **Atom|spreng|kopf** M atomic *or* nuclear warhead; **Atom|spreng|kör|per** M nuclear explosive; **Atom|staat** M nuclear power; **Atom|stopp** M nuclear ban; **Atom|strah|lung** F nuclear radiation; **Atom|streit|macht** F nuclear capability; **Atom|strom** M *(inf)* electricity generated by nuclear power; **Atom|tech|nik** F nuclear technology, nucleonics *sing*

Atom|test M nuclear test

Atom|test-: **Atom|test|stopp** M nuclear test ban; **Atom|test|stopp|ab|kom|men** NT nuclear test ban treaty

Atom-: **Atom|tod** M *(Press sl)* nuclear death; **Atom|trieb|werk** NT nuclear engine; **Atom-U-Boot** NT nuclear submarine; **Atom|uhr** F atomic clock; **Atom|ver|such** M nuclear test; **Atom|ver|suchs|stopp** M nuclear test ban

Atom|waf|fe F nuclear *or* atomic weapon

Atom|waf|fen-: **atom|waf|fen|frei** ADJ nuclear-free; **Atom|waf|fen|sperr|ver|trag** M nuclear *or* atomic weapons nonproliferation treaty; **Atom|waf|fen|test** M, **Atom|waf|fen|ver|such** M nuclear test

Atom-: **Atom|wirt|schaft** F nuclear industry; **Atom|wis|sen|schaft** F nuclear *or* atomic science; **Atom|wis|sen|schaft|ler(in)** M(F) nuclear *or* atomic scientist; **Atom|zeit** F nuclear time; **Atom|zeit|al|ter** NT atomic *or* nuclear age; **Atom|zer|fall** M atomic disintegration *or* decay; **Atom|zer|trüm|me|rung** F splitting of the atom

ato|nal ['atona:l, ato'na:l] ADJ atonal

Ato|na|li|tät [atonali'tɛ:t] F -, *no pl* atonality

Ato|pi|ker [a'to:pikɐ] M **-s, -**, **Ato|pi|ke|rin** [-ərɪn] F **-, -nen** *(Med)* atopy sufferer

ato|pisch [a'to:pɪʃ] ADJ *(Med)* atopic

ato|xisch ['atɔksɪʃ, a'tɔksɪʃ] ADJ *(form)* nontoxic

At|ra|zin [atra'tsi:n] NT **-s**, *no pl (Chem)* atrazine

At|ri|um ['a:triʊm] NT **-s, Atrien** [-riən] *(Archit, Anat)* atrium

At|ri|um|haus NT house built around an open court *or* atrium

Atro|phie [atro'fi:] F **-, -n** [-'fi:ən] *(Med)* atrophy

atro|phisch [a'tro:fɪʃ] ADJ atrophied

ätsch [ɛ:tʃ] INTERJ *(inf)* ha-ha

At|ta|ché [ata'ʃe:] M **-s, -s** attaché

At|tach|ment [ə'tɛtʃmɛnt] NT *(Comput: = an E-Mail angehänge Datei)* attachment

At|ta|cke [a'takə] F **-, -n** *(= Angriff)* attack; *(Mil Hist)* (cavalry) charge; **eine ~ gegen jdn/etw reiten** *(lit)* to charge sb/sth; *(fig)* to attack sb/sth

at|ta|ckie|ren [ata'ki:rən] *ptp* **attackiert** VT *(= angreifen)* to attack; *(Mil Hist)* to charge

At|ten|tat ['atnta:t, atn'ta:t] NT **-(e)s, -e** assassination; *(= Attentatsversuch)* assassination attempt; **ein ~ auf jdn verüben** to assassinate sb; *(bei gescheitertem Versuch)* to make an attempt on sb's life; **ich habe ein ~ auf dich vor** *(hum)* listen, I've got a great idea

At|ten|tä|ter(in) M(F) assassin; *(bei gescheitertem Versuch)* would-be assassin

At|ten|tis|mus [atɛn'tɪsmʊs] M -, *no pl (pej)* wait-and-see policy

At|test [a'tɛst] NT **-(e)s, -e** certificate

at|tes|tie|ren [atɛs'ti:rən] *ptp* **attestiert** VT *(form)* to certify; **jdm seine Dienstuntauglichkeit** *etc* **~** to certify sb as unfit for duty *etc*

At|ti|ka ['atika] NT **-s** *(Geog)* Attica

At|ti|ka|woh|nung F *(Sw)* penthouse (flat *(Brit) or* apartment)

at|tisch ['atɪʃ] ADJ Attic

At|ti|tü|de [ati'ty:də] F **-, -n** *(geh)* **a** attitude **b** *(= Geste)* gesture

At|trak|ti|on [atrak'tsio:n] F **-, -en** attraction

at|trak|tiv [atrak'ti:f] ADJ attractive

At|trak|ti|vi|tät [atraktivi'tɛ:t] F -, *no pl* attractiveness

At|trap|pe [a'trapə] F **-, -n** dummy; *(fig: = Schein)* sham; **die ~ eines ...** a dummy ...; **bei ihr ist alles ~** everything about her is false

At|tri|but [atri'bu:t] NT **-(e)s, -e** *(geh, Gram)* attribute *(auch Comput)*

At|tri|but|satz M *(Gram)* relative clause

atü [a'ty:] *abbr von* **Atmosphärenüberdruck**

aty|pisch ['aty:pɪʃ, a'ty:pɪʃ] ADJ *(geh)* atypical

at|zen ['atsn] VT *(Hunt)* to feed

ät|zen ['ɛtsn] VTI **a** *(auf Platte)* to etch **b** *(Säure)* to corrode **c** *(Med)* to cauterize

ät|zend ADJ **a** *(lit) Säure* corrosive; *(Med)* caustic **b** *Geruch* pungent; *Rauch* choking; *Spott, Kritik* caustic **c** *(inf: = furchtbar)* lousy *(inf)*; **der Typ ist echt ~** that guy really grates on you *(inf)*

Ätz-: **Ätz|mit|tel** NT *(Chem)* corrosive; *(Med)* cautery, caustic; **Ätz|nat|ron** NT caustic soda; **Ätz|stift** M *(Med)* cautery; *(bei Friseur)* styptic pencil

At|zung ['atsʊŋ] F **-, -en** *(Hunt, hum) (= Vorgang)* feeding; *(= Futter)* food, fodder; **wann gibt es ~?** *(hum)* when is it feeding time?

Ät|zung ['ɛtsʊŋ] F **-, -en** etching; *(mit Säure)* corrosion; *(Med)* cauterization, cautery

au [au] INTERJ **a** ow, ouch; **au, das war knapp!** oh *or* God, that was close! **b** *(Ausdruck der Begeisterung)* oh

AU [a:'lu:] F -, *no pl abbr von* **Abgasuntersuchung**

Au [au] F **-, -en** *(S Ger, Aus)* meadow, pasture

aua ['aua] INTERJ ow, ouch

au|ber|gi|ne [obɛr'ʒi:nə] ADJ *pred,* **au|ber|gi|ne|far|ben** [-farbn] ADJ aubergine

Au|ber|gi|ne [obɛr'ʒi:nə] F **-, -n** aubergine, eggplant *(esp US)*

auch [aux] ADV **a** *(= zusätzlich, gleichfalls)* also, too, as well; **die Engländer müssen ~ zugeben, dass ...** the English must admit too *or* as well that ..., the English must also admit that ...; **~ die Engländer müssen ...** the English too must ...; **das kann ich ~** I can do that too *or* as well; **das ist ~ möglich** that's possible too *or* as well, that's also possible; **ja, das ~** yes, that too; **~ gut** that's OK too; **du ~?** you too?, you as well?; **~ nicht** not ... either; **das ist ~ nicht richtig** that's not right either; **er kommt – ich ~** he's coming – so am I *or* me too; **ich will eins – ich ~** I want one – so do I *or* me too; **er kommt nicht – ich ~ nicht** he's not coming – nor *or* neither am I, he's not coming – I'm not either *or* me neither; **~ das noch!** that's all I needed!

b *(= tatsächlich)* too, as well; **und das tue/meine ich ~** and I'll do it/I mean it too *or* as well; **wenn sie sagt, sie geht, dann geht sie ~** if she says she's going then she'll go; **Frechheit! – ja, das ist es ~** what impudence! – you can say that again; **du siehst müde aus – das bin ich ~** you look tired – (so) I am; **das ist er ja ~** (and so) he is; **so ist es ~** (so) it is

c *(= sogar)* even; **~ wenn du Vorfahrt hast** even if you (do) have right of way; **ohne ~ nur zu fragen** without even asking

d *(emph)* **den Teufel ~!** damn it (all)! *(inf)*; **zum Donnerwetter ~!** blast it! *(inf)*; **so ein Dummkopf ~!** what an absolute blockhead! *(inf)*; **so was Ärgerliches aber ~!** it's really too annoying!; **wozu ~?** what on earth for? *(inf)*, whatever for?

e *(= auch immer)* **wie dem ~ sei** be that as it may; **was er ~ sagen mag** whatever he might say; **und mag er ~ noch so klug sein, wenn er ~ noch so klug ist** however clever he may be; **so schnell er ~ laufen mag** however fast he runs *or* he may run, no matter how fast he runs → **immer**

Au|di|enz [au'diɛnts] F **-, -en** *(bei Papst, König etc)* audience

Au|di|enz|saal M audience chamber

Au|di|max [audi'maks, 'audimaks] NT -, *no pl (Univ sl)* main lecture hall

au|dio-: **Au|dio|guide** M **-s, -s** audioguide, audio guide; **au|dio|phil** [audio'fi:l] ADJ audiophile; **Au|dio|phi|le(r)** [audio'fi:lə] MF *decl as adj* audiophile; **Au|dio|re|kor|der** M *(Comput)* sound recorder; **Au|dio|sche|ma** NT *(Comput)* sound scheme; **au|dio|vi|su|ell** [audiovi'zuɛl] ADJ audiovisual; **~er Unterricht** audiovisual instruction; **~e Medien** audiovisual media ADV audiovisually; *gestalten* using audiovisual aids; *werben* using audiovisual media

Au|dit ['au:dit] M OR NT **-s, -s** *(esp Sw)* audit

au|di|tiv [audi'ti:f] ADJ auditory

Au|di|to|ri|um [audi'to:riʊm] NT **-s, Auditorien** [-riən] **a** *(= Hörsaal)* lecture hall; **~ maximum** *(Univ)* main lecture hall **b** *(geh: = Zuhörerschaft)* audience

Aue ['auə] F **-, -n** **a** *(dial, poet)* meadow, pasture, lea *(poet)*, mead *(poet)* **b** *(dial: = Insel)* island

Au|en-: **Au|en|land|schaft** F pasture landscape, pastureland; **Au|en|wald** M riverside wood(s *pl*) *or* forest

Au|er|bach|sprung ['auɐbax-] M *(Sport)* backward *or* reverse somersault

Au|er|hahn ['auɐ-] M *pl* **Auerhähne** *or (Hunt)* **-en** capercaillie

Au|er|hen|ne F, **Au|er|huhn** NT capercaillie (hen)

Au|er|och|se M aurochs

auf [auf]

1 PRÄPOSITION (*+dat*) 3 ADVERB
2 PRÄPOSITION (*+acc*) 4 BINDEWORT

In Verbindung mit Substantiven, Verben etc siehe auch dort.

1 – PRÄPOSITION (*+dat*)

a [Ort] on; **das Buch lag auf dem Tisch** the book was lying on the table; **auf einem Stuhl sitzen** to sit on a chair; **auf (der Insel) Kos** on (the island of) Kos; **auf den Orkneyinseln** on *or* in the Orkney Islands; **auf See** at sea; **auf der Bank/Post®/dem Rathaus** at the bank/post office/town hall; **mein Geld ist auf der Bank** my money is in the bank; **auf meinem Zimmer** in my room; **auf der Straße** on *or* in the street; **Greenwich liegt auf 0 Grad** Greenwich lies at 0 degrees; **die Tachonadel steht auf 105** the speedometer is at *or* on 105

b [andere Wendungen] **auf der Fahrt/dem Weg** on the journey/way; **auf der Geige spielen** to play the violin; **etw auf dem Klavier spielen** to play sth on the piano; **auf einem Ohr taub sein** to be deaf in one ear; **das hat nichts auf sich, damit hat es nichts auf sich** it doesn't mean anything; **was hat es damit auf sich?** what does it mean?

2 – PRÄPOSITION (*+acc*)

a [Ort] on; **etw auf einen Zettel schreiben** to write sth on a piece of paper; **etw auf etw stellen** to put sth on(to) sth; **etw auf etw heben** to lift sth onto sth; **sich auf etw setzen/legen** to sit/lie (down) on sth; **sich auf die Straße setzen** to sit down in the road; **das Wrack ist auf den Meeresgrund gesunken** the wreck sank to the bottom of the sea; **er ist auf die Orkneyinseln gefahren** he has gone to the Orkney Islands; **er segelt auf das Meer hinaus** he is sailing out to sea; **man konnte nicht weiter als auf zehn Fuß herankommen** you couldn't get any nearer than ten feet; **geh mal auf die Seite** move aside; **Geld auf die Bank bringen** to take money to the bank; (*= einzahlen*) to put money in the bank; **auf sein Zimmer/die Post®/die Polizei gehen** to go to one's room/the post office/the police; **aufs Gymnasium gehen** ≈ to go to grammar school (*Brit*), ≈ to go to high school (*US*); **auf eine Party/eine Hochzeit gehen** to go to a party/wedding

b [Zeit] **die Uhr auf 10 stellen** to put *or* set the clock to 10; **Heiligabend fällt auf einen Dienstag** Christmas Eve falls on a Tuesday; **die Sitzung auf morgen verschieben** to postpone the meeting until tomorrow; **die Dauer auf ein Jahr reduzieren** to reduce the duration to one year; **auf drei Tage** for three days; **die Nacht (von Montag) auf Dienstag** Monday night; **auf morgen/bald!** see you tomorrow/soon!; **zwanzig auf sieben** (*dial*) twenty to seven

c [Häufung] **Niederlage auf Niederlage** defeat after *or* upon defeat; **Beleidigung auf Beleidigung** insult upon *or* after insult; **einer auf den anderen** one after another

d [= für] **auf 10 km** for 10 km; **auf eine Tasse Kaffee/eine Zigarette** *or* **Zigarettenlänge** for a cup of coffee/a smoke; **ein Manuskript auf Fehler prüfen** to check a manuscript for errors

e [= pro] **auf einen Polizisten kommen 1.000 Bürger** there is one policeman for *or* to every 1,000 citizens; **auf jeden kamen zwei Flaschen Bier** there were two bottles of beer (for) each

f [andere Wendungen] **auf ihn!** get him!; **auf unseren lieben Onkel Egon/ein glückliches Gelingen!** here's to dear Uncle Egon/a great success!; **auf deine Gesundheit!** (your very) good health!; **auf das** *or* **aufs schändlichste/liebenswürdigste** *or* **Schändlichste/Liebenswürdigste** (*geh*) most shamefully/kindly; **auf die elegante/ehrliche Art** elegantly/honestly; **auf die billige Tour** on the cheap

♦ **auf etw** (*acc*) **hin** (*als Reaktion*) at; **auf seinen Vorschlag/seine Bitte (hin)** at his suggestion/request; **auf meinen Brief hin** on receiving my letter

♦ **auf jdn/etw zu er kam auf mich zu und sagte ...** he came up to me and said ...; **während er auf mich zukam** as he was coming toward(s) me; **es geht auf Weihnachten zu** Christmas is approaching → *auch* **gehen 1 c**

3 – ADVERB

a [= offen] open; **die Tür/das Fenster ist auf** the door's/window's open; **ist das Fenster auf oder zu?** is the window open or shut?; **Mund/Fenster auf!** open your mouth/the window! → **auf sein**

b [andere Wendungen] **Helm auf!** helmets on!; **Handschuhe an, Mütze auf, so wird er sich nicht erkälten** with his gloves and hat on he won't catch cold; **nachmittags Unterricht, und dann noch so viel auf!** (*inf*) school in the afternoon, and all that homework too!; **auf, an die Arbeit!** right, let's get down to work!; **auf nach Chicago!** let's go to Chicago; **auf gehts!** let's go!; **auf und ab** up and down; **auf und nieder** (*geh*) up and down; **sie ist auf und davon** she has disappeared; **ihr Mann verließ sie und ging auf und davon** her husband just walked out and left her; **Sprung auf! marsch, marsch!** (*Mil*) jump to it!, at (*Brit*) *or* on (*US*) the double!; **die Jagd ist auf** the hunt is on

4 – BINDEWORT

♦ **auf dass** (*liter*) that (*old, liter*); **richtet nicht, auf dass ihr nicht gerichtet werdet** (*Bibl*) judge not, that ye be not judged (*Bibl*); **auf dass wir niemals vergessen mögen** lest we forget

Auf [auf] NT *inv* **das ~ und Ab** *or* **Nieder** the up and down; (*fig*) the ups and downs; **das ~ und Ab des Kolbens** the up(ward) and down(ward) movement of the piston

auf+ad|die|ren *ptp* **aufaddiert** VTR *sep* to add up

auf+ar|bei|ten VT *sep* **a** (*= erneuern*) to refurbish, to do up; *Möbel etc* to recondition **b** (*= auswerten*) *Literatur etc* to incorporate critically; *Vergangenheit* to reappraise **c** (*= erledigen*) *Korrespondenz, Liegengebliebenes* to catch up with *or* on, to clear **d** (*Phys*) *Brennelemente* to reprocess

Auf|ar|bei|tung F **-, -en** **a** (*= Erneuerung*) refurbishing; (*von Möbeln*) reconditioning **b** (*= Auswertung*) (*von Literatur*) critical incorporation; (*von Vergangenheit*) reappraisal **c** (*= Erledigung: von Korrespondenz etc*) catching up; **die ~ des Liegengebliebenen dauerte einige Zeit** it took some time to catch up with *or* clear the backlog **d** (*Phys: von Brennelementen*) reprocessing

auf+at|men VI *sep* (*lit, fig*) to breathe *or* heave a sigh of relief; **ein Aufatmen** a sigh of relief

auf+ba|cken VT *sep* to warm *or* crisp up

auf+bah|ren ['aufba:rən] VT *sep* *Sarg* to lay on the bier; *Leiche* to lay out; **einen Toten feierlich ~** to put a person's body to lie in state

Auf|bah|rung F **-, -en** laying out; (*feierlich*) lying in state

Auf|bau M *pl* **-bauten** **a** *no pl* (*= das Aufbauen*) construction, building; (*von neuem Staat*) building; (*von Netzwerk, System*) setting up; (*= das Wiederaufbauen*) reconstruction; **der wirtschaftliche ~** the building up of the economy; **der ~ Ost** the rebuilding of East Germany **b** (*= Aufgebautes, Aufgesetztes*) top; (*von Auto, LKW*) coachwork *no pl*, body → **Aufbauten** **c** *no pl* (*= Struktur*) structure

AUFBAU OST

Aufbau Ost is a colloquial term for the **Wirtschaftsförderung Ost**, by means of which the economic system of the former East Germany is being brought into line with the demands of the social market economy. Using funds from the **Solidaritätszuschlag**, the Federal Government seeks to subsidize investment in the East, to develop infrastructure and to support research, environmental conservation and the creation of new businesses.
→ SOLIDARITÄTSZUSCHLAG

Auf|bau|ar|beit F construction (work); (*= Wiederaufbau*) reconstruction (work)

auf+bau|en *sep* VT **a** (*= errichten*) to put up; *Verbindung, Netzwerk, System* to set up; (*= hinstellen*) *Ausstellungsstücke, kaltes Büfett, Brettspiel etc* to set *or* lay out; (*inf*) *Posten, Ordnungspersonal etc* to post; (*= zusammenbauen*) *elektrische Schaltung etc* to put together, to assemble
b (*= daraufbauen*) *Stockwerk* to add (on), to build on; *Karosserie* to mount
c (*fig: = gestalten*) *Organisation, Land, Armee, Geschäft, Angriff, Druck, Spannung, Verbindung* to build up; *Zerstörtes* to rebuild; *Theorie, Plan, System* to construct; **sich** (*dat*) **eine (neue) Existenz** *or* **ein Leben ~** to build (up) a new life for oneself
d (*fig: = fördern, weiterentwickeln*) *Gesundheit, Kraft* to build up; *Star, Politiker* to promote; *Beziehung* to build; **jdn/etw zu etw ~** to build sb/sth up into sth
e (*fig: = gründen*) **etw auf etw** (*dat or acc*) **~** to base *or* found sth on sth
f (*= strukturieren, konstruieren*) to construct; *Aufsatz, Rede, Organisation* to structure
VI **a** (*= sich gründen*) to be based *or* founded (*auf +dat or acc* on)
b **wir wollen ~ und nicht zerstören** we want to build and not destroy
VR **a** (*inf: = sich postieren*) to take up position; **sie bauten sich in einer Reihe auf** they formed (themselves) up into a line; **er baute sich vor dem Feldwebel/Lehrer auf und ...** he stood up in front of the sergeant/teacher and ...; **sich vor jdm drohend ~** to plant oneself in front of sb (*inf*)
b (*= sich bilden: Wolken, Hochdruckgebiet*) to build up
c (*= bestehen aus*) **sich aus etw ~** to be built up *or* composed of sth
d (*= sich gründen*) **sich auf etw** (*dat or acc*) **~** to be based *or* founded on sth

Auf|bau-: **Auf|bau|hil|fe** F development(al) aid *or* assistance; **Auf|bau|kurs** M continuation course

auf+bäu|men ['aufbɔymən] VR *sep* (*Tier*) to rear; **sich gegen jdn/etw ~** (*fig*) to rebel *or* revolt against sb/sth; **sich vor Schmerz ~** to writhe with pain

Auf|bau-: **Auf|bau|pha|se** F development(al) phase; **Auf|bau|prä|pa|rat** NT regenerative product; **Auf|bau|prin|zip** NT structural principle; **die Motoren sind alle nach demselben ~ konstruiert** the engines are all constructed on the same principle

auf+bau|schen *sep* VT to blow out; *Segel auch* to (make) billow out, to belly out; (*fig*) to blow up, to exaggerate VR to blow out; (*Segel auch*) to billow (out), to belly (out); (*fig*) to blow up (*zu* into)

Auf|bau-: **Auf|bau|stu|di|um** NT (*Univ*) course of further study; **Auf|bau|stu|fe** F (*Sch*) *school class leading to university entrance*, ≈ sixth form (*Brit*), ≈ twelfth grade (*US*)

Auf|bau|ten PL (*Naut*) superstructure

Auf|bau|trai|ning NT (*Sport*) stamina training

auf+be|geh|ren *ptp* **aufbegehrt** VI *sep* (*geh*) to rebel, to revolt (*gegen* against)

auf+be|hal|ten *ptp* **aufbehalten** VT *sep irreg* *Hut, Brille etc* to keep on; *Tür, Schrank etc* to leave *or* keep open; *Knopf* to leave *or* keep undone

auf+bei|ßen VT *sep irreg* *Verpackung etc* to bite open; *Nuss etc* to crack with one's teeth; **sich**

(dat) **die Lippe ~** to bite one's lip (and make it bleed)

auf+be|kom|men *ptp* **aufbekommen** VT *sep irreg (inf)* **a** *(= öffnen)* to get open **b** *Aufgabe* to get as homework; **habt ihr keine Hausarbeiten ~?** didn't you get any homework? **c** *Essen* to (manage to) eat up; **ich habe nur die halbe Portion ~** I could only manage (to eat) half a portion

auf+be|rei|ten *ptp* **aufbereitet** VT *sep* to process; *Trinkwasser auch* to purify; *Erze* to prepare, to dress; *Daten* to edit; *Text etc* to work up; **aufbereitetes Wasser** purified water; **etw literarisch ~** to turn sth into literature; **etw dramaturgisch ~** to adapt sth for the theatre *(Brit)* or theater *(US)*

Auf|be|rei|tung F -, -en processing; *(von Trinkwasser auch)* purification; *(von Erz, Kohle)* preparation, dressing; *(von Daten)* editing; *(von Texten)* working up; *(fürs Theater)* adaptation

Auf|be|rei|tungs|an|la|ge F processing plant

auf+bes|sern VT *sep* to improve; *Gehalt etc auch* to increase

Auf|bes|se|rung F, **Auf|bess|rung** ['aufbɛsrʊŋ] F -, -en improvement; *(von Gehalt auch)* increase

auf+be|wah|ren *ptp* **aufbewahrt** VT *sep* to keep; *Lebensmittel auch* to store; *(= behalten) alte Zeitungen etc auch* to save; *Wertsachen etc* to look after; **ein Dokument gut ~** to keep a document in a safe place; **Medikamente kühl ~** to keep medicines in a cool place; **jds Dokumente ~** to be looking after sb's documents, to have sb's documents in one's keeping; **kann ich hier meinen Koffer ~ lassen?** can I leave my suitcase here?

Auf|be|wah|rung F **a** *(= das Aufbewahren)* keeping; *(von Lebensmitteln)* storage; **jdm etw zur ~ übergeben** to give sth to sb for safekeeping, to put sth in(to) sb's safekeeping; **einen Koffer in ~ geben** to deposit a suitcase (at the left-luggage *(Brit)* or checkroom *(US)*) **b** *(= Stelle)* left luggage (office) *(Brit)*, checkroom *(US)*

Auf|be|wah|rungs|ort M *pl* -orte *place where something is to be kept;* **etw an einen sicheren ~ bringen** to put sth in a safe place; **das ist kein geeigneter ~ für Medikamente** that is not the right place to keep medicines; **einen ~ für etw finden** to find a place to keep sth, to find a home for sth *(inf)*

Auf|be|wah|rungs|schein M left-luggage receipt or ticket *(Brit)*, checkroom ticket *(US)*

auf+bie|gen *sep irreg* VT to bend open VR *(Ring etc)* to bend open

auf+bie|ten VT *sep irreg* **a** *Menschen, Mittel* to muster; *Kräfte, Fähigkeiten* to summon (up), to muster; *Militär, Polizei* to call in; *(old) Soldaten* to levy *(old)* **b** *Brautpaar* to call the banns of **c** *(bei Auktionen)* to put up

Auf|bie|tung F -, *no pl (von Menschen, Mitteln)* mustering; *(von Kräften, Fähigkeiten)* summoning (up); *(von Polizei, Militär)* calling in; **unter** or **bei ~ aller Kräfte ...** summoning (up) all his/her etc strength ...

auf+bin|den VT *sep irreg* **a** *(= öffnen) Schuh etc* to undo, to untie **b** *(= hochbinden) Haare* to put or tie up; *Pflanzen, Zweige etc* to tie (up) straight **c** *(= befestigen)* to tie on; **etw auf etw** *(acc)* **~** to tie sth on(to) sth **d** **lass dir doch so etwas nicht ~** *(fig)* don't fall for that; **jdm eine Lüge ~** to take sb in, to tell sb a lie **e** *(Typ) Buch* to bind

auf+blä|hen *sep* VT to blow out; *Segel auch* to fill, to billow out, to belly out; *(Med)* to distend, to swell; *(fig)* to inflate VR to blow out; *(Segel auch)* to billow or belly out; *(Med)* to become distended or swollen; *(fig pej)* to puff oneself up

Auf|blä|hung F *(Med)* distension

auf|blas|bar ADJ inflatable

auf+bla|sen *sep irreg* VT **a** *Ballon* to blow up; *Reifen etc* to inflate, to blow up; *Backen* to puff out, to blow out **b** *(= hochblasen)* to blow up VR *(fig pej)* to puff oneself up → *auch* **aufgeblasen**

auf+blät|tern *sep* VT *Buch etc* to open (up)

auf+blei|ben VI *sep irreg aux sein* **a** *(= nicht schlafen gehen)* to stay up; **wegen jdm ~** to wait up or to stay up for sb **b** *(= geöffnet bleiben)* to stay open

Auf|blen|de F *(Film)* fade-in

auf+blen|den *sep* VI *(Phot)* to open up the lens, to increase the aperture; *(Film)* to fade in; *(Aut)* to turn the headlights on full (beam); **er fährt aufgeblendet** he drives on full beam VT *(Aut) Scheinwerfer* to turn on full (beam); *(Film) Einstellung* to fade in

auf+bli|cken VI *sep* to look up; **zu jdm/etw ~** *(lit, fig)* to look up to sb/sth

auf+blin|ken VI *sep (lit, fig)* to flash; *(Aut inf: = kurz aufblenden)* to flash (one's headlights)

auf+blit|zen VI *sep* **a** *(Licht, Strahl, Blitz, Augen)* to flash **b** *aux sein (fig) (Emotion, Hass etc)* to flare up; *(Gedanke, Erinnerung)* to flash through one's mind

auf+blü|hen VI *sep aux sein* **a** *(Knospe)* to blossom (out); *(Blume)* to bloom **b** *(fig) (Mensch)* to blossom out; *(Wissenschaft, Kultur)* to (begin to) flourish; **das ließ sie/die Stadt ~** it allowed her/the town to flourish

auf+bo|cken VT *sep Auto* to jack up; *Motorrad* to put on its stand

auf+boh|ren VT *sep* to bore or drill a hole in; *Zahn auch* to drill

auf+bran|den VI *sep aux sein (geh)* to surge; *(fig: Beifall)* to burst forth; **Beifall brandete immer wieder auf** there was wave upon wave of applause

auf+bra|ten VT *sep irreg Essen* to warm up; *(in der Pfanne auch)* to fry up

auf+brau|chen *sep* VT to use up; **seine Geduld ist aufgebraucht** his patience is exhausted VR *(= sich verbrauchen)* to get used up; *(Reifen: = sich abnutzen)* to get worn out, to wear out

auf+brau|sen VI *sep aux sein* **a** *(Brandung etc)* to surge; *(Brausetablette, Brause etc)* to fizz up; *(fig: Beifall, Jubel)* to break out, to burst forth **b** *(fig: Mensch)* to flare up, to fly off the handle *(inf)*

auf|brau|send ADJ *Temperament* irascible; *Mensch auch* quick-tempered, liable to flare up

auf+bre|chen *sep irreg* VT to break or force open; *Tresor auch, Auto* to break into; *Deckel* to prise off; *Boden, Asphalt, Oberfläche* to break up; *(geh) Brief* to break open; *(fig) System, soziale Struktur etc* to break down VI *aux sein* **a** *(= sich öffnen) (Straßenbelag etc)* to break up; *(Knospen)* to (burst) open; *(Wunde)* to open **b** *(fig: Konflikte, Hass etc)* to break out **c** *(= sich auf den Weg machen)* to start out or off, to set out or off

auf+bren|nen *sep irreg* VT **a** **einem Tier ein Zeichen ~** to brand an animal; **jdm eins ~** *(inf) (= schlagen)* to wallop or clout *(Brit)* sb (one) *(inf)*; *(= anschießen)* to shoot sb, to put a slug into sb *(inf)*; **sie brannte dem Hund eins auf** *(inf: = schlug)* she hit the dog **b** *(= verbrennen) Kerze, Kohlen etc* to burn up VI *aux sein (Feuer, Leidenschaft)* to flare up

auf+brin|gen VT *sep irreg* **a** *(= beschaffen)* to find; *Geld* to raise, to find; *Kraft, Mut, Energie* to find, to summon up **b** *(= erzürnen)* to make angry, to irritate; **jdn gegen jdn/etw ~** to set sb against sb/sth → *auch* **aufgebracht** **c** *(= ins Leben rufen)* to start **d** *(Naut) Schiff* to seize; *(= in Hafen zwingen)* to bring in **e** *(= auftragen) Farbe etc* to put on, to apply; **etw auf etw** *(acc)* **~** to put sth on sth, to apply sth to sth **f** *(dial: = aufbekommen) Tür etc* to get open

Auf|bruch M **a** *no pl (= Abreise, das Losgehen)* departure; **das Zeichen zum ~ geben** to give the signal to set out or off; **der ~ ins 21. Jahrhundert** the emergence into the 21st century; **eine Zeit des ~s** a time of new departures **b** *(= aufgebrochene Stelle)* crack

Auf|bruchs-: **auf|bruchs|be|reit** ADJ ready to set off or go or depart; **Auf|bruchs|sig|nal** NT signal to set off; **hast du das ~ gehört?** did you hear the off?; **Auf|bruch(s)|stim|mung** F **a** **hier herrscht schon ~** *(bei Party etc)* it's all breaking up; *(in Gastwirtschaft)* they're packing up; **es herrschte allgemeine ~ (unter den Gästen)** the party was breaking up; **bist du schon in ~?** are you wanting or ready to go already? **b** *(= Euphorie)* euphoric mood; **es herrscht ~** there is a spirit of optimism

auf+brü|hen VT *sep* to brew up

auf+brül|len VI *sep* to shout or yell out; *(Tier)* to bellow

auf+brum|men *sep* VT *(inf)* **jdm etw ~** to give sb sth; **jdm die Kosten ~** to land sb with the costs *(inf)* VI **a** *(Motor)* to roar out **b** *aux sein (Aut inf)* to bang, to prang *(Brit inf)* *(auf +acc* into); *(Naut sl)* to run aground, to hit the bottom

auf+bü|geln VT *sep* **a** *Kleidungsstück* to iron out; *(fig inf)* to vamp up *(inf)* **b** *Flicken, Bild etc* to iron on; **Flicken zum Aufbügeln** iron-on patches

auf+bum|sen VI *sep (inf) aux sein* to bang; **etw auf etw** *(dat)* **~ lassen** to plump or plonk *(esp Brit inf)* sth down on sth; **mit dem Hinterkopf ~** to bump or bang the back of one's head

auf+bür|den VT *sep (geh)* **jdm etw ~** *(lit)* to load sth onto sb; *(fig)* to encumber sb with sth; **jdm die Schuld für etw ~** to put the blame for sth on sb

auf+bürs|ten VT *sep* **etw ~** to give sth a brush, to brush sth

auf dass CONJ → **auf 4**

auf+de|cken *sep* VT **a** *jdn* to uncover; *Bett(decke)* to turn down; *Gefäß* to open; *Spielkarten* to show **b** *(fig) Wahrheit, Verschwörung, Zusammenhänge* to discover, to uncover; *Verbrechen* to expose, to uncover; *Schwäche* to lay bare; *Geheimnis, Rätsel* to solve; *wahren Charakter* to disclose, to lay bare, to expose **c** *(= auf den Esstisch stellen)* to put on the table; **das Geschirr ~** to lay *(Brit)* or set the table VI to lay *(Brit)* or set the table

Auf|de|ckung F *(fig) (von Wahrheit, Verschwörung, Zusammenhängen)* uncovering; *(von Verbrechen)* exposing, exposure; *(von Schwäche)* laying bare; *(von Geheimnis, Rätsel)* solving; *(von wahrem Charakter)* disclosing, disclosure

auf+don|nern VR *sep (pej inf)* to tart oneself up *(Brit pej inf)*, to get dolled up *(Brit inf)*, to get tarted up *(Brit pej inf)*, to deck oneself out *(US inf)* → *auch* **aufgedonnert**

auf+drän|gen *sep* VT **jdm etw ~** to impose or force or push sth on sb VR to impose; **sich jdm ~** *(Mensch)* to impose oneself or one's company on sb; *(fig: Erinnerung)* to come involuntarily to sb's mind; **dieser Gedanke/Verdacht drängte sich mir auf** I couldn't help thinking/suspecting that

auf+dre|hen *sep* VT **a** *Wasserhahn, Wasser etc* to turn on; *Ventil* to open; *Schraubverschluss* to unscrew; *Schraube* to loosen, to unscrew; *Lautstärke* to turn up; *(Aus: = einschalten) Licht, Radio etc* to turn or switch on **b** *(= aufrollen) Haar* to put in rollers; *Schnurrbart* to turn or twist up VI *(inf) (= beschleunigen)* to put one's foot down hard, to open up; *(fig)* to get going, to start going like the clappers *(Brit inf)*; *(fig: = ausgelassen werden)* to get going, to let it all hang out *(inf)* → *auch* **aufgedreht**

auf+drin|gen VTR *sep irreg* = **aufdrängen**

auf|dring|lich ADJ *Mensch, Benehmen* pushing, pushy *(inf)*; *Farbe* loud, garish; *Geruch, Parfüm* overpowering; **die ~e Art meines Mitreisenden** the way my fellow passenger forced himself or his company upon me; **dieser ~e Kerl kam einfach auf mich zu** this guy just forced himself or his company on me *(inf)*; **beim Tanzen wurde er ~** when we/they were dancing he kept trying to get fresh *(esp US inf)*

Auf|dring|lich|keit F *(von Mensch)* pushiness; **die ~ meiner Nachbarin** the way my neighbour *(Brit)* or neighbor *(US)* forces herself or her company on you; **die ~ ihres Parfüms** her overpowering perfume; **die ~ der Tapete** the loud *or* garish wallpaper

auf+drö|seln ['aufdrø:zln] VT *sep (lit, fig)* to unravel; *Strickarbeit* to undo

Auf|druck M *pl* **-drucke** **a** *(= Aufgedrucktes)* imprint; *(auf Briefmarke)* overprint **b** *(Phys)* upward pressure

auf+dru|cken VT *sep* **etw auf etw** *(acc)* **~** to print sth on sth; **Postwertstempel auf Briefe ~** to stamp letters

auf+drü|cken *sep* VT **a** **etw (auf etw** *acc)* **~** to press sth on (sth); **den Bleistift nicht so fest ~!** don't press (on) your pencil so hard **b** *(= aufdrucken)* **etw auf etw** *(acc)* **~** to stamp sth on sth; **ein Siegel auf einen Brief ~** to impress a seal on a letter; **jdm einen ~** *(inf)* to give sb a kiss *or* a quick peck *(inf)* → **Stempel b** **c** *(= öffnen) Tür etc* to push open; *Pickel etc* to squeeze **d** *(inf: = durch Knopfdruck öffnen) Tür* to open *(by pressing the button)*; **er drückte die Tür auf** he pressed *or* pushed the button and the door opened VI **a** *(= drücken)* to press **b** *(inf: = die Tür elektrisch öffnen)* to open the door *(by pressing a button)* VR to leave an impression *(auf +acc* on)

auf|ei|nan|der [auflai'nandɐ] ADV **a** on (top of) each other *or* one another **b** **~ folgend** = **aufeinanderfolgend**; **sich ~ verlassen können** to be able to rely on each other *or* one another; **~ zufahren** to drive toward(s) each other

auf|ei|nan|der-: **auf|ei|nan|der+bei|ßen** *sep irreg*, **auf|ei|nan|der bei|ßen** △ *irreg* VT *Zähne* to clench, to bite together; **auf|ei|nan|der+drü|cken** *sep*, **auf|ei|nan|der drü|cken** △ VT to press together; **auf|ei|nan|der+fah|ren** *sep irreg aux sein*, **auf|ei|nan|der fah|ren** △ *irreg aux sein* VI to drive *or* crash into each other

Auf|ei|nan|der|fol|ge F, *no pl* sequence; *(zeitlich auch)* succession; **in schneller ~** in quick succession

auf|ei|nan|der+fol|gen *sep aux sein*, **auf|ei|nan|der fol|gen** *sep aux sein* VI to follow each other *or* one another, to come after each other *or* one another; **die beiden Termine folgten unmittelbar aufeinander** the two appointments followed *or* came one immediately after the other, one appointment came immediately after the other

auf|ei|nan|der|fol|gend ADJ *(zeitlich)* successive; **drei schnell ~e Tore** three goals in quick succession

auf|ei|nan|der-: **auf|ei|nan|der+hän|gen** *sep,*; **auf|ei|nan|der hän|gen** △ VI *irreg* **a** *(inf: Leute)* to hang around together *(inf)*; **die beiden Autos hängen zu nah aufeinander** the two cars are sticking too close (together); **in einer kleinen Wohnung hängt man immer zu eng aufeinander** in a small flat *(Brit) or* apartment you're always too much on top of each other *(inf)* **b** *(= übereinanderhängen)* to hang one over the other VT to hang on top of each other; **auf|ei|nan|der+het|zen** *sep*, **auf|ei|nan|der het|zen** △ VT to set on *or* at each other; **auf|ei|nan|der+ho|cken** *sep*, **auf|ei|nan|der ho|cken** △ VI *(inf)* = **aufeinanderhängen VI a**; **auf|ei|nan|der+knal|len** *sep*, **auf|ei|nan|der knal|len** △ *(inf)* VI *aux sein (lit, fig)* to collide VT to bang together; **auf|ei|nan|der+le|gen** *sep*, **auf|ei|nan|der le|gen** △ VT to lay on top of each other, to lay one on top of the other VR to lie on top of each other; **auf|ei|nan|der+lie|gen** *sep irreg (S Ger, Aus, Sw: aux sein)*, **auf|ei|nan|der lie|gen** △ *irreg (S Ger, Aus, Sw: aux sein)* VI to lie on top of each other; **auf|ei|nan|der+pas|sen** *sep*, **auf|ei|nan|der pas|sen** △ VI to fit on top of each other; **auf|ei|nan|der+pral|len** *sep aux sein*, **auf|ei|nan|der pral|len** △ *aux sein* VI *(Autos etc)* to collide; *(Truppen etc, Meinungen)* to clash; **auf|ei|nan|der+pres|sen** VT *sep*, **auf|ei|nan|der pres|sen** △ VT to press together; **auf|ei|nan|der+ra|sen** *sep aux sein*, **auf|ei|nan|der ra|sen** △ *aux sein* VI to hurtle into each other; **auf|ei|nan|der+schich|ten** *sep*, **auf|ei|nan|der schich|ten** △ VT to put in layers one on top of the other; **auf|ei|nan|der+schla|gen** *sep irreg*, **auf|ei|nan|der schla|gen** △ *irreg* VI *aux sein* to knock *or* strike against each other VT to knock *or* strike together; **auf|ei|nan|der+set|zen** *sep*, **auf|ei|nan|der set|zen** △ VT to put on top of each other VR *(Gegenstände)* to be placed one on top of the other *or* on top of each other; *(Bienen etc)* to settle on each other; **auf|ei|nan|der+sit|zen** *sep irreg (S Ger, Aus, Sw: aux sein)*, **auf|ei|nan|der sit|zen** △ *irreg (S Ger, Aus, Sw: aux sein)* VI **a** *(Gegenstände)* to lie on top of each other **b** *(inf)* **die Autos sitzen zu dicht aufeinander** the cars are too close together **c** *(inf: Menschen)* to sit on top of each other *(inf)*; *(= eng wohnen)* to live on top of each other *(inf)*; **auf|ei|nan|der+stel|len** *sep*, **auf|ei|nan|der stel|len** △ VT to put *or* place on top of each other VR to get on top of each other; **auf|ei|nan|der+sto|ßen** *sep irreg*, **auf|ei|nan|der sto|ßen** △ *irreg aux sein* VI to bump into each other, to collide; *(fig: Meinungen, Farben)* to clash; **auf|ei|nan|der+tref|fen** *sep irreg aux sein*, **auf|ei|nan|der tref|fen** △ *irreg aux sein* VI *(Mannschaften, Gruppen etc)* to meet; *(Meinungen)* to clash, to come into conflict; *(Kugeln, Gegenstände etc)* to hit each other; **auf|ei|nan|der+tür|men** *sep*, **auf|ei|nan|der tür|men** △ VT to pile on top of each other

Auf|ent|halt ['auflɛnthalt] M **a** *(= das Sichaufhalten)* stay; *(= das Wohnen)* residence; **der ~ im Aktionsbereich des Krans ist verboten** do not stand within the radius of the crane, keep well clear of the crane **b** *(= Aufenthaltszeit)* stay, sojourn *(liter)* **c** *(esp Rail)* stop; *(bei Anschluss)* wait; **der Zug hat 20 Minuten ~** the train stops for 20 minutes; **wie lange haben wir ~?** how long do we stop for?; *(bei Anschluss)* how long do we have to wait? **d** *(geh: = Verzögerung)* delay, wait **e** *(geh: = Aufenthaltsort)* abode *(form)*, domicile, place of residence; **~ nehmen** to take up residence

Auf|ent|hal|ter(in) M(F) *(Sw)* foreign resident, resident alien *(form)*

Auf|ent|halts-: **Auf|ent|halts|be|rech|ti|gung** F right of residence; **Auf|ent|halts|be|schrän|kung** F restriction on residence, limitation of (period of) residence; **Auf|ent|halts|be|wil|li|gung** F residence permit; **Auf|ent|halts|dau|er** F length *or* duration of stay; **Auf|ent|halts|er|laub|nis** F, **Auf|ent|halts|ge|neh|mi|gung** F residence permit; **Auf|ent|halts|ort** M *pl* **-orte** whereabouts *sing or pl*; *(Jur)* abode, residence; **man weiß nicht, was sein augenblicklicher ~ ist** his present whereabouts is *or* are not known; **Auf|ent|halts|raum** M day room; *(in Betrieb)* recreation room; *(auf Flughafen)* lounge; **Auf|ent|halts|ver|bot** NT **jdm ~ erteilen** to ban sb from staying (in a country *etc*); **er hat ~** he is not allowed to stay (in the country *etc*), he is banned

auf+er|le|gen *ptp* **auferlegt** VT *sep or insep (geh)* to impose *(jdm* on sb); *Strafe auch* to inflict *(jdm* on sb)

Auf|er|stan|de|ne(r) ['auflɛɐʃtandnə] M *decl as adj (Rel)* **der ~** the risen Christ

auf+er|ste|hen *ptp* **auferstanden** VI *sep or insep irreg aux sein* to rise from the dead, to rise again *(esp Rel)*; **Christus ist auferstanden** Christ is (a)risen

Auf|er|ste|hung ['auflɛɐʃte:ʊŋ] F **-, -en** resurrection; **(fröhliche) ~ feiern** *(hum)* to have been resurrected

Auf|er|ste|hungs|fest NT *(geh)* Feast of the Resurrection

auf+er|we|cken *ptp* **auferweckt** VT *sep or insep (geh)* to raise from the dead; *(fig)* to reawaken

Auf|er|we|ckung F raising from the dead

auf+es|sen *sep irreg* VT to eat up VI to eat (everything) up

auf+fä|chern *sep* VT to fan out; *(fig)* to arrange *or* order neatly VR to fan out

auf+fä|deln VT *sep* to thread *or* string (together)

auf+fah|ren *sep irreg* VI *aux sein* **a** *(= aufprallen)* **auf jdn/etw ~** to run *or* drive into sb/sth; **auf eine Sandbank ~** to run onto a sandbank, to run aground on a sandbank **b** *(= näher heranfahren)* to drive up, to move up; **zu dicht ~** to drive too close behind (the car in front); **mein Hintermann fährt dauernd so dicht auf** the car behind me is right on my tail all the time **c** *(= nach oben fahren) (Bergleute)* to go up; *(Rel)* to ascend **d** *(= hinauffahren)* **auf etw** *(acc)* **~** to drive onto sth; *(auf Autobahn)* to enter sth **e** *(= aufschrecken)* to start; **aus dem Schlaf ~** to awake with a start **f** *(= aufbrausen)* to flare up, to fly into a rage VT **a** *(= herbeischaffen) Truppen etc* to bring up; *Sand, Erde, Torf etc* to put down; *(inf) Getränke etc* to serve up; *Speisen, Argumente* to dish *(inf) or* serve up; **lass mal eine Runde ~** *(inf)* how about buying us a round? *(inf)* **b** *(= aufwühlen)* to churn *or* dig up

auf|fah|rend ADJ *Temperament* irascible, hasty; *Mensch auch* quick-tempered

Auf|fahrt F **a** *(= das Hinauffahren)* climb, ascent **b** *(= Zufahrt)* approach (road); *(bei Haus etc)* drive; *(= Rampe)* ramp **c** *(von Fahrzeugen)* driving up **d** *(Sw)* = **Himmelfahrt**

Auf|fahr|un|fall M *(von zwei Autos)* collision; *(von mehreren Autos)* pile-up

auf+fal|len *sep irreg* VI *aux sein* **a** *(= sich abheben)* to stand out; *(= unangenehm auffallen)* to attract attention; *(= sich hervortun)* to be remarkable *(durch* for); **er fällt durch seine roten Haare auf** his red hair makes him stand out; **er ist schon früher als unzuverlässig/Extremist aufgefallen** it has been noticed before that he is unreliable/an extremist; **angenehm/unangenehm ~** to make a good/bad impression; **man soll möglichst nicht ~** you should try to be as inconspicuous as possible, you should keep a low profile, you should try to avoid being noticed; **nur nicht ~!** just don't be conspicuous, just don't get yourself noticed **b** *(= bemerkt werden)* **jdm fällt etw auf** sb notices sth, sth strikes sb; **so etwas fällt doch sofort auf** that will be noticed immediately; **so etwas fällt doch nicht auf** that will never be noticed; **der Fehler fällt nicht besonders auf** the mistake is not all that noticeable, the mistake does not show all that much; **fällt es/der Fleck auf?** does it/the stain show?, is it/the stain noticeable?; **das muss dir doch aufgefallen sein!** surely you must have noticed (it)! **c** *(= auftreffen: Regen, Licht etc)* **auf etw** *(acc)* **~** to fall onto sth, to strike sth; **er fiel mit dem Knie (auf einen Stein) auf** he fell and hurt his knee (on a stone) **d** *aux haben (rare: = verletzen)* **sich** *(dat)* **etw ~** to fall and hurt sth, to fall on sth

auf|fal|lend ADJ conspicuous, noticeable; *Schönheit, Ähnlichkeit, Farbe, Kleider* striking; **das Auffallendste an ihr sind die roten Haare** her most striking feature is her red hair, the most striking thing about her is her red hair ADV conspicuously, noticeably; *(= besonders) schön, nett* remarkably, strikingly; **er ist ~ intelligent** he is strikingly *or* remarkably intelligent; **stimmt ~!** *(hum)* too true!, how right you are!

auf|fäl|lig ADJ conspicuous; *Farbe, Kleidung* striking; **~ werden** *(Mensch)* to get oneself noticed; **~ ist, dass/wie …** it's striking *or* quite amazing that/how …; **~ ist seine Vorliebe für …** his preference for … is very marked, he has a very marked preference for … ADV conspicuously; (= besonders) lang, kurz amazingly; **sich ~ verhalten** to get oneself noticed; **er hat sich ~ genau erkundigt** he made a point of inquiring precisely; **er hat ~ wenig mit ihr geredet** it was conspicuous how little he talked with her; **~er gehts nicht mehr** they/he etc couldn't make it more obvious or conspicuous if they/he etc tried

Auf|fäl|lig|keit F **a** (= etw Auffälliges) striking feature **b** no pl (= das Auffälligsein) **die ~ ihrer Kleidung** her striking clothes

auf+fal|ten sep VT to unfold; Fallschirm to open VR to unfold; (Fallschirm) to open; (Geol) to fold upward

Auf|fang|be|cken NT collecting tank; (fig) gathering place; (für Flüchtlinge) focal point

auf+fan|gen VT sep irreg **a** Ball, Gesprächsfetzen to catch; Wagen, Flugzeug to get or bring under control; Flugzeug to pull out; (Telec) Nachricht to pick up; **jds Blick ~** to catch sb's eye **b** (= abfangen) Aufprall etc to cushion, to absorb; Faustschlag to block; (fig) Preissteigerung, Verluste to offset, to counterbalance; **jdn ~** (fig: nach Niederlage, Schicksalsschlag) to support sb, to be there for sb **c** (= sammeln) Regenwasser etc to collect, to catch; (fig) Flüchtlinge etc to assemble

Auf|fang-: **Auf|fang|ge|sell|schaft** F (Fin) rescue company; **Auf|fang|la|ger** NT reception camp, reception centre (Brit) or center (US)

auf+fas|sen sep VT **a** (= interpretieren) to interpret, to understand; **etw als etw** (acc) **~** to take sth as sth; **die Planeten als Götter ~** to conceive of the planets as gods; **das Herz als (eine Art) Pumpe ~** to think or conceive of the heart as a (kind of) pump; **etw falsch/richtig ~** to take sth the wrong way/in the right way **b** (= geistig aufnehmen) to take in, to grasp VI to understand

Auf|fas|sung F **a** (= Meinung, Verständnis) opinion, view; (= Begriff) conception, view; **nach meiner ~** in my opinion, to my mind; **nach christlicher ~** according to Christian belief **b** (= Auffassungsgabe) perception

Auf|fas|sungs-: **auf|fas|sungs|fä|hig** ADJ intelligent; **Auf|fas|sungs|fä|hig|keit** F, **Auf|fas|sungs|ga|be** F **er hat eine große ~** he has a tremendous grasp of things; **Auf|fas|sungs|kraft** F intellectual or mental powers pl; **Auf|fas|sungs|sa|che** F (inf) question of interpretation; (= Ansichtssache) matter of opinion; **Auf|fas|sungs|ver|mö|gen** NT = **Auffassungsfähigkeit**; **Auf|fas|sungs|wei|se** F interpretation; **es hängt von der ~ ab** it depends (on) how you interpret it

auf+fe|gen sep VT to sweep up VI to sweep (up)

auf|fi ['aufi] ADV (Aus) = **herauf, hinauf**

auf|find|bar ADJ **es ist nicht/ist ~** it isn't/is to be found, it can't/can be found; **es ist schwer ~** it's hard to find

auf+fin|den VT sep irreg to find, to discover

auf+fi|schen VT sep **a** Gegenstand to fish up; (inf) Schiffbrüchige to fish out **b** (fig inf) to find; Menschen to find, to dig up (inf)

auf+fla|ckern VI sep aux sein (lit, fig) to flare up

auf+flam|men VI sep aux sein (lit, fig: Feuer, Unruhen etc) to flare up; **in seinen Augen flammte Empörung auf** his eyes flashed in indignation

auf+flat|tern VI sep aux sein (Vogel) to flutter up; (Buch) to rustle

auf+flie|gen VI sep irreg aux sein **a** (= hochfliegen) to fly up **b** (= sich öffnen) to fly open **c** (fig inf: = jäh enden) (Konferenz etc) to break up; (Rauschgiftring, Verbrecher etc) to be busted (inf); **einen Schmugglerring ~ lassen** to bust a ring of smugglers (inf); **eine Konferenz ~ lassen** to bust up (inf) or break up a meeting

auf+for|dern VT sep **a** (= ersuchen) to ask; **wir fordern Sie auf, …** you are required to … **b** (= bitten) to ask, to invite; (zum Wettkampf etc) to challenge **c** (= zum Tanz bitten) to ask to dance

auf|for|dernd ADJ inviting

Auf|for|de|rung F request; (nachdrücklicher) demand; (= Einladung) invitation; (Jur) incitement; **eine ~ zum Tanz** (fig) a challenge

Auf|for|de|rungs-: **Auf|for|de|rungs|cha|rak|ter** M (Psych) stimulative nature; **den ~ einer Äußerung nachweisen** (Jur) to prove that a statement constitutes incitement; **Auf|for|de|rungs|satz** M (Gram) (als Hauptsatz) imperative sentence, command (sentence); (als Teilsatz) imperative clause

auf+fors|ten sep VT Gebiet to reafforest; Wald to retimber, to restock VI **man ist dabei aufzuforsten** they are doing some reafforesting/retimbering

Auf|fors|tung ['aufɔrstʊŋ] F **-, -en** (von Gebiet) reafforestation; (von Wald) retimbering, restocking

auf+fres|sen sep irreg VT (lit, fig) to eat up; **ich könnte dich ~** (inf) I could eat you; **er wird dich deswegen nicht gleich ~** (inf) he's not going to eat you (inf) VI (Tier) to eat all its food up; (inf: = aufessen) to finish eating

auf+fri|schen sep VT to freshen (up); Anstrich, Farbe auch to brighten up; Möbel etc to renovate, to refurbish; (= ergänzen) Vorräte to replenish; (fig) Erinnerungen to refresh; Kenntnisse to polish up; Sprachkenntnisse to brush up; persönliche Beziehungen to renew; Impfung to boost VI aux sein or haben (Wind) to freshen VI impers aux sein to get fresher or cooler

Auf|fri|schung ['auffrɪʃʊŋ] F **-, -en** freshening (up); (von Farbe, Anstrich auch) brightening up; (von Möbeln) renovation, refurbishment; (= Ergänzung: von Vorräten) replenishment; (von Erinnerungen) refreshing; (von Kenntnissen) polishing up; (von Sprachkenntnissen) brushing up; (von Beziehungen) renewal; (von Impfung) boosting

Auf|fri|schungs-: **Auf|fri|schungs|imp|fung** F booster; **eine ~ vornehmen lassen** to have a booster; **Auf|fri|schungs|kurs** M refresher course

auf+fri|sie|ren VT sep **a** Haar to touch up, to titivate **b** (inf) Tisch, Auto etc to do up; Motor to soup up (inf)

auf|führ|bar ADJ (Mus) performable; (Theat auch) stageable; **Faust II ist praktisch gar nicht ~** it is practically impossible to perform or stage Faust II

auf+füh|ren sep VT **a** Theaterstück, Ballett to put on; Drama, Oper to stage, to perform, to put on; Musikwerk, Komponist to perform; **ein Theater ~** (fig) to make a scene **b** (= auflisten) to list; (= nennen) Beispiel to quote, to cite; **einzeln ~** to itemize VR to behave; **sich wie ein Betrunkener ~** to act like a drunkard; **wie er sich wieder aufgeführt hat!** what a performance!

Auf|füh|rung F **a** (Theat) putting on; (von Drama, Oper) staging, performance; (= Vorstellung) performance; **etw zur ~ bringen** (form) to perform sth; **zur ~ kommen** or **gelangen** (form) to be performed **b** (= Auflistung) listing; (= Liste) list; **einzelne ~** itemization

Auf|füh|rungs-: **Auf|füh|rungs|recht** NT performing rights pl; **auf|füh|rungs|reif** ADJ ready to be performed

auf+fül|len VT sep **a** (= vollständig füllen) to fill up; (= nachfüllen) to top up; Mulde etc to fill in or up; **darf ich Ihr Glas ~?** can I top you up? **b** (= ergänzen) Flüssigkeit to dilute; Vorräte to replenish; Öl to top up (Brit) or off (US); **Benzin ~** to tank up, to fill up with petrol (Brit) or gas (US) **c** Suppe, Essen to serve

auf+fut|tern VT sep (inf) to eat up, to polish off

Auf|ga|be F **a** (= Arbeit, Pflicht) job, task; **es ist deine ~, …** it is your job or task or responsibility to …; **es ist nicht ~ der Regierung, …** it is not the job or task or responsibility of the government to …; **sich** (dat) **etw zur ~ machen** to make sth one's job or business **b** (= Zweck, Funktion) purpose, job **c** (esp Sch) (= Problem) question; (zur Übung) exercise; (usu pl: = Hausaufgabe) homework no pl **d** (= Abgabe, Übergabe) (von Koffer, Gepäck) registering, registration; (Aviat) checking (in); (von Brief, Postsendung) handing in; (von Anzeige) placing no pl, insertion **e** (= Verzicht auf weiteren Kampf, weitere Anstrengungen) (Sport) retirement; (Mil etc) surrender; **er hat das Spiel durch ~ verloren** he lost the game by retiring; **die Polizei forderte die Geiselnehmer zur ~ auf** the police appealed to the kidnappers to give themselves up or to surrender **f** (von Gewohnheit, Geschäft) giving up; (von Plänen, Forderungen) dropping, giving up; (von Hoffnung, Studium) abandoning, abandonment; **unter ~ all ihrer Habe** abandoning all their property; **er riet ihm zur ~ seines Studiums** he advised him to give up or abandon or drop his studies **g** (= das Verlorengeben) giving up for lost **h** (Volleyball, Tennis etc) service, serve

auf+ga|beln VT sep Heu, Mist etc to fork up; (fig inf) jdn to pick up (inf); **wo hat er denn die aufgegabelt?** (inf) where did he dig her up? (inf)

Auf|ga|ben-: **Auf|ga|ben|be|reich** M, **Auf|ga|ben|ge|biet** NT area of responsibility; **Auf|ga|ben|heft** NT (Sch) homework book; **Auf|ga|ben|kreis** M (geh) area of responsibility; **Auf|ga|ben|samm|lung** F set of exercises or problems; (von Mathematikaufgaben) maths (Brit) or math (US) question book; **Auf|ga|ben|stel|lung** F **a** (= Formulierung) formulation **b** (= Aufgabe) type of problem; **Auf|ga|ben|ver|tei|lung** F allocation of responsibilities or tasks

Auf|ga|be-: **Auf|ga|be|ort** M pl **-orte** place where a letter etc was posted (Brit) or mailed (esp US); **Auf|ga|be|stem|pel** M postmark

Auf|gang M pl **-gänge** **a** (von Sonne, Mond, Stern) rising; (fig: von Stern) appearance, emergence **b** (= Treppenaufgang) stairs pl, staircase; **im ~** on the stairs or staircase **c** (= Aufstieg) ascent **d** (Sport) opening, beginning, start

Auf|gangs|punkt M (Astron) **der ~ eines Sterns** the point at which a star rises

auf+ge|ben sep irreg ✪ 47.2 VT **a** Hausaufgaben to give, to set; schwierige Frage, Problem to pose (jdm for sb); **jdm viel/nichts ~** (Sch) to give or set sb a lot of/no homework **b** (= übergeben, abgeben) Koffer, Gepäck to register, to check in; Fluggepäck to check in; Brief, Paket to post (Brit), to mail (esp US); Anzeige to put in, to place; Bestellung to place **c** Kampf, Hoffnung, Arbeitsstelle, Freund etc to give up; **gibs auf!** why don't you give up? **d** (= verloren geben) Patienten to give up; (fig) Sohn, Schüler to give up (with or on) **e** (inf) Essen to serve; **jdm etw ~** to give sb sth VI **a** (= sich geschlagen geben) to give up or in; (Mil) to surrender **b** (inf: bei Tisch) to serve (jdm sb); **kann ich dir noch mal ~?** can I give you some more?

auf|ge|bla|sen ['aufgəbla:zn] ADJ (fig) puffed-up, self-important → auch **aufblasen**

Auf|ge|bla|sen|heit F **-,** no pl (fig) self-importance

Auf|ge|bot NT **a** (Jur) public notice **b** (zur Eheschließung) notice of intended marriage; (Eccl) banns pl; **das ~ bestellen** to give notice of one's intended marriage; (Eccl) to put up or post the banns; **das ~ veröffentlichen** to publish the announcement of one's intended marriage; (Eccl) to call the banns **c** (= Ansammlung) (von Menschen) contingent; (von Material etc) array **d** (= Aufbietung) **mit dem ~** or **unter ~ aller Kräfte …** summoning all his/her etc strength …

auf|ge|bracht ['aufgəbraxt] ADJ outraged, incensed → auch **aufbringen**

auf|ge|don|nert ['aufgədɔnɐt] ADJ (pej inf) tarted-up (Brit pej inf), decked-out (US inf) → auch **aufdonnern**

auf|ge|dreht ['aufgədre:t] ADJ (inf) in high spirits → auch **aufdrehen**

auf|ge|dun|sen ADJ swollen, bloated; *Gesicht auch* puffy

auf+ge|hen VI *sep irreg aux sein* **a** *(Sonne, Mond, Sterne)* to come up, to rise **b** *(= sich öffnen)* to open; *(Theat: Vorhang)* to go up; *(Knopf, Knoten, Reißverschluss, Jacke etc)* to come undone **c** *(= aufkeimen, Med: Pocken)* to come up **d** *(Cook)* to rise **e** *(= klar werden)* **jdm geht etw auf** sb realizes sth, sth dawns on sb, sth becomes apparent to sb **f** *(Math: Rechnung etc)* to work out, to come out; *(fig)* to come off, to work (out); **wenn man 20 durch 6 teilt, geht das nicht auf** 20 divided by 6 doesn't go; **im Kriminalroman muss alles sauber ~** in a detective story everything has to work out *or* to be resolved neatly **g** *(= seine Erfüllung finden)* **in etw** *(dat)* **~** to be wrapped up in sth, to be taken up with sth; **er geht ganz in der Familie auf** his whole life revolves around his family **h** *(= sich auflösen)* **in Flammen** *etc* **~** to go up in flames *etc*; **in der Masse ~** to disappear *or* merge into the crowd **i** *(Hunt: Jagdzeit)* to begin

auf|ge|ho|ben ['aufgəho:bn] ADJ **(bei jdm) gut/schlecht ~ sein** to be/not to be in good hands (with sb) → *auch* **aufheben**

auf+gei|len ['aufgailən] VR *sep (sl)* **er geilt sich an diesen Fotos auf** he gets off on these photos *(inf)*

auf|ge|klärt ['aufgəklɛːɐt] ADJ **a** enlightened *(auch Philos)*; **der ~e Absolutismus** *(Hist)* Benevolent Despotism **b** *(sexualkundlich)* **~ sein** to know the facts of life → *auch* **aufklären**

Auf|ge|klärt|heit F -, *no pl* enlightenment; *(sexualkundlich)* knowledge of the facts of life

auf|ge|knöpft ['aufgəknœpft] ADJ *(inf: = mitteilsam)* chatty *(inf)* → *auch* **aufknöpfen**

auf|ge|kratzt ['aufgəkratst] ADJ *(inf)* in high spirits, full of beans *(Brit inf)*, boisterous → *auch* **aufkratzen**

Auf|ge|kratzt|heit F -, *no pl* high spirits *pl*, boisterousness

Auf|geld NT *(dial: = Zuschlag)* extra charge; *(old: = Anzahlung)* deposit, earnest (money) *(old)*

auf|ge|legt ['aufgəle:kt] ADJ **gut/schlecht** *etc* **~** in a good/bad *etc* mood; **(dazu) ~ sein, etw zu tun** to feel like doing sth; **zum Musikhören ~ sein** to be in the mood for listening to music, to feel like listening to music → *auch* **auflegen**

auf|ge|löst ['aufgəlø:st] ADJ **a** *(= außer sich)* beside oneself *(vor +dat* with), distraught; *(= bestürzt)* upset; **in Tränen ~** in tears **b** *(= erschöpft)* exhausted, drained, shattered *(inf)* → *auch* **auflösen**

auf|ge|räumt ['aufgərɔymt] ADJ *(geh: = gut gelaunt)* jovial, light-hearted → *auch* **aufräumen**

auf|ge|regt ['aufgəre:kt] ADJ *(= erregt)* excited; *(= nervös)* nervous; *(= durcheinander)* flustered ADV excitedly → *auch* **aufregen**

Auf|ge|regt|heit F -, *no pl (= Erregtheit)* excitement; *(= Nervosität)* nervousness; *(= Durcheinandersein)* flustered state

auf|ge|schlos|sen ['aufgəʃlɔsn] ADJ *(= nicht engstirnig)* open-minded *(für, gegenüber* as regards, about); *(= empfänglich)* receptive, open *(für, gegenüber* to); **ich bin Vorschlägen gegenüber** *or* **für Vorschläge jederzeit ~** I'm always open to suggestion(s); **einer Sache** *(dat)* **~ gegenüberstehen** to be open-minded as regards *or* about sth → *auch* **aufschließen**

Auf|ge|schlos|sen|heit F -, *no pl* open-mindedness *(für, gegenüber* as regards, about); *(= Empfänglichkeit)* receptiveness, openness *(für, gegenüber* to)

auf|ge|schmis|sen ['aufgəʃmɪsn] ADJ *pred (inf)* in a fix *(inf)*, stuck *(inf)* → *auch* **aufschmeißen**

auf|ge|schos|sen ['aufgəʃɔsn] ADJ **(hoch** *or* **lang) ~** *(Mensch)* who has shot up *or* grown; **ein lang ~er Junge** a tall lanky lad *(esp Brit) or* boy → *auch* **aufschießen**

auf|ge|schwemmt ['aufgəʃvɛmt] ADJ bloated, swollen; *Mensch* bloated → *auch* **aufschwemmen**

auf|ge|setzt ADJ **a sie tötete sich mit einem ~en Kopfschuss** she killed herself by shooting herself in the head **b** *(= geheuchelt) Sprüche* hypocritical, insincere; *Laune, Mimik* put on; **~ wirken** *(= unecht)* to seem false *or* put on → *auch* **aufsetzen**

auf|ge|stellt ADJ *(Sw: = frohsinnig, gute Laune verbreitend)* convivial → *auch* **aufstellen**

auf|ge|ta|kelt ['aufgəta:klt] ADJ *(pej)* dressed (up) to the nines *(inf)* → *auch* **auftakeln**

auf|ge|weckt ['aufgəvɛkt] ADJ bright, quick, sharp → *auch* **aufwecken**

Auf|ge|weckt|heit F -, *no pl* mental quickness, sharpness

auf|ge|wühlt ['aufgəvy:lt] ADJ *(geh)* agitated, in a turmoil *pred*; *Gefühle auch* turbulent; *Wasser, Meer* churning, turbulent; **völlig ~** *(fig)* in a complete turmoil → *auch* **aufwühlen**

auf+gie|ßen VT *sep irreg* **a etw (auf etw** *acc*) **~** to pour sth on (sth); **das angebräunte Mehl mit Brühe ~** to pour stock on(to) the browned flour **b** *Kaffee* to make; *Tee* to make, to brew

auf+glän|zen VI *sep aux sein (lit, fig)* to light up; *(Mond, Sonne, Sterne)* to come out; *(Strahlen reflektierend)* to (begin to) gleam

auf+glie|dern *sep* VT *(in +acc* into) to split up, to (sub)divide; *(= analysieren auch)* to break down, to analyse *(Brit)*, to analyze *(US)*; *(in Kategorien auch)* to categorize, to break down VR *(in +acc* into) to (sub)divide, to break down

Auf|glie|de|rung F division; *(= Analyse auch)* breakdown, analysis; *(in Kategorien)* categorization, breakdown

auf+glim|men VI *sep irreg aux sein* to light up, to begin to glow; *(fig)* to glimmer

auf+glü|hen VI *sep aux sein or haben* to light up, to begin to glow; *(fig) (Gesicht)* to light up, to glow; *(Hass, Neid)* to (begin to) gleam; *(Leidenschaft, Liebe)* to awaken

auf+gra|ben VT *sep irreg* to dig up

auf+grät|schen VI *sep aux sein or haben (Sport)* **auf etw** *(acc)* **~** to straddle sth

auf+grei|fen VT *sep irreg* **a** *(= festnehmen)* to pick up, to apprehend *(form)* **b** *(= weiterverfolgen) Thema, Gedanken* to take up, to pick up; *(= fortsetzen) Gespräch* to continue, to take up again

auf|grund [auf'grʊnt], **auf Grund** ✪ 44.1 PREP *+gen* on the basis of; **~ von Zeugenaussagen** on the basis *or* strength of the witnesses' testimonies; **~ einer Verwechslung/seiner Eifersucht** owing to *or* because of a mistake/his jealousy

auf+gu|cken VI *sep (inf)* to look up *(von* from)

Auf|guss M brew, infusion *(auch Sci)*; *(in Sauna)* pouring of water onto hot coals *(fig pej)* rehash

Auf|guss|beu|tel M sachet (containing coffee/herbs *etc*) for brewing; *(= Teebeutel)* tea bag

auf+ha|ben *sep irreg* VT **a** *Hut, Brille* to have on, to wear; **sie hat ihre Brille nicht aufgehabt** she didn't have her glasses on, she wasn't wearing her glasses **b** *Tür, Augen, Laden, Jacke* to have open **c** *(Sch: als Hausaufgabe)* **etw ~** to have sth (to do); **ich habe heute viel auf** I've got a lot of homework today **d** *(inf: = aufgemacht haben)* to have got *or* gotten *(US)* open **e** *(inf: = aufgegessen haben)* to have eaten up VI *(Laden etc)* to be open

auf+ha|cken VT *sep Straße* to break up; *(Vogel)* to break *or* peck open

auf+hal|sen ['aufhalzn] VT *sep (inf)* **jdm/sich etw ~** to saddle *or* land sb/oneself with sth *(inf)*, to land sth on sb/oneself *(inf)*; **sich** *(dat)* **etw ~ lassen** to get oneself saddled *or* landed with sth *(inf)*

auf+hal|ten *sep irreg* VT **a** *(= zum Halten bringen) Fahrzeug, Entwicklung* to stop, to halt; *Inflation etc* to check; *(= verlangsamen)* to hold up, to delay; *(= abhalten, stören) (bei* from) to hold back, to keep back; **ich will dich nicht länger ~** I don't want to keep *or* hold you back any longer **b** *(inf: = offen halten)* to keep open; **die Hand ~** to hold one's hand out VR **a** *(= an einem Ort bleiben)* to stay **b** *(= sich verzögern)* to stay on, to linger; *(bei der Arbeit etc)* to take a long time *(bei* over) **c** *(= sich befassen)* **sich bei etw ~** to dwell on sth, to linger over sth; **sich mit jdm/etw ~** to spend time dealing with sb/sth **d** *(= sich entrüsten)* **sich über etw** *(acc)* **~** to rail against sth

auf+hän|gen *sep* VT **a** *Kleidung, Bild* to hang up; *(Aut) Rad* to suspend **b** *(= töten)* to hang *(an +dat* from) **c** *(inf)* **jdm etw ~** *(= aufschwatzen)* to palm sth off on sb; *(= glauben machen)* to talk sb into believing sth; *(= aufbürden)* to land *or* saddle sb with sth *(inf)* **d etw an einer Frage/einem Thema ~** *(fig: = entwickeln)* to use a question/subject as a peg to hang sth on VR *(= sich töten)* to hang oneself *(an +dat* from); *(hum: = seine Kleider aufhängen)* to hang one's things up

Auf|hän|ger M tag, loop; **ein ~ für etw** *(fig inf)* a peg to hang sth on *(fig)*

Auf|hän|ge|vor|rich|tung F hanger, suspender; *(Tech)* suspension device

Auf|hän|gung ['aufhɛŋʊŋ] F -, -en *(Tech)* suspension

auf+har|ken VT *sep* to rake up

auf+hau|en *sep* VT *reg or (geh) irreg (= öffnen)* to knock open, to hew open *(liter)*; *Eis* to open up, to hew open *(liter)*; **sich** *(dat)* **den Kopf** *etc* **~** to gash one's head *etc* open VI *aux sein (inf: = auftreffen)* **mit dem Kopf** *etc* **auf etw** *(acc or dat)* **~** to bash *(inf) or* bump one's head *etc* against *or* on sth

auf+häu|fen *sep* VT to pile up, to accumulate; *(fig auch)* to amass VR to accumulate, to pile up

auf|heb|bar ADJ *Gesetz, Regelung* revocable

auf+he|beln ['aufhe:bln] VT *sep (inf, mit Brecheisen) Tür, Kiste* to force *or* break open

auf+he|ben *sep irreg* VT **a** *(vom Boden)* to pick up; *größeren Gegenstand* to lift up; *(= in die Höhe heben)* to raise, to lift (up); *Deckel* to lift off **b** *(= nicht wegwerfen)* to keep; **jdm etw ~** to put sth aside for sb, to keep sth (back) for sb → *auch* **aufgehoben** **c** *(= ungültig machen)* to abolish, to do away with; *Gesetz* to repeal, to abolish, to rescind; *Vertrag* to cancel, to annul, to revoke; *Urteil* to reverse, to quash; *Verlobung* to break off; **dieses Gesetz hebt das andere auf** this law supersedes the other **d** *(= beenden) Blockade, Belagerung* to raise, to lift; *Beschränkung* to remove, to lift; *Sitzung* to close; *Parlament* to dissolve → **Tafel c** **e** *(= ausgleichen)* to offset, to make up for; *Widerspruch* to resolve; *Schwerkraft* to neutralize, to cancel out **f** *(obs: = festnehmen)* to capture, to seize VR **a** *(old: = aufstehen)* to rise *(old, form)* **b** *(= sich ausgleichen)* to cancel each other out, to offset each other; *(Math)* to cancel (each other) out

Auf|he|ben NT -s, *no pl* fuss; **viel ~(s) (von** *or* **um etw) machen** to make a lot of fuss (about *or* over sth); **viel ~(s) von jdm** *or* **um jdn machen** to make a lot of fuss about sb; **ohne (jedes) ~** without any fuss; **ohne viel** *or* **großes ~** without much *or* a big fuss

Auf|he|bung F **a** *(= Abschaffung)* abolition; *(von Gesetz auch)* repeal, rescinding; *(von Vertrag)* cancellation, annulment, revocation; *(von Urteil)* reversal, quashing; *(von Verlobung)* breaking off **b** *(= Beendigung) (von Blockade etc)* raising, lifting; *(von Beschränkung)* removal; *(von Sitzung)* closing; *(von Parlament)* dissolving **c** *(von Widerspruch)* resolving, resolution; *(von Schwerkraft)* neutralization, cancelling out **d** *(obs: = Festnahme)* capture, seizure

Auf|he|bungs|ver|trag M termination agreement

auf+hei|tern ['aufhaitɐn] *sep* **VT** *jdn* to cheer up; *Rede, Leben* to brighten up (*jdm* for sb) **VR** *(Himmel)* to clear, to brighten (up); *(Wetter)* to clear up, to brighten up

auf|hei|ternd ADJ **a** *(Met)* becoming brighter, brightening up **b** *Buch etc* cheerful

Auf|hei|te|rung F -, -en (= *Erheiterung*) cheering up; *(von Rede, Leben)* brightening up; *(Met)* brighter period; **zunehmende ~** gradually brightening up

auf+hei|zen *sep* **VT** to heat (up); *(fig) Zuhörer* to inflame, to stir up; **die Stimmung ~** to whip *or* stir up feelings **VR** to heat up; *(fig)* to hot up *(inf)*, to intensify, to build up

auf+hel|fen VI *sep irreg* (*lit: beim Aufstehen*) to help up (*jdm* sb); **einer Sache** *(dat)* ~ (= *aufbessern*) to help sth (to) improve; *(stärker)* to help strengthen sth

auf+hel|len ['aufhɛlən] *sep* **VT** to brighten (up); *Haare* to lighten; *(fig:* = *klären)* to throw *or* shed light upon **VR** *(Himmel, Wetter, fig: Miene)* to brighten (up); *(fig: Sinn)* to become clear

Auf|hel|ler ['aufhɛlɐ] M -s, - *(in Reinigungsmitteln)* colour *(Brit) or* color *(US)* brightener; *(für Haare)* lightener

Auf|hel|lung F -, -en brightening; *(von Haaren)* lightening; *(fig:* = *Klärung)* clarification; **es kam zu zeitweisen ~en** from time to time the weather brightened up

auf+het|zen VT *sep* to stir up, to incite; **jdn gegen jdn/etw ~** to stir up sb's animosity against sb/sth; **jdn zu etw ~** to incite sb to (do) sth

Auf|het|ze|rei F *(inf)* agitation; *(esp durch Reden)* rabble-rousing

auf|het|ze|risch ADJ inflammatory, rabble-rousing

Auf|het|zung F -, -en incitement, agitation

auf+heu|len VI *sep* to give a howl (*vor* of), to howl (*vor* with); *(Sirene)* to (start to) wail; *(Motor, Menge)* to (give a) roar; (= *weinen*) to start to howl

auf+ho|cken VI *sep aux sein or haben* **a** *(Sport)* to crouch-jump (*auf +acc* on to) **b** *(dial)* **auf etw** *(acc)* ~ to sit on sth

auf+ho|len *sep* **VT** **a** *Zeit, Verspätung, Vorsprung* to make up; *Lernstoff* to catch up on; *Strecke* to make up, to catch up; **Versäumtes ~** to make up for lost time **b** *(Naut)* to haul up, to raise **VI** *(Wanderer, Mannschaft, Schüler, Arbeiter)* to catch up; *(Läufer, Rennfahrer etc auch)* to make up ground; *(Zug etc)* to make up time; (= *Versäumnisse aufholen)* to make up for lost time

Auf|hol|jagd F *(Sport)* pursuit race; *(fig)* race to catch up

auf+hor|chen VI *sep* to prick up one's ears, to sit up (and take notice); **das ließ ~** that made people sit up (and take notice)

auf+hö|ren VI *sep* to stop; *(Musik, Lärm, Straße auch, Freundschaft, Korrespondenz)* to (come to an) end; *(bei Arbeitsstelle)* to finish; **nicht ~/~, etw zu tun** to keep on/stop doing sth; **hör doch endlich auf!** (will you) stop it!; **mit etw ~** to stop sth; **da hört sich doch alles auf!** *(inf)* that's the (absolute) limit!; **da hört bei ihm der Spaß auf** *(inf)* he's not amused by that

auf+hüp|fen VI *sep aux sein (Mensch)* to jump *or* leap up; *(Vogel)* to hop; *(Ball etc)* to bounce; **vor Angst/Freude ~** to jump with fear/for joy

auf+ja|gen VT *sep (lit)* to disturb; *(fig)* to chase away

auf+jauch|zen VI *sep* to shout (out) (*vor* with)

auf+jau|len VI *sep* to give a howl (*vor* of), to howl (*vor* with)

auf+ju|beln VI *sep* to shout (out) with joy, to cheer

auf+juch|zen VI *sep* to whoop with joy, to give a whoop of joy

Auf|kauf M buying up

auf+kau|fen VT *sep* to buy up

Auf|käu|fer(in) M(F) buyer

auf+keh|ren VTI *sep (esp S Ger)* to sweep up

auf+kei|men VI *sep aux sein* to germinate, to sprout; *(fig) (Hoffnung, Liebe, Sympathie)* to bud, to burgeon *(liter)*; *(Zweifel)* to (begin to) take root; **~d** *(fig)* budding, burgeoning *(liter)*, nascent *(liter)*; *Zweifel* growing, nascent *(liter)*

auf+klaf|fen VI *sep aux sein or haben* to gape; *(Abgrund auch)* to yawn; **~d** *(lit, fig)* gaping

auf|klapp|bar ADJ *Fenster, Tafel* hinged; *Truhe, Schreibpult* with a hinged lid; *Klappe* which lets down; *Verdeck* which folds back, fold-back

Auf|klapp|buch NT pop-up book

auf+klap|pen *sep* **VT** to open up; *Klappe* to lift up; *Verdeck* to fold back; *Messer* to unclasp; *Fensterläden, Buch, Landkarte* to open **VI** *aux sein* to open

auf+kla|ren ['aufkla:rən] *sep (Met)* **VI** *impers* to clear (up), to brighten (up) *(auch fig)* **VI** *(Wetter)* to clear *or* brighten (up); *(Himmel)* to clear, to brighten (up)

auf+klä|ren *sep* **VT** **a** *Missverständnis, Irrtum* to clear up, to resolve; *Verbrechen, Rätsel* to solve, to clear up; *Ereignis, Vorgang* to throw *or* shed light upon, to elucidate
b *jdn* to enlighten; **Kinder ~** *(sexualkundlich)* to explain the facts of life to children, to tell children the facts of life; *(in der Schule)* to give children sex education; **jdn über etw** *(acc)* **~** to inform sb about sth; **klär mich mal auf, wie ...** *(inf)* (can you) enlighten me as to how ... → *auch* **aufgeklärt**
c *(Mil)* to reconnoitre *(Brit)*, to reconnoiter *(US)*
VR *(Irrtum, Geheimnis etc)* to resolve itself, to be cleared up; *(Himmel)* to clear, to brighten (up); *(fig: Miene, Gesicht)* to brighten (up)

Auf|klä|rer ['aufklɛ:rɐ] M -s, - *(Mil)* reconnaissance plane; *(klein)* scout (plane)

Auf|klä|rer ['aufklɛ:rɐ] M -s, -, **Auf|klä|re|rin** [-ərɪn] F -, -nen *(Philos)* philosopher of the Enlightenment

auf|klä|re|risch ['aufklɛ:rərɪʃ] ADJ *(Philos)* (of the) Enlightenment; (= *freigeistig)* progressive, striving to enlighten the people; (= *erzieherisch, unterrichtend)* informative; *(Pol)* educational

Auf|kla|rung ['aufkla:rʊŋ] F *(des Wetters)* clearing up; *(des Himmels)* clearing

Auf|klä|rung F **a** *(Philos)* **die ~** the Enlightenment **b** *(von Missverständnis)* clearing up, resolution; *(von Verbrechen, Rätsel)* solution; *(von Ereignis, Vorgang)* elucidation **c** (= *Information)* enlightenment; *(von offizieller Stelle)* informing *(über +acc* about); *(Pol)* instruction **d** **(sexuelle) ~** *(in Schulen)* sex education; **die ~ von Kindern** explaining the facts of life to children **e** *(Mil)* reconnaissance

Auf|klä|rungs-: **Auf|klä|rungs|ar|beit** F instructional *or* educational work; **Auf|klä|rungs|bro|schü|re** F informative pamphlet; *(sexualkundlich)* sex education pamphlet; **Auf|klä|rungs|buch** NT sex education book; **Auf|klä|rungs|film** M sex education film; **Auf|klä|rungs|flug** M *(Mil)* reconnaissance flight *or* mission; **Auf|klä|rungs|flug|zeug** NT reconnaissance plane; *(klein)* scout (plane); **Auf|klä|rungs|kam|pag|ne** F information campaign; **Auf|klä|rungs|li|te|ra|tur** F informative literature; *(Pol)* educational literature; *(sexualkundlich)* sex education literature; *(Philos)* literature of the Enlightenment; **Auf|klä|rungs|ma|te|ri|al** NT informational material; **Auf|klä|rungs|pflicht** F *(Jur) judge's duty to ensure that all the relevant facts of a case are clearly presented (Med) duty to inform the patient of the possible dangers of an operation/a course of treatment etc*; **Auf|klä|rungs|quo|te** F *(in Kriminalstatistik)* success rate (in solving cases), percentage of cases solved; **Auf|klä|rungs|sa|tel|lit** M spy satellite; **Auf|klä|rungs|schiff** NT *(Mil)* reconnaissance ship; **Auf|klä|rungs|schrift** F information pamphlet; *(Pol)* educational pamphlet; *(sexualkundlich)* sex education pamphlet; **Auf|klä|rungs|trup|pe** F *(Mil)* armoured reconnaissance troop(s *pl*); **Auf|klä|rungs|un|ter|richt** M *(Sch)* sex education (classes *pl*); **Auf|klä|rungs|zeit** F = **Aufklärungszeitalter**; **Auf|klä|rungs|zeit|al|ter** NT Age of Enlightenment; **Auf|klä|rungs|ziel** NT *(Mil)* reconnaissance object, object of reconnaissance

auf+klat|schen VI *sep aux sein* (*auf +acc* on) to land with a smack; *(auf Wasser auch)* to land with a splash

auf+klau|ben VT *sep (dial: lit, fig)* to pick up

Auf|kle|be|ad|res|se F (gummed *or* adhesive) address label

auf+kle|ben VT *sep* (*auf +acc* to) to stick on; *(mit Leim, Klebstoff auch)* to glue on; *(mit Kleister)* to paste on; *Briefmarke* to put *or* stick on, to affix *(form)* (*auf +acc* to)

Auf|kle|ber M sticker

auf+klin|gen VI *sep irreg aux sein* to ring out; *(fig)* to echo

auf+klin|ken ['aufklɪŋkn] VT *sep Tür* to open, to unlatch

auf+klop|fen VT *sep* (= *öffnen) Nuss* to crack open

auf+knab|bern VT *sep (inf)* to nibble up; **sie hat alle Chips aufgeknabbert** she gobbled up all the crisps *(Brit) or* potato chips *(US, inf)*

auf+kna|cken VT *sep Nüsse etc* to crack (open); *(inf) Tresor* to break into, to break open, to crack *(inf)*; *Auto* to break into

auf+knal|len *sep (inf)* **VI** *aux sein (Auto)* to crash; *(Gegenstand, Mensch)* to crash down; **auf etw** *(acc)* ~ (= *gegen etw knallen)* to crash into sth; (= *auf etw fallen)* to crash (down) onto sth; **mit dem Kopf (auf etw** *acc)* **~** to bang *or* hit one's head on sth **VT** *(als Strafe)* to give

auf+knöp|fen VT *sep* (= *öffnen)* to unbutton, to undo; **aufgeknöpft** *(Hemd)* unbuttoned; **etw auf etw** *(acc)* **~** to button sth to sth → *auch* **aufgeknöpft**

auf+kno|ten VT *sep* to untie, to undo

auf+knüp|fen *sep* **VT** **a** (= *aufhängen)* to hang (*an +dat* from), to string up *(inf)* (*an +dat* on) **b** (= *aufknoten)* to untie, to undo **VR** to hang oneself (*an +dat* from)

auf+ko|chen *sep* **VT** **a** (= *zum Kochen bringen)* to bring to the *(Brit) or* a *(US)* boil **b** (= *erneut kochen lassen)* to boil up again **VI** **a** *aux sein* to come to the *(Brit) or* a *(US)* boil; *(fig)* to begin to boil *or* seethe; **etw ~ lassen** to bring sth to the *(Brit) or* a *(US)* boil; **das Pulver in die ~de Milch schütten** sprinkle the powder in the milk as it comes to the *(Brit) or* a *(US)* boil **b** *(Aus)* to prepare a fine spread

auf+kom|men VI *sep irreg aux sein* **a** *(lit, fig:* = *entstehen)* to arise; *(Nebel)* to come down; *(Wind)* to spring *or* get up; (= *auftreten: Mode etc)* to appear (on the scene), to arise; **etw ~ lassen** *(fig, Zweifel, Kritik)* to give rise to sth; *üble Stimmung* to allow sth to develop
b **~ für** (= *Kosten tragen)* to bear the costs of, to pay for; (= *Verantwortung tragen)* to carry the responsibility for, to be responsible for; (= *Haftung tragen)* to be liable for; **für die Kinder ~** *(finanziell)* to pay for the children's upkeep; **für die Kosten ~** to bear *or* defray *(form)* the costs; **für den Schaden ~** to make good the damage, to pay for the damage
c **gegen jdn/etw ~** to prevail against sb/sth; **gegen jdn nicht ~ können** to be no match for sb
d **er lässt niemanden neben sich** *(dat)* **~** he won't allow anyone to rival him
e (= *aufsetzen, auftreffen)* to land (*auf +dat* on)
f *(dated)* (= *sich erheben)* to rise, to get up; (= *sich erholen)* to recover
g *(Naut:* = *herankommen)* to come up; *(Sport:* = *Rückstand aufholen) (bei Match)* to come back; *(bei Wettlauf, -rennen)* to catch up, to make up ground
h *(dial: Schwindel, Diebstahl etc)* to come out, to be discovered

Auf|kom|men NT -s, - **a** *no pl* (= *das Auftreten)* appearance; *(von Methode, Mode etc)* advent, emergence; ~ **frischer Winde gegen Abend** fresh winds will get up toward(s) evening **b** *(Fin) (= Summe, Menge)* amount; *(von Steuern)* revenue *(aus, +gen* from) **c** *no pl (von Flugzeug)* landing; **beim** ~ on touchdown

auf+kor|ken ['aufkɔrkn] VT *sep* to uncork

auf+krat|zen *sep* VT *(= zerkratzen)* to scratch; *(= öffnen) Wunde* to scratch open → *auch* **aufgekratzt** VR to scratch oneself sore

auf+krei|schen VI *sep (Mensch)* to scream, to shriek, to give a scream *or* shriek; *(Bremsen, Maschine)* to (give a) screech

auf+krem|peln VT *sep* **(jdm/sich) die Ärmel/Hose** ~ to roll up sb's/one's sleeves/trousers

auf+kreu|zen VI *sep* **a** *aux sein (inf: = erscheinen)* to turn *or* show up *(inf)* **b** *aux sein or haben* **gegen den Wind** ~ *(Naut)* to tack

auf+krie|gen VT *sep (inf)* = **aufbekommen**

auf+kün|den *(geh)*, **auf+kün|di|gen** VT *sep Vertrag etc* to revoke, to terminate; **jdm den Dienst** ~ to hand in one's notice to sb, to give notice to sb that one is leaving (one's employment); **jdm die Freundschaft** ~ *(geh)* to terminate one's friendship with sb; **jdm den Gehorsam** ~ to refuse obedience to sb

Auf|kün|di|gung F termination, revocation; *(von Freundschaft)* termination

Aufl. *abbr von* **Auflage**

auf+la|chen VI *sep* to (give a) laugh; *(schallend)* to burst out laughing; **laut/schrill** ~ to squeal with laughter

auf|lad|bar ADJ chargeable; *(= neu aufladbar)* rechargeable; **~e Geldkarte** electronic cash card

Auf|la|de|ge|rät NT charger

auf+la|den *sep irreg* VT **a etw (auf etw** *acc)* ~ to load sth on(to) sth; **jdm/sich etw** ~ to load sb/oneself down with sth, to burden sb/oneself with sth; *(fig)* to saddle sb/oneself with sth **b** *(elektrisch)* to charge; *(= neu aufladen)* to recharge; *Geldkarte* to reload; *Karte von Prepaid-Handy* to top up; **emotional aufgeladen** *(fig)* emotionally charged **c** *(Aut) Motor* to supercharge, to boost VR *(Batterie etc)* to be charged; *(neu)* to be recharged; *(= elektrisch/elektrostatisch geladen werden)* to become charged

Auf|la|dung F *(Elec) (= das Aufladen)* charging; *(= Ladung)* charge

Auf|la|ge F **a** *(= Ausgabe)* edition; *(= Druck)* impression; *(= Auflagenhöhe)* number of copies; *(von Zeitung)* circulation; **das Buch hat hohe ~n erreicht** a large number of copies of this book have been published; **die Zeitung hat hohe ~n erreicht** this paper has attained a large circulation

b *(Ind: = Fertigungsmenge)* production; **limitierte** ~ limited edition

c *(= Bedingung)* condition; **jdm etw zur ~ machen** to impose sth on sb as a condition; **jdm zur ~ machen, etw zu tun** to make it a condition for sb to do sth, to impose a condition on sb that he do sth; **er bekam die Genehmigung nur mit der ~, das zu tun** he obtained permission only on condition that he do that; **die ~ haben, etw zu tun** to be obliged to do sth

d *(= Stütze)* support, rest

e *(= Überzug)* plating *no pl*, coating; *(= Polsterung)* pad, padding *no pl*; **eine ~ aus Silber** silver plating *or* coating

Auf|la|ge-: **Auf|la|ge|flä|che** F supporting surface; **Auf|la|ge|hö|he** F *(von Buch)* number of copies published; *(von Zeitung)* circulation; **das Buch hatte eine ~ von 12.000** 12,000 copies of the book were published; **die Zeitung hatte eine ~ von ...** the paper had a circulation of ...

Auf|la|gen- = **Auflage-**

Auf|la|ge-: **Auf|la|ge|punkt** M point of support; **auf|la|ge|schwach** ADJ low-circulation *attr*; **auf|la|ge|stark** ADJ high-circulation *attr*; **Auf|la|ge|zif|fer** F circulation (figures *pl*); *(von Buch)* number of copies published

auf|lan|dig ['auflandɪç] ADJ *(Naut)* landward, coastward; *Wind auch* onshore *attr*

auf+las|sen VT *sep irreg* **a** *(inf: = offen lassen)* to leave open; *(= aufbehalten) Hut* to keep *or* leave on; **das Kind länger** ~ to let the child stay up (longer) **b** *(= schließen) (Min) Grube* to close *or* shut down; *(Aus, S Ger) Betrieb* to close *or* shut down; **eine aufgelassene Grube** a closed-down *or* an abandoned mine **c** *(Jur) Grundstück* to convey *(form)*, to transfer, to make over *(form)*

Auf|las|sung F -, -en **a** *(Min, Aus, S Ger: von Geschäft)* closing down, shutdown **b** *(Jur)* conveyancing *(form)*, conveyance *(form)*, transference

Auf|las|sungs|vor|mer|kung F *(Jur)* deed of conveyance

auf+las|ten VT *sep* = **aufbürden**

auf+lau|ern VI *sep +dat* to lie in wait for; *(und angreifen, ansprechen)* to waylay

Auf|lauf M **a** *(= Menschenauflauf)* crowd **b** *(Cook)* (baked) pudding *(sweet or savoury)*

auf+lau|fen VI *sep irreg aux sein* **a** *(= auf Grund laufen: Schiff)* to run aground *(auf +acc or dat* on); *(fig)* to run into trouble; **jdn ~ lassen** to drop sb in it *(inf)* **b** *(= aufprallen)* **auf jdn/etw** ~ to run into sb/sth, to collide with sb/sth; **jdn ~ lassen** *(Ftbl)* to bodycheck sb **c** *(= sich ansammeln)* to accumulate, to mount up; *(Zinsen)* to accrue **d** *(Wasser: = ansteigen)* to rise; **~des Wasser** flood tide, rising tide **e** *(dial: = anschwellen)* to swell (up)

Auf|lauf-: **Auf|lauf|form** F *(Cook)* ovenproof dish; **Auf|lauf|kind** F *(Ftbl; als Begleitung ins Stadion einlaufender Spieler)* mascot

auf+le|ben VI *sep aux sein* to revive; *(= munter, lebendig werden)* to liven up, to come to life again; *(= neuen Lebensmut bekommen)* to find a new lease of life; **Erinnerungen wieder ~ lassen** to revive memories → *auch* **wiederaufleben**

auf+le|cken VT *sep* to lick up

auf+le|gen *sep* ✪ 27.3, 27.6 VT **a** *Tischdecke, Schallplatte etc* to put on; *Gedeck* to set; *Kompresse* to apply, to put on; *Hörer* to put down, to replace; **jdm die Hand** ~ *(Rel)* to lay hands on sb

b *(= herausgeben) Buch* to bring out, to publish; **ein Buch neu** ~ to reprint a book; *(neu bearbeitet)* to bring out a new edition of a book

c *(zur Einsichtnahme)* to display, to put up

d *(Econ) Serie* to launch

e *(Fin) Aktien* to issue, to float; *Fonds* to set up

f *(Naut) Schiff* to lay up

g *(rare: = auferlegen)* **sich** *(dat)* **Entbehrungen** *etc* ~ to impose sacrifices *etc* on oneself, to suffer self-imposed privations *etc*

h → **aufgelegt**

VI **a** *(= Telefonhörer auflegen)* to hang up, to ring off *(Brit)*

b *(= Feuerholz/Kohle etc auflegen)* to put on more firewood/coal *etc*

auf|leh|nen *sep* VR **sich gegen jdn/etw** ~ to revolt *or* rebel against sb/sth VT *(dial)* **den Arm** ~ to lean on one's arm; **die Arme auf etw** *(acc or dat)* ~ to lean one's arms on sth

Auf|leh|nung F -, -en revolt, rebellion

auf+lei|men VT *sep* to glue on *(auf +acc* -to)

auf+le|sen VT *sep irreg (lit, fig inf)* to pick up; **jdn/etw von der Straße** ~ to pick sb/sth up off the street

auf+leuch|ten VI *sep aux sein or haben (lit, fig)* to light up

auf+lich|ten *sep* VT *(= aufhellen) Bild, Raum* to brighten up; *(fig) Hintergründe, Geheimnis* to clear up, to get to the bottom of VR *(Himmel)* to clear; *(fig: Hintergründe)* to be cleared up, to become clear

Auf|lich|tung F *(= Aufhellung)* brightening up; *(fig: von Hintergründen, Geheimnis)* clearing up

Auf|lie|fe|rer M -s, -, **Auf|lie|fe|rin** F -, -nen *(form)* sender; *(von Fracht)* consignor

auf+lie|fern VT *sep (form)* to dispatch; *Fracht* to consign (for delivery)

auf+lie|gen *sep irreg* VI **a** *(= auf etw sein)* to lie *or* rest on top; *(Schallplatte)* to be on the turntable; *(Hörer)* to be on; *(Tischdecke)* to be on (the table); **auf etw** *(dat)* ~ to lie *or* rest on sth, to be on sth **b** *(= ausliegen) (zur Ansicht)* to be displayed; *(zur Benutzung)* to be available **c** *(= erschienen sein: Buch)* to be published **d** *(Naut)* to be laid up VR *(inf: Patient)* to get bedsores VT *(inf)* **sich** *(dat)* **den Rücken** *etc* ~ to get bedsores on one's back *etc*

Auf|lie|ger ['aufliːgɐ] M -s, - *(von Lkw)* trailer

auf+lis|ten ['auflɪstn] VT *sep* to list

Auf|lis|tung F -, -en *(auch Comput)* listing; *(= Liste)* list

auf+lo|ckern *sep* VT **a** *Boden* to break up, to loosen (up) **b die Muskeln** ~ to loosen up (one's muscles); *(durch Bewegung auch)* to limber up **c** *(= abwechslungsreicher machen) Unterricht, Stoff, Vortrag* to make less monotonous, to give relief to *(durch* with); *(= weniger streng machen)* to make less severe; *Frisur, Muster* to soften, to make less severe **d** *(= entspannen, zwangloser machen)* to make more relaxed; *Verhältnis, Atmosphäre* to ease; **in aufgelockerter Stimmung** in a relaxed mood VR **a** *(Sport)* to limber *or* loosen up **b** *(Bewölkung)* to break up, to disperse

Auf|lo|cke|rung F **a** *(von Boden)* breaking up, loosening (up); *(von Muskeln)* loosening up; **... trägt zur ~ des Stoffes/des strengen Musters bei** ... helps to make the material less monotonous/the pattern less severe; **ihm gelang die ~ einer gespannten Atmosphäre** he succeeded in easing a tense atmosphere **b** *(Sport)* limbering *or* loosening up **c** *(von Bewölkung)* breaking up, dispersal, dispersing

Auf|lo|cke|rungs|übung F *(Sport)* limbering-up exercise

auf+lo|dern VI *sep aux sein (Flammen)* to flare up; *(= in Flammen aufgehen)* to go up in flames; *(= lodernd brennen)* to blaze; *(fig: Kämpfe, Hass, Leidenschaft)* to flare up

auf|lös|bar ADJ soluble; *Gleichung auch* solvable; *Ehe* dissoluble; *Verlobung* that can be broken off; *Vertrag* revocable, able to be cancelled *(Brit) or* canceled *(US)*

Auf|lös|bar|keit ['aufløːsbaːɐkait] F -, *no pl* solubility; *(von Gleichung)* solvability; *(von Ehe)* dissolubility; *(von Vertrag)* revocability

auf+lö|sen *sep* VT **a** *(in Flüssigkeit)* to dissolve; *(= in Bestandteile zerlegen, Phot)* to resolve *(in +acc* into); *(Math) Klammern* to eliminate; *Gleichung* to (re)solve; *(Mus) Vorzeichen* to cancel; *Dissonanz* to resolve *(in +acc* into) → *auch* **aufgelöst**

b *(= aufklären) Widerspruch, Missverständnis* to clear up, to resolve; *Rätsel* to solve

c *(= zerstreuen) Wolken, Versammlung* to disperse, to break up

d *(= aufheben)* to dissolve *(auch Parl)*; *Einheit, Gruppe* to disband; *Firma* to wind up; *Verlobung* to break off; *Vertrag* to cancel; *Konto* to close; *Haushalt* to break up

e *(geh) Haar* to let down; *geflochtenes Haar* to let loose; **mit aufgelösten Haaren** with one's hair loose

VR **a** *(in Flüssigkeit)* to dissolve; *(= sich zersetzen: Zellen, Reich, Ordnung)* to disintegrate; *(Zweifel, Probleme)* to disappear; **all ihre Probleme haben sich in nichts aufgelöst** all her problems have dissolved into thin air *or* have disappeared

b *(= sich zerstreuen)* to disperse; *(Wolken)* to break up, to disperse; *(Nebel)* to lift, to disperse

c *(= auseinandergehen) (Verband)* to disband; *(Firma)* to cease trading; *(= sich formell auflösen: esp Parl)* to dissolve

d *(= sich aufklären) (Missverständnis, Problem)* to resolve itself, to be resolved; *(Rätsel)* to be resolved *or* solved

e sich in etw *(acc)* ~ *(= verwandeln)* to turn into sth; *(= undeutlich werden)* to dissolve into sth

f (*geh: Schleife, Haar*) to become undone
g (*Phot*) to be resolved

Auf|lö|sung F **a** (*= das Auflösen*) (*in Flüssigkeit*) dissolving; (*in Bestandteile*) resolution; (*von Widerspruch, Missverständnis*) clearing up, resolving; (*von Rätsel*) solving; (*von Wolken, Versammlung*) dispersal; (*von Einheit, Gruppe*) disbanding; (*von Firma*) winding up; (*von Verlobung*) breaking off; (*von Vertrag*) cancellation; (*von Konto*) closing; (*von Haushalt*) breaking up; (*von Reich, Ordnung, Zellen*) disintegration; (*von Parlament*) dissolution; (*Math*) (*von Klammern*) elimination; (*von Gleichung*) (re)solving; (*Mus: von Vorzeichen*) cancellation
b (*= Lösung*) (*von Problem etc*) resolution; (*von Rätsel*) solution (+*gen*, *von* to)
c (*Phot, Comput, von Bildschirm*) resolution; **das eingebaute Display hat eine ~ von 800 mal 480 Pixel** the integrated display's resolution is set to 800 by 480 pixels
d (*= Verstörtheit*) distraction

Auf|lö|sungs-: **Auf|lö|sungs|er|schei|nung** F sign of breaking up; **Auf|lö|sungs|pro|zess** M process of disintegration; **Auf|lö|sungs|ver|trag** M (*Econ, Jur*) cancellation *or* termination contract; **Auf|lö|sungs|zei|chen** NT (*Mus*) natural

auf+ma|chen *sep* VT **a** (*= öffnen*) to open; (*= lösen, aufknöpfen, aufschnallen*) to undo; *Haar* to loosen; (*inf: = operieren*) to open up (*inf*), to cut open (*inf*)
b (*= eröffnen, gründen*) *Geschäft, Unternehmen* to open (up)
c (*= gestalten*) *Buch, Zeitung* to make *or* get up; (*= zurechtmachen*) *jdn* to dress, to get up (*inf*); (*in Presse*) *Ereignis, Prozess etc* to feature; **der Prozess wurde groß aufgemacht** the trial was given a big spread *or* was played up (in the press)
d (*dial: = anbringen*) *Plakat, Vorhänge* to put up, to hang (up)
VI (*= Tür öffnen*) to open up, to open the door; (*= Geschäft (er)öffnen*) to open (up)
VR **a** (*= sich zurechtmachen*) to get oneself up (*inf*)
b (*= sich anschicken*) to get ready, to make preparations; (*= aufbrechen*) to set out, to start (out); **sich zu einem Spaziergang ~** to set out on a walk

Auf|ma|cher M (*Press*) lead

Auf|ma|chung ['aufmaxʊŋ] F **-, -en a** (*= Kleidung*) turnout, rig-out (*inf*); **in großer ~ erscheinen** to turn up in full dress **b** (*= Gestaltung*) presentation, style; (*von Buch*) presentation, make-up; (*von Seite, Zeitschrift*) layout; **der Artikel erschien in großer ~** the article was given a big spread, the article was featured prominently **c** (*Press: = Artikel etc auf Titelseite*) lead feature

auf+ma|len VT *sep* to paint on (*auf etw acc* sth); (*inf*) to scrawl (*auf* +*acc* on)

Auf|marsch M **a** (*Mil*) (*= das Aufmarschieren*) marching up; (*in Stellung, Kampflinie*) deployment; (*= Parade*) march past **b** (*Sw*) attendance

Auf|marsch|ge|biet NT deployment zone

auf+mar|schie|ren *ptp* **aufmarschiert** VI *sep aux sein* (*= heranmarschieren*) to march up; (*= vorbeimarschieren*) to march past; (*Mil: = in Stellung gehen*) to deploy; **~ lassen** (*Mil: an Kampflinie etc*) to deploy; (*fig hum*) to have march up/past

Auf|maß NT (*Build*) dimension

auf+mei|ßeln VT *sep* (*Med*) to trephine

auf+mer|ken VI *sep* (*= aufhorchen*) to sit up and take notice; (*geh: = Acht geben*) to pay heed *or* attention (*auf* +*acc* to)

auf|merk|sam ['aufmɛrkza:m] ADJ **a** *Zuhörer, Beobachter, Schüler* attentive; *Augen* keen; (*= scharf beobachtend*) observant; **jdn auf etw** (*acc*) **~ machen** to draw sb's attention to sth; **jdn darauf ~ machen, dass ...** to draw sb's attention to the fact that ...; **auf jdn/etw ~ werden** to become aware of sb/sth; **~ werden** to sit up and take notice **b** (*= zuvorkommend*) attentive; **(das ist) sehr ~ von Ihnen** (that's) most kind of you
ADV *zusehen* carefully; *zuhören* attentively; **Felix beteiligt sich ~ am Unterrichtsgeschehen** Felix pays attention in class

Auf|merk|sam|keit F **-, -en a** *no pl* attention, attentiveness; **das ist meiner ~ entgangen** I failed to notice that, that escaped my notice *or* attention **b** *no pl* (*= Zuvorkommenheit*) attentiveness **c** (*= Geschenk*) token (gift); **(nur) eine kleine ~** (just) a little something *or* gift; **kleine ~en** little gifts

auf+mi|schen VT *sep* (*inf*) (*= in Unruhe versetzen*) to stir up; (*= verprügeln*) to beat up, to lay into (*inf*)

auf+mö|beln ['aufmø:bln] VT *sep* (*inf*) *Gegenstand* to do up (*inf*); *Kenntnisse* to polish up (*inf*); *jdn* (*= beleben*) to buck up (*inf*), to pep up (*inf*); (*= aufmuntern*) to buck up (*inf*), to cheer up

auf+mon|tie|ren *ptp* **aufmontiert** VT *sep* to mount, to fit (on); **etw auf etw** (*acc*) **~** to mount sth on sth, to fit sth on *or* to sth

auf+mot|zen *sep* VT (*inf*) to zap up (*inf*); *Theaterstück auch* to revamp (*inf*) VI to get cheeky (*Brit*) *or* fresh (*US*)

auf+mu|cken, auf+muck|sen VI *sep* (*inf*) to protest (*gegen* at, against)

auf+mun|tern ['aufmʊntɐn] VT *sep* (*= aufheitern*) to cheer up; (*= beleben*) to liven up, to ginger up (*inf*); (*= ermutigen*) to encourage; **jdn zu etw ~** to encourage sb to do sth; **ein ~des Lächeln** an encouraging smile

Auf|mun|te|rung F **-, -en a** *no pl* cheering up; (*= Belebung*) livening up, gingering up (*inf*) **b** (*= Ermutigung*) encouragement

auf|müp|fig ['aufmʏpfɪç] ADJ (*inf*) rebellious

Auf|müp|fig|keit F **-, -en** (*inf*) rebelliousness

auf+na|geln VT *sep* to nail on (*auf* +*acc* -to)

auf+nä|hen VT *sep* to sew on (*auf* +*acc* -to)

Auf|nä|her ['aufnɛːɐ] M **-s, -** (*auf Jacke*) (sew-on) badge (*Brit*) *or* patch (*US*)

Auf|nah|me ['aufna:mə] F **-, -n a** (*= Empfang, fig: = Reaktion*) reception; (*= Empfangsraum*) reception (area); **bei jdm freundliche ~ finden** (*lit, fig*) to meet with a warm reception from sb; **jdm eine freundliche ~ bereiten** to give sb a warm reception; **die ~ in ein Krankenhaus** admission (in)to hospital; **wie war die ~ beim Publikum?** how did the audience receive it *or* react?
b (*in Verein, Orden etc*) admission (*in* +*acc* to); (*= Aufgenommener*) recruit
c *no pl* (*lit, fig: = Absorption*) absorption; (*= Nahrungsaufnahme*) taking, ingestion (*form*)
d *no pl* (*= Einbeziehung*) inclusion, incorporation; (*in Liste, Bibliografie*) inclusion
e *no pl* (*von Geldern, Kapital, Hypothek*) raising
f *no pl* (*= Aufzeichnung*) (*von Protokoll, Diktat*) taking down; (*von Personalien*) taking (down); (*von Telegramm*) taking; **die ~ eines Unfalls** taking down details of an accident
g *no pl* (*= Beginn*) (*von Gespräch etc*) start, commencement; (*von Tätigkeit*) taking up; (*von Beziehung, Verbindung*) establishment
h *no pl* (*= das Fotografieren*) taking, photographing; (*= das Filmen*) filming, shooting; **Achtung, ~!** action!
i (*= Fotografie*) photo(graph), shot (*inf*); (*= Schnappschuss, Amateuraufnahme*) snap (*inf*); **eine ~ machen** to take a photo(graph) *etc*
j (*auf Tonband*) recording

Auf|nah|me-: **Auf|nah|me|an|trag** M application for membership *or* admission; **Auf|nah|me|be|din|gung** F condition of admission; **auf|nah|me|be|reit** ADJ *Boden* ready for planting; *Kamera* ready to shoot; (*fig*) receptive, open (*für* to); **Auf|nah|me|be|reit|schaft** F (*fig*) receptiveness, receptivity; **auf|nah|me|fä|hig** ADJ **a für etw ~ sein** to be able to take sth in; **ich bin nicht mehr ~** I can't take anything else in **b** *Markt* receptive; **Auf|nah|me|fä|hig|keit** F **a** ability to take things in **b** (*von Markt*) receptiveness; **Auf|nah|me|for|ma|li|tä|ten** PL admission formalities *pl*; **Auf|nah|me|ge|bühr** F enrolment (*Brit*) *or* enrollment (*US*) fee; (*in Verein*) admission fee; **Auf|nah|me|ge|rät** NT (*Film*) (film) camera; (*= Tonbandgerät*) recorder; **Auf|nah|me|la|ger** NT reception camp; **Auf|nah|me|land** NT host country (*für* to); **Auf|nah|me|lei|ter(in)** M(F) (*Film*) production manager; (*Rad, TV*) producer; **Auf|nah|me|prü|fung** F entrance examination; **Auf|nah|me|stopp** M (*für Flüchtlinge etc*) ban on immigration; **Auf|nah|me|stu|dio** NT (film) studio; (*für Tonaufnahmen*) (recording) studio; **Auf|nah|me|tech|nik** F (*Tonaufnahmen*) recording method; (*Phot, Film*) shooting *or* filming technique; **Auf|nah|me|ver|fah|ren** NT (*für Schule, Verein etc*) admission(s) procedure; (*für Tonaufnahmen*) recording technique; **Auf|nah|me|ver|mö|gen** NT **a** (*= Aufnahmefähigkeit*) receptiveness, receptivity (*für* to) **b** (*= Fassungsvermögen*) capacity; **Auf|nah|me|wa|gen** M (*Rad*) recording van; **auf|nah|me|wür|dig** ADJ (*für Verein*) worthy of admittance; (*für Wörterbuch etc*) worth including

Auf|nahms|prü|fung F (*Aus*) entrance examination

auf+neh|men VT *sep irreg* **a** (*vom Boden*) to pick up; (*= heben*) to lift up
b (*lit: = empfangen, fig: = reagieren auf*) to receive
c (*= unterbringen*) to take (in); (*= fassen*) to take, to hold; *Arbeitskräfte, Einwanderer* to absorb
d (*in Verein, Orden, Schule etc*) to admit (*in* +*acc* to); (*Aus: = anstellen*) to take on
e (*= absorbieren*) to absorb, to take up; (*= im Körper aufnehmen*) to take; (*fig*) (*= eindringen lassen*) *Eindrücke* to take in; (*= begreifen*) to grasp, to take in; **etw in sich** (*dat*) **~** to take sth in; **er nimmt (alles) schnell auf** he takes things in quickly, he grasps things quickly, he's quick on the uptake
f (*= mit einbeziehen*) to include, to incorporate; (*in Liste, Bibliografie*) to include; (*fig: = aufgreifen*) to take up
g (*esp Ftbl*) *Ball* to take, to receive
h (*dial*) (*= aufwischen*) to wipe up
i (*= beginnen*) to begin, to commence; *Tätigkeit, Studium* to take up, to begin; *Verbindung, Beziehung* to establish; **Kontakt** *or* **Fühlung mit jdm ~** to contact sb → **Kampf**
j *Kapital* to borrow; *Kredit, Hypothek* to take out
k (*= niederschreiben*) *Protokoll, Diktat* to take down; *Personalien* to take (down); *Telegramm* to take
l (*= fotografieren*) to take (a photograph *or* picture of), to photograph; (*= filmen*) to film, to shoot (*inf*)
m (*auf Tonband*) to record, to tape
n (*beim Stricken*) *Maschen* to cast on; (*zusätzliche*) to increase, to make
o es mit jdm/etw ~ können to be a match for sb/sth, to be able to match sb/sth; **es mit jdm/etw nicht ~ können** to be no match for sb/sth; **an Naivität kann es keiner mit ihm ~** where naivety is concerned there's no-one to beat him

auf|neh|mens|wert ADJ = **aufnahmewürdig**

Auf|neh|mer M (*dial*) **a** (*N Ger: = Scheuertuch*) cloth **b** (*= Müllschaufel*) shovel

äuf|nen ['ɔyfnən] VT (*Sw*) *Geld etc* to accumulate

auf+nes|teln VT *sep* (*inf*) *Knoten, Schnur* to undo; *Bluse, Haken auch* to unfasten

auf+no|tie|ren *ptp* **aufnotiert** VT *sep* **(sich** *dat*) **etw ~** to note sth down, to make a note of sth

auf+nö|ti|gen VT *sep* **jdm etw ~** (*Geld, Essen*) to force *or* press sth on sb; *Entscheidung, Meinung* to force *or* impose sth on sb; **die Lage nötigt (uns) Vorsicht auf** the situation requires *or* demands that we be cautious, the situation requires caution (on our part)

auf+okt|roy|ie|ren *ptp* **aufoktroyiert** VT *sep* **jdm etw ~** to impose *or* force sth on sb

auf+op|fern *sep* VR to sacrifice oneself VT to sacrifice, to give up

auf|op|fernd ADJ *Mensch* self-sacrificing; *Liebe, Tätigkeit, Arbeit* devoted; **ein ~es Leben** a life of self-sacrifice ADV selflessly, self-sacrificingly

Auf|op|fe|rung F a (= *Aufgabe*) sacrifice; **durch ~ einer Sache** *(gen)* by sacrificing sth; **unter ~ einer Sache** *(gen)* at the cost of sth b (= *Selbstaufopferung*) self-sacrifice; **mit ~** with devotion

Auf|op|fe|rungs-: **auf|op|fe|rungs|be|reit** ADJ self-sacrificing; **Auf|op|fe|rungs|be|reit|schaft** F self-sacrifice; **auf|op|fe|rungs|voll** ADJ self-sacrificing ADV selflessly, self-sacrificingly

auf+pa|cken VT *sep* **jdm/einem Tier etw ~** to load sth onto sb/an animal, to load sb/an animal with sth; **jdm etw ~** *(fig)* to burden *or* saddle *(inf)* sb with sth; **er packte sich** *(dat)* **den Rucksack auf** he put on his rucksack

auf+päp|peln VT *sep (inf) (mit Nahrung)* to feed up; *(durch Pflege)* to nurse back to health

auf+pas|sen ✪ 29.3 VI *sep* a (= *beaufsichtigen*) **auf jdn/etw ~** to watch sb/sth, to keep an eye on sb/sth; (= *hüten*) to look after *or* to mind sb/sth; (= *Aufsicht führen*) to supervise sb/sth; *(bei Examen)* to invigilate sb b (= *aufmerksam sein, Acht geben*) to pay attention; **pass auf!, aufgepasst!** look, watch; (= *sei aufmerksam*) pay attention; (= *Vorsicht*) watch out, mind (out)

Auf|pas|ser [ˈaufpasɐ] M **-s, -**, **Auf|pas|se|rin** [-ərɪn] F **-, -nen** *(pej:* = *Aufseher, Spitzel)* spy *(pej)*, watchdog *(inf)*; *(für VIP etc)* minder; (= *Beobachter*) supervisor; *(bei Examen)* invigilator; (= *Wächter*) guard

auf+peit|schen VT *sep Meer, Wellen* to whip up; *(fig) Sinne* to inflame, to fire; *Menschen* to inflame, to work up; *(stärker)* to whip up into a frenzy; **eine ~de Rede** a rabble-rousing *(pej) or* inflammatory speech

auf+pep|pen [ˈaufpɛpn] VT *sep (inf)* to jazz up *(inf)*

auf+pflan|zen *sep* VT to plant; *(Mil) Bajonett* to fix VR **sich vor jdm ~** to plant oneself in front of sb

auf+pfrop|fen VT *sep (lit)* to graft on (*+dat* -to); *(fig)* to superimpose (*+dat* on)

auf+pi|cken VT *sep* a *(Vogel)* to peck up; *(fig)* to glean, to pick up b (= *öffnen*) to peck open

auf+pin|seln VT *sep (inf:* = *hinschreiben)* to scrawl (*auf +acc* on)

auf+plat|zen VI *sep aux sein* to burst open; *(Lack)* to crack; *(Wunde)* to open up, to rupture

auf+plus|tern *sep* VT *Federn* to ruffle up; *(fig) Vorfall, Ereignis* to blow up, to exaggerate VR *(Vogel)* to ruffle (up) its feathers, to puff itself up; *(Mensch)* to puff oneself up

auf+po|lie|ren *ptp* **aufpoliert** VT *sep (lit, fig)* to polish up

auf|pop|pen VI *sep (Comput, Internet, Popup-Menü, Popup-Fenster)* to pop up

auf+prä|gen VT *sep* to emboss, to stamp; **einen Stempel auf etw** *(acc)* **~** to emboss sth with a stamp

Auf|prall M impact

auf+pral|len VI *sep aux sein* **auf etw** *(acc)* **~** to strike *or* hit sth; *(Fahrzeug auch)* to collide with sth, to run into sth

Auf|preis M extra *or* additional charge; **gegen ~** for an extra *or* additional charge

auf+pres|sen VT *sep* to press on (*auf +acc* -to); (= *öffnen*) to press open

auf+pro|bie|ren *ptp* **aufprobiert** VT *sep* to try (on)

auf+pum|pen VT *sep Reifen, Ballon* to pump up, to inflate; *Fahrrad* to pump up *or* inflate the tyres *(Brit) or* tires *(US)* of

auf+pus|ten VT *(inf)* = **aufblasen VT a**

auf+put|schen *sep* VT a (= *aufwiegeln*) to rouse; *Gefühle, öffentliche Meinung* to stir up (*gegen* against); **jdn zu etw ~** to incite sb to (do) sth b *(durch Reizmittel)* to stimulate; **~de Mittel** stimulants VR to pep oneself up *(inf)*, to dope oneself *(Sport inf)*

Auf|putsch|mit|tel NT stimulant

Auf|putz M get-up *(inf)*, rig-out *(inf)*; *(festlich geschmückt)* finery *(iro)*, attire *(iro)*

auf+put|zen VT *sep* a (= *schönmachen*) *jdn* to dress up, to deck out; *(fig:* = *aufpolieren) Gegenstand* to do up; *Image* to polish *or* brush up b *(dial:* = *aufwischen) Boden* to clean (up); *Flüssigkeit* to mop *or* wipe up

auf+quel|len VI *sep irreg aux sein* a (= *anschwellen*) to swell (up); **aufgequollen** swollen; *Gesicht auch* puffy, bloated; *Mensch* bloated (-looking); **etw ~ lassen** to soak sth (to allow it to swell up) b *(geh:* = *aufsteigen) (Rauch)* to rise

auf+raf|fen *sep* VR to pull oneself up; *(vom Boden auch)* to pick oneself up; **sich ~, etw zu tun** *(inf)* **sich zu etw ~** *(inf)* to rouse oneself to do sth VT *Rock, Papiere, Eigentum* to gather up; (= *schnell aufheben*) to snatch up

auf+ra|gen VI *sep aux sein or haben* (= *in die Höhe aufragen*) to rise; *(sehr hoch, groß auch)* to tower (up) (*über +dat* above, over); **die hoch ~den Türme** the soaring towers; **die hoch ~den Fabrikkamine/Tannen** the towering factory chimneys/fir trees

auf+rap|peln VR *sep (inf)* a = **aufraffen VR** b (= *wieder zu Kräften kommen*) to recover, to get over it; **er hat sich nach seiner Krankheit endlich wieder aufgerappelt** he at last recovered from *or* got over his illness

auf+rau|chen VT *sep* (= *zu Ende rauchen*) to finish (smoking); (= *aufbrauchen*) to smoke, to get through

auf+rau|en VT *sep* to roughen (up); *(Tex) Stoff* to nap; *Haut, Hände* to roughen, to make rough

auf+räu|men *sep* VT to tidy *or* clear up; (= *wegräumen auch*) to clear *or* put away; **aufgeräumt** *(Zimmer)* tidy → *auch* **aufgeräumt** VI a **mit etw ~** to do away with sth b *(pej:* = *dezimieren)* **unter der Bevölkerung (gründlich) ~** *(Seuche etc)* to decimate the population, to wreak havoc among the population; *(Tyrann etc)* to slaughter the population wholesale

Auf|räu|mungs|ar|bei|ten PL clear(ing)-up operations *pl*

auf+rech|nen VT *sep* a **jdm etw ~** to charge sth to sb *or* to sb's account; *(fig:* = *vorwerfen)* to throw sth in sb's face b **etw gegen etw ~** to set sth off against sth, to offset sth against sth

auf|recht [ˈaufrɛçt] ADJ *(lit, fig)* upright; *Körperhaltung, Gangart auch* erect; **in** *or* **mit ~em Gang** *(fig)* with one's head held high ADV **~ gehen/stehen** to walk/stand upright *or* erect; **~ sitzen** to sit up(right); **etw ~ hinstellen** to place sth upright, to place sth in an upright position; **halte dich ~!** stand up straight!

auf|recht+er|hal|ten *ptp* **aufrechterhalten** VT *sep irreg* to maintain; *Kontakt, Bräuche auch* to keep up; *Behauptung auch* to stick to; *Entschluss, Glauben auch* to keep *or* adhere to, to uphold; *Verein* to keep going; (= *moralisch stützen*) *jdn* to keep going, to sustain

Auf|recht|er|hal|tung F maintenance, maintaining; *(von Kontakten, Bräuchen auch)* keeping up

auf+re|den VT *sep* = **aufschwatzen**

auf+re|gen *sep* VT (= *ärgerlich machen*) to irritate, to annoy; (= *nervös machen*) to make nervous *or* edgy *(inf)*; (= *beunruhigen*) to agitate, to disturb; (= *bestürzen*) to upset; (= *erregen*) to excite; **du regst mich auf!** you're getting on my nerves; **er regt mich auf** he drives me mad *(inf)* VR to get worked up *(inf) or* excited (*über +acc* about) → *auch* **aufgeregt**

auf|re|gend ADJ exciting

Auf|re|gung F excitement *no pl*; (= *Beunruhigung*) agitation *no pl*; **nur keine ~!** don't get excited, don't get worked up *(inf) or* in a state *(inf)!*; **die Nachricht hat das ganze Land in ~ versetzt** the news caused a great stir throughout the country; **jdn in ~ versetzen** to put sb in a flurry, to get sb in a state *(inf)*; **alles war in heller ~** everything was in utter confusion, there was complete bedlam

auf+rei|ben *sep irreg* VT a (= *wund reiben*) *Haut etc* to chafe, to rub sore; **sich** *(dat)* **die Hände/Haut ~** to chafe one's hands/oneself, to rub one's hands/oneself sore b *(fig:* = *zermürben)* to wear down *or* out c *(Mil:* = *völlig vernichten)* to wipe out, to annihilate VR *(durch Sorgen etc)* to wear oneself out; *(durch Arbeit auch)* to work oneself into the ground

auf|rei|bend ADJ *(fig)* wearing, trying; *(stärker)* stressful; **nervlich ~** stressful

auf+rei|hen *sep* VT *(in Linie)* to line up, to put in a line/lines *or* a row/rows; *Perlen* to string; *(fig:* = *aufzählen)* to list, to enumerate VR to line up, to get in a line/lines *or* a row/rows

auf+rei|ßen *sep irreg* VT a (= *durch Reißen öffnen, aufbrechen*) to tear *or* rip open; *Straße* to tear *or* rip up b *Tür, Fenster* to fling open; *Augen, Mund* to open wide c (= *beschädigen*) *Kleidung* to tear, to rip; *Haut* to gash d *(Sport inf) Deckung, Abwehr* to open up e (= *in groben Zügen darstellen*) *Thema* to outline f *(inf) Mädchen* to pick up *(inf)* VI *aux sein (Naht)* to split, to burst; *(Hose)* to tear, to rip; *(Wunde)* to tear open; *(Wolkendecke)* to break up

auf+rei|ßen VT *sep irreg (Tech)* to draw the/an elevation of

auf+rei|zen VT *sep* a (= *herausfordern*) to provoke; (= *aufwiegeln*) to incite b (= *erregen*) to excite; *(stärker)* to inflame

auf|rei|zend ADJ provocative ADV provocatively

auf+rib|beln [ˈaufrɪbln] VT *sep (inf)* to unpick

Auf|rich|te [ˈaufrɪçtə] F **-, -n** *(Sw:* = *Richtfest)* topping-out ceremony

auf+rich|ten *sep* VT a (= *in aufrechte Lage bringen*) *Gegenstand* to put *or* set upright; *jdn* to help up; *Oberkörper* to raise (up), to straighten (up) b (= *aufstellen*) to erect, to put up; *(fig)* to set up c *(fig: moralisch)* to put new heart into, to give fresh heart to, to lift VR (= *gerade stehen*) to stand up (straight); (= *gerade sitzen*) to sit up (straight); *(aus gebückter Haltung)* to straighten up; *(fig: moralisch)* to pick oneself up, to get back on one's feet; **sich im Bett ~** to sit up in bed; **sich an jdm ~** *(fig)* to find new strength in sb, to take heart from sb

auf|rich|tig ADJ sincere (*zu, gegen* towards); (= *ehrlich auch*) honest ADV sincerely, honestly; *hassen, verabscheuen* truly

Auf|rich|tig|keit F sincerity (*zu, gegen* towards); (= *Ehrlichkeit auch*) honesty

auf+rie|geln [ˈaufriːgln] VT *sep* to unbolt

Auf|riss M a *(Tech)* elevation; **etw im ~ zeichnen** to draw the side/front elevation of sth b *(fig:* = *Abriss)* outline, sketch

Auf|riss|zeich|nung F *(Tech, Archit)* elevation

auf+rit|zen VT *sep* (= *öffnen*) to slit open; (= *verletzen*) to cut (open)

auf+rol|len *sep* VT a (= *zusammenrollen*) *Teppich, Ärmel* to roll up; *Kabel* to coil *or* wind up; *(auf Rolle)* to wind up b (= *entrollen*) to unroll; *Fahne* to unfurl; *Kabel* to uncoil, to unwind; *(von Rolle)* to unwind, to reel off c *(fig) Problem* to go into; **einen Fall/Prozess wieder ~** to reopen a case/trial d *(Mil, Comm:* = *angreifen) Stellung, Markt* to penetrate VR (= *sich zusammenrollen*) to roll up

auf+rü|cken VI *sep aux sein* a (= *weiterrücken, aufschließen*) to move up *or* along b (= *befördert werden*) to move up, to be promoted; *(Schüler)* to move *or* go up; **zum Geschäftsleiter ~** to be promoted to manager

Auf|ruf M a appeal (*an +acc* to); **einen ~ an jdn richten** to appeal to sb; **~ zum Streik/Handeln** call for a strike/for negotiations b *(von Namen)* **seinen ~ abwarten** to wait for one's name to be called, to wait to be called; **nach ~** on being called, when called; **letzter ~ für Flug LH 1615** last call for flight LH 1615 c *(Comput)* call d *(Fin: von Banknoten)* calling in

auf+ru|fen *sep irreg* VT a *Namen* to call; *Wartenden* to call (the name of); **Sie werden aufgerufen** your name *or* you will be called; **einen**

Schüler ~ to ask a pupil (to answer) a question **b** *(= auffordern)* **jdn zu etw** ~ *(zu Mithilfe, Unterstützung etc)* to appeal to *or* call upon sb for sth; **jdn ~, etw zu tun** to appeal to *or* call upon sb to do sth; **Arbeiter zum Streik/zu einer Demonstration** ~ to call upon workers to strike/ to attend a demonstration
c *(Jur) Zeugen* to summon
d *(Comput)* to call (up); **wieder** ~ to recall
VI zum Widerstand/Streik *etc* ~ to call for resistance/a strike *etc*, to call upon people to resist/strike *etc* **a** *(Fin: = einziehen) Banknoten* to call in

Auf|ruhr [ˈaufruːɐ] **M -(e)s, -e a** *(= Auflehnung)* revolt, rebellion, uprising **b** *(= Bewegtheit, fig: = Erregung)* tumult, turmoil; **ihr innerlicher** ~ the tumult *or* turmoil within her; **in ~ sein** to be in a tumult *or* turmoil; **in ~ geraten** to get into a state of turmoil; **jdn in ~ versetzen** to throw sb into a turmoil

auf+rüh|ren VT *sep* to stir up; *(fig auch) Gefühle* to rouse; **alte Geschichten wieder** ~ to rake *or* stir up old stories

Auf|rüh|rer [ˈaufryːrɐ] **M -s, -, Auf|rüh|re|rin** [-ərɪn] **F -, -nen** rabble-rouser

auf|rüh|re|risch [ˈaufryːrərɪʃ] **ADJ a** *(= aufwiegelnd) Rede, Pamphlet* rabble-rousing, inflammatory **b** *attr (= in Aufruhr)* rebellious; *(= meuternd)* mutinous **ADV** *fragen, sagen* provocatively

auf+run|den VT *sep Betrag, Zahl etc* to round up *(auf +acc* to)

auf+rüs|ten VT *sep* **a** *auch vi (Mil)* to arm; **ein Land atomar** ~ to give a country nuclear arms; **wieder** ~ to rearm **b** *(Tech) Gerät, Computer* to upgrade **c** *(fig)* **jdn moralisch** ~ to boost sb's morale

Auf|rüs|tung F a *(Mil)* arming; **atomare** ~ acquiring nuclear armaments **b** *(Tech, von Gerät, Computer)* upgrading

auf+rüt|teln VT *sep* to rouse *(aus* from); *(aus Lethargie etc auch)* to shake up *(aus* out of); **jdn/jds Gewissen** ~ to stir sb/sb's conscience; **jdn zum Handeln** ~ to rouse sb to action

Auf|rüt|te|lung F -, -en, Auf|rütt|lung [ˈaufrʏtlʊŋ] **F -, -en** *(fig) (= das Aufrütteln)* rousing; *(aus Lethargie etc auch)* shaking up; *(Zustand)* excitement

aufs [aufs] *contr von* **auf das**

auf+sa|gen VT *sep* **a** *Gedicht etc* to recite, to say **b** *(geh: = für beendet erklären)* **jdm die Freundschaft** ~ to break off one's friendship with sb; **jdm den Dienst/Gehorsam** ~ to refuse to serve/obey sb

auf+sam|meln VT *sep (lit, fig)* to pick up

auf|säs|sig [ˈaufzɛsɪç] **ADJ** rebellious; *esp Kind auch* recalcitrant, obstreperous

Auf|säs|sig|keit F -, *no pl* rebelliousness; *(esp von Kind auch)* recalcitrance, obstreperousness

auf+sat|teln VT *sep Pferd* to saddle (up)

Auf|satz M a *(= Abhandlung)* essay; *(Sch)* essay, composition **b** *(= oberer Teil)* top *or* upper part; *(zur Verzierung)* bit on top; *(von Kamera etc)* attachment; **ein Schrank mit abnehmbarem** ~ a cupboard with a removable top part *or* section **c** *(Mil: von Geschütz)* (gun) sight

Auf|satz-: Auf|satz|heft NT essay *or* composition book; **Auf|satz|samm|lung F** collection of essays; **Auf|satz|the|ma NT** essay subject

auf+sau|gen VT *sep irreg Flüssigkeit* to soak up; *(Sonne auch)* to absorb; *(fig)* to absorb; **etw mit dem Staubsauger** ~ to vacuum sth up; **etw in sich** *(dat)* ~ *(Mensch)* to absorb sth, to soak sth up

auf+schau|en VI *sep (dial)* = **aufblicken**

auf+schau|feln VT *sep* **a** *(= aufhäufen)* to pile up **b** *(= aufgraben)* to dig up

auf+schau|keln VR *sep (fig: Hass, Emotionen)* to build up

auf+schäu|men *sep* **VI** *aux sein (Meer)* to foam; *(Getränke)* to foam *or* froth up; **vor Zorn** ~ to boil with anger **VT** *Kunststoff* to foam

auf+schei|nen VI *sep irreg aux sein* **a** *(geh: = aufleuchten)* to light up; *(Licht)* to appear; *(fig liter)* to shine out **b** *(Aus: = erscheinen)* to appear

auf+scheu|chen VT *sep* to startle; *(inf) Öffentlichkeit* to startle, to shock; **jdn aus etw** ~ to jolt sb out of sth; **jdn von seiner Arbeit/Lektüre** ~ to disturb sb when he is working/reading

auf+scheu|ern *sep* **VT** *Fuß etc* to rub sore; *Haut* to chafe; **sich** *(dat)* **die Hände/Füße** ~ to take the skin off one's hands/feet **VR** to rub oneself sore

auf+schich|ten VT *sep* to stack, to pile up; *Stapel* to build up

Auf|schich|tung F stacking, piling up; *(von Stapel)* building

auf+schie|ben VT *sep irreg Fenster, Tür* to slide open; *Riegel* to push *or* slide back; *(fig: = verschieben)* to put off; **aufgeschoben ist nicht aufgehoben** *(prov)* putting something off doesn't mean it won't happen

auf+schie|ßen *sep irreg* **VI** *aux sein* **a** *(Saat, Jugendlicher)* to shoot up; *(Flammen, Fontäne etc)* to leap *or* shoot up; **wie Pilze** ~ *(Hochhäuser etc)* to mushroom → *auch* **aufgeschossen b** *(= emporschnellen, hochfahren)* to shoot *or* leap up **VT** *(Naut) Tau* to coil

auf+schim|mern VI *sep aux sein or haben (geh)* to flash; **in etw** *(dat)* ~ *(fig)* to illuminate sth

Auf|schlag M a *(= das Aufschlagen)* impact; *(= Geräusch)* crash **b** *(Tennis etc)* service, serve; **wer hat ~?** whose service *or* serve is it?; **sie hat** ~ she's serving, it's her service *or* serve **c** *(= Preisaufschlag)* surcharge, extra charge **d** *(= Ärmelaufschlag)* cuff; *(= Hosenaufschlag)* turn-up *(Brit)*, cuff *(US)*; *(= Mantelaufschlag etc)* lapel

Auf|schlag|ball M *(Tennis)* service, serve

auf+schla|gen *sep irreg* **VI a** *aux sein (= auftreffen)* **auf etw** *(dat)* ~ to hit sth; **das Flugzeug schlug in einem Waldstück auf** the plane crashed into a wood; **mit dem Kopf** *etc* **auf etw** *(acc or dat)* ~ to hit one's head *etc* on sth; **dumpf** ~ to thud *(auf +acc* onto); **sie fühlte, wie ihr Kopf hart aufschlug** she felt the hard crack on her head
b *aux sein (= sich öffnen)* to open
c *aux sein (Flammen)* to leap *or* blaze up *(aus* out of)
d *aux haben or (rare) sein (Waren, Preise)* to rise, to go up *(um* by)
e *(Tennis etc)* to serve; **du musst** ~ it's your service *or* serve
VT a *(= durch Schlagen öffnen)* to crack; *Nuss* to crack (open); *Eis* to crack a hole in; **jdm/sich den Kopf** ~ to crack *or* cut open sb's/one's head; **jdm/sich die Augenbraue** ~ to cut open sb's/one's eyebrow
b *(= aufklappen)* to open; *(= zurückschlagen) Bett, Bettdecke* to turn back; *(= hochschlagen) Kragen etc* to turn up; *Schleier* to lift up, to raise; **schlagt Seite 111 auf** open your books at page 111
c *Augen* to open
d *(= aufbauen) Bett, Liegestuhl* to put up; *Zelt* to pitch, to put up; *(Nacht)lager* to set up, to pitch; **er hat seinen Wohnsitz in Wien/einem alten Bauernhaus aufgeschlagen** he has taken up residence in Vienna/an old farmhouse
e *(Comm) Preise* to put up, to raise; **10% auf etw** *(acc)* ~ to put 10% on sth

Auf|schlä|ger(in) M(F) *(Tennis etc)* server

Auf|schlag-: Auf|schlag|feh|ler M service fault; **Auf|schlag|spiel NT** service game; **Auf|schlag|zün|der M** *(Mil)* percussion fuse

auf+schle|cken VT *sep (S Ger)* to lick up

auf+schlie|ßen *sep irreg* **VT a** *(= öffnen)* to unlock; *(geh: = erklären)* to elucidate *(jdm* to sb); **jdm die Tür** *etc* ~ to unlock the door *etc* for sb **b** *(geh: = offenbaren)* **jdm sein Herz** ~ to open one's heart to sb; **jdm sein Innerstes** ~ to tell sb one's innermost thoughts **c** *(Chem, Biol)* to break down **d** *Rohstoffvorkommen, Bauland* to develop **VR** *(geh)* **sich leicht** ~ to find it easy to be open *or* frank; **sich jdm** ~ to be open *or* frank with sb **VI a** *(= öffnen)* **(jdm)** ~ to unlock the door (for sb) **b** *(= heranrücken)* to close up; *(Sport)* to catch up *(zu* with) → *auch* **aufgeschlossen**

auf+schlit|zen VT *sep* to rip (open); *(mit Messer auch)* to slit (open); *Gesicht* to slash; *Bauch* to slash open

auf+schluch|zen VI *sep (geh)* to sob convulsively

Auf|schluss M a *(= Aufklärung)* information *no pl*; **(jdm)** ~ **über etw** *(acc)* **geben** to give (sb) information about sth; ~ **über etw** *(acc)* **verlangen** to demand an explanation of sth **b** *(Chem, Biol)* breaking down **c** *(Min: = Erschließung)* development

auf+schlüs|seln [ˈaufʃlʏsln] **VT** *sep* to break down *(nach* into); *(= klassifizieren)* to classify *(nach* according to)

Auf|schlüs|se|lung F -, -en, Auf|schlüss|lung [ˈaufʃlʏslʊŋ] *(rare)* **F -, -en** breakdown *(nach* into); *(= Klassifikation)* classification *(nach* according to)

auf|schluss|reich ADJ informative, instructive

auf+schmei|ßen VT *sep irreg* **a** *(Aus inf) jdn* to send up *(inf)* **b** → **aufgeschmissen**

auf+schmie|ren VT *sep (inf)* to spread on; *Farbe* to smear on

auf+schnal|len VT *sep* **a** *(= befestigen)* to buckle *or* strap on *(auf etw acc* (-to) sth) **b** *(= losschnallen)* to unbuckle, to unstrap

auf+schnap|pen *sep* **VT** to catch; *(inf) Wort etc* to pick up **VI** *aux sein* to snap *or* spring open

auf+schnei|den *sep irreg* **VT a** *(= öffnen)* to cut open; *(= tranchieren) Braten* to carve; *Buch* to cut; *(Med) Geschwür* to lance → **Pulsader b** *(= in Scheiben schneiden)* to slice **VI** *(inf: = prahlen)* to brag, to boast

Auf|schnei|der(in) M(F) *(inf)* boaster, braggart

Auf|schnei|de|rei F -, -en *(inf)* bragging *no pl*, boasting *no pl*

auf|schnei|de|risch [ˈaufʃnaidərɪʃ] **ADJ** *(inf)* boastful

auf+schnel|len VI *sep aux sein (= hochschnellen)* to leap *or* jump up

Auf|schnitt M, *no pl* (assorted) sliced cold meat, cold cuts *pl (US)*; *(= Käse)* (assorted) sliced cheeses *pl*; **kalter** ~ (assorted) sliced cold meat, cold cuts *pl (US)*

auf+schnü|ren VT *sep* **a** *(= lösen)* to untie, to undo **b** *(rare: = befestigen)* to tie on *(auf +acc* -to)

auf+schram|men VT *sep* = **aufschürfen**

auf+schrau|ben VT *sep* **a** *Schraube etc* to unscrew; *Flasche etc* to take the top off **b** *(= festschrauben)* to screw on *(auf +acc* -to)

auf+schre|cken *sep pret* **schreckte auf**, *ptp* **aufgeschreckt VT** to startle; *(aus Gleichgültigkeit)* to rouse *(aus* from), to jolt *(aus* out of); **jdn aus dem Schlaf** ~ to rouse sb from sleep **VI** *pret auch* **schrak auf** *aux sein* to start (up), to be startled; **aus dem Schlaf** ~ to wake up with a start; **aus seinen Gedanken** ~ to start

Auf|schrei M yell; *(schriller Aufschrei)* scream, shriek; **ein ~ der Empörung/Entrüstung** *(fig)* an outcry

auf+schrei|ben VT *sep irreg* **a** *(= niederschreiben)* **etw** ~ to write *or* note sth down **b** *(= notieren)* **sich** *(dat)* **etw** ~ to make a note of sth **c** *(= als Schulden anschreiben)* to put on the slate *(inf)*, to chalk up *(inf)* **d** *(inf: = verordnen)* to prescribe **e** *(inf: = polizeilich aufschreiben)* **jdn** ~ to take sb's particulars; **das Auto** ~ to take the car's number

auf+schrei|en VI *sep irreg* to yell out; *(schrill)* to scream *or* shriek out

Auf|schrift F *(= Beschriftung)* inscription; *(= Etikett)* label; **eine Flasche mit der ~ „Vorsicht Gift" versehen** to label a bottle "Danger - Poison"

Auf|schub M *(= Verzögerung)* delay; *(= Vertagung)* postponement; **die Sache duldet** *or* **lei-**

det *(old)* **keinen ~** *(geh)* the matter brooks no delay *(liter)*; **jdm ~ gewähren** *(= Zahlungsaufschub)* to give sb an extension of the payment deadline, to allow sb grace

auf+schür|fen VT *sep* **sich** *(dat)* **die Haut/das Knie ~** to graze *or* scrape oneself/one's knee

auf+schüt|teln VT *sep Kissen etc* to shake *or* plump up

auf+schüt|ten VT *sep* **a** *Flüssigkeit* to pour on; **Wasser auf etw** *(acc)* **~** to pour water on *or* over sth; **Kaffee ~** to make coffee **b** *(= nachfüllen) Kohle* to put on (the fire) **c** *Stroh, Steine* to spread; *Damm, Deich* to throw up; *Straße* to raise **d** *(Geol)* to deposit

Auf|schüt|tung F **-, -en a** *(= Damm)* bank of earth **b** *(Geol)* deposit

auf+schwat|zen, auf+schwät|zen *(dial)* VT *sep (inf)* **jdm etw ~** to talk sb into taking sth; **sie hat ihr ihren Sohn aufgeschwatzt** she talked her into marrying her son

auf+schwei|ßen VT *sep* to cut open (with an oxyacetylene torch)

auf+schwel|len *sep* VI *irreg aux sein* to swell (up)

auf+schwem|men VT *sep* **jdn ~** to make sb bloated; **jds Gesicht ~** to make sb's face bloated *or* puffy → *auch* **aufgeschwemmt**

auf+schwin|gen VR *sep irreg* to swing oneself up; *(Vogel)* to soar (up); *(fig: Gedanken)* to rise to higher realms; **sich zu etw ~** *(= sich aufraffen)* to bring oneself to do sth; *(= sich aufwerfen)* to set oneself up to be sth; *(= sich hocharbeiten)* to work one's way up to be(come) sth; *(hum: = etw kaufen)* to bring oneself to get sth

Auf|schwung M **a** *(= Antrieb)* lift; *(der Fantasie)* upswing; *(der Seele)* uplift; *(der Wirtschaft etc)* upturn, upswing (*+gen* in); **das gab ihr (einen) neuen ~** that gave her a lift; **der ~ Ost** *the economic upturn in Eastern Germany* **b** *(Turnen)* swing-up

auf+se|hen VI *sep irreg* to look up; **zu jdm/etw ~** *(lit)* to look up at sb/sth; *(fig)* to look up to sb/sth

Auf|se|hen NT **-s,** *no pl* sensation; **~ erregend = aufsehenerregend; großes ~ erregen** to cause a sensation *or* stir; **um etw viel ~ machen** to make a lot of fuss about sth; **ohne großes ~** without any to-do *(inf) or* fuss; **ich möchte jedes ~ vermeiden** I want to avoid any fuss; **bitte kein ~, meine Herren** no fuss please, gentlemen

auf|se|hen|er|re|gend ADJ sensational

Auf|se|her(in) M(F) *(allgemein)* supervisor; *(bei Prüfung)* invigilator; *(= Sklavenaufseher)* overseer; *(= Gefängnisaufseher)* warder *(Brit)*, guard *(US)*; *(= Parkaufseher, Museumsaufseher etc)* attendant

auf sein VI *irreg aux sein* **a** *(= aufgestanden sein)* to be up **b** *(= geöffnet sein)* to be open

auf|sei|ten [aufˈzaitn], **auf Sei|ten** PREP *+gen* on the part of

auf+set|zen *sep* VT **a** *(= auf etw setzen) Brille, Hut, Topf, Essen, Flicken* to put on; *Kegel* to set up; *Steine* to lay; *Tonarm* to lower; *Fuß* to put on the ground, to put down; *(fig) Lächeln, Miene etc* to put on; **ich kann den Fuß nicht richtig ~** I can't put any weight on my foot; **sich** *(dat)* **den Hut ~** to put on one's hat → *auch* **aufgesetzt, Dämpfer, Horn a b** *Flugzeug* to land, to bring down; *Boot* to pull up, to beach; *(unabsichtlich)* to ground, to run aground **c** *(= aufrichten) Kranken etc* to sit up **d** *(= verfassen)* to draft VR to sit up VI *(Flugzeug)* to touch down, to land; *(Tonarm)* to come down

Auf|set|zer [ˈaufzɛtsɐ] M **-s, -** *(Sport)* bouncing ball

auf+seuf|zen VI *sep* **(tief/laut) ~** to heave a (deep/loud) sigh

Auf|sicht [ˈaufzɪçt] F **-, -en a** *no pl (= Überwachung)* supervision *(über +acc* of); *(= Obhut)* charge; **unter jds ~** *(dat)* under the supervision of sb, in the charge of sb; **unter polizeilicher/ärztlicher ~** under police/medical supervision; **~ über jdn/etw führen** to be in charge of sb/sth; **bei einer Prüfung ~ führen** to invigilate an exam; **im Pausenhof ~ führen** to be on duty during break; **jdn ohne ~ lassen** to leave sb unsupervised *or* without supervision; **der Kranke darf niemals ohne ~ sein** the patient must be kept under constant supervision; **jdm obliegt die ~ über etw** *(acc) (form)* sb is in charge of *or* responsible for sth **b** *(= Aufsicht Führender)* person in charge; *(= Aufseher)* supervisor; **~ führend** *(Behörde)* supervisory; *Beamter* supervising; *Lehrer* on duty *pred*; *(bei Prüfung)* invigilating; **~ Führende(r) = Aufsichtführende(r) c** *(Math: = Draufsicht)* top view

Auf|sicht-: auf|sicht|füh|rend ADJ *attr* → **Aufsicht b**; **Auf|sicht|füh|ren|de(r)** [-fyːrəndə] MF *decl as adj* person in charge; *(= Aufseher)* supervisor; *(= Lehrer)* teacher on duty; *(in Examen)* invigilator

Auf|sichts-: Auf|sichts|amt NT board of control, inspectorate; **Auf|sichts|be|am|te(r)** M *decl as adj*, **Auf|sichts|be|am|tin** F *(in Museum, Zoo etc)* attendant; *(bei Gericht, Polizei)* warder *(Brit)*, guard *(US)*; **Auf|sichts|be|hör|de** F supervisory authority *or* body; **Auf|sichts|per|son** F supervisor, person in charge; **Auf|sichts|per|so|nal** NT supervisory staff; **Auf|sichts|pflicht** F *(Jur) legal responsibility to care for sb esp a child*; **die elterliche ~, die ~ der Eltern** (legal) parental responsibility; **Auf|sichts|rat** M (supervisory) board; **im ~ einer Firma sitzen** to be *or* sit on the board of a firm; **Auf|sichts|rat** M, **Auf|sichts|rä|tin** F member of the board; **Auf|sichts|rats|vor|sit|zen|de(r)** MF *decl as adj* chairman/chairwoman of the board

auf+sit|zen VI *sep irreg* **a** *(= aufgerichtet sitzen, aufbleiben)* to sit up **b** *aux sein (auf Reittier)* to mount; *(auf Fahrzeug)* to get on; **aufs Pferd ~** to mount the horse; **aufgesessen!** *(Mil)* mount! **c** *(= ruhen auf)* to sit on *(auf etw (dat)* sth) **d** *(Naut)* to run aground *(auf +dat* on) **e** *aux sein (inf: = hereinfallen)* **jdm/einer Sache ~** to be taken in by sb/sth **f** *aux sein (inf)* **jdn ~ lassen** *(= im Stich lassen)* to leave sb in the lurch *(inf)*, to let sb down; *(= Verabredung nicht einhalten)* to stand sb up *(inf)*

auf+spal|ten VTR *sep* to split; *(fig auch)* to split up; **eine Klasse in drei Gruppen ~** to split up *or* divide up a class into three groups

Auf|spal|tung F splitting; *(fig auch)* splitting up; **seit der ~ der Partei** since the party split up

auf+span|nen VT *sep* **a** *Netz, Sprungtuch* to stretch *or* spread out; *Schirm* to put up, to open **b** *(= aufziehen) Leinwand* to stretch *(auf +acc* onto); *Saite* to put on *(auf etw (acc)* sth)

auf+spa|ren VT *sep* to save (up), to keep; **sich** *(dat)* **eine Bemerkung bis zum Ende ~** to save *or* keep a remark until the end

auf+spei|chern VT *sep* to store (up); *Energie auch* to accumulate; *(fig) Zorn etc* to build up

Auf|spei|che|rung F storage; *(von Energie auch)* accumulation

auf+sper|ren VT *sep* **a** *(inf: = aufreißen) Tür, Schnabel* to open wide; **die Ohren ~** to prick up one's ears **b** *(S Ger, Aus: = aufschließen) Tür etc* to unlock

auf+spie|len *sep* VI *(dated)* to play; *(= anfangen)* to strike up; **die Mannschaft spielte glänzend auf** the team began playing brilliantly VR *(inf)* **a** *(= sich wichtigtun)* to give oneself airs **b** *(= sich ausgeben als)* **sich als etw ~** to set oneself up as sth; **sich als Boss ~** to play the boss

auf+spie|ßen VT *sep* to spear; *(= durchbohren)* to run through; *(mit Hörnern)* to gore; *Schmetterlinge* to pin; *Fleisch (mit Spieß)* to skewer; *(mit Gabel)* to prong

auf+split|ten [aufʃplɪtn, ˈaufsp-] VT *sep (fig inf: = spalten) Unternehmen, Einnahmen* to divide *or* split up

auf+split|tern *sep* VT to split (up) VR *(Gruppe etc)* to split (up)

auf+spre|chen VT *sep irreg (Telec: auf Anrufbeantworter)* to record

auf+spren|gen VT *sep* to force open; *(mit Sprengstoff)* to blow open

auf+sprie|ßen VI *sep irreg aux sein (geh)* to burst forth, to sprout

auf+sprin|gen VI *sep irreg aux sein* **a** *(= hochspringen)* to jump *or* leap to one's feet, to jump *or* leap up; **auf etw** *(acc)* **~** to jump onto sth **b** *(= auftreffen)* to bounce; *(Ski)* to land **c** *(= sich öffnen: Tür)* to burst *or* fly open; *(= platzen)* to burst; *(Rinde, Lack)* to crack; *(Haut, Lippen etc)* to crack, to chap; *(liter: Knospen)* to burst open

auf+sprit|zen *sep* VT **etw (auf etw** *acc)* **~** to spray sth on (sth) VI *aux sein* to spurt (up)

auf+spru|deln VI *sep aux sein* to bubble up

auf+sprü|hen *sep* VT **etw (auf etw** *acc)* **~** to spray sth on (sth) VI *aux sein* to spray up

Auf|sprung M *(Sport)* landing; *(von Ball)* bounce

auf+spu|len VT *sep* to wind on a spool; *Angelschnur, Garn auch* to wind on a reel

auf+spü|len VT *sep* **a** *(= anspülen) Sand, Schlick etc* to wash up **b** *(= aufwirbeln) Sand, Schlamm etc* to whirl up

auf+spü|ren VT *sep (lit, fig)* to track down

auf+sta|cheln VT *sep* to spur (on); *(= antreiben)* to goad on; **jdn ~, etw zu tun** *(= aufwiegeln)* to goad sb on to do sth *or* into doing sth

auf+stamp|fen VI *sep* to stamp; **mit dem Fuß ~** to stamp one's foot

Auf|stand M rebellion, revolt; **im ~** in rebellion *or* revolt; **den ~ proben** *(fig)* to flex one's muscles

auf|stän|disch ADJ rebellious, insurgent

Auf|stän|di|sche(r) [ˈaufʃtɛndɪʃə] MF *decl as adj* rebel, insurgent

auf+sta|peln VT *sep* to stack *or* pile up

auf+stau|en *sep* VT *Wasser* to dam; **etw in sich** *(dat)* **~** *(fig)* to bottle sth up inside (oneself) VR to accumulate, to collect; *(fig: Ärger)* to become bottled up

auf+ste|chen VT *sep irreg* to puncture; *(Med)* to lance, to pierce; *(dial: = aufdecken)* to bring into the open

auf+ste|cken *sep* VT **a** *(= auf etw stecken)* to put on *(auf +acc* -to); *Fahne* to put up *(auf +acc* on); *(Comput) Modul, Karte* to plug in; **sich** *(dat)* **einen Ring ~** to put on a ring; **jdm einen Ring ~** to put a ring on sb's finger; **Kerzen auf einen Leuchter/den Baum ~** to put candles in a candlestick/on the tree **b** *(mit Nadeln)* to pin up; *Haar* to put up **c** *(inf: = aufgeben)* to pack in *(inf)* VI *(inf: = aufgeben)* to pack it in *(inf)*; *(bei Rennen etc auch)* to retire

auf+ste|hen VI *sep irreg aux sein* **a** *(= sich erheben)* to get *or* stand up; *(morgens aus dem Bett)* to get up; *(fig: Persönlichkeit)* to arise; **aus dem Sessel ~** to get up out of the chair; **aus dem Bett ~** to get out of bed; **vor jdm/für jdn ~** to stand up for sb; **~ dürfen** *(Kranker)* to be allowed (to get) up; **er steht nicht mehr** *or* **wieder auf** *(fig inf)* he's a goner *(inf)*; **da musst du früher** *or* **eher ~!** *(fig inf)* you'll have to do better than that!

b *(inf: = offen sein)* to be open

c *(= sich auflehnen)* to rise (in arms)

d *aux haben (= auf dem Boden etc stehen)* to stand *(auf +dat* on); **der Tisch steht nur mit drei Beinen/nicht richtig auf** the table is only standing on three legs/is not standing firmly

auf+stei|gen VI *sep irreg aux sein* **a** *(auf Berg, Leiter)* to climb (up); *(Vogel, Drachen)* to soar (up); *(Flugzeug)* to climb; *(Stern, Sonne, Nebel)* to rise; *(Gewitter, Wolken)* to gather; *(Gefühl)* to rise; *(geh: = aufragen)* to tower, to rise up; *(drohend)* to loom; **zum Gipfel ~** to climb (up) to the summit; **einen Ballon ~ lassen** to release a balloon; **in einem Ballon ~** to go up in a balloon; **an die Oberfläche ~** to rise to the surface; **~de Linie** ascending line; **in jdm ~** *(Hass, Verdacht, Erinnerung etc)* to well up in sb

b auf ein Fahrrad/Motorrad ~ to get on(to) a

bicycle/motorbike; **auf ein Pferd ~** to mount a horse, to get on(to) a horse
c (*fig: im Rang etc*) to rise (*zu* to); (*esp beruflich*) to be promoted; (*Sport*) to go up, to be promoted (*in +acc* to); **zum Abteilungsleiter ~** to rise to be head of department; **das ~de Bürgertum** the rising middle classes

Auf|stei|ger(in) M(F) **a** (*Sport*) league climber; (*in höhere Liga*) promoted team **b** **(sozialer)** ~ social climber

auf+stel|len *sep* VT **a** (*= aufrichten, aufbauen*) to put up (*auf +dat* on); *etw Liegendes* to stand up; *Zelt* to pitch, to put up; *Schild, Mast, Denkmal* to erect, to put up; *Kegel* to set up; *Maschine* to put in, to install; *Falle* to set; (*Mil*) to deploy; (*= postieren*) *Wachposten* to post, to station; *Wagen* to line up; (*= hochstellen*) *Kragen* to turn up; (*= aufrichten*) *Ohren, Stacheln* to prick up
b *Essen etc (auf Herd)* to put on
c (*fig: = zusammenstellen*) *Truppe* to raise; (*Sport*) *Spieler* to select, to pick; *Mannschaft* to draw up
d (*= benennen*) *Kandidaten* to nominate
e (*= erzielen*) *Rekord* to set (up)
f *Forderung, Behauptung, Vermutung* to put forward; *System* to establish; *Programm, Satzungen, Rechnung* to draw up; *Liste* to make, to draw up
g (*Sw*) → **aufgestellt**
VR **a** (*= sich postieren*) to stand; (*hintereinander*) to line up; (*Soldaten*) to fall into line; **sich im Karree/Kreis** *etc* **~** to form a square/circle *etc*
b (*Ohren etc*) to prick up

Auf|stel|lung F **a** *no pl* (*= das Aufstellen*) putting up; (*von Zelt*) pitching; (*von Schild, Mast, Denkmal*) erection, putting up; (*von Verkehrsampel*) installation; (*von Maschine*) putting in, installation; (*von Falle*) setting; (*Mil*) deployment; (*von Wachposten*) posting, stationing; (*von Wagen*) lining up; **~ nehmen** (*Mil*) to take up position
b *no pl* (*= das Zusammenstellen*) (*von Truppen*) raising; (*von Spielern*) selecting, picking; (*von Mannschaft*) drawing up
c *no pl* (*von Kandidaten*) nominating; (*von Rekord*) setting
d *no pl* (*von Forderung, Behauptung, Vermutung*) putting forward; (*von System*) establishing; (*von Programm, Satzung, Rechnung, Liste*) drawing up
e (*= Liste*) list; (*= Tabelle*) table; (*= Inventar*) inventory
f (*= Mannschaft*) line-up (*inf*), team

auf+stem|men VT *sep* to force *or* pry open (with a chisel *etc*); (*mit der Schulter*) to force open

auf+stem|peln VT *sep* to stamp on; **etw auf etw** (*acc*) **~** to stamp sth on sth

auf+step|pen VT *sep* to sew *or* stitch on (*auf etw* (*acc*) -to sth)

auf+stie|ben VI *sep irreg aux sein* to fly up

Auf|stieg M **a** *no pl* (*auf Berg*) climb, ascent; (*von Flugzeug, Rakete*) climb; (*von Ballon*) ascent **b** (*fig*) (*= Aufschwung*) rise; (*beruflich, politisch, sozial*) advancement; (*Sport: von Mannschaft*) climb, rise; (*in höhere Liga*) promotion (*in +acc* to); **den ~ zu etw schaffen** to rise to (become) sth; **den ~ ins Management schaffen** to work one's way up into the management **c** (*= Weg*) way up (*auf etw* (*acc*) sth), ascent (*auf +acc* of)

Auf|stiegs-: **Auf|stiegs|chan|ce** F, **Auf|stiegs|mög|lich|keit** F prospect of promotion; **Auf|stiegs|run|de** F (*Sport*) qualifying round, round deciding promotion; **Auf|stiegs|spiel** NT (*Sport*) match deciding promotion

auf+stö|bern VT *sep Wild* to start, to flush; *Rebhühner etc auch* to put up; (*fig: = stören*) to disturb; (*inf: = entdecken*) to dig up (*inf*)

auf+sto|cken *sep* VT **a** *Haus* to build another storey (*Brit*) *or* story (*US*) onto **b** *Kapital, Kredit, Armee* to increase (*um* by); *Vorräte* to build *or* stock up VI to build another storey (*Brit*) *or* story (*US*)

Auf|sto|ckung F (*Archit*) storey (*Brit*) *or* story (*US*) extension; (*Econ*) accumulation of capital

auf+stöh|nen VI *sep* to groan loudly, to give a loud groan; **erleichtert ~** to give a loud sigh of relief

auf+stö|ren VT *sep* to disturb; *Wild* to start; **jdn aus dem** *or* **im Schlaf ~** to disturb sb while he/she is sleeping

auf+sto|ßen *sep irreg* VT **a** (*= öffnen*) to push open; (*mit dem Fuß*) to kick open
b (*rare*) **etw auf etw** (*acc*) **~** to strike sth on sth, to hit sth against sth; **er stieß den Stock (auf den Boden) auf** he tapped his stick on the ground
c (*= verletzen*) **sich** (*dat*) **das Knie ~** to graze one's knee
VI **a** *aux sein* **auf etw** (*acc*) **~** to hit (on *or* against) sth; **ich bin mit dem Ellbogen auf die Tischkante aufgestoßen** I hit my elbow on *or* against the edge of the table
b *aux haben* (*= rülpsen*) to burp
c *aux sein or haben* (*Speisen*) to repeat; **Radieschen stoßen mir auf** radishes repeat on me; **das könnte dir noch sauer** *or* **übel ~** (*fig inf*) you might have to pay for that; **das ist mir sauer aufgestoßen** (*fig inf*) it left a nasty taste in my mouth
d *aux sein* (*fig: = auffallen*) to strike (*jdm* sb)
VR to graze oneself

Auf|sto|ßen NT **-s**, *no pl* burping, flatulence (*form*)

auf+stre|ben VI *sep aux sein* (*geh: = aufragen*) to soar, to tower; **hoch ~de Türme/Berge** high soaring towers/mountains

auf|stre|bend ADJ (*fig*) *Land, Volk* striving for progress, aspiring; *Stadt* up-and-coming, striving; *Persönlichkeit* ambitious; *Bürgertum, Volkswirtschaft* rising

auf+strei|chen VT *sep irreg* to put on (*auf etw* (*acc*) sth); *Butter etc* to spread (*auf +acc* on)

auf+streu|en VT *sep* to sprinkle on; **etw auf etw** (*acc*) **~** to sprinkle sth on(to) *or* over sth; **Splitt/Salz auf die Straßen ~** to grit/salt the roads

Auf|strich M **a** (*auf Brot*) spread; **was möchten Sie als ~?** what would you like on your bread/toast *etc*? **b** (*Mus*) up-bow **c** (*beim Schreiben*) upstroke

auf+stül|pen VT *sep* (*= draufstülpen*) to put on; (*fig: = aufzwingen*) to force on; **etw auf etw** (*acc*) **~** to put sth on sth; **sich** (*dat*) **den Hut/eine Perücke ~** to put on one's hat/a wig

auf+stüt|zen *sep* VT *Kranken etc* to prop up; *Ellbogen, Arme* to rest (*auf +acc or dat* on); **den Kopf ~** to rest one's head on one's hand VR to support oneself; (*im Bett, beim Essen*) to prop oneself up; **sich auf die** *or* **der Hand ~** to support oneself with one's hand

auf+su|chen VT *sep* **a** *Bekannten* to call on; *Arzt, Ort, Toilette* to go to; **das Bett ~** (*geh*) to retire to bed **b** (*= aufsammeln*) to pick up; (*auf Landkarte, in Buch*) to find

auf+sum|men VTR *sep* to add up

auf+sum|mie|ren *ptp* **aufsummiert** VTR *sep* to add up

auf+ta|feln VTI *sep* to serve (up)

auf+ta|keln VT *sep* (*Naut*) to rig up; **sich ~** (*pej inf*) to tart oneself up (*Brit pej inf*), to do (*esp US*) *or* make oneself up (*inf*) → *auch* **aufgetakelt**

Auf|takt M **a** (*= Beginn*) start; (*= Vorbereitung*) prelude; **den ~ von** *or* **zu etw bilden** to mark the beginning *or* start of sth/to form a prelude to sth **b** (*Mus*) upbeat; (*Poet*) arsis (*form*)

auf+tan|ken VTI *sep* to fill up; (*Aviat*) to refuel; *500 Liter* to refuel with, to take on; *10 Liter* to put in; **Benzin ~** to fill up with petrol (*Brit*) *or* gas (*US*)

auf+tau|chen VI *sep aux sein* **a** (*aus dem Wasser*) to surface, to come up **b** (*fig*) (*= sichtbar werden*) to appear; (*aus Nebel etc*) to emerge, to appear; (*Zweifel, Problem*) to arise **c** (*= gefunden werden, sich zeigen, kommen*) to turn up

auf+tau|en *sep* VI *aux sein* to thaw; (*fig auch*) to unbend VT *Eis* to thaw; *Tiefkühlkost, Wasserleitung* to thaw (out)

Auf|tau|stu|fe F (*von Mikrowellengerät*) defrost setting

auf+tei|len VT *sep* **a** (*= aufgliedern*) to divide *or* split up (*in +acc* into) **b** (*= verteilen*) to share out (*an +acc* between)

Auf|tei|lung F (*= Aufgliederung*) division (*in +acc* into); (*= Verteilung*) sharing out (*an +acc* between)

auf+tip|pen VI *sep aux sein* to bounce

auf+ti|schen [ˈauftɪʃn] VT *sep* to serve up; (*fig inf*) to come up with; **jdm etw ~** (*lit*) to give sb sth, to serve sb (with) sth; **jdm Lügen** *etc* **~** (*inf*) to give *or* tell sb a lot of lies *etc*

Auf|trag [ˈauftraːk] M **-(e)s, Aufträge** [-trɛːgə] **a** *no pl* (*= Anweisung*) orders *pl*, instructions *pl*; (*= zugeteilte Arbeit*) job, task; (*Jur*) brief; **jdm den ~ geben, etw zu tun** to give sb the job of doing sth, to instruct sb to do sth; **einen ~ ausführen** to carry out an order; **ich habe den ~, Ihnen mitzuteilen ...** I have been instructed to tell you ...; **in jds ~** (*dat*) (*= für jdn*) on sb's behalf; (*= auf jds Anweisung*) on sb's instructions; **die Oper wurde im ~ des Königs komponiert** the opera was commissioned by the king; **i. A.** *or* **im ~ G. W. Kurz** pp G. W. Kurz
b (*Comm*) order (*über +acc* for); (*bei Künstlern, Freischaffenden etc*) commission (*über +acc* for); **etw in ~ geben** to order/commission sth (*bei* from); **im ~ und auf Rechnung von** by order and for account of
c *no pl* (*geh: = Mission, Aufgabe*) task
d (*von Farbe etc*) application

auf+tra|gen *sep irreg* VT **a** (*= servieren*) to serve; **es ist aufgetragen!** (*geh*) lunch/dinner *etc* is served! **b** *Farbe, Salbe, Schminke* to apply, to put on; **etw auf etw** (*acc*) **~** to apply sth to sth, to put sth on sth **c** **jdm etw ~** (*form*) to instruct sb to do sth; **er hat mir Grüße an Sie aufgetragen** he has asked me to give you his regards **d** *Kleider* to wear out VI **a** (*Kleider*) to make sb look fat; **die Jacke trägt auf** the jacket is not very flattering to your/her/his figure **b** (*= übertreiben*) **dick** *or* **stark ~** (*inf*) to lay it on thick (*inf*), to lay it on with a trowel (*Brit inf*)

Auf|trag-: **Auf|trag|ge|ber(in)** M(F) client; (*von Firma, Freischaffenden*) customer; **Auf|trag|neh|mer(in)** M(F) (*Comm*) firm accepting the order; (*Build*) contractor

Auf|trags-: **Auf|trags|ab|wick|lung** F order processing; **Auf|trags|ar|beit** F commissioned work; **Auf|trags|be|stän|de** [-bəʃtɛndə] PL backlog *sing* of oders; **Auf|trags|be|stä|ti|gung** F confirmation of order; **Auf|trags|buch** NT *usu pl* order book; **Auf|trags|dienst** M (*Telec*) ≈ (telephone) answering service; **Auf|trags|ein|bruch** M dramatic reduction *or* slump in orders; **Auf|trags|ein|gang** M **bei ~** on receipt of order; **hohe Auftragseingänge** a high number of orders; **Auf|trags|er|tei|lung** F placing of orders; (*bei einer Ausschreibung*) award; **Auf|trags|for|mu|lar** NT order form; **auf|trags|ge|mäß** ADJ ADV as instructed; (*Comm*) as per order; **Auf|trags|la|ge** F order situation, situation concerning orders; **Auf|trags|pols|ter** NT **wir haben ein dickes ~** our order books are well-filled; **Auf|trags|rück|gang** M drop in orders; **Auf|trags|ver|ga|be** F, *no pl* placing of orders; (*bei Ausschreibungen*) award of contract; **Auf|trags|vo|lu|men** NT volume of orders; **Auf|trags|wal|ze** F (*Typ*) inking roller; **Auf|trags|werk** NT commissioned work *or* piece

auf+tref|fen VI *sep irreg aux sein* **auf etw** (*dat or acc*) **~** to hit *or* strike sth; (*Rakete*) to land on sth; **er traf mit dem Kopf auf der Kante auf** he hit his head on the edge; **~de Strahlen** incident rays

auf+trei|ben VT *sep irreg* **a** (*inf*) (*= beschaffen*) *Geld, Heroin, Geräte* to get hold of; (*= ausfindig machen*) *Wohnung, Geschenk, Sponsor, Mieter, Täter* to find **b** *Leib* to distend, to bloat; **sein aufgetriebener Bauch** his swollen *or* distended stomach **c** *Vieh (zum Verkauf)* to drive to market; *(auf die Alm)* to drive up to the (Alpine) pastures

auf+tren|nen VT *sep* to undo

auf+tre|ten *sep irreg* VI *aux sein* **a** *(lit)* to tread; **der Fuß tut so weh, dass ich (mit ihm) nicht mehr ~ kann** my foot hurts so much that I can't walk on it *or* put my weight on it **b** *(= erscheinen)* to appear; **als Zeuge/Kläger ~** to appear as a witness/as plaintiff; **zum ersten Mal (im Theater) ~** to make one's début (appearance), to make one's first (stage) appearance; **er tritt zum ersten Mal in Köln auf** he is appearing in Cologne for the first time; **gegen jdn/etw ~** to stand up *or* speak out against sb/sth; **geschlossen ~** to put up a united front **c** *(fig: = eintreten)* to occur; *(Schwierigkeiten etc)* to arise **d** *(= sich benehmen)* to behave; **bescheiden/arrogant ~** to have a modest/arrogant manner; **vorsichtig ~** to tread warily **e** *(= handeln)* to act; **als Vermittler/Friedensstifter** *etc* **~** to act as (an) intermediary/(a) peacemaker *etc* VT *Tür etc* to kick open

Auf|tre|ten NT **-s,** *no pl* **a** *(= Erscheinen)* appearance **b** *(= Benehmen)* manner **c** *(= Vorkommen)* occurrence; **bei ~ von Schwellungen ...** in case swelling occurs ..., in the event of swelling ...

Auf|trieb M **a** *no pl (Phys)* buoyancy (force); *(Aviat)* lift **b** *no pl (fig) (= Aufschwung)* impetus; *(= Preisauftrieb)* upward trend (+*gen* in); *(= Ermunterung)* lift; **das wird ihm ~ geben** that will give him a lift **c** *(von Alpenvieh)* **der ~ findet Anfang Mai statt** the cattle are driven up to the (Alpine) pastures at the beginning of May **d** *(von Marktvieh)* **der ~ an Vieh/Kälbern** the number of cattle/calves (at the market)

Auf|triebs|kraft F buoyancy force; *(Aviat)* lift

Auf|tritt M **a** *(= Erscheinen)* entrance; **ich habe meinen ~ erst im zweiten Akt** I don't go *or* come on until the second act **b** *(Theat: = Szene)* scene **c** *(= Streit)* row

Auf|tritts|ver|bot NT stage ban; **~ bekommen/haben** to be banned from making a public appearance; **~ über jdn verhängen** *(inf)* to ban sb from appearing

auf+trump|fen VI *sep* to be full of oneself *(inf)*; *(= sich schadenfroh äußern)* to crow; *(= seine Leistungsstärke zeigen)* to show how good one is; **~d sagte er ...** ..., he crowed

auf+tun *sep irreg* VT **a** *(inf: = ausfindig machen)* to find **b** *(= öffnen) Tür, Tor* to open; **er hat den Mund nicht aufgetan** he didn't open his mouth **c** *(inf: = servieren)* **jdm/sich etw ~** to put sth on sb's/one's plate, to help sb/oneself to sth **d** *(dial: = aufsetzen)* to put on VR **a** *(= sich öffnen)* to open up **b** *(= sich ergeben) (Kluft)* to open up; *(Differenz, Möglichkeiten, Probleme, Widersprüche)* to arise VI *(= öffnen)* **jdm ~** to open the door to sb

auf+tür|men *sep* VT to pile *or* stack up; *(Geol)* to build up (in layers) VR *(Gebirge etc)* to tower *or* loom up; *(Schwierigkeiten)* to pile *or* mount up; **hoch aufgetürmte Felsen** towering cliffs

auf+wa|chen VI *sep aux sein (lit, fig)* to wake up; **aus seiner Lethargie ~** to snap out of one's lethargy; **aus einer Narkose ~** to come out of an anaesthetic *(Brit) or* anesthetic *(US)*

Auf|wach|raum M *(Med, nach Operation)* recovery room

auf+wach|sen VI *sep irreg aux sein* to grow up

auf+wal|len VI *sep aux sein* to bubble up; *(Cook)* to boil up; *(Leidenschaft etc)* to surge up; **die Soße einmal ~ lassen** bring the sauce to the *(Brit) or* a *(US)* boil; **seine ~de Wut** his seething rage; **seine ~de Leidenschaft** the passion surging up in him

Auf|wal|lung F *(fig) (von Leidenschaft)* surge; *(von Wut)* outburst, fit (of rage)

Auf|wand ['aufvant] M **-(e)s** [-dəs], *no pl* **a** *(von Geld)* expenditure *(an +dat* of); **das erfordert einen ~ von 10 Millionen Euro** that will cost *or* take 10 million euros; **das erfordert einen großen ~ (an Zeit/Energie/Geld)** that requires a lot of time/energy/money; **der dazu nötige ~ an Konzentration/Zeit** the concentration/time needed **b** *(= Luxus, Prunk)* extravagance; **(großen) ~ treiben** to be (very) extravagant; **was da für ~ getrieben wurde!** the extravagance!

auf|wän|dig ADJ, ADV = **aufwendig**

Auf|wands|ent|schä|di|gung F expense allowance

auf+wär|men *sep* VT to heat *or* warm up; *(inf: = wieder erwähnen)* to bring up, to drag up *(inf)* VR to warm oneself up; *(Sport)* to warm *or* limber up

Auf|wärm-: **Auf|wärm|pha|se** F *(Sport)* warm-up phase; **Auf|wärm|ü|bun|gen** PL warm-up *or* warming-up *or* limbering-up exercises *pl*

Auf|war|te|frau F char(woman) *(Brit)*, cleaner

auf+war|ten VI *sep* **a** *(geh: = bedienen)* to serve *(jdm* sb); **(bei Tisch) ~** to wait at table *(Brit)*, to wait a table *(US)*; **uns wurde mit Sekt aufgewartet** we were served champagne **b** *(= zu bieten haben)* **mit etw ~** to offer sth; **er hat viel Geld, damit kann ich nicht ~** he's very rich, I can't compete with that **c** *(dated: = besuchen)* **jdm ~** to wait (up)on sb *(old)*, to visit sb

auf|wärts ['aufvɛrts] ADV up, upward(s); *(= bergauf)* uphill; **den Fluss ~** upstream; **von einer Million ~** from a million up(wards); **vom Feldwebel ~** from sergeant up → **aufwärtsbiegen, aufwärtsgehen**

Auf|wärts-: **Auf|wärts|be|we|gung** F upward movement; *(Tech)* upstroke; **auf|wärts+bie|gen** VR *sep irreg* **die Ecken haben sich aufwärtsgebogen** the corners have curled up; **Auf|wärts|ent|wick|lung** F upward trend (+*gen* in); **auf|wärts+ge|hen** *sep impers irreg aux sein*,; **auf|wärts ge|hen** △ *impers irreg aux sein* VI **mit dem Staat/der Firma geht es aufwärts** things are looking up *or* getting better *or* improving for the country/firm; **mit ihm geht es aufwärts** *(finanziell, beruflich)* things are looking up for him; *(in der Schule, gesundheitlich)* he's doing *or* getting better; **mit seinen Leistungen geht es aufwärts** he's doing better; **Auf|wärts|ha|ken** M *(Boxen)* uppercut; **auf|wärts|kom|pa|ti|bel** ADJ *(Comput)* upward compatible; **Auf|wärts|kom|pa|ti|bi|li|tät** F *(Comput)* upward compatibility; **Auf|wärts|pfeil** M *(Comput)* up arrow; **Auf|wärts|trend** M upward trend

Auf|war|tung F **a** *no pl (dated) (= Bedienung)* waiting at table *(Brit)*, waiting a table *(US)*; *(= Reinemachen)* cleaning **b** *(geh: = Besuch)* **jdm seine ~ machen** to wait (up)on sb *(old)*, to visit sb **c** *(dial: = Aufwartefrau etc)* char(woman) *(Brit)*, cleaner

Auf|wasch ['aufvaʃ] M **-(e)s,** *no pl (dial)* = **Abwasch**

auf+wa|schen *sep irreg (dial)* VT *Geschirr* to wash, to wash up *(Brit)* VI to wash up *(Brit)*, to do the washing-up *(Brit)*, to wash the dishes

auf+we|cken VT *sep* to wake (up), to waken; *(fig)* to rouse → *auch* **aufgeweckt**

auf+we|hen *sep* VT **a** *(= in die Höhe wehen)* to blow up; *(= auftürmen)* to pile up; **der Wind hat Dünen aufgeweht** the wind has blown the sand into dunes **b** *(= öffnen)* to blow open VI *aux sein* to blow up

auf+wei|chen *sep* VT to make soft; *Weg, Boden* to make sodden; *Brot* to soak; *(durch Wärme)* to soften; *(fig: = lockern)* to weaken; *Doktrin, Gesetz* to water down; *Gegner* to soften up VI *aux sein* to become *or* get soft; *(Weg, Boden)* to become *or* get sodden; *(fig) (= sich lockern)* to be weakened; *(Doktrin, Gesetz)* to become *or* get watered down

auf+wei|sen VT *sep irreg* to show; **die Leiche wies keinerlei Verletzungen auf** the body showed no signs of injury; **das Buch weist einige Fehler auf** the book contains some mistakes *or* has some mistakes in it; **etw aufzuweisen haben** to have sth to show for oneself; **man muss schon einiges an Veröffentlichungen aufzuweisen haben** you have to have something to show in the way of publications

auf+wen|den VT *sep irreg* to use; *Zeit, Energie* to expend; *Mühe* to take; *Geld* to spend; **viel Mühe/Zeit ~, etw zu tun** to take a lot of trouble/spend a lot of time doing sth; **das wäre unnütz aufgewandte Zeit/Energie** that would be a waste of time/energy

auf|wen|dig ['aufvɛndɪç] ADJ *(= teuer)* costly; *(= üppig)* lavish ADV extravagantly

Auf|wen|dung F **a** *no pl* using; *(von Zeit, Energie)* expenditure; *(von Mühe)* taking; *(von Geld)* spending; **unter ~ von ...** by using/expending/taking/spending ... **b** **Aufwendungen** PL expenditure

auf+wer|fen *sep irreg* ✪ 53.2, 53.6 VT **a** *(= nach oben werfen)* to throw up; *(= aufhäufen)* to pile up; *Damm etc* to build (up) **b** *Kopf* to toss; *Lippen* to purse **c** *Tür* to throw open **d** *(= zur Sprache bringen) Frage, Probleme, Thema* to raise, to bring up; *Verdacht* to raise VR **sich zu etw ~** to set oneself up as sth; **sich zum Richter ~** to set oneself up as judge

auf+wer|ten VT *sep* **a** *auch vi Währung* to revalue **b** *(fig)* to increase the value of; *Menschen, Ideal* to enhance the status of

Auf|wer|tung F *(von Währung)* revaluation; *(fig)* increase in value; **das kommt einer ~ des Terrorismus gleich** that is tantamount to enhancing the status of terrorism

auf+wi|ckeln VT *sep (= aufrollen)* to roll up; *(inf) Haar* to put in curlers

auf Wie|der|se|hen [auf 'vi:dɐze:ən], **auf Wie|der|schau|en** [auf 'vi:dɐʃauən] *(geh, S Ger, Aus, Sw)* INTERJ goodbye

Auf|wie|ge|lei [aufvi:gə'lai] F **-, -en** incitement *no pl*

auf+wie|geln ['aufvi:gln] VT *sep* to stir up; **jdn zum Streik/Widerstand ~** to incite sb to strike/resist

Auf|wie|ge|lung ['aufvi:gəlʊŋ] F **-, -en** incitement *no pl*

auf+wie|gen VT *sep irreg (fig)* to offset; **das ist nicht mit Geld aufzuwiegen** that can't be measured in terms of money

Auf|wieg|ler ['aufvi:glɐ] M **-s, -**, **Auf|wieg|le|rin** [-ərɪn] F **-, -nen** agitator; *(= Anstifter)* instigator

auf|wieg|le|risch ['aufvi:glərɪʃ] ADJ seditious; *Rede, Artikel auch* inflammatory

Auf|wind M *(Aviat)* upcurrent; *(Met)* upwind; **guter ~** good upcurrents *pl*; **(durch etw) neuen ~ bekommen** *(fig)* to get new impetus (from sth); **einer Sache** *(dat)* **~ geben** *(fig)* to give sth impetus; **sich im ~ fühlen** to feel one is on the way up *or* in the ascendant

auf+wir|beln *sep* VI *aux sein (Staub, Schnee)* to swirl *or* whirl up VT to swirl *or* whirl up; *Staub auch* to raise; **(viel) Staub ~** *(fig)* to cause a (big) stir

auf+wi|schen *sep* VT *Wasser etc* to wipe *or* mop up; *Fußboden* to wipe; **die Küche (feucht) ~** to wash the kitchen floor; **das Bier vom Boden ~** to mop the beer up off the floor VI to wipe the floor(s); **feucht ~** to wash the floor(s)

Auf|wisch|lap|pen M, **Auf|wisch|tuch** NT cleaning cloth, floorcloth

auf+wo|gen VI *sep aux sein (liter)* to heave

auf+wöl|ben VR *sep* to swell, to buckle; *(Archit)* to arch

auf+wüh|len VT *sep* **a** *(lit) Erde, Meer* to churn (up) **b** *(geh)* to stir; *(schmerzhaft)* to churn up; *Leidenschaften* to rouse; **das hat seine Seele zutiefst aufgewühlt** that stirred him to the depths of his soul; **~d** stirring → *auch* **aufgewühlt**

auf+zah|len VT *sep (S Ger, Aus)* **50 Euro/einen Zuschlag ~** to pay an additional 50 euros/a surcharge (on top)

auf+zäh|len VT *sep* to list; *Beispiele, Details, Namen auch, Liste* to give; **er hat mir alle meine Fehler aufgezählt** he told me all my faults, he listed all my faults; **man kann die Fälle an den Fingern einer Hand ~** the instances can be counted on the fingers of one hand

Auf|zah|lung F *(S Ger, Aus)* additional charge

Auf|zäh|lung F list; *(von Gründen, Fehlern etc auch)* enumeration

Auf|zäh|lungs|zei|chen NT *(Comput)* bullet (point)

auf+zäu|men VT *sep* to bridle; **etw verkehrt ~** to go about sth the wrong way

auf+zeh|ren *sep* VT to exhaust; *(fig)* to sap VR to burn oneself out

Auf|zeh|rung F exhaustion; *(fig)* sapping

auf+zeich|nen VT *sep* **a** *Plan etc* to draw, to sketch **b** *(= notieren, Rad, TV)* to record

Auf|zeich|nung F **a** *(= Zeichnung)* sketch **b** *usu pl (= Notiz)* note; *(= Niederschrift)* record **c** *(= Magnetbandaufzeichnung, Filmaufzeichnung)* recording

auf+zei|gen *sep* VT to show; *(= nachweisen auch)* to demonstrate VI *(dated Sch: = sich melden)* to put one's hand up

auf+zie|hen *sep irreg* VT **a** *(= hochziehen)* to pull *or* draw up; *(mit Flaschenzug etc)* to hoist up; *Schlagbaum, Zugbrücke* to raise; *Flagge, Segel* to hoist; *Jalousien* to let up; *(Med) Spritze* to fill; *Flüssigkeit* to draw up
b *(= öffnen) Reißverschluss* to undo; *Schleife etc* to untie, to undo; *Schublade* to (pull) open; *Gardinen* to draw (back)
c *(= aufspannen) Foto etc* to mount; *Leinwand, Stickerei* to stretch; *Landkarte etc* to pull up; *Saite, Reifen* to fit, to put on; **Saiten/neue Saiten auf ein Instrument ~** to string/restring an instrument → **Saite b**
d *(= spannen) Feder, Uhr etc* to wind up
e *(= großziehen) Kind* to bring up, to raise; *Tier* to raise, to rear
f *(inf) (= veranstalten)* to set up; *Fest* to arrange; *(= gründen) Unternehmen* to start up
g *(= verspotten)* **jdn ~** *(inf)* to make fun of sb, to tease sb *(mit* about)
VI *aux sein (dunkle Wolke)* to come up; *(Gewitter, Wolken auch)* to gather; *(= aufmarschieren)* to march up; **die Wache zog vor der Kaserne auf** the soldiers mounted guard in front of the barracks
VR to wind; **sich von selbst ~** to be self-winding

Auf|zin|sung ['auftsɪnzʊŋ] F -, -en *(Fin)* accumulation

Auf|zucht F **a** *no pl (= das Großziehen)* rearing, raising **b** *(= Nachwuchs)* young family

Auf|zug M **a** *(= Fahrstuhl)* lift *(Brit)*, elevator *(US)* **b** *(Phot)* wind-on **c** *(= Marsch, Festzug)* parade; **der ~ der Wache** the mounting of the guard **d** *(von Gewitter etc)* gathering **e** *(Turnen)* pull-up **f** *(Theat)* act **g** *no pl (pej inf: = Kleidung)* get-up *(inf)*

Auf|zug- *in cpds* lift *(Brit)*, elevator *(US)*; **Auf|zug|füh|rer(in)** M(F) lift *(Brit)* or elevator *(US)* operator; **Auf|zug(s)|schacht** M lift *(Brit)* or elevator *(US)* shaft

auf+zwi|cken VT *sep (Aus inf)* **sich** *(dat)* **jdn ~** to chat sb up *(Brit inf)*, to put the moves on sb *(US inf)*

auf+zwin|gen *sep irreg* VT **jdm etw ~** to force sth on sb; **jdm seinen Willen ~** to impose one's will on sb VR to force itself on one; **sich jdm ~** to force itself on sb; *(Gedanke)* to strike sb forcibly; **das zwingt sich einem doch förmlich auf** the conclusion is unavoidable

auf+zwir|beln VT *sep Bart* to twirl up, to twist up; *Garn* to twist up, to roll between one's fingers

Aug|ap|fel M eyeball; **jdn/etw wie seinen ~ hüten** to cherish sb/sth like life itself

Au|ge ['augə] -s, -n

SUBSTANTIV (NT)

a [= Sehorgan] eye; **Auge um Auge, Zahn um Zahn** *(Bibl)* an eye for an eye and a tooth for a tooth; **wieder einmal waren meine Augen größer als der Bauch** as usual my eyes were bigger than my stomach; **ganz Auge und Ohr sein** to be all ears; **Augen zu und durch!** *(inf)* grit your teeth and get on with it!; **Augen rechts/links!** *(Mil)* eyes right/left!; **das Auge des Gesetzes** the eye of the law

♦ **Auge(n) + haben gute/schlechte Augen haben** to have good/bad eyesight; **ein sicheres Auge für etw haben** to have a good eye for sth; **da muss man seine Augen überall** *or* **hinten und vorn** *(inf)* **haben** you need eyes in the back of your head; **ich kann doch meine Augen nicht überall haben** I don't have eyes in the back of my head; **haben Sie keine Augen im Kopf?** *(inf)* haven't you got eyes in your head?, use your eyes!; **die Augen offen haben** to keep one's eyes open; **ich hab doch hinten keine Augen!** I don't have eyes in the back of my head!; **er hatte nur Augen für sie** he only had eyes for her; **ein Auge auf jdn/etw haben** *(= aufpassen)* to keep an eye on sb/sth; **ein Auge auf jdn/etw (geworfen) haben** to have one's eye on sb/sth

♦ **Auge(n) + andere Verben die Augen aufmachen** *or* **aufsperren** *(inf) or* **auftun** *(inf)* to open one's eyes; **sich** *(dat)* **die Augen ausweinen** to cry one's eyes out; **da blieb kein Auge trocken** *(hum)* there wasn't a dry eye in the house; *(vor Lachen)* everyone laughed till they cried; **dem fallen bald die Augen raus** *(sl)* his eyes will pop out of his head in a minute *(inf)*; **er guckte** *(inf)* **sich** *(dat)* **die Augen aus dem Kopf** his eyes were popping out of his head *(inf)*; **die Augen offenhalten** to keep one's eyes open; **er lässt kein Auge von ihr** he doesn't let her out of his sight; **große Augen machen** to be wide-eyed; **jdm schöne** *or* **verliebte Augen machen** to make eyes at sb; **die Augen öffnen** to open one's eyes; **jdm die Augen öffnen** *(fig)* to open sb's eyes; **so weit das Auge reicht** as far as the eye can see; **ein Auge riskieren** *(hum)* to have a peep *(inf)*; **die Augen schließen** *(lit)* to close one's eyes; *(euph)* to fall asleep; **die Augen vor etw** *(dat)* **verschließen** to close one's eyes to sth; **sich** *(dat)* **die Augen aus dem Kopf weinen** *(inf)* to cry one's eyes out; **ein Auge** *or* **beide Augen zudrücken** *(inf)* to turn a blind eye; **ich habe kein Auge zugetan** I didn't sleep a wink → **blau a, Luchs, vier b**

b [mit Präposition]

♦ **aufs Auge jdm etw aufs Auge drücken** *(inf)* to force sth on sb

♦ **aus + Augen aus den Augen, aus dem Sinn** *(Prov)* out of sight, out of mind *(Prov)*; **ich konnte kaum aus den Augen sehen** *or* **gucken** I could hardly see straight; **geh mir aus den Augen!** get out of my sight!; **sie ließen ihn nicht aus den Augen** they didn't let him out of their sight; **jdn/etw aus den Augen verlieren** to lose sight of sb/sth; *(fig)* to lose touch with sb/sth

♦ **fürs Auge etwas fürs Auge sein** *(Gegenstand)* to be nice to look at, to look nice; *(Mensch)* to be nice-looking; **nur fürs Auge** just nice to look at

♦ **im Auge etw im Auge haben** *(lit)* to have sth in one's eye; *(fig)* to have one's eye on sth; **jdn im Auge behalten** *(= beobachten)* to keep an eye on sb; *(= vormerken)* to keep *or* bear sb in mind; **etw im Auge behalten** to keep *or* bear sth in mind; **sein Ziel im Auge behalten** to keep one's objective in view

♦ **ins Auge dem Tod ins Auge sehen** to look death in the eye; **etw ins Auge fassen** to contemplate sth; **das springt** *or* **fällt einem gleich ins Auge** it strikes one immediately; **ins Auge stechen** *(fig)* to catch the eye; **das kann leicht ins Auge gehen** *(fig inf)* it might easily go wrong

♦ **in + Auge(n) in den Augen der Leute/Öffentlichkeit** in the eyes of most people/the public; **in meinen Augen** in my opinion *or* view; **jdm in die Augen sehen** to look sb in the eye(s); **ich schau dir in die Augen, Kleines** here's looking at you, kid; **Auge in Auge** face to face

♦ **mit + Auge(n) mit den Augen zwinkern** to wink; **mit den Augen blinzeln** to blink; **jdn/etw mit den Augen verschlingen** to devour sb/sth with one's eyes; **jdn/etw mit anderen Augen (an)sehen** to see sb/sth with different eyes; **etw mit eigenen Augen gesehen haben** to have seen sth with one's own eyes; **mit bloßem** *or* **nacktem Auge** with the naked eye; **du brauchst mich gar nicht mit großen Augen anzusehen** you needn't look at me with those big eyes; **mit offenen Augen schlafen** to daydream; **mit verbundenen Augen** *(lit, fig)* blindfold; **mit einem lachenden und einem weinenden Auge** with mixed feelings

♦ **unter + Augen unter jds Augen** before sb's very eyes; **komm mir nicht mehr unter die Augen!** keep out of my sight!; **wenn du mir noch einmal unter die Augen kommst, ...** if you let me see you again ...

♦ **vor + Auge(n) jdm etw vor Augen führen** *(fig)* to make sb aware of sth; **das muss man sich** *(dat)* **mal vor Augen führen!** just imagine it!; **es führt sich offenbar niemand richtig vor Augen, dass ...** it obviously isn't clear to everyone that ...; **etw noch genau** *or* **lebhaft vor Augen haben** to remember sth clearly *or* vividly; **etw steht** *or* **schwebt jdm vor Augen** sb has sth in mind; **etw/den Tod vor Augen sehen** to face sth/death; **vor aller Augen** in front of everybody; **vor meinem geistigen** *or* **inneren Auge** in my mind's eye

c [= Knospenansatz] *bei Kartoffel* eye; *(bei Zweig)* axil

d [= Fettauge] little globule of fat

e [bei Spielen] **wie viele Augen hat der König?** what is the king worth?; **wer zuerst sechs Augen würfelt** the person who first throws a six

f [in technischen Zusammenhängen] *von Hurrikan* eye; **magisches Auge** *(Rad)* magic eye

---

äu|gen ['ɔygn] VI to look

Au|gen-: **Au|gen|ab|stand** M interocular distance *(form)*, distance between the eyes; **Au|gen|arzt** M, **Au|gen|ärz|tin** F eye specialist, eye doctor, ophthalmologist; **au|gen|ärzt|lich** ADJ *attr Gutachten etc* ophthalmological; *Behandlung* eye *attr*, ophthalmic ADV *untersucht werden* by an ophthalmologist *or* eye doctor; **ein ~ interessanter Fall** an interesting ophthalmological case; **Au|gen|auf|schlag** M look; **Au|gen|aus|wi|sche|rei** [-ausvɪʃə'rai] F -, -en *(fig inf)* eyewash; **Au|gen|bad** NT eyebath; **ein ~ nehmen** to bathe one's eye(s); **Au|gen|bank** F *pl* **-banken** eyebank; **Au|gen|bin|de** F eye bandage; *(= Augenklappe)* eye patch

Au|gen|blick M moment; **alle ~e** constantly, all the time; **jeden ~** any time *or* minute *or* moment; **einen ~, bitte** one moment please!; **~ mal!** *(inf)* just a minute *or* second!, just a sec! *(inf)*; **im ~** at the moment; **in diesem** *or* **im selben ~...** at that moment ...; **im letzten/richtigen** *etc* **~** at the last/right *etc* moment; **im ersten ~** for a moment; **im nächsten ~** the (very) next moment; **er ist gerade im ~ gegangen** he just left this very moment; **er zögerte keinen ~** he didn't hesitate for a moment; **den ~ festhalten** to capture the moment

au|gen|blick|lich ['augnblɪklɪç, augn'blɪklɪç] ADJ **a** *(= sofortig)* immediate **b** *(= gegenwärtig)* present, current; **die ~e Lage** the present *or* current situation, the situation at the moment **c** *(= vorübergehend)* temporary; *(= einen Augen-*

blick dauernd) momentary **ADV** **a** *(= sofort)* at once, immediately, instantly **b** *(= zurzeit)* at the moment, presently

au|gen|blicks [-blɪks] **ADV** at once, immediately, instantly

Au|gen|blicks-: **Au|gen|blicks|auf|nah|me** F *(Phot)* snapshot; **Au|gen|blicks|er|folg** M short-lived success; **Au|gen|blicks|idee** F idea thought up on the spur of the moment; **Au|gen|blicks|mensch** M spontaneous *or* spur-of-the-moment person *or* type; **Au|gen|blicks|sa|che** F quick job; **das ist nur eine ~** it'll just take a moment; **das war eine ~** it was over in a flash; **Au|gen|blicks|stim|mung** F **aus einer ~ heraus** on the spur of the moment

Au|gen-: **Au|gen|blin|zeln** NT **-s**, *no pl* wink; **Au|gen|braue** F eyebrow; **Au|gen|brau|en|stift** M eyebrow pencil; **Au|gen|bren|nen** NT stinging eyes *pl*, stinging of *or* in the eyes; **Au|gen|de|ckel** M eyelid; **Au|gen|ent|zün|dung** F inflammation of the eyes; **au|gen|fäl|lig** ADJ conspicuous; *(= offensichtlich)* obvious; **Au|gen|far|be** F colour *(Brit) or* color *(US)* of eyes; **Menschen mit einer dunklen ~** people with dark eyes; **Au|gen|feh|ler** M eye defect; **Au|gen|flim|mern** NT **-s**, *no pl* flickering before the eyes; **au|gen|freund|lich** ADJ *Bildschirm, Größe der Buchstaben etc* easy on the eyes; **Au|gen|glas** NT *(dated)* monocle; **Au|gen|glä|ser** PL *(esp Aus)* glasses *pl*, spectacles *pl*; **Au|gen|gym|nas|tik** F eye exercises *pl*; **Au|gen|heil|kun|de** F ophthalmology; **Au|gen|hö|he** F **in ~** at eye level; **Au|gen|höh|le** F eye socket, orbit *(form)*; **Au|gen|klap|pe** F **a** eye patch **b** *(für Pferde)* blinker, blinder *(US)*; **Au|gen|kli|nik** F eye clinic *or* hospital; **Au|gen|krank|heit** F eye disease; **Au|gen|lei|den** NT eye complaint; **Au|gen|licht** NT, *no pl* (eye)sight; **Au|gen|lid** NT eyelid; **Au|gen|maß** NT, *no pl* eye; *(für Entfernungen)* eye for distance(s); *(fig)* perceptiveness; **nach ~** by eye; **~ haben** *(lit)* to have a good eye (for distance(s)); *(fig)* to be able to assess *or* gauge things *or* situations; **ein gutes/schlechtes ~ haben** to have a good eye/no eye (for distance(s)); **ein ~ für etw haben** *(fig)* to have an eye for sth; **Au|gen|mensch** M *(inf)* visual(ly oriented) person; **Au|gen|merk** [-mɛrk] NT **-s**, *no pl (= Aufmerksamkeit)* attention; **jds/sein ~ auf etw** *(acc)* **lenken** *or* **richten** to direct sb's/one's attention to sth; **einer Sache** *(dat)* **sein ~ zuwenden** to turn one's attention to a matter; **Au|gen|mit|tel** NT *(Med)* eye medication, ophthalmic agent *(spec)*; **Au|gen|nerv** M optic nerve; **Au|gen|ope|ra|ti|on** F eye operation; **Au|gen|op|ti|ker(in)** M(F) optician; **Au|gen|paar** NT pair of eyes; **Au|gen|par|tie** F eye area; **Au|gen|pro|the|se** F artificial eye; **Au|gen|pul|ver** NT *(fig inf: = Schrift, Buch etc)* tiny *or* microscopic print; **das ist ja das reinste ~** you'd strain your eyes trying to read that; **Au|gen|rän|der** PL rims *pl* of the/one's eyes; **er hatte rote ~, seine ~ waren gerötet** the rims of his eyes were red; **Au|gen|rei|zung** F *(Med)* eye irritation; **Au|gen|rin|ge** PL rings *pl* round *or* under the/one's eyes; **Au|gen|sal|be** F eye ointment; **Au|gen|schat|ten** PL shadows *pl* under the/one's eyes; **Au|gen|schein** M, *no pl* **a** *(= Anschein)* appearance; **dem ~ nach** by all appearances, to judge by appearances; **der ~ trügt** appearances are deceptive; **nach dem ~ urteilen** to judge by appearances **b jdn/etw in ~ nehmen** to look closely at sb/sth, to have a close look at sb/sth; **au|gen|schein|lich** ['augnʃainlɪç, augn'ʃainlɪç] **ADJ** obvious, evident **ADV** obviously; **die beiden sind ~ zerstritten** the two have obviously *or* clearly had a quarrel; **Au|gen|schmaus** M *(hum)* feast for the eyes; **Au|gen|schutz** M visor, vizor; **Au|gen|spie|gel** M ophthalmoscope; **Au|gen|spie|ge|lung** F ophthalmoscopy; **Au|gen|stern** M **a** *(Liter: = Pupille)* pupil, orb *(poet)* **b** *(dated: = Liebstes)* apple of one's eye, darling; **Au|gen|trop|fen** PL eye drops *pl*; **Au|gen|ver|let|zung** F eye injury *or* damage; **Au|gen|wei|de** F, *no pl* feast *or* treat for the eyes; **nicht gerade eine ~** *(iro)* a bit of an eyesore; **Au|gen|wim|per** F eyelash; **Au|gen|win|kel** M corner of the/one's eye; **Au|gen|wi|sche|rei** [-vɪʃə'rai] F **-, -en** *(fig)* eyewash; **Au|gen|zahl** F *(Cards etc)* number of points; **Au|gen|zahn** M eyetooth; **Au|gen|zeu|ge** M, **Au|gen|zeu|gin** F eyewitness *(bei* to); **ich war ~ dieses Unfalls** *or* **bei diesem Unfall** I was an eyewitness to this accident; **Au|gen|zeu|gen|be|richt** M eyewitness account; **Au|gen|zwin|kern** NT **-s**, *no pl* winking; **au|gen|zwin|kernd** **ADJ** winking *attr*; *(fig)* sly **ADV** with a wink; **er grinste mich ~ an** he grinned at me, winking; **sie sahen sich ~ an** they winked at each other; **jdm etw ~ zu verstehen geben** to let sb know sth with a wink

Au|gi|as|stall [au'gi:as-, 'augias-] M *(fig geh)* dunghill, Augean stables *pl (liter)*

-äu|gig [ɔygɪç] ADJ *suf* -eyed; **braunäugig** brown-eyed

Au|gur ['augʊr] M **-s** *or* **-en, -en** [au'gu:rən] *(Hist, fig geh)* augur

Au|gu|ren|lä|cheln NT *(pej geh)* knowing smile

Au|gust [au'gʊst] M **-(e)s** *or* **-, -e** August → *auch* **März**

Au|gust ['augʊst] M **-s** Augustus; **der dumme ~** *(inf)* the clown; **den dummen ~ spielen** to play *or* act the clown *or* fool

Au|gust|ap|fel M Laxton

Au|gust|fei|er F *(Sw)* August public holiday

Au|gus|ti|ner(mönch) [augʊs'ti:nɐ-] M **-s, -** Augustinian (monk)

Auk|ti|on [auk'tsio:n] F **-, -en** auction

Auk|ti|o|na|tor [auktsio'na:to:ɐ] M **-s, Auktionatoren** [-'to:rən], **Auk|ti|o|na|to|rin** [-'to:rɪn] F **-, -nen** auctioneer

auk|ti|o|nie|ren [auktsio'ni:rən] *ptp* **auktioniert** VT to auction

Auk|ti|ons-: **Auk|ti|ons|hal|le** F auction room; **Auk|ti|ons|haus** NT auction house *or* company, auctioneers *pl*

Au|la ['aula] F **-, Aulen** [-lən] *(Sch, Univ etc)* (assembly) hall; *(= Atrium)* atrium

Au-pair-: **Au-pair-Jun|ge** M, **Au|pair|jun|ge** △ M (male) au pair; **Au-pair-Mäd|chen** NT, **Au|pair|mäd|chen** △ NT au pair (girl); **als ~ arbeiten** to work (as an) au pair; **Au-pair-Stel|le** F, **Au|pair|stel|le** △ F au pair job

Au|ra ['aura] F **-**, *no pl (Med, geh)* aura

Au|re|o|le [aure'o:lə] F **-, -n** *(Art)* aureole, halo; *(Met)* corona, aureole; *(fig: rare)* aura

Au|ri|kel [au'ri:kl] F **-, -n** *(Bot)* auricula

Au|ro|ra [au'ro:ra] F **-s** *(Myth, liter)* Aurora

aus [aus] **PREP** *+dat* **a** *(räumlich)* from; *(= aus dem Inneren von)* out of; **~ dem Fenster/der Tür** out of the window/door; **~ unserer Mitte** from our midst; **~ der Flasche trinken** to drink from the bottle, to drink out of the bottle; **jdm ~ einer Verlegenheit helfen** to help sb out of a difficulty

b *(Herkunft, Quelle bezeichnend)* from; **~ dem Deutschen** from (the) German; **~ ganz Frankreich** from all over France; **~ guter Familie** from *or* of a good family; **ein Wort ~ dem Zusammenhang herausgreifen** to take a word out of (its) context

c *(auf Ursache deutend)* out of; **~ Hass/Gehorsam/Mitleid** out of hatred/obedience/sympathy; **~ Erfahrung** from experience; **~ Furcht vor/Liebe zu** for fear/love of; **~ dem Grunde, dass ...** for the reason that ...; **~ einer Laune heraus** on (an) impulse; **~ Spaß** for fun, for a laugh *(inf)*; **~ Unachtsamkeit** due to carelessness; **~ Versehen** by mistake; **~ sich heraus** of one's own accord, off one's own bat *(Brit inf)*; **ein Mord ~ Berechnung** a calculated murder; **ein Mord** *or* **ein Verbrechen ~ Leidenschaft** a crime of passion

d *(zeitlich)* from; **~ dem Barock** from the Baroque period

e *(= beschaffen aus)* (made out) of; **ein Herz ~ Stein** a heart of stone

f *(Herstellungsart)* out of, from; *(fig: Ausgangspunkt)* out of; **kann man ~ diesem Stoff noch etwas machen?** can something still be made out of *or* from this material?; **einen Soldaten/Pfarrer ~ jdm machen** to make a soldier/minister (out) of sb; **einen anständigen Menschen ~ jdm machen** to make sb into a decent person; **was ist ~ ihm/dieser Sache geworden?** what has become of him/this?; **~ der Sache ist nichts geworden** nothing came of it; **~ ihm wird einmal ein guter Arzt** he'll make a good doctor one day; **~ mir ist nichts geworden** I never got anywhere (in life)

g ~ dem Gleichgewicht out of balance; *Mensch, Gegenstand* off balance; **~ der Mode** out of fashion

h *(Aus: = in)* in; **eine Prüfung ~ Geschichte** an examination in *or* on history

i *(Typ)* **gesetzt ~ ...** set in ...

ADV → *auch* **aus sein a** *(Sport)* out; *(Ftbl, Rugby)* out (of play), in touch

b *(inf: = vorbei, zu Ende)* over; **~ jetzt!** that's enough!, that'll do now! *(inf)*; **~ und vorbei** over and done with

c *(= gelöscht)* out; *(an Geräten)* off; **Licht ~!** lights out!

d *(in Verbindung mit von)* **vom Fenster ~** from the window; **von München ~** from Munich; **von sich** *(dat)* **~** off one's own bat *(Brit inf)*, of one's own accord; **von ihm ~** as far as he's concerned; **ok, von mir ~** OK, if you like → **ein**

Aus [aus] NT **-, - a** *no pl (Ftbl, Rugby)* touch *no art*; **ins ~ gehen** to go out of play; *(seitlich)* to go into touch; **ins politische ~ geraten** to end up in the political wilderness **b** *no pl (= Ausscheiden)* exit *(für* of) **c** *(= Ende)* end; **das ~ für die Firma ist unabwendbar** the company is doomed to close down

aus+ar|bei|ten *sep* **VT** to work out; *(= errichten, entwerfen auch) System, Gedankengebäude* to elaborate, to draw up; *(= vorbereiten)* to prepare; *(= formulieren)* to formulate, to compose **VR** *(Sport)* to have a work-out

Aus|ar|bei|tung F **-, -en** working out; *(= Vorbereitung)* preparation; *(= Formulierung)* formulation, composition

aus+ar|ten VI *sep aux sein* **a** *(Party etc)* to get out of control; **~ in** *(+acc) or* **zu** to degenerate into **b** *(= ungezogen etc werden)* to get out of hand, to become unruly; *(= pöbelhaft, ordinär etc werden)* to misbehave; *(= fluchen)* to use bad language

aus+at|men VTI *sep* to breathe out, to exhale

aus+ba|cken VT *sep irreg* **a** *(= in Fett backen)* to fry **b** *(= zu Ende backen)* to bake (for) long enough; *(= durchbacken)* to bake (right) through

aus+ba|den VT *sep (fig inf)* to carry the can for *(Brit inf)*, to take the rap for *(inf)*, to pay for; **ich muss jetzt alles ~** I have to carry the can *(Brit inf)*, I have to take the rap *(inf)*

aus+bag|gern VT *sep Graben* to excavate; *Fahrrinne, Schlamm* to dredge (out)

aus+ba|lan|cie|ren *ptp* **ausbalanciert** *sep (lit, fig)* **VT** to balance (out) **VR** to balance (each other out)

aus+bal|do|wern *ptp* **ausbaldowert** VT *sep (inf)* to scout out *(inf)*; **~, ob ...** to scout *or* nose around to find out whether ... *(inf)*

Aus|ball M *(Sport)* **bei ~** when the ball goes out of play

Aus|bau M *no pl* **a** *no pl (= das Ausbauen)* removal; *(lit, fig: = Erweiterung)* extension *(zu* into); *(von Befestigungsanlagen)* reinforcement; *(= Umbau)* conversion *(zu* (in)to); *(von Beziehungen, Freundschaft)* building up, cultivation; *(= Festigung: von Position, Vorsprung)* consolidation, strengthening **b** *(am Haus)* extension **c** *(= Einzelgehöft)* (small) farmstead *(separated from main settlement)*

Aus|bau|ar|bei|ten PL extension *or* conversion work *sing*

aus+bau|en VT *sep* **a** *(= herausmontieren)* to remove *(aus* from) **b** *(lit, fig: = erweitern, vergrößern)* to extend *(zu* into); *Befestigungsanlagen* to reinforce; *(= umbauen)* to convert *(zu* (in)to); *(= innen ausbauen)* to fit out; *Beziehungen, Freundschaft* to build up, to cultivate; *Plan* to elaborate; *(= festigen) Position, Vorsprung* to consolidate, to strengthen; **ausgebaut** *(= umgebaut)* converted; *(= erweitert) Schul-, Verkehrssystem etc* fully developed; **ein ausgebautes Dachgeschoss** a loft conversion; **gut/nicht gut ausgebaut** well/badly planned

aus|bau|fä|hig ADJ *Position* with good prospects; *Geschäft, Produktion, Markt, Computer* expandable; *Beziehungen* that can be built up; *Machtstellung* that can be consolidated *or* strengthened; *(inf) Schüler, Mitarbeiter* promising

Aus|bau|fä|hig|keit F development potential; *(von Computer)* expandability

Aus|bau-: **Aus|bau|plan** M development plan; **Aus|bau|stre|cke** F *(Mot) section of improved road*; **„Ende der ~"** ≈ "road narrows"; **Aus|bau|stu|fe** F *(von Kraftwerk, Flughafen etc)* development stage; **Aus|bau|woh|nung** F extension flat *(esp Brit)*, granny annexe *(Brit inf)*, in-law apartment *(US)*

aus+be|din|gen *ptp* **ausbedungen** VT *sep irreg* **sich** *(dat)* **etw ~** to insist on sth, to make sth a condition; **sich** *(dat)* **~, dass ...** to stipulate that ..., to make it a condition that ...; **ich bin dazu bereit, aber ich bedinge mir aus, ...** I'm prepared to do it but (only) on condition that ...; **sich** *(dat)* **das Recht ~, etw zu tun** to reserve the right to do sth

aus+bei|ßen VT *sep irreg* **sich** *(dat)* **einen Zahn ~** to break *or* lose a tooth *(when biting into sth)*; **sich** *(dat)* **die Zähne an etw** *(dat)* **~** *(fig)* to have a tough time of it with sth

aus+be|kom|men *ptp* **ausbekommen** VT *sep irreg (inf)* to get off

aus+bes|sern VT *sep* to repair; *Gegenstand, Wäsche etc auch* to mend; *Roststelle etc* to remove; *Gemälde etc* to restore; *Fehler* to correct

Aus|bes|se|rung F repair; *(= das Flicken)* mending; *(von Gemälde)* restoration; *(von Fehler)* correction

Aus|bes|se|rungs-: **Aus|bes|se|rungs|ar|bei|ten** PL repair work *sing*; **aus|bes|se|rungs|be|dürf|tig** ADJ in need of repair *etc*; **Aus|bes|se|rungs|werk** NT *(Rail)* repair shop

aus+be|to|nie|ren *ptp* **ausbetoniert** VT *sep* to concrete

aus+beu|len *sep* VT **a** *Kleidung* to make baggy; *Hut* to make floppy; **ausgebeult** *(Kleidung)* baggy; *Hut* battered **b** *(= Beule entfernen)* to remove a dent/dents in; *(Tech: durch Hämmern)* to beat out VR *(Hose)* to go baggy; *(Hut)* to go floppy

Aus|beu|te F *(= Gewinn)* profit, gain; *(= Ertrag einer Grube etc)* yield *(an +dat* in); *(fig)* result(s) *pl*; *(= Einnahmen)* proceeds *pl*; **die ~ an verwertbaren Erkenntnissen war gering** the useful results (gleaned) were minimal

aus+beu|ten ['ausbɔytn] VT *sep (lit, fig)* to exploit; *(Min) eine Grube auch* to work; *(Agr) Boden* to overwork, to deplete

Aus|beu|ter ['ausbɔytɐ] M **-s, -**, **Aus|beu|te|rin** [-ərɪn] F **-, -nen** exploiter; **~ und Ausgebeutete** the exploiters and the exploited

Aus|beu|ter|be|trieb M *(pej)* sweatshop

Aus|beu|te|rei [ausbɔytə'rai] F **-, -en** *(pej)* exploitation

Aus|beu|ter|ge|sell|schaft F society based on exploitation

aus|beu|te|risch ['ausbɔytərɪʃ] ADJ exploitative ADV **die Arbeiter ~ zu Überstunden antreiben** to exploit the workers by forcing them to work overtime

Aus|beu|tung F **-, -en** *(lit, fig)* exploitation; *(Min, von Grube auch)* working

aus+be|zah|len *ptp* **ausbezahlt** VT *sep Geld* to pay out; *Arbeitnehmer* to pay off; *(= abfinden) Erben etc* to buy out, to pay off; **in bar ausbezahlt** paid in cash; **wie viel kriegst du pro Woche ausbezahlt?** what is your weekly take-home pay?

Aus|be|zah|lung F payment; *(von Erben etc)* buying out, paying off

aus+bie|ten VT *sep irreg* to put on offer, to offer (for sale); **ausgeboten werden** to be on offer; *(bei Versteigerung auch)* to be up for auction

aus+bil|den *sep* VT **a** *(beruflich, Sport, Mil)* to train; *(= unterrichten)* to instruct, to train; *(akademisch)* to educate; **sich in etw** *(dat)***/als** *or* **zu etw ~ lassen** *(esp Arbeiter, Lehrling)* to train in sth/as sth; *(= studieren)* to study sth/to study to be sth; *(= Qualifikation erwerben)* to qualify in sth/as sth; **sich am Klavier** *etc* **~ lassen** to have piano *etc* tuition *(Brit)*, to have private piano *etc* lessons; **jdn als Sänger ~ lassen** to have sb trained as a singer; **ein ausgebildeter Übersetzer** a trained/qualified translator

b *Fähigkeiten* to develop, to cultivate; *(Mus) Stimme* to train

c *(= formen)* to form; *(= gestalten)* to shape; *(= entwickeln)* to develop; **etw oval ~** to give sth an oval shape; *(Designer etc)* to design sth with an oval shape

VR **a** *(= sich entwickeln)* to develop; *(= sich bilden)* to form

b *(= sich schulen)* **sich in etw** *(dat)* **~** *(esp Arbeiter, Lehrling)* to train in sth; *(= studieren)* to study sth; *(= Qualifikation erwerben)* to qualify in sth

Aus|bil|der ['ausbɪldɐ] M **-s, -**, **Aus|bil|de|rin** [-ərɪn] F **-, -nen** instructor; *(Frau auch)* instructress

Aus|bild|ner ['ausbɪldnɐ] M **-s, -**, **Aus|bild|ne|rin** [-ərɪn] F **-, -nen** *(Aus Mil)* instructor; *(Frau auch)* instructress

Aus|bil|dung F **a** *(beruflich, Sport, Mil)* training; *(akademisch)* education; **er ist noch in der ~** he hasn't yet finished his education **b** *(= das Herausbilden: von Fähigkeiten)* development, cultivation; *(= Formung)* formation; *(= Gestaltung)* shaping; *(= Entwicklung)* development

Aus|bil|dungs-: **Aus|bil|dungs|bei|hil|fe** F *(für Schüler)* (education) grant; *(für Lehrling)* training allowance; **Aus|bil|dungs|be|ruf** M occupation that requires training; **Aus|bil|dungs|be|trieb** M *company that takes on trainees*; **Aus|bil|dungs|dau|er** F training *or* qualification period; **die ~ für einen Ingenieur beträgt sechs Jahre** it takes six years to become an engineer; **Aus|bil|dungs|för|de|rung** F promotion of training; *(akademisch)* promotion of education; *(= Stipendium)* grant; **Aus|bil|dungs|gang** M *pl* **-gänge** training; **Aus|bil|dungs|jahr** NT year of training; **Aus|bil|dungs|kom|pa|nie** F training unit *(for weapons training)*; **Aus|bil|dungs|kos|ten** PL cost *sing* of training *or* of a traineeship; *(für Studium)* cost *sing* of studying; **Aus|bil|dungs|kurs** M, **Aus|bil|dungs|kur|sus** M, **Aus|bil|dungs|lehr|gang** M training course; **Aus|bil|dungs|la|ger** NT training camp; **Aus|bil|dungs|lei|ter(in)** M(F) chief *or* head instructor, head trainer; **Aus|bil|dungs|me|tho|de** F training method, method of training; **Aus|bil|dungs|mög|lich|kei|ten** PL training opportunities; *(Studium)* opportunities for studying; **Aus|bil|dungs|mu|ni|ti|on** F blank ammunition *(used in training)*; **Aus|bil|dungs|of|fi|zier(in)** M(F) training officer; **Aus|bil|dungs|ord|nung** F training regulations *pl*; **Aus|bil|dungs|platz** M place to train; *(= Stelle)* training vacancy; **Aus|bil|dungs|stand** M level of training; **Aus|bil|dungs|stät|te** F place of training; **Aus|bil|dungs|ver|gü|tung** F payment made during training; **Aus|bil|dungs|ver|hält|nis** NT **sie steht noch im ~** she's still a trainee, she's still in training; **Aus|bil|dungs|ver|si|che|rung** F education insurance; **Aus|bil|dungs|ver|trag** M articles *pl* of apprenticeship; **Aus|bil|dungs|zeit** F period of training; **nach zweijähriger ~** after a two-year period of training *or* training period; **Aus|bil|dungs|ziel** NT aims *pl* of education; **die ~e der Schule** the aims of school education *or* education at school

aus+bit|ten VT *sep irreg* **sich** *(dat)* **(von jdm) etw ~** *(geh)* to ask (sb) for sth, to request sth (from sb) *(form)*; **das möchte ich mir (auch) ausgebeten haben!** I should think so too!; **ich bitte mir Ruhe aus!** I must *or* will have silence!

aus+bla|sen VT *sep irreg* to blow out; *Hochofen* to shut down, to extinguish; *Ei* to blow

aus+blei|ben VI *sep irreg aux sein (= fortbleiben)* to stay out; *(= nicht erscheinen: Gäste, Schüler, Schneefall)* to fail to appear; *(= nicht eintreten: Erwartung, Befürchtung)* to fail to materialize; *(= überfällig sein)* to be overdue; *(= aufhören: Puls, Atmung etc)* to stop; **die Strafe/ein Krieg wird nicht ~** punishment/a war is inevitable; **das blieb nicht lange aus** that wasn't long in coming; **es konnte nicht ~, dass ...** it was inevitable that ...; **bei manchen Patienten bleiben diese Symptome aus** in some patients these symptoms are absent *or* do not appear

Aus|blei|ben NT **-s**, *no pl (= Fehlen)* absence; *(= das Nichterscheinen)* nonappearance; **bei ~ von ...** in the absence of ...; **bei ~ der Periode** if your period doesn't come

aus+blei|chen VTI **sep irreg** *(vi: aux sein)* to fade, to bleach

aus+blen|den *sep* VTI *(TV etc)* to fade out; *(plötzlich)* to cut out; *(Comput) Fenster etc* to hide; *(= deaktivieren) Schaltfläche etc* to gray (out) VR **sich (aus einer Übertragung) ~** to leave a transmission

Aus|blen|dung F *(TV etc)* fade-out; *(plötzlich)* cutting out, cut

Aus|blick M **a** view *(auf +acc* of), outlook *(auf +acc* over, onto); **ein Zimmer mit ~ auf die Straße/aufs Meer** a room overlooking the street/with a view of the sea *or* overlooking the sea **b** *(fig)* prospect, outlook *(auf +acc, in +acc* for); **einen ~ auf etw** *(acc)* **geben** to give the prospects for sth

aus+bli|cken VI *sep (geh)* **nach jdm ~** to look for sb

aus+blu|ten *sep* VI *aux sein (= verbluten)* to bleed to death; *(fig)* to be bled white; **ein Schwein ~ lassen** to bleed a pig dry VT *(fig)* to bleed white

aus+boh|ren VT *sep* to bore; *(mit Bohrgerät, Med)* to drill; *(= herausbohren)* to bore/drill out

aus+bom|ben VT *sep* to bomb out; **die Ausgebombten** people who have been bombed out (of their homes)

aus+boo|ten ['ausbo:tn] *sep* VT **a** *(inf) jdn* to kick *or* boot out *(inf)* **b** *(Naut)* to disembark *(in boats)*; *(= abladen)* to unload VI *(Naut)* to disembark *(in boats)*

aus+bor|gen VT *sep (inf)* **sich** *(dat)* **etw (von jdm) ~** to borrow sth (from sb); **jdm etw ~** to lend sb sth, to lend sth (out) to sb

aus+bra|ten *sep irreg* VT *(= auslassen) Speck* to fry the fat out of VI *aux sein (Fett)* to run out *(aus* of); **ausgebratenes Fett** melted bacon *etc* fat

aus+bre|chen *sep irreg* VI **a** *(= beginnen, Krieg, Seuche, Feuer)* to break out; *(Konflikt, Gewalt, Hysterie, Unruhen)* to break out, to erupt; *(Jubel, Zorn, Frust)* to erupt, to explode; *(Zeitalter)* to arrive, to begin; **in Gelächter/Tränen** *or* **Weinen ~** to burst into laughter/tears, to burst out laughing/crying; **in Jubel ~** to erupt with jubilation; **in Beifall ~** to break into applause; **in den Ruf „..." ~** to burst out with the cry "..."; **in Schweiß ~** to break out in a sweat; **bei dir ist wohl der Wohlstand ausgebrochen** *(fig inf)* have you struck it rich? *(inf)*

b *(aus Gefangenschaft)* to break out *(aus* of); *(Tier)* to escape *(aus* from); *(fig: = sich befreien)* to get out *(aus* of), to escape *(aus* from); **aus dem Gefängnis ~** to escape from prison

c *(Vulkan)* to erupt

VT *Zahn* to break; *Steine* to break off; **sich** *(dat)* **einen Zahn** ~ to break a tooth

Aus|bre|cher [ˈausbrɛçɐ] **M -s, - a** *(inf: = Tier)* escaped animal, runaway **b** *(= Pferd)* horse that swerves round jumps

Aus|bre|cher [ˈausbrɛçɐ] **M -s, -, Aus|bre|che|rin** [-ərɪn] **F -, -nen** *(inf: = Gefangener)* escaped prisoner, escapee; *(= notorischer Ausbrecher)* jailbreaker *(inf)*

aus+brei|ten *sep* VT *Landkarte, Handtuch* to spread (out); *Flügel, Äste* to spread (out), to extend; *Arme* to stretch out, to extend; *(= ausstellen, fig: = zeigen)* to display; *Licht, Wärme* to spread; **einen Plan vor jdm** ~ to unfold a plan to sb; **sein Leben vor jdm** ~ to lay one's whole life before sb
VR **a** *(= sich verbreiten)* to spread
b *(= sich erstrecken)* to extend, to stretch (out), to spread out
c *(inf: = sich breitmachen)* to spread oneself out
d sich über etw *(acc)* ~ *(fig)* to dwell on sth; **sich in Einzelheiten** ~ to go into great detail; **darüber will ich mich jetzt nicht** ~ I'd rather not go into that now

Aus|brei|tung [ˈausbraitʊŋ] **F -, -en** *(= das Sichausbreiten)* spread; *(= das Ausbreiten)* spreading

aus+brem|sen VT *sep* **a** *(Aut)* **den Hintermann** ~ to brake, forcing the person behind to slow down **b** *(fig inf: = stoppen) Widersacher etc* to thwart; **jdn** ~ to put a spanner in sb's works *(inf)*

aus+bren|nen *sep irreg* VI *aux sein* **a** *(= zu Ende brennen)* to burn out; *(Vulkan)* to become extinct **b** *(= völlig verbrennen)* to be burned out, to be gutted; **ausgebrannt** burned-out; *Gebäude auch* gutted; *Brennstab* spent → *auch* **ausgebrannt** VT to burn out; *(Sonne: = ausdörren)* to scorch; *(Med)* to cauterize

aus+brin|gen VT *sep irreg* **a** *Trinkspruch* to propose **b** *(Naut) Boot, Anker* to lower **c** *(Typ) Zeile* to space out

Aus|bruch **M a** *(aus* from) *(aus Gefängnis)* break-out *(auch Mil)*, escape *(auch fig)* **b** *(= Beginn)* outbreak; *(von Vulkan)* eruption; **zum** ~ **kommen** to break out **c** *(fig) (= Gefühlsausbruch, Zornausbruch)* outburst; *(stärker)* eruption, explosion; **zum** ~ **kommen** to erupt, to explode

Aus|bruchs-: **Aus|bruchs|herd** **M** *(Geol)* focus *(of an earthquake)*; **Aus|bruchs|ver|such** **M** *(aus* from) attempted break-out *(auch Mil) or* escape, break-out *or* escape attempt; *(fig)* attempt at escape

aus+brü|ten VT *sep* to hatch; *(esp in Brutkasten)* to incubate; *(fig inf) Plan etc* to cook up *(inf)*, to hatch (up); **eine Erkältung** ~ to be coming down with a cold

aus+bu|chen VT *sep* → **ausgebucht**

aus+büch|sen [ˈausbʏksn] VI *sep (N Ger: = ausreißen)* to break out, to run away

aus+buch|ten [ˈausbʊxtn] *sep* VT *Ufer* to hollow out; *Straße* to make a curve in the side of; *Wand* to round out VR to bulge *or* curve out

Aus|buch|tung **F -, -en** bulge; *(von Strand)* (small) cove

aus+bud|deln VT *sep (inf)* to dig up *(auch fig inf)*

aus+bü|geln VT *sep* to iron out; *(inf) Fehler, Verlust, Mängel* to make good; *Missverständnis, Angelegenheit* to iron out *(inf)*

aus+bu|hen VT *sep (inf)* to boo

Aus|bund **M**, *no pl (von Tugend, Schönheit)* paragon, model, epitome; **ein** ~ **von Tugend** a paragon *or* model of virtue, the epitome of virtue; **er ist ein** ~ **an** *or* **von Gemeinheit/Frechheit** he is baseness/impudence itself *or* personified

aus+bür|gern [ˈausbʏrgɐn] VT *sep* **jdn** ~ to expatriate sb

Aus|bür|ge|rung [ˈausbʏrgərʊŋ] **F -, -en** expatriation

aus+bürs|ten VT *sep* to brush out *(aus* of); *Anzug* to brush

aus+bü|xen [ˈausbʏksn] VI *sep aux sein (hum inf)* to run off, to scarper *(inf)*; **jdm** ~ to run away from sb

aus+che|cken [ˈaustʃɛkn] VI *sep (Flug, Hotel etc)* to check out *(aus* of); **hast du schon (dein Gepäck) ausgecheckt?** have you picked up your luggage *(Brit) or* baggage yet?

aus+chil|len VI *sep (sl)* to chill out *(sl)*

Ausch|witz [ˈauʃvɪts] **NT -'** Auschwitz

Ausch|witz-Lü|ge **F** holocaust denial

Aus|dau|er **F**, *no pl* staying power, stamina; *(im Ertragen)* endurance; *(= Beharrlichkeit)* perseverance, persistence, tenacity; *(= Hartnäckigkeit)* persistence; **beim Lernen/Lesen keine** ~ **haben** to have no staying power when it comes to learning/reading

aus|dau|ernd ADJ **a** *Mensch* with staying power, with stamina; *(im Ertragen)* with endurance; *(= beharrlich)* persevering, tenacious; *(= hartnäckig)* persistent; *Bemühungen, Anstrengungen* untiring **b** *(Bot) Pflanze* perennial ADV diligently; ~ **lernen** to apply oneself to learning, to study diligently

Aus|dau|er|trai|ning **NT** stamina training

aus|dehn|bar **ADJ** expandable; *(= dehnbar) Gummi etc* elastic; *(fig)* extendable *(auf +acc* to), extensible

aus+deh|nen *sep* VT **a** *(= vergrößern)* to expand; *(= dehnen)* to stretch, to extend; *(= länger machen)* to elongate, to stretch **b** *(fig)* to extend; *(zeitlich)* to extend, to prolong *(auf +acc* to) VR **a** *(= größer werden)* to expand; *(durch Dehnen)* to stretch; *(= sich erstrecken)* to extend, to stretch *(bis* as far as); **die Seuche/der Krieg dehnte sich über das ganze Land aus** the epidemic/the war spread over the whole country **b** *(fig)* to extend *(über +acc* over, *bis* as far as, to); *(zeitlich)* to go on *(bis* until), to extend *(bis* until) → *auch* **ausgedehnt**

Aus|deh|nung **F a** *(= das Vergrößern)* expansion; *(= das Dehnen)* stretching, extension; *(fig, zeitlich)* extension **b** *(= Umfang)* expanse; *(Math: von Raum)* extension; **eine** ~ **von 10.000 Quadratmetern haben** to cover an area of 10,000 square metres *(Brit) or* meters *(US)*

Aus|deh|nungs-: **aus|deh|nungs|fä|hig** **ADJ** *(esp Phys)* capable of expansion, expansile, expansible; **Aus|deh|nungs|fä|hig|keit** **F** ability to expand; **Aus|deh|nungs|ver|mö|gen** **NT** *(esp Phys)* capacity to expand, expansibility

aus+den|ken VT *sep irreg* **sich** *(dat)* **etw** ~ *(= erfinden)* to think sth up; *Idee, Plan auch* to devise sth; *(in Einzelheiten)* to think sth out, to devise sth; *Wunsch* to think of sth; *Entschuldigung* to contrive sth, to think sth up; *Überraschung* to plan sth; *Geschichte* to make *or* think sth up; *(= sich vorstellen)* to imagine sth; *(= durchdenken)* to think sth through; **eine ausgedachte Geschichte** a made-up story; **das ist nicht auszudenken** *(= unvorstellbar)* it's inconceivable; *(= zu schrecklich etc)* it doesn't bear thinking about; **da musst du dir schon etwas anderes ~!** *(inf)* you'll have to think of something better than that!

aus+deu|ten VT *sep* to interpret; *Äußerung, Wort auch* to construe; **falsch** ~ to misinterpret, to misconstrue

aus+deut|schen [ˈausdɔytʃn] VT *sep (Aus inf)* **jdm etw** ~ to explain sth to sb in words of one syllable, to explain sth to sb in plain English

Aus|deu|tung **F** interpretation

aus+die|nen VI *sep* **ausgedient haben** *(Mil old)* to have finished one's military service; *(= im Ruhestand sein)* to have been discharged; *(fig inf)* to have had its day; *(Kugelschreiber etc)* to be used up, to be finished; **ein ausgedienter Soldat** *(dated)* a veteran, an ex-serviceman → *auch* **ausgedient**

aus+dis|ku|tie|ren *sep ptp* **ausdiskutiert** VT *Thema* to discuss fully VI *(= zu Ende diskutieren)* to finish discussing *or* talking

aus+dor|ren VI *sep aux sein* = **ausdörren VI**

aus+dör|ren *sep* VT to dry up; *Kehle* to parch; *Pflanzen* to shrivel VI *aux sein* to dry up; *(Boden auch)* to become parched; *(Pflanze auch)* to shrivel up → *auch* **ausgedörrt**

aus+dre|hen VT *sep (= ausschalten)* to turn *or* switch off; *Licht auch* to turn out

aus+dre|schen *sep irreg* VT to thresh (fully) VI *(das Dreschen beenden)* to finish (the) threshing

Aus|druck **M** *pl* **-drücke a** *no pl (= Gesichtsausdruck)* expression; **der** ~ **ihrer Gesichter** the expression(s) on their faces
b *no pl* **als** ~ **meiner Dankbarkeit** as an expression of my gratitude; **mit dem** ~ **des Bedauerns** *(form)* expressing regret, with an expression of regret; **ohne jeden** ~ **singen/spielen** to sing/play without any expression; **etw zum** ~ **bringen, einer Sache** *(dat)* ~ **geben** *or* **verleihen** *(form)* to express sth, to give expression to sth; **in seinen Worten/seinem Verhalten kam Mitleid zum** ~ his words expressed/his behaviour *(Brit) or* behavior *(US)* showed his sympathy
c *(= Wort)* expression; *(= Fachausdruck, Math)* term; **das ist gar kein ~!** that's not the word for it; **sich im** ~ **vergreifen** to use the wrong word

Aus|druck **M** *pl* **-drucke** *(von Computer etc)* printout, hard copy; ~ **in Datei** *(Druckoption)* print to file

aus+dru|cken *sep* VT **a** *(Comput)* to print out **b** *(Typ) (= fertig drucken)* to finish printing; *(= ungekürzt drucken)* to print in full; **ausgedruckte Exemplare** fully printed copies VI *(Buchstaben etc)* to come out

aus+drü|cken *sep* VT **a** *(= zum Ausdruck bringen)* to express *(jdm* to sb); *(Verhalten, Gesicht) Trauer etc* to reveal, to express; **um es anders/gelinde auszudrücken** to put it another way/mildly; **anders ausgedrückt** in other words; **einfach ausgedrückt** put simply, in simple terms, in words of one syllable
b *Frucht* to press out, to squeeze out; *Tube, Pickel* to squeeze; *Schwamm, Lappen* to squeeze out; *(= ausmachen)* to put out; *Zigarette* to stub out; **den Saft einer Zitrone** ~ to press *or* squeeze juice out of a lemon, to squeeze a lemon
VR *(Mensch)* to express oneself; *(Emotion)* to be expressed *or* revealed; **in ihrem Gesicht/Verhalten drückte sich Verzweiflung aus** her face/behaviour *(Brit) or* behavior *(US)* showed her despair; **er kann sich gewandt** ~ he is very articulate

aus|drück|lich [ˈausdrʏklɪç, ausˈdrʏklɪç] ADJ *attr Wunsch, Genehmigung* express ADV expressly; *(= besonders)* particularly; **etw** ~ **betonen** to emphasize sth particularly *or* specifically

Aus|drück|lich|keit **F -**, *no pl* **in aller** ~ expressly

Aus|drucks-: **Aus|drucks|be|dürf|nis** **NT** need to express oneself; **aus|drucks|fä|hig** **ADJ** expressive; *(= gewandt)* articulate; **Aus|drucks|fä|hig|keit** **F** expressiveness; *(= Gewandtheit)* articulateness; **Aus|drucks|form** **F** form of expression; **Aus|drucks|kraft** **F**, *no pl* expressiveness; *(von Schriftsteller)* articulateness, word power; **aus|drucks|leer** **ADJ** expressionless; **Aus|drucks|lee|re** **F** expressionlessness; **aus|drucks|los** **ADJ** inexpressive; *Gesicht, Blick auch* expressionless; **Aus|drucks|lo|sig|keit** **F -**, *no pl* inexpressiveness; *(von Gesicht, Blick)* expressionlessness; **Aus|drucks|mit|tel** **NT** means of expression; **Aus|drucks|mög|lich|keit** **F** mode of expression; **aus|drucks|schwach** **ADJ** inexpressive; **aus|drucks|stark** **ADJ** expressive; **Aus|drucks|stär|ke** **F** expressiveness; **Aus|drucks|tanz** **M** free dance; **aus|drucks|voll** **ADJ** expressive; **Aus|drucks|wei|se** **F** way of expressing oneself, mode of expression; **was ist denn das für eine ~!** what sort of language is that to use!

aus+dün|nen [ˈausdʏnən] *sep* VT **a** *Pflanzen, Haare* to thin out **b** *Verkehr, Kapital* to reduce VR *(Kursus)* to thin out

aus+düns|ten *sep* VT *Geruch* to give off; *(Med, Bot auch)* to transpire VI *(= Dunst/Geruch abson-*

dern) to give off vapour *(Brit)* or vapor *(US)*/a smell; *(Bot, Med)* to transpire

Aus|düns|tung F -, -en **a** *(= das Ausdünsten)* evaporation; *(von Körper, Pflanze)* transpiration **b** *(= Dampf)* vapour *(Brit)*, vapor *(US)*; *(= Geruch)* fume, smell; *(von Tier)* scent; *(von Mensch)* smell; *(fig)* emanation

aus|ei|nan|der [auslai'nandɐ] ADV **a** *(= voneinander entfernt, getrennt)* apart; **weit ~** far apart; *Augen, Beine etc* wide apart; *Zähne* widely spaced; *Meinungen* very different; **die beiden sind (im Alter) ein Jahr ~** there is a year between the two of them; **~ sein** *(inf: Paar)* to have broken or split up; **die Verlobung ist ~** *(inf)* the engagement is off **b** *(= jedes aus dem anderen)* from one another, one from another or the other; **diese Begriffe kann man nur ~ erklären** one can only explain these concepts in relation to one another

aus|ei|nan|der-: **aus|ei|nan|der+be|kom|men** *sep irreg*, **aus|ei|nan|der be|kom|men** △ *irreg* VT to be able to get apart; **aus|ei|nan|der+bie|gen** *sep irreg*, **aus|ei|nan|der bie|gen** △ *irreg* VT to bend apart; **aus|ei|nan|der+bre|chen** *sep irreg*, **aus|ei|nan|der bre|chen** △ *irreg* VT to break in two VI *aux sein (lit, fig)* to break up; **aus|ei|nan|der+brei|ten** *sep*, **aus|ei|nan|der brei|ten** △ VT to unfold; **aus|ei|nan|der+brin|gen** *sep irreg*, **aus|ei|nan|der brin|gen** △ *irreg* VT *(inf)* to manage to be able to get apart *(auch fig)*; **aus|ei|nan|der+di|vi|die|ren** *sep*, **aus|ei|nan|der di|vi|die|ren** △ VT to divide; **eine Gruppe ~** to create divisions within a group; **aus|ei|nan|der+drif|ten** *sep*, **aus|ei|nan|der drif|ten** △ VI to drift apart; **aus|ei|nan|der+ent|wi|ckeln** *sep*, **aus|ei|nan|der ent|wi|ckeln** △ VR to grow apart (from each other); *(Partner)* to drift apart; **aus|ei|nan|der+fal|len** *sep irreg aux sein*, **aus|ei|nan|der fal|len** △ *irreg aux sein* VI **a** *(= zerfallen)* to fall apart; *(fig)* to collapse, to fall apart **b** *(fig: = sich gliedern)* to divide up *(in +acc* into); **aus|ei|nan|der+fal|ten** *sep*, **aus|ei|nan|der fal|ten** △ VT to unfold; **aus|ei|nan|der+flie|gen** *sep irreg aux sein*, **aus|ei|nan|der flie|gen** △ *irreg aux sein* VI to fly apart; *(nach allen Seiten)* to fly in all directions; **aus|ei|nan|der+flie|ßen** *sep irreg aux sein*, **aus|ei|nan|der flie|ßen** △ *irreg aux sein* VI *(nach allen Seiten)* to flow in all directions; *(= zerfließen)* to melt; *(Farben)* to run; **aus|ei|nan|der+ge|hen** *sep irreg aux sein*, **aus|ei|nan|der ge|hen** △ *irreg aux sein* VI **a** *(lit, fig: = sich trennen) (Menschen, Vorhang)* to part, to separate; *(Menge)* to disperse; *(Versammlung, Ehe etc)* to break up; *(= auseinanderfallen: Schrank etc)* to fall apart **b** *(= sich verzweigen: Weg etc)* to divide, to branch, to fork; *(zwei Wege)* to diverge; *(fig: Ansichten etc)* to diverge, to differ **c** *(inf: = dick werden)* to get fat → **Hefeteig**; **aus|ei|nan|der+hal|ten** *sep irreg*, **aus|ei|nan|der hal|ten** △ *irreg* VT to keep apart; *(= unterscheiden) Begriffe* to distinguish between; *esp Zwillinge etc* to tell apart; **aus|ei|nan|der+ja|gen** *sep*, **aus|ei|nan|der ja|gen** △ VT to scatter; **aus|ei|nan|der+ken|nen** *sep irreg*, **aus|ei|nan|der ken|nen** △ *irreg* VT *(inf)* to tell apart; **aus|ei|nan|der+klaf|fen** *sep aux sein*, **aus|ei|nan|der klaf|fen** △ *aux sein* VI to gape open; *(fig: Meinungen)* to be far apart, to diverge (wildly); **aus|ei|nan|der+kla|mü|sern** *sep*, **aus|ei|nan|der kla|mü|sern** △ VT *(dial, hum)* to sort out; **jdm etw ~** to spell sth out for sb; **aus|ei|nan|der+klau|ben** *sep*, **aus|ei|nan|der klau|ben** △ VT *(esp S Ger, Aus, Sw)* to sort out; **aus|ei|nan|der+krie|gen** *sep*, **aus|ei|nan|der krie|gen** △ VT *(inf)* to be able to get apart; **aus|ei|nan|der+lau|fen** *sep irreg aux sein*, **aus|ei|nan|der lau|fen** △ *irreg aux sein* VI **a** *(= zerlaufen)* to melt; *(Farbe)* to run; *(= sich ausbreiten)* to spread **b** *(inf: = sich trennen)* to break up; *(Menge)* to disperse; *(= sich auseinanderentwickeln)* to go their separate ways **c** *(Wege)* to divide, to fork, to diverge; **aus|ei|nan|der+le|ben** *sep*, **aus|ei|nan|der le|ben** △ VR to drift apart *(mit* from); **aus|ei|nan|der+lie|gen** *sep irreg (S Ger, Aus, Sw: aux sein)*, **aus|ei|nan|der lie|gen** △ *irreg (S Ger, Aus, Sw: aux sein)* VI **die Ereignisse liegen (um) zwei Tage auseinander** the events are separated by two days or are two days apart; **aus|ei|nan|der+ma|chen** *sep*, **aus|ei|nan|der ma|chen** △ VT *(inf)* **a** *(= auseinandernehmen)* to take apart **b** *(= auseinanderfalten)* to unfold **c** *(= spreizen) Arme, Beine* to spread (apart), to open; **aus|ei|nan|der+neh|men** *sep irreg*, **aus|ei|nan|der neh|men** △ *irreg* VT to take apart; *Maschine etc auch* to dismantle; *(kritisch)* to tear apart or to pieces; **aus|ei|nan|der+pflü|cken** *sep*, **aus|ei|nan|der pflü|cken** △ VT *(lit, fig)* to pick to pieces; **aus|ei|nan|der+rei|ßen** *sep irreg*, **aus|ei|nan|der rei|ßen** △ *irreg* VT to tear or rip apart; *(fig) Familie* to tear apart; **aus|ei|nan|der+schrau|ben** *sep*, **aus|ei|nan|der schrau|ben** △ VT to unscrew; **aus|ei|nan|der+schrei|ben** *sep*, **aus|ei|nan|der schrei|ben** △ VT **etw ~** to write sth as two words; **aus|ei|nan|der+set|zen** *sep*, **aus|ei|nan|der set|zen** △ VT **a zwei Kinder ~** to separate two children **b** *(fig) erläutern (jdm* to sb) to explain; *(schriftlich auch)* to set out VR **a sich ~** to sit apart **b** *(fig)* **sich mit etw ~** *(= sich befassen)* to have a good look at sth; **sich kritisch mit etw ~** to have a critical look at sth; **sich damit ~, was/weshalb ...** to tackle the problem of what/why ...; **sich mit jdm ~** to talk *or (sich streiten)* to argue with sb; **sich mit jdm gerichtlich ~** to take sb to court

Aus|ei|nan|der|set|zung [auslai'nandɐzɛtsʊŋ] F -, -en **a** *(= Diskussion)* discussion, debate *(über +acc* about, on); *(= Streit)* argument; *(= feindlicher Zusammenstoß)* clash *(wegen* over) **b** *(= das Befassen)* examination *(mit* of); *(kritisch)* analysis *(mit* of)

aus|ei|nan|der-: **aus|ei|nan|der+sprei|zen** *sep*, **aus|ei|nan|der sprei|zen** △ VT to open, to spread apart; **aus|ei|nan|der+sprin|gen** *sep irreg aux sein*, **aus|ei|nan|der sprin|gen** △ *irreg aux sein* VI to shatter; **aus|ei|nan|der+stie|ben** *sep irreg aux sein*, **aus|ei|nan|der stie|ben** △ *irreg aux sein* VI to scatter; **aus|ei|nan|der+stre|ben** *sep aux sein*, **aus|ei|nan|der stre|ben** △ *aux sein* VI *(geh fig: Meinungen, Tendenzen)* to diverge; **aus|ei|nan|der+trei|ben** *sep irreg*, **aus|ei|nan|der trei|ben** △ *irreg* VT *(= trennen)* to drive apart; *(= auseinanderjagen)* to scatter; *Demonstranten* to disperse VI *aux sein* to drift apart; **aus|ei|nan|der+zie|hen** *sep irreg*, **aus|ei|nan|der zie|hen** △ *irreg* VT **a** *(= dehnen)* to stretch **b** *(= trennen)* to pull apart; *Gardinen auch* to pull open VI *aux sein (= gemeinsame Wohnung aufgeben)* to separate (and live apart) VR to spread out; *(Kolonne auch)* to string out

aus+er|kie|sen *ptp* **auserkoren** VT *sep irreg (liter)* to choose; *(Gott)* to ordain *(liter)*; **zu etw auserkoren (worden) sein** to be chosen or selected for sth

aus|er|ko|ren ['auslɛɐko:rən] ADJ *(liter)* chosen, selected; **jds Auserkorene(r)** *(hum)* sb's intended *(inf)*

aus|er|le|sen ADJ *(= ausgesucht)* select; *Speisen, Weine auch* choice *attr* PTP **zu etw ~ (worden) sein** to be chosen or selected for sth ADV *(verstärkend)* particularly, especially

aus+er|se|hen *ptp* **ausersehen** VT *sep irreg (geh)* to choose; *(für Amt auch)* to designate *(zu* as); **dazu ~ sein, etw zu tun** to be chosen to do sth

aus+er|wäh|len *ptp* **auserwählt** VT *sep (geh)* to choose

aus|er|wählt ADJ *(geh)* chosen; *(= ausgesucht)* select; **das ~e Volk** the Chosen People

Aus|er|wähl|te(r) ['auslɛɐvɛ:ltə] MF *decl as adj (geh)* chosen one; **die ~n** the elect, the chosen (ones); **seine ~** *(hum)* his intended *(Brit inf)*, the woman of his choice *(US inf)*; **ihr ~r** *(hum)* her intended *(Brit inf)*, the man of her choice *(US inf)*

aus+es|sen *sep irreg* VT *Speise* to eat up, to finish (eating); *Schüssel* to empty, to clear; *Pampelmuse* to eat VI to finish eating

aus+fä|deln VR *sep* **sich ~ aus** *(Aut)* to slip out of or from

aus|fahr|bar ADJ extensible, extendable; *Antenne, Fahrgestell, Klinge* retractable

aus+fah|ren *sep irreg* VT **a** *jdn (im Kinderwagen)* to take for a walk (in the pushchair *(Brit)* or stroller *(US)*); *(im Rollstuhl)* to take for a walk (in his/her wheelchair); *(im Auto)* to take for a drive or ride
b *(= ausliefern) Waren* to deliver
c *(= abnutzen) Weg* to rut, to wear out; **sich in ausgefahrenen Bahnen bewegen** *(fig)* to keep to well-trodden paths
d *(Aut) Kurve* to (drive) round; *(mit aux sein) Rennstrecke* to drive round
e *(= austragen) Rennen* to hold
f ein Auto *etc* **(voll) ~** to drive a car *etc* flat out *(esp Brit)* or at full speed
g *(Tech)* to extend; *Fahrgestell etc* to lower
VI *aux sein* **a** *(= spazieren fahren)* to go for a ride or *(im Auto auch)* drive; **mit dem Baby ~** to take the baby out in the pushchair *(Brit)* or stroller *(US)*
b *(= abfahren) (Zug)* to pull out *(aus* of), to leave; *(Schiff)* to put to sea, to sail; **aus dem Hafen ~** to sail out of the harbour *(Brit)* or harbor *(US)*, to leave harbour *(Brit)* or harbor *(US)*
c *(Min: aus dem Schacht)* to come up
d *(= Straße verlassen)* to turn off, to leave a road/motorway *(Brit)* or highway *(US)*
e *(Tech: Fahrgestell, Gangway)* to come out
f *(= eine heftige Bewegung machen)* to gesture; **mit ~den Bewegungen** with expansive gestures
g *(böser Geist)* to come out *(aus* of)

Aus|fah|rer(in) M(F) *(Aus, S Ger)* delivery man/woman

Aus|fahrt F **a** *no pl (= Abfahrt)* departure; *(Min: aus Schacht)* ascent *(aus* from); **der Zug hat keine ~** the train has not been cleared for departure **b** *(= Spazierfahrt)* drive, ride; **eine ~ machen** to go for a ride or *(im Auto auch)* drive **c** *(= Ausgang, Autobahnausfahrt)* exit; **~ Gütersloh** Gütersloh exit, exit for Gütersloh; **„Ausfahrt frei halten"** "keep clear"

Aus|fahrt(s)-: **Aus|fahrt(s)|schild** NT *pl* **-schilder** exit sign; **Aus|fahrt(s)|sig|nal** NT *(Rail)* departure signal; **Aus|fahrt(s)|stra|ße** F exit road

Aus|fall M **a** *(= Verlust, Fehlbetrag, Mil)* loss; *(= das Versagen) (Tech, Med)* failure; *(von Motor)* breakdown; *(= Produktionsstörung)* stoppage; **bei ~ des Stroms ...** in case of a power failure ...
b *no pl (= das Herausfallen)* loss
c *no pl (von Sitzung, Unterricht etc)* cancellation; **wir hatten einen hohen ~ an** or **von Schulstunden** a lot of school lessons were cancelled *(Brit)* or canceled *(US)*
d *no pl (= das Ausscheiden)* dropping out; *(im Rennen)* retirement; *(= Abwesenheit)* absence
e *(Ling)* dropping, omission
f *(Mil: = Ausbruch)* sortie, sally
g *(Sport) (Fechten)* thrust, lunge; *(Gewichtheben)* jerk
h *(fig: = Angriff)* attack

Aus|fall|bürg|schaft F *(Fin: = Haftungssumme)* security

aus+fal|len VI *sep irreg aux sein* **a** *(= herausfallen)* to fall out; *(Chem)* to be precipitated; *(Ling)* to be dropped or omitted; **mir fallen die Haare aus** my hair is falling out
b *(= nicht stattfinden)* to be cancelled *(Brit)* or canceled *(US)*; **etw ~ lassen** to cancel sth; **die Schule/die erste Stunde fällt morgen aus** there's no school/first lesson tomorrow
c *(= nicht funktionieren)* to fail; *(Motor)* to break down; *(Computer, System)* to go down
d *(= wegfallen: Verdienst)* to be lost
e *(= ausscheiden)* to drop out; *(= fernbleiben)* to

be absent
f gut/schlecht *etc* ~ to turn out well/badly *etc*; **die Rede ist zu lang ausgefallen** the speech was too long, the speech turned out to be too long; **die Bluse fällt zu eng aus** the blouse is too tight
g *(Mil)* to fall, to be lost (*bei* in); (*old*: = *einen Ausfall machen*) to make a sortie
h *(Fechten)* to thrust, to lunge
i → **ausgefallen**

aus+fäl|len VT *sep (Chem)* to precipitate

aus|fal|lend, aus|fäl|lig ADJ abusive; ~ **werden** to become abusive ADV abusively

Aus|fall|stra|ße F arterial road

Aus|fall(s)|win|kel M *(Phys)* angle of reflection

Aus|fall|zeit F *(Insur) time which counts toward(s) pension although no payments were made*

aus+fa|sern VI *sep aux sein or haben* to fray

aus+fech|ten VT *sep irreg (fig)* to fight (out)

aus+fe|gen VT *sep Schmutz* to sweep up; *Zimmer* to sweep out

aus+fei|len VT *sep* to file (out); *(= glätten)* to file down; *(fig)* to polish → *auch* **ausgefeilt**

aus+fer|ti|gen VT *sep (form)* **a** *Dokument* to draw up; *Rechnung, Lieferschein* to make out; *Pass* to issue **b** *(= unterzeichnen)* to sign

Aus|fer|ti|gung F *(form)* **a** *no pl (von Dokument)* drawing up; *(von Rechnung, Lieferschein)* making out; *(von Pass)* issuing **b** *(= Abschrift)* copy; **die erste** ~ the top copy; **ein Dokument in einfacher** ~ one copy *or* a single copy of a document; **in doppelter/dreifacher** ~ in duplicate/triplicate; **Zeugnisse in vierfacher** *etc* ~ four *etc* copies of references

Aus|fer|ti|gungs|da|tum NT *(von Pass, Urkunde)* date of issue

aus|fin|dig ADJ ~ **machen** to find, to discover; *(= Aufenthaltsort feststellen)* to locate, to trace

aus+fi|schen VT *sep Karpfen etc* to catch; *Teich* to fish dry *or* out

aus+flag|gen VT *sep* **a** *Schiff (= schmücken)* to dress; *(= unter Billigflagge fahren lassen)* to allow to sail under a flag of convenience **b** *Weg, Piste* to mark out (with flags)

aus+flen|nen VR *sep (inf)* = **ausheulen VR**

aus+flie|gen *sep irreg* VI *aux sein (= wegfliegen)* to fly away *or* off; *(aus Gebiet etc)* to fly out (*aus* of); *(= flügge werden)* to leave the nest; *(fig inf: = weggehen)* to go out; **ausgeflogen sein** *(fig inf)* to be out, to have gone out; **der Vogel ist ausgeflogen** *(fig inf)* the bird has *or* is flown VT *(Aviat)* **a** *Verwundete etc* to evacuate (by air), to fly out (*aus* from) **b** *Flugzeug* to fly full out

aus+flie|sen VT *sep* to tile

aus+flie|ßen VI *sep irreg aux sein (= herausfließen)* to flow out (*aus* of); *(Eiter etc)* to be discharged; *(= auslaufen: Öl etc, Fass)* to leak (*aus* out of)

aus+flip|pen ['ausflɪpn] VI *sep aux sein (inf)* to freak out *(inf)* → *auch* **ausgeflippt**

aus+flo|cken ['ausflɔkn] VTI *sep (vi: aux sein) (Chem)* to precipitate

Aus|flucht ['ausflʊxt] F -, **Ausflüchte** [-flʏçtə] excuse; *(geh: = Flucht)* escape (*in +acc* into); **Ausflüchte machen** to make excuses; **keine Ausflüchte!** (I want) no excuses!

Aus|flug M **a** trip, outing; *(esp mit Reisebüro)* excursion; *(= Betriebsausflug, Schulausflug)* outing; *(= Wanderung)* walk, hike; *(fig)* excursion; **einen ~ machen** to go on *or* for a trip *etc*; **einen ~ in die Politik machen** to make an excursion into politics **b** *(von Vögeln etc)* flight; *(von Bienen)* swarming **c** *(am Bienenstock)* hive exit

Aus|flüg|ler ['ausfly:glɐ] M **-s, -, Aus|flüg|le|rin** [-ərɪn] F **-, -nen** tripper; **Fahrkarte für** ~ excursion ticket

Aus|flug|schnei|se F *(Aviat)* takeoff path

Aus|flugs-: **Aus|flugs|damp|fer** M pleasure steamer; **Aus|flugs|fahrt** F pleasure trip, excursion; **Aus|flugs|lo|kal** NT tourist café; *(am Meer)* seaside café; **Aus|flugs|ort** M *pl* **-orte** place to go for an outing; **Aus|flugs|ver|kehr** M *(an Feiertagen)* holiday *(esp Brit) or* vacation *(US)* traffic; *(am Wochenende)* weekend holiday *(esp Brit) or* vacation *(US)* traffic; **Aus|flugs|ziel** NT destination *(of one's outing)*

Aus|fluss M **a** *(= das Herausfließen)* outflow; *(= das Auslaufen)* leaking **b** *(= Ausflussstelle)* outlet **c** *(Med)* discharge **d** *(fig geh)* product, result

aus+fol|gen VT *sep (Aus form)* to hand over *(jdm* to sb)

aus+for|men *sep* VT to mould *(Brit)*, to mold *(US)*, to shape *(zu* into); *Manuskript etc* to polish, to refine VR to take shape, to be formed

aus+for|mu|lie|ren *ptp* **ausformuliert** VT *sep* to formulate; *Rede* to tidy up

Aus|for|mung F **a** *(= das Formen)* moulding *(Brit)*, molding *(US)*, shaping; *(von Manuskript etc)* polishing, refining **b** *(= Form)* shape, form

aus+for|schen VT *sep* **a** *Sache* to find out; *(= erforschen)* to investigate **b** *(Aus) Täter* to apprehend

Aus|for|schung F **a** *(= Erforschung)* investigating **b** *(= Befragung)* questioning **c** *(Aus: von Täter)* apprehension

aus+fra|gen VT *sep* to question, to quiz *(inf)* *(nach* about); *(strenger)* to interrogate; **so fragt man die Leute aus** *(inf)* that would be telling *(inf)*

aus+fran|sen *sep* VIR *(vi: aux sein)* to fray, to become frayed VT to fray

aus+frat|scheln ['ausfra:tʃln] VT *sep (Aus inf)* to quiz *(inf)*

aus+fres|sen VT *sep irreg* **a** *(= auffressen)* to eat up **b** *(= ausspülen: Wasser, Fluss)* to erode, to eat away **c** *(inf: = anstellen)* **etwas** ~ to do something wrong; **was hat er denn wieder ausgefressen?** what's he (gone and) done now? *(inf)*

Aus|fuhr ['ausfu:ɐ] F **-, -en** **a** *no pl (= das Ausführen)* export; *(= Ausfuhrhandel)* exports *pl* **b** **Ausfuhren** PL *(= Ausfuhrgüter)* exports *pl*

Aus|fuhr- *in cpds* → *auch* **Export-** export; **Aus|fuhr|ar|ti|kel** M export

aus|führ|bar ADJ **a** *Plan* feasible, practicable, workable; *(Comput) Programm* executable; **schwer** ~ difficult to carry out **b** *(Comm)* exportable

Aus|führ|bar|keit ['ausfy:ɐba:ɐkait] F -, *no pl* feasibility, practicability

Aus|fuhr-: **Aus|fuhr|be|schrän|kung** F export restriction; **Aus|fuhr|be|stim|mun|gen** PL export regulations *pl*; **Aus|fuhr|be|wil|li|gung** F export licence *(Brit) or* license *(US) or* permit

aus+füh|ren VT *sep* **a** *(zu Spaziergang, ins Theater etc)* to take out; *Hund* to take for a walk; *(hum) Kleid* to parade **b** *(= durchführen) Anweisung* to carry out; *Aufgabe* to perform, to carry out; *Auftrag, Plan, Befehl, Bewegung* to execute, to carry out; *Operation (Mil)* to execute, to carry out; *(Med)* to perform, to carry out; *Gesetz* to implement; *Bauarbeiten* to undertake; *(Sport) Freistoß etc* to take; *(Comput) Programm* to execute **c** *(= gestalten) Plan, Entwurf, Bild etc* to execute **d** *(= erklären)* to explain; *(= darlegen)* to set out; *(argumentierend)* to argue; *(= sagen)* to say **e** *(Comm) Waren* to export

aus|füh|rend ADJ *Künstler* performing; *Organe* executive; **die ~e Baufirma** the firm carrying out the building work; **die ~e Gewalt** *(Pol)* the executive

Aus|füh|ren|de(r) ['ausfy:rəndə] MF *decl as adj* **a** *(= Künstler)* performer **b** *(= Handelnder)* executive

Aus|fuhr-: **Aus|fuhr|ge|neh|mi|gung** F export licence *(Brit) or* license *(US) or* permit; **Aus|fuhr|gü|ter** PL export goods *pl*, exports *pl*; **Aus|fuhr|ha|fen** M port of exportation; **Aus|fuhr|han|del** M export trade; **Aus|fuhr|land** NT **a** *(= Land, das ausführt)* exporting country; **ein ~ für Jute** a jute-exporting country **b** *(= Land, in das ausgeführt wird)* export market

aus|führ|lich ['ausfy:ɐlɪç, *(Aus)* aus'fy:ɐlɪç] ADJ detailed; *Informationen, Gespräche, Katalog auch* full ADV in detail, in full; **sehr** ~ in great detail; **~er** in more *or* greater detail

Aus|führ|lich|keit F -, *no pl* detail; **in aller** ~ in (great) detail

Aus|fuhr-: **Aus|fuhr|lis|te** F export list; **Aus|fuhr|prä|mie** F export premium; **Aus|fuhr|quo|te** F export quota; **Aus|fuhr|sper|re** F export ban *or* embargo; **Aus|fuhr|über|schuss** M export surplus

Aus|füh|rung F **a** *no pl (= Durchführung)* carrying out; *(von Operation, Aufgabe)* performance, carrying out; *(von Auftrag, Plan, Befehl, Bewegung)* execution, carrying out; *(von Gesetz)* implementation; *(von Freistoß)* taking; **zur ~ gelangen** *or* **kommen** to be carried out **b** *(= Gestaltung: von Plan, Entwurf, Bild)* execution **c** *(= Erklärung)* explanation; *(von Thema etc)* exposition; *(= Bemerkung)* remark; *(usu pl: = Bericht)* report **d** *(von Waren)* design; *(Tech: = äußere Ausführung)* finish; *(= Qualität)* quality; *(= Modell)* model

Aus|fuhr-: **Aus|fuhr|ver|bot** NT ban on exports, export embargo; **Aus|fuhr|vo|lu|men** NT volume of exports; **Aus|fuhr|wa|ren** PL exports *pl*, export goods *pl*; **Aus|fuhr|zoll** M export duty

aus+fül|len VT *sep* to fill; *Loch* to fill (up *or* out); *Ritze* to fill in; *Platz* to take up; *Formular* to fill in *(Brit) or* out; *Posten* to fill; **jdn (voll** *or* **ganz)** ~ *(= befriedigen)* to give sb (complete) fulfilment *(Brit) or* fulfillment *(US)*, to satisfy sb (completely); *(= Zeit in Anspruch nehmen)* to take (all) sb's time; **er füllt den Posten nicht/gut aus** he is not fitted/well-fitted for the position; **der Gedanke an dich füllt mich ganz aus** the thought of you occupies my every minute; **seine Zeit mit etw** ~ to pass one's time doing sth, to fill up one's time with sth; **ein ausgefülltes Leben** a full life

aus+füt|tern VT *sep (Sew)* to line

Aus|ga|be F **a** *no pl (= Austeilung) (von Proviant, Decken etc)* distribution, giving out; *(von Befehl, Fahrkarten, Dokumenten etc)* issuing; *(von Essen)* serving **b** *(= Schalter)* issuing counter; *(in Bibliothek)* issue desk; *(in Kantine)* serving counter; *(= Stelle, Büro)* issuing office **c** *(von Buch, Zeitung, Sendung)* edition; *(von Zeitschrift)* edition, issue; *(von Aktien)* issue **d** *(= Ausführung)* version **e** *(= Geldaufwand)* expense, expenditure *no pl* **f** **Ausgaben** PL *(= Geldverbrauch)* expenditure *sing* (*für* on); *(= Kosten)* expenses *pl*, costs *pl* **g** *(Comput) (= Ausdruck)* print-out; *(am Bildschirm)* output

Aus|ga|be-: **Aus|ga|be|da|tei** F *(Comput)* output file; **Aus|ga|be|da|ten** PL *(Comput)* output data; **Aus|ga|be|ge|rät** NT *(Comput)* output device; **Aus|ga|be|kurs** M *(Fin)* rate of issue

Aus|ga|ben-: **Aus|ga|ben|be|gren|zung** F limit on expenditure; **Aus|ga|ben|be|leg** M receipt for expenditure; **Aus|ga|ben|buch** NT cash-book; **Aus|ga|ben|kür|zung** F expenditure cut, cut in expenditure; **Aus|ga|ben|po|li|tik** F expenditure policy; **Aus|ga|ben|sei|te** F expenditure column

Aus|ga|be|schal|ter M issuing counter; *(in Bibliothek etc)* issue desk

Aus|ga|be|ter|min M date of issue

Aus|gang M *pl* **-gänge** **a** *(= Auslass, Weg nach draußen)* exit, way out (*+gen, von* from); *(= Dorfausgang)* end; *(von Wald)* edge; *(Med, von Organ)* opening (*+gen* out of); *(Aviat)* gate
b *(= Erlaubnis zum Ausgehen)* permission to go out; *(Mil)* pass; ~ **haben** to have the day off *or (am Abend)* the evening off; *(Mil)* to have a pass; **bis 10 Uhr ~ haben** to be allowed out/to have a pass till 10 o'clock
c *(= Spaziergang)* walk *(under supervision)*
d *no pl (= Ende)* end; *(esp von Epoche)* close; *(von Roman, Film)* ending, end; *(= Ergebnis)* outcome, result; **ein Unfall mit tödlichem** ~ a fatal accident; **ein Ausflug mit tragischem** ~ an ex-

cursion with a tragic outcome
e no pl (= Ausgangspunkt) starting point; (von Reise auch) point of departure; (= Anfang) beginning; **von hier nahm diese weltweite Bewegung ihren ~** this was where this worldwide movement started
f no pl (= Abschicken von Post) mailing, sending off
g **Ausgänge** PL (Post) outgoing mail sing; (Waren) outgoing goods pl

aus|gangs ['ausgaŋs] PREP +gen at the end of; (der Schlusskurve etc) coming out of; **eine Frau ~ der Siebziger** a woman in her late seventies ADV **~ (von) Hamburg** on the outskirts of Hamburg, just outside Hamburg

Aus|gangs-: **Aus|gangs|ba|sis** F starting point, basis; **Aus|gangs|fra|ge** F initial question; **Aus|gangs|la|ge** F initial or starting position; **Aus|gangs|ma|te|ri|al** NT source material; **Aus|gangs|po|si|ti|on** F initial or starting position; **Aus|gangs|punkt** M starting point; (von Reise auch) point of departure; **Aus|gangs|si|tu|a|ti|on** F starting or initial situation, point of departure; **Aus|gangs|sper|re** F ban on going out; (esp bei Belagerungszustand) curfew; (für Soldaten) confinement to barracks; **~ haben** (Soldat) to be confined to barracks; (Schüler) to be banned from going out, to be gated (Brit); **Aus|gangs|spra|che** F source language; **Aus|gangs|stel|lung** F (Sport) starting position; (Mil) initial position; **Aus|gangs|text** M (einer Übersetzung) source text; **Aus|gangs|tür** F exit (door); **Aus|gangs|ver|bot** NT = **Ausgangssperre**; **Aus|gangs|zei|le** F (Typ) club line, widow; **Aus|gangs|zu|stand** M initial or original condition; (= Lage) initial or original position; (esp Pol) status quo

aus+ge|ben sep irreg VT **a** (= austeilen) Proviant, Decken etc to distribute, to give out; (= aushändigen) Dokumente, Fahrkarten, Aktien etc to issue; Befehl to issue, to give; Essen to serve; (Cards) to deal; (= ausdrucken) Text to print out
b Geld to spend (für on); **eine Runde ~** to stand a round (inf); **ich gebe heute Abend einen aus** (inf) it's my treat this evening; **unser Chef hat einen ausgegeben** our boss treated us; **darf ich dir einen/einen Whisky ~?** may I buy you a drink/a whisky?; **er gibt nicht gern einen aus** he doesn't like buying people drinks
c **jdn/etw als** or **für jdn/etw ~** to pass sb/sth off as sb/sth; **sich als jd/etw ~** to pose as sb/sth, to pass oneself off as sb/sth
VR to exhaust oneself; (= sein Geld ganz ausgeben) to spend all one's money

Aus|ge|beu|te|te(r) ['ausgəbɔytətə] MF decl as adj **die ~n** the exploited pl

aus|ge|brannt ADJ (fig) burned-out (inf); **geistig ~** mentally exhausted; **er ist ~** he's burned out (inf) → auch **ausbrennen**

aus|ge|bucht ['ausgəbu:xt] ADJ Reise etc booked up; (inf) Person booked up

Aus|ge|burt F (pej) (der Fantasie etc) monstrous product or invention; (= Geschöpf, Kreatur, Institution) monster; **eine ~ der Hölle** a fiend from hell, a fiendish monster; **sie ist eine ~ von Eitelkeit und Dummheit** she is a monstrous combination of vanity and stupidity

aus|ge|dehnt ['ausgəde:nt] ADJ Gummiband (over)stretched; (= breit, groß, fig: = weitreichend) extensive; (zeitlich) lengthy, extended; Spaziergang long, extended → auch **ausdehnen**

aus|ge|dient ADJ (inf: = unbrauchbar) Auto, Maschine clapped-out (Brit inf), worn-out (inf); **meine ~en Sachen/Bücher** etc the things/books etc I don't have any further use for → auch **ausdienen**

aus|ge|dörrt ['ausgədœrt] ADJ dried up; Boden, Kehle parched; Pflanzen shrivelled (Brit), shriveled (US); Land, Gebiet arid; (fig) Hirn ossified, dull; **mein Hirn ist völlig ~** (fig) I can't think straight any more → auch **ausdörren**

aus|ge|fal|len ['ausgəfalən] ADJ **a** Unterrichtsstunde etc cancelled (Brit), canceled (US) **b** (= ungewöhnlich) unusual; (= übertrieben) extravagant; Mensch eccentric; (= überspannt) odd, weird → auch **ausfallen**

Aus|ge|fal|len|heit F -, -en **a** (= Ungewöhnlichkeit) unusualness **b** (= Übertriebenheit) extravagance; (von Mensch) eccentricity; (= Überspanntheit) oddness, weirdness

aus|ge|feilt ['ausgəfailt] ADJ (fig) polished; Schrift stylized → auch **ausfeilen**

Aus|ge|feilt|heit F -, no pl (von Stil) polished nature, polish

aus|ge|flippt ['ausgəflɪpt] ADJ (inf) freaky (inf), freaked-out (inf), flipped-out (inf); (aus der Gesellschaft) dropout (inf); **er ist ein richtig ~er Typ** he's really freaky (inf), he's a real dropout (inf) → auch **ausflippen**

Aus|ge|flipp|te(r) ['ausgəflɪptə] MF decl as adj (inf) freak (inf); (aus der Gesellschaft) dropout (inf)

aus|ge|fuchst ['ausgəfʊkst] ADJ (inf) clever; (= listig) crafty (inf); Kartenspieler cunning

aus|ge|gli|chen ['ausgəglɪçn] ADJ balanced; Spiel, Klima even; Torverhältnis equal; (= gleichbleibend) consistent → auch **ausgleichen**

Aus|ge|gli|chen|heit F -, no pl balance; (von Spiel, Klima) evenness; **ihre ~** her even nature

aus|ge|go|ren ['ausgəgo:rən] ADJ Most fully fermented; (fig inf) Pläne worked out; **wenig ~** half-baked (inf)

aus+ge|hen sep irreg aux sein VI **a** (= weggehen, zum Vergnügen) to go out; (= spazieren gehen) to go out (for a walk); **er geht selten aus** he doesn't go out much; **wir gehen heute Abend ganz groß aus** we're going out for a big celebration tonight
b (= ausfallen: Haare, Federn, Zähne) to fall out; (Farbe) to run; (dial: Stoff) to fade; **ihm gehen die Haare aus** his hair is falling out; **ihm gehen die Zähne aus** he is losing his teeth
c (= seinen Ausgang nehmen) to start (von at); (= herrühren: Idee, Anregung etc) to come (von from); **von dem Platz gehen vier Straßen aus** four streets lead or go off (from) the square; **etw geht von jdm/etw aus** (= wird ausgestrahlt) sb/sth radiates sth; **von der Rede des Ministers ging eine große Wirkung aus** the minister's speech had a great effect
d (= abgeschickt werden: Post) to be sent off; **die ~de Post** the outgoing mail
e (= zugrunde legen) to start out (von from); **gehen wir einmal davon aus, dass ...** let us assume that ..., let us start from the assumption that ...; **wovon gehst du bei dieser Behauptung aus?** on what are you basing your statement?; **davon kann man nicht ~** you can't go by that
f **auf etw** (acc) **~** to be intent on sth; **auf Gewinn ~** to be intent on making a profit; **auf Eroberungen ~** (hum inf) to be out to make a few conquests
g (= einen bestimmten Ausgang haben: esp Sport) to end; (= ausfallen) to turn out; **gut/schlecht ~** to turn out well/badly; (Film etc) to end happily/unhappily; (Abend, Spiel) to end well/badly
h (Ling: = enden) to end
i **straffrei** or **straflos ~** to receive no punishment, to get off scot-free (inf); **leer ~** (inf) to come away empty-handed
j (= zu Ende sein: Vorräte etc) to run out; (dial: Vorstellung, Schule etc) to finish; **mir ging die Geduld aus** I lost (my) patience; **mir ging das Geld aus** I ran out of money; **ihm ist die Luft** or **die Puste** or **der Atem ausgegangen** (inf) (lit) he ran out of breath or puff (Brit inf); (fig) he ran out of steam (inf); (finanziell) he ran out of funds
k (= aufhören zu brennen) to go out
l (inf: = sich ausziehen lassen) to come off; **die nassen Sachen gehen so schwer aus** these wet things are so hard to take off
VR (Aus) **es geht sich aus** it works out all right; (Vorräte, Geld etc) there is enough

aus|ge|hend ADJ attr **im ~en Mittelalter** toward(s) the end of the Middle Ages; **das ~e 20. Jahrhundert** the end or close of the 20th century

Aus|geh|er|laub|nis F permission to go out; (Mil) pass

aus|ge|hun|gert ['ausgəhʊŋɐt] ADJ starved; (= abgezehrt) Mensch etc emaciated; **wie ~e Wölfe** like starving wolves; **nach etw ~ sein** (fig) to be starved of sth → auch **aushungern**

Aus|geh-: **Aus|geh|uni|form** F walking-out uniform; **Aus|geh|ver|bot** NT **jdm ~ erteilen** to forbid sb to go out; (Mil) to confine sb to barracks; **~ haben/bekommen** to be forbidden to go out; (Mil) to be confined to barracks

aus|ge|klü|gelt ['ausgəkly:glt] ADJ (inf) System cleverly thought-out; (= genial) ingenious → auch **ausklügeln**

aus|ge|kocht ['ausgəkɔxt] ADJ (pej inf) (= durchtrieben) cunning; **er ist ein ~er Bursche** he's a thoroughly bad character → auch **auskochen**

aus|ge|las|sen ['ausgəlasn] ADJ (= heiter) lively; Stimmung happy; (= wild) Kinder boisterous; Stimmung, Party mad ADV wildly, boisterously; **dort geht es ~ zu** things are wild there → auch **auslassen**

Aus|ge|las|sen|heit F (= Heiterkeit) liveliness; (= Wildheit: von Kindern) boisterousness

aus|ge|las|tet ['ausgəlastət] ADJ Mensch fully occupied; Maschine, Anlage working to capacity; **mit dem Job ist er nicht (voll) ~** he is not fully stretched in that job (esp Brit), he is not working at his full capacity in that job; **mit den vier Kindern ist sie voll ~** her four children keep her fully occupied, she has her hands full with her four children; **unsere Kapazitäten sind voll ~** we're working at full capacity → auch **auslasten**

aus|ge|latscht ['ausgəla:tʃt] ADJ (inf) Schuhe worn; **meine Schuhe sind völlig ~** my shoes have gone completely out of shape

aus|ge|lei|ert ['ausgəlaiɐt] ADJ Gummiband, Gewinde, Feder worn; Hosen, Pullover baggy; Redensart hackneyed (Brit), trite → auch **ausleiern**

aus|ge|lernt ['ausgəlɛrnt] ADJ (inf) qualified → auch **auslernen**

aus|ge|le|sen ['ausgəle:zn] ADJ (fig geh) Ware select, choice → auch **auslesen**

Aus|ge|lie|fert|sein ['ausgəli:fɐtzain] NT subjection (an +acc to); **unser ~ an die Gesellschaft** the fact that we are at the mercy of society

aus|ge|lutscht ['ausgəlʊtʃt] ADJ (lit, fig inf: = alt, verbraucht) Kaugummi, Floskel stale; Technik, Witz old hat pred (inf); Thema etc done to death (inf) → auch **auslutschen**

aus|ge|macht ADJ **a** (= abgemacht) agreed; **es ist eine ~e Sache, dass ...** it is agreed that ... **b** attr (inf: = vollkommen) complete, utter → auch **ausmachen**

aus|ge|mer|gelt ['ausgəmɛrglt] ADJ Körper, Gesicht, Tier emaciated → auch **ausmergeln**

aus|ge|nom|men ['ausgənɔmən] CONJ except, apart from; **niemand/alle, ~ du** or **dich ~** no-one/everyone except (for) you or apart from yourself or save yourself; **täglich ~ sonntags** daily except for or excluding Sundays; **~ wenn/dass ...** except when/that ... → auch **ausnehmen**

aus|ge|picht ['ausgəpɪçt] ADJ (inf) (= raffiniert) Mensch, Plan cunning; (= verfeinert) Geschmack refined

aus|ge|pow|ert ['ausgəpauɐt] ADJ (inf) Mensch washed-out (inf), done in (inf)

aus|ge|prägt ['ausgəprɛ:kt] ADJ Gesicht distinctive; Eigenschaft, Charakter auch distinct; Interesse marked, pronounced; **ein (stark) ~er Sinn für alles Schöne** a well-developed sense for everything beautiful → auch **ausprägen**

Aus|ge|prägt|heit F -, no pl distinctiveness

aus|ge|pumpt ['ausgəpʊmpt] ADJ (inf) whacked (Brit inf), worn-out (inf) → auch **auspumpen**

aus|ge|rech|net ['ausgərɛçnət] ADV **~ du/er** etc you/he etc of all people; **~ mir muss das passie-**

ren why does it have to happen to me (of all people)?; ~ **heute/gestern** today/yesterday of all days; **muss das ~ heute sein?** does it have to be today (of all days)?; ~ **jetzt kommt er** he would have to come just now; ~ **dann kam er** he would have to come just at that moment; **~, als wir spazieren gehen wollten, …** just when we wanted to go for a walk … → *auch* **ausrechnen**

aus|ge|schamt [ˈausɡəʃaːmt] ADJ *(dial)* = **unverschämt**

aus|ge|schlos|sen ADJ *pred (= unmöglich)* impossible; *(= nicht infrage kommend)* out of the question; **es ist nicht ~, dass …** it's just possible that …; **diese Möglichkeit ist nicht ~** it's not impossible; **jeder Irrtum ist ~** there is no possibility of a mistake → *auch* **ausschließen**

aus|ge|schnit|ten [ˈausɡəʃnɪtn] ADJ *Bluse, Kleid* low-cut; **sie geht heute tief ~** *(inf)* she's wearing a very low-cut dress/blouse *etc* today; **ein weit** *or* **tief ~es Kleid** a dress with a plunging neckline → *auch* **ausschneiden**

aus|ge|spielt [ˈausɡəʃpiːlt] ADJ **~ haben** to be finished; **er hat bei mir ~** *(inf)* he's had it as far as I am concerned *(inf)*, I'm finished *or* through with him → *auch* **ausspielen**

aus|ge|spro|chen [ˈausɡəʃprɔxn] ADJ *(= besonders) Schönheit, Qualität, Vorliebe* definite; *(= ausgeprägt) Trinkernase etc* pronounced; *Begabung* particular; *Ähnlichkeit* marked; *Geiz, Großzügigkeit* extreme; *(= groß) Pech, Freundlichkeit, Hilfsbereitschaft etc* real; **eine ~e Frohnatur** a very sunny person; **ein ~er Chauvi** *(inf)* an out-and-out male chauvinist; **~es Pech haben** to have really bad luck, to be really unlucky ADV really; *schön, begabt, groß, hilfsbereit etc auch* extremely; *geizig, frech etc auch* terribly → *auch* **aussprechen**

aus|ge|spro|che|ner|ma|ßen [ˈausɡəʃprɔxnəˈmaːsn] ADV = **ausgesprochen ADV**

aus+ge|stal|ten *ptp* **ausgestaltet** VT *sep (künstlerisch, musikalisch)* to arrange; *(= planend gestalten)* to organize; *(= dekorieren, einrichten)* to decorate; *(= ausbauen) Theorie, Begriff, Methode* to build up; **Bücher künstlerisch ~** to do the art work for books

Aus|ge|stal|tung F **a** *(künstlerisch, musikalisch)* arranging; *(= Planung)* organizing; *(= Einrichtung, Dekoration)* decorating; *(von Theorie, Begriff, Methode)* building up **b** *(= Gestalt, Form)* form

aus|ge|stellt ADJ *Rock etc* flared → *auch* **ausstellen**

aus|ge|stor|ben [ˈausɡəʃtɔrbn] ADJ *Tierart* extinct; *(fig)* deserted; **der Park war wie ~** the park was deserted → *auch* **aussterben**

Aus|ge|sto|ße|ne(r) [ˈausɡəʃtoːsnə] MF *decl as adj* outcast

aus|ge|sucht ADJ **a** *(= besonders groß)* extreme, exceptional **b** *(= erlesen) Wein, Aktien* choice, select; *Gesellschaft* select; *Worte* well-chosen ADV *(= überaus, sehr)* extremely, exceptionally → *auch* **aussuchen**

aus|ge|tre|ten [ˈausɡətreːtn] ADJ *Schuhe* well-worn; *Pfad* well-trodden; *Stufe* worn down; **~e Wege gehen** *(fig)* to tread a beaten track → *auch* **austreten**

aus|ge|wach|sen ADJ fully grown; *(inf) Blödsinn* utter, complete; *Skandal* huge → *auch* **auswachsen**

aus|ge|wählt ADJ select; *Satz etc* well-chosen; *Werke* selected → *auch* **auswählen**

Aus|ge|wan|der|te(r) [ˈausɡəvandətə] MF *decl as adj* emigrant

aus|ge|wie|sen [ˈausɡəviːzn] ADJ **a** *(= namhaft)* well-known, renowned **b** *(Sw: = nachgewiesen)* identified; *Fachmann* qualified → *auch* **ausweisen**

Aus|ge|wie|se|ne(r) [ˈausɡəviːznə] MF *decl as adj* expellee

aus|ge|wo|gen ADJ balanced; *Maß* equal; **ein ~es Kräfteverhältnis** a balance of powers → *auch* **auswiegen**

Aus|ge|wo|gen|heit F balance

aus|ge|zeich|net ADJ excellent ADV excellently; **sie kann ~ schwimmen/tanzen** she is an excellent swimmer/dancer; **es geht mir ~** I'm feeling marvellous *(Brit) or* marvelous *(US)* → *auch* **auszeichnen**

aus|gie|big [ˈausɡiːbɪç] ADJ *Mahlzeit etc* substantial, large; *Mittagsschlaf, Gespräch* (good) long; *Gebrauch* extensive; **~en Gebrauch von etw machen** to make full *or* good use of sth ADV **~ frühstücken** to have a substantial breakfast; **~ schlafen/schwimmen** to have a (good) long sleep/swim; **~ einkaufen** to buy a lot of things; **etw ~ gebrauchen** to use sth extensively

Aus|gie|big|keit F -, *no pl* **in aller ~ frühstücken** to have a substantial breakfast; **in aller ~ schlafen/baden** to have a (good) long sleep/bath; **in aller ~ die Zeitung lesen** to take one's time reading the newspaper

aus+gie|ßen VT *sep irreg* **a** *(aus einem Behälter)* to pour out; *(= weggießen)* to pour away; *Behälter* to empty; *(= verschütten)* to spill; *(= über jdn/etw gießen)* to pour *(über +acc* over); **seinen Spott über jdn ~** *(geh)* to pour scorn on sb *(esp Brit)*; **seinen Hohn über jdn ~** *(geh)* to mock sb **b** *(= füllen) Gussform* to fill; *Ritzen, Fugen* to fill in

Aus|gleich [ˈausɡlaiç] M **-(e)s,** *(rare)* **-e a** *(= Gleichgewicht)* balance; *(von Konto)* balancing; *(von Schulden)* settling; *(von Verlust, Fehler, Mangel)* compensation; *(von Abweichung, Unterschieden)* balancing out; *(von Meinungsverschiedenheiten, Konflikten)* evening out; **zum** *or* **als ~ für etw** in order to compensate for sth; **er treibt zum ~ Sport** he does sport for exercise; **Tennisspielen ist für mich ein guter ~** I like playing tennis, it gives me a change; **wenn er ins Ausland geht, bekommt sie zum ~ ein Auto** when he goes abroad, she gets a car to even things out; **dieses Jahr fährt er zum ~ ans Meer** this year he's going to the seaside for a change; **zum ~ Ihres Kontos** to balance your account

b *no pl (Ballspiele)* equalizer *(Brit)*, tie; *(Tennis)* deuce

aus+glei|chen *sep irreg* VT *Ungleichheit, Unterschiede* to even out; *Unebenheit* to level out; *Konto* to balance; *Schulden* to settle; *Verlust, Fehler* to make good; *Mangel* to compensate for; *Meinungsverschiedenheiten, Konflikte* to reconcile; **etw durch etw ~** to compensate for sth with sth/by doing sth; **~de Gerechtigkeit** poetic justice → *auch* **ausgeglichen**

VI **a** *(Sport)* to equalize; **zum 1:1 ~** to equalize the score at 1 all *(Brit)*, to even up the score to 1 all *(US)*

b *(= vermitteln)* to act as a mediator; **~des Wesen** conciliatory manner

VR to balance out; *(Einnahmen und Ausgaben)* to balance; **das gleicht sich wieder aus** it balances itself out; **das gleicht sich dadurch aus, dass …** it's balanced out by the fact that …

Aus|gleichs-: Aus|gleichs|ab|ga|be F *(Jur)* countervailing duty *or* charge; **Aus|gleichs|fonds** [-fõː] M *(Econ)* equalization fund; **Aus|gleichs|for|de|rung** F equalization claim; **Aus|gleichs|ge|trie|be** NT *(Tech)* differential gear; **Aus|gleichs|gym|nas|tik** F exercises *pl*; **Aus|gleichs|leis|tung** F *(Jur)* compensatory payment; **Aus|gleichs|sport** M keep-fit activity; **als ~** to keep fit; **Aus|gleichs|tor** NT, **Aus|gleichs|tref|fer** M equalizer *(Brit)*, equalizing *(Brit) or* tying *(US)* goal; **Aus|gleichs|zah|lung** F compensation

aus+glei|ten VI *sep irreg aux sein* **a** *(= ausrutschen)* to slip *(auf +dat* on); **es ist ihm ausgeglitten** it slipped from his hands *or* grasp **b** *(Boot, Skifahrer)* to coast in

aus+glie|dern VT *sep* to exclude

Aus|glie|de|rung F exclusion; *(Econ: einer Firma)* spin-off, hiving off *(Brit)*

aus+glit|schen VI *sep aux sein (= ausrutschen)* to slip *(auf +dat* on)

aus+glü|hen VT *sep (Tech) Metall* to anneal; *(Med)* to sterilize *(by heating)*

aus+gra|ben VT *sep irreg* to dig up; *Grube, Loch* to dig out; *Altertümer* to excavate; *(fig)* to dig up; *(= hervorholen)* to dig out; *alte Geschichten* to bring up

Aus|gra|bung F *(= das Ausgraben)* excavation; *(Ort)* excavation site; *(= Fund)* (archaeological *(Brit) or* archeological *(US))* find

Aus|gra|bungs-

Aus|gra|bungs|fund M archaeological *(Brit) or* archeological *(US)* find

Aus|gra|bungs|ort M, **Aus|gra|bungs|stät|te** F excavation site, (archaeological *(Brit) or* archeological *(US))* dig

aus+grä|ten [ˈausɡrɛːtn] VT *sep Fisch* to fillet, to bone

aus+grei|fen VI *sep irreg (Pferd)* to lengthen its stride; *(beim Gehen)* to stride out; *(fig: Redner)* to go far afield; **weit ~d** *(Schritte)* long, lengthy; *Bewegung* striding

aus+gren|zen VT *sep* to exclude

Aus|gren|zung F **-, -en** exclusion

aus+grün|den VT *sep (Econ)* to establish

Aus|guck [ˈausɡʊk] M **-(e)s, -e** lookout; **~ halten** to keep a lookout

aus+gu|cken *sep* VI **a** *(= Ausschau halten)* to look out *(nach* for) **b** *(= auskundschaften)* to have a look VT *(inf)* **a** *(suchend)* **sich** *(dat)* **die Augen nach jdm ~** to look everywhere for sb **b** *(= aussuchen, entdecken)* **sich** *(dat)* **jdn ~** to set one's sights on sb, to pick sb out

Aus|guss M **a** *(= Becken)* sink; *(= Abfluss)* drain; *(dial: = ausgegossene Flüssigkeit)* waste (water *etc*); *(= Tülle)* spout **b** *(Tech)* tap hole

Aus|guss|be|cken NT sink

aus+ha|ben *sep irreg (inf)* VT *(= fertig sein mit) Buch, Essen etc* to have finished; *(= ausgezogen haben)* to have taken off VI *(Arbeit, Schule etc: = beendet haben)* to finish

aus+ha|cken VT *sep* **a** *Unkraut* to hoe; *Rüben etc* to hoe out **b** *(Vogel) Augen* to peck out; *Federn* to tear out → **Krähe**

aus+ha|ken *sep* VT *Fensterladen, Kette* to unhook; *Reißverschluss* to undo VI *(inf)* **es hat bei ihm ausgehakt** *(= nicht begreifen)* he gave up *(inf)*; *(= wild werden)* something in him snapped *(inf)* VR *(Reißverschluss)* to come undone

aus+hal|ten *sep irreg* VT **a** *(= ertragen können)* to bear, to stand, to endure; *(= standhalten) Gewicht etc* to bear; *Druck* to stand, to withstand; *jds Blick* to return; **den Vergleich mit etw ~** to bear comparison with sth; **es lässt sich ~** it's bearable; **hier lässt es sich ~** this is not a bad place; **das ist nicht auszuhalten** *or* **zum Aushalten** it's unbearable; **ich halte es vor Hitze/zu Hause nicht mehr aus** I can't stand the heat/being at home any longer; **er hält es in keiner Stellung lange aus** he never stays in one job for long; **wie kann man es bei der Firma bloß ~?** how can anyone stand working for that firm?; **es bis zum Ende ~** *(auf Party etc)* to stay until the end; **hältst dus noch bis zur nächsten Tankstelle aus?** *(inf)* can you hold out till the next garage?; **er hält viel aus** he can take a lot; **er hält nicht viel aus** he can't take much; **ein Stoff, der viel ~ muss** a material which has to take a lot of wear (and tear)

b *Ton* to hold

c *(inf: = unterhalten)* to keep; **sich von jdm ~ lassen** to be kept by sb

VI **a** *(= durchhalten)* to hold out; **hältst du noch aus?** can you hold out (any longer)?

b auf einem Ton ~ to hold a note

aus+häm|mern VT *sep Beule* to hammer out; *Gefäß* to beat out

aus+han|deln VT *sep Vertrag, Lösung* to negotiate; *bessere Bedingungen, höhere Löhne* to negotiate for; *(erfolgreich)* to negotiate

aus+hän|di|gen [ˈaushɛndɪɡn] VT *sep* **jdm etw ~** to hand sth over to sb; **jdm einen Preis ~** to give sb a prize; **wann können Sie mir die Ware ~?** when can you deliver (the goods)?

Aus|hän|di|gung F **-, -en** handing over; *(von Gütern etc)* delivery; **nach ~ seiner Papiere** after his papers had been handed over to him; **die ~ der Preise nimmt der Direktor vor** the headmaster will be giving out the prizes

Aus|hang M *(= Bekanntmachung)* notice, announcement; *(= das Aushängen)* posting; **etw durch ~ bekannt geben** to put up a notice about sth; **etw im ~ lesen** to read a notice of *or* about sth

Aus|hän|ge|kas|ten M (glass-fronted) notice *(Brit) or* bulletin *(US)* board

aus+hän|gen *sep* VT **a** *(= bekannt machen) Nachricht etc* to put up; *Plakat* to post, to put up; *(inf: = ausstellen)* to show **b** *(= herausheben) Tür* to unhinge; *Haken* to unhook VI *irreg (Anzeige, Aufgebot)* to have been put up; *(inf: Brautleute)* to have the banns up *(Brit)*, to have the official wedding notice up *(US)*; **am Schwarzen Brett ~** to be on the notice *(Brit) or* bulletin *(US)* board VR *(= sich glätten: Falten, Locken)* to drop out; **das Kleid wird sich ~** the creases will drop *or* hang out of the dress

Aus|hän|ger M *(von Buch)* folded section

Aus|hän|ge|schild NT *pl* **-schilder** *(lit: = Reklametafel)* sign; *(fig: = Reklame)* advertisement

aus+har|ren VI *sep (geh)* to wait; **auf seinem Posten ~** to stand by one's post *(Brit)*, to stay at one's post *(US)*

aus+hau|chen VT *sep (geh) Luft, Atem, Rauch* to exhale; *(fig) Worte, Seufzer* to breathe; *(= ausströmen) Geruch, Dünste* to emit; **sein Leben ~** to breathe one's last (breath)

aus+hau|en VT *sep irreg* **a** *Loch, Stufen* to cut out; *Weg, Durchgang* to hew out **b** *(= roden) Wald, Weinberg* to clear; *(= einzelne Bäume fällen)* to cut down; *(= Zweige entfernen)* to prune

aus|häu|sig ['aushɔyzɪç] ADJ *(= außer Haus)* outside the home; *(= unterwegs)* away from home; **du warst doch letzte Woche wieder ~?** you were out gallivanting again last week, weren't you?

aus+he|beln ['aushe:bln] VT *sep* **a** *(Ringen)* to lever **b** *(fig) Vorhaben, Gesetz* to annul, to cancel **c** *(fig: aus leitender Position)* to lever out

aus+he|ben VT *sep irreg* **a** *Tür etc* to take off its hinges; **sich** *(dat)* **die Schulter ~** *(dial inf)* to put out one's shoulder *(inf)* **b** *Erde* to dig out; *Graben, Grab* to dig **c** *Vogelnest* to rob; *Vogeleier, Vogeljunge* to steal; *(fig) Diebesnest* to raid; *Bande* to make a raid on; *(Aus: = leeren) Briefkasten* to empty **d** *(old) Truppen* to levy *(old)*

Aus|he|bung F *(old: von Truppen)* levying

aus+he|cken ['aushɛkn] VT *sep (inf) Plan* to cook up *(inf)*, to hatch; **neue Streiche ~** to think up new tricks

aus+hei|len *sep* VT *Krankheit* to cure; *Organ, Wunde* to heal VI *aux sein (Krankheit)* to be cured; *(Organ, Wunde)* to heal VR to recover

Aus|hei|lung F *(von Organ, Wunde)* healing; **nach völliger ~ der Krankheit** after a complete recovery from the illness; **nach völliger ~ der Wunde** after the wound is completely healed

aus+hel|fen VI *sep irreg* to help out *(jdm* sb)

aus+heu|len *sep (inf)* VI *(= aufhören)* to stop crying; *(Sirene)* to stop sounding VR to have a good cry; **sich bei jdm ~** to have a good cry on sb's shoulder

Aus|hil|fe F **a** help, aid; *(= Notbehelf)* temporary *or* makeshift substitute; **jdn zur ~ haben** to have sb to help out; **Stenotypistin zur ~ gesucht** shorthand typist wanted for temporary work **b** *(Mensch)* temporary worker; *(esp im Büro)* temp *(inf)*; **als ~ arbeiten** to help out; *(im Büro auch)* to temp *(inf)*

Aus|hilfs-: **Aus|hilfs|ar|beit** F temporary work, temporary jobs *pl*; **Aus|hilfs|job** M temporary job; *(im Büro)* temping job; **Aus|hilfs|kell|ner** M stand-in waiter; **Aus|hilfs|kell|ne|rin** F stand-in waitress; **Aus|hilfs|koch** M, **Aus|hilfs|kö|chin** F stand-in cook; **Aus|hilfs|kraft** F temporary worker; *(esp im Büro)* temp *(inf)*; **Aus|hilfs|leh|rer(in)** M(F) supply *(Brit) or* substitute *(US)* teacher; **Aus|hilfs|per|so|nal** NT temporary staff; **Aus|hilfs|tä|tig|keit** F temporary job; **aus|hilfs|wei|se** ADV on a temporary basis; *(= vorübergehend)* temporarily; **sie kocht ab und zu ~** she sometimes cooks to help out

aus+höh|len ['aushø:lən] VT *sep* to hollow out; *Ufer, Steilküste* to erode; *(fig) (= untergraben)* to undermine; *(= erschöpfen)* to weaken

Aus|höh|lung F **a** *(= ausgehöhlte Stelle)* hollow **b** *no pl (= das Aushöhlen)* hollowing out; *(von Ufer, Steilküste)* erosion; *(fig: = Untergrabung)* undermining

aus+ho|len VI *sep* **a** *(zum Schlag)* to raise one's hand/arm *etc*; *(zum Wurf)* to reach back; *(mit Schläger, Boxer)* to take a swing; **weit ~** *(zum Schlag, beim Tennis)* to take a big swing; *(zum Wurf)* to reach back a long way; *(fig: Redner)* to go far afield; **bei einer Erzählung weit ~** to go a long way back in a story; **mit dem Arm/der Hand zum Wurf/Schlag ~** to raise one's arm/hand ready to throw/strike; **zum Gegenschlag ~** *(lit, fig)* to prepare for a counterattack **b** *(= ausgreifen)* to stride out; **er ging mit weit ~den Schritten** he walked with long strides

aus+hor|chen VT *sep (inf) jdn* to sound out

aus+hül|sen ['aushʏlzn] VT *sep Erbsen* to shell, to pod

aus+hun|gern VT *sep* to starve out → *auch* **ausgehungert**

aus+hus|ten *sep* VT to cough up VI *(= zu Ende husten)* to finish coughing; *(Schleim/Blut aushusten)* to cough up phlegm/blood VR to finish coughing; **er hustete sich aus, bis ...** he coughed and coughed until ...

aus+ixen ['auslɪksn] VT *sep (inf)* to cross *or* ex out

aus+jam|mern VR *sep* to have a good moan, to gripe *(inf)*

aus+jä|ten VT *sep Blumenbeet* to weed; **im Garten Unkraut ~** to weed the garden

aus+käm|men VT *sep* **a** *(= entfernen) Staub, Haare* to comb out **b** *(= frisieren)* to comb out **c** *(fig: = durchsuchen)* to comb

aus+ke|geln *sep* VT **den Pokal ~** to bowl for the cup VI to finish bowling

aus+keh|ren *sep* VT *Schmutz* to sweep away; *Zimmer* to sweep out VI to do the sweeping

aus+kei|len VI *sep* **a** *(= ausschlagen)* to kick out **b** *(= keilförmig auslaufen)* to taper off

aus+kei|men VI *sep aux sein (Getreide)* to germinate; *(Kartoffeln)* to sprout

aus+ken|nen VR *sep irreg (an einem Ort)* to know one's way around; *(auf einem Gebiet)* to know a lot *(auf or in +dat* about); **sich in der Stadt ~** to know one's way around the town; **sich bei Männern/Frauen (gut) ~** to know (a lot) about men/women; **man kennt sich bei ihm nie aus** you never know where you are with him

aus+ker|nen ['auskɛrnən] VT *sep Obst* to stone *(Brit)*, to remove the pit of *(US)*

aus+kip|pen VT *sep (inf)* to empty (out); *Flüssigkeit* to pour out

aus+klam|mern VT *sep Problem* to leave aside, to ignore; *(Math) Zahl* to put outside the brackets

aus+kla|mü|sern *ptp* **ausklamüsert** VT *sep (inf)* to work out

Aus|klang M *(geh)* conclusion, end; *(esp Mus)* finale; **zum ~ des Abends ...** to conclude the evening ...

aus|klapp|bar ADJ folding; *Blatt* fold-out; **dieser Tisch ist ~** this table can be opened out; **diese Fußstütze ist ~** this footrest can be pulled out

aus+klap|pen VT *sep* to open out; *Fußstütze etc* to pull out

aus+klau|ben VT *sep (dial)* to pick out, to sort out; *Erz* to select

aus+klei|den *sep* VT **a** *(geh: = entkleiden)* to undress **b** *(= beziehen)* to line VR *(geh)* to get undressed

Aus|klei|dung F lining

aus+klin|gen VI *sep irreg* **a** *(Glocken)* to finish ringing **b** *aux sein (Lied)* to finish; *(Abend, Feier etc)* to end *(in +dat* with); **die Verhandlungen klangen in die hoffnungsvolle Note aus, dass ...** the negotiations ended on the hopeful note that ...; **das ~de Jahrhundert** *(geh)* the close of the century

aus+klin|ken ['ausklɪŋkn] *sep* VT *Scanner, Bombe, Seil* to release VI *(= innerlich abschalten)* to switch off VR *(= sich zurückziehen, nicht mehr mitmachen)* to withdraw; **sich aus etw ~** to withdraw from sth; *aus dem Alltag, dem Beruf* to get away from sth; *aus dem Solidaritätsprinzip* to reject sth; **sich aus seiner Zeit ~** to reject modern technology

aus+klop|fen VT *sep Teppich* to beat; *Pfeife* to knock out; *Kleider* to beat the dust out of

Aus|klop|fer M carpet beater

aus+klü|geln VT *sep* to work out → *auch* **ausgeklügelt**

aus+knei|fen VI *sep irreg aux sein (inf)* to run away (*+dat, von* from)

aus+knip|sen VT *sep (inf) Licht, Lampe* to turn out *or* off, to switch off; *Gerät* to turn *or* switch off

aus|kno|beln VT *sep* **a** *(inf) Plan* to figure *(inf) or* work out **b** *(= durch Knobeln entscheiden)* ≈ to toss for

aus+kno|cken ['ausnɔkn] VT *sep (Boxen, fig)* to knock out

aus|knöpf|bar ADJ *Futter* detachable

aus+ko|chen VT *sep* **a** *(Cook) Knochen* to boil; *(dial) Fett, Speck* to melt **b** *Wäsche* to boil; *(Med) Instrumente* to sterilize *(in boiling water)*; *(fig inf: = sich ausdenken)* to cook up *(inf)* → *auch* **ausgekocht**

aus+kom|men VI *sep irreg aux sein* **a** *(= genügend haben, zurechtkommen)* to get by *(mit* on), to manage *(mit* on, with); **das Auto kommt mit sieben Litern auf 100 km aus** the car only uses seven litres *(Brit) or* liters *(US)* every 100 kilometres *(Brit) or* kilometers *(US)*; **ohne jdn/etw ~** to manage *or* do without sb/sth **b mit jdm (gut) ~** to get on *or* along (well) with sb; **mit ihm ist nicht auszukommen** he's impossible to get on *or* along with

Aus|kom|men NT **-s**, *no pl (= Einkommen)* livelihood; **sein ~ haben/finden** to get by; **mit ihr ist kein ~** she's impossible to get on *or* along with

aus|kömm|lich ['auskœmlɪç] ADJ *Gehalt* adequate; *Verhältnisse* comfortable ADV **~ leben** to live comfortably

aus+kos|ten VT *sep* **a** *(= genießen)* to make the most of; *Leben* to enjoy to the full **b** *(geh: = erleiden)* **etw ~ müssen** to have to suffer sth

aus+kot|zen *sep (vulg)* VT to throw up *(inf)*; *(fig inf) Wissen* to spew out *(inf)* VR to throw up *(inf)*; *(fig inf: = sich aussprechen)* to have a bloody good moan *(Brit inf) or* a really good gripe *(inf)*

aus+kra|men VT *sep (inf: = hervorholen) Gegenstand* to dig out, to unearth; *(fig) alte Geschichten etc* to bring up; *Schulkenntnisse* to dig up

aus+krat|zen VT *sep* to scrape out; *(Med) Gebärmutter* to scrape; *Patientin* to give a scrape; **jdm die Augen ~** to scratch sb's eyes out

Aus|krat|zung F **-, -en** *(Med)* scrape

aus+krie|chen VI *sep irreg aux sein* to hatch out

aus+krie|gen VT *sep (inf) Buch* to finish; *Flasche etc* to empty

Aus|kris|tal|li|sa|ti|on F crystallization

aus+kris|tal|li|sie|ren *ptp* **auskristallisiert** VTIR *sep (vi: aux sein)* to crystallize

Aus|kuck ['auskʊk] M **-(e)s, -e** *(N Ger)* = **Ausguck**

aus+ku|cken VTI *sep (N Ger)* = **ausgucken**

aus+ku|geln VT *sep* **sich** *(dat)* **den Arm/die Schulter ~** to dislocate one's arm/shoulder

aus+küh|len *sep* VT *Speise* to cool; *Ofen etc* to cool down; *Körper, Menschen* to chill through VI *aux sein (= abkühlen)* to cool down; *(Körper, Menschen)* to chill through; **etw ~ lassen** to leave sth to cool

Aus|küh|lung F cooling; *(von Mensch)* loss of body heat

aus+kund|schaf|ten *sep* VT *Weg, Lage* to find out; *Versteck* to spy out; *Geheimnis* to ferret out; *(esp Mil)* to reconnoitre *(Brit)*, to reconnoiter *(US)*, to scout VI to find out; **jdn zum Auskundschaften vorschicken** to send sb ahead to reconnoitre *(Brit)* or reconnoiter *(US)*

Aus|kunft ['auskʊnft] ✪ 27.1 F -, **Auskünfte** a [-kʏnftə] *(= Mitteilung)* information *no pl* *(über +acc* about); **nähere ~** more information, further details; **jdm eine ~ erteilen** *or* **geben** to give sb some information; **wo bekomme ich ~?** where can I get some information?; **eine ~** *or* **Auskünfte einholen** *or* **einziehen** to make (some) inquiries *(über +acc* about) b *(= Informationsstelle)* information office; *(= Schalter)* information desk; *(am Bahnhof)* inquiry office/desk; *(Telec)* directory inquiries *no art* c *(inf: = Auskunftsperson)* information man/woman *(inf)*

Aus|kunf|tei [auskʊnf'tai] F -, -en credit inquiry agency

Aus|kunfts-: **Aus|kunfts|be|am|te(r)** M *decl as adj*, **Aus|kunfts|be|am|tin** F information officer; *(am Bahnhof)* information clerk; **Aus|kunfts|bü|ro** NT enquiry office, information office; **Aus|kunfts|dienst** M information service; **aus|kunfts|freu|dig** ADJ informative; **Aus|kunfts|per|son** F informer; *(= Beamter)* information clerk; **Aus|kunfts|pflicht** F *(Jur)* obligation to give information; **die Bank hat gegenüber der Polizei ~** the bank has a duty *or* is obliged to inform the police authorities; **die ~ des Arbeitgebers gegenüber der Polizei** the employer's duty to inform the police; **aus|kunfts|pflich|tig** [-pflɪçtɪç] ADJ *(Jur)* required to give information; **Aus|kunfts|schal|ter** M information desk; *(am Bahnhof)* inquiry desk; **Aus|kunfts|stel|le** F information office

aus+kun|geln VT *sep (inf)* **etw ~** to work sth out on the q.t. *(inf)*

aus+kup|peln VI *sep* to disengage the clutch

aus+ku|rie|ren *ptp* **auskuriert** *sep (inf)* VT to cure; *Krankheit auch* to get rid of *(inf)* VR to get better

aus+la|chen *sep* VT *jdn* to laugh at; **lass dich nicht ~** don't make a fool of yourself VR to have a good laugh VI to stop laughing

aus+la|den *sep irreg* VT a *Ware, Ladung* to unload; *(Naut)* to discharge, to unload b *(inf)* **jdn ~** to tell sb not to come, to uninvite sb *(hum)* VI *(Äste)* to spread; *(Dach, Balkon)* to protrude, to jut out

aus|la|dend ADJ *Kinn etc* protruding; *Gebäudekomplex auch* projecting; *Dach* overhanging, projecting; *Kleid* wide; *Gebärden, Bewegung, Ansprüche* sweeping

Aus|la|ge F a *(von Waren)* display; *(= Schaufenster)* (shop) window; *(= Schaukasten)* showcase b *(Sport)* basic stance; *(Fechten)* on guard position c *usu pl* expense; **seine ~n für Verpflegung** his outlay for food

aus+la|gern VT *sep* to evacuate; *(= aus dem Lager bringen)* to take out of store

Aus|land NT, *no pl* foreign countries *pl*; *(fig: = die Ausländer)* foreigners *pl*; **ins/im ~** abroad; **aus dem** *or* **vom ~** from abroad; **wie hat das ~ darauf reagiert?** what was the reaction abroad?; **Handel mit dem ~** foreign trade, trade with other countries; **das feindliche/nichtkapitalistische** *or* **nicht kapitalistische ~** enemy/noncapitalist countries; **im benachbarten/europäischen ~** in neighbouring *(Brit)* or neighboring *(US)*/other European countries; **im ~ lebende Deutsche** expatriate Germans, Germans living abroad

Aus|län|der ['auslɛndɐ] M -s, -, **Aus|län|de|rin** [-ərɪn] F -, -nen foreigner; *(höflicher)* non-German or British *etc*; *(Admin, Jur)* alien

Aus|län|der-: **Aus|län|der|amt** NT foreigners' registration office; **Aus|län|der|an|teil** M proportion or percentage of foreigners/foreign workers *etc*; **Aus|län|der|be|auf|trag|te(r)** MF *decl as adj* official looking after foreign immigrants; **Aus|län|der|be|hör|de** F ≈ immigration authority; **aus|län|der|feind|lich** ADJ hostile to foreigners, xenophobic; *Anschlag* on foreigners ADV **~ motivierte Straftaten** crimes with a racist motive; **Aus|län|der|feind|lich|keit** F hostility toward(s) foreigners, xenophobia; **aus|län|der|freund|lich** ADJ *Land, Politik* friendly to foreigners; **Aus|län|der|ge|setz** NT *(Jur)* law on immigrants; **Aus|län|der|hass** M xenophobia

Aus|län|de|rin [-ərɪn] F → **Ausländer**

Aus|län|der-: **Aus|län|der|kind** NT child of immigrants *or* from an immigrant family; **Aus|län|der|kri|mi|na|li|tät** F crime *or* criminality among immigrants; **Aus|län|der|po|li|tik** F policy on immigrants; **Aus|län|der|wahl|recht** NT **allgemeines/kommunales ~** aliens' right to vote in general/local elections; **Aus|län|der|wohn|heim** NT immigrant hostel

aus|län|disch ['auslɛndɪʃ] ADJ a *attr* foreign; *(Bot)* exotic b *(fig: = fremdländisch)* exotic

Aus|lands- *in cpds* foreign; **Aus|lands|ab|tei|lung** F *(Econ)* export *or* foreign sales department; **Aus|lands|amt** NT *(an Universität etc)* international students' office; **Aus|lands|an|lei|he** F foreign loan; **Aus|lands|auf|ent|halt** M stay abroad; **Aus|lands|auf|klä|rung** F *(= Spionage)* reconnaissance abroad; **Aus|lands|be|tei|li|gung** F *(Econ)* foreign investment; **Aus|lands|be|zie|hun|gen** PL foreign relations *pl*; **Aus|lands|brief** M overseas *(Brit)* or foreign letter; *(ins Ausland auch)* letter going abroad; *(aus dem Ausland auch)* letter from abroad; **Aus|lands|deut|sche(r)** MF *decl as adj* expatriate German, German national (living abroad); **Aus|lands|dienst** M foreign service; **Aus|lands|ein|satz** M *(von Soldaten, Journalisten etc)* deployment abroad; *(für mehrere Monate/Jahre)* foreign posting; **Aus|lands|flug** M international flight; **Aus|lands|ge|schäft** NT foreign business *or* trade; **Aus|lands|ge|spräch** NT international call; **Aus|lands|in|ves|ti|ti|on** F foreign investment; **Aus|lands|ka|pi|tal** NT *(Econ)* foreign capital; **Aus|lands|kon|to** NT *(Econ)* foreign account, account abroad *or* overseas *(US)*; **Aus|lands|kor|res|pon|dent(in)** M(F) foreign correspondent; **Aus|lands|kran|ken|schein** M *(Med)* certificate of entitlement to benefits in kind *(during a stay abroad)*; **Aus|lands|rei|se** F journey *or* trip abroad; **Aus|lands|schul|den** PL foreign exchange debts *pl*; **Aus|lands|schu|le** F British/German *etc* school (abroad); **die ~n in Brüssel** the foreign schools in Brussels; **Aus|lands|schutz|brief** M international travel cover; *(= Dokument)* certificate of entitlement for international travel cover; **Aus|lands|stu|di|um** NT (course of) studies *pl* abroad; **ein ~ machen** to study abroad; **Aus|lands|ver|tre|tung** F agency abroad; *(von Firma)* foreign branch; **Aus|lands|zu|la|ge** F *(auf Gehalt)* overseas *or* expatriation allowance, foreign allowance *(US)*

aus+las|sen *sep irreg* VT a *(= weglassen, aussparen, übergehen)* to leave *or* miss out; *(= versäumen) Chance, Gelegenheit* to miss; **er lässt kein Geschäft aus** he doesn't miss a chance to make a deal b *(= abreagieren)* to vent *(an +dat* on); **seine Gefühle ~** to vent one's feelings, to let off steam *(inf)* c *Butter, Fett* to melt; *Speck* to render (down) d *Kleider etc* to let out; *Saum* to let down e *(inf) Radio, Motor, Ofen etc* to leave off; *Licht* to leave off, to leave out; *(= nicht anziehen) Kleidung* to leave off f *(Aus) (= los-, freilassen)* to let go; *(= in Ruhe lassen)* to leave alone g → **ausgelassen** VR to talk *(über +acc* about); **sich über jdn/etw ~** *(pej)* to go on about sb/sth *(pej)*; **er hat sich nicht näher darüber ausgelassen** he didn't say any more about it VI a *(Aus: = loslassen)* to let go b *(= versagen)* to fail

Aus|las|sung F -, -en a *(= Weglassen)* omission b **Auslassungen** PL *(pej: = Äußerungen)* remarks *pl*

Aus|las|sungs-: **Aus|las|sungs|punk|te** PL suspension points *pl*, ellipsis *sing*; **Aus|las|sungs|zei|chen** NT apostrophe

aus+las|ten VT *sep* a *Fahrzeug* to make full use of; *Maschine auch* to use to capacity b *jdn* to occupy fully → *auch* **ausgelastet**

Aus|las|tung F -, -en *(von Maschine)* full *or* capacity utilization

aus+lat|schen VT *sep (inf)* to wear *or* stretch out of shape; **latsch deine Schuhe nicht so aus** don't walk on your shoes like that → *auch* **ausgelatscht**

Aus|lauf M a *no pl (= Bewegungsfreiheit)* exercise; *(für Kinder)* room to run about b *(Gelände)* run c *(Sport) (Leichtathletik)* slowing down; *(Ski: = Strecke)* out-run d *no pl (= das Auslaufen)* discharge; *(= das Lecken)* leakage e *(Stelle)* outlet

aus+lau|fen *sep irreg* VI *aux sein* a *(Flüssigkeit)* to run out *(aus* of); *(Behälter)* to empty; *(= undicht sein)* to leak; *(Wasserbett, Blase, Auge)* to drain; *(Eiter)* to drain, to discharge b *(Naut: Schiff, Besatzung)* to sail c *(= nicht fortgeführt werden: Modell, Serie)* to be discontinued; *(= ausgehen: Vorräte, Lager)* to run out; **etw ~ lassen** *(Produkt etc)* to phase sth out d *(= aufhören: Straße, Vertrag etc)* to run out e *(= ein bestimmtes Ende nehmen)* to turn out f *(= zum Stillstand kommen) (Motor, Förderband)* to come to a stop; *(Sport) (Läufer)* to ease off, to slow down; *(Skifahrer)* to coast to a stop g *(= übergehen in)* to run; *(fig: Streit etc)* to turn *(in +acc* into); **die Berge laufen in die Ebene/spitz aus** the mountains run into the plain/come to a point; **in eine Bucht ~** to open out into a bay h *(Farbe, Stoff)* to run VR to have some exercise; **sich ~ können** *(Kinder)* to have room to run about

aus|lau|fend ADJ *Vertrag, Frist* expiring; **im ~en Jahr** in the year about to end; **~es Modell** = **Auslaufmodell**

Aus|läu|fer M a *(Bot)* runner b *(Met) (von Hoch)* ridge; *(von Tief)* trough c *(= Vorberge)* foothill *usu pl* d *(von Stadt)* suburb e *(Sw: = Bote)* delivery boy/man

Aus|läu|fe|rin F *(Sw: = Botin)* delivery girl/woman

Aus|lauf|mo|dell NT a *(lit)* discontinued model b *(fig, inf: Person)* old model *(hum inf)*; **ein ~ sein** *(fig inf: Konzept, Idee)* to be old hat *(inf)*

aus|lauf|si|cher ADJ leak-proof

aus+lau|gen ['auslaugn] VT *sep (lit) Boden* to exhaust; *(Regen)* to wash the goodness out of; *Haut* to dry out; *(fig)* to exhaust, to wear out

Aus|laut M *(Ling)* final position

aus+lau|ten VI *sep* to end *(auf +dat* in); **~der Konsonant** final consonant

aus+läu|ten *sep* VT to ring out; *Gottesdienst* to ring out the end of VI to finish *or* cease ringing

aus+le|ben *sep* VR *(Mensch)* to live it up; *(Fantasie etc)* to run free VT *(geh)* to realize

aus+le|cken VT *sep* to lick out

aus+lee|ren VT *sep Flüssigkeit* to pour out, to empty; *Gefäß* to empty

aus+le|gen *sep* VT a *(= ausbreiten)* to lay out; *Waren etc* to display; *Köder* to put down; *Reusen* to drop; *Kabel, Minen* to lay; *Saatgut* to sow; *Kartoffeln* to plant b *(= bedecken)* to cover; *(= auskleiden)* to line; *(mit Einlegearbeit)* to inlay; **den Boden/das Zimmer (mit Teppichen) ~** to carpet the floor/room c *(= erklären)* to explain; *(= deuten)* to interpret; **etw richtig ~** to interpret sth correctly; **etw falsch ~** to interpret sth wrongly, to misinterpret sth; **jds Scherz/Tat übel ~** to take sb's joke/action badly

d *Geld* to lend (*jdm etw* sb sth); **sie hat die 5 Euro für mich ausgelegt** she paid the 5 euros for me
e *(Tech)* to design (*auf +acc, für* for); **straff ausgelegt sein** *(Federung)* to be tightly set
VI *(dial inf: = dicklich werden)* to put (it) on a bit *(inf)*
VR *(Fechten)* to adopt the on guard position

Aus|le|ger ['ausle:gɐ] **M -s, - a** *(von Kran etc)* jib, boom **b** *(an Ruderboot)* rowlock; *(= Kufe gegen Kentern)* outrigger

Aus|le|ger ['ausle:gɐ] **M -s, -, Aus|le|ge|rin** [-ərın] **F -, -nen** *(= Deuter)* interpreter

Aus|le|ge|ware F floor covering; *(= Teppiche)* carpeting

Aus|le|gung ['ausle:gʊŋ] **F -, -en** *(= Deutung)* interpretation; *(= Erklärung)* explanation (*zu* of); **falsche ~** misinterpretation

Aus|le|gungs-: Aus|le|gungs|fra|ge F question *or* matter of interpretation; **Aus|le|gungs|me|tho|de F** method of interpretation; **Aus|le|gungs|sa|che F** matter of interpretation

Aus|leg|wa|re F = Auslegeware

aus+lei|den VI *sep irreg* **sie hat ausgelitten** her suffering is at an end

aus+lei|ern *sep* **VT** *(inf)* **etw ~** *(Gummiband, Gewinde, Feder)* to wear sth out; *Hosen, Pullover* to make sth go baggy **VI** *aux sein* to wear out; *(Pullover)* to go baggy → *auch* **ausgeleiert**

Aus|leih|bib|lio|thek F, Aus|leih|bü|che|rei F lending library

Aus|lei|he F *(= das Ausleihen)* lending; *(= Schalter)* issue desk; **eine ~ ist nicht möglich** it is not possible to lend out anything

aus+lei|hen VT *sep irreg (= verleihen)* to lend (*jdm, an jdn* to sb); *(= von jdm leihen)* to borrow; **sich** *(dat)* **etw ~** to borrow sth (*bei, von* from)

aus+ler|nen VI *sep (Lehrling)* to finish one's apprenticeship; *(inf: Schüler, Student etc)* to finish school/college *etc*; **man lernt nie aus** *(prov)* you live and learn *(prov)* → *auch* **ausgelernt**

Aus|le|se F a *no pl (= Auswahl)* selection; *(Liter: verschiedener Autoren)* anthology; **natürliche ~** natural selection; **eine ~ treffen** *or* **vornehmen** to make a selection **b** *(= Elite)* **die ~** the élite **c** *(= Wein) high-quality wine made from selected grapes*

aus+le|sen *sep irreg* **VT a** *(= auswählen)* to select; *(= aussondern) Schlechtes* to pick out; *Erbsen, Linsen etc* to pick over **b** *Buch etc* to finish reading; **er legte das ausgelesene Buch beiseite** he put away the book he had finished reading **VI** *(= zu Ende lesen)* to finish reading; **hast du bald ausgelesen?** will you finish (reading) it soon?

Aus|le|se-: Aus|le|se|pro|zess M selection process; **Aus|le|se|ver|fah|ren NT** selection procedure

aus+leuch|ten VT *sep* to illuminate; *(fig)* to throw light on

Aus|leuch|tung F -, -en illumination

aus+lich|ten VT *sep* to thin out

aus+lie|fern VT *sep* **a** *Waren* to deliver **b** *jdn* to hand over (*an +acc* to); *(an anderen Staat)* to extradite (*an +acc* to); *(fig: = preisgeben)* to leave (*jdm* in the hands of); **sich der Polizei/Justiz ~** to give oneself up *or* surrender oneself to the police/to justice; **jdm/einer Sache ausgeliefert sein** to be at sb's mercy/the mercy of sth

Aus|lie|fe|rung F a *(von Ware)* delivery **b** *(von Menschen)* handing over; *(von Gefangenen)* extradition

Aus|lie|fe|rungs-: Aus|lie|fe|rungs|ab|kom|men NT *(Pol)* extradition treaty; **Aus|lie|fe|rungs|an|trag M** *(Jur)* application for extradition; **Aus|lie|fe|rungs|be|geh|ren NT** *(Jur)* extradition request; **ein ~ stellen** to make an extradition request; **Aus|lie|fe|rungs|haft F** *(Jur)* extradition custody; **Aus|lie|fe|rungs|la|ger NT** *(Comm)* distribution centre *(Brit)* or center *(US)*; **Aus|lie|fe|rungs|ver|fah|ren NT** *(Jur)* extradition proceedings *pl*; **Aus|lie|fe|rungs|ver|trag M** *(Jur)* extradition treaty

aus+lie|gen VI *sep irreg (Waren)* to be displayed; *(Zeitschriften, Liste etc)* to be available (to the public); *(Schlinge, Netz etc)* to be down

Aus|li|nie F *(Sport) (Ftbl)* touchline; *(bei Tennis, Hockey etc)* sideline; **die ~n** *(Tennis)* the tramlines *pl*

aus+lo|ben VT *sep (form) (= als Belohnung aussetzen) Geldbetrag* to offer as a reward; *(= als Preis aussetzen)* to offer as a prize

Aus|lo|bung F -, -en *(= Belohnung)* reward

aus+löf|feln VT *sep Suppe etc* to eat up completely; *Teller* to empty; **etw ~ müssen** *(inf)* to have to take the consequences of sth; **~ müssen, was man sich eingebrockt hat** *(inf)* to have to take the consequences

aus|log|gen ['auslɔgn] **VR** *(Comput)* to log out *or* log off; **sich aus dem System ~** to log out of the system

aus+lö|schen VT *sep* **a** *Feuer* to put out, to extinguish; *Kerze auch* to snuff out; *(geh) Licht* to extinguish **b** *(= auswischen) Spuren* to obliterate; *(mit Schwamm etc)* to wipe out; *Schrift* to erase (*an +dat* from); *Erinnerung, Schmach* to blot out; **ein Menschenleben ~** *(geh)* to destroy *or* blot out a human life

aus+lo|sen VT *sep* to draw lots for; *Preis, Gewinner* to draw; **es wurde ausgelost, wer beginnt** lots were drawn to see who would start

aus+lö|sen VT *sep* **a** *Mechanismus, Alarm, Reaktion* to set *or* trigger off, to trigger; *Kameraverschluss, Bombe* to release; *(fig) Wirkung* to produce; *Begeisterung, Mitgefühl, Überraschung* to arouse; *Aufstand, Beifall* to trigger off **b** *(dated: = einlösen) Gefangene* to release; *(durch Geld)* to ransom; *Wechsel, Pfand* to redeem **c** *(dial) Knochen etc* to take out

Aus|lö|ser ['auslø:zɐ] **M -s, - a** trigger; *(für Bombe)* release button; *(Phot)* shutter release **b** *(= Anlass)* cause; **der ~ für etw sein** to trigger sth off **c** *(Psych)* trigger mechanism

Aus|lo|sung F draw

Aus|lö|sung F a *(von Gefangenen)* release; *(von Wechsel, Pfand)* redemption; *(= Lösegeld)* ransom **b** *(= Entschädigung)* travel allowance

aus+lo|ten VT *sep (Naut) Fahrrinne* to sound the depth of; *Tiefe* to sound; *(Tech) Mauer* to plumb; *(fig geh)* to plumb; *jds Wesen, Charakter* to plumb the depths of; **die Sache muss ich doch mal ~** *(fig inf)* I'll have to try to get to the bottom of the matter, I'll have to try to fathom it out

aus+lüf|ten VTI *sep* to air; **lüfte dein Gehirn ein bisschen aus** *(inf)* get your thoughts *or* ideas straightened out

aus+lut|schen VT *sep (inf) Orange, Zitrone etc* to suck; *Saft* to suck out; *(fig)* to suck dry

aus+ma|chen ✪ 28.1, 31, 34.5 **VT** *sep* **a** *Feuer, Kerze, Zigarette* to put out; *elektrisches Licht, Radio, Gas* to turn off
b *(= ermitteln, sichten)* to make out; *(= ausfindig machen)* to locate; *(= feststellen)* to determine; **es lässt sich nicht mehr ~, warum ...** it can no longer be determined why ...
c *(= vereinbaren)* to agree; *Streitigkeiten* to settle; **einen Termin ~** to agree (on) a time; **wir müssen nur noch ~, wann wir uns treffen** we only have to arrange when we should meet; **etw mit sich selbst ~ (müssen)** to (have to) sort sth out for oneself → *auch* **ausgemacht**
d *(= bewirken, darstellen)* (to go) to make up; **alles, was das Leben ausmacht** everything that is a part of life; **all der Luxus, der ein angenehmes Leben ausmacht** all the luxuries which (go to) make up a pleasant life; **ihm fehlt alles, was einen Musiker ausmacht** he has none of the qualities which (go to) make up a musician; **der Hintergrund macht den Reiz an diesem Bild aus** the background makes this picture attractive
e *(= betragen) Summe, Unterschied* to come to; *(zeitlich)* to make up
f *(= bedeuten)* **viel ~** to make a big difference; **wenig** *or* **nicht viel ~** not to make much difference; **das macht nichts aus** that doesn't matter; *(= ist egal auch)* that doesn't make any difference
g *(= stören)* to matter (*jdm* to); **macht es Ihnen etwas aus, wenn ...?** would you mind if ...?; **es macht mir nichts aus, den Platz zu wechseln** I don't mind changing places
h *(dial) Kartoffeln, Rüben* to dig up

aus+mah|len VT *sep* to grind (down)

aus+ma|len VT *sep* **sich** *(dat)* **etw ~** to imagine sth; **sich** *(dat)* **sein Leben ~** to picture one's life

aus+ma|növ|rie|ren *ptp* **ausmanövriert VT** *sep* to outmanoeuvre *(Brit)*, to outmaneuver *(US)*

aus+mä|ren ['ausmɛ:rən] **VR** *sep (dial inf) (= langsam arbeiten)* to dawdle *(inf)*; *(= viel erzählen)* to rattle on (*über +acc* about) *(inf)*; **mär dich endlich aus!** stop dawdling! *(inf)*

Aus|marsch M departure

aus+mar|schie|ren *ptp* **ausmarschiert VI** *sep aux sein* to march out

Aus|maß NT a *(= Größe: von Gegenstand, Fläche)* size; *(= Umfang: von Katastrophe)* extent; *(= Grad)* degree, extent; *(von Liebe etc)* extent; *(= Größenordnung: von Änderungen, Verlust etc)* scale; **ein Verlust in diesem ~** a loss on this scale; **das Feuer war nur von geringem ~** the fire was only on a small scale **b Ausmaße PL** proportions *pl*; **erschreckende ~e annehmen** to assume alarming proportions

aus+mer|geln ['ausmɛrgln] **VT** *sep Gesicht, Körper etc* to emaciate; *Boden* to exhaust → *auch* **ausgemergelt**

aus+mer|zen ['ausmɛrtsn] **VT** *sep (= ausrotten) Ungeziefer, Unkraut* to eradicate; *(= aussondern) schwache Tiere* to cull; *(fig) schwache Teilnehmer* to sort *or* weed out; *Fehler, Missstände* to eradicate; *Erinnerungen* to obliterate

aus+mes|sen VT *sep irreg Raum, Fläche etc* to measure (out); **das Zimmer ~** *(fig)* to pace up and down the room

Aus|mes|sung F a *(= das Messen)* measuring (out) **b** *(= Maße)* dimensions *pl*

aus+mis|ten *sep* **VT** *Stall* to muck out *(Brit)*, to clear *(US)*; *(fig inf) Schrank etc* to tidy *(esp Brit)* *or* clean out; *Zimmer* to clean out **VI** *(lit)* to muck out *(Brit)*, to clear of dung *(US)*; *(fig)* to have a clean-out

aus+mon|tie|ren *ptp* **ausmontiert VT** *sep* to take out

aus+mus|tern VT *sep Maschine, Fahrzeug etc* to take out of service; *(Mil: = entlassen)* to invalid out *(Brit)*, to discharge

Aus|nah|me ['ausna:mə] **F -, -n** exception; **mit ~ von** *or* **+gen** with the exception of; **mit ~ von ihm** with the exception of him, except (for) him; **ohne ~** without exception; **~n bestätigen die Regel** *(prov)* **keine Regel ohne ~** *(prov)* the exception proves the rule *(prov)*

Aus|nah|me-: Aus|nah|me|be|stim|mung F special regulation; **Aus|nah|me|er|schei|nung F** exception; **Aus|nah|me|fall M** exception, exceptional case; **Aus|nah|me|fehler M** *(Comput)* exception (error); **Aus|nah|me|ge|neh|mi|gung F** special (case) authorization; **Aus|nah|me|si|tu|a|ti|on F** special *or* exceptional situation; **Aus|nah|me|stel|lung F** special position; **Aus|nah|me|zu|stand M** *(Pol)* state of emergency; **den ~ verhängen** to declare a state of emergency

aus|nahms|los ADV without exception **ADJ** *Bewilligung, Zustimmung* unanimous; **das ~e Erscheinen der ganzen Belegschaft** the appearance of all the staff without exception

aus|nahms|wei|se ADV darf ich das machen? – ~ may I do that? – just this once; **wenn er ~ auch mal einen Fehler macht** when he makes a mistake too just for once; **sie hat es mir ~ einmal erlaubt** she let me do it once as a special exception; **er darf heute ~ früher von der Arbeit weggehen** as an exception he may leave work earlier today

aus+neh|men *sep irreg* VT **a** *(fig) Verbrecherbande, Diebesnest etc* to raid; *(Mil) Stellung* to take out; **das Nest ~** to remove the eggs from the nest **b** *Fisch, Kaninchen* to gut, to dress; *Geflügel* to draw; *Hammel, Rind etc* to dress; *Eingeweide, Herz etc* to take out, to remove **c** *(= ausschließen) jdn* to make an exception of; *(= befreien)* to exempt; **ich nehme keinen aus** I'll make no exceptions → *auch* **ausgenommen d** *(inf: finanziell) jdn* to fleece *(inf)*; *(beim Kartenspiel)* to clean out *(inf)* **e** *(Aus: = erkennen)* to make out VR *(geh: = wirken)* **sich schön** *or* **gut/schlecht ~** to look good/bad

aus|neh|mend ADJ *(geh)* exceptional ADV exceptionally; **das gefällt mir ~ gut** I like that very much indeed

aus+nüch|tern [ˈausnʏçtn] VTIR *sep* to sober up

Aus|nüch|te|rung F -, -en sobering up

Aus|nüch|te|rungs|zel|le F drying-out cell

aus+nut|zen, *(esp S Ger, Aus, Sw)* **aus+nüt|zen** VT *sep* to use, to make use of; *jdn* to use; *(= ausbeuten)* to exploit; *Gelegenheit* to make the most of; *jds Gutmütigkeit, Leichtgläubigkeit etc* to take advantage of

Aus|nut|zung F -, *no pl, (esp S Ger, Aus, Sw)* **Aus|nüt|zung** F -, *no pl* use; *(= Ausbeutung)* exploitation

aus+pa|cken *sep* VTI *Koffer* to unpack; *Geschenk* to unwrap VI *(inf) (= alles sagen)* to talk *(inf)*; *(= seine Meinung sagen)* to speak one's mind

aus+par|ken *sep* VI to get out of a/the parking space

aus+peit|schen VT *sep* to whip

aus+pel|len *sep (inf)* VT to peel; *Nuss, Erbsen* to shell VR to strip off

Aus|pend|ler(in) M(F) commuter

aus+pen|nen VIR *sep (inf)* to have a (good) kip *(Brit inf) or* nap

aus+pfei|fen VT *sep irreg* to boo *or* hiss at; *Stück, Schauspieler* to boo off the stage

aus+pflan|zen VT *sep (Hort)* to plant out

Aus|pi|zi|um [ausˈpiːtsiʊm] NT -s, **Auspizien** [-tsiən] *usu pl (geh)* auspice

aus+plap|pern VT *sep (inf)* to blurt out *(inf)*

aus+plau|dern *sep* VT to let out VR *(dial)* to have a good chat

aus+plün|dern VT *sep Dorf etc* to plunder, to pillage; *Kasse, Laden* to raid; *(hum) Speisekammer etc* to raid; *jdn* to plunder *(inf)*, to clean out *(inf)*

aus+pols|tern VT *sep Mantel etc* to pad (out); *Kiste, Raum etc* to line, to pad

aus+po|sau|nen *ptp* **ausposaunt** VT *sep (inf)* to broadcast *(inf)*

aus+po|wern [ˈaʊspoːvɐn] VT *sep (= verarmen)* to impoverish; *(= ausbeuten) Massen, Boden* to exploit; **ein wirtschaftlich ausgepowertes Land** an impoverished country

aus|pow|ern [ˈaʊspauɐn] VR *(inf, in Fitness-Studio etc)* to have a good work-out

Aus|po|we|rung F -, -en impoverishment; *(= Ausbeutung)* exploitation

aus+prä|gen VT *Münzen etc* to mint; **Metall zu Münzen ~** to stamp coins out of metal VR *sep (Begabung, Charaktereigenschaft etc)* to reveal *or* show itself; **die Erziehung prägt sich im Charakter/Verhalten aus** one's upbringing leaves its stamp on one's character/behaviour *(Brit) or* behavior *(US)* → *auch* **ausgeprägt**

Aus|prä|gung F **a** *no pl (von Charakter)* shaping, moulding *(Brit)*, molding *(US)* **b** *no pl (= das Ausgeprägtsein)* markedness; **in einer derart starken ~ ist mir diese Krankheit noch nicht untergekommen** I have never come across this illness to such a marked degree **c** *(= Ausdruck)* expression

aus+prei|sen VT *sep Waren* to price

aus+pres|sen VT *sep* **a** *(= herauspressen) Saft, Schwamm etc* to squeeze out; *Zitrone etc* to squeeze **b** *(fig: = ausbeuten)* to squeeze dry, to bleed white **c** *(fig: = ausfragen)* to press; **jdn wie eine Zitrone ~** to squeeze sb like a lemon (for information)

aus+pro|bie|ren *ptp* **ausprobiert** VT *sep* to try out; *Auto auch* to test-drive; **alles mal ~** to give everything a go *(inf)*

Aus|puff M *pl* **-puffe** exhaust

Aus|puff-: **Aus|puff|ga|se** PL exhaust fumes *pl*; **Aus|puff|krüm|mer** [-krʏmɐ] M -s, - *(Aut)* exhaust manifold; **Aus|puff|rohr** NT exhaust pipe; **Aus|puff|topf** M silencer *(Brit)*, muffler *(US)*

aus+pum|pen VT *sep* **a** *(= leeren)* to pump out **b** *(inf: = erschöpfen)* to drain

aus+punk|ten [ˈauspʊŋktn] VT *sep (Boxen)* to outpoint, to beat on points

aus+pus|ten VT *sep (inf)* to blow out; **die Luft kräftig ~** to blow out hard; **jdm das Lebenslicht ~** to snuff out sb's life

aus+put|zen *sep* VT **a** *(esp S Ger, Aus: = reinigen)* to clean out; *Kleider* to clean; *Flecken* to get out **b** *(Ftbl) Ball* to clear **c** *(dial: = ausnutzen)* to use VI *(Ftbl)* to clear (the ball); *(= Ausputzer sein)* to act as *or* be the sweeper

Aus|put|zer [ˈausputsɐ] M -s, -, **Aus|put|ze|rin** [-ərɪn] F -, -nen *(Ftbl)* sweeper; *(fig inf)* troubleshooter

aus+quar|tie|ren [ˈauskvartiːrən] *ptp* **ausquartiert** VT *sep* to move out; *(Mil)* to billet out

Aus|quar|tie|rung F -, -en moving out; *(Mil)* billeting out

aus+quat|schen [ˈauskvatʃn] VR *sep (inf)* to have a heart-to-heart *(bei jdm* with sb), to get a load off one's chest

aus+quet|schen VT *sep Saft etc* to squeeze out; *Zitrone etc* to squeeze; *(inf: = ausfragen) (Polizei etc)* to grill *(inf)*; *(aus Neugier)* to pump *(inf)*

aus+ra|die|ren *ptp* **ausradiert** VT *sep* to rub out, to erase; *(fig: = vernichten)* to wipe out; **etw aus dem Gedächtnis ~** to erase sth from one's mind *or* memory

aus+ran|gie|ren *ptp* **ausrangiert** VT *sep (inf) Kleider* to throw out; *Maschine, Auto* to scrap; **ein altes ausrangiertes Auto** an old disused car

aus+ra|sie|ren *ptp* **ausrasiert** VT *sep* to shave; *Koteletten* to trim; **jdm/sich die Haare im Nacken ~** to shave sb's/one's neck

aus+ras|ten *sep* VI *aux sein* **a** *(Tech)* to come out **b** *(hum inf: = zornig werden)* to blow one's top *(inf)*, to do one's nut *(Brit inf)* VR *(Aus, S Ger: = ausruhen)* to have a rest VI *impers (inf)* **es rastet bei jdm aus** something snaps in sb *(inf)*

aus+rau|ben VT *sep* to rob

aus+räu|bern VT *sep (auch hum)* to plunder, to raid; **jdn ~** to clean sb out *(inf)*

aus+rau|chen *sep* VT *Zigarette etc* to finish (smoking) VI **a** *(= zu Ende rauchen)* to finish smoking **b** *aux sein (Aus) (= verdunsten)* to evaporate; *(= Geschmack verlieren)* to lose its taste

aus+räu|chern VT *sep Zimmer* to fumigate; *Tiere, Schlupfwinkel, Bande* to smoke out

aus+rau|fen VT *sep* to tear *or* pull out; **ich könnte mir die Haare ~** I could kick myself

aus+räu|men VT *sep* to clear out; *Möbel* to move out; *Magen, Darm* to purge; *(fig) Missverständnisse, Konflikt* to clear up; *Vorurteile, Bedenken* to dispel; *(inf: = ausrauben)* to clean out *(inf)*

aus+rech|nen VT *sep* to work out; *(= ermitteln) Gewicht, Länge etc* to calculate; **sich** *(dat)* **etw ~ können** *(fig)* to be able to work sth out (for oneself); **sich** *(dat)* **große Chancen/einen Vorteil ~** to reckon *or* fancy that one has a good chance/an advantage → *auch* **ausgerechnet**

Aus|rech|nung F working out; *(von Gewicht, Länge etc)* calculation

aus+re|cken VT *sep* to stretch (out); **sich** *(dat)* **den Hals ~** to crane one's neck

Aus|re|de F excuse

aus+re|den *sep* VI to finish speaking; **er hat mich gar nicht erst ~ lassen** he didn't even let me finish (speaking) VT **jdm etw ~** to talk sb out of sth VR *(esp Aus) (= sich aussprechen)* to have a heart-to-heart (talk); *(= Ausflüchte machen)* to make excuses; **er versucht sich immer auf irgendwas auszureden** he is always trying to make some excuse

aus+reg|nen VIR *impers sep* to stop raining

aus+rei|ben VT *sep irreg Fleck etc* to rub out; *Topf etc* to scour; *Gläser* to wipe out; **sich** *(dat)* **die Augen ~** to rub one's eyes

aus+rei|chen VI *sep* to be sufficient *or* enough; **die Zeit reicht nicht aus** there is not sufficient time; **mit etw ~** *(dial)* to manage on sth

aus|rei|chend ADJ sufficient, enough; *(Sch)* satisfactory ADV sufficiently

aus+rei|fen VI *sep aux sein* to ripen; *(fig)* to mature

Aus|rei|se F **bei der ~** on leaving the country; *(= Grenzübertritt)* on crossing the border; **jdm die ~ verweigern** to prohibit sb from leaving the country

Aus|rei|se-: **Aus|rei|se|an|trag** M application for an exit visa; **Aus|rei|se|er|laub|nis** F, **Aus|rei|se|ge|neh|mi|gung** F exit permit

aus+rei|sen VI *sep aux sein* to leave (the country); **ins Ausland/nach Frankreich ~** to go abroad/to France

Aus|rei|se-: **Aus|rei|se|sper|re** F ban on leaving the country; **Aus|rei|se|ver|bot** NT ban on leaving a/the country; **Aus|rei|se|ver|kehr** M traffic leaving the country; **Aus|rei|se|vi|sum** NT exit visa; **Aus|rei|se|wel|le** F wave of departures, emigration wave; **aus|rei|se|wil|lig** ADJ *Ausländer* waiting to leave the country, keen to emigrate; **Aus|rei|se|wil|li|ge(r)** [ˈausraizəvɪlɪgə] MF *decl as adj* prospective emigrant

aus|reiß|bar ADJ *Ärmel, Jackenfutter* detachable

aus+rei|ßen *sep irreg* VT *Haare, Blatt* to tear out; *Unkraut, Blumen, Zahn* to pull out; **einem Käfer die Flügel/Beine ~** to pull a beetle's wings/legs off; **er hat sich** *(dat)* **kein Bein ausgerissen** *(inf)* he didn't exactly overstrain himself, he didn't exactly bust a gut *(inf)*; **ich könnte Bäume ~** *(inf)* I feel full of beans *(inf)* → **Fliege a** VI *aux sein* **a** *(= sich lösen) (Ärmel etc)* to come away; *(= einreißen) (Naht)* to come out; *(Knopfloch)* to tear **b** (+dat from) *(inf: = davonlaufen)* to run away; *(Sport)* to break away

Aus|rei|ßer [ˈausraisɐ] M -s, - **a** *(Mil)* stray bullet **b** *(= Ausnahme)* anomaly, aberration; **ein statistischer ~** a statistical anomaly

Aus|rei|ßer [ˈausraisɐ] M -s, -, **Aus|rei|ße|rin** [-ərɪn] F -, -nen *(inf)* runaway; *(Sport)* runner who breaks away; *(Radfahrer)* cyclist who breaks away

aus+rei|ten *sep irreg* VI *aux sein* to ride out, to go riding, to go for a ride VT *Pferd* to take out, to exercise; **ein Pferd voll ~** to ride a horse to its limit

aus+rei|zen VT *sep Karten* to bid up to strength; *Kontrahenten* to outbid; *(fig: = ausschöpfen) Möglichkeiten, Potenzial, Thema* to exhaust; *Mittel* to exploit, to exhaust

aus+ren|ken [ˈausrɛŋkn] VT *sep* to dislocate; **sich/jdm den Arm ~** to dislocate one's/sb's arm; **sich** *(dat)* **(fast) den Hals ~** *(inf)* to crane one's neck

aus+rich|ten *sep* ✪ 27.6, 49 VT **a** *(= aufstellen)* to line up; *(Comput)* to align; **jdn/etw auf etw** *(acc)* **~** *(= einstellen)* to orientate sb/sth to sth, to align sb/sth with sth; *(= abstellen)* to gear sb/sth to sth

b *(= veranstalten)* to organize; *Hochzeit, Fest* to arrange, to organize

c *(= erreichen)* to achieve; **ich konnte bei ihr nichts ~** I couldn't get anywhere with her

d *(= übermitteln)* to tell; *Nachricht* to pass on; **jdm ~, dass ...** to tell sb (that) ...; **jdm etwas ~** to give sb a message; **kann ich etwas ~?** can I give him/her *etc* a message?; **bitte richten Sie ihm einen Gruß aus** please give him my regards

e *(Aus: = schlechtmachen)* to run down

VR to line up in a straight row; *(Mil)* to dress

ranks; **sich nach dem Nebenmann/Vordermann/Hintermann ~** to line up (exactly) with the person next to/in front of/behind one; **ausgerichtet in einer Reihe stehen** to stand next to one another in a straight line; **sich an etw** *(dat)* **~** *(fig)* to orientate oneself to sth

Aus|rich|tung F **a** *(fig) (auf Ideologie etc)* orientation *(auf +acc* towards), alignment *(auf +acc* with); *(auf Bedürfnisse etc)* gearing *(auf +acc* to); *(an einer Ideologie)* orientation *(an +dat* to) **b** *(von Veranstaltung)* organization; *(von Hochzeit, Fest)* arrangement, organization **c** *(= Aufstellung)* lining up; *(= Einstellung)* alignment *(auf +acc* with); *(Comput)* alignment; *(= Druckausrichtung)* orientation

aus+rin|gen VT *sep irreg (dial: = auswringen)* to wring out

Aus|ritt M ride (out); *(= das Ausreiten)* riding out

aus+rol|len *sep* **VT** *Teig, Teppich* to roll out; *Kabel* to run out **VI** *aux sein (Flugzeug)* to taxi to a standstill *or* stop; *(Fahrzeug)* to coast to a stop

aus+rot|ten ['ausrɔtn] VT *sep* to wipe out; *Wanzen etc* to destroy; *Religion, Ideen* to stamp out, to eradicate

Aus|rot|tung F **-, -en** wiping out; *(von Wanzen etc)* destruction; *(von Religion, Ideen)* stamping out, eradication

aus+rü|cken *sep* **VI** *aux sein* **a** *(Mil)* to move *or* set out; *(Polizei, Feuerwehr)* to turn out **b** *(inf: = ausreißen)* to make off; *(von zu Hause)* to run away; *(aus Gefängnis)* to run away, to get out **VT** **a** *(Tech)* to disengage, to release **b** *(Typ) Zeilen etc* to reverse-indent *(spec)*, to move out

Aus|ruf M **a** *(= Ruf)* cry, shout **b** *(= Bekanntmachung)* proclamation; **etw durch ~ bekannt machen** to proclaim sth

aus+ru|fen VT *sep irreg* to exclaim; *Schlagzeilen* to cry out; *Waren* to cry; *(auf Auktion)* to start; *(= verkünden)* to call out; *Haltestellen, Streik* to call; **die Stunden ~** *(Hist)* to call the hours; **jdn zum** *or* **als König ~** to proclaim sb king; **jdn** *or* **jds Namen ~ (lassen)** *(über Lautsprecher etc)* to put out a call for sb; *(im Hotel)* to page sb

Aus|ru|fer ['ausru:fɐ] M **-s, -**, **Aus|ru|fe|rin** [-ərın] F **-, -nen** *(Hist)* (town) crier; *(von Waren)* crier

Aus|ru|fe-: **Aus|ru|fe|satz** M exclamation; **Aus|ru|fe|wort** NT *pl* **-wörter** exclamation, interjection; **Aus|ru|fe|zei|chen** NT exclamation mark *(Brit)*, exclamation point *(US)*

Aus|ru|fung F **-, -en** proclamation; **die ~ eines Streiks** a strike call

Aus|ru|fungs|zei|chen NT exclamation mark *(Brit)*, exclamation point *(US)*

aus+ru|hen VTIR *sep* to rest; *(Mensch)* to take *or* have a rest; **ausgeruht** (well) rested; **meine Augen müssen (sich) ein wenig ~** I shall have to rest my eyes a little; **seine Augen ~ (lassen)** to rest one's eyes → **Lorbeer b**

aus+rup|fen VT *sep* to pull out; *Federn* to pluck out

aus+rüs|ten VT *sep (lit, fig)* to equip; *Fahrzeug, Schiff* to fit out; *Tuch* to treat; **ein Fahrzeug mit etw ~** to fit a car with sth

Aus|rüs|ter ['ausrʏstɐ] M **-s, -**, **Aus|rüs|te|rin** [-ərın] F **-, -nen** *(Sport: = Sponsor)* sponsor

Aus|rüs|tung F **a** *no pl (= das Ausrüsten)* equipping; *(von Fahrzeug, Schiff)* fitting out; *(von Tuch)* treating **b** *(= Ausrüstungsgegenstände)* equipment; *(= esp Kleidung)* outfit

Aus|rüs|tungs|ge|gen|stand M, **Aus|rüs|tungs|stück** NT piece of equipment

aus+rut|schen VI *sep aux sein* to slip; *(fig inf) (= sich schlecht benehmen)* to drop a clanger *(Brit inf)*, to put one's foot in it; *(= straffällig werden)* to get into trouble; **das Messer/die Hand ist mir ausgerutscht** my knife/my hand slipped

Aus|rut|scher M *(inf) (lit, fig)* slip; *(= schlechte Leistung)* slip-up

Aus|saat F **a** *no pl (= das Säen)* sowing **b** *(= Saat)* seed

aus+sä|en VT *sep (lit, fig)* to sow

Aus|sa|ge F statement; *(= Behauptung)* opinion; *(= Bericht)* report; *(Jur) (eines Beschuldigten, Angeklagten)* statement; *(= Zeugenaussage)* evidence *no pl*, testimony; *(fig: von Roman etc)* message; **eine eidliche/schriftliche ~** a sworn/written statement; **hier steht ~ gegen ~** it's one person's word against another's; **der Angeklagte verweigerte die ~** the accused refused to make a statement; **der Zeuge verweigerte die ~** the witness refused to give evidence *or* testify; **eine ~ machen** to make a statement, to give evidence; **nach ~ seines Chefs** according to his boss

Aus|sa|ge-: **Aus|sa|ge|kraft** F, *no pl* meaningfulness; **aus|sa|ge|kräf|tig** ADJ meaningful

aus+sa|gen *sep* **VT** to say *(über +acc* about); *(= behaupten)* to state; *(unter Eid)* to testify; **was will der Roman ~?** what message does this novel try to convey?; **etw über jdn ~** *(Jur)* to give sth in evidence about sb **VI** *(Jur) (Zeuge)* to give evidence; *(Angeklagter, schriftlich)* to make a statement; *(unter Eid)* to testify; **eidlich** *or* **unter Eid ~** to give evidence under oath; **für/gegen jdn ~** to give evidence *or* to testify for/against sb; **schriftlich ~** to make a written statement

aus+sä|gen VT *sep* to saw out

Aus|sa|ge-: **Aus|sa|ge|satz** M statement; **aus|sa|ge|stark** ADJ powerful; *Bewerbung* strong; **Aus|sa|ge|ver|wei|ge|rung** F *(Jur)* refusal to give evidence *or* to testify; **ein Recht auf ~ haben** to have a right to refuse to give evidence *or* to testify

Aus|satz M, *no pl (Med)* leprosy; *(fig)* pestilence

aus|sät|zig ADJ *(Med)* leprous

Aus|sät|zi|ge(r) ['auszɛtsıgə] MF *decl as adj (lit, fig)* leper

aus+sau|fen *sep irreg* VT *(Tier) Wasser* to drink up; *Napf* to empty

aus+sau|gen VT *sep Saft etc* to suck out; *Frucht* to suck (dry); *Wunde* to suck the poison out of; *(fig: = ausbeuten)* to drain dry; **jdn bis aufs Blut** *or* **Mark ~** to bleed sb white

aus+scha|ben VT *sep* to scrape out; *(Med)* to curette

Aus|scha|bung F **-, -en** *(Med)* curettage, scrape

aus+schach|ten ['ausʃaxtn] VT *sep* to dig, to excavate; *Brunnen* to sink

Aus|schach|tung F **-, -en** **a** *no pl (= das Ausschachten)* digging, excavation; *(von Erde)* digging up **b** *(= Grube etc)* excavation

Aus|schach|tungs|ar|bei|ten PL excavation work

aus+schaf|fen VT *sep (Sw form: = abschieben)* to deport

Aus|schaf|fung F *(Sw form: = Abschiebung)* deportation

aus+scha|len ['ausʃa:lən] VT *sep (Build)* = **verschalen**

Aus|schalt|au|to|ma|tik F auto *or* automatic stop

aus+schal|ten VT *sep* **a** *(= abstellen)* to switch off, to turn off; *(Comput) Gerät* to switch *or* power off; *Warnsignal etc* to disable; **sich (automatisch) ~** to switch *or* turn (itself) off (automatically) **b** *(fig)* to eliminate

Aus|schal|tung F **a** *(= das Abstellen)* switching off, turning off **b** *(fig)* elimination

Aus|schank M **-(e)s, Ausschänke** [-ʃɛŋkə] **a** *(= Schankraum)* bar, pub *(Brit)*; *(= Schanktisch)* bar, counter **b** *(no pl: = Getränkeausgabe)* serving of drinks; **„Ausschank von 9.00 Uhr bis 14.00 Uhr"** "open from 9.00 to 14.00"; **~ über die Straße** ≈ off-sales *pl (Brit)*, *selling of drinks for consumption off the premises*; **„kein ~ an Jugendliche unter 16 Jahren"** "drinks not sold to persons under the age of 16"

Aus|schank F **-, Ausschänke** *(Aus)* = **Ausschank a**

Aus|schank|er|laub|nis F licence *(Brit)*, license *(US)*

Aus|schau F, *no pl* **~ halten** to look out, to be on the lookout, to keep a lookout

aus+schau|en VI *sep* **a** *(geh) (nach* for) to look out, to be on the lookout, to keep a lookout **b** *(dial)* = **aussehen**; **wie schauts aus?** *(inf)* how's things? *(esp Brit inf)*, how are things going?

aus+schau|feln VT *sep Grube, Grab* to dig; *Erde* to dig out; *Leiche* to dig up

aus+schäu|men VT *sep (Tech)* to foam

aus+schei|den *sep irreg* **VT** *(= aussondern)* to take out; *esp Menschen* to remove; *(Physiol)* to excrete **VI** *aux sein* **a** *(aus einem Amt)* to retire *(aus* from); *(aus Club, Firma)* to leave *(aus etw* sth); *(Sport)* to be eliminated; *(in Wettkampf)* to drop out; **wer unfair kämpft, muss ~** whoever cheats will be disqualified **b** *(= nicht in Betracht kommen: Plan, Möglichkeit etc)* to be ruled out; **das/er scheidet aus** that/he has to be ruled out

Aus|schei|dung F **a** *no pl (= das Aussondern)* removal; *(Physiol)* excretion **b** **Ausscheidungen** PL *(Med)* excretions *pl* *(Sport)* elimination; *(= Vorkampf)* qualifying contest *(Brit)*, preliminary (round)

Aus|schei|dungs- *in cpds (Physiol)* excretory; *(Sport)* qualifying *(Brit)*, preliminary; **Aus|schei|dungs|kampf** M *(Sport)* qualifying contest *(Brit)*, preliminary (round); *(Leichtathletik, Schwimmen)* heat; **Aus|schei|dungs|or|gan** NT excretory organ; **Aus|schei|dungs|pro|dukt** NT excretory product; **Aus|schei|dungs|run|de** F *(Sport)* qualifying round; **Aus|schei|dungs|spiel** NT qualifying match *or* game; **Aus|schei|dungs|wett|kampf** M *(Sport)* qualifying contest, qualifier; *(bei Leichtathletik)* (qualifying) heat

aus+schei|ßen VR *sep irreg (vulg)* to have a good shit *(sl)*

aus+schel|ten VT *sep irreg (geh)* to scold

aus+schen|ken VTI *sep* to pour (out); *(am Ausschank)* to serve

aus+sche|ren VI *sep aux sein (aus Kolonne) (Soldat)* to break rank; *(Fahrzeug, Schiff)* to leave the line *or* convoy; *(Flugzeug)* to break formation, to peel off; *(zum Überholen)* to pull out; *(= ausschwenken, von gerader Linie abweichen)* to swing out; *(fig)* to step out of line; **aus der Parteilinie ~** to deviate from the party line

aus+schi|cken VT *sep* to send out

aus+schie|ßen *sep irreg* **VT** **a** **jdm ein Auge ~** to shoot out sb's eye **b** *(in Wettbewerb)* to shoot for **c** *(old: = aussondern)* to reject, to throw out **d** *(Typ)* to impose **VI** *aux sein* **a** *(Pflanzen)* to shoot up **b** *(S Ger, Aus: = verbleichen)* to fade

aus+schif|fen *sep* **VT** to disembark; *Ladung, Waren* to unload, to discharge **VR** to disembark

Aus|schif|fung F **-, -en** disembarkation; *(von Ladung)* unloading, discharging

aus+schil|dern VT *sep* to signpost

aus+schimp|fen VT *sep* to tell off

aus+schir|ren ['ausʃırən] VT *sep Pferd* to unharness; *Ochsen* to unyoke

ausschl. *abbr von* **ausschließlich** excl.

aus+schlach|ten VT *sep* **a** *Tier, Beute* to gut, to dress **b** *(fig) Fahrzeuge, Maschinen etc* to cannibalize **c** *(fig inf: = ausnutzen) Skandal, Ereignis* to exploit; *Buch, Werk etc* to get everything out of

aus+schla|fen *sep irreg* **VT** *Rausch etc* to sleep off **VIR** to have a good sleep

Aus|schlag M **a** *(Med)* rash; **(einen) ~ bekommen** to come out in *or* get a rash **b** *(von Zeiger etc)* swing; *(von Kompassnadel)* deflection **c** *(fig)* decisive factor; **den ~ geben** *(fig)* to be the decisive factor; **die Stimme des Vorsitzenden gibt den ~** the chairman has the casting vote

aus+schla|gen *sep irreg* **VT** **a** *(= herausschlagen)* to knock out; *(dial: = ausschütteln) Staubtuch etc* to shake out; **jdm die Zähne ~** to knock sb's teeth out **b** *Feuer* to beat out

c *(= verkleiden)* to line; *(mit Kacheln, Tapete)* to cover
d *(= ablehnen)* to turn down; *Erbschaft* to waive; **jdm etw ~** to refuse sb sth
VI **a** *aux sein or haben (Baum, Strauch)* to come out, to start to bud, to burgeon (out) *(liter)*
b *(= los-, zuschlagen)* to hit *or* lash out; *(Pferd)* to kick
c *aux sein or haben (Zeiger, Nadel, Pendel)* to swing; *(Kompassnadel)* to be deflected; *(Wünschelrute etc)* to dip; **nach oben/unten ~** *(Börsenkurse etc)* to go up/down
d **ausgeschlagen haben** *(Turmuhr)* to have finished striking; *(liter: Herz)* to have beat its last *(liter)*
e *aux sein* **günstig/nachteilig ~** to turn out well *or* favourably *(Brit) or* favorably *(US)*/badly; **zu jds Schaden ~** to turn out badly for sb; **zum Guten ~** to turn out all right

aus|schlag|ge|bend ADJ decisive; *Stimme auch* deciding; **~ sein** to be the decisive factor; **das ist von ~er Bedeutung** that is of prime importance

aus+schle|cken VT *sep (S Ger)* to lick out

aus+schlei|fen VT *sep irreg (Tech)* to grind out

aus+schlie|ßen ✪ 43.3, 53.4, 53.6 VT *sep irreg* **a** *(= aussperren)* to lock out **b** *(= entfernen)* to exclude; *(aus Gemeinschaft)* to expel; *(vorübergehend)* to suspend; *(Sport)* to disqualify; *(Typ)* to justify; *Panne, Fehler, Möglichkeit etc* to rule out; **das eine schließt das andere nicht aus** the one does not exclude the other; **ich will nicht ~, dass er ein Dieb ist, aber ...** I don't want to rule out the possibility that he's a thief but ...; **die Öffentlichkeit ~** *(Jur)* to exclude the public → *auch* **ausgeschlossen**

aus|schließ|lich ['ausʃli:slɪç, 'aus'ʃl-, aus'ʃl-] ADJ *attr* exclusive; *Rechte* exclusive, sole ADV exclusively PREP *+gen* exclusive of, excluding

Aus|schließ|lich|keit F -, *no pl* exclusiveness

Aus|schließ|lich|keits|an|spruch M claim to sole rights

Aus|schlie|ßung F = **Ausschluss**

aus+schlüp|fen VI *sep aux sein* to slip out; *(aus Ei, Puppe)* to hatch out

Aus|schluss M *(= Entfernung)* exclusion; *(aus Gemeinschaft)* expulsion; *(vorübergehend)* suspension; *(Sport)* disqualification; *(Typ)* spacing material; **mit ~ von** *(dated)* with the exception of; **unter ~ der Öffentlichkeit stattfinden** to be closed to the public → **Rechtsweg**

Aus|schluss-: **Aus|schluss|frist** F time limit; **Aus|schluss|ver|fah|ren** NT disqualification system *or* procedure

aus+schmü|cken VT *sep* to decorate; *(fig) Erzählung* to embroider, to embellish; **~de Details** embellishments

Aus|schmü|ckung F -, -en decorating, decoration; *(fig: von Erzählung)* embroidery, embellishment

Aus|schnei|de|bo|gen M cutout sheet

aus+schnei|den VT *sep irreg* **a** *(= herausschneiden)* to cut out; *Zweige etc* to cut away; **~ und einfügen** *(Comput)* to cut and paste **b** *Baum etc* to prune → *auch* **ausgeschnitten**

Aus|schnitt M **a** *(= Zeitungsausschnitt)* cutting, clipping **b** *(Math)* sector **c** *(= Kleidausschnitt)* neck; **ein tiefer ~** a low neckline; **er versuchte, ihr in den ~ zu schauen** he was trying to look down her dress **d** *(fig: = Teil)* part; *(aus einem Bild)* detail; *(aus einem Roman)* excerpt, extract; *(aus einem Film)* clip; **ich kenne das Buch/den Film nur in ~en** I only know parts of the book/film

aus|schnitt|wei|se ADJ partial; *Veröffentlichung* in extracts; **bei ~m Lesen** by reading sections ADV *wahrnehmen, vermitteln, erfassen* partially; **etw ~ sehen/hören/zitieren** to see/hear/quote parts of sth

aus+schnit|zen VT *sep* to carve out

aus+schnüf|feln VT *sep (inf)* to ferret *or* nose out *(Brit inf)*, to sniff out

aus+schöp|fen VT *sep* **a** *(= herausschöpfen) Wasser etc* to ladle out *(aus of)*; *(aus Boot)* to bale out *(aus of)* **b** *(= leeren)* to empty; *Fass etc* to drain, to empty; *Boot* to bale out; *(fig)* to exhaust; **die Kompetenzen voll ~** to do everything within one's power

aus+schrei|ben VT *sep irreg* **a** *(in Buchstaben) Zahlen* to write out; *(= ungekürzt schreiben) Namen, Abkürzung* to write (out) in full **b** *(= ausstellen) Rechnung etc* to make out; *Rezept, Überweisung* to write out **c** *(= bekannt machen)* to announce; *Versammlung, Wahlen* to call; *Stellen* to advertise; *Projekt, Auftrag* to invite tenders for; *Grundstück (zum Verkauf)* to advertise; **etw öffentlich/europaweit ~** *(Stelle)* to advertise sth to the general public/throughout Europe; **jdn zur Fahndung/Festnahme ~** to put sb on the wanted list; **einen Haftbefehl auf jdn ~** to make out a warrant for sb's arrest

Aus|schrei|bung F **a** *(= Bekanntmachung)* announcement; *(von Versammlung, Wahlen)* calling; *(von Projekt)* invitation of tenders *(+gen* for); *(von Stellen)* advertising **b** *(= Ausstellung) (von Rechnung)* making out

aus+schrei|en *sep irreg* VT **a** = **ausrufen** **b** *(= schreien)* **sich** *(dat)* **die Kehle** *or* **Lunge ~** *(inf)* to shout one's head off *(inf)* **c** *(= ausbuhen)* to shout down VR *(inf: = zu Ende schreien)* to finish shouting VI to finish shouting

aus+schrei|ten *sep irreg* VI *aux sein (geh)* to stride out, to step out VT to pace

Aus|schrei|tung F -, -en *usu pl (= Aufruhr)* riot, rioting *no pl*; *(dated: = Ausschweifung)* excess

aus+schu|len *sep* VT **ausgeschult werden** to leave school VI *aux sein (Aus)* to leave school

Aus|schuss M **a** *no pl (Comm)* rejects *pl*; *(fig inf)* trash **b** *(= Komitee)* committee **c** *(eines Geschosses)* exit point; *(= Wunde)* exit wound

Aus|schuss-: **Aus|schuss|mit|glied** NT committee member; **Aus|schuss|öff|nung** F point of exit, exit point; *(= Wunde)* exit wound; **Aus|schuss|sit|zung** F committee meeting; **Aus|schuss|wa|re** F *(Comm)* rejects *pl*

aus+schüt|teln VT *sep* to shake out

aus+schüt|ten *sep* VT **a** *(= auskippen)* to tip out; *Eimer, Glas, Füllhorn* to empty; **jdm sein Herz ~** *(fig)* to pour out one's heart to sb → **Kind** **b** *(= verschütten)* to spill **c** *(Fin) Dividende etc* to distribute VR **sich (vor Lachen) ~** *(inf)* to split one's sides laughing

Aus|schüt|tung F -, -en **a** *(Fin)* distribution; *(von Dividende)* dividend **b** *(Phys)* fallout

aus+schwär|men VI *sep aux sein (Bienen, Menschen)* to swarm out; *(Mil)* to fan out

aus+schwe|feln VT *sep* to sulphur *(Brit)*, to sulfur *(US)*, to fumigate (with sulphur *(Brit) or* sulfur *(US)*)

aus+schwei|fen *sep* VI *aux sein (Redner)* to digress; *(Fantasie)* to run riot; *(in Lebensweise)* to lead a dissipated life VT *Möbelstück* to curve

aus|schwei|fend ADJ *Leben* dissipated; *Fantasie* wild

Aus|schwei|fung F *(= Maßlosigkeit)* excess; *(in Lebensweise)* dissipation

aus+schwei|gen VR *sep irreg* to remain silent *(über +acc, zu* about); **sich eisern ~** to maintain a stony silence

aus+schwem|men VT *sep* to wash out; *Giftstoffe* to flush out *(aus* of); *(= aushöhlen)* to hollow out

aus+schwen|ken *sep* VT *(= ausspülen)* to rinse out VI *aux sein* **a** *(Mil)* to wheel; **nach links/rechts ~** to wheel left/right **b** *(Kran, Boot)* to swing out

aus+schwit|zen *sep* VT to sweat out; *(Wände)* to sweat VI *aux sein* to sweat

aus+seg|nen VT *sep (Eccl) Toten* to give the last blessing to

Aus|seg|nungs|hal|le F chapel of rest

aus+se|hen VI *sep irreg* **a** to look; **gut ~** to look good; *(hübsch)* to be good looking; *(gesund)* to look well; **gesund/elend ~** to look healthy/wretched; **zum Fürchten ~** to look frightening; **es sieht nach Regen aus** it looks like rain, it looks as if it's going to rain; **wie jd/etw ~** to look like sb/sth; **weißt du, wie ein Gnu aussieht?** do you know what a gnu looks like?; **wie siehts aus?** *(inf: = wie stehts)* how's things? *(esp Brit inf)*, how are things going?; **wie siehst du denn (bloß) aus?** what DO you look like?, just look at you!; **ich habe (vielleicht) ausgesehen!** you should have seen me!; **er sieht nach nichts aus** he doesn't look (like) anything special; **es soll nach etwas ~** it's got to look good; **es sieht danach** *or* **so aus, als ob ...** it looks as if ...; **ihr seht mir danach aus** *(iro)* I bet!; **seh ich so** *or* **danach aus?** *(inf)* what do you take me for?; **so siehst du (gerade) aus!** *(inf)* that's what you think!; **er sieht ganz so** *or* **danach aus** he looks it; **es sieht nicht gut mit ihm aus** things don't look good for him; **bei mir sieht es gut aus** I'm doing fine
b *(geh: = Ausschau halten)* to look out *(nach* for)

Aus|se|hen NT -s, *no pl* appearance; **dem ~ nach** to go by appearances, by the looks of it; **etw dem ~ nach beurteilen** to judge sth by appearances

aus sein *irreg aux sein* VI *(inf)* **a** *(= zu Ende sein) (Schule)* to be out, to have finished; *(Krieg, Stück)* to have ended; *(= nicht an sein) (Feuer, Ofen)* to be out; *(Radio, Fernseher etc)* to be off; *(Sport) (= außerhalb sein: Ball)* to be out (of play); *(= ausgeschieden sein: Spieler)* to be out
b **auf etw** *(acc)* **~** to be (only) after sth *or* interested in sth *or* out for sth; **auf jdn ~** to be after sb *(inf)*; **nur auf Männer/auf eins ~** to be interested only in men/one thing
c *(= ausgehen)* **ich war gestern Abend (mit ihr) aus** I went out (with her) last night
VI *impers* **es ist aus (und vorbei) zwischen uns** it's (all) over between us; **es ist aus mit ihm** he is finished, he has had it *(inf)*; **es ist aus (und vorbei) mit dem bequemen Leben** the life of leisure is (all) over; **daraus ist nichts geworden, damit ist es aus** nothing came of it, it's finished *or* all over

au|ßen ['ausn] ADV **a** **die Tasse ist ~ bemalt** the cup is painted on the outside; **~ an der Windschutzscheibe** on the outside of the windscreen *(Brit) or* windshield *(US)*; **von ~ sieht es gut aus** outwardly *or* on the outside it looks good; **er läuft ~** he's running on the outside; **er spielt ~** he's playing on the wing; **das Fenster geht nach ~ auf** the window opens outwards; **nach ~ hin** *(fig)* outwardly; **etw nach ~ tragen** *(fig)* to make sth public; **~ stehend** *(Beobachter etc)* outside *attr* **b** **~ vor sein** to be left out; **etw ~ vor lassen** *(= etw ausschließen)* to leave sth out, to exclude sth **c** *(Aus)* = **draußen**

Au|ßen ['ausn] M -, - *(Sport)* wing; **~ spielen** to play on the wing

Au|ßen NT -, *no pl* outside

Au|ßen-: **Au|ßen|ab|mes|sung** F external dimensions *pl*; **Au|ßen|an|sicht** F exterior, view of the outside; **Au|ßen|an|ten|ne** F outdoor aerial *(Brit) or* antenna *(esp US)*; **Au|ßen|ar|bei|ten** PL work on the exterior; **Au|ßen|auf|nah|me** F outdoor shot, exterior; **Au|ßen|bahn** F outside lane; **Au|ßen|be|leuch|tung** F exterior lighting; **Au|ßen|be|zirk** M outlying district; **Au|ßen|bor|der** ['ausnbɔrdɐ] M -s, - *(inf)* outboard; **Au|ßen|bord|mo|tor** M outboard motor; **au|ßen|bords** ['ausnbɔrts] ADV *(Naut)* outboard; **Au|ßen|deich** M outside dyke

aus+sen|den VT *sep irreg* to send out

Au|ßen|dienst M external duty; **im ~ sein** to work outside the office; **~ machen** *or* **haben** to work outside the office

Au|ßen|dienst|mit|ar|bei|ter(in) M(F) sales representative

Au|ßen-: **Au|ßen|flä|che** F outside, outside *or* exterior surface; *(= Flächeninhalt)* external surface area; **Au|ßen|ha|fen** M outer harbour *(Brit) or* harbor *(US)*; *(= Hafenstadt)* port

Au|ßen|han|del M foreign trade

Au|ßen|han|dels-: **Au|ßen|han|dels|be|zie|hun|gen** PL foreign trade relations *pl*; **Au|ßen|han|dels|bi|lanz** F balance of trade; **Au|ßen|han|dels|po|li|tik** F foreign trade policy

Au|ßen-: **Au|ßen|haut** F outer skin; **Au|ßen|kur|ve** F outside bend; **Au|ßen|li|nie** F *(Sport)* boundary (line); **Au|ßen|mi|nis|ter(in)** M(F) foreign minister, foreign secretary *(Brit)*, secretary of state *(US)*; **Au|ßen|mi|nis|te|ri|um** NT foreign ministry, Foreign Office *(Brit)*, State Department *(US)*; **Au|ßen|netz** NT *(Ftbl)* side netting; **Au|ßen|po|li|tik** F *(Gebiet)* foreign politics *sing*; *(bestimmte)* foreign policy; **Au|ßen|po|li|ti|ker(in)** M(F) foreign affairs politician; **au|ßen|po|li|tisch** ADJ *Debatte, Einfluss, Sprecher* on foreign affairs; *Schaden* to foreign affairs; *Fehler* as regards foreign affairs; *Berichterstattung* of foreign affairs; *Schulung, Erfahrung* in foreign affairs; **~e Angelegenheiten** foreign affairs; **aus ~er Sicht** from the point of view of foreign affairs; **ein Experte auf ~em Gebiet** an expert on foreign affairs ADV in terms of foreign policy; **~ sinnvoll sein** to be sensible foreign policy; **~ gesehen** from the point of view of foreign affairs; **Au|ßen|sei|te** F outside; **die vordere ~ des Hauses** the front of the house

Au|ßen|sei|ter ['ausnzaitɐ] M **-s, -**, **Au|ßen|sei|te|rin** [-ərɪn] F **-, -nen** *(Sport, fig)* outsider

Au|ßen|sei|ter-: **Au|ßen|sei|ter|rol|le** F role as an outsider; **eine ~ spielen** to play the role of an outsider; **Au|ßen|sei|ter|tum** ['ausnzaitɐtu:m] NT **-s**, *no pl* being an outsider; **das ~ als literarisches Thema** the outsider as a literary theme

Au|ßen-: **Au|ßen|spie|gel** M *(Aut)* outside mirror; **Au|ßen|stän|de** PL *(esp Comm)* outstanding debts *pl*, arrears *pl*; **wir haben noch 2.000 Euro ~** we still have *or* there are still 2,000 euros outstanding; **au|ßen|ste|hend** ADJ → **außen a**; **Au|ßen|ste|hen|de(r)** ['ausnʃte:əndə] MF *decl as adj* outsider; **Au|ßen|stel|le** F branch; **Au|ßen|stür|mer(in)** M(F) *(Ftbl)* wing; **Au|ßen|ta|sche** F outside pocket; **Au|ßen|tem|pe|ra|tur** F outside temperature; *(außerhalb Gebäude)* outdoor temperature; **wir haben 20° ~** the temperature outdoors is 20°; **Au|ßen|tem|pe|ra|tur|an|zei|ge** F *(Aut)* external temperature gauge; **Au|ßen|toi|let|te** F outside toilet; *(auf dem Flur)* shared toilet; **Au|ßen|trep|pe** F outside staircase; **Au|ßen|wand** F outer wall; **Au|ßen|welt** F outside world; **Au|ßen|wer|bung** F outdoor advertising; **Au|ßen|win|kel** M *(Math)* exterior angle; **Au|ßen|wirt|schaft** F foreign trade; **Au|ßen|zoll** M external tariff

au|ßer ['ausɐ] PREP +*dat or (rare) gen* **a** *(räumlich)* out of; **~ Sicht/Gefecht/Kurs** *etc* out of sight/action/circulation *etc*; **~ sich** *(acc)* **geraten** to go wild; **~ sich** *(dat)* **sein** to be beside oneself; **~ Haus** *or* **Hauses sein/essen** to be/eat out; **~ Atem** out of breath → **Acht**, **Betrieb b**, **Land c** **b** *(= ausgenommen)* except (for); *(= abgesehen von)* apart from, aside from *(esp US)*; **~ ihm habe ich keine Verwandten mehr** I have no relatives left apart from him *or* left but him **c** *(= zusätzlich zu)* in addition to CONJ except; **~ dass ...** except that ...; **~ wenn ...** except when...; **~ sonntags** except Sundays

Au|ßer-: **Au|ßer|acht|las|sung** [ausɐ'laxtlasʊŋ] F **-**, *no pl* disregard; **unter ~ der Regeln** in total disregard of the rules, with total disregard for the rules; **au|ßer|amt|lich** ADJ unofficial; **au|ßer|be|trieb|lich** ADJ *Veranstaltung, Regelung* private; *Tätigkeiten, Arbeitsplätze* outside; *Berufsbildungsstätte* external ADV *veranstalten, regeln* privately; *ausbilden* externally; **sie treffen sich auch ~** they also meet outside work

au|ßer|dem ['ausɐde:m, ausɐ'de:m] ADV besides; *(= dazu)* in addition, as well; *(= überdies)* anyway; **ich kann ihn nicht leiden, (und) ~ lügt er immer** I can't stand him and besides *or* anyway he always tells lies; **er ist Professor und ~ noch Gutachter** he's a professor and a consultant besides *or* as well

au|ßer|dienst|lich ADJ *(= nicht dienstlich) Telefonat, Angelegenheit* private; *(= außerhalb der Arbeitszeit)* social ADV **ich bin heute ~ unterwegs** I'm not on business today; **dürfte ich Sie mal ~ sprechen?** could I speak to you privately?

au|ßer|ehe|lich ADJ extramarital; *Kind* illegitimate; **ein ~es Verhältnis haben** to have an extramarital affair ADV outside marriage; **das Kind war ~ gezeugt worden** the child had been conceived out of wedlock

äu|ße|re(r, s) ['ɔysərə] ADJ *(= außerhalb gelegen, Geog)* outer; *Durchmesser, Verletzung* external; *(= außenpolitisch)* external; *Schein, Eindruck* outward

Äu|ße|re(s) ['ɔysərə] NT *decl as adj* exterior; *(fig: = Aussehen auch)* outward appearance; **das ~ täuscht oft** appearances are often deceptive; **Minister des ~n** *(form)* foreign minister, foreign secretary *(Brit)*, secretary of state *(US)*

Au|ßer-: **au|ßer|eu|ro|pä|isch** ADJ *attr* non-European; *Raum* outside Europe; **au|ßer|fahr|plan|mä|ßig** ADJ nonscheduled ADV **dieser Zug verkehrt ~** this train is running outside of the normal timetable; **au|ßer|ge|richt|lich** ADJ, ADV out of court; **au|ßer|ge|setz|lich** ADJ extralegal; *(= gesetzbrecherisch)* illegal; **au|ßer|ge|wöhn|lich** ADJ unusual, out of the ordinary; *(= sehr groß)* remarkable; **Außergewöhnliches leisten** to do some remarkable things ADV *(= sehr)* extremely

au|ßer|halb ['ausɐhalp] PREP +*gen* outside; **~ der Stadt** outside the town, out of town; **~ der Dienststunden** out of *or* outside office hours; **~ der Legalität** outside the law ADV *(= außen)* outside; *(= außerhalb der Stadt)* out of town; **~ wohnen/arbeiten** to live/work out of town; **nach ~** outside; *(der Stadt)* out of town; **von ~** from outside/out of town; **~ stehen** *(fig)* to be on the outside

Au|ßer-: **au|ßer|ir|disch** ADJ extraterrestrial; **Au|ßer|ir|di|sche(r)** ['ausɐlɪrdɪʃə] MF *decl as adj* extraterrestrial; **au|ßer|kirch|lich** ADJ nonecclesiastic(al); *Trauung* civil; **Au|ßer|kraft|set|zung** [ausɐ'kraftzɛtsʊŋ] F **-, -en** repeal; **Au|ßer|kurs|set|zung** [ausɐ'kʊrszɛtsʊŋ] F **-, -en** *(von Währung)* withdrawal (from circulation); *(fig)* rejection

äu|ßer|lich ['ɔysɐlɪç] ADJ **a** external; **„nur ~!"**, **„nur zur ~en Anwendung!"** for external use only **b** *(fig: = oberflächlich)* superficial; *(= scheinbar)* outward; *(esp Philos) Wahrnehmung* external; **einer Sache** *(dat)* **~ sein** *(geh)* to be extrinsic to sth ADV **a** externally; **~ schien er unverletzt** he seemed to have no external injuries **b** *(fig)* *(= oberflächlich)* outwardly, superficially; **sie wirkt ~ jung** in terms of appearance she seems young; **rein ~ betrachtet** on the face of it

Äu|ßer|lich|keit F **-, -en** **a** *(fig)* triviality; *(= Oberflächlichkeit)* superficiality; *(= Formalität)* formality **b** *(lit)* external characteristic; **~en** *pl* (outward) appearances

äu|ßerln ['ɔysɐln] VTI *infin only (Aus)* **einen Hund ~ (führen)** to take a dog for a walk

äu|ßern ['ɔysɐn] ✪ 33.3 VT *(= sagen)* to say; *Wunsch etc* to express; *Worte* to utter; *Kritik* to voice; **seine Meinung ~** to give one's opinion *or* views VR *(Mensch)* to speak; *(Krankheit, Symptom)* to show *or* manifest itself; **sich dahin gehend ~, dass ...** to make a comment to the effect that ...; **ich will mich dazu nicht ~** I don't want to say anything about that

Au|ßer-: **au|ßer|or|dent|lich** ['ausɐ'ɔrdntlɪç] ADJ extraordinary; *(= ungewöhnlich)* exceptional; *(= bemerkenswert)* remarkable, exceptional; *Professor* associate; **~e Hauptversammlung** extraordinary general meeting; **Außerordentliches leisten** to achieve some remarkable things ADV *(= sehr)* exceptionally, extremely, extraordinarily; **au|ßer|orts** ['ausɐlɔrts] ADV *(Sw, Aus)* out of town; **au|ßer|par|la|men|ta|risch** ADJ extraparliamentary; **au|ßer|plan|mä|ßig** ADJ *Besuch, Treffen, Sitzung* unscheduled; *Mahlzeit* additional; *Ausgaben* unbudgeted; *Defizit* unplanned ADV **sie trafen sich ~** they had an unscheduled meeting; **dieser Bus verkehrt ~** this bus is running outside of the normal timetable; **au|ßer|schu|lisch** ADJ *Aktivitäten, Interessen* extracurricular; **au|ßer|sinn|lich** ADJ extrasensory; **~e Wahrnehmung** extrasensory perception

äu|ßerst ['ɔysɛst] ADV extremely, exceedingly ADJ → **äußerste(r, s)**

au|ßer|stan|de, **au|ßer Stan|de** [ausɐ'ʃtandə, 'ausɐʃtandə] ADV *(= unfähig)* incapable; *(= nicht in der Lage)* unable; **~ sein, etw zu tun** to be incapable of doing sth, to be unable to do sth → *auch* **Stand**

äu|ßers|ten|falls ADV at most

äu|ßers|te(r, s) ['ɔysɛstə] ADJ *superl von* **äußere(r, s)** *(räumlich)* furthest; *Planet, Schicht* outermost; *Norden etc* extreme; *(zeitlich)* latest possible; *(fig)* utmost, extreme; **der ~ Preis** the last price; **mein ~s Angebot** my final offer; **im ~n Falle** if the worst comes to the worst, if worst comes to worst *(US)*; **mit ~r Kraft** with all one's strength; **von ~r Dringlichkeit/Wichtigkeit** of (the) utmost urgency/importance

Äu|ßers|te(s) ['ɔysɛstə] NT *decl as adj* **bis zum ~n gehen** to go to extremes; **er geht bis zum ~n** he would go to any extreme; **er hat sein ~s gegeben** he gave his all; **das ~ wagen** to risk everything; **ich bin auf das ~ gefasst** I'm prepared for the worst

au|ßer-: **au|ßer|ta|rif|lich** ADJ *Regelung* nonunion; *Zuschlag* supplementary to agreed union rates ADV **~ bezahlt werden** to be paid nonunion rates; **au|ßer|tour|lich** [-tu:ɐlɪç] *(Aus, S Ger)* ADJ additional; **ein ~er Bus** a special ADV in addition; **und ich mache ~ noch Überstunden** and I do overtime as well *or* on top

Äu|ße|rung ['ɔysərʊŋ] F **-, -en** *(= Bemerkung)* remark, comment; *(Ling: = Behauptung)* statement; *(= Zeichen)* expression; **Tränen als ~ der Trauer** tears as an expression of mourning

Äu|ße|rungs|form F manifestation

aus+set|zen *sep* VT **a** *Kind, Haustier* to abandon; *Wild, Fische* to release; *Pflanzen* to plant out; *(Naut) Passagiere* to maroon; *Boot* to lower **b** *(= preisgeben)* **jdn/etw einer Sache** *(dat)* **~** to expose sb/sth to sth; **jdm/einer Sache ausgesetzt sein** *(= ausgeliefert)* to be at the mercy of sb/sth; **jdn dem Gelächter ~** to expose sb to ridicule **c** *(= festsetzen) Belohnung, Preis* to offer; *(in Testament)* to bequeath, to leave; **auf jds Kopf** *(acc)* **1000 Dollar ~** to put 1,000 dollars on sb's head; **für Hinweise, die zur Ergreifung der Täter führen, sind 5.000 Euro Belohnung ausgesetzt** a reward of 5,000 euros is being offered for information leading to the arrest of the suspects **d** *(= unterbrechen)* to interrupt; *Debatte, Prozess* to adjourn; *Zahlung* to break off **e** *(= vertagen) Strafvollstreckung, Verfahren* to suspend; *Urteilsverkündung* to defer; **eine Strafe zur Bewährung ~** to give a suspended sentence **f** **an jdm/etw etwas auszusetzen haben** to find fault with sb/sth; **daran ist nichts auszusetzen** there is nothing wrong with it; **daran habe ich nur eines auszusetzen** I've only one objection to make to that; **was haben Sie daran auszusetzen?** what don't you like about it? **g** *Billardkugel* to place **h** *(Eccl)* to expose VI *(= aufhören)* to stop; *(Mensch)* to break off, to stop; *(bei Spiel)* to sit out; *(Herz)* to stop (beating); *(Motor)* to fail, to stop; *(= versagen)* to give out; **mit etw ~** to stop sth; **mit der Pille ~** to stop taking the pill; **mit der Behandlung ~** to interrupt the treatment; **zwei Wochen mit der Arbeit ~** to interrupt one's work for two weeks; **ich setze besser mal aus** I'd better have a break; *(bei Spiel)* I'd better sit this one out;

einen Tag ~ to take a day off; **ohne auszusetzen** without a break

Aus|set|zung F -, -en **a** *(von Kind, Tier)* abandonment; *(von Fischen, Wild)* release; *(von Pflanzen)* planting out; *(Naut) (von Passagieren)* marooning; *(von Boot)* lowering
b *(= Festsetzung) (von Belohnung)* offer; *(in Testament)* bequest; **durch ~ einer Belohnung** by offering a reward, by the offer of a reward
c *(= Unterbrechung)* interruption; *(von Debatte, Prozess)* adjournment; *(von Zahlung)* breaking off
d *(Jur) (von Vollstreckung, Verfahren)* suspension; *(von Urteilsverkündung)* deferment; **die ~ der Strafe zur Bewährung war in diesem Falle nicht möglich** it was impossible to give a suspended sentence in this case
e *(Eccl: des Allerheiligsten)* exposition

Aus|sicht F -, -en **a** *(= Blick)* view *(auf +acc* of); **ein Zimmer mit ~ auf den Park** a room overlooking the park; **jdm die ~ nehmen/verbauen** to block *or* obstruct sb's view
b *(fig)* prospect *(auf +acc* of); **die ~, dass etw geschieht** the chances of sth happening; **gute ~en haben** to have good prospects; **unser Plan hat große ~en auf Erfolg** our plan has every prospect *or* chance of succeeding; **keine ~** no prospect *or* chance; **nicht die geringste ~** not the slightest prospect *or* chance; **etw in ~ haben** to have good prospects of sth; **jdn/etw in ~ nehmen** *(form)* to take sb/sth into consideration; **jdm etw in ~ stellen** to promise sb sth; **in ~ stehen** to be in prospect; **das sind ja schöne ~en!** *(iro inf)* what a prospect!

Aus|sichts-: **aus|sichts|los** ADJ hopeless; *(= zwecklos)* pointless; **eine ~e Sache** a lost cause; **Aus|sichts|lo|sig|keit** F -, *no pl* hopelessness; *(= Zwecklosigkeit)* pointlessness; **Aus|sichts|platt|form** F viewing *or* observation platform *or* deck; **Aus|sichts|punkt** M viewpoint; *(fig)* vantage point; **aus|sichts|reich** ADJ promising; *Stellung* with good prospects; **Aus|sichts|turm** M observation *or* lookout tower; **aus|sichts|voll** ADJ promising; **Aus|sichts|wa|gen** M *(Rail)* observation car

aus+sie|ben VT *sep (lit, fig)* to sift out

aus+sie|deln VT *sep* to resettle; *(= evakuieren)* to evacuate

Aus|sied|ler(in) M(F) *(= Auswanderer)* emigrant; *(= Evakuierter)* evacuee

> **AUSSIEDLER**
>
> **Aussiedler** are people of German extraction in Eastern Europe and former Soviet Union countries who exercise their right to come and live in Germany. To help them integrate, **Aussiedler** are given financial support and up to six months of language classes. To limit the number of **Aussiedler**, local schemes are now being set up to help with housing, jobs and German-language education, to encourage people to stay where they are.

Aus|sied|ler|heim NT emigrant hostel

Aus|sied|lung F resettlement; *(= Evakuierung)* evacuation

aus+sit|zen VT *sep irreg Problem* to sit out

aus+söh|nen ['auszø:nən] *sep* VT **jdn mit jdm/etw ~** to reconcile sb with sb/to sth; **jdn ~** to appease sb VR **sich mit jdm/etw ~** to become reconciled with sb/to sth; **wir haben uns wieder ausgesöhnt** we have made it up again VI **mit etw ~** to compensate for sth

Aus|söh|nung F -, -en reconciliation *(mit jdm* with sb, *mit etw* to sth)

aus+son|dern VT *sep* **a** *(= auslesen)* to select; *Schlechtes* to pick out; *(euph) Menschen* to single out; **die ausgesonderte Ware wird billig abgegeben** the reject goods are sold cheaply **b** *(Physiol)* to secrete

Aus|son|de|rung F -, -en **a** selection; *(von Schlechtem)* picking out; *(euph: von Menschen)* singling out **b** *(Physiol)* secretion

aus+sor|gen VI *sep* **ausgesorgt haben** to have no more money worries, to be set up for life

aus+sor|tie|ren *ptp* **aussortiert** VT *sep* to sort out

aus+spä|hen *sep* VI **nach jdm/etw ~** to look out for sb/sth VT to spy out; *(Mil)* to reconnoitre

aus+span|nen *sep* VT **a** *Tuch, Netz* to spread out; *Schnur, Leine* to put up **b** *(= ausschirren)* to unharness, to unhitch; *Ochsen* to unyoke; *(aus Schreibmaschine) Bogen* to take out **c** *(fig inf)* **jdm etw ~** to do sb out of sth *(inf)*; **jdm die Freundin** *etc* **~** to pinch *(Brit inf) or* steal sb's girlfriend *etc* VI **a** *(= sich erholen)* to have a break **b** *(Pferde ausspannen)* to unharness the horses; *(Ochsen ausspannen)* to unyoke the oxen

Aus|span|nung F, *no pl (fig)* relaxation; **zur ~** for relaxation

aus+spa|ren VT *sep Fläche* to leave blank; *(fig)* to omit

Aus|spa|rung F -, -en *(= Lücke)* gap; *(= unbeschriebene Stelle)* blank space

aus+spei|en *sep irreg* VT *(= ausspucken)* to spit out; *(= erbrechen)* to bring up, to disgorge *(form)*; *(fig: = herausschleudern)* to spew out *or* forth VI to spit out; **das Ausspeien** spitting

aus+sper|ren VT *sep* to lock out

Aus|sper|rung F *(Ind)* lockout; **mit ~ drohen** to threaten (the workers with) a lockout; **die ~ sollte illegal sein** lockouts should be made illegal

aus+spie|len *sep* VT **a** *Karte* to play; *(am Spielanfang)* to lead with; **einen Trumpf ~** *(lit)* to play a trump (card); *(fig)* to play a *or* one's trump card; **seinen letzten Trumpf ~** *(fig)* to play one's last card
b *Rolle, Szene* to act out; **er hat (seine Rolle) ausgespielt** *(fig)* he's finished *or* through *(inf)*, he's played out *(inf)*
c *(= zu Ende spielen)* to finish playing
d *(fig: = einsetzen) Überlegenheit etc* to display
e *(fig)* **jdn/etw gegen jdn/etw ~** to play sb/sth off against sb/sth
f *(Sport) Pokal, Meisterschaft* to play for; *Gegner* to outplay
g *Gewinne* to give as a prize/as prizes
VI **a** *(Cards)* to play a card; *(als erster)* to lead; **wer spielt aus?** whose lead is it?, who has the lead?
b *(= zu Ende spielen)* to finish playing → *auch* **ausgespielt**

Aus|spie|lung F -, -en *(im Lotto)* payout

aus+spin|nen VT *sep irreg* to spin out; *(= sich ausdenken)* to think up

aus+spi|o|nie|ren *ptp* **ausspioniert** VT *sep Pläne etc* to spy out; *Person* to spy (up)on

aus+spot|ten VT *sep (S Ger, Sw, Aus)* = **verspotten**

Aus|spra|che F **a** pronunciation; *(= Art des Artikulierens)* articulation; *(= Akzent)* accent **b** *(= Meinungsaustausch)* discussion; *(= Gespräch)* talk; **es kam zu einer offenen ~ zwischen den beiden** they talked things out; **eine ~ herbeiführen** to bring things out into the open

Aus|spra|che-: **Aus|spra|che|an|ga|be** F, **Aus|spra|che|be|zeich|nung** F *(Ling)* phonetic transcription; **Aus|spra|che|wör|ter|buch** NT dictionary of pronunciation, pronouncing dictionary

aus|sprech|bar ADJ pronounceable; **leicht/schwer ~** easy/difficult to pronounce; **nicht ~** unpronounceable

aus+spre|chen *sep irreg* VT *Wort, Urteil etc* to pronounce; *Scheidung* to grant; *(= zu Ende sprechen) Satz* to finish; *(= äußern)* to express *(jdm* to sb); *Verdächtigung* to voice; *Warnung* to give, to deliver; **jdm ein Lob ~** to give sb a word of praise; **der Regierung sein Vertrauen ~** to pass a vote of confidence in the government
VR **a** *(Partner)* to talk things out; *(= sein Herz ausschütten, seine Meinung sagen)* to say what's on one's mind; **sich mit jdm (über etw** *acc***) ~** to have a talk with sb (about sth); *(= jdm sein Herz ausschütten)* to have a heart-to-heart (talk) with sb (about sth); **sich für/gegen etw ~** to declare *or* pronounce oneself in favour *(Brit) or* favor *(US)* of/against sth, to come out in favour *(Brit) or* favor *(US)* of/against sth; **sich entschieden gegen Doping ~** to take a firm anti-doping line
b *(Wort)* to be pronounced; **dieses Wort spricht sich leicht/schwer aus** this word is easy/difficult to pronounce
VI *(= zu Ende sprechen)* to finish (speaking) → *auch* **ausgesprochen**

aus+spren|gen VT *sep (mit Sprengstoff)* to blast out

aus+sprit|zen VT *sep* **a** *Flüssigkeit* to squirt out; *(sprühend)* to spray out **b** *Bottich* to flush (out); *(Med) Zahn etc* to rinse out; *Ohr* to syringe **c** *Feuer* to put out

Aus|spruch M remark; *(= geflügeltes Wort)* saying

aus+spu|cken *sep* VT to spit out; *(fig) Produkte* to pour *or* spew out; *(hum inf) Geld* to cough up *(inf)*; *Gelerntes* to regurgitate; **sie hat das ganze Essen wieder ausgespuckt** *(inf: = erbrochen)* she vomited *or* spewed *(inf)* the whole meal back up again VI to spit; **vor jdm ~** to spit at sb's feet; *(fig)* to spit upon sb

aus+spü|len VT *sep* to rinse (out); *(kräftiger)* to flush (out); *(Med, Geol)* to wash out; **sich** *(dat)* **den Mund ~** to rinse one's mouth (out)

Aus|spü|lung F *(Med)* irrigation; *(Geol)* erosion

aus+staf|fie|ren ['ausʃtafi:rən] *ptp* **ausstaffiert** VT *sep (inf)* to equip, to fit out; *jdn* to rig *or* kit *(Brit)* out; *(= herausputzen)* to dress up; **sein Roman ist mit sämtlichen Klischees ausstaffiert** his novel is peppered with clichés

Aus|staf|fie|rung F -, -en *(inf)* equipment, fittings *pl*; *(= Kleidung)* rig(-out) *(inf)*, outfit

Aus|stand M **a** *(= Streik)* strike, industrial action *(Brit)*; **im ~ sein** to be on strike; **in den ~ treten** to (go on) strike, to take industrial action *(Brit)* **b** *usu pl (Comm)* outstanding debt **c** **seinen ~ geben** to throw a leaving party

aus|stän|dig ADJ *(esp Aus)* outstanding

aus+stan|zen VT *sep Metallteil* to stamp out; *Loch* to punch (out)

aus+stat|ten ['ausʃtatn] VT *sep* to equip; *(= versorgen)* to provide, to furnish; *(mit Rechten)* to vest *(esp Jur)*; *(= möblieren)* to furnish; *Buch* to produce; **mit Intelligenz** *etc* **ausgestattet sein** to be endowed with intelligence *etc*; **ein Zimmer neu ~** to refurbish a room

Aus|stat|ter ['ausʃtatɐ] M -s, -, **Aus|stat|te|rin** [-ərɪn] F -, -nen **a** *(= Herrenausstatter)* gentleman's outfitter, haberdasher *(US)* **b** *(= Raumausstatter)* interior decorator; *(Firma)* (firm of) interior decorators *pl*, interior decorating company **c** *(Film, Theat etc)* set designer; *(Kostüme)* wardrobe designer

Aus|stat|tung F -, -en **a** *(= Ausrüstung)* equipment; *(Tech auch)* fittings *pl*; *(= Kapital)* provisions *pl*; *(von Zimmer etc)* furnishings *pl*; *(Theat)* décor and costumes *pl*; *(= Mitgift)* dowry; *(von Buch)* presentation **b** *(= das Ausstatten)* equipping; *(= Versorgung)* provision; *(mit Rechten)* vesting; *(= das Möblieren)* furnishing; *(von Buch)* production

Aus|stat|tungs-: **Aus|stat|tungs|film** M spectacular (film); **Aus|stat|tungs|stück** NT **a** *(Theat)* spectacular (show) **b** *(= Möbelstück)* piece of furniture

aus+ste|chen VT *sep irreg* **a** *Pflanzen, Unkraut* to dig up; *Torf, Plätzchen* to cut out; *Apfel* to core; *Graben* to dig (out) **b** *Augen (esp als Strafe)* to gouge out, to put out **c** *(fig) jdn (= verdrängen)* to push out; *(= übertreffen)* to outdo; **jdn bei einem Mädchen ~** to take sb's place in a girl's affections; **jdn beim Chef ~** to push sb out of favour *(Brit) or* favor *(US)* with the boss

Aus|stech|form F, **Aus|stech|förm|chen** NT *(Cook)* cutter

aus+ste|hen *sep irreg* VT *(= ertragen)* to endure; *(= erdulden auch)* to put up with; *Sorge, Angst* to

go through, to suffer; **ich kann ihn/so etwas nicht ~** I can't bear *or* stand him/anything like that; **jetzt ist es ausgestanden** now it's all over; **mit jdm viel auszustehen haben** to have to go through a lot with sb, to have to put up with a lot from sb
VI a *(= fällig sein)* to be due; *(Antwort)* to be still to come; *(Buch)* to be still to appear; *(Entscheidung)* to be still to be taken; *(Lösung)* to be still to be found; *(= noch zu erwarten sein)* to be still expected
b *(Schulden, Zahlung)* to be outstanding; **Geld ~ haben** to have money owing; **~de Forderungen** outstanding demands

aus+stei|gen VI *sep irreg aux sein* **a** *(aus Fahrzeug)* to get out *(aus* of); *(aus Bus, Zug etc auch)* to get off *(aus etw* sth), to alight *(aus* from) *(form)*; *(Comput inf)* to quit, to exit, to leave; *(Aviat sl)* to bale *or* bail out *(aus* of); *(fig: aus Gesellschaft)* to opt out; **alles ~!** everybody out!; *(von Schaffner)* all change!; **das Aussteigen während der Fahrt ist verboten** do not alight while train *etc* is in motion
b *(Sport: = aufgeben)* to give up, to retire *(aus* from); *(bei Wettrennen auch)* to drop out *(aus* of); **einen Gegenspieler ~ lassen** *(esp Ftbl)* to outplay an opponent
c *(inf: aus Geschäft etc)* to get out *(aus* of)

Aus|stei|ger(in) M(F) *(aus Gesellschaft)* person who opts out, dropout *(esp pej)*; *(aus Terroristenszene, Sekte, Prostitution)* dropout

aus+stel|len *sep* **VT a** *(= zur Schau stellen)* to display; *(auf Messe, in Museum etc)* to exhibit **b** *(= ausschreiben)* to make out *(jdm* to sb), to write (out) *(jdm* sb); *(= behördlich ausgeben)* to issue *(jdm etw* sb with sth, sth to sb); **einen Scheck auf jdn ~** to make out a cheque *(Brit)* or check *(US)* to sb, to make a cheque *(Brit)* or check *(US)* payable to sb; **eine Rechnung über EUR 500 ~** to make out a bill for EUR 500 **c** *(= ausschalten) Gerät* to turn *or* switch off **d** → **ausgestellt VI** to exhibit

Aus|stel|ler ['ausʃtɛlɐ] M **-s, -**, **Aus|stel|le|rin** [-ərın] F **-, -nen a** *(auf Messe)* exhibitor **b** *(von Dokument)* issuer; *(von Scheck)* drawer

Aus|stell|fens|ter NT *(Aut)* quarterlight *(Brit)*, vent (window) *(US)*

Aus|stel|lung F **a** *(= Kunstausstellung, Messe)* exhibition; *(= Blumenausstellung, Hundeausstellung etc)* show **b** *no pl (von Scheck, Rezept, Rechnung etc)* making out; *(behördlich)* issuing

Aus|stel|lungs-: **Aus|stel|lungs|be|su|cher(in)** M(F) visitor (to an/the exhibition); **Aus|stel|lungs|da|tum** NT date of issue; **Aus|stel|lungs|flä|che** F exhibition area; **Aus|stel|lungs|ge|län|de** NT exhibition site *or* area; **Aus|stel|lungs|hal|le** F exhibition hall; **Aus|stel|lungs|ka|ta|log** M exhibition catalogue *(Brit)* or catalog *(US)*; **Aus|stel|lungs|stand** M exhibition stand; **Aus|stel|lungs|stück** NT *(in Ausstellung)* exhibit; *(in Schaufenster etc)* display item; **Aus|stel|lungs|tag** M day of issue

Aus|stel|lungs|zent|rum NT exhibition centre *(Brit)* or center *(US)*

aus+stem|peln VI *sep (bei Arbeitsende)* to clock out *or* off

Aus|ster|be|etat M *(hum)* **auf dem ~ stehen** *or* **sein** to be being phased out; **etw auf den ~ setzen** to phase sth out

aus+ster|ben VI *sep irreg aux sein* to die out; *(esp Spezies, Geschlecht auch)* to become extinct; **die Dummen sterben nie aus** there's one born every minute → *auch* **ausgestorben**

Aus|ster|ben NT extinction; **im ~ begriffen** dying out, becoming extinct; **vom ~ bedroht sein** to be threatened by extinction

Aus|steu|er F dowry

aus+steu|ern VT *sep* **a** *(Insur)* to disqualify **b** *Gerät, Sound* to balance; **schlecht ausgesteuerte Musik** music with poor sound balance

Aus|steu|e|rung F *(Insur)* disqualification

Aus|steu|e|rungs|au|to|ma|tik F automatic tuning

Aus|steu|er|ver|si|che|rung F endowment insurance *(for one's daughter's wedding etc)*

Aus|stieg M **a** *no pl (= das Aussteigen)* climbing out *(aus* of); *(aus Bus, Zug etc)* getting out *or* off, alighting *(aus* from) *(form)*; *(fig: aus Gesellschaft)* opting out *(aus* of); **der ~ aus der Kernenergie** abandoning nuclear energy; **der ~ aus einer Organisation** withdrawal from an organization **b** *(= Ausgang)* exit **c** *(auch* **Ausstiegluke**) exit *or* escape hatch

Aus|stiegs|lu|ke F *(Tech: aus Raumfahrzeug etc)* exit hatch; *(für Notfall)* escape hatch

aus+stop|fen VT *sep Kissen etc, Tiere* to stuff; *Ritzen* to fill; **sich** *(dat)* **den Bauch ~** to pad one's stomach

aus+stöp|seln VT *sep (Elec)* to unplug

Aus|stoß M **a** *(esp Phys, Tech: = das Ausstoßen)* expulsion, ejection, discharge; *(von Torpedo, Geschoss)* firing **b** *(= Ausschluss: aus Verein etc)* expulsion **c** *(= Produktion)* output, production

aus+sto|ßen VT *sep irreg* **a** *(= äußern)* to utter; *Schrei* to give; *Seufzer* to heave
b *(= ausschließen: aus Verein, Armee etc)* to expel *(aus* from); *(= verbannen)* to banish *(aus* from); **jdn aus der Gesellschaft ~** to banish sb from society, to cast sb out from society → **Ausgestoßene(r)**
c *(= herausstoßen)* to eject, to discharge; *Atem, Plazenta* to expel; *Gas etc* to give off, to emit; *(Naut) Torpedo* to fire; *(= herstellen) Teile, Stückzahl* to put *or* turn out, to produce
d sich *(dat)* **ein Auge/einen Zahn ~** to lose an eye/a tooth; **jdm ein Auge ~** to put sb's eye out; **jdm einen Zahn ~** to knock sb's tooth out
e *(Ling) Laut* to drop

Aus|stoß|rohr NT *(Naut)* torpedo tube

Aus|sto|ßung ['ausʃto:sʊŋ] F **-, -en a** *(aus* from) *(= Ausschließung)* expulsion; *(aus der Gesellschaft)* banishment; *(aus einer Gemeinschaft)* exclusion **b** *(Ling: eines Lautes)* dropping

aus+strah|len *sep* **VT** to radiate *(auch fig)*; *esp Licht, Wärme auch* to give off; *(Rad, TV)* to transmit, to broadcast **VI** *aux sein* to radiate; *(esp Licht, Wärme auch)* to be given off; *(Schmerz)* to extend, to spread *(bis in +acc* as far as); **seine Freude strahlte auf die Zuhörer aus** his joy was communicated to the listeners

Aus|strah|lung F radiation; *(Rad, TV)* transmission, broadcast(ing); *(fig: von Ort)* aura; *(von Mensch)* charisma

aus+stre|cken *sep* **VT** to extend *(nach* towards); *Fühler auch* to put out; *Hand auch, Beine etc* to stretch out; *Zunge* to stick out *(nach* at); **mit ausgestreckten Armen** with arms extended **VR** to stretch (oneself) out

aus+strei|chen VT *sep irreg* **a** *Geschriebenes* to cross *or* strike *(Brit)* out, to delete; *(fig)* to obliterate; **jds Namen auf einer Liste ~** to cross *or* strike *(Brit)* sb's name off a list, to delete sb's name from a list **b** *(= glätten) Falten* to smooth out **c** *Backform (mit Fett)* to grease

aus+streu|en VT *sep* to scatter, to spread; *(fig) Gerücht* to spread, to put about; **die Garage mit Holzspänen ~** to cover the garage floor with wood shavings

aus+strö|men *sep* **VI** *aux sein* **a** *(= herausfließen)* to stream *or* pour out *(aus* of); *(= entweichen)* to escape *(aus* from) **b** *(= ausstrahlen)* **die Hitze, die vom Ofen ausströmt** the heat which is radiated from the stove; **etw strömt von jdm/etw aus** *(fig)* sb/sth radiates sth **VT** *Duft, Gas* to give off; *(= ausstrahlen) Wärme, Ruhe etc* to radiate

aus+stu|die|ren *ptp* **ausstudiert** VI *sep (inf)* to finish studying

aus+su|chen VT *sep* **a** *(= auswählen)* to choose; *(esp iro)* to pick; **such dir was aus!** choose *or* pick what you want, take your pick → *auch* **ausgesucht b** *(old: = durchsuchen)* to search

aus+tä|feln VT *sep* to panel

aus+ta|pe|zie|ren *ptp* **austapeziert** VT *sep* to paper

aus+ta|rie|ren *ptp* **austariert** VT *sep* **a** *(= ins Gleichgewicht bringen)* to balance **b** *(Aus: = Leergewicht feststellen)* to determine the tare weight of

Aus|tausch M exchange; *(= Ersatz)* replacement; *(Sport)* substitution; **im ~ für** *or* **gegen** in exchange for

aus|tausch|arm ADJ **~e Wetterlage** *weather situation with a rather limited exchange of air masses*

aus|tausch|bar ADJ exchangeable; *(= untereinander austauschbar)* interchangeable; *(= ersetzbar)* replaceable

Aus|tausch|bar|keit ['austauʃba:ɐkait] F **-,** *no pl* interchangeability; *(= Ersetzbarkeit)* replaceability

Aus|tausch|do|zent(in) M(F) exchange lecturer, visiting faculty member *(US)*

aus+tau|schen VT *sep (lit, fig)* to exchange *(gegen* for); *(= untereinander austauschen)* to interchange; *(= ersetzen)* to replace *(gegen* with); **er ist wie ausgetauscht** *(fig)* he's (become) a different person, he's completely changed

Aus|tausch-: **Aus|tausch|leh|rer(in)** M(F) exchange teacher; **Aus|tausch|mo|tor** M replacement engine; **Aus|tausch|pro|fes|sor(in)** M(F) exchange *(Brit)* or visiting *(US)* professor; **Aus|tausch|pro|gramm** NT *(für Schüler-, Studentenaustausch)* exchange programme *(Brit)* or program *(US)*; **Aus|tausch|schü|ler(in)** M(F) exchange student *or* pupil; **Aus|tausch|stu|dent(in)** M(F) exchange student; **aus|tausch|wei|se** ADV as part of an exchange; *(bei Studenten etc)* on an exchange basis

aus+tei|len VT *sep* to distribute *(unter +dat, an +acc* among); *(= aushändigen auch)* to hand out *(unter +dat, an +acc* to); *Spielkarten* to deal (out); *Essen* to serve; *Sakrament* to administer, to dispense; *Befehle* to give, to issue; *Prügel* to hand out, to administer

Aus|tei|lung F distribution; *(= Aushändigung auch)* handing out; *(von Essen etc)* serving; *(von Sakrament)* administration, dispensation

Aus|ter ['austɐ] F **-, -n** oyster

Aus|tern-: **Aus|tern|bank** F *pl* **-bänke** oyster bed *or* bank; **Aus|tern|fi|scher** M *(Orn)* oystercatcher; **Aus|tern|fi|sche|rei** F oyster fishing; **Aus|tern|park** M oyster farm *or* park; **Aus|tern|pilz** M oyster mushroom; **Aus|tern|scha|le** F oyster shell; **Aus|tern|so|ße** F oyster sauce; **Aus|tern|zucht** F oyster farm; *(= Austernzüchtung)* oyster farming

aus+tes|ten ['austɛstn] VT *sep* to test; *(Comput) Programm etc* to debug

Aus|til|gung F eradication; *(von Schädlingen auch, von Menschen)* extermination; *(von Erinnerung)* obliteration

aus+to|ben *sep* **VT** to work off *(an +dat* on) **VR a** *(Mensch)* to let off steam; *(= sich müde machen)* to tire oneself out; *(= ein wildes Leben führen)* to have one's fling; **ein Garten, wo sich die Kinder ~ können** a garden where the children can romp about; **hat sie sich jetzt ausgetobt?** has she cooled down now? **b** *(= abebben: Leidenschaft, Sturm, Fieber etc)* to die down

aus+tol|len VR *sep (= umherspringen etc)* to have a good romp; *(= Energie loswerden)* to let off steam; *(= sich amüsieren)* to let one's hair down

Aus|trag ['austra:k] M **-(e)s** [-gəs], *no pl* settlement, resolution; **zum ~ kommen** to be up for settlement; **zum ~ gelangen** to be settled *or* decided

aus+tra|gen *sep irreg* **VT a** *Problem, Frage* to deal with; *Duell, Wettkampf etc* to hold; **einen Streit mit jdm ~** to have it out with sb **b** *Waren, Post etc* to deliver **c ein Kind ~** to carry a child (through) to full term; *(= nicht abtreiben)* to have a child **d** *(= abmelden)* to sign out; *(= löschen) Zahlen, Daten* to take out; *(aus Liste, bei*

Buchung) jdn to cancel sb's name VR to sign out

Aus|trä|ger M delivery man/boy; *(von Zeitungen)* newspaper man/boy; **wir suchen Studenten als ~** we are looking for students to deliver newspapers

Aus|trä|ge|rin F delivery woman/girl; *(von Zeitungen)* newspaper woman/girl → *auch* **Austräger**

Aus|trag(s)|haus NT *(S Ger, Aus)* ≈ small house for farmers in retirement

Aus|tra|gung ['austra:gʊŋ] F **-, -en** *(Sport)* holding

Aus|tra|gungs|ort M *pl* **-orte** *(Sport)* venue

aus|trai|niert ['austreni:ɐt, 'austreni:ɐt] ADJ *(Sport)* well-prepared

Aust|ra|li|de(r) [austra'li:də] MF *decl as adj* Australoid

Aust|ra|li|en [aus'tra:liən] NT **-s** Australia; **~ und Ozeanien** Australasia

Aust|ra|li|er [aus'tra:liɐ] M **-s, -**, **Aust|ra|li|e|rin** [-iərɪn] F **-, -nen** Australian

aust|ra|lisch [aus'tra:lɪʃ] ADJ Australian; **Australischer Bund** the Commonwealth of Australia

Aust|ral|ne|ger(in) [aus'tra:l-] M(F) *(dated, neg!)* Australoid

aus+träu|men VT *sep* to finish dreaming; **sein Traum von Reichtümern ist ausgeträumt** *(fig)* his dream of riches is over

aus+trei|ben *sep irreg* VT **a** *(= vertreiben)* to drive out; *Teufel etc* to exorcise, to drive out; **..., dass es mir den Schweiß austrieb** ... until the sweat was pouring off me; **jdm etw ~** to cure sb of sth; *(esp durch Schläge)* to knock sth out of sb **b** *(Typ) Zeilen* to space out **c** *Vieh* to drive *or* turn out VI *(= sprießen)* to sprout

Aus|trei|bung ['austraibʊŋ] F **-, -en** expulsion; *(von Teufel etc)* exorcism, driving out, casting out *(esp old, liter)*

aus+tre|ten *sep irreg* VI *aux sein* **a** *(= herauskommen)* to come out *(aus* of); *(esp Blut)* to issue *(aus* from); *(= entweichen: Gas etc)* to escape *(aus* from, through) **b** *(Med: bei Bruch)* to protrude **c** *(= zur Toilette gehen)* to go to the toilet; *(Sch)* to be excused *(euph)* **d** *(= ausscheiden)* to leave *(aus etw* sth); *(formell)* to resign *(aus* from); *(aus politischer Gemeinschaft)* to withdraw *(aus* from) **e** *(Hunt)* to come out (into the open); **aus der Deckung ~** to break cover VT *Spur, Feuer etc* to tread out; *Schuhe* to wear out of shape → *auch* **ausgetreten**

Aus|tri|a|zis|mus [austria'tsɪsmʊs] M **-, Austriazismen** [-'tsɪsmən] *(Ling)* Austriacism

aus+trick|sen VT *sep (inf: Sport, fig)* to trick

aus+trin|ken VTI *sep irreg* to finish; **trink (deine Milch) aus!** drink (your milk) up

Aus|tritt M **a** *no pl (= das Heraustreten) (von Flüssigkeit)* outflow; *(= das Entweichen)* escape; *(von Kugel)* exit; *(esp von Eiter)* discharge; *(von Blut)* issue; *(Med: von Bruch)* protrusion **b** *(= das Ausscheiden)* leaving *no art (aus etc* sth); *(formell)* resignation *(aus* from); *(aus politischer Gemeinschaft)* withdrawal *(aus* from); **die ~e aus der Kirche häufen sich** there are more and more people leaving the church

Aus|tritts|er|klä|rung F (notice of) resignation

aust|ro-, Aust|ro- ['austro] *in cpds* Austro-; **aust|ro|ame|ri|ka|nisch** ADJ Austro-American

aus+trock|nen *sep* VI *aux sein* to dry out; *(Fluss etc)* to dry up; *(Kehle)* to become parched VT to dry out; *Fluss etc* to dry up; *Kehle* to make parched; *(= trockenlegen) Sumpf* to drain

Aus|trock|nung F **-n, -en** *usu sing* drying up; *(Med)* dehydration

aus+trom|meln VT *sep (Hist)* to announce on the drum; *(fig)* to shout from the rooftops

aus+trom|pe|ten *ptp* **austrompetet** VT *sep (inf)* to broadcast *(inf)*

aus+tüf|teln VT *sep (inf)* to work out; *(= ersinnen)* to think up

aus+üben VT *sep* **a** *Beruf, Kunst* to practise *(Brit)*, to practice *(US)*; *Aufgabe, Funktion, Amt* to perform; *(= innehaben) Amt* to hold **b** *Druck, Einfluss* to exert *(auf +acc* on); *Macht, Recht* to exercise; *Wirkung* to have *(auf +acc* on); **einen Reiz auf jdn ~** to have *or* hold an attraction for sb

aus|übend ADJ *Arzt, Rechtsanwalt, Künstler* practising *(Brit)*, practicing *(US)*; *Gewalt* executive

Aus|übung F **a** *(von Beruf, Kunst)* practice; *(von Aufgabe, Funktion, Amt)* performance; *(= das Innehaben: von Amt)* holding; **in ~ seines Dienstes/seiner Pflicht** *(form)* in the execution of his duty; **in ~ seines Berufs** *(form)* in pursuance of one's profession *(form)* **b** *(von Druck)* exertion; *(von Macht)* exercising

aus+ufern ['auslu:fɐn] VI *sep aux sein (Fluss)* to burst *or* break its banks; *(fig)* to get out of hand; *(Konflikt etc)* to escalate *(zu* into)

Aus|ver|kauf M (clearance) sale; *(wegen Geschäftsaufgabe)* closing-down sale; *(fig: = Verrat)* sellout; **etw im ~ kaufen** to buy sth at the sale(s)

aus+ver|kau|fen *ptp* **ausverkauft** VT *sep* to sell off, to clear

Aus|ver|kaufs|wa|re F sale goods *pl*, sale merchandise *(US)*

aus|ver|kauft ['ausfɛɐkauft] ADJ sold out; **vor ~em Haus spielen** to play to a full house

aus|ver|schämt ADJ, ADV *(dial)* = **unverschämt**

aus+wach|sen *sep irreg* VR **a** *(= verschwinden)* to disappear **b** *(= sich entwickeln)* **sich zu etw ~** *(fig: Streit etc)* to turn into sth VI *aux sein* **a das ist (ja) zum Auswachsen** *(inf)* it's enough to drive you mad *(Brit inf) or* crazy, it's enough to drive you round the bend *(Brit inf) or* up a tree *(US inf)*; **zum Auswachsen langweilig** *(inf)* incredibly boring → *auch* **ausgewachsen b** *(= herauswachsen: gefärbte Haare)* to grow out

Aus|wahl F selection *(an +dat* of); *(= Angebot auch)* range; *(= Wahl)* choice; *(= die Besten)* pick; *(= Vielfalt)* variety; *(Sport)* representative team; **ohne ~** indiscriminately; **viel/eine reiche ~** a large/wide selection *or* range; **hier gibt es keine ~** there is no choice; **viele Sachen zur ~ haben** to have many things to choose from; **drei Bewerber stehen zur ~** there are three applicants to choose from, there is a choice of three applicants; **jdm drei Sachen zur ~ vorlegen** to offer sb a choice of three things; **eine ~ treffen** *(= eines auswählen)* to make a choice; *(= einige auswählen)* to make a selection

Aus|wahl-: **Aus|wahl|ant|wort** F answer (to a/the multiple choice question); **Aus|wahl|band** [-bant] M *pl* **-bände** selection

aus+wäh|len VT *sep* to select, to choose *(unter +dat* from among); **sich** *(dat)* **etw ~** to select *or* choose sth (for oneself) → *auch* **ausgewählt**

Aus|wahl-: **Aus|wahl|kom|mis|si|on** F selection committee *or* commission; **Aus|wahl|kri|te|ri|um** F selection criterion; **Aus|wahl|mann|schaft** F representative team; **Aus|wahl|mög|lich|keit** F choice; **Aus|wahl|prin|zip** NT selection principle, criterion; **Aus|wahl|sen|dung** F (selection of) samples; **Aus|wahl|spie|ler(in)** M(F) representative player; **Aus|wahl|ver|fah|ren** NT selection procedure

aus+wal|zen VT *sep* **a** *Metall* to roll out **b** *(fig)* to go to town on; *Thema auch* to drag out

Aus|wan|de|rer M, **Aus|wan|de|rin** F emigrant

Aus|wan|de|rer-: **Aus|wan|de|rer|schiff** NT emigrant ship; **Aus|wan|de|rer|vi|sum** NT emigration visa

aus+wan|dern VI *sep aux sein* to emigrate *(nach, in +acc* to); *(Volk)* to migrate

Aus|wan|de|rung F emigration; *(= Massenauswanderung)* migration

aus|wär|tig ['ausvɛrtɪç] ADJ *attr* **a** *(= nicht ansässig)* nonlocal; *Schüler, Mitglied* from out of town **b** *(Pol)* foreign; **der ~e Dienst** the foreign service; **das Auswärtige Amt** the Foreign Ministry, the Foreign Office *(Brit)*, the State Department *(US)*; **der Minister des Auswärtigen** *(form)* the foreign minister, the foreign secretary *(Brit)*, the secretary of state *(US)*

Aus|wär|ti|ge(r) ['ausvɛrtɪgə] MF *decl as adj* non-local (person), stranger

aus|wärts ['ausvɛrts] ADV **a** *(= nach außen)* outwards **b** *(= außerhalb des Hauses)* away from home; *(= außerhalb der Stadt)* out of town; *(Sport)* away; **von ~ anrufen** to call long distance; **~ essen** to eat out; **~ sprechen** *(hum inf)* to speak foreign *(hum inf)*

Aus|wärts-: **Aus|wärts|nie|der|la|ge** F *(Sport)* away defeat; **Aus|wärts|sieg** M *(Sport)* away win *or* victory; **Aus|wärts|spiel** NT *(Sport)* away (match *or* game); **Aus|wärts|tor** NT *(Ftbl)* away goal

aus+wa|schen *sep irreg* VT to wash out; *(= spülen)* to rinse (out); *(Geol)* to erode VR *(Farbe)* to wash out

aus|wech|sel|bar ADJ (ex)changeable; *(= untereinander auswechselbar)* interchangeable; *(= ersetzbar)* replaceable

aus+wech|seln *sep* VT to change; *(esp gegenseitig)* to exchange; *(= ersetzen)* to replace; *(Sport)* to substitute *(gegen* for); **er ist wie ausgewechselt** *(fig)* he's a changed *or* different person VI *(Sport)* to bring on a substitute, to make a substitution

Aus|wech|sel|spie|ler(in) M(F) substitute

Aus|wech|se|lung ['ausvɛksəlʊŋ] F **-, -en**, **Aus|wechs|lung** ['ausvɛkslʊŋ] F **-, -en** exchange; *(= Ersatz)* replacement; *(Sport)* substitution

Aus|weg M way out; *(fig: = Lösung auch)* solution; **der letzte ~** a last resort; **er sieht** *or* **weiß keinen anderen ~ als ...** he can see no other way out but ...; **sich** *(dat)* **einen ~ offenlassen** *or* **offenhalten** to leave oneself an escape route *or* a way out

Aus|weg-: **aus|weg|los** ADJ *(fig)* hopeless; **Aus|weg|lo|sig|keit** F **-**, *no pl (fig)* hopelessness

aus+wei|chen VI *sep irreg aux sein* **a** *(= Hindernis, Gefahr umgehen)* to get out of the way *(+dat* of); *(= Platz machen)* to make way *(+dat* for); **nach rechts ~** to get out of the way/to make way by going to the right **b** *(= zu entgehen versuchen) (lit)* to get out of the way; *(fig)* to evade the issue; **einer Sache** *(dat)* **~** *(lit)* to avoid sth; *(fig)* to evade *or* dodge *(inf)* sth; **jdm/einer Begegnung ~** to avoid sb/a meeting; **dem Feind ~** to avoid (contact with) the enemy; **eine ~de Antwort** an evasive answer **c auf etw** *(acc)* **~** *(fig)* to switch to sth

Aus|weich-: **Aus|weich|flug|ha|fen** M alternative airport; **Aus|weich|gleis** NT *(Rail)* siding; **Aus|weich|la|ger** NT reserve depot *or* store; **Aus|weich|ma|nö|ver** NT evasive action *or* manoeuvre *(Brit) or* maneuver *(US)*; **Aus|weich|mög|lich|keit** F *(fig)* alternative; *(auf Straße)* possibility of getting out of the way; **Aus|weich|quar|tier** NT alternative accommodation; **Aus|weich|stel|le** F *(auf Straßen)* passing place; **Aus|weich|stre|cke** F *(Mot)* alternative road *or* route; *(kurz)* passing point *or* place

aus+wei|den VT *sep (Hunt)* to break up; *Opfertier etc* to disembowel

aus+wei|nen *sep* VR to have a (good) cry; *(= zu Ende weinen)* to finish crying; **sich bei jdm ~** to have a cry on sb's shoulder VI to finish crying VT **seinen Kummer** *etc* **~** to weep *(bei jdm* on sb's shoulder); **sich** *(dat)* **die Augen ~** to cry one's eyes *or* heart out *(nach* over)

Aus|weis ['ausvais] M **-es, -e** [-zə] **a** *(= Mitglieds-/Leser-/Studentenausweis etc)* (membership/library/student *etc)* card; *(= Personalausweis)* identity card; *(= Berechtigungsnachweis)* pass; **~, bitte** your papers please **b** *(= Beleg)* proof; *(von Identität)* proof of identity, identification; **nach ~ +gen** *(form)* according to **c** *(= Bankaus-*

weis) bank return **d** *(dated Aus Sch: = Zeugnis)* report

aus+wei|sen *sep irreg* VT **a** *(aus dem Lande)* to expel, to deport → **Ausgewiesene(r) b** *(= Identität nachweisen)* to identify **c** *(= zeigen)* to reveal **d** *(= für bestimmten Zweck vorsehen) Gebiet, Fläche* to designate; **ein Gebiet als Naturschutzgebiet/zur gewerblichen Nutzung ~** to designate an area as a nature reserve/for commercial purposes VR **a** *(mit Ausweis, Pass)* to identify oneself; **können Sie sich ~?** do you have any means of identification? **b** *(= sich erweisen)* **sich als etw ~** to prove oneself to be sth → *auch* **ausgewiesen**

Aus|weis-: **Aus|weis|kar|te** F = **Ausweis**; **Aus|weis|kon|trol|le** F identity check

aus|weis|lich ['ausvaislıç] PREP *+gen (geh)* according to

Aus|weis-: **Aus|weis|pa|pie|re** PL identity papers *pl*; **Aus|weis|pflicht** F obligation to carry an identity card

Aus|wei|sung F expulsion, deportation

Aus|wei|sungs|be|fehl M, **Aus|wei|sungs|ver|fü|gung** F *(form)* expulsion *or* deportation order

aus+wei|ten *sep* VT to widen; *esp Dehnbares* to stretch; *(fig)* to expand *(zu* into) VR to widen; *(esp Dehnbares)* to stretch; *(fig) (Thema, Bewegung)* to expand *(zu* into); *(= sich verbreiten)* to spread

Aus|wei|tung F **-, -en** widening; *(= Ausdehnung)* stretching; *(fig)* expansion; *(von Konflikt etc)* widening; *(= Verbreitung)* spreading

aus|wen|dig ADV by heart, from memory; **etw ~ können/lernen** to know/learn sth (off) by heart; **das kann ich schon ~** *(fig inf)* I know it backwards *(inf) or* by heart; **ein Musikstück ~ spielen** to play a piece (of music) from memory → **inwendig**

Aus|wen|dig|ler|nen NT **-s,** *no pl (von Geschichtszahlen, Fakten)* learning by heart, memorizing; **ein Gedicht zum ~** a poem to learn by heart

aus+wer|fen VT *sep irreg* **a** *Anker, Netz, Leine* to cast **b** *(= hinausschleudern) Lava, Asche* to throw out, to eject; *Geschosshülsen* to eject **c** *(= ausspucken) Schleim, Blut* to cough up **d** *(= herausschaufeln)* to shovel out; *Graben* to dig out **e** *(= verteilen) Dividende* to pay out; *(= zuteilen) Mittel, Summen* to allocate **f** *(= produzieren)* to produce, to put *or* turn out **g jdm ein Auge ~** to put out sb's eye

aus+wer|ten VT *sep* **a** *(= bewerten)* to evaluate; *(= analysieren)* to analyse **b** *(= nutzbar machen)* to utilize

Aus|wer|tung F **a** *(= Bewertung)* evaluation; *(= Analyse)* analysis **b** *(= Nutzbarmachung)* utilization

aus+wet|zen VT *sep* to grind out

aus+wi|ckeln VT *sep Paket, Bonbon etc* to unwrap; **ein Kind ~** to take a child out of its blankets *etc*; *(Hist: = Windeln entfernen)* to unswaddle a child

aus+wie|gen VT *sep irreg* to weigh (out) → *auch* **ausgewogen**

aus+wil|dern VT *sep Tiere* to release *or* to set free into the wild

aus+wir|ken VR *sep* to have an effect *(auf +acc* on); **sich günstig/negativ ~** to have a favourable *(Brit) or* favorable *(US)*/negative effect; **sich in etw** *(dat)* **~** to result in sth; **sich zu jds Vorteil ~** to work *or* turn out to sb's advantage

Aus|wir|kung F *(= Folge)* consequence; *(= Wirkung)* effect; *(= Rückwirkung)* repercussion

aus+wi|schen VT *sep* to wipe out; *Glas etc, Wunde* to wipe clean; *Schrift etc* to rub *or* wipe out; **sich** *(dat)* **die Augen ~** to rub *or* wipe one's eyes; **jdm eins ~** *(inf)* to get *(Brit) or* pull *(esp US)* one over on sb *(inf)*; *(aus Rache)* to get one's own back on sb *(esp Brit)*, to get back at sb

aus+wrin|gen VT *sep irreg* to wring out

Aus|wuchs ['ausvu:ks] M **-es, Auswüchse** [-vy:ksə] **a** (out)growth; *(Med, Bot auch)* excrescence *(form)*; *(= Missbildung)* deformity **b** *(fig) (= Erzeugnis)* product; *(= Missstand, Übersteigerung)* excess

aus+wuch|ten VT *sep Räder* to balance

Aus|wurf M, *no pl* **a** *(von Lava etc)* ejection, eruption; *(= ausgeworfene Lava etc auch)* ejecta *pl (Geol)* **b** *(Med)* sputum; **~ haben** to bring up phlegm; **blutigen ~ haben** to be coughing up blood **c** *(pej) (= Abschaum)* scum; *(= Schund)* trashy product; **der ~ der Menschheit** the dregs *pl or* scum of humanity

aus+wür|feln *sep* VI to throw dice; *(= das Glück entscheiden lassen)* to draw lots VT to throw *(Brit) or* roll *(US)* dice for

aus+za|cken VT *sep* to serrate

aus+zah|len *sep* VT *Geld etc* to pay out; *Arbeiter, Gläubiger* to pay off; *Kompagnon, Miterben* to buy out; **er bekommt EUR 500 die Woche ausgezahlt** his net pay is 500 euros a week VR *(= sich lohnen)* to pay (off)

aus+zäh|len *sep* VT *Stimmen* to count (up); *(= durch Zählen wählen) Person* to choose *or* select (by counting); *(Boxen)* to count out VI *(bei Kinderspielen)* to count out

Aus|zähl|reim M = **Abzählreim**

Aus|zah|lung F *(von Geld)* paying out; *(von Arbeiter, Gläubiger)* paying off; *(von Kompagnon)* buying out; **zur ~ kommen** *(form) or* **gelangen** *(form)* to be paid out

Aus|zäh|lung F *(von Stimmen etc)* counting (up), count

Aus|zah|lungs-: **Aus|zah|lungs|an|wei|sung** F order to pay; **Aus|zah|lungs|stel|le** F payments *(Brit) or* payment *(US)* office

Aus|zähl|vers M = **Abzählreim**

aus+zah|nen VT *sep (Tech)* to tooth

aus+zan|ken VI *sep (= zu Ende zanken)* to finish quarrelling

aus+zeh|ren VT *sep* to drain, to exhaust; *Land* to drain; **~de Krankheit** wasting disease

Aus|zeh|rung F **a** *(= Kräfteverfall)* emaciation; **unter personeller ~ leiden** *(fig)* to be short-staffed **b** *(obs Med)* consumption *(old)*

aus+zeich|nen *sep* VT **a** *(= mit Zeichen versehen)* to mark; *Waren* to label; *(Typ) Manuskript* to mark up; **etw mit einem Preis(schild) ~** to price sth
b *(= ehren)* to honour *(Brit)*, to honor *(US)*; **jdn mit einem Orden ~** to decorate sb (with a medal); **jdn mit einem Preis/Titel ~** to award a prize/title to sb
c *(= hervorheben)* to distinguish (from all others); *(= kennzeichnen)* to be a feature of
VR to stand out *(durch* due to), to distinguish oneself *(durch* by) *(auch iro)*; **dieser Wagen zeichnet sich durch gute Straßenlage aus** one of the remarkable features of this car is its good roadholding, what makes this car stand out is its good roadholding → *auch* **ausgezeichnet**

Aus|zeich|nung F **a** *(no pl: = das Auszeichnen) (von Baum etc)* marking; *(von Waren)* labelling *(Brit)*, labeling *(US)*; *(mit Preisschild)* pricing; *(Typ: von Manuskript)* mark up **b** *(no pl: = das Ehren)* honouring *(Brit)*, honoring *(US)*; *(mit Orden)* decoration; **seine ~ mit einem Preis** his being awarded a prize **c** *(= Markierung)* marking *(+gen, an +dat* on); *(an Ware)* ticket; *(Typ: auf Manuskript)* mark up **d** *(= Ehrung)* honour *(Brit)*, honor *(US)*, distinction; *(= Orden)* decoration; *(= Preis)* award, prize; **mit ~ bestehen** to pass with distinction

Aus|zeit F *(Sport)* time out

aus|zieh|bar ADJ extendible, extensible; *Antenne* telescopic; *Wäscheleine* retractable; **ein ~er Tisch** a pull-out table

aus+zie|hen *sep irreg* VT **a** *Kleider, Schuhe, Handschuhe* to take off, to remove; *jdn* to undress; **jdm die Jacke** *etc* **~** to take off sb's jacket *etc*; **sich** *(dat)* **etw ~** to take off sth; **die Uniform ~** *(fig)* to retire from the services; **das zieht einem ja die Schuhe** *or* **Socken** *or* **Stiefel aus!** *(dated sl)* it's enough to make you cringe!
b *(= herausziehen)* to pull out; *(= verlängern auch)* to extend; *Metall (zu Draht)* to draw out *(zu* into)
c *Wirkstoffe (aus Kräutern)* to extract
d *(= ausbleichen) Farbe* to bleach (out), to take out
e *(= nachzeichnen) Linie* to trace *(mit Tusche* in ink)
VR *(= sich entkleiden)* to undress, to take off one's clothes; **sich nackt ~** to take off one's clothes; *(bei Leibesvisitation)* to strip naked
VI *aux sein (= aufbrechen, abreisen)* to set out; *(demonstrativ)* to walk out; *(aus einer Wohnung)* to move *(aus* out of); **auf Abenteuer ~** to set off *or* out in search of adventure; **auf Raub ~** to set off *or* out to rob and steal; **zur Jagd ~** to set off for the hunt; **zum Kampf ~** to set off to battle

Aus|zieh-: **Aus|zieh|fe|der** F drawing pen; **Aus|zieh|lei|ter** F extension ladder; **Aus|zieh|plat|te** F *(von Tisch)* leaf; **Aus|zieh|tisch** M extending *or* pull-out table; **Aus|zieh|tu|sche** F drawing ink

aus+zi|schen VT *sep (Theat)* to hiss (off)

Aus|zu|bil|den|de(r) ['austsubıldndə] MF *decl as adj* trainee

Aus|zug M **a** *(= das Weggehen)* departure; *(demonstrativ)* walkout; *(zeremoniell)* procession; *(aus der Wohnung)* move; **der ~ der Kinder Israel** *(Bibl)* the Exodus (of the Children of Israel) **b** *(= Ausschnitt, Exzerpt)* excerpt; *(aus Buch)* extract, excerpt; *(= Zusammenfassung)* abstract, summary; *(= Kontoauszug)* statement; *(Chem)* extract; *(Mus)* arrangement; **etw in Auszügen drucken** to print extracts of sth **c** *(= ausziehbarer Teil)* extension

Aus|zugs-: **Aus|zugs|mehl** NT superfine flour; **aus|zugs|wei|se** ADV in extracts, in excerpts; *(= gekürzt)* in an/the abridged version; **~ aus etw lesen** to read extracts from sth

au|tark [au'tark] ADJ self-sufficient *(auch fig)*, autarkic *(Econ)*

Au|tar|kie [autar'ki:] F **-, -n** [-'ki:ən] self-sufficiency *(auch fig)*, autarky *(Econ)*

Au|then|ti|fi|zie|rung [autɛntifi'tsi:rʊŋ] F **-, -en** *(als Sicherheitsmaßnahme)* authentication *(auch Comput)*

au|then|tisch [au'tɛntıʃ] ADJ authentic; *(Mus) Kadenz* perfect

Au|then|ti|zi|tät [autɛntitsi'tɛ:t] F **-,** *no pl* authenticity

Au|tis|mus [au'tısmʊs] M **-,** *no pl* autism

Au|tist [au'tıst] M **-en, -en**, **Au|tis|tin** [au'tıstın] F **-, -nen** autistic child/person, autistic *(form)*

au|tis|tisch [au'tıstıʃ] ADJ autistic ADV autistically

Au|to ['auto] NT **-s, -s** car, automobile *(esp US, dated)*; **~ fahren** *(selbst)* to drive (a car); *(als Mitfahrer)* to go by car; **mit dem ~ fahren** to go by car; **er guckt wie ein ~** *(inf)* his eyes are popping out of his head *(inf)*

Au|to-: **Au|to|ab|ga|se** PL *(Mot)* car exhaust fumes *pl*, car emissions *pl*; **Au|to|apo|the|ke** F first-aid kit (for the car); **Au|to|at|las** M road atlas; **Au|to|auf|kle|ber** M bumper sticker

Au|to|bahn F motorway *(Brit)*, interstate (highway *or* freeway) *(US)*; *(esp in Deutschland)* autobahn; *(gebührenpflichtig)* turnpike *(US)*

AUTOBAHN

There is no general speed limit on German **Autobahnen** (motorways), although there is a recommended limit of 130kph (80mph). However, there are actually not many sections of road that are not subject to speed restrictions, introduced for safety and environmental reasons. German **Autobahnen** are free, while in Austria and Switzerland drivers have to buy a **Vignette**. An additional toll, a **Maut**, is payable on some sections. → VIGNETTE

Au|to|bahn- *in cpds* motorway *(Brit)*, interstate (highway *or* freeway) *(US)*; **Au|to|bahn|auf|fahrt** F motorway *etc* access road, slip road, freeway on-ramp *(US)*; **Au|to|bahn|aus|fahrt** F motorway *etc* exit, freeway off-ramp *(US)*; **Au|to|bahn|drei|eck** NT motorway *etc* merging point; **Au|to|bahn|ge|bühr** F toll; **Au|to|bahn|kreuz** NT motorway *etc* intersection; **Au|to|bahn|meis|te|rei** F **-, -en** motorway *etc* maintenance authority; **Au|to|bahn|po|li|zei** F motorway *etc* police; **Au|to|bahn|po|li|zist(in)** M(F) motorway *etc* policeman/-woman; **Au|to|bahn|rast|hof** M, **Au|to|bahn|rast|stät|te** F motorway service area *(Brit)*, motorway services *pl (Brit)*, rest area *(US)*; **Au|to|bahn|ring** M motorway *etc* ring road; **Au|to|bahn|vig|net|te** F motorway *etc* toll disc *or* badge, tollway smart card *(US)*; **Au|to|bahn|zu|brin|ger** M motorway approach road *(Brit)*, motorway feeder *(Brit)*, highway *or* freeway approach *(US)*

Au|to-: **Au|to|bat|te|rie** F car battery; **Au|to|bio|graf(in)** M(F) autobiographer; **Au|to|bio|gra|fie** F autobiography; **au|to|bio|gra|fisch** ADJ autobiographical ADV autobiographically; **Au|to|bio|graph** *etc* = **Autobiograf** *etc*; **Au|to|bom|be** F car bomb

Au|to|bus M bus; *(= Reiseomnibus)* coach *(Brit)*, bus; **einstöckiger/zweistöckiger ~** single-decker/double-decker (bus)

Au|to|cam|ping NT driving and camping

Au|to|car M *(Sw)* coach *(Brit)*, bus

au|toch|thon [autɔx'to:n] ADJ *(geh)* autochthonous *(form)*

Au|to-: **Au|to-Cross** ['autokrɔs] NT **-, -**, **Au|to|cross** NT **-, -** autocross; **Au|to|da|fé** [autoda'fe:] NT **-s, -s** *(geh)* auto-da-fé;; **Au|to|deck** NT *(auf Fähren)* car deck; **Au|to|di|dakt** [autodi'dakt] M **-en, -en**, **Au|to|di|dak|tin** [-'daktɪn] F **-, -nen** autodidact *(form)*, self-educated person; **Au|to|di|dak|ten|tum** [autodi'daktntu:m] NT **-s**, *no pl* autodidacticism *(form)*; **au|to|di|dak|tisch** [autodi'daktɪʃ] ADJ autodidactic *(form)*, self-taught *no adv* ADV **sich ~ bilden** to educate oneself; **Au|to|dieb(in)** M(F) car thief; **Au|to|dieb|stahl** M car theft; **Au|to|drom** [auto'dro:m] NT **-s, -e** a motor-racing circuit b *(Aus)* Dodgems® *pl*, bumper cars *pl*; **Au|to|drosch|ke** F *(dated)* taxicab; **Au|to|elekt|rik** F (car) electrics *pl*; **Au|to|ero|tik** F autoeroticism; **Au|to|fab|rik** F car factory *or* plant; **Au|to|fäh|re** F car ferry; **Au|to|fah|ren** NT **-s**, *no pl* driving (a car); *(als Mitfahrer)* driving in a car; **Au|to|fah|rer(in)** M(F) (car) driver; **Au|to|fah|rer|gruß** M *(iro inf)* **jdm den ~ bieten** ≈ to give sb a V sign *(Brit)* or the finger *(US)*; **Au|to|fahrt** F drive; **Au|to|fal|le** F *(bei Überfällen)* road trap; *(= Radarkontrolle)* speed *or* radar trap; **Au|to|fo|kus|ka|me|ra** ['autofo:kʊs-] F autofocus camera; **au|to|frei** ADJ *Innenstadt, Urlaubsort, Sonntag* car-free; **Au|to|fried|hof** M *(inf)* car dump; **Au|to|gas** NT liquefied petroleum gas

au|to|gen [auto'ge:n] ADJ autogenous; **~es Training** *(Psych)* relaxation through self-hypnosis

Au|to|gen|schwei|ßen NT **-s**, *no pl* autogenous welding

au|to|ge|recht ADJ *(speziell für Autos gebaut) Straßen etc* car-friendly

Au|to|graf [auto'gra:f] NT **-s, -en** autograph

Au|to|gramm [auto'gram] NT *pl* **-gramme** autograph

Au|to|gramm-: **Au|to|gramm|jä|ger(in)** M(F) autograph hunter; **Au|to|gramm|stun|de** F autograph(ing) session; **eine ~ geben** to hold an autograph(ing) session

Au|to-: **Au|to|graph** NT = **Autograf**; **Au|to|händ|ler(in)** M(F) car *or* automobile *(US)* dealer; **Au|to|hyp|no|se** F autohypnosis; **Au|to|im|mun|er|kran|kung** F, **Au|to|im|mun|krank|heit** F *(Med)* autoimmune disease; **Au|to|in|dust|rie** F car industry; **Au|to|kar|te** F road map; **Au|to|ki|no** NT drive-in cinema *(Brit)*, drive-in movie theater *(US)*; **Au|to|kna|cker(in)** M(F) *(inf)* car thief; **Au|to|ko|lon|ne** F line of cars; **Au|to|krat** [auto'kra:t] M **-en, -en**, **Au|to|kra|tin** [-'kra:tɪn] F **-, -nen** autocrat; **Au|to|kra|tie** [autokra'ti:] F **-, -n** [-'ti:ən] autocracy; **au|to|kra|tisch** [auto'kra:tɪʃ] ADJ autocratic ADV autocratically; **Au|to|kun|de** M, **Au|to|kun|din** F customer with a car; **Au|to|len|ker(in)** M(F) *(Sw)* (car) driver; **Au|to|mar|der** M a *(= Tier)* marten *(that chews brake pipes etc)* b *(inf: = Autoknacker)* car thief; **Au|to|mar|ke** F make (of car)

Au|to|mat [auto'ma:t] M **-en, -en** *(auch fig: = Mensch)* machine; *(= Verkaufsautomat)* vending machine; *(= Roboter)* automaton, robot; *(= Musikautomat)* jukebox; *(= Spielautomat)* slot machine; *(= Rechenautomat)* calculator; *(rare: = Telefonautomat)* payphone; *(Elec: = selbsttätige Sicherung)* cutout

Au|to|ma|ten-: **Au|to|ma|ten|buf|fet** NT *(esp Aus)* automat; **Au|to|ma|ten|kna|cker(in)** M(F) *(inf)* vandal *(who breaks into vending machines)*; **Au|to|ma|ten|pa|ckung** F vending-machine pack; **Au|to|ma|ten|res|tau|rant** NT automat; **Au|to|ma|ten|stra|ße** F vending machines *pl*

Au|to|ma|tik [auto'ma:tɪk] M **-s, -s** *(Aut)* automatic

Au|to|ma|tik F **-, -en** a automatic mechanism *(auch fig)* b *(= Gesamtanlage)* automatic system; *(Rad)* automatic frequency control, AFC; *(Aut)* automatic transmission

Au|to|ma|tik-: **Au|to|ma|tik|ge|trie|be** NT *(Aut)* automatic transmission; **Au|to|ma|tik|gurt** NT inertia(-reel) seat belt; **Au|to|ma|tik|schal|tung** F automatic transmission; **Au|to|ma|tik|wa|gen** M automatic

Au|to|ma|ti|on [automa'tsio:n] F **-**, *no pl* automation

au|to|ma|tisch [auto'ma:tɪʃ] ADJ automatic ADV automatically

au|to|ma|ti|sie|ren [automati'zi:rən] *ptp* **automatisiert** VT to automate

au|to|ma|ti|siert [automati'zi:ɐt] ADJ automated

Au|to|ma|ti|sie|rung F **-, -en** automation

Au|to|ma|tis|mus [automa'tɪsmʊs] M **-, Automatismen** [-mən] automatism

Au|to-: **Au|to|me|cha|ni|ker(in)** M(F) car *or* motor mechanic; **Au|to|mi|nu|te** F minute by car, minute's drive

Au|to|mo|bil [automo'bi:l] NT **-s, -e** *(dated, geh)* motorcar, automobile *(esp US, dated)*

Au|to|mo|bil-: **Au|to|mo|bil|aus|stel|lung** F motor show; *(= ständige Automobilausstellung)* car exhibition; **Au|to|mo|bil|bau** M, *no pl* car *or* automobile *(US)* manufacture

Au|to|mo|bi|list [automobi'lɪst] M **-en, -en**, **Au|to|mo|bi|lis|tin** [-'lɪstɪn] F **-, -nen** *(Sw geh)* (car) driver

Au|to|mo|bil-: **Au|to|mo|bil|klub** M automobile association; **Au|to|mo|bil|sa|lon** M motor show

Au|to-: **Au|to|mo|dell** NT (car) model; *(= Miniaturauto)* model car; **au|to|nom** [auto'no:m] ADJ autonomous *(auch fig)*; *Nervensystem* autonomic; **Au|to|no|me(r)** [auto'no:mə] MF *decl as adj (Pol)* independent; **Au|to|no|mie** [autono'mi:] F **-, -n** [-'mi:ən] autonomy *(auch fig)*; **Au|to|no|mist** [autono'mɪst] M **-en, -en**, **Au|to|no|mis|tin** [-'mɪstɪn] F **-, -nen** autonomist; **Au|to|num|mer** F (car) number; **Au|to|öl** NT motor oil; **Au|to|pi|lot** M *(Aviat)* autopilot; **vom ~en gesteuert werden** to be on autopilot

Au|top|sie [autɔ'psi:] F **-, -n** [-'psi:ən] *(Med)* autopsy

Au|tor ['auto:ɐ] M **-s, Autoren** [au'to:rən] author

Au|to-: **Au|to|ra|dio** NT car radio; **Au|to|rei|fen** M car tyre *(Brit) or* tire *(US)*; **Au|to|rei|se|zug** M *train carrying holidaymakers' cars*, ≈ motorail train *(Brit)*; **mit dem ~ fahren** to go by motorail *(Brit)*

Au|to|ren-: **Au|to|ren|film** M ≈ film written and directed by the same person; **Au|to|ren|kol|lek|tiv** NT team of authors

Au|to-: **Au|to|renn|bahn** F motor-racing circuit; **Au|to|ren|nen** NT (motor) race; *(Rennsport)* motor racing; **Au|to|renn|sport** M motor racing; **Au|to|re|pa|ra|tur|werk|statt** F garage, car repair shop *(US)*

Au|to|ren|re|gis|ter NT index of authors

Au|to|re|verse-Funk|ti|on ['autorivø:ɐs-, 'autorivœrs-] F auto-reverse (function)

Au|to|rin [au'to:rɪn] F **-, -nen** author, authoress

Au|to|ri|sa|ti|on [autoriza'tsio:n] F **-, -en** *(geh)* authorization

au|to|ri|sie|ren [autori'zi:rən] *ptp* **autorisiert** VT to authorize

au|to|ri|tär [autori'tɛ:ɐ] ADJ authoritarian ADV in an authoritarian manner; **ein ~ geführtes Land** a country ruled by an authoritarian government

Au|to|ri|tät [autori'tɛ:t] F **-, -en** *(alle Bedeutungen)* authority

au|to|ri|ta|tiv [autorita'ti:f] ADJ *(geh)* authoritative

Au|to|ri|täts-: **au|to|ri|täts|gläu|big** ADJ trusting in authority; **Au|to|ri|täts|gläu|big|keit** F trust in authority; **au|to|ri|täts|hö|rig** ADJ slavishly following authority; **~ sein** to be a slave to authority

Au|tor|kor|rek|tur F *(= Korrekturfahne)* author's proof; *(= Änderung)* author's correction

Au|tor|schaft ['auto:ɐʃaft] F **-, -en** authorship

Au|to-: **Au|to|sa|lon** ['autozalɔŋ, *(esp S Ger, Aus)* -zalo:n, *(esp Sw)* -salõ:] M motor show, auto (-mobile) show *(US)*; **Au|to|schal|ter** M drive-in counter; **Au|to|schlan|ge** F queue *(Brit) or* line of cars; **Au|to|schlos|ser(in)** M(F) panel beater; **Au|to|schlos|se|rei** F body shop; **Au|to|schlüs|sel** M car key; **Au|to|skoo|ter** ['autosku:tɐ] M **-s, -** Dodgem® *(Brit) or* bumper car; **Au|to|speng|ler(in)** M(F) *(S Ger, Aus, Sw)* panel beater; **Au|to|speng|le|rei** [-ʃpɛŋlə'rai] F **-, -en** *(S Ger, Aus, Sw)* body shop; **Au|to|sport** M motor sport; **Au|to|stell|platz** M (car) parking space; **Au|to|stopp** M hitchhiking, hitching *(esp Brit inf)*; **~ machen, per ~ fahren** to hitchhike; **Au|to|stra|ße** F main road, highway *(esp US)*; **Au|to|strich** M *(inf) prostitution to car drivers (= Gegend)* kerb-crawling *(Brit) or* curb-crawling *(US)* area *(inf)*; **Au|to|stun|de** F hour's drive; **Au|to|sug|ges|ti|on** F autosuggestion; **Au|to|te|le|fon** NT car phone; **Au|to|ty|pie** [autoty'pi:] F **-, -n** [-'pi:ən] autotypy; **Au|to|un|fall** M car accident; **Au|to|ver|kehr** M (motor) traffic; **Au|to|ver|leih** M, **Au|to|ver|mie|tung** F car hire *or* rental; *(= Firma)* car hire *or* rental firm; **Au|to|ver|si|che|rung** F car *or* motor insurance; **Au|to|wasch|an|la|ge** F car wash; **Au|to|werk|statt** F garage, car repair shop *(US)*; **Au|to|wrack** NT (car) wreck, wrecked car; **Au|to|zoom** NT *(Phot)* automatic zoom (lens); **Au|to|zu|be|hör** NT car *or* motor accessories *pl*; **Au|to|zug** M *train carrying holidaymakers' cars*, ≈ motorail train *(Brit)*; **mit dem ~ fahren** to go by motorail *(Brit)*

autsch [autʃ] INTERJ *(inf)* ouch, ow

Au|wald M riverside wood(s *pl*) *or* forest

au|weh [au've:], **au|wei(a)** [au'vai,a,] INTERJ oh dear

AV *abbr von* **audiovisuell** AV

Avan|ce [a'vã:sə] F **-, -n jdm ~n machen** *(geh)* to make approaches to sb

avan|cie|ren [avã'si:rən] *ptp* **avanciert** VI *aux sein (dated, geh)* to advance *(zu* to)

Avant-: **Avant|gar|de** [a'vã:gardə, avã'gardə] F *(geh) (Art)* avant-garde; *(Pol)* vanguard; **Avant|gar|dis|mus** [avãgar'dɪsmʊs, avant-] M **-**, *no pl* avant-gardism; **Avant|gar|dist** [avãgar'dɪst, avant-] M **-en, -en**, **Avant|gar|dis|tin** [-'dɪstɪn]

F -, -nen member of the avant-garde, avant-gardist; **avant|gar|dis|tisch** [avãgar'dıstıʃ, avant-] ADJ avant-garde

AvD [a:fau'de:] *abbr von* **Automobilclub von Deutschland**

Ave-Ma|ria ['a:vema'ri:a] NT **-(s), -(s)** Ave Maria; *(Gebet auch)* Hail Mary

Avers [a'vɛrs] M **-es, -e** face, obverse

Aver|si|on [avɛr'zio:n] F **-, -en** aversion *(gegen* to)

Avi|a|ri|um [avi'a:rium] **-s, Aviarien** [-riən] NT aviary

Avis [a'vi:s] [a'vi:] M OR NT **-** *or* **-es, -** *or* **-e** *(Comm)* advice; *(schriftlich)* advice note

avi|sie|ren [avi'zi:rən] *ptp* **avisiert** VT to send notification of, to advise of

Avi|so [a'vi:zo] NT **-s, -s** (*Aus Comm*) advice; *(schriftlich)* advice note

Avi|ta|mi|no|se [avitami'no:zə] F **-, -n** *(Med)* avitaminosis

AV-Me|di|en PL AV media *pl*

Avo|ca|do [avo'ka:do] F **-, -s** avocado

Avo|ca|to [avo'ka:to] F **-, -s** = **Avocado**

A-Waf|fe ['a:-] F *abbr von* **atomare Waffe**

Axel ['aksl] M **-s, -** *(Sport)* axel

axi|al [a'ksia:l] ADJ axial

Axi|al|la|ger NT *(Tech)* axial *or* thrust bearing

Axi|om [a'ksio:m] NT **-s, -e** axiom

Axi|o|ma|tik [aksio'ma:tık] F **-,** *no pl* axiomatics *sing*

axi|o|ma|tisch [aksio'ma:tıʃ] ADJ axiomatic

Axt [akst] F **-, ⸚e** ['ɛkstə] axe *(Brit)*, ax *(US)*; **sich wie eine** *or* **die ~ im Wald benehmen** *(fig inf)* to behave like a peasant *or* boor; **die ~ im Haus erspart den Zimmermann** *(Prov)* self-help is the best help; **die ~ an etw** *(acc) or* **an die Wurzel einer Sache** *(gen)* **legen** *(fig)* to tear up the very roots of sth

Axt|hieb M blow of the/an axe *(Brit) or* ax *(US)*

Aya|tol|lah [aja'tɔla] M **-s, -s** ayatollah

Aza|lee [atsa'le:ə] F **-, -n**, **Aza|lie** [a'tsa:liə] F **-, -n** *(Bot)* azalea

Aze|tat [atse'ta:t] NT **-s, -e** acetate

Aze|tat|sei|de F acetate silk

Aze|ton [atse'to:n] NT **-s,** *no pl (Chem)* acetone

Aze|ty|len [atsety'le:n] NT **-s,** *no pl (Chem)* acetylene

Azi|mut [atsi'mu:t] NT **-s, -e** *(Astron)* azimuth

Azo|ren [a'tso:rən] PL *(Geog)* Azores *pl*

Azo|ren|hoch NT *(Met)* high over the Azores

Az|te|ke [ats'te:kə] M **-n, -n**, **Az|te|kin** [-'te:kın] F **-, -nen** Aztec

Az|te|ken|reich NT Aztec empire

az|te|kisch [ats'te:kıʃ] ADJ Aztec

Azu|bi [a'tsu:bi:, 'a(:)tsubi] M **-s, -s** *or f* **-, -s** *abbr von* **Auszubildende(r)**

Azur [a'tsu:ɐ] M **-s,** *no pl (poet)* azure sky; *(= Farbe)* azure

azur|blau [a'tsu:ɐ-], **azurn** [a'tsu:ɐn] *(poet)* ADJ azure (blue)

azyk|lisch ['atsy:klıʃ, a'tsy:klıʃ] ADJ acyclic

B

B, b [beː] NT -, - B, b; *(Mus) (= Ton)* B flat; *(= Versetzungszeichen)* flat; **B-Dur** (the key of) B flat major; **b-Moll** (the key of) B flat minor

Baas [baːs] M **-es, -e** [ˈbaːzə] *(Naut)* boss

bab|beln [ˈbabln] VI *(inf)* to babble; *(Schwätzer auch)* to chatter

Ba|bel [ˈbaːbl] NT **-s** *(Bibl)* Babel; *(fig) (= Sündenbabel)* sink of iniquity; *(von Sprachen)* melting pot

Ba|by [ˈbeːbi] NT **-s, -s** baby

Ba|by- *in cpds* baby; **Ba|by|aus|stat|tung** F layette; **Ba|by|boom** M baby boom; **Ba|by|doll** [ˈbeːbidɔl, beːbiˈdɔl] NT **-(s), -s** baby-dolls *pl*, baby-doll pyjamas *pl*; **Ba|by|jog|ger** M baby jogger *or* stroller; **Ba|by|jahr** NT *(für Mutter nach Geburt)* maternity leave *(for one year)*; *(Insur) year of pension contributions credited to women for each child*; **Ba|by|klap|pe** F baby flap *(for safe, legal surrender of unwanted newborn babies)*; **Ba|by|korb** M bassinet; **Ba|by|kost** F baby food

Ba|by|lon [ˈbaːbylɔn] NT **-s** Babylon

ba|by|lo|nisch [babyˈloːnɪʃ] ADJ Babylonian; **eine ~e Sprachverwirrung** a Babel of languages; **der Babylonische Turm** the Tower of Babel; **die Babylonische Gefangenschaft** the Babylonian captivity

Ba|by-: **Ba|by|nah|rung** F baby food; **Ba|by|pau|se** F *(der Mutter)* maternity leave; *(des Vaters)* paternity leave; **eine ~ einlegen** to have *or* take *or* go on maternity *or* paternity leave; **sie will eine zweijährige ~ einlegen** she wants to take a two-year break to have a baby; **Ba|by|schwim|men** NT baby swimming; **ba|by|sit|ten** [ˈbeːbizɪtn] VI *insep* to babysit; **Ba|by|sit|ter** [ˈbeːbizɪtɐ] M **-s, -**, **Ba|by|sit|te|rin** [-ərɪn] F **-, -nen** babysitter; **Ba|by|speck** M *(inf)* puppy fat *(Brit)*, baby fat *(US)*; **Ba|by|spra|che** F baby talk; **Ba|by|strich** M child prostitution *no art*; *(= Gegend)* pick-up place for child prostitutes; **Ba|by|tra|ge|ta|sche** F carrycot *(Brit)*, traveling baby bed *(US)*; **Ba|by|waa|ge** F scales *pl* for weighing babies; **Ba|by|wip|pe** F bouncy chair; **Ba|by|zel|le** F *(Elec: = Kleinstbatterie)* round cell

Bac|ca|ra [ˈbakara] NT **-s**, *no pl (Cards)* baccarat

Bac|cha|nal [baxaˈnaːl] NT **-s, -e** *or* **-ien** [-liən] **a** *(in der Antike)* Bacchanalia **b** *(geh: = Gelage)* bacchanal, drunken orgy

Bac|chant [baˈxant] M **-en, -en**, **Bac|chan|tin** [-ˈxantɪn] F **-, -nen** bacchant

bac|chan|tisch [baˈxantɪʃ] ADJ bacchanalian

bac|chisch [ˈbaxɪʃ] ADJ *(Myth)* Bacchic

Bac|chus [ˈbaxʊs] M **-'** *(Myth)* Bacchus; **dem ~ huldigen** *(geh)* to imbibe *(form)*

Bach [bax] M **-(e)s, ¨-e** [ˈbɛçə] stream *(auch fig)*, brook; *(Naut, Aviat: sl: = Gewässer)* drink *(inf)*; **den ~ heruntergehen** *(inf: Firma etc)* to go down the tubes *(inf)*

bach|ab [baxˈlap] ADV *(Sw)* downstream; **etw ~ schicken** *(fig inf)* to throw sth away; **~ gehen** *(fig inf)* to go up the creek *(inf) or* spout *(inf)*

Bach|bett NT stream bed

Bach|blü|ten PL *(Med)* Bach flower extracts *pl*

Bach|blü|ten|the|ra|pie F *(Med)* Bach *or* Bach's flower remedy (therapy); **eine ~ machen** to take Bach's flower remedy *or* remedies

Ba|che [ˈbaxə] F **-, -n** (wild) sow

Bä|chel|chen [ˈbɛçlçən] NT **-s, -** *dim von* **Bach**

Bach|fo|rel|le F brown trout

Bäch|lein [ˈbɛçlain] NT **-s, -** *dim von* **Bach** (small) stream, brooklet; **ein ~ machen** *(baby-talk)* to do a wee-wee *(baby-talk)*

Bach|stel|ze F wagtail

back [bak] ADV *(Naut)* back

Back [bak] F **-, -en** *(Naut)* **a** *(= Deck)* forecastle, fo'c'sle **b** *(= Schüssel)* dixie, mess tin, mess kit *(US)*; *(= Tafel)* mess table; *(= Besatzung)* mess

Back|blech NT baking tray *(Brit)*, baking pan *(US)*

Back|bord NT, *no pl (Naut)* port (side); **von ~ nach Steuerbord** from port to starboard; **über ~** over the port side

back|bord(s) [ˈbakbɔrt(s)] ADV *(Naut)* on the port side; **(nach) ~** to port

Back|brett NT baking board

Bäck|chen [ˈbɛkçən] NT **-s, -** (little) cheek

Ba|cke [ˈbakə] F **-, -n** **a** *(= Wange)* cheek; **mit vollen ~n kauen** to chew *or* eat with bulging cheeks; *(mit Genuss)* to eat heartily; **au ~!** *(dated inf)* oh dear! **b** *(inf: = Hinterbacke)* buttock, cheek; **auf einer ~** *(inf: = mit Leichtigkeit)* easily, no problem *(inf)* **c** *(von Schraubstock)* jaw; *(= Bremsbacke) (bei Auto)* shoe; *(bei Fahrrad)* block; *(von Skibindung)* toe-piece; *(von Gewehr)* cheekpiece

ba|cken [ˈbakn] *pret* **backte** *or (old)* **buk** [ˈbaktə, buːk], *ptp* **gebacken** [gəˈbakn] VT to bake; *Brot, Kuchen* to make, to bake; **frisch/knusprig gebackenes Brot** fresh/crusty bread; **wir ~ alles selbst** we do all our own baking; **gebackener Fisch** fried fish; *(im Ofen)* baked fish VI *(Brot, Kuchen)* to bake; **der Kuchen muss noch 20 Minuten ~** the cake will have to be in the oven *or* will take another 20 minutes; **sie bäckt gern** she enjoys baking

ba|cken *(dial inf)* VI *(= kleben: Schnee etc)* to stick *(an +dat* to), to cake *(an +dat* on, onto) VT **etw an etw** *(acc)* **~** to stick sth onto sth

Ba|cken-: **Ba|cken|bart** M sideboards *pl (Brit)*, sideburns *pl*, (side) whiskers *pl*; **Ba|cken|brem|se** F *(bei Auto)* shoe brake; *(bei Fahrrad)* block brake; **Ba|cken|kno|chen** M cheekbone; **Ba|cken|ta|sche** F *(Zool)* cheek pouch; **Ba|cken|zahn** M molar

Bä|cker [ˈbɛkɐ] M **-s, -**, **Bä|cke|rin** [-ərɪn] F **-, -nen** baker; **~ lernen** to learn the baker's trade, to be an apprentice baker; **~ werden** to be *or* become a baker; **beim ~** at the baker's; **zum ~ gehen** to go to the baker's

Back|erb|sen PL *(S Ger, Aus)* ≈ small pasta balls put into soups

Bä|cke|rei [bɛkəˈrai] F **-, -en** **a** *(= Bäckerladen)* baker's (shop); *(= Backstube)* bakery **b** *(= Gewerbe)* bakery, baking trade **c** *(Aus) (= Gebäck)* pastries *pl*; *(= Kekse)* biscuits *pl (Brit)*, cookies *pl (US)*

Bä|cker|ge|sel|le M, **Bä|cker|ge|sel|lin** F (trained) baker

Bä|cke|rin [-ərɪn] F → **Bäcker**

Bä|cker|jun|ge M baker's boy; *(= Lehrling)* baker's apprentice

Bä|cker|la|den M baker's (shop)

Bä|cker|meis|ter(in) M(F) master baker

Bä|ckers|frau F baker's wife

Back-: **Back|fei|ge** F *(dial)* = **Ohrfeige**; **back|fer|tig** ADJ oven-ready; **Back|fett** NT cooking fat; **Back|fisch** M **a** fried fish **b** *(dated)* teenager, teenage girl; **Back|form** F baking tin *(Brit) or* pan *(US)*; *(für Kuchen)* cake tin *(Brit) or* pan *(US)*

Back|gam|mon [bɛkˈgɛmən] NT **-(s)**, *no pl* backgammon

Back|ground [ˈbɛkgraunt] M **-s, -s** background

Back-: **Back|hähn|chen** NT, **Back|hendl** NT *(S Ger, Aus)*, **Back|huhn** NT, **Back|hühn|chen** NT roast chicken; **Back|mi|schung** F cake mix; **Back|mul|de** F kneading *or* dough trough, dough tray, hutch; **Back|obst** NT dried fruit; **Back|ofen** M oven; **es ist heiß wie in einem ~** it's like an oven; **back|ofen|fest** ADJ ovenproof; **Back|pa|pier** NT baking parchment, grease-proof paper; **Back|pfei|fe** F *(dial)* slap on *or* round *(inf)* the face; **Back|pflau|me** F prune; **Back|pul|ver** NT baking powder; **Back|röh|re** F, *(Aus)* **Back|rohr** NT oven

Back|slash [ˈbɛkslɛʃ] M **-s, -s** *(Typ: = umgekehrter Schrägstrich)* backslash

Back|space|tas|te [ˈbɛkspeːs-] F, **Back|space-Tas|te** F *(Comput)* backspace key

Back|stein M brick

Back|stein-: **Back|stein|bau** M *pl* **-bauten** brick building; **Back|stein|bau|wei|se** F brick (building) style; **ein Haus in ~** a brick (-built) house; **Back|stein|go|tik** F *Gothic architecture built in brick*

Back|stu|be F bakery

bäckt [bɛkt] 3. PERS SING *pres von* **backen**

Back|trog M kneading *or* dough trough, dough tray, hutch

Back-up [ˈbɛkap] NT **-s, -s** *(Comput)* backup

Back-up-Pro|gramm NT *(Comput)* backup program

Back-: **Back|vor|schrift** F baking instructions *pl*; **Back|wa|ren** PL bread, cakes and pastries *pl*; **Back|werk** NT *(old)* cakes and pastries *pl*; **Back|zeit** F baking time

Bad [baːt] NT **-(e)s, ¨-er** [ˈbɛːdɐ] **a** *(= Wannenbad, Badewanne, Phot)* bath; *(= das Baden)* bathing; **ein ~ nehmen** to have *or* take a bath; **(sich** *dat***) ein ~ einlaufen lassen** to run (oneself) a bath; **jdm Bäder verschreiben** *(Med)* to prescribe sb a course of (therapeutic) baths; **~ in der Menge** *(fig)* walkabout; **ein ~ in der Menge nehmen** to go (on a) walkabout

b *(im Meer etc)* bathe, swim; *(= das Baden)* bathing, swimming

c *(= Badezimmer)* bathroom; **Zimmer mit ~** room with (private) bath

d *(= Schwimmbad)* (swimming) pool *or* bath(s); **die städtischen Bäder** the public baths *(Brit) or* pools *(US)*; **türkisches ~** Turkish *or* Russian bath

e *(= Heilbad)* spa; *(= Seebad)* (seaside) resort; **~ Doberan** Bad Doberan

Ba|de-: **Ba|de|an|stalt** F (public) swimming baths *(Brit) or* pools *(US) pl*; **Ba|de|an|zug** M swimsuit, bathing suit *(esp US)*; **Ba|de|arzt** M, **Ba|de|ärz|tin** F spa doctor; **Ba|de|gast** M **a** *(im Kurort)* spa visitor **b** *(im Schwimmbad)*

bather, swimmer; **Ba|de|ge|le|gen|heit** F **gibt es dort eine ~?** can you swim there?; **Ba|de|hand|tuch** NT bath towel; **Ba|de|hau|be** F *(dated)* swimming cap *or* hat, bathing cap; **Ba|de|ho|se** F (swimming *or* bathing) trunks *pl*; **eine ~** a pair of (swimming *or* bathing) trunks; **Ba|de|ka|bi|ne** F changing cubicle; **Ba|de|kap|pe** F swimming cap *or* hat, bathing cap; **Ba|de|kos|tüm** NT *(geh)* swimming *or* bathing costume *(Brit)*, bathing suit *(esp US)*; **Ba|de|la|ken** NT bath sheet; **Ba|de|lus|ti|ge(r)** MF *decl as adj; usu pl* bather, swimmer; **Ba|de|man|tel** M beach robe; *(= Morgenmantel)* bathrobe, dressing gown *(Brit)*; **Ba|de|mat|te** F bath mat; **Ba|de|meis|ter(in)** M(F) *(im Schwimmbad)* (pool) attendant; **Ba|de|mo|de** F swimwear, beachware; **Ba|de|müt|ze** F swimming cap *or* hat, bathing cap

ba|den ['ba:dn] VI **a** *(in der Badewanne)* to have a bath, to bath *(Brit)*, to bathe *(US)*; **hast du schon gebadet?** have you had your bath already?; **warm/kalt ~** to have a hot/cold bath
b *(im Meer, Schwimmbad etc)* to swim, to bathe; **sie hat im Meer gebadet** she swam *or* bathed in the sea, she had a swim in the sea; **die Badenden** the bathers; **~ gehen** to go swimming; *(einmal)* to go for a swim
c *(inf)* **~ gehen** to come a cropper *(inf)*; **wenn das passiert, gehe ich ~** I'll be (in) for it if that happens *(inf)*
VT **a** *Kind etc* to bath *(Brit)*, to bathe *(US)*; **er ist als Kind zu heiß gebadet worden** *(hum)* he was dropped on the head as a child *(hum)*; **in Schweiß gebadet** bathed *or* drenched in sweat
b *Augen, Wunde etc* to bathe
VR to bathe, to have a bath

Ba|den ['ba:dn] NT **-s** *(Geog)* Baden

Ba|de|ner ['ba:dənɐ] M **-s, -**, **Ba|de|ne|rin** [-ərɪn] F **-, -nen** person *or* man/woman from Baden; **er ist ~** he comes from Baden

Ba|de|ni|xe F *(hum)* bathing beauty *or* belle *(dated)*

Ba|den|ser [ba'dɛnzɐ] M **-s, -**, **Ba|den|se|rin** [-ərɪn] F **-, -nen** *(inf)* = **Badener**

Ba|den-Würt|tem|berg ['ba:dn'vʏrtəmbɛrk] NT **-s** Baden-Württemberg

Ba|de-: **Ba|de|ofen** M boiler; **Ba|de|ort** M *pl* **-orte** *(= Kurort)* spa; *(= Seebad)* (seaside) resort; **Ba|de|platz** M place for bathing

Ba|der ['ba:dɐ] M **-s, -** *(old)* barber *(old)*; *(dial: = Arzt)* village quack *(hum)*

Bä|der|be|hand|lung F *medical treatment using therapeutic baths*

Ba|de|rei|se F *(dated)* trip to a spa

Bä|der-: **Bä|der|kun|de** F balneology; **Bä|der|kur** F *medical treatment using therapeutic baths*

Ba|de-: **Ba|de|sa|chen** PL swimming gear, swimming *or* bathing things *pl*; **Ba|de|sai|son** F swimming season; *(in Kurort)* spa season; **Ba|de|salz** NT bath salts *pl*; **Ba|de|schaum** M bubble bath; **Ba|de|schuh** M sandal; *(= Latschen)* flip flop; **Ba|de|schwamm** M sponge; **Ba|de|see** M (bathing) lake; **Ba|de|strand** M (bathing) beach; **Ba|de|stu|be** F *(N Ger)* bathroom; **Ba|de|tuch** NT *pl* **-tücher** bath towel; **Ba|de|ur|laub** M holiday at the seaside, beach *or* seaside holiday, vacation by the sea *(US)*; **~ machen** to go to the seaside for one's holiday *(Brit)* *or* vacation *(US)*; **Ba|de|ver|bot** NT ban on bathing; **Ba|de|wan|ne** F bath(tub); **Ba|de|was|ser** NT, *no pl* bath water; **Ba|de|wet|ter** NT weather warm enough for bathing *or* swimming; **Ba|de|zeit** F bathing *or* swimming season; **Ba|de|zeug** NT, *no pl* swimming gear, swimming *or* bathing things *pl*; **Ba|de|zim|mer** NT bathroom; **Ba|de|zu|satz** M *bath salts, bubble bath etc*

ba|disch ['ba:dɪʃ] ADJ Baden *attr*; *Wein etc auch* from Baden; *Dialekt auch* of Baden; *Landschaft auch* around Baden; **das Dorf ist ~** *or* **im Badischen** the village is in Baden

Bad|min|ton ['bɛtmɪntən] NT **-**, *no pl* badminton

Bad|rei|ni|ger M bath cleaner

baff [baf] ADJ *pred (inf)* **~ sein** to be flabbergasted

BA|föG ['ba:føk] NT **-**, *no pl*, **Ba|fög** NT **-**, *no pl abbr von* **Bundesausbildungsförderungsgesetz**; **er kriegt ~** he gets a grant

> **BAFÖG**
>
> BAföG stands for **Bundesausbildungsförderungsgesetz**, the regulation governing financial assistance for students of higher education. **BAföG** is generally used as a name for the allowance students get. Awards are means-tested and usually given in the form of a loan.

BA|föG-Emp|fän|ger(in) ['ba:føk-] M(F) recipient of a (state) grant

Ba|ga|ge [ba'ga:ʒə] F **-**, *no pl* **a** *(old, Sw: = Gepäck)* luggage, baggage **b** *(dated inf) (= Gesindel)* crowd, crew *(inf)*, gang *(inf)*; *(= Familie)* pack *(inf)*; **die ganze ~** the whole bloody lot *(Brit inf)*, the whole darn group *(US)*

Ba|ga|tell [baga'tɛl] F **-, -en** *(Aus inf)* trifle, bagatelle

Ba|ga|tell|de|likt NT *(Jur)* petty *or* minor offence *(Brit)* *or* offense *(US)*

Ba|ga|tel|le [baga'tɛlə] F **-, -n** trifle, bagatelle; *(Mus)* bagatelle

Ba|ga|tell|fall M *(Jur)* petty lawsuit

ba|ga|tel|li|sie|ren [bagatɛli'zi:rən] *ptp* **bagatellisiert** VT to trivialize, to minimize VI to trivialize

Ba|ga|tell-: **Ba|ga|tell|sa|che** F *(Jur)* petty *or* minor case; **Ba|ga|tell|scha|den** M minor *or* superficial damage; **Ba|ga|tell|ver|let|zung** F minor *or* superficial injury

Bag|dad ['bakdat, bak'da:t] NT **-s** Baghdad

Bag|ger ['bagɐ] M **-s, -** excavator; *(für Schlamm)* dredger

Bag|ger|füh|rer(in) M(F) → **Bagger** driver of an/the excavator, driver of a/the dredger

bag|gern ['bagɐn] VTI *Graben* to excavate, to dig; *Fahrrinne* to dredge VI *(sl: = Mädchen/Jungen anmachen)* to pull *(Brit inf)*, to pick up *(inf)*

Bag|ger-: **Bag|ger|schau|fel** F excavator shovel; **Bag|ger|see** M *artificial lake in quarry etc*

> **BAGGERSEE**
>
> Many German towns and villages have a local **Baggersee** which can be used for bathing in summer. This is an old quarry which has filled up with water. It is usually free, although this means there is no supervision for bathers. Increasingly, larger **Baggerseen** are being converted into **Strandbäder**, with facilities such as changing rooms, showers and supervision. They then have fixed opening times and charge an entrance fee.

Ba|guette [ba'gɛt] NT OR F **-s, -s** baguette

bah [ba:], **bäh** [bɛ:] INTERJ **a** *(aus Schadenfreude)* hee-hee *(inf)*; *(vor Ekel)* ugh **b** **~ machen** *(baby-talk: Schaf)* to baa, to go baa

Ba|ha|ma|in|seln [ba'ha:ma-] PL, **Ba|ha|mas** [ba'ha:mas] PL Bahamas *pl*

Bäh|lamm ['bɛ:lam] NT *(baby-talk)* baa-lamb *(baby-talk)*

Bahn [ba:n] F **-, -en** **a** *(= Weg)* path, track; *(von Fluss)* course; *(fig)* path; *(= Fahrbahn)* carriageway; **~ frei!** make way!, (get) out of the way!; **jdm/einer Sache die ~ ebnen/frei machen** *(fig)* to pave/clear the way for sb/sth; **die ~ ist frei** *(fig)* the way is clear; **sich** *(dat)* **~ brechen** *(lit)* to force one's way; *(fig)* to make headway; *(Mensch)* to forge ahead; **einer Sache** *(dat)* **~ brechen** to blaze the trail for sth; **sich auf neuen ~en bewegen** to break new *or* fresh ground; **in gewohnten ~en verlaufen** *(fig)* to go on in the same old way, to continue as before; **von der rechten ~ abkommen** *(geh)* to stray from the straight and narrow; **jdn auf die rechte ~ bringen** *(fig)* to put sb on the straight and narrow; **etw in die richtige ~** *or* **die richtigen ~en lenken** *(fig)* to channel sth properly; **jdn aus der ~ werfen** *or* **schleudern** *(fig)* to throw sb off the track → **schief**
b *(= Eisenbahn)* railway *(Brit)*, railroad *(US)*; *(= Straßenbahn)* tram *(esp Brit)*, streetcar *(US)*; *(= Zug) (der Eisenbahn, U-Bahn)* train; *(der Straßenbahn)* tram *(esp Brit)*, streetcar *(US)*; *(= Bahnhof)* station; *(Verkehrsnetz, Verwaltung)* railway *usu pl (Brit)*, railroad *(US)*; **mit der** *or* **per ~** by train *or* rail/tram *(esp Brit)* *or* streetcar *(US)*; **frei ~** *(Comm)* free on rail; **er ist** *or* **arbeitet bei der ~** he's with the railways *(Brit)* *or* railroad *(US)*, he works for *or* on the railways *(Brit)*
c *(Sport)* track; *(für Pferderennen auch)* course; *(in Schwimmbecken)* pool; *(= Kegelbahn)* (bowling) alley; *(für einzelne Teilnehmer)* lane; *(= Schlittenbahn, Bobbahn)* run
d *(Phys, Astron)* orbit, path; *(= Raketenbahn, Geschossbahn)* (flight) path, trajectory
e *(= Stoffbahn, Tapetenbahn)* length, strip
f *(Tech: von Werkzeug)* face

Bahn-: **bahn|amt|lich** ADJ *Tarife etc* official railway *(Brit)* *or* *(US)* railroad *attr*; **Bahn|an|schluss** M railway *(Brit)* *or* railroad *(US)* connection *or* link; **~ haben** to be connected *or* linked to the railway *(Brit)* *or* railroad *(US)* (system); **Bahn|ar|bei|ter(in)** M(F) rail worker, railroader *(US)*; **Bahn|be|am|te(r)** M *decl as adj*, **Bahn|be|am|tin** F railway *(Brit)* *or* railroad *(US)* official; **Bahn|be|triebs|werk** NT railway *(Brit)* *or* railroad *(US)* depot; **bahn|bre|chend** ADJ pioneering; **Bahnbrechendes leisten** to pioneer new developments; **~ sein** to be pioneering; *(Erfinder etc)* to be a pioneer ADV **~ wirken** to be pioneering; *(Erfinder etc)* to be a pioneer; **Bahn|bre|cher(in)** M(F) pioneer; **Bahn|bus** M *bus run by railway company*; **Bahn|Card®** [-ka:ɐd] F **-, -s** ≈ railcard, *entitling the holder to reduced fares*

> **BAHNCARD**
>
> The **BahnCard®** is a card issued by German railways allowing half-price travel throughout Germany for one year. Since rail travel is generally quite expensive, a **BahnCard®**, although not exactly cheap, can pay for itself within a short time.

Bähn|chen ['bɛ:nçən] NT **-s, -** *dim von* **Bahn**

Bahn|damm M (railway) embankment

bah|nen ['ba:nən] VT *Pfad* to clear; *Flussbett* to carve *or* channel out; **jdm/einer Sache den/einen Weg ~** to clear the/a way for sb/sth; *(fig)* to pave *or* prepare the way for sb/sth; **sich** *(dat)* **einen Weg ~** to fight one's way

bah|nen|wei|se ADV in lengths *or* strips

Bah|ner ['ba:nɐ] M **-s, -**, **Bah|ne|rin** [-ərɪn] F **-, -nen** *(inf)* railway *(Brit)* *or* railroad *(US)* employee

Bahn-: **Bahn|fahrt** F rail journey; **Bahn|fracht** F rail freight; **bahn|frei** ADJ, ADV *(Comm)* free on rail; **Bahn|ge|län|de** NT railway *(Brit)* *or* railroad *(US)* area; **Bahn|gleis** NT railway *(Brit)* *or* railroad *(US)* line; *(von Straßenbahn)* tram *(esp Brit)* *or* streetcar *(US)* line

Bahn|hof M (railway *(Brit)* *or* railroad *(US)*) station; *(= Busbahnhof)* bus station; *(dated: = Straßenbahndepot)* tram *(esp Brit)* *or* streetcar *(US)* depot; **am** *or* **auf dem ~** at the station; **~ Schöneberg** Schöneberg station; **ich verstehe nur ~** *(hum inf)* it's as clear as mud (to me) *(Brit inf)*, it's all Greek to me *(inf)*; **er wurde mit großem ~ empfangen** he was given the red carpet treatment, they rolled the red carpet out for him; **es wurde auf einen großen ~ verzichtet** they didn't bother with the red carpet treatment

Bahn|hof- *in cpds (esp Sw)* = **Bahnhofs-**: **Bahn|hof|buf|fet** NT *(Sw)* station buffet

Bahn|hofs- *in cpds* station; **Bahn|hofs|buch|hand|lung** F (railway *(Brit) or* railroad *(US)*) station bookshop; **Bahn|hofs|buf|fet** NT *(esp Aus)* station buffet; **Bahn|hofs|gast|stät|te** F station restaurant; **Bahn|hofs|hal|le** F (station) concourse; **in der ~** in the station; **Bahn|hofs|mis|si|on** F *charitable organization for helping needy passengers*, traveller's *(Brit) or* traveler's *(US)* aid

> **BAHNHOFSMISSION**
>
> Founded in 1897 by the Protestant and Catholic Churches, the **Bahnhofsmission** is a charity offering help in every sizeable railway station. It provides assistance to passengers in difficulty and to others, such as the homeless. Many of those working in the **Bahnhofsmission** are volunteers.

Bahn|hofs-: **Bahn|hofs|platz** M station square; **Bahn|hofs|uhr** F station clock; **Bahn|hofs|vier|tel** NT (seedy) area around the main station; **Bahn|hofs|vor|platz** M station forecourt; **sich auf dem ~ versammeln** to meet in front of the station; **Bahn|hofs|vor|stand** M *(Aus)*, **Bahn|hofs|vor|ste|her(in)** M(F) stationmaster; **Bahn|hofs|wirt|schaft** F station bar; *(= Bahnhofsrestaurant)* station restaurant

Bahn-: **Bahn|ki|lo|me|ter** M kilometre *(Brit) or* kilometer *(US)* travelled *(Brit) or* traveled *(US)* by rail, ≈ passenger mile; **Bahn|kör|per** M track; **bahn|la|gernd** ADJ, ADV *(Comm)* to be collected from *(esp Brit) or* picked up at the station; **etw ~ schicken** to send sth to be collected from *(esp Brit) or* picked up at the station

Bähn|ler ['bɛːnlɐ] M **-s, -**, **Bähn|le|rin** [-ərɪn] F **-, -nen** *(Sw)* railway *(Brit) or* railroad *(US)* employee

Bahn-: **Bahn|li|nie** F (railway *(Brit) or* railroad *(US)*) line *or* track; **Bahn|meis|te|rei** [-maistə'rai] F **-, -en** railway *(Brit) or* railroad *(US)* board; **Bahn|netz** NT rail(way) *(Brit) or* railroad *(US)* network; **Bahn|po|li|zei** F railway *(Brit) or* railroad *(US)* police; **Bahn|rei|sen|de(r)** MF *decl as adj* rail traveller *(Brit) or* traveler *(US)*, rail passenger; **Bahn|schran|ke** F, *(Aus)* **Bahn|schran|ken** M level *(Brit) or* grade *(US)* crossing barrier *or* gate; **Bahn|steig** M platform; **Bahn|steig|kar|te** F platform ticket; **Bahn|stre|cke** F railway *(Brit) or* railroad *(US)* route *or* line; **Bahn|sur|fen** NT, **Bahn-Sur|fen** NT train surfing; **Bahn|trans|port** M rail transport; *(= Güter)* consignment sent by rail; **Bahn|über|füh|rung** F railway *(Brit) or* railroad *(US)* footbridge; **Bahn|über|gang** M level *(Brit) or* grade *(US)* crossing; **beschrankter ~** level *(Brit) or* grade *(US)* crossing with gates; **unbeschrankter ~** unguarded level *(Brit) or* grade *(US)* crossing; **Bahn|un|ter|füh|rung** F railway *(Brit) or* railroad *(US)* underpass; **Bahn|ver|bin|dung** F train service; **nach einer ~ fragen** to inquire about a train connection; **Bahn|wär|ter(in)** M(F) *(an Bahnübergängen)* gatekeeper, (level *(Brit) or* grade *(US)* crossing) attendant; *(= Streckenwärter)* platelayer *(Brit)*, trackman *(US)*

Bah|re ['baːrə] F **-, -n** *(= Krankenbahre)* stretcher; *(= Totenbahre)* bier

Bah|rein [ba'rain, bax'rain] NT **-s** Bahrain

Bahr|tuch NT *pl* **-tücher** pall

Bai [bai] F **-, -en** bay

bai|risch ['bairɪʃ] ADJ *(Hist, Ling)* Bavarian

Bai|ser [bɛ'zeː] NT **-s, -s** meringue

Bais|se ['bɛːs(ə)] F **-, -n** *(St Ex)* fall; *(plötzliche)* slump; **auf (die) ~ spekulieren** to bear

Bais|se|spe|ku|lant(in) ['bɛːs(ə)-] M(F), **Bais|sier** [bɛ'sieː] M **-s, -s** *(St Ex)* bear

Ba|ja|de|re [baja'deːrə] F **-, -n** bayadere

Ba|jaz|zo [ba'jatso] M **-s, -s** clown

Ba|jo|nett [bajo'nɛt] NT **-(e)s, -e** bayonet

Ba|jo|nett-: **Ba|jo|nett|fas|sung** F *(Elec)* bayonet fitting; **Ba|jo|nett|ver|schluss** M *(Elec)* bayonet socket *or* mount

Ba|ju|wa|re [baju'vaːrə] M **-n, -n**, **Ba|ju|wa|rin** [-'vaːrɪn] F **-, -nen** *(old, hum)* Bavarian

ba|ju|wa|risch [baju'vaːrɪʃ] ADJ *(old, hum)* Bavarian

Ba|ke ['baːkə] F **-, -n** *(Naut)* marker buoy; *(Aviat)* beacon; *(= Verkehrszeichen)* distance warning signal; *(Surv)* marker pole

Ba|ke|lit® [bakə'liːt] NT **-(e)s**, *no pl* Bakelite®

Bak|ka|rat ['bakara(t), baka'ra] NT **-s**, *no pl (Cards)* baccarat

Bak|schisch ['bakʃɪʃ] NT **-s, -e** *or* **-s** baksheesh; *(= Bestechungsgeld)* bribe, backhander *(inf)*; **~ geben** to give baksheesh/a bribe *or* backhander *(inf)*

Bak|te|rie [bak'teːriə] F **-, -n** *usu pl* germ, bacterium *(spec)*; **~n** *pl* germs *pl*, bacteria *pl*

bak|te|ri|ell [bakte'riɛl] ADJ bacterial ADV bacterially; **~ verursacht** caused by germs *or* bacteria

Bak|te|ri|en- *in cpds* bacteria; **Bak|te|ri|en|kul|tur** F bacteria culture; **Bak|te|ri|en|stamm** M strain of bacteria; **Bak|te|ri|en|trä|ger(in)** M(F) carrier; **Bak|te|ri|en|züch|tung** F growing *or* culturing of bacteria

Bak|te|rio|lo|ge [bakterio'loːgə] M **-n, -n**, **Bak|te|rio|lo|gin** [-'loːgɪn] F **-, -nen** bacteriologist

Bak|te|rio|lo|gie [bakteriolo'giː] F **-**, *no pl* bacteriology

bak|te|rio|lo|gisch [bakterio'loːgɪʃ] ADJ *Forschung, Test* bacteriological; *Krieg* biological

Bak|te|ri|um [bak'teːriʊm] NT **-s**, **Bakterien** [-'teːriən] *(form)* = **Bakterie**

bak|te|ri|zid [bakteri'tsiːt] ADJ germicidal, bactericidal

Bak|te|ri|zid [bakteri'tsiːt] NT **-s, -e** [-də] germicide, bactericide

Ba|la|lai|ka [bala'laika] F **-, -s** *or* **Balalaiken** [-'laikn] balalaika

Ba|lan|ce [ba'lãːs(ə)] F **-, -n** balance, equilibrium; **die ~ halten/verlieren** to keep/lose one's balance

Ba|lan|ce-: **Ba|lan|ce|akt** [ba'lãːs(ə)-] M *(lit)* balancing *or* tightrope *or* high-wire act; *(fig)* balancing act; **Ba|lan|ce|reg|ler** [ba'lãːs(ə)-] M *(Tech)* balance control

ba|lan|cie|ren [balã'siːrən] *ptp* **balanciert** VI *aux sein* to balance; *(fig)* to achieve a balance *(zwischen +dat* between); **über etw** *(acc)* **~** to balance one's way across sth VT to balance

Ba|lan|cier|stan|ge F (balancing) pole

bal|bie|ren [bal'biːrən] *ptp* **balbiert** VT *(inf)* **jdn über den Löffel ~** to pull the wool over sb's eyes, to lead sb by the nose *(inf)*

bald [balt] ADV *comp* **eher** *or* **≃er** ['bɛldɐ] *(old, dial) superl* **am ehesten** **a** *(= schnell, in Kürze)* soon; **er kommt ~** he'll be coming soon; **~ ist Weihnachten/Winter** it will soon be Christmas/winter; **~ darauf** soon afterwards, a little later; **(all)zu ~** (all) too soon; **so ~ wie** *or* **als möglich, möglichst ~** as soon as possible; **das gibt es so ~ nicht noch einmal** you won't find one of those again in a hurry; *(besonderes Ereignis)* that won't happen again in a hurry; **wirst du wohl ~ ruhig sein?** will you just be quiet!; **wirds ~?** get a move on; **bis ~!** see you soon

b *(= fast)* almost, nearly; **das ist ~ nicht mehr schön** that is really beyond a joke *(Brit)*, that's going too far

CONJ *(geh)* **~ …, ~ …** one moment …, the next …, now …, now …; **~ hier, ~ da** now here, now there; **~ so, ~ so** now this way, now that

Bal|da|chin ['baldaxiːn, balda'xiːn] M **-s, -e** canopy, baldachin; *(Archit)* baldachin, baldaquin

Bäl|de ['bɛldə] F **in ~** in the near future

bal|dig ['baldɪç] ADJ *attr no comp* quick, speedy; *Antwort, Wiedersehen* early; **wir hoffen auf Ihr ~es Kommen** we hope you will come soon; **auf ~es Wiedersehen!** (hope to) see you soon!

bal|digst ['baldɪçst] ADV *superl von* **baldig** *(form)* as soon as possible, without delay

bald|mög|lichst ADV as soon as possible

bal|do|wern [bal'doːvɐn] *ptp* **baldowert** VT *(inf)* = **ausbaldowern**

Bald|ri|an ['baldriaːn] M **-s, -e** valerian

Bald|ri|an|trop|fen PL valerian (drops *pl*)

Bal|dur ['baldʊr] M **-s** *(Myth)* Balder

Ba|le|a|ren [bale'aːrən] PL **die ~** the Balearic Islands *pl*

Balg [balk] M **-(e)s, ≃e** ['bɛlgə] **a** *(= Tierhaut)* pelt, skin; *(von Vogel)* skin; *(inf: = Bauch)* belly *(Brit inf)*, stomach; *(einer Puppe)* body; **einem Tier den ~ abziehen** to skin an animal; **sich** *(dat)* **den ~ vollschlagen** *or* **vollstopfen** *(inf)* to stuff oneself *(inf)*; **ich habe eine Wut im ~** *(inf)* I'm mad *or* livid → **rücken VI b** *(= Blasebalg, Phot, Rail)* bellows *pl*; **die Bälge treten** to work the bellows

Balg M OR NT **-(e)s, ≃er** ['bɛlgɐ] *(pej inf: = Kind)* brat *(pej inf)*

bal|gen ['balgn] VR to scrap (*um* over)

Bal|gen ['balgn] M **-s, -** *(Phot)* bellows *pl*

Bal|ge|rei [balgə'rai] F **-, -en** scrap, tussle; **hört jetzt auf mit der ~!** stop scrapping!

Bal|kan ['balkaːn] M **-s** **a** *(= Balkanhalbinsel, Balkanländer)* **der ~** the Balkans *pl*; **auf dem ~** in the Balkans; **vom ~** from the Balkans; **dort herrschen Zustände wie auf dem ~** *(fig inf)* things are in a terrible state there **b** *(= Balkangebirge)* Balkan Mountains *pl*

Bal|kan|halb|in|sel F Balkan Peninsula

bal|ka|nisch [bal'kaːnɪʃ] ADJ Balkan

bal|ka|ni|sie|ren [balkani'ziːrən] *ptp* **balkanisiert** VT to Balkanize

Bal|ka|ni|sie|rung F **-, -en** Balkanization

Bal|kan-: **Bal|kan|län|der** PL Balkan States; **Bal|kan|staat** M Balkan state

Bälk|chen ['bɛlkçən] NT **-s, -** *dim von* **Balken**

Bal|ken ['balkn] M **-s, -** **a** *(= Holzbalken, Schwebebalken)* beam; *(= Stützbalken)* prop, shore; *(= Querbalken)* joist, crossbeam; *(Sport: bei Hürdenlauf)* rail; **der ~ im eigenen Auge** *(Bibl)* the beam in one's own eye; **lügen, dass sich die ~ biegen** *(inf)* to lie through one's teeth, to tell a pack of lies; **Wasser hat keine ~** *(Prov)* not everyone can walk on water **b** *(= Strich)* bar; *(Her)* fess(e); *(= Uniformstreifen)* stripe **c** *(an Waage)* beam

Bal|ken-: **Bal|ken|brü|cke** F girder bridge; **Bal|ken|code** M barcode *(Brit)*, universal product code *(US)*; **Bal|ken|de|cke** F ceiling with wooden beams; **Bal|ken|di|a|gramm** NT bar chart; **Bal|ken|holz** NT (piece of) (squared) timber; *(= Balkengerüst)* timbers *pl*, beams *pl*; **Bal|ken|kode** M = **Balkencode**; **Bal|ken|konst|ruk|ti|on** F timber frame construction; **Bal|ken|über|schrift** F *(Press)* banner headline; **Bal|ken|waa|ge** F (beam) balance; **Bal|ken|werk** NT timbering, timbers *pl*, beams *pl*

Bal|kon [bal'kɔŋ, bal'koːn] M **-s, -s** *or (bei dt. Aussprache)* **-e** balcony; *(Theat)* (dress) circle *(esp Brit)*, balcony; **~ sitzen** *(Theat)* to have seats in the (dress) circle *(esp Brit) or* balcony

Bal|kon-: **Bal|kon|blu|me** F balcony plant; **Bal|kon|mö|bel** PL garden furniture *sing*; **Bal|kon|pflan|ze** F balcony plant; **Bal|kon|tür** F French window(s *pl*); **Bal|kon|zim|mer** NT room with a balcony

Ball [bal] M **-(e)s, ≃e** ['bɛlə] ball; **~ spielen** to play (with a) ball; **am ~ sein** *(lit)* to have the ball, to be in possession of the ball; **immer am ~ sein** *(fig)* to be on the ball; **am ~ bleiben** *(lit)* to keep (possession of) the ball; *(fig: = auf dem neuesten Stand bleiben)* to stay on the ball; **bei jdm am ~ bleiben** *(fig)* to keep in with sb; **er bemüht sich, bei ihr am ~ zu bleiben** he is trying to keep in the running with her; **hart am ~ bleiben** to stick at it; **jdm den ~ zuspielen** *(lit)* to pass (the ball) to sb; **jdm/sich gegenseitig**

die Bälle zuspielen *or* **zuwerfen** *(fig)* to feed sb/ each other lines; **den ~ aufgreifen** *or* **aufnehmen** *(fig)* to take up the theme; **einen ~ machen** *(Billard)* to pocket a ball; **der glutrote ~ der Sonne** *(poet)* the sun's fiery orb *(poet)*

Ball M -(e)s, ⸚e ['bɛlə] *(= Tanzfest)* ball; **auf dem ~** at the ball

bal|la|bal|la [bala'bala] ADJ *pred (dated inf)* mad, crazy *(inf)*, nuts *(inf)*

Ball|ab|ga|be F *(Sport)* pass; **bei der ~** when the ball was played, when he/she *etc* played the ball

Bal|la|de [ba'la:də] F -, -n ballad

bal|la|den|haft ADJ balladic, ballad-like ADV in a balladic *or* ballad-like way *or* manner

Bal|la|den|sän|ger(in) M(F) balladeer, ballad singer

bal|la|desk [bala'dɛsk] ADJ, ADV = **balladenhaft**

Ball|an|nah|me F *(Sport)* stopping and controlling the ball; *(aus der Luft)* bringing down the ball

Bal|last ['balast, ba'last] M -(e)s, *(rare)* -e *(Naut, Aviat)* ballast; *(fig)* burden, encumbrance; *(in Büchern)* padding; **~ abwerfen, ~ über Bord werfen** *(lit)* to discharge *or* shed ballast; *(fig)* to get rid of a burden *or* an encumbrance; **mit ~ beladen** *or* **beschweren** to ballast, to load with ballast; **jdn/etw als ~ empfinden** to find sb/sth (to be) a burden *or* an encumbrance

Bal|last|stof|fe PL *(Med)* roughage *sing*, dietary fibre *(Brit) or* fiber *(US)*

bal|last|stoff|reich ADJ high-fibre *(Brit) or* -fiber *(US)*; **~e Nahrung** *or* **Ernährung** high-fibre *(Brit) or* -fiber *(US)* food(s *pl*) *or* diet

Ball-: **Ball|be|herr|schung** F *(Sport)* ball control; **Ball|be|sitz** M *(Sport)* **im ~ sein** to have possession (of the ball), to be in possession of the ball

Bäll|chen ['bɛlçən] NT -s, - *dim von* **Ball**

bal|len ['balən] VT *Faust* to clench; *Papier* to crumple (into a ball); *Lehm etc* to press (into a ball) → *auch* **geballt, Faust** VR *(Menschenmenge)* to crowd; *(Wolken)* to gather, to build up; *(Verkehr)* to build up; *(Faust)* to clench

Bal|len ['balən] M -s, - **a** bale; *(= Kaffeeballen)* sack; **in ~ verpacken** to bale **b** *(Anat: an Daumen, Zehen)* ball; *(an Pfote)* pad **c** *(Med: am Fußknochen)* bunion

bal|len|wei|se ADV in bales

Bal|le|rei [balə'rai] F -, -en *(inf)* shoot-out *(inf)*, shoot-up *(inf)*

Bal|le|ri|na [balə'ri:na] F -, **Balleri|nen** [-'ri:nən] ballerina, ballet dancer

Bal|le|ri|na M -s, -s *(= Schuh)* pump

Bal|le|ri|nas PL *(Fashion)* ballerina shoes *pl*

Bal|ler|mann ['baleman] M *pl* **-männer** *(dated sl)* iron *(inf)*, gun

bal|lern ['balen] VI *(inf)* to shoot, to fire; *(Schuss)* to ring out; **gegen die Tür ~** to hammer *or* beat on the door VT *Stein etc* to hurl; *Tür etc* to slam

Bal|lett [ba'lɛt] NT -(e)s, -e ballet; **beim ~ sein** *(inf)* to be (a dancer) with the ballet, to be a ballet dancer; **zum ~ gehen** to become a ballet dancer

Ballettänzer(in) △ M(F) → **Balletttänzer**

Bal|let|teu|se [balɛ'tø:zə] F -, -n *(usu pej)* ballet dancer

Bal|lett- *in cpds* ballet; **Bal|lett|meis|ter(in)** M(F) ballet master/mistress; **Bal|lett|rat|te** F *(inf)* ballet pupil; **Bal|lett|röck|chen** NT tutu; **Bal|lett|schuh** M ballet shoe; **Bal|lett|tän|zer(in)** M(F) ballet dancer; **Bal|lett|trup|pe** F ballet (company)

Ball-: **ball|för|mig** ADJ ball-shaped, round; **Ball|füh|ren|de(r)** MF *(Sport)* ball carrier, man *or* woman on the ball; **Ball|füh|rung** F *(Sport)* ball control; **Ball|ge|fühl** NT *(Sport)* feel for the ball

Bal|lis|tik [ba'lɪstɪk] F -, *no pl* ballistics *sing*

bal|lis|tisch [ba'lɪstɪʃ] ADJ ballistic

Ball-: **Ball|jun|ge** M *(Tennis)* ball boy; **Ball|kleid** NT ball dress *or* gown; **Ball|kö|ni|gin** F belle of the ball; **Ball|künst|ler(in)** M(F) *(Ftbl)* artist with the ball; **Ball|mäd|chen** NT *(Tennis)* ball girl

Bal|lon [ba'lɔŋ, ba'lo:n, ba'lõ:] M -s, -s *or (bei deutscher Aussprache)* -e **a** balloon **b** *(Chem)* carboy, demijohn

Bal|lon-: **Bal|lon|di|la|ta|ti|on** F -, -en *(Med)* balloon dilatation; **Bal|lon|fah|rer(in)** M(F) balloonist; **Bal|lon|fahrt** F balloon ride *or* trip; **eine ~ machen** to go up in a/one's balloon; **Bal|lon|müt|ze** F baker's boy cap; **Bal|lon|rei|fen** M balloon tyre *(Brit) or* tire *(US)*

Ball-: **Ball|saal** M ballroom; **Ball|scha|ni** ['balʃa:ni] M -s, - *(Aus inf)* ball boy; **Ball|schuh** M evening *or* dancing shoe; **Ball|spiel** NT ball game; **Ball|spie|len** NT -s, *no pl* playing ball; **„Ballspielen verboten"** "no ball games"; **Ball|tech|nik** F *(Sport)* technique with the ball; **Ball|tre|ter(in)** M(F) *(inf)* footballer *(Brit)*, soccer player *(US)*

Bal|lung ['balʊŋ] F -, -en concentration; *(von Truppen auch)* massing

Bal|lungs-: **Bal|lungs|ge|biet** NT, **Bal|lungs|raum** M conurbation; **Bal|lungs|zent|rum** NT centre *(Brit) or* center *(US, of population, industry etc)*

Ball-: **ball|ver|liebt** ADJ *(Sport) Fußballspieler* selfish; **~ sein** to hold onto the ball, to refuse to let go of the ball; **M. ist einfach zu ~** M. won't pass the ball; **Ball|ver|lust** M ball loss; **Ball|wech|sel** M *(Sport)* rally

Bal|neo|lo|gie [balneolo'gi:] F -, *no pl* balneology

Bal pa|ra|dox ['bal para'dɔks] M - -, -s - *ball at which women ask men to dance*

Bal pa|ré ['bal pa're:] M - -, -s -s grand ball

Bal|sa|holz ['balza-] NT balsa wood

Bal|sam ['balza:m] M -s, -e balsam, balm *(liter)*; *(fig)* balm; **~ in jds Wunden** *(acc)* **träufeln** *(liter)* to pour balm on sb's wounds; **die Zeit ist ein heilender ~** *(liter)* time is a great healer

Bal|sam|es|sig M balsamic vinegar

bal|sa|mie|ren [balza'mi:rən] *ptp* **balsamiert** VT to embalm

bal|sa|misch [bal'za:mɪʃ] ADJ *(liter)* **a** *(= duftend)* balmy *(liter)*, fragrant **b** *(= lindernd)* soothing

Bal|te ['baltə] M -n, -n, **Bal|tin** [-tɪn] F -, -nen person *or* man/woman from the Baltic; **er ist ~** he comes from the Baltic

Bal|ten|re|pub|lik F Baltic republic

Bal|ten|staat M Baltic state

Bal|ti|kum ['baltikʊm] NT -s **das ~** the Baltic States *pl*

Bal|tin [-tɪn] F → **Balte**

bal|tisch ['baltɪʃ] ADJ Baltic *attr*

Ba|lust|ra|de [balʊs'tra:də] F -, -n balustrade

Balz [balts] F -, -en **a** *(= Paarungsspiel)* courtship display **b** *(= Paarungszeit)* mating season

bal|zen ['baltsn] VI to perform the courtship display; *(pej: Sänger)* to croon

Balz-: **Balz|ruf** M mating call *or* cry; **Balz|ver|hal|ten** NT mating *or* courtship display *or* behaviour *(Brit) or* behavior *(US)*; **Balz|zeit** F mating season

Bam|bi ['bambi] NT -s, -s *(inf: = Rehkitz)* young deer

Bam|bi M -s, -s Bambi *(German film award)*

Bam|bu|le [bam'bu:lə] F -, -n *(sl)* ructions *pl (inf)*; **~ machen** to go on the rampage

Bam|bus ['bambʊs] M -ses *or* -, -se bamboo

Bam|bus- *in cpds* bamboo; **Bam|bus|rohr** NT bamboo cane; **Bam|bus|spros|sen** PL bamboo shoots *pl*; **Bam|bus|stab** M *(Sport)* bamboo (vaulting) pole; **Bam|bus|vor|hang** M *(Pol)* bamboo curtain

Bam|mel ['baml] M -s, *no pl (inf)* **(einen) ~ vor jdm/etw haben** to be nervous *or (stärker)* scared of sb/sth

bam|meln ['bamln] VI *(inf)* to swing, to dangle *(an +dat, von* from)

ba|nal [ba'na:l] ADJ banal, trite ADV banally, tritely; **~ klingen, sich ~ anhören** to sound banal *or* trite

ba|na|li|sie|ren [banali'zi:rən] *ptp* **banalisiert** VT to trivialize

Ba|na|li|tät [banali'tɛ:t] F -, -en **a** *no pl* banality, triteness **b** *usu pl (Äußerung)* platitude; **~en äußern** to utter platitudes

Ba|na|ne [ba'na:nə] F -, -n banana

Ba|na|nen-: **Ba|na|nen|damp|fer** M banana boat; **Ba|na|nen|flan|ke** F *(Ftbl inf)* curving cross; **Ba|na|nen|re|pub|lik** F *(Pol pej)* banana republic; **Ba|na|nen|scha|le** F banana skin; **Ba|na|nen|stau|de** F banana tree; **Ba|na|nen|ste|cker** M jack plug

Ba|nau|se [ba'nauzə] M -n, -n, **Ba|nau|sin** [-'nauzɪn] F -, -nen *(pej)* peasant *(inf)*; *(= Kulturbanause auch)* Philistine

Ba|nau|sen-: **ba|nau|sen|haft** ADJ Philistine ADV *sich äußern, sich benehmen* like a Philistine; **Ba|nau|sen|tum** [ba'nauzntu:m] NT -s, *no pl (pej)* Philistinism

band *pret von* **binden**

Band [bant] NT -(e)s, ⸚er ['bɛndɐ] **a** *(= Seidenband etc)* ribbon; *(= Isolierband, Maßband, Zielband)* tape; *(= Haarband, Hutband)* band; *(= Schürzenband)* string; *(Tech: zur Verpackung)* (metal) band; *(= Fassband)* hoop; *(Art: = Ornament)* band; **das Blaue ~** the Blue Riband; **das silberne ~ des Nils** *(liter)* the silver ribbon of the Nile

b *(= Tonband)* (recording) tape; **etw auf ~ aufnehmen** to tape *or* (tape-)record sth; **etw auf ~ sprechen** to record sth on tape; **etw auf ~ diktieren** to dictate sth onto tape

c *(= Fließband)* conveyor belt; *(als Einrichtung)* production line; *(= Montageband)* assembly line; *(in Autowerk)* track *(inf)*; **am ~ arbeiten** *or* **stehen** to work on the production line *etc*; **vom ~ laufen** to come off the conveyor belt *etc*; **ein neues Auto auf ~ legen** *(Ind inf)* to put a new car into production; **durchs ~ (weg)** *(Sw)* every single one (without exception); **am laufenden ~** *(fig)* nonstop, continuously; **es gab Ärger am laufenden ~** there was nonstop *or* continuous trouble; **etw am laufenden ~ tun** to keep on doing sth

d *(Rad)* wavelength, frequency band; **auf dem 44m-~ senden** to broadcast on the 44m band

e *(Anat) usu pl* ligament

f *(= Baubeschlag)* hinge

Band NT -(e)s, -e [-də] *(liter)* **a das ~ der Freundschaft/Liebe** *etc* the bonds *or* ties of friendship/love *etc*; **familiäre ~e** family ties; **mit jdm freundschaftliche ~e anknüpfen** to become *or* make friends with sb; **zarte ~e knüpfen sich an** Cupid is at work; **zarte ~e knüpfen** to start a romance **b Bande** PL *(= Fesseln)* bonds *pl*, fetters *pl*; *(fig auch)* shackles *pl*; **jdn in ~e schlagen** to clap *or* put sb in irons

Band M -(e)s, ⸚e *(= Buchband)* volume; **ein gewaltiger ~** a mighty tome; **darüber könnte man Bände schreiben** *or* **erzählen** you could write volumes *or* a book about that; **mit etw Bände füllen** to write volumes about sth; **das spricht Bände** that speaks volumes

Band [bɛnt] F -, -s *(Mus)* band; *(= Beatband auch)* group

Ban|da|ge [ban'da:ʒə] F -, -n bandage; **mit harten ~n kämpfen** *(fig inf)* to fight with no holds barred

ban|da|gie|ren [banda'ʒi:rən] *ptp* **bandagiert** VT to bandage (up)

Band-: **Band|auf|nah|me** F tape recording; **Band|auf|nah|me|ge|rät** NT tape recorder; **Band|brei|te** F **a** *(Rad)* waveband, frequency range **b** *(fig)* range **c** *(Fin)* (range of) fluctuation *or* variation *(Comput)* bandwidth

Bänd|chen ['bɛntçən] NT -s, - *dim von* **Band a**, *von* **Band**

Ban|de ['bandə] F -, -n gang; *(= Schmugglerbande)* band; *(inf: = Gruppe)* bunch *(inf)*, crew *(inf)*

Ban|de F -, -n *(Sport) (von Eisbahn, Reitbahn)* barrier; *(Billard)* cushion; *(von Kegelbahn)* edge; **die Kugel an die ~ spielen** to play the ball off the cushion/edge

Ban|deau|top NT *(Fashion)* bandeau top
Band|ei|sen NT metal hoop
Bän|del ['bɛndl] M OR NT **-s, -** *(dial)* ribbon; *(= Schnürsenkel)* shoelace; **jdn am ~ haben** *or* **führen** *(dated inf)* to be able to twist sb round one's little finger *(inf)*
Ban|den-: **Ban|den|be|kämp|fung** F *(Mil sl)* guerilla warfare; **Ban|den|chef(in)** M(F) *(inf)* gang leader; **Ban|den|dieb|stahl** M *(Jur)* gang robbery; **Ban|den|füh|rer(in)** M(F) gang leader; **Ban|den|krieg** M gang war; **Ban|den|kri|mi|na|li|tät** F gang crime; **Ban|den|mit|glied** NT member of a/the gang, gang member, gangbanger *(sl)*; **Ban|den|wer|bung** F pitch-perimeter advertising; **Ban|den|we|sen** NT gangsterism
Ban|de|ro|le [bandə'ro:lə] F **-, -n** tax *or* revenue seal
Bän|der- *(Med)*: **Bän|der|riss** M torn ligament; **Bän|der|zer|rung** F pulled ligament
Band-: **Band|fil|ter** M OR NT *(Rad)* band-pass filter; **Band|för|de|rer** M conveyor belt
-bän|dig [bɛndɪç] ADJ *suf* -volume; **eine dreibändige Ausgabe** a three-volume edition, an edition in three volumes
bän|di|gen ['bɛndɪgn] VT *(= zähmen)* to tame; *(= niederhalten) Menschen, Tobenden etc* to (bring under) control, to subdue; *(= zügeln) Leidenschaften etc* to (bring under) control, to master; *Wut* to control; *Naturgewalten* to harness; *Kinder* to (bring under) control; **du musst lernen, dich zu ~** you must learn to control yourself
Bän|di|ger ['bɛndɪgɐ] M **-s, -, Bän|di|ge|rin** [-ərɪn] F **-, -nen** (animal) tamer
Bän|di|gung F **-, -en** *(= Zähmung)* taming; *(von Menschen)* subduing; *(von Leidenschaften)* mastering; *(von Naturgewalten)* harnessing
Ban|dit [ban'di:t] M **-en, -en, Ban|di|tin** [-'di:tɪn] F **-, -nen** bandit, brigand; *(fig pej)* brigand; **einarmiger ~** one-armed bandit
Ban|di|ten|tum [ban'di:tntu:m] NT **-s,** *no pl,* **Ban|di|ten|(un)|we|sen** NT banditry
Band|ke|ra|mik F *(Archeol)* ribbon ware, band ceramics *pl*
Bändl ['bɛndl] NT **-s, -** = **Bändel**
Band|lauf|werk NT *(Comput)* tape drive
Band|lea|der ['bɛntli:dɐ] M **-s, -, Band|lea|de|rin** [-ərɪn] F **-, -nen** band leader
Band-: **Band|maß** NT tape measure; **Band|nu|deln** PL ribbon noodles *pl*
Ban|dog ['bɛndɔk] M **-s, -s** bandog
Ban|do|ne|on [ban'do:neɔn] NT **-s, -s, Ban|do|ni|on** [ban'do:niɔn] NT **-s, -s** bandoneon, bandonion
Band-: **Band|sä|ge** F band saw; **Band|sa|lat** M *(inf)* **dann bekommen Sie ~** then your tape gets tangled up, then your tape gets into a tangle; **Band|schei|be** F *(Anat)* (intervertebral) disc; **er hats an** *or* **mit der ~** *(inf)* he has slipped a disc, he has a slipped disc; **Band|schei|ben|scha|den** M, **Band|schei|ben|vor|fall** M slipped disc; **Band|stahl** M strip *or* band steel; **Band|werk** NT *(Art)* interlace; **Band|wurm** M tapeworm; **ein ~ von einem Satz** *(hum)* an endless *or* never-ending sentence; **Band|wurm|satz** M *(inf)* long *or* lengthy sentence
bang [baŋ] ADJ *comp* **-er** *or* **⸚er** ['bɛŋɐ], *superl* **-ste(r, s)** *or* **⸚ste(r, s)** ['bɛŋstə] **a** *attr (= ängstlich)* scared, frightened; **mir ist ~ vor ihm** I'm scared *or* frightened *or* afraid of him; **mir ist ~ vor der Prüfung** I'm scared *or* frightened of the exam; **das wird schon klappen, da ist mir gar nicht ~** it will be all right, I am quite sure of it → **angst, Angst**
b *(geh: = beklommen)* uneasy; *Augenblicke, Stunden auch* anxious, worried (*um* about); **es wurde ihr ~ ums Herz** her heart sank, she got a sinking feeling; **ihr wurde ~ und bänger** she became more and more afraid; **eine ~e Ahnung** a sense of foreboding
c *(S Ger)* **ihr war ~ nach dem Kinde** she longed *or* yearned *(liter)* for the child, she longed *or* yearned *(liter)* to be with the child
Bang|büx ['baŋbʏks] F **-, -en** *(N Ger inf)* scaredy-cat *(inf)*
ban|ge ['baŋə] ADJ *comp* **-r** *or* **⸚r** ['bɛŋɐ], *superl* **bangste(r, s)** *or* **bängste(r, s)** ['bɛŋstə] = **bang**
Ban|ge ['baŋə] F **-,** *no pl (esp N Ger)* **~ haben** to be scared *or* frightened (*vor +dat* of); **jdm ~ machen** to scare *or* frighten sb; **~ machen gilt nicht** *(inf)* you can't scare me, you won't put the wind up me *(Brit inf)*; **nur keine ~!** *(inf)* don't worry
Ban|ge-: **Ban|ge|ma|chen** NT **-s,** *no pl* scaremongering *(esp Brit)*; **~ gilt nicht** *(inf)* you can't scare me, you won't put the wind up me *(Brit inf)*; **Ban|ge|ma|cher(in)** M(F) scaremonger *(esp Brit)*, alarmist
ban|gen ['baŋən] *(geh)* **VI** **a** *(= Angst haben)* to be afraid (*vor +dat* of); **es bangt mir vor ihm, mir bangt vor ihm** I'm afraid *or* frightened of him, I fear him **b** *(= sich sorgen)* to worry, to be worried (*um* about); **um jds Leben ~** to fear for sb's life **c** *(dial, liter)* **nach jdm/etw ~** to long *or* yearn *(liter)* for sb/sth **VR** to be worried *or* anxious (*um* about)
Ban|gig|keit ['baŋɪçkait] F **-,** *no pl (= Furcht)* nervousness; *(= Sorge)* anxiety; *(= Beklemmung)* apprehension
Bang|la|desch [baŋgla'dɛʃ] NT **-s** Bangladesh
Bang|la|de|scher [baŋgla'dɛʃɐ] M **-s, -, Bang|la|de|sche|rin** [-ərɪn] F **-, -nen** Bangladeshi
Bang|la|desh [baŋgla'dɛʃ] NT **-s, -** Bangladesh
Bang|la|de|shi [baŋgla'dɛʃi] MF **-, -** Bangladeshi
bäng|lich ['bɛŋlɪç] ADJ *(geh)* nervous
Ban|jo ['banjo, 'bɛndʒo, 'bandʒo] NT **-s, -s** banjo
Bank [baŋk] F **-, ⸚e** ['bɛŋkə] **a** bench; *(mit Lehne)* seat; *(= Kirchenbank)* pew; *(= Parlamentsbank)* bench; *(= Anklagebank)* dock; **auf** *or* **in der ersten/letzten ~** on the front/back bench *etc*; **er predigte vor leeren Bänken** he preached to an empty church; **die Debatte fand vor leeren Bänken statt** the debate took place in an empty house; **(alle) durch die ~ (weg)** *(inf)* every single *or* last one, the whole lot (of them) *(inf)*; **etw auf die lange ~ schieben** *(inf)* to put sth off
b *(= Arbeitstisch)* (work)bench; *(= Drehbank)* lathe
c *(= Sandbank)* sandbank, sandbar; *(= Nebelbank, Wolkenbank)* bank; *(= Austernbank)* bed; *(= Korallenbank)* reef; *(Geol)* layer, bed
d *(Ringen)* crouch (position)
Bank F **-, -en** **a** *(Fin, Comm)* bank; **Geld auf der ~ liegen haben** to have money in the bank; **bei der ~** at the bank; **ein Konto bei einer ~ eröffnen** to open an account with a bank; **bei der ~ arbeiten** *or* **sein** *(inf)* to work for the bank, to be with the bank **b** *(bei Glücksspielen)* bank; **(die) ~ halten** *(inf)* to hold *or* be the bank, to be banker; **die ~ sprengen** to break the bank
Bank-: **Bank|an|ge|stell|te(r)** MF *decl as adj* bank employee; **Bank|an|wei|sung** F banker's order; **Bank|auf|sicht** F = **Bankenaufsicht**; **Bank|auf|sichts|be|hör|de** F = **Bankenaufsichtsbehörde**; **Bank|au|to|mat** M cash dispenser *(Brit)*, money machine *(US)*, ATM; **Bank|be|am|te(r)** M *decl as adj (dated)*, **Bank|be|am|tin** F *(dated)* bank employee; **Bank|bürg|schaft** F *(Fin)* bank guarantee
Bänk|chen ['bɛŋkçən] NT **-s, -** *dim von* **Bank a**
Bank|di|rek|tor(in) M(F) director of a/the bank
Bank|drü|cken NT *(Sport)* bench press
Bank|ein|bruch M bank raid
Bank|ein|la|ge F *(Comm)* bank deposit
Bank|ein|zug M *(Comm)* direct debit, automatic payment *(US) or* draft *(US)*; **per ~ zahlen** to pay by direct debit *or* automatic draft *(US)*
Bank|ein|zugs|ver|fah|ren NT *(Comm)* direct debiting, automatic payment transfer *(US)*
Bän|kel-: **Bän|kel|lied** NT street ballad; **Bän|kel|sang** M **-(e)s,** *no pl* ballad; **Bän|kel|sän|ger** M ballad singer, minstrel
Ban|ken-: **Ban|ken|auf|sicht** F *(Fin)* **a** *(Behörde)* banking regulatory authority **b** *(Kontrolle)* banking regulation; **Ban|ken|auf|sichts|be|hör|de** F banking regulatory authority; **Ban|ken|kon|sor|ti|um** NT banking syndicate *or* group; **Ban|ken|platz** M banking *or* financial centre *(Brit) or* center *(US)*; **Ban|ken|vier|tel** NT banking area
Ban|ker ['bɛŋkɐ] M **-s, -, Ban|ke|rin** [-ərɪn] F **-, -nen** *(inf)* banker
Ban|kert ['baŋkɐt] M **-s, -e** *(old pej)* bastard
Ban|kett [baŋ'kɛt] NT **-(e)s, -e** *(= Festessen)* banquet
Ban|kett NT **-(e)s, -e, Ban|ket|te** [baŋ'kɛtə] F **-, -n** **a** *(an Straßen)* verge *(Brit)*, shoulder *(US)*; *(an Autobahnen)* (hard) shoulder; **„Bankette nicht befahrbar", „weiche ~e"** "soft verges *(Brit) or* shoulder *(US)*" **b** *(Build)* footing
Bank-: **Bank|fach** NT **a** *(= Beruf)* banking, banking profession; **im ~** in banking, in the banking profession **b** *(= Schließfach)* safety-deposit box; **Bank|fi|li|a|le** F branch of a bank; **Bank|ge|bäu|de** NT bank; **Bank|ge|bühr** F bank charge; **Bank|ge|heim|nis** NT confidentiality in banking; **Bank|ge|schäft** NT **a** banking transaction **b** *no pl (= Bankwesen)* banking world; **Bank|ge|wer|be** NT banking industry; **Bank|gut|ha|ben** NT bank balance; **Bank|hal|ter(in)** M(F) *(bei Glücksspielen)* bank, banker; **Bank|haus** NT **~ Grün & Co** Grün & Co, Bankers
Ban|ki|er [baŋ'kie:] M **-s, -s** banker
Ban|king ['bɛŋkɪŋ] NT **-s,** *no pl (Fin)* banking
Bank-: **Bank|kar|te** F bank card; **Bank|kauf|frau** F, **Bank|kauf|mann** M (qualified) bank clerk; **Bank|kon|to** NT bank account; **Bank|kre|dit** [-kredi:t] M bank loan; **Bank|krei|se** [-kraizə] PL banking circles *pl*, the banking community *sing*; **Bank|leh|re** F training as a bank clerk; **eine ~ machen** to train as a bank clerk; **Bank|leit|zahl** F bank code number, (bank) sort code *(Brit)*, A.B.A. *or* routing number *(US)*; **Bank|nach|bar(in)** M(F) *(Sch)* **sie ist meine ~in** I sit next to her (at school); **Bank|no|te** F banknote, bill *(US)*
Ban|ko|mat [baŋko'ma:t] M **-en, -en** cash dispenser, hole-in-the-wall *(inf)*, ATM *(US)*
Ban|ko|mat|kar|te F cash card, ATM card *(US)*
Bank-: **Bank|platz** M = **Bankenplatz**; **Bank|pro|vi|si|on** F *(Fin)* bank commission; **Bank|ra|te** M official discount rate; **Bank|raub** M bank robbery; **Bank|räu|ber(in)** M(F) bank robber
bank|rott [baŋ'krɔt] ADJ bankrupt; *Mensch, Politik* discredited; *Kultur* debased; *(moralisch)* bankrupt; **jdn ~ machen** to make sb (go) bankrupt, to bankrupt sb; **er ist politisch/innerlich ~** he is a politically discredited/a broken man
Bank|rott [baŋ'krɔt] M **-(e)s, -e** bankruptcy; *(fig)* breakdown, collapse; *(moralisch)* bankruptcy; **~ machen** to become *or* go bankrupt; **den ~ anmelden** *or* **ansagen** *or* **erklären** to declare oneself bankrupt → **bankrottgehen**
Bank|rott|er|klä|rung F declaration of bankruptcy; *(fig)* sellout *(inf)*
Bank|rot|teur [baŋkrɔ'tø:ɐ] M **-s, -e, Bank|rot|teu|rin** [-'tø:rɪn] F **-, -nen** *(lit, fig)* bankrupt; *(fig)* moral bankrupt
bank|rott+ge|hen VI *sep irreg aux sein* to become *or* go bankrupt
Bank-: **Bank|schal|ter** M bank counter *or* window; **Bank|scheck** M cheque *(Brit)*, check *(US)*; **Bank|schließ|fach** NT safety-deposit box *(in bank)*; **Bank|schuld|ver|schrei|bung** F *(Fin)* (bank) bond; **Bank|spe|sen** PL bank (-ing) charges *pl*; **Bank|über|fall** M bank raid; **Bank|über|wei|sung** F bank transfer; **bank|üb|lich** ADJ **es ist ~** it is normal bank-

ing practice; **Bank|ver|bin|dung** F banking arrangements *pl*; **geben Sie bitte Ihre ~ an** please give your account details; **Bank|ver|kehr** M bank transactions *pl*; **Bank|we|sen** NT **das ~** banking

Bann [ban] M -(e)s, -e **a** no pl (geh: = magische Gewalt) spell; **im ~ eines Menschen/einer Sache stehen** or **sein** to be under sb's spell/the spell of sth; **jdn in seinen ~ schlagen** to captivate sb; **sie zog** or **zwang ihn in ihren ~** she cast her spell over him **b** (Hist: = Kirchenbann) excommunication; **jdn in den ~ tun, jdn mit dem ~ belegen, den ~ über jdn aussprechen** to excommunicate sb; **jdn vom ~ lösen** to absolve sb

Bann|brief M, **Bann|bul|le** F (Hist) letter of excommunication

ban|nen ['banən] VT **a** (geh: = bezaubern) to bewitch, to captivate, to entrance; **jdn/etw auf die Platte** (inf)/**die Leinwand ~** (geh) to capture sb/sth on film/canvas → auch **gebannt** **b** (= vertreiben) böse Geister, Teufel to exorcize; (= abwenden) Gefahr to avert, to ward off **c** (Hist) to excommunicate

Ban|ner ['banɐ] NT -s, - (geh) banner; (fig auch) flag; (Internet) banner ad; **das ~ des Sozialismus hochhalten** to fly the flag of socialism, to wave the banner of socialism

Ban|ner-: **Ban|ner|trä|ger(in)** M(F) (geh) standard-bearer; (fig) vanguard *no pl*; **Ban|ner|wer|bung** F (Internet) (= Anzeige) banner ad; (das Werben) banner advertising

Bann|fluch M excommunication

ban|nig ['banıç] ADV (N Ger inf) terribly, really; **das hat ~ Spaß gemacht** that was great fun

Bann-: **Bann|kreis** M (fig) **in jds ~ (dat) stehen** to be under sb's influence; **Bann|mei|le** F inviolable precincts *pl (of city, Parliament etc)*; **Bann|spruch** M excommunication; **Bann|strahl** M (liter) excommunication; **Bann|wald** M (Aus, Sw) *protected forest that acts as a shield against avalanches etc*; **Bann|wart** ['banwart] M -(e)s, -e, **Bann|war|tin** [-tın] F -, -nen (Sw) forester

Ban|tam ['bantam] NT -s, -s bantam

Ban|tam-: **Ban|tam|ge|wicht** NT bantamweight; **Ban|tam|ge|wicht|ler** [-gəvıçtlɐ] M -s, -, **Ban|tam|ge|wicht|le|rin** [-ərın] F -, -nen bantamweight; **Ban|tam|huhn** NT bantam

Ban|tu ['bantu] M -(s), -(s) Bantu

Ban|tu-: **Ban|tu|frau** F Bantu woman; **Ban|tu|ne|ger(in)** M(F) (neg!) Bantu; **Ban|tu|spra|che** F Bantu language

Bap|tist [bap'tıst] M -en, -en, **Bap|tis|tin** [-'tıstın] F -, -nen Baptist

Bap|tis|te|ri|um [baptıs'te:rium] NT -s, **Baptisterien** [-riən] (Eccl) baptistry; (= Taufbecken) font

bar [ba:ɐ] ADJ no comp **a** cash; **~es Geld** cash; **(in) ~ bezahlen** to pay (in) cash; **~ auf die Hand** cash on the nail; **(Verkauf) nur gegen ~** cash (sales) only; **etw für ~e Münze nehmen** (fig) to take sth at face value **b** attr (= rein) Zufall pure; Unsinn auch utter, absolute **c** pred +gen (liter) devoid of, utterly or completely without; **~ aller Hoffnung, aller Hoffnung ~** devoid of hope, completely or utterly without hope **d** (liter: = bloß) bare; **~en Hauptes** bareheaded

Bar [ba:ɐ] F -, -s **a** (= Nachtlokal) nightclub, bar **b** (= Theke) bar

Bar NT -s, -s (Met) bar

Bär [bɛ:ɐ] M -en, -en **a** bear; **stark wie ein ~** (inf) (as) strong as an ox or a horse; **der Große/Kleine ~** (Astron) the Great/Little Bear (Brit), Ursa Major/Minor, the Big/Little Dipper; **jdm einen ~en aufbinden** (inf) to have (Brit) or put (US) sb on (inf) → **schlafen VI** **b** (Tech) (= Schlagbär) hammer; (= Rammbär) rammer

Ba|ra|ber [ba'ra:bɐ] M -s, -, **Ba|ra|be|rin** [-ərın] F -, -nen (Aus inf) labourer (Brit), laborer (US); (= Straßenarbeiter) navvy (inf)

ba|ra|bern [ba'ra:bɐn] ptp **barabert** VI (Aus inf) to labour (Brit), to labor (US)

Bar|ab|gel|tung F (Fin) cash settlement

Bar|ab|he|bung F cash withdrawal

Ba|ra|cke [ba'rakə] F -, -n hut, shack

Ba|ra|cken|la|ger NT, **Ba|ra|cken|sied|lung** F camp (made of huts); (für Flüchtlinge) refugee camp

Bar-: **Bar|aus|gleich** F (Fin) cash settlement; **Bar|aus|schüt|tung** F (Fin) cash distribution; **Bar|aus|zah|lung** F cash payment

Bar|bar [bar'ba:ɐ] M -en, -en, **Bar|ba|rin** [-'ba:rın] F -, -nen **a** (pej) barbarian; (= Rohling auch) brute **b** (Hist) Barbarian

Bar|ba|ra|zweig ['barbara-] M usu pl *sprig cut on St. Barbara's Day (4 Dec.) to flower for Christmas*

Bar|ba|rei [barba'rai] F -, -en (pej) **a** (= Unmenschlichkeit) barbarity **b** (no pl: = Kulturlosigkeit) barbarism

bar|ba|risch [bar'ba:rıʃ] ADJ **a** (pej) (= unmenschlich) Grausamkeit, Folter, Sitten barbarous, savage, brutal; (= ungebildet) Benehmen, Mensch barbaric, uncivilized **b** (Hist) Volk, Stamm barbarian ADV **a** misshandeln, quälen brutally, savagely **b** (= entsetzlich) heiß, kalt terribly, horribly

Bar|ba|ris|mus [barba'rısmus] M -, **Barbarismen** [-mən] (Liter) barbarism

Bar|be ['barbə] F -, -n (Zool) barbel

Bar|be|cue ['ba:bikju:] NT -(s), -s barbecue

bär|bei|ßig ['bɛ:ɐbaisıç] ADJ (inf) Gesicht, Miene, Mensch grouchy (inf), grumpy; Antwort etc gruff, grumpy; Manieren surly

Bar-: **Bar|be|stand** M (Comm) cash; (Buchführung) cash in hand; **Bar|be|trag** M cash sum or amount

Bar|bie® ['barbi] F -, -s Barbie®

Bar|bie-Pup|pe® F, **Bar|bie|pup|pe®** F Barbie® doll

Bar|bier [bar'bi:ɐ] M -s, -e (old, hum) barber

bar|bie|ren [bar'bi:rən] ptp **barbiert** VT (old, hum) **jdn ~** to shave sb; (= Bart beschneiden) to trim sb's beard; (= die Haare schneiden) to cut sb's hair; **sich (dat) ~ lassen** to go to the barber's → **balbieren**

Bar|bi|tu|rat [barbitu'ra:t] NT -s, -e barbiturate

Bar|bi|tur|säu|re [barbi'tu:ɐ-] F barbituric acid

bar|brüs|tig [-brʏstıç], **bar|bu|sig** [-bu:zıç] ADJ topless ADV auftreten, bedienen, tanzen topless

Bar|code ['ba:ɐko:t] M barcode

Bar|da|me F barmaid; (euph: = Prostituierte) hostess (euph)

Bar|de ['bardə] M -n, -n (Liter) bard; (iro) minstrel

Bar-: **Bar|ein|gän|ge** [-aingɛŋə] PL (Fin) cash receipts *pl*; **Bar|ein|la|ge** [-ainla:gə] F (Fin) cash deposit

Bä|ren-: **Bä|ren|dienst** M **jdm/einer Sache einen ~ erweisen** to do sb/sth a bad turn, to do sb/sth a disservice; **Bä|ren|dreck** M (S Ger, Aus, Sw: inf) liquorice; **Bä|ren|fang** M (= Likör) ≈ mead; **Bä|ren|fell** NT bearskin; **Bä|ren|fell|müt|ze** F bearskin (hat); (hohe Mütze) bearskin (cap), busby (Brit Mil); **Bä|ren|füh|rer(in)** M(F) bear trainer; (hum) (tourist) guide; **Bä|ren|hatz** F bear hunt; **Bä|ren|haut** F **auf der ~ liegen, sich auf die ~ legen** (dated) to laze or loaf about; **Bä|ren|hun|ger** M (inf) **einen ~ haben** to be famished (inf) or ravenous (inf); **Bä|ren|jagd** F bear hunt; **Bä|ren|jun|ge(s)** NT decl as adj (Zool) (bear) cub; **Bä|ren|klau** F -, - or m -s, - (Bot) (= Heracleum) hogweed; (= Akanthus) bear's-breech; **Bä|ren|kräf|te** PL the strength *sing* of an ox; **Bä|ren|markt** M (St Ex) bear market; **Bä|ren|müt|ze** F bearskin, busby; **Bä|ren|na|tur** F **eine ~ haben** (inf) to be (physically) tough; **bä|ren|stark** ADJ **a** strapping, strong as an ox **b** (inf) terrific; **ein ~es Buch** an amazing book; **Bä|ren|tat|ze** F bear's paw

Ba|rents|see ['ba:rənts-] F (Geog) Barents Sea

Bä|ren|zwin|ger M bear cage

Ba|rett [ba'rɛt] NT -(e)s, -e or -s cap; (für Geistliche, Richter etc) biretta; (Univ) mortarboard; (= Baskenmütze) beret

Bar|frau F barmaid

bar|fuß ['ba:ɐfu:s] ADJ pred barefoot(ed); **~ gehen** to go/walk barefoot(ed); **ich bin ~** I've got nothing on my feet, I am barefoot(ed)

bar|fü|ßig ADJ barefooted

barg pret von **bergen**

Bar-: **Bar|geld** NT cash; **bar|geld|los** ADJ cashless, without cash; **~er Zahlungsverkehr** payment by money transfer ADV without using cash; **Bar|gut|ha|ben** NT cash balance, ready money; **bar|haupt** ['ba:ɐhaupt] ADJ pred (liter), **bar|häup|tig** ['ba:ɐhɔyptıç] ADJ (geh) bareheaded; **Bar|ho|cker** M (bar) stool

bä|rig ['bɛ:rıç] (Aus inf) ADJ tremendous, fantastic ADV tremendously, fantastically

Bä|rin ['bɛ:rın] F -, -nen (she-)bear

Ba|ri|ton ['ba:rıtɔn] M -s, -e [-to:nə] baritone

Ba|ri|um ['ba:rium] NT -s, no pl (abbr **Ba**) barium

Bark [bark] F -, -en (Naut) barque

Bar|ka|ro|le [barka'ro:lə] F -, -n (Mus) barcarol(l)e

Bar|kas|se [bar'kasə] F -, -n launch; (= Beiboot auch) longboat

Bar|kauf M cash purchase; **~ ist billiger** it is cheaper to pay (in) cash

Bar|ke ['barkə] F -, -n (Naut) skiff; (liter) barque (liter)

Bar|kee|per ['ba:ɐki:pɐ] M -s, - barman, bartender

Bar-: **Bar|code, Bar|kode** ['ba:ɐko:t] M barcode; **Bar|kre|dit** [-kredi:t] M cash loan

Bär|lapp ['bɛ:ɐlap] M -s, -e (Bot) lycopod(ium)

Bär|lauch ['bɛ:ɐlaux] M -s, -e usu sing (Bot, Cook) ramsons *usu sing*, bear's or wild garlic

Bar|mann M pl **-männer** barman

bar|men ['barmən] VI (dial) to moan, to grumble (über +acc about) VT (liter) **er barmt mich** I feel pity for him

barm|her|zig [barm'hɛrtsıç] ADJ (liter, Rel) merciful; (= mitfühlend) compassionate; **~er Himmel!** (old, dial) good heavens above!; **der ~e Samariter** (lit, fig) the good Samaritan; **Barmherzige Schwestern** Sisters of Charity

Barm|her|zig|keit F -, no pl (liter, Rel) mercy, mercifulness; (= Mitgefühl) compassion; **~ (an jdm) üben** to show mercy (to sb)/compassion (towards sb); **Herr, übe ~ an mir!** Lord, have mercy on me! → **Gnade**

Bar|mit|tel PL cash (reserves *pl*)

Bar|mi|xer M barman

Bar|mi|xe|rin F barmaid

ba|rock [ba'rɔk] ADJ baroque; (fig) (= überladen auch, verschnörkelt) ornate; Sprache florid; (= seltsam) Einfälle bizarre, eccentric; **sie hat eine sehr ~e Figur** (hum) she has a very ample figure (esp Brit)

Ba|rock [ba'rɔk] NT OR M -(s), no pl baroque; **das Zeitalter des ~** the baroque age

Ba|rock- in cpds baroque; **Ba|rock|bau** M pl **-bauten** baroque building; **Ba|rock|stil** M (Archit) baroque (style); **eine Kirche im ~** a baroque church; **Ba|rock|zeit** F baroque style

Ba|ro|me|ter [baro'me:tɐ] NT -s, - (lit, fig) barometer; **das ~ steht auf Sturm** the barometer is on stormy; (fig) things look stormy

Ba|ro|me|ter|stand M barometer reading

ba|ro|met|risch [baro'me:trıʃ] ADJ attr barometric

Ba|ron [ba'ro:n] M -s, -e **a** baron; **~ (von) Schnapf** Baron or Lord Schnapf; **Herr ~** my lord **b** (fig: = Industriebaron etc) baron, magnate

Ba|ro|ness [baro'nɛs] F -, -en (dated), **Ba|ro|nes|se** [baro'nɛsə] F -, -n daughter of a baron; **Fräulein ~** my lady

Ba|ro|nin [ba'ro:nın] F -, -nen baroness; **Frau ~** my lady

Bar|ras ['baras] M -, no pl (dated sl) army; **beim ~** in the army; **zum ~ gehen** to join up (inf), to join the army; **er muss nächstes Jahr zum ~** he's got to do his military service next year, he'll be drafted next year *(US)*

Bar|rel ['bɛrəl] NT -s, -s *or* - barrel

Bar|ren ['barən] M -s, - **a** *(= Metallbarren)* bar; *(= esp Goldbarren)* ingot **b** *(Sport)* parallel bars *pl* **c** *(S Ger, Aus: = Futtertrog)* trough

Bar|ren|gold NT gold bullion

Bar|re|ser|ven PL cash reserves *pl*

Bar|ri|e|re [ba'rie:rə] F -, -n *(lit, fig)* barrier

Bar|ri|ka|de [bari'ka:də] F -, -n barricade; **auf die ~n gehen** *(lit, fig)* to go to the barricades

Bar|ri|ka|den-: **Bar|ri|ka|den|kampf** M street battle; *(= das Kämpfen)* street fighting *no pl*; **Bar|ri|ka|den|stür|mer(in)** M(F) *(fig)* revolutionary

bar|ri|ka|die|ren [barika'di:rən] *ptp* **barrikadiert** VT to barricade

barsch [barʃ] ADJ brusque, curt; **jdm eine ~e Abfuhr erteilen** to give sb short shrift ADV brusquely, curtly; **jdn ~ anfahren** to snap at sb

Barsch [barʃ] M -(e)s, -e bass; *(= Flussbarsch)* perch

Bar|schaft ['ba:ɐʃaft] F -, *(rare)* -en cash; **meine ganze ~ bestand aus 10 Euro** all I had on me was 10 euros

Bar|scheck M open *or* uncrossed cheque *(Brit)*, open check *(US)*

Barsch|heit F -, -en brusqueness, curtness; *(von Befehl auch)* peremptoriness

Bar|soi [bar'zɔy] M -s, -s borzoi

Bar|sor|ti|ment NT book wholesaler's

barst *pret von* **bersten**

Bart [ba:ɐt] M -(e)s, ⸚e ['bɛ:ɐtə] **a** *(von Mensch, Ziege, Vogel, Getreide)* beard; *(von Katze, Maus, Robbe etc)* whiskers *pl*; **sich** *(dat)* **einen ~ wachsen** *or* **stehen lassen** to grow a beard; **ein drei Tage alter ~** three days' growth (on one's chin) **b** *(fig inf)* **(sich** *dat*) **etwas in den ~ murmeln** *or* **brumme(l)n** to murmur *or* mutter sth in one's boots *or* beard *(inf)*; **jdm um den ~ gehen, jdm Honig um den ~ streichen** *or* **schmieren** to butter sb up *(inf)*, to soft-soap sb *(inf)*; **der Witz hat einen ~** that's a real oldie *(inf)*, that's an old chestnut; **der ~ ist ab** that's that!, that's the end of it *or* that **c** *(= Schlüsselbart)* bit

Bart|bin|de F *device for keeping a moustache in shape*

Bärt|chen ['bɛ:ɐtçən] NT -s, - *(= Kinnbärtchen)* (small) beard; *(= Oberlippenbärtchen)* toothbrush moustache *(Brit)* *or* mustache *(US)*; *(= Menjoubärtchen)* pencil moustache *(Brit)* *or* mustache *(US)*

Bar|teln ['bartln] PL *(Zool)* barbels *pl*

Bar|ten|wal ['bartn-] M whalebone *or* baleen whale

Bart-: **Bart|fä|den** PL *(Zool)* barbels *pl*; **Bart|flech|te** F **a** *(Med)* sycosis, barber's itch **b** *(Bot)* beard lichen *or* moss; **Bart|haar** NT facial hair; *(= Bart auch)* beard

Bar|thel ['bartl] M **wissen, wo (der) ~ den Most holt** *(inf)* to know what's what *(inf)*

Bar|tho|lo|mä|us [bartolo'mɛ:ʊs] M -' Bartholomew

Bar|tho|lo|mä|us|nacht F *(Hist)* Massacre of St. Bartholomew

bär|tig ['bɛ:ɐtɪç] ADJ bearded

Bär|ti|ge(r) M *decl as adj* bearded man, man with a beard

Bart-: **bart|los** ADJ beardless; *(= glatt rasiert)* clean-shaven; **Bart|nel|ke** F sweet william; **Bart|stop|pel** F piece of stubble; **Bart|stop|peln** PL stubble *sing*; **Bart|tas|se** F moustache cup; **Bart|tracht** F beard style; **Bart|wisch** M -(e)s, -e *(S Ger, Aus)* hand brush; **Bart|wuchs** M beard; *(esp weiblicher)* facial hair *no indef art*; **er hat starken ~** he has a strong *or* heavy growth of beard; **Bart|zot|teln** PL wispy beard *sing*

Bar-: **Bar|über|wei|sung** F *(Fin)* cash transfer; **Bar|ver|kauf** M cash sales *pl*; **ein ~** a cash sale; **Bar|ver|mö|gen** NT cash *or* liquid assets *pl*; **Bar|wert** M *(Fin)* (actual) cash value; **Bar|zah|lung** F payment by *or* in cash; **(Verkauf) nur gegen ~** cash (sales) only; **bei ~ 3% Skonto** 3% discount for cash; **Bar|zah|lungs|ra|batt** M *(Comm)* cash discount

Ba|salt [ba'zalt] M -(e)s, -e basalt

ba|sal|ten [ba'zaltn], **ba|sal|tig** [ba'zaltɪç] ADJ basaltic

Ba|sar [ba'za:ɐ] M -s, -e **a** *(= orientalischer Markt)* bazaar; **auf dem ~** in the bazaar **b** *(= Wohltätigkeitsbasar)* bazaar

Bäs|chen ['bɛ:sçən] NT -s, - *dim von* **Base**

Ba|se ['ba:zə] F -, -n *(old, dial)* cousin; *(= Tante)* aunt

Ba|se F -, -n *(Chem)* base

Base|ball ['be:sbo:l] M -s, *no pl* baseball

Base|ball-: **Base|ball|müt|ze** ['be:sbo:l-] F baseball cap; **Base|ball|schlä|ger** ['be:sbo:l-] M baseball bat

Ba|se|dow ['ba:zədo] M -s, *no pl (inf)*, **Ba|se|dow|krank|heit** F, **ba|se|dow|sche Krank|heit** ['ba:zədoʃə] F (exophthalmic) goitre *(Brit)* *or* goiter *(US)*

Ba|sel ['ba:zl] NT -s Basle, Basel

Ba|se|ler ['ba:zlɐ] ADJ *attr* = **Basler**

Ba|sen *pl von* **Basis, Base**

ba|sie|ren [ba'zi:rən] *ptp* **basiert** VI *(auf +dat on)* to be based, to rest VT to base *(auf +acc or (rare) +dat* on)

Ba|si|li|ka [ba'zi:lika] F -, **Basiliken** [-kn] basilica

Ba|si|li|kum [ba'zi:likʊm] NT -s, *no pl* basil

Ba|si|lisk [bazi'lɪsk] M -en, -en basilisk

Ba|si|lis|ken|blick M *(liter)* baleful glare

Ba|sis ['ba:zɪs] F -, **Basen** ['ba:zn] basis; *(Archit, Mil, Math)* base; **auf breiter ~** on a broad basis; **auf einer festen** *or* **soliden ~ ruhen** to be firmly established; **sich auf gleicher ~ treffen** to meet on an equal footing, to meet on equal terms; **~ und Überbau** *(Pol, Sociol)* foundation and superstructure; **die ~** *(inf)* the grass roots (level); *(= die Leute)* (those at) the grass roots

Ba|sis-: **Ba|sis|ar|beit** F *(Pol)* groundwork; **Ba|sis|camp** NT base camp

ba|sisch ['ba:zɪʃ] *(Chem)* ADJ basic ADV **~ reagieren** to show a basic reaction

Ba|sis-: **Ba|sis|de|mo|kra|tie** F grass-roots democracy; **ba|sis|de|mo|kra|tisch** ADJ grass-roots *attr* ADV **der ~ gewählte Kandidat** the candidate elected by the grass roots; **~ organisierter Verein** grass-roots organization; **Ba|sis|grup|pe** F action group; **Ba|sis|la|ger** NT base camp; **Ba|sis|preis** M *(Fin: von Kaufoption)* call exercise price; **Ba|sis|wis|sen** NT basic knowledge; **Ba|sis|zins** M *(Fin)* base (interest) rate

Bas|ke ['baskə] M -n, -n, **Bas|kin** ['baskɪn] F -, -nen Basque

Bas|ken|land NT Basque region

Bas|ken|müt|ze F beret

Bas|ket|ball ['ba:skət-, 'baskət-] M -s, *no pl* basketball

Bas|kin ['baskɪn] F -, -nen Basque

bas|kisch ['baskɪʃ] ADJ Basque

Bas|kisch(e) ['baskɪʃ] NT Basque → *auch* **Deutsch(e)**

Bas|ler ['ba:zlɐ] ADJ *attr* Basle *attr*

Bas|ler ['ba:zlɐ] M -s, -, **Bas|le|rin** [-ərɪn] F -, -nen native of Basle; *(= Einwohner)* inhabitant of Basle

Bas|re|li|ef ['bareliɛf, bare'liɛf] NT *(Archit, Art)* bas-relief

bass [bas] ADV *(old, hum)* **~ erstaunt** much *or* uncommonly *(old)* amazed

Bass [bas] M -es, ⸚e ['bɛsə] **a** *(= Stimme, Sänger)* bass; **hoher/tiefer** *or* **schwarzer ~** basso cantante/profundo; **einen hohen/tiefen ~ haben** to be a basso cantante/profundo **b** *(= Instrument)* double bass; *(im Jazz auch)* bass **c** *(= Basspartie)* bass (part)

Bass|ba|ri|ton M bass baritone

Bas|sett|horn [ba'sɛt-] NT basset horn

Bass-: **Bass|gei|ge** F *(inf)* (double) bass; **Bass|gi|tar|re** F bass guitar

Bas|sin [ba'sɛ̃:] NT -s, -s *(= Schwimmbassin)* pool; *(= Gartenbassin)* pond

Bas|sist [ba'sɪst] M -en, -en *(= Sänger)* bass (singer)

Bas|sist [ba'sɪst] M -en, -en, **Bas|sis|tin** [-'sɪstɪn] F -, -nen *(im Orchester etc)* (double) bass player; **~ sein** to be a (double) bass player, to play the (double) bass

Bass-: **Bass|kla|ri|net|te** F bass clarinet; **Bass|par|tie** F bass part; **Bass|sän|ger** M bass (singer); **Bass|schlüs|sel** M bass clef; **Bass|stimme** F bass (voice); *(= Partie)* bass (part)

Bast [bast] M -(e)s, *(rare)* -e **a** *(zum Binden, Flechten)* raffia; *(Bot)* bast, phloem **b** *(an Geweih)* velvet

bas|ta ['basta] INTERJ **(und damit) ~!** (and) that's that

Bas|tard ['bastart] M -(e)s, -e [-də] **a** *(Hist: = uneheliches Kind)* bastard **b** *(Biol: = Kreuzung) (= Pflanze)* hybrid; *(= Tier)* crossbreed, cross; *(= Mensch)* half-caste, half-breed

Bas|tei [bas'tai] F -, -en bastion

Bas|tel-: **Bas|tel|ar|beit** F piece of handcraft, handicraft; *(= das Basteln)* (doing) handcraft *or* handicrafts; **etw in langer ~ bauen** to spend a long time making *or* building sth; **sich viel mit ~en beschäftigen** to do a lot of handcraft *or* handicrafts; **Bas|tel|e|cke** F *(in Zimmer)* handicraft corner; *(in Zeitschrift)* hobbies corner *or* page

Bas|te|lei [bastə'lai] F -, -en *(inf)* handcraft, handicraft; *(= Stümperei)* botched job *(inf)*

bas|teln ['bastln] VI **a** *(als Hobby)* to make things with one's hands; *(= Handwerksarbeiten herstellen)* to do handcraft *or* handicrafts; **sie kann gut ~** she is good with her hands **b an etw** *(dat)* **~** to make sth, to work on sth; *an Modellflugzeug etc* to build *or* make sth; *(= an etw herumbasteln)* to mess around with sth, to tinker with sth VT to make; *Geräte etc auch* to build

Bas|teln NT -s, *no pl* handicraft, handicrafts *pl*

Bas|tel|raum M workroom

Bast|fa|ser F bast fibre *(Brit)* *or* fiber *(US)*

Bas|til|le [bas'ti:jə, -'tɪljə] F - *(Hist)* **der Sturm auf die ~** the storming of the Bastille

Bas|ti|on [bas'tio:n] F -, -en bastion, ramparts *pl*; *(fig)* bastion, bulwark

Bast|ler ['bastlɐ] M -s, -, **Bast|le|rin** [-ərɪn] F -, -nen *(von Modellen etc)* modeller *(Brit)*, modeler *(US)*; *(von Möbeln etc)* do-it-yourselfer; **ein guter ~ sein** to be good *or* clever with one's hands, to be good at making things

Bas|to|na|de [basto'na:də] F -, -n bastinado

Bast|sei|de F wild silk, shantung (silk)

bat *pret von* **bitten**

BAT [be:la:'te:] *abbr von* **Bundesangestelltentarif**

> **BAT**
>
> **BAT** stands for **Bundesangestelltentarif** and refers to the salary scale for public service employees. Private firms also use these rates as a guide: wording such as **Bezahlung nach BAT** can often be seen in job advertisements.

Ba|tail|le [ba'ta:jə, ba'taljə] F -, -n *(old)* battle

Ba|tail|lon [batal'jo:n] NT -s, -e *(Mil, fig)* battalion

Ba|tail|lons|füh|rer(in) M(F), **Ba|tail|lons|kom|man|deur(in)** M(F) battalion commander

Ba|ta|te [ba'ta:tə] F -, -n sweet potato, yam *(esp US)*, batata

Batch [bɛtʃ] M -, -es *(Comput)* batch

Batch- [bɛtʃ] *(Comput)*: **Batchbefehl** M batch command; **Batchbetrieb** M batch processing; **Batchdatei** F batch file

Ba|tik ['ba:tɪk] F -, -en *or m* -s, -en batik

ba|ti|ken ['ba:tɪkn] VI to do batik VT to decorate with batik; **eine gebatikte Bluse** a batik blouse

Ba|tist [ba'tɪst] M -(e)s, -e batiste, cambric

Bat|te|rie [batəˈriː] F -, -n [-ˈriːən] *(Elec, Mil: = Legebatterie)* battery; *(= Mischbatterie etc)* regulator; *(= Reihe: von Flaschen etc)* row, battery

Bat|te|rie-: **Bat|te|rie|an|zei|ger** M battery display *or* meter; **Bat|te|rie|be|trieb** M **das Radio ist für ~ eingerichtet** the radio takes batteries, the radio can be battery-powered; **bat|te|rie|be|trie|ben** [-bətriːbn] ADJ battery-powered; **Bat|te|rie|fach** NT battery compartment; **Bat|te|rie|ge|rät** NT battery-powered radio *etc*; **Bat|te|rie|huhn** NT battery hen *or* chicken; **Bat|te|rie|la|de|ge|rät** NT battery charger; **Bat|te|rie|zün|dung** F battery ignition (system)

Bat|zen [ˈbatsn] M -s, - **a** *(dated: = Klumpen)* clod, lump **b** *(obs: = Münze)* batz *(silver coin)*; **ein (schöner) ~ Geld** *(inf)* a tidy sum *(inf)*, a pretty penny *(inf)*

Bau [bau] M **a** -(e)s, *no pl (= das Bauen)* building, construction; **im** *or* **in ~** under construction; **sich im ~ befinden** to be under construction; **das im ~ befindliche Kraftwerk** the power station which is under construction; **der ~ des Hauses dauerte ein Jahr** it took a year to build the house; **mit dem ~ beginnen, an den ~ gehen** to begin building *or* construction; **den ~ beenden, mit dem ~ fertig sein** to finish building, to complete construction
b -(e)s, *no pl (= Aufbau)* structure; *(von Satz, Maschine, Apparat auch)* construction; *(= Körperbau)* **von kräftigem/schwächlichem ~ sein** to be powerfully/slenderly built, to have a powerful/slender build *or* physique
c -s, *no pl (= Baustelle)* building site; **auf dem ~ arbeiten, beim ~ sein** to be a building worker, to work on a building site; **vom ~ sein** *(fig inf)* to know the ropes *(inf)*
d -(e)s, -ten [-tn] *(= Gebäude)* building; *(= Bauwerk)* construction; **~ten** *(Film)* sets
e -(e)s, -e *(= Erdhöhle)* burrow, hole; *(= Biberbau)* lodge; *(= Fuchsbau)* den; *(= Dachsbau)* set(t); **heute gehe ich nicht aus dem ~** *(inf)* I'm not sticking my nose out of doors today *(inf)*; **zu ~ gehen** *(Hunt)* to go to earth
f -(e)s, -e *(Min)* workings *pl*; **im ~ sein** to be down the pit *or* mine
g -(e)s, *no pl (Mil sl)* guardhouse; **4 Tage ~** 4 days in the guardhouse
h -(e)s, -e *(inf: = Gefängnis)* **in den ~ wandern** to end up in the slammer *(inf)*

Bau-: **Bau|ab|nah|me** F building inspection; **Bau|ab|schnitt** M stage *or* phase of construction; **Bau|amt** NT planning department and building control office *(Brit)*, Board of Works *(US)*; **Bau|an|lei|tung** F construction manual; **Bau|ar|bei|ten** PL building *or* construction work *sing*; *(= Straßenbau)* roadworks *pl (Brit)*, road construction *(US)*; **Bau|ar|bei|ter(in)** M(F) building *or* construction worker, building labourer *(Brit) or* laborer *(US)*; **Bau|art** F construction, design; *(= Stil)* style; **Bau|auf|sicht** F supervision of building *or* construction; **die ~ liegt bei der Flughafenverwaltung** the airport authority is supervising the construction; **Bau|aus|füh|rung** F construction, building; **~ Firma Meyer** builders *or* constructors Meyer and Co; **Bau|be|ginn** M start of construction (work); **Bau|be|hör|de** F planning department and building control office *(Brit)*, Board of Works *(US)*; **Bau|be|wil|li|gung** F planning permission; **Bau|bio|lo|ge** M, **Bau|bio|lo|gin** F building biologist; **Bau|bio|lo|gie** F building biology; **bau|bio|lo|gisch** ADJ *attr* building biology ADV **~ unbedenkliche Wohnungen** *apartments built safely according to the principles of building biology*; **Bau|block** M *pl* **-blocks** block; **Bau|bran|che** F building trade, construction industry; **Bau|bu|de** F building workers' hut

Bauch [baux] M -(e)s, **Bäuche** [ˈbɔyçə] **a** *(von Mensch)* stomach, tummy *(inf)*; *(Anat)* abdomen; *(von Tier)* stomach, belly; *(= Fettbauch)* paunch, potbelly *(inf)*; **ihm tat der ~ weh** he had stomach ache *or* tummy ache *(inf)*; **sich** *(dat)* **den ~ vollschlagen** *(inf)* to stuff oneself *(inf)*; **ein voller ~ studiert nicht gern** *(Prov)* you can't study on a full stomach; **sich** *(dat)* **(vor Lachen) den ~ halten** *(inf)* to split one's sides (laughing) *(inf)*; **einen dicken ~ haben** *(sl: = schwanger sein)* to have a bun in the oven *(inf)*; **vor jdm auf dem ~ rutschen** *(inf) or* **kriechen** *(inf)* to grovel *or* kowtow to sb *(inf)*, to lick sb's boots *(inf)*; **etw aus dem ~ heraus entscheiden** to decide sth according to (a gut) instinct; **mit etw auf den ~ fallen** *(inf)* to come a cropper with sth *(Brit inf)*, to fall flat on one's face with sth *(inf)* → **Wut a, Loch, Bein**
b *(= Wölbung, Hohlraum)* belly; *(= Innerstes: von Schiff auch, von Erde)* bowels *pl*

Bauch-: **Bauch|an|satz** M beginning(s) of a paunch; **Bauch|bin|de** F **a** *(für Frack)* cummerbund; *(Med)* abdominal bandage *or* support **b** *(um Zigarre, Buch)* band; **Bauch|de|cke** F abdominal wall; **Bauch|fell** NT **a** *(Anat)* peritoneum **b** *(= Fell am Bauch)* stomach *or* belly fur; **Bauch|fell|ent|zün|dung** F peritonitis; **Bauch|fleck** M *(Aus inf)* belly flop *(inf)*; **Bauch|flos|se** F ventral fin; **Bauch|ge|gend** F abdominal region; **Bauch|grim|men** NT -s, *no pl (inf)* stomach ache, tummy ache *(inf)*; **Bauch|höh|le** F abdominal cavity, abdomen; **Bauch|höh|len|schwan|ger|schaft** F ectopic pregnancy

bau|chig [ˈbauxɪç] ADJ *Gefäß* bulbous; *Schrift* rounded

Bauch|klat|scher M *(inf)* belly flop *(inf)*

Bauch|la|den M sales tray *(carried round the neck)*

Bauch|lan|dung F *(inf) (Aviat)* belly landing; *(bei Sprung ins Wasser)* belly flop *(inf)*; **mit dem neuen Stück/mit der neuen Firma haben wir eine ~ gemacht** *(fig)* the new play/the new company was a flop

Bäuch|lein [ˈbɔyçlain] NT -s, - tummy *(inf)*; *(hum: = Fettbäuchlein)* bit of a stomach *or* tummy *(inf)*

bäuch|lings [ˈbɔyçlɪŋs] ADV on one's front, face down

Bauch-: **Bauch|mus|kel** M stomach *or* abdominal muscle; **Bauch|mus|ku|la|tur** F stomach *or* abdominal muscles *pl*; **Bauch|na|bel** M navel, bellybutton *(inf)*; **bauch|pin|seln** VT *(inf)* → **gebauchpinselt**; **Bauch|pres|sen** PL *(Sport)* crunches *pl*; **bauch+re|den** VI *sep usu infin* to ventriloquize; **Bauch|red|ner(in)** M(F) ventriloquist; **Bauch|schmer|zen** PL stomach ache, tummy ache *(inf)*; *(fig)* discomfort, anguish; **jdm ~ bereiten** *(fig)* to cause sb major problems; **wegen etw ~ haben** *(fig)* to feel uncomfortable because of sth; **Bauch|schuss** M shot in the stomach; *(= Verletzung)* stomach wound; **einen ~ abbekommen** to be shot in the stomach; **Bauch|speck** M *(Cook)* belly of pork; *(hum)* spare tyre *(Brit inf) or* tire *(US inf)*; **Bauch|spei|chel|drü|se** F pancreas; **Bauch|tanz** M belly dancing; *(einzelner Tanz)* belly dance; **bauch+tan|zen** VI *sep usu infin* to belly-dance; **Bauch|tän|ze|rin** F belly dancer; **Bauch|um|fang** M stomach girth, wasteline

Bau|chung [ˈbauxʊŋ] F -, -en bulge

Bauch-: **Bauch|wand** F stomach *or* abdominal wall; **Bauch|weh** NT stomach ache, tummy ache *(inf)*; **Bauch|wel|le** F *(Sport)* circle on the beam

Bau|con|tai|ner M Portakabin®, prefabricated hut

Baud [baut, bɔːt] NT -(s), - *(Comput)* baud

Bau-: **Bau|dar|le|hen** NT building loan; **Bau|denk|mal** NT historical monument

Baud-Ra|te [ˈbaut-, ˈbɔːt-] F *(Comput)* baud rate

Bau|ele|ment NT component part

bau|en [ˈbauən] VT **a** *(= erbauen)* to build, to construct; *(= anfertigen auch)* to make; *Satz* to construct; *Höhle* to dig, to make; **sich** *(dat)* **ein Haus ~** to build oneself a house; **sich** *(dat)* **ein Nest ~** to make *or* build oneself a nest *(auch fig)*; **seine Hoffnung auf jdn/etw ~** to build one's hopes on sb/sth; **die Betten ~** *(esp Mil)* to make the beds → *auch* **gebaut**
b *(inf: = verursachen) Unfall* to cause; **da hast du Scheiße gebaut** *(inf)* you really messed *(inf) or* cocked *(Brit inf)* that up; **bleib ruhig, bau keine Scheiße** *(inf)* cool it, don't make trouble *(inf)*
c *(inf: = machen, ablegen) Prüfung etc* to pass; **den Führerschein ~** to pass one's driving test; **seinen Doktor ~** to get one's doctorate
VI **a** *(= Gebäude errichten)* to build; **wir haben neu/auf Sylt gebaut** we built a new house/a house on Sylt; **nächstes Jahr wollen wir ~** we're going to build *or* to start building next year; **an etw** *(dat)* **~** to be working on sth, to be building sth *(auch fig)*; **hier wird viel gebaut** there is a lot of building *or* development going on round *(Brit) or* around here; **hoch ~** to build high-rise buildings
b *(= vertrauen)* to rely, to count *(auf +acc* on)

Bau|ent|wurf M building plans *pl*

Bau|er [ˈbauɐ] M -n *or (rare)* -s, -n **a** *(= Landwirt)* farmer; *(als Vertreter einer Klasse)* peasant; *(pej: = ungehobelter Mensch)* (country) bumpkin, yokel; **die dümmsten ~n haben die größten** *or* **dicksten Kartoffeln** *(prov inf)* fortune favours *(Brit) or* favors *(US)* fools *(prov)*; **was der ~ nicht kennt, das frisst er nicht** *(prov inf)* some people won't try anything new **b** *(Chess)* pawn; *(Cards)* jack, knave

Bau|er [ˈbauɐ] M -s, -, **Bau|e|rin** [-ərɪn] F -, -nen *(= Erbauer)* builder; *(fig auch)* architect

Bau|er NT OR M -s, - *(= Käfig)* (bird)cage

Bäu|er|chen [ˈbɔyɐçən] NT -s, - **a** *dim von* **Bauer b** *(baby-talk)* burp; **(ein) ~ machen** to (do a) burp

Bäu|e|rin [ˈbɔyərɪn] F -, -nen **a** *(= Frau des Bauern)* farmer's wife **b** *(= Landwirtin)* farmer; *(als Vertreterin einer Klasse)* peasant (woman)

bäu|e|risch [ˈbɔyərɪʃ] ADJ = **bäurisch**

Bäu|er|lein [ˈbɔyɐlain] NT -s, - *(liter, hum)* farmer

bäu|er|lich [ˈbɔyɐlɪç] ADJ rural; *(= ländlich) Fest, Bräuche, Sitten* rustic, country *attr*; **~e Klein- und Großbetriebe** small and large farms ADV **~ geprägt sein** to be rural; **~ eingerichtet** rustically furnished

Bäu|er|lich|keit F -, *no pl* rurality

Bau|ern-: **Bau|ern|auf|stand** M peasants' revolt *or* uprising; **Bau|ern|brot** NT coarse rye bread; **Bau|ern|dorf** NT farming *or* country village; **Bau|ern|fang** M **auf ~ ausgehen** *(inf)* to play con tricks *(inf)*; **Bau|ern|fän|ger** M *(inf)* con man *(inf)*, swindler; **Bau|ern|fän|ge|rei** [-fɛŋəˈrai] F -, -en *(inf)* con *(inf)*, swindle; **Bau|ern|fän|ge|rin** F *(inf)* swindler, con woman *(inf)*; **Bau|ern|frau** F farmer's wife; **Bau|ern|früh|stück** NT bacon and potato omelette; **Bau|ern|gut** NT farm(stead); **Bau|ern|haus** NT farmhouse; **Bau|ern|hoch|zeit** F country wedding; **Bau|ern|hof** M farm; **Bau|ern|jun|ge** M country boy, country lad *(esp Brit inf)*; **Bau|ern|ka|len|der** M country almanac; **Bau|ern|krie|ge** PL *(Hist)* Peasant War(s); **Bau|ern|le|gen** NT -s, *no pl (Hist, Pol pej)* expropriation of peasants' land; **Bau|ern|mäd|chen** NT country girl, country lass *(esp Brit inf)*; **Bau|ern|magd** F farmer's maid; **Bau|ern|mö|bel** PL farmhouse furniture *sing*; **Bau|ern|op|fer** NT *(fig) (= Mensch)* fall guy; *(= Sache)* necessary sacrifice; **Bau|ern|par|tei** F *(Pol)* country party; **Bau|ern|re|gel** F country saying; **Bau|ern|schä|del** M (large) head; *(pej)* thick skull *(inf)*; **Bau|ern|schaft** [ˈbauɐnʃaft] F -, *no pl* farming community; *(ärmlich)* peasantry; **Bau|ern|schläue** F native *or* low cunning, craftiness, shrewdness; **Bau|ern|schrank** M farmhouse cupboard, cupboard in rustic style; **Bau|ern|stand** M farming community, farmers *pl*; **Bau|ern|stu|be** F farmhouse parlour *(Brit) or* parlor *(US)*; *(in Gast-*

haus) country-style dining room; **Bau|ern|the|a|ter** NT rural folk theatre *(Brit) or* theater *(US)*; **Bau|ern|töl|pel** M *(pej)* country bumpkin, yokel; **Bau|ern|tum** ['bauɐntu:m] NT **-s,** *no pl (= Bauernstand)* farming community, farmers *pl*; **er ist stolz auf sein ~** he is proud of coming from farming stock; **Bau|ern|ver|band** M farmers' organization

Bau|ers-: **Bau|ers|frau** F farmer's wife; **Bau|ers|leu|te** PL farm(ing) folk, farmers *pl*; **Bau|ers|mann** M *pl* **-leute** *(old, liter)* farmer

Bau-: **Bau|er|war|tungs|land** NT *(Admin)* development area; **Bau|fach** NT construction industry; **Bau|fahr|zeug** NT construction vehicle; **bau|fäl|lig** ADJ dilapidated; *Decke, Gewölbe* unsound, unsafe; **Bau|fäl|lig|keit** F dilapidation; **wegen ~ gesperrt** closed because building unsafe; **Bau|fi|nan|zie|rung** F construction *or* mortgage financing, construction *or* building finance; **Bau|fir|ma** F building contractor *or* firm; **Bau|flucht** F line; **Bau|form** F form *or* shape (of a building); **Bau|ge|län|de** NT land for building; *(= Baustelle)* building site; **Bau|geld** NT building capital; **Bau|ge|neh|mi|gung** F planning and building permission; **Bau|ge|nos|sen|schaft** F housing association; **Bau|ge|rüst** NT scaffolding; **Bau|ge|schäft** NT building firm; **Bau|ge|sell|schaft** F property company; **Bau|ge|wer|be** NT building and construction trade; **bau|gleich** ADJ *Modell, Ausführung* structurally identical; **Bau|glied** NT *(Archit)* part of a building; **Bau|gru|be** F excavation, construction pit; **Bau|grund** M *(= Gelände)* building land, development site; *(= Grundstück)* site, (building) plot; **Bau|grund|stück** NT (building) plot, plot of land for building; **Bau|hand|werk** NT building trade; **Bau|hand|wer|ker(in)** M(F) (trained) building worker; **Bau|haus** NT *(Archit, Art)* Bauhaus; **Bau|herr(in)** M(F) client *(for whom sth is being built)*; **seitdem er ~ ist ...** since he has been having a house built ...; **~in ist die Stadt** the clients are the town authorities; **~ Ministerium des Innern** under construction for the Ministry *(Brit) or* Department *(US)* of the Interior; **Bau|her|ren|mo|dell** NT *scheme by which tax relief is obtained on investment in building projects*; **Bau|holz** NT building timber; **Bau|hüt|te** F **a** *(= Baubude)* building workers' hut **b** *(Hist, Archit)* church masons' guild; **Bau|in|dust|rie** F building and construction industry; **Bau|in|ge|ni|eur(in)** M(F) civil engineer

Bauj. *abbr von* **Baujahr**

Bau-: **Bau|jahr** NT year of construction; *(von Gebäude auch)* year of building; *(von Auto)* year of manufacture; **VW ~ 98** 1998 VW; **welches ~?** what year?; **Bau|kas|ten** M building *or* construction kit; *(mit Holzklötzen)* box of bricks; *(= Chemiebaukasten)* set; **Bau|kas|ten|prin|zip** NT building-block principle; **Bau|kas|ten|sys|tem** NT *(Tech)* modular *or* unit construction system; **Bau|klotz** M (building) brick *or* block; **Bauklötze(r) staunen** *(inf)* to gape (in astonishment); **Bau|klötz|chen** NT (building) block; **Bau|ko|lon|ne** F gang of building workers; *(bei Straßenbau)* gang of navvies *(Brit inf)*, construction unit *(US)*; **Bau|kos|ten** PL building *or* construction costs *pl*; **Bau|kos|ten|zu|schuss** M building subsidy *or* grant; **Bau|kran** M construction *or* builder's crane; **Bau|kunst** F *(geh)* architecture; **Bau|land** NT building land; *(für Stadtplanung)* development area; **einen Acker als ~ verkaufen** to sell a field for building; **Bau|lei|ter(in)** M(F) (building) site manager; **Bau|lei|tung** F **a** *(= Aufsicht)* (building) site supervision; *(= Büro)* site office **b** *(= die Bauleiter)* (building) site supervisory staff; **bau|lich** ['baulɪç] ADJ structural; **in gutem/schlechtem ~em Zustand** structurally sound/unsound ADV structurally; **das Gebäude ist in einem ~ schlechten Zustand** structurally, the building is in bad condition; **Bau|lö|we** M building speculator; **Bau|lü|cke** F empty site, gap site

Baum [baum] M **-(e)s, Bäume** ['bɔymə] tree; **auf dem ~** in the tree; **der ~ der Erkenntnis** *(Bibl)* the tree of knowledge; **er ist stark wie ein ~** he's as strong as an ox; **zwischen ~ und Borke stecken** *or* **stehen** to be in two minds; **die Bäume wachsen nicht in den Himmel** *(prov)* all good things come to an end; **einen alten ~** *or* **alte Bäume soll man nicht verpflanzen** *(prov)* you can't teach an old dog new tricks *(prov)*; **ein Kerl wie ein ~** *(inf)* a tall, athletic guy *(inf)* → **ausreißen VT, Wald**

Bau-: **Bau|man|gel** M *usu pl* construction defect; *(strukturell)* structural defect; **Bau|markt** M property market; *(= Geschäft für Heimwerker)* DIY superstore; **Bau|ma|schi|ne** F piece of building machinery; **Bau|ma|schi|nen** PL building machinery *or* plant *sing*; **Bau|maß|nah|men** PL building operations *pl*; **Bau|ma|te|ri|al** NT building material

Baum-: **Baum|be|stand** M tree population *no pl*, stock of trees; **Baum|blü|te** F blossom

Bäum|chen ['bɔymçən] NT **-s, -** small tree; *(= junger Baum auch)* sapling; **~, wechsle dich spielen** to play tag; *(hum: = Partnertausch)* to swap partners

Baum|chi|rurg(in) M(F) tree surgeon

Bau|meis|ter(in) M(F) **a** master builder; *(= Bauunternehmer)* building contractor; *(= Architekt)* architect **b** *(= Erbauer)* builder

bau|meln ['bauml̩n] VI to dangle *(an +dat* from); **die Haarsträhnen baumelten ihm ins Gesicht** the strands of hair hung in his face; **jdn ~ lassen** *(sl)* to let sb swing *(inf)*

Baum-: **Baum|farn** M tree fern; **Baum|fäu|le** F *(in Holz)* dry rot; *(in Baum)* rot in a/the living tree; **Baum|fre|vel** M *(form)* malicious damage to trees; **Baum|gren|ze** F tree *or* timber line; **Baum|grup|pe** F coppice, cluster of trees; **Baum|haus** NT tree house; **baum|hoch** ADJ tree-high; **Baum|kro|ne** F treetop; **Baum|ku|chen** M *(Cook)* ≈ cylindrical cake built up from horizontal layers baked successively; **baum|lang** ADJ **ein ~er Kerl** *(inf)* a beanpole *(inf)*; **Baum|läu|fer** M tree creeper; **baum|los** ADJ treeless; **baum|reich** ADJ wooded; **Baum|rie|se** M *(liter)* giant tree; **Baum|rin|de** F tree bark; **Baum|sche|re** F (tree) pruning shears *pl*, secateurs *pl*; **Baum|schu|le** F tree nursery; **Baum|stamm** M tree trunk; **baum|stark** ADJ *Arme, Beine* massive; *Mann* beefy *(inf)*, hefty; **Baum|step|pe** F scrub; **Baum|ster|ben** NT tree death; **Baum|struk|tur** F *(Comput)* tree structure; **Baum|strunk** M, **Baum|stumpf** M tree stump; **Baum|wip|fel** M treetop

Baum|woll- *in cpds* cotton

Baum|wol|le F cotton; **ein Hemd aus ~** a cotton shirt

baum|wol|len ADJ *attr* cotton

Baum|woll-: **Baum|woll|hemd** NT (100%) cotton shirt; **Baum|woll|spin|ne|rei** F cotton mill; **Baum|woll|strauch** M cotton plant

Baum|wuchs M tree growth

Bau-: **Bau|ord|nung** F building regulations *pl*; **Bau|plan** M building plan; *(= Vorhaben auch)* building project; *(Biol: genetischer, biologischer etc)* blueprint; **Bau|pla|nung** F planning (of a building); **Bau|plas|tik** F architectural sculpture; **Bau|platz** M site (for building); **Bau|po|li|zei** F building control department *(Brit)*, Board of Works *(US)*; **bau|po|li|zei|lich** ADJ building control *attr (Brit)* ADV **~ genehmigt** covered by a building permit; **Bau|preis** M building price; **Bau|rat** M, **Bau|rä|tin** F head of the planning department and building control office *(Brit)*, head of the Board of Works *(US)*; **Bau|recht** NT planning and building laws and regulations; **bau|reif** ADJ *Grundstück* available for building; **Bau|rei|he** F *(von Auto)* model range; *(von Flugzeug, Computer)* series

bäu|risch ['bɔyrɪʃ] ADJ *(pej)* boorish, rough

Bau-: **Bau|ru|i|ne** F *(inf)* unfinished building; **Bau|sach|ver|stän|di|ge(r)** MF *decl as adj* quantity surveyor; **Bau|satz** M kit

Bausch [bauʃ] M **-es, Bäusche** *or* **-e** **a** *(= Wattebausch)* ball; *(Med auch)* swab **b** *(= Krause) (an Vorhang)* pleat; *(an Kleid)* bustle; *(an Ärmel)* puff **c in ~ und Bogen** lock, stock and barrel

Bäusch|chen ['bɔyʃçən] NT **-s, -** *dim von* **Bausch**

bau|schen ['bauʃn̩] VR **a** *(= sich aufblähen)* to billow (out) **b** *(Kleidungsstück)* to puff out; *(ungewollt)* to bunch (up) VT **a** *Segel, Vorhänge* to fill, to swell **b** *(= raffen)* to gather; **gebauschte Ärmel** puffed sleeves VI *(Kleidungsstück)* to bunch (up), to become bunched

Bau|schen ['bauʃn̩] M **-s, -** *(S Ger, Aus: = Wattebausch)* ball; *(Med auch)* swab

bau|schig ['bauʃɪç] ADJ *Wolken* billowing; *Rock, Vorhänge* full; *Watte* fluffy

Bau-: **Bau|schlos|ser(in)** M(F) fitter on a building site; **Bau|schutt** M building rubble; **Bau|schutt|mul|de** F skip; **Bau|sek|tor** M building *or* construction sector

Bau|spar|dar|le|hen ['bauʃpa:ɐ-] M building society loan *(Brit)*, loan from a/one's building and loan association *(US)*

bau+spa|ren VI *sep usu infin* to save with a building society *(Brit) or* building and loan association *(US)*

Bau|spa|rer(in) M(F) saver with a building society *(Brit) or* building and loan association *(US)*

Bau|spar-: **Bau|spar|kas|se** F building society *(Brit)*, building and loan association *(US)*; **Bau|spar|ver|trag** M savings contract with a building society *(Brit) or* building and loan association *(US)*

Bau-: **Bau|stahl** M mild *or* structured steel; **Bau|stein** M stone (for building); *(Spielzeug)* brick; *(= elektronischer Baustein)* chip; *(fig: = Bestandteil)* building block; *(Tech)* module; **Bau|stel|le** F building *or* construction site; *(bei Straßenbau)* roadworks *pl (Brit)*, road construction *(US)*; *(bei Gleisbau)* railway *(Brit) or* railroad *(US)* construction site; **„Achtung, ~!"** "danger, roadworks *(Brit) or* road construction *(US)*"; **„Betreten der ~ verboten"** "unauthorized entry prohibited", "trespassers will be prosecuted"; **die Strecke ist wegen einer ~ gesperrt** the road is closed because of roadworks *(Brit) or* road construction *(US)*; *(Bahnstrecke)* the line is closed because of (railway *(Brit) or* railroad *(US)*) construction work; **Bau|stel|len|ver|kehr** M heavy traffic (from a building site); **„Achtung, ~!"** "construction traffic"; **Bau|stil** M architectural style; **Bau|stoff** M building material; **Bau|stopp** M **einen ~ verordnen** to impose a halt on building (projects); **Bau|stu|fe** F construction stage *or* phase, stage *pr* phase of construction; **Bau|sub|stanz** F fabric, structure; **die ~ ist gut** the house is structurally sound; **Bau|sum|me** F total building cost; **Bau|tä|tig|keit** F building; **eine rege ~** a lot of building; **Bau|tech|ni|ker(in)** M(F) site engineer; **bau|tech|nisch** ADJ structural; **eine ~e Glanzleistung** a superb feat of structural engineering; **Bau|teil** M *(= Gebäudeteil)* part (of a building); **Bau|teil** NT *(= Bauelement)* component

Bau|ten *pl von* **Bau d**

Bau-: **Bau|tisch|ler(in)** M(F) joiner; **Bau|trä|ger(in)** M(F) builder, building contractor; **Bau|un|ter|neh|men** NT **a** *(= Firma)* building contractor **b** *(= Bauvorhaben)* building project *or* scheme; **Bau|un|ter|neh|mer(in)** M(F) building contractor, builder; **Bau|vo|lu|men** NT volume of building; **Bau|vor|ha|ben** NT building project *or* scheme; **Bau|wei|se** F type *or* method of construction; *(= Stil)* style; **in konventioneller ~** built in the conventional way/style; **offene ~** detached houses; **geschlossene ~** terraced *(Brit) or* row *(US)* houses; **Bau|werk** NT construction; *(= Gebäude auch)* edifice, building; **Bau|we|sen** NT, *no pl* building and construction industry; **ein Ausdruck aus dem ~** a building term; **Bau|wich** ['bauvɪç] M -(e)s, -e *(Archit)* space between two neighbouring *(Brit)* or neighboring *(US)* buildings; **Bau|wirt|schaft** F building and construction industry; **Bau|wut** F building frenzy *or* craze

Bau|xit [bau'ksi:t] M -s, -e bauxite

bauz [bauts] INTERJ wham, crash, bang; **~ machen** *(baby-talk)* to go (crash bang) wallop

Bau-: **Bau|zaun** M hoarding, fence; **Bau|zeich|nung** F building plan *usu pl*; **Bau|zeit** F time taken for building *or* construction; **die ~ betrug drei Jahre** it took three years to build

b. a. w. *abbr von* **bis auf weiteres** until further notice

b. a. W. *abbr von* **bis auf Weiteres** until further notice

Bay|er ['baiɐ] M -n, -n, **Bay|e|rin** ['baiərɪn] F -, -nen Bavarian

bay|e|risch ['baiərɪʃ] ADJ Bavarian; **der Bayerische Wald** the Bavarian Forest

Bay|e|risch(e) ['baiərɪʃ] NT Bavarian (dialect) → *auch* **Deutsch(e)**

Bay|ern ['baiɐn] NT -s Bavaria

bay|risch ['bairɪʃ] ADJ = **bayerisch**

Bay|risch(e) ['bairɪʃ] NT = **Bayerisch(e)**

Ba|zar [ba'za:ɐ] M -s, -e = **Basar**

Ba|zi ['ba:tsi] M -, - *(Aus inf)* blighter *(Brit inf)*, scoundrel

Ba|zil|le [ba'tsɪlə] F -, -n **a** *(inf: = Bazillus)* bacillus; *(= Krankheitserreger)* germ **b** **linke ~** *(sl: = übler Typ)* sly git *(sl)*

Ba|zil|len-: **Ba|zil|len|furcht** F germ phobia; **Ba|zil|len|schleu|der** F *(inf: = Mensch, Klimaanlage etc) germ-spreading person or thing*; **Ba|zil|len|trä|ger(in)** M(F) carrier

Ba|zil|lus [ba'tsɪlʊs] M -, **Bazillen** [-'tsɪlən] **a** bacillus; *(= Krankheitserreger)* germ **b** *(fig)* cancer, growth

Ba|zoo|ka [ba'zu:ka] F -, -s bazooka

BBS [bi:bi:'ɛs] NT *abbr von* **bulletin board system** *(Comput)* BBS

Bd. *abbr von* **Band**

BDA [be:de:'la:] F - **a** *abbr von* **Bundesvereinigung der Arbeitgeberverbände** *employers' association*, ≈ CBI *(Brit)* **b** *abbr von* **Bund deutscher Architekten**

Bde. *abbr von* **Bände**, → **Band**

BDI [be:de:'li:] M -, *no pl abbr von* **Bundesverband der Deutschen Industrie** *manufacturing industries' association*, ≈ CBI *(Brit)*

BDM [be:de:'lɛm] M -, *no pl (NS) abbr von* **Bund Deutscher Mädel**

BE *abbr von* **Broteinheit**

be|ab|sich|ti|gen [bə'lapzɪçtɪgn] ✪ 35.1, 35.2, 45.4 *ptp* **beabsichtigt** VT to intend; **eine Reise/Steuererhöhung ~** *(form)* to intend to go on a journey/to increase taxes; **das hatte ich nicht beabsichtigt** I didn't mean it to happen, I didn't intend that to happen; **das war beabsichtigt** that was deliberate *or* intentional; **die beabsichtigte Wirkung** the desired *or* intended effect

be|ach|ten *ptp* **beachtet** VT **a** *(= befolgen)* to heed; *Ratschlag auch* to follow; *Vorschrift, Verbot, Verkehrszeichen* to observe, to comply with; *Regel* to observe, to follow; *Gebrauchsanweisung* to follow; **etw besser ~** to pay more attention to sth → **Vorfahrt**
b *(= berücksichtigen)* to take into consideration *or* account; **es ist zu ~, dass ...** it should be taken into consideration *or* account that ...
c *(= Aufmerksamkeit schenken) jdn* to notice, to pay attention to; *(bei Bilderklärungen, Reiseführung etc)* to observe; **jdn nicht ~** to ignore sb, to take no notice of sb; **von der Öffentlichkeit kaum beachtet** scarcely noticed by the public; **das Ereignis wurde in der Öffentlichkeit kaum/stark beachtet** the incident aroused little/considerable public attention

be|ach|tens|wert [bə'laxtnsve:ɐt] ADJ noteworthy, remarkable

be|acht|lich [bə'laxtlɪç] ADJ **a** *(= beträchtlich)* considerable; *Verbesserung, Zu- or Abnahme* marked; *Erfolg* notable; *Talent* remarkable **b** *(= bedeutend) Ereignis* significant; *(= lobenswert) Leistung* considerable, excellent; *(= zu berücksichtigend)* relevant; **~!** *(dated)* well done; **er hat im Leben/Beruf Beachtliches geleistet** he has achieved a considerable amount in life/his job ADV *(= sehr)* significantly, considerably

Be|ach|tung F **a** *(= das Befolgen)* heeding; *(von Ratschlag, Gebrauchsanweisung)* following; *(von Vorschrift, Regel, Verbot, Verkehrszeichen)* observance, compliance (+*gen* with); **die ~ der Vorschriften** observance *of or* compliance with the regulations; **unter ~ der Vorschriften** in accordance with the regulations
b *(= Berücksichtigung)* consideration; **unter ~ aller Umstände** taking into consideration *or* considering all the circumstances
c *(= das Beachten)* notice, attention (+*gen* to); **„zur ~"** please note; **~ finden/verdienen** to receive/deserve attention; **jdm/einer Sache ~ schenken** to pay attention to sb/sth, to take notice of sb/sth; **jdm keine ~ schenken** to ignore sb, to take no notice of sb

Beach|vol|ley|ball ['bi:tʃvɔli-] M beach volleyball

be|ackern *ptp* **beackert** VT **a** *Feld* to till, to work **b** *(inf) Thema, Wissensgebiet* to go into, to examine

Bea|gle ['bi:gl] M -s, -(s) beagle

bea|men ['bi:mən] VT to beam VR to beam oneself

Bea|mer ['bi:mɐ] M -s, - *(Tech, Opt)* digital *or* data projector, LCD *or* DLP projector

Be|am|te M = **Beamte(r)**

Be|am|ten-: **Be|am|ten|an|wär|ter(in)** M(F) civil service trainee; **Be|am|ten|ap|pa|rat** M bureaucracy; **Be|am|ten|be|lei|di|gung** F insulting an official; **Be|am|ten|be|ste|chung** F bribing an official; **Be|am|ten|da|sein** NT *(usu pej)* life of *or* as a minor official *or* civil servant; **ein eintöniges ~ führen** to lead the routine-bound life of a minor official; **Be|am|ten|deutsch** NT officialese; **Be|am|ten|lauf|bahn** F career in the civil service; **die ~ einschlagen** to enter *or* join the civil service; **Be|am|ten|men|ta|li|tät** F bureaucratic mentality; **Be|am|ten|recht** NT civil service law; **Be|am|ten|schaft** [bə'lamtnʃaft] F -, *no pl* civil servants *pl*, civil service; **Be|am|ten|see|le** F *(pej)* petty official; **Be|am|ten|stand** M *(dated)* civil service; **Be|am|ten|sta|tus** M civil servant status; **~ haben** to have civil servant status, to be a civil servant; **Be|am|ten|tum** [bə'lamtntu:m] NT -s, *no pl* **a** civil service; *(= Beamtenschaft auch)* civil servants *pl* **b** *(Wesen)* **sein ~** the civil servant in him; **es ist Kennzeichen des ~s, dass ...** it is the mark of civil servants that ...; **Be|am|ten|ver|hält|nis** NT **im ~ stehen** to be a civil servant; **ins ~ übernommen werden** to become a civil servant; **Be|am|ten|will|kür** F arbitrariness of officials; **das war ~** that was an arbitrary bureaucratic decision

Be|am|te(r) [bə'lamtə] M *decl as adj*, **Be|am|tin** [bə'lamtɪn] F -, -nen official; *(= Staatsbeamte)* civil servant; *(= Zollbeamte)* official, officer; *(= Polizeibeamte)* officer; *(dated: = Bürobeamte, Schalterbeamte)* clerk; **politischer ~r** politically-appointed civil servant; **er ist ~r** *(bei Land, Bund)* he is a civil servant, he is in the civil service; **~r auf Widerruf** *(Ger) civil servant employed by the state for a probationary period*; **~r auf Zeit** *civil servant on a temporary contract*; **~r auf Lebenszeit** *civil servant on a life-term contract, person retaining civil service status for life*; **er ist ein typischer ~r** *(pej)* he is a typical petty official *or* bureaucrat; **ein kleiner ~r** a minor *or (esp pej)* petty official

be|am|tet [bə'lamtət] ADJ *(form)* established, appointed on a permanent basis *(by the state)*

be|ängs|ti|gen *ptp* **beängstigt** VT *(geh)* to alarm, to frighten, to scare

be|ängs|ti|gend ADJ alarming, frightening; **sein Zustand ist ~** his condition is giving cause for concern ADV alarmingly, frighteningly

Be|ängs|ti|gung [bə'lɛŋstɪgʊŋ] F -, -en alarm, fear; **in großer ~** in (a state of) great alarm

be|an|spru|chen [bə'lanʃprʊxn] *ptp* **beansprucht** VT **a** *(= fordern)* to claim; *Gebiet auch* to lay claim to; **etw ~ können** to be entitled to sth
b *(= erfordern)* to take; *Zeit auch* to take up; *Platz auch* to take up, to occupy; *Kräfte auch, Aufmerksamkeit* to demand; *(= benötigen)* to need
c *(= ausnützen)* to use; *jds Gastfreundschaft* to take advantage of; *jds Geduld* to demand; *jds Hilfe* to ask for; **ich möchte Ihre Geduld nicht zu sehr ~** I don't want to try your patience
d *(= strapazieren) Maschine etc* to use; *jdn* to occupy, to keep busy; **jdn stark** *or* **sehr ~** to keep sb very busy *or* occupied; **eine höchst beanspruchte Maschine** a heavily used machine; **ihr Beruf beansprucht sie ganz** her job is very demanding, her job takes up all her time and energy

Be|an|spru|chung F -, -en **a** *(= Forderung)* claim (+*gen* to); *(= Anforderung)* demand **b** *(= Ausnutzung: von jds Geduld, Hilfe etc)* demand (*von* on) **c** *(= Belastung, Abnutzung)* use; *(beruflich)* demands *pl*

be|an|stan|den [bə'lanʃtandn] *ptp* **beanstandet** VT to query, to complain about; **das ist beanstandet worden** there has been a query *or* complaint about that; **er hat an allem etwas zu ~** he has complaints about everything; **die beanstandete Ware** the goods complained about *or* queried

Be|an|stan|dung F -, -en complaint (+*gen* about); **zu ~en Anlass geben** *(form)* to give cause for complaint; **er hat jahrelang ohne jede ~ seine Pflicht getan** for years he did his duty without giving any cause for complaint

be|an|tra|gen [bə'lantra:gn] *ptp* **beantragt** VT to apply for (*bei* to); *(Jur) Strafe* to demand, to ask for; *(= vorschlagen: in Debatte etc)* to move, to propose; **er beantragte, versetzt zu werden** he applied for a transfer, he applied to be transferred; **etw bei der Behörde ~** to apply to the authorities for sth

Be|an|tra|gung F -, -en application (+*gen* for); *(von Strafe)* demand (+*gen* for); *(= Vorschlag)* proposal

be|ant|wort|bar ADJ answerable; **das ist nicht so einfach ~** there's no easy answer to that (question)

be|ant|wor|ten *ptp* **beantwortet** VT to answer; *Anfrage, Brief auch* to reply to; *Gruß, Beleidigung, Herausforderung auch* to respond to; **jdm eine Frage ~** to answer sb's question; **eine Frage mit Nein ~** to answer a question in the negative; **leicht zu ~** easily answered

Be|ant|wor|tung [bə'lantvɔrtʊŋ] F -, -en (+*gen* to) answer; *(von Anfrage, Brief auch)* reply; *(von Gruß, Beleidigung, Herausforderung auch)* response

be|ar|bei|ten *ptp* **bearbeitet** VT **a** *(= behandeln)* to work on; *Stein, Holz* to work, to dress; *(inf: mit Chemikalien)* to treat; **etw mit dem Hammer/Meißel ~** to hammer/chisel sth
b *(= sich befassen mit)* to deal with; *Fall* to handle, to deal with; *Bestellungen etc* to process
c *(= redigieren)* to edit *(auch Comput)*; *(= neu bearbeiten)* to revise; *(= umändern) Roman etc* to adapt; *Musikstück* to arrange; **etw für die Drucklegung ~** to prepare sth for press
d *(inf: = einschlagen auf) Klavier, Trommel etc* to hammer *or* bash away at; *Geige* to saw away at; **jdn mit Fußtritten ~** to kick sb about *(inf)*; **jdn mit Fäusten ~** to thump sb
e *(inf: = einreden auf) jdn* to work on
f *Land* to cultivate

Be|ar|bei|ter(in) M(F) **a** *(von Angelegenheit)* person dealing with sth; *(von Fall auch)* person handling sth; *(von Bestellung)* person processing sth; **wer war der ~ der Akte?** who dealt with the file? **b** *(= Redakteur)* editor; *(von Neubearbeitung)* reviser; *(von Umänderung)* adapter; *(von Musik)* arranger

Be|ar|bei|tung [bəˈlarbaitʊŋ] **F -, -en a** *(= Behandlung)* working (on); *(von Stein, Holz)* dressing; *(mit Chemikalien)* treating; **die ~ von Granit ist schwierig** it is difficult to work *or* dress granite
b *(von Angelegenheit, Antrag etc)* dealing with; *(von Fall)* handling; *(von Bestellung)* processing; **die ~ meines Antrags hat lange gedauert** it took a long time to deal with my claim
c *(= Redigieren)* editing; *(= Neubearbeitung)* revising; *(= Umänderung)* adapting; *(von Musik)* arrangement; *(= bearbeitete Ausgabe etc)* edition; revision; revised edition; adaptation; arrangement; **neue ~** *(von Film etc)* new version; **die deutsche ~** the German version; **ein polnisches Volkslied in der ~ von Chopin** a Polish folk song as arranged by Chopin

Be|ar|bei|tungs-: **Be|ar|bei|tungs|ge|bühr** **F** handling charge; **Be|ar|bei|tungs|modus** **M** *(Comput)* editing mode; **Be|ar|bei|tungs|zeit** **F** *(Admin)* (time for) processing; **die ~ beträgt zwei Wochen** processing will take two weeks

be|arg|wöh|nen *ptp* **beargwöhnt** **VT** to be suspicious of

Beat [biːt] **M -(s),** *no pl* **a** *(= Musik)* beat *or* pop music **b** *(= Rhythmus)* beat

Beat|band [ˈbiːtbɛnt] **F** *pl* **-bands** beat *or* pop group

Beat|ge|ne|ra|ti|on **F** beat generation

Be|a|ti|fi|ka|ti|on [beatifikaˈtsioːn] **F -, -en** *(Eccl)* beatification

be|a|ti|fi|zie|ren [beatifiˈtsiːrən] *ptp* **beatifiziert** **VT** *(Eccl)* to beatify

be|at|men *ptp* **beatmet** **VT** *Ertrunkenen* to give artificial respiration to; *Gewässer* to oxygenate; **jdn künstlich ~** to keep sb breathing artificially

Be|at|mung **F -, -en** artificial respiration; *(von Gewässer)* oxygenation

Be|at|mungs|ge|rät **NT** respirator, ventilator

Beat|mu|sik [ˈbiːt-] **F** beat *or* pop music

Beat|nik [ˈbiːtnɪk] **M -s, -s** beatnik

Beat|schup|pen [ˈbiːt-] **M** *(inf)* beat club

Beau [boː] **M -, -s** good-looker *(inf)*

Beau|fort|ska|la, Beau|fort-Ska|la [boˈfoːɐskaːla, ˈboːfɐt-] **F** *(Met)* Beaufort scale

be|auf|sich|ti|gen [bəˈlaufzɪçtɪgn] *ptp* **beaufsichtigt** **VT** *Arbeit, Bau* to supervise; *Klasse, Schüler, Häftlinge auch* to keep under supervision; *Kind* to mind *(Brit)*, to look after; *Prüfung* to invigilate at; **jdn bei einer Arbeit/beim Arbeiten ~** to supervise sb's work/sb working; **staatlich beaufsichtigt** state-controlled, under state control

Be|auf|sich|ti|gung **F -, -en** supervision, supervising; *(von Kind)* minding *(Brit)*, supervision; *(bei Prüfung)* invigilation; **die ~ von drei Kindern unter 10 Jahren ist nicht leicht** looking after three children under 10 is not easy

be|auf|tra|gen [bəˈlauftraːgn] *ptp* **beauftragt** **VT** **a** *(= heranziehen)* to engage; *Firma auch* to hire; *Architekten, Künstler etc, Forschungsinstitut* to commission; *Ausschuss etc* to appoint, to set up; **jdn mit etw ~** to engage *etc* sb to do sth **b** *(= anweisen) Untergebenen etc* to instruct; **wir sind beauftragt, das zu tun** we have been instructed to do that

Be|auf|trag|te(r) [bəˈlauftraːktə] **MF** *decl as adj* representative

be|aug|ap|feln [bəˈlauklapfln] *ptp* **beaugapfelt** **VT** *(hum)* to eye

be|äu|geln [bəˈlɔygln] *ptp* **beäugelt** **VT** *(hum)* to make eyes at *(inf)*, to ogle

be|äu|gen [bəˈlɔygn] *ptp* **beäugt** **VT** *(inf)* to gaze *or* look at

Beau|té [boˈteː] **F -, -s** *(geh)*, **Beau|ty** [ˈbjuːti] **F -, -s** *(Press sl)* stunner *(inf)*, beauty

Beau|ty-Case [ˈbjuːtikeːs] **NT OR M -, -s** make-up case *or* bag; *(zum Reisen)* vanity case

Beau|ty|farm [ˈbjuːtifarm] **F** beauty farm

be|bän|dern [bəˈbɛndɐn] *ptp* **bebändert** **VT** *usu ptp* to decorate with ribbons, to beribbon *(liter)*

be|bar|tet [bəˈbaːɐtət] **ADJ** *(usu hum)* bearded

be|bau|bar **ADJ** **a** *Boden* cultiv(at)able **b** *Grundstück* suitable for building; *(= zum Bau freigegeben)* available for building

Be|bau|bar|keit [bəˈbaubaːɐkait] **F -,** *no pl (von Grundstück)* suitability for building

be|bau|en *ptp* **bebaut** **VT** **a** *Grundstück* to build on, to develop; **das Grundstück ist jetzt mit einer Schule bebaut** the piece of land has had a school built on it; **das Viertel war dicht bebaut** the area was heavily built-up; **ein Gelände mit etw ~** to build sth on a piece of land **b** *(Agr)* to cultivate; *Land* to farm

Be|bau|ung [bəˈbauʊŋ] **F -, -en a** *(= Vorgang)* building (*+gen* on); *(von Gelände)* development; *(= Bauten)* buildings *pl*; **Viertel mit dichter ~** densely built-up area **b** *(Agr)* cultivation; *(von Land)* farming

Be|bau|ungs-: **Be|bau|ungs|dich|te** **F** density of building *or* development; **für geringere ~ sorgen** to ensure development is less dense; **Be|bau|ungs|plan** **M** development plan *or* scheme

Bé|bé [beˈbeː] **NT -s, -s** *(Sw)* baby

be|ben [ˈbeːbn] **VI** to shake, to tremble; *(Stimme auch)* to quiver *(vor +dat* with); **am ganzen Leib** *or* **an allen Gliedern ~** to tremble *or* shake all over; **vor jdm ~** *(liter)* to be in fear and trembling of sb; **um jdn ~** *(liter)* to tremble for sb

Be|ben [ˈbeːbn] **NT -s, -** *(= Zittern)* shaking, trembling; *(von Stimme auch)* quivering; *(= Erdbeben)* earthquake

be|bil|dern [bəˈbɪldɐn] *ptp* **bebildert** **VT** *Buch, Vortrag* to illustrate

Be|bil|de|rung **F -, -en** illustrations *pl* (*+gen* in)

be|brillt [bəˈbrɪlt] **ADJ** *(hum inf)* bespectacled

be|brü|ten *ptp* **bebrütet** **VT** *Eier* to incubate; **die Lage ~** *(fig inf)* to brood over the situation

Bé|cha|mel|so|ße [beʃaˈmɛl-] **F** *(Cook)* béchamel (sauce)

Be|cher [ˈbɛçɐ] **M -s, - a** cup; *(old: = Kelch)* goblet; *(= Glasbecher)* glass, tumbler; *(= esp aus Porzellan, Ton, mit Henkel)* mug; *(= Joghurtbecher etc)* carton, tub; *(= Eisbecher) (aus Pappe)* tub; *(aus Metall)* sundae dish; **ein ~ Eis** a tub of ice cream/an ice-cream sundae **b** *(Bot: = Eichelbecher)* cup, cupule *(spec)*

Be|cher-: **be|cher|för|mig** **ADJ** cup-shaped; **Be|cher|glas** **NT** **a** *(= Trinkglas)* glass, tumbler **b** *(Chem)* glass, beaker

be|chern [ˈbɛçɐn] **VI** *(hum inf)* to have a few *(inf)*

be|cir|cen [bəˈtsɪrtsn] *ptp* **becirct** **VT** = **bezirzen**

Be|cken [ˈbɛkn] **NT -s, - a** *(= Brunnenbecken, Hafenbecken, Waschbecken, Geol)* basin; *(= Abwaschbecken)* sink; *(= Toilettenbecken)* bowl, pan; *(= Schwimmbecken)* pool; *(= Staubecken)* reservoir; *(= Fischbecken)* pond; *(= Taufbecken)* font **b** *(Anat)* pelvis, pelvic girdle; **ein breites ~** broad hips **c** *(Mus)* cymbal

Be|cken- *(Anat, Med)*: **Be|cken|bo|den** **M** pelvic floor; **Be|cken|bo|den|gym|nas|tik** **F** pelvic floor exercises *pl*; **Be|cken|bruch** **M** fractured pelvis, pelvic fracture; **Be|cken|end|la|ge** **F** breech position *or* presentation; **Be|cken|kno|chen** **M** hipbone; **Be|cken|rand** **M** *(von Schwimmbecken)* edge of the pool

Beck|mes|ser [ˈbɛkmɛsɐ] **M -s, -** *(pej)* caviller, carper

Beck|mes|se|rei [bɛkmɛsəˈrai] **F -, -en** *(pej)* cavilling *(Brit)*, caviling *(US)*, carping

beck|mes|se|risch [ˈbɛkmɛsərɪʃ] **ADJ** *(pej)* carping, cavilling *(Brit)*, caviling *(US)*

beck|mes|sern [ˈbɛkmɛsɐn] **VI** *(pej)* to cavil, to carp

Bec|que|rel [bɛkəˈrɛl] **NT -(s), -** becquerel

be|da|chen [bəˈdaxn] *ptp* **bedacht** **VT** to roof

be|dacht [bəˈdaxt] **ADJ** **a** *(= überlegt)* prudent, careful, cautious **b auf etw** *(acc)* **~ sein** to be concerned about sth; **er ist nur auf sich ~** he only thinks about himself; **darauf ~ sein, etw zu tun** to be concerned to do sth, to be concerned to do sth → *auch* **bedachen, bedenken**

Be|dacht [bəˈdaxt] **M -s,** *no pl (geh)* **mit ~** *(= vorsichtig)* prudently, carefully, with care; *(= absichtlich)* deliberately; **voll ~** very prudently *or* carefully, with great care; **ohne ~** without thinking, imprudently; **etw mit (gutem) ~ tun** to do sth (quite) deliberately

Be|dach|te(r) [bəˈdaxtə] **MF** *decl as adj (Jur)* beneficiary

be|däch|tig [bəˈdɛçtɪç] **ADJ** *(= gemessen) Schritt, Sprache* measured *no adv*, deliberate; *Wesen* deliberate, steady; *(= besonnen)* thoughtful, reflective; **mit ~en Schritten** *or* **~en Schrittes** *(liter)* **gehen** to walk with measured *or* deliberate steps **ADV** *gehen* with measured *or* deliberate steps; **langsam und ~ sprechen** to speak in slow, measured tones

Be|däch|tig|keit **F -,** *no pl (= Gemessenheit) (von Schritten, Sprache)* measuredness, deliberateness; *(= Besonnenheit)* thoughtfulness, reflectiveness; **etw mit großer ~ tun** to do sth very thoughtfully *or* reflectively

be|dacht|sam [bəˈdaxtzaːm] *(geh)* **ADJ** careful, deliberate **ADV** carefully, deliberately

Be|dacht|sam|keit **F -,** *no pl (geh)* care, deliberation

Be|da|chung **F -, -en** roofing; *(= Dach auch)* roof

be|dan|ken ✪ 47.5, 49, 52.1 *ptp* **bedankt** **VR** **a** to say thank you, to express one's thanks *(form)*; **sich bei jdm (für etw) ~** to thank sb (for sth), to say thank you to sb (for sth); **ich bedanke mich herzlich** thank you very much, (very) many thanks; **dafür können Sie sich bei Herrn Weitz ~** *(iro inf)* you've got Mr Weitz to thank for that *(iro)*, you can thank Mr Weitz for that *(iro)*
b *(iro inf)* **ich bedanke mich, dafür bedanke ich mich (bestens)** no thank you (very much); **dafür** *or* **für dergleichen wird er sich ~** he'll just love that *(iro)*
VT *(form)* **seien Sie (herzlich) bedankt!** please accept my/our (grateful *or* deepest) thanks *(form)*

Be|darf [bəˈdarf] **M -(e)s, -e,** *no pl* **a** *(= Bedürfnis)* need *(an +dat* for); *(= Bedarfsmenge)* requirements *pl*, requisites *pl*; **bei ~** as *or* when required; **bei dringendem ~** in cases of urgent need; **der Bus hält hier nur bei ~** the bus stops here only on request; **Dinge des täglichen ~s** basic *or* everyday necessities; **alles für den häuslichen ~** all household requirements *or* requisites; **seinen ~ an Wein/Lebensmitteln** *etc* **einkaufen** to buy one's supply of wine/food *etc*, to buy the wine/food *etc* one needs; **einem ~ abhelfen** to meet a need; **an etw** *(dat)* **~ haben** to need sth, to be in need of sth; **danke, kein ~** *(iro inf)* no thank you, not on your life *(inf)* → **decken VT e**
b *(Comm: = Nachfrage)* demand *(an +dat* for); **(je) nach ~** according to demand; **den ~ übersteigen** to exceed demand; **über ~** in excess of demand

Be|darfs-: **Be|darfs|ampel** **F** traffic lights *pl* operated by pedestrians, pelican crossing *(Brit)*; **Be|darfs|ana|ly|se** **F** *(Comm etc)* demand analysis; **Be|darfs|ar|ti|kel** **M** requisite; **Be|darfs|be|frie|di|gung** **F**, **Be|darfs|de|ckung** **F** satisfaction of the/sb's needs; **Be|darfs|fall** **M** *(form)* need; **im ~** if necessary; *(= wenn gebraucht)* as necessary *or* required; **für den ~ vorsorgen** to provide for a time of need; **wir wissen nicht, wann der ~ eintritt** we don't know when the need will arise; **be|darfs|ge|recht** **ADJ** *Politik* designed to meet people's needs; **ein ~es Warenangebot** a range of goods which meets consumer demands **ADV** as needed; **~ produzieren** to match production to demand; **Be|darfs|gü|ter** **PL** consumer goods *pl*; **Be|darfs|hal|te|stel|le** F request (bus) stop; **Be|darfs|len|kung** F *(Comm etc)* demand management, consumption control; **Be|darfs|trä|ger(in)** M(F) *(Comm)* consumer; **Be|darfs|we|ckung** F -, *no pl* stimulation of demand

be|dau|er|lich [bəˈdauɐlɪç] ADJ regrettable, unfortunate; **~!** how unfortunate

be|dau|er|li|cher|wei|se ADV regrettably, unfortunately

be|dau|ern [bəˈdauɐn] ✪ 39.2, 45.3 *ptp* **bedauert** VT **a** *etw* to regret; **einen Irrtum ~** to regret one's mistake, to regret having made a mistake; **wir ~, Ihnen mitteilen zu müssen, …** we regret to have to inform you …; **er hat sehr bedauert, dass …** he was very sorry that …; **er schüttelte ~d den Kopf** he shook his head regretfully; **(ich) bedau(e)re!** I am sorry **b** *(= bemitleiden) jdn* to feel *or* be sorry for; **sich selbst ~** to feel sorry for oneself; **er ist zu ~** he is to be pitied, one *or* you should feel sorry for him; **er lässt sich gerne ~, er will immer bedauert sein** he always wants people to feel sorry for him

Be|dau|ern ✪ 45.3, 51.4, 52.1, 52.4 NT [bəˈdauɐn] **-s**, *no pl* regret; **(sehr) zu meinem ~** (much) to my regret; **zu meinem ~ kann ich nicht kommen** I regret that I will not be able to come, to my regret I will not be able to come; **zu meinem größten ~ muss ich Ihnen mitteilen …** it is with the deepest regret that I must inform you …; **mit ~ habe ich …** it is with regret that I …

be|dau|erns|wert, **be|dau|erns|wür|dig** *(geh)* ADJ *Mensch* pitiful; *Zustand* deplorable

be|de|cken *ptp* **bedeckt** VT **a** *(= zudecken)* to cover; **von etw bedeckt sein** to be covered in sth; **mit einem Tuch/mit Papieren/Pickeln/Staub bedeckt sein** to be covered with a cloth/with *or* in papers/spots/dust; **sie hat ihre Familie mit Schande bedeckt** *(liter)* she brought shame upon her family **b** *(Astron) Stern* to eclipse, to occult *(spec)* VR **a** *(= sich zudecken)* to cover oneself **b** *(Himmel)* to become overcast, to cloud over; **der Himmel bedeckte sich mit Wolken** it *or* the sky clouded over *or* became overcast → *auch* **bedeckt**

be|deckt [bəˈdɛkt] ADJ **a** *(= zugedeckt)* covered; **~en Hauptes** *(old)* with one's head covered **b** *(= bewölkt)* overcast, cloudy; **bei ~em Himmel** when the sky *or* it is overcast *or* cloudy **c sich ~ halten** *(fig)* to keep a low profile → *auch* **bedecken**

Be|deckt|sa|mer [bəˈdɛktza:mɐ] M, **Be|deckt|sa|mi|ge** [-za:mɪgə] PL *decl as adj (Bot)* Angiospermae *pl*

Be|de|ckung F **-, -en a** *(= das Bedecken)* covering **b** *(= Deckendes)* cover, covering **c** *(Mil) (= Geleitschutz)* guard, escort; *(= Leibwache)* guard; **der Konvoi hatte drei Fregatten zur ~** the convoy was escorted by three frigates, the convoy had an escort of three frigates **d** *(Astron: von Stern)* eclipse, occultation *(spec)*

be|den|ken *ptp* **bedacht** [bəˈdaxt] *irreg* VT **a** *(= überlegen) Sache, Lage, Maßnahme etc* to consider, to think about; **das will wohl bedacht sein** *(geh)* that calls for careful consideration; **wenn man es recht bedenkt, …** if you think about it properly … **b** *(= in Betracht ziehen) Umstand, Folgen etc* to consider, to take into consideration; **man muss ~, dass …** one must take into consideration the fact that …; **das hättest du früher** *or* **vorher ~ sollen** you should have thought about that sooner *or* before; **ich gebe zu ~, dass …** I would ask you to consider that …; **bedenke, dass du sterben musst** remember you are mortal **c** *(in Testament)* to remember; **jdn mit einem Geschenk ~** *(geh)* to give sb a present; **jdn reich ~** *(geh)* to be generous to sb; **ich wurde auch diesmal reich bedacht** *(geh)* I did very well this time; **mit etw bedacht werden** to receive sth; **auch ich wurde bedacht** I was not forgotten (either), there was something for me too → **Bedachte(r)** VR *(geh)* to think (about it), to reflect; **bedenke dich gut, ehe du …** think well before you …; **ohne sich lange zu ~** without stopping to think *or* reflect → *auch* **bedacht**

Be|den|ken [bəˈdɛŋkn] NT **-s, - a** *usu pl (= Zweifel, Einwand)* doubt, reservation, misgiving; **moralische ~** moral scruples; **~ haben** *or* **tragen** *(geh)* to have one's doubts *(bei* about); **ihm kommen ~** he is having second thoughts; **ohne ~ vorgehen** to act relentlessly *or* unrelentingly **b** *no pl (= das Überlegen)* consideration (+*gen* of), reflection (+*gen* (up)on); **nach langem ~** after much thought; **ohne ~** without thinking

be|den|ken|los ADJ **a** *(= ohne Zögern) Zustimmung* unhesitating, prompt **b** *(= skrupellos)* heedless of others; *(= unüberlegt)* thoughtless ADV **a** *(= ohne Zögern)* unhesitatingly, with no reservations; **ich würde ~ hingehen** I would not hesitate to go, I would have no reservations about going; **~ zustimmen** to agree with no reservations **b** *(= skrupellos)* unscrupulously; **etw ~ tun** *(= unüberlegt)* to do sth without thinking

Be|den|ken|lo|sig|keit F **-,** *no pl* **a** *(= Bereitwilligkeit)* readiness, promptness **b** *(= Skrupellosigkeit)* unscrupulousness, lack of scruples; *(= Unüberlegtheit)* thoughtlessness, lack of thought

be|den|kens|wert ADJ worth thinking about *or* considering

Be|den|ken|trä|ger M **die ~** all those who object

be|denk|lich [bəˈdɛŋklɪç] ADJ **a** *(= zweifelhaft) Geschäfte, Mittel etc* dubious, questionable **b** *(= besorgniserregend) Lage, Verschlimmerung etc* serious, disturbing, alarming; *Gesundheitszustand* serious; **der Zustand des Kranken ist ~** the patient's condition is giving cause for concern; **der Himmel sah ~ aus** the sky looked ominous **c** *(= besorgt)* apprehensive, anxious; **ein ~es Gesicht machen** to look apprehensive ADV **a** *(= zweifelhaft)* **sie handelten ~** their behaviour *(Brit)* *or* behavior *(US)* was questionable *or* dubious **b** *(= besorgniserregend)* seriously, disturbingly, alarmingly; **~ hohe Schulden** alarmingly high debts; **~ zunehmen** to rise alarmingly; **der Termin rückt ~ nahe** the date is getting alarmingly close **c** *(= besorgt)* apprehensively, anxiously; **~ mit dem Kopf schütteln** to shake one's head apprehensively; **jdn ~ stimmen** to make sb (feel) apprehensive

Be|denk|lich|keit F **-,** *no pl* **a** *(= Zweifelhaftigkeit)* dubiousness **b** *(= besorgniserregende Natur)* seriousness; *(= Besorgtheit)* apprehension, anxiety

Be|denk|zeit F **jdm zwei Tage/bis Freitag ~ geben** *or* **einräumen** to give sb two days/until Friday to think about it; **sich** *(dat)* **(eine) ~ ausbitten** *or* **erbitten, um ~ bitten** to ask for time to think about it

be|dep|pert [bəˈdɛpɐt] ADJ *(inf)* **a** *(= ratlos)* dazed, stunned **b** *(= trottelig)* dopey *(inf)*, gormless *(Brit inf)*

be|deu|ten ✪ 53.3 *ptp* **bedeutet** VT **a** *(= gleichzusetzen sein mit, heißen, bezeichnen)* to mean; *(Math, Ling)* to stand for, to denote; *(= versinnbildlichen)* to signify, to symbolize; **was bedeutet dieses Wort?** what does this word mean?, what's the meaning of this word?; **was soll das ~?** what does that mean?; **was soll denn das ~?** what's the meaning of that?; **das hat nichts zu ~** it doesn't mean anything; *(= macht nichts aus)* it doesn't matter **b** *(= ankündigen, zur Folge haben)* to mean; **diese Wolken ~ schlechtes Wetter** these clouds mean *or* spell bad weather; **das bedeutet nichts Gutes** that spells trouble, that bodes ill *(form)* **c** *(= gelten)* to mean (+*dat*, *für* to); **Geld bedeutet mir nichts** money doesn't mean anything *or* means nothing to me; **sein Name bedeutet etwas in der Medizin** his name means something in the field of medicine, he is a name in the field of medicine **d** *(geh: = einen Hinweis geben)* to indicate, to intimate; *(mit Geste)* to indicate, to gesture; *Abneigung, Zustimmung* to indicate; **ich bedeutete ihm, das zu tun** I indicated *or* intimated that he should do that; **man bedeutete mir, dass …** I was given to understand that …

be|deu|tend ADJ **a** *(= wichtig, bemerkenswert) Persönlichkeit* important, distinguished, eminent; *Leistung, Rolle, Kunstwerk* significant, important; **etwas Bedeutendes leisten** to achieve something important *or* significant **b** *(= groß) Summe, Erfolg* considerable, significant ADV *(= beträchtlich)* considerably

be|deut|sam [bəˈdɔytza:m] ADJ **a** *(= wichtig) Gespräch, Fortschritt etc* important; *(= folgenschwer)* significant *(für* for) **b** *(= vielsagend)* meaningful, significant; *Rede* eloquent; *Blick* meaningful ADV meaningfully; **jdm ~ zulächeln** to smile meaningfully at sb

Be|deut|sam|keit F **-,** *no pl* **a** *(= Wichtigkeit)* importance; *(= Folgenschwere)* significance **b** *(geh) (= Bedeutung)* meaningfulness, significance; *(von Rede, Blick)* eloquence

Be|deu|tung F **a** *(= Sinn, Wortsinn)* meaning; **in wörtlicher/übertragener ~** in the literal/figurative sense **b** *(= Wichtigkeit)* importance, significance; *(= Tragweite)* significance; **von ~ sein** to be important *or* significant, to be of significance; **von (großer** *or* **tiefer/geringer) ~ sein** to be of (great/little) importance, to be (very/not very) important; **ein Mann von ~** an important figure; **nichts von ~** nothing of any importance; **ohne ~** of no importance; **große ~ besitzen** to be of great importance; **an ~ gewinnen/verlieren** to gain/lose in importance

Be|deu|tungs-: **Be|deu|tungs|er|wei|te|rung** F *(Ling)* extension of meaning; **Be|deu|tungs|ge|halt** M meaning; **be|deu|tungs|gleich** ADJ synonymous, identical in meaning; **Be|deu|tungs|leh|re** F *(Ling)* semantics *sing*, science of meaning *(old)*; **be|deu|tungs|los** ADJ **a** *(= unwichtig)* insignificant, unimportant **b** *(= nichts besagend)* meaningless; **Be|deu|tungs|lo|sig|keit** F **-,** *no pl* insignificance, unimportance; **zur ~ verurteilt sein** to be condemned to insignificance; **be|deu|tungs|schwan|ger** ADJ *(geh)* pregnant with meaning; **be|deu|tungs|schwer** ADJ *(geh)* meaningful, laden *or* pregnant with meaning; *(= folgenschwer)* momentous; **Be|deu|tungs|un|ter|schied** M difference in meaning; **Be|deu|tungs|ver|en|gung** F *(Ling)* narrowing of meaning; **Be|deu|tungs|ver|schie|bung** F *(Ling)* shift of meaning, sense *or* semantic shift; **be|deu|tungs|ver|wandt** ADJ *(Ling)* semantically related; **be|deu|tungs|voll** ADJ, ADV = **bedeutsam**; **Be|deu|tungs|wan|del** M *(Ling)* change in meaning, semantic change; **Be|deu|tungs|wör|ter|buch** NT (defining) dictionary

be|dien|bar ADJ **leicht/schwer ~** easy/hard to use; **elektrisch ~** electrically operated

Be|dien|bar|keit [bəˈdi:nba:ɐkait] F **-,** *no pl* usability; **leichte ~** ease of use

be|die|nen *ptp* **bedient** VT **a** *(Verkäufer)* to serve, to attend to; *(Kellner, Diener etc)* to wait on, to serve; **werden Sie schon bedient?** are you being attended to *or* served?; **hier wird man gut bedient** the service is good here; **er lässt sich gern ~** he likes to be waited on; **mit diesem Ratschlag war ich schlecht bedient** I was ill-served by that advice; **mit dieser Ware/damit sind Sie sehr gut bedient** these goods/that should serve you very well; **ich bin bedient!** *(inf)* I've had enough, I've had all I can take; *(Aus sl)* I'm pissed *(Brit inf)* or smashed *(inf)* **b** *(Verkehrsmittel)* to serve; **diese Flugroute wird**

von X bedient X operate (on) this route
c *(= handhaben) Maschine, Geschütz etc* to operate; *Telefon* to answer
d *(Fin) Schulden* to service
e *(Sport)* to pass *or* feed (the ball) to
f *(Cards)* **(eine) Farbe ~** to follow suit; **Karo ~** to follow suit in diamonds
VI **a** *(in Geschäft, bei Tisch)* to serve; *(Kellner auch)* to wait (at table *(Brit)* *or* a table *(US)*); *(als Beruf)* to wait, to be a waiter/waitress
b *(Cards)* **du musst ~** you must follow suit; **falsch ~** to revoke, to fail to follow suit
VR **a** *(bei Tisch)* to help *or* serve oneself *(mit* to); **bitte ~ Sie sich** please help *or* serve yourself
b *(geh: = gebrauchen)* **sich jds/einer Sache ~** to use sb/sth

Be|die|ner M **-s, -, Be|die|ne|rin** F **-, -nen** *(Comput)* operator

Be|die|ner-: **be|die|ner|freund|lich** ADJ user-friendly; **Be|die|ner|füh|rung** F, *no pl* *(Comput)* context-sensitive help; **Be|die|ner|hand|buch** NT *(Comput)* user's handbook, user manual

Be|die|ne|rin F **a** *(Comput)* operator **b** *(Aus: = Aufwartefrau)* charwoman *(Brit)*, cleaner

Be|die|ner|ober|flä|che F *(Comput)* user interface

be|diens|tet [bəˈdiːnstət] ADJ **bei jdm ~ sein** to be in service with sb; **~ sein** *(Aus: im öffentlichen Dienst)* to be in the civil service

Be|diens|te|te(r) [bəˈdiːnstətə] MF *decl as adj* **a** *(im öffentlichen Dienst)* public employee **b** *(old: = Diener)* servant

Be|die|nung [bəˈdiːnʊŋ] F **-, -en a** *no pl (in Restaurant etc)* service; *(von Maschinen)* operation; **die ~ der Kunden** serving the customers; **eine Tankstelle mit ~** a petrol station with forecourt service; **ein Restaurant mit ~** a restaurant with waiter service; **zur freien** *or* **gefälligen** *(old)* **~** please take one, please help yourself; **die ~ des Geräts erlernen** to learn how to operate the machine
b *(Fin: von Schulden)* servicing
c *(= Bedienungsgeld)* service (charge)
d *(= Bedienungspersonal)* staff; *(= Kellner etc)* waiter; *(weiblich)* waitress; **kommt denn hier keine ~?** isn't anyone serving here?; **hallo, ~!, ~ bitte!** waiter/waitress!
e *(Mil: = Bedienungsmannschaft)* crew

Be|die|nungs-: **Be|die|nungs|an|lei|tung** F, **Be|die|nungs|an|wei|sung** F operating instructions *pl* *or* directions *pl*; **Be|die|nungs|auf|schlag** M NT service charge; **Be|die|nungs|feh|ler** M mistake in operating a/the machine; **be|die|nungs|freund|lich** ADJ user-friendly; **Be|die|nungs|geld** NT service charge; **Be|die|nungs|he|bel** M operating lever; **Be|die|nungs|kom|fort** M *(Comput, Tech)* ease of operation; **Be|die|nungs|mann|schaft** F *(Mil)* crew; **Be|die|nungs|vor|schrift** F operating instructions *pl*; **Be|die|nungs|zu|schlag** M service charge

be|din|gen *ptp* **bedingt** VT **a** *(= bewirken)* to cause; *(= notwendig machen)* to necessitate; *(Psych, Physiol)* to condition; *(= logisch voraussetzen)* to presuppose; **sich gegenseitig ~** to be mutually dependent; **~de Konjunktion** conditional conjunction → *auch* **bedingt b** *(= voraussetzen, verlangen)* to call for, to demand

be|dingt [bəˈdɪŋt] ADJ **a** *(= eingeschränkt)* limited; *Lob auch* qualified **b** *(= an Bedingung geknüpft) Annahme, Straferlass, Strafaussetzung* conditional **c** *(Physiol) Reflex* conditioned ADV **a** *(= eingeschränkt)* partly, partially; **~ tauglich** *(Mil)* fit for limited duties; **gefällt es Ihnen hier? – ~!** do you like it here? – with some reservations; **(nur) ~ richtig** (only) partly *or* partially valid; **(nur) ~ gelten** to be (only) partly *or* partially valid → *auch* **bedingen b** *(Sw, Aus)* conditionally

Be|din|gung [bəˈdɪŋʊŋ] F **-, -en a** *(= Voraussetzung)* condition; *(= Erfordernis)* requirement; **die erste ~ für etw** the basic requirement for sth; **mit** *or* **unter der ~, dass ...** on condition that ..., with the proviso that ...; **unter keiner ~** in *or* under no circumstances, on no condition; **(nur) unter einer ~** (only) on one condition; **unter jeder anderen ~** in any other circumstances; **von einer ~ abhängen** *or* **abhängig sein** to be conditional on one thing; **~ (für meine Zustimmung) ist, dass ...** it is a condition (of my consent) that ...; **etw zur ~ machen** to make sth a condition; **es zur ~ machen, dass ...** to stipulate that ...; **~en (für etw) stellen** to place conditions (on sth)
b *(= Forderung)* term, condition; **zu günstigen ~en** *(Comm)* on favourable *(Brit)* *or* favorable *(US)* terms
c Bedingungen PL *(= Umstände)* conditions *pl*; **unter guten/harten ~en arbeiten** to work in good/under *or* in difficult conditions

Be|din|gungs-: **Be|din|gungs|form** F *(Gram)* conditional (form); **be|din|gungs|los** ADJ *Kapitulation* unconditional; *Hingabe, Gehorsam, Gefolgschaft* unquestioning ADV unconditionally; **~ für etw eintreten** to support sth without reservation; **Be|din|gungs|lo|sig|keit** F **-,** *no pl* *(von Hingabe, Gehorsam, Gefolgschaft)* unquestioning nature; **Be|din|gungs|satz** M conditional clause

be|drän|gen *ptp* **bedrängt** VT *Feind* to attack; *gegnerische Mannschaft* to put pressure on, to pressurize; *(= belästigen)* to plague, to badger; *Schuldner* to press (for payment); *Passanten, Mädchen* to pester; *(= bedrücken: Sorgen)* to beset; *(= heimsuchen)* to haunt; **ein bedrängtes Herz** *(liter)* a troubled heart; **sich in einer bedrängten Lage/in bedrängten Verhältnissen finden** to be in dire *or* desperate straits; **die Bedrängten und Verzweifelten** people in distress and despair

Be|dräng|nis [bəˈdrɛŋnɪs] F **-ses, -se** *(geh)* *(= seelische Bedrängnis)* distress, torment; **in arger** *or* **großer ~, in einer argen** *or* **großen ~** in dire *or* desperate straits; **jdn/etw in ~ bringen** to get sb/sth into trouble; **in ~ geraten** to get into difficulties

Be|drän|gung [bəˈdrɛŋʊŋ] F **-, -en a** *(= das Bedrängen)* attacking; *(der gegnerischen Mannschaft)* pressurizing; *(= Belästigung)* plaguing, badgering; *(von Schuldner)* pressing; *(von Passanten, Mädchen)* pestering; *(durch Sorgen)* distress **b** = **Bedrängnis**

be|dripst [bəˈdrɪpst] ADJ *(N Ger)* stunned, dazed

be|dro|hen *ptp* **bedroht** VT to threaten; *(= gefährden)* to endanger; **den Frieden ~** to be a threat to peace; **vom Tode bedroht** in mortal danger; **von Überschwemmung bedroht** in danger of being flooded; **vom Aussterben bedroht** threatened with extinction, in danger of becoming extinct

be|droh|lich [bəˈdroːlɪç] ADJ *(= gefährlich)* alarming; *(= Unheil verkündend)* menacing, threatening; **in ~e Nähe rücken** *or* **kommen** to get dangerously *or* perilously close; **Aids ist eine ~e Krankheit** AIDS is a dangerous illness ADV dangerously, alarmingly; **sich ~ verschlechtern** to deteriorate alarmingly; **der Himmel war ~ schwarz** the sky was an ominous *or* a menacing black

Be|droh|lich|keit F **-,** *no pl* *(= Gefährlichkeit)* dangerousness; **seine ~ verlieren** to become less of a threat

Be|dro|hung F threat *(+gen* to); *(= das Bedrohen auch)* threatening *(+gen* of); **in ständiger ~ leben** to live under a constant threat

Be|dro|hungs|ana|ly|se F *(Mil)* threat analysis

be|dröp|pelt [bəˈdrœplt] ADJ *(N Ger inf)* **~ dastehen** *or* **dreinschauen** *(= niedergeschlagen)* to look crestfallen; *(= verlegen)* to look sheepish

be|dru|cken *ptp* **bedruckt** VT to print on; **ein bedrucktes Kleid** a print dress; **bedruckter Stoff** print, printed fabric; **etw mit einem Muster ~** to print a pattern on sth

be|drü|cken *ptp* **bedrückt** VT **a** *(= belasten)* to depress; **jdn ~** to depress sb, to make sb feel depressed; **was bedrückt dich?** what is (weighing) on your mind?; **Sorgen bedrückten ihn** cares were weighing upon him → *auch* **bedrückt b** *(old: = unterdrücken)* to oppress

be|drü|ckend ADJ *Anblick, Nachrichten, Vorstellung* depressing; *(= lastend)* oppressive; *Sorge, Not* pressing

Be|drü|cker [bəˈdrʏkɐ] M **-s, -, Be|drü|cke|rin** [-ərɪn] F **-, -nen** *(old)* oppressor

be|drückt [bəˈdrʏkt] ADJ *(= niedergeschlagen)* depressed, dejected; *Schweigen* oppressive → *auch* **bedrücken**

Be|drü|ckung [bəˈdrʏkʊŋ] F **-, -en a** *(= Niedergeschlagenheit)* depression, dejection **b** *(old: = Unterdrückung)* oppression

Be|du|i|ne [beduˈiːnə] M **-n, -n, Be|du|i|nin** [-ˈiːnɪn] F **-, -nen** Bedouin

be|dür|fen *ptp* **bedurft** VI *irreg +gen (geh)* to need, to require; **das bedarf keiner weiteren Erklärung** there's no need for any further explanation; **es hätte nur eines Wortes bedurft, um ...** it would only have taken a word to ...; **es bedarf nur eines Wortes von Ihnen** you only have to *or* need to say the word; **es bedarf einiger Mühe** some effort is called for *or* required; **ohne dass es eines Hinweises bedurft hätte, ...** without having to be asked ...

Be|dürf|nis [bəˈdʏrfnɪs] NT **-ses, -se a** *(= Notwendigkeit)* need; *(no pl: = Bedarf auch)* necessity; **die ~se des täglichen Lebens** everyday needs; **dafür liegt kein ~ vor, dafür besteht kein ~** there is no need *or* necessity for that
b *no pl (= Verlangen)* need; *(form: = Anliegen)* wish, desire; **es war ihm ein ~, ...** it was his wish *or* desire to ..., he wished *or* desired to ...; **es ist mir ein wirkliches ~** it is my sincere wish/desire; **ich hatte das ~/das dringende ~, das zu tun** I felt the need/an urgent need to do that; **das ~ nach Schlaf haben** *or* **fühlen** to be *or* feel in need of sleep
c *(old: = Notdurft)* call of nature; **(s)ein ~ verrichten** to relieve oneself

Be|dürf|nis-: **Be|dürf|nis|an|stalt** F *(dated form, hum)* **öffentliche ~** public convenience *or* restroom *(US)*; **Be|dürf|nis|be|frie|di|gung** F satisfaction of one's/sb's needs; **be|dürf|nis|los** ADJ *Mensch etc* modest in one's needs; **ein ~es Leben** a modest lifestyle; **Be|dürf|nis|lo|sig|keit** F, *no pl (von Mensch)* modest lifestyle; **die ~ eines mönchischen Lebens** a monk's modest lifestyle

be|dürf|tig [bəˈdʏrftɪç] ADJ **a** *(= hilfsbedürftig)* needy, in need; **die Bedürftigen** the needy *pl*, those in need **b einer Sache** *(gen)* **~ sein** *(geh)* to be *or* stand in need of sth, to have need of sth

Be|dürf|tig|keit F **-,** *no pl* need; **jds ~ (amtlich) feststellen** to give sb a means test

be|du|seln [bəˈduːzln] *ptp* **beduselt** VR *(inf)* to get sozzled *(Brit inf)* *or* tipsy *(inf)*

be|du|selt [bəˈduːzlt] ADJ *(inf)* *(= angetrunken)* sozzled *(Brit inf)*, tipsy *(inf)*; *(= benommen)* bemused, befuddled

Beef|bur|ger [ˈbiːfbøːrgɐ] M (beef)burger

Beef|steak [ˈbiːfsteːk] NT steak; **deutsches ~** hamburger, beefburger

be|eh|ren *ptp* **beehrt** VT *(geh)* to honour *(Brit)*, to honor *(US)*; **wann ~ Sie uns (mit einem Besuch)?** when will you hono(u)r us with a visit?; **bitte ~ Sie uns bald wieder** *(Kellner etc)* I hope you'll do us the hono(u)r of coming again soon VR **sich ~, etw zu tun** *(form)* to have the hono(u)r *or* privilege of doing sth *(form)*

be|ei|den [bəˈlaidn] *ptp* **beeidet** VT *(= beschwören) Sache, Aussage* to swear to; *(= vereidigen) Dolmetscher, Experten* to swear in

be|ei|di|gen [bəˈlaidɪgn] *ptp* **beeidigt** VT **a** *(= beeiden)* to swear to **b** *(Jur: = vereidigen)* to swear in; **jdn auf etw** *(acc)* ~ to have *or* make sb swear on sth; **beeidigte Dolmetscherin** sworn interpreter

be|ei|len *ptp* **beeilt** VR to hurry (up), to get a move on *(inf)*; **sich sehr** *or* **mächtig** *(inf)* ~ to get a real move on *(inf)*; **er beeilte sich hinzuzufügen ...** *(form)* he hastened to add ...

Be|ei|lung [bəˈlailʊŋ] INTERJ *(inf)* get a move on! *(inf)*, step on it! *(inf)*

be|ein|dru|cken [bəˈlaindrʊkn] *ptp* **beeindruckt** VT to impress; *(= Eindruck hinterlassen auch)* to make an impression on; **davon lasse ich mich nicht ~** I won't be impressed by that

be|ein|dru|ckend ADJ impressive ADV impressively

be|ein|fluss|bar ADJ *Mensch* impressionable, suggestible; **er ist nur schwer ~** he is hard to influence *or* sway; **diese Vorgänge sind nicht ~** these events cannot be influenced *or* changed

be|ein|flus|sen [bəˈlainflʊsn] *ptp* **beeinflusst** VT *jdn* to influence; *Urteil, Meinung, Aussage auch* to sway; *Ereignisse, Vorgänge auch* to affect; **jdn günstig/nachhaltig ~** to have a favourable *(Brit) or* favorable *(US) or* good/lasting influence on sb; **er ist leicht/schwer zu ~** he is easily influenced/hard to influence; **kannst du deinen Freund nicht ~?** can't you persuade your friend?; **durch etw beeinflusst sein** to be *or* to have been influenced *or* affected by sth

Be|ein|flus|sung F -, -en *(= das Beeinflussen)* influencing; *(= Einfluss)* influence *(durch* of); ~ **der Rechtspflege** *(Jur)* prejudicing the outcome of a trial

be|ein|träch|ti|gen [bəˈlaintrɛçtɪgn] *ptp* **beeinträchtigt** VT **a** *(= stören)* to spoil; *Vergnügen, Genuss* to detract from, to spoil; *Rundfunkempfang* to interfere with, to impair; **sich gegenseitig ~** *(Empfangsgeräte)* to interfere with one another **b** *(= schädigen) jds Ruf* to damage, to harm; *(= vermindern) Gesundheit, Sehvermögen etc* to impair; *Appetit, Energie, Qualität, Absatz, Wert* to reduce; **dadurch wird der Wert erheblich beeinträchtigt** that reduces the value considerably; **den Wettbewerb ~** to restrict competition; **sich gegenseitig ~** *(Entwicklungen, Interessen)* to have an adverse effect on one another; **das beeinträchtigt schottische Interessen/die Interessen unserer Firma** this is detrimental to Scottish interests/to our firm's interests **c** *(= hemmen) Entscheidung* to interfere with; *(= einschränken) Freiheit, Entschlusskraft* to restrict, to interfere with, to curb; **jdn in seiner Freiheit** *or* **jds Freiheit ~** to restrict *or* interfere with *or* curb sb's freedom; **jdn in seinen Rechten ~** *(Jur)* to infringe sb's rights

Be|ein|träch|ti|gung F -, -en **a** *(= Stören)* spoiling; *(von Genuss, Vergnügen)* detracting (+*gen* from), spoiling (+*gen* of); *(von Konzentration)* disturbance; *(von Rundfunkempfang)* interference (+*gen* with) **b** *(= Schädigen: von Ruf)* damage, harm (+*gen* to); *(= Verminderung: von Appetit, Energie, Qualität)* reduction (+*gen* of, in); *(von Gesundheit, Sehvermögen, Leistung, Reaktion)* impairment **c** *(= Einschränken: von Freizeit, Entschlusskraft)* restriction, curbing (+*gen* of); **ohne ~ von jds Rechten** *(Jur)* without detriment to sb's rights

be|elen|den [bəˈleːlɛndn] *ptp* **beelendet** VT *(Sw)* to upset, to distress

Beel|ze|bub [beˈɛltsəbuːp, ˈbeːltsə-] M -s *(Bibl)* Beelzebub → **Teufel a**

be|en|den *ptp* **beendet**, **be|en|di|gen** *ptp* **beendigt** VT to end; *Arbeit, Aufgabe etc* to finish, to complete; *Vortrag, Brief, Schulstunde, Versammlung* to end, to bring to an end, to conclude; *Streik, Streit, Krieg, Verhältnis* to end, to bring to an end; *Studium* to complete; *(Comput) Programm* to quit; *(als Menüpunkt)* to exit; *(in Startmenü)* to shut down; **der Abend wurde mit einer Diskussion beendet** the evening ended with *or* finished with a discussion; **etw vorzeitig ~** to cut sth short; **sein Leben ~** *(geh)* to end one's days; *(durch Selbstmord)* to take one's life; **damit ist unser Konzert/unser heutiges Programm beendet** that brings to an end *or* concludes our concert/our programmes *(Brit) or* programs *(US)* for today

Be|en|di|gung [bəˈlɛndɪgʊŋ] F -, *no pl*, **Be|en|dung** F, *no pl* ending; *(= Ende)* end; *(= Fertigstellung)* completion; *(= Schluss)* conclusion; **zur ~ dieser Arbeit ...** to finish this piece of work ...; **zur ~ des heutigen Abends ...** to round off this evening ...; **nach ~ des Unterrichts** after school (ends)

be|en|gen [bəˈlɛŋən] *ptp* **beengt** VT *(lit) Bewegung* to restrict, to cramp; *(Möbel etc) Zimmer* to make cramped; *(fig)* to stifle, to inhibit; **das Zimmer beengt mich** the room is too cramped for me; **das Kleid beengt mich** the dress is too tight for me; **~de Kleidung** tight *or* restricting clothing

be|engt [bəˈɛŋt] ADJ cramped, confined; *(fig auch)* stifled; **sich ~ fühlen** to feel confined *etc*; **~e Verhältnisse** *(fig)* restricted circumstances ADV **~ wohnen** to live in cramped conditions

Be|engt|heit F -, *no pl* confinement; *(von Räumen)* cramped conditions *pl*; **ein Gefühl der ~ haben** to feel restricted *or* confined; *(fig auch)* to feel stifled

be|er|ben *ptp* **beerbt** VT **jdn ~** to inherit sb's estate, to be heir to sb; *(inf: bezüglich Stelle, Posten)* to succeed sb

be|er|di|gen [bəˈleːɐdɪgn] *ptp* **beerdigt** VT to bury; **jdn kirchlich ~** to give sb a Christian burial

Be|er|di|gung F -, -en burial; *(= Beerdigungsfeier)* funeral

Be|er|di|gungs- *in cpds* → *auch* **Bestattungs-** funeral; **Be|er|di|gungs|fei|er** F funeral service; **Be|er|di|gungs|ins|ti|tut** NT undertaker's, funeral director's *(form)*, funeral home *(US)*; *(Schild)* Undertakers, Funeral Directors; **Be|er|di|gungs|kos|ten** PL funeral expenses *pl*

Bee|re [ˈbeːrə] F -, -n berry; *(= Weinbeere)* grape; **~n tragen** to bear fruit; **~n sammeln, in die ~n gehen** *(dial)* to go berry-picking; *(Brombeeren)* to go blackberrying *(Brit)*, to go blackberry-picking *(US)*

Bee|ren-: **Bee|ren|aus|le|se** F *(= Wein) wine made from specially selected grapes*; **Bee|ren|frucht** F berry; **Bee|ren|le|se** F fruit picking; **Bee|ren|obst** NT soft fruit

Beet [beːt] NT -(e)s, -e *(= Blumenbeet, Spargelbeet)* bed; *(= Gemüsebeet)* patch; *(= Rabatte)* border *(mit* of)

Bee|te [ˈbeːtə] F -, -n = **Bete**

be|fä|hi|gen [bəˈfɛːɪgn] *ptp* **befähigt** VT to enable; *(Ausbildung)* to qualify, to equip; **jdn zu etw ~** to enable sb to do sth; to qualify *or* equip sb to do sth

be|fä|higt [bəˈfɛːɪçt] ADJ capable, competent; *(durch Ausbildung)* qualified; **sie ist zum Richteramt ~** she is qualified to be *or* become a judge; **zu etw ~ sein** to be capable of doing sth, to be competent to do sth

Be|fä|hi|gung F -, *no pl* **a** *(durch Ausbildung, Voraussetzung)* qualifications *pl*; **die ~ zum Richteramt** the qualifications to be *or* become a judge **b** *(= Können, Eignung)* capability, ability; **er hat nicht die ~ dazu** he does not have the ability to do that; **~ zu etw zeigen** to show talent *or* a gift for sth

Be|fä|hi|gungs|nach|weis M certificate of qualifications

be|fahl *pret von* **befehlen**

be|fahr|bar ADJ *Straße, Weg* passable; *Seeweg, Fluss* navigable; **~ sein** *(Straße)* to be open to traffic; **nicht ~ sein** *(Straße, Weg)* to be closed (to traffic); *(wegen Schnee etc auch)* to be impassable; *(Seeweg, Fluss)* to be unnavigable → **Bankette, Seitenstreifen**

Be|fahr|bar|keit [bəˈfaːɐbaːɐkait] F -, *no pl (von Seeweg, Fluss)* navigability; **die ~ der Straße ist beeinträchtigt** the road is only passable with care

be|fah|ren [bəˈfaːrən] *ptp* **befahren** VT *irreg* **a** *Straße, Weg* to use, to drive on *or* along; *Passstraße* to drive over; *Gegend, Land* to drive *or* travel through; *Kreuzung, Seitenstreifen* to drive onto; *Eisenbahnstrecke* to travel on; **der Pass kann nur im Sommer ~ werden** the pass is only open to traffic *or* passable in summer; **die Straße darf nur in einer Richtung ~ werden** this road is only open in one direction; **dieser Weg kann nur mit dem Fahrrad ~ werden** you can only use a bicycle on this path; **die Straße darf nicht ~ werden** the road is closed; **diese Straße wird stark/wenig ~** this road is used a lot/isn't used much, there is a lot of/not much traffic on this road **b** *(Schiff, Seemann)* to sail; *Fluss* to sail up/down; *Seeweg* to navigate; *Küste* to sail along; **diese Route wird nicht mehr von Schiffen ~** ships no longer sail this route **c** *(Min) Schacht* to go down; **die Grube wird nicht mehr ~** the mine is not worked any more **d** *(= abladen auf)* to spread; **ein Feld mit Dung ~** to spread manure on a field

be|fah|ren ADJ **a** *Straße, Seeweg, Kanal* used; **eine viel** *or* **stark/wenig ~e Straße** *etc* a much/little used road *etc* **b** *(Naut: = erprobt)* seasoned *attr*, experienced; **(ein) ~es Volk** seasoned *or* experienced sailors *pl or* seamen *pl* **c** *(Hunt: = bewohnt)* inhabited

Be|fah|ren NT -s, *no pl* use (+*gen* of); *(= Vorgang)* using; **beim ~ der Brücke** when using the bridge; **„Befahren verboten"** "road closed"; **„Befahren der Brücke verboten"** "bridge closed"

Be|fall M, *no pl* attack; *(mit Schädlingen)* infestation; **es kam zum ~ aller Organe** all organs were affected; **der ~ (des Kohls) mit Raupen** the blight of caterpillars (on the cabbage)

be|fal|len [bəˈfalən] *ptp* **befallen** VT *irreg* **a** *(geh: = überkommen)* to overcome; *(Angst)* to grip, to overcome; *(Durst, Hunger)* to grip, to seize; *(Fieber, Krankheit, Seuche)* to attack, to strike; *(Missgeschick, Schicksal etc)* to befall, to affect; **eine Schwäche befiel sie** she felt faint; **eine Ohnmacht befiel sie** she fainted **b** *(= angreifen, infizieren)* to affect; *(Schädlinge, Ungeziefer)* to infest

be|fal|len ADJ affected *(von* by); *(von Schädlingen)* infested *(von* with)

be|fan|gen [bəˈfaŋən] ADJ **a** *Mensch, Lächeln* diffident; *Schweigen, Stille* awkward **b** *(esp Jur: = voreingenommen)* prejudiced, bias(s)ed; **als ~ gelten** to be considered (to be) prejudiced *or* bias(s)ed; *(Jur)* to be considered (to be) an interested party; **sich für ~ erklären** *(Jur)* to declare oneself disqualified due to a conflict of interests; **jdn als ~ erklären** to claim that sb is not qualified due to a conflict of interests; **jdn als ~ ablehnen** *(Jur)* to object to sb on grounds of suspected bias **c** *(geh: = verstrickt)* **in der Vorstellung ~ sein, dass ...** *or* **... zu ...** to have the impression that ...; **er ist in seinen eigenen Anschauungen ~** he can only see his own point of view; **in einem Irrtum ~ sein** to labour *(Brit) or* labor *(US)* under a misapprehension

Be|fan|gen|heit F -, *no pl* **a** *(= Verlegenheit) (von Mensch, Lächeln)* diffidence; *(von Schweigen, Stille)* awkwardness **b** *(= Voreingenommenheit)* bias, prejudice; *(Jur)* interest; **jdn wegen (Besorgnis der) ~ ablehnen** *(Jur)* to object to sb on grounds of suspected bias

be|fas|sen *ptp* **befasst** VR **a** *(= sich beschäftigen)* **sich mit etw ~** to deal with sth; *mit Problem, Frage auch* to look into sth; *mit Fall, Angelegenheit auch* to attend to sth; *mit Arbeit auch, mit Forschungsbereich etc* to work on sth; **sich mit jds Vorleben ~** to look into sb's past; **damit haben wir uns jetzt lange genug befasst** we have spent long enough on *or* over that; **er hat sich lange damit befasst, alle Einzelheiten auszuarbeiten** he spent a long time working out all the details; **mit solchen Kleinigkeiten hat er sich nie befasst** he has never bothered with *or* concerned himself with such trivialities

b *(= sich annehmen)* **sich mit jdm ~** to deal with sb, to attend to sb; *mit Kindern auch* to see to sb; **sich mit jdm sehr ~** to give sb a lot of attention

VT **a** *(dial: = anfassen)* to touch

b *(form)* **jdn mit etw ~** to get sb to deal with sth; **mit etw befasst sein** to be dealing with sth; **die mit diesem Fall befassten Richter** the judges engaged on this case

be|feh|den [bəˈfeːdn] *ptp* **befehdet** VT *(Hist)* to be feuding with; *(fig)* to attack VR to be feuding; **sich mit Worten ~** to attack each other verbally

Be|fehl [bəˈfeːl] M **-(e)s, -e** **a** *(= Anordnung)* order, command *(an +acc* to, *von* from); *(Comput, Physiol)* command; **einen ~ verweigern** to refuse to obey an order *etc*; **er gab (uns) den ~, ...** he ordered us to ...; **wir hatten den ~, ...** we had orders to ..., we were ordered to ...; **wir haben ~, Sie festzunehmen** we have orders *or* have been ordered to arrest you; **auf seinen ~ (hin)** on his orders, at his command; **auf ~** to order; *(= sofort)* at the drop of a hat *(inf)*; **auf ~ handeln** to act under *or* according to orders; **auf höheren ~** on orders from above; **zu ~, Herr Hauptmann** *(Mil)* yes, sir; *(nach erhaltenem Befehl auch)* very good, sir; **zu ~, Herr Kapitän** aye aye, sir; **~ ausgeführt!** mission accomplished; **~ ist ~** orders are orders; **~ von oben** orders from above; **~ vom Chef!** boss's orders; **dein Wunsch ist mir ~** *(hum)* your wish is my command

b *(= Befehlsgewalt)* command; **den ~ haben** *or* **führen** to have command, to be in command *(über +acc* of); **den ~ übernehmen** to take *or* assume command

be|feh|len [bəˈfeːlən] *pret* **befahl** [bəˈfaːl], *ptp* **befohlen** [bəˈfoːlən] VT **a** *(= anordnen)* to order; **er befahl Stillschweigen** *or* **zu schweigen** he ordered them/us *etc* to be silent; **sie befahl ihm Stillschweigen** *or* **zu schweigen** she ordered him to be silent; **er befahl, den Mann zu erschießen, er befahl die Erschießung des Mannes** he ordered the man to be shot; **sie befahl, dass ...** she ordered *or* gave orders that ...; **du hast mir gar nichts zu ~, von dir lasse ich mir nichts ~** I won't take orders from you; **gnädige Frau ~?** *(old form)*, **was ~ gnädige Frau?** *(old form)* yes, Madam?, what can I do for you, Madam?

b *(= beordern) (an die Front etc)* to order, to send; *(zu sich auch)* to summon

c *(liter: = anvertrauen)* to entrust, to commend *(liter)*; **seine Seele Gott/in die Hände Gottes ~** to commend *or* entrust one's soul to God/into God's hands

VI **a** *(= Befehle erteilen)* to give orders; **schweigen Sie, befahl er** be quiet, he ordered; **er befiehlt gern** he likes giving orders; **hier habe nur ich zu ~** I give the orders around here; **wie Sie ~** as you wish; **wer ~ will, muss erst gehorchen lernen** *(prov)* if you wish to command you must first learn to obey

b *(Mil: = den Befehl haben)* to be in command, to have command *(über +acc* of); **über Leben und Tod ~** to be in absolute command

be|feh|le|risch [bəˈfeːlərɪʃ] ADJ *Ton, Wesen* imperious, dictatorial

be|feh|li|gen [bəˈfeːlɪgn] *ptp* **befehligt** VT *(Mil)* to command, to be in command of, to have command of *or* over

Be|fehls-: **Be|fehls|aus|ga|be** F *(Mil)* issuing of orders; **um 15 Uhr ist ~** orders will be issued at 1500 hours; **Be|fehls|be|reich** M *(Mil)* (area of) command; **Be|fehls|code** M *(Comput)* command code; **Be|fehls|emp|fän|ger(in)** M(F) recipient of an order; **~ sein** to follow orders (*+gen* from); **jdn zum ~ degradieren** *(fig)* to lower sb to the level of just following orders; **Be|fehls|fol|ge** F *(Comput)* command sequence; **Be|fehls|form** F *(Gram)* imperative; **be|fehls|ge|mäß** ADJ, ADV as ordered, in accordance with (sb's) orders; **er muss sich ~ um 9 Uhr dort einfinden** his orders are to report there at 9 o'clock; **Be|fehls|ge|walt** F *(Mil)* command; **~ haben** to be in *or* to have command *(über +acc* over); **jds ~** *(dat)* **unterstehen** to be under sb's command; **Be|fehls|ha|ber** [-haːbɐ] M **-s, -**, **Be|fehls|ha|be|rin** [-ərɪn] F **-, -nen** commander; **be|fehls|ha|be|risch** [-haːbərɪʃ] ADJ dictatorial; **Be|fehls|kode** M = **Befehlscode**; **Be|fehls|me|nü** NT *(Comput)* command menu; **Be|fehls|not|stand** M *(Jur)* compulsion *or* necessity to obey orders; **unter ~ handeln** to be acting under orders; **Be|fehls|satz** M *(Gram)* imperative, command; **Be|fehls|schalt|flä|che** F *(Comput)* command button; **Be|fehls|spra|che** F *(Comput)* command language; **Be|fehls|tas|te** *(Comput)* command key; **Be|fehls|ton** M, *no pl* peremptory tone; **Be|fehls|ver|wei|ge|rung** F *(Mil)* refusal to obey orders; **be|fehls|wid|rig** ADJ, ADV contrary to orders, against orders; **Be|fehls|zei|le** F *(Comput)* command line

be|fein|den [bəˈfaindn] *ptp* **befeindet** VT *(geh) Land* to be hostile towards; *Ideologie, Schriften, Schriftsteller* to attack VR to be hostile (towards each other)

be|fes|ti|gen *ptp* **befestigt** VT **a** *(an +dat* to) *(= anbringen)* to fasten; *Boot* to tie up; **etw durch Nähen/Kleben** *etc* **~** to sew/glue *etc* sth; **etw an der Wand/Tür ~** to attach *or* fix sth to the wall/door; **die beiden Enden/Teile werden (aneinander) befestigt** the two ends/parts are fastened together; **die Wäsche mit Klammern an der Leine ~** to peg the washing on the line; **ein loses Brett ~** to fasten down *or* secure a loose board

b *(= fest, haltbar machen) Böschung, Deich* to reinforce; *Fahrbahn, Straße* to make up; **eine Straße gut ~** to make up a road with good foundations

c *(Mil: = mit Festungsanlagen versehen)* to fortify

VR *(Fin) Preis, Börsenkurs* to stabilize

Be|fes|ti|gung F **a** *(= das Befestigen)* fastening; *(von Boot)* tying up; **zur ~ des Plakats ...** in order to attach the poster ... **b** *(= Vorrichtung zum Befestigen)* fastening, catch **c** *(= das Haltbarmachen)* reinforcement; *(fig: = Stärkung)* consolidation; **zur ~ der Macht des ...** in order to consolidate the power of ... **d** *(Mil)* fortification

Be|fes|ti|gungs|an|la|ge F, **Be|fes|ti|gungs|bau** M *pl* **-bauten**, **Be|fes|ti|gungs|werk** NT fortification, defence *(Brit)*, defense *(US)*

be|feuch|ten [bəˈfɔyçtn] *ptp* **befeuchtet** VT to moisten; *Finger auch* to wet; *Wäsche* to damp(-en); **das vom Tau befeuchtete Gras** the grass moistened by the dew

be|feu|ern *ptp* **befeuert** VT **a** *(= beheizen)* to fuel **b** *(Naut, Aviat) Wasserstraße, Untiefen* to light *or* mark with beacons; *Start- und Landebahn* to light, to mark with lights **c** *(lit, fig: mit Geschossen)* to bombard **d** *(geh: = anspornen)* to fire with enthusiasm

Be|feu|e|rung F *(Aviat, Naut)* lights *pl*, beacons *pl*

Beff|chen [ˈbɛfçən] NT **-s, -** Geneva band

be|fie|dert [bəˈfiːdɐt] ADJ feathered

be|fiehlt [bəˈfiːlt] 3. PERS SING *pres von* **befehlen**

be|fin|den *ptp* **befunden** [bəˈfʊndn] *irreg* VR **a** *(= sein)* to be; *(= liegen auch)* to be situated; *(in Maschine, Körper etc)* to be (situated *or* located); **sich auf Reisen ~** to be away; **unter ihnen befanden sich einige, die ...** there were some amongst them who ...; **die Abbildung befindet sich in diesem Buch** the illustration can be found *or* is in this book; **sich in Verwirrung/guter Laune/im Irrtum ~** to be confused/in a good mood/mistaken; **sich auf dem Weg der Besserung ~** to be on the road to recovery; **wenn man sich in schlechter Gesellschaft befindet ...** if you find yourself in bad company ...

b *(form: = sich fühlen)* to feel; **wie ~ Sie sich heute?** how are you (feeling) today?, how do you feel today?

VT *(form: = erachten)* to deem *(form)*, to find; **etw für nötig/angemessen/für** *or* **als gut ~** to deem *or* find sth (to be) necessary/appropriate/good; **Ihre Papiere wurden in Ordnung befunden** your papers were found to be in order; **jdn für schuldig ~** to find sb guilty → **wiegen**

VI *(geh: = entscheiden)* to come to *or* make a decision, to decide *(über +acc* about, *in +dat* on); **darüber hat der Arzt zu ~** that is for the doctor to decide; **darüber habe ich nicht zu ~** that is not for me to decide; **über jdn/etw ~** to pass judgement on sb/sth, to reach a verdict on sb/sth

Be|fin|den [bɐˈfɪndn] NT **-s**, *no pl* **a** *(form: = Gesundheitszustand)* (state of) health; *(eines Kranken)* condition; **seelisches ~** mental state *or* condition; **wie ist das (werte)** *or* **Ihr (wertes) ~?** *(form)* how are you (feeling)? **b** *(geh: = das Dafürhalten)* view, opinion; **nach meinem ~** in my view *or* opinion; **nach eigenem ~ entscheiden** to decide according to one's own judgement

be|find|lich [bəˈfɪntlɪç] ADJ *usu attr (form)* **a** *(an einem Ort) Gebäude, Park* situated, located; *(in Behälter)* contained; **der hinter dem Hause ~e Garten** the garden (situated) behind the house; **alle in der Bibliothek ~en Bücher** all the books in the library **b** *(in einem Zustand)* **das im Umbau ~e Hotel** the hotel which is being renovated; **das im Umlauf ~e Geld** the money in circulation; **die in Kraft ~e Verordnung** the regulation which is in force

Be|find|lich|keit F **-, -en** sensitivities *pl*; **nationale ~en** national sensitivities

be|fin|gern [bəˈfɪŋɐn] *ptp* **befingert** VT *(inf) (= betasten)* to finger

be|fi|schen [bəˈfɪʃn] *ptp* **befischt** VT *Gewässer, Meer* to fish

be|flag|gen *ptp* **beflaggt** VT *Häuser* to (be)deck *or* decorate with flags; *Schiff* to dress; **die beflaggten Straßen** the flag-decked streets, the streets (be)decked *or* decorated with flags; **anlässlich seines Todes wurden alle öffentlichen Gebäude beflaggt** flags were flown on all public buildings to mark his death

Be|flag|gung [bəˈflagʊŋ] F **-, -en** **a** *(= das Beflaggen) (von Gebäuden)* decoration with flags; *(von Schiffen)* dressing **b** *(= Fahnenschmuck)* flags *pl*

be|fle|cken [bɐˈflɛkn] *ptp* **befleckt** VT **a** *(lit)* to stain; **er hat seinen Anzug mit Farbe befleckt** he got paint on his suit; **er hat sich** *or* **seine Hände mit Blut befleckt** *(fig)* he has blood on his hands **b** *(fig geh) Ruf, Ehre* to cast a slur on, to besmirch, to sully; *Heiligtum* to defile, to desecrate

be|fleckt [bəˈflɛkt] ADJ **a** stained; **sein mit Blut ~er Anzug** his bloodstained suit **b** *Ruf, Ehre* sullied, besmirched

Be|fle|ckung F **-, -en** **a** *(= Beschmutzen)* staining **b** *(von Ruf, Ehre)* besmirching, sullying; *(von Heiligtum)* defilement, desecration

be|flei|ßen [bəˈflaisn] *pret* **befliss** [bəˈflɪs], *ptp* **beflissen** [bəˈflɪsn] VR *(old)* = **befleißigen**

be|flei|ßi|gen [bəˈflaisɪgn] *ptp* **befleißigt** VR *(geh)* **sich einer Sache** *(gen)* **~** to cultivate sth; **sich ~, etw zu tun** to make a great effort to do sth; **sich größter** *or* **der größten Höflichkeit ~** to go out of one's way to be polite

be|flie|gen *ptp* **beflogen** [bəˈfloːgn] VT *irreg (Aviat) Strecke* to fly, to operate (on); *Gegend* to fly over; *Raum* to fly through *or* in; **eine viel beflogene Strecke** a heavily used route

be|fliss *pret von* **befleißen**

be|flis|sen [bəˈflɪsn] PTP *von* **befleißen** ADJ *(geh: = bemüht)* zealous; *(pej: = unterwürfig)* obsequious; **um etw ~ sein** to be concerned for sth; **er war sehr um die Zufriedenheit seiner Gäste ~** he was very anxious *or* concerned to please his guests; **~ sein, etw zu tun** to be concerned to do sth; **ängstlich ~** anxious ADV zealously; *(pej)* obsequiously

Be|flis|sen|heit F -, *no pl (= Bemühtheit)* zeal; *(= Unterwürfigkeit)* obsequiousness

be|flis|sent|lich [bəˈflɪsntlɪç] ADV = **geflissentlich**

be|flü|geln [bəˈfly:gln] *ptp* **beflügelt** VT *(geh)* to inspire, to fire; **die Angst beflügelte seine Schritte** *(liter)* fear winged his steps *(liter)*; **der Gedanke an Erfolg beflügelte ihn** the thought of success spurred him on

be|foh|len *ptp von* **befehlen**

be|fol|gen *ptp* **befolgt** VT *Vorschrift, Befehl etc* to obey, to comply with; *grammatische Regel* to follow, to obey; *Ratschlag* to follow, to take

Be|fol|gung [bəˈfɔlgʊŋ] F -, *no pl* obeying, compliance *(+gen* with); *(von grammatischer Regel)* following, obeying; *(von Ratschlag)* following, taking; ~ **der Vorschriften** obeying the rules, compliance with the rules

Be|för|de|rer M, **Be|för|de|rin** F *(form)* carrier

be|för|dern *ptp* **befördert** VT **a** *Waren, Gepäck* to transport, to carry; *Personen* to carry; *Post* to handle; **etw mit der Post®/per Luftpost/Bahn/Schiff** ~ to send sth by mail/airmail/rail/ship; to ship sth; **jdn/etw von A nach B** ~ to transport *or* convey sb/sth from A to B; **jdn an die (frische) Luft** *or* **zur Tür hinaus** *or* **ins Freie** ~ *(fig)* to fling *or* chuck sb out *(inf)*; **jdn ins Jenseits** ~ *(inf)* to bump sb off *(inf)*, to do sb in *(inf)* **b** *(= dienstlich aufrücken lassen)* to promote; **er wurde zum Major befördert** he was promoted to (the rank of) major

Be|för|de|rung F **a** *(= Transport)* transportation, carriage; *(von Personen)* carriage; *(von Post)* handling; **die ~ der Post/eines Briefes dauert drei Tage** the post/a letter takes three days (to arrive); **für die ~ von 35 Personen zugelassen** permitted to carry 35 persons; **für die ~ der Kursteilnehmer wird gesorgt** transport will be arranged for course participants; ~ **zu Lande/zur Luft/per Bahn** land/air/rail transportation **b** *(beruflich)* promotion

Be|för|de|rungs-: **Be|för|de|rungs|aus|sich|ten** PL *(= Aufstiegschancen)* promotion prospects *pl*, chances *pl or* prospects *pl* of promotion; **Be|för|de|rungs|be|din|gun|gen** PL terms *pl or* conditions *pl* of carriage; **Be|för|de|rungs|dau|er** F delivery time; **Be|för|de|rungs|kos|ten** PL transport costs *pl*; **Be|för|de|rungs|lis|te** F promotion list; **Be|för|de|rungs|mit|tel** NT means of transport; **Be|för|de|rungs|pflicht** F *obligation of taxis, buses etc to accept passengers*; **Be|för|de|rungs|stau** M *(im Beruf)* promotion bottleneck; **Be|för|de|rungs|steu|er** F transport tax; **Be|för|de|rungs|stopp** M *(im Beruf)* promotion moratorium, moratorium on promotion(s); **Be|för|de|rungs|ta|rif** M transportation *or (bei Postbeförderung)* postage charge

be|frach|ten [bəˈfraxtn] *ptp* **befrachtet** VT *Fahrzeug, Schiff* to load; *(fig geh auch)* to burden; **ein schwer befrachtetes Schiff** a heavily laden ship; **seine übermäßig mit Emotionen befrachtete Rede** his speech, overladen with emotion

Be|frach|ter [bəˈfraxtɐ] M -s, -, **Be|frach|te|rin** [-ərɪn] F -, -nen shipper, freighter

Be|frach|tung F -, -en loading

be|frackt [bəˈfrakt] ADJ in tails, tail-coated *(Brit)*, in tail coat *(US)*

be|fra|gen *ptp* **befragt** VT **a** *(über +acc, zu, nach* about) to question; *Zeugen auch* to examine; **jdn im Kreuzverhör** ~ to cross-question *or (esp Jur)* to cross-examine sb; **auf Befragen** when questioned **b** *(= um Stellungnahme bitten)* to consult *(über +acc, nach* about); **jdn um Rat/nach seiner Meinung** ~ to ask sb for advice/his opinion, to ask sb's advice/opinion; **jdn in einer Angelegenheit** ~ to consult sb about *or* on a matter VR *(dated)* to consult; *(= sich erkundigen)* to make inquiries; **sich bei jdm/etw** ~ to consult sb/sth

Be|frag|te(r) [bəˈfra:ktə] MF *decl as adj* person asked; *(in Umfrage auch)* interviewee; **alle ~n** all those asked

Be|fra|gung [bəˈfra:gʊŋ] F -, -en **a** *(= das Befragen)* questioning; *(von Zeugen auch)* examining, examination **b** *(von Fachmann)* consultation (+*gen* with *or* of) **c** *(= Umfrage)* survey

be|franst [bəˈfranst] ADJ fringed, with a fringe

be|frei|en *ptp* **befreit** VT **a** *(= frei machen)* to free, to release; *Volk, Land* to liberate, to free; *(= freilassen) Gefangenen, Tier, Vogel* to set free, to free; **jdn aus einer schwierigen Lage** ~ to rescue sb from a tricky situation, to get sb out of a tricky situation

b *(= freistellen) (von* from) to excuse; *(von Militärdienst, Steuern)* to exempt; *(von Eid etc)* to absolve; *(von Pflicht)* to release; **sich vom Religionsunterricht ~ lassen** to be excused religious instruction

c *(= erlösen: von Schmerz etc)* to release, to free; **jdn von einer Last** ~ to take a weight off sb's mind; **ein ~des Lachen** a healthy *or* an unrepressed laugh → *auch* **befreit**

d *(= reinigen) (von* of) *(von Ungeziefer etc)* to rid; *(von Schnee, Eis)* to free; **seine Schuhe von Schmutz** ~ to remove the dirt from one's shoes

VR **a** *(Volk, Land)* to free oneself; *(= entkommen)* to escape *(von, aus* from); **sich aus einer schwierigen Lage** ~ to get oneself out of a difficult situation

b *(= erleichtern)* to rid oneself *(von* of), to free oneself *(von* from)

Be|frei|er [bəˈfraiɐ] M -s, -, **Be|frei|e|rin** [-ərɪn] F -, -nen liberator

be|freit [bəˈfrait] ADJ *(= erleichtert)* relieved ADV *lächeln* with relief; ~ **aufatmen/aufseufzen** to heave *(Brit) or* breathe a sigh of relief; **die Bevölkerung kann endlich ~ aufatmen** the people can finally breathe easy again → *auch* **befreien**

Be|frei|ung [bəˈfraiʊŋ] F -, -en **a** *(= das Befreien)* freeing, releasing; *(von Volk, Land)* liberation, freeing; *(von Gefangenen, Tieren)* setting free, freeing **b** *(= Freistellung)* excusing; *(von Militärdienst, Steuern)* exemption; *(von Eid)* absolving; *(von Pflichten)* releasing; **um ~ von etw bitten** to ask to be excused/exempted from sth **c** *(von Schmerz)* releasing **d** *(von Ungeziefer)* ridding; *(von Schnee, Eis)* freeing

Be|frei|ungs-: **Be|frei|ungs|ak|ti|on** F liberation campaign; **Be|frei|ungs|be|we|gung** F liberation movement; **Be|frei|ungs|front** F liberation front; **Be|frei|ungs|kampf** M struggle for liberation; **Be|frei|ungs|krieg** M war of liberation; **Be|frei|ungs|or|ga|ni|sa|ti|on** F liberation organization; **Be|frei|ungs|schlag** M *(Eishockey, Ftbl)* clearance; *(fig)* coup; **Be|frei|ungs|theo|lo|ge** M liberation theologian; **Be|frei|ungs|theo|lo|gie** F liberation theology; **Be|frei|ungs|theo|lo|gin** F liberation theologian; **Be|frei|ungs|ver|such** M escape attempt

be|frem|den [bəˈfrɛmdn] *ptp* **befremdet** VT to disconcert; **es befremdet mich, dass ...** I'm rather taken aback that ...; **das befremdet mich an ihr** that (side of her) disconcerts me → *auch* **befremdet** VI to cause disconcertment

Be|frem|den [bəˈfrɛmdn] NT -s, *no pl* disconcertment; **nicht ohne ~ ...** it is with some disconcertment that ...

be|frem|dend ADJ disconcerting

be|frem|det [bəˈfrɛmdət] ADJ disconcerted, taken aback → *auch* **befremden**

be|fremd|lich [bəˈfrɛmtlɪç] ADJ *(geh)* = **befremdend**

Be|frem|dung F -, *no pl* = **Befremden**

be|freun|den [bəˈfrɔyndn] *ptp* **befreundet** VR **a** *(= sich anfreunden)* to make *or* become friends; **ich habe mich schnell mit ihm befreundet** I quickly made friends with him, he and I quickly became friends; **die beiden haben sich (miteinander) befreundet** the pair made *or* became friends **b** *(fig) (mit Gedanken etc)* **sich mit etw** ~ to get used to sth, to get *or* grow accustomed to sth

be|freun|det [bəˈfrɔyndət] ADJ **wir/sie sind schon lange (miteinander)** ~ we/they have been friends *or* friendly for a long time; **gut** *or* **eng ~ sein** to be good *or* close friends; **alle ~en Familien** all the families we *etc* are friendly with; **ein uns ~er Staat** a friendly nation; **das ~e Ausland** friendly (foreign) countries; **ein uns ~er Arzt** a doctor (who is a) friend of ours; **~e Zahlen** *(Math)* amicable numbers

be|frie|den [bəˈfri:dn] *ptp* **befriedet** VT *(geh)* to pacify

be|frie|di|gen [bəˈfri:dɪgn] *ptp* **befriedigt** VT to satisfy; *Gläubiger auch* to pay; *Gelüste auch* to gratify; *Ansprüche, Forderungen, Verlangen auch* to meet; **jdn (sexuell)** ~ to satisfy sb (sexually); **er ist leicht/schwer zu** ~ he's easily/not easily satisfied, he's easy/hard to satisfy → *auch* **befriedigt** VI to be satisfactory; **Ihre Leistung hat nicht befriedigt** your performance was unsatisfactory VR **sich (selbst)** ~ to masturbate

be|frie|di|gend ADJ satisfactory; *Verhältnisse, Leistung, Arbeit, Antwort auch* adequate; *Lösung auch* acceptable; *Gefühl* satisfying; *(als Schulnote)* fair; **nicht ~ sein** to be unsatisfactory/inadequate/unacceptable ADV satisfactorily

be|frie|digt [bəˈfri:dɪçt] ADJ satisfied, contented; **bist du nun endlich ~?** are you satisfied at last? ADV with satisfaction; **er lächelte ~** he smiled with satisfaction → *auch* **befriedigen**

Be|frie|di|gung F -, -en **a** *(= das Befriedigen)* satisfaction, satisfying; **sexuelle ~** sexual satisfaction; **zur ~ deiner Neugier ...** to satisfy your curiosity ... **b** *(= Genugtuung)* satisfaction; **seine ~ in etw** *(dat)* **suchen** to look for *or* seek satisfaction in sth

Be|frie|dung F -, -en *(geh)* pacification

be|fris|ten [bəˈfrɪstn] *ptp* **befristet** VT to limit, to restrict *(auf +acc* to); *Aufgabe, Projekt* to put a time limit on

be|fris|tet [bəˈfrɪstət] ADJ *Genehmigung, Visum* restricted, limited *(auf +acc* to); *Arbeitsverhältnis, Anstellung* temporary; **~ sein** *(Pass etc)* to be valid for a limited time; **auf zwei Jahre ~ sein** *(Visum etc)* to be valid for two years; **mein Arbeitsverhältnis ist auf zwei Jahre ~** my appointment is limited *or* restricted to two years

Be|fris|tung F -, -en limitation, restriction *(auf +acc* to)

be|fruch|ten *ptp* **befruchtet** VT **a** *(lit) Eizelle* to fertilize; *Blüte* to pollinate; **künstlich** ~ to inseminate artificially **b** *(fig: = fruchtbar machen)* to make fertile **c** *(fig: = geistig anregen)* to stimulate, to have a stimulating effect on

be|fruch|tend [bəˈfrʊxtnd] ADJ *(fig)* fruitful, stimulating ADV **~ wirken** to have a stimulating effect *(auf +acc* on) → *auch* **befruchten**

Be|fruch|tung [bəˈfrʊxtʊŋ] F -, -en fertilization; *(von Blüte)* pollination; **künstliche ~** artificial insemination

be|fu|gen [bəˈfu:gn] *ptp* **befugt** VT *(form)* to authorize; **wer hat Sie dazu befugt?** who authorized you to do that?

Be|fug|nis [bəˈfu:knɪs] F -, -se *(form)* authority *no pl*; *(= Erlaubnis)* authorization *no pl*; **eine ~ erhalten/erteilen** to receive/give authorization *or* authority; **besondere ~se erhalten** to receive *or* be given special authority; **Zutritt ohne ~ nicht gestattet** no entry to unauthorized persons

be|fugt [bəˈfu:kt] ADJ *(form)* **~ sein(, etw zu tun)** to have the authority *or (= ermächtigt worden sein)* be authorized (to do sth)

be|füh|len *ptp* **befühlt** VT to feel; *(= hinstreichen über auch)* to run one's hands over

be|fum|meln *ptp* **befummelt** VT *(inf: = betasten)* to paw *(inf)*

Be|fund M results *pl*, findings *pl*; **der ~ war positiv/negativ** *(Med)* the results were positive/negative; **ohne ~** *(Med)* (results) negative

be|fürch|ten *ptp* **befürchtet** VT to fear, to be afraid of; **ich befürchte das Schlimmste** I fear the worst; **es ist** *or* **steht zu ~, dass ...** it is (to be) feared that ...; **dabei sind Komplikationen zu ~** it is feared there may be complications;

dabei ist gar nichts zu ~ there's nothing to fear with that

Be|fürch|tung [bəˈfʏrçtʊŋ] F -, -en fear *usu pl*; **~en** *or* **die ~ haben, dass ...** to fear *or* be afraid that ...; **die schlimmsten ~en haben** *or* **hegen** *(geh)* to fear the worst

be|für|wor|ten [bəˈfyːɐvɔrtn] ✪ 40.1, 40.2 *ptp* **befürwortet** VT to approve

Be|für|wor|ter [bəˈfyːɐvɔrtɐ] M -s, -, **Be|für|wor|te|rin** [-ərɪn] F -, -nen supporter; *(von Idee auch)* advocate

Be|für|wor|tung F -, -en approval, support

be|ga|ben [bəˈgaːbn] *ptp* **begabt** VT *usu pass (liter)* to endow; **mit etw begabt sein** to be endowed with sth

be|gabt [bəˈgaːpt] ADJ talented; *(esp geistig, musisch auch)* gifted; **für etw ~ sein** to be talented at sth; *für Musik, Kunst etc auch* to have a gift for sth

Be|gab|ten-: **Be|gab|ten|aus|le|se** F selection of the most gifted *or* talented people; **Be|gab|ten|för|de|rung** F **a** *(= Zuschuss)* (educational) grant **b** *(= System)* scholarship system **c** *(= Unterricht)* extra *or* specialized tuition for gifted students

Be|gab|te(r) [bəˈgaːptə] MF *decl as adj* talented *or* gifted person/man/woman *etc*

Be|ga|bung F -, -en **a** *(= Anlage)* talent; *(geistig, musisch)* gift, talent; **er hat eine ~ dafür, immer das Falsche zu sagen** he has a gift for *or* a knack of always saying the wrong thing; **er hat ~ zum Lehrer** he has a gift for teaching; **mangelnde ~** a lack of talent, insufficient talent **b** *(= begabter Mensch)* talented person; **sie ist eine musikalische ~** she has a talent for music

be|gaf|fen *ptp* **begafft** VT *(pej inf)* to gape *or* goggle at *(inf)*

be|gann *pret von* **beginnen**

be|ga|sen [bəˈgaːzn] *ptp* **begast** VT *(Agr)* to gas

be|gat|ten [bəˈgatn] *ptp* **begattet** *(esp Zool)* VT to mate *or* copulate with; *(geh, hum)* to copulate with VR to mate, to copulate; *(geh, hum)* to copulate

Be|gat|tung F -, -en *(esp Zool)* mating, copulation; *(geh, hum)* copulation

Be|gat|tungs|or|ga|ne PL reproductive organs *pl*

be|gau|nern [bəˈgaunɐn] *ptp* **begaunert** VT to swindle, to cheat

be|geb|bar [bəˈgeːpbaːɐ] ADJ *(Fin) Wertpapiere (= übertragbar)* transferable; *(= verkäuflich)* negotiable

be|ge|ben *ptp* **begeben** *irreg* VR **a** *(geh: = gehen)* to betake oneself *(liter)*, to go; **sich nach Hause ~, sich auf den Heimweg ~** to wend *(liter) or* make one's way home; **sich auf eine Reise ~** to undertake a journey; **sich zu Bett ~** to retire to one's bed *(liter)*; **sich zur Ruhe ~** to retire; **sich an seinen Platz ~** to take one's place; **sich in ärztliche Behandlung ~** to undergo medical treatment; **sich an die Arbeit ~** to commence work
b *(= sich einer Sache aussetzen)* **sich in Gefahr ~** to expose oneself to danger, to put oneself in danger; **sich in jds Schutz** *(acc)* **~** to place oneself under sb's protection → **Gefahr a**
c *(old liter: = geschehen)* to come to pass *(old liter)*; **es begab sich aber zu der Zeit, dass ...** *(Bibl)* and it came to pass at that time that ...; **es hatte sich vieles ~** many things had happened
d *(geh: = aufgeben)* +gen to relinquish, to renounce
VT *(Fin)* to issue

Be|ge|ben|heit [bəˈgeːbnhait] F -, -en *(geh)*, **Be|geb|nis** [bəˈgeːpnɪs] NT -ses, -se *(old)* occurrence, event

be|geg|nen [bəˈgeːgnən] *ptp* **begegnet** VI *aux sein* +dat **a** *(= treffen)* to meet; **sich** *or* **einander** *(geh)* **~** to meet; **ihre Augen** *or* **Blicke begegneten sich** their eyes met; **unsere Wünsche ~ sich** *(liter)* our wishes coincide *(form)*
b *(= stoßen auf)* **einer Sache** *(dat)* **~** to encounter sth; *Schwierigkeiten* to encounter sth, to run into sth; **dieses Wort wird uns später noch einmal ~** we will encounter this word again later
c *(= widerfahren)* **jdm ist etw begegnet** sth has happened to sb; **es war mir schon einmal begegnet, dass ...** it had happened to me once before that ...
d *(geh: = behandeln)* to treat; **man begegnete mir nur mit Spott** I only met with derision
e *(geh) (= entgegentreten) einer Krankheit, Seuche, der Not* to combat; *einem Übel, Angriff, Unrecht auch* to oppose, to resist; *(= überwinden) einer Gefahr, Schwierigkeiten, dem Schicksal* to confront, to meet, to face; *(= reagieren auf) einem Wunsch, Vorschlag, einer Ansicht* to meet, to respond to; **man begegnete seinen Vorschlägen mit Zurückhaltung** his suggestions met with reserve
f *(geh: = einwenden gegen) Behauptungen etc* to counter

Be|geg|nung F -, -en **a** *(= Treffen)* meeting, encounter; *(fig: mit Idee etc)* encounter; **bei der ersten/letzten ~ der beiden** at the first/last meeting between the two; **ein Ort internationaler ~** an international meeting place **b** *(Sport)* encounter, match; **die ~ Spanien-Italien findet nächsten Monat statt** Spain and Italy meet next month

Be|geg|nungs|stät|te F meeting place

be|geh|bar ADJ **a** *(lit) Weg* passable; *Schrank, Skulptur* walk-in *attr* **b** *(fig) Weg, Pfad* practical

be|ge|hen *ptp* **begangen** VT *irreg* **a** *(= verüben) Selbstmord, Ehebruch, Sünde* to commit; *Verbrechen* to commit, to perpetrate *(form)*; *Fehler* to make; **eine Indiskretion (gegenüber jdm) ~** to be indiscreet (about sb); **einen Mord an jdm ~** to murder sb; **eine Dummheit/Taktlosigkeit/Unvorsichtigkeit ~** to do something stupid/tactless/careless; **die Dummheit/Taktlosigkeit/Unvorsichtigkeit ~, ...** to be so stupid/tactless/careless as to ...; **an jdm ein Unrecht ~** to wrong sb, to be unjust to sb; **Verrat an jdm/etw ~** to betray sb/sth; **ein oft begangener Fehler** a frequent mistake
b *(= entlanggehen) Weg* to use; **der Weg wird viel begangen** the path is used a lot, it is a much-used path; **„Begehen der Brücke auf eigene Gefahr"** "persons using this bridge do so at their own risk", "cross bridge at own risk"
c *(= abschreiten) Bahnstrecke, Felder, Baustelle* to inspect (on foot)
d *(geh: = feiern)* to celebrate

Be|gehr [bəˈgeːɐ] M OR NT -s, *no pl (old)* wish, desire; **er fragte nach meinem ~** he inquired after my wishes

be|geh|ren [bəˈgeːrən] *ptp* **begehrt** VT **a** *(geh: = Verlangen haben nach)* to desire, to crave; *Frau* to desire; *Gegenstände, Besitz eines andern* to covet; **ein Mädchen zur Frau ~** *(liter)* to desire a girl's hand in marriage; **sie bekam die von ihr so begehrte Rolle** she was given the role she desired so much; **du sollst nicht ~ ...** *(Bibl)* thou shalt not covet ... *(Bibl)* → *auch* **begehrt**
b *(old: = wollen)* to desire

Be|geh|ren [bəˈgeːrən] NT -s, *(rare)* - **a** *(geh: = Verlangen)* desire *(nach* for); **das ~ fühlen** *or* **haben, etw zu tun** to feel the *or* a desire to do sth; **heißes ~** burning desire **b** *(old: = Wunsch, Forderung)* wish; **nach jds ~ fragen** to inquire after sb's wishes, to ask what sb wants; **auf mein ~ (hin)** at my request

be|geh|rens|wert ADJ desirable, attractive; *Frau* desirable

be|gehr|lich [bəˈgeːɐlɪç] *(geh)* ADJ covetous ADV longingly, yearningly

Be|gehr|lich|keit F -, -en *(geh)* **a** *no pl* covetousness **b** *(= Verlangen)* desire *(nach* for)

be|gehrt [bəˈgeːɐt] ADJ much *or* very sought-after; *Posten auch* desirable; *Partner etc auch, Ferienziel* popular; *Junggeselle* eligible → *auch* **begehren**

Be|ge|hung [bəˈgeːʊŋ] F -, -en **a** *(form) (einer Sünde)* committing; *(eines Verbrechens)* committing, perpetrating *(form)*; **nach ~ des Verbrechens** after committing *etc* the crime **b** *(= das Abschreiten)* inspection (on foot)

be|gei|fern *ptp* **begeifert** VT *(fig pej)* to run down, to slam *(inf)*; *(lit)* to dribble on

be|geis|tern *ptp* **begeistert** VT *jdn* to fill with enthusiasm; *(= inspirieren)* to inspire; **er begeistert alle durch sein** *or* **mit seinem Talent** everybody is enthusiastic about his talent; **er ist für nichts zu ~** he's never enthusiastic about anything VR to be *or* feel enthusiastic *(an +dat, für* about) → *auch* **begeistert**

be|geis|ternd ADJ inspiring; *Rede auch* stirring ADV inspiringly; **~ wirken** to be inspiring

be|geis|tert [bəˈgaistɐt] ✪ 34.3, 40.2, 41 ADJ enthusiastic *(von* about) ADV enthusiastically → *auch* **begeistern**

Be|geis|te|rung [bəˈgaistərʊŋ] F -, *no pl* enthusiasm *(über +acc* about, *für* for); **etw mit ~ tun** to do sth enthusiastically *or* with enthusiasm; **in ~ geraten** to become enthusiastic, to be filled with enthusiasm; **sich in ~ reden** to get carried away with what one is saying

Be|geis|te|rungs-: **be|geis|te|rungs|fä|hig** ADJ able to get enthusiastic; *Publikum etc* quick to show one's enthusiasm; **sie ist zwar ~, aber ...** her enthusiasm is easily aroused but ...; **Be|geis|te|rungs|fä|hig|keit** F capacity for enthusiasm; **ein Pessimist, dem jegliche ~ abgeht** a pessimist who never shows enthusiasm for anything; **Be|geis|te|rungs|sturm** M storm of enthusiasm; **Be|geis|te|rungs|tau|mel** M frenzy of enthusiasm

Be|gier [bəˈgiːɐ] F -, *no pl (liter)*, **Be|gier|de** [bəˈgiːɐdə] F -, -n *(geh)* desire *(nach* for); *(= Sehnsucht)* longing, yearning; **vor ~ brennen, etw zu tun** to be longing *or* burning to do sth

be|gie|rig [bəˈgiːrɪç] ADJ *(= voll Verlangen)* hungry, greedy; *(= gespannt)* eager, keen; *Leser* avid; **auf etw** *(acc)* **~ sein** to be eager for sth; **~ (darauf) sein, etw zu tun** to be eager *or* keen to do sth ADV *(= verlangend)* greedily; *(= gespannt)* eagerly

be|gie|ßen *ptp* **begossen** [bəˈgɔsn] VT *irreg* **a** *(mit Wasser)* to pour water on; *Blumen, Beet* to water; *(mit Fett) Braten etc* to baste → *auch* **begossen b** *(fig inf) freudiges Ereignis, Vereinbarung* to celebrate; **das muss begossen werden!** that calls for a drink!

Be|ginn [bəˈgɪn] M -(e)s, *no pl* beginning, start; **am** *or* **bei** *or* **zu ~** at the beginning; **mit ~ der Verhandlungen** at the beginning *or* start of the negotiations; **gleich zu ~** right at the beginning *or* start, at the very beginning *or* start

be|gin|nen [bəˈgɪnən] ✪ 53.1, 53.2 *pret* **begann**, [bəˈgan] *ptp* **begonnen** VI [bəˈgɔnən] to start, to begin, to commence *(form)*; *(in Beruf etc auch)* to start off; **mit einer Arbeit ~** to start *or* begin (to do) a job; **mit der Arbeit ~** to start *or* begin work; **es beginnt zu regnen** it's starting *or* beginning to rain; **er hat als Lehrling/mit nichts begonnen** he started (off) *or* began as an apprentice/with nothing
VT **a** *(= anfangen)* to start, to begin; *Gespräch, Verhandlungen, Rede auch* to open; **~, etw zu tun** to start *or* begin to do sth, to start doing sth
b *(= anpacken) Aufgabe etc* to tackle, to go *or* set about
c *(geh: = unternehmen)* to do; **ich wusste nicht, was ich ~ sollte** I didn't know what to do

Be|gin|nen [bəˈgɪnən] NT -s, *no pl (geh: = Vorhaben)* enterprise, plan, scheme

be|gin|nend ADJ *attr* incipient *(form)*; **eine ~e Erkältung** the beginnings of a cold; **bei ~er Dämmerung/Nacht** at dusk/nightfall; **im ~en 19. Jahrhundert** in the early 19th century

be|glän|zen *ptp* **beglänzt** VT *(poet)* to light up, to illumine *(poet)*

be|glau|bi|gen [bəˈglaubɪgn] *ptp* **beglaubigt** VT **a** *Testament, Unterschrift* to witness; *Zeugnisabschrift* to authenticate; *Echtheit* to attest (to); **etw behördlich/notariell ~ lassen** to have sth witnessed *etc* officially/by a notary **b** *Gesandten, Botschafter* to accredit *(bei* to)

be|glau|bigt [bəˈglaubɪçt] ADJ certified; **~e Abschrift** certified copy; *(als Vermerk)* true copy → *auch* **beglaubigen**

Be|glau|bi|gung F -, -en **a** *(von Testament, Unterschrift)* witnessing; *(von Zeugnisabschrift)* authentication; *(von Echtheit)* attestation **b** *(von Gesandtem, Botschafter)* accrediting, accreditation *(form)*

Be|glau|bi|gungs|schrei|ben NT credentials *pl*

be|glei|chen ✪ 47.5 *ptp* **beglichen** VT [bəˈglɪçn] *irreg (lit: = bezahlen) Rechnung, Zeche* to settle, to pay; *Schulden auch* to discharge *(form)*; *(fig) Schuld* to pay (off), to discharge; **mit Ihnen habe ich noch eine Rechnung zu ~** *(fig)* I've a score to settle with you

Be|glei|chung ✪ 47.5 F *(von Rechnung, Zeche)* settlement, payment; *(von Schulden auch)* discharging; **vollständige ~** payment in full; **teilweise ~** part *(Brit)* or partial *(US)* payment

Be|gleit-: **Be|gleit|ad|res|se** F dispatch note; **Be|gleit|brief** M covering letter *(Brit)*, cover letter *(US)*; **Be|gleit|do|ku|men|te** PL accompanying documents *pl*

be|glei|ten *ptp* **begleitet** VT **a** *(= mitgehen, mitfahren mit)* to accompany; *(zu Veranstaltung auch)* to go/come with; *(zum Schutz auch)* to escort; *esp Schiff auch* to escort, to convoy; **er wurde stets von seinem Hund begleitet** his dog always went everywhere with him; **ein paar ~de Worte** a few accompanying words; **meine Wünsche ~ Sie** my best wishes go with you; **~de Umstände** attendant *or* accompanying circumstances *(form)* **b** *(Mus)* to accompany *(an or auf +dat* on)

Be|glei|ter [bəˈglaitɐ] M -s, -, **Be|glei|te|rin** [-ərɪn] F -, -nen **a** companion; *(zum Schutz)* escort; *(von Reisenden)* courier; **ständiger ~** constant companion **b** *(Mus)* accompanist

Be|gleit-: **Be|gleit|er|schei|nung** F concomitant *(form)*; *(Med)* side effect; **ist Jugendkriminalität eine ~ der Wohlstandsgesellschaft?** does juvenile delinquency go hand in hand with an affluent society?; **Be|gleit|fahr|zeug** NT escort vehicle; **Be|gleit|flug|zeug** NT escort plane; **Be|gleit|in|stru|ment** NT accompanying instrument; **Be|gleit|ma|te|ri|al** NT backup *or* accompanying material(s *pl*); **Be|gleit|mu|sik** F accompaniment; *(in Film etc)* incidental music; **Be|gleit|pa|pie|re** PL *(Comm)* accompanying documents *pl*; **Be|gleit|per|son** F escort; **die ~ eines Jugendlichen** the person accompanying a minor; **Be|gleit|per|so|nal** NT escort; **Be|gleit|schein** M dispatch note; **Be|gleit|schiff** NT *(Mil)* escort (ship); **Be|gleit|schrei|ben** NT covering letter *(Brit)*, cover letter *(US)*; *(für Waren auch)* advice note; **Be|gleit|schutz** M escort; **Be|gleit|text** M (accompanying) text; **Be|gleit|um|stän|de** PL attendant circumstances *pl*

Be|glei|tung [bəˈglaitʊŋ] F -, -en **a** *no pl* company; **er bot ihr seine ~ an** he offered to accompany *or (zum Schutz auch)* escort her; **in ~ seines Vaters** accompanied by his father; **in ~ Peters ~** accompanied by Peter; **ich bin in ~ hier** I'm with someone **b** *(= Begleiter)* companion; *(zum Schutz)* escort; *(= Gefolge)* entourage, retinue; **ohne ~** unaccompanied **c** *(Mus) (= Begleitmusik)* accompaniment; *(= das Begleiten auch)* accompanying; *(= Begleitstimme)* harmony; **ohne ~ spielen** to play unaccompanied

be|glot|zen *ptp* **beglotzt** VT *(inf)* to goggle *or* gape at *(inf)*, to gawp *(Brit) or* gawk at *(inf)*

be|glü|cken *ptp* **beglückt** VT **jdn ~** to make sb happy; **er hat uns gestern mit seinem Besuch beglückt** *(iro)* he honoured *(Brit) or* honored *(US)* us with a visit yesterday; **Casanova hat tausende** *or* **Tausende von Frauen beglückt** *(hum)* Casanova bestowed his favours *(Brit) or* favors *(US)* upon thousands of women; **ein ~des Gefühl/Erlebnis** a cheering feeling/experience; **er ist sehr beglückt darüber** he's very happy *or* pleased about it; **beglückt lächeln** to smile happily

Be|glü|cker [bəˈglʏkɐ] M -s, - *(liter, iro)* benefactor; **er fühlt sich als ~ aller Frauen** *(hum)* he thinks he's God's gift (to women)

Be|glü|cke|rin [bəˈglʏkərɪn] F -, -nen *(liter, iro)* benefactress

be|glück|wün|schen [bəˈglʏkvʏnʃn] *ptp* **beglückwünscht** VT to congratulate, to offer one's congratulations *(form)* *(zu* on); **lass dich ~!** congratulations!

be|gna|den [bəˈgnaːdn] *ptp* **begnadet** VT *(liter)* to bless *(liter)*, to endow; **ein begnadeter Künstler/Musiker** a gifted artist/musician

be|gna|di|gen [bəˈgnaːdɪgn] *ptp* **begnadigt** VT to reprieve; *(= Strafe erlassen)* to pardon

Be|gna|di|gung F -, -en reprieve; *(= Straferlass)* pardon; **um (jds) ~ ersuchen** to seek a reprieve (for sb)

Be|gna|di|gungs-: **Be|gna|di|gungs|ge|such** NT plea for (a) reprieve; **Be|gna|di|gungs|recht** NT right of reprieve

be|gnü|gen [bəˈgnyːgn] *ptp* **begnügt** VR **sich mit etw ~** to be content *or* satisfied with sth, to content oneself with sth; **sich damit ~, etw zu tun** to be content *or* satisfied with doing sth *or* to do sth, to content oneself with doing sth; **damit begnüge ich mich nicht** that doesn't satisfy me, I'm not satisfied with that

Be|go|nie [beˈgoːniə] F -, -n begonia

be|gon|nen *ptp von* **beginnen**

be|gos|sen ADJ **er stand da wie ein ~er Pudel** *(inf)* he looked that small, he looked so sheepish → *auch* **begießen**

be|gra|ben *ptp* **begraben** VT *irreg* **a** *(= beerdigen)* to bury; **dort möchte ich nicht ~ sein** *(inf)* I wouldn't like to be stuck in that hole *(inf)*; **der kann sich ~ lassen** *(inf)* he is worse than useless → **Hund a b** *(= verschütten)* to bury; **beim Einsturz begrub das Gebäude alle Bewohner unter sich** when the building collapsed all the residents were buried **c** *(= aufgeben) Hoffnung, Wunsch* to abandon, to relinquish; *(= beenden) Streit, Angelegenheit, Feindschaft* to end; **ein längst ~er Wunsch** a long-abandoned wish; **diese Angelegenheit ist längst ~** this matter was over (and done with) long ago

Be|gräb|nis [bəˈgrɛːpnɪs] NT -ses, -se burial; *(= Begräbnisfeier)* funeral

Be|gräb|nis-: **Be|gräb|nis|fei|er** F funeral (ceremony), obsequies *pl (form)*; **Be|gräb|nis|kos|ten** PL funeral costs *pl*; **Be|gräb|nis|stät|te** F *(geh)* burial place

be|grab|schen VT *(inf)* to grope *(inf)*

be|gra|di|gen [bəˈgraːdɪgn] *ptp* **begradigt** VT to straighten

Be|gra|di|gung F -, -en straightening

be|grap|schen VT *(inf)* to grope *(inf)*

be|grast [bəˈgraːst] ADJ grassy, grass-covered

be|greif|bar ADJ conceivable

Be|greif|bar|keit [bəˈgraifbaːɐkait] F -, *no pl* conceivability

be|grei|fen *ptp* **begriffen** [bəˈgrɪfn] *irreg* VT **a** *(= verstehen)* to understand; *Aufgabe, Problemstellung, Zusammenhang* to understand, to grasp, to comprehend; *jdn, jds Handlung or Haltung* to understand, to comprehend; *Sinn, Notwendigkeit, (Schwierigkeit einer) Lage auch* to see, to appreciate; **~, dass ...** *(= einsehen)* to realize that ...; **er begriff nicht, worum es ging** he didn't understand *or* comprehend what it was about; **hast du mich begriffen?** did you understand what I said?; **es ist kaum zu ~** it's almost incomprehensible; **es lässt sich leicht ~, dass ...** it's easy to understand that ...; **wie kann man Gott/die Unendlichkeit ~?** how can one comprehend God/infinity?; **ich begreife mich selbst nicht** I don't understand myself **b** *(= auffassen, interpretieren)* to view, to see **c** *(geh: = einschließen)* **etw in sich** *(dat)* **~** to encompass *or* include sth **d** *(dial: = anfassen)* to touch

VI to understand, to comprehend; **leicht** *or* **schnell ~** to be quick on the uptake; **schwer** *or* **langsam ~** to be slow on the uptake

VR to be understandable; **eine solche Tat lässt sich nicht leicht ~** such an action cannot be easily understood → *auch* **begriffen**

be|greif|lich [bəˈgraiflɪç] ADJ understandable; **es wird mir allmählich ~, warum ...** I'm beginning to understand why ...; **ich kann mich ihm nicht ~ machen** I can't make myself clear to him; **ich habe ihm das ~ gemacht** I've made it clear to him

be|greif|li|cher|wei|se ADV understandably

be|gren|zen *ptp* **begrenzt** VT **a** *(= Grenze sein von)* to mark *or* form the boundary of *no pass*; *Horizont* to mark; *Straße etc* to line; **das Gebiet wird durch einen** *or* **von einem Wald begrenzt** a forest marks *or* forms the boundary of the area **b** *(= beschränken)* to restrict, to limit *(auf +acc* to)

be|grenzt [bəˈgrɛntst] ADJ *(= beschränkt)* restricted, limited; *(= geistig beschränkt)* limited; **meine Aufenthaltsdauer ist nicht zeitlich ~** there's no time limit on (the length of) my stay; **eine genau ~e Aufgabe** a clearly defined task ADV *(zeitlich)* for a limited time; **sich nur ~ bewegen können** to be restricted in one's movements; **~ Einfluss nehmen** to exert limited influence

Be|grenzt|heit F -, *no pl (von Menschen)* limitations *pl*; **die ~ der Mittel/des Einkommens** the limited means/income; **die ~ ihres Talents** her limited talents

Be|gren|zung [bəˈgrɛntsʊŋ] F -, -en **a** *(= das Begrenzen) (von Gebiet, Straße etc)* demarcation; *(von Horizont)* marking; *(von Geschwindigkeit, Redezeit)* restriction **b** *(= Grenze)* boundary

Be|griff M **a** *(objektiv) (= Bedeutungsgehalt)* concept; *(= Terminus)* term; **etw in ~e fassen** to put sth into words; **in neuen ~en denken** to think in new terms; **sein Name ist mir ein/kein ~** his name means something/doesn't mean anything to me; **sein Name ist in aller Welt ein ~** his name is known all over the world; **ein ~ für Qualität!** a byword for quality **b** *(subjektiv: = Vorstellung, Eindruck)* idea; **sein ~ von** *or* **der Freiheit** his idea *or* conception of freedom; **falsche ~e von etw haben** to have the wrong ideas about sth; **sich** *(dat)* **einen ~ von etw machen** to imagine sth; **du machst dir keinen ~ (davon)** *(inf)* you've no idea (about it) *(inf)*; **das geht über meine ~e** that's beyond me; **es war über alle ~e schön** it was incredibly beautiful; **nach unseren heutigen ~en** by today's standards; **nach menschlichen ~en** in human terms; **für meine ~e** in my opinion **c im ~ sein** *or* **stehen** *(form)*, **etw zu tun** to be on the point of doing sth, to be about to do sth **d schwer** *or* **langsam/schnell von ~ sein** *(inf)* to be slow/quick on the uptake; **sei doch nicht so schwer von ~!** *(inf)* don't be so dense *(inf)*

be|grif|fen ADJ **in etw** *(dat)* **~ sein** *(form)* to be in the process of doing sth; **ein noch in der Entwicklung ~er Plan** a plan still in the process of being developed → *auch* **begreifen**

be|griff|lich [bəˈgrɪflɪç] ADJ **a** *attr (= bedeutungsmäßig)* conceptual; **~e Klärung** clarification of one's terms **b** *(= gedanklich, abstrakt)* abstract ADV **a** *(= bedeutungsmäßig)* conceptually; **~ bestimmen** to define (in clear terms); **~ ordnen** to arrange according to conceptual groups; **das Wort ist mir ~ unklar** the meaning of that word is not clear to me; **mit dem Wort kann ich ~ nichts anfangen** I have no idea what that word means **b** *(= gedanklich)* abstractly; **etw ~ erfassen** to understand sth in the abstract

Be|griff|lich|keit F -, -en **~en** (abstract) concepts

Be|griffs-: **Be|griffs|be|stim|mung** F definition; **Be|griffs|bil|dung** F formation of a concept/concepts; **Be|griffs|in|halt** M meaning; *(in der Logik)* connotation; **be|griffs|mä|ßig**

ADJ conceptual; **be|grifs|stut|zig**, *(Aus)* **be|grifs|stüt|zig** [-ʃtʏtsɪç] ADJ *(inf)* thick *(inf)*; **Be|grifs|stut|zig|keit** F -, *no pl (inf)* **von einer unglaublichen ~** unbelievably thick *(inf)*; **~ mimen** to act dumb *(inf)*; **ich kann mich nur über deine ~ wundern** I can't believe how thick you are! *(inf)*; **Be|grifs|sys|tem** NT system of concepts; **Be|grifs|ver|mö|gen** NT understanding; **das ging über ihr ~** that was beyond her grasp *or* understanding; **Be|grifs|ver|wir|rung** F confusion of concepts; *(von Termini)* confusion of terms; **Be|grifs|welt** F *(einer Person)* conceptual range

be|grün|den *ptp* **begründet** VT **a** *(= Gründe anführen für)* to give reasons for; *(rechtfertigend) Forderung, Meinung, Ansicht* to justify; *Verhalten* to account for; *Verdacht, Behauptung* to substantiate; **wie** *or* **womit begründete er seine Ablehnung?** how did he account for *or* justify his refusal?, what reason(s) did he give for his refusal?; **etw eingehend/näher ~** to give detailed/specific reasons for sth; **ein ~der Satz** *(Gram)* a causal clause → **begründet b** *(= beginnen, gründen)* to establish

Be|grün|der(in) M(F) founder

be|grün|det [bəˈgrʏndət] ADJ well-founded; *(= berechtigt)* justified; *(= bewiesen) Tatsache etc* proven; **es besteht ~e/keine ~e Hoffnung, dass ...** there is reason/no reason to hope that ...; **das halte ich für nicht ~** I think that's unfounded/unjustified; **sachlich ~** founded on fact; **etw liegt** *or* **ist in etw** *(dat)* **~** sth has its roots in sth

Be|grün|det|heit F -, *no pl* well-foundedness

Be|grün|dung ✪ 44.1 F **a** reason *(für, +gen* for), grounds *pl (für, +gen* for); *(von Anklage, Behauptung etc)* grounds *pl (+gen* for); **etwas zur** *or* **als ~ sagen** to say something in explanation **b** *(= Gründung)* establishment; *(von Schule, Verein, Geschäft auch)* foundation; *(von Hausstand)* setting up

Be|grün|dungs|satz M *(Gram)* causal clause

be|grü|nen *ptp* **begrünt** VT *Hinterhöfe, Plätze* to cover with greenery, to landscape

be|grünt [bəˈgryːnt] PTP *von* **begrünen** ADJ green; *(= bepflanzt)* planted with grass *or* trees, bushes *etc*; **~e Flächen** *pl* green areas *pl or* spaces *pl* → *auch* **begrünen**

Be|grü|nung [bəˈgryːnʊŋ] F -, -en planting with trees and grass, landscaping

be|grü|ßen ✪ 31, 38.1, 38.2, 52.2 *ptp* **begrüßt** VT **a** *jdn* to greet; *(als Gastgeber)* to greet, to welcome; **jdn herzlich ~** to greet sb heartily, to give sb a hearty welcome; **es ist mir eine große Ehre, Sie bei mir ~ zu dürfen** *(form)* it's a great honour *(Brit)* or honor *(US)* to (be able to) welcome you here; **wir würden uns freuen, Sie bei uns ~ zu dürfen** *(form)* we would be delighted to have the pleasure of your company *(form)*

b *(= gut finden) Kritik, Entschluss etc* to welcome; *(esp iro, form)* to appreciate; **es ist zu ~, dass ...** it's a good thing that ...

c *(Sw: = um Erlaubnis fragen)* to ask *(um* for, *wegen* about)

be|grü|ßens|wert ADJ welcome; **es wäre ~, wenn ...** it would be desirable if ...

Be|grü|ßung [bəˈgryːsʊŋ] F -, -en greeting; *(der Gäste) (= das Begrüßen)* welcoming; *(= Zeremonie)* welcome; **er nickte zur ~ mit dem Kopf** he nodded his head in greeting; **jdm einen Blumenstrauß zur ~ überreichen** to welcome sb with a bouquet of flowers; **jdm die Hand zur ~ reichen** to hold out one's hand to sb in welcome; **jdn zur ~ küssen** to kiss sb hello

Be|grü|ßungs-: **Be|grü|ßungs|an|spra|che** F welcoming speech; **Be|grü|ßungs|for|mel** F welcoming words *pl*, words *pl* of welcome; *(Anrede)* salutation; **Be|grü|ßungs|kuss** M welcoming kiss; **Be|grü|ßungs|trank** M welcoming drink; **Be|grü|ßungs|worte** PL welcoming words *pl*, words *pl* of welcome

be|gu|cken *ptp* **beguckt** VT *(inf)* to look at; **lass dich mal ~** let's (have *or* take a) look at you!

be|güns|ti|gen [bəˈgʏnstɪgn] *ptp* **begünstigt** VT **a** *(= förderlich sein für)* to favour *(Brit)*, to favor *(US)*; *Wachstum, Handel* to encourage; *Pläne, Beziehungen* to further; *(Jur)* to aid and abet; **vom Schicksal begünstigt** smiled upon by fate; **durch die Dunkelheit begünstigt** assisted by the darkness **b** *(= bevorzugen)* **jdn ~** to favour *(Brit) or* favor *(US)* sb; **von jdm begünstigt werden** to be favo(u)red by sb, to be shown favo(u)r by sb

Be|güns|tig|te(r) [bəˈgʏnstɪçtə] MF *decl as adj (Jur)* beneficiary

Be|güns|ti|gung F -, -en **a** *(Jur)* aiding and abetting; **persönliche ~** aiding and abetting; **sachliche ~** (acting as an) accessory; **~ im Amt** connivance **b** *(= Bevorzugung)* preferential treatment; *(= Vorteil)* advantage **c** *(= Förderung)* favouring *(Brit)*, favoring *(US)*; *(von Wachstum, Handel)* encouragement; *(von Plänen, Beziehungen)* furthering

be|gut|ach|ten *ptp* **begutachtet** VT *(= beurteilen, Gutachten abgeben)* to give expert advice about; *Kunstwerk, Stipendiaten* to examine; *Projekte, Leistung* to judge; *Gelände, Haus* to survey; *(inf: = ansehen)* to have *or* take a look at; **etw ~ lassen** to get *or* obtain expert advice about sth

Be|gut|ach|ter(in) M(F) expert; *(von Haus, Gelände)* surveyor

Be|gut|ach|tung [bəˈguːtlaxtʊŋ] F -, -en (expert) assessment; *(von Haus, Gelände)* survey; *(= das Begutachten)* surveying; **psychologische/grafologische** *etc* **~** (expert) psychological/graphological *etc* assessment

be|gü|tert [bəˈgyːtɐt] ADJ **a** *(dated: = Landgüter besitzend)* landed *attr*, propertied **b** *(= reich)* wealthy, affluent; **die ~e Klasse/Schicht** the rich *pl*

be|gü|ti|gen [bəˈgyːtɪgn] *ptp* **begütigt** VT to pacify, to placate, to appease

be|gü|ti|gend ADJ *Worte etc* soothing ADV soothingly; **~ auf jdn einreden** to calm sb down

be|haart [bəˈhaːɐt] ADJ hairy, hirsute; **stark ~** very hairy; **dicht ~** (thickly) covered with hair; **schwarz ~** covered with black hair

Be|haa|rung [bəˈhaːrʊŋ] F -, -en covering of hair, hairs *pl (+gen, an +dat* on)

be|hä|big [bəˈhɛːbɪç] ADJ **a** *Mensch* portly; *(= phlegmatisch, geruhsam)* stolid; *(fig) Leben, Möbel, Auto* comfortable; *Architektur* solid; *Sprache, Ton* complacent **b** *(old liter, Sw: = wohlhabend)* well-to-do, affluent ADV **(breit und) ~ herumsitzen** to sit on one's fat backside *(inf)*

Be|hä|big|keit F -, *no pl (von Mensch)* portliness; *(= Geruhsamkeit)* stolidity; *(von Architektur)* solidness; *(von Sprache, Ton)* complacency

be|haf|tet [bəˈhaftət] ADJ **mit etw ~ sein** *(mit Krankheit etc)* to be afflicted with sth; *mit Fehlern, Vorurteilen etc* to be full of sth; *mit einer schweren Last, mit Sorgen, Schulden etc* to be encumbered with sth; *mit Makel* to be tainted with sth

be|ha|gen [bəˈhaːgn] *ptp* **behagt** VI **etw behagt jdm** sth pleases sb, sb likes sth; **etw behagt jdm nicht** *(= nicht gefallen)* sth doesn't please sb, sb doesn't like sth; *(= beunruhigen)* sb feels uneasy about sth; **er behagt ihr nicht** she doesn't like him

Be|ha|gen [bəˈhaːgn] NT -s, *no pl* contentment; **mit sichtlichem ~** with visible *or* obvious pleasure; **mit ~ essen** to eat with relish *or* pleasure

be|hag|lich [bəˈhaːklɪç] ADJ cosy; *(= heimelig auch)* snug, homely; *(= bequem)* comfortable; *(= zufrieden)* contented ADV *(= gemütlich)* comfortably; *(= genussvoll)* contentedly; **~ warm** comfortably warm; **es sich** *(dat)* **~ machen** to make oneself comfortable; **~ in der Sonne sitzen** to sit comfortably in the sun; **die Katze streckte sich ~** the cat stretched contentedly

Be|hag|lich|keit F -, *no pl* cosiness; *(= Heimeligkeit auch)* snugness, homeliness; *(= Bequemlichkeit)* comfort; *(= Zufriedenheit)* contentment

be|hal|ten *ptp* **behalten** VT *irreg* **a** *(= nicht weggeben, nicht zurückgeben)* to keep

b *(= lassen, wo es ist)* to keep; **~ Sie (doch) Platz!** please don't get up!; **den Hut auf dem Kopf ~** to keep one's hat on; **jdn an der Hand ~** to keep hold of sb's hand; **der Kranke kann nichts bei sich ~** the patient can't keep anything down → **Auge a**

c *(= nicht verlieren)* to keep; *Wert auch* to retain; **die Ruhe ~** to keep one's cool *(inf)*; **die Nerven ~** to keep one's nerve *(Brit)*, to keep one's nerves under control *(US)*; **wenn wir solches Wetter ~** if this weather lasts → **Fassung c**, **Kopf d**, **Zügel** *etc*

d *(= nicht vergessen)* to remember; **im Gedächtnis/im Kopf ~** to remember, to keep in one's head; **er behielt die Melodie im Ohr** he kept the tune in his head; **ich habe die Zahl/seine Adresse nicht ~** I've forgotten the number/his address

e *(= nicht weitersagen)* **etw für sich ~** to keep sth to oneself

f *(= nicht weggehen lassen)* to keep; *Mitarbeiter* to keep on; **jdn bei sich ~** to keep sb with one; **einen Gast zum Abendbrot bei sich ~** to invite a guest to stay to *(esp Brit) or* for supper

g *(= nicht aufgeben) Stellung, Namen, Staatsangehörigkeit* to keep; **sie muss immer ihren Willen ~** she always has to have her own way

h *(= aufbewahren, versorgen) Kinder, Katze, Gegenstand* to look after; *(= nicht wegwerfen) Briefe etc* to keep; **jdn/etw in guter/schlechter Erinnerung ~** to have happy/unhappy memories of sb/sth → **Andenken a**

i *(= zurückbehalten, nicht loswerden)* to be left with; *Schock, Schaden* to suffer; **vom Unfall hat er ein steifes Knie ~** after the accident he was left with a stiff knee

Be|häl|ter [bəˈhɛltɐ] M -s, - **a** container, receptacle *(form)* **b** *(= Container)* container

Be|häl|ter|schiff NT container ship

be|häm|mern *ptp* **behämmert** VT *(lit, fig)* to hammer

be|häm|mert [bəˈhɛmɐt] ADJ *(inf)* screwy *(inf)*

be|händ [bəˈhɛnt], **be|hän|de** [bəˈhɛndə] *(geh)* ADV *(= flink)* swiftly, quickly; *(= gewandt)* nimbly, agilely ADJ *(= flink)* swift, quick; *(= gewandt)* nimble, agile

be|han|deln *ptp* **behandelt** VT **a** *Material, Stoff, Materie* to treat **b** *Thema, Frage, Problem, Antrag* to deal with **c** *(= in bestimmter Weise umgehen mit)* to treat; *(= verfahren mit)* to handle; **jdn/etw gut/schlecht ~** to treat sb/sth well/badly; **er weiß, wie man Kinder/die Maschine ~ muss** he knows how to handle children/the machine; **eine Angelegenheit diskret ~** to treat *or* handle a matter with discretion; **jdn/etw ungeschickt ~** to handle sb/sth clumsily **d** *(ärztlich) Patienten, Krankheit* to treat; *Zähne* to attend to; **jdn/etw operativ ~** to operate on sb/sth; **der ~de Arzt** the doctor in attendance

be|hän|di|gen [bəˈhɛndɪgn] *ptp* **behändigt** VT *(Sw: = an sich nehmen)* to take; *(= stehlen auch)* to steal

Be|hän|dig|keit [bəˈhɛndɪçkait] F -, *no pl (geh, = Flinkheit)* swiftness, quickness; *(= Gewandtheit)* nimbleness, agility

Be|hand|lung F **a** *(von Material)* treatment

b *(von Frage, Problem)* treatment; **wir sind jetzt bei der ~ dieses Themas** we are now dealing with this subject; **um schnelle ~ des Antrags wird gebeten** please deal with the application as quickly as possible

c *(= Umgang mit Menschen)* treatment; *(von Angelegenheit)* handling; **die schlechte ~ seiner Frau und Kinder** the ill-treatment *or* maltreatment of his wife and children

d *(ärztlich)* treatment; *(von Zähnen)* attention *(+gen* to); **waren Sie deswegen schon früher in ~?** have you had treatment *or* been treated for this before?; **bei wem sind Sie in ~?** who's treating you?

Be|hand|lungs-: **Be|hand|lungs|art** F type of treatment; **be|hand|lungs|be|dürf|tig** ADJ in need of treatment; **Be|hand|lungs|form** F form of treatment; **Be|hand|lungs|kos|ten** PL cost *sing* of treatment; **Be|hand|lungs|me|tho|de** F (method of) treatment; **Be|hand|lungs|raum** M treatment room; **Be|hand|lungs|schein** M *(= Krankenschein)* health insurance certificate; *(= Überweisungsschein)* referral (note); **Be|hand|lungs|stuhl** M doctor's chair; *(von Zahnarzt)* dentist's chair; **Be|hand|lungs|ver|fah|ren** NT therapy; **Be|hand|lungs|wei|se** F treatment; **Be|hand|lungs|zim|mer** NT consulting room, surgery *(Brit)*, (doctor's) office *(US)*

be|hand|schuht [bəˈhantʃuːt] ADJ gloved

Be|hang M **a** curtain; *(= Wandbehang)* hanging; *(= Schmuck)* decorations *pl*; **der Birnbaum hat einen guten ~** the pear tree promises a good crop **b** *(Hunt: von Hund)* lop-ears *pl*

be|han|gen [bəˈhaŋən] ADJ **ein mit Sternen ~er Weihnachtsbaum** a Christmas tree laden with stars; **ein mit Goldketten ~er Mann** a man decked out with gold chains

be|hän|gen *ptp* **behängt** *or* **behangen** VT to decorate; *Wände auch* to hang VR *(pej)* to deck oneself out (*mit* in *or* with)

be|har|ken *ptp* **beharkt** VT *(inf)* to set about *(inf)*, to have a go at *(inf)* VR to have a go at each other *(inf)*

be|har|ren [bəˈharən] *ptp* **beharrt** VI **a** *(= hartnäckig sein)* to insist (*auf +dat* on); *(= nicht aufgeben)* to persist, to persevere (*bei* in) **b** *(= bleiben)* **in etw** *(dat)* **~** *(in Zustand)* to persist in sth; *(an Ort)* to remain in sth

Be|har|ren NT **-s**, *no pl* **a** *(auf Meinung, Anrecht etc)* insistence (*auf* on); *(= Ausdauer)* persistence, perseverance (*bei* in) **b** *(= das Bleiben)* (*in +dat* in) *(in Zustand)* persistence, perseverance; *(an Ort)* remaining

be|harr|lich [bəˈharlɪç] ADJ *(= hartnäckig)* insistent; *(= ausdauernd)* persistent; *Glaube, Liebe* steadfast, unwavering; **~er Fleiß** perseverance ADV *(= hartnäckig)* insistently; *(= ausdauernd)* persistently; *glauben* steadfastly; **~ fortfahren, etw zu tun** to persist in doing sth

Be|harr|lich|keit F **-**, *no pl (= Hartnäckigkeit)* insistence; *(= Ausdauer)* persistence; *(von Glaube, Liebe)* steadfastness

Be|har|rung F **-**, *no pl (Phys)* inertia

Be|har|rungs|ver|mö|gen NT *(Phys)* inertia

be|hau|chen *ptp* **behaucht** VT to breathe on; *(Ling)* to aspirate; **behauchte Laute** *(Ling)* aspirates

be|hau|en *ptp* **behauen** VT *irreg Holz* to hew; *Stein* to cut; *(mit dem Meißel)* to carve

be|haup|ten [bəˈhauptn] ✪ 42.3, 53 *ptp* **behauptet** VT **a** *(= sagen)* to claim; *(= bestimmte Aussage aufstellen)* to maintain; **steif und fest ~** to insist; **von jdm ~, dass …** to say of sb that …; **es wird behauptet, dass …** it is said *or* claimed that … **b** *(= erfolgreich verteidigen) Stellung, Recht* to maintain; *Meinung* to assert; *Markt* to keep one's share of → **Feld e** VR to assert oneself; *(bei Diskussion)* to hold one's own *or* one's ground (*gegenüber, gegen* against); **sich auf dem Markt ~** to maintain one's hold on the market

Be|haup|tung ✪ 53.6 F **-**, **-en** **a** claim; *(= esp unerwiesene Behauptung)* assertion **b** *(= Aufrechterhaltung)* assertion; *(von Stellung)* successful defence *(Brit) or* defense *(US)* **c** *(= das Sichbehaupten)* assertion; **die ~ der Firma auf dem Markt** the firm's ability to maintain its hold on the market

Be|hau|sung [bəˈhauzʊŋ] F **-**, **-en** **a** *no pl (liter. = das Behausen)* accommodation, housing **b** *(geh, hum: = Wohnung)* dwelling

Be|ha|vi|o|ris|mus [biheviəˈrɪsmʊs] M **-**, *no pl* behaviourism *(Brit)*, behaviorism *(US)*

Be|ha|vi|o|rist [biheviəˈrɪst] M **-en**, **-en**, **Be|ha|vi|o|ris|tin** [-ˈrɪstɪn] F **-**, **-nen** behaviourist *(Brit)*, behaviorist *(US)*

be|ha|vi|o|ris|tisch [biheviəˈrɪstɪʃ] ADJ behaviouristic *(Brit)*, behavioristic *(US)*

be|he|ben *ptp* **behoben** [bəˈhoːbn] VT *irreg* **a** *(= beseitigen)* to remove; *Mängel, Missstände* to rectify, to remedy; *Schaden* to repair, to put right; *Störung* to clear **b** *(Aus: = abheben) Geld* to withdraw

Be|he|bung F, *no pl* **a** *(= Beseitigung)* removal; *(von Mangel, Missstand)* rectification, remedying; *(von Schaden)* repairing, putting right; *(von Störung)* clearing **b** *(Aus: von Geld)* withdrawal

be|hei|ma|ten [bəˈhaimatn] *ptp* **beheimatet** VT to find a home for

be|hei|ma|tet [bəˈhaimatət] ADJ *(= ansässig)* resident (*in +dat* in); *(= heimisch) Pflanze, Tier, Volk* indigenous, native (*in +dat* to); **wo sind Sie ~?** where is your home?; **eine in Schottland ~e Pflanze** a plant (that is) indigenous to Scotland

be|heiz|bar ADJ heatable; *Heckscheibe, Außenspiegel* heated

be|hei|zen *ptp* **beheizt** VT to heat

Be|hei|zung F **-**, *no pl* heating

Be|helf [bəˈhɛlf] M **-(e)s**, **-e** **a** *(= Ersatz)* substitute; *(= Notlösung)* makeshift; **als ~ dienen** to serve *or* act as a substitute/makeshift **b** *(Jur. = Rechtsbehelf)* (legal) remedy

be|hel|fen *ptp* **beholfen** [bəˈhɔlfn] VR *irreg* **a** *(= Ersatz verwenden)* to manage, to make do; **sich mit Ausreden ~** to resort to excuses; **sich mit Ausflüchten ~** to be evasive **b** *(= auskommen)* to manage, to get by; **er weiß sich allein nicht zu ~** he can't manage alone, he can't get by alone

Be|helfs- *in cpds* temporary; **Be|helfs|aus|fahrt** F *(auf Autobahn)* temporary exit; **Be|helfs|bau** F **-s**, **-bauten** temporary building; *(improvisiert)* makeshift building; **Be|helfs|heim** NT temporary accommodation; **be|helfs|mä|ßig** ADJ makeshift; *(zeitlich begrenzt) Straßenbelag, Ausweis* temporary ADV temporarily; **etw ~ reparieren** to make makeshift repairs to sth; **Be|helfs|maß|nah|men** PL stopgap *or* temporary emergency measures *pl*; **Be|helfs|un|ter|kunft** F temporary accommodation *no pl*; *(für Notfall auch)* emergency accommodation *no pl*; **be|helfs|wei|se** ADV temporarily; **er hat sich ~ eingerichtet** his furnishings are only makeshift

be|hel|li|gen [bəˈhɛlɪgn] *ptp* **behelligt** VT to bother

Be|hel|li|gung F **-**, **-en** bother *no pl*; **jds ~ mit Fragen** *(= das Behelligen)* bothering sb with questions; *(= das Behelligtwerden)* sb being bothered with questions

be|helmt [bəˈhɛlmt] ADJ helmeted

be|hend △ [bəˈhɛnt], **be|hen|de** △ [bəˈhɛndə] → **behänd**

Be|hen|dig|keit △ [bəˈhɛndɪçkait] F **-**, *no pl* → **Behändigkeit**

be|her|ber|gen [bəˈhɛrbɛrgn] *ptp* **beherbergt** VT *(lit, fig)* to house; *Gäste* to accommodate

Be|her|ber|gung F **-**, **-en** housing; *(= Unterkunft)* accommodation

Be|her|ber|gungs|ge|wer|be NT hotel trade, (tourist) accommodation industry

be|herr|schen *ptp* **beherrscht** VT **a** *(= herrschen über)* to rule, to govern; *(fig: Gefühle, Vorstellungen)* to dominate **b** *(fig: = das Übergewicht haben) Stadtbild, Landschaft, Ebene, Markt* to dominate → **Feld d**, **Szene a** **c** *(= zügeln)* to control; *Zunge* to curb **d** *(= gut können) Handwerk, Sprache, Instrument, Tricks, Spielregeln* to master **e** *(= bewältigen) Situation* to have control of VR to control oneself; **ich kann mich ~!** *(iro inf)* not likely! *(inf)* → *auch* **beherrscht**

be|herr|schend [bəˈhɛrʃənt] ADJ *(fig: = vorherrschend)* dominating; **~es Thema der Verhandlungen war …** topic number one *or* the leading topic of the talks was … → *auch* **beherrschen**

Be|herr|scher(in) M(F) *(liter)* ruler

be|herrscht [bəˈhɛrʃt] ADJ *(fig)* self-controlled ADV with self-control → *auch* **beherrschen**

Be|herrscht|heit F **-**, *no pl (fig)* self-control

Be|herr|schung [bəˈhɛrʃʊŋ] F **-**, *no pl* control; *(= Selbstbeherrschung)* self-control; *(des Markts)* domination; *(eines Fachs)* mastery; **die ~ verlieren** to lose one's temper

be|her|zi|gen [bəˈhɛrtsɪgn] *ptp* **beherzigt** VT to take to heart, to heed

Be|her|zi|gung F **-**, *no pl* heeding; **dies zur ~!** *(old)* heed this!, take heed!

be|herzt [bəˈhɛrtst] *(geh)* ADJ courageous, brave ADV courageously, bravely

Be|herzt|heit F **-**, *no pl (geh)* courage, bravery

be|he|xen *ptp* **behext** VT to bewitch

be|hielt *pret von* **behalten**

be|hilf|lich [bəˈhɪlflɪç] ADJ helpful; **jdm (bei etw) ~ sein** to help sb (with sth)

be|hin|dern *ptp* **behindert** VT to hinder; *Sicht* to impede; *(bei Sport, im Verkehr)* to obstruct; **jdn bei etw ~** to hinder sb in sth

be|hin|dert ADJ **a** *(mit einer Behinderung)* disabled; **geistig/körperlich ~** mentally/physically handicapped **b** *(sl: = blöd)* stupid; **~es Auto** shitheap *(sl)*; **ein ~er Typ** a tosser *(sl)*

Be|hin|der|ten-: **Be|hin|der|ten|ar|beit** F work with the disabled; **Be|hin|der|ten|aus|weis** M *disabled person card or ID*; **be|hin|der|ten|ge|recht** ADJ adapted to the needs of the disabled; **etw ~ umbauen/gestalten** to alter/design sth to fit the needs of the disabled; **Be|hin|der|ten|olym|pi|a|de** F Paralympics *pl*; **Be|hin|der|ten|sport** M disabled sport; **Be|hin|der|ten|toi|let|te** F disabled *or* handicapped toilet, toilet for the disabled *or* handicapped; **Be|hin|der|ten|werk|statt** F sheltered workshop

Be|hin|der|te(r) [bəˈhɪndɐtə] MF *decl as adj* disabled *or* handicapped person/man/woman; **die ~n** the handicapped *pl or* disabled *pl*

Be|hin|de|rung F hindrance; *(im Sport, Verkehr)* obstruction; *(körperlich, = Nachteil)* handicap; **mit ~en muss gerechnet werden** delays *or* hold-ups are likely to occur

Be|hör|de [bəˈhøːɐdə] F **-**, **-n** authority *usu pl*; *(= Amtsgebäude)* office *usu pl*; **die ~n** the authorities; **die zuständige ~** the appropriate *or* proper authorities

Be|hör|den-: **Be|hör|den|ap|pa|rat** M *(pej)* administrative machinery, bureaucratic machine, bureaucracy; **Be|hör|den|deutsch** NT *(pej)* (German) officialese *(pej)*; **Be|hör|den|gang** M *visit to the authorities*; **Be|hör|den|spra|che** F bureaucratic language; **Be|hör|den|un|we|sen** NT sprawling bureaucracy; **Be|hör|den|ver|tre|ter(in)** M(F) official; **Be|hör|den|weg** M administrative procedure; **auf dem ~** following the proper administrative channels; **Be|hör|den|we|sen** NT bureaucracy; **Be|hör|den|will|kür** F **die deutsche ~** the arbitrary nature of German authorities

be|hörd|lich [bəˈhøːɐtlɪç] ADJ official ADV officially

be|hörd|li|cher|seits [bəˈhøːɐtlɪçɐzaits] ADV *(form)* by the authorities; *(= auf behördlicher Seite)* on the part of the authorities

Be|huf [bəˈhuːf] M *(old form)* **zu diesem ~** to this end, for this purpose

be|huft [bəˈhuːft] ADJ hoofed

be|hü|ten *ptp* **behütet** VT *(= beschützen, bewachen)* to look after; *(esp Engel etc)* to watch over; **jdn vor etw ~** *(dat)* to save *or* protect sb from sth; **(Gott) behüte!** *(inf)* God *or* Heaven forbid!; **behüt dich Gott!** *(old, S Ger)* (may) God be with you! → *auch* **behütet**

Be|hü|ter [bəˈhyːtɐ] M **-s**, **-**, **Be|hü|te|rin** [-ərɪn] F **-**, **-nen** *(geh)* protector; *(Frau auch)* protectress

be|hü|tet [bəˈhyːtət] ADJ *Mädchen* carefully brought up; *Jugend, Alltag* sheltered ADV **~ auf-**

wachsen to have a sheltered upbringing → *auch* **behüten**

be|hut|sam [bə'huːtzaːm] ADJ cautious, careful; *(= zart auch)* gentle ADV carefully; *streicheln* gently; **man muss es ihr ~ beibringen** it will have to be broken to her gently

Be|hut|sam|keit F -, *no pl* care(fulness), cautiousness; *(= Zartheit auch)* gentleness; *(= Feingefühl)* delicacy

bei [bai]

PRÄPOSITION *(+dat)*

a Nähe near; **sie wohnt beim Rathaus** she lives near the town hall; **wir treffen uns beim Leuchtturm/bei der Kirche** we'll meet by the lighthouse/the church; **dicht bei dem Ort, wo …** very near the place where …; **die Völkerschlacht bei Leipzig** the Battle of the Nations near Leipzig; **Altdorf bei Nürnberg** Altdorf near Nuremberg; **ich stand/saß bei ihm** I stood/sat beside him *or* next to him; **er bot sich an, beim Gepäck zu bleiben** he offered to stay by the luggage; **ich bleibe bei den Kindern, dann kannst du einkaufen gehen** I'll stay with the children so you can go shopping; **bei X schneiden sich die beiden Geraden** the two lines bisect at X; **der Wert liegt bei tausend Euro** the value is around a thousand euros; **nicht bei sich sein** *(inf)* to be out of one's mind *(inf)*

b Aufenthalt at; **ich war bei meiner Tante** I was at my aunt's; **ich bin bei Gabriele zum Kaffee eingeladen** I'm invited to Gabriele's for coffee; **er wohnt bei seinen Eltern** he lives with his parents; **bei jdm übernachten** to spend the night at sb's; **bei Müller** *(auf Briefen)* care of *or* c/o Müller; **bei uns zu Hause** *(im Haus)* at our house; *(im Land, in Familie)* at home, back home *(US)*; **bei uns in Deutschland** in Germany; **bei uns fängt man um 8 Uhr zu arbeiten an** (here) we start work at 8 o'clock; **bei uns ist um 12.30 Uhr Mittagspause** we have our lunch break at 12.30; **bei jdm arbeiten** to work for sb; **bei Siemens angestellt sein** to work at Siemens; **er ist** *or* **arbeitet bei der Post®** he works for the post office; **beim Film/Fernsehen sein** to be in films/TV; **beim Fleischer/Friseur** at the butcher's/hairdresser's; **beim Militär** in the army; **ein Konto bei der Bank** an account at the bank; **bei Collins erschienen** published by Collins; **bei jdm Unterricht haben** to have lessons with sb; **bei Shakespeare liest man …** Shakespeare says …; **ich habe keine Taschentücher bei mir** I haven't got a hanky; **hast du Geld bei dir?** have you any money with *or* on you?; **bei Tisch** at table

c Berührung by; **er nahm mich bei der Hand** he took me by the hand; **jdn beim Arm/bei den Schultern packen** to grab sb by the arm/shoulder

d = zusammen mit among; **bei den Briefen lag auch das Schreiben mit meiner Kündigung** among the letters was one giving me notice; **bei meiner Post sind immer mehr Rechnungen als Privatbriefe** there are always more bills than letters in my mail

e Teilnahme at; **bei einer Hochzeit sein** to be at a wedding; **bei einer Aufführung anwesend sein** to be present at a performance; **bei einer Ausstellungseröffnung eine Rede halten** to give a speech at the opening of an exhibition; **machst du bei der Demonstration mit?** are you taking part in the demonstration?; **ich habe bei der Party mitgeholfen** I helped with the party; **er hat bei der Aufführung der Elektra mitgewirkt** he took part in the performance of Elektra

f = betreffend **bei ihm ist es 8 Uhr** he makes it *or* he has *(US)* 8 o'clock; **bei mir ist Schluss für heute** I've had enough for today; **das war bei ihm der Fall** that was the case with him; **man weiß nicht, woran man bei ihm ist** *(inf)* you never know where you are with him; **bei mir hast du damit kein Glück** you won't get anywhere with me; **bei Kühen findet man Maul- und Klauenseuche** you get foot-and-mouth in cows; **bei den Franzosen isst man die Schnecken mit Knoblauchbutter** the French eat snails with garlic butter → **weit 2 f, Wort g, Name**

g Zeit **beim letzten Ton des Zeitzeichens …** at the last pip …; **beim letzten Gewitter** during the last storm; **bei meiner Ankunft** on my arrival; **Vorsicht bei der Abfahrt (des Zuges)!** stand clear, the train is about to leave!; **beim Erwachen** on waking; **beim Erscheinen der Königin** when the queen appeared; **bei Beginn und Ende der Vorstellung** at the beginning and end of the performance; **bei Nacht** by night; **bei Tag** by day; **bei Tag und Nacht** day and night

h Umstand **bei dieser Schlacht** in *or* during this battle; **bei dem Zugunglück starben viele Menschen** a lot of people died in the train crash; **ich habe ihm beim Arbeiten** *or* **bei der Arbeit geholfen** I helped him with the work; **bei der Arbeit solltest du keine Musik hören** you shouldn't listen to music while you're working; **beim Fernsehen stricken** to knit while watching television; **er verliert beim Kartenspiel immer** he always loses at cards; **ich gehe gerne bei Regen spazieren** I love walking in the rain; **bei Kerzenlicht essen** to eat by candlelight; **bei offenem Fenster schlafen** to sleep with the window open; **etw bei einer Flasche Wein bereden** to discuss sth over a bottle of wine; **bei zehn Grad unter null** when it's ten degrees below zero; **das Schönste bei der Sache** the best thing about it; **bei guter Gesundheit sein** to be in good health → **Bewusstsein b, Kraft a, Verstand** *etc*

i Bedingung in case of; **bei Feuer Scheibe einschlagen** in case of fire break glass; **bei Gefahr Notbremse ziehen** in case of emergency pull the communication cord; **bei Nebel und Glatteis muss man vorsichtig fahren** when there is fog and ice you have to drive carefully; **bei Regen findet die Veranstaltung im Saale statt** if it rains the event will take place in the hall; **bei einer Erkältung sollte man sich warm halten** when you've got a cold you should keep warm

j Grund with; **bei seinem Talent** with his talent; **bei dieser Sturheit/so vielen Schwierigkeiten** with this stubbornness/so many difficulties; **bei reiflicher Überlegung** upon mature reflection; **bei solcher Hitze braucht man sich nicht zu wundern, dass niemand auf der Straße ist** when it's as hot as this it's no wonder there's nobody in the streets

k Einschränkung in spite of, despite; **bei aller Vorsicht** in spite of *or* despite all one's caution; **bei all seinen Bemühungen hat er es trotzdem nicht geschafft** despite all his efforts he still didn't manage it; **es geht beim besten Willen nicht** with the best will in the world, it's not possible

l in Schwurformeln by; **bei Gott** by God; **bei meiner Ehre** (up)on my honour *(Brit)* or honor *(US)*; **beim Zeus!** by Jove!

bei+be|hal|ten *ptp* **beibehalten** VT *sep irreg* to keep; *Bräuche, Regelung auch* to retain; *Leitsatz, Richtung* to keep to; *Gewohnheit* to keep up

Bei|be|hal|tung F, *no pl* keeping; *(von Bräuchen, Regelung auch)* retention; *(von Leitsatz, Richtung)* keeping to; *(von Gewohnheit)* keeping up

bei+bie|gen VT *sep irreg* **jdm etw ~** *(inf)* to get sth through to sb *(inf)*

Beibl. *abbr von* **Beiblatt**

Bei|blatt NT *(Press)* insert, supplement

Bei|boot NT *(Naut)* dinghy

bei+brin|gen VT *sep irreg* **a jdm etw ~** *(= mitteilen)* to break sth to sb; *(= zu verstehen geben)* to get sth across to sb, to get sb to understand sth **b** *(= unterweisen in)* to teach *(jdm etw* sb sth) **c** *(= zufügen) Verluste, Wunde, Niederlage, Schläge* to inflict *(jdm etw* sth on sb) **d** *(= herbeischaffen)* to produce; *Dokumente, Beweis, Geld etc* to furnish, to supply

Bei|brin|gung ['baibrɪŋʊŋ] F -, *no pl (von Verlusten, Wunde, Niederlage)* infliction; *(= das Herbeischaffen)* production; *(von Dokumenten, Beweis, Geld)* furnishing, supplying

Beich|te ['baiçtə] F -, **-n** confession; **zur ~ gehen** to go to confession; **(bei jdm) die ~ ablegen** to make one's confession (to sb); **eine ~ ablegen** *(fig)* to make a confession; **jdm die ~ abnehmen** to hear sb's confession; **~ hören** *or* **sitzen** *(inf)* to hear *or* take confession

beich|ten ['baiçtn] *(lit, fig)* VT to confess *(jdm etw* sth to sb) VI to confess; **~ gehen** to go to confession

Beicht-: **Beicht|for|mel** F *form of words used at confession*; **Beicht|ge|heim|nis** NT seal of confession *or* of the confessional; **das ~ wahren** to observe the seal of confession *or* of the confessional; **beicht+hö|ren** VI *sep (inf, Aus)* to hear confession; **Beicht|sie|gel** NT = **Beichtgeheimnis**; **Beicht|stuhl** M confessional; **Beicht|va|ter** M father confessor; **Beicht|zet|tel** M *(= Aufstellung)* list of sins; *(= Bescheinigung)* absolution

beid-: **beid|ar|mig** ADJ with both arms; *Lähmung* of *or* in both arms ADV **ein ~ gelähmter Mann** a man paralyzed in both arms; **er war ~ amputiert** he had had both arms amputated; **beid|bei|nig** ADJ with both legs; *Lähmung* of *or* in both legs; *Absprung* double-footed ADV **~ abspringen** to take off with both feet; **ein ~ gelähmter Mann** a man paralyzed in both legs; **er war ~ amputiert** he had had both legs amputated

bei|de ['baidə] PRON **a** *(adjektivisch) (ohne Artikel)* both; *(mit Artikel)* two; **alle ~n Teller** both plates; **seine ~n Brüder** both his brothers, his two brothers; **~ Mal** both times

b *(als Apposition)* both; **ihr ~(n)** the two of you; **euch ~** the two of you; **euch ~n herzlichen Dank** many thanks to both of you; **wer von uns ~n** which of us (two); **wie wärs denn mit uns ~n?** *(inf)* how about it? *(inf)*

c *(substantivisch) (ohne Artikel)* both (of them); *(mit Artikel)* two (of them); **alle ~** both (of them); **alle ~ wollten gleichzeitig Geld haben** both of them *or* they both wanted money at the same time; **keiner/keines** *etc* **von ~n** neither of them; **ich habe ~ nicht gesehen** I haven't seen either of them, I've seen neither of them

d ~s *(substantivisch: zwei verschiedene Dinge)* both; **(alles) ~s ist erlaubt** both are permitted

bei|de|mal △ ['baidəmaːl] ADV → **beide a**

bei|der-: **bei|der|lei** ['baidɐlai] ADJ *attr inv* both; **bei|der|sei|tig** ['baidɐzaitɪç] ADJ *(= auf beiden Seiten)* on both sides; *(= gegenseitig) Abkommen, Vertrag etc* bilateral; *Versicherungen, Einverständnis etc* mutual; **bei|der|seits** ['baidɐ'zaits] ADV on both sides; **sie haben ~ versichert …** they have given mutual assurances *or* assurances on both sides … PREP *+gen* on both sides of

Bei|der|wand ['baidɐvant] F OR NT **-(e)s** [-dəs] *no pl (Tex)* linsey-woolsey

Beid-: **beid|fü|ßig** ADJ two-footed; *Absprung* double-footed ADV **~ abspringen** to take off with both feet; **Beid|hän|der** ['baithɛndɐ] M **-s, -** *(= Schwert)* two-handed sword; **Beid|hän|der** ['baithɛndɐ] M **-s, -**, **Beid|hän|de|rin** [-ərɪn] F **-, -nen** ambidextrous person; **beid|hän|dig** ADJ *(= mit beiden Händen gleich geschickt)* ambidextrous; *(= mit beiden Händen zugleich)* two-handed ADV **~ schießen/schreiben können** to be able to shoot/write with either hand *or* both hands

bei+dre|hen VI *sep (Naut)* to heave to

beid-: **beid|sei|tig** ['baitzaitıç] ADJ (= *auf beiden Seiten*) on both sides; (= *gegenseitig*) mutual; **~e Zufriedenheit** satisfaction on both sides; mutual satisfaction ADV on both sides; **beid|seits** ['baitzaits] PREP +*gen* (*Sw, S Ger*) on both sides of

bei|ei|nan|der [bailai'nandɐ] ADV together

bei|ei|nan|der-: **bei|ei|nan|der+ha|ben** *sep irreg*, **bei|ei|nan|der ha|ben** △ *irreg* VT (*inf*) to have together; **du hast sie nicht richtig** *or* **alle beieinander** you can't be all there (*inf*); **bei|ei|nan|der+hal|ten** *sep irreg*, **bei|ei|nan|der hal|ten** △ *irreg* VT to keep together; **bei|ei|nan|der sein** VI *irreg aux sein* (*inf*) (*gesundheitlich*) to be in good shape (*inf*); (*geistig*) to be all there (*inf*); **gut ~** to be in good shape; to be all there; (*S Ger*: = *dick sein*) to be a bit chubby (*inf*); **Bei|ei|nan|der|sein** NT being together *no art*; (*von Gruppe*) get-together

Bei|fah|rer(in) M(F) (*Aut*) (front-seat) passenger; (*bei einem Motorrad*) (*im Beiwagen*) sidecar passenger; (*auf dem Soziussitz*) pillion rider *or* passenger; (= *berufsmäßiger Mitfahrer, Sport*) co-driver

Bei|fah|rer-: **Bei|fah|rer|air|bag** M (*Aut*) passenger airbag; **Bei|fah|rer|platz** M passenger seat; **Bei|fah|rer|sitz** M passenger seat; (*auf Motorrad*) pillion

Bei|fall M, *no pl* (= *Zustimmung*) approval; (= *das Händeklatschen*) applause; (= *Zuruf*) cheering, cheers *pl*; **~ finden** to meet with approval; **~ heischend** looking for approval; (= *Applaus wollend*) looking for applause; **~ spenden/klatschen/klopfen** *etc* to applaud; **~ spendend** applauding

bei|fall|hei|schend ADJ → **Beifall**

bei|fäl|lig ADJ approving; **~e Worte/Laute** words/noises of approval ADV approvingly; **er nickte ~ mit dem Kopf** he nodded his head approvingly *or* in approval; **dieser Vorschlag wurde ~ aufgenommen** this suggestion was favourably (*Brit*) *or* favorably (*US*) received, this suggestion met with approval

Bei|falls-: **Bei|falls|äu|ße|rung** F expression of (one's) approval; **Bei|falls|be|kun|dung** F show *or* demonstration of (one's) approval; **Bei|falls|be|zei|gung** [-bətsaigʊŋ] F **-, -en**, **Bei|falls|kund|ge|bung** F applause *no pl*

bei|fall|spen|dend ADJ → **Beifall**

Bei|falls-: **Bei|falls|ruf** M cheer; **Bei|falls|sturm** M storm of applause

Bei|fang M, *no pl* (*Fishing*) unwanted catch

Bei|fang|quo|te F (*Fishing*) quota of unwanted catch

Bei|film M supporting film

bei+fü|gen VT *sep* (= *mitschicken*) to enclose (+*dat* with); (= *beiläufig sagen*) to add

Bei|fü|gung F **a** *no pl* (*form*) enclosure; **unter ~ eines Fotos** enclosing a photo **b** (*Gram*) attribute

Bei|fü|gungs|satz M (*Gram*) attributive clause

Bei|fuß M, *no pl* (*Bot*) mugwort

Bei|fut|ter NT supplementary fodder

Bei|ga|be F **a** (= *das Beigeben*) addition; **eine ~ von etw empfehlen** to recommend adding sth, to recommend the addition of sth; **unter ~ eines Löffels Senf** adding a spoonful of mustard **b** (= *Beigefügtes, Begleiterscheinung*) addition; (= *Beilage*: *Gemüse, Salat etc*) side dish; (*Comm*: = *Zugabe*) free gift; (= *Grabbeigabe*) burial gift

beige [be:ʃ, 'be:ʒə, 'bɛ:ʒə] ADJ (*geh*: *inv*) beige

Beige [be:ʃ, 'be:ʒə, 'bɛ:ʒə] NT **-, -** *or* (*inf*) **-s** beige

Bei|ge ['baigə] F **-, -n** (*S Ger, Aus, Sw*) pile

bei+ge|ben *sep irreg* VT (= *zufügen*) to add (+*dat* to); (= *mitgeben*) *jdn* to assign (*jdm* to sb) VI **klein ~** (*inf*) to give in

bei|ge|bun|den ['baigəbʊndn] ADJ (*Typ*) bound in

beige|far|ben ['be:ʃfarbn-, 'be:ʒə-, 'bɛ:ʒə-] ADJ beige(-coloured) (*Brit*), beige(-colored) (*US*)

bei+ge|hen VI *sep irreg aux sein* (*dial*) to start

bei|ge|ord|net ADJ (*Gram*) *Nebensatz* coordinate → *auch* **beiordnen**

Bei|ge|ord|ne|te(r) ['baigəlɔrdnətə] MF *decl as adj* (town) councillor (*Brit*), councilor (*US*)

Bei|ge|schmack M aftertaste; (*fig*: *von Worten*) flavour (*Brit*), flavor (*US*); **es hat einen unangenehmen ~** (*lit, fig*) it has a nasty *or* an unpleasant taste (to it)

bei+ge|sel|len *ptp* **beigesellt** *sep* (*geh*) VT **ihr wurde ein Beschützer beigesellt** she was provided with an escort VR **sich jdm ~** to join sb

Beig|net [bɛn'je:] M **-s, -s** (*Cook*) fritter

Bei|heft NT supplement; (= *Lösungsheft*) answer book

bei+hef|ten VT *sep* to append, to attach

Bei|hil|fe F **a** (= *finanzielle Unterstützung*) financial assistance *no indef art*; (= *Zuschuss, Kleidungsbeihilfe*) allowance; (*für Arztkosten*) contribution; (= *Studienbeihilfe*) grant; (= *Subvention*) subsidy **b** (*Jur*) abetment; **wegen ~ zum Mord** because of being an *or* acting as an accessory to the murder

bei|hil|fe|fä|hig ADJ (*form*) → **Beihilfe** eligible for financial assistance/a contribution/contributions *etc*

bei+ho|len VT *sep* (*Naut*) to take in (the sail)

Bei|jing [bei'dʒɪŋ] NT **-s** Beijing, Peking

Bei|klang M (*lit*) (accompanying) sound; (*fig*) overtone *usu pl*

bei+kom|men VI *sep irreg aux sein* **a jdm ~** (= *zu fassen bekommen*) to get hold of sb; (= *fertig werden mit*) to get the better of sb; **einer Sache** (*dat*) **~** (= *bewältigen*) to deal with sth **b** (*old inf*: = *einfallen*) **jdm ~** to occur to sb; **lass dir das ja nicht ~!** don't even think of it! **c** (*dial*: = *herkommen*) to come **d** (*dial*: = *heranreichen*) **ich komme da nicht bei** I can't reach it

Bei|kost F supplementary diet

Beil [bail] NT **-(e)s, -e** axe (*Brit*), ax (*US*); (*kleiner*) hatchet; (= *Fleischerbeil*) cleaver; (*zum Hinrichten*) axe (*Brit*), ax (*US*); (= *Fallbeil*) blade (of a/the guillotine)

beil. *abbr von* **beiliegend**

bei+la|den VT *sep irreg* **a** *Ladung* to add (+*dat* to) **b** (*Jur*) to call in

Bei|la|dung F **a** (= *das Beiladen*) additional loading; (= *zusätzliche Ladung*) extra *or* additional load **b** (*Jur*) calling in; **notwendige ~** subpoena

Bei|la|ge F **a** (= *Gedrucktes*) insert; (= *Beiheft*) supplement **b** (= *das Beilegen*) enclosure; (*in Buch*) insertion; (*Aus*: = *Anlage zu Brief*) enclosure **c** (*Cook*) side dish; (= *Gemüsebeilage*) vegetables *pl*; (= *Salatbeilage*) side salad; **Erbsen und Kartoffeln als ~ zum Hähnchen** chicken with peas and potatoes

Bei|la|ger NT (*Hist*) consummation; (*obs*: = *Beischlaf*) sexual relations *pl*

bei|läu|fig ADJ **a** casual; *Bemerkung, Erwähnung* casual, passing *attr* **b** (*Aus*: = *ungefähr*) approximate ADV **a** (= *nebenbei*) *erwähnen, bemerken* casually, in passing **b** (*Aus*) approximately, about

Bei|läu|fig|keit F **-, -en a** (*in Benehmen etc*) casualness; (= *Nebensächlichkeit*) triviality; **mit einer erstaunlichen ~** amazingly casually **b Beiläufigkeiten** PL trivia *pl*

bei+le|gen VT *sep* **a** (= *hinzulegen*) to insert (+*dat* in); (*einem Brief, Paket*) to enclose (+*dat* with, in) **b** (= *beimessen*) to attribute, to ascribe (+*dat* to); **einer Sache** (*dat*) **Bedeutung** *or* **Gewicht/Wert ~** to attach importance/value to sth **c** (= *schlichten*) to settle **d** (*Naut*: = *anlegen*) to moor

Bei|le|gung ['baile:gʊŋ] F **-, -en** (= *Schlichtung*) settlement

bei|lei|be [bai'laibə] ADV **~ nicht!** certainly not; **das darf ~ nicht passieren** that mustn't happen under any circumstances; **~ kein ...** by no means a ..., certainly no ...

Bei|leid ✪ 51.4 NT condolence(s), sympathy; **jdm sein ~ aussprechen** *or* **ausdrücken** *or* **bezeigen** to offer sb one's condolences, to express one's sympathy with sb; **mein ~!** (*iro*) you have my sympathy!

Bei|leids- *in cpds* of condolence *or* sympathy; **Bei|leids|be|kun|dung** F expression of sympathy; **Bei|leids|be|such** M visit of condolence; **Bei|leids|be|zei|gung** [-bətsaigʊŋ] F **-, -en**, **Bei|leids|be|zeu|gung** F expression of sympathy; (*Brief, Telegramm etc*) condolence(s); **Bei|leids|kar|te** F sympathy *or* condolence card; **Bei|leids|schrei|ben** NT letter of condolence

Beil|hieb M blow with *or* from an axe (*Brit*) *or* ax (*US*)

bei+lie|gen VI *sep irreg* **a** (= *beigefügt sein*) to be enclosed (+*dat* with, in); (*einer Zeitschrift etc*) to be inserted (+*dat* in) **b** (*Naut*) to lie to **c** (*obs*) **jdm ~** to lie with sb (*obs*)

bei|lie|gend ADJ enclosed ADV enclosed; **~ senden wir Ihnen ...** please find enclosed ...

beim [baim] *contr von* **bei dem**

bei+ma|chen VR *sep* (*dial*) to get down to it

bei+men|gen VT *sep* to add (+*dat* to)

bei+mes|sen VT *sep irreg* **jdm/einer Sache Bedeutung** *or* **Gewicht/Wert ~** to attach importance/value to sb/sth

bei+mi|schen VT *sep* to add (+*dat* to); **unserer Freude war eine leichte Traurigkeit beigemischt** our joy was tinged with sadness

Bei|mi|schung F addition; **eine leichte ~ von ...** (*fig*) a touch of ...

Bein [bain] NT **-(e)s, -e a** leg; **mit übereinandergeschlagenen ~en** cross-legged; **von einem ~ aufs andere treten** to shift from one leg *or* foot to the other; **sich kaum auf den ~en halten können** to be hardly able to stay *or* stand on one's feet; **er ist noch gut auf den ~en** he's still sprightly; **schwach auf den ~en sein** to be a bit shaky; **jdm ein ~ stellen** (*lit, fig*) to trip sb up; **jdm wieder auf die ~e helfen** (*lit, fig*) to help sb back on his feet; **auf den ~en sein** (= *nicht krank, in Bewegung*) to be on one's feet; (= *unterwegs sein*) to be out and about; **sich auf die ~e machen** (*inf*) to make tracks (*inf*); **jdm ~e machen** (*inf*) (= *antreiben*) to make sb get a move on (*inf*); (= *wegjagen*) to make sb clear off (*inf*); **die ~e unter den Arm** *or* **in die Hand nehmen** (*inf*) to take to one's heels; **meine Tasche hat ~e bekommen** (*fig*) my bag has vanished into thin air, my bag seems to have grown legs and walked; **sich** (*dat*) **die ~e in den Bauch** *or* **Leib stehen** (*inf*) to stand around until one is fit to drop (*inf*); **mit beiden ~en im Leben** *or* **auf der Erde stehen** (*fig*) to have both feet (firmly) on the ground; **mit einem ~ im Grab stehen** (*fig*) to have one foot in the grave; **mit einem ~ im Gefängnis stehen** to be likely to end up in jail; **das steht auf schwachen ~en** (*fig*) that isn't very sound; **auf eigenen ~en stehen** (*fig*) to be able to stand on one's own two feet; **auf einem ~ kann man nicht stehen!** (*fig inf*) you can't stop at one!; **er fällt immer wieder auf die ~e** (*fig*) he always falls on his feet; **wieder auf die ~e kommen** (*fig*) to get back on one's feet again; **jdn wieder auf die ~e bringen** *or* **stellen** (*fig*) to get sb back on his/her feet again; **etw auf die ~e stellen** (*fig*) to get sth off the ground; *Geld etc* to raise sth; **die ~e breit machen** (*sl*: *zum Geschlechtsverkehr*) to spread one's legs (*sl*); **sich** (*dat*) **etw ans ~ binden** (*fig*) to saddle oneself with sth; **jdn/etw am ~ haben** (*fig inf*) to have sb/sth (a)round one's neck (*inf*) → **ausreißen** VT, **Knüppel, Lüge, Klotz**

b (= *Knochen*) bone; **der Schreck ist ihm in die ~e gefahren** the shock went right through him; **Fleisch am ~** (*old*) meat on the bone → **Stein c, Mark**

c (= *Elfenbein*) ivory

d (*dial*: = *Fuß*) foot

bei|nah ['baina:, 'bai'na:], **bei|na|he** ['baina:ə, 'bai'na:ə, bai'na:ə] ADV almost, nearly; **~(e) in allen Fällen, in ~(e) allen Fällen** in almost *or* nearly every case; **das kommt ~(e) auf dasselbe heraus** that comes to almost *or* nearly the same thing

Bei|na|he|ka|ta|stro|phe F near disaster *or* catastrophe
Bei|na|he|zu|sam|men|stoß M *(Aviat)* near miss
Bei|na|me M epithet; *(= Spitzname)* nickname
Bein-: **Bein|am|pu|ta|ti|on** F leg amputation; **bein|am|pu|tiert** [-lamputi:ɐt] ADJ with an amputated leg/amputated legs; ~ **sein** to have had a leg/both legs amputated; **Bein|am|pu|tier|te(r)** MF *decl as adj* leg amputee; **Bein|ar|beit** F *(Sport)* footwork; *(beim Schwimmen)* legwork; **Bein|bruch** M fracture of the leg; **das ist kein ~** *(fig inf)* it could be worse *(inf)* → **Hals- und Beinbruch**
bei|nern ['bainɐn] ADJ *(= aus Knochen)* made of bone; *(= aus Elfenbein)* ivory
Bein|frei|heit F, *no pl* legroom
be|in|hal|ten [bə'ınhaltn] *ptp* **beinhaltet** VT *insep (form)* to comprise
bein|hart ADJ *Mensch* hard as nails; *Erde, Piste, Kuchen* rock-hard; *Wettstreit, Kampf* fierce; *Geschäft* very hard; *Druck, Stress* intense; *Argument, Bemerkung* scathing ADV *verhandeln, spielen* fiercely; **die Gewerkschaft ging den Minister ~ an** the union gave the minister a rough ride; ~ **gegen Schuldner vorgehen** to give debtors a rough time *or* ride; **die Vertragsbedingungen sind ~ formuliert** the terms of the contract are really harsh
Bein|haus NT charnel house
-bei|nig [bainıç] ADJ *suf* -legged; **zweibeinig** two-legged
Bein-: **Bein|kleid** NT *usu pl (old, hum)* breeches *pl (old)*; **Bein|ling** ['bainlıŋ] M **-s, -e** leg; **Bein|pres|se** F leg press; **Bein|pro|the|se** F artificial leg; **Bein|raum** M leg room; **Bein|schie|ne** F *(Hist)* greave; *(Sport)* shin pad; *(bei Cricket)* (leg) pad; *(Med)* splint; **Bein|schüt|zer** [-ʃʏtsɐ] M *(Sport)* shin pad; **Bein|stumpf** M stump
bei+ord|nen VT *sep* **a** *(Gram)* to coordinate → *auch* **beigeordnet** **b** *(= beigeben)* **jdm/einer Sache beigeordnet sein** to be assigned to sb/appointed to sth; **bei einer Prüfung beigeordnet sein** to sit in on an examination
Bei|pack M additional consignment *or* order; *(= Frachtgut)* part load *(zu* with)
bei+pa|cken VT *sep* to enclose; *Frachtgut* to add (+*dat* to)
Bei|pack|zet|tel M instruction leaflet; *(= Inhaltsverzeichnis)* list *(Brit) or* table of contents
bei+pflich|ten VI *sep* **jdm/einer Sache in etw** *(dat)* ~ to agree with sb/sth on sth
Bei|pro|gramm NT supporting programme *(Brit) or* program *(US)*
Bei|rat M *(= Körperschaft)* advisory council *or* committee *or* body
Bei|rat M, **Bei|rä|tin** F adviser
Bei|rat|schaft ['baira:tʃaft] F **-, -en** *(Sw Jur)* (legal) care and protection
Bei|ried ['bairi:t] NT **-s,** *no pl* (*Aus: Cook*) piece of beef loin
be|ir|ren [bə'ırən] *ptp* **beirrt** VT *(= verwirren)* to disconcert; **sich nicht in etw** *(dat)* **~ lassen** not to let oneself be shaken *or* swayed in sth; **sich (durch etw) ~/nicht ~ lassen** to let/not to let oneself be put off (by sth); **er lässt sich nicht ~** he won't be put off; **nichts konnte ihn (in seinem Vorhaben) ~** nothing could shake him (in his intentions)
bei|sam|men [bai'zamən] ADV together
bei|sam|men- PREF together; **bei|sam|men+blei|ben** VI *sep irreg aux sein (inf) Gruppe, Leute etc* to stay *or* remain together; **bei|sam|men+ha|ben** VT *sep irreg (inf) Geld, Leute* to have got together; **seine Gedanken ~** to have one's wits about one; **seinen Verstand** *or* **seine fünf Sinne ~** to have all one's wits about one; **(sie) nicht alle ~** not to be all there; **Bei|sam|men|le|ben** NT, *no pl* living together; **bei|sam|men sein** VI *irreg aux sein (fig) (körperlich)* to be in good shape; *(geistig)* to be all there; **gut ~** to be in good shape; *(= kräftig gebaut sein)* to be well built; **Bei|sam|men|sein** NT get-together
Bei|sas|se ['baizasə] M **-n, -n** *(Hist) citizen without full civic rights*
Bei|satz M *(Gram)* appositive
bei+schaf|fen VT *sep (dial)* to bring
bei+schie|ßen VT *sep irreg (inf)* to chip in with *(inf)*
Bei|schlaf M *(Jur)* sexual intercourse *or* relations *pl*
bei+schla|fen VI *sep irreg (form)* to have sexual intercourse *or* relations (+*dat* with)
bei+schlie|ßen VT *sep irreg (Aus)* to enclose (+*dat* with)
Bei|schluss M *(Aus)* enclosure; **unter ~ von ...** enclosing ...
Bei|se|gel NT studdingsail
Bei|sein NT presence; **in jds ~** in sb's presence; **ohne jds ~** without sb being present
bei|sei|te [bai'zaitə] ADV aside *(auch Theat)*; **Spaß** *or* **Scherz ~!** joking aside *or* apart!
beiseite-: **bei|sei|te+brin|gen** VT *sep irreg* = **beiseiteschaffen**; **bei|sei|te+drän|gen** VT *sep* push aside; **bei|sei|te+ge|hen** VI *sep irreg aux sein* = **beiseitetreten**; **bei|sei|te+las|sen** VT *sep irreg* to leave aside *or* on one side; *(= nicht beachten)* to ignore, to disregard; **bei|sei|te+le|gen** VT *sep* to put aside *or* on one side; *(= weglegen)* to put away; *Geld* to put *or* set aside; **bei|sei|te+neh|men** VT *sep irreg* to take aside; **bei|sei|te+schaf|fen** VT *sep* **etw ~** to hide sth away; **jdn ~** to get rid of sb
Bei|sei|te|schaf|fung F removal
beiseite-: **bei|sei|te+schie|ben** VT *sep irreg* **Bedenken ~** to push doubts aside; **bei|sei|te+ste|hen** VI *sep irreg (S Ger, Aus, Sw: aux sein)* to stand aside *or* to one side; **bei|sei|te+tre|ten** VI *sep irreg aux sein* to step aside *or* to one side
Bei|sel ['baizl] NT **-s, -n** *(Aus inf)* pub *(Brit)*, bar
bei+set|zen VT *sep* **a** *(= beerdigen)* to inter *(form)*, to bury; *Urne* to install (in its resting place) **b** *(Naut) Segel* to set, to spread **c** *(old)* = **zusetzen**
Bei|set|zung ['baizɛtsʊŋ] F **-, -en** funeral; *(von Urne)* installing in its resting place
Bei|set|zungs|fei|er|lich|kei|ten PL funeral ceremony *sing*, obsequies *pl (form)*
bei+sit|zen VI *sep irreg (in Versammlung)* to attend; *(einem Ausschuss)* to have a seat (+*dat* on), to sit (+*dat* on); *(bei Prüfung)* to sit in *(bei* on)
Bei|sit|zer ['baizıtsɐ] M **-s, -**, **Bei|sit|ze|rin** [-ərın] F **-, -nen** **a** *(Jur)* assessor **b** *(= Ausschussmitglied)* committee member; *(bei Prüfung)* observer
Beisl ['baizl] NT **-s, -n** *(Aus inf)* pub *(Brit)*, bar
Bei|spiel ✪ 53.1, 53.5 NT example; **zum ~** for example *or* instance; **wie zum ~** such as; **jdm als ~ dienen** to be an example to sb; **jdm ein ~ geben** to set sb an example; **sich** *(dat)* **ein ~ an jdm nehmen** to take a leaf out of sb's book; **sich** *(dat)* **ein ~ an etw** *(dat)* **nehmen** to take sth as an example; **mit gutem ~ vorangehen** to set a good example
Bei|spiel-: **bei|spiel|ge|bend** ADJ exemplary; **~ für etw sein** to serve as an example for sth; **bei|spiel|haft** ADJ exemplary ADV exemplarily; **bei|spiel|hal|ber** ADV *(= als Beispiel)* by way of example; *(= zum Beispiel)* for example, for instance; **bei|spiel|los** ADJ unprecedented; *(= unerhört)* outrageous; **Bei|spiel|satz** M example
bei|spiels|hal|ber ADV *(= als Beispiel)* by way of example; *(= zum Beispiel)* for example, for instance
bei|spiels|wei|se ADV for example *or* instance
bei+sprin|gen VI *sep irreg aux sein* **jdm ~** to rush to sb's aid; *(mit Geldbeträgen)* to help sb out
bei|ßen ['baisn] *pret* **biss** [bıs], *ptp* **gebissen** [gə'bısn] VTI to bite; *(= brennen: Geschmack, Geruch, Schmerzen)* to sting; *(= kauen)* to chew; **in den Apfel ~** to bite into the apple, to take a bite out of the apple; **ich kann dieses Brot nicht ~** this bread is too hard for me; **der Hund hat mich** *or* **mir ins Bein gebissen** the dog has bitten my leg *or* me in the leg; **der Rauch/Wind beißt in den Augen/mich in die Augen** *(inf)* the smoke/wind makes one's/my eyes sting; **er wird dich schon nicht ~** *(fig)* he won't eat *or* bite you; **etwas/nichts zu ~** *(inf: = essen)* something/nothing to eat; **an etw** *(dat)* **zu ~ haben** *(fig)* to have sth to chew over *(Brit) or* on → **Gras**
VR *(Farben)* to clash; **sich** *(acc or dat)* **auf die Zunge/Lippen ~** to bite one's tongue/lips; **sich in den Arsch** *(vulg) or* **Hintern** *(sl)* **~** to kick oneself *(inf)*
bei|ßend ADJ *(lit, fig)* biting; *Wind auch, Bemerkung* cutting; *Geschmack, Geruch* pungent, sharp; *Schmerz* gnawing; *Ironie, Hohn, Spott* bitter
Bei|ßer|chen ['baisɐçən] PL *(baby-talk)* toothy-pegs *pl (baby-talk)*
Beiß-: **Beiß|korb** M *(für Hunde)* muzzle; **Beiß|ring** M teething ring; **Beiß|zan|ge** ['bais-] F (pair of) pincers *pl or* pliers *pl*; *(pej inf)* shrew; **das würde ich nicht mit der ~ anfassen** *or* **anpacken** *(inf)* I wouldn't touch that with a barge pole *(Brit inf) or* a 10-foot pole *(US inf)*
Bei|stand M **a** *no pl (= Hilfe)* help, assistance; *(= Unterstützung)* support; *(von Priester)* attendance, presence; **jdm ~ leisten** to give sb help *or* assistance; to give *or* lend sb one's support; to attend sb **b** *(Jur)* legal adviser *or* representative; *(in Duell)* aid, representative, second; **einen ~ stellen** *(Jur)* to appoint a legal adviser *or* representative
Bei|stands-: **Bei|stands|ab|kom|men** NT, **Bei|stands|pakt** M mutual assistance pact; **Bei|stands|ver|trag** M treaty of mutual assistance
bei+ste|hen VI *sep irreg* **jdm ~** to stand by sb
bei+stel|len VT *sep* **a** *(= daneben stellen)* to put *or* place beside **b** *(Aus: = zur Verfügung stellen)* (+*dat* for) to make available, to provide **c** *(Rail: = bereitstellen)* to put on
Bei|stell-: **Bei|stell|herd** M auxiliary cooker *(Brit) or* kitchen range *(US)*; **Bei|stell|mö|bel** PL occasional *(Brit) or* extra *(US)* furniture *sing*; **Bei|stell|tisch** M occasional table
bei+steu|ern VT *sep* to contribute
bei+stim|men VI *sep* = **zustimmen**
Bei|strich M *(esp Aus)* comma
Bei|tel ['baitl] M **-s, -** chisel
Bei|trag ['baitra:k] M **-(e)s, ¨-e** [-trɛ:gə] **a** *(= Anteil)* contribution; *(= Aufsatz auch)* article; **einen ~ zu etw leisten** to make a contribution to sth, to contribute to sth **b** *(= Betrag)* contribution; *(= Versicherungsbeitrag)* premium; *(= Mitgliedsbeitrag)* fee *(Brit)*, dues *pl*
bei+tra|gen VTI *sep irreg* to contribute *(zu* to); *(= mithelfen auch)* to help *(zu* to); **das trägt nur dazu bei, die Lage zu verschlimmern** that only helps to make the position worse
Bei|trags-: **Bei|trags|be|mes|sungs|gren|ze** F *(Insur)* income threshold *(for insurance contributions)*; **Bei|trags|er|hö|hung** F increase in contributions, premium increase, increased contributions *pl or* premiums *pl*; **bei|trags|frei** ADJ noncontributory; *Person* not liable to pay contributions; **Bei|trags|frei|heit** F non-liability to pay contributions; **Bei|trags|grup|pe** F, **Bei|trags|klas|se** F insurance group; *(bei Verein etc)* class of membership; **Bei|trags|mar|ke** F stamp; **Bei|trags|pflicht** F liability to pay contributions; **bei|trags|pflich|tig** [-pflıçtıç] ADJ *Arbeitsentgelt* contributory; **~ sein** *(Mensch)* to have to pay contributions; **Bei|trags|rück|er|stat|tung** F contribution *or* premium refund; **Bei|trags|rück|stand** M arrears *pl*; **Bei|trags|satz** M membership rate; **Bei|trags|schlüs|sel** M, **Bei|trags|sys|tem** NT contributory system; **Bei|trags|zah|len|de(r)** [-tsa:ləndə] MF *decl as adj*, **Bei|trags|-**

zah|ler(in) M(F) contributor; **Bei|trags|zah|lung** F premium *or* contribution payment, payment of the contribution *or* of contributions

bei+trei|ben VT *sep irreg Steuern* to collect; *Schulden auch* to recover; *(esp Jur)* to enforce (the) payment of

Bei|trei|bung ['baitraibʊŋ] F -, -en *(Jur)* collection

bei+tre|ten VI *sep irreg aux sein +dat* to join; *einem Pakt, Abkommen* to enter into; *einem Vertrag* to accede to

Bei|tritt M joining (*zu etw* sth); *(zu einem Pakt, Abkommen)* agreement (*zu* to); *(zu einem Vertrag)* accession (*zu* to); **seinen ~ erklären** to become a member

Bei|tritts-: **Bei|tritts|er|klä|rung** F confirmation of membership; **Bei|tritts|ge|such** NT application for membership; **Bei|tritts|kri|te|ri|en** PL *(für EU-Beitritt etc)* accession criteria *pl*; **Bei|tritts|ver|hand|lun|gen** PL membership talks *pl or* negotiations *pl*

Bei|wa|gen M **a** *(beim Motorrad)* sidecar **b** *(dated: = Anhänger)* carriage

Bei|wa|gen|ma|schi|ne F *(inf: = Motorrad mit Beiwagen)* (motorcycle) sidecar combination

Bei|werk NT additions *pl*; *(bei Aufsatz etc)* details *pl*; *(modisch)* accessories *pl*

bei+wil|li|gen ['baivılıgn] VI *sep (Sw)* = **zustimmen**

bei+woh|nen VI *sep +dat (geh)* **a** *(= dabei sein)* to be present at **b** *(dated euph)* to have sexual relations with

Bei|woh|nung F **a** *(form: = Anwesenheit)* presence **b** *(Jur)* intimacy *no art*

Bei|wort NT *pl* **-wörter** **a** *(= Adjektiv)* adjective **b** *(= beschreibendes Wort)* epithet

Beiz [baits] F -, -en *(Sw, S Ger: inf)* pub *(Brit)*, bar

Bei|ze ['baitsə] F -, -n **a** *(= Beizmittel)* corrosive fluid; *(= Metallbeize)* pickling solution, pickle; *(= Holzbeize)* stain; *(zum Gerben)* lye; *(= Tabakbeize)* sauce; *(Agr)* disinfectant; *(= Färbemittel, Typ)* mordant; *(Cook)* marinade **b** *(= das Beizen)* steeping in a/the corrosive fluid *etc* **c** *(Hunt)* hawking

Bei|ze F -, -n *(dial)* pub *(Brit)*, bar

bei|zei|ten [bai'tsaitn] ADV in good time

bei|zen ['baitsn] VT **a** *Holz* to stain; *Häute* to bate, to master; *Tabak* to steep in sauce; *Saatgut* to disinfect, to treat; *Kupfer* to etch; *Metal* to pickle; *(Cook)* to marinate **b** *(Hunt)* to hawk

bei+zie|hen ['baitsi:ən] VT *sep irreg (esp S Ger, Aus, Sw) Experten etc* to call in; *Bücher, Unterlagen* to consult

Bei|zie|hung ['baitsi:ʊŋ] F -, -en *usu sing (von Experten etc)* consultation, consulting (*+gen* a/an)

Beiz-: **Beiz|jagd** F hawking, falconry; **Beiz|mit|tel** NT = **Beize a**; **Beiz|vo|gel** M falcon, hawk

be|ja|gen VT *(Hunt) Wild* to hunt; *Gebiet* to hunt in

be|ja|hen [bə'ja:ən] *ptp* **bejaht** VT to answer in the affirmative; *(= gutheißen)* to approve of; **das Leben ~** to have a positive attitude toward(s) life VI to answer in the affirmative

be|ja|hend ADJ positive, affirmative; *Einstellung* positive ADV affirmatively; **etw ~ beantworten** *(form)* to answer sth in the affirmative

be|jahrt [bə'ja:ɐt] ADJ elderly, advanced in years

Be|ja|hung F -, -en affirmative answer (*+gen* to); *(= Gutheißung)* approval

Be|ja|hungs|fall M *(form)* **im ~e** in the event of an affirmative answer

be|jam|mern *ptp* **bejammert** VT to lament; *Schicksal, Los auch* to bewail *(liter)*; *jdn* to lament for

be|jam|merns|wert, **be|jam|merns|wür|dig** *(rare)* ADJ deplorable, lamentable; *Mensch* pitiable; *Schicksal* pitiable, dreadful

be|ju|beln *ptp* **bejubelt** VT to cheer; *Ereignis* to rejoice at; **sie wurden als Befreier bejubelt** they were acclaimed as liberators

be|ka|keln [bə'ka:kln] *ptp* **bekakelt** VT *(N Ger inf)* to talk over, to discuss

be|kal|men [bə'kalmən] *ptp* **bekalmt** VT *(Naut)* to becalm

be|kam *pret von* **bekommen**

be|kämp|fen *ptp* **bekämpft** VT to fight; *(fig auch)* to combat; *Ungeziefer* to control; **sich gegenseitig ~** to fight one another

Be|kämp|fung [bə'kɛmpfʊŋ] F -, *(rare)* -en fight, battle (*von, +gen* against); *(von Ungeziefer)* controlling; **zur ~ der Terroristen** to fight *or* combat the terrorists

Be|kämp|fungs|mit|tel NT *(= Insektenbekämpfungsmittel)* pesticide, insecticide; *(= Unkrautbekämpfungsmittel)* weedkiller

be|kannt [bə'kant] ADJ **a** *(= allgemein gekannt, gewusst)* well-known (*wegen* for); *Mensch auch* famous; **die ~eren Spieler** the better-known *or* more famous players; **die ~esten Spieler** the best-known *or* most famous players; **wie ist er ~ geworden?** how did he become famous?; **sie ist in Wien ~** she is (well-)known in Vienna; **er ist ~ dafür, dass er seine Schulden nicht bezahlt** he is well-known for not paying his debts; **das ist mir ~** I know about that; **sie ist mir ~** I know her, she is known to me; **es ist allgemein/durchaus ~, dass ...** it is common knowledge/a known fact that ...; **ich darf diese Tatsachen als ~ voraussetzen** I assume that these facts are known

b *(= nicht fremd)* familiar; **jdn mit etw ~ machen** *(mit Aufgabe etc)* to show sb how to do sth; *mit Gebiet, Fach etc* to introduce sb to sth; *mit Problem* to familiarize sb with sth; **sich mit etw ~ machen** to familiarize *or* acquaint oneself with sth; **jdn/sich (mit jdm) ~ machen** to introduce sb/oneself (to sb); **wir sind miteinander ~** we already know each other, we have already met → *auch* **bekennen**

Be|kann|ten|kreis M circle of acquaintances

Be|kann|te(r) [bə'kantə] MF *decl as adj* friend; *(= entfernter Bekannter)* acquaintance

be|kann|ter|ma|ßen [bə'kantɐ'ma:sn] ADV *(form)* as is known

Be|kannt|ga|be F announcement; *(in Zeitung etc)* publication

be|kannt ge|ben ✪ 51.2, 51.3 *irreg*, **be|kannt+ge|ben** *sep irreg* VT to announce; *(in Zeitung etc)* to publish; **ihre Verlobung geben bekannt ...** the engagement is announced between ...

Be|kannt|heit F -, *no pl* fame; *(von Fakten)* knowledge; **aufgrund der ~ dieser Tatsachen** because these facts are known

Be|kannt|heits|grad M **einen hohen/niedrigen ~ haben** to be well-known/little-known

be|kannt|lich [bə'kantlıç] ADV **~ gibt es ...** it is known that there are ...; **er hat ~ eine Schwäche für Frauen** he is known to have a weakness for women; **London ist ~ die Hauptstadt Englands** London is known to be the capital of England

be|kannt ma|chen, **be|kannt+ma|chen** *sep* VT to announce; *(= der Allgemeinheit mitteilen)* to publicize → **bekannt b**

Be|kannt|ma|chung [bə'kantmaxʊŋ] F -, -en **a** *(= das Bekanntmachen)* announcement; *(= Veröffentlichung)* publicizing **b** *(= Anschlag etc)* announcement, notice

Be|kannt|schaft [bə'kantʃaft] F -, -en **a** *(= das Bekanntwerden)* acquaintance; *(mit Materie, Gebiet)* knowledge (*mit* of); **jds ~ machen** to make sb's acquaintance; **mit etw ~ machen** to come into contact with sth; **bei näherer ~** on closer acquaintance **b** *(inf: = Bekannte)* acquaintance; **meine ganze ~** all my acquaintances; **ich habe gestern eine nette ~ gemacht** I met a nice person yesterday

Be|kannt|schafts|an|zei|ge F personal ad; **~n** *pl (Zeitungsrubrik)* personal ads *pl or* column *sing*, lonely hearts column *sing (inf)*

be|kannt wer|den *irreg aux sein*, **be|kannt+wer|den** *sep irreg aux sein* VI to become known; *(Geheimnis)* to leak out → **bekannt a**

be|keh|ren *ptp* **bekehrt** VT to convert (*zu* to) VR to be(come) converted (*zu* to); **er hat sich endlich bekehrt** *(fig)* he has finally turned over a new leaf, he has finally mended his ways

Be|keh|rer [bə'ke:rɐ] M -s, -, **Be|keh|re|rin** [-ərın] F -, -nen apostle (*+gen* to); *(= Missionar)* missionary (*+gen* to); *(fig)* proselytizer

Be|kehr|te(r) [bə'ke:ɐtə] MF *decl as adj* convert, proselyte

Be|keh|rung [bə'ke:rʊŋ] F -, -en conversion

be|ken|nen *ptp* **bekannt** [bə'kant] *irreg* VT to confess, to admit; *Sünde* to confess; *Wahrheit* to admit; *(Rel) Glauben* to bear witness to VR **sich (als or für) schuldig ~** to admit *or* confess one's guilt; **sich zum Christentum/zu einem Glauben/zu Jesus ~** to profess Christianity/a faith/one's faith in Jesus; **sich zu jdm/etw ~** to declare one's support for sb/sth; **sich nicht zu jdm ~** to deny sb

be|ken|nend ADJ *Katholik, Homosexueller* professed; **die Bekennende Kirche** the (German) Confessional Church

Be|ken|ner(in) M(F) confessor

Be|ken|ner-: **Be|ken|ner|an|ruf** M call claiming responsibility; **Be|ken|ner|brief** M *(nach Anschlag, Attentat etc)* letter claiming responsibility, written responsibility claim; **Be|ken|ner|geist** M, **Be|ken|ner|mut** M courage of one's convictions

Be|ken|ne|rin F confessor

Be|ken|ner|schrei|ben NT *(nach Anschlag, Attentat etc)* letter claiming responsibility, written responsibility claim

Be|kennt|nis [bə'kɛntnıs] NT -ses, -se **a** *(= Geständnis)* confession (*zu* of); *(zum religiösen Glauben auch)* profession (*zu* to); **ein ~ zu den Menschenrechten** a declaration of belief in human rights; **sein ~ zum Sozialismus** his declared belief in socialism; **ein ~ zur Demokratie ablegen** to declare one's belief in democracy; **ein ~ zum Christentum ablegen** to profess one's Christianity **b** *(Rel: = Konfession)* denomination

Be|kennt|nis-: **Be|kennt|nis|christ(in)** M(F) member of the Confessional Church; **Be|kennt|nis|frei|heit** F freedom of religious belief; **be|kennt|nis|freu|dig** ADJ eager to make confessions; **Be|kennt|nis|kir|che** F (German) Confessional Church; **be|kennt|nis|los** ADJ uncommitted to any religious denomination; **Be|kennt|nis|schu|le** F denominational school

be|kie|ken *ptp* **bekiekt** *(N Ger inf)* VT to look at VR to (have a) look at oneself; *(gegenseitig)* to look at each other

be|kiest [bə'ki:st] ADJ gravelled *(Brit)*, graveled *(US)*, gravel *attr*

be|kif|fen *ptp* **bekifft** VR *(inf)* to get stoned *(inf)*; **bekifft sein** to be stoned *(inf)*

be|kin|dert [bə'kındɐt] ADJ *(form)* with children

be|kla|gen *ptp* **beklagt** VT **a** to lament; *Los* to bewail; *Tod, Verlust* to mourn; **Menschenleben sind nicht zu ~** there are no casualties **b** → **beklagt** VR to complain (*über +acc, wegen* about); **sich bei jdm über etw** *(acc)* **~** to complain *or* make a complaint to sb about sth; **ich kann mich nicht ~** I can't complain, I've nothing to complain about

be|kla|gens|wert, **be|kla|gens|wür|dig** *(geh)* ADJ *Mensch* pitiful; *Zustand* lamentable, deplorable; *Misserfolg, Vorfall, Scheitern* regrettable, unfortunate; *Unfall* terrible

be|klagt [bə'kla:kt] ADJ *(Jur)* **die ~e Partei** the defendant; *(bei Scheidung)* the respondent; **der ~e Ehegatte** the respondent → *auch* **beklagen**

Be|klag|te(r) [bə'kla:ktə] MF *decl as adj (Jur)* defendant; *(bei Scheidung)* respondent

be|klat|schen *ptp* **beklatscht** VT **a** *(= applaudieren)* to clap, to applaud **b** *(inf: = Klatsch verbreiten über)* to gossip about

be|klau|en *ptp* **beklaut** VT *(inf) jdn* to rob

be|kle|ben *ptp* **beklebt** VT **etw (mit Papier/Plakaten** *etc***)** ~ to stick paper/posters *etc* on(to) sth; **etw mit Etiketten** ~ to stick labels on(to) sth, to label sth

be|kle|ckern *ptp* **bekleckert** *(inf)* VT to stain; **ich habe mir das Kleid bekleckert** I've made a mess on my dress VR **sich (mit Saft** *etc***)** ~ to spill juice *etc* all down *or* over oneself; **er hat sich nicht gerade mit Ruhm bekleckert** *(inf)* he didn't exactly cover himself with glory

be|kleck|sen *ptp* **bekleckst** VT *(inf)* to splatter *(mit* with); **etw (mit Tinte/Farbe)** ~ to splatter ink/paint on sth; **du bist ja von oben bis unten bekleckst!** *(inf)* you're covered in ink/paint *etc*! VR to splatter oneself with ink/paint *etc*

be|klei|den *ptp* **bekleidet** *(geh)* VT **a** *(= anziehen)* to dress *(mit* in); *(= Kleidung geben)* to clothe; **er war nur mit einer Hose bekleidet** he was only wearing a pair of trousers; **etw mit etw** ~ *(geh)* to cover sth in sth **b** *(= innehaben) Amt etc* to occupy, to hold; **jdn mit einem Amt/einer Würde** ~ to bestow an office/a title on sb VR to get dressed

be|klei|det [bəˈklaidət] ADJ dressed, clad *(mit* in); **sie war nur leicht** ~ she was only lightly *or (spärlich)* scantily dressed *or* clad; **nur mit einer Hose** ~ **sein** to be clad in *or* wearing only a pair of trousers

Be|klei|dung F **a** *(= Kleider)* clothes *pl*, clothing; *(= Aufmachung)* dress, attire; **ohne** ~ without any clothes on **b** *(form: eines Amtes)* tenure; *(rare: mit einem Amt)* honouring *(Brit)*, honoring *(US)*

Be|klei|dungs-: **Be|klei|dungs|amt** NT *(Mil)* quartermaster's store; **Be|klei|dungs|ar|ti|kel** M, **Be|klei|dungs|ge|gen|stand** M garment, article of clothing; **Be|klei|dungs|ge|wer|be** NT clothing *or* garment *(esp US)* trade; **Be|klei|dungs|in|dust|rie** F clothing *or* garment industry, rag trade *(inf)*; **Be|klei|dungs|stück** NT garment, article of clothing; **Be|klei|dungs|vor|schrif|ten** PL clothing regulations *pl*; *(bezüglich Uniform)* uniform regulations *pl*

be|kleis|tern *ptp* **bekleistert** VT **a** *Tapete etc* to paste **b** *(= bekleben)* **eine Wand (mit Plakaten)** ~ to stick posters all over a wall

be|klem|men *ptp* **beklemmt** VT *(fig)* to oppress; *(Schuld auch)* to weigh upon

be|klem|mend ADJ *(= beengend)* oppressive, constricting; *(= beängstigend)* tormenting, oppressive ADV oppressively; **der Raum war** ~ **eng** the room was so small it was oppressive; ~ **wirken** to be oppressive

Be|klemm|nis [bəˈklɛmnɪs] F -, -se feeling of oppressiveness; *(= Gefühl der Angst)* feeling of apprehension *or* trepidation

Be|klem|mung [bəˈklɛmʊŋ] F -, -en *usu pl* feeling of oppressiveness; *(= Gefühl der Angst)* feeling of apprehension *or* trepidation; **~en haben** to feel oppressed; to be full of apprehension *or* trepidation; *(bei enger Kleidung)* to feel restricted

be|klom|men [bəˈklɔmən] ADJ apprehensive, anxious; *Mensch auch* full of trepidation; *Schweigen* uneasy ADV apprehensively; **sie saß da und schwieg** ~ she sat there in uneasy silence; ~ **klingen** to sound troubled

Be|klom|men|heit F -, *no pl* trepidation, apprehensiveness

be|klö|nen *ptp* **beklönt** VT *(N Ger inf)* to talk over

be|klop|fen *ptp* **beklopft** VT to tap; *Brust auch* to sound

be|kloppt [bəˈklɔpt] ADJ *(inf) Mensch* loony, crazy, mad *(all inf)*; *Sache* lousy, stupid, crappy *(all inf)*

be|knackt [bəˈknakt] *(sl)* ADJ *Mensch, Frage, Idee* daft *(Brit inf)*, stupid; *Spruch, Frage* idiotic ADV *sich verhalten, sich anstellen* like a total idiot *(inf)*; ~ **fragen** to ask daft *(Brit inf) or* stupid questions

be|knien *ptp* **bekniet** VT *(inf) jdn* to beg

be|ko|chen *ptp* **bekocht** VT *(inf)* to cook for

be|kö|dern *ptp* **beködert** VT to bait

be|kom|men *ptp* **bekommen** *irreg* VT **a** *(= erhalten)* to get; *Genehmigung, Stimmen, Nachricht* to get, to obtain; *Geschenk, Brief, Lob, Belohnung* to get, to receive; *Zug, Bus, Krankheit* to get, to catch; *Schlaganfall, Junges, ein Kind, Besuch* to have; *Spritze, Tadel* to be given; **ein Jahr Gefängnis** ~ to be given one year in prison; **wir** ~ **Kälte/anderes Wetter** the weather is turning cold/is changing; **wir** ~ **Regen/Schnee** we're going to have rain/snow; **einen Stein/Ball** *etc* **an den Kopf** ~ to be hit on the head by a stone/ball *etc*; **kann ich das schriftlich ~?** can I have that in writing?; **wir haben das große Bett nicht nach oben** ~ we couldn't get the big bed upstairs; **jdn ins/aus dem Bett** ~ to get sb into/out of bed; **was ~ Sie(, bitte)?** what will you have, sir/madam?; **ich bekomme bitte ein Glas Wein** I'll have a glass of wine, please; **was ~ Sie dafür?** how much is that?; **was ~ Sie von mir?** how much do I owe you?; **jdn dazu ~, etw zu tun** to get sb to do sth; **er bekam es einfach nicht über sich, ...** he just could not bring himself to ...; **ich bekomme den Deckel nicht abgeschraubt** *(inf)* I can't unscrew the lid

b *(= entwickeln) Fieber, Schmerzen, Vorliebe, Komplexe* to get, to develop; *Zähne* to get, to cut; *Übung, neue Hoffnung* to gain; **Rost/Risse** ~ to get *or* become rusty/cracked, to develop rust/cracks; **Heimweh** ~ to get *or* become homesick; **Sehnsucht** ~ to develop a longing *(nach* for); **graue Haare/eine Glatze** ~ to go grey *(Brit) or* gray *(US)*/bald; **Hunger/Durst** ~ to get *or* become hungry/thirsty; **Angst** ~ to get *or* become afraid; **einen roten Kopf** ~ to go red

c *(mit Infinitivkonstruktion)* to get; **etw zu essen** ~ to get sth to eat; **etw zu sehen/hören** ~ to get to see/hear sth; **was muss ich denn da zu hören ~?** what's all this I've been hearing?; **es mit jdm zu tun** ~ to get into trouble with sb; **etw zu fassen** ~ to catch hold of sth; **wenn ich ihn zu fassen bekomme ...** if I get my hands on him ...

d *(mit ptp oder adj siehe auch dort)* **etw gemacht** ~ to get *or* have sth done; **seine Arbeit fertig** *or* **gemacht** *(inf)* ~ to get one's work finished *or* done; **etw geschenkt** ~ to be given sth (as a present); **ich habe das Buch geliehen** ~ I have been lent the book; **etw bezahlt** ~ to get paid for sth; **einen Wunsch erfüllt** ~ to have a wish fulfilled; **das Haus sauber** ~ to get the house clean; **etw satt** ~ → **sattbekommen**

e *(in Verbindung mit n siehe auch dort)* **Lust ~, etw zu tun** to feel like doing sth; **es mit der Angst/Wut** ~ to become afraid/angry; **Ärger** ~ to get into trouble; **eine Ohrfeige** *or* **eine** *(inf)* ~ to catch *(Brit) or* get it *(inf)*; **Prügel** *or* **sie** *(inf) or* **es** *(inf)* ~ to be given *or* to get a hiding

VI **a** *aux sein +dat (= zuträglich sein)* **jdm (gut)** ~ to do sb good; *(Essen)* to agree with sb; **jdm nicht** *or* **schlecht** ~ not to do sb any good; *(Essen)* to disagree with sb, not to agree with sb; **wie ist Ihnen das Bad ~?** how was your bath?; **wie bekommt ihm die Ehe?** how is he enjoying married life?; **es ist ihm schlecht ~, dass er nicht gearbeitet hat** not working did him no good; **wohl bekomms!** your health!

b *(= bedient werden)* ~ **Sie schon?** are you being attended to *or* served?

be|kömm|lich [bəˈkœmlɪç] ADJ *Mahlzeit, Speisen* (easily) digestible; *Luft, Klima* beneficial; **leicht** ~ **sein** to be easily digestible; **schwer/besser** ~ **sein** to be difficult/easier to digest

Be|kömm|lich|keit F -, *no pl (von Mahlzeit, Speisen)* digestibility; *(von Luft, Klima)* beneficial qualities *pl*

be|kös|ti|gen [bəˈkœstɪgn] *ptp* **beköstigt** VT to cater for

Be|kös|ti|gung F -, -en *(= das Beköstigen)* catering (+*gen* for); *(= Kost)* food

be|kräf|ti|gen *ptp* **bekräftigt** VT to confirm; *Vorschlag* to support, to back up; **etw nochmals** ~ to reaffirm sth; **seine Aussage mit einem Eid** ~ to reinforce one's evidence by swearing an oath; **eine Vereinbarung mit einem Handschlag** ~ to seal an agreement by shaking hands; **er nickte ~d** he nodded in support

Be|kräf|ti|gung F confirmation; *(= Versicherung)* assurance; **zur** ~ **seiner Worte** to reinforce his words

be|krän|zen *ptp* **bekränzt** VT to crown with a wreath; *(mit Blumen)* to garland

be|kreu|zen *ptp* **bekreuzt** VT *(Eccl)* to bless (with the sign of the cross) VR to cross oneself

be|kreu|zi|gen *ptp* **bekreuzigt** VR to cross oneself

be|krie|gen *ptp* **bekriegt** VT to wage war on; *(fig)* to fight; **sie ~ sich (gegenseitig) schon seit Jahren** they have been at war with one another for years; **bekriegt werden** to be attacked

be|krit|teln *ptp* **bekrittelt** VT to criticize; *Arbeit auch* to find fault with

be|krit|zeln *ptp* **bekritzelt** VT to scribble over; **das Buch mit Bemerkungen** ~ to scribble comments all over the book

be|krö|nen *ptp* **bekrönt** VT to crown *(auch fig)*; *(Archit)* to surmount

be|ku|cken *ptp* **bekuckt** VT *(N Ger)* = **begucken**

be|küm|mern *ptp* **bekümmert** VT to worry; **das braucht dich nicht zu** ~ there is no need for you to worry about that VR **sich über etw** *(acc)* ~ to worry about sth; **sich um etw** ~ to concern oneself with sth → *auch* **bekümmert**

Be|küm|mer|nis F *(geh)* distress

be|küm|mert [bəˈkʏmɐt] ADJ worried *(über +acc* about)

be|kun|den [bəˈkʊndn] *ptp* **bekundet** VT to show, to express; *(in Worten auch)* to state; *(Jur: = bezeugen)* to testify to; **~, dass ...** *(Jur)* to testify that ... VR *(geh)* to manifest itself

Be|kun|dung F -, -en expression, manifestation; *(in Worten auch)* statement; *(Jur)* testimony

be|la|bern *ptp* **belabert** VT *(inf)* **jdn** ~ to keep on at sb; **er hat mich belabert** *(= überreden)* he talked me into it

be|lä|cheln *ptp* **belächelt** VT to smile at

be|la|chen *ptp* **belacht** VT to laugh at

be|la|den [bəˈlaːdn] *ptp* **beladen** *irreg* VT *Schiff, Zug* to load (up); *(fig: mit Sorgen etc) jdn* to burden; **etw mit Holz** *etc* ~ to load sth with wood *etc*, to load wood *etc* onto sth; **ein Tier mit einer schweren Last** ~ to put a heavy load on an animal VR *(mit Gepäck etc)* to load oneself up; **sich mit Verantwortung/Sorgen** ~ to take on responsibilities/worries; **sich mit Schuld** ~ to incur guilt

be|la|den [bəˈlaːdn] ADJ loaded; *Mensch* laden; *(mit Schuld)* laden, burdened; **mit etw ~ sein** to be loaded with sth; *(Mensch)* to be loaded down *or* laden with sth; *(mit Schuld etc)* to be weighed down *or* laden *or* burdened with sth

Be|la|dung [bəˈlaːdʊŋ] F -, -en *usu sing* loading (up)

Be|lag [bəˈlaːk] M -(e)s, ¨-e [-ˈlɛːgə] coating; *(= Schicht)* layer; *(= Ölfilm etc)* film; *(auf Pizza, Brot)* topping; *(auf Tortenboden, zwischen zwei Brotscheiben)* filling; *(auf Zahn)* film; *(= Zungenbelag)* fur; *(= Bremsbelag)* lining; *(= Fußbodenbelag)* covering; *(= Straßenbelag)* surface

Be|la|ge|rer [bəˈlaːgərɐ] M -s, -, **Be|la|ge|rin** [-ərɪn] F -, -nen besieger

be|la|gern *ptp* **belagert** VT *(Mil)* to besiege *(auch fig)*, to lay siege to

Be|la|ge|rung F siege

Be|la|ge|rungs-: **Be|la|ge|rungs|krieg** M siege warfare; **Be|la|ge|rungs|ma|schi|ne** F siege engine; **Be|la|ge|rungs|zu|stand** M state of siege; **den** ~ **ausrufen** to declare a state of siege

Be|la|mi [bɛla'mi:] M **-(s), -s** *(dated)* lady-killer *(inf)*

be|läm|mert [bə'lɛmɐt] ADJ *(= betreten)* sheepish; *(= niedergeschlagen)* miserable; *(= scheußlich) Wetter, Angelegenheit* lousy *(inf)* ADV *(= dumm)* like an idiot

Be|lang [bə'laŋ] M **-(e)s, -e** **a** *(no pl: = Wichtigkeit)* importance, significance; **von/ohne ~ (für jdn/etw) sein** to be of importance/of no importance (to sb/for *or* to sth) **b** **Belange** PL interests **c** *(form: = Sache)* matter; **in diesem ~** as regards this matter

be|lan|gen *ptp* **belangt** VT **a** *(Jur)* to prosecute (*wegen* for); *(wegen Beleidigung, Verleumdung)* to sue; **dafür kann man belangt werden** you could be prosecuted for that **b** *(dated: = betreffen)* **was mich belangt** as far as I am concerned

be|lang|los ADJ inconsequential, trivial; **das ist für das Ergebnis ~** that is irrelevant to the result

Be|lang|lo|sig|keit F **-, -en** triviality

Be|lang|sen|dung F *(Aus: TV, Rad)* party political broadcast

Be|lan|gung [bə'laŋʊŋ] F **-, -en** prosecution; *(wegen Beleidigung, Verleumdung)* suing

be|lang|voll ADJ relevant (*für* to)

be|las|sen *ptp* **belassen** VT *irreg* to leave; **wir wollen es dabei ~** let's leave it at that; **jdn in dem Glauben ~, dass …** to allow sb to go on believing that …; **jdn in seinem Amt ~** to allow sb to remain in office; **etw an seinem Ort ~** to leave sth in its place; **das muss ihm ~ bleiben** that must be left up to him

be|last|bar ADJ **a** *(mit Last, Gewicht)* **bis zu 50 Tonnen ~ sein** to have a maximum load of *or* load-bearing capacity of 50 tons; **wie hoch ist diese Brücke ~?** what is the maximum load of this bridge?
b *(fig)* **daran habe ich bemerkt, wie ~ ein Mensch ist** that made me see how much a person can take; **das Gedächtnis ist nur bis zu einem gewissen Grad ~** the memory can only absorb a certain amount; **weiter waren seine Nerven nicht ~** his nerves could take no more, his nerves were at breaking point
c *(= beanspruchbar) (Med) Mensch, Körper, Organe, Kreislauf* resilient; **der Steuerzahler ist nicht weiter ~** the tax payer cannot be burdened any more; **die Atmosphäre ist nicht unbegrenzt (durch Schadstoffe) ~** the atmosphere cannot stand an unlimited degree of contamination; **da wird sich zeigen, wie ~ das Stromnetz/unser Wasserhaushalt ist** that will show how much pressure our electricity/water supply will take
d **wie hoch ist mein Konto ~?** what is the limit on my account?; **der Etat ist nicht unbegrenzt ~** the budget is not unlimited

Be|last|bar|keit [bə'lastba:ɐkait] F **-, -en** **a** *(von Brücke, Aufzug)* load-bearing capacity **b** *(von Menschen, Nerven)* ability to cope with stress; *(von Gedächtnis)* capacity **c** *(von Stromnetz etc)* maximum capacity; *(von Mensch, Organ)* maximum resilience; **die höhere physische ~ eines Sportlers** an athlete's higher degree of physical resilience **d** *(von Haushalt)* (maximum) limit (*+gen* of, on)

be|las|ten *ptp* **belastet** VT **a** *(lit) (mit Gewicht) Brücke, Balken, Träger, Ski* to put weight on; *(mit Last) Fahrzeug, Fahrstuhl* to load; **etw mit 50 Tonnen ~** to put a 50 ton load on sth, to put a weight of 50 tons on sth; **den Träger gleichmäßig ~** to distribute weight evenly over the girder; **das darf nur mit maximal 5 Personen/Tonnen belastet werden** its maximum load is 5 people/tons; **die Brücke zu sehr ~** to put too much weight on the bridge; **das Fahrzeug zu sehr ~** to overload the vehicle
b *(fig)* **jdn mit etw ~** *(mit Arbeit)* to load sb with sth; *mit Verantwortung, Sorgen, Wissen* to burden sb with sth; **das Gedächtnis mit unnützem Wissen ~** to burden one's memory with useless knowledge; **jdn ~** *(mit Arbeit, Verantwortung, Sorgen)* to burden sb; *(= nervlich, körperlich anstrengen)* to put a strain on sb; **jdn mit zu viel Arbeit ~** to overload sb with work; **jdn mit zu viel Verantwortung** *etc* **~** to overburden sb with responsibility *etc*; **~d sein** to be a strain → **erblich**
c *(fig: = bedrücken)* **jdn/jds Gewissen/Seele mit etw ~** *(Mensch)* to burden sb/sb's conscience/soul with sth; **jdn ~** *(Schuld etc)* to weigh on sb *or* sb's mind; **jds Gewissen ~** to weigh on sb's conscience; **das belastet ihn sehr** it weighs heavily on his mind; **mit einer Schuld belastet sein** to be weighed down *or* burdened by guilt; **von Sorgen belastet** weighed down with cares
d *(= beanspruchen) Wasserhaushalt, Stromnetz, Leitung* to put pressure on, to stretch; *Atmosphäre* to pollute; *(Med) Kreislauf, Magen, Organe, Körper, Mensch* to put a strain on, to strain; *Nerven* to strain, to tax; *Steuerzahler* to burden; **jdn/etw zu sehr** *or* **stark ~** to overstrain sb/sth; *Wasserhaushalt etc* to put too much pressure on sth, to overstretch sth
e *(Jur) Angeklagten* to incriminate; **~des Material** incriminating evidence
f *(Fin) Konto* to charge; *Etat* to be a burden on; *(steuerlich) jdn* to burden; **etw (mit einer Hypothek) ~** to mortgage sth; **das Konto mit einem Betrag ~** to debit the account with a sum, to debit a sum to the account; **jdn mit den Kosten ~** to charge the costs to sb; **dafür werden wir Sie mit 50 Euro ~** we will charge you 50 euros for that
VR **a** **sich mit etw ~** *(mit Arbeit)* to take sth on; *mit Verantwortung* to take sth upon oneself; *mit Sorgen* to burden oneself with sth; **sich mit Schuld ~** to incur guilt; **damit belaste ich mich nicht** *(mit Arbeit, Verantwortung)* I don't want to take that on; **ich will mich nicht ~** *(mit Wissen)* I don't want to know (about it)
b *(Jur)* to incriminate oneself

be|läs|ti|gen [bə'lɛstɪgn] *ptp* **belästigt** VT *(= zur Last fallen)* to bother; *(= zudringlich werden)* to pester; *(körperlich)* to molest; *(= nachstellen) Ex-Freundin etc* to stalk; *(Licht, Geräusch, Geruch)* to irritate

be|läs|ti|gend ADJ annoying, aggravating; *Licht, Geruch etc* irritating

Be|läs|ti|gung F **-, -en** annoyance; *(durch Lärm etc)* irritation; *(= Zudringlichkeit)* pestering; **etw als eine ~ empfinden** to find sth a nuisance; **sie beklagte sich über die ~en durch ihren Chef** she complained about being harassed by her boss; **sexuelle ~** sexual harassment

Be|las|tung [bə'lastʊŋ] F **-, -en** **a** *(= das Belasten)* putting weight on; *(von Fahrzeug, Fahrstuhl)* loading; *(= Last, Gewicht)* weight; *(in Fahrzeug, Fahrstuhl etc)* load; **die erhöhte ~ der Brücke** the increased weight put on the bridge; **maximale ~ der Brücke** weight limit of the bridge; **maximale ~ des Fahrstuhls** maximum load of the lift
b *(fig) (= das Belasten) (mit Arbeit)* loading; *(mit Verantwortung etc)* burdening; *(= Anstrengung)* strain; *(= Last, Bürde)* burden
c *(= Bedrückung)* burden (*+gen* on)
d *(= Beeinträchtigung)* pressure (*+gen* on); *(von Atmosphäre)* pollution (*+gen* of); *(von Kreislauf, Magen)* strain (*+gen* on)
e *(Jur)* incrimination
f *(Fin) (von Konto)* charge (*+gen* on); *(von Etat, steuerlich)* burden (*+gen* on); *(mit Hypothek)* mortgage (*+gen* on)

Be|las|tungs-: **Be|las|tungs|elekt|ro|kar|dio|gramm** NT, **Be|las|tungs-EKG** NT *(Med)* exercise electrocardiogram *or* ECG; **be|las|tungs|fä|hig** ADJ = **belastbar**; **Be|las|tungs|fä|hig|keit** F **-,** *no pl* **a** *(von Brücke, Aufzug)* load-bearing capacity **b** *(von Menschen, Nerven)* ability to cope with stress; *(von Gedächtnis)* capacity **c** *(von Stromnetz etc)* maximum capacity; *(von Mensch, Organ)* maximum resilience; **die höhere physische ~ eines Sportlers** an athlete's higher greater physical resilience **d** *(von Haushalt)* (maximum) limit (*+gen* of, on); **Be|las|tungs|gren|ze** F *(von Brücke, Balken etc)* weight limit; *(von Fahrzeug)* maximum load; *(von Atmosphäre, Wasserhaushalt)* maximum capacity; *(seelisch, physisch)* limit; *(Elec)* level of peak load; **ich habe meine ~ erreicht** I've reached my limit, I've had enough; **ich habe meine ~ überschritten** I've overdone it; **Be|las|tungs|ma|te|ri|al** NT *(Jur)* incriminating evidence; **Be|las|tungs|pro|be** F endurance test; **Be|las|tungs|spit|ze** F *(Elec)* peak load; **Be|las|tungs|zeu|ge** M, **Be|las|tungs|zeu|gin** F *(Jur)* witness for the prosecution

be|lat|schern [bə'la:tʃɐn] *ptp* **belatschert** VT *(dial inf)* to talk round *(Brit)*, to persuade

be|lau|ben [bə'laubn] *ptp* **belaubt** VR to come into leaf; **spärlich/dicht belaubt sein** to have sparse/thick foliage

Be|lau|bung F **-,** *no pl (= Laub)* leaves *pl*, foliage; *(= das Sichbelauben)* coming into leaf

be|lau|ern *ptp* **belauert** VT to watch (secretly); **jdn misstrauisch ~** to eye sb suspiciously VR to eye each other *or* one another

be|lau|fen *ptp* **belaufen** *irreg* VR **sich auf etw** *(acc)* **~** to come *or* amount to sth VT *(rare: = begehen)* to walk; **ein viel ~er Weg** a well-trodden path VI *aux sein (dial)* = **beschlagen**

be|lau|schen *ptp* **belauscht** VT to eavesdrop on; *(= genau beobachten)* to observe

be|le|ben *ptp* **belebt** VT **a** *(= anregen)* to liven up; *(= neu beleben) Natur* to revive; *(= aufmuntern)* to brighten up, to liven up; *Absatz, Konjunktur, jds Hoffnungen* to stimulate; **eine kalte Dusche wird dich neu ~** a cold shower will refresh you **b** *(= lebendiger gestalten)* to brighten up; *Unterhaltung auch* to animate **c** *(= zum Leben erwecken)* to bring to life VR *(Konjunktur)* to be stimulated; *(Augen, Gesicht)* to light up; *(Natur, Stadt)* to come to life; *(= geschäftiger werden)* to liven up → *auch* **belebt** VI **das belebt** that livens you up

be|le|bend ADJ invigorating; **ein ~es Element in etw** *(acc)* **einbringen** to liven sth up ADV **~ wirken** to have a stimulating effect

be|lebt [bə'le:pt] ADJ **a** *Straße, Stadt etc* busy **b** *(= lebendig)* living; **die ~e Natur** the living world; **~er Schlamm** activated sludge → *auch* **beleben**

Be|lebt|heit F **-,** *no pl (von Straße, Stadt etc)* bustle

Be|le|bung [bə'le:bʊŋ] F **-, -en** revival; *(der Wirtschaft, Konjunktur)* stimulation; **zur ~ trank er einen starken Kaffee** he drank a cup of strong coffee to revive himself

Be|le|bungs|ver|such M *(Med)* resuscitation attempt

be|le|cken *ptp* **beleckt** VT to lick

Be|leg [bə'le:k] M **-(e)s, -e** [-gə] **a** *(= Beweis)* instance, piece of evidence; *(= Quellennachweis)* reference; **~e für den Gebrauch eines Wortes** instances of the use of a word **b** *(= Quittung)* receipt

Be|leg|arzt M, **Be|leg|ärz|tin** F *general practitioner who also looks after a certain number of patients in a hospital*

be|leg|bar ADJ verifiable

Be|leg|bett NT *hospital bed at the disposal of a general practitioner*, GP bed

be|le|gen *ptp* **belegt** VT **a** *(= bedecken)* to cover; *Brote, Tortenboden* to fill; **etw mit Fliesen/Teppich ~** to tile/carpet sth; **mit Beschuss ~** to bombard; **mit Bomben ~** to bomb, to bombard → *auch* **belegt**
b *(= besetzen) Wohnung, Hotelbett, Sitzplatz* to occupy; *(= reservieren)* to reserve, to book; *(Univ) Fach* to take; *Seminar, Vorlesung* to enrol *(Brit) or* enroll *(US)* for; **den fünften Platz ~** to take fifth place, to come fifth
c *(= beweisen)* to verify
d *(= auferlegen)* **jdn mit etw ~** to impose sth on sb; **jdn mit dem Bann ~** to proscribe sb; *(Eccl)* to excommunicate sb; **etw mit einem Namen ~** to give sth a name

Be|leg-: **Be|leg|exemp|lar** NT specimen copy; **Be|leg|frist** F *(Univ)* enrolment *(Brit) or* enrollment *(US)* period; **Be|leg|kran|ken|haus** NT ≈ hospital providing wards for non-resident doctors, general practitioners' hospital *(Brit)*; **Be|leg|le|ser** M OCR reader; **Be|leg|ma|te|ri|al** NT documentation

Be|leg|schaft [bə'le:kʃaft] F -, -en **a** *(= Beschäftigte)* staff; *(esp in Fabriken etc)* workforce **b** *(inf: = die Anwesenden)* **die ganze ~** the whole mob *(inf)* or gang *(inf)*

Be|leg|schafts-: **Be|leg|schafts|ak|ti|en** PL employees' shares; **Be|leg|schafts|mit|glied** NT employee; **Be|leg|schafts|ra|batt** M staff discount; **Be|leg|schafts|ver|samm|lung** F meeting of employees

Be|leg-: **Be|leg|stel|le** F reference; **Be|leg|stück** NT piece of evidence

be|legt [bə'le:kt] ADJ *Zunge* furred; *Stimme* hoarse; *Zimmer, Bett, Wohnung* occupied; *(Telec) Telefon, Nummer, Leitung* busy, engaged; *(Comput) Speicherplatz* used; **~e Brote** open *(Brit)* or open-faced *(US)* sandwiches → *auch* **belegen**

Be|legt|zei|chen NT *(Telefon)* engaged *(Brit)* or busy *(esp US)* tone

be|leh|nen *ptp* **belehnt** VT **a** *(Hist)* to enfeoff **b** *(Sw) Haus* to mortgage

be|lehr|bar ADJ teachable

be|leh|ren *ptp* **belehrt** VT *(= unterweisen)* to teach, to instruct; *(= aufklären)* to inform, to advise *(form)* *(über +acc* of); **jdn eines anderen ~** to teach sb otherwise; **sich eines anderen ~ lassen** to learn or be taught otherwise; **da musste ich mich ~ lassen** I realized I was wrong; **er ist nicht zu ~, er lässt sich nicht ~** he won't be told; **ich bin belehrt!** I've learned my lesson → **besser ADJ a**

be|leh|rend ADJ didactic; **der ~e Zeigefinger** *(fig)* a lecturing or moralizing tone ADV **auf jdn ~ einreden** to give sb a lecture; **~ sprechen** to lecture

Be|leh|rung [bə'le:rʊŋ] F -, -en explanation, lecture *(inf)*; *(= Anweisung)* instruction *(über +acc* about); *(von Zeugen, Angeklagten)* caution; **deine ~en kannst du dir sparen** there's no need to lecture me

be|leibt [bə'laipt] ADJ stout, corpulent, portly

Be|leibt|heit F -, *no pl* corpulence, stoutness

be|lei|di|gen [bə'laidɪgn] *ptp* **beleidigt** VT *jdn* to insult; *(Verhalten, Anblick, Geruch etc)* to offend; *(Jur) (mündlich)* to slander; *(schriftlich)* to libel

be|lei|digt [bə'laidɪçt] ADJ insulted; *(= gekränkt)* offended; *Gesicht, Miene* hurt; **er fühlt sich in seiner Ehre ~** he feels his honour *(Brit)* or honor *(US)* has been insulted; **die ~e Leberwurst spielen** *(inf)* to be in a huff *(inf)*; **bist du jetzt ~?** have I offended you?; **jetzt ist er ~** now he's in a huff *(inf)* ADV in a huff *(inf)*, offended; **~ weggehen** to go off in a huff *(inf)*

Be|lei|di|gung F -, -en insult; *(Jur) (mündliche)* slander; *(schriftliche)* libel; **eine ~ für den Geschmack** an insult to one's taste; **eine ~ für das Auge** an eyesore; **etw als ~ auffassen** to take sth as an insult, to take offence *(Brit)* or offense *(US)* at sth

Be|lei|di|gungs-: **Be|lei|di|gungs|kla|ge** F → **Beleidigung** *(Jur)* slander/libel action, action for slander/libel; **Be|lei|di|gungs|pro|zess** M *(Jur)* → **Beleidigung** slander/libel trial

be|leih|bar [bə'laibaːɐ] ADJ *(Fin)* eligible as collateral; *Sicherheit* pledgeable; *Immobilie* mortgageable

be|lei|hen *ptp* **beliehen** [bə'li:ən] VT *irreg* **a** *(Comm)* to lend money on; *Haus, Grundstück* to give a mortgage on **b** *(Hist: belehnen)* to enfeoff

Be|lei|hung [bə'laiʊŋ] F -, -en *(Fin)* raising of a loan or mortgage *(+gen* on)

Be|lei|hungs|gren|ze F *(Fin)* lending limit

be|lem|mert △ [bə'lɛmɐt] ADJ, ADV → **belämmert**

be|le|sen [bə'le:zn] ADJ well-read

Be|le|sen|heit F -, *no pl* **eine gewisse ~** wide reading

Bel|eta|ge [bɛle'ta:ʒə] F *(old)* first floor *(Brit)*, second floor *(US)*

be|leuch|ten *ptp* **beleuchtet** VT *(= Licht werfen auf)* to light up, to illuminate; *(= mit Licht versehen) Straße, Bühne etc* to light; *(fig: = betrachten)* to examine

Be|leuch|ter(in) M(F) lighting technician

Be|leuch|ter|brü|cke F lighting bridge

be|leuch|tet [bə'lɔyçtət] PTP von **beleuchten** ADJ lit up, illuminated; **gut/schlecht ~** well-lit/badly lit *attr*, well/badly lit *pred*

Be|leuch|tung [bə'lɔyçtʊŋ] F -, -en **a** *(= das Beleuchten)* lighting; *(= das Bestrahlen)* illumination; *(fig)* examination, investigation **b** *(= Licht)* light; *(= das Beleuchtetsein)* lighting; *(= Lichter)* lights *pl*; **die ~ der Straßen** street lighting; **die ~ der Fahrzeuge** lights *pl* on vehicles

Be|leuch|tungs-: **Be|leuch|tungs|an|la|ge** F lighting (installation); **Be|leuch|tungs|kör|per** M lighting appliance; **Be|leuch|tungs|stär|ke** F intensity of light; **Be|leuch|tungs|tech|nik** F lighting engineering

be|leum|det [bə'lɔymdət], **be|leu|mun|det** [bə'lɔymʊndət] ADJ **gut/schlecht ~ sein** to have a good/bad reputation; **ein schlecht ~es Etablissement** an establishment with a bad reputation

bel|fern ['bɛlfɐn] VI to bark; *(Kanone)* to boom

Bel|gi|en ['bɛlgiən] NT -s Belgium

Bel|gi|er ['bɛlgiɐ] M -s, -, **Bel|gi|e|rin** [-iərɪn] F -, -nen Belgian

bel|gisch ['bɛlgɪʃ] ADJ Belgian

Bel|grad ['bɛlgra:t] NT -s Belgrade

Bel|gra|der ['bɛlgra:dɐ] ADJ *attr* Belgrade

Bel|gra|der ['bɛlgra:dɐ] M -s, -, **Bel|gra|de|rin** [-ərɪn] F -, -nen native of Belgrade; *(= Einwohner)* inhabitant of Belgrade

be|lich|ten *ptp* **belichtet** VT *(Phot)* to expose; **wie lange muss ich das Bild ~?** what exposure should I give the shot?

Be|lich|tung F *(Phot)* exposure

Be|lich|tungs-: **Be|lich|tungs|au|to|ma|tik** F automatic exposure; **Be|lich|tungs|dau|er** F exposure (time); **Be|lich|tungs|mes|ser** M -s, - light meter; **Be|lich|tungs|ta|bel|le** F exposure chart or table; **Be|lich|tungs|zeit** F exposure (time)

be|lie|ben *ptp* **beliebt** VI *impers (geh)* **wie es Ihnen beliebt** as you like or wish; **was beliebt?** *(old: = wird gewünscht)* what can I do for you? VT *(old, iro)* **es beliebt jdm, etw zu tun** *(= jd hat Lust)* sb feels like doing sth; *(iro)* sb deigns or condescends to do sth; **jd beliebt, etw zu tun** *(= jd neigt dazu)* sb likes doing sth; **er beliebt zu scherzen** *(iro)* he must be joking

Be|lie|ben [bə'li:bn] NT -s, *no pl* **nach ~** just as you/they *etc* like, any way you *etc* want (to); **das steht** or **liegt in Ihrem ~** that is up to you, that is left to your discretion

be|lie|big [bə'li:bɪç] ADJ any; **(irgend)eine/jede ~e Zahl** any number at all or whatever or you like; **nicht jede ~e Zahl** not every number; **jeder Beliebige** anyone at all; **eine ganz ~e Reihe von Beispielen** a quite arbitrary series of examples; **in ~er Reihenfolge** in any order whatever; **alles Beliebige** anything whatever; **die Auswahl ist ~** the choice is open or free ADV as you *etc* like; **Sie können ~ lange bleiben** you can stay as long as you like; **die Zahlen können ~ ausgewählt werden** you can choose any number you like

Be|lie|big|keit F -, *no pl* randomness, arbitrariness

be|liebt [bə'li:pt] ADJ popular *(bei* with); **sich bei jdm ~ machen** to make oneself popular with sb

Be|liebt|heit F -, *no pl* popularity

Be|liebt|heits|ska|la F -, -skalen *usu sing* popularity scale

be|lie|fern *ptp* **beliefert** VT to supply; **jdn (mit etw) ~** to supply sb (with sth)

Be|lie|fe|rung F supplying; **die ~ einer Firma einstellen** to stop supplying a firm

Bel|la|don|na [bɛla'dɔna] F -, **Belladonnen** [-'dɔnən] deadly nightshade, belladonna; *(= Extrakt)* belladonna

bel|len ['bɛlən] VI to bark VT to bark; *Befehle* to bark out; **etw ins Telefon/Mikrofon ~** to yell or shout sth into the telephone/microphone

bel|lend ADJ *Husten* hacking; *Stimme* gruff

Bel|let|ris|tik [bɛle'trɪstɪk] F -, *no pl* fiction and poetry, belles lettres *pl*

bel|let|ris|tisch [bɛle'trɪstɪʃ] ADJ *Zeitschrift, Neigung* literary; **~e Literatur** fiction and poetry; **~e Bücher** books of fiction and poetry; **~e Abteilung** department for fiction and poetry

be|lo|bi|gen [bə'lo:bɪgn] *ptp* **belobigt** VT to commend, to praise

Be|lo|bi|gung F -, -en *(form)* commendation

Be|lo|bi|gungs|schrei|ben NT commendation

be|loh|nen *ptp* **belohnt**, *(Sw)* **be|löh|nen** *ptp* **belöhnt** VT to reward; **starker Beifall belohnte den Schauspieler** the actor received hearty applause

Be|loh|nung [bə'lo:nʊŋ] F -, -en *(Sw)*, **Be|löh|nung** [bə'lø:nʊŋ] F -, -en reward; *(= das Belohnen)* rewarding; **zur** or **als ~ (für)** as a reward (for); **eine ~ aussetzen** to offer a reward; **zur ~ der Kinder für ihr gutes Benehmen** in order to reward the children for their good behaviour *(Brit)* or behavior *(US)*

Belt [bɛlt] M -s, -e **der Große/Kleine ~** the Great/Little Belt

be|lüf|ten *ptp* **belüftet** VT to ventilate

Be|lüf|tung F **a** *(= das Belüften)* ventilating, airing **b** *(inf: = ganze Anlage)* ventilation

Be|lüf|tungs-: **Be|lüf|tungs|an|la|ge** F ventilation (system); **Be|lüf|tungs|ven|til** NT *(Tech)* ventilation valve

Be|lu|ga [be'lu:ga] M -s, -s *(Zool)* beluga (whale)

be|lü|gen *ptp* **belogen** [bə'lo:gn] VT *irreg* to lie or tell lies/a lie to; **sich selbst ~** to deceive oneself

be|lus|ti|gen [bə'lʊstɪgn] *ptp* **belustigt** VT to amuse VR *(geh)* **sich über jdn/etw ~** to make fun of sb/sth; **sich an etw** *(dat)* **~** to laugh at sth; **sich mit etw ~** to amuse oneself by (doing) sth

be|lus|tigt [bə'lʊstɪçt] ADJ *Gesichtsausdruck, Ton, Stimme* amused ADV in amusement

Be|lus|ti|gung F -, -en *(geh: = Veranstaltung)* entertainment; *(= das Belustigtsein)* amusement

Bel|ze|bub ['bɛltsəbu:p] M -s *(Bibl)* Beelzebub → **Teufel**

be|ma|chen *ptp* **bemacht** VR *(inf)* **a** *(= sich beschmutzen)* to make oneself dirty or filthy **b** *(= sich aufregen)* to get het up *(Brit inf)* or worked up

be|mäch|ti|gen [bə'mɛçtɪgn] *ptp* **bemächtigt** VR *(geh)* **a** *(= in seine Gewalt bringen)* **sich eines Menschen/einer Sache ~** to take or seize hold of sb/sth; **sich des Thrones ~** to seize or take the throne; *(durch Intrige)* to usurp the throne **b** *(Gefühl, Gedanke)* **sich jds ~** to come over sb

be|mähnt [bə'mɛ:nt] ADJ *Tier* maned; *(hum) Jugendliche* shaggy-haired

be|mä|keln *ptp* **bemäkelt** VT to find fault with, to pick holes in

be|ma|len *ptp* **bemalt** VT to paint; *(= verzieren auch)* to decorate; **etw mit Blumen ~** to paint flowers on sth; **bemalt sein** *(pej)* to be heavily made up VR to paint oneself; *(pej: = schminken)* to put on one's war paint *(inf)*

Be|ma|lung [bə'ma:lʊŋ] F -, -en *(= das Bemalen, Farbschicht)* painting; *(zur Verzierung auch)* decoration

be|män|geln [bə'mɛŋln] *ptp* **bemängelt** VT to find fault with, to fault; **was die Kritiker an dem Buch ~, ist …** the fault the critics find with the book is …

Be|män|ge|lung F -, -en finding fault *(+gen* with), faulting *(+gen* of)

be|man|nen [bəˈmanən] *ptp* **bemannt** VT *U-Boot, Raumschiff* to man; **sie ist seit Neuestem wieder bemannt** *(inf)* she has just recently got herself a man again *or* a new boyfriend

Be|man|nung F -, -en manning; *(rare: = Mannschaft)* crew

be|män|teln [bəˈmɛntln] *ptp* **bemäntelt** VT to cover up

Be|män|te|lung F -, -en covering up

Bem|bel [ˈbɛmbl] M -s, - *(dial)* pitcher

be|merk|bar ADJ noticeable, perceptible; **sich ~ machen** *(= sich zeigen)* to make itself felt, to become noticeable; *(= auf sich aufmerksam machen)* to draw attention to oneself, to attract attention; **mach dich ~, wenn du etwas brauchst** let me know if you need anything

be|mer|ken ✪ 38.1 *ptp* **bemerkt** VT **a** *(= wahrnehmen)* to notice; *Schmerzen auch* to feel; **er bemerkte rechtzeitig/zu spät, dass ...** he realized in time/too late that ... **b** *(= äußern)* to remark, to comment *(zu* on); **ganz richtig, bemerkte sie** quite right, she said; **nebenbei bemerkt** by the way; **ich möchte dazu ~, dass ...** I would like to say *or* add, that ...; **er hatte einiges zu ~** he had quite a few comments *or* remarks to make

Be|mer|ken [bəˈmɛrkn] NT *(form)* **mit dem ~** with the observation

be|mer|kens|wert ADJ remarkable ADV remarkably

Be|mer|kung [bəˈmɛrkʊŋ] F -, -en **a** remark, comment *(zu* on) **b** *(old: = Wahrnehmung)* observation

be|mes|sen *ptp* **bemessen** *irreg* VT *(= zuteilen)* to allocate; *(= einteilen)* to calculate; **der Raum ist für eine kleine Gruppe ~** the room is designed for a small group of people; **reichlich ~** generous; **knapp ~** not very generous; **meine Zeit ist kurz** *or* **knapp ~** my time is limited *or* restricted VR *(form)* to be proportionate *(nach* to)

Be|mes|sung F **a** *(= Zuteilung)* allocation; *(= Einteilung)* calculation **b** *(Build)* building specification

Be|mes|sungs-: **Be|mes|sungs|grund|la|ge** F *(Fin)* basis of assessment; **Be|mes|sungs|zeit|raum** M *(Fin, von Steuern)* assessment period

be|mit|lei|den [bəˈmɪtlaidn] *ptp* **bemitleidet** VT to pity, to feel pity for, to feel sorry for; **er ist zu ~** he is to be pitied; **sich selbst ~** to feel sorry for oneself

be|mit|lei|dens|wert [bəˈmɪtlaidnsveːɐt] ADJ pitiable, pitiful

be|mit|telt [bəˈmɪtlt] ADJ well-to-do, well-off

Bem|me [ˈbɛmə] F -, -n *(dial)* slice of buttered bread; *(zusammengeklappt)* sandwich

be|mo|geln *ptp* **bemogelt** VT *(inf)* to cheat

be|moo|sen [bəˈmoːzn] *ptp* **bemoost** VR to become overgrown with moss

be|moost [bəˈmoːst] ADJ mossy, moss-covered; **~es Haupt** *(inf)* old fogey *(inf)*; *(= Student)* perpetual student

be|mü|hen [bəˈmyːən] *ptp* **bemüht** VT to trouble, to bother; *Rechtsanwalt etc* to engage; **jdn zu sich ~** to call in sb, to call upon the services of sb; **die Bibel** *or* **Bibelstellen ~** to quote from the Bible VR **a** *(= sich Mühe geben)* to try hard, to endeavour *(Brit)*, to endeavor *(US)*; **sich um gute Beziehungen/eine Stelle ~** to try to establish good relations/get a job; **sich um jds Wohl ~** to take trouble over sb's wellbeing; **sich um jds Vertrauen ~** to try to win sb's trust; **sich um jds Gunst ~** to court sb's favour *(Brit) or* favor *(US)*; **sich um eine Verbesserung der Lage ~** to try to improve the situation; **sich um jdn ~** *(für eine Stelle)* to try to get sb; *(um Kranken etc)* to look after sb; *(um jds Gunst)* to court sb; **bitte ~ Sie sich nicht** please don't trouble yourself *or* put yourself out; **sich redlich ~** to make a genuine effort → *auch* **bemüht** **b** *(geh: = gehen)* to go, to proceed *(form)*; **sich ins Nebenzimmer ~** to proceed to the next room *(form)*; **sich zu jdm ~** to go to sb; **sich auf die Polizei ~** to go to the police

Be|mü|hen [bəˈmyːən] NT -s, *no pl (geh)* efforts *pl*, endeavours *(Brit) or* endeavors *(US) pl (um* for)

be|müht [bəˈmyːt] ADJ **~ sein, etw zu tun** to try hard to do sth, to endeavour *(Brit) or* endeavor *(US)* to do sth; **um etw ~ sein, darum ~ sein, etw zu tun** to be at pains to do sth, to endeavour *(Brit) or* endeavor *(US)* to do sth → *auch* **bemühen**

Be|mü|hung F -, -en effort, endeavour *(Brit)*, endeavor *(US)*; **vielen Dank für Ihre (freundlichen) ~en** *(form)* thank you for your efforts *or* trouble

be|mü|ßi|gen [bəˈmyːsɪgn] *ptp* **bemüßigt** VR *(geh)* **sich einer Sache** *(gen)* **~** to avail oneself of sth

be|mü|ßigt [bəˈmyːsɪçt] ADJ **sich ~ fühlen/sehen/finden** *(geh, usu iro)* to feel called upon *or* obliged

be|mut|tern [bəˈmʊtɐn] *ptp* **bemuttert** VT to mother

Be|mut|te|rung F -, -en *usu sing* mothering; **ihre ständige ~ geht mir auf die Nerven** I hate the way she keeps nannying me *or* people

be|mützt [bəˈmʏtst] ADJ wearing a cap; **weiß ~e Bergkuppen** snow-capped mountains

be|nach|bart [bəˈnaxbaːɐt] ADJ neighbouring *attr (Brit)*, neighboring *attr (US)*; *Haus, Familie auch* next door; *Staat auch* adjoining; **die Häuser sind ~** the houses are next (door) to one another

be|nach|rich|ti|gen [bəˈnaːxrɪçtɪgn] *ptp* **benachrichtigt** VT to inform *(von* of); *(amtlich auch)* to notify *(von* of)

Be|nach|rich|ti|gung F -, -en *(= Nachricht)* notification *(auch Comput)*; *(Comm)* advice note; **die ~ der Eltern ist in solchen Fällen vorgeschrieben** the parents must be notified in such cases

Be|nach|rich|ti|gungs|schrei|ben NT letter of notification

be|nach|tei|li|gen [bəˈnaːxtailɪgn] *ptp* **benachteiligt** VT to put at a disadvantage; *(wegen Geschlecht, Klasse, Rasse, Glauben etc)* to discriminate against; **benachteiligt sein** to be at a disadvantage; to be discriminated against

Be|nach|tei|lig|te(r) [bəˈnaːxtailɪçtə] MF *decl as adj* **der/die ~ sein** to be at a disadvantage

Be|nach|tei|li|gung F -, -en *(= das Benachteiligen)* disadvantaging; *(wegen Geschlecht, Rasse, Glauben)* discrimination *(+gen* against); *(Zustand)* disadvantage; discrimination *no pl*

be|na|geln *ptp* **benagelt** VT **eine Wand/das Dach** *etc* **mit etw ~** to nail sth onto a wall/the roof *etc*

be|na|gen *ptp* **benagt** VT to gnaw at

be|nä|hen *ptp* **benäht** VT **das Kleid** *etc* **mit etw ~** to sew sth onto the dress

be|näs|sen *ptp* **benässt** VT *(geh)* to moisten

Bench|mark [ˈbɛntʃmaːk] F -, -s *(Econ etc)* benchmark

Ben|del △ [ˈbɛndl] M OR NT -s, - → **Bändel**

be|ne|beln [bəˈneːbln] *ptp* **benebelt** VT *(inf)* **jdn** *or* **jds Sinne** *or* **jds Kopf ~** to make sb's head swim *or* reel; *(Narkose, Sturz)* to daze sb, to make sb feel dazed; **benebelt sein** to be feeling dazed *or (von Alkohol)* woozy *(inf)*

be|ne|dei|en [beneˈdaiən] VT *(Eccl)* to bless; *Gott* to glorify

Be|ne|dik|ti|ner [benedɪkˈtiːnɐ] M -s, - *(= Likör)* Benedictine

Be|ne|dik|ti|ner M -s, - *(Eccl)* Benedictine (friar/monk)

Be|ne|dik|ti|ne|rin [benedɪkˈtiːnərɪn] F -, -nen *(Eccl)* Benedictine (nun)

Be|ne|dik|ti|ner- *in cpds* Benedictine; **Be|ne|dik|ti|ner|klos|ter** NT Benedictine monastery

Be|ne|dik|tus [beneˈdɪktʊs] NT -, - *(Eccl)* Benedictus

Be|ne|fiz [beneˈfiːts] NT -es, -e benefit

Be|ne|fi|zi|um [beneˈfiːtsiʊm] NT -s, **Benefizien** [-tsiən] **a** benefice **b** *(Hist)* fee, feoff

Be|ne|fiz-: **Be|ne|fiz|kon|zert** NT charity *or* benefit concert; **Be|ne|fiz|spiel** NT benefit match; **Be|ne|fiz|vor|stel|lung** F charity performance

be|neh|men *ptp* **benommen** [bəˈnɔmən] *irreg* VR to behave; *(in Bezug auf Umgangsformen auch)* to behave oneself; **benimm dich!** behave yourself!; **sich gut ~** to behave oneself, to behave well; **sich schlecht ~** to behave (oneself) badly, to misbehave VT *(geh)* **a** *(= rauben)* to take away; **jdm den Atem ~** to take sb's breath away **b** *(rare: = die Sinne trüben)* **jdm die Sinne** *or* **den Kopf** *or* **jdn ~** to make sb feel dazed → *auch* **benommen**

Be|neh|men [bəˈneːmən] NT -s, *no pl* **a** behaviour *(Brit)*, behavior *(US)*; **kein ~ haben** to have no manners, to be bad-mannered **b** *(form: = Einvernehmen)* **sich mit jdm ins ~ setzen** to get in touch with sb; **im ~ mit jdm** in conjunction with sb

be|nei|den *ptp* **beneidet** VT to envy; **jdn um etw ~** to envy sb sth; **er ist nicht zu ~** I don't envy him

be|nei|dens|wert [bəˈnaidnsveːɐt] ADJ enviable ADV wonderfully; *reich* enviably; **~ naiv** *(iro)* amazingly naïve

Be|ne|lux [ˈbeːnelʊks, beneˈlʊks] *abbr von* **Belgien, Niederlande, Luxemburg**

Be|ne|lux|län|der [ˈbeːnelʊks-, beneˈlʊks-] PL, **Be|ne|lux|staa|ten** PL Benelux countries *pl*

be|nen|nen *ptp* **benannt** [bəˈnant] VT *irreg* to name; *jdn auch* to call; **jdn/etw nach jdm ~** to name *or* call sb/sth after *or* for *(US)* sb

Be|nen|nung F *(= das Benennen)* naming; *(von Mensch auch)* calling; *(= Bezeichnung)* name, designation *(form)*

be|net|zen *ptp* **benetzt** VT *(geh)* to moisten; *(Tau, Tränen auch)* to cover

Ben|ga|le [bɛŋˈgaːlə] M -n, -n, **Ben|ga|lin** [-ˈgaːlɪn] F -, -nen Bengalese, Bengali

Ben|ga|len [bɛŋˈgaːlən] NT -s Bengal

ben|ga|lisch [bɛŋˈgaːlɪʃ] ADJ **a** Bengalese; *Mensch, Sprache auch* Bengali **b ~es Feuer** Bengal light; **~es Hölzchen** Bengal match; **~e Beleuchtung** subdued multicoloured *(Brit) or* multicolored *(US)* lighting

Ben|gel [ˈbɛŋl] M -s, -(s) **a** boy, lad *(Brit inf)*; *(= frecher Junge)* rascal; **ein süßer ~** *(inf)* a dear little boy **b** *(dial: = Knüppel)* stick; **den ~ wegwerfen** *(dial)* to lose courage

Be|nimm [bəˈnɪm] M -s, *no pl (inf)* manners *pl*

Be|nimm|re|gel F *usu pl* etiquette *sing*; **eine ~** a rule of etiquette

Be|nin [beˈniːn] M -s Benin

Ben|ja|min [ˈbɛnjamiːn] M -s, -e Benjamin; **er ist der ~** he is the baby of the family

be|nom|men [bəˈnɔmən] ADJ dazed; *(von Ereignissen auch)* bemused → *auch* **benehmen**

Be|nom|men|heit F -, *no pl* daze, dazed state

be|no|ten [bəˈnoːtn] *ptp* **benotet** VT to mark *(Brit)*, to grade *(esp US)*; **etw mit „gut" ~** to mark *(Brit) or* grade *(esp US)* sth "good"

be|nö|ti|gen ✪ 37.1 *ptp* **benötigt** VT to need, to require; **das benötigte Geld** *etc* the necessary money *etc*, the money *etc* needed

Be|no|tung F -, -en mark *(Brit)*, grade *(esp US)*; *(= das Benoten)* marking *(Brit)*, grading *(esp US)*

be|nutz|bar ADJ usable; *Weg* passable

Be|nutz|bar|keit [bəˈnʊtsbaːɐkait] F -, *no pl* usability

be|nut|zen *ptp* **benutzt**, *(esp S Ger, Aus, Sw)* **be|nüt|zen** *ptp* **benützt** VT *(= verwenden)* to use; *Gelegenheit auch* to make use of, to take advantage of; *Literatur* to consult; **etw als Schlafzimmer/Vorwand ~** to use sth as a bedroom/an excuse; **das benutzte Geschirr** the dirty dishes

Be|nut|zer M -s, -, **Be|nut|ze|rin** F -, -nen user; *(von Leihbücherei)* borrower

Be|nüt|zer [bəˈnʏtsɐ] M **-s, -**, **Be|nüt|ze|rin** [-ərɪn] F **-, -nen** *(esp S Ger, Aus, Sw)* user; *(von Leihbücherei)* borrower

Be|nut|zer-: **Be|nut|zer|da|tei** F user-file; **be|nut|zer|de|fi|niert** ADJ *(Comput)* custom, user-defined; **be|nut|zer|freund|lich** ADJ *Computer, Telefonsystem* user-friendly ADV **etw ~ gestalten** to make sth user-friendly; **~ konzipiert/designt sein** to be conceived/designed to be user-friendly; **Be|nut|zer|freund|lich|keit** F user-friendliness; **Be|nut|zer|hand|buch** NT user's guide, user handbook

Be|nut|ze|rin F, **Be|nüt|ze|rin** [-ərɪn] F → **Benutzer, Benützer**

Be|nut|zer-: **Be|nut|zer|ken|nung** F *(Comput)* user identification, user ID; **Be|nut|zer|kenn|wort** NT *(Comput)* user password; **Be|nut|zer|kreis** M users *pl*; **Be|nut|zer|na|me** M *(Comput)* user name; **Be|nut|zer|ober|flä|che** F *(Comput)* user *or* system interface; **Be|nut|zer|pro|fil** NT *(Comput)* user profile; **Be|nut|zer|schnitt|stel|le** F *(Comput)* user interface; **Be|nut|zer|spra|che** F *(Comput)* user language; **Be|nut|zer|un|ter|stüt|zung** F *(Comput)* user support

Be|nut|zung F, *(esp S Ger, Aus, Sw)* **Be|nüt|zung** [bəˈnʏtsʊŋ] F **-, -en** use; **etw in ~ haben/nehmen** to be/start using sth; **jdm etw zur ~ überlassen** to put sth at sb's disposal; **etw zur ~ freigeben** *or* **bereitstellen** to open sth

Be|nut|zungs|ge|bühr F charge; *(= Leihgebühr)* hire charge

ben|zen [ˈbɛntsn] VI *(Aus inf)* **a** *(= betteln)* to beg **b** *(= klagen)* to complain

Ben|zin [bɛnˈtsiːn] NT **-s, -e** *(für Auto)* petrol *(Brit)*, gasoline *(US)*, gas *(US)*; *(= Reinigungsbenzin)* benzine; *(= Feuerzeugbenzin)* lighter fuel

Ben|zin-: **Ben|zin|ab|schei|der** [-lapʃaidɐ] M **-s, -** petrol *(Brit) or* gasoline *(US)* separator; **Ben|zin|ein|sprit|zung** F fuel injection

Ben|zi|ner [bɛnˈtsiːnɐ] M **-s, -** *(inf)* car which runs on petrol *(Brit) or* gasoline *(US)*

Ben|zin-: **Ben|zin|feu|er|zeug** NT petrol lighter *(Brit)*, gasoline lighter *(US)*; **Ben|zin|fres|ser** M *(inf)* petrol *or* fuel guzzler *(Brit)*, gas guzzler *(US)*; **Ben|zin|gut|schein** M petrol coupon *(Brit)*, gasoline coupon *(US)*; **Ben|zin|hahn** M fuel cock; **den ~ zudrehen** *(fig)* to stop the supply of petrol *(Brit) or* gasoline *(US)*; **Ben|zin|ka|nis|ter** M petrol can *(Brit)*, gasoline can *(US)*; **Ben|zin|kos|ten** PL fuel costs *pl*, petrol *(Brit) or* gas *(US)* costs *pl*; **Ben|zin|kos|ten|be|tei|li|gung** F **(gegen) ~** *(in Annonce)* share petrol *(Brit) or* gas *(US)* costs; **Ben|zin|lei|tung** F fuel pipe, petrol pipe *(Brit)*, gasoline pipe *(US)*; **Ben|zin|mo|tor** M petrol engine *(Brit)*, gasoline engine *(US)*; **Ben|zin|preis** M cost of petrol *(Brit) or* gas(oline) *(US)*, petrol *(Brit) or* gas *(US)* prices *pl*, cost *or* price of fuel; **Ben|zin|pum|pe** F *(Aut)* fuel pump; *(an Tankstellen)* petrol pump *(Brit)*, gasoline pump *(US)*; **Ben|zin|tank** M petrol *(Brit) or* gas *(US)* tank, fuel tank; **Ben|zin|uhr** F fuel gauge; **Ben|zin|ver|brauch** M fuel consumption, petrol consumption *(Brit)*, gasoline consumption *(US)*

Ben|zoe [ˈbɛntsoe] F **-**, *no pl* benzoin

Ben|zoe|säu|re F benzoic acid

Ben|zol [bɛnˈtsoːl] NT **-s, -e** benzol(e)

be|ob|acht|bar ADJ observable

be|ob|ach|ten [bəˈloːbaxtn] *ptp* **beobachtet** VT to observe; *(= bemerken auch)* to notice, to see; *(= genau verfolgen, betrachten auch)* to watch; **etw an jdm ~** to notice sth in sb; **jdn ~ lassen** *(Polizei etc)* to put sb under surveillance; **er wird von der Polizei beobachtet** he's under police surveillance; **sich beobachtet fühlen** to feel (as if) one is being watched

Be|ob|ach|ter [bəˈloːbaxtɐ] M **-s, -**, **Be|ob|ach|te|rin** [-ərɪn] F **-, -nen** observer

Be|ob|ach|ter-: **Be|ob|ach|ter|sta|tus** M *(form)* observer status; **bei einer Konferenz** *etc* **~ haben** to take part in a conference *etc* as an observer; **Be|ob|ach|ter|trup|pen** PL *(Mil)* observer force *sing*

Be|ob|ach|tung F **-, -en** observation; *(polizeilich)* surveillance; **die ~ habe ich oft gemacht** I've often noticed that; **bei der ~ der Vorgänge ...** as I *etc* observed *or* watched these developments ...

Be|ob|ach|tungs-: **Be|ob|ach|tungs|bal|lon** M observation balloon; **Be|ob|ach|tungs|ga|be** F talent for observation; **er hat eine gute ~** he has a very observant eye; **Be|ob|ach|tungs|pos|ten** M *(Mil)* observation post; *(= Mensch)* lookout; **auf ~ sein** to be on lookout duty; **Be|ob|ach|tungs|sa|tel|lit** M *(Mil)* observation satellite; **Be|ob|ach|tungs|sta|ti|on** F **a** *(Med)* observation ward; *(nach Operation)* postoperative ward **b** *(Met)* weather station; **Be|ob|ach|tungs|zeit|raum** M period of observation

be|or|dern *ptp* **beordert** VT to order; *(= kommen lassen)* to summon, to send for; *(an andern Ort)* to instruct *or* order to go; **jdn zu sich ~** to send for sb

be|pa|cken *ptp* **bepackt** VT to load (up); **jdn/etw mit etw ~** to load sb/sth up with sth VR to load oneself up

be|pflan|zen *ptp* **bepflanzt** VT to plant; **das Blumenbeet mit etw ~** to plant sth in the flower bed

Be|pflan|zung F **a** *(= das Bepflanzen)* planting **b** *(= Gesamtheit der Pflanzen)* plants *pl* (+*gen* in)

be|pflas|tern *ptp* **bepflastert** VT *Straße* to pave; *(fig: = behängen)* to plaster

be|pin|keln *ptp* **bepinkelt** *(inf)* VT to pee on *(inf)* VR to wet oneself *(inf)*

be|pin|seln *ptp* **bepinselt** VT to paint *(auch fig)*; *(Cook, Med)* to brush; *Zahnfleisch* to paint; *Wand* to brush down; *(= vollschreiben)* to scribble on

be|pis|sen *ptp* **bepisst** VT *(vulg)* to piss on *(sl)* VR **a** *(vulg: = urinieren)* to piss *(Brit sl) or* wet oneself **b** *(sl: = sich amüsieren)* to piss oneself (laughing) *(sl)*

Be|plan|kung [bəˈplaŋkʊŋ] F **-, -en** *(Tech)* planking

be|pu|dern *ptp* **bepudert** VT to powder *(auch fig)*

be|quas|seln *ptp* **bequasselt** VT *(inf)* to talk over

be|quat|schen [bəˈkvatʃn] *ptp* **bequatscht** VT *(inf)* **a** *etw* to talk over **b** *(= überreden) jdn* to persuade; **wir haben sie bequatscht, dass sie kommt** we talked her into coming

be|quem [bəˈkveːm] ADJ *(= angenehm)* comfortable; *Gast, Schüler etc* easy; *(= leicht, mühelos) Weg, Methode* easy; *Ausrede* convenient; *(= träge) Mensch* idle; **es ~ haben** to have an easy time of it; **es sich** *(dat)* **~ machen** to make oneself comfortable; **machen Sie es sich ~** make yourself at home ADV *(= leicht)* easily; *(= angenehm)* comfortably; **sich ~ tragen** to be comfortable to wear; **auf dem Stuhl sitzt es sich ~** this chair is comfortable to sit in

be|que|men [bəˈkveːmən] *ptp* **bequemt** VR **sich zu etw ~, sich (dazu) ~, etw zu tun** to bring oneself to do sth; **endlich bequemten sie sich nach Hause** they finally forced themselves to go home

be|quem|lich [bəˈkveːmlɪç] ADJ *(dated)* = **bequem**

Be|quem|lich|keit F **-, -en** **a** *no pl (= Behaglichkeit)* comfort; *(= Trägheit)* laziness; **aus (reiner) ~** out of (sheer) laziness **b** *(Einrichtung)* convenience

be|rap|pen [bəˈrapn] *ptp* **berappt** VTI *(inf)* to fork *or* shell out *(inf)*; **er musste schwer ~** he had to fork out a lot *(inf)*

be|ra|ten ✪ 29.2 *ptp* **beraten** *irreg* VT **a jdn ~** to advise sb, to give sb advice; **gut/schlecht ~ sein** to be well-advised/ill-advised; **jdn gut/schlecht ~** to give sb good/bad advice; **sich von jdm ~ lassen(, wie ...)** to ask sb's advice (on how ...), to consult sb (about how ...) **b** *(= besprechen)* to discuss VI to discuss; **mit jdm über etw** *(acc)* **~** to discuss sth with sb; **sie ~ noch** they are still in discussion, they are still discussing it VR *(= gegenseitig Rat spenden)* to give each other advice; *(= sich besprechen)* to discuss; **sich mit jdm ~** to consult (with) sb *(über +acc* about); **das Kabinett tritt heute zusammen, um sich zu ~** the cabinet meets today for talks

be|ra|tend ADJ advisory, consultative; *Ingenieur* consultant; **~es Gespräch** consultation; **er hat nur eine ~e Stimme** he is only in an advisory capacity ADV in an advisory capacity; **jdm ~ zur Seite stehen** to act in an advisory capacity to sb; **~ an einer Konferenz teilnehmen** to attend a conference in a consultative *or* an advisory capacity

Be|ra|ter [bəˈraːtɐ] M **-s, -**, **Be|ra|te|rin** [-ərɪn] F **-, -nen** adviser

Be|ra|ter-: **Be|ra|ter|fir|ma** F consulting *or* consultancy firm, firm of consultants; **Be|ra|ter|funk|ti|on** F advisory function; **Be|ra|ter|stab** M team of advisers, think tank *(inf)*; **Be|ra|ter|tä|tig|keit** F consultancy work; **Be|ra|ter|ver|trag** M consultancy contract

be|rat|schla|gen *ptp* **beratschlagt** VTI *insep* to discuss

Be|rat|schla|gung F **-, -en** discussion

Be|ra|tung [bəˈraːtʊŋ] F **-, -en** **a** *(= das Beraten)* advice; *(bei Rechtsanwalt, Arzt etc)* consultation **b** *(= Besprechung)* discussion; **eine ~ haben** *or* **abhalten** to have *or* hold talks *or* discussions

Be|ra|tungs-: **Be|ra|tungs|dienst** M advice *or* advisory service; *(esp Comm, Fin auch)* consultancy; **Be|ra|tungs|fir|ma** F consulting *or* consultancy firm, consultants *pl*; **Be|ra|tungs|ge|bühr** F consultancy fee; **Be|ra|tungs|ge|spräch** NT consultation; **Be|ra|tungs|stel|le** F advice centre *(Brit) or* center *(US)*; **Be|ra|tungs|zim|mer** NT consultation room

be|rau|ben *ptp* **beraubt** VT to rob; **jdn einer Sache** *(gen)* **~** to rob sb of sth; *seiner Freiheit, seines Rechtes* to deprive sb of sth; **aller Hoffnung beraubt** having lost all hope

be|rau|schen *ptp* **berauscht** VT *(= trunken machen)* to intoxicate; *(Alkohol etc auch)* to inebriate; *(Droge auch)* to make euphoric; *(= in Verzückung versetzen)* to intoxicate, to enrapture *(liter)*; *(Geschwindigkeit)* to exhilarate; *(Blut, Gräueltat etc)* to put in a frenzy; **der Erfolg hat ihn völlig berauscht** he was carried away *or* drunk with success; **von Glück/Leidenschaft berauscht ...** in transports of happiness/passion ...; **berauscht von dem Wein** intoxicated by the wine; **berauscht von der Poesie/den Klängen** intoxicated *or* enraptured by the poetry/the sounds VR **sich an etw** *(dat)* **~** *(an Wein, Drogen)* to become intoxicated with sth; *an Geschwindigkeit* to be exhilarated by sth; *an Blut, Gräueltat etc* to be in a frenzy over sth

be|rau|schend ADJ *Getränke, Drogen* intoxicating; **das war nicht sehr ~** *(iro)* that wasn't very enthralling *or* exciting

Ber|ber [ˈbɛrbɐ] M **-s, -** *(auch* **Berberteppich***)* Berber carpet

Ber|ber [ˈbɛrbɐ] M **-s, -**, **Ber|be|rin** [-ərɪn] F **-, -nen** **a** *(in Nordafrika)* Berber **b** *(sl: = Penner)* tramp, bum *(esp US inf)*, hobo *(US)*

Ber|be|rit|ze [bɛrbəˈrɪtsə] F **-, -n** *(Bot)* berberis

Ber|ber|tep|pich M Berber carpet

be|re|chen|bar ADJ *Kosten* calculable; *Verhalten etc* predictable

Be|re|chen|bar|keit [bəˈrɛçnbaːɐkait] F **-**, *no pl (von Kosten)* calculability; *(von Verhalten etc)* predictability

be|rech|nen *ptp* **berechnet** VT **a** *(= ausrechnen)* to calculate; *(= schätzen)* to estimate; *Worte, Gesten* to calculate the effect of; **alles, was sie tut, ist berechnet** everything she does is calculated **b** *(= in Rechnung stellen)* to charge; **das ~ wir Ihnen nicht** we will not charge you for it; **das hat er mir mit 75 Euro berechnet** he charged me 75 euros for it **c** *(= vorsehen)* to intend, to mean; **alle Rezepte sind für 4 Personen berechnet** all the recipes are (calculated) for 4 persons; **auf eine bestimmte Wirkung berechnet sein** to be intended *or* calculated to have a particular effect

be|rech|nend ADJ *(pej) Mensch* calculating

Be|rech|nung F **a** *(= das Berechnen)* calculation; *(= Schätzung)* estimation; **meiner ~ nach, nach meiner ~** according to my calculations, by my reckoning

b *(Comm: = Aufführen auf Rechnung)* charge; **ohne ~** without any charge

c *(pej: = Eigennutz)* **aus ~ handeln** to act in a calculating manner, to act calculatingly; **mit kühler ~ vorgehen** to act in a cool and calculating manner; **es war alles genaue ~** it was all calculated exactly; **er ist nur aus ~ so freundlich** *(= weil er etwas will)* he's only being so friendly because he wants something; **sie hat mir viel geholfen, aber nur aus ~** she helped me a lot, but only because she wanted something

Be|rech|nungs|grund|la|ge F basis of calculation; *(von Steuer)* basis of assessment

be|rech|ti|gen [bəˈrɛçtɪgn] *ptp* **berechtigt** VTI to entitle; **(jdn) zu etw ~** to entitle sb to sth; **diese Karte berechtigt nicht zum Eintritt** this ticket does not entitle the bearer to admittance; **er/seine Begabung berechtigt zu den größten Hoffnungen** he/his talent gives grounds for the greatest hopes; **das berechtigt zu der Annahme, dass …** this justifies the assumption that …

be|rech|tigt [bəˈrɛçtɪçt] ADJ justifiable; *Vorwurf auch* just; *Forderung, Einwand auch* justified; *Frage, Hoffnung* legitimate; *Anspruch* legitimate, rightful; **~ sein, etw zu tun** to be entitled to do sth; **einen ~en Anspruch auf etw** *(acc)* **haben** to have a legitimate *or* rightful claim to sth, to be fully entitled to sth

be|rech|tig|ter|wei|se [bəˈrɛçtɪçtɐˈvaizə] ADV legitimately; *(= verständlicherweise)* justifiably

Be|rech|ti|gung F -, -en **a** *(= Befugnis)* entitlement; *(= Recht)* right; **die ~/keine ~ haben, etw zu tun** to be entitled/not to be entitled to do sth **b** *(= Rechtmäßigkeit)* legitimacy; *(= Verständlichkeit)* justifiability

Be|rech|ti|gungs|schein M authorization

be|re|den *ptp* **beredet** VT **a** *(= besprechen)* to discuss, to talk over **b** *(= überreden)* **jdn zu etw ~** to talk sb into sth; **jdn dazu ~, etw zu tun** to talk sb into doing sth **c** *(inf: = beklatschen)* to gossip about VR **sich mit jdm über etw** *(acc)* **~** to talk sth over with sb, to discuss sth with sb; **die beiden haben sich miteinander beredet** the two of them talked it over

be|red|sam [bəˈreːtzaːm] ADJ *(geh)* eloquent; *(iro: = redselig)* talkative; **ein ~es Stück Geschichte** a telling period of history

Be|red|sam|keit F -, *no pl (geh)* eloquence

be|redt [bəˈreːt] *(geh)* ADJ eloquent; **mit ~en Worten** eloquently ADV eloquently; **~ Zeugnis von etw ablegen** to bear eloquent witness to sth

Be|redt|heit F -, *no pl (geh)* eloquence

be|reg|nen *ptp* **beregnet** VT to water, to sprinkle; *(vom Flugzeug aus)* to spray (with water); **beregnet werden** to be watered *etc*; *(natürlich)* to get rain

Be|reg|nung [bəˈreːgnʊŋ] F -, -en watering, sprinkling; *(vom Flugzeug aus)* spraying (with water); *(natürliche)* rain(fall)

Be|reg|nungs|an|la|ge F sprinkler

Be|reich [bəˈraiç] M -(e)s, -e **a** area; **in nördlicheren ~en** in more northerly regions; **im ~ der Kaserne** inside the barracks; **im ~ des Domes** in the precincts of the cathedral; **im ~ der Innenstadt** in the city centre *(Brit)* or center *(US)* (area) **b** *(= Einflussbereich, Aufgabenbereich)* sphere; *(= Sachbereich)* area, sphere, field; *(= Sektor)* sector; **im ~ des Möglichen liegen** to be within the realms *or* bounds of possibility; **Musik aus dem ~ der Oper** music from the realm of opera; **in jds ~** *(acc)* **fallen** to be within sb's province

be|rei|chern [bəˈraiçɐn] *ptp* **bereichert** VT *(lit, fig)* to enrich; *(= vergrößern)* to enlarge; **das Gespräch hat mich sehr bereichert** I gained a great deal from the conversation VR to make a lot of money *(an +dat* out of); **sich auf Kosten anderer ~** to feather one's nest at the expense of other people

Be|rei|che|rung F -, -en **a** *(= das Bereichern)* enrichment; *(= Vergrößerung)* enlargement; **persönliche ~** *(Jur)* personal gain; **~ im Amt** *(Jur)* exploiting one's position for personal gain **b** *(= das Reichwerden)* moneymaking; **seine eigene ~** making money for oneself **c** *(= Gewinn)* boon; **das Gespräch mit Ihnen war mir eine ~** I gained a lot from my conversation with you; **das ist eine wertvolle ~** that is a valuable addition

be|rei|fen *ptp* **bereift** VT *(Aut) Wagen* to put tyres *(Brit)* or tires *(US)* on; *Rad* to put a tyre *(Brit)* or tire *(US)* on; *Fass* to hoop; **gut/richtig bereift sein** *(Auto)* to have good/the right tyres *(Brit)* or tires *(US)*

Be|rei|fung [bəˈraifʊŋ] F -, -en *(Aut)* set of tyres *(Brit)* or tires *(US)*; **eine neue ~** new tyres *(Brit)* or tires *(US)*, a new set of tyres *(Brit)* or tires *(US)*; **die ~ bei diesem Auto** the tyres *(Brit)* or tires *(US)* on this car

be|rei|ni|gen *ptp* **bereinigt** VT to clear up, to resolve; *Meinungsverschiedenheiten auch* to settle; **ich habe mit ihr noch etwas zu ~** I have something to clear up with her; **die Sache hat sich von selbst bereinigt** the matter resolved itself, the matter cleared itself up; **den Markt ~** *(Comm euph)* to remove the competition from the market

be|rei|nigt [bəˈrainɪçt] ADJ *(= korrigiert) Statistik, Quote* adjusted

Be|rei|ni|gung F clearing up, resolving; *(von Meinungsverschiedenheit)* settling

be|rei|sen *ptp* **bereist** VT *ein Land* to travel around; *(Comm) Gebiet* to travel, to cover; **die Welt/fremde Länder ~** to travel the world/in foreign countries

be|reit [bəˈrait] ADJ *usu pred* **a** *(= fertig)* ready; *(= vorbereitet auch)* prepared; **es ist alles zum Essen ~** the meal is all ready *or* prepared; **es ist alles zum Aufbruch ~** we're all ready to go; **zum Einsatz ~e Truppen** troops ready *or* prepared to go into action → **bereithaben, bereithalten VR**

b *(= willens)* willing, prepared; **zu Zugeständnissen/Verhandlungen ~ sein** to be prepared to make concessions/to negotiate; **~ sein, etw zu tun** to be willing *or* prepared to do sth; **sich ~ zeigen, etw zu tun** to show oneself willing *or* prepared *or* ready to do sth; **sich ~ erklären, etw zu tun** to agree to do sth; **sich zu etw ~ finden** to be willing *or* prepared to do sth → **Schandtat**

be|rei|ten [bəˈraitn] *ptp* **bereitet** VT **a** *(= zubereiten)* (+dat for) to prepare; *Arznei* to make up; *Bett* to make (up) **b** *(= verursachen)* to cause; *Überraschung, Empfang, Freude, Kopfschmerzen* to give; **jdm Kummer/Ärger ~** to cause sb grief/trouble; **er hat mir Schwierigkeiten bereitet** he made difficulties for me; **das bereitet mir Schwierigkeiten** it causes me difficulties; **einer Sache** *(dat)* **ein Ende ~** to put an end to sth; **es bereitet mir (viel** *or* **ein großes) Vergnügen** *(form)* it gives me (the greatest) pleasure VR **sich zu etw ~** *(geh)* to prepare oneself for sth

be|rei|ten *ptp* **beritten** [bəˈrɪtn] VT *irreg Gebiet* to ride over

be|reit-: **be|reit+er|klä|ren** VR *sep* → **bereit b**; **be|reit+fin|den** VR *sep* → **bereit b**; **be|reit+ha|ben** VT *sep irreg* **eine Antwort/Ausrede ~** to have an answer/excuse ready, to have a ready answer/excuse; **be|reit+hal|ten** *sep irreg* VT *Fahrkarten etc* to have ready; *(für den Notfall)* to keep ready; *Überraschung* to have in store; **wer weiß, was das Schicksal für uns bereithält?** who knows what fate has in store for us? VR **sich ~** to be ready *or* prepared; **be|reit+le|gen** VT *sep* to lay out ready; **be|reit+lie|gen** VI *sep irreg* to be ready; **be|reit ma|chen**, **be|reit+ma|chen** *sep* VT to get ready

be|reits [bəˈraits] ADV already; **~ vor drei Wochen/vor 100 Jahren** even three weeks/100 years ago; **~ damals/damals, als …** even then/when …; **das haben wir ~ gestern** *or* **gestern ~ gemacht** we did that yesterday; **er ist ~ vor zwei Stunden angekommen** he arrived two hours ago; **ich warte ~ seit einer Stunde** I've (already) been waiting for an hour; **der Bus ist ~ abgefahren** the bus has already left; **das hat man mir ~ gesagt** I've been told that already; **~ am nächsten Tage** on the very next day

Be|reit|schaft [bəˈraitʃaft] F -, -en **a** *no pl* readiness; *(= Bereitwilligkeit auch)* willingness, preparedness; **in ~ sein** to be ready; *(Polizei, Feuerwehr, Soldaten etc)* to be on stand-by; *(Arzt)* to be on call *or (im Krankenhaus)* on duty; **etw in ~ haben** to have sth ready *or* in readiness **b** *no pl (= Bereitschaftsdienst)* **~ haben** *(Arzt etc)* to be on call *or (im Krankenhaus)* on duty; *(Apotheke)* to provide emergency *or* after-hours service; *(Polizei etc)* to be on stand-by **c** *(= Mannschaft)* squad

Be|reit|schafts-: **Be|reit|schafts|arzt** M, **Be|reit|schafts|ärz|tin** F doctor on call; *(im Krankenhaus)* duty doctor; **Be|reit|schafts|dienst** M emergency service; **~ haben** → **Bereitschaft b**; **Be|reit|schafts|po|li|zei** F riot police

Be|reit-: **be|reit+ste|hen** VI *sep irreg* to be ready; *(Flugzeug auch, Truppen)* to stand by; **die Truppen stehen bereit** the troops are standing by; **etw ~ haben** to have sth ready; **Ihr Wagen steht bereit** your car is waiting; **zur Abfahrt ~** to be ready to depart; **be|reit+stel|len** VT *sep* to get ready; *Material, Fahrzeug, Mittel* to provide, to supply; *(Rail)* to make available; *Truppen* to put on stand-by; **Be|reit|stel|lung** F preparation; *(von Auto, Material, Mitteln)* provision, supply; *(von Truppen)* putting on stand-by

Be|rei|tung [bəˈraitʊŋ] F -, -en preparation

Be|reit-: **be|reit|wil|lig** ADJ *(= entgegenkommend)* willing; *(= eifrig)* eager; **~e Auskunft erteilen** to give information willingly ADV willingly; *annehmen, Auskunft erteilen* gladly; **Be|reit|wil|lig|keit** F *(= Entgegenkommen)* willingness; *(= Eifer)* eagerness

be|ren|nen *ptp* **berannt** VT *irreg (Mil)* to charge, to assault; *(Sport)* to rush, to storm

be|ren|ten [bəˈrɛntn] *ptp* **berentet** VT *(Admin sl)* **berentet werden** to retire and receive a pension; **sich ~ lassen** to retire with a pension

Bé|ret [beˈrɛ] NT -s, -s, **Be|ret** NT -s, -s *(Sw)* beret

be|reu|en *ptp* **bereut** VT to regret; *Schuld, Sünden* to repent of; **~, etw getan zu haben** to regret having done sth; **das wirst du noch ~!** you will be sorry (for that)! VI to repent

Berg [bɛrk] M -(e)s, -e [-gə] **a** hill; *(größer)* mountain; **wenn der ~ nicht zum Propheten kommt, muss der Prophet zum ~ kommen** *(Prov)* if the mountain won't come to Mahomet, then Mahomet must go to the mountain *(Prov)*; **~e versetzen (können)** to (be able to) move mountains; **~e versetzend** *(Glaube)* colossal; **mit etw hinterm ~ halten** *(fig)* to keep sth to oneself, to keep quiet about sth; *mit seinem Alter* to be cagey about sth; **in die ~e fahren** to go to the hills *etc*; **über ~ und Tal** up hill and down dale; **über den ~ sein** *(inf)* to be out of the woods; **über alle ~e sein** *(inf)* to be long gone, to be miles away *(inf)*; **jdm goldene ~e versprechen** to promise sb the moon; **die Haare standen ihm zu ~e** his hair stood on end; **da stehen ei-**

nem ja die Haare zu ~e it's enough to make your hair stand on end; **am ~ sein** *(Sw fig: = ratlos)* to be in the dark → **Ochs a**
b *(= große Menge)* heap, pile; *(von Sorgen)* mass; *(von Papieren)* mountain, heap, pile
c *(inf: = Bergwerk)* pit; **im ~ arbeiten** to work down the pit

Bẹrg- *in cpds* mountain; *(= Bergbau-)* mining; **bẹrg|ab** [bɛrkˈlap] ADV downhill; **es geht mit ihm ~** *(fig)* he is going downhill; **Bẹrg|ab|hang** M side of a mountain, mountainside; **Bẹrg|ab|satz** M ledge; **Bẹrg|ab|sturz** M drop; **bẹrg|ab|wärts** [bɛrkˈlapvɛrts] ADV downhill; **Bẹrg|ahorn** M sycamore (tree); **Bẹrg|aka|de|mie** F mining college

Ber|ga|mọt|te [bɛrgaˈmɔtə] F **-, -n** bergamot

Bẹrg-: **Bẹrg|amt** NT mining authority; **berg|ạn** [bɛrkˈlan] ADV = **bergauf(wärts)**; **Bẹrg|ar|bei|ter(in)** M(F) miner; **berg|auf|(wärts)** [bɛrkˈlauf(vɛrts)] ADV uphill; **es geht wieder bergauf** *(fig)* things are getting better *or* looking up; **es geht mit seinem Geschäft/seiner Gesundheit wieder bergauf** his business/health is looking up; **Bẹrg|bahn** F mountain railway; *(= Seilbahn)* funicular *or* cable railway; **Bẹrg|bau** M, *no pl* mining; **Bẹrg|bau|er** M mountain farmer; **Bẹrg|bäu|e|rin** F (female) mountain farmer; **Bẹrg|be|woh|ner(in)** M(F) mountain dweller; **Bẹrg|dorf** NT mountain village

bẹr|ge|hoch ADJ, ADV = **berghoch**

Bẹr|ge|lohn M *(Naut)* salvage (money)

bẹr|gen [ˈbɛrgn] *pret* **barg** [bark], *ptp* **geborgen** [gəˈbɔrgn] VT **a** *(= retten) Menschen* to save, to rescue; *Leichen* to recover; *Ladung, Schiff, Fahrzeug* to salvage; *Ernte* to get *or* gather (in); *(Naut) Segel* to furl; **aus dem Wasser tot/lebend geborgen werden** to be brought out of the water dead/alive; **25 Passagiere konnten lebend geborgen werden** *(nach Flugzeugabsturz)* 25 passengers were brought out alive
b *(geh: = enthalten)* to hold; *Schätze auch* to hide; **das birgt viele Gefahren in sich** that holds many dangers; **diese Möglichkeit birgt die Gefahr/das Risiko in sich, dass ...** this possibility involves the danger/risk that ...
c *(liter: = verbergen) Gesicht* to hide; *Verfolgten etc* to shelter; **sie barg ihren Kopf an seiner Schulter** she buried her face in his shoulder → *auch* **geborgen**

bẹr|ge-: **bẹr|ge|ver|set|zend** ADJ → **Berg a**; **bẹr|ge|weise** ADV by the ton

Bẹrg-: **Bẹrg|fach** NT mining; **Bẹrg|fahrt** F **a** mountaineering *or* climbing expedition; **auf ~ gehen** to go mountaineering *etc or* on a mountaineering *etc* expedition **b** *(auf Fluss)* upstream passage; *(von Seilbahn)* uphill *or* upward journey; **Bẹrg|fex** M *(inf)* mountaineering enthusiast *or* freak *(inf)*; **Bẹrg|fried** [ˈbɛrkfriːt] M **-(e)s, -e** [-də] keep; **Bẹrg|füh|rer(in)** M(F) mountain guide; **Bẹrg|geist** M mountain troll; **Bẹrg|gip|fel** M mountain top; **Bẹrg|grat** M mountain ridge; **Bẹrg|hang** M mountain slope; **bẹrg|hoch** ADJ *Wellen, Haufen* mountainous; **berghoher Müll** mountains of rubbish ADV **die Wellen stiegen ~** the waves reached mountainous heights; **der Müll türmt sich ~** mountains of rubbish are piling up; **die Akten stapeln sich schon ~** the files are already piling up a mile high; **Bẹrg|hüt|te** F mountain hut *or* refuge, bothy *(Scot)*

bẹr|gig [ˈbɛrgɪç] ADJ hilly; *(= mit hohen Bergen)* mountainous

Bẹrg-: **Bẹrg|in|ge|ni|eur(in)** M(F) mining engineer; **Bẹrg|kamm** M mountain crest; **Bẹrg|kes|sel** M cirque, corrie; **Bẹrg|ket|te** F mountain range *or* chain, range *or* chain of mountains; **bẹrg|krank** ADJ affected by mountain sickness; **Bẹrg|krank|heit** F mountain sickness; **Bẹrg|krax|ler** [-kraksle] M **-s, -**, **Bẹrg|krax|le|rin** [-ərɪn] F **-, -nen** *(esp Aus inf)* mountaineer; **Bẹrg|kris|tall** M rock crystal; **Bẹrg|kup|pe** F (round) mountain top; **Bẹrg|land** NT hilly *or (= Gebirgsland)* mountainous country; *(= Gegend)* hilly/mountainous region; *(= Landschaft)* hilly/mountainous scenery; **Bẹrg|luft** F mountain air

Bẹrg|mann M *pl* **-leute** miner

bẹrg|män|nisch [-mɛnɪʃ] ADJ miner's *attr*

Bẹrg|manns-: **Bẹrg|manns|gruß** M miner's greeting; **Bẹrg|manns|spra|che** F mining terminology

Bẹrg-: **Bẹrg|not** F **in ~ sein/geraten** to be in/get into difficulties while climbing; **jdn aus ~ retten** to rescue sb who was in difficulties while climbing; **Bẹrg|pfad** M mountain path; **Bẹrg|pla|teau** NT mountain plateau; **Bẹrg|pre|digt** F *(Bibl)* Sermon on the Mount; **bẹrg|reich** ADJ mountainous; **Bẹrg|ren|nen** NT *(Sport)* hill climbing; **ein ~** a hill climb; **Bẹrg|ret|tungs|dienst** M mountain rescue service; **Bẹrg|rie|se** M gigantic mountain; **Bẹrg|rü|cken** M mountain ridge *or* crest; **Bẹrg|rutsch** M landslide *(auch fig)*, landslip; **Bẹrg|sat|tel** M (mountain) saddle, col; **Bẹrg|schrund** M bergschrund *(spec)*; **Bẹrg|schuh** M climbing boot; **bẹrg|seits** [ˈbɛrkzaits], **bẹrg|sei|tig** ADV on the mountain side; **Bẹrg|spit|ze** F mountain peak; **Bẹrg|sport** M mountaineering, mountain climbing; **Bẹrg|sta|ti|on** F top station, summit station; **bẹrg+stei|gen** VI *sep irreg aux sein or haben, infin and ptp only* to go mountain climbing *or* mountaineering, to mountaineer; **~ gehen** to go mountain climbing *or* mountaineering; **(das) Bergsteigen** mountaineering, mountain climbing; **Bẹrg|stei|ger(in)** M(F) mountaineer, mountain climber; **Bẹrg|stei|ge|rei** [bɛrkʃtaigəˈrai] F **-, -en** *(inf)* mountaineering, mountain climbing; **bẹrg|stei|ge|risch** [ˈbɛrkʃtaigərɪʃ] ADJ mountaineering, mountain-climbing ADV from a mountaineering point of view; **Bẹrg|stock** M **a** *(= Wanderstock)* hiking pole, alpenstock **b** *(Geol)* massif; **Bẹrg|stra|ße** F mountain road; **die ~** *(Geog) wine-producing area north of Heidelberg*

> **BERGSTRASSE**
>
> The **Bergstraße** is a region on the western edge of the Odenwald between Darmstadt and Wiesloch (near Heidelberg). The Romans built a road here and even today the B3 road follows its route. Most of the settlements along the **Bergstraße** date back to Roman and Frankish times. The area is remarkable for its extremely mild climate and fertile soil, and is consequently renowned for the cultivation of fruit and vegetables. As the name suggests, the **Bergstraße** runs along the foot of a mountain range, whose slopes provide ideal conditions for wine-growing. Attractive countryside and picturesque towns and villages have made the **Bergstraße** a popular tourist destination.

Bẹrg-: **Bẹrg|sturz** M landslide, landslip; **Bẹrg|tour** F trip round the mountains; *(= Bergbesteigung)* (mountain) climb; **Bẹrg-und-Tạl-Bahn** F roller coaster, big dipper *(Brit)*, switchback *(Brit)*; **Bẹrg-und-Tạl-Fahrt** F ride on the roller coaster *etc*; **das war die reinste ~** *(fig)* it was like being on a roller coaster

Bẹr|gung F **-, -en a** *(von Menschen)* saving, rescue; *(von Leiche)* recovery; *(von Ladung, Schiff, Fahrzeug)* salvage, salvaging; *(von Ernte)* gathering (in) **b** *(liter: von Verfolgten)* sheltering

Bẹr|gungs-: **Bẹr|gungs|ak|ti|on** F rescue operation; *(bei Schiffen etc)* salvage operation; **Bẹr|gungs|ar|bei|ten** PL rescue work *sing*; *(bei Schiffen etc)* salvage work *sing or* operation *sing*; **Bẹr|gungs|damp|fer** M salvage vessel; **Bẹr|gungs|fahr|zeug** NT rescue vehicle; *(bei Flugzeugabsturz auch)* crash vehicle; *(Naut)* salvage vessel; **Bẹr|gungs|hub|schrau|ber** M rescue helicopter; **Bẹr|gungs|kom|man|do** NT *(esp Mil)*, **Bẹr|gungs|mann|schaft** F rescue team; **Bẹr|gungs|schiff** NT salvage vessel, **Bẹr|gungs|trupp** M rescue team

Bẹrg-: **Bẹrg|volk** NT **a** mountain race **b** *(rare: = Bergleute)* miners *pl*; **Bẹrg|vor|sprung** M (mountain) ledge; **Bẹrg|wacht** F mountain rescue service; **Bẹrg|wald** M mountain forest *or* wood(s *pl*); **Bẹrg|wand** F mountain face; **Bẹrg|wan|dern** NT mountain hiking; **Bẹrg|wan|de|rung** F walk *or* hike in the mountains; **bẹrg|wärts** [ˈbɛrkvɛrts] ADV uphill; **Bẹrg|welt** F mountains *pl*; **Bẹrg|werk** NT mine; **im ~ arbeiten** to work down the mine; **Bẹrg|wie|se** F mountain pasture; **Bẹrg|zin|ne** F *(geh)* mountain pinnacle

Be|ri|be|ri [beriˈbeːri] F **-**, *no pl (Med)* beriberi

Be|rịcht [bəˈrɪçt] M **-(e)s, -e** report *(von* on, *über +acc* about, on); *(= Erzählung auch)* account; *(= Zeitungsbericht auch)* story; *(Sch: = Aufsatzform)* commentary; **der ~ eines Augenzeugen** an eyewitness account; **~e zum Tagesgeschehen** news reports; **eigener ~** from our correspondent; **(über etw** *acc***) ~ erstatten** to report (on sth), to give a report (on sth); **jdm über etw** *(acc)* **~ erstatten** to give sb a report on sth

be|rịch|ten *ptp* **berichtet** VTI to report; *(= erzählen)* to tell; **jdm über etw** *(acc)* **~** to report to sb about sth; *(= erzählen)* to tell sb about sth; **mir ist (darüber) berichtet worden, dass ...** I have received reports that ..., I have been told that ...; **uns wird soeben berichtet, dass ...** *(Rad, TV)* news is just coming in that ...; **wie unser Korrespondent berichtet** according to our correspondent; **wie soeben berichtet wird, sind die Verhandlungen abgebrochen worden** we are just receiving reports that negotiations have been broken off; **gibt es Neues zu ~?** has anything new happened?; **sie berichtete, dass ...** she said *or* reported that ...; **sie hat bestimmt viel(es) zu ~** she is sure to have a lot to tell us

Be|rịcht-: **Be|rịcht|er|stat|ter** [bəˈrɪçtlɛɐʃtatɐ] M **-s, -**, **Be|rịcht|er|stat|te|rin** [-ərɪn] F **-, -nen** reporter; *(= Korrespondent)* correspondent; **~ ist ...** *(bei Jahresversammlung etc)* the report will be given by ...; **Be|rịcht|er|stat|tung** F reporting; **eine objektive ~** objective reporting; **~ durch Presse/Rundfunk** press/radio reporting; **die ~ über diese Vorgänge in der Presse** press coverage of these events; **zur ~ zurückgerufen werden** to be called back to report *or* to make a report

be|rịch|ti|gen [bəˈrɪçtɪgn] ✪ 47.5 *ptp* **berichtigt** VT to correct; *Fehler auch* to rectify; *(Jur)* to rectify; *Text, Aussage auch* to amend

Be|rịch|ti|gung F **-, -en** correction; *(von Fehler auch, Jur)* rectification; *(von Text, Aussage auch)* amendment

Be|rịch|ti|gungs|ak|tie F *(St Ex)* bonus share

Be|rịchts-: **Be|rịchts|heft** NT apprentice's record book; **Be|rịchts|jahr** NT *(Comm)* year under review *or* report; **Be|rịchts|zeug|nis** NT *(Sch)* (school) report *(giving a written assessment of the pupil's work rather than grades)*, report card *(US, Scot)*

be|rie|chen *ptp* **berochen** [bəˈrɔxn] VT *irreg* to sniff at, to smell; **sich (gegenseitig) ~** *(fig inf)* to size each other up

be|rie|seln *ptp* **berieselt** VT **a** *(mit Flüssigkeit)* to spray with water *etc*; *(durch Sprinkleranlage)* to sprinkle **b** *(fig inf)* **von etw berieselt werden** *(fig)* to be exposed to a constant stream of sth; **sich von Musik ~ lassen** to have (a constant stream of) music going on in the background

Be|rie|se|lung [bəˈriːzəlʊŋ] F **-, -en** watering; **die ständige ~ der Kunden mit Musik/Werbung** exposing the customers to a constant stream of music/advertisements; **die ~ mit** *or* **durch etw** *(fig)* the constant stream of sth

Be|rie|se|lungs|an|la|ge F sprinkler (system)

be|rịn|gen *ptp* **beringt** VT to put a ring on; *Vogel auch* to ring; **mit Diamanten beringte Finger** fingers ringed with diamonds

Be|ring|meer [ˈbeːrɪŋ-] NT Bering Sea

Be|ring|stra|ße [ˈbeːrɪŋ-] F Bering Strait(s *pl*)

Be|rin|gung [bəˈrɪŋʊŋ] F -, -en putting a ring on; *(von Vogel auch)* ringing; *(= Ring)* ring

be|rit|ten [bəˈrɪtn] ADJ mounted, on horseback; **~e Polizei** mounted police

Ber|ke|li|um [bɛrˈkeːliʊm] NT -s, *no pl* (*abbr* **Bk**) berkelium

Ber|lin [bɛrˈliːn] NT -s Berlin

Ber|li|ner [bɛrˈliːnɐ] ADJ *attr* Berlin; **~ Weiße (mit Schuss)** *light, fizzy beer (with fruit juice added)*

Ber|li|ner [bɛrˈliːnɐ] M -s, - *(auch* **Berliner Pfannkuchen***)* doughnut *(Brit)*, donut *(US)*

Ber|li|ner [bɛrˈliːnɐ] M -s, -, **Ber|li|ne|rin** [-ərɪn] F -, -nen Berliner

ber|li|ne|risch [bɛrˈliːnərɪʃ] ADJ *(inf) Dialekt* Berlin *attr*; **er spricht Berlinerisch** he speaks the Berlin dialect

ber|li|nern [bɛrˈliːnɐn] *ptp* **berlinert** VI *(inf)* to speak in the Berlin dialect

ber|li|nisch [bɛrˈliːnɪʃ] ADJ Berlin *attr*

Ber|mu|da|drei|eck [bɛrˈmuːda-] NT Bermuda triangle

Ber|mu|da|in|seln [bɛrˈmuːda-] PL, **Ber|mu|das** [bɛrˈmuːdas] PL Bermuda *sing, no def art*; **auf den ~** in Bermuda, in the Bermudas

Ber|mu|das [bɛrˈmuːdas] PL, **Ber|mu|da|shorts** [bɛrˈmuːda-] PL Bermuda shorts *pl*, Bermudas *pl*

Bern [bɛrn] NT -s Bern(e)

Ber|ner [ˈbɛrnɐ] ADJ *attr* Berne(se)

Ber|ner [ˈbɛrnɐ] M -s, -, **Ber|ne|rin** [-ərɪn] F -, -nen Bernese

Bern|har|di|ner [bɛrnharˈdiːnɐ] M -s, - Saint Bernard (dog)

Bern|stein [ˈbɛrnʃtain] M, *no pl* amber

bern|stein|far|ben [-farbn], **bern|stein|gelb** ADJ amber(-coloured) *(Brit)*, amber(-colored) *(US)*

be|rockt [bəˈrɔkt] ADJ *(hum)* (dressed) in a skirt

Ber|ser|ker [bɛrˈzɛrkɐ, ˈbɛrzɛrkɐ] M -s, - *(Hist)* berserker; **wie ein ~ arbeiten/kämpfen** to work/fight like mad *(inf)* or fury; **wie ein ~ toben** to go berserk; **auf jdn einschlagen wie ein ~** to go berserk and attack sb

bers|ten [ˈbɛrstn] *pret* **barst** [barst], *ptp* **geborsten** [gəˈbɔrstn] VI *aux sein (geh)* to crack; *(= aufbersten, zerbrechen)* to break; *(= zerplatzen)* to burst; *(fig: vor Wut etc)* to burst *(vor* with*)*; **als wollte ihm das Herz in der Seele ~** as if his heart would burst; **die Erde barst** the earth broke asunder *(liter)*; **vor Ungeduld/Neugier/Zorn** *etc* **~** to be bursting with impatience/curiosity/anger *etc*; **zum Bersten voll** *(auch inf)* full to bursting

Berst|schutz M *(im Kernreaktor)* safety containment

be|rüch|tigt [bəˈrʏçtɪçt] ADJ notorious, infamous

be|rü|cken *ptp* **berückt** VT *(geh)* to charm, to enchant

be|rü|ckend ADJ charming, enchanting; **das ist nicht gerade ~** *(iro inf)* it's not exactly stunning

be|rück|sich|ti|gen [bəˈrʏkzɪçtɪgn] *ptp* **berücksichtigt** VT *(= beachten, bedenken)* to take into account *or* consideration; *Mangel, Alter, geringe Erfahrung, körperliches Leiden* to make allowances for; *(= in Betracht ziehen) Antrag, Bewerbung, Bewerber* to consider; **das ist zu ~** that must be taken into account *or* consideration; **meine Vorschläge wurden nicht berücksichtigt** my suggestions were disregarded

Be|rück|sich|ti|gung F -, -en consideration; **in** *or* **unter ~ der Umstände/der Tatsache, dass …** in view of the circumstances/the fact that …; **eine ~ Ihres Antrags ist zurzeit nicht möglich** it is impossible for us to consider your application at present

Be|ruf [bəˈruːf] M *(= Tätigkeit)* occupation; *(akademischer auch)* profession; *(handwerklicher)* trade; *(= Stellung)* job; **freie ~e** independent professions; **was sind Sie von ~?** what is your occupation *etc*?, what do you do for a living?; **von ~ Arzt/Bäcker/Hausfrau sein** to be a doctor by profession/a baker by *or* to *(Brit)* trade/a housewife by occupation; **ihr stehen viele ~e offen** many careers are open to her; **seinen ~ verfehlt haben** to have missed one's vocation; **im ~ stehen** to be working; **von ~s wegen** on account of one's job

be|ru|fen [bəˈruːfn] *ptp* **berufen** *irreg* VT **a** *(= ernennen, einsetzen)* to appoint; **jdn auf einen Lehrstuhl/zu einem Amt ~** to appoint sb to a chair/an office **b** *(old: = kommen lassen)* **jdn zu sich/an einen Ort ~** to call *or* summon sb to one/to a place; **Gott hat ihn zu sich ~** he has been called to his Maker **c** *(inf: = beschwören)* **ich will/wir wollen** *etc* **es nicht ~** touch wood *(Brit inf)*, knock on wood *(US inf)*; **ich will es nicht ~, aber …** I don't want to tempt fate, but … **d** *(dial: = ermahnen)* to tell off, to reproach
VR **sich auf jdn/etw ~** to refer to sb/sth
VI *(Aus Jur: = Berufung einlegen)* to appeal

be|ru|fen [bəˈruːfn] ADJ **a** *(= befähigt) Kritiker* competent, capable; **von ~er Seite, aus ~em Mund** from an authoritative source; **zu etw ~ sein, ~ sein, etw zu tun** to be competent to do sth **b** *(= ausersehen)* **zu etw ~ sein** to have a vocation for sth; *(esp Rel)* to be called to sth; **viele sind ~** *(Bibl)* many are called; **sich zu etw ~ fühlen** to feel one has a mission to be/do sth

be|ruf|lich [bəˈruːflɪç] ADJ *(esp auf akademische Berufe bezüglich)* professional; *Weiterbildung auch* job- *or* career-orientated; **sein ~er Werdegang** his career; **im ~en Leben** in my *etc* working life, in my *etc* career; **meine ~en Probleme** my problems at work *or* in my job; **was das Berufliche betrifft, bin ich zufrieden** as far as my job is concerned I am satisfied
ADV professionally, jobwise; **~ ist sie sehr erfolgreich** she is very successful in her career; **sich ~ weiterbilden** to undertake further job- *or* career-orientated *or* professional training; **er ist ~ viel unterwegs** he is away a lot on business; **sich ~ verbessern** to get a better job; **was machen Sie ~?** what do you do for a living?; **er ist ~ Elektriker** he's an electrician by *or* to *(Brit)* trade

Be|rufs- *in cpds* professional; **Berufs|all|tag** M (everyday) working life; **Be|rufs|an|fän|ger(in)** M(F) **sie ist ~in** she has just entered the job market; **wir suchen Lexikografen, keine ~** vacancies for lexicographers, experience necessary; **Be|rufs|auf|bau|schu|le** F *vocational school preparing adult learners for technical college*; **Be|rufs|aus|bil|dung** F training *(for an occupation)*; *(für Handwerk)* vocational training; **Be|rufs|aus|bil|dungs|bei|hil|fe** F *supplementary allowance for people on vocational training courses*; **Be|rufs|aus|sich|ten** PL job prospects *pl*; **Be|rufs|aus|ü|bung** F pursuit of one's career; **jdm die ~ untersagen** not to allow sb to pursue his *or* her career, to exclude sb from his *or* her profession; **Be|rufs|be|am|ten|tum** NT civil service with tenure; **Be|rufs|be|am|te(r)** M *decl as adj*, **Be|rufs|be|am|tin** F civil servant with tenure; **be|rufs|be|dingt** ADJ occupational, caused by one's occupation; **be|rufs|be|glei|tend** ADJ in tandem with work; **ein ~es Studium absolvieren** to complete a course of study while working; **Be|rufs|be|ra|ter(in)** M(F) careers adviser; **Be|rufs|be|ra|tung** F careers guidance; **Be|rufs|be|zeich|nung** F job title; **be|rufs|be|zo|gen** [-bətsoːgn] ADJ relevant to one's job; *Unterricht* vocationally orientated ADV practically orientated; **Be|rufs|bild** NT job outline; **be|rufs|bil|dend** ADJ **~e Schulen** vocational schools; **Be|rufs|bil|dungs|zen|trum** NT job training centre *(Brit) or* center *(US)*; **Be|rufs|boxen** NT professional boxing; **Be|rufs|chan|cen** [-ʃãːsn] PL job *or* career prospects *pl*; **be|rufs|er|fah|ren** ADJ (professionally) experienced; **Be|rufs|er|fah|rung** F (professional) experience; **Be|rufs|ethos** NT professional ethics *pl*; **Be|rufs|fach|schu|le** F training college *(attended full-time)*; **Be|rufs|feu|er|wehr** F fire service; **Be|rufs|frei|heit** F freedom to choose and carry out one's career; **be|rufs|fremd** ADJ *Tätigkeit* unconnected with one's occupation; *Mensch* from outside the/a profession/trade; **eine ~e Tätigkeit** a job outside one's profession; *(handwerklich)* a job outside one's trade; **Be|rufs|frem|de(r)** MF *decl as adj* person from outside the/a profession/trade; **Be|rufs|fuß|ball** M professional football *(Brit) or* soccer *(US)*; **Be|rufs|ge|heim|nis** NT professional secret; *(= Schweigepflicht)* professional secrecy, confidentiality; **das ~ wahren** to observe professional secrecy *or* confidentiality; **Be|rufs|ge|nos|sen|schaft** F → **Beruf** professional/trade association; **Be|rufs|grup|pe** F occupational group; **Be|rufs|heer** NT professional *or* regular army; **Be|rufs|klei|dung** F working clothes *pl*; **Be|rufs|krank|heit** F occupational disease; **Be|rufs|kri|mi|na|li|tät** F professional crime; **Be|rufs|le|ben** NT working *or* professional life; **im ~ stehen** to be working, to be in employment; **be|rufs|los** ADJ → **Beruf** without a profession/trade; **be|rufs|mä|ßig** ADJ professional ADV professionally; **etw ~ betreiben** to do sth professionally, to do sth on a professional basis; **Be|rufs|of|fi|zier(in)** M(F) regular officer; **Be|rufs|per|spek|ti|ve** F job *or* career prospects *pl*; **Be|rufs|pflicht** F professional duty; **Be|rufs|po|li|ti|ker(in)** M(F) professional *or* career politician; **Be|rufs|prak|ti|kum** NT (practical) work experience; *(von Arzt, Lehrer etc)* practical *(Brit)*; **Be|rufs|re|vo|lu|ti|o|när(in)** M(F) *(esp pej)* professional revolutionary; **Be|rufs|ri|si|ko** NT occupational hazard *or* risk; **Be|rufs|schu|le** F vocational school, ≈ technical college *(Brit)*; **Be|rufs|schü|ler(in)** M(F) student at a vocational school, ≈ student at a technical college *(Brit)*; **Be|rufs|sol|dat(in)** M(F) regular *or* professional soldier; **Be|rufs|spie|ler(in)** M(F) professional player; **Be|rufs|sport** M professional sport; **Be|rufs|sport|ler(in)** M(F) professional sportsman/-woman; **Be|rufs|stand** M profession, professional group; *(= Gewerbe)* trade; **Be|rufs|start** M **ein erfolgreicher ~** a successful start to his/her *etc* career; **be|rufs|tä|tig** ADJ working; **~ sein** to be working, to work; **halbtags ~ sein** to work part-time; **ich bin auch ~** I go out to work too; **nicht mehr ~ sein** to have left work; **Be|rufs|tä|ti|ge(r)** [-tɛːtɪgə] MF *decl as adj* working person; **Be|rufs|tä|tig|keit** F *(= Ausübung eines Berufs)* occupation; **während meiner ~** during my working life; **Frauen** *(dat)* **die ~ ermöglichen** to enable women to go out to work; **Bewerber sollten eine dreijährige ~ nachweisen können** applicants should be able to provide proof of three years' work experience; **be|rufs|un|fä|hig** ADJ occupationally disabled; **Be|rufs|un|fä|hig|keit** F inability to practise one's profession; **Be|rufs|un|fä|hig|keits|ren|te** F disability pension *(Brit)*, disability *(US)*; **Be|rufs|un|fall** M occupational accident; **Be|rufs|ver|band** M → **Beruf** professional/trade organization *or* association; **Be|rufs|ver|bot** NT *exclusion from a civil service profession by government ruling*; **jdm ~ erteilen** to ban sb from a profession; **unter das ~ fallen** to be banned from a profession; **Be|rufs|ver|bre|cher(in)** M(F) professional criminal; **Be|rufs|ver|kehr** M commuter traffic; **Be|rufs|vor|be|rei|tungs|jahr** NT *year in which students gain practical skills in preparation for entry into the job market*; **Be|rufs|wahl** F → **Beruf** choice of occupation/profession/trade; **Be|rufs|wech|sel** M change of occupation/profession/trade; **Be|rufs|wunsch** M preferred choice of job *or* career; **Be|rufs|ziel** NT occupation/profession/trade one is aiming for; **Be|rufs|zweig** M → **Beruf** branch of an occupation/profession/trade; *(= Berufsgruppe)* occupation/profession/trade

Be|ru|fung [bəˈruːfʊŋ] F -, -en **a** *(Jur)* appeal; **in die ~ gehen, ~ einlegen** to appeal *(bei* to) **b** *(in ein Amt etc)* appointment *(auf or an +acc* to) **c** *(= innerer Auftrag)* vocation; *(Rel)* mission, vocation, calling; **die ~ zu etw in sich** *(dat)* **fühlen** to feel one has a vocation *etc* to be sth **d** *(form)* **die ~ auf jdn/etw** reference to sb/sth; **unter ~ auf etw** *(acc)* with reference to sth

Be|ru|fungs-: **Be|ru|fungs|an|trag** M petition for appeal; **einen ~ stellen** to file a petition for appeal; **Be|ru|fungs|aus|schuss** M appeal tribunal; **Be|ru|fungs|frist** F period in which an appeal must be submitted; **Be|ru|fungs|ge|richt** NT appeal court, court of appeal; **Be|ru|fungs|in|stanz** F court of appeal; **Be|ru|fungs|kla|ge** F appeal; **Be|ru|fungs|klä|ger(in)** M(F) appellant; **Be|ru|fungs|ver|fah|ren** NT appeal proceedings *pl*

be|ru|hen *ptp* **beruht** VI to be based *or* founded *(auf +dat* on); **das beruht auf Gegenseitigkeit** *(inf)* the feeling is mutual; **etw auf sich ~ lassen** to let sth rest

be|ru|hi|gen [bəˈruːɪgn] *ptp* **beruhigt** VT to calm (down); *Baby* to quieten *(Brit)*, to quiet *(US)*; *(= trösten)* to soothe, to comfort; *(= versichern)* to reassure; *Magen* to settle; *Nerven* to soothe, to calm; *Verkehr* to calm; *Gewissen* to soothe, to ease; *Schmerzen* to ease, to relieve; **na, dann bin ich ja beruhigt** well I must say I'm quite relieved; **dann kann ich ja beruhigt schlafen/nach Hause gehen** then I can go to sleep/go home with my mind at rest; **~d** *(körperlich, = beschwichtigend)* soothing; *(= tröstlich)* reassuring; **es ist ~d zu wissen, dass ...** it is reassuring to know that ...
VR to calm down; *(Krise auch)* to ease off, to lessen; *(Gewissen)* to be eased; *(Andrang, Verkehr, Kämpfe)* to subside, to lessen; *(Börse, Preise, Magen)* to settle down; *(Krämpfe, Schmerzen)* to lessen, to ease; *(Meer)* to become calm; *(Sturm)* to die down, to abate; **sie konnte sich gar nicht darüber ~, dass ...** she could not get over the fact that ...; **beruhige dich doch!** calm down!

Be|ru|hi|gung F -, *no pl* **a** *(= das Beruhigen)* calming (down); *(von Baby)* quietening *(Brit)*, quieting *(US)*; *(= das Trösten)* soothing, comforting; *(= das Versichern)* reassuring; *(von Magen)* settling; *(von Nerven)* soothing; *(von Verkehr)* calming; *(von Gewissen)* soothing, easing; *(von Schmerzen)* easing, relieving; **zu Ihrer ~ kann ich sagen ...** you'll be reassured to know that ...
b *(= das Sichberuhigen)* calming down; *(von Krise auch)* easing off, lessening; *(von Gewissen)* easing; *(von Andrang, Verkehr, Kämpfen)* subsiding, lessening; *(von Börse, Preisen, Magen)* settling down; *(von Meer)* calming; *(von Sturm)* abatement; **ein Gefühl der ~** a reassuring feeling

Be|ru|hi|gungs-: **Be|ru|hi|gungs|mit|tel** NT sedative, tranquillizer *(Brit)*, tranquilizer *(US)*; **Be|ru|hi|gungs|pil|le** F, **Be|ru|hi|gungs|tab|let|te** F sedative (pill), tranquillizer *(Brit)*, tranquilizer *(US)*, downer *(inf)*; **Be|ru|hi|gungs|sprit|ze** F sedative (injection)

be|rühmt [bəˈryːmt] ADJ famous; **wegen** *or* **für etw ~ sein** to be famous *or* renowned for sth; **das war nicht ~** *(inf)* it was nothing to write home about *(inf)*

be|rühmt-be|rüch|tigt ADJ infamous, notorious

Be|rühmt|heit F -, -en **a** fame; **~ erlangen** to become famous; **zu trauriger ~ gelangen** to become notorious *or* infamous **b** *(= Mensch)* celebrity

be|rüh|ren *ptp* **berührt** VT **a** *(= anfassen, streifen, Math)* to touch; *(= grenzen an)* to border on; *(= auf Reise streifen) Länder* to touch; *Hafen* to stop at; *(= erwähnen) Thema, Punkt* to touch on; **Berühren verboten** do not touch
b *(= seelisch bewegen)* to move; *(= auf jdn wirken)* to affect; *(= betreffen)* to affect, to concern; **das berührt mich gar nicht!** that's nothing to do with me; **von etw peinlich/schmerzlich berührt sein** to be embarrassed/pained by sth; **es berührt mich angenehm/seltsam, dass ...** I am pleased/surprised that ...
VR to touch; *(Menschen auch)* to touch each other; *(Drähte etc)* to be in contact, to touch; *(Ideen, Vorstellungen, Interessen)* to coincide

Be|rüh|rung F -, -en touch; *(zwischen Drähten etc, = menschlicher Kontakt)* contact; *(= Erwähnung)* mention; **mit jdm/etw in ~ kommen** to come into contact with sb/sth; **jdn mit jdm/etw in ~ bringen** to bring sb into contact with sb/sth; **körperliche ~** physical *or* bodily contact; **die ~ der Instrumente ist zu vermeiden** avoid touching the instruments; **bei ~ Lebensgefahr!** danger – do not touch!; **Ansteckung durch ~** contagion, infection by contact

Be|rüh|rungs-: **Be|rüh|rungs|angst** F *usu pl* reservation *(mit* about); **die Berührungsängste vor diesem Thema sind noch groß** there is still great reluctance to deal with this subject; **Be|rüh|rungs|bild|schirm** M touch screen; **Be|rüh|rungs|gift** NT contact poison; **Be|rüh|rungs|punkt** M point of contact; *(Math auch)* tangential point; **be|rüh|rungs|sen|si|tiv** ADJ *(Comput)* touch-sensitive; **~er Bildschirm** touch screen

Be|ryl|li|um [beˈryliʊm] NT -s, *no pl* (*abbr* **Be**) beryllium

bes. *abbr von* **besonders**

be|sab|bern *ptp* **besabbert** *(inf)* VT to slobber all over *or* on VR to slobber all over oneself

be|sä|en *ptp* **besät** VT *(lit)* to sow → *auch* **besät**

be|sa|gen *ptp* **besagt** VT to say; *(= bedeuten)* to mean, to imply; **das besagt nichts** that does not mean anything; **das besagt viel** that means a lot; **das besagt nicht, dass ...** that does not mean (to say) that ...

be|sagt [bəˈzaːkt] ADJ *attr (form)* said *(form)*, aforementioned *(form)*

be|sai|ten [bəˈzaitn] *ptp* **besaitet** VT to string; **etw neu ~** to restring sth → **zart**

be|sa|men [bəˈzaːmən] *ptp* **besamt** VT to fertilize; *(künstlich)* to inseminate; *(Bot)* to pollinate

be|sam|meln *ptp* **besammelt** VR *(esp Sw)* to assemble, to gather

Be|samm|lung F *(esp Sw)* assembly

Be|sa|mung F -, -en fertilization; *(künstlich)* insemination; *(Bot)* pollination

Be|san [beˈzaːn, ˈbeːzaːn] M -s, -e *(Naut)* mizzen; *(= Segel auch)* mizzen sail; *(= Mast auch)* mizzenmast

be|sänf|ti|gen [bəˈzɛnftɪgn] *ptp* **besänftigt** VT to calm down, to soothe; *Menge auch* to pacify; *jds Zorn, Erregung, Gemüt* to soothe; **er war nicht zu ~** it was impossible to calm him down VR *(Mensch)* to calm down; *(Meer, Elemente)* to become calm

Be|sänf|ti|gung F -, -en calming (down), soothing; *(von Menge auch)* pacifying; *(von Zorn, Erregung, Gemüt)* soothing

Be|san|mast M *(Naut)* mizzenmast

be|sät [bəˈzɛːt] ADJ covered; *(mit Blättern etc)* strewn; *(iro: mit Orden)* studded; **der mit Sternen ~e Himmel** the star-spangled sky *(liter)* → *auch* **besäen**

Be|satz M **a** edging, trimming; *(an Tischtuch auch)* border; **einen ~ aus etw haben** to be trimmed with sth **b** *(= Bestand)* stock

Be|sat|zer [bəˈzatsɐ] M -s, - *(pej inf: = Soldat)* occupying soldier; *(pl: = Armee)* occupying forces *pl*

Be|sat|zung F **a** *(= Mannschaft)* crew; *(= Verteidigungstruppe)* garrison **b** *(= Besatzungsarmee)* occupying army *or* forces *pl*

Be|sat|zungs-: **Be|sat|zungs|ar|mee** F occupying army, army of occupation; **Be|sat|zungs|kind** NT *illegitimate child of member of the occupying forces*; **Be|sat|zungs|macht** F occupying power; **Be|sat|zungs|sol|dat(in)** M(F) soldier in/of the occupying army *or* forces; **Be|sat|zungs|sta|tut** NT statute of occupation; **Be|sat|zungs|streit|kräf|te** PL, **Be|sat|zungs|trup|pen** PL occupying forces *pl*; **Be|sat|zungs|zo|ne** F occupation zone; **die amerikanische ~** the American(-occupied) zone

be|sau|fen *ptp* **besoffen** [bəˈzɔfn] VR *irreg (inf)* to get plastered *(inf) or* pissed *(Brit inf)* → *auch* **besoffen**

Be|säuf|nis [bəˈzɔyfnɪs] NT -ses, -se *(inf)* booze-up *(inf)*, chug-a-lug *(US inf)*

be|säu|seln *ptp* **besäuselt** VR *(inf)* to get merry *(Brit inf) or* tipsy; **besäuselt** tipsy, merry *(Brit inf)*

be|schä|di|gen *ptp* **beschädigt** VT to damage; **beschädigt** damaged; *Schiff auch* disabled; *Datei, Festplattensektor* corrupted, damaged

Be|schä|dig|te(r) [bəˈʃɛːdɪçtə] MF *decl as adj* disabled person/man/woman

Be|schä|di|gung F damage *(von* to); **das Auto hat mehrere ~en** the car is damaged in several places

be|schaf|fen [bəˈʃafn] *ptp* **beschafft** VT to procure *(form)*, to get (hold of), to obtain; **jdm etw ~** to get (hold of) *or* obtain sth for sb; **jdm/sich eine Stelle ~** to get sb/oneself a job; **das ist schwer zu ~** that is difficult to get (hold of)

be|schaf|fen ADJ *(form)* **wie ist es mit seiner Gesundheit ~?** what about his health?; **mit jdm/damit ist es gut/schlecht ~** sb/it is in a good/bad way; **so ~ sein wie ...** to be the same as ...; **das ist so ~, dass ...** that is such that ...

Be|schaf|fen|heit F -, *no pl* composition; *(von Mensch) (körperlich)* constitution; *(seelisch)* nature, qualities *pl*; **die glatte ~ des Steins** the smoothness of the stone; **er hat für diesen Beruf nicht die seelische/körperliche ~** he doesn't have the right sort of psychological make-up/physique for this job; **je nach ~ der Lage** according to the situation

Be|schaf|fung F, *no pl* procuring, obtaining

Be|schaf|fungs-: **Be|schaf|fungs|kos|ten** PL procurement costs *pl*, cost *sing* of acquisition; **Be|schaf|fungs|kri|mi|na|li|tät** F drug-related crime; **Be|schaf|fungs|pros|ti|tu|ti|on** F drug-related prostitution

be|schäf|ti|gen [bəˈʃɛftɪgn] ✪ 33.3 *ptp* **beschäftigt** VR **sich mit etw ~** to occupy oneself with sth; *(= sich befassen, abhandeln)* to deal with sth; **sich mit dem Tod ~** to think about death; **sich mit Literatur ~** to study literature; **sich mit der Frage ~, ob ...** to consider the question of whether ...; **sich mit jdm ~** to devote one's attention to sb; **sie beschäftigt sich viel mit den Kindern** she devotes a lot of her time to the children; **sie beschäftigt sich gerade mit den Kindern** she is busy with the children just now
VT **a** *(= innerlich beschäftigen)* **jdn ~** to be on sb's mind; **die Frage beschäftigt sie sehr** she is very preoccupied with that question, that question has been on her mind a lot
b *(= anstellen)* to employ
c *(= eine Tätigkeit geben)* to occupy, to keep occupied; **jdn mit etw ~** to give sb sth to do

be|schäf|tigt [bəˈʃɛftɪçt] ADJ **a** busy; **mit dem Nähen/jdm ~ sein** to be busy sewing/with sb; **mit sich selbst/seinen Problemen ~ sein** to be preoccupied with oneself/one's problems **b** *(= angestellt)* employed *(bei* by, at)

Be|schäf|tig|te(r) [bəˈʃɛftɪçtə] MF *decl as adj* employee

Be|schäf|ti|gung F -, -en **a** *(= berufliche Arbeit)* work *no indef art*, job; *(= Anstellung, Angestelltsein)* employment; **eine ~ suchen** to be looking for work *or* a job, to seek employment *(form)*; **einer ~ nachgehen** *(form)* to be employed; **ohne ~ sein** to be unemployed, to be out of work
b *(= Tätigkeit)* activity, occupation; **jdm eine ~ geben** to give sb something to do; **~ haben** to have something to do
c *(= geistige Beschäftigung)* preoccupation; *(mit*

Frage) consideration; *(mit Thema)* treatment *(mit* of); *(mit Literatur)* study *(mit* of); *(mit sich, seinen Problemen)* preoccupation
d *(von Kindern, Patienten etc)* occupying, keeping occupied; **die ~ der Patienten** keeping the patients occupied

Be|schäf|ti|gungs-: **Be|schäf|ti|gungs|ge|sell|schaft** F *local or regional job creation scheme in areas with high unemployment*; **Be|schäf|ti|gungs|la|ge** F employment situation; **be|schäf|ti|gungs|los** ADJ unoccupied; *(= arbeitslos)* unemployed, out-of-work; **Be|schäf|ti|gungs|nach|weis** M proof of employment; **Be|schäf|ti|gungs|of|fen|si|ve** F job creation campaign; **Be|schäf|ti|gungs|pro|gramm** NT job creation scheme; **Be|schäf|ti|gungs|the|ra|peut(in)** M(F) occupational therapist; **Be|schäf|ti|gungs|the|ra|pie** F occupational therapy; **Be|schäf|ti|gungs|ver|hält|nis** NT *(form)* employment, employment status; **in was für einem ~ stehen Sie?** what type of employment are you in?

be|schä|len *ptp* **beschält** VT *(form)* to cover, to serve

Be|schä|ler [bəˈʃɛːlɐ] M **-s, -** *(form)* stallion, stud

be|schal|len [bəˈʃalən] *ptp* **beschallt** VT **a** *(mit Lautsprechern)* to fill with sound **b** *(Med, Tech, mit Ultraschall)* **jdn ~** *(zur Behandlung)* to treat sb with ultrasound; *(zur Diagnose)* to give sb an ultrasound scan

Be|schä|lung [bəˈʃɛːlʊŋ] F **-, -en** *(form)* covering, service

be|schä|men *ptp* **beschämt** VT to shame; *(jds Großzügigkeit)* to embarrass; **es beschämt mich, zu sagen ...** I feel ashamed to have to say ...; **beschämt** ashamed, abashed; **ich fühle mich durch deine Großzügigkeit beschämt** I am embarrassed by your generosity

be|schä|mend ADJ **a** *(= schändlich)* shameful; **es war ~ für seine ganze Familie** it brought shame on *or* to his whole family **b** *(= vorbildlich)* shaming; *Großzügigkeit* embarrassing **c** *(= demütigend)* humiliating, shaming ADV *(= schändlich)* disgracefully, shamefully

Be|schä|mung [bəˈʃɛːmʊŋ] F **-,** *(rare)* **-en** shame; *(= Verlegenheit)* embarrassment; **zu meiner ~** to my shame; **in tiefer ~ ging er nach Hause** he went home feeling very ashamed

be|schat|ten [bəˈʃatn] *ptp* **beschattet** VT **a** *(geh) (= Schatten geben)* to shade; *(fig: = trüben)* to overshadow **b** *(= überwachen)* to shadow, to tail; **jdn ~ lassen** to have sb shadowed *or* tailed **c** *(Sport)* to mark closely

Be|schat|ter [bəˈʃatɐ] M **-s, -, Be|schat|te|rin** [-ərɪn] F **-, -nen a** *(= Polizist etc)* tail **b** *(Sport)* marker

Be|schat|tung F **-, -en a** *(= Überwachung)* shadowing, tailing **b** *(Sport)* marking

Be|schau F **-,** *no pl* inspection

be|schau|en *ptp* **beschaut** VT **a** *Fleisch etc* to inspect **b** *(dial: = betrachten)* to look at; **sich** *(dat)* **etw ~** to look at sth

Be|schau|er [bəˈʃauɐ] M **-s, -, Be|schau|e|rin** [-ərɪn] F **-, -nen a** inspector **b** *(= Betrachter)* spectator; *(von Bild)* viewer

be|schau|lich [bəˈʃaulɪç] ADJ **a** *(= geruhsam) Leben, Abend* quiet, tranquil; *Charakter, Mensch* pensive, contemplative **b** *(Rel)* contemplative ADV *(= geruhsam)* quietly, tranquilly; **~ dasitzen** to sit contemplating; **~ leben** to lead a simple life

Be|schau|lich|keit F **-,** *no pl (= Geruhsamkeit) (von Leben, Abend)* tranquillity; *(von Charakter, Mensch)* pensiveness

Be|schau|ung [bəˈʃauʊŋ] F **-, -en** inspection

Be|scheid [bəˈʃait] M **-(e)s, -e** [-də] **a** *(= Auskunft)* information; *(= Nachricht)* notification; *(= Entscheidung auf Antrag etc)* decision; **wir erwarten Ihren ~** we look forward to hearing from you; **ich warte noch auf ~** I am still waiting to hear, I still have not heard anything; **jdm (über etw** *(acc) or* **von etw) ~ sagen** *or* **geben** to let sb know (about sth), to tell sb (about sth); **jdm ordentlich ~ sagen, jdm gründlich ~ stoßen** *(inf)* to tell sb where to get off *(inf)*; **~ hinterlassen** to leave word
b **(über etw** *acc or* **in etw** *dat)* **~ wissen** to know (about sth); **weißt du ~ wegen Samstagabend?** do you know about Saturday evening?; **weißt du ~ mit den Maschinen?** do you know how to deal with these machines?, do you know about these machines?; **ich weiß hier nicht ~** I don't know about things around here; **er weiß gut ~** he is well informed; **auf dem Gebiet weiß ich nicht ~** I don't know much about that sort of thing; **weißt du schon ~?** do you know?, have you heard?; **sag ihr, Egon habe angerufen, dann weiß sie schon ~** if you tell her Egon phoned she'll understand

be|schei|den [bəˈʃaidn] *pret* **beschied** [bəˈʃiːt], *ptp* **beschieden** [bəˈʃiːdn] VT **a** *(form: = bestellen)* to summon *(form)* *(zu jdm* to sb)
b *(form: = entscheiden) Gesuch, Antrag* to decide upon; **etw abschlägig ~** to turn sth down
c *(form: = informieren)* **jdn dahin gehend ~, dass ...** to inform *or* notify sb that ...
d *(geh: = zuteilwerden lassen)* **jdm etw ~** to grant sb sth; **es war ihr nicht beschieden, den Erfolg zu genießen** she was not granted the opportunity to enjoy the success, it was not given to her to enjoy the success *(liter)*
VR *(geh)* to be content; **sich mit wenigem ~** to be content *or* to content oneself with little

be|schei|den [bəˈʃaidn] ADJ **a** modest; *Mensch, Verhalten* modest, unassuming; **in ~en Verhältnissen leben** to live modestly; **eine ~e Frage** one small question; **aus ~en Anfängen** from humble beginnings **b** *(euph: = beschissen)* awful, terrible; *(inf: = mäßig)* mediocre ADV **a** *leben* modestly; **darf ich mal ~ fragen, ob ...** may I venture to ask whether ... **b** *(euph) sich fühlen* terrible; *spielen* terribly; **ich habe in der Englischarbeit ~ abgeschnitten** I got a terrible mark *(Brit) or* grade *(esp US)* in English

Be|schei|den|heit F **-,** *no pl* modesty; **nur keine falsche ~** no false modesty now; **~ ist eine Zier, doch weiter kommt man ohne ihr** *(hum inf)* modesty is fine but it doesn't get you very far

be|schei|nen *ptp* **beschienen** [bəˈʃiːnən] VT *irreg* to shine on; *(Feuer)* to light up; **vom Mond beschienen** moonlit; **von der Sonne beschienen** sunlit

be|schei|ni|gen [bəˈʃainɪgn] *ptp* **bescheinigt** VT to certify; *Gesundheit, Tauglichkeit* to confirm in writing; *Empfang* to confirm, to acknowledge; *(durch Quittung)* to sign for, to give a receipt for; *(inf: = mündlich bestätigen)* to confirm; **sich** *(dat)* **die Arbeit/Überstunden ~ lassen** to get written confirmation of having done the work/overtime; **können Sie mir ~, dass ...** can you confirm in writing that ..., can you give me written confirmation that ...; **hiermit wird bescheinigt, dass ...** this is to certify that ...; **jdm äußerste Kompetenz ~** to confirm sb's extreme competence

Be|schei|ni|gung F **-, -en** *(= das Bescheinigen)* certification; *(der Gesundheit, Tauglichkeit)* confirmation; *(= Schriftstück)* certificate; written confirmation; *(= Quittung)* receipt

be|schei|ßen *ptp* **beschissen** [bəˈʃɪsn] *irreg (inf)* VT *jdn* to swindle, to cheat, to do *(um* out of) → *auch* **beschissen** VI to cheat

be|schen|ken *ptp* **beschenkt** VT *jdn* to give presents/a present to; **jdn mit etw ~** to give sb sth (as a present); **sich (gegenseitig) ~** to give each other presents; **jdn reich ~** to shower sb with presents; **damit bin ich reich beschenkt** that's very generous

be|sche|ren *ptp* **beschert** VTI **a** **jdn ~** to give sb a Christmas present/presents; **jdn mit etw ~** to give sb sth for Christmas; **um 5 Uhr wird beschert** the Christmas presents will be given out at 5 o'clock; **jdm eine Überraschung ~** to give sb a nice surprise **b** *(= zuteilwerden lassen)* **jdm etw ~** to grant sb sth, to bestow sth upon sb; *(Gott)* to bless sb with sth

Be|sche|rung [bəˈʃeːrʊŋ] F **-, -en a** *(= Feier)* giving out of Christmas presents **b** *(iro inf)* **das ist ja eine schöne ~!** this is a nice mess; **die (ganze) ~** the (whole) mess; **da haben wir die ~!** I told you so!, what did I tell you!

be|scheu|ert [bəˈʃɔyɐt] *(inf)* ADJ stupid; *Mensch auch* dumb *(inf)* ADV **sich ~ anstellen** to act stupidly; **wie ~ putzen** to clean like crazy *(inf)*; **~ aussehen** to look idiotic *or* ridiculous; **~ fragen** to ask idiotic *or* stupid questions

be|schich|ten *ptp* **beschichtet** VT *(Tech)* to coat, to cover; **mit Kunststoff beschichtet** laminated; **PVC-beschichtet** PVC-coated

Be|schich|tung [bəˈʃɪçtʊŋ] F **-, -en a** *(= Schicht)* coat(ing) **b** *(Tech: = das Beschichten)* coating

be|schi|cken *ptp* **beschickt** VT **a** *(= Vertreter schicken auf)* to send representatives to; *(= Exemplare schicken auf)* to send exhibits to; **eine Ausstellung mit jdm/etw ~** to send sb/sth to an exhibition; **die Firma hat die Messe beschickt** the firm exhibited at the fair; **der Kongress wurde von den meisten Ländern beschickt** most countries sent representatives to the congress **b** *(Tech) Hochofen* to charge; *Kessel* to fire

be|schi|ckert [bəˈʃɪkɐt] ADJ *(inf)* tipsy

Be|schi|ckung [bəˈʃɪkʊŋ] F **-, -en** *(Tech) (von Hochofen)* charging; *(von Kessel)* firing; *(= Ladung)* load

be|schied *pret von* **bescheiden**

be|schie|den *ptp von* **bescheiden**

be|schie|ßen *ptp* **beschossen** [bəˈʃɔsn] VT *irreg* **a** *Gebäude, Stadt, Menschen* to shoot at, to fire on *or* at; *(mit Geschützen)* to bombard **b** *(Phys) Atomkern* to bombard

Be|schie|ßung [bəˈʃiːsʊŋ] F **-, -en a** shooting (+*gen* at), firing (+*gen* on, at); *(mit Geschützen)* bombardment (+*gen* of) **b** *(Phys: von Atomkern)* bombarding

be|schil|dern *ptp* **beschildert** VT to put a sign *or* notice/signs *or* notices on; *(mit Schildchen) Ausstellungsgegenstand, Käfig etc* to label; *(mit Verkehrsschildern)* to signpost

Be|schil|de|rung F **-, -en** *(mit Schildchen)* labelling *(Brit)*, labeling *(US)*; *(mit Verkehrsschildern)* signposting; *(= Schilder)* signs *pl*; *(= Schildchen)* labels *pl*; *(= Verkehrsschilder)* signposts *pl*

be|schimp|fen *ptp* **beschimpft** VT *jdn* to swear at, to abuse; **jdn als Nazi ~** to accuse sb of being a Nazi

Be|schimp|fung [bəˈʃɪmpfʊŋ] F **-, -en a** *(= das Beschimpfen)* abusing, swearing (+*gen* at); *(Jur)* slander (+*gen* on) **b** *(= Schimpfwort)* insult

be|schir|men *ptp* **beschirmt** VT **a** *(geh: = beschützen)* to shield, to protect **b** *(geh: = sich breiten über)* to shade **c** *(= mit Schirm versehen)* **ich werde dich ~** *(hum inf)* I'll let you share my umbrella

Be|schiss [bəˈʃɪs] M **-es, -e** *(inf)* swindle, rip off *(inf)*; **das ist ~** it's a swindle *or* swizz *(Brit inf)*

be|schis|sen [bəˈʃɪsn] *(inf)* ADJ bloody awful *(Brit inf)*, lousy *(inf)*, shitty *(inf)* ADV **das schmeckt ~** that tastes lousy *(inf)*; **mir gehts ~** I feel bloody awful *(Brit inf) or* shitty *(sl)*; **sich ~ verhalten** to behave like a louse *(inf)*; **jdn ~ behandeln** to treat sb like (a piece of) shit *(sl)*; **wir werden ~ bezahlt** our pay is bloody awful *(Brit)*, our pay is lousy *or* shitty *(inf)*; **ich komme mir echt ~ vor** I feel really shitty *(inf)* → *auch* **bescheißen**

be|schla|fen *ptp* **beschlafen** VT *irreg (inf)* **a** *Sache* to sleep on **b** *Mädchen* to sleep with

Be|schlag M **a** *(an Koffer, Truhe, Buch)* (ornamental) fitting; *(an Tür, Fenster, Möbelstück, Sattel)* (ornamental) mounting; *(= Scharnier/Schließe)* ornamental hinge/clasp; *(von Pferd)* shoes *pl* **b** *(= das Beschlagen: von Pferd)* shoeing **c** *(auf Metall)* tarnish; *(auf Speisen)* layer of mould *(Brit) or* mold *(US)*; *(auf Glas, Spiegel etc)* condensation; **der Löffel hat einen ~** the spoon is tarnished **d** **jdn/etw mit ~ belegen, jdn/etw in**

~ nehmen to monopolize sb/sth; **mit ~ belegt sein** to be being used; *(Mensch)* to be occupied

be|schla|gen *ptp* **beschlagen** *irreg* VT **a** *(= mit Beschlägen versehen) Truhe, Möbel, Tür* to put (metal) fittings on; *Huftier* to shoe; *Schuhe* to put metal tips on; *(mit Ziernägeln)* to stud; **ist das Pferd ~?** is the horse shod? **b** *(Hunt) Wild* to cover, to serve **c** *(Sw: = betreffen)* to concern VI|R *(vi: aux sein) (Brille, Glas, Fenster)* to steam up, to get steamed up, to mist up *or* over; *(Wand)* to get covered in condensation, to get steamed up; *(Silber etc)* to tarnish; **würden Sie bitte die ~en Scheiben abwischen?** the windows are getting steamed up *etc*, could you give them a wipe?

be|schla|gen ADJ *(= erfahren)* well-versed; **in etw** *(dat)* **(gut) ~ sein** to be well-versed in sth; **auf einem Gebiet ~ sein** to be well-versed in a subject

Be|schla|gen|heit F -, *no pl* sound knowledge *(in +dat* of)

Be|schlag|nah|me [bəˈʃlaːknaːmə] F -, -n = **Beschlagnahmung**

be|schlag|nah|men [bəˈʃlaːknaːmən] *ptp* **beschlagnahmt** VT *insep* **a** *(= konfiszieren)* to confiscate; *Vermögen, Grundbesitz, Drogen* to seize; *Kraftfahrzeug, Boot* to impound **b** *(inf: = in Anspruch nehmen) (Mensch)* to monopolize, to hog *(inf)*; *(Arbeit) Zeit* to take up

Be|schlag|nah|mung F -, -en *(von Eigentum, Pass)* confiscation; *(von Vermögen, Grundbesitz, Drogen)* seizure; *(von Kraftfahrzeug, Boot)* impounding

be|schlei|chen *ptp* **beschlichen** [bəˈʃlɪçn] VT *irreg* to creep *or* steal up to *or* up on; *Wild* to stalk; *(fig)* to creep over

be|schleu|ni|gen [bəˈʃlɔynɪgn] *ptp* **beschleunigt** VT to accelerate, to speed up; *Arbeit, Lieferung etc auch* to expedite; *Tempo auch* to increase; *Atem, Puls auch* to quicken; *Verfall, wirtschaftlichen Zusammenbruch etc* to precipitate, to hasten, to accelerate; **die Angst beschleunigte ihre Schritte** fear quickened *or* hastened her steps → *auch* **beschleunigt** VR to accelerate, to speed up; *(Tempo auch)* to increase; *(Atem, Puls auch)* to quicken; *(Verfall, Zusammenbruch)* to be precipitated *or* hastened VI *(Fahrzeug, Fahrer)* to accelerate

Be|schleu|ni|ger [bəˈʃlɔynɪgɐ] M -s, - *(Phys, Chem)* accelerator

be|schleu|nigt [bəˈʃlɔynɪçt] ADJ faster; **~es Verfahren** *(Jur)* summary proceedings *pl* ADV **~ gestiegene Preise** an accelerated increase in prices; **eine sich ~ fortsetzende Entwicklung** a continuously accelerating development → *auch* **beschleunigen**

Be|schleu|ni|gung F -, -en **a** acceleration *(auch Aut, Phys)*, speeding up; *(von Tempo auch)* increase; *(von Atem, Puls auch)* quickening; *(von Verfall etc)* precipitation, hastening; **wir tun alles, was zur ~ der Arbeit führen könnte** we are doing everything we can toward(s) speeding up *or* in order to speed up the work **b** *(= Eile)* speed

Be|schleu|ni|gungs-: **Be|schleu|ni|gungs|an|la|ge** F, **Be|schleu|ni|gungs|ma|schi|ne** F accelerator; **Be|schleu|ni|gungs|ver|mö|gen** NT accelerating power, acceleration; **Be|schleu|ni|gungs|wert** M *(Aut)* acceleration ratio

be|schlie|ßen ✪ 35.2 *ptp* **beschlossen** *irreg* [bəˈʃlɔsn] VT **a** *(= Entschluss fassen)* to decide on; *Gesetz* to pass; *Statuten* to establish; **~, etw zu tun** to decide *or* resolve to do sth **b** *(= beenden)* to end; *Brief, Abend, Programm* to end, to conclude, to wind up VI **über etw** *(acc)* **~** to decide on sth → *auch* **beschlossen**

be|schlos|sen [bəˈʃlɔsn] ADJ *(= entschieden)* decided, agreed; **das ist ~e Sache** that's settled → *auch* **beschließen**

Be|schluss M **a** *(= Entschluss)* decision, resolution; **einen ~ fassen** to pass a resolution; **auf ~ des Gerichts** by order of the court; **wie lautete der ~ des Gerichts?** what was the court's decision? **b** *(obs: = Schluss)* conclusion, end

Be|schluss-: **be|schluss|fä|hig** ADJ **a ~ sein** to have a quorum; **~e Anzahl** quorum **b** *Dokument* ready for a decision; **Be|schluss|fä|hig|keit** F, *no pl* quorum; **Be|schluss|fas|sung** F (passing of a) resolution; **Be|schluss|la|ge** F *(esp Pol)* policy position; **Be|schluss|recht** NT competence (to pass *or* make a resolution); **be|schluss|reif** ADJ *Gesetz* ready to be voted on, ready for the vote; **Be|schluss|rei|fe** F readiness for the vote; **~ haben** to be ready for the vote *or* to be voted on; **be|schluss|un|fä|hig** ADJ **~ sein** not to have a quorum; **Be|schluss|un|fä|hig|keit** F lack of a quorum

be|schmei|ßen *ptp* **beschmissen** [bəˈʃmɪsn] VT *irreg (inf)* to pelt, to bombard

be|schmie|ren *ptp* **beschmiert** VT **a** *(= bestreichen) Brot* to spread; *Körperteil, Maschinenteil* to smear, to cover; **Brot mit Butter ~** to butter bread; **Brot mit Käse ~** to spread cheese on bread **b** *Kleidung* to (be)smear; *Wand* to smear, to bedaub; *Tafel* to scribble *or* scrawl all over; **ein Buch mit Bemerkungen ~** to scrawl comments all over a book VR to get (all) dirty, to get oneself in a mess; **sich von oben bis unten mit etw ~** to get sth all over oneself, to cover oneself with sth

be|schmun|zeln *ptp* **beschmunzelt** VT to smile (quietly) at; **der alte Scherz wird immer noch beschmunzelt** the old joke still raises *(Brit)* or gets a smile

be|schmut|zen *ptp* **beschmutzt** VT to (make *or* get) dirty, to soil; *(fig) Ruf, Namen* to besmirch, to sully; *Ehre* to stain → **Nest c** VR to make *or* get oneself dirty

Be|schmut|zung [bəˈʃmʊtsʊŋ] F -, -en dirtying, soiling; *(von Namen, Ruf)* besmirching, sullying; *(von Ehre)* staining

be|schna|cken *ptp* **beschnackt** VT *(esp N Ger inf)* **a** *(= besprechen)* to talk over, to discuss **b** *(= überreden)* to talk round, to persuade; **jdn ~, etw zu tun** to talk sb into doing sth

be|schnei|den *ptp* **beschnitten** [bəˈʃnɪtn] VT *irreg* **a** *(= zurechtschneiden, stutzen)* to trim; *Sträucher, Reben* to prune; *Bäume* to prune, to trim, to lop; *Flügel* to clip **b** *(Med, Rel)* to circumcise **c** *(fig: = beschränken) Rechte, Ansprüche* to cut back, to curtail

Be|schnei|dung [bəˈʃnaidʊŋ] F -, -en **a** *(Med, Rel)* circumcision **b** *(von Sträuchern, Reben)* pruning; *(von Bäumen)* pruning, lopping; *(von Flügeln)* clipping **c** *(von Finanzen)* cutback; *(von Rechten)* curtailing, curtailment

be|schnei|en *ptp* **beschneit** VT to cover with artificial snow

be|schneit [bəˈʃnait] ADJ snow-covered; *Berge auch* snowcapped

Be|schnei|ungs|an|la|ge [bəˈʃnaiʊŋs-] F artificial snowblower

be|schnüf|feln *ptp* **beschnüffelt** VT to sniff at; *(fig) (= vorsichtig untersuchen)* to sniff out, to suss out *(inf)*; *jdn* to size up; *(= bespitzeln)* to spy out VR *(Hunde)* to have a sniff at each other, to sniff each other; *(fig)* to size each other up

be|schnup|pern *ptp* **beschnuppert** VTR = **beschnüffeln**

be|schö|ni|gen [bəˈʃøːnɪgn] *ptp* **beschönigt** VT to gloss over; **~der Ausdruck** euphemism; **... sagte er ~d** ... he said, trying to make things seem better

Be|schö|ni|gung F -, -en glossing over; **was er zur ~ angeführt hat, ...** what he said to make things seem better ...

be|schot|tern *ptp* **beschottert** VT *Straße* to macadamize, to metal; *(Rail)* to ballast

be|schrän|ken [bəˈʃrɛŋkn] ✪ 53.2 *ptp* **beschränkt** VT *(auf +acc* to) to limit, to restrict; *Anzahl, Ausgaben, Bedeutung eines Wortes etc auch* to confine VR *(auf +acc* to) to limit, to restrict; *(esp Jur, Rede, Aufsatz etc auch)* to confine oneself; *(= sich einschränken)* to restrict oneself; **das Wort beschränkt sich auf regionalen Gebrauch** the word is limited *or* restricted *or* confined to regional usage

be|schrankt [bəˈʃraŋkt] ADJ *Bahnübergang* with gates

be|schränkt [bəˈʃrɛŋkt] ADJ **a** *(= eingeschränkt, knapp)* limited; *Gebrauch* limited, restricted; **wir sind räumlich/zeitlich/finanziell ~** we have only a limited amount of space/time/money; **~e Haftung** limited liability; **Gesellschaft mit ~er Haftung** limited company *(Brit)*, corporation *(US)* **b** *(pej) (geistig) Mensch, Intelligenz* limited; *(= engstirnig auch)* narrow; **wie kann man nur so ~ sein?** how can anyone be so dim *(inf) or* stupid? ADV **a** *(= knapp)* **~ leben** to live on a limited income; **~ wohnen** to live in cramped conditions; **jdn ~ unterstützen** to give sb limited support **b** *(pej)* like an idiot

Be|schränkt|heit F -, *no pl* **a** *(= Knappheit)* **die ~ der Plätze/unserer Mittel** the limited (number of) places/our limited means **b** *(geistig, von Mensch)* limited intelligence; *(= Engstirnigkeit)* narrowness; **er konnte in seiner ~ nicht begreifen, dass ...** his simple mind could not grasp that ...

Be|schrän|kung F -, -en **a** *(= das Beschränken)* limitation, restriction; *(von Anzahl, Ausgaben, Bedeutung auch)* confinement; **eine ~ der Teilnehmerzahl scheint unvermeidbar zu sein** it seems unavoidable that the number of participants will have to be limited *or* restricted **b** *(= das Sichbeschränken) (auf +acc* to) limitation, restriction; *(esp Jur: von Rede, Aufsatz)* confinement **c** *(Maßnahme)* restriction, limitation; **jdm ~en auferlegen** to impose restrictions on sb

be|schreib|bar ADJ *CD, DVD* recordable

be|schrei|ben *ptp* **beschrieben** [bəˈʃriːbn] VT *irreg* **a** *(= darstellen)* to describe, to give a description of; **sein Glück/Schmerz war nicht zu ~** his happiness/pain was indescribable *or* was beyond (all) description; **ich kann dir nicht ~, wie erleichtert ich war** I can't tell you how relieved I was; **~de Psychologie/Grammatik** descriptive psychology/grammar **b** *(= vollschreiben)* to write on **c** *Kreis, Bahn* to describe

Be|schrei|bung F **a** description **b** *(= Gebrauchsanweisung)* instructions *pl*

be|schrei|en *ptp* **beschrien** VT *irreg (inf)* = **berufen** VT **c**

be|schrei|ten *ptp* **beschritten** [bəˈʃrɪtn] VT *irreg (lit geh) Pfad* to walk *or* step along; *Brücke* to walk *or* step across; *(fig) neue Wege* to follow, to pursue, to take; *neue Methode* to follow, to pursue

be|schrif|ten [bəˈʃrɪftn] *ptp* **beschriftet** VT to write on; *Grabstein, Sockel etc* to inscribe; *(mit Aufschrift)* to label; *Umschlag* to address; *Karikatur* to give a caption (to); **etw mit seinem Namen ~** to write one's name on sth; **die Funde waren mit Tusche beschriftet** the finds were marked with ink

Be|schrif|tung F -, -en **a** *(= das Beschriften)* inscribing; *(mit Etikett)* labelling *(Brit)*, labeling *(US)*; *(von Umschlag)* addressing; *(von Karikatur)* giving a caption to; *(von Funden)* marking; **bei der ~ der Etiketten** while filling in the labels **b** *(= Aufschrift)* writing; *(auf Grabstein, Sockel)* inscription; *(von Karikatur)* caption; *(= Etikett)* label

be|schu|hen [bəˈʃuːən] *ptp* **beschuht** VT to shoe; *(Tech) Pfahl, Spitze etc* to tip with metal

be|schuht [bəˈʃuːt] ADJ wearing shoes, shod

be|schul|di|gen [bəˈʃʊldɪgn] *ptp* **beschuldigt** VT to accuse; *(esp Jur)* to accuse, to charge; *(liter)* to charge; **jdn einer Sache** *(gen)* **~** to accuse sb of sth, to charge sb with sth

Be|schul|dig|te(r) [bəˈʃʊldɪçtə] MF *decl as adj* accused

Be|schul|di|gung F -, -en accusation; *(esp Jur auch, liter)* charge

Be|schu|lung F, *no pl* provision of school(ing) facilities *(+gen* for)

be|schum|meln *ptp* **beschummelt** VTI *(inf)* to cheat; **jdn um etw ~** to cheat *or* diddle *(inf)* sb out of sth

be|schuppt [bəˈʃʊpt] ADJ scaly; **dick ~** thick--scaled, with thick scales

be|schup|sen *ptp* **beschupst** VTI *(inf)* = **beschummeln**

Be|schuss M **-es**, *no pl (Mil)* fire; *(mit Granaten auch)* shelling, bombardment; *(Phys)* bombardment, bombarding; **jdn/etw unter ~ nehmen** *(Mil)* to (start to) bombard *or* shell sb/sth; *Stellung auch* to fire on sth; *(fig)* to attack sb/sth, to launch an attack on sb/sth; **unter ~ stehen** *or* **liegen** *(Mil)* to be under fire; **unter ~ geraten** *(Mil, fig)* to come under fire

be|schüt|ten *ptp* **beschüttet** VT *(mit Sand etc)* to cover; **jdn/etw (mit Wasser** *etc***) ~** to pour water *etc* on *or* over sb/sth; **die Straße mit Sand ~** to throw *or* put sand on the road; **ein Feld mit Jauche ~** to put liquid manure on a field

be|schüt|zen *ptp* **beschützt** VT to protect, to shield, to shelter *(vor +dat* from); **~d** protective

Be|schüt|zer [bəˈʃʏtsɐ] M **-s, -**, **Be|schüt|ze|rin** [-ərɪn] F **-, -nen** protector; *(Frau auch)* protectress

be|schwat|zen *ptp* **beschwatzt**, *(esp S Ger)* **be|schwät|zen** *ptp* **beschwätzt** VT *(inf)* **a** *(= überreden)* to talk over; **jdn zu etw ~** to talk sb into sth; **sich zu etw ~ lassen** to get talked into sth **b** *(= bereden)* to chat about, to have a chat about

Be|schwer [bəˈʃveːɐ] F - *or* NT **-s**, *no pl (obs)* hardship

Be|schwer|de [bəˈʃveːɐdə] F **-, -n** **a** *(= Klage)* complaint; *(Jur)* appeal; **eine ~ gegen jdn** a complaint about sb; **wenn Sie eine ~ haben** if you have a complaint *or* grievance; **~ führen** *or* **einlegen** *or* **erheben** *(form)* to lodge a complaint; **jdm Grund zur ~ geben** to give sb grounds *or* cause for complaint **b Beschwerden** PL *(= Leiden)* trouble; **das macht mir immer noch ~n** it's still causing *or* giving me trouble; **mit etw ~n haben** to have trouble with sth; **wenn Sie wieder ganz ohne ~n sind** when the trouble's cleared up completely **c** *(= Mühe)* hardship

Be|schwer|de-: **Be|schwer|de|brief** M letter of complaint, written complaint; **Be|schwer|de|buch** NT complaints book; **be|schwer|de|frei** ADJ *(Med)* fit and healthy; **er war nie wieder ganz ~** the symptoms never completely disappeared; **Be|schwer|de|frist** F *(Jur) period of time during which an appeal may be lodged or filed*; **be|schwer|de|füh|rend** ADJ **die ~e Partei** *(Jur)* the appealing party, the appellant; **Be|schwer|de|füh|ren|de(r)** [-fyːrəndə] MF *decl as adj*, **Be|schwer|de|füh|rer(in)** M(F) *(form)* person who lodges a complaint; *(Jur)* appellant; **Be|schwer|de|schrift** F written *or* formal complaint, petition; **Be|schwer|de|weg** M *(form) possibility of lodging a complaint with sb (in authority)* **auf dem ~** by (means of) lodging *or* making a complaint; **den ~ beschreiten** to lodge a complaint

be|schwe|ren [bəˈʃveːrən] *ptp* **beschwert** VT *(mit Gewicht)* to weigh(t) down; *(fig: = belasten: Problem, Kummer)* to weigh on; **von Kummer beschwert** weighed down with sorrow VR **a** *(= sich beklagen)* to complain **b** *(= sich belasten) (lit)* to weigh oneself down; *(fig)* to encumber oneself

be|schwer|lich [bəˈʃveːɐlɪç] ADJ laborious, arduous; *Reise* arduous; **jdm ~ fallen/werden** *(old)* to be/become a burden to sb; **das Gehen/Atmen ist für ihn ~** he finds walking/breathing hard work

Be|schwer|lich|keit F **-, -en** arduousness *no pl*; **die ~en des Alters** the heavy weight of years; **die ~en des Lebens** life's burdens; **die ~en der Reise** the difficulties of the journey

Be|schwer|nis [bəˈʃveːɐnɪs] F **-, -se** *or nt* **-ses, -se** *(geh: = Mühsal)* hardship

Be|schwe|rung F **-, -en** **a** *(= das Beschweren)* weigh(t)ing down **b** *(Gegenstand)* weight

be|schwich|ti|gen [bəˈʃvɪçtɪgn] *ptp* **beschwichtigt** VT *jdn* to appease, to pacify; *Kinder* to calm down, to soothe; *jds Zorn, Gewissen* to soothe, to appease, to calm

Be|schwich|ti|gung F **-, -en** appeasement, pacification; *(von Kindern)* calming down, soothing; *(von Gewissen, Zorn)* soothing, appeasement, calming; *(= beschwichtigende Worte)* calming *or* soothing words *pl*

Be|schwich|ti|gungs-: **Be|schwich|ti|gungs|for|mel** F reassuring words *pl*, words *pl* of reassurance; **diplomatische ~n** diplomatic words of reassurance; **Be|schwich|ti|gungs|po|li|tik** F policy of appeasement

be|schwin|deln *ptp* **beschwindelt** VT *(inf)* **a** *(= belügen)* **jdn ~** to tell sb a lie *or* a fib *(inf)* **b** *(= betrügen)* to cheat, to swindle, to do *(inf)*

be|schwin|gen *ptp* **beschwingt** VT to exhilarate, to elate

be|schwingt [bəˈʃvɪŋt] ADJ elated, exhilarated; *Musik, Mensch* vibrant; **sich ~ fühlen** to walk on air; **ein ~es Gefühl** a feeling of elation *or* exhilaration; **~en Schrittes** *(geh) or* **Fußes** *(liter)* with a spring *or* bounce in one's step, lightly tripping *(liter)*

Be|schwingt|heit F **-**, *no pl* elation, exhilaration; *(von Mensch, Musik)* vibrancy

be|schwip|sen [bəˈʃvɪpsn] *ptp* **beschwipst** *(inf)* VT to make tipsy, to go to sb's head VR to get tipsy

be|schwipst [bəˈʃvɪpst] ADJ *(inf)* tipsy

be|schwö|ren *ptp* **beschworen** [bəˈʃvoːrən] VT *irreg* **a** *(= beeiden)* to swear to; *(Jur auch)* to swear on oath **b** *(= anflehen)* to implore, to beseech; **sie hob ~d die Hände** she raised her hands imploringly *or* beseechingly **c** *(= erscheinen lassen)* to conjure up; *Verstorbene* to raise, to call up; *Schlangen* to charm **d** *(geh: = hervorrufen) Erinnerung etc* to conjure up; **das beschwor Erinnerungen in mir** that conjured up memories

Be|schwö|rung [bəˈʃvøːrʊŋ] F **-, -en** **a** *(= das Flehen)* entreaty **b** *(= das Heraufbeschwören)* conjuring up, conjuration; *(von Verstorbenen)* raising, calling up; *(von Schlangen)* charming **c** *(auch* **Beschwörungsformel***)* incantation

be|see|len [bəˈzeːlən] *ptp* **beseelt** VT **a** *(lit: = mit Seele versehen)* to give a soul to; *Natur, Kunstwerk* to breathe life into; **das beseelte Spiel des Pianisten** *(geh)* the pianist's inspired playing **b** *(= erfüllen)* to fill; **neuer Mut beseelte ihn** he was filled *or* imbued with fresh courage; **ein neuer Geist beseelt unser Jahrhundert** a new spirit pervades *or* informs *(liter)* our century

be|se|hen *ptp* **besehen** *irreg* VT *(auch* **sich** *dat* **besehen***)* to take a look at, to look at VR to (take a) look at oneself

be|sei|beln [bəˈzaibln] *ptp* **beseibelt**, **be|sei|bern** [bəˈzaibɐn] *ptp* **beseibert** VT *(dial)* to dribble all over, to slobber all over

be|sei|ti|gen [bəˈzaitɪgn] *ptp* **beseitigt** VT **a** *(= entfernen)* to remove, to get rid of; *Abfall, Schnee* to clear (away); *Atommüll* to dispose of; *Schwierigkeiten* to sort *or* smooth out; *Fehler* to eliminate; *Missstände* to get rid of, to do away with **b** *(euph: = umbringen)* to get rid of, to eliminate

Be|sei|ti|gung F **-**, *no pl* **a** *(= das Entfernen)* removal, getting rid of; *(von Abfall, Schnee)* clearing (away); *(von Atommüll)* disposal; *(von Schwierigkeiten)* sorting *or* smoothing out; *(von Fehlern)* elimination; *(von Missständen)* doing away with **b** *(euph: von Menschen)* getting rid of, elimination

be|se|li|gen [bəˈzeːlɪgn] *ptp* **beseligt** VT to make blissfully happy; **~d/beseligt** blissful

Be|sen [ˈbeːzn] M **-s, -** **a** *(= Kehrbesen)* broom; *(= Reisigbesen)* besom; *(zum Rühren)* whisk; *(von Hexe)* broomstick; **ich fresse einen ~, wenn das stimmt** *(inf)* if that's right, I'll eat my hat *(inf)*; **neue ~ kehren gut** *(Prov)* a new broom sweeps clean *(Prov)* **b** *(pej inf: = Frau)* old bag *(inf)*, old boot *(Brit inf)*, besom *(dial pej inf)*

Be|sen-: **Be|sen|bin|der(in)** M(F) broom-maker; **Be|sen|kam|mer** F broom cupboard; **Be|sen|ma|cher(in)** M(F) broom-maker; **be|sen|rein** ADJ well-swept ADV **eine Wohnung ~ verlassen** to leave an apartment in a clean and tidy condition (for the next tenant); **Be|sen|schrank** M broom cupboard; **Be|sen|stiel** M broomstick, broom handle; **steif wie ein ~** as stiff as a poker; **er sitzt da als hätte er einen ~ verschluckt** *(inf)* he's sitting there as stiff as a board

> **BESENWIRTSCHAFT**
>
> **Besenwirtschaften** are found in Germany's wine regions. They are private bars opened by wine-growers as soon as the new wine (known as **Federweißer**) has fermented and is ready to drink. A broom is placed in front of the door - or in some regions a bunch of flowers is hung over the door, giving rise to the name **Straußwirtschaft** - as a sign that the **Besenwirtschaft** is open. As well as home-produced wine, substantial cold snacks are also normally available. In Austria such places are called **Buschenschenken**.

be|ses|sen [bəˈzɛsn] ADJ *(von bösen Geistern)* possessed *(von* by); *(von einer Idee, Leidenschaft etc)* obsessed *(von* with); **wie ~** like a thing possessed, like one possessed → *auch* **besitzen**

Be|ses|se|ne(r) [bəˈzɛsənə] MF *decl as adj* one possessed *no art*; **die ~n** the possessed; **wie ein ~r** like one possessed

Be|ses|sen|heit F **-**, *no pl (mit bösen Geistern)* possession; *(mit Idee, Leidenschaft etc)* obsession

be|set|zen *ptp* **besetzt** VT **a** *(= belegen)* to occupy; *(= reservieren)* to reserve; *(= füllen) Plätze, Stühle* to fill; **ist hier** *or* **dieser Platz besetzt?** is this place taken?; **irgendjemand hat die (Telefon)leitung stundenlang besetzt** somebody was on the line for hours, somebody was keeping the line busy for hours → *auch* **besetzt** **b** *(mit Person) Stelle, Amt, Posten* to fill; *(Theat) Rolle* to cast; *(mit Tieren)* to stock; **eine Stelle** *etc* **neu ~** to find a new person to fill a job **c** *(esp Mil: = eingenommen haben)* to occupy; *(Hausbesetzer)* to squat in **d** *(= dekorieren)* to trim; *(mit Edelsteinen)* to stud

Be|set|zer(in) M(F) *(= Hausbesetzer)* squatter

be|setzt [bəˈzɛtst] ✪ 27.3 ADJ *(= belegt) Telefon, Nummer, Leitung* engaged *(Brit)*, busy *(esp US)*; *(= in Gebrauch) Spielautomat etc* being used, taken, busy; *WC* occupied, engaged; *Abteil, Tisch* taken; *Hörsaal* being used; *Gebiet* occupied; *(= vorgebucht)* booked; *(voll) Bus, Wagen, Abteil etc* full (up); *(= anderweitig beschäftigt, verplant) Mensch* busy; **Freitag ist schon ~** Friday I'm/he's *etc* busy, Friday's out; **eine international ~e Jury** an international jury; **ein negativ ~es Thema** a very negative subject → *auch* **besetzen**

Be|setzt|ton M *pl* **-töne**, **Be|setzt|zei|chen** NT *(Telec)* engaged *(Brit) or* busy *(esp US)* tone

Be|set|zung [bəˈzɛtsʊŋ] F **-, -en** **a** *(= das Besetzen) (von Stelle)* filling; *(von Rolle)* casting; *(mit Tieren)* stocking; *(Theat: = Schauspieler)* cast; *(Mus: = Arrangement)* arrangement; *(Sport: = Mannschaft)* team, side; **die Nationalelf in der neuen ~** the new line-up for the international team; **das Stück in der neuen ~** the play with the new cast; **zweite ~** *(Theat)* understudy **b** *(Mil, von Gebäude, durch Hausbesetzer)* occupation

Be|set|zungs|couch F *(hum inf)* casting couch

Be|set|zungs|lis|te F *(Theat, Film)* cast list

be|sich|ti|gen [bəˈzɪçtɪgn] *ptp* **besichtigt** VT *(= ansehen) Kirche, Sehenswürdigkeit* to have a look at, to visit; *Stadt* to visit; *Betrieb* to tour, to have a look over *or* (a)round; *(zur Prüfung) Haus* to view, to have a look at, to look over; *Ware* to have a look at, to inspect; *Schule* to inspect; *(= inspizieren) Truppen* to inspect, to review; *(hum) Baby, zukünftigen Schwiegersohn etc* to inspect

Be|sich|ti|gung F **-, -en** *(von Sehenswürdigkeiten)* sightseeing tour; *(von Museum, Kirche, Betrieb)* tour; *(zur Prüfung) (von Haus)* viewing; *(von Wa-*

ren, Schule, Baby) inspection; *(von Truppen)* inspection, review; **nach einer kurzen ~ der Kirche/des Museums/Betriebs** *etc* after a short look (a)round the church/museum/factory *etc*; **die Waren liegen zur ~ aus** the goods are on display

Be|sich|ti|gungs-: Be|sich|ti|gungs|rei|se F, **Be|sich|ti|gungs|tour** F *(zum Vergnügen)* sightseeing tour *or* trip; *(zur Überprüfung)* tour of inspection; **Be|sich|ti|gungs|zei|ten** PL hours *pl* of opening

be|sie|deln *ptp* **besiedelt** VT *(= ansiedeln)* to populate, to settle *(mit* with); *(= sich niederlassen in)* to settle; *(= kolonisieren)* to colonize; *(Tiere)* to populate, to inhabit; *(Pflanzen)* to be found in, to inhabit; **dicht/dünn/schwach besiedelt** densely/thinly/sparsely populated

Be|sie|de|lung [bəˈziːdəlʊŋ] F -, -en, **Be|sied|lung** F -, -en settlement; *(= Kolonisierung)* colonization; **dichte/dünne/schwache ~** dense/thin/sparse population

Be|sied|lungs|dich|te F population density

be|sie|geln *ptp* **besiegelt** VT to seal

Be|sie|ge|lung [bəˈziːgəlʊŋ] F -, -en sealing

be|sie|gen *ptp* **besiegt** VT *(= schlagen)* to defeat, to beat; *Feind auch* to conquer, to vanquish *(liter)*; *(= überwinden)* to overcome, to conquer

Be|sieg|te(r) [beˈziːktə] MF *decl as adj* **die ~n** the conquered

Be|sie|gung [bəˈziːgʊŋ] F -, *no pl* defeat; *(von Feind auch)* conquest, vanquishing; *(= Überwindung)* overcoming

be|sin|gen *ptp* **besungen** [bəˈzʊŋən] VT *irreg* **a** *(= rühmen)* to sing of, to sing *(poet)*; **jdn/etw ~** to sing the praises of sb/sth **b** *Schallplatte, Tonband* to record

be|sin|nen *ptp* **besonnen** [bəˈzɔnən] VR *irreg (= überlegen)* to reflect, to think; *(= erinnern)* to remember *(auf jdn/etw* sb/sth); *(= es sich anders überlegen)* to have second thoughts; **besinne dich, mein Kind!** take thought, my child; **sich anders** *or* **eines anderen ~** to change one's mind; **sich eines Besseren ~** to think better of it; **er hat sich besonnen** he has seen the light; **ohne sich (viel) zu ~, ohne langes Besinnen** without a moment's thought *or* hesitation; **wenn ich mich recht besinne** if I remember correctly → *auch* **besonnen**

VT *(geh: = bedenken)* to reflect on, to ponder, to consider

be|sinn|lich ADJ contemplative; *Texte, Worte* reflective; **eine ~e Zeit** a time of contemplation; **~ werden** to become thoughtful *or* pensive

Be|sinn|lich|keit F reflection

Be|sin|nung [bəˈzɪnʊŋ] F -, *no pl* **a** *(= Bewusstsein)* consciousness; **bei/ohne ~ sein** to be conscious/unconscious; **die ~ verlieren** to lose consciousness; *(fig)* to lose one's head; **wieder zur ~ kommen** to regain consciousness, to come to; *(fig)* to come to one's senses; **jdn zur ~ bringen** to bring sb round *(Brit)* or around *(US)*; *(fig)* to bring sb to his senses **b** *(= das Sichbesinnen)* contemplation *(auf +acc* of), reflection *(auf +acc* upon) **c** *(= das Nachdenken)* reflection; **ich brauche Zeit, zur ~ zu kommen** I need time to reflect *or* for reflection

Be|sin|nungs-: Be|sin|nungs|auf|satz M discursive essay; **be|sin|nungs|los** ADJ unconscious, insensible; *(fig)* blind; *Wut* blind, insensate; **~ werden** to lose consciousness; **Be|sin|nungs|lo|sig|keit** F -, *no pl (lit)* unconsciousness

Be|sitz [bəˈzɪts] M, *no pl* **a** *(= das Besitzen)* possession; **im ~ von etw sein** to be in possession of sth; **ich bin im ~ Ihres Schreibens** I am in receipt of your letter; **etw in ~ nehmen** to take possession of sth; **von etw ~ ergreifen** to seize possession of sth; **von jdm ~ ergreifen** to take *or* seize hold of sb; *(Zweifel, Wahnsinn etc)* to take possession of sb's mind; **in privatem ~** in private ownership **b** *(= Eigentum)* property; *(= Landgut)* estate; **in jds ~ übergehen** to become sb's property

Be|sitz|an|spruch M claim of ownership; *(Jur)* title; **einen ~ auf etw** *(acc)* **haben** to have a claim to sth; **seine Besitzansprüche (auf etw** *acc)* **anmelden** to make one's claims (to sth), to lay claim to sth

be|sitz|an|zei|gend ADJ *(Gram)* possessive

Be|sitz|bür|ger|tum NT middle-class property owners *pl*, property-owning bourgeoisie

be|sit|zen *ptp* **besessen** [bəˈzɛsn] VT *irreg* to have, to possess; *käufliche Güter* to have, to own; *Vermögen* to possess, to own; *Wertpapiere* to have, to possess, to hold; *Narbe, grüne Augen* to have; *Rechte, jds Zuneigung etc* to enjoy, to have, to possess; **große Schönheit/Fähigkeiten** *etc* **~** to be possessed of great beauty/abilities *etc*; **die ~den Klassen** the propertied classes → *auch* **besessen**

Be|sit|zer(in) M(F) owner; *(von Wertpapieren auch, von Führerschein etc)* holder; *(= Inhaber auch)* proprietor; **den ~ wechseln** to change hands

Be|sit|zer|grei|fung [-lɛɐgraifʊŋ] F -, *(rare)* -en seizure

Be|sit|zer-: Be|sit|zer|stolz M pride of possession; **voller ~** proudly; **Be|sit|zer|wech|sel** M change of ownership

Be|sitz-: Be|sitz|ge|mein|schaft F *(= Gütergemeinschaft)* community of property; **Be|sitz|gier** F acquisitive greed, acquisitiveness; **be|sitz|los** ADJ without possessions; **Be|sitz|lo|se(r)** [-loːzə] MF *decl as adj* unpropertied person; *(entwurzelt)* dispossessed person; **Be|sitz|lo|sig|keit** F -, *no pl* lack of possessions; **Be|sitz|nah|me** [-naːmə] F -, *no pl* seizure; **Be|sitz|stand** M *(form)* assets *pl*; *(fig)* vested rights *pl*; **Be|sitz|stands|wah|rung** F *(fig)* protection of vested rights

Be|sitz|tum [bəˈzɪtstuːm] NT -s, -tümer [-tyːmɐ] *(= Eigentum)* possession, property *no pl*; *(= Grundbesitz)* estate(s *pl*), property

Be|sit|zung F possession; *(= privater Land- und Grundbesitz)* estate(s *pl*)

Be|sitz-: Be|sitz|ver|hält|nis|se PL property situation *or* conditions *pl*; **Be|sitz|ver|tei|lung** F distribution of property

be|sof|fen [bəˈzɔfn] ADJ *(inf: = betrunken)* pissed *(Brit sl)*, smashed *(inf)* → *auch* **besaufen**

Be|sof|fe|ne(r) [bəˈzɔfnə] MF *decl as adj (inf)* drunk

be|soh|len *ptp* **besohlt** VT to sole; *(= neu besohlen)* to resole

Be|soh|lung [bəˈzoːlʊŋ] F -, -en soling *no pl*; *(= Neubesohlung)* resoling

be|sol|den [bəˈzɔldn] *ptp* **besoldet** VT to pay

Be|sol|dung F -, -en pay

Be|sol|dungs-: Be|sol|dungs|grup|pe F pay *or* salary group; **Be|sol|dungs|ord|nung** F pay *or* salary regulations *pl*

be|son|de|re(r, s) [bəˈzɔndərə] ADJ **a** *(= ungewöhnlich, eine Ausnahme bildend)* special; *(= hervorragend) Qualität, Schönheit etc* exceptional; **er ist ein ganz ~r Freund** he is a very special friend; **es ist eine ~ Freude** it is a special *or* particular pleasure; **das sind ~ Umstände** those are special circumstances; **das ist ein ganz ~s Gemälde** that is a very unusual painting **b** *(= speziell)* special, particular; *(= bestimmt)* particular; **unser ~s Interesse gilt ...** we are particularly *or* (e)specially interested in ...; **wir legen ~n Wert auf ...** we place particular *or* special emphasis on ...; **ohne ~ Begeisterung** without any particular enthusiasm; **er hat sich mit ~m Eifer darangemacht** he set about it with particular enthusiasm; **es ist mein ganz ~r Wunsch, dass ...** it is my very special wish that ..., I particularly wish that ...; **in diesem ~n Fall** in this particular case; **keine ~n Vorlieben** no special *or* particular preferences; **das ist von ~r Bedeutung** it is of special *or* particular importance **c** *(= zusätzlich, separat, gesondert)* special, separate

Be|son|de|re(s) [bəˈzɔndərə] NT *decl as adj* **a das ~ und das Allgemeine** the particular and the general; **im ~n** *(= im Einzelnen)* in particular cases; *(= vor allem)* in particular **b etwas/nichts ~s** something/nothing special; **er möchte etwas ~s sein** he thinks he's something special; **das ist doch nichts ~s** that's nothing special, that's nothing out of the ordinary, what's special about that?; **das ~ daran** the special thing about it

Be|son|der|heit [bəˈzɔndɐhait] F -, -en unusual quality *or* feature; *(= besondere Eigenschaft)* peculiarity

be|son|ders [bəˈzɔndɐs] ADV *gut, hübsch, teuer etc* particularly, (e)specially; *(= ausdrücklich, vor allem)* particularly, in particular, (e)specially; *(= gesondert)* separately, individually; *(= speziell) anfertigen etc* specially; **~ du müsstest das wissen** you particularly *or* in particular *or* especially should know that; **nicht ~ (lustig/kalt)** not particularly *or* not (e)specially (funny/cold); **nicht ~ viel Geld** not a particularly *or* not an especially large amount of money; **ich habe nicht ~ wenig Geld** I'm not particularly badly off; **das Essen/der Film war nicht ~** *(inf)* the food/film was nothing special, the food/film was nothing to write home about *(inf)*; **wie gehts dir? – nicht ~** *(inf)* how are you? – not too hot *(inf)*; **~ wenig Fehler** an exceptionally *or* a particularly low number of mistakes; **er hat ~ viel/wenig gearbeitet** he did a particularly large/small amount of work; **er hat ~ viel gegessen** he ate a particularly large amount of food; **er hat ~ wenig gegessen** he ate particularly little

be|son|nen [bəˈzɔnən] ADJ level-headed; *Politik, Urteil auch* considered; **ihre ruhige, ~e Art** her calm and collected way ADV *(= mit vorsichtiger Bedachtsamkeit)* in a careful and thoughtful manner; **die Polizei ist ~ vorgegangen** the police proceeded in a careful and thoughtful way → *auch* **besinnen**

Be|son|nen|heit F -, *no pl* level-headedness; **durch seine ~ hat er eine Katastrophe verhindert** by staying calm and collected he avoided a disaster; **zur ~ aufrufen/mahnen** to call for/urge calm; **jdn zur ~ mahnen** to urge sb to stay calm

be|sonnt [bəˈzɔnt] ADJ sunny; **vom Glück ~** blessed with luck

be|sor|gen *ptp* **besorgt** VT **a** *(= kaufen, beschaffen etc)* to get; *(euph inf: = stehlen)* to acquire *(euph inf)*; **jdm/sich etw ~** to get sth for sb/oneself, to get sb/oneself sth; **jdm eine Stelle ~** to get *or* find a job for sb, to fix sb up with a job

b *(= erledigen)* to attend *or* see to; **was du heute kannst ~, das verschiebe nicht auf morgen** *(Prov)* never put off until tomorrow what you can do today

c *(= versorgen)* to take care of, to look after

d *(inf)* **es jdm ~** to sort sb out *(inf)*, to fix sb *(inf)*

e *(sl: sexuell)* **es jdm ~** to have it off with sb *(inf)*, to give sb one *(inf)*; **es sich** *(dat)* **selber ~** to bring oneself off *(sl)*

Be|sorg|nis [bəˈzɔrknɪs] F -, -se anxiety, worry, apprehension; **~ erregend** = **besorgniserregend**

be|sorg|nis|er|re|gend ADJ alarming, disquieting ADV alarmingly

be|sorgt [bəˈzɔrkt] ADJ **a** *(= voller Sorge)* anxious, worried *(wegen* about) **b um jdn/etw ~ sein** to be concerned about sb/sth ADV anxiously

Be|sorgt|heit F -, *no pl* concern, solicitude *(form)*

Be|sor|gung [bəˈzɔrgʊŋ] F -, -en **a** *(= das Kaufen)* purchase; **er wurde mit der ~ von ... beauftragt** he was asked to get ... **b** *(= Erledigung)* **jdn mit der ~ seiner Geschäfte betrauen** to entrust sb with looking after one's affairs **c** *(= Einkauf)* errand; **~en** shopping; **~en machen** to do some shopping

be|spạn|nen *ptp* **bespạnnt** VT **a** *(= überziehen) (mit Material)* to cover; *(mit Saiten, Fäden etc)* to string **b** *(mit Zugtieren) Wagen* to harness up; **den Wagen mit zwei Pferden ~** to harness two horses to the cart

Be|spạn|nung F **a** *no pl (= das Bespannen)* covering; *(mit Saiten etc)* stringing; *(mit Pferden)* harnessing **b** *(= Material)* covering; *(= Saiten, Fäden etc)* strings *pl*

be|spa|ßen *ptp* **bespaßt** VT *(inf)* to entertain, to keep amused; **er musste am Nachmittag seine Eltern ~** he had to keep his parents amused for the afternoon

be|spei|en *ptp* **bespie(e)n** [bəˈʃpi:(ə)n] VT *irreg (geh)* to spit at *or* (up)on

be|spi|cken *ptp* **bespi̦ckt** VT *(mit Fett)* to lard; *(mit Nägeln)* to stud, to spike; *(fig: = dicht bestecken)* to cover; **seine mit Orden bespickte Brust** his chest bristling with medals

be|spie|geln *ptp* **bespie̦gelt** VR *(lit: im Spiegel)* to look at oneself in a/the mirror; *(fig: = Selbstbetrachtung machen)* to contemplate oneself, to contemplate one's own navel *(hum)* VT *(geh) das eigene Ich* to contemplate; *(= darstellen, verarbeiten) Vergangenheit, Gefühle, Nöte* to portray, to give a picture of

be|spiel|bar ADJ *Rasen etc* playable; *Kassette, Tonträger* recordable

be|spie|len *ptp* **bespie̦lt** VT **a** *Schallplatte, Tonband* to record on, to make a recording on; **das Band ist mit klassischer Musik bespielt** the tape has a recording of classical music on it **b** *(Theat) Ort* to play **c** *(Sport)* to play on

be|spit|zeln *ptp* **bespi̦tzelt** VT to spy on

Be|spit|ze|lung [bəˈʃpɪtsəlʊŋ] F **-, -en**, **Be|spitz|lung** [bəˈʃpɪtslʊŋ] F **-, -en** spying

be|spöt|teln *ptp* **bespö̦ttelt** VT to mock (at), to scoff at, to ridicule

be|spre|chen *ptp* **bespro̦chen** [bəˈʃprɔxn] *irreg* VT **a** *(= über etw sprechen)* to discuss, to talk about; **wie besprochen** as arranged **b** *(= rezensieren)* to review **c** *Schallplatte, Tonband* to make a recording on; **ein besprochenes Band** a tape of sb's voice *or* of sb talking **d** *(= beschwören)* to (attempt a) cure by magic *or* incantation VR **sich mit jdm ~** to confer with sb, to consult (with) sb *(über +acc* about); **sich über etw** *(acc)* **~** to discuss sth

Be|spre|chung [bəˈʃprɛçʊŋ] F **-, -en** **a** *(= Unterredung)* discussion, talk; *(= Konferenz)* meeting; **nach ~ mit ...** after discussion with ..., after talking with ...; **er ist bei einer ~, er hat eine ~** he's in a meeting **b** *(= Rezension)* review, notice **c** *(von Tonbändern, Schallplatten)* recording **d** *(= Beschwörung)* conjuring away

Be|spre|chungs-: **Be|spre|chungs|exemp|lar** NT review copy; **Be|spre|chungs|zim|mer** NT meeting room

be|spren|gen *ptp* **bespre̦ngt** VT to sprinkle

be|spren|keln *ptp* **bespre̦nkelt** VT *(mit Farbe, Schmutz)* to speckle; *(fig: = übersäen)* to stud

be|sprin|gen *ptp* **bespru̦ngen** [bəˈʃprʊŋən] VT *irreg (Tier)* to mount, to cover

be|sprit|zen *ptp* **bespri̦tzt** VT to spray; *(= beschmutzen)* to (be)spatter, to splash VR to spray oneself; *(= sich beschmutzen)* to (be)spatter oneself, to splash oneself

be|sprü|hen *ptp* **besprü̦ht** VT to spray VR to spray oneself

be|spu|cken *ptp* **bespu̦ckt** VT to spit at *or* (up)on

bes|ser [ˈbɛsɐ] ✪ 28.1, 29.2 ADJ *comp von* **gut** **a** better; **~e Kreise/Gegend** better circles/area; **~e Leute** better class of people; **er hat ~e Tage** *or* **Zeiten gesehen** *(iro)* he has seen better days; **du willst wohl etwas Besseres sein!** *(inf)* I suppose you think you're better than other people, I suppose you think yourself superior; **soll es etwas Besseres sein?** did you have something of rather better quality in mind?; **~ werden** to improve, to get better; **das ist auch ~ so** it's better that way; **das wäre noch ~** *(iro)* no way; **Besseres zu tun haben** *(inf)* to have better things to do; **eine Wendung zum Besseren nehmen** to take a turn for the better; **jdn eines Besseren belehren** to teach sb otherwise *or* better → **besinnen**
b das Essen war nur ein ~er Imbiss the meal was just a glorified snack
ADV *comp von* **gut, wohl** **a** better; **~ ist ~** (it is) better to be on the safe side; **umso ~!** *(inf)* so much the better!; **~ (gesagt)** or rather, or better; **~ gestellt** → **bessergestellt**; **sie will immer alles ~ wissen** she always thinks she knows better; **das macht nichts ~** that doesn't improve matters, that doesn't make things any (the) better; **es kommt noch ~** *(iro)* there's worse *or* more to come *or* follow; **es ~ haben** to have a better life
b *(= lieber)* **lass das ~ bleiben** you had better leave well alone; **das solltest du ~ nicht tun** you had better not do that; **du tätest ~ daran ...** you would do better to ..., you had better ...; **dann geh ich ~** then I'd better go

bes|ser ge|hen *impers irreg aux sein*, **bes|ser+ge|hen** *sep impers irreg aux sein* VI **es geht jdm besser** sb is feeling better; **jetzt gehts der Firma wieder besser** the firm is doing better again now, things are going better again for the firm now → *auch* **gehen 1 g, 3 a**

bes|ser|ge|stellt ADJ better-off; **~ sein** to be better off

Bes|ser|ge|stell|te(r) [-gəʃtɛltə] MF *decl as adj* **die ~n** *pl* those who are better off, the better-off (people), the well-to-do

bes|sern [ˈbɛsɐn] VT **a** *(= besser machen)* to improve, to (make) better; *Verbrecher etc* to reform **b** *(old) (= ausbessern)* to mend; *(= verbessern)* to improve VR *(moralisch, im Benehmen)* to mend one's ways; **bessere dich** *(hum inf)* mend your ways!

bes|ser-: **bes|ser+ste|hen** *sep irreg (S Ger, Aus, Sw: aux sein)*, **bes|ser ste|hen** △ *irreg (S Ger, Aus, Sw: aux sein)* VR *(inf)* to be better off; **bes|ser+stel|len** *sep*, **bes|ser stel|len** △ VT **jdn ~** to improve sb's financial position VR to be better off

Bes|ser|stel|lung F **-, -n** (financial/social *etc*) betterment

Bes|se|rung [ˈbɛsərʊŋ] ✪ 50.4 F **-,** *no pl* improvement; *(von Verbrecher etc)* reformation; *(= Genesung)* recovery; **(ich wünsche dir) gute ~!** I wish you a speedy recovery, I hope you get better soon; **auf dem Wege der ~ sein** to be getting better, to be improving; *(Patient auch)* to be on the road to recovery

Bes|se|rungs-: **Bes|se|rungs|an|stalt** F *(dated)* reformatory *(dated)*, approved *(Brit dated)* *or* reform school; **bes|se|rungs|fä|hig** ADJ improvable; *Verbrecher* capable of being reformed, reformable; **Bes|se|rungs|maß|nah|me** F *(Jur)* corrective measure; **bes|se|rungs|wil|lig** ADJ willing to reform (oneself)

Bes|ser-: **Bes|ser|ver|die|nen|de(r)** [-vɛɐdi:nəndə] MF *decl as adj* **die ~n** *pl* those earning more, those on higher incomes, the upper income bracket(s *pl*); **Bes|ser|wes|si** [ˈbɛsɐvɛsi] M **-s, -s** *(pej inf)* West German know-all *or* know-it-all *(US)*; **Bes|ser|wis|ser** [ˈbɛsɐvɪsɐ] M **-s, -**, **Bes|ser|wis|se|rin** [-ərɪn] F **-, -nen** *(inf)* know-all *(Brit inf)*, know-it-all *(US inf)*, smart aleck *(inf)*, smart-ass *(esp US inf)*; **Bes|ser|wis|se|rei** [bɛsɐvɪsəˈrai] F **-,** *no pl (inf)* know-all *etc* manner; **bes|ser|wis|se|risch** [ˈbɛsɐvɪsərɪʃ] *(inf)* ADJ *Einstellung, Art, Beifahrer etc* know(-it)-all *attr* ADV in a superior *or* know(-it)-all manner

best- [bɛst] *in cpds mit adj* best

be|stal|len [bəˈʃtalən] *ptp* **bestạllt** VT *(form)* to install, to appoint *(zu* as)

Be|stal|lung F **-, -en** *(form)* installation, appointment

Be|stal|lungs|ur|kun|de F certificate of appointment

Be|stand M **a** *(= Fortdauer)* continued existence, continuance; **von ~ sein, ~ haben** to be permanent, to endure; **das Gesetz hat noch immer ~** the law still continues to exist; **zum 100-jährigen ~ des Vereins** *(Aus)* on the (occasion of the) 100th anniversary of the society **b** *(= vorhandene Menge, Tiere)* stock *(an +dat* of); *(= Forstbestand)* forest *or* timber *(US)* stand; **~ aufnehmen** to take stock **c** *(Aus: = Pacht)* lease, tenure; **in ~ geben** to let (out) *or* put out on lease

be|stan|den [bəˈʃtandn] ADJ **a** *(= bewachsen)* covered with trees; *Allee* lined with trees; **mit Bäumen ~** *(Allee)* tree-lined; *Abhang* tree-covered; **der Wald ist gut ~** the forest is well stocked **b nach ~er Prüfung** after passing the/an exam; **bei nicht ~er Prüfung** if you *etc* don't pass the exam; **sie feiert die ~e Prüfung** she's celebrating passing her exam **c** *(Sw: = alt)* advanced (in years) → *auch* **bestehen**

be|stän|dig [bəˈʃtɛndɪç] ADJ **a** *no pred (= dauernd)* constant, continual **b** *(= gleichbleibend)* constant; *Mitarbeiter* steady; *Wetter* settled **c** *(= widerstandsfähig)* resistant *(gegen* to); *Farbe* fast; *(= dauerhaft) Freundschaft, Beziehung* lasting, durable ADV **a** *(= dauernd)* constantly, continually; **ich mache mir ~ Sorgen** I am constantly *or* continually worried **b** *(= gleichbleibend)* consistently, steadily

-be|stän|dig ADJ *suf* -resistant; **hitzebeständig** heat-resistant

Be|stän|dig|keit F **-,** *no pl* **a** *(= gleichbleibende Qualität)* constant standard; *(von Mitarbeiter)* steadiness; *(von Liebhaber)* constancy; *(von Wetter)* settledness **b** *(= Widerstandsfähigkeit)* resistance; *(von Farbe)* fastness; *(= Dauerhaftigkeit: von Freundschaft)* durability

Be|stands-: **Be|stands|auf|nah|me** F stocktaking; **Be|stands|ka|ta|log** M *(in Bibliothek etc)* catalogue *(Brit) or* catalog *(US)* of holdings; **Be|stands|lis|te** F inventory, stock list

Be|stand|teil M component, part, element; *(fig)* essential *or* integral part; **sich in seine ~e auflösen** to fall to pieces, to come apart; **etw in seine ~e zerlegen** to take sth apart *or* to pieces

be|stär|ken *ptp* **bestärkt** VT to confirm; *Verdacht auch* to reinforce; **jdn in seinem Vorsatz/Wunsch ~** to confirm sb in his intention/desire, to make sb's intention/desire firmer *or* stronger; **das hat mich nur darin bestärkt, es zu tun** that merely made me all the more determined to do it

Be|stär|kung F confirmation; *(von Verdacht auch)* reinforcement

be|stä|ti|gen [bəˈʃtɛ:tɪgn] ✪ 38.1, 39.1, 47.2, 47.3, 48.3, 53.2 *ptp* **bestä̦tigt** VT **a** *Aussage, Verdacht, jdn* to confirm; *Theorie, Alibi etc* to bear out, to corroborate; *(Jur) Urteil* to uphold; *(Comput) Kennwort etc* to validate; **sich in etw** *(dat)* **bestätigt finden** to be confirmed in sth; **ich hatte angenommen, dass ... und fand mich darin bestätigt** I had assumed that ... and my assumption was confirmed *or* borne out; **~d** confirmative, confirmatory; **ein ~des Kopfnicken** a nod of confirmation; **... sagte er ~d** ... he said in confirmation
b *(Comm) Empfang, Brief* to acknowledge (receipt of)
c *(= beurkunden)* to confirm, to certify, to attest; **hiermit wird bestätigt, dass ...** this is to confirm *or* certify that ...; **jdn (im Amt) ~** to confirm sb's appointment
d *(= anerkennen)* to acknowledge, to recognize
VR to be confirmed, to prove true, to be proved true; **das tut er nur, um sich selbst zu ~** he only does it to boost his ego

Be|stä|ti|gung ✪ 53.2 F **-, -en** **a** confirmation *(auch Dokument)*; *(Comput) (von Kennwort etc)* validation; *(von Theorie, Alibi)* bearing out, corroboration; *(Jur: von Urteil)* upholding **b** *(= Empfangsbestätigung)* acknowledgement (of receipt) **c** *(= Beurkundung)* confirmation, certification, attestation; *(im Amt)* confirmation of appointment **d** *(= Anerkennung)* recognition

Be|stä|ti|gungs|schrei|ben NT letter of confirmation

be|stat|ten [bəˈʃtatn] *ptp* **bestattet** VT to bury; **bestattet liegen** to be *or* lie buried (*in +dat* in); **wann wird er bestattet?** when is the funeral (service)?

Be|stat|ter [bəˈʃtatɐ] M **-s, -**, **Be|stat|te|rin** [-ərɪn] F **-, -nen** undertaker, mortician *(US)*

Be|stat|tung F **-, -en** burial; *(= Feuerbestattung)* cremation; *(= Feier)* funeral; **kirchliche/weltliche ~** Christian/secular burial

Be|stat|tungs-: **Be|stat|tungs|in|sti|tut** NT, **Be|stat|tungs|un|ter|neh|men** NT undertaker's, mortician's *(US)*; **Be|stat|tungs|kos|ten** PL funeral expenses *pl*; **Be|stat|tungs|un|ter|neh|mer(in)** M(F) undertaker, funeral director, mortician *(US)*

be|stäu|ben *ptp* **bestäubt** VT to dust *(auch Cook)*, to sprinkle; *(Bot)* to pollinate; *(Agr)* to dust, to spray

Be|stäu|bung [bəˈʃtɔybʊŋ] F **-, -en** dusting, sprinkling; *(Bot)* pollination; *(Agr)* dusting, spraying

be|stau|nen *ptp* **bestaunt** VT to marvel at, to gaze at in wonder *or* admiration; *(verblüfft)* to gape at, to stare at in astonishment; **lass dich ~** let's have a good look at you; **sie wurde von allen bestaunt** they all gazed at her in admiration/gaped at her

best-: **best|be|mit|telt** ADJ *(Aus)* extremely well-off; **best|be|währt** ADJ *attr* well-proven; **best|be|zahlt** ADJ *attr* best-paid

bes|te → **beste(r, s)**

be|ste|chen *ptp* **bestochen** [bəˈʃtɔxn] *irreg* VT **a** *(mit Geld, Geschenken etc)* to bribe; *Beamte* to bribe, to corrupt; **ich lasse mich nicht ~** I'm not open to bribery; *(mit Geld etc auch)* I don't take bribes **b** *(= beeindrucken)* to captivate VI *(= Eindruck machen)* to be impressive *(durch* because of); **ein Mädchen, das durch Schönheit besticht** a girl of captivating beauty

be|ste|chend ADJ *Schönheit, Eindruck* captivating; *Angebot* tempting, enticing; *Klarheit* irresistible; *Geist, Kondition* winning ADV *(= beeindruckend) einfach, elegant, klar* impressively; *schön, logisch* incredibly

be|stech|lich [bəˈʃtɛçlɪç] ADJ bribable, corruptible, venal

Be|stech|lich|keit F **-**, *no pl* corruptibility, venality

Be|ste|chung [bəˈʃtɛçʊŋ] F **-, -en** bribery; *(von Beamten etc auch)* corruption; **aktive ~** *(Jur)* offering of bribes/a bribe (to an official); **passive ~** *(Jur)* taking of bribes/a bribe (by an official)

Be|ste|chungs-: **Be|ste|chungs|af|fä|re** F corruption *or* bribery scandal; **Be|ste|chungs|geld** NT *usu pl* bribe; **Be|ste|chungs|skan|dal** M corruption *or* bribery scandal; **Be|ste|chungs|sum|me** F bribe; **Be|ste|chungs|ver|such** M attempted bribery

Be|steck [bəˈʃtɛk] NT **-(e)s, -e** **a** *(= Essbesteck)* knives and forks *pl*, cutlery *sing (Brit)*, flatware *sing (US)*; *(= Set, für ein Gedeck)* set of cutlery *(Brit) or* flatware *(US)*; **ein silbernes ~** a set of silver cutlery *(Brit) or* flatware *(US)*; **Herr Ober, ich habe kein ~** waiter, I haven't any cutlery *(Brit) or* flatware *(US)* **b** *(= Instrumentensatz)* set of instruments; *(= Raucherbesteck)* pipe-cleaning implements *pl*, smoker's set; *(= Drogenbesteck)* needles; **chirurgisches ~** (set of) surgical instruments **c** *(Naut)* reckoning, ship's position

be|ste|cken *ptp* **besteckt** VT to decorate

Be|steck-: **Be|steck|kas|ten** M cutlery *(Brit) or* flatware *(US)* tray; *(mit Deckel)* cutlery canteen, flatware chest *(US)*; **Be|steck(schub)|fach** NT cutlery *(Brit) or* flatware *(US)* drawer

be|ste|hen ✪ 35.2, 35.4, 42.2, 42.3, 43.2, 43.3, 46.1, 53.2 *ptp* **bestanden** *irreg* [bəˈʃtandn] VT **a** *Examen, Probe* to pass; **eine Prüfung mit Auszeichnung/„sehr gut" ~** to get a distinction/"very good" (in an exam), to pass an exam with distinction/"very good" → *auch* **bestanden**

b *(= durchstehen) Schicksalsschläge* to withstand; *schwere Zeit* to come through, to pull through; *Gefahr* to overcome; *Kampf* to win

VI **a** *(= existieren)* to exist, to be in existence; *(Brauch auch)* to be extant; *(Zweifel, Hoffnung, Aussicht, Gefahr, Probleme etc)* to exist; **~ bleiben** *(Frage, Hoffnung etc)* to remain; **die Universität/Firma besteht seit hundert Jahren** the university/firm has been in existence *or* has existed for a hundred years; **es besteht die Aussicht/der Verdacht/die Hoffnung, dass …** there is a prospect/a suspicion/(a) hope that …

b *(= Bestand haben)* to continue to exist; *(Zweifel, Problem etc)* to continue to exist, to persist

c *(= sich zusammensetzen)* to consist *(aus* of); **in etw** *(dat)* **~** to consist in sth; *(Aufgabe)* to involve sth; **seine einzige Chance besteht darin, …** his only chance is to …; **die Schwierigkeit/das Problem besteht darin, dass …** the difficulty/problem consists *or* lies in the fact that …, the difficulty/problem is that …; **das Problem besteht darin, zu zeigen …** the problem consists in showing …

d *(= standhalten, sich bewähren)* to hold one's own *(in +dat* in); **vor etw** *(dat)* **~** to stand up to *or* against sth

e *(= durchkommen)* to pass; **(in einer Prüfung) mit „sehr gut" ~** to get a "very good" (in an exam)

f auf etw *(dat)* **~** to insist on sth; **ich bestehe darauf** I insist

Be|ste|hen NT **-s**, *no pl* **a** *(= Vorhandensein, Dauer)* existence; **seit ~ der Firma/des Staates** ever since the firm/state has existed *or* came into existence; **das 100-jährige ~ von etw feiern** to celebrate the hundredth anniversary *or* first hundred years of (the existence of) sth **b** *(= Beharren)* insistence *(auf +dat* on) **c** *(von Prüfung)* passing; *(von Schicksalsschlägen)* withstanding; *(von schwerer Zeit)* coming *or* pulling through; *(von Gefahr)* overcoming; **bei ~ der Prüfung** on passing the exam

be|ste|hen blei|ben VI *irreg aux sein* to last, to endure; *(Hoffnung)* to remain; *(Versprechen, Vereinbarungen)* to hold good

be|ste|hend ADJ existing; *Gesetze auch* present, current; *Umstände, Verhältnisse auch* prevailing; *Preise* current; **die seit 1887 ~en Gesetze** the laws which have existed since 1887

be|ste|hen las|sen *ptp* **bestehen lassen** VT *irreg* to keep, to retain

be|steh|len *ptp* **bestohlen** [bəˈʃtoːlən] VT *irreg* to rob; **jdn (um etw) ~** *(lit, fig)* to rob sb of sth

be|stei|gen *ptp* **bestiegen** [bəˈʃtiːgn] VT *irreg* **a** *Berg, Turm, Leiter* to climb (up), to ascend *(liter)*; *Fahrrad, Pferd* to mount, to get *or* climb on(to); *Bus, Flugzeug* to get on, to enter; *Auto, Segelflugzeug, Hubschrauber* to get into; *Schiff* to go on *or* aboard; *Thron* to ascend **b** *(= bespringen)* to mount, to cover; *(sl: Mensch)* to mount *(inf)*

Be|stei|gung F *(von Berg)* climbing, ascent; *(von Thron)* accession *(+gen* to)

Be|stell-: **Be|stell|block** M *pl* **-blöcke** *or* **-blocks** order pad, pad of order forms; **Be|stell|buch** NT order book

be|stel|len ✪ 47.2 *ptp* **bestellt** VT **a** *(= anfordern, in Restaurant)* to order; *(= abonnieren auch)* to subscribe to; **sich** *(dat)* **etw ~** to order sth; **das Material ist bestellt** the material has been ordered, the material is on order; **wie bestellt und nicht abgeholt** *(hum inf)* like orphan Annie *(inf)*

b *(= reservieren)* to book, to reserve

c *(= ausrichten)* **bestell ihm (von mir), dass …** tell him (from me) that …; **soll ich irgendetwas ~?** can I take a message?, can I give him/her a message?; **~ Sie ihm schöne Grüße von mir** give him my regards; **er hat nicht viel/nichts zu ~** he doesn't have much/any say here

d *(= kommen lassen) jdn* to send for, to summon; **jdn zu jdm/an einen Ort ~** to summon sb to sb/a place, to ask sb to come to sb/a place; **ich bin um** *or* **für 10 Uhr bestellt** I have an appointment for *or* at 10 o'clock

e *(= einsetzen, ernennen)* to nominate, to appoint

f *(= bearbeiten) Land* to till

g *(fig)* **es ist schlecht um ihn/mit seinen Finanzen bestellt** he is/his finances are in a bad way; **damit ist es schlecht bestellt** that's rather difficult

VI *(= anfordern: in Restaurant)* to order

Be|stel|ler [bəˈʃtɛlɐ] M **-s, -**, **Be|stel|le|rin** [-ərɪn] F **-, -nen** customer; *(= Abonnent)* subscriber; **Hinweise für den ~** ordering instructions, instructions on how to order

Be|stell|geld NT price including postage and packing; *(für Zeitungen etc)* subscription rate *or* charge

Bestelliste △ F → **Bestellliste**

Be|stell-: **Be|stell|kar|te** F order form; **Be|stell|lis|te** F order list; **Be|stell|men|ge** F order quantity; **Be|stell|num|mer** F order number *or* code; **Be|stell|pra|xis** F *(Med)* appointments-only surgery *(Brit)*, surgery *(Brit) or* doctor's office *(US)* with an appointments system; **Be|stell|schein** M order form *or* slip

Be|stel|lung ✪ 47.2, 47.3, 47.4 F **a** *(= Anforderung, das Angeforderte)* order; *(= das Bestellen)* ordering **b** *(= das Reservieren)* booking, reservation **c** *(= Nachricht)* message **d** *(= Ernennung)* nomination, appointment **e** *(von Acker, Land)* tilling

Be|stell|zet|tel M order form *or* slip

bes|ten ADV **am ~** → **beste(r, s)** ADV

bes|ten|falls [ˈbɛstnfals] ADV at best

bes|tens [ˈbɛstns] ADV *(= sehr gut)* very well; *(= herzlich) danken* very warmly; **sie lässt ~ grüßen** she sends her best regards

bes|te(r, s) [ˈbɛstə] ✪ 29.2 ADJ *superl von* **gut** **a** *attr* best; **im ~n Fall** at (the) best; **im ~n Alter, in den ~n Jahren** in the prime of (one's) life; **er hat seine ~n Jahre hinter sich** *(inf: = ist alt geworden)* he's over the hill *(inf)*; **mit (den) ~n Grüßen/Wünschen** with best wishes; **in ~n Händen** in the best of hands; **aus ~m Hause sein** to come from the very best of homes; **das kommt in den ~n Familien vor** *(hum)* that can happen in the best of families; **jds ~s Stück, jds ~r Freund** *(hum sl: = Penis)* sb's John Thomas *(Brit hum inf)*, sb's Johnnie *(US hum sl)*

b der/die/das Beste the best; **der/die Beste sein** to be the best; *(in der Klasse auch)* to be top (of the class); **meine Beste!** *(dated inf)* (my) dear lady; **mein Bester!** *(dated inf)* (my) dear fellow; **zu deinem Besten** for your good; **ich will nur dein Bestes** I've your best interests at heart; **sein Bestes tun** to do one's best; **sein Bestes geben** to give of one's best; **wir wollen das Beste hoffen** let's hope for the best; **der/die/das erste** *or* **nächste Beste** the first (person/job *etc*) that comes along; the first (hotel/cinema *etc*) one comes to; **ich hielte es für das Beste, wenn …** I thought it (would be) best if …; **das Beste wäre, wir …** the best thing would be for us to …, it would be best for us to …; **aufs** *or* **auf das Beste** very well; **zum Besten** for the best; **es steht nicht zum Besten** it does not look too promising *or* good *or* hopeful; **jdn zum Besten haben** *or* **halten** to pull sb's leg, to have sb on *(Brit inf)*; **etw zum Besten geben** *(= erzählen)* to tell sth; **jdm eine Geschichte/ein Liedchen zum Besten geben** to entertain sb with a story/song

ADV **am ~n** best; **ich hielt es für am ~n, wenn …** I thought it (would be) best if …; **am ~n würden wir gleich gehen** we'd be best to go immediately; **am ~n gehe ich jetzt** I'd *or* I had best go *or* be going now

be|sternt [bəˈʃtɛrnt] ADJ *(geh)* star-studded, starry

Bes|te(s) [ˈbɛstə] NT → **beste(r, s)** ADJ **b**

be|steu|ern *ptp* **besteuert** VT to tax; **Luxusartikel sind sehr hoch besteuert** there is a high tax on luxury goods, luxury goods are heavily taxed

Be|steu|e|rung F taxation; *(= Steuersatz)* tax

Best-: **Best|form** F *(esp Sport)* top *or* best form; **in ~ sein** to be in top form, to be on one's best form; **best|ge|hasst** [-gəhast] ADJ *attr (iro)* most hated; **best|ge|klei|det** [-gəklaidət] ADJ *attr* best-dressed

bes|ti|a|lisch [bɛs'tia:lɪʃ] ADJ bestial; *(inf)* awful, beastly *(inf)* ADV *(inf)* terribly, incredibly; *stinken, zurichten* dreadfully; *wehtun* like hell *(inf)*; *zurichten* brutally; **~ kalt** incredibly cold; **~ stinken** to stink to high heaven *(inf)*

Bes|ti|a|li|tät [bɛstiali'tɛ:t] F **-, -en** bestiality

be|sti|cken *ptp* **bestickt** VT to embroider

Bes|tie ['bɛstiə] F **-, -n** beast; *(fig)* animal

be|stimm|bar ADJ determinable; **schwer ~ sein** to be difficult to determine

be|stim|men *ptp* **bestimmt** VT **a** *(= festsetzen)* to determine; *Grenze, Ort, Zeit etc auch* to fix, to set; *(= entscheiden auch)* to decide; **sie will immer alles ~** she always wants to decide the way things are to be done → *auch* **bestimmt**
b *(= prägen) Stadtbild, Landschaft* to characterize; *(= beeinflussen) Preis, Anzahl* to determine; *Entwicklung, Werk, Stil etc* to have a determining influence on; *(Gram) Kasus, Tempus* to determine; **näher ~** *(Gram)* to qualify
c *(= wissenschaftlich feststellen) Alter, Standort* to determine, to ascertain; *Pflanze, Tier, Funde* to classify; *(= definieren) Wort, Bedeutung* to define
d *(= vorsehen)* to intend, to mean *(für* for); **jdn zu etw ~** to choose *or* designate sb as sth; **er ist zu Höherem bestimmt** he is destined for higher things; **wir waren füreinander bestimmt** we were meant for each other
VI **a** *(= entscheiden)* to decide *(über +acc* on); **du hast hier nicht zu ~** you don't make the decisions here
b *(= verfügen)* **er kann über sein Geld allein ~** it is up to him what he does with his money; **du kannst nicht über ihn/seine Zeit ~** it's not up to you to decide what he's going to do/how his time is to be spent
VR **sich nach etw ~** to be determined by sth

be|stim|mend ADJ *(= entscheidend) Faktor, Einfluss* determining, decisive, determinant; **die ~e Figur innerhalb der Partei** the most influential figure within the party; **für etw ~ sein** to be characteristic of sth; *(= entscheidend)* to have a determining influence on sth ADV decisively; **an etw** *(dat)* **~ mitwirken** to play a determining *or* decisive part in sth

be|stimmt [bə'ʃtɪmt] ADJ **a** *(= gewiss, nicht genau genannt) Leute, Dinge, Vorstellungen, Aussagen etc* certain; *(= speziell, genau genannt)* particular, definite; *(= festgesetzt) Preis, Tag* set, fixed; *(= klar, deutlich) Angaben, Ausdruck* definite, precise; *(Gram) Artikel, Zahlwort* definite; **suchen Sie etwas Bestimmtes?** are you looking for anything in particular?; **den ganz ~en Eindruck gewinnen, dass ...** to get *or* have a definite *or* the distinct impression that ... → *auch* **bestimmen**
b *(= entschieden) Auftreten, Ton, Mensch* firm, resolute, decisive; **höflich, aber ~** polite but firm
ADV **a** *(= sicher)* definitely, certainly; **ich weiß ganz ~, dass ...** I know for sure *or* for certain that ...; **kommst du? – ja – ~?** are you coming? – yes – definitely?; **ich schaffe es ~** I'll manage it all right; **er schafft es ~ nicht** he definitely won't manage it
b *(= wahrscheinlich)* no doubt; **das hat er ~ verloren** he's bound to have lost it; **er kommt ~ wieder zu spät** he's bound to be late again

Be|stimmt|heit F **-,** *no pl* **a** *(= Sicherheit)* certainty; **ich kann mit ~ sagen, dass ...** I can say definitely *or* with certainty that ...; **ich weiß aber mit ~, dass ...** but I know for sure *or* for certain that ... **b** *(= Entschiedenheit)* firmness; **in** *or* **mit aller ~** quite categorically

Be|stim|mung F **a** *(= Vorschrift)* regulation; **gesetzliche ~en** legal requirements
b *no pl (= Zweck)* purpose; **eine Brücke/Straße/Anlage ihrer ~ übergeben** to open a new bridge/road/plant officially
c *(= Schicksal)* destiny
d *(old: = Ort)* destination
e *(Gram)* modifier; **adverbiale ~** adverbial modifier
f *(= das Bestimmen)* determination, determining; *(von Grenze, Zeit etc)* fixing, setting; *(Gram, von Preis, Anzahl)* determining, determination; *(von Alter, Standort)* determining, determination, ascertaining, ascertainment; *(von Pflanze, Tier, Funden)* classification; *(= Definition)* definition; **seine ~ zu dieser Aufgabe** choosing him for this task; **nähere ~** *(durch Adverb)* qualifying, qualification

Be|stim|mungs-: **Be|stim|mungs|bahn|hof** M (station of) destination; **be|stim|mungs|ge|mäß** ADJ, ADV in accordance with the requirements; **Be|stim|mungs|glei|chung** F *(Math)* conditional equation; **Be|stim|mungs|grö|ße** F *(Math, Phys)* defining quantity; **Be|stim|mungs|ha|fen** M (port of) destination; **Be|stim|mungs|land** NT (country of) destination; **Be|stim|mungs|ort** M *pl* **-orte** (place of) destination; **Be|stim|mungs|wort** NT *pl* **-wör|ter** *(Gram)* modifier

Best-: **best|in|for|miert** ADJ *attr* best-informed; **Best|leis|tung** F *(esp Sport)* best performance; **seine persönliche ~** his personal best; **Best|mar|ke** F record; **best|mög|lich** ADJ *no pred* best possible; **wir haben unser Bestmögliches getan** we did our (level *(Brit)*) best ADV in the best way possible

Best. Nr. *abbr von* **Bestellnummer**

be|sto|cken *ptp* **bestockt** VT to stock; **der Wald ist gut bestockt** the forest is well timbered

Be|sto|ckung F *(= das Bestocken)* stocking; *(= Bestand)* stock

be|stra|fen *ptp* **bestraft** VT to punish; *(Jur) jdn* to sentence *(mit* to); *(Sport) Spieler, Foul* to penalize; **der Schiedsrichter bestrafte das Foul mit einem Elfmeter** the referee awarded *or* gave a penalty for the foul

Be|stra|fung F **-, -en** punishment; *(Jur)* sentencing; *(Sport)* penalization; **wir fordern eine strengere ~ von ...** we demand more severe punishments *or (Jur auch)* sentences for ...

be|strah|len *ptp* **bestrahlt** VT to shine on; *(= beleuchten) Gebäude, Bühne* to light up, to illuminate; *(Med)* to give radiotherapy *or* ray *or* radiation treatment to; *Lebensmittel* to irradiate; **er ließ sich von der Sonne ~** he was soaking up the sun

Be|strah|lung F illumination; *(Med)* radiotherapy, ray *or* radiation treatment; *(= von Lebensmitteln)* irradiation; **Pflanzen der direkten ~ der Sonne aussetzen** to expose plants to direct sunlight, to expose plants directly to the sun's rays; **15 ~en verordnen** to prescribe (a course of) 15 doses of radiotherapy

Be|strah|lungs-: **Be|strah|lungs|ka|no|ne** F *(Med)* radiation gun; **Be|strah|lungs|lam|pe** F radiation *or* ray lamp

Be|stre|ben NT endeavour *(Brit)*, endeavor *(US)*; **im** *or* **in seinem ~, dem Fußgänger auszuweichen** in his efforts *or* attempts *or* endeavo(u)rs to avoid the pedestrian

be|strebt [bə'ʃtre:pt] ADJ **~ sein, etw zu tun** to endeavour *(Brit)* *or* endeavor *(US)* to do sth; **wir waren immer ~, ...** we have always endeavo(u)red ..., it has always been our endeavo(u)r ...

Be|stre|bung F *usu pl* endeavour *(Brit)*, endeavor *(US)*, attempt, effort

be|strei|chen *ptp* **bestrichen** [bə'ʃtrɪçn] VT *irreg* **a** *(mit Salbe, Flüssigkeit)* to spread; *(mit Butter)* to spread, to butter; *(Cook, mit Milch etc)* to coat; *(mit Farbe)* to paint; **etw mit Butter/Fett/Öl ~** to butter/grease/oil sth; **etw mit Butter/Salbe/Klebstoff ~** to spread butter/ointment/glue on sth; **etw mit Farbe ~** to put a coat of paint on sth **b** *(Mil)* to rake, to sweep **c** *(Scheinwerfer, Strahl)* to sweep (over); *(in der Elektronik: = abtasten)* to scan

be|strei|ken *ptp* **bestreikt** VT to black *(Brit)*, to boycott; **bestreikt** strikebound; **die Fabrik wird zurzeit bestreikt** there's a strike on in the factory at the moment; **„dieser Betrieb wird bestreikt"** "please do not cross the picket line"

Be|strei|kung [bə'ʃtraikʊŋ] F **-, -en** blacking *(Brit)*, boycotting; **die ~ einer Fabrik beschließen** to decide to take strike action against a factory, to decide to black *(Brit)* *or* boycott a factory

be|streit|bar ADJ disputable, contestable

be|strei|ten *ptp* **bestritten** [bə'ʃtrɪtn] VT *irreg* **a** *(= abstreiten)* to dispute, to contest, to challenge; *(= leugnen)* to deny; **jdm das Recht auf ... ~** to dispute *etc* sb's right to ...; **das möchte ich nicht ~** I'm not disputing *or* denying it **b** *(= finanzieren)* to pay for, to finance; *Kosten* to carry, to defray *(form)* **c** *(= tragen, gestalten)* to provide for, to carry; **er hat das ganze Gespräch allein bestritten** he did all the talking

Be|strei|tung [bə'ʃtraitʊŋ] F **-, -en** **a** *(= das Leugnen)* denial **b** *(= Finanzierung)* financing; *(von Kosten)* carrying, defrayal *(form)*

best|re|nom|miert ['bɛst-] ADJ *attr* most renowned

be|streu|en *ptp* **bestreut** VT to cover *(mit* with); *(Cook)* to sprinkle

be|stri|cken *ptp* **bestrickt** VT **a** *(fig)* to charm, to captivate; **~der Charme** alluring charms **b** *(hum inf)* to knit things for

be|strumpft [bə'ʃtrʊmpft] ADJ in stockings; *Beine* stockinged

Best|sel|ler ['bɛstzɛlɐ] M **-s, -** bestseller

Best|sel|ler-: **Best|sel|ler|au|tor(in)** M(F) bestselling author, bestseller; **Best|sel|ler|lis|te** F bestseller list; *(von Schallplatten)* charts *pl*

best|si|tu|iert ['bɛst-] ADJ *attr (esp Aus)* well-to-do, well-off

be|stü|cken [bə'ʃtʏkn] *ptp* **bestückt** VT to fit, to equip; *(Mil)* to arm; *Lager* to stock; **sie ist gut bestückt** *(hum inf)* she's pretty well-stacked *(inf)*

Be|stü|ckung F **-, -en** **a** *(= das Bestücken)* fitting, equipping; *(Mil)* arming; *(von Lager)* stocking **b** *(= Ausstattung)* equipment; *(= Geschütze)* guns *pl*, armaments *pl*

Be|stuh|lung [bə'ʃtu:lʊŋ] F **-, -en** seating *no indef art*

be|stür|men *ptp* **bestürmt** VT to storm; *(mit Fragen, Bitten)* to bombard; *(mit Anfragen, Briefen, Anrufen)* to inundate

Be|stür|mung [bə'ʃtʏrmʊŋ] F **-, -en** storming; *(mit Fragen, Bitten)* bombardment; *(mit Anfragen, Briefen, Anrufen)* inundation

be|stür|zen *ptp* **bestürzt** VT to shake, to fill with consternation → *auch* **bestürzt**

be|stür|zend ADJ alarming; **ich finde es ~, wie wenig die Schüler wissen** it fills me with consternation *or* it dismays me to see how little the children know ADV *hoch, niedrig* alarmingly

be|stürzt [bə'ʃtʏrtst] ADJ filled with consternation; **sie machte ein ~es Gesicht** a look of consternation came over her face ADV in consternation; **er sah mich ~ an** he looked at me in consternation → *auch* **bestürzen**

Be|stürzt|heit F **-,** *no pl* consternation

Be|stür|zung [bə'ʃtʏrtsʊŋ] F **-,** *no pl* consternation

be|stusst [bə'ʃtʊst] ADJ *(inf) Kerl, Ausrede, Behauptung* crazy

Best-: **Best|wert** M *(Fin)* top value; *(Tech, Sport)* best performance; **Best|zeit** F *(esp Sport)* best time; **Best|zu|stand** M perfect condition

Be|such [bə'zu:x] M **-(e)s, -e** **a** *(= das Besuchen)* visit *(des Museums etc* to the museum *etc)*; *(von Schule, Veranstaltung)* attendance *(+gen* at); **ein ~ (von) meiner Tante** a visit from my aunt; **zu seinen Aufgaben gehört auch der ~ der Klienten** his jobs include visiting clients; **bei jdm auf** *or* **zu ~ sein** to be visiting sb; **(von jdm) ~**

erhalten *or* **bekommen** to have *or* get a visit (from sb); **jdm einen ~ abstatten, einen ~ bei jdm machen** to pay sb a visit
b *(= Besucher)* visitor; visitors *pl*; **ist dein ~ wieder abgefahren?** have your visitors/has your visitor gone?; **er hat ~** he has company *or* visitors/a visitor; **er bekommt viel ~** he has a lot of visitors, he often has visitors

be|su|chen *ptp* **besucht** VT *jdn* to visit, to pay a visit to; *(Arzt) Patienten* to visit; *Vortrag, Schule, Seminar, Gottesdienst* to attend, to go to; *Kino, Theater, Lokal* to go to; *Bordell, Museum* to go to, to visit; **du kannst mich mal am Abend** *or* **im Mondschein ~** *(euph inf)* you know what you can do *(inf)* → *auch* **besucht**

Be|su|cher(in) M(F) visitor; *(von Kino, Theater)* patron *(form)*; **etwa 1.000 ~ waren zu der Veranstaltung/dem Vortrag/der Ausstellung gekommen** about 1,000 people attended *or* went to the function/lecture/visited the exhibition; **ein regelmäßiger ~ der Oper** a regular opera-goer, an habitué of the opera

Be|su|cher-: **Be|su|cher|aus|weis** M visitor's pass; **Be|su|cher|re|kord** M record number of visitors; *(Sport)* record attendance; **die Ausstellung verzeichnete einen ~** the exhibition broke all attendance records; **Be|su|cher|rit|ze** F *(hum inf) crack between the two mattresses of twin beds*; **Be|su|cher|schar** F crowd of visitors; **Be|su|cher|ter|ras|se** F *(von Flughafen etc)* observation terrace; **Be|su|cher|zahl** F attendance figures *pl*; *(bei Schloss, Museum, Ausstellung etc)* number of visitors

Be|suchs-: **Be|suchs|er|laub|nis** F visitor's card; *(für Land)* visitor's visa; **~ haben** to be allowed to receive visitors; **~ bekommen** to obtain permission to visit sb; **Be|suchs|recht** NT *(Jur, nach Scheidung)* (right of) access; **das ~ bei ihrem Sohn** the right to visit her son; **Be|suchs|tag** M visiting day; **be|suchs|wei|se** ADV on a visit; **Be|suchs|zeit** F visiting time; **jetzt ist keine ~** it's not visiting time; **Be|suchs|zim|mer** NT visitor's room

be|sucht [bə'zu:xt] ADJ **gut/schlecht/schwach ~ sein** to be well/badly/poorly attended; *(Schloss etc)* to get a lot of/not many/only a handful of visitors → *auch* **besuchen**

be|su|deln *ptp* **besudelt** *(geh)* VT *Wände* to besmear; *Kleidung, Hände* to soil; *(fig) Andenken, Namen, Ehre* to besmirch, to sully VR **sich mit Blut ~** *(fig)* to get blood on one's hands

Be|ta ['be:ta] NT **-(s), -s** beta

Be|ta|blo|cker M *(Med)* beta-blocker

be|tagt [bə'ta:kt] ADJ *(geh)* aged, well advanced in years

Be|tagt|heit F **-,** *no pl (geh)* advancing years *pl*

be|ta|keln *ptp* **betakelt** VT *(Aus: = betrügen)* to swindle

be|tan|ken *ptp* **betankt** VT *Fahrzeug* to fill up; *Flugzeug* to refuel

Be|tan|kung F **-, -en** *(von Fahrzeug)* filling-up *(Brit)*, refueling *(US)*; *(von Flugzeug, Rennwagen)* refuelling *(Brit)*, refueling *(US)*

be|tas|ten *ptp* **betastet** VT to feel; *(Med auch)* to palpate *(form)*

Be|ta-: **Be|ta|strah|len** PL beta rays *pl*; **Be|ta|strah|lung** F beta radiation; **Be|ta|teil|chen** NT beta particle

be|tä|ti|gen *ptp* **betätigt** VT **a** *Muskeln, Gehirn, Darm, Auslöser* to activate; *Bremse* to apply, to put on; *Mechanismus* to operate, to work, to activate, to actuate *(form)*; *Taste, Knopf* to press; *(= drehen)* to turn; *Schalter, Blinker* to turn on; *Hebel* to move, to operate; *Sirene* to operate, to sound
b *(liter. = bewirken)* to bring about, to effect
c *(liter. = einsetzen)* to put into effect
VR to busy oneself; *(körperlich)* to get some exercise; **sich politisch ~** to be active in politics; **sich als etw ~** *(beruflich)* **sich wissenschaftlich/literarisch ~** to do (some) scientific work/some writing; **sich künstlerisch ~** to do (some) painting/sculpture *etc*; **sich sportlich ~** to do sport; **sich geistig und körperlich ~** to stay active in body and mind; **wenn man sich längere Zeit nicht geistig betätigt hat** if you haven't used your mind for months

Be|tä|ti|gung F **a** *(= Tätigkeit)* activity; **an ~ fehlt es mir nicht** I've no lack of things to do
b *(= Aktivierung)* operation; *(von Muskel, Gehirn, Darm)* activation; *(von Bremsen)* applying, application; *(von Mechanismus)* operation, activation, actuation *(form)*; *(von Knopf)* pressing; *(durch Drehen)* turning; *(von Schalter)* turning on; *(von Hebel)* moving; *(von Sirene)* sounding; **etw zur ~ der Muskeln tun** to do sth to exercise one's muscles; **die ~ des Mechanismus erfolgt durch Knopfdruck** pressing the button activates the mechanism *or* sets the mechanism in motion

Be|tä|ti|gungs-: **Be|tä|ti|gungs|drang** M need for activity; **Be|tä|ti|gungs|feld** NT sphere *or* field of activity

Be|ta|tron ['be:tatro:n] NT **-s, -e** betatron

be|tat|schen *ptp* **betatscht** VT *(inf)* to paw *(inf)*

be|täu|ben [bə'tɔybn] *ptp* **betäubt** VT *(= unempfindlich machen) Körperteil* to (be)numb, to deaden; *Nerv* to deaden; *Schmerzen* to kill, to deaden; *(durch Narkose)* to anaesthetize; *(mit einem Schlag)* to stun, to daze; *(fig) Kummer, Gewissen* to ease; *(fig: = benommen machen)* to stun; **er versuchte, seinen Kummer mit Alkohol zu ~** he tried to drown his sorrows with alcohol; **~der Lärm** deafening noise; **ein ~der Duft** an overpowering smell; **der Duft betäubte mich fast** I was almost overcome by the smell

Be|täu|bung F **-, -en** **a** *(= das Betäuben)* (be)numbing, deadening; *(von Nerv, Schmerz)* deadening; *(von Schmerzen)* killing; *(durch Narkose)* anaesthetization; *(durch Schlag)* stunning, dazing; *(von Gewissen, Kummer)* easing **b** *(= Narkose)* anaesthetic; **örtliche** *or* **lokale ~** local anaesthetic

Be|täu|bungs|mit|tel NT anaesthetic; *(= Droge)* narcotic

Be|täu|bungs|mit|tel|ge|setz NT *law concerning drug abuse*, narcotics law *(US)*

be|taut [bə'taut] ADJ dewy, bedewed

Be|ta|ver|si|on F *(Comput)* beta release, beta version

Bet- ['be:t-]: **Bet|bank** F *pl* **-bänke** kneeler; **Bet|bru|der** M *(pej inf)* churchy type, Holy Joe *(Brit pej inf)* *or* Roller *(US pej inf)*

Be|te ['be:tə] F **-,** *(rare)* **-n** beet; **Rote ~** beetroot

be|tei|len *ptp* **beteilt** VT *(Aus)* to give presents to; *Flüchtlinge etc* to give gifts to; **jdn mit etw ~** to give sb sth

be|tei|li|gen [bə'tailɪgn] *ptp* **beteiligt** VT **jdn an etw** *(dat)* **~** to let sb take part in sth, to involve sb in sth; *(finanziell)* to give sb a share in sth VR to take part, to participate (*an +dat* in); *(finanziell)* to have a share (*an +dat* in); **sich an den Unkosten ~** to contribute to the expenses; **ich möchte mich bei** *or* **an dem Geschenk ~** I would like to put something toward(s) the present

be|tei|ligt [bə'tailɪçt] ADJ **an etw** *(dat)* **~ sein/werden** to be involved in sth, to have a part in sth; *(finanziell)* to have a share in sth; *am Gewinn* to have a slice of sth *or* a share in sth; **an einem Unfall/einer Schlägerei ~ sein** to be involved in an accident/a fight; **an einer Tat/Sache ~ sein** to be party to a deed/cause; **er war an dem Gelingen der Aktion maßgeblich ~** he made a major contribution to the success of the campaign; **er ist an dem Geschäft (mit 250.000 Euro) ~** he has a (250,000-euro) share in the business

Be|tei|lig|te(r) [bə'tailɪçtə] MF *decl as adj* person involved; *(= Teilhaber)* partner; *(Jur)* party; **die an der Diskussion ~n** those taking part in *or* involved in the discussion; **die am Unfall ~n** those involved in the accident; **an alle ~n** to all concerned

Be|tei|li|gung F **-, -en** **a** *(= Teilnahme)* (*an +dat* in) participation; *(finanziell)* share; *(an Unfall)* involvement **b** *(= das Beteiligen)* involvement *(an +dat* in); **die ~ der Arbeiter am Gewinn** giving the workers a share in the profits

Be|tei|li|gungs|ge|sell|schaft F *(Fin, Comm)* holding company

Be|tei|lung F *(Aus)* giving; **die ~ der Armen mit ...** the giving of ... to the poor

Be|tel ['be:tl] M **-s,** *no pl* betel

Be|tel|nuss F betel nut

be|ten ['be:tn] VI to pray (*um, für, zu* to), to say one's prayers; *(bei Tisch)* to say grace VT to say

be|teu|ern [bə'tɔyɐn] *ptp* **beteuert** VT to declare, to aver, to asseverate *(liter)*; *Unschuld auch* to protest, to affirm; **er beteuerte mir seine Liebe** he declared his love to me, he professed his love for me

Be|teu|e|rung F declaration, averment, asseveration *(liter)*; *(von Unschuld auch)* protestation

be|tex|ten *ptp* **betextet** VT *Bild* to write a caption for; *Lied* to write the words *or* lyric(s) for

Bet-: **Bet|glo|cke** F church bell; **Bet|haus** NT temple

be|ti|teln *ptp* **betitelt** VT to entitle; *(= anreden) jdn* to address as, to call; *(= beschimpfen)* to call; **die Sendung ist betitelt ...** the broadcast is entitled ...; **wie ist das Buch betitelt?** what is the book called?, what's the book's title?; **er betitelte seinen Artikel ...** he called his article ..., he gave his article the title ..., he entitled his article ...

Be|ti|te|lung [bə'ti:təlʊŋ] F **-, -en** **a** *no pl (= das Betiteln)* **eine andere ~ des Films wäre besser** it would be better to call the film something else, it would be better to find a different title for the film **b** *(= Titel)* title; *(= Anrede)* form of address; *(= Benennung)* name; **ich verbitte mir eine solche ~** I refuse to be called names like that

Be|ton [be'tɔŋ, be'tõ:, *(esp Aus)* be'to:n] M **-s,** *(rare)* **-s** concrete

Be|ton- *in cpds* concrete; **Be|ton|bau** M **a** *pl* **-bauten** concrete building *or* structure **b** *no pl (= Bauweise)* concrete construction; **Be|ton|bau|er(in)** M(F) *pl* **-bauer(innen)** builder; **Be|ton|bau|wei|se** F concrete construction; **ein Gebäude in ~ errichten** to erect a building as a concrete construction; **Be|ton|bun|ker** M **a** *(lit)* concrete bunker; *(= Luftschutzbunker)* concrete air-raid shelter **b** *(fig pej: = Betonhochhaus)* concrete block *(pej)*; **Be|ton|burg** F *(pej)* pile of concrete; **Be|ton|de|cke** F concrete ceiling; *(von Straße)* concrete surface

be|to|nen ✪ 53.6 *ptp* **betont** VT **a** *(= hervorheben)* to emphasize; *Hüften, Augen auch* to accentuate; *(= Gewicht legen auf auch)* to stress; **ich möchte noch einmal ~, dass ...** I want to stress *or* emphasize once again that ... → *auch* **betont**
b *(Ling, Mus: = einen Akzent legen auf)* to stress; *(= Tonfall gebrauchen)* to intonate *(form)*; **ein Wort falsch ~** to give a word the wrong stress, to stress a word wrongly; **du musst den Satz anders ~** you must stress the sentence differently; *(mit Tonfall)* you must say the sentence with a different intonation

Be|ton|frak|ti|on [be'tɔŋ-, be'tõ:-, *(esp Aus)* be'to:n-] F *(Pol inf)* hardline faction

be|to|nie|ren [beto'ni:rən] *ptp* **betoniert** VT **a** *(lit)* to concrete; **betoniert** concrete **b** *(fig: = festlegen)* to firm up VI **a** *(lit)* to concrete **b** *(Sport sl)* to block the goal (area)

Be|to|nie|rung F **-, -en** *(= das Betonieren)* concreting; *(= Betondecke auch)* concrete surface

Be|ton-: **Be|ton|klotz** M *(lit)* block of concrete, concrete block; *(fig pej)* concrete block; **Be|ton|kopf** M *(pej inf)* reactionary die-hard; **Be|ton|mi|scher** M; **Be|ton|misch|ma|schi|ne** F cement mixer; **Be|ton|pfei|ler** M concrete pillar; **Be|ton|plat|te** F concrete slab; **Be|ton|rie|ge** F *(Pol inf)* hardline faction; **Be|ton|si|lo** M *(pej inf)* high-rise block, concrete block *(pej)*

be|tont [bə'to:nt] ADJ *Höflichkeit* emphatic, deliberate; *Kühle, Sachlichkeit* pointed; *Eleganz* pronounced ADV *knapp, kühl* deliberately, pointedly, emphatically; **~ sparsam leben** to live a markedly modest life; **sich ~ einfach kleiden** to dress with marked *or* pronounced simplicity → *auch* **betonen**

Be|to|nung F -, -en **a** *no pl (= das Betonen)* emphasis; *(von Hüften, Augen)* accentuation; *(= Unterstreichung)* stressing **b** *(= Akzent)* stress; *(fig: = Gewicht)* emphasis, stress, accent; **die ~ liegt auf der ersten Silbe** the stress is on the first syllable

Be|to|nungs|zei|chen NT stress mark

Be|ton|wüs|te F *(pej)* concrete jungle

be|tö|ren [bəˈtøːrən] *ptp* **betört** VT to bewitch, to beguile

be|tö|rend ADJ bewitching; *Worte auch* beguiling; *(stärker)* seductive

Be|tö|rer [bəˈtøːrɐ] M -s, -, **Be|tö|re|rin** [-ərɪn] F -, -nen *(geh)* bewitcher, beguiler

Be|tö|rung F -, -en bewitchment

Bet|pult NT prie-dieu, kneeler

betr. *abbr von* **betreffend, betrifft, betreffs**

Betr. *abbr von* **Betreff, betrifft**

Be|tracht [bəˈtraxt] M -(e)s, *no pl* **a außer ~ bleiben** to be left out of consideration, to be disregarded; **etw außer ~ lassen** to leave sth out of consideration, to disregard sth; **in ~ kommen** to be considered; **nicht in ~ kommen** to be out of the question; **jdn in ~ ziehen** to take sb into consideration, to consider sb; **etw in ~ ziehen** to take sth into account *or* consideration **b** *(dated: = Hinsicht)* **in diesem ~** in this respect; **in gewissem ~** in certain respects

be|trach|ten ✪ 40.2, 48.3, 53.1, 53.2, 53.4 *ptp* **betrachtet** VT **a** *(= sehen, beurteilen)* to look at; *Verhältnisse, Situation etc* to look at, to view; **sich** *(dat)* **etw ~** to have a look at sth; **bei näherem Betrachten** on closer examination **b** *(= halten für)* **als jd** *or* **jdn/etw ~** to look upon *or* regard *or* consider as sb/sth; **ich betrachte ihn als Freund** I regard *etc* him as a friend

Be|trach|ter [bəˈtraxtɐ] M -s, -, **Be|trach|te|rin** [-ərɪn] F -, -nen *(von Anblick)* observer, beholder *(liter)*; *(von Situation)* observer; **der aufmerksame ~ wird bei diesem Bild festgestellt haben ...** to the alert eye it will have become apparent that in this picture ...

be|trächt|lich [bəˈtrɛçtlɪç] ADJ considerable; **um ein ~es** considerably ADV *(= in starkem Maße) höher, niedriger* considerably

Be|trach|tung [bəˈtraxtʊŋ] ✪ 53.2 F -, -en **a** *(= das Betrachten)* contemplation; **bei näherer ~** on closer examination, when you look more closely; **eine neuartige ~ des Problems** a new way of looking at the problem **b** *(= Überlegung, Untersuchung)* reflection; **über etw** *(acc)* **~en anstellen** to reflect on sth, to contemplate sth; **in ~en versunken** lost in thought *or* meditation

Be|trach|tungs|wei|se F **verschiedene ~n der Lage** different ways of looking at the situation; **er hat eine völlig andere ~** he has a completely different way of looking at things

Be|trag [bəˈtraːk] ✪ 47.5 M -(e)s, ⸗e amount, sum [-ˈtrɛːgə]; **der gesamte ~** the total (amount); **~ dankend erhalten** (payment) received with thanks

be|tra|gen *ptp* **betragen** *irreg* VI to be; *(Kosten, Rechnung auch)* to come to, to amount to; **die Entfernung 25 km** the distance was 25 km; **der Unterschied beträgt 100 Euro** the difference amounts to *or* is 100 euros VR to behave; **sich gut/schlecht ~** to behave (oneself) well/badly; **sich unhöflich ~** to behave impolitely

Be|tra|gen NT -s, *no pl* behaviour *(Brit)*, behavior *(US)*; *(esp im Zeugnis)* conduct

be|trau|en *ptp* **betraut** VT **jdn mit etw ~** to entrust sb with sth; **jdn damit ~, etw zu tun** to give sb the task of doing sth; **jdn mit einem öffentlichen Amt ~** to appoint sb to public office

be|trau|ern *ptp* **betrauert** VT to mourn; *jdn auch* to mourn for

be|träu|feln *ptp* **beträufelt** VT **den Fisch mit Zitrone ~** to sprinkle lemon juice over the fish; **die Wunde mit der Lösung ~** to put drops of the solution on the wound

Be|trau|ung F entrustment, entrusting

Be|treff [bəˈtrɛf] M -(e)s, -e *(form)* **~: Ihr Schreiben vom ...** re your letter of ...; **den ~ angeben** to state the reference *or* subject matter; **in ~ dieser Frage** with respect *or* regard to this question; **in diesem ~** *(old)* in this regard *(old)* or respect

be|tref|fen ✪ 33.2, 38.1, 53.2 *ptp* **betroffen** VT [bəˈtrɔfn] *irreg* **a** *(= angehen)* to concern; **das betrifft dich** it concerns you; **von dieser Regelung werde ich nicht betroffen** this rule does not concern *or* affect me; **was mich betrifft ...** as far as I'm concerned ...; **was das betrifft ...** as far as that goes *or* is concerned ...; **betrifft** re → *auch* **betreffend, betroffen b** *(geh: = widerfahren)* to befall **c** *(geh: = seelisch treffen)* to affect, to touch; **jdn schwer ~** to affect sb deeply

be|tref|fend ADJ *attr (= erwähnt)* in question; *(= zuständig, für etw relevant)* relevant; **das ~e Wort richtig einsetzen** to insert the appropriate word in the right place; **alle (mein Fach) ~en Artikel** all the articles relevant to my subject, all the relevant articles

Be|tref|fen|de(r) [bəˈtrɛfndə] MF *decl as adj* person concerned; **die ~n** those concerned

be|treffs [bəˈtrɛfs] PREP *+gen (form)* concerning, re *(esp Comm)*

Be|treff|zei|le F *(in E-Mail, Anschreiben etc)* subject line

be|trei|ben *ptp* **betrieben** [bəˈtriːbn] VT *irreg* **a** *(= vorantreiben)* to push ahead *or* forward; **auf jds Betreiben** *(acc)* **hin** at sb's instigation **b** *(= ausüben) Gewerbe, Handwerk* to carry on; *Geschäft* to conduct; *Handel auch, Sport* to do; *Studium, Politik* to pursue **c** *(Tech)* to operate **d** *(Sw)* to obtain a writ of account against

Be|trei|ber(in) M(F) operating authority

Be|trei|bung [bəˈtraibʊŋ] F -, -en *(= Ausübung)* carrying on; *(von Geschäft)* conduct; **bei der ~ einer Klage** in the pursuit of a legal action

be|tresst [bəˈtrɛst] ADJ braided

be|tre|ten [bəˈtreːtn] *ptp* **betreten** VT *irreg (= hineingehen in)* to enter, to go/come into; *(= auf etw treten) Rasen, Spielfeld etc* to walk on; *feuchten Zementboden* to step *or* walk on; *Bühne, Brücke* to walk *or* step onto; *Podium* to step (up) onto; **wir ~ damit ein noch unerforschtes Gebiet** we are here entering unknown *or* unexplored territory; **„Betreten (des Rasens) verboten!"** "keep off (the grass)"; **„Betreten für Unbefugte verboten"** "no entry to unauthorized persons"

be|tre|ten ADJ embarrassed ADV with embarrassment; **er sah ~ zu Boden** he looked at the floor, embarrassed

Be|tre|ten|heit F -, *no pl* embarrassment

be|treu|en [bəˈtrɔyən] *ptp* **betreut** VT to look after; *Reisegruppe, Abteilung auch* to be in charge of; **betreutes Wohnen** assisted living, sheltered housing

Be|treu|er [bəˈtrɔyɐ] M -s, -, **Be|treu|e|rin** [-ərɪn] F -, -nen person who is in charge of *or* looking after sb; *(= Kinderbetreuer)* child minder *(Brit)*, babysitter *(US)*; *(von alten Leuten, Kranken)* nurse; **wir suchen noch ~ für ...** we are still looking for people to look after *or* take charge of ...; **der medizinische ~ der Nationalelf** the doctor who looks after the international team

Be|treu|ung F -, -en looking after; *(von Patienten, Tieren etc)* care; **er wurde mit der ~ der Gruppe beauftragt** he was put in charge of the group, the group was put in his care

Be|trieb M **a** *(= Firma)* business, company, concern; *(= Fabrik)* factory, works *sing or pl*; *(= Arbeitsstelle)* place of work; **wir kommen um 5 Uhr aus dem ~** we leave work at 5 o'clock; **der Direktor ist heute nicht im ~** the director isn't at work *or* in (the office) today

b *(= Tätigkeit)* work; *(von Maschine, Fabrik)* working, operation; *(von Eisenbahn)* running; *(von Bergwerk)* working; **den ~ stören** to be disruptive, to cause disruption; **er hält den ganzen ~ auf** he's holding everything up; **der ganze ~ stand still** everything stopped *or* came to a stop; **außer ~** out of order; **die Maschinen sind in ~** the machines are running; **eine Maschine in ~ setzen** to start a machine up; **eine Maschine außer ~ setzen** to stop a machine; **eine Fabrik außer ~ setzen** to put a factory out of operation; **eine Maschine/Fabrik in ~ nehmen** to put a machine/factory into operation, to start operating a machine/in a factory; **einen Bus in ~ nehmen** to put a bus into service; **etw dem ~ übergeben** to open sth

c *(= Betriebsamkeit)* bustle; **in den Geschäften herrscht großer ~** the shops are very busy; **auf den Straßen ist noch kein ~** there is nobody about in the streets yet; **bei dem ~ soll sich ein Mensch konzentrieren können!** how can anybody concentrate with all that (bustle) going on?

d *(inf)* **ich habe den ganzen ~ satt!** I'm fed up with the whole business! *(inf)*; **ich schmeiß den ganzen ~ hin!** I'm going to chuck it all up! *(Brit inf)*, I'm going to chuck the whole business in *(inf)*

be|trieb|lich [bəˈtriːplɪç] ADJ *attr* company *attr*; *Nutzungsdauer etc* operational ADV **eine Sache ~ regeln** to settle a matter within the company; **~ bedingte Entlassungen/Rationalisierungen** redundancies/rationalization measures caused by company restructuring

Be|triebs- *in cpds (= Fabrik-)* factory, works; *(= Firmen-)* company

be|trieb|sam [bəˈtriːpzaːm] ADJ busy, bustling *no adv* ADV **seine Assistenten huschten ~ herum** his assistants bustled around

Be|trieb|sam|keit F -, *no pl* bustle; *(von Mensch)* active nature; **wegen der ständigen ~ meiner Mutter ...** because my mother is a very busy *or* active person ...

Be|triebs-: **Be|triebs|an|ge|hö|ri|ge(r)** MF *decl as adj* employee; **Be|triebs|an|lei|tung** F, **Be|triebs|an|wei|sung** F operating instructions *pl*, operating *or* user's manual; **Be|triebs|art** F operating mode; **Be|triebs|arzt** M, **Be|triebs|ärz|tin** F company doctor; **Be|triebs|aus|flug** M (annual) works *(Brit) or* company *(esp US)* outing; **be|triebs|be|dingt** ADJ **es gab 50 ~e Kündigungen** 50 people were made redundant because of restructuring; **Be|triebs|be|ge|hung** F round of inspection; **Be|triebs|be|ra|tung** F management consultancy; **be|triebs|be|reit** ADJ operational; **Be|triebs|be|reit|schaft** F operational readiness; **Be|triebs|be|sich|ti|gung** F tour of a/the factory *or* firm; **be|triebs|blind** ADJ blind to the shortcomings of one's (own) company; **Be|triebs|blind|heit** F blindness to the shortcomings of one's (own) company; **Be|triebs|da|ten** PL operational data *sing*; **be|triebs|ei|gen** ADJ company *attr*; **Be|triebs|er|geb|nis** NT *(Fin)* trading result; **Be|triebs|er|laub|nis** F operating licence *(Brit) or* license *(US)*; **be|triebs|fä|hig** ADJ in working condition, operational; **Be|triebs|fä|hig|keit** F operational capability; **Be|triebs|fe|ri|en** PL (annual) holiday *(esp Brit)*, vacation close-down *(US)*; **wegen ~ geschlossen** closed for holidays *(esp Brit) or* vacation *(US)*; **be|triebs|fremd** ADJ outside; **~e Personen** people visiting a/the company; **Be|triebs|frie|den** M industrial peace; **Be|triebs|füh|rung** F management; **Be|triebs|ge|heim|nis** NT trade secret; **Be|triebs|ge|mein|schaft** F staff and management *pl*; **Be|triebs|ge|neh|mi|gung** F operating licence *(Brit) or* license *(US)*; **Be|triebs|in|ge|ni|eur(in)** M(F) production engineer; **be|triebs|in|tern** ADJ internal company *attr*; *Ausbildung, Kenntnisse* in-house *attr* ADV **etw ~**

regeln to settle sth within the company; **Be|triebs|ka|pi|tal** NT *(= laufendes Kapital)* working capital; *(= Anfangskapital)* initial capital; **Be|triebs|kin|der|gar|ten** M company kindergarten *or* daycare (center) *(US)*; **Be|triebs|kli|ma** NT atmosphere at work, working atmosphere; **Be|triebs|kos|ten** PL *(von Firma etc)* overheads *pl*, overhead expenses *pl*; *(von Maschine)* running costs *pl*; **Be|triebs|kran|ken|kas|se** F company health insurance scheme; **Be|triebs|lei|ter(in)** M(F) (works *or* factory) manager; **Be|triebs|lei|tung** F management; **Be|triebs|mit|tel** NT means of production *pl*; **Be|triebs|nu|del** F *(inf)* live wire *(inf)*; *(= Witzbold)* office/club *etc* clown; **Be|triebs|prak|ti|kum** NT work placement *(Brit)*, internship *(US)*; **ein ~ absolvieren** to go on *or* to do a work placement *(Brit) or* internship *(US)*; **Be|triebs|prü|fung** F (government) audit; **Be|triebs|psy|cho|lo|gie** F industrial psychology; **Be|triebs|rat** M *(= Gremium)* works *or* factory committee, employee organization *(US)*; **Be|triebs|rat** M, **Be|triebs|rä|tin** F works *or* factory committee member, employee representative *(US)*; **Be|triebs|rats|vor|sit|zen|de(r)** MF *decl as adj* chair of works *or* factory committee; **Be|triebs|rats|wahl** F works committee *(Brit) or* employee organization *(US)* elections *pl*; **Be|triebs|rente** F company pension; **Be|triebs|ru|he** F shutdown; **Be|triebs|schlie|ßung** F (complete) shutdown (of a/the factory), (factory) closure; **Be|triebs|schluss** M *(von Firma)* end of business hours; *(von Fabrik)* end of factory hours; **nach ~** after business/factory hours; **was macht der Durchschnittsbürger nach ~?** what does the average citizen do after work?; **Be|triebs|schutz** M *(von Anlagen)* factory *or* works security; *(= Arbeitsschutz)* industrial safety; **be|triebs|si|cher** ADJ safe (to operate); **Be|triebs|si|cher|heit** F **a** (operational) safety **b** *(von Betrieb)* factory *or* works security; **Be|triebs|so|zio|lo|gie** F industrial sociology; **Be|triebs|still|le|gung** F (complete) shutdown (of a/the factory), (factory) closure; **es gab viele ~en** many factories had to close down; **Be|triebs|sto|ckung** F hold-up (in production); **Be|triebs|stoff** M **a** *(= Treibstoff etc)* fuel **b** *(= Rohstoff)* raw *or* working materials *pl*; **Be|triebs|stö|rung** F breakdown; **Be|triebs|sys|tem** NT *(Comput)* operating system; **Be|triebs|treue** F faithful service to the company; **Be|triebs|un|fall** M industrial accident; *(hum inf)* accident; **Be|triebs|ur|laub** M company holiday *or* vacation *(US)*; **Be|triebs|ver|ein|ba|rung** F internal agreement; **Be|triebs|ver|fas|sung** F *regulations governing industrial relations within a company*; **Be|triebs|ver|fas|sungs|ge|setz** NT *law governing industrial relations within a company*; **Be|triebs|ver|samm|lung** F company meeting; **Be|triebs|wirt(in)** M(F) management expert, graduate in business management *or* administration; *(Student)* student of business management *or* administration; **Be|triebs|wirt|schaft** F, *no pl* business management *or* administration; **Be|triebs|wirt|schaft|ler(in)** M(F) management expert, graduate in business management *or* administration; *(Student)* student of business management *or* administration; **be|triebs|wirt|schaft|lich** ADJ business management *or* administration *attr* ADV in terms of business management *or* administration; **Be|triebs|wirt|schafts|leh|re** F business management *or* administration; **Be|triebs|zu|ge|hö|rig|keit** F **nach zehnjähriger ~** after ten years of employment with the company

be|trin|ken *ptp* **betrunken** [bəˈtrʊŋkn] VR *irreg* to get drunk → *auch* **betrunken**

be|trof|fen [bəˈtrɔfn] ADJ **a** affected *(von* by) **b** *(= bestürzt)* sad; *Schweigen* embarrassed, awkward ADV *(= bestürzt)* in consternation; *(= betrübt)* sadly, in dismay; **jdn ~ ansehen** to look at sb in consternation → *auch* **betreffen**

Be|trof|fe|ne(r) [bəˈtrɔfnə] MF *decl as adj* person affected; **schließlich sind wir die ~n** after all we are the ones who are affected *or* who are on the receiving end *(inf)*

Be|trof|fen|heit F -, *no pl* sadness; **stumme ~** embarrassed *or* awkward silence

be|trog *pret von* **betrügen**

be|tro|gen *ptp von* **betrügen**

be|trü|ben *ptp* **betrübt** VT to sadden, to distress; **es betrübt mich sehr ...** it grieves *or* saddens me greatly ... → **betrübt** VR *(dated, hum)* to grieve *(über +acc* over)

be|trüb|lich [bəˈtryːplɪç] ADJ sad, distressing; *Zustände, Unwissenheit, Unfähigkeit* deplorable ADV **die Lage sieht ~ aus** things look bad

be|trüb|li|cher|wei|se [bəˈtryːplɪçɐˈvaizə] ADV lamentably

Be|trüb|nis [bəˈtryːpnɪs] F -, **-se** *(geh)* grief, sadness *no pl*, distress *no pl*; **~se** sorrows

be|trübt [bəˈtryːpt] ADJ saddened, distressed

Be|trübt|heit F -, *no pl* sadness, distress, grief

Be|trug M deceit, deception; *(Jur)* fraud; **das ist ja (alles) ~** it's (all) a cheat *(Brit) or* fraud; **das ist ja ~, du hast geguckt!** that's cheating, you looked! → **fromm d**

be|trü|gen [bəˈtryːgn] *pret* **betrog** [bəˈtroːk], *ptp* **betrogen** [bəˈtroːgn] VT to deceive; *(geschäftlich auch)* to cheat; *Freund, Ehepartner* to be unfaithful to, to cheat (on); *(Jur)* to defraud; **jdn um etw ~** to cheat *or* swindle sb out of sth; *(Jur)* to defraud sb of sth; **sie betrügt mich mit meinem besten Freund** she is having an affair with my best friend; **ich fühle mich betrogen** I feel betrayed; **sich um etw betrogen sehen** to feel deprived of sth, to feel done out of sth *(Brit)*; **ich sah mich in ihm betrogen** he disappointed me, he let me down, I was deceived in him; **sich in seinen Hoffnungen betrogen sehen** to be disappointed in one's hopes; **sich in seinem Vertrauen zu jdm betrogen sehen** to be proved wrong in trusting sb
VR to deceive oneself

Be|trü|ger [bəˈtryːgɐ] M **-s, -**, **Be|trü|ge|rin** [-ərɪn] F **-, -nen** *(beim Spiel)* cheat; *(geschäftlich)* swindler; *(Jur)* defrauder; *(= Hochstapler)* confidence trickster *(esp Brit)*, con man/woman

Be|trü|ge|rei [bətryːgəˈrai] F **-, -en** deceit; *(geschäftlich)* cheating *no pl*, swindling *no pl*; *(von Ehepartner)* deceiving *no pl*; *(Jur)* fraud; **seine Frau ist nie hinter seine ~en gekommen** *(inf)* his wife never found out that he was deceiving her *or* being unfaithful to her

be|trü|ge|risch [bəˈtryːgərɪʃ] ADJ deceitful; *(Jur)* fraudulent; **in ~er Absicht** with intent to defraud

be|trun|ken [bəˈtrʊŋkn] ADJ drunk *no adv*, drunken *attr*; **er torkelte ~ nach Hause** he staggered home drunk, he staggered drunkenly home; **Fahren in ~em Zustand** driving while under the influence of drink *(Brit) or* alcohol *(form)*, drunk driving → *auch* **betrinken**

Be|trun|ke|ne(r) [bəˈtrʊŋknə] MF *decl as adj* drunk

Be|trun|ken|heit F -, *no pl* drunkenness

Bet-: **Bet|sche|mel** M kneeler; **Bet|schwes|ter** F *(pej)* churchy type, Holy Roller *(US pej inf)*; **Bet|stuhl** M prie-dieu, kneeler; **Bet|stun|de** F prayer meeting

Bett [bɛt] NT **-(e)s, -en** *(alle Bedeutungen)* bed; *(= Federbett)* (continental) quilt, duvet; **das ~ machen** to make the bed; **~en bauen** *(esp Mil)* to make the beds; **Frühstück ans ~** breakfast in bed; **an jds ~** *(dat)* **sitzen** to sit at sb's bedside, to sit by sb's bed; **im ~** in bed; **ins** *or* **zu ~ gehen** to go to bed; **jdn ins** *or* **zu ~ bringen** to put sb to bed; **mit jdm ins ~ gehen/steigen** *(euph)* to go to/jump into bed with sb; **mit jdm das ~ teilen** to share sb's bed; **er hat sich ins gemachte ~ gelegt** *(fig)* he had everything handed to him on a plate → **französisch**

Bet|tag [ˈbeːttaːk] M → **Buß- und Bettag**

Bett-: **Bett|an|zug** M *(Sw)* duvet *or* (continental) quilt cover; **Bett|bank** F *pl* **-bänke** *(Aus)* bed settee *(Brit)*, pullout couch *(US)*; **Bett|be|zug** M duvet *or* (continental) quilt cover; **Bett|couch** F bed settee *(Brit)*, pullout couch *(US)*; **Bett|de|cke** F blanket; *(gesteppt)* (continental) quilt, duvet; **sich unter der ~ verstecken** to hide under the bedclothes *(Brit) or* bedcovers *(US)*

Bet|tel [ˈbɛtl] M **-s**, *no pl* **a** *(obs: = das Betteln)* begging **b** *(dial) (= Gerümpel)* rubbish, lumber, junk; **den (ganzen) ~ hinschmeißen** *(inf)* to chuck the whole thing *or* business *(inf)*

Bet|tel-: **bet|tel|arm** ADJ destitute; **Bet|tel|brief** M begging letter; **Bet|tel|bru|der** M **a** *(= Bettelmönch)* mendicant *or* begging friar **b** *(pej: = Bettler)* beggar, panhandler *(US inf)*

Bet|te|lei [bɛtəˈlai] F **-, -en** begging

Bet|tel-: **Bet|tel|geld** NT *(pej)* pittance; **Bet|tel|kram** M = **Bettel b**; **Bet|tel|lohn** M *(pej)* pittance; **Bet|tel|mönch** M mendicant *or* begging monk; **Bet|tel|mu|si|kant(in)** M(F) *(dated)* street musician

bet|teln [ˈbɛtln] VI to beg; **um ein Almosen ~** to beg (for) alms; **„Betteln verboten"** "no begging"; **(bei jdm) um etw ~** to beg (sb) for sth

Bet|tel-: **Bet|tel|or|den** M mendicant order; **Bet|tel|sack** M beggar's sack; **Bet|tel|schwes|ter** F *(pej: = Bettlerin)* beggar, panhandler *(US inf)*; **Bet|tel|stab** M **an den ~ kommen** to be reduced to beggary; **jdn an den ~ bringen** to reduce sb to beggary; **Bet|tel|weib** NT *(old)* beggar woman *(dated)*

bet|ten [ˈbɛtn] VT *(= legen)* to make a bed for, to bed down *(Brit)*; *Unfallopfer* to lay *or* bed *(Brit)* down; *Kopf* to lay; **jdn weich ~** to put sb on a soft bed; **jdn flach ~** to lay sb down flat; **die Patienten werden zweimal am Tag gebettet** the patients have their beds made up twice a day; **das Dorf liegt ins** *or* **im Tal gebettet** *(liter)* the village nestles *or* lies nestling in the valley → **Rose a**
VR to make a bed for oneself, to bed oneself down *(Brit)*; **wie man sich bettet, so liegt man** *(Prov)* as you make your bed so you must lie on it *(Brit Prov)*, you make the bed you lie in *(US Prov)*; **sich weich ~** to sleep on a soft mattress; **er hat sich schön weich gebettet** *(mit Heirat)* he's feathered his nest very nicely; *(in Stellung)* he's got a nice cushy little number for himself *(inf)*

Bet|ten-: **Bet|ten|burg** F *(pej inf) (= riesiges Hotel)* large concrete hotel; *(= Urlaubsort)* large concrete tourist development; **Bet|ten|man|gel** M (a) shortage of beds

Bett-: **Bett|fe|der** F bedspring; **Bett|fe|dern** PL *(= Daunen)* bed feathers *pl*; **Bett|fla|sche** F hot-water bottle; **Bett|ge|flüs|ter** NT pillow talk; **Bett|ge|nos|se** M, **Bett|ge|nos|sin** F *(dated, iro)* bedfellow; **Bett|ge|schich|te** F (love) affair; **~n** bedroom antics; **Bett|ge|stell** NT bedstead; **Bett|häs|chen** [-hɛːsçən] NT, **Bett|ha|se** M *(inf)* sexy piece *(Brit inf) or* thing *(inf)*; **Bett|him|mel** M canopy; **Bett|hup|ferl** [-hʊpfɐl] NT **-s, -** *(S Ger)* bedtime sweets; **Bett|ja|cke** F bed jacket; **Bett|kan|te** F edge of the bed; **Bett|kas|ten** M linen drawer; **Bett|la|de** F *(S Ger, Aus)* bedstead; **bett|lä|ge|rig** [-lɛːgərɪç] ADJ bedridden, confined to bed; **Bett|lä|ge|rig|keit** F -, *no pl* confinement to bed; **Bett|la|ken** NT sheet; **Bett|lek|tü|re** F bedtime reading

Bett|ler [ˈbɛtlɐ] M **-s, -**, **Bett|le|rin** [-ərɪn] F **-, -nen** beggar, mendicant *(form)*

Bett-: **Bett|nach|bar(in)** M(F) neighbour *(Brit)*, neighbor *(US)*, person in the next bed; **Bett|näs|sen** NT **-s**, *no pl* bed-wetting; **Bett|näs|ser** [ˈbɛtnɛsɐ] M **-s, -**, **Bett|näs|se|rin** [-ərɪn] F **-, -nen** bed-wetter; *(sl: Schimpfwort)* tosser *(sl)*; **Bett|pfan|ne** F bedpan; **Bett|pfos|ten** M bedpost; **Bett|platz** M *(Rail)* sleeping berth; **Bett|rand** M edge of the bed;

bett|reif ADJ ready for bed; **Bett|rost** M (bed) base; **Bett|ru|he** F confinement to bed, bed rest; **der Arzt hat eine Woche ~ verordnet** the doctor ordered him *etc* to stay in bed for one week; **Bett|schüs|sel** F bedpan; **Bett|schwe|re** F *(inf)* **die nötige ~ haben/bekommen** to be/get tired enough to sleep; **Bett|statt** F *pl* **-stätten** *or (Sw)* **-statten, Bett|stel|le** F bed; **Bett|sze|ne** F bedroom scene; **Bett|tuch** NT *pl* **-tücher** sheet; **Bett|über|wurf** M bedspread, counterpane; **Bett|über|zug** M duvet *or* (continental) quilt cover

Bettuch △ NT → **Betttuch**

Bett|um|ran|dung F bed surround

Bet|tung ['bɛtʊŋ] F -, -en *(Tech)* bed(ding); *(Rail)* ballast; *(Mil: = Geschützbettung)* platform

Bett-: **Bett|vor|la|ge** F *(dial)*, **Bett|vor|le|ger** M bedside rug; **Bett|wan|ze** F bedbug; **Bett|wär|me** F warmth of one's bed; **Bett|wä|sche** F bed linen; **Bett|zeug** NT, *no pl* bedding; **Bett|zip|fel** M corner of the bed cover; **nach dem ~ schielen** *(hum)* to be longing for one's bed

be|tucht [bə'tuːxt] ADJ *(inf)* well-to-do

be|tu|lich [bə'tuːlɪç] ADJ **a** *(= übertrieben besorgt)* fussing *attr; Redeweise* old-womanish; **sei doch nicht so ~** don't be such an old mother hen *(inf)* **b** *(= beschaulich)* leisurely *no adv* ADV **a** *(= überbesorgt)* fussily; *reden* like an old woman; **tu nicht so ~** don't be such an old woman **b** *(= gemächlich)* in a calm, unhurried fashion

Be|tu|lich|keit F -, *no pl* **a** *(= übertriebene Besorgtheit)* fussing; **er redet mit einer schrecklichen ~** he talks in such a dreadfully old-womanish way **b** *(= Gemächlichkeit)* leisureliness; *(= Biederkeit)* staidness

be|tun *ptp* **betan** [bə'taːn] VR *irreg (inf)* **a** *(= sich zieren)* to make a song and dance *(inf)* **b** *(= übertrieben besorgt sein)* to make a fuss, to fuss about

be|tup|fen *ptp* **betupft** VT to dab; *(Med)* to swab

be|tup|pen [bə'tʊpn] *ptp* **betuppt** VT *(dial inf)* to cheat, to trick

be|tü|tern [bə'tyːtɐn] *ptp* **betütert** *(N Ger inf)* VT to mollycoddle *(esp Brit)*, to pamper VR to get tipsy

be|tü|tert [bə'tyːtɐt] ADJ *(N Ger inf: = betrunken)* tipsy; *(= verwirrt)* dazed

beug|bar ADJ *(Gram) Substantiv, Adjektiv etc* declinable; *Verb* conjugable

Beu|ge ['bɔygə] F -, -n bend; *(von Arm auch)* crook; *(= Rumpfbeuge)* forward bend; *(seitlich)* sideways bend; *(= Kniebeuge)* knee bend; **in die ~ gehen** to bend

Beu|ge|haft F *(Jur)* coercive detention

Beu|gel ['bɔygl] M -s, - *(Aus)* croissant

Beu|ge|mus|kel M flexor

beu|gen ['bɔygn] VT **a** *(= krümmen)* to bend; *(Phys) Wellen* to diffract; *Strahlen, Licht* to deflect; *(fig) Stolz, Starrsinn* to break; **das Recht ~** to pervert the course of justice; **vom Alter gebeugt** bent *or* bowed by age; **von der Last gebeugt** bowed down with the weight; **von Kummer/Gram gebeugt** bowed down with grief/sorrow → *auch* **gebeugt**

b *(Gram) Substantiv, Adjektiv etc* to decline; *Verb* to conjugate

VR to bend; *(fig)* to submit, to bow (+*dat* to); **sich nach vorn ~** to bend *or* lean forward; **sich aus dem Fenster ~** to lean out of the window; **er beugte sich zu mir herüber** he leaned across to me; **über seine Bücher/seinen Teller gebeugt** hunched over his books/his plate; **sich der Mehrheit ~** to bow *or* submit to the will of the majority

Beu|ger ['bɔygɐ] M -s, - *(Anat)* flexor

Beu|ge|stel|lung F bent position

Beu|gung F -, -en **a** *(= Krümmung)* bending; *(Phys, von Wellen)* diffraction; *(von Strahlen, Licht)* deflection; *(von Stolz, Starrsinn)* breaking; **eine ~ des Rechts** a perversion of (the course of) justice **b** *(Gram)* declension; *(von Verb)* conjugation

Beu|le ['bɔylə] F -, -n *(von Stoß etc)* bump; *(eiternd)* boil; *(= Delle)* dent

beu|len ['bɔylən] VI to bag

Beu|len|pest F bubonic plague

be|un|ru|hi|gen [bə'ʊnruːɪgn] *ptp* **beunruhigt** VT to worry; *(Nachricht etc auch)* to disquiet, to disturb; *(Mil)* to harass; **über etw** *(acc)* **beunruhigt sein** to be worried *or* disturbed about sth; **es ist ~d** it's worrying *or* disturbing, it gives cause for concern VR to worry (oneself) *(über +acc, um, wegen* about)

Be|un|ru|hi|gung F -, -en concern, disquiet; *(Mil)* harassment

be|ur|kun|den [bə'luːɐkʊndn] *ptp* **beurkundet** VT **a** *(= mit Urkunde bestätigen)* to certify; *Vertrag* to record; *Geschäft* to document **b** *(old: = bezeugen) Gefühle, Gesinnung, Haltung* to give evidence of

Be|ur|kun|dung F -, -en **a** *(= das Beurkunden)* certification; *(von Vertrag)* recording; *(von Geschäft)* documentation **b** *(= Dokument)* documentary proof *or* evidence *no indef art, no pl*

be|ur|lau|ben *ptp* **beurlaubt** VT to give *or* grant leave (of absence); *(Univ) Studenten* to give time off; *Lehrpersonal* to give *or* grant sabbatical leave; *(= von Pflichten befreien)* to excuse *(von* from); **beurlaubt sein** to be on leave, to have leave of absence; to have time off; to be on sabbatical leave; *(= suspendiert sein)* to have been relieved of one's duties; **sich ~ lassen** to take leave (of absence)/time off/sabbatical leave VR *(dated: = sich zurückziehen)* to excuse oneself

Be|ur|lau|bung [bə'uːɐlaubʊŋ] F -, -en *(+gen* to) granting of leave (of absence); *(von Studenten)* giving time off; *(von Lehrpersonal)* granting of sabbatical leave; *(= das Beurlaubtsein)* leave (of absence); *(von Studenten)* time off; *(von Lehrpersonal)* sabbatical leave; **seine ~ vom Dienst** *(= Befreiung)* his being excused (from) his duties; *(= Suspendierung)* his being relieved of his duties

be|ur|tei|len *ptp* **beurteilt** VT to judge *(nach* by, from); *Buch, Bild etc* to give an opinion of; *Leistung, Wert* to assess; **etw richtig ~** to judge sth correctly; **etw falsch ~** to misjudge sth; **du kannst das doch gar nicht ~** you are not in a position to judge

Be|ur|tei|ler(in) M(F) judge

Be|ur|tei|lung F **a** *(= das Beurteilen)* judging, judgement; *(von Leistung, Wert)* assessing, assessment; *(= Urteil)* assessment; *(= Kritik: von Stück etc)* review

Be|ur|tei|lungs-: **Be|ur|tei|lungs|ge|spräch** NT appraisal interview; **Be|ur|tei|lungs|maß|stab** M criterion

Beu|schel ['bɔyʃl] NT -s, - *(Aus)* **a** *dish made of offal* **b** *(sl)* lungs *pl*; *(= Eingeweide)* entrails *pl*

Beu|te ['bɔytə] F -, *no pl* **a** *(= Kriegsbeute, auch fig hum)* spoils *pl*, booty, loot *no indef art*; *(= Diebesbeute)* haul, loot *(inf)*; *(von Raubtieren etc)* prey; *(getötete)* kill; *(= Jagdbeute)* bag; *(beim Fischen)* catch; **reiche** *or* **fette ~ machen** to capture a lot of booty/make a good haul/a good kill/get a good bag/a good catch; **ohne ~** *(Hunt, fig)* empty-handed **b** *(liter: = Opfer)* prey; **eine leichte ~** easy prey; **jdm/einer Sache zur ~ fallen** *(liter)* to fall (a) prey to sb/sth

Beu|te F -, -n *(= Bienenkasten)* (bee)hive

beu|te|gie|rig ADJ *Tier* eager for the kill, ravening *attr*; *(fig)* eager for booty *or* a haul

Beu|te|kunst F, *no pl* looted art, trophy *or* booty art

Beu|tel ['bɔytl] M -s, - **a** *(= Behälter)* bag; *(= Tasche)* (drawstring) bag *or* purse; *(= Tragetasche)* carrier bag; *(= Tabaksbeutel, Zool)* pouch; *(dial) (= Tüte)* paper bag; *(= Päckchen)* packet **b** *(inf: = Geldbeutel) (von Frau)* purse; *(von Mann)* wallet; **tief in den ~ greifen** to put one's hand in one's pocket, to dig deep into one's pocket(s); **jds ~ ist leer** sb has no money, sb is broke *(inf)*; *(von Staat etc)* sb's coffers are empty; **das geht an den ~** that costs money!; **die Hand auf dem ~ haben** *(dated)*, **den ~ zuhalten** *(dated)* to be tightfisted → **Loch**

beu|teln ['bɔytln] VT *(dial)* to shake; *(fig)* to shake about; **mich hats gebeutelt!** *(= bin gefallen)* I fell, I came a cropper *(Brit inf)*; *(= bin krank geworden)* I've come down with it/with flu *etc*

Beu|tel-: **Beu|tel|rat|te** F opossum; **Beu|tel|schnei|der(in)** M(F) *(obs: = Gauner)* cutpurse *(obs)*, pickpocket; *(dated geh: = Wucherer)* swindler; **Beu|tel|schnei|de|rei** F *(obs)* theft, thievery *(old)*; *(geh: = Nepp)* swindling; **Beu|tel|tier** NT marsupial

Beu|te-: **Beu|te|recht** NT right of plunder; **Beu|te|stück** NT booty; **Beu|te|tier** NT prey, quarry; **Beu|te|zug** M raid *(auch fig)*; **auf ~ durch die Geschäfte gehen** *(fig)* to go on a foray of the shops

Beut|ler ['bɔytlɐ] M -s, - *(Zool)* marsupial

be|völ|kern [bə'fœlkɐn] *ptp* **bevölkert** VT **a** *(= bewohnen)* to inhabit; *(= beleben)* to crowd, to fill; **schwach/stark** *or* **dicht bevölkert** thinly *or* sparsely/densely *or* thickly populated; **tausende** *or* **Tausende bevölkerten den Marktplatz** the marketplace was crowded with thousands of people **b** *(= besiedeln)* to populate VR to become inhabited; *(fig)* to fill up

Be|völ|ke|rung F -, -en **a** *(= die Bewohner)* population **b** *no pl (= das Bevölkern)* peopling, populating

Be|völ|ke|rungs-: **Be|völ|ke|rungs|ab|nah|me** F fall *or* decrease in population; **Be|völ|ke|rungs|be|we|gung** F population movement; **Be|völ|ke|rungs|dich|te** F density of population, population density; **Be|völ|ke|rungs|ex|plo|si|on** F population explosion; **Be|völ|ke|rungs|grup|pe** F section of the population; **Be|völ|ke|rungs|po|li|tik** F population policy; **Be|völ|ke|rungs|py|ra|mi|de** F population pyramid; **Be|völ|ke|rungs|rück|gang** M fall *or* decline in population; **Be|völ|ke|rungs|schicht** F class of society, social stratum *or* class; **Be|völ|ke|rungs|sta|tis|tik** F population statistics *pl*; **Be|völ|ke|rungs|struk|tur** F population structure; **Be|völ|ke|rungs|wachs|tum** NT population growth, rise *or* increase in population; **Be|völ|ke|rungs|zahl** F (total) population; **Be|völ|ke|rungs|zu|nah|me** F rise *or* increase in population

be|voll|mäch|ti|gen [bə'fɔlmɛçtɪgn] ✪ 36.2 *ptp* **bevollmächtigt** VT to authorize *(zu etw* to do sth)

Be|voll|mäch|tig|te(r) [bə'fɔlmɛçtɪçtə] MF *decl as adj* authorized representative; *(Pol)* plenipotentiary

Be|voll|mäch|ti|gung F -, -en authorization *(durch* from)

be|vor [bə'foːɐ] CONJ before; **~ Sie (nicht) die Rechnung bezahlt haben** until you pay *or* you have paid the bill

be|vor|mun|den *ptp* **bevormundet** VT to treat like a child; **jdn ~** to make sb's decisions (for him/her), to make up sb's mind for him/her; **ich lasse mich von niemandem ~** I shan't *(esp Brit) or* won't let anyone make my decisions (for me) *or* make up my mind for me

Be|vor|mun|dung [bə'foːɐmʊndʊŋ] F -, -en **seine Schüler/Untergebenen** *etc* **wehren sich gegen die ständige ~** his pupils/subordinates *etc* object to his constantly making up their minds for them; **unsere ~ durch den Staat** the State's making up our minds for us

be|vor|ra|ten [bə'foːɐraːtn] *ptp* **bevorratet** VT *insep (form)* to stock up

Be|vor|ra|tung [bə'foːɐraːtʊŋ] F -, -en *usu sing (form)* stockingup, stockpiling

be|vor|rech|tigt [bə'foːɐrɛçtɪçt] ADJ *(= privilegiert)* privileged; *(= wichtig)* high-priority; *(Fin) Gläubiger, Verbindlichkeiten* preferential

Be|vor|rech|ti|gung [bəˈfoːɐrɛçtɪgʊŋ] F -, -en preferential treatment no pl

be|vor|schus|sen [bəˈfoːɐʃʊsn] ptp **bevorschusst** VT insep (rare) to make an advance to

be|vor+ste|hen VI sep irreg to be imminent; (Winter etc) to be near, to approach; **jdm ~** to be in store for sb; **ihm steht eine Überraschung bevor** there's a surprise in store for him; **das Schlimmste steht uns noch bevor** the worst is yet or still to come; **die Prüfung stand ihm noch bevor** the exam was yet or still to come, the exam still lay ahead

be|vor|ste|hend ADJ forthcoming; Gefahr, Krise imminent; Winter approaching

be|vor|zu|gen [bəˈfoːɐtsuːgn] ptp **bevorzugt** VT to prefer; (= begünstigen) to favour (Brit), to favor (US), to give preference to, to give preferential treatment to; **keines unserer Kinder wird bevorzugt** we don't give preference to any of our children; **hier wird niemand bevorzugt** there's no favouritism (Brit) or favoritism (US) here

be|vor|zugt [bəˈfoːɐtsuːkt] ADJ preferred; Behandlung preferential; (= privilegiert) privileged; **die von mir ~en Bücher** the books I prefer ADV **jdn ~ abfertigen/bedienen** etc to give sb preferential treatment; **etw ~ abfertigen/bedienen** etc to give sth priority

Be|vor|zu|gung F -, -en preference (+gen for); (= vorrangige Behandlung) preferential treatment (bei in)

be|wa|chen ptp **bewacht** VT to guard; (Sport) Tor to guard; Spieler to mark

Be|wa|cher [bəˈvaxɐ] M -s, -, **Be|wa|che|rin** [-ərɪn] F -, -nen guard; (Sport: von Spieler) marker

be|wach|sen [bəˈvaksn] ptp **bewachsen** VT irreg to grow over, to cover

be|wach|sen [bəˈvaksn] ADJ overgrown, covered (mit in, with)

Be|wa|chung [bəˈvaxʊŋ] F -, -en guarding; (= Wachmannschaft) guard; (Sport) marking; **jdn unter ~ halten/stellen** to keep/put sb under guard

be|waff|nen ptp **bewaffnet** VT to arm VR (lit, fig) to arm oneself

be|waff|net [bəˈvafnət] ADJ armed; **bis an die Zähne ~** armed to the teeth

Be|waff|ne|te(r) [bəˈvafnətə] MF decl as adj armed man/woman/person

Be|waff|nung [bəˈvafnʊŋ] F -, -en **a** no pl (= das Bewaffnen) arming; **man hat die ~ der Polizei beschlossen** it was decided to arm the police **b** (= Waffen) weapons pl

be|wah|ren ptp **bewahrt** VT **a** (= beschützen) to protect (vor +dat from); **jdn vor etw ~** to protect or save or preserve sb from sth; **(i** or **Gott) bewahre!** (inf) heaven or God forbid!, heaven or saints preserve us! **b** (geh: = aufbewahren) to keep; **jdn/etw in guter Erinnerung ~** to have happy memories of sb/sth **c** (= beibehalten) to keep, to retain, to preserve; Denkmal to conserve; **sich (dat) etw ~** to keep or retain or preserve sth

be|wäh|ren ptp **bewährt** VR (Mensch) to prove oneself, to prove one's worth; (Gerät etc) to prove itself, to prove its worth; (Methode, Plan, Investition, Sparsamkeit, Fleiß) to pay off, to prove (to be) worthwhile; (Auto) to prove (to be) a good investment; **sich im Leben ~** to make something of one's life; **wenn sich der Straftäter bewährt** if the offender proves he has reformed; **die Methode hat sich gut/schlecht bewährt** the method proved/didn't prove (to be) very worthwhile; **das Gerät hat sich gut/schlecht bewährt** the appliance proved/didn't prove (to be) a very good investment; **es bewährt sich immer, das zu tun** it's always worthwhile doing that; **ihre Freundschaft hat sich bewährt** their friendship stood the test of time → auch **bewährt**

Be|wah|rer [bəˈvaːrɐ] M -s, -, **Be|wah|re|rin** [-ərɪn] F -, -nen (rare) guardian, custodian, keeper

be|wahr|hei|ten [bəˈvaːɐhaitn] ptp **bewahrheitet** VR (Befürchtung, Hoffnung, Gerücht) to prove (to be) well-founded; (Prophezeiung) to come true

be|währt [bəˈvɛːɐt] ADJ proven, tried and tested, reliable; Geldanlage worthwhile; Rezept tried and tested; **vielfach ~** tried and tested; **seit Langem ~** well-established → auch **bewähren**

Be|währt|heit F -, no pl reliability

Be|wah|rung F **a** (= das Beschützen) protection (vor +dat from) **b** (= das Aufbewahren) keeping **c** (= Wahrung) keeping

Be|wäh|rung F **a** (von Menschen) proving oneself or one's worth; (von Gerät) proving itself or its worth; (von Methode, Plan, Investition) proving itself worthwhile; **bei ~ der Methode …** if the method proves (to be) worthwhile … **b** (Jur) probation; **eine Strafe zur ~ aussetzen** to impose a suspended sentence; **ein Jahr Gefängnis mit ~** a suspended sentence of one year; **10 Monate Freiheitsstrafe ohne ~** a 10-month prison sentence without probation; **er hat noch ~** he is still on probation; **er ist nur auf ~ auf freiem Fuß** he is only out on probation **c** (Bewährungsfrist) (period of) probation, probation(ary) period

Be|wäh|rungs-: **Be|wäh|rungs|auf|la|ge** F (Jur) probation order; **Be|wäh|rungs|frist** F (Jur) probation(ary) period, (period of) probation; **Be|wäh|rungs|heim** NT home for young offenders; **Be|wäh|rungs|hel|fer(in)** M(F) probation officer; **Be|wäh|rungs|hil|fe** F probation service; **Be|wäh|rungs|pro|be** F test; **etw einer ~ (dat) unterziehen** to put sth to the test; **Be|wäh|rungs|stra|fe** F (Jur) suspended sentence, (period of) probation; **Be|wäh|rungs|zeit** F time spent on probation

be|wal|den [bəˈvaldn] ptp **bewaldet** VT to plant with trees, to afforest (form) VR **allmählich bewaldet sich das Gebiet** trees are gradually beginning to grow in the area

be|wal|det [bəˈvaldət] ADJ wooded

Be|wal|dung F -, -en (= das Bewalden) planting with trees, afforestation (form); (= Baumbestand) trees pl, woodlands pl; **spärliche ~** few trees; **dichte ~** dense woodlands

be|wäl|ti|gen [bəˈvɛltɪgn] ptp **bewältigt** VT (= meistern) Schwierigkeiten, Problem to cope with; Arbeit, Aufgabe auch, Strecke to manage; (= überwinden) Vergangenheit, Erlebnis etc to get over; Schüchternheit to overcome, to get over; (= erledigen, beenden) to deal with; (= aufessen) to manage

Be|wäl|ti|gung F -, no pl **die ~ der Schwierigkeiten** coping with the difficulties; **die ~ der Arbeit** managing the work; **die ~ eines Erlebnisses** getting over an experience

be|wan|dert [bəˈvandɐt] ADJ experienced; **in etw (dat) ~ sein** to be familiar with or well-versed in sth; **auf einem Gebiet ~ sein** to be experienced or well-versed in a field

be|wandt [bəˈvant] ADJ (old) **es ist so ~, dass …** the situation or position is such that …; **wie ist es damit ~?** how does the matter lie?

Be|wandt|nis [bəˈvantnɪs] F -, -se reason, explanation; **damit hat es** or **das hat eine andere ~** there's another reason or explanation for that; **damit hat es** or **das hat seine eigene ~** that's a long story; **damit hat es** or **das hat folgende ~** the fact of the matter is this/the facts of the matter are these

be|wäs|sern ptp **bewässert** VT to irrigate; (mit Sprühanlage) to water

Be|wäs|se|rung [bəˈvɛsərʊŋ] F, no pl irrigation; (mit Berieselungsanlage) watering

Be|wäs|se|rungs-: **Be|wäs|se|rungs|an|la|ge** F irrigation plant; **Be|wäs|se|rungs|gra|ben** M irrigation channel, feeder; **Be|wäs|se|rungs|ka|nal** M irrigation canal; **Be|wäs|se|rungs|sys|tem** NT irrigation system

be|weg|bar ADJ = **beweglich a**

be|we|gen [bəˈveːgn] ptp **bewegt** VT **a** (= Lage verändern, regen) to move; Erdmassen, Möbelstück to move, to shift; Hund, Pferd to exercise **b** (= innerlich bewegen) to move; (= beschäftigen, angehen) to concern; **dieser Gedanke bewegt mich seit Langem** this has been on my mind a long time; **~d** moving → **bewegt** **c** (= bewirken, ändern) to change VR **a** (= in Bewegung sein) to move; **beide Reden bewegten sich in der gleichen Richtung** both speeches were along the same lines **b** (= Bewegung haben: Mensch) to get some exercise; (inf: = spazieren gehen) to stretch one's legs, to get some exercise **c** (fig: = variieren, schwanken) to vary, to range (zwischen between); **der Preis bewegt sich um die 50 Euro** the price is about 50 euros; **die Verluste ~ sich in den tausenden** or **Tausenden** losses are in the thousands **d** (= sich ändern, Fortschritte machen) to change; **es bewegt sich etwas** things are beginning to happen **e** (= auftreten, sich benehmen) to behave, to act → auch **bewegt**

be|we|gen pret **bewog** [bəˈvoːk], ptp **bewogen** [bəˈvoːgn] VT **jdn zu etw ~** to induce or persuade sb to do sth; **was hat dich dazu bewogen?** what induced you to do that?; **sich dazu ~ lassen, etw zu tun** to allow oneself to be persuaded to do sth

Be|weg|grund M motive

be|weg|lich [bəˈveːklɪç] ADJ **a** (= bewegbar) movable; Hebel, Griff movable, mobile; Truppe mobile **b** (= wendig) agile; Fahrzeug manoeuvrable (Brit), maneuverable (US); (= geistig beweglich) agile-minded, nimble-minded; (fig) Geist nimble; **mit einem Kleinwagen ist man in der Stadt ~er** you're more mobile in town with a small car

Be|weg|lich|keit F -, no pl **a** (von Hebel, Griff etc) mobility **b** (= Wendigkeit) agility; (von Fahrzeug) manoeuvrability (Brit), maneuverability (US); (geistig) mental agility; (körperlich) agility; (von Gliedmaßen) flexibility; **die neue ~** the new mobility of the population

be|wegt [bəˈveːkt] ADJ **a** (= unruhig) Wasser, See choppy; Zeiten, Vergangenheit, Leben eventful; Jugend eventful, turbulent; **die See war stark ~/kaum ~** the sea was rough/fairly calm **b** (= gerührt) Stimme, Worte, Stille emotional; **~ sein** to be moved → auch **bewegen**

Be|wegt|heit F -, no pl emotion

Be|we|gung [bəˈveːgʊŋ] F -, -en **a** movement; (= Handbewegung auch) gesture; (Sci, Tech) movement, motion; **eine falsche ~!** one false move!; **keine ~!** freeze! (inf), don't move!; **in ~ sein** (Fahrzeug) to be moving, to be in motion; (Menge) to mill around; **sich in ~ setzen** to start moving, to begin to move; **etw in ~ setzen** or **bringen** to set sth in motion, to start sth moving; **jdn in ~ bringen** to get sb moving; **Himmel und Hölle** or **alle Hebel in ~ setzen** to move heaven and earth; **jdn in ~ halten** to keep sb moving, to keep sb on the go (inf) **b** (= körperliche Bewegung) exercise; **sich (dat) ~ verschaffen** or **machen** to get (some) exercise **c** (= Unruhe) agitation; **in ~ geraten** to get into a state of agitation; **diese Nachricht ließ die ganze Stadt in ~ geraten** this news threw the whole town into a state of agitation; **plötzlich kam ~ in die Menschenmenge** the crowd suddenly became agitated **d** (= Entwicklung) progress; **etw kommt in ~** sth gets moving; **endlich kam ~ in die Verhandlungen** at last there was some progress in the negotiations **e** (= Ergriffenheit) emotion **f** (Pol, Art etc) movement

Be|we|gungs-: **Be|we|gungs|ap|pa|rat** M, no pl (Anat) locomotor system; **Be|we|gungs|ar|mut** F, no pl lack of exercise; **Be|we|gungs|bild** NT (Admin) record of (sb's) movements; **Be|we|gungs|drang** M urge or impulse to be active; **Be|we|gungs|ener|gie** F kinetic energy; **be|we|gungs|fä|hig** ADJ mobile; **Be|we|gungs|fä|hig|keit** F mobility; **Be|we|gungs|frei|heit** F freedom of movement; *(fig)* freedom of action; **Be|we|gungs|krieg** M mobile warfare; **be|we|gungs|los** ADJ motionless, immobile ADV without moving; *liegen, sitzen, stehen* motionless; **Be|we|gungs|lo|sig|keit** F -, *no pl* motionlessness, immobility; **Be|we|gungs|man|gel** M, *no pl* lack of exercise; **Be|we|gungs|mel|der** M motion detector, passive infrared detector; **Be|we|gungs|nerv** M motor nerve; **Be|we|gungs|spiel** NT *(Sport)* active game; **Be|we|gungs|stö|rung** F *(Med)* motor disturbance, akinesia *(spec)*; **Be|we|gungs|stu|die** F **a** *(Ind)* time and motion study **b** *(Art)* study in movement; **Be|we|gungs|the|ra|pie** F *(aktiv)* therapeutic exercise; *(passiv)* manipulation; **Be|we|gungs|trieb** M urge *or* impulse to be active; **be|we|gungs|un|fä|hig** ADJ unable to move; *(= gehunfähig)* unable to move about, unable to get about; **Be|we|gungs|un|fä|hig|keit** F inability to move; *(= Gehunfähigkeit)* inability to move about *or* get about; **Be|we|gungs|un|schär|fe** F *(Phot)* camera shake; **Be|we|gungs|zu|stand** M state of motion

be|weh|ren *ptp* **bewehrt** *(old)* VT to fortify; *(= bewaffnen)* to arm VR *(auch iro)* to arm oneself

Be|weh|rung [bəˈveːrʊŋ] F -, **-en** *(old)* **a** *(= Befestigung)* fortifying; *(= Bewaffnung)* arming **b** *(= Wehranlagen)* fortifications *pl*; *(= Waffen)* arms *pl*

be|wei|ben [bəˈvaibn] *ptp* **beweibt** VR *(dated)* to take a wife *(dated)*, to wed *(dated)*

be|wei|den *ptp* **beweidet** VT *(Agr) Land* to pasture; *(Kühe)* to graze on

be|weih|räu|chern [bəˈvairɔyçɐn] *ptp* **beweihräuchert** VT to (in)cense; *(fig)* to heap praise on; **sich (selbst) ~** to indulge in self-adulation

be|wei|nen *ptp* **beweint** VT to mourn (for), to weep for

be|wei|nens|wert [bəˈvainənsveːɐt] ADJ *(geh)* lamentable

Be|wei|nung [bəˈvainʊŋ] F -, *(rare)* **-en** mourning; **die ~ Christi** *(Art)* the Mourning of Christ

Be|weis [bəˈvais] M **-es, -e** [-zə] proof *(für of)*; *(= Zeugnis)* evidence *no pl*; **als** *or* **zum ~** as proof *or* evidence; **das ist kein ~ für das, was du behauptest** that doesn't prove *or* that's no proof of what you have been claiming; **ein eindeutiger ~** clear evidence; **sein Schweigen ist ein ~ seines Schuldgefühls** his silence is proof *or* evidence of his feeling of guilt; **etw unter ~ stellen** to prove sth; **den ~ antreten, einen/den ~ führen** to offer evidence *or* proof; **den ~ für etw/seiner Unschuld erbringen** to produce *or* supply evidence *or* proof of sth/of one's innocence; **~ erheben** *(Jur)* to hear *or* take evidence; **jdm einen ~ seiner Hochachtung geben** to give sb a token of one's respect

Be|weis-: **Be|weis|an|trag** M *(Jur)* motion to take *or* hear evidence; **Be|weis|auf|nah|me** F *(Jur)* taking *or* hearing of evidence; **be|weis|bar** ADJ provable, demonstrable, capable of being proved

Be|weis|bar|keit [bəˈvaisbaːɐkait] F -, *no pl* demonstrability

be|wei|sen ✪ 53.4 *ptp* **bewiesen** *irreg* [bəˈviːzn] VT **a** *(= nachweisen)* to prove; **was zu ~ war** QED, quod erat demonstrandum; **was noch zu ~ wäre** that remains to be seen **b** *(= erkennen lassen, dated: = erweisen)* to show VR to prove oneself/itself

Be|weis-: **be|weis|er|heb|lich** ADJ *(Jur)* evidentiary *(spec)*;; **Be|weis|er|he|bung** F *(Jur)* taking (or) hearing of evidence; **Be|weis|füh|rung** F *(Jur)* presentation of one's case; *(Math)* proof; *(= Argumentation)* (line of) argumentation *or* reasoning *(Brit)*, line of argument; **Be|weis|gang** M *pl* **-gänge** argumentation *(in proving sth)*; **Be|weis|ge|gen|stand** M *(esp Jur)* point at issue; **Be|weis|grund** M argument; **Be|weis|ket|te** F chain of proof; *(Jur auch)* chain of evidence; **Be|weis|kraft** F evidential *(Brit) or* evidentiary *(US)* value, value as evidence; **be|weis|kräf|tig** ADJ evidential *(Brit)*, evidentiary *(US)*, probative *(form)*; **Be|weis|la|ge** F *(Jur)* body of evidence; **Be|weis|last** F *(Jur)* onus, burden of proof; **Be|weis|ma|te|ri|al** NT (body of) evidence; **Be|weis|mit|tel** NT evidence *no pl*; **Be|weis|not** F *(Jur)* lack of evidence; **in ~ sein** to be lacking evidence; **Be|weis|pflicht** F *(Jur)* onus, burden of proof; **Be|weis|stück** NT exhibit; **Be|weis|wür|di|gung** F *(Jur)* assessment of the evidence

be|wen|den VT *impers* **es bei** *or* **mit etw ~ lassen** to be content with sth; **wir wollen es dabei ~ lassen** let's leave it at that

Be|wen|den NT **damit hatte es sein/die Angelegenheit ihr ~** the matter rested there, that was the end of the matter

Be|werb [bəˈvɛrp] M **-(e)s, -e** [-bə] *(Aus Sport)* = **Wettbewerb**

be|wer|ben ✪ 46.1 *ptp* **beworben** *irreg* [bəˈvɔrbn] VR to apply *(um* for, *als* for the position *or* job of); **sich bei einer Firma ~** to apply to a firm (for a job); **sich um jdn ~** *(dated)* to ask for sb's hand in marriage VT *Produkte, Firmen* to promote

Be|wer|ber(in) M(F) applicant; *(dated: = Freier)* suitor *(dated)*

Be|wer|bung F application; *(dated: um Mädchen)* wooing *(dated)*, courting *(dated)*

Be|wer|bungs-: **Be|wer|bungs|bo|gen** M, **Be|wer|bungs|for|mu|lar** NT application form; **Be|wer|bungs|frist** F application deadline, deadline for applications; **Be|wer|bungs|ge|spräch** NT (job) interview; **Be|wer|bungs|schrei|ben** NT (letter of) application; **Be|wer|bungs|un|ter|la|gen** PL application documents *pl*; **Be|wer|bungs|ver|fah|ren** NT application procedure

be|wer|fen *ptp* **beworfen** [bəˈvɔrfn] VT *irreg* **a** **jdn/etw mit etw ~** to throw sth at sb/sth; *mit Steinen, Eiern auch* to pelt sb with sth; *(fig)* to hurl sth at sb/sth; **jdn/jds guten Namen mit Schmutz** *or* **Dreck ~** to throw *or* sling mud at sb/sb's good name **b** *(Build)* to face, to cover; *(mit Rauputz)* to roughcast; **mit Kies beworfen** pebble-dashed

be|werk|stel|li|gen [bəˈvɛrkʃtɛlɪgn] *ptp* **bewerkstelligt** VT to manage; *Geschäft* to effect, to bring off; **es ~, dass jd etw tut** to manage *or* contrive to get sb to do sth

Be|werk|stel|li|gung F -, *no pl* managing

be|wer|ten *ptp* **bewertet** VT *jdn* to judge; *Leistung auch, Schularbeit* to assess; *Gegenstand* to value, to put a value on; **etw zu hoch/niedrig ~** to overvalue/undervalue sth; **jdn/etw nach einem Maßstab ~** to judge sb/measure sth against a yardstick; **etw mit der Note 5 ~** to give sth a mark *(Brit) or* grade *(US)* of 5; **eine Arbeit mit (der Note) „gut" ~** to mark *(Brit) or* grade *(US)* a piece of work "good"

Be|wer|tung F judgement; *(von Leistung auch, von Schularbeit)* assessment; *(von Gegenstand)* valuation

Be|wer|tungs-: **Be|wer|tungs|kri|te|ri|um** NT criterion; **Be|wer|tungs|maß|stab** M set of criteria; **Be|wer|tungs|ska|la** F scale of assessment *or* valuation

be|wie|sen ADJ *(= nachgewiesen)* proven → *auch* **beweisen**

be|wie|se|ner|ma|ßen [bəˈviːznɐˈmaːsn] ADV **was er sagt, ist ~ unwahr** it has been proved that what he is saying is untrue, there is evidence to show that what he is saying is untrue; **er ist ~ ein Betrüger** he has been proved to be a fraud

be|wil|li|gen *ptp* **bewilligt** VT to allow; *Mittel, Geld, Darlehen etc auch* to grant; *Planstelle auch, Etat, Steuererhöhung etc* to approve; *Stipendium* to award; **jdm etw ~** to allow/grant/award sb sth

Be|wil|li|gung [bəˈvɪlɪgʊŋ] F -, **-en** allowing; *(von Planstelle auch, von Etat, Steuererhöhung)* approving, approval; *(von Geldern auch)* granting; *(von Stipendium)* awarding; *(= Genehmigung)* approval; **dafür brauchen Sie eine ~** you need approval for that; **die ~ für einen Kredit bekommen** to be allowed *or* granted credit

Be|wil|li|gungs-: **Be|wil|li|gungs|be|scheid** M approval; **be|wil|li|gungs|pflich|tig** [-pflɪçtɪç] ADJ subject to approval

be|will|komm|nen [bəˈvɪlkɔmnən] *ptp* **bewillkommnet** VT *insep (geh)* to welcome

Be|will|komm|nung F -, **-en** *(rare)* welcoming *no pl*, reception

be|wim|pert [bəˈvɪmpɐt] ADJ *Auge* lashed; *(Zool)* ciliate(d) *(spec)*

be|wir|ken *ptp* **bewirkt** VT **a** *(= verursachen)* to cause, to bring about, to produce; **~, dass etw passiert** to cause sth to happen **b** *(= erreichen)* to achieve; **mit so einem Auftreten kannst du bei ihm nichts ~** you won't get anywhere *or* achieve anything with him if you behave like that; **damit bewirkst du bei ihm nur das Gegenteil** that way you'll only achieve the opposite effect

be|wir|ten [bəˈvɪrtn] *ptp* **bewirtet** VT **jdn ~** to feed sb; *(bei offiziellem Besuch etc)* to entertain sb *(by giving them a meal)*; **wir wurden während der ganzen Zeit köstlich bewirtet** we were very well fed all the time, we were given excellent food all the time; **jdn mit Kaffee und Kuchen ~** to entertain sb to coffee and cakes; **wenn man so viele Leute zu ~ hat** if you have so many people to cater for *or* to feed

be|wirt|schaf|ten *ptp* **bewirtschaftet** VT **a** *Betrieb etc* to manage, to run; **die Berghütte wird im Winter nicht/wird von Herrn und Frau X bewirtschaftet** the mountain hut is not serviced in the winter/is managed *or* run by Mr and Mrs X **b** *Land* to farm, to cultivate, to work **c** *(= staatlich kontrollieren) Waren* to ration; *Devisen, Wohnraum* to control

Be|wirt|schaf|tung [bəˈvɪrtʃaftʊŋ] F -, **-en** **a** *(von Betrieb)* management, running **b** *(von Land)* farming, cultivation, working **c** *(= staatliche Kontrolle)* rationing; *(von Devisen, Wohnraum)* control

Be|wir|tung F -, **-en** *(= das Bewirten)* hospitality; *(im Hotel)* (food and) service; *(rare: = Essen und Getränke)* food (and drink); **die ~ so vieler Gäste** catering for *or* feeding so many guests

Be|wir|tungs|kos|ten PL entertainment expenses *pl*

be|wit|zeln *ptp* **bewitzelt** VT to make fun of

be|wog *pret von* **bewegen**

be|wo|gen *ptp von* **bewegen**

be|wohn|bar ADJ **a** *Gegend, Land etc* habitable **b** *Haus, Wohnung etc* habitable, fit to live in; *(= beziehbar)* habitable, ready to live in

be|woh|nen *ptp* **bewohnt** VT to live in; *Haus, Zimmer, Bau, Nest auch* to occupy; *(Volk)* to inhabit; **das Zimmer/das Haus war jahrelang nicht bewohnt** the room was unoccupied/the house was uninhabited *or* unoccupied for years → *auch* **bewohnt**

Be|woh|ner [bəˈvoːnɐ] M **-s, -**, **Be|woh|ne|rin** [-ərɪn] F **-, -nen** *(von Land, Gebiet)* inhabitant; *(von Haus etc)* occupier; **dieser Vogel ist ein ~ der Wälder** this bird is a forest dweller, this bird is a denizen of the forest *(liter)*

Be|woh|ner|schaft [bəˈvoːnɐʃaft] F -, **-en** occupants *pl*

be|wohnt [bəˈvoːnt] ADJ *Land, Gebiet, Planet* inhabited; *Haus etc auch* occupied → *auch* **bewohnen**

be|wöl|ken [bəˈvœlkn] *ptp* **bewölkt** VR *(lit, fig)* to cloud over, to darken

be|wölkt [bəˈvœlkt] ADJ cloudy; **~ bis bedeckt** *(Met)* cloudy, perhaps overcast

Be|wöl|kung F -, **-en** *(= das Bewölken)* clouding over, darkening; **wechselnde bis zunehmende ~** *(Met)* variable amounts of cloud, becoming cloudier

Be|wöl|kungs-: **Be|wöl|kungs|auf|lo|cke|rung** F break-up of the cloud; **Be|wöl|kungs|zu|nah|me** F increase in cloud

be|wu|chern *ptp* **bewuchert** VT to grow over, to cover

Be|wuchs M, *no pl* vegetation

Be|wun|de|rer [bəˈvʊndərɐ] M **-s, -**, **Be|wun|de|rin** [bəˈvʊndərɪn] F **-, -nen** admirer

be|wun|dern *ptp* **bewundert** VT to admire (*wegen* for); **~d** admiring; **ein überall bewunderter Künstler** a universally admired artist

be|wun|derns|wert, be|wun|derns|wür|dig ADJ admirable ADV admirably

Be|wun|de|rung [bəˈvʊndərʊŋ] ✪ 40.4 F **-,** (*rare*) **-en** admiration

be|wun|de|rungs|wert, be|wun|de|rungs|wür|dig ADJ admirable ADV admirably

Be|wund|rer [bəˈvʊndrɐ] M **-s, -**, **Be|wund|re|rin** [-ərɪn] F **-, -nen** admirer

Be|wurf M **a** (*Build*) facing, covering; (*= Rauputz*) roughcast; (*= Kiesbewurf*) pebble dash **b** (*= das Bewerfen*) **der ~ der Feinde/Mauern mit Steinen** throwing stones at the enemy/walls, pelting the enemy/walls with stones

be|wur|zeln *ptp* **bewurzelt** VR to root, to grow roots

be|wusst [bəˈvʊst] ADJ **a** *usu attr* (*Philos, Psych*) conscious

b *attr* (*= überlegt*) conscious; *Mensch* self-aware; **er führte ein sehr ~es Leben** he lived a life of total awareness

c *pred* **sich** (*dat*) **einer Sache** (*gen*) **~ sein/werden** to be/become aware *or* conscious of sth, to realize sth; **etw ist jdm ~** sb is aware *or* conscious of sth; **es wurde ihm allmählich ~, dass ...** he gradually realized (that) ..., it gradually dawned on him (that) ...

d *attr* (*= willentlich*) deliberate, intentional; *Lüge* deliberate

e *attr* (*= überzeugt*) convinced; **er ist ein ~er Kommunist** he is a convinced communist

f *attr* (*= bekannt, besagt*) in question; *Zeit* agreed; **die ~e Kreuzung** the crossroads in question

ADV **a** consciously; *leben* in total awareness

b (*= willentlich*) deliberately, intentionally

Be|wusst|heit F **-,** *no pl* awareness; (*= Absichtlichkeit*) deliberateness

Be|wusst-: **be|wusst|los** ADJ unconscious, senseless; **~ werden** to lose consciousness, to become unconscious; **in ~em Zorn** in a blind rage ADV **jdn ~ prügeln/schlagen** to beat sb unconscious *or* senseless; **~ zusammenbrechen** to fall senseless, to collapse unconscious; **Be|wusst|lo|se(r)** [bəˈvʊstloːzə] MF *decl as adj* unconscious man/woman/person *etc*; **die ~n** the unconscious; **Be|wusst|lo|sig|keit** F **-,** *no pl* unconsciousness; **bis zur ~** (*inf*) ad nauseam; **be|wusst ma|chen, be|wusst+ma|chen** *sep* VT **jdm etw ~** to make sb aware *or* conscious of sth, to make sb realize sth; **sich** (*dat*) **etw ~** to realize sth

Be|wusst|sein NT **a** (*= Wissen*) awareness, consciousness; **etw kommt jdm zu(m) ~** sb becomes aware *or* conscious of sth, sb realizes sth; **jdm etw zu ~ bringen, jdm etw ins ~ rufen** to make sb (fully) conscious *or* aware of sth; **etw tritt in jds ~** (*acc*) sth occurs to sb; **jdm etw ins ~ rücken** to make sb aware of sth; **das allgemeine ~** general awareness; **im ~** (*+gen*)**/, dass ...** in the knowledge of/that ...

b (*Philos, Psych, Med*) consciousness; **das ~ verlieren/wiedererlangen** to lose/regain consciousness; **bei ~ sein** to be conscious; **zu(m) ~ kommen** to regain consciousness; **bei vollem ~** fully conscious; **jdm schwindet das ~** (*geh*) sb faints *or* swoons (*liter*)

c er tat es mit (vollem)/ohne ~ he was (fully) aware/he was not aware of what he was doing

d (*= Anschauungen*) convictions *pl*

Be|wusst|seins-: **Be|wusst|seins|bil|dung** F (*Pol*) shaping of political ideas; **Be|wusst|seins|e|be|ne** F plane of consciousness; **be|wusst|seins|er|wei|ternd** ADJ **~e Drogen** mind-expanding drugs; **Be|wusst|seins|er|wei|te|rung** F heightening of (one's) awareness; **Be|wusst|seins|in|halt** M *usu pl* (*Philos*) content of consciousness; **Be|wusst|seins|kunst** F (*Liter*) stream-of-consciousness technique; **Be|wusst|seins|la|ge** F (*Pol*) state of political awareness; **Be|wusst|seins|len|kung** F (*Sociol*) manipulation of consciousness; **Be|wusst|seins|schwel|le** F (*Psych*) threshold of consciousness; **Be|wusst|seins|spal|tung** F (*Med, Psych*) splitting of the consciousness; **Be|wusst|seins|stö|rung** F (*Psych*) disturbance of consciousness; **Be|wusst|seins|strom** M (*Liter*) stream of consciousness; **Be|wusst|seins|trü|bung** F (*Psych*) dimming of consciousness; **be|wusst|seins|ver|än|dernd** ADJ (*Psych*) **~e Drogen** drugs which alter one's (state of) awareness; **~e Erfahrungen** experiences which alter one's outlook; **Be|wusst|seins|ver|än|de|rung** F change in the state of mind; (*durch Erfahrungen*) change in outlook; **(politische) ~** change in political outlook

be|wusst+wer|den VI *sep irreg aux sein* → **bewusst ADJ c**

Be|wusst|wer|dung [-veːɐdʊŋ] F **-,** *no pl* dawning of consciousness

bez. *abbr* **a** *von* **bezahlt** paid **b** *von* **bezüglich** with reference to, re

Bez. *abbr von* **Bezirk**

be|zahl|bar ADJ payable; **das ist zwar recht teuer, aber für die meisten doch durchaus ~** although it's quite expensive most people can certainly afford it

be|zah|len *ptp* **bezahlt** VT **a** *Menschen, Betrag* to pay; *Rechnung, Schuld* to pay (off), to settle; **jdm 10 Euro ~** to pay sb 10 euros; **etw an jdn ~** to pay sb sth

b *Sache, Leistung, Schaden* to pay for; *Zeche* to pay, to foot (*inf*); **etw bezahlt bekommen** *or* **kriegen** (*inf*) to get paid for sth; **für etw nichts bezahlt bekommen** *or* **kriegen** (*inf*) not to get paid for sth; **jdm etw ~** (*= für jdn kaufen*) to pay for sth for sb; (*= Geld geben für*) to pay sb for sth; **lass mal, ich bezahl das** it's OK, I'll pay for that *or* I'll get that; **er hat seinen Fehler mit dem Leben bezahlt** he paid for his mistake with his life; **... als ob er es bezahlt bekäme** (*inf*) like mad *or* crazy (*inf*), like hell (*inf*); **Liebe ist nicht mit Geld zu ~** money can't buy love, love cannot be bought

VI to pay; **Herr Ober, ~ bitte!** waiter, the bill (*Brit*) *or* check (*US*) please!

Be|zahl|fern|se|hen NT, *no pl* pay TV

be|zahlt [bəˈtsaːlt] ADJ paid; **sich ~ machen** to be worth it, to pay off

Be|zah|lung F **a** (*= das Bezahlen*) payment; (*von Rechnung, Schulden*) paying off, settlement; (*von Leistung, Schaden*) paying for (*einer Sache* (*gen*) sth) **b** (*= Lohn, Gehalt*) pay; (*für Dienste*) payment; **ohne/gegen** *or* **für ~** without/for payment

be|zäh|men *ptp* **bezähmt** VT **a** (*fig geh*) *Begierden, Leidenschaften* to master, to control, to curb **b** (*lit obs*: *= zähmen*) to tame VR to control *or* restrain oneself

be|zau|bern *ptp* **bezaubert** VT (*fig*) to charm, to captivate VI to be bewitching *or* captivating

be|zau|bernd ADJ enchanting, charming

Be|zau|be|rung [bəˈtsaubərʊŋ] F **-, -en** bewitchment, captivation; (*= Entzücken*) enchantment, delight

be|ze|chen *ptp* **bezecht** VR (*inf*) to get drunk

be|zecht [bəˈtsɛçt] (*inf*) ADJ drunk; **völlig ~** dead (*Brit*) *or* completely drunk (*inf*)

be|zeich|nen *ptp* **bezeichnet** VT **a** (*= kennzeichnen*) (*durch, mit* by) to mark; *Takt, Tonart* to indicate

b (*= genau beschreiben*) to describe; **er bezeichnete uns den Weg** he described the way to us

c (*= benennen*) to call, to describe; **ich weiß nicht, wie man das bezeichnet** I don't know what that's called; **das würde ich schlicht als eine Unverschämtheit ~** I would describe that as sheer effrontery *or* impudence, I would call that sheer effrontery *or* impudence; **so kann man es natürlich auch ~** of course, you can call it that *or* describe it that way too; **jd/etw wird mit dem Wort ... bezeichnet** sb/sth is described by the word ..., the word ... describes sb/sth; **er bezeichnet sich gern als Künstler** he likes to call himself an artist

d (*= bedeuten*) to mean, to denote

e (*geh*: *= typisch sein für*) to epitomize

be|zeich|nend ADJ (*für* of) characteristic, typical; **es ist ~ für ihre Unfähigkeit, dass ...** (*= ist ein Beweis für*) it's indicative of her incompetence that ...

be|zeich|nen|der|wei|se [bəˈtsaiçnəndɐˈvaizə] ADV **die Regierung hat ~ die Wahlversprechen wieder nicht eingehalten** typically (enough), the government hasn't kept its election promises again

Be|zeich|ner M (*Comput*) identifier

Be|zeich|nung F **a** (*= Kennzeichnung*) marking; (*von Tonart, Takt*) indication; (*= Beschreibung, Benennung*) description **b** (*= Ausdruck*) expression, term

Be|zeich|nungs|leh|re F (*Ling*) onomastics *sing*

be|zeu|gen *ptp* **bezeugt** VT **a** (*Sache*) to attest; (*Person auch*) to testify to; **~, dass ...** to attest the fact that ...; to testify that ... **b** (*geh*) **jdm etw ~** to show sb sth

Be|zeu|gung F attestation; **urkundliche ~** documentary proof *or* evidence

be|zich|ti|gen [bəˈtsɪçtɪgn] *ptp* **bezichtigt** VT to accuse; **jdn einer Sache** (*gen*) **~** to accuse sb of sth, to charge sb with sth; **jdn ~, etw getan zu haben** to accuse sb of having done sth

Be|zich|ti|gung F **-, -en** accusation, charge

be|zieh|bar ADJ **a** (*= bezugsfertig*) *Wohnung etc* ready to move into **b** (*= erhältlich*) *Waren etc* obtainable **c** relatable, referable; **das ist auf einen Vorfall in seiner Jugend ~** that can be related to an incident in his youth

be|zie|hen *ptp* **bezogen** [bəˈtsoːgn] *irreg* VT **a** (*= überziehen*) *Polster, Regenschirm* to (re)cover; *Bettdecke, Kissen* to put a cover on; (*mit Saiten*) *Geige etc* to string; **die Betten frisch ~** to put clean sheets on the beds, to change the beds

b (*= einziehen in*) *Wohnung* to move into

c (*esp Mil*: *= einnehmen*) *Posten, Position, Stellung* to take up; (*old*) *Universität* to enter, to go up to; (*fig*) *Standpunkt* to take up, to adopt; **ein Lager ~** to encamp; **Wache ~** to mount guard, to go on guard

d (*= sich beschaffen*) to get, to obtain; *Zeitungen etc* to take, to get

e (*= erhalten*) to get, to receive; *Einkommen, Rente* to get, to draw; *Prügel etc* to get

f (*= in Beziehung setzen*) **etw auf jdn/etw ~** to apply sth to sb/sth; **warum bezieht er (bloß) immer alles auf sich?** why does he always take everything personally?; **auf jdn/etw bezogen** referring to sb/sth

g (*Sw*: *= einfordern*) *Steuern* to collect

VR **a** (*= sich bedecken*: *Himmel*) to cloud over, to darken

b (*= betreffen*) **sich auf jdn/etw ~** to refer to sb/sth; **diese Bemerkung bezog sich nicht auf dich** this remark wasn't meant to refer to you *or* wasn't intended for you

c (*= sich berufen*) **sich ~ auf** (*+acc*) to refer to

Be|zie|her [bəˈtsiːɐ] M **-s, -**, **Be|zie|he|rin** [-ərɪn] F **-, -nen** (*von Zeitung*) regular reader; (*= Abonnent, von Aktien*) subscriber; (*von Waren*) purchaser; (*von Einkommen, Rente*) drawer

Be|zie|hung F **a** (*= Verhältnis*) relationship; (*Philos, Math*) relation

b *usu pl* (*= Kontakt*) relations *pl*; **diplomatische ~en aufnehmen/abbrechen** to establish/break off diplomatic relations; **intime ~en zu jdm haben** to have intimate relations with sb; **menschliche ~en** human relations *or* intercourse

c *(= Zusammenhang)* connection *(zu* with), relation; **etw zu etw in ~ setzen** to relate sth to sth; **zwischen den beiden Dingen besteht keinerlei ~** there is absolutely no connection between the two (things), the two (things) are totally unconnected *or* unrelated; **in keiner ~ zueinander stehen** to have no connection (with each other); **etw hat keine ~ zu etw** sth has no bearing on sth, sth has no relationship to sth; **jd verliert die ~ zur Wirklichkeit** sb feels cut off from reality
d *usu pl (= Verbindung)* connections *pl* (*zu* with); **er hat die Stelle durch ~en bekommen** he got the position through his connections *or* through knowing the right people; **seine ~en spielen lassen** to pull strings; **~en haben** to have connections, to know the right people; **~en muss/müsste man haben** you need to know the right people, you need to be able to pull strings
e *(= Sympathie) (zu etw)* feeling (*zu* for); *(zu jdm)* affinity (*zu* for), rapport (*zu* with); **ich habe keine ~ zu abstrakter Malerei** I have no feeling for abstract art, abstract painting doesn't do anything for me; **er hat überhaupt keine ~ zu seinen Kindern** he just doesn't relate to his children, he has no affinity for his children
f = **Bezug g**
g *(= Hinsicht)* **in einer/keiner ~** in one/no respect *or* way; **in jeder ~** in every respect, in all respects; **in mancher ~** in some *or* certain respects; **in dieser ~** in this respect

Be|zie|hungs-: **Be|zie|hungs|angst** F *(Psych)* fear of relationships; **Be|zie|hungs|ge|flecht** NT network of connections; **Be|zie|hungs|kis|te** F *(inf)* relationship; **be|zie|hungs|los** ADJ **a** unrelated, unconnected **b** *(= ohne menschliche Beziehungen)* devoid of relationships; **Be|zie|hungs|lo|sig|keit** F -, *no pl* **a** unrelatedness, unconnectedness **b** *(= Mangel an menschlichen Beziehungen)* lack of relationships; **be|zie|hungs|reich** ADJ rich in associations; **be|zie|hungs|voll** ADJ suggestive; **Be|zie|hungs|wahn** M *(Psych)* paranoia

be|zie|hungs|wei|se CONJ **a** *(= oder aber)* or **b** *(= im anderen Fall)* and … respectively; **zwei Briefmarken, die 25 ~ 55 Cent kosten** two stamps costing 25 and 55 cents respectively; **geben Sie in Ihrer Bestellung rot ~ blau als gewünschte Farbe an** state your choice of colour *(Brit)* or color *(US)* in your order: red or blue **c** *(= genauer gesagt)* or rather, or that is to say

Be|zie|hungs|wort NT *pl* **-wörter** *(Gram)* antecedent

be|zif|fer|bar [bəˈtsɪfɐbaːɐ] ADJ quantifiable; **nicht ~** unquantifiable

be|zif|fern [bəˈtsɪfɐn] *ptp* **beziffert** VT **a** *(= mit Ziffern versehen)* to number; *Bass* to figure **b** *(= angeben)* to estimate (*auf +acc, mit* at); **man bezifferte den Schaden auf 500.000 Euro** the damage was estimated at *or* was put at 500,000 euros VR **sich ~ auf** *(+acc) (Verluste, Schaden, Gewinn)* to amount to, to come to; *(Teilnehmer, Besucher)* to number

be|zif|fert [bəˈtsɪfɐt] ADJ *(Mus) Bass* figured; **ein Zuschuss in nicht ~er Höhe** a subsidy of an unspecified amount

Be|zif|fe|rung F -, **-en** **a** *(= das Beziffern)* numbering; *(Mus)* figuring **b** *(= Zahlen)* numbers *pl*, figures *pl*

Be|zirk [bəˈtsɪrk] M **-(e)s, -e** **a** *(= Gebiet)* district; *(fig: = Bereich)* sphere, realm **b** *(= Verwaltungseinheit) (von Stadt)* ≈ district; *(von Land)* ≈ region

Be|zirks-: **Be|zirks|arzt** M, **Be|zirks|ärz|tin** F district medical officer; **Be|zirks|be|am|te(r)** M *decl as adj*, **Be|zirks|be|am|tin** F local government officer; **Be|zirks|ge|richt** NT *(Aus, Sw)* district court; **Be|zirks|haupt|mann** M *(Aus) head official of local government*; **Be|zirks|klas|se** F *(Sport)* regional division; **Be|zirks|kran|ken|haus** NT regional hospital; *(= psychiatrische Klinik)* psychiatric clinic *or* hospital, mental hospital; **Be|zirks|li|ga** F *(Sport)* regional league; **Be|zirks|re|gie|rung** F regional administration; **Be|zirks|rich|ter(in)** M(F) *(Aus, Sw)* district court judge; **Be|zirks|spi|tal** NT *(esp Sw)* district hospital; **Be|zirks|stadt** F ≈ county town

be|zir|zen [bəˈtsɪrtsn] *ptp* **bezirzt** VT *(inf)* to bewitch

Be|zo|ge|ne(r) [bəˈtsoːgənə] MF *decl as adj (Fin) (von Scheck)* drawee; *(von Wechsel)* acceptor

be|zug △ → **Bezug h**

Be|zug M **a** *(= Überzug) (für Kissen, Polster etc)* cover; *(für Kopfkissen)* pillowcase, pillowslip
b *(= Bespannung)* strings *pl*
c *(= Erwerb) (von Waren etc)* buying, purchase; *(von Zeitung)* taking; **der ~ der diversen Magazine kostet uns …** the various magazines we subscribe to cost (us) …
d *(= Erhalt: von Einkommen, Rente etc)* drawing
e **Bezüge** PL *(= Einkünfte)* income, earnings *pl*; **Bezüge aus Nebenerwerb** income *or* earnings from secondary sources **f** *(= Zusammenhang)* = **Beziehung c**
g *(form: = Berufung)* reference; **~ nehmen auf** *(+acc)* to refer to, to make reference to; **~ nehmend auf** *(+acc)* referring to, with reference to; **mit** *or* **unter ~ auf** *(+acc)* with reference to
h *(= Hinsicht)* **in ~ auf** *(+acc)* regarding, with regard to, concerning; **in ~ darauf** regarding that

Be|zü|ger [bəˈtsyːgɐ] M **-s, -**, **Be|zü|ge|rin** [-ərɪn] F -, **-nen** *(Sw)* **a** = **Bezieher b** *(von Steuern)* collector

be|züg|lich [bəˈtsyːklɪç] PREP *+gen (form)* regarding, with regard to, concerning, re *(Comm)* ADJ *(= sich beziehend)* **das ~e Fürwort** *(Gram)* the relative pronoun; **auf etw** *(acc)* **~** relating to sth; **alle darauf ~en Fragen** all questions relating to that

Be|zug|nah|me [-naːmə] F -, **-n** *(form)* reference; **unter ~ auf** *(+acc)* with reference to

Be|zugs-: **Be|zugs|be|din|gun|gen** PL *(von Zeitschriften)* terms *pl* of delivery *or* subscription; *(bei Katalogbestellungen etc)* conditions *pl* of purchase; **be|zugs|be|rech|tigt** ADJ entitled to draw; **Be|zugs|be|rech|tig|te(r)** [-bərɛçtɪçtə] MF *decl as adj (von Rente etc)* authorized drawer; *(von Versicherung)* beneficiary; **be|zugs|be|reit** ADJ *Haus etc* ready to move into, ready for occupation

Be|zug|schein M = **Bezugsschein**

Be|zugs-: **be|zugs|fer|tig** ADJ *Haus etc* ready to move into, ready for occupation; **Be|zugs|grö|ße** F standard for comparison; **Be|zugs|per|son** F **die wichtigste ~ des Kleinkindes** the person to whom the small child relates most closely; **Be|zugs|preis** M *(von Zeitungsabonnement etc)* subscription charge *(Brit)* or price *(US)*; **Be|zugs|punkt** M *(lit, fig)* point of reference; **Be|zugs|quel|le** F source of supply; **Be|zugs|rah|men** M terms *pl* of reference; **Be|zugs|recht** NT *(Fin)* option (on a new share issue), subscription right; **Be|zugs|satz** M *(Gram)* relative clause; **Be|zugs|schein** M (ration) coupon; **etw auf** *or* **durch ~ bekommen** to get sth on coupons; **be|zugs|schein|pflich|tig** [-pflɪçtɪç] ADJ rationed, available only on coupons; **Be|zugs|sys|tem** NT frame of reference; *(Statistik)* reference system; **Be|zugs|wort|satz** M relative clause

be|zu|schus|sen [bəˈtsuːʃʊsn] *ptp* **bezuschusst** VT to subsidize

Be|zu|schus|sung F -, **-en** subsidizing; *(= Betrag)* subsidy

be|zwe|cken [bəˈtsvɛkn] *ptp* **bezweckt** VT to aim at; *(Regelung, Maßnahme auch)* to have as its object; **etw mit etw ~** *(Mensch)* to intend sth by sth; **das bezweckt doch gar nichts** that doesn't get you anywhere (at all); **was soll das ~?** what's the point of that?

be|zwei|feln ✪ 43.1 *ptp* **bezweifelt** VT to doubt, to question, to have one's doubts about; **das ist nicht zu ~** that's unquestionable, that's beyond question; **~, dass …** to doubt that …, to question whether …

be|zwing|bar ADJ conquerable; *Feind auch* defeatable; *(Sport auch)* beatable

be|zwin|gen *ptp* **bezwungen** [bəˈtsvʊŋən] *irreg* VT to conquer; *Feind auch* to defeat, to overcome, to vanquish *(liter)*; *(Sport)* to beat, to defeat; *Festung* to capture; *Zorn, Gefühle* to master, to overcome; *Berg* to conquer, to vanquish *(liter)*; *Strecke* to do VR *(= seine Gefühle/Wünsche etc beherrschen)* to overcome *or* master one's emotions/desires *etc*

be|zwin|gend ADJ compelling; *Charme, Ausstrahlung* captivating, irresistible

Be|zwin|ger [bəˈtsvɪŋɐ] M **-s, -**, **Be|zwin|ge|rin** [-ərɪn] F -, **-nen** *(von Berg, Feind)* conqueror, vanquisher *(liter)*; *(Sport)* winner (*+gen* over); *(von Festung, Burg)* captor

Be|zwin|gung [bəˈtsvɪŋʊŋ] F -, **-en** conquering, conquest; *(von Feind auch)* defeat(ing), overcoming, vanquishing *(liter)*; *(Sport)* beating, defeat(-ing); *(von Festung)* capture, capturing; *(von Zorn, Gefühlen)* mastering, overcoming; *(von Berg)* conquering, vanquishing *(liter)*

Bf. *abbr von* **Bahnhof, Brief**

BfA [beːlɛfˈlaː] F - *abbr von* **Bundesversicherungsanstalt für Angestellte** *federal pensions office for salaried employees*

BGB [beːgeːˈbeː] NT -, *no pl abbr von* **Bürgerliches Gesetzbuch**

BGBl [beːgeːbeːˈlɛl] NT -, *no pl abbr von* **Bundesgesetzblatt**

BGH [beːgeːˈhaː] M **-s** *abbr von* **Bundesgerichtshof**

BGS [beːgeːˈlɛs] M - *abbr von* **Bundesgrenzschutz**

BH [beːˈhaː] M **-(s), -(s)** *abbr von* **Büstenhalter** bra

Bhag|wan [ˈbagvan] M **-s**, *no pl* Bhagwan

Bhf. *abbr von* **Bahnhof**

bi [biː] ADJ *pred (inf)* ac/dc *(inf)*, bi *(inf)*

bi- [biː], **Bi-** PREF bi-; **bidirektional** *(Comput)* bidirectional

Bi|ath|let(in) M(F) biathlete

Bi|ath|lon [ˈbiːatlɔn] NT **-s, -s** *(Sport)* biathlon

bib|bern [ˈbɪbɐn] VI *(inf) (vor Angst)* to tremble, to shake; *(vor Kälte)* to shiver; **um jdn/etw ~** to fear for sb/sth

Bi|bel [ˈbiːbl] F **-, -n** *(lit)* Bible; *(fig)* bible

Bi|bel|aus|le|gung F interpretation of the Bible

Bi|be|les|käs [ˈbɪbələs-] M, **Bi|be|les|kä|se** M *(dial: = Quark)* quark

Bi|bel-: **bi|bel|fest** ADJ well versed in the Bible; **Bi|bel|fes|tig|keit** F thorough knowledge of the Bible; **Bi|bel|for|scher(in)** M(F) *(dated)* Jehovah's witness; **Bi|bel|kom|men|tar** M Bible commentary; **Bi|bel|spra|che** F biblical language; **Bi|bel|spruch** M biblical saying, quotation from the Bible; **Bi|bel|stel|le** F passage *or* text from the Bible; **Bi|bel|stun|de** F Bible study *no pl*; **Bi|bel|text** M text of the Bible; *(= Auszug)* text *or* passage from the Bible; **Bi|bel|über|set|zung** F translation of the Bible, Bible translation; **Bi|bel|vers** M verse from the Bible; **Bi|bel|wort** NT *pl* **-worte** biblical saying

Bi|ber [ˈbiːbɐ] M **-s, -** **a** *(= Tier, Pelz, Tuch)* beaver **b** AUCH NT *(= Tuch)* flannelette sheet *(esp Brit)* **c** *(inf) (= Vollbart)* full beard; *(= Mensch)* man with a beard, bearded man

Bi|ber-: **Bi|ber|bau** M *pl* **-baue** beaver's lodge; **Bi|ber|bett|tuch** NT flannelette sheet *(esp Brit)*; **Bi|ber|burg** F beaver's lodge; **Bi|ber|geil** [-gail] NT **-(e)s**, *no pl* castor(eum)

bi|bern [ˈbiːbɐn] VI *(inf)* to stink, to smell like a fox

Bi|ber-: **Bi|ber|pelz** M beaver (fur); **Bi|ber|schwanz** M **a** beaver's tail **b** *(Build: = Dachziegel)* flat tile, plain tile; **Bi|ber|tuch** NT, *no pl* flannelette sheet *(esp Brit)*

Bib|lio|graf [biblioˈgraːf] M **-en, -en**, **Bib|lio|gra|fin** [-ˈgraːfɪn] F -, **-nen** bibliographer

Bib|lio|gra|fie [bibliogra'fiː] F -, -n [-'fiːən] bibliography
bib|lio|gra|fie|ren [bibliogra'fiːrən] *ptp* **bibliografiert** *insep* VT **a** *(= verzeichnen)* to record in a/the bibliography **b** *(= einordnen)* to take (the) bibliographical details of VI to take bibliographical details
bib|lio|gra|fisch [biblio'graːfɪʃ] ADJ bibliographic(al) ADV bibliographically
Bib|lio|graph *etc* = **Bibliograf** *etc*
Bib|lio|ma|ne [biblio'maːnə] M -n, -n, **Bib|lio|ma|nin** [-'maːnɪn] F -, -nen bibliomaniac
Bib|lio|ma|nie [biblioma'niː] F bibliomania
bib|lio|ma|nisch [biblio'maːnɪʃ] ADJ bibliomaniac(al) *(form)*
bib|lio|phil [biblio'fiːl] ADJ *Mensch* bibliophilic *(form)*, bibliophil(e) *(form)*, book-loving *attr*; *Ausgabe* for bibliophil(e)s, for book-lovers ADV *ausgestattet* for collectors of books, for book-lovers
Bib|lio|phi|le(r) [biblio'fiːlə] MF *decl as adj* book-lover, bibliophil(e)
Bib|lio|phi|lie [bibliofi'liː] F -, *no pl* love of books, bibliophily *(form)*
Bib|lio|thek [biblio'teːk] F -, -en library
Bib|lio|the|kar [bibliote'kaːɐ] M -s, -e, **Bib|lio|the|ka|rin** [-'kaːrɪn] F -, -nen librarian
bib|lio|the|ka|risch [bibliote'kaːrɪʃ] ADJ library *attr*; **~e Ausbildung** training in librarianship, training as a librarian ADV **~ ausgebildet sein** to be a trained/qualified librarian
Bib|lio|theks-: **Bib|lio|theks|ka|ta|log** M library catalogue *(Brit)* or catalog *(US)*; **Bib|lio|theks|kun|de** F librarianship; **bib|lio|theks|kund|lich** [-kʊntlɪç] ADJ library *attr*; **Bib|lio|theks|leh|re** F (practical aspects of) librarianship; **Bib|lio|theks|saal** M (library) reading room; **Bib|lio|theks|we|sen** NT, *no pl* libraries *pl*; *(als Fach)* librarianship; **Bib|lio|theks|wis|sen|schaft** F librarianship
bib|lisch ['biːblɪʃ] ADJ biblical; **ein ~es Alter** a great age, a ripe old age
Bick|bee|re ['bɪk-] F *(N Ger)* bilberry, blueberry *(esp US)*
Bi|det [bi'deː] NT -s, -s bidet
bi|di|rek|ti|o|nal ['biːdirɛktsionaːl] ADJ bidirectional *(auch Comput)*
bie|der ['biːdɐ] ADJ **a** *(= rechtschaffen)* honest; *Mensch, Leben auch* upright **b** *(pej)* conventional, conservative; *Miene* worthy *(iro)* ADV *(pej)* conventionally, conservatively
Bie|der|keit F -, *no pl* **a** *(= Rechtschaffenheit)* honesty; *(von Mensch, Leben auch)* uprightness **b** *(pej)* conventionality, conservatism; *(von Miene)* worthiness
Bie|der-: **Bie|der|mann** M *pl* **-männer a** *(dated, iro)* honest man **b** *(pej geh)* petty bourgeois; **bie|der|män|nisch** [-mɛnɪʃ] ADJ **a** *(dated)* honest **b** *(pej geh)* petty bourgeois; *Geschmack, Gesinnung auch* Philistine
Bie|der|mei|er ['biːdɐmaiɐ] NT -s, *no pl* Biedermeier period
Bie|der|mei|er- *in cpds* Biedermeier; **Bie|der|mei|er|stil** M, *no pl* Biedermeier style; **Bie|der|mei|er|sträuß|chen** NT posy (with paper frill); **Bie|der|mei|er|zeit** F, *no pl* Biedermeier period
Bie|der-: **Bie|der|mie|ne** F *(geh)* worthy air; **Bie|der|sinn** M, *no pl (geh)* **a** *(dated)* honest mentality **b** *(pej)* middle-class or petty-bourgeois mentality
bieg|bar ADJ flexible; *Material auch* pliable
Bie|ge ['biːgə] F -, -n *(dial)* bend, curve; **eine ~ drehen/fahren/fliegen** *(inf)* to go for a walk/a short ride or a spin *(inf)*/a short flight or a spin *(inf)*; **die ~ machen** *(inf)* to disappear
Bie|ge|fes|tig|keit F *(Tech)* bending strength
bie|gen ['biːgn] *pret* **bog** [boːk], *ptp* **gebogen** [gə'boːgn] VT **a** *Draht, Rohr etc* to bend; *Glieder* to bend, to flex; *(fig: = manipulieren)* to wangle *(inf)*; **das Recht ~** *(fig dated)* to bend the law; **auf Biegen und** or **oder Brechen** *(inf)* by hook or by crook *(inf)*, come hell or high water *(inf)* → *auch* **gebogen**
b *(Aus Gram: = flektieren)* to inflect
VI *aux sein (Mensch, Wagen)* to turn; *(Weg, Straße auch)* to curve
VR to bend; *(= sich verziehen) (Schallplatte, Holz)* to warp; *(Metall)* to buckle; **seine Nase biegt sich leicht nach oben** his nose turns up slightly, his nose is slightly turned-up; **sich vor Lachen ~** *(fig)* to double up or crease up *(inf)* with laughter
bieg|sam ['biːkzaːm] ADJ flexible; *Material auch* pliable; *Glieder, Körper* supple, lithe; *(fig)* pliable, pliant
Bieg|sam|keit F -, *no pl* flexibility; *(von Material auch)* pliability; *(von Gliedern, Körper)* suppleness, litheness
Bie|gung F -, -en **a** bend; *(von Weg, Fluss)* bend, curve *(+gen* in); *(von Wirbelsäule)* curve *(+gen* in); **die ~en der Straße** the (twists and) turns or the curves in the road; **der Fluss/die Straße macht eine ~** the river/road curves or bends **b** *(Aus Gram)* inflection
Bie|ne ['biːnə] F -, -n **a** bee **b** *(inf: = Mädchen)* bird *(Brit inf)*, chick *(esp US inf)*
Bie|nen-: **bie|nen|ar|tig** ADJ *Insekt* bee-like; *(fig)* bustling *attr*; **Bie|nen|fleiß** M bustling industriousness; **bie|nen|flei|ßig** ADJ industrious; **Bie|nen|gift** NT bee poison; **Bie|nen|hal|tung** F beekeeping; **Bie|nen|hau|be** F bee veil(s); **Bie|nen|haus** NT apiary; **Bie|nen|ho|nig** M real or natural honey; **Bie|nen|kas|ten** M (bee)hive; **Bie|nen|kö|ni|gin** F queen bee; **Bie|nen|korb** M (bee)hive; **Bie|nen|schwarm** M swarm (of bees); **Bie|nen|spra|che** F language of bees; **Bie|nen|staat** M bee colony; **Bie|nen|stich** M **a** bee sting **b** *(Cook) cake coated with sugar and almonds and filled with custard or cream*; **Bie|nen|stock** M (bee)hive; **Bie|nen|volk** NT bee colony, colony of bees; **Bie|nen|wa|be** F honeycomb; **Bie|nen|wachs** NT beeswax; **Bie|nen|zucht** F beekeeping, apiculture; **Bie|nen|züch|ter(in)** M(F) beekeeper, apiarist
Bi|en|na|le [biɛ'naːlə] F -, -n biennial film/art festival
Bier [biːɐ] NT -(e)s, -e beer; **zwei ~, bitte!** two beers, please; **zwanzig verschiedene ~e** twenty different kinds of beer, twenty different beers; **dunkles/helles ~** dark/light beer; **~ vom Fass** draught *(Brit)* or draft *(US)* beer; **das ist mein** *etc* **~** *(fig inf)* that's my *etc* business

> **BIER**
>
> Beer has a long tradition in Germany and is of two main types: top-fermented beers (**Weizenbier**, made from wheat and barley) and bottom-fermented beers (lager beers that are stored in the barrel for four to six weeks). Each type can be light, medium or dark. Some beers, such as **Kölsch** or **Berliner Weiße**, are drunk mainly in the region in which they are produced, but **Pilsener** or **Pils** – a light beer with a strong bitter taste, served in traditional tulip glasses – is found everywhere. Light beers such as **Dortmunder**, which is also called **Helles** or **Export** depending on the region and the brewing method, have a slightly bitter taste. Medium beers include **Märzen** and **Wiener Bier**. Dark beers taste more strongly of malt and are sweeter.

Bier- *in cpds* beer; **Bier|bass** M *(inf)* deep bass voice; **Bier|bauch** M *(inf)* beer gut *(inf)*, beer belly *(inf)*, potbelly; **Bier|brau|e|rei** F *(= das Brauen)* (beer-)brewing; *(= Betrieb)* brewery
Bier|chen ['biːɐçən] NT -s, - (glass of) beer
Bier-: **Bier|de|ckel** M beer mat *(Brit)* or coaster *(US)*; **Bier|do|se** F beer can; **Bier|durst** M *(inf)* **~ haben** to feel like a beer; **Bier|ei|fer** M, **Bier|ernst** M *(inf)* deadly *(Brit)* or complete seriousness; **bier|ernst** *(inf)* ADJ deadly *(Brit)* or completely serious, solemn ADV solemnly; **Bier|fass** NT keg; **Bier|filz** M beer mat; **Bier|fah|ne** F beery or beery breath; **eine ~ haben** to smell of beer; **Bier|fla|sche** F beer bottle; **Bier|gar|ten** M beer garden

> **BIERGARTEN**
>
> **Biergärten** are unpretentious open-air bars that serve mainly beer and simple food. Most of them are located in the gardens and backyards of pubs. However, some bars operate exclusively as **Biergärten** and these are closed in the winter. **Biergärten** are originally a Bavarian institution but can now be found all over Germany.

Bier-: **Bier|glas** NT beer glass; **Bier|hal|le** F *(auf Volksfest etc)* beer hall; **Bier|kas|ten** M beer crate; **Bier|kel|ler** M *(= Lager)* beer cellar; *(= Gaststätte auch)* bierkeller; **Bier|krug** M tankard *(esp Brit)*, beer mug; *(aus Steingut)* (beer) stein; **Bier|krü|gel** NT *(Aus)* half-litre *(Brit)* or half-liter *(US)* beer mug; **Bier|kut|scher** M **a** brewer's drayman **b** *(inf)* beer-lorry *(Brit)* or beer-truck *(US)* driver; **Bier|lau|ne** F *(inf)* **in einer ~, aus einer ~ heraus** after a few beers; **Bier|lei|che** F *(inf)* drunk; **es lagen noch einige ~n herum** there were still a few drunks lying around dead to the world; **Bier|rei|se** F *(hum)* pub-crawl; **Bier|ru|he** F *(inf)* cool *(inf)*; **Bier|schin|ken** M ham sausage; **Bier|sei|del** NT tankard *(esp Brit)*, beer mug; **bier|se|lig** ADJ *Mensch* boozed up *(inf)*; **er kam in einer ~en Stimmung nach Hause** he came home pretty merry *(Brit inf)* or a bit drunk; **Bier|ulk** M *(inf)* drunken prank; **Bier|ver|lag** M, **Bier|ver|trieb** M beer wholesaler's; **Bier|wär|mer** [-vɛrmɐ] M -s, - beer-warmer; **Bier|wurst** F ham sausage; **Bier|zei|tung** F *(inf)* comic newspaper; **Bier|zelt** NT beer tent
Bie|se ['biːzə] F -, -n **a** *(an Hose)* braid **b** *(Sew)* tuck; *(an Schuh)* decorative seam
Biest [biːst] NT -(e)s, -er ['biːstɐ] *(pej inf)* **a** *(= Tier)* creature; *(= Insekt)* bug **b** *(= Mensch)* (little) wretch; *(= Frau)* bitch *(sl)*, cow *(inf)*; **sie ist ein süßes ~** she looks like a sweet little thing but she can be a bitch at times *(sl)* **c** *(= Sache)* beast (of a thing) *(inf)*
Bies|te|rei [biːstə'rai] F -, -en *(inf)* **a** *(= Gemeinheit)* horrible thing **b** *(= Anstoßendes)* obscenity **c** *(= Schinderei)* beast of a job *(inf)*
bies|tig ['biːstɪç] ADJ *(inf)* beastly *(inf)*, horrible; *(= schlechter Laune)* ratty *(Brit inf)*, grumpy
Biet [biːt] NT -(e)s, -e *(Sw)* area
bie|ten ['biːtn] ✪ 40.2, 53.1 *pret* **bot**, [boːt] *ptp* **geboten** [gə'boːtn] VT **a** *(= anbieten)* to offer *(jdm etw* sb sth, sth to sb); *(bei Auktion)* to bid *(auf +acc* for); *Möglichkeit, Gelegenheit* to offer, to give *(jdm etw* sb sth, sth to sb); **jdm die Hand ~** to hold out one's hand to sb, to offer sb one's hand; *(fig auch)* to make a conciliatory gesture to sb; **jdm die Hand zur Versöhnung ~** *(fig)* to hold out the olive branch to sb; **jdm den Arm ~** to offer sb one's arm; **wer bietet mehr?** will anyone offer me *etc* more?; *(bei Auktion)* any more bids?; **mehr bietet dir niemand** no-one will give or offer you more, no-one will make you a higher offer; **diese Stadt/dieser Mann hat nichts zu ~** this town/man has nothing to offer
b *(= geben)* to give *(jdm etw* sb sth); *Gewähr, Sicherheit, Anlass etc auch* to provide *(etw* sth, *jdm etw* sb with sth); *Asyl* to grant *(jdm etw* sb sth)
c *(= haben, aufweisen)* to have; *Problem, Schwierigkeit* to present; **das Hochhaus bietet Wohnungen für fünfzig Familien** the tower block *(Brit)* or apartment building *(US)* provides accommodation for fifty families
d *(= zeigen, darbieten) Anblick, Bild* to present; *Film* to show; *Leistung* to give; **die Mannschaft bot den Zuschauern ein hervorragendes Spiel** the team put on an excellent game for the

spectators → **Blöße b**, **Stirn**, **Trotz**
e (= *zumuten*) **sich** (*dat*) **etw ~ lassen** to stand for sth; **so etwas könnte man mir nicht ~** I wouldn't stand for that sort of thing; **ist dir so etwas schon einmal geboten worden?** have you ever known the like (*inf*) *or* anything like it?
f (*geh*: = *sagen*) **jdm einen Gruß ~** to greet sb; **jdm einen guten Morgen ~** to bid sb good morning (*old, liter*) → **Paroli**, **geboten**
VI (*Cards*) to bid; (*bei Auktion auch*) to make a bid (*auf +acc* for)
VR (*Gelegenheit, Lösung, Anblick etc*) to present itself (*jdm* to sb); **ein grauenhaftes Schauspiel bot sich unseren Augen** a terrible scene met our eyes

bie|ten+las|sen VT *sep irreg* → **bieten VT e**

Bie|ter ['bi:tɐ] M **-s, -**, **Bie|te|rin** [-ərɪn] F **-, -nen** bidder

bi|fo|kal [bifo'ka:l] ADJ bifocal

Bi|fo|kal|bril|le [bifo'ka:l-] F bifocals *pl*

Bi|ga|mie [biga'mi:] F **-, -n** [-'mi:ən] bigamy

Bi|ga|mist [biga'mɪst] M **-en, -en**, **Bi|ga|mis|tin** [-'mɪstɪn] F **-, -nen** bigamist

bi|ga|mis|tisch [biga'mɪstɪʃ] ADJ bigamous ADV *leben* bigamously

Big Bang ['bɪg 'bɛŋ] M **- -s, - -s** (*Astron, Fin, fig*) big bang

bi|gott [bi'gɔt] ADJ overly pious

Bi|got|te|rie [bigɔtə'ri:] F **-, -n** [-'ri:ən] (*pej*) **a** *no pl* excessive piousness **b** (= *Handlung*) overly pious behaviour (*Brit*) *or* behavior (*US*) *no pl*; (= *Bemerkung*) overly pious remark

Bi|jou|te|rie [biʒutə'ri:] F **-, -n** [-'ri:ən] **a** (= *Schmuck*) jewellery (*Brit*), jewelry (*US*) **b** (*Sw obs*: = *Geschäft*) jeweller's shop

Bi|kar|bo|nat ['bi:karbona:t, bikarbo'na:t] NT bicarbonate

Bi|ker ['baikɐ] M **-s, -**, **Bi|ke|rin** ['baikərɪn] F **-, -nen** (*inf*: = *Motorradfahrer*) biker

Bi|ki|ni [bi'ki:ni] M **-s, -s** bikini

Bi|ki|ni-: **Bi|ki|ni|hös|chen** M bikini bottoms *pl*; **Bi|ki|ni|li|nie** F bikini line *or* zone; **Bi|ki|ni|ober|teil** NT bikini top; **Bi|ki|ni|zo|ne** F bikini zone *or* line

bi|kon|kav [bikɔn'ka:f, bikɔŋ'ka:f] ADJ biconcave

bi|kon|vex [bikɔn'vɛks] ADJ biconvex

bi|la|bi|al [bilabi'a:l] ADJ (*Ling*) bilabial

Bi|lanz [bi'lants] F **-, -en** **a** (*Econ, Comm*) (= *Lage*) balance; (= *Abrechnung*) balance sheet; **eine ~ aufstellen** to draw up a balance sheet; **~ machen** (*fig inf*) to check one's finances **b** (*fig*: = *Ergebnis*) end result; **(die) ~ ziehen** to take stock (*aus* of)

Bi|lanz-: **Bi|lanz|buch|hal|ter(in)** M(F) company accountant (*who balances end-of-year accounts*); **Bi|lanz|fäl|schung** F accounting fraud, window dressing of accounts (*inf*), cooking the books (*inf*)

bi|lan|zie|ren [bilan'tsi:rən] *ptp* **bilanziert** VTI to balance; (*fig*) to assess

Bi|lanz-: **Bi|lanz|prü|fer(in)** M(F) auditor; **Bi|lanz|sum|me** F balance

bi|la|te|ral ['bi:latera:l, bilate'ra:l] ADJ bilateral

Bild [bɪlt] NT **-(e)s, -er** ['bɪldɐ] **a** (*lit, fig*) picture; (= *Fotografie*) photo, picture; (*Film*) frame; (*Art*) (= *Zeichnung*) drawing; (= *Gemälde*) painting; (*Cards*) court *or* face (*US*) card, picture card (*inf*); **~ oder Wappen** heads or tails; **ein ~ machen** to take a photo *or* picture; **etw im ~ festhalten** to photograph/paint/draw sth as a permanent record; **sie ist ein ~ von einer Frau** she's a fine specimen of a woman; **ein ~ des Elends** a picture of misery; **~: Hans Schwarz** (*TV, Film*) camera: Hans Schwarz → **schwach**
b (= *Abbild*) image; (= *Spiegelbild auch*) reflection; **Gott schuf den Menschen ihm zum ~e** (*Bibl*) God created man in His own image
c (= *Anblick, Ansicht*) sight; **das äußere ~ der Stadt** the appearance of the town
d (*Opt*) image
e (*Theat*: = *Szene*) scene → **lebend**
f (= *Metapher*) metaphor, image; **um mit einem** *or* **im ~ zu sprechen ...** to use a metaphor ...; **etw mit einem ~ sagen** to say *or* express sth metaphorically; **im ~ bleiben** to use the same metaphor
g (= *Erscheinungsbild*) character; **sie gehören zum ~ dieser Stadt** they are part of the scene in this town
h (*fig*: = *Vorstellung*) image, picture; **im ~e sein** to be in the picture (*über +acc* about); **jdn ins ~ setzen** to put sb in the picture (*über +acc* about); **sich** (*dat*) **von jdm/etw ein ~ machen** to get an idea of sb/sth; **du machst dir kein ~ davon, wie schwer das war** you've no idea *or* conception how hard it was; **das ~ des Deutschen/Amerikaners** the image of the German/American

Bild-: **Bild|ab|tas|tung** F (*Tech*) scanning; **Bild|ar|chiv** NT picture library; **Bild|at|las** M pictorial atlas; **Bild|auf|lö|sung** F (*TV, Comput*) resolution; **Bild|aus|fall** M (*TV*) loss of vision; **Bild|aus|schnitt** M detail; **Bild|au|tor(in)** M(F) photographer; **Bild|band** [-bant] M *pl* **-bände** illustrated book, coffee-table book

bild|bar ADJ (*lit, fig*) malleable; **der Charakter des Kindes ist noch ~** the child's character can still be shaped

Bild-: **Bild|bei|la|ge** F colour (*Brit*) *or* color (*US*) supplement; **Bild|be|richt** M photographic report; **Bild|be|schrei|bung** F (*Sch*) description of a picture; **Bild|be|trach|tung** F art appreciation

Bild|chen ['bɪltçən] NT **-s, -** *dim von* **Bild**

Bild-: **Bild|do|ku|ment** NT → **Bild a** photograph/drawing/painting of documentary value; **Bild|ebe|ne** F (*Phot*) focal plane; **Bild|emp|fän|ger** M (*Tech*) picture receiver

bil|den ['bɪldn] VT **a** (= *formen*) to form; *Figuren etc auch* to fashion; (*fig*) *Charakter auch* to shape, to mould (*Brit*), to mold (*US*); *Körper, Figur* to shape; **sich** (*dat*) **ein Urteil/eine Meinung ~** to form a judgement/an opinion
b (= *hervorbringen, Gram*) to form; **der Magen hat ein Geschwür gebildet** an ulcer formed in the stomach, the stomach developed an ulcer
c (= *einrichten*) *Fonds, Institution etc* to set up
d (= *zusammenstellen*) *Kabinett, Regierung* to form; *Ausschuss, Gruppe auch* to set up; *Vermögen* to acquire
e (= *ausmachen*) *Höhepunkt, Regel, Ausnahme, Problem, Gefahr etc* to constitute; *Dreieck, Kreis etc* to form; **die Teile ~ ein Ganzes** the parts make up *or* form a whole; **die drei ~ ein hervorragendes Team** the three of them make (up) an excellent team
f (= *erziehen*) to educate
VR **a** (= *entstehen*) to form, to develop; **damit sich keine Vorurteile ~ ...** so that no prejudices are allowed to form ...
b (= *lernen*) to educate oneself; (*durch Lesen etc*) to improve one's mind; (*durch Reisen etc*) to broaden one's mind → *auch* **gebildet**
VI (= *der Bildung dienen*) to be educational; (*Lesen*) to improve the *or* one's mind; (*Reisen*) to broaden the *or* one's mind

bil|dend ADJ **die ~e Kunst** art; **die ~en Künste** the fine arts; **~er Künstler** artist

Bil|der|bo|gen M illustrated broadsheet

Bil|der|buch NT picture book; **a** picture book; **eine Landschaft wie im ~** a picturesque landscape **b** (*rare*: = *Bildband*) illustrated book, coffee-table book

Bil|der|buch- *in cpds* (*lit*) picture-book; (*fig*) perfect; **Bil|der|buch|lan|dung** F **eine ~** a perfect *or* textbook landing; **Bil|der|buch|ver|lag** M publisher of picture books

Bil|der-: **Bil|der|ge|schich|te** F **a** picture story **b** (*in Comic, Zeitung*) strip cartoon; (*lustig auch*) comic strip; **Bil|der|kult** M (*Rel*) image worship, iconolatry (*form*); **Bil|der|rah|men** M picture frame; **Bil|der|rät|sel** NT picture puzzle; **bil|der|reich** ADJ *Buch etc* full of pictures; (*fig*) *Sprache* rich in imagery ADV **~ sprechen** to use a lot of images; **Bil|der|reich|tum** M wealth of pictures; (*fig*) richness of imagery; **Bil|der|schrift** F pictographic writing system; **Bil|der|spra|che** F metaphorical language; **Bil|der|streit** M (*Eccl Hist*) controversy over image worship, iconographic controversy; **Bil|der|sturm** M (*Eccl Hist*) iconoclasm; **Bil|der|stür|mer(in)** M(F) (*lit, fig*) iconoclast; **bil|der|stür|me|risch** [-ʃtʏrmərɪʃ] ADJ (*lit, fig*) iconoclastic; **Bil|der|ver|eh|rung** F (*Rel*) image worship, iconolatry (*form*)

Bild-: **Bild|fern|spre|cher** M videophone; **Bild|flä|che** F **a** (= *Leinwand*) projection surface; (*von Fotoapparat*) film plane **b** (*fig inf*) **auf der ~ erscheinen** to appear on the scene; **von der ~ verschwinden** to disappear (from the scene); **Bild|fol|ge** F sequence of pictures; (*Film*) sequence of shots; **Bild|for|mat** NT picture size; (*Quer-/Längsformat*) picture *or* image format; (*Film*) frame size; **Bild|fre|quenz** F picture *or* image frequency; (*Kameraeinstellung auch*) filming speed; **Bild|funk** M radio photography; **Bild|ge|schich|te** F strip cartoon; **bild|haft** ADJ pictorial; *Beschreibung, Vorstellung, Sprache* vivid ADV vividly; **Bild|haf|tig|keit** ['bɪlthaftɪçkait] F **-**, *no pl* pictorial nature; (*von Beschreibung, Vorstellung, Sprache*) vividness; **Bild|hau|er(in)** M(F) sculptor; (*Frau auch*) sculptress; **Bild|hau|e|rei** [bɪlthauə'rai] F **-**, *no pl* sculpture; **bild|hau|e|risch** ['bɪlthauərɪʃ] ADJ sculptural; **Bild|hau|er|kunst** F sculpture; **Bild|hau|er|werk|statt** F sculptor's workshop *or* studio; **bild|hau|ern** ['bɪlthauən] VTI *insep* (*inf*) to sculpt; **bild|hübsch** ADJ *Mädchen* (as) pretty as a picture; *Kleid, Garten etc* really lovely; **Bild|jour|na|list(in)** M(F) photojournalist; **Bild|kar|te** F court *or* face (*US*) card, picture card (*inf*); **Bild|kon|ser|ve** F film recording; **Bild|lauf** M (*Comput*) scroll; **bild|lauf|fä|hig** ADJ (*Comput*) scrollable; **Bild|lauf|feld** NT (*Comput*) scroll box; **Bild|lauf|leis|te** F (*Comput*) scroll bar

bild|lich ['bɪltlɪç] ADJ pictorial; *Ausdruck etc* metaphorical, figurative ADV pictorially, vividly; *meinen, gebrauchen, verwenden* metaphorically, figuratively; **sich** (*dat*) **etw ~ vorstellen** to picture sth in one's mind's eye; **stell dir das mal ~ vor!** just picture it

Bild|lich|keit F **-**, *no pl* (*von Beschreibung*) graphicness; **die große ~ seiner Sprache** his highly figurative language

Bild-: **Bild|ma|te|ri|al** NT pictures *pl*; (*für Vortrag*) visual material, photographic and film material; (*für Buch*) pictorial material; (*Sch*) visual aids *pl*; **Bild|mi|scher** [-mɪʃɐ] M **-s, -**, **Bild|mi|sche|rin** [-ərɪn] F **-, -nen** (*TV*) vision mixer; **Bild|nach|weis** M (*Typ*: *für Abbildungen in Medien*) photo credits *pl*

Bild|ner ['bɪltnɐ] M **-s, -**, **Bild|ne|rin** [-ərɪn] F **-, -nen** (*geh*: = *Schöpfer*) creator

bild|ne|risch ['bɪltnərɪʃ] ADJ *Begabung, Fähigkeit, Wille, Werk* artistic; *Element, Mittel, Gestaltung* visual

Bild|nis ['bɪltnɪs] NT **-ses, -se** (*liter*) portrait

Bild-: **Bild|plat|te** F video disc; **Bild|plat|ten|spie|ler** M video disc player; **Bild|punkt** M (*TV, Phot, Comput*) pixel; **Bild|qua|li|tät** F (*TV, Film*) picture quality; (*Phot*) print quality; **Bild|re|dak|teur(in)** M(F) picture editor; **Bild|re|por|ta|ge** F (*in Zeitschrift etc*) picture story; (*TV, Film*) film documentary; **Bild|röh|re** F (*TV*) picture tube; **Bild|schär|fe** F definition *no indef art*

Bild|schirm M (*TV, Comput*) screen; **geteilter ~** split screen

Bild|schirm-: **Bild|schirm|ab|strah|lung** F, *no pl* screen radiation; **Bild|schirm|ar|bei|ter(in)** M(F) VDU operator; **Bild|schirm|ar|beits|platz** M work station; **Bild|schirm|fens|ter** NT (*Comput*) window; **Bild|schirm|fil|ter** M (*Comput*) screen filter; **Bild|schirm|ge|rät** NT visual display unit, VDU; **Bild|schirm|scho|ner** M (*Comput*) screen saver; **Bild|schirm|-**

sei|te F *(TV: Teletext; Internet)* screen page; **Bild|schirm|text** M Viewdata® *sing*, Prestel®

Bild-: **Bild|schnit|zer(in)** M(F) woodcarver; **Bild|schnit|ze|rei** F (wood) carving; **bild|schön** ADJ beautiful; **Bild|sei|te** F **a** face, obverse *(form)* **b** *(von Buch)* picture page; **Bild|stel|le** F educational film hire service; **Bild|stock** M **a** wayside shrine **b** *(Typ)* block; **Bild|stö|rung** F *(TV)* interference (on vision *or* on the picture); **Bild|such|lauf** M picture search; **Bild|sym|bol** NT pictogram; *(Comput)* icon; **bild|syn|chron** ADJ *(Film, TV)* synchronized (with the picture); **Bild|ta|fel** F plate; **Bild|te|le|fon** NT videophone; **Bild|te|le|gramm** NT phototelegram; **Bild|text** M caption

Bil|dung ['bɪldʊŋ] F -, -en **a** *(= Erziehung)* education; *(= Kultur)* culture; **zu seiner ~ macht er Abendkurse** he does evening classes to try and educate himself; **zu seiner ~ liest er viel** he reads to improve his mind; **die allgemeine ~** general education; *(eines Menschen)* one's general education; **höhere ~** higher education; **~ haben** to be educated
b *no pl (= das Formen)* formation, forming; *(von Figuren etc)* fashioning; *(fig: von Charakter etc)* shaping; **zur ~ des Passivs** to form the passive
c *(= Form: von Baum, Hand etc, Ling: = Wort etc)* form
d *no pl (= Entstehung: von Rost etc)* formation
e *no pl (= Einrichtung)* setting up
f *no pl (= Zusammenstellung) (von Kabinett, Regierung)* formation, forming; *(von Ausschuss, Gruppe)* setting up, forming; *(von Vermögen)* acquisition

Bil|dungs-: **Bil|dungs|ab|schluss** M (educational) qualifications *pl*; **Bil|dungs|an|stalt** F *(form)* educational establishment; **Bil|dungs|ar|beit** F work in the field of education; **bil|dungs|be|flis|sen** ADJ eager to improve one's mind; **Bil|dungs|be|flis|sen|heit** F eagerness to improve one's mind; **Bil|dungs|bür|ger(in)** M(F) member of the educated classes; **Bil|dungs|bür|ger|tum** NT educated classes *pl*; **Bil|dungs|chan|cen** PL educational opportunities *pl*; **Bil|dungs|drang** M desire for education; **Bil|dungs|dün|kel** M intellectual snobbery; **Bil|dungs|ei|fer** M desire to be educated; **bil|dungs|eif|rig** ADJ eager to be educated; **Bil|dungs|ein|rich|tung** F educational institution; *(= Kulturstätte)* cultural institution; **Bil|dungs|fab|rik** F *(pej)* educational mill, diploma mill *(US)*; **bil|dungs|fä|hig** ADJ educable; **bil|dungs|feind|lich** ADJ anti-education; **Bil|dungs|gang** M *pl* **-gänge** school (and university) career; **Bil|dungs|grad** M level of education; **Bil|dungs|gut** NT, *no pl* established part of one's general education; **das gehört zum deutschen ~** that is part of the German cultural heritage; **Bil|dungs|hun|ger** M thirst for education; **bil|dungs|hung|rig** ADJ thirsting for education; **der ~e Student** the eager student; **Bil|dungs|ide|al** NT educational ideal; **Bil|dungs|in|sti|tut** NT educational institution; *(= Kulturstätte)* cultural institution; **Bil|dungs|lü|cke** F gap in one's education; **Bil|dungs|mi|se|re** F **die ~** the lamentable state of (higher) education; **Bil|dungs|mo|no|pol** NT monopoly on education; **Bil|dungs|ni|veau** NT standard *or* level of education; **Bil|dungs|not|stand** M chronic shortage of educational facilities; **Bil|dungs|pla|nung** F education(al) planning *no indef art*; **Bil|dungs|po|li|tik** F education policy; **Bil|dungs|po|li|ti|ker(in)** M(F) *politician with a special interest in or responsibility for education*; **bil|dungs|po|li|tisch** ADJ *Maßnahmen, Fehlentscheidung* with regard to educational policy; *Sprecher* on educational policy ADV in terms of educational policy; **Bil|dungs|re|form** F educational reform; **Bil|dungs|rei|se** F educational trip *or* journey; **Bil|dungs|ro|man** M *(Liter)* Bildungsroman *(form), novel concerned with the intellectual or spiritual development of the main character*; **Bil|dungs|stand** M level of education, educational level; **Bil|dungs|stät|te** F *(geh)* place *or* seat of learning; **Bil|dungs|stre|ben** NT striving after education; **Bil|dungs|stu|fe** F level of education; **eine hohe/niedrige ~ haben** to be highly/not very educated; **Bil|dungs|ur|laub** M educational holiday *(esp Brit) or* vacation *(US)*; *(in Firma)* study leave; **Bil|dungs|weg** M **jds ~** the course of sb's education; **auf dem zweiten ~** through night school; **einen anderen ~ einschlagen** to opt for a different type of education

> **ZWEITER BILDUNGSWEG**
>
> The German school system is strictly regulated and rather inflexible. If students fail to get the qualifications necessary for their chosen career the **zweiter Bildungsweg** gives them a second chance. The courses on offer include the **Abitur** which is taught in evening and half-day classes, as well as with distance learning. Shorter courses are also available.
> →ABITUR

Bil|dungs|we|sen NT education system

Bild-: **Bild|un|ter|schrift** F caption; **Bild|ver|ar|bei|tung** F *(Comput)* **digitale ~** image processing; **Bild|vor|la|ge** F *(für Gemälde, Zeichnung)* subject for a/the picture; **Bild|wand** F projection wall; **Bild|wer|fer** M projector; **Bild|wie|der|hol|fre|quenz** F, **Bild|wie|der|hol|ra|te** F *(TV, Comput)* refresh *or* scan rate; **Bild|win|kel** M *(Opt, Phot)* angle of view; **Bild|wör|ter|buch** NT pictorial *or* picture dictionary; **Bild|zei|le** F *(TV etc)* (scanning) line; **Bild|zu|schrift** F reply enclosing photograph

Bil|ge ['bɪlgə] F -, -n *(Naut)* bilge

Bil|har|zi|o|se [bɪlhar'tsio:zə] F -, -n *(Med)* bilharzia

bi|lin|gu|al [biliŋ'gua:l], **bi|lin|gu|isch** [bi'lɪŋguɪʃ] *(form)* ADJ bilingual ADV **an der Uni Biel wird ~ unterrichtet** at the University of Biel courses are taught in two languages; **sie erzieht ihre Kinder ~** she is bringing her children up to be bilingual

Bi|li|ru|bin [biliru'bi:n] NT -s, *no pl* bilirubin

Bil|lard ['bɪljart] NT -s, -e *or (Aus)* -s [-də] **a** *(= Spiel)* billiards *sing* **b** *(inf: = Spieltisch)* billiard table

Bil|lard- *in cpds* billiard; **Bil|lard|ball** M, **Bil|lard|ku|gel** F billiard ball; **Bil|lard|queue** NT OR (AUS INF) M, **Bil|lard|stock** M billiard cue; **Bil|lard|tisch** M billiard table

Bil|le|teur [bɪlje'tø:ɐ] M -s, -e **a** *(Aus: = Platzanweiser)* usher **b** *(Sw: = Schaffner)* conductor

Bil|le|teu|rin [bɪlje'tø:rɪn] F -, -nen *(Aus: Platzanweiserin)* usherette

Bil|le|teu|se [bɪlje'tø:zə] F -, -n *(Sw: = Schaffnerin)* conductress

Bil|lett [bɪl'jɛt] NT -(e)s, -e *or* -s **a** *(Sw dated: = Fahrbillett, Eintrittskarte)* ticket **b** *(Aus obs: = Schreiben)* note; *(= Briefkarte)* letter *(Brit) or* correspondence *(US)* card

Bil|lett|steu|er F *(Sw)* entertainment tax

Bil|li|ar|de [bɪ'liardə] F -, -n million billion *(Brit)*, thousand trillion *(US)*

bil|lig ['bɪlɪç] ADJ **a** *(= preisgünstig)* cheap; *Preis* low; *(= minderwertig)* cheap, cheapo *(inf)*; **~ abzugeben** going cheap; **~es Geld** *(inf: = leicht verdient)* easy money; **etw für ~es Geld kaufen** to buy sth cheap; **~ davonkommen** *(inf)* to get off lightly **b** *(pej: = primitiv)* cheap; *Trick, Masche* cheap, shabby; *Ausrede* feeble; **ein ~er Trost** cold comfort **c** *(old) (= angemessen)* proper, meet *(old)*; *(= gerecht, berechtigt)* just, fair → **recht**

Bil|lig- *in cpds* cheap; **Bil|lig|an|bie|ter(in)** M(F) supplier of cheap goods; **Bil|lig|an|ge|bot** NT cut-price offer

bil|li|gen ['bɪlɪgn] VT to approve; **etw stillschweigend ~** to condone sth; **~, dass jd etw tut** to approve of sb's doing sth

bil|li|ger|ma|ßen ['bɪlɪge'ma:sn], **bil|li|ger|wei|se** ADV *(old) (= mit Recht)* rightly; *(= gerechterweise)* by rights

Bil|lig-: **Bil|lig|flag|ge** F *(Naut)* flag of convenience; **unter ~ fahren** to sail under a flag of convenience; **Bil|lig|flug** M cheap *or* bargain flight; **Billigflüge** *pl* cheap *or* cut-price air travel; **Bil|lig|job** M low-paid job

Bil|lig|keit F -, *no pl* **a** *(= Preisgünstigkeit)* cheapness; *(von Preis)* lowness **b** *(pej: = Primitivität)* cheapness; *(von Ausrede)* feebleness; **die ~ dieser Masche** this cheap trick; **die ~ der Aufmachung** the cheap presentation **c** *(old) (= Angemessenheit)* properness, meetness *(old)*; *(= Gerechtigkeit, Berechtigung, Jur)* justness, fairness

Bil|lig-: **Bil|lig|land** NT country with low production costs; **Bil|lig|lohn|land** NT low-wage country; **Bil|lig|preis** M low price; **Bil|lig|preis|land** NT low-cost country; **Bil|lig|rei|se** F cheap holiday *(Brit) or* vacation *(US)*; **~n** *pl (Firmenangebote)* cut-price *or* bargain travel; **Bil|lig|ta|rif** M *(Telec etc)* cheap rate; **zum ~ reisen/telefonieren** to travel cut-price/to make cheap-rate phone calls; **Reisen zum ~** *(Angebot)* cut-price *or* bargain travel (offers *pl*)

Bil|li|gung F -, -en approval; **jds ~ finden** to meet with sb's approval

Bil|li|on [bɪ'lio:n] F -, -en thousand billion *(Brit)*, trillion *(US)*

bim [bɪm] INTERJ ding

bim|bam ['bɪm'bam] INTERJ ding-dong

Bim|bam ['bɪm'bam] M **ach, du heiliger ~!** *(inf)* hell's bells! *(inf)*

Bim|bim ['bɪm'bɪm] F -, -s *(baby-talk)* tram *(esp Brit)*, streetcar *(US)*

Bim|bo ['bɪmbo] M -s, -s *(pej sl: = Schwarzer)* wog *(Brit pej sl)*, nigger *(pej sl)*

Bi|me|tall ['bi:-] NT *(= Material)* bimetal; *(= Bimetallstreifen)* bimetal strip

Bim|mel ['bɪml] F -, -n *(inf)* bell

Bim|mel|bahn F *(inf) small train with a warning bell*

Bim|me|lei [bɪmə'lai] F -, *no pl (pej)* ringing

bim|meln ['bɪmln] VI *(inf)* to ring

Bims [bɪms] M -es, -e **a** pumice stone **b** *(Build)* breeze block

Bim|se ['bɪmzə] F -, *no pl (inf)* **~ kriegen** to get a walloping *(esp Brit inf) or* a beating

bim|sen ['bɪmzn] VT *(inf)* **a** *(= drillen)* to drill **b** *(= einüben) Vokabeln etc* to swot *(Brit inf)*, to cram *(inf)*; *Griffe etc* to practise *(Brit)*, to practice *(US)*

Bims|stein M **a** pumice stone **b** *(Build)* breeze block

bin [bɪn] *1. pers sing pres von* **sein**

bi|när [bi'nɛ:ɐ], **bi|nar**, **bi|na|risch** ADJ binary

Bi|när-: **Bi|när|kode** M binary code; **Bi|när|zahl** F binary number

Bin|de ['bɪndə] F -, -n **a** *(Med)* bandage; *(= Schlinge)* sling **b** *(= Band)* strip of material; *(= Schnur)* cord; *(= Armbinde)* armband; *(= Augenbinde)* blindfold **c** *(= Monatsbinde)* (sanitary) towel *or (esp US)* napkin **d** *(dated: = Krawatte)* tie; **sich** *(dat)* **einen hinter die ~ gießen** *or* **kippen** *(inf)* to put a few drinks away

Bin|de-: **Bin|de|ge|we|be** NT *(Anat)* usu sing connective tissue; **Bin|de|ge|webs|schwä|che** F, *no pl (Med)* connective tissue weakness; **Bin|de|glied** NT connecting link; **Bin|de|haut** F *(Anat)* conjunctiva; **Bin|de|haut|ent|zün|dung** F conjunctivitis; **Bin|de|mit|tel** NT binder

bin|den ['bɪndn] *pret* **band** [bant], *ptp* **gebunden** [gə'bʊndn] VT **a** *(= zusammenbinden)* to tie; *(= festbinden)* to bind; *(fig geh)* to bind, to unite; **etw zu etw** *or* **in etw** *(acc)* **~** to tie *or* bind sth into sth
b *(= durch Binden herstellen)* to bind; *Strauß, Kranz* to make up; *Knoten etc* to tie; *Fass* to hoop

c *(= zubinden) Schal* to tie; *Krawatte* to knot; **sich** *(dat)* **die Schuhe ~** to tie (up) one's shoelaces

d *(= fesseln, befestigen) (an +acc* to) to tie (up); *Ziege, Pferd auch* to tether; *Boot* to moor; *(fig) Menschen* to bind, to tie; *(an einen Ort)* to tie; *Geldmittel* to tie up; *(Versprechen, Vertrag, Eid etc)* to bind; **jdn an Händen und Füßen ~** to tie *or* bind sb hand and foot; **jdm die Hände auf den Rücken ~** to tie sb's hands behind his back; **mir sind die Hände gebunden** *(fig)* my hands are tied; **nichts bindet mich an Glasgow** I have no special ties to keep me in Glasgow; **sie versuchte, ihn an sich zu ~** she tried to tie him to her → *auch* **gebunden, Nase a**

e *(= festhalten) Staub, Erdreich* to bind; *(Chem) (= aufnehmen)* to absorb; *(= sich verbinden mit)* to combine with

f *(= zusammenhalten, auch Cook) Farbe, Soße* to bind

g *(= verbinden) (Poet)* to bind; *(fig geh auch)* to unite; *(Mus) Töne* to slur; *gleiche Note* to tie; **was Gott gebunden hat, soll der Mensch nicht trennen** what God has joined together let no man put asunder

VI *(Mehl, Zement, Soße etc)* to bind; *(Klebstoff)* to bond; *(fig)* to be tying, to tie one down; *(Erlebnisse)* to create a bond

VR *(= sich verpflichten)* to commit oneself *(an +acc* to); **ich will mich nicht ~** I don't want to get involved

bin|dend ADJ binding *(für* on); *Zusage* definite

Bin|der [ˈbɪndɐ] M **-s, - a** *(= Krawatte)* tie **b** *(Agr) (= Bindemaschine)* binder; *(= Mähbinder)* reaper *(Brit) or* grain *(US)* binder **c** *(Build) (= Stein)* header; *(= Balken)* truss beam **d** *(= Bindemittel)* binder

Bin|der [ˈbɪndɐ] M **-s, -, Bin|de|rin** [-ərɪn] F **-, -nen** *(S Ger, Aus: = Böttcher)* cooper

Bin|de|rei [bɪndəˈrai] F **-, -en** *(= Buchbinderei)* bindery; *(= Blumenbinderei)* wreath and bouquet department

Bin|de-: **Bin|de|strich** M hyphen; **Bin|de|strich|frau** F *(hum, pej) woman with hyphenated surname made up of her husband's name and her own*; **Bin|de|vo|kal** M thematic vowel; **Bin|de|wort** NT *pl* **-wörter** *(Gram)* conjunction

Bind|fa|den M string; **ein (Stück) ~** a piece of string; **es regnet Bindfäden** *(inf)* it's sheeting down *(Brit inf)*, it's coming down in buckets *(US inf)*

-bin|dig [bɪndɪç] ADJ *suf (Chem)* **dieses Element ist vierbindig** this element has a valency of four

Bin|dig|keit F **-**, *no pl (Chem)* valency

Bin|dung [ˈbɪndʊŋ] F **-, -en a** *(= Beziehung zu einem Partner)* relationship *(an +acc* with); *(= Verbundenheit mit einem Menschen, Ort)* tie, bond *(an +acc* with); *(= Verpflichtung: an Beruf etc, durch Vertrag)* commitment *(an +acc* to); **seine enge ~ an die Heimat** his close ties with his home country **b** *(= Skibindung)* binding **c** *(Chem)* bond **d** *(Tex)* weave

Bin|dungs-: **Bin|dungs|angst** F *usu pl (Psych)* fear of commitment *no pl*; **bin|dungs|fä|hig** ADJ capable of commitment; **nicht ~ sein** to be incapable of having a (personal) relationship

bin|go [ˈbɪŋgo] INTERJ *(inf) (= ok)* OK; *(= aha)* bingo

Bin|go [ˈbɪŋgo] NT **-(s)**, *no pl* bingo

Bin|kel [ˈbɪŋkl] M **-s, -(n)** *(Aus inf)* **a** = **Bündel b** *(= Dummkopf)* twit *(inf)* **c** = **Beule**

bin|nen [ˈbɪnən] PREP *+dat or (geh) +gen (form)* within; **~ Kurzem** shortly

Bin|nen-: **bin|nen|bords** [-bɔrts] ADV *(Naut)* inboard; **Bin|nen|deich** M inner dyke *(Brit) or* dike *(esp US)*; **bin|nen|deutsch** ADJ *Ausdruck, Wort* used in Germany; *Sprache, Dialekt* spoken in Germany; **Bin|nen|deut|sche(r)** MF *decl as adj* German living in Germany; **Bin|nen|fi|sche|rei** F freshwater fishing; **Bin|nen|ge|wäs|ser** NT inland water; **Bin|nen|gren|ze** F internal border; **Bin|nen|ha|fen** M river port; **Bin|nen|han|del** M domestic trade; **Bin|nen|land** NT **a** *(= Landesinneres)* interior **b** *(N Ger: = eingedeichtes Gebiet)* dyked *(Brit) or* diked *(esp US)* land; **Bin|nen|län|der** [-lɛndɐ] M **-s, -, Bin|nen|län|de|rin** [-ərɪn] F **-, -nen** inlander; **bin|nen|län|disch** [-lɛndɪʃ] ADJ inland; **Bin|nen|markt** M home market; *(von EU)* single market; **der europäische ~** the European Single Market; **Bin|nen|meer** NT **a** inland sea **b** *(= Binnensee)* lake, continental lake *(form)*; **Bin|nen|reim** M *(Poet)* internal rhyme; **Bin|nen|schif|fer(in)** M(F) sailor on inland waterways; *(auf Schleppkahn)* bargeman/-woman; **Bin|nen|schiff|fahrt** F inland navigation; **Bin|nen|see** M lake, continental lake *(form)*; **Bin|nen|staat** M landlocked country *or* state; **Bin|nen|ver|kehr** M inland traffic; **Bin|nen|wäh|rung** F internal currency; **Bin|nen|was|ser|stra|ße** F inland waterway; **Bin|nen|wirt|schaft** F domestic economy; **Bin|nen|zoll** M internal duty

Bi|nom [biˈnoːm] NT **-s, -e** binomial

bi|no|misch [biˈnoːmɪʃ] ADJ binomial

Bin|se [ˈbɪnzə] F **-, -n** *usu pl* rush; **in die ~n gehen** *(fig inf) (= misslingen)* to be a washout *(inf)*; *(= verloren gehen)* to go west *(inf)*, to go for a burton *(Brit inf)*; *(= kaputtgehen)* to give out *(inf)*

Bin|sen|wahr|heit F, **Bin|sen|weis|heit** F truism

bio [ˈbiːo] ADJ *(inf) Nahrungsmittel, Anbau etc* organic; **das ist alles ~** it's all organic food

Bio [ˈbiːo] F **-**, *no pl (Sch inf)* biol *(inf)*, bio *(esp US inf)*, bilge *(hum sl)*

bio-, Bio- *in cpds* bio-; **Bio|ab|fall** M biological waste; **bio|ak|tiv** [biolakˈtiːf, ˈbiːo-] ADJ *Waschmittel* biological; **Bio|bau|er** M, **Bio|bäu|e|rin** F organic farmer; **Gemüse vom ~n** organic vegetables *pl*; **Bio|che|mie** [bioçeˈmiː] F biochemistry; **bio|che|misch** ADJ biochemical ADV biochemically; **Bio|chi|rur|gie** F *(Med)* biosurgery; **Bio|die|sel** [ˈbiːo-] M biodiesel; **bio|dy|na|misch** [biodyˈnaːmɪʃ] ADJ biodynamic ADV biodynamically; **Gemüse ~ anbauen** to grow vegetables biodynamically; **Bio|ener|ge|tik** [bioleneɐˈgeːtɪk] F, *no pl* bioenergetics *sing*; **Bio|ethik** [ˈbiːoleːtɪk] F, *no pl* bioethics *sing or pl*; **Bio|ethi|ker(in)** [ˈbiːoleːtɪkɐ, -ərɪn] M(F) bioethicist; **Bio|gas** [ˈbiːo-] NT methane gas; **Bio|ge|ne|se** [biogeˈneːzə] F biogenesis; **bio|ge|ne|tisch** [biogeˈneːtɪʃ] ADJ biogenetic

Bio|graf [bioˈgraːf] M **-en, -en, Bio|gra|fin** [-ˈgraːfɪn] F **-, -nen** biographer

Bio|gra|fie [biograˈfiː] F **-, -n** [-ˈfiːən] biography

bio|gra|fisch [bioˈgraːfɪʃ] ADJ biographical ADV biographically

Bio|graph *etc* = **Biograf** *etc*

Bio-: **Bio|kost** F, *no pl* organic food; **Bio|kraft|stoff** M organic fuel; **Bio|la|den** [ˈbiːo-] M wholefood *or* health-food shop

> **BIOLADEN**
>
> A **Bioladen** is a shop that mainly sells organic food. You can also buy environmentally-friendly goods such as recycled-paper products and bleach-free detergents. Vegetarians are well catered for by **Bioläden**, which stock food guaranteed to be of purely vegetable origin.

Bio|lo|ge [bioˈloːgə] M **-n, -n, Bio|lo|gin** [-ˈloːgɪn] F **-, -nen** biologist

Bio|lo|gie [biologiː] F **-**, *no pl* biology

bio|lo|gisch [bioˈloːgɪʃ] ADJ biological; *Anbau* organic; **~-technische Assistentin, ~-technischer Assistent** laboratory technician; **~e Uhr** biological clock ADV biologically; *anbauen* organically

Bio-: **Bio|mas|se** [ˈbiːo-] F, *no pl (Chem)* organic substances *pl*; **Bio|met|rie** [biomeˈtriː] F **-**, *no pl*, **Bio|met|rik** [bioˈmeːtrɪk] F **-**, *no pl* biometrics *sing*; **bio|met|risch** [bioˈmeːtrɪʃ] ADJ *Risiken, Werte, Systeme, Verfahren etc* biometric; **Bio|müll** [ˈbiːo-] M organic waste

Bio|nik [biˈoːnɪk] F **-**, *no pl* bionics *sing*

Bio|phy|sik [biofyˈziːk, ˈbiːo-] F biophysics *sing*

bio|phy|si|ka|lisch [biofyziˈkaːlɪʃ] ADJ biophysical

Bi|op|sie [bioˈpsiː] F **-, -n** [-ˈpsiːən] *(Med)* biopsy

Bio-: **Bio|re|ak|tor** [ˈbiːo-] M bioreactor; **Bio|re|so|nanz** F bioresonance, bio-resonance; **Bio|rhyth|mus** [ˈbiːo-] M biorhythm; **das verlangt mein ~** my internal clock tells me it's necessary

BIOS [ˈbiːɔs] NT **-**, *no pl (Comput) abbr von* **basic input output system** BIOS

Bio-: **Bio|sphä|re** [bioˈsfɛːrə, ˈbiːo-] F, *no pl* biosphere; **Bio|sphä|ren|re|ser|vat** NT biosphere reserve; **Bio|tech|nik** [bioˈtɛçnɪk, ˈbiːo-] F biotechnology; **Bio|tech|ni|ker(in)** [bioˈtɛçnikɐ, ˈbiːo-, -ərɪn] M(F) bioengineer; **bio|tech|nisch** [bioˈtɛçnɪʃ, ˈbiːo-] ADJ biotechnological; **Bio|tech|no|lo|gie** [bioteçnoloˈgiː, ˈbiːo-] F **a** *no pl (Wissenschaft)* biotechnology **b** *(Verfahren)* biotechnological method *or* process; **Bio|ton|ne** [ˈbiːo-] F organic waste bin; **Bio|top** [bioˈtoːp] NT **-s, -e** biotope; **Bio|wasch|mit|tel** [ˈbiːo-] NT biological detergent; **Bio|wis|sen|schaft** [ˈbiːo-] F biological science; **Bio|wis|sen|schaft|ler(in)** M(F) bioscientist

BIP [beːliːˈpeː] NT **-** *abbr von* **Bruttoinlandsprodukt** GDP

bi|quad|ra|tisch [bikvaˈdraːtɪʃ, ˈbiː-] ADJ biquadratic

Bir|cher|mü|es|li [ˈbɪrçɐ-] NT *(Sw)*, **Bir|cher|müs|li** NT muesli *(with fresh fruit)*

birgt [bɪrkt] 3. PERS SING *pres von* **bergen**

Bir|ke [ˈbɪrkə] F **-, -n** birch; *(= Baum auch)* birch tree

Bir|ken-: **Bir|ken|pilz** M boletus (scaber); **Bir|ken|wald** M birch wood *or* forest; **Bir|ken|was|ser** NT *pl* **-wässer** hair lotion *(made from birch sap)*

Birk-: **Birk|hahn** M black cock; **Birk|huhn** NT black grouse

Bir|ma [ˈbɪrma] NT **-s** Burma

Bir|ma|ne [bɪrˈmaːnə] M **-n, -n, Bir|ma|nin** [-ˈmaːnɪn] F **-, -nen** Burmese

bir|ma|nisch [bɪrˈmaːnɪʃ] ADJ Burmese

Birn|baum M *(Baum)* pear tree; *(Holz)* pear wood

Bir|ne [ˈbɪrnə] F **-, -n a** pear **b** *(= Glühlampe)* (light) bulb **c** *(inf: = Kopf)* nut *(inf)*

Bir|nen-: **Bir|nen|fas|sung** F *(= Lampenfassung)* light-bulb socket; **bir|nen|för|mig** ADJ pear-shaped; **Bir|nen|was|ser** NT *(= Birnenschnaps)* pear brandy

birst 3. PERS SING *pres von* **bersten**

bis[1] [bɪs] ADV *(Mus)* bis, twice

bis[2] [bɪs]

1 PRÄPOSITION	2 BINDEWORT

1 – PRÄPOSITION *(+acc)*

a zeitlich until; *(= bis spätestens)* by

> Im Sinne von *bis spätestens* wird *bis* meist mit *by* übersetzt.

bis 5 Uhr mache ich Hausaufgaben, und dann … I do my homework until 5 o'clock, and then …; **das muss bis Ende Mai warten** that will have to wait until *or* till the end of May; **ich kann nur (noch) bis nächste Woche warten** I can only wait until next week, no longer; **er ist bis gegen 5 Uhr noch da** he'll be there (up) until *or* till about 5 o'clock; **bis zum Schluss war unklar, wie der Prozess ausgehen würde** the outcome of the trial was in doubt right up to the end; **es dauert mindestens/höchstens bis nächste Woche** it will take until next week at the very least/most; **bis jetzt hat er nichts gesagt** up to now *or* so far he has said nothing; **bis spätestens Montag darfst du es behalten** you can keep it until Monday, no longer; **die Wäsche ist frühestens bis nächsten Montag fertig** the laundry won't be ready until *or* before next Monday at the earliest; **bis zu diesem Zeitpunkt** up to this time; **dieser Brauch hat sich bis ins 19. Jahrhundert gehalten** this custom continued into the 19th century; **bis in den Sommer/die Nacht hinein** into the summer/night; **bis 5 Uhr kann ich das unmöglich machen/gemacht haben** I can't possibly do it/get it done by 5 o'clock; **bis Ende Mai bin ich wieder in Berlin** I'll be in Berlin again by the end of May; **das sollte bis zum nächsten Sommer fertig sein** it should be finished by next summer; **das hätte eigentlich bis jetzt fertig sein müssen** that should really have been finished by now; **bis spätestens Montag brauche ich das Geld** I need the money by Monday at the latest; **bis gegen 5 Uhr ist das fertig** it'll be ready by about 5 o'clock; **Montag bis Freitag** Monday to *or* through *(US)* Friday; **bis einschließlich 5. Mai** up to and including 5th May; **bis ausschließlich 5. Mai** up to but not including 5th May; **bis bald/später/morgen!** see you soon/later/tomorrow!; **bis wann gilt der Fahrplan?** when is the timetable valid till?; **bis wann bleibt ihr hier?** how long are you staying here?; **bis wann ist das fertig?** when will that be finished?; **bis wann können Sie das machen?** when can you do it by?; **bis dato** *(form)* to date; **bis anhin** *(Sw)* hitherto; **bis auf Weiteres** until further notice; **bis auf Weiteres halten wir die Regelung so** until further notice we'll make this the arrangement; **sie geht bis auf Weiteres auf die Schule in der Kantstraße** for the time being, she'll continue going to the school on Kantstraße

♦ **bis dahin** *or* **dann bis dahin** *or* **dann muss die Arbeit fertig sein** the work must be finished by then; **bis dahin hatte sie noch nie etwas von Schröder gehört** up to then she hadn't heard anything about Schröder; **bis dahin ist noch viel Zeit** that's still a long time off; **bis dahin bin ich alt und grau** I'll be old and grey *(Brit)* *or* gray *(US)* by then; **bis dahin ist er längst weg** he will have gone long before then; **bis dann!** see you then!

♦ **von ... bis ...** from ... to *or* till *or* through *(US)* ...; *(mit Uhrzeiten)* from ... till *or* to ...; **vom 10. Mai bis 12. Oktober** from 10th May until 12th October; **vom 10. Mai bis einschließlich 12. Oktober** from 10th May until 12th October inclusive; **von 10 Uhr bis 17 Uhr** from 10am till 5pm

b [räumlich] to; *(in Buch, Film, Erzählung)* up to; **bis durch/über/unter** right through/over/under; **ich fahre nur bis München** I'm only going to Munich *or* as far as Munich; **ich habe nur bis Seite 35 gelesen** I've only read up to *or* as far as page 35; **bis an unsere Mauer** up to *or* right to our wall; **bis vor den Baum** (up) to the tree; **bis hinter den Baum** (to) beyond the tree; **es sind noch 10 km bis nach Schlüchtern** it's another 10 km to Schlüchtern; **bis ins Letzte** *or* **Kleinste** down to the smallest detail; **er hat alles bis ins Kleinste ausgearbeitet** he's worked everything out down to the smallest detail; **bis wo/wohin?** how far?; **bis wohin ist Ihnen der Mann gefolgt?** how far did the man follow you?; **bis dort** *or* **dorthin** *or* **dahin** (to) there; **wie weit ist es zum nächsten Supermarkt? – bis dorthin sind es nur 5 km** how far is the nearest supermarket? – it's only 5km (away); **bis hierher** this far; **bis hierher hast du ja recht gehabt** so *or* this far you've been right; **bis hierher und nicht weiter** *(lit, fig)* this far and no further; **ich gehe bis hierher, aber nicht weiter** I'll go as far as that, but no further; **höchstens bis Carlisle** to Carlisle at the furthest; **bis mindestens Carlisle** at least as far as Carlisle; **bis einschließlich** up to and including; **bis einschließlich Kapitel 3** up to the end of chapter 3; **bis ausschließlich** up to but not including

c [mit Maßangaben] up to; **Kinder bis sechs Jahre, bis sechs Jahre alte Kinder** children up to the age of six; **für Wagen bis sechs Tonnen** for vehicles up to six tons; **bieten Sie bis 100 Euro** offer up to 100 euros

d [andere Wendungen]

♦ **bis zu** *(= bis zu einer oberen Grenze von)* up to; *(= bis zu einer unteren Grenze von)* (down) to; **Totschlag wird mit Gefängnis bis zu 8 Jahren bestraft** manslaughter is punishable by up to 8 years imprisonment; **er ist genau bis zur Haarspalterei** he is exact to the point of hair-splitting

♦ **bis auf** *(+acc)* *(= außer)* except (for); *(= einschließlich)* (right) down to; **es sind alle gekommen, bis auf Sandra** they all came, except Sandra; **das Schiff ging unter und sie ertranken alle, bis auf den letzten Mann** the ship sank and every single one of them drowned

2 – BINDEWORT

a [beiordnend] to; **zehn bis zwanzig Stück** ten to twenty; **bewölkt bis bedeckt** cloudy or overcast

b [unterordnend zeitlich] until, till; *(= nicht später als)* by the time; **ich warte noch, bis es dunkel wird** I'll wait until *or* till it gets dark; **bis es dunkel wird, möchte ich zu Hause sein** I want to get home before it gets dark; **das muss gemacht sein, bis ich nach Hause komme** it must be done by the time I come home; **bis das einer merkt!** it'll be ages before anyone realizes *(inf)*; **du gehst hier nicht weg, bis das (nicht) gemacht ist** you're not leaving until *or* before it's done; **bis dass der Tod euch scheide(t)** *(form)* until *or* till death do you part *(form)*

c [= sobald] *Aus inf* when; **gleich bis er kommt** the moment he comes *(inf)*, as soon as he comes

Bi|sam ['bi:zam] **M -s, -e** *or* **-s** **a** *(= Pelz)* musquash **b** *no pl (= Moschus)* musk

Bi|sam|rat|te **F** muskrat (beaver)

Bi|schof ['bɪʃɔf, 'bɪʃo:f] **M -s, ⸚e** ['bɪʃœfə, 'bɪʃø:fə], **Bi|schö|fin** ['bɪʃœfɪn, 'bɪʃø:fɪn] **F -, -nen** bishop

bi|schöf|lich ['bɪʃœflɪç, 'bɪʃø:flɪç] **ADJ** episcopal

Bi|schofs-: **Bi|schofs|amt** **NT** episcopate; **Bi|schofs|müt|ze** **F** **a** (bishop's) mitre *(Brit)* *or* miter *(US)* **b** *(= Kaktus)* bishop's mitre *(Brit)* *or* miter *(US)*; **Bi|schofs|sitz** **M** diocesan town; **Bi|schofs|stab** **M** crosier, (bishop's) crook; **Bi|schofs|stuhl** **M** cathedra, bishop's seat

Bi|se|xu|a|li|tät [bizɛksuali'tɛ:t, 'bi:-] **F** bisexuality, bisexualism

bi|se|xu|ell [bizɛ'ksuɛl, 'bi:-] **ADJ** bisexual

bis|her [bɪs'he:ɐ] **ADV** until *or* till now, hitherto; *(= und immer noch)* up to now; **~ nicht** not until *or* till now, not before; *(= und immer noch nicht)* not as yet; **das wusste ich ~ nicht** I didn't know that before; **~ habe ich es ihm nicht gesagt** I haven't told him as yet; **ein ~ unbekannter Stern** a hitherto *or* previously unknown star, a star unknown until *or* till now; **alle ~ bekannten Sterne** all the known stars; **die ~ heftigsten Kämpfe** the worst *or* heaviest fighting yet

bis|he|rig [bɪs'he:rɪç] **ADJ** *attr (= vorherig)* previous; *(= momentan)* present, up to now; **der ~e Stellvertreter ist jetzt Vorsitzender** the previous deputy is now chairman; **der ~e Stellvertreter wird jetzt Vorsitzender** the present deputy will become chairman; **wegen unserer ~en Arbeitsweise war das unmöglich** because of our previous way of working *or* because of the way we worked before that wasn't possible; **wegen unserer ~en Arbeitsweise ist das unmöglich** because of our present way of working *or* because of the way we have worked up to now that isn't possible; **wir müssen unsere ~en Anschauungen revidieren** we will have to revise our present views; **das ist mir in meiner ~en Karriere noch nicht vorgekommen** I've never known that in my career up to now; **die ~en Bestimmungen gelten seit letzter Woche nicht mehr** the regulations previously in force ceased to be valid last week; **die ~en Bestimmungen gelten ab nächster Woche nicht mehr** the regulations presently in force cease to be valid next week

Bis|ka|ya [bɪs'ka:ja] **F - die ~** (the) Biscay; **Golf von ~** Bay of Biscay

Bis|kuit [bɪs'kvi:t, bɪs'kui:t] **NT OR M -(e)s, -s** *or* **-e** (fatless) sponge

Bis|kuit|ge|bäck **NT** sponge cake/cakes; **Bis|kuit|rol|le** **F** Swiss roll; **Bis|kuit|teig** **M** sponge mixture

bis|lang [bɪs'laŋ] **ADV** = **bisher**

Bis|marck|he|ring ['bɪsmark-] **M** Bismarck herring, *filleted pickled herring*

Bi|son ['bi:zɔn] **M -s, -s** bison

biss *pret von* **beißen**

Biss [bɪs] **M -es, -e** bite; *(Zahnmedizin auch)* occlusion; *(fig)* vigour *(Brit)*, vigor *(US)*, spirit; **mit einem ~ war das Törtchen verschwunden** the tart disappeared in one mouthful; **Spag(h)etti/Bohnen mit ~** spaghetti/beans al dente; **~ haben** *(dated inf)* to have punch; **einer Sache den ~ nehmen** to take the sting out of sth

biss|chen ['bɪsçən] **ADJ** *inv* **ein ~ Geld/Liebe/Wärme** a bit of *or* a little money/love/warmth; **ein ~ Milch/Wasser** a drop *or* bit of milk/water, a little milk/water; **ein klein ~ ...** a little bit/drop of ...; **kein ~ ...** not one (little) bit/not a drop of ...; **das ~ Geld/Whisky** that little bit of money/drop of whisky; **ich habe kein ~ Hunger** I'm not a bit hungry

ADV **ein ~** a bit, a little; **ein klein ~** a little bit; **ein ~ wenig** not very much; **ein ~ mehr/viel/teuer** *etc* a bit more/much/expensive *etc*; **ein ~ zu wenig** not quite enough; **ein ~ sehr** *(inf)* a little bit too much; **ein ~ sehr teuer** *etc (inf)* a (little) bit too expensive *etc*

NT *inv* **ein ~** a bit, a little; *(von Flüssigkeit)* a drop, a little; **ein ganz ~** *(inf)* just a tiny bit/drop → **lieb**

bis|sel ['bɪsl] *(dial)* = **bisschen**

Bis|sen ['bɪsn] **M -s, -** mouthful; *(= Imbiss)* bite (to eat); **er will keinen ~ anrühren** he won't eat a thing; **einen ~ zu sich nehmen** to have a bite to eat; **sich** *(dat)* **jeden ~ vom** *or* **am Munde absparen** to watch every penny one spends

bis|sen|wei|se **ADV** mouthful by mouthful; *(fig)* bit by bit

bis|serl ['bɪsɐl] *(dial)* = **bisschen**

biss|fest **ADJ** firm, crisp; *Nudeln* al dente

bis|sig ['bɪsɪç] **ADJ** **a** *(lit, fig)* vicious; **~ sein** to bite; **„Vorsicht, ~er Hund"** "beware of the dog" **b** *(= übellaunig)* waspish; **du brauchst nicht gleich ~ zu werden** there's no need to bite my *etc* head off

Bis|sig|keit **F -, -en** **a** *(lit, fig)* viciousness; *(Bemerkung)* vicious remark **b** *(= Übellaunigkeit)* waspishness; *(Bemerkung)* waspish remark

bissl ['bɪsl] **ADJ, ADV, NT** *inv (dial)* = **bisschen**

Biss|wun|de **F** bite

bist [bɪst] *2. pers sing pres von* **sein**

bis|te ['bɪstə] *(dial inf) contr von* **bist du**

Bist|ro ['bɪstro, bɪs'tro:] **NT -s, -s** bistro

Bis|tum ['bɪstu:m] **NT -s, ⸚er** [-ty:mɐ] diocese, bishopric

bis|wei|len [bɪs'vailən] **ADV** *(geh)* from time to time, now and then

Bit [bɪt] **NT -(s), -(s)** *(Comput)* bit; **... ~ pro Sekunde** ... bits per second

Bit-: **Bit|dich|te** **F** *(Comput)* bit density; **Bit|map** ['bɪtmɛp] **F** *(Comput)* bitmap; **Bit|map-Grafik** **F** *(Comput)* bitmap; **Bit|ra|te** **F** *(Comput)* bit rate

Bitt|brief **M** petition

bit|te ['bɪtə] **INTERJ** **a** *(bittend, auffordernd)* please; **~ schön** please; **nun hör mir doch mal ~ zu** listen to me please; **~ sei so gut und ruf mich an** would you phone me, please?, would

you please phone me?; **wo ist ~ das nächste Telefon?** could you please tell me where the nearest telephone is?; **~ nicht!** no, please!, please don't!; **ja ~!**, **~ ja!** yes please; **~ ~ machen** *(inf) (Kind)* ≈ to say pretty please; *(Hund)* to (sit up and) beg; **~ zahlen, zahlen ~!** (could I/we have) the bill *(Brit)* or check *(US)*, please; **~ nach Ihnen!** after you
b *(bei höflicher Frage, Aufforderung; meist nicht übersetzt)* **~ schön?, ~(, was darf es sein)?** *(in Geschäft)* can I help you?; *(in Gaststätte)* what would you like?; **~ (, Sie wünschen)?** what can I do for you?; **~ (schön** or **sehr)(, Ihr Bier/Kaffee)!** your beer/coffee, here you are *(inf)*; **ja ~?** yes?; **~(, treten Sie ein)!** come in!, come!; **~(, nehmen Sie doch Platz)!** *(form)* please or do sit down; **~ hier, hier ~!** (over) here, please; **Entschuldigung! – ~!** I'm sorry! – that's all right; **~, mit (dem größten) Vergnügen!** *(form)* with pleasure; **aber ~!** sure *(inf)*, go (right) ahead *(inf)*, please do; **~, nur zu!** help yourself; **na ~!** there you are!
c *(sarkastisch: = nun gut)* all right; **~, wie du willst** (all right,) just as you like; **~, soll er doch kommen, mir ist das egal** (all right,) let him come, it's all the same to me
d *(Dank erwidernd)* you're welcome, not at all *(Brit)*, sure *(US inf)*; **~ sehr** or **schön** you're welcome, not at all *(Brit)*; **~(, gern geschehen)** (not at all,) my pleasure; **~, keine Ursache** it was nothing; **~, nichts zu danken** don't mention it; **aber ~!** there's no need to thank me
e *(nachfragend)* **(wie) ~?** (I beg your) pardon? *(auch iro)*, sorry(, what did you say)?

Bit|te ['bɪtə] **F -, -n** request; *(inständig)* plea; **auf jds ~** *(acc)* at sb's request; **auf seine ~ hin** at his request; **ich habe eine große ~ an dich** I have a (great) favour *(Brit)* or favor *(US)* to ask you; **sich mit einer ~ an jdn wenden** to make a request to sb; **er kann ihr keine ~ ausschlagen** or **abschlagen** he can't refuse her anything; **er gab den ~n der Kinder nach** he gave in to the children's pleas

bit|ten ['bɪtn] ✪ 31, 46.1, 46.5, 46.6, 48.3 *pret* **bat**, [ba:t] *ptp* **gebeten** VT [gə'be:tn] **a** *jdn* to ask; *(inständig)* to beg; *(Eccl)* to beseech; **jdn um etw ~** to ask/beg/beseech sb for sth; **jdn (darum) ~, etw zu tun** or **dass er etw tut** to ask *etc* sb to do sth; **jdn etw** *(acc)* **~** *(dated)* to ask sth of sb; **darf ich Sie um Ihren Namen ~?** might I ask your name?; **um Ruhe wird gebeten** silence is requested; *(auf Schild)* silence please; **darf ich Sie um den nächsten Tanz ~?** may I have the pleasure of the next dance?; **wir ~ dich, erhöre uns!** *(Eccl)* we beseech Thee to hear us; *(katholisch, anglikanisch)* Lord hear us; **ich bitte dich um alles in der Welt** I beg or implore you; **er lässt sich gerne ~** he likes people to keep asking him; **er lässt sich nicht (lange) ~** you don't have to ask him twice; **aber ich bitte dich!** not at all; **ich bitte dich, wie kann man nur so dumm sein?** I ask you, how can anyone be so stupid?; **wenn ich ~ darf** *(form)* if you please, if you wouldn't mind; **ich bitte darum** *(form)* I'd be glad if you would, if you wouldn't mind; **(keineswegs,) ich bitte sogar darum** *(form)* (not at all,) I should be glad; **darum möchte ich doch sehr gebeten haben!** *(form)* I should hope so indeed; **ich muss doch (sehr) ~!** well I must say!
b *(= einladen)* to ask, to invite; **jdn auf ein Glas Wein ~** to invite sb to have a glass of wine; **jdn zum Abendessen (zu sich) ~** to ask or invite sb to dinner; **jdn zu Tisch ~** to ask sb to come to table; **jdn ins Zimmer ~** to ask or invite sb to come in
c *(= bestellen)* **jdn an einen Ort ~** to ask sb (to come) somewhere; **jdn zu sich ~** to ask sb to come and see one
VI **a** *(= eine Bitte äußern)* to ask; *(inständig)* to plead, to beg; **um etw ~** to ask (for) or request sth; *(inständig)* to plead or beg for sth; **bei jdm um etw ~** to ask sb for sth; **~ und betteln** to beg and plead
b *(= einladen)* **der Herr Professor lässt ~** the Professor will see you now; **ich lasse ~** he/she can come in now, would you ask him/her to come in now?; **darf ich zu Tisch ~?** lunch/dinner is served; **darf ich (um den nächsten Tanz) ~?** may I have the pleasure (of the next dance)?

Bit|ten NT **-s,** *no pl* pleading; **sich aufs ~ verlegen** to resort to pleas or pleading; **auf ~ von** at the request of

bit|tend ADJ pleading; **mit ~en Augen** with a look of pleading ADV pleadingly

bit|ter ['bɪtɐ] ADJ **a** bitter; *Schokolade* plain; *(fig) Geschmack* nasty → **Pille**
b *(fig) Enttäuschung, Erfahrung, Ironie* bitter; *Wahrheit, Lehre, Verlust* hard, painful; *Zeit, Schicksal* hard; *Ernst, Feind* deadly; *Hohn, Spott* cruel; **ein ~es Gefühl** a feeling of bitterness; **bis zum ~en Ende** to the bitter end
c *(fig: = verbittert)* bitter; **jdn ~ machen** to embitter sb, to make sb bitter; **~e Klagen führen** to complain bitterly
d *(= stark) Kälte, Frost, Reue, Tränen* bitter; *Not, Notwendigkeit* dire; *Leid, Unrecht* grievous
ADV **a ~ schmecken** to taste bitter
b *(= sehr) bereuen* bitterly; *bezahlen, büßen* dearly; **jdn/etw ~ entbehren/vermissen** to miss sb/sth terribly; **etw ~ nötig haben** to be in dire need of sth; **~ wenig Geld haben** to be desperately short of money; **solche Fehler rächen sich ~** one pays dearly for mistakes like that

Bit|ter ['bɪtɐ] **M -s, -** bitters *pl*

bit|ter|bö|se ADJ furious ADV furiously

Bit|te|re(r) ['bɪtərə] **M** *decl as adj* bitters *pl*

Bit|ter-: **bit|ter|ernst** ADJ *Situation etc* extremely serious; *Mensch* deadly *(Brit)* or very serious; **damit ist es mir ~** I am deadly *(Brit)* or very serious, I am in deadly *(Brit)* or complete earnest; **bit|ter|kalt** ADJ *attr* bitterly cold, bitter; **Bit|ter|keit** **F -,** *no pl (lit, fig)* bitterness; **bit|ter|lich** ['bɪtɐlɪç] ADJ bitter ADV bitterly; **Bit|ter|man|del** **F** bitter almond

Bit|ter|nis ['bɪtɐnɪs] **F -, -se** *(geh)* bitterness *no pl*; *(fig: von Mensch auch)* embitterment *no pl*; *(= Leiden)* adversity, hardship

Bit|ter-: **Bit|ter|oran|ge** **F** Seville or bitter orange; **Bit|ter|salz** NT Epsom salts *pl*; **Bit|ter|scho|ko|la|de** **F** plain chocolate; **Bit|ter|stoff** **F** *usu pl* bitter constituent; **bit|ter|süß** ADJ *(lit, fig)* bittersweet

Bit|te|schön ['bɪtəʃø:n] NT **-s, -s** *(bittend, auffordernd)* please; *(Dank erwidernd)* not at all; *(anbietend) (von Verkäufer)* can I help you?; *(von Kellner)* what would you like?

Bitt-: **Bitt|gang** **M** *pl* **-gänge a** *(geh)* **einen ~ zu jdm machen** to go to sb with a request; **das war ein schwerer ~** it was hard (for him *etc*) to ask that **b** *(Eccl)* pilgrimage; *(= Bittprozession)* rogation procession; **Bitt|ge|bet** NT (prayer of) supplication; **Bitt|ge|such** NT petition; **Bitt|got|tes|dienst** **M** rogation service

bitt|schön ['bɪtʃø:n] INTERJ = **bitte schön**, → **bitte a, b, d**

Bitt-: **Bitt|schrift** **F** *(dated)* petition; **Bitt|stel|ler** ['bɪtʃtɛlɐ] **M -s, -**, **Bitt|stel|le|rin** [-ərɪn] **F -, -nen** petitioner, supplicant

Bi|tu|men [bi'tu:mən] NT **-s, -** or **Bitumina** [-'tu:mina] bitumen

bi|va|lent [biva'lɛnt] ADJ bivalent

Bi|wak ['bi:vak] NT **-s, -s** or **-e** bivouac

bi|wa|kie|ren [biva'ki:rən] *ptp* **biwakiert** VI to bivouac

bi|zarr [bi'tsar] ADJ bizarre; *Form, Gestalt etc auch* fantastic ADV *geformt, gestaltet* bizarrely, fantastically

Bi|zar|re|rie [bitsarə'ri:] **F -, -n** [-'ri:ən] *(geh)* **a** *no pl* bizarreness **b** *(= Gedanke)* bizarre idea; *(= Verhalten)* bizarre behaviour *(Brit)* or behavior *(US) no pl*; *(= Bemerkung)* bizarre comment

Bi|zeps ['bi:tsɛps] **M -(es), -e** biceps

Bj. *abbr von* **Baujahr**

BK [be:'ka:] **F -,** *no pl abbr von* **bildende Kunst** *(Sch inf)* art

BKA [be:ka:'la:] NT **-** *abbr von* **Bundeskriminalamt**

BKB [be:ka:'be:] **F -** *abbr (in Annoncen) von* **Benzinkostenbeteiligung**

BKK **F -, -s** *abbr von* **Betriebskrankenkasse**

bla|bla [bla'bla:] INTERJ *(inf)* blah blah blah *(inf)*

Bla|bla [bla'bla:] NT **-s,** *no pl (inf)* waffle *(inf)*

Bla|che ['blaxə] **F -, -n** *(esp Sw)* = **Plane**

Black|box ['blɛkbɔks] **F -, -es**, **Black Box** **F -, -es** *(Aviat, Telec, Comput)* black box

Black|out [blɛk'aut] NT OR M **-(s), -s**, **Black-out** NT OR M **-(s), -s** blackout

blaf|fen ['blafn], **bläf|fen** ['blɛfn] VI to yelp; *(= schimpfen)* to snap

Blag [bla:k] NT **-s, -en** [-gn], **Bla|ge** ['bla:gə] **F -, -n** *(pej inf)* brat

blä|hen ['blɛ:ən] VT to swell; *Segel auch* to belly (out), to fill; *Anorak, Gardine, Windsack* to fill; *Nasenflügel, Nüstern* to flare; **voller Stolz blähte er seine Brust** his chest swelled with pride VR to swell; *(Segel auch)* to belly out, to billow; *(Anorak, Gardine)* to billow; *(Nasenflügel, Nüstern)* to flare; *(fig: Mensch)* to puff oneself up *(inf)* VI to cause flatulence or wind or *(US)* gas

blä|hend ADJ *(Med)* flatulent *(form)*

Blä|hung **F -, -en** *usu pl (Med)* wind *no pl*, flatulence *no pl*; **eine ~ abgehen lassen** to break wind

bla|kig ['bla:kɪç] ADJ *(= verrußt)* sooty; *(= rußend)* smoky

bla|ma|bel [bla'ma:bl] ADJ shameful

Bla|ma|ge [bla'ma:ʒə] **F -, -n** disgrace

bla|mie|ren [bla'mi:rən] *ptp* **blamiert** VT to disgrace → **Innung** VR to make a fool of oneself; *(durch Benehmen)* to disgrace oneself

blan|chie|ren [blã'ʃi:rən] *ptp* **blanchiert** VT *(Cook)* to blanch

blank [blaŋk] ADJ **a** *(= glänzend, sauber)* shiny, shining; *(= abgescheuert) Hosenboden etc* shiny; **etw scheuern/polieren, bis es ~ wird** to clean/polish sth till it shines; **der ~e Hans** *(poet)* the wild North Sea
b *(poet: = strahlend) Licht* bright; *Augen* bright, shining; **der ~e Tag** broad daylight
c *(= nackt)* bare; *Schwert etc auch* naked; *(Aus: = ohne Mantel)* coatless; *(inf: = ohne Geld)* broke; *(Cards: = einzeln)* single
d *(= rein)* pure, sheer; *Hohn* utter
ADV **a** *(= glänzend) scheuern, polieren* till it shines; **~ gewetzt** (worn) shiny; **~ poliert** brightly polished
b eine Karte ~ haben to have only one card of a suit; **die Herzzehn habe ich ~** the ten of hearts is the only heart I have

Blan|kett [blaŋ'kɛt] NT **-s, -e** *(Fin)* blank form

blank|ge|wetzt [-gəvɛtst] ADJ *attr* → **blank ADV a**

blan|ko ['blaŋko] ADJ *pred* **a** *Papier* plain **b** *Scheck etc* blank

Blan|ko- *in cpds* blank; **Blan|ko|ak|zept** NT *(Fin)* blank acceptance; **Blan|ko|kre|dit** [-kre-di:t] **M** open or blank credit; **Blan|ko|scheck** **M** blank cheque *(Brit)* or check *(US)*; **jdm einen ~ ausstellen** *(fig)* to give sb carte blanche or *(US)* a blank check; **Blan|ko|un|ter|schrift** **F** blank signature; **Blan|ko|voll|macht** **F** carte blanche, unlimited power(s)

blank-: **blank+po|lie|ren** *ptp* **blankpoliert** VT *sep* → **blank ADV a**; **blank|po|liert** [-poli:ɐt] ADJ *attr* → **blank ADV a**; **blank+scheu|ern** VT *sep* → **blank ADV a**

Blank|vers **M** blank verse

Bläs|chen ['blɛ:sçən] NT **-s, - a** *dim von* **Blase** **b** *(Med)* vesicle *(form)*, small blister

Bläs|chen|aus|schlag **M** herpes *sing*, blistery rash *(inf)*

Bla|se ['bla:zə] **F -, -n a** *(= Seifenblase, Luftblase)* bubble; *(= Sprechblase)* balloon; **~n werfen** or **ziehen** *(Farbe)* to blister; *(Teig)* to become light and frothy **b** *(Med)* blister; *(= Fieberblase auch)* vesicle *(form)*; **sich** *(dat)* **~n laufen** to get blisters from walking *etc* **c** *(Anat)* bladder; **sich** *(dat)* **die ~ erkälten** to get a chill on the bladder **d** *(pej inf: = Clique)* gang *(inf)*, mob *(inf)*

Bla|se|balg M (pair of) bellows

bla|sen ['bla:zn] *pret* **blies** [bli:s], *ptp* **geblasen** [gə'bla:zn] VI to blow; *(Posaunenbläser etc)* to play; *(auf Essen)* to blow on it; *(auf Wunde etc)* ≈ to kiss it better; **zum Rückzug ~** *(lit, fig)* to sound the retreat; **zum Aufbruch ~** *(lit)* to sound the departure; *(fig)* to say it's time to go; **es bläst** *(inf)* it's blowy *(inf)* or windy, there's a wind blowing → **tuten, Horn b**

VT **a** to blow

b *Melodie, Posaune etc* to play

c *(inf)* **dir/ihm werd ich was ~!** I'll give you/him a piece of my mind → **Marsch b, Trübsal**

d *(inf: = mitteilen)* to tell; **jdm etw ins Ohr ~** to whisper sth in sb's ear

e *(sl: = fellieren)* **jdm einen ~** to give sb a blow job *(sl)*

Bla|sen-: **Bla|sen|bil|dung** F formation of bubbles; *(bei Anstrich, an Fuß etc)* blistering; **Bla|sen|ent|zün|dung** F, **Bla|sen|ka|tarr(h)** M cystitis *(spec)*; **Bla|sen|lei|den** NT bladder trouble *no art*; **Bla|sen|schwä|che** F weakness of the bladder; **unter ~ leiden** suffer from a weak bladder; **Bla|sen|spie|ge|lung** F *(Med)* cystoscopy *(spec)*; **Bla|sen|stein** M bladder stone; **Bla|sen|tee** M *herb tea beneficial in cases of bladder trouble*

Blä|ser ['blɛ:zɐ] M **-s, -**, **Blä|se|rin** [-ərɪn] F **-, -nen** *(Mus)* wind player; **die ~** the wind (section)

Blä|ser|quar|tett NT wind quartet

bla|siert [bla'zi:ɐt] ADJ *(pej geh)* blasé

Bla|siert|heit F **-, -en** *(pej geh)* blasé attitude

bla|sig ['bla:zɪç] ADJ full of bubbles; *Flüssigkeit etc* aerated; *Teig* light and frothy; *(Med)* blistered

Blas-: **Blas|in|stru|ment** NT wind instrument; **Blas|ka|pel|le** F brass band; **Blas|mu|sik** F brass band music

Blas|phe|mie [blasfe'mi:] F **-, -n** [-'mi:ən] blasphemy

blas|phe|misch [blas'fe:mɪʃ] ADJ blasphemous

Blas|rohr NT **a** *(= Waffe)* blowpipe **b** *(Tech)* blast pipe

blass [blas] ADJ **a** *Gesicht, Haut etc* pale; **~ werden** to go *(Brit)* or grow pale, to pale; *(vor Schreck auch)* to blanch; **~ wie der Tod** *(geh)* deathly pale; **~ wie Kreide** white as chalk *(Brit)* or a sheet; **~ vor Neid werden** to go green with envy; **etw macht jdn ~** sth makes sb look pale

b *Farbe, Schrift etc* pale

c *(geh) Licht, Mond* pale, wan

d *(fig)* faint; *Ahnung, Vorstellung auch* vague; *Erinnerung auch* dim, vague; *Ausdruck, Sprache, Schilderung* colourless *(Brit)*, colorless *(US)*; **ich habe keinen ~en Schimmer** or **Dunst (davon)** *(inf)* I haven't a clue or the faintest (idea) (about it) *(inf)*

e *(rare: = pur)* sheer, pure

blass-: **blass-** *in cpds* pale; **blass|blau** ADJ pale blue

Bläs|se ['blɛsə] F **-, -n** paleness; *(von Haut, Gesicht etc)* pallor; *(von Licht)* paleness, wanness; *(fig: von Ausdruck, Schilderung etc)* colourlessness *(Brit)*, colorlessness *(US)*

blass|grün ADJ pale green

Bläss|huhn ['blɛs-] NT coot

bläss|lich ['blɛslɪç] ADJ palish, rather pale

blass|ro|sa ADJ pale pink

bläst [blɛ:st] 3. PERS SING *pres von* **blasen**

Blatt [blat] NT **-(e)s, ¨-er** ['blɛtɐ] **a** *(Bot)* leaf; **kein ~ vor den Mund nehmen** not to mince one's words

b *(Papier etc)* sheet; **ein ~ Papier** a sheet of paper; **(noch) ein unbeschriebenes ~ sein** *(= unerfahren)* to be inexperienced; *(= ohne Image)* to be an unknown quantity; **er ist kein unbeschriebenes ~** he's been around *(inf)*; *(Krimineller)* he's got a record

c *(= Seite)* page; **das steht auf einem anderen ~** *(fig)* that's another story; **ein neues ~ in der Geschichte** or **im Buch der Geschichte** a new chapter of history

d *(= Notenblatt)* sheet; **vom ~ singen/spielen** to sight-read

e *(= Kunstblatt)* print; *(= Reproduktion)* reproduction

f *(bei Landkartenserien)* sheet

g *(= Zeitung)* paper

h *(von Messer, Ruder, Propeller)* blade

i *(Cards)* hand; *(= Einzelkarte)* card; **das ~ hat sich gewendet** *(fig)* the tables have been turned

j *(Hunt, Cook)* shoulder

Blatt|ader F *(Bot)* leaf vein

Blätt|chen ['blɛtçən] NT **-s, -** *dim von* **Blatt** *(pej: = Zeitung)* rag *(inf)*

Blat|ter ['blatɐ] F **-, -n** **a** *(dated Med: = Pocke)* pock, pustule **b** **Blattern** PL *(= Krankheit)* smallpox

blät|te|rig ['blɛtərɪç] ADJ *Teig* flaky; *Farbe etc* flaking; **~ werden** *(Farbe etc)* to start flaking

-blät|te|rig ADJ *suf* -leaved; **ein vierblätteriges Kleeblatt** a four-leaved clover

Blät|ter|ma|gen M *(Zool)* omasum *(spec)*

blät|tern ['blɛtɐn] VI **a** *(in Buch)* to leaf or *(schnell)* flick through it/them; *(Comput)* to scroll; **in etw** *(dat)* **~** to leaf or flick through sth **b** *aux sein (rare) (= in Schichten zerfallen)* to flake; *(= abblättern)* to flake off VT *Geldscheine, Spielkarten* to put down one by one; **er blätterte mir die 100 Euro auf den Tisch** he put the 100 euros down note by note *(Brit)* or bill by bill *(US)* on the table for me

Blat|ter-: **Blat|ter|nar|be** F *(dated)* pockmark; **blat|ter|nar|big** ADJ *(dated)* pockmarked

Blät|ter-: **Blät|ter|pilz** M agaric; **Blät|ter|schmuck** M *(poet)* beautiful foliage; **Blät|ter|teig** M puff pastry or paste *(US)*, filo pastry; **Blät|ter|teig|ge|bäck** NT puff pastry; *(= Gebäckstück)* ≈ Danish pastry; **Blät|ter|teig|pas|te|te** F vol-au-vent; **Blät|ter|wald** M *(Press hum)* press; **es rauscht im deutschen ~** there are murmurings in the German press; **Blät|ter|werk** NT, *no pl* foliage

Blatt-: **Blatt|fe|der** F *(Tech)* leaf spring; **Blatt|form** F *(Bot)* leaf shape; **blatt|för|mig** ADJ leaf-shaped, foliar *(form)*; **Blatt|ge|mü|se** NT greens *pl*, green or leaf *(form)* vegetables *pl*; **ein ~** a leaf vegetable; **Blatt|ge|wächs** NT foliate plant; **Blatt|gold** NT gold leaf; **Blatt|grün** NT chlorophyll; **Blatt|knos|pe** F leaf bud; **Blatt|laus** F greenfly, aphid; **blatt|los** ADJ leafless; **Blatt|pflan|ze** F foliate plant

blätt|rig ['blɛtrɪç] ADJ = **blätterig**

-blätt|rig ADJ *suf* = **-blätterig**

Blatt-: **Blatt|rip|pe** F *(Bot)* (leaf) rib or vein; **Blatt|sä|ge** F pad saw; **Blatt|sa|lat** M green salad; **Blatt|schuss** M *(Hunt)* shot through the shoulder to the heart; **Blatt|sil|ber** NT silver leaf; **Blatt|spi|nat** M leaf spinach; **Blatt|stän|gel** M petiole, leafstalk; **Blatt|stel|lung** F leaf arrangement; **Blatt|stiel** M petiole, leafstalk; **Blatt|trieb** M leaf shoot; **Blatt|ver|gol|dung** F gilding; **blatt|wei|se** ADV leaf by leaf; *(bei Papier)* sheet by sheet; **Blatt|werk** NT, *no pl* foliage

Blätz [blɛts] M **-, -** *(Sw)* cloth

Blätz|li ['blɛtsli] NT **-(s), -(s)** *(Sw)* cutlet

blau [blau] ADJ **a** blue; **Forelle** *etc* **~** *(Cook)* trout *etc* au bleu; **~er Anton** *(inf)* boiler suit *(Brit)*, workman's overalls; **ein ~es Auge** *(inf)* a black eye; **ich tu das nicht wegen deiner schönen ~en Augen** *(fig)* I'm not doing it for the sake of your bonny blue eyes; **mit einem ~en Auge davonkommen** *(fig)* to get off lightly; **die ~e Blume** *(Liter)* the Blue Flower; **~es Blut in den Adern haben** to have blue blood in one's veins; **ein ~er Fleck** a bruise; **~e Flecken haben** to be bruised; **die ~en Jungs** *(inf)* the boys in blue *(inf)*, the navy; **der Blaue Nil** the Blue Nile; **der Blaue Planet** the blue planet; **der Blaue Reiter** *(Art)* the Blaue Reiter; **die ~e Stunde** *(poet)* the twilight hour; **er wird sein ~es Wunder erleben** *(inf)* he won't know what's hit him *(inf)* → **Dunst**

b *usu pred (inf: = betrunken)* drunk, tight *(inf)*, canned *(inf)* → **Veilchen**

c *(inf: = geschwänzt)* **einen ~en Montag machen** to skip work on Monday *(inf)*; **der letzte Freitag war für mich ~** I skipped work last Friday *(inf)*

d **ein ~er Brief** *(Sch) letter informing parents that their child must repeat a year (von Hauswirt)* notice to quit; *(von der Firma)* one's cards

> **BLAUER BRIEF**
>
> A **blauer Brief** is a letter from a school telling parents that their child is in danger of having to repeat a year. Until the mid-1970s it was actually delivered in a blue envelope. **Blauer Brief** is also a colloquial term for the dismissal notice issued by a firm. This dates from the time when officers were sent a letter in a blue envelope to tell them they were going to be discharged from the army.

Blau [blau] NT **-s, -** or *(inf)* **-s** blue

Blau-: **Blau|al|gen** PL blue-green algae *pl*; **blau+är|gern** VR *sep* **sich grün- und ~** *(inf)* to be furious; **blau|äu|gig** ADJ blue-eyed; *(fig)* naïve; **Blau|äu|gig|keit** F **-,** *no pl (lit)* blue eyes *pl*; *(fig)* naïvety; **Blau|bart** M *(geh)* Bluebeard; **Blau|bee|re** F bilberry, blueberry *(esp US)*; **blau|blü|tig** ADJ blue-blooded; **Blau|blü|tig|keit** F **-,** *no pl* blue blood

Blaue ['blauə] M = **Blaue(r), Blaue(s)**

Bläue ['blɔyə] F **-,** *no pl* blueness; *(des Himmels auch)* blue

blau|en ['blauən] VI *(liter: Himmel)* to turn blue

bläu|en ['blɔyən] VT **a** *(= blau färben)* to dye blue; *Lackmuspapier etc* to turn blue **b** *Wäsche* to blue **c** *(= schlagen)* to beat

Blaue(r) ['blauə] M *decl as adj* **a** *(inf: = Polizist)* cop *(inf)*, copper *(inf)* **b** *(sl Hist: = Hundertmarkschein)* hundred-mark note *(Brit)* or bill *(US)*

Blaue(s) ['blauə] NT *decl as adj* **a** **das ~** *(= Farbe)* the blue; **es spielt ins ~** it has a touch of blue in it; **das ~ vom Himmel (herunter)lügen** *(inf)* to tell a pack of lies; **das ~ vom Himmel (herunter)reden** *(inf)* to talk one's head off *(inf)*, to prattle away nineteen to the dozen *(Brit inf)*, to talk a mile a minute *(US inf)*; **jdm das ~ vom Himmel (herunter)versprechen** *(inf)* to promise sb the moon

b *(ohne Ziel)* **ins ~ hinein** *(inf)* at random; *arbeiten* with no particular goal; **wir wollen ins ~ fahren** we'll just set off and see where we end up; **eine Fahrt ins ~** a trip to nowhere in particular; *(= Veranstaltung)* a mystery tour

Blau-: **Blau|fel|chen** M whitefish, powan *(spec)*; **Blau|fil|ter** M OR NT *(Phot)* blue filter; **Blau|fuchs** M arctic fox; **blau|grau** ADJ blue-grey *(Brit)*, blue-gray *(US)*, bluish or bluey grey *(Brit)* or gray *(US)*; **blau|grün** ADJ blue-green, bluish or bluey green; **Blau|helm** M *(Press sl)* UN soldier, blue helmet; **Blau|hemd** NT *(DDR)* **a** blue shirt *(worn by members of the Free German Youth)* **b** *(inf: = Mensch)* member of the Free German Youth; **Blau|ja|cke** F *(inf)* bluejacket *(inf)*, sailor; **Blau|kohl** M *(dial)*, **Blau|kraut** NT *(S Ger, Aus)* red cabbage; **Blau|kreuz|ler** [-krɔytslɐ] M **-s, -**, **Blau|kreuz|le|rin** [-ərɪn] F **-, -nen** member of the Blue Cross Temperance League

bläu|lich ['blɔylɪç] ADJ bluish, bluey

Blau-: **Blau|licht** NT *(von Polizei etc)* flashing blue light; *(= Lampe)* blue light; **mit ~** with its blue light flashing; **blau+ma|chen** *sep (inf)* VI to skip work VT **den Freitag/zwei Tage ~** to skip work on Friday/for two days; **Blau|mann** M *pl* **-männer** *(inf)* boiler suit *(Brit)*, workman's overalls; **Blau|mei|se** F bluetit; **Blau|pa|pier** NT carbon paper; **Blau|pau|se** F blueprint; **blau|rot** ADJ purple; **Blau|säu|re** F prussic or hydrocyanic acid; **Blau|schim|mel** M blue mould *(Brit)* or mold *(US)*; **Blau|schim|mel|kä|se** M blue cheese; **blau+schla|gen** VT *sep irreg* **jdn grün- und ~** *(inf)* to beat sb black and blue; **blau|schwarz** ADJ blue-black, bluey black; **Blau|stich** M *(Phot)* blue cast; **blau|sti|chig** [-ʃtɪçɪç] ADJ *(Phot)* with a blue cast; **Blau|stift** M blue pencil; *(zum Malen)* blue crayon; **Blau|strumpf** M bluestocking; **blau|strümp|fig** [-ʃtrʏmpfɪç] ADJ bluestocking *attr*; **Blau|sucht** F, *no pl (Med)* cyanosis; **Blau|tan|ne** F blue *or* Colorado spruce; **blau|vi|o|lett** ADJ (dark) bluish *or* bluey purple; **Blau|wal** M blue whale

Bla|zer ['ble:zɐ] M **-s, -**, **Bla|zer|ja|cke** F blazer

Blech [blɛç] NT **-(e)s, -e** **a** *no pl* (sheet) metal; *(von Auto)* body; **eine Dose aus ~** a tin *(Brit)*, a metal container; **das ist doch nur ~** it's just ordinary metal **b** *(= Blechstück)* metal plate **c** *(= Backblech)* (baking) tray *(Brit)*, baking sheet **d** *no pl (inf: = Blechinstrumente)* brass **e** *no pl (pej inf: = Orden etc)* gongs *pl (inf)*, fruit salad *(US inf)* **f** *no pl (inf: = Unsinn)* rubbish *no art (inf)*, trash *no art (inf)*; **red kein ~** don't talk crap *(inf)*

Blech-: **Blech|blä|ser(in)** M(F) brass player; **die ~** the brass (section); **Blech|blas|in|stru|ment** NT brass instrument; **Blech|büch|se** F tin *(Brit)*, can; **Blech|do|se** F tin container; *(esp für Konserven)* tin *(Brit)*, can

ble|chen ['blɛçn] VTI *(inf)* to cough *or* pay up *(inf)*, to fork out *(inf)*

ble|chern ['blɛçɐn] ADJ **a** *attr* metal **b** *Geräusch, Stimme etc* tinny; *(fig: = hohl)* hollow, empty ADV tinnily; *klingen, tönen, scheppern* tinny; **das klingt ~** that sounds tinny

Blech-: **Blech|ge|schirr** NT metal pots and pans *pl*, metal utensils *pl (form)*; **Blech|in|stru|ment** NT brass instrument; **Blech|ka|nis|ter** M metal can; **Blech|kis|te** F *(pej inf)* (old) crate *(inf)*; **Blech|la|wi|ne** F *(pej inf)* vast column of cars; **Blech|leh|re** F metal gauge; **Blech|mu|sik** F *(usu pej)* brass (band) music; **Blech|napf** M metal bowl; **Blech|scha|den** M damage to the bodywork; **Blech|sche|re** F (pair of) metal shears; *(= Maschine)* metal shearer; **Blech|trom|mel** F tin drum; **Blech|walz|werk** NT sheet (rolling) mill

ble|cken ['blɛkn] VT **die Zähne ~** to bare *or* show one's teeth

Blei [blai] NT **-(e)s, -e** **a** *no pl (abbr* **Pb***)* lead; **jdm wie ~ in den Gliedern** *or* **Knochen liegen** *(Schreck)* to paralyze sb; *(Depression)* to weigh sb down; **die Müdigkeit/Anstrengung lag ihm wie ~ in den Gliedern** *or* **Knochen** his whole body ached with tiredness/the exertion → **Magen** **b** *(= Lot)* plumb, (plumb) bob **c** *(= Munition)* lead; *(Typ)* hot metal

Blei- *in cpds* lead; **Blei|ader** F lead vein

Blei|be ['blaibə] F **-, -n** **a** *(= Unterkunft)* place to stay; **eine/keine ~ haben** to have somewhere/nowhere to stay **b** *(= Institution)* remand home

blei|ben ['blaibn] *pret* **blieb** [bli:p], *ptp* **geblieben** [gə'bli:bn] VI *aux sein* **a** *(= sich nicht verändern)* to stay, to remain; **unbelohnt/unbestraft ~** to go unrewarded/unpunished; **unbeachtet ~** to go unnoticed, to escape notice; **unbeantwortet ~** to be left *or* to remain unanswered; **unvergessen ~** to continue to be remembered; **an Samstagen bleibt unser Geschäft geschlossen** this shop is closed on Saturdays; **in Verbindung ~** to keep *or* stay *or* remain in touch; **in Übung/Form ~** to keep in practice/form; **jdm in** *or* **in jds Erinnerung ~** to stay *or* remain in sb's mind; **ruhig/still ~** to keep calm/quiet; **wach ~** to stay *or* keep awake; **Freunde ~** to stay *or* remain friends, to go on being friends

b *(= sich nicht bewegen, zu Besuch bleiben)* to stay; *(= nicht weggehen, nicht zurückkommen)* to stay, to remain; **sitzen/stehen ~** to stay sitting down/standing up, to remain seated/standing; **bitte, ~ Sie doch sitzen** please don't get up; **jdn zum Bleiben einladen** *or* **auffordern** to invite sb to stay; **von etw ~** to stay *or* keep away from sth; **wo bleibst du so lange?** *(inf)* what's keeping you (all this time)?; **wo bleibt er so lange?** *(inf)* where has he got to?; **wo sind denn all die alten Häuser geblieben?** what (has) happened to all the old houses?, where have all the old houses gone (to)?; **hier ist meines Bleibens nicht (mehr** *or* **länger)** *(geh)* I cannot remain here (any longer) → **Ball**, **Land c**, **Apparat c**

c *(fig)* **bei etw ~** to keep *or* stick *(inf)* to sth; **das bleibt unter uns** that's (just) between ourselves; **wir möchten für** *or* **unter uns ~** we want to keep ourselves to ourselves → **dabei g**, **Sache e**

d *(= übrig bleiben)* to be left, to remain; **es blieb mir keine andere Wahl/Möglichkeit** I had no other choice/possibility; **es blieb keine andere Wahl/Möglichkeit** there was no other choice/possibility; **es blieb mir keine Hoffnung** I lost all hope

e *(= sein)* **es bleibt abzuwarten** it remains to be seen; **es bleibt zu hoffen** *or* **wünschen, dass ...** I/we can only hope that ...

f *(inf: = versorgt werden)* **sie können (selber) sehen, wo sie ~** they'll just have to look out for themselves *(inf)*; **und wo bleibe ich?** and what about me?; **sieh zu, wo du bleibst!** you're on your own! *(inf)*, you'd better look out for yourself! *(inf)*

g *(euph: = umkommen)* **er ist auf See geblieben** he died at sea; **er ist im Krieg geblieben** he didn't come back from the war

blei|bend ADJ *Wert, Erinnerung etc* lasting; *Schaden, Zähne* permanent

blei|ben las|sen *ptp* **bleiben lassen** *irreg*, **blei|ben+las|sen** *ptp* **bleibenlassen** *sep irreg* VT *(inf)* **a** *(= unterlassen)* **etw ~** to give sth a miss *(inf)*; **das werde ich/wirst du ganz schön ~** I'll/you'll do nothing of the sort! **b** *(= aufgeben)* to give up; **das Rauchen/Nägelkauen ~** to give up *or* to stop smoking/biting one's nails

Blei|be|recht NT, *no pl* **a** *(Jur) law concerning temporary residence status* **b** *(= Berechtigung)* right of residence, right to stay

bleich [blaiç] ADJ pale; *(fig) Grauen, Entsetzen* sheer; **~ wie der Tod** deathly pale, pale as death

Blei|che ['blaiçə] F **-, -n** **a** *no pl* paleness; *(von Mensch auch)* pallor **b** *(= Bleichplatz)* bleachery *(obs), green where sheets etc were laid out to be bleached by the sun*

blei|chen ['blaiçn] VT to bleach VI *pret* **bleichte** *or (old)* **blich** ['blaiçtə, blɪç], *ptp* **gebleicht** *or (old)* **geblichen** to be *or* become bleached; **in der Sonne ~** to be bleached by the sun

Bleich-: **Bleich|ge|sicht** NT **a** *(inf: = blasser Mensch)* pasty-face *(inf)*, pale-faced person **b** *(= Weißer)* paleface; **bleich|ge|sich|tig** [-gəzɪçtɪç] ADJ *(inf)* pale-faced, pasty-faced *(inf)*; **Bleich|mit|tel** NT bleach, bleaching agent; **Bleich|sucht** F *(old Med)* anaemia; **bleich|süch|tig** ADJ *(old Med)* anaemic

blei|ern ['blaiɐn] ADJ **a** *attr (= aus Blei)* lead; *(fig) Farbe, Himmel* leaden; **wie eine ~e Ente schwimmen** *(hum)* to swim like a brick **b** *(fig)* leaden; *Beine* like lead; *Müdigkeit* heavy; *Verantwortung* onerous ADV *(fig)* heavily; **die Verantwortung lastete ~ auf ihm/seiner Seele** the responsibility weighed heavily upon him/his mind; **es lag ihr ~ in den Gliedern** her limbs were like lead → **Magen**

Blei-: **Blei|erz** NT lead ore; **Blei|far|be** F lead paint; **blei|far|big**, **blei|far|ben** [-farbn] ADJ lead-coloured *(Brit)*, lead-colored *(US)*, lead-grey *(Brit)*, lead-gray *(US)*; *Himmel* leaden; **blei|frei** ADJ *Benzin etc* lead-free, unleaded ADV **~ fahren** to use lead-free *or* unleaded petrol *(Brit)* or gas *(US)*; **mein Auto fährt ~** my car runs on lead-free *or* unleaded petrol *(Brit)* or gas *(US)*; **Blei|frei** NT **-s**, *no pl (= bleifreies Benzin)* lead-free; **Blei|fuß** M **mit ~ fahren** *(inf)* to keep one's foot down, to drive with *or* to have a lead foot *(US)*; **Blei|ge|halt** M lead content; **Blei|ge|wicht** NT lead weight; *(Angeln)* sinker; **Blei|gie|ßen** NT **-s**, *no pl New Year's Eve custom of telling fortunes by the shapes made by molten lead dropped into cold water*; **Blei|glanz** M galena, galenite; **blei|grau** ADJ lead-grey *(Brit)*, lead-gray *(US)*; **blei|hal|tig** ADJ containing lead; *Erz, Gestein* plumbiferous *(spec)*; *Benzin etc* leaded; **~/zu ~ sein** to contain lead/too much lead; **Blei|hüt|te** F lead works *pl*; **Blei|kris|tall** NT lead crystal; **Blei|ku|gel** F lead bullet, lead ball; **Blei|lot** NT plumb line; **Blei|men|ni|ge** F minium, red lead; **Blei|oxid** NT, **Blei|oxyd** NT lead oxide; **gelbes ~** lead monoxide; **rotes ~** red lead; **Blei|satz** M *(Typ)* hot-metal setting; **Blei|schür|ze** F lead apron; **blei|schwer** ADJ, ADV = **bleiern** ADJ **b** ADV; **Blei|sol|dat** M ≈ tin soldier

Blei|stift M pencil; *(zum Malen)* crayon; **mit/in ~** with a/in pencil

Blei|stift- *in cpds* pencil; **Blei|stift|ab|satz** M stiletto heel; **Blei|stift|spit|zer** M pencil sharpener

Blei-: **Blei|ver|gif|tung** F lead poisoning; **blei|ver|glast** ADJ leaded; **Blei|ver|gla|sung** F lead glazing; **Fenster mit ~** leaded windows; **blei|ver|seucht** [-fɛɐzɔyçt] ADJ lead-polluted; **Blei|weiß** NT white lead

Blen|de ['blɛndə] F **-, -n** **a** *(= Lichtschutz)* shade, screen; *(Aut)* (sun) visor; *(an Fenster)* blind **b** *(Opt)* filter **c** *(Phot) (= Öffnung)* aperture; *(= Einstellungsposition)* f-stop; *(= Vorrichtung)* diaphragm; **die ~ schließen** to stop down; **bei** *or* **mit ~ 2.8** at (an aperture setting of) f/2.8 **d** *(Film, TV, Tontechnik: = Aufblende, Abblende)* fade **e** *(Naut)* deadlight **f** *(Archit) (= Fenster)* blind window; *(= Bogen)* blind arch **g** *(Sew)* trim **h** *(= Verkleidung)* cover **i** *(Geol)* blende

blen|den ['blɛndn] VT **a** *(lit, fig: = bezaubern)* to dazzle; *(fig geh: = täuschen auch)* to blind, to hoodwink **b** *(= blind machen)* to blind VI **a** *(Licht, Scheinwerfer)* to be dazzling; **~d weiß (sein)** (to be) shining *or* dazzling white **b** *(fig: = täuschen)* to dazzle

Blen|den|au|to|ma|tik F *(Phot)* automatic diaphragm

blen|dend ADJ splendid; *Pianist, Schüler etc* brilliant; *Laune, Stimmung* sparkling ADV splendidly; **es geht mir ~** I feel wonderful; **sich ~ amüsieren** to have a splendid *or* wonderful time

blen|dend|weiß △ ADJ *attr* → **blenden VI a**

Blen|den- *(Phot)*: **Blen|den|ein|stel|lung** F aperture (setting); *(= Vorrichtung)* aperture control; **Blen|den|öff|nung** F aperture; **Blen|den|vor|wahl** F aperture priority

Blen|der ['blɛndɐ] M **-s, -**, **Blen|de|rin** [-ərɪn] F **-, -nen** phoney *(Brit inf)*, phony *(US inf)*

Blend-: **blend|frei** ADJ dazzle-free; *Glas, Fernsehschirm* nonreflective; **Blend|gra|na|te** F *(Mil)* stun grenade; **Blend|la|ter|ne** F signalling *(Brit)* or signaling *(US)* lantern; **Blend|rah|men** M **a** *(Art)* canvas-stretcher **b** *(Build)* frame; **Blend|schutz** M **a** protection against dazzle *(Brit)* or glare **b** *(= Vorrichtung)* antidazzle *(Brit)* or antiglare *(US)* device; **Blend|schutz|git|ter** NT, **Blend|schutz|zaun** M antidazzle *(Brit)* or antiglare *(US)* barrier

Blen|dung F **-, -en** **a** *(= das Blindmachen, Täuschen)* blinding **b** *(= das Geblendetsein)* blindness

Blend-: **Blend|werk** NT *(liter)* illusion; *(= Vortäuschung)* deception; **hinter einem ~ schöner Worte** *or* **aus schönen Worten** behind a screen of pretty words; **ein ~ des Teufels** *or* **der Hölle** a trap set by the devil; **Blend|zaun** M antidazzle *(Brit)* or antiglare *(US)* barrier

Bles|se ['blɛsə] F **-, -n** **a** *(= Fleck)* blaze **b** *(= Tier) horse with a blaze*

Bless|huhn ['blɛs-] NT coot → *auch* **Blässhuhn**

bles|sie|ren [blɛ'siːrən] *ptp* **blessiert** VT *(old: = verwunden)* to wound

Bles|sur [blɛ'suːɐ] F **-, -en** *(old)* wound

bleu [bløː] ADJ *inv (Fashion)* light blue

bleu|en △ ['blɔyən] VT → **bläuen c**

blich *(old) pret von* **bleichen VI**

Blick [blɪk] ✪ 44.1 M **-(e)s, -e** a *(= das Blicken)* look; *(= flüchtiger Blick)* glance; **auf den ersten ~** at first glance; **Liebe auf den ersten ~** love at first sight; **auf den zweiten ~** when one looks (at it) again, the second time one looks (at it); **mit einem ~, auf einen ~** at a glance; **jds ~ (dat) ausweichen** to avoid sb's eye; **jds ~ erwidern** to return sb's gaze; **~e miteinander wechseln** to exchange glances; **jdn mit (seinen) ~en verschlingen** to devour sb with one's eyes; **er folgte ihr mit ~en** *or* **mit dem ~** his eyes followed her; **sie zog alle ~e auf sich** everybody's eyes were drawn to her; **einen ~ auf etw** *(acc)* **tun** *or* **werfen** to throw a glance at sth; **einen ~ hinter die Kulissen tun** *or* **werfen** *(fig)* to take a look behind the scenes; **sie würdigte ihn keines ~es** she did not deign to look at him; **jdm einen ~ schenken** to look at sb; **jdm keinen ~ schenken** not to spare sb a glance; **wenn ~e töten könnten!** if looks could kill! → **durchbohren**

b *(= Blickrichtung)* eyes *pl*; **mein ~ fiel auf sein leeres Glas** my eye fell on his empty glass; **von hier aus fällt der ~ auf den Dom** from here one can see the cathedral; **den ~ heben** to raise one's eyes, to look up; **den ~ senken** to look down

c *(= Augenausdruck)* expression *or* look in one's eyes; **den bösen ~ haben** to have the evil eye; **in ihrem ~ lag Verzweiflung** there was a look of despair in her eyes; **er musterte sie mit durchdringendem/finsterem ~** he looked at her penetratingly/darkly

d *(= Ausblick)* view; **ein Zimmer mit ~ auf den Park** a room with a view of the park, a room overlooking the park; **dem ~ entschwinden** *(geh)* to disappear from view *or* sight, to go out of sight; **etw aus dem ~ verlieren** to lose sight of sth; **mit ~ auf, im ~ auf** *(= hinsichtlich)* in view of

e *(= Verständnis)* **seinen ~ für etw schärfen** to increase one's awareness of sth; **einen klaren ~ haben** to see things clearly; **einen (guten) ~ für etw haben** to have an eye *or* a good eye for sth; **er hat keinen ~ dafür** he doesn't see *or* notice that sort of thing; **etw in den ~ nehmen** *(= berücksichtigen)* to take account of sth

blick|dicht ADJ *Strümpfe* opaque

bli|cken ['blɪkn] VI *(auf +acc* at) to look; *(= flüchtig blicken)* to glance; *(fig: = hervorsehen)* to peep; **sich ~ lassen** to put in an appearance; **lass dich hier ja nicht mehr ~!** don't let me see you here again!, don't show your face here again!; **lass dich doch mal wieder ~!** why don't you drop in some time?; **danach hat er sich nie wieder ~ lassen** after that he was never seen again; **das lässt tief ~** that's very revealing VT *(inf: = verstehen)* to get

bli|cken+las|sen *ptp* **blickenlassen** VR *sep irreg* → **blicken VI**

Blick-: **Blick|fang** M eye-catcher; **als ~** to catch the eye; **Blick|feld** NT field of vision; **ein enges ~ haben** *(fig)* to have narrow horizons; **ins ~ (der Öffentlichkeit) rücken** to become the focus of (public) attention; **Blick|kon|takt** M eye contact; **Blick|punkt** M a *(= Zentrum der Aufmerksamkeit)* centre *(Brit) or* center *(US)* of one's field of vision; *(fig)* limelight; **im ~ der Öffentlichkeit stehen** to be in the public eye b *(fig: = Standpunkt)* viewpoint, point of view; **Blick|rich|tung** F line of vision *or* sight; *(fig)* outlook; **in ~ (nach) links** looking to the left; **Blick|wech|sel** M exchange of glances; *(fig)* change in one's viewpoint; **Blick|win|kel** M angle of vision; *(fig)* viewpoint

blind [blɪnt] ADJ a *(lit, fig)* blind *(für* to); *Zufall* pure, sheer; *Alarm* false; **~ für etw sein, ~ in Bezug auf etw** *(acc)* **sein** *(fig)* to be blind to sth; **ich bin doch nicht ~!** *(fig)* I'm not blind; **~ geboren** blind from birth; **jdn ~ machen** *(lit, fig)* to blind sb, to make sb blind; **ein ~es Huhn findet auch mal ein Korn** *(Prov)* anyone can be lucky now and again; **~er Fleck** *(Anat)* blind spot; **in ~er Liebe** blinded with love; **ihr Blick war von** *or* **vor Tränen ~** she was blinded with tears; **~e Gewalt** brute force; **~er Eifer** blind enthusiasm; **~er Eifer schadet nur** *(Prov)* it's not a good thing to be overenthusiastic; **ein ~er Schuss** *(= nicht scharf)* a shot with a blank cartridge; *(= nicht gezielt)* a blind shot

b *(= getrübt)* dull; *Spiegel, Glasscheibe* clouded; *Fleck* blind

c *(= verdeckt) Naht etc* invisible; *(= vorgetäuscht, Archit)* false; *Fenster* blind, false; **ein ~er Passagier** a stowaway

d *(sl: = betrunken)* pissed *(Brit inf)*, plastered *(inf)*

ADV a *(= wahllos)* at random, indiscriminately; **etw ~ herausgreifen** to take *or* pick sth at random; **~ in etw** *(acc)* **hineingreifen** to put one's hand in sth without looking

b *(= ohne zu überlegen) folgen, vertrauen, glauben* blindly; **jdm ~ gehorchen** to obey sb blindly

c *(= ohne zu sehen)* without being able to see; **~ Schach spielen** to play chess blind; **der Nebel war so dicht, dass ich ~ fahren musste** the fog was so thick that I had to drive without being able to see anything

Blind-: **Blind|band** [-bant] M *pl* **-bände** *(Typ)* dummy; **Blind|be|wer|bung** F speculative *(Brit) or* unsolicited *or* cold *(US inf)* application; **Blind|bo|den** M *(Archit)* subfloor

Blind|darm M *(Anat)* caecum *(Brit)*, cecum *(US)*; *(inf: = Wurmfortsatz)* appendix

Blind|darm-: **Blind|darm|ent|zün|dung** F appendicitis; **Blind|darm|ope|ra|ti|on** F appendic(ic)ectomy; **Blind|darm|rei|zung** F grumbling appendix

Blin|de|kuh *no art (= Spiel)* blind man's buff

Blin|den-: **Blin|den|an|stalt** F home for the blind; **Blin|den|füh|rer(in)** M(F) blind person's guide; **Blin|den|hund** M guide dog; **Blin|den|schrift** F braille; **Blin|den|schu|le** F school for the blind; **Blin|den|sen|dung** F *(Post)* mail *no pl* for the blind

Blin|de(r) ['blɪndə] MF *decl as adj* blind person/man/woman *etc*; **die ~n** the blind; **die ~n und die Lahmen** *(Bibl)* the lame and the blind; **das sieht doch ein ~r (mit dem Krückstock)** *(hum inf)* any fool can see that; **unter den ~n ist der Einäugige König** *(Prov)* in the country of the blind the one-eyed man is king *(prov)*; **der ~ verlacht den Lahmen** *(Prov)* the pot calling the kettle black; **von etw reden, wie der ~ von der Farbe** *(prov)* to talk about sth when one knows nothing about it

Blind-: **Blind|fens|ter** NT false window; **blind+flie|gen** *sep irreg aux sein*, **blind flie|gen** △ *irreg aux sein* VI to fly blind; **Blind|flug** M blind flight; *(= das Blindfliegen)* blind flying; **das kann ich im ~ machen** *(fig inf)* I can do that in my sleep *(fig)*; **Blind|gän|ger** [-gɛŋɐ] M **-s, -** *(Mil)* dud (shot); **Blind|gän|ger** [-gɛŋɐ] M **-s, -**, **Blind|gän|ge|rin** [-ərɪn] F **-, -nen** *(inf: = Versager)* dud *(inf)*, dead loss *(inf)*; **blind|ge|bo|ren** ADJ *attr* → **blind ADJ a**; **Blind|ge|bo|re|ne(r)** [-gəboːrənə] MF *decl as adj* person blind from birth; **blind|gläu|big** ADJ credulous ADV *folgen, vertrauen* blindly; **Blind|heit** F **-,** *no pl (lit, fig)* blindness; **jdn mit ~ schlagen** *(Bibl, liter)* to strike sb blind; **wie mit ~ geschlagen** *(fig)* as though blind; **mit ~ geschlagen sein** *(fig)* to be blind; **blind+lan|den** *sep aux sein*, **blind lan|den** △ *aux sein* VI *(Aviat)* to make a blind landing, to land blind; **Blind|lan|dung** F blind *or* instrument landing; **blind|lings** ['blɪntlɪŋs] ADV blindly; **Blind|ma|te|ri|al** NT *(Typ)* leads *pl*; **Blind|schlei|che** [-ʃlaiçə] F **-, -n** slowworm; **blind+schrei|ben** *sep irreg*, **blind schrei|ben** △ *irreg* VTI to touch-type; **Blind|schreib|ver|fah|ren** NT touch-typing; **Blind|spiel** NT *(Chess)* blind game; **blind+spie|len** *sep*, **blind spie|len** △ VI to play blind; **Blind|start** M *(Aviat)* blind takeoff; **Blind|ver|such** M *(Med, Psych)* blind test; **blind|wü|tig** ADJ *Mensch* in a blind rage; *Angriff* furious ADV in a blind rage, furiously

blin|ken ['blɪŋkn] VI a *(= funkeln)* to gleam b *(= Blinkzeichen geben) (Boje, Leuchtturm)* to flash; *(Aut)* to indicate VT *Signal* to flash; **SOS ~** to flash an SOS (signal); **rechts/links ~** to indicate right/left; **er hat mir geblinkt, dass ich überholen kann** he signalled for me to overtake *(Brit)*, he signaled for me to pass *(US)*

Blin|ker ['blɪŋkɐ] M **-s, -** a *(Aut)* indicator *(esp Brit)*, winker *(Brit inf)*, turn signal *(US)*, blinker *(US inf)* b *(Angeln)* spinner

blin|kern ['blɪŋkɐn] VI a *(inf: = blinken)* to flash; **er blinkerte mit den Augen** he blinked b *(Angeln)* to use a spinner

Blink-: **Blink|feu|er** NT flashing light; **Blink|leuch|te** F indicator *(esp Brit)*, turn signal *(US)*; **Blink|licht** NT flashing light; *(inf: = Blinkleuchte)* indicator *(esp Brit)*, winker *(Brit inf)*, turn signal *(US)*, blinker *(US inf)*; **Blink|licht|an|la|ge** F warning light system; **Blink|zei|chen** NT signal

blin|zeln ['blɪntslṇ], **blin|zen** ['blɪntsn] *(dated)* VI to blink; *(= zwinkern)* to wink; *(geblendet)* to squint

Blitz [blɪts] M **-es, -e** a *(= das Blitzen)* lightning *no pl, no indef art*; *(= Blitzstrahl)* flash of lightning; *(= Lichtstrahl)* flash (of light); **vom ~ getroffen/erschlagen werden** to be struck by lightning; **wie vom ~ getroffen** *(fig)* thunderstruck; **aus ihren Augen schossen** *or* **sprühten ~e** her eyes flashed; **einschlagen wie ein ~** *(fig)* to be a bombshell; **die Nachricht schlug überall wie ein ~ ein** the news came as a bombshell to everyone; **wie ein ~ aus heiterem Himmel** *(fig)* like a bolt from the blue; **wie der ~** *(inf)* like lightning; **laufen wie ein geölter ~** *(inf)* to run like greased lightning; **die Antwort kam wie ein geölter ~** *(inf)* the answer came in a flash b *(Phot inf)* flash; *(= Blitzlichtgerät)* flash(gun)

Blitz- *in cpds (esp Mil: = schnell)* lightning; **Blitz|ab|lei|ter** M lightning conductor; **jdn als ~ benutzen** *or* **missbrauchen** to vent one's anger on sb; **Blitz|ak|ti|on** F lightning operation; **Blitz|an|griff** M *(Mil)* lightning attack; **der ~ auf London** the London Blitz; **blitz|ar|tig** ADJ lightning *attr* ADV *(= schnell) reagieren* like lightning; *(= plötzlich) verschwinden* in a flash; **Blitz|be|such** M *(inf)* flying *or* lightning visit

blit|ze|blank ['blɪtsə'blaŋk], **blitz|blank** ['blɪts'blaŋk] *(inf)* ADJ spick and span ADV *putzen, polieren* until it shines

Blitz|ein|bruch M *(inf: = Verbrechen)* ram raid

blit|zen ['blɪtsn] VI *impers* **es blitzt** there is lightning; *(mehrmals auch)* there are flashes of lightning; **es blitzt und donnert** there is thunder and lightning; **hat es eben geblitzt?** was that (a flash of) lightning?; **es fing an zu ~** lightning began; **bei dir blitzt es** *(hum inf)* your slip is showing, Charlie's dead *(Brit inf)*

VI a *(= strahlen)* to flash; *(Gold, Zähne)* to sparkle; **vor Sauberkeit ~** to be sparkling clean; **Zorn blitzte aus seinen Augen** his eyes flashed with anger

b *(inf: = unbekleidet flitzen)* to streak

c *(Phot inf)* to use (a) flash

d *(Phot inf)* to use (a) flash

VT *(Phot inf)* to take a flash photograph of; *(inf: in Radarfalle)* to flash

Blit|zer ['blɪtsɐ] M **-s, -**, **Blit|ze|rin** [-ərɪn] F **-, -nen** *(inf)* streaker

Blit|zes|schnel|le F lightning speed; **mit ~** at lightning speed; **in ~** in a flash

Blitz-: **Blitz|ge|rät** NT *(Phot)* flash(gun); **blitz|ge|scheit** ADJ *(inf)* brilliant; **Blitz|ge|spräch** NT special priority telephone call; **Blitz|kaf|-**

fee M *(Sw)* instant coffee; **Blitz|kar|ri|e|re** F rapid rise; **eine ~ machen** to rise rapidly; **Blitz|krieg** M blitzkrieg

Blitz|licht NT *(Phot)* flash(light)

Blitz|licht-: **Blitz|licht|auf|nah|me** F flash shot; **Blitz|licht|bir|ne** F flashbulb; **Blitz|licht|ge|wit|ter** NT popping of flashbulbs; **Blitz|licht|wür|fel** M flashcube

Blitz-: **Blitz|mer|ker** [-mɛrkɐ] M **-s, -**, **Blitz|mer|ke|rin** [-ərɪn] F **-, -nen** *(inf: usu iro)* bright spark *(inf)*; **Blitz|rei|se** F flying visit; **blitz|sau|ber** ADJ spick and span ADV *putzen, polieren* until it shines; **Blitz|scha|den** M damage caused by lightning; **Blitz|schlag** M flash of lightning; **vom ~ getroffen** struck by lightning; **blitz|schnell** ADJ lightning *attr* ADV like lightning; *(= plötzlich) verschwinden* in a flash; **Blitz|schutz|an|la|ge** F lightning protection equipment; **Blitz|sieg** M lightning victory; **Blitz|start** M lightning *or* jump start; **Blitz|strahl** M flash of lightning; **Blitz|um|fra|ge** F quick poll; **Blitz|wür|fel** M *(Phot)* flashcube

Bliz|zard [ˈblɪzɐt] M **-s, -s** blizzard

Bloch [blɔx] M OR NT **-(e)s, -e** *or* **≃er** [ˈblœçɐ] *(S Ger, Aus)* log

Block [blɔk] M **-(e)s, -s** *or* **≃e** [ˈblœkə] **a** block *(von, aus* of); *(von Seife, Schokolade)* bar
b *pl auch* **-s** *(= Häuserblock, Haus, Reaktorblock)* block
c *pl auch* **-s** *(= Papierblock)* pad; *(= Briefmarkenblock)* block; *(von Fahrkarten)* book
d *pl* **-s** *(Rail)* block
e *(= Zusammengefasstes)* block; **etw im ~ kaufen** to buy sth in bulk
f *pl auch* **-s** *(Pol) (= Staatenblock)* bloc; *(= Fraktion)* faction
g *(NS) smallest organizational unit of Nazi party based on a block of houses*
h *(Sport)* wall
i *pl auch* **-s** *(inf: = Blockierung)* (mental) block
j *(= Folterblock)* stocks *pl*
k *(Comput)* block

Blo|cka|de [blɔˈkaːdə] F **-, -n** *(= Absperrung)* blockade; **eine ~ brechen** to run *or* break a blockade

Blo|cka|de|bre|cher(in) M(F) blockade runner

Block-: **Block|bau** M **a** *pl* **-bauten** *(= Gebäude)* log cabin **b** *no pl (auch* **Blockbauweise**) method of building houses from logs; **Block|bil|dung** F *(Pol)* formation of blocs; *(= Fraktionsbildung)* formation of factions; **Block|buch|sta|be** M block letter *or* capital; **Block|dia|gramm** NT block diagram

blo|cken [ˈblɔkn] VTI **a** *(Rail)* to block **b** *(Hunt)* to perch **c** *(= abfangen)* to block, to stop; *(= verhindern)* to block, to stall **d** *(Sport: = sperren)* to block **e** *(dial: = bohnern)* to polish **f** *(Comput)* to block

Blo|cker [ˈblɔkɐ] M **-s, -** *(S Ger: = Bohner)* floor-polishing brush

Block|flö|te F recorder; *(Pol sl: = Person)* fellow traveller *(Brit) or* traveler *(US)*, comrade

block|frei ADJ nonaligned

Block|frei|heit F nonalignment

Block|haus NT log cabin

Block|heiz|kraft|werk NT block heating and generating plant

Block|hüt|te F log cabin

blo|ckie|ren [blɔˈkiːrən] *ptp* **blockiert** VT **a** *(= sperren, hemmen)* to block; *Verkehr, Verhandlung* to obstruct; *Flugverkehr* to halt; *Gesetz* to block the passage of; *Rad, Lenkung* to lock **b** *(= mit Blockade belegen)* to blockade VI to jam; *(Bremsen, Rad etc)* to lock

Blo|ckie|rung F **-, -en** blocking; *(von Verkehr, Verhandlung)* obstruction; *(von Rad, Lenkung)* locking; *(= Blockade)* blockade

Block-: **Block|lei|ter(in)** M(F) *(NS)* block leader; **Block|malz** NT *type of cough drop*; **Block|par|tei** F *(esp DDR)* party in a faction; **Block|po|li|tik** F joint policy; **Block|satz** M *(Typ)* justification; **Block|scho|ko|la|de** F, *no pl* cooking chocolate; **Block|schrift** F block capitals *pl or* letters *pl*; **Block|staat** M aligned state; **Block|sta|ti|on** F, **Block|stel|le** F *(Rail)* block signal; **Block|stun|de** F *(Sch)* double period; **Block|sys|tem** NT **a** *(Rail)* block system **b** *(Pol)* system of factions; **Block|un|ter|richt** M *(Sch)* teaching by topics; **Block|wart** [-vart] M **-(e)s, -e**, **Block|war|tin** [-vartɪn] F **-, -nen** *(NS)* block leader; **Block|werk** NT *(Rail)* block signal

blöd [bløːt], **blö|de** [ˈbløːdə] *(inf)* ADJ **a** *(= dumm)* silly, stupid, idiotic; *Wetter* terrible; *Gefühl* funny; **das Blöde daran ist, dass ...** the silly etc thing about it is that ... **b** *(Med: = schwachsinnig)* imbecilic **c** *(Sw: = schüchtern)* shy **d** *(S Ger: = abgescheuert)* worn ADV *(= dumm)* stupidly, idiotically; **~ fragen** to ask stupid questions

Blö|del [ˈbløːdl] M **-s, -** *(inf)* stupid fool *(inf) or* idiot *(inf)*; *(= ungeschickter Mensch)* clumsy fool *(inf) or* idiot *(inf)*

Blö|de|lei [bløːdəˈlai] F **-, -en** *(inf) (= Albernheit)* messing *(inf) or* fooling around; *(= Witz)* joke; *(= dumme Streiche)* pranks *pl*; **lass die ~** stop messing *(inf) or* fooling around

blö|deln [ˈbløːdln] VI *(inf)* to mess *(inf) or* fool around; *(= Witze machen)* to make jokes; **mit jdm ~** to have fun with sb

blö|der|wei|se [ˈbløːdɐˈvaizə] ADV *(inf)* stupidly

Blöd|heit F **-, -en a** *(= Dummheit)* stupidity **b** *(= blödes Verhalten)* stupid thing; *(= alberne Bemerkung)* silly *or* stupid remark; **es ist eine ~, das zu machen** it's stupid to do that **c** *(Med: = Schwachsinnigkeit)* imbecility **d** *(Sw: = Schüchternheit)* shyness

Blö|di|an [ˈbløːdiaːn] M **-(e)s, -e** *(inf)* idiot

Blöd|mann M *pl* **-männer** *(inf)* stupid fool *(inf)*

Blöd|sinn M, *no pl* **a** *(= Unsinn)* nonsense, rubbish; *(= Unfug)* stupid tricks *pl*; **so ein ~** what nonsense *or* rubbish/how stupid; **das ist doch ~** that's nonsense *or* rubbish/stupid; **~ machen** to fool *or* mess around; **wer hat diesen ~ hier gemacht?** what fool did this?; **mach keinen ~** don't fool *or* mess around **b** *(= Schwachsinn)* imbecility

blöd|sin|nig ADJ **a** stupid, idiotic **b** *(Med)* imbecilic

Blöd|sin|nig|keit F **-, -en** *(inf)* **a** *(= Eigenschaft)* stupidity, idiocy **b** *(= Verhalten)* stupid thing; **lass diese ~en** stop being stupid

Blog [blɔg] NT *OR* M **-(s), -s** *(Internet)* blog

blog|gen [ˈblɔgn] VI to blog

Blog|ger [ˈblɔgɐ] M **-(s), -**, **Blog|ge|rin** [ˈblɔgərɪn] F **-, -nen** *(Internet)* blogger

blö|ken [ˈbløːkn] VI *(Schaf)* to bleat; *(geh: Rinder)* to low

blond [blɔnt] ADJ **a** *(= blondhaarig) Frau* blonde, fair(-haired); *Mann, Menschenrasse* blond, fair-haired; **~es Gift** *(hum inf)* blonde bombshell *(inf)* **b** *(hum inf: = hellfarbig)* light-coloured *(Brit)*, light-colored *(US)*; *Bier* light, pale ADV **~ gefärbt** dyed blond; *(bei Frauen auch)* dyed blonde; **sich** *(dat)* **die Haare ~ färben** to dye one's hair blond *or (Frau auch)* blonde; **~ gelockt** with fair curly hair; *Haar* fair curly *attr*; **~ gelockt sein** to have fair curly hair

Blond [blɔnt] NT **-s**, *no pl* blonde, blond

Blon|de(s) [ˈblɔndə] NT *decl as adj (inf: = Bier)* ≈ lager

Blond-: **blond+fär|ben** VT *sep* → **blond** ADV; **blond|ge|färbt** ADJ *attr* → **blond** ADV; **blond|ge|lockt** ADJ → **blond** ADV; **blond|haa|rig** ADJ fair-haired; *Frau auch* blonde; *Mann, Rasse auch* blond

blon|die|ren [blɔnˈdiːrən] *ptp* **blondiert** VT to bleach; **blondiert** *(Haare)* bleached

Blon|die|rung F **-, -en a** *(= Vorgang)* bleaching **b** *(= Zustand)* bleachedness

Blon|di|ne [blɔnˈdiːnə] F **-, -n** blonde

Blond|kopf M **a** *(von Frau)* fair *or* blonde hair *or* head; *(von Mann)* fair *or* blond hair *or* head **b** *(Frau/Mädchen)* fair-haired *or* blonde woman/girl; *(Mann/Junge)* fair-haired *or* blond man/boy

blond|lo|ckig ADJ *Frau* with fair *or* blonde curly hair; *Mann* with fair *or* blond curly hair

Blond|schopf M = **Blondkopf**

bloß [bloːs] ADJ **a** *(= unbedeckt)* bare; **etw auf der ~en Haut tragen** to wear sth without anything on underneath; **mit ~en Füßen** barefooted, barefoot; **mit der ~en Hand** with one's bare hand → **Oberkörper**
b *attr (= alleinig)* mere; *Neid, Dummheit* sheer; *(= allein schon) Gedanke, Anblick* very, mere; **er kam mit dem ~en Schrecken davon** he got off with no more than a fright
ADV only; **ich möchte es schon machen, ~ weiß ich nicht wie** I'd like to but *or* only I don't know how; **wie kann so etwas ~ geschehen?** how on earth can something like that happen?; **was er ~ hat?** what on earth *or* whatever is wrong with him?; **tu das ~ nicht wieder!** don't you dare do that again; **geh mir ~ aus dem Weg** just get out of my way; **nicht ~ ..., sondern auch ...** not only ... but also ...

Blö|ße [ˈbløːsə] F **-, -n a** *(geh) (= Unbedecktheit)* bareness; *(= Nacktheit)* nakedness **b** *(im Wald)* clearing **c** *(Sport)* opening; **jdm eine ~ bieten** *(lit)* to drop one's guard with sb; *(fig)* to show sb one's ignorance; **sich** *(dat)* **eine ~ geben** *(fig)* to reveal *or* show one's ignorance

Bloß-: **bloß+le|gen** VT *sep (fig) Geheimnis* to reveal; *Hintergründe* to bring to light; **bloß le|gen**, **bloß+le|gen** *sep* VT to uncover; *(= ausgraben auch, Med)* to expose; **bloß lie|gen** *irreg (S Ger, Aus, Sw: aux sein)*, **bloß+lie|gen** *sep irreg (S Ger, Aus, Sw: aux sein)* VI to be *or* lie uncovered; *(Ausgegrabenes auch, Med)* to be exposed; *(fig geh, Geheimnis)* to be revealed; **bloß+stel|len** *sep* VT *jdn* to show up; *Lügner, Betrüger* to unmask, to expose VR to show oneself up, to expose oneself; **Bloß|stel|lung** F showing up; *(von Lügner, Betrüger)* unmasking; **bloß stram|peln**, **bloß+stram|peln** △ *sep* VR to kick one's covers off

Blou|son [bluˈzõː] M OR NT **-(s), -s** blouson *(Brit)*, bomber jacket

Blow-out [ˈbloaut] M **-s, -s**, **Blow|out** M **-s, -s** *(von Bohrinsel etc)* blowout

blub|bern [ˈblubɐn] VI *(inf)* to bubble; *(dial: = undeutlich sprechen)* to gabble; *(= Blödsinn reden)* to waffle *(inf)*

Blü|cher [ˈblyːçɐ] M **er geht ran wie ~** *(inf)* he doesn't hang about *(inf)*

Blue|jeans [ˈbluː dʒiːns] PL, **Blue Jeans** △ PL (pair of) (blue) jeans *or* denims

Blues [bluːs] M **-, -** blues *sing or pl*; **(einen) ~ tanzen** to smooch *(inf)*

Bluff [bluf, *(dated)* blœf] M **-(e)s, -s** bluff

bluf|fen [ˈblufn, *(dated)* ˈblœfn] VTI to bluff

blü|hen [ˈblyːən] VI **a** *(Blume)* to be in flower *or* bloom, to bloom, to flower; *(Bäume)* to be in blossom, to blossom; *(Garten, Wiese)* to be full of flowers; *(fig: = gedeihen)* to flourish, to thrive; **weiß ~** to have *or* bear white flowers **b** *(inf: = bevorstehen)* to be in store *(jdm* for sb); **... dann blüht dir aber was** ... then you'll be in for it *(inf)*; **das kann mir auch noch ~** that may happen to me too VI *impers* **es blüht** there are flowers

blü|hend ADJ *Baum* blossoming; *Blume, Pflanze auch* blooming; *Garten, Wiese, Feld* full of flowers; *(fig) Aussehen* radiant; *Geschäft, Handel, Industrie, Kultur, Stadt* flourishing, thriving; *Fantasie* vivid, lively; *Unsinn* absolute; *Zukunft* glowing; **~e Landschaften** green pastures; **ein wirtschaftlich ~es Land** a country with a thriving economy; **wie das ~e Leben aussehen, ~ aussehen** to look the very picture of health

Blüm|chen [ˈblyːmçən] NT **-s, -** *dim von* **Blume**

Blüm|chen-: **Blüm|chen|kaf|fee** M *(hum)* weak coffee; **Blüm|chen|mus|ter** NT (small) floral pattern

Blu|me [ˈbluːmə] F **-, -n a** *(= Blüte, Pflanze)* flower; *(= Topfblume)* (flowering) pot plant; *(poet: =*

Frau) pearl; **vielen Dank für die ~n** *(iro)* thanks for nothing, thank you very much *(iro)*; **jdm etw durch die ~ sagen/zu verstehen geben** to say/put sth in a roundabout way to sb; **die blaue ~ der Romantik** the blue flower *(symbol of German Romanticism)* **b** *(von Wein, Weinbrand)* bouquet; *(von Bier)* head **c** *(Hunt) (von Kaninchen, Hasen)* scut; *(von Fuchs)* tag

Blu|men- *in cpds* flower; **Blu|men|bank** F *pl* **-bänke** *(am Fenster)* windowsill; *(= Blumenständer)* flower stand; **Blu|men|beet** NT flowerbed; **Blu|men|bin|der(in)** M(F) florist; **Blu|men|blatt** NT petal; **Blu|men|bou|quet**, **Blu|men|bu|kett** NT *(old)* bouquet (of flowers); **Blu|men|draht** M florist's wire; **Blu|men|dün|ger** M plant feed; **Blu|men|er|de** F potting compost; **Blu|men|fens|ter** NT window full of flowers; *(Archit) window for keeping and displaying flowers and pot plants*; **Blu|men|flor** M *(liter)* abundance of flowers; **Blu|men|frau** F flower woman; **Blu|men|ge|schäft** NT flower shop; *(Brit auch)* florist('s); *(US auch)* florist; **blu|men|ge|schmückt** [-gəʃmʏkt] ADJ adorned with flowers; **Blu|men|gruß** M **jdm einen ~ übermitteln** to send sb flowers; **Blu|men|händ|ler(in)** M(F) florist; **Blu|men|igel** M pinholder; **Blu|men|kas|ten** M window box; **Blu|men|kind** NT *(inf)* flower child, hippie; **~er** flower children *or* people, hippies; **Blu|men|kohl** M, *no pl* cauliflower; **Blu|men|kohl|ohr** NT *(inf)* cauliflower ear; **Blu|men|kor|so** M flower carnival; **Blu|men|kranz** M floral wreath; **Blu|men|kü|bel** M flower tub; **Blu|men|la|den** M flower shop, florist('s) *(esp Brit)*, florist *(esp US)*; **Blu|men|mäd|chen** NT flower girl; **Blu|men|meer** NT sea of flowers; **Blu|men|mus|ter** NT floral pattern; **Blu|men|pracht** F brilliant display of flowers; **Blu|men|ra|bat|te** F herbaceous border; **blu|men|reich** ADJ full of flowers, flowery; *(fig) Stil, Sprache etc* flowery, ornate ADV *(fig) sprechen* in a flowery way; *schreiben* in a flowery style; **Blu|men|schmuck** M flower arrangement(s *pl*), floral decoration(s *pl*); **Blu|men|spra|che** F language of flowers; **Blu|men|stän|der** M flower stand; **Blu|men|stock** M flowering plant; **Blu|men|strauß** M *pl* **-sträuße** bouquet *or* bunch of flowers; **Blu|men|stück** NT *(Art)* flower painting; **Blu|men|tep|pich** M carpet of flowers; **Blu|men|topf** M flowerpot; *(= Pflanze)* flowering plant; **damit ist kein ~ zu gewinnen** *(inf)* that's nothing to write home about *(inf)*; **Blu|men|topf|er|de** F potting compost; **Blu|men|va|se** F (flower) vase; **Blu|men|zucht** F growing of flowers, floriculture *(form)*; **Blu|men|züch|ter(in)** M(F) flower grower, floriculturist *(form)*; **Blu|men|zwie|bel** F bulb

blü|me|rant [blymə'rant] ADJ *Gefühl* strange; **jdm wird es ~** sb feels strange

blu|mig ['blu:mɪç] ADJ *Parfüm* flowery; *Wein auch* with a flowery bouquet; *(fig) Stil, Sprache* ornate, flowery

Blu|mig|keit F -, *no pl* floweriness; *(fig auch)* ornateness

Blüs|chen ['bly:sçən] NT **-s, -** *dim von* **Bluse**

Blu|se ['blu:zə] F **-, -n** blouse

Blü|se ['bly:zə] F **-, -n** *(Naut)* flare

blu|sig ['blu:zɪç] ADJ bloused, blouse *attr*

Blut [blu:t] NT **-(e)s,** *no pl (lit, fig)* blood; **~ bildend** = **blutbildend**; **jdm ~ abnehmen** to take blood from sb; **er lag in seinem ~** he lay in a pool of blood; **es ist viel ~ vergossen worden** *or* **geflossen** there was a lot of bloodshed; **nach ~ lechzen** *or* **dürsten** to thirst for blood; **er kann kein ~ sehen** he can't stand the sight of blood; **~ lecken** *(lit: Hund)* to taste blood; *(fig)* to develop a taste *or* liking for it; **etw mit seinem ~ besiegeln** to lay down one's life for sth; **böses ~ machen** *or* **schaffen** *or* **geben** to cause bad blood *or* ill feeling; **jdm steigt das ~ in den Kopf** the blood rushes to sb's head; **ihnen gefror** *or* **stockte** *or* **gerann das ~ in den Adern** their blood froze; **ihm kocht das ~ in den Adern** his blood is boiling; **vor Scham/Zorn schoss ihr das ~ ins Gesicht** she blushed with shame/went red with anger; **alles ~ wich aus ihrem Gesicht** she went deathly pale; **blaues ~ haben** *(= adelig sein)* to have blue blood; **heißes** *or* **feuriges ~ haben** to be hot-blooded; **etw im ~ haben** to have sth in one's blood; **das liegt mir im ~** it's in my blood; **kaltes ~ bewahren** to remain unmoved; **kalten ~es** cold-bloodedly; **(nur) ruhig ~** keep your shirt on *(inf)*; **jdn bis aufs ~ hassen** to loathe (and detest) sb; **jdn/sich bis aufs ~ bekämpfen** to fight sb/fight bitterly; **jdn bis aufs ~ reizen** *(inf)* to make sb's blood boil; **ein junges ~** *(liter)* a young blood *(dated) or (Mädchen)* thing; **frisches ~** *(fig)* new blood; **~ und Eisen** blood and iron; **~ und Boden** *(NS)* blood and soil, *idea that political stability and power depend on unification of race and territory*; **~ und Wasser schwitzen** *(inf)* to sweat blood; **die Stimme des ~es** the call of the blood; **es geht (einem) ins ~** it gets into your blood

Blut-: **Blut|acker** M *(Bibl)* field of blood; **Blut|ader** F vein; **Blut|al|gen** PL red algae *pl*; **Blut|al|ko|hol** M, **Blut|al|ko|hol|ge|halt** M; **Blut|al|ko|hol|spie|gel** M blood alcohol level *or* content; **Blut|ana|ly|se** F *(Med)* blood analysis; **Blut|an|drang** M congestion; **Blut|ap|fel|si|ne** F blood orange; **blut|arm** ADJ **a** ['blu:tlarm] *(Med)* anaemic *(Brit)*, anemic *(US)*; *(fig auch)* colourless *(Brit)*, colorless *(US)* **b** [blu:t'larm] *(liter)* very poor, penniless; **Blut|ar|mut** F *(Med)* anaemia *(Brit)*, anemia *(US)*; **Blut|auf|fri|schung** F blood replacement; **Blut|aus|tausch** M *(Med)* exchange transfusion; **Blut|bad** NT bloodbath; **Blut|bahn** F bloodstream; **Blut|bank** F *pl* **-banken** blood bank; **Blut|bann** M power over life and death; **blut|be|fleckt** ADJ *(lit, fig)* bloodstained; **blut|be|schmiert** [-bəʃmi:ɐt] ADJ smeared with blood; **blut|be|spritzt** [-bəʃprɪtst] ADJ blood-spattered; **Blut|beu|tel** M *(Med)* blood bag; **Blut|bild** NT blood count; **blut|bil|dend** ADJ haematinic *(Brit spec)*, hematinic *(US spec)*; *Nahrung* full of iron; **Blut|bil|dung** F formation of blood, blood formation; **Blut|bla|se** F blood blister; **Blut|bu|che** F copper beech

Blut|druck M, *no pl* blood pressure

Blut|druck-: **blut|druck|er|hö|hend** ADJ, ADV = **blutdrucksteigernd**; **Blut|druck|mes|ser** M **-s, -**, **Blut|druck|mess|ge|rät** NT *(Med)* blood pressure gauge; **Blut|druck|mes|sung** F blood pressure reading; **eine stündliche ~ wäre ratsam** taking an hourly blood pressure reading would be advisable; **blut|druck|sen|kend** ADJ hypotensive; *Mittel* antihypertensive ADV **~ sein** *or* **wirken** to reduce high blood pressure; **blut|druck|stei|gernd** ADJ hypertensive; *Mittel* antihypotensive ADV **~ sein** *or* **wirken** to increase low blood pressure

Blut-: **Blut|durst** M *(geh)* blood lust; **blut|dürs|tig** [-dʏrstɪç] ADJ *(geh)* bloodthirsty

Blü|te ['bly:tə] F **-, -n a** *(Bot: = Pflanzenteil) (von Blume)* flower, bloom; *(von Baum)* blossom; **~n treiben** to be in flower *or* bloom, to be flowering *or* blooming; *(Baum)* to be blossoming *or* in blossom; **seltsame ~n treiben** to produce strange effects; *(Fantasie, Angst)* to produce strange ideas; **eine ~ seiner Fantasie** a figment of his imagination **b** *(= das Blühen, Blütezeit)* **zur ~ des Klees** when the clover is in flower *or* bloom; **zur ~ der Kirschbäume** when the cherry trees are blossoming *or* in blossom; **die ~ beginnt** the flowers are coming into bloom; *(bei Bäumen)* the trees are coming into blossom; **die ~ der Apfelbäume ist vorüber** the apple trees are no longer blossoming *or* in blossom; **in (voller) ~ stehen** to be in (full) flower *(esp Brit) or* blossom; *(Bäume)* to be in (full) blossom; *(Kultur, Geschäft)* to be flourishing; **sich zur vollen ~ entfalten** to come into full flower; *(Mädchen, Kultur)* to blossom; **seine ~ erreichen** *or* **erleben** *(Kultur etc)* to reach its peak; **ein Zeitalter kultureller ~** an age of cultural ascendency; **in der ~ seiner Jahre** in his prime, in the prime of his life; **eine neue ~ erleben** to undergo a revival **c** *(Med: = Ausschlag)* rash, efflorescence *(spec)* **d** *(inf: = gefälschte Note)* dud *(inf)*

Blut|egel M leech

blu|ten ['blu:tn] VI to bleed *(an +dat, aus* from); **mir blutet das Herz** my heart bleeds; **~den Herzens** with heavy heart; **für etw (schwer) ~** *(inf)* to cough up a lot of money for sth *(inf)*

Blü|ten-: **Blü|ten|blatt** NT petal; **Blü|ten|ho|nig** M honey *(made from flowers)*; **Blü|ten|kelch** M calyx; **Blü|ten|knos|pe** F flower bud; **blü|ten|los** ADJ nonflowering; **Blü|ten|meer** NT sea of blossom(s); **Blü|ten|pflan|ze** F flowering plant; **Blü|ten|ran|ke** F blossom tendril; **Blü|ten|stand** M inflorescence; **Blü|ten|staub** M pollen

Blut|ent|nah|me F taking of a blood sample

Blü|ten|zweig M flowering twig

Blu|ter ['blu:tɐ] M **-s, -** *(Med)* haemophiliac *(Brit)*, hemophiliac *(US)*

Blut|er|guss ['blu:tlɛɐgʊs] M haematoma *(Brit spec)*, hematoma *(US spec)*; *(= blauer Fleck)* bruise

Blu|ter|krank|heit ['blu:tɐ-] F haemophilia *(Brit)*, hemophilia *(US)*

Blü|te|zeit F **a die ~ der Obstbäume ist vorbei** the fruit trees are no longer in blossom **b** *(fig)* heyday; *(von Mensch)* prime

Blut-: **Blut|farb|stoff** M haemoglobin *(Brit)*, hemoglobin *(US)*; **Blut|fa|ser|stoff** M fibrin; **Blut|feh|de** F blood feud; **Blut|fett** NT blood fat, blood lipids *pl*; **Blut|fett|wer|te** PL *(Physiol)* blood lipid level(s *pl*); **Blut|fett|sen|ker** M **-s, -** *(Pharm)* blood-fat-lowering drug; **Blut|fett|spie|gel** M *(Med)* blood-fat level; **Blut|fleck** M bloodstain; **Blut|flüs|sig|keit** F blood plasma; **Blut|ge|fäß** NT blood vessel; **Blut|geld** NT blood money; **Blut|ge|rinn|sel** NT blood clot; **Blut|ge|rin|nung** F clotting of the blood; **Blut|ge|rin|nungs|fak|tor** M *(Med)* blood clotting factor; **Blut|ge|rüst** NT *(liter)* scaffold; **blut|ge|tränkt** [-gətrɛŋkt] ADJ blood-soaked, soaked in blood; **Blut|gier** F blood lust; **blut|gie|rig** ADJ bloodthirsty; **Blut|grup|pe** F blood group; **die ~ 0 haben** to be blood group 0; **jds ~ bestimmen** to type *or* group sb's blood

Blut|grup|pen-: **Blut|grup|pen|be|stim|mung** F blood-typing; **Blut|grup|pen|un|ter|su|chung** F *(Jur)* blood test *(to determine paternity)*

Blut-: **Blut|hoch|druck** M high blood pressure; **Blut|hoch|zeit** F *(Hist)* Massacre of St. Bartholomew; **Blut|hund** M *(lit, fig)* bloodhound; **Blut|hus|ten** M haemoptysis *(Brit spec)*, hemoptysis *(US spec)*; **er hat ~** he is coughing (up) blood

blu|tig ['blu:tɪç] ADJ **a** *(lit, fig)* bloody; **sich ~ machen** to get blood on oneself; **~e Tränen weinen** *(liter)* to shed bitter tears **b** *(inf) Anfänger* absolute; *Ernst* unrelenting ADV bloodily; **er wurde ~ geschlagen/gepeitscht** he was beaten/whipped until he bled

-blü|tig [bly:tɪç] ADJ *suf* **a** *Tier, Mensch* -blooded; **kaltblütig** cold-blooded **b** *Pflanze* **eine rotblütige Tulpe** a red tulip

Blut-: **blut|jung** ADJ very young; **Blut|kon|ser|ve** F unit *or* pint of stored blood; **Blut|kon|takt** M contact through blood; **Blut|kör|per|chen** [-kœrpɐçən] NT **-s, -** blood corpuscle; **Blut|krank|heit** F blood disease; **Blut|krebs** M leukaemia *(Brit)*, leukemia *(US)*; **Blut|kreis|lauf** M blood circulation; **Blut|la|che** [-laxə, -la:xə] F pool of blood; **blut|leer** ADJ bloodless; **Blut|lee|re** F, *no pl* lack of blood; **blut|los** ADJ bloodless; *(fig) Stil* colourless *(Brit)*, colorless *(US)*, anaemic *(Brit)*, anemic *(US)*; **Blut|op|fer** NT **a** *(= Op-*

ferung) blood sacrifice **b** *(= Geopferter)* victim; *(fig)* casualty; **Blut|oran|ge** F blood orange; **Blut|pass** M *card giving blood group etc*; **Blut|pfropf** M clot of blood; **Blut|plas|ma** NT blood plasma; **Blut|plätt|chen** NT platelet; **Blut|pro|be** F blood test; *(= entnommene Blutmenge)* blood sample; **Blut|ra|che** F blood feud; **Blut|rausch** M frenzy; **blut|rei|ni|gend** ADJ blood-cleansing, depurative *(spec)* ADV **~ sein** *or* **wirken** to cleanse the blood; **Blut|rei|ni|gung** F cleansing of the blood; **Blut|rei|ni|gungs|tee** M blood-cleansing tea; **blut|rot** *(liter)* ADJ blood-red ADV **~ gefärbt** blood-red; **blut|rüns|tig** [-rʏnstɪç] ADJ bloodthirsty; **Blut|sau|ger(in)** M(F) *(lit, fig)* bloodsucker; *(= Vampir)* vampire

Bluts-: **Bluts|ban|de** PL *(geh)* bonds *pl* or ties *pl* of blood; **Bluts|bru|der** M blood brother; **Bluts|brü|der|schaft** F blood brotherhood

Blut-: **Blut|schan|de** F incest; **Blut|schuld** F *(liter)* blood guilt; **eine ~ auf sich** *(acc)* **laden** to sully one's hands with blood *(liter)*; **Blut|schwamm** M *(Med)* strawberry mark; **Blut|sen|kung** F *(Med)* sedimentation of the blood; **eine ~ machen** to test the sedimentation rate of the blood; **Blut|se|rum** NT, *no pl* blood serum; **Blut|spen|de** F unit *or* pint of blood *(given by a donor)*; **Blut|spen|den** NT **-s**, *no pl* giving blood *no art*; **zum ~ aufrufen** to appeal for blood donors; **Blut|spen|de|pass** M blood donor card; **Blut|spen|der(in)** M(F) blood donor; **Blut|spur** F trail of blood; **~en** traces of blood; **Blut|stau|ung** F congestion; **Blut|stein** M haematite *(Brit)*, hematite *(US)*; **blut|stil|lend** ADJ styptic ADV **~ wirken** to have a styptic effect; **Blut|strahl** M stream of blood; **Blut|strom** M bloodstream; *(aus Wunde)* stream of blood

Bluts|trop|fen M drop of blood

Blut-: **Blut|stuhl** M, *no pl (Med)* blood in the faeces *(Brit)* or feces *(US)*; **Blut|sturz** M haemorrhage *(Brit)* or hemorrhage *(US)*

Bluts-: **bluts|ver|wandt** ADJ related by blood; **Bluts|ver|wand|te(r)** MF *decl as adj* blood relation *or* relative; **Bluts|ver|wandt|schaft** F blood relationship

blutt [blʊt] ADJ *(Sw: = nackt)* bare

Blut-: **Blut|tat** F bloody deed; **Blut|test** M blood test; **Blut|trans|fu|si|on** F blood transfusion; **blut|trie|fend** ADJ *attr* bloody, dripping with blood; **blut|über|strömt** [-ly:bɐʃtrø:mt] ADJ streaming with blood; **Blut|über|tra|gung** F blood transfusion

Blu|tung ['blu:tʊŋ] F **-, -en** bleeding *no pl*; *(starke)* haemorrhage *(Brit)*, hemorrhage *(US)*; *(monatliche)* period; **eine/die ~ stillen** to stop the bleeding

Blut-: **blut|un|ter|lau|fen** ADJ suffused with blood; *Augen* bloodshot; **Blut|un|ter|su|chung** F blood test; **Blut|ver|dün|nungs|mit|tel** NT anticoagulant *(spec)*; **Blut|ver|gie|ßen** NT **-s**, *no pl* bloodshed *no indef art*; **Blut|ver|gif|tung** F blood poisoning *no indef art*; **Blut|ver|lust** M loss of blood; **blut|ver|schmiert** ADJ bloody, smeared with blood; **blut|voll** ADJ vivid, lively; **Blut|wal|lung** F congestion; *(bei Frau)* hot flush *or (US)* flash; **Blut|wä|sche** F *(Med)* detoxification of the blood; **Blut|was|ser** NT, *no pl* blood serum; **Blut|wurst** F blutwurst *(US)*, blood sausage; *(zum Warmmachen)* black *(Brit)* or blood *(US)* pudding; **Blut|zel|le** F blood corpuscle *or* cell; **Blut|zeu|ge** M, **Blut|zeu|gin** F *(old)* martyr; **Blut|zir|ku|la|ti|on** F blood circulation; **Blut|zoll** M *(geh)* toll (of lives); **Blut|zu|cker** M blood sugar; **Blut|zu|cker|spie|gel** M blood sugar level; **Blut|zu|fuhr** F blood supply

BLZ [be:lɛl'tsɛt] F **-, -s** *abbr von* **Bankleitzahl**

BMX-Rad [be:lɛm'lɪks-] NT BMX bike

BND [be:lɛn'de:] M **-(s)** *abbr von* **Bundesnachrichtendienst**

Bö [bø:] F **-, -en** ['bø:ən] gust (of wind); *(stärker, mit Regen)* squall

Boa ['bo:a] F **-, -s** *(= Schlange, Schal)* boa

Board|mar|ker ['bo:ɐtma:ɐkɐ] M **-s, -** *(= Faserschreiber für Weißwandtafeln)* whiteboard pen

Bob [bɔp] M **-s, -s** bob(sleigh) *(Brit)*, bobsled

Bob-: **Bob|bahn** F bob(sleigh) *(Brit)* or bobsled run; **Bob|fah|rer(in)** M(F) bobber *(inf)*; **Bob|schlit|ten** M bobsleigh, bobsled

Boc|cia ['bɔtʃa] NT **-(s)** *or f* **-**, *no pl* bowls *sing*

Bock [bɔk] M **-(e)s, ¨-e** ['bœkə] **a** *(= Rehbock, Kaninchenbock)* buck; *(= Schafsbock)* ram; *(= Ziegenbock)* he-goat, billy goat; **alter ~** *(inf)* old goat *(inf)*; **sturer ~** *(inf)* stubborn old devil *(inf)*; **geiler ~** *(inf)* randy *(Brit)* or horny old goat *(inf)*; **wie ein ~ stinken** to smell like a pig *(inf)*, to stink to high heaven *(inf)*; **die Böcke von den Schafen scheiden** *or* **trennen** *(fig)* to separate the sheep from the goats; **den ~ zum Gärtner machen** *(fig)* to be asking for trouble; **einen ~ schießen** *(fig inf)* to (make a) boob *(Brit inf)* or blunder *(inf)*; *(= Fauxpas)* to drop a clanger *(Brit inf)*, to make a blunder *(inf)*
b *(inf: = Trotz)* stubbornness; **(s)einen ~ haben** to be awkward *(esp Brit)* or difficult, to play up *(inf)*
c *(= Gestell)* stand; *(= Stützgerät)* support; *(für Auto)* ramp; *(aus Holzbalken, mit Beinen)* trestle; *(= Sägebock)* sawhorse
d *(Sport)* vaulting horse; **den** *or* **einen ~ machen** to bend over *(for someone to vault over)*
e *(= Schemel)* (high) stool
f *(= Kutschbock)* box (seat)
g *(= Ramme)* (battering) ram
h *(sl: = Lust, Spaß)* **null ~!** couldn't be buggered! *(Brit sl)*, I don't feel like it; **Böcke** *or* **~ auf etw** *(acc)* **haben** to fancy sth *(inf)*, to be bent on sth; **Böcke** *or* **~ haben, etw zu tun** to fancy doing sth *(inf)*, to be bent on doing sth; **ich hab keinen** *or* **null ~, das zu tun** I can't be buggered doing that *(Brit sl)*, I just don't feel like doing that; **null ~ auf nichts** pissed off with everything *(inf)*

Bock NT OR M **-s, -** bock (beer) *(type of strong beer)*

Bock-: **bock|bei|nig** ADJ *(inf)* contrary, awkward; **Bock|bier** NT bock (beer) *(type of strong beer)*

bo|cken ['bɔkn] VI **a** *(Zugtier etc)* to refuse to move; *(= nicht springen wollen: Pferd)* to refuse; *(fig inf: Auto, Motor etc) (= nicht anspringen)* to refuse to start; *(= nicht richtig funktionieren)* to refuse to go properly; **vor einer Hürde ~** to refuse a jump **b** *(inf: = trotzen)* to play *or* act up *(inf)* **c** *(sl: = Spaß machen)* **das bockt** that's the business *(sl)*

bo|ckig ['bɔkɪç] ADJ *(inf)* stubborn, awkward

Bo|ckig|keit F **-, -en** stubbornness, awkwardness; **noch so ein paar ~en und ...** any more of your stubbornness and ...

Bock-: **Bock|lei|ter** F stepladder; **Bock|mist** M *(inf) (= dummes Gerede)* bullshit *(sl)*; **~ machen** to make a balls-up *(Brit inf)*, to make a big blunder *(inf)*

Bocks-: **Bocks|beu|tel** M *wide, rounded bottle containing Franconian wine*; **Bocks|horn** NT **jdn ins ~ jagen** to put the wind up sb *(Brit inf)*; **sich von jdm ins ~ jagen lassen** to let sb upset one; **sie ließ sich nicht ins ~ jagen** she didn't let herself get into a state

Bock-: **Bock|sprin|gen** NT **-s**, *no pl* leapfrog; *(Sport)* vaulting; **~ machen** to play leapfrog; **Bock|sprung** M **a** *(= Sprung über Menschen)* leapfrog; *(Sport)* vault **b** *(= ungeschickter Sprung)* leap, bound; **Bock|wurst** F bockwurst *(type of sausage)*

Bod|den ['bɔdn] M **-s, -** *(Geol)* ≈ shallow bay

Bo|den ['bo:dn] M **-s, ¨-** ['bø:dn] **a** *(= Erde, Grundfläche)* ground; *(= Erdreich auch)* soil; *(= Fußboden)* floor; *(= Grundbesitz)* land; *(no pl: = Terrain)* soil; **auf spanischem ~** on Spanish soil; **zu ~ fallen** to fall to the ground; **jdn zu ~ schlagen** *or* **strecken** to knock sb down, to floor sb; **festen ~ unter den Füßen haben, auf festem ~ sein** to be *or* stand on firm ground, to be on terra firma; *(fig) (= finanziell abgesichert)* to be secure; *(= fundierte Argumente haben)* to be on firm ground; **den ~ unter den Füßen verlieren** *(lit)* to lose one's footing; **keinen Fuß auf den ~ bekommen** *(fig)* to be unable to find one's feet; *(fig: in Diskussion)* to get out of one's depth; **der ~ brannte ihm unter den Füßen** *(fig)* **ihm wurde der ~ (unter den Füßen) zu heiß** *(fig)* things were getting too hot for him; **jdm den ~ unter den Füßen wegziehen** *(fig)* to cut the ground from under sb's feet *(Brit)*, to pull the carpet out from under sb's feet; **ich hätte (vor Scham) im ~ versinken können** *(fig)* I was so ashamed that I wished the ground would (open and) swallow me up; **am ~ zerstört sein** *(inf)* to be shattered *(Brit fig inf)* or devastated; **(an) ~ gewinnen/verlieren** *(fig)* to gain/lose ground; **~ gutmachen** *or* **wettmachen** *(fig)* to make up ground, to catch up; **etw aus dem ~ stampfen** *(fig)* to conjure sth up out of nothing; *Häuser auch* to build overnight; **er stand wie aus dem ~ gewachsen vor mir** he appeared in front of me as if by magic; **auf fruchtbaren ~ fallen** *(fig)* to fall on fertile ground; **jdm/einer Sache den ~ bereiten** *(fig)* to prepare the ground for sb/sth; **durch alle Böden (hindurch)** *(Sw: = um jeden Preis)* at any price → **Fass, Grund a, schießen VI b**
b *(= unterste Fläche) (von Behälter)* bottom; *(von Meer auch)* seabed; *(von Hose)* seat; *(= Tortenboden)* base → **doppelt ADJ**
c *(Raum) (= Dachboden, Heuboden)* loft; *(= Trockenboden) (für Getreide)* drying floor; *(für Wäsche)* drying room
d *(fig: = Grundlage)* **auf dem ~ der Wissenschaft/Tatsachen/Wirklichkeit stehen** to base oneself on scientific fact/on fact/on reality; *(Behauptung)* to be based *or* founded on scientific fact/on fact/on reality; **sie wurde hart auf den ~ der Wirklichkeit zurückgeholt** she was brought down to earth with a bump; **auf dem ~ der Tatsachen bleiben** to stick to the facts; **den ~ der Tatsachen verlassen** to go into the realm of fantasy; **sich auf unsicherem ~ bewegen** to be on shaky ground; **er steht auf dem ~ des Gesetzes** *(= nicht ungesetzlich)* he is within the law; *(= hat Gesetz hinter sich)* he has the backing of the law; **einem Gerücht den ~ entziehen** to show a rumour *(Brit)* or rumor *(US)* to be unfounded

Bo|den-: **Bo|den|ab|stand** M *(Mot)* (ground) clearance; **Bo|den|ab|wehr** F ground defence *(Brit)* or defense *(US)*; **Bo|den|be|ar|bei|tung** F cultivation of the land *or* soil, tillage; **Bo|den|be|lag** M floor covering; **Bo|den|be|schaf|fen|heit** F condition of the ground; *(von Acker etc)* condition of the soil; **Bo|den|brü|ter** M *(Orn)* ground nester, ground-nesting bird; **Bo|den|de|cker** [-dɛkɐ] M **-s, -** *(Bot)* ground-cover plant; **Bo|den|er|he|bung** F elevation; **Bo|den|ero|si|on** F soil erosion; **Bo|den|er|trag** M *(Agr)* crop yield; **Bo|den|feuch|te** F, **Bo|den|feuch|tig|keit** F *(Hort, Agr)* soil *or* ground humidity; *(im Haus)* rising damp; **Bo|den|flä|che** F *(Agr)* area of land; *(von Zimmer)* floor space *or* area; **Bo|den|frost** M ground frost; **bo|den|ge|stützt** [-gəʃtʏtst] ADJ *Flugkörper* ground-launched; **Bo|den|grup|pe** F *(Aut)* substructure, floorpan; **Bo|den|haf|tung** F *(Aut)* road holding *no indef art*; **Bo|den|hal|tung** F *(Agr, von Hühnern etc) keeping (of hens etc) in free-range conditions*; **„aus ~"** "free-range"; **Bo|den|hei|zung** F underfloor (central) heating; **Bo|den|kam|mer** F attic; **Bo|den|kon|trol|le** F *(Space)* ground control; **Bo|den|le|ger** [-le:gɐ] M **-s, -**, **Bo|den|le|ge|rin** [-ərɪn] F **-, -nen** floor layer; **bo|den|los** ADJ bottomless; *(inf: = unerhört)* indescribable, incredible; **ins Bodenlose fallen** to fall into an abyss ADV *(inf) frech, unverschämt, gemein* unbelievably, incredibly; **Bo|den|ne|-**

bel M ground mist; **Bo|den|nut|zung** F land utilization; **Bo|den|or|ga|ni|sa|ti|on** F *(Aviat)* ground organization; **Bo|den|per|so|nal** NT *(Aviat)* ground personnel *pl or* staff *pl*; **Bo|den|plat|te** F *(Build)* floor slab; *(Tech)* base plate; **Bo|den|pro|be** F soil sample *or* specimen; **Bo|den|re|form** F land *or* agrarian reform; **Bo|den|satz** M sediment; *(von Kaffee)* grounds *pl*, dregs *pl*; *(fig: Menschen)* dregs; *(fig: von Gefühlen)* hidden reservoir; **Bo|den|schät|ze** PL mineral resources *pl*; **Bo|den|schicht** F layer of soil; *(Geol)* stratum; **Bo|den|schwel|le** F speed bump *or* ramp; **Bo|den|see** M **der ~** Lake Constance; **Bo|den|sen|ke** F depression, hollow; **Bo|den|sicht** F *(Aviat)* ground visibility; **Bo|den|spe|ku|la|ti|on** F land speculation; **bo|den|stän|dig** ADJ *(= lang ansässig)* long-established; *(fig: = unkompliziert)* down-to-earth; **Bo|den|sta|ti|on** F *(Space)* ground station; **Bo|den|streit|kräf|te** PL ground forces *pl*; **Bo|den|struk|tur** F soil structure; **Bo|den|tur|nen** NT floor exercises *pl*; **Bo|den|übung** F *(Sport)* floor exercise; **Bo|den|va|se** F floor vase; **Bo|den|ver|bes|se|rung** F *(Agr, Hort)* soil improvement; **Bo|den|wel|le** F **a** bump **b** *(Rad)* ground wave

Bod|me|rei [boːdmə'rai] F -, -en *(Naut)* bottomry

Bo|dy ['bɔdɪ] M -s, -s body

Bo|dy-: **Bo|dy|buil|der** ['bɔdibɪldɐ] M -s, -, **Bo|dy|buil|de|rin** [-ərɪn] F -, -nen bodybuilder; **Bo|dy|buil|ding** ['bɔdibɪldɪŋ] NT -s, *no pl* bodybuilding; **~ machen** to do bodybuilding exercises; **Bo|dy|check** ['bɔditʃɛk] M -s, -s *(Sport)* bodycheck; **Bo|dy|guard** ['bɔdigaːɐt] M -s, -s *(= Leibwächter)* bodyguard; **Bo|dy|lo|ti|on** ['bɔdiloːʃn] F body lotion; **Bo|dy|suit** ['bɔdisuːt] M -(s), -s body stocking *or* suit

Böe ['bøːə] F -, -n gust (of wind); *(stärker, mit Regen)* squall

bog *pret von* **biegen**

Bo|gen ['boːgn] M -s, - *or* ⸚ ['bøːgn] **a** *(= gekrümmte Linie)* curve; *(= Kurve)* bend; *(= Umweg)* detour; *(Math)* arc; *(Mus) (zwischen zwei Noten gleicher Höhe)* tie; *(zur Bindung von verschiedenen Noten)* slur (mark); *(Ski)* turn; **einen ~ fahren** *(Ski)* to do *or* execute a turn; **den ~ heraushaben** *(inf)* to have got the hang of it *(inf)*; **den ~ heraushaben, wie …** *(inf)* to have got the hang of how … *(inf)*; **einen ~ machen** *(Fluss etc)* to curve, to describe a curve *(form)*; *(= einen Umweg machen)* to make a detour; **einen großen ~ um jdn/etw machen** *(= meiden)* to keep well clear of sb/sth, to give sb/sth a wide berth; **jdn in hohem ~ hinauswerfen** *(inf)* to send sb flying out; **der Ball flog in hohem ~ ins Tor** with a lob the ball flew into the net
b *(Archit)* arch
c *(= Waffe, Mus: = Geigenbogen etc)* bow; **den ~ überspannen** *(fig)* to overstep the mark, to go too far
d *(= Papierbogen)* sheet (of paper)

Bo|gen-: **Bo|gen|fens|ter** NT bow window; **bo|gen|för|mig** ADJ arched ADV in the shape of an arch; **Bo|gen|füh|rung** F *(Mus)* bowing; **Bo|gen|gang** M *pl* **-gänge** **a** *(Archit)* arcade **b** *(Anat: von Ohr)* semicircular canal; **Bo|gen|lam|pe** F arc lamp *or* light; **Bo|gen|maß** NT *(Math)* radian *or* circular measure; **Bo|gen|mi|nu|te** F *(Math)* arc minute; **Bo|gen|pfei|ler** M pillar, column *(supporting an arch)*; **Bo|gen|schie|ßen** NT -s, *no pl* archery; **Bo|gen|schüt|ze** M, **Bo|gen|schüt|zin** F archer; **Bo|gen|seh|ne** F bowstring; **Bo|gen|se|kun|de** F *(Math)* arc second; **Bo|gen|strich** M *(Mus)* bowing

Bo|hei M -s, *no pl (inf)* hype

Bo|heme [bo'eːm, bo'ɛːm] F -, *no pl* Bohemian world

Bo|he|mi|en [boe'miɛ̃ː, bohe'miɛ̃ː] M -s, -s, **Bo|he|mi|enne** [boemi'ɛn, bohemi'ɛn] F -, -s Bohemian

Boh|le ['boːlə] F -, -n (thick) board; *(Rail)* sleeper

böh|ma|keln ['bøːmakln] VI *(Aus inf)* to speak with a dreadful accent

Böh|me ['bøːmə] M -n, -n, **Böh|min** ['bøːmɪn] F -, -nen Bohemian *(inhabitant of Bohemia)*

Böh|men ['bøːmən] NT -s Bohemia

Böh|mer|wald ['bøːmɐ-] M Bohemian Forest

böh|misch ['bøːmɪʃ] ADJ Bohemian; **die Böhmischen Brüder** *(Rel)* the Bohemian Brethren; **das sind für mich ~e Dörfer** *(inf)* that's all Greek to me *(inf)* ADV **~ einkaufen** *(Aus inf)* to shoplift

Böhn|chen ['bøːnçən] NT -s, - *dim von* **Bohne**

Boh|ne ['boːnə] F -, -n bean; *(inf: = Kot des Kaninchens, Rehs)* droppings *pl*; **dicke/grüne/weiße ~n** broad/green *or* French *or* runner/haricot *(Brit) or* string *or* navy *(US)* beans; **rote ~n** kidney beans; **blaue ~** *(dated Mil sl)* bullet; **nicht die ~** *(inf)* not a scrap *(inf)*, not one little bit; **das kümmert mich nicht die ~** I don't care a fig about that *(Brit inf)*, I don't give a hoot about that; **du hast wohl ~n in den Ohren** *(inf)* are you deaf?

Boh|nen-: **Boh|nen|ein|topf** M bean stew; **Boh|nen|kaf|fee** M real coffee; **gemahlener ~** ground coffee; **Boh|nen|kraut** NT savo(u)ry; **Boh|nen|ran|ke** F tendril; **Boh|nen|sa|lat** M *(Cook)* (French) bean salad; **Boh|nen|stan|ge** F bean support; *(fig inf)* beanpole *(inf)*; **Boh|nen|stroh** NT **dumm wie ~** *(inf)* (as) thick as two (short) planks *(inf)*; **Boh|nen|sup|pe** F bean soup

Boh|ner ['boːnɐ] M -s, -, **Boh|ner|be|sen** M, **Boh|ner|bürs|te** F floor-polishing brush

boh|nern ['boːnɐn] VTI to polish

Boh|ner|wachs NT floor polish *or* wax

Bohr|ar|bei|ten PL drillings *pl*

boh|ren ['boːrən] VT to bore; *(mit Bohrer, Bohrmaschine auch)* to drill; *Brunnen* to sink; *(= hineindrücken) Stange, Pfahl, Schwert etc* to sink *(in +acc* into); **ein Schiff in den Grund ~** to send a ship to the bottom (of the sea)
VI **a** *(mit Bohrer)* to bore *(in +dat* into), to drill *(nach* for); **in einem Zahn ~** to drill a tooth; **in der Nase ~** to pick one's nose
b *(fig) (= drängen)* to keep on; *(= peinigen: Schmerz, Zweifel etc)* to gnaw; **er bohrte und bohrte, bekam aber keine Antwort** he kept on and on but got no reply; **der Schmerz bohrte ihm im Magen** he had a gnawing pain in his stomach
VR **sich in/durch etw** *(acc)* **~** to bore its way into/through sth; **ein grelles Licht bohrte sich durchs Dunkel** a glaring light pierced the darkness

boh|rend ADJ *(fig) Blick* piercing; *Schmerz, Zweifel, Hunger, Reue* gnawing; *Frage* probing

Boh|rer ['boːrɐ] M -s, - *(elektrisch, = Drillbohrer)* drill; *(= Handbohrer)* gimlet, auger

Boh|rer ['boːrɐ] M -s, -, **Boh|re|rin** [-ərɪn] F -, -nen driller

Bohr-: **Bohr|feld** NT oil/gas field; **Bohr|fut|ter|schlüs|sel** M chuck key; **Bohr|in|sel** F drilling rig; *(für Öl auch)* oil rig; **Bohr|kopf** M drilling *or* boring head, bit; **Bohr|loch** NT borehole; *(in Holz, Metall etc)* drill hole; **Bohr|ma|schi|ne** F drill; **Bohr|mei|ßel** M boring tool, drill bit, cutter; **Bohr|pro|be** F drilling; **Bohr|schrau|ber** M drilldriver, drill driver; **Bohr|stan|ge** F drill rod; **Bohr|turm** M derrick

Boh|rung F -, -en **a** *(= das Bohren)* boring; *(mit Bohrer, Bohrmaschine auch)* drilling; *(von Brunnen)* sinking **b** *(= Loch)* bore(hole); *(in Holz, Metall etc)* drill hole

bö|ig ['bøːɪç] ADJ gusty; *(stärker, mit Regen)* squally

Boi|ler ['bɔylɐ] M -s, - (hot-water) tank; **den ~ anstellen** to put the water heater on

Bo|je ['boːjə] F -, -n buoy

Bo|le|ro [bo'leːro] M -s, -s *(= Tanz, Jäckchen)* bolero

Bo|li|de [bo'liːdə] M -n, -n **a** *(Aut: = Rennwagen)* (high-performance) racing car **b** *(Comput)* high-performance computer; *(= Superrechner)* supercomputer

Bo|li|vi|a|ner [bolivi'aːnɐ] M -s, -, **Bo|li|vi|a|ne|rin** [-ərɪn] F -, -nen Bolivian

bo|li|vi|a|nisch [bolivi'aːnɪʃ] ADJ Bolivian

Bo|li|vi|en [bo'liːviən] NT -s Bolivia

Bölk|stoff ['bœlk-] M *(sl: = Bier)* wallop *(Brit sl)*

Böl|ler ['bœlɐ] M -s, - (small) cannon *(for ceremonial use)*

bol|lern ['bɔlɐn] VI **a** *aux sein (dial: = poltern)* to thud **b** *(Ftbl sl)* to fire the ball blindly at the goal

böl|lern ['bœlɐn] VI to fire; **es böllert** there is firing

Böl|ler|schuss M gun salute; **5 Böllerschüsse** 5 shots from the cannon

Bol|ler|wa|gen ['bɔlɐ-] M handcart

Boll|werk ['bɔl-] NT *(lit, fig)* bulwark *(usu fig)*, bastion, stronghold; *(= Kai)* bulwark

Bol|sche|wik [bɔlʃe'vɪk] M -en, -en *or* -i, **Bol|sche|wi|kin** [-'vɪkɪn] F -, -nen Bolshevik

Bol|sche|wis|mus [bɔlʃe'vɪsmʊs] M -, *no pl* Bolshevism

Bol|sche|wist [bɔlʃe'vɪst] M -en, -en, **Bol|sche|wis|tin** [-'vɪstɪn] F -, -nen Bolshevist

bol|sche|wis|tisch [bɔlʃe'vɪstɪʃ] ADJ Bolshevist, Bolshevik *attr*

bol|zen ['bɔltsn] *(inf)* VI to kick about; **es wurde mehr gebolzt als gespielt** they just kicked (the ball) about instead of playing football *(Brit) or* soccer *(US)* VT *Ball* to slam

Bol|zen ['bɔltsn] M -s, - **a** *(Tech)* pin; *(esp mit Gewinde)* bolt **b** *(= Geschoss)* bolt

Bol|zen-: **bol|zen|ge|ra|de** ADJ (as) straight as a poker; *(vertikal)* bolt upright

Bol|zen|schnei|der M bolt cutters *pl*

Bol|zen|schuss|ap|pa|rat M *(für Schlachtung)* bolt apparatus, humane killer *(inf)*

Bolz|platz M *piece of ground where children play football*

Bom|bar|de|ment [bɔmbardə'mãː, *(Aus)* bɔmbard'mãː] NT -s, -s bombardment; *(mit Bomben)* bombing; **ein ~ von** *(fig)* a deluge *or* shower of

bom|bar|die|ren [bɔmbar'diːrən] *ptp* **bombardiert** VT *(= mit Bomben belegen)* to bomb; *(= mit Granaten beschießen, fig)* to bombard

Bom|bar|die|rung F -, -en *(mit Bomben)* bombing; *(mit Granaten, fig)* bombardment

Bom|bast [bɔm'bast] M -(e)s, *no pl* bombast

bom|bas|tisch [bɔm'bastɪʃ] ADJ *Sprache* bombastic; *Architektur, Hauseinrichtung* overdone *pred*; *Aufwand* ostentatious ADV *(= schwülstig)* bombastically; *(= pompös) eingerichtet, gebaut* ostentatiously

Bom|bay ['bɔmbe] NT -s *(Hist)* Bombay *(Hist)* → **Mumbai**

Bom|be ['bɔmbə] F -, -n bomb; *(dated: = Könner)* ace *(in +dat* at); *(Sport inf: = Schuss)* cracker *(inf)*; **mit ~n belegen** to bomb; **wie eine ~ einschlagen** to come as a (real) bombshell; **eine/die ~ platzen lassen** *(fig)* to drop a/the bombshell

bom|ben ['bɔmbn] VT *(Sport inf) Ball* to smash *(inf)*, to slam *(inf)*

Bom|ben- *in cpds (Mil)* bomb; *(inf: = hervorragend)* fantastic *(inf)*, great *(inf)*; **Bom|ben|alarm** M bomb scare; **Bom|ben|an|griff** M bomb attack *or* raid; **Bom|ben|an|schlag** M bomb attack; **Bom|ben|at|ten|tat** NT bomb attempt; **Bom|ben|be|set|zung** F *(inf)* fantastic *or* great cast *(inf)*; **Bom|ben|dro|hung** F bomb threat *or* scare; **Bom|ben|er|folg** M *(inf)* smash hit *(inf)*; **bom|ben|fest** ADJ **a** *(Mil)* bombproof **b** *(inf) Klebestelle, Naht* absolutely secure; *Entschluss* unshakeable ADV *(inf)* **etw ~ zusammenkleben** to stick sth securely together; **Bom|ben|flug|zeug** NT bomber; **Bom|ben|form** F *(Sport; inf)* **in ~ sein** to be in great shape; **Bom|ben|ge|schä|dig|te(r)** MF *decl as adj* bomb victim; **Bom|ben|ge|schäft**

NT *(inf)* **ein ~ sein** to be a gold mine *(fig inf)*; **ein ~ machen** to do a roaring trade *(inf)* *(mit* in); **Bom|ben|ge|schwa|der** NT bomber squadron; **Bom|ben|hit|ze** F *(inf)* sweltering heat *no indef art*; **Bom|ben|kra|ter** M bomb crater; **Bom|ben|le|ger** [-le:gɐ] M **-s, -**, **Bom|ben|le|ge|rin** [-ərɪn] F **-, -nen** bomber; **Bom|ben|nacht** F night of bombing; **Bom|ben|schacht** M *(Mil: in Flugzeug)* bomb bay; **Bom|ben|scha|den** M bomb damage; **Bom|ben|schuss** M *(inf)* unstoppable shot; **bom|ben|si|cher** ADJ **a** *(Mil)* bombproof **b** *(inf)* dead certain *(inf)*; *Landung* absolutely safe; **eine ~e Geschäftsidee** an absolute winner of a business idea ADV **a** *(Mil) lagern, unterbringen* in a bombproof place **b** *(inf)* **das steht ~ fest** that's absolutely certain; **Bom|ben|split|ter** M bomb fragment; **Bom|ben|stel|lung** F *(inf)* job in a million *(inf)*, fantastic job *(inf)*; **Bom|ben|stim|mung** F, *no pl (inf)* terrific *or* tremendous atmosphere; **sie waren in ~** they were *or* felt on top of the world *(inf)*; **Bom|ben|tep|pich** M **einen ~ legen** to blanket-bomb an/the area; **Bom|ben|ter|ror** M terror bombing; **Bom|ben|trich|ter** M bomb crater

Bom|ber ['bɔmbɐ] M **-s, -** *(= Bombenflugzeug)* bomber

Bom|ber ['bɔmbɐ] M **-s, -**, **Bom|be|rin** [-ərɪn] F **-, -nen** **a** *(= Attentäter)* bomber **b** *(Ftbl inf)* powerful striker

Bom|ber|ja|cke F bomber jacket

Bom|mel ['bɔml] F **-, -n** bobble

Bon [bɔŋ, bõ:] M **-s, -s** voucher, coupon; *(= Kassenzettel)* receipt, (sales) slip

Bon|bon [bɔŋ'bɔŋ, bõ'bõ:] NT OR M **-s, -s** sweet *(Brit)*, candy *(US)*; *(fig)* treat

bon|bon|far|ben [bɔŋ'bɔŋfarbn, bõ'bõ:-], **bon|bon|far|big** ADJ candy-coloured *(Brit)*, candy-colored *(US)*

Bon|bon|ni|e|re [bɔŋbɔ'nie:rə, bõ-] F **-, -n** box of chocolates

Bon|bon|pa|pier [bɔŋ'bɔŋ-, bõ'bõ:-] NT sweet *(Brit)* or candy *(US)* wrapper

Bond [bɔnt] M **-s, -s** *(Fin)* bond; **festverzinsliche ~s** *pl* fixed-income bonds *pl*

bon|gen ['bɔŋən] VT *(inf) Betrag etc* to ring up; **das ist gebongt** *(inf)* okey-doke, righto *(inf)*

Bon|go ['bɔŋgo] NT **-(s), -s** F **-, -s**, **Bon|go|trom|mel** F bongo (drum)

Bo|ni|fi|ka|ti|on [bonifika'tsio:n] F **-, -en** *(Fin)* *(= Bonus)* bonus; *(= Provision)* commission

bo|ni|fi|zie|ren [bonifi'tsi:rən] *ptp* **bonifiziert** VTI *(Comm)* to reimburse, to remunerate

Bo|ni|tät [boni'tɛ:t] F **-, -en** *(Fin)* financial standing, creditworthiness

Bo|ni|täts|prü|fung F *(Fin)* credit investigation

Bon|mot [bõ'mo:] NT **-s, -s** bon mot

Bonn [bɔn] NT **-s** Bonn

Bon|ner ['bɔnɐ] ADJ *attr* Bonn

Bon|ner ['bɔnɐ] M **-s, -**, **Bon|ne|rin** [-ərɪn] F **-, -nen** native of Bonn; *(= Einwohner)* inhabitant of Bonn

Bon|sai ['bɔnzai] NT **-s, -s** bonsai

Bo|nus ['bo:nʊs] M **- or -ses, - or -se** *(Comm, fig)* bonus; *(Univ, Sport: = Punktvorteil)* bonus points *pl*

Bo|nus|mei|le F air mile *(Brit)*, bonus mile *(US)*

Bo|nus|sys|tem NT bonus system

Bon|vi|vant [bõvi'vã:] M **-s, -s** *(= Lebemann)* bon vivant; *(Theat)* rake, roué

Bon|ze ['bɔntsə] M **-n, -n** **a** *(Rel)* bonze **b** *(pej)* bigwig *(inf)*, big shot *(inf)*

Boo|gie(-Woo|gie) ['bʊgi('vʊgi)] M **-(s), -s** boogie-woogie

Books on de|mand PL *no art* books on demand

Boom [bu:m] M **-s, -s** boom

boo|men ['bu:mən] VI to boom

Boos|ter ['bu:stɐ] M **-s, -** *(an Triebwerk)* booster rocket; *(Elec)* booster; *(Med)* booster (injection)

Boot [bo:t] NT **-(e)s, -e** boat; **~ fahren** to go out in a boat; *(zum Vergnügen)* to go boating; **wir sitzen alle in einem** *or* **im selben** *or* **im gleichen ~** *(fig)* we're all in the same boat

boo|ten ['bu:tn] VTI *(Comput)* to boot (up)

Boo|ten ['bu:tn] NT *(Comput)* booting, bootstrapping

Boots-: **Boots|an|hän|ger** M boat trailer; **Boots|bau|er(in)** M(F) *pl* **-bauer(innen)** boatbuilder; **Boots|deck** NT boat deck; **Boots|fahrt** F boat trip; **Boots|flücht|lin|ge** PL boat people; **Boots|haus** NT boathouse; **Boots|län|ge** F *(Sport)* (boat's) length; **Boots|mann** M *pl* **-leute** *(Naut)* bo'sun, boatswain; *(= Dienstgrad)* petty officer; **Boots|ren|nen** NT boat race; **Boots|schup|pen** M boatshed; **Boots|steg** M landing stage; **Boots|ver|leih** M boat hire (business); **Boots|ver|lei|her(in)** M(F) boat hirer

Bor ['bo:ɐ] NT **-s**, *no pl (abbr* **B)** boron

Bo|rax ['bo:raks] M **-(es)**, *no pl* borax

Bord [bɔrt] M **-(e)s** [-dəs], *no pl* **an ~ (eines Schiffes/der „Bremen")** aboard *or* on board (a ship/the "Bremen"); **alle Mann an ~!** all aboard!; **frei an ~** *(Comm)* free on board, f.o.b.; **an ~ gehen** to board *or* to go aboard (the ship/plane), to go on board; **über ~** overboard; **Mann über ~!** man overboard!; **über ~ gehen** to go overboard; *(fig)* to go by the board; **über ~ werfen** *(lit, fig)* to throw overboard, to jettison; **die Vorsicht über ~ werfen** to throw caution to the winds; **von ~ gehen** to leave (the) ship/the plane; *(esp Passagiere am Ziel)* to disembark

Bord NT **-(e)s, -e** *(= Wandbrett)* shelf

Bord NT **-(e)s, -e** *(Sw)* *(= Rand)* ledge, raised edge; *(= Böschung)* embankment, bank

Bord-: **Bord|buch** NT log(book); **Bord|case** [-keɪs] NT OR M **-, -s** [-keɪsɪz] flight *or* carry-on case; **Bord|com|pu|ter** M on-board computer; **bord|ei|gen** ADJ ship's/plane's *etc*; **Bord|e|lek|tro|nik** F *(Aviat)* avionics *pl*, on-board electronics *pl*

Bor|dell [bɔr'dɛl] NT **-s, -e** brothel

Bor|del|li|er [bɔrdə'lie:] M **-s, -s** brothel keeper

Bor|dell-: **Bor|dell|vier|tel** NT red-light district; **Bor|dell|wir|tin** F brothel keeper, madam

Bord-: **Bord|funk** M *(Naut)* (ship's) radio; *(Aviat)* (aircraft) radio equipment; **Bord|fun|ker(in)** M(F) *(Naut, Aviat)* radio operator; **Bord|ge|päck** NT *(Aviat)* hand luggage *or* baggage *(esp US)*, carry-on baggage *(esp US)*; **Bord|in|ge|ni|eur(in)** M(F) *(Aviat)* flight engineer; *(Naut)* ship's engineer; **Bord|ka|me|ra** F *(Mil)* on-board camera; **Bord|ka|no|ne** F *(Mil)* *(an Flugzeug)* aircraft cannon; *(an Panzer)* gun; **Bord|kan|te** F kerb *(Brit)*, curb *(US)*; **Bord|kar|te** F boarding pass *or* card; **Bord|me|cha|ni|ker(in)** M(F) ship's/aircraft mechanic; **Bord|mit|tel** PL **mit ~n** *(lit)* with our/their *etc* on-board equipment; *(fig)* with the means we have *or* had at our disposal/they *etc* have *or* had at their *etc* disposal; **Bord|stein** M kerb *(Brit)*, curb *(US)*; **den ~ mitnehmen** *(inf)* to hit the kerb *(Brit)* or curb *(US)*; **Bord|stein|kan|te** F, **Bord|stein|rand** M kerb *(Brit)*, curb *(US)*

bor|die|ren [bɔr'di:rən] *ptp* **bordiert** VT *(Sew)* to edge, to border

Bor|dü|re [bɔr'dy:rə] F **-, -n** edging, border

Bord-: **Bord|waf|fen** PL *(Mil)* *(von Flugzeug)* aircraft armaments *pl*; *(von Panzer)* tank armaments *pl*; *(von Schiff)* ship armaments *pl*; **Bord|wand** F *(Naut)* ship's side; *(Aviat)* side of the aircraft

bo|re|al [bore'a:l] ADJ *Nadelwald etc* boreal

bor|gen ['bɔrgn] VTI **a** *(= erhalten)* to borrow *(von* from) **b** *(= geben)* to lend, to loan *(jdm etw* sb sth, sth to sb)

Bor|ke ['bɔrkə] F **-, -n** bark

Bor|ken-: **Bor|ken|flech|te** F *(Med)* ringworm; **Bor|ken|kä|fer** M bark beetle; **Bor|ken|krepp** M *(Tex)* crepe

Born [bɔrn] M **-(e)s, -e** *(old, liter)* *(= Brunnen)* well; *(= Quelle)* spring; *(fig)* fountain, fount *(liter)*

bor|niert [bɔr'ni:ɐt] ADJ bigoted

Bor|niert|heit F **-,** *no pl* bigotry

Bor|re|li|o|se [bɔre'lio:zə] F **-, -n** *usu sing (Med)* borreliosis *(spec)*, Lyme disease

Bor|retsch ['bɔrɛtʃ] M **-(e)s**, *no pl* borage

Bor|sal|be F boric acid ointment

Bor|sa|li|no [bɔrza'li:no] M **-s, -s** fedora

Bör|se ['bœrzə, 'bø:ɐzə] F **-, -n** **a** *(= Geldbörse)* *(für Frauen)* purse; *(für Männer)* wallet *(Brit)*, billfold *(US)* **b** *(= Wertpapierhandel)* stock market; *(Ort)* stock exchange; **an die ~ gehen** to be floated on the stock market *or* stock exchange

Bör|sen- *(St Ex)*: **Bör|sen|auf|sicht** F **a** *(Behörde)* stock exchange supervisory board, stock market regulator, ≈ Securities and Investments Board *(Brit)*, ≈ Securities and Exchange Commission *(US)* **b** *no pl (Kontrolle)* regulation of the stock market; **Bör|sen|auf|sichts|be|hör|de** F = **Börsenaufsicht a**; **Bör|sen|ba|ro|me|ter** NT *(inf fig)* (stock) market barometer; **Bör|sen|be|ginn** M opening of the stock market; **bei ~** when the stock market opens; **Bör|sen|be|richt** M stock market report; **Bör|sen|crash** M *(inf)* stock market crash; **Bör|sen|ein|füh|rung** F flotation on the stock exchange; **bör|sen|fä|hig** ADJ negotiable on the stock exchange; **Bör|sen|fä|hig|keit** F negotiability on the stock exchange; **Bör|sen|gang** M (stock market) flotation, initial public offering *(spec)*; **Bör|sen|ge|schäft** NT *(= Wertpapierhandel)* stockbroking; *(= Transaktion)* stock market transaction; **Bör|sen|han|del** M stock exchange trading; **Bör|sen|in|dex** M stock exchange index; **Bör|sen|job|ber(in)** M(F) *(inf)* (stock) jobber; **Bör|sen|krach** M stock market crash; **Bör|sen|kri|se** F crisis on the stock market; **Bör|sen|kurs** M stock market price; **Bör|sen|mak|ler(in)** M(F) stockbroker; **Bör|sen|nach|rich|ten** PL financial news *sing or* report *sing*; **bör|sen|no|tiert** [-noti:ɐt] ADJ *Firma* listed; **Bör|sen|no|tie|rung** F quotation (on the stock exchange); **Bör|sen|ord|nung** F stock exchange rules *pl*; **Bör|sen|platz** M stock exchange; **Bör|sen|pros|pekt** M (stock exchange) prospectus; **Bör|sen|schluss** M, *no pl* close of the stock market; **Bör|sen|schwan|kun|gen** PL fluctuations on the stock market; **Bör|sen|schwin|del** M stock market swindle *or* fiddle *(inf)*; **Bör|sen|spe|ku|lant(in)** M(F) speculator on the stock market; **Bör|sen|spe|ku|la|ti|on** F speculation on the stock market; **Bör|sen|spiel** NT *(= Wettbewerb mit fiktiven Börsengeschäften)* stock market simulation game; **Bör|sen|sturz** M collapse of the market; **Bör|sen|ten|denz** F stock market trend; **Bör|sen|tipp** M market tip; **Bör|sen|um|satz|steu|er** F stock exchange tax; **Bör|sen|ver|kehr** M stock market dealings *pl or* transactions *pl*; **Bör|sen|we|sen** NT stock market

Bör|si|a|ner [bœr'zia:nɐ] M **-s, -**, **Bör|si|a|ne|rin** [-ərɪn] F **-, -nen** *(inf)* *(= Makler)* broker; *(= Spekulant)* speculator

Bors|te ['bɔrstə] F **-, -n** bristle

Bors|ten-: **Bors|ten|tier** NT pig, swine; **Bors|ten|vieh** NT pigs *pl*, swine *pl*

bors|tig ['bɔrstɪç] ADJ bristly; *(fig)* snappish

Bor|te ['bɔrtə] F **-, -n** braid trimming

Bor|was|ser NT, *no pl* boric acid lotion

bös [bø:s] ADJ, ADV = **böse**

bös|ar|tig ADJ *Mensch, Wesen* malicious, nasty; *Tier* vicious; *(Med) Geschwür* malignant

Bös|ar|tig|keit F **-, -en** maliciousness, nastiness; *(von Tier, stärker: von Mensch, Wesen)* viciousness; *(Med: von Geschwür)* malignancy

Bö|schung ['bœʃʊŋ] F **-, -en** *(von Straße)* bank, embankment; *(von Bahndamm)* embankment; *(von Fluss)* bank

Bö|schungs|win|kel M gradient

bö|se ['bø:zə] ADJ **a** *(= sittlich schlecht)* bad; *(stärker)* evil, wicked; *(inf: = unartig)* naughty, bad; **die ~ Fee/Stiefmutter** the Wicked Fairy/Stepmother; **ein ~r Geist** an evil spirit; **das war keine ~ Absicht** there was no harm intended; **eine ~ Zunge haben, ein ~s Mundwerk haben** to have a malicious *or* wicked tongue → **Blick**
b *no pred (= unangenehm, übel)* *Traum, Angelegenheit, Krankheit* bad; *Überraschung, Streich, Geschichte* nasty; **ein ~s Erwachen** a rude awakening; **~ Folgen** dire consequences; **~ Zeiten** bad times → **Blut, Ende**
c *(= verärgert)* angry, cross (+*dat*, *auf* +*acc*, *mit* with); **ein ~s Gesicht machen** to scowl
d *(inf) (= schmerzend, entzündet)* bad *attr*, sore; *(= krank, schlimm)* bad; *Wunde, Husten* nasty, bad
e *(inf: verstärkend)* real *(inf)*; *Enttäuschung, Gewitter, Sturz* bad, terrible
ADV **a** *(= übel gesinnt)* nastily; *(stärker)* evilly; **das war nicht ~ gemeint** I/he *etc* didn't mean it nastily
b *(= schlimm)* nastily; *verprügeln* badly; **er ist ~ dran** life's not easy for him; *(gesundheitlich)* he's in a bad way; **das/es sieht ~ aus** things look/it looks bad
c *(inf: = sehr)* badly, terribly; **er hat ~ geschimpft** he didn't half curse *(Brit inf)*, he cursed like hell *(inf)*

Bö|se(r) ['bø:zə] MF *decl as adj* wicked *or* evil person; *(Film, Theat)* villain, baddy *(inf)*; **die ~n** the wicked; **der ~** *(= Teufel)* the Evil One

Bö|se(s) ['bø:zə] NT *decl as adj* evil; *(= Schaden, Leid)* harm; **jdm ~s antun** to do sb harm; **ich will dir doch nichts ~s** I don't mean you any harm; **im ~n auseinandergehen** to part on bad terms; **mir schwant ~s** it sounds/looks ominous (to me); **ich dachte an gar nichts ~s, als …** I was quite unsuspecting when …; **ich habe mir gar nichts ~s dabei gedacht, als ich das sagte** I didn't mean any harm when I said that; **und erlöse uns von dem ~n** *(Eccl)* and deliver us from evil → **ahnen VT**

Bö|se|wicht ['bø:zəvɪçt] M **-(e)s, -e** *or* **-er** *(old, hum)* villain

bos|haft ['bo:shaft] ADJ malicious, nasty ADV *grinsen, lächeln* maliciously, spitefully, nastily

Bos|haf|tig|keit ['bo:shaftɪçkait] F **-, -en a** *no pl* maliciousness, nastiness **b** *(Bemerkung)* malicious *or* nasty remark

Bos|heit ['bo:shait] F **-, -en** malice; *(Bemerkung)* malicious remark; *(Handlung)* malicious thing to do; **er hat es mit konstanter ~ getan** maliciously he kept on doing it; **aus lauter ~** from pure malice

Bos|kop ['bɔskɔp] M **-s, -** ≈ russet

Bos|ni|en ['bɔsniən] NT **-s** Bosnia

Bos|ni|en und Her|ze|go|wi|na ['bɔsniənʊnthɛrtseˈgo:vina, -hɛrtsegoˈvi:na] NT **-s** Bosnia and Herzegovina

Bos|ni|er ['bɔsniɐ] M **-s, -**, **Bos|ni|e|rin** [-ərɪn] F **-, -nen** Bosnian

bos|nisch ['bɔsnɪʃ] ADJ Bosnian

Bos|po|rus ['bɔspɔrʊs] M **- der ~** the Bosporus

Boss [bɔs] M **-es, -e** *(inf)* boss *(inf)*

Bos|sa No|va ['bɔsa 'no:va] M **- -, - -s** bossa nova

bos|seln ['bɔsln] *(inf)* VI to tinker *or* fiddle about *(inf)* (*an* +*dat* with) VT *(= zusammenbasteln)* to rig up *(inf)* (*jdm* for sb)

bös|wil|lig ADJ malicious; *(Jur auch)* wilful; **in ~er Absicht** with malicious intent ADV *(= mit böser Absicht)* maliciously; *(Jur auch)* wilfully

Bös|wil|lig|keit F **-**, *no pl* malice

bot *pret von* **bieten**

Bo|ta|nik [bo'ta:nɪk] F **-**, *no pl* botany

Bo|ta|ni|ker [bo'ta:nikɐ] M **-s, -**, **Bo|ta|ni|ke|rin** [-ərɪn] F **-, -nen** botanist

bo|ta|nisch [bo'ta:nɪʃ] ADJ botanic

bo|ta|ni|sie|ren [botani'zi:rən] *ptp* **botanisiert** VI to collect and study plants, to botanize *(rare)*

Bo|ta|ni|sier|trom|mel F (botanist's) specimen container

Böt|chen ['bø:tçən] NT **-s, -** *dim von* **Boot** little boat

Bo|te ['bo:tə] M **-n, -n a** *(usu mit Nachricht)* messenger; *(= Kurier)* courier; *(= Postbote)* postman *(esp Brit)*, mailman *(US)*; *(= Zeitungsbote)* paperboy; *(= Laufbursche)* errand boy; *(= Gerichtsbote)* messenger-at-arms **b** *(fig: = Anzeichen)* herald, harbinger *(liter)*

Bo|ten-: **Bo|ten|be|richt** M *(Liter)* report by messenger; **Bo|ten|dienst** M errand; *(= Einrichtung)* messenger service; **Bo|ten|gang** M *pl* **-gänge** errand; **einen ~ machen** to run an errand; **Bo|ten|lohn** M delivery fee; *(= Bezahlung des Boten)* messenger's fee; *(von Laufbursche)* errand boy's fee; **Bo|ten|stoff** M *(Med)* neurotransmitter

Bo|tin ['bo:tɪn] F **-, -nen** messenger; *(= Kurierin)* courier; *(= Postbotin)* postwoman *(esp Brit)*, mailwoman *(US)*; *(= Zeitungsbotin)* papergirl; *(für Botengänge)* errand girl; *(= Gerichtsbotin)* messenger-at-arms

bot|mä|ßig ADJ *(old, geh) (= untertänig)* compliant, submissive; *(= gehorsam)* obedient; **jdm ~ sein** to be at sb's command

Bot|mä|ßig|keit F, *no pl (old, geh)* **a** *(= Herrschaft)* dominion, rule **b** *(= Untertänigkeit)* compliance, submissiveness; *(= Gehorsamkeit)* obedience

Bot|schaft ['bo:tʃaft] F **-, -en a** *(= Mitteilung)* message; *(esp amtlich)* communication; *(= Neuigkeit)* piece of news, news *no indef art, no pl*; *(= Aussage)* message; **eine freudige ~** good news, glad tidings *pl (liter, hum)*; **die ~ in ihren Protestliedern** the message in her protest songs → **froh b b** *(Pol: = Vertretung)* embassy

Bot|schaf|ter ['bo:tʃaftɐ] M **-s, -**, **Bot|schaf|te|rin** [-ərɪn] F **-, -nen** ambassador

Bot|schaf|ter|ebe|ne F **auf ~** at ambassadorial level

Bot|schafts-: **Bot|schafts|an|ge|hö|ri|ge(r)** MF *decl as adj* ambassadorial employee; **Bot|schafts|be|set|zung** F occupation of an/the embassy; **Bot|schafts|sek|re|tär(in)** M(F) secretary *(in the diplomatic service)*

Bott [bɔt] NT **-(e)s, -e** *(Sw)* general meeting

Bött|cher ['bœtçɐ] M **-s, -**, **Bött|che|rin** [-ərɪn] F **-, -nen** cooper

Bött|che|rei [bœtçə'rai] F **-, -en a** *no pl (= Gewerbe)* cooper's trade, cooperage **b** *(= Werkstatt)* cooper's (work)shop, cooperage

Bot|tich ['bɔtɪç] M **-(e)s, -e** tub

Bot|tle|par|ty ['bɔtl-] F, **Bot|tle-Par|ty** F bottle party

Bo|tu|lis|mus [botu'lɪsmʊs] M **-**, *no pl (Med: = Lebensmittelvergiftung)* botulism *(spec)*

Bouc|lé [bu'kle:] NT **-s, -s** bouclé (yarn)

Bou|doir [bu'doa:ɐ] NT **-s, -s** *(dated geh)* boudoir

Bou|gain|vil|lea [bugɛ̃'vɪlea] F **-, Bougainvilleen** [-leən] *(Bot)* bougainvillea

Bouil|lon [bʊl'jɔn, bʊl'jõ:, *(Aus)* bu'jõ:] F **-, -s** stock, bouillon; *(auf Speisekarte)* bouillon, consommé

Bouil|lon|wür|fel M stock *or* bouillon cube

Boule [bu:l] NT **-(s)**, *no pl* boules *sing*

Bou|le|vard [bulə'va:ɐ, bul'va:ɐ] M **-s, -s** boulevard

Bou|le|vard-: **Bou|le|vard|blatt** NT *(inf)* popular daily, tabloid *(auch pej)*; **Bou|le|vard|pres|se** F *(inf)* popular press; **Bou|le|vard|stück** NT *(Theat)* light comedy; **Bou|le|vard|the|a|ter** NT light theatre *(Brit) or* theater *(US)*; **Bou|le|vard|zei|tung** F popular daily *(Brit)*, tabloid *(auch pej)*

Bou|quet [bu'ke:] NT **-s, -s a** *(= Strauß)* bouquet **b** *(von Wein)* bouquet, nose

bour|geois [bʊr'ʒoa] ADJ *(geh)* bourgeois, middle-class

Bour|geois [bʊr'ʒoa] M **-, -** *(geh)* bourgeois

Bour|geoi|sie [bʊrʒoa'zi:] F **-, -n** [-'zi:ən] *(geh)* bourgeoisie

Bou|tique [bu'ti:k] F **-, -n** boutique

Bo|vist [bo'vɪst, 'bo:vɪst] M **-s, -e** *(Bot)* puffball, bovista *(spec)*

Bow|le ['bo:lə] F **-, -n a** *(= Getränk)* punch; **eine ~ ansetzen** to prepare (some) punch **b** *(= Gefäß, Schüssel)* punchbowl; *(= Garnitur)* punch set (punchbowl and cups)

Bow|len-: **Bow|len|schüs|sel** F punchbowl; **Bow|len|ser|vice** [-zɛrvi:s] NT punch set (punchbowl and cups)

Bow|ling ['bo:lɪŋ] NT **-s, -s** *(= Spiel)* (tenpin) bowling; *(= Ort)* bowling alley; **~ spielen gehen** to go bowling

Bow|ling-: **Bow|ling|bahn** F bowling alley; **Bow|ling|ku|gel** F bowl

Box [bɔks] F **-, -en a** *(= abgeteilter Raum)* compartment; *(für Pferde)* box; *(in Großgarage)* (partitioned-off) parking place; *(für Rennwagen)* pit; *(bei Ausstellungen)* stand **b** *(= Kamera)* box camera **c** *(= Behälter)* box **d** *(= Lautsprecherbox)* speaker (unit)

Box|calf ['bɔkskalf] NT **-s**, *no pl* box calf

bo|xen ['bɔksn] VI *(Sport)* to box; *(zur Übung)* to spar; *(= mit Fäusten zuschlagen)* to hit out, to punch; **um einen Titel ~** to fight for a title; **gegen jdn ~** to fight sb VT **a** *(= schlagen) jdn* to punch, to hit **b** *(Sport sl: = antreten gegen)* to fight **c** *(mit der Faust) Ball* to punch, to thump **d** *(fig: = durchsetzen)* to push, to force; **ein Produkt auf den Markt ~** to push a product VR **a** *(inf: = sich schlagen)* to have a punch-up *(Brit inf) or* a fight **b** *(= sich einen Weg bahnen)* to fight one's way; **sich durchs Leben/nach oben ~** *(fig inf)* to fight one's way through life/up

Bo|xen NT **-s**, *no pl (Sport)* boxing

Bo|xen|stopp M pit stop

Bo|xer ['bɔksɐ] M **-s, -** *(= Hund)* boxer

Bo|xer ['bɔksɐ] M **-s, -**, **Bo|xe|rin** [-ərɪn] F **-, -nen** *(= Sportler)* boxer

Bo|xer-: **Bo|xer|auf|stand** M *(Hist)* Boxer Rebellion; **Bo|xer|mo|tor** M *(Tech)* opposed cylinder engine *(Brit)*, boxer engine *(US)*; **Bo|xer|na|se** F boxer's nose, broken nose; **Bo|xer|shorts** PL boxer shorts *pl*; **Bo|xer|stel|lung** F boxer's stance

Box-: **Box|hand|schuh** M boxing glove; **Box|kalf** ['bɔkskalf] NT **-s**, *no pl* = **Boxcalf**; **Box|ka|me|ra** F box camera; **Box|kampf** M *(= Disziplin)* boxing *no art*; *(= Einzelkampf)* fight, bout, (boxing) match; **Box|ring** M boxing ring; **Box|sport** M (sport of) boxing

Boy [bɔy] M **-s, -s** pageboy *(Brit)*, bellhop *(esp US)*

Boy|kott [bɔy'kɔt] M **-(e)s, -e** *or* **-s** boycott

Boy|kott|dro|hung [bɔy'kɔt-] F threat of a boycott

boy|kot|tie|ren [bɔykɔ'ti:rən] *ptp* **boykottiert** VT to boycott

BP [be:'pe:] *abbr von* **Bundespost**

B-Pro|be F *(bei Dopingkontrolle)* B test

bps [bi:pi:'ɛs] *abbr von* **bits per second**

brab|beln ['brabln] VI *(inf)* to mumble, to mutter; *(Baby)* to babble

brach *pret von* **brechen**

brach [bra:x] ADJ *attr (old)* fallow

Bra|che ['bra:xə] F **-, -n** *(old) (= Land)* fallow (land); *(= Zeit)* fallow period

Brach|feld NT fallow field

Bra|che|jahr NT *(Agr)* fallow year; *(nach EU-Regelung)* set-aside

bra|chi|al [bra'xia:l] ADJ *Mittel, Methode* primitive; **mit ~er Gewalt** by brute force

Bra|chi|al|ge|walt F brute force

Brach-: **Brach|land** NT fallow (land); **brach+le|gen** VT *sep* to leave fallow; **brach+lie|gen** VI *sep irreg (S Ger, Aus, Sw: aux sein)* to lie fallow; *(fig)* to be left unexploited; **~de Kenntnisse/Kräfte** unexploited knowledge/powers; **Brach|mo|nat** M, **Brach|mond** *(obs)* M June

brach|te *pret von* **bringen**

Brach|vo|gel M curlew

Brack [brak] NT **-s, -s** brackish water

bra|ckig ['brakɪç] ADJ brackish

Brack|was|ser NT *pl* **-wasser** brackish water
Brah|man ['bra:man] NT **-s**, *no pl* Brahma
Brah|ma|ne [bra'ma:nə] M **-n, -n**, **Brah|ma|nin** [-'ma:nɪn] F **-, -nen** Brahman, Brahmin
brah|ma|nisch [bra'ma:nɪʃ] ADJ Brahminical, Brahman *attr*
Brah|ma|nis|mus [brama'nɪsmʊs] M **-**, *no pl* Brahmanism
Braille|schrift [braj-] F, *no pl* Braille, braille
Brain|drain ['bre:ndre:n] M **-s**, *no pl*, **Brain-Drain** △ M **-s**, *no pl* brain drain *(inf)*
Brain|stor|ming ['bre:nstɔ:mɪŋ] NT **-s, -s** brainstorming session
Brain|trust ['bre:ntrast] M **-(s), -s**, **Brain-Trust** M **-(s), -s** brains *(Brit)* *or* brain *(US)* trust
bra|mar|ba|sie|ren [bramarba'zi:rən] *ptp* **bramarbasiert** VI *(geh)* to brag *(von* about), to boast *(von* about), to swagger
Bram- ['bra:m-]: **Bram|se|gel** NT topgallant sail; **Bram|sten|ge** [-ʃtɛŋə] F **-, -n** topgallant stay
Bran|che ['brã:ʃə] F **-, -n** *(= Fach)* field, department; *(= Gewerbe)* trade; *(= Geschäftszweig)* area of business, trade; *(= Wirtschaftszweig)* (branch of) industry; **das gehört in seine ~** that's in his line *or* department *or* field
Bran|chen-: **Bran|chen|ad|ress|buch** NT, **Bran|chen|buch** NT *(Telec)* classified directory, Yellow Pages®; **bran|chen|fremd** ADJ → **Branche** *Waren* foreign to the trade/industry; *Kollege* not familiar with the trade; **Bran|chen|füh|rer(in)** M(F) market leader; **Bran|chen|ken|ner(in)** M(F) market expert, person with a good knowledge of the trade/business; **er ist ~** he knows the trade/business; **Bran|chen|kennt|nis** F → **Branche** knowledge of the trade/industry; **bran|chen|kun|dig** ADJ → **Branche** experienced *or* well-versed in the trade/industry; **Bran|chen|lea|der** [-li:dɐ] M **-s, -**, **Bran|chen|lea|de|rin** [-ərɪn] F **-, -nen** market leader; **bran|chen|üb|lich** ADJ → **Branche** usual in the trade/industry; **bran|chen|un|üb|lich** ADJ → **Branche** not usual in the trade/industry; **Bran|chen|ver|zeich|nis** NT *(Telec)* classified directory, Yellow Pages®
Brand [brant] M **-(e)s, ¨-e** ['brɛndə] **a** *(= Feuer)* fire; *(lodernd)* blaze, conflagration *(liter)*; **in ~ geraten** to catch fire; *(in Flammen aufgehen)* to burst into flames; **in ~ stehen** to be on fire, to be ablaze; **etw in ~ setzen** *or* **stecken** to set fire to sth, to set sth alight *or* on fire; **einen ~ legen** to set a fire
b *usu pl (= brennendes Holz etc)* firebrand
c *(fig geh, der Liebe, des Hasses)* burning passion
d *(= das Brennen, von Porzellan etc)* firing
e *(fig inf: = großer Durst)* raging thirst
f *(dial inf) (= Brennstoff)* fuel; *(= Holz auch)* firewood
g *(Med)* gangrene *no art*
h *(= Pflanzenkrankheit)* blight
Brand-: **brand|ak|tu|ell** ADJ *(inf) Thema, Frage* red-hot *(inf)*; *Buch* hot from the presses; *Platte etc* the latest thing *(inf)*; **Brand|an|schlag** M arson attack; **Brand|be|kämp|fung** F fire-fighting; **Brand|bin|de** F bandage for burns; **Brand|bla|se** F (burn) blister; **Brand|bom|be** F firebomb, incendiary bomb *or* device; **Brand|brief** M *(inf) (= Bettelbrief)* begging letter; *(= Mahnbrief)* urgent reminder; **Brand|di|rek|tor(in)** M(F) ≈ fire chief; **brand|ei|lig** ADJ *(inf)* extremely urgent; **brand|heiß** ADJ *(inf)* = **brandaktuell**
bran|den ['brandn] VI to surge *(auch fig)*; **an** *or* **gegen etw** *(acc)* **~** to break against sth; **~der Beifall** thunderous applause
Bran|den|burg ['brandnbʊrk] NT **-s** Brandenburg
Brand-: **Brand|fa|ckel** F firebrand; **Brand|fleck** M burn; **Brand|gans** F shelduck; **Brand|ge|fahr** F danger of fire; **bei ~** when there is danger of fire; **Brand|ge|ruch** M smell of burning; **Brand|herd** M source of the fire *or* blaze; *(fig)* source
bran|dig ['brandɪç] ADJ **a** *(Bot)* suffering from blight; *(Med)* gangrenous **b ~ riechen** to smell of burning; *(bei ausgegangenem Brand)* to have a burnt smell
Brand-: **Brand|in|spek|tor(in)** M(F) fire inspector; **Brand|kas|se** F fire insurance company; **Brand|ka|ta|stro|phe** F fire disaster; **Brand|le|ger** [-le:gɐ] M **-s, -**, **Brand|le|ge|rin** [-ərɪn] F **-, -nen** *(esp Aus)* fire raiser *(esp Brit)*, arsonist *(esp Jur)*, incendiary *(Jur)*; **Brand|loch** NT burn hole; **Brand|mal** NT *pl* **-male** brand; *(fig)* stigma; **Brand|ma|le|rei** F *(Art)* **a** *no pl (= Kunstrichtung)* pyrography, pokerwork *(Brit)* **b** *(= eingebranntes Bild)* (piece of) pyrography *or* pokerwork *(Brit)*; **brand|mar|ken** ['brantmarkn] VT *insep* to brand; *(fig)* to denounce; **jdn als etw ~** *(fig)* to brand sb (as) sth; **Brand|mau|er** F fire(proof) wall; **Brand|meis|ter(in)** M(F) fire chief; **brand|neu** ADJ *(inf)* brand-new, spanking new *(inf)*; **Brand|op|fer** NT **a** *(Rel)* burnt offering **b** *(= Mensch)* fire victim; **Brand|re|de** F harangue; **Brand|ro|dung** F slash-and-burn; **Brand|sal|be** F ointment for burns; **Brand|satz** M incendiary compound; **Brand|scha|den** M fire damage; **brand|schat|zen** ['brantʃatsn] VT *insep* to sack, to lay waste to; **die ~den Horden** the pillaging mob; **Brand|schat|zung** F **-, -en** sack, pillage; **Brand|schutz** M protection against fire; **Brand|soh|le** F insole; **Brand|stel|le** F *(= Ort des Brandes)* fire, blaze; *(= verbrannte Stelle)* burned patch; **Brand|stif|ter(in)** M(F) fire raiser *(esp Brit)*, arsonist *(esp Jur)*, incendiary *(Jur)*; **Brand|stif|tung** F arson *(auch Jur)*, fire raising *(esp Brit)*; **Brand|teig** M choux pastry
Bran|dung ['brandʊŋ] F **-, -en** surf, breakers *pl*; *(fig geh)* surge
Bran|dungs|wel|le F breaker
Brand-: **Brand|ur|sa|che** F cause of a/the fire *or* blaze; **Brand|wa|che** F **a** *(= Überwachung der Brandstelle)* firewatch **b** *(= Personen)* firewatch team; **Brand|wun|de** F burn; *(durch Flüssigkeit)* scald; **Brand|zei|chen** NT brand
brann|te *pret von* **brennen**
Brannt|wein M spirits *pl*, (hard) liquor *(esp US)*, schnap(p)s; **jede Art von ~** all types *or* every type of spirit(s) *or (esp US)* liquor; **Whisky ist ein ~** whisky is a (type of) spirit *or (esp US)* liquor
Brannt|wein-: **Brannt|wein|bren|ner(in)** M(F) distiller; **Brannt|wein|bren|ne|rei** F distillery; *(= Branntweinbrennen)* distilling *or* distillation of spirits *or (esp US)* liquor; **Brannt|wein|schank** [-ʃaŋk] F **-, -en** *(Aus)* ≈ public house *(Brit)*, ≈ bar; **Brannt|wein|steu|er** F tax on spirits *or (esp US)* liquor
brä|sig ['brɛ:zɪç] ADJ *(esp N Ger: = behäbig, untätig)* complacent; **faul und ~ herumsitzen** to sit around on one's backside *(inf)*
Bra|sil [bra'zi:l] F **-, -(s)** Brazil cigar
Bra|sil M **-s, -e** *or* **-s** *(= Tabak)* Brazil(ian) tobacco
Bra|sil|holz NT brazil wood
Bra|si|li|a|ner [brazi'lia:nɐ] M **-s, -**, **Bra|si|li|a|ne|rin** [-ərɪn] F **-, -nen** Brazilian
bra|si|li|a|nisch [brazi'lia:nɪʃ] ADJ Brazilian
Bra|si|li|en [bra'zi:liən] NT **-s** Brazil
Bras|se ['brasə] F **-, -n** **a** *(Naut)* brace **b** *(= Fisch)* bream
bras|sen ['brasn] VT *(Naut)* to brace
brät [brɛ:t] 3. PERS SING *pres von* **braten**
Brät [brɛ:t] NT **-s**, *no pl* sausage meat
Brat|ap|fel M baked apple
bra|ten ['bra:tn] *pret* **briet** [bri:t], *ptp* **gebraten** [gə'bra:tn] VTI *(am Spieß, im Ofen: mit Fett)* to roast; *(im Ofen: ohne Fett)* to bake; *(in der Pfanne)* to fry; **etw braun ~** to roast/fry sth until it is brown; **etw knusprig ~** to roast/fry sth until it is crispy VI *(inf: in der Sonne)* to roast *(inf)*; **sich ~ lassen** to roast oneself *(inf)*
Bra|ten ['bra:tn] M **-s, -** ≈ pot roast meat *no indef art, no pl*; *(im Ofen gebraten)* joint *(Brit)*, roast, roast meat *no indef art, no pl*; **kalter ~** cold meat; **ein fetter ~** *(fig)* a prize catch; **den ~ riechen** *or* **schmecken** *(inf)* to smell a rat *(inf)*, to get wind of it/something; **einen ~ in der Röhre haben** *(inf)* to have a bun in the oven *(inf)*
Bra|ten-: **Bra|ten|fett** NT meat fat and juices *pl*, drippings *(esp US)*; **Bra|ten|fleisch** NT meat for roasting, roasting meat; *(für die Pfanne)* meat for frying, frying meat; **Bra|ten|rock** M frock coat, Prince Albert (coat) *(US)*; **Bra|ten|saft** M meat juices *pl*, meat drippings *pl (esp US)*, juices *pl or* drippings *pl (esp US)* from the meat; **Bra|ten|so|ße** F gravy; **Bra|ten|wen|der** [-vɛndɐ] M **-s, -** fish slice
Brat-: **brat|fer|tig** ADJ oven-ready; **Brat|fett** NT fat for roasting; *(für die Pfanne)* fat for frying; **Brat|fisch** M fried fish; **Brat|hähn|chen** NT, *(Aus, S Ger)* **Brat|hendl** NT roast chicken; **Brat|he|ring** M fried herring *(sold cold)*; **Brat|huhn** NT, **Brat|hühn|chen** NT roast chicken; *(= Huhn zum Braten)* roasting chicken; **Brat|kar|tof|feln** PL fried *or* sauté potatoes; **Brat|kar|tof|fel|ver|hält|nis** NT *(hum)* **er hat ein ~ mit ihr** he only sees her because she feeds and waters him *(hum)*; **er sucht ein ~** he's looking for a meal ticket
Brat|ling ['bra:tlɪŋ] M **-s, -e** *(Cook)* veggieburger, Vegeburger®, vegetarian rissole
Brat-: **Brat|ofen** M oven; **Brat|pfan|ne** F frying pan; **Brat|röh|re** F oven; **Brat|rost** M grill; *(über offenem Feuer auch)* gridiron
Brat|sche ['bra:tʃə] F **-, -n** viola
Brat|scher ['bra:tʃɐ] M **-s, -**, **Brat|sche|rin** [-ərɪn] F **-, -nen**, **Brat|schist** [bra'tʃɪst] M **-en, -en**, **Brat|schis|tin** [-'tʃɪstɪn] F **-, -nen** violist, viola player
Brat-: **Brat|spieß** M skewer; *(= Teil des Grills)* spit; *(= Gericht)* kebab; **Brat|wurst** F, **Brat|würst|chen** NT *(zum Braten)* (frying) sausage; *(gebraten)* (fried) sausage
Bräu [brɔy] NT **-(e)s, -e** *(esp S Ger) (= Biersorte)* brew, beer; *(= Brauerei)* brewery; *(rare: = Schenke)* inn *(old)*, pub *(Brit)*
Brauch [braux] M **-(e)s, Bräu|che** ['brɔyçə] custom, tradition; **nach altem ~** according to (established) custom *or* tradition; **etw ist ~** sth is traditional, sth is the custom; **so ist es ~, so will es der ~** that's the tradition *or* custom; **das ist bei uns so ~** *(inf)* that's traditional with us
brauch|bar ADJ **a** *(= benutzbar)* useable; *Plan* workable; *(= nützlich)* useful **b** *(= ordentlich) Schüler, Idee* decent, reasonable; *Arbeit, Arbeiter etc auch* useful *attr (inf)*
Brauch|bar|keit ['brauxba:ɐkait] F **-**, *no pl* usefulness; *(von Plan)* workability
brau|chen ['brauxn] VT **a** *(= nötig haben)* to need, to require *(form)* *(für, zu* for)
b *(bei Zeitangaben)* **Zeit/zwei Minuten** *etc* **~** to need time/two minutes *etc*; **normalerweise brauche ich zwei Stunden dafür** I normally take two hours to do it; **wenn 5 Männer 3 Stunden ~, …** if 5 men take 3 hours …; **es braucht alles seine Zeit** everything takes time; **das braucht seine Zeit** that takes time; **wie lange braucht man, um …?** how long does it take to …?; **er hat zwei Tage dafür gebraucht** he took two days over it *(Brit)*, he needed two days to do it
c *(inf: = nützlich finden)* **das könnte ich ~** I could do with that, I could use that; **wir können das/ihn nicht ~** we could *or* can do without that/him, we don't need that/him; **das kann ich gerade ~!** *(iro)* that's all I need!; **kannst du die Sachen ~?** have you any use for the things?, are the things of any use to you?; **er ist zu allem zu ~** *(inf)* he's a really useful type (to have around) *(inf)*; **heute bin ich zu nichts zu ~** *(inf)* I'm useless today *(inf)*
d *(= benutzen) Waffe, Verstand, Gerät* to use → *auch* **gebraucht**
e *(inf: = verbrauchen)* to use (up); *Strom etc* to use
VI *impers (dated, geh: = bedürfen)* **es braucht ei-**

ner Sache *(gen)* sth is necessary **V AUX** to need; **du brauchst das nicht tun** you needn't do that, you've no need to do that, you don't have *or* need to do that; **du brauchst es ihm nicht (zu) sagen** you needn't tell him that, you don't need to tell him that; *(= er weiß das schon)* you don't need to tell him that; **du hättest das nicht (zu) tun ~** you needn't have done that, you didn't need to do that, you had no need to do that; **du brauchst nur an(zu)rufen** you only have *or* need to call, you need only call; **es braucht nicht besonders betont zu werden, dass ...** there's no need to stress the fact that ...; **es hätte nicht sein ~** there was no need for that; *(= das hätte nicht geschehen müssen)* that needn't have happened

Brauch|tum ['brauxtu:m] **NT -s,** *(rare)* **-tümer** [-ty:mɐ] customs *pl,* traditions *pl;* **zum ~ in diesem Land gehört ...** one of the customs in this country is ...

Brauch|was|ser **NT** process water

Braue ['brauə] **F -, -n** (eye)brow

brau|en ['brauən] **VT** *Bier* to brew; *(inf: = zubereiten) Tee* to brew up; *Kaffee* to make; *Zaubertrank, Punsch etc* to concoct **VI** **a** *(= Bier brauen)* to brew **b** *(old liter, Nebel)* to build up

Brau|er ['brauɐ] **M -s, -, Brau|e|rin** [-ərɪn] **F -, -nen** brewer

Brau|e|rei [brauə'rai] **F -, -en** **a** brewery **b** *no pl (= das Brauen)* brewing

Brau|e|rei|we|sen **NT** brewing trade *or* industry

Brau-: **Brau|haus** **NT** brewery; **Brau|meis|ter(in)** **M(F)** master brewer

braun [braun] **ADJ** brown; *(von Sonne auch) Mensch, Haut* (sun)tanned; *(inf: = braunhaarig)* brown-haired; *(pej: = Nazibraun)* Nazi; **~ werden** *(Mensch)* to get a (sun)tan, to go *(Brit) or* get brown, to tan; **~ gebrannt** (sun)tanned, bronzed, brown; **von der Sonne ~ gebrannt sein** to be tanned (by the sun); **die Braunen** *(old: = Pferde)* the brown *or* bay horses; *(= Nazis)* the Brownshirts

Braun [braun] **NT -s, -** brown

Braun-: **braun|äu|gig** **ADJ** brown-eyed; **Braun|bär** **M** brown bear

Brau|ne(r) ['braunə] **M** *decl as adj* **a** *(= Pferd)* bay (horse) **b** *(Aus: = Kaffee)* **ein großer/kleiner ~r** a large/small white coffee, a large/small coffee with milk

Bräu|ne ['brɔynə] **F -,** *no pl (= braune Färbung)* brown(ness); *(von Sonne)* (sun)tan

bräu|nen ['brɔynən] **VT** *(Cook)* to brown; *(Sonne etc)* to tan → *auch* **gebräunt** **VI** *(Cook)* to go *or* turn brown; *(Mensch)* to tan, to go brown *(Brit); (Sonne)* to tan; **sich in der Sonne ~ lassen** to get a (sun)tan **VR** *(Haut)* to get *or (Brit)* go brown; *(Mensch auch)* to tan

Braun-: **Braun|fäu|le** **F** *(Bot, Agr)* blight; **braun|ge|brannt** **ADJ** *attr* → **braun**; **braun|haa|rig** **ADJ** brown-haired; *Frau auch* brunette; **Braun|hemd** **NT** *usu pl (Hist: = Nazi)* (Nazi) brownshirt *or* Brownshirt; **Braun|kohl** **M** *(dial)* (curly) kale; **Braun|koh|le** **F** brown coal

bräun|lich ['brɔynlɪç] **ADJ** brownish, browny

braun|rot **ADJ** reddish brown

Braun|sche Röh|re ['braunʃə-] **F** *(Tech)* cathode-ray tube

Braun|schweig ['braunʃvaik] **NT -s** Brunswick

Bräu|nung **F -, -en** browning; *(von Haut)* bronzing; **eine tiefe ~ der Haut** a deep (sun)tan

Bräu|nungs|creme **F** (quick-)tanning lotion

Bräu|nungs|stu|dio **NT** tanning studio

Braus [braus] **M** → **Saus**

Brau|se ['brauzə] **F -, -n** **a** *(= Dusche, Duschvorrichtung)* shower; **sich unter die ~ stellen** to have a shower **b** *(= Brauseaufsatz)* shower attachment; *(an Schlauch, Gießkanne)* rose, spray (attachment) **c** *(= Getränk)* pop; *(= Limonade)* (fizzy) lemonade; *(= Brausepulver)* lemonade powder

Brau|se-: **Brau|se|bad** **NT** shower (bath); **Brau|se|kopf** **M** *(dated)* hothead

brau|sen ['brauzn] **VI** **a** *(= tosen)* to roar; *(Orgel, Beifall)* to thunder; *(Jubel)* to ring out; *(Ohren)* to ring, to buzz; *(= sprudeln) (Wasser, Brandung)* to foam; *(geh, Blut)* to pound; **es brauste mir in den Ohren, es brauste in meinen Ohren** my ears were ringing *or* buzzing; **~der Beifall** thunderous applause **b** *aux sein (= rasen, rennen, schnell fahren)* to race **c** *auch vr (= duschen)* to (have a) shower **VT** *(= abspülen) Gegenstände* to rinse (off); *(= abduschen) Körperteil, Kinder* to put under the shower

Brau|se-: **Brau|se|pul|ver** **NT** sherbet; **Brau|se|tab|let|te** **F** effervescent tablet; **Brau|se|wür|fel** **M** tablet of lemonade powder

Braut [braut] **F -, Bräute** ['brɔytə] **a** *(bei Hochzeit)* bride; *(dated) (= Verlobte)* fiancée, betrothed *(old),* bride-to-be; *(= Freundin)* girl(friend); **~ Christi** bride of Christ **b** *(sl: = Frau, Mädchen)* bird *(esp Brit inf),* chick *(esp US inf)*

Braut-: **Braut|bett** **NT** nuptial *or* marital bed; **Braut|füh|rer** **M** ≈ person who gives away the bride; **Braut|ge|mach** **NT** *(Hist)* nuptial chamber

Bräu|ti|gam ['brɔytɪgam, 'brɔytigam] **M -s, -e** (bride)groom; *(dated: = Verlobter)* fiancé, betrothed *(old),* husband-to-be

Braut-: **Braut|jung|fer** **F** bridesmaid; **Braut|kleid** **NT** wedding dress; **Braut|kranz** **M** *headdress of myrtle leaves traditionally worn by a bride*; **Braut|leu|te** **PL** = **Brautpaar**; **Braut|mo|den|ge|schäft** **NT** bridal shop *or* store; **Braut|mut|ter** **F** *pl* **-mütter** bride's mother; **Braut|paar** **NT** bride and (bride)groom, bridal pair *or* couple; *(dated: = Verlobte)* engaged couple; **Braut|schau** **F** **auf (die) ~ gehen** to go looking for a bride *or* wife; **auf ~ sein** to be looking for a bride *or* wife; *(hum sl)* to be out to make a kill *(inf)*; **Braut|schlei|er** **M** wedding *or* bridal veil; **Braut|schmuck** **M** wedding jewellery *(esp Brit) or* jewelry *(esp US)*; **Braut|staat** **M** wedding finery; **Braut|stand** **M,** *no pl (dated)* engagement; **Braut|suche** **F** = **Brautschau**; **Braut|un|ter|richt** **M** *in RC church, religious instruction of engaged couple prior to marriage*; **Braut|va|ter** **M** bride's father; **Braut|wer|bung** **F** courtship, wooing; **Braut|zeit** **F** last few weeks before the wedding

Brau|we|sen **NT,** *no pl* brewing (industry)

brav [bra:f] **ADJ** **a** *(= gehorsam) Kind* good, well-behaved; **sei schön ~!** be a good boy/girl **b** *(= rechtschaffen)* upright, worthy; *(= bieder) Frisur, Kleid* plain **c** *(dated: = tapfer)* brave **ADV** **a** *(= artig)* **~ (gemacht)!** *(zu Tier)* good boy!, well done; **iss das ~ leer** be a good boy/girl and eat it up, eat it up like a good boy/girl **b** *(= ganz ordentlich)* **~ seine Pflicht tun** to do one's duty without complaining; **etw zu ~ spielen** *(pej)* to give an uninspired rendition of sth

Brav|heit **F -,** *no pl* **a** *(= Gehorsamkeit: von Kind)* good behaviour *(Brit) or* behavior *(US)* **b** *(= Rechtschaffenheit)* uprightness, worthiness; *(= Biederkeit: von Frisur, Kleid)* plainness **c** *(dated: = Tapferkeit)* bravery

bra|vo ['bra:vo] **INTERJ** well done; *(für Künstler)* bravo

Bra|vo|ruf **M** cheer

Bra|vour [bra'vu:ɐ] **F -,** *no pl (geh)* bravura; *(old: = Kühnheit)* bravery, daring; **mit ~** with style

Bra|vour|leis|tung [bra'vu:ɐ-] **F** *(geh)* brilliant performance

bra|vou|rös [bravu'rø:s] *(geh)* **ADJ** **a** *(= meisterhaft)* brilliant **b** *(= forsch)* **mit ~em Tempo** with verve **ADV** **a** *(= meisterhaft)* brilliantly **b** *(= kühn)* boldly; **etw ~ in Angriff nehmen** to attack *or* tackle sth with verve *or* gusto

Bra|vour|stück [bra'vu:ɐ-] **NT** *(geh)* brilliant coup; *(Mus)* bravura

Bra|vur [bra'vu:ɐ] **F** *(etc)* → **Bravour** *etc*

BRD [be:|ɛr'de:] **F -** *abbr von* **Bundesrepublik Deutschland** FRG

> **BRD**
>
> **BRD** is the official abbreviation for **Bundesrepublik Deutschland**. Formerly this name distinguished West Germany from East Germany (**DDR**). Since re-unification on October 3rd 1990 the **BRD** has consisted of 16 **Länder**, whose powers are subordinate to those of the Federal Government. The constitution of the **BRD** is set by the **Grundgesetz**.

Break [bre:k] **NT OR M -s, -s** *(Tennis)* break

Break-even-Point [bre:k'li:vnpɔint] **M -s, -s** *(Econ)* breakeven point

Brech-: **brech|bar** **ADJ** *(lit, fig)* breakable; **Brech|boh|nen** **PL** French beans *pl (Brit),* green *or* wax beans *(US)*; **Brech|durch|fall** **M** diarrhoea *(Brit) or* diarrhea *(US)* and sickness; **Brech|ei|sen** **NT** crowbar; *(von Dieb)* jemmy, jimmy *(US)*

bre|chen ['brɛçn] *pret* **brach** [bra:x], *ptp* **gebrochen** [gə'brɔxn] **VT** **a** *(= zerbrechen, herausbrechen)* to break; *Schiefer, Stein, Marmor* to cut; *Widerstand* to overcome, to break; *Licht* to refract; *(geh: = pflücken) Blumen* to pluck, to pick; **sich/jdm den Arm ~** to break one's/sb's arm; **einer Flasche den Hals ~** to crack (open) a bottle; **das wird ihm das Genick** *or* **den Hals ~** *(fig)* that will bring about his downfall; **jdm die Treue ~** to break trust with sb; *(Liebhaber etc)* to be unfaithful to sb → *auch* **gebrochen, Bahn a, Eis a, Ehe**

b *(= erbrechen)* to vomit (up), to throw up

VI **a** *aux sein* to break; **seine Augen brachen** *(old, liter)* he passed away; **mir bricht das Herz** it breaks my heart; **zum Brechen** *or* **~d voll sein** to be full to bursting

b **mit jdm/etw ~** to break with sb/sth

c *(= sich erbrechen)* to be sick, to throw up

VR *(Wellen)* to break; *(Lichtstrahl)* to be refracted; *(Schall)* to rebound *(an +dat* off)

Bre|cher ['brɛçɐ] **M -s, -** **a** *(= Welle)* breaker **b** *(Tech)* crusher

Brech-: **Brech|mit|tel** **NT** emetic; **er/das ist das reinste ~ (für mich)** he/it makes me feel ill *or* sick; **Brech|reiz** **M** nausea; **ein leichter ~** a slight touch of nausea; **Brech|stan|ge** **F** crowbar; **mit der ~** *(fig)* using the sledgehammer approach

Bre|chung ['brɛçʊŋ] **F -, -en** **a** *(der Wellen)* breaking; *(des Lichts)* refraction; *(des Schalls)* rebounding **b** *(Ling)* mutation

Bre|chungs|win|kel **M** angle of refraction

Bre|douil|le [bre'dʊljə] **F -,** *no pl* **in der ~ sein** *or* **sitzen** to be in a scrape *(inf)*; **in die ~ geraten** *or* **kommen** to get into a scrape *(inf)*

Brei [brai] **M -(e)s, -e** mush, paste, goo *(inf)*; *(für Kinder, Kranke)* mash *(Brit),* mush *(esp US),* semi-solid food; *(= Haferbrei)* porridge; *(= Grießbrei)* semolina; *(= Reisbrei)* rice pudding; *(= Papierbrei)* pulp; **verrühren Sie die Zutaten zu einem dünnen ~** mix the ingredients to a thin paste; **die Lava fließt wie ein zäher ~** the lava flows like a sluggish pulp; **jdn zu ~ schlagen** *(inf)* to beat sb to a pulp *(inf)*; **um den heißen ~ herumreden** *(inf)* to beat about *(Brit) or* around the bush *(inf)*; **jdm ~ um den Mund** *or* **ums Maul schmieren** *(inf)* to soft-soap sb *(inf)* → **Katze, Koch**

brei|ig ['braiɪç] **ADJ** mushy; **eine ~e Masse** a paste, a paste-like substance

breit [brait] **ADJ** **a** broad; *(esp bei Maßangabe)* wide; *Bekanntenkreis, Publikum* wide; *Interessen* broad, wide; *Schrift* broadly spaced, sprawling; **etw ~er machen** to broaden *or* widen sth; **~es Lachen** guffaw; **er hat ein ~es Lachen** he guffaws; **die ~e Masse** the masses *pl,* the broad mass of the population; **die ~e Öffentlichkeit** the public at large; **ein ~es Angebot** a broad *or* wide selection; **~e Streuung des Eigentums** widespread distribution of property, distribution of property on a broad basis; **er hat einen ~en Rücken** *or* **Buckel** *(fig inf)* he has a broad back, his shoulders are broad

b *(sl: = betrunken, unter Drogen)* high
ADV **den Stoff ~ nehmen** to take the material widthways; **~ lachen** to guffaw; **~ sprechen** to speak with a broad accent; **~ gebaut** sturdily built; **~ gefächert** *(Firmengruppe, Messe, Kritik)* wide-ranging; **ein ~ gefächertes Angebot** a wide range; **die Schuhe ~ treten** to wear one's shoes out of shape; **der Stoff liegt doppelt ~** the material is double width; **sich ~ hinsetzen** to sit down squarely; **setz dich doch nicht so ~ hin** don't take up so much room

Breit|band-: **Breit|band|an|ti|bio|ti|kum** NT *(Pharm)* broad-spectrum antibiotic; **Breit|band|ka|bel** NT broadband cable; **Breit|band|(kom|mu|ni|ka|ti|ons)|netz** NT *(Telec)* broadband (communications) network; **Breit|band|laut|spre|cher** M *(Tech)* full-range loudspeaker; **Breit|band|ver|tei|ler** M broadband distributor

breit-: **breit|bei|nig** ADJ **in ~er Stellung** with one's legs apart; **~er Gang** rolling gait ADV with one's legs apart; **Breit|cord** M **-(e)s, -e** *or* **-s** *(Tex)* jumbo cord; **breit drü|cken**, **breit+drü|cken** *sep* VT to press flat

Brei|te ['braitə] F **-, -n** **a** breadth; *(von Dialekt, Aussprache)* broadness; *(esp bei Maßangaben)* width; *(von Angebot)* breadth; *(von Interessen)* breadth, wide range; **der ~ nach** widthways; **etw in aller ~ erklären** to explain sth in great detail; **in voller ~ vor jdm** smack in front of sb *(inf)*; **in die ~ gehen** to go into detail; *(inf: = dick werden)* to put on weight, to put it on a bit *(inf)* **b** *(Geog)* latitude; *(= Gebiet)* part of the world; **in südlichere ~n fahren** *(inf)* to travel to more southerly climes *or* parts; **es liegt (auf) 20° nördlicher/südlicher ~** it lies 20° north/south; **in unseren ~n** in our area

brei|ten ['braitn] VTR to spread; **jdm etw über die Beine** *etc* **~** to spread sth across sb's legs *etc*; **sich über das Tal/jds Gesicht ~** to spread across the valley/across *or* over sb's face

Brei|ten-: **Brei|ten|ar|beit** F, *no pl* broader *or* more general work; **Brei|ten|grad** M (degree of) latitude; **Brei|ten|kreis** M parallel; **Brei|ten|sport** M popular sport; **Brei|ten|wir|kung** F *(von Roman etc)* large *or* widespread impact

Breit-: **breit|flä|chig** ADJ *Gesicht* wide; *Ausbreitung* over a wide area ADV over a wide area; **~ malen** to paint with broad strokes; **breit|ge|fä|chert** [-gəfɛçɐt] ADJ → **breit** ADV; **Breit|kord** [-kɔrt] M **-(e)s, -s** *or* **-e** [-də] = **Breitcord**; **breit|krem|pig** [-krɛmpɪç] ADJ broad-brimmed

Breit|ling M whitebait

Breit-: **breit+ma|chen**, **breit ma|chen** △ VR *(inf, Mensch)* to make oneself at home; *(Gefühl, Angst, Skepsis, Befürchtung)* to spread; **wenn er sich auf dem Sofa breitmacht …** when he plants himself on the sofa …; **mach dich doch nicht so breit!** don't take up so much room; **die Touristen haben sich im Hotel breitgemacht** the tourists in the hotel are behaving as if they owned the place → **Bein a**; **breit|na|sig** ADJ *Mensch* broad-nosed, flat-nosed; **breit|ran|dig** ADJ *Hut* broad-brimmed; *Schwimmbecken, Gefäß, Brille* broad-rimmed; **Breit|rei|fen** M *(Mot)* wide tyre *(Brit)* or tire *(US)*; **breit+schla|gen** VT *sep irreg (inf)* **jdn (zu etw) ~** to talk sb round *(Brit)* or around *(US)* (to sth); **sich ~ lassen** to let oneself be talked round *(Brit) or* around *(US)*; **breit|schul|te|rig**, **breit|schult|rig** ADJ broad-shouldered; **Breit|schwanz** M, *no pl* caracul; **Breit|sei|te** F *(Naut, auch fig)* broadside; *(von Tisch)* short end; **eine ~ abgeben** to fire a broadside *(auch fig)*; **Breit|spur|bahn** F broad-gauge railway; **breit|spu|rig** [-ʃpuːrɪç] ADJ *Bahn* broad-gauge *attr*; *Straße* wide-laned ADV *(fig)* flashily, showily; **~ reden/auftreten** to speak/behave in a showy manner; **breit+tre|ten** VT *sep irreg (inf)* to go on about *(inf)*; *Thema, Witz* to flog to death *(inf)*; **Breit|wand** F wide screen; **etw in ~ drehen** to film sth for the wide screen; **Breit|wand|film** M film for the wide screen

Bre|men ['breːmən] NT **-s** Bremen

Bre|mer ['breːmɐ] ADJ *attr* Bremen

Bre|mer ['breːmɐ] M **-s, -**, **Bre|me|rin** [-ərɪn] F **-, -nen** native of Bremen; *(= Einwohner)* inhabitant of Bremen

bre|misch ['breːmɪʃ] ADJ Bremen *attr*

Brems-: **Brems|ab|stand** M *(Mot)* braking distance; **Brems|an|la|ge** F braking system; **Brems|ba|cke** F brake block; **Brems|be|lag** M brake lining

Brem|se ['brɛmzə] F **-, -n** *(bei Fahrzeugen)* brake; **auf die ~(n) treten/steigen** *(inf)* to put on *or* apply/slam on *(inf)* the brake(s)

Brem|se F **-, -n** *(= Insekt)* horsefly

brem|sen ['brɛmzn] VI **a** *(Fahrer, Auto)* to brake; *(Vorrichtung)* to function as a brake; **der Dynamo bremst** the dynamo acts as a brake; **der Wind bremst** the wind slows you *etc* down **b** *(inf: = zurückstecken)* to ease off, to put on the brakes *(inf)*; **mit etw ~** to cut down (on) sth; **jetzt sollten wir mit den Ausgaben ~** it's time to apply the (financial) brakes
VT **a** *Fahrzeug* to brake **b** *(fig)* to restrict, to limit; *Entwicklung* to slow down; *Begeisterung* to dampen; *(inf) jdn* to check; **er ist nicht zu ~** *(inf)* there's no stopping him
VR *(inf)* **sich in seiner Ausdrucksweise ~** to moderate one's language; **ich kann** *or* **werd mich ~** not likely!, no fear!

Brem|sen|stich M horsefly bite

Brem|ser ['brɛmzɐ] M **-s, -** *(Rail, Sport)* brakeman

Brem|se|rin ['brɛmzərɪn] F **-, -nen** *(Rail, Sport)* brakewoman

Brems-: **Brems|fall|schirm** M brake parachute; **Brems|flüs|sig|keit** F brake fluid; **Brems|griff** M brake lever; **Brems|he|bel** M brake lever; **Brems|klap|pe** F *(Aviat)* brake flap; **Brems|klotz** M *(Aut)* brake pad; **Brems|kraft** F braking power; **Brems|kraft|ver|stär|ker** M servo brake; **Brems|leis|tung** F braking efficiency; **Brems|leuch|te** F, **Brems|licht** NT brake light; **Brems|pe|dal** NT brake pedal; **Brems|pro|be** F brake test; **eine ~ machen** to test one's brakes; **Brems|prüf|stand** M brake test stand; **Brems|ra|ke|te** F retrorocket; **Brems|schlauch** M brake hose; **Brems|schuh** M brake shoe; **Brems|seil** NT brake cable; **Brems|spur** F skid mark *usu pl*; **Brems|stre|cke** F braking *or* stopping distance

Brem|sung F **-, -en** braking

Brems-: **Brems|vor|rich|tung** F brake mechanism; **Brems|weg** M braking *or* stoppng distance

Brenn-: **brenn|bar** ADJ combustible, inflammable, flammable; **leicht ~** highly combustible *or* inflammable; **Brenn|bar|keit** ['brɛnbaːɐkait] F **-**, *no pl* combustibility, inflammability, flammability; **Brenn|dau|er** F *(von Glühbirnen)* life; **Brenn|ele|ment** NT fuel element

bren|nen ['brɛnən] *pret* **brannte** ['brantə], *ptp* **gebrannt** [gə'brant] VI to burn; *(Haus, Wald auch)* to be on fire; *(elektrisches Gerät, Glühbirne etc)* to be on; *(Zigarette, Sparflamme)* to be alight; *(Stich)* to sting; *(Füße)* to hurt, to be sore; **das Streichholz/Feuerzeug brennt nicht** the match/lighter won't light; **auf der Haut/in den Augen ~** to burn *or* sting the skin/eyes; **das Licht ~ lassen** to leave the light on; **im Zimmer brennt noch Licht** the light is still on in the room; **es brennt!** fire, fire!; *(fig)* it's urgent; **wo brennts denn?** *(inf)* what's the panic?; **darauf ~, etw zu tun** to be dying to do sth; **das brennt mir auf der Seele** that is preying on my mind; **es brennt mir unter den Nägeln, zu erfahren, ob …** I am itching *(inf)* or dying to know if … → **Boden a**
VT **a** to burn; *Branntwein* to distil *(Brit)*, to distill *(US)*; *Mandeln, Kaffee* to roast; *Porzellan, Ton, Ziegel* to fire, to bake **b** *(Comput)* CD, DVD to burn, to record
VR *(lit)* to burn oneself *(an +dat* on); *(inf: = sich täuschen)* to be very much mistaken

bren|nend ADJ *(lit, fig)* burning; *Zigarette* lighted; *Durst* raging; *Hass* consuming ADV *(inf: = sehr)* terribly; **sich ~ für etw interessieren** to be really *or* incredibly interested in sth; **ich wüsste ja ~ gern …** I'm dying *or* itching *(inf)* to know …

Bren|ner ['brɛnɐ] M **-s, -** *(Tech)* burner

Bren|ner ['brɛnɐ] M **-s, -**, **Bren|ne|rin** [-ərɪn] F **-, -nen** *(= Branntweinbrenner)* distiller; *(= Kaffeebrenner)* coffee roaster; *(= Ziegelbrenner)* brick-firer

Bren|ne|rei [brɛnə'rai] F **-, -en** distillery; *(= Kaffeebrennerei)* coffee-roasting plant; *(= Ziegelbrennerei)* brickworks *sing or pl*

Brennessel △ F = **Brennnessel**

Brenn-: **Brenn|glas** NT burning glass; **Brenn|holz** NT firewood; **Brenn|kam|mer** F combustion chamber; **Brenn|ma|te|ri|al** NT fuel (for heating); **Brenn|nes|sel** F stinging nettle; **Brenn|ofen** M kiln; **Brenn|punkt** M *(Math, Opt)* focus; **im ~ des Interesses stehen** to be the focal point *or* the focus of attention; **etw in den ~ rücken** *(fig)* to focus attention on sth; **Brenn|sche|re** F curling tongs *pl (Brit)*, curling iron *(US)*; **Brenn|schluss** M *(von Rakete)* burnout; **Brenn|spie|gel** M burning glass; **Brenn|spi|ri|tus** [-ʃpiːritʊs] M methylated spirits *sing or pl*; **Brenn|stab** M fuel rod; **Brenn|stoff** M fuel; **Brenn|stoff|kreis|lauf** M *(in Atomkraftwerk)* (nuclear) fuel cycle; **Brenn|wei|te** F *(Opt)* focal length; **Brenn|wert** M *(Tech, Physiol)* calorific value

brenz|lig ['brɛntslɪç] ADJ **a** **ein ~er Geruch** a smell of burning **b** *(inf) Situation, Angelegenheit* precarious, dicey *(Brit inf)*; **die Sache/die Lage wurde ihm zu ~** things got too hot for him ADV **~ riechen** to smell of burning

Bre|sche ['brɛʃə] F **-, -n** breach, gap; **in etw** *(acc)* **eine ~ schießen** to breach sth; **in die ~ springen** *(fig)* to step into *or* fill the breach; **für jdn/etw eine ~ schlagen** *(fig)* to stand up for sb/sth

Bre|tag|ne [bre'tanjə] F **- die ~** Brittany

Bre|to|ne [bre'toːnə] M **-n, -n**, **Bre|to|nin** [-'toːnɪn] F **-, -nen** Breton

bre|to|nisch [bre'toːnɪʃ] ADJ Breton

Brett [brɛt] NT **-(e)s, -er** ['brɛtɐ] **a** *(= Holzplatte)* board; *(länger und dicker)* plank; *(= Spielbrett, Sprungbrett)* board; *(= Bücherbrett, Gewürzbrett)* shelf; *(inf: = Tablett)* tray; *(= Frühstücksbrett)* platter, wooden plate; **Schwarzes ~** notice board *(Brit)*, bulletin board *(US)*; **etw mit ~ern vernageln** to board sth up; **hier ist die Welt mit ~ern vernagelt** this is a parochial little place; **ich habe heute ein ~ vor dem Kopf** *(inf)* I can't think straight today → **Stein a**
b **Bretter** PL *(fig)* (= *Bühne)* stage, boards *pl*, planks *pl (inf)*; *(= Boden des Boxrings)* floor, canvas; *(= Skier)* planks *pl (sl)*; **über die ~er gehen** *(Theat)* to be put on; **die ~er, die die Welt bedeuten** the stage; **auf den ~ern stehen** to be on the stage; *(auf Skiern)* to ski; **jdn auf die ~er schicken** *(Sport)* to send sb to the canvas, to floor sb, to knock sb down

Brett|chen ['brɛtçən] NT **-s, -** *(inf)* platter, wooden plate; *(zum Schneiden)* board

Bret|ter-: **Bret|ter|bo|den** M wooden floor *(made from floorboards)*; **Bret|ter|bu|de** F booth; *(pej)* shack

bret|tern ['brɛtɐn] VI *(inf, Fahrzeug, Fahrer)* to race (along); **über die Autobahn ~** to tear along the motorway *(Brit)* or freeway *(US)*

Bret|ter-: **Bret|ter|wand** F wooden wall; *(= Trennwand)* wooden partition; *(= Zaun, für Reklame)* hoarding; **Bret|ter|ver|schlag** M *(= Schuppen)* (wooden) shed; *(angebaut)* (wooden) lean-to; *(= Trennwand)* wooden partition; **Bret|ter|zaun** M wooden fence; *(an Baustellen auch)* hoarding

Brett|spiel NT board game

Bret|zel F -, -n *(Sw)* pretzel

Bre|vier [bre'viːɐ] NT -s, -e **a** *(Eccl)* breviary **b** *(= Auswahl von Texten)* extracts *pl*; *(= Leitfaden)* guide (+*gen* to)

Bre|ze ['breːtsə] F -, -n *(S Ger)* pretzel

Bre|zel ['breːtsl] F -, -n pretzel; **das geht wies ~ backen** it's no trouble at all

brich [brɪç] IMPER *sing von* **brechen**

Bridge [brɪtʃ] NT -, *no pl (Cards)* bridge

Brief [briːf] M -(e)s, -e **a** letter; *(Bibl)* epistle; **aus seinen ~en** from his letters *or* correspondence; **etw als ~ schicken** to send sth (by) letter post *(esp Brit)*; **jdm ~ und Siegel auf etw** *(acc)* **geben** to give sb one's word **b** *(St Ex: = Briefkurs)* selling rate, offer price

Brief- *in cpds* letter; **Brief|ab|la|ge** F letter file; **Brief|adel** M title conferred by letters patent; *(= Leute)* nonhereditary nobility; **Brief|be|schwe|rer** [-bəʃveːrɐ] M -s, - paperweight; **Brief|block** M *pl* **-blöcke** *or* **-blocks** writing *or* letter pad; **Brief|bo|gen** M (sheet of) writing *or* letter *or* note paper; **Brief|bom|be** F letter bomb

Brief|chen ['briːfçən] NT -s, - **a** note **b** *(für Shampoo, Creme, Pulver)* sachet; *(für Streichhölzer)* book; *(für Nadeln)* packet, paper; *(für Rauschgift)* small packet *(containing drugs)*

Brief-: **Brief|druck|sa|che** F circular; **Brief|ein|wurf** M *(in Tür)* letter box *(Brit)*, mailbox *(US)*; *(in Postamt etc)* postbox *(Brit)*, mailbox *(US)*

brie|fen [briːfn] VT *(= informieren, einweisen)* to brief

Brief-: **Brief|fach** NT pigeonhole; **Brief|form** F **in ~** in letter form; *(= mittels Brief)* by letter; **Brief|freund(in)** M(F) pen friend, pen pal *(inf)*; **Brief|freund|schaft** F correspondence with a pen friend; **eine ~ mit jdm haben** to be pen friends with sb; **Brief|ge|heim|nis** NT privacy of the post *(Brit) or* mail

Brie|fing ['briːfɪŋ] NT -s, -s briefing

Brief|kar|te F correspondence card

Brief|kas|ten M *(am Haus)* letter box *(Brit)*, mailbox *(US)*; *(der Post®)* postbox *(Brit)*, pillar box *(dated Brit)*, mailbox *(US)*; *(in Zeitungen)* problem column, agony column; **elektronischer ~** *(Comput)* electronic mailbox → **tot b**

Brief|kas|ten-: **Brief|kas|ten|fir|ma** F **das ist nur eine ~** that firm is just an accommodation address; **Brief|kas|ten|on|kel** M *(inf)* agony columnist *or* uncle *(inf)*; **Brief|kas|ten|tan|te** F *(inf)* agony columnist *or* aunt *(inf)*

Brief-: **Brief|kon|takt** M written contact; **in ~ stehen** to correspond with; **sie stehen in ~** they correspond (with each other), they write to each other; **Brief|kopf** M letterhead; *(handgeschrieben)* heading; **Brief|kurs** M *(St Ex)* selling rate, offer price; **Brief|ku|vert** NT envelope

brief|lich ['briːflɪç] ADJ by letter; **wir bitten um ~e Mitteilung** please inform us by letter; **~er Verkehr** correspondence ADV by letter; **mit jdm ~ verkehren** to correspond with sb

Brief|mar|ke F stamp

Brief|mar|ken- *in cpds* stamp; **Brief|mar|ken|al|bum** NT stamp album; **Brief|mar|ken|au|to|mat** M stamp machine; **Brief|mar|ken|bo|gen** M sheet of stamps; **Brief|mar|ken|kun|de** F philately; **Brief|mar|ken|samm|ler(in)** M(F) stamp collector, philatelist; **Brief|mar|ken|samm|lung** F stamp collection

Brief-: **Brief|öff|ner** M letter opener, paper knife; **Brief|pa|pier** NT letter *or* writing *or* note paper; **Brief|por|to** NT postage; *(= Gebühr)* postage rate for letters, letter rate; **Brief|post** F letter post *(esp Brit)*; **Brief|qua|li|tät** F *(Comput)* letter quality; **Brief|ro|man** M epistolary novel, novel in letter form; **Brief|sen|dung** F letter, item sent by letter post *(esp Brit)*; **Brief|ta|sche** F wallet, billfold *(US)*; **Brief|tau|be** F carrier pigeon; **Brief|trä|ger** M postman *(Brit)*, mailman *(US)*; **Brief|trä|ge|rin** F postwoman *(Brit)*, mailwoman *(US)*; **Brief|um|schlag** M envelope; **Brief|ver|kehr** M correspondence; **Brief|waa|ge** F letter scales *pl*; **Brief|wahl** F postal vote; **seine Stimme durch ~ abgeben** to use the postal vote, to vote by post *(Brit)*; **Brief|wäh|ler(in)** M(F) postal voter; **Brief|wech|sel** M correspondence; **im ~ mit jdm stehen, einen ~ mit jdm führen** to be in correspondence with sb, to be corresponding with sb; **Brief|zu|stel|ler** M *(form)* postman *(Brit)*, mailman *(US)*; **Brief|zu|stel|le|rin** F *(form)* postwoman *(Brit)*, mailwoman *(US)*

Brie|kä|se ['briː-] M brie

Bries [briːs] NT -es, -e [-zə] *(Physiol)* thymus; *(Cook)* sweetbread

briet *pret von* **braten**

Bri|ga|de [bri'gaːdə] F -, -n **a** *(Mil)* brigade **b** *(DDR)* (work) team *or* group

Bri|ga|de|ge|ne|ral(in) M(F) brigadier *(Brit)*, brigadier general *(US)*; *(in Luftwaffe)* air commodore *(Brit)*, brigadier general *(US)*

Bri|ga|dier [briga'diːɐ] M -s, -e *(DDR)* (work) team leader

Brigg [brɪk] F -, -s *(Naut: = Schiff)* brig

Bri|kett [bri'kɛt] NT -s, -s *or (rare)* -e briquette

Bri|kett|zan|ge F fire tongs *pl*

bril|lant [brɪl'jant] ADJ brilliant ADV brilliantly; **~ aussehen** to look beautiful

Bril|lant [brɪl'jant] M -en, -en brilliant, diamond

Bril|lant- *in cpds* diamond; **Bril|lant|feu|er|werk** NT cascade; **Bril|lant|kol|li|er** NT diamond necklace; **Bril|lant|ring** M diamond ring; **Bril|lant|schmuck** M diamonds *pl*

Bril|lanz [brɪl'jants] F -, *no pl* brilliance

Bril|le ['brɪlə] F -, -n **a** *(Opt)* glasses *pl*, spectacles *pl*, specs *(inf) pl*; *(= Schutzbrille)* goggles *pl*; *(= Sonnenbrille)* glasses *pl*; **eine ~** a pair of glasses *or* spectacles; **eine ~ tragen** to wear glasses → **rosa b** *(= Klosettbrille)* (toilet) seat

Bril|len-: **Bril|len|etui** NT, **Bril|len|fut|te|ral** NT glasses *or* spectacle case; **Bril|len|fas|sung** F, **Bril|len|ge|stell** NT spectacle frames *pl*; **Bril|len|glas** NT lens; **Bril|len|schlan|ge** F *(pej)* four-eyes *(pej inf)*, woman who wears glasses; **Bril|len|trä|ger(in)** M(F) person who wears glasses; **er ist ~** he wears glasses

Bril|li ['brɪli] M -s, -s *(inf)* diamond, rock *(inf)*

bril|lie|ren [brɪl'jiːrən] *ptp* **brilliert** VI *(geh)* to be brilliant; **sie brillierte mit ihrem Gesang** her singing was brilliant

Brim|bo|ri|um [brɪm'boːriʊm] NT -s, *no pl (inf)* fuss

brin|gen ['brɪŋən]
pret **brachte** ['braxtə], *ptp* **gebracht** [gə'braxt]

TRANSITIVES VERB

Im Sinne von *herbringen* wird *bringen* im Englischen mit *to bring* übersetzt, im Sinne von *woanders hinbringen* mit *to take.*

a [= herbringen] to bring; *(= holen)* to bring, to get *(jdm* for *sb)*; **bring mir bitte meine Schuhe** please bring me my shoes; **der Besuch hat mir Blumen gebracht** my visitors brought me flowers; **was für Nachricht bringen Sie?** what news have you got?; **sich** *(dat)* **etw bringen lassen** to have sth brought to one; **der letzte Sommer brachte uns viel Regen** last summer brought us a lot of rain; **Schäfchenwolken bringen schönes Wetter** fleecy clouds bring fine weather; **jdn/etw unter** *or* **in seine Gewalt bringen** to gain control over *or* of sb/sth; **er bringt es nicht übers Herz** *or* **über sich** he can't bring himself to do it; **etw an sich** *(acc)* **bringen** to acquire sth

♦ **etw mit sich bringen der Frühling bringt viele prächtige Blüten mit sich** spring brings lots of wonderful flowers; **seine Vergesslichkeit bringt viele Probleme mit sich** his forgetfulness causes a lot of problems; **die Liebe bringt es mit sich, dass man alles durch eine rosarote Brille sieht** love means you see everything through rose-coloured spectacles *(Brit) or* rose-colored glasses *(US)*

b [= woanders hinbringen] to take; **jdn ins Krankenhaus/zum Bahnhof/nach Hause bringen** to take sb to hospital/to the station/home; **kannst du mich zum Bahnhof bringen?** can you give me a lift to the station?; **bring das Auto in die Garage** put the car in the garage; **die Kinder zu** *or* **ins Bett bringen** to put the children to bed; **das Essen auf den Tisch bringen** to serve the food; **jdm eine Nachricht bringen** to give sb some news; **etw hinter sich** *(acc)* **bringen** to get sth over and done with

c [= einbringen] *Geld, Gewinn* to bring in, to make; *(Boden, Mine etc)* to produce; *Ärger* to cause; *Vorteile* to bring; **das Bild brachte 500 Euro** the picture went for 500 euros; **Freude bringen** to bring joy; **Vergnügen bringen** to give pleasure; **(jdm) Glück/Unglück bringen** to bring (sb) luck/bad luck; **Unglück über jdn bringen** to bring sb unhappiness; **das bringt nichts** *(inf)* it's pointless

d [= lenken, versetzen] **in die richtige Form bringen** to get *or* put in the right form; **jdn/sich in Gefahr bringen** to put sb/oneself in danger; **das bringt dich vors Gericht/ins Gefängnis** you'll end up in court/prison if you do that; **das Gespräch/die Rede auf etw** *(acc)* **bringen** to bring the conversation/talk round to sth; **jdn auf die schiefe Bahn bringen** to lead sb astray; **jdn wieder auf den rechten Weg bringen** *(fig)* to get sb back on the straight and narrow; **jdn außer sich** *(acc)* **bringen** to upset sb; **zum Stillstand bringen** *(Verkehr, Verhandlungen)* to bring to a standstill; *Fahrzeug* to bring to a halt; **jdn zum Lachen/Weinen bringen** to make sb laugh/cry; **jdn zur Verzweiflung bringen** to drive sb to despair; **jdn dazu bringen, etw zu tun** to get sb to do sth

♦ **so weit bringen, dass sie bringt ihn mit ihrer Nörgelei noch so weit, dass er kündigt** her nagging will make him hand in his notice; **wir bringen ihn mit ständigen Ermunterungen noch so weit, dass er sich als Kandidat aufstellen lässt** if we keep on encouraging him we'll get him to put himself forward as a candidate; **du wirst es noch so weit bringen, dass man dich hinauswirft** you will make them throw you out

e [= veröffentlichen] *Verlag* to publish; *(Zeitung)* to print; *(= senden) Bericht etc* to broadcast; **etw in die Zeitung bringen** to publish sth in the paper; *Verlobung, Angebot* to announce sth in the paper; **die Zeitung/das Fernsehen brachte nichts darüber** there was nothing in the paper/on television about it; **die Zeitung brachte einen Artikel darüber** there was an article in the paper about it; **alle Zeitungen brachten es auf der ersten Seite** all the papers had it on the front page; **wir bringen einen Sonderbericht aus Kuba** we now have a special report from Cuba; **wir bringen Nachrichten** here is the news; **um zehn Uhr bringen wir Nachrichten** at ten o'clock we have the news; **die nächsten Nachrichten bringen wir um 10 Uhr** the next news will be at 10 o'clock; **was bringt das Fernsehen/Radio heute Abend?** what's on television/the radio tonight?

f [= aufführen] *Stück* to do; **welche Lieder bringt sie auf ihrer Tournee?** what songs is she doing on her tour?

g [= schaffen, leisten] *sl* **ich bringe diese Übung nicht** I can't do this exercise; **das bringt er nicht** he's not up to it; **hat er das tatsächlich gebracht?** did he really do it?; **er bringts** he's got what it takes; **das Auto bringt 180 km/h** *(inf)* the car can do 180 km/h; **der Motor bringts nicht mehr** the engine has had it *(inf)*; **ihr Typ bringts nicht mehr** her boyfriend can't stand the pace any more *(inf)*; **das kannst du doch nicht bringen** that's not on *(inf)*

h [andere Wendungen]

♦ **es bringen** *(= erreichen)* **es auf 80 Jahre bringen** to reach the age of 80; **der Motor hat es**

auf 180.000 km gebracht the engine has done 180,000 km; **das Auto hat es auf 180.000 km gebracht** the car has clocked up 180,000 km; **er hat es auf 25 Punkte gebracht** he got 25 points; **es zu etwas/nichts bringen** to get somewhere/nowhere; **es (im Leben) weit bringen** to do very well; **es zu Ehren bringen** to win honours *(Brit) or* honors *(US)*; **er hat es bis zum Hauptmann/Direktor gebracht** he made it to captain/director, he got to be captain/director → *auch* **g**

♦ **jdn um etw bringen** to do sb out of sth; **das bringt mich noch um den Verstand** it's driving me mad *(Brit) or* crazy; **der Lärm hat mich um den Schlaf gebracht** the noise stopped me getting any sleep; **jdn/sich ums Leben bringen** to kill sb/oneself

Brin|ger ['brɪŋɐ] **M -s, -** *(inf) (Sache)* the cat's whiskers *(Brit)*; *(Person)* the bee's knees; **das ist auch nicht gerade der ~** it's not exactly brilliant; **er ist auch nicht gerade der ~** he's hardly the bee's knees (himself)

Bring|schuld **F** *(Jur) obligation to be performed at creditor's habitual residence (fig)* obligation to fulfil *(Brit) or* fulfill *(US)*

bri|sant [bri'zant] **ADJ** *(lit, fig)* explosive

Bri|sanz [bri'zants] **F -, -en** explosive force; *(fig)* explosive nature; **ein Thema von äußerster ~** an extremely explosive subject

Bri|se ['bri:zə] **F -, -n** breeze

Bri|tan|ni|en [bri'tanian] **NT -s** *(Hist)* Britain, Britannia *(Hist)*; *(Press: = Großbritannien)* Britain

bri|tan|nisch [bri'tanɪʃ] **ADJ** *(Hist)* Britannic

Bri|te ['brɪtə, 'bri:tə] **M -n, -n**, **Bri|tin** ['brɪtɪn, 'bri:tɪn] **F -, -nen** Briton, Brit *(inf)*; **er ist ~** he is British; **die ~n** the British

bri|tisch ['brɪtɪʃ, 'bri:tɪʃ] **ADJ** British; **die Britischen Inseln** the British Isles

Bröck|chen ['brœkçən] **NT -s, -** *dim von* **Brocken**

brö|cke|lig ['brœkəlɪç] **ADJ** crumbly; *Mauer, Putz* crumbling; **~ werden** to (start to) crumble

brö|ckeln ['brœkln] **VI** *aux sein* **a** *(Haus, Fassade)* to crumble; *(Gestein auch)* to crumble away; *(Preise, Kurse)* to tumble; *(Streikfront)* to crumble; *(Argwohn, Vertrauen etc)* to disintegrate **b** *(sl: = sich übergeben)* to puke *(inf)*

bro|cken ['brɔkn] **VT** *Brot* to break

Bro|cken ['brɔkn] **M -s, -** lump, chunk; *(fig: = Bruchstück)* scrap; *(Hunt)* bait; *(inf: Person)* lump *(inf)*; **das Baby ist ein richtiger ~** the baby's a regular little dumpling *(Brit inf)*, the baby's as plump as a dumpling *(US inf)*; **ein paar ~ Spanisch** a smattering of Spanish; **er schnappte den anderen die besten ~ weg** he snapped up all the best titbits *(Brit) or* tidbits *(US)*; **ein harter ~** *(= Person)* a tough/hard nut *(inf)*, a tough cookie *(inf)*; **das ist ein harter** *or* **dicker ~** that's a tough nut to crack; **die ~ hinschmeißen** *(inf)* to chuck it all in *(inf)*

bro|cken|wei|se **ADV** bit by bit

bro|deln ['bro:dln] **VI** *(Wasser, Suppe)* to bubble; *(in Krater auch)* to seethe; *(Dämpfe, liter: Nebel)* to swirl, to seethe; **es brodelt** *(fig)* there is seething unrest

Bro|dem ['bro:dəm] **M -s, -** *(liter)* foul-smelling vapour *(Brit) or* vapor *(US)*

Broi|ler ['brɔylɐ] **M -s, -** *(dial)* roast chicken

Bro|kat [bro'ka:t] **M -(e)s, -e** brocade

Bro|ker ['bro:kɐ] **M -s, -**, **Bro|ke|rin** [-ərɪn] **F -, -nen** *(St Ex)* (stock)broker; *(Comm)* broker

Bro|ker|fir|ma **F** *(St Ex)* brokerage firm

Bro|ker|haus **NT** *(St Ex)* brokerage house

Brok|ko|li ['brɔkoli] **PL** broccoli *sing*

Brom [bro:m] **NT -s,** *no pl (abbr* **Br***)* bromine

Brom|bee|re ['brɔm-] **F** blackberry, bramble

Brom|beer|strauch **M** blackberry *or* bramble bush

Brom|sil|ber ['bro:m-] **NT** silver bromide

bron|chi|al [brɔn'çia:l] **ADJ** bronchial

Bron|chi|al-: **Bron|chi|al|asth|ma** **NT** bronchial asthma; **Bron|chi|al|ka|tarr(h)** **M** bronchial catarrh; **Bron|chi|al|tee** **M** bronchial tea

Bron|chie ['brɔnçiə] **F -, -n** *usu pl* bronchial tube, bronchus *(form)*

Bron|chi|tis [brɔn'çi:tɪs] **F -, Bronchitiden** [-çi-'ti:dn] bronchitis

Bronn [brɔn] **M -s, -en**, **Bron|nen** ['brɔnən] **M -s, -** *(obs, liter)* fount *(liter)*

Bron|to|sau|rus [brɔnto'zaurus] **M -, -se**, **Bron|to|sau|ri|er** **M** brontosaurus

Bron|ze ['brõ:sə] **F -, -n** bronze

Bron|ze-: **Bron|ze|me|dail|le** ['brõ:sə-] **F** bronze medal; **bron|ze|far|ben** ['brõ:səfarbn] **ADJ** bronze, bronze-coloured *(Brit) or* -colored *(US)*

bron|zen ['brõ:sn] **ADJ** bronze **ADV** **~ schimmern** to glint like bronze

Bron|ze-: **Bron|ze|plas|tik** ['brõ:sə-] **F** *(Art)* bronze sculpture, bronze; **Bron|ze|zeit** ['brõ:sə-] **F,** *no pl* Bronze Age

Bro|sa|me ['bro:za:mə] **F -, -n** *(liter)* crumb

Bro|sche ['brɔʃə] **F -, -n** brooch

bro|schiert [brɔ'ʃi:ɐt] **ADJ** *Ausgabe* paperback; *(= geheftet)* sewn; *(= geklammert)* wire-stitched; **jetzt auch ~ erhältlich** now also available in paperback; **~es Heftchen** booklet

Bro|schur [brɔ'ʃu:ɐ] **F -, -en** *(Typ)* cut flush binding

Bro|schur|ar|beit **F** *(Typ)* cut flush work

Bro|schü|re [brɔ'ʃy:rə] **F -, -n** brochure

Bro|schur|ein|band **M** *(Typ)* cut flush binding

Brö|sel ['brø:zl] **M -s, -** crumb

brö|se|lig ['brø:zəlɪç] **ADJ** crumbly; **~ werden** to (start to) crumble

brö|seln ['brø:zln] **VI** *(Kuchen, Stein)* to crumble; *(Mensch)* to make crumbs

brös|lig ['brø:zlɪç] **ADJ** = **bröselig**

Brot [bro:t] **NT -(e)s, -e** bread; *(= Laib)* loaf (of bread); *(= Scheibe)* slice (of bread); *(= Butterbrot)* bread and butter *no art, no pl*, slice *or* piece of bread and butter; *(= Stulle)* sandwich; *(fig: = Unterhalt)* daily bread *(hum)*, living; **ein ~ mit Käse** a slice of bread and cheese; **belegte ~e** open *(Brit) or* open-face *(US)* sandwiches; **das ist ein hartes** *or* **schweres ~** *(fig)* that's a hard way to earn one's living; **wes ~ ich ess, des Lied ich sing** *(Prov)* he who pays the piper calls the tune *(Prov)*; **der Mensch lebt nicht vom ~ allein** *(Prov)* man does not live by bread alone → **täglich ADJ**

> **BROT**
>
> Bread is an important food in German-speaking countries – at least one meal a day is based on bread or rolls – and there are many different varieties of bread. There are two basic sorts: white bread made from wheat, and darker bread made from rye. **Vollkornbrot** is produced using wholemeal flour and has a coarse texture. Another speciality is **Laugengebäck**: pretzels, rolls and crescent shapes that are made from a special wheat dough and dipped in caustic soda before baking, to give them a brown crust and distinctive taste.

Brot-: **Brot|auf|strich** **M** spread *(for bread)*; **Brot|be|lag** **M** topping *(for bread)*; **Brot|be|ruf** **M** bread and butter job; **Brot|beu|tel** **M** haversack

Bröt|chen ['brø:tçən] **NT -s, -** roll; **(sich** *dat***) seine ~ verdienen** *(inf)* to earn one's living, to earn one's daily bread *(hum)*; **kleine ~ backen** *(inf)* to set one's sights lower

Bröt|chen|ge|ber(in) **M(F)** *(inf)* employer, provider *(hum)*

Brot-: **Brot|ein|heit** **F** carbohydrate exchange *(Brit)*, bread unit *(US)*; **Brot|er|werb** **M** (way of earning one's) living; **etw zum ~ betreiben** to do sth for a living; **Brot|ge|ber(in)** **M(F)** *(hum)*, **Brot|herr(in)** **M(F)** *(obs)* employer, provider *(hum)*; **Brot|ge|trei|de** **NT** bread grain, bread cereals *pl*; **Brot|kas|ten** **M** bread bin; **Brot|korb** **M** bread basket; **jdm den ~ höher hängen** *(fig)* to keep sb short; **Brot|kru|me** **F** breadcrumb; **Brot|krus|te** **F** crust; **brot|los** **ADJ** unemployed, out of work; **jdn ~ machen** to put sb out of work → **Kunst d**; **Brot|ma|schi|ne** **F** bread slicer; **Brot|mes|ser** **NT** bread knife; **Brot|neid** **M** envy of other people's incomes; *(in Bezug auf Arbeitsplatz)* envy of other people's jobs; **das ist der reine ~** he *etc* is just jealous of your *etc* salary/job; **Brot|rin|de** **F** crust; **Brot|schnei|de|ma|schi|ne** **F** bread slicer; **Brot|schnit|te** **F** slice of bread; **Brot|sup|pe** **F** *soup made from bread, stock etc*; **Brot|teig** **M** bread dough; **Brot|ver|die|ner(in)** **M(F)** breadwinner; **Brot|ver|meh|rung** **F** **die wunderbare ~** *(Bibl)* the miracle of the loaves and fishes; **Brot|zeit** **F** **a** *(S Ger: = Pause)* tea break *(Brit)*, snack break *(US)* **b** *(= Essen)* sandwiches *pl*

brow|sen ['brauzn] **VI** *(Comput)* to browse

Brow|ser ['brauzɐ] **M -s, -** *(Comput)* browser

Brow|ser-Soft|ware ['brauzɐ-] **F**, **Brow|ser|soft|ware** **F** *(Comput)* browser software

brr [br] **INTERJ** *(Befehl an Zugtiere)* whoa; *(Zeichen des Ekels)* ugh, yuck; *(bei Kälte)* brr

Bruch [brʊx] **M -(e)s, ¨-e** ['brʏçə] **a** *(= Bruchstelle)* break; *(in Porzellan etc)* crack; *(in Damm)* breach; *(= das Brechen)* breaking; *(von Fels)* breaking off; *(von Damm)* breaching; **das führte zu einem ~ an der Achse** it caused the axle to break; **zu ~ gehen** to get broken; **zu ~ fahren** to smash; **~ machen** *(inf) (mit Flugzeug, Auto)* to crash *(mit etw* sth); *(beim Abwaschen)* to break something

b *(fig) (von Vertrag, Eid etc)* breaking; *(von Gesetz, Abkommen)* violation, infringement, breaking; *(mit Vergangenheit, Partei, in einer Entwicklung)* break; *(des Vertrauens)* breach; *(von Freundschaft)* break-up; *(von Verlöbnis)* breaking off; *(im Stil)* discontinuity, break; **in die Brüche gehen** *(Ehe, Freundschaft)* to break up; **es kam zum ~ zwischen ihnen** they broke up

c *(= zerbrochene Ware)* broken biscuits/chocolate *etc*; *(= Porzellan)* breakage

d *(Med) (= Knochenbruch)* fracture, break; *(= Eingeweidebruch)* hernia, rupture; **sich** *(dat)* **einen ~ heben** to rupture oneself (by lifting something), to give oneself a hernia

e *(= Steinbruch)* quarry

f *(Geol)* fault

g *(= Knick)* fold

h *(Math)* fraction

i *(sl: = Einbruch)* break-in; **(einen) ~ in einem Geschäft machen** to break into a shop; **einen ~ machen** to do a break-in

Bruch [brʊx, bru:x] **M OR NT -(e)s, ¨-e** ['brʏçə, 'bry:çə] marsh(land), bog

Bruch-: **Bruch|band** [-bant] **NT** *pl* **-bänder** truss; **Bruch|bu|de** **F** *(pej)* hovel; **bruch|fest** **ADJ** unbreakable; **Bruch|fes|tig|keit** **F** robustness; *(von Knochen)* strength; **Bruch|flä|che** **F** surface of the break; **die ~n zusammendrücken** press the two broken edges together

brü|chig ['brʏçɪç] **ADJ** *Material, Knochen* brittle, fragile; *Gestein, Mauerwerk* crumbling; *Leder* cracked, split; *Fingernägel* brittle; *(fig) Stimme* cracked, rough; *Verhältnisse, Ehe* unstable, crumbling; *Moral* crumbling; *Frieden* fragile; *Annahme* shaky; **~ werden** *(Gestein, Macht etc)* to (begin to) crumble; *(Ehe, Verhältnisse auch)* to (begin to) break up; *(Leder)* to crack, to split

Brü|chig|keit **F -,** *no pl (von Material, Knochen)* brittleness, fragility; *(von Gestein etc)* crumbliness; *(fig) (von Stimme)* roughness; *(von Ehe, Verhältnissen)* instability

Bruch-: **Bruch|kan|te** **F** edge (of break); **Bruch|lan|dung** **F** crash-landing; **eine ~ machen** to crash-land; **bruch|rech|nen** **VI** *infin only* to do fractions; **Bruch|rech|nen** **NT** fractions *sing or pl*; **Bruch|rech|nung** **F** fractions *sing or pl*; *(= Aufgabe)* sum with fractior **Bruch|schrift** **F** Gothic script; **Bruch|s** **M** rough, undressed stone; **Bruch|s**

break; *(von Knochen auch)* fracture; **Bruch|strich** M *(Math)* line (of a fraction), fraction line *or* bar; **Bruch|stück** NT fragment; *(von Lied, Rede etc auch)* snatch; **bruch|stück|haft** ADJ fragmentary ADV in a fragmentary way; **ich kenne die Geschichte nur ~** I only know parts *or* fragments of the story; **Bruch|teil** M fraction; **im ~ einer Sekunde** in a split second; **Bruch|zahl** F *(Math)* fraction; **Bruch|zo|ne** F *(Geol)* fault *or* rift zone

Brü|cke ['brʏkə] F **-, -n** **a** *(lit, fig)* bridge; **alle ~n hinter sich** *(dat)* **abbrechen** *(fig)* to burn one's boats *(Brit) or* bridges; **jdm eine ~ bauen** *(fig)* to give sb a helping hand; **jdm goldene ~n bauen** to make things easy for sb; **eine ~ schlagen** *(liter)* to build *or* throw *(liter)* a bridge *(über +acc* across); **~n schlagen** *(fig)* to forge links **b** *(Turnen)* crab; *(Ringen)* bridge **c** *(Anat)* pons (Varolii) **d** *(Naut)* bridge; *(= Landungsbrücke)* gangway, gangplank **e** *(= Zahnbrücke)* bridge **f** *(Elec)* bridge **g** *(= Teppich)* rug

Brü|cken-: **Brü|cken|bau** M **a** *no pl* bridge-building **b** *pl* **-bauten** *(= Brücke)* bridge; **Brü|cken|bo|gen** M arch (of a/the bridge); **Brü|cken|ge|bühr** F toll; **Brü|cken|ge|län|der** NT parapet; **Brü|cken|kopf** M *(Mil, fig)* bridgehead; **Brü|cken|pfei|ler** M pier (of a/the bridge); **Brü|cken|schlag** M *(fig)* **das war der erste ~** that forged the first link; **Brü|cken|steg** M footbridge; **Brü|cken|tag** M extra day off *(taken between two public holidays or a public holiday and a weekend)*; **Brü|cken|waa|ge** F platform scale; **Brü|cken|zoll** M bridge toll

Bru|der ['bru:dɐ] M **-s, ⸚** ['bry:dɐ] **a** brother; **Brüder** *pl (Rel)* brothers *pl*, brethren *pl*; **der große ~** *(fig)* Big Brother; **die Brüder Müller** the Müller brothers; **die Brüder Grimm** the Brothers Grimm; **unter Brüdern** *(inf)* between friends; **Brüder im Geiste** *(geh)* spiritual brothers; **und willst du nicht mein ~ sein, so schlag ich dir den Schädel ein** *(prov)* if you're not prepared to agree with me, then you'd better watch out! **b** *(= Mönch)* friar, brother; *(= Diakon)* deacon; **~ Franziskus** *(als Anrede)* Brother Francis; **die Brüder** *pl* the brothers *pl*, the brethren *pl* **c** *(inf: = Mann)* guy *(inf)*, bloke *(Brit inf)*; **ein zwielichtiger ~** a shady character *or* customer *(inf)*; **das sind alles ganz windige Brüder** *(pej)* they're a shady lot *(Brit) or* crew *(Brit inf) or* bunch *(inf)*; **euch Brüder kenn ich** *(pej)* I know YOU lot *(Brit) or* bunch *(inf)*

Bru|der|bund M *pl* **-bünde** *(geh)* (link of) comradeship, fraternal *or* brotherly link

Brü|der|chen ['bry:dɐçən] NT **-s, -** little brother, baby brother

Bru|der-: **Bru|der|hand** F *(liter)* hand of brotherhood; **Bru|der|hass** M fraternal hatred, hatred between brothers; **Bru|der|herz** NT *(hum)* dear brother; **na ~, wie gehts?** well, brother dear *or* dear brother, how are you?; **Bru|der|krieg** M war between brothers, fratricidal war; **Bru|der|kuss** M *(fig)* fraternal *or* brotherly kiss; **Bru|der|land** NT *(sozialistisch)* brother nation

Brü|der|lein ['bry:dɐlain] NT **-s, -** little brother

brü|der|lich ['bry:dɐlɪç] ADJ fraternal, brotherly *no adv* ADV like brothers; **ich bin ihm ~ verbunden** he's like a brother to me; **~ teilen** to share and share alike; **mit jdm ~ teilen** to share generously with sb

Brü|der|lich|keit F **-,** *no pl* brotherliness → **Freiheit**

Bru|der-: **Bru|der|lie|be** F brotherly love; **Bru|der|mord** M fratricide; **Bru|der|mör|der(in)** M(F) fratricide; **Bru|der|par|tei** F *(sozialistisch)* brother party

Brü|der|schaft ['bry:dɐʃaft] F **-, -en**, **Bru|der|schaft** ['bru:dɐʃaft] F **-, -en** *(esp Eccl)* **a** *(Eccl)* brotherhood **b** *(= Freundschaft)* close *or* intimate friendship *(in which the familiar "du" is used)*; **mit jdm ~ trinken** to agree over a drink to use the familiar "du"

Bru|der-: **Bru|der|volk** NT *(geh)* sister nation; **unser ~ in Kuba** our Cuban brothers; **Bru|der|zwist** M *(liter)* fraternal feud

Brüg|ge ['brʏgə] NT **-s** Bruges

Brü|he ['bry:ə] F **-, -n** *(= Suppe)* (clear) soup; *(als Suppengrundlage)* stock; *(dial: von Gemüse)* vegetable water; *(pej) (= schmutzige Flüssigkeit)* sludge; *(= Getränk)* dishwater *(inf)*, muck *(inf)*

brü|hen ['bry:ən] VT **a** *(= mit heißem Wasser begießen)* to blanch, to pour boiling water over **b** *Tee* to brew; *Kaffee* to make in the jug *or* pot

Brüh-: **brüh|heiß** ADJ scalding (hot), boiling hot; **Brüh|kar|tof|feln** PL potatoes *pl* boiled in meat stock; **brüh|warm** *(inf)* ADJ hot from the press *(inf)* ADV **er hat das sofort ~ weitererzählt** he promptly went straight off and spread it around; **Brüh|wür|fel** M stock cube; **Brüh|wurst** F sausage *(to be heated in water)*

Brüll|af|fe M howling monkey, howler; *(inf: = Mensch)* loudmouth *(inf)*

brül|len ['brʏlən] VI to shout, to roar; *(pej: = laut weinen)* to yell, to bawl; *(Stier)* to bellow; *(Elefant)* to trumpet; **brüll doch nicht so!** don't shout!; **er brüllte vor Schmerzen** he screamed with pain; **vor Lachen ~** to roar *or* howl *or* scream with laughter; **~des Gelächter** roars *or* howls *or* screams of laughter *(all pl)*; **~ wie am Spieß** to cry *or* scream blue *(Brit) or* bloody murder *(inf)*; **das ist zum Brüllen** *(inf)* it's a scream *(inf)* VT to shout, to roar; **jdm seine Wut ins Gesicht ~** to shout furiously at sb

Brül|ler M *(inf)* **a** *(= komisches Ereignis)* hoot *(inf)* **b** *(= Hit, Schlager)* smash hit *(inf)*

Brumm-: **Brumm|bär** M *(inf)* **a** *(baby-talk)* teddy bear *(baby-talk)* **b** *(= brummiger Mann)* crosspatch *(Brit inf)*, grouch *(inf)*; **Brumm|bart** M *(inf)* crosspatch *(Brit inf)*, grouch *(inf)*; **Brumm|bass** M *(inf: = Bassgeige)* (double) bass; *(= Bassstimme)* deep bass (voice)

brum|meln ['brʊmln] VTI *(inf)* to mumble, to mutter

brum|men ['brʊmən] VI **a** *(Insekt)* to buzz; *(Bär)* to growl; *(Motor, Bass)* to drone; *(Kreisel etc)* to hum; **mir brummt der Kopf** *or* **Schädel** my head is throbbing **b** *(beim Singen)* to drone **c** *(= murren)* to grumble, to grouch *(inf)*, to grouse *(inf)* **d** *(= brummeln)* to mumble, to mutter **e** *(inf) (= in Haft sein)* to be locked up *(inf)*; *(Sch: = nachsitzen)* to be kept in; **vier Monate ~** to do four months *(inf)* **f** *(Wirtschaft, Geschäft)* to boom, to flourish VT **a** *(= brummeln)* to mumble, to mutter **b** *(beim Singen)* to drone

Brum|mer ['brʊmɐ] M **-s, -** **a** *(= Schmeißfliege)* bluebottle; *(hum inf: = Sänger)* droner **b** *(inf) (= etwas Großes)* whopper *(inf)*; *(= Lastwagen)* juggernaut *(Brit)*, semi *(US)*

Brum|mi ['brʊmi] M **-s, -s** *(inf: = Lastwagen)* lorry *(Brit)*, truck

Brum|mi|fah|rer(in) M(F) lorry *(Brit) or* truck driver

brum|mig ['brʊmɪç] ADJ grumpy, grouchy *(inf)*, sour-tempered

Brumm-: **Brumm|krei|sel** M *(inf)* humming top; **Brumm|schä|del** M *(inf)* thick head *(inf)*; **Brumm|ton** M low(-pitched) hum, humming sound *or* noise

Brunch [brantʃ, branʃ] M **-(e)s, -(e)s** *or* **-e** brunch

brü|nett [bry'nɛt] ADJ dark(-haired); **~es Mädchen** dark-haired girl, brunette; **sie ist ~** she is (a) brunette

Brü|net|te [bry'nɛtə] F **-, -n** brunette

Brunft [brʊnft] F **-, ⸚e** ['brʏnftə] *(Hunt)* rut; *(= Brunftzeit auch)* rutting season; **in der ~ sein** to be rutting

brunf|ten ['brʊnftn] VI *(Hunt)* to rut

brunf|tig ['brʊnftɪç] ADJ *(Hunt)* rutting

Brunft-: **Brunft|platz** M rutting ground; **Brunft|schrei** M bell, mating *or* rutting call *(auch fig)*; **Brunft|zeit** F rutting season, rut

Brun|nen ['brʊnən] M **-s, -** **a** well; *(fig liter)* fountain, fount *(liter)*; **den ~ erst zudecken, wenn das Kind hineingefallen ist** *(fig)* to lock the stable door after the horse has bolted *(prov)*; **erst, wenn das Kind in den ~ gefallen ist** *(fig)* but not until things had gone wrong **b** *(= Springbrunnen)* fountain **c** *(= Heilquelle)* spring; **~ trinken** to take the waters

Brun|nen-: **Brun|nen|bau|er(in)** M(F) *pl* **-bauer(innen)** well digger, well borer; **Brun|nen|be|cken** NT basin (of a well); *(von Springbrunnen)* basin (of a fountain); **Brun|nen|fi|gur** F (decorative) sculpture on a fountain; **Brun|nen|haus** NT pump room; **Brun|nen|kres|se** F watercress; **Brun|nen|kur** F (course of) spa treatment, cure; **Brun|nen|schacht** M well shaft; **Brun|nen|ver|gif|ter** [-fɛɐgɪftɐ] M **-s, -**, **Brun|nen|ver|gif|te|rin** [-ərɪn] F **-, -nen** **a** well poisoner **b** *(fig pej)* (political) troublemaker; **Brun|nen|ver|gif|tung** F well poisoning; **politische ~** political calumny; **Brun|nen|was|ser** NT *pl* **-wässer** well water

Brünn|lein ['brʏnlain] NT **-s, -** *dim von* **Brunnen**

Brunst [brʊnst] F **-, ⸚e** ['brʏnstə] *(von männlichen Tieren)* rut; *(von weiblichen Tieren)* heat; *(= Brunstzeit)* rutting season; heat; *(hum: von Mensch)* lust, sexual appetite; **in der ~** rutting; on *(Brit) or* in *(esp US)* heat

brüns|tig ['brʏnstɪç] ADJ **a** *(von männlichen Tieren)* rutting; *(von weiblichen Tieren)* on *(Brit) or* in *(esp US)* heat; *(hum: von Mensch)* (feeling) sexy *(hum)* **b** *(liter: = inbrünstig)* ardent, fervent

Brunst-: **Brunst|schrei** M mating call; **Brunst|zeit** F rutting season

brun|zen ['brʊntsn] VI *(S Ger inf)* to (have a) piss *(sl) or* slash *(Brit inf)*

brüsk [brʏsk] ADJ brusque, abrupt, curt ADV brusquely, abruptly, curtly; **sich ~ abwenden** to turn away abruptly *or* brusquely

brüs|kie|ren [brʏs'ki:rən] *ptp* **brüskiert** VT to snub

Brüs|kie|rung F **-, -en** snub

Brüs|sel ['brʏsl] NT **-s** Brussels

Brüs|se|ler ['brʏsəlɐ], **Brüss|ler** ['brʏslɐ] ADJ *attr* Brussels; **~ Spitzen** Brussels lace; **~ Salat** *(Sw: = Chicorée)* chicory

Brüs|se|ler ['brʏsəlɐ] M **-s, -**, **Brüs|se|le|rin** [-ərɪn] F **-, -nen**, **Brüss|ler** ['brʏslɐ] M **-s, -**, **Brüss|le|rin** [-ərɪn] F **-, -nen** inhabitant *or (gebürtiger)* native of Brussels; **er ist ~** he lives in Brussels; *(dort geboren)* he comes from Brussels

Brust [brʊst] F **-, ⸚e** ['brʏstə] **a** *(= Körperteil)* chest; *(fig: = Inneres)* breast, heart; **einen zur ~ nehmen** *(inf)* to have a quick drink *or* a quickie *(inf)*; **~ (he)raus!** chest out!; **~ an ~** face to face; **sich an jds ~** *(dat)* **ausweinen** to cry on sb's shoulder; **sich** *(dat)* **an die ~ schlagen** *(fig)* to beat one's breast; **sich in die ~ werfen** *(fig)* to puff oneself up; **sich** *(dat)* **jdn zur ~ nehmen** to have a word with sb; **sich** *(dat)* **etw zur ~ nehmen** to criticize sth harshly; **mit geschwellter ~** *(fig)* as proud as Punch *or* a peacock; **schwach auf der ~ sein** *(inf)* to have a weak chest; *(hum: = an Geldmangel leiden)* to be a bit short *(inf)* **b** *(= weibliche Brust)* breast; **einem Kind die ~ geben, ein Kind an die ~ legen** to feed a baby *(at the breast)*, to nurse a baby **c** *(Cook)* breast **d** *(= Brustschwimmen)* breaststroke

Brust-: **Brust|am|pu|ta|ti|on** F *(Med)* mastectomy *(spec)*; **Brust|bein** NT *(Anat)* breastbone, sternum; **Brust|beu|tel** M money bag *(worn around the neck)*; **Brust|bild** NT half-length portrait; **Brust|brei|te** F **um ~** by a whisker

Brüst|chen ['brʏstçən] NT **-s, -** *dim von* **Brust**

Brust|drü|se F mammary gland

brüs|ten ['brʏstn] VR to boast, to brag *(mit* about)

Brust-: **Brust|fell** NT *(Anat)* pleura; **Brust|fell|ent|zün|dung** F pleurisy; **Brust|flos|se** F pectoral fin; **Brust|ge|gend** F thoracic region; **Brust|haar** NT hair on the chest, chest hair;

Brust|har|nisch M breastplate; **brust|hoch** ADJ chest-high; **Brust|hö|he** F **in ~** chest high; **Brust|höh|le** F thoracic cavity; **Brust|kas|ten** M *(inf, Anat)* thorax; **Brust|kind** NT breastfed baby; **Brust|korb** M *(Anat)* thorax; **Brust|krebs** M breast cancer, cancer of the breast; **Brust|kreuz** NT *(Eccl)* pectoral cross; **Brust|la|ge** F prone position; **in ~ schwimmen** to swim in the prone position; **Brust|mus|kel** M pectoral muscle; **Brust|o|pe|ra|ti|on** F *(Med)* breast operation; *(= Schönheitsoperation)* breast enhancement, boob job *(inf)*; **Brust|pan|zer** M breastplate; **Brust|plas|tik** F cosmetic breast surgery; **Brust|schutz** M *(esp Fechten)* breast *or* chest protector, plastron; **brust|schwim|men**, **Brust schwim|men** VI *infin only* to swim *or* do the breaststroke; **Brust|schwim|men** NT breaststroke; **Brust|schwim|mer(in)** M(F) breaststroke swimmer; **Brust|stim|me** F chest voice; **Brust|stück** NT *(Cook)* breast; **Brust|ta|sche** F breast pocket; *(= Innentasche)* inside (breast) pocket; **Brust|tee** M herbal tea *(for infections of the respiratory tract)*; **brust|tief** ADJ chest-deep, up to one's chest; **Brust|ton** M *pl* **-töne** *(Mus)* chest note; **im ~ der Überzeugung, (dass ...)** in a tone of utter conviction (that ...); **Brust|um|fang** M chest measurement; *(von Frau)* bust measurement

Brüs|tung [ˈbrʏstʊŋ] F **-, -en** parapet; *(= Balkonbrüstung etc auch)* balustrade; *(= Fensterbrüstung)* breast

Brust-: **Brust|wand** F *(Anat)* thoracic *or* chest wall; **Brust|war|ze** F nipple; **Brust|wehr** F *(Mil)* breastwork; *(Hist)* parapet; **Brust|wei|te** F chest measurement; *(von Frau)* bust measurement; **Brust|wi|ckel** M chest compress; **Brust|wir|bel** M thoracic *or* dorsal vertebra

Brut [bru:t] F **-, -en** **a** *no pl (= das Brüten)* brooding, sitting, incubating **b** *(= die Jungen)* brood; *(pej)* lot, mob *(inf)* **c** *(bei Pflanzen)* offset, offshoot

bru|tal [bruˈta:l] ADJ brutal; *(= gewalttätig auch)* violent ADV **a** *zuschlagen* brutally; *behandeln* cruelly; **jdm etw ganz ~ sagen** to be brutally *or* cruelly frank to sb about sth, to tell sb sth (quite) brutally **b** *(inf: = sehr)* incredibly; **das tut ~ weh** *(inf)* that hurts like hell *(inf)*

bru|ta|li|sie|ren [brutaliˈzi:rən] *ptp* **brutalisiert** VT to brutalize

Bru|ta|li|sie|rung F **-, -en** brutalization

Bru|ta|li|tät [brutaliˈtɛ:t] F **-, -en** **a** *no pl* brutality; *(= Gewalttätigkeit auch)* violence **b** *(= Gewalttat)* act of violence *or* brutality; **~en** *pl* brutalities, acts of violence *or* brutality

Bru|ta|lo [bruˈta:lo] M **-s, -s** *(inf)* bruiser *(inf)*, thug

Brut|ap|pa|rat M incubator

brü|ten [ˈbry:tn] VI to brood, to sit, to incubate; *(fig)* to ponder *(über +dat* over); **~de Hitze** oppressive *or* stifling heat; **~d heiß** sweltering, boiling (hot) *(inf)* VT **a** *(künstlich)* to incubate; *(Tech)* to breed **b** *(geh) Rache, Verrat* to plot

brü|tend|heiß △ ADJ *attr* → **brüten VI**

Brü|ter [ˈbry:tɐ] M **-s, -** *(Tech)* breeder (reactor); **Schneller ~** fast-breeder (reactor)

Brut-: **Brut|hen|ne** F sitting hen; **Brut|hit|ze** F *(inf)* stifling *or* sweltering heat; **Brut|kas|ten** M *(Med)* incubator; **hier ist eine Hitze wie in einem ~** *(inf)* it's like an oven *or* a furnace in here *(inf)*; **Brut|ofen** M *(fig)* furnace; **Brut|pfle|ge** F care of the brood; **Brut|platz** M breeding ground; **Brut|re|ak|tor** M breeder (reactor); **Brut|schrank** M *(Med, Agr etc)* incubator; **Brut|stät|te** F breeding ground *(+gen* for); *(fig auch)* hotbed *(+gen* of); **Brut|teich** M spawning pond

brut|to [ˈbrʊto] ADV gross; **~ EUR 1000, EUR 1000 ~** EUR 1000 gross

Brut|to-: **Brut|to|be|trag** M gross amount; **Brut|to|ein|kom|men** NT gross *or* before-tax income; **Brut|to|er|trag** M gross *or* before-tax profit; **Brut|to|ge|halt** NT gross salary; **Brut|to|ge|wicht** NT gross weight; **Brut|to|ge|winn** M gross *or* before-tax profit; **Brut|to|in|lands|pro|dukt** NT gross domestic product, GDP; **Brut|to|lohn** M gross *or* before-tax wage(s); **Brut|to|na|ti|o|nal|pro|dukt** NT *(Aus Econ)* gross national product, GNP; **Brut|to|preis** M gross price; **Brut|to|re|gis|ter|ton|ne** F register ton; **Brut|to|so|zi|al|pro|dukt** NT gross national product, GNP; **Brut|to|ver|dienst** M gross *or* before-tax earnings *pl*

Brut|zeit F incubation (period)

brut|zeln [ˈbrʊtsln] *(inf)* VI to sizzle (away) VT to fry (up)

Bru|yère [bryˈjɛ:r] NT **-s**, *no pl*, **Bru|yère|holz** [bryˈjɛ:r-] NT briar *or* brier (wood)

Bru|yère [bryˈjɛ:r] F **-, -s**, **Bru|yère|pfei|fe** [bryˈjɛ:r-] F briar *or* brier (pipe)

BSE [be:lɛsˈle:] *abbr von* **Bovine Spongiforme Enzephalopathie** BSE

BSE- *in cpds* BSE; **BSE-Er|re|ger** M BSE virus; **BSE-frei** ADJ *Betrieb, Fleisch, Tiere* free from BSE

B-Sei|te [ˈbe:-] F *(von Schallplatte)* B-side

BSE-: **BSE-Kri|se** F BSE crisis; **BSE-Ri|si|ko|ma|te|ri|al** NT Specified Risk Material, SRM; **BSE-Seu|che** F BSE epidemic; **BSE-ver|seucht** [be:lɛsˈle:-] ADJ *Fleisch* BSE-contaminated, contaminated with BSE *pred*

BTA [be:te:ˈla:] M **-s, -s** F **-, -s** *abbr von* **biologisch-technische Assistentin, biologisch-technischer Assistent**

Btx [be:te:ˈlɪks] M **-**, *no pl abbr von* **Bildschirmtext**

Bub [bu:p] M **-en, -en** [-bn] *(S Ger, Aus, Sw)* boy, lad *(Brit)*

Büb|chen [ˈby:pçən] NT **-s, -** *dim von* **Bub**

Bu|be [ˈbu:bə] M **-n, -n** **a** *(old)* rogue, knave *(old)* **b** *(Cards)* jack, knave

bu|ben|haft [-haft] ADJ boyish ADV boyishly

Bu|ben|streich M, **Bu|ben|stück** NT, **Bü|be|rei** [byːbəˈrai] F **-, -en** **a** *(old)* piece of knavery *(old) or* villainy, knavish trick *(old)* **b** *(= Streich)* silly *or* foolish *or* childish prank

Bu|bi [ˈbu:bi] M **-s, -s** *(inf)* little boy *or* lad *(Brit)*, laddie *(Brit inf)*; *(pej inf)* (school)boy; *(als Anrede)* laddie *(Brit inf)*, (little) boy

Bu|bi-: **Bu|bi|kopf** M bobbed hair *no pl*, bob; **sich** *(dat)* **einen ~ machen lassen** to have one's hair bobbed, to have one's hair cut in a bob; **Bu|bi|kra|gen** M Peter Pan collar

bü|bisch [ˈby:bɪʃ] ADJ **a** *(old: = schurkenhaft)* villainous, knavish *(old)* **b** *(= verschmitzt)* roguish, mischievous ADV *(= verschmitzt) grinsen, lächeln, sagen* roguishly, mischievously

Bu|bi|strich M, **Bu|bi-Strich** M *(= Prostitution)* prostitution by rent boys; *(= Gebiet)* red-light district for rent boys, rent-boy area

Buch [bu:x] NT **-(e)s, ¨-er** [ˈby:çɐ] **a** book *(auch Bibl)*; *(= Band)* volume; *(= Drehbuch)* script; **über den Büchern sitzen** to pore over one's books; **er redet wie ein ~** *(inf)* he never stops talking; **ein Gentleman, wie er im ~e steht** a perfect example of a gentleman; **ein Tor, wie es im ~e steht** a textbook *or* copybook goal; **das erste ~ Mose** *(Bibl)* Genesis; **das ~ der Bücher** the Book of Books; **das Goldene ~ der Stadt** the VIP visitor's book; **ein ~ mit sieben Siegeln** *(fig)* a closed book; **er ist für mich ein offenes** *or* **aufgeschlagenes ~** I can read him like a book; **sich ins ~ der Geschichte eintragen** *(geh)* to enter one's name in the annals *or* book of history; **~ machen** *(Pferderennen)* to make a book
b *usu pl (Comm: = Geschäftsbuch)* books *pl*, accounts *pl*; **über etw** *(acc)* **~ führen** to keep a record of sth; **jdm die Bücher führen** to keep sb's accounts *or* books; **zu ~ (e) schlagen** to make a (significant) difference; **das schlägt mit 1000 Euro zu ~(e)** that gives you 1000 euros; **zu ~ stehen mit** to be valued at

Buch-: **Buch|be|spre|chung** F book review; **Buch|bin|der(in)** M(F) bookbinder; **Buch|bin|de|rei** F *(= Betrieb)* bookbindery; *(= Handwerk)* bookbinding; **Buch|block** M *pl* **-blocks** book block; **Buch|de|ckel** M book cover; **Buch|druck** M, *no pl* letterpress (printing); **Buch|dru|cker(in)** M(F) printer; **Buch|dru|cke|rei** F *(= Betrieb)* printing works *sing or pl*; *(= Handwerk)* printing; **Buch|dru|cker|kunst** F art of printing

Bu|che [ˈbu:xə] F **-, -n** *(= Baum)* beech (tree); *(= Holz)* beech(wood)

Buch|ecker [ˈbu:xlɛkɐ] F **-, -n** beechnut

Buch|ein|band M binding, (book) cover

bu|chen [ˈbu:xn] ✪ 48.3 VT **a** *(Comm)* to enter, to post *(spec)*; *(Kasse)* to register; *(fig: = registrieren)* to register, to record; **einen Erfolg für sich ~** to chalk up *(inf) or* mark up a success (for oneself); **etw als Erfolg ~** to put sth down as a success **b** *(= vorbestellen)* to book, to reserve

bu|chen ADJ *(rare)* (made) of beech(wood), beech

Bu|chen-: **Bu|chen|holz** NT beechwood; **Bu|chen|wald** M beech wood

Bü|cher-: **Bü|cher|ba|sar** M book sale; **Bü|cher|bord** NT, **Bü|cher|brett** NT bookshelf; **Bü|cher|bus** M mobile library

Bü|che|rei [by:çəˈrai] F **-, -en** (lending) library

Bü|cher-: **Bü|cher|freund(in)** M(F) book-lover, bibliophile; **Bü|cher|ge|stell** NT bookcase; **Bü|cher|gut|schein** M book token; **Bü|cher|markt** M book market; **Bü|cher|narr** M, **Bü|cher|när|rin** F book-fan, book freak *(inf)*; **er ist ein richtiger ~** he's book mad *(inf)*, he's crazy about books, he's a real book freak *(inf)*; **Bü|cher|reff** NT case for transporting books; **Bü|cher|re|gal** NT bookshelf; **Bü|cher|re|vi|si|on** F audit; **Bü|cher|schrank** M bookcase; **Bü|cher|sen|dung** F consignment of books; *(im Postwesen)* books (sent) at printed paper rate; **Bü|cher|stu|be** F bookshop; **Bü|cher|stüt|ze** F book end; **Bü|cher|ver|bot** NT ban on books; **Bü|cher|ver|bren|nung** F burning of books; **Bü|cher|ver|zeich|nis** NT bibliography; **Bü|cher|wand** F wall of book shelves; *(als Möbelstück)* (large) set of book shelves; **Bü|cher|weis|heit** F book learning; **Bü|cher|wurm** M *(lit, fig hum)* bookworm

Buch|fink M chaffinch

Buch-: **Buch|form** F **in ~** in book form; **Buch|for|mat** NT format for a book; **Buch|füh|rung** F book-keeping, accounting; **einfache/doppelte ~** single/double entry book-keeping; **Buch|geld** NT *(Fin)* bank deposit money; **Buch|ge|lehr|sam|keit** F book-learning; **Buch|ge|mein|schaft** F book club; **Buch|ge|winn** M *(St Ex, Fin)* paper profit(s *pl*), profit(s *pl*) on paper; **Buch|hal|ter(in)** M(F) book-keeper; **buch|hal|te|risch** [-haltərɪʃ] ADJ book-keeping ADV **sich ~ ausbilden lassen** to be trained in book-keeping *or* as a book-keeper; **ein Problem ~ sehen** to see something as a book-keeping problem, to view a problem in terms of book-keeping; **Ihre Abrechnung ist ~ korrekt** your book-keeping is correct; **sie ist ~ versiert** she is good at book-keeping; **~ kompliziert** complicated in terms of book-keeping; **Buch|hal|tung** F **a** book-keeping, accounting **b** *(Abteilung einer Firma)* accounts department; **Buch|han|del** M book trade; **im ~ erhältlich** available *or* on sale in bookshops; **Buch|händ|ler(in)** M(F) bookseller; **buch|händ|le|risch** [-hɛndlərɪʃ] ADJ of *or* connected with the book trade; **eine ~e Ausbildung haben** to be a trained bookseller ADV **~ tätig sein** to be a bookseller; **Buch|hand|lung** F bookshop, bookstore *(US)*; **Buch|hül|le** F dust jacket *or* cover; **Buch|klub** M book club; **Buch|kri|tik** F **a** *(= das Rezensieren)* book reviewing; *(= Rezension)* book review **b** *no pl (= die Rezensenten)* book reviewers *pl or* critics *pl*; **Buch|la|den** M bookshop, bookstore *(US)*; **Buch|ma|cher(in)** M(F) bookmaker, bookie *(inf)*; **Buch|ma|le|rei** F illumination; **Buch|-**

mes|se F book fair; **Buch|prü|fer(in)** M(F) auditor; **Buch|prü|fung** F audit; **Buch|rü|cken** M spine

Buchs ['bʊks] M **-es, -e, Buchs|baum** M box (tree)

Büchs|chen ['bʏksçən] NT **-s, -** *dim von* **Büchse**

Buch|se ['bʊksə] F **-, -n** *(Elec)* socket; *(Tech) (von Zylinder)* liner; *(von Lager)* bush

Büch|se ['bʏksə] F **-, -n** **a** tin; *(= Konservenbüchse)* can, tin *(Brit)*; *(= Sammelbüchse)* collecting box; **die ~ der Pandora** *(Myth, liter)* Pandora's box **b** *(= Gewehr)* rifle, (shot)gun

Büch|sen-: **Büch|sen|fleisch** NT canned *or* tinned *(Brit)* meat; **Büch|sen|ma|cher(in)** M(F) gunsmith; **Büch|sen|milch** F tinned *(Brit) or* evaporated milk; **Büch|sen|öff|ner** M can-opener, tin-opener *(Brit)*

Buch|sta|be ['bu:xʃta:bə] M **-n(s), -n** letter; *(= esp Druckbuchstabe)* character; **kleiner ~** small letter; **großer ~** capital (letter); **ein fetter ~** a bold character, a character in bold (face); **in fetten ~n** in bold (face); **Betrag in ~n** amount in words; **dem ~n nach** *(fig)* literally; **auf den ~n genau** *(fig)* **bis auf den letzten ~n** *(fig)* to the letter; **nach dem ~n des Gesetzes ist das verboten, aber ...** according to the letter of the law that's illegal but ... → **vier b**

Buch|sta|ben-: **Buch|sta|ben|fol|ge** F *(alphabetisch)* alphabetical order; *(= Aneinanderreihung von Buchstaben)* sequence of letters; **buch|sta|ben|ge|treu** ADJ literal ADV **etw ~ befolgen** to follow sth to the letter; **Buch|sta|ben|glau|be** M literalism; **buch|sta|ben|gläu|big** ADJ literalist(ic); **Buch|sta|ben|kom|bi|na|ti|on** F combination (of letters); **Buch|sta|ben|rät|sel** NT word puzzle, anagram; **Buch|sta|ben|schrift** F alphabetic script; **Buch|sta|ben|treue** F adherence to the letter

buch|sta|bie|ren [bu:xʃta'bi:rən] *ptp* **buchstabiert** VT **a** *Wort, Namen* to spell **b** *(= mühsam lesen)* to spell out

Buch|sta|bier-: **Buch|sta|bier|me|tho|de** F alphabetical method; **Buch|sta|bier|ta|fel** F word spelling alphabet

buch|stäb|lich ['bu:xʃtɛ:plɪç] ADJ literal ADV literally

Buch|stüt|ze F book-end

Bucht [bʊxt] F **-, -en** **a** *(im Meer)* bay; *(kleiner)* cove **b** *(für Schweine etc)* stall

Buch|teln ['bʊxtln] PL *(Aus Cook) sweet bread roll with jam filling*

buch|ten|reich, buch|tig ['bʊxtɪç] ADJ *Küste* indented

Buch-: **Buch|ti|tel** M (book) title; **Buch|um|schlag** M dust jacket *or* cover

Bu|chung ['bu:xʊŋ] F **-, -en** *(Comm)* entry; *(= Reservierung)* booking, reservation

Bu|chungs-: **Bu|chungs|be|leg** M *(Econ, Fin)* accounting record, (bookkeeping) voucher; *(für Reisebuchung)* booking receipt; **Bu|chungs|com|pu|ter** M computerized booking system; **ich kann Sie im ~ nicht finden** I can't find your booking on the computer; **Bu|chungs|kar|te** F charge card; **Bu|chungs|ma|schi|ne** F accounting machine; **Bu|chungs|num|mer** F *(Econ, Fin)* entry number; *(für Reisebuchung)* booking number; **Bu|chungs|sys|tem** NT booking system

Buch|ver|lag M (book) publisher(s *pl*), (book) publisher's

Buch|wei|zen M buckwheat

Buch-: **Buch|wert** M *(Comm)* book value; **Buch|wis|sen** NT *(pej)* book learning

Bu|ckel ['bʊkl] M **-s, -** **a** hump(back), hunchback; *(inf: = Rücken)* back; **einen ~ machen** *(Katze)* to arch its back; **steh gerade, mach nicht so einen ~!** stand up (straight), don't hunch your back *or* shoulders like that!; **einen krummen ~ machen** *(fig inf)* to bow and scrape, to kowtow; **den ~ vollkriegen** *(inf)* to get a good hiding, to get a belting *(inf)*; **er kann mir den ~ (he)runterrutschen** *(inf)* he can (go and) take a running jump, he can get lost *or* knotted *(all inf)*; **viel/genug auf dem ~ haben** *(inf)* to have a lot/enough on one's plate *(inf)*; **den ~ voll Schulden haben** *(inf)* to be up to one's neck *or* eyes in debt *(inf)*; **den ~ hinhalten** *(fig inf)* to carry the can *(inf)*; **seine 80 Jahre auf dem ~ haben** *(inf)* to be 80 (years old), to have seen 80 summers → **jucken VTI, breit ADJ** **b** *(inf: = Hügel)* hummock, hillock **c** *(inf: = Auswölbung)* bulge, hump **d** *(von Schild)* boss

bu|cke|lig ['bʊkəlɪç] ADJ hunchbacked, humpbacked; *(inf) Straße* bumpy; *Landschaft* undulating, hilly

Bu|cke|li|ge(r) ['bʊkəlɪgə] MF *decl as adj* hunchback, humpback

bu|ckeln ['bʊkln] VI *(pej)* to bow and scrape, to kowtow; **nach oben ~ und nach unten treten** to bow to superiors and tread inferiors underfoot

Bu|ckel-: **Bu|ckel|pis|te** F *(Ski)* mogul piste; **Bu|ckel|rind** NT zebu; **Bu|ckel|wal** M humpback whale

bü|cken ['bʏkn] VR to bend (down), to stoop; **sich nach etw ~** to bend down *or* to stoop to pick sth up → *auch* **gebückt**

Bu|ckerl ['bʊkɐl] NT **-s, -(n)** *(Aus inf)* bow

buck|lig ['bʊklɪç] ADJ ETC = **buckelig**

Buck|li|ge(r) ['bʊklɪgə] MF *decl as adj* hunchback, humpback

Bück|ling ['bʏklɪŋ] M **-s, -e** **a** *(Cook)* smoked herring **b** *(hum inf: = Verbeugung)* bow

Bu|da|pest ['bu:dapɛst] NT **-s** Budapest

Büd|chen ['by:tçən] NT **-s, -** *dim von* **Bude a**

Bud|del ['bʊdl] F **-, -n** *(N Ger inf)* bottle

Bud|de|lei [bʊdə'lai] F **-, -en** *(im Sand)* digging; *(inf: = Tiefbauarbeiten)* constant digging (up) *(of road etc)*

Bud|del|kas|ten M *(dial)* sandbox

bud|deln ['bʊdln] VI *(inf)* to dig; **in der Straße wird dauernd gebuddelt** they're always digging up the road VT *(dial) (= ausgraben) Kartoffeln* to dig up; *Loch* to dig

Bud|dha ['bʊda] M **-s, -s** Buddha

Bud|dhis|mus [bʊ'dɪsmʊs] M **-,** *no pl* Buddhism

Bud|dhist [bʊ'dɪst] M **-en, -en, Bud|dhis|tin** [-'dɪstɪn] F **-, -nen** Buddhist

bud|dhis|tisch [bʊ'dɪstɪʃ] ADJ Buddhist(ic) ADV **jdn ~ erziehen** to bring sb up (as) a Buddhist; **~ beeinflusst** influenced by Buddhism; **~ heiraten** to marry in a Buddhist ceremony

Bu|de ['bu:də] F **-, -n** **a** *(= Bretterbau)* hut; *(= Baubude)* (workmen's) hut; *(= Marktbude, Verkaufsbude)* stall, stand, booth; *(= Zeitungsbude)* kiosk **b** *(pej inf: = Laden, Lokal etc)* dump *(inf)* **c** *(inf) (= Zimmer)* room; *(= Wohnung)* pad *(inf)*; **Leben in die ~ bringen** to liven *or* brighten up the place; **jdm die ~ einrennen** *or* **einlaufen** to pester *or* badger sb; **jdm auf die ~ rücken** *(als Besucher)* to drop in on sb, to land on sb *(inf)*; *(aus einem bestimmten Grund)* to pay sb a visit, to go/come round to sb's place *(inf)*; **jdm die ~ auf den Kopf stellen** to turn sb's place upside down *(inf)*

Bu|del ['bu:dl] F **-, -n** *(Aus inf)* (shop) counter

Bu|den-: **Bu|den|be|sit|zer(in)** M(F) (market) stallholder; **Bu|den|zau|ber** M *(dated inf)* knees-up *(dated sl)*, jamboree *(dated inf)*

Bud|get [bʏ'dʒe:] NT **-s, -s** budget

bud|ge|tär [bʏdʒe'tɛ:ɐ] ADJ budgetary

Bud|get- *(Pol)*: **Bud|get|be|ra|tung** F budget debate; **Bud|get|ent|wurf** M draft budget

bud|ge|tie|ren [bʏdʒe'ti:rən] *ptp* **budgetiert** [bʏdʒe'ti:ɐt] VTI *(Pol, Comm, Fin)* to budget

Bud|get|vor|la|ge [bʏ'dʒe:-] F presentation of the budget

Bu|di|ke [bu'di:kə] F **-, -n** *(dial)* bar, pub *(Brit)*, saloon *(US)*

Bu|di|ker [bu'di:kɐ] M **-s, -, Bu|di|ke|rin** [-ərɪn] F **-, -nen** *(dial)* bar keeper, landlord/landlady *(Brit)*

Bu|e|nos Ai|res ['bue:nɔs 'airɛs] NT **- -** Buenos Aires

Bü|fett [by'fɛt] NT **-(e)s, -e** *or* **-s** **a** *(= Geschirrschrank)* sideboard **b** *(= Schanktisch)* bar; *(= Verkaufstisch)* counter **c** **kaltes ~** cold buffet **d** *(Sw: = Bahnhofsgaststätte)* (station) buffet

Bü|fett|da|me F, **Bü|fett|fräu|lein** NT, **Bü|fett|mam|sell** F *(dated) (in Gastwirtschaft)* barmaid; *(in Konditorei)* (counter) assistant

Bü|fet|ti|er [byfɛ'tie:] M **-s, -s** barman

Büf|fel ['bʏfl] M **-s, -** buffalo

Büf|fe|lei [bʏfə'lai] F **-, -en** *(inf)* swotting *(Brit inf)*, cramming *(inf)*

Büf|fel-: **Büf|fel|her|de** F herd of buffalo; **Büf|fel|le|der** NT buff (leather), buffalo skin

büf|feln ['bʏfln] *(inf)* VI to swot *(Brit inf)*, to cram *(inf)* VT *Lernstoff* to swot up *(Brit inf)*, to bone up on *(US inf)*

Buf|fet [by'fe:] NT **-s, -s, Büf|fet** [bʏ'fe:] NT **-s, -s** *(esp Aus)* = **Büfett**

Buf|fo ['bʊfo] M **-s, -s** *or* **Buffi** ['bʊfi] buffo

Bug [bu:k] M **-(e)s, ⸗e** *or* **-e** ['by:gə, 'bu:gə] **a** *(= Schiffsbug)* bow *usu pl*; *(= Flugzeugbug)* nose; **jdm eins vor den ~ knallen** *(inf)* to sock sb one *(inf)* **b** *(Cook: = Schultergegend)* shoulder **c** *(Tech)* brace, strut

Bü|gel ['by:gl] M **-s, -** **a** *(= Kleiderbügel)* (coat) hanger **b** *(= Steigbügel)* stirrup **c** *(= Stromabnehmer)* bow (collector) **d** *(von Säge, Handtasche)* frame; *(= Brillenbügel)* side piece, earpiece, bow; *(von Gewehr)* trigger guard; *(für Einweckgläser)* clip, clamp; *(am Lift)* T-bar

Bü|gel-: **Bü|gel|au|to|mat** M rotary iron; **Bü|gel-BH** M underwire(d) bra; **Bü|gel|brett** NT ironing board; **bü|gel|echt** ADJ ironable; **Bü|gel|ei|sen** NT iron; **Bü|gel|fal|te** F crease in one's trousers *(esp Brit) or* pants *(esp US)*; **bü|gel|fer|tig** ADJ ready for ironing; **Bü|gel|fla|sche** F flip-top bottle; **bü|gel|frei** ADJ noniron; **Bü|gel|ma|schi|ne** F rotary iron

bü|geln ['by:gln] VT *Wäsche* to iron; *Hose* to press VI to iron

Bü|gel-: **Bü|gel|sä|ge** F hacksaw; **Bü|gel|schloss** NT *(für Zweiräder)* U-lock; **Bü|gel|tisch** F ironing table; **Bü|gel|wäsche** F ironing

Bug|frau F *(Rudern)* bow

Bug|gy ['bagi] M **-s, -s** buggy

Büg|ler ['by:glɐ] M **-s, -, Büg|le|rin** [-ərɪn] F **-, -nen** ironer

Bug-: **Bug|mann** M *pl* **-männer** *or* **-leute** *(Rudern)* bow(man); **Bug|rad** NT *(Aviat)* nose wheel; **Bug|see** F *(Naut)* bow wave

Bug|sier|damp|fer M, **Bug|sier|schlep|per** M *(Naut)* tug(boat)

bug|sie|ren [bʊ'ksi:rən] *ptp* **bugsiert** VT **a** *(Naut)* to tow **b** *(inf) Möbelstück etc* to manoeuvre *(Brit)*, to maneuver *(US)*, to edge; **jdn aus dem Zimmer ~** to steer *or* hustle sb out of the room **c** *(inf: = lancieren)* **jdn in einen Posten ~** to wangle *or* fiddle *or* finagle *(US)* a job for sb *(inf)* VI *(Naut)* to tow; **Schlepper, die im Hafen ~** tugs that do the towing in the port

Bug|sie|rer [bʊ'ksi:rɐ] M **-s, -** *(Naut)* tug(boat)

Bug|sier|tau NT, **Bug|sier|tros|se** F *(Naut)* towline, towrope

Bug- *(Naut)*: **Bug|spriet** NT bowsprit; **Bug|wel|le** F bow wave

buh [bu:] INTERJ boo

Buh [bu:] NT **-s, -s** *(inf)* boo

Bü|hel ['by:əl] M **-s, -, Bühl** [by:l] M **-s, -** *(S Ger, Aus, Sw)* hill

bu|hen ['bu:ən] VI *(inf)* to boo

Buh|frau F **-, -en** bogeywoman *(inf)*

Buh|le ['bu:lə] M **-n, -n** *(old liter)* paramour *(obs, liter)*, lover

Buh|le F **-, -n** *(old liter)* paramour *(obs, liter)*, mistress

buh|len ['bu:lən] VI **a** *(pej: = werben)* **um jdn/Anerkennung ~** to woo sb/recognition; **um jds Gunst ~** to woo *or* court sb's favour *(Brit) or* favor *(US)* **b** *(obs)* **mit jdm ~** to have a love affair with sb

Buh|ler ['bu:lɐ] M **-s, -, Buh|le|rin** [-ərɪn] F **-, -nen** **a** *(old liter)* paramour *(obs, liter)*; *(Mann*

auch) lover; *(Frau auch)* mistress **b** *(pej: = Werbender)* wooer
Buh|le|rei [bu:lə'rai] F -, *no pl (pej)* wooing *(um jdn/etw* of sb/sth)
Buh|mann ['bu:man] M *pl* **-männer** *(inf)* bogeyman *(inf)*
Buh|ne ['bu:nə] F -, **-n** groyne, breakwater
Büh|ne ['by:nə] F -, **-n** **a** *(lit, fig)* stage; *(von Konzertsaal, Aula etc)* stage, platform; **über die ~ gehen** *(fig inf)* to go *or* pass off; **etw über die ~ bringen** *(fig inf)* to stage sth; **wie haben Sie Ihren ersten Elternabend/Ihre Antrittsvorlesung über die ~ gebracht?** how did you manage your first parents' evening/your inaugural lecture?; **hinter der ~** *(lit, fig)* behind the scenes; **von der ~ abtreten** *or* **verschwinden** *(inf)* **die ~ verlassen** to make one's exit, to leave the scene **b** *(= Theater)* theatre *(Brit)*, theater *(US)*; **Städtische ~n** Municipal Theatres *(Brit)* or Theaters *(US)*; **zur ~ gehen** to go on the stage, to go into the theatre *(Brit) or* theater *(US)*; **an** *or* **bei der ~ sein** to be on the stage, to be in the theatre *(Brit) or* theater *(US)*; **sie steht seit zwanzig Jahren auf der ~** she has been on the stage *or* in the theatre *(Brit) or* theater *(US)* for twenty years; **das Stück ging über alle ~n** the play was put on *or* staged everywhere *or* in all the theatres *(Brit) or* theaters *(US)*
c *(dial: = Dachboden)* loft
d *(Tech: = Hebebühne)* ramp
Büh|nen-: **Büh|nen|an|wei|sung** F stage direction; **Büh|nen|ar|bei|ter(in)** M(F) stage hand; **Büh|nen|aus|bil|dung** F dramatic training; **Büh|nen|aus|spra|che** F standard *or* received pronunciation; **Büh|nen|aus|stat|tung** F stage property *or* props *pl*; **Büh|nen|au|tor(in)** M(F) playwright, dramatist; **Büh|nen|be|ar|bei|tung** F stage adaptation; **Büh|nen|be|leuch|ter(in)** M(F) lighting man/woman; **Büh|nen|be|leuch|tung** F stage lighting; **Büh|nen|bild** NT (stage) set; **Büh|nen|bild|ner(in)** M(F) set designer; **Büh|nen|dich|ter(in)** M(F) playwright, dramatist; **Büh|nen|dich|tung** F dramatic verse; **Büh|nen|ef|fekt** M stage effect; **Büh|nen|er|fah|rung** F stage experience; **Büh|nen|er|folg** M success; *(= Stück auch)* (stage) hit; **Büh|nen|fas|sung** F stage adaptation; **büh|nen|ge|recht** ADJ suitable for the stage ADV **etw ~ bearbeiten** to adapt sth for the stage; **Büh|nen|ge|stalt** F (dramatic) character; **Büh|nen|haus** NT fly tower; **Büh|nen|held** M stage hero; **Büh|nen|hel|din** F stage heroine; **Büh|nen|him|mel** M cyclorama; **Büh|nen|ma|ler(in)** M(F) scene painter; **Büh|nen|ma|le|rei** F scene painting; **Büh|nen|meis|ma|nu|skript** NT script; **Büh|nen|meis|ter(in)** M(F) stage manager; **Büh|nen|mu|sik** F incidental music; **Büh|nen|per|so|nal** NT theatre *(Brit) or* theater *(US)* staff; **Büh|nen|prä|senz** F stage presence; **Büh|nen|raum** M stage and backstage area; **büh|nen|reif** ADJ ready for the stage; **Büh|nen|schaf|fen|de(r)** [-ʃafndə] MF *decl as adj (geh)* dramatic artist; **Büh|nen|spra|che** F standard *or* received pronunciation; **Büh|nen|stück** NT (stage) play; **Büh|nen|tech|nik** F stage technique; **Büh|nen|tech|ni|ker(in)** M(F) stage technician; **Büh|nen|werk** NT stage entertainment, dramatic work; **büh|nen|wirk|sam** ADJ effective on the stage ADV *bearbeiten, umgestalten* effectively for the stage; **lässt sich dieser Stoff ~ gestalten?** would this material be effective on the stage?; **Büh|nen|wirk|sam|keit** F effectiveness on the stage; **Büh|nen|wir|kung** F dramatic effect
Buh-: **Buh|ruf** M boo, catcall; **Buh|ru|fer(in)** M(F) **der Redner wurde von ~n empfangen** the speaker was booed, the speaker was greeted by boos *or* booing; **die ~ wurden aus dem Saal entfernt** those who had booed were removed from the auditorium
buk *(old) pret von* **backen**
Bu|ka|rest ['bu:karɛst] NT **-s** Bucharest
Bu|kett [bu'kɛt] NT **-s, -s** *or* **-e** *(geh)* **a** *(= Blumenbukett)* bouquet **b** *(von Wein)* bouquet, nose
Buk|lee [bu'kle:] NT **-s, -s** bouclé (yarn)
Bu|ko|lik [bu'ko:lɪk] F -, *no pl (Liter)* bucolic *or* pastoral poetry
bu|ko|lisch [bu'ko:lɪʃ] ADJ *(Liter)* bucolic, pastoral
Bu|let|te [bu'lɛtə] F -, **-n** *(dial)* meat ball; **ran an die ~n** *(inf)* go right ahead!
Bul|ga|re [bʊl'ga:rə] M **-n, -n**, **Bul|ga|rin** [-'ga:rɪn] F -, **-nen** Bulgarian
Bul|ga|ri|en [bʊl'ga:riən] NT **-s** Bulgaria
bul|ga|risch [bʊl'ga:rɪʃ] ADJ Bulgarian
Bul|ga|risch(e) [bʊl'ga:rɪʃ] NT Bulgarian → *auch* **Deutsch(e)**
Bu|li|mie [buli'mi:] F -, *no pl (Med)* bulimia
Bulk|la|dung ['bʊlk-] F *(Naut)* bulk cargo
Bull|au|ge ['bʊl-] NT *(Naut)* porthole
Bull|dog|ge ['bʊl-] F bulldog
Bull|do|zer ['bʊldo:zɐ] M **-s, -** bulldozer
Bul|le ['bʊlə] M **-n, -n** **a** bull **b** *(inf: = starker Mann)* great ox of a man **c** *(pej sl: = Polizist)* cop *(inf)*; **die ~n** the fuzz *(pej sl)*, the cops *(inf)*
Bul|le F -, **-n** *(Hist, Eccl)* bull
Bul|len-: **Bul|len|bei|ßer** [-baisɐ] M **-s, -** *(= Hund)* bulldog; **Bul|len|bei|ßer** [-baisɐ] M **-s, -**, **Bul|len|bei|ße|rin** [-ərɪn] F -, **-nen** *(pej)* cantankerous *or* sour-tempered *(esp Brit)* character; **Bul|len|hit|ze** F *(inf)* sweltering *or* boiling *(inf)* heat; **Bul|len|markt** M *(St Ex inf)* bull market *(inf)*; **bul|len|stark** ADJ *(inf)* beefy *(inf)*, brawny, strong as an ox
Bul|le|rei [bʊlə'rai] F -, *no pl (sl)* cop-shop *(Brit inf)*, police station
bul|le|rig ['bʊlərɪç] ADJ *(dial)* sour-tempered *(esp Brit)*, cantankerous
bul|lern ['bʊlɐn] VI *(inf)* **a** *(= poltern)* to thud, to rumble; *(Wasser, Flüssigkeit)* to bubble; *(Ofen)* to roar **b** *(dial: = schimpfen)* to bellyache *(inf)*, to moan and groan *(inf)*
Bul|le|tin [bʏl'tɛ̃:] NT **-s, -s** bulletin
Bulle|tin|board ['bʊlətɪnbɔ:ɐd] NT **-s, -s**, **Bulle|tin-Board** NT **-s, -s** *(Comput)* bulletin board
bul|lig ['bʊlɪç] ADJ *(inf)* **a** brawny, beefy *(inf)* **b** *Hitze* sweltering, boiling *(inf)*
Bul|lig|keit F -, *no pl* brawniness, beefiness *(inf)*
bull|rig ['bʊlrɪç] ADJ = **bullerig**
Bull|ter|ri|er ['bʊl-] M bull terrier
bum [bʊm] INTERJ bang; *(tiefer)* boom
Bu|me|rang ['bu:məraŋ, 'bʊməraŋ] M **-s, -s** *or* **-e** *(lit, fig)* boomerang
Bu|me|rang|ef|fekt M boomerang effect
Bum|mel ['bʊml] M **-s, -** stroll; *(durch Lokale)* wander (*durch* around), tour (*durch* of); **einen ~ machen, auf einen ~ gehen** to go for *or* take a stroll; **einen ~ durch die Stadt machen** to go for *or* take a stroll (a)round (the) town, to (go for a) wander (a)round (the) town; **einen ~ durch die Nachtlokale machen** to take in a few nightclubs
Bum|me|lant [bʊmə'lant] M **-en, -en**, **Bum|me|lan|tin** [-'lantɪn] F -, **-nen** *(inf)* **a** *(= Trödler)* slowcoach *(Brit inf)*, slowpoke *(US inf)*, dawdler **b** *(= Faulenzer)* loafer *(inf)*, idler
Bum|me|lan|ten|tum [bʊmə'lantntu:m] NT **-s**, *no pl (pej)* absenteeism
Bum|me|lei [bʊmə'lai] F -, **-en** *(inf)* *(= Trödelei)* dawdling; *(= Faulenzerei)* loafing about *(inf)*, idling
Bum|mel|frit|ze M *(inf)* loafer *(inf)*, idler
bum|me|lig ['bʊməlɪç] ADJ *(= trödelnd)* slow; *(= faul)* idle
Bum|mel|le|ben NT *(inf)* life of idleness
bum|meln ['bʊmln] VI **a** *aux sein (= spazieren gehen)* to stroll; *(= Lokale besuchen)* to go (a)round the pubs/bars *etc*; *(= ausgehen)* to go out on the town; **im Park ~ gehen** to go for *or* take a stroll in the park **b** *(= trödeln)* to dawdle, to hang about *(inf)* **c** *(= faulenzen)* to idle *or* fritter one's time away, to take it easy
Bum|mel-: **Bum|mel|streik** M go-slow; **Bum|mel|zug** M *(inf)* slow *or* stopping train
Bum|merl ['bʊmɐl] NT **-s, -(n)** *(Aus inf)* point against
bum|mern ['bʊmɐn] VI *(dial)* to hammer, to bang
Bumm|ler ['bʊmlɐ] M **-s, -**, **Bumm|le|rin** [-ərɪn] F -, **-nen** **a** *(= Spaziergänger)* stroller **b** *(= Trödler)* slowcoach *(Brit inf)*, slowpoke *(US inf)*, dawdler
bumm|lig ['bʊmlɪç] ADJ *(inf)* = **bummelig**
bums [bʊms] INTERJ thump, thud; **~, da fiel der Kleine hin** bang! down went the little one
Bums [bʊms] M **-es, -e** *(inf: = Schlag)* bang, thump
Bums|bom|ber M *(sl)* plane carrying sex tourists
bum|sen ['bʊmzn] VI *impers (inf: = dröhnen)* **..., dass es bumste** ... with a bang; **er schlug gegen die Tür, dass es bumste** he hammered *or* thumped on the door; **es bumste, als ...** there was a thump *or* thud when ...; **es hat gebumst** *(von Fahrzeugen)* there's been a smash-up *(esp Brit inf) or* crash
VI **a** *(= schlagen)* to thump, to hammer; *(Ftbl sl)* to kick
b *aux sein (= prallen, stoßen)* to bump, to bang, to clout *(inf)*; *(= fallen)* to fall with a bang *or* bump; **mit dem Kopf gegen etw ~** to bump *or* bang *or* clout *(inf)* one's head on sth
c *(inf: = koitieren)* to have it off *(Brit inf)*, to have sex *or* nookie *(hum inf)*
VT *(inf)* **jdn ~** to lay sb *(sl)*, to have it off with sb *(Brit inf)*, to have sex *or* a bit of nookie *(hum inf)* with sb; **gebumst werden** to get laid *(sl)*
Bum|se|rei [bʊmzə'rai] F -, **-en** *(inf)* screwing *(sl)*
Bums-: **Bums|knei|pe** F *(pej inf)*, **Bums|lo|kal** NT *(pej inf)* (low) dive; **Bums|mu|sik** F *(inf)* loud (vulgar) music; **bums|voll** ADJ *(inf)* full to bursting
Bund [bʊnt] M **-(e)s, ⸚e** ['bʏndə] **a** *(= Vereinigung, Gemeinschaft)* bond; *(= Bündnis)* alliance; **der Alte/Neue ~** *(Bibl)* the Old/New Testament *or* Covenant; **mit jdm im ~e stehen** *or* **sein** to be in league with sb; **sich (dat) die Hand zum ~e reichen** *(geh)* to enter into a bond of friendship; **den ~ der Ehe eingehen** to enter (into) the bond of marriage; **ein ~ der Freundschaft** a bond of friendship; **den ~ fürs Leben schließen** to take the marriage vows → **australisch**
b *(= Organisation)* association, (con)federation; *(= Staatenbund)* league, alliance
c *(Pol: = Bundesstaat)* Federal Government; **~ und Länder** the Federal Government and the/its Länder
d *(inf: = Bundeswehr)* **der ~** the army, the services *pl*
e *(an Kleidern)* waistband
f *(Mus: bei Saiteninstrumenten)* fret
Bund NT **-(e)s, -e** ['bʊndə] *(von Stroh, Flachs, Reisig etc)* bundle; *(von Radieschen, Spargel etc)* bunch
BUND [bʊnt] -, *no pl abbr von* **Bund für Umwelt und Naturschutz Deutschland** ≈ German union for environmental and nature concerns
Bünd|chen ['bʏntçən] NT **-s, -** *(am Hals)* neckband; *(am Ärmel)* sleeve band
Bün|del ['bʏndl] NT **-s, -** bundle, sheaf; *(= Strohbündel)* sheaf; *(von Banknoten)* wad, bundle; *(von Karotten, Radieschen etc)* bunch; *(Opt: = Strahlenbündel)* pencil; *(Math)* sheaf; *(fig) (von Fragen, Problemen etc)* cluster; *(von Vorschlägen etc)* set; **ein hilfloses/schreiendes ~** a helpless/howling (little) bundle; **sein ~ schnüren** *or* **packen** *(dated)* to pack one's bags; **jeder hat sein ~ zu tragen** everybody has his cross to bear
Bün|del|funk M *(Telec)* trunking *(Brit)*
bün|deln ['bʏndln] VT *Zeitungen etc* to bundle up, to tie into bundles/a bundle; *Garben, Stroh*

to sheave; *Karotten etc* to tie into bunches/a bunch; *(Opt) Strahlen* to focus, to concentrate; *(fig) Widerstand, Aktionen* to consolidate → *auch* **gebündelt**

bün|del|wei|se ADV by the bundle, in bundles; **er holte ~ Banknoten aus der Tasche** he pulled wads of banknotes out of his pocket

Bün|den ['byndn] NT -s (= *Graubünden*) the Grisons

Bun|des- *in cpds* federal; **Bun|des|ad|ler** M *(Ger)* Federal Eagle; **Bun|des|agen|tur** F ~ **für Arbeit** (State) Department of Employment; **Bun|des|amt** NT Federal Office; **Bun|des|an|ge|stell|ten|ta|rif** M *(Ger)* statutory salary scale; **Bun|des|an|lei|he** F *(Ger)* government bond; **Bun|des|an|stalt** F *(Ger)* Federal Institute; ~ **für Arbeit** Federal Institute of Labour *(Brit) or* Labor *(US)*; **Bun|des|an|walt** M, **Bun|des|an|wäl|tin** F **a** *(Ger)* attorney of the Federal Supreme Court **b** *(Sw)* ≈ Public Prosecutor; **Bun|des|an|walt|schaft** F *(Ger)* Federal Prosecutor's Office; (= *Gesamtheit der Anwälte*) Federal bar; **Bun|des|an|zei|ger** M *(Ger)* Federal legal gazette; **Bun|des|ärz|te|kam|mer** F *(Ger) professional organization of German doctors,* ≈ General Medical Council *(Brit),* ≈ State Medical Board of Registration *(US)*; **Bun|des|auf|sicht** F *(Ger)* Government supervision; **Bun|des|auf|sichts|amt** NT Federal Regulator; **Bun|des|aus|bil|dungs|för|de|rungs|ge|setz** NT *law regarding grants for higher education*; **Bun|des|au|to|bahn** F *(Ger, Aus)* Federal autobahn *(maintained by the Federal Government)*; **Bun|des|bahn** F *(Aus, Sw)* Federal Railway(s *pl*); **Bun|des|bank** F, *no pl (Ger)* Federal bank; **Deutsche ~** Federal Bank of Germany; **Bun|des|be|auf|trag|te(r)** MF *decl as adj* Federal representative *or* official; **~r für Datenschutz** federal commissioner for data protection; **Bun|des|be|hör|de** F Federal authority; **Bun|des|blatt** NT *(Sw)* Federal Law Gazette; **Bun|des|bru|der** M *(Univ)* fellow member (of a/the student fraternity); **Bun|des|bür|ger(in)** M(F) *(Ger)* German, citizen of Germany; **bun|des|deutsch** ADJ German; *(Hist: = westdeutsch)* West German; **Bun|des|deut|sche(r)** MF *decl as adj* German; *(Hist: = Westdeutsche(r))* West German; **Bun|des|ebe|ne** F **auf ~** at a national level; **bun|des|ei|gen** ADJ Federal (-owned), national; **bun|des|ein|heit|lich** ADJ Federal, national ADV nationally; **etw ~ regeln** to regulate sth at national level

> **BUNDESFEIER**
>
> The **Bundesfeier** is celebrated in Switzerland on the evening of August 1st, the national holiday. It commemorates the so-called **Rütlischwur**, a pledge under which the very first cantons – Uri, Schwyz and Unterwalden – formed an alliance. This is regarded as the official founding of modern Switzerland.

Bun|des-: **Bun|des|fern|stra|ße** F *(Ger)* trunk *(Brit) or* main road *(maintained by the Federal Government)*; **Bun|des|fi|nanz|hof** M *(Ger)* Federal Fiscal Court; **Bun|des|ge|biet** NT *(Ger)* Federal territory; **Bun|des|ge|nos|se** M, **Bun|des|ge|nos|sin** F ally, confederate; **Bun|des|ge|richt** NT **a** *(Ger, Aus)* Federal Court **b** *(Sw)* Federal Appeal Court; **Bun|des|ge|richts|hof** M, *no pl (Ger)* Federal Supreme Court; **Bun|des|ge|schäfts|füh|rer(in)** M(F) *(von Partei, Verein)* general secretary; **Bun|des|ge|setz|blatt** NT *(Ger, Aus)* Federal Law Gazette; **Bun|des|grenz|schutz** M *(Ger)* Federal Border Guard; **Bun|des|haupt|stadt** F Federal capital; **Bun|des|haus** NT *(Ger, Sw)* Federal Houses of Parliament; **Bun|des|haus|halt** M Federal budget; **Bun|des|heer** NT *(Aus)* services *pl*, army, (federal) armed forces; **Bun|des|ka|bi|nett** NT *(Ger)* Federal cabinet; **Bun|des|kanz|lei** F *(Sw)* Federal Chancellery; **Bun|des|kanz|ler(in)** M(F) **a** *(Ger, Aus)* Chancellor **b** *(Sw)* Head of the Federal Chancellery; **Bun|des|kanz|ler|amt** NT *(Ger, Aus)* Federal Chancellery

> **BUNDESKANZLER**
>
> The **Bundeskanzler** of the Federal Republic of Germany is the head of government. In 2005 Angela Merkel became the first **Bundeskanzlerin**. The Chancellor is responsible for the government's general policy and by means of recommendations to the **Bundespräsident** appoints and dismisses ministers. The **Bundeskanzler** is generally elected for a period of four years (corresponding to the four-year **Bundestag** mandate) by a majority of members of parliament and on the recommendation of the **Bundespräsident**.
> In Austria, too, the **Bundeskanzler** is the head of government, appointed by the **Bundespräsident**. The Chancellor has no legal responsibility for general policy, but nominates ministers and thereby determines the composition of the government.
> In Switzerland, on the other hand, the **Bundeskanzler** is the head of the Federal Chancellery, a department of the **Bundesversammlung** and the **Bundesrat**. The responsibilities of the office include the organization of Federal elections and ballots and the publication of Federal laws. → BUNDESPRÄSIDENT, BUNDESRAT, BUNDESTAG, BUNDESVERSAMMLUNG

Bun|des-: **Bun|des|kri|mi|nal|amt** NT *(Ger)* Federal Criminal Police Office; **Bun|des|la|de** F *(Bibl)* Ark of the Covenant; **Bun|des|land** NT state; *(Ger auch)* Land of the Federal Republic of Germany; **die neuen Bundesländer** the former East German states; **die alten Bundesländer** the former West German states; **Bun|des|li|ga** F *(Ger Sport)* national league; **Bun|des|li|gist** [-ligɪst] M **-en, -en** *(Ger Sport)* national league team; **Bun|des|mi|nis|ter(in)** M(F) *(Ger, Aus)* Federal Minister; **Bun|des|mi|nis|te|ri|um** NT *(Ger, Aus)* Federal Ministry; **Bun|des|mit|tel** PL Federal funds *pl*; **Bun|des|nach|rich|ten|dienst** M *(Ger)* Federal Intelligence Service; **Bun|des|post** F *(Ger Hist)* **die (Deutsche) ~** the (German) Federal Post (Office); **Bun|des|prä|si|dent(in)** M(F) *(Ger, Aus)* (Federal) President; *(Sw)* President of the Federal Council

> **BUNDESPRÄSIDENT**
>
> The **Bundespräsident**, elected by the **Bundesversammlung**, is the head of state of the Federal Republic of Germany. The term of office is five years and the President can be re-elected only once. The **Bundespräsident's** main task is to represent Germany at home and abroad. Since the office is non-party political, presidents can make use of their status to draw attention to social problems and abuses of power.
> The Austrian **Bundespräsident** is also the head of state, but is elected by the people. The term of office is six years, with a possible second term. The President can dissolve the **Nationalrat** and appoints and dismisses the **Bundeskanzler**.
> In Switzerland the **Bundespräsident** is the chairman of the **Bundesrat** and is in office for a period of one year only. The President is not head of state, but he represents the country abroad. → BUNDESKANZLER, BUNDESRAT, BUNDESVERSAMMLUNG, NATIONALRAT

Bun|des-: **Bun|des|pres|se|amt** NT *(Ger)* Federal Government's Press and Information Office; **Bun|des|rat** M *(Ger)* Bundesrat, *upper house of the German Parliament (Sw)* Council of Ministers; **Bun|des|rat** M, **Bun|des|rä|tin** F *(Sw)* Minister of State

> **BUNDESRAT**
>
> The **Bundesrat** is the second chamber of the Federal Republic of Germany, representing the **Länder**. It has 69 members, who are not elected but delegated by the 16 **Land** governments. The most important of the **Bundesrat's** duties concerns legislation: Federal laws that impinge upon the responsibilities of the **Länder** require its approval. The **Bundesrat** may also object to other laws, although the **Bundestag** can overrule the objection. As a result, Federal policy can be influenced by parties who are in opposition in the **Bundestag** if these parties hold a majority in most of the **Land** parliaments.
> In Austria the **Bundesrat** has 63 members. Apart from being able to introduce its own proposals for legislation, the **Bundesrat** has certain rights of veto and approval with regard to laws passed by the **Nationalrat**.
> In Switzerland, however, the **Bundesrat** is the executive body, i.e. the government. The **Bundesversammlung** appoints seven **Bundesräte** (ministers), who must come from different cantons, for a period of four years. Each of these ministers is then placed in charge of a **Departement**. → BUNDESTAG, BUNDESVERSAMMLUNG, NATIONALRAT

Bun|des-: **Bun|des|rech|nungs|hof** M, *no pl (Ger)* Federal Audit Office, Federal Accounting Office; **Bun|des|recht** NT Federal law; **Bun|des|re|gie|rung** F *(Ger, Aus)* Federal Government; **Bun|des|re|pub|lik** F Federal Republic; **~ Deutschland** Federal Republic of Germany; **Bun|des|re|pub|li|ka|ner(in)** M(F) *(Ger)* citizen of the Federal Republic of Germany; **bun|des|re|pub|li|ka|nisch** ADJ *(Ger)* German; **Bun|des|schatz|brief** M *(Ger Fin)* Federal treasury bill; **Bun|des|schul|den|ver|wal|tung** F *(Fin)* Federal Debt Administration; **Bun|des|staat** M (= *Staatenbund, Gliedstaat*) federal state; **bun|des|staat|lich** ADJ federal ADV **die USA sind ~ organisiert** the US is divided into federal states; **Bun|des|stra|ße** F *(Ger)* Federal road *(maintained by the Federal Government)*; **Bun|des|tag** M, *no pl (Ger)* Bundestag, *lower house of the German Parliament (Hist)* Diet of the German Confederation

> **BUNDESTAG**
>
> The German **Bundestag** is the representative body of the Federal Republic of Germany and is elected by the people every four years. There are at least 598 elected representatives, of whom half are directly elected (**Erststimme**) and half taken from the parties' **Landeslisten** (**Zweitstimme**). The **Bundestag** passes Federal laws, elects the **Bundeskanzler**, exercises parliamentary control over the Federal government and sets the Federal budget. Although the General Assembly is its public face, the **Bundestag** carries out most of its work in committees, whose composition reflects that of the **Bundestag**.
> At the **Land** level there is usually a similar body, the **Landtag**. → BUNDESKANZLER, ERSTSTIMME/ZWEITSTIMME

Bun|des|tags- *(Ger)*: **Bun|des|tags|ab|ge|ord|ne|te(r)** MF *decl as adj* German member of Parliament, member of the Bundestag; **Bun|des|tags|frak|ti|on** F group *or* faction in the Bundestag; **Bun|des|tags|mit|glied** NT member of the Bundestag, member of (the German) parliament; **Bun|des|tags|prä|si|dent(in)** M(F) President of the Bundestag *or* German Parliament; **Bun|des|tags|wahl** F (federal) parliamentary elections *pl*

Bun|des-: **Bun|des|trai|ner(in)** M(F) *(Ger Sport)* national coach; **Bun|des|ver|band** M (= *bundesweite Vereinigung*) federal association;

Bun|des|ver|dienst|kreuz NT *(Ger)* order of the Federal Republic of Germany, ≈ OBE *(Brit)*; **Bun|des|ver|fas|sung** F Federal constitution; **Bun|des|ver|fas|sungs|ge|richt** NT *(Ger)* Federal Constitutional Court; **Bun|des|ver|samm|lung** F **a** *(Ger, Aus)* Federal Convention **b** *(Sw)* Federal Assembly

BUNDESVERSAMMLUNG

In Germany the **Bundesversammlung** is the body that elects the **Bundespräsident**. Half of the **Bundesversammlung** is made up of members of the **Bundestag**; the other half are delegates from the **Landtage**.
In Austria the **Bundesversammlung** is the joint body of the **Nationalrat** and **Bundesrat**. Its most important function is to swear-in the **Bundespräsident**.
The Swiss **Bundesversammlung** is a two-chamber parliament (**Nationalrat** and **Ständerat**) responsible for legislation. It also elects the **Bundesrat**, the **Bundeskanzler** and, every year, the **Bundespräsident**. The two chambers discuss the various bills independently of one another. → BUNDESKANZLER, BUNDESPRÄSIDENT, BUNDESRAT, BUNDESTAG, NATIONALRAT, STÄNDERAT

Bun|des-: **Bun|des|ver|si|che|rungs|an|stalt** F ~ **für Angestellte** federal pensions office for salaried employees; **Bun|des|ver|wal|tungs|ge|richt** NT *(Ger)* Supreme Administrative Court; **Bun|des|wehr** F, *no pl (Ger)* services *pl*, army, (German) Federal Armed Forces *pl*; **bun|des|weit** ADJ nationwide ADV nationwide, nationally; **sie bewarb sich ~ bei verschiedenen Firmen** she applied to different companies all over the country; **Bun|des|zent|ral|re|gis|ter** NT central criminal register

BUNDESWEHR

The **Bundeswehr** is the name for the German armed forces. It came into being in 1955, originally as a volunteer army. Since 1956, however, every male between the ages of 18 and 30 has been liable for **Wehrdienst** (military service), or a non-military alternative. Currently the **Bundeswehr** is composed of men performing their military service, soldiers serving voluntarily for a set period of between 2 and 15 years, and professional soldiers. Women are not liable for military service but since 2001 have been able to join the forces as volunteers. → BUNDESKANZLER, WEHRDIENST

Bund-: **Bund|fal|te** F pleat; **Hose mit ~** pleated trousers *pl*; **Bund|fal|ten|ho|se** F pleated trousers *pl (esp Brit)* or pants *pl (esp US)*; **Bund|ho|se** F knee breeches *pl*

bün|dig [ˈbʏndɪç] ADJ **a** *(= schlüssig)* conclusive; *(= kurz, bestimmt)* concise, succinct **b** *(= in gleicher Ebene)* flush *pred*, level ADV *fassen, formulieren* concisely, succinctly → **kurz**

Bün|dig|keit F -, *no pl (= Schlüssigkeit)* conclusiveness; *(= Kürze, Bestimmtheit)* conciseness, succinctness

bün|disch [ˈbʏndɪʃ] ADJ **die ~e Jugend** *(Hist)* members of the "free youth movement"

Bünd|nis [ˈbʏntnɪs] NT **-ses, -se** alliance; *(= Nato)* (NATO) Alliance; **~ 90** *political alliance of civil rights campaigners from the former GDR*; **~ für Arbeit** *informal alliance between employers and unions to help create jobs*

BÜNDNIS 90/DIE GRÜNEN

In 1993 the West German party **Die Grünen** joined forces with the East German grouping **Bündnis 90**, which had emerged from civil rights groups of the former **DDR**. The present party **Bündnis 90/Die Grünen** sees itself as a party of ecological reform. In addition to its environmental concerns, the party aims to increase social justice through a restructuring of the tax, social security and pension systems. It also demands an equitable sharing of burdens and interests between West and East Germany.

Bünd|nis-: **Bünd|nis|block** M *pl* **-blöcke** allied bloc; **Bünd|nis|grü|ne(r)** MF *(Pol)* member of Bündnis 90/Die Grünen; **Bünd|nis|part|ner** M *(Pol)* ally; **Bünd|nis|po|li|tik** F policy vis-à-vis one's allies; **Bünd|nis|sys|tem** NT system of alliances; **Bünd|nis|treue** F loyalty to the alliance; **die ~ der Ruritanier** the loyalty of the Ruritanians to the *or* their alliance; **Bünd|nis|ver|pflich|tung** F commitment to one's allies; **Bünd|nis|ver|trag** M pact of alliance

Bund-: **Bund|steg** M *(Typ, Comput)* gutter; **Bund|wei|te** F waist measurement; **Bund|zei|chen** NT jointing mark

Bun|ga|low [ˈbʊŋgalo] M **-s, -s** bungalow

Bun|gee-Sprin|gen [ˈbandʒi-] NT, **Bun|gee|sprin|gen** NT bungee jumping

Bun|ker [ˈbʊŋkɐ] M **-s, - a** *(Mil)* bunker; *(= Luftschutzbunker)* air raid shelter **b** *(= Sammelbehälter)* bin; *(= Kohlenbunker)* bunker; *(= Getreidebunker)* silo **c** *(Golf)* bunker **d** *(Mil sl: = Gefängnis)* clink *(inf)*, jankers *(Brit Mil sl)*

bun|kern [ˈbʊŋkɐn] VTI **a** *Kohle* to bunker; *Öl* to refuel **b** *(sl: = anhäufen, verwahren)* to stash (away) *(inf)*

Bun|ker|öl NT bunker oil *or* fuel

Bun|sen|bren|ner [ˈbʊnzn-] M Bunsen burner

bunt [bʊnt] ADJ **a** *(= farbig)* coloured *(Brit)*, colored *(US)*; *(= mehrfarbig)* colo(u)rful; *(= vielfarbig)* multicolo(u)red, many-colo(u)red; *(= gefleckt)* mottled, spotted; **zu ~e Kleidung** loud *or* gaudy clothing; **~e Farben** bright *or* gay colo(u)rs; **~es Glas** stained glass; **Abzüge in Bunt** *(Phot)* **~e Abzüge** *(Phot)* colo(u)r prints; **ich sehe lieber Filme in Bunt** I prefer seeing films in colo(u)r → **Hund**
b *(fig: = abwechslungsreich)* varied; **eine ~e Menge** an assorted *or* a motley crowd; **ein ~es Bild** a colourful *(Brit)* or colorful *(US)* picture; **in ~er Reihenfolge** in a varied sequence; **ein ~er Teller** a plate of cakes and sweets *(Brit)* or candy *(US)*; **ein ~er Abend** a social; *(Rad, TV)* a variety programme *(Brit)* or program *(US)*
c *(fig: = wirr)* confused, higgledy-piggledy
ADV **a** *(= farbig) anstreichen, anmalen* colourfully *(Brit)*, colorfully *(US)*; *gekleidet* brightly, colo(u)rfully; *bemalt, bemalen* brightly, gaily, in bright colo(u)rs; **etw ~ bekleben** to stick colo(u)red paper on sth; **~ fotografieren** *(inf)* to photograph in colo(u)r; **~ geblümt** *(Stoff, Kleid)* with a colo(u)rful flower design *or* pattern; **~ gefärbt** multicolo(u)red, many-colo(u)red; **~ gefiedert** with multi-colo(u)red *or* bright feathers *or* plumage; **~ gefleckt** *(Tier)* spotted, mottled; **~ gemischt** *(Programm)* varied; *Truppe, Team* diverse; **~ kariert** with a colo(u)red check (pattern); **~ gestreift** with colo(u)red stripes; **~ schillernd** iridescent; *(= farbig, fig)* colo(u)rful; *Vergangenheit auch* chequered *(Brit)*, checkered *(US)*
b *(= ungeordnet)* **~ durcheinander** *(= unordentlich)* higgledy-piggledy; **es geht ~ durcheinander** it's all a complete mess
c *(inf: = wild)* **jetzt wird es mir zu ~** I've had enough of this; **jetzt wirds mir aber zu ~!** that's going too far!, I've had enough!; **es geht hier ~ zu** it's lively here, this is some sort of madhouse *(pej inf)*; **es zu ~ treiben** to carry things too far, to overstep the mark

Bunt-: **bunt|be|malt** [-bəmaːlt] ADJ → **bunt ADV a**; **Bunt|druck** M *pl* **-drucke** colour *(Brit)* or color *(US)* print; **bunt|far|big** ADJ colourful *(Brit)*, colorful *(US)*, brightly coloured *(Brit)* or colored *(US)*; **Bunt|film** M *(inf)* colour *(Brit)* or color *(US)* film; **bunt|ge|blümt** ADJ → **bunt ADV a**; **bunt|ge|färbt** ADJ → **bunt ADV a**; **bunt|ge|fie|dert** ADJ → **bunt ADV a**; **bunt|ge|fleckt** ADJ → **bunt ADV a**; **bunt|ge|klei|det** ADJ → **bunt ADV a**; **bunt|ge|mischt** ADJ → **bunt ADV a**; **bunt|ge|streift** ADJ → **bunt ADV a**; **Bunt|heit** F -, *no pl* colourfulness *(Brit)*, colorfulness *(US)*, gay *or* bright colours *(Brit)* or colors *(US) pl*; **bunt|ka|riert** ADJ → **bunt ADV a**; **Bunt|me|tall** NT nonferrous metal; **Bunt|pa|pier** NT coloured *(Brit)* or colored *(US)* paper; **Bunt|sand|stein** M new red sandstone; **bunt|sche|ckig** ADJ spotted; *Pferd* dappled; *(fig)* motley; **bunt|schil|lernd** ADJ → **bunt ADV a**; **Bunt|specht** M spotted woodpecker; **Bunt|stift** M coloured *(Brit)* or colored *(US)* pencil; **Bunt|wä|sche** F coloureds *pl (Brit)*, coloreds *pl (US)*

Bür|de [ˈbʏrdə] F **-, -n** *(geh)* load, weight; *(fig)* burden; **jdm eine ~ aufladen** *(fig)* to impose a burden on sb

bür|den [ˈbʏrdn] VT *(dated geh)* **etw auf jdn ~** *(lit, fig)* to load sth upon sb

Bu|re [ˈbuːrə] M **-n, -n**, **Bu|rin** [ˈbuːrɪn] F **-, -nen** Boer

Bu|ren|krieg M Boer War

Burg [bʊrk] F **-, -en** [-gn] **a** castle; *(= Strandburg)* wall of sand *(built on beach by holiday-maker to demarcate his chosen spot)* **b** *(= Biberbau)* (beaver's) lodge

Burg-: **Burg|an|la|ge** F castle buildings *pl or* complex; **Burg|berg** M castle hill *or* mound

Bür|ge [ˈbʏrgə] M **-n, -n** *(fig)* guarantee *(für* of)

Bür|ge [ˈbʏrgə] M **-n, -n**, **Bür|gin** [ˈbʏrgɪn] F **-, -nen** guarantor; **für jdn ~ sein** to be sb's guarantor, to stand surety for sb; **einen ~n stellen** *(Fin)* to offer surety

bür|gen [ˈbʏrgn] VI **für etw ~** to guarantee sth, to vouch for sth; *(fig)* to guarantee sth, to be a guarantee of sth; **für jdn ~** *(Fin)* to stand surety for sb; *(fig)* to vouch for sb; **Sie ~ mir persönlich dafür, dass ...** you are personally responsible *or* answerable to me that ...

Bur|ger M *(Cook)* burger

Bür|ger [ˈbʏrgɐ] M **-s, -**, **Bür|ge|rin** [-ərɪn] F **-, -nen** *(von Staat, Gemeinde)* citizen, burgher *(Hist)*; *(Sociol, pej)* bourgeois; **die ~ von Ulm** the townsfolk of Ulm

Bür|ger-: **Bür|ger|ak|ti|on** F citizens' initiative, citizens' action group; **Bür|ger|be|auf|trag|te(r)** MF *decl as adj* ombudsman/-woman; **Bür|ger|be|geh|ren** NT *(Ger)* public petition; **Bür|ger|be|ra|tungs|stel|le** F citizens' advice bureau; **Bür|ger|block** M *pl* **-blöcke** conservative alliance; **Bür|ger|brief** M patent *(Brit)* or certificate *(US)* of citizenship; **Bür|ger|eid** M civic oath; **Bür|ger|ent|scheid** M *(Ger)* citizens' *or* public decision; **Bür|ger|fa|mi|lie** F merchant family; **bür|ger|fern** ADJ nonpopulist; **Bür|ger|fo|rum** NT open *or* public debate; **Bür|ger|haus** NT **a** town house *or* residence **b** *(dated: = Bürgerfamilie)* merchant family

Bür|ge|rin [-ərɪn] F → **Bürger**

Bür|ger-: **Bür|ger|ini|ti|a|ti|ve** F citizens' initiative *or* action group; **Bür|ger|ko|mi|tee** NT citizens' committee; **Bür|ger|krieg** M civil war; **bür|ger|kriegs|ähn|lich** ADJ civil war-like *attr*; **~e Zustände** civil war conditions

bür|ger|lich [ˈbʏrgɐlɪç] ADJ **a** *attr Ehe, Recht etc* civil; *Pflicht* civic; **Bürgerliches Gesetzbuch** Civil Code **b** *(= dem Bürgerstand angehörend)* middle-class *(auch pej)*, bourgeois *(esp pej)*; *(Hist)* bourgeois; **aus guter ~er Familie** from a good respectable *or* middle-class family; **~es Essen/Küche** good plain food/cooking; **~es Trauerspiel** *(Liter)* domestic tragedy ADV **diese Stadt ist ~ geprägt** this town is very middle-class; **ein ~ orientierter Politiker** a politician who aims for the middle-class vote; **~ essen** to eat good plain food

Bür|ger|li|che(r) [ˈbʏrgɐlɪçə] MF *decl as adj* commoner

Bür|ger|lich|keit F -, *no pl (von Lebensstil)* middle-class way of life; *(von Denkweise)* middle-class mentality

Bür|ger-: **Bür|ger|meis|ter** M mayor; **Bür|ger|meis|ter|amt** NT **a** *(= Aufgabe)* office of mayor **b** *(= Behörde, Gebäude)* town hall; **Bür|ger|meis|te|rei** [-maistə'rai] F -, **-en** *(old)* **a** district council; *(= Gebäude)* district council offices *pl* **b** *(dial: = Bürgermeisteramt)* town hall; **Bür|ger|meis|te|rin** F mayor(ess); *(= Frau eines Bürgermeisters)* mayoress; **bür|ger|nah** ADJ populist; **Bür|ger|nä|he** F populism; **Bür|ger|pflicht** F civic duty; **Ruhe ist die erste ~** law and order is the citizen's first duty, the first duty of the citizen is law and order; **Bür|ger|recht** NT *usu pl* civil rights *pl*; **jdm die ~e aberkennen** *or* **entziehen** to strip sb of his civil rights; **Bür|ger|recht|ler** [-rɛçtlɐ] M **-s, -**, **Bür|ger|recht|le|rin** [-ərɪn] F **-, -nen** civil rights campaigner

Bür|ger|rechts-: **Bür|ger|rechts|be|we|gung** F civil rights movement; **Bür|ger|rechts|kämp|fer(in)** M(F) civil rights campaigner

Bür|ger|schaft ['bʏrgɐʃaft] F -, **-en** citizens *pl*; *(= Vertretung)* City Parliament

Bür|ger|schafts|wahl F metropolitan council election *(in Hamburg and Bremen)*

Bür|ger|schreck M bog(e)y of the middle classes

Bür|gers|frau ['bʏrgɐs-] F *(old)* middle-class woman, bourgeoise *(Hist)*

Bür|gers|mann ['bʏrgɐs-] M *pl* **-leute** *(old)* citizen, bourgeois *(Hist)*

Bür|ger(s)|sohn M *(usu iro)* son of the middle classes

Bür|ger|stand M *(old)* middle class(es), bourgeoisie *(Hist)*

Bür|ger|steig M pavement *(Brit)*, sidewalk *(US)*; **die ~e hochklappen** *(inf)* to shut up *or* down (for the night)

Bür|gers|toch|ter ['bʏrgɐs-] F *(usu iro)* daughter of the middle classes

Bür|ger|tum ['bʏrgɐtu:m] NT **-s**, *no pl (Hist)* bourgeoisie *(Hist)*

Bür|ger|ver|samm|lung F town *or* citizens' meeting

Bür|ger|wehr F *(Hist)* militia

Burg-: **Burg|fräu|lein** NT damsel of the/a castle *(old)*; **Burg|fried** [-fri:t] M **-(e)s, -e** [-də] keep; **Burg|frie|de(n)** M **a** *(fig)* truce **b** *(Hist)* castle precincts *pl*, castellany; **Burg|herr** M lord of the/a castle; **Burg|her|rin** F lady of the/a castle

Bür|gin ['bʏrgɪn] F → **Bürge**

Burg|ru|i|ne F ruined castle, castle ruins *pl*

Bürg|schaft ['bʏrkʃaft] F -, **-en** *(Jur) (gegenüber Gläubigern)* security, surety; *(= Haftungssumme)* penalty; *(old liter)* pledge *(old liter)*; **~ für jdn leisten** to stand surety for sb, to act as guarantor for sb; *(fig)* to vouch for sb; **er verlangte eine ~** he demanded (a) security *or* surety

Bürg|schafts-: **Bürg|schafts|er|klä|rung** F declaration of suretyship; **Bürg|schafts|neh|mer(in)** M(F) creditor

Bur|gund [bʊr'gʊnt] NT **-s** Burgundy

Bur|gun|der [bʊr'gʊndɐ] M **-s, -** *(auch* **Burgunderwein***)* Burgundy

Bur|gun|der [bʊr'gʊndɐ] M **-s, -**, **Bur|gun|de|rin** [-ərɪn] F **-, -nen** Burgundian

bur|gun|der|far|ben [-farbn], **bur|gun|der|rot** ADJ burgundy (red)

bur|gun|disch [bʊr'gʊndɪʃ] ADJ Burgundian; **die Burgundische Pforte** the Belfort Gap

Burg|ver|lies NT (castle) dungeon

Bu|rin ['bu:rɪn] F **-, -nen** Boer

Bur|ka ['bʊrka] F **-, -s** chador

Bur|ki|na Fa|so [bʊr'ki:na 'fa:zo] NT **-s** Burkina-Faso

bur|lesk [bʊr'lɛsk] ADJ burlesque *no adv*

Bur|les|ke [bʊr'lɛskə] F **-, -n** burlesque

Bur|ma ['bʊrma] NT **-s** Burma

Bur|me|se [bʊr'me:zə] M **-n, -n**, **Bur|me|sin** [-'me:zɪn] F **-, -nen** Burmese

bur|me|sisch [bʊr'me:zɪʃ] ADJ Burmese

Burn-out ['bœrnaut, 'bø:ɐnaut] M **-s**, *no pl*, **Burn|out** M **-s**, *no pl (Med)* burnout

Burn-out-Syn|drom ['bœrnaut-, 'bø:ɐnaut-] NT *(Med)* burnout syndrome

Bur|nus ['bʊrnʊs] M **-** *or* **-ses, -se** burnous(e)

Bü|ro [by'ro:] NT **-s, -s** office

Bü|ro- *in cpds* office; **Bü|ro|an|ge|stell|te(r)** MF *decl as adj* office worker; **Bü|ro|ar|beit** F office work; **Bü|ro|ar|ti|kel** M item of office equipment; *(pl)* office supplies *pl or* equipment; **Bü|ro|au|to|ma|ti|on** F office automation; **Bü|ro|be|darf** M office supplies *pl or* equipment; **Bü|ro|dreh|stuhl** M swivel (desk) chair; **Bü|ro|ein|rich|tung** F office equipment *or* setup; **Bü|ro|flä|che** F office space *no pl*; **Bü|ro|ge|bäu|de** NT office building; **Bü|ro|ge|hil|fe** M, **Bü|ro|ge|hil|fin** F (office) junior; **Bü|ro|haus** NT office block; **Bü|ro|hengst** M *(pej inf)* office worker; **all die ~e** all the office crowd; **Bü|ro|hoch|haus** NT multistorey *(Brit) or* multistory *(US) or* high-rise office block; **Bü|ro|kauf|frau** F, **Bü|ro|kauf|mann** M office administrator; **Bü|ro|klam|mer** F paper clip; **Bü|ro|kom|mu|ni|ka|ti|on** F, *no pl* office communication; **Bü|ro|kraft** F (office) clerk; **Bü|ro|kram** M *(inf pej)* odd bits *pl* of paperwork

Bü|ro|krat [byro'kra:t] M **-en, -en**, **Bü|ro|kra|tin** [-'kra:tɪn] F **-, -nen** bureaucrat

Bü|ro|kra|tie [byrokra'ti:] F -, *no pl* bureaucracy

bü|ro|kra|tisch [byro'kra:tɪʃ] *(usu pej)* ADJ bureaucratic ADV bureaucratically

bü|ro|kra|ti|sie|ren [byrokrati'zi:rən] *ptp* **bürokratisiert** VT to bureaucratize

Bü|ro|kra|tis|mus [byrokra'tɪsmʊs] M -, *no pl* bureaucracy

Bü|ro-: **Bü|ro|land|schaft** F office environment *no pl*; **Bü|ro|lei|ter(in)** M(F) office manager; **Bü|ro|ma|schi|ne** F office machine; **Bü|ro|ma|te|ri|al** NT office supplies *pl*; *(= Schreibwaren)* stationery *no pl*; **Bü|ro|mensch** M *(inf)* office worker, pen pusher *(pej inf)*; **Bü|ro|mö|bel** PL office furniture *sing*; **Bü|ro|schluss** M office closing time; **nach ~** after office hours; **Bü|ro|stun|den** PL office hours *pl*; **Bü|ro|tä|tig|keit** F office work; **Bü|ro|tech|nik** F office technology; **Bü|ro|turm** M office block; **Bü|ro|vor|ste|her(in)** M(F) *(dated)* senior *or* chief *or* head clerk; **Bü|ro|zeit** F office hours *pl*

Bürsch|chen ['bʏrʃçən] NT **-s, -** *dim von* **Bursche** little lad *(Brit) or* fellow; **freches ~** cheeky *(Brit) or* fresh *(US)* little devil; **mein ~!** laddie! *(Brit)*, young man!

Bur|sche ['bʊrʃə] M **-n, -n** **a** *(old, dial)* boy, lad *(Brit)*; **ein toller ~** quite a lad *(Brit) or* young man **b** *(inf: = Kerl)* fellow, guy *(inf)*, so-and-so *(pej inf)*; **ein übler ~** a bad lot *(Brit)*, a shady character *(US)* **c** *(Univ: = Verbindungsmitglied)* member of a student fraternity **d** *(= Laufbursche)* boy **e** *(old Mil)* batman *(Brit)*, orderly **f** *(inf: = großes Exemplar)* **das ist vielleicht ein ~** what a whopper! *(inf)*; **da haben wir den ~n** that's got it *or* him! *(inf)*

Bur|schen-: **Bur|schen|herr|lich|keit** F good old student days; **Bur|schen|schaft** ['bʊrʃnʃaft] F **-, -en** student fraternity; **Bur|schen|schaf|ter** [-ʃaftɐ] M **-s, -**, **Bur|schen|schaft|ler** [-ʃaftlɐ] M **-s, -** member of a student fraternity; **bur|schen|schaft|lich** [-ʃaftlɪç] ADJ *attr* of a/the (student) fraternity; **~e Verbindung** student fraternity

BURSCHENSCHAFT

Burschenschaften are student organizations similar to American fraternities. They continue a tradition going back to the early 19th century, when they were politically very active and influential. Before the 1980s they were either banned or – during times of student unrest – marginalized, since they were regarded as conservative and nationalistic. Typical **Burschenschaftler** are recognizable by their bright sashes and peaked caps and are most often seen in university cities such as Heidelberg or Tübingen. Many **Burschenschaftler** remain loyal to their **Burschenschaft** after their student days are over. In so-called **schlagende Verbindungen**, the **Mensur**, a duel, is compulsory.

bur|schi|kos [bʊrʃi'ko:s] ADJ **a** *(= jungenhaft)* (tom)boyish **b** *(= unbekümmert)* casual ADV (tom)boyishly; **benimm dich doch nicht so ~** stop behaving like a tomboy

Bur|schi|ko|si|tät [bʊrʃikozi'tɛ:t] F **-, -en** **a** *(= Jungenhaftigkeit)* (tom)boyishness **b** *(= Unbekümmertheit)* casualness

Bur|se ['bʊrzə] F **-, -n** hostel

Bürs|te ['bʏrstə] F **-, -n** brush; *(inf: = Bürstenfrisur)* crew cut

bürs|ten ['bʏrstn] VT to brush; *(vulg: = koitieren)* to screw *(sl)*

Bürs|ten-: **Bürs|ten|bin|der(in)** M(F) brush-maker; **wie ein ~** *(inf)* like mad *(inf)* → **saufen**; **Bürs|ten|fri|sur** F, **Bürs|ten|haar|schnitt** M crew cut; **Bürs|ten|ma|cher(in)** M(F) brush-maker; **Bürs|ten|mas|sa|ge** F brush massage; **Bürs|ten|schnitt** M crew cut

Bu|run|di [bu'rʊndi] NT **-s** Burundi

Bu|run|di|er [bu'rʊndiɐ] M **-s, -**, **Bu|run|di|e|rin** [-iərɪn] F **-, -nen** Burundian

bu|run|disch [bu'rʊndɪʃ] ADJ Burundian

Bür|zel ['bʏrtsl] M **-s, -** **a** *(Orn)* rump **b** *(Hunt)* tail **c** *(Cook)* parson's nose

Bus [bʊs] M **-ses, -se** bus; *(= Privat- und Überlandbus)* bus, coach *(Brit)*

Bus M **-, -se** *(Comput)* bus

Bus|bahn|hof M → **Bus** bus/coach *(Brit)* station

Busch [bʊʃ] M **-(e)s, ¨-e** ['bʏʃə] **a** *(= Strauch)* bush, shrub; **etwas ist im ~** *(inf)* there's something up; **mit etw hinter dem ~ halten** *(inf)* to keep sth quiet *or* to oneself; **auf den ~ klopfen** *(inf)* to fish (about) for information *(inf)*; **bei jdm auf den ~ klopfen** *(inf)* to sound sb out; **sich (seitwärts) in die Büsche schlagen** *(inf)* to slip away; *(euph hum)* to go behind a tree *(euph hum)* **b** *(Geog: in den Tropen)* bush; *(inf: = Wildnis)* jungle **c** *(= Strauß)* bunch; *(rare: = Büschel)* tuft

Busch|boh|ne F dwarf bean

Bü|schel ['bʏʃl] NT **-s, -** *(von Gras, Haaren)* tuft; *(von Heu, Stroh)* bundle; *(von Blumen, Rettichen)* bunch; **in ~n wachsen** to grow in tufts; *(Blumen)* to grow in clumps

bü|sche|lig ['bʏʃəlɪç] ADJ in tufts; *Blüten* in clusters

bü|scheln ['bʏʃln] VT *(S Ger, Sw)* to tie into bunches

bü|schel|wei|se ADV *(von Gras, Haaren)* in tufts; *(von Heu, Stroh)* in bundles; *(von Blumen, Rettichen)* in bunches; *(von Blumenpflanzen)* in clumps

Bu|schen ['bʊʃn] M **-s, -** *(dial)* bunch of leaves *etc*

Bu|schen|schän|ke F, **Bu|schen|schen|ke** F *(Aus)* ≈ inn

Busch|feu|er NT *(lit)* bush fire; **sich wie ein ~ ausbreiten** to spread like wildfire

Bu|schi ['bʊʃi] NT **-s, -s** *(Sw)* baby

bu|schig ['bʊʃɪç] ADJ bushy

büsch|lig ['bʏʃlɪç] ADJ = **büschelig**

Busch-: **Busch|mann** M *pl* **-männer** *or* **-leute** bushman; **Busch|mann|frau** F bushwoman; **Busch|mes|ser** NT machete; **Busch|ne|ger(in)** M(F) maroon; **Busch|werk** NT bushes *pl*; **Busch|wind|rös|chen** [-rø:sçən] NT (wood) anemone

Bu|sen ['bu:zn] M **-s, -** *(von Frau)* bust, bosom; *(old: = Oberteil des Kleides)* bodice; *(liter: von Mann)* breast *(liter)*; *(fig geh: = Innerstes, von Natur)* bosom *(liter)*; **ein Geheimnis in seinem ~ wahren** to keep a secret deep in one's heart *(liter)*

Bu|sen-: **bu|sen|frei** ADJ topless ADV **sich ~ sonnen** to sunbathe topless; **Bu|sen|freund(in)** M(F) *(iro)* bosom friend; **Bu|sen|grab|scher** M -s, - *(inf)* groper *(inf)*; **Bu|sen|star** M *(inf)* busty film star *(inf)*

Bus-: **Bus|fah|rer(in)** M(F) → **Bus** bus/coach *(Brit)* driver; **Bus|fahr|plan** M bus timetible *(Brit)* or schedule *(US)*; **Bus|fahrt** F → **Bus** bus/coach *(Brit)* ride; **Bus|hal|te|stel|le** F bus stop

Bu|si|ness|class ['bɪznɪsklaːs] F -, *no pl*, **Bu|si|ness|klas|se** ['bɪznɪs-] F -, *no pl* business class

Bus|li|nie F bus route; **welche ~ fährt zum Bahnhof?** which bus goes to the station?

Bus|sard ['bʊsart] M -s, -e [-də] buzzard

Bu|ße ['buːsə] F -, -n **a** *(Rel) (= Reue)* repentance, penitence; *(= Bußauflage)* penance; *(= tätige Buße)* atonement; **~ tun** to do penance; **zur ~** as a penance; **zur ~ bereit sein** to be ready to do penance *or* to atone; **das Sakrament der ~** the sacrament of penance **b** *(Jur) (= Schadenersatz)* damages *pl*; *(= Geldstrafe)* fine; **eine ~ von 100 Euro** a 100-euro fine; **jdn zu einer ~ verurteilen** to make sb pay (the) damages; to fine sb, to impose a fine on sb

Bus|sel ['bʊsl] NT -s, -(n) *(Aus)* kiss

bus|seln ['bʊsln], **bus|sen** ['bʊsn] VTI *(S Ger, Aus)* to kiss

bü|ßen ['byːsn] VT to pay for; *Sünden* to atone for, to expiate; **das wirst** *or* **sollst du mir ~** I'll make you pay for that, you'll pay for that VI **für etw ~** *(auch Rel)* to atone for sth; *(= wiedergutmachen)* to make amends for sth; *für Leichtsinn etc* to pay for sth; **schwer (für etw) ~ müssen** to have to pay dearly (for sth)

Bü|ßer ['byːsɐ] M -s, -, **Bü|ße|rin** [-ərɪn] F -, -nen penitent

Bü|ßer|ge|wand NT, **Bü|ßer|hemd** NT penitential robe, hair shirt

Bus|se(r)l ['bʊs(ɐ)l] NT -s, -(n) *(S Ger, Aus)* kiss

bus|se(r)ln ['bʊs(ɐ)ln] VTI *(S Ger, Aus)* to kiss

Bü|ßer|schnee M *(spec)* penitent snow *(spec)*

Buß-: **buß|fer|tig** ADJ repentant, contrite; *(Rel auch)* penitent; **Buß|fer|tig|keit** F repentance, contrition; **Buß|gang** M *pl* **-gänge** penitential pilgrimage; **einen ~ antreten** *(fig)* to don sackcloth and ashes; **Buß|ge|bet** NT prayer of repentance

Buß|geld NT fine

Buß|geld-: **Buß|geld|be|scheid** M notice of payment due *(for traffic violation etc)*; **Buß|geld|ka|ta|log** M list of offences punishable by fines; **Buß|geld|stel|le** F fine payment office *(for traffic offenders)*; **Buß|geld|ver|fah|ren** NT fining system

Buß|ge|sang ['buːs-] M, **Buß|lied** NT penitential hymn

Bus|si ['bʊsi] NT -s, -s *(S Ger)* kiss

Bus|so|le [bʊ'soːlə] F -, -n compass; *(Elec)* galvanometer

Buß-: **Buß|pre|di|ger(in)** M(F) preacher of repentance; **Buß|pre|digt** F sermon calling to repentance

Bus|spur F bus lane

Buß-: **Buß|sa|kra|ment** NT sacrament of penance; **Buß|tag** M **a** day of repentance **b** = **Buß- und Bettag**; **Buß- und Bet|tag** M day of prayer and repentance; **Buß|übung** F act of penance

Büs|te ['bʏstə] F -, -n bust; *(= Schneiderbüste)* tailor's dummy; *(weibliche)* dressmaker's dummy

Büs|ten|hal|ter M bra, brassière *(dated)*

Bus|ti|er [bʏs'tieː] NT -s, -s *(ohne Träger)* bustier, boob tube *(Brit inf)*; *(mit Trägern)* bra top

Bu|su|ki [bu'zuːki] F -, -s bouzouki

Bus|un|glück NT → **Bus** bus/coach accident

Bus|ver|bin|dung F → **Bus** bus/coach connection

Bu|tan [bu'taːn] NT -s, -e, **Bu|tan|gas** NT butane (gas)

Butt [bʊt] M -(e)s, -e flounder, butt; **die ~e** the bothidae *(form)*, flounders

Bütt [bʏt] F -, -en *(dial)* speaker's platform; **in die ~ steigen** to mount the platform

But|te ['bʊtə] F -, -n **a** *(= Bütte)* vat; *(= Wanne)* tub **b** *(für Trauben)* grape container

Büt|te ['bʏtə] F -, -n vat; *(dial: = Wanne)* tub

But|tel ['bʊtl] F -, -n *(N Ger inf)* bottle

Büt|tel ['bʏtl] M -s, - *(old)* bailiff; *(pej)* henchman *(pej)*; *(= Polizist)* cop(per) *(inf)*; **die ~** the law *(inf)*, the cops *pl (inf)*; **ich bin doch nicht dein ~** *(inf)* I'm not going to do your dirty work *(pej inf)*, I'm not your henchman

Büt|tel|dienst M dirty work *(pej inf)*

Büt|ten|(pa|pier) ['bʏtn-] NT -s, *no pl* handmade paper *(with deckle edge)*

Büt|ten-: **Büt|ten|rand** M deckle edge; **Büt|ten|re|de** F carnival speech; **Büt|ten|red|ner(in)** M(F) *speaker on the platform at carnival*

But|ter ['bʊtɐ] F -, *no pl* butter; **braune ~** browned (melted) butter; **gute ~** real butter; **es schmolz wie ~ in der Sonne** *(fig)* it vanished into thin air; **alles (ist) in ~** *(inf)* everything is fine *or* OK *or* hunky-dory *(inf)*; **sein Herz ist weich wie ~** his heart is as soft as butter; **jdm die ~ auf dem Brot nicht gönnen** *(fig inf)* to begrudge sb the very air he/she breathes; **wir lassen uns (dat) nicht die ~ vom Brot nehmen** *(inf)* we're not going to let somebody put one over on us *(inf)*, we're going to stick up for our rights

But|ter- *in cpds* butter; **But|ter|bem|me** F *(dial)* bread and butter *no art, no pl*, slice *or* piece of bread and butter; *(inf: = Sandwich)* sandwich; **But|ter|berg** M *(inf)* butter mountain; **But|ter|blu|me** F buttercup; **But|ter|brot** NT bread and butter *no art, no pl*, slice *or* piece of bread and butter; *(inf: = Sandwich)* sandwich; **für ein ~** *(inf)* for next to nothing; *kaufen, verkaufen auch* for a song; **das musst du mir nicht ständig aufs ~ streichen** *or* **schmieren** there's no need to keep rubbing it in; **But|ter|brot|pa|pier** NT greaseproof paper; **But|ter|creme** F butter cream; **But|ter|creme|tor|te** F cream cake; **But|ter|damp|fer** M *(dated inf)* **a** *ferry sailing to another country to allow purchase of cheap goods* **b** *boat which sells duty-free goods once outside a country's territorial waters*; **But|ter|do|se** F butter dish; **But|ter|fahrt** F *(pej) boat/bus trip to buy cheap or duty-free goods*; **But|ter|fass** NT butter churn; **But|ter|fett** NT butterfat; **But|ter|flöck|chen** NT *(Cook)* (small knob of) butter

But|ter|fly|(stil) ['batɐflai-] M -s, *no pl* butterfly (stroke)

But|ter|fly|mes|ser ['batɐflai-] NT butterfly knife

But|ter-: **but|ter|gelb** ADJ butter yellow; **But|ter|gelb** NT **a** *(= Farbe)* butter yellow **b** *(= Farbstoff)* butter colour *(Brit)* or color *(US)*

but|te|rig ['bʊtərɪç] ADJ buttery

But|ter-: **But|ter|kä|se** M (full fat) hard cheese; **But|ter|keks** M ≈ rich tea biscuit *(Brit)*, ≈ butter cookie *(US)*; **But|ter|krem** F butter cream; **But|ter|mes|ser** NT butter knife; **But|ter|milch** F buttermilk

but|tern ['bʊtɐn] VT **a** *Brot* to butter **b** *Milch* to make into butter **c** *(inf: = investieren)* to put *(in +acc* into) VI to make butter

But|ter-: **But|ter|pilz** M boletus luteus *(form)*; **But|ter|säu|re** F butyric acid; **But|ter|schmalz** NT clarified butter; **But|ter|sei|te** F *(lit)* buttered side; **auf die ~ fallen** *(fig inf)* to fall on one's feet *(inf)*; **But|ter|toast** M buttered toast; **but|ter|weich** ADJ *Frucht, Landung* beautifully soft; *(Sport inf) Abgabe, Pass, Aufschlag* gentle ADV *landen, aufkommen* softly, gently; **~ formulierte Regelungen** vaguely worded regulations

Butt|je(r) ['bʊtjə] M -s, -s *(N Ger)* kid *(inf)*, child

Bütt|ner ['bʏtnɐ] M -s, -, **Bütt|ne|rin** [-ərɪn] F -, -nen *(dial)* cooper

But|ton ['batn] M -s, -s badge

But|ton-down-Kra|gen [batn'daun-] M button-down collar

butt|rig ['bʊtrɪç] ADJ = **butterig**

Butz [bʊts] M -en, -en *(dial) (= Zwerg)* hobgoblin; *(= Schreckgestalt)* bog(e)y(man)

Butz M -en, -en *(dial)* (apple) core

But|ze|mann ['bʊtsə-] M *pl* **-männer** *(= Zwerg)* hobgoblin; *(= Schreckgestalt)* bog(e)yman

But|zen ['bʊtsn] M -s, - *(dial)* **a** *(= Kerngehäuse)* (apple) core **b** *(in Butzenscheibe)* bulge *(in a bull's-eye pane)*

büt|zen ['bʏtsn] VTI *(dial)* to kiss

But|zen|schei|be ['bʊtsn-] F bulls'-eye (window) pane

Büx [bʏks] F -, -en, **Bu|xe** ['bʊksə] F -, -n *(N Ger)* trousers *pl (esp Brit)*, pants *pl (esp US)*; **fünf ~en** five pairs of trousers *(esp Brit)* or pants *(esp US)*

Bux|te|hu|de [bʊkstə'huːdə] NT -s **a** Buxtehude *(town near Hamburg)* **b** *(inf)* **aus/nach ~** from/to the back of beyond *(inf)*; **in ~ leben** to live in the back of beyond *(inf)*; **das macht man vielleicht noch in ~** perhaps they still do that in the provincial backwaters

Buy-out ['baiaut] M -s, -s, **Buy|out** M -s, -s buyout

BVG [beːfau'geː] NT - *abbr von* **Bundesverfassungsgericht**

Bw *abbr von* **Bundeswehr**

b. w. *abbr von* **bitte wenden** pto

B-Waf|fe ['beː-] F *von* **biologische Waffe**

BWL [beːveː'lɛl] F - *abbr von* **Betriebswirtschaftslehre**

BWV [beːveː'fau] NT -(s) *abbr von* **Bachwerkeverzeichnis** ≈ list of J. S. Bach's works

By|pass ['baipas] M -(es), -es *or* **Bypässe** [-pɛsə] *(Med)* bypass; **dreifacher/vierfacher ~** triple/quadruple bypass

By|pass|ope|ra|ti|on ['baipas-] F bypass operation

Byte ['bait] NT -s, -s byte

By|zan|ti|ner [bytsan'tiːnɐ] M -s, -, **By|zan|ti|ne|rin** [-ərɪn] F -, -nen Byzantine

by|zan|ti|nisch [bytsan'tiːnɪʃ] ADJ **a** Byzantine **b** *(= üppig)* extravagant

By|zan|ti|nist [bytsanti'nɪst] M -en, -en, **By|zan|ti|nis|tin** [-'nɪstɪn] F -, -nen Byzantine scholar

By|zan|ti|nis|tik [bytsanti'nɪstɪk] F -, *no pl* Byzantine studies *pl*

By|zanz [by'tsants] NT -' Byzantium

B-Zel|le ['beː-] F *(Med)* B-cell, B-lymphocyte

bzgl. *abbr von* **bezüglich**

bzw. *abbr von* **beziehungsweise**

C

C, c [tseː] **NT -, -** C, c
C *abbr von* **Celsius**
ca. *abbr von* **circa** approx
Cab|rio ['kaːbrio] **NT -s, -s** (*Aut inf*) convertible
Cab|ri|o|let [kabrio'leː] **NT -s, -s** (*Aut*) convertible
Cache [kɛʃ] **M -, -s** (*Comput*) cache; **externer ~** secondary *or* external cache; **interner ~** primary *or* internal cache
Cache-Spei|cher ['kɛʃ-] **M** (*Comput*) cache memory → *auch* **Cache**
Ca|chou [ka'ʃuː] **NT -s, -s, Ca|chou|bon|bon** [ka'ʃuː-] **NT** cachou
CAD [tseːlaː'deː] **NT -s,** *no pl abbr von* **computer aided design** CAD
Cad|die ['kɛdi] **M -s, -s** (*Golf*) caddie, caddy; (= *Einkaufswagen*) trolley, caddy (*US*)
Cad|mi|um ['katmiʊm] **NT -s,** *no pl* (*abbr* **Cd**) cadmium
Cae|sar ['tsɛːzar] **M -s** Caesar
Ca|fé [ka'feː] **NT -s, -s** café
Ca|fe|te|ria [kafeta'riːa] **F -, -s** cafeteria
Ca|fe|tier [kafe'tieː] **M -s, -s, Ca|fe|tie|re** [kafe'tieːrə] **F -, -n** (*old, Aus*) coffee house proprietor
Cai|pi **M -s, -s** (*inf*), **Cai|pi|rin|ha** **M -s, -s** caipirinha
cal *abbr von* **(Gramm)kalorie** (gram) calorie
Ca|lais [ka'lɛː] **NT -'** Calais; **die Straße von ~** the Straits of Dover
Cal|ci|um ['kaltsiʊm] **NT -s,** *no pl* calcium
Ca|li|for|ni|um [kali'fɔrniʊm] **NT -s,** *no pl* (*abbr* **Cf**) californium
Call-: **Call|box** ['kɔːl-] **F** (*Telec*) voicemail *no art*; **Call|boy** ['kɔːl-] **M** male prostitute; **Call|cen|ter** ['kɔːl-] **NT** (*Comm*) call centre (*Brit*) *or* center (*US*); **Call|girl** ['kɔːl-] **NT** call girl
Cal|va|dos [kalva'doːs] **M -, -** Calvados
cal|vi|nisch **ADJ ETC** = **kalvinisch**
Ca|lyp|so [ka'lɪpso] **M -(s), -s** calypso
CAM [tseːlaː'lɛm] **NT -s,** *no pl abbr von* **computer-aided manufacture** CAM
Cam|cor|der ['kamkɔrdɐ] **M -s, -** camcorder
Ca|mem|bert ['kaməmbeːɐ, kamã'bɛːɐ] **M -s, -s** Camembert
Ca|mi|on ['kamiõː] **M -s, -s** (*Sw*) lorry (*Brit*), truck
Ca|mor|ra [ka'mɔra] **F -,** *no pl* Camorra
Ca|mouf|la|ge [kamu'flaːʒə] **F -, -n** (*dated, geh*) camouflage
Camp [kɛmp] **NT -s, -s** camp; (= *Gefangenenlager auch*) compound
cam|pen ['kɛmpn] **VI** to camp
Cam|per ['kɛmpɐ] **M -s, -, Cam|pe|rin** ['kɛmpərɪn] **F -, -nen** camper
Cam|per ['kɛmpɐ] **M -s, -** (*Wohnmobil*) camper van (*Brit*), camper (*US*); (*größer*) motorhome
cam|pie|ren [kam'piːrən] *ptp* **campiert** **VI** **a** = **kampieren** **b** (*Aus, Sw:* = *campen*) to camp
Cam|ping ['kɛmpɪŋ] **NT -s,** *no pl* camping *no art*; **zum ~ fahren** to go camping
Cam|ping- *in cpds* camping; **Cam|ping|an|hän|ger** **M** (*für Fahrzeug*) camping trailer, travel trailer (*US*); **Cam|ping|ar|ti|kel** **M** piece *or* item of camping equipment; (*pl*) camping equipment *sing*; **Cam|ping|bus** **M** Dormobile® (*Brit*), camper (*esp US*); **Cam|ping|füh|rer** **M** camping *or* camper's guide(book); **Cam|ping|gas** **NT** camping gas; **Cam|ping|ko|cher** **M** camping stove; **Cam|ping|platz** **M** camp site; **Cam|ping|ur|laub** **M** camping holiday *or* trip (*Brit*), camping vacation (*US*); **~ machen** to go on a camping holiday (*Brit*) *or* trip (*Brit*) *or* vacation (*US*), to go camping; **Cam|ping|zu|be|hör** **NT** camping equipment
Cam|pus ['kampʊs] **M -,** *no pl* (*Univ*) campus; **auf dem ~** on (the) campus
Ca|nas|ta [ka'nasta] **NT -s,** *no pl* canasta
Can|can [kã'kãː] **M -s, -s** cancan
cand. *abbr von* **candidatus**, → **Kandidat**; **~ phil./med** *etc* final year arts/medical *etc* student
Can|na|bis ['kanabɪs] **M -,** *no pl* cannabis
Can|nel|lo|ni [kanɛ'loːni] **PL** cannelloni *sing or pl*
Ca|nos|sa [ka'nɔsa] **NT -s** (*fig*) humiliation; **nun muss er nach ~ gehen** he now has to eat humble pie → **Gang** **b**
Ca|nos|sa|gang **M** *pl* **-gänge einen ~ machen** *or* **antreten müssen** to eat humble pie
Can|to ['kanto] **M -s, -s** (*Liter*) canto
Can|yo|ning **NT -(s),** *no pl* (*Sport*) canyoning
Ca|ñon ['kanjɔn] **M -s, -s** canyon
Cape [keːp] **NT -s, -s** cape
Cap|puc|ci|no [kapu'tʃiːno] **M -s, -s** cappuccino
Cap|ric|cio [ka'prɪtʃo] **NT -s, -s** (*Mus*) caprice, capriccio
Car [kaːɐ] **M -s, -s** (*Sw*) *abbr von* **Autocar**
Ca|ra|van ['ka(ː)ravan, kara'vaːn] **M -s, -s** **a** (= *Kombiwagen*) estate car (*Brit*), station wagon **b** (= *Wohnwagen*) caravan (*Brit*), trailer (*US*)
Ca|ra|va|ning ['ka(ː)ravaːnɪŋ] **NT -s,** *no pl* caravanning (*Brit*), trailer camping (*US*)
CARE-Pa|ket ['kɛːə-], **Care|pa|ket** ['kɛːə-] **NT** CARE packet *or* parcel *or* package (*esp US*)
Ca|ret-Zei|chen **NT** (*Typ*) caret
Car|pool ['kaːɐpuːl] **M** car pool
Car|port ['kaːɐpɔrt] **M -s, -s** carport
car|ra|risch [ka'raːrɪʃ] **ADJ** *Marmor* Carrara
Car|rier ['kɛriɐ] **M -s, -s** (*Aviat, Comm, Telec*) carrier
Car|sha|ring ['kaːɐʃɛːrɪŋ] **NT -s,** *no pl*, **Car-Sha|ring** **NT -s,** *no pl* car sharing
car|te|si|a|nisch [karte'ziaːnɪʃ] **ADJ ETC** = **kartesianisch**
Car|toon [kar'tuːn] **M OR NT -(s), -s** cartoon; (= *Bildergeschichte auch*) strip cartoon
Car|too|nist [kartu'nɪst] **M -en, -en, Car|too|nis|tin** [-'nɪstɪn] **F -, -nen** cartoonist
Car|ving ['kaːɐvɪŋ] **NT -s,** *no pl* (*Ski*) carving
Car|ving|ski ['kaːɐvɪŋʃiː] **M** (*Ski*) carver (ski)
Ca|sa|no|va [kaza'noːva] **M -s, -s** (*fig*) Casanova
Cä|sar ['tsɛːzar] **M -s** Caesar
Cä|sar ['tsɛːzar] **M -en, -en** [tsɛ'zaːrən] (= *Titel*) Caesar
Cä|sa|ren- [tsɛ'zaːrən-]: **Cä|sa|ren|herr|schaft** **F** autocratic rule, dictatorship; **Cä|sa|ren|wahn|(sinn)** **M** megalomania
Cä|sa|ris|mus [tsɛza'rɪsmʊs] **M -,** *no pl* Caesarism, autocracy
cash [kɛʃ] **ADV** (*inf*) cash; **~ zahlen** to pay in cash
Cash [kɛʃ] **NT -,** *no pl* (*inf*) cash
Ca|shew|nuss ['kɛʃu-] **F** cashew (nut)
Cash|flow ['kɛʃfloː] **M -s,** *no pl* cash flow
Ca|si|no [ka'ziːno] **NT -s, -s** (*Aus*) = **Kasino**
Cä|si|um ['tsɛːziʊm] **NT -s,** *no pl* (*abbr* **Cs**) caesium (*Brit*), cesium (*US*)
Cas|set|te [ka'sɛtə] **F -, -n** (*etc*) → **Kassette**
Cas|ting ['kaːstɪŋ] **NT -s, -s** (*für Filmrolle etc*) casting session
Cas|tor® ['kastoːɐ] **M -s, -, Cas|tor|be|häl|ter** **M** spent fuel rod container

> **CASTOR**
>
> **CASTOR** containers are special containers for the transport and temporary storage of radioactive waste or fuel elements. The word is an abbreviation of the English "cask for storage and transport of radioactive material". Since nuclear energy is extremely controversial in Germany, demonstrations against the transport of **CASTOR** containers to temporary storage sites are a regular occurrence.

Cas|tor|trans|port ['kastoːɐ-] **M -s, -e** Castor transport, spent fuel rod transport
Ca|sus Bel|li ['kaːzʊs 'bɛli] **M - -, - -** ['kaːzuːs] (*geh*) casus belli (*form*)
CAT *abbr von* **computer-assisted trading** CAT
Catch-as-catch-can ['kɛtʃəz'kɛtʃ'kɛn] **NT -,** *no pl* (*lit*) catch-as-catch-can, all-in wrestling (*esp Brit*); (*fig*) free-for-all
cat|chen ['kɛtʃn] **VI** to do catch(-as-catch-can) wrestling, to do all-in wrestling (*esp Brit*); **er catcht gegen X** he has an all-in (*esp Brit*) *or* catch bout against X; **er catcht gut** he's a good all-in (*esp Brit*) *or* catch wrestler
Cat|cher ['kɛtʃɐ] **M -s, -, Cat|che|rin** ['kɛtʃərɪn] **F -, -nen** catch(-as-catch-can) wrestler, all-in wrestler (*esp Brit*)
Ca|te|ring ['keːtərɪŋ] **NT -(s),** *no pl* catering
Ca|te|ring-: **Ca|te|ring-Ser|vice** ['keːtərɪŋzøːɐvɪs, -zœrvɪs] **M, Ca|te|ring|ser|vice** **M** catering service; **Ca|te|ring-Un|ter|neh|men** **NT** catering firm *or* company
Ca|tull [ka'tʊl] **M -s** Catullus
Cause cé|lè|bre [koz se'lɛbr] **F - -, -s -s** (*geh*) cause célèbre
Ca|yenne|pfef|fer [ka'jɛn-] **M** cayenne (pepper)
CB-Funk [tseː'beː-] **M,** *no pl* Citizens' Band, CB (radio)
CB-Fun|ker(in) [tseː'beː-] **M(F)** CB (radio) user
cbm *abbr von* **Kubikmeter** cubic metre (*Brit*) *or* meter (*US*)
ccm *abbr von* **Kubikzentimeter** cc, cubic centimetre (*Brit*) *or* centimeter (*US*)
CD [tseː'deː] **F -, -s** *abbr von* **Compact Disc** CD
CD- *in cpds* CD; **CD-Bren|ner** **M** CD writer *or* burner; **CD-Ge|rät** **NT** CD player; **CD-I** [tseːdeː'liː] **F** *abbr von* **Compact Disc - Interactive** (*Comput*) CD-I; **CD-Lauf|werk** **NT** CD drive; **CD-Play|er** [-pleːɐ] **NT** CD player; **CD-R** [tseːdeː'lɛr] **F** *abbr von* **Compact Disc - Readable** (*Comput*) CD-R; **CD-Re|kor|der** **M** CD recorder; **CD-Roh|ling** **M** blank CD, recordable CD; **CD-ROM** [tseːdeː'rɔm] **F -, -s** CD-ROM; **CD-ROM-Lauf|werk** [tseːdeː'rɔm-] **NT** CD-ROM drive; **CD-RW** [tseːdeːɛr'veː] **F** *abbr von* **Compact Disc - Rewritable** (*Comput*) CD-RW; **CD-Spie|-**

ler M CD player; **CD-Stän|der** M CD rack; *(Turm auch)* CD tower

CDU [tseːdeːˈluː] F - *abbr von* **Christlich-Demokratische Union** Christian Democratic Union

> **CDU**
>
> The **CDU** **(Christlich-Demokratische Union Deutschlands)**, founded in 1945, is a political party in Germany standing for conservative Christian values and a social market economy. It contests elections in all **Länder** except Bavaria, where its sister party, the **CSU**, represents conservative voters. → CSU

CD-: **CD-Vi|deo** F video disc; **CD-Vi|deo|ge|rät** NT video disc player, CD video; **CD-Wechs|ler** M CD changer

Ce|dil|le [seˈdiːj(ə)] F -, -n cedilla

Ce|les|ta [tʃeˈlɛsta] F -, -s *or* **Celesten** [-ˈlɛstn] celeste, celesta

Cel|list [tʃɛˈlɪst] M -en, -en, **Cel|lis|tin** [-ˈlɪstɪn] F -, -nen cellist

Cel|lo [ˈtʃɛlo] NT -s, -s *or* **Celli** [ˈtʃɛli] cello

Cel|lo|phan® [tsɛloˈfaːn] NT -s, *no pl*, **Cel|lo|phan|pa|pier** NT *(inf)* cellophane® (paper)

Cel|lu|li|te [tsɛluˈliːtə] F -, *no pl*, **Cel|lu|li|tis** [tsɛluˈliːtɪs] F -, *no pl (Med)* cellulite → *auch* **Zellulitis**

Cel|lu|loid [tsɛluˈlɔyt, tsɛluloˈiːt] NT -s, *no pl* celluloid → *auch* **Zelluloid**

Cel|si|us [ˈtsɛlziʊs] *no art inv* Celsius, centigrade

Cel|si|us|ska|la F centigrade scale

Cem|ba|lo [ˈtʃɛmbalo] NT -s, -s cembalo, harpsichord

Cent [(t)sɛnt] M -(s), - cent; **30 ~** 30 cents; **mit dem** *or* **jedem ~ rechnen müssen** *(fig)* to have to watch *or* count every penny *(Brit) or* cent *(US)*; **jeden ~ (dreimal) umdrehen** *(fig inf)* to think twice about every penny *(Brit) or* cent *(US)* one spends

Cent|be|trag M **es war nur ein ~** it was only a matter of pennies *(Brit) or* cents *(US)*

Cen|ter [ˈsɛntɐ] NT -s, - *(= Einkaufscenter)* shopping centre *(Brit) or* center *(US)*

Cen|ter [ˈsɛntɐ] M -s, -(s), **Cen|te|rin** [-ərɪn] F -, -nen *(Sw Sport: = Mittelstürmer)* centre *(Brit) or* center *(US)* forward

Cent-: **Cent|stück** NT cent (piece); **cent|wei|se** ADV cent by cent, one cent at a time

Cer [tseːɐ] NT -s, *no pl (abbr* **Ce***)* cerium

ce|ri|se [səˈriːz] ADJ *inv (Fashion)* cerise, cherry

Cer|ve|lat [tsɛrvəˈlaːt] M -s, -s *(Sw)* cervelat, German salami

ces [tsɛs] NT -, -, **Ces** NT -, - *(Mus)* C flat

Cey|lon [ˈtsailɔn] NT -s Ceylon

Cey|lo|ne|se [tsailoˈneːzə] M -n, -n, **Cey|lo|ne|sin** [-ˈneːzɪn] F -, -nen Ceylonese, Sin(g)halese

cey|lo|ne|sisch [tsailoˈneːzɪʃ] ADJ Ceylonese, Sin(g)halese

Cha-Cha-Cha [ˈtʃaˈtʃaˈtʃa] M -(s), -s cha-cha (-cha)

Chag|rin|le|der [ʃaˈgrɛ̃ː-] NT shagreen

Chai|se [ˈʃɛːzə] F -, -n **a** *(old) (= Kutsche)* (post) chaise *(old)*; *(= Stuhl)* chair **b** *(inf)* jalopy *(inf)*, banger *(Brit inf)*

Chai|se|longue [ʃɛzəˈlɔŋ] F -, -s chaise longue

Cha|let [ʃaˈleː] NT -s, -s chalet

Cha|mä|le|on [kaˈmɛːleɔn] NT -s, -s *(lit, fig)* chameleon

cha|mä|le|on|ar|tig ADJ *(lit, fig)* chameleon-like ADV like a chameleon

Chamb|re sé|pa|rée [ʃɑ̃brəsepaˈre] NT - -, -s -s *(dated)* private room

Cha|mois [ʃaˈmoa] NT -, *no pl* **a** *(= Farbe)* buff (colour *(Brit) or* color *(US)*), (light) tan (colour *(Brit) or* color *(US)*) **b** *(auch* **Chamoisleder***)* chamois (leather)

Champ [tʃɛmp] M -s, -s *(inf: Sport, fig)* champ

Cham|pag|ner® [ʃamˈpanjɐ] M -s, - champagne

cham|pag|ner|far|ben [ʃamˈpanjɐfarbn] ADJ champagne, champagne-coloured *(Brit)*, champagne-colored *(US)*

Cham|pig|non [ˈʃampɪnjɔŋ, ˈʃɑ̃ːpɪnjõː] M -s, -s mushroom

Cham|pig|non-: **Cham|pig|non|kul|tur** F mushroom culture; **Cham|pig|non|zucht** F mushroom cultivation *or* growing

Cham|pi|on [ˈtʃɛmpiən] M -s, -s champion; *(= Mannschaft)* champions *pl*

Chan|ce [ˈʃɑ̃ːsə, *(Aus)* ʃɑ̃ːs] F -, -n **a** chance; *(bei Wetten)* odds *pl*; **keine ~ haben** not to have *or* stand a chance; **nicht die geringste ~ haben** not to have an earthly (chance) *(inf)*; **ich sehe keine ~, das noch rechtzeitig zu schaffen** I don't see any chance of being able to do it in time; **die ~n, von einem Auto überfahren zu werden** the chances of being run over by a car; **jdm eine letzte ~ geben** to give sb one last chance; **die ~n stehen nicht schlecht, dass...** there's a good chance that...; **wie sieht es mit deiner Beförderung aus? – na ja, die ~n stehen nicht schlecht** what about your promotion? – well, I'm in with a good chance *(Brit) or* well, the odds are in my favor *(US)*; **die ~n stehen 100:1** the odds are a hundred to one; **die ~n verringern sich/steigen** the odds are lengthening/shortening; *(fig auch)* the chances are getting worse/improving **b Chancen** PL *(= Aussichten)* prospects *pl*; **im Beruf ~n haben** to have good career prospects; **(bei jdm) ~n haben** *(inf)* to stand a chance (with sb) *(inf)*

Chan|cen-: **chan|cen|gleich** ADJ *Aufstiegsmöglichkeiten* equal; **sie waren ~** they had equal opportunities; **Chan|cen|gleich|heit** F equal opportunities *pl*; **chan|cen|los** ADJ *Spieler, Partei* bound to lose; *Plan, Produkt* bound to fail; **Chan|cen|lo|sig|keit** F -, *no pl* lack of prospects for success; **Chan|cen|ver|wer|tung** F *(Sport)* finishing

chan|gie|ren [ʃɑ̃ˈʒiːrən, ʃaŋˈʒiːrən] *ptp* **changiert** VI **a** *(= schillern)* to be iridescent; **~de Seide** shot silk **b** *(Pferd)* to change step

Chan|son [ʃɑ̃ˈsõː] NT -s, -s (political/satirical) song

Chan|so|net|te [ʃɑ̃soˈnɛtə] F -, -n, **Chan|son|net|te** [ʃɑ̃sɔˈnɛtə] F -, -n singer of political/satirical songs

Chan|son|ni|er [ʃɑ̃sɔˈnieː] M -s, -s singer of political/satirical songs; *(= Dichter)* political/satirical songwriter

Cha|os [ˈkaːɔs] NT -, *no pl* chaos; **einem ~ gleichen, ein einziges ~ sein** to be in utter chaos

Cha|os-: **Cha|os|for|schung** [ˈkaːɔs-] F research into the chaos theory; **Cha|os|ta|ge** [ˈkaːɔs-] PL *(inf)* **a** chaos days *pl*, chaotic period **b** *(Pol sl)* meeting of the lunatic fringe; **Cha|os|the|o|rie** [ˈkaːɔs-] F *(Math, Phys)* chaos theory

Cha|ot [kaˈoːt] M -en, -en, **Cha|o|tin** [kaˈoːtɪn] F -, -nen *(Pol pej)* anarchist *(pej)*; *(= unordentlicher Mensch)* scatterbrain *(pej)*; **er ist ein richtiger ~** he's completely chaotic

cha|o|tisch [kaˈoːtɪʃ] ADJ chaotic; **~e Zustände** a state of (utter) chaos ADV chaotically; **es geht ~ zu** there is utter chaos; **in deinem Zimmer sieht es ~ aus** your room looks chaotic

Cha|peau claque [ʃapo ˈklak] M - -, -x -s opera hat

Cha|rak|ter [kaˈraktɐ] M -s, -e [-ˈteːrə] **a** *(= Wesen, Eigenart)* character; **er ist ein Mann von ~** he is a man of character; **etw prägt den ~** sth is character-forming; **keinen ~ haben** *(ohne Prägung)* to have no character, to lack character; *(nicht ehrenhaft auch)* to have no principles; **die Party bekam immer mehr den ~ einer Orgie** the party became more and more like an orgy; **seine Warnung hatte mehr den ~ einer Drohung** his warning was more like a threat; **der vertrauliche ~ dieses Gespräches** the confidential nature of this conversation **b** *(= Person)* character, personality; *(Liter, Theat)* character; **sie sind ganz gegensätzliche ~e** their characters are entirely different, they have entirely different personalities **c** *(dated Typ)* character

Cha|rak|ter-: **Cha|rak|ter|an|la|ge** F characteristic, trait; **angeborene ~n** innate characteristics; **jds gute ~n fördern** to encourage sb's good qualities *or* (character) traits; **Cha|rak|ter|bild** NT character (image); *(= Charakterschilderung)* character study; **cha|rak|ter|bil|dend** ADJ character-forming; **Cha|rak|ter|bil|dung** F character formation; **Cha|rak|ter|dar|stel|ler(in)** M(F) character actor/actress; **Cha|rak|ter|ei|gen|schaft** F character trait; **Cha|rak|ter|feh|ler** M character defect; **cha|rak|ter|fest** ADJ strong-minded, of firm *or* strong character; **ein ~er Mann** a man of firm *or* strong character; **Cha|rak|ter|fes|tig|keit** F strength of character, strong-mindedness

cha|rak|te|ri|sie|ren [karakteriˈziːrən] *ptp* **charakterisiert** VT to characterize; **jdn als etw ~** to portray *or* characterize sb as sth

Cha|rak|te|ri|sie|rung F -, -en characterization

Cha|rak|te|ris|tik [karakteˈrɪstɪk] F -, -en **a** description; *(= typische Eigenschaften)* characteristics *pl* **b** *(Tech)* characteristic curve

Cha|rak|te|ris|ti|kum [karakteˈrɪstikʊm] NT -s, **Charakteristika** [-ka] *(geh)* characteristic (feature)

cha|rak|te|ris|tisch [karakteˈrɪstɪʃ] ADJ characteristic *(für* of)

cha|rak|te|ris|ti|scher|wei|se ADV characteristically

Cha|rak|ter-: **Cha|rak|ter|kopf** M *(= Kopf)* distinctive *or* striking features *pl*; **cha|rak|ter|lich** [kaˈraktɐlɪç] ADJ (of) character; **~e Stärke** strength of character; **~e Mängel** character defects; **~e Qualitäten** personal qualities; **~e Anforderungen stellen** to make demands on one's character ADV in character; **sie hat sich ~ sehr verändert** her character has changed a lot; **jdn ~ stark prägen** to have a strong influence on sb's character; **cha|rak|ter|los** ADJ **a** *(= niederträchtig) Mensch, Verhalten etc* unprincipled **b** *(= ohne Prägung)* characterless; *Spiel, Vortrag* colourless *(Brit)*, colorless *(US)* ADV in an unprincipled way; **Cha|rak|ter|lo|sig|keit** F -, -en **a** *(= Niederträchtigkeit)* lack of principles; *(Handlung)* unprincipled behaviour *(Brit) or* behavior *(US) no pl* **b** *no pl (= Prägungslosigkeit)* characterlessness; *(von Spiel, Vortrag)* colourlessness *(Brit)*, colorlessness *(US)*; **Cha|rak|ter|merk|mal** NT characteristic

Cha|rak|te|ro|lo|ge [karakteroˈloːgə] M -n, -n, **Cha|rak|te|ro|lo|gin** [-ˈloːgɪn] F -, -nen characterologist

Cha|rak|te|ro|lo|gie [karakteroloˈgiː] F -, *no pl* characterology

cha|rak|te|ro|lo|gisch [karakteroˈloːgɪʃ] ADJ characterological

Cha|rak|ter-: **Cha|rak|ter|rol|le** F character part *or* role; **Cha|rak|ter|sa|che** F *(inf)* **das ist ~** it's a matter of character; **Cha|rak|ter|schau|spie|ler(in)** M(F) character actor/actress; **cha|rak|ter|schwach** ADJ weak, of weak character; **Cha|rak|ter|schwä|che** F weakness of character; **Cha|rak|ter|schwein** NT *(inf)* unprincipled character; **cha|rak|ter|stark** ADJ strong, of strong character; **Cha|rak|ter|stär|ke** F strength of character; **Cha|rak|ter|stück** NT *(Mus)* mood piece; **Cha|rak|ter|stu|die** F character study; **cha|rak|ter|voll** ADJ **a** *(= anständig) Verhalten* which shows character; **dazu ist er zu ~** he has too much character for that **b** *(= ausgeprägt)* full of character; **eine ~e Stadt** a town (full) of character; **Cha|rak|ter|zug** M characteristic; *(von Menschen auch)* (character) trait; **es ist kein sehr schöner ~ von ihm, ...** it is not very nice of him ...

Char|ge [ˈʃarʒə] F -, -n **a** *(Mil, fig: = Dienstgrad, Person)* rank; **die unteren ~n** the lower ranks *or* echelons **b** *(Theat)* minor character part

char|gie|ren [ʃarˈʒiːrən] *ptp* **chargiert** VI *(Theat)* (= *übertreiben*) to overact, to ham *(inf)*; (= *eine Charge spielen*) to play a minor character part

Cha|ris|ma [ˈçaːrɪsma, ˈçarɪsma, kaˈrɪsma] NT **-s, Charismen** *or* **Charismata** [-mən, -mata] *(Rel, fig)* charisma

Cha|ris|ma|ti|ker [çarɪsˈmaːtikɐ] M **-s, -, Cha|ris|ma|ti|ke|rin** [-ərɪn] F **-, -nen** *(Rel)* member of the charismatic movement; *(fig)* charismatic person

cha|ris|ma|tisch [çarɪsˈmaːtɪʃ] ADJ charismatic ADV charismatically

Charles|ton [ˈtʃarlstn] M **-, -s** charleston

Char|lot|ten|bur|ger [ʃarˈlɔtnbʊrgɐ] M **-s, - einen ~ machen** *(dial sl) to blow out snot using one's fingers and flick it away*

char|mant [ʃarˈmant] ADJ charming ADV *lächeln, sich verhalten* charmingly

Charme [ʃarm] M **-s,** *no pl* charm

Char|meur [ʃarˈmøːɐ] M **-s, -e** charmer; (= *Schmeichler*) flatterer; **du alter ~!** you old smoothy! *(inf)*

Char|meuse [ʃarˈmøːz] F **-,** *no pl (Tex)* Charmeuse®

Chart [tʃart] M OR NT **-, -s** a *(Comput)* chart; (= *grafische Darstellung*) chart, graph b **die ~s** (= *Hitparade*) the charts

Char|ta [ˈkarta] F **-, -s** charter; **Magna ~** Magna Carta

Char|ter [ˈtʃartɐ] M **-s, -s** charter

Char|ter-: **Char|ter|flug** M charter flight; **Char|ter|(flug)|ge|sell|schaft** F charter (flight) company; **Char|ter|ma|schi|ne** F charter plane

char|tern [ˈtʃartɐn] VT *Schiff, Flugzeug* to charter; *(fig inf) Taxi, Arbeitskräfte etc* to hire

Char|ter|ver|kehr M charter flights *pl*

Chas|sis [ʃaˈsiː] NT **-, -** [-iːs, -iːs] *(Aut, Rad, TV)* chassis

Chat [tʃɛt] M *(Internet inf)* chat

Chat|i|quet|te [tʃɛtɪˈkɛtə] F *(Internet)* chatiquette

Chat- [ˈtʃɛt]: **Chat|pro|gramm** M M chat program; **Chat|raum** M, **Chat|room** [ˈtʃɛtruːm] M **-s, -s** chat room

chat|ten [ˈtʃɛtn] VI *(Internet inf)* to chat

Chauf|feur [ʃɔˈføːɐ] M **-s, -e, Chauf|feu|rin** [-ˈføːrɪn] F **-, -nen** chauffeur

chauf|fie|ren [ʃɔˈfiːrən] *ptp* **chauffiert** VTI *(dated)* to chauffeur, to drive

Chaus|see [ʃoˈseː] F **-, -n** [-ˈseːən] *(dated)* high road; *(in Straßennamen)* Avenue

Chaus|see-: **Chaus|see|baum** M *(dated)* roadside tree; **Chaus|see|gra|ben** M *(dated)* ditch

Chau|vi [ˈʃoːvi] M **-s, -s** *(inf)* male chauvinist pig *(pej inf)*, MCP *(Brit pej inf)*

Chau|vi|nis|mus [ʃoviˈnɪsmʊs] M **-, Chauvinismen** [-mən] chauvinism; (= *männlicher Chauvinismus*) male chauvinism; (= *Benehmen/Äußerung*) chauvinist(ic) action/remark

Chau|vi|nist [ʃoviˈnɪst] M **-en, -en, Chau|vi|nis|tin** [-ˈnɪstɪn] F **-, -nen** *(Pol)* chauvinist; (= *männlicher Chauvinist*) male chauvinist (pig)

chau|vi|nis|tisch [ʃoviˈnɪstɪʃ] ADJ a *(Pol)* chauvinist(ic); **er ist sehr ~** he is a real chauvinist b (= *männlich-chauvinistisch*) male chauvinist(ic) ADV a *(Pol)* chauvinistically; **~ klingende Wahlpropaganda** chauvinistic election propaganda; **~ angehauchte Politiker** politicians with chauvinistic tendencies b (= *männlich-chauvinistisch*) in a male chauvinist way; **sich ~ verhalten** to behave like a male chauvinist

Cheat M **-s, -s** *(Comput)* cheat (code)

che|cken [ˈtʃɛkn] VT a (= *überprüfen*) to check b *(inf: = verstehen)* to get *(inf)* c *(inf: = merken)* to cotton *(Brit) or* catch on to *(inf)*, to wise up to *(inf)*; **er hat das nicht gecheckt** he didn't cotton *(Brit) or* catch on *(inf)*, he didn't wise up to it *(inf)* VTI *(Eishockey)* to block; (= *anrempeln*) to barge

Check-: **Check|lis|te** F check list; **Check|point** [-pɔynt] M **-s, -s** checkpoint; **Check-up** [ˈtʃɛkap] M OR NT **-(s), -s** *(Med)* checkup

Chef [ʃɛf, *(Aus)* ʃeːf] M **-s, -s** boss; *(von Bande, Delegation etc)* leader; *(von Organisation, inf: = Schuldirektor)* head; *(der Polizei)* chief; *(Mil: von Kompanie)* commander; **~ des Stabes** Chief of Staff; **er ist der ~ vom Ganzen** he's in charge *or* the boss here; **hallo ~!** *(inf)* hey, gov(ernor) *or* chief *or* squire *(all Brit inf) or* mac *(US inf)*

Chef|an|klä|ger(in) M(F) *(Jur)* chief prosecutor

Chef|arzt M, **Chef|ärz|tin** F senior consultant

Chef|eta|ge F management *or* executive floor; *(fig: = Unternehmensleitung)* management

Chef-: **Chef|ideo|lo|ge** M, **Chef|ideo|lo|gin** F *(inf)* chief ideologist

Che|fin [ˈʃɛfɪn, *(Aus)* ˈʃeːfɪn] F **-, -nen** a boss; *(Sch)* head; *(von Delegation etc)* head b *(inf: = Frau des Chefs)* boss's wife; **Frau ~!** ma'am *(US)*, ≈ excuse me

Chef-: **Chef|koch** M, **Chef|kö|chin** F chef, head cook; **Chef|re|dak|teur(in)** M(F) editor in chief; *(einer Zeitung)* editor; **Chef|re|dak|ti|on** F a (= *Aufgabe*) (chief) editorship b (= *Büro*) main editorial office c (= *Personal*) main editorial staff; **Chef|sa|che** F **etw zur ~ erklären** to make sth a matter for decision at the top level; **das ist ~** it's a matter for the boss; **Chef|sek|re|tär(in)** M(F) personal assistant; **Chef|ses|sel** M *(inf, fig)* boss's job; **auf dem ~ sitzen** to be the boss; **es auf den ~ abgesehen haben** to have one's eye on the boss's job; **Chef|un|ter|händ|ler(in)** M(F) chief negotiator; **Chef|vi|si|te** F *(Med)* consultant's round

chem. *abbr von* **chemisch**

Che|mie [çeˈmiː, *(esp S Ger)* keˈmiː] F **-,** *no pl (lit, fig)* chemistry; *(inf: = Chemikalien)* chemicals *pl*; **was die so essen, ist alles ~** they just eat synthetic food

Che|mie-: **Che|mie|ar|bei|ter(in)** M(F) chemical worker; **Che|mie|be|ruf** M job in industrial chemistry; **Che|mie|fa|ser** F synthetic *or* man-made fibre *(Brit) or* fiber *(US)*; **Che|mie|klo** NT *(inf)* chemical toilet; **Che|mie|kon|zern** M chemicals group; **Che|mie|to|i|let|te** F chemical toilet; **Che|mie|un|fall** M chemical accident; **Che|mie|un|ter|richt** M chemistry; **Che|mie|waf|fe** F *usu pl* chemical weapon; **che|mie|waf|fen|frei** ADJ free of chemical weapons; **~e Zone** chemical-weapon-free zone

Che|mi|kal [çemiˈkaːl, *(esp S Ger)* ke-] NT **-s, -ien** [-liən] = **Chemikalie**

Che|mi|ka|lie [çemiˈkaːliə, *(esp S Ger)* ke-] F **-, -n** *usu pl* chemical

Che|mi|ker [ˈçeːmikɐ, *(esp S Ger)* ˈkeː-] M **-s, -, Che|mi|ke|rin** [-ərɪn] F **-, -nen** chemist

Che|mi|née [ˈʃmineː] NT **-s, -s** *(Sw)* fireplace

che|misch [ˈçeːmɪʃ, *(esp S Ger)* ˈkeː-] ADJ chemical → **Reinigung** ADV *behandeln, untersuchen* chemically; **etw ~ reinigen** to dry-clean sth

Che|mo-: **Che|mo|tech|nik** F chemical engineering, technochemistry; **Che|mo|tech|ni|ker(in)** M(F) chemical engineer; **Che|mo|the|ra|peu|ti|kum** [-teraˈpɔytikʊm] NT **-s, -therapeutika** [-ka] *(Pharm)* chemotherapeutic drug; **che|mo|the|ra|peu|tisch** ADJ chemotherapeutic ADV **jdn ~ behandeln** to give sb chemotherapy; **Che|mo|the|ra|pie** F chemotherapy

-chen [çən] NT *suf dim* little; **Hündchen** little dog; **ein Löffelchen** a small spoon

Che|rub [ˈçeːrʊp] M **-s, -im** *or* **-inen** [ˈçeːrubiːm] cherub [çeruˈbiːnən]

che|va|le|resk [ʃəvaləˈrɛsk] ADJ *(geh)* chivalrous

Chi|as|mus [ˈçiasmʊs] M **-, Chiasmen** [-mən] *(Ling)* chiasmus

Chic [ʃɪk] M = **Schick**

chic [ʃɪk] ADJ, ADV = **schick**

Chi|ca|na [tʃiˈkaːna] F **-, -s** chicana

Chi|ca|no [tʃiˈkaːno] M **-s, -s** chicano

Chi|co|rée [ˈʃɪkore, ʃikoˈreː] F **-** *or m* **-s,** *no pl* chicory → *auch* **Schikoree**

Chif|fon [ˈʃɪfõ, ʃɪˈfõː] M **-s, -s** chiffon

Chiff|re [ˈʃɪfɐ, ˈʃɪfrə] F **-, -n** a cipher b *(in Zeitung)* box number

Chiff|re-: **Chiff|re|an|zei|ge** F advertisement with a box number; **Chiff|re|num|mer** F *(für Zeitungsannonce)* box number; **Chiff|re|schrift** F cipher, code

chiff|rie|ren [ʃɪˈfriːrən] *ptp* **chiffriert** VTI to encipher, to code; **chiffriert** coded

Chi|le [ˈtʃiːle, ˈçiːlə] NT **-s** Chile

Chi|le|ne [tʃiˈleːnə, çiˈleːnə] M **-n, -n, Chi|le|nin** [-ˈleːnɪn] F **-, -nen** Chilean

chi|le|nisch [tʃiˈleːnɪʃ, çiˈleːnɪʃ] ADJ Chilean

Chi|le|sal|pe|ter M chile saltpetre *(Brit) or* saltpeter *(US)*, sodium nitrate

Chi|li [ˈtʃiːli] M **-s,** *no pl* chil(l)i (pepper)

Chi|li-: **Chi|li|pul|ver** [ˈtʃiːli-] NT *usu sing* chil(l)i powder; **Chi|li|so|ße** [ˈtʃiːli-] F chil(l)i sauce

chil|len [ˈtʃɪlən] VI *(sl)* to chill out *(sl)*

chil|lig [ˈtʃɪlɪç] ADJ *(sl)* chillin' *(sl)*, laid-back

Chi|mä|re [çiˈmɛːrə] F **-, -n** a *(Zool, Biol)* chimaera b *(Myth)* = **Schimäre**

Chi|na [ˈçiːna, *(esp S Ger)* ˈkiːna] NT **-s** China

Chi|na-: **Chi|na|cra|cker** M banger *(Brit)*, firecracker *(US)*; **Chi|na|kohl** M Chinese cabbage; **Chi|na|kra|cher** M banger *(Brit)*, firecracker *(US)*; **Chi|na|krepp** M crêpe de Chine; **Chi|na|res|tau|rant** NT Chinese restaurant

Chin|chil|la [tʃɪnˈtʃɪla] F **-, -s** (= *Tier*) chinchilla

Chin|chil|la NT **-s, -s** a (= *Pelz*) chinchilla b *(auch* **Chinchillakaninchen**) chinchilla rabbit

Chi|ne|se [çiˈneːzə, *(esp S Ger)* ki-] M **-n, -n** Chinese (man); **zum ~n gehen** to go to a/the Chinese restaurant

Chi|ne|sen|vier|tel [çiˈneːzn-, *(esp S Ger)* ki-] NT (= *Wohngebiet*) Chinatown

Chi|ne|sin [çiˈneːzɪn, *(esp S Ger)* ki-] F **-, -nen** Chinese (woman)

chi|ne|sisch [çiˈneːzɪʃ, *(esp S Ger)* ki-] ADJ Chinese; **die Chinesische Mauer** the Great Wall of China

Chi|ne|sisch(e) [çiˈneːzɪʃ, *(esp S Ger)* ki-] NT *(Ling)* Chinese; **das ist ~ für mich** *(inf)* that's all Greek *or* Chinese to me *(inf)* → *auch* **Deutsch(e)**

Chi|nin [çiˈniːn] NT **-s,** *no pl* quinine

Chi|noi|se|rie [ʃinoazəˈriː] F **-, -n** [-ˈriːən] chinoiserie

Chip [tʃɪp] M **-s, -s** a (= *Spielchip*) chip b *(usu pl: = Kartoffelchip)* (potato) crisp *(Brit)*, potato chip *(US)* c *(Comput)* chip

Chip|kar|te F smart card

Chi|ro-: **Chi|ro|mant** [çiroˈmant] M **-en, -en, Chi|ro|man|tin** [-ˈmantɪn] F **-, -nen** chiromancer; **Chi|ro|man|tie** [çiromanˈtiː] F **-,** *no pl* chiromancy; **Chi|ro|prak|tik** F, *no pl* chiropractic; **Chi|ro|prak|ti|ker(in)** M(F) chiropractor; **Chi|ro|the|ra|peut(in)** M(F) chiropractor

Chi|rurg [çiˈrʊrk] M **-en, -en** [-gn], **Chi|rur|gin** [çiˈrʊrgɪn] F **-, -nen** surgeon

Chi|rur|gie [çirʊrˈgiː] F **-, -n** [-ˈgiːən] surgery; **er liegt in der ~** he's in surgery

chi|rur|gisch [çiˈrʊrgɪʃ] ADJ surgical; **ein ~er Eingriff** surgery ADV surgically; *tätig sein* to be a surgeon, to do surgical work

Chi|tin [çiˈtiːn] NT **-s,** *no pl* chitin

Chlor [kloːɐ] NT **-s,** *no pl (abbr* **Cl**) chlorine

Cli|ent [ˈklaiənt] M **-(s), -s** *(Comput)* client

Chlor|ak|ne F chloracne

chlo|ren [ˈkloːrən], **chlo|rie|ren** [kloˈriːrən] *ptp* **chloriert** VT to chlorinate

chlor-: **chlor|frei** ADJ *Papier, Kunststoff* chlorine-free ADV **~ gebleichtes Papier** paper bleached without the use of chlorine; **chlor|hal|tig** [-haltɪç] ADJ *Wasser* chlorinated

Chlo|rid [kloˈriːt] NT **-s, -e** [-də] chloride

chlo|rig [ˈkloːrɪç] *(Chem)* ADJ chlorous ADV **~ riechen** to smell of chlorine

Chlor|koh|len|was|ser|stoff M *(Chem)* chlorinated hydrocarbon

Chlo|ro-: **Chlo|ro|form** [-ˈfɔrm] NT **-s**, *no pl* chloroform; **chlo|ro|for|mie|ren** [-fɔrˈmiːrən] *ptp* **chloroformiert** VT to chloroform; **Chlo|ro|phyll** [-ˈfʏl] NT **-s**, *no pl* chlorophyll

Chlor|was|ser NT, *no pl* a *(Chem)* chlorine water b *(im Hallenbad)* chlorinated water

Choke [tʃoːk] M **-s, -s**, **Cho|ker** [ˈtʃoːkɐ] M **-s, -** choke

Cho|le|ra [ˈkoːlera] F **-**, *no pl* cholera

Cho|le|ri|ker [koˈleːrikɐ] M **-s, -**, **Cho|le|ri|ke|rin** [-ərɪn] F **-, -nen** choleric person; *(fig)* irascible *or* hot-tempered person

cho|le|risch [koˈleːrɪʃ] ADJ choleric

Cho|les|te|rin [çolɛstəˈriːn, ko-] NT **-s**, *no pl* cholesterol

Cho|les|te|rin-: **Cho|les|te|rin|ge|halt** M cholesterol content; **Cho|les|te|rin|hem|mer** M *(Med)* cholesterol inhibitor; **Cho|les|te|rin|spie|gel** M cholesterol level

Chor [koːɐ] M **-(e)s, ⸚e** [ˈkøːrə] a *(= Sängerchor)* choir; *(= Bläserchor etc)* section; **im ~ singen** to sing in the choir; *(= zusammen singen)* to sing in chorus, to chorus; **im ~ sprechen/rufen** to speak/shout in chorus; **ja** *or* **Ja, riefen sie im ~** yes, they chorused b *(Theat)* chorus c *(= Komposition)* choral work *or* composition d *(bei Orgel)* rank e *(bei Klavier, Laute etc)* group of strings tuned in unison *or* to the same pitch

Chor [koːɐ] M OR (RARE) NT **-(e)s, -e** *or* **⸚e** [ˈkøːrə] *(Archit)* a *(= Altarraum)* chancel, choir b *(= Chorempore)* loft, gallery

Cho|ral [koˈraːl] M **-s, Cho|rä|le** [-ˈrɛːlə] *(Mus)* a *(Gregorianischer)* chant, plainsong b *(= Kirchenlied)* hymn

Cho|reo-: **Cho|reo|graf** [-ˈgraːf] M **-en, -en**, **Cho|reo|gra|fin** [-ˈgraːfɪn] F **-, -nen** choreographer; **Cho|reo|gra|fie** [-graˈfiː] F **-, -n** [-ˈfiːən] choreography; **cho|reo|gra|fie|ren** [-graˈfiːrən] *ptp* **choreografiert** VT to choreograph, to write *or* do the choreography for VI to write *or* do (the) choreography; **cho|reo|gra|fisch** [-ˈgraːfɪʃ] ADJ choreographic(al); **Cho|reo|graph** *etc* = **Choreograf** *etc*

Chor-: **Chor|frau** F *(Eccl)* canoness; **Chor|ge|bet** NT Divine Office; **Chor|ge|sang** M *(= Lied)* choral music; *(= das Singen)* choral singing; **Chor|ge|stühl** NT choir stalls *pl*; **Chor|herr** M *(Eccl)* canon

cho|risch [ˈkoːrɪʃ] ADJ choral

Cho|rist [koˈrɪst] M **-en, -en**, **Cho|ris|tin** [-ˈrɪstɪn] F **-, -nen** = **Chorsänger(in)**

Chor-: **Chor|kna|be** M choirboy; **Chor|lei|ter** M choirmaster; **Chor|lei|te|rin** F choirmistress; **Chor|sän|ger(in)** M(F) member of a choir; *(im Kirchenchor)* chorister; *(im Opernchor etc)* member of the chorus; **Chor|schran|ke** F choir *or* rood screen; **Chor|stuhl** M choir stall

Cho|rus [ˈkoːrʊs] M **-, -se** a *(obs: = Altarraum)* chancel, choir b *(Jazz: = Variationsthema)* theme

Cho|se [ˈʃoːzə] F **-, -n** *(inf)* a *(= Angelegenheit)* business, thing b *(= Zeug)* stuff; **die ganze ~** the whole lot

Chow-Chow [tʃauˈtʃau] M **-s, -s** chow

Chr. *abbr von* **Christus**

Christ [krɪst] M **-s** *(old, geh: = Christus)* Christ

Christ [krɪst] M **-en, -en**, **Chris|tin** [ˈkrɪstɪn] F **-, -nen** Christian

Christ|baum [ˈkrɪst-] M Christmas tree; *(Mil inf)* flares *pl*

Christ|baum- *in cpds*: **Christ|baum|ku|gel** F Christmas tree ball; **Christ|baum|schmuck** M a Christmas tree decorations *pl* b *(iro: = Orden)* gongs *pl (Brit inf)*, fruit salad *(US inf)*

Christ-: **Christ|de|mo|krat(in)** M(F) Christian Democrat; **christ|de|mo|kra|tisch** ADJ Christian Democratic ADV **eine ~ geführte Regierung** a Christian Democrat-led government; **~ wählen** to vote Christian Democrat

Chris|ten-: **Chris|ten|ge|mein|de** F Christian community; **Chris|ten|glau|be(n)** M Christian faith; **Chris|ten|heit** F **-**, *no pl* Christendom; **Chris|ten|pflicht** F (one's) duty as a Christian, (one's) Christian duty; **Chris|ten|tum** [ˈkrɪstntuːm] NT **-s**, *no pl* Christianity; **Chris|ten|ver|fol|gung** F persecution of the Christians

Christ|fest NT *(dated, dial)* Christmas

Chris|ti *gen von* **Christus**

chris|ti|a|ni|sie|ren [krɪstianiˈziːrən] *ptp* **christianisiert** VT to convert to Christianity, to Christianize VI to convert people to Christianity

Chris|ti|a|ni|sie|rung F **-, -en** conversion to Christianity, Christianization

Chris|tin [ˈkrɪstɪn] F Christian

Christ-: **Christ|kind|(chen)** NT, *no pl* baby *or* infant Jesus, Christ Child; *(= Sinnbild für Weihnachten)* Christmas; *(das Geschenke bringt)* ≈ Father Christmas; *(fig inf: = Dummerchen)* little innocent; **Christ|kindl** NT, **Christ|kind|le** NT *(dial)* a = **Christkind(chen)** b *(dial: = Geschenk)* Christmas present; **zum ~** as a Christmas present, for Christmas

Christ|kind|les|markt [ˈkrɪstkɪndləs-] M *(Fränkisch)* Christmas market

Christ|kindl|markt M *(S Ger, Aus)* Christmas market

christ|lich [ˈkrɪstlɪç] ADJ Christian; **er ist bei der ~en Seefahrt** *(hum)* he is a seafaring man; **Christlicher Verein Junger Menschen** Young Men's Christian Association ADV like *or* as a Christian; **~ leben** to live a Christian life; **~ handeln** to act like a Christian; **~ aufwachsen** to grow up as a Christian; **jdn ~ erziehen** to bring sb up as a Christian; **eine ~ orientierte Moral** a Christian(-orientated) morality; **etw ~ teilen** to let the other person have the larger share of sth

Christ|lich|keit F **-**, *no pl* Christianity

Christ-: **Christ|mes|se** F Midnight Mass; **Christ|met|te** F *(katholisch)* Midnight Mass; *(evangelisch)* Midnight Service

Chris|toph [ˈkrɪstɔf] M **-s** Christopher

Chris|to|pho|rus [krɪsˈtoːforʊs] M **-ˈ** Saint Christopher

Christ|ro|se F Christmas rose

Christ|so|zi|a|le(r) [-zotsiaːlə] MF *decl as adj* member of the CSU

Christ|stol|len M *(Cook)* (Christmas) stollen, fruit loaf

Chris|tus [ˈkrɪstʊs] M *gen* **Christi** [ˈkrɪsti], *dat* **-** *or (form)* **Christo** [ˈkrɪsto], *acc* **-** *or (form)* **Christum** [ˈkrɪstʊm] Christ; *(= Christfigur auch)* figure of Christ; **vor Christi Geburt, vor Christo** *(form) or* **~** before Christ, BC; **nach Christi Geburt, nach Christo** *(form) or* **~** AD, Anno Domini, in the year of our Lord *(liter)*; **Christi Himmelfahrt** the Ascension of Christ; *(= Himmelsfahrtstag)* Ascension Day

Chrom [kroːm] NT **-s**, *no pl* chrome; *(Chem) (abbr* **Cr***)* chromium

Chro|ma|tik [kroˈmaːtɪk] F **-**, *no pl* a *(Mus)* chromaticism b *(Opt)* chromatics *sing*

chro|ma|tisch [kroˈmaːtɪʃ] ADJ *(Mus, Opt)* chromatic

chrom|blit|zend ADJ gleaming with chrome

Chro|mo|som [kromoˈzoːm] NT **-s, -en** chromosome

Chro|mo|so|men-: **Chro|mo|so|men|paar** NT pair of chromosomes; **Chro|mo|so|men|satz** M set of chromosomes; **Chro|mo|so|men|zahl** F chromosome count, number of chromosomes

Chro|nik [ˈkroːnɪk] F **-, -en** chronicle; **etw in einer ~ aufzeichnen** to chronicle sth, to record sth in a chronicle

chro|nisch [ˈkroːnɪʃ] ADJ *(Med, fig)* chronic ADV chronically; **~ krank sein** to be chronically ill; **ein ~ defizitäres Unternehmen** a company which is chronically in deficit

Chro|nist [kroˈnɪst] M **-en, -en**, **Chro|nis|tin** [-ˈnɪstɪn] F **-, -nen** chronicler

Chro|no|lo|gie [kronoloˈgiː] F **-, -n** [-ˈgiːən] chronology

chro|no|lo|gisch [kronoˈloːgɪʃ] ADJ chronological ADV chronologically

Chro|no|me|ter [kronoˈmeːtɐ] NT **-s, -** chronometer

Chry|san|the|me [kryzanˈteːmə] F **-, -n** chrysanthemum

chtho|nisch [ˈçtoːnɪʃ] ADJ *(liter)* chthonian *(liter)*, chthonic *(liter)*

Chuz|pe [ˈxʊtspə] F **-**, *no pl (inf)* chutzpa(h) *(sl)*, audacity

CIA [ˈsiːaiˈeː] F **-** *or m* **-s** CIA

Ci|ce|ro [ˈtsiːtsero] M **-s** Cicero

Ci|ce|ro F OR M **-**, *no pl (Typ)* twelve-point type, pica

Ci|ce|ro|ne [tʃitʃeˈroːnə] M **-(s), -s** *or (geh)* **Ciceroni** [-ni] a *(= Mensch)* cicerone *(form)*, guide b *(= Buch)* (travel) guide(book)

Cie. *abbr von* **Kompanie**

Cinch|buch|se [ˈsɪntʃbʊksə] F *(Tech)* cinch socket

Cinch|ste|cker [ˈsɪntʃ-] M *(Tech)* cinch connector *or* jack *or* plug

Ci|ne|ast [sineˈast] M **-en, -en**, **Ci|ne|as|tin** [-ˈastɪn] F **-, -nen** cineaste

Ci|ne|ma|thek [sinemaˈteːk] F **-, -en** film library *or* archive

cir|ca [ˈtsɪrka] ADV = **zirka**

Cir|ce [ˈtsɪrtsə] F **-, -n** *(Myth)* Circe; *(fig geh)* femme fatale

cir|cen|sisch [tsɪrˈtsɛnzɪʃ] ADJ = **zirzensisch**

Cir|cu|lus vi|ti|o|sus [ˈtsɪrkulʊs viˈtsioːzʊs] M **-, Circuli vitiosi** [ˈtsɪrkuli viˈtsioːzi] *(geh)* *(= Teufelskreis)* vicious circle; *(= Zirkelschluss auch)* circular argument, petitio principii *(form)*

cis [tsɪs] NT, **Cis** NT **-, -** *(Mus)* C sharp

Ci|ty [ˈsɪti] F **-, -s** city centre *(Brit) or* center *(US)*

Ci|ty-: **Ci|ty|bahn** F express commuter train; **Ci|ty|la|ge** F central location; **in ~** central, (situated) in the town *or* city centre *(Brit) or* center *(US)*, downtown *(US)*; **ci|ty|nah** ADJ close to the town *or* city centre *(Brit) or* center *(US)*, central; **Ci|ty|nä|he** F central location; **in ~** central(ly), close to the town *or* city centre *(Brit) or* center *(US)*

CJK [tseːjɔtˈkaː] *abbr von* **Creuzfeldt-Jakob-Krankheit** CJD

Claim [kleːm] NT **-(s), -s** *(lit, fig)* claim; **seine ~s abstecken** to stake one's claim

Clair-obs|cur [klɛrɔpsˈkyːɐ] NT **-s**, *no pl (Art)* chiaroscuro

Clan [klaːn] M **-s, -s** *or (rare)* **-e** *(lit, fig)* clan

Cla|queur [klaˈkøːɐ] M **-s, -e**, **Cla|queu|rin** [-ˈkøːrɪn] F **-, -nen** hired applauder, claqueur

Cla|vi|cem|ba|lo [klaviˈtʃɛmbalo] NT **-s, -s** *or* **Clavicembali** [-li] clavicembalo, harpsichord

clean [kliːn] ADJ *pred (inf)* clean *(inf)*, off drugs; **~ werden** to kick the habit *(inf)*, to get clean *(inf)*

Clea|ring [ˈkliːrɪŋ] NT **-s, -s** *(Econ)* clearing

Clea|ring|stel|le [ˈkliːrɪŋ-] F *(Fin)* clearing house

Cle|ma|tis [kleˈmaːtɪs, ˈkleːmatɪs] F **-, -** *(Bot)* clematis

Cle|men|ti|ne [klemɛnˈtiːnə] F **-, -n** clementine

cle|ver [ˈklɛvɐ] ADJ clever; *(= raffiniert)* sharp, shrewd; *(= gerissen)* crafty, cunning ADV *(= raffiniert)* sharply; *(= gerissen)* craftily; **sich ~ verhalten** to be crafty

Cle|ver|ness [ˈklɛvɐnɛs] F **-**, *no pl* cleverness; *(= Raffiniertheit)* sharpness, shrewdness; *(= Gerissenheit)* craftiness, cunning

Cliff|han|ger [ˈklɪfhɛŋɐ] M **-s, -**, **Cliff|hän|ger** M *(inf)* cliffhanger

Clinch [klɪntʃ] M **-(e)s**, *no pl (Boxen, fig)* clinch; **in den ~ gehen** *(lit, fig)* to go into a clinch; *(fig: Verhandlungspartner)* to get stuck into each other *(inf)*; **jdn in den ~ nehmen** *(lit)* to go into a clinch with sb; *(fig)* to get stuck into sb *(inf)*; **sich aus dem ~ lösen, den ~ lösen** to break the clinch; **mit jdm im ~ liegen** *(fig)* to be at loggerheads with sb

clin|chen [ˈklɪntʃn] VI to clinch

Clip [klɪp] M **-s, -s** *(= Haarclip, am Füller etc)* clip; *(= Brosche)* clip-on brooch; *(= Ohrclip)* (clip-on) earring
Clip|art NT **-s, -s** *(Comput)* clip art, clipart
Clip|board ['klɪpbɔːɐd] NT **-s, -s** *(Comput)* clipboard
Clips [klɪps] M **-, -e** (clip-on) earring
Cli|que ['klɪkə] F **-, -n** **a** *(= Freundeskreis)* group, set; **wir fahren mit der ganzen ~ weg** the whole gang *or* crowd of us are going away together; **Thomas und seine ~** Thomas and his set **b** *(pej)* clique
Cli|quen-: **Cli|quen|bil|dung** F forming of cliques; **da kam es natürlich zur ~** then of course it started getting cliquey *(inf)*, then of course people started forming cliques; **Cli|quen(un)|we|sen** NT *(pej)* cliquishness; **Cli|quen|wirt|schaft** F *(pej inf)* cliquey setup *(inf)*
Clo|chard [klɔ'ʃaːr] M **-s, -s** tramp
Clou [kluː] M **-s, -s** *(von Geschichte)* (whole) point; *(von Show)* highlight, high spot; *(von Begebenheit)* show stopper; *(= Witz)* real laugh *(inf)*; **und jetzt kommt der ~ der Geschichte** and now, wait for it, ...; **das ist doch gerade der ~** but that's just it, but that's the whole point; **das wäre der ~** that'd be a real laugh *(inf)*
Clown [klaun] M **-s, -s** *(lit, fig)* clown; **den ~ spielen** to clown around, to play the fool; **sich/jdn zum ~ machen** to make a clown of oneself/sb
Clow|ne|rie [klaunə'riː] F **-, -n** [-'riːən] clowning (around) *no pl*
clow|nesk [klau'nɛsk] ADJ clownish
Clow|nin ['klaunɪn] F **-, -nen** *(lit, fig)* clown
Club [klʊb] *etc* = **Klub** *etc*
cm *abbr von* **Zentimeter** cm
C-Netz ['tseː-] NT *(Telec)* cellular (analogue) network
Co-, co- ['koː] *in cpds* co-
Co. *abbr von* **Kompagnon, Kompanie** Co
CO_2-Fuß|ab|druck [tseloː'tsvai,fuːslapdrʊk] M carbon footprint
CO_2-neut|ral [tseloː,tsvainɔy'traːl] ADJ carbon neutral
Coach [koːtʃ] M **-(s), -s** *(Sport)* coach
coa|chen ['koːtʃn] VTI *(Sport)* to coach
Co|au|tor(in) ['koː-] M(F) coauthor
Co|ca ['koːka] F **-, -s** *(inf)* ≈ Coke® *(inf)*
Co|cker|spa|ni|el ['kɔkɐ-] M cocker spaniel
Cock|pit ['kɔkpɪt] NT **-s, -s** cockpit
Cock|tail ['kɔkteːl] M **-s, -s** **a** *(= Getränk, fig)* cocktail **b** *(= Empfang)* reception **c** *(= Cocktailparty)* cocktail party; **jdn zum ~ einladen** to invite sb for cocktails, to invite sb to a cocktail party
Cock|tail-: **Cock|tail|kleid** NT cocktail dress; **Cock|tail|par|ty** F cocktail party; **Cock|tail|to|ma|te** F cherry tomato
Co|com ['koːkɔm] NT **-** Cocom
Code [koːt] M **-s, -s** code → *auch* **Kode**
Co|de|in [kode'iːn] NT **-s**, *no pl* codeine
Co|dex ['koːdɛks] M **-es** *or* **-, -e** *or* **Codizes** ['koːditseːs] = **Kodex**
co|die|ren [ko'diːrən] *ptp* **codiert** VT to (en)code → *auch* **kodieren**
Co|dier|ge|rät NT *(Comput)* encoder
Co|die|rung F **-, -en** coding, encoding → *auch* **Kodierung**
Cog|nac® ['kɔnjak] M **-s, -s** cognac
Coif|feur [koa'føːɐ] M **-s, -e**, **Coif|feu|se** [-'føːzə] F **-, -n** *(Sw)* hairdresser; *(geh)* hair stylist
Coif|fure [koa'fyːɐ] F **-, -n** **a** *(geh)* hairstyling **b** *(Sw)* hairdressing salon
Co|la ['koːla] F **-, -s** *(inf)* ≈ Coke® *(inf)*
Co|la|do|se F ≈ Coke® can
Co|la|nuss F cola nut
Col|la|ge [kɔ'laːʒə] F **-, -n** *(Art, fig)* collage; *(Mus)* medley
Col|lege ['kɔlɪtʃ, -ɪdʒ] NT **-(s), -es** [-ɪz] *(Univ)* college
Col|lie ['kɔli] M **-s, -s** collie
Col|li|er [kɔ'lieː] NT **-s, -s** necklet, necklace
Col|lo|qui|um [kɔ'lɔkviʊm] NT **-s, Colloquien** [-kviən] colloquium; *(Aus Univ: = Prüfung)* examination
Co|lo|nia-: **Co|lo|ni|a|kü|bel** M *(Aus)* dustbin *(Brit)*, trash *or* garbage can *(US)*; **Co|lo|ni|a|wa|gen** M *(Aus)* refuse lorry *(Brit) or* truck
co|lor ['koːloːɐ, ko'loːɐ] ADV *(inf)* in colour *(Brit) or* color *(US)*
Co|lor ['koːloːɐ, ko'loːɐ] NT **in ~** in colour *(Brit) or* color *(US)*
Co|lor- *in cpds* colour *(Brit)*, color *(US)*; **Co|lor|film** M colour *(Brit) or* color *(US)* film
Colt® [kɔlt] M **-s, -s** Colt®
Com|bo ['kɔmbo] F **-, -s** combo
Come|back [kam'bɛk] NT **-(s), -s**, **Come-back** NT **-(s), -s** comeback
Co|me|con ['kɔmekɔn] M OR NT, **COMECON** M OR NT **-** *(Hist)* Comecon
Co|me|dy|se|rie ['kɔmədi-] F *(TV)* (television) comedy series; *(mit Situationskomödie)* sitcom *(inf)*
Co|mic ['kɔmɪk] M **-s, -s** comic strip
Co|mic-: **Co|mic|fi|gur** F cartoon character; **Co|mic|heft** NT comic, comic book *(US)*
Co|ming-out ['kamɪŋaut] NT **-s**, *no pl (inf, als Homosexueller)* coming out; **er erlebte sein ~ als Schlagersänger** he emerged as a pop singer
Com|mu|ni|qué [kɔmyni'keː] NT **-s, -s** communiqué
Com|pact Disc, Com|pact Disk [kɔm'pakt 'dɪsk] F **-, -s**, **Com|pact|disc** △ F **-, -s**, **Com|pact Plat|te** F compact disc
Com|pi|ler [kɔm'pailɐ] M **-s, -** *(Comput)* compiler
Com|pu|ter [kɔm'pjuːtɐ] M **-s, -** computer; **auf ~** on computer; **per ~** by computer; **sich mit ~n auskennen** to be computer-literate; **am ~ entworfen** computer-designed
Com|pu|ter- *in cpds*: **Com|pu|ter|ab|sturz** M computer crash; **Com|pu|ter|a|ni|ma|ti|on** F computer animation; **com|pu|ter|a|ni|miert** ADJ computer-animated; **Com|pu|ter|ar|beits|platz** M computer work station; **Com|pu|ter|blitz** M *(Phot)* electronic flash; **Com|pu|ter|bran|che** F computing; **Com|pu|ter|di|ag|nos|tik** F *(Med)* computer diagnosis; **Com|pu|ter|fach|frau** F, **Com|pu|ter|fach|mann** M computer *or* IT consultant *or* expert; **Com|pu|ter|feh|ler** M computer error; **Com|pu|ter|freak** M computer freak; **Com|pu|ter|fuz|zi** M *(inf)* computer nerd *or* freak; **Com|pu|ter|ge|ne|ra|ti|on** F computer generation; **com|pu|ter|ge|ne|riert** ADJ computer-generated; **com|pu|ter|ge|recht** **ADJ** computer-compatible **ADV** *übertragen* in computer-compatible form; **com|pu|ter|ge|steu|ert** [-gəʃtɔyɐt] ADJ controlled by computer, computer-controlled; **com|pu|ter|ge|stützt** [-gəʃtʏtst] ADJ computer-aided *or* -controlled; **~es Design** computer-aided *or* -assisted design, CAD; **~es Lernen** computer-assisted instruction, CAI; **~es Sprachenlernen** computer-assisted language learning, CALL; **Com|pu|ter|gra|fik, Com|pu|ter|gra|phik** F computer graphics *pl*; **Com|pu|ter|her|stel|ler** M computer manufacturer(s *pl*)
com|pu|te|ri|sie|ren [kɔmpjutəri'ziːrən] *ptp* **computerisiert** VT to computerize
Com|pu|te|ri|sie|rung [kɔmpjutəri'ziːrʊŋ] F **-**, *no pl* computerization
Com|pu|ter-: **Com|pu|ter|jar|gon** M computerese ; **Com|pu|ter|kas|se** F computer cash register; **Com|pu|ter|kennt|nis|se** PL computer skills *or* literacy; **Com|pu|ter|kri|mi|na|li|tät** F computer crime; **com|pu|ter|les|bar** ADJ machine-readable; **Com|pu|ter|lin|gu|is|tik** F computational linguistics *sing*; **Com|pu|ter|mes|se** F computer fair; **Com|pu|ter|mo|dell** NT computer model; **Com|pu|ter|sa|bo|ta|ge** F computer sabotage; **Com|pu|ter|satz** M computer typesetting; **Com|pu|ter|sex** M computer sex; **Com|pu|ter|si|cher|heit** F computer security; **Com|pu|ter|si|mu|la|ti|on** F computer simulation; **Com|pu|ter|spiel** NT computer game; **Com|pu|ter|spra|che** F computer language; **Com|pu|ter|sys|tem** NT computer system; **Com|pu|ter|to|mo|graf** M CT scanner, computer tomograph; **Com|pu|ter|to|mo|gra|fie** F computed *or* computer*or* computerized tomography; **Com|pu|ter|to|mo|graph** *etc* = **Computertomograf** *etc*; **Com|pu|ter|to|mo|gramm** NT computed tomogram, CT; **com|pu|ter|un|ter|stützt** [-ʊntɐʃtʏtst] ADJ computer-aided; **Com|pu|ter|vi|rus** NT OR M computer virus; **Com|pu|ter|wis|sen|schaft** F computer science; **Com|pu|ter|zeit|al|ter** NT computer age
Com|tes|se [kɔm'tɛsə] F **-, -n** countess
Con|di|tio si|ne qua non [kɔn'diːtsio 'ziːnə 'kvaː 'noːn] F **- - - -**, *no pl (geh)* sine qua non
Con|do|me|rie [kɔndomə'riː] F **-, -n** [-'riːən] *(inf)* = **Kondomerie**
Con|fé|ren|ci|er [kõferã'sieː] M **-s, -s** compère, MC
Con|fi|se|rie [kɔnfizə'riː] F **-, -n** [-'riːən] *(Sw)* **a** *(= Konfekt)* confectionery **b** *(= Konditorei)* cake shop; *(mit Café)* café
Con|nais|seur [kɔnɛ'søːɐ] M **-s, -e**, **Con|nais|seu|rin** [-'søːrɪn] F **-, -nen** *(geh)* connoisseur
Con|sen|sus [kɔn'zɛnzʊs] M **-, -** [-zuːs] *(geh)* agreement, assent, consent
Con|tai|ner [kɔn'teːnɐ] M **-s, -** container; *(= Blumentrog)* plant box; *(= Bauschuttcontainer)* skip; *(= Müllcontainer)* waste container; *(= Transportcontainer)* container; *(= Wohncontainer)* prefabricated hut, Portakabin®
Con|tai|ner- *in cpds* container; **Con|tai|ner|bahn|hof** M container depot; **Con|tai|ner|dorf** NT village of prefabricated huts; **Con|tai|ner|ha|fen** M container port; **Con|tai|ner|schiff** NT container ship; **Con|tai|ner|show** F *(TV inf) term to describe the Big Brother reality TV show*; **Con|tai|ner|ter|mi|nal** M OR NT container terminal; **Con|tai|ner|ver|kehr** M container traffic; **auf ~ umstellen** to containerize
Con|tain|ment [kɔn'teːnmənt] NT **-s, -s** containment
Con|te|nance [kõtə'nãːs(ə)] F **-**, *no pl (geh)* composure; **die ~ bewahren** to keep one's composure *or* countenance
Con|ter|gan® [kɔntɛr'gaːn] NT **-s** ≈ thalidomide
Con|ter|gan|kind NT *(inf)* thalidomide child
Con|tra ['kɔntra] M **-s, -s** *(Pol)* Contra
Con|trol|ler[1] [kɔn'troːlɐ] M **-s, -** *(Comput)* controller
Con|trol|ler[2] [kɔn'troːlɐ] M **-s, -**, **Con|trol|le|rin** [-ərɪn] F **-, -nen** *(Fin: = Finanzbuchhalter)* cost controller
Con|trol|ling [kɔn'troːlɪŋ] NT **-s**, *no pl (Fin)* cost control
Con|trol|tas|te [kɔn'troːl-] F *(Comput)* control key
Coo|kie ['kʊkɪ] NT **-s, -s** *(Comput)* cookie
cool [kuːl] ADJ **a** *(inf: = gefasst)* cool *(inf)*, laid-back *(inf)*; **du musst ~ bleiben** you must keep your cool *(inf)*, you must stay cool *(inf)*; **ganz ~ agieren** to play it cool *(inf)* **b** *(sl: = angenehm)* cool *(inf)*; **die Party war ~** the party was (real) cool *(inf)*
Cool|ness ['kuːlnɛs] F **-**, *no pl (inf)* coolness
Co|pi|lot(in) ['koː-] M(F) copilot
Co|py|right ['kɔpirait] NT **-s, -s** copyright
Co|py|shop ['kɔpiʃɔp] M **-s, -s** copy shop
co|ram pub|li|co ['koːram 'puːbliko] ADV *(geh)* publicly
Cord [kɔrt] M **-s, -e** *or* **-s** [-də] *(Tex)* cord, corduroy
Cord- *in cpds* cord, corduroy → *auch* **Kord** *etc*; **Cord|ho|se** F cord trousers *pl (esp Brit) or* pants *pl (esp US)*, cords *pl*; **Cord|ja|cke** F cord(uroy) jacket; **Cord|jeans** PL cords *pl*; **eine ~** (a pair of) cord(uroy) jeans *pl*

Cor|don bleu [kɔrdõ'blø:] NT - -, -s -s *(Cook)* veal cordon bleu
Cord|samt M cord velvet
Cor|ner ['ko:ɐnɐ] M -s, - *(Aus Sport)* corner
Corn|flakes® ['ko:ɐnfle:ks] PL, **Corn Flakes®** PL cornflakes *pl*
Cor|ni|chon [kɔrni'ʃõ:] NT -s, -s gherkin
Cor|po|ra De|lic|ti *pl von* **Corpus delicti**
Cor|po|rate I|den|ti|ty ['kɔ:pərɪt ai'dɛntəti] F - -, - -s corporate identity
Corps [ko:ɐ] NT -, - *(Mil)* corps; *(Univ)* (duelling *(Brit)* or dueling *(US)*) corps
Cor|pus ['kɔrpʊs] NT -, **Corpora** ['kɔrpora] *(Ling)* corpus
Cor|pus De|lic|ti ['kɔrpʊs de'lɪkti] NT - -, **Corpora** - ['kɔrpora] corpus delicti; *(hum)* culprit *(inf)*
cos *abbr von* **Kosinus** cos
Co|sa Nost|ra ['ko:za 'nɔstra] F - -, *no pl* Cosa Nostra
Cos|ta Ri|ca ['kɔsta 'ri:ka] NT -s Costa Rica
Cos|ta-Ri|ca|ner [kɔstari'ka:nɐ] M -s, -, **Cos|ta-Ri|ca|ne|rin** [-ərɪn] F -, -nen Costa Rican
cos|ta-ri|ca|nisch [kɔstari'ka:nɪʃ] ADJ Costa Rican
Couch [kautʃ] F -, -s or -en or *(Sw)* m -s, -(e)s couch
Couch-: **Couch|gar|ni|tur** F three-piece suite; **Couch|po|ta|to** [-pote:to] F -, -es *(inf)* couch potato *(inf)*; **Couch|tisch** M coffee table
Cou|leur [ku'lø:ɐ] F -, -s **a** *(geh)* kind, sort; **Faschisten/Sozialisten jeder** ~ fascists/socialists of every shade **b** *(Univ)* colours *pl (Brit)*, colors *pl (US)*; ~ **tragen** to wear the colours of one's student society *(Brit)*, to wear the colors of one's fraternity *(US)*
Count|down ['kaunt'daun] M OR NT -s, -s, **Count-down** M OR NT -s, -s *(Space, fig)* countdown
Coup [ku:] M -s, -s coup; **einen ~ (gegen jdn/etw) landen** to bring *or* pull *(inf)* off a coup (against sb/sth)
Cou|pé [ku'pe:] NT -s, -s coupé
Coup|let [ku'ple:] NT -s, -s cabaret song
Cou|pon [ku'põ:] M -s, -s **a** *(= Zettel)* coupon **b** *(Fin)* (interest) coupon **c** *(= Stoffcoupon)* length (of material)
Cour [ku:ɐ] F *(dated)* **einem Mädchen die ~ machen** *or* **schneiden** to court a young lady *(dated)*
Cou|ra|ge [ku'ra:ʒə] F -, *no pl (geh)* courage, pluck
cou|ra|giert [kura'ʒi:ɐt] *(geh)* ADJ courageous ADV courageously
Cour|ta|ge [kʊr'ta:ʒə] F -, -n *(Fin)* commission
Cous|cous ['kʊskʊs] M OR NT -, - *(Cook)* couscous
Cous|in [ku'zɛ̃:] M -s, -s, **Cou|si|ne** [ku'zi:nə] F -, -n cousin
Cou|vert [ku've:ɐ, ku'vɛ:ɐ] NT -s, -s **a** *(= Briefumschlag)* envelope **b** *(= Gedeck)* cover
Co|ver ['kavɐ] NT -s, -s cover
Co|ver-: **Cover|girl** ['kavɐ-] NT cover girl; **Cover|ver|si|on** ['kavɐ-] F *(Mus)* cover (version)
Cow|boy ['kaubɔy] M cowboy
Cow|boy|stie|fel ['kaubɔy-] M cowboy boot
Cox Oran|ge ['kɔks o'rã:ʒə] M OR F - -, - - or - -n Cox's (Orange) Pippin, Cox
C-Par|tei ['tse:-] F *(Pol inf)* **die ~en** the CDU and CSU

Crack¹ [krɛk] M -s, -s *(= Sportler)* ace
Crack² NT -, *no pl (= Droge)* crack
cra|cken ['krɛkn] VT *(Chem)* = **kracken**
Cra|cker ['krɛkɐ] M -s, -(s) **a** *(= Keks)* cracker **b** *(= Feuerwerkskörper)* banger *(Brit)*, firecracker *(US)*
Cra|que|lé [krakə'le:] NT -s, -s crackle
Crash [krɛʃ] M -s, -s *(inf: = Unfall, St Ex, Comput)* crash
Crash-: **Crash|kid** NT -s, -s *(inf)* joyrider; **Crash|kurs** M crash course; **Crash|pro|gramm** NT *(= Schnelllernprogramm)* crash program(me); **Crash|test** M *(Aut)* crash test
Cre|do ['kre:do] NT -s, -s *(lit, fig)* creed, credo
creme [kre:m, krɛ:m] ADJ *pred (Fashion)* cream
Creme [kre:m, krɛ:m] F -, -s *(= Hautcreme, Cook, fig)* cream; **die ~ der Gesellschaft** the cream of society, the crème de la crème *(liter)*; **die ~ de la ~** the crème de la crème
creme-: **creme|ar|tig** ADJ cream-like; **creme|far|ben** [-farbn] ADJ cream-coloured *(Brit)*, cream-colored *(US)*
Crème fraîche [krɛm 'frɛʃ] F -, *no pl (Cook)* crème fraîche
Creme|tor|te F cream gateau
cre|mig ['kre:mɪç] ADJ creamy ADV like cream; *rühren* until creamy; ~ **schmecken** to taste creamy
Crêpe¹ [krɛp] F -, -s *(Cook)* crêpe
Crêpe² [krɛp] M -s, -e or -s crepe
Crêpe de Chine [krɛp də 'ʃin] M - - -, -s - - crêpe de Chine
Cre|scen|do [kre'ʃɛndo] NT -s, -s or **Crescendi** [-di] **a** *(Mus)* crescendo **b** *(Sport)* final spurt
Creutz|feldt-Ja|kob-Krank|heit [krɔytsfɛlt-'jakɔp-] F Creutzfeldt-Jakob disease
Creutz|feldt-Ja|kob-Syn|drom NT Creutzfeldt-Jakob syndrome
Crew [kru:] F -, -s crew; *(= Kadettenjahrgang)* cadets *pl* of the same year/age
Crois|sant [kroa'sã:] NT -s, -s croissant
Cro|mar|gan® [kromar'ga:n] NT -s, *no pl* stainless steel
Cross [krɔs] M -, *no pl*, **Cross-Count|ry** NT -, *no pl (Sport)* cross-country; *(= Motorradrennen)* motocross
Cross|(ball) ['krɔs-] M -, - *(Tennis)* cross-court shot
Cross-over M *(Mus)* crossover
Crou|pier [kru'pie:] M -s, -s croupier
Croû|ton M *(Cook: = Suppeneinlage)* crouton
Crou|ton|we|cken [kru'tõ:-] M *(Aus)* French bread; *(= Laib)* French loaf
Cruise-Mis|sile, Cruise|mis|sile [kru:z'mɪsail, -'mɪsl] NT -s, -s *(Mil)* cruise missile
Crux [krʊks] F -, *no pl* **a** *(= Last)* nuisance **b** *(= Schwierigkeit)* trouble, problem; **die ~ bei der Sache ist, ...** the trouble *or* problem (with that) is ...
C-Schlüs|sel ['tse:-] M alto *or* C clef
CSFR [tʃe:lɛslɛf'lɛr] F - *(Hist)* = **Tschechoslowakei**
CS-Gas [tse:'lɛs-] NT CS gas
CSSR [tʃe:lɛslɛs'lɛr] F - *(Hist)* = **Tschechoslowakei**
CSU [tse:lɛs'lu:] F - *abbr von* **Christlich-Soziale Union** Christian Social Union

> **CSU**
>
> The **CSU (Christlich-Soziale Union)**, founded in 1945, is the sister party of the **CDU** and contests elections only in Bavaria. It stands for conservative Christian values and a social market economy. It also champions the sovereignty of the **Länder**, especially Bavaria. The **CSU** frequently receives an absolute majority in **Landtag** elections and so can rely on a broad basis of support. → **CDU**

c. t. [tse:'te:] *abbr von* **cum tempore** ADV within fifteen minutes of the time stated; **18.30 ~** 6.30 for 6.45
cum gra|no sa|lis [kʊm 'gra:no 'za:lɪs] ADV *(geh)* with a pinch of salt
cum lau|de [kʊm 'laudə] ADV *(Univ)* cum laude *(form)*, with distinction
Cun|ni|lin|gus [kʊni'lɪŋgʊs] M -, **Cunnilingi** [-gi] cunnilingus, cunnilinctus
Cup [kap] M -s, -s *(Sport)* cup
Cu|pi|do [ku'pi:do] M -s Cupid
Cu|rie [ky'ri:] NT -, - *(abbr* **Ci***)* Curie
Cu|ri|um ['ku:riʊm] NT -s, *no pl (abbr* **Cu***)* curium
Cur|ling ['kø:ɐlɪŋ, 'kœrlɪŋ] NT -s, *no pl* curling
Cur|ri|cu|la *(geh) pl von* **Curriculum**
cur|ri|cu|lar [kʊriku'la:ɐ] ADJ *attr (geh)* curricular
Cur|ri|cu|lum [kʊ'ri:kulʊm] NT -s, **Curricula** [-la] *(geh)* **a** *(= Lehrplan)* curriculum **b** *(obs: = Lebenslauf)* curriculum vitae *(Brit)*, résumé *(US)*
Cur|ri|cu|lum|for|schung F curriculum development
Cur|ry ['kari] M OR NT -s, -s curry; **mit ~ zubereitet** curried
Cur|ry|wurst ['kari-] F curried sausage
Cur|sor ['kø:ɐsɐ, 'kœrsɐ] M -s, -s *(Comput)* cursor
Cur|sor- ['kø:ɐsɐ, 'kœrsɐ] *(Comput)*: **Cur|sor|block** M cursor pad; **Cur|sor|steu|e|rung** F cursor control; *(Taste)* cursor control key; **Cur|sor|tas|te** F arrow key
Cut [kœt, kat] M -s, -s, **Cut|away** ['kœtəve, 'kat-] M -s, -s *(dated)* cutaway
cut|ten ['katn] VTI *(Film, Rad, TV)* to cut, to edit
Cut|ter ['katɐ] M -s, -, **Cut|te|rin** ['katərɪn] F -, -nen *(Film, Rad, TV)* editor
CVJF [tse:faujɔt'lɛf] M -s *abbr von* **Christlicher Verein Junger Frauen** YWCA
CVJM [tse:faujɔt'lɛm] M -s *abbr von* **Christlicher Verein Junger Menschen** YMCA
C-Waf|fe ['tse:-] F *abbr von* **chemische Waffe**
Cy|an [tsy'a:n] NT -s, *no pl* cyan
Cy|a|nid [tsya'ni:t] NT -s, -e [-də] cyanide
Cy|ber- ['saibɐ] *in cpds* cyber-; **Cy|ber|an|griff** M *(Comput)* cyberattack; **Cy|ber|ca|fé** ['saibɐkafe:] NT *(Comput)* cybercafé, Internet café; **Cy|ber|freak** M *(inf)* cyberfreak; **Cy|ber|geld** NT cybermoney; **Cy|ber|mall** F -, -s cybermall; **Cy|ber|mob|bing** NT *(Internet)* cyberbullying; **Cy|ber|müll** M cyberjunk; **Cy|ber|naut** ['saibɐnɔ:t] M -en, -en, **Cy|ber|nau|tin** [-nɔ:tɪn] F -, -nen cybernaut; **Cy|ber|sex** M cybersex; **Cy|ber|shop|per** M -s, -(s), **Cy|ber|shop|pe|rin** F -, -nen *(inf)* cybershopper; **Cy|ber|space** ['saibɐspe:s] M -, *no pl (Comput)* cyberspace; **Cy|ber|welt** F *(Comput)* cyberspace
Cyc|la|mat® [tsykla'ma:t] NT -s, -e cyclamate
Cy|pern ['tsy:pɐn] NT -s = **Zypern**
cys|tisch ['tsʏstɪʃ] ADJ = **zystisch**

D

D, d [de:] **NT -, -** D, d

da [da:] ✪ 44.1 ADV **a** *(örtlich) (= dort)* there; *(= hier)* here; **es liegt da draußen/drinnen/drüben/vorn** it's out there/in there/over there/there in front; **das liegt etwa da herum** it's somewhere round about there, it's somewhere thereabouts; **geh da herum** go round there; **da und da** what's-its-name *(inf)*; **hier und da, da und dort** here and there; **wer da?** who goes there?; **he, Sie da!** hey, you there!; **die Frau da** that woman (over) there; **da bin ich/sind wir** here I am/we are; **da bist du ja!** there you are!; **da kommt er ja** here he comes; **wir sind gleich da** we'll soon be there, we're almost there; **da, wo …** where …; **wo die Straße über den Fluss geht, da fängt Schottland an** Scotland begins where the road crosses the river, where the road crosses the river, that's where Scotland begins; **ach, da war der Brief!** so that's where the letter was; **da möchte ich auch einmal hinfahren** *(inf)* I'd like to go there one day; **geben Sie mir ein halbes Pfund von dem da** give me half a pound of that one (there); **da haben wirs** *or* **den Salat** *(inf)* that had to happen; **da hast du deinen Kram/dein Geld!** (there you are,) there's your stuff/money; **da, nimm schon!** here, take it! → **da sein**
b *(zeitlich: = dann, damals)* then; **ich ging gerade aus dem Haus, da schlug es zwei** I was just going out of the house when the clock struck two; **vor vielen, vielen Jahren, da lebte ein König** *(liter)* long, long ago there lived a king *or* there once was a king; **da werden wir uns den Schaden mal ansehen** *(inf)* let's have a look at the damage; **da kommen Sie mal gleich mit** *(inf)* you just come along with me; **da siehst du, was du angerichtet hast** now see what you've done
c *(= daraufhin) sagen* to that; *lachen* at that; **sie weinte, da ließ er sich erweichen** when she started to cry he softened, she started to cry, whereupon he softened *(liter)*; **als er das Elend der Leute sah, da nahm er sich vor …** when he saw the people's suffering he decided …
d *(= folglich)* so; *(= dann)* then; **es war niemand im Zimmer, da habe ich …** there was nobody in the room, so I …; **wenn ich schon gehen muss, da gehe ich lieber gleich** if I have to go, (then) I'd rather go straight away
e *(inf: = in diesem Fall)* there; **da haben wir aber Glück gehabt!** we were lucky there!; **da muss man vorsichtig sein** you've got to be careful there; **was gibts denn da zu lachen?** what's funny about that?; **was gibts denn da zu fragen?** what is there to ask?; **da kann man nichts mehr machen** there's nothing more to be done (there *or* about it); **da kann man** *or* **lässt sich nichts machen** nothing can be done about it; **da könnte man aus der Haut fahren** it would drive you mad *(esp Brit) or* crazy *(inf)*; **da kann man nur lachen/sich nur fragen, warum** you can't help laughing/asking yourself why; **da kann man sich nur wundern** you can't help being amazed; **da kann man nur noch still sein** you can't say anything; **und da fragst du noch?** and you still have to ask?; **und da soll einer** *or* **ein Mensch wissen, warum!** and you're meant to know why!; **da fragt man sich (doch), ob der Mann noch normal ist** it makes you wonder if the man's normal; **da hat doch jemand gelacht/alle Kirschen gegessen** somebody laughed/has eaten all the cherries
f *(zur Hervorhebung)* **wir haben da eine neue Mitschülerin/Ausführung des Artikels** we've got this new girl in our school/this new model; **da fällt mir gerade ein …** it's just occurred to me …
g *(N Ger)* → **dabei, dafür** *etc*
CONJ **a** *(= weil)* as, since, seeing that
b *(liter: = als)* when; **die Stunde, da du …** the hour when you …; **nun** *or* **jetzt, da** now that

d. Ä. *abbr von* **der Ältere** sen

DAAD [de:|a:|a:'de:] **M -** *abbr von* **Deutscher Akademischer Austauschdienst** German Academic Exchange Service

da+be|hal|ten *ptp* **dabehalten** VT *sep irreg* to keep (here/there); *(in Haft auch)* to detain (there); *Schüler* to keep behind

da|bei [da'bai, *(emph)* 'da:bai] ADV **a** *(örtlich)* with it; *(bei Gruppe von Menschen, Dingen)* there; **ein Häuschen mit einem Garten ~** a little house with a garden (attached to it *or* attached); **ist die Lösung ~?** is the solution given (there)?; **nahe ~** nearby
b *(zeitlich) (= gleichzeitig)* at the same time; *(= währenddessen, wodurch)* in the course of this; **er aß weiter und blätterte ~ in dem Buch** he went on eating, leafing through the book as he did so *or* at the same time; **warum arbeiten Sie im Stehen? Sie können doch auch ~ sitzen** why are you working standing up? you can sit down while you're doing it; **nach der Explosion entstand eine Panik; ~ wurden drei Kinder verletzt** there was a general panic after the explosion, in the course of which *or* during which three children were injured; **… orkanartige Winde; ~ kam es zu schweren Schäden** … gale-force winds, which have resulted in serious damage
c *(= außerdem)* as well, into the bargain *(inf)*, with it *(inf)*; **sie ist schön und ~ auch noch klug** she's pretty, and clever as well
d *(wenn, während man etw tut)* in the process; *ertappen, erwischen* at it; **er wollte helfen und wurde ~ selbst verletzt** he wanted to help and got injured in the process *or* (in) doing so *or* while he was about it *(inf)*; **du warst bei einem Jugendtreffen? hast du denn ~ etwas gelernt?** you were at a youth meeting? did you learn anything there *or* from it?; **~ darf man nicht vergessen, dass …** it shouldn't be forgotten that …; *(Einschränkung eines Arguments)* it should not be forgotten here that …; **die ~ entstehenden Kosten** the expenses arising from this/that; **als er das tat, hat er ~ …** when he did that he …; **wenn man das tut, muss man ~ …** when you do that you have to …; **wir haben ihn ~ ertappt, wie er über den Zaun stieg** we caught him in the act of climbing over the fence
e *(= in dieser Angelegenheit)* **das Schwierigste ~** the most difficult part of it; **wichtig ~ ist …** the important thing here *or* about it is …; **mir ist nicht ganz wohl ~** I don't really feel happy about it; **~ kann man viel Geld verdienen** there's a lot of money in that; **er hat ~ einen Fehler gemacht** he's made a mistake; **sie hat sich ~ sehr dumm benommen** she behaved very stupidly; **es kommt doch nichts ~ heraus** nothing will come of it
f *(einräumend: = doch)* (and) yet; **er hat mich geschlagen, ~ hatte ich gar nichts gemacht** he hit me and I hadn't even done anything *or* and yet I hadn't done anything; **ich habe fünf Stück gegessen, ~ hatte ich gar keinen Hunger** I've eaten five pieces, and I wasn't even hungry
g **du gehst sofort nach Hause, und ~ bleibt es!** you're going straight home and that's that *or* that's the end of it!; **es bleibt ~, dass ihr morgen alle mitkommt** we'll stick to that *or* keep it like that, you're all coming tomorrow; **ich bleibe ~** I'm not changing my mind; **er bleibt ~, dass er es nicht gewesen ist** he still insists that he didn't do it, he's still sticking to his guns that he didn't do it; **aber ~ sollte es nicht bleiben** but it shouldn't stop there *or* at that; **lassen wir es ~** let's leave it at that!; **was ist schon ~?** so what? *(inf)*, what of it? *(inf)*; **was ist schon ~, wenn man das tut?** what harm is there in doing that?; **ich finde gar nichts ~** I don't see any harm in it; **es ist nichts ~, wenn man das tut** *(= schadet nichts)* there's no harm in doing that; *(= will nichts bedeuten)* doing that doesn't mean anything; **nimm meine Bemerkung nicht so ernst, ich habe mir nichts ~ gedacht** don't take my remark so seriously, I didn't mean anything by it; **ich habe mir nichts ~ gedacht, als ich den Mann aus der Bank kommen sah** I didn't think anything of it when I saw the man coming out of the bank; **was hast du dir denn ~ gedacht?** what were you thinking of?; **~ kann er sich nicht viel gedacht haben** he can't have thought about it much

da|bei+blei|ben VI *sep irreg aux sein* to stay *or* stick *(inf)* with it; *(bei Firma, Stelle, Armee etc)* to stay on → *auch* **dabei g**

da|bei+ha|ben VT *sep irreg (inf)* to have with one; *Geld, Pass, Schirm etc auch* to have on one

da|bei sein VI *irreg aux sein* **a** *(= anwesend sein)* to be there *(bei* at); *(= mitmachen)* to be involved *(bei* in); **ich bin dabei!** count me in!; **er war bei der Flugzeugentführung dabei** he was there when the plane was hijacked, he was there at the hijacking; **ein wenig Furcht ist immer dabei** I'm/you're *etc* always a bit scared; **er will überall ~** he wants to be in on everything
b *(= im Begriff sein)* **~, etw zu tun** to be just doing sth; **ich bin (gerade) dabei** I'm just doing it

Da|bei|sein NT **~ ist alles** it's all about taking part

da|bei+sit|zen VI *sep irreg aux haben or (S Ger, Aus, Sw) sein* to sit there; **bei einer Besprechung ~** to sit in on a discussion

da|bei+ste|hen VI *sep irreg aux haben or (S Ger, Aus, Sw) sein* to stand there

da+blei|ben VI *sep irreg aux sein* to stay (on); *(= nachsitzen)* to stay behind; **(jetzt wird) dageblieben!** (you just) stay right there!

da ca|po [da 'ka:po] ADV da capo; **~ rufen** to call for an encore

Dach [dax] NT **-(e)s, ⸚er** ['dɛçɐ] **a** roof; **das ~ der Welt** the roof of the world; **ein/kein ~ über dem Kopf haben** *(inf)* to have a/no roof over one's head; **mit jdm unter einem ~ wohnen** to live under the same roof as sb; **jdm das ~ überm Kopf anzünden** to burn down sb's house; **unterm ~ juchhe** *(inf)* right under the eaves; **unterm ~ wohnen** *(inf)* to live in an attic room/flat *(Brit)* or apartment; *(im obersten Stock)* to live right on the top floor; **unter einem ~** under one roof; **unter ~ und Fach sein** *(= abgeschlossen)* to be all wrapped up, to be all in the bag *(inf)*; *(Vertrag, Geschäft auch)* to be signed and sealed; *(= in Sicherheit)* to be safely under cover; *(Ernte)* to be safely in; **etw unter ~ und Fach bringen** to get sth all wrapped up/signed and sealed/safely under cover
b *(fig inf)* **jdm eins aufs ~ geben** *(= schlagen)* to smash sb on the head *(inf)*; *(= ausschimpfen)* to give sb a (good) talking-to; **eins aufs ~ bekommen** or **kriegen** *(= geschlagen werden)* to get hit on the head; *(= ausgeschimpft werden)* to be given a (good) talking-to; **jdm aufs ~ steigen** *(inf)* to get onto sb *(inf)*; **unter dem ~** *+gen* under the umbrella of

Dach- *in cpds* roof; **Dach|an|ten|ne** F roof aerial *or* antenna; **Dach|bal|ken** M roof joist *or* beam; **Dach|be|de|ckung** F, **Dach|be|lag** M roofing; **Dach|bo|den** M attic, loft; *(von Scheune)* loft; **auf dem ~** in the attic; **Dach|de|cker** [-dɛkɐ] M **-s, -**, **Dach|de|cke|rin** [-ərın] F **-, -nen** roofer; *(mit Ziegeln)* tiler; *(mit Schiefer)* slater; *(mit Stroh)* thatcher; **das kannst du halten wie ein ~** *(fig inf)* it doesn't matter two ha'pence *(Brit inf)* or one jot *(esp Brit inf)*; **Dach|de|cker|ar|bei|ten** PL roofing; tiling; slating; thatching

da|chen ['daxn] VT *(obs)* to roof

Dach-: **Dach|er|ker** M dormer window; **Dach|fens|ter** NT skylight; *(ausgestellt)* dormer window; **Dach|first** M ridge of the roof; **dach|för|mig** ADJ rooflike; **Dach|gar|ten** M roof garden; **Dach|ge|bälk** NT roof timbers *pl*; **Dach|ge|päck|trä|ger** M *(Aut)* roof rack; **Dach|ge|schoss** NT, **Dach|ge|schoß** *(Aus, S Ger)* NT attic (storey *(Brit)* or story *(US)*); *(= oberster Stock)* top floor or storey *(Brit)* or story *(US)*; **Dach|ge|sell|schaft** F parent company; **Dach|ge|sims** NT (roof) cornice; **Dach|ge|stühl** NT roof truss; **Dach|gie|bel** M gable; **Dach|glei|che** [-glaiçə] F *decl as adj*, **Dach|glei|chen|fei|er** F *(Aus)* topping-out ceremony; **Dach|hal|se** M *(hum)* cat; **Dach|kam|mer** F attic room, garret *(dated)*; **Dach|lat|te** F tile or roof batten *or* lath; **Dach|la|wi|ne** F snowfall from a/the roof; **Dach|lu|ke** F skylight; **Dach|nei|gung** F slope of the roof; **Dach|or|ga|ni|sa|ti|on** F umbrella *or (Comm)* parent organization; **Dach|pap|pe** F roofing felt *(Brit)* or paper; **Dach|pfan|ne** F (roof) tile; **Dach|rei|ter** M *(Archit)* roof or ridge turret; **Dach|rin|ne** F gutter

Dachs [daks] M **-es, -e** **a** *(Zool)* badger; **schlafen wie ein ~** *(inf)* to sleep like a log *(inf)* **b** *(inf: = Mensch)* **ein frecher ~!** a cheeky devil! *(Brit)*, a smart-alec!; **ein junger ~** a young whippersnapper *(dated inf)*

Dachs|bau M *pl* **-baue** badger's sett

Dach-: **Dach|scha|den** M **a** *(lit)* damage to the roof **b** *(inf)* **einen (kleinen) ~ haben** to have a slate loose *(inf)*; **Dach|schie|fer** M roofing slate; **Dach|schin|del** F (roof) shingle

Dachs|hund M dachshund

Dach|sil|hou|et|te F outline of the roof

Däch|sin ['dɛksın] F **-, -nen** female badger

Dach-: **Dach|spar|ren** M rafter; **Dach|stein** M (cement) roofing slab; **Dach|stroh** NT thatch; **Dach|stu|be** F, **Dach|stüb|chen** NT attic room, garret *(dated)*; **Dach|stuhl** M roof truss; **Dach|stuhl|brand** M roof fire

dach|te *pret von* **denken**

Dach-: **Dach|ter|ras|se** F roof terrace; **Dach|trä|ger** M *(Aut)* roof rack; **Dach|trau|fe** F rain spout; *(dial: = Dachrinne)* gutter; **Dach|ver|band** M umbrella organization; **Dach|woh|nung** F attic flat *(Brit)* or apartment; **Dach|zie|gel** M roofing tile; **Dach|zim|mer** NT attic room, garret *(dated)*

Da|ckel ['dakl] M **-s, -** dachshund, sausage dog *(inf)*; *(inf: = Person)* silly clot *(Brit inf)*, ninny *(US inf)*

Da|ckel|bei|ne PL *(inf)* short stumpy legs *pl*

Da|da|is|mus [dada'ısmʊs] M **-**, *no pl* Dadaism, Dada

Da|da|ist [dada'ıst] M **-en, -en**, **Da|da|is|tin** [-'ıstın] F **-, -nen** Dadaist; **die ~en** the Dada group, the Dadaists

da|da|is|tisch [dada'ıstıʃ] ADJ Dadaist

Dad|del|au|to|mat ['dadl-] M *(inf)* fruit machine

Dad|del|hal|le F *(inf)* amusement arcade

dad|deln ['dadln] VI *(inf)* to play the fruit machines

da|durch [da'dʊrç, *(emph)* 'da:dʊrç] ADV **a** *(örtlich)* through there; *(wenn Bezugsobjekt vorher erwähnt)* through it; *(geh: in Relativsatz)* through which
b *(kausal)* thereby *(form)*; *(= mithilfe von, aus diesem Grund auch)* because of this/that, through this/that; *(= durch diesen Umstand, diese Tat etc auch)* by *or* with that; *(= auf diese Weise)* in this/that way; **was willst du ~ gewinnen?** what do you hope to gain by *or* from that?; **meinst du, ~ wird alles wieder gut?** do you think that will make everything all right again?; **~ kam es, dass er nicht dabei sein konnte** that was why he couldn't be there
c ~, dass er das tat, hat er ... *(= durch diesen Umstand, diese Tat)* by doing that he ...; *(= deswegen, weil)* because he did that he ...; **~, dass ich das tat, hat er ...** by my doing that he ..., because I did that he ...; **~, dass er den zweiten Satz gewonnen hat, sind seine Chancen wieder gestiegen** his chances improved again with him *or* his winning the second set; **~, dass das Haus isoliert ist, ist es viel wärmer** the house is much warmer because it's insulated *or* for being insulated

Daff|ke ['dafkə] **aus ~** *(dial inf)* *(= aus Trotz)* out of spite; *(= aus Spaß)* for fun, for the fun of it

da|für [da'fy:ɐ, *(emph)* 'da:fy:ɐ] ADV **a** *(= für das, diese Tat etc)* for that/it; **wir haben kein Geld ~** we've no money for that; **~ haben wir kein Geld** we've no money for that sort of thing; **der Grund ~ ist, dass ...** the reason for that is (that) ...; **warum ist er so böse? er hat doch keinen Grund ~** why is he so angry? there's no reason for it *or* he has no reason to be; **~ war er nicht zu haben** it wasn't his scene *(inf)*; *(= erlaubte es nicht)* he wouldn't have it; **~ ist er immer zu haben** he never says no to that; **ich bin nicht ~ verantwortlich, was mein Bruder macht** I'm not responsible for what my brother does; **~ bin ich ja hier** that's what I'm here for, that's why I'm here; **er ist ~ bestraft worden, dass er frech zum Lehrer war** he was punished for being cheeky to *(Brit)* or sassy with *(US)* the teacher
b *(Zustimmung)* for that/it, in favour *(Brit)* or favor *(US)* (of that/it); **ich bin ganz ~** I'm all for it *(inf)*, I'm all in favo(u)r; **ich bin (ganz) ~, dass wir/sie das machen** I'm (all) for *or* in favo(u)r of doing that/them doing that; **~ stimmen** to vote for it; **ich bin nicht ~, dass das so gemacht wird** I don't think it should be done like that, I'm not in favo(u)r of it being done that way
c *(als Ersatz)* instead, in its place; *(als Bezahlung)* for that/it; *(bei Tausch)* in exchange; *(als Gegenleistung)* in return; **... ich mache dir ~ deine Hausaufgaben** ... and I'll do your homework in return
d *(zum Ausgleich)* but ... to make up; **in Physik ist er schlecht, ~ kann er gut Golf spielen** he's very bad at physics but he makes up for it at golf *or* but he's good at golf to make up; **ich hatte diesmal immer nur Kurzferien, ~ habe ich umso mehr gesehen** I've only had short holidays *(Brit)* or a short vacation *(US)* this time but I've seen a lot more for all that
e *(= im Hinblick darauf)* **der Junge ist erst drei Jahre, ~ ist er sehr klug** the boy is only three, (so) considering that he's very clever; **~, dass er erst drei Jahre ist, ist er sehr klug** seeing *or* considering that he's only three he's very clever
f *(in Verbindung mit n, vb etc siehe auch dort)* **er interessiert sich nicht ~** he's not interested in that/it; **~ interessiert er sich nicht** he's not interested in that sort of thing; **er gibt sein ganzes Geld ~ aus** he spends all his money on that/it; **ein Beispiel ~ wäre ...** an example of that would be ...; **ich kann mich nicht ~ begeistern** I can't get enthusiastic about it, I can't rouse any enthusiasm for it; **sie ist dreißig/sehr intelligent – ~ hätte ich sie nicht gehalten** she's thirty/very intelligent – I would never have thought it *or* thought she was; **~ werde ich schon sorgen** I'll see to that, I'll take care of that; **ich werde ~ sorgen, dass ...** I'll see to it that ...

da|für-: **da|für+hal|ten** VI *sep irreg (geh)* to be of the opinion; **ich halte dafür, dass wir zu Hause bleiben** I am of the opinion that we should stay at home; **nach meinem Dafürhalten** in my opinion; **da|für+kön|nen** *sep irreg*, **da|für kön|nen** △ *irreg* VT **er kann nichts dafür** he can't help it, it's not his fault; **er kann nichts dafür, dass er dumm ist** he can't help being stupid, it's not his fault that he's stupid; **er kann nichts dafür, dass es kaputtgegangen ist** it's not his fault that it broke, he couldn't help it breaking; **er kann etwas dafür, dass es kaputtgegangen ist** it was his fault that it broke; **was kann ich dafür, dass es heute regnet?** it's not my fault (that) *or* I can't help it that it's raining today; **als ob ich was dafürkönnte!** as if I could help it!, as if it were my fault!; **da|für+ste|hen** VIR *sep irreg (Aus)* to be worth it, to be worthwhile

DAG [de:la:'ge:] F **-** *abbr von* **Deutsche Angestellten-Gewerkschaft** Trade Union of German Employees

da|ge|gen [da'ge:gn, *(emph)* 'da:ge:gn] ✪ 36.1, 36.2, 39.2 ADV **a** *(örtlich)* against it → **dagegenhalten, dagegenpochen, dagegenprallen**
b *(als Einwand, Ablehnung)* against that/it; **~ sein** to be against it, to be opposed (to it); **etwas ~ haben** to object; **nichts ~ haben** not to object; **ich habe etwas ~** I object to that; **was hat er ~, dass wir früher anfangen?** what has he got against us starting earlier?, why does he object to us *or* our starting earlier?; **haben Sie was ~, wenn ich rauche?** do you mind if I smoke?, would you mind *or* object if I smoked?; **sollen wir ins Kino gehen? – ich hätte nichts ~ (einzuwenden)** shall we go to the cinema? – that's okay by me *(inf)*; **ich hätte nichts ~, wenn er nicht kommen würde** I wouldn't mind at all if he didn't come; **ich werde ~ protestieren** I will protest against that/it; **ich werde ~ protestieren, dass das gemacht wird** I will protest against that being done
c *(als Gegenmaßnahme) tun, unternehmen* about it; *Medikamente einnehmen etc* for it; **~ lässt sich nichts machen** nothing can be done about it; **bei mir regnet es herein, aber ich kann nichts ~ machen** the rain comes in, but I can't do anything to stop it *or* about it
d *(= verglichen damit)* compared with that/it/them, in comparison; **die Stürme letztes Jahr waren furchtbar, ~ sind die jetzigen nicht so schlimm** the gales last year were terrible, compared with them *or* those, these aren't so bad *or* these aren't so bad in comparison
e *(als Ersatz, Gegenwert)* for that/it/them
CONJ *(= im Gegensatz dazu)* on the other hand, however; **er sprach fließend Französisch, ~ konnte er kein Deutsch** he spoke French flu-

ently, but (on the other hand) he could not speak any German

da|ge|gen-: da|ge|gen+hal|ten VT *sep irreg* **a** **mache das Licht an und halte das Dia dagegen** put the light on and hold the slide up to it *or* against it **b** *(= vergleichen)* to compare it/them with; **wenn wir das Original ~ ...** if we compare the original with it ... **c** *(= einwenden)* = **dagegensetzen**; **da|ge|gen+po|chen** VI *sep* **die Tür war verschlossen, also pochte er dagegen** the door was locked, so he hammered on it; **da|ge|gen+pral|len** VI *sep* **es stand ein Baum im Weg und der Vogel/Wagen prallte dagegen** there was a tree in the way and the bird/car crashed into it; **da|ge|gen+set|zen** VT *sep (fig)* **seine eigene Meinung ~** to put forward one's own opinion in opposition; **das Einzige, was Sie ~ könnten, wäre ...** the only objection you could put forward would be ...; **er setzte dagegen, dass ...** he put forward the objection that ...; **da|ge|gen+spre|chen** VI *sep irreg* to be against it; **was spricht dagegen?** what is there against it?; **was spricht dagegen, dass wir es so machen?** what is there against us doing it that way?, why shouldn't we do it that way?; **es spricht nichts dagegen, es so zu machen** there's no reason not to do it that way; **da|ge|gen+stel|len** VR *sep* to oppose it; **warum musst du dich immer ~?** why must you always oppose everything?; **da|ge|gen+stem|men** VR *sep* to fight it, to oppose it bitterly; **da|ge|gen+wir|ken** VI *sep* to act against it

da|ge|we|sen ADJ → **da sein**

Da|ge|we|se|ne(s) NT *decl as adj* **das übertrifft alles bisher ~** that beats everything

da+ha|ben VT *sep irreg* **a** *(= vorrätig haben)* to have here/there; *(in Geschäft etc)* to have in stock **b** *(= zu Besuch haben)* to have here/there; *(zum Essen etc)* to have in

da|heim [da'haim] ADV *(esp S Ger, Aus, Sw)* at home; *(nach prep)* home; **bei uns ~** back home (where I/we come from); **das Buch liegt bei mir ~** *or* **~ bei mir** I've got the book at home; **wir haben bei mir ~** *or* **~ bei mir gefeiert** we had a celebration at my place; **~ sein** *(lit, fig)* to be at home; *(nach Reise)* to be home; **wo bist du ~?** where's your home?; **ich bin für niemanden ~** I'm not at home to anybody; **~ ist ~** *(Prov)* east, west, home's best *(prov)*, there's no place like home *(prov)*

Da|heim NT, *no pl (esp S Ger, Aus, Sw)* home

Da|heim-: Da|heim|ge|blie|be|ne(r) [-gəbli:bnə] MF *decl as adj* **die/alle ~n** those/all those at home; **Da|heim|sein** NT **das ~ ist auch schön** being (at) home is nice too, it's nice being (at) home

da|her [da'he:ɐ, *(emph)* 'da:he:ɐ] ✪ 44.1 ADV **a** *(= von dort)* from there; **von ~** from there; **~ habe ich das** that's where I got it from **b** *(dial: = hierher)* here **c** *(= durch diesen Umstand)* that is why; **~ weiß ich das** that's how *or* why I know that; **~ die große Eile/all der Lärm** that's why there's all this hurry/noise, that's the reason for all this hurry/noise; **~ der Name X** that's why it's/he's *etc* called X; **~ kommt es, dass ...** that is (the reason) why ...; **ich bin überzeugt, dass seine Krankheit ~ kommt** I'm sure that's why he's ill; **das kommt** *or* **rührt ~, dass ...** that is because ...

CONJ *(= deshalb)* that is why; **~ die Verspätung** that's what is causing the delay, hence the delay

da|her-: da|her+brin|gen VT *sep irreg (Aus)* to produce, to bring along; **da|her+flie|gen** VI *sep irreg aux sein* to fly along; **da|her|ge|lau|fen** ADJ **jeder Dahergelaufene, jeder ~e Kerl** any Tom, Dick or Harry, any guy who comes/came along; **diese ~en Kerle in der Politik** these self-important nobodies in politics; **sie hat so einen ~en Kerl geheiratet** she married some fellow who just happened along *(inf)*; **da|her+kom|men** VI *sep irreg aux sein* to come along; **da kommt so einer daher ...** this guy comes along ... *(inf)*; **wie kann man nur so geschminkt/schlampig ~?** *(inf)* how can anybody go around with make-up like that/looking so scruffy?; **da|her+lau|fen** VI *sep irreg aux sein (gehen)* to walk up; *(laufen)* to run up; **dahergelaufen kommen** to come running up → *auch* **dahergelaufen**; **da|her+re|den** *sep* VI to talk away; **red doch nicht so (dumm) daher!** don't talk such rubbish *(Brit inf)* *or* nonsense! VT to say without thinking; **was er alles/für ein blödes Zeug daherredet** the things/the rubbish *(inf)* *or* nonsense he comes out with! *(inf)*; **das war nur so dahergeredet** I/he *etc* just said that; **da|her+sa|gen** VT *sep* to say without thinking

da|he|rum ['da:hɛrʊm] ADV (a)round there

da|hin [da'hɪn, *(emph)* 'da:hɪn] ADV **a** *(räumlich)* there; *(= hierhin)* here; **kommst du auch ~?** are you coming too?; **~ und dorthin blicken** to look here and there; **~ gehe ich nie wieder, da gehe ich nie wieder hin** *(inf)* I'm never going there again; **bis ~** as far as there, up to that point; **ist es noch weit bis ~?** is it still a long way?; **bis ~ dauert es noch zwei Stunden** it'll take us another two hours to get there; **es steht mir bis ~** I've had it up to here *(inf)* **b** *(fig: = so weit)* **~ kommen** to come to that, to reach such a pass; **es ist ~ gekommen, dass ...** things have got to the stage where ..., things have reached such a pass that ...; **du wirst es ~ bringen, dass ...** you'll bring things to such a pass that ...
c *(= in dem Sinne, in die Richtung)* **er äußerte sich ~ gehend, dass ...** he said something to the effect that ...; **eine ~ gehende Aussage/Änderung** *etc* a statement/change *etc* to that effect; **ein ~ gehender Befehl, dass ...** an order to the effect that ...; **wir sind ~ gehend verblieben, dass ...** we agreed that ...; **er hat den Bericht ~ (gehend) interpretiert, dass ...** he interpreted the report as saying ...; **wir haben uns ~ geeinigt/abgesprochen, dass ...** we have agreed that ...; **alle meine Hoffnungen/Bemühungen gehen ~, dass ich dieses Ziel bald erreiche** all my hopes/efforts are directed toward(s) (my) reaching this goal soon; **seine Meinung geht ~, dass ...** he tends to feel that ..., he tends to the opinion that ...
d *(zeitlich)* then → **bis**
ADJ *pred* **~ sein** to have gone; **sein Leben** *or* **er ist ~** *(geh)* his life is over; **das Auto ist ~** *(hum inf)* the car has had it *(inf)*

da-: da|hi|nab [dahɪ'nap] ADV = **dorthinab**; **da|hi|nauf** [dahɪ'nauf] ADV = **dorthinauf**; **da|hi|naus** [dahɪ'naus] ADV there; *transportieren, bringen* out that way; **~ muss der Dieb entkommen sein** that must be where the thief escaped; **~ will er also!** *(fig)* so that's what he's getting at!

da|hin-: da|hin+be|we|gen *ptp* **dahinbewegt** VR *sep* to move on one's way; *(Fluss)* to flow on its way; **da|hin+däm|mern** VI *sep aux sein* to lie/sit there in a stupor; **da|hin+ei|len** VI *sep aux sein (liter)* to hurry along; *(Zeit)* to pass swiftly

da|hi|nein [dahɪ'nain] ADV = **dorthinein**

da|hin-: da|hin+fah|ren VI *sep irreg aux sein (liter: = sterben)* to pass away *or* over; **da|hin+flie|gen** VI *sep irreg aux sein (liter) (= wegfliegen)* to fly off; *(fig: = schnell fahren, vergehen)* to fly along *or* past; **da|hin+ge|ben** VT *sep irreg (liter) Leben, Gut, Besitz* to give up; **Da|hin|ge|gan|ge|ne(r)** [-gəgaŋənə] MF *decl as adj (liter)* departed

da|hin|ge|gen [dahɪn'ge:gn] ADV on the other hand

da|hin+ge|hen VI *sep irreg aux sein (geh)* **a** *(= vergehen: Zeit, Jahre)* to pass *(jdm* for sb) **b** *(= vorbeigehen, entlanggehen)* to pass **c** *(= sterben)* to pass away *or* on

da|hin|ge|hend ADJ, ADV → **dahin c**

da|hin-: Da|hin|ge|schie|de|ne(r) [-gəʃi:dənə] MF *decl as adj (liter)* departed; **da|hin|ge|stellt** ADJ **~ sein lassen, ob ...** to leave it open whether ...; **es bleibt** *or* **sei ~, ob ...** it is an open question whether ...; **da|hin+le|ben** VI *sep* to exist, to vegetate *(pej)*; **da|hin+raf|fen** VT *sep (liter)* to carry off; **da|hin+re|den** VI *sep* to say the first thing that comes into one's head; **da|hin+sa|gen** VT *sep* to say without (really) thinking; **das war nur so dahingesagt** I/he *etc* just said that (without thinking); **da|hin+schei|den** VI *sep irreg aux sein (geh)* to pass away; **da|hin+schlep|pen** VR *sep (lit: = sich fortbewegen)* to drag oneself along; *(fig: Verhandlungen, Zeit)* to drag on; **da|hin+schwin|den** VI *sep irreg aux sein (geh) (Vorräte, Geld, Kraft)* to dwindle (away); *(Interesse, Gefühle etc)* to dwindle; *(= vergehen: Zeit)* to go past; **da|hin+sie|chen** VI *sep aux sein (geh)* to waste away; **vor Kummer ~** to pine away; **jahrelang siechte er in einem dunklen Keller dahin** for years he languished in a dark cellar; **da|hin+ste|hen** VI *sep irreg* to be debatable

da|hin|ten [da'hɪntn, *(emph)* 'da:hɪntn] ADV over there; *(hinter Sprecher)* back there; **ganz weit ~** right *or* way *(inf)* over there

da|hin|ter [da'hɪntɐ, *(emph)* 'da:hɪntɐ] ADV **a** *(räumlich)* behind (it/that/him *etc*); **was sich wohl ~ verbirgt?** *(lit, fig)* I wonder what's behind that?; **da ist schon etwas ~** *(fig)* there's something in that; **(da ist) nichts ~** *(fig)* there's nothing behind it **b** *(= danach)* beyond

da|hin|ter|her [dahɪntɐ'he:ɐ] ADJ **~ sein** *(inf)* to push *(dass* to see that); **die Polizei ist ~, die Jugendkriminalität einzudämmen** the police are pretty hot on keeping juvenile delinquency under control *(inf)*

da|hin|ter-: da|hin|ter+klem|men *sep*, **da|hin|ter klem|men** △, **da|hin|ter+knien** *sep*, **da|hin|ter knien** △ VR *(inf)* to put one's back into it, to get *or* pull one's finger out *(inf)*; **klemm** *or* **knie dich mal ein bisschen dahinter** make a bit of an effort; **da|hin|ter+kom|men** *sep irreg aux sein*, **da|hin|ter kom|men** △ *irreg aux sein* VI *(inf)* to find out; *(= langsam verstehen)* to get it *(inf)*; **da|hin|ter+set|zen** *sep*, **da|hin|ter set|zen** △ VR = **dahinterklemmen**; **da|hin|ter+ste|cken** *sep*, **da|hin|ter ste|cken** △ VI *(inf)* to be behind it/that; **da steckt doch etwas dahinter** there's something behind it; **da steckt doch etwas dahinter, dass er jetzt gehen will** there's something behind his *or* him wanting to go now; **da werden die Eltern ~, dass er nicht mehr kommen will** his parents must be behind his *or* him not wanting to come any more; **er redet viel, es steckt aber nichts dahinter** he talks a lot but there's nothing behind it; **da|hin|ter+ste|hen** *sep irreg (S Ger, Aus, Sw: aux sein)*, **da|hin|ter ste|hen** △ *irreg (S Ger, Aus, Sw: aux sein)* VI **a** *(= unterstützen)* to back it/that, to be behind it/that **b** *(= zugrunde liegen)* to underlie it/that

da|hi|nun|ter [dahɪ'nʊntɐ, *(emph)* 'da:hɪnʊntɐ] ADV = **dorthinunter**

da|hin+ve|ge|tie|ren *ptp* **dahinvegetiert** VI *sep* to vegetate

Dah|lie ['da:liə] F **-, -n** dahlia

DAK [de:la'ka:] F **-** *abbr von* **Deutsche Angestellten-Krankenkasse** German Employees' Health Insurance

Da|ka|po [da'ka:po] NT **-s, -s** encore

Da|ka|po|ruf M call for an encore

dak|ty|lisch [dak'ty:lɪʃ] ADJ *(Poet)* dactylic

Dak|ty|lo-: Dak|ty|lo|gra|fie [-gra'fi:] F **-, -n** [-'fi:ən] *(Sw)* typing; **Dak|ty|lo|gramm** [-'gram] NT *pl* **-gramme** *(von einem Finger)* fingerprint; *(von ganzer Hand)* fingerprints *pl*; **Dak|ty|lo|gra|phie** [-gra'fi:] F **-, -n** [-'fi:ən] = **Daktylografie**; **Dak|ty|lo|sko|pie** [-sko'pi:] F **-, -n** [-'pi:ən] fingerprinting

Dak|ty|lus ['daktylʊs] M **-, Daktylen** [-lən] *(Poet)* dactyl

Da|lai-La|ma ['da:lai'la:ma] M -(s), -s (Rel) Dalai Lama
da-: **da+las|sen** VT sep irreg to leave (here/there); **da+lie|gen** VI sep irreg to lie there; **... sonst liegst du nachher da mit einer schweren Grippe** (inf) ... otherwise you'll be in bed with a bad dose of (the) flu
Dalk [dalk] M -(e)s, -e (Aus inf) (= Dummkopf) fathead (Brit inf), blockhead (inf); (= ungeschickter Mensch) clumsy oaf (inf)
dal|ke(r)t ['dalkət, 'dalkɐt] ADJ (Aus inf) daft (inf)
dal|li ['dali] ADV (inf) **~, ~!** on the double! (inf), look smart! (inf); **mach ein bisschen ~!** get a move on! (inf); **verzieh dich, aber ~!** beat it, go on, quick!
Dal|ma|ti|en [dal'ma:tsiən] NT -s Dalmatia
Dal|ma|ti|ner [dalma'ti:nɐ] M -s, - (Hund) dalmatian
da|ma|lig ['da:ma:lıç] ADJ attr at that or the time; Inhaber eines Amtes auch then attr; Sitten auch in those days
da|mals ['da:ma:ls] ADV at that time, then; **seit ~** since then, since that time; **von ~** of that time; **~, als ...** at the time when ...; **wenn ich daran denke, was ~ war** when I think of that time, when I think of what things were like then
Da|mas|kus [da'maskus] NT - Damascus
Da|mast [da'mast] M -(e)s, -e damask
da|mas|ten [da'mastn] ADJ attr (liter) damask
Da|mas|ze|ner|klin|ge [damas'tse:nɐ-] F damascene sword
Dam|bock ['dam-] M fallow deer
Däm|chen ['dɛ:mçən] NT -s, - (pej) precocious young madam; (= Dirne) tart (Brit inf), floozy (inf)
Da|me ['da:mə] F -, -n **a** lady; **sehr verehrte** (form) or **meine ~n und Herren!** ladies and gentlemen!; **guten Abend, die ~n** (old, hum) good evening, ladies; **„Damen"** (= Toilette) "Ladies"; **die ~ wünscht?** (old) can I be of assistance, madam? (form); **ganz ~ sein** to be the perfect lady, to be every inch a lady
b (allgemein gesehen: = Tanzpartnerin, Begleiterin) lady; (auf einen bestimmten Herrn bezogen) partner; (bei Cocktailparty, Theaterbesuch etc) (lady) companion; **seine ~ ist eben mit einem anderen weggegangen** the lady he came with has just left with someone else; **bringen Sie ruhig Ihre ~n mit** do by all means bring your wives and girlfriends
c (Sport) woman, lady; **Hundert-Meter-Staffel der ~n** women's or ladies' hundred metre (Brit) or meter (US) relay
d (Spiel) draughts sing (Brit), checkers sing (US); (= Doppelstein) king
Da|me|brett NT draughtboard (Brit), checkerboard (US)
Da|men- in cpds ladies'; **Da|men|bart** M facial hair; **Da|men|be|glei|tung** F **~ erwünscht** please bring a lady or (bei Ball) partner; **in ~** in the company of a lady; **Da|men|be|kannt|schaft** F female acquaintance (inf); **eine ~ machen** to make the acquaintance of a lady; **Da|men|be|such** M lady visitor/visitors; **Da|men|bin|de** F sanitary towel or napkin (US); **Da|men|dop|pel** NT (Tennis etc) ladies' doubles sing; **Da|men|ein|zel** NT (Tennis etc) ladies' singles sing; **Da|men|fahr|rad** NT ladies' bicycle or bike (inf); **Da|men|fri|seur** M, **Da|men|fri|seu|rin** F ladies' hairdresser; (= Geschäft) ladies' hairdresser's, beauty salon (US); **Da|men|fuß|ball** M women's football (esp Brit) or soccer; **Da|men|ge|sell|schaft** F **a** no pl (= Begleitung von Dame) company of ladies/a lady **b** (= gesellige Runde) ladies' gathering; **Da|men|grö|ße** F (= Konfektionsgröße) ladies' size; **da|men|haft** ADJ ladylike no adv ADV sich benehmen, sich kleiden in a ladylike way; **Da|men|kon|fek|ti|on** F ladies' wear (department); **Da|men|man|gel** M shortage of ladies; **Da|men|ober|be|klei|dung** F ladies' wear; **Da|men|rad** NT ladies' bicycle or bike (inf); **Da|men|ra|sie|rer** M (inf) women's razor; **Da|men|sat|tel** M side-saddle; **im ~ reiten** to ride side-saddle; **Da|men|schnei|der(in)** M(F) dressmaker; **Da|men|schnei|de|rei** F **a** dressmaking **b** (= Werkstatt) dressmaker's; **Da|men|sitz** M side-saddle style of riding; **im ~** side-saddle; **Da|men|to|i|let|te** F **a** (= WC) ladies, ladies' toilet or restroom (US) **b** (= Kleidung) ladies' toilette; **Da|men|un|ter|wä|sche** F ladies' underwear, lingerie; **Da|men|wahl** F ladies' choice; **Da|men|welt** F, no pl (dated hum) ladies pl; **in** or **bei der ~ beliebt** popular with the ladies
Da|me-: **Da|me|spiel** NT draughts sing (Brit), checkers sing (US); **Da|me|stein** M draughtsman (Brit), checker (US)
Dam|hirsch ['dam-] M fallow deer
da|misch ['da:mıʃ] (S Ger, Aus) ADJ **a** (= dämlich) daft (inf) **b** (pred: = schwindelig) dizzy, giddy ADV (= sehr) terribly (inf)
da|mit [da'mıt, (emph) 'da:mıt] ADV → auch **mit**, vbs +mit **a** (= mit diesem Gegenstand, dieser Tätigkeit, mithilfe davon) with it/that; **sie hatte zwei Koffer und stand ~ am Bahnhof** she had two (suit)cases and was standing there with them in the station; **sie hat Ärger mit der Waschmaschine – ~ habe ich auch Probleme** she's having trouble with her washing machine – I've got problems with mine too; **was will er ~?** what does he want that for?, what does he want with that?; **was soll ich ~?** what am I meant to do with that?; **ist Ihre Frage ~ beantwortet?** does that answer your question?; **~ kann er mich ärgern** I get really annoyed when he does that
b (= mit, in dieser Angelegenheit) **meint er mich ~?** does he mean me?; **weißt du, was er ~ meint?** do you know what he means by that?; **was ist ~?** what about it?; **wie wäre es ~?** how about it?; **er konnte mir nicht sagen, was es ~ auf sich hat** he couldn't tell me what it was all about; **wie sieht es ~ aus?** what's happening about or with (esp US) it?; **muss er denn immer wieder ~ ankommen?** (= davon reden) must he keep on about it?; (mit Bitten, Forderungen etc) must he keep coming back about it?; **das/er hat gar nichts ~ zu tun** that/he has nothing to do with it; **~ ist nichts** (inf) it's no go (inf); **hör auf ~!** (inf) lay off! (inf); **~ hat es noch Zeit** there's no hurry for that
c (bei Verben) → vb +mit; **was willst du ~ sagen?** what's that supposed or meant to mean?; **~ will ich nicht sagen, dass ...** I don't mean to say that ...; **sind Sie ~ einverstanden?** do you agree to that?; **er hatte nicht ~ gerechnet** he hadn't reckoned on or with that; **~, dass du dich jetzt aufregst, machst du den Schaden auch nicht wieder gut** you're not making anything better by getting excited; **sie fangen schon ~ an** they're already starting on it; **sie fangen schon ~ an, das Haus abzureißen** they're already starting to pull down the house; **~ fing der Streit an** the argument started with that; **der Streit fing ~ an, dass er behauptete ...** the argument started when he said ...; **er fing ~ an, dass er ... sagte** he began by saying that ...
d (bei Befehlen) with it; **weg/heraus ~!** away/out with it; **her ~!** give it here! (inf); **Schluss** or **genug ~!** that's enough (of that)!
e (begründend) therefore; **er verlor den zweiten Satz und ~ das Spiel** he lost the second set and therefore the match; **~ ist es klar, dass er es war** from that it's clear that it was he (form) or him
f (= daraufhin, dann, jetzt) with that; **~ schließe ich für heute** I'll close with that for today; **~ kommen wir zum Ende des Programms** that brings us to the end of our programmes (Brit) or programs (US)
CONJ so that; **~ er nicht fällt** so that he does not fall, lest he (should) fall (old)
däm|lich ['dɛ:mlıç] (inf) ADJ stupid, dumb (inf) ADV stupidly; **guck nicht so ~** don't give me that dumb look (inf); **komm mir nicht so ~!** don't give me that! (inf), don't come that with me! (Brit inf); **er ist mir vielleicht ~ gekommen** he acted really dumb (inf) or stupid; **~ fragen** to ask stupid or dumb (inf) questions/a stupid or dumb (inf) question
Däm|lich|keit F -, -en **a** no pl stupidity, dumbness (inf) **b** (= dumme Handlung) stupid or dumb (inf) thing
Damm [dam] M -(e)s, **=e** ['dɛmə] **a** (= Deich) dyke (Brit), dike (esp US); (= Staudamm) dam; (= Hafendamm) wall; (= Uferdamm) embankment, levee (esp US); (= Verkehrsverbindung zu Insel) causeway; (fig) barrier; **einen ~ gegen etw aufbauen** (fig) **einer Sache** (dat) **einen ~ (entgegen)setzen** (fig) to check sth; **wenn wir das kleinste bisschen nachgeben, werden alle Dämme brechen** if we give way at all, the floodgates will open
b (= Bahndamm, Straßendamm) embankment
c (dial: = Fahrdamm) road
d (Anat) perineum
e (fig inf) **wieder auf dem ~ sein** to be back to normal; **geistig auf dem ~ sein** to be with it (inf); **nicht recht auf dem ~ sein** not to be up to the mark (inf)
Damm|bruch M breach in a/the dyke (Brit) or dike (esp US) etc
däm|men ['dɛmən] VT **a** (Tech) Wärme to keep in; Schall to absorb **b** (fig: = eindämmen) Abfallflut, Überfluss to contain
Däm|mer ['dɛmɐ] M -s, no pl **a** (poet) = **Dämmerung b** (fig geh) nebulousness
däm|me|rungs|ak|tiv ADJ (Zool) twilight-active, active at twilight pred
däm|mer|haft ADJ (liter) hazy, nebulous
däm|me|rig ['dɛmərıç] ADJ Licht dim, faint; Zimmer gloomy; Stunden twilight attr; **es wird ~** (abends) dusk is falling; (morgens) dawn is breaking
Däm|mer|licht NT twilight; (abends auch) dusk; (= Halbdunkel) half-light, gloom
däm|mern ['dɛmɐn] VI **a** (Tag, Morgen) to dawn; (Abend) to fall; **als der Tag** or **Morgen/Abend dämmerte ...** as dawn was breaking/dusk was falling ...; **die Erkenntnis** or **es dämmerte ihm, dass ...** (inf) he began to realize that ... **b** (= im Halbschlaf sein) to doze; (Kranker) to be dopey; **vor sich hin ~** (= im Halbschlaf sein) to doze; (= nicht bei klarem Verstand sein) to be dopey VI impers **es dämmert** (morgens) dawn is breaking; (abends) dusk is falling; **jetzt dämmerts (bei) mir!** (inf) now it's dawning (on me)!
Däm|mer-: **Däm|mer|schein** M (liter) glow; **Däm|mer|schlaf** M doze; **ich war nur im ~** I was only dozing; **Däm|mer|schop|pen** M early evening drink; **Däm|mer|stun|de** F twilight, dusk
Däm|me|rung ['dɛmərʊŋ] F -, -en twilight; (= Abenddämmerung auch) dusk; (= Morgendämmerung auch) dawn; (= Halbdunkel) half-light; **bei** or **mit Anbruch der ~** when dusk began/begins to fall; when dawn began/begins to break; **in der ~** at dusk/dawn
Däm|mer|zu|stand M (= Halbschlaf) dozy state; (= Bewusstseinstrübung) dopey state
Dämm-: **Dämm|ma|te|ri|al** NT (Build, Tech) insulating or insulation material; **Dämm|plat|te** F (Build, Tech) insulating board, softboard
dämm|rig ['dɛmrıç] ADJ = **dämmerig**
Damm-: **Damm|riss** M (Med) tear of the perineum; **Damm|rutsch** M landslide which destroys a dyke etc; **Damm|schnitt** M (Med) episiotomy
Dämm|stof|fe PL insulating materials pl
Däm|mung ['dɛmʊŋ] F -, -en insulation
Damm|weg M causeway
Dam|num ['damnʊm] NT -s, **Dam|na** [-na] (Fin) debt discount
Da|mok|les|schwert ['da:moklɛs-] NT (lit, fig) sword of Damocles

Dä|mon ['dɛːmɔn] **M -s, Dämonen** [dɛ'moːnən] demon; **ein böser ~** an evil spirit, a demon

Dä|mo|nie [dɛmo'niː] **F -, -n** [-'niːən] demonic nature

dä|mo|nisch [dɛ'moːnɪʃ] **ADJ** demonic **ADV** demonically

dä|mo|ni|sie|ren [dɛmoni'ziːrən] *ptp* **dämonisiert** **VT** to demonize

Dä|mo|nis|mus [dɛmo'nɪsmʊs] **M -,** *no pl (Rel)* demonism

Dampf [dampf] **M -(e)s, ⸗e** ['dɛmpfə] **a** vapour *(Brit)*, vapor *(US)*; *(= Wasserdampf)* steam; **~ ablassen** *or* **abblasen** *(lit, fig)* to let off steam; **unter ~ sein** *or* **stehen** to have (its) steam up; **aus dem Schornstein quoll der ~ in weißen Wolken** clouds of white smoke poured from the chimney **b** *(inf: = Wucht, Schwung)* force; **jdm ~ machen** *(inf)* to make sb get a move on *(inf)*; **~ dahintermachen** *or* **-setzen** to get a move on *(inf)*; **mit ~** *(inf)* at full tilt; **vorm Chef hat sie unheimlich ~** the boss really puts the wind up her *(inf)*; **~ draufhaben** *(dated inf)* to be going at full steam

Dampf- *in cpds* steam; **Dampf|an|trieb** **M** steam drive; **Maschine mit ~** steam-driven engine; **Dampf|bad** **NT** steam bath; **Dampf|boot** **NT** steamboat; **Dampf|bü|gel|ei|sen** **NT** steam iron; **Dampf|druck** **M** *pl* **-drücke** steam pressure

damp|fen ['dampfn] **VI** **a** *(= Dampf abgeben)* to steam; *(Badezimmer etc)* to be full of steam; *(Pferd)* to be in a lather; **ein ~des Bad/Essen** a steaming hot bath/meal **b** *aux sein (Zug, Schiff)* to steam **c** *aux sein (inf) (= mit Dampfer fahren)* to sail, to steam; *(= mit Zug fahren)* to go by (steam) train

dämp|fen ['dɛmpfn] **VT** **a** *(= abschwächen)* to muffle; *Geräusch, Lärm, Schall auch* to deaden, to dampen; *Geige, Trompete, Farbe* to mute; *Licht, Stimme* to lower; *Wut* to calm; *Freude, Begeisterung, Stimmung* to dampen; *Aufprall* to deaden; *(fig) jdn* to subdue; *Konjunktur* to depress → *auch* **gedämpft** **b** *(Cook)* to steam **c** *(= bügeln)* to press with a damp cloth; *(mit Dampfbügeleisen)* to press with a steam iron

Damp|fer ['dampfɐ] **M -s, -** steamer, steamship; **auf dem falschen ~ sein** *or* **sitzen** *(fig inf)* to have got the wrong idea

Dämp|fer ['dɛmpfɐ] **M -s, -** **a** *(Mus: bei Klavier)* damper; *(bei Geige, Trompete)* mute; **dadurch hat er/sein Optimismus einen ~ bekommen** that dampened his spirits/optimism; **jdm einen ~ aufsetzen** to dampen sb's spirits; **einer Sache** *(dat)* **einen ~ aufsetzen** *(inf)* to put a damper on sth *(inf)* **b** *(Cook: = Dampfkochtopf)* steamer

Damp|fer-: **Damp|fer|an|le|ge|stel|le** **F** steamer jetty; **Damp|fer|fahrt** **F** boat trip; **Damp|fer|li|nie** **F** steamship line

Dampf-: **dampf|för|mig** **ADJ** vaporous; **Dampf|ham|mer** **M** steam hammer; **Dampf|hei|zung** **F** steam heating

damp|fig ['dampfɪç] **ADJ** steamy

dämp|fig ['dɛmpfɪç] **ADJ** **a** *(Vet)* broken-winded **b** *(dial: = schwül)* muggy

Dampf-: **Dampf|kes|sel** **M** *(Tech)* steam-boiler; *(Cook)* steamer; **Dampf|ko|cher** **M**, **Dampf|koch|topf** **M** pressure cooker; **Dampf|kraft** **F** steam power; **Dampf|kraft|werk** **NT** steam power station; **Dampf|lo|ko|mo|ti|ve** **F**, **Dampf|lok** **F** *(inf)* steam engine *or* locomotive; **Dampf|ma|schi|ne** **F** steam(-driven) engine; **Dampf|nu|del** **F** *(Cook)* sweet yeast dumpling cooked in milk and sugar; **aufgehen wie eine ~** *(fig inf)* to blow up like a balloon *(inf)*; **Dampf|pfei|fe** **F** steam whistle; *(von Schiff)* siren; **Dampf|ram|me** **F** steam-operated pile driver; **Dampf|rei|ni|ger** **M** *(für Teppiche etc)* steam cleaner; **Dampf|schiff** **NT** steamship, steamer; **Dampf|schiff|fahrt** **F** steam navigation; **Dampf|schiff|fahrt|ge|sell|schaft** **F** steamship company; **Dampf|strahl|rei|ni|ger** **M** *(für Steinböden, Fliesen etc)* steam cleaner; **Dampf|tur|bi|ne** **F** steam turbine

Dämp|fung ['dɛmpfʊŋ] **F -, -en** *(Mus)* damping; *(Phys, Rad, TV)* attenuation

Dampf|wal|ze **F** steamroller

Dam|wild ['dam-] **NT** fallow deer

da|nach [da'naːx, *(emph)* 'daːnaːx] **ADV** **a** *(zeitlich)* after that/it; *(= nachher auch)* afterwards, after *(inf)*; **ich habe einen Whisky getrunken, ~ fühlte ich mich schon besser** I had a whisky and after that *or* afterwards felt better, I had a whisky and felt better after that *or* afterwards *or* after *(inf)*; **ich las das Buch zu Ende, erst ~ konnte ich einschlafen** only when I had finished reading the book could I get to sleep; **zehn Minuten ~ war sie schon wieder da** ten minutes later she was back; **um die Zwanziger und ~** around the twenties and after **b** *(in der Reihenfolge) (örtlich)* behind that/it/him/them *etc*; *(zeitlich)* after that/it/him/them *etc*; **als Erster ging der Engländer durchs Ziel und gleich ~ der Russe** the Englishman finished first, immediately followed by the Russian *or* and the Russian immediately after him; **bei ihm kommt als erstes die Arbeit, ~ lange nichts und dann das Privatleben** work comes first with him, and then, a long, long way behind, his private life **c** *(= dementsprechend)* accordingly; *(= laut diesem)* according to that; *(= im Einklang damit)* in accordance with that/it; **wir haben hier einen Bericht; ~ war die Stimmung damals ganz anders** we have a report here, according to which the atmosphere at the time was quite different; **~ sein** *(Wetter, Bedingungen, Stimmung etc)* to be right; **sie hat den Aufsatz in zehn Minuten geschrieben – ~ ist er auch** *(inf)* she wrote the essay in ten minutes – it looks like it too; **sie sieht auch/nicht ~ aus** she looks/doesn't look (like) it; *(= als ob sie so was getan hätte)* she looks/doesn't look the type; **~ siehst du gerade aus** *(iro)* I can just see that *(iro)*; **lesen Sie Paragraf 218; ~ ist es verboten** read paragraph 218, under that it is illegal; **~ zu urteilen** judging by *or* from that; **mir war nicht ~** *(inf) or* **~ zumute** *or* **zu Mute** I didn't feel like it; **mir steht der Sinn nicht ~** *(geh)* I don't feel inclined to **d** *(in bestimmte Richtung)* toward(s) it; **er griff schnell ~** he grabbed at it, he made a grab for it; **hinter ihm war etwas, aber er hat sich nicht ~ umgesehen** there was something behind him, but he didn't look round *(Brit) or* around to see what it was **e** *(in Verbindung mit n, vb etc siehe auch dort)* **sie sehnte sich ~** she longed for that/it; **sie sehnte sich ~, ihren Sohn wiederzusehen** she longed to see her son again; **er hatte großes Verlangen ~** he felt a great desire for it; **er hatte großes Verlangen ~, wieder einmal die Heimat zu sehen** he felt a great desire to see his home again; **~ kann man nicht gehen** you can't go by that; **wenn es ~ ginge, was ich sage/was mir Spaß macht, dann ...** if it were a matter of what I say/enjoy then ...; **sich ~ erkundigen, ob ...** to inquire whether ...

Da|na|er|ge|schenk ['daːnaɐ-] **NT** *(fig)* two-edged gift

dan|cen ['dɛnsn] **VI** *(sl)* to dance, to boogie

Dan|dy ['dɛndi] **M -s, -s** dandy

dan|dy|haft ['dɛndihaft] **ADJ** *(pej)* dandyish

Dä|ne ['dɛːnə] **M -n, -n** Dane, Danish man/boy

da|ne|ben [da'neːbn, *(emph)* 'daːneːbn] **ADV** **a** *(räumlich) (= in unmittelbarer Nähe von jdm/etw)* next to him/her/that/it *etc*; *(zum Vergleich)* beside him/her/that/it *etc*; **links/rechts ~** *(neben Sache)* to the left/right of it; *(neben Mensch)* to his/her *etc* left/right; → **danebenfallen, danebengreifen** *etc* **b** *(= verglichen damit)* compared with that/it/him/them *etc*, in comparison **c** *(= außerdem)* besides that, as well as that, in addition (to that); *(= gleichzeitig)* at the same time

da|ne|ben-: **da|ne|ben+be|neh|men** *ptp* **danebenbenommen** **VR** *sep irreg (inf)* to make an exhibition of oneself; **da|ne|ben+fal|len** **VI** *sep irreg aux sein* to miss (it *or* one's mark); **da|ne|ben+ge|hen** **VI** *sep irreg aux sein* **a** *(= verfehlen: Schuss etc)* to miss; **der Ball ging knapp daneben** the ball went just wide **b** *(inf: = scheitern)* to go wrong; *(Witz)* to fall flat; **da|ne|ben+ge|ra|ten** *ptp* **danebengeraten** **VI** *sep irreg aux sein* to go wrong; *(Übersetzung)* not to hit the mark; **da|ne|ben+grei|fen** **VI** *sep irreg* **a** *(= verfehlen) (auf dem Klavier etc)* to play a wrong note/some wrong notes; *(beim Fangen)* to miss (the mark), to be wide of the mark **b** *(fig inf, mit Schätzung, Prognose etc)* to be wide of the mark, to be way out *(inf)*; **im Ton ~** to strike the wrong note; **im Ausdruck ~** to put things the wrong way; **mit seiner Bemerkung hat er aber ganz schön danebengegriffen** he really put his foot in it with that remark *(inf)*; **da|ne|ben+hal|ten** *sep irreg* **VT** **jdn/etw ~** to compare him/her/it *etc* with sb/sth **VI** *(= danebenzielen)* to aim to miss; **da|ne|ben+hau|en** **VI** *sep irreg* **a** *(beim Schlagen)* to miss; *(beim Klavierspielen)* to play a wrong note/some wrong notes **b** *(inf: = sich irren)* to miss the mark, to be wide of the mark; *(beim Berechnen, Raten, Schätzen auch)* to be way out *(inf)*; **da|ne|ben+lie|gen** **VI** *sep irreg (inf: = sich irren)* to be quite wrong, to be way out *(inf)*; **da|ne|ben+ra|ten** **VI** *sep irreg (inf)* to guess wrong; **da|ne|ben+schie|ßen** **VI** *sep irreg* **a** *(= verfehlen)* to miss **b** *(= absichtlich vorbeischießen)* to shoot to miss; **da|ne|ben+schla|gen** **VI** *sep irreg* to miss; **da|ne|ben sein** **VI** *irreg aux sein (inf)* **a** *(= verwirrt sein)* to be completely confused; *(= sich nicht wohlfühlen)* not to feel up to it *(inf)* **b** *(= unangebracht sein)* to be out of order *(inf)*; **da|ne|ben+ste|hen** **VI** *sep irreg (S Ger, Aus, Sw: aux sein)* **ich stand direkt daneben, als die Bombe losging** the bomb went off right next to me; **da|ne|ben+tip|pen** **VI** *sep (inf)* to guess wrong; **da|ne|ben+tref|fen** **VI** *sep irreg* to miss; **da|ne|ben+woh|nen** **VI** *sep* **wir wohnen im Haus daneben** we live in the house next door; **da|ne|ben+zie|len** **VI** *sep* to aim to miss

Dä|ne|mark ['dɛːnəmark] **NT -s** Denmark

da|nie|den [da'niːdn] **ADV** *(obs)* down below; **~ auf Erden** on earth below

da|nie|der+lie|gen **VI** *sep irreg* **a** *(old liter: = krank sein)* to be laid low *(Brit) or* up *(inf)*, to be ill **b** *(fig geh: = schwach sein)* to be depressed

Dä|nin ['dɛːnɪn] **F -, -nen** Dane, Danish woman/girl

dä|nisch ['dɛːnɪʃ] **ADJ** Danish

Dä|nisch(e) ['dɛːnɪʃ] **NT** Danish → *auch* **Deutsch(e)**

dank [daŋk] **PREP** *+gen or dat* thanks to

Dank [daŋk] ✪ 48.1, 49, 52.3 **M -(e)s,** *no pl (ausgedrückt)* thanks *pl*; *(= Gefühl der Dankbarkeit)* gratitude; **besten** *or* **herzlichen** *or* **schönen** *or* **vielen ~** many thanks, thank you very much, thanks a lot *(inf)*; **vielen herzlichen/tausend ~!** many/very many thanks!, thanks a million! *(inf)*; **~ sei dem Herrn** *(Eccl)* thanks be to God; **haben Sie/hab ~!** *(geh)* thank you!; *(für Hilfe auch)* I'm much obliged to you; **jdm für etw ~ sagen** *(liter)* to express one's *or* give *(esp Eccl)* thanks to sb for sth; **~ sagen** *(Aus)* to express one's thanks; *(Eccl)* to give thanks; **jdm ~ schulden** *(form)* to owe sb a debt of gratitude; **jdm für etw ~ wissen** *(form)* to be indebted to sb for sth; **etw mit ~ annehmen** to accept sth with thanks; **mit bestem ~ zurück!** many thanks for lending it/them to me; *(iro: = Retourkutsche)* thank you, the same to you!; **das war ein schlechter ~** that was poor thanks; **das ist der (ganze) ~ dafür** that's all the thanks one gets; **als ~ für seine Dienste** in grateful recognition of his service; **zum ~ (dafür)** as a way of saying thank you; **das ist der ~ des Vaterlandes!** *(iro)* that's all the thanks one gets!; **der ~ des Vaterlandes ist dir gewiss** *(iro)* you'll get a medal for that

Dank|ad|res|se F official letter of thanks

dank|bar ✪ 29.1, 31, 46.5, 47.1, 47.5, 49 ADJ **a** *(= dankerfüllt)* grateful; *(= erleichtert, froh)* thankful; *Publikum, Zuhörer* appreciative; **jdm ~ sein** to be grateful to sb *(für* for); **sich ~ erweisen** *or* **zeigen** to show one's gratitude *(gegenüber* to); **ich wäre dir ~, wenn du ...** I would be grateful if you ..., I would appreciate it if you ... **b** *(= lohnend) Arbeit, Aufgabe, Rolle* rewarding; *Stoff* easy-care *attr*; *(= haltbar)* hard-wearing; *Opfer* worthwhile; **eine ~e Pflanze** a plant which doesn't need much attention ADV *(= voller Dank)* gratefully

Dank|bar|keit [ˈdaŋkbaːɐkait] ✪ 49 F -, *no pl* gratitude *(gegen, gegenüber* to); *(= Gefühl der Erleichterung)* thankfulness

Dank|brief M thank-you letter

dan|ke [ˈdaŋkə] INTERJ **a** thank you, thanks *(inf)*, ta *(Brit inf)*; *(ablehnend)* no thank you; **~ ja, ja, ~** yes please, yes, thank you; **~ nein, nein, ~** no thank you; **~ schön** *or* **sehr** thank you *or* thanks *(inf)* very much; **(zu jdm) ~ (schön) sagen** to say thank you (to sb); **ich soll dir von meiner Schwester ~ schön sagen** my sister sends (you) her thanks; **~ vielmals** many thanks; *(iro)* thanks a million *(inf)*; **~ der Nachfrage** *(form)* thank you for your concern; **wie gehts? – ~, ich kann nicht klagen** how's it going? – (I) can't complain; **soll ich helfen? – ~, ich glaube, ich komme allein zurecht** can I help? – thanks (all the same), but I think I can manage → *auch* **danken**
b *(inf)* **mir gehts ~** I'm OK *(inf)*; **sonst gehts dir (wohl) ~!** *(iro)* are you feeling all right?

dan|ken [ˈdaŋkn] ✪ 47.1, 47.2, 49 VI **a** *(= Dankbarkeit zeigen)* to express one's thanks; **jdm ~** to thank sb *(für* for); **mit überschwänglichen Worten ~** to be effusive in one's thanks; **mit einem Strauß Blumen ~** to express one's thanks with a bunch of flowers; **ich danke dir für das Geschenk/die Gastfreundschaft** *etc* thank you for your *or* the present/your hospitality *etc*; **wir ~ für die Einladung** thank you for your *or* the invitation; **(ich) danke!** yes please; *(ablehnend)* no thank you, no thanks *(inf)*; **(ich) danke bestens** *(iro)* thanks a million *(inf)*, thanks for nothing *(inf)*; **man dankt** *(inf)* thanks *(inf)*, ta *(Brit inf)*; **ich danke Ihnen (dafür), dass Sie mir den Betrag überwiesen haben** thank you for transferring the money (to me); **jdm ~ lassen** to send sb one's thanks; **bestellen Sie bitte Ihrem Vater, ich lasse herzlich ~** please give your father my thanks; **nichts zu ~** don't mention it, not at all *(Brit)*, you're welcome; **dafür danke ich, für so was danke ich** *(iro)* not on your life!, not a chance! *(inf)*; **na, ich danke** *(iro)* no thank you; **etw ~d annehmen/ablehnen** to accept/decline sth with thanks
b *(= ablehnen)* to decline
c *(= Gruß erwidern)* to return a/the greeting
VT **a** *(geh: = verdanken)* **jdm/einer Sache etw ~** to owe sth to sb/sth; **ihm danke ich es, dass ...** I owe it to him that ...; **nur dem rechtzeitigen Erscheinen der Polizei ist es zu ~, dass ...** it was only thanks to the prompt turnout of the police that ...
b jdm etw ~ *(= jdm dankbar sein für)* to thank sb for sth; *(= jdm etw lohnen)* to repay sb for sth; **man wird es dir nicht ~** you won't be thanked for it; **man wird es nicht zu ~ wissen** it won't be appreciated; **sie werden es mir später einmal ~, dass ich das getan habe** they'll thank me for doing that one day; **all meine Hilfe wurde mir mit keinem Wort gedankt** I didn't get a single word of thanks for all my help; **man hat es mir schlecht gedankt, dass ich das getan habe** I got small thanks for doing it, I didn't get a lot of thanks for doing it; **wie kann ich Ihnen das jemals ~?** how can I ever thank you?

dan|kens|wert ADJ *Bemühung, Hingabe* commendable; *Hilfe* kind; *(= lohnenswert) Aufgabe, Arbeit* rewarding; **in ~er Weise** *(= löblich)* (most) commendably; *(= freundlicherweise)* very kindly

dan|kens|wer|ter|wei|se [ˈdaŋknsveːɐtɐˈvaizə] ADV thankfully; **Herr Kopleck hat uns ~ informiert** Mr Kopleck was kind enough to inform us

dank|er|füllt [-lɐfʏlt] ADJ *(liter)* grateful

Dan|kes-: **Dan|kes|be|zei|gung** [-bətsaigʊŋ] F -, **-en** demonstration of one's gratitude *or* thanks; **Dan|kes|brief** M thank-you letter, letter of thanks

Dan|ke|schön ✪ 49 NT **-s**, *no pl* thank you

Dan|kes-: **Dan|kes|re|de** F speech of thanks, words *pl* of thanks; **Dan|kes|wor|te** PL words *pl* of thanks; *(von Redner)* vote *sing* of thanks

Dank-: **Dank|ge|bet** NT prayer of thanksgiving; **Dank|got|tes|dienst** M service of thanksgiving; **Dank|op|fer** NT thanks offering; **dank|sa|gen** *pret* **danksagte**, *ptp* **dankgesagt**, *infin auch* **dankzusagen** VI *(geh)* to express one's thanks *(jdm* to sb); *(Eccl)* to give thanks *(jdm* to sb); **Dank|sa|gung** [ˈdaŋkzaːgʊŋ] F -, **-en a** *(Eccl)* thanksgiving **b** *(= Brief)* note of thanks; **Dank|schrei|ben** NT letter of thanks

dann [dan] ADV **a** *(Reihenfolge ausdrückend, = später)* then; **~ und ~** (a)round about then; **von ~ bis ~** for some time (a)round then; **~ und wann** now and then; **gerade ~, wenn ...** just when ...; **wenn das gemacht ist, ~ kannst du gehen** when that's done you can go; **noch eine Woche, ~ ist Weihnachten** another week till Christmas, another week and (then) it's Christmas → **bis**
b *(= unter diesen Umständen)* then; **wenn ..., ~ if ...,** (then); **wenn du was brauchst, ~ sagst dus mir, nicht?** just tell me if you need anything, if you need anything (then) just tell me; **ja, selbst ~** yes, even then; **nein, selbst ~ nicht** no, not even then; **selbst ~/selbst ~ nicht, wenn ...** even/not even if ...; **erst ~, wenn ...** only when ...; **ja, ~!** (oh) well then!; **ich habe keine Lust mehr – ~ hör doch auf!** I'm not in the mood any more – well stop then!; **und wie es ~ so geht** *or* **ist, kommt natürlich Besuch** and as was bound to happen, I got visitors, but you know how it is, I got visitors; **wenn er seine Gedichte selbst nicht versteht, wer ~?** if he can't understand his own poems, who else could (understand them)?; **wenn man nicht einmal in Schottland echten Whisky bekommt, wo ~?** if you can't get real whisky in Scotland, where *can* you expect to find it?; **wenn ich nicht einmal das Einmaleins bei euch voraussetzen kann, was ~?** if I can't even assume you know your (multiplication) tables, what can I assume you know?; **~ eben nicht** well, in that case (there's no more to be said); **~ erst recht nicht!** in that case no way *(inf)* or not a chance! *(inf)*; **~ ist ja alles in Ordnung** (oh well,) everything's all right then, in that case everything's all right; **~ will ich lieber gehen** well, I'd better be getting along (then); **ja ~, auf Wiedersehen** well then, goodbye; **also ~ bis morgen** right then, see you tomorrow, see you tomorrow then
c *(= außerdem)* **~ ... noch** on top of that; **strohdumm und ~ auch noch frech** as thick as they come and cheeky into the bargain *(Brit)*, as dumb as they come and a smart alec too *(esp US)*; **kommandiert mich herum und meint ~ auch noch ...** orders me around and then on top of that thinks ...

dan|nen [ˈdanən] ADV **von ~** *(obs: = von woher)* thence *(old)*, from thence *(Eccl)*; *(liter: = weg)* away

dan|tesk [danˈtɛsk] ADJ Dantesque

dan|tisch [ˈdantɪʃ] ADJ Dantean

da|ran [daˈran, *(emph)* ˈdaːran] ADV **a** *(räumlich: = an dieser Stelle, diesem Ort, Gegenstand)* on it/that; *schieben, lehnen, stellen* against it/that; *legen* next to it/that; *kleben, befestigen, machen, gehen* to it/that; *sich setzen* at it/that; **nahe** *or* **dicht ~** right up against it, up close against it; **nahe ~ sein** *(fig)* to be on the point of it, to be just about to; **nahe ~ sein, etw zu tun** to be on the point of doing sth, to be just about to do sth; **zu nahe ~** too close (to it); **~ vorbei** past it; **er hat dicht ~ vorbeigeschossen** his shot just missed it; **~ kommen** *or* **fassen/riechen/schlagen** to touch/smell/hit it/that; **er hielt seine Hand ~** he touched it with his hand; **die Kinder sind wieder ~ gewesen** *(inf)* the children have been at it again
b *(zeitlich: = danach anschließend)* **im Anschluss ~, ~ anschließend** following that/this; **im Anschluss ~ findet eine Diskussion statt** it/this/that will be followed by a discussion; **erst fand ein Vortrag statt, ~ schloss sich eine Diskussion** first there was a lecture which was followed by a discussion *or* and after that a discussion
c *(inf)* **er ist schlecht ~** *(gesundheitlich, finanziell)* he's in a bad way *(inf)*; **er ist gut ~** *(gesundheitlich, finanziell)* he's OK *(inf)*; **ich weiß nie, wie ich (bei ihm) ~ bin** I never know where I am with him; **sie sind sehr arm ~** *(= haben wenig Geld)* they're not at all well-off; *(= sind bedauernswert)* they are poor creatures
d *(in Verbindung mit n, adj, vb siehe auch dort) arbeiten* on it/that; *sterben, erinnern, Bedarf, Mangel* of it/that; *interessieren, sich beteiligen, arm, reich* in it/that; *sich klammern* to it/that; **~ sticken/bauen** to embroider/build it/that; **was macht der Aufsatz? – ich bin zurzeit ~** how's the essay doing? – I'm (working) on it now; **er war ~ interessiert** he was interested in it; **er war ~ interessiert, es zu tun** he was interested in doing it; **ich zweifle nicht ~** I don't doubt it; **ich zweifle nicht ~, dass ...** I don't doubt that ...; **erinnere mich ~** remind me about *or* of that; **erinnere mich ~, dass ich das machen soll** remind me to do that, remind me that I must do that; **~ wird er zugrunde** *or* **zu Grunde gehen** that will be the ruin of him; **wir haben großen Anteil ~ genommen** we sympathized deeply; **wird sich etwas ~ ändern?** will that change at all?; **wir können nichts ~ machen** we can't do anything about it; **~ sieht man, wie ...** there you (can) see how ...; **Sie würden gut ~ tun, dieses Angebot anzunehmen** you would do well *or* would be well-advised to accept this offer; **das Beste/Schönste/Schlimmste** *etc* **~** the best/nicest/worst *etc* thing about it; **es ist kein wahres Wort ~** there isn't a word of truth in it, not a word of it is true; **es ist nichts ~** *(= ist nicht fundiert)* there's nothing in it; *(= ist nichts Besonderes)* it's nothing special → *auch* **dran**

da|ran-: **da|ran+ge|ben** VT *sep irreg (geh)* to sacrifice; **da|ran+ge|hen** VI *sep irreg aux sein* to set about it; **~, etw zu tun** to set about doing sth; **da|ran+ma|chen** VR *sep (inf)* to set about it; *(= endlich in Angriff nehmen)* to get down to it; **sich ~, etw zu tun** to set about doing sth; to get down to doing sth; **da|ran+set|zen** *sep* VT *(= einsetzen)* to exert; *(= aufs Spiel setzen)* to stake, to risk; **seine ganzen Kräfte ~, etw zu tun** to spare no effort to do sth VR to sit down to it; **da|ran+wen|den** VT *sep irreg (geh)* to exert; **seine ganzen Kräfte ~, etw zu tun** to spare no effort to do sth

da|rauf [daˈrauf, *(emph)* ˈdaːrauf] ADV **a** *(räumlich)* on it/that/them *etc*; *(in Richtung)* toward(s) it/that/them *etc*; *schießen, zielen, losfahren* at it/that/them *etc*; *(fig) fußen, basieren, aufbauen* on it/that; *zurückführen, beziehen* to it/that; **da er es nicht wagte herunterzuklettern, musste er ~ sitzen bleiben** since he didn't dare climb down he just had to sit (up) there; **er hielt den Nagel fest und schlug mit dem Hammer ~** he held the nail in place and hit it with the hammer; **seine Behauptungen stützen sich ~, dass der Mensch von Natur aus gut ist** his claims are based on the supposition that man is naturally good
b *(Reihenfolge: zeitlich, örtlich)* after that; **die Tage, die ~ folgten** the days which followed; ~

folgte ... that was followed by ..., after that came ...; **~ folgend** after him/it/that *etc*; *Tag etc* following; *Wagen etc* behind *pred*; **zuerst kam der Wagen des Premiers, ~ folgten Polizisten** the prime minister's car came first, followed by policemen; **am Tag/Abend/Jahr ~** the next day/evening/year, the day/evening/year after (that)
c *(= infolgedessen)* because of that; **er hat gestohlen und wurde ~ von der Schule verwiesen** he was caught stealing and because of that was expelled
d *(als Reaktion) sagen, reagieren* to that; **~ antworten** to answer that; **eine Antwort ~** an answer to that; **er hat ein Gedicht ~ geschrieben** that prompted him to write a poem; **~ wurde er ganz beschämt** that made him feel quite ashamed; **~ haben sich viele Interessenten gemeldet** a lot of people have shown an interest in it/that; **nimm die Marke, ~ bekommst du ein Essen in der Kantine** take this token, you'll get a meal in the canteen for *or* with it; **~ steht die Todesstrafe/stehen mindestens fünf Jahre Gefängnis** that carries the death penalty/a minimum sentence of five years' imprisonment
e *(in Verbindung mit n, adj, vb siehe auch dort) bestehen, verlassen, wetten, Zeit/Mühe verschwenden, Einfluss* on that/it; *hoffen, warten, sich vorbereiten, gefasst sein, reinfallen* for that/it; *trinken* to that/it; *stolz sein* of that/it; **ich bin stolz ~, dass sie gewonnen hat** I'm proud that she won, I'm proud of her winning; **ich bestehe ~, dass du kommst** I insist that you come, I insist on your coming; **wir müssen ~ Rücksicht nehmen/Rücksicht ~ nehmen, dass ...** we must take that into consideration/take into consideration that ...; **ich möchte ~ hinweisen, dass ...** I would like to point out that ...; **gib mir die Hand ~** shake on it; **~ freuen wir uns schon** we're looking forward to it already; **~ kommen** *(= auffinden)* to come (up)on that/it; *(= sich erinnern)* to think of that/it; **wir kamen auch ~ zu sprechen** we talked about that too; **wie kommst du ~?** what makes you think that?, how do you work that out? *(inf)*; **~ willst du hinaus!** that's what you're getting at!; **er war nur ~ aus** he was only after that, he was only interested in that; **er war nur ~ aus, möglichst viel Geld zu verdienen** he was only interested in earning as much money as possible

da|rauf|fol|gend ADJ *attr* → **darauf b**

da|rauf|hin [daraufhɪn, *(emph)* 'da:raufhɪn] ADV **a** *(= aus diesem Anlass, deshalb)* as a result (of that/this); *(= danach)* after that, thereupon **b** *(= im Hinblick darauf)* with regard to that/this; **wir müssen es ~ prüfen, ob es für unsere Zwecke geeignet ist** we must test it with a view to whether it is suitable for our purposes

da|raus [da'raus, *(emph)* 'da:raus] ADV **a** *(räumlich)* out of that/it/them; **~ kann man nicht trinken!** you can't drink out of that/it! **b** *(= aus diesem Material etc)* from *or* out of that/it/them; **~ kann man Wein herstellen** you can make wine from that **c** *(= aus dieser Sache, Angelegenheit)* from that/it/them; **~ ergibt sich/folgt, dass ...** it follows from that that ...; **~ sieht man ...** from this it can be seen ...

dar|ben ['darbn] VI *(geh)* *(= entbehren)* to live in want; *(= hungern)* to starve

dar+bie|ten ['da:ɐ-] *sep irreg (geh)* **VT** **a** *(= vorführen) Tänze, Schauspiel* to perform; *(= vortragen) Lehrstoff* to present **b** *(= anbieten)* to offer; *Speisen* to serve; *(= reichen) Hand, Geschenk etc* to offer, to proffer *(form)* **VR** to present itself; *(Gelegenheit, Möglichkeit auch)* to offer itself; **dort bot sich (ihnen) ein schauerlicher Anblick dar** a horrible sight met their eyes, they were faced with a horrible sight

Dar|bie|tung ['da:ɐbi:tʊŋ] F -, -en *(= das Darbieten)* performance; *(= das Dargebotene)* act

dar+brin|gen ['da:ɐ-] VT *sep irreg (geh) Opfer* to offer

Dar|da|nel|len [darda'nɛlən] PL **die ~** the Dardanelles *pl*

da|rein [da'rain, *(emph)* 'da:rain] ADV **a** *(räumlich: = hinein)* in there; *(wenn Bezugsobjekt vorher erwähnt)* in it/them; **hierein? – nein, ~!** in here? – no, in there **b** *(old: = in diese Lage) einwilligen, sich ergeben* to that

da|rein- PREF → *auch* **drein-**: **da|rein+fin|den** VR *sep irreg (geh)* to come to terms with it, to learn to accept it; **sich ~, etw zu tun** to come to terms with doing sth, to learn to accept doing sth; **da|rein+fü|gen** VR *sep (geh)* **wir müssen uns ~** we must accept that, we must bow to that; **da|rein+le|gen** VT *sep (fig geh)* = **dareinsetzen**; **da|rein+re|den** VI *sep (in Angelegenheiten)* to interfere *(jdm* in sb's affairs); **da|rein+set|zen** VT *sep (fig geh) Energie* to put into it, to devote to it; **seine ganze Energie ~, etw zu tun** to put all one's energy into doing sth, to devote all one's energy to doing sth; **er setzte seinen ganzen Stolz darein** it was a matter of pride with him

darf [darf] 3. PERS SING *pres von* **dürfen**

da|rin [da'rɪn, *(emph)* 'da:rɪn] ADV **a** *(räumlich)* in there; *(wenn Bezugsobjekt vorher erwähnt)* in it/them; *(fig)* in that/it; **~ liegt ein Widerspruch** there is a contradiction in that
b *(= in dieser Beziehung)* in that respect; **~ ist er ganz groß** *(inf)* he's very good at that; **~ unterscheiden sich die beiden** the two of them differ in that (respect); **die beiden unterscheiden sich ~, dass ...** the two of them differ in that ...; **~ liegt der Unterschied** that is the difference, that is where the difference is; **der Unterschied liegt ~, dass ...** the difference is that ...; **wir stimmen ~ überein, dass ...** we agree that ...
c *(old: = worin)* in which

da|rin|nen [da'rɪnən] ADV *(old)* therein *(old)*

Dark|room ['darkru:m] M -s, -s *darkened room for anonymous sex*

dar+le|gen ['da:ɐ-] VT *sep* to explain *(jdm* to sb); *Theorie, Plan, Ansichten auch* to expound *(jdm* to sb)

Dar|le|gung ['da:ɐle:gʊŋ] F -, -en explanation

Dar|le|hen ['da:ɐle:ən] NT -s, - loan; **als ~** as a loan

Dar|le|hens-: **Dar|le|hens|bank** F *pl* **-banken** lending *or* credit bank; **Dar|le|hens|ge|ber(in)** M(F) lender; **Dar|le|hens|kas|se** F credit bank; **Dar|le|hens|kon|to** NT loan account; **Dar|le|hens|neh|mer(in)** M(F) borrower; **Dar|le|hens|schuld** F loan; **Dar|le|hens|sum|me** F **die ~** the amount of the/a loan; **eine ~** a loan; **Dar|le|hens|zin|sen** PL interest *sing* on loans, lending rate(s *pl*)

Dar|lehn ['da:ɐle:n] NT -s, - loan; **als ~** as a loan

Darm [darm] M -(e)s, ⸚e ['dɛrmə] intestine(s *pl*), bowel(s *pl*), gut(s *pl*); *(für Wurst)* (sausage) skin *or* case; *(= Material: für Saiten, Schläger etc)* gut; **Wurst in echtem/künstlichem ~** sausage in real/synthetic skin

Darm- *in cpds* intestinal; **Darm|aus|gang** M anus; **Darm|bak|te|rie** F *usu pl (Physiol)* intestinal *or* gut bacterium; **die ~n** *pl* the intestinal flora *sing*; **Darm|be|we|gung** F peristalsis *no art, no pl*, peristaltic movement; **Darm|ent|lee|rung** F evacuation of the bowels; **Darm|flo|ra** F *(Physiol)* intestinal flora; **Darm|grip|pe** F gastric influenza *or* 'flu; **Darm|ka|tarr(h)** M enteritis; **Darm|krebs** M cancer of the intestine; **Darm|lei|den** NT intestinal trouble *no art*; **Darm|sai|te** F gut string; **Darm|spie|ge|lung** F enteroscopy *(spec)*; *(des Dickdarms)* colonoscopy *(spec)*; **Darm|spü|lung** F enema; **Darm|tä|tig|keit** F peristalsis *no art*; **die ~ fördern/regulieren** to stimulate/regulate the movement of the bowels; **Darm|träg|heit** F underactivity of the intestines; **Darm|ver|schlin|gung** F volvulus *(form)*, twisting of the intestine; **Darm|ver|schluss** M obstruction of the bowels *or* intestines

dar|nach [dar'nax, 'darna:x] ADV *(old)* = **danach**

dar|ne|ben [dar'ne:bn] ADV *(old)* = **daneben**

da|rob [da'rɔp, *(emph)* 'da:rɔp] ADV *(old)* **a** = **darüber** **b** *(= deswegen)* **er war ~ sehr erstaunt** he was very surprised by that; **er wurde ~ sehr bewundert** he was much admired for that *or* on that account

Dar|re ['darə] F -, -n drying kiln *or* oven; *(= Hopfendarre, Malzdarre)* oast

dar+rei|chen ['da:ɐ-] VT *sep (liter)* *(= anbieten)* to offer *(jdm etw* sb sth, sth to sb); *(= reichen auch)* to proffer *(form)* *(jdm etw* sth to sb)

Dar|rei|chungs|form ['da:rraiçʊŋs-] F presentation; *(von Medikamenten)* (form of) administration

dar|ren ['darən] VT to (kiln-)dry; *Malz, Hopfen* to (oast-)dry

Darr|ofen M drying kiln *or* oven; *(für Hopfen, Malz)* oast

dar|stell|bar ['da:ɐ-] ADJ *(in Literaturwerk etc)* portrayable; *(in Bild etc auch)* depictable; *(durch Diagramm etc)* representable; *(= beschreibbar)* describable; **schwer/leicht ~** hard/easy to portray/depict/show/describe; **dieses Phänomen ist grafisch ~** this phenomenon can be shown on a graph; **das ist auf dem Bildschirm nicht ~** this can't be displayed *or* shown on screen

dar+stel|len ['da:ɐ-] *sep* **VT** **a** *(= abbilden)* to show; *(= ein Bild entwerfen von)* to portray, to depict; *(Theat)* to portray; *Rolle* to play; *(= beschreiben)* to describe; *(auf Bildschirm)* to display, to show; **etw in einem möglichst günstigen Licht ~** to show sth in the best possible light; **etw kurz** *or* **knapp ~** to give a short description of sth; **was sollen diese verworrenen Striche ~?** what are these confused lines supposed to show *or (in Zeichnung)* be?; **die ~den Künste** *(= Theater)* the dramatic *or* performing arts; *(= Malerei, Plastik)* the visual arts; **er stellt etwas/nichts dar** *(fig)* he has a certain air/doesn't have much of an air about him
b *(Math) Funktion* to plot; *(Chem)* to produce; **~de Geometrie** projective geometry
c *(= bedeuten)* to constitute, to represent
VR *(= Eindruck vermitteln)* to appear *(jdm* to sb); *(= sich erweisen)* to show oneself; **die Sache stellte sich (als) sehr fragwürdig dar** the matter appeared (to be) very dubious; **bei dem Talentwettbewerb stellte er sich als begabter Sänger dar** at the talent competition he showed himself to be a gifted singer

Dar|stel|ler ['da:ɐʃtɛlɐ] M -s, - *(Theat)* actor; **der ~ des Hamlet** the actor playing Hamlet; **ein hervorragender ~ tragischer Rollen** an excellent actor in tragic roles

Dar|stel|le|rin ['da:ɐʃtɛlərɪn] F -, -nen *(Theat)* actress → *auch* **Darsteller**

dar|stel|le|risch ['da:ɐʃtɛlərɪʃ] **ADJ** dramatic; **eine ~e Höchstleistung** a magnificent piece of acting **ADV** *(= in darstellerischer Hinsicht)* in terms of acting; **~ war die Weber der Klein weit überlegen** as an actress Weber was much superior to Klein

Dar|stel|lung ['da:ɐ-] F **a** portrayal; *(in Buch, Bild auch)* depiction; *(durch Diagramm etc)* representation; *(= Beschreibung)* description; *(= Bericht)* account; **an den Wänden fand man ~en der Heldentaten des Königs** on the walls one could see the King's heroic deeds depicted; **eine falsche ~ der Fakten** a misrepresentation of the facts; **er gab eine großartige ~ des Hamlet** his performance as Hamlet was superb; **der Stoff war in** *or* **durch ~en von Wanderbühnen bekannt geworden** the material became known through being performed by travelling theatre *(Brit) or* traveling theater *(US)* groups
b *(Math)* **grafische ~** graph
c *(Chem)* preparation

Dar|stel|lungs-: **Dar|stel|lungs|form** F form of expression; *(Theat)* dramatic art form; **Dar|stel|lungs|kunst** F skills *pl* of portrayal; *(von Schauspieler)* acting technique; **Dar|stel|lungs|mit|tel** NT technique (of representation)

Darts [da:ɐts] NT -, *no pl* darts *sing*

dar+tun ['da:ɐ-] VT *sep irreg (geh)* to set forth; *Überlegenheit* to demonstrate

da|rü|ber [da'ry:bɐ, *(emph)* 'da:ry:bɐ] ✪ 53.3 ADV **a** *(räumlich)* over that/it/them; *(= quer darüber)* across *or* over there; *(wenn Bezugsobjekt vorher erwähnt)* across *or* over it/them; *(= höher als etw)* above (there/it/them); *(= direkt auf etw)* on top (of it/them); **geh ~, nicht hierüber!** go across *or* over there, not here!; **die Aufgabe war sehr schwer, ich habe lange ~gesessen** the exercise was very difficult, I sat over it for a long time; **~ hinweg sein** *(fig)* to have got over it; **~ hinaus** apart from this/that, in addition; **~ hinaus kann ich nichts sagen** over and above that I can't say anything; **~ hinaus log sie mich auch noch an** on top of that she also lied to me; **jetzt ist er ~ hinaus** *(fig)* he is past that now
b *(= deswegen, in dieser Beziehung)* about that/it; **sich ~ beschweren/beklagen** *etc* to complain/moan *etc* about it; **sich ~ beschweren/beklagen** *etc*, **dass ...** to complain/moan *etc* that ...; **wir wollen nicht ~ streiten, ob ...** we don't want to argue *or* disagree about whether ...
c *(= davon)* about that/it; **Rechenschaft ~ ablegen** to account for it; **sie führt eine Liste ~** she keeps a list of it
d *(= währenddessen)* in the meantime; **Wochen gingen ~ hin** meanwhile *or* in the meantime weeks went past
e *(= mehr, höher)* above *or* over that; **21 Jahre/4 Euro und ~** 21 years/4 euros and above *or* over; **kein Cent ~** not a penny over (that) *or* more; **~ hinaus** over and above that; **es geht nichts ~** there is nothing to beat it

da|rü|ber-: **da|rü|ber+fah|ren** *sep irreg aux sein*, **da|rü|ber fah|ren** △ *irreg aux sein* VI *(fig)* to run over it; **wenn du mit der Hand darüberfährst, ...** if you run your hand over it ...; **da|rü|ber+lie|gen** *sep irreg (S Ger, Aus, Sw: aux sein)*, **da|rü|ber lie|gen** △ *irreg (S Ger, Aus, Sw: aux sein)* VI *(fig)* to be higher; **da|rü|ber+schrei|ben** *sep irreg*, **da|rü|ber schrei|ben** △ *irreg* VT to write above it; **da|rü|ber+ste|hen** *sep irreg (S Ger, Aus, Sw: aux sein)*, **da|rü|ber ste|hen** △ *irreg (S Ger, Aus, Sw: aux sein)* VI *(fig)* to be above such things

da|rum [da:'rʊm, *(emph)* 'da:rʊm] ADV **a** *(räumlich)* (a)round that/it/him/her/them; **~ herum** (a)round about (it/him/her/them); **~, wo ...** (a)round where ...
b *(= um diese Angelegenheit) (in Verbindung mit n, vb siehe auch dort)* **es geht ~, dass ...** the thing is that ...; **~ geht es gar nicht** that isn't the point; **~ geht es** that is what it is about, that's it; **~ geht es mir** that's my point; **~ geht es mir nicht** that's not the point for me; **es geht mir ~, Ihnen das klarzumachen** I'm trying to make it clear to you; **wir kommen leider nicht ~ herum, die Preise heraufzusetzen** unfortunately we cannot avoid raising prices; **wir wollen nicht lange ~ herumreden** we don't want to spend a long time talking around the subject; **ich gäbe viel ~, die Wahrheit zu erfahren** I would give a lot to learn the truth; **ich habe ihn schon ein paar Mal ~ gebeten, aber ...** I've asked him a few times (for it/to do it), but ...; **könntest du ihn ~ bitten, zu mir zu kommen?** could you ask him to come to me?; **sie haben sich ~ gestritten** they argued over it; **sie haben sich ~ gestritten, wer ...** they argued over who ...
c *(liter. = darüber, davon)* about that/it; **nur wenige wissen ~, wie ...** *(geh)* few people know how ...
d *(= deshalb)* that's why, because ...; **~, dass** *or* **weil ...** because ...; **eben ~** that is exactly why; **ach ~!** so that's why!; **~?** because of that?; **warum willst du nicht mitkommen? – ~!** *(inf)* why don't you want to come? – (just) 'cos! *(inf)*; **er ist faul, aber ~ nicht dumm** he's lazy but that doesn't mean he's stupid → *auch* **drum**

da|rum-: **da|rum+kom|men** VI *sep irreg aux sein* to lose it/them; **~, etw zu tun** to lose the opportunity of doing sth; **da|rum+le|gen** VT *sep* to put around it/them; **da|rum+ste|hen** VI *sep irreg aux haben or sein* to stand around; **da|rum+wi|ckeln** VT *sep* to wrap round *(Brit) or* around *(US)* it/them

da|run|ter [da'rʊntɐ, *(emph)* 'da:rʊntɐ] ADV **a** *(räumlich)* under that/it/them, underneath *or* beneath (that/it/them); *(= niedriger als etw)* below *or* under(neath) (that/it/them); **~ hervorkommen** to appear from underneath; **als weitere Belastung kam der Tod seiner Mutter, ~ ist er dann zusammengebrochen** his mother's death was an added burden and he broke down under this strain
b *(= weniger)* under that; **Leute im Alter von 35 Jahren und ~** people aged 35 and under; **der Preis beträgt 50 Euro, ~ kann ich die Ware nicht abgeben** the price is 50 euros, I can't sell for less; **kein Cent ~** not a penny under that *or* less; **~ macht sies nicht** *(inf)* she won't do it for less
c *(= dabei)* among them; **~ waren viele Ausländer** there were a lot of foreigners among them
d *(= unter dieser Angelegenheit) (in Verbindung mit n, vb siehe auch dort)* **was verstehen Sie ~?** what do you understand by that/it?; **~ kann ich mir nichts vorstellen** that doesn't mean anything to me → *auch* **drunter**

da|run|ter-: **da|run|ter+blei|ben** *sep irreg aux sein*, **da|run|ter blei|ben** △ *irreg aux sein* VI *(fig)* to be lower; **Sie kennen die Anforderungen, wenn Sie mit** *or* **in Ihrer Leistung ~, werden Sie entlassen** you are aware of the requirements, if you fail to meet them you will be dismissed; **da|run|ter+fal|len** *sep irreg aux sein*, **da|run|ter fal|len** △ *irreg aux sein* VI *(fig) (= dazugerechnet werden)* to be included; *(= davon betroffen werden)* to come *or* fall under it/them; **da|run|ter+ge|hen** *sep irreg aux sein*, **da|run|ter ge|hen** △ *irreg aux sein* VI *(= darunterpassen)* to fit underneath; **da|run|ter+lie|gen** *sep irreg (S Ger, Aus, Sw: aux sein)*, **da|run|ter lie|gen** △ *irreg (S Ger, Aus, Sw: aux sein)* VI **a** *(lit)* to lie underneath **b** *(fig)* = **darunterbleiben**; **da|run|ter+mi|schen** *sep*, **da|run|ter mi|schen** △ VT *Mehl etc* to mix in VR *(Mensch)* to mingle with them; **da|run|ter+schrei|ben** *sep irreg*, **da|run|ter schrei|ben** △ VT to write underneath; *Namen auch* to sign at the bottom; **da|run|ter+set|zen** *sep*, **da|run|ter set|zen** △ VT *Unterschrift* to put to it

das [das] [das] → **der**

da sein VI *irreg aux sein (lit, fig inf)* to be there; **noch ~** to be still there; *(= übrig sein auch)* to be left; **wieder ~** to be back; **ich bin gleich wieder da** I'll be right *or* straight back; **sind Sie schon lange da?** have you been here/there long?; **ist Post/sind Besucher für mich da?** is there any mail/are there visitors for me?; **war der Briefträger schon da?** has the postman *(Brit) or* mailman *(US)* been yet?; **für jdn ~** to be there *or* available for sb; **wir sind immer für Sie da** we're there when you need us; **ein Arzt, der immer für seine Patienten da ist** a doctor who always has time for his patients; **voll ~** *(inf)* to be all there *(inf)*; **so etwas ist noch nie da gewesen** it's quite unprecedented; **es ist alles schon mal da gewesen** it's all been done before; **ein nie da gewesener Erfolg** an unprecedented success; **das da Gewesene** = **Dagewesene**

Da|sein NT *(= Leben, Existenz, Philos)* existence; *(= das Anwesendsein)* presence; **der Kampf ums ~** the struggle for existence; **etw ins ~ rufen** *(liter)* to bring sth into existence, to call sth into being

Da|seins-: **Da|seins|angst** F *(Philos)* existential fear, angst; **Da|seins|be|din|gun|gen** PL living conditions *pl*; **Da|seins|be|rech|ti|gung** F right to exist; **hat die UNO noch eine ~?** can the UN still justify its existence?; **Da|seins|form** F form of life *or* existence; **Da|seins|freu|de** F zest for life, joie de vivre; **Da|seins|kampf** M struggle for survival; **Da|seins|wei|se** F mode of being; **Da|seins|zweck** M reason for existence, raison d'être *(spec)*

da|selbst [da'zɛlpst] ADV *(old)* in said place; *(bei Quellenangaben)* ibidem, ibid *abbr*; **geboren 1714 zu Florenz, gestorben 1768 ~** born in Florence 1714, died there 1768

da+sit|zen VI *sep irreg aux haben or sein* to sit there; **wie die Kinder heutzutage ~!** the way children sit nowadays!; **ohne Hilfe/einen Cent ~** *(inf)* to be left without any help/without a penny *(Brit) or* cent *(US)*

das|je|ni|ge ['dasje:nɪgə] DEM PRON → **derjenige**

dass [das] CONJ **a** *(mit Subjektsatz)* that; **~ wir alle sterben müssen, ist sicher** that we all must die is certain *(liter)*, it is certain (that) we all must die
b *(mit Objektsatz)* (that); **ich bin überzeugt, ~ du das Richtige getan hast** I'm sure (that) you have done the right thing; **ich verstehe nicht, ~ man ihn als Bewerber abgelehnt hat** I don't understand why he was turned down; **ich sehe nicht ein, ~ wir hungern sollen** I don't see why we should starve
c *(mit Attributivsatz)* that; **angenommen/vorausgesetzt, ~ ...** given/provided that ...; **ich bin mir dessen bewusst, ~ ...** I am aware (that) ..., I am aware of the fact that ...; **unter der Bedingung, ~ ...** on (the) condition that ...
d *(mit Kausalsatz)* that; **ich war böse, ~ ...** I was annoyed that ...; **ich freue mich darüber, ~ ...** I'm glad (that) ...; **das kommt daher, ~ ...** that comes because ...; **das liegt daran, ~ ...** that is because ...; **das kommt davon, ~ er niemals aufpasst** that comes from him *or* his never paying attention
e *(mit Konsekutivsatz)* that; **er fuhr so schnell, ~ er sich überschlug** he drove so fast that he overturned
f *(geh: mit Finalsatz)* so that; **ich gab ihm den Brief, ~ er ihn selbst lesen konnte** I gave him the letter so that he could read it himself
g *(als Einleitung eines Instrumentalsatzes)* **er verbringt seine Freizeit damit, ~ er Rosen züchtet** he spends his free time breeding roses
h *(geh) (mit Wunschsatz)* if only, would that *(liter)*; *(in Befehl)* see that; **~ er immer da wäre!** would that he were always there *(liter)*, if only he were always there; **~ du es mir nicht verlierst!** see that you don't lose it!

das|sel|be [das'zɛlbə], **das|sel|bi|ge** [das'zɛlbɪgə] DEM PRON → **derselbe**

da+ste|hen VI *sep irreg aux haben or sein* **a** *(= da sein)* to stand there; **wie stehst denn du wieder da!** what sort of a way do you call that to stand!; **steh nicht so dumm da!** don't just stand there looking stupid
b *(fig)* **anders/glänzend/gut/schlecht ~** to be in a different/splendid/good/bad position; **die Firma/Regierung steht wieder gut da** the company/government is doing all right again *(inf)* *or* is in a good position again; **allein ~** to be on one's own; **einzig ~** to be unique *or* unparalleled; **jetzt stehe ich ohne Mittel/als Lügner da** now I'm left with no money/looking like a liar; **wenn die Sache schiefgeht, stehst du dumm da** if things go wrong you'll be left looking stupid; **wie stehe ich jetzt da!** *(Selbstlob)* just look at me now!; *(Vorwurf)* what kind of fool do I look now!

DAT [de:la:'te:, dat] NT **-, -s** DAT

Date NT **-(s), -s** **a** *(= Treffen, Termin)* date; **ein ~ haben** to have a date, to go (out) on a date **b** *(= Person)* date

Da|tei [da'tai] F **-, -en** *(Comput)* file; **eine ~ öffnen/schließen** to open/close a file; **eine ~ aufrufen/einfügen/anhängen** to activate/insert/attach a file

Da|tei- *in cpds (Comput)* file; **Da|tei|at|tri|but** NT file attribute; **Da|tei|ver|wal|tung** F file management; **Da|tei|en|dung**, **Da|tei|er|weite|rung** F extension; **Da|tei|grö|ße** F file size; **Da|tei|ma|na|ger** M file manager; **Da|tei|na|me** M file name; **Da|tei|sys|tem** NT file system; **Da|tei|trans|fer|pro|to|koll** NT file transfer protocol; **Da|tei|ver|wal|tung** F file management; **Da|tei|ver|wal|tungs|pro|gramm** NT file manager; **Da|tei|ver|zeich|nis** NT directory; **Da|tei|zu|ord|nungs|ta|bel|le** F file allocation table, FAT

Da|ten ['da:tn] **a** *pl von* **Datum** **b** *pl (Comput)* data *sing*

Da|ten- *in cpds* data; **Da|ten|ab|fra|ge** F (data) query; **Da|ten|ab|ruf** M data retrieval; **Da|ten|auf|be|rei|tung** F data preparation; **Da|ten|aus|ga|be** F data output; **Da|ten|aus|tausch** M data exchange *or* interchange; **Da|ten|au|to|bahn** F information (super)highway; **Da|ten|band** [-bant] NT *pl* **-bänder** data tape; **Da|ten|bank** F *pl* **-banken** database; *(= Zentralstelle)* data bank; **multidimensionale/relationale ~** multidimensional/relational database; **da|ten|bank|ge|stützt** [-gəʃtʏtst] ADJ database-supported; **Da|ten|bank|pfle|ge** F database management *or* maintenance; **Da|ten|bank|ver|wal|tung** F database management; **Da|ten|be|stand** M database; **Da|ten|bit** NT data bit; **Da|ten|bus** M *(Comput)* bus; **Da|ten|ein|ga|be** F data input *or* entry; **Da|ten|er|fas|sung** F data capture; **Da|ten|er|he|bung** F survey; **Da|ten|feld** NT array; **Da|ten|fern|über|tra|gung** F remote data transmission; **Da|ten|fern|ver|ar|bei|tung** F teleprocessing; **Da|ten|fluss|plan** M data flowchart; **Da|ten|for|mat** NT data format; **Da|ten|hand|schuh** M data glove; **Da|ten|klau** [-klau] M **-s, -s** *(inf)* theft of data; **Da|ten|kap|se|lung** F embedding; **Da|ten|kom|pres|si|on** F data compression; **Da|ten|kom|pres|si|ons|pro|gramm** NT data compression program; **Da|ten|kom|pri|mie|rung** F data compression; **Da|ten|miss|brauch** M misuse of data, data abuse; **Da|ten|müll** M *(inf)* rubbish data; **Da|ten|netz** NT data network; **Da|ten|ra|te** F data rate; **Da|ten|satz** M record; **Da|ten|schrott** M *(inf) (= fehlerhafte Daten)* corrupt data; *(= überflüssige Daten)* rubbish data rubbish data; **Da|ten|schutz** M data protection; **Da|ten|schutz|be|auf|trag|te(r)** MF *decl as adj* data protection official; **Da|ten|schüt|zer** [-ʃʏtsɐ] M **-s, -**, **Da|ten|schüt|ze|rin** [-ərın] F **-, -nen** data protectionist; **Da|ten|schutz|ge|setz** NT data protection act; **Da|ten|si|che|rung** F data backup; **Da|ten|sicht|ge|rät** NT VDU, visual display unit; **Da|ten|spei|cher** M data memory; *(= Speichermedium)* data storage medium; **Da|ten|strom** M data stream; **Da|ten|trä|ger** M data carrier; **Da|ten|trä|ger|be|rei|ni|gung** F disk cleanup; **Da|ten|trä|ger|be|zeich|nung** F volume label; **Da|ten|trans|fer** M data transfer; **Da|ten|ty|pist** [-typıst] M **-en, -en**, **Da|ten|ty|pis|tin** [-pıstın] F **-, -nen** keyboarder; **Da|ten|über|mitt|lung** F data communication; **Da|ten|über|tra|gung** F data transmission; **Da|ten|ver|ar|bei|tung** F data processing; **Da|ten|ver|ar|bei|tungs|an|la|ge** F data processing equipment; **Da|ten|ver|ar|bei|tungs|kauf|frau** F, **Da|ten|ver|ar|bei|tungs|kauf|mann** M data processing clerk; **Da|ten|ver|bund** M data network; **Da|ten|ver|kehr** M data traffic; **Da|ten|ver|lust** M loss of data, data loss; **Da|ten|ver|schlüs|se|lung** F data (en)coding; **Da|ten|ver|wal|tung** F data management; **Da|ten|zent|ra|le** F, **Da|ten|zent|rum** NT data centre *(Brit) or* center *(US)*

da|tie|ren [da'ti:rən] *ptp* **datiert** VT *Brief, Fund* to date; **der Brief ist vom 20. April datiert** the letter is dated 20th April VI *(= stammen)* to date (*aus* from); **dieser Brief datiert vom 1. Januar** this letter is dated January 1st; **unsere Freundschaft datiert seit einer Reise vor zehn Jahren** our friendship dates from *or* dates back to a trip ten years ago

Da|tiv ['da:ti:f] M **-s, -e** [-və] *(Gram)* dative (case)

Da|tiv|ob|jekt NT *(Gram)* indirect object

DAT-Kas|set|te ['dat-] F DAT *or* digital audio tape cassette

DAT-Lauf|werk ['dat-] NT DAT *or* digital audio tape drive

da|to ADV **bis ~** *(Comm, inf)* to date

Da|to|wech|sel M *(Comm)* time bill

DAT-Re|kor|der ['dat-] M DAT *or* digital audio tape recorder

Dat|scha ['datʃa] F **-, Datschen** ['datʃn], **Dat|sche** ['datʃə] F **-, -n** country cottage; **auf seiner ~** in his country cottage

DAT-Strea|mer ['dat-] M DAT *or* digital audio tape streamer

Dat|tel ['datl] F **-, -n** date

Dat|tel- *in cpds* date; **Dat|tel|pal|me** F date palm

Dat|te|rich ['datərıç] M *(inf)* **den ~ haben/bekommen** to have/get the shakes *(inf)*

Da|tum ['da:tʊm] NT **-s, Daten** ['da:tn] **a** date; **was für ein ~ haben wir heute?** what is the date today?; **das heutige/gestrige/morgige ~** today's/yesterday's/tomorrow's date; **sich im ~ irren** to get the date wrong; **ein Brief gleichen ~s** a letter of the same date; **gleichen ~s übersandten wir Ihnen …** *(form)* on the same date we sent you …; **etw mit dem ~ versehen** to date sth; **der Brief trägt das ~ vom 1. April** the letter is dated 1st April; **ein Brief ohne ~** an undated letter; **~ des Poststempels** date as postmark; **ein Nachschlagewerk neueren/älteren ~s** a recent/an old reference work
b *usu pl (= Faktum)* fact; *(= statistische Zahlenangabe etc)* datum *(form)*, piece of data; **technische Daten** technical data *pl*

Da|tums-: **Da|tums|for|mat** NT *(Comput)* date style, date format; **Da|tums|gren|ze** F *(Geog)* (international) date line; **Da|tums|stem|pel** M date stamp

Dau|be ['daubə] F **-, -n** stave; *(beim Eisschießen)* tee

Dau|er ['dauɐ] F **-,** *no pl (= das Andauern)* duration; *(= Zeitspanne)* period, term; *(= Länge: einer Sendung etc)* length; **während der ~ des Vertrages/Krieges** for the duration of the contract/war; **für die ~ eines Monats** *or* **von einem Monat** for a period of one month; **ein Gefängnisaufenthalt von zehnjähriger ~** a ten-year term of imprisonment; **von ~ sein** to be long-lasting; **seine Begeisterung war nicht von ~** his enthusiasm was short-lived, his enthusiasm wasn't long-lasting; **keine ~ haben** to be short-lived; **von langer ~ sein** to last a long time; **von kurzer ~ sein** not to last long; **auf die ~** in the long term; **auf die ~ wird das langweilig** it gets boring in the long run; **das kann man auf die ~ nicht ertragen** you can't stand it for any length of time; **das kann auf die ~ nicht so weitergehen** it can't go on like that indefinitely; **auf ~** permanently; **auf ~ gearbeitet** made to last; **für die ~ Ihres Aufenthaltes in unserem Hause** as long as you stay with us, for the period *or* duration of your stay with us *(form)*; **man konnte sich nicht über die ~ der Regelung einigen** they could not decide on the duration of the agreement

Dau|er- *in cpds* permanent; **Dau|er|ar|beits|lo|se(r)** MF *decl as adj* long-term unemployed person; **die ~n** the long-term unemployed; **Dau|er|ar|beits|lo|sig|keit** F long-term unemployment; **Dau|er|auf|trag** M *(Fin)* standing order; **Dau|er|aus|weis** M (permanent) identity card; *(= Fahrkarte etc)* season ticket; **Dau|er|be|las|tung** F continual pressure *no indef art*; *(von Maschine)* constant load; **unter ~** under continual pressure/a constant load; **Dau|er|be|schäf|ti|gung** F *(= Stellung)* permanent position; **Dau|er|be|trieb** M continuous operation; **Dau|er|be|zie|hung** F permanent relationship; **Dau|er|brand|ofen** M slow-burning stove; **Dau|er|bren|ner** M **a** *(= Dauerbrandofen)* slow-burning stove **b** *(inf) (= Dauererfolg)* long runner; *(= Dauerthema)* long-running issue; *(hum: = Kuss)* long passionate kiss; **Dau|er|bü|gel|fal|te** F permanent crease; **Dau|er|ein|rich|tung** F permanent institution; **Dau|er|ein|satz** M **im ~ sein** to be working nonstop *or* round the clock; **Dau|er|emit|tent** [-emitɛnt] M **-en, -en**, **Dau|er|emit|ten|tin** [-tɛntın] F **-, -nen** constant issuer; **Dau|er|er|folg** M long-running success; **Dau|er|fes|tig|keit** F *(Tech)* fatigue strength; **Dau|er|feu|er** NT *(Mil)* sustained fire; **Dau|er|flug** M *(Aviat)* long haul flight; **Dau|er|frost** M freeze-up; **Dau|er|frost|bo|den** M permafrost; **Dau|er|funk|ti|on** F *(bei Schreibmaschine etc)* locking function; **Dau|er|gast** M permanent guest; *(= häufiger Gast)* regular visitor, permanent fixture *(hum)*; **er scheint sich hier als ~ einrichten zu wollen** *(iro inf)* he seems to be settling down for a long stay; **Dau|er|ge|schwin|dig|keit** F cruising speed

dau|er|haft ADJ *Zustand, Einrichtung, Farbe* permanent; *Bündnis, Frieden, Beziehung* lasting *attr*, long-lasting, durable ADV *(= für immer)* permanently, lastingly; **durch eine Impfung sind Sie gegen diese Krankheit ~ geschützt** one vaccination gives you lasting immunity to this disease

Dau|er|haf|tig|keit ['dauɐhaftıçkait] F **-,** *no pl* permanence; *(von Material, Bündnis, Beziehung, Frieden)* durability

Dau|er-: **Dau|er|kar|te** F season ticket; **Dau|er|lauf** M *(Sport)* jog; *(= das Laufen)* jogging; **im ~** at a jog *or* trot; **einen ~ machen** to jog, to go jogging, to go for a jog; **Dau|er|laut** M *(Phon)* continuant; **Dau|er|leih|ga|be** F *(Art: für Museum)* permanent loan; **es ist eine ~** it's on permanent loan (*gen* from); **Dau|er|lut|scher** M lollipop; **Dau|er|marsch** M *(Mil)* forced march; **Dau|er|mie|te** F long lease *or* tenancy; **er hat das Haus in ~** he has the house on a long lease; **Dau|er|mie|ter(in)** M(F) long-term tenant; **Dau|er|milch** F long-life milk

dau|ern ['dauɐn] VI **a** *(= andauern)* to last, to go on; **das Gewitter dauerte zwei Stunden** the thunderstorm lasted (for) *or* went on for two hours; **die Verhandlungen ~ schon drei Wochen** the negotiations have already been going on for three weeks; **wie lange soll dieser Zustand noch ~?** how long will this situation last *or* go on (for) *or* continue?
b *(= Zeit benötigen)* to take a while *or* some time; *(lange)* to take a long time; **das dauert noch** *(inf)* it'll be a while *or* some time yet; **warum dauert das Anziehen bei dir immer so lange?** why do you always take so long to get dressed?; **es dauerte lange, bis er sich befreit hatte** it took him a long time to get free; **das dauert mir zu lange** it takes too long for me; **muss das so lange ~?** does it have to take so long?; **das dauert immer, bis er fertig ist** *(inf)* it always takes ages for him to get ready *(inf)*; **das dauert und dauert** *(inf)* it takes forever *(inf)*; **es dauert jetzt nicht mehr lange** it won't take much longer; **das dauert heute vielleicht wieder einmal** *(inf)* it's taking ages again today *(inf)*
c *(geh: = dauerhaft sein)* to last

dau|ern VT *(old, liter)* **etw dauert jdn** sb regrets sth; **er/sie dauert mich** I feel sorry for him/her; **es dauert mich, dass …** I regret *or* I'm sorry that …; **es dauerte ihn im Alter, seine Jugend so vergeudet zu haben** in his old age he regretted having squandered his youth like that; **das arme Tier kann einen ~** you can't help feeling sorry for the poor animal

dau|ernd ADJ *(= anhaltend) Frieden, Regelung* lasting; *(= ständig) Wohnsitz, Ausstellung* permanent; *(= fortwährend) Unterbrechung, Nörgelei, Sorge* constant, perpetual ADV **etw ~ tun** to keep doing sth; *(stärker)* to be always *or* forever *(inf)* doing sth, to do sth the whole time *(inf)*; **sie musste ~ auf die Toilette** she had to keep going to the toilet *(Brit) or* bathroom *(esp US)*; **er beschwert sich ~ darüber** he's always *or* forever *(inf)* complaining about it, he complains about it the whole time *(inf)*; **frag nicht ~ so dumm!** don't keep asking stupid questions

Dau|er-: **Dau|er|obst** NT fruit suitable for storing; **Dau|er|par|ker** [-parkɐ] M **-s, -**, **Dau|er|par|ke|rin** [-ərɪn] F **-, -nen** long-stay *(Brit) or* long-term *(US)* parker; **Parkplatz für ~** long-stay car park *(Brit)*, long-term parking lot *(US)*; **Dau|er|prob|lem** NT constant *or* permanent *or* ongoing problem; **Dau|er|red|ner(in)** M(F) *(pej)* interminable speaker; **Dau|er|re|gen** M continuous rain; **ein mehrtägiger ~** several days of continuous rain; **Dau|er|schlaf** M prolonged sleep; **ich fiel in einen 24-stündigen ~** I fell asleep for 24 hours solid; **Dau|er|schwing|fes|tig|keit** F *(Tech)* fatigue strength; **Dau|er|schwin|gung** F continuous oscillation; **Dau|er|sit|zung** F prolonged *or* lengthy session; **Dau|er|span|nung** F *(Elec)* continuous voltage; **Dau|er|spei|cher** M *(Comput)* permanent memory; **Dau|er|stel|lung** F permanent position; **in ~ beschäftigt** employed on a permanent basis; **Dau|er|streit** M permanent conflict; **Dau|er|stress** M **im ~ sein** to be in a state of permanent stress; **Dau|er|strom** M, *no pl (Elec)* constant current; **Dau|er|test** M long-term test; **Dau|er|the|ma** NT long-running issue; **Dau|er|ton** M *pl* **-töne** continuous tone; **Dau|er|wald** M permanent forest; **Dau|er|wel|le** F perm, permanent wave; **Dau|er|wir|kung** F (long-)lasting effect; **Dau|er|wohn|recht** NT permanent right of tenure; **Dau|er|wurst** F German salami; **Dau|er|zu|stand** M permanent state of affairs; **ich möchte das nicht zum ~ werden lassen** I don't want that to become permanent

Däum|chen [ˈdɔymçən] NT **-s, -** **a** *dim von* **Daumen** **b** *(inf)* **~ drehen** to twiddle one's thumbs; **und da mussten wir ~ drehen** and we were left twiddling our thumbs

Dau|men [ˈdaumən] M **-s, -** thumb; **am ~ lutschen** to suck one's thumb; **jdm** *or* **für jdn die ~ drücken** *or* **halten** to keep one's fingers crossed for sb; **den ~ auf etw** *(acc)* **halten** *(inf)* to hold on to sth → **peilen**

Dau|men-: **Dau|men|ab|druck** M thumbprint; **Dau|men|bal|len** M ball of the/one's thumb; **dau|men|breit** ADJ as broad as your thumb; **Dau|men|brei|te** F thumb's width; **Dau|men|in|dex** M thumb index; **Dau|men|ki|no** NT flicker book; **Dau|men|lut|scher(in)** M(F) thumb-sucker; **Dau|men|na|gel** M thumbnail; **Dau|men|re|gis|ter** NT thumb index; **Dau|men|schrau|be** F *(Hist)* thumbscrew; **jdm die ~n anlegen** *(lit, fig inf)* to put the (thumb)screws on sb; **die ~n ansetzen** *(fig)* to put the screws on

Däum|ling [ˈdɔymlɪŋ] M **-s, -e** **a** *(im Märchen)* **der ~** Tom Thumb **b** *(von Handschuh)* thumb; *(Med)* thumbstall

Dau|ne [ˈdaunə] F **-, -n** down feather; **~n** down *sing*; **ich schlief dort wie auf ~n** it was like sleeping on air; **weich wie ~n** as soft as down

Dau|nen-: **Dau|nen|ano|rak** M down jacket, down parka *(US)*; **Dau|nen|bett** NT, **Dau|nen|de|cke** F (down-filled) duvet *(Brit) or* quilt; **Dau|nen|fe|der** F down feather; **Dau|nen|ja|cke** F quilted jacket; **Dau|nen|kis|sen** NT down-filled cushion; *(= Kopfkissen)* down pillow; **Dau|nen|schlaf|sack** M down(-filled) sleeping bag; **dau|nen|weich** ADJ as soft as down

Dau|phin [doˈfɛ̃ː] M **-s, -s** *(Hist)* dauphin

Daus [daus] M **(ei) der ~!** *(old)* **was der ~!** *(old)* what the devil *or* deuce! *(dated)*

Daus NT **-es, Däuse(r)** [ˈdɔyzə, ˈdɔyzɐ] **a** *(beim Würfel)* deuce **b** *(Cards)* ace *(in German pack)*

Da|vid(s)|stern [ˈdaːfɪt(s)-, ˈdaːvɪt(s)-] M star of David

Da|vis|cup [ˈdeːvɪskap] M, **Da|vis|po|kal** [ˈdeːvɪs-] M Davis cup

da|von [daˈfɔn, *(emph)* ˈdaːfɔn] ADV **a** *(räumlich)* from there; *(wenn Bezugsobjekt vorher erwähnt)* from it/them; *(mit Entfernungsangabe)* away (from there/it/them); **weg ~!** *(inf)* get away from there/it/them; **~ zweigt ein Weg ab** a path branches off it → **auf**
b *(fig) (in Verbindung mit n, vb siehe auch dort)* **es unterscheidet sich ~ nur in der Länge** it only differs from it in the length; **nein, weit ~ entfernt!** no, far from it!; **ich bin weit ~ entfernt, Ihnen Vorwürfe machen zu wollen** the last thing I want to do is reproach you; **wenn wir einmal ~ absehen, dass ...** if for once we overlook the fact that ...; **wir möchten in diesem Fall ~ absehen, Ihnen den Betrag zu berechnen** in this case we shall not invoice you; **in ihren Berechnungen sind sie ~ ausgegangen, dass ...** they made their calculations on the basis that ...
c *(fig: = dadurch) leben, abhängen* on that/it/them; *sterben* of that/it; *krank/braun werden* from that/it/them; **... und ~ kommt das hohe Fieber** ... and that's where the high temperature comes from, ... and the high temperature comes from that; **das kommt ~!** that's what you get; **... und ~ hängt es ab** and it depends on that; **das hängt ~ ab, ob ...** that depends on whether ...; **~ hat man nur Ärger** you get nothing but trouble with it; **~ wird man müde** that makes you tired; **gib ihr ein bisschen mehr, ~ kann sie doch nicht satt werden** give her a bit more, that won't fill her up; **~ stirbst du nicht** it won't kill you; **was habe ICH denn ~?** what do I get out of it?; **was HABE ich denn ~?** why should I?; **was hast du denn ~, dass du so schuftest?** what do you get out of slaving away like that?
d *(mit Passiv)* by that/it/them; **~ betroffen werden** *or* **sein** to be affected by that/it/them
e *(Anteil, Ausgangsstoff)* of that/it/them; **~ essen/trinken/nehmen** to eat/drink/take some of that/it/them; **nehmen Sie doch noch etwas ~!** do have some more!; **die Hälfte ~** half of that/it/them; **das Doppelte ~** twice *or* double that; **zwei/ein Viertelpfund ~, bitte!** would you give me two of those/a quarter of a pound of that/those, please; **er hat drei Schwestern, ~ sind zwei älter als er** he has three sisters, two of whom are older than he is; **früher war er sehr reich, aber nach dem Krieg ist ihm nichts ~ geblieben** he used to be very rich but after the war nothing was left of his earlier wealth
f *(= darüber) hören, wissen, sprechen* about that/it/them; *verstehen, halten* of that/it/them; **genug ~!** enough of this!; **ich habe keine Ahnung ~** I've no idea about that/it; **nichts mehr ~!** no more of that!; **nichts ~ halten** not to think much of it; **ich halte viel ~** I think it is quite good; **was wissen Sie ~!** what do you know about it anyway?

da|von-: **da|von+blei|ben** VI *sep irreg aux sein* *(inf)* to keep away; *(= nicht anfassen)* to keep one's hands off; **da|von+ei|len** VI *sep aux sein* *(geh)* to hurry *or* hasten away; **da|von+fah|ren** VI *sep irreg aux sein* **a** *(Fahrer, Fahrzeug)* to drive away; *(auf Fahrrad etc)* to ride away; *(Zug)* to pull away **b** **jdm ~** to pull away from sb; **da|von+flie|gen** VI *sep irreg aux sein* to fly away; **da|von+ge|hen** VI *sep irreg aux sein (geh)* to walk away; **da|von+ja|gen** VT *sep* to chase off *or* away; **da|von+kom|men** VI *sep irreg aux sein* *(= entkommen)* to get away, to escape; *(= nicht bestraft werden)* to get away with it; *(= freigesprochen werden)* to get off; **mit dem Schrecken/dem Leben ~** to escape with no more than a shock/with one's life; **mit einer Geldstrafe ~** to get off with a fine; **da|von+las|sen** VT *sep irreg* **die Hände** *or* **Finger ~** *(inf)* to leave it/them well alone; **du sollst die Hände** *or* **Finger ~** keep your hands *or* fingers off (it/them); **da|von+lau|fen** VI *sep irreg aux sein* **a** *(= weglaufen)* to run away *(jdm/vor jdm* from sb); *(= verlassen)* to walk out *(jdm* on sb); **den Eltern** *or* **von zu Hause ~** to run away from home; **das Hausmädchen/ihr Mann ist ihr davongelaufen** *(inf)* the maid/her husband walked out on her; **es ist zum Davonlaufen!** *(inf)* it's all too much! **b** *(= außer Kontrolle geraten)* to get out of hand; **die Preise sind davongelaufen** prices have got out of hand; **die Preise sind uns/den Löhnen davongelaufen** prices are beyond our control/have surpassed wages; **da|von+ma|chen** VR *sep* to make off; **da|von+ren|nen** VI *sep irreg aux sein (inf)* = **davonlaufen a**; **da|von+schlei|chen** VIR *sep irreg (vi: aux sein)* to creep *or* slink away *or* off; **da|von+schwim|men** VI *sep irreg aux sein* **jdm ~** to outswim *or* outstrip sb; **da|von+steh|len** VR *sep irreg (geh)* to steal away; **da|von+tra|gen** VT *sep irreg* **a** *(= wegtragen) Gegenstände, Verletzte* to carry away **b** *(= erringen) Preis* to carry off; *Sieg, Ruhm* to win **c** *(= erleiden) Schaden, Verletzung* to suffer; **da|von+zie|hen** VI *sep irreg aux sein (liter)* to leave; *(Prozession etc)* to move off; *(Sport inf)* to pull away *(jdm* from sb)

da|vor [daˈfoːɐ, *(emph)* ˈdaːfoːɐ] ADV **a** *(räumlich)* in front (of that/it/them); *(wenn Bezugsobjekt vorher erwähnt)* in front of it/them; **ein Haus mit einem großen Rasen ~** a house with a big front lawn, a house with a big lawn in front
b *(zeitlich) (= vor einem bestimmten Datum)* before that; *(= bevor man etw tut)* beforehand; **ist er 1950 ausgewandert? – nein, schon ~** did he emigrate in 1950? – no, before that
c *(in Verbindung mit n, vb siehe auch dort) bewahren, schützen* from that/it; *warnen* of *or* about that/it; *Angst haben* of that/it; *sich ekeln* by that/it; **ich habe Angst ~, das zu tun** I'm afraid of doing that; **ich habe Angst ~, dass der Hund beißen könnte** I'm afraid that the dog might bite; **sein Ekel ~** his disgust of it; **ich warne Sie ~!** I warn you!; **ich habe ihn ~ gewarnt, sich in Gefahr zu begeben** I warned him not to get into danger

da|vor-: **da|vor+hän|gen** *sep*, **da|vor hän|gen** △ VT to hang in front of it/them; **sie hängte das Schloss davor** she put the lock on it; **da|vor+le|gen** *sep*, **da|vor le|gen** △ VT to put in front of it/them; **leg doch eine Kette davor** put a chain on it/them VR to lie down in front of it/them; **da|vor+lie|gen** *sep irreg (S Ger, Aus, Sw: aux sein)*, **da|vor lie|gen** △ *irreg (S Ger, Aus, Sw: aux sein)* VI to lie in front of it/them; **da|vor+ste|hen** *sep irreg (S Ger, Aus, Sw: aux sein)*, **da|vor ste|hen** △ *irreg (S Ger, Aus, Sw: aux sein)* VI to stand in front of it/them; **da|vor+stel|len** *sep*, **da|vor stel|len** △ VT to put in front of it/them VR to stand in front of it/them

da|wi|der [daˈviːdɐ, *(emph)* ˈdaːviːdɐ] ADV *(old)* against it; **dafür und ~** for and against

DAX® [daks] M **-**, *no pl abbr von* **Deutscher Aktienindex** DAX® index

DAX

The **DAX** is the German share index, introduced in 1988 and comprising the 30 strongest German shares. Once a year the evaluation and selection of these shares is checked and, if necessary, updated.

DAX-Wert [daks-] M *(= Einzelaktie im DAX)* DAX share

da|zu [daˈtsuː, *(emph)* ˈdaːtsuː] ADV **a** *(räumlich)* there; **wozu gehört das? – ~!** where does that belong? – there!
b *(= dabei, damit)* with it; *(= außerdem, obendrein auch)* into the bargain *(inf)*, at the same time; **er ist dumm und ~ auch noch faul** he's stupid and lazy with it *or* into the bargain *(inf) or* as well; **sie ist hübsch und ~ nicht unintelligent** she's pretty and not unintelligent either; **noch ~** as well, too; **noch ~, wo ...** when ...

too; ~ **reicht** *or* **serviert man am besten Reis** it's best to serve rice with it; **er singt und spielt Gitarre** ~ he sings and accompanies himself on the guitar
c *(= dahin)* to that/it; **auf dem besten Wege ~ sein, etw zu tun** to be well on the way to doing sth; **er ist auf dem besten Wege ~** he's well on the way to it; **das führt ~, dass weitere Forderungen gestellt werden** that will lead to further demands being made; **~ führt das dann** that's what it leads to; **wie konnte es nur ~ kommen?** how could that happen?; **wer weiß, wie sie ~ gekommen ist** *(zu diesem Auto etc)* who knows how she came by it; **wie komme ich ~?** *(empört)* why on earth should I?; **… aber ich bin nicht ~ gekommen** … but I didn't get (a)round to it
d *(= dafür, zu diesem Zweck)* for that/it; **~ bin ich zu alt** I'm too old for that; **ich bin zu alt ~, noch tanzen zu gehen** I'm too old to go dancing; **~ habe ich dich nicht studieren lassen, dass du …** I didn't send you to university so that you could … *or* for you to …; **ich habe ihm ~ geraten** I advised him to (do that); **Sie sind/die Maschine ist ~ wie geschaffen** it's as if you were/the machine was made for it; **~ fähig sein, etw zu tun** to be capable of doing sth; **~ bereit sein, etw zu tun** to be prepared to do sth; **er war nicht ~ fähig/bereit** he wasn't capable of it/prepared to; **~ gehört viel Geld** that takes a lot of money; **~ ist er da** that's what he's there for, that's why he's there; **die Erlaubnis/die Mittel/das Recht ~** permission/the means/the right to do it; **ich habe keine Lust ~** I don't feel like it; **ich habe keine Lust ~, mitzugehen** I don't feel like going along; **~ habe ich keine Zeit** I haven't the time (for that); **ich habe keine Zeit ~, die Fenster zu putzen** I haven't (the) time to clean the windows; **ich bin nicht ~ in der Lage** I'm not in a position to
e *(= darüber, zum Thema)* about that/it; **was sagst/meinst du ~?** what do you say to/think about that?; **meine Gedanken/Meinung ~** my thoughts about/opinion of that; **…, ~ hören Sie jetzt einen Kommentar** … we now bring you a commentary; **das Hauptthema war die Inflation; ~ schreibt die Zeitung …** the main subject was inflation – the paper has this to say about it …; **er hat sich nur kurz ~ geäußert** he only commented briefly on that/it
f *(in Wendungen)* **im Gegensatz ~** in contrast to that; **im Vergleich ~** in comparison with that; **früher war sie nicht so hysterisch, er hat sie ~ gemacht** she never used to be so hysterical, he made her like that; **er war nicht immer Lord, er wurde erst ~ gemacht** he wasn't born a Lord, he was made *or* created one; **~ wird man nicht gewählt, sondern ernannt** one is appointed rather than elected to that

da|zu-: **da|zu+ge|ben** VT *sep irreg* to add → **Senf**; **da|zu+ge|hö|ren** *ptp* **dazugehört** VI *sep* to belong (to it/us *etc*); *(als Ergänzung)* to go with it/them; *(= eingeschlossen sein)* to be included (in it/them); **bei einer Familienfeier gehört Onkel Otto auch dazu** Uncle Otto should be part of any family gathering too; **das gehört mit dazu** that belongs to/goes with/is included in it; *(= versteht sich von selbst)* it's all part of it; **es gehört schon einiges dazu** that takes a lot; **es gehört schon einiges dazu, das zu tun** it takes a lot to do that; **da|zu|ge|hö|rig** ADJ *attr* which goes/go with it/them; *Schlüssel etc* belonging to it/them; *(= zu dieser Arbeit gehörend) Werkzeuge, Material* necessary; **da|zu+kom|men** VI *sep irreg aux sein* **a** *(= ankommen)* to arrive (on the scene); **er kam zufällig dazu** he happened to arrive on the scene **b** *(= hinzugefügt werden)* to be added; **es kommen laufend neue Bücher dazu** new books are always being added; **es kamen noch mehrere Straftaten dazu** there were several other offences *(Brit) or* offenses *(US)*; **kommt noch etwas dazu?** is there *or* will there be anything else?; **es kommt noch dazu, dass er faul ist** on top of that he's lazy, in addition to that he's lazy **c** *(Aus, Sw: = Zeit dafür finden)* to get (a)round to it; **da|zu+kön|nen** *sep irreg* VT *(inf)* **ich kann nichts dazu** I can't do anything about it; **da|zu+le|gen** *sep* VT to add to it; **jdm/sich noch ein Stückchen Fleisch ~** to give sb/oneself another piece of meat; **leg die Sachen ruhig dazu** just put the things with it/them VR to lie down with him/them *etc*; **da|zu+ler|nen** VT *sep* **viel/nichts ~** to learn a lot more/nothing new; **man kann immer was ~** there's always something to learn; **schon wieder was dazugelernt!** you learn something (new) every day!

da|zu|mal ['da:tsuma:l] ADV *(old)* in those days → **anno**

da|zu-: **da|zu+rech|nen** VT *sep* **a** *Kosten, Betrag, Zahl* to add on **b** *(= mit berücksichtigen)* to consider also; **da|zu+schau|en** VI *sep (Aus)* = **zusehen**; **da|zu+schrei|ben** VT *sep irreg* to add; **da|zu+set|zen** *sep* VT **a können wir den Jungen hier noch ~?** could the boy sit here too? **b** *(= dazuschreiben)* to add VR to join him/us *etc*; **komm, setz dich doch dazu** come and sit with us, come and join us; **da|zu+tun** VT *sep irreg (inf)* to add; **Da|zu|tun** NT **er hat es ohne dein ~ geschafft** he managed it without your doing/saying anything; **ohne dein ~ hätte er es nicht geschafft** he wouldn't have managed it if you hadn't done/said something *or* without your doing/saying anything; **da|zu+ver|die|nen** VTI *sep* to earn *sth* extra; **seine Frau muss ~** his wife has to earn a bit on the side as well

da|zwi|schen [da'tsvɪʃn, *(emph)* 'da:tsvɪʃn] ADV *(räumlich, zeitlich)* in between; *(in der betreffenden Menge, Gruppe)* amongst them, in with them; **die Betten standen dicht nebeneinander, es hing nur ein Vorhang ~** the beds were very close together, there was only a curtain between them

da|zwi|schen-: **da|zwis|chen+fah|ren** VI *sep irreg aux sein* **a** *(= eingreifen)* to step in and put a stop to things, to intervene **b** *(= unterbrechen)* to break in, to interrupt; **jdm ~** to interrupt sb; **da|zwi|schen+fun|ken** VI *sep (Rad)* to jam the signal; *(inf: = eingreifen)* to put one's oar in *(inf)*; *(= etw vereiteln)* to put a spoke in it *(inf)*; **da|zwi|schen+kom|men** VI *sep irreg aux sein* **a mit der Hand/der Hose** *etc* **~** to get one's hand/trousers *etc* caught in it/them **b** *(= störend erscheinen)* to get in the way; **… wenn nichts dazwischenkommt!** … if all goes well; **leider ist** *or* **mir ist leider etwas dazwischengekommen, ich kann nicht dabei sein** something has come *or* cropped up, I'm afraid I can't be there; **da|zwi|schen+le|gen** VT *sep* to put in between; **da|zwi|schen|lie|gend** ADJ *attr* **die ~en Seiten/Monate/Bahnhöfe/Farbtöne** *etc* the pages/months/stations/shades *etc* in between; **da|zwi|schen+re|den** VI *sep* **a** *(= unterbrechen)* to interrupt *(jdm* sb) **b** = **dreinreden**; **da|zwi|schen+ru|fen** VTI *sep irreg* to yell out; **da|zwi|schen+schla|gen** VI *sep irreg* to wade in, to lam in *(esp US inf)*; **da|zwi|schen+ste|hen** VI *sep irreg aux haben or sein* **a** *(lit)* to be amongst *or (zwischen zweien)* between them **b** *(zwischen den Parteien)* to be neutral **c** *(geh: hindernd)* to be in the way; **da|zwi|schen+tre|ten** VI *sep irreg aux sein* **a** *(schlichtend)* to intervene; **sein Dazwischentreten** his intervention **b** *(geh: störend)* to come between them

DB [de:'be:] F - *abbr von* **Deutsche Bahn, Deutsche Bundesbahn**

DCC [de:tse:'tse:] F -, -s *abbr von* **Digitale Compact Cassette** DCC®

DD-Dis|ket|te [de:'de:-] F *(Comput)* DD diskette

DDR [de:de:'ɛr] F - *(Hist) abbr von* **Deutsche Demokratische Republik** GDR, German Democratic Republic, East Germany

> **DDR**
>
> **DDR** is the abbreviated name of the former East Germany (**Deutsche Demokratische Republik**). The **DDR** was created in 1949 out of the Soviet-occupied zone of Germany and evolved into a Warsaw Pact state. Its economy, government and society were closely based on those of the Soviet Union.
> In 1961 the **DDR** cut itself off even further from West Germany and the West in general with the construction of the Berlin Wall. By the end of the 1980s increasing numbers of civil rights groups were protesting against its harsh regime, and demanding reforms. The huge pressure exerted by this "velvet revolution" brought about the collapse of the economically weak socialist system in the autumn of 1989. On October 3rd 1990 Germany was re-unified and the **DDR** became part of the **Bundesrepublik Deutschland**. → BRD

DDR-Bür|ger(in) [de:de:'ɛr-] M(F) *(Hist)* East German, citizen of the German Democratic Republic

DDT® [de:de:'te:] NT - *abbr von* **Dichlordiphenyltrichloräthan** DDT®

Dead|line ['dɛdlain] F -, -s *(= letztmöglicher Termin)* deadline

de|ak|ti|vie|ren [de|akti'vi:rən] *ptp* **deaktiviert** VT to deactivate;.*(Comput: = ausschalten)* to disable; *Kontrollkästchen* to uncheck

Deal [di:l] M -s, -s (= *Geschäft etc, inf: = Drogengeschäft*) deal

dea|len ['di:lən] *(inf)* VI **er dealt** he is a dealer; **mit etw ~** to deal in sth; **mit Drogen ~** to deal (in) drugs VT to deal in; *Drogen auch* to push

Dea|ler ['di:lɐ] M -s, -, **Dea|le|rin** ['di:lərɪn] F -, -nen *(inf)* (drug) dealer, pusher; *(international)* trafficker, dealer

De|ba|kel [de'ba:kl] NT -s, - debacle; **ein ~ erleiden** *(Stück etc)* to be a debacle; **damit hat die Regierung ein ~ erlitten** that turned into something of a debacle for the government

De|bat|te [de'batə] F -, -n debate; **etw in die ~ werfen** to throw sth into the discussion; **etw zur ~ stellen** to put sth up for discussion *or (Parl)* debate; **was steht zur ~?** what is being discussed *or* is under discussion?; *(Parl)* what is being debated?; **das steht hier nicht zur ~** that's not the issue; **sich in** *or* **auf eine ~ (über etw** *acc*) **einlassen** to enter into a discussion (about sth)

de|bat|te|los ADJ *(Parl)* without debate

de|bat|tie|ren [deba'ti:rən] *ptp* **debattiert** VTI to debate; **über etw** *(acc)* **(mit jdm) ~** to discuss sth (with sb); **mit ihm kann man schlecht ~** you can't have a good discussion with him

De|bat|tier|klub M debating society

De|bet ['de:bɛt] NT -s, -s *(Fin)* debits *pl*

De|bet|sei|te F *(Fin)* debit side

de|bil [de'bi:l] ADJ *(Med)* feeble-minded

De|bi|li|tät [debili'tɛ:t] F -, *no pl (Med)* feeble-mindedness

de|bi|tie|ren [debi'ti:rən] *ptp* **debitiert** VT *(Fin)* to debit; **jdn mit einem Betrag ~** to debit an amount to sb, to debit sb with an amount

De|bi|tor ['de:bito:ɐ] M -s, **Debitoren** [-'to:rən], **De|bi|to|rin** [-'to:rɪn] F -, -nen *(Fin)* debtor

De|bi|to|ren [debi'to:rən] PL *(Econ, Fin)* accounts *pl* receivable

de|bug|gen VTI *(Comput)* to debug

De|bug|ger M *(Comput: = Programm)* debugger

De|büt [de'by:] NT -s, -s debut; **sein ~ als etw geben** to make one's debut as sth

De|bü|tant [deby'tant] M -en, -en *person making his debut (fig: = Anfänger, Neuling)* novice

De|bü|tan|tin [deby'tantɪn] F -, -nen **a** *person making her debut (fig: = Anfängerin)* novice **b** *(in der Gesellschaft)* debutante, deb *(inf)*

De|bü|tan|tin|nen|ball M debutantes' ball

de|bü|tie|ren [deby'ti:rən] *ptp* **debütiert** VI *(Theat, fig)* to make one's debut

De|cha|nat [deça'na:t] NT -(e)s, -e (Eccl) deanery

De|cha|nei [deça'nai] F -, -en (Eccl) deanery, dean's residence

De|chant [dɛ'çant, 'dɛçant] M -en, -en (Eccl) dean

de|chif|frie|ren [deʃɪ'fri:rən] ptp dechiffriert VT to decode; Text, Geheimschrift auch to decipher

De|chif|frie|rung F -, -en decoding; (von Text, Geheimschrift) deciphering

Deck [dɛk] NT -(e)s, -s deck; (in Parkhaus) level; auf ~ on deck; an ~ gehen to go on deck; alle Mann an ~! all hands on deck!; unter or von ~ gehen to go below deck

Deck-: **Deck|ad|res|se** F, **Deck|an|schrift** F accommodation or cover (US) address; **Deck|an|strich** M top or final coat; **Deck|auf|bau|ten** PL (Naut) superstructure sing; **Deck|bett** NT feather quilt; **Deck|blatt** NT (Bot) bract; (von Zigarre) wrapper; (= Schutzblatt) cover; (= Einlageblatt) overlay; (Comput) cover page

Deck|chen ['dɛkçən] NT -s, - mat; (auf Tablett) tray cloth; (= Tortendeckchen) doily; (auf Sessel etc) antimacassar; (für Lehne) arm cover

Deck|dienst M (Naut) deck duty

De|cke ['dɛkə] F -, -n **a** cloth; (= Wolldecke) blanket; (kleiner) rug; (= Steppdecke) quilt; (= Bettdecke) cover; unter die ~ kriechen to pull the bedclothes (Brit) or bedcovers up over one's head; sich nach der ~ strecken (fig) to cut one's coat according to one's cloth; mit jdm unter einer ~ stecken (fig) to be in league or in cahoots (inf) or hand in glove with sb **b** (= Zimmerdecke) ceiling; (Min) roof; es tropft von der ~ there's water coming through the ceiling; an die ~ gehen (inf) to hit the roof (inf); vor Freude an die ~ springen (inf) to jump for joy; mir fällt die ~ auf den Kopf (fig inf) I don't like my own company **c** (= Schicht) layer; (= Schneedecke, Staubdecke etc) blanket; (= Straßendecke) surface; (= Reifendecke) outer tyre (Brit) or tire (US) or cover or casing **d** (Hunt) skin

De|ckel ['dɛkl] M -s, - lid; (von Schachtel, Glas auch, von Flasche) top; (= Buchdeckel, Uhrdeckel) cover; (inf: = Hut, Mütze) titfer (Brit inf), hat; eins auf den ~ kriegen (inf) (= geschlagen werden) to get hit on the head; (= ausgeschimpft werden) to be given a (good) talking-to (inf); jdm eins auf den ~ geben (inf) (= schlagen) to hit sb on the head; (= ausschimpfen) to give sb a (good) talking-to (inf); etw unter dem or unterm ~ halten to keep the lid on sth → Topf

de|ckeln ['dɛkln] VT **a** (= mit einem Deckel versehen) to put a/the lid on; (fig: = nach oben begrenzen) to impose an upper limit on; wir müssen die Kosten ~ we'll have to keep a lid on the costs **b** (inf: = rügen) jdn ~ to carpet sb (Brit inf), to tear sb off a strip (Brit inf), to chew sb out (US inf)

de|cken ['dɛkn] VT **a** (= zudecken) to cover; ein Dach mit Schiefer/Ziegeln ~ to roof a building with slate/tiles; ein Dach mit Stroh/Reet ~ to thatch a roof (with straw/reeds) → auch gedeckt **b** (= zurechtmachen) Tisch, Tafel to set, to lay; es ist für vier Personen gedeckt the table is laid or set for four (people); sich an einen gedeckten Tisch setzen (lit) to find one's meal ready and waiting; (fig) to be handed everything on a plate **c** (= breiten) die Hand/ein Tuch über etw (acc) ~ to cover sth with one's hand/a cloth, to put one's hand/a cloth over sth **d** (= schützen) to cover; (Ftbl) Spieler auch to mark; Komplizen to cover up for **e** Kosten, Schulden, Bedarf to cover, to meet; mein Bedarf ist gedeckt I have all I need; (fig inf) I've had enough (to last me some time); damit ist unser Bedarf gedeckt that will meet or cover our needs **f** (Comm, Fin: = absichern) Scheck, Darlehen to cover; Defizit to offset; der Schaden wird voll durch die Versicherung gedeckt the cost of the damage will be fully met by the insurance **g** (= begatten) Stute, Ziege to cover

VI to cover; (Ftbl: = Spieler decken) to mark; (Boxen) to guard; (= Tisch decken) to lay a/the table; du musst besser ~ (Ftbl) you must mark your opponent better; (Boxen) you must improve your guard; es ist gedeckt luncheon/dinner etc is served

VR **a** (Standpunkte, Interessen, Begriffe) to coincide; (Aussagen) to correspond, to agree; (Math: Dreiecke, Figur) to be congruent; sich ~de Dreiecke congruent triangles; sich ~de Begriffe/Interessen concepts/interests which coincide **b** (= sich schützen) to defend oneself; (mit Schild etc) to protect oneself; (Boxer etc) to cover oneself; (= sich absichern) to cover oneself

De|cken-: **De|cken|bal|ken** M ceiling beam; **De|cken|be|leuch|tung** F ceiling lighting; **De|cken|flu|ter** M -s, - torchiere (lamp); **De|cken|ge|mäl|de** NT ceiling fresco; **De|cken|ge|wöl|be** NT (Archit) vaulting; **De|cken|hei|zung** F overhead heating; **De|cken|kon|struk|ti|on** F roof construction; **De|cken|lam|pe** F ceiling light; **De|cken|ma|le|rei** F ceiling fresco; **De|cken|strah|ler** M uplighter; **De|cken|trä|ger** M ceiling girder

Deck-: **Deck|far|be** F opaque watercolour (Brit) or watercolor (US); **Deck|flü|gel** M (Zool) wing case; **Deck|fracht** F (Naut) deck cargo; **Deck|geld** NT (Agr) stud fee; **Deck|glas** NT (Opt) cover glass; **Deck|haar** NT top hair; **Deck|haus** NT (Naut) deckhouse; **Deck|hengst** M stud (horse), stallion; **Deck|man|tel** M (fig) mask, blind; unter dem ~ von ... under the guise of ...; **Deck|na|me** M assumed name; (Mil) code name; **Deck|of|fi|zier(in)** M(F) (Naut) ≈ warrant officer; **Deck|pas|sa|gier(in)** M(F) (Naut) first-class passenger; **Deck|pla|ne** F (Aut) tarpaulin; **Deck|plat|te** F (Build) slab; (von Mauer) coping stone; (von Grab) covering stone or slab; **Deck|sa|lon** M (Naut) first-class lounge; **Deck|schicht** F surface layer; (von Straße) surface; (Geol) top layer or stratum; **Deck|sta|ti|on** F stud (farm); **Deck|stein** M (Build) coping stone; (von Grab) covering stone

De|ckung ['dɛkʊŋ] F -, (rare) -en **a** (= Schutz) cover; (Ftbl, Chess) defence (Brit), defense (US); (Boxen, Fechten) guard; in ~ gehen to take cover; ~ suchen to seek cover; volle ~! (Mil) take cover!; jdm ~ geben to cover sb; (= Feuerschutz auch) to give sb cover **b** (= Verheimlichung) die ~ von etw covering up of sth; er kann mit ~ durch den Minister rechnen he can count on the minister covering up for him **c** (Comm, Fin) (von Scheck, Wechsel) cover; (von Darlehen) security; (= das Decken) covering; (= das Begleichen) meeting; der Scheck ist ohne ~ the cheque (Brit) or check (US) is not covered; ein Darlehen ohne ~ an unsecured loan; zur ~ seiner Schulden to meet or cover his debts; als ~ für seine Schulden as security or surety for his debts; dafür ist auf meinem Konto keine ~ there are no funds to cover that in my account; die Versicherung übernahm die ~ des Schadens the insurance company agreed to meet or cover the cost of the damage **d** (= Befriedigung) meeting; eine ~ der Nachfrage ist unmöglich demand cannot possibly be met **e** (= Übereinstimmung) (Math) congruence; zur ~ bringen (Math) to make congruent; lassen sich diese Standpunkte/Interessen zur ~ bringen? can these points of view/interests be made to coincide?; diese beiden Zeugenaussagen lassen sich schwer zur ~ bringen these two statements can't be made to agree

De|ckungs-: **De|ckungs|auf|la|ge** F (Typ) breakeven quantity; **De|ckungs|bei|trag** M (Econ) contribution margin, profit contribution; **De|ckungs|bei|trags|rech|nung** F (Econ, Fin) **a** break-even analysis, direct costing **b** (= Rechnung) contribution margin accounting, direct or marginal costing; **De|ckungs|feh|ler** M (Ftbl) error by the defence (Brit) or defense (US); **De|ckungs|feu|er** NT (Mil) covering fire; im ~ der Kameraden under covering fire from their etc comrades; **de|ckungs|gleich** ADJ (Math) congruent; ~ sein (fig) to coincide; (Aussagen) to agree; **De|ckungs|gleich|heit** F (Math) congruence; wegen der ~ der Ansichten/Aussagen because of the degree to which these views coincide/these statements agree; **De|ckungs|gra|ben** M (Mil) shelter trench; **De|ckungs|ka|pi|tal** NT (Insur) covering funds pl; **De|ckungs|loch** NT (Mil) foxhole; **De|ckungs|lü|cke** F (Fin) shortfall no pl, deficit; **De|ckungs|sum|me** F (Insur) sum or amount insured; **De|ckungs|zu|sa|ge** F (von Versicherung) cover note

Deck-: **Deck|weiß** NT opaque white; **Deck|wort** NT pl -wörter code word

De|co|der [de'ko:dɐ] M -s, - decoder

de|co|die|ren [deko'di:rən] ptp decodiert VT to decode

De|co|die|rung F -, -en decoding

Dé|col|le|té [dekɔl'te:] NT -s, -s = Dekolleté

de|cou|ra|giert [dekura'ʒi:ɐt] ADJ (dated geh) disheartened, dispirited

De|cres|cen|do [dekre'ʃɛndo] NT (Mus) diminuendo

De|di|ka|ti|on [dedika'tsio:n] F -, -en (geh) **a** (= Widmung) dedication **b** (= Schenkung) gift

De|di|ka|ti|ons|ex|emp|lar NT presentation copy

de|di|zie|ren [dedi'tsi:rən] ptp dediziert VT (geh) **a** (= widmen) to dedicate **b** (= schenken) jdm etw ~ to present sth to sb

De|duk|ti|on [dedʊk'tsio:n] F -, -en deduction

de|duk|tiv [dedʊk'ti:f] ADJ deductive ADV deductively

de|du|zie|ren [dedu'tsi:rən] ptp deduziert VT to deduce (aus from)

Deern [de:ɐn] F -, -s (N Ger inf) lass(ie) (dial inf), girl

De|es|ka|la|ti|on [deleskala'tsio:n] F (Mil) de-escalation

de|es|ka|lie|ren [deleska'li:rən] ptp deeskaliert VT to de-escalate VI aux sein to de-escalate

Deez [de:ts] M -es, -e (hum inf) bonce (Brit inf), head

de fac|to [de 'fakto] ADV de facto

De-fac|to-An|er|ken|nung F (Pol) de facto recognition

de|fä|kie|ren [defɛ'ki:rən] ptp defäkiert VI (form) to defecate

De|fä|tis|mus [defɛ'tɪsmʊs] M -, no pl defeatism

De|fä|tist [defɛ'tɪst] M -en, -en, **De|fä|tis|tin** [-'tɪstɪn] F -, -nen defeatist

de|fä|tis|tisch [defɛ'tɪstɪʃ] ADJ defeatist no adv

De|fault [di'fɔ:lt] M -(s), -s (Comput) default

de|fä|zie|ren [defɛ'tsi:rən] ptp defäziert VI (form) to defecate

de|fekt [de'fɛkt] ADJ Gerät etc faulty, defective; Gen defective; geistig/moralisch ~ sein to be mentally/morally deficient

De|fekt [de'fɛkt] M -(e)s, -e fault, defect; (Med) deficiency; körperlicher ~ physical defect; geistiger ~ mental deficiency; einen ~ haben to be faulty or defective; (inf: Mensch) to be a bit lacking (inf)

de|fek|tiv [defɛk'ti:f] ADJ (Gram) defective

De|fek|ti|vum [defɛk'ti:vʊm] NT -s, Defektiva [-va] (Gram) defective

de|fen|siv [defɛn'zi:f] ADJ Maßnahmen, Taktik defensive; Fahrweise non-aggressive; Forschungen into defensive systems ADV defensively; sich ~ verhalten to be on the defensive

De|fen|siv- in cpds defensive; **De|fen|siv|bünd|nis** NT defence (Brit) or defense (US) alliance

De|fen|si|ve [defɛn'zi:və] F -, (rare) -n defensive; in der ~ bleiben to remain on the defensive;

jdn in die ~ drängen to force sb onto the defensive

De|fen|si|vi|tät [defɛnzivi'tɛ:t] F -, *no pl* defensiveness; *(von Fahrweise)* lack of aggression (*+gen* in), defensiveness *(US)* (*+gen* of)

De|fen|siv-: **De|fen|siv|krieg** M defensive warfare; **De|fen|siv|spiel** NT defensive game; **De|fen|siv|stel|lung** F defensive position, position of defence *(Brit)* or defense *(US)*

De|fi|bril|la|tor [defibri'la:to:ɐ] M -s, -en [-la'to:rən] *(Med)* defibrillator

De|fi|lee [defi'le:] NT -s, -s *or* -n [-'le:ən] *(Mil)* march past; *(fig)* parade

de|fi|lie|ren [defi'li:rən] *ptp* **defiliert** VI *aux haben or sein (Mil)* to march past; *(fig)* to parade past

de|fi|nier|bar ADJ definable; **frei ~** *(Comput)* free(ly) definable; **schwer/leicht ~** hard/easy to define

de|fi|nie|ren [defi'ni:rən] *ptp* **definiert** VT to define; **etw neu ~** to redefine sth; **frei definiert** *(Comput)* free(ly) defined

De|fi|ni|ti|on [defini'tsio:n] F -, -en definition

de|fi|ni|tiv [defini'ti:f] ADJ definite ADV *(= bestimmt)* definitely

de|fi|ni|to|risch [defini'to:rɪʃ] *(geh)* ADJ *Frage, Problem* of definition ADV **ein ~ schwieriges Problem** a problem which is hard to define

de|fi|zi|ent [defi'tsiɛnt] ADJ deficient

De|fi|zit ['de:fitsɪt] NT -s, -e *(= Fehlbetrag)* deficit; *(= Mangel)* deficiency (*an +dat* of)

de|fi|zi|tär [defitsi'tɛ:ɐ] ADJ in deficit; **die ~e Entwicklung der Organisation** the trend in the organization to run to a deficit; **eine ~e Haushaltspolitik führen** to follow an economic policy which can only lead to deficit ADV **das Bankwesen entwickelt sich immer ~er** the banks have a larger deficit every year

De|fla|ti|on [defla'tsio:n] F -, -en *(Econ)* deflation

de|fla|ti|o|när [deflatsio'nɛ:ɐ], **de|fla|ti|o|nis|tisch** [deflatsio'nɪstɪʃ] ADJ deflationary *no adv*

De|fla|ti|ons|po|li|tik F deflationary policy

de|fla|to|risch [defla'to:rɪʃ] ADJ *(Econ)* = **deflationär**

De|flo|ra|ti|on [deflora'tsio:n] F -, -en defloration

de|flo|rie|ren [deflo'ri:rən] *ptp* **defloriert** VT to deflower

De|for|ma|ti|on [defɔrma'tsio:n] F deformation, distortion; *(= Missbildung)* deformity; *(= Entstellung)* disfigurement

de|for|mie|ren [defɔr'mi:rən] *ptp* **deformiert** VT *(Tech)* to deform, to contort; *(lit, fig: = missbilden)* to deform; *(= entstellen)* to disfigure; **in einer Schlägerei haben sie ihm die Nase deformiert** they flattened his nose (for him) in a fight; **eine deformierte Nase** a misshapen nose

De|for|mie|rung F **a** *(= das Deformieren)* deformation; *(= Entstellung)* disfigurement **b** = **Deformation**

De|for|mi|tät [defɔrmi'tɛ:t] F -, -en *(Med)* deformity

de|frag|men|tie|ren [de:fragmɛn'ti:rən] *ptp* **defragmentiert** VT *(Comput)* to defragment

De|fros|ter [de'frɔstɐ] M -s, - *(Aut)* heated windscreen *(Brit)* or windshield *(US)*, defroster *(US)*; *(= Sprühmittel)* de-icer; *(im Kühlschrank)* defroster

def|tig ['dɛftɪç] ADJ **a** *(= derb, urwüchsig) Witz, Humor* ribald **b** *(= kräftig) Lüge* whopping *(inf)*, huge; *Mahlzeit, Wurst etc* substantial, good solid *attr*; *Ohrfeige* cracking *(inf)*; *Preis* extortionate; **~e Hausmannskost** good plain cooking, good honest fare *(esp Brit)* ADV *(= tüchtig)* really; **~ schmecken** to taste well-seasoned; **sich ~ ausdrücken** to speak bluntly

Def|tig|keit F -, *no pl (= Derbheit, Urwüchsigkeit)* ribaldry

de|ga|gie|ren [dega'ʒi:rən] *ptp* **degagiert** VT *(Fechten)* to disengage

De|gen ['de:gn] M -s, - rapier; *(Sportfechten)* épée; **mit bloßem** *or* **nacktem ~** with one's rapier drawn → **kreuzen VT**

De|ge|ne|ra|ti|on [degenera'tsio:n] F degeneration

De|ge|ne|ra|ti|ons|er|schei|nung F sign of degeneration

de|ge|ne|ra|tiv [degenera'ti:f] ADJ *Schäden, Krankheit* degenerative

de|ge|ne|rie|ren [degene'ri:rən] *ptp* **degeneriert** VI *aux sein* to degenerate (*zu* into)

de|ge|ne|riert [degene'ri:ɐt] ADJ degenerate

De|gen-: **De|gen|fech|ten** NT -s, *no pl* épée fencing; **De|gen|klin|ge** F rapier blade; **De|gen|knauf** M pommel; **De|gen|korb** M guard; **De|gen|stoß** M thrust from one's/a rapier

de|gou|tant [degu'tant] ADJ *(geh)* distasteful, disgusting

de|gou|tie|ren [degu'ti:rən] *ptp* **degoutiert** VT *(geh)* to disgust

De|gra|da|ti|on [degrada'tsio:n] F *(Phys)* ~ **der Energie** degradation of energy

de|gra|die|ren [degra'di:rən] *ptp* **degradiert** VT *(Mil)* to demote (*zu* to); *(fig: = herabwürdigen)* to degrade; **jdn/etw zu etw ~** *(fig)* to lower sb/sth to the level of sth

De|gra|die|rung F -, -en *(Mil)* demotion (*zu* to); *(fig)* degradation; **diese Behandlung empfand er als (eine) ~** he felt such treatment to be degrading

De|gres|si|on [degrɛ'sio:n] F -, -en *(Fin)* degression

de|gres|siv [degrɛ'si:f] ADJ *(Fin)* degressive

De|gus|ta|ti|on [degusta'tsio:n] F -, -en *(esp Sw)* tasting

de|gus|tie|ren [degʊs'ti:rən] *ptp* **degustiert** VTI *(esp Sw) Wein* to taste

dehn|bar ADJ *(lit)* elastic; *(fig auch)* flexible; *Stoff* stretch *attr*, stretchy *(inf)*, elastic; *Metall* ductile; **ein ~er Vokal** a vowel which can be lengthened

Dehn|bar|keit ['de:nba:ɐkait] F -, *no pl (lit)* elasticity; *(fig auch)* flexibility; *(von Stoff)* stretchiness *(inf)*, elasticity; *(von Metall)* ductility; **Eisen hat eine geringere ~ als Blei** iron is less ductile than lead; **die ~ der Vokale** the degree *or* extent to which the vowels can be lengthened

deh|nen ['de:nən] VT to stretch; *(Med auch)* to dilate; *Laut, Silbe* to lengthen; **seine gedehnte Sprechweise** his drawling way of speaking; **Vokale gedehnt aussprechen** to pronounce one's vowels long VR to stretch; **er dehnte und streckte sich** he had a good stretch; **die Minuten dehnten sich zu Stunden** *(geh)* the minutes seemed like hours; **vor ihnen dehnte sich der Ozean** *(geh)* the ocean stretched out before them; **der Weg dehnte sich endlos** the road seemed to go on for ever

Dehn- *(Ling)*: **Dehn|strich** M length mark; **Dehn|stu|fe** F lengthened grade, dehnstufe *(form)*

Deh|nung F -, -en stretching; *(Med auch)* dilation; *(von Laut, Silbe)* lengthening

Deh|nungs- *(Ling)*: **Deh|nungs-h** [-ha:] NT h with a lengthening effect on the preceding vowel; **Deh|nungs|strich** M length mark

de|hyd|rie|ren [dehy'dri:rən] *ptp* **dehydriert** VT *(Chem)* to dehydrate

De|hyd|rie|rung F -, -en *(Chem)* dehydration

Dei|bel ['daibl] M -s, - *(N Ger inf)* → **Teufel, pfui**

Deich [daiç] M -(e)s, -e dyke *(Brit)*, dike *(esp US)*

Deich-: **Deich|bau** M, *no pl* dyke *(Brit)*, dike *(esp US)*; *(= das Bauen)* dyke *(Brit)* or dike *(esp US)* building; **Deich|bruch** M breach in the dyke *(Brit)* or dike *(esp US)*; **Deich|ge|nos|sen|schaft** F *association of owners of dyked land*; **Deich|graf** M, **Deich|haupt|mann** M dyke *(Brit)* or dike *(esp US)* reeve *(old)* or warden; **Deich|kro|ne** F dyke *(Brit)* or dike *(esp US)* top

Deich|sel ['daiksl] F -, -n shaft, whiffletree *(US)*; *(= Doppeldeichsel)* shafts *pl*; **ein Pferd in der ~** a horse in *or* between the shafts; **Ochsen an die ~ spannen** to yoke oxen into *or* between the shafts

Deich|sel-: **Deich|sel|bruch** M broken shaft/shafts; **Deich|sel|kreuz** NT **a** handle **b** *(Rel)* Y-shaped cross

deich|seln ['daiksln] VT *(inf)* to wangle *(inf)*; **das werden wir schon ~** we'll wangle it somehow *(inf)*

Deich-: **Deich|ver|band** M *association of owners of dyked land*; **Deich|vogt** M *(old)* dyke *(Brit)* or dike *(esp US)* reeve *(old)*; **Deich|vor|land** NT *land to the seaward side of a dyke*

De|i|fi|ka|ti|on [deifika'tsio:n] F -, -en *(Philos)* deification

de|i|fi|zie|ren [deifi'tsi:rən] *ptp* **deifiziert** VT *(Philos)* to deify

dein [dain] POSS PRON **a** *(adjektivisch)* your, thy *(obs, dial)*; **~ doofes/schönes Gesicht** that stupid/beautiful face of yours, your stupid/beautiful face; **rauchst du immer noch ~e 20 Zigaretten pro Tag?** are you still smoking your 20 cigarettes a day?; **herzliche Grüße, Deine Elke** with best wishes, yours *or (herzlicher)* love Elke; **stets** *or* **immer Dein Otto** yours ever, Otto; **Dein Wille geschehe** *(Bibl)* Thy will be done **b** *(old: substantivisch)* yours; **behalte, was ~ ist** keep what is yours PERS PRON *gen von* **du** *(old, poet)* **ich werde ewig ~ gedenken** I shall remember you forever

dei|ner ['dainɐ] PERS PRON *gen von* **du** *(geh)* of you; **wir werden ~ gedenken** we will remember you

dei|ne(r, s) ['dainə] POSS PRON *(substantivisch)* yours; **der/die/das ~** *or* **Deine** *(geh)* yours; **tu du das ~** *or* **Deine** *(geh)* you do your bit *or* part *(esp US)*; **stets** *or* **immer der ~** *or* **Deine** *(form)* yours ever; **die ~n** *or* **Deinen** *(geh)* your family, your people; **du und die ~n** *or* **Deinen** *(geh: = Familie)* you and yours; **das ~** *or* **Deine** *(geh: = Besitz)* what is yours

dei|ner|seits ['dainɐ'zaits] ADV *(= auf deiner Seite)* for your part; *(= von deiner Seite)* on your part; **den Vorschlag hast du ~ gemacht** you made the suggestion yourself

dei|nes|glei|chen ['dainəs'glaiçn] PRON *inv* people like you *or* yourself; *(pej auch)* your sort *or* type, the likes of you; **an Schönheit ist keine ~** *(liter)* in beauty there is none to equal you *(liter)*

dei|net-: **dei|net|hal|ben** ['dainət'halbn] *(dated)* ADV = **deinetwegen**; **dei|net|we|gen** ['dainət've:gn] ADV *(= wegen dir)* because of you, on account of you, on your account; *(= dir zuliebe)* for your sake; *(= um dich)* about you; *(= für dich)* on your behalf; **dei|net|wil|len** ['dainət'vɪlən] ADV **um ~** for your sake

dei|ni|ge ['dainɪgə] POSS PRON *(old, geh)* **der/die/das ~** *or* **Deinige** yours; **die ~n** *or* **Deinigen** your family *or* people; **das ~** *or* **Deinige** *(= Besitz)* what is yours; **tu du das ~** *or* **Deinige** you do your bit *or* part *(esp US)*

deins [dains] POSS PRON yours

De|in|stal|la|ti|on [de:ɪnstala'tsio:n] F -, -en *(Comput: von Software)* de-installation

de|in|stal|lie|ren [de:ɪnsta'li:rən] *ptp* **deinstalliert** VT *(Comput) Software* to uninstall, to de-install

De|is|mus [de'ɪsmʊs] M -, *no pl (Philos)* deism

De|ist [de'ɪst] M -en, -en, **De|is|tin** [-'ɪstɪn] F -, -nen *(Philos)* deist

de|is|tisch [de'ɪstɪʃ] ADJ *(Philos)* deistic

Dei|wel ['daivl] M -s, - *(N Ger)*, **Dei|xel** ['daiksl] M -s, - *(S Ger)* = **Teufel**

Déjà-vu-Er|leb|nis [deʒa'vy:-] NT *(Psych)* sense *or* feeling of déjà vu

de ju|re [de: 'ju:rə] ADV de jure

De-ju|re-An|er|ken|nung F de jure recognition

De|ka ['dɛka] NT -(s), - *(Aus)* = **Dekagramm**

De|ka|de [de'ka:də] F -, -n (= 10 Tage) ten days, ten-day period; (= 10 Jahre) decade

de|ka|dent [deka'dɛnt] ADJ decadent

De|ka|denz [deka'dɛnts] F -, no pl decadence

De|ka|denz|er|schei|nung F sign of decadence

de|ka|disch [de'ka:dɪʃ] ADJ *Zahlensystem* decimal; **~er Logarithmus** common logarithm

De|ka-: **De|ka|eder** [deka'le:dɐ] M -s, - decahedron; **De|ka|gon** [deka'go:n] NT -s, -e decagon; **De|ka|gramm** ['deka-, 'dɛka-] NT decagram(me); **10 ~ Schinken** (Aus) 100 grams of ham; **De|ka|li|ter** ['deka-, 'dɛka-] M decalitre (Brit), decaliter (US)

De|ka|log [deka'lo:k] M -(e)s [-gəs] (Bibl) decalogue

De|ka|me|ron [de'ka:merɔn] NT -s Decameron

De|ka|me|ter ['deka-, 'dɛka-] M decametre (Brit), decameter (US)

De|kan [de'ka:n] M -s, -e (Univ, Eccl) dean

De|ka|nat [deka'na:t] NT -(e)s, -e **a** (Univ, Eccl: = Amt, Amtszeit) deanship **b** (= Amtssitz) (Univ) office of the dean; (Eccl) deanery

De|ka|nei [deka'nai] F -, -en (Eccl) deanery

De|ka|nin [de'ka:nɪn] F -, -nen (Univ) dean

de|kan|tie|ren [dekant'i:rən] ptp **dekantiert** VT *Wein* to decant

de|kar|bo|ni|sie|ren [dekarboni'zi:rən] ptp **dekarbonisiert** VT to decarbonize; (Aut) to decoke

de|kar|tel|lie|ren [dekartɛ'li:ən] ptp **dekartelliert**, **de|kar|tel|li|sie|ren** [dekartɛli'zi:rən] ptp **dekartellisiert** VT to decartelize

De|kla|ma|ti|on [deklama'tsio:n] F -, -en declamation; **~en** (pej) (empty) rhetoric *sing*

de|kla|ma|to|risch [deklama'to:rɪʃ] ADJ declamatory, rhetorical

de|kla|mie|ren [dekla'mi:rən] ptp **deklamiert** VTI to declaim

De|kla|ra|ti|on [deklara'tsio:n] F -, -en (alle Bedeutungen) declaration

de|kla|rie|ren [dekla'ri:rən] ptp **deklariert** VT (alle Bedeutungen) to declare

De|kla|rie|rung F -, -en declaration

de|klas|sie|ren [dekla'si:rən] ptp **deklassiert** VT **a** (Sociol: = herabsetzen) to downgrade **b** (Sport: = weit übertreffen) to outclass

De|klas|sie|rung F -, -en (Sociol) downgrading; (Sport) outclassing

de|kli|na|bel [dekli'na:bl] ADJ (Gram) declinable

De|kli|na|ti|on [deklina'tsio:n] F -, -en **a** (Gram) declension **b** (Astron, Phys) declination

de|kli|nier|bar ADJ (Gram) declinable

de|kli|nie|ren [dekli'ni:rən] ptp **dekliniert** VT (Gram) to decline

de|ko|die|ren [deko'di:rən] ptp **dekodiert** VT = **dekodieren**

De|ko|die|rung F -, -en = **Dekodierung**

De|kol|le|té [dekɔl'te:] NT -s, -s, **De|kol|le|tee** NT -s, -s low-cut or décolleté neckline, décolletage; **ein Kleid mit einem tiefen/gewagten ~** a very/daringly low-cut or décolleté dress; **ihr ~ war so tief, ...** she was wearing such a low-cut or plunging neckline ...

de|kol|le|tie|ren [dekɔl'ti:rən] ptp **dekolletiert** VT to give a or cut with a low neckline

de|kol|le|tiert [dekɔl'ti:ɐt] ADJ *Kleid* low-cut, décolleté; **eine ~e Dame** a woman in a low-cut dress

De|ko|lo|ni|sa|ti|on [dekoloniza'tsio:n] F decolonization

de|ko|lo|ni|sie|ren [dekoloni'zi:rən] ptp **dekolonisiert** VT to decolonize

De|kom|po|si|ti|on [dekɔmpozi'tsio:n] F decomposition

De|kom|po|si|tum [dekɔm'po:zitum] NT (Ling) (= zusammengesetztes Wort) mutiple compound, decomposite (form), decompound (form); (= Ableitung) compound derivative

De|kom|pres|si|on [dekɔmpre'sio:n] F decompression

De|kom|pres|si|ons|kam|mer F decompression chamber

de|kom|pri|mie|ren [dekɔmpri'mi:rən] ptp **dekomprimiert** VT (Comput) to decompress, to uncompress

De|kon|ta|mi|na|ti|on [dekɔntamina'tsio:n] F decontamination

de|kon|ta|mi|nie|ren [dekɔntami'ni:rən] ptp **dekontaminiert** VT to decontaminate

De|kon|zent|ra|ti|on [dekɔntsɛntra'tsio:n] F deconcentration, decentralization

De|kor [de'ko:ɐ] M OR NT -s, -s or -e **a** decoration; (von Raum auch) décor; (= Muster) pattern **b** (Theat, Film etc) décor

De|ko|ra|teur [dekora'tø:ɐ] M -s, -e, **De|ko|ra|teu|rin** [-'tø:rɪn] F -, -nen (= Schaufensterdekorateur) window-dresser; (von Innenräumen) interior designer

De|ko|ra|ti|on [dekora'tsio:n] F -, -en **a** no pl (= das Ausschmücken) decorating, decoration **b** (= Einrichtung) décor *no pl*; (= Fensterdekoration) window-dressing or decoration; (Theat: = Bühnenbild) set; **zur ~ dienen** to be decorative; **zu Weihnachten haben viele Kaufhäuser schöne ~en** many department stores are beautifully decorated for Christmas **c** (= Orden, Ordensverleihung) decoration

De|ko|ra|ti|ons-: **De|ko|ra|ti|ons|ar|bei|ten** PL decorating *no pl*; **De|ko|ra|ti|ons|ma|ler(in)** M(F) (interior) decorator; (Theat) scene painter; **De|ko|ra|ti|ons|stoff** M (Tex) furnishing fabric; **De|ko|ra|ti|ons|stück** NT piece of the décor; **das ist nur ein ~** that's just for decoration

de|ko|ra|tiv [dekora'ti:f] ADJ decorative ADV decoratively; **~ wirken** or **aussehen** to look decorative

de|ko|rie|ren [deko'ri:rən] ptp **dekoriert** VT to decorate; *Schaufenster* to dress

De|ko|rie|rung F -, -en decoration; (von Schaufenster) dressing

De|ko|rum [de'ko:rum] NT -s, no pl (liter) propriety, decorum; **das ~ wahren** to maintain or observe the proprieties; **das ~ verletzen** to go against or infringe the proprieties

De|ko|stoff ['deko-] M furnishing fabric

Dek|ret [de'kre:t] NT -(e)s, -e decree

dek|re|tie|ren [dekre'ti:rən] ptp **dekretiert** VT to decree

de|kuv|rie|ren [deku'vri:rən] ptp **dekuvriert** (geh) VT *Skandal, Machenschaften* to expose, to uncover; *Person, Betrüger etc* to expose VR to reveal oneself

De|le|a|tur(zei|chen) [dele'a:tur-] NT -s, - (Typ) deletion mark

De|le|gat [dele'ga:t] M -en, -en, **De|le|ga|tin** [-'ga:tɪn] F -, -nen delegate

De|le|ga|ti|on [delega'tsio:n] F -, -en (alle Bedeutungen) delegation

De|le|ga|ti|ons|chef(in) M(F) head of a delegation; **der koreanische ~** the head of the Korean delegation

de|le|gie|ren [dele'gi:rən] ptp **delegiert** VT (alle Bedeutungen) to delegate (an +acc to)

De|le|gier|ten|kon|fe|renz F, **De|le|gier|ten|ver|samm|lung** F delegates' conference

De|le|gier|te(r) [dele'gi:ɐtə] MF decl as adj delegate

de|lek|tie|ren [delɛk'ti:rən] ptp **delektiert** (geh) VR **sich an etw** (dat) **~** to delight in sth VT **jdn mit etw ~** to delight sb with sth; **sie delektierten den Sultan mit Tänzen** they danced for the sultan's delectation (liter)

De|lete-Taste F (Comput) delete key

Del|fin M -s, -e (Zool) dolphin

Del|fin NT -s, no pl (= Delfinschwimmen) butterfly (stroke)

Del|fi|na|ri|um [dɛlfi'na:rium] NT -s, **Delfinarien** [-riən] dolphinarium

Del|fin|schwim|men NT butterfly (stroke)

Delf|ter ['dɛlftɐ] ADJ *attr Porzellan etc* Delft

de|li|kat [deli'ka:t] ADJ **a** (= wohlschmeckend) exquisite, delicious **b** (= behutsam) delicate; *Andeutung auch* gentle **c** (= heikel) *Problem, Frage* delicate, sensitive; (= gewagt) risqué **d** (geh: = empfindlich) delicate ADV *zubereitet* exquisitely; **~ schmecken** to taste exquisite or delicious

De|li|ka|tess- [delika'tɛs] in cpds (top-)quality

De|li|ka|tes|se [delika'tɛsə] F -, -n **a** (= Leckerbissen, fig) delicacy; **ein Geschäft für Obst und ~n** a fruit shop and delicatessen **b** no pl (geh: = Feinfühligkeit) delicacy, sensitivity

De|li|ka|tes|sen|ge|schäft NT delicatessen, deli (inf)

De|li|ka|tess-: **De|li|ka|tess|gur|ke** F gherkin; **De|li|ka|tess|la|den** M = **Delikatessengeschäft**; **De|li|ka|tess|senf** M (top-)quality mustard

De|likt [de'lɪkt] NT -(e)s, -e (Jur) offence (Brit), offense (US); (schwerer) crime

De|li|mi|ter [dɪ'lɪmɪtɐ] M -(s), - (Comput) delimiter

de|lin|quent [delɪŋ'kvɛnt] ADJ (Sociol, Psych) delinquent

De|lin|quent [delɪŋ'kvɛnt] M -en, -en, **De|lin|quen|tin** [-'kvɛntɪn] F -, -nen (geh) offender

De|lin|quenz [delɪŋ'kvɛnts] F -, no pl (Sociol, Psych) delinquency

de|li|rie|ren [deli'ri:rən] ptp **deliriert** VI (geh, Med) to be delirious; **er delirierte im Fieber** he was delirious with fever

De|li|ri|um [de'li:rium] NT -s, **Delirien** [-riən] delirium; **im ~ sein** to be delirious, to be in a state of delirium; (inf: = betrunken) to be paralytic (inf); **im ~ redete der Kranke wirr und konfus** the sick man raved deliriously; **in seinen Delirien** whenever he was delirious; (= betrunken) whenever he was paralytic (inf); **~ tremens** delirium tremens, the DT's

de|li|zi|ös [deli'tsiø:s] (liter) ADJ most delectable ADV *schmecken, duften* delectable, delicious

Del|le ['dɛlə] F -, -n **a** (inf) dent; **eine ~ bekommen** to get a dent, to get or be dented **b** (= Bodendelle) hollow, dip

de|lo|gie|ren [delo'ʒi:rən] ptp **delogiert** VT (Aus) *Mieter* to evict

De|lo|gie|rung F -, -en (Aus) eviction

Del|phi ['dɛlfi] NT -s Delphi; **das Orakel von ~** the Delphic oracle, the oracle of Delphi

Del|phin [dɛl'fi:n] etc = **Delfin** etc

del|phisch ['dɛlfɪʃ] ADJ Delphic; **das Delphische Orakel** the Delphic oracle

Del|ta ['dɛlta] NT -s, -s or **Del|ten** ['dɛltn] (Geog) delta

Del|ta NT -(s), -s (= Buchstabe) delta

Del|ta-: **del|ta|för|mig** ADJ delta-shaped, deltaic (rare); *Muskel* deltoid; **Del|ta|mün|dung** F delta estuary; **Del|ta|mus|kel** M deltoid; **Del|ta|strah|len** PL (Phys) delta rays *pl*

de Luxe [də 'lyks] ADJ (Comm) de luxe

De-Luxe-Aus|füh|rung F (Comm) de luxe version

dem [de:m] DEF ART dat von **der, das** **a** to the; (mit Präposition) the **b** **es ist nicht an ~** that is not the case, that is not how it is; **wenn ~ so ist** if that is the way it is; **wie ~ auch sei** be that as it may DEM PRON dat von **der, das** **a** attr to that; (mit Präposition) that **b** (substantivisch) to that one; that one; (Menschen) to him; him; (von mehreren) to that one; that one REL PRON dat von **der, das** to whom, that or who(m) ... to; (mit Präposition) who(m); (von Sachen) to which, which or that ... to; which; **~ der Fehler unterlaufen ist, ...** whoever made that mistake ...

De|ma|go|ge [dema'go:gə] M -n, -n, **De|ma|go|gin** [-'go:gɪn] F -, -nen demagogue

De|ma|go|gie [demago'gi:] F -, -n [-'gi:ən] demagogy, demagoguery

de|ma|go|gisch [dema'go:gɪʃ] ADJ *Rede etc* demagogic ADV **leider lassen sich die Wähler immer noch ~ beeinflussen** sadly voters can still be swayed by demagogues or by demagogic ploys; **er hat in seiner Rede die Tatsachen ~ verzerrt** in his speech he twisted the facts to demagogic ends

de|man|ten [de'mantn] ADJ *(poet)* = **diamanten**
De|mar|che [de'marʃə] F -, -n *(Pol)* (diplomatic) representation, démarche; **eine ~ unternehmen** to lodge a diplomatic protest
De|mar|ka|ti|on [demarka'tsio:n] F -, -en demarcation
De|mar|ka|ti|ons|li|nie F *(Pol, Mil)* demarcation line; **die ~ des Waffenstillstands** the cease-fire line
de|mar|kie|ren [demar'ki:rən] *ptp* **demarkiert** VT *Grenze, Bereiche* to demarcate
de|mas|kie|ren [demas'ki:rən] *ptp* **demaskiert** VT to unmask, to expose; **jdn als etw ~** to expose sb as sth VR to unmask oneself, to take off one's mask; **sich als etw ~** to show oneself to be sth
De|men|ti [de'mɛnti] NT -s, -s denial
de|men|tie|ren [demɛn'ti:rən] *ptp* **dementiert** VT to deny VI to deny it
De|men|tie|rung F -, -en denial, denying
dem|ent|spre|chend ['de:mlɛnt'ʃprɛçnt] ADV correspondingly; *(= demnach)* accordingly; *bezahlt* commensurately ADJ appropriate; *Bemerkung auch* apposite *(form)*; *Gehalt* commensurate; *Vertrag* on this matter; **er nennt sich Christ, aber sein Verhalten ist nicht ~** he says he is a Christian but he does not behave accordingly *or* correspondingly
De|menz [de'mɛnts] F -, -en *(Med)* dementia
De|menz|kran|ke(r) MF *(Med)* dementia sufferer; *(im Krankenhaus)* dementia patient
dem-: **dem|ge|gen|über** ['de:mge:gn'ly:bɐ] ADV *(= wohingegen)* on the other hand; *(= im Vergleich dazu)* in contrast; **dem|ge|mäß** ['de:mgəmɛ:s] ADV ADJ = **dementsprechend**
de|mi|li|ta|ri|sie|ren [demilitari'zi:rən] *ptp* **demilitarisiert** VT to demilitarize
De|mi|li|ta|ri|sie|rung F -, -en demilitarization
De|mi|mon|de [dəmi'mõ:d] F -, *no pl (pej geh)* demimonde
De|mis|si|on [demɪ'sio:n] F *(Pol) (= Rücktritt)* resignation; *(= Entlassung)* dismissal; **um seine ~ bitten** to ask to be relieved of one's duties; **er wurde zur ~ gezwungen** he was forced to resign
de|mis|si|o|nie|ren [demɪsio'ni:rən] *ptp* **demissioniert** VI *(Pol, Sw: = kündigen)* to resign
De|mis|si|ons|an|ge|bot NT offer of resignation *or* to resign
De|mi|urg [demi'ʊrk] M -en *or* -s, *no pl (Myth, liter)* demiurge
dem-: **dem|nach** ['de:mna:x] ADV therefore; *(= dementsprechend)* accordingly; **dem|nächst** ['de:mnɛ:çst, de:m'nɛ:çst] ADV soon; **~ (in diesem Kino)** coming soon
De|mo ['de:mo] F -, -s *(inf)* demo *(inf)*
De|mo|bi|li|sa|ti|on [demobiliza'tsio:n] F -, -en *(Mil)* demobilization
de|mo|bi|li|sie|ren [demobili'zi:rən] *ptp* **demobilisiert** VT to demobilize; *Soldaten* to demobilize, to demob *(Brit inf)* VI to demobilize; *(Soldat)* to demobilize, to get *or* be demobbed *(Brit inf)*
De|mo|bi|li|sie|rung F -, -en demobilization; *(von Soldaten)* demobilization, demob *(Brit inf)*
De|mo-CD F *(inf)* demo CD
dé|mo|dé [de:mo'de:] ADJ *attr (geh)* outmoded
De|mo|dis|ket|te ['de:mo-] F *(Comput)* demo disk
De|mo|du|la|ti|on [demodula'tsio:n] F -, -en *(Tech)* demodulation
De|mo|graf [demo'gra:f] M -en, -en, **De|mo|gra|fin** [-'gra:fɪn] F -, -nen demographer
De|mo|gra|fie [demogra'fi:] F -, -n [-'fi:ən] demography
de|mo|gra|fisch [demo'grafɪʃ] ADJ demographic
De|mo|graph *etc* = **Demograf** *etc*
De|mo|krat [demo'kra:t] M -en, -en, **De|mo|kra|tin** [-'kra:tɪn] F -, -nen democrat; *(US Pol)* Democrat

De|mo|kra|tie [demokra'ti:] F -, -n [-'ti:ən] democracy
De|mo|kra|tie-: **De|mo|kra|tie|be|griff** M concept of democracy; **De|mo|kra|tie|ver|ständ|nis** NT understanding of (the meaning of) democracy
de|mo|kra|tisch [demo'kra:tɪʃ] ADJ democratic ADV democratically
de|mo|kra|ti|sie|ren [demokrati'zi:rən] *ptp* **demokratisiert** VT to democratize, to make democratic
De|mo|kra|ti|sie|rung F -, -en democratization
De|mo|kra|ti|sie|rungs|pro|zess M democratization *or* democratic process
de|mo|lie|ren [demo'li:rən] *ptp* **demoliert** VT to wreck, to smash up; *(Rowdy auch)* to vandalize; **nach dem Unfall war das Auto total demoliert** after the accident the car was a complete wreck; **er sah ganz schön demoliert aus** *(inf)* he was a real mess, he looked pretty badly bashed about *(inf)*
De|mo|lie|rung F -, -en wrecking, smashing-up; *(durch Rowdy auch)* vandalizing
De|monst|rant [demɔn'strant] M -en, -en, **De|monst|ran|tin** [-'strantɪn] F -, -nen demonstrator
De|monst|ra|ti|on [demɔnstra'tsio:n] F -, -en *(alle Bedeutungen)* demonstration; **zur ~ seiner Friedfertigkeit ...** as a demonstration of *or* to demonstrate his peaceful intentions ...; **eine ~ für/gegen etw** a demonstration in support of/against sth
De|monst|ra|ti|ons-: **De|monst|ra|ti|ons|frei|heit** F freedom *or* right to demonstrate, freedom to hold demonstrations; **De|monst|ra|ti|ons|marsch** M march; **De|monst|ra|ti|ons|ma|te|ri|al** NT teaching material *or* aids *pl*; **De|monst|ra|ti|ons|ob|jekt** NT teaching aid; **De|monst|ra|ti|ons|recht** NT right to demonstrate, right to hold demonstrations; **De|monst|ra|ti|ons|straf|recht** NT criminal law as it relates to demonstrations; **De|monst|ra|ti|ons|ver|bot** NT ban on demonstrations; **De|monst|ra|ti|ons|zug** M demonstration, (protest) march
de|monst|ra|tiv [demɔnstra'ti:f] ADJ demonstrative *(auch Gram)*; *Beifall* acclamatory; *Protest, Fehlen* pointed; *Beispiel* clear; **war seine Abwesenheit ~ oder reiner Zufall?** was his absence a deliberate *or* pointed gesture or pure chance? ADV pointedly; **der Botschafter verließ während der Rede ~ den Saal** during the speech the ambassador pointedly left the room; **~ Beifall spenden** to make a point of applauding
De|monst|ra|tiv|pro|no|men NT *(Gram)* demonstrative pronoun
de|monst|rie|ren [demɔn'stri:rən] *ptp* **demonstriert** VTI *(alle Bedeutungen)* to demonstrate; **für/gegen etw ~** to demonstrate in support of/against sth; **die Regierung hat ihre Entschlossenheit demonstriert** the government gave a demonstration of *or* demonstrated its determination
De|mon|ta|ge [demɔn'ta:ʒə] F *(lit, fig)* dismantling
de|mon|tie|ren [demɔn'ti:rən] *ptp* **demontiert** VT *(lit, fig)* to dismantle; *Räder* to take off
De|mo|ra|li|sa|ti|on [demoraliza'tsio:n] F -, *(rare)* -en *(= Entmutigung)* demoralization; *(= Sittenverfall)* moral decline
de|mo|ra|li|sie|ren [demorali'zi:rən] *ptp* **demoralisiert** VT *(= entmutigen)* to demoralize; *(= korrumpieren)* to corrupt; **die römische Gesellschaft war am Ende so demoralisiert, dass ...** ultimately Roman society had suffered such a moral decline that ...
De|mo|ra|li|sie|rung F -, -en *(= Entmutigung)* demoralization
De|mo|skop [demo'sko:p] M -en -en, **De|mo|sko|pin** [-'sko:pɪn] F -, -nen (opinion) pollster

De|mo|sko|pie [demosko'pi:] F -, *no pl* (public) opinion research
de|mo|sko|pisch [demo'sko:pɪʃ] ADJ *Daten, Erkenntnisse* opinion poll *attr*; *Veränderungen* in (public) opinion research; **~es Institut** (public) opinion research institute; **alle ~en Voraussagen waren falsch** all the predictions in the opinion polls were wrong; **eine ~e Untersuchung** a (public) opinion poll
De|mo|ver|si|on F *(von Software)* demo version
dem-: **dem|sel|ben** [de:m'zɛlbn] *dat von* **derselbe, dasselbe**; **dem|un|er|ach|tet** △ ['de:mlʊnlɛɐ'laxtət, 'de:m'lʊn-], **dem|un|ge|ach|tet** △ ['de:mlʊngə'laxtət, 'de:m'lʊn-] ADV *(old)* → **dessen REL PRON**
De|mut ['de:mu:t] F -, *no pl* humility; **in ~** with humility
de|mü|tig ['de:my:tɪç] ADJ *Bitte, Blick* humble ADV humbly
de|mü|ti|gen ['de:my:tɪgn] VT *Gefangenen, Besiegten, Volk* to humiliate; *(= eine Lektion erteilen) stolzen Menschen etc* to humble VR to humble oneself *(vor +dat* before)
De|mü|ti|gung F -, -en humiliation; **jdm ~en/eine ~ zufügen** to humiliate sb
De|muts-: **De|muts|ge|bär|de** F, **De|muts|hal|tung** F *(esp Zool)* submissive posture; **de|muts|voll** ADJ *Person, Geste, Entschuldigung, Respekt* humble
dem|zu|fol|ge ['de:mtsu'fɔlgə] ADV therefore
den [de:n] DEF ART **a** *acc von* **der** the **b** *dat pl von* **der, die, das** the; to the DEM PRON *acc von* **der** **a** *attr* that **b** *(substantivisch)* that one; *(Menschen)* him; *(von mehreren)* that one REL PRON *acc von* **der** who(m), that; *(von Sachen)* which, that
de|na|tu|ra|li|sie|ren [denaturali'zi:rən] *ptp* **denaturalisiert** VT to denaturalize
de|na|tu|rie|ren [denatu'ri:rən] *ptp* **denaturiert** VT to denature VI **zu etw ~** *(fig geh)* to degenerate into sth
Dend|rit [dɛn'dri:t] M -en, -en *(Geol, Med)* dendrite
de|nen ['de:nən] DEM PRON *dat pl von* **der, die, das** to them; *(mit Präposition)* them REL PRON *dat pl von* **der, die, das** to whom, that *or* who(m) ... to; *(mit Präposition)* whom; *(von Sachen)* to which, that *or* which ... to; which
den|geln ['dɛŋln] VT *Sense* to sharpen, to hone
Den Haag [de:n 'ha:k] NT -s *(= Stadt)* The Hague
De|nim® ['de:nɪm, de'ni:m] M OR NT -(s), *no pl (Tex)* denim
Denk-: **Denk|an|satz** M starting point; **Denk|an|stoß** M something to start one thinking; **jdm Denkanstöße geben** to give sb something to think about, to give sb food for thought; **Denk|art** F way of thinking; **eine edle ~** high-mindedness; **eine niedrige ~** low-mindedness; **Denk|auf|ga|be** F brain-teaser; **denk|bar** ADJ conceivable; **es ist durchaus ~, dass er kommt** it's very possible *or* likely that he'll come ADV extremely; *(= ziemlich)* rather; **den ~ schlechtesten/besten Eindruck machen** to make the worst/best possible impression; **Denk|bla|se** F *(in Comic)* thought bubble
Den|ke ['dɛŋkə] F -, *no pl (inf)* (way of) thinking, mentality

den|ken ['dɛŋkn]
pret **dachte** ['daxtə], *ptp* **gedacht** [gə'daxt]
28.1, 29, 33.1, 39.1, 48.1

1 INTRANSITIVES VERB 2 TRANSITIVES VERB

1 – INTRANSITIVES VERB

a [= überlegen] to think; **das gibt einem zu denken** it makes you think; **das gab mir zu denken** it made me think; **ich denke, also bin ich** I think, therefore I am; **langsam/schnell denken** to be a slow/quick thinker; **bei sich denken** to think to oneself; **solange ich denken kann** (for) as long as I can remember; **sie dachte hin**

und her und kam schließlich zu dem Ergebnis, sich doch noch für die Prüfung anzumelden she thought a lot about it *or* she had a good think about it, and finally decided to sit *(Brit) or* take the exam after all; **wo denken Sie hin!** what an idea!; **der Mensch denkt, (und) Gott lenkt** *(Prov)* man proposes, God disposes *(Prov)*

b = urteilen to think *(über +acc* about); **was denken Sie über die Lage im Balkan?** what do you think about the situation in the Balkans?; **wie denken Sie darüber?** what do you think about it?; **schlecht von jdm** *or* **über jdn denken** to think badly of sb; **ich denke genauso** I think the same (way); **so darf man eben nicht denken** you shouldn't think like that; **wie viel soll ich spenden? – wie Sie denken** how much should I give? – it's up to you; **ich dächte, …** I would have thought …; **ich denke schon** I think so; **ich denke nicht** I don't think so

c = gesinnt sein to think; **edel denken** to be noble-minded; **kleinlich denken** to be petty-minded; **alle, die liberal denken** all liberally-minded people; **da muss man etwas großzügiger denken** one must be more generous-minded

♦ **denken an** to think of *or* about; **ich denke an eine rote Decke für mein Sofa** I'm thinking of *or* about (getting) a red cover for my sofa; **ich denke oft an meine alte Tante und frage mich, wie es ihr wohl geht** I often think about my old aunt and wonder how she is; **denk mal an mich, wenn du wieder einmal nach Paris fährst** think of me when you go back to Paris; **an das Geld habe ich gar nicht mehr gedacht** I had forgotten about the money; **denken Sie zum Beispiel an England im 19. Jahrhundert** look at England in the 19th century, for example; **wenn ich so an früher denke** when I think back; **und dann dachte sie an Josef als Babysitter** and then she thought of Josef as a baby-sitter; **an die Prüfung morgen denke ich mit gemischten Gefühlen** I've got mixed feelings about the exam tomorrow; **das Erste, woran ich dachte** the first thing I thought of; **daran ist gar nicht zu denken** that's (quite) out of the question; **ich denke nicht daran!** no way! *(inf)*; **ich denke nicht daran, das zu tun** there's no way I'm going to do that *(inf)*; **die viele Arbeit, ich darf gar nicht daran denken** all that work, it doesn't bear thinking about *(esp Brit) or* I don't dare think about it; **denk daran!** don't forget!

2 – TRANSITIVES VERB

a to think; **sagen was man denkt** to say what one thinks; **was denkst du jetzt?** what are you thinking (about)?; **ich denke gar nichts** I'm not thinking about anything; **was sie dafür bezahlt hat, das wage ich kaum zu denken** I hardly dare think how much she paid for it; **er war der Erste, der diesen Gedanken gedacht hat** he was the first to have this idea; **wie viel Trinkgeld gibt man? – so viel, wie Sie denken** how big a tip does one give? – it's up to you

♦ **für jdn/etw gedacht sein** *(= vorgesehen)* to be intended *or* meant for sb/sth; **so war das nicht gedacht** that wasn't what I/he *etc* had in mind

b = annehmen, glauben to think; **was sollen bloß die Leute denken!** what will people think!; **wer hätte das (von ihr) gedacht!** who'd have thought it (of her)!; **(nur) Schlechtes/Gutes von jdm denken** to think ill/well of sb; **denkste!** *(inf)* that's what you think!

♦ **sich** *(dat)* **etw denken** to imagine sth; **ich denke mir einen schönen Garten** I imagine a beautiful garden; **sich** *(dat)* **etw bei etw denken** to mean sth by sth; **was hast du dir bei dieser Bemerkung bloß gedacht?** what did you mean by that remark?; **ich habe mir nichts Böses dabei gedacht** I meant no harm (by it); **das kann ich mir denken** I can imagine; **wie viel soll ich Ihnen zahlen? – was Sie sich** *(dat)* **so gedacht haben** how much shall I pay you? – whatever you think; **ich könnte ihn mir gut als Direktor denken** I can just imagine him as director; **wie denkst du dir das eigentlich?** *(inf)* what's the big idea? *(inf)*; **ich habe mir das so gedacht …** this is what I'd thought …; **das habe ich mir gleich gedacht** I thought that from the first; **das habe ich mir gedacht** I thought so; **das habe ich mir beinahe gedacht** I thought as much; **dachte ich mirs doch!** I knew it!; **ich denke mir mein Teil** I have my own thoughts on the matter; **das lässt sich denken** that's very likely; **sie läuft zu Hause immer nackt herum und denkt sich nichts dabei** she runs around the house with no clothes on and thinks nothing of it → **gedacht**

Den|ken NT **-s,** *no pl* **a** *(= Gedankenwelt)* thought; *(= Denkweise)* thinking; **ich kann seinem ~ nicht folgen** I can't follow his thinking *or* his train of thought; **im ~ Goethes** in Goethe's thought; **im ~ der Aufklärung** in the thinking of the Enlightenment; **abstraktes ~** abstract thought *or* thinking; **klares ~** clear thinking, clarity of thought; **positives ~** positive thinking **b** *(= Gedanken)* thoughts *pl*, thinking **c** *(= Denkvermögen)* mind

Den|ker ['dɛŋkɐ] M **-s, -, Den|ke|rin** [-ərɪn] F **-, -nen** thinker; **das Volk der Dichter und ~** the nation of poets and philosophers

Den|ker|fal|te F *usu pl (hum)* furrow on one's brow; **er zog seine Stirn in ~n** *(acc)* he furrowed his brow

den|ke|risch ['dɛŋkərɪʃ] ADJ intellectual

Den|ker|stirn F *(hum)* lofty brow

Denk-: **Denk|fab|rik** F think tank; **denk|fä|hig** ADJ capable of thinking; **nicht mehr ~** incapable of thinking (straight) (any more); **als ~er Mensch** as an intelligent person; **Denk|fä|hig|keit** F ability to think; **denk|faul** ADJ (mentally) lazy; **sei nicht so ~!** get your brain working!; **Denk|faul|heit** F mental laziness; **Denk|feh|ler** M mistake in the/one's logic, flaw in the/one's reasoning; **ein ~ in der Beurteilung der Lage** an error in the assessment of the situation; **Denk|ge|wohn|heit** F *usu pl* habitual way of thinking; **Denk|hem|mung** F mental block; **Denk|hil|fe** F clue, hint; *(= Merkhilfe)* reminder; **Denk|ho|ri|zont** M mental horizon; **Denk|in|halt** M idea; **Denk|ka|te|go|rie** F *usu pl* thought category; **in veralteten ~n erzogen** brought up to think in outmoded categories; **Denk|kraft** F mental capacity

Denk|mal ['dɛŋkma:l] NT **-s, -e** *(liter) or* **=er** [-mɛ:lɐ] **a** *(= Gedenkstätte)* monument, memorial *(für* to); *(= Standbild)* statue; **die Stadt hat ihm ein ~ gesetzt** the town put up *or* erected a memorial/statue to him; **er hat sich** *(dat)* **ein ~ gesetzt** he has left a memorial (to himself) **b** *(= Zeugnis: literarisch etc)* monument *(+gen* to)

denk|mal|ge|schützt ADJ *Gebäude, Monument* listed (on a historic register); *Baum etc* protected; **das ist ein ~es Haus** this (house) is a listed building, this house is listed on a historic register *(US)*

Denk|mal(s)-: **Denk|mal(s)|kun|de** F study of historical monuments; **Denk|mal(s)|pfle|ge** F preservation of historical monuments; **Denk|mal(s)|pfle|ger(in)** M(F) curator of monuments; **Denk|mal(s)|schän|dung** F defacing a monument *no art*; **~en** defacing monuments; **Denk|mal(s)|schutz** M protection of historical monuments; **etw unter ~ stellen** to classify sth as a historical monument; **unter ~ stehen** to be listed *or* under a preservation order *or* classified as a historical monument; **Denk|mal(s)|schüt|zer(in)** M(F) preservationist

Denk-: **Denk|mo|dell** NT *(= Entwurf)* plan for further discussion; *(wissenschaftlich)* working hypothesis; *(= Denkmuster)* thought pattern; **Denk|mus|ter** NT thought pattern; **Denk|pau|se** F break, adjournment; **eine ~ einlegen** to have a break *or* to adjourn to think things over; **Denk|pro|zess** M thought-process; **Denk|psy|cho|lo|gie** F psychology of thought; **Denk|schab|lo|ne** F *(pej)* (set *or* hackneyed) thought pattern; **Denk|sche|ma** NT thought pattern; **Denk|schrift** F memorandum, memo *(inf)*; **Denk|schritt** M step (in one's/sb's thinking); **Denk|spiel** NT mental *or* mind game; **Denk|sport** M mental exercise; **„Denksport"** "puzzle corner"; **er ist ein Liebhaber des ~s** he loves doing puzzles and brain-teasers; **Denk|sport|auf|ga|be** F brain-teaser; **Denk|spruch** M motto

denks|te ['dɛŋkstə] INTERJ → **denken 2 b**

Denk-: **Denk|sys|tem** NT system of thought; **Denk|übung** F mental exercise

Den|kungs|art F, **Den|kungs|wei|se** F = **Denkart**

Denk-: **Denk|ver|mö|gen** NT capacity for thought, intellectual capacity; **Denk|vers** M mnemonic (verse); **Denk|vor|gang** M thought process; **Denk|wei|se** F = **Denkart**; **denk|wür|dig** ADJ memorable, notable; **Denk|wür|dig|keit** ['dɛŋkvʏrdɪçkait] F **-, -en a** *no pl (von Ereignis)* memorability, notability **b** *(liter: = Ereignis)* memorable *or* notable event; **Denk|zent|rum** NT thought centre *(Brit) or* center *(US)*; **Denk|zet|tel** M *(inf)* warning; **jdm einen ~ verpassen** to give sb a warning

denn [dɛn] CONJ **a** *(kausal)* because, for *(esp liter)* **b** *(geh: vergleichend)* than; **schöner ~ je** more beautiful than ever **c** *(konzessiv)* **es sei ~, (dass)** unless; **…, du segnest mich ~** *(Bibl)* … except thou blessest me *(obs, Bibl)* → **geschweige**

ADV **a** *(verstärkend)* **wann/woran/wer/wie/wo ~?** when/why/who/how/where?; **ich habe ihn gestern gesehen – wo ~?** I saw him yesterday – oh, where?; **wieso ~?** why?, how come?; **warum ~ nicht?** why not?; **wie gehts ~?** how are you *or* things then?, how's it going then?; **wo bleibt er ~?** where has he got to?; **was soll das ~?** what's all this then?; **das ist ~ doch die Höhe!** (well,) that really is the limit! **b** *(N Ger inf: = dann)* then; **na, ~ man los!** right then, let's go!; **na, ~ prost!** well, cheers (then)

den|noch ['dɛnɔx] ADV nevertheless, nonetheless, still; **~ liebte er sie** yet he still loved her, he loved her nevertheless; **er hat es ~ getan** (but *or* yet) he still did it, he did it nonetheless *or* nevertheless; **und ~, …** and yet …; **schön und ~ hässlich** beautiful and yet ugly

De|no|mi|na|tiv [de:nomina'ti:f] NT **-s, -e** [-və] *(Ling)* denominative

De|no|tat [deno'ta:t] NT **-s, -e** *(Ling)* denotation

De|no|ta|ti|on [denota'tsio:n] F *(Ling)* denotation

den|sel|ben [de:n'zɛlbn] DEM PRON *acc von* **derselbe** *dat von* **dieselben**

den|tal [dɛn'ta:l] ADJ *(Med, Ling)* dental

Den|tal(laut) [dɛn'ta:l-] M **-s, -e** *(Ling)* dental

Den|tal|la|bor [dɛn'ta:l-] NT *(Med)* dental laboratory

Den|tist [dɛn'tɪst] M **-en, -en, Den|tis|tin** [-'tɪstɪn] F **-, -nen** *(dated)* dentist

De|nun|zi|ant [denʊn'tsiant] M **-en, -en, De|nun|zi|an|tin** [-'tsiantɪn] F **-, -nen** *(pej)* informer

De|nun|zi|an|ten|tum [denʊn'tsiantntu:m] NT **-s,** *no pl (pej)* informing

De|nun|zi|a|ti|on [denʊntsia'tsio:n] F **-, -en** *(pej)* informing *no pl* *(von* on, against); *(= Anzeige)* denunciation *(von* of)

de|nun|zie|ren [denʊn'tsi:rən] *ptp* **denunziert** VT *(pej)* **a** *(= verraten)* to inform on *or* against, to denounce *(bei* to) **b** *(geh: = verunglimpfen)* to denounce, to condemn

Deo ['de:o] NT **-(s), -s** *abbr von* **Deodorant**

De|o|do|rant [delodo'rant] NT **-s, -s** *or* **-e** deodorant

De|o|do|rant|spray NT OR M deodorant spray

de|o|do|rie|rend [delodo'ri:rənt] ADJ deodorant

Deo-: **Deo|rol|ler** M roll-on (deodorant); **Deo|spray** NT OR M deodorant spray; **Deo|stift** M stick deodorant

De|par|te|ment [departə'mã:] NT -s, -s *(esp Sw)* department

De|pen|dance [depã'dã:s] F -, -n **a** *(geh)* branch **b** *(= Hoteldependance)* annexe *(Brit)*, annex *(US)*

De|pen|denz [depɛn'dɛnts] F -, -en *(Philos)* dependence

De|pen|denz|gram|ma|tik F dependence grammar

De|per|so|na|li|sa|ti|on [depɛrzonaliza'tsio:n] F -, -en *(Psych)* depersonalization

De|pe|sche [de'pɛʃə] F -, -n *(dated)* dispatch

de|pla|ciert [depla'si:ɐt] ADJ *(old)* = **deplatziert**

de|plat|ziert [depla'tsi:ɐt], **de|pla|ziert** △ [depla'tsi:ɐt] ADJ out of place

De|po|nie [depo'ni:] F -, -n [-'ni:ən] dump, disposal site

de|po|nie|ren [depo'ni:rən] *ptp* **deponiert** VT *(geh)* to deposit

De|po|nie|rung F -, -en *(geh)* depository

De|por|ta|ti|on [depɔrta'tsio:n] F -, -en deportation

de|por|tie|ren [depɔr'ti:rən] *ptp* **deportiert** VT to deport

De|por|tier|te(r) [depɔr'ti:ɐtə] MF *decl as adj* deportee

De|po|si|tar [depozi'ta:ɐ] M -s, -e, **De|po|si|ta|rin** [-'ta:rɪn] F -, -nen, **De|po|si|tär** [depozi'tɛ:ɐ] M -s, -e, **De|po|si|tä|rin** [-'tɛ:rɪn] F -, -nen *(Fin)* depositary

De|po|si|ten [depo'zi:tn] PL *(Fin)* deposits *pl*

De|po|si|ten- *(Fin)*: **De|po|si|ten|bank** F *pl* -banken deposit bank; **De|po|si|ten|gel|der** PL deposits *pl*, deposit(ed) money; **De|po|si|ten|ge|schäft** NT deposit banking; **De|po|si|ten|kon|to** NT deposit account

De|pot [de'po:] NT -s, -s **a** depot; *(= Aufbewahrungsort auch, Wertpapierdepot)* depository; *(in Bank)* strongroom; *(= Wertpapierkonto)* securities account; *(= aufbewahrte Gegenstände)* deposits *pl*; *(= Guthaben)* deposit; *(= Schließfach)* safety deposit box; *(Med)* deposit **b** *(Sw: = Pfand)* deposit

De|pot-: **De|pot|aus|zug** M *(Fin)* statement of deposited securities; **De|pot|be|hand|lung** F *(Med)* depot treatment; **De|pot|ef|fekt** M *(Pharm)* controlled release; **De|pot|fett** NT *(Med)* adipose fat; **De|pot|ge|bühr** F *(Fin)* safe custody charge(s *pl*); **De|pot|ge|schäft** NT *(Fin)* security deposit business; **De|pot|stimm|recht** NT *(Fin)* voting power for deposited shares

Depp [dɛp] M -en *or* -s, -e(n) *(S Ger, Aus, Sw: pej)* twit *(inf)*

dep|pert ['dɛpɐt] *(S Ger, Aus: inf)* ADJ dopey *(inf)* ADV **sich ~ benehmen** to be dopey *(inf)*; **~ fragen** to ask dopey questions *(inf)*; **~ schauen** to have a dopey look on one's face *(inf)*

dep|ra|viert [depra'vi:ɐt] ADJ *(geh)* depraved

De|pres|si|on [deprɛ'sio:n] F *(alle Bedeutungen)* depression; **~en haben** to suffer from depression

de|pres|siv [deprɛ'si:f] ADJ depressive; *(Econ)* depressed

De|pres|si|vi|tät [deprɛsivi'tɛ:t] F -, *no pl* depressiveness

de|pri|mie|ren [depri'mi:rən] *ptp* **deprimiert** VT to depress

de|pri|mie|rend ADJ depressing ADV depressingly

de|pri|miert [depri'mi:ɐt] ADJ depressed

De|pri|miert|heit F -, *no pl* depression

De|pri|va|ti|on [depriva'tsio:n] F -, -en *(Psych)* deprivation

de|pri|vie|ren [depri'vi:rən] *ptp* **depriviert** VT *(Psych)* to deprive

De|pu|tat [depu'ta:t] NT -(e)s, -e **a** *(esp Agr)* payment in kind **b** *(Sch)* teaching load

De|pu|ta|ti|on [deputa'tsio:n] F -, -en deputation

de|pu|tie|ren [depu'ti:rən] *ptp* **deputiert** VT to deputize

De|pu|tier|ten|kam|mer F *(Pol)* Chamber of Deputies

De|pu|tier|te(r) [depu'ti:ɐtə] MF *decl as adj* deputy

der [de:ɐ] DEF ART **a** *gen sing, pl von* **die** of the; **das Miauen ~ Katze** the miaowing of the cat, the cat's miaowing **b** *dat sing von* **die** to the; *(mit Präposition)* the DEM PRON *dat sing von* **die** **a** *(adjektivisch)* to that; *(mit Präpositionen)* that **b** *(substantivisch)* to her; her REL PRON *dat sing von* **die** to whom, that *or* who(m) … to; *(mit Präposition)* who(m); *(von Sachen)* to which, which … to; which

der [de:ɐ], **die, das** *pl* **die** DEF ART *gen* **des, der, des**, *pl* **der**; *dat* **dem, der, dem**, *pl* **den**; *acc* **den, die, das**, *pl* **die** the; **~/die Arme!** the poor man/woman *or* girl; **die Toten** the dead *pl*; **die Engländer** the English *pl*; **~ Engländer** *(dated inf: = die Engländer)* the Englishman; **~ Faust** Faust; **~ Hans** *(inf)* Hans; **~ kleine Hans** little Hans; **~ Rhein** the Rhine; **~ Michigansee** Lake Michigan; **die Domstraße** Cathedral Street; **die „Bismarck"** the "Bismarck"; **~ Lehrer/die Frau** *(im Allgemeinen)* teachers *pl*/women *pl*; **~ Tod/die Liebe/das Leben** death/love/life; **~ Tod des Sokrates** the death of Socrates; **das Viktorianische England** Victorian England; **in dem England, das ich kannte** in the England (that *or* which) I knew; **er liebt den Jazz/die Oper/das Kino** he likes jazz/(the) opera/the cinema; **das Singen macht ihm Freude** singing gives him pleasure; **das Singen meines Opas** my grandpa's singing; **mir fiel das Atmen schwer** I found breathing difficult; **das Herstellen von Waffen ist …** manufacturing weapons is …, the manufacturing of weapons is …; **die Callas** Callas; **~ spätere Wittgenstein** the later Wittgenstein; **er war nicht mehr ~ Hans, ~ …** he was no longer the Hans who …; **er hat sich den Fuß verletzt** he has hurt his foot; **wascht euch** *(dat)* **mal das Gesicht!** wash your faces; **er nimmt den Hut ab** he takes his hat off; **ein Euro das Stück** one euro apiece *or* each; **20 Euro die Stunde** 20 euros an *or* per hour; **~ und ~ Wissenschaftler** such and such a scientist

DEM PRON *gen* **dessen** *or (old)* **des, deren, dessen**, *pl* **deren**; *dat* **dem, der, dem**, *pl* **denen**; *acc* **den, die, das**, *pl* **die** **a** *(attr) (= jener, dieser)* that; *(pl)* those, them *(inf)*; **zu ~ und ~ Zeit** at such and such a time; **an dem und dem Ort** at such and such a place

b *(substantivisch)* he/she/it; *(pl)* those, them *(inf)*; **~/die war es** it was him/her; **~/die mit ~ großen Nase** the one *or* him/her *(inf)* with the big nose; **die** *pl* **mit den roten Haaren** those *or* them *(inf)* with red hair; **deine Schwester, die war nicht da** *(inf)* your sister, she wasn't there; **~ und schwimmen?** him, swimming?, swimming, (what) him?; **~/die hier** *(von Menschen)* he/she, this man/woman *etc*; *(von Gegenständen)* this (one); *(von mehreren)* this one; **~/die da** *(von Menschen)* he/she, that man/woman *etc*; *(von Gegenständen)* that (one); *(von mehreren)* that one; **die hier/da** *pl* they, these/those men/women *etc*, these/those, them *(inf)*; **~, den ich meine** the one I mean; **~ und ~/die und die** so-and-so; **das und das** such and such

REL PRON *decl as dem pron (Mensch)* who, that; *(Gegenstand, Tier)* which, that

REL + DEM PRON *decl as dem pron* **~/die dafür verantwortlich war, …** the man/woman who was responsible for it; **die so etwas tun, …** those *or* people who do that sort of thing …

de|ran|giert [derã'ʒi:ɐt] ADJ *(geh) Kleidung* untidy, messed up; *Haar auch* dishevelled *(Brit)*, disheveled *(US)*, mussed up *(inf)*

der|art ['de:ɐ'la:ɐt] ADV **a** *(Art und Weise)* in such a way; **er hat sich ~ benommen, dass …** he behaved so badly that …; **sein Benehmen war ~, dass …** his behaviour *(Brit) or* behavior *(US)* was so bad that …; **~ vorbereitet, …** thus prepared … **b** *(Ausmaß) (vor adj)* so; *(vor vb)* so much, to such an extent; **ein ~ unzuverlässiger Mensch** such an unreliable person, so unreliable a person; **er hat mich ~ geärgert, dass …** he annoyed me so much that …; **es hat ~ geregnet, dass …** it rained so much that …

der|ar|tig ['de:ɐ'la:ɐtɪç] ADJ such, of that kind; **bei ~en Versuchen** in such experiments, in experiments of that kind; **(etwas) Derartiges** something like that, something of the kind ADV = **derart**

derb [dɛrp] ADJ **a** *(= kräftig)* strong; *Stoff, Leder auch* tough; *Schuhe auch* stout; *Kost* coarse **b** *(= grob)* coarse; *Manieren, Kerl auch* uncouth; *Sprache, Witz, Ausdrucksweise* crude **c** *(= unfreundlich)* gruff ADV **a** *(= heftig)* roughly; **jdn ~ anfassen** to manhandle sb; *(fig)* to be rough with sb **b** *(= grob)* crudely; **um mich einmal ~ auszudrücken …** to put it crudely …

Derb|heit F -, -en **a** *(= Kräftigkeit)* strength; *(von Stoff, Leder)* toughness, strength **b** *(= Grobheit)* coarseness; *(von Manieren, Kerl)* uncouthness, coarseness; *(von Witz, Sprache, Ausdrucksweise)* crudeness; **~en** crudities **c** *(= Unfreundlichkeit)* gruffness

Der|by ['dɛrbi] NT -s, -s horse race for three-year-olds, derby *(US)*; *(fig: = sportliche Begegnung)* derby; **das (englische) ~** the Derby

Der|by|ren|nen NT = **Derby**

de|re|gu|lie|ren [deregu'li:rən] *ptp* **dereguliert** VT *(Econ)* to deregulate

De|re|gu|lie|rung F *(Econ)* deregulation

der|einst [de:ɐ'lainst] ADV *(liter)* **a** *(= in der Zukunft)* one day **b** *(rare: = früher)* at one time, once

der|eins|tig [de:ɐ'lainstɪç] ADJ *(liter)* **a** *(= künftig)* future, tomorrow's; **im ~en vereinten Europa** in tomorrow's united Europe, in the united Europe of tomorrow **b** *(= damalig)* of former times

de|ren ['de:rən] DEM PRON *gen pl von* **der, die, das** their REL PRON **a** *gen sing von* **die** whose **b** *gen pl von* **der, die, das** whose, of whom; *(von Sachen)* of which

de|rent|hal|ben ['de:rənt'halbn] *(dated)* ADV = **derentwegen**

de|rent|we|gen ['de:rənt've:gn] ADV *(= weswegen)* because of whom, on whose account; *(von Sachen)* because of which, on account of which; *(= welcher zuliebe auch)* for whose sake; *(von Sachen)* for the sake of which; *(= um welche)* about whom; *(von Sachen)* about which; *(= für welche)* on whose behalf

de|rent|wil|len ['de:rənt'vɪlən] ADV **a** **um ~** *(rel)* for whose sake; *(von Sachen)* for the sake of which **b** **um ~** *(dem) (sing)* for her/its sake; *(pl)* for their sake

de|rer ['de:rɐ] DEM PRON *gen pl von* **der, die, das** of those; **das Geschlecht ~ von Hohenstein** *(geh)* the von Hohenstein family

de|ret- *in cpds* = **derent-**

der|ge|stalt ['de:ɐgə'ʃtalt] ADV *(geh)* in such a way; *(Ausmaß)* to such an extent; **~ ausgerüstet, …** thus equipped …; **dann gab er dem Pferde die Sporen ~, dass …** then he spurred his horse on so forcefully that …

der|glei|chen ['de:ɐ'glaiçn] *inv* DEM PRON **a** *(adjektivisch)* of that kind, such, like that; **~ Dinge** things of that kind, things like that, such things **b** *(substantivisch)* that sort of thing; **nichts ~** nothing of that kind, nothing like it; **er tat nichts ~** he did nothing of the kind; **und ~ (mehr)** and suchlike REL PRON *(old)* of the kind that; **Juwelen, ~ man selten sieht** jewels whose like *or* the like of which one rarely sees

De|ri|vat [deri'va:t] NT -(e)s, -e *(Chem, Ling, Fin)* derivative

De|ri|va|ti|on [deriva'tsio:n] F -, -en *(Ling)* derivation

De|ri|va|tiv [deriva'ti:f] NT -s, -e [-və] *(Ling)* derivative

der|je|ni|ge ['de:ɐje:nɪgə], **die|je|ni|ge, das|je|ni|ge** *pl* **diejenigen** DEM PRON **a** *(substantivisch)* the one; *(pl)* those; **sie ist immer diejenige, welche** *(inf)* it's always her; **du warst also ~, welcher!** *(inf)* so it was you!, so you're the one! **b** *(adjektivisch)* the; *(pl)* those

der|lei ['de:ɐ'lai] DEM PRON *inv* **a** *(adjektivisch)* such, like that, that kind of; **~ Probleme** problems like that, that kind of problems, such problems **b** *(substantivisch)* that sort *or* kind of thing; **und ~ (mehr)** and suchlike

der|mal|en ['de:ɐma:lən, de:ɐ'ma:lən] ADV *(old, Aus form)* presently, at present, now

der|ma|lig ['de:ɐma:lɪç, de:ɐ'ma:lɪç] ADJ *(old, Aus form)* present, actual

der|ma|ßen ['de:ɐ'ma:sn] ADV *(mit adj)* so; *(mit vb)* so much; **~ dumm** so stupid; **ein ~ dummer Kerl** such a stupid fellow; **sie hatte ~ Angst, dass ...** she was so afraid that ...; **er hat sich geärgert und zwar ~, dass ...** he was angry, so much so that ...

Der|ma|to|lo|ge [dɛrmato'lo:gə] M -en, -en, **Der|ma|to|lo|gin** [-'lo:gɪn] F -, -nen dermatologist

Der|ma|to|lo|gie [dɛrmatolo'gi:] F -, *no pl* dermatology

Der|ma|to|plas|tik [dɛrmato'plastɪk] F plastic surgery, dermatoplasty *(spec)*

Der|nier Cri [dɛrnje 'kri] M - -, -s -s dernier cri

de|ro ['de:ro] POSS PRON *(obs)* her; *(pl)* their; **Dero Gnaden** Your Grace

der|sel|be [de:ɐ'zɛlbə], **die|sel|be, das|sel|be** *pl* **dieselben** DEM PRON **a** *(substantivisch)* the same; *(old: = er, sie, es)* he/she/it; *(inf: = der, die, das gleiche)* the same; **er sagt in jeder Vorlesung dasselbe** he says the same (thing) in every lecture; **jedes Jahr kriegen dieselben mehr Geld** every year the same people get more money; **sie ist immer noch ganz dieselbe** she is still exactly the same; **es sind immer dieselben** it's always the same ones *or* people; **noch mal dasselbe, bitte!** *(inf)* same again, please **b** *(adjektivisch)* the same; **ein und ~ Mensch** one and the same person

der|sel|bi|ge *etc* [de:ɐ'zɛlbɪgə] DEM PRON *(old)* = **derselbe** *etc*

der|weil ['de:ɐ'vail], **der|wei|len** ['de:ɐ'vailən] ADV in the meantime, meanwhile CONJ *(old)* whilst, while

Der|wisch ['dɛrvɪʃ] M -es, -e dervish

der|zeit ['de:ɐ'tsait] ADV **a** *(= jetzt)* at present, at the moment **b** *(dated: = damals)* at that *or* the time, then

der|zei|tig ['de:ɐ'tsaitɪç] ADJ *attr* **a** *(= jetzig)* present, current **b** *(dated: = damalig)* of that *or* the time

des [dɛs] DEF ART **a** *gen von* **der, das** of the; **das Bellen ~ Hundes** the barking of the dog, the dog's barking **b** *(old)* = **dessen**

des [dɛs] NT -, -, **Des** NT -, - *(Mus)* D flat

De|sas|ter [de'zastɐ] NT -s, - disaster

de|sas|trös [deza'strø:s] ADJ *(geh)* disastrous

des|avou|ie|ren [dɛslavu'i:rən, deza-] *ptp* **desavouiert** VT *(geh)* to disavow; *Bemühungen, Pläne* to compromise

De|sen|si|bi|li|sa|tor [dezɛnzibili'za:to:ɐ] M *(Phot)* desensitizer

de|sen|si|bi|li|sie|ren [dezɛnzibili'zi:rən] *ptp* **desensibilisiert** VT *(Phot, Med)* to desensitize

De|ser|teur [dezɛr'tø:ɐ] M -s, -e, **De|ser|teu|rin** [-'tø:rɪn] F -, -nen *(Mil, fig)* deserter

de|ser|tie|ren [dezɛr'ti:rən] *ptp* **desertiert** VI *aux sein or (rare) haben (Mil, fig)* to desert

De|ser|ti|on [dezɛr'tsio:n] F -, -en *(Mil, fig)* desertion

des|glei|chen ['dɛs'glaiçn] ADV *(= ebenso)* likewise, also; **er ist Vegetarier, ~ seine Frau** he is a vegetarian, as is his wife DEM PRON *inv (old: = dasselbe)* the same; **~ habe ich noch nie gehört** I have never heard the like REL PRON *inv (old)* the like of which

des|halb ['dɛs'halp] ADV CONJ therefore; *(= aus diesem Grunde, darüber)* because of that; *(= dafür)* for that; **es ist schon spät, ~ wollen wir anfangen** it is late, so let us start; **~ bin ich hergekommen** that is what I came here for, that is why I came here; **ich bin ~ hergekommen, weil ich dich sprechen wollte** what I came here for was to speak to you, the reason I came here was that I wanted to speak to you; **~ also!** so that's why *or* the reason!; **~ muss er nicht dumm sein** that does not (necessarily) mean (to say) he is stupid; **~ frage ich ja** that's exactly why I'm asking

de|si|de|ra|bel [dezide'ra:bl] ADJ *(geh)* desirable

De|si|de|rat [dezide'ra:t] NT -(e)s, -e, **De|si|de|ra|tum** [dezide'ra:tʊm] NT -s, **Desiderata** [-ta] desideratum; *(= Anschaffungsvorschlag)* suggestion

De|sign [di'zain] NT -s, -s design

De|sig|nat [dezɪ'gna:t] NT -(e)s, -e *(Philos, Ling)* referendum

De|sig|na|ti|on [dezɪgna'tsio:n] F -, -en designation

De|sig|na|tor [dezɪ'gna:to:ɐ] M -s, **Designatoren** [-'to:rən] *(Philos, Ling)* referens

de|sig|nen [di'zainən] *ptp* **designt** [di'zaint] VT to design

De|sig|ner [di'zainɐ] M -s, -, **De|sig|ne|rin** [di'zainərɪn] F -, -nen designer

De|sig|ner- *in cpds* designer *attr;* **De|sig|ner|bril|le** F designer glasses *pl or* spectacles *pl,* designer specs *pl (inf);* **De|sig|ner|dro|ge** F designer drug; **De|sig|ner|food** NT designer food; **De|sig|ner|jeans** PL designer jeans *pl;* **De|sig|ner|kla|mot|ten** PL designer clothes *pl;* **De|sig|ner|la|bel** NT designer label; **De|sig|ner|mö|bel** PL designer furniture *sing;* **De|sig|ner|mo|de** F designer fashion

de|sig|nie|ren [dezɪ'gni:rən] *ptp* **designiert** VT to designate *(jdn zu etw* sb as sth)

de|sig|niert [dezɪ'gni:ɐt] ADJ *attr* **der ~e Vorsitzende** the chairman elect *or* designate

des|il|lu|si|o|nie|ren [dɛsɪluzio'ni:rən, dezɪ-] *ptp* **desillusioniert** VT to disillusion

Des|il|lu|si|o|nie|rung F -, -en disillusionment

Des|in|fek|ti|on [dɛsɪnfɛk'tsio:n, dezɪ-] F disinfection

Des|in|fek|ti|ons-: Des|in|fek|ti|ons|lö|sung F antiseptic solution; **Des|in|fek|ti|ons|mit|tel** NT disinfectant

des|in|fi|zie|ren [dɛsɪnfi'tsi:rən, dezɪ-] *ptp* **desinfiziert** VT *Zimmer, Bett etc* to disinfect; *Spritze, Gefäß etc* to sterilize

des|in|fi|zie|rend *prp von* **desinfizieren** ADJ disinfectant; **eine ~e Wirkung haben** to act as a disinfectant

Des|in|fi|zie|rung F -, -en *(von Zimmer, Bett)* disinfection; *(von Spritze, Gefäß)* sterilization

Des|in|for|ma|ti|on [dɛsɪnfɔrma'tsio:n, dezɪ-] F *(Pol)* disinformation *no pl*

Des|in|for|ma|ti|ons|kam|pag|ne F campaign of disinformation

Des|in|teg|ra|ti|on [dɛsɪntegra'tsio:n, dezɪ-] F *(Sociol, Psych)* disintegration

Des|in|te|res|se [dɛsɪntə'rɛsə, dezɪ-] NT lack of interest *(an +dat* in)

des|in|te|res|siert [dɛsɪntərɛ'si:ɐt, dezɪ-] ADJ uninterested; *Gesicht* bored

De|skrip|ti|on [deskrɪp'tsio:n] F *(geh)* -, -en description

de|skrip|tiv [deskrɪp'ti:f] ADJ descriptive

Desk|top ['dɛsktɔp] M -(s), -s *(Comput)* desktop

Desk|top-Pub|li|shing ['dɛsktɔp'pablɪʃɪŋ] NT -, *no pl,* **Desk|top|pub|li|shing** NT -, *no pl* desktop publishing, DTP

Des|odo|rant [dɛslodo'rant, dezo-] NT -s, -s *or* -e deodorant

de|so|lat [dezo'la:t] ADJ *(geh)* desolate; *Zustand, wirtschaftliche Lage* desperate; **die ~en Staatsfinanzen** the desperate state of the public finances

Des|or|ga|ni|sa|ti|on [dɛslɔrganiza'tsio:n, dezɔ-] F disorganization; *(= Auflösung auch)* disruption; **auf der Tagung herrschte eine völlige ~** there was complete chaos at the conference

des|or|ga|ni|sie|ren [dɛslɔrgani'zi:rən, dezɔ-] *ptp* **desorganisiert** VT to disorganize

des|ori|en|tie|ren [dɛslorien'ti:rən, dezo-] *ptp* **desorientiert** VT to disorient(ate)

Des|ori|en|tiert|heit F -, *no pl,* **Des|ori|en|tie|rung** F disorientation

Des|oxy|ri|bo|nuk|le|in|säu|re [dɛslɔksyribonukle'i:nzɔyrə, dezɔ-] F *(abbr* **DNS**) deoxyribonucleic acid, DNA

des|pek|tier|lich [despɛk'ti:ɐlɪç] ADJ *(old, hum)* disrespectful

Des|pek|tier|lich|keit F -, -en *(old, hum)* disrespect; **~en** disrespectful comments

Des|pe|ra|do [dɛspe'ra:do] M -s, -s desperado

des|pe|rat [dɛspe'ra:t] ADJ *(geh)* desperate

Des|pe|ra|ti|on [dɛspera'tsio:n] F -, -en *(geh)* desperation

Des|pot [dɛs'po:t] M -en, -en, **Des|po|tin** [-'po:tɪn] F -, -nen despot

Des|po|tie [dɛspo'ti:] F -, -n [-'ti:ən] despotism

des|po|tisch [dɛs'po:tɪʃ] ADJ despotic ADV despotically

Des|po|tis|mus [dɛspo'tɪsmʊs] M -, *no pl* despotism

des|sel|ben [dɛs'zɛlbn] DEM PRON *gen von* **derselbe, dasselbe**

des|sen ['dɛsn] DEM PRON *gen von* **der**, *von* **das** his; *(von Sachen, Tieren)* its REL PRON *gen von* **der**, *von* **das** whose; *(von Sachen)* of which, which ... of; **~ ungeachtet** *(geh)* nevertheless, notwithstanding (this)

des|sent|hal|ben ['dɛsnt'halbn] *(dated),* **des|sent|we|gen** ['dɛsnt've:gn] = **derenthalben** *etc*

des|sent|wil|len ['dɛsnt'vɪlən] ADV **a um ~** *(rel)* for whose sake **b um ~** *(dem)* for his/its sake

des|sen|un|ge|ach|tet △ ['dɛsnlʊngə'laxtət, 'dɛsn'lʊngəlaxtət] ADV → **dessen REL PRON**

Des|sert [dɛ'se:ɐ] NT -s, -s dessert

Des|sert- *in cpds* dessert; **Des|sert|löf|fel** M dessertspoon; **Des|sert|wein** M dessert *or* pudding wine

Des|sin [dɛ'sɛ̃:] NT -s, -s *(Tex)* pattern, design

Des|sous [dɛ'su:] NT -, - [dɛ'su:s] *usu pl (dated)* undergarment, underwear *no pl*

de|sta|bi|li|sie|ren [destabili'zi:rən, -ʃt-] *ptp* **destabilisiert** VT to destabilize

De|sta|bi|li|sie|rung F -, -en destabilization

Des|til|lat [dɛstɪ'la:t] NT -(e)s, -e *(Chem)* distillation, distillate; *(fig)* distillation

Des|til|la|teur [dɛstɪla'tø:ɐ] M -s, -e, **Des|til|la|teu|rin** [-'tø:rɪn] F -, -nen distiller

Des|til|la|ti|on [dɛstɪla'tsio:n] F -, -en **a** *(Chem)* distillation **b** *(= Branntweinbrennerei)* distillery **c** *(dated dial: = Großgaststätte)* drinking establishment, ≈ gin palace *(old),* ≈ brandy shop *(old)*

Des|til|la|ti|ons-: Des|til|la|ti|ons|an|la|ge F distilling *or* distillation plant; **Des|til|la|ti|ons|pro|dukt** NT distillate

Des|til|le [dɛs'tɪlə] F -, -n **a** *(dial inf: = Gaststätte)* (big) pub *(Brit),* bar **b** *(= Brennerei)* distillery

des|til|lie|ren [dɛstɪ'li:rən] *ptp* **destilliert** VT to distil *(Brit),* to distill *(US); (fig)* to condense

Des|til|lier|kol|ben [dɛstɪ'li:ɐ-] M *(Chem)* retort

des|to ['dɛsto] CONJ **~ mehr/besser** all the more/better; **~ grausamer** all the more cruel; **~ schneller** all the faster; **~ wahrscheinlicher ist es, dass wir ...** that makes it all the more probable that we ... → **je CONJ a**

De|struk|ti|on [destrʊk'tsio:n] F -, -en destruction

De|struk|ti|ons|trieb M *(Psych)* destructive instinct

de|struk|tiv [destrʊk'ti:f] ADJ destructive

De|struk|ti|vi|tät [destrʊktiviˈtɛːt] F -, no pl destructiveness

des|un|ge|ach|tet △ [ˈdɛslʊngəˈlaxtət, ˈdɛsˈlʊngəlaxtət] ADV (old) = **dessen ungeachtet**, → **dessen REL PRON**

des|we|gen [ˈdɛsˈveːgn] ADV = **deshalb**

des|zen|dent [destsɛnˈdɛnt] ADJ (Astron) descendent (spec), setting

Des|zen|dent [destsɛnˈdɛnt] M **-en, -en im ~en sein** (Astrol) to be in the descendent

Des|zen|denz [destsɛnˈdɛnts] F -, **-en** **a** (= Abstammung) descent; (= Nachkommenschaft) descendants pl **b** (Astron) descendence (spec), setting

Des|zen|denz|the|o|rie F (Biol) theory of evolution

des|zen|die|ren [destsɛnˈdiːrən] ptp **deszendiert** VI aux sein (Astron, liter) to descend

De|tail [deˈtai, deˈtaːj] NT **-s, -s** detail; (= Filmeinstellung) big close-up; **ins ~ gehen** to go into detail(s); **im ~** in detail; **bis ins kleinste ~** (right) down to the smallest or last detail; **in allen ~s** in the greatest detail; **etw mit allen ~s berichten** to report sth in full detail, to give a fully detailed account of sth; **die Schwierigkeiten liegen im ~** it is the details that are most difficult → **Teufel b**

De|tail-: **De|tail|be|richt** M detailed report; **De|tail|fra|ge** F question of detail; **de|tail|ge|nau, de|tail|ge|treu** ADJ accurate in every detail pred, accurate down to the last detail pred ADV **etw ~ nachbauen** to make or build an exact or a faithful copy of sth; **De|tail|han|del** M (dated) = **Einzelhandel**; **De|tail|händ|ler(in)** M(F) (dated) retailer, retail trader; **De|tail|kennt|nis|se** PL detailed knowledge no pl

de|tail|lie|ren [detaˈjiːrən] ptp **detailliert** VT (= genau beschreiben) to specify, to give full particulars of; **etw genauer ~** to specify sth more precisely

de|tail|liert [detaˈjiːɐt] ADJ detailed ADV in detail; **~er** in greater or more detail

De|tail|liert|heit F -, no pl detail

De|tail-: **de|tail|reich** ADJ highly detailed ADV **etw ~ schildern** to describe sth in great detail; **De|tail|reich|tum** M wealth of detail; **De|tail|schil|de|rung** F detailed account; **die beiden Versionen unterscheiden sich in der ~** the two versions differ in their account of the details; **De|tail|ver|kauf** M (dated Comm) retail sale; (= das Verkaufen) retailing, retail selling; **De|tail|zeich|nung** F detail drawing

De|tek|tei [detɛkˈtai] F -, **-en** (private) detective agency, firm of (private) investigators; **„Detektei R. B. von Halske"** "R.B. von Halske, private investigator"

De|tek|tiv [detɛkˈtiːf] M **-s, -e** [-və], **De|tek|ti|vin** [-ˈtiːvɪn] F -, **-nen** private investigator or detective or eye (inf)

De|tek|tiv|bü|ro NT = **Detektei**

de|tek|ti|visch [detɛkˈtiːvɪʃ] ADJ Arbeit, Aufgabe detective attr; **man braucht dazu ~en Scharfsinn/~e Neugierde** you need the astuteness/inquisitiveness of a detective for this; **in ~er Kleinarbeit** with detailed detective work ADV like a detective; aufdecken through detailed detective work; **bei etw ~ vorgehen** to go about sth like a detective

De|tek|tiv|ro|man M detective novel

De|tek|tor [deˈtɛktoːɐ] M **-s, Detektoren** [-ˈtoːrən] (Tech) detector

De|tek|tor|emp|fän|ger M (Rad) crystal set

Dé|tente [deˈtãːt] F -, no pl (rare: Pol) détente

De|ter|mi|nan|te [detɛrmiˈnantə] F -, **-n** (Math, Biol) determinant

de|ter|mi|nie|ren [detɛrmiˈniːrən] ptp **determiniert** VT to (pre)determine; (Gram) to govern

De|ter|mi|nis|mus [detɛrmiˈnɪsmʊs] M -, no pl (Philos) determinism

De|ter|mi|nist [detɛrmiˈnɪst] M **-en, -en**, **De|ter|mi|nis|tin** [-ˈnɪstɪn] F -, **-nen** (Philos) determinist

de|ter|mi|nis|tisch [detɛrmiˈnɪstɪʃ] ADJ (Philos) deterministic

De|to|na|ti|on [detonaˈtsioːn] F -, **-en** explosion, blast; **etw (acc) zur ~ bringen** to detonate sth

De|to|na|ti|ons|wel|le F blast, shock wave(s pl); (Auswirkung) impact of the blast

de|to|nie|ren [detoˈniːrən] ptp **detoniert** VI aux sein to explode, to go off

Deu|bel [ˈdɔybl] M **-s, -** (dial) = **Teufel**

deucht [dɔyçt] 3. pers sing pres von **dünken**

De|us ex Ma|chi|na [ˈdeːʊs ɛks ˈmaxina] M - -, **Dei - -** [ˈdeːi] (rare) deus ex machina

Deut [dɔyt] M **um keinen ~** not one jot (Brit) or iota; **seine Ratschläge sind keinen ~ wert** his advice is not worth tuppence (Brit) or a dime (US); **er versteht nicht einen ~ davon** he does not know the first thing about it; **daran ist kein ~ wahr** there is not a grain of truth in it; **du bist keinen ~ besser** you're not one jot (Brit) or iota better

deut|bar ADJ interpretable; **..., ob Nietzsche theologisch ~ ist** ... whether Nietzsche can be interpreted or understood theologically; **nicht/schwer ~** impossible/difficult to interpret; **es ist nicht anders ~** it cannot be explained in any other way

Deu|te|lei [dɔytəˈlai] F -, **-en** (pej geh) quibbling, quibbles pl, cavilling (Brit), caviling (US)

deu|teln [ˈdɔytln] VI (geh) to quibble, to cavil; **an jedem Wort ~** to quibble over every word; **daran gibt es nichts zu ~!** there are no ifs and buts about it! (Brit), there are no ifs, ands or buts about it! (US)

deu|ten [ˈdɔytn] VT (= auslegen) to interpret; Zukunft auch to read; **sich (dat) etw ~** (geh) to understand sth; **etw falsch ~** to misinterpret sth VI **a** (= zeigen) **(mit dem Finger) auf etw** (acc) **~** to point (one's finger) at sth **b** (fig: = hinweisen) to indicate; **alles deutet auf Regen/Schnee** all the signs are that it is going to rain/snow, everything points to rain/snow; **alles deutet darauf, dass ...** all the indications are that ..., everything indicates that ...

Deu|ter [ˈdɔytɐ] M **-s, -** (Aus: = Wink) sign

Deu|ter [ˈdɔytɐ] M **-s, -**, **Deu|te|rin** [-ərɪn] F -, **-nen** interpreter

deut|lich [ˈdɔytlɪç] ADJ **a** (= klar) clear **b** (= unmissverständlich) clear, plain; **eine ~e Sprache mit jdm reden** to speak plainly or bluntly with sb; **~ werden** to make oneself clear or plain; **das war ~!** (= taktlos) that was clear or plain enough; **muss ich ~er werden?** have I not made myself clear or plain enough?
ADV **a** (= klar) sehen, unterscheiden, sprechen clearly; erkennbar, hörbar, wahrnehmbar clearly, plainly; **~ zu erkennen/sehen/hören** easy to recognize/see/hear; **~ fühlen** to feel distinctly; **ich fühle ~, dass ...** I have the distinct feeling that ...
b (= unmissverständlich) sich ausdrücken, sagen explicitly; **jdm etw ~ vor Augen führen** to make sth perfectly clear or plain to sb; **sich ~ ausdrücken** to make oneself clear or plain; **ich muss es einmal ~ sagen** let me make myself perfectly clear; **jdm ~ zu verstehen geben, dass ...** to make it clear or plain to sb that ...

Deut|lich|keit F -, no pl clarity; **etw mit aller ~ sagen** to make sth perfectly clear or plain; **seine Antwort ließ an ~ nichts zu wünschen übrig** his answer was perfectly clear or plain and left no possible doubt

deut|lich|keits|hal|ber ADV for the sake of clarity

deutsch [dɔytʃ] ADJ **a** German; **~e Schrift** Gothic script; **Deutscher Schäferhund** Alsatian (Brit), German shepherd; **~e Gründlichkeit** etc German or Teutonic efficiency etc; **die Deutsche Bucht** the German Bight; **Deutsche Mark** (Hist) Deutschmark, German mark; **der Deutsche Orden** (Hist) the Teutonic Order (of Knights)
b (in Bezug auf Sprache) German; **er hat ~ nicht englisch gesprochen** he spoke German not English; **mit jdm ~ reden** (fig inf: deutlich) to speak bluntly with sb
ADV **etw ~ aussprechen** to pronounce sth as it is said in German, to give sth a German pronunciation; **~ denken** to think in German; **sich ~ unterhalten** to speak (in) German; **der Text ist ~ geschrieben** the text is written in German

Deutsch [dɔytʃ] NT **-(s)**, dat -, no pl German; **das ~ Thomas Manns** Thomas Mann's German; **gut(es) ~ sprechen** to speak good German; (Ausländer auch) to speak German well; **~ sprechend** German-speaking; **~ lernen/verstehen** to learn/understand German; **sich auf ~ unterhalten** to speak (in) German; **auf** or **zu ~ heißt das ...** in German it means ...; **der Text ist in ~ geschrieben** the text is written in German; **der Vortrag wird in** or **auf ~ gehalten** the lecture will be given in German; **der Unterricht in ~** German lessons pl; **die Schulnote in ~** school mark (Brit) or grade (US) in or for German; **auf gut ~ (gesagt)** (fig inf) in plain English → auch **deutsch ADJ b**

Deutsch-: **Deutsch|ame|ri|ka|ner(in)** M(F) German American; **deutsch|ame|ri|ka|nisch** ADJ German-American; **deutsch-deutsch** ADJ Vereinigung etc German; **die ~e Grenze** (Hist) the intra-German border

Deutsch(e) NT **-n**, dat **-n**, no pl **a** (Ling) German; **aus dem ~en/ins ~e übersetzt** translated from/into (the) German; **das ~(e) des Mittelalters** medieval German, the German of the Middle Ages; **die Aussprache des ~en** the pronunciation of German, German pronunciation **b** (= Charakteristik) Germanness; **manchmal kommt noch das ~e in ihm durch** sometimes the German in him or his Germanness shows through

Deut|sche De|mo|kra|ti|sche Re|pub|lik F (abbr **DDR**) (Hist) German Democratic Republic, East Germany no art, GDR

Deut|schen-: **Deut|schen|feind(in)** M(F), **Deut|schen|fres|ser(in)** M(F) (inf) anti-German, Germanophobe; **Deut|schen|freund(in)** M(F) Germanophile

deutsch-eng|lisch ADJ **a** (Pol) Anglo-German **b** (Ling) German-English

Deut|schen-: **Deut|schen|hass** M Germanophobia; **Deut|schen|has|ser** [-hasɐ] M **-s, -**, **Deut|schen|has|se|rin** [-ərɪn] F -, **-nen** Germanophobe, German-hater

Deut|sche(r) [ˈdɔytʃə] MF decl as adj **er ist ~r** he is (a) German; **die ~n** the Germans; **der hässliche ~** the obnoxious German

> **DEUTSCHE WELLE**
>
> **Deutsche Welle** is a radio station controlled by the Federal Government and financed exclusively from Federal funds. It makes programmes to be broadcast in foreign countries. The aim is to provide a comprehensive picture of political, cultural and economic life in Germany, and to present and explain Germany's position on important national and international questions.

Deutsch-: **deutsch|feind|lich** ADJ anti-German, Germanophobic; **Deutsch|feind|lich|keit** F Germanophobia; **deutsch-fran|zö|sisch** ADJ **a** (Pol) Franco-German; **der Deutsch-Französische Krieg** the Franco-Prussian war **b** (Ling) German-French; **deutsch|freund|lich** ADJ pro-German, Germanophile; **Deutsch|freund|lich|keit** F Germanophilia; **deutsch|ge|sinnt** ADJ **~ sein** to feel oneself to be German, to think of oneself as being German; **Deutsch|her|ren** [ˈdɔytʃhɛrən] PL (Hist) Teutonic Knights pl; **Deutsch|her|ren|or|den** M (Hist) Teutonic Order of Knights; **Deutsch|kennt|nis|se** PL (a knowledge sing of) German, German language skills pl; **gute ~** a good command of German, fluent German; **gute ~ Voraussetzung** (in Annoncen) German essential; **Deutsch|kurs** M German course, German lessons *pl*; **einen ~ machen** to do a German course, to take German lessons

Deutsch|land ['dɔytʃlant] NT **-s** Germany; **die beiden ~(s)** *(Hist)* the two Germanys

Deutsch|land-: **Deutsch|land|bild** NT *(fig, von Ausländern)* image of the Germans; **Deutsch|land|fra|ge** F *(Pol Hist)* German question; **Deutsch|land|lied** NT (West) German national anthem; **Deutsch|land|po|li|tik** F home *or* domestic policy; *(von fremdem Staat)* policy on *or* toward(s) Germany; **Deutsch|land|tour|nee** F tour of Germany

Deutsch-: **Deutsch|leh|rer(in)** M(F) German teacher; **deutsch|na|ti|o|nal** ADJ *(Hist)* German National; **Deutsch|or|dens|rit|ter** M *(Hist)* Teutonic Knight; **Deutsch|rit|ter|or|den** M *(Hist)* Teutonic Order of Knights; **Deutsch|schweiz** F **die ~** German-speaking Switzerland; **Deutsch|schwei|zer(in)** M(F) German Swiss; **deutsch|schwei|ze|risch** ADJ German-Swiss; **deutsch|spra|chig** ADJ *Bevölkerung, Gebiete* German-speaking; *Zeitung, Ausgabe* German language; *Literatur* German; **Deutsch|spra|chig|keit** F **-**, *no pl* use of the German language; *(= Fähigkeit)* ability to speak German; **deutsch|sprach|lich** ADJ German(-language); **Deutsch|spre|chen** NT **-s**, *no pl* speaking German; **deutsch|spre|chend** ADJ German-speaking; **deutsch|stäm|mig** ADJ of German origin *or* stock; **Deutsch|stäm|mi|ge(r)** [-ʃtɛmɪgə] MF *decl as adj* ethnic German; **Deutsch|stun|de** F German lesson; **Deutsch|tum** ['dɔytʃtu:m] NT **-s**, *no pl* Germanness; *(= die Deutschen)* Germans *pl*; **Deutsch|tü|me|lei** [dɔytʃty:mə'lai] F **-**, **-en** *(pej)* hyper-Germanness; **Deutsch|un|ter|richt** M German lessons *pl*, German classes *pl*; *(= einzelne Stunde)* German lesson *or* class; *(= das Unterrichten)* teaching German, the teaching of German

Deu|tung ['dɔytʊŋ] F **-**, **-en** interpretation; **eine falsche ~** a misinterpretation

Deu|tungs|ver|such M attempt at an interpretation; **er unternimmt einen neuen ~ des ...** he attempts a new interpretation of ...

De|vi|se [de'vi:zə] F **-**, **-n** **a** *(= Wahlspruch)* maxim, motto; *(Her auch)* device **b** **Devisen** PL *(Fin)* foreign exchange *or* currency

De|vi|sen-: **De|vi|sen|ab|kom|men** NT foreign exchange agreement; **De|vi|sen|aus|gleich** M foreign exchange offset; **De|vi|sen|be|schrän|kun|gen** PL foreign exchange restrictions *pl*; **De|vi|sen|be|stim|mun|gen** PL foreign exchange control regulations *pl*; **De|vi|sen|be|wirt|schaf|tung** F foreign exchange control; **De|vi|sen|bi|lanz** F foreign exchange balance; **De|vi|sen|bör|se** F foreign exchange market; **De|vi|sen|brin|ger** [-brɪŋɐ] M **-s**, **-** *(= Geschäft etc)* earner of foreign exchange *or* currency; **De|vi|sen|ein|nah|men** PL (foreign currency) receipts *pl*; **De|vi|sen|ge|schäft** NT foreign exchange dealing; **De|vi|sen|han|del** M foreign currency *or* exchange dealings *pl*, sale and purchase of currencies; **De|vi|sen|knapp|heit** F shortage of foreign exchange; **De|vi|sen|kurs** M exchange rate, rate of exchange; **De|vi|sen|markt** M foreign exchange market; **De|vi|sen|po|li|tik** F foreign exchange policy; **De|vi|sen|re|ser|ven** PL foreign exchange reserves *pl*; **De|vi|sen|schmug|gel** M currency smuggling; **de|vi|sen|schwach** ADJ **~e Länder** countries with limited foreign currency reserves; **De|vi|sen|ter|min|ge|schäft** NT forward exchange; **De|vi|sen|ver|ge|hen** NT breach of exchange control regulations; **De|vi|sen|vor|schrif|ten** PL foreign exchange control regulations *pl*

de|vot [de'vo:t] ADJ *(geh)* **a** *(pej: = unterwürfig)* obsequious **b** *(old: = demütig)* humble

De|vo|ti|on [devo'tsio:n] F **-**, **-en** *(geh)* **a** *(pej: = Unterwürfigkeit)* obsequiousness **b** *(old: = Demut)* humility

De|vo|ti|o|na|li|en [devotsio'na:liən] PL devotional objects *pl*

Dext|ro|se [dɛks'tro:zə] F **-**, *no pl (Chem)* dextrose

Dez [de:ts] M **-es**, **-e** *(dial inf)* bonce *(Brit inf)*, head

De|zem|ber [de'tsɛmbɐ] M **-(s)**, **-** December → *auch* **März**

De|zen|ni|um [de'tsɛniʊm] NT **-s**, **Dezennien** [-niən] *(geh)* decade, decennium *(form)*

de|zent [de'tsɛnt] ADJ discreet; *Kleidung* subtle; *Einrichtung* refined ADV *andeuten, hinweisen* discreetly; **~ gekleidet sein** to be dressed unobtrusively; **~ eingerichtet sein** to have refined furnishings

de|zent|ral [detsɛn'tra:l] ADJ decentralized ADV *verwalten* decentrally; **Müll ~ entsorgen** to have a decentralized waste disposal system

De|zent|ra|li|sa|ti|on [detsɛntraliza'tsio:n] F decentralization

de|zent|ra|li|sie|ren [detsɛntrali'zi:rən] *ptp* **dezentralisiert** VT to decentralize

De|zent|ra|li|sie|rung F decentralization

De|zenz [de'tsɛnts] F **-**, *no pl (geh)* **a** *(old: = Anstand)* sense of decency **b** *(von Geschmack, Kleidung etc)* discreetness; *(von Benehmen auch)* discretion

De|zer|nat [detsɛr'na:t] NT **-(e)s**, **-e** *(Admin)* department

De|zer|nent [detsɛr'nɛnt] M **-en**, **-en**, **De|zer|nen|tin** [-'nɛntɪn] F **-**, **-nen** *(Admin)* head of department

De|zi|bel ['de:tsibɛl, -'bɛl] NT **-s**, **-** *(Phys)* decibel

de|zi|diert [detsi'di:ɐt] *(geh)* ADJ firm, determined ADV firmly

De|zi- *(Aus)*: **De|zi|gramm** NT decigram(me); **De|zi|li|ter** M OR NT decilitre *(Brit)*, deciliter *(US)*

de|zi|mal [detsi'ma:l] ADJ decimal

De|zi|mal|bruch M decimal fraction

De|zi|ma|le [detsi'ma:lə] F **-(n)**, **-n** decimal

de|zi|ma|li|sie|ren [detsimali'zi:rən] *ptp* **dezimalisiert** VT to decimalize; **als in Großbritannien dezimalisiert wurde** when Great Britain went decimal

De|zi|ma|li|sie|rung F **-**, **-en** decimalization

De|zi|mal-: **De|zi|mal|klas|si|fi|ka|ti|on** F decimal classification; **De|zi|mal|kom|ma** NT *(englischsprachige Länder)* decimal point; *(deutschsprachige Länder etc)* decimal comma; **De|zi|mal|maß** NT decimal measure; **De|zi|mal|rech|nung** F decimals *pl*; **De|zi|mal|stel|le** F decimal place; **auf zwei ~n genau** correct to two decimal places; **De|zi|mal|sys|tem** NT decimal system; **De|zi|mal|trenn|zei|chen** NT *(Comput: für Zahlen, Währungen)* decimal symbol; **De|zi|mal|waa|ge** F decimal balance; **De|zi|mal|zahl** F decimal number

De|zi|me ['de:tsimə, de'tsi:mə] F **-**, **-n** *(Mus)* tenth

De|zi|me|ter [detsi'me:tɐ, 'de:tsime:tɐ] M OR NT decimetre *(Brit)*, decimeter *(US)*

de|zi|mie|ren [detsi'mi:rən] *ptp* **dezimiert** *(fig)* VT to decimate VR to be decimated

De|zi|mie|rung F **-**, **-en** *(fig)* decimation

DFB [de:ɛf'be:] M **-s** *abbr von* **Deutscher Fußball-Bund** German Football Association

DFÜ [de:ɛf'y:] F **-** *abbr von* **Datenfernübertragung**

DGB [de:ge:'be:] M **-s** *abbr von* **Deutscher Gewerkschaftsbund** Federation of German Trade Unions

> **DGB**
>
> The **DGB** – short for **Deutscher Gewerkschaftsbund** – is the largest trade union organization in Germany: it is an alliance of several unions. It was founded in 1949 and is governed by the **Industrieverbandsprinzip**. This means that all employees in a company, regardless of their particular job, are covered by the trade union corresponding to the core business of the company. Thus a secretary or an accountant in a car-manufacturing company belongs to the union "IG Metall". Matters relating to specific occupational groups are taken up by the individual trade unions, which also negotiate pay agreements.

dgl. *abbr von* **dergleichen, desgleichen** the like

d. Gr. *abbr von* **der Große**

d. h. *abbr von* **das heißt** i.e.

d. i. *abbr von* **das ist** i.e.

Dia ['di:a] NT **-s**, **-s** *(Phot)* slide, transparency

Di|a|be|tes [dia'be:tɛs] M **-**, *no pl* diabetes

Di|a|be|ti|ker [dia'be:tikɐ] M **-s**, **-**, **Di|a|be|ti|ke|rin** [-ərɪn] F **-**, **-nen** diabetic

Di|a|be|ti|ker|kost F diabetic food

di|a|be|tisch [dia'be:tɪʃ] ADJ diabetic

Dia|be|trach|ter M slide viewer

Di|a|bo|lik [dia'bo:lɪk] F **-**, *no pl (geh)* diabolicalness, fiendishness

di|a|bo|lisch [dia'bo:lɪʃ] *(geh)* ADJ diabolical, fiendish ADV diabolically

dia|chron [dia'kro:n] ADJ diachronic

Dia|chro|nie [diakro'ni:] F **-**, *no pl (Ling)* diachrony

dia|chro|nisch [dia'kro:nɪʃ] ADJ diachronic

Di|a|dem [dia'de:m] NT **-s**, **-e** diadem

Di|a|do|chen [dia'dɔxn] PL *(Hist)* diadochi *pl*; *(fig)* rivals *pl* in a power struggle

Di|a|do|chen|kämp|fe PL *(fig)* power struggle

Di|ag|no|se [dia'gno:zə] F **-**, **-n** diagnosis; **eine ~ stellen** to make a diagnosis

Di|ag|no|se-: **Di|ag|no|se|pro|grammnt** *(Comput)* diagnostics program; **Di|ag|no|se|stand** M diagnostic test bay; **Di|ag|no|se|sys|tem** NT diagnostic system; **Di|ag|no|se|ver|fah|ren** NT diagnostic method, method of diagnosis; **Di|ag|no|se|zent|rum** NT diagnostic centre *(Brit) or* center *(US)*

Di|ag|nos|tik [dia'gnɔstɪk] F **-**, *no pl* diagnosis

Di|ag|nos|ti|ker [dia'gnɔstikɐ] M **-s**, **-**, **Di|ag|nos|ti|ke|rin** [-ərɪn] F **-**, **-nen** diagnostician

di|ag|nos|tisch [dia'gnɔstɪʃ] ADJ diagnostic

di|ag|nos|ti|zie|ren [diagnɔsti'tsi:rən] *ptp* **diagnostiziert** VTI *(Med, fig)* to diagnose; **(auf) etw** *(acc)* **~** to diagnose sth

dia|go|nal [diago'na:l] ADJ diagonal ADV diagonally; **ein Buch ~ lesen** *(inf)* to skim *or* flick through a book

Dia|go|na|le [diago'na:lə] F **-**, **-n** diagonal

Dia|go|nal|rei|fen M *(Aut)* cross-ply (tyre *(Brit) or* tire *(US)*)

Dia|gramm NT *pl* **-gramme** diagram

Dia|gramm-: **Dia|gramm|form** F **in ~** diagrammatically; **Dia|gramm|pa|pier** NT graph paper

Di|a|kon [dia'ko:n, *(Aus)* 'di:ako:n] M **-s** *or* **-en**, **-e(n)** *(Eccl)* deacon

Di|a|ko|nat [diako'na:t] NT **-(e)s**, **-e** *(Eccl)* **a** *(= Amt)* deaconry, deaconship, diaconate **b** *(= Wohnung)* deacon's house

Di|a|ko|nie [diako'ni:] F **-**, *no pl (Eccl)* social welfare work

Di|a|ko|nie|sta|ti|on F (church) community care centre *(Brit) or* center *(US)*

Di|a|ko|nin [dia'ko:nɪn] F **-**, **-nen** *(Eccl)* deacon(-ess)

Di|a|ko|nis|se [diako'nɪsə] F **-**, **-n**, **Di|a|ko|nis|sin** [-'nɪsɪn] F **-**, **-nen** *(Eccl)* deaconess

dia|kri|tisch [dia'kri:tɪʃ] ADJ diacritic; **~e Zeichen** diacritics, diacritic(al) marks *or* signs

Di|a|lekt [dia'lɛkt] M **-(e)s**, **-e** dialect

di|a|lek|tal [dialɛk'ta:l] ADJ dialectal

Di|a|lekt-: **Di|a|lekt|fär|bung** F accent, dialect features *pl*; **Di|a|lekt|for|scher(in)** M(F) dialectologist, dialectician; **Di|a|lekt|for|schung** F dialect research, dialectology; **di|a|lekt|frei** ADJ dialect-free ADV **~ sprechen** to speak standard German/English *etc*

Di|a|lek|tik [dia'lɛktɪk] F **-**, *no pl (Philos)* dialectics *sing or pl*

Di|a|lek|ti|ker [dia'lɛktikɐ] M **-s, -**, **Di|a|lek|ti|ke|rin** [-ərɪn] F **-, -nen** *(Philos)* dialectician

di|a|lek|tisch [dia'lɛktɪʃ] ADJ **a** *(Philos)* dialectic(al); **~er Materialismus** dialectical materialism **b** *(Ling)* = **dialektal**

Di|a|lek|tis|mus [dialɛk'tɪsmʊs] M **-**, *no pl (Ling)* dialecticism

Di|a|ler M **-s, -** *(Telec, Internet)* dialer

Di|a|log [dia'lo:k] M **-(e)s, -e** [-gə] dialogue *(Brit)*, dialog *(US)*

Di|a|log-: **Di|a|log|au|tor(in)** M(F) *(Film)* scriptwriter; **di|a|log|be|reit** ADJ **~ sein** to be willing to negotiate *or* to have talks; **Di|a|log|be|reit|schaft** F willingness to negotiate *or* to have talks, openness for talks; **Di|a|log|be|trieb** M *(Comput)* conversation mode; **di|a|log|fä|hig** ADJ *(Comput)* **~ sein** to be capable of two-way communication; **Di|a|log|fä|hig|keit** F ability to engage in meaningful conversation; *(Comput)* two-way communication capability; **Di|a|log|feld** NT, **Di|a|log|fens|ter** NT *(Comput)* dialogue *(Brit) or* dialog *(US)* box; **Di|a|log|form** F dialogue *(Brit) or* dialog *(US)* form

di|a|lo|gisch [dia'lo:gɪʃ] ADJ dialogue *attr (Brit)*, dialog *attr (US)*

Di|a|log-: **Di|a|log|re|gie** F *(Film)* script supervision; **Di|a|log|stück** NT *(Theat)* dialogue *(Brit) or* dialog *(US)* play

Di|a|ly|se [dia'ly:zə] F **-, -n** *(Med)* dialysis

Di|a|ly|se-: **Di|a|ly|se|ge|rät** [dia'ly:zə-] NT *(Med)* dialysis *or* kidney machine; **Di|a|ly|se|zent|rum** NT *(Med)* (kidney) dialysis centre *(Brit) or* center *(US)*, (kidney) dialysis clinic

Dia|ma|ga|zin NT *(Phot)* slide tray

Di|a|mant [dia'mant] M **-en, -en** diamond

Di|a|mant F **-**, *no pl (Typ)* four-point, diamond *(4½ point)*

di|a|mant|be|setzt ADJ *attr* diamond-studded

di|a|man|ten [dia'mantn] ADJ *attr* diamond; **von ~er Härte** as hard as diamond; **~er Glanz** adamantine lustre *(Brit liter) or* luster *(US liter)*; **~e Hochzeit** diamond wedding

Di|a|mant-: **Di|a|mant|kol|li|er** [-kɔ'lie:] NT diamond necklace; **Di|a|mant|na|del** F **a** diamond brooch **b** *(an Tonarm)* diamond (stylus); **Di|a|mant|schlei|fer(in)** M(F) diamond polisher; **Di|a|mant|schliff** M diamond polishing; **Di|a|mant|schmuck** M diamonds *pl*, diamond jewellery *(Brit) or* jewelry *(US)*; **Di|a|mant|stahl** M diamond plate; **Di|a|mant|staub** M diamond dust

Dia|me|ter [dia'me:tɐ] M *(Geometrie)* diameter

dia|met|ral [diame'tra:l] ADJ diametral; *(fig) Ansichten* diametrically opposed; *Gegensatz* exact ADV **~ entgegengesetzt sein, sich ~ gegenüberliegen** to be diametrically opposite; **~ entgegengesetzt** *(fig)* diametrically opposed

Di|a|na ['dia:na] F **-s** *(Myth)* Diana

Dia|phrag|ma [dia'fragma] NT **-s, Diaphragmen** [-mən] *(Tech, Med)* diaphragm

Dia- *(Phot)*: **Dia|po|si|tiv** NT slide, transparency; **Dia|pro|jek|tor** M slide projector; **Dia|rah|men** M slide frame; **Dia|show** F slide show; *(= Diavortrag)* slide talk

Di|ar|rhö(e) [dia'rø:] F **-, -(e)n** *(Med)* diarrhoea *(Brit)*, diarrhea *(US)*

Di|as|po|ra F **-**, *no pl (Eccl)* diaspora

Dias|to|le [di'astole, dia'sto:lə] F **-, -n** *(Med)* diastole

dias|to|lisch [dia'sto:lɪʃ] ADJ diastolic

Di|ät [di'ɛ:t] F **-, -en** *(Med)* diet; **~ kochen** to cook according to a diet; **~ essen** to eat according to a diet; **~ halten** to keep to *or* observe a diet; **nach einer ~ leben** to be on a diet *or (wegen Krankheit)* special diet; **jdn auf ~ setzen** *(inf)* to put sb on a diet; **auf ~ sein** *(inf)* to be on a diet

di|ät △ [di'ɛ:t] ADV → **Diät**

Di|ät-: **Di|ät|as|sis|tent(in)** M(F) dietician; **Di|ät|bier** NT diet beer

Di|ä|ten PL *(Parl)* parliamentary allowance

Di|ä|ten-: **Di|ä|ten|an|pas|sung** F *(euph)* adjustment of parliamentary *(Brit) or* congressional *(US)* allowances; **Di|ä|ten|er|hö|hung** F increase in parliamentary *(Brit) or* congressional *(US)* allowances

Di|ä|te|tik [diɛ'te:tɪk] F **-, -en** dietetics *sing*

di|ä|te|tisch [diɛ'te:tɪʃ] ADJ dietetic

Di|ät|fahr|plan M *(hum)* dieting course *or* schedule

Dia|thek [dia'te:k] F **-, -en** slide collection *or* library

Di|ä|tist [diɛ'tɪst] M **-en, -en**, **Di|ä|tis|tin** [-'tɪstɪn] F **-, -nen** dietician

Di|ät-: **Di|ät|kost** F dietary foods *pl*; **~ bekommen** to be on a special diet; **Di|ät|kur** F dietary *or* dietetic treatment

Dia|to|nik [dia'to:nɪk] F **-**, *no pl (Mus)* diatonicism

dia|to|nisch [dia'to:nɪʃ] ADJ *(Mus)* diatonic

Dia|vor|trag M slide presentation *or* talk *or* show

dich [dɪç] PERS PRON *acc von* **du** you; *(obs, dial)* thee REFL PRON yourself; **wie fühlst du ~?** how do you feel?

Di|cho|to|mie [dɪçoto'mi:] F **-, -n** [-'mi:ən] dichotomy

dicht [dɪçt] ADJ **a** *Gefieder, Haar, Hecke* thick; *Laub, Nebel* thick, dense; *Wald, (Menschen)menge, Gewühl* dense; *Verkehr* heavy, dense; *Gewebe* close; *Stoff* closely-woven; *(fig: = konzentriert) Stil* dense; *Szene* full, compact; **in ~er Folge** in rapid *or* quick succession; **sie standen in ~en Reihen** they were standing row upon row close together

b *(= undurchlässig) Vorhänge* thick, heavy; *Rollladen* heavy; *(= wasserdicht)* watertight; *(= luftdicht)* airtight; **~ machen** to seal, to make watertight/airtight; *Fenster* to seal → *auch* **dichtmachen**; **er ist nicht ganz ~** *(inf)* he's crackers *(Brit inf) or* nuts *(inf)*

c *(inf: = zu)* shut, closed

d *(sl: = betrunken, high)* off one's face *(Brit inf)*, out of it *(inf)*

ADV **a** *(= nahe)* closely; **(~ an) ~ stehen** to stand close together; **~ gefolgt von** closely followed by

b *(= fest) zuziehen, schließen* tightly; *weben* densely; **~ halten** to be watertight; **~ verhängen** to curtain heavily

c *(= sehr stark) bevölkert, bepflanzt* densely; *bewaldet* densely, thickly; **~ bevölkert** densely populated; **~ bewachsen** *Baumstämme* grown over with moss and lichen; *Ufer* thickly covered with vegetation; *Landstrich* rich in vegetation; **~ mit Efeu bewachsen** overgrown with ivy; **~ mit etw übersät** covered with sth; **~ behaart** very hairy; **~ belaubt** thick with leaves, densely foliated; **~ bewölkt** heavily overcast; **~ gedrängt** closely packed; *Programm* packed

d *(mit Präpositionen)* **~ an/bei** close to; **~ dahinter/darüber/davor** right behind/above/in front; **~ daneben** right *or* close beside it; **~ bevor** right before; **~ daran** hard by it; **~ hintereinander** close(ly) *or* right behind one another; **~ beieinander** *or* **beisammen** close together; **~ am Winde halten** *(Naut)* to sail close to the wind, to hug the wind; **~ hinter jdm her sein** to be right *or* hard *or* close behind sb

dicht-: **dicht|auf** ['dɪçt'lauf] ADV closely; **~ folgen** to follow close behind *or* closely; **dicht|be|haart** [-bəha:ɐt] ADJ → **dicht ADV c**; **dicht|be|laubt** [-bəlaupt] ADJ → **dicht ADV c**; **dicht|be|völ|kert** [-bəfœlkɐt] ADJ → **dicht ADV c**; **dicht|be|wach|sen** ADJ → **dicht ADV c**; **dicht|be|wölkt** ADJ → **dicht ADV c**

Dich|te ['dɪçtə] F **-, -n**, *no pl* **a** *(von Gefieder, Haar, Hecke)* thickness; *(von Laub, Nebel, Wald, Menschenmenge)* denseness; *(von Verkehr)* heaviness; *(von Gewebe)* closeness; *(von Stoff)* close weave; *(fig: = Konzentriertheit, von Stil)* denseness **b** *(Phys)* density **c** *(Comput)* **Diskette mit einfacher/doppelter ~** single-density/double-density diskette

Dich|te|mes|ser M **-s, -** *(Phys)* densimeter

dich|ten ['dɪçtn] VT to write, to compose; **sein Glückwunsch war gedichtet** his congratulations were (written) in verse VI to write poems/a poem

dich|ten VT *(= undurchlässig machen)* to seal; *(Naut auch)* to caulk

Dich|ter ['dɪçtɐ] M **-s, -**, **Dich|te|rin** [-ərɪn] F **-, -nen** poet; *(= Schriftsteller)* writer, author

Dich|ter|fürst(in) M(F) prince/princess among poets

dich|te|risch ['dɪçtərɪʃ] ADJ poetic; *(= schriftstellerisch)* literary; **~e Freiheit** poetic licence *(Brit) or* license *(US)*

Dich|ter-: **Dich|ter|kreis** M circle of poets; **Dich|ter|le|sung** F reading *(by a poet/writer from his own works)*; **Dich|ter|ling** ['dɪçtelɪŋ] M **-s, -e** *(pej)* rhymester *(pej)*, poetaster *(pej)*; **Dich|ter|schu|le** F → **Dichter** school of poets/writers; **Dich|ter|spra|che** F poetic language; **Dich|ter|wort** NT *pl* **-worte** (literary) quotation

Dicht-: **dicht|ge|drängt** ADJ *attr* → **dicht ADV c**; **dicht+hal|ten** VI *sep irreg (inf)* to hold one's tongue *(inf)*, to keep one's mouth shut *(inf)*; **Dicht|heit** F **-**, *no pl* = **Dichte a**; **Dicht|kunst** F art of poetry; *(= Schriftstellerei)* creative writing; **dicht+ma|chen** VTI *sep* **a** *(inf) Laden etc* to shut up, to close; *Fabrik, Betrieb etc* to close *or* shut down; **(den Laden) ~** to shut up shop (and go home) *(inf)*; **er hat (sich) völlig dichtgemacht** *(fig inf)* he's pulled down the shutters *(inf)* **b** *Boot, Fenster etc* → **dicht ADJ b**

Dich|tung ['dɪçtʊŋ] F **-, -en** **a** *no pl (= Dichtkunst, Gesamtwerk)* literature; *(in Versform)* poetry; **~ und Wahrheit** *(Liter)* poetry and truth; *(fig)* fact and fantasy *or* fiction **b** *(= Dichtwerk)* poem, poetic work; literary work; **dramatische ~** dramatic poem

Dich|tung F **-, -en** *(Tech)* seal; *(in Wasserhahn etc)* washer; *(Aut: von Zylinder, Vergaser)* gasket; *(= das Abdichten)* sealing

Dich|tungs-: **Dich|tungs|art** F, **Dich|tungs|gat|tung** F literary genre; **Dich|tungs|man|schet|te** F seal; **Dich|tungs|mas|se** F sealant; **Dich|tungs|ma|te|ri|al** NT, **Dich|tungs|mit|tel** NT sealing compound; **Dich|tungs|ring** M, **Dich|tungs|schei|be** F seal, sealing ring; *(in Wasserhahn)* washer

dick [dɪk] ADJ **a** thick; *Mensch, Körperteil, Band, Buch, Brieftasche* fat; *Baum, Stamm* big, large, thick; *(inf) Gehalt, Belohnung, Rechnung, Gewinn* fat, hefty; *(inf) Tränen, Geschäft* big; **einen ~en Mercedes fahren** *(inf)* to drive a big Mercedes; **eine ~e Zigarre** a big fat cigar; **die ~e Berta** Big Bertha; **ein ~er Brocken** *(inf)* a hard *or* tough nut (to crack); **~e Dinger** *(sl: = Busen)* knockers *pl (Brit inf)*, hooters *pl (US inf)*; **ein ~es Fell haben** *(inf)* to have (a) thick skin, to be thick-skinned; **eine ~e Lippe riskieren** *(inf)* to be cheeky *(Brit)*, to act fresh *(US inf)*; **~ machen** *Speisen* to be fattening; **~ werden** *(Mensch: = zunehmen)* to get fat

b *(nach Maßangaben)* thick; *Erdschicht* deep; **3 m ~e Wände** walls 3 metres *(Brit) or* meters *(US)* thick, 3-metre *(Brit) or* meter *(US)* thick walls

c *(inf: = schwerwiegend) Fehler, Verweis* big; **das ist ein ~er Tadel/ein ~es Lob** that's heavy criticism/high praise; **das ist ein ~er Hund** *or* **ein ~es Ei** *(inf: = unerhört)* that's a bit much *(inf)*; **ach, du ~es Ei!** *(inf)* for goodness' sake! *(inf)*; **das ~e Ende kommt noch** *(prov)* the worst is yet to come

d *(= geschwollen) Backe, Beine, Finger, Mandeln* swollen; *Beule* big; **ein ~er Kopf** *(inf)* a thick head *(inf)* → **Bauch**

e *(= zähflüssig, dicht)* thick; **eine ~e Suppe** *(inf: = Nebel)* a real peasouper *(Brit inf)*, very thick fog; **~e Milch** sour milk; **durch ~ und dünn** through thick and thin → **Luft**

f *(inf: = herzlich) Freundschaft, Freund* close; **mit jdm ~e sein** to be thick with sb *(inf)*

ADV **a** *(= warm)* warmly; **sich/jdn ~ anziehen** to wrap up/sb up warmly
b *anstreichen, unterstreichen* heavily
c *(= reichlich) auftragen, schmieren, bestreichen* thickly; **etw ~ mit Butter bestreichen** to spread butter thickly on sth; **~(e)** *(inf: = ausreichend)* easily; **er hat es ~(e)** *(= hat es satt)* he's had enough of it; *(= hat viel)* he's got enough and to spare; **jdn/etw ~(e) haben** *(= von jdm/etw genug haben)* to have had one's fill of sb/sth *(inf)*, to have had sb/sth up to here *(inf)* → **auftragen VI b, Faxen a**
d *(inf: = sehr)* **~ satt sein** to be stuffed *(inf)*; **jdm etw ~ ankreiden** to hold sth against sb; **~ im Geschäft sein** to make it big *(inf)*; **~(e) kommen** *(inf)* to come thick and fast
e *(inf: = eng)* **mit jdm ~ befreundet sein** to be thick with sb *(inf)*

Dick-: **dick|bau|chig** ADJ *Vase, Krug* bulbous; *Mann* potbellied; **dick|bäu|chig** [-bɔyçıç] ADJ *Mensch* potbellied; *(krankhaft auch)* swollen-bellied; **Dick|darm** M *(Anat)* colon

di|cke ['dıkə] ADV *(inf)* → **dick ADJ f ADV c, d**

Di|cke ['dıkə] F **-, -n a** *(= Stärke, Durchmesser)* thickness; *(bei Maßangaben auch)* depth **b** *(von Menschen, Körperteilen)* fatness

Di|cken-: **Di|cken|mes|ser** M **-s, -** thickness gauge; **Di|cken|wachs|tum** NT lateral growth

Di|cke(r) ['dıkə] MF *decl as adj (inf)* fatty *(inf)*, fatso *(inf)*

Di|cker|chen ['dıkɐçən] NT **-s, -** *(inf)* chubby chops *(Brit inf)*, chubby

di|cke+tun VR *sep irreg (inf)* = **dicktun**

Dick-: **dick|fel|lig** [-fɛlıç] ADJ *(inf)* thick-skinned; **Dick|fel|lig|keit** F **-,** *no pl (inf)* insensitivity, rhinoceros hide *(inf)*; **dick|flüs|sig** ADJ thick, viscous *(Tech)*; **Dick|flüs|sig|keit** F thickness, viscosity *(Tech)*; **Dick|häu|ter** [-hɔytɐ] M **-s, -** pachyderm; *(fig)* thick-skinned person; **dick|häu|tig** ADJ *(fig)* thick-skinned

Di|ckicht ['dıkıçt] NT **-(e)s, -e** *(= Gebüsch)* thicket; *(fig)* jungle, maze

Dick-: **Dick|kopf** M **a** *(= Starrsinn)* obstinacy, stubbornness, mulishness; **einen ~ haben** to be obstinate *or* stubborn *or* mulish; **sie setzt ihren ~ immer durch** she always gets what she wants **b** *(= Mensch)* mule *(inf)*; **dick|köp|fig** ADJ *(fig)* stubborn; **Dick|köp|fig|keit** F **-,** *no pl* stubbornness; **dick|lei|big** [-laibıç] ADJ *Buch* massive; *Mensch* corpulent; **Dick|lei|big|keit** F **-,** *no pl (von Mensch)* corpulence; **dick|lich** ['dıklıç] ADJ plump; *Mensch auch* plumpish, tubby *(inf)*; **dick+ma|chen** VI *sep* → **dick ADJ a**; **Dick|milch** F *(Cook)* sour milk; **Dick|schä|del** M *(inf)* = **Dickkopf**; **dick|scha|lig** [-ʃa:lıç] ADJ thick-skinned, with a thick skin *or* peel; **Dick|sein** NT fatness; **Dick|tu|e|rei** F *(inf)* swanking *no pl*; **dick+tun** VR *sep irreg (inf)* to swank *(inf)*; **(sich) mit etw ~** to swank about sth *(inf)*; **dick|wan|dig** ADJ *Gebäude, Bunker etc* with thick walls, thick-walled; *Gefäß, Schale* with thick sides, thick; **Dick|wanst** M *(pej inf)* fatso *(inf)*

Di|dak|tik [di'daktık] F **-, -en** didactics *sing (form)*, teaching methods *pl*

Di|dak|ti|ker [di'daktikɐ] M **-s, -**, **Di|dak|ti|ke|rin** [-ərın] F **-, -nen** *(Univ)* lecturer in teaching methods; **er ist ein miserabler ~** his teaching methods are terrible

di|dak|tisch [di'daktıʃ] ADJ didactic ADV didactically

di|del|dum [di:dl'dʊm], **di|del|dum|dei** [di:dldʊm'dai] INTERJ tum-ti-tum

die [di:] [di:] → **der**

Dieb [di:p] M **-(e)s, -e** [-bə], **Die|bin** ['di:bın] F **-, -nen** thief; **haltet den ~!** stop thief!; **sich wie ein ~ davonschleichen** to steal *or* slink away like a thief in the night

Die|be|rei [di:bə'rai] F **-, -en** thievery *no pl*, thieving *no pl*

Die|bes-: **Die|bes|ban|de** F gang of thieves; **Die|bes|ge|sin|del** NT *(pej)* thieving riff-raff *(pej)*; **Die|bes|gut** NT, *no pl* stolen property *or* goods *pl*; **Die|bes|höh|le** F thieves' den; **Die|bes|nest** NT den of thieves; **Die|bes|pack** NT *(pej)* thieving riffraff *(pej) or* trash *(pej)*; **die|bes|si|cher** ADJ thief-proof

Die|bin ['di:bın] F **-, -nen** thief

die|bisch ['di:bıʃ] ADJ **a** *Gesindel, Elster* thieving *attr* **b** *(inf) Freude, Vergnügen* impish, mischievous

Dieb|stahl ['di:pʃta:l] M **-(e)s, ¨-e** [-ʃtɛ:lə] theft; *(Jur auch)* larceny; **einfacher/schwerer ~** petty/grand larceny; **bewaffneter ~** armed robbery; **geistiger ~** plagiarism

Dieb|stahl-: **dieb|stahl|si|cher** ADJ theft-proof; **Dieb|stahl|si|che|rung** F *(Aut)* anti-theft device; **Dieb|stahl|ver|si|che|rung** F insurance against theft

die|je|ni|ge ['di:je:nıgə] DEM PRON → **derjenige**

Die|le ['di:lə] F **-, -n a** *(= Fußbodenbrett)* floorboard **b** *(= Vorraum)* hall, hallway → **Eisdiele, Tanzdiele c** *(N Ger: = Tenne)* threshing floor

die|len ['di:lən] VT *Zimmer* to lay floorboards in

Die|len|brett NT floorboard

die|nen ['di:nən] VI **a** *(= Dienste tun, sich einsetzen)* to serve *(jdm* sb); *(old: = angestellt sein)* to be in service *(bei* with); **bei Hof ~** to serve *or* wait at court; **bei der Messe** *or* **am Altar ~** to serve at mass
b *(Mil) (= beim Militär sein)* to serve; *(= Militärdienst leisten)* to do (one's) military service; **bei der Kavallerie/unter jdm ~** to serve in the cavalry/under sb; **ein gedienter Soldat** an ex-soldier → *auch* **Pike**
c *(= fördern) (einer Sache (dat)* sth) to serve; *dem Fortschritt, der Erforschung* to aid; *dem Verständnis* to promote; *(= nützlich sein)* to be of use *or* service *(jdm* to sb); **es dient einem guten Zweck** it serves a useful purpose; **es dient einer guten Sache** it is in *or* for a good cause; **der Verbesserung der Arbeitsbedingungen ~** to serve to improve working conditions; **das wird dir später ~** that will be *or* come in useful to you later
d *(= behilflich sein)* to help *(jdm* sb), to be of help *or* service *(jdm* to sb); **womit kann ich Ihnen ~?** what can I do for you?; *(im Geschäft auch)* can I help you?; **damit kann ich leider nicht ~** I'm afraid I can't help you there; **damit ist mir wenig gedient** that's no use *or* good to me
e *(= verwendet werden)* **als/zu etw ~** to serve *or* be used as/for sth; **lass dir das als Warnung ~!** let that serve as *or* be a warning to you!

Die|ner ['di:nɐ] M **-s, - a** *(= Mensch) (lit, fig)* servant; *(= Lakai auch)* valet; **~ Gottes** servant of God; **Ihr ergebenster ~** *(old: in Briefen)* your (most) obedient servant → **stumm ADJ a b** *(inf: = Verbeugung)* bow

Die|ne|rin ['di:nərın] F **-, -nen** maid, maidservant *(old)*

die|nern ['di:nɐn] VI *(vor +dat* to) *(lit)* to bow; *(fig pej)* to bow and scrape

Die|ner|schaft ['di:nɐʃaft] F **-, -en** servants *pl*, domestic staff

dien|lich ['di:nlıç] ADJ useful, helpful; *(= ratsam)* expedient, advisable; **jdm/einer Sache ~ sein** to help sb/sth, to be of use *or* help to sb/sth

Dienst [di:nst] M **-(e)s, -e a** *(= Arbeitsverhältnis, Tätigkeitsbereich)* service; *(= Arbeitsstelle)* position; **diplomatischer/öffentlicher ~** diplomatic/civil service; **bei jdm in ~(en) sein** *or* **stehen, in jds ~(en)** *(dat)* **sein** *or* **stehen** to be in sb's service; **jdn in (seinen) ~ nehmen** to engage sb; **in jds ~(e)** *(acc)* **treten** to enter sb's service; **Oberst** *etc* **außer ~** *(abbr* **a. D.***)* retired colonel *etc*; **den ~ quittieren, aus dem ~ (aus)scheiden** to resign one's post; *(Mil)* to leave the service; **nicht mehr ~ mit der Waffe** *(Mil)* armed service; **nicht mehr im ~ sein** to have left the service; **im ~ ergraut sein** to have many years of faithful service behind one
b *(= Berufsausübung, Amtspflicht)* duty; *(= Arbeit, Arbeitszeit)* work; **im ~ sein, ~ haben** *(Arzt, Feuerwehrmann etc)* to be on duty; *(Apotheke)* to be open; **~ habend** = **diensthabend**; **im ~ sein** *(Angestellter etc)* to be working; **außer ~ sein** to be off duty; **nach ~** after work; **zum ~ gehen** to go to work; **~ tun** to serve *(bei* in, *als* as); **~ tuend** = **diensttuend**; **jdn vom ~ beurlauben** to grant sb leave of absence; **jdn vom ~ befreien** to exempt sb from his duties; **Tellerwäscher/Kindermädchen vom ~** *(hum)* resident dishwasher/babysitter *(hum)*; **~ nach Vorschrift** work to rule; **~ ist ~ und Schnaps ist Schnaps** *(Prov inf)* you can't mix business with pleasure, there's a time for everything
c *(= Tätigkeit, Leistung, Hilfe)* service; **im ~(e) einer Sache/der Menschheit** in the service of sth/humanity; **sich in den ~ der Sache stellen** to embrace the cause; **jdm einen ~/einen schlechten ~ erweisen** to do sb a good/bad turn, to do sb a service/disservice; **jdm gute ~e leisten** *or* **tun** to serve sb well; **jdm den ~ verweigern** to refuse to work for sb; **die Stimme** *etc* **versagte ihr den ~** her voice *etc* failed (her) *or* gave way; **~ am Vaterland** service to one's country; **~ am Kunden** customer service; **etw in ~ stellen** to put sth into commission *or* service; **jdm zu ~en** *or* **zu jds ~en stehen** to be at sb's disposal; *(Mensch auch)* to be at sb's service; **(ich stehe) zu ~en!** *(old)* at your service!; **was steht zu ~en?** *(old)* you wish, sir/madam?
d *(= Einrichtung)* service
e *(Archit)* engaged column *or* shaft

-dienst M *suf in cpds* service; *(für Hausarbeit etc)* duty; **Militärdienst** military service; **Küchendienst haben** to be on kitchen duty

Dienst-: **Dienst|ab|teil** NT *(Rail)* ≈ guard's compartment, ≈ conductor's car *(US)*; **Dienst|adel** M *(Hist) nobility whose titles derive from being in the king's service*

Diens|tag ['di:nsta:k] M Tuesday; **am ~** on Tuesday; **an einem ~, eines ~s** one Tuesday; **hast du ~ Zeit?** have you time on Tuesday?; **heute ist ~, der 10. Juni** today is Tuesday the tenth of June *or* Tuesday June the tenth; **jeden ~, alle ~e** every Tuesday; **des ~s** *(geh)* on Tuesdays; **die Nacht von ~ auf** *or* **zum Mittwoch** the night of Tuesday to Wednesday; **den (ganzen) ~ über** all (day) Tuesday, the whole of Tuesday *(esp Brit)*; **ab nächsten** *or* **nächstem ~** from next Tuesday; **~ in acht Tagen** *or* **in einer Woche** a week on Tuesday, Tuesday week *(esp Brit)*; **seit letzten** *or* **letztem ~** since last Tuesday; **~ vor einer Woche** *or* **vor acht Tagen** a week (ago) last Tuesday

Diens|tag-: **Diens|tag|abend** M (on) Tuesday evening; **diens|tag|abends** ADV on Tuesday evenings; **Diens|tag|mit|tag** M (on) Tuesday around noon, midday Tuesday, Tuesday (at) midday, Tuesday lunchtime; **diens|tag|mit|tags** ADV on Tuesdays around noon, Tuesday lunchtime; **Diens|tag|mor|gen** M (on) Tuesday morning; **diens|tag|mor|gens** ADV on Tuesday mornings; **Diens|tag|nach|mit|tag** M (on) Tuesday afternoon; **diens|tag|nach|mit|tags** ADV on Tuesday afternoons; **Diens|tag|nacht** F (on) Tuesday night; **diens|tag|nachts** ADV on Tuesday nights

diens|tags ['di:nsta:ks] ADV on Tuesdays, on a Tuesday; **~ abends** on Tuesday evenings, on a Tuesday evening

Dienstag-: **Diens|tag|vor|mit|tag** M (on) Tuesday morning; **diens|tag|vor|mit|tags** ADV on Tuesday mornings

Dienst-: **Dienst|al|ter** NT length of service; **Dienst|äl|tes|te(r)** MF *decl as adj* longest-serving member of staff; **dienst|äl|tes|te(r, s)** ADJ longest-serving; **Dienst|an|bie|ter** M *(Comput, Internet)* provider; **Dienst|an|tritt** M assumption of one's duties; *(jeden Tag)* commencement of work; **bei ~** on taking up one's duties; on commencing work; **Dienst|an|wei|sung** F instructions *pl*, regulations *pl*;

Dienst|an|zug M *(Mil)* service uniform *or* dress; **Dienst|auf|fas|sung** F conception of one's duties; **was ist denn das für ~!** have you no sense of duty?; **Dienst|auf|sicht** F supervision; **die ~ über etw** *(acc)* **haben** to be in charge of sth; **Dienst|auf|sichts|be|schwer|de** F complaint about a ruling; **Dienst|aus|weis** M company ID (card); **dienst|bar** ADJ **a** *(Hist)* subject **b** *(fig: = helfend)* **~er Geist** helpful soul; **~e Geister** willing hands; **sich** *(dat)* **etw ~ machen** to utilize sth;; **Dienst|bar|keit** [ˈdiːnstbaːɐkait] F **-, -en a** *(Jur, Hist)* servitude; **etw in seine ~ bringen** *(fig geh)* to utilize sth **b** *(= Gefälligkeit, Tätigsein als Diener)* service; **dienst|be|flis|sen** ADJ zealous, assiduous; **Dienst|be|flis|sen|heit** F zealousness, assiduity; **Dienst|be|frei|ung** F *(Mil)* leave, furlough *(US)*; **Dienst|be|ginn** M start of work; **~ ist um 8 Uhr** work starts at 8 o'clock; **dienst|be|reit** ADJ **a** *(= geöffnet) Apotheke* open *pred*; *Arzt* on call *pred*; *Mitarbeiter* on duty *pred* **b** *(= hilfsbereit)* willing to be of service, obliging; **Dienst|be|reit|schaft** F **a ~ haben** *(Arzt)* to be on call; *(Mitarbeiter)* to be on duty; **in ~ sein** *(Apotheke)* to be open; **welche Apotheke hat dieses Wochenende ~?** which chemist *(Brit) or* pharmacy is open this weekend? **b** *(= Hilfsbereitschaft)* helpfulness, willingness to be of service; **Dienst|be|spre|chung** F (official) meeting; **Dienst|be|zü|ge** PL salary *sing*; **Dienst|bo|te** M, **Dienst|bo|tin** F servant; **Dienst|bo|ten|ein|gang** M tradesmen's *or* service entrance; **Dienst|eid** M oath of service; **Dienst|ei|fer** M zeal; **dienst|eif|rig** ADJ zealous, assiduous; **dienst|fä|hig** ADJ fit for work; *(Mil)* fit for duty; **Dienst|fä|hig|keit** F fitness for work; *(Mil)* fitness for duty; **Dienst|fahrt** F business trip; *(von Beamten auch)* official trip; **dienst|fer|tig** ADJ zealous, assiduous; **dienst|frei** ADJ free; **~er Tag** day off, free day; **~ haben/bekommen** to have/be given a day off; **Dienst|ge|brauch** M *(Mil, Admin)* **nur für den ~** for official use only; **Dienst|ge|heim|nis** NT official secret; **Dienst|ge|spräch** NT business call; *(von Beamten)* official call; **Dienst|grad** M *(Mil)* **a** *(= Rangstufe)* rank **b** *(= Mensch)* **ein höherer ~** a person of higher rank, a higher ranking person; **Dienst|grad|ab|zei|chen** NT *(Mil)* insignia; **dienst|ha|bend** ADJ *attr (Arzt, Offizier etc)* duty *attr*, on duty; **Dienst|ha|ben|de(r)** MF *decl as adj* **der ~** *(Mil)* the duty officer; **Dienst|herr(in)** M(F) employer; **Dienst|jahr** NT *usu pl (Mil, Admin)* year of service; **Dienst|klei|dung** F working dress, uniform; *(Mil)* service dress; **Dienst|leis|ter** M **-s, -** *(= Firma)* service company; **wir arbeiten viel mit ~n** we use a lot of contractors; **die Datenerfassung haben wir an ~ vergeben** we've outsourced our data acquisition; **Dienst|leis|ter** M **-s, -**, **Dienst|leis|te|rin** F *(Person)* service provider; **Dienst|leis|tung** F service; **Dienst|leis|tungs|abend** M late-closing night; **Dienst|leis|tungs|be|reich** M service sector *or* industry; **Dienst|leis|tungs|be|ruf** M job in a service industry; **Dienst|leis|tungs|be|trieb** M service company; **Dienst|leis|tungs|ge|sell|schaft** F service society; **Dienst|leis|tungs|ge|wer|be** NT services trade; **Dienst|leis|tungs|sek|tor** M service sector *or* industry; **dienst|lich** [ˈdiːnstlɪç] **ADJ** *Angelegenheiten* business *attr*; *Schreiben, Befehl* official; **~ werden** *(inf)* to become businesslike **ADV** on business; **wir haben hier ~ zu tun** we have business here; **Dienst|mäd|chen** NT maid; **Dienst|mann** M **a** *pl* **-männer** *or* **-leute** *(= Gepäckträger)* porter **b** *pl* **-mannen** *or* **-leute** *(Hist: = Vasall)* liegeman, vassal; **Dienst|mar|ke** F ID badge; **Dienst|müt|ze** F uniform cap; **Dienst|ord|nung** F *(Admin)* official regulations *pl*; *(Mil)* service regulations *pl*; **Dienst|per|so|nal** NT staff, personnel; **Dienst|pflicht** F compulsory service; **dienst|pflich|tig** [-pflɪçtɪç] ADJ liable for compulsory service; **Dienst|pflich|ti|ge(r)** MF *decl as adj* person/man/woman liable for compulsory service; **Dienst|pis|to|le** F service revolver *or* pistol; **Dienst|plan** M duty rota *(Brit) or* roster; **Dienst|pro|gramm** NT *(Comput)* utility, tool; **Dienst|rang** M grade; *(Mil)* rank; **Dienst|rei|se** F business trip; *(von Beamtem auch)* official trip; **auf ~** on a business trip; **Dienst|sa|che** F *(Post)* **gebührenfreie ~** official matter sent postage paid; **Dienst|schluss** M end of work; **nach ~** *(von Arbeiter etc)* after work; *(von Büro, Firma etc auch)* after working hours; **wir haben jetzt ~** we finish work now; **Dienst|sie|gel** NT, **Dienst|stem|pel** M official stamp; **Dienst|stel|le** F *(Admin)* department; *(Mil)* section; **Dienst|stun|den** PL working hours *pl*; **dienst|taug|lich** ADJ *(Mil)* fit for duty; **Dienst|taug|lich|keit** F *(Mil)* fitness for duty; **dienst|tu|end** [-tuənt] ADJ *attr (Arzt)* duty *attr*, on duty; **dienst|un|fä|hig** ADJ unfit for work; *(Mil)* unfit for duty; **Dienst|un|fä|hig|keit** F unfitness for work; *(Mil)* unfitness for duty; **dienst|un|taug|lich** ADJ *(Mil)* unfit for duty; **Dienst|un|taug|lich|keit** F *(Mil)* unfitness for duty; **Dienst|ver|ge|hen** NT breach of duty; **Dienst|ver|hält|nis** NT **im ~ stehen** to be a public employee; **in ein ~ übernommen werden** to become a public employee; **dienst|ver|pflich|ten** *ptp* **dienstverpflichtet** VT *insep* to call up *or* draft *(US)* for essential service; **Dienst|ver|trag** M contract of employment; **Dienst|vor|schrift** F official regulations *pl*; *(Mil)* service regulations *pl*; **Dienst|waf|fe** F service weapon; **Dienst|wa|gen** M company car; *(von Beamten)* official car; *(Mil)* staff car; *(Rail)* ≈ guard's carriage, ≈ conductor's car *(US)*; **Dienst|weg** M **den ~ einhalten** to go through the proper *or* official channels *pl*; **dienst|wil|lig** ADJ willing to be of service; *(Mil)* willing to do one's duty; **Dienst|woh|nung** F police/army *etc* house, house provided by the police/army *etc*; **Dienst|zeit** F **a** period of service **b** *(= Arbeitszeit)* working hours *pl*; *(Mil)* hours *pl* of duty; **Dienst|zeug|nis** NT testimonial

dies [diːs] DEM PRON *inv* this; *(pl)* these; **~ sind** these are; **~ und das** this and that; **~ alles, alles ~** all this/that → **dieser**

dies|be|züg|lich *(form)* **ADJ** relating to *or* regarding this **ADV sich ~ äußern** to give one's views regarding this *or* on this matter

die|se [ˈdiːzə] DEM PRON → **dieser**

Die|sel [ˈdiːzl] M **-s, -** *(inf)* diesel; **mf**

Die|sel|an|trieb M diesel drive; **mit ~** diesel-driven

die|sel|be [diːˈzɛlbə], **die|sel|bi|ge** [diːˈzɛlbɪgə] DEM PRON → **derselbe**

Die|sel-: **die|sel|elek|trisch** ADJ diesel-electric; **Die|sel|lok** F, **Die|sel|lo|ko|mo|ti|ve** F diesel locomotive; **Die|sel|mo|tor** M diesel engine; **Die|sel|öl** NT diesel oil

die|ser [ˈdiːzɐ], **die|se, die|ses** *pl* **diese** DEM PRON **a** *(substantivisch)* this; *(pl)* these; *(= dieser dort, da)* that; *(pl)* those; **diese(r, s) hier** this (one); **diese hier** *pl* these (ones); **diese(r, s) da** that (one); **diese da** *pl* those (ones); **wer hat es getan? – ~!** which one did it? – this/that one!; **~ ist es!** this/that is the one!; **~ ..., jener ...** the latter ..., the former ...; **schließlich fragte ich einen Polizisten; ~ sagte mir ...** in the end I asked a policeman, he told me ...; **dieses und jenes** this and that; **~ und jener** this person and that; **~ oder jener** someone or other; **... oder dem Überbringer dieses** *(form)* ... or to the bearer of this
b *attr* this; *(pl)* these; *(= dieser dort, da)* that; *(pl)* those; **gib mir dieses Buch** give me that book; **dieses Jahr** this year; **~ Monat** this month; **Anfang dieses Jahres/Monats** at the beginning of the *or* this *or* the current *(form)* year/month; **in diesen Wochen/Jahren habe ich viel erlebt** I experienced a lot in those weeks/years; **ich fahre diese Woche/dieses Jahr noch weg** I'm going away this week/year; **am 5. dieses Monats** on the 5th of this month; *(in Briefen auch)* on the 5th inst *(form)*; **~ Tage** *(vergangen)* the other day; *(zukünftig)* one of these days; **(nur) dieses eine Mal** just this/that once; **~ Maier** *(inf)* that *or* this Maier → **Nacht**

die|ser|art [ˈdiːzɐlaːɐt] ADV *(Aus, old)* thus, in this way

die|ses [ˈdiːzəs] DEM PRON → **dieser**

die|sig [ˈdiːzɪç] ADJ *Wetter, Luft* hazy, misty

Die|sig|keit F **-,** *no pl* haziness, mistiness

dies-: **dies|jäh|rig** ADJ *attr* this year's; **die ~e Ernte** this year's harvest; **dies|mal** ADV this time; **dies|ma|lig** [-maːlɪç] ADJ *attr* **der ~e Preis** the price this time; **dies|sei|tig** [-zaitɪç] ADJ **a** *Ufer* near(side) *attr*, (on) this side **b** *(= irdisch)* of this world; *Leben* in this world; **dies|seits** [ˈdiːszaits] PREP *+gen* on this side of; **Dies|seits** [ˈdiːszaits] NT **-,** *no pl* **das ~** this life; **im ~** in this life, on earth

Diet|rich [ˈdiːtrɪç] M **-s, -e** picklock, skeleton key

die|weil [diːˈvail] *(obs)* **ADV** meanwhile, in the meantime, the while *(dial)* **CONJ** whilst, while

Dif|fa|ma|ti|on [dɪfamaˈtsioːn] F **-, -en** *(= das Diffamieren)* defamation (of character); *(= Bemerkung etc)* defamatory statement

dif|fa|mie|ren [dɪfaˈmiːrən] *ptp* **diffamiert** VT to defame

dif|fa|mie|rend ADJ defamatory

Dif|fa|mie|rung F **-, -en** *(= das Diffamieren)* defamation (of character); *(= Bemerkung etc)* defamatory statement

Dif|fa|mie|rungs|kam|pag|ne F smear campaign

Dif|fe|ren|ti|al [dɪfərɛnˈtsiaːl] NT **-s, -e** = **Differenzial**

Dif|fe|ren|ti|al- *in cpds* = **Differenzial-**: **Dif|fe|ren|ti|al|rech|nung** F = **Differenzialrechnung**

Dif|fe|renz [dɪfəˈrɛnts] F **-, -en a** *(= Unterschied, fehlender Betrag, Math)* difference; *(= Abweichung)* discrepancy **b** *usu pl (= Meinungsverschiedenheit)* difference (of opinion), disagreement

Dif|fe|renz|be|trag M difference, balance

Dif|fe|ren|zi|al [dɪfərɛnˈtsiaːl] NT **-s, -e a** *(Math)* differential **b** *(Aut: auch* **Differenzialgetriebe***)* differential (gear)

Dif|fe|ren|zi|al- *in cpds (Tech, Math)* differential; **Dif|fe|ren|zi|al|glei|chung** F *(Math)* differential equation; **Dif|fe|ren|zi|al|rech|nung** F *(Math)* differential calculus

dif|fe|ren|zie|ren [dɪfərɛnˈtsiːrən] *ptp* **differenziert VT a** *(= unterscheiden)* to make distinctions/a distinction in; *Behauptung, Urteil* to be discriminating in; *(= abändern)* to make changes/a change in, to modify; **die Gesetze wurden immer stärker differenziert** the laws became more and more sophisticated
b *(Math)* to differentiate
VI to make distinctions/a distinction *(zwischen +dat* between, *bei* in); *(= den Unterschied verstehen)* to differentiate *(zwischen +dat* between, *bei* in); *(bei Behauptung, Urteil)* to be discriminating, to discriminate *(bei* in); **~de Methoden** discriminative methods; **zwischen zwei Dingen ~** to differentiate between two things; **genau ~** to make a precise distinction
VR to become sophisticated; *(= sich auseinanderentwickeln)* to become differentiated

dif|fe|ren|ziert [dɪfərɛnˈtsiːɐt] **ADJ** *(= fein unterscheidend)* subtly differentiated; *(= verfeinert)* sophisticated; *Charakter, Mensch, Gefühlsleben* complex; *(= verschiedenartig) Farbgebung, Anschauungen* subtly diversified; *Warenangebot* diverse **ADV** *gestalten, sich ausdrücken* in a sophisticated manner; **ein Problem ~ sehen/betrachten** to look at/examine a problem from all angles; **ich sehe das etwas ~er** I think it's a bit more complex than that

Dif|fe|ren|ziert|heit F **-,** *no pl* differentiation, sophistication; *(von Charakter, Mensch, Gefühlsle-*

ben) complexity; (= *Verschiedenartigkeit: von Warenangebot)* diversity

Dif|fe|ren|zie|rung F -, -en **a** (= *Unterscheidung)* distinction; *(zwischen zwei Dingen)* differentiation; (= *Abänderung)* modification **b** *(Math)* differentiation

dif|fe|rie|ren [dɪfəˈriːrən] *ptp* **differiert** VI *(geh)* to differ

dif|fi|zil [dɪfiˈtsiːl] ADJ *(geh)* difficult, awkward; *Mensch* complicated

dif|fus [dɪˈfuːs] ADJ *Licht* diffuse; *Gedanken, Ausdrucksweise* confused; *Rechtslage* unclear

Dif|fu|si|on [dɪfuˈzioːn] F diffusion

Di|gi|cam F -, -s digicam

di|gi|tal [digiˈtaːl] ADJ digital ADV digitally

Di|gi|tal- *in cpds* digital; **Di|gi|tal-Ana|log-Wand|ler** [-vantlɐ] M *(Tech)* digital-analog converter; **Di|gi|tal|auf|nah|me** F *(Tech)* digital recording; *(= Foto)* digital photo *or* shot; **Di|gi|tal|band** [-bant] NT *pl* **-bänder** digital tape; **Di|gi|tal|bau|stein** M integrated circuit element; **Di|gi|tal|fern|se|hen** NT digital television

Di|gi|tal|funk M digital broadcasting

di|gi|ta|li|sie|ren [digitaliˈziːrən] *ptp* **digitalisiert** VT to digit(al)ize

Di|gi|ta|li|sie|rer M -s, - *(Comput)* digitizer

Di|gi|ta|li|sie|rung F -, -en digit(al)ization

Di|gi|tal-: **Di|gi|tal|ka|me|ra** F *(Tech)* digital camera; **Di|gi|tal|rech|ner** M *(Comput)* digital calculator; **Di|gi|tal|tech|nik** F *(Comput)* digital technology; **Di|gi|tal|te|le|fon** NT digital (tele)phone; **Di|gi|tal|ton|band** NT *(abbr* **DAT**) digital audio tape; **Di|gi|tal|uhr** F digital clock; *(= Armbanduhr)* digital watch

Dik|ta *(geh) pl von* **Diktum**

Dik|ta|fon [diktaˈfoːn] NT -s, -e, **Dik|ta|phon** NT -s, -e Dictaphone®

Dik|tat [dɪkˈtaːt] NT -(e)s, -e **a** dictation *(also Sch)*; **ein ~ schreiben** *(Sch)* to do (a) dictation; **etw nach ~ schreiben** to write sth from dictation; **Frau Wengel, bitte zum ~!** take a letter please, Ms Wengel; **nach ~ verreist** dictated by X and signed in his/her absence **b** *(fig: = Gebot)* dictate; *(Pol)* dictate, diktat

Dik|ta|tor [dɪkˈtaːtoːɐ] M -s, **Diktatoren** [-ˈtoːrən], **Dik|ta|to|rin** [-ˈtoːrɪn] F -, -nen dictator

dik|ta|to|risch [dɪktaˈtoːrɪʃ] ADJ dictatorial

Dik|ta|tur [dɪktaˈtuːɐ] F -, -en dictatorship

dik|tie|ren [dɪkˈtiːrən] *ptp* **diktiert** VT *(lit, fig) Brief, Bedingungen* to dictate

Dik|tier|ge|rät NT, **Dik|tier|ma|schi|ne** F dictating machine

Dik|ti|on [dɪkˈtsioːn] F -, -en style

Dik|ti|o|när [dɪktsioˈnɛːɐ] NT OR M -s, -e *(old)* dictionary

Dik|tum [ˈdɪktʊm] NT -s, **Dikta** [-ta] *(geh)* dictum, adage

Di|la|ta|ti|on [dilataˈtsioːn] F -, -en *(Med)* dilatation, dilation

Dil|do [ˈdɪldo] M -s, -s dildo

Di|lem|ma [diˈlɛma] NT -s, -s *or (geh)* **-ta** [-ta] dilemma

Di|let|tant [dileˈtant] M -en, -en, **Di|let|tan|tin** [-ˈtantɪn] F -, -nen amateur; *(pej auch)* dilettante

di|let|tan|tisch [dileˈtantɪʃ] ADJ amateurish ADV amateurishly; **~ vorgehen** to act like an amateur

Di|let|tan|tis|mus [dilɛtanˈtɪsmʊs] M -, *no pl* amateurism

di|let|tie|ren [dilɛˈtiːrən] *ptp* **dilettiert** VI *(geh)* to dabble *(in +dat* in)

Dill [dɪl] M -(e)s, -e, **Dil|le** [dɪlə] F -, -en *(Aus) (Bot, Cook)* dill

di|lu|vi|al [diluˈviaːl] ADJ *(Geol)* diluvial

Di|lu|vi|um [diˈluːviʊm] NT -s, *no pl (Geol)* glacial epoch, ice age

Di|men|si|on [dimɛnˈzioːn] F -, -en *(Phys, Math, fig)* dimension

-di|men|si|o|nal [dimɛnzionaːl] ADJ *suf* -dimensional; **dreidimensional** three-dimensional

Di|mi|nu|en|do [dimiˈnuɛndo] NT -s, -s *(Mus)* diminuendo

di|mi|nu|tiv [diminuˈtiːf] ADJ *Form, Endung* diminutive *(zu, von* of)

Di|mi|nu|tiv [diminuˈtiːf] NT -s, -e [-və] diminutive *(zu, von* of)

Di|mi|nu|tiv|form F diminutive form

Di|mi|nu|ti|vum [diminuˈtiːvʊm] NT -s, **Diminutiva** [-va] diminutive *(zu, von* of)

Dim|mer [ˈdɪmɐ] M -s, - dimmer (switch)

DIN® [dɪn, diːn] F -, *no pl abbr von* **Deutsche Industrie-Norm** German Industrial Standard; **~ A4** A4; **~-Format** German standard paper size

DIN [diːn] NT -(s), *no pl (Phot)* DIN; **~-Grad** DIN-speed

di|na|risch [diˈnaːrɪʃ] ADJ *Rasse* Dinaric; **Dinarisches Gebirge** Dinaric Alps

Di|ner [diˈneː] NT -s, -s *(form)* (= *Mittagessen)* luncheon; (= *Abendessen)* dinner

Ding [dɪŋ] NT -(e)s, -e *or (inf)* -er **a** (= *Sache, Gegenstand)* thing; **Gläser, Flaschen und ähnliche ~e** glasses, bottles and that sort of thing *or* and things of that kind; **die Welt der ~e** *(Philos)* the world of material objects; **das ~ an sich** *(Philos)* the thing-in-itself; **das ist ein ~ der Unmöglichkeit** that is quite impossible; **das ist nicht sein ~** *(inf)* that's not really his thing *(inf)*; **guter ~e sein** *(geh)* to be in good spirits, to be of good cheer *(old)*; **die ~e beim (rechten) Namen nennen** to call a spade a spade *(Brit prov)*, to be frank; **jedes ~ hat zwei Seiten** *(prov)* there are two sides to everything; **gut ~ will Weile haben** *(Prov)* it takes time to do a thing well → **drei**

b (= *Gegebenheit)* thing; (= *Angelegenheit, Thema auch)* matter; (= *Ereignis auch)* event; **in diesen ~en** about these things *or* matters; **vergangene ~e** past events; **berufliche ~e** professional matters; **reden wir von andern ~en** let's talk about something else; **wir harrten der ~e, die da kommen sollten** we waited to see what would happen; **die ~e sind nun mal nicht so** things aren't like that; **so wie die ~e liegen** as things are, as matters lie; **wie ich die ~e sehe** as I see things *or* matters; **über den ~en stehen** to be above things; **die ~e stehen schlecht** things are bad; **nach Lage der ~e** the way things are; **vor allen ~en** above all (things), first and foremost; **es müsste nicht mit rechten ~en zugehen, wenn ...** it would be more than a little strange if ... → **Lauf b, Natur d, unverrichtet** *etc*

c *(inf: auch* **Dings**) (= *unbestimmtes Etwas)* thing; (= *Vorrichtung auch)* gadget; **was ist das für ein ~?** what's that thing?; **das ~(s) da** *(inf)* that thing (over) there; **das ist ein ~!** now there's a thing! *(inf)*; **ein tolles ~!** great! *(inf)*; **das ~ ist gut!** that's a good one! *(inf)* → *auch* **Dings**

d *pl* **-er** *(inf: = Verbrechen)* job; **sich** *(dat)* **ein ~ leisten** to get *(Brit) or* be up to something; **da hast du dir aber ein ~ geleistet** that was quite something you got *(Brit) or* were up to *(inf)*; **~er machen** to get *(Brit) or* be up to all sorts of tricks *(inf)*; **was macht ihr bloß für ~er?** the things you do! *(inf)*; **das war vielleicht ein ~** *(inf)* that was quite something *(inf)* → **drehen VT, krumm b**

e (= *Mädchen)* thing, creature

f *(inf: = Penis)* tool *(sl)*, dong *(US sl)*

g *(sl: = Busen)* pair *(hum inf)*, boobs *pl (inf)*

Ding NT -(e)s, -e *(Hist)* thing

din|gen [ˈdɪŋən] *pret* **dingte** [ˈdɪŋtə], *ptp* **gedungen** [gəˈdʊŋən] VT *(old) Diener* to hire, to engage; **gedungener Mörder** hired assassin

Din|gens [ˈdɪŋəns] NT -, - *(dial inf)* = **Ding a, c**

ding|fest ADJ **jdn ~ machen** to take sb into custody, to arrest sb

Din|gi [ˈdɪŋgi] NT -s, -s dinghy

ding|lich [ˈdɪŋlɪç] ADJ material; **~er Anspruch** *(Jur)* claim in rem; **~e Klage** *(Jur)* action in rem; **~er Arrest** *(Jur)* distraint ADV *(Fin)* **~ gesicherte Forderungen** claims *pl* covered by assets

Ding|lich|keit F -, *no pl* materiality

Dings [dɪŋs] NT -, *no pl*, **Dings|bums** [ˈdɪŋsbʊms] NT -, *no pl*, **Dings|da** [ˈdɪŋsdaː] NT -, *no pl (inf)* (= *Sache)* whatsit, doodah, thingummy (-bob), thingummyjig *(all inf)*; **der/die ~** (= *Person)* what's-his/her-name *(inf)*

Ding|wort NT *pl* **-wörter** *(Gram)* noun

di|nie|ren [diˈniːrən] *ptp* **diniert** VI *(geh)* to dine *(form)*

Din|kel [ˈdɪŋkl] M -s, - *(Bot)* spelt

Din|ner [ˈdɪnɐ] NT -s, - *(geh)* dinner

Di|no|sau|ri|er [dino-] M *(lit, fig)* dinosaur

Di|o|de [diˈloːdə] F -, -n diode

di|o|ny|sisch [dioˈnyːzɪʃ] ADJ Dionysian

Di|op|ter [diˈɔptɐ] NT -s, - *(old) (Phot)* viewfinder; *(am Gewehr)* (peep) sight

Di|opt|rie [diɔpˈtriː] F -, -n [-ˈtriːən] *(Opt) (abbr* **dpt**) diopter; **wie viel ~n hast du?** what's your diopter strength?, what strength of glasses do you need?

Di|o|ra|ma [dioˈraːma] NT -s, **Dioramen** [-mən] diorama

Di|os|ku|ren [diɔsˈkuːrən] PL *(Myth)* heavenly twins *pl (auch fig)*, Dioscuri *pl (form)*

Di|oxid [diɔˈksiːt] NT -s, -e [-də] dioxide

Di|oxin [diɔˈksiːn] NT -s, -e dioxin

di|oxin-: **di|oxin|be|las|tet** ADJ dioxin-contaminated *attr*, dioxin-polluted *attr*, contaminated *or* polluted with dioxin *pred*; **di|oxin|hal|tig** ADJ dioxinated

Di|oxyd [ˈdiːɔksyːt, diɔˈksyːt] NT -s, -e [-də] dioxide

Di|ö|ze|san [diøtseˈzaːn] M -en, -en diocesan

Di|ö|ze|san|bi|schof [diøtseˈzaːn-] M *(Eccl; katholisch)* diocesan bishop, bishop of a/the diocese

Di|ö|ze|se [diøˈtseːzə] F -, -n diocese; **die ~ Münster** the diocese of Münster

Diph|the|rie [dɪfteˈriː] F -, -n [-ˈriːən] diphtheria

Diph|the|rie|(schutz)|imp|fung F diphtheria immunization; *(eine Impfung)* diphtheria injection

Diph|thong [dɪfˈtɔŋ] M -s, -e diphthong

diph|thon|gie|ren [dɪftɔŋˈgiːrən] *ptp* **diphthongiert** VT to diphthongize

Diph|thon|gie|rung F -, -en diphthongization

diph|thon|gisch [dɪfˈtɔŋɪʃ] ADJ diphthongized ADV **~ aussprechen** to pronounce as a diphthong

Dipl. *abbr von* **Diplom**

Dipl.-Ing. *abbr von* **Diplomingenieur**

Dipl.-Kfm. *abbr von* **Diplomkaufmann**

Dip|lom [diˈploːm] NT -s, -e diploma; (= *Zeugnis auch)* certificate; **ein ~ machen** to take *(esp Brit) or* do one's diploma

DIPLOM

The **Diplom** is an academic degree in natural sciences, technology, social sciences or economics. To attain the **Diplom**, students must undertake a period of study lasting at least eight semesters, submit a substantial dissertation, and take a final examination. The **Diplom** is presented at a fairly informal ceremony which varies from university to university. The holder is permitted to use the title **Dipl.-Ing., Dipl.-Kfm.** etc.

In the former East Germany the **Diplom** was the standard degree for all subjects.

Dip|lom- *in cpds (vor Berufsbezeichnung)* qualified

Dip|lo|mand [diploˈmant] M -en, -en [-dn], **Dip|lo|man|din** [-ˈmandɪn] F -, -nen *student about to do his/her diploma*

Dip|lom|ar|beit F dissertation *(submitted for a diploma)*

Dip|lo|mat [diploˈmaːt] M -en, -en, **Dip|lo|ma|tin** [-ˈmaːtɪn] F -, -nen diplomat

Dip|lo|ma|ten-: **Dip|lo|ma|ten|kof|fer** M executive case; **Dip|lo|ma|ten|vier|tel** NT (= *Wohngebiet)* diplomatic quarter

Dip|lo|ma|tie [diplomaˈtiː] F -, *no pl (lit, fig)* diplomacy

dip|lo|ma|tisch [diplo'ma:tɪʃ] *(Pol, fig)* ADJ diplomatic ADV diplomatically; **sie hat sich nicht sehr ~ verhalten** she wasn't very diplomatic; **ein Land ~ anerkennen** to recognize a country diplomatically

dip|lo|miert [diplo'mi:ɐt] ADJ qualified

Dip|lom-: **Dip|lom|in|ge|ni|eur(in)** M(F) qualified engineer; **Dip|lom|kauf|frau** F, **Dip|lom|kauf|mann** M business school graduate

Di|pol ['di:po:l] M **-s, -e** **a** *(Phys)* dipole **b** *(auch* **Dipolantenne)** dipole (aerial *(esp Brit)* *or* antenna)

dip|pen ['dɪpn] VT *(Naut) Flagge* to dip

DIP-Schal|ter ['dɪp-] M *(Comput)* dip switch

dir [di:ɐ] PERS PRON *dat von* **du** to you; *(obs, dial)* to thee; *(nach Präpositionen)* you; *(obs, dial)* thou → *auch* **ihm**

Dir. *abbr von* **Direktion, Direktor, Dirigent**

di|rekt [di'rɛkt] ADJ **a** *(= unmittelbar, gerade)* direct; *Erledigung* immediate; **eine ~e Verbindung** *(mit Zug)* a through train; *(mit Flugzeug)* a direct flight; **~e Rede** direct speech
b *(= unverblümt) Mensch, Frage, Ausdrucksweise* direct, blunt; *(= genau) Hinweis* plain; *Vorstellungen, Antwort, Auskunft* clear; **~ sein/werden** to be/become upfront
c *(inf: = ausgesprochen)* perfect, sheer; **es war keine ~e Katastrophe** it wasn't exactly a catastrophe
ADV **a** *(= unmittelbar)* directly; *(= geradewegs auch)* straight; **~ aus** *or* **von/zu** *or* **nach** straight *or* direct from/to; **~ an/neben/unter/über** directly *or* right by/next to/under/over; **~ gegenüber** right *or* directly *or* straight opposite; **jdm ~ ins Gesicht/in die Augen sehen** to look sb straight in the face/the eyes; **~ übertragen** *or* **senden** to transmit live
b *(= unverblümt)* bluntly; **jdm etw ~ ins Gesicht sagen** to tell sb sth (straight) to his face; **~ fragen** to ask outright, to ask straight out
c *(inf: = geradezu)* really; **nicht ~** not exactly *or* really

Di|rekt- *in cpds* direct; *(Rad, TV)* live; **Di|rekt|bank** F *pl* **-banken** *(Fin)* direct bank; **Di|rekt|flug** M direct flight; **Di|rekt|heit** F **-,** *no pl* directness

Di|rek|ti|on [dirɛk'tsio:n] F **-, -en** **a** *(= Leitung)* management, administration; *(von Schule)* headship *(Brit)*, principalship *(esp US)* **b** *(= Direktoren, Vorstand)* management **c** *(= Direktionsbüro)* manager's office

Di|rek|ti|ons|recht NT right to give directives

Di|rek|ti|ve F **-, -n** *(geh)* directive

Di|rekt-: **Di|rekt|kan|di|dat(in)** M(F) *(Pol)* candidate with a direct mandate; **Di|rekt|man|dat** NT *(Pol)* direct mandate; **Di|rekt|mar|ke|ting** NT *(Comm)* direct marketing

Di|rek|tor [di'rɛkto:ɐ] M **-s, Direktoren** [-'to:rən], **Di|rek|to|rin** [-'to:rɪn] F **-, -nen** director; *(von Gefängnis)* governor, warden *(US)*; *(von Krankenhaus)* ≈ senior consultant; *(von Hochschule)* principal; *(von Schule)* head (teacher), headmaster/-mistress *(esp Brit)*, principal *(esp US)*; **geschäftsführender ~** *(Univ)* head of department; **~ der Bank von England** governor of the Bank of England

Di|rek|to|rat [direkto'ra:t] NT **-(e)s, -e** **a** *(= Amt)* directorship; *(von Schule)* headship *(Brit)*, principalship *(esp US)*; *(von Gefängnis)* governorship, wardenship *(US)* **b** *(= Diensträume)* *(von Firma, Museum)* director's office; *(von Hochschule etc)* principal's office; *(von Schule)* head(-master/mistress)'s *or* principal's *(esp US)* study *or* room; *(von Gefängnis)* governor's *or* warden's *(US)* office **c** *(= Abteilung)* department

Di|rek|to|ri|um [dirɛk'to:riʊm] NT **-s, Direktorien** [-riən] **a** board of directors, directorate **b** *(Hist)* Directory, Directoire *(Brit)*

Di|rekt|ri|ce [dirɛk'tri:sə] F **-, -n** manageress

Di|rekt-: **Di|rekt|strah|lung** F direct radiation; **Di|rekt|über|tra|gung** F *(Rad, TV)* live transmission; **Di|rekt|ver|bin|dung** F *(Rail)* through train; *(Aviat)* direct flight; **Di|rekt|ver|mark|tung** F *(Comm)* direct marketing; **Di|rekt|ver|si|che|rung** F *(Insur)* direct insurance; *(= Police)* direct insurance policy; **Di|rekt|ver|trieb** M direct marketing; **Di|rekt|zu|griff** M direct access; **Di|rekt|zu|griffs|spei|cher** M random access memory, RAM

Di|rex ['di:rɛks] M **-, -e** *(Sch sl)* head, principal *(esp US)*

Di|ri|gent [diri'gɛnt] M **-en, -en**, **Di|ri|gen|tin** [-'gɛntɪn] F **-, -nen** *(Mus)* conductor; *(fig)* leader

Di|ri|gen|ten-: **Di|ri|gen|ten|pult** NT conductor's stand *or* desk; **Di|ri|gen|ten|stab** M *(inf)*, **Di|ri|gen|ten|stock** M (conductor's) baton

di|ri|gie|ren [diri'gi:rən] *ptp* **dirigiert** VT **a** *auch vi (Mus)* to conduct; *(fig)* to lead **b** *(= leiten, einweisen) Verkehr etc* to direct

Di|ri|gis|mus [diri'gɪsmʊs] M **-,** *no pl (Pol)* dirigism

di|ri|gis|tisch [diri'gɪstɪʃ] ADJ *Maßnahmen* dirigiste

Dirn [dɪrn] F **-, -en** **a** *(S Ger, Aus: = Magd)* maid **b** *(N Ger: = Mädchen)* girl, lass *(dial inf)*

Dirndl ['dɪrndl] NT **-s, -** **a** *(auch* **Dirndlkleid)** dirndl **b** *(S Ger, Aus: = Mädchen)* girl, lass *(dial inf)*

Dir|ne ['dɪrnə] F **-, -n)** **a** *(= Prostituierte)* prostitute, hooker *(esp US inf)* **b** *(obs: = Mädchen)* lass *(old, dial)*

Dir|nen-: **Dir|nen|mi|li|eu** NT red light district, prostitution scene; **im ~** *(auch)* among prostitutes; **Dir|nen|vier|tel** NT red light district

dis NT **-, -**, **Dis** [dɪs] NT **-, -** *(Mus)* D sharp

Dis|agio [dɪs'la:dʒo, dɪs'la:ʒio] NT **-s, -s** *or* **Disagien** [-'la:dʒən, -la:ʒiən] *(Fin)* discount

Disc|jo|ckey ['dɪskdʒɔke] M **-s, -s** disc jockey, deejay *(inf)*, DJ *(inf)*

Disc|man® ['dɪskmən] M **-s, -s** Discman®

Dis|co ['dɪsko] F **-, -s** disco

Dis|count- [dɪs'kaunt] *in cpds* discount

Dis|coun|ter [dɪs'kauntɐ] M **-s, -** *(inf)* **a** *(= Laden)* discount shop **b** *(= Billigfluganbieter)* no--frills airline

Dis|coun|ter [dɪs'kauntɐ] M **-s, -**, **Dis|coun|te|rin** [-ərɪn] F **-, -nen** *(inf: = Händler)* discount *or* cut-price retailer, discounter *(US)*

Dis|count-: **Dis|count|händ|ler(in)** M(F) discount dealer; **Dis|count|la|den** M discount shop

Di|seur [di'zø:ɐ] M **-s, -e** diseur

Di|seu|se [di'zø:zə] F **-, -n** diseuse

Dis|har|mo|nie [dɪs-] F *(Mus)* discord, dissonance, disharmony; *(fig: = Unstimmigkeit)* discord *no pl*, friction *no pl*, disagreement; *(von Farben)* clash

dis|har|mo|nie|ren [dɪs-] *ptp* **disharmoniert** VI *(geh) (Mus)* to be discordant *or* dissonant; *(Farben)* to clash; *(Menschen)* to be at variance, to disaccord *(form)*; **die beiden ~ so offensichtlich** the two of them are so obviously out of tune with one another

dis|har|mo|nisch [dɪs-] ADJ *Akkord* discordant, dissonant, disharmonious; *Farbzusammenstellung* clashing; *Ehe, Verbindung, Atmosphäre* discordant

Dis|kant [dɪs'kant] M **-s, -e** *(= Stimmlage)* treble; *(= Gegenstimme)* descant

Dis|kant|schlüs|sel M soprano clef

Dis|ket|te [dɪs'kɛtə] F **-, -n** disk, diskette

Dis|ket|ten|lauf|werk NT disk drive

Disk|jo|ckey ['dɪskdʒɔke] M **-s, -s** = **Discjockey**

Disk|ka|me|ra ['dɪsk-] F disc camera

Dis|ko ['dɪsko] F **-, -s** disco

Dis|kont [dɪs'kɔnt] M **-s, -e** *(Fin)* discount

Dis|kon|ten [dɪs'kɔntn] PL *(Fin)* discounted bills *pl*

dis|kon|tie|ren [dɪskɔn'ti:rən] *ptp* **diskontiert** VT *(Fin)* to discount

dis|kon|ti|nu|ier|lich [dɪs-] ADJ *(geh)* discontinuous

Dis|kon|ti|nu|i|tät [dɪs-] F *(geh)* discontinuity

Dis|kont|satz M *(Fin)* discount rate *(Brit)*, bank rate *(US)*

Dis|ko|thek [dɪsko'te:k] F **-, -en** **a** *(= Tanzbar)* discotheque, disco **b** *(= Plattensammlung)* record collection

dis|kre|di|tie|ren [dɪs-] *ptp* **diskreditiert** VT *(geh)* to discredit

Dis|kre|panz [dɪskre'pants] F **-, -en** discrepancy

dis|kret [dɪs'kre:t] ADJ **a** *(= taktvoll, unaufdringlich)* discreet; *(= vertraulich) Angelegenheit, Gespräch* confidential; **er ist sehr ~** *(= verschwiegen)* he's not one to betray a confidence *or* to betray something told in confidence; **du musst lernen, etwas ~er zu sein** you must learn to be more discreet about confidential matters **b** *(Math)* discrete ADV discreetly

Dis|kre|ti|on [dɪskre'tsio:n] F **-,** *no pl* discretion; *(= vertrauliche Behandlung)* confidentiality; **~ üben** to be discreet; **strengste ~ wahren** to preserve the strictest confidence; **jdn um ~ in einer Angelegenheit bitten** to ask sb to treat an affair as a matter of confidence; **~ ist Ehrensache!** you can count on my discretion

Dis|kri|mi|nan|te [dɪskrimi'nantə] F **-, -n** *(Math)* discriminant

dis|kri|mi|nie|ren [dɪskrimi'ni:rən] *ptp* **diskriminiert** VT to discriminate against

dis|kri|mi|nie|rend ADJ discriminatory

Dis|kri|mi|nie|rung F **-, -en** discrimination

Dis|kri|mi|nie|rungs|ver|bot NT ban on discrimination

Dis|kurs [dɪs'kʊrs] M *(geh)* discourse

dis|kur|siv [dɪskʊr'zi:f] ADJ *(Philos)* discursive

Dis|kus ['dɪskʊs] M **-, -se** *or* **Disken** ['dɪskn] discus

Dis|kus|si|on [dɪskʊ'sio:n] F **-, -en** discussion; **zur ~ stehen** to be under discussion; **etw zur ~ stellen** to put *or* bring sth up for discussion; **sich mit jdm auf eine ~ einlassen** to be drawn *or* to get into discussion with sb; **da gibts gar keine ~, du …** I'm not having any discussion about it, you …

Dis|kus|si|ons-: **Dis|kus|si|ons|be|darf** M need for discussion; **es besteht ~** we *etc* need to talk about this; **Dis|kus|si|ons|bei|trag** M contribution to the discussion; **Dis|kus|si|ons|lei|ter(in)** M(F) moderator, anchorman/-woman/-person *(US)*; **Dis|kus|si|ons|red|ner(in)** M(F) speaker (in a discussion); **Dis|kus|si|ons|run|de** F round of discussions; *(= Personen)* discussion group *or* panel; **Dis|kus|si|ons|stoff** M something to talk about; **~ liefern** to provide a subject/subjects for discussion; **für ~ war gesorgt** there was plenty to discuss *or* talk about; **Dis|kus|si|ons|teil|neh|mer(in)** M(F) participant (in a discussion)

Dis|kus-: **Dis|kus|wer|fen** NT **-s,** *no pl* throwing the discus; **Dis|kus|wer|fer(in)** M(F) discus thrower

dis|ku|ta|bel [dɪsku'ta:bl], **dis|ku|tier|bar** ADJ worth discussing; **das ist überhaupt nicht ~** that's not even worth talking about

Dis|ku|tant [dɪsku'tant] M **-en, -en**, **Dis|ku|tan|tin** [-'tantɪn] F **-, -nen** participant (in a discussion)

dis|ku|tie|ren [dɪsku'ti:rən] *ptp* **diskutiert** VTI to discuss; **über etw** *(acc)* **~** to discuss sth; **darüber lässt sich ~** that's debatable; **er diskutiert gern** he's a great one for discussing (everything); **wir haben stundenlang diskutiert** we've spent hours in discussion; **was gibts denn da zu ~?** what is there to talk about *or* to discuss?

Dis|ney|land® ['dɪzni-] NT Disneyland®

Dis|pa|ri|tät [dɪs-] F disparity

Dis|pat|cher [dɪs'pɛtʃɐ] M **-s, -**, **Dis|pat|che|rin** [dɪs'pɛtʃərɪn] F **-, -nen** *(Comm)* dispatcher

Dis|pens [dɪs'pɛns] F **-, -en** *or m* **-es, -e** [-zə] *(Eccl)* dispensation

dis|pen|sie|ren [dɪspɛn'zi:rən] *ptp* **dispensiert** VT **a** *jdn* to excuse *(von* from); *(Eccl)* to dispense **b** *(= zubereiten) Arznei* to dispense

Dis|per|si|on [dɪspɛr'zio:n] F **-, -en** *(Chem, Opt)* dispersion

Dis|per|si|ons|far|be F emulsion (paint)

Dis|play [dɪs'pleː] **NT -s, -s** (*Comput, von Waren*) display; **monochromes ~** monochrome display

Dis|po|kre|dit ['dɪspokrediːt] **M** (*Fin inf*) overdraft

Dis|po|nent [dɪspo'nɛnt] **M -en, -en**, **Dis|po|nen|tin** [-'nɛntɪn] **F -, -nen** (*bei Transportunternehmen*) dispatcher; (*Comm*) managing clerk (*Brit*), manager; (*Theat*) manager

dis|po|ni|bel **ADJ** available

dis|po|nie|ren [dɪspo'niːrən] *ptp* **disponiert** **VI** (*geh*) **a** (*= verfügen*) **über jdn ~** to command sb's services (*form*); **willkürlich über jdn ~** to deal with sb high-handedly; **ich kann nicht über sie ~** I can't tell her what to do; **über etw** (*acc*) (**frei**) **~** to do as one wishes *or* likes with sth; **über etw** (*acc*) **~ können** (*= zur Verfügung haben*) to have sth at one's disposal; **ich kann über meine Zeit frei ~** my time is my own (to do with as I wish) **b** (*= planen*) to make arrangements *or* plans

dis|po|niert [dɪspo'niːɐt] **ADJ** **a** (*geh*) **gut/schlecht ~ sein** to be on/off form (*Brit*), to be in good/bad form, to be in/out of form; **zu** *or* **für etw ~ sein** (*Med*) to be prone to sth; **so ~e Leute** people with this kind of disposition **b** *Gelder* available

Dis|po|si|ti|on [dɪs-] **F** (*geh*) **a** (*= Verfügung*) **zur ~ stehen** to be up for consideration; **jdm zur** *or* **zu jds ~ stehen** to be at sb's disposal; **jdm etw zur ~ stellen** to place sth at sb's disposal; **etw zur ~ stellen** to put sth up for consideration; **etw zur ~ haben** to have sth at one's disposal **b** (*= Anordnung*) arrangement, provision; **seine ~en treffen** to make (one's) arrangements *or* plans **c** (*= Gliederung*) layout, plan **d** (*Med*: *= Anlage*) susceptibility, proneness (*zu* to)

Dis|po|si|ti|ons|kre|dit [-krediːt] **M** (*Fin*) overdraft

dis|pro|por|ti|o|niert [dɪsprɔpɔrtsio'niːɐt] **ADJ** ill-proportioned

Dis|put [dɪs'puːt] **M -(e)s, -e** (*geh*) dispute

dis|pu|ta|bel [dɪspu'taːbl] **ADJ** (*dated*) disputable

Dis|pu|tant [dɪspu'tant] **M -en, -en**, **Dis|pu|tan|tin** [-'tantɪn] **F -, -nen** disputant

Dis|pu|ta|ti|on [dɪsputa'tsioːn] **F -, -en** (*old*) disputation

dis|pu|tie|ren [dɪspu'tiːrən] *ptp* **disputiert** **VI** (*geh*) to dispute (*über etw acc* sth)

Dis|qua|li|fi|ka|ti|on [dɪs-] **F** disqualification

dis|qua|li|fi|zie|ren [dɪs-] *ptp* **disqualifiziert** **VT** to disqualify

Dis|qua|li|fi|zie|rung **F -, -en** disqualification

dis|sen **VT** (*sl*) to diss (*sl*)

Dis|sens [dɪ'sɛns] **M -es, -e** [-zə] (*Jur*) dissent, disagreement *no indef art*

Dis|ser|ta|ti|on [dɪserta'tsioːn] **F -, -en** dissertation; (*= Doktorarbeit*) (doctoral) thesis

dis|ser|tie|ren [dɪsɛr'tiːrən] *ptp* **dissertiert** **VI** → **Dissertation** to write a dissertation/(doctoral) thesis (*über +acc* on)

Dis|si|dent [dɪsi'dɛnt] **M -en, -en**, **Dis|si|den|tin** [-'dɛntɪn] **F -, -nen** dissident

Dis|si|den|ten|be|we|gung **F** dissident movement

Dis|si|mi|la|ti|on [dɪsimila'tsioːn] **F -, -en** (*Ling*) dissimilation; (*Biol auch*) catabolism

dis|si|mi|lie|ren [dɪsimi'liːrən] *ptp* **dissimiliert** **VT** (*Ling*) *Laut* to dissimilate; (*Biol*) *Stoffe* to break down

dis|so|nant [dɪso'nant] **ADJ** dissonant; (*fig*) *Persönlichkeit* lacking harmony

Dis|so|nanz [dɪso'nants] **F -, -en** (*Mus*) dissonance; (*fig*) (note of) discord

dis|so|zi|al [dɪso'tsiaːl] **ADJ** (*Psych*) (socially) dysfunctional

Dis|tanz [dɪs'tants] **F -, -en** **a** (*lit*) distance; (*fig*) (*= Abstand, Entfernung*) detachment; (*= Zurückhaltung*) reserve; **~ halten** *or* **wahren** (*lit, fig*) to keep one's distance; **(zu jdm/etw) auf ~ gehen** (*fig*) to distance oneself (from sb/sth); **die nötige ~ zu etw finden/haben** to become/be sufficiently detached from sth **b** (*Sport*) distance

dis|tan|zie|ren [dɪstan'tsiːrən] *ptp* **distanziert** **VR** **sich von jdm/etw ~** to distance oneself from sb/sth; (*= jdn/etw zurückweisen*) to dissociate oneself from sb/sth **VT** (*Sport*) to outdistance

dis|tan|ziert [dɪstan'tsiːɐt] **ADJ** *Verhalten* distant **ADV** **sich ~ verhalten** to act distant; **~ wirken** to seem distant

Dis|tan|ziert|heit **F -,** *no pl* distance

Dis|tanz|waf|fe **F** (*Mil*) long-range weapon

Dis|tel ['dɪstl] **F -, -n** thistle

Dis|tel|fink **M** goldfinch

Dis|ti|chon ['dɪstɪxɔn] **NT -s, Distichen** [-çn] (*Poet*) distich

dis|tin|gu|iert [dɪstɪŋ'giːɐt, dɪstɪŋgu'iːɐt] **ADJ** (*geh*) distinguished

Dis|tin|gu|iert|heit [dɪstɪŋ'giːɐt-, dɪstɪŋgu'iːɐt-] **F -,** *no pl* distinction

dis|tinkt [dɪs'tɪŋkt] **ADJ** (*old*) distinct, clear

Dis|tink|ti|on [dɪstɪŋk'tsioːn] **F -, -en** (*geh*) **a** (*= Auszeichnung*) distinction **b** (*= Rang*) distinction; (*Aus*: *= Rangabzeichen*) insignia *pl*

Dis|tri|bu|ti|on [dɪstribu'tsioːn] **F -, -en** distribution

dis|tri|bu|tiv [dɪstribu'tiːf] **ADJ** (*Gram, Math*) distributive

Dis|trikt [dɪs'trɪkt] **M -(e)s, -e** district

Dis|zip|lin [dɪstsi'pliːn] **F -, -en** **a** *no pl* (*= Zucht, Ordnung*) discipline; **~ halten** (*Lehrer*) to keep *or* maintain discipline; (*Klasse*) to behave in a disciplined manner **b** (*= Fachrichtung, Sportart*) discipline

Dis|zip|li|nar- *in cpds* disciplinary; **Dis|zip|li|nar|ge|setz** **NT** disciplinary code; **Dis|zip|li|nar|ge|walt** **F** disciplinary powers *pl*

dis|zip|li|na|risch [dɪstsipli'naːrɪʃ] **ADJ** disciplinary **ADV** **jdn ~ bestrafen, ~ gegen jdn vorgehen** to take disciplinary action against sb; **sein Regelverstoß wurde ~ geahndet** he was disciplined for an infringement of the rules; **jdm ~ unterstellt sein** to be answerable to sb

Dis|zip|li|nar-: **Dis|zip|li|nar|maß|nah|me** **F** disciplinary measure *or* action; **Dis|zip|li|nar|stra|fe** **F** punishment; **mit einer ~ rechnen** to expect disciplinary action; **eine ~ bekommen** to be disciplined; **Dis|zip|li|nar|ver|fah|ren** **NT** disciplinary proceedings *pl*

dis|zip|li|nie|ren [dɪstsipli'niːrən] *ptp* **diszipliniert** **VT** to discipline **VR** to discipline oneself

dis|zip|li|niert [dɪstsipli'niːɐt] **ADJ** disciplined **ADV** in a disciplined manner

Dis|zip|li|niert|heit **F -,** *no pl* discipline

Dis|zip|lin-: **dis|zip|lin|los** **ADJ** undisciplined **ADV** in an undisciplined manner; **Dis|zip|lin|lo|sig|keit** **F -, -en** lack *no pl* of discipline

di|to ['diːto] **ADV** (*Comm, hum*) ditto

Di|va ['diːva] **F -, -s** *or* **Diven** ['diːvn] star; (*Film*) screen goddess

di|ver|gent [divɛr'gɛnt] **ADJ** divergent

Di|ver|genz [divɛr'gɛnts] **F -, -en** **a** *no pl* divergence **b** *usu pl* (*= Meinungsverschiedenheit*) difference (of opinion)

di|ver|gie|ren [divɛr'giːrən] *ptp* **divergiert** **VI** to diverge

di|ver|gie|rend [divɛr'giːrənd] *prp von* **divergieren** diverging **PREP** *von* **divergieren** diverging **ADJ** divergent

di|vers [di'vɛrs] **ADJ** *attr* various; **die ~esten ...** the most diverse ...; **~es Angebot von ...** an assortment of ...; **~e** (*= mehrere der gleichen Art*) several; **„Diverses"** "miscellaneous"; **wir haben noch Diverses zu erledigen** we still have various *or* several things to see to

Di|ver|sant [divɛr'zant] **M -en, -en**, **Di|ver|san|tin** [-'zantɪn] **F -, -nen** (*Hist*) subversive

Di|ver|si|fi|ka|ti|on [divɛrzifika'tsioːn] **F -, -en** diversification

di|ver|si|fi|zie|ren [divɛrzifi'tsiːrən] *ptp* **diversifiziert** **VTI** to diversify

Di|ver|ti|men|to [divɛrti'mɛnto] **NT -s, -s** *or* **Divertimenti** [-ti], **Di|ver|tis|se|ment** [divɛrtɪsə'mãː] **NT -s, -s** (*Mus*) divertimento, divertissement

Di|vi|dend [divi'dɛnt] **M -en, -en** [-dn] (*Math*) dividend

Di|vi|den|de [divi'dɛndə] **F -, -n** (*Fin*) dividend

Di|vi|den|den-: **Di|vi|den|den|aus|schüt|tung** **F** (*Fin*) distribution of dividends; **Di|vi|den|den|er|trag** **M** (*Fin*) dividend yield

di|vi|die|ren [divi'diːrən] *ptp* **dividiert** **VTI** to divide (*durch* by)

di|vi|na|to|risch [divina'toːrɪʃ] **ADJ** (*geh*) divinatory

Di|vis [di'viːs] **NT -es, -e** [-zə] (*Typ*) hyphen

Di|vi|si|on [divi'zioːn] **F -, -en** (*Math, Mil*) division

Di|vi|si|o|när [divizio'nɛːɐ] **M -s, -e**, **Di|vi|si|o|nä|rin** [-'nɛːrɪn] **F -, -nen** (*Sw*) divisional commander

Di|vi|si|ons- *in cpds* (*Math*) division; (*Mil*) divisional; **Di|vi|si|ons|stab** **M** (*Mil*) divisional headquarters *pl*; **Di|vi|si|ons|zei|chen** **NT** (*Math*) division sign

Di|vi|sor [di'viːzoːɐ] **M -s, Divisoren** [-'zoːrən] (*Math*) divisor

Di|wan ['diːvaːn] **M -s, -e** divan

DJ (*inf*) *abbr von* **Discjockey** DJ (*inf*), deejay (*inf*)

d. J. *abbr* **a** *von* **dieses Jahres** of this year **b** *von* **der Jüngere** jun.

DJH [deːjɔt'haː] **NT -(s)** *abbr von* **Deutsches Jugendherbergswerk** German Youth Hostel Association

DKP [deːkaː'peː] **F -** *abbr von* **Deutsche Kommunistische Partei**

DLG [deːlɛl'geː] **F -** *abbr von* **Deutsche Landwirtschafts-Gesellschaft** German Agricultural Society

DM [deː'lɛm] *no art* **-, -** (*Hist*) *abbr von* **Deutsche Mark** DM

d. M. *abbr von* **dieses Monats** inst

D-Mark ['deːmark] **F** *pl* **-Mark** (*Hist*) Deutschmark, German mark

DNA [deːlɛn'laː] **F - = DNS**

DNA [deːlɛn'laː] *abbr von* **Deutscher Normenausschuss** German Committee of Standards

D-Netz ['deː-] **NT** (*Telec*) digital cellular phone network

DNS [deːlɛn'lɛs] **F -** *abbr von* **Desoxyribonukleinsäure** DNA

DNS [diːlɛn'lɛs] **M -** (*Comput*) *abbr von* **Domain Name Server** DNS

DNS-: **DNS-Code, DNS-Kode** **M** DNA code; **DNS-Strick|lei|ter** **F** DNA ladder; **DNS--Zei|le** **F** line of DNA

Do|ber|mann ['doːbɛrman] **M -(s), -männer** Doberman (Pinscher)

doch [dɔx] **CONJ** (*= aber, allein*) but; (*= jedoch, trotzdem*) but still, yet; **und ~ hat er es getan** but he still did it, but still he did it

ADV **a** (*betont*) (*= dennoch*) after all; (*= trotzdem*) anyway, all the same; (*= sowieso*) anyway; **jetzt ist er ~ nicht gekommen** now he hasn't come after all; **..., aber ich bin ~ hingegangen** ... but I went anyway *or* all the same *or* after all; **du weißt es ja ~ besser** you always know better than I do anyway; **das geht denn ~ zu weit!** that really is going too far; **und ~, ...** and yet ...

b (*betont*: *= tatsächlich*) really; **ja ~!** of course!, sure! (*esp US*); **nein ~!** of course not!, certainly not!; **also ~!** so it IS/so he DID! *etc*; **er hat es gestohlen – also ~!** he stole it – so it WAS him!; **er hat es also ~ gesagt** so he DID say it; **es ist ~ so, wie ich vermutet hatte** so it (really) IS as I thought; **das ist er ~!** (why,) that IS him!; **das ist ~ interessant, was er da sagt** what he's saying is really interesting; **was es ~ alles für Leute gibt!** the people you get!

c (*als bejahende Antwort*) yes I do/it does *etc*; **hat es dir nicht gefallen? – (~,) ~!** didn't you like it? – (oh) yes I did! *or* oh I did, I did!; **will er nicht mitkommen? – ~!** doesn't he want to come? – (oh) yes, he does; **~, schon, aber ...** yes it does/I do *etc*, but ...

d *(auffordernd: nicht übersetzt, aber emphatisches „to do" wird oft gebraucht)* **komm ~** do come; **kommen Sie ~ bitte morgen wieder** won't you come back tomorrow?; **gib ~ mal her** (come on,) give it to me; **seid ~ endlich still!** do keep quiet!, keep quiet, can't you?; **sei ~ nicht so frech!** don't you be so cheeky *(Brit)* or fresh *(US inf)!*; **lass ihn ~!** just leave him!; **soll er ~!** well let him!, let him then!; **nicht ~!** don't (do that)!

e *(verstärkend)* but; *(Bestätigung erwartend)* isn't it/haven't you *etc*?; **sie ist ~ noch so jung** but she's still so young; **es wäre ~ schön, wenn ...** (but) it WOULD be nice if ...; **dass sie ~ immer widersprechen muss!** why must she always contradict everything?; **das ist ~ die Höhe** or **das Letzte!** well, that's the limit!, that really is the limit!; **das ist ~ gar nicht wahr!** (but) that's just not true!; **das ist ~ wohl nicht wahr?** that's not true, is it?; **du hast ~ nicht etwa ...?** you haven't ..., have you?, surely you haven't or you haven't by any chance ...(, have you)?; **ich habe ~ (aber) gefragt** (but) I did ask

f *(= eigentlich)* really, actually; **es war ~ ganz interessant** it was really or actually quite interesting; **hier ist es ~ ganz nett** it's actually quite nice here

g *(als bekannt Angenommenes wiederholend: nicht übersetzt)* **Sie wissen ~, wie das so ist** (well,) you know how it is, don't you?; **du kennst dich ~ hier aus, wo ist denn ...?** you know your way around here, where is ...?; **wie war ~ Ihr Name?** (I'm sorry,) WHAT was your name?; **hier darf man ~ nicht rauchen** you can't smoke here(, you know)

h *(in Wunschsätzen)* **wenn ~** if only; **o wäre es ~ schon Frühling!** oh if only it were spring!; **dass dich ~ der Teufel holte!** (oh) go to blazes! *(inf)*, the devil take you *(old)*

i *(geh: begründet)* but then; **er sprach etwas verwirrt, war er ~ eben erst aus dem Bett aufgestanden** he spoke in a somewhat confused manner, but then he had only just got out of bed

Docht [dɔxt] **M -(e)s, -e** wick

Docht-: **Docht|hal|ter M** wick holder; **Docht|sche|re F** wick trimmer

Dock [dɔk] **NT -s, -s** or **-e** dock

Dock|ar|bei|ter(in) M(F) docker, dockworker

Do|cke ['dɔkə] **F -, -n** **a** *(aus Korn)* stook; *(aus Wolle, Garn)* hank, skein; *(aus Tabak)* bundle **b** *(dial: = Puppe)* doll

do|cken ['dɔkn] **VTI** to dock

do|cken VT *Korn etc* to stook; *Wolle etc* to wind into a hank or skein; *Tabak* to bundle

Do|cker ['dɔkɐ] **M -s, -, Do|cke|rin** [-ərɪn] **F -, -nen** docker

Do|cking ['dɔkɪŋ] **NT -s, -s** *(Space)* docking

Do|ge ['do:ʒə] **M -n, -n** *(Hist)* doge

Do|gen|pa|last M Doge's Palace

Dog|ge ['dɔgə] **F -, -n** mastiff; **Englische ~** (English) mastiff; **Deutsche ~** great Dane

Dog|ger ['dɔgɐ] **M -s, -** *(Naut)* dogger

Dog|ger M -s *(Geol)* Middle Jurassic, Dogger; *(= Gestein)* dogger

Dog|ger|bank F, *no pl (Geog)* **die ~** the Dogger Bank

Dog|ma ['dɔgma] **NT -s, Dog|men** [-mən] dogma; **etw zum ~ erheben** to make sth into dogma

Dog|ma|tik [dɔ'gma:tɪk] **F -, -en** dogmatics *sing*; *(fig: usu pej)* dogmatism

Dog|ma|ti|ker [dɔ'gma:tikɐ] **M -s, -, Dog|ma|ti|ke|rin** [-ərɪn] **F -, -nen** dogmatist

dog|ma|tisch [dɔ'gma:tɪʃ] **ADJ** *(Rel, fig)* dogmatic

dog|ma|ti|sie|ren [dɔgmati'zi:rən] *ptp* **dogmatisiert** **VT** to make into a dogma, to dogmatize **VI** *(fig pej)* to be dogmatic

Dog|ma|tis|mus [dɔgma'tɪsmʊs] **M -,** *no pl (pej)* dogmatism

Doh|le ['do:lə] **F -, -n** *(Orn)* jackdaw

Doh|le F -, -n *(= Abfluss)* drain

Döhn|kes ['dø:nkəs] **PL** *(N Ger)* stories *pl*, anecdotes *pl*

Dok|tor ['dɔkto:ɐ] **M -s, Doktoren** [-'to:rən], **Dok|to|rin** [-'to:rɪn, 'dɔktorɪn] **F -, -nen** *(auch inf: = Arzt)* doctor; **ja, Herr/Frau ~** yes, Doctor; **er ist ~ der Philosophie/Theologie** he is a doctor of philosophy/theology; **sie hat den ~, sie ist ~** she has a doctorate or PhD, she is a PhD; **den** or **seinen ~ machen** or **bauen** *(inf)* to do a doctorate or PhD; **zum ~ promoviert werden** to receive one's doctorate or PhD; **~ spielen** *(inf)* to play doctors and nurses

Dok|to|rand [dɔkto'rant] **M -en, -en** [-dn], **Dok|to|ran|din** [-'randɪn] **F -, -nen** graduate student studying for a doctorate

Dok|tor|ar|beit F doctoral or PhD thesis

Dok|to|rat [dɔkto'ra:t] **NT -(e)s, -e** **a** *(dated)* doctorate **b** *(Aus: = Prüfung)* examination for a/one's doctorate

Dok|tor-: **Dok|tor|dip|lom NT** doctor's diploma; **Dok|tor|exa|men NT** examination for a/one's doctorate; **Dok|tor|grad M** doctorate, doctor's degree, PhD; **den ~ erwerben** to obtain one's doctorate; **Dok|tor|hut M** doctor's cap; *(fig)* doctorate

Dok|to|rin [-'to:rɪn, 'dɔktorɪn] **F** doctor → *auch* **Doktor**

Dok|tor-: **Dok|tor|prü|fung F** examination for a/one's doctorate; **Dok|tor|schrift F** *(inf: = Handschrift)* doctor's or illegible handwriting; **Dok|tor|spie|le PL** doctors and nurses *sing*; **Dok|tor|ti|tel M** doctorate; **den ~ führen** to have the title of doctor; **jdm den ~ verleihen** to confer a doctorate or the degree of doctor (up)on sb; **Dok|tor|va|ter M** *(Univ)* supervisor; **Dok|tor|wür|de F** doctorate; **jdm die ~ verleihen** to confer a doctorate or the degree of doctor (up)on sb

Dokt|rin [dɔk'tri:n] **F -, -en** doctrine

dokt|ri|när [dɔktri'nɛ:ɐ] **ADJ** doctrinal; *(pej: = stur)* doctrinaire

Do|ku|ment [doku'mɛnt] **NT -(e)s, -e** document; *(fig: = Zeugnis)* record

Do|ku|men|tar [dokumen'ta:ɐ] **M -s, -e, Do|ku|men|ta|rin** [-'ta:rɪn] **F -, -nen** documentalist

Do|ku|men|tar- *in cpds* documentary; **Do|ku|men|tar|film M** documentary (film)

do|ku|men|ta|risch [dokumen'ta:rɪʃ] **ADJ** documentary **ADV** **a** *(= mit Dokumenten)* with documents; **etw ~ belegen/festhalten** to provide documentary evidence for or of sth; **etw ~ festhalten** to document sth

Do|ku|men|tar-: **Do|ku|men|tar|li|te|ra|tur F** documentary literature; **Do|ku|men|tar|sen|dung F** documentary; **Do|ku|men|tar|se|rie F** *(TV)* documentary series; **Do|ku|men|tar|spiel NT** docudrama

Do|ku|men|ta|ti|on [dokumenta'tsio:n] **F -, -en** documentation; *(= Sammlung auch)* records *pl*

Do|ku|men|ten-: **do|ku|men|ten|echt, do|ku|men|ten|fest ADJ** *Tinte* waterproof; **~e Computerausdrucke** document-quality computer print-outs; **~es Papier = Dokumentenpapier**; **Do|ku|men|ten|echt|heit F** *(von Drucker)* document quality; **Do|ku|men|ten|pa|pier NT** *good quality paper used for documents, certificates etc*

do|ku|men|tie|ren [dokumen'ti:rən] *ptp* **dokumentiert** **VT** to document; *(fig: = zu erkennen geben)* to reveal, to show **VR** *(fig)* to become evident

Do|ku|ment|typ M *(Comput)* document type

Do|ku|ment|typ|de|fi|ni|ti|on F *(Comput)* document type definition, DTD

Do|ku|ment|vor|la|ge F *(Comput)* template

Dol|ce Vi|ta ['dɔltʃə 'vi:ta] **NT OR F - -,** *no pl* life of ease, dolce vita; **~ machen** *(inf)* to live a life of ease

Dolch [dɔlç] **M -(e)s, -e** dagger; *(inf: = Messer)* knife

Dolch|stich M, Dolch|stoß *(esp fig)* **M** stab *(auch fig)*, dagger thrust; **ein ~ (von hinten)** *(fig)* a stab in the back

Dolch|stoß|le|gen|de F *(Hist)* myth of the stab in the back *(betrayal of Germany in the first World War by its own politicians)*

Dol|de ['dɔldə] **F -, -n** umbel

Dol|den-: **Dol|den|blüt|ler** [-bly:tlɐ] **M -s, -** umbellifer, umbelliferous plant; **dol|den|för|mig ADJ** umbellate; **Dol|den|ge|wächs NT** umbellifer; **die ~e** the Umbelliferae

Do|le ['do:lə] **F -, -n** drain

Do|li|ne [do'li:nə] **F -, -n** *(Geol)* doline, dolina, sinkhole

doll [dɔl] *(dial, inf)* **ADJ** **a** = **toll ADJ** **b** *(= unerhört)* incredible **ADV** **a** = **toll ADV** **b** *(= sehr)* really; **das hat ~ wehgetan** that hurt like hell *(inf)*

Dol|lar ['dɔlar] **M -(s), -s** or *(nach Zahlenangaben)* **-** dollar; **hundert ~** a hundred dollars

Dol|lar-: **Dol|lar|kurs M** dollar rate; **Dol|lar|no|te F** dollar bill; **dol|lar|sen|si|bel ADJ** dollar-sensitive; **dollarsensible Werte** *pl* dollar-sensitive securities *pl*; **Dol|lar|zei|chen NT** dollar sign

Doll|bord ['dɔl-] **NT** *(Naut)* gunwale

Dol|le ['dɔlə] **F -, -n** *(Naut)* rowlock, oarlock *(US)*

Dol|ly ['dɔli] **M -(s), -s** *(Film)* dolly

Dolm [dɔlm] **M -s, -** *(Aus)* idiot, clot *(Brit inf)*

Dol|men ['dɔlmən] **M -s, -** *(Archeol)* dolmen

Dol|metsch ['dɔlmɛtʃ] **M -(e)s, -e** **a** *(Aus, old)* interpreter **b** *(geh: = Fürsprecher)* spokesman (+*gen, von* for)

dol|met|schen ['dɔlmɛtʃn] **VTI** to interpret; **jdm** or **für jdn ~** to interpret for sb

Dol|met|scher ['dɔlmɛtʃɐ] **M -s, -, Dol|met|sche|rin** [-ərɪn] **F -, -nen** interpreter

Dol|met|scher-: **Dol|met|scher|in|sti|tut NT** school or institute of interpreting; **Dol|met|scher|ka|bi|ne F** interpreter's booth; **Dol|met|scher|schu|le F** school or institute of interpreting

Do|lo|mit [dolo'mi:t] **M -s, -e** *(Geol, Chem)* dolomite

Do|lo|mi|ten [dolo'mi:tn] **PL** *(Geog)* **die ~** the Dolomites *pl*

Dom [do:m] **M -(e)s, -e** **a** cathedral **b** *(fig poet)* vault *(poet)*, dome *(poet)*

Do|main [do'me:n] **F -, -s** *(Comput, Internet)* domain; **eine ~ (auf seinen Namen) registrieren lassen** to register a domain (in one's name)

Do|main|na|me [do'me:n-] **M** *(Comput, Internet)* domain name

Do|mä|ne [do'mɛ:nə] **F -, -n** *(Hist, Jur)* demesne; *(Comput, Internet)* domain; *(fig)* domain, province

Do|mä|nen|na|me M *(Comput, Internet)* domain name

Do|mes|tik [domɛs'ti:k] **M -en, -en = Domestike**

Do|mes|ti|ka|ti|on [domɛstika'tsio:n] **F -, -en** domestication

Do|mes|ti|ke [domɛs'ti:kə] **M -n, -n** **a** *(pej old)* (domestic) servant, domestic **b** *(Sport)* pacemaker

do|mes|ti|zie|ren [domɛsti'tsi:rən] *ptp* **domestiziert** **VT** to domesticate; *(fig auch)* to tame

Dom-: **Dom|frei|heit F** *(Hist)* cathedral close or precincts *pl*; **Dom|herr M** *(Eccl)* canon

Do|mi|na ['do:mina] **F -, -s** dominatrix

do|mi|nant [domi'nant] **ADJ** dominant *(auch Biol)*, dominating

Do|mi|nant- *in cpds (Mus)* dominant

Do|mi|nant|ak|kord M *(Mus)* dominant chord

Do|mi|nan|te [domi'nantə] **F -, -n** **a** *(Mus)* dominant **b** *(= wichtigster Faktor)* dominant or dominating feature

Do|mi|nanz [domi'nants] **F -, -en** *(Biol, Psych)* dominance

do|mi|nie|ren [domi'ni:rən] *ptp* **dominiert** **VI** *(= vorherrschen)* to be (pre)dominant, to predominate; *(Mensch)* to dominate **VT** to dominate

do|mi|nie|rend ADJ dominating, dominant

Do|mi|ni|ka|ner [domini'ka:nɐ] M **-s, -**, **Do|mi|ni|ka|ne|rin** [-ərɪn] F **-, -nen** **a** *(Eccl)* Dominican **b** *(Geog)* Dominican

Do|mi|ni|ka|ner-: **Do|mi|ni|ka|ner|klos|ter** NT Dominican monastery; **Do|mi|ni|ka|ner|or|den** M Order of St Dominic, Dominicans *pl*

do|mi|ni|ka|nisch [domini'ka:nɪʃ] ADJ **a** *(Eccl)* Dominican **b** *(Geog)* **die Dominikanische Republik** the Dominican Republic

Do|mi|no ['do:mino] M **-s, -s** domino

Do|mi|no NT **-s, -s** *(= Spiel)* dominoes *sing*

Do|mi|no-: **Do|mi|no|ef|fekt** M domino effect; **dann tritt ein ~ ein** then the domino theory comes into play; **einen ~ auslösen** to have a knock-on *(Brit)* or domino effect; **Do|mi|no|spiel** NT dominoes *sing; (= Spielmaterial)* set of dominoes; *(= Partie)* game of dominoes; **Do|mi|no|stein** M **a** domino **b** *(Cook) small chocolate biscuit with layers of marzipan and gingerbread*

Do|mi|zil [domi'tsi:l] NT **-s, -e** domicile *(form)*

Dom-: **Dom|ka|pi|tel** NT cathedral chapter; **Dom|ka|pi|tu|lar** [-kapitula:ɐ] M **-s, -e** canon; **Dom|propst** M dean of a/the cathedral

Dom|pfaff ['do:mpfaf] M **-en** or **-s, -en** *(Orn)* bullfinch

Domp|teur [dɔmp'tø:ɐ] M **-s, -e**, **Domp|teu|rin** [-'tørɪn] F **-, -nen**, **Domp|teu|se** [-'tø:zə] F **-, -n** trainer; *(von Raubtieren)* tamer

Don [dɔn] M **-(s)** *(Geog)* Don

Do|nar ['do:nar] M **-s** Thor

Do|nau ['do:nau] F **- die ~** the (river) Danube

Do|nau|mo|nar|chie F *(Hist)* Austria-Hungary, Austro-Hungarian Empire

Do|nau|schwa|ben PL *Swabian settlers on the Danube in Hungary*

Dö|ner ['dø:nɐ] M **-s, -** doner kebab

Dö|ner-: **Dö|ner|bu|de** F *(inf)* kebab shop or bar; **Dö|ner|ke|bab** [dø:nɐke'bap] M **-(s), -s** *(inf)* doner kebab

Don Ju|an [dɔn 'xuan, dɔn 'ju:an] M **- -s, - -s** Don Juan

Dön|kes ['dœŋkəs] PL *(N Ger)* stories *pl*, anecdotes *pl*

Don|ko|sa|ken ['dɔn-] PL Don Cossacks *pl*

Don|ner ['dɔnɐ] M **-s,** *(rare)* **-** *(lit, fig)* thunder *no indef art, no pl; (= Donnerschlag)* peal or clap of thunder; **wie vom ~ gerührt** *(fig inf)* thunderstruck; **~ und Doria** or **Blitz!** *(dated inf)* by thunder! *(dated inf)*, by Jove! *(dated inf)*

Don|ner-: **Don|ner|bal|ken** M *(Mil sl)* thunderbox *(sl)*; **Don|ner|blech** NT *(Theat)* thunder sheet; **Don|ner|büch|se** F *(hum dated)* shotgun; **Don|ner|ge|pol|ter** NT, **Don|ner|ge|tö|se** NT thunderous or deafening crash; **mit Donnergetöse** with a thunderous or deafening crash; **Don|ner|gott** M god of thunder; **Don|ner|grol|len** NT **-s**, *no pl* rolling thunder; **Don|ner|keil** M *(Geol)* thunderstone; *(Archeol)* flintstone; *(Myth, poet)* thunderbolt; **~!** *(dated)*, **Donnerkiel!** *(dated)* my word!, heavens!; **Don|ner|ma|schi|ne** F *(Theat)* thunder machine

don|nern ['dɔnɐn] VI *impers* to thunder; **es donnerte in der Ferne** there was (the sound of) thunder in the distance VI *aux haben or (bei Bewegung) sein* to thunder; **gegen etw ~** *(= prallen)* to crash into sth; *(= schlagen)* to hammer on sth; *(= schimpfen)* to thunder against sth; **er hat furchtbar gedonnert** he really thundered on VT *(inf) (= brüllen)* to thunder out; *(= schleudern, schlagen)* to slam, to crash; **jdm eine ~** to thump *(Brit inf)* or pound *(esp US inf)* sb

don|nernd ADJ *(fig) Beifall, Gesänge* thunderous; *Hufe* thundering

Don|ner-: **Don|ner|rol|len** NT **-s**, *no pl* rolling of thunder; **Don|ner|schlag** M clap or peal of thunder, thunderclap; **die Nachricht traf mich wie ein ~** the news left me thunderstruck

Don|ners|tag ['dɔnɐsta:k] M Thursday → *auch* **Dienstag**

don|ners|tags ['dɔnɐsta:ks] ADV on Thursdays

Don|ner-: **Don|ner|stim|me** F thunderous voice; **Don|ner|wet|ter** NT *(lit old)* thunderstorm; *(fig inf: = Schelte)* row; **das wird ein schönes ~ geben** or **setzen** *(inf)* all hell will be let loose *(inf)*; **~!** *(inf: anerkennend)* my word!; **(zum) ~!** *(inf: zornig)* damn or blast (it)! *(inf)*

Don Qui|chotte [dɔn ki'ʃɔt] M **- -s, - -s** *(Liter, fig)* Don Quixote

Don|qui|chot|te|rie [dɔnkiʃɔtə'ri:] F **-, -n** [-'ri:ən] *(geh)* quixotism; *(= Handlung)* quixotic gesture or act

Don Qui|jo|te [dɔn ki'xo:tə] M **- -s, - -s**, **Don Qui|xo|te** [dɔn ki'xo:tə] M **- -s, - -s** *(Liter, fig)* Don Quixote

Dönt|jes ['dœntjəs, 'dø:ntjəs] PL *(N Ger)* stories *pl*, anecdotes *pl*

doof [do:f] *(inf)* ADJ daft *(esp Brit inf)*, dumb *(inf)* ADV *aussehen* dumb; **~ fragen** to ask a dumb question; **~ lächeln** to give a dumb smile

Doof|heit F **-**, *no pl (inf)* daftness *(esp Brit inf)*, dumbness *(inf)*

Doo|fi ['do:fi] M **-(s), -s** *(inf)* thicky, dummy, dumb-dumb *(all inf)*; **wie Klein ~ mit Plüschohren aussehen** to look a proper charlie *(Brit inf)* or fool

Doof|kopp [-kɔp] M **-s, Doofköppe** [-kœpə] *(sl)*, **Doof|mann** M *pl* **-männer** *(inf)* thickhead *(Brit inf)*, blockhead *(inf)*

Do|pa|min [dopa'mi:n] NT **-s**, *no pl (Med)* dopamine

Dope [do:p] NT **-s, -s** *(sl)* dope *(inf)*

do|pen ['dɔpn, 'do:pn] *(Sport)* VT to dope; **er war gedopt** he had taken drugs VR to take drugs

Do|ping ['dɔpɪŋ, 'do:pɪŋ] NT **-s, -s** *(Sport)* drug-taking; *(bei Pferden)* doping

Do|ping-: **Do|ping|kon|trol|le** F *(Sport)* drug(s) test; **Do|ping|mit|tel** F *(Sport)* drug, doping substance; **Do|ping|prob|lem** NT doping problem; **Do|ping|skan|dal** M *(Sport)* doping scandal; **Do|ping|sün|der(in)** M(F) *(Sport)* drug-taker; **Do|ping|test** M *(Sport)* drug(s) test; **Do|ping|ver|dacht** M *(Sport)* **bei ihm besteht ~** he is suspected of having taken drugs; **Do|ping|vor|wurf** M *(Sport)* doping charge

Dop|pel ['dɔpl] NT **-s, -** **a** *(= Duplikat)* duplicate (copy) *(+gen, zu* of) **b** *(Tennis etc)* doubles *sing; (= Mannschaft)* doubles pair

Dop|pel- *in cpds* double; **Dop|pel|ad|ler** M double eagle; **Dop|pel|agent(in)** M(F) double agent; **Dop|pel-b** [-be:] NT *(Mus)* double flat; **Dop|pel|band** [-bant] M *pl* **-bände** *(von doppeltem Umfang)* double-sized volume; *(= zwei Bände)* two volumes *pl*; **Dop|pel|bau|er** M *(Chess)* doubled pawn; **Dop|pel|be|las|tung** F double or dual load or burden *(+gen* on); **steuerliche ~** double taxation; **Dop|pel|be|schluss** M *(Pol)* two-track or twin-track decision; **Dop|pel|be|steu|e|rung** F double taxation; **Dop|pel|be|steu|e|rungs|ab|kom|men** NT double taxation agreement; **Dop|pel|bett** NT double bed; *(= zwei Betten)* twin beds *pl*; **Dop|pel|bil|der** PL *(Med)* **~ wahrnehmen** or **sehen** to have double vision; **Dop|pel|blind|ver|such** M *(Psych)* experiment using a double blind; **Dop|pel|bock** NT OR M double (-strength) bock beer; **dop|pel|bö|dig** [-bø:dɪç] ADJ *Koffer etc* false-bottomed; *(= doppeldeutig)* ambiguous; **Dop|pel|bö|dig|keit** F **-, -en** *(fig)* ambiguity; **Dop|pel|bo|gen** M double sheet (of paper); **Dop|pel|brief** M *letter weighing over 20 g*; **Dop|pel|bruch** M *(Math)* compound fraction; **Dop|pel|büch|se** F double-barrelled *(Brit)* or double-barreled *(US)* gun or *(Schrotbüchse)* shotgun; **Dop|pel|buch|sta|be** M double letter; **Dop|pel|de|cker** [-dɛkɐ] M **-s, -** **a** *(Aviat)* biplane **b** *(auch* **Doppeldeckerbus)** double-decker (bus); **dop|pel|deu|tig** [-dɔytɪç] ADJ ambiguous; **Dop|pel|deu|tig|keit** F **-, -en** ambiguity; **Dop|pel|ehe** F bigamous marriage; *(= Tatbestand)* bigamy *no pl*; **eine ~ führen** to live bigamously; **Dop|pel|feh|ler** M *(Tennis)* double fault; *(Sch)* double mistake; **einen ~ machen** *(Tennis)* to serve a double fault, to double-fault; **Dop|pel|fens|ter** NT double window; **~ haben** to have double glazing; **Dop|pel|flin|te** F double-barrelled *(Brit)* or double-barreled *(US)* gun or *(Schrotflinte)* shotgun; **Dop|pel|funk|ti|on** F dual or twin function; **Dop|pel|gän|ger** [-gɛŋɐ] M **-s, -**, **Dop|pel|gän|ge|rin** [-ərɪn] F **-, -nen** double, doppelgänger *(esp Liter)*; **ein ~ von Boris Becker** a Boris Becker lookalike, a double of Boris Becker; **dop|pel|ge|schlech|tig** [-gəʃlɛçtɪç] ADJ *(Bot)* hermaphrodite; **Dop|pel|ge|sicht** NT two faces *pl*; *(fig)* two sides *pl*; **dop|pel|ge|sich|tig** [-gəzɪçtɪç] ADJ two-faced, having two faces; *(fig)* two-sided; **Dop|pel|ge|stirn** NT double star; **dop|pel|glei|sig** ADJ *(Rail)* double-track, twin-track; *(fig)* double; **~ sein** *(lit)* to have two tracks ADV **~ fahren** *(fig)* to play a double game; **Dop|pel|griff** M *(Mus)* double stop; **Dop|pel|haus** NT semidetached house *(Brit)*, semi *(Brit inf)*, duplex (house) *(US)*; **er bewohnt eine Hälfte eines ~es** he lives in a semi (-detached house *etc*); **Dop|pel|haus|hälf|te** F semidetached house *(Brit)*, duplex (house) *(US)*; **Dop|pel|heft** NT *(von Zeitschrift)* double number or edition; *(Sch)* exercise book of double thickness; **Dop|pel|hoch|zeit** F double wedding; **Dop|pel|ka|bi|ne** F double or twin cabin or *(von LKW)* cab; **Dop|pel|kinn** NT double chin; **Dop|pel|kle|be|band** NT double-sided adhesive tape; **Dop|pel|klick** [-klɪk] M **-s, -s** *(Comput)* double click *(auf* on); **dop|pel+kli|cken** VI *sep (Comput)* to double-click *(auf* on); **Dop|pel|kol|ben|mo|tor** M two-cylinder engine; **Dop|pel|kon|so|nant** M double or geminate *(spec)* consonant; **Dop|pel|kopf** M *German card game*; **Dop|pel|korn** M *type of schnapps*; **Dop|pel|kreuz** NT *(Mus)* double sharp; *(Typ)* double dagger; **Dop|pel|lauf** M double barrel; **dop|pel|läu|fig** ADJ double-barrelled *(Brit)*, double-barreled *(US)*; **Dop|pel|laut** M *(Ling) (Konsonant)* double or geminate *(spec)* consonant; *(Vokal)* double vowel; *(= Diphthong)* diphthong; **Dop|pel|le|ben** NT double life; **Dop|pel|mo|ral** F double (moral) standard(s *pl*); **Dop|pel|mord** M double murder

dop|peln ['dɔpln] VT **a** *(= verdoppeln)* to double **b** *(Aus: = besohlen)* to resole

Dop|pel-: **Dop|pel|naht** F double-stitched seam; **Dop|pel|na|me** M *(= Nachname)* double-barrelled *(Brit)* or double-barreled *(US)* name; *(= Vorname)* double name; **Dop|pel|na|tur** F dual nature; **Dop|pel|nel|son** M *(Ringen)* full nelson; **Dop|pel|num|mer** F *(von Zeitschrift)* double issue; **Dop|pel|pack** M twin pack; **im ~** as a twin pack; **Dop|pel|part|ner(in)** M(F) *(Sport)* doubles partner; **Dop|pel|pass** M **a** *(Ftbl)* one-two **b** *(für doppelte Staatsbürgerschaft)* second passport; **einen ~ haben** to have dual citizenship; **Dop|pel|punkt** M colon; **Dop|pel|rahm|kä|se** M full-fat cheese; **dop|pel|rei|hig** ADJ in two rows; *Jacke* double-breasted; **~e Perlenkette** double string of pearls; **~e Nietung** two rows of rivets; **Dop|pel|rol|le** F *(Theat)* double role; *(fig)* dual capacity; **dop|pel|schläf|rig** ADJ *Bett* double; **Dop|pel|schlag** M *(Mus)* turn; **Dop|pel|schräg|strich** M *(Typ)* double (forward) slash; **umgekehrter ~** double backslash; **dop|pel|sei|tig** [-zaitɪç] ADJ two-sided, double-sided; *Diskette* double-sided; *Lungenentzündung* double; **~e Anzeige** double page spread; **~e Lähmung** diplegia; **Dop|pel|sieg** M double victory, one-two (victory); **Dop|pel|sinn** M double meaning, ambiguity; **dop|pel|sin|nig** ADJ ambiguous; **Dop|pel|spiel** NT **a** *(Tennis)* (game of) doubles *sing* **b** *(fig)* double game; **Dop|pel|spiel|feld** NT *(Tennis)* doubles court; **Dop|pel|spit|ze** F **a** *(Pol, Admin) joint occupation of (high) office by two people* **b**

(Ftbl) two-pronged attack; **dop|pel|spu|rig** [-ʃpuːrɪç] ADJ = **zweispurig**; **Dop|pel|steck|do|se** F double socket; **Dop|pel|ste|cker** M two-way adaptor; **Dop|pel|stern** M double star; **Dop|pel|steu|er|ab|kom|men** NT reciprocal taxation agreement; **dop|pel|stö|ckig** ADJ *Haus* two-storey *(Brit)*, two-story *(US)*, twin-storey *(Brit)*, twin-story *(US)*; *Bus* double-decker *attr*; *(hum inf) Schnaps* double; **ein ~es Bett** bunk beds *pl*; **Dop|pel|stock|wa|gen** M *(Rail)* double-deck carriage *(Brit) or* car *(US)*; **Dop|pel|stock|zug** M *(Rail)* double-deck train; **Dop|pel|stra|te|gie** F dual strategy; **Dop|pel|strich** M *(Mus)* double bar; **Dop|pel|stu|di|um** NT joint course (of study) *(Brit)*, double major *(US)*; **Dop|pel|stun|de** F *(esp Sch)* double period

dop|pelt ['dɔplt] **ADJ** double; *(= verstärkt) Enthusiasmus* redoubled; *(= mit zwei identischen Teilen)* twin *attr*; *(= zweimal so viel)* twice; *(Comm) Buchführung* double-entry; *Staatsbürgerschaft* dual; **die ~e Freude/Länge/Menge** double *or* twice the pleasure/length/amount; **~e Negation** *or* **Verneinung** double negative; **~er Boden** *(von Koffer)* false bottom; *(von Boot)* double bottom; **~e Moral, eine Moral mit ~em Boden** double standards *pl*, a double standard; **in ~er Hinsicht** in two respects; **ein ~es Spiel spielen** *or* **treiben** to play a double game → **Ausfertigung**
ADV *sehen, zählen* double; *(= zweimal)* twice; *(direkt vor Adjektiv)* doubly; **~ so schön/so viel** twice as nice/much; **sie ist ~ so alt wie ich** she is twice as old as I am, she is twice my age; **das/die Karte habe ich ~** I have two of them/these cards; **das freut mich ~** that gives me double *or* twice the pleasure; **~ gemoppelt** *(inf)* saying the same thing twice over; **sich ~ in Acht nehmen** to be doubly careful; **~ und dreifach** *(bereuen, leidtun)* deeply; *sich entschuldigen* profusely; *prüfen* thoroughly; *versichern* absolutely; **seine Schuld ~ und dreifach bezahlen** to pay back one's debt with interest; **der Stoff liegt ~** the material is double width; **~ (genäht) hält besser** *(prov)* ≈ better safe than sorry *(prov)*

Dop|pel|te(r) ['dɔpltə] M *decl as adj (inf)* double

Dop|pel|te(s) ['dɔpltə] NT *decl as adj* double; **um das ~ größer** twice as large; *(Gegenstand auch)* double the size; **auf das ~ steigen** to double; **das ~ bezahlen** to pay twice as much, to pay double the amount; **etw um das ~ erhöhen** to double sth

Dop|pelt-: **dop|pelt|ge|mop|pelt** ADJ → **doppelt ADV**; **dop|pelt|koh|len|sau|er** ADJ **doppeltkohlensaures Natron** sodium bicarbonate, bicarbonate of soda; **Dop|pelt|se|hen** NT double vision

Dop|pe|lung ['dɔpəlʊŋ] F **-, -en** doubling

Dop|pel-: **Dop|pel|ver|die|ner(in)** M(F) person with two incomes; *(pl: = Paar)* couple with two incomes, two-income *or* double-income family; **Dop|pel|ver|ga|ser** M twin carburettors *pl (Brit) or* carburetors *pl (US) or* carbs *pl (inf)*; **Dop|pel|ver|gla|sung** F double glazing; **Fenster mit ~** double-glazed window; **Dop|pel|ver|si|che|rung** F double insurance; *(= Police)* double insurance policy; **Dop|pel|vie|rer** M *(Sport)* quadruple skulls *pl*; **Dop|pel|vo|kal** M double vowel; **Dop|pel|wäh|rung** F bimetallism; **Dop|pel|zent|ner** M 100 kilos, (metric) quintal; **Dop|pel|zim|mer** NT double room; **dop|pel|zün|gig** [-tsʏŋɪç] **ADJ** *(fig)* devious; *(stärker)* deceitful; *Mensch* two-faced, devious **ADV ~ reden** to say one thing and mean another; **Dop|pel|zün|gig|keit** F **-, -en** **a** *no pl (fig)* deviousness; *(stärker)* deceitfulness **b** *(Äußerung)* devious remark; **Dop|pel|zwei|er** M *(Sport)* double skulls *pl*

Dopp|ler|ef|fekt ['dɔplɐ-] M *(Phys)* Doppler effect

Do|ra|do [do'raːdo] NT **-s, -s** El Dorado

Dorf [dɔrf] NT **-(e)s, =er** ['dœrfɐ] village; *(fig)* backwater; **auf dem ~(e)** *(= in einem bestimmten Dorf)* in the village; *(= auf dem Land)* in the country; **das Leben auf dem ~e** village life; **er ist vom ~(e)** he's from the/our village; *(= vom Lande)* he's from the country; **nie aus seinem ~ herausgekommen sein** *(fig)* to be parochial *or* insular; **das olympische ~** the Olympic Village → **böhmisch, Kirche**

Dorf- *in cpds* village; **Dorf|äl|tes|te(r)** MF *decl as adj* village elder; **Dorf|an|ger** M *(dated)* village green; **Dorf|be|woh|ner(in)** M(F) villager

Dörf|chen ['dœrfçən] NT **-s, -** *dim von* **Dorf** small village, hamlet

Dorf-: **Dorf|er|neu|e|rung** F village regeneration (scheme); **Dorf|gast|haus** NT, **Dorf|gast|hof** M village inn; **Dorf|ge|mein|de** F village community; *(Admin)* rural district; *(Eccl)* village parish; **Dorf|ge|schich|te** F **a** *(Liter: = Erzählung)* story of village life **b** *no pl* village history; **Dorf|hel|fe|rin** F *domestic help employed when a farmer's wife is ill*; **Dorf|ju|gend** F young people *pl* of the village, village youth *pl*; **Dorf|krug** M village inn *or* pub *(Brit)*

Dörf|lein ['dœrflain] NT **-s, -** *dim von* **Dorf**

Dörf|ler ['dœrflɐ] M **-s, -**, **Dörf|le|rin** [-ərɪn] F **-, -nen** *(dated)* villager

Dorf|leu|te PL villagers *pl*

dörf|lich ['dœrflɪç] ADJ village *attr*; *(= ländlich)* rustic, rural

Dorf-: **Dorf|pfar|rer(in)** M(F) *(bes katholisch)* village priest, country vicar *(Brit)*; **Dorf|platz** M village square; **Dorf|schaft** ['dɔrfʃaft] F **-, -en** *(Sw)* hamlet; **Dorf|schö|ne** F, **Dorf|schön|heit** F *(iro)* village beauty; **Dorf|schul|ze** M *(Hist)* village mayor; **Dorf|trot|tel** M *(inf)* village idiot

Do|ria ['doːria] INTERJ → **Donner**

do|risch ['doːrɪʃ] ADJ *(Archit)* Doric; *(Hist auch, Mus)* Dorian

Dor|mi|to|ri|um [dɔrmi'toːriʊm] NT **-s, Dormi|to|rien** [-riən] *(Eccl)* dormitory

Dorn [dɔrn] **M -(e)s, -en** *or (inf)* **-e** *or* **=er** ['dœrnɐ] **a** *(Bot, fig)* thorn; **das ist mir ein ~ im Auge** *(fig)* that is a thorn in my flesh *(esp Brit) or* side; *(Anblick)* I find that an eyesore **b PL -e** *(poet: = Dornbusch)* briar, thornbush **c PL -e** *(= Sporn)* spike; *(von Schnalle)* tongue; *(von Scharnier)* pin; *(Tech: = Werkzeug)* awl

Dorn|busch M briar, thornbush; **der brennende ~** *(Bibl)* the burning bush

Dor|nen-: **dor|nen|ge|krönt** [-gəkrøːnt] ADJ *(Bibl)* wearing a crown of thorns, crowned with thorns; **Dor|nen|ge|strüpp** NT thorny bushes *pl or* undergrowth; **Dor|nen|he|cke** F thorn(y) hedge; **Dor|nen|kro|ne** F *(Bibl)* crown of thorns; **Dor|nen|pfad** M thorny path; *(fig)* path fraught with difficulties, path of tribulation; **dor|nen|reich** ADJ thorny; *(fig)* fraught with difficulty; **dor|nen|voll** ADJ *(fig)* fraught with difficulty

Dorn|fort|satz M *(Anat)* spiny *or* spinous *(spec)* process

dor|nig ['dɔrnɪç] ADJ thorny; *(fig auch)* fraught with difficulty

Dorn-: **Dorn|rös|chen** [-'røːsçən] NT Sleeping Beauty; **Dorn|rös|chen|schlaf** [-'røːsçən-] F *(fig)* torpor, slumber; **Dorn|strauch** M briar, thornbush

Dör|re ['dœrə] F **-, -n** *(dial)* drying kiln *or* oven; *(= Höpfendörre, Malzdörre)* oast

dor|ren ['dɔrən] VI *aux sein (geh)* to dry; *(= austrocknen)* to dry up

dör|ren ['dœrən] **VT** to dry **VI** *aux sein* to dry; *(= austrocknen)* to dry up

Dörr- *in cpds* dried; **Dörr|fisch** M dried fish; **Dörr|fleisch** NT dried meat; **Dörr|obst** NT dried fruit; **Dörr|pflau|me** F prune

dor|sal [dɔr'zaːl] ADJ *(Zool, Ling)* dorsal; *Verkrümmung, Schwäche* spinal

Dor|sal [dɔr'zaːl] M **-s, -e**, **Dor|sal|laut** M *(Ling)* dorsal (consonant)

Dorsch [dɔrʃ] M **-(e)s, -e** fish of the cod group; *(= Kabeljau)* cod(fish)

Dorsch|le|ber F cod liver

dort [dɔrt] ADV there; **~ zu Lande** in that country, (over) there → **da ADV a**

dort-: **dort+be|hal|ten** *sep irreg*, **dort be|hal|ten** △ *irreg* VT to keep there; **dort+blei|ben** *sep irreg aux sein*, **dort blei|ben** △ *irreg aux sein* VI to stay *or* remain there

dor|ten ['dɔrtn] ADV *(old, Aus)* there

dort-: **dort|her** ['dɔrt'heːɐ, dɔrt'heːɐ, *(emph)* 'dɔrtheːɐ] ADV **von ~** from there, thence *(old, liter)*; **dort|he|rum** ['dɔrthɛ'rʊm, dɔrthɛ'rʊm, *(emph)* 'dɔrthɛrʊm] ADV (a)round (there), thereabouts; **dort|hin** ['dɔrt'hɪn, dɔrt'hɪn, *(emph)* 'dɔrthɪn] ADV there, thither *(old, liter)*; **bis ~** as far as there, up to that place; **wie komme ich ~?** how do I get there?; **dort|hi|nab** ['dɔrthɪ'nap, dɔrthɪ'nap, *(emph)* 'dɔrthɪnap] ADV down there; **dort|hi|nauf** ['dɔrthɪ'nauf, dɔrthɪ'nauf, *(emph)* 'dɔrthɪnauf] ADV up there; **dort|hi|naus** ['dɔrthɪ'naus, dɔrthɪ'naus, *(emph)* 'dɔrthɪnaus] ADV out there; **frech bis ~** *(inf)* really cheeky *(Brit) or* fresh *(US inf)*; **das ärgert mich bis ~** *(inf)* that really gets me *(inf)*, that doesn't half annoy me *(Brit inf)*; **dort|hi|nein** ['dɔrthɪ'nain, dɔrthɪ'nain, *(emph)* 'dɔrthɪnain] ADV in there; **dort|hi|nun|ter** ['dɔrthɪ'nʊntɐ, dɔrthɪ'nʊntɐ, *(emph)* 'dɔrthɪnʊntɐ] ADV down there

dor|tig ['dɔrtɪç] ADJ there *(nachgestellt)*; **die ~en Behörden** the authorities there

dort|zu|lan|de ['dɔrttsulandə] ADV in that country, (over) there

DOS [dɔs] NT **-**, *no pl abbr von* **Disk Operating System** *(Comput)* DOS

Dös|chen ['døːsçən] NT **-s, -** *dim von* **Dose**

Do|se ['doːzə] F **-, -n** **a** *(= Blechdose)* tin; *(= Konservendose)* can, tin *(Brit)*; *(= Bierdose)* can; *(esp aus Holz)* box; *(mit Deckel)* jar; *(= Pillendose, für Schmuck)* box; *(= Butterdose)* dish; *(= Zuckerdose)* bowl; *(für Gesichtspuder)* compact; *(= Plastikdose, Streudose)* pack *(inf)*; **in ~n** *(Konserven)* canned, tinned *(Brit)* **b** *(Elec)* socket **c** *(Pharm: = Dosis)* dose **d** *(sl: = Vagina)* hole *(sl)*

dö|sen ['døːzn] VI *(inf)* to doze

Do|sen- *in cpds* canned, tinned *(Brit)*; **Do|sen|bier** NT canned beer; **Do|sen|blech** NT tin for making cans *or* tins *(Brit)*; **Do|sen|milch** F canned *or* tinned *(Brit)* milk, condensed milk; **Do|sen|öff|ner** M can-opener, tin-opener *(Brit)*; **Do|sen|pfand** NT deposit on (drinks) cans, can deposit

do|sier|bar ADJ **leichter ~ sein** to be more easily measured into exact doses; **etw in ~en Mengen verabreichen** to administer sth in exact doses

do|sie|ren [do'ziːrən] *ptp* **dosiert** VT *Arznei* to measure into doses; *Menge* to measure out; *(fig) Rat, Liebe, Geschenke, Lob* to dispense, to measure *or* hand out; *Stoff, Hinweise* to dispense; **ein Medikament genau ~** to measure out an exact dose of a medicine; **etw dosiert verteilen** *(fig)* to dispense *etc* sth in small amounts *or* doses

Do|sie|rung F **-, -en** **a** *(= Dosis)* dosage, dose **b** *(von Arznei)* measuring into doses; *(von Menge)* measuring out

dö|sig ['døːzɪç] ADJ *(inf)* dozy *(inf)*, drowsy

Do|si|me|ter [dosi'meːtɐ] NT **-s, -** dosage meter, dosimeter

Do|sis ['doːzɪs] F **-, Do|sen** ['doːzn] dose; **in kleinen Dosen** *(lit, fig)* in small doses

Dös|kopp ['døːskɔp] M **-s, Dös|köp|pe** [-kœpə] *(N Ger inf)* dozy *(Brit inf) or* stupid idiot

Dos|si|er [dɔ'sieː] NT OR (DATED) M **-s, -s** dossier

Do|ta|ti|on [dota'tsioːn] F **-, -en** endowment

Dot|com ['dɔtkɔm] F **-, -s** *(Comm sl: = Internetfirma)* dotcom

do|tie|ren [do'tiːrən] *ptp* **dotiert** VT *Posten* to remunerate *(mit* with); *Preis* to endow *(mit* with); **eine gut dotierte Stellung** a remunerative position

Do|tie|rung F -, -en endowment; *(von Posten)* remuneration

Dot|ter ['dɔtɐ] M OR NT -s, - yolk

Dot|ter-: **Dot|ter|blu|me** F globe flower; *(= Sumpfdotterblume)* marsh marigold; **dot|ter|gelb** ADJ golden yellow; **Dot|ter|sack** M *(Zool)* yolk sac

dou|beln ['du:bln] VT *jdn* to stand in for; *Szene* to shoot with a stand-in; **er lässt sich nie ~** he never has a stand-in; **ein Stuntman hat die Szene für ihn gedoubelt** a stuntman doubled for him in the scene VI to stand in; *(= als Double arbeiten)* to work as a stand-in

Dou|ble ['du:bl] NT -s, -s *(Film etc)* stand-in; *(für Gesang)* dubber

Doub|lé [du'ble:] NT -s, -s rolled gold *no pl*; *(= Gegenstand)* article made of rolled gold

Doub|lé|gold NT rolled gold

Doub|let|te [du'blɛtə] F -, -n = **Dublette**

doub|lie|ren [du'bli:rən] *ptp* **doubliert** VT *Metall* to coat with gold; *Garn* to twist

Doug|la|sie [du'gla:ziə] F -, -n, **Doug|las|fich|te** ['du:glas-] F, **Doug|las|tan|ne** ['du:glas-] F Douglas fir *or* pine

Dow-Jones-In|dex ['dau'dʒo:nz-] M, *no pl* *(Econ)* Dow-Jones Index

down [daun] ADJ *pred (inf)* **~ sein** to be (feeling) down *or* blue *(inf)*

Down|load ['daunlo:t] -s, -s M *(Comput)* download

down|loa|den ['daunlo:dn] *ptp* **downgeloadet** VTI *(Comput, Internet)* to download

Down|si|zing ['daunsaizɪŋ] NT -s, *no pl (= Verkleinerung durch Abbau von Arbeitsplätzen)* downsizing

Down|syn|drom ['daun-] NT, *no pl (Med)* Down's syndrome; **ein Kind mit ~** a Down's (syndrome) child

Do|yen [doa'jɛ̃:] M -s, -s *(lit, fig)* doyen

Do|yenne [doa'jɛn] F -, -n doyenne

Doz. *abbr von* **Dozent**

Do|zent [do'tsɛnt] M -en, -en, **Do|zen|tin** [-'tsɛntɪn] F -, -nen lecturer *(für* in), (assistant) professor *(US)* *(für* of)

Do|zen|tur [dotsɛn'tu:ɐ] F -, -en lectureship *(für* in), (assistant) professorship *(US)* *(für* of)

do|zie|ren [do'tsi:rən] *ptp* **doziert** *(Univ)* VI to lecture *(über +acc* on, *an +dat* at); *(pej auch)* to hold forth *(über +acc* on), to pontificate *(über +acc* about) VT to lecture in

do|zie|rend ADJ *(pej)* pontificating, lecturing

Do|zier|ton M *pl* **-töne** *(pej)* pontificating tone

dpa [de:pe:'la:] F - *abbr von* **Deutsche Presse-Agentur**

dpi *abbr von* **dots per inch** dpi

dpt *abbr von* **Dioptrie**

Dr. *abbr von* **Doktor**; **~ rer. nat./rer. pol./phil.** PhD; **~ theol./jur.** DD/LLD; **~ med.** MD

Dra|che ['draxə] M -n, -n → *auch* **Drachen** **a** *(Myth)* dragon **b** *(Astron)* Draco

Dra|chen ['draxn] M -s, - **a** *(= Papierdrachen)* kite; *(Sport: = Fluggerät)* hang-glider; **einen ~ steigen lassen** to fly a kite **b** *(pej inf: = zänkisches Weib)* dragon *(inf)*, battle-axe *(Brit inf)*, battle-ax *(US inf)* **c** *(= Wikingerschiff)* longship; *(= Segelschiff)* dragon class yacht

Dra|chen-: **Dra|chen|blut** NT *(Myth)* dragon's blood; **Dra|chen|flie|gen** NT -s, *no pl (Sport)* hang-gliding; **Dra|chen|flie|ger(in)** M(F) *(Sport)* hang-glider; **Dra|chen|saat** F *(pej geh)* seeds of discord *pl*; **Dra|chen|tö|ter** [-tø:tɐ] M -s, - dragon-killer

Drach|me ['draxmə] F -, -n *(Hist: = Währung)* drachma; *(Pharm old)* drachm

Drag & Drop [,drɛgɛnt'drɔp] M -s, *no pl (Comput)* drag and drop

Dra|gee [dra'ʒe:] NT -s, -s, **Dra|gée** [dra'ʒe:] NT -s, -s **a** *(= Bonbon)* sugar-coated chocolate sweet; *(= Nussdragee, Mandeldragee)* dragee **b** *(Pharm)* dragee, sugar-coated pill *or* tablet

Dra|gee|form F **in ~** coated with sugar, in sugar-coated form

dra|gie|ren [dra'ʒi:rən] *ptp* **dragiert** VT *(Pharm)* to sugar-coat, to coat with sugar

Dra|go|man ['dra:goma:n] M -s, -e dragoman

Dra|go|ner [dra'go:nɐ] M -s, - *(Hist)* dragoon; *(pej: Frau)* battle-axe, dragon; **fluchen wie ein ~** *(inf)* to swear like a trooper *(inf)*

Drags|ter ['drɛgstɐ] M -s, - dragster

Draht [dra:t] M -(e)s, ≈e ['drɛ:tə] wire; **per** *or* **über ~** by wire *or (ins Ausland)* cable; **auf ~ sein** *(inf)* to be on the ball *(inf)*; *(wissensmäßig auch)* to know one's stuff; **du bist wohl heute nicht ganz auf ~** *(inf)* you're not quite with it today *(inf)*; **jdn auf ~ bringen** *(inf)* to bring sb up to scratch *(Brit) or* speed; **einen guten ~ zu jdm haben** to be on good terms with sb, to have a good relationship with sb → **heiß ADJ e**

Draht- *in cpds* wire; **Draht|aus|lö|ser** M *(Phot)* cable release; **Draht|bürs|te** F wire brush

drah|ten ['dra:tn] VT *(dated)* to wire, to cable

Draht-: **Draht|esel** M *(dated hum)* trusty bicycle; *(alt auch)* boneshaker *(inf)*; **Draht|fern|se|hen** NT cable television; **Draht|funk** M wire *or* line broadcasting; **Draht|ge|flecht** NT wire mesh; **Draht|ge|we|be** NT wire gauze; **Draht|git|ter** NT wire netting; **Draht|haar|(da|ckel)** M wire-haired dachshund; **draht|haa|rig** ADJ wire-haired; **Draht|haar|ter|ri|er** M wire-haired terrier

drah|tig ['dra:tɪç] ADJ *Haar, Mensch* wiry

Draht-: **draht|los** ADJ *Telegrafie* wireless; *Telefon, Nachrichtenübermittlung* cordless; **Draht|rol|le** F wire coil; **Draht|sai|te** F *(Mus)* steel string; **Draht|sche|re** F wire cutters *pl*; **Draht|schnei|der** M wire cutters *pl*

Draht|seil NT wire cable; **Nerven wie ~e** *(inf)* nerves of steel

Draht|seil-: **Draht|seil|akt** M *(lit, fig)* balancing act; **Draht|seil|bahn** F cable railway; **Draht|seil|künst|ler(in)** M(F) *(= Seiltänzer)* tightrope artist *or* walker

Draht-: **Draht|sieb** NT wire sieve; **Draht|stift** M panel pin; **Draht|ver|hau** M wire entanglement; *(= Käfig)* wire enclosure; **Draht|zan|ge** F wire cutters *pl*; **Draht|zaun** M wire fence; **Draht|zie|hen** NT -s, *no pl* wiredrawing; **Draht|zie|her** [-tsi:ɐ] M -s, -, **Draht|zie|he|rin** [-ərɪn] F -, -nen wiredrawer; *(fig)* wirepuller *(esp US)*

Drai|na|ge [drɛ'naʒə, drɛ'na:ʒ] F -, -n *(esp Aus, Sw)* drainage *(auch Med etc)*

drai|nie|ren [drɛ'ni:rən] *ptp* **drainiert** VTI *(esp Aus, Sw)* to drain *(auch Med)*

Drai|si|ne [drai'zi:nə, drɛ'zi:nə] F -, -n *(Rail)* trolley; *(= Fahrrad)* dandy horse *(old)*

dra|ko|nisch [dra'ko:nɪʃ] ADJ Draconian

drall [dral] ADJ *Mädchen, Arme* strapping, sturdy; *Busen, Hintern* ample; *Backen* rounded

Drall [dral] M -(e)s, -e **a** *(von Kugel, Ball)* spin; *(um Längsachse auch)* twist; *(= Abweichung von Bahn)* swerve; *(inf: von Auto)* pull; **einem Ball einen ~ geben** to give a ball (some) spin, to spin a ball; **einen ~ nach links haben** *(Auto)* to pull to the left **b** *(fig: = Hang)* tendency, inclination; **sie hat einen ~ nach links** she inclines *or* leans to the left

Dra|lon® ['dra:lɔn] NT -(s), *no pl* Dralon®

Dra|ma ['dra:ma] NT -s, **Dramen** [-mən] *(lit: = Stück, Gattung, fig: = dramatisches Geschehen)* drama; *(fig) (= Katastrophe)* disaster; *(= Aufheben)* to-do *(inf)*

Dra|ma|tik [dra'ma:tɪk] F -, *no pl (lit, fig)* drama

Dra|ma|ti|ker [dra'ma:tikɐ] M -s, -, **Dra|ma|ti|ke|rin** [-ərɪn] F -, -nen dramatist

dra|ma|tisch [dra'ma:tɪʃ] *(lit, fig)* ADJ dramatic ADV dramatically; **machs nicht so ~!** don't be so dramatic!

dra|ma|ti|sie|ren [dramati'zi:rən] *ptp* **dramatisiert** VT *(lit, fig)* to dramatize

Dra|ma|ti|sie|rung F -, -en dramatization

Dra|ma|turg [drama'tʊrk] M -en, -en [-gn], **Dra|ma|tur|gin** [-'tʊrgɪn] F -, -nen dramaturge *(form)*, literary manager

Dra|ma|tur|gie [dramatʊr'gi:] F -, -n [-'gi:ən] dramaturgy; *(= Abteilung)* drama department

dra|ma|tur|gisch [drama'tʊrgɪʃ] ADJ dramatic, dramaturgical *(rare)*; *Abteilung* drama *attr*

dran [dran] ADV *(inf)* → *auch* **daran** **a** *(= an der Reihe)* **jetzt bist du ~** it's your turn now; *(beim Spielen auch)* it's your go now; **(wenn er erwischt wird,) dann ist er ~** *or (hum)* **am ~sten** (if he gets caught) he'll be for it *(inf)*, (if he gets caught) he'll be for the high jump *(Brit inf)*; **er war ~** *(= musste sterben)* his time had come; **morgen ist Englisch ~** we've got English tomorrow → **drauf, drum, glauben**

b **schlecht ~ sein** to be in a bad way; *(= unglücklich auch)* to be unfortunate; **gut ~ sein** to be well off; *(= glücklich)* to be fortunate; *(gesundheitlich)* to be well; **früh/spät ~ sein** to be early/late

c **an ihm ist nichts ~** *(= sehr dünn)* he's nothing but skin and bone; *(= nicht attraktiv, nicht interessant)* there is nothing to him; **an dem Hühnchen ist nichts ~** there is no meat on that chicken; **was ist an ihm ~, dass ...?** what is there about him that ...?; **da ist alles ~!** that's got everything; **da wird schon etwas (Wahres) ~ sein** there must be some truth *or* something in that; **an den Gerüchten ist nichts ~** there's nothing in those rumours; **an dem Auto ist irgendetwas ~** there is something wrong *or* the matter with the car; **ich weiß nicht, wie ich (bei ihm) ~ bin** I don't know where I stand (with him)

Drä|na|ge [drɛ'na:ʒə] F -, -n drainage

dran+blei|ben VI *sep irreg aux sein (inf)* **a** *(= sich nicht entfernen)* to stay close; *(am Apparat)* to hang on; *(an der Arbeit)* to stick at it; **am Gegner/an der Arbeit ~** to stick to one's opponent/at one's work **b** *(= sterben)* to kick the bucket *(inf)*; **er ist bei der Operation drangeblieben** the operation did for him *(inf)*

drang *pret von* **dringen**

Drang [draŋ] M -(e)s, ≈e ['drɛŋə] **a** *(= Antrieb)* urge *(auch Physiol)*, impulse; *(= Sehnsucht)* yearning *(nach* for); *(nach Wissen)* thirst *(nach* for); **~ nach Bewegung** urge *or* impulse to move; **ich habe einen ~** *(inf: zur Toilette)* I'm dying to go *(inf)* → **Sturm a** **b** **der ~ zum Tor** *(Sport)* the surge *(Brit) or* drive *(US)* toward(s) the goal; **der ~ nach Osten** the drive toward(s) the East **c** *(geh: = Druck)* pressure; **im ~ der Ereignisse** under the pressure of events

dran+ge|ben VT *sep irreg (inf)* **a** *(= zufügen)* to add *(an +acc* to); **ich geb noch 10 Minuten dran** I'll wait another ten minutes, I'll give you/him *etc* another ten minutes **b** *(= opfern)* to give up; *Leben auch* to sacrifice; *Geld* to fork out *(inf)*; **sein Leben für etw ~** to give one's life for sth

dran+ge|hen VI *sep irreg aux sein (inf)* **a** *(= berühren, sich zu schaffen machen an)* to touch *(an etw acc* sth); **an etw** *(acc)* **(zu nahe) ~** *(= sich nähern)* to go (too) close to sth; **das Telefon klingelte, er ging aber nicht dran** the phone rang but he didn't answer it **b** *(= in Angriff nehmen)* **~, etw zu tun** to get down to doing sth; **es wird Zeit, dass ich drangehe** it's time I got down to it

Drän|ge|lei [drɛŋə'lai] F -, -en *(inf)* pushing, jostling; *(im Verkehr)* jostling; *(= Bettelei)* pestering

drän|geln ['drɛŋln] *(inf)* VI to push, to jostle; *(im Verkehr)* to jostle VTI *(= betteln)* to pester VR **sich nach vorne** *etc* **~** to push one's way to the front *etc*; **sich ~, etw zu tun** *(fig)* to fall over oneself to do sth *(inf)*

drän|gen ['drɛŋən] VI **a** *(in Menge)* to push, to press; **die Menge drängte zum Ausgang** the crowd pressed toward(s) the exit

b *(Sport: = offensiv spielen)* to press *or* push forward

c *(= fordern)* to press *(auf +acc* for); **darauf ~, eine Antwort zu erhalten, auf Antwort ~** to

press for an answer; **darauf ~, dass jd etw tut/dass etw getan wird** to press for sb to do sth/for sth to be done; **zum Aufbruch/zur Eile ~** to be insistent that one should leave/hurry **d** *(zeitlich)* to be pressing, to press; **die Zeit drängt** time is pressing, time presses; **es drängt (nicht)** it's (not) pressing *or* urgent
VT **a** *(mit Ortsangabe)* to push **b** *(= auffordern)* to press, to urge; **es drängt mich, das zu tun** I feel moved *or* the urge to do that
VR *(Menge)* to throng *or* crowd; *(fig: Termine etc)* to mount up; **sich nach vorn/durch die Menge ~** to push *or* force one's way to the front/through the crowd → *auch* **gedrängt**

Drän|gen NT **-s,** *no pl* urging; *(= Bitten)* requests *pl*; *(= Bestehen)* insistence

drän|gend ADJ pressing, urgent

Dräng|ler M **-s, -**, **Dräng|le|rin** F **-, -nen** *(pej)* pushy person; *(Aut)* pushy driver, road hog *(inf)*

Drang|sal ['draŋza:l] F **-, -e** *(old, liter)* (= *Not)* hardship; *(= Leiden)* suffering, distress

drang|sa|lie|ren [draŋza'li:rən] *ptp* **drangsaliert** VT *(= plagen)* to pester, to plague; *(= unterdrücken)* to oppress

drang|voll ADJ **~e Enge** *(geh)* terrible crush (of people)

dran+hal|ten *sep irreg (inf)* **VT** to hold up (*+dat, an +acc* to); **etw näher an etw** *(acc)* **~** to hold sth closer to sth **VR** *(= sich beeilen)* to hurry up, to get a move on *(inf)*; *(= sich anstrengen)* to make an effort, to get one's *or* the finger out (*Brit inf*); *(= nahe dranbleiben)* to keep close to it

dran+hän|gen *sep (inf)* **VT** **etw an etw** *(acc)* **~** to hang sth onto sth; **viel Zeit** *etc* **~, etw zu tun** to put a lot of time *etc* into doing sth **VI** *irreg* **an etw** *(dat)* **~** to hang from sth; **es hing ein Zettel dran** a tag was attached (*an +dat* to) **VR** to hang on; *(= verfolgen)* to stay close behind; *(= ständig begleiten)* to latch on (*bei* to); *(= jds Beispiel folgen)* to follow suit

drä|nie|ren [drɛ'ni:rən] *ptp* **dräniert** VT to drain

dran+kom|men VI *sep irreg aux sein (inf)* **a** *(= berühren)* to touch **b** *(= erreichen können)* to be able to reach *(an etw (acc)* sth) **c** *(= an die Reihe kommen)* to have one's turn; *(bei Spielen)* to have one's turn *or* go; *(Sch) (beim Melden)* to be called; *(Frage, Aufgabe etc)* to come up; **jetzt kommst du dran** now it's your turn/go; **du kommst als Erster/Nächster dran** you're first/next; **nun kommt das Schlafzimmer dran** it's the bedroom next

dran+krie|gen VT *sep (inf)* **jdn ~** to get sb *(inf)*; *(zu einer Arbeit)* to get sb to do it/sth; *(mit Witz, Streich)* to catch sb out

Drank|ton|ne ['draŋk-] F *(N Ger)* swill bucket; *(fig inf)* walking dustbin *(hum)*

dran+las|sen VT *sep irreg (inf)* **etw (an etw** *dat*) **~** to leave sth on (sth)

dran+ma|chen *sep (inf)* **VR** = **daranmachen VT** **etw (an etw** *acc*) **~** to put sth on (sth)

dran+neh|men VT *sep irreg (inf) Schüler* to ask, to question; *Patienten* to take, to see

dran+set|zen *sep (inf)* **VT** **a** *(= anfügen)* **ein Stück/ein Teil (an etw** *acc*) **~** to add a piece/part (to sth) **b** *(= einsetzen)* **seine Kraft/sein Vermögen ~** to put one's effort/money into it; **alles ~** to make every effort; **jdn ~** to put sb onto the job *or* it **VR** **a** *(nahe an etw)* **sich (an etw** *acc*) **~** to sit (down) next to sth **b** *(= Arbeit anfangen)* to get down to work *or* it

drans|ten ['dranstn] ADV *(hum)* **am ~** → **dran**

dran+wol|len VI *sep (inf) (= drankommen wollen)* to want to have one's turn; *(= probieren wollen)* to want to have a go

Dra|pe|rie [drapə'ri:] F **-, -en** [-'ri:ən] *(old)* drapery; *(= Faltenwurf)* drapes *pl*

dra|pie|ren [dra'pi:rən] *ptp* **drapiert** VT to drape; *(fig)* to cloak

Dra|pie|rung F **-, -en** **a** *(= das Drapieren)* draping; *(fig)* cloaking **b** *(= Schmuck, kunstvolle Falten)* drape; **~en** *(fig: = beschönigende Worte)* fine phrases *pl*

Dras|tik ['drastɪk] F **-,** *no pl (= Derbheit)* drasticness; *(= Deutlichkeit)* graphicness; **etw mit besonderer ~ beschreiben** to describe sth particularly graphically

dras|tisch ['drastɪʃ] **ADJ** *(= derb)* drastic; *(= deutlich)* graphic **ADV** *(= energisch) kürzen* drastically; *(= deutlich) zeigen, verdeutlichen* explicitly; **~ vorgehen** to take drastic measures; **~ sparen** to cut spending drastically; **sich ~ ausdrücken** to use strong language

dräu|en ['drɔyən] VI *(poet)* = **drohen VI c**

drauf [drauf] ADV *(inf)* → *auch* **darauf**; **immer feste ~!** get stuck in there! *(inf)*, let him have it! *(inf)*; **~ und dran sein, etw zu tun** to be on the point *or* verge of doing sth → **draufhaben**

Drauf-: **drauf+be|kom|men** *ptp* **draufbekommen** VT *sep irreg (inf)* **eins ~** to be given a smack; **Drauf|ga|be** F **a** *(Comm)* deposit **b** *(Aus)* = **Zugabe**; **Drauf|gän|ger** [-gɛŋɐ] M **-s, -**, **Drauf|gän|ge|rin** [-ərɪn] F **-, -nen** daredevil, adventurous type; *(= Mann: bei Frauen)* predator; **drauf|gän|ge|risch** [-gɛŋərɪʃ] ADJ daring, adventurous; *(negativ)* reckless; *(bei Frauen)* predatory, wolfish; **Drauf|gän|ger|tum** NT **-s,** *no pl* daring, adventurousness; *(negativ)* recklessness; *(bei Frauen)* predatory ways *pl*; **drauf+ge|ben** VT *irreg sep* **a** **jdm eins ~** *(inf)* to give sb a smack **b** *(= dazugeben)* **noch etwas ~** to add some extra *(inf)* **c** *(Aus: = als Zugabe anfügen)* to sing/play *etc* as an encore; **drauf+ge|hen** VI *sep irreg aux sein (inf) (= entzweigehen)* to fall apart *or* to bits; *(= sterben)* to bite the dust *(inf)*; *(Geld)* to disappear; **Drauf|geld** NT extra payment; **drauf+ha|ben** VT *sep irreg (inf) Sprüche, Antwort* to come out with; **er hat es drauf** he knows his stuff *(inf)*; **jetzt hat sie es endlich drauf** she's finally got it; **zeigen, was man draufhat** to show what one is made of; **den Chauvi ~** to be a real chauvinist; **etw ~** *(sl) (= können)* to be able to do sth no bother *(inf)*; *Kenntnisse* to be well up on sth *(inf)*; *Witze, Sprüche* to have sth off pat *(inf)*; **schwer was ~** *(sl)* to know one's stuff *(inf) or* onions (*Brit inf*); **160 Sachen ~** *(inf)* to be doing 160; **drauf+hal|ten** *sep irreg (inf)* **VT** **etw (auf etw** *acc*) **~** to hold sth on (sth) **VI** *(= als Ziel angehen)* to aim for it; **drauf+hau|en** *sep irreg* **VI** *(inf: = schlagen)* to hit hard; **drauf+kom|men** VI *sep irreg aux sein (inf) (= sich erinnern)* to remember; *(= begreifen)* to catch on, to get it *(inf)*; **jdm ~** to get on to sb *(inf)*; **drauf+krie|gen** VT *sep (inf)* **etw (auf etw** *acc*) **~** to get *or* fit sth on(to sth); **eins ~** to be given what for (*Brit inf*), to be told off; *(= geschlagen werden)* to be given a smack; *(= Schicksalsschlag erhalten)* to receive a blow; *(= besiegt werden)* to be given a thrashing *(inf)*; **drauf+las|sen** VT *sep irreg (inf)* **etw (auf etw** *dat*) **~** to leave sth on (sth); **drauf+le|gen** *sep (inf)* **VT** **a** to lay out; **20 Euro ~** to lay out an extra 20 euros **b** **etw (auf etw** *acc*) **~** to put *or* lay sth on(to sth) **VI** *(= mehr bezahlen)* to pay more

drauf|los [drauf'lo:s] ADV **(nur) immer feste** *or* **munter ~!** (just) keep at it!, keep it up!

drauf|los-: **drauf|los+ar|bei|ten** VI *sep (inf)* to work away, to beaver away (*Brit inf*); *(= anfangen)* to start working; **drauf|los+fah|ren** VI *sep irreg aux sein (inf) (auf ein Ziel)* to make *or* head straight for it; *(ohne Ziel)* to just set off (in any direction); **drauf|los+ge|hen** VI *sep irreg aux sein (inf) (auf ein Ziel)* to make straight for it; *(ohne Ziel)* to set off (with no special destination); *(= nicht zögern)* to set to work; **drauf|los+ma|len** VI *sep (inf)* to paint away; *(= anfangen)* to start painting; **drauf|los+re|den** VI *sep (inf)* to talk away; *(= anfangen)* to start talking; **drauf|los+schie|ßen** VI *sep irreg (inf)* to fire away; **drauf|los+schla|gen** VI *sep irreg (inf)* to hit out, to let fly *(inf)*

drauf-: **drauf+ma|chen** VT *sep (inf)* **etw (auf etw** *acc*) **~** to put sth on(to sth); **einen ~** to make a night of it *(inf)*; **drauf+sat|teln** VT *sep (inf)* to slap on (top); **drauf sein** VI *irreg aux sein (inf)* **schlecht/gut ~** to be in a bad/good mood; **wie ist der denn drauf?** what kind of trip is he on? *(inf)*; **drauf+set|zen** VT *sep (fig inf)* **eins** *or* **einen ~** to go one step further; **Drauf|sicht** F top view; **drauf+ste|hen** VI *sep irreg (inf) aux haben or (dial) sein* **etw steht drauf** sth is on it; **auf etw** *(dat)* **~** *(Mensch, Sache)* to stand on sth; *(Aufschrift)* to be on sth; **(da) stehe ich nicht drauf** *(fig sl)* it doesn't turn me on *(inf)*; **drauf+sto|ßen** *sep irreg (inf)* **VI** *aux sein* to come *or* hit upon it; *(= gegen etw stoßen)* to bump *or* run into it; *(= finden)* to come across it **VT** **jdn ~** to point it out to sb; **drauf+stür|zen** VR *sep (inf)* to swoop *or* pounce on it/them, to rush to get one's hands on it/them; **drauf+zah|len** *sep (inf)* **VT** = **drauflegen VT a** **VI** **a** = **drauflegen VI** **b** *(fig: = Einbußen erleiden)* to pay the price

draus [draus] ADV = **daraus**

draus-: **draus+brin|gen** VT *sep irreg (dial)* **jdn ~** *(= Konzentration stören)* to make sb lose track, to distract sb; *(= irremachen)* to put sb off; **draus+kom|men** VI *sep irreg aux sein* **a** *(dial, Aus: = aus dem Konzept kommen)* to lose track **b** *(Sw: = verstehen)* to see, to get it *(inf)*

drau|ßen ['drausn] ADV outside; *(= im Freien auch)* out of doors, outdoors; *(= da draußen, weit weg von hier)* out there; *(= im Ausland)* abroad; **~ (an der Front)** out there (on the front); **~ auf dem Lande/dem Balkon/im Garten** out in the country/on the balcony/in the garden; **~ (auf dem Meer)** out at sea; **da/hier ~** out there/here; **ganz da ~** way out there; **~ (vor der Tür)** at the door; **nach ~** outside; *(ferner weg)* out there; **weit/weiter ~** far/further out; **~ bleiben/lassen** to stay/leave out *(auch fig inf) or* outside; **„Hunde müssen ~ bleiben"** "no dogs (please)", "please leave your dog outside"; **etw ~ tragen** to wear sth outside

Drech|sel|bank F *pl* **-bänke** wood(turning) lathe

drech|seln ['drɛksln] **VT** to turn *(on a wood lathe)*; *(fig pej)* to overelaborate; *Vers* to turn → *auch* **gedrechselt** **VI** to work the (wood) lathe

Drechs|ler ['drɛkslɐ] M **-s, -**, **Drechs|le|rin** [-ərɪn] F **-, -nen** (wood)turner

Drechs|ler|ar|beit F (wood)turning; *(= Gegenstand)* piece turned on the lathe

Drechs|le|rei [drɛkslə'rai] F **-, -en** *(= Werkstatt)* (wood)turner's workshop; *(= Handwerk)* (wood)turning

Dreck [drɛk] M **-(e)s,** *no pl* **a** dirt; *(esp ekelhaft)* filth; *(= Schlamm)* mud; *(= Kot)* muck; *(fig) (= Schund)* rubbish; *(= Schmutz, Obszönes)* dirt, muck; *(stärker)* filth; *(inf: = schlimme Lage)* mess, jam *(inf)*; **~ machen** to make a mess; **in/mit ~ und Speck** *(= ungewaschen)* unwashed; **im ~ sitzen** *or* **stecken** *(inf)* to be in a mess *or* jam *(inf)*; **aus dem größten** *or* **gröbsten ~ heraus sein** *(inf)* to be through *or* past the worst; **jdn wie den letzten ~ behandeln** *(inf)* to treat sb like dirt; **der letzte ~ sein** *(inf: Mensch)* to be the lowest of the low; **~ am Stecken haben** *(fig)* to have a skeleton in the cupboard; **etw in den ~ ziehen** *or* **treten** *(fig)* to drag sth through the mud → **Karren b**, **bewerfen a**
b *(inf) (= Angelegenheit, Kram)* business, stuff *(inf)*; *(= Kleinigkeit)* little thing; **sich einen ~ um jdn/etw kümmern** *or* **scheren** not to care *or* give a damn about sb/sth *(inf)*; **mach deinen ~ alleine!** do it yourself; **die Nase in jeden ~ stecken** *(inf)* to poke one's nose into everyone's business *or* into everything; **das geht ihn einen ~ an** that's none of his business, that's got damn all to do with him *(inf)*; **einen ~ ist er/hast du** like hell he is/you have *(inf)*

Dreck-: **Dreck|ar|beit** F *(inf)* **a** *(lit, fig: = schmutzige Arbeit)* dirty work **b** *(pej: = niedere Arbeit)* drudgery *no pl*; **Dreck|ei|mer** M *(inf) (im Haus)* rubbish bin *(Brit)*, trash can *(US)*; *(im Freien)* dustbin, trash can *(US)*; **Dreck|fin|-**

ger PL *(inf: lit, fig)* dirty fingers *pl*; **Dreck|fink** M *(inf)* = **Dreckspatz**

dre|ckig [ˈdrɛkɪç] ADJ *(lit, fig)* dirty; *(stärker)* filthy ADV *(inf)* ~ **lachen** to give a dirty laugh; **es geht mir** ~ I'm in a bad way; *(finanziell)* I'm badly off; **wenn man ihn erwischt, geht es ihm** ~ if they catch him, he'll be sorry *or* he'll be in for it *(inf)*

Dreck-: **Dreck|loch** NT *(pej)* hole *(inf)*, hovel; **Dreck|nest** NT *(pej)* dump *(inf)*, hole *(inf)*; **Dreck|pfo|ten** PL *(inf: lit, fig)* dirty *or* filthy paws *pl*; **Dreck|sack** M *(pej inf)* dirty bastard *(sl)*; **Dreck|sau** F *(vulg)* filthy swine *(inf)*; **Dreck|schleu|der** F *(pej)* (= *Mundwerk*) foul mouth; (= *Mensch*) foul-mouthed person; (= *Kraftwerk, Auto*) environmental hazard; **Dreck|schwein** NT *(inf)* dirty pig *(inf)*

Drecks|kerl M *(inf)* dirty swine *(inf)*, louse *(inf)*

Dreck|spatz M *(inf)* (= *Kind*) mucky pup *(Brit inf)*, grubby kid; *(Schimpfwort)* filthy beggar *(inf)*

Dreck(s)|zeug NT *(inf)* damn *or* blasted stuff *(inf)*; **das ist doch ein** ~ damn this stuff *(inf)*

Dreck|wet|ter NT *(inf)* filthy weather *(inf)*

Dreh [dreː] M **-s, -s** *or* **-e** **a** (= *List*) dodge; (= *Kunstgriff*) trick; **den ~ heraushaben, etw zu tun** to have got the knack of doing sth; **den (richtigen) ~ heraushaben** *or* **weghaben** *(inf)* to have got the hang of it **b** = **Drehe**

Dreh-: **Dreh|ach|se** F axis of rotation; **Dreh|ar|beit** F **a** *(von Dreher)* lathe work; (= *Gegenstand*) piece turned on the lathe **b** **Dreh|ar|bei|ten** PL *(Film)* shooting *sing*; **Dreh|bank** F *pl* **-bänke** lathe; **dreh|bar** ADJ *(rundum)* rotating, revolving *attr*; *(um einen Festpunkt)* swivelling *attr (Brit)*, swiveling *attr (US)*; (= *drehgelagert*) pivoted; ~ **sein** to rotate *or* revolve/swivel; **Dreh|be|ginn** M *(Film)* start of shooting; **Dreh|be|we|gung** F turn(ing motion); *(esp Tech)* rotation, rotary motion; **eine ~ machen** to turn/rotate; **Dreh|blei|stift** M propelling *(Brit) or* mechanical *(US)* pencil; **Dreh|brü|cke** F swing bridge; **Dreh|buch** NT *(Film)* screenplay, (film) script; **Dreh|buch|au|tor(in)** M(F) scriptwriter, screenplay writer; **Dreh|büh|ne** F revolving stage

Dre|he [ˈdreːə] F -, *no pl (inf)* **(so) um die** ~ *(zeitlich)* or thereabouts, (a)round about then; **(so) in der** ~ *(örtlich)* (there) or thereabouts, (a)round about there

dre|hen [ˈdreːən] VT to turn *(auch Tech: auf Drehbank)*; *(um eine Achse auch)* to rotate; *(um Mittelpunkt auch)* to revolve, to rotate; *Stuhl* to swivel; *Kreisel* to spin; *Kopf auch* to twist; *Zwirne* to twist; *Zigaretten, Pillen* to roll; *Film* to shoot; *(fig:* = *verdrehen)* to twist; *(inf:* = *schaffen)* to fix *(inf)*, to work *(inf)*; **das Gas hoch/auf klein** ~ to turn the gas up high/down low; **Fleisch durch den Wolf** ~ to put meat through the mincer *(Brit) or* meat grinder *(US)*; **ein Ding** ~ *(sl)* to play a prank, to pull off a prank; *(Verbrecher)* to pull a job *(inf) or* caper *(inf)*; **wie man es auch dreht und wendet** no matter how you look at it → **Däumchen b**, **Runde c**, **Strick a**

VI to turn; *(Wind)* to shift, to change; *(Film)* to shoot, to film; (= *Zigaretten drehen*) to roll one's own; **an etw** *(dat)* ~ to turn sth; **am Radio** ~ to turn a knob on the radio; **daran ist nichts zu ~ und deuteln** *(fig)* there are no two ways about it

VR **a** (= *sich umdrehen, kreisen*) to turn (*um* about); *(um Mittelpunkt auch)* to revolve, to rotate; *(um Achse auch)* to rotate; *(sehr schnell: Kreisel)* to spin; *(Wind)* to shift, to change; **sich auf den Rücken** ~ to turn on(to) one's back; **sich um etw** ~ to revolve *or* rotate around sth; **sich um sich (selbst)** ~ to rotate, to revolve on its own axis; *(Mensch)* to turn round *(Brit)*, to turn around *(US)*; *(Auto)* to spin; **sich im Kreise** ~ to turn round and round *(Brit)*, to turn around and around *(US)*; **mir drehte sich alles** everything's spinning about me; **mir dreht sich alles im Kopf** my head is spinning *or* swimming; **sich ~ und winden** *(fig)* to twist and turn

b **sich um etw** ~ (= *betreffen*) to concern sth, to be about sth; *(um zentrale Frage)* to centre *(Brit) or* center *(US)* on sth; **alles dreht sich um sie** everything revolves (a)round her; *(steht im Mittelpunkt)* she's the centre *(Brit) or* center *(US)* of attention *or* interest; **es dreht sich darum, dass ...** the point is that ...; **meine Frage dreht sich darum, ob ...** my question is whether ...; **in dieser Sendung drehte es sich um ..., die Sendung drehte sich um ...** the broadcast concerned ... *or* was about ...

Dre|her [ˈdreːɐ] M **-s, -** (= *Tanz*) country waltz

Dre|her [ˈdreːɐ] M **-s, -**, **Dre|he|rin** [-ərɪn] F **-, -nen** lathe operator; (= *Drechsler auch*) (wood) turner

Dreh-: **Dreh|er|laub|nis** F *(Film)* *(allgemein)* filming permission; *(konkret)* filming permit; **keine ~ erhalten** not to be granted *or* not to get permission to film *or* shoot; **Dreh|feld** NT *(Comput)* spin box; **Dreh|ge|schwin|dig|keit** F rotary *or* rotating speed; **Dreh|ge|stell** NT *(Rail)* bogie; **Dreh|im|puls** M angular momentum; **Dreh|knopf** M knob; **Dreh|kran** M slewing *or* rotary crane; **Dreh|kreuz** NT turnstile; **Dreh|lei|er** F barrel-organ, hurdy-gurdy; **Dreh|lei|ter** F turntable ladder; **Dreh|ma|schi|ne** F motorized (metal-turning) lathe; **Dreh|mo|ment** NT torque; **Dreh|or|gel** F barrel organ, hurdy-gurdy; **Dreh|or|gel|spie|ler(in)** M(F) organ-grinder, hurdy-gurdy man/woman; **Dreh|ort** M *pl* **-orte** *(Film)* location; **Dreh|pau|se** F *(Film)* break in shooting; **Dreh|punkt** M pivot; **Dreh|res|tau|rant** NT revolving restaurant; **Dreh|schal|ter** M rotary switch; **Dreh|schei|be** F **a** *(Rail)* turntable **b** (= *Töpferscheibe*) potter's wheel **c** *(fig)* nerve centre *(Brit) or* center *(US)*; **Dreh|spieß** M *(von Grill)* revolving spit; **Dreh|strom** M three-phase current; **Dreh|stuhl** M swivel chair; **Dreh|tag** M *(Film)* day of shooting; **Dreh|tür** F revolving door; **Dreh- und An|gel|punkt** M → **Angelpunkt**

Dre|hung [ˈdreːʊŋ] F **-, -en** **a** turn; (= *ganze Drehung um eigene Achse auch*) rotation; *(um einen Punkt auch)* revolution; **eine halbe/ganze** ~ a half/complete turn; **eine ~ um 180°** a 180° turn, a turn through 180° **b** (= *das Drehen*) turning; *(um eigene Achse auch)* rotation; *(um einen Punkt auch)* revolving

Dreh|wurm M *(inf)* **einen** *or* **den ~ kriegen/haben** to get/feel giddy

Dreh|zahl F number of revolutions *or* revs; *(pro Minute)* revolutions *or* revs *pl* per minute, rpm

Dreh|zahl-: **Dreh|zahl|be|reich** M *(Aut)* engine speed range; **im niederen/hohen** ~ at low/high revs; **Dreh|zahl|mes|ser** M **-s, -** rev counter

drei [drai] NUM three; **von uns ~en** from the three of us; **die (Heiligen) Drei Könige** the Three Kings, the Magi; **die ~ Weisen aus dem Morgenland** the Three Wise Men from the East; **die ~ tollen Tage** *the last three days of Fasching in Germany*; **aller guten Dinge sind ~!** *(prov)* all good things come in threes!; *(nach zwei missglückten Versuchen)* third time lucky!; **er arbeitet/isst für** ~ *(inf)* he does the work of/eats enough for three; **etw in ~ Worten erklären** *(inf)* to explain sth briefly *or* in a few words; **ehe man bis ~ zählen konnte** *(inf)* in a trice *(esp Brit)*, before you could say Jack Robinson *(inf)*; **sie sieht aus, als ob sie nicht bis ~ zählen könnte** *(inf)* she looks pretty empty-headed; (= *unschuldig*) she looks as if butter wouldn't melt in her mouth → *auch* **vier**

Drei [drai] F **-, -en** three → *auch* **Vier**

drei-, Drei- *in cpds* three-, tri-; **Drei|ach|tel|takt** M three-eight time; **drei|ad(e)|rig** [ˈdrailad(ə)rɪç] ADJ *(Elec)* three-core; **drei|bei|nig** ADJ three-legged; **Drei|bett|zim|mer** NT three-bed room, room with three beds; **drei|blätt|rig** [ˈdraiblɛtrɪç] ADJ *(Bot)* three-leaved; **~es Kleeblatt** three-leav(ed) clover; **Drei|bund** M, *no pl (Hist)* Triple Alliance *(between Germany, Austria-Hungary and Italy in 1882)*

Drei-D- *in cpds* 3-D; **Drei-D-Bril|le** F 3-D glasses *pl or* specs *pl*

Drei-: **Drei|de|cker** [-dɛkɐ] M **-s, -** *(Aviat)* triplane; *(Naut)* three-decker; **drei|di|men|si|o|nal** ADJ three-dimensional; **Drei|di|men|si|o|na|li|tät** [-dimɛnzionalitɛːt] F **-**, *no pl* three-dimensionality

Drei|eck [ˈdrailɛk] NT **-(e)s, -e** triangle; (= *Zeichendreieck*) set square; *(Sport:* = *Winkel)* top left/right hand corner of the goal; **das Goldene** ~ the golden triangle

drei|eckig ADJ triangular, three-sided

Drei|ecks-: **Drei|ecks|ge|schäft** NT *(Econ)* three-way deal, triangular transaction *(spec)*; **Drei|ecks|tuch** NT *pl* **-tücher** triangular scarf; *(um die Schultern getragen)* triangular shawl; *(Med)* triangular bandage; **Drei|ecks|ver|hält|nis** NT (eternal) triangle; **ein ~ haben** to be involved in an eternal triangle

drei|ei|nig [draiˈlainɪç] ADJ triune, three in one *pred*; **der ~e Gott** the Holy Trinity, the Triune God

Drei|ei|nig|keit F Trinity; **die ~ Gottes** the Holy Trinity

Drei|er [ˈdraiɐ] M **-s, -** **a** *(Aus, S Ger:* = *Ziffer, Note)* three **b** *(Sport)* *(Eislauf etc)* three; *(Golf)* threesome; **ein flotter** ~ *(inf: Sex)* a threesome *(inf)* **c** *(Hist:* = *Münze)* three pfennig piece, ≈ thrupence *(Brit)*

Drei|er-: **Drei|er|grup|pe** F group of three; **Drei|er|kon|fe|renz** F *(Telec)* three-way calling; **Drei|er|pack** NT three-pack, triple pack; **Drei|er|rei|he** F row of three; **in ~n** *(von Personen)* three abreast

drei|fach [ˈdraifax] ADJ triple, threefold *(liter)*; **die ~e Menge** three times *or* triple *or* treble the amount; **ein ~es Hoch!** three cheers! → **Ausfertigung** ADV three times; ~ **abgesichert/verstärkt** three times as *or* trebly secure/reinforced → **vierfach**

Drei|fa|che(s) [ˈdraifaxə] NT *decl as adj* **das Dreifache** three times *or* triple *or* treble the amount, three times as much; **9 ist das Dreifache von 3** 9 is *or* equals three times 3; **ein Dreifaches kosten** to cost three times as much; **er verdient das Dreifache von dem, was ich bekomme** he earns three times as much as I do *or* treble the amount that I do; **etw um das Dreifache vermehren** to multiply sth three times *or (Zahl auch)* by three; **auf das Dreifache steigen** to treble, to triple

Drei|fach-: **Drei|fach|sieg** M *(Sport)* triple victory, one-two-three victory; **Drei|fach|steck|do|se** F *(Elec)* three-way *or* triple socket; **Drei|fach|ste|cker** M three-way adapter

Drei-: **drei|fal|tig** [-ˈfaltɪç] ADJ = **dreieinig**; **drei|fäl|tig** [-ˈfɛltɪç] ADJ = **dreifach**; **Drei|fal|tig|keit** F **-**, *no pl* Trinity; **Drei|fal|tig|keits|fest** NT, **Drei|fal|tig|keits|sonn|tag** M Trinity Sunday; **Drei|far|ben|druck** M **a** (= *Verfahren*) three-colour *(Brit) or* three-color *(US)* printing **b** (= *Gedrucktes*) three-colour *(Brit) or* three-color *(US)* print; **drei|far|big**, **drei|fär|big** [-fɛrbɪç] *(Aus)* ADJ three-colour *attr (Brit)*, three-color *attr (US)*, three-coloured *(Brit)*, three-colored *(US)*, trichromatic *(form)*; **Drei|fel|der|wirt|schaft** F three-field system; **Drei|fuß** M tripod; (= *Gestell für Kessel*) trivet; (= *Schemel*) three-legged stool; **drei|fü|ßig** ADJ *Vers* three-foot *attr*

Drei|gang M, *no pl (inf)* = **Dreigangschaltung**

Drei|gang-: **Drei|gang|ge|trie|be** NT three-speed gear; **Drei|gang|rad** NT three-speed bike; **Drei|gang|schal|tung** F three-speed gear; **ein Fahrrad mit ~** a three-speed bicycle

Drei-: **Drei|ge|spann** NT troika; *(fig)* threesome; *(an leitender Stelle)* triumvirate; **Drei|ge|stirn** NT *(lit)* triple star; *(fig geh)* big three; **drei|ge|stri|chen** ADJ *(Mus)* **das ~e C/F** the

C/F two octaves above middle C; **drei|ge|teilt** [-gətailt] ADJ divided into three (parts); **drei|glie|de|rig** ADJ *System* three-tier *attr*; *(Math)* trinomial; **Drei|glie|de|rung** F *(= das Gegliedertsein)* three-part *or* tripartite structure; *(= das Gliedern)* division into three (parts); **drei|glied|rig** [-gli:drɪç] ADJ *(Math)* trinomial; **Drei|gro|schen|heft|(chen)** NT, **Drei|gro|schen|ro|man** M *(pej)* penny-dreadful *(dated Brit inf)*, trashy paperback, dime novel *(US)*

Drei|heit F -, *no pl* trinity

Drei-: **drei|hun|dert** ['drai'hʊndɐt] NUM three hundred → *auch* **vierhundert**; **Drei|kampf** M three-part competition *(100m sprint, long jump and shot put)*; **Drei|kant** ['draikant] NT OR M -(e)s, -e trihedron; **Drei|kant|schlüs|sel** M *(Tech)* (male) triangular spanner *(Brit) or* wrench *(US)*; **Drei|kä|se|hoch** [drai'kɛ:zəho:x] M -s, -s *(inf)* tiny tot *(inf)*; **Drei|klang** M *(Mus)* triad; **Drei|klas|sen|wahl|sys|tem** NT *(Hist)* three-class electoral system *(in Prussia 1850-1918)*; **Drei|kö|ni|ge** PL Epiphany *sing*; **Drei|kö|nigs|fest** NT (feast of) Epiphany; **Drei|kö|nigs|tag** M feast of Epiphany; **Drei|län|der|eck** NT place where three countries meet; **Drei|li|ter|au|to**, **Drei-Li|ter-Au|to** NT three-litre *(Brit) or* three-liter *(US)* car; **Drei|mäch|te|pakt** M *(Hist)* three-power *or* tripartite pact *(between Germany, Italy and Japan)*, Axis pact

drei|mal ['draima:l] ADV three times, thrice *(old)* → *auch* **viermal**

Drei-: **Drei|mas|ter** ['draimastɐ] M -s, - three-master; **Drei|mei|len|gren|ze** F three-mile limit; **Drei|mei|len|zo|ne** F three-mile zone; **Drei|me|ter|brett** NT three-metre *(Brit) or* three-meter *(US)* board

drein [drain] ADV *(inf)* = **darein**

drein- *in cpds* → *auch* **darein-**: **drein+bli|cken** VI *sep* **traurig** *etc* ~ to look sad *etc*; **drein+fah|ren** VI *sep irreg aux sein (dial)* to intervene; **drein+fin|den** VR *sep irreg (inf)* → **dareinfinden**; **drein+fü|gen** VR *sep* to resign oneself (to it), to come to terms with it; **drein+re|den** VI *sep (inf) (= dazwischenreden)* to interrupt; *(= sich einmischen)* to interfere (*bei* in, with); **ich lasse mir in dieser Angelegenheit von niemandem** ~ I won't have anyone interfering (with this); **er ließ sich nirgends** ~ he would never be told; **drein+schau|en** VI *sep (esp dial)* **traurig** *etc* ~ to look sad *etc*; **drein+schi|cken** VI *sep* **schließlich schickte er sich drein** eventually he became reconciled to this; **drein+schla|gen** VI *sep irreg (dial)* to weigh in *(inf)*

Drei-: **Drei|pha|sen|strom** M three-phase current; **drei|po|lig** [-po:lɪç] ADJ three-pole *attr*, with three poles; *Kabel* three-core; *Steckdose, Stecker* three-pin; **Drei|punkt|(si|cher|heits)|gurt** M lap and diagonal seat belt; **Drei|rad** NT tricycle; *(inf: = Auto)* three-wheeler; **drei|rä|de|rig**, **drei|räd|rig** ADJ three-wheeled; **Drei|rad|wa|gen** M three-wheeled vehicle, three-wheeler; **drei|sai|tig** ADJ *(Mus) Instrument* three-stringed; **Drei|satz** M *(Math)* rule of three

Drei|satz-: **Drei|satz|auf|ga|be** F problem using the rule of three; **Drei|satz|rech|nung** F calculation using the rule of three; **Drei|satz|tisch** M nest of tables

Drei-: **drei|schif|fig** [-ʃɪfɪç] ADJ *Kirche* with three naves; **drei|spal|tig** [-ʃpaltɪç] ADJ *(Typ) Seite etc* three-column *attr*, with three columns *(nachgestellt)*; **Drei|spitz** M three-cornered hat, tricorn; **Drei|sprin|ger(in)** M(F) triple jumper; **Drei|sprung** M triple jump, hop, step and jump; **drei|spu|rig** [-ʃpu:rɪç] ADJ *(Mot) Fahrbahn, Verkehr etc* three-lane *attr*

drei|ßig ['draisɪç] NUM thirty → *auch* **vierzig**

drei|ßig- *in cpds* → *auch* **vierzig-**

Drei|ßi|ger ['draisɪgɐ] M -s, -, **Drei|ßi|ge|rin** [-ərɪn] F -, -nen thirty-year-old; *(zwischen 30 und 40)* man in his/woman in her thirties → *auch* **Vierziger**

drei|ßig|jäh|rig ADJ *(= dreißig Jahre dauernd)* thirty years' *attr*, lasting thirty years; *(= dreißig Jahre alt)* thirty years old, thirty-year-old *attr*; **der Dreißigjährige Krieg** the Thirty Years' War

Drei|ßigs|tel ['draisɪçstl] NT -s, - thirtieth → *auch* **Viertel**

Drei|ßigs|tel F -, *no pl (Phot inf)* thirtieth (of a second)

drei|ßigs|te(r, s) ['draisɪçstə] ADJ thirtieth

dreist [draist] ADJ bold; *Handlung auch* audacious

Dreis|tig|keit ['draistɪçkait] F -, -en **a** *no pl* boldness; *(von Handlung auch)* audacity **b** *(= Bemerkung)* bold remark; *(= Handlung)* bold *or* audacious act

Drei-: **Drei|stu|fen|plan** M three-stage *or* three-phase plan; **Drei|stu|fen|ra|ke|te** F three-stage rocket; **drei|stu|fig** ADJ *Rakete* three-stage *attr*, with three stages; *Plan auch* three-phase *attr*; **eine ~e Treppe** three steps; **Drei|ta|ge|bart** M stubble, three-day growth *(esp Brit)*; **Drei|tau|sen|der** M *(Berg)* 3000-metre *(Brit) or* -meter *(US)* peak; **drei|tei|lig** ADJ *(= aus 3 Teilen) Kostüm etc* three-piece *attr*; *(= in 3 Teile geteilt)* three-part *attr*, tripartite *(form)*; **Drei|tei|lung** F division into three; **die ~ der Streitkräfte** dividing the armed forces into three

drei vier|tel ['drai 'fɪrtl] ADJ ADV → **viertel, Viertel**

Drei|vier|tel ['drai'fɪrtl] NT three-quarters; **in einem ~ der Zeit** in three-quarters of the time; **das Saal war zu einem ~ leer** the room was three-quarters empty

Drei|vier|tel-: **Drei|vier|tel|arm** M *(inf)*, **Drei|vier|tel|är|mel** M three-quarter(-length) sleeve; **Drei|vier|tel|ja|cke** F three-quarter-length coat; **Drei|vier|tel|jahr** NT nine months *pl*, nine-month period; **drei|vier|tel|lang** ADJ three-quarter-length; **Drei|vier|tel|li|ter|fla|sche** F 75 cl bottle; **Drei|vier|tel|mehr|heit** F three-quarters majority; **Drei|vier|tel|spie|ler(in)** M(F) *(Rugby)* three-quarter; **Drei|vier|tel|stun|de** F three-quarters of an hour *no indef art*; **Drei|vier|tel|takt** M three-four time; **im ~** in three-four time

Drei|weg- *in cpds (Elec)* three-way; **Drei|we|ge|ka|ta|ly|sa|tor** M *(Aut)* three-way catalytic converter; **geregelter ~** computer-controlled *or* feedback three-way catalytic converter; **ungeregelter ~** open-loop three-way catalytic converter; **Drei|weg|(laut|spre|cher)|box** F three-way loudspeaker system; **Drei|weg|schal|ter** M three-way switch; **Drei|weg|ste|cker** M three-way adapter

Drei-: **drei|wer|tig** ADJ *(Chem)* trivalent; *(Ling)* three-place; **drei|wö|chent|lich** ADJ *attr* three-weekly ADV every three weeks, at three-weekly intervals; **drei|wö|chig** [-vœçɪç] ADJ *attr* three-week; **Drei|zack** [-tsak] M -s, -e trident; **drei|za|ckig** ADJ three-pointed

drei|zehn ['draitse:n] NUM thirteen; **jetzt schlägts aber ~** *(inf)* that's a bit much *or* thick *(inf)* → *auch* **vierzehn**

Drei|zim|mer|woh|nung F three-room *or* two-bedroom(ed) flat *(Brit) or* apartment

Dresch|bo|den M, **Dresch|die|le** F threshing floor

Dre|sche ['drɛʃə] F -, *no pl (inf)* thrashing; **~ kriegen** to get a thrashing

dre|schen ['drɛʃn] *pret* **drosch** [drɔʃ], *ptp* **gedroschen** [gə'drɔʃn] VT **a** *Korn* to thresh; *(inf) Phrasen* to bandy; **leeres Stroh ~** *(fig)* to talk a lot of hot air *(inf)*, to talk/write a lot of claptrap *(inf)*; **Skat ~** *(inf)* to play skat **b** *(inf: = prügeln)* to thrash **c** *(Sport inf: = treten, schlagen)* to slam *(inf)*, to wallop *(inf)* VI **a** *(= Korn dreschen)* to thresh **b** *(inf: = schlagen, treten)* to hit violently; **auf die Tasten ~** to thump *or* pound the keys VR *(inf: = sich prügeln)* to have a fight

Dre|scher ['drɛʃɐ] M -s, -, **Dre|sche|rin** [-ərɪn] F -, -nen thresher

Dresch-: **Dresch|fle|gel** M flail; **Dresch|ma|schi|ne** F threshing machine; **Dresch|ten|ne** F threshing floor

Dress [drɛs] M -es, -e, *or (Aus)* f -, -en *(Sport)* (sports) kit; *(für Fußball auch)* strip

Dres|seur [drɛ'sø:ɐ] M -s, -e, **Dres|seu|rin** [-'sø:rɪn] F -, -nen trainer

dres|sier|bar ADJ *Tier* trainable; *(pej) Mensch auch* susceptible to conditioning; **leicht/schwer ~** easy/difficult to train/condition

dres|sie|ren [drɛ'si:rən] *ptp* **dressiert** VT **a** *Tier* to train; *(pej) Menschen auch* to condition, to discipline; **auf jdn/etw dressiert sein** to be trained to respond to sb/sth; **auf den Mann dressiert sein** to be trained to attack people; **auf das Zusammentreiben von Tieren dressiert** trained to round up animals; **zu etw dressiert sein** to be trained *etc* to do sth **b** *(Cook) Geflügel* to dress; *Braten* to prepare; *(esp Aus) Torte etc* to decorate; *Teig, Creme* to pipe

Dres|sing ['drɛsɪŋ] NT -s, -s *(Cook)* dressing; **grüner Salat ohne ~** undressed green salad

Dress|man ['drɛsmən] M -s, **Dressmen** male model

Dres|sur [drɛ'su:ɐ] F -, -en training; *(für Dressurreiten)* dressage; *(fig)* conditioning

Dres|sur-: **Dres|sur|akt** M performing animal act; **Dres|sur|prü|fung** F dressage test; **Dres|sur|rei|ten** NT -s, *no pl* dressage; **Dres|sur|rei|ter(in)** M(F) dressage rider

drib|beln ['drɪbln] VI to dribble; **mit dem Ball ~** to dribble the ball

Dribb|ling ['drɪblɪŋ] NT -s, -s dribbling; **ein ~** a piece of dribbling

Drift [drɪft] F -, -en *(Naut)* drift

drif|ten ['drɪftn] VI *aux sein (Naut, fig)* to drift

Drill [drɪl] M -(e)s, *no pl (Mil, fig)* drill; *(Sch auch)* drills *pl*

Drill|boh|rer M drill

dril|len ['drɪlən] VTI **a** *(Mil, fig)* to drill; **jdn auf etw** *(acc)* **~** to drill sb in sth; **auf etw** *(acc)* **gedrillt sein** *(fig inf)* to be practised *(Brit) or* practiced *(US)* at doing sth **b** *Loch* to drill **c** *(Agr)* to drill, to sow *or* plant in drills **d** *(beim Angeln)* to play

Dril|lich ['drɪlɪç] M -s, -e drill; *(für Matratzen etc)* ticking; *(für Markisen)* canvas

Dril|lich-: **Dril|lich|an|zug** M overalls *pl*, dungarees *pl*; **Dril|lich|zeug** NT, *no pl* overalls *pl*

Dril|ling ['drɪlɪŋ] M -s, -e **a** triplet **b** *(= Angelhaken)* three-pronged hook **c** *(= Jagdgewehr)* triple-barrelled *(Brit) or* triple-barreled *(US)* shotgun

Dril|lings|ge|burt F triple birth

Drill-: **Drill|ma|schi|ne** F *(Agr)* seed drill; **Drill|übung** F drill

drin [drɪn] ADV **a** *(inf)* = **darin a**, **drinnen b** *(inf)* **da ~** = **darin b c** in it; **er/es ist da ~** he/it is in there; **in der Flasche ist noch etwas ~** there's still something in the bottle; **hallo, ist da jemand ~?** hello, is (there) anyone in there? → **drinsitzen** *etc* **d** *(inf: in Redewendungen)* **das ist** *or* **liegt bei dem alles ~** anything's possible with him; **bis jetzt ist** *or* **liegt noch alles ~** everything is still quite open; **~ sein** *(in der Arbeit)* to be into it; **für sie ist doch (gegen ihn) nichts ~** she hasn't a hope (against him); **das ist doch nicht ~** *(= geht nicht)* that's not on *(inf)*

drin|gen ['drɪŋən] *pret* **drang** [draŋ], *ptp* **gedrungen** [gə'drʊŋən] VI **a** *aux sein* to penetrate, to come through; *(fig: Nachricht, Geheimnis)* to penetrate, to get through *(an or in +acc* to); **(durch etw) ~** to come through (sth), to penetrate (sth); **jdm ans Herz ~** *(liter)* to go to *or* touch sb's heart; **an** *or* **in die Öffentlichkeit ~** to leak *or* get out, to become public knowledge; **der Pfeil drang ihm in die Brust** the arrow penetrated (into) his chest; **durch eine Menschenmenge ~** to push (one's way) through a crowd of people; **hinter die Ursache/ein Rätsel ~** to get to the bottom of this/a puzzle

b *aux sein (geh)* **in jdn ~** to press *or* urge sb; **mit Bitten/Fragen in jdn ~** to ply *or* press sb with requests/questions **c auf etw** *(acc)* ~ to insist on sth; **er drang darauf, einen Arzt zu holen** *or* **dass man einen Arzt holte** he insisted that a doctor should be sent for

drin|gend ['drɪŋənt] ADJ *(= eilig, wichtig)* urgent, pressing; *(= nachdrücklich, zwingend)* strong; *Abraten, Anraten* strong, strenuous; *Gründe* compelling; **etw ~ machen** *(inf)* to treat sth as urgent; **ein ~er Fall** *(Med)* an emergency ADV *(= unbedingt)* urgently; *(= nachdrücklich) warnen, empfehlen, abraten* strongly; **ich muss Sie ~ sprechen** I must speak to you urgently; **jdn ~ bitten, etw zu unterlassen** to ask sb in the strongest terms *or* to urge sb to stop doing sth; **~ notwendig** *or* **erforderlich** urgently needed, essential; **~ verdächtig** strongly suspected

dring|lich ['drɪŋlɪç] ADJ urgent, pressing

Dring|lich|keit F -, *no pl* urgency

Dring|lich|keits-: **Dring|lich|keits|an|fra|ge** F *(Parl)* emergency question; **Dring|lich|keits|an|trag** M *(Parl)* emergency motion; **Dring|lich|keits|stu|fe** F priority; **~ 1** top priority

drin+hän|gen VI *sep irreg (inf)* = **drinstecken b, c**

Drink [drɪŋk] M **-s, -s** drink

drin|nen ['drɪnən] ADV *(= in geschlossenem Raum)* inside; *(= im Haus auch)* indoors; *(fig: = im Inland)* internally, at home; **~ und draußen** inside and outside; *(im Inland etc)* at home and abroad; **hier/dort ~** in here/there; **ich gehe nach ~** *(inf)* I'm going in(side)

drin+sit|zen VI *sep irreg (inf)* to be in trouble

drin+ste|cken VI *sep (inf)* **a** *(= verborgen sein)* to be (contained); **auch bei ihm muss ein guter Kern ~** there must be some good even in him **b** *(= investiert sein)* **da steckt eine Menge Geld/Arbeit** *etc* **drin** a lot of money/work *etc* has gone into it **c** *(= verwickelt sein)* to be involved in it; **er steckt bis über die Ohren drin** he's up to his ears in it **d** *(= voraussehen können)* **da steckt man nicht drin** one never knows *or* one can never tell (what will happen)

drin+ste|hen VI *sep irreg aux haben or (dial) sein (inf)* to be in it

drischt [drɪʃt] *3. pers sing pres von* **dreschen**

dritt [drɪt] ADV **wir kommen zu ~** three of us are coming together → *auch* **viert**

dritt- *in cpds* third; **dritt|äl|tes|te(r, s)** ADJ third oldest

Drit|tel ['drɪtl] NT **-s, -** third → *auch* **Viertel**

drit|teln ['drɪtln] VT to divide into three (parts); *Zahl* to divide by three

Drit|tel|pa|ri|tät F equal say in decision-making for each of three groups; **die ~ verlangen** to demand an equal say in decision-making

drit|tel|pa|ri|tä|tisch ADJ *Ausschuss, Gremium* made up of equal numbers from each of three groups ADV *entscheiden* by giving each of three groups an equal vote; **~ zusammengesetzt** made up of equal numbers from each of three groups

Drit|ten|ab|schla|gen NT **-s**, *no pl children's game,* ≈ tag

drit|tens ['drɪtns] ADV thirdly → **viertens**

Drit|te(r) ['drɪtə] MF *decl as adj* third person, third man/woman *etc*; *(= Unbeteiligter)* third party; **der lachende ~** *the third party who benefits from a division between two others*; **in dieser Angelegenheit ist er der lachende ~** he comes off best from this matter; **wenn zwei sich streiten, freut sich der ~** *(prov)* when two people quarrel a third one rejoices; **der ~ im Bunde** the third in *or* of the trio → *auch* **Vierte(r)**

drit|te(r, s) ['drɪtə] ADJ third; **der ~ Fall** *(Gram)* the dative case; **an einem ~n Ort** on neutral territory; **von ~r Seite (eine Neuigkeit erfahren)** (to learn a piece of news) from a third party; **Menschen ~r Klasse** third-class citizens; **ein Drittes** a third thing → **vierte(r, s), Reich a, Welt**

Drit|te-Welt- *in cpds* Third World; **Drit|te-Welt-Be|we|gung** F Third World movement; **Drit|te-Welt-La|den** M ≈ OXFAM shop *(Brit)*, ≈ thrift store *(US)*, ≈ charity shop for the Third World; **Drit|te-Welt-Land** NT, **Drit|te-Welt-Staat** M Third World country

Dritt-: **dritt|größ|te(r, s)** ADJ third-biggest, third-largest; **dritt|höchs|te(r, s)** ADJ third-highest; **Dritt|in|te|res|se** NT interest of a third party; **dritt|klas|sig** ADJ third-rate *(pej)*, third-class; **Dritt|kläss|ler** M **-s, -**, **Dritt|kläss|le|rin** F **-, -nen** *(Sch)* third-former *(Brit)*, third-grader *(US)*; **Dritt|land** NT third country; **dritt|letz|te(r, s)** ADJ third from last, last but two; **an ~r Stelle** third from last, last but two; **Dritt|mit|tel** PL *(Fin)* external funds *pl*; **Dritt|per|son** F third person *or* party; **dritt|ran|gig** [-raŋɪç] ADJ third-rate; **Dritt|scha|den** M damage suffered by a third party; **Dritt|staat** M third country

Drive [draif] M **-s, -s** drive

DRK [de:ɛr'ka:] NT - *abbr von* **Deutsches Rotes Kreuz**

drob [drɔp] ADV *(obs)* = **darob**

dro|ben ['dro:bn] ADV *(old, dial)* up there; **dort ~** up there

Dro|ge ['dro:gə] F **-, -n** drug

drö|ge ['drø:gə] ADJ *(N Ger)* = **trocken a b**

Drö|ge|ler ['drø:gəlɐ] M **-s, -**, **Drö|ge|le|rin** [-ərɪn] F **-, -nen** *(Sw)* drug addict

Dro|gen-: **dro|gen|ab|hän|gig** ADJ addicted to drugs; **er ist ~** he's a drug addict; **Dro|gen|ab|hän|gi|ge(r)** MF *decl as adj* drug addict; **Dro|gen|ab|hän|gig|keit** F drug addiction *no art*; **Dro|gen|ba|ron** M *(inf)* drug baron *(inf)*; **Dro|gen|be|nut|zer(in)** M(F) drug user; **Dro|gen|be|ra|tungs|stel|le** F drugs advice centre *(Brit)* *or* center *(US)*; **Dro|gen|boss** M *(inf)* drug(s) boss; **Dro|gen|fahn|der** [-fa:ndɐ] M **-s, -**, **Dro|gen|fahn|de|rin** [-ərɪn] F **-, -nen** drug squad officer, narcotics officer; **Dro|gen|fahn|dungs|be|hör|de** F drug squad; **Dro|gen|ge|schäft** NT drug trade; **Dro|gen|han|del** M drug traffic *or* trade; **Dro|gen|händ|ler(in)** M(F) drug trafficker *or* dealer; **Dro|gen|kon|sum** [-kɔnzu:m] M drug consumption; **Dro|gen|ku|rier(in)** M(F) drug courier; **Dro|gen|la|bor** NT drug laboratory; **Dro|gen|miss|brauch** M drug abuse *no art*; **Dro|gen|prä|ven|ti|on** F drug abuse prevention; **Dro|gen|prob|lem** NT drug (dependency) problem; **er hat ~e** he has a drug problem; **Dro|gen|sucht** F drug addiction; **dro|gen|süch|tig** ADJ addicted to drugs; **er ist ~** he's a drug addict; **Dro|gen|süch|ti|ge(r)** MF *decl as adj* drug addict; **Dro|gen|sze|ne** F drug scene; **Dro|gen|to|te(r)** MF *decl as adj* person who died from drug abuse; **200 ~ pro Jahr** 200 drug deaths per year; **Dro|gen|um|schlag|platz** M drug-dealing *or* drug-trafficking area

Dro|ge|rie [drogə'ri:] F **-, -n** [-'ri:ən] chemist's (shop) *(nondispensing)*, drugstore *(US)*

Dro|gist [dro'gɪst] M **-en, -en**, **Dro|gis|tin** [-'gɪstɪn] F **-, -nen** chemist, druggist *(US)*

Drög|ler ['drø:glɐ] M **-s, -**, **Drög|le|rin** [-ərɪn] F **-, -nen** *(Sw)* drug addict

Droh|brief M threatening letter

dro|hen ['dro:ən] VI **a** *(= Drohung aussprechen)* to threaten *(jdm* sb); **er drohte dem Kind mit erhobenem Zeigefinger** he raised a warning finger to the child **b (jdm) mit etw ~** to threaten (sb with) sth; **er droht mit Selbstmord** he threatens to commit suicide; **(jdm) ~, etw zu tun** to threaten to do sth **c** *(= bevorstehen) (Gefahr)* to threaten; *(Gewitter)* to be imminent, to be in the offing; *(Streik, Krieg)* to be imminent *or* looming; **jdm droht etw** sb is being threatened by sth; **jdm droht Gefahr/der Tod** sb is in danger/in danger of dying; **es droht Gefahr/ein Streik** there is the threat of danger/a strike V AUX to threaten; **das Schiff drohte zu sinken** the ship threatened to sink, the ship was in danger of sinking

dro|hend ADJ **a** *Handbewegung, Haltung, Blick, Wolken* threatening, menacing **b** *(= bevorstehend) Unheil, Gefahr, Krieg, Krise* imminent, impending

Droh|ge|bär|de F threatening gesture

Drohn [dro:n] M **-en, -en** *(form)* = **Drohne a**

Droh|ne [dro:nə] F **-, -n a** drone; *(fig pej auch)* idler, parasite **b** *(Mil)* drone

dröh|nen ['drø:nən] VI **a** *(Flugzeug, Motor, Straßenlärm)* to roar; *(Donner)* to rumble; *(Lautsprecher, Musik, Bass, Stimme, Fernseher)* to boom; **etw dröhnt jdm in den Ohren/im Kopf** sth roars *etc* in sb's ears/head **b** *(Raum etc)* to resound, to echo; **mir ~ die Ohren/dröhnt der Kopf** my ears are/head is ringing **c** *aux sein (= sich dröhnend fortbewegen: Lkw etc)* to rumble **d** *(sl: = high machen)* to give a buzz *(inf)*

dröh|nend ADJ *Lärm, Applaus* resounding, echoing; *Musik, Stimme* booming; *Gelächter* roaring ADV **~ lachen** to roar with laughter

Droh|nen-: **Droh|nen|da|sein** NT *(fig pej)* idle *or* parasitic life; **droh|nen|haft** ADJ drone-like; *(fig auch)* idle, parasitic; **Droh|nen|schlacht** F *(Zool)* slaughter of the drones

Dröh|nung ['drø:nʊŋ] F **-, -en** *(sl)* **a** *(= laute Musik)* booming music **b** *(= Rausch)* high *(inf)*; *(= Dosis)* fix *(inf)*; **sich** *(dat)* **voll die ~** *or* **die volle ~ geben** to get stoned *(sl)*

Dro|hung ['dro:ʊŋ] F **-, -en** threat

Droh-: **Droh|ver|hal|ten** NT threatening *or* aggressive behaviour *(Brit)* *or* behavior *(US)*; **Droh|wort** NT *pl* **-worte** threat

drol|lig ['drɔlɪç] ADJ **a** funny, comical, droll **b** *(= seltsam)* odd, strange; **werd nicht ~!** don't be funny!; **ein ~er Kauz** an odd bod *(Brit inf)*, an oddball *(esp US inf)*

Dro|me|dar [drome'da:ɐ, 'dro:-] NT **-s, -e** dromedary

Drop-down-Menü NT *(Comput)* drop-down menu

Drop-out ['drɔpaut] M **-s, -s**, **Drop|out** M **-s, -s a** *(= Mensch)* dropout **b** *(in Bandaufzeichnung)* fade

Drops [drɔps] M OR NT **-, -** *or* **-e** fruit drop

drosch *pret von* **dreschen**

Drosch|ke ['drɔʃkə] F **-, -n a** *(= Pferdedroschke)* (hackney) cab, hackney carriage **b** *(dated: = Taxi)* (taxi)cab

Drosch|ken-: **Drosch|ken(hal|te)|platz** M *(dated)* cab rank; **Drosch|ken|kut|scher(in)** M(F) cab driver

Dro|so|phi|la [dro'zo:fila] F **-, Drosophilae** [-lɛ] *(Biol)* drosophila

Dros|sel ['drɔsl] F **-, -n** *(Orn)* thrush

Dros|sel F **-, -n** *(= Drosselspule)* choking coil; *(= Drosselventil)* throttle valve

Dros|sel|klap|pe F *(Tech)* throttle valve

dros|seln ['drɔsln] VT **a** *Motor, Dampf etc* to throttle, to choke; *Heizung, Wärme* to turn down; *Strom* to reduce; *Tempo, Produktion etc* to cut down **b** *(dated: = würgen)* to throttle, to strangle

Dros|sel|spu|le F *(Elec)* choking coil

Dros|se|lung F **-, -en** *(von Motor, Dampf)* throttling, choking; *(von Heizung, Wärme)* turning down; *(von Strom)* reducing; *(von Tempo, Produktion)* cutting down

Dros|sel|ven|til NT throttle valve

Dross|lung ['drɔslʊŋ] F **-, -en** = **Drosselung**

drü|ben ['dry:bn] ADV over there; *(= auf der anderen Seite)* on the other side; *(inf: auf Amerika bezogen)* over the water; **hier/dort** *or* **da ~** over here/there; **nach ~** over there; *(inf: auf die DDR/die BRD bezogen)* to the other side; **von ~** from over there; *(inf: auf die DDR/die BRD bezogen)* from the other side; **bei dem Nachbarn ~** over at my neighbour's *(Brit)* *or* neighbor's *(US)*; **~ über dem Rhein** on the other side of the Rhine → **hüben**

Drü|ben ['dry:bn] NT **-s**, *no pl (= Jenseits)* hereafter, next world

drü|ber ['dry:bɐ] ADV (inf) **a** = **darüber, hinüber** **b da ~ = darüber**

Druck [drʊk] M **-(e)s, ⸚e** ['drʏkə] **a** (Phys, fig) pressure; **unter ~ stehen** (lit, fig) to be under pressure; **jdn unter ~ setzen** (fig) to put pressure on sb, to pressurize sb; **unter ~ geraten** to come under pressure; **(fürchterlich) in ~ sein** (fig) to be under (terrible) pressure; **~ auf jdn/etw ausüben** (lit, fig) to exert or put pressure on sb/sth; **~ machen** (inf) to put the pressure on (inf); **~ hinter etw** (acc) **machen** (inf) to put some pressure on sth; **~ und Gegendruck** pressure and resistance; **ein ~ im Kopf/Magen** a feeling of pressure in one's head/stomach; **einen ~ haben** (sl: = Lust auf Sex) to be choking (Brit) or gagging (Brit) or dying for it (sl)
b (= das Drücken) pressure (+gen from) no indef art; **durch einen ~ auf den Knopf** by pressing the button
c (Drogen sl) fix (inf); **sich** (dat) **einen ~ verpassen** to have a fix (inf)

Druck M **-(e)s, -e** **a** (= das Drucken) printing; (Art des Drucks, = Schriftart) print; (= Druckwerk) copy; **~ und Satz** setting and printing; **das Buch ist im ~** the book is in the press or is being printed; **im ~ erscheinen** to appear in print; **in ~ gehen** to go into print; **etw in ~ geben** to send sth to press or to be printed; **~ und Verlag von ...** printed and published by ... **b** (= Kunstdruck) print **c** PL **-s** (Tex) print

Druck-: **Druck|ab|fall** M drop or fall in pressure; **Druck|an|stieg** M rise in pressure; **Druck|an|zug** M pressure suit; **Druck|auf|trag** M (Comput) print job; **Druck|aus|gleich** M pressure balance; **Druck|be|häl|ter** M pressure vessel; **Druck|be|las|tung** F pressure load; **Druck|be|reich** M (Comput) print range, print area; **Druck|blei|stift** M retractable pencil; **Druck|bo|gen** M (Typ) printed sheet; **Druck|buch|sta|be** M printed character or letter; **in ~n schreiben** to print

Drü|cke|ber|ger ['drʏkəbɛrgɐ] M **-s, -**, **Drü|cke|ber|ge|rin** [-ərɪn] F **-, -nen** (pej inf) (= fauler Mensch) shirker; (in der Schule) shirker, skiver (Brit inf); (= Feigling) coward

Drü|cke|ber|ge|rei [drʏkəbɛrgə'rai] F **-, -en** (pej inf) shirking; (in der Schule) shirking, skiving (Brit inf)

drü|cke|ber|ge|risch ['drʏkəbɛrgərɪʃ] ADJ (pej inf) Mensch, Einstellung idle; **sein ~es Verhalten** his idling or shirking

druck|emp|find|lich ADJ sensitive (to pressure); (Comput) touch-sensitive

dru|cken ['drʊkn] VTI **a** (Typ, Tex) to print; **ein Buch ~ lassen** to have a book printed; **ein Buch in 1000 Exemplaren/einer hohen Auflage ~** to print 1000 copies/a large edition of a book → **gedruckt** **b** (dial) = **drücken**

drü|cken ['drʏkn] VT **a** Hand, Klinke, Hebel to press; Knopf to press, to push; (Comput) Taste to hit, to press; Obst, Saft, Eiter to squeeze; **jdm etw in die Hand ~** to press or slip sth into sb's hand; **jdn ~** to squeeze sb; (= umarmen) to hug sb; **jdn/etw an sich/ans Herz ~** to press or clasp sb/sth to one/one's breast; **jdn zur Seite/nach hinten/in einen Stuhl ~** to push sb aside/back/into a chair; **den Hut in die Stirn ~** to pull one's hat down over one's brow or forehead; **~ Sie eine beliebige Taste, um fortzufahren** (Comput) hit any key to continue; **die rechte Maustaste gedrückt halten** (Comput) to press and hold down the right mouse button
b (geh: = bedrücken) to weigh heavily upon; **was drückt dich denn?** what's on your mind?
c (= Druckgefühl erzeugen: Schuhe, Korsett etc) to pinch, to nip; **jdn im Magen ~** (Essen) to lie or weigh heavily on sb's stomach; **mich drückt der Magen** my stomach feels full
d (= verringern, herabsetzen) to force down; Rekord to beat; Leistung, Niveau to lower; Steuern to bring down
e (inf: = unterdrücken) jdn to keep down; Stimmung to dampen
f (Sport) Gewicht to press; Handstand to press into
g (Aviat) to point down
h (Cards) to discard
i (Econ) **etw in** or **auf den Markt ~** to push sth
VI **a** (auf Gegenstand, Klinke, Knopf etc) to press; (Wetter, Hitze) to be oppressive; (Brille, Schuhe, Korsett etc) to pinch; (Essen) to weigh (on one's stomach); **„bitte ~"** "push"; **auf etw** (acc)**/an etw** (acc) **~** to press sth; **aufs Gemüt ~** to dampen or depress one's spirits, to get one down; **auf die Stimmung ~** to dampen one's mood → auch **gedrückt**
b (= drängeln, stoßen) to push
c (bei Stuhlentleerung) to strain, to push
d (inf: = Heroin injizieren) to shoot up
VR **a** (mit Ortsangabe) (in +acc into) (an +acc against) (= sich quetschen) to squeeze; (Schutz suchend) to huddle; **sich aus dem Zimmer ~** to slip out of the room
b (inf: = kneifen) to shirk, to dodge; (vor Militärdienst) to dodge; **sich vor etw** (dat) **~** to shirk or dodge sth; **sich (um etw) ~** to get out of sth; (esp in Schule auch) to skive off (sth) (Brit inf), to avoid sth

drü|ckend ADJ Last, Steuern heavy; Sorgen, Probleme serious; Verantwortung weighty; Armut grinding; Wetter, Hitze oppressive, close; Enge, Atmosphäre oppressive ADV **(es ist) ~ heiß** (it's) oppressively hot

drü|ckend|heiß △ ['drʏknt'hais] ADJ attr → **drückend**

Dru|cker ['drʊkɐ] M **-s, -** (Comput) printer

Dru|cker ['drʊkɐ] M **-s, -**, **Dru|cke|rin** [-ərɪn] F **-, -nen** (= Beruf) printer

Drü|cker ['drʏkɐ] M **-s, -** **a** (= Knopf) (push) button; (inf: von Pistole etc) trigger; (von Klingel) push; **die Hand am ~ haben** (fig inf) to be ready to act; **am ~ sein** or **sitzen** (fig inf) (in Machtposition) to be in a key position; (an der Quelle) to be ideally placed, to be in an ideal position; **auf den letzten ~** (fig inf) at the last minute **b** (= Türklinke) handle; (von Schnappschloss) latch

Drü|cker ['drʏkɐ] M **-s, -**, **Drü|cke|rin** [-ərɪn] F **-, -nen** (inf: = Hausierer) hawker (inf)

Dru|cke|rei [drʊkə'rai] F **-, -en** **a** printing works pl, printery; (= Firma) printer's **b** (= Druckwesen) printing no art

Drü|cker|ko|lon|ne F (inf) door-to-door sales team

Druck|er|laub|nis F imprimatur

Dru|cker-: **Dru|cker|pres|se** F printing press; **Dru|cker|schwär|ze** F printer's ink; **Dru|cker|spoo|ler** [-spu:lɐ] M (Comput) print spooler; **Dru|cker|spra|che** F printer's language; **Dru|cker|sta|tus** M (Comput) printer status; **Dru|cker|trei|ber** M (Comput) printer driver; **Dru|cker|war|te|schlan|ge** F (Comput) printer queue; **Dru|cker|zei|chen** NT printer's mark

Druck-: **Druck|er|zeug|nis** NT printed material; **Druck|fah|ne** F galley (proof), proof; **Druck|far|be** F coloured (Brit) or colored (US) printing ink; **Druck|feh|ler** M misprint, typographical or printer's error; **Druck|feh|ler|teu|fel** M (hum) gremlin (which causes misprints); **druck|fer|tig** ADJ ready to print, ready for the press; **druck|fest** ADJ Werkstoff pressure-resistant; **Druck|fes|tig|keit** F pressure resistance; **Druck|form** F (Typ) printing form(e), quoin; **Druck|for|mat** NT (Typ) format; **druck|frisch** ADJ hot off the press; Geldscheine newly printed; **Druck|ge|fäl|le** NT (Phys) difference in pressure; **Druck|ge|fühl** NT feeling of pressure; **Druck|ge|schwin|dig|keit** F (Comput) print speed; **Druck|ka|bi|ne** F pressurized cabin; **Druck|knopf** M **a** (Sew) press stud, snap fastener **b** (Tech) push button; **Druck|kopf** M (Comput) print head

Druck|kos|ten PL printing costs pl

Druck|le|gung [-le:gʊŋ] F **-, -en** printing; **mit der ~ beginnen** to begin printing, to go to press

Druck|luft F compressed air

Druck|luft-: **Druck|luft|boh|rer** M pneumatic drill; **Druck|luft|brem|se** F air brake

Druck-: **Druck|ma|schi|ne** F (Typ) printing press; **Druck|me|nü** NT (Comput) print menu; **Druck|mes|ser** M **-s, -** pressure gauge; **Druck|mit|tel** NT (fig) form of pressure, means of exerting pressure; **als politisches ~** as a form of political pressure, as a means of exerting political pressure; **Druck|mus|ter** NT print(ed pattern or design); **Stoffe mit ~** prints, printed materials; **Druck|ort** M pl **-orte** place of printing; **Druck|pa|pier** NT printing paper; **Druck|plat|te** F printing plate; **Druck|pos|ten** M (inf) cushy job or number (inf); **Druck|pres|se** F printing press; **Druck|pum|pe** F pressure pump; **Druck|qua|li|tät** F print quality; **druck|reif** ADJ ready for printing, passed for press; (fig) polished ADV **~ sprechen** to speak in a polished style; **Druck|rei|hen|fol|ge** F printing order; **Druck|sa|che** F **a** (Post) business letter; (= Werbematerial) circular; (als Portoklasse) printed matter; **„Drucksache"** "printed matter"; **etw als ~ schicken** ≈ to send sth at printed-paper rate **b** (Typ: = Auftrag) stationery printing job **c** **Drucksachen** PL (= Akzidenz) stationery printing sing; **Druck|schal|ter** M push-button switch; **Druck|schott** NT (Aviat) bulkhead; **Druck|schrift** F **a** (= Schriftart) printing; **in ~ schreiben** to print; **die ~ lernen** to learn printing, to learn to print **b** (= gedrucktes Werk) pamphlet; **Druck|sei|te** F printed page

druck|sen ['drʊksn] VI (inf) to hum and haw (inf)

Druck-: **Druck|sor|ten** PL (Aus) printed forms pl; **Druck|stel|le** F place or (Mal) mark (where pressure has been applied); (= Fleck auf Pfirsich, Haut) bruise; **Druck|stock** M (Typ) relief plate; **Druck|tas|te** F push button; **Druck|tech|nik** F printing technology or (= Verfahren) technique; **druck|tech|nisch** ADJ typographical; (in Bezug auf mechanischen Vorgang) printing attr ADV from a typographical/printing point of view; **~ verfeinert** improved from the printing point of view; **Druck|trom|mel** F (Comput) print drum; **Druck|ty|pe** F type; **druck|un|emp|find|lich** ADJ insensitive to pressure; **Druck|un|ter|schied** M difference in pressure; **Druck|ver|band** M (Med) pressure bandage; **Druck|ver|bot** NT printing ban; **Druck|ver|fah|ren** NT printing process; **Druck|ver|lust** M (Tech) loss of pressure, reduction in pressure; **Druck|vor|la|ge** F (Typ) setting copy; **Druck|vor|schau** F (Comput) print preview; **Druck|was|ser|re|ak|tor** M pressurized water reactor; **Druck|wel|le** F shock wave; **Druck|werk** NT printed work, publication; **Druck|we|sen** NT, no pl printing no art; **Druck|zei|le** F line of print

Dru|de ['dru:də] F **-, -n** (Myth) witch

Dru|den|fuß M (Myth) pentagram

druff [drʊf] ADV (dial inf) = **drauf**

Dru|i|de [dru'i:də] M **-n, -n**, **Dru|i|din** [dru'i:dɪn] F **-, -nen** Druid

dru|i|disch [dru'i:dɪʃ] ADJ druidic(al), druid attr

drum [drʊm] ADV (inf) around, round (Brit); **~ (he)rum** all (a)round; **~ (he)rumreden** to beat about the bush; **da wirst du nicht ~ (he)rumkommen** there's no getting out of it; **seis ~!** (geh) never mind; **das (ganze) Drum und Dran** the paraphernalia; (= Begleiterscheinungen) the fuss and bother; **mit allem Drum und Dran** with all the bits and pieces (inf); Mahlzeit with all the trimmings pl → **darum**

Drum|he|rum [drʊmhe'rʊm] NT **-s**, no pl trappings pl

Drum|mer ['dramɐ] M **-s, -**, **Drum|me|rin** ['dramərɪn] F **-, -nen** (Mus) drummer

drun|ten ['drʊntn] ADV (old, dial) down there

drun|ter ['drʊntɐ] ADV under(neath); **da kann ich mir nichts ~ vorstellen** that means nothing to me; ~ **und drüber** upside down, topsy-turvy *(inf)*; **alles ging** *or* **es ging alles ~ und drüber** everything was upside down *or* topsy-turvy *(inf)*; **das Drunter und Drüber** the confusion, the muddle → **darunter**

Drusch [drʊʃ] M **-(e)s, -e** *(Agr)* threshing; *(= Produkt)* threshed corn

Drü|se ['dry:zə] F **-, -n** gland

Dru|se ['dru:zə] F **-, -n** *(Min, Geol)* druse

Dru|se ['dru:zə] M **-n, -n**, **Dru|sin** ['dru:zɪn] F **-, -nen** *(Rel)* Druse

Drü|sen-: **drü|sen|ar|tig** ADJ glandular; **Drü|sen|fie|ber** NT glandular fever, mono(nucleosis) *(US)*; **Drü|sen|funk|ti|on** F glandular function; **Drü|sen|krank|heit** F, **Drü|sen|lei|den** NT glandular disorder; **Drü|sen|schwel|lung** F glandular swelling, swollen glands *pl*; **Drü|sen|über|funk|ti|on** F hyperactivity *or* overactivity of the glands; **Drü|sen|un|ter|funk|ti|on** F underactivity of the glands

Dru|sin ['dru:zɪn] F **-, -nen** *(Rel)* Druse

DSB [de:lɛs'be:] M **-s** *abbr von* **Deutscher Sportbund** German Sports Association

Dschun|gel ['dʒʊŋl] M **-s, -** *(lit, fig)* jungle; **sich im ~ der Paragrafen zurechtfinden** to wade one's way through the verbiage

Dschun|gel-: **dschun|gel|ar|tig** ADJ *Wald* jungle-like; **Dschun|gel|fie|ber** NT yellow fever; **Dschun|gel|ge|setz** NT law of the jungle; **Dschun|gel|krieg** M jungle warfare

Dschun|ke ['dʒʊŋkə] F **-, -n** *(Naut)* junk

DSG [de:lɛs'ge:] F **-** *abbr von* **Deutsche Schlafwagen- und Speisewagen-Gesellschaft**

DTD [de:te:'de:] F *abbr von* **Document Type Definition, Dokumenttypdefinition** DTD

DTP [de:te:'pe:] NT *abbr von* **Desktop Publishing** DTP

DTP- *in cpds* DTP; **DTP-An|wen|der(in)** M(F) DTP user; **DTP-Fach|frau** F, **DTP-Fach|mann** M DTP specialist; **DTP-Pro|fi** M *(inf)* DTP pro *(inf) or* expert; **DTP-Soft|ware** F DTP software

dt(sch). *abbr von* **deutsch**

Dtzd. *abbr von* **Dutzend**

du [du:] PERS PRON *gen* **deiner**, *dat* **dir**, *acc* **dich** you *(familiar form of address)*, thou *(obs, dial)*; *(= man)* you; **ich gehe heute ins Kino und du?** I'm going to the cinema today, how about you?; **du (zu jdm) sagen, jdn mit Du anreden** to use the familiar form of address (with sb), to say "du" (to sb); **du, der du es erlebt hast** you who have experienced it; **mit jdm auf Du und Du stehen** to be pals with sb; **mit jdm per du sein** to be on familiar *or* friendly terms with sb; **du bist es** it's you; **bist du es** *or* **das?** is it *or* that you?; **Vater unser, der Du bist im Himmel** our Father, who *or* which art in heaven; **mach du das doch!** YOU do it!, do it yourself!; **du, meine Heimat!** *(poet)* thou, my homeland!; **du Glücklicher!** lucky you, you lucky thing; **du Idiot!** you idiot; **du Schlingel/Schuft(, du)!** you rascal/scoundrel(, you)!; **ach du lieber Gott** *or* **liebe Güte** good Lord!, good heavens!; **du (Mutti), kannst du mir mal helfen?** hey (mummy), can you help me?; **du, ich muss jetzt aber gehen** listen, I have to go now; **du, du!** *(hum: drohend)* naughty, naughty → **mir**

Du [du:] NT **-(s), -(s)** "du", familiar form of address; **jdm das Du anbieten** to suggest that sb uses "du" *or* the familiar form of address

du|al [du'a:l] ADJ dual

> **DUALES SYSTEM**
>
> The **duales System** is a waste disposal system which has operated in Germany since 1991. Packaging materials that can be recycled –paper, glass, metal, plastics – are marked with the **Grüner Punkt**. Licences for using this symbol must be obtained from **DSD (Duales System Deutschland GmbH)**, the company responsible for operating the system. The recyclable waste thus marked is collected separately, then sorted and sent for recycling. Although there is no charge for collecting waste for recycling, the cost of obtaining the licence from **DSD** is often included in the retail price. Austria has a similar system, for which the company **ARA (Altstoff Recycling Austria AG)** is responsible. → GRÜNER PUNKT

Du|al [du'a:l] M **-s, -e**, **Du|a|lis** [du'a:lɪs] M **-, Duale** [-lə] dual

Du|a|lis|mus [dua'lɪsmʊs] M **-**, *no pl* *(Philos, Pol, geh)* dualism

Du|a|list [dua'lɪst] M **-en, -en**, **Du|a|lis|tin** [-'lɪstɪn] F **-, -nen** *(Philos)* dualist

du|a|lis|tisch [dua'lɪstɪʃ] ADJ *(Philos, Pol, geh)* dualistic

Du|a|li|tät [duali'tɛ:t] F **-, -en** *(geh)* duality

Du|al|sys|tem NT *(Math)* binary system

Du|ath|lon NT *(Sport)* duathlon

Dub [dab] M **-**, *no pl* *(Mus)* dub

Dü|bel ['dy:bl] M **-s, -** Rawlplug®; *(= Holzdübel)* dowel

Dü|bel|mas|se F plugging compound, filler

dü|beln ['dy:bln] VTI to plug

du|bi|os [du'bio:s], **du|bi|ös** [du'biø:s] ADJ *(geh)* dubious

Dub|lee [du'ble:] NT **-s, -s** = **Doublé**

Dub|let|te [du'blɛtə] F **-, -n** **a** *(= doppelt vorhandenes Stück, Kopie)* duplicate **b** *(Hunt)* right and left **c** *(= Edelstein)* doublet **d** *(Boxen)* one-two

dub|lie|ren [du'bli:rən] *ptp* **dubliert** VT = **doublieren**

Dub|lin ['dablɪn] NT **-s** Dublin

Dub|li|ner ['dablinɐ] ADJ *attr* Dublin

Dub|li|ner ['dablinɐ] M **-s, -**, **Dub|li|ne|rin** [-ərɪn] F **-, -nen** Dubliner

du|cken ['dʊkn] VR to duck; *(fig pej)* to cringe, to cower; *(fig: Bäume, Häuser)* to nestle; **ich duckte mich vor dem Hieb** I ducked the blow; **sich in eine Ecke/hinter eine Deckung ~** to duck *or* dodge into a corner/behind cover → *auch* **geduckt** VT *Kopf, Menschen* to duck; *(fig)* to humiliate VI *(fig pej)* to cower

Duck|mäu|ser ['dʊkmɔyzɐ] M **-s, -**, **Duck|mäu|se|rin** [-ərɪn] F **-, -nen** *(pej)* moral coward

Duck|mäu|se|rei [dʊkmɔyzə'rai] F **-, -en** *(pej)* moral cowardice; **Erziehung zur ~** bringing up to be moral cowards

duck|mäu|se|risch ['dʊkmɔyzərɪʃ] *(pej)* ADJ showing moral cowardice ADV **sich ~ verhalten** to act without integrity

duck|mäu|sern ['dʊkmɔyzɐn] VI *insep (pej)* to be moral cowards/a moral coward

Duck|mäu|ser|tum ['dʊkmɔyzɐtu:m] NT **-s**, *no pl (pej)* moral cowardice; **jdn zum ~ erziehen** to bring sb up to be a moral coward

Du|de|lei [dudə'lai] F **-, -en** *(pej)* humming; *(auf Flöte)* tootling

Du|del|kas|ten M *(pej inf)* noise box

du|deln ['du:dln] *(pej inf)* VI to hum; *(auf Flöte)* to tootle (auf +*dat* on) VT **a** *Lied* to hum; *(auf Flöte)* to tootle **b** *(dial)* **einen ~** to have a nip *or* a wee dram *(Brit dial)*

Du|del|sack M bagpipes *pl*

Du|del|sack|pfei|fer(in) M(F), **Du|del|sack|spie|ler(in)** M(F) (bag)piper

Due Di|li|gence [dju: 'dɪlɪtʃənts, dju: 'dɪlɪdʒəns] F **-**, *no pl (Econ)* due diligence

Du|ell [du'ɛl] NT **-s, -e** *(lit, fig)* duel *(um* over); **ein ~ auf Degen** a duel with swords; **ein ~ (mit jdm) austragen** to fight *or* have a duel (with sb); **jdn zum ~ (heraus)fordern, jdn ins ~ fordern** to challenge sb to a duel

Du|el|lant [duɛ'lant] M **-en, -en**, **Du|el|lan|tin** [-'lantɪn] F **-, -nen** dueller, duellist

du|el|lie|ren [duɛ'li:rən] **duelliert** VR to (fight a) duel

Du|ell|pis|to|le F duelling pistol

Du|ett [du'ɛt] NT **-(e)s, -e** **a** *(Mus, fig)* duet; **im ~ singen** to sing a duet; **etw im ~ singen** to sing sth as a duet **b** *(fig inf: = Paar)* duo *(inf)*

duff [dʊf] ADJ *(N Ger)* matt; *Glas, Fenster* dull

Duf|fle|coat ['daflko:t] M **-s, -s** duffel coat

Duft [dʊft] M **-(e)s, ¨e** ['dʏftə] **a** (pleasant) smell, scent; *(von Blumen, Parfüm)* smell, scent, fragrance; *(von Essen, Kaffee etc)* smell, aroma; *(= Absonderung von Tieren)* scent; *(fig)* allure; **den ~ der großen weiten Welt verspüren** *(usu iro)* to get a taste of the big wide world **b** *(liter: = Dunst)* haze

Duft|drü|se F scent gland

duf|te ['dʊftə] ADJ ADV *(dated inf)* smashing *(Brit inf)*, great *(inf)*

duf|ten ['dʊftn] VI to smell; **nach etw ~** to smell of sth, to have a smell of sth VI *impers* **hier duftet es nach Kaffee** there is a smell of coffee here, it smells of coffee here

duf|tend ADJ *attr* nice-smelling; *Parfüm, Blumen etc* fragrant; *Kaffee, Kräuter* aromatic

duf|tig ['dʊftɪç] ADJ **a** *Kleid, Stoff* gossamery; *Spitzen* frothy; *Wolken* fluffy **b** *(poet: = zart dunstig)* hazy

Duf|tig|keit F **-**, *no pl (von Kleid, Stoff)* gossamer lightness; *(von Spitzen)* frothiness; *(von Wolken)* fluffiness

Duft-: **Duft|kis|sen** NT scented sachet; *(= parfümiertes Kopfkissen)* scented pillow; **duft|los** ADJ odourless *(Brit)*, odorless *(US)*, unscented; **Duft|mar|ke** F scent mark; **Duft|no|te** F *(von Parfüm)* scent; *(von Mensch)* smell; **Duft|or|gan** NT scent gland; **Duft|pro|be** F **a** *(= Vorgang)* perfume test **b** *(= Probeflasche)* free sample of perfume; **Duft|stoff** M scent; *(für Parfüm, Waschmittel etc)* fragrance; **Duft|was|ser** NT *pl* **-wässer** toilet water; *(hum: = Parfüm)* perfume, scent; **Duft|wol|ke** F *(iro)* fragrance *(iro)*; *(von Parfüm)* cloud of perfume

duhn [du:n] ADJ *(N Ger inf)* sloshed *(esp Brit inf)*

Du|ka|ten [du'ka:tn] M **-s, -** ducat

Du|ka|ten-: **Du|ka|ten|esel** M *(hum)* = **Dukatenscheißer(in)**; **Du|ka|ten|gold** NT fine gold; **Du|ka|ten|schei|ßer(in)** M(F) *(inf)* **ein ~ sein** to be a gold mine, to be made of money

Dü|ker ['dy:kɐ] M **-s, -** *(Straßenbau)* drain, culvert

Duk|tus ['dʊktʊs] M **-**, *no pl (geh)* characteristic style; *(von Handschrift)* characteristics *pl*, flow

dul|den ['dʊldn] VI *(geh: = leiden)* to suffer VT **a** *(= zulassen)* to tolerate; *Widerspruch auch* to countenance; **ich dulde das nicht** I won't tolerate that; **die Sache duldet keinen Aufschub** the matter cannot be delayed *or* postponed; **etw stillschweigend ~** to connive at sth **b** *(= nicht vertreiben)* to tolerate; **er ist hier nur geduldet** he's only tolerated here, he's only here on sufferance **c** *(geh: = erdulden) Not, Schmerz* to suffer

Dul|der ['dʊldɐ] M **-s, -**, **Dul|de|rin** [-ərɪn] F **-, -nen** silent sufferer

Dul|der|mie|ne F *(iro)* air of patient suffering; **mit ~** with an air of patient suffering

duld|sam ['dʊltza:m] ADJ tolerant *(gegenüber* of, *jdm gegenüber* towards sb); *(= geduldig)* forbearing ADV tolerantly; *(= geduldig)* with forbearance

Duld|sam|keit F **-**, *no pl* tolerance; *(= Geduld)* forbearance

Dul|dung F **-**, *(rare)* **-en** **a** toleration; **solche Zustände erlauben keine weitere ~** such conditions can be tolerated no longer; **unter** *or* **bei** *or* **mit stillschweigender ~ der Behörden** *etc* with the (tacit) connivance of the authorities *etc* **b** *(= Aufenthaltsgenehmigung)* short-term residence permit

Dul|li|äh [dʊli'ɛ:] M **-**, *no pl (Aus inf)* tipsiness *(inf)*; **im ~** (when one is/was) tipsy

Dult [dʊlt] F **-, en** *(S Ger, Aus: = Jahrmarkt)* fair

Dul|zi|nea [dʊltsi'ne:a] F **-, Dulzineen** [-'ne:ən] *(hum)* ladylove

Dum|dum [dʊm'dʊm] NT **-(s), -(s)**, **Dum|dum|ge|schoss** NT dumdum (bullet)

dumm [dʊm] [dʊm] ADJ *comp* **¨er** ['dʏmɐ] ['dʏmɐ], *superl* **¨ste(r, s)** ['dʏmstə] ['dʏmstə] **a**

stupid, dumb *(esp US)*; *Mensch* stupid, thick *(inf)*, dumb *(esp US)*; *(= unklug, unvernünftig)* stupid, silly, foolish; **der ~e August** *(inf)* the clown; **~e Gans** silly goose; **~es Zeug (reden)** (to talk) rubbish *(Brit)* or nonsense; **ein ~es Gesicht machen** to look stupid; **jdn wie einen ~en Jungen behandeln** *(inf)* to treat sb like a child; **jdn für ~ verkaufen** *(inf)* to think sb is stupid; **du willst mich wohl für ~ verkaufen** you must think I'm stupid; **ich lasse mich nicht für ~ verkaufen** I'm not so stupid *(inf)*; **das ist gar nicht (so) ~** that's not a bad idea; **er ist dümmer als die Polizei erlaubt** *(inf)* he's as stupid as they come *(inf)*; **das war dümmer als die Polizei erlaubt** *(inf)* that was as stupid as you can get *(inf)*; **jetzt wirds mir zu ~** I've had enough; **der Krach macht mich ganz ~ (im Kopf)** the noise is making my head spin → **Bohnenstroh, Bauer a**, → **Wäsche b**

b *(= ärgerlich, unangenehm)* annoying; *Gefühl auch* nagging; *Sache, Geschichte, Angelegenheit auch* silly; **es ist zu ~, dass er nicht kommen kann** it's too bad that he can't come; **etwas Dummes** a silly *or* stupid thing; **so etwas Dummes** how silly *or* stupid; *(= wie ärgerlich)* what a nuisance

ADV *comp* **¨er**, *superl* **am ¨sten ~ gucken** to look stupid; **dümmer hättest du dich wirklich nicht anstellen können** you couldn't have made things worse if you'd tried; **sich ~ anstellen** to behave stupidly; **sich ~ stellen** to act stupid, to play dumb *(esp US)*; **~ fragen** to ask a silly question/silly questions; **~ dastehen** to look stupid *or* foolish; **sich ~ und dämlich reden** *(inf)* to talk till one is blue in the face *(inf)*; **sich ~ und dämlich suchen** *(inf)* to search high and low; **sich ~ und dämlich verdienen** *(inf)* to earn the earth *(inf)*; **~ geboren, nichts dazugelernt** *(prov)* he/she *etc* hasn't got the sense he/she *etc* was born with *(prov)*; **jdm ~ kommen** *(inf)* to get funny with sb *(inf)*

Dụmm-: **Dụmm|bach** NT **-s**, *no pl (inf)* **ich bin doch nicht aus ~** you can't fool me that easily, I'm not stupid; **Dụmm|bart** M, **Dụmm|beu|tel** M *(inf)* fool *(inf)*, dumbbell *(US inf)*

Dụmm|chen [ˈdʊmçən] NT **-s, -** *(inf)* silly-billy *(Brit inf)*, ninny *(inf)*

dụmm|dreist ADJ insolent; *Idee* impertinent ADV *grinsen, antworten* insolently, impertinently

Dụmm|dreis|tig|keit F insolence

Dum|me|jun|gen|streich M silly *or* foolish *or* childish prank

Dụm|men|fang M **das ist der reinste ~** that's just a con *(inf)*; **auf ~ ausgehen** to try to catch fools

Dụm|me(r) [ˈdʊmə] MF *decl as adj (inf)* mug *(inf)*, fool, sucker *(inf)*; **der ~ sein** to be left to carry the can *(inf)*, to be left holding the baby *(inf)*; **einen ~n finden** to find a mug *(inf) or a* sucker *(inf)*

Dụm|mer|chen [ˈdʊmɐçən] NT **-s, -** *(inf)* silly-billy *(Brit inf)*, ninny *(inf)*; **mein ~** you silly-billy *(Brit inf) or* ninny *(inf)*

Dụm|mer|jan [ˈdʊmɐjaːn] M **-s, -e** *(inf)* silly dope *(inf)*

dụm|mer|wei|se ADV unfortunately; *(= aus Dummheit)* stupidly, foolishly

Dụmm|heit F **-, -en a** *no pl* stupidity; **vor ~ brüllen** *or* **schreien** to be incredibly stupid *or* thick *(inf)* **b** *(= dumme Handlung)* stupid thing; **mach bloß keine ~en!** just don't do anything stupid

dụmm+kom|men VI *sep irreg aux sein* → **dumm ADV**

Dụmm|kopf M *(inf)* idiot, fool

dụ̈mm|lich [ˈdʏmlɪç] ADJ silly, stupid; *Mensch auch* foolish, dumb *(esp US)*; **eine ~e Blondine** a dumb blonde

Dụ̈mm|ling [ˈdʏmlɪŋ] M **-s, -e** fool

Dụmm|schwät|zer(in) M(F) *(inf)* hot-air merchant *(inf)*, bullshitter *(vulg)*

Dum|my [ˈdami] M **-s, -s a** *(= Attrappe, bei Unfalltests)* dummy **b** *(= Probeband)* demo (tape) *(inf)*

Dump [ˈdamp] M **-s, -s** *(Comput)* dump

dụ̈m|peln [ˈdʏmpln] VI **a** *(Naut)* to bob up and down **b** *(fig)* to hover; **die Partei dümpelt bei 40%** the party is hovering around the 40% mark

dụmpf [dʊmpf] ADJ **a** *Geräusch, Ton* muffled **b** *Luft, Geruch, Keller, Geschmack etc* musty; *(fig) Atmosphäre* stifling **c** *Gefühl, Ahnung, Erinnerung* vague; *Schmerz* dull; *(= bedrückend)* gloomy **d** *(= stumpfsinnig)* dull ADV **a** *(= hohl) aufprallen* with a thud; **~ klingen** to sound dull; *(weil hohl)* to sound hollow **b** *(= stumpfsinnig)* **~ glotzen** to have a mindless look on one's face; **~ vor sich hin brüten** to be completely apathetic

Dụmpf|ba|cke F *(sl)* nerd *(inf)*

Dụmpf|heit F **-,** *no pl* **a** *(von Geräusch, Ton)* muffled quality **b** *(von Luft, Geruch, Keller, Geschmack etc)* mustiness; **die ~ der Provinzatmosphäre** *(fig)* the stifling atmosphere of the provinces **c** *(von Gefühl, Ahnung, Erinnerung)* vagueness; *(von Schmerz)* dullness; *(= Bedrücktheit)* gloominess **d** *(= Stumpfsinnigkeit)* dullness

dụmp|fig [ˈdʊmpfɪç] ADJ *(= feucht)* dank, damp; *(= muffig)* musty; *(= moderig)* mouldy *(Brit)*, moldy *(US)*

Dụmp|fig|keit F **-,** *no pl (= Feuchte)* dankness, dampness; *(= Muffigkeit)* mustiness; *(= Moderigkeit)* mouldiness *(Brit)*, moldiness *(US)*

Dum|ping [ˈdampɪŋ] NT **-s**, *no pl (Econ)* dumping

Dum|ping|preis [ˈdampɪŋ-] M giveaway price

dụn [duːn] ADJ *(N Ger inf)* sloshed *(inf)*

Dü|ne [ˈdyːnə] F **-, -n** (sand) dune

Dü|nen-: **Dü|nen|bil|dung** F formation of dunes; **Dü|nen|gras** NT marram (grass); **Dü|nen|sand** M dune sand

Dụng [dʊŋ] M **-(e)s**, *no pl* dung, manure

Dün|ge|mit|tel NT fertilizer

dụ̈n|gen [ˈdʏŋən] VT to fertilize VI *(Stoff)* to act as a fertilizer; *(Mensch)* to apply fertilizer; **im Garten ~** to put fertilizer on the garden

Dụ̈n|ger [ˈdʏŋɐ] M **-s, -** fertilizer

Dụng-: **Dụng|flie|ge** F dung fly; **Dụng|gru|be** F manure pit; **Dụng|hau|fen** M dung *or* manure heap

Dụ̈n|gung F **-, -en a** *(= das Düngen)* fertilizing **b** *(= Dünger)* fertilizer

dụn|kel [ˈdʊŋkl] ADJ **a** *(= finster)* dark; *(fig auch)* black; **im Dunkeln** in the dark; **in dunkler Nacht** at dead of night; **im Zimmer ~ machen** *(inf)* to make the room dark, to darken the room

b *(farblich)* dark; **ein Dunkles, bitte!** ≈ a brown ale *(Brit) or* dark beer, please

c *(= tief) Stimme, Ton* deep

d *(= unbestimmt, unklar)* vague; *Erinnerung* vague, dim; *Textstelle* unclear; **in dunkler Vergangenheit** *or* **Vorzeit** in the dim and distant past; **im Dunkeln tappen** *(fig)* to grope (about) in the dark; **jdn im Dunkeln lassen** to leave sb in the dark; **das liegt noch im Dunkeln** that remains to be seen

e *(pej: = zweifelhaft, zwielichtig)* shady *(inf)*, dubious

ADV **a** *(= in dunklen Farben)* in a dark colour *(Brit) or* color *(US)*, in dark colours *(Brit) or* colors *(US)*; **~ gefärbt sein** to be a dark colo(u)r; **sich ~ kleiden** to dress in dark colo(u)rs; **~ gekleidet** dressed in dark(-coloured) *(Brit) or* dark(-colored) *(US)* clothes; **etw ~ anmalen** to paint sth a dark colo(u)r

b sich ~ erinnern to remember vaguely

Dụn|kel [ˈdʊŋkl] NT **-s**, *no pl (lit, fig)* darkness; **im ~ der Vergangenheit** in the dim and distant past; **das verliert sich im ~ der Geschichte** it is lost in the mists of history; **in ~ gehüllt sein** *(fig)* to be shrouded in mystery; **im ~ der Nacht** at dead of night

Dü̈n|kel [ˈdʏŋkl] M **-s**, *no pl (pej geh)* conceit, arrogance

dụn|kel- *in cpds* dark; **dụn|kel|blau** ADJ dark blue; **dụn|kel|blond** ADJ light brown; **dụn|kel|braun** ADJ dark brown; **dụn|kel|far|ben** ADJ dark-coloured *(Brit)*, dark-colored *(US)*; **dụn|kel|ge|klei|det** ADJ → **dunkel ADV a**; **dụn|kel|grau** ADJ dark grey *(Brit)*, dark gray *(US)*; **dụn|kel|grün** ADJ dark green; **dụn|kel|haa|rig** ADJ dark-haired

dụ̈n|kel|haft ADJ *(pej geh)* arrogant, conceited

Dụ̈n|kel|haf|tig|keit F **-,** *no pl (pej geh)* arrogance, conceit

Dụn|kel-: **dụn|kel|häu|tig** ADJ dark-skinned; **Dụn|kel|heit** F **-,** *(rare)* **-en** *(lit, fig)* darkness; **bei Einbruch** *or* **Eintritt der ~** at nightfall; **Dụn|kel|kam|mer** F *(Phot)* darkroom; **Dụn|kel|kam|mer|leuch|te** F, **Dụn|kel|kam|mer|lam|pe** F safelight; **Dụn|kel|mann** M *pl* **-männer** *(pej)* **a** shady character **b** *(liter)* obscurant(ist)

dụn|keln [ˈdʊŋkln] VI *impers* **es dunkelt** *(geh)* darkness is falling, it is growing dark VI **a** *(poet: Nacht, Abend)* to grow dark **b** *aux sein (= dunkel werden)* to become darker, to darken

Dụn|kel-: **dụn|kel|rot** ADJ dark red; **dụn|kel|weiß** ADJ *(hum)* off-white; **Dụn|kel|wer|den** NT nightfall; **Dụn|kel|zif|fer** F *estimated number of unreported/undetected cases*; **Dụn|kel|zo|ne** F twilight zone

dụ̈n|ken [ˈdʏŋkn] *(geh) pret* **dünkte** *or (obs)* **deuchte** [ˈdʏŋktə, ˈdɔyçtə], *ptp* **gedünkt** *or (obs)* **gedeucht** [gəˈdʏŋkt, gəˈdɔyçt] VTI *impers* **das dünkt mich gut, das dünkt mich** *or* **mir gut zu sein, mich dünkt, dass das gut ist** it seems good to me; **mich dünkt, er kommt nicht mehr** methinks *(obs) or* I think he will not come VI to seem, to appear VR to think *or* imagine (oneself); **sie dünkt sich sehr klug** she thinks herself very clever

dụ̈nn [dʏn] ADJ thin; *Suppe, Bier auch* watery; *Kaffee, Tee* watery, weak; *(= fein) Schleier, Regen, Strümpfe* fine; *Haarwuchs, Besiedlung* thin, sparse; *(fig: = dürftig)* thin; **sich ~ machen** *(hum)* to breathe in → **dick, dünnmachen** ADV *besiedelt, bevölkert* sparsely; **~ behaart** *(Mensch)* with thin hair; *Haupt* thinly covered in hair; **~ gesät** *(fig)* thin on the ground, few and far between

Dụ̈nn-: **dụ̈nn|be|haart** ADJ → **dünn ADV**; **dụ̈nn|be|sie|delt** [-bəziːdlt], **dụ̈nn|be|völ|kert** [-bəfœlkɐt] ADJ → **dünn ADV**; **Dụ̈nn|bier** NT weak beer; **Dụ̈nn|brett|boh|rer(in)** M(F) *(pej inf)* slacker, skiver *(Brit inf)*; **geistiger ~** dimwit *(inf)*; **Dụ̈nn|darm** M small intestine; **Dụ̈nn|druck|aus|ga|be** F India paper edition; **Dụ̈nn|druck|pa|pier** NT India paper

dụ̈n|ne [ˈdʏnə] ADJ *pred (dial)* = **dünn**

Dụ̈n|ne [ˈdʏnə] F **-,** *no pl* thinness

dụ̈n|ne+ma|chen VR *sep (dial, inf)* to make oneself scarce *(inf)*

dụn|ne|mals [ˈdʊnəmaːls] ADV *(dated, hum)* = **damals**

Dụ̈nn-: **dụ̈nn|flüs|sig** ADJ *Farbe, Öl* thin; *Teig, Honig* runny; *Stuhlgang* loose; **Dụ̈nn|flüs|sig|keit** F *(von Farbe, Öl)* thinness; *(von Teig, Honig)* runniness; *(von Stuhlgang)* looseness; **dụ̈nn|ge|sät** [-gəzɛːt] ADJ *attr* → **dünn ADV**; **dụ̈nn|häu|tig** ADJ thin-skinned; *(fig auch)* sensitive; **dụ̈nn|lip|pig** [-lɪpɪç] ADJ thin-lipped; **dụ̈nn+ma|chen** VR *sep (inf: = weglaufen)* to make oneself scarce; **Dụ̈nn|pfiff** M *(inf)* the runs *(inf)*; **Dụ̈nn|säu|re** F dilute acid; **Dụ̈nn|säu|re|ver|klap|pung** F dumping of dilute acids; **dụ̈nn|scha|lig** [-ʃaːlɪç] ADJ *Obst* thin-skinned; *Nüsse, Ei etc* thin-shelled; **Dụ̈nn|schiss** M *(inf)* the runs *(inf)*; **dụ̈nn|wan|dig** ADJ *Haus, Behälter, Blutgefäße* thin-walled

Dụnst [dʊnst] M **-(e)s, ¨e** [ˈdʏnstə] *(= leichter Nebel)* mist, haze; *(= Dampf)* steam; *(= Smog)* smog; *(= dumpfe Luft)* fug; *(= Geruch)* smell; **blauer ~** *(fig inf)* sheer invention; **jdm blauen ~ vormachen** *(inf)* to throw dust in sb's eyes; **sich in ~ auflösen** to go up in smoke → **blass d**

Dụnst-: **Dụnst|ab|zugs|hau|be** F extractor hood *(over a cooker)*; **dụnst|ar|tig** ADJ

Rauch, Nebel vapoury *(Brit)*, vapory *(US)*, vaporous

dụns|ten ['dʊnstn] VI **a** *(= dampfen)* to steam **b** *(= Dunst ausströmen)* to give off a smell, to smell

dụ̈ns|ten ['dʏnstn] VT *(Cook) Gemüse, Fisch, Fleisch* to steam; *Obst* to stew

Dụnst|glo|cke F, **Dụnst|hau|be** F *(= Nebel)* haze; *(= Smog)* pall of smog

dụns|tig ['dʊnstɪç] ADJ **a** hazy, misty; *Licht* hazy **b** *(= schlecht belüftet)* stuffy; *(= verräuchert)* smoky

Dụnst-: **Dụnst|kreis** M atmosphere; *(von Mensch)* society; **Dụnst|schicht** F layer of haze *or* mist; **Dụnst|schlei|er** M veil of haze *or* mist; **Dụnst|schwa|den** PL clouds *pl* of haze; *(= Nebel)* haze *sing*; *(= Dampf)* clouds *pl* of steam; *(= Rauch)* clouds *pl* of smoke; **Dụnst|wol|ke** F cloud of smog

Dụ̈nst|obst NT *(Cook)* stewed fruit

Dü|nung ['dyːnʊŋ] F -, -en *(Naut)* swell

Duo ['duːo] NT -s, -s **a** *(Mus) (= Musikstück)* duet, duo; *(= Ausführende)* duo **b** *(= Paar)* duo

Duo|dez-: **Duo|dez|aus|ga|be** F duodecimo edition; **Duo|dez|band** [-bant] M *pl* -bände duodecimo volume; **Duo|dez|fürst** M *(pej geh)* princeling, minor *or* petty prince; **Duo|dez|fürs|ten|tum** NT *(pej geh)* minor *or* petty princedom

Duo|de|zi|mal|sys|tem [duodetsi'maːl-] NT duodecimal system

Duo|dez|staat [duo'deːts-] M *(pej geh)* miniature state

dü|pie|ren [dy'piːrən] *ptp* **düpiert** VT *(geh)* to dupe

dü|piert [dy'piːɐt] ADJ *(geh)* duped

Dup|li|kat [dupli'kaːt] NT -(e)s, -e duplicate (copy)

Dup|li|ka|ti|on [duplika'tsioːn] F -, -en *(geh)* duplication

dup|li|zie|ren [dupli'tsiːrən] *ptp* **dupliziert** VT *(geh)* to duplicate

Dup|li|zi|tät [duplitsi'tɛːt] F -, -en *(geh)* duplication

Dup|lo|stein® ['duplo-] M Duplo® brick

Dur [duːɐ] NT -, *no pl (Mus)* major; **ein Stück in ~/in G-~** a piece in a major key/in G major

du|ra|bel [du'raːbl] ADJ *(geh)* durable

Dur|ak|kord M major chord

durch [dʊrç] PREP +*acc* **a** *(räumlich: = hindurch)* through; **quer ~** right across; **mitten ~ die Stadt** through the middle of the town; **~ den Fluss waten** to wade across the river; **~ die ganze Welt reisen** to travel all over the world *or* throughout the world **b** *(= mittels, von)* through, by (means of); *(in Passivkonstruktion: = von)* by; *(= über jdn/etw, mit jds Hilfe)* through, via; *(den Grund, die Ursache nennend)* through, because of; **Tod ~ Ertrinken/den Strang** death by drowning/hanging; **Tod ~ Erfrieren/Herzschlag** *etc* death from exposure/a heart attack *etc*; **neun (geteilt) ~ drei** nine divided by three, three into nine; **~ Zufall/das Los** by chance/lot; **~ die Post®** by post *(Brit)* *or* mail; **etw ~ die Zeitung bekannt geben** to announce sth in the press; **~ den Lautsprecher** through the loudspeaker **c** *(= aufgrund, infolge von)* due *or* owing to **d** *(Aus: zeitlich)* for

ADV **a** *(= hindurch)* through; **die ganze Nacht ~** all through the night, throughout the night; **es ist 4 Uhr ~** it's past *or* gone 4 o'clock; **~ und ~** *(kennen)* through and through; *verlogen, überzeugt* completely, utterly; **~ und ~ ehrlich** honest through and through; **~ und ~ nass** wet through; **das geht mir ~ und ~** that goes right through me **b** *(Cook inf) Steak* well-done; **das Fleisch ist noch nicht ~** the meat isn't done yet → *auch* **durch sein**

dụrch- *(in Verbindung mit Verben)* through

dụrch+ackern *sep (inf)* VT to plough *(Brit) or* plow *(US)* through VR to plough *(Brit) or* plow *(US)* one's way through *(durch etw* sth)

dụrch+ar|bei|ten *sep* VT **a** *Buch, Stoff etc* to work *or* go through **b** *(= ausarbeiten)* to work out (in detail) **c** *(= durchkneten) Teig, Knetmasse* to work *or* knead thoroughly; *Muskeln* to massage *or* knead thoroughly VI to work through VR **sich durch etw ~** to work one's way through sth

dụrch|ar|bei|tet ['dʊrç'larbaitət] ADJ **nach fünf ~en Nächten** after being up working five whole nights

dụrch+at|men ['dʊrçlatmən] VI *sep* to breathe deeply, to take deep breaths

durch|ạt|men [dʊrç'laːtmən] *ptp* **durchatmet** VT *insep (poet)* to pervade, to inform *(liter)*

durch|aus [dʊrç'laus, 'dʊrç'laus, 'dʊrçlaus] ADV **a** *(in bejahten Sätzen: = unbedingt)* **das muss ~ sein** that definitely has to be; **sie wollte ~ mitgehen/ein neues Auto haben** she insisted on going too/having a new car; **wenn du das ~ willst** if you insist, if you absolutely must; **das ist ~ nötig** that is absolutely necessary; **du musst ~ mitkommen** you really must come; **muss das sein? – ja ~** is that necessary? – yes, definitely *or* absolutely; **hat er sich anständig benommen? – ja ~** did he behave himself properly? – yes, perfectly *or* absolutely; **es musste ~ dieses Kleid sein** it absolutely had to be this dress; **er will ~ recht haben** he (absolutely) insists that he is right **b** *(bekräftigend in bejahten Sätzen) quite; verständlich, richtig, korrekt, möglich* quite, perfectly; *passen, annehmen* perfectly well; *sich freuen, gefallen* really; **das könnte man ~ machen, das lässt sich ~ machen** that sounds feasible, I/we *etc* could do that; **ich bin ~ Ihrer Meinung** I quite *or* absolutely agree with you; **ich hätte ~ Lust ...** I would like to ...; **ich hätte ~ Zeit** I would have time; **es ist mir ~ ernst damit** I am quite *or* perfectly *or* absolutely serious about it; **es ist ~ anzunehmen, dass sie kommt** it's highly likely that she'll be coming; **das ist zwar ~ möglich, aber ...** that is quite *or* perfectly possible, but ... **c** *(in bejahten Sätzen: = ganz und gar) ehrlich, zufrieden, unerfreulich* thoroughly, completely; **ein ~ gelungener Abend** a thoroughly successful evening; **ein ~ beneidenswerter Mensch** a thoroughly enviable person **d** *(in verneinten Sätzen)* **~ nicht** *(als Verstärkung)* by no means; *(als Antwort)* not at all; *(stärker)* absolutely not; **~ nicht reich/so klug** by no means rich/as clever; **etw ~ nicht tun wollen** to refuse absolutely to do sth; **das braucht ~ nicht schlecht zu sein** that does not HAVE to be bad; **das ist ~ kein Witz** that's no joke at all; **er ist ~ kein schlechter Mensch** he is by no means a bad person; **es ist ~ nicht so einfach wie ...** it is by no means as easy as ...

dụrch+ba|cken *sep* VT *Kuchen* to bake through VI *(Kuchen)* to bake thoroughly

durch|be|ben [dʊrç'beːbn] *ptp* **durchbebt** VT *insep (geh)* to run through

dụrch+bei|ßen ['dʊrçbaisn] *sep irreg* VT *(in zwei Teile)* to bite through VR *(inf) (durch etw* sth) to struggle through; *(mit Erfolg)* to win through

durch|bei|ßen [dʊrç'baisn] *ptp* **durchbissen** [dʊrç'bɪsn] VT *insep irreg* **jdm die Kehle ~** to tear sb's throat open

dụrch+be|kom|men *ptp* **durchbekommen** VT *sep irreg (inf)* to get through

dụrch+bet|teln VR *sep* to beg one's way

dụrch+beu|teln VT *sep (S Ger inf)* to shake thoroughly *(auch fig)*, to give a good shaking

dụrch+bie|gen *sep irreg* VT *Knie* to bend VR to sag

dụrch+bla|sen ['dʊrçblaːzn] *sep irreg* VT **a** *(= Luft etc hindurchblasen)* to blow through *(durch etw* sth); *Eileiter, Rohr, Ohren etc* to clear (by blowing) **b** *(Wind)* to blow VI to blow through *(durch etw* sth)

durch|bla|sen [dʊrç'blaːzn] *ptp* **durchblasen** VT *insep irreg* to blow (through)

dụrch+blät|tern ['dʊrçblɛtɐn] ['dʊrçblɛtɐn] VT *sep Buch etc* to leaf *or* flick through

dụrch+bläu|en VT *sep (inf)* to beat black and blue

Dụrch|blick M vista *(auf +acc* of); *(= Ausblick)* view *(auf +acc* of); *(fig inf: = Verständnis, Überblick)* knowledge; **den ~ haben** *(inf)* to know what's what *(inf)*; **den ~ verlieren** to lose track *(bei* of)

dụrch+bli|cken VI *sep* **a** *(lit)* to look through *(durch etw* sth); *(= zum Vorschein kommen)* to shine through **b** *(fig)* **etw ~ lassen** to hint at sth, to intimate sth **c** *(fig inf: = verstehen)* to understand; **blickst du da durch?** do you get it? *(inf)*

durch|blịt|zen *ptp* **durchblitzt** VT *insep* to flash through; **jdn ~** to flash through sb's mind

durch|blu|ten [dʊrç'bluːtn] *ptp* **durchblutet** VT *insep* to supply with blood → *auch* **durchblutet**

dụrch+blu|ten ['dʊrçbluːtn] VTI *sep* **die Wunde hat durchgeblutet** the wound has bled through (the bandage), blood from the wound has soaked through (the bandage); **es blutet durch** the blood is soaking through; **der Verband ist durchgeblutet** the bandage is soaked through with blood

durch|blu|tet [dʊrç'bluːtət] ADJ supplied with blood; **gut/schlecht ~e Körperteile** parts of the body in which circulation is good/bad; **sie hat schlecht ~e Finger** she's got bad circulation in her fingers

Durch|blu|tung [dʊrç'bluːtʊŋ] F circulation (of the blood) (+*gen* to)

Durch|blu|tungs|stö|rung F circulatory disturbance, disturbance of the circulation

durch|boh|ren [dʊrç'boːrən] *ptp* **durchbohrt** VT *insep Wand, Brett* to drill through; *(mit Schwert etc)* to run through; *(Kugel)* to go through; **jdn mit Blicken ~** *(fig)* to look piercingly at sb; *(hasserfüllt)* to look daggers at sb

dụrch+boh|ren ['dʊrçboːrən] *sep* VT **etw durch etw ~** *(Loch, Tunnel)* to drill sth through sth; *Schwert etc* to run sth through sth; *Nagel* to pierce sth through sth VI to drill through *(durch etw* sth) VR *(durch etw* sth) to bore one's way through; *(Speer)* to go through

durch|boh|rend ADJ piercing; *Blicke auch* penetrating

dụrch+bo|xen *sep (fig inf) (durch etw* sth) VT to push *or* force through VR to fight one's way through

dụrch+bra|ten VTI *sep irreg* to cook through; **durchgebraten** well done

dụrch+brau|sen VI *sep aux sein* to tear *or* roar through *(durch etw* sth)

dụrch+bre|chen ['dʊrçbrɛçn] *sep irreg* VT *(in zwei Teile)* to break (in two) VI *aux sein* **a** *(in zwei Teile)* to break (in two) **b** *(= einbrechen: Mensch)* to fall through *(durch etw* sth) **c** *(= hervorbrechen) (Knospen)* to appear; *(Zahn)* to come through; *(Sonne)* to break through, to appear *(durch etw* sth); *(Charakter)* to reveal itself **d** *(Med: Blinddarm etc)* to burst, to perforate

durch|bre|chen [dʊrç'brɛçn] *ptp* **durchbrochen** [dʊrç'brɔxn] VT *insep irreg Schallmauer* to break; *Mauer, Blockade etc* to break through; *(fig)* to break

Durch|bre|chung [dʊrç'brɛçʊŋ] F *(der Schallmauer)* breaking; *(von Mauer, Blockade)* breaking through

dụrch+bren|nen VI *sep irreg* **a** *(= nicht ausgehen: Ofen, Feuer, Licht etc)* to stay alight **b** *aux sein (Sicherung, Glühbirne)* to blow, to burn out; *(inf: = davonlaufen)* to run off *or* away, to abscond; **jdm ~** *(inf)* to run away from sb

Dụrch|bren|ner(in) M(F) *(inf)* runaway

dụrch+brin|gen *sep irreg* VT **a** *(durch etw* sth) *(= durchsetzen) (durch Prüfung, Kontrolle)* to get through; *(durch Krankheit)* to pull through; *(= für Unterhalt sorgen)* to provide for, to support **b** *Geld* to get through, to blow *(inf)* **c** *(dial: = durchbekommen)* to get through **VR** to get by; **sich kümmerlich ~** to scrape by

durch|bro|chen [dʊrç'brɔxn] **ADJ** open; *Stickerei etc* openwork *attr*

Durch|bruch **M** **a** *(durch etw* sth) *(durch Eis)* falling through *no art*; *(von Knospen)* appearance; *(von Zahn)* coming through; *(von Sonne)* breaking through; *(von Charakter)* revelation; *(von Blinddarm etc)* bursting, perforation; **zum ~ kommen** *(fig) (Gewohnheit etc)* to assert *or* show itself; *(Natur)* to reveal itself **b** *(Mil)* breakthrough; *(Sport auch)* break; *(fig: = Erfolg)* breakthrough; **eine Idee kommt zum ~** an idea comes to the fore, an idea emerges; **jdm/einer Sache zum ~ verhelfen** to help sb/sth on the road to success **c** *(= durchbrochene Stelle)* breach; *(= Öffnung)* opening; *(Geog: von Fluss)* rise, resurgence

durch+buch|sta|bie|ren *ptp* **durchbuchstabiert** **VT** *sep* to spell out

durch+bum|meln ['dʊrçbʊmln] **VI** *sep aux sein (inf) (= durchschlendern)* to stroll through *(durch etw* sth); **die Nacht ~** to spend the night on the tiles *(inf)*

durch|bum|meln [dʊrç'bʊmln] *ptp* **durchbummelt** **VT** *insep Nacht* to spend on the tiles *(inf)*

durch+bürs|ten **VT** *sep* to brush thoroughly

durch+che|cken **VT** *sep* **a** *Gepäck* to check through **b** *(inf: = überprüfen)* to check through

durch|dacht [dʊrç'daxt] **ADJ** properly thought-out; **gut/schlecht ~** well/badly thought-out

durch|den|ken ['dʊrçdɛŋkn] [dʊrç'dɛŋkn] *ptp* **durchdacht** [dʊrç'daxt] **VT** *insep*, **durch+den|ken** ['dʊrçdɛŋkn] [dʊrç'dɛŋkn] **VT** *sep irreg* [dʊrç'daxt] to think out *or* through

durch+dis|ku|tie|ren *ptp* **durchdiskutiert** **VT** *sep* to discuss thoroughly, to talk through

durch+drän|geln *(inf)*, **durch+drän|gen** **VR** *sep* to push *or* force one's way through *(durch etw* sth)

durch+dre|hen *sep* **VT** *Fleisch etc* to mince **VI** **a** *(Rad)* to spin **b** *(inf)* to do one's nut *(Brit inf)*, to flip *(inf)*; *(nervlich)* to crack up *(inf)*; **ganz durchgedreht sein** *(inf)* to be really uptight *(inf) or (aus dem Gleichgewicht)* confused

durch+drin|gen ['dʊrçdrɪŋən] **VI** *sep irreg aux sein* **a** *(= hindurchkommen)* to penetrate *(durch etw* sth); *(Flüssigkeit, Kälte, Sonne)* to come through *(durch etw* sth); *(Stimme, Geräusch)* to be heard *(durch etw* through sth); **bis zu jdm ~** *(fig)* to go *or* get as far as sb **b** *(= sich durchsetzen, sich verständlich machen)* to get through; **zu jdm ~** to get through to sb; **mit einem Vorschlag ~** to get a suggestion accepted *(bei, in +dat* by)

durch|drin|gen [dʊrç'drɪŋən] *ptp* **durchdrungen** [dʊrç'drʊŋən] **VT** *insep irreg Materie, Dunkelheit etc* to penetrate; *(Gefühl, Idee, Gedanke)* to pervade → *auch* **durchdrungen**

durch|drin|gend ['dʊrçdrɪŋənt] **ADJ** piercing; *Kälte, Wind auch* biting; *Stimme, Geräusch, Blick auch* penetrating; *Geruch* pungent, sharp

Durch|drin|gung [dʊrç'drɪŋʊŋ] **F -, -en** **a** penetration; *(= Sättigung)* saturation; *(= Verschmelzung)* fusion **b** *(fig: = Erfassen)* investigation, exploration

durch+drü|cken *sep* **VT** **a** *(durch Sieb)* to rub through; *(durch Presse)* to press through; *Creme, Teig* to pipe **b** *(fig) Gesetz, Reformen, Neuerungen etc* to push *or* force through; *seinen Willen* to get; **es ~, dass ...** to get the decision through that ... **c** *Knie, Ellbogen etc* to straighten **d** *Wäsche* to wash through **VR** to squeeze *or* push (one's way) through *(durch etw* sth); **sich in der Menge ~** to squeeze *or* push (one's way) through the crowd

Durch|drück|pa|ckung ['dʊrçdrʏk-] **F** *(einzelne Packung)* blister pack; **~en** *pl* blister packaging *sing*

durch|drun|gen [dʊrç'drʊŋən] **ADJ** *pred* imbued *(von* with); **ganz von einer Idee ~ sein** to be taken with an idea; **von einem Gefühl der Freude ~ sein** to be full of *or* imbued with a feeling of joy → *auch* **durchdringen**

durch+dür|fen **VI** *sep irreg (inf)* to be allowed through; **darf ich mal durch?** can I get through?; **Sie dürfen hier nicht durch** you can't come through here

durch|ei|nan|der [dʊrçlai'nandɐ] **ADV** mixed *or* muddled up, in a muddle *or* mess; **Gemüse ~** vegetable stew **ADJ** *pred* **~ sein** *(inf) (Mensch)* to be confused; *(= aufgeregt)* to be in a state *(inf)*; *(Zimmer, Papier)* to be in a mess *or* muddle

Durch|ei|nan|der [dʊrçlai'nandɐ, 'dʊrçlainandɐ] **NT -s**, *no pl (= Unordnung)* mess, muddle; *(= Wirrwarr)* confusion; **in dem Zimmer herrscht ein wüstes ~** the room is in a terrible mess *or* muddle

durch|ei|nan|der-: **durch|ei|nan|der+brin|gen** *sep irreg*, **durch|ei|nan|der brin|gen** △ *irreg* **VT** to muddle *or* mix up; *(= in Unordnung bringen auch)* to get into a mess *or* muddle; *(= verwirren) jdn* to confuse; **durch|ei|nan|der+es|sen** *sep irreg*, **durch|ei|nan|der es|sen** △ *irreg* **VT** **alles ~** to eat indiscriminately; **durch|ei|nan|der+ge|hen** *sep irreg aux sein*, **durch|ei|nan|der ge|hen** △ *irreg aux sein* **VI** to get confused, to get into a muddle; **durch|ei|nan|der+ge|ra|ten** *sep irreg aux sein*, **durch|ei|nan|der ge|ra|ten** △ *irreg aux sein* **VI** to get mixed *or* muddled up; **jetzt bin ich mit dem Datum völlig ~** now I've got completely mixed *or* muddled up about the date; **durch|ei|nan|der+kom|men** *sep irreg aux sein*, **durch|ei|nan|der kom|men** △ *irreg aux sein* **VI** **a** *(= vermischt werden)* to get mixed *or* muddled up **b** *(inf)* = **durcheinandergeraten**; **durch|ei|nan|der+lau|fen** *sep irreg aux sein*, **durch|ei|nan|der lau|fen** △ *irreg aux sein* **VI** to run about *or* around all over the place; **durch|ei|nan|der+lie|gen** *sep irreg (S Ger, Aus, Sw: aux sein)*, **durch|ei|nan|der lie|gen** △ *irreg (S Ger, Aus, Sw: aux sein)* **VI** to be in a muddle, to be all over the place; **durch|ei|nan|der+men|gen** *sep*, **durch|ei|nan|der men|gen** △, **durch|ei|nan|der+mi|schen** *sep*, **durch|ei|nan|der mi|schen** △ **VT** to mix (up); **durch|ei|nan|der+re|den** *sep*, **durch|ei|nan|der re|den** △ **VI** to all speak *or* talk at once *or* at the same time; **durch|ei|nan|der+ren|nen** *sep irreg aux sein*, **durch|ei|nan|der ren|nen** △ *irreg aux sein* **VI** to run about *or* around all over the place; **durch|ei|nan|der+ru|fen** *sep irreg*, **durch|ei|nan|der ru|fen** △ *irreg*, **durch|ei|nan|der+schrei|en** *sep irreg*, **durch|ei|nan|der schrei|en** △ *irreg* **VI** to all shout out at once *or* at the same time; **durch|ei|nan|der+trin|ken** *sep irreg*, **durch|ei|nan|der trin|ken** △ *irreg* **VT** **alles ~** to drink indiscriminately; **durch|ei|nan|der+wer|fen** *sep irreg*, **durch|ei|nan|der wer|fen** △ *irreg* **VT** to muddle up; *(fig inf: = verwechseln)* to mix up, to confuse; **durch|ei|nan|der+wir|beln** *sep*, **durch|ei|nan|der wir|beln** △ **VT** *Blätter* to whirl around; *(fig)* to shake up

durch+es|sen **VR** *sep irreg* **a** **sich bei jdm ~** to eat at sb's expense **b** **sich durch etw ~** to eat one's way through sth

durch+ex|er|zie|ren *ptp* **durchexerziert** **VT** *sep* to rehearse, to run *or* go through

durch+fah|ren ['dʊrçfa:rən] **VI** *sep irreg aux sein* **a** *(durch einen Ort, Tunnel etc)* to go through *(durch etw* sth) **b** *(= nicht anhalten/umsteigen)* to go straight through (without stopping/changing); **er ist bei Rot durchgefahren** he jumped the lights; **die Nacht ~** to travel through the night

durch|fah|ren [dʊrç'fa:rən] *ptp* **durchfahren** **VT** *insep irreg* to travel through; *(fig: Schreck, Zittern etc)* to shoot through; **ein Gedanke durchfuhr ihn blitzartig** a (sudden) thought flashed through his mind

Durch|fahrt **F** **a** *(= Durchreise)* way through; **auf der ~ sein** to be passing through; **auf** *or* **bei der ~ sieht man ja nicht viel** one doesn't see much when one is just passing through **b** *(= Passage)* thoroughfare; *(Naut)* thoroughfare, channel; **~ bitte frei halten!** please keep access free **c** *(= das Durchfahren)* thoroughfare; **~ verboten!** no through road, no thoroughfare; **der Polizist gab endlich die ~ frei/gab das Zeichen zur ~** the policeman finally allowed/signalled the traffic through

Durch|fahrts-: **Durch|fahrts|hö|he** **F** headroom, clearance; **Durch|fahrts|recht** **NT** right of way; **Durch|fahrts|stra|ße** **F** through road; **Durch|fahrts|ver|bot** **NT** **seit wann besteht hier ~?** since when has this been a no through road?; **die Anwohner haben das ~ durchgesetzt** the residents managed to get through traffic banned

Durch|fall **M** **a** *(Med)* diarrhoea *no art (Brit)*, diarrhea *no art (US)* **b** *(= Misserfolg)* failure; *(von Theaterstück auch)* flop

durch+fal|len **VI** *sep irreg aux sein* **a** *(durch Loch, Lücke etc)* to fall through *(durch etw* sth) **b** *(inf: = nicht bestehen)* to fail; *(Theaterstück etc auch)* to (be a) flop; *(Wahlkandidat)* to lose, to be defeated; **in** *or* **bei der Prüfung ~** to fail the exam; **jdn ~ lassen** to fail sb; **beim Publikum/bei der Kritik ~** to be a failure *or* flop with the public/critics; **bei der Wahl ~** to lose the election, to be defeated in the election

Durch|fall|quo|te **F** *(Sch etc)* failure rate

durch+fär|ben *sep* **VT** to dye *or* colour *(Brit) or* color *(US)* (evenly) **VI** to come *or* seep through *(durch etw* sth)

durch+fau|len **VI** *sep aux sein* to rot through

durch+fech|ten *sep irreg* **VT** **etw ~** to fight to get sth through **VR** **sich (im Leben) ~** to struggle through (in life)

durch+fe|dern **VI** *sep* to bend one's knees

durch+fe|gen ['dʊrçfe:gn] *sep* **VT** to sweep out **VI** to sweep up

durch|fe|gen [dʊrç'fe:gn] *ptp* **durchfegt** **VT** *insep* to sweep through

durch+fei|ern ['dʊrçfaiɐn] **VI** *sep* to stay up all night celebrating

durch|fei|ern [dʊrç'faiɐn] *ptp* **durchfeiert** **VT** *insep* **die Nacht ~** to stay up all night celebrating; **nach durchfeierter Nacht** after celebrating all night

durch+fei|len [dʊrç'failən] ['dʊrçfailən] *sep*, **durch|fei|len** [dʊrç'failən] ['dʊrçfailən] *ptp* **durchfeilt** *insep* **VT** to file through

durch|feuch|ten [dʊrç'fɔyçtn] *ptp* **durchfeuchtet** **VT** *insep* to soak; **von etw durchfeuchtet sein** to be soaked (through) with sth

durch+fin|den **VIR** *sep irreg (lit, fig)* to find one's way through *(durch etw* sth); **ich finde (mich) hier nicht mehr durch** *(fig)* I am simply lost; **ich kann mich bei diesem Kram nicht ~** *(fig)* I can't make head nor tail of this mess

durch|flech|ten [dʊrç'flɛçtn] *ptp* **durchflochten** [dʊrç'flɔxtn] **VT** *insep irreg* **etw mit etw ~** *(lit)* to thread *or* weave sth through sth, to intertwine sth with sth; *(fig)* to interweave sth with sth

durch+flie|gen ['dʊrçfli:gn] **VI** *sep irreg aux sein* **a** *(mit Flugzeug)* to fly through *(durch etw* sth); *(ohne Landung)* to fly nonstop *or* direct **b** *(inf, durch Prüfung)* to fail, to flunk *(inf) (durch etw, in etw (dat)* (in) sth)

durch|flie|gen [dʊrç'fli:gn] *ptp* **durchflogen** [dʊrç'flo:gn] **VT** *insep irreg Luft, Wolken* to fly through; *Luftkorridor* to fly along; *Strecke* to cover; *(= flüchtig lesen)* to skim through

durch+flie|ßen ['dʊrçfli:sn] **VI** *sep irreg aux sein* to flow *or* run through *(durch etw* sth)

durch|flie|ßen [dʊrç'fli:sn] *ptp* **durchflossen** [dʊrç'flɔsn] **VT** *insep irreg (lit, fig)* to flow *or* run through

Durch|flug **M** flight through; *(= das Durchfliegen)* flying through *(durch etw* sth)

Durch|flugs|recht **NT** *usu sing* overflying rights *pl*, air transit rights *pl*

Durch|fluss **M** *(= das Fließen, Durchflussmenge)* flow; *(= Öffnung)* opening

durch+flu|ten ['dʊrçflu:tn] VI *sep aux sein (geh)* to flow through (*durch etw* sth)

durch|flu|ten [dʊrç'flu:tn] *ptp* **durchflutet** VT *insep (geh) (Fluss)* to flow through; *(fig) (Licht, Sonne)* to flood; *(Wärme, Gefühl)* to flow or flood through; **Licht durchflutete das Zimmer** the room was flooded with *or* bathed in light, light flooded the room

durch+for|men VT *sep* to work out (down) to the last detail

durch|for|schen [dʊrç'fɔrʃn] *ptp* **durchforscht** VT *insep Gegend* to search; *Land, Wissensgebiet* to explore; *Akten, Bücher* to search through

durch|fors|ten ['dʊrçfɔrstn] [dʊrç'fɔrstn] *ptp* **durchforstet** VT *insep Wald* to thin out; *(fig) Bücher, Akten etc* to go through

durch+fra|gen VR *sep* to ask one's way

durch+fres|sen ['dʊrçfrɛsn] *sep irreg* VR (*durch etw* sth) *(Säure, Rost, Tier)* to eat (its way) through; **sich (bei jdm) ~** *(pej inf)* to live on sb's hospitality; **sich durch ein Buch ~** *(inf)* to plough *(Brit)* or plow *(US)* or wade through a book VT *(Rost, Maus)* to eat (its way) through; *(Motten)* to eat holes in; **ein Loch durch etw ~** to eat a hole in sth

durch|fres|sen [dʊrç'frɛsn] *ptp* **durchfressen** VT *insep irreg* to eat through; *(Motten)* to eat holes in; **ein von Motten ~er Pullover** a moth-eaten pullover

durch+fret|ten VR *sep (Aus, S Ger)* to eke out an existence

durch+frie|ren VI *sep irreg aux sein (See, Fluss)* to freeze through, to freeze solid; *(Mensch)* to get frozen stiff, to get chilled to the bone

durch|fro|ren [dʊrç'fro:rən] ADJ = **durchgefroren**

Durch|fuhr ['dʊrçfu:ɐ] F -, **-en** transit, passage

durch|führ|bar ADJ practicable, feasible, workable

Durch|führ|bar|keit ['dʊrçfy:ɐba:ɐkait] F -, *no pl* feasibility, practicability, workability

Durch|führ|bar|keits|stu|die F feasibility study

durch+füh|ren *sep* VT **a** *(= durchleiten)* (*durch etw* sth) *jdn* to lead through, to take through; *Fluss* to lead through; *Leitung, Rohr* to run through; *Straße* to build through, to lay through; *Kanal, Tunnel* to dig through; **etw durch etw ~** to lead *etc* sth through sth; **jdn durch eine Stadt/ein Haus ~** to show sb (a)round a town/a house
b *(= verwirklichen) Vorhaben, Beschluss, Plan* to carry out; *Gesetz* to implement, to enforce; *(= unternehmen, veranstalten) Experiment, Haussuchung, Sammlung, Untersuchung, Reform* to carry out; *Test* to run, to carry out; *Expedition, Reise* to undertake; *Messung* to take; *Kursus* to run; *Wahl, Prüfung* to hold; *Unterrichtsstunde* to take, to give
c *(= konsequent zu Ende bringen)* to carry through; *Gedankengang* to carry through (to its conclusion)
VI (*durch etw* sth) to lead through; *(Straße)* to go through; **zwischen etw** *(dat)* **~** to lead between sth; **unter etw** *(dat)* **~** to go under sth

Durch|fuhr-: **Durch|fuhr|er|laub|nis** F transit permit; **Durch|fuhr|han|del** M transit trade; **Durch|fuhr|land** NT country of transit

Durch|füh|rung F **a** *(= das Verwirklichen)* carrying out; *(von Gesetz)* implementation, enforcement; *(von Experiment, Untersuchung, Reise, Expedition)* undertaking; *(von Messung)* taking; *(von Kursus, Test)* running; *(von Wahl, Prüfung)* holding; *(von Unterrichtsstunde)* giving; **zur ~ kommen** *(form, Reform, Gesetz, Maßnahme)* to come into force; **zur ~ bringen** *(form, Reform, Gesetz, Maßnahme)* to bring into force **b** *(= konsequentes Beenden)* carrying through **c** *(= das Durchleiten)* leading; *(von Rohr)* running; *(von Straße)* building; *(von Kanal, Tunnel)* digging **d** *(Mus) (von Sonate)* development; *(von Fuge)* exposition

Durch|fuhr-: **Durch|fuhr|ver|bot** NT transit embargo; **Durch|fuhr|zoll** M transit duty

durch|fur|chen [dʊrç'fʊrçn] *ptp* **durchfurcht** VT *insep (geh) Land* to plough *(Brit)*, to plow *(US)*; *Wogen* to plough *(Brit)* or plow *(US)* through

durch+füt|tern VT *sep (inf)* to feed; **sich von jdm ~ lassen** to live off sb

Durch|ga|be F **a** *(von Nachricht, Lottozahlen etc)* announcement; *(von Hinweis, Bericht)* giving; **bei der ~ von Zahlen übers Telefon kommen oft Fehler vor** when numbers are given over the telephone mistakes are often made **b** *(= Nachricht, Ankündigung)* announcement; *(telefonisch)* message (over the telephone)

Durch|gang M *pl* **-gänge a** *(= Weg, Passage)* way; *(schmal)* passage(way); *(= Torweg)* gateway **b** *(= das Durchgehen)* **kein ~!, ~ verboten!** no right of way; **beim ~ durch das Tal** going through the valley; **der ~ zur Höhle/zum anderen Tal ist beschwerlich** it's difficult to get through to the cave/other valley; **er hat mir den ~ versperrt** he blocked my passage **c** *(von Experiment, bei Arbeit, Parl)* stage **d** *(bei Wettbewerb, von Wahl, Sport)* round; *(beim Rennen)* heat **e** *(Astron)* transit

Durch|gän|ger [-gɛŋɐ] M **-s, -** *(= Pferd)* bolter

durch|gän|gig ADJ universal, general; **eine ~e Eigenschaft in seinen Romanen** a constant feature in *or* of his novels ADV generally; *feststellbar* universally; **die Kandidaten wurden ~ abgelehnt** every single one of the candidates was rejected

Durch|gän|gig|keit F **a** *(von Stil, Prozess etc)* consistency **b** *(Tech, Med)* ability to penetrate

Durch|gangs-: **Durch|gangs|bahn|hof** M through station; **Durch|gangs|han|del** M transit trade; **Durch|gangs|la|ger** NT transit camp; **Durch|gangs|sta|di|um** NT transition stage; **Durch|gangs|sta|ti|on** F *(fig)* stopping-off place; **Durch|gangs|stra|ße** F through road, thoroughfare; **Durch|gangs|ver|kehr** M *(Mot)* through traffic; *(= Transitverkehr)* transit traffic

durch+ga|ren *sep* VT to cook thoroughly VI *aux sein* to cook through

durch|ge|ba|cken *ptp von* **durchbacken** ADJ *Kuchen* baked through; **nicht richtig** *or* **ganz ~** not properly cooked (through)

durch+ge|ben VT *sep irreg* **a** *(= durchreichen)* to pass through (*durch etw* sth) **b** *(Rad, TV) Hinweis, Meldung, Wetter, Straßenzustandsbericht* to give; *Nachricht, Lottozahlen* to announce; **jdm etw telefonisch ~** to let sb know sth by telephone, to telephone sth to sb; **ein Telegramm telefonisch ~** to telephone a telegram; **jdm ~, dass ...** to let sb know that ..., to tell sb that ...; **es wurde im Radio durchgegeben** it was announced on the radio; **wir geben (Ihnen) nun den Wetterbericht durch** and now we bring you the weather forecast

durch|ge|bra|ten *ptp von* **durchbraten** ADJ *Fleisch etc* well-done *attr*, well done *pred*; **es ist noch nicht ~** it isn't (properly) done yet → **durchbraten**

durch|ge|fro|ren ADJ *Mensch* frozen stiff, perishing (cold) *(inf) pred*

durch+ge|hen *sep irreg aux sein* VI **a** *(lit)* (*durch etw* sth) to go through, to walk through; *(durch Kontrolle, Zoll)* to pass through; *(= weitergehen, inf: = sich durchstecken lassen)* to go through; **bitte ~!** *(im Bus)* move right down (the bus) please!
b *(Fluss, Weg, Linie etc)* (*durch etw* sth) to run through, to go through; *(fig: Thema)* to run through
c *(= durchdringen)* to come through (*durch etw* sth)
d *(= nicht zurückgewiesen werden) (Gesetz)* to be passed, to go through; *(Antrag)* to be carried, to be passed, to go through
e *(= toleriert werden)* to be allowed (to pass), to be tolerated; **jdm etw ~ lassen** to let sb get away with sth, to overlook sth; **das lasse ich noch mal ~** I'll let it pass
f *(= gehalten werden für)* **für etw ~** to pass for sth, to be taken for sth
g *(= durchpassen)* to go through (*durch etw* sth); **zwischen/unter etw** *(dat)* **~** to go (through) between/under sth
h *(ohne Unterbrechung)* to go straight through; *(Fußgänger)* to walk *or* go straight through; *(Flug)* to be nonstop or direct; *(zeitlich: Party, Unterricht; örtlich: Straße, Linie)* to run (right) through, to go straight through; **die ganze Nacht ~** *(Mensch)* to walk all night (long), to walk throughout the night; *(Party)* to last all night (long)
i *(Pferd etc)* to bolt; *(inf: = sich davonmachen)* to run off *or* away; **mit jdm ~** to run *or* go off with sb, to elope with sb; **jdm ~** to run away from sb; **seine Frau ist ihm durchgegangen** his wife has run off and left him; **mit etw ~** to run *or* make off with sth
j *(= außer Kontrolle geraten)* **mit jdm ~** *(Temperament, Nerven)* to get the better of sb; *(Gefühle auch)* to run away with sb
VT *auch aux haben (= durchsehen, -sprechen etc)* to go *or* run through, to go *or* run over
VI *impers* **es geht durch/nicht durch** there's a/no way through; **wo geht es durch?** where's the way through?

durch|ge|hend ADJ *Öffnungszeiten* round-the-clock *attr (Brit)*, around-the-clock *attr (US)*, continuous; *Straße* straight; *Verkehrsverbindung* direct; *Zug* nonstop, through *attr*, direct; *Fahrkarte* through *attr*; *Muster* continuous; *Eigenschaft* constant; **~e Güter** goods in transit ADV throughout, right through; **~ geöffnet** open right through, open 24 hours; **~ gefüttert** fully lined, lined throughout

durch|geis|tigt [dʊrç'gaistɪçt] ADJ cerebral

durch|ge|knallt [-gəknalt] ADJ *(inf: = verrückt)* cuckoo *(inf)*, loopy *(Brit inf)*, crazy *(inf)*

durch|ge|le|gen [-gəle:gn] *ptp von* **durchliegen** ADJ *Bett, Matratze* sagging, saggy, worn (down); *Rücken etc* bedsore, suffering from bedsores *pred* → *auch* **durchliegen**

durch|ge|reg|net [-gəre:gnət] ADJ soaked; **ich war völlig ~** I was soaked to the skin, I was soaked through → *auch* **durchregnen**

durch|ge|schwitzt [-gəʃvɪtst] ADJ *Mensch* bathed in sweat; *Kleidung* soaked in sweat, sweat-soaked *attr* → *auch* **durchschwitzen**

durch+ge|stal|ten *ptp* **durchgestaltet** VT *sep* to work out (down) to the last detail

durch|ge|stri|chen ADJ struck out, deleted; *(Comput: Schriftoption)* strikeout

durch+gie|ßen VT *sep irreg* to pour through (*durch etw* sth); **etw durch ein Sieb ~** to strain sth, to pour sth through a sieve

durch+glie|dern VT *sep* to subdivide

durch+glü|hen ['dʊrçgly:ən] *sep* VI *aux sein* to glow red-hot; *(Lampe, Draht, Sicherung)* to burn out VT *Eisen* to heat until red-hot, to heat to red heat

durch|glü|hen [dʊrç'gly:ən] *ptp* **durchglüht** VT *insep (liter: Gefühl)* to glow through; **von Begeisterung durchglüht** aglow with enthusiasm

durch+gra|ben *sep irreg* VT to dig through (*durch etw* sth) VR to dig one's way through (*durch etw* sth)

durch+grei|fen VI *sep irreg* to reach through (*durch etw* sth); *(fig)* to take vigorous action, to resort to drastic measures; **hier muss viel strenger durchgegriffen werden** much more vigorous action is needed here

durch|grei|fend ADJ *Änderung, Maßnahme* drastic; *(= weitreichend) Änderung* far-reaching, radical, sweeping *attr*

durch+gu|cken VI *sep* **a** (*durch etw* sth) *(Mensch)* to look through, to peep through; *(= durchscheinen)* to show through **b** *(fig inf: = verstehen)* to understand (*durch etw* sth); **guckst du da durch?** do you get it? *(inf)*

durch+ha|ben VT *sep irreg (inf)* **etw ~** *(= hindurchbekommen haben)* to have got *(Brit)* or gotten *(US)* sth through (*durch etw* sth); *(= durchgelesen etc haben)* to have got *(Brit)* or gotten

(US) through sth, to have finished sth; *(= zerteilt haben)* to have got *(Brit)* or gotten *(US)* through sth, to be through sth

durch+ha|cken VT *sep* to chop *or* hack through

Durch|hal|te|ap|pell M appeal to hold out, rallying call

durch+hal|ten *sep irreg* VT *(= durchstehen) Zeit, Ehe, Kampf etc* to survive; *Streik* to hold out till the end of, to see through; *Belastung* to (with)-stand; *(Sport) Strecke* to stay; *Tempo (= beibehalten)* to keep up; *(= aushalten)* to stand; **das Rennen ~** to stay the course VI to hold out, to stick it out *(inf)*; *(= beharren)* to persevere, to stick it out *(inf)*; *(bei Rennen)* to stay the course; **bis zum Äußersten ~** to hold out *or* stick it out *(inf)* to the last; **eisern ~** to hold out grimly

Durch|hal|te-: **Durch|hal|te|pa|ro|le** F appeal to hold out, rallying call; **Durch|hal|te|ver|mö|gen** NT, *no pl* staying power, (powers *pl* of) endurance *no indef art*

Durch|hang M sag, slack

durch+hän|gen VI *sep irreg aux haben or sein* to sag; *(fig inf) (= deprimiert sein)* to be down (in the mouth) *(inf)*; *(= schlappmachen)* to wilt, to flag; *(= erschöpft sein)* to be shattered *(inf)* or knackered *(Brit inf)*; **du solltest dich nicht so ~ lassen** you shouldn't let yourself go like that

Durch|hän|ger M **-s, -** *(inf: = schlechte Phase)* bad patch; *(an bestimmtem Tag)* off day *(inf)*; **einen ~ haben** to be off form

durch+hau|en ['dʊrçhauən] *sep irreg or (inf) reg* VT **a** *(= entzweischlagen)* to chop *or* hack in two; *(= spalten)* to split, to cleave **b** *(inf: = verprügeln)* **jdn ~** to give sb a thrashing *or* walloping *(inf)*, to thrash *or* wallop *(inf)* sb VR *(lit)* to hack one's way through *(durch etw* sth); *(fig: = sich durchschlagen)* to get by

durch|hau|en [dʊrç'hauən] *ptp* **durchhauen** VT *insep irreg* to chop *or* hack in two

durch+he|cheln VT *sep* **a** *Flachs etc* to hackle **b** *(fig inf)* to gossip about, to pull to pieces *(inf)*; **in allen Zeitungen durchgehechelt** dragged through all the papers

durch+hei|zen *sep* VT *(= gründlich heizen)* to heat right through; *(= ohne Unterbrechung heizen)* to heat continuously, to heat day and night VI *(ohne Unterbrechung)* to keep the heating on

durch+hel|fen *sep irreg* VI **jdm (durch etw) ~** to help sb through (sth) VR to get by, to get along, to manage

durch+hö|ren VT *sep* **a etw (durch etw) ~** *(lit, Lärm)* to hear sth (through sth); *(fig) Gefühl, Enttäuschung auch* to discern sth (through sth); **ich konnte ~, dass ...** I could hear *or* tell that ... **b** *Schallplatte, Konzert etc* to hear (all the way) through, to hear all of

durch+hun|gern VR *sep* to struggle along on the breadline, to scrape by

durch|ir|ren [dʊrç'ɪrən] *ptp* **durchirrt** VT *insep* to wander *or* rove *or* roam through

durch+ixen VT *sep (inf)* to ex out

durch+ja|gen ['dʊrçja:gn] *sep* VT **a** *(= durcheilen)* to chase through *(durch etw* sth) **b** *(fig) Gesetz, Prozess etc* to rush *or* push through VI *aux sein* to race *or* tear through; **zwischen/unter etw** *(dat)* **~** to race *or* tear between/under sth

durch|ja|gen [dʊrç'ja:gn] *ptp* **durchjagt** VT *insep Land etc* to race *or* tear through

durch+käm|men ['dʊrçkɛmən] VT *sep* **a** *Haare* to comb out **b** *(= absuchen)* to comb (through)

durch|käm|men [dʊrç'kɛmən] *ptp* **durchkämmt** VT *insep (= absuchen)* to comb (through)

durch+kämp|fen *sep* VT *(= durchsetzen)* to push *or* force through VR **a** *(durch etw* sth) to fight *or* battle one's way through; *(fig)* to struggle through **b** = **durchringen** VI *(= Kampf nicht aufgeben) (Soldaten)* to carry on fighting; *(Sportler, Bergsteiger)* to battle on, to carry on the battle *or* struggle; **es wurde selbst über die Weihnachtszeit durchgekämpft** the fighting continued even over Christmas

durch+kau|en VT *sep Essen* to chew (thoroughly); *(inf: = besprechen)* to go over *or* through

durch+klet|tern VI *sep aux sein* to climb through *(durch etw* sth)

durch+klin|gen ['dʊrçklɪŋən] VI *sep irreg aux haben or sein (durch etw* sth) to sound through; *(fig)* to come through *(durch etw* sth), to come across *(durch etw* through sth); **die Musik klang durch den Lärm durch** the music could be heard above the noise

durch|klin|gen [dʊrç'klɪŋən] *ptp* **durchklungen** [dʊrç'klʊŋən] VT *insep irreg* to ring through

durch+knei|fen VT *sep irreg Draht* to snip through

durch+kne|ten VT *sep Teig etc* to knead thoroughly; *(bei Massage)* to massage thoroughly; **sich ~ lassen** to have a thorough massage

durch+knöp|fen VT *sep* to button all the way up; **ein durchgeknöpftes Kleid** a button-through *(Brit) or* button-up dress

durch+ko|chen VTI *sep* to boil thoroughly

durch+kom|men VI *sep irreg aux sein* **a** *(durch etw* sth) *(= durchfahren)* to come through; *(= vorbeikommen, passieren auch)* to come past; **er ist durch diese Straße/Stadt/unter dieser Brücke durchgekommen** he came through this street/town/under *or* through this bridge **b** *(durch etw* sth) to get through; *(Sonne, Wasser etc)* to come through; *(Sender, Farbe)* to come through; *(Charakterzug)* to show through, to come out *or* through; *(= sichtbar werden) (Sonne)* to come out; *(Blumen)* to come through; **kommst du durch?** can you get through?; **es kommt immer wieder durch, dass sie Ausländerin ist** the fact that she is a foreigner keeps showing *or* coming through **c** *(lit, fig: = mit Erfolg durchkommen)* to succeed *(durch etw* in sth), to get through *(durch etw* sth); *(= sich durchsetzen) (telefonisch)* to get through; *(finanziell)* to get by; **ich komme mit meiner Hand nicht (durch das Loch) durch** I can't get my hand through (the hole); **mit etw ~** *(mit Forderungen etc)* to succeed with sth; *mit Betrug, Schmeichelei etc* to get away with sth; **er kam (bei dem Lärm) mit seiner Stimme nicht durch** he couldn't make his voice heard (above the noise); **damit kommt er bei mir nicht durch** he won't get away with that with me **d** *(= Prüfung bestehen)* to get through, to pass **e** *(= überleben)* to come through; *(Patient auch)* to pull through **f** *(im Radio)* to be announced

durch+kom|po|nie|ren *ptp* **durchkomponiert** VT *sep* **a** *(Mus) Libretto* to set to music; *Gedicht* to set to music *(with a different setting for each stanza)* **b** *(fig) Bild, Text* to work out in detail **c** *(ohne Unterbrechung)* to compose right through

durch+kön|nen VI *sep irreg (inf)* to be able to get through *(durch etw* sth)

durch+kon|stru|ie|ren *ptp* **durchkonstruiert** VT *sep* **gut durchkonstruiert** well put together throughout

durch+kos|ten VT *sep (geh)* to taste (one after the other); *(fig) Freuden* to taste; *Leiden* to endure, to experience

durch|kreu|zen [dʊrç'krɔytsn] *ptp* **durchkreuzt** VT *insep* **a** *Land, Wüste, Ozean* to cross, to travel across **b** *(fig) Pläne etc* to thwart, to foil, to frustrate

durch+kreu|zen ['dʊrçkrɔytsn] VT *sep (mit Strichen)* to cross out, to cross through

Durch|kreu|zung [dʊrç'krɔytsʊŋ] F **a** *(von Land etc)* crossing **b** *(von Plänen etc)* thwarting, foiling, frustrating

durch+krie|chen VI *sep irreg aux sein* to crawl through, to creep through *(durch etw* sth)

durch+krie|gen VT *sep (inf)* to get through

durch+la|den VTI *sep irreg Gewehr* to reload

durch+lan|gen *sep (inf)* VI *(durch etw* sth) to reach through, to put one's hand through VT *(= durchreichen)* to pass through

Durch|lass ['dʊrçlas] M **-es, Durchlässe** [-lɛsə] **a** *(= Durchgang)* passage, way through; *(für Wasser)* duct **b** *no pl (geh)* permission to pass; **jdm ~ verschaffen** to obtain permission for sb to pass; *(mit Gewalt)* to force a way through for sb; **sich ~ verschaffen** to obtain permission to pass; *(mit Gewalt)* to force one's way through

durch+las|sen VT *sep irreg (durch etw* sth) *(= passieren lassen)* to allow *or* let through; *Licht, Wasser etc (= durchdringen lassen)* to let through; *(= eindringen lassen)* to let in; *(inf: durch Prüfung)* to let through, to pass; *(inf: = durchgehen lassen) Fehler etc* to let pass, to overlook

durch|läs|sig ADJ *Material* permeable; *(= porös)* porous; *Zelt, Regenmantel, Schuh* that lets water in; *Zelt, Schuh* leaky; *Krug, Vase* that lets water out *or* through; *Grenze* open; **eine ~e Stelle** *(fig)* a leak; **die Bildungswege ~ machen** to make the elements of the education programme *(Brit) or* program *(US)* interchangeable

Durch|läs|sig|keit F permeability; *(= Porosität)* porosity; **die ~ des Zelts/Krugs** the fact that the tent/jug leaks *or* lets water through; **die ~ der Bildungswege** the interchangeability of the elements of the education programme *(Brit) or* program *(US)*

Durch|laucht ['dʊrçlauxt, dʊrç'lauxt] F **-, -en** serenity; **Seine ~** His (Serene) Highness; **(Euer) ~** Your Highness

durch|lauch|tig [dʊrç'lauxtɪç] ADJ *attr (old)* serene

Durch|lauf M **a** *(= das Durchlaufen)* flow **b** *(TV, Rad, Comput)* run, run-through **c** *(Sport)* heat

durch+lau|fen ['dʊrçlaufn] *sep irreg* VT *Schuhe, Sohlen* to go *or* wear through VI *aux sein* **a** *(durch etw* sth) *(= durch Straße/Öffnung etc gehen)* to go through; *(Straße, Rohr etc)* to run through; *(Flüssigkeit)* to run through **b** *(ohne Unterbrechung: Mensch)* to run without stopping; **8 Stunden lang ohne Pause ~** to run for 8 hours without stopping; **der Fries/das Geländer läuft von der einen Seite des Gebäudes zur anderen durch** the frieze/railing runs uninterrupted *or* without a break from one end of the building to the other

durch|lau|fen [dʊrç'laufn] *ptp* **durchlaufen** VT *insep irreg* **a** *Gebiet* to run through; *Strecke* to cover, to run; *(Astron) Bahn* to describe; *Lehrzeit, Schule, Phase* to pass *or* go through **b** *(= erfassen, erfüllen) (Gerücht)* to spread through; *(Gefühl)* to run through; **es durchlief mich heiß** I felt hot all over

durch|lau|fend ['dʊrçlaufnt] ADJ continuous

Durch|lauf-: **Durch|lauf|er|hit|zer** [-lɛɐhɪtsɐ] M **-s, -** continuous-flow water heater; **Durch|lauf|zeit** F *(Comput)* length of a/the run

durch+la|vie|ren *ptp* **durchlaviert** VR *sep* to steer *or* manoeuvre *(Brit) or* maneuver *(US)* one's way through *(durch etw* sth)

durch|le|ben [dʊrç'le:bn] *ptp* **durchlebt** VT *insep Jugend, Gefühl* to go through, to experience; *Zeit* to go *or* live through

durch|lei|den [dʊrç'laidn] *ptp* **durchlitten** [dʊrç'lɪtn] VT *insep irreg* to suffer, to endure

durch+lei|ten VT *sep* to lead through *(durch etw* sth)

durch+le|sen VT *sep irreg* to read through; **etw ganz ~** to read sth all the way through; **etw flüchtig ~** to skim *or* glance through sth; **etw auf Fehler (hin) ~** to read sth through (looking) for mistakes; **sich** *(dat)* **etw ~** to read sth through

durch|leuch|ten [dʊrç'lɔyçtn] *ptp* **durchleuchtet** VT *insep* **a** *(= untersuchen) Patienten* to X-ray; *Eier* to candle; *(fig) Angelegenheit etc* to investigate, to probe; **jdm die Lunge ~** to X-ray sb's lungs; **sich ~ lassen** to have an X-ray **b** *(geh: Schein, Sonne etc)* to light up, to flood with light

durch+leuch|ten ['dʊrçlɔyçtn] VI *sep* to shine through *(durch etw* sth)

Durch|leuch|tung [dʊrçˈlɔyçtʊŋ] **F -, -en** *(Med: mit Röntgenstrahlen)* X-ray examination; *(fig: von Angelegenheit etc)* investigation

dụrch+lie|gen *sep irreg* **VT** *Matratze, Bett* to wear down (in the middle) **VR** to get *or* develop bedsores

durch|lö̱|chern [dʊrçˈlœçɐn] *ptp* **durchlö̱chert VT** *insep* to make holes in; *(Motten auch, Rost)* to eat holes in; *Socken etc* to wear holes in; *(fig)* to undermine completely; *Argumente* to shoot down, to undermine completely; **(mit Schüssen) ~** to riddle with bullets; **eine völlig durchlöcherte Leiche** a corpse riddled with bullet holes; **er hatte völlig durchlöcherte Socken/Kleidung an** his socks/clothes were full of holes; **von Würmern durchlöchert** worm-eaten; **von Rost durchlöchert** eaten away with rust

dụrch+lot|sen VT *sep (durch etw* sth) *Schiff* to pilot through; *Autofahrer* to guide through; *(fig)* to steer through; **jdn durch etw ~** to pilot *etc* sb through sth

dụrch+lüf|ten [ˈdʊrçlʏftn] **VTI** *sep* to air thoroughly; *Wäsche auch* to air through; **ich muss mich mal wieder ~ lassen** *(inf)* I must (go and) get some fresh air

durch|lụ̈f|ten [dʊrçˈlʏftn] **durchlụ̈ftet VT** *insep* to air thoroughly

Durch|lụ̈f|tung F -, *no pl* ventilation

dụrch+lü|gen VR *sep irreg (inf)* to lie one's way through *(durch etw* sth)

dụrch+ma|chen *sep* **VT a** *(= erdulden)* to go through; *Krankheit* to have; *Operation* to undergo, to have; **er hat viel durchgemacht** he has been *or* gone through a lot
b *(= durchlaufen)* to go through; *Lehre* to serve; *(fig) Entwicklung* to undergo; *Wandlung* to undergo, to experience
c *(inf: = durchbewegen, durchstecken etc) Faden, Nadel, Stange etc* to put through *(durch etw* sth)
d *(inf: = durchtrennen)* **(in der Mitte) ~** to cut in half
e *(inf) (= durcharbeiten)* to work through; **eine ganze Nacht/Woche ~** *(= durchfeiern)* to have an all-night/week-long party, to make a night/week of it *(inf)*
VI *(inf) (= durcharbeiten)* to work right through; *(= durchfeiern)* to keep going all night

dụrch+ma|nö̱v|rie|ren *ptp* **dụrchmanö̱vriert VT** *sep* to manoeuvre *(Brit) or* maneuver *(US)* through *(durch etw* sth)

Dụrch|marsch M a march(ing) through; *(fig: = problemloser Durchbruch) (Sport, von Politiker)* walkover; *(von Partei)* landslide; **der ~ durch die Stadt** the march through the town; **auf dem ~** when marching through; **sich zum ~ entschließen** *(fig)* to resolve to push (on) through **b** *(inf: = Durchfall)* the runs *pl (inf)*; **den ~ haben** to have the runs *(inf)* **c** *(Cards)* grand slam

dụrch+mar|schie|ren *ptp* **dụrchmarschiert VI** *sep aux sein* to march through *(durch etw* sth)

dụrch+men|gen VT *sep* to mix thoroughly

durch|mẹs|sen [dʊrçˈmɛsn] *ptp* **durchmẹssen VT** *insep irreg (geh) Raum* to stride across; *Strecke* to cover

Dụrch|mes|ser M -s, - diameter; **120 cm im ~** 120 cm in diameter

dụrch+mi|schen [ˈdʊrçmɪʃn] **VT** *sep* to mix thoroughly

durch|mị|schen [dʊrçˈmɪʃn] *ptp* **durchmịscht VT** *insep* to (inter)mix; **etw mit etw ~** to mix sth with sth

dụrch+mo|geln *sep (inf)* **VR** to wangle *(inf) or* fiddle *(inf)* one's way through **VT** to fiddle through *(inf) (durch etw* sth)

dụrch+müs|sen VI *sep irreg (inf) (durch etw* sth) to have to go *or* get through; *(fig) (durch schwere Zeit)* to have to go through; *(durch Unangenehmes)* to have to go through with *(inf)*; **da musst du eben durch** *(fig)* you'll just have to see it through

dụrch+na|gen *sep* **VT** to gnaw through **VR** to gnaw one's way through *(durch etw* sth)

durch|nạ̈s|sen [dʊrçˈnɛsn] *ptp* **durchnạ̈sst VT** *insep* to soak, to drench, to make wet through; **völlig durchnässt** wet through, soaking wet, drenched

dụrch+näs|sen [ˈdʊrçnɛsn] **VI** *sep (Flüssigkeit)* to come *or* seep through *(durch etw* sth); **die Zeltplane nässt durch** wet is coming *or* seeping through the canvas; **die Wunde nässt durch** moisture from the wound is coming *or* seeping through

dụrch+neh|men VT *sep irreg* **a** *(Sch)* to go through, to do *(inf)* **b** *(pej inf)* to gossip about

dụrch+num|me|rie|ren *ptp* **dụrchnummeriert VT** *sep* to number consecutively (all the way through)

dụrch+or|ga|ni|sie|ren *ptp* **dụrchorganisiert VT** *sep* to organize down to the last detail

dụrch+or|geln VT *sep (sl) Frau* to ride *(sl)*

dụrch+pas|sie|ren *ptp* **dụrchpassiert VT** *sep* to (rub through a) sieve

dụrch+pau|ken VT *sep (inf)* **a** *(Schüler)* to cram *(inf)*, to swot up *(Brit inf)*; **etw mit jdm ~** to drum sth into sb *(inf)* **b** *(= durchsetzen) Gesetz, Änderungen* to force *or* push through **c** *(= durch Schwierigkeiten bringen) Schüler* to push through; **dein Anwalt wird dich schon irgendwie ~** your lawyer will get you off somehow

dụrch+pau|sen VT *sep* to trace

dụrch+peit|schen VT *sep* to flog; *(fig)* to rush through, to railroad through *(inf)*

dụrch+pflü|gen [ˈdʊrçpfly:gn] *sep* **VT** to plough *(Brit) or* plow *(US)* thoroughly **VR** to plough *(Brit) or* plow *(US)* (one's way) through *(durch etw* sth)

durch|pflü̱|gen [dʊrçˈpfly:gn] *ptp* **durchpflü̱gt VT** *insep* to plough *(Brit) or* plow *(US)* through

dụrch+pla|nen VT *sep* to plan (down) to the last detail

dụrch+plump|sen VI *sep aux sein (inf) (lit)* to fall through *(durch etw* sth); *(bei Prüfung)* to fail, to flunk *(inf) (durch etw, in etw (dat)* (in) sth)

dụrch+pres|sen VT *sep* to press through, to squeeze through; *Knoblauch* to crush; *Kartoffeln* to mash *(by pushing through a press)*; *Teig* to pipe

dụrch+pro|ben VT *sep* to rehearse right through

dụrch+pro|bie|ren *ptp* **dụrchprobiert VT** *sep* to try one after the other

dụrch+prü|geln VT *sep* to thrash, to beat

durch|pụl|sen [dʊrçˈpʊlzn] *ptp* **durchpụlst VT** *insep (geh)* to pulsate through; **von etw durchpulst sein** to be pulsating *or* vibrating with sth; **von Leben durchpulst** pulsating *or* throbbing with life

dụrch+pus|ten VT *sep (inf) Rohr, Düse* to blow through; **etw (durch etw) ~** to blow sth through (sth); **der Wind hat uns kräftig durchgepustet** the wind blew right through us

durch|que̱|ren [dʊrçˈkve:rən] *ptp* **durchque̱rt VT** *insep* to cross; *Land, Gebiet auch* to pass through, to traverse *(form)*

Durch|que̱|rung F -, -en *usu sing* crossing

dụrch+quet|schen *sep (inf)* **VT** = **durchpressen VR** *(inf)* to squeeze (one's way) through

dụrch+ra|sen [ˈdʊrçra:zn] **VI** *sep aux sein (durch etw* sth) to race *or* tear through; *(inf: = durchrennen auch)* to dash through

durch|ra̱|sen [dʊrçˈra:zn] *ptp* **durchra̱st VT** *insep* to race through, to tear through; *(liter: Schmerz)* to shoot through

dụrch+ras|seln VI *sep aux sein (inf)* to fail, to flunk *(inf) (durch etw, in etw (dat)* (in) sth)

dụrch+rau|schen VI *sep aux sein (inf) (durch etw* sth) **a** *(durch einen Raum)* to sweep through **b** *(bei Prüfung)* to fail, to flunk *(inf) (durch etw, in etw (dat)* (in) sth)

dụrch+rech|nen VT *sep* to calculate; **eine Rechnung noch einmal ~** to go over *or* through a calculation (again)

dụrch+reg|nen VI *impers sep* **a** *(= durchkommen)* **hier regnet es durch** the rain is coming through here; **es regnet durchs Dach durch** the rain is coming through the roof **b** *(= ununterbrochen regnen)* to rain continuously; **während des ganzen Festivals hat es durchgeregnet** it rained throughout the whole festival; **es hat die Nacht durchgeregnet** it rained all night long, it rained all through the night

dụrch+rei|ben *sep irreg* **VT** to rub through; *Material* to wear through **VR** *(Material)* to wear through

Dụrch|reic|he [ˈdʊrçraiçə] **F -, -n** (serving) hatch, pass-through *(US)*

dụrch+rei|chen VT *sep* to pass *or* hand through *(durch etw* sth)

Dụrch|rei|se F journey through; **auf der ~ sein** to be on the way through, to be passing through

Dụrch|rei|se|er|laub|nis F permission to travel through

dụrch+rei|sen [ˈdʊrçraizn] **VI** *sep aux sein (durch etw* sth) to travel through, to pass through; **wir reisen nur durch** we are just passing through, we are just on the way through

durch|rei̱|sen [dʊrçˈraizn] *ptp* **durchrei̱st VT** *insep* to travel through, to traverse *(form)*

Dụrch|rei|sen|de(r) MF *decl as adj* traveller *(Brit) or* traveler *(US)* (passing through), transient *(US)*; **~ nach München** through passengers to Munich

Dụrch|rei|se|vi|sum NT transit visa

dụrch+rei|ßen *sep irreg* **VT** to tear in two *or* in half; **etw (in der Mitte) ~** to tear sth in two *or* in half *or* down the middle **VI** *aux sein* to tear in two *or* in half; *(Seil)* to snap (in two *or* in half)

dụrch+rei|ten [ˈdʊrçraitn] *sep irreg* **VI** *aux sein* to ride through *(durch etw* sth); **die Nacht ~** to ride through(out) the night, to ride all night long **VT** *Hose* to wear out (through riding)

durch|rei̱|ten [dʊrçˈraitn] *ptp* **durchrịtten** [dʊrçˈrɪtn] **VT** *insep irreg* to ride through; *Land auch* to ride across

dụrch+ren|nen [ˈdʊrçrɛnən] **VI** *sep irreg aux sein* to run *or* race through *(durch etw* sth)

durch|rẹn|nen [dʊrçˈrɛnən] *ptp* **durchrạnnt** [dʊrçˈrant] **VT** *insep irreg* to run *or* race through

dụrch+rie|seln [ˈdʊrçri:zln] **VI** *sep aux sein* to trickle through *(durch etw* sth); **jdm zwischen den Fingern ~** to trickle between *or* through sb's fingers

durch|rie̱|seln [dʊrçˈri:zln] *ptp* **durchrie̱selt VT** *insep (fig: Gefühl, Schauer)* to run through

dụrch+rin|gen VR *sep irreg* to make up one's mind finally; **er hat sich endlich durchgerungen** after much hesitation, he has finally made up his mind *or* come to a decision; **sich zu einem Entschluss ~** to force oneself to make a decision; **sich dazu ~, etw zu tun** to bring *or* force oneself to do sth

dụrch+rin|nen VI *sep irreg aux sein* to run through *(durch etw* sth); *(= durchsickern)* to trickle through; **zwischen etw** *(dat)* **~** to run between sth; **das Geld rinnt mir nur so zwischen den Fingern durch** *(fig inf)* money just runs through my fingers

Dụrch|ritt M ride through; **beim ~, auf dem ~** on the ride through

dụrch+ros|ten VI *sep aux sein* to rust through

dụrch+ruf|en VI *sep irreg (inf)* to ring

dụrch+rüh|ren VT *sep* to mix thoroughly

dụrch+rut|schen VI *sep aux sein (lit)* to slip through *(durch etw* sth); *(fig) (Fehler etc)* to slip through; *(bei Prüfung)* to scrape through; **zwischen etw** *(dat)* **~** to slip between sth; **einige Fehler sind ihm durchgerutscht** a few mistakes slipped past him, he let a few mistakes slip through

dụrch+rüt|teln VT *sep* to shake about

dụrchs [dʊrçs] *contr von* **durch das**

dụrch+sä|beln VT *sep (inf)* to hack through

dụrch+sa|cken VI *sep aux sein* **a** *(= durchhängen) (Bett etc)* to sag; *(= durchbrechen) (Dach, Sitz)* to give way; *(= nach unten sinken)* to sink; **durch**

etw ~ *(Mensch)* to fall (down) through sth **b** *(Aviat: Flugzeug)* to pancake

Durch|sa|ge F message; *(im Radio)* announcement; **eine ~ der Polizei** a police announcement

durch+sa|gen VT *sep* **a** = **durchgeben b b** *Parole, Losung* to pass on

durch+sä|gen VT *sep* to saw through

Durch|satz M *(Ind, Comput)* throughput

durch+sau|fen [ˈdʊrçzaufn] *sep irreg (inf)* **VI** to booze the whole night long *(inf)*; **die Nacht ~** to booze all night long *(inf)* **VR** to booze at somebody else's expense *(inf)*; **sich durch etw ~** to booze one's way through sth *(inf)*

durch|sau|fen [dʊrçˈzaufn] *ptp* **durchsoffen** [dʊrçˈzɔfn] VT *insep irreg (inf)* → **durchsoffen**

durch+sau|sen VI *sep aux sein (inf)* **a** *(= durchflitzen)* to rush *or* whizz *(inf)* through *(durch etw* sth) **b** *(inf: = nicht bestehen)* to fail, to flunk *dat (durch etw, in etw (inf)* (in) sth)

durch+schal|ten *sep* **VT** *(Elec)* to connect through **VI a** *(Elec)* to connect through **b** *(Aut)* to change through the gears

durch|schau|bar [dʊrçˈʃaubaːɐ] ADJ *(fig) Hintergründe, Plan, Ereignisse* clear; *Lüge* transparent; **gut** *or* **leicht ~** *(= verständlich)* easily comprehensible *or* understood; *(= erkennbar, offensichtlich)* perfectly clear; **eine leicht ~e Lüge** a lie that is easy to see through; **schwer ~er Charakter/Mensch** inscrutable *or* enigmatic character/person

Durch|schau|bar|keit F -, *no pl (von Hintergründen, Plan, Ereignissen)* clearness; *(von Lüge)* transparency

durch|schau|en [dʊrçˈʃauən] *ptp* **durchschaut** VT *insep (= erkennen) Absichten, Lüge, jdn, Spiel* to see through; *Sachlage* to see clearly; *(= begreifen)* to understand, to comprehend; **du bist durchschaut!** I've/we've seen through you, I/we know what you're up to *(inf)*, I/we know what your little game is *(inf)*

durch+schau|en [ˈdʊrçʃauən] VTI *sep (esp dial)* = **durchsehen VI VT a b**

durch|schau|ern [dʊrçˈʃauɐn] *ptp* **durchschauert** VT *insep* to run through; **es durchschauert mich** a shiver *or* shudder runs through me

durch+schei|nen [ˈdʊrçʃainən] VI *sep irreg (durch etw* sth) *(Licht, Sonne)* to shine through; *(Farbe, Muster)* to show through; *(fig)* to shine through

durch|schei|nen [dʊrçˈʃainən] *ptp* **durchschienen** [dʊrçˈʃiːnən] VT *insep irreg (Sonne)* to flood with light

durch|schei|nend [ˈdʊrçʃainənt] ADJ transparent; *Porzellan, Papier auch* translucent; *Stoff auch* diaphanous; *Bluse etc* see-through

durch+scheu|ern *sep* **VT** to wear through; **sich** *(dat)* **die Haut ~** to graze one's skin; **durchgescheuert sein** to be *or* have worn through **VR** to wear through

durch+schie|ben *sep irreg* **VT** to push *or* shove *(inf)* through *(durch etw* sth) **VR** to push *or* shove *(inf)* (one's way) through *(durch etw* sth)

durch+schie|ßen [ˈdʊrçʃiːsn] VI *sep irreg* **a durch etw ~** to shoot through sth; **zwischen etw** *(dat)* **~** to shoot between sth **b** *aux sein (= schnell fahren, rennen)* to shoot *or* flash through; **zwischen etw** *(dat)* **~** to shoot between sth

durch|schie|ßen [dʊrçˈʃiːsn] *ptp* **durchschossen** [dʊrçˈʃɔsn] VT *insep irreg* **a** *(mit Kugeln)* to shoot through; *(fig)* to shoot *or* flash through; **die Lunge ~** to shoot through the lung; **ein Gedanke durchschoss mich/mein Gehirn** a thought flashed through my mind **b** *(Typ: = leere Seiten einfügen)* to interleave **c** *auch vi (Typ: = Zeilenabstand vergrößern)* to set *or* space out **d** *(Tex) Stoff* to interweave

durch|schif|fen [dʊrçˈʃɪfn] *ptp* **durchschifft** VT *insep* to sail across, to cross

durch+schim|mern VI *sep (durch etw* sth) to shimmer through; *(Farbe, fig)* to show through

durch+schla|fen VI *sep irreg* to sleep through (the night)

Durch|schlaf|prob|lem NT *usu pl* sleep problem, problem with sleeping through (the night)

Durch|schlag M **a** *(= Kopie)* carbon (copy), copy **b** *(= Küchengerät)* sieve, strainer **c** *(= Lochgerät)* punch **d** *(Elec)* disruptive discharge

durch+schla|gen [ˈdʊrçʃlaːgn] *sep irreg* **VT etw ~** *(= entzweischlagen)* to chop through sth; *(= durchtreiben)* to knock sth through *(durch etw* sth); *(Cook)* to rub sth through a sieve, to sieve sth

VI a *aux sein (= durchkommen) (durch etw* sth) to come through; *(fig: Charakter, Eigenschaft, Untugend)* to show through; **bei ihm schlägt der Vater durch** you can see his father in him

b *aux sein (= Loch verursachen)* to go through *(durch etw* sth)

c *aux haben (= abführen)* to have a laxative effect; **grüne Äpfel schlagen (bei mir/ihm) durch** *(inf)* green apples run *or* go straight through me/him

d *aux sein (= Wirkung haben)* to catch on; **auf etw** *(acc)* **~** to make one's/its mark on sth; **auf jdn ~** to rub off on sb; **alte Werte schlagen wieder voll durch** old values are reasserting themselves in a big way; **Investitionen schlagen auf die Nachfrage durch** investments have a marked effect on demand

e *aux sein (Sicherung)* to blow, to go

f *aux sein (Tech: Federung, Stoßdämpfer)* to seize up; **das Auto schlug durch** the suspension went

VR a *(= sich durchbringen)* to fight one's way through; *(im Leben)* to struggle through *or* along

b *(= ein Ziel erreichen)* to fight one's way through

VT *impers (Elec)* **es hat die Sicherung durchgeschlagen** the fuse has blown *or* gone

durch|schla|gen [dʊrçˈʃlaːgn] *ptp* **durchschlagen** VT *insep irreg* to blast a hole in

durch|schla|gend [ˈdʊrçʃlaːgnt] ADJ *Sieg, Erfolg* sweeping; *Maßnahmen* effective, decisive; *Argument, Beweis* decisive, conclusive; *Grund* compelling, cogent; **eine ~e Wirkung haben** to be totally effective

Durch|schlag|pa|pier NT copy paper; *(= Kohlepapier)* carbon paper

Durch|schlags-: **Durch|schlags|kraft** F *(von Geschoss)* penetration; *(fig) (von Argument)* decisiveness, conclusiveness; *(von Maßnahmen)* effectiveness; *(von Grund)* cogency; **durch|schlags|kräf|tig** ADJ *(fig) Argument, Beweis* decisive, conclusive; *Grund* compelling, cogent; *Maßnahme* effective, decisive

durch+schlän|geln VR *sep (durch etw* sth) *(Fluss)* to wind (its way) through, to meander through; *(Mensch)* to thread one's way through; *(fig)* to manoeuvre *(Brit)* or maneuver *(US)* one's way through

durch+schlei|chen VIR *sep irreg (vi: aux sein)* to slip through *(durch etw* sth)

durch+schlep|pen *sep* **VT** to drag *or* haul through *(durch etw* sth); *(fig) jdn* to drag along; *Kollegen, Mitglied etc* to carry (along) (with one) **VR** *(lit: = mühsam gehen)* to drag oneself along; *(fig)* to struggle through *(durch etw* sth)

durch+schleu|sen VT *sep* **a ein Schiff ~** to pass a ship through a lock **b** *(fig) (durch etw* sth) *(durch schmale Stelle)* to guide *or* lead through; *(= durchschmuggeln) Menschen, Gegenstand* to smuggle *or* get through

Durch|schlupf [ˈdʊrçʃlʊpf] M **-(e)s, Durchschlüpfe** [-ʃlʏpfə] way through

durch+schlüp|fen VI *sep aux sein* to slip through, to creep through *(durch etw* sth); **er ist der Polizei durchgeschlüpft** he slipped through the fingers of the police; **durch Lücken im Gesetz ~** to slip through loopholes in the law

durch+schme|cken *sep* **VT** to taste; **man kann den Essig ~** one can taste the vinegar through the other flavours *(Brit)* or flavors *(US)* **VI** to come through; **der Knoblauch schmeckt deutlich durch** the taste of the garlic comes through strongly

durch+schmug|geln VT *sep* to smuggle through *(durch etw* sth)

durch+schnei|den [ˈdʊrçʃnaidn] VT *sep irreg* to cut through, to cut in two; **etw in der Mitte ~** to cut sth (down) through the middle; **etw mitten ~** to cut sth in two *or* in half

durch|schnei|den [dʊrçˈʃnaidn] *ptp* **durchschnitten** [dʊrçˈʃnɪtn] VT *insep irreg* to cut through, to cut in two; *(Schiff) Wellen* to plough *(Brit)* or plow *(US)* through; *(Straße, Weg)* to cut through; *(fig: Schrei)* to pierce; **Wasserwege ~ das Land** the country is crisscrossed by waterways

Durch|schnitt M **a** *(= Mittelwert, Mittelmaß)* average; *(in Statistik)* mean; *(Math)* average, (arithmetic) mean; **der ~** *(= normale Menschen)* the average person; *(= die Mehrheit)* the majority; **im ~** on average; **im ~ 100 km/h fahren** to average 100 kmph; **im ~ 8 Stunden täglich arbeiten** to work on average 8 hours a day, to average 8 hours a day; **über/unter dem ~** above/below average; **~ sein** to be average; **guter ~ sein, zum guten ~ gehören** to be a good average **b** *(form: = Querschnitt)* (cross) section

durch|schnitt|lich [ˈdʊrçʃnɪtlɪç] **ADJ** average; *Wert auch* mean *attr*; *(= mittelmäßig auch)* ordinary **ADV** *(= im Durchschnitt) verdienen, schlafen, essen etc* on (an) average; **~ begabt/groß** *etc* of average ability/height *etc*; **~ gut** good on average; **die Mannschaft hat sehr ~ gespielt** the team played a very average game

Durch|schnitt|lich|keit F -, *no pl* ordinariness

Durch|schnitts- *in cpds* average; **Durch|schnitts|al|ter** NT average age; **Durch|schnitts|bil|dung** F average education; **Durch|schnitts|bür|ger(in)** M(F) average citizen; **Durch|schnitts|ehe** F average *or* normal marriage; **Durch|schnitts|ein|kom|men** NT average income; **Durch|schnitts|ge|schwin|dig|keit** F average speed; **Durch|schnitts|ge|sicht** NT ordinary *or* nondescript *(pej)* face; **Durch|schnitts|leis|tung** F average performance; **Durch|schnitts|le|ser(in)** M(F) average reader; **Durch|schnitts|mensch** M average person; **Durch|schnitts|no|te** F average mark *(Brit)* or grade *(esp US)*; **Durch|schnitts|schü|ler(in)** M(F) average pupil; **Durch|schnitts|tem|pe|ra|tur** F average *or* mean *(spec)* temperature; **Durch|schnitts|typ** M *(Person)* average sort of person; **er ist ein ~** he's your average sort of guy *(inf)*; **Durch|schnitts|wert** M average *or* mean *(Math)* value; **Durch|schnitts|zeich|nung** F sectional drawing; **Durch|schnitts|zeit** F average time

durch+schnüf|feln [dʊrçˈʃnʏfln] [ˈdʊrçʃnʏfln] VT *sep (pej inf) Post, Tasche* to nose through *(inf)*; *Wohnung* to sniff *or* nose around in *(inf)*; **alle Winkel ~** to poke one's nose into every corner *(inf)*

durch|schos|sen [dʊrçˈʃɔsn] ADJ *(Typ) Buch* interleaved; *Satz* spaced → *auch* **durchschießen**

Durch|schrei|be|block M *pl* **-blöcke** *or* **-blocks** duplicating pad

durch+schrei|ben *sep irreg* **VT** to make a (carbon) copy of; **alles wird durchgeschrieben** copies are *or* a copy is made of everything **VI a** *(= Kopie anfertigen)* to make a (carbon) copy **b** *(= Kopie liefern)* to print through, to produce a copy

Durch|schrei|be-: **Durch|schrei|be|pa|pier** NT carbon paper; **Durch|schrei|be|satz** M carbon pad

durch+schrei|ten [ˈdʊrçʃraitn] VI *sep irreg aux sein (geh)* to stride through

durch|schrei|ten [dʊrçˈʃraitn] *ptp* **durchschritten** [dʊrçˈʃrɪtn] VT *insep irreg (geh)* to stride through

Durch|schrift F (carbon) copy

Durch|schuss M **a** *(= durchgehender Schuss)* shot passing right through; **bei einem ~ ...** when a shot passes right through ... **b** (=

Loch) bullet hole; *(= Wunde)* gunshot wound *(where the bullet has passed right through)*; **ein ~ durch den Darm** a gunshot wound right through the intestine **c** *(Tex: = Schussfaden)* weft **d** *(Typ: = Zwischenraum)* leading; **ohne ~** unspaced, unleaded; **mit viel/wenig ~** widely/lightly leaded *or* spaced

durch+schüt|teln VT *sep Mischung* to shake thoroughly; *jdn (zur Strafe)* to give a good shaking; *(in Auto, Bus etc)* to shake about

durch|schwär|men [dʊrçˈʃvɛrmən] *ptp* **durchschwärmt** VT *insep (geh) Gebäude, Gelände* to swarm through; **die Nacht ~** to make a merry night of it

durch+schwe|ben [ˈdʊrçʃveːbn] VI *sep aux sein (Vogel)* to glide through; *(Wolken auch, Ballon)* to float through

durch|schwe|ben [dʊrçˈʃveːbn] *ptp* **durchschwebt** VT *insep (poet) (Vogel)* to glide through; *(Wolken auch)* to float through

durch|schwei|fen [dʊrçˈʃvaifn] *ptp* **durchschweift** VT *insep (liter)* to roam *or* wander through

durch+schwei|ßen VT *sep* to through-weld

durch+schwim|men [ˈdʊrçʃvɪmən] VI *sep irreg aux sein* **a** *(durch etw* sth) to swim through; *(Dinge)* to float through; **unter/zwischen etw** *(dat)* **~** to swim/float under/between sth **b** *(= ohne Pause schwimmen)* to swim without stopping

durch|schwim|men [dʊrçˈʃvɪmən] *ptp* **durchschwommen** [dʊrçˈʃvɔmən] VT *insep irreg* to swim through; *Strecke* to swim

durch+schwin|deln VR *sep* to trick *or* cheat one's way through

durch+schwit|zen [dʊrçˈʃvɪtsn] [ˈdʊrçʃvɪtsn] VT *sep* to soak with *or* in sweat → *auch* **durchgeschwitzt**

durch+se|geln [ˈdʊrçzeːgln] VI *sep aux sein* **a** *(Schiff)* to sail through *(durch etw* sth); **unter/zwischen etw** *(dat)* **~** to sail under/between sth **b** *(inf: = nicht bestehen)* to fail, to flunk *(inf) (durch etw, bei etw* sth) **c** *(inf: = durchlaufen)* to sail *or* sweep through *(durch etw* sth)

durch|se|geln [dʊrçˈzeːgln] *ptp* **durchsegelt** VT *insep Meer, See* to sail across; **die Meere ~** to sail (across) the seas

durch+se|hen *sep irreg* VI *(= hindurchschauen)* to look through *(durch etw* sth); **ein Stoff, durch den man ~ kann** material one can see through VT **a** *(= nachsehen, überprüfen)* **etw ~** to look *or* check sth through *or* over, to have a look through sth, to go through *or* over sth *(auf +acc* for); **etw flüchtig ~** to glance *or* skim through sth **b** *(durch etw hindurch)* to see through *(durch etw* sth)

durch+sei|hen VT *sep (Cook)* to strain

durch sein VI *irreg aux sein (inf)* **a** *(= hindurchgekommen sein)* to be through *(durch etw* sth); *(= vorbeigekommen sein)* to have gone
b *(= fertig sein)* to have finished, to be through *(esp US)*; **durch etw ~** to have got *(Brit) or* gotten *(US)* through sth, to have finished sth
c *(= durchgetrennt sein)* to be through, to be in half; *(= durchgescheuert sein)* to have worn *or* gone through
d *(Gesetz, Antrag)* to have gone through
e *(= eine Krankheit überstanden haben)* to have pulled through; *(= eine Prüfung bestanden haben)* to be through, to have got *(Brit) or* gotten *(US)* through; **durch die Krise ~** to be over the crisis
f *(Cook) (Steak, Gemüse, Kuchen)* to be done

durch|setz|bar [-zɛtsbaːɐ] ADJ **schwer ~** hard to enforce; **nicht ~** unenforceable, impossible to enforce *pred*

durch+set|zen [ˈdʊrçzɛtsn] *sep* VT *Maßnahmen, Reformen* to put *or* carry through; *Anspruch, Forderung* to push through; *Vorschlag, Plan, Vorhaben* to carry through; *Ziel* to achieve, to accomplish; **etw bei jdm ~** to get sb to agree to sth; **etw beim Aufsichtsrat ~** to get sth through the board; **seinen Willen (bei jdm) ~** to impose one's will (on sb), to get one's (own) way (with sb) → **Dickkopf, Kopf d**
VR **a** *(Mensch)* to assert oneself *(bei jdm* with sb); *(Partei etc)* to be successful, to win through; **sich gegen etw ~** to win through against sth; **sich gegen jdn ~** to assert oneself against sb, to have one's way despite sb; **sich mit etw ~** to be successful with sth; **sich im Leben ~** to make one's way in life, to be a success in life
b *(Idee, Meinung, Neuheit)* to be (generally) accepted, to gain acceptance, to catch on

durch|set|zen [dʊrçˈzɛtsn] *ptp* **durchsetzt** VT *insep* **etw mit etw ~** to intersperse sth with sth; **ein Land mit Spionen ~** to infiltrate spies into a country; **die Armee war von subversiven Elementen durchsetzt** the army was infiltrated by subversive elements

durch|setzt [-ˈsɛtst] *ptp von* **durchsetzen** ADJ **ein mit Unkraut ~er Rasen** a weed-ridden lawn → *auch* **durchsetzen**

Durch|set|zung [ˈdʊrçzɛtsʊŋ] F **-,** *no pl (von Maßnahmen, Reformen)* putting *or* carrying through; *(von Anspruch, Forderung)* pushing through; *(von Vorschlag, Plan, Vorhaben)* carrying through; *(von Ziel)* achievement, accomplishment

Durch|set|zung [dʊrçˈzɛtsʊŋ] F **-, -en die ~ des Laubwaldes mit Nadelbäumen** the fact that the deciduous forest is interspersed with conifers

Durch|set|zungs|kraft [ˈdʊrç-] F, *no pl*, **Durch|set|zungs|ver|mö|gen** [ˈdʊrç-] NT, *no pl* ability to assert oneself, powers *pl* of self-assertion

durch|seu|chen [dʊrçˈzɔyçn] *ptp* **durchseucht** VT *insep (= verseuchen)* to infect

Durch|seu|chung [dʊrçˈzɔyçʊŋ] F **-, -en** spread of infection; **die ~ der Bevölkerung** the spread of the infection throughout the population

Durch|seu|chungs-: **Durch|seu|chungs|grad** M degree of infection; **Durch|seu|chungs|ra|te** F rate of infection

Durch|sicht F examination, inspection, check; *(von Examensarbeiten)* checking through; **jdm etw zur ~ geben/vorlegen** to give sb sth to look through *or* over, to give sb sth to check (through) *or* to examine; **bei ~ der Bücher** on checking the books

durch|sich|tig [-zɪçtɪç] ADJ *Material* transparent; *Bluse etc auch* see-through; *Wasser, Luft* clear; *(fig)* transparent; *Stil* clear, lucid

Durch|sich|tig|keit F **-,** *no pl (von Material)* transparency; *(von Wasser, Luft)* clarity; *(fig)* transparency; *(von Stil)* clarity, lucidity

durch+si|ckern VI *sep aux sein (lit, fig)* to trickle through, to seep through; *(fig: trotz Geheimhaltung)* to leak out *or* through; **Informationen ~ lassen** to leak information

durch+sie|ben [ˈdʊrçziːbn] VT *sep* to sieve, to sift

durch|sie|ben [dʊrçˈziːbn] *ptp* **durchsiebt** VT *insep (inf)* **etw (mit etw) ~** to riddle sth with sth

durch+sit|zen *sep irreg* VT *Sessel* to wear out (the seat of); **ich habe mir die Hose durchgesessen** I've worn out *or* through the seat of my trousers VR *(Sessel, Polster)* to wear out; **der neue Sessel hat sich schon durchgesessen** the seat of the new armchair is *or* has already worn out

durch|sof|fen [dʊrçˈzɔfn] ADJ *attr (inf)* boozy *(inf)*; **eine ~e Nacht** a night of boozing *(inf)*, a boozy night *(inf)*

durch|sonnt [dʊrçˈzɔnt] ADJ *(poet)* sunny, sun-drenched, sun-soaked

durch+spie|len *sep* VT *Szene, Spiel, Stück* to play through; *Rolle* to act through; *(fig)* to go through VI *(= zu Ende spielen)* to play through VR *(Sport)* to get through

durch+spre|chen *sep irreg* VI **a durch etw ~** to speak *or* talk through sth **b** *(= durchgehend sprechen)* to speak without a break, to speak solidly VT **a** *Problem, Möglichkeiten, Taktik* to talk over *or* through, to go over *or* through **b** *(Theat) Rolle* to read through

durch+sprin|gen [ˈdʊrçʃprɪŋən] VI *sep irreg aux sein* to jump *or* leap *or* spring through *(durch etw* sth)

durch|sprin|gen [dʊrçˈʃprɪŋən] *ptp* **durchsprungen** [dʊrçˈʃprʊŋən] VT *insep irreg* to jump *or* leap *or* spring through

durch+spü|len VT *sep* to rinse *or* flush *or* wash (out) thoroughly; *Mund, Wäsche* to rinse (out) thoroughly

durch+star|ten *sep* VI *(Aviat)* to overshoot; *(Aut)* to accelerate off again; *(beim, vorm Anfahren)* to rev up; *(fig)* to get going again VT *Flugzeug* to pull up; *Motor, Auto* to rev (up)

durch+ste|chen [ˈdʊrçʃtɛçn] *sep irreg* VT *Nadel, Spieß* to stick through *(durch etw* sth); *Ohren* to pierce; *Deich, Damm, Grassode* to cut through; *Kanal, Tunnel* to build *or* put through *(durch etw* sth) VI to pierce; *(mit einer dünnen Nadel)* to prick; **die Nadel sticht durch** the needle is sticking through

durch|ste|chen [dʊrçˈʃtɛçn] *ptp* **durchstochen** [dʊrçˈʃtɔxn] VT *insep irreg* to pierce; *(mit Degen, Spieß etc)* to run through; *(mit Nadel)* to prick

Durch|ste|che|rei [dʊrçʃtɛçəˈrai] F *(inf)* sharp practice

durch+ste|cken VT *sep (durch etw* sth) to put *or* stick through; *Nadel etc* to stick through

durch+ste|hen [ˈdʊrçʃteːən] [ˈdʊrçʃtandn] **durch|ste|hen** [dʊrçˈʃteːən] [ˈdʊrçʃteːən] *ptp* **durchstanden** [dʊrçˈʃtandn] *insep* VT *irreg Zeit, Prüfung* to get through; *Krankheit* to pull *or* come through, to get over; *Tempo, Test, Qualen* to (with)stand; *Abenteuer* to have; *Schwierigkeiten, Situation* to get through

Durch|steh|ver|mö|gen NT, *no pl* endurance, staying power

durch+stei|gen VI *sep irreg aux sein* to climb through *(durch etw* sth); *(fig inf)* to get *(inf)*, to see; **da steigt doch kein Mensch durch** *(fig inf)* you couldn't expect anyone to get that *(inf)*

durch+stel|len ✪ 27.4 VT *sep* to put through; *(= durchreichen auch)* to pass through; **einen Moment, ich stelle durch** one moment, I'll put you through

Durch|stich M *(= Vorgang)* cut(ting); *(= Öffnung)* cut

Durch|stieg M passage

durch|stö|bern [ˈdʊrçʃtøːbɐn] [dʊrçˈʃtøːbɐn] *ptp* **durchstöbert** VT *insep* to hunt through *(nach* for), to rummage through *(nach* for); *Stadt, Gegend* to scour *(nach* for); *(= durchwühlen)* to ransack *(nach* looking for, in search of)

Durch|stoß M breakthrough

durch|sto|ßen [dʊrçˈʃtoːsn] *ptp* **durchstoßen** VT *insep irreg* to break through; *(Mil auch)* to penetrate

durch+sto|ßen [ˈdʊrçʃtoːsn] *sep irreg* VI *aux sein (zu einem Ziel gelangen)* to break through *(esp Mil)* VT *(= durchbrechen)* to break through; **etw (durch etw) ~** to push sth through (sth); *Tunnel* to drive sth through (sth)

durch+strei|chen [ˈdʊrçʃtraiçn] VT *sep irreg* to cross out *or* through, to strike out, to delete

durch|strei|chen [dʊrçˈʃtraiçn] *ptp* **durchstrichen** [dʊrçˈʃtrɪçn] VT *insep irreg (liter)* to roam *or* wander *or* rove through

durch|strei|fen [dʊrçˈʃtraifn] *ptp* **durchstreift** VT *insep (geh)* to roam *or* wander *or* rove through

durch+strö|men [ˈdʊrçʃtrøːmən] VI *sep aux sein (geh)* to flow *or* run through; *(Menschenmenge)* to stream *or* pour through

durch|strö|men [dʊrçˈʃtrøːmən] *ptp* **durchströmt** VT *(geh) insep (lit, fig)* to flow *or* run through

durch+struk|tu|rie|ren *ptp* **durchstrukturiert** VT *sep Aufsatz* to give a good structure to; *Gesetzesvorlage* to work out in detail; **ein gut durchstrukturierter Aufsatz** a well-structured essay

durch+sty|len VT *sep* to give style to; **durchgestylt** fully styled

durch|su|chen [dʊrçˈzuːxn] ptp **durchsucht** VT insep (nach for) to search (through); Stadt, Gegend auch to scour; jdn to search, to frisk; (Comput) to browse

durch+su|chen [ˈdʊrçzuːxn] VT sep to search (through)

Durch|su|chung [dʊrçˈzuːxʊŋ] F -, -en search (auf +dat for)

Durch|su|chungs|be|fehl M search warrant; **richterlicher ~** official search warrant

durch+tan|zen [ˈdʊrçtantsn] sep VI to dance through; **die Nacht ~** to dance through the night, to dance all night, to dance the night away VT Schuhe to wear out (by or with) dancing

durch|tan|zen [dʊrçˈtantsn] ptp **durchtanzt** VT insep to dance through; **eine durchtanzte Nacht** a night of dancing

durch+tas|ten VR sep to feel or grope one's way through (durch etw sth)

durch+tes|ten VT sep to test out

durch+tra|gen VT sep irreg to carry or take through (durch etw sth)

durch+trai|nie|ren ptp **durchtrainiert** sep VT Sportler, Mannschaft, Körper, Muskeln to get fit; **(gut) durchtrainiert** (Sportler) completely or thoroughly fit; Muskeln, Körper in superb condition VI (= ohne Pause trainieren) to train without a break, to train nonstop

durch|trän|ken [dʊrçˈtrɛŋkn] ptp **durchtränkt** VT insep to soak or saturate (completely); **mit/von etw durchtränkt sein** (fig geh) to be imbued with sth

durch+trei|ben VT sep irreg **etw (durch etw) ~** to drive sth through (sth)

durch+tren|nen [dʊrçˈtrɛnən] [ˈdʊrçtrɛnən] VT sep Stoff, Papier to tear (through), to tear in two; (= schneiden) to cut (through), to cut in two; Nerv, Sehne to sever; Nabelschnur to cut (through)

Durch|tren|nung F usu sing (= Zerteilung) division; (= Schneiden: von Nerv, Kabel etc) cutting, severing, severance (form)

durch+tre|ten sep irreg VT **a** Pedal to step on; (am Fahrrad) to press down; Starter to kick **b** (= abnutzen) Teppich, Schuh, Sohle to go or wear through **c** (= durchkicken) to kick through (durch etw sth) VI **a** (Aut: = Gas geben) to step on the accelerator; (Radfahrer) to pedal (hard) **b** (Ftbl) to kick out **c** aux sein (= durchsickern, durchdringen) to come through (durch etw sth) **d** aux sein (form: = weitergehen) to go or walk through VR to wear through

durch|trie|ben [dʊrçˈtriːbn] ADJ cunning, sly

Durch|trie|ben|heit F -, no pl cunning, slyness

Durch|tritt M (= das Durchtreten) passage; (= Durchtrittsstelle) place where the gas/water etc comes through

durch+trop|fen VI sep aux sein to drip through (durch etw sth)

durch|wa|chen [dʊrçˈvaxn] ptp **durchwacht** VT insep **die Nacht ~** to stay awake all through the night

durch+wach|sen [ˈdʊrçvaksn] VI sep irreg aux sein to grow through (durch etw sth)

durch|wach|sen [dʊrçˈvaksn] ADJ **a** (lit) Speck streaky; Fleisch, Schinken with fat running through (it) **b** pred (hum inf: = mittelmäßig) so-so (inf), fair to middling (Brit); **ihm geht es ~** he's having his ups and downs

durch+wa|gen VR sep to venture through (durch etw sth)

Durch|wahl F (Telec) **a** (= Wählen) direct dialling **b** (= Nebenstelle) extension

durch+wäh|len ✪ 27.1, 27.3 VI sep to dial direct; **nach London ~** to dial London direct, to dial through to London (direct)

Durch|wahl|num|mer F dialling code (Brit), dial code (US); (in Firma) extension

durch+wal|ken VT sep (inf) **a** (= verprügeln) **jdn ~** to give sb a belting (inf) or hammering (inf), to belt sb (inf) **b** (dated: = durchkneten) to knead thoroughly

durch+wan|dern [ˈdʊrçvandɐn] VI sep aux sein (durch Gegend) to hike through (durch etw sth); (= ohne Unterbrechung wandern) to carry on or continue hiking

durch|wan|dern [dʊrçˈvandɐn] ptp **durchwandert** VT insep Gegend to walk through; (hum) Zimmer, Straßen etc to wander through; **die halbe Welt ~** to wander halfway round the world

durch+wa|schen VT sep irreg to wash through

durch+wa|ten [ˈdʊrçvaːtn] VI sep aux sein to wade through (durch etw sth)

durch|wa|ten [dʊrçˈvaːtn] ptp **durchwatet** VT insep to wade through

durch|we|ben [dʊrçˈveːbn] ptp **durchwebt** or (liter) **durchwoben** [dʊrçˈvoːbn] VT insep irreg (mit, von with) to interweave; (fig liter auch) to intersperse

durch|weg [ˈdʊrçvɛk, dʊrçˈvɛk], (esp Aus) **durch|wegs** [ˈdʊrçveːks, dʊrçˈveːks] ADV (bei adj) (= ausnahmslos) without exception; (= in jeder Hinsicht) in every way or respect; (bei n) without exception; (bei vb) (= völlig) totally; (= ausnahmslos) without exception; **~ gut** good without exception/in every way or respect

durch|we|hen [dʊrçˈveːən] ptp **durchweht** VT insep (geh) to waft through

durch+we|hen [ˈdʊrçveːən] VTI sep to blow through; **(etw) durch etw ~** to blow (sth) through sth

durch+wei|chen [ˈdʊrçvaiçn] sep VI aux sein (= sehr nass werden) to get wet through, to get soaked or drenched; (= weich werden: Karton, Boden) to go soggy VT Kleidung, jdn to soak, to drench; Boden, Karton to make soggy

durch|wei|chen [dʊrçˈvaiçn] ptp **durchweicht** VT insep (geh) Boden, Karton to soften

durch+wer|fen VT sep irreg to throw through (durch etw sth)

durch+wet|zen VTR sep to wear through

durch+win|den VR sep irreg (Fluss) to wind its way, to meander (durch etw through sth); (Mensch) to thread or worm one's way through (durch etw sth); (fig) to worm one's way through (durch etw sth); **sich zwischen etw** (dat) **~** to wind its way/to thread or worm one's way between sth

durch|wir|ken [dʊrçˈvɪrkn] ptp **durchwirkt** VT insep (geh) Gewebe to interweave

durch+wit|schen [-vɪtʃn] VI sep aux sein (inf) to slip through (durch etw sth)

durch|wo|gen [dʊrçˈvoːgn] ptp **durchwogt** VT insep (fig geh) to surge through

durch+wol|len VI sep (inf) to want to go/come through (durch etw sth); **zwischen/unter etw** (dat) **~** to want to pass between/under sth; **der Bohrer/Faden will nicht (durch den Beton/das Öhr) durch** the drill/thread doesn't want to go through (the concrete/eye)

durch+wüh|len [ˈdʊrçvyːlən] sep VT to rummage through, to rummage about in (nach for); Zimmer, Haus auch to ransack (nach looking for, in search of) VR (durch etw sth) to burrow through; (fig) to work one's way through, to plough (Brit) or plow (US) through

durch|wüh|len [dʊrçˈvyːlən] ptp **durchwühlt** VT insep to rummage through, to rummage about in (nach for); Zimmer auch to ransack (nach looking for, in search of); Boden to dig up

durch+wursch|teln [-vʊrʃtln], **durch+wurs|teln** VR sep (inf) to muddle through

durch+zäh|len sep VT to count through or up VI to count or number off

durch+ze|chen [ˈdʊrçtsɛçn] VI sep to carry on drinking

durch|ze|chen [dʊrçˈtsɛçn] ptp **durchzecht** VT insep **die Nacht ~** to drink through the night, to carry on drinking all night; **eine durchzechte Nacht** a night of drinking

durch+zeich|nen VT sep to trace

durch+zie|hen [ˈdʊrçtsiːən] sep irreg VT **a** (= durch etw hindurchziehen) to pull or draw through (durch etw sth) **b** (inf: = erledigen, vollenden) to get through **c** (= durchbauen) (durch etw sth) Graben to dig through; Mauer to build through VI **a** aux sein (= durchkommen) (durch etw sth) to pass or go through; (Truppe) to march through; (Schmerz) to go through; (Kälte) to come through **b** aux sein to soak; **etw in etw** (dat) **~ lassen** to steep or soak sth in sth; (in Marinade) to marinate sth in sth **c** aux haben (sl) **kräftig ~** (= Sex haben) to have a good shag (sl) VR to run through (durch etw sth)

durch|zie|hen [dʊrçˈtsiːən] ptp **durchzogen** [dʊrçˈtsoːgn] VT insep irreg (= durchwandern) to pass through, to go through; (Straße, Fluss, fig: Thema) to run through; (Geruch) to fill, to pervade; (Graben) to cut through; **sein Haar ist von grauen Fäden durchzogen** his hair is streaked with grey (Brit) or gray (US); **die Welt ~** to travel (a)round the world; **ein Feld mit Gräben ~** to crisscross a field with ditches; **ein mit Goldfäden durchzogener Stoff** material with a gold thread running through it

durch|zu|cken [dʊrçˈtsʊkn] ptp **durchzuckt** VT insep (Blitz) to flash across; (fig: Gedanke) to flash through

Durch|zug M **a** no pl (= Luftzug) draught (Brit), draft (US); **~ machen** to create a draught (Brit) or draft (US); (zur Lüftung) to get the air moving; **(die Ohren) auf ~ stellen** or **schalten** (fig) to switch off (inf) **b** (durch ein Gebiet) passage; (von Truppen) march through; **auf dem/beim ~ durch ein Land** while passing through a country

Durch|zugs|recht NT right of passage

durch+zwän|gen sep (durch etw sth) VT to force or squeeze through VR to force one's way through, to squeeze (one's way) through

dür|fen [ˈdʏrfn] ✪ 27.5, 28.1, 29.2, 30, 36.1, 36.3, 37.4, 45.2, 46.5, 52.2 pret **durfte**, [ˈdʊrftə] ptp **gedurft** or (bei modal aux vb) **dürfen** VI, MODAL AUX VB [gəˈdʊrft, ˈdʏrfn] **a** (= Erlaubnis haben) **etw tun ~** to be allowed to do sth, to be permitted to do sth; **darf ich/man das tun?** may I/one do it?, am I/is one allowed to do it?; **darf ich? – ja, Sie ~** may I? – yes, you may; **darf ich ins Kino?** may I go to the cinema?; **er hat nicht gedurft** he wasn't allowed to

b (verneint) **man darf etw nicht (tun)** (= sollte, muss nicht) one must not or mustn't do sth; (= hat keine Erlaubnis) one isn't allowed to do sth, one may not do sth; (= kann nicht) one may not do sth; **hier darf man nicht rauchen** (= ist verboten) smoking is prohibited here, it is prohibited to smoke here; **diesen Zug darf ich nicht verpassen** I must not miss this train; **du darfst ihm das nicht übel nehmen** you must not take offence (Brit) or offense (US) at him; **die Kinder ~ hier nicht spielen** the children aren't allowed to or may not play here; **der Patient darf noch nicht transportiert werden** the patient may not be moved yet; **das darf doch nicht wahr sein!** that can't be true!; **da darf er sich nicht wundern** that shouldn't surprise him

c (in Höflichkeitsformeln) **darf ich das tun?** may I do that?; **Ruhe, wenn ich bitten darf!** quiet, (if you) please!, will you please be quiet!; **darf ich um den nächsten Tanz bitten?** may I have (the pleasure of) the next dance?; **darf ich Sie bitten, das zu tun?** may or could I ask you to do that?; **was darf es sein?** can I help you?, what can I do for you?; (vom Gastgeber gesagt) what can I get you?, what'll you have?; **dürfte ich bitte Ihren Ausweis sehen** (als Aufforderung) may or might I see your identity card, please

d (= Veranlassung haben, können) **wir freuen uns, Ihnen mitteilen zu ~** we are pleased to be able to tell you; **ich darf wohl sagen, dass ...** I think I can say that ...; **man darf doch wohl fragen** one can or may ask, surely?; **Sie ~ mir das ruhig glauben** you can or may take my word for it

e (im Konjunktiv) **das dürfte ...** (als Annahme) that must ...; (= sollte) that should or ought to …; *(= könnte)* that could …; **das dürfte Emil sein** that must be Emil; **das dürfte wohl das Beste sein** that is probably the best thing; **das dürfte reichen** that should be enough, that ought to be enough; **das Essen dürfte stärker gewürzt sein** the food could have been more highly spiced

dürf|tig ['dʏrftɪç] ADJ **a** *(= ärmlich)* wretched, miserable; *Essen auch* meagre *(Brit)*, meager *(US)* **b** *(pej: = unzureichend)* miserable, pathetic *(inf)*; *Kenntnisse* sketchy, scanty; *Ausrede* feeble, lame, pathetic *(inf)*; *Ersatz* poor *attr*; *(= spärlich) Haarwuchs, Pflanzenwuchs* sparse; *Bekleidung* scanty, skimpy; **ein paar ~e Tannen** a few scrawny fir trees ADV *(= kümmerlich) beleuchtet* poorly; *gekleidet* scantily; **die Ernte ist ~ ausgefallen** the harvest turned out to be quite meagre *(Brit)* or meager *(US)*

Dürf|tig|keit F -, *no pl* **a** *(= Ärmlichkeit)* wretchedness; *(von Essen)* meagreness *(Brit)*, meagerness *(US)* **b** *(von Kenntnissen)* sketchiness, scantiness; *(von Ausrede)* feebleness, lameness; *(von Ersatz)* poorness; *(von Haarwuchs, Pflanzenwuchs)* sparseness; *(von Bekleidung)* skimpiness; **die ~ seines Einkommens/seiner Leistung** *(pej)* his miserable *or* pathetic *(inf)* salary/performance

dürr [dʏr] ADJ **a** *(= trocken)* dry; *(= ausgetrocknet) Boden* arid, barren; *Ast, Strauch* dried up, withered **b** *(pej: = mager)* scrawny, scraggy **c** *(fig: = knapp, dürftig) Auskunft* meagre *(Brit)*, meager *(US)*; *Handlung einer Oper etc* thin; **mit ~en Worten** in plain terms, plainly, bluntly; **die ~en Jahre** *(Bibl, fig)* the lean years

Dür|re ['dʏrə] F -, -n **a** *(= Zeit der Dürre)* drought **b** = **Dürrheit**

Dür|re-: **Dür|re|jahr** NT year of drought; **Dür|re|ka|ta|stro|phe** F catastrophic *or* disastrous drought; **Dür|re|op|fer** NT *(Person)* drought victim; **Dür|re|pe|ri|o|de** F (period of) drought; *(fig)* barren period

Dürr|heit F -, *no pl* **a** *(= Trockenheit)* dryness; *(von Boden auch)* aridity, barrenness **b** *(pej: = Magerkeit)* scrawniness, scragginess

Durst [dʊrst] M -(e)s, *no pl (lit, fig)* thirst *(nach* for); **~ haben** to be thirsty; **~ bekommen** *or* **kriegen** *(inf)* to get *or* become thirsty; **den ~ löschen** *or* **stillen** to quench one's thirst; **das macht ~** that makes you thirsty, that gives you a thirst; **ein Glas** *or* **einen über den ~ getrunken haben** *(inf)* to have had one too many *(inf)*

durs|ten ['dʊrstn] VI **a** *(geh)* to be thirsty, to thirst *(liter)*; **er musste ~** he had to go thirsty **b** *(fig)* = **dürsten VI** VT *impers (liter)* = **dürsten VT**

dürs|ten ['dʏrstn] VT *impers (liter)* **es dürstet mich, mich dürstet** I thirst *(liter)*; **es dürstet ihn nach Rache/Wissen/Wahrheit** he thirsts for revenge/knowledge/(the) truth → **Blut** VI *(fig)* **er dürstet nach Rache/Wahrheit** he is thirsty for revenge/truth

Durst|ge|fühl NT feeling of thirst

durs|tig ['dʊrstɪç] ADJ thirsty; **jdn ~ machen** to make sb thirsty, to give sb a thirst; **diese Arbeit macht ~** this is thirsty work *(inf)*, this work makes you thirsty; **nach etw ~ sein** *(fig geh)* to be thirsty for sth, to thirst for sth *(liter)*; **sie ist eine ~e Seele** *(hum inf)* she likes the bottle *(Brit hum)*, she likes to tip the bottle *(US hum inf)*

Durst-: **durst|lö|schend, durst|stil|lend** ADJ thirst-quenching; **Durst|stre|cke** F hard times *pl*; *(= Mangel an Inspiration)* barren period; **Durst|streik** M thirst strike

Dur-: **Dur|ton|art** ['du:ɐto:n-] F major key; **Dur|ton|lei|ter** F major scale

Dusch|bad NT **a** shower (bath); **ein ~ nehmen** to have *or* take a shower (bath) **b** *(= Gel)* shower gel

Du|sche ['dʊʃə] F -, -n shower; **unter der ~ sein** *or* **stehen** to be in the shower, to be taking a shower; **eine ~ nehmen** to have *or* take a shower; **das war eine kalte ~** *(fig)* that really brought him/her *etc* down to earth (with a bump); **bei ihrem Enthusiasmus wirkten seine Worte wie eine kalte ~** *(fig)* his words poured cold water on her enthusiasm

Dusch|ecke F shower (cubicle)

du|schen ['dʊʃn] VIR to have *or* take a shower, to shower; **(sich) kalt ~** to have *or* take a cold shower VT **jdn ~** to give sb a shower; **jdm/sich den Kopf/Rücken ~** to spray sb's/one's head/back

Dusch-: **Dusch|gel** NT shower gel; **Dusch|ge|le|gen|heit** F shower facilities *pl*; **Dusch|hau|be** F shower cap; **Dusch|ka|bi|ne** F shower (cubicle); **Dusch|kopf** M shower head; **Dusch|raum** M shower room, showers *pl*; **Dusch|vor|hang** M shower curtain; **Dusch|wand** F shower screen; **Dusch|wan|ne** F shower tray

Dü|se ['dy:zə] F -, -n nozzle; *(Mech auch)* jet; *(von Flugzeug)* jet

Du|sel ['du:zl] M -s, *no pl (inf)* **a** *(= Glück)* luck; **~ haben** to be lucky; **da hat er (einen) ~ gehabt** his luck was in *(Brit inf)*, he was lucky; **so ein ~!** that was lucky!, that was a fluke! *(inf)* **b** *(= Trancezustand)* daze, dream; *(durch Alkohol)* fuddle; **im ~** in a daze *or* dream; in a fuddle

du|se|lig ['du:zəlɪç] ADJ *(= schlaftrunken)* drowsy; *(= benommen)* dizzy, giddy; *(esp durch Alkohol)* (be)fuddled; **mir ist ganz ~ (im Kopf), ich habe ein ~es Gefühl** my head is swimming, I feel quite dizzy *or* giddy

du|seln ['du:zln] VI *(inf)* to doze

dü|sen ['dy:zn] VI *aux sein (inf)* to dash; *(mit Flugzeug)* to jet; **nach Hause ~** to dash *or* whizz off home; **durch die Welt ~** to jet (a)round the world

Dü|sen-: **Dü|sen|an|trieb** M jet propulsion; **mit ~** jet-propelled, with jet propulsion; **Dü|sen|bom|ber** M jet bomber; **Dü|sen|flug|zeug** NT jet aircraft *or* plane, jet; **dü|sen|ge|trie|ben** [-gətri:bn] ADJ jet-propelled, jet-powered; **Dü|sen|jä|ger** M **a** *(Mil)* jet fighter **b** *(inf: = Düsenflugzeug)* jet aircraft *or* plane, jet; **Dü|sen|klip|per** [-klɪpɐ] M -s, - jet airliner; **Dü|sen|ma|schi|ne** F jet (aircraft *or* plane); **Dü|sen|mo|tor** M jet engine; **Dü|sen|treib|stoff** M jet fuel; **Dü|sen|trieb|werk** NT jet power-unit

dus|lig ['du:zlɪç] ADJ *(inf)* = **duselig**

Dus|sel ['dʊsl] M -s, - *(inf)* twit *(Brit inf)*, twerp *(inf)*, dope *(inf)*

Dus|se|lei [dʊsə'lai] F -, -en *(inf)* stupidity

dus|se|lig ['dʊsəlɪç], **duss|lig** ['dʊslɪç] *(inf)* ADJ stupid ADV **a** *(= dumm)* **sich ~ anstellen** to be stupid **b** *(= sehr viel)* **sich ~ reden** to talk till one is blue in the face *(inf)*; **sich ~ verdienen** to make a killing *(inf)*; **sich ~ arbeiten** to work like a horse

Dus|se|lig|keit F -, -en, **Duss|lig|keit** F -, -en *(inf)* stupidity

dus|ter ['du:stɐ] ADJ = **dunkel**

düs|ter ['dy:stɐ] ADJ gloomy; *Nacht auch* murky; *Tag, Wetter auch* dismal, murky; *Musik auch* funereal, lugubrious; *Farbe, Gesicht auch* sombre *(Brit)*, somber *(US)*, dismal; *Bild, Gedanken, Zukunftsvisionen auch* sombre *(Brit)*, somber *(US)*, dismal, dark; *Miene, Stimmung* dark, black, gloomy; *(= unheimlich) Gestalten, Stadtteil* sinister, (dark and) forbidding

Düs|te|re(s) ['dy:stərə] NT *decl as adj (poet)* gloom, dark(ness); *(fig: von Gedanken, Stimmung)* gloominess

Düs|ter|keit F -, *no pl* gloominess; *(= Unheimlichkeit: von Stadtteil)* sinister character; *(= Dunkelheit)* gloom, darkness

Dutt [dʊt] M -(e)s, -s *or* -e *(dial)* bun

Dut|te ['dʊtə] F -, -n *(Aus)* teat, nipple

Duty-free-Shop ['dju:tɪ'fri:ʃɔp] M -s, -s, **Du|ty|free|shop** M -s, -s duty-free shop

Dut|zend ['dʊtsnt] NT -s, -e [-də] dozen; **ein halbes ~** half-a-dozen, a half-dozen; **zwei/drei ~** two/three dozen; **ein ~ frische** *or* **frischer** *(geh)* **Eier kostet** *or* **kosten …** a dozen fresh eggs cost(s) …; **das ~ kostet 2 Euro** they cost 2 euros a dozen; **~e** *pl (inf)* dozens *pl*; **sie kamen in** *or* **zu dutzenden** *or* **~en** they came in (their) dozens; **im ~ billiger** *(inf) (bei größerer Menge)* the more you buy, the more you save; *(bei mehr Leuten)* the more you are, the more you save *(inf)*; **dutzend(e) Mal** dozens of times → **zwölf**

Dut|zend-: **dut|zend|fach** ADJ dozens of; **in ~en Variationen** in dozens of variations ADV in dozens of ways; **dut|zend|mal** △ ADV *(inf)* → **Dutzend**; **Dut|zend|mensch** M *(pej)* ordinary *or* run-of-the-mill sort of person; **Dut|zend|preis** M price per dozen; **Dut|zend|wa|re** F *(pej)* (cheap) mass-produced item; **~n** (cheap) mass-produced goods; **dut|zend|wei|se** ADV in dozens, by the dozen

Duz|bru|der M good friend *or* pal *(inf)*; **alte Duzbrüder** old friends *or* pals *(inf)*

du|zen ['du:tsn] VT to address with the familiar "du"-form; **wir ~ uns** we use "du" *or* the "du"-form (to each other)

> **DUZEN/SIEZEN**
>
> There are two ways of addressing people in German: the familiar **du** and the polite **Sie**. **Duzen** means that people say "du" to each other and use first names; **siezen** means that people say "Sie" and "Herr/Frau…". **Du** is reserved for family, children and close friends, otherwise **Sie** is used. **Du** is often introduced by the elder of two people as a token of friendship. Nowadays, however, etiquette is becoming less strict, and young people especially say **du** to one another almost as a matter of course. Sometimes different forms of address are combined, for example when colleagues use first names but the polite **Sie**.

Duz-: **Duz|freund(in)** M(F) good friend; **alte ~e** old friends; **Duz|fuß** M **mit jdm auf dem ~ stehen** *(inf)* to be on familiar terms with sb

DV [de:'fau] F - *abbr von* **Datenverarbeitung** DP

DVD [de:fau'de:] F -, -s *abbr von* **digital versatile** *or* **video disc** DVD

DVD: **DVD-Play|er** [de:fau'de:ple:ɐ] M -s, - DVD player; **DVD-Bren|ner** M DVD recorder *or* writer; **DVD-Lauf|werk** NT DVD drive; **DVD-Re|kor|der** M DVD recorder

d. Verf. *abbr von* **der Verfasser**

dwars [dvars] ADV *(N Ger Naut)* abeam

Dy|na|mik [dy'na:mɪk] F -, *no pl* **a** *(Phys)* dynamics *sing* **b** *(fig)* dynamism; **Menschen mit einer solchen ~** people with such dynamism

Dy|na|mi|ker [dy'na:mikɐ] M -s, -, **Dy|na|mi|ke|rin** [-ərɪn] F -, -nen go-getter

dy|na|misch [dy'na:mɪʃ] ADJ **a** dynamic; **~e Gesetze** laws of dynamics **b** *(fig)* dynamic; *Renten* ≈ index-linked ADV *(= schwungvoll)* dynamically

dy|na|mi|sie|ren [dynami'zi:rən] *ptp* **dynamisiert** VT *(geh)* to make dynamic; *Debatte* to enliven; *Gesellschaft* to revitalize; *(= vorantreiben) Prozess, Reform* to speed up; *Renten, Sozialhilfe* ≈ to index-link

Dy|na|mi|sie|rung F -, -en *(geh) (von Reform etc)* speeding up; *(von Renten)* ≈ index-linking; **sie streben eine ~ ihrer Politik an** they are seeking to make their policies more dynamic

Dy|na|mit [dyna'mi:t] NT -s, *no pl (lit, fig)* dynamite

Dy|na|mo(|ma|schi|ne) [dy'na:mo-, 'dy:namo-] M(F) -s, -s dynamo; *(fig)* powerhouse

Dy|nast [dy'nast] M -en, -en dynast

Dy|nas|tie [dynas'ti:] F -, -n [-'ti:ən] dynasty

dy|nas|tisch [dy'nastɪʃ] ADJ dynastic

Dys|pro|si|um [dʏs'pro:ziʊm] NT -s, *no pl (abbr* **Dy)** dysprosium

D-Zug ['de:-] M fast *(Brit) or* express train; *(hält nur in großen Städten)* non-stop *or* through train; **ein alter Mann/eine alte Frau ist doch kein ~** *(inf)* I am going as fast as I can, I can't go any faster

D-Zug-: **D-Zug-Tem|po** NT *(inf)* fantastic speed *(inf)*; **im ~** like greased lightning *(inf)*, in double-quick time *(inf)*; **D-Zug-Zu|schlag** M express travel supplement *(Brit)*, additional fare payable on express trains *(US)*; *(inf: = Karte)* supplementary ticket, additional fare *(US)*

E

E, e [eː] **NT -, -** E, e
Eau de Co|log|ne ['oː də ko'lɔnjə] **NT - - -,** *no pl* eau de Cologne
Eau de Toi|let|te ['oː də toa'lɛt] **NT - - -,** *no pl* eau de toilette
Eb|be ['ɛbə] **F -, -n** **a** *(= ablaufendes Wasser)* ebb tide; *(= Niedrigwasser)* low tide; **~ und Flut** the tides, ebb and flow; **bei ~ baden** to swim when the tide is going out; *(bei Niedrigwasser)* to swim at low tide; **bei ~ auslaufen** to go out on the (ebb) tide; *(bei Niedrigwasser)* to go out at low tide; **mit der ~** on *or* with the ebb tide; **die ~ tritt um 15.30 Uhr ein** the tide starts to go out *or* turns at 3.30 p.m; **es ist ~** the tide is going out; *(= es ist Niedrigwasser)* it's low tide, the tide is out
b *(fig)* **bei mir** *or* **in meinem Geldbeutel ist** *or* **herrscht ~** I'm a bit hard up *(inf) or* my finances are at a pretty low ebb at the moment; **in den Beziehungen der beiden Staaten herrscht zurzeit ~** relations between the two countries are at a low ebb at the moment *or* have fallen off recently
ebd. *abbr von* **ebenda**
eben ['eːbn] **ADJ** *(= glatt)* smooth; *(= gleichmäßig)* even; *(= gleich hoch)* level; *(= flach)* flat; *(Math)* plane; **zu ~er Erde** at ground level; **auf ~er Strecke** on the flat
ADV **a** *(zeitlich) (= soeben)* just; *(= schnell, kurz)* for a minute *or* second; **das wollte ich ~ sagen** I was just about to say that; **mein Bleistift war doch ~ noch da** my pencil was there (just) a minute ago; **kommst du ~ mal mit?** will you come with me for a minute *or* second?; **ich gehe ~ zur Bank** I'll just pop to *(Brit) or* by *(US)* the bank *(inf)*
b *(= gerade or genau das)* exactly, precisely; **(na) ~!** exactly!, quite!, precisely!; **das ist es ja ~!** that's just *or* precisely it!; **das ~ nicht!** no, not that!; **das ist es ~ nicht!** that's just *or* exactly what it isn't!; **~ das wollte ich sagen** that's just *or* exactly what I wanted to say; **nicht ~ billig/viel/angenehm** *etc* not exactly cheap/a lot/pleasant *etc*
c *(= gerade noch)* just; **das reicht so** *or* **nur ~ aus** it's only just enough; **wir haben den Zug ~ noch erreicht** we just caught the train
d *(= nun einmal, einfach)* just, simply; **das ist ~ so** that's just the way it is *or* things are; **dann bleibst du ~ zu Hause** then you'll just have to stay at home → **dann**
Eben|bild **NT** image; **dein ~** the image of you; **das genaue ~ seines Vaters** the spitting image of his father
eben|bür|tig ['eːbnbʏrtɪç] **ADJ** **a** *(= gleichwertig)* equal; *Gegner* evenly matched; **jdm an Kraft/Ausdauer ~ sein** to be sb's equal in strength/endurance; **sie war ihm an Kenntnissen ~** her knowledge equalled *(Brit) or* equaled *(US)* his, her knowledge was equal to his; **wir sind einander ~** we are equal(s) **b** *(Hist: = gleichrangig)* of equal birth
Eben|bür|tig|keit **F -,** *no pl* **a** *(= Gleichwertigkeit)* equality; **die ~ dieser beiden Gegner wurde deutlich** it became clear that the two opponents were evenly matched **b** *(Hist)* equality of birth
eben-: **eben|da** ['eːbn'daː, *(emph)* eːbn'daː] **ADV** **a** *(= gerade dort)* **~ will auch ich hin** that is exactly where I am bound too **b** *(bei Zitat)* ibid, ibidem; **eben|da|hin** ['eːbnda'hɪn, *(emph)* eːbn'daːhɪn] **ADV** **~ zieht es auch mich** that is exactly where *or* whither *(old)* I am bound too; **eben|dann** ['eːbn'dan, *(emph)* eːbn'dan] **ADV** **~ soll ich zum Arzt** that is exactly when I have to go to the doctor; **eben|da|rum** ['eːbnda'rʊm, *(emph)* eːbn'daːrʊm] **ADV** that is why, for that reason; **~!** *(zu Kind)* because I say so!; **eben|der, eben|die, eben|das** **PRON** he; she; it; **~ hat auch gesagt, dass ...** he was also the one who said that ..., it was he who also said that ...; **eben|des|halb, eben|des|we|gen** ['eːbndɛs'veːgn, *(emph)* eːbn'dɛsveːgn] **ADV** that is exactly why; **eben|die** **PRON** → **ebender**; **eben|die|se(r, s)** ['eːbn'diːzə, *(emph)* eːbn'diːzə] **PRON** *(liter)* he; she; it; **und ~r wurde später ermordet** and this same man was later murdered **ADJ** this very *or* same; **und ~n Mann hat sie geheiratet** and this was the very man she married; **eben|dort** ['eːbn'dɔrt, *(emph)* eːbn'dɔrt] **ADV** *(old)* at that very *or* same place
Ebe|ne ['eːbənə] **F -, -n** *(= Tiefebene)* plain; *(= Hochebene)* plateau; *(Math, Phys)* plane; *(fig)* level; **auf höchster/der gleichen ~** *(fig)* at the highest/the same level; **seine Beleidigungen liegen auf der gleichen ~ wie ...** his insults are on a par with ... → **schief**
eben|er|dig **ADJ** at ground level
eben|falls **ADV** as well, likewise; *(bei Verneinungen)* either; **er hat ~ nichts davon gewusst** he knew nothing about it either; **danke, ~!** thank you, the same to you!
Eben|heit **F -,** *no pl (= Glattheit)* smoothness; *(= Gleichmäßigkeit)* evenness; *(= gleiche Höhe)* levelness; *(= Flachheit)* flatness
Eben|holz **NT** ebony
Eben-: **eben|je|ne(r, s)** ['eːbn'jeːnə, *(emph)* eːbn'jeːnə] *(liter)* **PRON** he; she; it; **~r wurde später Präsident** this same man later became president **ADJ** that very *or* same; **Eben|maß** **NT** *(von Gestalt, Gesichtszügen)* elegant proportions *pl*; *(von Zähnen)* evenness; *(von Versen)* even flow; **eben|mä|ßig** **ADJ** *Gestalt, Gesichtszüge* elegantly proportioned; *Zähne* even; *Verse* evenly flowing **ADV** **~ geformt** elegantly proportioned; **Eben|mä|ßig|keit** **F** = **Ebenmaß**
eben|so ['eːbnzoː] **ADV** *(= genauso)* just as; *(= auch, ebenfalls)* as well; **das kann doch ~ eine Frau machen** a woman can do that just as well; **die Geschäfte sind geschlossen, ~ alle Büros** the shops are closed, as are all the offices; **viele Leute haben sich ~ wie wir beschwert** a lot of people complained just like we did *or* just as we did *or* just like us; **er freute sich ~ wie ich** he was just as pleased as I was; **er hat ein ~ großes Zimmer wie wir** he has just as big a room as we have; **ich mag sie ~ gern** I like her just as much, I like her equally well; **ich esse ~ gern Reis** I like rice just as much, I'd just as soon eat rice; **ich komme ~ gern morgen** I'd just as soon come tomorrow; **~ gut** (just) as well; **ich kann ~ gut Französisch wie Italienisch** I can speak French (just) as well as I can speak Italian, my French is (just) as good as my Italian; **~ lang** just as long; **~ oft** *or* **häufig** just as often *or* frequently; **~ sehr** just as much; **~ wenig** just as little; **~ wenig, wie man dies sagen kann, kann man behaupten, ...** there is just as little ground for saying this as for claiming ...; **~ viel** just as much
eben|sol|che(r, s) ['eːbn'zɔlçə] **ADJ** (exactly) the same
eben|so-: **eben|so|oft** △ ['eːbnzoɔft] **ADV** → **ebenso**; **eben|so|sehr** △ ['eːbnzozeːɐ] **ADV** → **ebenso**; **eben|so|viel** △ ['eːbnzofiːl] **ADV** → **ebenso**; **eben|so|we|nig** △ ['eːbnzoveːnɪç] **ADV** → **ebenso**
Eber ['eːbɐ] **M -s, -** boar
Eber|esche **F** rowan, mountain ash
EBK *abbr von* **Einbauküche**
eb|nen ['eːbnən] **VT** to level (off), to make level; **jdm/einer Sache den Weg ~** *(fig)* to smooth the way for sb/sth
Ebo|la-: **Ebo|la|epi|de|mie** **F**, **Ebo|la|seu|che** **F** Ebola epidemic; **Ebo|la|vi|rus** **M OR NT** Ebola virus
E-Book-Rea|der ['iːbʊkˌriːdɐ] **M -s, -** e-reader
EC [eː'tseː] **M -, -s** *(Rail) abbr von* **Euro-City-Zug**
echauf|fie|ren [eʃɔ'fiːrən] *ptp* **echauffiert** **VR** *(dated)* to get into a taking *(dated)*, to get het-up *(Brit) or* worked up
Echo ['ɛço] **NT -s, -s** echo *(auch Comput)*; *(fig)* response *(auf +acc* to); **er war nur das ~ seines Chefs** *(fig)* he was only an echo of his boss; **ein starkes** *or* **lebhaftes ~ finden** *(fig)* to meet with *or* attract a lively *or* positive response *(bei* from)
echo|en ['ɛçoən] **VI** *(rare)* to echo; **hallooo ...!, echote es** hallooo ...!, came the echo
Echo-: **Echo|kar|dio|gra|fie**, **Echo|kar|dio|gra|phie** [ɛçokardiogra'fiː] **F -, -n** [-'fiːən] *(Med)* echocardiography; **Echo|lot** ['ɛçoloːt] **NT** *(Naut)* echo sounder, sonar; *(Aviat)* sonic altimeter; **Echo|or|tung** **F** echolocation
Ech|se ['ɛksə] **F -, -n** *(Zool)* lizard
echt [ɛçt] **ADJ, ADV** **a** real, genuine; *Gefühle* real, genuine, sincere; *Haar, Perlen, Gold* real; *Unterschrift, Geldschein, Gemälde* genuine; *Haarfarbe* natural; **das Gemälde war nicht ~** the painting was a forgery, the painting was forged
b *(= typisch)* typical; **ein ~er Bayer** a real *or* typical Bavarian
c *Farbe* fast
d *(Math)* **~er Bruch** proper fraction
ADV **a** *(= typisch)* typically; **~ Tiroler Trachten** original Tyrolean costumes; **~ englisch** typically English; **~ Shakespeare** typical of Shakespeare, typically Shakespearean; **~ Franz/Frau** typical of *or* just like Franz/a woman, Franz/a woman all over *(inf)*
b *(= rein)* **der Ring ist ~ golden/silbern** the ring is real gold/silver; **~ silbern** real silver
c *(inf: = wirklich)* really; **meinst du das ~?** do you really *or* honestly mean that?; **der spinnt doch ~** he must be out of his mind, he must be cracked *(Brit inf)*, he must be round the bend *(Brit inf)*; **ich habs ~ eilig** I'm really in a hurry
Echt-: **echt|gol|den** **ADJ** *attr* → **echt ADV b**; **Echt|haar|pe|rü|cke** **F** real hair wig

Echt|heit F -, *no pl* genuineness; *(von Unterschrift, Dokument auch)* authenticity; *(von Gefühlen, Glauben auch)* sincerity; *(von Haarfarbe)* naturalness; *(von Farbe)* fastness

Echt|heits|be|stä|ti|gung F *(Comput)* authentication

Echt-: **echt|sil|bern** ADJ *attr* → **echt ADV b**; **Echt|zeit** F *(Comput)* real time; **Echt|zeit|uhr** F *(Comput)* real-time clock; **Echt|zeit|ver|ar|bei|tung** F *(Comput)* real time processing

Eck [ɛk] NT -(e)s, -e **a** *(esp Aus, S Ger)* = **Ecke a** **b** *(Sport)* **das kurze/lange ~** the near/far corner of the goal **c über ~** diagonally across *or* opposite; **die Schrauben über ~ anziehen** to tighten the nuts working diagonally across; **im ~ sein** *(Aus)* to be out of form; **da hats ein ~** *(Aus inf)* you've/she's *etc* got problems there

Eckart ['ɛkart] M -s **der getreue ~** *(liter)* the faithful Eckart *(mythical figure in medieval German literature)*; *(fig)* the old faithful

ec-Kar|te, EC-Kar|te [e:'tse:-] F = **Euroscheckkarte**

Eck-: **Eck|ba|de|wan|ne** F corner bath (unit); **Eck|ball** M *(Sport)* corner; **einen ~ schießen** *or* **treten/geben** to take/give a corner; **Eck|bank** F *pl* **-bänke** corner seat; **Eck|da|ten** PL key figures *pl*

Ecke ['ɛkə] F -, -n **a** corner; *(= Kante)* edge; *(von Kragen)* point; *(Sport: = Eckball)* corner; **Kantstraße ~ Goethestraße** at the corner of Kantstraße and Goethestraße; **er wohnt gleich um die ~** he lives just (a)round the corner; **ein Kind in die ~ stellen** to make a child stand in the corner; **er wurde in die reaktionäre ~ gestellt** he was pigeon-holed as a reactionary; **etw in allen ~n und Winkeln suchen** to search *or* look high and low for sth; **jdn in die ~ drängen** *(fig)* to push sb into the background; **an allen ~n und Enden sparen** to pinch and scrape *(inf)*; **jdn um die ~ bringen** *(inf)* to bump sb off *(inf)*, to do away with sb *(inf)*; **mit jdm um ein paar** *or* **um sieben ~n herum verwandt sein** *(inf)* to be distantly related to sb, to be sb's second cousin twice removed *(hum inf)*; **die neutrale ~** *(Boxen)* the neutral corner; **~n und Kanten** *(fig)* rough edges → **fehlen VI** *impers*
b *(= Käseecke, Kuchenecke)* wedge
c *(inf) (= Gegend)* corner, area; *(von Stadt)* quarter, area; *(= Strecke)* way; **eine ~** *(fig: = viel)* quite a bit; **eine ganze ~ entfernt** quite a (long) way away, a fair way away; **eine (ganze) ~ älter/billiger/größer** (quite) a bit older/cheaper/bigger; **aus welcher ~ kommst du?** what part of the world are you from?

Ecken-: **Ecken|ste|her(in)** M(F) *(inf)* loafer *(inf)*; **Ecken|ver|hält|nis** NT *(Ftbl)* number of corners per team; **sie liegen nach dem ~ vorn** they're ahead on corners

Ecker ['ɛkɐ] F -, -n *(Bot)* beechnut

Eck-: **Eck|fah|ne** F *(Sport)* corner flag; **Eck|fens|ter** NT corner window; **Eck|grund|stück** NT corner plot; **Eck|haus** NT house at *or* on the corner; *(= Reiheneckhaus)* end house

eckig ['ɛkɪç] ADJ angular; *Tisch, Brot, Klammer, Kinn, Mund* square; *(= spitz)* sharp; *(fig) Bewegung, Gang* jerky

-eckig ADJ *suf (fünf- und mehreckig)* -cornered; **achteckig** eight-cornered → **dreieckig, viereckig**

Eck-: **Eck|knei|pe** F *(inf)* pub *(Brit)* or bar on the corner; **Eck|la|den** M shop on a corner, corner shop; **Eck|lohn** M basic rate of pay; **Eck|pfei|ler** M corner pillar; *(fig)* cornerstone; **Eck|pfos|ten** M corner post; **Eck|platz** M *(in Zug etc)* corner seat; *(in Theater etc)* end seat, seat at the end of a row; **Eck|schrank** M corner cupboard; **Eck|stein** M **a** *(lit, fig)* cornerstone **b** *(Cards)* diamonds *pl*; **Eck|stoß** M *(Sport)* corner; **einen ~ ausführen** to take a corner; **Eck|stun|de** F *(Sch)* first/last lesson of the day; **~n** lessons at the start and end of the day; **Eck|tisch** M corner table; **Eck|turm** M corner tower; **Eck|wert** M *(Econ)* benchmark figure; *(fig)* basis; **Eck|wurf** M *(beim Handball)* corner (throw); **Eck|zahn** M canine tooth; **Eck|zim|mer** NT corner room; **Eck|zins** M *(Fin)* minimum lending rate

Ec|lair [e'klɛ:ɐ] NT -s, -s *(Cook)* eclair

Eco|no|my|klas|se [i'kɔnəmɪ-] F economy class; *(Aviat auch)* coach class *(esp US)*; **~ fliegen** to fly coach

EC-Scheck [e:'tse:-] M = **Euroscheck**

Ecs|ta|sy ['ɛkstəzi] NT -, *no pl (= Droge)* ecstasy

Ecs|ta|sy: **Ecs|ta|sy|pil|le** F ecstasy pill; **Ecs|ta|sy|sze|ne** F ecstasy scene; **Ecs|ta|sy|tab|let|te** F ecstasy tablet

Ecu [e'ku:] M -(s), -(s) ecu

Ecu|a|dor [ekua'do:ɐ] NT -s Ecuador

ecu|a|do|ri|a|nisch [ekuado'ria:nɪʃ] ADJ Ecuadorian

Ed. *abbr von* **Edition**

ed. *abbr von* **edidit** = **herausgegeben**

Eda|mer (Kä|se) ['e:damɐ] M -s, - Edam (cheese)

edc-Ser|vice [e:de:'tse:zø:ɐvɪs, -zœrvɪs] M *(Fin)* edc service

Ed|da ['ɛda] F -, **Ed|den** ['ɛdn] *(Liter)* Edda

edel ['e:dl] ADJ **a** *(attr: = vornehm, adlig)* noble **b** *(= hochwertig)* precious; *Hölzer* precious, fine; *Rosen, Speisen* fine; *Wein* noble, fine; *Pferd* thoroughbred **c** *(= edel geformt, harmonisch)* noble; *Nase* regal, aristocratic **d** *(fig) Gesinnung, Mensch, Tat* noble; *(= großherzig)* noble, generous → **Spender(in)** ADV *eingerichtet* classically; *dinieren* exclusively; **~ gestylt** with a classic design; **~ geformte Züge** classic features; **er denkt ~** he has noble thoughts

Edel- *in cpds (= hochwertig)* high-grade; *(pej)* fancy *(pej inf)*, posh *(inf)*; **Edel|fäu|le** F *(bei Weintrauben)* noble rot; *(bei Käse)* (veins *pl* of) mould *(Brit) or* mold *(US)*; **Edel|frau** F *(Hist)* noblewoman; **Edel|fräu|lein** NT *(Hist)* unmarried noblewoman; **Edel|gas** NT rare gas; **Edel|holz** NT high-grade wood; **Edel|kas|ta|nie** F sweet *or* Spanish chestnut; **Edel|kitsch** M *(iro)* pretentious rubbish *or* kitsch; **Edel|mann** M *pl* **-leute** *(Hist)* noble(man); **Edel|me|tall** NT precious metal; **Edel|mut** M *(liter)* magnanimity; **edel|mü|tig** [-my:tɪç] ADJ *(liter)* magnanimous; **Edel|nut|te** F *(iro)* high-class tart; **Edel|pilz** M mushroom; *(in Käse, auf Weintrauben)* mould *(Brit)*, mold *(US)*; **Edel|pilz|kä|se** M blue (vein) cheese, mould-ripened *(Brit) or* mold-ripened *(US)* cheese *(spec)*; **Edel|rost** M patina; **Edel|schnul|ze** F *(iro)* sentimental ballad; **Edel|stahl** M high-grade steel; **Edel|stein** M precious stone; *(geschliffener auch)* jewel, gem; **edel|süß** ADJ **~er Wein/Paprika** sweet wine/paprika; **Edel|tan|ne** F noble fir; **Edel|weiß** ['e:dlvais] NT -(es), -e edelweiss

Ede|ling ['e:dəlɪŋ] M -s, -e *(Hist)* (Germanic) nobleman

Edel-: **Edel|knap|pe** M *(Hist)* squire; **Edel|reis** NT scion

Eden ['e:dn] NT -s, *no pl* Eden; **der Garten ~** *(Bibl)* the Garden of Eden

edie|ren [e'di:rən] *ptp* **ediert** VT to edit

Edikt [e'dɪkt] NT -(e)s, -e *(Hist)* edict

edi|tier|bar ADJ editable

edi|tie|ren [edi'ti:rən] *ptp* **editiert** VT to edit

Edi|tier|funk|ti|on F *(Comput)* editing function

Edi|tier|mo|dus M *(Comput)* editing mode

Edi|ti|on [edi'tsio:n] F -, -en *(= das Herausgeben)* editing; *(= die Ausgabe)* edition

Edi|tor ['ɛdito:ɐ] M -s, -en [-'to:rən] *(Comput)* editor

Edi|tor ['e:dito:ɐ] M -s, -en [-'to:rən], **Edi|to|rin** [-'to:rɪn] F -, -nen editor

Edi|to|ri|al [edi'to:ria:l] NT -s, -s editorial

edi|to|risch [edi'to:rɪʃ] ADJ editorial

Ed|le(r) ['e:dlə] MF *decl as adj* **a** *(= Mann)* noble(man); *(= Frau)* noblewoman **b** *(in Namen)* **Ulf ~r von Trautenau** Lord Ulf von Trautenau; **Johanna ~ von Fürstenberg** Lady Johanna von Fürstenberg **c** *(fig geh: = edler Mensch)* noble person

Edu|ard ['e:duart] M -s Edward

Edu|tain|ment [edu'te:nmənt] NT -s, *no pl* edutainment

EDV [e:de:'fau] F - *abbr von* **elektronische Datenverarbeitung** EDP

EDV-: **EDV-An|la|ge** F EDP *or* computer system; **EDV-Bran|che** F data-processing business; **EDV-Fach|frau** F, **EDV-Fach|mann** M computer specialist; **EDV-Kennt|nis|se** PL computing expertise *sing or* know-how *sing (inf)*; **~ haben** to be computer-literate

EEG [e:le:'ge:] NT -, -s *abbr von* **Elektroenzephalogramm** EEG

Efeu ['e:fɔy] M -s, *no pl* ivy; **mit ~ bewachsen** covered in ivy, ivy-clad *(liter)*, ivy-covered

efeu|be|wach|sen ADJ ivy-covered, covered in ivy *pred*, ivy-clad *(liter)*

Eff|eff [ɛf'lɛf, 'ɛf'lɛf, 'ɛflɛf] NT -, *no pl (inf)* **etw aus dem ~ können** to be able to do sth standing on one's head *(inf) or* just like that *(inf)*; **etw aus dem ~ beherrschen/kennen** to know sth inside out

Ef|fekt [ɛ'fɛkt] M -(e)s, -e effect; **der ~ war gleich null** the effect was absolutely nil *(Brit) or* zero *(US)*, it had no effect whatsoever

Ef|fekt|be|leuch|tung F special lighting; *(Theat)* special effect lighting

Ef|fek|ten [ɛ'fɛktn] PL *(Fin)* stocks and bonds *pl*

Ef|fek|ten-: **Ef|fek|ten|bör|se** F stock exchange; **Ef|fek|ten|han|del** M stock dealing; **im ~ lässt sich viel Geld verdienen** there's a lot of money to be made in dealing on the stock exchange; **Ef|fek|ten|mak|ler(in)** M(F) stockbroker; **Ef|fek|ten|markt** M stock market

Ef|fekt|ha|sche|rei [-haʃə'rai] F -, -en *(inf)* cheap showmanship

ef|fek|tiv [ɛfɛk'ti:f] ADJ **a** effective **b** *(= tatsächlich)* actual; **~e Verzinsung** *or* **Rendite** net yield ADV *(= bestimmt)* actually; **ich weiß ~, dass ...** I know for a fact that ...; **~ nicht/kein** absolutely not/no

Ef|fek|tiv|ge|schäft NT *(Comm)* spot transaction

Ef|fek|ti|vi|tät [ɛfɛktivi'tɛ:t] F -, *no pl* effectiveness

Ef|fek|tiv-: **Ef|fek|tiv|lohn** M actual wage; **Ef|fek|tiv|ver|zin|sung** F redemption yield

ef|fekt|voll ADJ effective

ef|fe|mi|niert [ɛfemi'ni:ɐt] ADJ *(geh)* effeminate

Ef|fet [ɛ'fe:] M OR NT -s, -s *(Billard)* side; **den Ball mit ~ schießen** to put side on a ball

ef|fi|zi|ent [ɛfi'tsiɛnt] ADJ efficient ADV efficiently

Ef|fi|zi|enz [ɛfi'tsiɛnts] F -, -en efficiency

EFTA ['ɛfta] F *abbr von* **European Free Trade Association** EFTA

EG [e:'ge:] F - *abbr von* **Europäische Gemeinschaft** EC

egal [e'ga:l] ✪ 34.5 ADJ, ADV **a** *pred (= gleichgültig)* **das ist ~** that doesn't matter, that doesn't make any difference; **das ist mir ganz ~** it's all the same to me; *(= beides ist mir gleich)* I don't mind (either way), it doesn't make any difference to me; *(= es kümmert mich nicht)* I don't care, I couldn't care less; **ob du willst oder nicht, das ist mir ganz ~** I don't care whether you want to or not; **~ ob/wo/wie** it doesn't matter whether/where/how, no matter whether/where/how; **ihm ist alles ~** he doesn't care about anything
b *(inf) (= gleichartig)* the same, identical; *(= gleich groß)* the same size; *(= gleichmäßig) Rocksaum* even; **~ gearbeitet sein** to be the same, to match; **die Bretter ~ schneiden** to cut the planks (to) the same size
c *(inf: = glatt) Holzfläche* smooth
ADV *(dial inf: = ständig)* non-stop

ega|li|sie|ren [egali'zi:rən] *ptp* **egalisiert** VT *(Sport) Rekord* to equal; **er egalisierte den Vorsprung des Gegners** he levelled *(Brit) or* lev-

eled *(US)* with his opponent, he closed his opponent's lead
ega|li|tär [egali'tɛːɐ] ADJ *(geh)* egalitarian
Ega|li|tät [egali'tɛːt] F -, *no pl (liter)* equality
egal|weg ADV *(dial inf)* = **egal ADV**
EG- [eː'geː-]: **EG-Be|am|te(r)** M *decl as adj*, **EG-Be|am|tin** F EC official; **EG-Be|hör|de** F EC institution; **EG-ein|heit|lich** ADJ harmonized within the EC
Egel ['eːgl] M **-s, -** *(Zool)* leech
Eger|ling ['eːgɐlɪŋ] **-s, -e** *(Bot: = Champignon)* mushroom; **brauner ~** chestnut *or* brown-cap mushroom
Eg|ge ['ɛgə] F **-, -n** **a** *(Agr)* harrow **b** *(Tex)* selvedge
eg|gen ['ɛgn] VT *(Agr)* to harrow
EG- [eː'geː-]: **EG-Kom|mis|si|on** F EC Commission; **EG-Mi|nis|ter|rat** M Council of Ministers; **EG-Mit|glieds|land** NT EC member state; **EG-Norm** F EC standard
Ego ['eːgo] NT **-s, -s** *(Psych)* ego
Ego|is|mus [ego'ɪsmʊs] M **-, Egoismen** [-mən] ego(t)ism
Ego|ist [ego'ɪst] M **-en, -en**, **Ego|is|tin** [-'ɪstɪn] F **-, -nen** ego(t)ist
ego|is|tisch [ego'ɪstɪʃ] ADJ ego(t)istical ADV ego(t)istically, like an egoist
Ego-: **Ego|ma|ne** [ego'maːnə] M **-n, -n**, **Ego|ma|nin** [-'maːnɪn] F **-, -nen** egomaniac; **Ego|ma|nie** [egoma'niː] F, *no pl* egomania; **Ego|trip** ['eːgo-] M *(inf)* ego trip *(inf)*; **Ego|zent|rik** [ego'tsɛntrɪk] F **-**, *no pl* egocentricity; **Ego|zent|ri|ker** [ego'tsɛntrikɐ] M **-s, -**, **Ego|zent|ri|ke|rin** [-ərɪn] F **-, -nen** egocentric; **ego|zent|risch** [ego'tsɛntrɪʃ] ADJ egocentric; **Ego|zent|ris|mus** M **-**, *no pl* egocentrism
EG-Staat [eː'geː-] M EC country
eh [eː] INTERJ hey CONJ = **ehe** ADV **a** *(= früher, damals)* **seit eh und je** since the year dot *(Brit inf)*, for ages *(inf)*; **wie eh und je** just as *or* like before; **es war alles wie eh und je** everything was just as it always had been **b** *(esp S Ger, Aus: = sowieso)* anyway; **ich komme eh nicht dazu** I won't get (a)round to it anyway
e. h., eh. *abbr von* **ehrenhalber**
ehe ['eːə] CONJ *(= bevor)* before, ere *(old, liter)*; **~ ich es vergesse ...** before I forget ...; **wir können nichts tun, ~ wir (nicht) Nachricht haben** we can't do anything until *or* before we get some news; **~ (dass) ich mich auf andere verlasse, mache ich lieber alles selbst** rather than rely on others, I would prefer to do everything myself
Ehe ['eːə] F **-, -n** marriage; **er versprach ihr die ~** he promised to marry her; **in den Stand der ~ treten** *(form)* **die ~ eingehen** *(form)* to enter into matrimony *(form)*; **mit jdm die ~ eingehen** *or* **schließen** *(form)* to marry sb, to enter into marriage with sb *(form)*; **die ~ vollziehen** to consummate a/their/the marriage; **eine glückliche/unglückliche ~ führen** to have a happy/an unhappy marriage; **die ~ brechen** *(form)* to commit adultery; **~ zur linken Hand** *(Hist)*, **morganatische ~** *(Hist)* morganatic *or* left-handed marriage; **sie hat drei Kinder aus erster ~** she has three children from her first marriage; **Kinder in die ~ mitbringen** to bring children into the marriage; **ein außerhalb der ~ geborenes Kind** a child born out of wedlock; **er ist in zweiter ~ mit einer Adligen verheiratet** his second wife is an aristocrat; **in zweiter ~ war er mit Uta Schwarz verheiratet** his second marriage was to Uta Schwarz, his second wife was Uta Schwarz; **ihre ~ ist 1975 geschieden worden** they were divorced in 1975; **sie leben in wilder ~** *(dated, hum)* they are living in sin; **~ ohne Trauschein** common-law marriage; **sie leben in einer ~ ohne Trauschein** they live together; **eine offene ~** an open marriage → **Hafen b**, **Bund a**
Ehe-: **ehe|ähn|lich** ADJ *(form)* similar to marriage; **in einer ~en Gemeinschaft leben** to cohabit *(form)*, to live together as man and wife; **Ehe|an|bah|nung** F marriage-broking; *(= Institut)* marriage bureau; **Ehe|an|bah|nungs|in|sti|tut** NT marriage bureau; **Ehe|be|ra|ter(in)** M(F) marriage guidance counsellor *(Brit) or* counselor *(US)*; **Ehe|be|ra|tung** F *(= das Beraten)* marriage guidance (counselling *(Brit) or* counseling *(US)*), couples therapy *(US)*; *(= Stelle)* marriage guidance council *(Brit)*, marriage counseling center *(US)*; **Ehe|be|ra|tungs|stel|le** F marriage guidance council *(Brit)*, marriage counseling center *(US)*; **Ehe|bett** NT double bed; *(fig)* marital bed; **ehe|bre|chen** VI *(infin only)* to commit adultery; **Ehe|bre|cher** M adulterer; **Ehe|bre|che|rin** F adulteress; **ehe|bre|che|risch** [-brɛçərɪʃ] ADJ adulterous; **Ehe|bruch** M adultery; **Ehe|bund** M *pl* **-bünde**, **Ehe|bünd|nis** NT *(form)* bond of matrimony; **ehe|fä|hig** ADJ *(Jur)* marriageable, fit to marry *pred*; **Ehe|fä|hig|keit** F, *no pl (Jur)* marriageability; **Ehe|fä|hig|keits|zeug|nis** NT *(Jur)* certificate of marriageability; **Ehe|frau** F wife; **~en haben es nicht leicht** married women have a hard time; **Ehe|gat|te** M *(form)* husband, spouse *(form)*; **Ehe|gat|ten|split|ting** NT *(Steuerrecht) taxation of the total income of a married couple on the basis of equal halves*; **Ehe|gat|tin** F *(form)* wife, spouse *(form)*; **Ehe|ge|lüb|de** NT wedding vows *pl*; **Ehe|ge|mein|schaft** F *(form)* wedlock *(form)*, matrimony; **Ehe|glück** NT married bliss *or* happiness; **Ehe|ha|fen** M *(hum)* **in den ~ einlaufen** to plight one's troth *(old, hum)*; **Ehe|hin|der|nis** NT *(Jur)* impediment to marriage; **Ehe|kan|di|dat(in)** M(F) *(inf)* prospective husband/wife; *(kurz vor Eheschließung)* husband-to-be/wife-to-be; **Ehe|ko|mö|die** F marital comedy; **Ehe|krach** M marital row; **Ehe|krieg** M marital feud; **Ehe|kri|se** F marital crisis; **Ehe|krüp|pel** M *(hum inf)* casualty of married life *(hum)*; **Ehe|le|ben** NT married life; **Ehe|leu|te** PL *(form)* married couple; **ich vermiete diese Wohnung an die ~ A. und P. Meier** I hereby let this apartment to Mr and Mrs Meier; **die jungen ~** the young couple
ehe|dem ['eːə'deːm] ADV *(old)* formerly; **seit ~** since time immemorial
Ehe-: **Ehe|ge|spons** M OR NT *(hum)* spouse *(hum)*;; **Ehe|hälf|te** F *(hum inf)* **meine bessere ~** my better half *(inf)*
ehe|lich ['eːəlɪç] ADJ marital; *Pflichten, Rechte auch* conjugal; *Kind* legitimate; **für ~ erklären** to (declare or make) legitimate; **das ~e Leben** married life; **die ~en Freuden** the joys of marriage
ehe|li|chen ['eːəlɪçn] VT *(old, hum)* to wed *(old)*, to espouse *(old, form)*
Ehe|lich|keit F **-**, *no pl (von Kind)* legitimacy
Ehe|lich|keits|er|klä|rung F *(Jur)* declaration of legitimacy
ehe|los ADJ unmarried, single
Ehe|lo|sig|keit F **-**, *no pl* unmarried state; *(Rel)* celibacy; **~ hat auch ihre Vorteile** being single *or* unmarried also has its advantages
ehem., ehm. *abbr von* **ehemals**
ehe|ma|lig ['eːəmaːlɪç] ADJ *attr* former; **die Ehemaligen einer Schulklasse** the ex-pupils *or* former pupils of a class; **die Ehemaligen seiner Klasse** his former classmates; **ein ~er Häftling** an ex-convict; **ein Ehemaliger** *(inf)* an old lag *(Brit inf)*, an ex-con *(inf)*; **mein Ehemaliger/meine Ehemalige** *(hum inf)* my ex *(inf)*
ehe|mals ['eːəmals] ADV *(form)* formerly, previously; **die ~ deutschen Ostgebiete** the eastern territories which were formerly German
Ehe-: **Ehe|mann** M *pl* **-männer** husband; **seitdem er ~ ist** since he has been married; **ehe|mü|de** ADJ tired of married life *pred*; **ehe|mün|dig** ADJ *(Jur)* of marriageable age; **Ehe|mün|dig|keit** F, *no pl (Jur)* marriageable age; **die ~ tritt im Alter von 18 Jahren ein** a person becomes legally marriageable at the age of 18; **Ehe|na|me** M married name; **Ehe|paar** NT (married) couple; **Ehe|part|ner(in)** M(F) *(= Ehemann)* husband; *(= Ehefrau)* wife; **beide ~** both partners (in the marriage)
eher ['eːɐ] ADV **a** *(= früher)* earlier, sooner; **je ~, je** *or* **desto lieber** the sooner the better; **nicht ~ als bis/als** not until/before **b** *(= lieber)* rather, sooner; *(= wahrscheinlicher)* more likely; *(= leichter)* more easily; **alles ~ als das!** anything but that!; **~ verzichte ich** *or* **will ich verzichten, als dass ...** I would rather *or* sooner do without than ...; **umso ~, als** the more so *or* all the more because *or* as; **das lässt sich schon ~ hören** that sounds more like it *(inf)*, that sounds better; **das könnte man schon ~ sagen, das ist ~ möglich** that is more likely *or* probable; **diese Prüfung kannst du ~ bestehen** this exam will be easier for you to pass **c** *(= vielmehr)* more; **er ist ~ faul als dumm** he's more lazy than stupid, he's lazy rather than stupid; **er ist alles ~ als das/ein Engel/dumm** he's anything but that/an angel/stupid
Ehe-: **Ehe|recht** NT marriage law; **Ehe|ring** M wedding ring
ehern ['eːɐn] ADJ *(liter) (lit)* made of ore; *(fig)* iron; **mit ~er Stirn** boldly; *(= tollkühn auch)* brazenly
Ehe-: **Ehe|ro|man** M *novel about marriage*; **Ehe|sa|che** F *(Jur)* matrimonial matter; **Ehe|sak|ra|ment** NT marriage sacrament, sacrament of marriage; **Ehe|schei|dung** F divorce; **Ehe|schei|dungs|kla|ge** F *(= Prozess)* divorce case; **die ~ einreichen** to file a divorce petition, to file a petition for divorce; **ehe|scheu** ADJ marriage-shy, not keen on marriage *or* getting married *pred*, wedding-shy *(US inf)*; **Ehe|schlie|ßung** F marriage ceremony, wedding
ehest [eːəst] ADV *(Aus)* as soon as possible
Ehe|stand M, *no pl* matrimony, marriage
Ehe|stands|dar|le|hen NT *low interest bank loan given to newly married couples*
ehes|tens ['eːəstns] ADV **a** *(= frühestens)* **~ morgen** tomorrow at the earliest; **ich kann ~ heute Abend kommen** the earliest I can come is this evening **b** *(Aus: = baldigst)* as soon as possible, at the earliest opportunity
ehes|te(r, s) ['eːəstə] ADJ **bei ~r Gelegenheit** at the earliest opportunity ADV **am ~n** *(= am liebsten)* best of all; *(= am wahrscheinlichsten)* most likely; *(= am leichtesten)* the easiest; *(= zuerst)* first; **am ~n würde ich mir ein Auto kaufen** what I'd like best (of all) would be to buy myself a car; **keins der Kleider gefällt mir so richtig, am ~n würde ich noch das rote nehmen** I don't really like any of the dresses, but if I had to choose I'd take the red one; **das geht wohl am ~n** that's probably the best way; **er ist am ~n gekommen** he was the first (person) to come
Ehe-: **Ehe|stif|ter(in)** M(F) matchmaker; **Ehe|streit** M marital row *or* argument; **Ehe|tra|gö|die** F marital tragedy; **Ehe|ver|kün|di|gung** F, **Ehe|ver|kün|dung** F *(Sw)* marriage announcement; **Ehe|ver|mitt|ler(in)** M(F) *(= Person)* marriage broker; *(= Büro)* marriage bureau; **Ehe|ver|mitt|lung** F marriage-broking; *(= Büro)* marriage bureau; **Ehe|ver|mitt|lungs|in|sti|tut** NT marriage bureau; **Ehe|ver|spre|chen** NT *(Jur)* promise to marry; **Bruch des ~s** breach of promise; **Ehe|ver|trag** M marriage contract, prenuptial agreement, prenups *(US inf)*; **Ehe|weib** NT *(old: = Ehefrau)* wife; *(hum inf)* old woman *(inf)*; **ehe|wid|rig** ADJ *(form) Beziehungen* extramarital, adulterous; *Verhalten* constituting a matrimonial offence *(Brit) or* offense *(US)*
Ehr|ab|schnei|der(in) M(F) calumniator *(form)*
Ehr|auf|fas|sung F concept of honour *(Brit) or* honor *(US)*
ehr|bar ADJ *(= achtenswert)* respectable; *(= ehrenhaft)* honourable *(Brit)*, honorable *(US)*; *Beruf* reputable, respectable
Ehr|bar|keit ['eːɐbaːɐkait] F **-**, *no pl (= Geachtetheit)* respectability; **die ~ dieses Mannes steht**

außer Zweifel there can be no doubt that this is an honourable *(Brit) or* honorable *(US)* man

Ehr|be|griff M sense of honour *(Brit) or* honor *(US)*

Eh|re [ˈeːrə] ✪ 52.1 F -, -n honour *(Brit)*, honor *(US)*; *(= Ruhm)* glory; **etw in ~n halten** to treasure *or* cherish sth; **damit/mit ihm können Sie ~ einlegen** that/he does you credit, that/he is a credit to you; **er wollte mit dieser Rede ~ einlegen** he was wanting to gain kudos with this speech; **für jdn/etw ~ einlegen** to bring hono(u)r on sb/sth; **bei jdm mit etw ~ einlegen** to make a good impression on sb with sth; **jdm ~ machen** to do sb credit; **jdm wenig ~ machen** not to do sb any credit; **jdm/einer Sache zur ~ gereichen** to do sb/sth credit; **auf ~!** *(obs)*, **bei meiner ~!** *(obs)* by my troth! *(obs)*, 'pon my oath! *(obs)*; **auf ~ und Gewissen** on my/his *etc* hono(u)r; **auf ~ und Gewissen?** cross your heart? *(inf)*, on your hono(u)r?; **auf ~ und Gewissen: ich bin es nicht gewesen!** cross my heart *(inf) or* I promise you, it wasn't me; **zu seiner ~ muss ich sagen, dass ...** in his favour *(Brit) or* favor *(US)* I must say (that) ...; **etw um der ~ willen tun** to do sth for the hono(u)r of it; **das musst du schon um deiner ~ willen machen** you should do that as a matter of hono(u)r; **ein Mann von ~** a man of hono(u)r; **keine ~ im Leib haben** *(dated)* to have not a shred of self-respect; **er ist in ~n ergraut** *(geh)* **er ist in ~n alt geworden** he has had a long and hono(u)rable life; **sein Wort/seine Kenntnisse in allen ~n, aber ...** I don't doubt his word/his knowledge, but ...; **sich** *(dat)* **etw zur ~ anrechnen** to count sth an hono(u)r; **sich** *(dat)* **es zur ~ anrechnen, dass ...** to feel hono(u)red that ..., to count it an hono(u)r that ...; **das rechne ich ihm zur ~ an** I consider that a point in his favour *(Brit) or* favor *(US)*; **mit wem habe ich die ~?** *(iro, form)* with whom do I have the pleasure of speaking? *(form)*; **was verschafft mir die ~?** *(iro, form)* to what do I owe the hono(u)r (of your visit)?; **es ist mir eine besondere ~, ...** *(form)* it is a great hono(u)r for me ...; **um der Wahrheit die ~ zu geben ...** *(geh)* to be perfectly honest ..., to tell you the truth ...; **wir geben uns die ~, Sie zu ... einzuladen** *(form)* we request the hono(u)r of your company at ... *(form)*; **zu ~n** *(+gen)* in hono(u)r of; **darf ich um die ~ bitten, Sie zu begleiten?** *(form)* may I have the hono(u)r of accompanying you? *(form)*, would you do me the hono(u)r of allowing me to accompany you? *(form)*; **Habe die ~!** *(dated Aus)* *(als Gruß)* hello; *(beim Abschied)* goodbye; *(als Ausdruck des Erstaunens)* good heavens; **~, wem ~ gebührt** *(prov)* credit where credit is due *(prov)*; **~ sei Gott in der Höhe** *(Bibl)* glory to God in the highest → **letzte(r, s) a, militärisch**

eh|ren [ˈeːrən] VT *(= Achtung erweisen, würdigen)* to honour *(Brit)*, to honor *(US)*; **etw ehrt jdn** sth does sb credit *or* hono(u)r; **dein Besuch/Ihr Vertrauen ehrt mich** I am hono(u)red by your visit/trust; **der Präsident ehrte den Preisträger in einer Rede** the president made a speech in hono(u)r of the prizewinner; **der Preisträger wurde in einer Rede geehrt** a speech was made *or* there was a speech in hono(u)r of the prizewinner; **jdm ein ~des Andenken bewahren** to treasure sb's memory; **du sollst Vater und Mutter ~** *(Bibl)* hono(u)r thy father and thy mother → *auch* **geehrt**

Eh|ren-: **Eh|ren|amt** NT honorary office *or* position; **eh|ren|amt|lich** ADJ honorary; *Helfer, Tätigkeit* voluntary; **~er Richter** ≈ member of the jury ADV in an honorary capacity; **Eh|ren|amt|lich|keit** F *(= ehrenamtlicher Charakter)* voluntary nature; **Eh|ren|be|zei|gung** [-bətsaiɡʊŋ] F -, -en, **Eh|ren|be|zeu|gung** [-bətsɔyɡʊŋ] F -, -en *(Mil)* salute; **jdm die ~ erweisen/verweigern** to salute/refuse to salute sb

Eh|ren|bür|ger(in) M(F) freeman *(Brit)*, honorary citizen; **er wurde zum ~ der Stadt ernannt** he was given the freedom of the city

Eh|ren|bür|ger|recht NT freedom; **die Stadt verlieh ihm das ~** he was given the freedom of the city

Eh|ren-: **Eh|ren|dok|tor(in)** M(F) honorary doctor; **Eh|ren|dok|tor|wür|de** F honorary doctorate; **ihm wurde die ~ der Universität Wien verliehen** he was made an honorary doctor of *or* given an honorary doctorate by the University of Vienna; **Eh|ren|er|klä|rung** F *(von Beleidiger)* (formal) apology; *(von dritter Seite)* statement in defence (of sb's honour); **ich werde eine ~ für Sie abgeben** I will make a statement in your defence *(Brit) or* defense *(US)*; *(nach erfolgter Beleidigung)* I will make (you) a formal apology; **Eh|ren|for|ma|ti|on** F guard of honour *(Brit) or* honor *(US)*, honour *(Brit) or* honor *(US)* guard; **Eh|ren|gar|de** F guard of honour *(Brit) or* honor *(US)*; **Eh|ren|gast** M guest of honour *(Brit) or* honor *(US)*; **Eh|ren|ge|leit** NT guard of honour *(Brit) or* honor *(US)*; **Eh|ren|ge|richt** NT tribunal; **eh|ren|haft** ADJ honourable *(Brit)*, honorable *(US)*; **Eh|ren|haf|tig|keit** [ˈeːrənhaftɪçkait] F -, *no pl* sense of honour *(Brit) or* honor *(US)*; **eh|ren|hal|ber** ADV **er wurde ~ zum Vorsitzenden auf Lebenszeit ernannt** he was made honorary president for life; **Doktor ~** *(abbr* **e. h.***)* Doctor honoris causa *(form)*, honorary doctor; **Eh|ren|han|del** M *pl* **-händel** *(old)* **eine Form des ~s war das Duell** the duel was one way of settling an affair of honour *(Brit) or* honor *(US)*;; **Eh|ren|kar|te** F complimentary ticket; **Eh|ren|ko|dex** M code of honour *(Brit) or* honor *(US)*; **Eh|ren|kom|pa|nie** F *(Mil)* guard of honour *(Brit) or* honor *(US)*; **Eh|ren|krän|kung** F insult, affront; **Eh|ren|le|gi|on** F legion of honour *(Brit) or* honor *(US)*; **Eh|ren|lo|ge** F VIP box; *(für königliche Gäste)* royal box; *(in Stadion)* directors' box; **Eh|ren|mal** NT *pl* **-male** *or* **-mäler** memorial; **Eh|ren|mann** M *pl* **-männer** man of honour *(Brit) or* honor *(US)*; **ein sauberer ~** *(pej)* a blackguard *(pej)*, a scoundrel; **Eh|ren|me|dail|le** F medal of honour *(Brit) or* honor *(US)*; **Eh|ren|mit|glied** NT honorary member; **Eh|ren|mit|glied|schaft** F honorary membership; **Eh|ren|mord** M honour *(Brit) or* honor *(US)* killing; **Eh|ren|na|del** F badge of honour *(Brit) or* honor *(US)*; **Eh|ren|pflicht** F bounden duty; **Eh|ren|platz** M *(lit)* place *or* seat of honour *(Brit) or* honor *(US)*; *(fig)* special place; **Eh|ren|prä|si|dent(in)** M(F) honorary president; **Eh|ren|preis** M *(= Auszeichnung)* prize; *(= Anerkennung)* consolation prize; **Eh|ren|preis** M OR NT **-es, -** *(Bot)* speedwell, veronica; **Eh|ren|rech|te** PL *(Jur)* civil rights *pl*; **Verlust/Aberkennung der bürgerlichen ~** loss/forfeiture of one's civil rights; **Eh|ren|ret|tung** F, *no pl* retrieval of one's honour *(Brit) or* honor *(US)*; **eine ~ versuchen** to attempt to retrieve one's hono(u)r; **zu seiner ~ sei gesagt, dass ...** in his favour *(Brit) or* favor *(US)* it must be said that ...; **eh|ren|rüh|rig** ADJ defamatory; **etw als ~ empfinden** to regard sth as an insult to one's honour *(Brit) or* honor *(US)*; **Eh|ren|run|de** F *(Sport)* lap of honour *(Brit) or* honor *(US)*; *(fig inf: = wiederholtes Schuljahr)* repeat year; **Eh|ren|sa|che** F matter of honour *(Brit) or* honor *(US)*; **~!** *(inf)* you can count on me; **das ist für mich ~!** that's a matter of hono(u)r for me; **Eh|ren|sa|lut** M, **Eh|ren|sal|ve** F salute; **Eh|ren|schuld** F debt of honour *(Brit) or* honor *(US)*; **Eh|ren|sold** M honorarium; **Eh|ren|ta|fel** F **a** *(= Tisch)* top table **b** *(= Gedenktafel)* roll of honour *(Brit) or* honor *(US)*; **Eh|ren|tag** M *(= Geburtstag)* birthday; *(= großer Tag)* big *or* great day; **zum heutigen ~** on this special day; **Eh|ren|ti|tel** M honorary title; **Eh|ren|tor** NT, **Eh|ren|tref|fer** M *(Sport)* consolation goal; **Eh|ren|tri|bü|ne** F VIP rostrum *(Brit) or* platform; **Eh|ren|ur|kun|de** F certificate *(for outstanding performance in sport)*; **eh|ren|voll** ADJ *Friede, Beruf, Niederlage* honourable *(Brit)*, honorable *(US)*; *Aufgabe auch* noble; **Eh|ren|vor|sit|zen|de(r)** MF *decl as adj* honorary chairman/-woman; **Eh|ren|wa|che** F guard of honour *(Brit) or* honor *(US)*; **eh|ren|wert** ADJ *Mensch, Absichten* honourable *(Brit)*, honorable *(US)*, worthy; **die ~e Gesellschaft** *(hum)* the Mafia; **Eh|ren|wort** NT *pl* **-worte** word of honour *(Brit) or* honor *(US)*; **(großes) ~!** *(inf)* cross my heart (and hope to die)! *(inf)*; **~?** *(inf)* cross your heart? *(inf)*; **mein ~!** you have my word; **sein ~ geben/halten/brechen** to give/keep/break one's word; **Urlaub auf ~** parole; **eh|ren|wört|lich** ADJ *Versprechen* solemn, faithful ADV on one's honour *(Brit) or* honor *(US)*; **Eh|ren|zei|chen** NT decoration

ehr|er|bie|tig [ˈeːɐ̯lɛɐ̯biːtɪç] ADJ respectful, deferential

Ehr|er|bie|tung [ˈeːɐ̯lɛɐ̯biːtʊŋ] F -, *no pl* respect, deference

Ehr|furcht F great *or* deep respect *(vor +dat* for); *(= fromme Scheu)* reverence *(vor +dat* for); **vor jdm/etw ~ haben** to respect/revere sb/sth, to have (great) respect for sb/sth; **von ~ ergriffen** overawed; **~ gebietend** awe-inspiring; *Stimme, Geste* authoritative; **er ist eine ~ gebietende Persönlichkeit** he's the kind of person who commands (one's) respect

ehr|furcht|ge|bie|tend [-ɡəbiːtnt] ADJ → **Ehrfurcht**

ehr|fürch|tig [-fʏrçtɪç], **ehr|furchts|voll** ADJ reverent; *Distanz* respectful

ehr|furchts|los ADJ irreverent

Ehr|furchts|lo|sig|keit F -, -en irreverence

Ehr|ge|fühl NT sense of honour *(Brit) or* honor *(US)*; *(= Selbstachtung)* self-respect; **etw aus falschem ~ heraus tun** to do sth out of a misplaced sense of hono(u)r

Ehr|geiz ✪ 35.2, 35.4 M ambition

ehr|gei|zig ADJ ambitious

Ehr|geiz|ling [ˈeːɐ̯ɡaitslɪŋ] M -s, -e *(pej inf)* pusher *(inf)*

ehr|lich [ˈeːɐ̯lɪç] ADJ, ADV honest; *Name* good; *Absicht, Zuneigung* sincere; **der ~e Finder bekommt 50 Euro** a reward of 50 euros will be given to anyone finding and returning this; **eine ~e Haut** *(inf)* an honest soul; **ich hatte die ~e Absicht zu kommen** I honestly did intend to come; **er hat ~e Absichten** *(inf)* his intentions are honourable *(Brit) or* honorable *(US)*; **~ währt am längsten** *(Prov)* honesty is the best policy *(Prov)*

ADV **a** *(= ohne Betrug)* **~ verdientes Geld** hard-earned money; **~ teilen** to share fairly; **~ gesagt ...** quite frankly *or* honestly ..., to be quite frank ...; **er meint es ~ mit uns** he is being honest with us; **~ spielen** *(Cards)* to play straight

b *(= wirklich)* honestly, really (and truly), truly; **ich bin ~ begeistert** I'm really thrilled; **~, ich habe nichts damit zu tun** honestly, I've got nothing to do with it; **~!** honestly!, really!

ehr|li|cher|wei|se [ˈeːɐ̯lɪçɐˈvaizə] ADV honestly, truly, in all honesty

Ehr|lich|keit F -, *no pl* honesty; *(von Absicht, Zuneigung)* sincerity; **sie zweifelte an der ~ seiner Absichten** she doubted the sincerity of his intentions; *(in Bezug auf Heirat)* she doubted that his intentions were honourable *(Brit) or* honorable *(US)*

Ehr-: **ehr|los** ADJ dishonourable *(Brit)*, dishonorable *(US)*; **Ehr|lo|sig|keit** F -, *no pl* *(= Schlechtigkeit)* infamy; **die ~ seines Verhaltens** his dishonourable *(Brit) or* dishonorable *(US)* conduct; **ehr|pus|se|lig** [-pʊsəlɪç], **ehr|puss|lig** [-pʊslɪç] ADJ *(inf)* sensitive about one's reputation; **ehr|sam** [ˈeːɐ̯zaːm] ADJ *(old)* = **ehrbar**; **Ehr|sucht** F *(old)* inordinate ambitiousness *or* ambition; **ehr|süch|tig** ADJ *(old)* inordinately ambitious

Eh|rung ['e:rʊŋ] F -, -en honour *(Brit)*, honor *(US)*

Ehr-: **ehr|ver|let|zend** ADJ *(geh)* insulting; **Ehr|ver|let|zung** F *(geh)* insult (to one's honour *(Brit)* or honor *(US)*); **Ehr|ver|lust** M loss of honour *(Brit)* or honor *(US)*; *(Jur)* loss of one's civil rights

Ehr|wür|den ['e:ɐvʏrdn] M -s, *no pl* Reverend; **Euer ~** Reverend Father; *(zu Äbtissin)* Reverend Mother

ehr|wür|dig ['e:ɐvʏrdɪç] ADJ venerable; **~e Mutter** *(Eccl)* Reverend Mother; **~er Vater** *(Eccl)* Reverend Father

Ehr|wür|dig|keit F venerability

ei [ai] INTERJ *(zärtlich)* there (there); *(old) (spöttisch)* well; *(bekräftigend)* oh; **(bei einem Kind/Tier) ei ei machen** to pet a child/an animal; **ei freilich** or **gewiss!** *(old)* but of course!

Ei [ai] NT -(e)s, -er **a** *(= Vogelei, Schlangenei)* egg; *(Physiol)* egg, ovum; **das Ei des Kolumbus finden** to come up with just the thing; **das ist das Ei des Kolumbus** that's just the thing or just what we want; **das Ei will klüger sein als die Henne** you're trying to teach your grandmother to suck eggs *(prov)*; **jdn wie ein rohes Ei behandeln** *(fig)* to handle sb with kid gloves; **wie auf Eiern gehen** *(inf)* to step gingerly; **wie aus dem Ei gepellt aussehen** *(inf)* to look spruce; **sie gleichen sich** or **einander wie ein Ei dem anderen** they are as alike as two peas (in a pod); **kümmere dich nicht um ungelegte Eier!** *(inf)* don't cross your bridges before you come to them! *(prov)*; **das sind ungelegte Eier!** *(inf)* we'll cross that bridge when we come to it *(prov)* → **dick**
b Eier PL *(dated sl) (= Geld)* euros; *(in GB)* quid *(inf)*; *(in US)* bucks *(inf)*; **das kostet seine 50 Eier** that'll cost a good 50 euros **c Eier** PL *(sl)* *(= Hoden)* balls *pl (sl)*; **ein Tritt in die Eier** a kick in the balls *(sl)*; **dicke Eier haben** *(sl: = Lust auf Sex)* to be choking *(Brit)* or gagging *(Brit)* or dying for it *(sl)* **d** *(Rugby sl)* ball, pill *(inf)*

eia|po|peia [aiapo'paia, 'aiapo'paia] INTERJ lullaby baby

EIB *abbr von* **Europäische Investitionsbank**

Ei|be ['aibə] F -, -n *(Bot)* yew

Ei|bisch ['aibɪʃ] M -(e)s, -e *(Bot)* marshmallow

Eich-: **Eich|amt** NT ≈ Weights and Measures Office *(Brit)*, ≈ Bureau of Standards *(US)*; **Eich|baum** M oak tree; **Eich|blatt|sa|lat** M oak-leaf lettuce

Ei|che ['aiçə] F -, -n oak; *(= Baum auch)* oak tree

Ei|chel ['aiçl] F -, -n **a** *(Bot)* acorn **b** *(Anat)* glans **c** *(Cards) suit in German playing cards equivalent to clubs*

Ei|chel|hä|her M jay

ei|chen ['aiçn] ADJ oak, oaken *(old)*

ei|chen VT to calibrate; **darauf bin ich geeicht!** *(inf)* that's right up my street *(inf)*

Ei|chen-: **Ei|chen|baum** M oak tree; **Ei|chen|holz** NT oak; **ein Tisch aus ~** an oak table; **Ei|chen|laub** NT oak leaves *pl* → **Ritterkreuz**; **Ei|chen|sarg** M oak(en) coffin; **Ei|chen|wald** M oakwood

Eich|hörn|chen NT, **Eich|kätz|chen** NT squirrel; **mühsam nährt sich das ~** *(inf)* one struggles on and little by little

Eich-: **Eich|maß** NT standard measure; *(= Gewicht)* standard weight; **Eich|pfahl** M *calibrated pole marking the maximum safe water level of a reservoir etc*; **Eich|stem|pel** M verification stamp; **Eich|strich** M official calibration; *(an Gläsern)* line measure; **ein Glas mit ~** a lined glass

Ei|chung ['aiçʊŋ] F -, -en calibration

Eid [ait] M -(e)s, -e [-də] oath; **einen ~ ablegen** or **leisten** or **schwören** to take or swear an oath; **einen ~ auf die Bibel/Verfassung leisten** to swear an oath on the Bible/the constitution; **darauf kann ich einen ~ schwören** I can swear to that, I can take my oath on that; **ich nehme es auf meinen ~, dass ...** I would be prepared to swear that ...; **jdm den ~ abnehmen** to administer the oath to sb, to take the oath from sb; **unter ~** under or on oath; **eine Erklärung an ~es statt abgeben** *(Jur)* to make a declaration in lieu of oath; **ich erkläre an ~es statt, dass ...** I do solemnly declare that ...

Ei|dam ['aidam] M -(e)s, -e *(obs)* son-in-law

Eid-: **Eid|bruch** M breach of one's oath; **einen ~ begehen** to break one's oath; **eid|brü|chig** ADJ **~ werden** to break one's oath

Ei|dech|se ['aidɛksə] F *(Zool)* lizard; *(Astron)* Lacerta; *(inf: = Hubwagen)* fork-lift truck

Ei|der-: **Ei|der|dau|nen** PL eiderdown *no pl*; **Ei|der|en|te** F eider (duck)

Ei|des-: **Ei|des|be|leh|rung** F *(Jur) caution as to the consequences of committing perjury*; **Ei|des|for|mel** F wording of the oath; **die ~ nachsprechen** to repeat the oath; **Ei|des|leis|tung** F swearing of the oath; **niemand kann zur ~ gezwungen werden** no-one can be forced to swear or take the oath; **ei|des|statt|lich** ADJ **eine ~e Erklärung** or **Versicherung abgeben** to make a declaration in lieu of an oath, to declare in lieu of an oath ADV **etw ~ erklären** to declare sth in lieu of an oath

Ei|de|tik [ai'de:tɪk] F -, *no pl (Psych)* eidetic ability

Ei|de|ti|ker [ai'de:tikɐ] M -s, -, **Ei|de|ti|ke|rin** [-ərɪn] F -, -nen eidetic, eidetiker

ei|de|tisch [ai'de:tɪʃ] ADJ eidetic

Eid|ge|nos|se ['ait-] M, **Eid|ge|nos|sin** F confederate; *(= Schweizer Eidgenosse)* Swiss citizen

Eid|ge|nos|sen|schaft F confederation; **Schweizerische ~** Swiss Confederation

eid|ge|nös|sisch [-gənœsɪʃ] ADJ confederate; *(= schweizerisch)* Swiss

eid|lich ['aitlɪç] ADJ sworn *attr*, given on or under oath; **er gab eine ~e Erklärung ab** he made a declaration on or under oath; *(schriftlich)* he swore an affidavit ADV on or under oath; **~ gebunden** bound by (one's) oath

Ei|dot|ter M OR NT egg yolk

Ei|er-: **Ei|er|be|cher** M eggcup; **Ei|er|bri|kett** NT ovoid *(of coal)*; **Ei|er|far|be** F *paint used to decorate Easter eggs*; **Ei|er|frucht** F *(Bot)* aubergine, eggplant *(US)*; **Ei|er|hand|gra|na|te** F *(Mil)* (pineapple) hand grenade, pineapple *(inf)*; **Ei|er|ko|cher** M egg boiler; **Ei|er|kog|nak** M advocaat; **Ei|er|kopf** M *(inf: hum or pej)* **a** *(lit)* egg-shaped head **b** *(= Intellektueller)* egghead *(inf)*, boffin *(esp Brit inf)*; **Ei|er|ku|chen** M pancake; *(= Omelette) omelette made with a mixture containing flour*; **Ei|er|lau|fen** NT -s, *no pl* egg and spoon race; **~ machen** to have an egg and spoon race; **Ei|er|li|kör** M advocaat; **Ei|er|löf|fel** M eggspoon

ei|ern ['aiɐn] VI *(inf)* to wobble

Ei|er-: **Ei|er|nu|deln** PL *(Cook)* (egg) noodles *pl*; **Ei|er|pflau|me** F (large oval) plum; **Ei|er|scha|le** F eggshell; **er hat noch die ~n hinter den Ohren** *(inf)* he's still wet behind the ears *(inf)*; **ei|er|scha|len|far|ben** ADJ cream, off-white; **Ei|er|schaum** M, **Ei|er|schnee** M *(Cook)* beaten egg white; **Ei|er|schnei|der** M egg slicer; **Ei|er|schwamm** M *(esp Aus)*, **Ei|er|schwam|merl** NT *(S Ger, Aus) (Bot)* chanterelle; **Ei|er|spei|se** F **a** egg dish **b** *(Aus: = Rührei)* scrambled egg; **Ei|er|stock** M *(Anat)* ovary; **Ei|er|tanz** M tortuous manoeuvring *(Brit)* or maneuvering *(US)*; **einen regelrechten ~ aufführen** *(fig inf)* to go through all kinds of contortions; **Ei|er|uhr** F egg timer; **Ei|er|wär|mer** [-vɛrmɐ] M -s, - egg cosy

Ei|fer ['aife] M -s, *no pl (= Begeisterung)* enthusiasm; *(= Eifrigkeit)* eagerness, keenness; **mit ~** enthusiastically; eagerly, keenly; **mit ~ arbeiten** to work with a will, to work with great zeal; **in ~ geraten** to get agitated, to get into a state; **mit großem ~ bei der Sache sein** to put one's heart into it; **im ~ des Gefechts** *(fig inf)* in the heat of the moment → **blind ADJ a**

Ei|fe|rer ['aifərɐ] M -s, -, **Ei|fe|rin** [-ərɪn] F -, -nen *(liter)* fanatic; *(Rel auch)* zealot

ei|fern ['aifɐn] VI *(liter)* **a gegen jdn/etw ~** to rail or inveigh *(liter)* against sb/sth; **für etw ~** to crusade or campaign for sth **b** *(= streben)* **nach etw ~** to strive for sth **c** *(= wetteifern)* **um etw ~** to compete or vie for sth

Ei|fer|sucht F jealousy *(auf +acc* of); **aus/vor (lauter) ~** out of/for (pure) jealousy

Ei|fer|süch|te|lei [aifɐzʏçtə'lai] F -, -en petty jealousy

ei|fer|süch|tig ADJ jealous *(auf +acc* of)

Ei|fer|suchts-: **Ei|fer|suchts|sze|ne** F **ihr Mann hat ihr wieder eine ~ gemacht** her husband's jealousy caused another scene; **Ei|fer|suchts|tat** F act of jealousy, jealous act; **Ei|fer|suchts|tra|gö|die** F **„Eifersuchtstragödie in München"** "jealousy causes tragedy in Munich"

ei|för|mig ADJ egg-shaped, oval

eif|rig ['aifrɪç] ADJ eager; *Befürworter auch* keen; *Leser, Sammler, Kinobesucher* keen, avid; *Schüler* industrious; **die Eifrigen** the eager beavers *(inf)* ADV *üben* religiously; *an die Arbeit gehen* enthusiastically; *teilnehmen* gladly; **~ lernen** to apply oneself; **~ bemüht sein** to make a sincere effort; **er putzte gerade ~ sein Auto, als ich ankam** he was busy or busily cleaning his car when I arrived; **sie diskutierten ~** they were involved in an animated discussion

Eif|rig|keit F -, *no pl (von Schüler)* industriousness

Ei|gelb NT -s, -e or *(bei Zahlenangabe)* - egg yolk; **vier ~** the yolks of four eggs, four egg yolks

ei|gen ['aign] ADJ **a** own; *(= selbstständig)* separate; **seine ~e Wohnung/Meinung haben** to have a flat/an opinion of one's own, to have one's own flat/opinion; **etw sein Eigen nennen** *(geh)* to have sth to one's name, to have sth to call one's own; **er ist stolz, zwölf Kinder sein Eigen nennen zu können** he is proud of having been blessed with twelve children; **jdm etw zu ~ geben** *(liter)* to give sb sth; **meiner Mutter zu ~** *(liter)* for or (dedicated) to my mother; **~er Bericht** *(Press)* from or by our (own) correspondent; **Zimmer mit ~em Eingang** room with its own or a separate entrance; **San Marino ist ein ~er Staat** San Marino is an independent or a separate state; **sich** *(dat)* **etw zu ~ machen** to adopt sth; *(= zur Gewohnheit machen)* to make sth a habit, to make a habit of sth; **übergeben Sie diesen Brief dem Anwalt zu ~en Händen** *(form)* give this letter to the lawyer in person; **ich habe das Papier auf ~e Rechnung gekauft** I paid for the paper myself; **ich möchte kurz in ~er Sache sprechen** I would like to say something on my own account → **Fuß, Nest, Tasche**
b *(= typisch, kennzeichnend)* typical; **das ist ihm ~** that is typical of him; **er antwortete mit dem ihm ~en Zynismus** he answered with (his) characteristic cynicism; **ein Menschenschlag von ganz ~er Prägung** a race apart
c *(= seltsam)* strange, peculiar; **es ist eine Landschaft von ganz ~em Reiz** the country is strangely attractive in its own way or has its own strange attraction
d *(= ordentlich)* particular; *(= übergenau)* fussy; **in Gelddingen** or **was Geld anbetrifft ist er sehr ~** he is very particular about money matters

Ei|gen-: **Ei|gen|an|teil** M *(Insur)* own share, excess *(Brit)*; **Ei|gen|an|trieb** M **Fahrzeuge mit ~** self-propelled vehicles; **~ haben** to be self-propelled; **Ei|gen|art** F *(= Besonderheit)* peculiarity; *(= Eigenschaft)* characteristic; *(= Individualität)* individuality; *(= Eigentümlichkeit von Personen)* idiosyncrasy; **das gehört zur ~ der Bayern** that's a typically Bavarian characteristic; **ei|gen|ar|tig** ADJ peculiar; *(= sonderbar auch)* strange; *(= persönlich kennzeichnend)* idiosyncratic ADV peculiarly, strangely; **~ aussehen/klingen** to look/sound strange or peculiar; **ei|gen|ar|ti|ger|wei|se** ADV strangely or oddly enough; **Ei|gen|ar|tig|keit** F **a** *no pl* strangeness **b** *(= Gebaren)* idiosyncrasy; **Ei|gen|bau** M, *no pl* **Tabak/Gemüse im ~ züchten** to grow one's own tobacco/vegetables; **er fährt ein Fahrrad Marke ~** *(hum inf)* he rides a home-made bike; **er raucht Zigaretten Marke ~** *(hum inf)* he smokes home-grown cigarettes *(hum)*; **Ei|gen|be|darf** M *(von Mensch)* personal use; *(von Staat)* domestic requirements *pl*; **zum ~** for (one's own) personal use; **der Hausbesitzer machte ~ geltend** the landlord showed that he needed the house/flat *(Brit)* or apartment for himself; **Ei|gen|be|richt** M *(Press)* **diese Zeitung bringt kaum ~e** this paper rarely carries articles by its own journalists; **Ei|gen|be|tei|li|gung** F *(Insur)* own share, excess *(Brit)*; **Ei|gen|be|we|gung** F *(Astron)* proper motion; **Ei|gen|blut** NT *(Med)* (own) blood; **dem Patienten wird ~ abgenommen** some of the patient's (own) blood is taken; **Ei|gen|blut|be|hand|lung** F *(Med)* autohaemotherapy *(Brit)*, autohemotherapy *(US)*; **Ei|gen|blut|trans|fu|si|on** F *(Med)* own *or* autologous *(spec)* blood transfusion; **Ei|gen|brö|te|lei** [aignbrøːtəˈlai] F -, -en *(inf)* eccentricity; *(= Einzelgängertum)* solitary ways *pl*; **Ei|gen|bröt|ler** [ˈaignbrøːtlɐ] M -s, -, **Ei|gen|bröt|le|rin** [-ərɪn] F -, -nen *(inf)* loner, lone wolf; *(= komischer Kauz)* queer fish *(inf)*, oddball *(esp US inf)*; **ei|gen|bröt|le|risch** [ˈaignbrøːtlərɪʃ] ADJ *(inf)* solitary; *(= komisch)* eccentric; **Ei|gen|dün|kel** M sense of superiority; **Ei|gen|dy|na|mik** F momentum; **eine ~ entwickeln** to gather momentum; **Ei|gen|fi|nan|zie|rung** F self-financing; **wir bauen die neue Fabrik in ~** we are financing the building of the new factory ourselves; **ei|gen|ge|nutzt** ADJ *(form) Wohnung etc* owner-occupied; **ei|gen|ge|setz|lich** ADJ autonomous ADV **jede Revolution entwickelt sich ~** every revolution develops according to laws of its own; **Ei|gen|ge|setz|lich|keit** F autonomous laws *pl*; **sein Handeln folgte einer geheimnisvollen ~** his behaviour *(Brit)* or behavior *(US)* followed its own mysterious laws; **Ei|gen|ge|wicht** NT *(von LKW etc)* unladen weight; *(Comm)* net weight; *(Sci)* dead weight; **Ei|gen|goal** NT *(Aus Sport)* own goal; **Ei|gen|grup|pe** F *(Sociol)* in-group; **ei|gen|hän|dig** ADJ *Brief, Unterschrift etc* in one's own hand, handwritten; *Übergabe* personal; **ein ~es Werk Rembrandts** a work from Rembrandt's own hand *or* by Rembrandt himself ADV oneself, with one's own hands; **eine Arbeit ~ machen** to do a job oneself *or* personally *or* with one's own hands

Ei|gen|heim NT one's own home; **sparen Sie für ein ~!** save for a home of your own!

Ei|gen|heim-: **Ei|gen|heim|för|de|rung** F ≈ state support for home-buying; **Ei|gen|heim|zu|la|ge** F ≈ state subsidy available to people buying a home

Ei|gen|heit [ˈaignhait] F -, -en = **Eigenart**

Ei|gen-: **Ei|gen|in|i|ti|a|ti|ve** F initiative of one's own; **auf ~** on one's own initiative; **Ei|gen|in|te|res|se** NT vested interest, self-interest; *(von Firma)* **aus ~** out of self-interest, to serve one's own interests; **Ei|gen|ka|pi|tal** NT *(von Person)* personal capital; *(von Firma)* company capital; **10.000 Euro ~** 10,000 euros of one's own capital; **Ei|gen|le|ben** NT, *no pl* one's own life; *(= selbstständige Existenz)* independent existence; *(= Privatleben)* private life; **Ei|gen|leis|tung** F *(Fin: bei Hausbau)* borrower's own funding, personal contribution; **Ei|gen|lie|be** F amour-propre; *(= Selbstverliebtheit)* self-love, love of self; **Ei|gen|lob** NT self-importance, vaingloriousness; **~ stinkt!** *(inf)* don't blow your own trumpet! *(prov)*; **ei|gen|mäch|tig** ADJ *(= selbstherrlich)* high-handed; *(= eigenverantwortlich)* taken/done *etc* on one's own authority; *(= unbefugt)* unauthorized; **~e Abwesenheit** *(Mil)* absence without leave ADV high-handedly; (entirely) on one's own authority; without any authorization; **ei|gen|mäch|ti|ger|wei|se** ADV *(= selbstherrlich)* high-handedly; *(= unbefugt)* without any authorization; **Ei|gen|mäch|tig|keit** F -, -en *(= Selbstherrlichkeit)* high-handedness *no pl*; *(= unbefugtes Handeln)* unauthorized behaviour *(Brit)* or behavior *(US) no pl*; **die ~ seines Vorgehens wurde von allen kritisiert** everyone criticized him for having acted high-handedly/without authorization; **Ei|gen|mit|tel** PL *(form)* one's own resources; **die ~ der Körperschaft** the corporation's (own) resources; **man braucht nur 20% ~** you only need to find 20% yourself *or* from your own resources; **Ei|gen|na|me** M proper name; **Ei|gen|nutz** [-nʊts] M -es, *no pl* self-interest; **das habe ich ohne jeden ~ getan** I did that with no thought of myself *or* of furthering my own interests; **ei|gen|nüt|zig** [-nʏtsɪç] ADJ selfish; **Ei|gen|nüt|zig|keit** F -, *no pl* = **Eigennutz**; **Ei|gen|nut|zung** F -, *no pl (von Wohnung etc)* owner-occupation; **Ei|gen|pro|duk|ti|on** F **das ist eine ~** we/they *etc* made it ourselves/themselves *etc*; **etw in ~ herstellen** to make sth oneself, to make one's own sth; **aus ~** *(= hausgemacht)* home-made; *Tabak etc* home-grown; **das war eine ~ des Irischen Fernsehens** that was one of Irish Television's own productions

ei|gens [ˈaigns] ADV (e)specially; *(= ausdrücklich auch)* specifically

Ei|gen|schaft [ˈaignʃaft] F -, -en *(= Attribut)* quality; *(Chem, Phys etc)* property; *(= Merkmal)* characteristic, feature; *(= Funktion)* capacity; **~en** *(Comput)* properties

Ei|gen|schafts|wort NT *pl* **-wörter** adjective

Ei|gen-: **Ei|gen|schwin|gung** F *(Sci)* free vibration; **Ei|gen|sinn** M, *no pl* stubbornness, obstinacy; *(inf: = Trotzkopf)* stubborn child; **ei|gen|sin|nig** ADJ stubborn, obstinate; **Ei|gen|sin|nig|keit** [-zɪnɪçkait] F -, -en stubbornness, obstinacy; **~en** *pl* stubborn *or* obstinate behaviour *(Brit) or* behavior *(US)*; **ei|gen|staat|lich** ADJ sovereign; **Ei|gen|staat|lich|keit** [-ʃtaːtlɪçkait] F -, *no pl* sovereignty; **ei|gen|stän|dig** ADJ original; *(= unabhängig)* independent; *(= eigengesetzlich)* autonomous; *(Comput) Gerät* stand-alone *pred*; **Ei|gen|stän|dig|keit** [-ʃtɛndɪçkait] F -, *no pl* originality; *(= Unabhängigkeit)* independence; *(= Eigengesetzlichkeit)* autonomy; **Ei|gen|sucht** F, *no pl* selfishness; *(= Egotismus auch)* self-centredness *(Brit)*, self-centeredness *(US)*; **ei|gen|süch|tig** ADJ selfish; *(= zum Egotismus neigend)* self-centred *(Brit)*, self-centered *(US)*

ei|gent|lich [ˈaigntlɪç] ADJ *(= wirklich, tatsächlich)* real, actual; *Wert* true, real; *(= ursprünglich)* original; **im ~en Sinne bedeutet das ...** that really means ...; **im ~en Sinne des Wortes ...** in the original meaning of the word ...

ADV actually; *(= tatsächlich, wirklich)* really; *(= überhaupt)* anyway; **~ wollte ich nur fünf Minuten bleiben** actually I was only *or* I was really only going to stay five minutes; **was willst du ~ hier?** what do you want here anyway?; **wissen Sie ~, wer ich bin?** do you know who I am?; **was ist ~ mit dir los?** what's the matter with you (anyway)?; **ich bin ~ froh, dass ...** really *or* actually I'm happy that ...; **~ müsstest du das wissen** you should really know that; **~ dürftest du das nicht tun** you shouldn't really do that

Ei|gent|lich|keit F -, *no pl (Philos)* essentiality

Ei|gen|tor NT *(Sport, fig)* own goal; **ein ~ schießen** to score an own goal

Ei|gen|tum [ˈaigntuːm] NT -s, *no pl* property; **bewegliches ~** movables *pl*, movable property; **unbewegliches ~** immovables *pl*, real property; **~ an etw** *(dat)* **erwerben** to acquire possession of sth; **~ an den Produktionsmitteln** ownership of the means of production

Ei|gen|tü|mer [ˈaigntyːmɐ] M -s, -, **Ei|gen|tü|me|rin** [-ərɪn] F -, -nen owner

ei|gen|tüm|lich [ˈaigntyːmlɪç] ADJ **a** *(= sonderbar, seltsam)* strange, curious, odd **b** *(geh: = typisch)* **jdm/einer Sache ~ sein** to be characteristic *or* typical of sb/sth

ei|gen|tüm|li|cher|wei|se ADV strangely *or* curiously *or* oddly enough

Ei|gen|tüm|lich|keit F -, -en **a** *(= Kennzeichen, Besonderheit)* characteristic **b** *(= Eigenheit)* peculiarity

Ei|gen|tums-: **Ei|gen|tums|an|spruch** M claim of ownership; **einen ~ auf etw** *(acc)* **geltend machen** to claim ownership of sth; **Ei|gen|tums|be|griff** M concept of property; **Ei|gen|tums|bil|dung** F private acquisition of property; **Ei|gen|tums|de|likt** NT *(Jur) offence against property*; **Ei|gen|tums|denken** NT *(= Theorie)* property ethic; *(= Gesinnung)* property-mindedness; **Ei|gen|tums|recht** NT right of ownership; *(= Urheberrecht)* copyright; **Ei|gen|tums|streu|ung** F dispersal of property; **Ei|gen|tums|über|tra|gung** F *(Jur)* transfer of ownership *or* title; **Ei|gen|tums|ur|kun|de** F *(Jur)* title deed; **Ei|gen|tums|ver|ge|hen** NT *(Jur) offence against property*; **Ei|gen|tums|ver|hält|nis|se** PL distribution *sing* of property; **Ei|gen|tums|vor|be|halt** M *(Jur)* reservation of proprietary rights; **Ei|gen|tums|woh|nung** F owner-occupied flat *(Brit)* or apartment, ≈ condominium *(US)*; **er kaufte sich** *(dat)* **eine ~** he bought a flat *(Brit) or* an apartment (of his own); **~en bauen** to build flats *(Brit) or* apartments for owner-occupation

Ei|gen-: **ei|gen|ver|ant|wort|lich** ADJ autonomous ADV on one's own authority; **~ für etw sorgen müssen** to be personally responsible for sth; **er hat ~ dafür gesorgt** he saw to it personally *or* himself; **Ei|gen|ver|ant|wort|lich|keit** F autonomy; **jds ~ für etw** sb's personal responsibility for sth; **Ei|gen|ver|lag** M private publisher; **sein im ~ erschienenes Buch** the book which he published himself; **Ei|gen|wär|me** F body heat; **Ei|gen|wer|bung** F self-advertising *or* -publicity; **~ treiben** to promote oneself; **Ei|gen|wert** M intrinsic value; **ei|gen|wil|lig** ADJ with a mind of one's own; *(= eigensinnig)* self-willed; *(= unkonventionell)* unconventional, original; **sie ist in allem recht ~** she has a mind of her own in everything; **Ei|gen|wil|lig|keit** [-vɪlɪçkait] F -, -en independence of mind; *(= Eigensinnigkeit)* self-will; *(= Unkonventionalität)* unconventionality, originality; **Ei|gen|zeit** F *(Phys)* proper time

eig|nen [ˈaignən] VR to be suitable *(für, zu* for, *als* as); **er würde sich nicht zum Lehrer ~** he wouldn't make a good teacher → *auch* **geeignet** VI *(geh)* **ihm eignet der Charme des Österreichers** he has *or* possesses all the charm of an Austrian; **seinen Büchern eignet ein präziser Prosastil** his books are characterized by a precise narrative style

Eig|ner [ˈaignɐ] M -s, -, **Eig|ne|rin** [-ərɪn] F -, -nen *(form)* owner

Eig|nung [ˈaignʊŋ] F -, -en suitability; *(= Befähigung)* aptitude

Eig|nungs|prü|fung F, **Eig|nungs|test** M aptitude test

eigtl. *abbr von* **eigentlich**

Ei|klar [ˈaiklaːɐ] NT -s, - *(Aus, S Ger)* egg white

Ei|land [ˈailant] NT -(e)s, -e [-də] *(liter)* isle *(liter)*

Eil-: **Eil|an|ge|bot** NT *(Comm)* express offer; **Eil|auf|trag** M *(Comm)* rush order; **Eil|bo|te** M, **Eil|bo|tin** F messenger; **per** *or* **durch ~n** express; **Eil|brief** M express letter; **ich schicke diesen Brief als ~** I am sending this letter express

Ei|le [ˈailə] F -, *no pl* hurry; **in ~ sein** to be in a hurry; **~ haben** *(Mensch)* to be in a hurry *or* rush; *(Sache)* to be urgent; **damit hat es keine ~, das hat keine ~** there is no hurry *or* rush about it, it's not urgent; **er trieb uns zur ~ an** he hurried us up; **in aller ~** hurriedly, hastily; **in höchster ~ laufen/fahren** to rush/drive in a tremendous hurry; **mit ~/mit fieberhafter ~ arbeiten** to work very quickly/feverishly; **in der ~** in the hurry; **in meiner ~** in my haste; **nur keine ~!** don't rush!

Ei|lei|ter M *(Anat)* Fallopian tube
Ei|lei|ter|schwan|ger|schaft F ectopic pregnancy
ei|len ['ailən] VI **a** *aux sein* to rush, to hasten *(liter)*, to hurry; **er eilte dem Ertrinkenden zu Hilfe** he rushed *or* hastened to help the drowning man; **eile mit Weile** *(Prov)* more haste less speed *(Prov)* **b** *(= dringlich sein)* to be urgent *or* pressing; **eilt!** *(auf Briefen etc)* urgent; **die Sache eilt** it's urgent, it's an urgent matter VR *(inf)* to rush VI *impers* **es eilt** it's urgent *or* pressing; **damit eilt es nicht** there's no great hurry *or* rush about it; **mit dieser Arbeit eilt es sehr/nicht** this work is very/is not urgent
ei|lends ['ailənts] ADV hurriedly, hastily
Eil-: **eil|fer|tig** ADJ *(geh)* zealous; **Eil|fer|tig|keit** F, *no pl (geh)* zeal, zealousness; **Eil|fracht** F, **Eil|gut** NT, *no pl* express freight; **etw als ~ senden** to send sth express freight
ei|lig ['ailıç] ADJ **a** *(= schnell, rasch)* quick, hurried, hasty; **es ~ haben** to be in a hurry *or* rush; **nur nicht so ~!** don't be in such a hurry *or* rush! **b** *(= dringend)* urgent; **er hatte nichts Eiligeres zu tun, als ...** *(iro)* he had nothing better to do than ... *(iro)* ADV as quickly as possible; **sich ~ auf den Weg machen** to hurry; **er bat den Arzt, ~st zu kommen** he asked the doctor to come as quickly as possible
Eil-: **Eil|marsch** M *(Mil)* fast march; **Eil|mel|dung** F *(Press)* flash; **Eil|pa|ket** NT express parcel; **Eil|sen|dung** F express delivery *or* letter/parcel; **~en** *pl* express mail *or* post *(Brit)*; **Eil|tem|po** NT **etw im ~ machen** to do sth in a real rush; **er kam im ~ auf mich zugerannt** he came rushing *or* tearing up to me; **Eil|ver|fah|ren** NT *(Jur)* summary proceeding(s *pl*); **etw im ~ durchnehmen** *(fig)* to rush through sth; **etw im ~ herstellen** *or* **produzieren** to rush sth off; **Eil|zug** M *(Aus)* fast stopping train; **Eil|zu|stel|lung** F special delivery; **mit ~** (by) special delivery
Ei|mer ['aimɐ] M **-s, -** **a** bucket, pail; *(= Milcheimer)* pail; *(= Mülleimer)* (rubbish) bin *(Brit)*, garbage can *(US)*; **ein ~ (voll) Wasser** a bucket(ful) of water; **es gießt wie mit** *or* **aus ~n** *(inf)* it's bucketing down *(Brit inf)*, it's coming down in buckets *(US inf)*, it's raining cats and dogs *(inf)* **b** **im ~ sein** *(inf)* to be up the spout *(Brit inf)*, to be down the drain *or* tubes *(US inf)*; *(= kaputt sein auch)* to be bust *(inf)*
ei|mer|wei|se ADV in bucketfuls, by the bucket(ful)
ein [ain] ADV *(an Geräten)* **Ein/Aus** on/off; **~ und aus gehen** to come and go; **er geht bei uns ~ und aus** he is always (a)round at our place; **ich weiß (mit ihm) nicht mehr ~ noch aus** I'm at my wits' end (with him)
ein, **ei|ne**, **ein** NUM one; **das kostet nur ~en Euro** it only costs one euro; **~ Uhr** one (o'clock); **~ Uhr zwanzig** twenty past one; **~ für alle Mal** once and for all; **~ und derselbe/dieselbe/dasselbe** one and the same; **er ist ihr Ein und Alles** he means *or* is everything to her → *auch* **eins**
INDEF ART a; *(vor Vokalen)* an; **~ Mann** a man; **~e Frau** a woman; **~ Kind** a child; **~ Europäer** a European; **~ Hotel** a *or* an hotel; **der Sohn ~es Lehrers** the son of a teacher, a teacher's son; **nur ~ Hegel konnte das schreiben** only a Hegel could have written that; **~e Hitze ist das hier!** the *or* some heat here!; **was für ~ Wetter/Lärm!** some weather/noise, what a noise; **wir hatten ~en Durst!** *(inf)* we were parched!, were we thirsty! → *auch* **eine(r, s)**
ein|ach|sig ['ainlaksıç] ADJ two-wheeled, single-axle *attr*
Ein|ak|ter ['ainlaktɐ] M **-s, -** *(Theat)* one-act play
ei|nan|der [ai'nandɐ] PRON one another, each other; **zwei ~ widersprechende Zeugenberichte** two (mutually) contradictory eyewitness reports
ein+ar|bei|ten *sep* VR to get used to the work; **sie muss sich in ihr neues Gebiet ~** she has to get used to her new area of work VT **a** *jdn* to train **b** *(= einfügen)* to incorporate, to include **c** *(= einnähen)* to sew in; *Futter, Polster auch* to attach
Ein|ar|bei|tung ['ainlarbaitʊŋ] F **-, -en** **a** *(von Menschen)* training **b** *(= Einfügung)* incorporation, inclusion **c** *(= das Einnähen)* sewing in; *(von Futter, Polster auch)* attachment
Ein|ar|bei|tungs|zeit F training period
ein|ar|mig ADJ one-armed; *Turnübungen* single-arm; **~er Bandit** one-armed bandit
ein+äschern ['ainlɛʃɐn] VT *sep Leichnam* to cremate; *Stadt etc* to burn to the ground, to burn down, to reduce to ashes
Ein|äsche|rung F **-, -en** *(von Leichnam)* cremation; *(von Stadt etc)* burning down
ein+at|men VTI *sep* to breathe in
ein+ät|zen VT *sep* to etch (in)
ein|äu|gig ADJ one-eyed; *Spiegelreflexkamera* single-lens
Ein|äu|gi|ge(r) MF *decl as adj* one-eyed person/man/woman *etc*
Ein|bahn-: **Ein|bahn|stra|ße** F one-way street; **Ein|bahn|ver|kehr** M one-way traffic
ein+bal|sa|mie|ren *ptp* **einbalsamiert** VT *sep* to embalm
Ein|bal|sa|mie|rung F **-, -en** embalming, embalmment
Ein|band [-bant] M *pl* **-bände** book cover, case *(spec)*
ein|bän|dig ADJ one-volume *attr*, in one volume
ein|ba|sisch ADJ *(Chem)* monobasic
Ein|bau M *pl* **-bauten** **a** *no pl (= das Einbauen)* installation **b** *(usu pl: = Schrank etc)* fixture
ein+bau|en VT *sep* to install, to put in; *Motor auch* to fit; *(inf: = einfügen) Zitat etc* to work in, to incorporate; **eingebaute Möbel** built-in furniture; **eingebauter Belichtungsmesser** built-in exposure meter
Ein|bau|kü|che F (fully-)fitted kitchen
Ein|baum M dug-out (canoe)
Ein|bau-: **Ein|bau|mö|bel** PL built-in *or* fitted furniture; *(= Schränke)* fitted cupboards *pl*; **Ein|bau|schrank** M built-in *or* fitted cupboard
ein|be|grif|fen ['ainbəgrıfn] ADJ included
ein+be|hal|ten *ptp* **einbehalten** VT *sep irreg* to keep back
ein|bei|nig ADJ one-legged
Ein|be|kennt|nis NT *(geh)* admission
ein+be|rech|nen *ptp* **einberechnet** VT *sep* to allow for (in one's calculations); **~, dass ...** to allow for the fact that ...
ein+be|ru|fen *ptp* **einberufen** VT *sep irreg Parlament* to summon; *Versammlung* to convene, to call; *(Mil)* to call up, to conscript, to draft *(US)*; **Leute zu einer Versammlung ~** to summon *or* call people to a meeting
Ein|be|ru|fe|ne(r) ['ainbəru:fənə] MF *decl as adj (Mil)* conscript, draftee *(US)*
Ein|be|ru|fung F **a** *(einer Versammlung)* convention, calling; *(des Parlaments)* summoning **b** *(Mil)* conscription; *(= Einberufungsbescheid)* call-up, draft call *(US)*
Ein|be|ru|fungs|be|scheid M, **Ein|be|ru|fungs|be|fehl** M *(Mil)* call-up *or* draft *(US)* papers *pl*
ein|be|schrie|ben ['ainbəʃri:bn] ADJ *(Math) Kreis* inscribed; **einer Sache** *(dat)* **~** encompassed by sth
ein+be|to|nie|ren *ptp* **einbetoniert** VT *sep* to cement in (*in +acc* -to)
ein+bet|ten VT *sep* to embed (*in +acc* in); *Rohr, Kabel* to lay (*in +acc* in) → *auch* **eingebettet**
Ein|bett-: **Ein|bett|ka|bi|ne** F *(Naut)* single-berth cabin; **Ein|bett|zim|mer** NT single room
ein+beu|len VT *sep* to dent (in)
ein+be|zie|hen *ptp* **einbezogen** VT *sep irreg* to include (*in +acc* in)
Ein|be|zie|hung F inclusion; **unter ~ von etw** including sth; **unter ~ sämtlicher Gesichtspunkte** having regard to all points
ein+bie|gen *sep irreg* VI *aux sein* to turn (off) (*in +acc* into); **du musst hier links ~** you have to turn (off to the) left here; **diese Straße biegt in die Hauptstraße ein** this road joins the main road VT to bend in
ein+bil|den VT *sep* **a** **sich** *(dat)* **etw ~** to imagine sth; **er bildet sich** *(dat)* **ein, dass ...** he's got hold of the idea that ...; **sich** *(dat)* **steif und fest ~, dass ...** *(inf)* to get it fixed in one's head that ... *(inf)*; **das bildest du dir nur ein** that's just your imagination; **ich bilde mir nicht ein, ich sei ...** I don't have any illusions about being ..., I'm not pretending to be ...; **er bildet sich** *(dat)* **viel ein!** he imagines a lot of things!; **bilde dir (doch) nichts ein!** don't kid *(inf)* *or* delude yourself!; **was bildest du dir eigentlich ein?** what's got *(Brit)* *or* gotten *(US)* into you?; **bilde dir bloß nicht ein, dass ich das glaube!** don't kid yourself *(inf)* *or* don't go thinking that I believe that!
b *(= stolz sein)* **sich** *(dat)* **viel auf etw** *(acc)* **~** to be conceited about *or* vain about sth; **darauf kann ich mir etwas ~** *(iro)* praise indeed!; **darauf können Sie sich etwas ~!** that's something to be proud of!, that's a feather in your cap!; **darauf brauchst du dir nichts einzubilden!** that's nothing to crow about *(inf)* *or* be proud of; **auf diesen bescheidenen Erfolg brauchst du dir nichts einzubilden** don't go getting any big ideas just because of this little success → *auch* **eingebildet**
Ein|bil|dung F **a** *(= Vorstellung)* imagination; *(= irrige Vorstellung)* illusion; **das sind ~en** that's pure imagination; **das ist alles nur ~** it's all in the mind, it's just (your/his) imagination; **krank ist er bloß in seiner ~** he just imagines *or* thinks he's ill **b** *(= Dünkel)* conceit; **an ~en leiden** *(hum inf)* to be (pretty) stuck on oneself *(esp US inf)*, to really fancy oneself *(Brit inf)*; **~ ist auch eine Bildung** *(hum inf)* he's/she's too conceited for words
Ein|bil|dungs|kraft F, **Ein|bil|dungs|ver|mö|gen** NT, *no pl* (powers *pl* of) imagination
ein+bim|sen VT *sep (inf)* **jdm etw ~** to drum *or* din sth into sb *(inf)*
ein+bin|den VT *sep irreg Buch* to bind; *(in Schutzhülle)* to cover; *(fig: = einbeziehen)* to integrate; **neu ~** to rebind
Ein|bin|dung F *(fig)* integration
ein+bla|sen VT *sep irreg* to blow in (*in +acc* -to); *Kaltluft auch* to blast in (*in +acc* -to); *(Mus) Blasinstrument* to play *or* blow *(inf)* in; **Gott blies Adam den Lebenshauch ein** God breathed the breath of life into Adam; **jdm etw ~** *(fig inf)* to whisper sth to sb
ein+bläu|en VT *sep (inf)* **jdm etw ~** *(durch Schläge)* to beat sth into sb; *(= einschärfen)* to drum sth into sb, to ram sth into sb's head *(inf)*; **ich habe ihm eingebläut, das ja nicht zu vergessen** I told him time and again not to forget it
ein+blen|den *sep (Film, TV, Rad)* VT to insert, to slot in; *(allmählich)* to fade in; *(nachträglich) Musik etc* to dub over; *(Comput) Dialog, Zweig* to expand VR **sich in etw** *(acc)* **~** to link up with sth; **sich bei jdm/etw ~** to go over to sb/sth
Ein|blen|dung F *(Film, TV, Rad)* insert; *(= das Einblenden)* insertion; *(von Musik)* overdub
ein+bleu|en △ VT *sep* → **einbläuen**
Ein|blick M **a** *(rare: = Blick in etw hinein)* view (*in +acc* of) **b** *(fig: = Kenntnis)* insight; **~ in etw** *(acc)* **gewinnen** to gain an insight into sth; **~ in die Akten nehmen** to look at *or* examine the files; **jdm ~ in etw** *(acc)* **gewähren** to allow sb to look at sth; **er hat ~ in diese Vorgänge** he has some knowledge of these events; **~e in etw** *(acc)* **eröffnen** to give insights *or* an insight into sth
ein+bre|chen *sep irreg* VT *Tür, Wand etc* to break down

VI **a** *aux sein (= einstürzen)* to fall *or* cave in; **er ist (auf dem Eis) eingebrochen** he went *or* fell through the ice
b *aux sein or haben (= Einbruch verüben)* to break in; **in unser** *or* **unserem Haus sind Diebe eingebrochen** thieves broke into our house; **bei mir ist eingebrochen worden, man hat bei mir eingebrochen** I've had a break-in, I've been burgled *or (US)* burglarized; **in neue Absatzmärkte** *etc* **~** to make inroads into new markets *etc*
c *aux sein (Nacht, Dämmerung, Dunkelheit)* to fall; *(Winter)* to set in; **bei ~der Nacht** at nightfall
d *aux sein (inf: = Verluste machen)* to come a cropper *(Brit inf)*, to fall apart *(US)*

Ein|bre|cher(in) M(F) burglar

Ein|bre|cher|ban|de F gang of burglars

ein+bren|nen *sep irreg* VT *Mal* to brand; **Buchstaben/Muster in Holz ~** to burn letters/patterns into wood VR *(liter)* to engrave *or* etch itself

ein+brin|gen VT *sep irreg* **a** *(Parl) Gesetz* to introduce
b *(= Ertrag bringen) Geld, Nutzen* to bring in; *Ruhm* to bring; *Zinsen* to earn; **jdm etw ~** to bring/earn sb sth; **das bringt nichts ein** *(fig)* it's not worth it
c etw in die Ehe ~ to bring sth into the marriage; **etw in die Firma ~** to put sth into the firm
d *(= hineinbringen, -schaffen)* to put in *(in +acc* -to); *Schiff* to bring in *(in +acc* -to); *Ernte* to bring *or* gather in
e *(Typ) Zeilen* to take in
f sich in etw *(acc)* **~** to play a part in sth; **jdn in etw** *(acc)* **~** to get sb involved in sth; **sie brachte ihre Kenntnisse in die Diskussion ein** she brought her knowledge to bear in the discussion

ein+bro|cken VT *sep* to crumble *(in +acc* into); **jdm/sich etwas ~** *(inf)* to land sb/oneself in it *(inf) or* in the soup *(inf)*; **da hast du dir etwas Schönes eingebrockt!** *(inf)* you've really let yourself in for it there; **was man sich eingebrockt hat, das muss man auch auslöffeln** *(prov)* you've made your bed, now you must lie on *(Brit) or* in it *(prov)* → **Suppe**

Ein|bruch M **a** *(= Einbruchdiebstahl)* burglary *(in +acc* in), breaking and entering *(form)*; **ein ~** a break-in, a burglary; **der ~ in die Bank** the bank break-in **b** *(von Wasser)* penetration; **~ kühler Meeresluft** *(Met)* a stream of cold air moving inland **c** *(= Einsturz: einer Mauer etc)* collapse; *(Geol)* rift valley; *(= Verlust)* setback; **~ der Kurse/der Konjunktur** *(Fin)* stock exchange/economic crash **d** *(fig) (der Nacht)* fall; *(des Winters)* onset; **bei/vor ~ der Nacht/Dämmerung** at/before nightfall/dusk

Ein|bruch(s)-: **Ein|bruch(s)|dieb|stahl** M *(Jur)* burglary, breaking and entering *(form)*; **Ein|bruch(s)|se|rie** F series of break-ins *or* burglaries; **ein|bruch(s)|si|cher** ADJ burglar-proof; **Ein|bruch(s)|stel|le** F *(im Damm)* breach; *(im Eis)* hole; **Ein|bruch(s)|tal** NT *(Geol)* rift valley; **Ein|bruch(s)|ver|si|che|rung** F burglary insurance; **Ein|bruch(s)|werk|zeug** NT housebreaking *or* burglary tool

ein|bu|chen VR *(Telec)* to register VTI *(Comput)* to book VT *(fig) Erfolg etc* to chalk up *(inf)*

ein+buch|ten ['ainbʊxtn] VT *sep (lit)* to indent; *(inf)* to put away *(inf)*, to lock up

Ein|buch|tung F **-, -en** indentation; *(= Bucht)* inlet, bay

ein+bud|deln *sep (inf)* VT to bury *(in +acc* in) VR **sich (in den Sand) ~** to dig oneself in(to the sand)

ein+bür|gern ['ainbʏrgɐn] *sep* VT *Person* to naturalize; *Fremdwort, Gewohnheit, Pflanze* to introduce; **er ist in die** *or* **der Türkei eingebürgert worden** he has become a naturalized Turk VR *(Person)* to become *or* be naturalized; *(Brauch, Tier, Pflanze)* to become established; *(Fremdwort)* to gain currency, to become established; **das hat sich so eingebürgert** *(Brauch)* it's just the way we/they *etc* have come to do things; *(Wort)* it's been adopted into the language; **es hat sich bei uns so eingebürgert, dass wir uns abwechseln** we've got into the habit of taking turns

Ein|bür|ge|rung F **-, -en** *(von Menschen)* naturalization; *(von Fremdwort, Pflanze)* introduction

Ein|bür|ge|rungs|an|trag M application *or* petition for naturalization; **einen ~ stellen** to apply for naturalization

Ein|bu|ße F loss *(an +dat* to); **der Skandal hat seinem Ansehen schwere ~ getan** he lost a considerable amount of respect because of the scandal

ein+bü|ßen *sep* VT to lose; *(durch eigene Schuld)* to forfeit VI to lose something; **an Klarheit** *(dat)* **~** to lose some of its clarity

Ein|cent|stück [ain'(t)sɛnt-] NT one-cent piece

ein+che|cken VTI *sep (am Flughafen)* to check in *(an +dat* at); *(im Hotel auch)* to register

Ein|che|cken NT **-s**, *no pl (am Flughafen)* checking in, check-in; *(im Hotel auch)* registration; **beim ~** as I *etc* was checking in; **das ~ dauert immer furchtbar lange** it always takes ages to check in

ein+cre|men ['ainkre:mən] VT *sep* to put cream on; *Gesicht etc auch* to cream

ein+däm|men VT *sep Fluss* to dam; *(fig) (= halten, vermindern)* to check, to stem; *(= im Zaum halten)* to contain

Ein|däm|mung F **a** *(= Damm)* dam **b** *(= das Eindämmen)* damming; *(= Verminderung)* checking, stemming; *(von Gefühlen)* containing

ein+damp|fen VT *sep* to evaporate

ein+de|cken *sep* VR **sich (mit etw) ~** to stock up (with sth); *(für den Haushalt)* to get in supplies (of sth); **wir haben uns ausreichend mit Geld eingedeckt** we've got enough money; **ich bin gut eingedeckt, ich habe mich eingedeckt** I am well supplied VT **a** *(Build, Mil, fig)* to cover; **ein Dach mit Ziegeln/Stroh ~** to tile/thatch a roof **b** *(inf: = überhäufen)* to inundate; **mit Arbeit eingedeckt sein** to be snowed under with *or* inundated with work

Ein|de|cker ['aindɛkɐ] M **-s, -** *(Aviat)* monoplane; *(= Autobus)* single decker

ein+dei|chen ['aindaiçn] VT *sep* to dyke *(Brit)*, to dike *(US)*; *Fluss auch* to embank

ein+del|len ['aindɛlən] VT *sep (inf)* to dent (in)

ein|deu|tig ['aindɔytɪç] ADJ clear; *Beweis auch* definite; *(= nicht zweideutig)* unambiguous; *Witz* explicit; *(Comput) Adresse, Variable, Datensatz* unique ADV **a** *(= unmissverständlich) formulieren* unambiguously; *sich ausdrücken* clearly; **jdm etw ~ sagen** to tell sb sth quite plainly, to tell sb sth straight *(inf)* **b** *(= klar)* clearly; **das ist ~ der Fall** it's clearly *or* obviously the case

Ein|deu|tig|keit F **-**, *no pl* clearness; *(= Unzweideutigkeit)* unambiguity; *(von Witz)* explicitness

ein+deut|schen ['aindɔytʃn] VT *sep Fremdwort* to Germanize; **Clips, ~d auch Klips** Clips, sometimes Germanized as Klips

Ein|deut|schung F **-, -en** Germanization

ein+di|cken ['aindɪkn] VTI *sep (vi: aux sein)* to thicken

ein|di|men|si|o|nal ADJ one-dimensional, unidimensional

Ein|di|men|si|o|na|li|tät F **-**, *no pl* one-dimensionality

ein+do|sen ['aindo:zn] VT *sep* to can, to tin *(Brit)*

ein+dö|sen VI *sep aux sein (inf)* to doze off, to drop off *(inf)*

ein+drän|gen *sep* VR to crowd in *(in +acc* -to); *(fig)* to intrude *(in +acc* upon); *(= sich einmischen) (in +acc* in) to interfere, to meddle *(inf)* VI *aux sein (lit, fig)* to crowd in *(auf +acc* on)

ein+dre|cken ['aindrɛkn] VT *sep (inf)* to get dirty *or* muddy

ein+dre|hen VT *sep* **a** *(= einschrauben)* to screw in *(in +acc* -to) **b** *Haar* to put in rollers

ein+dre|schen VI *sep irreg (inf)* **auf jdn ~** to lay into sb *(inf)*

ein+dril|len VT *sep (inf)* **jdm etw ~** to drill sb in sth; *Verhalten, Manieren etc* to din *or* drum sth into sb *(inf)*

ein+drin|gen VI *sep irreg aux sein* **a** *(= einbrechen)* **in etw** *(acc)* **~** to force one's way into sth; *(Dieb etc auch)* to force an entry into sth; **in unsere Linien/das Land ~** *(Mil)* to penetrate our lines/into the country
b in etw *(acc)* **~** to go into sth, to penetrate (into) sth; *(Wasser, Gas auch)* to get into *or* find its way into sth; *(Fremdwort, Amerikanismus)* to find its way into sth; **der Nagel drang tief ins Holz ein** the nail went deep into the wood; **eine Stimmung in sich ~ lassen** to let oneself be carried away by a mood
c *(= bestürmen)* **auf jdn ~** to go for *or* attack sb *(mit* with); *(mit Fragen, Bitten etc)* to besiege sb

ein|dring|lich ✪ ADJ *(= nachdrücklich)* insistent; *(= dringend auch)* urgent; *Schilderung* vivid; **mit ~en Worten** insistently, with insistence; vividly, in vivid words ADV *warnen* urgently, strongly; **ich habe ihn ~ gebeten, zu Hause zu bleiben** I urged him to stay at home; **jdm ~ nahelegen, etw zu tun** to urge sb *or* advise sb most strongly to do sth

Ein|dring|lich|keit F *(= Nachdrücklichkeit)* insistence; *(= Dringlichkeit auch)* urgency; *(von Schilderung)* vividness

Ein|dring|ling ['aindrɪŋlɪŋ] M **-s, -e** intruder; *(in Gesellschaft etc)* interloper

Ein|druck ✪ 33.2, 45.4, 53.4 M *pl* **-drücke** **a** impression; **den ~ erwecken, als ob** *or* **dass ...** to give the impression that ...; **die Eindrücke, die wir gewonnen hatten** our impressions; **ich habe den ~, dass ..., ich kann mich des ~s nicht erwehren, dass ...** *(geh)* I have the impression that ..., I can't help thinking that ... *(inf)*; **großen ~ auf jdn machen** to make a great *or* big impression on sb; **er macht einen heiteren ~/den ~ eines heiteren Menschen** he gives the impression of being cheerful/of being a cheerful person; **die Rede hat ihren ~ auf ihn nicht verfehlt** the speech made a strong impression on him; **er will ~ (bei ihr) machen** *or* **schinden** *(inf)* he's out to impress (her); **ich stehe noch ganz unter dem ~ der Ereignisse** I'm still too close to it all; **viele (neue) Eindrücke sammeln** to gain a whole host of new impressions; **du solltest einmal neue Eindrücke sammeln** you should broaden your horizons
b *(rare: = Spur)* impression, imprint

ein+drü|cken *sep* VT **a** *Fenster* to break; *Tür, Mauer* to push down; *(Sturm, Explosion)* to blow in/down; *(= einbeulen)* to dent, to bash in *(inf)*; *Brustkorb* to crush; *Nase* to flatten **b** *Fußspuren etc* to impress VR to make *or* leave an impression

Ein|drucks-: **ein|drucks|fä|hig** ADJ receptive; **Ein|drucks|fä|hig|keit** F, *no pl* receptiveness; **ein|drucks|los** ADJ unimpressive; **ein|drucks|voll** ADJ impressive

ein+dru|seln ['aindru:zln] VI *sep aux sein (inf)* to doze off, to drop off *(inf)*

ein+dü|beln VT *sep Haken* to plug *(in +acc* into)

ein+du|seln VI *sep aux sein (inf)* to doze off, to drop off *(inf)*

ei|ne ['ainə] → **ein**, **eine(r,s)**

ein+eb|nen VT *sep (lit)* to level (off); *(fig)* to level (out)

Ein|eb|nung F **-, -en** levelling *(Brit)*, leveling *(US)*

Ein|ehe F monogamy

ein|ei|ig ['ainlaiɪç] ADJ *Zwillinge* identical

ein|ein|halb ['ainlain'halp] NUM one and a half; **~ Mal** one and a half times → *auch* **anderthalb**

ein|ein|halb|mal ['ainlain'halpma:l] ADV → **eineinhalb**

Ein|el|tern|(teil)|fa|mi|lie F single-parent family

ei|nen ['ainən] VTR *(geh)* to unite

ein+en|gen ['ainlɛŋən] VT *sep (lit)* to constrict; *(fig) Begriff* to restrict, to narrow down; *Freiheit* to curb, to restrict; **sich (in seiner Freiheit) eingeengt fühlen** to feel cramped *or* restricted; **jdn in seiner Freiheit ~** to curb sb's freedom; **eingeengt sitzen/stehen/liegen** to sit/stand/lie (all) squashed up

ein|en|gend ADJ *(lit)* constricting; *(fig)* restrictive ADV **einen Begriff ~ interpretieren** to interpret a concept narrowly

Ein|en|gung F -, -en *(lit)* constriction; *(fig)* restriction

ei|ner ['ainɐ] ADV *(Aus)* = **herein**

Ei|ner ['ainɐ] M -s, - **a** *(Math)* unit **b** *(= Ruderboot)* single scull; **Weltmeister im ~** world champion in the single sculls

ei|ne(r, s) ['ainə] INDEF PRON **a** one; *(= jemand)* somebody, someone; **der/die/das Eine** the one; **das ~ Buch habe ich schon gelesen** I've already read one of the books *or* the one book; **das ~ Gute war ...** the one good thing was ...; **sein ~r Sohn** *(inf)* one of his sons; **weder der ~ noch der andere** neither (one) of them; **die ~n sagen so, die anderen gerade das Gegenteil** some (people) say one thing and others *or* some say just the opposite; **~r für alle, alle für ~n** *(Prov)* all for one and one for all *(Prov)*; **dumm/intelligent** *etc* **wie nur ~r** *(dated)* thick/intelligent *etc* as they come *(inf)*; **das ist ~r!** *(inf)* he's a (right) one! *(inf)*; **du bist mir vielleicht ~r!** *(inf)* you're a fine *or* right one *(inf)*; **sieh mal ~r an!** *(iro)* well what do you know! *(inf)*, surprise, surprise! *(inf)*; **alles in ~m abmachen** to do everything in one go; **in ~m fort** *(inf)* **in ~r Tour** *(inf)* non-stop → **ande|re(r, s)**
b *(= man)* one *(form)*, you; **und das soll ~r glauben!** *(inf)* and we're/you're meant to believe that!; **wie kann ~r nur so unklug sein!** how could anybody be so stupid!; **wenn ~m so etwas gegeben wird** if such a thing is given (to) one *(form) or* (to) you
c ~s *(auch* **eins***)* one thing; **~s gefällt mir nicht an ihm** (there's) one thing I don't like about him; **~s sag ich dir** I'll tell you one thing; **noch ~s!** another one!; *(Lied etc)* more!; **noch ~s, bevor ichs vergesse** (there's) something else *or* one other thing before I forget; **es kam ~s nach dem** *or* **zum anderen** it was (just) one thing after another; **es läuft alles auf ~s hinaus, es kommt alles auf ~s heraus** it all comes to the same (thing) in the end
d *(inf)* **sich** *(dat)* **~n genehmigen** to have a quick one *(inf) or* drink; **jdm ~ kleben** to thump sb one *(Brit inf)*, to punch sb → **abbrechen VT a**

Ei|ner|ka|jak M single seater *or* one-man canoe *or* kayak; *(= Disziplin)* single kayak *or* canoe

ei|ner|lei ['ainɐ'lai] ADJ *inv* **a** *pred (= gleichgültig)* all the same; **das ist mir ganz ~** it's all the same *or* all one to me; **was du machst ist mir ~** it's all the same to me what you do; **~ ob er kommt** no matter whether he comes or not; **~ was/wer ...** it doesn't matter what/who ... **b Stoff von ~ Farbe** self-coloured *(Brit) or* self-colored *(US)* material; **sie kocht immer nur ~ Essen** she always cooks the same kind *or* sort of food; **es gab für alle nur ~ zu essen** everyone had to eat the same thing

Ei|ner|lei ['ainɐ'lai] NT -s, *no pl* monotony

ei|ner|seits ['ainɐzaits] ✪ 53.5 ADV **~ ... andererseits ...** on the one hand ... on the other hand ...

Ei|ner|stel|le F *(Math)* unit (place)

ei|nes|teils ['ainəstails] ADV **~ ... ander(e)nteils** on the one hand ... on the other hand

Ein|eu|ro|stück [ain'ɔyro-] NT one-euro piece

Ei|ne-Welt-La|den M ≈ OXFAM shop *(Brit)*, ≈ thrift store *(US)*, ≈ charity shop for the Third World

ein|fach ['ainfax] ADJ **a** simple; *Mensch* ordinary; *Essen* plain
b *(nicht doppelt) Knoten, Schleife* simple; *Fahrkarte, Fahrt* one-way, single *(Brit)*; *Rockfalten* knife; *Buchführung* single-entry; **einmal ~!** *(in Bus etc)* single please *(Brit)*, one-way ticket please *(US)*; **~e Anführungszeichen** *pl* single quotation marks; **das ist nicht so ~ zu verstehen** that is not so easy to understand, that is not so easily understood
ADV **a** *(= schlicht) leben, essen, sich kleiden* simply
b *(= nicht doppelt)* once, simply; **~ gefaltet** folded once; **die Wolle ~ nehmen** to use one strand of wool
c *(verstärkend: = geradezu)* simply, just; **~ gemein** downright mean; **das ist doch ~ dumm** that's (just) plain stupid
d *(= ohne Weiteres)* just
e *(= mit Verneinung)* just

Ein|fach|heit F -, *no pl* simplicity; *(von Mensch)* ordinariness; *(von Essen)* plainness; **der ~ halber** for the sake of simplicity

ein+fä|deln *sep* VT **a** *Nadel, Faden* to thread *(in +acc* through); *Nähmaschine* to thread up; *Film* to thread **b** *(inf) Intrige, Plan etc* to set up *(inf)* VR **sich in eine Verkehrskolonne ~** to filter into a stream of traffic

ein+fah|ren *sep irreg* VI *aux sein (Zug, Schiff)* to come in *(in +acc* -to); *(Hunt: Fuchs, Dachs etc)* to go to earth; **in die Grube/den Schacht ~** *(Min)* to go down (to the face); **auf Bahnsteig 2 fährt der Zug aus München ein** the train from Munich is arriving at *or* coming in at platform 2
VT **a** *(= kaputt fahren) Mauer, Zaun* to knock down
b *Ernte* to bring in
c *Fahrgestell, Periskop* to retract
d *(= ans Fahren etc gewöhnen)* to break in; *Wagen* to run in *(Brit)*, to break in *(US)*; **„wird eingefahren"** "running in" *(Brit)*, "being broken in" *(US)*
e *Verluste* to make; *Gewinne auch* to bring in
VR to get used to driving; **ich muss mich erst mit dem neuen Auto ~** I have to get used to (driving) the new car; **das hat sich so eingefahren** *(fig)* it has just become a habit → *auch* **eingefahren**

Ein|fahr|sig|nal NT *(Rail)* home signal

Ein|fahrt F **a** *no pl (= das Einfahren)* entry *(in +acc* to); *(Min)* descent; **Vorsicht bei (der) ~ des Zuges!** stand well back, the train is arriving; **der Schnellzug hat ~ auf Gleis 3** the express is arriving at platform 3; **der Zug hat noch keine ~** the train can't enter the station **b** *(= Eingang)* entrance; *(= Toreinfahrt)* entry; *(Hunt)* tunnel; **„Einfahrt frei halten"** "keep clear"

Ein|fall M **a** *(fig) (= plötzlicher Gedanke)* idea; *(= Grille, Laune)* notion; **jdn auf den ~ bringen, etw zu tun** to give sb the idea of doing sth; **auf den ~ kommen, etw zu tun** to get the idea of doing sth; **es war ein bloßer** *or* **nur so ein ~** it was just an idea; **er hat Einfälle wie ein altes Haus** *(hum inf)* he has some weird ideas **b** *(Mil)* invasion *(in +acc* of) **c** *(des Lichts)* incidence *(spec)*; **je nach (dem) ~ des Lichts** according to how the light falls **d** *(liter) (der Nacht)* fall; *(des Winters)* onset; **vor ~ der Nacht** before nightfall

ein+fal|len ✪ 39.3, 41 VI *sep irreg aux sein* **a** *(Gedanke)* **jdm ~** to occur to sb; **das ist mir nicht eingefallen** I didn't think of that, that didn't occur to me; **mir fällt nichts ein, was ich schreiben kann** I can't think of anything to write; **jetzt fällt mir ein, wie/warum ...** I've just thought of how/why ..., it's just occurred to me how/why ...; **ihm fällt immer eine Ausrede ein** he can always think of an excuse; **das fällt mir nicht im Traum ein!** I wouldn't dream of it!; **sich** *(dat)* **etw ~ lassen** to think of sth, to come up with sth; **hast du dir etwas ~ lassen?** have you had any ideas?, have you thought of anything?; **da musst du dir schon etwas anderes/Besseres ~ lassen!** you'll really have to think of something else/better; **was fällt Ihnen ein!** what are you thinking of!
b *(= in Erinnerung kommen)* **jdm ~** to come to sb; **dabei fällt mir mein Onkel ein, der ...** that reminds me of my uncle, who ...; **es fällt mir jetzt nicht ein** I can't think of it at the moment, it won't come to me at the moment; **es wird Ihnen schon wieder ~** it will come back to you
c *(= einstürzen)* to collapse, to cave in; *(Gesicht, Wangen)* to become sunken *or* haggard → *auch* **eingefallen**
d *(= eindringen)* **in ein Land ~** to invade a country; **in die feindlichen Reihen ~** to penetrate the enemy lines; **Wölfe sind in die Schafherde eingefallen** *(liter)* wolves fell upon the flock of sheep *(liter)*
e *(Lichtstrahlen)* to fall, to be incident *(spec)*; *(in ein Zimmer etc)* to come in *(in +acc* -to)
f *(= mitsingen, mitreden)* to join in; *(= einsetzen: Chor, Stimmen)* to come in; *(= dazwischenreden)* to break in *(in +acc* on)
g *(liter) (Nacht)* to fall; *(Winter)* to set in
h *(Hunt: Federwild)* to come in, to settle

Ein|falls-: **ein|falls|los** ADJ unimaginative; **Ein|falls|lo|sig|keit** F -, *no pl* unimaginativeness; **ein|falls|reich** ADJ imaginative; **Ein|falls|reich|tum** M, *no pl* imaginativeness; **Ein|falls|tor** NT gateway

Ein|fall|stra|ße F access road

Ein|falls|win|kel M *(Phys)* angle of incidence

Ein|falt ['ainfalt] F -, *no pl (= Arglosigkeit)* simplicity, naivety; *(= Dummheit)* simple-mindedness, simpleness

ein|fäl|tig ['ainfɛltɪç] ADJ *(= arglos)* simple, naive; *(= dumm)* simple(-minded)

Ein|fäl|tig|keit F -, *no pl* simple-mindedness, simpleness

Ein|falts|pin|sel M *(inf)* simpleton

Ein|fa|mi|li|en|haus NT single-family house

ein+fan|gen VT *sep irreg (lit, fig)* to catch, to capture

ein+fär|ben VT *sep* **a** *Stoff, Haar* to dye **b** *(Typ) Druckwalze* to ink

ein|far|big, *(Aus)* **ein|fär|big** ADJ all one colour *(Brit) or* color *(US)*; *(Tex)* self-coloured *(Brit)*, self-colored *(US)*

ein+fas|sen VT *sep* **a** *(= umsäumen) Beet, Grab* to border, to edge; *Kleid, Naht, Knopfloch* to trim **b ein Grundstück (mit einem Zaun/einer Mauer/Hecke) ~** to put a fence/wall/hedge (a)round a plot of land **c** *Edelstein* to set *(mit* in); *Bild* to mount; *Quelle* to put a wall (a)round

Ein|fas|sung F **a** *(von Beet, Grab)* border, edging; *(von Kleid, Naht, Knopfloch)* trimming **b** *(= Zaun)* fence; *(= Mauer)* wall; *(= Hecke)* hedge **c** *(von Edelstein)* setting; *(von Bild)* mount

ein+fet|ten VT *sep* to grease; *Leder, Schuhe* to dubbin; *Haut, Gesicht* to cream, to rub cream into

ein+fin|den VR *sep irreg* to come; *(= eintreffen)* to arrive; *(zu Prüfung etc)* to present oneself; **ich bitte alle, sich pünktlich in meinem Büro einzufinden** I would ask you all to be in my office punctually; **ich werde mich also um 10 Uhr bei euch ~** I'll be *or* arrive at your place at 10 o'clock

ein+flech|ten VT *sep irreg Band, Blumen* to twine; *(fig: ins Gespräch etc)* to work in *(in +acc* -to), to introduce *(in +acc* in, into); **darf ich an dieser Stelle kurz ~, dass ...** I would just like to say at this point that ...; **in das Buch sind viele witzige Anekdoten eingeflochten** many amusing anecdotes have been woven into the book

ein+flie|gen *sep irreg* VT **a** *Flugzeug* to test-fly **b** *Proviant, Truppen* to fly in *(in +acc* -to) **c** *Verluste* to make; *Gewinne* to bring in, to make VI *aux sein* to fly in *(in +acc* -to)

ein+flie|ßen VI *sep irreg aux sein* to flow in; *(Gelder auch)* to pour in; *(Wasser auch)* to run in; *(fig)* to have some influence *(in +acc* on), to leave its mark *(in +acc* on); **er ließ nebenbei ~,**

dass er Professor sei he let it drop that he was a professor

ein+flö|ßen VT *sep* **jdm etw ~** to pour sth down sb's throat; *Medizin auch* to give sb sth; *Ehrfurcht, Mut etc* to instil *(Brit)* or instill *(US)* sth into sb, to instil *(Brit)* or instill *(US)* sb with a sense of sth

Ein|flug M **er beobachtete das Flugzeug beim ~** he watched the plane coming in; **er wurde beim ~ in Feindgebiet abgeschossen** he was shot down when flying into enemy territory

Ein|flug|schnei|se F *(Aviat)* approach path

Ein|fluss M **a** influence; **unter dem ~ von jdm/etw** under the influence of sb/sth; **~ auf jdn haben/ausüben** to have/exert an influence on sb; **~ nehmen** to bring an influence to bear; **seinen ~ geltend machen** to make one's influence felt; **das Wetter steht unter dem ~ eines atlantischen Tiefs** the weather is being affected *or* influenced by an Atlantic depression; **auf die Entscheidung hat es keinen ~** it has no influence *or* bearing on the decision, it won't influence the decision; **darauf habe ich keinen ~** I can't influence that, I've no influence over that **b** *(lit: = das Einfließen) (von Luft, fig)* influx; *(von Gas, Abwässern)* inflow

Ein|fluss-: **Ein|fluss|be|reich** M, **Ein|fluss|ge|biet** NT sphere of influence; **England liegt im ~ eines atlantischen Tiefs** England is being affected by an Atlantic depression; **ein|fluss|los** ADJ uninfluential; **Ein|fluss|lo|sig|keit** F -, *no pl* lack of influence; **Ein|fluss|mög|lich|keit** F influence; **unsere ~en sind begrenzt** we don't have much scope for influence; **Ein|fluss|nah|me** [-na:mə] F -, *(rare)* **-n** exertion of influence *(+gen* by); **ein|fluss|reich** ADJ influential; **Ein|fluss|sphä|re** F sphere of influence

ein+flüs|tern VT *sep* **jdm etw ~** to whisper sth to sb; *(fig)* to insinuate sth to sb

Ein|flüs|te|rung ['ainflʏstərʊŋ] F -, **-en** *(fig)* insinuation

ein+for|dern VT *sep Schulden* to demand payment of, to call (in); *Recht* to demand; *Versprechen, Zusage* to demand fulfilment *(Brit)* or fulfillment *(US)* of; *Unterstützung, Gerechtigkeit* to demand, to call for

ein|för|mig ADJ uniform; *(= eintönig)* monotonous

Ein|för|mig|keit F -, **-en** uniformity; *(= Eintönigkeit)* monotony

ein+fres|sen VR *sep irreg* to eat in *(in +acc* -to); **der Hass hatte sich tief in ihn eingefressen** hate had eaten deep into his heart

ein+frie|den ['ainfri:dn] VT *sep (geh)* to enclose

Ein|frie|dung F -, **-en** *(geh)* fence; wall; hedge

ein+frie|ren *sep irreg* VI *aux sein* to freeze; *(Wasserleitung, Schiff)* to freeze up; **im Eis eingefroren** frozen into the ice; **die Beziehungen ~ lassen** to suspend relations VT *(lit, fig) Nahrungsmittel, Löhne etc* to freeze; *(Pol) Beziehungen* to suspend; **sich ~ lassen** to allow oneself to be put into deep-freeze

Ein|frie|rung ['ainfri:rʊŋ] F -, **-en** *(fig) (von Löhnen etc)* freezing; *(von Beziehungen)* suspension

Ein|fü|ge|mar|ke F *(Comput)* insertion point

Ein|fü|ge|mo|dus M *(Comput)* insert mode

ein+fü|gen *sep* VT *Steine, Maschinenteile* to fit *(in +acc* into); *(Comput)* to insert *(in +acc* in); *ausgeschnittenen Text* to paste *(in +acc* in); *(= nachtragen)* to add *(in +acc* in); **darf ich an dieser Stelle ~, dass ...** may I add at this point that ... VR to fit in *(in +acc* -to); *(= sich anpassen)* to adapt *(in +acc* to); *(Haus in Umgebung etc)* to fit in *(in +acc* with)

Ein|fü|ge|tas|te F *(Comput)* insert key

Ein|fü|gung F insertion, addition

ein+füh|len VR *sep* **sich in jdn ~** to empathize with sb; *(Theat)* to feel oneself into (the role of) sb; **er kann sich gut in andere Leute ~** he's good at putting himself in other people's shoes *(inf)* or places, he's good at empathizing with other people; **sich in etw** *(acc)* **~** to understand sth; **sich in die Atmosphäre des 17. Jahrhunderts ~** to get into *or* project oneself into the atmosphere of the 17th century; **sich in ein Gedicht ~** to experience a poem

ein|fühl|sam ['ainfy:lza:m] ADJ *Interpretation* sensitive; *Mensch auch* understanding, empath(et)ic *(form)* ADV sensitively

Ein|fühl|sam|keit F -, *no pl* sensitivity; *(von Mensch auch)* understanding

Ein|füh|lung F understanding *(in +acc* of); *(in einen Menschen auch)* empathy *(in +acc* with); *(einer Interpretation)* sensitivity

Ein|füh|lungs|ver|mö|gen NT, *no pl* capacity for understanding, empathy; **ein Buch mit großem ~ interpretieren** to interpret a book with a great deal of sensitivity

Ein|fuhr ['ainfu:ɐ] F -, **-en** import; *(= das Einführen)* importing

Ein|fuhr- *in cpds* import; **Ein|fuhr|ar|ti|kel** M import; **ein ~ sein** to be imported; **Ein|fuhr|be|schrän|kun|gen** PL import restrictions *pl*; **Ein|fuhr|be|stim|mun|gen** PL import regulations *pl*

ein+füh|ren *sep* VT **a** *(= hineinstecken)* to insert, to introduce *(in +acc* into) **b** *(= bekannt machen)* to introduce *(in +acc* into); *(Comm) Firma, Artikel* to establish; **jdn in sein Amt ~** to install sb (in office); **jdn in seine Arbeit ~** to introduce sb to his work; **jdn bei Hofe ~** to present sb at court; **~de Worte** introductory words, words of introduction **c** *(als Neuerung)* to introduce, to bring in; *neue Mode* to set, to start; *Sitte* to start **d** *(Comm) Waren, Devisen* to import **e** *(St Ex)* to list, to introduce *(an +dat* on) VR to introduce oneself; **sich gut/nicht gut ~** to make a good/bad (initial) impression, to get off to a good/bad start *(inf)*

Ein|fuhr-: **Ein|fuhr|er|laub|nis** F, **Ein|fuhr|ge|neh|mi|gung** F import licence *(Brit)* or license *(US)*; **Ein|fuhr|ha|fen** M port of entry; **Ein|fuhr|kon|tin|gent** NT import quota; **Ein|fuhr|land** NT importing country; **Ein|fuhr|sper|re** F = **Einfuhrstopp**; **Ein|fuhr|stopp** M ban on imports, import ban; **ein ~ für etw** a ban on the import of sth

Ein|füh|rung ✪ 53.1 F introduction *(in +acc* to); *(von Produkt, Währung)* launch; *(= Amtseinführung)* installation; *(bei Hof)* presentation; *(= Börseneinführung)* listing, introduction; *(= das Hineinstecken)* insertion *(in +acc* into)

Ein|füh|rungs- *in cpds* introductory; **Ein|füh|rungs|an|ge|bot** NT *(Comm: bei Ladeneröffnung, neuer Ware etc)* introductory offer; **Ein|füh|rungs|kurs** M *(Univ etc)* introductory course; *(St Ex)* introductory rate; **Ein|füh|rungs|preis** M introductory price

Ein|fuhr-: **Ein|fuhr|ver|bot** NT ban on imports; **ein ~ für etw** a ban on the import of sth; **Ein|fuhr|zoll** M import duty

ein+fül|len VT *sep* to pour in; **etw in Flaschen/Säcke/Fässer ~** to put sth into bottles/sacks/barrels, to bottle/sack/barrel sth

Ein|füll-: **Ein|füll|öff|nung** F opening; **Ein|füll|stut|zen** M *(Aut)* filler pipe

Ein|ga|be F **a** *(form: = Gesuch)* petition *(an +acc* to) **b** *(von Medizin)* administration **c** *(Comput: von Daten)* input

Ein|ga|be-: **Ein|ga|be|auf|for|de|rung** F *(Comput)* command *or* system prompt; **Ein|ga|be|da|ten** PL input data *sing*; **Ein|ga|be|feh|ler** M *(Comput)* input error; **Ein|ga|be|frist** F time limit for the filing of petitions; **Ein|ga|be|ge|rät** NT input device; **Ein|ga|be|mas|ke** F *(Comput)* input mask; **Ein|ga|be|port** M **-s, -s** *(Comput)* input port; **Ein|ga|be|tas|te** F *(Comput)* enter key

Ein|gang M *pl* **-gänge a** entrance *(in +acc* to); *(= Zutritt, Aufnahme)* entry; **„kein ~!"** "no entrance"; **sich ~ in etw** *(acc)***/zu etw verschaffen** to gain entry into/to sth; **in etw** *(acc)* **~ finden** to find one's way into sth **b** *(Comm) (= Wareneingang, Posteingang)* delivery; *(= Erhalt)* receipt; **wir bestätigen den ~ Ihres Schreibens vom ...** we acknowledge receipt of your communication of the ...; **die Waren werden beim ~ gezählt** the goods are counted on delivery; **den ~ or die Eingänge bearbeiten** to deal with the in-coming post *(Brit)* or mail **c** *(= Beginn)* start, beginning; **zum ~ möchte ich bemerken ...** I would like to start by saying ...

ein|gän|gig ADJ *Melodie, Spruch* catchy; *Theorie* neat

Ein|gän|gig|keit F -, *no pl (von Melodie, Spruch)* catchiness

ein|gangs ['aingaŋs] ADV at the start *or* beginning PREP *+gen (form)* at the start *or* beginning of

Ein|gangs-: **Ein|gangs|be|reich** M *(von Gebäude)* entrance area, lobby; *(von Theater, Oper etc)* foyer; **Ein|gangs|be|stä|ti|gung** F *(Comm)* acknowledgement of receipt; **Ein|gangs|buch** NT *(Comm)* receipt book, book of receipts; **Ein|gangs|da|tum** NT date of receipt; **Ein|gangs|for|mel** F *(Jur)* preamble; *(in Brief)* opening phrase; **Ein|gangs|hal|le** F entrance hall; **Ein|gangs|pfor|te** F *(lit, fig)* gateway; **Ein|gangs|stem|pel** M *(Comm)* receipt stamp; **mit einem ~ versehen** stamped with the date of receipt; **Ein|gangs|tor** NT entrance, main gate; **Ein|gangs|tür** F entrance, door; **Ein|gangs|ver|merk** M *(Comm)* notice of receipt

ein+ge|ben VT *sep irreg* **a** *(= verabreichen)* to give; **jdm das Essen ~** to feed sb **b** *(Comput) Text, Befehl* to enter; *(= eintippen auch)* to key in; **Daten in den Computer ~** to feed *or* enter data into the computer **c** *(dated: = einreichen) Gesuch etc* to submit *(an +acc* to) **d** *(liter)* **jdm etw ~** *(Gedanken etc)* to inspire sb with sth; **das hat uns Gott eingegeben** it comes from God

ein|ge|bet|tet [-gəbɛtət] ADJ embedded *(auch Comput)*; **in** *or* **zwischen Wäldern/Hügeln ~** nestling among the woods/hills → *auch* **einbetten**

ein|ge|bil|det ADJ **a** *(= hochmütig)* conceited **b** *(= imaginär)* imaginary; *Schwangerschaft* phantom; **ein ~er Kranker** a hypochondriac → *auch* **einbilden**

Ein|ge|bil|det|heit F -, *no pl* conceit

ein|ge|bo|ren ADJ *(= einheimisch)* native; *(= angeboren)* innate, inborn *(+dat* in); **Gottes ~er Sohn** the only begotten Son of God

Ein|ge|bo|re|nen|spra|che F native language

Ein|ge|bo|re|ne(r) ['aingəbo:rənə] MF *decl as adj* native *(auch hum)*

Ein|ge|bo|re|nen|stamm M native *or* indigenous tribe *or* people

Ein|ge|bung ['ainge:bʊŋ] F -, **-en** inspiration

ein|ge|denk ['aingədɛŋk] *(old, liter)* PREP *+gen* bearing in mind, remembering; **~ dessen, dass ...** bearing in mind that ..., remembering that ... ADJ *pred* **einer Sache** *(gen)* **~ sein** to bear sth in mind, to be mindful of sth *(old liter)*

ein|ge|fah|ren [-gəfa:rən] ADJ *Verhaltensweise* well-worn; **die Diskussion bewegte sich in ~en Gleisen** the discussion stayed in the same old groove *or* covered the same old well-worn topics → *auch* **einfahren**

ein|ge|fal|len ADJ *Wangen* hollow, sunken; *Augen* sunken, deep-set; *Gesicht* haggard, gaunt; *Schultern* drooping → *auch* **einfallen**

ein|ge|fleischt [-gəflaiʃt] ADJ **a** *attr (= überzeugt)* confirmed; *(= unverbesserlich)* dyed-in-the-wool; *(hum)* confirmed bachelor **b** *(= zur zweiten Natur geworden)* ingrained, deep-rooted

ein+ge|hen ✪ 53.2 *sep irreg aux sein* VI **a** *(= ankommen) (Briefe, Waren etc)* to arrive, to be received; *(Meldung, Spenden, Bewerbungen)* to come in, to be received; **~de Post/Waren** incoming mail/goods; **eingegangene Post/Spenden** mail/donations received

b (*old*: = *eintreten*) to enter (*in +acc* into); (= *Aufnahme finden: Wort, Sitte*) to be adopted (*in +acc* in); **in die Geschichte ~** to go down in (the annals of) history; **in die Unsterblichkeit ~** to attain immortality; **zur ewigen Ruhe** *or* **in den ewigen Frieden ~** to go to (one's) rest **c etw geht jdm ein** (= *wird verstanden*) sb grasps *or* understands sth; **wann wird es dir endlich ~, dass ...?** when will it finally sink in *or* when will you finally understand that ...?; **es will mir einfach nicht ~, wie ...** it's beyond me how ..., I just cannot understand how ... **d** (= *wirken*) **diese Musik geht einem leicht ein** this music is very catchy; **diese Worte gingen ihm glatt ein** these words were music to his ears **e** (*fig*: = *einfließen*) to leave its mark, to have some influence (*in +acc* on); **die verschiedensten Einflüsse sind in das Werk eingegangen** there have been the most diverse influences on his work **f** (= *einlaufen: Stoff*) to shrink **g** (= *sterben: Tiere, Pflanze*) to die (*an +dat* of); (*inf: Firma etc*) to fold; **bei dieser Hitze/Kälte geht man ja ein!** (*inf*) this heat/cold is just too much (*inf*) *or* is killing (*inf*) **h auf etw** (*acc*) **~** (= *behandeln, auf Frage, Punkt etc*) to go into sth; **darauf gehe ich noch näher ein** I will go into that in more detail; **niemand ging auf meine Frage/mich ein** nobody took any notice of my question/me **i** (= *sich widmen, einfühlen*) **auf jdn/etw ~** to give (one's) time and attention to sb/sth **j** (= *zustimmen*) **auf einen Vorschlag/Plan ~** to agree to *or* fall in with a suggestion/plan

VT (= *abmachen, abschließen*) to enter into; *Risiko* to take; *Wette* to make; **er gewinnt, darauf gehe ich jede Wette ein** I bet you anything he wins; **einen Vergleich ~** (*Jur*) to reach a settlement

ein|ge|hend **ADJ** (= *ausführlich*) detailed; (= *gründlich*) thorough; *Bericht, Studien, Untersuchungen* in-depth *attr* **ADV** (= *ausführlich*) in detail; (= *gründlich*) thoroughly

ein|ge|keilt ['aingəkailt] **ADJ** hemmed in; *Auto* hemmed in, boxed in; (*Sport*) boxed in; (*fig*) trapped → *auch* **einkeilen**

ein|ge|legt ['aingəlekt] *ptp von* **einlegen** **ADJ** **a** (*Cook*) *Gemüse* preserved; (*in Essig*) *auch Hering* pickled **b** (= *mit Intarsien verziert*) **~er Schrank** inlaid cupboard **c** (*Mot*) **mit ~em Gang parken** to park with the car *etc* in gear → *auch* **einlegen**

Ein|ge|mach|te(s) ['aingəmaxtə] **NT** *decl as adj* bottled fruit/vegetables; (= *Marmelade*) preserves *pl*; (*inf*: = *Erspartes*) one's own resources *pl*; **ans ~ gehen** (*fig inf*) to dig deep into one's reserves

ein+ge|mein|den ['aingəmaindn] *ptp* **eingemeindet** **VT** *sep* to incorporate (*in +acc, nach* into)

Ein|ge|mein|dung **F -, -en** incorporation

ein|ge|nom|men ['aingənɔmən] **ADJ** **für jdn/etw ~ sein** to be taken with sb/sth, to be enamoured (*Brit*) *or* enamored (*US*) of sb/sth; **gegen jdn/etw ~ sein** to be prejudiced *or* biased against sb/sth; **er ist sehr von sich** (*dat*) **selbst ~** he thinks a lot of himself, he really fancies himself (*Brit inf*) → *auch* **einnehmen**

Ein|ge|nom|men|heit **F -,** *no pl* partiality (*für, von* to)

ein|ge|schlech|tig ['aingəʃlɛçtɪç] **ADJ** (*Bot*) unisexual, diclinous (*form*)

ein|ge|schlecht|lich **ADJ** *Gruppe* single-sex

ein|ge|schlos|sen [-gəʃlɔsn] *ptp von* **einschließen** **ADJ** **a** (= *eingesperrt*) *Wertsachen etc* locked up; *Person* locked in **b** (= *umgeben*) *Grundstück, Haus etc* enclosed **c** (= *umzingelt*) surrounded, encircled **d** (= *nicht extra zu zahlen*) **im Preis ~** included in the price; **es ist alles mit ~** it's all-inclusive → *auch* **einschließen**

ein|ge|schnappt [-gəʃnapt] **ADJ** (*inf*) cross; **~ sein** to be in a huff; **sie ist immer gleich ~** she always goes into a huff → *auch* **einschnappen**

ein|ge|schos|sig, ein|ge|scho|ßig (*Aus, S Ger*) **ADJ** *Haus* single-storey (*Brit*), single-story (*US*)

ein|ge|schränkt [-gəʃrɛŋkt] **ADJ** (= *eingeengt*) restricted, limited; (= *sparsam*) careful; **in ~en Verhältnissen leben** to live in straitened circumstances → *auch* **einschränken**

Ein|ge|schränkt|heit **F -,** *no pl* restriction; (*finanziell*) straitened circumstances *pl*

ein|ge|schrie|ben [-gəʃri:bn] **ADJ** *Mitglied, Brief* registered → *auch* **einschreiben**

ein|ge|schwo|ren [-gəʃvo:rən] **ADJ** confirmed; *Gemeinschaft* close; **auf etw** (*acc*) **~ sein** to swear by sth; **auf eine Politik ~ sein** to be committed to a policy; **er ist auf diese Art von Malerei ~** he is a great fan of this type of painting; **die beiden sind aufeinander ~** the two of them are very close (to one another) → *auch* **einschwören**

ein|ge|ses|sen [-gəzɛsn] **ADJ** established; **die Firma/Familie ist dort seit Generationen ~** the firm/family has been (established) there for generations; **die Eingesessenen** the established inhabitants/families *etc* → *auch* **einsitzen**

Ein|ge|sot|te|ne(s) ['aingəzɔtənə] **NT** *decl as adj* (*Aus*) bottled fruit

ein|ge|spannt **ADJ** busy → *auch* **einspannen**

ein|ge|spielt [-gəʃpi:lt] **ADJ** *Mannschaft* used to playing together; *Arbeitsteam, Kollegen* used to working together; **aufeinander ~ sein** to be used to one another → *auch* **einspielen**

ein|ge|stan|de|ner|ma|ßen ['aingəʃtandənɐ'ma:sn], **ein|ge|stand|ner|ma|ßen** ['aingəʃtandnɐ'ma:sn] **ADV** admittedly

Ein|ge|ständ|nis **NT** admission, confession

ein+ge|ste|hen *ptp* **eingestanden** **VT** *sep irreg* to admit, to confess; **sie hat den Diebstahl eingestanden** she admitted (to) *or* confessed to the theft; **sich** (*dat*) **~, dass ...** to admit to oneself that ...

ein|ge|stellt **ADJ** **materialistisch/fortschrittlich ~ sein** to be materialistically/progressively minded, to be materialistic/progressive; **links/rechts ~ sein** to have leanings to the left/right; **die links/rechts Eingestellten** leftists/rightists, left-/right-wingers; **wer so ~ ist wie er** anyone who thinks as he does, anyone like him; **gegen jdn ~ sein** to be set against sb; **ich bin im Moment nicht auf Besuch ~** I'm not prepared for visitors; **wir sind nur auf kleinere Reisegesellschaften ~** we can only cater for small parties; **auf Export ~ sein** to be geared to exports, to be tailored to the export market → *auch* **einstellen**

ein|ge|stri|chen [-gəʃtrɪçn] **ADJ** (*Mus*) **das ~e C** middle C; **das ~e A** the A above middle C

ein|ge|tra|gen [-gətra:gn] **ADJ** *Mitglied, Warenzeichen, Verein* registered → *auch* **eintragen**

Ein|ge|wei|de ['aingəvaidə] **NT -s, -** *usu pl* entrails *pl*, innards *pl*; **der Schreck fuhr mir bis in die ~** (*liter*) my blood froze

Ein|ge|wei|de|bruch **M** (*Med*) hernia

Ein|ge|weih|te(r) ['aingəvaitə] **MF** *decl as adj* initiate; **seine Lyrik ist nur ~n verständlich** his poetry can only be understood by the initiated; **ein paar ~** a chosen few

ein+ge|wöh|nen *ptp* **eingewöhnt** **VR** *sep* to settle down *or* in (*in +dat* in)

Ein|ge|wöh|nung **F** settling down *or* in

Ein|ge|wöh|nungs|zeit **F** settling-in *or* settling-down period

ein|ge|wur|zelt [-gəvʊrtslt] **ADJ** deep-rooted, deep-seated; **tief bei jdm ~ sein** to be deeply ingrained in sb

Ein|ge|zo|ge|ne(r) ['aingətso:gənə] **MF** *decl as adj* (*Mil*) conscript, draftee (*US*)

ein|ge|zwängt [-gətsvɛŋt] *ptp von* **einzwängen** **ADJ** packed *or* jammed (*in +dat* into); (*fig*) straitjacketed; **sich ~ fühlen** (*in Ehe*) to feel constricted *or* trapped; (*in Kleidung*) to feel constricted → *auch* **einzwängen**

ein+gie|ßen **VT** *sep irreg* (= *hineinschütten*) to pour in (*in +acc* -to); (= *einschenken*) to pour (out); **darf ich Ihnen noch Kaffee ~?** can I give you or pour you some more coffee?

ein+gip|sen **VT** *sep Arm, Bein* to put in plaster; *Dübel etc* to plaster in (*in +acc* -to)

Ein|glas **NT** (*dated*) monocle

ein|glei|sig **ADJ** single-track **ADV** **der Zug fährt hier nur ~** the railway (*Brit*) *or* railroad (*US*) line is only single-track here; **die Straßenbahn fährt hier nur ~** the tram (*Brit*) *or* streetcar (*US*) line is only single-track here; **er denkt sehr ~** (*fig*) he's completely single-minded

Ein|glei|sig|keit ['ainglaizɪçkait] **F -,** *no pl* (*fig*) single-mindedness

ein+glie|dern *sep* **VT** *Firma, Gebiet* to incorporate (*+dat* into, with); *jdn* to integrate (*in +acc* into); (= *einordnen*) to include (*unter +acc* under, in) **VR** to fit in (*+dat, in +acc* -to, in), to integrate oneself (*+dat, in +acc* into) (*form*)

Ein|glie|de|rung **F** (*von Firma, Gebiet*) incorporation; (*von Behinderten, Straffälligen*) integration

Ein|glie|de|rungs|hil|fe **F** (*für Behinderte, Spätaussiedler etc*) assistance with social integration

ein+gra|ben *sep irreg* **VT** *Pfahl, Pflanze* to dig in (*in +acc* -to); (= *vergraben*) *Schatz, Leiche* to bury (*in +acc* in); **eine Inschrift in Granit ~** (*geh*) to carve an inscription into granite **VR** to dig oneself in (*auch Mil*); **der Fluss hat sich ins Gestein eingegraben** the river carved itself a channel in the rock; **dieses Erlebnis hat sich seinem Gedächtnis eingegraben** this experience has carved itself on his memory

ein+gra|vie|ren *ptp* **eingraviert** **VT** *sep* to engrave (*in +acc* in)

ein+grei|fen **VI** *sep irreg* **a** (*Tech*) to mesh (*in +acc* with) **b** (= *einschreiten, Mil*) to intervene; **in jds Rechte** (*acc*) **~** to intrude (up)on sb's rights; **wenn nicht sofort ein Arzt eingreift, ...** without immediate medical intervention ...; **Eingreifen** intervention

Ein|greif|trup|pe **F** (*Mil*) strike force

ein+gren|zen **VT** *sep* (*lit*) to enclose; (*fig*) *Problem, Thema* to delimit, to circumscribe; (= *verringern*) to narrow *or* cut down

Ein|gren|zung ['aingrɛntsʊŋ] **F -, -en** enclosure; (*von Problem, Thema*) delimitation, circumscription; (= *Verringerung*) narrowing down

Ein|griff **M** **a** (*Med*) operation; **ein verbotener ~** an illegal abortion **b** (= *Übergriff*) intervention; **ein ~ in jds Rechte/Privatsphäre** an intrusion (up)on sb's rights/privacy **c** (*von Herrenunterhose*) fly

Ein|griffs|mög|lich|keit **F** possibility of intervention

ein+grup|pie|ren *ptp* **eingruppiert** **VT** *sep* to group (*in +acc* in)

Ein|grup|pie|rung **F** grouping

ein+ha|cken **VI** *sep* to peck (*auf +acc* at); **auf jdn ~** (*fig*) to pick on sb

ein+ha|ken *sep* **VT** to hook in (*in +acc* -to) **VI** (*inf*: = *Punkt aufgreifen*) to intervene; (*in Unterhaltung auch*) to break in; **wenn ich an diesem Punkt vielleicht ~ darf** if I might just take up that point **VR** **sie hakte sich bei ihm ein** she put *or* slipped her arm through his; **eingehakt gehen** to walk arm in arm

Ein|halt **M**, *no pl* **jdm/einer Sache ~ gebieten** to stop *or* halt sb/sth; *einem Missbrauch auch* to put an end *or* a stop to sth

ein+hal|ten *sep irreg* **VT** **a** (= *beachten*) to keep; *Spielregeln* to follow; *Diät, Vertrag* to keep to; *Verpflichtungen* to carry out; **die Zeit ~** to keep to time *or* schedule; **den Kurs ~** (*Aviat, Naut*) to maintain (its/one's) course, to stay on course; **er hält seine Zahlungsverpflichtungen immer pünktlich ein** he's always prompt about payments **b** (*old*: = *aufhalten*) *Schwungrad* to stop **c** (*Sew*) to gather **VI** **a** (*geh*) (= *aufhören*) to stop, to halt; (= *innehalten*) to pause; **halt ein!** stop! **b** (*dial*: = *Harn, Stuhlgang zurückhalten*) to wait

Ein|hal|tung **F** (= *Beachtung*) keeping (*+gen* of); (*von Spielregeln*) following (*+gen* of); (*von Diät, Vertrag*) keeping (*+gen* to); (*von Verpflichtungen*)

carrying out (+*gen* of); **ich werde ihn zur ~ des Vertrages zwingen** I will force him to keep (to) the contract

ein+häm|mern *sep* VT *Nagel etc* to hammer in (*in +acc* -to); *Inschrift etc* to chisel in (*in +acc* -to), to engrave (*in +acc* into); **jdm etw ~** (*fig*) to hammer *or* drum sth into sb VI **auf etw** (*acc*) **~** to hammer on sth; **auf jdn ~** (*lit, fig*) to pound sb

ein+hams|tern VT *sep* (*inf*) to collect

ein+han|deln VT *sep* **a** (*gegen, für* for) to trade, to swap, to exchange **b** (*= bekommen*) **sich** (*dat*) **etw ~** (*inf*) to get sth

ein|hän|dig ADJ one-handed

ein+hän|di|gen ['ainhɛndɪgn] VT *sep* (*form*) to hand in, to submit (*form*)

Ein|hän|di|gung F -, -en (*form*) handing in, submission (*form*)

Ein|hand|seg|ler M (*= Boot*) single-handed yacht, single-hander

Ein|hand|seg|ler (in) M(F) single-handed yachtsman/-woman; **als ~ um die Welt fahren** to sail single-handed (a)round the world

ein+hän|gen *sep* VT *Tür* to hang; *Fenster* to put in VR **sich bei jdm ~** to slip *or* put one's arm through sb's; **sie gingen eingehängt** they walked arm in arm

ein+hau|chen VT *sep* (*liter*) **jdm/einer Sache etw ~** to breathe sth into sb/sth; **einer Sache** (*dat*) **neues Leben ~** to breathe new life into sth, to bring new life to sth

ein+hau|en *sep irreg* VT **a** *Nagel etc* to knock *or* drive *or* bash (*inf*) in (*in +acc* -to) **b** (*= zertrümmern*) to smash *or* bash (*inf*) in **c** (*= einmeißeln*) *Kerbe* to cut in (*in +acc* -to); *Inschrift etc auch* to carve in (*in +acc* -to) VI **a auf jdn ~** to lay into sb, to go for sb; **auf etw** (*acc*) **~** to go at sth **b** (*inf: beim Essen*) to tuck *or* pitch in (*inf*)

ein+he|ben VT *sep irreg* (*esp Aus*) *Steuern* to levy; *Geld* to collect

Ein|he|bung F (*esp Aus*) (*von Steuern*) levying; (*von Geldern*) collection

ein+hef|ten VT *sep* **a** *Buchseiten* to stitch in; (*mit Heftmaschine*) to staple in; (*Sew*) *Futter* to tack in **b** (*= einordnen*) *Akten etc* to file

ein+he|gen VT *sep* to enclose

ein|hei|misch ['ainhaimɪʃ] ADJ *Mensch, Tier, Pflanze* native, indigenous; *Produkt, Industrie, Mannschaft* local

Ein|hei|mi|sche(r) ['ainhaimɪʃə] MF *decl as adj* local

ein+heim|sen ['ainhaimzn] VT *sep* (*inf*) to collect; *Erfolg, Ruhm auch* to walk off with; *Geld auch* to rake in (*inf*); **er hat den Ruhm für sich allein eingeheimst** he took the credit himself

Ein|hei|rat F marriage (*in +acc* into)

ein+hei|ra|ten VI *sep* **in einen Betrieb ~** to marry into a business

Ein|heit ['ainhait] F -, -en **a** (*von Land etc, Einheitlichkeit*) unity; (*= das Ganze*) whole; **die drei ~en** (*Liter*) the three unities; **eine geschlossene ~ bilden** to form an integrated whole; **~ von Forschung und Lehre** indivisibility of teaching and research; **die (deutsche) ~** (German) unity **b** (*Mil, Sci, Telec*) unit

> **TAG DER DEUTSCHEN EINHEIT**
>
> The **Tag der deutschen Einheit** is the national holiday of the Federal Republic of Germany. It is celebrated on October 3rd, the day on which the two parts of Germany were re-unified in 1990. The tone of the day is political – serious speeches are made at official commemorative events – although people try to make it a day of rejoicing. The national holiday was formerly on June 17th, a day when the victims of the division of Germany were commemorated.

ein|heit|lich ['ainhaitlɪç] ADJ (*= gleich*) the same, uniform; (*= genormt*) standard(ized); (*= in sich geschlossen*) unified ADV uniformly; **~ gekleidet** dressed alike *or* the same; **wir müssen ~ vorgehen** we must act consistently with one another; **alle Spielplätze sind ~ gestaltet** all the playgrounds are built on the same lines; **die Pausenzeiten sind in allen Werken ~ geregelt** the times of breaks are laid down to be the same in all the works

Ein|heit|lich|keit F -, *no pl* (*= Gleichheit*) uniformity; (*= Genormtheit*) standardization; (*= innere Geschlossenheit*) unity

Ein|heits-: **Ein|heits|brei** M (*pej*) **es ist so ein ~** it's all so samey (*pej*); **Ein|heits|for|mat** NT standard format; **Ein|heits|fraß** M (*pej*) **wir bekommen einen ~** we all get the same disgusting food; **Ein|heits|front** F (*Pol*) united front; (*= Volksfront*) popular front; **Ein|heits|ge|werk|schaft** F unified trade *or* labor (*US*) union; **Ein|heits|klei|dung** F uniform; **Ein|heits|kurz|schrift** F standard shorthand; **Ein|heits|lis|te** F (*Pol*) single *or* unified list of candidates; **Ein|heits|par|tei** F united party; **in einigen Staaten gibt es nur eine ~** in some countries there is only a single *or* only one political party; **Ein|heits|preis** M standard *or* flat price; **Ein|heits|schu|le** F comprehensive (school); **Ein|heits|so|zi|a|list(in)** M(F) (*DDR*) SED member; **Ein|heits|staat** M (*Pol*) united state; **Ein|heits|ta|rif** M flat rate; **Ein|heits|wert** M (*von Immobilien*) ≈ rateable value

ein+hei|zen *sep* VI to put the heating on; **bei dieser Kälte muss man tüchtig ~** you have to have the heating going full blast in this cold weather; **jdm (tüchtig) ~** (*inf*) (*= die Meinung sagen*) to haul sb over the coals; (*= zu schaffen machen*) to make things hot for sb VT *Ofen* to put on; *Zimmer* to heat (up)

ein+hel|fen VI *sep irreg* (*dial*) to help out

ein|hel|lig ['ainhɛlɪç] ADJ unanimous ADV unanimously

Ein|hel|lig|keit F unanimity

ein|her [ain'heːɐ] ADV (*Aus*) = **herein**

ein|her- PREF (*= entlang*) along; (*= hin und her*) up and down; **einherreiten** to ride along/up and down

ein|her+ge|hen VI *sep irreg aux sein* (*= umhergehen*) to go around; **mit etw ~** (*fig: = mit sich bringen*) to be accompanied by sth

ein|her+re|den VTI *sep* = **daherreden**

ein|her+stol|zie|ren *ptp* **einherstolziert** VI *sep aux sein* (*dated*) to strut along; (*auf jdn zu*) to come strutting along

ein|hin [ain'hɪn] ADV (*Aus*) = **hinein**

ein|hö|cke|rig, **ein|höck|rig** ADJ *Kamel* one-humped

ein+ho|len VT *sep* **a** (*= einziehen*) *Boot, Netz, Tau* to pull *or* haul in; *Fahne, Segel* to lower, to take down **b** *Rat, Gutachten, Erlaubnis* to obtain; **bei jdm Rat ~** to obtain sb's advice *or* advice from sb **c** (*= erreichen, nachholen*) *Laufenden, Auto* to catch up; *Vorsprung, Versäumtes, Zeit* to make up; *Verlust* to make good; **der Alltag/die Vergangenheit hat mich eingeholt** the daily routine/the past has caught up with me **d** *auch vi* (*dial*) = **einkaufen**

Ein|hol- (*dial*): **Ein|hol|netz** NT string bag; **Ein|hol|ta|sche** F shopping bag

Ein|ho|lung ['ainhoːlʊŋ] F -, -en **a** (*von Fahne*) lowering **b** (*von Rat, Gutachten etc*) obtaining

Ein|horn NT (*Myth, Astron*) unicorn

Ein|hu|fer ['ainhuːfɐ] M -s, - (*Zool*) solidungulate (*spec*)

ein|hu|fig [-huːfɪç] ADJ solidungulate (*spec*)

ein+hül|len *sep* VT *Kind, Leichnam* to wrap (up), to swathe (*liter*) (*in +acc* in); **in Nebel/Wolken eingehüllt** shrouded *or* enveloped in mist/clouds VR (*geh*) to wrap oneself up

ein|hun|dert ['ain'hʊndɐt] NUM (*form*) = **hundert**

ein+hü|ten VI *sep* (*N Ger*) to keep house (*bei* for); (*= Kinder hüten*) to babysit (*bei* for)

ei|ni ['aini] ADV (*Aus*) = **hinein**

ei|nig ['ainɪç] ✪ 38.1 ADJ **a** (*= geeint*) united **b** (*= einer Meinung*) agreed, in agreement (*über +acc* on, about, *in +dat* on); **ich weiß mich in dieser Sache mit ihm ~** (*geh*) I know I am in agreement with him on this; **sich** (*dat*) **über etw** (*acc*) **~ werden** to agree on sth; **darüber** *or* **darin sind wir uns ~, dass …** we are agreed that …; **wir werden schon miteinander ~ werden** we will manage to come to an agreement; **ich bin mir selbst noch nicht ganz ~, was …** I am still somewhat undecided as to what …

ei|ni|ge ['ainɪgə] INDEF PRON = **einige(r, s)**

ein+igeln ['ainliːgln] VR *sep* (*Mil*) to take up a position of all-round defence (*Brit*) *or* all-around defense (*US*); (*fig*) to hide (oneself) away

ei|ni|ge|mal △ ['ainɪgəmaːl, 'ainɪgə'maːl] ADV → **einige(r, s) b**

ei|ni|gen ['ainɪgn] VT *Volk etc* to unite; *Streitende* to reconcile VR to reach (an) agreement (*über +acc* about); **sich über den Preis/eine gemeinsame Politik ~** to reach agreement *or* to agree on the price/a common policy; **sich auf einen Kompromiss/Vergleich ~** to agree to a compromise/settlement; **sich dahin (gehend) ~, dass …** to agree that …

Ei|ni|ger ['ainɪgɐ] M -s, -, **Ei|ni|ge|rin** [-ərɪn] F -, -nen (*geh*) unifier

ei|ni|ge(r, s) ['ainɪgə] INDEF PRON **a** *sing* (*= etwas*) some; (*= ziemlich viel*) (quite) some; **in ~r Entfernung** some distance away; **nach ~r Zeit** after a while *or* some time; **ich könnte dir ~s über ihn erzählen, was …** I could tell you a thing or two about him that …; **das wird ~s kosten** that will cost something; **dazu ist noch ~s zu sagen** there are still one or two things to say about that; **dazu gehört schon ~s** that really takes something; **dazu gehört schon ~ Frechheit/~r Mut** that takes some cheek (*Brit*) *or* nerve/some courage; **mit ~m guten Willen** (*= mit Anstrengung*) with a bit of effort; **mit ~m guten Willen hätte der Richter ihn freisprechen können** the judge could have given him the benefit of the doubt and acquitted him **b** *pl* some; (*= mehrere*) several; (*= ein paar*) a few, some; **mit ~n anderen** with several/a few others; **~ wenige** a few; **mit Ausnahme ~r weniger** with a few exceptions; **~ Mal(e)** a few times, several times; **~ hundert** *or* **Hundert Menschen** a few hundred people; **~ hunderte** *or* **Hunderte von Flaschen** hundreds of bottles, several hundred bottles; **an ~n Stellen** in some places; **in ~n Tagen** in a few days; **vor ~n Tagen** the other day, a few days ago

ei|ni|ger|ma|ßen ['ainɪgɐ'maːsn] ADV (*= ziemlich*) rather, somewhat; (*vor adj*) fairly; (*= ungefähr*) to some extent *or* degree; **ein ~ gutes Angebot** a fairly good offer, not a bad offer; **~ Bescheid wissen** to have a fair idea; **er hat die Prüfung so ~ geschafft** he did so-so in (*Brit*) *or* on (*US*) the exam; **wie gehts dir? – ~** how are you? – all right *or* so-so *or* not too bad ADJ *pred* (*inf: = leidlich*) all right, fair, reasonable; **wie ist denn das Hotel? – na ja, ~** what's the hotel like? – oh, fair *or* all right

ei|ni|ges ['ainɪgəs] INDEF PRON = **einige(r, s)**

ei|nig+ge|hen *sep irreg aux sein*, **ei|nig ge|hen** △ *irreg aux sein* VI to agree, to be agreed (*in +dat* on); **ich gehe mit ihm darin einig, dass …** I am agreed with him that …; **wir gehen einig in der Überzeugung, dass …** we are one in our conviction that …

Ei|nig|keit F -, *no pl* (*= Eintracht*) unity; (*= Übereinstimmung*) agreement; **in diesem** *or* **über diesen Punkt herrschte** *or* **bestand ~** there was agreement on this point; **~ macht stark** (*Prov*) unity gives strength, strength through unity (*prov*)

Ei|ni|gung F -, -en **a** (*Pol*) unification **b** (*= Übereinstimmung*) agreement; (*Jur: = Vergleich*) settlement; **über etw** (*acc*) **~ erzielen** to come to *or* reach agreement on sth

Ei|ni|gungs-: **Ei|ni|gungs|be|stre|bun|gen** PL (*Pol*) unification efforts *pl*, unification movement *sing*; **Ei|ni|gungs|pro|zess** M (*bei*

Wiedervereinigung etc) unification process; **Ei|ni|gungs|ver|such** M attempt to reach agreement; **Ei|ni|gungs|ver|trag** M (Pol) Unification Treaty

ein+imp|fen VT sep **jdm etw ~** (lit) to inject or inoculate sb with sth; **er hat seinen Kindern diese Ansichten eingeimpft** he drummed these ideas into his children

ein+ja|gen VT sep **jdm Furcht ~** to frighten sb; **jdm einen Schrecken ~** to give sb a fright or a shock

ein|jäh|rig ADJ Kind, Tier one-year-old; Pflanze annual; Amtszeit, Studium one-year attr; **nach ~er Pause** after a break of one or a year; **eine ~e Frist/Dauer** a period of one or a year

Ein|jäh|ri|ge(r) ['ainjɛːrɪgə] M decl as adj, **Ein|jäh|rig-Frei|wil|li|ge(r)** ['ainjɛːrɪgə] M decl as adj (Mil Hist) one-year army volunteer

Ein|jäh|ri|ge(s) ['ainjɛːrɪgə] NT decl as adj (old Sch) ≈ lower school certificate (old)

ein+kal|ku|lie|ren ptp **einkalkuliert** VT sep to reckon with or on; Kosten to include, to take into account

Ein|kam|mer|sys|tem NT (Pol) single-chamber or unicameral (form) system

ein+kap|seln ['ainkapsln] VR sep (Med) to encapsulate (form); (fig) to withdraw or go into one's shell

ein+kas|sie|ren ptp **einkassiert** VT sep **a** Geld, Schulden to collect; **die Polizei hat den Dieb einkassiert** the police nabbed the criminal (inf); **er hat eine Ohrfeige einkassiert** he earned himself a clip on the ear **b** (inf: = wegnehmen) to take

ein+kas|teln ['ainkastln] VT sep (inf: Aus, S Ger) Straftäter to put away (inf), to lock up

Ein|kauf M **a** (= das Einkaufen) buying (auch Comm), purchase; **der Sommer ist die beste Zeit für den ~ von Kohlen** summer is the best time to buy or for buying (in) coal; **Einkäufe machen** to go shopping; **ich muss noch ein paar Einkäufe machen** I still have a few things to buy, I still have a few purchases to make **b** (usu pl: = Gekauftes) purchase; **ein guter** or **vorteilhafter/schlechter ~** a good/bad buy; **sie packte ihre Einkäufe aus** she unpacked her shopping **c** no pl (Comm: = Abteilung) buying (department) **d** (in Altersheim, Firma etc) **durch den ~ in ein Seniorenheim** by buying oneself into an old people's home; **er versucht durch Einkäufe in diese Firma in Europa Fuß zu fassen** he is trying to get a foothold in Europe by buying up shares in this firm **e** (Ftbl) transfer

ein+kau|fen sep **VT** to buy; Vorräte to buy (in) **VI** to shop; (Comm) to buy, to do the buying; **~ gehen** to go shopping; **ich kaufe nur bei Müller ein** I only shop at Müllers **VR** to buy one's way (in +acc into)

Ein|käu|fer(in) M(F) (Comm) buyer

Ein|kaufs- in cpds shopping; **Ein|kaufs|bum|mel** M shopping spree; **einen ~ machen** to go on a shopping spree; **Ein|kaufs|ge|nos|sen|schaft** F consumers' cooperative society; **Ein|kaufs|korb** M shopping basket; **Ein|kaufs|lei|ter(in)** M(F) (Comm) chief buyer; **Ein|kaufs|lis|te** F shopping list; **Ein|kaufs|mög|lich|keit** F **mit guten ~en** with good shopping facilities; **Ein|kaufs|netz** NT string bag, shopping net; **Ein|kaufs|pas|sa|ge** F shopping arcade; **Ein|kaufs|preis** M wholesale price; (= Kaufpreis) purchase price; **Ein|kaufs|quel|le** F **eine gute ~ für etw** a good place to buy sth; **Ein|kaufs|stra|ße** F shopping street; **Ein|kaufs|ta|sche** F shopping bag; **Ein|kaufs|tü|te** F shopping bag; (= Plastiktüte) plastic bag; **Ein|kaufs|vier|tel** NT shopping area; **Ein|kaufs|wa|gen** M shopping trolley (Brit) or cart (US); **Ein|kaufs|zent|rum** NT shopping centre (Brit) or center (US); **Ein|kaufs|zet|tel** M shopping list

Ein|kehr ['ainkeːɐ] F -, no pl **a** (in Gasthaus) stop; **in einem Gasthaus ~ halten** to (make a) stop at an inn **b** (geh: = Besinnung) self-examination, reflection; **bei sich ~ halten** to look into or search one's heart

ein+keh|ren VI sep aux sein **a** (in Gasthof) to (make a) stop, to stop off (in +dat at); (bei Freunden) to call in (bei on) **b** (Ruhe, Friede) to come (bei to); (Not, Sorge) to come (bei upon, to); **wieder ~** to return (bei to)

ein+kei|len VT sep to hem in; Mensch auch, Auto to box in; (fig) to box in, to trap → auch **eingekeilt**

ein+kel|lern ['ainkɛlɐn] VT sep to store in a cellar

ein+ker|ben VT sep to cut a notch/notches in, to notch; (= schnitzen) to cut, to chip

Ein|ker|bung F notch

ein+ker|kern ['ainkɛrkɐn] VT sep to incarcerate

Ein|ker|ke|rung F -, -en incarceration

ein+kes|seln ['ainkɛsln] VT sep to encircle, to surround

Ein|kes|se|lung F -, -en encirclement, surrounding

ein+kit|ten VT sep to fix with putty (in +acc in)

ein|klag|bar ADJ Schulden (legally) recoverable; Anspruch, Recht (legally) enforceable

ein+kla|gen VT sep Schulden to sue for (the recovery of); Anspruch, Recht to take legal action to enforce

ein+klam|mern VT sep to put in brackets or parentheses, to put brackets (a)round; (fig) Thema, Frage to leave aside

Ein|klang M **a** (Mus) unison **b** (geh: = Übereinstimmung) harmony; **in ~ bringen** to bring into line; **in** or **im ~ mit etw stehen** to be in accord with sth; **seine Worte und Taten stehen nicht miteinander im** or **in ~** his words and deeds were at variance or not in accord with one another

Ein|klas|sen|schu|le F one-class school

ein|klas|sig ADJ Schule one-class attr

ein+kle|ben VT sep to stick in (in +acc -to)

ein+klei|den VT sep Soldaten to fit or kit out (with a uniform); Novizen to accept (as a novice); (fig) Gedanken to couch; **jdn/sich völlig neu ~** to buy sb/oneself a completely new wardrobe

Ein|klei|dung F **a** (= das Einkleiden) fitting out; acceptance as a novice; (von Gedanken) couching **b** (= Verhüllung) veil; **in mystischer ~** veiled in mysticism

ein+klem|men VT sep **a** (= quetschen) to jam; Finger etc to catch, to get caught; **er hat sich/mir die Hand in der Tür eingeklemmt** he caught his/my hand in the door; **der Fahrer war hinter dem Steuer eingeklemmt** the driver was pinned behind the wheel **b** (= festdrücken) to clamp; **der Hund klemmte den Schwanz ein** the dog put its tail between its legs; **eingeklemmter Bruch** (Med) strangulated hernia

ein+klin|ken ['ainklɪŋkn] sep **VT** Tür etc to latch; Segelflugzeug, Leine to hitch up; **die Tür ist eingeklinkt** the door is on the latch **VI** (Verschluss, Sicherheitsgurt) to click shut; (Tech: = einrasten) to engage **VR sich in etw** (acc) **~** to link up with sth

ein+klop|fen VT sep Nagel etc to knock in (in +acc -to); Hautcreme etc to pat in (in +acc -to)

ein+knei|fen VT sep irreg Schwanz (lit) to put between its legs; **mit eingekniffenem Schwanz** (lit, fig inf) with his etc tail between his etc legs

ein+kni|cken sep **VT** Papier to crease (over); Streichholz, Äste to snap **VI** aux sein (Strohhalm) to get bent; (Äste) to snap; (Knie) to give way, to buckle; (fig: = umfallen) to give way; **er knickt immer mit den Knien ein** his knees are always giving way; **mein Knöchel** or **Fuß knickt dauernd ein** I'm always going over on my ankle (Brit), I'm always turning my ankle (esp US)

ein|knöpf|bar ADJ Futter attachable

ein+knöp|fen VT sep Futter to button in

ein+knüp|peln VI sep **auf jdn ~** to beat sb (up) with cudgels; (Polizei) to beat sb (up) with batons or truncheons; (fig) to lash sb

ein+ko|chen sep **VT** Gemüse to preserve; Marmelade to make **VI** aux sein (Marmelade etc) to boil down; (Wasser) to boil away; (Soße) to thicken

Ein|koch|topf M preserving pan

ein+kom|men VI sep irreg aux sein (form) **a** **(bei jdm) um etw ~** to apply (to sb) for sth **b** (Sport, Naut) to come in

Ein|kom|men ['ainkɔmən] NT -s, - income

Ein|kom|mens-: **Ein|kom|mens|aus|fall** M loss of income no pl; **Ein|kom|mens|ein|bu|ße** F usu pl loss of income no pl; **Ein|kom|mens|ge|fäl|le** NT income differential; **Ein|kom|mens|gren|ze** F income limit; **Ein|kom|mens|grup|pe** F income bracket; **Ein|kom|mens|klas|se** F income bracket; **ein|kom|mens|los** ADJ (form) without an income; **~ sein** to have no income, to be without an income; **Ein|kom|mens|schicht** F income bracket; **ein|kom|mens|schwach** ADJ low-income attr; **ein|kom|mens|stark** ADJ high-income attr; **die Einkommensstarken** people in a high-income bracket

Ein|kom|men(s)|steu|er F income tax

Ein|kom|men(s)|steu|er-: **Ein|kom|men(s)|steu|er|be|scheid** M income tax assessment; **Ein|kom|men(s)|steu|er|er|klä|rung** F income tax return; **ein|kom|men(s)|steu|er|frei** ADJ free of income tax; **ein|kom|men(s)|steu|er|pflich|tig** [-pflɪçtɪç] ADJ liable to income tax; **Ein|kom|men(s)|steu|er|ver|an|la|gung** F income tax coding

Ein|kom|mens-: **Ein|kom|mens|ver|hält|nis|se** PL (level of) income; **Ein|kom|mens|ver|tei|lung** F distribution of income; **Ein|kom|mens|zu|wachs** M increase in income

ein+köp|fen VTI sep (Ftbl) to head in (in +acc -to); **Müller köpfte zum 1:0 ein** Müller's header made the score 1-0

ein+kra|chen VI sep aux sein (inf) to crash down

ein+krei|sen VT sep Feind, Wild to surround; (fig) Frage, Problem to consider from all sides; (Pol) to isolate

Ein|krei|sung ['ainkraizʊŋ] F -, -en surrounding; (von Frage, Problem) systematic consideration; (Pol) isolation

Ein|krei|sungs|po|li|tik F policy of isolation

ein+kre|men ['ainkreːmən] VT sep = **eincremen**

ein+krie|gen sep (inf) **VT** to catch up **VR sie konnte sich gar nicht mehr darüber ~, wie/dass ...** she couldn't get over how/the fact that ...; **krieg dich mal wieder ein!** control yourself!

Ein|künf|te ['ainkʏnftə] PL income sing; (einer Firma auch) receipts pl

ein+kup|peln sep **VI** (Aut) to let the clutch in, to engage the clutch **VT** Eisenbahnwaggon to couple (up)

ein+la|den ✪ 52 VT sep irreg **a** Waren to load (in +acc into) **b** to invite; **jdn zu einer Party ~** to invite or ask sb to a party; **jdn ins Kino ~** to ask sb to the cinema; **jdn auf ein Bier ~** to invite sb for a beer; **lass mal, ich lade dich ein** come on, this one's on me; **wir sind heute Abend eingeladen** we've been invited out this evening; **er traut sich nicht, das Mädchen einzuladen** he doesn't dare ask the girl out; **dieses hübsche Plätzchen lädt zum Bleiben ein** it's very tempting to linger in this pretty spot; **das lädt ja geradezu zum Stehlen/Einbrechen ein** that's inviting theft/a break-in, that's asking to be stolen/broken into **c** (Sw) = **auffordern**

ein|la|dend ADJ inviting; Speisen appetizing

Ein|la|dung ✪ 52 F **a** invitation; **einer ~ Folge leisten** (form) to accept an invitation; **eine ~ aussprechen** (sl: = aufs Klo gehen) to go for a

Jimmy *(Brit) or* Jerry *(US)* Riddle *(sl)* **b** *(Sw)* = **Aufforderung**

Ein|la|dungs-: **Ein|la|dungs|kar|te** F invitation (card); **Ein|la|dungs|schrei|ben** NT (official) invitation

Ein|la|ge F **a** *(= Zahneinlage)* temporary filling **b** *(= Schuheinlage)* insole; *(zum Stützen)* (arch) support **c** *(Sew)* padding; *(= Versteifung)* interfacing **d** *(in Brief, Paket)* enclosure; **einen Prospekt als ~ beilegen** to enclose a pamphlet **e** *(Cook) noodles, vegetables, egg etc added to a clear soup* **f** *(= Zwischenspiel)* interlude **g** *(Fin: = Kapitaleinlage)* investment; *(= Spareinlage auch)* deposit; *(= Spieleinlage)* stake

ein+la|gern *sep* **VT** to store **VR** to become deposited *(in +acc or dat* in); *(Met)* to settle

Ein|la|ge|rung F **a** storage **b** *(Geol)* deposit

ein|la|gig ADJ one-ply *attr*

ein+lan|gen VI *sep aux sein (Aus)* to arrive

Ein|lass ['ainlas] M **-es, ¨-e** [-lɛsə] **a** *no pl (= Zutritt)* admission; **jdm ~ gewähren** to admit sb; **sich** *(dat)* **~ in etw** *(acc)* **verschaffen** to gain entry *or* admission to sth **b** *(Tech: = Öffnung)* inlet, opening

ein+las|sen *sep irreg* **VT** **a** *(= eintreten lassen)* to let in, to admit **b** *(= einlaufen lassen) Wasser* to run *(in +acc* into); **er ließ sich** *(dat)* **ein Bad ein** he ran himself a bath **c** *(= einpassen, einfügen)* to let in *(in +acc* -to); *(in Holz, Metall auch)* to set in *(in +acc* -to); **ein eingelassener Schrank** a built-in cupboard, a cupboard built into the wall; **eingelassene Schraube** countersunk screw **d** *(Aus) Boden, Möbel* to varnish **VR** **a** **sich auf etw** *(acc)* **~** *(auf Angelegenheit, Abenteuer, Diskussion, Liebschaft)* to get involved in sth; *auf Streit, zwielichtiges Unternehmen auch* to get mixed up in sth, to get into sth; *(= sich zu etw verpflichten)* to let oneself in for sth; **sich auf einen Kompromiss ~** to agree to a compromise; **sich in ein Gespräch ~** to get into (a) *or* get involved in a conversation; **ich lasse mich auf keine Diskussion ein** I'm not having any discussion about it; **darauf lasse ich mich nicht ein!** *(bei Geschäft, Angelegenheit)* I don't want anything to do with it; *(bei Kompromiss, Handel etc)* I'm not agreeing to that; **lasse dich in keine Schlägerei ein!** don't you go getting mixed up in any rough stuff; **da habe ich mich aber auf etwas eingelassen!** I've let myself in for something there! **b** **sich mit jdm ~** *(pej: = Umgang pflegen mit)* to get mixed up *or* involved with sb; **er ließ sich mit diesem Flittchen ein** he was carrying on with this floozy *(pej inf) or* tarty little bit *(Brit pej inf)*; **sie lässt sich mit jedem ein!** she'll go with anyone **c** *(Jur: = sich äußern)* to testify *(zu on)*

Ein|las|sung ['ainlasʊŋ] F **-, -en** statement; *(Jur)* testimony

Ein|lass|zeit F opening time; *(für Veranstaltung)* timed entry; *(bei vorgebuchter Zeit)* entry time; *(= Öffnungszeit)* opening hours *pl*; **~ 9.30 Uhr** doors open at 9.30 a.m.

Ein|lauf M **a** *no pl (Sport) (am Ziel)* finish; *(ins Stadion etc)* entry; **beim ~ in die Zielgerade ...** coming into the final straight ... **b** *(Med)* enema; **jdm einen ~ machen** to give sb an enema **c** *(Cook) (= Einlaufsuppe) soup with egg and/or beurre manié added* **d** *(Comm: = Post)* = **Eingang b** **e** *(rare: = Einlauföffnung)* opening

ein+lau|fen *sep irreg* **VI** *aux sein* **a** *(= hineinlaufen)* to come in *(in +acc* -to); *(= ankommen auch)* to arrive *(in +acc* in); *(Sport) (ins Stadion)* to come *or* run in *(in +acc* -to), to enter *(in etw acc* sth); *(durchs Ziel)* to finish; **das Schiff läuft (in den Hafen) ein** the ship is coming into *or* entering the harbour *(Brit) or* harbor *(US)* **b** *(= hineinlaufen: Wasser)* to run in *(in +acc* -to) **c** *(= eintreffen) (Post)* to arrive; *(Bewerbungen, Spenden)* to be received, to come in **d** *(= eingehen: Stoff)* to shrink; **garantiert kein Einlaufen** guaranteed non-shrink **VT** *Schuhe* to wear in **VR** *(Motor, Maschine)* to run in *(Brit)*, to be broken in *(US)*; *(Sport)* to warm *or* limber up

Ein|lauf|wet|te F *(Pferderennen)* three-way bet

ein+läu|ten VT *sep Sonntag etc* to ring in; *(Sport) Runde* to sound the bell for; *(fig: = den Anfang darstellen von) Revolution* to herald the start of; *Wende* to usher in

ein+le|ben VR *sep* to settle down *(in or an +dat* in); *(fig: = sich hineinversetzen)* to immerse oneself *(in +acc* in)

Ein|le|ge|ar|beit F inlay work *no pl*

ein+le|gen VT *sep* **a** *(in Holz etc)* to inlay; **eingelegte Arbeit** inlay work **b** *(= hineintun)* to insert *(in +acc* in), to put in *(in +acc* -to); *Film* to load *(in +acc* into); *(in Brief)* to enclose *(in +acc* in); **einen Pfeil (in den Bogen) ~** to fit an arrow (into the bow) **c** *(= einfügen) Sonderschicht, Spurt, Sonderzug* to put on; *Lied, Kunststück, Pause* to have; *(Aut) Gang* to engage; *(Hist) Lanze* to couch **d** *(Fin: = einzahlen)* to pay in, to deposit **e** *(fig: = geltend machen) Protest* to register; **ein gutes Wort für jdn ~** to put in a good word for sb *(bei* with); **sein Veto ~** to exercise *or* use one's veto → **Ehre, Berufung** **f** *(Cook) Heringe, Gurken etc* to pickle **g** *Haare* to set, to put in rollers

Ein|le|ger ['ainle:gɐ] M **-s, -**, **Ein|le|ge|rin** [-ərɪn] F **-, -nen** investor

Ein|le|ge-: **Ein|le|ge|soh|le** F insole; **Ein|le|ge|tisch** M inlaid table

ein+lei|ten *sep* **VT** **a** *(= in Gang setzen)* to initiate; *Maßnahmen, Schritte* to introduce, to take; *neues Zeitalter* to mark the start of, to inaugurate; *(Jur) Verfahren* to institute; *(Med) Geburt* to induce **b** *(= beginnen)* to start; *(= eröffnen)* to open **c** *Buch (durch Vorwort)* to write an introduction to, to introduce; *(Mus)* to prelude **d** *Abwässer etc* to discharge *(in +acc* into) **VI** to give an introduction *(in +acc* to)

ein|lei|tend **ADJ** introductory; *Worte auch* of introduction **ADV** **er sagte ~, dass ...** he said by way of introduction that ...

Ein|lei|ter M *(= Einleitungsrohr)* discharge pipe; *(= Einleitungsverursacher)* discharger

Ein|lei|tung F **a** *(= Vorwort)* introduction; *(Mus)* prelude **b** *(= das Einleiten)* initiation; *(von Maßnahmen auch, von Schritten)* introduction; *(von neuem Zeitalter)* inauguration; *(von Verfahren)* institution; *(von Geburt)* induction **c** *(von Abwässern)* discharge *(in +acc* into)

Ein|lei|tungs|teil M *(von Buch, Vortrag etc)* introductory section

ein+len|ken VI *sep (= nachgeben)* to yield, to give way; **jdn zum Einlenken bewegen** to get sb to change his/her mind

ein+le|sen *sep irreg* **VR** **sich in ein Buch/Gebiet** *etc* **~** to get into a book/subject *etc* **VT** *Daten* to read in *(in +acc* -to)

ein+leuch|ten VI *sep* to be clear *(jdm* to sb); **der Grund seiner Abneigung leuchtet mir nicht ein** I don't see *or* understand *or* it's not clear to me why he doesn't like me; **ja, das leuchtet mir ein!** yes, I see that, yes, that's clear (to me); **das will mir nicht ~** I just don't understand *or* see that

ein|leuch|tend ADJ reasonable, plausible

ein+lie|fern VT *sep Waren* to deliver; **jdn ins Krankenhaus ~** to admit sb to hospital; **jdn ins Gefängnis ~** to put sb in prison, to commit sb to prison; **ein Paket bei der Post ~** to take a parcel to the post *(Brit)*, to take a package to the post office

Ein|lie|fe|rung F *(von Waren)* delivery; *(ins Krankenhaus)* admission *(in +acc* to); *(ins Gefängnis)* committal *(in +acc* to); *(von Briefen etc)* sending; **die ~ von Paketen ist nur bis 17.00 Uhr möglich** parcels *(Brit) or* packages are not accepted after 5 pm

Ein|lie|fe|rungs|schein M certificate of posting *(Brit) or* mailing *(esp US)*

ein|lie|gend ADJ *pred (form)* enclosed; **~ erhalten Sie ...** please find enclosed ...

Ein|lie|ger|woh|nung F granny annexe *(Brit) or* flat *(Brit)*, in-law apartment *(US)*

ein+lo|chen VT *sep* **a** *(inf: = einsperren)* to lock up, to put behind bars **b** *(Golf)* to hole out

ein+log|gen ['ainlɔgn] VR *(Comput)* to log in *or* on; **sich in das System ~** to log into *or* onto the system

ein+lo|gie|ren ['ainloʒi:rən] *ptp* **einlogiert** *sep* **VT** to put up, to lodge **VR** **sich (bei jdm) ~** to lodge (with sb); *(Mil)* to be billeted (with *or* on sb)

ein|lös|bar ADJ redeemable; **Versprechen, die nicht ~ sind** promises that can't be kept

ein+lö|sen VT *sep Pfand* to redeem; *Scheck, Wechsel* to cash (in); *(fig) Wort, Versprechen* to keep; **in der Praxis lässt sich das nicht problemlos ~** in practice that cannot easily be realized

Ein|lö|sung F *(von Pfand)* redemption; *(von Scheck, Wechsel)* cashing (in); *(von Wort, Versprechen)* keeping

ein+lö|ten VT *sep* to solder in *(in +acc* -to)

ein+lul|len ['ainlʊlən] VT *sep (inf) Kind* to lull to sleep; *(fig) Misstrauen, Wachsamkeit* to allay, to quiet; **jdn mit Versprechungen/schönen Worten ~** to lull sb with (soothing) promises/soft words

Ein|mach ['ainmax] F **-**, *no pl*, **Ein|ma|che** ['ainmaxə] F **-**, *no pl (Aus Cook)* roux

ein+ma|chen VT *sep Obst, Gemüse* to preserve; *(in Gläser auch)* to bottle; *(in Dosen)* to can, to tin *(Brit)*

Ein|mach-: **Ein|mach|glas** NT bottling *or* preserving jar, canning jar *(US)*; **Ein|mach|gum|mi** M *(inf)* rubber ring *(for a preserving or canning jar)*; **Ein|mach|topf** M preserving pan; **Ein|mach|zu|cker** M preserving sugar

ein+mah|nen VT *sep (form)* to demand payment of

ein|mal ['ainma:l] ADV **a** *(= ein einziges Mal)* once; *(= erstens)* first of all, firstly, for a start; **~ eins ist eins** once one is one, one times one is one; **~ sagt er dies, ~ das** sometimes he says one thing, sometimes another; **~ sagte sie, wir sollten bleiben, ~ wir sollten gehen** first of all she says that we should stay, then that we should go; **auf ~** *(= plötzlich)* suddenly, all of a sudden, all at once; *(= zugleich)* at once; **~ mehr** once again; **~ und nicht** *or* **nie wieder** once and never again; **noch ~** again; **versuchs noch ~** *(= wieder)* try once more, try again; **noch ~ so groß wie** as big again as; **wenn sie da ist, ist es noch ~ so schön** it's twice as nice when she's there; **~ ist keinmal** *(Prov) (= schadet nicht)* once won't hurt *or* do any harm; *(= zählt nicht)* once doesn't count **b** *(= früher, vorher)* once; *(= später, in Zukunft)* one *or* some day; **waren Sie schon ~ in Rom?** have you ever been to Rome?; **er hat schon ~ bessere Zeiten gesehen** he has seen better days; **sie waren ~ glücklich, aber jetzt ...** they were happy once *or* at one time, but now ...; **es war ~ ...** once upon a time there was ...; **das war ~!** that was then; **besuchen Sie mich doch ~!** come and visit me some time!; **das wird ~ anders werden** things will be different some *or* one day **c** *(verstärkend, eingrenzend: meist nicht übersetzt)* **nicht ~** not even; **auch ~** also, too; **wieder ~** again; **ich bin/die Frauen sind nun ~ so** that's the way I am/women are, I'm just/women are like that; **wie die Lage nun ~ ist** with things as or the way they are; **wenn er nun ~ hier ist ...** seeing he's here ...; **alle ~ herhören!** listen everyone!; **sag ~, ist das wahr?** tell me, is it true? → **erst a**

Ein|mal|eins [ainma:l'ains] NT **-**, *no pl* (multiplication) tables *pl*; *(fig)* ABC, basics *pl*; **das ~ lernen/aufsagen** to learn/say one's tables; **das kleine/große ~** (multiplication) tables up to/over ten

Ein|mal-: **Ein|mal|hand|schu|he** PL disposable gloves *pl*; **Ein|mal|hand|tuch** NT disposable towel

ein|ma|lig ['ainma:lɪç, (*emph*) 'ain'ma:lɪç] ADJ **a** *Gelegenheit, Angebot, Fall, Leistung* unique **b** (*= nur einmal erforderlich*) single; *Anschaffung, Zahlung* one-off *attr*; **beim ~en Durchlesen des Textes** on a single reading of the text, on reading the text through once **c** (*inf: = hervorragend*) fantastic, amazing; **dieser Film ist etwas Einmaliges** this film is really something (*inf*); **der Bursche ist wirklich ~** that guy is really something (*inf*) ADV (*inf: = besonders*) absolutely; **~ gut/schlecht** incredibly good/bad

Ein|ma|lig|keit ['ainma:lɪçkait] F -, *no pl* uniqueness; **alle lobten die ~ dieses Films** everyone said how fantastic the film was

Ein|mal-: **Ein|mal|ka|me|ra** F disposable *or* single-use camera; **Ein|mal|sprit|ze** F = **Einwegspritze**; **Ein|mal|zah|lung** F flat fee, lump sum; **eine ~ leisten** to make a lump-sum payment

Ein|mann-: **Ein|mann|be|trieb** M **a** one-man business *or* band (*inf*) **b** **die Busse auf ~ umstellen** to convert the buses for one-man operation; **Ein|mann|bus** M one-man bus, driver-operated bus; **Ein|mann|ka|pel|le** F one-man band; **Ein|mann|wa|gen** M one-man tram (*esp Brit*) *or* streetcar (*US*)

Ein|mark|stück [ain'mark-] NT (*Hist*) one-mark piece

Ein|marsch M entry (*in +acc* into); (*in ein Land*) invasion (*in +acc* of)

ein+mar|schie|ren *ptp* **einmarschiert** VI *sep aux sein* to march in (*in +acc* -to)

ein+mas|sie|ren *ptp* **einmassiert** VT *sep* to massage *or* rub in (*in +acc* -to)

Ein|mas|ter ['ainmastɐ] M -s, - (*Naut*) single-masted ship, single-master

ein|mas|tig [-mastɪç] ADJ single-masted

ein+mau|ern VT *sep* **a** (*= ummauern*) to wall in, to immure (*liter*) (*in +acc* in) **b** (*= einfügen*) to fix into the wall

ein+mei|ßeln VT *sep* to chisel in (*in +acc* -to)

Ein|me|ter|brett [ain'me:tɐ-] NT one-metre (*Brit*) *or* one-meter (*US*) (diving) board

ein+mie|ten *sep* VT (*Agr*) to clamp VR **sich bei jdm ~** to take lodgings with sb; **er hat sich in der Wohnung unter uns eingemietet** he has taken the apartment below us

ein+mi|schen VR *sep* to interfere (*in +acc* in), to stick one's oar in (*inf*); **sie muss sich bei allem ~** she has to interfere *or* meddle in everything; **wenn ich mich kurz ~ darf ...** if I can butt in a moment ...

Ein|mi|schung F interference, meddling (*in +acc* in)

ein|mo|na|tig ADJ *attr* one-month

ein|mo|nat|lich ADJ monthly

ein+mon|tie|ren *ptp* **einmontiert** VT *sep* to slot in (*in +acc* -to); (*Tech*) to fit in (*in +acc* -to)

ein|mo|to|rig ADJ *Flugzeug* single-engine(d)

ein+mot|ten ['ainmɔtn] VT *sep Kleider etc* to put in mothballs; (*fig auch*) to mothball; *Schiff, Flugzeug* to mothball

ein+mum|meln ['ainmʊmln], **ein+mum|men** ['ainmʊmən] VT *sep* (*inf*) to muffle up

ein+mün|den VI *sep aux sein* (*Fluss*) to flow in (*in +acc* -to); (*Straße*) to run *or* lead in (*in +acc* -to); **in etw** (*acc*) **~** to join sth; (*fig*) to end up in sth; (*Elemente, Einflüsse*) to go into sth

Ein|mün|dung F (*von Fluss*) confluence; (*von Straße*) junction; **die ~ der Isar in die Donau** the confluence of the Isar and the Danube

ein|mü|tig ['ainmy:tɪç] ADJ unanimous ADV unanimously; **~ zusammenstehen** to stand together as one

Ein|mü|tig|keit F -, *no pl* unanimity; **darüber besteht ~** there is complete agreement on that

ein+nach|ten VI *impers sep* (*Sw*) **es nachtet ein** it's getting dark

ein+na|geln VT *sep* to nail in (*in +acc* -to); (*= einhämmern*) to hammer in (*in +acc* -to)

ein+nä|hen VT *sep* to sew in (*in +acc* -to); (*= enger machen*) to take in

Ein|nah|me ['ainna:mə] F -, -n **a** (*Mil*) seizure; (*einer Stellung, Stadt auch*) capture **b** (*= Ertrag*) receipt **c** **Einnahmen** PL income *sing*; (*= Geschäftseinnahme*) takings *pl*; (*aus Einzelverkauf*) proceeds *pl*; (*= Gewinn*) earnings *pl*; (*eines Staates*) revenue *sing*; **~n und Ausgaben** income and expenditure **d** (*= das Einnehmen*) taking; **durch ~ von etw** by taking sth

Ein|nah|me-: **Ein|nah|me|aus|fall** M loss of income; (*von Geschäften*) drop in takings (*Brit*) *or* revenue (*US*); (*des Staates*) revenue shortfall; **Ein|nah|me|buch** NT (*Comm*) book of receipts, receipt book; **Ein|nah|me|pos|ten** M item of receipt; **Ein|nah|me|quel|le** F source of income; (*eines Staates*) source of revenue

ein+näs|sen *sep* (*form*) VT to wet VR to wet oneself; (*nachtsüber*) to wet the bed

ein+ne|beln *sep* VT (*Mil*) to put up a smokescreen (a)round; (*fig*) to befog, to obfuscate (*liter*) VR (*Mil*) to put up a smokescreen (around oneself); **es nebelt sich ein** (*Met*) it's getting misty, there's a mist coming down

ein+neh|men VT *sep irreg* **a** *Geld* (*Geschäft etc*) to take; (*Freiberufler*) to earn; *Steuern* to collect; **die eingenommenen Gelder** the takings **b** (*Mil: = erobern*) to take; *Stadt, Festung* to capture, to take **c** (*lit, fig*) *Platz etc* to take (up), to occupy; *Stelle* (*= innehaben*) to have, to occupy (*form*); *Haltung, Standpunkt etc* to take up; **er nimmt vorübergehend die Stelle des Chefs ein** he is acting for the boss; **bitte, nehmen Sie Ihre Plätze ein!** (*form*) please take your seats!; **die Plätze ~** (*Sport*) to take one's marks **d** (*= zu sich nehmen*) *Mahlzeit, Arznei* to take **e** **er nahm uns alle für sich ein** he won us all over; **er hat alle für seine Pläne eingenommen** he won everyone over to his plans; **jdn gegen sich/jdn/etw ~** to set *or* put sb against oneself/sb/sth; **das nimmt mich sehr für sie ein** that makes me think highly of her → *auch* **eingenommen**

ein|neh|mend ADJ likeable (*Brit*), likable; *Atmosphäre* agreeable, pleasant; **er hat etwas Einnehmendes** there is something lik(e)able about him; **er hat ein ~es Wesen** (*= gewinnend*) he's a lik(e)able character; (*hum inf: = habgierig*) he likes to acquire things

Ein|neh|mer(in) M(F) (*old*) collector

ein+ni|cken VI *sep aux sein* (*inf*) to doze *or* nod off

ein+nis|ten VR *sep* (*lit*) to nest; (*Parasiten, Ei*) to lodge; (*fig*) to park oneself (*bei* on); **in unserem Land haben sich so viele Kriminelle eingenistet** so many criminals have settled in our country; **in ihm hatte sich tiefes Misstrauen eingenistet** he was filled with a deep mistrust

Ein|öd ['ainlø:t] F -, -en [-dn] (*Aus*) = **Einöde**

Ein|öd|bauer M *pl* **-bauern**, **Ein|öd|bäu|e|rin** F farmer of an isolated farm

Ein|öde ['ainlø:də] F **Moore und ~** moors and wasteland; **Wüsten und ~** deserts and barren wastes *pl*; **die weiße ~ der Antarktis** the white wastes of the Antarctic; **er lebt in der ~ des schottischen Hochlands** he lives in the wilds of the Scottish Highlands; **er verließ die ~ seines Schwarzwaldhofes** he left the isolation of his Black Forest farm

Ein|öd|hof M ≈ croft

ein+ölen *sep* VT to oil VR to rub oneself with oil, to oil oneself

ein+ord|nen *sep* VT **a** (*der Reihe nach*) *Bücher etc* to (put in) order; *Akten, Karteikarten* to file **b** (*= klassifizieren*) to classify; *Begriff, Theorie, Denker auch* to categorize VR **a** (*in Gemeinschaft etc*) to fit in (*in +acc* -to) **b** (*Aut*) to get in(to) lane; **sich links/rechts ~** to get into the left/right lane; **„Einordnen"** "get in lane"

ein+pa|cken *sep* VT **a** (*= einwickeln*) to wrap (up) (*in +acc* in); **jdn warm ~** (*fig*) to wrap sb up warmly **b** (*= hineintun*) to pack (*in +acc* in) **c** (*= packen*) *Paket* to pack up VI to pack, to do one's packing; **dann können wir ~** (*inf*) in that case we may as well pack it all in (*inf*) *or* give up

ein+par|ken VTI *sep* to park; **(in eine Parklücke) ~** to get into a parking space; **eingeparkt** (*Auto, = abgestellt*) parked; (*= zugeparkt*) blocked in (by parked cars)

Ein|par|tei|en- *in cpds* one-party, single-party; **Ein|par|tei|en|staat** M one-party *or* single-party state

ein+pas|sen *sep* VT to fit in (*in +acc* -to) VR to adjust, to adapt oneself (*in +acc* to)

ein+pau|ken VT *sep* (*inf*) to mug up (on) (*Brit inf*), to cram; **jdm etw ~** to drum sth into sb

Ein|pau|ker(in) M(F) (*inf*) crammer (*pej*)

Ein|peit|scher ['ainpaitʃɐ] M -s, -, **Ein|peit|sche|rin** [-ərɪn] F -, -nen (*Pol*) whip (*Brit*), floor leader (*US*); (*inf: = Antreiber*) slave driver (*inf*)

ein+pen|deln *sep* VI to commute in (*in +acc* -to) VR (*fig*) to settle down; (*Währung, Preise etc*) to find its level, to level off

Ein|pend|ler(in) M(F) commuter

ein+pen|nen VI *sep aux sein* (*sl*) to doze off, to drop off (*inf*)

Ein|per|so|nen-: **Ein|per|so|nen|haus|halt** M single-person household; **Ein|per|so|nen|stück** NT (*Theat*) one-man play

Ein|pfen|nig|stück [ain'pfɛnɪç-] NT (*Hist*) one-pfennig piece

ein+pfer|chen VT *sep Vieh* to pen in (*in +acc* -to); (*fig*) to coop up (*in +acc* in); **eingepfercht stehen** to be hemmed in

ein+pflan|zen VT *sep* to plant (*in +dat* in); (*Med*) to implant (*jdm* in(to) sb); **jdm eine fremde Niere ~** to give sb a kidney transplant; **jdm etw ~** (*fig*) to imbue sb with a sense of sth, to instil (*Brit*) *or* instill (*US*) (a sense of) sth into sb

Ein|pha|sen|strom [ain'fa:zn-] M, **Ein|pha|sen|wech|sel|strom** M single-phase current

ein|pha|sig ADJ single-phase

ein+pin|seln VT *sep Wunde, Mandeln* to paint; (*Cook*) to brush

ein+pla|nen VT *sep* to plan (on), to include in one's plans; *Verzögerungen, Verluste* to allow for; *Baby* to plan

ein+pö|keln VT *sep Fisch, Fleisch* to salt; **eingepökeltes Rindfleisch** salt beef

ein|po|lig ['ainpo:lɪç] ADJ single-pole

ein+prä|gen *sep* VT *Muster, Spuren* to imprint, to impress; *Inschrift* to stamp; **ein Muster in Papier ~** to emboss paper with a pattern; **sich** (*dat*) **etw ~** to remember sth; (*= auswendig lernen*) to memorize sth, to commit sth to memory VR **sich jdm ins Gedächtnis ~** to make an impression on sb's mind; **sich jdm ~** to make an impression on sb; **die Worte haben sich mir unauslöschlich eingeprägt** the words made an indelible impression on me

ein|präg|sam ['ainprɛ:kza:m] ADJ easily remembered; *Slogan, Melodie auch* catchy ADV **er kann sehr ~ formulieren** he can put things in a way that is easy to remember

ein+pras|seln VI *sep aux sein* **auf jdn ~** to rain down on sb, to come pouring down on sb; (*Fragen*) to be showered upon sb; **von allen Seiten prasselten Geschosse auf uns ein** we were caught in a hail of shots from all sides

ein+pres|sen VT *sep* to press in (*in +acc* -to)

ein+pro|ben VT *sep* to rehearse

ein+pro|gram|mie|ren *ptp* **einprogrammiert** VT *sep Daten* to feed in; (*fig*) to take into account; **jdm etw ~** (*fig*) to inculcate sth in sb

ein+prü|geln *sep* (*inf*) VT **jdm etw ~** to din (*inf*) *or* drum sth into sb VI **auf jdn ~** to lay into sb

ein+pu|dern *sep* VR to powder oneself VT to powder

ein+pup|pen ['ainpʊpn] VR *sep* (*Zool*) to pupate

ein+quar|tie|ren ['ainkvarti:rən] *ptp* **einquartiert** *sep* VT to quarter; (*Mil auch*) to billet; **Gäs-**

te bei Freunden ~ to put visitors up with friends VR to be quartered *(bei* with); *(Mil auch)* to be billeted *(bei* on); *(Gäste)* to stop *(bei* with) *(inf)*; **er hat sich bei uns anscheinend für ewig einquartiert** he seems to have dumped himself on us for good *(inf)*

Ein|quar|tie|rung F -, -en **a** *(= das Einquartieren)* quartering; *(Mil auch)* billeting **b wir haben ~** *(inf) (= Soldaten)* we have soldiers billeted on us; *(= Besuch)* we've got people staying *or* stopping *(inf)* (with us)

ein+quet|schen VT *sep* = **einklemmen a**

Ein|rad NT unicycle

ein|rä|de|rig, ein|räd|rig ADJ one-wheeled

ein+rah|men VT *sep (lit, fig)* to frame; **von zwei Schönen eingerahmt** with a beauty on either side; **das kannst du dir ~ lassen!** *(inf)* you ought to get that framed!

ein+ram|men VT *sep Stadttor* to batter down *or* in; *Pfähle* to ram in *(in +acc* -to)

ein+ras|ten VTI *sep (vi: aux sein)* to engage

ein+räu|chern VT *sep* **a** *(= in Rauch hüllen)* to envelop in smoke; **die Polizei räucherte die Demonstranten mit Tränengas ein** the police used tear gas against the demonstrators **b** *(inf) Zimmer* to fill with smoke, to smoke up; *Gardinen* to make reek of smoke

ein+räu|men VT *sep* **a** *Wäsche, Bücher etc* to put away; *Schrank, Regal etc* to fill; *Wohnung, Zimmer* to arrange; *Möbel* to move in *(in +acc* -to); **Bücher ins Regal/in den Schrank ~** to put books on the shelf/in the cupboard; **er war mir beim Einräumen behilflich** he helped me sort things out; *(der Wohnung)* he helped me move in **b** *(= zugestehen)* to concede, to admit; *Freiheiten etc* to allow; *Frist, Kredit* to give, to grant, to allow; **jdm das Recht ~, etw zu tun** to give *or* grant sb the right to do sth, to allow sb to do sth; **~de Konjunktion** concessive conjunction

Ein|räu|mungs|satz M *(Gram)* concessive clause

ein+rech|nen VT *sep* to include; **ihn (mit) eingerechnet** including him; **Mehrwertsteuer eingerechnet** including VAT, inclusive of VAT

Ein|re|de F *(form)* objection

ein+re|den *sep* VT **jdm etw ~** to talk sb into believing sth, to persuade sb of sth; **sie hat ihm eingeredet, er sei dumm** she persuaded him that *or* talked him into believing that he was stupid; **das lasse ich mir nicht ~** you're not going to make me believe that; **wer hat dir denn diesen Unsinn eingeredet?** who put that rubbish *(Brit inf) or* nonsense into your head?; **er will mir ~, dass ...** he'd have me believe that ..., he wants me to believe that ...; **sich** *(dat)* **etw ~** to talk oneself into believing sth, to make oneself believe sth; **das redest du dir nur ein!** you're only imagining it

VI **auf jdn ~** to keep on and on at sb

ein+reg|nen *sep* VI *aux sein (Mensch)* to get soaked (through) VR **es hat sich eingeregnet** the rain has set in

ein+rei|ben VT *sep irreg* **er rieb sich** *(dat)* **das Gesicht mit Schnee/Creme ein** he rubbed snow over/cream into his face

Ein|rei|bung F **~en verordnen** to prescribe embrocation *or* liniment

ein+rei|chen VT *sep* **a** *Antrag, Unterlagen* to submit *(bei* to); *(Jur) Klage* to file → **Abschied b b** *(= bitten um) Versetzung, Pensionierung* to apply for, to request

Ein|rei|chung ['ainraiçʊŋ] F -, *(rare)* **-en** *(von Antrag, Unterlagen)* submission; *(Jur: von Klage)* filing

ein+rei|hen *sep* VT *(= einordnen, einfügen)* to put in *(in +acc* -to); *(= klassifizieren)* to class, to classify; **dieses Buch verdient, in die bedeutendste medizinische Fachliteratur eingereiht zu werden** this book deserves to be awarded a place amongst the most important works of medical literature; **er wurde in den Arbeitsprozess eingereiht** he was fitted into *or* given a place in the work process VR **sich in etw** *(acc)* **~** to join sth

Ein|rei|her ['ainraiɐ] M -s, - *(= Anzug)* single-breasted suit; *(= Jackett)* single-breasted jacket; *(= Mantel)* single-breasted coat

ein|rei|hig ADJ *Anzug, Jackett, Mantel* single-breasted

Ein|rei|se F entry *(in +acc* into, to); **bei der ~ in die Schweiz** when entering Switzerland, on entry to Switzerland

Ein|rei|se-: Ein|rei|se|er|laub|nis F entry permit; **Ein|rei|se|for|ma|li|tä|ten** PL entry formalities *pl*; **Ein|rei|se|for|mu|lar** NT form for entry into the country; **Ein|rei|se|ge|neh|mi|gung** F entry permit

ein+rei|sen VI *sep aux sein* to enter the country; **er reiste in die Schweiz ein** he entered Switzerland; **ein- und ausreisen** to enter and leave the country

Ein|rei|se-: Ein|rei|se|ver|bot NT refusal of entry; **~ haben** to have been refused entry; **Ein|rei|se|vi|sum** NT entry visa

ein+rei|ßen *sep irreg* VT **a** *Papier, Stoff, Nagel* to tear; **ich habe mir einen Splitter in den Zeh eingerissen** I've got a splinter in my toe **b** *Gebäude, Zaun, Barrikaden* to tear *or* pull down VI *aux sein (Papier)* to tear; *(fig inf: Unsitte etc)* to catch on *(inf)*, to get to be a habit *(inf)*

ein+rei|ten *sep irreg* VT *Pferd* to break in VI *aux sein (in die Manege etc)* to ride in *(in +acc* -to) VR to warm up; **sich mit einem Pferd ~** to get used to riding a particular horse

ein+ren|ken ['ainrɛŋkn] *sep* VT *Gelenk, Knie* to put back in place, to reduce *(spec)*; *(fig inf)* to sort out VR *(fig inf)* to sort itself out

ein+ren|nen VT *sep irreg (inf) Mauer, Tür etc* to batter *or* break down; **sich** *(dat)* **den Kopf an der Wand ~** to bang *or* bash *(inf)* one's head against the wall

ein+rich|ten *sep* VT **a** *(= möblieren) Wohnung, Zimmer* to furnish; *(= ausstatten) Hobbyraum, Spielzimmer, Praxis, Labor* to equip, to fit out *(Brit)*; **ein Haus antik/modern ~** to furnish a house in an old/a modern style; **sein Haus neu ~** to refurnish one's house; **Wohnungen im Dachgeschoss ~** to convert the attic into flats *(Brit) or* apartments

b *(= gründen, eröffnen)* to set up; *Lehrstuhl* to establish; *Konto* to open; *Buslinie etc* to start

c *(= einstellen) Maschine, Computer* to set up; *Motor* to set *(auf +acc* for); *(Mil) Geschütz* to aim *(auf +acc* at); **Seite ~** *(Comput: Menübefehl)* page setup;

d *(= bearbeiten) Musikstück* to arrange; *Theaterstück* to adapt

e *(fig: = arrangieren)* to arrange, to fix *(inf)*; **ich werde es ~, dass wir um zwei Uhr da sind** I'll see to it that we're there at two; **das lässt sich ~** that can be arranged; **auf Tourismus eingerichtet sein** to be geared to tourism; **auf warme Speisen eingerichtet sein** to be equipped for hot meals

f *(Med) Arm, Knochen* to set

VR **a** *(= sich möblieren)* **sich ~/neu ~** to furnish/refurnish one's house/one's flat *(Brit) or* apartment → **häuslich**

b *(= sich der Lage anpassen)* to get along *or* by, to manage; *(= sparsam sein)* to cut down; **er hat sich im bürgerlichen Leben eingerichtet** he has settled down into middle-class life

c sich auf etw *(acc)* **~** to prepare oneself for sth; **sich auf eine lange Wartezeit ~** to be prepared for a long wait

Ein|rich|tung F **a** *(= das Einrichten) (von Wohnung, Zimmer)* furnishing; *(von Hobbyraum, Spielzimmer, Labor, Praxis)* equipping, fitting-out *(Brit)*; *(von Maschine)* setting-up; *(von Computer)* set-up; *(von Geschütz)* aiming; *(Med)* setting

b *(= Bearbeitung) (Mus)* arrangement; *(Theat)* adaptation

c *(= Wohnungseinrichtung)* furnishings *pl*; *(= Geschäftseinrichtung etc)* fittings *pl*; *(= Laboreinrichtung etc)* equipment *no pl*

d *(= Gründung, Eröffnung)* setting-up; *(von Lehrstuhl)* establishment; *(von Konto)* opening; *(von Katalog, Busverkehr)* starting

e *(behördlich, wohltätig, = Gewohnheit)* institution; *(= Schwimmbäder, Transportmittel etc)* facility; **zur ständigen ~ werden** *(= Gewohnheit)* to become an institution

Ein|rich|tungs-: Ein|rich|tungs|da|tei F *(Comput)* setup file; **Ein|rich|tungs|ge|gen|stand** M item of furniture; *(= Geschäftseinrichtung)* fitment *(Brit)*, fixture; **Ein|rich|tungs|haus** NT furnishing house

ein+rie|geln ['ainri:gln] VTR *sep* **jdn/sich ~** to lock sb/oneself in *(in +dat* -to)

Ein|ritt M entry *(in +acc* into)

ein+rit|zen VT *sep* to carve in *(in +acc* -to)

ein+rol|len *sep* VT *(= einwickeln)* to roll up *(in +acc* in); *(Hockey)* to roll on *(in +acc* -to) VI *aux sein* to roll in *(in +acc* -to) VR to roll up; *(Tier etc auch)* to roll oneself up

ein+ros|ten VI *sep aux sein* to rust up; *(fig: Glieder)* to stiffen up; **mein Latein ist ziemlich eingerostet** my Latin has got pretty rusty

ein+rü|cken *sep* VT *Zeile* to indent; *Anzeige (in Zeitung)* to insert VI *aux sein (Mil)* **a** *(in ein Land)* to move in *(in +acc* -to); *(= wieder einrücken)* to return *(in +acc* to) **b** *(= eingezogen werden)* to report for duty; *(nach Urlaub etc)* to report back

ein+rüh|ren VT *sep* to stir *or* mix in *(in +acc* -to); *(Cook) Ei* to beat in *(in +acc* -to)

ein+rüs|ten VT *sep Haus* to put scaffolding around

eins [ains] NUM one; **es ist/schlägt ~** it's one/just striking one (o'clock); **um ~** at one (o'clock); **gegen ~** at around one (o'clock); **~, zwei, drei** *(lit)* one, two, three; *(fig)* in a trice *(Brit)*, in an instant, in no time; **das ist ~, zwei, drei geschehen** *(fig)* it doesn't take a second; **~ zu ~** *(Sport)* one all; **~ mit jdm sein** to be one with sb; *(= übereinstimmen)* to be in agreement with sb; **sich mit jdm ~ wissen** to know one is in agreement with sb; **das ist doch alles ~** *(inf)* it's all one, it's all the same; **es ist mir alles ~** *(inf)* it's all one *or* all the same to me; **sehen und handeln waren ~** to see was to act; **~ a** *(inf)* A 1 *(inf)*, first-rate *(inf)* → *auch* **ein, eine(r, s), vier**

Eins [ains] F -, **-en** one; *(Sch auch)* A, alpha; **er würfelte zwei ~en** he threw *(Brit) or* rolled two ones; **eine ~ schreiben/bekommen** to get an A *or* alpha *or* a one → *auch* **Vier**

ein+sa|cken VT *sep* **a** *(= in Säcke füllen)* to put in sacks, to sack **b** *(inf) (= erbeuten)* to grab *(inf)*; *Geld, Gewinne* to rake in *(inf)*

ein+sa|cken VI *sep aux sein (= einsinken)* to sink; *(Bürgersteig, Boden etc auch)* to subside

ein+sa|gen *sep (dial)* VI **jdm ~** to prompt sb VT **jdm etw ~** to whisper sth to sb

ein+sal|ben VT *sep* to rub with ointment; *Wunde, Hände auch* to rub ointment into

ein+sal|zen VT *sep irreg Fisch, Fleisch* to salt

ein|sam ['ainza:m] ADJ **a** *Mensch, Leben, Gefühl (= allein, verlassen)* lonely; *(= einzeln)* solitary; **sich ~ fühlen** to feel lonely *or* lonesome *(esp US)*; **ein ~es Boot** a lone *or* solitary boat; **ein ~er Schwimmer** a lone *or* solitary swimmer; **um sie wird es ~** she is becoming a lonely figure

b *(= abgelegen) Haus, Insel* secluded; *Dorf* isolated; *(= menschenleer)* empty; *Strände* lonely, empty

c *(inf: = hervorragend)* **~e Klasse** *or* **Spitze** absolutely fantastic *(inf)*, really great *(inf)*

ADV **a** *(= allein)* lonely; **~ leben** to live a lonely/solitary life; **~ überragt dieser Gipfel die anderen** this peak towers over the others in solitary grandeur

b *(= abgelegen)* isolated; **~ liegen** to be secluded/isolated

Ein|sam|keit F -, *no pl* **a** *(= Verlassenheit)* loneliness; *(= das Einzelnsein)* solitariness; **er liebt die ~** he likes solitude; **die ~ vieler alter Leute** the loneliness of many old people **b** *(= Abgele-*

genheit) (von Haus, Insel) seclusion; *(von Dorf)* isolation; *(= Menschenleere)* emptiness; *(von Strand)* loneliness; **die ~ der Bergwelt** the solitude of the mountains

Ein|sam|keits|ge|fühl NT feeling of loneliness

ein+sam|meln VT *sep* to collect (in); *Obst* to gather (in)

ein+sar|gen ['ainzargn] VT *sep* to put in a coffin; **lass dich (doch) ~!** *(inf)* (go and) take a running jump! *(inf)*, get stuffed! *(Brit inf)*

Ein|satz M **a** *(= Einsatzteil)* inset; *(= Schubladeneinsatz, Koffereinsatz)* tray; *(= Topfeinsatz)* compartment; *(= Bluseneinsatz) false blouse collar and neck to wear under pullover; (= Hemdeinsatz)* dicky *(dated)*
b *(= Spieleinsatz)* stake; *(= Kapitaleinsatz)* investment; **den ~ erhöhen** to raise the stakes; **den ~ heraushaben** *(inf)* to recover one's stake
c *(Mus)* entry; *(Theat)* entrance; **der Dirigent gab den ~** the conductor raised his baton and brought in the orchestra/solist *etc*; **der Dirigent gab den Geigern den ~** the conductor brought in the violins; **der ~ der Streicher war verfrüht** the strings came in too early
d *(= Verwendung)* use; *(esp Mil)* deployment; *(von Arbeitskräften)* employment; **im ~** in use; **die Ersatzspieler kamen nicht zum ~** the reserves weren't put in *or* used; **unter ~ von Schlagstöcken** using truncheons; **unter ~ aller Kräfte** by making a supreme effort
e *(= Aktion) (Mil)* action, operation; *(von Polizei, Feuerwehr)* operation; **im ~** in action; **wo war er im ~?** where did he see action?; **zum ~ kommen** to go into action; **bei seinem ersten ~** the first time he went into action; **sich zum ~ melden** to report for duty; **die Pfadfinder halfen in freiwilligen Einsätzen** the scouts helped on a voluntary basis
f *(= Hingabe)* commitment; **in selbstlosem ~ ihres Lebens** with a complete disregard for her own life; **etw unter ~ seines Lebens tun** to risk one's life to do sth, to do sth at the risk of one's life; **den ~ des eigenen Lebens nicht scheuen** *(geh)* not to hesitate to sacrifice one's own life

Ein|satz-: **Ein|satz|be|fehl** M order to go into action; **ein|satz|be|reit** ADJ ready for use; *(Mil)* ready for action; *Rakete etc* operational; **Ein|satz|be|reit|schaft** F readiness for use; *(Mil)* readiness for action; *(= Bereitschaftsdienst)* stand-by (duty); **Ein|satz|be|spre|chung** F briefing; *(nach dem Einsatz)* debriefing; **ein|satz|fä|hig** ADJ fit for use; *(Mil)* fit for action; *Sportler* fit; **Ein|satz|fä|hig|keit** F fitness for use; *(Mil)* fitness for action; *(von Sportler)* fitness; **Ein|satz|fahr|zeug** NT = **Einsatzwagen**; **Ein|satz|freu|de** F willing application; **ein|satz|freu|dig** ADJ eager (for action), enthusiastic; **Ein|satz|ge|biet** NT *(Mil)* operational area; *(= Betätigungsfeld)* field of activity; **Ein|satz|grup|pe** F, **Ein|satz|kom|man|do** *(Mil)* NT task force; **mobiles Einsatzkommando** mobile task force; **Ein|satz|lei|ter(in)** M(F) head of operations; **Ein|satz|ort** M place of action; *(von Diplomat etc)* posting; **Ein|satz|plan** M plan of action; **Ein|satz|stück** NT *(Tech)* insert; *(= Zubehörteil)* attachment; **Ein|satz|wa|gen** M *(von Polizei)* police car; *(von Feuerwehr)* fire engine; *(= Krankenwagen)* ambulance; *(= Straßenbahn/Bus)* extra tram *(esp Brit) or* streetcar *(US)*/bus; **Ein|satz|zent|ra|le** F centre *(Brit) or* center *(US)* of operations, nerve centre *(Brit) or* center *(US, inf)*

ein+sau|gen VT *sep (lit, fig)* to soak up, to absorb; *(durch Strohhalm etc)* to suck; *(= einatmen)* to breathe in; *frische Luft* to draw *or* suck in → **Muttermilch**

ein+säu|men VT *sep (Sew)* to hem; *(fig)* to edge, to line

ein+scan|nen ['ainskɛnən] VT *sep (Comput)* to scan in; **ein Bild in den Computer ~** to scan a picture into the computer

ein+scha|len [-ʃaːlən] VT *sep (Build)* to board, to shutter

ein+schal|ten *sep* VT **a** *Licht, Radio, Gerät, Computer* to switch *or* turn *or* put on; *Sender* to tune in to **b** *(= einfügen)* to interpolate; *Zitat, Erklärung etc auch* to include (in +*acc* in) **c** *jdn* ~ to call sb in; **jdn in etw** *(acc)* ~ to bring sb into sth *or* in on sth VR to intervene; *(= teilnehmen)* to join in; **wir schalten uns jetzt in die Sendungen von Radio Bremen ein** we now go over to *or* join Radio Bremen

Ein|schalt-: **Ein|schalt|he|bel** M starting lever *or* handle; **Ein|schalt|quo|te** F *(Rad, TV)* viewing figures *pl*

Ein|schal|tung F **a** *(von Licht, Motor etc)* switching *or* turning on **b** *(von Nebensatz etc)* interpolation; *(von Zitat)* inclusion **c** *(von Person, Organisation)* calling *or* bringing in

Ein|scha|lung F, **Ein|scha|lungs|ar|beit** F *(Build)* formwork

ein+schär|fen VT *sep* **jdm etw ~** to impress sth (up)on sb; *Höflichkeit, Rücksichtnahme etc* to inculcate sth in sb; **er hat uns Vorsicht eingeschärft** he impressed on us the need for caution; **ich habe den Kindern eingeschärft, Fremden gegenüber vorsichtig zu sein** I have impressed upon the children to be careful of strangers; **schärf dir das ein!** get that firmly fixed in your mind

ein+schar|ren VT *sep* to cover with earth

ein+schät|zen ✪ 33.1 VT *sep* to assess *(auch Fin)*, to evaluate; *(= schätzen auch)* to estimate; **falsch ~** to misjudge; *(= falsch schätzen)* to miscalculate; **wie ich die Lage einschätze** as I see the situation; **jdn sehr hoch/niedrig ~** to have a very high/low opinion of sb; **etw zu hoch/niedrig ~** to overestimate/underestimate sth; **jdn/sich zu hoch/niedrig ~** to overrate/underrate sb/oneself, to have too high/low an opinion of sb/oneself

Ein|schät|zung F assessment *(auch Fin)*, evaluation; *(= Schätzung auch)* estimation; **falsche ~** misjudgement; *(= falsche Schätzung)* miscalculation; **nach meiner ~** in my estimation

ein+schäu|men *sep* VT **a** *(= mit Schaum behandeln)* to lather **b** *(Tech)* to pack in plastic foam VR to lather oneself

ein+schen|ken VT *sep* to pour (out); **darf ich Ihnen noch Wein ~?** can I give *or* pour you some more wine?

ein+sche|ren *sep* VI *aux sein* to get back VT *Tau* to reeve

ein|schich|tig [-ʃɪçtɪç] ADJ **a** single-layered **b** *Arbeitstag* single-shift ADV **unsere Fabrik arbeitet ~** our factory works a single shift

ein+schi|cken VT *sep* to send in (*an* +*acc* to)

ein+schie|ben VT *sep irreg* **a** *(= hineinschieben)* to put in (*in* +*acc* -to) **b** *(= einfügen)* to put in; *Sonderzüge* to put on; *(= dazwischenschieben) Diskussion, Schüler, Patienten* to fit *or* squeeze *(inf)* in (*in* +*acc* -to); **eine Pause ~** to have a break

Ein|schieb|sel ['ainʃiːpsl] NT **-s, -** insertion

Ein|schie|nen|bahn ['ainʃiːnən-] F monorail

ein+schie|ßen *sep irreg* VT **a** *(= zertrümmern) Fenster* to shoot in; *(mit Ball etc)* to smash (in)
b *Gewehr* to try out and adjust
c *(Tech) Dübel etc* to insert
d *Fäden* to weave in; **ein Gewebe mit eingeschossenen Goldfäden** a fabric shot with gold (thread)
e *(Typ) Seiten, Blätter* to interleave
f *Fußball* to kick in; **Müller schoss den Ball zum 2:0 ein** Müller scored to make it 2-0
g *(Comm) Geld* to inject (*in* +*acc* into)
VR to find one's range, to get one's eye in; **sich auf ein Ziel ~** to get the range of a target; **sich auf jdn ~** *(fig)* to line sb up for the kill
VI **a** *(Sport)* to score; **er schoss zum 1:0 ein** he scored to make it 1-0
b *aux sein (Med)* **die Milch schießt in die Brust ein** the milk comes in
c **auf jdn ~** to shoot at sb

ein+schif|fen *sep* VT to ship VR to embark; **er schiffte sich in London nach Amerika ein** he boarded a ship in London for America

Ein|schif|fung ['ainʃɪfʊŋ] F **-, -en** *(von Personen)* boarding, embarkation; *(von Gütern)* loading

ein+schir|ren ['ainʃɪrən] VT *sep Pferd* to harness

einschl. *abbr von* **einschließlich** incl

ein+schla|fen VI *sep irreg aux sein* to fall asleep, to go to sleep, to drop off *(inf)*; *(Bein, Arm)* to go to sleep; *(euph: = sterben)* to pass away; *(fig: Gewohnheit, Freundschaft)* to peter out, to tail off; **ich kann nicht ~** I can't get to sleep; **bei** *or* **über seiner Arbeit ~** to fall asleep over one's work; **vor dem Einschlafen zu nehmen** *(Medizin)* to be taken before retiring

ein|schlä|fe|rig [-ʃlɛːfərɪç] ADJ *Bett* single

ein+schlä|fern ['ainʃlɛːfɐn] VT *sep* **a** *(= zum Schlafen bringen)* to send to sleep; *(= schläfrig machen)* to make sleepy *or* drowsy; *(fig) Gewissen* to soothe, to quiet; **das kann unsere Wachsamkeit nicht ~** that won't lull us into a false sense of security **b** *(= narkotisieren)* to give a soporific **c** *(= töten) Tier* to put to sleep, to put down

ein|schlä|fernd ADJ soporific; *(= langweilig)* monotonous; **ein ~es Mittel** a soporific (drug)

Ein|schlaf|stö|rung F problem in getting to sleep

Ein|schlag M **a** *(von Geschoss)* impact; *(von Blitz)* striking; **dieses Loch ist der ~ eines Geschosses** this hole was made by a bullet; **der ~ der Granate war deutlich zu sehen** the place where the grenade had landed was clearly visible
b *(Sew)* hem
c *(Tex)* weft, woof
d *(von Bäumen)* felling; *(= gefällte Bäume)* timber
e *(Aut: des Lenkrads)* lock; **das Lenkrad bis zum (vollen) ~ drehen** to put the wheel on full lock
f *(= Zusatz, Beimischung)* element; **einen stark(en) autoritären/südländischen ~ haben** to have more than a hint of authoritarianism/the Mediterranean about it/him/her *etc*

ein+schla|gen *sep irreg* VT **a** *Nagel* to hammer *or* knock in; *Pfahl* to drive in
b *(= zertrümmern)* to smash (in); *Tür* to smash down; *Schädel* to smash (in), to bash in *(inf)*; *Zähne* to knock out; **mit eingeschlagenem Schädel** with one's head bashed in *(inf)*
c *Bäume* to fell
d *(= einwickeln) Ware* to wrap up; *Buch* to cover
e *(= umlegen) Stoff, Decke* to turn up
f *(Aut) Räder* to turn
g *(= wählen) Weg* to take; *Kurs (lit)* to follow; *(fig)* to pursue, to adopt; *Laufbahn etc* to enter on; **das Schiff änderte den eingeschlagenen Kurs** the ship changed from its previous course; **die Regierung schlägt einen weicheren/härteren Kurs ein** the government is taking a softer/harder line
VI **a** **(in etw** *acc*) ~ *(Blitz)* to strike (sth); *(Geschoss etc auch)* to hit (sth); **es muss irgendwo eingeschlagen haben** something must have been struck by lightning; **gut ~** *(inf)* to go down well, to be a big hit *(inf)*; *(Schüler, Arbeiter)* to get on all right
b **auf jdn/etw ~** to hit out at sb/sth
c *(zur Bekräftigung)* to shake on it

ein|schlä|gig ['ainʃlɛːgɪç] ADJ **a** appropriate; *Literatur, Paragraf auch, Erfahrung* relevant **b** *(= zwielichtig) Lokal* dubious ADV **er ist ~ vorbestraft** *(Jur)* he has a previous conviction for a similar offence *(Brit) or* offense *(US)*; **in der Drogenszene ~ bekannt** well-known especially on the drugs scene

Ein|schlag|kra|ter M *(von Meteorit)* impact crater

ein+schlei|chen VR *sep irreg (in +acc* -to) to creep in; *(lit auch)* to steal *or* sneak *(inf)* in; *(fig: Fehler auch)* to slip in; **sich in jds Vertrauen ~** *(fig)* to worm one's way into sb's confidence

ein+schlei|fen VT *sep irreg* to grind; *(= eingravieren)* to cut in (*in* +*acc* -to); **eingeschliffene**

Reaktionen/Verhaltensweisen *(Psych, geh)* established reactions/patterns of behaviour *(Brit)* or behavior *(US)*

ein+schlei|men VR *sep (inf)* **sich bei jdm ~** to creep (up) to sb

ein+schlep|pen VT *sep (Naut) Schiff* to tow in *(in +acc* -to); *(fig) Krankheit, Ungeziefer* to bring in

Ein|schlep|pung [ˈainʃlɛpʊŋ] F -, **-en** *(fig)* introduction, bringing-in

ein+schleu|sen VT *sep* to smuggle in *(in +acc, nach* -to)

ein+schlie|ßen VT *sep irreg* **a** *(= wegschließen)* to lock up *(in +acc* in); *(Mil)* to confine to quarters; **er schloss sich/mich in dem** *or* **das Zimmer ein** he locked himself/me in the room **b** *(= umgeben)* to surround; *(Mil) Stadt, Feind auch* to encircle; **einen Satz in Klammern ~** to put a sentence in brackets *or* parentheses **c** *(fig: = einbegreifen, beinhalten)* to include

ein|schließ|lich [ˈainʃliːslɪç] PREP +gen including, inclusive of; **~ Porto** postage included; **Preis ~ Porto** price including postage, price inclusive of postage ADV **er hat das Buch bis S. 205 ~ gelesen** he has read up to and including p205; **vom 1. bis ~ 31. Oktober** *or* **bis 31. Oktober ~ geschlossen** closed from 1st to 31st October inclusive

Ein|schlie|ßung F *(esp Mil)* confinement

ein+schlum|mern VI *sep aux sein (geh)* to fall asleep; *(euph: = sterben)* to pass away

Ein|schluss M **a** *(von Gefangenen)* locking of the cells **b** **mit** *or* **unter ~ von** *(form)* with the inclusion of, including **c** *(Geol)* inclusion

ein+schmei|cheln VR *sep* **sich bei jdm ~** to ingratiate oneself with sb, to insinuate oneself into sb's good graces; **~de Musik** enticing music; **~de Stimme** silky voice

Ein|schmei|che|lung [ˈainʃmaiçəlʊŋ] F -, **-en**, **Ein|schmeich|lung** [ˈainʃmaiçlʊŋ] F -, **-en** attempt to ingratiate oneself

ein+schmei|ßen VT *sep irreg* **a** *(inf) Fenster* to smash (in) **b** *(sl: = nehmen)* **eine Pille ~** to take *or* pop a pill *(inf)*; **Ecstasy ~** to do *(inf)* or drop *(sl)* ecstasy

ein+schmel|zen *sep irreg* VT to melt down; *(fig: = integrieren)* to put in the melting pot VI *aux sein* to melt

Ein|schmel|zung [ˈainʃmɛltsʊŋ] F -, **-en** melting (down); *(fig)* coalescence

ein+schmie|ren VT *sep* **a** *(mit Fett)* to grease; *(mit Öl)* to oil; *Gesicht (mit Creme)* to cream, to put cream on; **er schmierte mir den Rücken mit Heilsalbe/Sonnenöl ein** he rubbed my back with ointment/suntan lotion **b** *(inf: = beschmutzen)* to get dirty; **er hat sich ganz mit Dreck/Marmelade eingeschmiert** he has covered himself in dirt/jam

ein+schmug|geln VT *sep* to smuggle in *(in +acc* -to); **er hat sich in den Saal eingeschmuggelt** he sneaked into the hall

ein+schnap|pen VI *sep aux sein* **a** *(Schloss, Tür)* to click shut **b** *(inf: = beleidigt sein)* to take offence *(Brit)* or offense *(US)*, to go into a huff *(inf)*; **er schnappt wegen jeder Kleinigkeit ein** he takes offence *(Brit)* or offense *(US)* at every little thing → *auch* **eingeschnappt**

ein+schnei|den *sep irreg* VT **a** *Stoff, Papier* to cut; **er schnitt das Papier an den Ecken einige Zentimeter ein** he cut a few centimetres *(Brit)* or centimeters *(US)* into the corners of the paper; **die Fesseln schneiden mir die Handgelenke ein** the bonds are cutting into my wrists **b** *(= einkerben) Namen, Zeichen* to carve *(in +acc* in, into); **der Fluss hat ein Tal in das Gestein eingeschnitten** the river has carved out *or* cut a valley in the rock; **tief eingeschnittene Felsen** steep cliffs; **eine tief eingeschnittene Schlucht** a deep ravine **c** *(Cook)* **Zwiebeln in die Suppe ~** to cut up some onions and put them in the soup **d** *(Film)* to cut in *(in +acc* -to) VI to cut in *(in +acc* -to)

ein|schnei|dend ADJ *(fig)* drastic, radical; *Maßnahmen auch* trenchant; *Bedeutung, Wirkung, Folgen* far-reaching

ein+schnei|en VI *sep aux sein* to get snowed up; *(Auto, Mensch auch)* to get snowed in; **eingeschneit sein** to be snowed up/in

Ein|schnitt M cut; *(Med)* incision; *(im Tal, Gebirge)* cleft; *(= Zäsur)* break; *(im Leben)* decisive point

ein+schnit|zen VT *sep* to carve *(in +acc* into)

ein+schnü|ren *sep* VT **a** *(= einengen)* to cut into; *Taille (mit Mieder)* to lace in; **dieser Kragen schnürt mir den Hals ein** this collar is nearly choking *or* strangling me **b** *(= zusammenbinden) Paket* to tie up VR to lace oneself up *or* in

ein+schrän|ken [ˈainʃrɛŋkn] *sep* VT to reduce, to cut back *or* down; *Bewegungsfreiheit, Recht* to limit, to restrict; *Wünsche* to moderate; *Behauptung* to qualify; **jdn in seinen Rechten ~** to limit *or* restrict sb's rights; **das Rauchen/Trinken/Essen ~** to cut down on smoking/on drinking/on what one eats VR *(= sparen)* to economize; **sich im Essen/Trinken ~** to cut down on what one eats/on one's drinking → *auch* **eingeschränkt**

ein+schrän|kend [ˈainʃrɛŋknd] *prp von* **einschränken** ADJ qualifying; *(Ling)* restrictive ADV **~ möchte ich sagen, dass ...** I'd like to qualify that by saying ... → *auch* **einschränken**

Ein|schrän|kung F -, **-en** **a** *(= das Einschränken)* reduction; *(von Bewegungsfreiheit, Recht)* limitation, restriction; *(von Wünschen)* moderation; *(von Behauptung)* qualification; *(= Vorbehalt)* reservation; **ohne ~** without reservation, unreservedly **b** *(= Sparmaßnahme)* economy; *(= das Einsparen)* economizing

ein+schrau|ben VT *sep* to screw in *(in +acc* -to)

Ein|schreib- = **Einschreibe-**

Ein|schrei|be-: **Ein|schrei|be|brief** M recorded delivery *(Brit)* or certified *(US)* letter; **Ein|schrei|be|ge|bühr** F **a** *(Post)* charge for recorded delivery *(Brit)* or certified mail *(US)* **b** *(Univ)* registration fee **c** *(für Verein)* membership fee

ein+schrei|ben *sep irreg* VT *(= eintragen)* to enter; *Post* to send recorded delivery *(Brit)* or certified mail *(US)* → *auch* **eingeschrieben** VR *(in Verein, für Abendkurse etc)* to enrol *(Brit)*, to enroll *(US)*; *(Univ)* to register; **er schrieb sich in die Liste ein** he put his name on the list

Ein|schrei|ben NT recorded delivery *(Brit)* or certified *(US)* letter/parcel *(Brit)* or package; **~** *pl* recorded delivery *(Brit)* or certified *(US)* mail *sing*; **einen Brief als** *or* **per ~ schicken** to send a letter recorded delivery *(Brit)* or certified mail *(US)*

Ein|schrei|be|sen|dung F letter/package sent recorded delivery *(Brit)* or certified mail *(US)*

Ein|schrei|bung F enrolment *(Brit)*, enrollment *(US)*; *(Univ)* registration

ein+schrei|en VI *sep irreg* **auf jdn ~** to yell *or* bawl at sb

ein+schrei|ten VI *sep irreg aux sein* to take action *(gegen* against); *(= dazwischentreten)* to intervene, to step in

Ein|schrei|ten NT **-s**, *no pl* intervention

ein+schrum|peln *(inf)*, **ein+schrump|fen** VI *sep aux sein* to shrivel (up)

Ein|schub M insertion

ein+schüch|tern [ˈainʃʏçtɐn] VT *sep* to intimidate

Ein|schüch|te|rung F -, **-en** intimidation

Ein|schüch|te|rungs-: **Ein|schüch|te|rungs|tak|tik** F scare *or* intimidatory tactics *pl*; **Ein|schüch|te|rungs|ver|such** M attempt at intimidation

ein+schu|len VT *sep* **eingeschult werden** *(Kind)* to start school; **wir müssen unseren Sohn dieses Jahr ~** our son has to start school this year; **wir schulen dieses Jahr weniger Kinder ein** we have fewer children starting school this year

Ein|schu|lung F first day at school; **die ~ findet im Alter von 6 Jahren statt** children start school at the age of 6

Ein|schuss M **a** *(= Einschussstelle)* bullet hole; *(Med)* point of entry; **Tod durch ~ in die Schläfe** death caused by a shot *or* a bullet through the side of the head **b** *(Space)* **nach ~ der Rakete in die Erdumlaufbahn** after the rocket had been launched into orbit (a)round the earth **c** *(Ftbl)* shot into goal **d** *(Tex)* weft, woof **e** *(St Ex)* margin

Ein|schuss-: **Ein|schuss|loch** NT bullet hole; **Ein|schuss|stel|le** F bullet hole; *(Med)* point of entry; **Ein|schuss|win|kel** M **a** *(Ftbl, Hockey etc)* shooting *or* scoring angle; **ein günstiger/ungünstiger ~** an easy/difficult shooting angle **b** *(von Geschoss)* entry angle, angle of entry

ein+schüt|ten VT *sep* to tip in *(in +acc* -to); *Flüssigkeiten* to pour in *(in +acc* -to); **dem Pferd Futter ~** to give the horse some fodder; **er hat sich** *(dat)* **noch etwas Kaffee eingeschüttet** *(inf)* he poured himself (out) *or* gave himself some more coffee

ein+schwär|zen VT *sep* to blacken, to make black

ein+schwe|ben VI *sep aux sein* to glide in *(in +acc* -to)

ein+schwei|ßen VT *sep (Tech)* *(= hineinschweißen)* to weld in *(in +acc* -to); *(= zuschweißen) Buch, Schallplatte* to shrink-wrap, to heat-seal *(spec)*

Ein|schweiß|fo|lie F shrink-wrapping

ein+schwen|ken VI *sep aux sein* to turn *or* swing in *(in +acc* -to); **links/rechts ~** *(Mil)* to wheel left/right; **auf etw** *(acc)* **~** *(fig)* to fall in with sth, to go along with sth

ein+schwö|ren VT *sep irreg* **jdn auf etw** *(acc)* **~** to swear sb to sth → *auch* **eingeschworen**

ein+seg|nen VT *sep* **a** *(= konfirmieren)* to confirm **b** *Altar, Kirche* to consecrate; *Feld, Haus, Gläubige* to bless

Ein|seg|nung F *(= Konfirmation)* confirmation; *(von Altar, Kirche)* consecration; *(von Feld, Haus, Gläubigen)* blessing

ein|seh|bar ADJ **a** *(= verständlich)* understandable **b** *Akten, Dateien etc* accessible; *Straße, Kreuzung, Eingang* visible

ein+se|hen *sep irreg* VT **a** *Gelände* to see; *(Mil)* to observe **b** *(= prüfen) Akte* to see, to look at **c** *(= verstehen, begreifen)* to see; *Fehler, Schuld auch* to recognize; **das sehe ich nicht ein** I don't see why; *(= verstehe ich nicht)* I don't see that; **es ist schwer einzusehen, warum/dass ...** it is hard to see why/that ...; **es ist nicht einzusehen, warum/dass ...** it is incomprehensible why/that ... VI **a** **in etw** *(acc)* **~** to see sth; *(Mil)* to observe sth **b** *(= prüfen)* to look *(in +acc* at)

Ein|se|hen NT **ein ~ haben** to have some understanding *(mit, für* for); *(= Vernunft, Einsicht)* to see reason *or* sense; **hab doch ein ~!** have a heart!, be reasonable!; **hast du kein ~?** can't you see sense?

ein+sei|fen VT *sep* **a** to soap; **jdm den Rücken ~** to soap sb's back **b** *(inf: = betrügen)* to con *(inf)*, to take for a ride *(inf)* **c** *(inf: mit Schnee)* to rub with snow

ein|sei|tig [ˈainzaitɪç] ADJ **a** on one side; *(Jur, Pol) Erklärung, Kündigung, Maßnahmen* unilateral; *(Comput)* single-sided; **~e Lungenentzündung** single pneumonia; **~e Lähmung** hemiplegia *(form)*, paralysis of one side of the body **b** *Freundschaft, Zuneigung* one-sided **c** *(= beschränkt) Ausbildung* one-sided; *(= parteiisch) Bericht, Standpunkt, Zeitung* biased; *Ernährung* unbalanced; **~e Kürzungen im Etat** reductions in one area of the budget only ADV **a** *(= auf einer Seite)* on one side **b** *(= unausgewogen)* **sich ~ ernähren** to have an unbalanced diet; **jdn ~ ausbilden** to give sb a one-sided education; **etw ~ schildern** to give a one-sided portrayal of sth, to portray sth one-

sidedly
c *(= parteiisch)* subjectively; **jdn ~ informieren** to give sb biased information

Ein|sei|tig|keit F -, *(rare)* **-en** *(fig)* one-sidedness; *(von Ernährung)* imbalance

ein+sen|den VT *sep irreg* to send in, to submit (*an +acc* to)

Ein|sen|der(in) M(F) sender; *(bei Preisausschreiben)* competitor; **wir bitten die ~ von Artikeln ...** we would ask those (people) who send in *or* submit articles ...

Ein|sen|de|schluss M last date for entries, closing date

Ein|sen|dung F **a** *no pl (= das Einsenden)* sending in, submission **b** *(= das Eingesandte)* letter/article/manuscript *etc*; *(bei Preisausschreiben)* entry

ein+sen|ken *sep* VT *sep* to sink in (*in +acc* -to) VR *(liter)* **dieses Bild senkte sich tief in seine Seele ein** this image made a deep impression on him *or* his mind

Ein|ser ['ainzɐ] M **-s, -** *(esp S Ger inf)* *(Sch)* A (grade), alpha, one; *(Autobus)* (number) one; **er hat einen ~ geschrieben** he got an A

ein+set|zen *sep* VT **a** *(= einfügen)* to put in (*in +acc* -to); *Maschinenteil* to put in (*in +acc* -to), to insert (*in +acc* into), to fit in (*in +acc* -to); *Ärmel* to set in (*in +acc* -to); *Stück Stoff* to let in (*in +acc* -to); *(= einschreiben)* to enter (*in +acc* in), to put in (*in +acc* -to); *Stiftzahn* to put on (*in +acc* -to); *Gebiss* to fit; **Fische in einen Teich ~** to stock a pond with fish; **jdm einen Goldzahn ~** to give sb a gold tooth; **eingesetzte Taschen** pockets let *or* set into the seams
b *(= ernennen, bestimmen)* to appoint; *Ausschuss* to set up, to appoint; *Erben, Nachfolger* to name; **jdn in ein Amt ~** to appoint sb to an office; **jdn als** *or* **zum Richter ~** to appoint sb judge
c *(= verwenden)* to use *(auch Sport)*, to employ; *Truppen, Polizei, Feuerwehr* to deploy, to bring into action; *Schlagstöcke* to use; *Busse, Sonderzüge* to put on; *(Chess) König etc* to bring into play; **etw als** *or* **zum Pfand ~** to give sth as a deposit
d *(beim Glücksspiel)* to stake; *(geh) Leben* to risk; **seine ganze Energie** *or* **Kraft für etw ~** to devote all one's energies to sth
VI *(= beginnen)* to start, to begin; *(Mus)* to come in; *(am Anfang)* to start to play/sing; **die Ebbe/Flut setzt um 3 Uhr ein** the tide turns at 3 o'clock, the tide starts to go out/come in at 3 o'clock; **kurz vor Spielbeginn setzte leichter Regen ein** *(Ftbl)* it began to rain lightly shortly before kick-off; **gegen Abend setzte stärkeres Fieber ein** the fever increased toward(s) evening
VR **a sich (voll) ~** to show (complete) commitment (*in +dat* to); **die Mannschaft setzte sich bis an den Rand ihrer Kraft ein** the team did their absolute utmost
b sich für jdn ~ to fight for sb, to support sb's cause; *(= sich verwenden für)* to give *or* lend sb one's support; **sie hat sich so sehr für ihn eingesetzt** she did so much for him; **sie hat sich voll für die Armen/Verwundeten eingesetzt** she lent her aid unreservedly to the poor/wounded; **sich für etw ~** to support sth; **ich werde mich dafür ~, dass ...** I will do what I can to see that ...; **er setzte sich für die Freilassung seines Bruders ein** he did what he could to secure the release of his brother

Ein|set|zung ['ainzɛtsʊŋ] F **-, -en** appointment (*in +acc* to); **die ~ des Bischofs in sein Amt** the Bishop's investiture → *auch* **Einsatz**

Ein|sicht F **a** *(in Akten, Bücher)* **~ in etw** *(acc)* **haben/nehmen/verlangen** to look/take a look/ask to look at sth; **jdm ~ in etw** *(acc)* **gewähren** to allow sb to look at *or* to see sth; **sie legte ihm die Akte zur ~ vor** she gave him the file to look at
b *(= Vernunft)* sense, reason; *(= Erkenntnis)* insight; *(= Kenntnis)* knowledge; *(= Verständnis)* understanding; *(euph: = Reue)* remorse; **zur ~ kommen** to come to one's senses; **ich bin zu der ~ gekommen, dass ...** I have come to the conclusion that ...; **~ ist der erste Schritt zur Besserung** *(prov)* a fault confessed is half redressed *(Prov)*; **haben Sie doch ~!** have a heart!; *(= seien Sie vernünftig)* be reasonable!; **jdn zur ~ bringen** to bring sb to his/her senses; **er hat ~ in die internen Vorgänge der Firma** he has some knowledge of the internal affairs of the firm

ein|sich|tig ['ainzɪçtɪç] ADJ **a** *(= vernünftig)* reasonable; *(= verständnisvoll)* understanding; **er war so ~, seinen Fehler zuzugeben** he was reasonable enough to admit his mistake **b** *(= verständlich, begreiflich)* understandable, comprehensible; **etw ~ erklären** to explain sth clearly; **jdm etw ~ machen** to make sb understand *or* see sth

Ein|sicht|nah|me [-na:mə] F **-, -n** *(form)* inspection; **er bat um ~ in die Akten** he asked to see the files; **nach ~ in die Akten** after seeing *or* inspecting the files; **„zur ~"** "for inspection"

ein|sichts-: **ein|sichts|los** ADJ *(= unvernünftig)* unreasonable; *(= verständnislos)* lacking in understanding; **Ein|sichts|lo|sig|keit** F **-, -en** *(= Unvernünftigkeit)* unreasonableness; *(= Verständnislosigkeit)* lack of understanding; **ein|sichts|voll** ADJ = **einsichtig a**

ein+si|ckern VI *sep aux sein* to seep in (*in +acc* -to); *(fig)* to filter in (*in +acc* -to); **Spione sickerten in unser Land ein** spies infiltrated (into) our country

Ein|sie|de|lei [ainzi:də'lai] F **-, -en** hermitage; *(fig hum: = einsames Haus)* country retreat *or* hideaway

ein+sie|den VT *sep irreg (S Ger, Aus) Obst* to bottle; *Marmelade* to make

Ein|sied|ler(in) M(F) hermit; *(fig auch)* recluse

ein|sied|le|risch ['ainzi:dlərɪʃ] ADJ hermit-like ADV *leben* like a hermit

Ein|sied|ler-: **Ein|sied|ler|krebs** M hermit crab; **Ein|sied|ler|le|ben** NT hermit's life, life of a hermit *or* recluse

Ein|sil|ber ['ainzɪlbɐ] M **-s, -** monosyllable

ein|sil|big ADJ **a** *Wort* monosyllabic; *Reim* masculine, single **b** *(fig) Mensch* uncommunicative; *Antwort, Erklärung* monosyllabic

Ein|sil|big|keit ['ainzɪlbɪçkait] F **-,** *no pl (lit)* monosyllabism; *(von Reim)* masculinity; *(fig: von Mensch)* uncommunicativeness

Ein|silb|ler M **-s, -** monosyllable

ein+sin|gen VR *sep irreg* to get oneself into voice

ein+sin|ken VI *sep irreg aux sein (im Morast, Schnee)* to sink in (*in +acc or dat* -to); *(Boden etc)* to subside, to cave in; **er sank bis zu den Knien im Schlamm ein** he sank up to his knees in the mud; **ein Stück eingesunkenen Bodens** an area where the ground has caved in *or* subsided; **eingesunkene Schläfen/Wangen** sunken *or* hollow temples/cheeks

ein+sit|zen VI *sep irreg (form)* to serve a prison sentence; **drei Jahre ~** to serve three years, to serve a three-year sentence → *auch* **eingesessen**

Ein|sit|zer M single-seater

ein|sit|zig [-zɪtsɪç] ADJ *Fahrzeug, Flugzeug* single-seater *attr*

ein+sor|tie|ren *ptp* **einsortiert** VT *sep* to sort and put away; *Dokumente* to file away; **in Schachteln/Körbe ~** to sort into boxes/baskets

ein|spal|tig [-ʃpaltɪç] ADJ *(Typ)* single-column ADV **etw ~ setzen** to set sth in a single column/in single columns

ein+span|nen VT *sep* **a** *(in Rahmen) Leinwand* to fit *or* put in (*in +acc* -to); **Saiten in einen Schläger ~** to string a racket **b** *(in Schraubstock)* to clamp in (*in +acc* -to) **c** *(in Kamera)* to put in (*in +acc* -to); *(in Schreibmaschine)* to put in (*in +acc* -to), to insert (*in +acc* in, into) **d** *Pferde* to harness **e** *(fig: = arbeiten lassen)* to rope in (*für etw* to do sth); **jdn für seine Zwecke ~** to use sb for one's own ends → *auch* **eingespannt**

Ein|spän|ner M one-horse carriage; *(hum: = Junggeselle)* bachelor; *(Aus) black coffee served in a glass with whipped cream*

ein|spän|nig ADJ *Wagen* one-horse; **der Wagen ist/fährt ~** the carriage is pulled by one horse

ein+spa|ren VT *sep* to save; *Energie, Strom auch* to save *or* economize on; *Kosten, Ausgaben* to cut down on, to reduce; *Posten* to dispense with, to eliminate

Ein|spar|po|ten|ti|al NT = **Einsparpotenzial**

Ein|spar|po|ten|zi|al NT *(esp Econ)* potential for economies

Ein|spa|rung F **-, -en** economy; *(= das Einsparen)* saving (*von* of); *(von Kosten, Ausgaben)* reduction; *(von Posten)* elimination

ein+spei|cheln ['ainʃpaiçln] VT *sep* to insalivate

ein+spei|chern VT *sep Daten* to feed in (*in +acc* -to), to enter (*in +acc* into)

ein+spei|sen VT *sep* to feed in (*in +acc* -to); *Daten auch* to enter (*in +acc* into)

ein+sper|ren VT *sep* to lock up (*in +acc or dat* in), to lock in (*in +acc or dat* -to); *(versehentlich)* to lock in (*in +acc or dat* -to); *(inf: ins Gefängnis)* to put away *(inf)*, to lock up

ein+spie|len *sep* VR *(Mus, Sport)* to warm up; *(nach Sommerpause etc)* to get into practice; *(Regelung, Arbeit)* to work out; **... aber das spielt sich alles noch ein** ... but things should sort themselves out all right; **ich fahre jetzt mit dem Bus, das hat sich gut eingespielt** I come by bus now, it's working out well; **sich aufeinander ~** to become attuned to one another, to get used to one another → *auch* **eingespielt**
VT **a** *(Mus, Sport) Instrument, Schläger* to play in **b** *(Film, Theat)* to bring in, to gross; *Kosten* to recover
c *(= aufnehmen) Lied* to record; *Schallplatte* to record, to cut
d *(= einblenden) Bild, Video* to insert; *Musik* to play
e *(Comput) Daten, Software* to load

Ein|spiel|er|geb|nis NT *(von Film)* box-office takings *pl or* receipts *pl*

Ein|spie|lung F *(von Musikstück, Oper etc)* recording (*von* by)

ein+spin|nen *sep irreg* VR *(Spinne)* to spin a web (a)round itself; *(Larve)* to spin a cocoon (a)round itself VT *(Spinne)* to spin a web (a)round

Ein|spra|che F *(Aus, Sw)* = **Einspruch**

ein|spra|chig ADJ monolingual

Ein|spra|chig|keit F **-,** *no pl* monolingualism

ein+spre|chen VI *sep irreg* **auf jdn ~** to harangue sb

ein+spren|gen VT *sep (mit Wasser)* to sprinkle with water, to dampen

Ein|spreng|sel ['ainʃprɛŋzl] NT **-s, -** *(Geol)* xenocryst *(spec)*, embedded crystal; **ein Buch mit einigen lyrischen ~n** a book with the odd moment of lyricism

ein+sprin|gen *sep irreg* VI *aux sein* **a** *(Tech)* to lock shut, to lock into place; *(Maschinenteile)* to engage **b** *(inf: = aushelfen)* to stand in; *(mit Geld etc)* to help out VR *(Sport)* to do some practice jumps

Ein|spritz- *in cpds (Aut, Med)* injection

Ein|spritz|dü|se F *(Aut)* injector

ein+sprit|zen VT *sep* **a** *(Aut, Med)* to inject; **er spritzte ihr/sich Insulin ein** he gave her/himself an insulin injection, he injected her/himself with insulin **b** *(= einsprengen) Wäsche* to dampen, to sprinkle with water **c** *(inf: mit Schmutz)* to splash, to spray

Ein|sprit|zer M *(Aut)* fuel injection engine

Ein|spritz-: **Ein|spritz|mo|tor** M *(Aut)* fuel injection engine; **Ein|spritz|pum|pe** F *(Aut)* fuel injection pump

Ein|sprit|zung ['ainʃprɪtsʊŋ] F **-, -en** injection

Ein|spruch M objection *(auch Jur)*; **~ einlegen** *(Admin)* to file an objection, to register a protest; **gegen etw ~ erheben** to object to sth, to raise an objection to sth; **ich erhebe ~!** *(Jur)* objection!; ~ **abgelehnt!** *(Jur)* objection overruled!; **(dem) ~ (wird) stattgegeben!** *(Jur)* objection sustained!

Ein|spruchs-: Ein|spruchs|frist F *(Jur)* period for filing an objection; **Ein|spruchs|recht** NT right to object *or* protest

ein|spu|rig [-ʃpu:rɪç] ADJ *(Rail)* single-track; *(Aut)* single-lane; *Fahrzeug* two-wheeled *(with the wheels one behind the other)* ADV **die Straße ist nur ~ befahrbar** only one lane of the road is open; **er denkt sehr ~** he has a one-track mind

Eins|sein NT *(liter)* oneness

einst [ainst] ADV **a** *(= früher, damals)* once; **Preußen ~ und heute** Prussia past and present *or* yesterday and today *or* then and now; **das Einst und das Heute** *or* **Jetzt** the past and the present **b** *(geh: = in ferner Zukunft)* one *or* some day

ein+stamp|fen VT *sep Papier, Buch, Auflage* to pulp

Ein|stand M **a ein guter ~** a good start to a new job; **er hat gestern seinen ~ gegeben** *or* **gefeiert** yesterday he celebrated starting his new job **b** *(Tennis)* deuce

Ein|stands-: Ein|stands|fei|er F *(in Firma)* celebration of a/the new job; **Ein|stands|preis** M *(Comm)* introductory price

ein+stan|zen VT *sep* to stamp in *(in +acc* -to)

ein+stau|ben *sep* VI *aux sein* to get covered in dust; **eingestaubt sein** to be covered in dust VT *(Aus)* **sich** *(dat)* **das Gesicht (mit Puder) ~** to powder one's face, to dust one's face with powder

ein+stäu|ben VT *sep (mit Puder)* to dust with powder, to powder; *(mit Parfüm etc)* to spray

ein+ste|chen *sep irreg* VT to pierce; *Gummi, Haut, Membran* to puncture, to pierce; *Nadel* to put *or* stick *(inf)* in *(in +acc* -to), to insert *(in +acc* in, into); *(Cook)* to prick; *(= eingravieren)* to engrave VI **auf jdn/etw ~** to stab at sb/sth

Ein|steck|al|bum NT (stamp) stock book *(spec)*, stamp album

ein+ste|cken VT *sep* **a** *(= in etw stecken)* to put in *(in +acc* -to); *Stecker auch, Gerät* to plug in; *Schwert* to sheathe **b** *(in die Tasche etc)* **(sich** *dat***) etw ~** to take sth; **hast du deinen Pass/ein Taschentuch eingesteckt?** have you got your passport/a handkerchief with you?; **er steckte (sich) die Zeitung ein und ging los** he put the paper in his pocket *etc* and left, he took the paper and left; **warte mal, ich habe mir meine Zigaretten noch nicht eingesteckt** hang on, I haven't got my cigarettes yet *(inf)*; **ich habe kein Geld eingesteckt** *or (incorrect)* ~ I haven't any money on me; **kannst du meinen Lippenstift für mich ~?** can you take my lipstick for me?; **steck deine Pistole wieder ein** put your pistol away **c** *(in den Briefkasten)* to post *(Brit)*, to mail *(esp US)* **d** *(inf) Kritik etc* to take; *Beleidigung* to swallow, to take; *(= verdienen) Geld, Profit* to pocket *(inf)*; **der Boxer musste viel ~** the boxer had to take a lot of punishment; **er steckt sie alle ein** he beats all of them *(inf)*

Ein|steck-: Ein|steck|kamm M (decorative) comb; **Ein|steck|kar|te** F *(Comput)* expansion card; **Ein|steck|tuch** NT *pl* **-tücher** breast pocket handkerchief

ein+ste|hen VI *sep irreg aux sein* **a** *(= sich verbürgen)* **für jdn/etw ~** to vouch for sb/sth; **ich stehe dafür ein, dass ...** I will vouch that ...; **er stand mit seinem Wort dafür ein** he vouched for it personally **b für etw ~** *(= Ersatz leisten)* to make good sth; *(= sich bekennen)* to answer for sth, to take responsibility for sth; **für jdn ~** to assume liability *or* responsibility for sb; **ich habe das immer behauptet und dafür stehe ich auch ein** I've always said that, and I'll stand by it

Ein|stei|ge|kar|te F *(Aviat)* boarding pass *or* card

ein+stei|gen VI *sep irreg aux sein* **a** *(in ein Fahrzeug etc)* to get in *(in +acc* -to); *(umständlich, mit viel Gepäck etc auch)* to climb *or* clamber in *(in +acc* -to); *(in Zug auch, in Bus)* to get on *(in +acc* -to); **~!** *(Rail etc)* all aboard!; **in eine Felswand ~** to attack a rock face; **er ist in die Problematik dieses Buchs noch nicht so richtig eingestiegen** he hasn't really got *(Brit) or* come to grips with the problems in this book **b** *(in ein Haus etc)* to climb *or* get in *(in +acc* -to) **c** *(inf)* **in die Politik/ins Verlagsgeschäft ~** to go into politics/publishing; **er ist mit einer Million in diese Firma eingestiegen** he put a million into this firm; **er ist ganz groß in dieses Geschäft eingestiegen** he's (gone) into that business in a big way *(inf)*; **der Verlag ist jetzt in Wörterbücher eingestiegen** the publishing company has branched out into dictionaries *or* into the dictionary market

Ein|stei|ger(in) M(F) *(inf)* beginner; **ein Modell für PC-~** an entry-level PC

Ein|stei|ni|um [ain'ʃtainiʊm] NT **-s**, *no pl (abbr* **Es)** einsteinium

ein|stell|bar ADJ adjustable

Ein|stell|be|reich M *(Aut)* adjustment range

ein+stel|len *sep* VT **a** *(= hineinstellen)* to put in; **das Auto in die** *or* **der Garage ~** to put the car in(to) the garage; **das Buch ist falsch eingestellt** the book has been put in the wrong place **b** *(= anstellen) Arbeitskräfte* to take on; **„wir stellen ein: Sekretärinnen"** "we have vacancies for secretaries", "we are looking for secretaries" **c** *(= beenden)* to stop; *Expedition, Suche* to call off; *(Mil) Feindseligkeiten, Feuer* to cease; *(Jur) Prozess, Verfahren* to abandon; **die Arbeit ist eingestellt worden** work has stopped; *(vorübergehend auch)* work has been halted; **die Zeitung hat ihr Erscheinen eingestellt** the paper has ceased publication; **die Arbeit ~** *(Kommission etc)* to stop work; *(= in den Ausstand treten)* to withdraw one's labour *(Brit) or* labor *(US)* **d** *(= regulieren)* to adjust *(auf +acc* to); *Kanone* to aim *(auf +acc* at); *Fernglas, Fotoapparat (auf Entfernung)* to focus *(auf +acc* on); *Wecker, Zünder* to set *(auf +acc* for); *Radio* to tune (in) *(auf +acc* to); *Sender* to tune in to; **die Steuerung auf Automatik ~** to switch over to *or* to put the plane on automatic pilot; **den Hebel auf Start ~** to set the lever to start **e** *(fig: = abstimmen)* to tailor *(auf +acc* to) **f** *(Sport) Rekord* to equal VR **a** *(Besucher etc)* to appear, to present oneself; *(Fieber, Regen)* to set in; *(Symptome)* to appear; *(Folgen)* to become apparent, to appear; *(Wort, Gedanke)* to come to mind; *(Jahreszeiten)* to come, to arrive; **wenn es kalt ist, stellen sich bei mir regelmäßig heftige Kopfschmerzen ein** I always suffer from bad headaches when it's cold **b sich auf jdn/etw ~** *(= sich richten nach)* to adapt oneself to sb/sth; *(= sich vorbereiten auf)* to prepare oneself for sb/sth → *auch* **eingestellt** VI to take on staff; *(Fabrik)* to take on workers

ein|stel|lig ADJ *Zahl* single-digit; **ein Verlust im ~en Millionenbereich** *or* **in ~er Millionenhöhe** a loss of between 1 and 10 million

Ein|stell-: Ein|stell|knopf M *(an Radio etc)* tuning knob; **Ein|stell|platz** M *(auf Hof)* carport; *(in großer Garage)* (covered) parking accommodation *no indef art*; **Ein|stell|schrau|be** F adjustment screw

Ein|stel|lung F **a** *(= Anstellung)* employment **b** *(= Beendigung)* stopping; *(von Expedition, Suche)* calling-off; *(Mil)* cessation; *(Jur)* abandonment; **der Sturm zwang uns zur ~ der Suche/Bauarbeiten** the storm forced us to call off *or* abandon the search/to stop work on the building; **die Lackierer beschlossen die ~ der Arbeit** the paint-sprayers decided to withdraw their labour *(Brit) or* labor *(US) or* to down tools **c** *(= Regulierung)* adjustment; *(von Fernglas, Fotoapparat)* focusing; *(von Wecker, Zünder)* setting; *(von Radio)* tuning (in); *(Film: = Szene)* take; **~en** *pl (Comput)* settings **d** *(= Gesinnung, Haltung)* attitude; *(politisch, religiös etc)* views *pl*; **er hat eine falsche ~ zum Leben** he doesn't have the right attitude to *or* outlook on life; **das ist doch keine ~!** what kind of attitude is that!, that's not the right attitude!

Ein|stel|lungs-: Ein|stel|lungs|ge|spräch NT interview; **Ein|stel|lungs|pra|xis** F policy for taking on staff *(Brit)*, hiring policy *(US)*; **Ein|stel|lungs|stopp** M halt in recruitment; **Ein|stel|lungs|ter|min** M starting date; **Ein|stel|lungs|test** M recruitment test; **Ein|stel|lungs|un|ter|su|chung** F *medical examination when starting a new job*; **Ein|stel|lungs|vo|raus|set|zung** F job requirement

ein+stem|peln VI *sep (bei Arbeitsantritt)* to clock in *or* on

eins|tens ['ainstns] ADV *(obs)* = **einst**

Ein|stich M *(= Einstichstelle)* puncture; *(= Vorgang)* insertion

Ein|stich|stel|le F puncture

Ein|stieg M **a** *no pl (= das Einsteigen)* getting in; *(in Bus)* getting on; *(von Dieb: in Haus etc)* entry; *(fig: zu einem Thema etc)* lead-in *(zu* to); **~ nur vorn!** enter only at the front; **kein ~** exit only; **er stürzte beim ~ in die Eigernordwand ab** he fell during the assault on the north face of the Eiger **b** *(von Bahn)* door; *(von Bus)* door, entrance

Ein|stiegs|dro|ge F starter drug, drug leading to further addiction

Ein|stiegs|mo|dell NT *(für Anfänger)* starter model

eins|tig ['ainstɪç] ADJ *attr* former

ein+stim|men *sep* VI *(in ein Lied)* to join in; *(fig) (= beistimmen)* to agree *(in +acc* with); *(= zustimmen)* to agree *(in +acc* to); **in den Gesang/die Buhrufe (mit) ~** to join in the singing/booing VT *(Mus) Instrument* to tune; **jdn/sich auf etw** *(acc)* **~** *(fig)* to get *or* put sb/oneself in the (right) mood for sth; *auf eine Atmosphäre etc* to attune sb/oneself to sth

ein|stim|mig ADJ **a** *Lied* for one voice **b** *(= einmütig)* unanimous ADV **a ~ singen** to sing in unison; **..., riefen sie ~** ..., they called in unison **b** *(= einmütig)* unanimously

Ein|stim|mig|keit F **-, -en** unanimity

Ein|stim|mig|keits|prin|zip NT unanimity rule

Ein|stim|mung F *(Mus: von Instrumenten)* tuning; **für die richtige ~ der Zuhörer sorgen** *(fig)* to get the audience in the right mood

ein+stip|pen VT *sep (dial)* to dunk

einst|mals ['ainstma:ls] ADV = **einst**

ein|stö|ckig ADJ *Haus* two-storey *(Brit)*, two-story *(US)*; **~ (gebaut) sein** to have two storeys *(Brit) or* stories *(US)*

ein+stöp|seln VT *sep (Elec)* to plug in *(in +acc* -to)

ein+sto|ßen VT *sep irreg Tür, Mauer* to knock *or* break down; *Scheibe* to push in, to break

ein+strah|len VI *sep* to irradiate *(spec)*, to shine

Ein|strah|lung F *(= Sonneneinstrahlung)* irradiation *(spec)*, shining

ein+strei|chen VT *sep irreg* **a eine Wunde (mit Salbe) ~** to put ointment on a wound; **eine Kuchenform (mit Fett) ~** to grease a baking tin *(Brit) or* pan *(US)* **b** *(inf) Geld, Gewinn* to pocket *(inf)*

ein+streu|en VT *sep* to sprinkle in *(in +acc* -to); *(fig) Bemerkung etc* to slip in *(in +acc* -to)

ein+strö|men VI *sep aux sein* to pour *or* flood in *(in +acc* -to); *(Licht, fig auch)* to stream in *(in +acc* -to); **kältere Luftschichten strömen nach Bayern ein** a stream of cooler air is moving in towards *(Brit) or* toward *(US)* Bavaria; **~de Kaltluft** a stream of cold air

ein|stro|phig ADJ one-verse *attr*

ein+stu|die|ren *ptp* **einstudiert** VT *sep Lied, Theaterstück* to rehearse; **einstudierte Antworten** *(fig)* well-rehearsed answers

Ein|stu|die|rung ['ainʃtudiːrʊŋ] F -, -en *(Theat)* production

ein+stu|fen VT *sep* to classify; **in eine Klasse/Kategorie** *etc* ~ to put into a class/category *etc*

ein|stu|fig ADJ *Rakete* single-stage; *Verfahren auch* single-phase

Ein|stu|fung F classification; *(auf Lernniveau etc)* placement; **nach seiner ~ in eine höhere Gehaltsklasse** after he was put on a higher salary grade *(Brit) or* into a higher salary bracket

Ein|stu|fungs|test M placement test

ein|stün|dig ADJ *attr* one-hour; **mehr als ~e Verspätungen** delays of more than an hour; **nach ~er Pause** after an hour's *or* a one-hour break, after a break of an hour

ein+stür|men VI *sep aux sein* **auf jdn ~** *(Mil)* to storm sb; *(fig)* to assail sb; **mit Fragen auf jdn ~** to bombard *or* besiege sb with questions

Ein|sturz M collapse; *(von Mauer, Boden, Decke auch)* caving-in

ein+stür|zen VI *sep aux sein* to collapse; *(Mauer, Boden, Decke auch)* to cave in; *(Theorie, Gedankengebäude auch)* to crumble; **auf jdn ~** *(fig)* to overwhelm sb; **es stürzte viel auf ihn ein** he was overwhelmed by events

Ein|sturz|ge|fahr F danger of collapse

ein|sturz|ge|fähr|det F in danger of collapsing *pred*

einst|wei|len ['ainst'vailən] ADV in the meantime; *(= vorläufig)* temporarily

einst|wei|lig ['ainst'vailɪç] ADJ *attr* temporary; **~e Verfügung/Anordnung** *(Jur)* temporary *or* interim injunction/order; **~ verfügen** *(Jur)* to issue a temporary *or* an interim injunction

ein+sug|ge|rie|ren *ptp* **einsuggeriert** VT *sep* **jdm etw ~** to suggest sth to sb; *(inf)* to brainwash sb into believing sth

Eins|wer|den NT *(geh)* becoming one *no art*

ein|tä|gig ADJ *attr* one-day → **viertägig**

Ein|tags|flie|ge F *(Zool)* mayfly; *(fig)* nine-day wonder; *(= Mode, Idee)* passing craze

ein+tan|zen VR *sep* to get used to dancing with sb; *(vor Turnier etc)* to dance a few practice steps

Ein|tän|zer M gigolo *(dated)*, dancing partner

ein+tä|to|wie|ren *ptp* **eintätowiert** VT *sep* to tattoo (*in/auf +acc* on)

ein+tau|chen *sep* **VT** to dip (*in +acc* in, into); *(völlig)* to immerse (*in +acc* in); *Brot (in Kaffee etc)* to dunk (*in +acc* in) **VI** *aux sein (Schwimmer)* to dive in; *(Springer)* to enter the water; *(U-Boot)* to dive; **das U-Boot ist jetzt ganz eingetaucht** the submarine is now completely submerged

Ein|tausch M exchange, swap *(inf)*; **„Eintausch von Gutscheinen"** "coupons exchanged here"

ein+tau|schen VT *sep* to exchange, to swap *(inf)* (*gegen, für* for); *(= umtauschen) Devisen* to change

ein|tau|send ['ain'tauznt] NUM *(form)* = **tausend**

ein+tei|len *sep* **VT** **a** *(= aufteilen)* to divide (up) (*in +acc* into); *(= aufgliedern)* to split (up) (*in +acc* into); *(in Grade) Thermometer* to graduate, to calibrate **b** *(= sinnvoll aufteilen) Zeit, Arbeit* to plan (out), to organize; *Geld auch* to budget; **wenn ich mir eine Flasche gut einteile, reicht sie eine Woche** if I plan it well a bottle lasts me a week **c** *(= dienstlich verpflichten)* to detail (*zu* for); **er ist heute als Aufseher eingeteilt** he has been allocated the job of supervisor today **VI** *(inf: = Haus halten)* to budget

Ein|tei|ler M *(Fashion)* one-piece (swimsuit)

ein|tei|lig ADJ *Badeanzug* one-piece *attr*

Ein|tei|lung F **a** *(= das Aufteilen)* division; *(in Grade)* gradation, calibration **b** *(von Zeit, Arbeit)* planning, organization; *(von Geld)* budgeting **c** *(= dienstliche Verpflichtung)* detailment *(esp Mil)*, assignment

Ein|tel ['aintl] NT (SW AUCH M) -s, - *(Math)* whole

ein+tip|pen VT *sep* to type in (*in +acc* -to)

ein|tö|nig ['aintøːnɪç] **ADJ** monotonous **ADV** monotonously; **~ reden** to talk in a monotone

Ein|tö|nig|keit F -, *no pl* monotony; *(von Stimme)* monotonousness

Ein|topf M stew

Ein|topf|es|sen NT, **Ein|topf|ge|richt** NT stew

Ein|tracht F, *no pl* harmony, concord; **er hat zwischen den beiden wieder ~ gestiftet** he restored peaceful relations between the two of them; **~ X** *(Sport)* ≈ X United

ein|träch|tig **ADJ** peaceable **ADV** peaceably

Ein|trag ['aintraːk] M -(e)s, ⸚e [-trɛːgə] **a** *(schriftlich, in Wörterbuch etc)* entry (*in +acc* in) **b** *(geh)* **das tut der Sache keinen ~** that does no harm **c** *(Tex)* weft, woof **d** *(= Schadstoffeinleitung)* discharge

ein+tra|gen *sep irreg* **VT** **a** *(in Liste, auf Konto etc)* to enter; *(= amtlich registrieren)* to register; **sich ~ lassen** to have one's name put down → *auch* **eingetragen**; **nicht im Telefonbuch eingetragen sein** to be ex-directory *(Brit)*, to be unlisted *(US)* **b** **jdm Hass/Undank/Gewinn ~** to bring sb hatred/ingratitude/profit; **das trägt nur Schaden ein** that will only do harm **VR** to sign; *(= sich vormerken lassen)* to put one's name down; **er trug sich ins Gästebuch ein** he signed the visitors' book; **er trug sich in die Warteliste ein** he put his name (down) on the waiting list

ein|träg|lich ['aintrɛːklɪç] ADJ profitable; *Geschäft, Arbeit auch* lucrative, remunerative

Ein|träg|lich|keit F -, -en profitability

Ein|tra|gung ['aintraːgʊŋ] F -, -en entry (*in +acc* in)

ein+trai|nie|ren *ptp* **eintrainiert** VT *sep* to practise *(Brit)*, to practice *(US)*

ein+träu|feln VT *sep* **jdm Medizin in die Nase/ins Ohr ~** to put drops up sb's nose/in sb's ear; **jdm Hass ~** *(geh)* to infuse sb with hatred

ein+tref|fen VI *sep irreg aux sein* **a** *(= ankommen)* to arrive; **„Bananen frisch eingetroffen"** "bananas - just in" **b** *(fig: = Wirklichkeit werden)* to come true; *(Prophezeiung)* to come true, to be fulfilled

ein|treib|bar ADJ *Schulden* recoverable; *Steuern, Zinsen* exactable

ein+trei|ben VT *sep irreg* **a** *Vieh, Nagel, Pfahl* to drive in (*in +acc* -to) **b** *(= einziehen) Geldbeträge* to collect; *Schulden* to recover, to collect

Ein|trei|bung ['aintraibʊŋ] F -, -en *(von Geldbeträgen)* collection; *(von Schulden auch)* recovery

ein+tre|ten *sep irreg* **VI** **a** *aux sein (= hineingehen) (ins Zimmer etc)* to go/come in (*in +acc* -to); *(in Verein, Partei etc)* to join (*in etw (acc)* sth); **ins Haus ~** to go into *or* enter the house; **in eine Firma ~** to go into *or* join a firm; **in die Politik/den diplomatischen Dienst ~** to go into *or* enter politics/the diplomatic service; **ins Heer ~** to join the army, to join up; **in den Krieg ~** to enter the war; **in Verhandlungen ~** *(form)* to enter into negotiations; **ins 30. Lebensjahr ~** *(form)* to enter upon *(form) or* go into one's 30th year; **die Verhandlungen sind in eine kritische Phase eingetreten** the negotiations have entered a critical phase; **die Rakete trat in ihre Umlaufbahn ein** the rocket went into its orbit; **bitte treten Sie ein!** *(form)* (please) do come in

b **auf jdn ~** to boot *or* kick sb, to put the boot in on sb *(inf)*

c *aux sein (= sich ereignen) (Tod)* to occur; *(Zeitpunkt)* to come; *(= beginnen) (Dunkelheit, Nacht)* to fall; *(Besserung, Tauwetter)* to set in; **bei Eintreten der Dunkelheit** at nightfall; **gegen Abend trat starkes Fieber ein** toward(s) evening the patient started to run a high temperature; **es ist eine Besserung eingetreten** there has been an improvement; **wenn der Fall eintritt, dass ...** if it happens that ...; **es ist der Fall eingetreten, den wir befürchtet hatten** what we had feared has in fact happened

d *aux sein* **für jdn/etw ~** to stand *or* speak up for sb/sth; **sein mutiges Eintreten für seine Überzeugung** his courageous defence *(Brit) or* defense *(US)* of his conviction *or* belief

e *(Sw)* **auf etw** *(acc)* **~** to follow sth up

VT **a** *(= zertrümmern)* to kick in; *Tür* to kick down *or* in

b *(= hineintreten) Stein etc* to tread in (*in +acc* -to)

c *Schuhe* to wear *or* break in

d **sich** *(dat)* **etw (in den Fuß) ~** to run sth into one's foot

ein+trich|tern ['aintrɪçtɐn], **ein+trim|men** VT *sep (inf)* **jdm etw ~** to drum sth into sb; **jdm ~, dass ...** to drum it into sb that ...

Ein|tritt M **a** *(= das Eintreten)* entry (*in +acc* (in)to); *(ins Zimmer etc)* entry, entrance; *(in Verein, Partei etc)* joining (*in +acc* of); **beim ~ ins Zimmer** when *or* on entering the room; **„Eintritt im Sekretariat"** "entrance through the office"; **seine Beziehungen erleichterten ihm den ~ ins Geschäftsleben** his connections made it easier for him to get into the business world; **der ~ in den Staatsdienst** entry (in)to the civil service; **die Schule soll auf den ~ ins Leben vorbereiten** school should prepare you for going out into life; **der ~ in die EU** entry to the EU; **der ~ ins Gymnasium** starting at grammar school *(Brit) or* high school *(US)*; **seit seinem ~ in die Armee** since joining the army, since joining up

b *(= Eintrittsgeld)* admission (*in +acc* to); *(= Einlass)* admission, admittance (*in +acc* to); **was kostet der ~?** how much *or* what is the admission?; **~ frei!** admission free; **~ EUR 10** admission EUR 10; **„Eintritt verboten"** "no admittance"; **jdm ~ in etw** *(acc)* **gewähren** *(form)* to allow *or* permit sb to enter sth, to grant sb admission to sth *(form)*

c *(von Winter, Dunkelheit)* onset; **bei ~ eines solchen Falles** in such an event; **der ~ des Todes** the moment when death occurs; **bei ~ der Dunkelheit** at nightfall, as darkness fell/falls

Ein|tritts-: **Ein|tritts|geld** NT entrance money, admission charge; **die Zuschauer verlangten ihr ~ zurück** the audience asked for their money back; **Ein|tritts|kar|te** F ticket (of admission), entrance ticket; **Ein|tritts|preis** M admission charge

ein+trock|nen VI *sep aux sein (Fluss, Farbe)* to dry up; *(Wasser, Blut)* to dry

ein+trom|meln *sep (inf)* **VT** = **eintrichtern** **VI** **auf jdn ~** *(lit, fig)* to pound sb

ein+trü|ben VR *sep (Met)* to cloud over, to become overcast

Ein|trü|bung F *(Met)* cloudiness *no pl*

ein+tru|deln VI *sep aux sein (inf)* to drift in *(inf)*; **... bis alle eingetrudelt sind** ... until everyone has turned up

ein+tun|ken VT *sep Brot* to dunk (*in +acc* in)

ein+tü|ten ['ainty:tn] VT *sep (form)* to put into (paper) bags

ein+üben VT *sep* to practise *(Brit)*, to practice *(US)*; *Theaterstück, Rolle etc* to rehearse; *Rücksichtnahme, Solidarität* to learn *or* acquire (through practice); **sich** *(dat)* **etw ~** to practise *(Brit) or* practice *(US)* sth

Ein|übung F practice; *(Theat etc)* rehearsal

Ei|nung ['ainʊŋ] F -, -en *(geh)* unification

ein+ver|lei|ben ['ainfɛɐlaibn] *ptp* **einverleibt** VT *sep and insep* **a** *Gebiet, Land* to annex (*dat* to); *Firma, Ministerium* to incorporate (*dat* into) **b** *(hum inf)* **sich** *(dat)* **etw ~** *(= essen, trinken)* to put sth away *(inf)*, to polish sth off *(inf)*; *(= sich aneignen, begreifen)* to assimilate sth, to take sth in

Ein|ver|lei|bung F -, -en *(von Gebiet, Land)* annexation; *(von Firma, Ministerium)* incorporation

Ein|ver|nah|me ['ainvɛɐnaːmə] F -, -n *(Jur: esp Aus, Sw)* = **Vernehmung**

ein|ver|neh|men *ptp* **einvernommen** VT *insep irreg (Jur: esp Aus, Sw)* = **vernehmen**

Ein|ver|neh|men NT *(= Eintracht)* amity, harmony; *(= Übereinstimmung)* agreement; **in gutem** *or* **bestem ~ leben** to live in perfect amity *or* harmony; **wir arbeiten in gutem ~ (miteinander)** we work in perfect harmony (together); **im ~ mit jdm** in agreement with sb; **in gegenseitigem** *or* **beiderseitigem ~** by mutual agreement; **sich mit jdm ins ~ setzen** *(form)* to come to *or* reach an agreement *or* understanding with sb

ein|ver|nehm|lich *(form)* ADJ *Regelung, Lösung* consensual ADV consensually

Ein|ver|nehm|lich|keit F -, *no pl* consensus, agreement

Ein|ver|neh|mung F *(Jur: esp Aus, Sw)* = **Vernehmung**

ein|ver|stan|den ['ainfɛɐʃtandn] ✪ 41 ADJ **~!** okay! *(inf)*, agreed!; **~ sein** to agree, to consent, to be agreed; **ich bin ~** that's okay *or* all right by me *(inf)*, I'm agreed; **mit jdm/etw ~ sein** to agree to sb/sth; *(= übereinstimmen)* to agree *or* be in agreement with sb/sth; **sie ist damit ~, dass sie nur 10% bekommt** she has agreed *or* consented to take only 10%; **ich bin mit deinem Verhalten/mit dir gar nicht ~** I don't approve of your behaviour *(Brit) or* behavior *(US)*; **sich mit etw ~ erklären** to give one's agreement to sth

ein|ver|ständ|lich ADJ mutually agreed; *Ehescheidung* by mutual consent ADV **diese Frage wurde ~ geklärt** this question was settled to the satisfaction of both/all parties

Ein|ver|ständ|nis NT agreement; *(= Zustimmung)* consent; **wir haben uns in gegenseitigem ~ scheiden lassen** we were divorced by mutual consent; **er erklärte sein ~ mit dem Plan** he gave his agreement to the plan; **das geschieht mit meinem ~** that has my consent *or* agreement; **im ~ mit jdm handeln** to act with sb's consent

Ein|ver|ständ|nis|er|klä|rung F declaration of consent; **die schriftliche ~ der Eltern** the parents' written consent

Einw. *abbr von* **Einwohner**

Ein|waa|ge F, *no pl (Comm)* **a** *(= Reingewicht)* *weight of contents of can or jar excluding juice etc*; **Frucht-~/Fleisch-~ 200 g** fruit/meat content 200g **b** *(Comm: = Gewichtsverlust)* weight loss

ein+wach|sen VT *sep Boden, Skier* to wax

ein+wach|sen VI *sep irreg aux sein (Baum, Staude)* to establish itself; *(Finger-, Zehennagel)* to become ingrown; **der Zehennagel ist mir eingewachsen** I have an ingrowing *(Brit) or* ingrown toenail

Ein|wahl F *(Telec, ins Internet)* dial-up; **bei der ~** when dialling *(Brit) or* dialing *(US)* in

ein+wäh|len *sep* VR *(Telec)* to dial in *(in +acc* -to); **sich in ein Telefonnetz ~** to dial into a telephone network; **sich ins Internet ~** to log onto the Internet

Ein|wahl|kno|ten, Ein|wähl|kno|ten M *(Telec, Comput)* point of presence, POP

Ein|wand ['ainvant] ✪ 28.1, 36.1, 36.2, 38.1 M -(e)s, ⸗e objection [-vɛndə]; **einen ~ erheben** *or* **vorbringen** *or* **geltend machen** *(form)* to put forward *or* raise an objection

Ein|wan|de|rer M, **Ein|wan|de|rin** F immigrant

ein+wan|dern VI *sep aux sein (nach, in +acc* to) to immigrate; *(Volk)* to migrate

Ein|wan|de|rung F immigration *(nach, in +acc* to); **vor seiner ~ in die USA** before he came *or* immigrated to the USA

Ein|wan|de|rungs- *in cpds* immigration; **Ein|wan|de|rungs|be|hör|de** F immigration authorities *pl*; **Ein|wan|de|rungs|de|bat|te** F immigration policy debate; **Ein|wan|de|rungs|land** NT immigration country; **Ein|wan|de|rungs|po|li|tik** F immigration policy

ein|wand|frei ADJ **a** *(= ohne Fehler)* perfect; *Sprache, Arbeit, Betrieb eines Systems auch* faultless; *Benehmen, Leumund* irreproachable, impeccable; *Lebensmittel* perfectly fresh; **er spricht ein ~es Spanisch** he speaks perfect Spanish, he speaks Spanish perfectly; **ethisch ~** ethically acceptable

b *(= unzweifelhaft)* indisputable; *Beweis auch* definite

ADV **a** *(= fehlerlos) Deutsch sprechen, funktionieren* perfectly; *sich verhalten* impeccably; **er arbeitet sehr genau und ~** his work is very precise and absolutely faultless; **~ funktionieren** *(Gerät, Maschine etc)* to work perfectly

b *(= unzweifelhaft)* indisputably; *beweisen auch* definitely; **etw ~ beweisen** to prove sth beyond doubt, to give definite proof of sth; **es steht ~ fest, dass ...** it is beyond question *or* quite indisputable that ...; **das ist ~ Betrug/Unterschlagung** that is a clear case of fraud/embezzlement

ein|wärts ['ainvɛrts] ADV inwards

ein|wärts|ge|bo|gen ADJ bent inwards

ein+wäs|sern VT *sep (Cook)* to steep

ein+we|ben VT *sep irreg* to weave in *(in +acc* -to); *(fig auch)* to work in *(in +acc* -to)

ein+wech|seln VT *sep Geld* to change *(in +acc, gegen* into); **jdm Geld ~** to change money for sb

ein+we|cken VT *sep* to preserve; *Obst etc auch* to bottle; *(rare: in Büchsen)* to can, to tin *(Brit)*

Ein|weck-: Ein|weck|glas NT preserving jar; **Ein|weck|gum|mi** M OR NT, **Ein|weck|ring** M rubber seal *(for preserving jar)*

Ein|weg- *in cpds (= Wegwerf-)* disposable; **Ein|weg|fla|sche** F non-returnable bottle; **Ein|weg|ka|me|ra** F disposable camera; **Ein|weg|schei|be** F one-way glass; **Ein|weg|spie|gel** M one-way mirror; **Ein|weg|sprit|ze** F disposable syringe; **Ein|weg|ver|pa|ckung** F disposable packaging

ein+wei|chen VT *sep* to soak

ein+wei|hen VT *sep* **a** *(= feierlich eröffnen)* to open (officially); *(fig)* to christen, to baptize **b** **jdn in etw** *(acc)* **~** to initiate sb into sth; **er ist eingeweiht** he knows all about it → **Eingeweihte(r)**

Ein|wei|hung ['ainvaiʊŋ] F -, -en, **Ein|wei|hungs|fei|er** F (official) opening

ein+wei|sen VT *sep irreg* **a** *(in Wohnung, Haus)* to send, to assign *(in +acc* to) **b** *(in Krankenhaus, Heilanstalt)* to admit *(in +acc* to) **c** *(= in Arbeit unterweisen)* **jdn ~** to introduce sb to his job *or* work; **er wurde von seinem Vorgänger (in die Arbeit) eingewiesen** his predecessor showed him what the job involved **d** *(in ein Amt)* to install *(in +acc* in) **e** *(Aut)* to guide in *(in +acc* -to)

Ein|wei|sung F **a** *(in Wohnung, Haus)* accommodation *(in +acc* in) **b** *(in Krankenhaus, Anstalt)* admission *(in +acc* in) **c** **die ~ der neuen Mitarbeiter übernehmen** to assume responsibility for introducing new employees to their jobs *or* work **d** *(in ein Amt)* installation *(in +acc* in)

Ein|wei|sungs|schein M *(in Krankenhaus, Anstalt)* referral

ein+wen|den VT *sep irreg* **etwas/nichts gegen etw einzuwenden haben** to have an objection/no objection to sth, to object/not to object to sth; **dagegen lässt sich ~, dass ...** one objection to this is that ...; **dagegen lässt sich nichts ~** there can be no objection to that; **er wandte ein, dass ...** he objected *or* raised the objection that ...; **er hat immer etwas einzuwenden** he always finds something to object to, he always has some objection to make

Ein|wen|dung F objection *(auch Jur)*; **gegen etw ~en erheben** *or* **haben** *or* **vorbringen** to raise objections to sth

ein+wer|fen *sep irreg* VT **a** *Fensterscheibe etc* to break, to smash **b** *(Sport) Ball* to throw in **c** *Brief* to post *(Brit)*, to mail *(esp US)*; *Münze* to insert **d** *(fig) Bemerkung* to make, to throw in; **er warf ein, dass ...** he made the point that ...; **ja, warf er ein** yes, he interjected VI *(Sport)* to throw in, to take the throw-in; **er hat falsch eingeworfen** he fouled when he was throwing in

ein|wer|tig ADJ *(Chem)* monovalent; *(Ling)* one place

ein+wi|ckeln VT *sep* **a** *(= einpacken)* to wrap (up); **er wickelte sich fest in seinen Mantel ein** he wrapped himself up well in his coat **b** *(inf: = übervorteilen, überlisten)* to fool *(inf)*, to take in; *(durch Schmeicheleien)* to butter up *(inf)*

Ein|wi|ckel|pa|pier NT wrapping paper

ein+wie|gen VT *sep irreg (Comm) Mehl etc* to weigh out

ein+wil|li|gen VI *sep (in +acc* to) to consent, to agree

Ein|wil|li|gung ['ainvɪlɪgʊŋ] F -, -en *(in +acc* to) consent, agreement

ein+win|ken VT *sep* to guide *or* direct in

ein+win|tern VT *sep* to winter

ein+wir|ken *sep* VI **auf jdn/etw ~** to have an effect on sb/sth; *(= beeinflussen)* to influence sb/sth; **diese Maßnahmen wirken günstig auf die Marktsituation ein** these measures are having a favourable *(Brit) or* favorable *(US)* effect on the market situation; **etw ~ lassen** *(Med)* to let sth work in; *(Chem)* to let sth react; *Beize* to let sth soak *or* work in; **einen Anblick auf sich** *(acc)* **~ lassen** to take a sight in VT to work in *(in +acc* -to)

Ein|wir|kung F influence; *(einer Sache auch)* effect; *(eines Katalysators)* effect; **Bayern steht unter ~ eines atlantischen Hochs** Bavaria is being affected by an anticyclone over the Atlantic; **unter (der) ~ von Drogen** *etc* under the influence of drugs *etc*; **unter (der) ~ eines Schocks stehen** to be suffering (from) the effects of shock; **nach ~ der Salbe ...** when the ointment has worked in ...

Ein|wir|kungs|mög|lich|keit F influence; **dadurch haben wir eine gute ~** this has made it possible for us to bring some influence to bear *or* to have some influence

ein|wö|chig [-vœçɪç] ADJ one-week *attr*

Ein|woh|ner ['ainvoːnɐ] M -s, -, **Ein|woh|ne|rin** [-ərɪn] F -, -nen inhabitant

Ein|woh|ner-: Ein|woh|ner|mel|de|amt NT *residents' registration office*; **sich beim ~ (an)melden** ≈ to register with the police; **Ein|woh|ner|schaft** ['ainvoːnɐʃaft] F -, *(rare)* -en population, inhabitants *pl*; **Ein|woh|ner|ver|zeich|nis** NT *list of inhabitants' names and addresses*; **Ein|woh|ner|zahl** F population, number of inhabitants

Ein|wurf M **a** *(= das Hineinwerfen) (von Münze)* insertion; *(von Brief)* posting *(Brit)*, mailing *(esp US)*; **~ 2 Euro** insert 2 euros **b** *(Sport)* throw-in; **falscher ~** foul throw **c** *(= Schlitz)* slot; *(von Briefkasten)* slit **d** *(fig)* interjection; *(= Einwand)* objection

ein+wur|zeln VIR *sep (vi: aux sein) (Pflanzen)* to take root; *(fig auch)* to become rooted *(bei* in) → **eingewurzelt**

Ein|zahl F singular

ein+zah|len VT *sep* to pay in; **Geld auf ein Konto ~** to pay money into an account

Ein|zah|lung F payment; *(auf Bankkonto auch)* deposit *(auf +acc* into)

Ein|zah|lungs-: Ein|zah|lungs|be|leg M paying-in counterfoil, deposit receipt *(US)*; **Ein|zah|lungs|for|mu|lar** NT paying-in form, deposit form *(US)*; **Ein|zah|lungs|schal|ter** M *(Post)* paying-in counter; **Ein|zah|lungs|schein** M paying-in slip, deposit slip *(US)*

ein+zäu|nen ['aintsɔynən] VT *sep* to fence in

Ein|zäu|nung F -, -en *(= Zaun)* fence, fencing; *(= das Umzäunen)* fencing-in

ein+zeich|nen VT *sep* to draw *or* mark in; **ist der Ort eingezeichnet?** is the place marked?

Ein|zeich|nung F **a** *no pl (= das Einzeichnen)* drawing *or* marking in **b** *(= Markierung)* marking

Ein|zei|ler ['aintsailɐ] M -s, - *(Liter)* one-line poem, one-liner *(inf)*, monostich *(form)*

ein|zei|lig ADJ one-line *attr* ADV **~ geschriebene Schreibmaschinenseiten** single-spaced typewritten pages

Ein|zel ['aintsl] NT -s, - *(Tennis)* singles *sing*

Ein|zel-: **Ein|zel|ak|ti|on** F independent action; *(Sport)* solo performance *or* effort; **Ein|zel|an|trieb** M *(Tech)* independent drive; **Ein|zel|auf|hän|gung** F *(Aut)* independent suspension; **Ein|zel|auf|stel|lung** F *(Comm)* itemized list; **Ein|zel|aus|ga|be** F separate edition; **Ein|zel|be|hand|lung** F individual treatment; **Ein|zel|bei|spiel** NT isolated *or* one-off example; **Ein|zel|bett** NT single bed; **Ein|zel|bild** NT *(Comput etc)* frame; **Ein|zel|blatt|ein|zug** M cut-sheet feed; **Ein|zel|dar|stel|lung** F individual treatment; **eine Geschichte unseres Jahrhunderts in ~en** a history of our century in individual portraits; **Ein|zel|er|schei|nung** F isolated occurrence; **Ein|zel|ex|emp|lar** NT unique specimen; *(von Buch etc)* unique copy; *(von Auto)* unique model, one-off (model *or* car); **Ein|zel|fah|rer(in)** M(F) *(Motorradrennen)* solo rider; **Ein|zel|fahr|schein** M single *(Brit) or* one-way ticket

Ein|zel|fall M individual case; *(= Sonderfall)* isolated case, exception

Ein|zel|fall|stu|die F *(Sociol, Psych)* (individual) case study

Ein|zel-: **Ein|zel|fer|ti|gung** F special order; **in ~ hergestellt** made to order, custom-made; **Ein|zel|gän|ger** [-gɛŋɐ] M **-s, -**, **Ein|zel|gän|ge|rin** [-ərɪn] F **-, -nen** loner, lone wolf; *(= Elefant)* rogue; **Ein|zel|haft** F solitary confinement

Ein|zel|han|del M retail trade; **das ist im ~ teurer als im Großhandel** that is dearer (to buy) retail than wholesale; **im ~ erhältlich** available retail; **im ~ kostet das …** it retails at …

Ein|zel|han|dels-: **Ein|zel|han|dels|ge|schäft** NT retail shop; **Ein|zel|han|dels|kauf|frau** F trained retail saleswoman; **Ein|zel|han|dels|kauf|mann** M trained retail salesman; **Ein|zel|han|dels|ket|te** F *(von Läden)* retail chain; **Ein|zel|han|dels|preis** M retail price; **Ein|zel|han|dels|span|ne** F retail profit margin

Ein|zel-: **Ein|zel|händ|ler(in)** M(F) retailer, retail trader; **Ein|zel|haus** NT detached house *(Brit)*, self-contained house *(US)*; **Ein|zel|heit** ['aintslhait] F **-, -en** detail, particular; **auf ~en eingehen** to go into detail(s); **etw in allen/bis in die kleinsten ~en schildern** to describe sth in great detail/right down to the last detail; **sich in ~en verlieren** to get bogged down in details; **Ein|zel|hof** M isolated farm; **Ein|zel|ka|bi|ne** F (individual) cubicle; **Ein|zel|kampf** M **a** *(Mil)* single combat **b** *(Sport)* individual competition; **Ein|zel|kämp|fer(in)** M(F) **a** *(Mil, Sport)* single *or* solo combatant **b** *(fig)* lone wolf, loner; **Ein|zel|kauf|frau** F small businesswoman; **Ein|zel|kauf|mann** M small businessman; **Ein|zel|kind** NT only child

Ein|zel|ler ['aintsɛlɐ] M **-s, -** *(Biol)* single-cell(ed) *or* unicellular organism

ein|zel|lig [-tsɛlɪç] ADJ single-cell(ed) *attr*, unicellular

ein|zeln ['aintsln] ADJ **a** individual; *(= getrennt)* separate; *(von Paar)* odd; **~e Teile des Bestecks kann man nicht kaufen** you cannot buy individual *or* separate *or* single pieces of this cutlery; **die ~en Städte, die wir besucht haben** the individual cities which we visited; **im ~en Fall** in the particular case

b *Mensch* individual

c *(= alleinstehend) Baum, Haus* single, solitary; **~ stehend** solitary; **ein paar ~ stehende Bäume** a few scattered trees, a few trees here and there; **ein ~ stehender Baum** a tree (standing) all by itself, a solitary tree

d *(mit pl n: = einige, vereinzelte)* some; *(Met) Schauer* scattered; **~e Firmen haben …** some firms have …, the odd firm has …, a few odd firms have …; **~e Besucher kamen schon früher** a few *or* one or two visitors came earlier

ADJ *(substantivisch)* **a** *(Mensch)* **der/die Einzelne** the individual; **ein Einzelner** an individual, a single person; *(= ein einziger Mensch)* one single person; **Einzelne** some (people), a few (people), one or two (people); **jeder Einzelne/jede Einzelne** each individual; **jeder Einzelne muss dabei helfen** (each and) every one of you/them *etc* must help; **als Einzelner kann man nichts machen** as an individual one can do nothing

b **Einzelnes** some; **Einzelnes hat mir gefallen** I liked parts *or* some of it; **Einzelne haben mir gefallen** I liked some of them

c **das Einzelne** the particular; **er kam vom Einzelnen zum Allgemeinen** he went from the particular to the general; **jedes Einzelne** each one; **im Einzelnen auf etw** *(acc)* **eingehen** to go into detail(s) *or* particulars about sth; **etw im Einzelnen besprechen** to discuss sth in detail; **bis ins Einzelne** right down to the last detail

ADV **a** *(= separat)* separately, individually; **~ aufführen** to list separately *or* individually *or* singly

b *(= nicht zusammen)* individually; **wir kamen ~** we came separately; **die Gäste kamen ~ herein** the guests came in separately *or* singly *or* one by one; **bitte ~ eintreten** please come in one (person) at a time

ein|zeln|ste|hend ADJ *attr* → **einzeln ADJ c**

Ein|zel-: **Ein|zel|num|mer** F *(von Zeitung)* single issue; **Ein|zel|per|son** F single person; **für eine ~ kochen** to cook for one (person) *or* a single person; **~en haben es auf Reisen meist schwer, ein Hotelzimmer zu bekommen** people travelling *(Brit) or* traveling *(US)* alone usually find it hard to get a hotel room; **Ein|zel|preis** M price, unit price *(Comm)*; *(von Zeitung)* price per copy; **Ein|zel|rad|auf|hän|gung** F *(Aut)* independent suspension; **Ein|zel|rei|sen|de(r)** MF *decl as adj* single traveller *(Brit) or* traveler *(US)*; **Ein|zel|rich|ter(in)** M(F) judge sitting singly; **Ein|zel|sie|ger(in)** M(F) individual winner; **Ein|zel|spiel** NT *(Tennis)* singles *sing*; **Ein|zel|staat** M individual state; **Ein|zel|ste|hen|de(r)** ['aintslʃte:əndə] MF *decl as adj* single person; **Ein|zel|stück** NT **ein schönes ~** a beautiful piece; **~e verkaufen wir nicht** we don't sell them singly; **Ein|zel|stun|de** F private *or* individual lesson; **Ein|zel|teil** NT individual *or* separate part; *(= Ersatzteil)* spare *or* replacement part; **etw in seine ~e zerlegen** to take sth to pieces, to take sth apart piece by piece *(esp US)*; **Ein|zel|the|ra|pie** F individual therapy; **Ein|zel|un|ter|richt** M private lessons *pl or* tuition; **Ein|zel|ver|bin|dungs|nach|weis** M *(Telec)* itemized call listing; **Ein|zel|ver|kauf** M *(Comm)* retail sale; *(das Verkaufen)* retailing, retail selling; **Ein|zel|ver|pa|ckung** F individual packing; **Ein|zel|wer|tung** F *(Sport)* individual placings *pl*; *(bei Kür)* individual marks *pl*; **Ein|zel|we|sen** NT individual; **Ein|zel|wett|be|werb** M *(Sport)* individual competition; **Ein|zel|zel|le** F single cell *(auch Biol)*; **Ein|zel|zim|mer** NT single room; **Ein|zel|zim|mer|zu|schlag** M *(auf Hotelpreis bei Pauschalreise)* single(-room) supplement

ein+ze|men|tie|ren *ptp* **einzementiert** VT *sep Stein* to cement; *Safe* to build *or* set into (the) concrete; *Kachel* to cement on

Ein|zieh-: **ein|zieh|bar** ADJ retractable; *Schulden* recoverable; **Ein|zieh|de|cke** F duvet, (continental) quilt

ein+zie|hen *sep irreg* VT **a** *(= hineinziehen, einfügen) Gummiband, Faden* to thread; *(in einen Bezug etc)* to put in; *(Build: = einbauen) Wand, Balken* to put in; *(Kopiergerät) Papier* to take in

b *(= einsaugen) Flüssigkeit* to soak up; *(durch Strohhalm)* to draw up; *Duft* to breathe in; *Luft, Rauch* to draw in

c *(= zurückziehen) Fühler, Krallen, Fahrgestell* to retract, to draw in; *Bauch, Netz* to pull *or* draw in; *Antenne* to retract; *Schultern* to hunch; *Periskop, Flagge, Segel* to lower, to take down; *Ruder* to ship, to take in; **den Kopf ~** to duck (one's head); **zieh den Bauch ein!** keep *or* tuck *(inf)* your tummy in; **der Hund zog den Schwanz ein** the dog put his tail between his legs; **mit eingezogenem Schwanz** *(lit, fig)* with its/his/her tail between its/his/her legs

d *(Mil)* (zu into) *Personen* to conscript, to call up, to draft *(US)*; *Fahrzeuge etc* to requisition

e *(= kassieren) Steuern, Gelder* to collect; *(fig) Erkundigungen* to make *(über +acc* about)

f *(= aus dem Verkehr ziehen) Banknoten, Münzen* to withdraw (from circulation), to call in; *(= beschlagnahmen) Führerschein* to take away, to withdraw; *Vermögen* to confiscate

g *(Typ) Wörter, Zeilen* to indent

VI *aux sein* **a** *(in Wohnung, Haus)* to move in; **wer ist im dritten Stock eingezogen?** who has moved into the third floor?; **er zog bei Bekannten ein** he moved in with friends; **ins Parlament ~** *(Partei)* to enter parliament; *(Abgeordneter)* to take one's seat (in parliament)

b *(auch Mil: = einmarschieren)* to march in *(in +acc* -to)

c *(= einkehren)* to come *(in +dat* to); **mit ihm zog eine fröhliche Stimmung bei uns ein** he brought a happy atmosphere with him; **wenn der Friede im Lande einzieht** when peace comes to our country, when we have peace; **Ruhe und Ordnung zogen wieder ein** law and order returned

d *(= eindringen)* to soak in *(in +acc* -to)

Ein|zie|hung F **a** *(Mil) (von Personen)* conscription, call-up, drafting *(US)*; *(von Fahrzeugen)* requisitioning **b** *(= Beschlagnahme) (von Vermögen, Publikationen)* confiscation; *(= Rücknahme: von Banknoten, Führerschein etc)* withdrawal **c** *(= Eintreiben: von Steuern etc)* collection

ein|zig ['aintsɪç] ADJ **a** *attr* only, sole; **ich sehe nur eine ~e Möglichkeit** I can see only one (single) possibility; **ich habe nicht einen ~en Brief bekommen** I haven't had a single *or* solitary letter; **kein** *or* **nicht ein ~es Mal** not once, not one single time

b *(emphatisch)* absolute, complete; **dieses Rugbyspiel war eine ~e Schlammschlacht** this rugby match was just one big mudbath

c *pred (= einzigartig)* unique; **es ist ~ in seiner Art** it is quite unique; **sein Können steht ~ da** his skill is unmatched, his skill is second to none

ADJ *(substantivisch)* **der/die Einzige** the only one; **das Einzige** the only thing; **das ist das Einzige, was wir tun können** that's the only thing we can do; **ein Einziger hat geantwortet** only one (person) answered; **kein Einziger wusste es** nobody knew, not a single *or* solitary person knew; **die Einzigen, die es wussten …** the only ones who knew …; **er hat als Einziger das Ziel erreicht** he was the only one *or* the sole person to reach the finish; **Hans ist unser Einziger** Hans is our only child, Hans is our one and only

ADV **a** *(= allein)* only, solely; **seine Beförderung hat er ~ dir zu verdanken** he owes his promotion entirely to you; **die ~ mögliche Lösung** the only possible solution, the only solution possible; **~ und allein** solely; **~ und allein deshalb hat er gewonnen** he owes his victory solely *or* entirely to that, that's the only *or* sole reason he won; **das ~ Wahre** *or* **Senkrechte** *(inf)* the only thing; *(= das beste)* the real McCoy *(inf)*; **jetzt Ferien machen/ein Bier trinken, das wäre das ~ Wahre** *etc* to take a holiday *(esp Brit) or* vacation *(US)*/have a beer, that's just what the doctor ordered *or* that would be just the job *(inf)*

b *(inf: = außerordentlich)* fantastically

ein|zig|ar|tig ADJ unique ADV *beleidigend, gerissen* incredibly, tremendously; **die Landschaft war ~ schön** the scenery was astoundingly beautiful

Ein|zig|ar|tig|keit F uniqueness

Ein|zig|keit F **-**, *no pl* uniqueness

Ein|zim|mer- *in cpds* one-room; **Ein|zim|mer|ap|par|te|ment** NT, **Ein|zim|mer|woh|nung** F one-room flat *(Brit) or* apartment, studio flat *(Brit)*, efficiency *or* studio apartment *(US)*, bedsit *(Brit inf)*

Ein|zug M **a** *(in Haus etc)* move *(in +acc* into); **vor dem ~** before moving in, before the move; **der ~ in das neue Haus** moving *or* the move into the new house; **der ~ ins Parlament** *(von Partei)* entering parliament; *(von Abgeordnetem)* taking one's seat (in parliament)
b *(= Einmarsch)* entry *(in +acc* into)
c *(fig: von Stimmung, Winter etc)* advent; **~ halten** to make an entrance; **der Winter hielt seinen ~ mit Schnee und Frost** winter arrived amid snow and frost; **der Frühling** *etc* **hält seinen ~** spring *etc* is coming
d *(von Feuchtigkeit)* penetration; **der ~ kühlerer Meeresluft ...** a low trough moving in from the sea ...
e *(von Steuern, Geldern)* collection; *(von Banknoten)* withdrawal, calling-in
f *(Typ)* indentation

Ein|zugs-: **Ein|zugs|auf|trag** M *(Fin)* direct debit; **Ein|zugs|be|reich** M catchment area *(Brit)*, service area *(US)*; **Ein|zugs|er|mäch|ti|gung** F *(Fin)* direct debit instruction; **eine ~ erteilen** to set up a direct debit; **Ein|zugs|fei|er** F house-warming (party); **Ein|zugs|ge|biet** NT *(lit, fig)* catchment area *(Brit)*, service area *(US)*; **Ein|zugs|ver|fah|ren** NT *(Fin)* direct debit

ein+zwän|gen VT *sep (lit)* to squeeze *or* jam *or* wedge in; *(fig)* **jdn** to constrain, to constrict

Ein|zy|lin|der|mo|tor M one-cylinder *or* single-cylinder engine

Ei|pul|ver NT dried *or* powdered egg

Eis [ais] NT **-es, - a** *no pl (= gefrorenes Wasser)* ice; **zu ~ gefrieren** to freeze, to turn to ice; **vom ~ eingeschlossen sein** to be iced in, to be icebound; **~ laufen** → **eislaufen**; **das ~ brechen** *(fig)* to break the ice; **etw auf ~ legen** *(lit)* to chill sth, to put sth on ice; *(fig inf)* to put sth on ice, to put sth into cold storage **b** *(= Speiseeis)* ice (cream); **er kaufte 3 ~** he bought 3 ice creams *or* ices; **gemischtes ~** assorted ice cream; *(mit selbstgewählten Sorten auch)* your choice of ice cream; **~ am Stiel** ice(d) lolly *(Brit)*, Popsicle® *(US)*

Eis-: **Eis|bahn** F ice rink; **Eis|bär** M polar bear; **Eis|be|cher** M *(aus Pappe)* ice-cream tub; *(aus Metall)* sundae dish; *(= Eis)* sundae; **eis|be|deckt** ADJ *attr* ice-covered, covered in ice; **Eis|bein** NT **a** *(Cook)* knuckle of pork *(boiled and served with sauerkraut)* **b** *(hum inf)* **wenn ich noch länger hier in dieser Kälte stehe, bekomme ich ~e** if I stand around here in this cold any longer my feet will turn to ice; **Eis|berg** M iceberg; **die Spitze des ~s** *(fig)* the tip of the iceberg; **Eis|berg|sa|lat** M *(Salatpflanzensorte)* iceberg lettuce; **Eis|beu|tel** M ice pack; **Eis|bil|dung** F **es kam zur ~ auf den Flüssen** ice formed on the rivers; **zur Verhinderung der ~ auf Fahrbahndecken** to prevent icing on *or* ice forming on road surfaces; **eis|blau** ADJ ice-blue; **Eis|blau** NT ice blue; **Eis|block** M *pl* **-blöcke** block of ice; **Eis|blu|me** F *usu pl* frost pattern; **Eis|bom|be** F *(Cook)* bombe glacée; **Eis|bre|cher** M icebreaker; **Eis|bu|de** F ice-cream stall

Ei|schnee ['ai-] M *(Cook)* beaten white of egg

Eis-: **Eis|creme** F ice (cream); **Eis|de|cke** F ice sheet, sheet of ice; **Eis|die|le** F ice-cream parlour *(Brit) or* parlor *(US)*

ei|sen ['aizn] VT *Tee, Wodka* to ice, to chill → *auch* **geeist**

Ei|sen ['aizn] NT **-s, - a** *no pl (Chem) (abbr* **Fe**) iron; **~ verarbeitend** iron-processing; **ein Mann aus ~** a man of iron; **mehrere/noch ein ~ im Feuer haben** *(fig)* to have more than one/another iron in the fire; **Muskeln von** *or* **aus ~ haben** to have muscles of steel; **zum alten ~ gehören** *or* **zählen** *(fig)* to be on the scrap heap; **jdn/etw zum alten ~ werfen** *(fig)* to throw sb/sth on the scrap heap; **man muss das ~ schmieden, solange es heiß** *or* **warm ist** *(Prov)* one must strike while the iron is hot *(prov)* → **heiß ADJ d**
b *(= Bügeleisen, Golfschläger)* iron; *(= Eisenbeschlag)* iron fitting; *(= Eisenband)* iron band *or* hoop; *(= Hufeisen)* shoe; *(= Fangeisen)* trap; *(obs: = Fesseln)* fetters *pl (obs)*, irons *pl*; *(obs: = Schwert)* iron *(obs)*; **jdn in ~ legen** *(obs)* to put *or* clap sb in irons
c *(no pl: Med)* iron

Ei|sen-: **Ei|sen|ader** F vein of iron ore; **ei|sen|ar|tig** ADJ ironlike

Ei|sen|bahn F railway *(Brit)*, railroad *(US)*; *(= Eisenbahnwesen)* railways *pl (Brit)*, railroad *(US)*; *(inf: = Zug)* train; *(= Spielzeugeisenbahn)* toy train; *(= Spielzeugeisenbahnanlage)* train set; **ich fahre lieber (mit der) ~ als (mit dem) Bus** I prefer to travel by train *or* rail than by bus; **Onkel Alfred arbeitet bei der ~** uncle Alfred works for the railways *(Brit) or* railroad *(US)*; **es ist (aller)höchste ~** *(inf)* it's getting late

Ei|sen|bahn-: **Ei|sen|bahn|ab|teil** NT (railway *(Brit) or* railroad *(US)*) compartment; **Ei|sen|bahn|an|la|gen** PL railway *(Brit) or* railroad *(US)* installations *pl*; **Ei|sen|bahn|brü|cke** F railway *(Brit) or* railroad *(US)* bridge

Ei|sen|bah|ner [-ba:nɐ] M **-s, -**, **Ei|sen|bah|ne|rin** [-ərın] F **-, -nen** railway employee *(Brit)*, railroader *(US)*

Ei|sen|bahn-: **Ei|sen|bahn|fäh|re** F train ferry; **Ei|sen|bahn|fahr|kar|te** F rail ticket; **Ei|sen|bahn|fahrt** F train *or* rail journey *or* ride; **Ei|sen|bahn|ge|sell|schaft** F railway *(Brit) or* railroad *(US)* company; **Ei|sen|bahn|gleis** NT railway *(Brit) or* railroad *(US)* track; **Ei|sen|bahn|kno|ten|punkt** M railway *(Brit) or* railroad *(US)* junction; **Ei|sen|bahn|netz** NT railway *(Brit) or* railroad *(US)* network; **Ei|sen|bahn|schaff|ner(in)** M(F) (railway) guard *(Brit)*, (railroad) conductor *(US)*; **Ei|sen|bahn|schie|ne** F railway *(Brit) or* railroad *(US)* track; **Ei|sen|bahn|schwel|le** F railway sleeper *(Brit)*, (railroad) tie *(US)*; **Ei|sen|bahn|sig|nal** NT railway *(Brit) or* railroad *(US)* signal; **Ei|sen|bahn|sta|ti|on** F railway *(Brit) or* railroad *(US)* station; **Ei|sen|bahn|stre|cke** F railway line *(Brit)*, railroad *(US)*; **Ei|sen|bahn|über|füh|rung** F (railway *(Brit) or* railroad *(US)*) footbridge; **Ei|sen|bahn|un|glück** NT railway *(Brit) or* railroad *(US)* accident, train crash; **Ei|sen|bahn|un|ter|füh|rung** F railway *(Brit) or* railroad *(US)* underpass; **Ei|sen|bahn|ver|bin|dung** F rail link; *(= Anschluss)* connection; **Ei|sen|bahn|ver|kehr** M railway *(Brit) or* railroad *(US)* traffic; **Ei|sen|bahn|wa|gen** M *(= Personenwagen)* railway carriage *(Brit)*, railroad car *(US)*; *(= Güterwagen)* goods wagon *or* truck *(Brit)*, freight car *(US)*; **Ei|sen|bahn|we|sen** NT railway *(Brit) or* railroad *(US)* system; **Ei|sen|bahn|zug** M railway *(Brit) or* railroad *(US)* train

Ei|sen|bart(h) ['aiznba:ɐt] M **Doktor ~** *(fig)* quack, horse doctor *(inf)*

Ei|sen-: **Ei|sen|be|rei|fung** F iron hooping; *(= Reif)* iron hoop; **Ei|sen|berg|werk** NT iron mine; **Ei|sen|be|schlag** M ironwork *no pl*; *(zum Verstärken)* iron band; **ei|sen|be|schla|gen** ADJ with iron fittings; *Stiefel* steel-tipped; **Ei|sen|be|ton** M *(dated)* ferroconcrete, reinforced concrete; **Ei|sen|blech** NT sheet iron; **Ei|sen|block** M *pl* **-blöcke** iron block, block of iron; **Ei|sen|boh|rer** M *(Tech)* iron *or* steel drill; **Ei|sen|chlo|rid** NT *(FeCl)* ferrous chloride; *(FeCl)* ferric chloride; **Ei|sen|draht** M steel wire; **Ei|sen|erz** NT iron ore; **Ei|sen|fei|le** F iron file; **Ei|sen|feil|spä|ne** PL iron filings *pl*; **Ei|sen|fle|cken** PL *(in Kartoffeln)* discoloured *(Brit) or* discolored *(US)* patches *pl*; **Ei|sen|fres|ser** M *(pej)* tough guy; **Ei|sen|garn** NT steel thread; **Ei|sen|ge|halt** M iron content; **Ei|sen|gie|ße|rei** F *(= Vorgang)* iron smelting; *(= Werkstatt)* iron foundry; **Ei|sen|glanz** M, **Ei|sen|glim|mer** M ferric oxide, iron glance; **Ei|sen|guss** M iron casting; **ei|sen|hal|tig** ADJ *Gestein* iron-bearing, ferruginous *(form)*; *Medikament* containing iron; **das Wasser ist ~** the water contains iron; **Ei|sen|ham|mer** M steam hammer; *(= Werkstatt)* forge; **ei|sen|hart** ADJ *(lit)* as hard as iron; **ein ~er Mann/Wille** a man/will of iron; **Ei|sen|hut** M **a** *(Bot)* monk's hood, aconite **b** *(Hist)* iron helmet; **Ei|sen|hüt|te** F ironworks *pl or sing*, iron foundry; **Ei|sen|in|dust|rie** F iron industry; **Ei|sen|kar|bid** NT cementite; **Ei|sen|kern** M iron core; **Ei|sen|kies** M iron pyrites *sing*; **Ei|sen|kitt** M iron-cement; **Ei|sen|kur** F course of iron treatment; **Ei|sen|le|gie|rung** F iron alloy; **Ei|sen|man|gel** M iron deficiency; **Ei|sen|oxid** NT, **Ei|sen|oxyd** NT ferric oxide; **Ei|sen|prä|pa|rat** NT *(Med) (flüssig)* iron tonic; *(Tabletten)* iron tablets *pl*; **Ei|sen|sä|ge** F hacksaw; **ei|sen|schüs|sig** [-ʃʏsıç] ADJ *Boden* iron-bearing, ferruginous *(form)*; **Ei|sen|spä|ne** PL iron filings *pl*; **Ei|sen|stan|ge** F iron bar; **Ei|sen|sul|phat** NT ferric sulphate; **Ei|sen|trä|ger** M iron girder; **ei|sen|ver|ar|bei|tend** ADJ *attr* → **Eisen a**; **Ei|sen|ver|bin|dung** F *(Chem)* iron compound; **Ei|sen|ver|hüt|tung** F *(Metal)* iron production, iron smelting; **Ei|sen|vit|ri|ol** NT iron *or* ferrous sulphate, green vitriol; **Ei|sen|wa|ren** PL ironmongery *sing (Brit)*, hardware *sing*; **Ei|sen|wa|ren|händ|ler(in)** M(F) ironmonger *(Brit)*, hardware dealer; **Ei|sen|wa|ren|hand|lung** F ironmonger's (shop) *(Brit)*, hardware store; **Ei|sen|werk** NT **a** *(Art)* ironwork **b** *(= Eisenhütte)* ironworks *pl or sing*, iron foundry; **Ei|sen|zeit** F, *no pl (Hist)* Iron Age

ei|sern ['aizɐn] ADJ **a** *attr (= aus Eisen)* iron; **das Eiserne Kreuz** *(Mil)* the Iron Cross; **der Eiserne Kanzler** the Iron Chancellor; **der ~e Vorhang** *(Theat)* the safety curtain; **der Eiserne Vorhang** *(Pol)* the Iron Curtain; **~e Lunge** *(Med)* iron lung; **die ~e Jungfrau** *(Hist)* the Iron Maiden; **~e Hochzeit** 65th wedding anniversary
b *(= fest, unnachgiebig) Disziplin* iron *attr*, strict; *Wille* iron *attr*, of iron; *Energie* unflagging, indefatigable; *Ruhe* unshakeable; **~e Gesundheit** iron constitution; **sein Griff war ~** his grip was like iron; **mit ~er Stirn** *(= unverschämt)* brazenly; *(= unerschütterlich)* resolutely; **mit ~er Faust** with an iron hand; **es ist ein ~es Gesetz, dass ...** it's a hard and fast rule that ...; **ein ~es Regiment führen** to rule with a rod of iron *(Brit)*, to rule with an iron fist; **in etw** *(dat)* **~ sein/bleiben** to be/remain resolute about sth; **da bin** *or* **bleibe ich ~!** *(inf)* that's definite; **mit ~em Besen (aus)kehren** to make a clean sweep, to be ruthless in creating order
c *attr (= unantastbar) Reserve* emergency; **~e Ration** emergency *or* iron rations *pl*
ADV resolutely; *trainieren* with iron determination; **er schwieg ~** he remained resolutely silent; **er ist ~ bei seinem Entschluss geblieben** he stuck steadfastly *or* firmly to his decision; **(aber) ~!** *(inf)* (but) of course!, absolutely!

Ei|ses|käl|te F icy cold

Eis-: **Eis|fach** NT freezer compartment, icebox; **Eis|fi|sche|rei** F fishing through ice; **Eis|flä|che** F (surface of the) ice; **die ~ des Sees** the (sheet of) ice covering the lake; **eis|frei** ADJ ice-free *attr*, free of ice *pred*; **Eis|gang** M, *no pl* ice drift; **eis|gän|gig** ADJ *Schiff* ice-breaking; *Gewässer* ice-bound; **eis|ge|kühlt** ADJ chilled; **Eis|ge|tränk** NT iced drink; **eis|glatt** ADJ *Straße* icy, slippery; **Eis|glät|te** F black ice; **eis|grau** ADJ *(liter)* steel(y) grey *(Brit) or* gray *(US)*; **Eis|hal|le** F *(Sport)* ice stadium, ice rink; **Eis|hei|li|gen** PL **die drei ~** *three Saints' Days, 12th-14th May, which are usually particularly cold and after which further frost is rare*; **Eis|ho|ckey** NT ice hockey, hockey *(US)*

ei|sig ['aizɪç] ADJ **a** *(= kalt) Wasser, Wind* icy (cold); *Kälte* icy **b** *(= jäh) Schreck, Grauen* chilling **c** *(fig: = abweisend)* icy, glacial; *Schweigen auch* frosty, chilly; *Ablehnung* cold; *Blick* icy, cold; *Lächeln, Empfang* frosty ADV **a** *(= abweisend)* icily, coldly; ~ **lächeln** to give a frosty smile; **er wurde ~ empfangen** he was given a frosty reception **b** *(= jäh)* **es durchzuckte mich ~** a cold shiver ran through me

Eis-: **Eis|jacht** F ice yacht; **Eis|kaf|fee** M iced coffee; **eis|kalt** ADJ **a** icy-cold **b** = **eisig ADJ b c** *(fig) (= abweisend)* icy, cold, frosty; *(= kalt und berechnend)* cold-blooded, cold and calculating; *(= dreist)* cool ADV **a** *(= kalt)* **es durchzuckte mich ~** an icy shiver ran through me **b** = **eisig ADV a c** *(= kalt und berechnend)* cold-blooded; **sie hat auf seine Drohung ~ reagiert** her reaction to his threat was ice cool **d** *(inf: = glattweg)* simply, just like that; **dem sag ich ~ die Meinung** I'll just tell him exactly what I think; **davor habe ich keine Angst, das mache ich ~** I'm not afraid of that, I can do it without turning a hair *(Brit) or* without batting an eyelash *(US)*; **machst du das? – ja! ~** will you do it? – no problem; **Eis|kap|pe** F icecap; **Eis|kas|ten** M *(S Ger, Aus)* refrigerator, fridge *(Brit)*, icebox *(US)*; **Eis|kel|ler** M cold store, cold room; **unser Schlafzimmer ist ein ~** our bedroom is like an icebox; **Eis|kon|fekt** NT *(aus Eiscreme)* ice cream confectionery; **Eis|krem** F, **Eis|kre|me** F = **Eiscreme**; **Eis|kris|tall** NT ice crystal; **Eis|kunst|lauf** M figure skating; **Eis|kunst|läu|fer(in)** M(F) figure skater; **Eis|lauf** M ice-skating; **eis+lau|fen** VI *sep irreg aux sein* to ice-skate; **sie läuft eis** she ice-skates; **Eis|läu|fer(in)** M(F) ice-skater; **Eis|män|ner** PL *(S Ger, Aus)* = **Eisheiligen**; **Eis|ma|schi|ne** F ice-cream machine; **Eis|meer** NT polar sea; **Nördliches/Südliches ~** Arctic/Antarctic Ocean; **Eis|mo|nat** M, **Eis|mond** M *(obs)* January; **Eis|na|deln** PL ice needles *pl*; **Eis|ne|bel** M freezing fog; **Eis|pa|ckung** F *(Med)* ice pack; **Eis|pa|last** M ice rink; *(hum inf)* icebox; **Eis|pi|ckel** M ice axe *(Brit)*, ice pick

Ei|sprung ['ai-] M *(Physiol)* ovulation *no art*

Eis-: **Eis|pul|ver** NT *(Cook)* ice-cream mix; **Eis|punkt** M *(Phys)* freezing point; **Eis|re|gen** M sleet; **Eis|re|vue** F ice revue, ice show; **Eis|rie|gel** M ice-cream bar; **Eis|schie|ßen** NT -s, *no pl* curling; **Eis|schmel|ze** F thaw; **Eis|schnell|lauf** M speed skating; **Eis|schnell|läu|fer(in)** M(F) speed skater; **Eis|schol|le** F ice floe; **Eis|schrank** M refrigerator, fridge *(Brit)*, icebox *(US)*; **Eis|se|geln** NT ice-sailing; **Eis|sport** M ice sports *pl*; **Eis|sport|hal|le** F ice rink; **Eis|(sport)|sta|di|on** NT (ice) rink; **Eis|stock** M *(Sport)* curling stone; **Eis|stock|schie|ßen** NT -s, *no pl* curling; **Eis|sur|fen** NT ice surfing; **Eis|tanz** M, **Eis|tan|zen** NT ice dancing; **Eis|tor|te** F ice-cream cake; **Eis|ver|käu|fer(in)** M(F) ice-cream seller *or* vendor; *(Mann auch)* ice-cream man *(inf)*; **Eis|vo|gel** M **a** kingfisher **b** *(= Schmetterling)* white admiral; **Eis|was|ser** NT, *no pl* icy water; *(= Getränk)* iced water

EISWEIN

Eiswein is a very sweet, alcoholic wine, made – as the name suggests – from grapes which have been exposed to frost. Selected grapes are left on the vine in autumn. Then, if there have been constant temperatures of below -5°C for at least a week, the frozen grapes are picked at night and immediately pressed. Care is taken that they do not thaw, so that only the best part of the grape goes into the wine. Since the yield from this process is very small, and tit is not certain that temperatures will be low enough for the process to take place, **Eiswein** is very expensive.

Eis-: **Eis|wür|fel** M ice cube; **Eis|wüs|te** F *(Geog)* frozen wastes *pl*, frozen wilderness; **Eis|zap|fen** M icicle; **Eis|zeit** F Ice Age, glacial epoch *(form)*; *(fig)* cold war; **eis|zeit|lich** ADJ ice-age, of the Ice Age

ei|tel ['aitl] ADJ **a** *Mensch* vain; *(= eingebildet auch)* conceited; **~ wie ein Pfau** vain as a peacock **b** *(liter) Hoffnung, Wahn, Versuch, Gerede* vain; **seine Hoffnungen erwiesen sich als ~** his hopes proved to be all in vain; **alles ist ~** *(Bibl)* all is vanity **c** *inv (obs: rein) Gold* pure; **es herrschte ~ Freude** there was absolute joy; **er denkt, das ganze Leben sei ~ Freude und Sonnenschein** he thinks the whole of life is nothing but a bed of roses

Ei|tel|keit F -, -en *(von Mensch)* vanity; *(liter: von Hoffnung, Wahn, Versuch)* vainness

Ei|ter ['aitɐ] M -s, *no pl* pus

Ei|ter-: **Ei|ter|beu|le** F boil; *(fig)* canker; **Ei|ter|bläs|chen** [-blɛːsçən] NT, **Ei|ter|bla|se** F pustule; **Ei|ter|er|re|ger** M pyogenic organism *(spec)*; **Ei|ter|herd** M suppurative focus *(spec)*

ei|te|rig ['aitərɪç] ADJ *Ausfluss* purulent; *Wunde* festering, suppurating; *Binde* pus-covered

ei|tern ['aiten] VI to fester, to discharge pus, to suppurate

Ei|ter-: **Ei|ter|pfropf** M core *(of a boil)*; *(von Pickel)* head; **Ei|ter|pi|ckel** M pimple (containing pus)

Ei|te|rung ['aitərʊŋ] F -, -en discharge of pus, suppuration

eit|rig ['aitrɪç] ADJ = **eiterig**

Ei|weiß ['aivais] NT -es, -e *or* - (egg) white, white of egg, albumen *(spec)*; *(Chem)* protein

Ei|weiß-: **ei|weiß|arm** ADJ low in protein; **~e Kost** a low-protein diet; **Ei|weiß|be|darf** M protein requirement; **Ei|weiß|ge|halt** M protein content; **ei|weiß|hal|tig** ADJ protein-containing *attr*; **Fleisch ist sehr ~** meat is high in protein, meat contains a lot of protein; **Ei|weiß|haus|halt** M *(Physiol)* protein metabolism; **Ei|weiß|man|gel** M protein deficiency; **Ei|weiß|prä|pa|rat** NT protein preparation; **ei|weiß|reich** ADJ protein-rich *attr*, rich in protein *pred*; **~e Kost** high-protein diet; **Ei|weiß|stoff|wech|sel** M protein metabolism

Ei|zel|le F *(Biol)* egg cell

Eja|ku|lat [ejaku'laːt] NT -(e)s, -e *(Med)* ejaculated semen, ejaculate *(spec)*

Eja|ku|la|ti|on [ejakula'tsioːn] F -, -en ejaculation

eja|ku|lie|ren [ejaku'liːrən] *ptp* **ejakuliert** VI to ejaculate

EK [eː'kaː] NT -s, -s *abbr von* **Eisernes Kreuz**; **EK I/II** Iron Cross First/Second Class

EKD [eːkaː'deː] F - *abbr von* **Evangelische Kirche in Deutschland**

Ekel ['eːkl] M -s, *no pl* disgust, revulsion, loathing; *(= Übelkeit)* nausea; **vor jdm/etw einen ~ haben** *or* **empfinden** to have a loathing of sb/sth, to loathe sb/sth; **dabei empfinde ich ~** it gives me a feeling of disgust; **~ erregend** = **ekelerregend**; **~ überkommt mich** a feeling of disgust *etc* overcomes me; **diese Heuchelei ist mir ein ~** this hypocrisy is just nauseating *or* disgusting, I find this hypocrisy nauseating *or* disgusting; **er hat das Essen vor ~ ausgespuckt** he spat out the food in disgust *or* revulsion; **er musste sich vor ~ übergeben** he was so nauseated that he vomited

Ekel NT -s, - *(inf)* obnoxious person, horror *(inf)*

ekel|er|re|gend ADJ nauseating, revolting, disgusting

ekel|haft, **eke|lig** ['eːkəlɪç] ADJ disgusting, revolting; *(inf) Schmerzen, Problem, Chef* nasty, horrible ADV *(= widerlich) riechen, schmecken* disgusting, revolting; *(inf: = unangenehm) sich benehmen* horribly, terribly; **sei nicht so ~ zu ihr!** don't be so nasty to her

Ekel|haf|tig|keit F -, -en **a** *no pl (von Person)* nastiness **b** *usu pl* nasty behaviour *(Brit) or* behavior *(US) no pl*

ekeln ['eːkln] VT to disgust, to revolt, to nauseate VT *impers* **es ekelt mich vor diesem Geruch/Anblick, mich** *or* **mir ekelt vor diesem Geruch/Anblick** the smell/sight of it fills me with disgust *or* revulsion, this smell/sight is disgusting *or* revolting *or* nauseating VR to be *or* feel disgusted *or* revolted *or* nauseated; **sich vor etw** *(dat)* **~** to find sth disgusting *or* revolting *or* nauseating

EKG, Ekg [eːkaː'geː] NT -s, -s *abbr von* **Elektrokardiogramm** ECG; **ein ~ machen lassen** to have an ECG

Ek|lat [e'kla(ː)] M -s, -s *(geh) (= Aufsehen)* sensation, stir; *(= Zusammenstoß)* row, (major) altercation *(form)*; **mit großem ~** causing a great stir *or* sensation, spectacularly; **mit (großem) ~ durchfallen** to be a resounding flop *or* a spectacular failure

ek|la|tant [ekla'tant] ADJ *(= aufsehenerregend) Fall* sensational, spectacular; *(= offenkundig) Beispiel* striking; *Verletzung* flagrant

Ek|lek|ti|ker [ɛk'lɛktikɐ, e'klɛktikɐ] M -s, -, **Ek|lek|ti|ke|rin** [-ərɪn] F -, -nen eclectic

ek|lek|tisch [ɛk'lɛktɪʃ, e'klɛktɪʃ] ADJ eclectic

Ek|lek|ti|zis|mus [ɛklɛkti'tsɪsmʊs, eklɛ-] M -, *no pl* eclecticism

ek|lig ['eːklɪç] ADJ, ADV = **ekelig**

Ek|lip|se [ɛk'lɪpsə, e'klɪpsə] F -, -n eclipse

Ek|lip|tik [ɛk'lɪptɪk, e'klɪptɪk] F -, -en ecliptic

ek|lip|tisch [ɛk'lɪptɪʃ, e'klɪptɪʃ] ADJ ecliptical

Eks|ta|se [ɛk'staːzə, ɛks'taːzə] F -, -n ecstasy; **in ~ geraten** to go into ecstasies; **jdn in ~ versetzen** to send sb into ecstasies

eks|ta|tisch [ɛk'staːtɪʃ, ɛks'taːtɪʃ] ADJ ecstatic, full of ecstasy ADV ecstatically

Ek|zem [ɛk'tseːm] NT -s, -e *(Med)* eczema

EL *abbr von* **Esslöffel** tbs, tbsp

Ela|bo|rat [elabo'raːt] NT -(e)s, -e *(pej)* concoction *(pej)*

Elan [e'laːn, e'lãː] M -s, *no pl* élan, zest, vigour *(Brit)*, vigor *(US)*

Elast [e'last] M -(e)s, -e rubber, elastomer *(spec)*

Elas|tik|bin|de [e'lastɪk-] F elasticated bandage

elas|tisch [e'lastɪʃ] ADJ elastic; *Gang* springy; *Metall, Holz* springy, flexible; *Stoff* elastic, stretchy; *Binde* elasticated; *(fig) (= spannkräftig) Muskel, Mensch* strong and supple; *(= flexibel)* flexible, elastic ADV supply, lithely; **der Baum bog sich ~ im Wind** the tree bent supply in the wind; **er federte ~** he bent supply at the knees; **der Bügel schnellte ~ zurück** the bow sprang back

Elas|ti|zi|tät [elastitsi'tɛːt] F -, *(rare)* -en elasticity; *(von Metall, Holz)* flexibility; *(= Flexibilität)* flexibility, elasticity; **die ~ seines Körpers** the supple strength of his body

Ela|tiv ['eːlatiːf] M -s, -e [-və] *(Gram)* absolute superlative

El|be ['ɛlbə] F - **die ~** the (river) Elbe

Elb|käh|ne ['ɛlp-] PL *(N Ger hum)* beetle-crushers *pl (inf)*, clodhoppers *pl (inf)*

Elch [ɛlç] M -(e)s, -e elk; *(in Nordamerika)* moose

Elch-: **Elch|bul|le** M bull elk; *(in Nordamerika)* bull moose; **Elch|kalb** NT elk calf; *(in Nordamerika)* moose calf; **Elch|kuh** F cow elk; *(in Nordamerika)* cow moose; **Elch|test** M *(inf) (Aut)* high-speed swerve *(to test a car's road-holding)*; *(fig: = entscheidender Test)* make-or-break test

El|do|ra|do [ɛldo'raːdo] NT -s, -s *(lit, fig)* eldorado

Elect|ro|nic Ban|king [elɛk'trɔnɪk 'bɛŋkɪŋ] NT -, *no pl* electronic banking

Elect|ro|nic Cash [elɛk'trɔnɪk 'kɛʃ] NT -, *no pl* electronic cash

Ele|fant [ele'fant] M -en, -en elephant; **wie ein ~ im Porzellanladen** *(inf)* like a bull in a china shop *(prov)* → **Mücke**

Ele|fan|ten-: **Ele|fan|ten|ba|by** NT *(inf)* baby elephant *(auch fig hum)*; **Ele|fan|ten|bul|le**

M bull elephant; **Ele|fan|ten|ge|dächt|nis** NT *(fig)* elephant's memory; **Ele|fan|ten|hoch|zeit** F *(Comm inf)* mega-merger *(inf)*; **Ele|fan|ten|kalb** NT elephant calf; **Ele|fan|ten|kuh** F cow elephant; **Ele|fan|ten|ren|nen** NT *(hum inf)* duel between two lorries *(Brit)* or trucks; **Ele|fan|ten|rob|be** F elephant seal; **Ele|fan|ten|run|de** F *(Pol) (= Koalitionsrunde)* top-level meeting of coalition members; *(im Fernsehen)* debate between party leaders; **Ele|fan|ten|rüs|sel** M elephant's trunk; **Ele|fan|ten|schlacht** F *(fig)* battle of the giants

Ele|fan|ti|a|sis [elefan'ti:azɪs] F -, **Elefantiasen** [-'tia:zn] *(Med)* elephantiasis

ele|gant [ele'gant] ADJ elegant; **die ~e Welt** *(dated)* high society ADV elegantly

Ele|ganz [ele'gants] F -, *no pl* elegance

Ele|gie [ele'gi:] F -, -n [-'gi:ən] elegy

Ele|gi|en|dich|ter(in) [ele'gi:ən-] M(F), **Ele|gi|ker** [e'le:gikɐ] M -s, -, **Ele|gi|ke|rin** [-ərɪn] F -, -nen elegist

ele|gisch [e'le:gɪʃ] ADJ elegiac; *(= melancholisch auch)* melancholy ADV **~ gestimmt** in a melancholy mood

Elei|son [e'laizɔn] NT -s, -s *(Eccl)* Kyrie eleison

Elekt|ri|fi|ka|ti|on [elɛktrifika'tsio:n] F -, -en *(Sw)* electrification

elekt|ri|fi|zie|ren [elɛktrifi'tsi:rən] *ptp* **elektrifiziert** VT to electrify

Elekt|ri|fi|zie|rung F -, -en electrification

Elekt|rik [e'lɛktrɪk] F -, -en **a** *(= elektrische Anlagen)* electrical equipment **b** *no pl (inf: = Elektrizitätslehre)* electricity

Elekt|ri|ker [e'lɛktrikɐ] M -s, -, **Elekt|ri|ke|rin** [-ərɪn] F -, -nen electrician

elekt|risch [e'lɛktrɪʃ] ADJ electric; *Entladung, Feld, Widerstand* electrical; **~e Geräte** electrical appliances; **~er Schlag/Strom** electric shock/current; **der ~e Stuhl** the electric chair; **bei uns ist alles ~** we're all electric ADV electrically, by or with electricity; **sich ~ rasieren** to use an electric razor; **~ betrieben** electrically driven, driven or run by electricity, electric; **wir kochen/heizen ~** we cook/heat by or with electricity; **das geht alles ~** *(inf)* it's all automatic

Elekt|ri|sche [e'lɛktrɪʃə] F *decl as adj (dated)* tram *(esp Brit)*, streetcar *(US)*

elekt|ri|sie|ren [elɛktri'zi:rən] *ptp* **elektrisiert** VT *(lit, fig)* to electrify; *(= aufladen)* to charge with electricity; *(Med)* to treat with electricity; **ich habe mich elektrisiert** I gave myself or I got an electric shock; **die elektrisierte Atmosphäre** the electrically-charged atmosphere; **wie elektrisiert** (as if) electrified VI to give an electric shock

Elekt|ri|sier|ma|schi|ne F electrostatic generator

Elekt|ri|zi|tät [elɛktritsi'tɛ:t] F -, *no pl* electricity

Elekt|ri|zi|täts-: **Elekt|ri|zi|täts|ge|sell|schaft** F electric power company; **Elekt|ri|zi|täts|leh|re** F (science of) electricity; **Elekt|ri|zi|täts|ver|sor|gung** F (electric) power supply; **Elekt|ri|zi|täts|ver|sor|gungs|un|ter|neh|men** NT electricity supplier or provider; **Elekt|ri|zi|täts|werk** NT (electric) power station; *(= Gesellschaft)* electric power company; **Elekt|ri|zi|täts|zäh|ler** M *(form)* electricity meter

Elekt|ro- *in cpds* electro- *(auch Sci)*, electric; **elekt|ro|akus|tisch** [elɛktrola'kustɪʃ, e'lɛktro-] ADJ electroacoustic(al); **Elekt|ro|ana|ly|se** [elɛktrolana'ly:zə, e'lɛktro-] F electroanalysis; **Elekt|ro|an|trieb** M electric drive; **Elekt|ro|ar|ti|kel** M electrical appliance; **Elekt|ro|au|to** NT electric car; **Elekt|ro|che|mie** [elɛktroçe'mi:, e'lɛktro-] F electrochemistry; **elekt|ro|che|misch** [elɛktro'çemɪʃ, e'lɛktro-] ADJ electrochemical

Elekt|ro|de [elɛk'tro:də] F -, -n electrode

Elekt|ro|den|span|nung F electrode potential

Elekt|ro-: **Elekt|ro|di|ag|nos|tik** [elɛktrodia'gnɔstɪk, e'lɛktro-] F *(Med)* electrodiagnosis; **Elekt|ro|dy|na|mik** [elɛktrody'na:mɪk, e'lɛktro-] F electrodynamics *sing*; **elekt|ro|dy|na|misch** [elɛktrody'na:mɪʃ, e'lɛktro-] ADJ electrodynamic; **Elekt|ro|en|ze|pha|lo|gramm** [elɛktrolɛtsefalo'gram] NT *(Med)* electroencephalogram, EEG; **Elekt|ro|fahr|zeug** NT electric vehicle; **Elekt|ro|ge|rät** NT electrical appliance; **Elekt|ro|ge|schäft** NT electrical shop *(Brit)* or store *(US)*; **Elekt|ro|gi|tar|re** F *(Mus)* electric guitar; **Elekt|ro|grill** M electric grill; **Elekt|ro|herd** M electric cooker; **Elekt|ro|in|dust|rie** F electrical industry; **Elekt|ro|in|ge|ni|eur(in)** M(F) electrical engineer; **Elekt|ro|in|stal|la|teur(in)** M(F) electrician; **Elekt|ro|kar|di|o|gramm** [elɛktrokardio'gram] NT *(Med)* electrocardiogram, ECG; **Elekt|ro|kar|ren** M small electric truck; *(des Milchmannes etc)* electric float; **Elekt|ro|lok** F, **Elekt|ro|lo|ko|mo|ti|ve** F electric locomotive; **Elekt|ro|ly|se** [elɛktro'ly:zə] F -, -n electrolysis; **Elekt|ro|lyt** [elɛktro'ly:t] M -en, -en electrolyte; **elekt|ro|ly|tisch** [elɛtro'ly:tɪʃ] ADJ electrolytic; **Elekt|ro|lyt|lö|sung** [elɛktro'ly:t-] F electrolytic solution, electrolyte; **Elekt|ro|mag|net** [elɛktroma'gne:t, e'lɛktro-] M electromagnet; **elekt|ro|mag|ne|tisch** [elɛktroma'gne:tɪʃ, e'lɛktro-] ADJ electromagnetic; **Elekt|ro|me|cha|ni|ker(in)** M(F) electrician; **elekt|ro|me|cha|nisch** [elɛktrome'ça:nɪʃ, e'lɛktro-] ADJ electromechanical; **Elekt|ro|meis|ter(in)** [e'lɛktro-] M(F) qualified electrician; **Elekt|ro|mes|ser** NT electric carving knife; **Elekt|ro|me|ter** [elɛktro'me:tɐ] NT -s, - electrometer; **Elekt|ro|mo|tor** M electric motor

Elekt|ron ['e:lɛktrɔn, e'lɛktrɔn, elɛk'tro:n] NT -s, -en [elɛk'tro:nən] electron

Elekt|ro|nen-: **Elekt|ro|nen|blitz** M, **Elekt|ro|nen|blitz|ge|rät** NT *(Phot)* electronic flash; **Elekt|ro|nen|(ge)|hirn** NT electronic brain; **Elekt|ro|nen|hül|le** F *(Phys)* electron shell or cloud; **Elekt|ro|nen|la|ser** M electron laser; **Elekt|ro|nen|mik|ro|skop** NT electron microscope; **Elekt|ro|nen|or|gel** F *(Mus)* electronic organ; **Elekt|ro|nen|rech|ner** M (electronic) computer; **Elekt|ro|nen|röh|re** F valve, electron tube *(US)*; **Elekt|ro|nen|scha|le** F electron shell; **Elekt|ro|nen|schleu|der** F *(Phys)* electron accelerator, betatron *(spec)*; **Elekt|ro|nen|strah|len** PL electron or cathode rays *pl*; **Elekt|ro|nen|the|o|rie** F electron theory

Elekt|ro|nik [elɛk'tro:nɪk] F -, -en electronics *sing*; *(= elektronische Teile)* electronics *pl*

Elekt|ro|nik- *in cpds* electronic; **Elekt|ro|nik|ge|rät** NT electronic device; **Elekt|ro|nik|schrott** M electronic waste; **Elekt|ro|nik|spiel|zeug** NT electronic toys *pl*

elekt|ro|nisch [elɛk'tro:nɪʃ] ADJ electronic; **~e Post** electronic mail, E-mail, e-mail; **~er Briefkasten** electronic mailbox; **~e Geldbörse** smartcard-based electronic wallet; **~es Banking** electronic banking; **~er Handel** e-commerce; **~er Kunde** e-shopper; **~e Verkaufsstelle** electronic point of sale, EPOS; **~e Währung** digital currency or cash ADV **~ gesteuert** electronically controlled

Elekt|ro-: **Elekt|ro|ofen** M *(Metal)* electric furnace; *(= Heizofen)* electric heater; **Elekt|ro|ra|sen|mä|her** M electric lawn mower; **Elekt|ro|ra|sie|rer** M electric shaver or razor; **Elekt|ro|schock** M *(Med)* electric shock, electroshock; **Elekt|ro|schock|be|hand|lung** F electric shock treatment; **Elek|tro|scho|cker** M stun gun; **Elekt|ro|schwei|ßen** NT electric arc welding; **Elekt|ro|schwei|ßung** F electric welding; **Elekt|ro|smog** M electromagnetic radiation; **Elekt|ro|stahl** M *(Metal)* electrosteel, electric steel; **Elekt|ro|sta|tik** [elɛktro'ʃta:tɪk] F *(Phys)* electrostatics *sing*; **elekt|ro|sta|tisch** [elɛktro'ʃta:tɪʃ] ADJ electrostatic ADV electrostatically; **Elekt|ro|tech|nik** [elɛktro'tɛçnɪk, e'lɛktro-] F electrical engineering; **Elekt|ro|tech|ni|ker(in)** [elɛktro'tɛçnikɐ, e'lɛktro-, -ərɪn] M(F) electrician; *(= Ingenieur)* electrical engineer; **elekt|ro|tech|nisch** [elɛktro'tɛçnɪʃ, e'lɛktro-] ADJ electrical, electrotechnical *(rare)*; **Elekt|ro|the|ra|pie** [elɛktrotera'pi:, e'lɛktro-] F *(Med)* electrotherapy; **Elekt|ro|zaun** [e'lɛktro-] M electric fence

Ele|ment [ele'mɛnt] NT -(e)s, -e **a** element *(auch Chem)*; *(Elec)* cell, battery; **kriminelle ~e** *(pej)* criminal elements; **in seinem ~ sein** to be in one's element **b** **Elemente** PL *(fig: = Anfangsgründe)* elements *pl*, rudiments *pl*; **das Toben der ~e** *(liter)* the raging of the elements

ele|men|tar [elemɛn'ta:ɐ] ADJ *(= grundlegend, wesentlich)* elementary; *(= naturhaft, urwüchsig) Gewalt, Trieb* elemental; *Hass* strong, violent ADV **~ hervorbrechen** to erupt with elemental force

Ele|men|tar- *in cpds (= grundlegend)* elementary; *(= naturhaft)* elemental; **Ele|men|tar|be|griff** M elementary or basic concept; **Ele|men|tar|er|eig|nis** NT natural disaster; **Ele|men|tar|ge|walt** F *(liter)* elemental force; **Ele|men|tar|kennt|nis|se** PL elementary knowledge *sing*; **Ele|men|tar|la|dung** F *(Phys)* elementary charge; **Ele|men|tar|schu|le** F *(rare)* primary or elementary school; **Ele|men|tar|teil|chen** NT *(Phys)* elementary particle

Elen ['e:lɛn] M OR NT -s, - *(rare: = Elch)* elk

elend ['e:lɛnt] ADJ **a** *(= unglücklich, jämmerlich, pej: = gemein)* wretched, miserable; *(= krank)* wretched, awful *(inf)*, ill *pred*; **mir ist ganz ~** I feel really awful *(inf)* or wretched; **mir wird ganz ~, wenn ich daran denke** I feel quite ill when I think about it, thinking about it makes me feel quite ill **b** *(inf: = sehr groß) Hunger, Hitze* awful, dreadful; *(= sehr schlecht) Wetter, Kälte, Leistung* wretched, dreadful, miserable ADV **a** *(= schlecht)* wretchedly, miserably; **~ aussehen** to look awful *(inf)* or wretched; **sich ~ fühlen** to feel awful *(inf)* or wretched **b** *(inf: = schlimm)* dreadfully, terribly; **ich habe ~ gefroren** I was miserably or terribly cold; **da bin ich ~ betrogen worden** I was cheated terribly; **es war ~ heiß/kalt** it was awfully or dreadfully hot/miserably or dreadfully or terribly cold

Elend ['e:lɛnt] NT -(e)s [-dəs], *no pl (= Unglück, Not)* misery, distress; *(= Verwahrlosung)* squalor; *(= Armut)* poverty, penury; **ein Bild des ~s** a picture of misery/squalor; **ins ~ geraten** to fall into poverty, to be reduced to penury, to become destitute; **im (tiefsten) ~ leben** to live in (abject) misery/squalor/poverty; **jdn/sich (selbst) ins ~ stürzen** to plunge sb/oneself into misery/poverty; **wie das leibhaftige ~ aussehen** *(inf)* to look really awful *(inf)* or terrible *(inf)*; **(wie) ein Häufchen ~** *(inf)* (looking) a picture of misery; **das heulende ~** *(inf)* the blues *pl (inf)*; **da kann man das heulende ~ kriegen** *(inf)* it's enough to make you scream *(inf)*; **es ist ein ~ mit ihm** *(inf)* he makes you want to weep *(inf)*, he's hopeless; **es ist ein ~, …** *(inf)* it's heartbreaking … → **lang ADJ b**

elen|dig(lich) ['e:lɛndɪk(lɪç), *(emph)* e:'lɛndɪk(-lɪç)] ADV *(geh)* miserably, wretchedly; **~ zugrunde** or **zu Grunde gehen** or **verrecken** *(sl)* to come to a wretched or miserable or dismal end

Elends-: **Elends|ge|stalt** F (poor) wretch, wretched figure; **Elends|quar|tier** NT slum (dwelling), squalid dwelling; **Elends|vier|tel** NT slums *pl*, slum area

Ele|phan|ti|a|sis [elefan'ti:azɪs] F -, **Elephantiasen** [-'tia:zn] *(Med)* elephantiasis

Ele|ve [e'le:və] M -n, -n, **Ele|vin** [e'le:vɪn] F -, -nen *(Theat)* student; *(old: = Schüler)* pupil

elf NUM eleven → *auch* **vier**

Elf [ɛlf] F -, -en *(Sport)* team, eleven

Elf [ɛlf] M -en, -en, **El|fe** ['ɛlfə] F -, -n elf

Elf-: **Elf|eck** NT undecagon, eleven-sided figure; **elf|eckig** ADJ eleven-sided

El|fen|bein ['ɛlfnbain] NT ivory

El|fen|bein|ar|beit F ivory (carving)

el|fen|bei|nern ADJ ivory, made of ivory; **~er Turm** *(Rel)* Tower of Ivory ADV ivory-like

El|fen|bein-: **el|fen|bein|far|ben** [-farbn], **el|fen|bein|far|big** ADJ ivory-coloured *(Brit)*, ivory-colored *(US)*; **El|fen|bein|küs|te** F Ivory Coast; **El|fen|bein|schnit|ze|rei** F ivory carving; *(Produkt auch)* ivory; **El|fen|bein|turm** M *(fig)* ivory tower

El|fen-: **el|fen|haft** ADJ *(liter)* elfish, elfin; **El|fen|reich** NT fairyland

El|fer ['ɛlfɐ] M **-s, -** *(Ftbl inf)* = **Elfmeter**

El|fer-: **El|fer|pro|be** F *(Math)* casting out of elevens; **El|fer|rat** M committee of eleven

elf-: **elf|fach** ['ɛlffax] ADJ elevenfold → *auch* **vierfach**; **elf|mal** ['ɛlfma:l] ADV eleven times → *auch* **viermal**

Elf|me|ter [ɛlf'me:tɐ] M *(Ftbl)* penalty (kick) *(für* to, for); **einen ~ schießen** to take a penalty

Elf|me|ter-: **Elf|me|ter|mar|ke** F, **Elf|me|ter|punkt** M *(Ftbl)* penalty spot; **Elf|me|ter|schie|ßen** NT **-s, -** *(Ftbl)* penalty shoot-out; **durch ~ entschieden** decided on penalties; **Elf|me|ter|schuss** M *(Ftbl)* penalty (kick); **Elf|me|ter|schüt|ze** M, **Elf|me|ter|schüt|zin** F *(Ftbl)* penalty-taker; **Elf|me|ter|tö|ter(in)** M(F) *(Ftbl, inf)* penalty killer *(inf)*

Elf|tel ['ɛlftl] NT **-s, -** eleventh → *auch* **Viertel**

elf|tens ['ɛlftns] ADV eleventh, in the eleventh place

elf|te(r, s) ['ɛlftə] ADJ eleventh → **vierte(r, s)**

Eli|mi|na|ti|on [elimina'tsio:n] F **-, -en** elimination *(auch Math)*

eli|mi|nie|ren [elimi'ni:rən] *ptp* **eliminiert** VT to eliminate *(auch Math)*

Eli|mi|nie|rung F **-, -en** elimination

eli|sa|be|tha|nisch [elizabe'ta:nɪʃ] ADJ Elizabethan

Eli|si|on [eli'zio:n] F **-, -en** *(Gram)* elision

eli|tär [eli'tɛ:ɐ] ADJ elitist ADV in an elitist fashion

Eli|te [e'li:tə] F **-, -n** elite

Eli|te-: **Eli|te|den|ken** NT elitism; **Eli|te|trup|pe** F *(Mil)* crack *or* elite troops *pl*

Eli|xier [elɪ'ksi:ɐ] NT **-s, -e** elixir *(liter)*, tonic

Ell|bo|gen ['ɛlbo:gn] M = **Ellenbogen**

El|le ['ɛlə] F **-, -n** **a** *(Anat)* ulna *(spec)* **b** *(Hist) (Measure)* cubit; *(= Maßstock)* ≈ yardstick; **alles mit der gleichen** *or* **mit gleicher ~ messen** *(fig)* to measure everything by the same yardstick *or* standards

El|len|bo|gen ['ɛlənbo:gn] M elbow; *(fig)* push; **er bahnte sich seinen Weg mit den ~ durch die Menge** he elbowed his way through the crowd; **die ~ gebrauchen** *(fig)* to use one's elbows, to be ruthless; **er hat keine ~** *(fig)* he's not ruthless enough, he has no push *(inf)*

El|len|bo|gen-: **El|len|bo|gen|frei|heit** F *(fig)* elbow room; **El|len|bo|gen|ge|sell|schaft** F dog-eat-dog society; **El|len|bo|gen|mensch** M ruthless *or* pushy *(inf)* person, pusher *(inf)*; **El|len|bo|gen|schüt|zer** M elbow pad; **El|len|bo|gen|tak|tik** F pushiness *(inf)*; **~ anwenden** to be pushy *(inf)*

el|len-: **el|len|lang** ADJ *(fig inf)* incredibly long *(inf)*; *Liste, Weg auch* mile-long *attr (inf)*, a mile long *pred (inf)*; *Geschichte etc auch* lengthy, interminable; *Kerl* incredibly tall *(inf)*; **el|len|wei|se** ADV ≈ by the yard

El|lip|se [ɛ'lɪpsə] F **-, -n** *(Math)* ellipse; *(Gram)* ellipsis

el|lip|tisch [ɛ'lɪptɪʃ] ADJ *(Math, Gram)* elliptic(al)

Elms|feu|er ['ɛlms-] NT *(Met)* St Elmo's fire, corposant

Elo|ge [e'lo:ʒə] F **-, -n** eulogy

E-Lok ['e:lɔk] F *abbr von* **elektrische Lokomotive** electric locomotive *or* engine

elo|quent [elo'kvɛnt] *(geh)* ADJ eloquent ADV eloquently

Elo|quenz [elo'kvɛnts] F **-,** *no pl (geh)* eloquence

El|sass ['ɛlzas] NT **-** *or* **-es das ~** Alsace

El|säs|ser ['ɛlzɛsɐ] ADJ Alsatian

El|säs|ser ['ɛlzɛsɐ] M **-s, -**, **El|säs|se|rin** [-ərɪn] F **-, -nen** Alsatian, inhabitant of Alsace

el|säs|sisch ['ɛlzɛsɪʃ] ADJ Alsatian

El|sass-Loth|rin|gen ['ɛlzas'lo:trɪŋən] NT Alsace-Lorraine

el|sass-loth|rin|gisch ['ɛlzas'lo:trɪŋɪʃ] ADJ Alsace-Lorraine *attr*, of Alsace-Lorraine

Els|ter ['ɛlstɐ] F **-, -n** magpie; **wie eine ~ stehlen** to be always stealing things, to have sticky fingers *(Brit inf)*; **eine diebische ~ sein** *(fig)* to be a thief *or* pilferer; **geschwätzig wie eine ~ sein** to chatter like a magpie

El|ter ['ɛltɐ] M OR NT **-s, -n** *(Sci)* parent

el|ter|lich ['ɛltɐlɪç] ADJ parental

El|tern ['ɛltɐn] PL parents *pl*; **nicht von schlechten ~ sein** *(inf)* to be quite something *(inf)*, to be a good one *(inf)*

El|tern-: **El|tern|abend** M *(Sch)* parents' evening; **El|tern|bei|rat** M ≈ PTA, parent-teacher association; **El|tern|haus** NT *(lit, fig)* (parental) home; **aus gutem ~ stammen** to come from a good home; **El|tern|ini|ti|a|ti|ve** F parents' action group, parent pressure group; **El|tern|lie|be** F parental love; **el|tern|los** ADJ orphaned, parentless ADV **~ aufwachsen** to grow up an orphan *or* without parents; **El|tern|pflicht** F parental duty; **die ~en** *pl (auch)* one's duties as a parent; **El|tern|schaft** ['ɛltɐnʃaft] F **-, -en** *(= alle Eltern zusammen)* parents *pl*; *(= das Elternsein)* parenthood; **El|tern|sprech|stun|de** F *(Sch)* consultation hour (for parents); **El|tern|sprech|tag** M open *or* visiting day (for parents); **El|tern|teil** M parent; **El|tern|ur|laub** M *unpaid leave given to new mother or father*; **El|tern|ver|tre|ter(in)** M(F) *(Sch)* parent governor, *member of the school's governing body*

El|tern|zeit F parental leave; **in ~ sein** to be on parental leave

Ely|si|um [e'ly:ziʊm] NT **-s**, *no pl (Myth, fig)* **das ~** Elysium

Email [e'mai, e'ma:j] NT **-s, -s** enamel

E-Mail ['i:me:l] F **-, -s** *(Comput)* E-mail, e-mail

E-Mail-Ad|res|se ['i:me:l-] F *(Comput)* E-mail *or* e-mail address

Email|lack [e'mailak, e'ma:j-] M enamel paint

Email|le [e'maljə, e'mai, e'ma:j] F **-, -n** enamel

email|lie|ren [ema'ji:rən, emal'ji:rən] *ptp* **emailliert** VT to enamel

Email- [e'mai-, e'ma:j-]: **Email|ma|le|rei** F enamel painting, enamelling *(Brit)*, enameling *(US)*; **Email|schmuck** M enamel jewellery *(Brit) or* jewelry *(US)*

Ema|na|ti|on [emana'tsio:n] F **-, -en** *(Philos, Chem)* emanation

Eman|ze [e'mantsə] F **-, -n** *(usu pej)* women's libber *(inf)*

Eman|zi|pa|ti|on [emantsipa'tsio:n] F **-, -en** emancipation

Eman|zi|pa|ti|ons|be|we|gung F emancipation movement

eman|zi|pa|to|risch [emantsipa'to:rɪʃ] ADJ emancipatory

eman|zi|pie|ren [emantsi'pi:rən] *ptp* **emanzipiert** VT to emancipate VR to emancipate oneself

Eman|zi|pie|rung F **-, -en** emancipation

Em|bar|go [ɛm'bargo] NT **-s, -s** embargo; **etw mit einem ~ belegen, ein ~ über etw** *(acc)* **verhängen** to put *or* place an embargo on sth

Emb|lem [ɛm'ble:m, ã'ble:m] NT **-(e)s, -e** emblem; *(= Firmenemblem)* logo

emb|le|ma|tisch [ɛmble'ma:tɪʃ, ãble'ma:tɪʃ] ADJ emblematic

Em|bo|lie [ɛmbo'li:] F **-, -n** [-'li:ən] *(Med)* embolism

Emb|ryo ['ɛmbryo] M (AUS AUCH NT) **-s, -s** *or* **-nen** [-'o:nən] embryo

Emb|ryo|lo|ge [ɛmbryo'lo:gə] M **-n, -n**, **Emb|ryo|lo|gin** [-'lo:gɪn] F **-, -nen** embryologist

Emb|ryo|lo|gie [ɛmbryolo'gi:] F **-,** *no pl* embryology

emb|ry|o|nal [ɛmbryo'na:l] ADJ *attr (Biol, fig)* embryonic

Emb|ry|o|nen|schutz|ge|setz NT embryo protection law

Emen|da|ti|on [emɛnda'tsio:n] F **-,** *no pl (Liter)* emendation

eme|ri|tie|ren [emeri'ti:rən] *ptp* **emeritiert** VT *(Univ)* to give emeritus status (to); **emeritierter Professor** emeritus professor

Eme|ri|tus [e'me:ritʊs] M **-, Emeriti** [-ti] *(Univ)* emeritus

Emig|rant [emi'grant] M **-en, -en**, **Emig|ran|tin** [-'grantɪn] F **-, -nen** emigrant; *(= politischer Flüchtling)* émigré

Emig|ran|ten|schick|sal NT **sein** *etc* **~** his *etc* fate as an exile *or* refugee *or* émigré

Emig|ra|ti|on [emigra'tsio:n] F **-, -en** emigration; *(= die Emigranten)* emigrant community; **in der ~ leben** to live in (self-imposed) exile; **in die ~ gehen** to emigrate → **innere(r, s) a**

emig|rie|ren [emi'gri:rən] *ptp* **emigriert** VI *aux sein* to emigrate

emi|nent [emi'nɛnt] *(geh)* ADJ *Person* eminent; *Kenntnis* remarkable; **von ~er Bedeutung** of the utmost significance; **er hat Eminentes geleistet** he is a man of eminent achievements ADV eminently; **~ wichtig** of the utmost importance

Emi|nenz [emi'nɛnts] F **-, -en** *(Eccl)* **(Seine/Eure) ~** (His/Your) Eminence → **grau**

Emir ['e:mɪr, e'mi:ɐ] M **-s, -e** emir

Emi|rat [emi'ra:t] NT **-(e)s, -e** emirate

Emis|sär [emi'sɛ:ɐ] M **-s, -e**, **Emis|sä|rin** [-'sɛ:rɪn] F **-, -nen** *(old)* emissary

Emis|si|on [emi'sio:n] F **a** *(Fin)* issue **b** *(Phys)* emission **c** *(Sw: = Radiosendung)* (radio) broadcast

Emis|si|ons-: **Emis|si|ons|bank** F *pl* **-banken** issuing bank; **Emis|si|ons|kurs** M rate of issue, issuing price; **Emis|si|ons|schutz** M emission(s) control; *(bei Auto)* exhaust emission(s) control

Emit|tent [emi'tɛnt] M **-en, -en**, **Emit|ten|tin** [emi'tɛntɪn] F **-, -nen** *(Fin: von Wertpapieren)* issuer, issuing company

emit|tie|ren [emi'ti:rən] *ptp* **emittiert** VT **a** *(Fin)* to issue **b** *(Phys)* to emit

Emm|chen ['ɛmçən] NT **-s, -** *(hum inf, Hist)* mark, ≈ quid *(Brit inf)*, ≈ buck *(US inf)*

Em|men|ta|ler ['ɛmənta:lɐ] M **-s, -** *(= Käse)* Emment(h)aler

Emo|ti|con [e'mo:tikɔn] NT **-s, -s** *(Comput, E-Mail: = Zeichenkombination zum Ausdruck von Gefühlen)* emoticon; *(positives Gefühl)* smiley

Emo|ti|on [emo'tsio:n] F **-, -en** emotion

emo|ti|o|nal [emotsio'na:l] ADJ emotional; *Ausdrucksweise* emotive ADV emotionally

emo|ti|o|na|li|sie|ren [emotsionali'zi:rən] *ptp* **emotionalisiert** VT to emotionalize

Emo|ti|o|na|li|tät F **-, -en** emotionality

emo|ti|o|nell [emotsio'nɛl] ADJ = **emotional ADJ**

emo|ti|ons-: **emo|ti|ons|arm** ADJ lacking in emotion, unfeeling; **emo|ti|ons|frei** ADJ, ADV = **emotionslos**; **emo|ti|ons|ge|la|den** ADJ emotionally charged; **emo|ti|ons|los** ADJ emotionless, free of emotion, unemotional ADV unemotionally; **Emo|ti|ons|lo|sig|keit** F **-,** *no pl* lack of emotion

Empf. *abbr von* **Empfänger, Empfohlen(er Preis)**

emp|fahl *pret von* **empfehlen**

emp|fand *pret von* **empfinden**

Emp|fang [ɛm'pfaŋ] M **-(e)s, ⚠e** [-'pfɛŋə] reception; *(von Brief, Ware etc)* receipt; *(von Sakramenten)* receiving; **jdm einen herzlichen ~ bereiten** to give sb a warm reception; **zu jds ~ kommen** *(= jdn begrüßen)* to (come to) receive sb; **einen ~ geben** *or* **veranstalten** to give *or* hold a reception; **jdn/etw in ~ nehmen** to receive sb/sth; *(Comm)* to take delivery of sth; **(zahlbar) nach/**

bei ~ *(+gen)* (payable) on receipt (of); **auf ~ bleiben** *(Rad)* to stand by; **auf ~ schalten** *(Rad)* to switch over to "receive"

emp|fan|gen [ɛm'pfaŋən] *pret* **empfing** [ɛm'pfɪŋ], *ptp* **empfangen** VT *auch Sender, Daten* to receive; *(= begrüßen)* to greet, to receive *(form)*; *(herzlich)* to welcome; *(= abholen) Besuch* to meet; **die Weihen ~** *(Eccl)* to take Holy Orders; **die Polizisten wurden mit einem Steinhagel ~** the police were greeted by a shower of stones VTI *(= schwanger werden)* to conceive

Emp|fän|ger [ɛm'pfɛŋɐ] M **-s, -** *(Rad)* receiver

Emp|fän|ger [ɛm'pfɛŋɐ] M **-s, -**, **Emp|fän|ge|rin** [-ərɪn] F **-, -nen** recipient, receiver; *(= Adressat)* addressee; *(= Warenempfänger)* consignee; **~ unbekannt** *(auf Briefen)* not known at this address; **~ verzogen** gone away

Emp|fän|ger|ab|schnitt M receipt slip

emp|fäng|lich [ɛm'pfɛŋlɪç] ADJ *(= aufnahmebereit)* receptive *(für* to); *(= beeinflussbar, anfällig)* susceptible *(für* to)

Emp|fäng|lich|keit F **-, -en** *(= Aufnahmebereitschaft)* receptivity *(für* to); *(= Beeinflussbarkeit, Anfälligkeit)* susceptibility *(für* to)

Emp|fäng|nis [ɛm'pfɛŋnɪs] F **-, -se** conception

Emp|fäng|nis-: **emp|fäng|nis|ver|hü|tend** ADJ contraceptive; **~e Mittel** *pl* contraceptives *pl*; **Emp|fäng|nis|ver|hü|tung** F contraception; **Emp|fäng|nis|ver|hü|tungs|mit|tel** NT contraceptive

Emp|fangs-: **Emp|fangs|an|ten|ne** F receiving aerial *(Brit)* or antenna; **emp|fangs|be|rech|tigt** ADJ authorized to receive payment/goods *etc*; **Emp|fangs|be|rech|tig|te(r)** [-bərɛçtɪçtə] MF *decl as adj* authorized recipient; **Emp|fangs|be|reich** M *(Rad, TV)* reception area; **Emp|fangs|be|schei|ni|gung** F, **Emp|fangs|be|stä|ti|gung** F (acknowledgment of) receipt; **Emp|fangs|chef(in)** M(F) *(von Hotel)* head porter; **Emp|fangs|da|me** F receptionist; **Emp|fangs|ge|rät** NT *(Rad, TV)* (radio/TV) set, receiver; **Emp|fangs|ko|pie** F incoming document; **Emp|fangs|schüs|sel** F *(TV, Rad, Telec)* receiving dish; **Emp|fangs|sta|ti|on** F *(Rad)* receiving station; *(Space)* tracking station; *(Comm)* destination; **Emp|fangs|stö|rung** F *(Rad, TV)* interference *no pl*; **Emp|fangs|zim|mer** NT reception room

emp|feh|len [ɛm'pfe:lən] ✪ 29.1, 40.4, 46.5 *pret* **empfahl**, [ɛm'pfa:l] *ptp* **empfohlen** VT [ɛm'pfo:lən] to recommend; *(liter: = anvertrauen)* to commend *(form)*, to entrust; **(jdm) etw/jdn ~** to recommend sth/sb (to sb); **~, etw zu tun** to recommend or advise doing sth; **jdm ~, etw zu tun** to recommend *or* advise sb to do sth; **diese Methode/dieses Restaurant ist sehr zu ~** I would recommend this method/restaurant, this method/restaurant is to be recommended; **ich würde dir Vorsicht/Geduld ~** I would recommend caution/patience, I would advise *or* recommend you to be cautious/patient; **seinen Geist (dem Herrn) ~** *(liter)* to commend one's soul to the Lord; **bitte, ~ Sie mich Ihrer Frau Gemahlin** *(form)* please convey my respects to your wife *(form)* → *auch* **empfohlen**

VR **a sich für Reparaturen/als Experte** *etc* **~** to offer one's services for repairs/as an expert *etc*; **diese Ware empfiehlt sich von selbst** this product is its own recommendation; **es empfiehlt sich, das zu tun** it is advisable to do that

b *(dated, hum: = sich verabschieden)* to take one's leave; **ich empfehle mich!** I'll take my leave; **ich empfehle mich Ihnen** *(am Briefende)* please be sure of my best wishes *(dated form)* → **französisch**

emp|feh|lens|wert ADJ to be recommended, recommendable

Emp|feh|lung F **-, -en** recommendation; *(= Referenz)* testimonial, reference; *(form: = Gruß)* regards *pl*, respects *pl*; **auf ~ von** on the recommendation of; **mit freundlichen** *or* **den besten ~en** *(am Briefende)* with best regards; **meine ~ an Ihre Frau Gemahlin!** *(form)* my regards *or* respects to your wife *(form)*

Emp|feh|lungs|schrei|ben NT letter of recommendation, testimonial *(esp Brit)*

emp|fiehlt [ɛm'pfi:lt] *3. pers sing pres von* **empfehlen**

emp|fin|den [ɛm'pfɪndn] *pret* **empfand** [ɛm'pfant], *ptp* **empfunden** [ɛm'pfʊndn] VT to feel; **etw als kränkend** *or* **als Beleidigung ~** to feel sth as an insult, to find sth insulting; **er hat noch nie Hunger empfunden** he has never experienced *or* known hunger; **er empfand einen solch starken Hunger, dass ...** his hunger was so great that ...; **bei Musik Freude ~** to experience pleasure from music; **ich habe dabei viel Freude empfunden** it gave me great pleasure; **viel/nichts für jdn ~** to feel a lot/nothing for sb; **jdn als (einen) Störenfried ~** to think of sb as a troublemaker, to feel sb to be a troublemaker

Emp|fin|den [ɛm'pfɪndn] NT **-s**, *no pl* feeling; **meinem ~ nach** to my mind, the way I feel about it

emp|find|lich [ɛm'pfɪntlɪç] ADJ **a** sensitive *(auch Phot, Tech)*; *Gesundheit, Stoff, Glas, Keramik etc* delicate; *(= leicht reizbar)* touchy *(inf)*, (over)sensitive; **~e Stelle** *(lit)* sensitive spot; *(fig auch)* sore point; **gegen etw ~ sein** to be sensitive to sth; **Kupfer ist sehr ~** copper is easily damaged

b *(= spürbar, schmerzlich) Verlust, Kälte, Strafe, Niederlage* severe; *Mangel* appreciable

ADV **a** *(= sensibel)* sensitively; **~ reagieren** to be sensitive *(auf +acc* to); **wenn man ihren geschiedenen Mann erwähnt, reagiert sie sehr ~** she is very sensitive to references to her ex-husband

b *(= spürbar)* severely; **deine Kritik hat ihn ~ getroffen** your criticism cut him to the quick *(esp Brit)* or bone *(US)*; **es ist ~ kalt** it is bitterly cold

Emp|find|lich|keit F **-, -en** sensitivity *(auch Phot, Tech)*, sensitiveness; *(von Gesundheit, Stoff, Glas, Keramik)* delicateness; *(= leichte Reizbarkeit)* touchiness *(inf)*, (over)sensitivity

emp|find|sam [ɛm'pfɪntza:m] ADJ *Mensch, Seele, Musik* sensitive; *(= gefühlvoll, Liter)* sentimental

Emp|find|sam|keit F **-**, *no pl* *(= Empfindlichkeit: von Mensch, Seele, Musik)* sensitivity; *(mit starkem Gefühlsausdruck)* sentimentality; **das Zeitalter der ~** *(Liter)* the age of sentimentalism

Emp|fin|dung [ɛm'pfɪndʊŋ] F **-, -en** feeling; *(= Sinnesempfindung auch)* sensation; *(= Eindruck, Ahnung auch)* impression

Emp|fin|dungs-: **emp|fin|dungs|los** ADJ *(lit, fig)* insensitive *(für, gegen* to); *Glieder* numb, without sensation; **Emp|fin|dungs|lo|sig|keit** F **-**, *no pl* *(lit, fig)* insensitivity; *(der Glieder)* numbness, loss of sensation; **Emp|fin|dungs|ner|ven** PL *(Physiol)* sensory nerves *pl*; **Emp|fin|dungs|ver|mö|gen** NT, *no pl* faculty of sensation; *(in Gliedern)* sensation; *(fig)* sensitivity, ability to feel; **~ für etw** ability to feel *or* sense sth; *(fig)* sensitivity to sth; **Emp|fin|dungs|wort** NT *pl* **-wörter** *(Gram)* interjection

emp|fing *pret von* **empfangen**

emp|foh|len *ptp von* **empfehlen** ADJ **(sehr** *or* **gut) ~** (highly) recommended

emp|fun|den *ptp von* **empfinden**

Em|pha|se [ɛm'fa:zə] F *(geh)* emphasis

em|pha|tisch [ɛm'fa:tɪʃ] *(geh)* ADJ emphatic ADV emphatically

Em|phy|sem [ɛmfy'ze:m] NT **-s, -e** *(Med)* emphysema

Em|pire [ã'pi:ɐ] NT **-(s)**, *no pl* *(Hist)* Empire; *(= Empirestil)* Empire style

Em|pire ['ɛmpaɪə] NT **-(s)**, *no pl* (British) Empire

Em|pire|stil [ã'pi:ɐ-] M Empire style

Em|pi|rik [ɛm'pi:rɪk] F **-**, *no pl* empirical experience

Em|pi|ri|ker [ɛm'pi:rikɐ] M **-s, -**, **Em|pi|ri|ke|rin** [-ərɪn] F **-, -nen** empiricist

em|pi|risch [ɛm'pi:rɪʃ] ADJ empirical

Em|pi|ris|mus [ɛmpi'rɪsmʊs] M **-**, *no pl* *(Philos, Sci)* empiricism

em|por [ɛm'po:ɐ] ADV *(liter)* upwards, up; **zum Licht ~** up(wards) toward(s) the light; **~ die Herzen/Blicke!** lift up your hearts/eyes! *(liter)* → *auch* **hinauf**

em|por-: **em|por+ar|bei|ten** VR *sep (geh)* to work one's way up; **em|por+bli|cken** VI *sep (liter)* to raise one's eyes; *(fig)* to look up *(zu* to)

Em|po|re [ɛm'po:rə] F **-, -n** *(Archit)* gallery

em|pö|ren [ɛm'pø:rən] *ptp* **empört** VT to fill with indignation, to outrage; *(stärker)* to incense → *auch* **empört** VR **a** *(über +acc* at) to be indignant *or* outraged; *(stärker)* to be incensed; **„das ist unerhört!", empörte sich der Schulmeister** „that's scandalous!", said the schoolmaster indignantly **b** *(liter: = sich auflehnen)* to rise (up) *or* rebel *(gegen* against)

em|pö|rend ADJ outrageous, scandalous

Em|pö|rer [ɛm'pø:rɐ] M **-s, -**, **Em|pö|re|rin** [-ərɪn] F **-, -nen** *(liter)* rebel, insurrectionist

em|pö|re|risch [ɛm'pø:rərɪʃ] ADJ *(liter)* rebellious, insurrectionary

em|por-: **em|por+he|ben** VT *sep irreg (geh)* to raise, to lift up; **jdn über andere ~** *(fig)* to raise *or* elevate sb above others; **em|por+kom|men** VI *sep irreg aux sein (geh)* to rise (up); *(fig) (= aufkommen)* to come to the fore; *(= vorankommen)* to go up *or* rise in the world, to get on; **nur an sein Emporkommen denken** *(fig)* to think only of one's advancement; **Em|por|kömm|ling** [ɛm'po:ɐkœmlɪŋ] M **-s, -e** *(pej)* upstart, parvenu; **em|por+lo|dern** VI *sep aux sein or haben (liter)* to blaze *or* flare upwards; **em|por+ra|gen** VI *sep aux haben or sein (geh: lit, fig)* to tower *(über +acc* above); **em|por+re|cken** *sep* VT *(liter) Faust* to raise aloft VR to stretch upwards; **em|por+schau|en** VI *sep (geh)* to raise one's eyes; *(fig)* to look up *(zu* to); **em|por+schie|ßen** VI *sep irreg aux sein (geh)* **a** *(= häufig werden)* to shoot up, to spring up; *(Neubauten etc auch)* to mushroom **b** *(= aufspringen, Person, Tier)* to jump *or* spring *or* leap up *or* to one's feet **c** *(= schnell an Höhe gewinnen, Wasserstrahl)* to gush up; *(Flugzeug etc)* to shoot up; **em|por+schwe|ben** VI *sep aux sein (geh)* to float upwards *or* aloft *(liter)*; **em|por+schwin|gen** VR *sep irreg (geh)* to soar upwards *or* aloft *(liter)*; *(Turner)* to swing upwards; **sich zu etw ~** *(fig)* to (come to) achieve sth; *zu einer Stellung* to reach sth; **em|por+stei|gen** *sep irreg aux sein (geh)* VT to climb (up) VI to climb (up); *(Mond, Angst etc)* to rise (up); *(fig: = Karriere machen)* to climb, to rise; **em|por+stre|ben** VI *sep aux sein (geh)* to soar upwards; *(fig) aux haben* to be ambitious

em|pört [ɛm'pø:ɐt] ADJ **a** (highly) indignant, outraged *(über +acc* at); *(= schockiert)* outraged, scandalized **b** *(liter: in Auflehnung)* rebellious ADV indignantly → *auch* **empören**

em|por+trei|ben VT *sep irreg (geh)* to drive up

Em|pö|rung [ɛm'pø:rʊŋ] F **-, -en a** *no pl* *(= Entrüstung)* indignation *(über +acc* at); **über etw in ~ geraten** to become *or* get indignant about sth **b** *(liter: = Aufstand)* rebellion, uprising

em|por-: **em|por+zie|hen** *sep irreg (geh)* VT to draw *or* pull up VI *aux sein* to drift upwards; **em|por+zün|geln** VI *sep aux sein (liter: Flammen)* to leap up(wards) *or* aloft *(liter)*

em|sig ['ɛmzɪç] ADJ busy, industrious; *(= eifrig)* eager, keen; *(= geschäftig)* bustling *attr*, busy ADV industriously, busily; *(= eifrig)* eagerly

Em|sig|keit F **-**, *no pl* industry, industriousness; *(= Eifrigkeit)* eagerness, zeal; *(= Geschäftigkeit)* bustle

Emu ['e:mu] M **-s, -s** emu

Emu|la|ti|on [emula'tsio:n] F **-, -en** *(esp Comput)* emulation

Emul|ga|tor [emʊl'ga:to:ɐ] M **-s, Emulgatoren** [-'to:rən] *(Chem)* emulsifier, emulsifying agent

emul|gie|ren [emʊl'gi:rən] *ptp* **emulgiert** VTI to emulsify

emu|lie|ren [emu'li:rən] *ptp* **emuliert** VT *(esp Comput)* to emulate
Emul|si|on [emʊl'zio:n] F -, -en emulsion
Emul|si|ons-: **Emul|si|ons|far|be** F emulsion (paint); **Emul|si|ons|mit|tel** NT emulsifier
E-Mu|sik ['e:-] F serious music
en bloc [ã 'blɔk] ADV en bloc
End- *in cpds* final; **End|ab|neh|mer(in)** M(F) end buyer; **End|ab|rech|nung** F final account; **End|an|wen|der(in)** M(F) *(Comput)* end user; **End|aus|schei|dung** F *(Sport)* final elimination (round); **End|bahn|hof** M terminus, terminal; **End|be|nut|zer(in)** M(F) end user; **end|be|tont** ADJ *Wort* with final stress; **End|be|trag** M final amount
End|chen ['ɛntçən] NT -s, - *(inf)* (small) piece, bit; *(eines Weges)* short distance, little way
En|de ['ɛndə] ✪ 53.4 NT -s, -n end; *(eines Jahrhunderts etc auch)* close; *(= Ausgang, Ergebnis)* outcome, result; *(= Ausgang eines Films, Romans etc)* ending; *(Hunt: = Geweihende)* point; *(inf: = Stückchen)* (small) piece; *(inf: = Strecke)* way, stretch; *(Naut: = Tau)* (rope's) end; **~ Mai/der Woche** at the end of May/the week; **~ der zwanziger Jahre** *or* **Zwanzigerjahre** in the late twenties; **er ist ~ vierzig** he is in his late forties; **das ~ der Welt** the end of the world; **er wohnt am ~ der Welt** *(inf)* he lives at the back of beyond, he lives in the middle of nowhere; **bis ans ~ der Welt** to the ends of the earth; **das ~ vom Lied** the final outcome; **das ~ der Fahnenstange** *(fig inf)* the end of the road; **ein ~ mit Schrecken** a terrible *or* dreadful end; **lieber ein ~ mit Schrecken als ein Schrecken ohne ~** *(Prov)* it's best to get unpleasant things over and done with; **Probleme ohne ~** endless problems; **letzten ~s** when all is said and done, after all; *(= am Ende)* in the end, at the end of the day; **einer Sache** *(dat)* **ein ~ machen** to put an end to sth; **(bei** *or* **mit etw) kein ~ finden** *(inf)* to be unable to stop (sth *or* telling/doing *etc* sth); **damit muss es jetzt ein ~ haben** there has to be an end to this now, this must stop now; **ein ~ nehmen** to come to an end; **das nimmt** *or* **findet gar kein ~** *(inf)* there's no sign of it stopping, there's no end to it; **ein böses ~ nehmen** to come to a bad end; **kein ~ ist abzusehen** there's no end in sight; **da ist das ~ von weg!** *(N Ger inf)* it's incredible! *(inf)*; **... und kein ~** ... with no end in sight, ... without end; **es war des Staunens/Jubels** *etc* **kein ~** *(old, liter)* there was no end to the surprise/celebrations *etc*; **es ist noch ein gutes** *or* **ganzes ~** *(inf)* there's still quite a way to go (yet); **am ~** at the end; *(= schließlich)* in the end; *(inf: = möglicherweise)* perhaps; **(am) ~ des Monats** at the end of the month; **am ~ sein** *(fig)* to be at the end of one's tether *(Brit)* or rope *(US)*; **mit etw am ~ sein** to be at the end of sth, to have reached the end of sth; *(Vorrat)* to have run out of sth; **ich bin mit meiner Weisheit am ~** I'm at my wits' end; **meine Geduld ist am ~** my patience is at an end; **ein Problem am richtigen/falschen** *or* **verkehrten ~ anfassen** to tackle a problem from the right/wrong end; **Leiden ohne ~** endless suffering, suffering without end; **das ist eine Kette** *or* **Schraube ohne ~** *(fig)* it's an endless spiral; **zu ~** finished, over, at an end; **etw zu ~ bringen** *or* **führen** to finish (off) sth; **ein Buch/einen Brief zu ~ lesen/schreiben** to finish (reading/writing) a book/letter; **etw zu einem guten ~ bringen** *or* **führen** to bring sth to a satisfactory conclusion; **zu ~ gehen** to come to an end; *(Vorräte)* to run out; **zu dem ~, dass ...** *(obs)* to the end that ... *(form)*; **zu diesem ~** *(obs)* to this end *(form)*; **~ gut, alles gut** *(Prov)* all's well that ends well *(Prov)*; **es hat alles einmal ein ~** *(Prov)* **alles hat einmal ein ~** *(Prov)* everything must come to an end some time; *(angenehme Dinge)* all good things must come to an end *(Prov)* → **dick ADJ c**
End|ef|fekt M **im ~** *(inf)* in the end, in the final analysis
en|deln ['ɛndln] VT *(Aus) Saum* to whip, to oversew
En|de|mie [ɛnde'mi:] F -, -n [-'mi:ən] *(Med)* endemic disease
en|de|misch [ɛn'de:mɪʃ] ADJ *(Med)* endemic
en|den ['ɛndn] VI to end, to finish; *(Frist auch)* to run out, to expire; *(Zug)* to terminate; *(= sterben)* to meet one's end; **auf etw** *(acc) or* **mit etw ~** *(Wort)* to end with sth; **mit den Worten ... ~** *(bei Rede)* to close with the words ...; **es endete damit, dass ...** the outcome was that ...; **der Streit endete vor Gericht** the quarrel ended up in court; **er endete im Gefängnis** he ended up in prison; **wie wird das noch mit ihm ~?** what will become of him?; **das wird böse ~!** no good will come of it!; **er wird schlimm ~** he will come to a bad end; **nicht ~ wollend** unending
End|er|geb|nis NT final result
En|de|tas|te F *(Comput)* end key
End-: **End|fas|sung** F *(von Text, Film)* final version; **End|ge|halt** NT final salary; **end|geil** ADJ *(sl)* shit-hot *(Brit sl)*, wicked *(sl)*; **End|ge|rät** NT *(Telec etc)* terminal; **End|ge|schwin|dig|keit** F terminal velocity
end|gül|tig ADJ final; *Beweis auch* conclusive; *Antwort* definite; **etwas Endgültiges lässt sich noch nicht sagen** I/we *etc* cannot say anything definite at this stage ADV finally; **sich ~ entscheiden** to make the final decision; **damit ist die Sache ~ entschieden** that settles the matter once and for all; **das ist ~ aus** *or* **vorbei** that's (all) over and done with; **sie haben sich jetzt ~ getrennt** they've separated for good; **jetzt ist ~ Schluss!** that's the end!, that's it!
End|gül|tig|keit F, *no pl* finality; *(von Antwort)* definitiveness
End|hal|te|stel|le F terminus, terminal, final stop *(US)*
En|di|vie [ɛn'di:viə] F -, -n endive
En|di|vi|en|sa|lat [ɛn'di:viən-] M **a** *(Pflanze)* endive **b** *(Salat)* endive salad
End-: **End|kampf** M *(Mil)* final battle; *(Sport)* final; *(= Endphase) (Mil)* final stages *pl* (of a battle); *(Sport)* final stages *pl* (of a contest); **End|kun|de** M *(Comm)* end customer; **End|la|ger** NT *(für Atommüll etc)* permanent (waste) disposal site; **end|la|gern** VT *insep Atommüll etc* to dispose of *sth* permanently; **End|la|ge|rung** F *(von Atommüll etc)* permanent (waste) disposal; **End|lauf** M final; **End|lauf|teil|neh|mer(in)** M(F) finalist
end|lich ['ɛntlɪç] ADJ **a** *(Math, Philos)* finite **b** *(rare: = lang erwartet, schließlich)* eventual ADV finally, at last; *(= am Ende)* eventually, in the end, finally; **na ~!** at (long) last!; **hör ~ damit auf!** will you stop that!; **komm doch ~!** come on, get a move on!; **~ kam er doch** he eventually came after all, in the end he came (after all)
End|lich|keit F -, *no pl (Math, Philos)* finiteness, finite nature
end|los ADJ endless; *(= langwierig auch)* interminable; **(sich) bis ins Endlose (erstrecken)** (to stretch) to infinity ADV forever; **ich musste ~ lange warten** I had to wait for an interminably long time, I had to wait for ages *(inf)*
End|lo|sig|keit F -, *no pl* endlessness, infinite nature; *(= Langwierigkeit)* interminable nature
End-: **End|los|pa|pier** NT, *no pl* continuous paper; **End|lö|sung** F **die ~** the Final Solution *(extermination of the Jews by the Nazis)*; **End|mon|ta|ge** F final assembly; **End|mo|rä|ne** F terminal moraine; **End|nut|zer(in)** M(F) end user
En|do- *in cpds* endo-; **en|do|gen** [ɛndo'ge:n] ADJ *(Biol, Psych)* endogenous; **en|do|krin** [ɛndo'kri:n] ADJ *(Med)* endocrine; **En|do|kri|no|lo|gie** [ɛndokrinolo'gi:] F -, *no pl (Med)* endocrinology
En|dor|phin [ɛndɔr'fi:n] NT -s, -e endorphin
En|do|skop [ɛndo'sko:p] NT -s, -e *(Med)* endoscope
En|do|sko|pie [ɛndosko'pi:] F -, -n [-'pi:ən] *(Med)* endoscopy; **operative ~** endosurgery
en|do|sko|pisch [ɛndo'sko:pɪʃ] *(Med)* ADJ endoscopic ADV **jdn ~ operieren/untersuchen** to operate on/examine sb using endoscopy *or* an endoscope
End-: **End|pha|se** F final stage(s *pl*); **End|preis** M final price; **End|pro|dukt** NT end *or* final product; **End|punkt** M *(lit, fig)* end; *(von Buslinie etc auch)* terminus, terminal, final stop *(US)*; **End|reim** M *(Liter)* end rhyme; **End|re|sul|tat** NT final result
End|run|de F *(Sport)* finals *pl*; *(Leichtathletik, Autorennen)* final lap; *(Boxen, fig)* final round
End|run|den-: **End|run|den|spiel** NT final (match); **End|run|den|teil|neh|mer(in)** M(F) finalist
End-: **End|see** M *(Geog)* lake without an outlet; **End|sieg** M final *or* ultimate victory; **End|sil|be** F final syllable; **End|spiel** NT *(Sport)* final; *(Chess)* end game; **End|spurt** M *(Sport, fig)* final spurt; **End|sta|di|um** NT final *or* *(Med)* terminal stage; **End|stand** M *(Sport: = Punktstand)* final result *or* score; *(Rennen etc)* final positions *pl*, final ranking(s *pl*); **End|sta|ti|on** F *(Rail etc)* terminus, terminal; *(fig)* end of the line; **End|stel|le** F *(Tech)* terminal apparatus; **End|stu|fe** F final stage; **End|sum|me** F (sum) total
En|dung ['ɛndʊŋ] F -, -en *(Gram)* ending
en|dungs|los ADJ *(Gram)* without an ending
En|du|ro [ɛn'du:ro] F -, -s enduro bike
End-: **End|ur|sa|che** ['ɛntlu:ɐzaxə] F ultimate cause; *(Philos)* final cause; **End|ur|teil** ['ɛntlurtail] NT final verdict *or* judgement; **End|ver|brau|cher(in)** M(F) consumer, end user; **End|vier|zi|ger(in)** M(F) *(inf)* man/woman in his/her late forties; **End|zeit** F last days *pl*; **end|zeit|lich** ADJ *attr Phase* final; *Stimmung, Prophezeiung* apocalyptic; **End|zeit|stim|mung** F apocalyptic mood; **End|ziel** NT ultimate goal *or* aim; **End|zif|fer** F final number; **End|zu|stand** M final state; **End|zweck** M ultimate aim *or* purpose
Ener|ge|tik [enɛr'ge:tɪk] F -, *no pl (Phys)* energetics *sing*
ener|ge|tisch [enɛr'ge:tɪʃ] ADJ *(Phys)* energetic
Ener|gie [enɛr'gi:] F -, -n [-'gi:ən] *(Sci, fig)* energy; *(= Schwung auch)* vigour *(Brit)*, vigor *(US)*, vitality; **~ sparend** = **energiesparend**; **seine ganze ~ für etw einsetzen** *or* **aufbieten** to devote all one's energies to sth; **mit aller** *or* **ganzer ~** with all one's energy *or* energies; **kriminelle ~** criminal resolve
Ener|gie-: **Ener|gie|an|zei|gef** *(von Notebook etc)* battery meter; **ener|gie|arm** ADJ *Nahrung* low-energy *attr*; **ein ~es Land** a country with few sources of energy; **Ener|gie|auf|wand** M energy expenditure, expenditure of energy, (amount of) energy involved; **der ~ lohnt (sich) nicht** it's not worth the effort (involved); **Ener|gie|be|darf** M energy requirement; **ener|gie|be|wusst** ADJ energy-conscious; **Ener|gie|bi|lanz** F *(Phys)* energy budget *or* balance; **Ener|gie|dich|te** F *(Phys)* energy density; **Ener|gie|drink** M energy drink; **ener|gie|ef|fi|zi|ent** ADJ energy-efficient; **Ener|gie|ef|fi|zi|enz** F energy efficiency; **Ener|gie|farm** F *(Tech)* energy farm; **ener|gie|ge|la|den** ADJ full of energy, energetic; **Ener|gie|ge|win|nung** F generation of energy; **Ener|gie|haus|halt** M *(Physiol)* energy balance; **ener|gie|in|ten|siv** ADJ energy-intensive; **Ener|gie|knapp|heit** F energy shortage; **Ener|gie|kri|se** F energy crisis; **ener|gie|los** ADJ lacking in energy, weak; **Ener|gie|lo|sig|keit** F -, *no pl* lack of energy; **Ener|gie|po|li|tik** F energy policy; **ener|gie|po|li|tisch** ADJ energy-policy *attr*; *Konsens, Parteilinie, Sprecher* on energy policy; **Ener|gie|prin|zip** NT principle of the conservation of energy; **Ener|gie|quel|le** F energy source; **ener|gie|reich** ADJ *Strahlung, Partikel* energy-rich; **Ener|gie|re|ser|ven** PL *(Sport etc)* energy reserves *pl*; *(von Person)* spare ener-

gy *sing*, physical reserves *pl*; **Ener|gie|satz** M *(Phys)* principle of the conservation of energy; **Ener|gie|spa|ren** NT **-s**, *no pl* energy saving; *(Maßnahmen)* energy saving measures *pl*; **ener|gie|spa|rend** ADJ energy-saving

Ener|gie|spar-: **Ener|gie|spar|funk|ti|on** F energy-saving feature; **Ener|gie|spar|lam|pe** F energy-saving bulb; **Ener|gie|spar|maß|nah|men** PL energy-saving measures *pl*; **Ener|gie|spar|pro|gramm** NT energy-saving scheme *or* programme *(Brit) or* program *(US)*; **Ener|gie|spar|tas|te** F *(von Waschmaschine, Geschirrspüler etc)* energy-saving switch

Ener|gie-: **Ener|gie|steu|er** F energy tax; **Ener|gie|tech|nik** F energy-producing technique; **Ener|gie|trä|ger** M energy source; **Ener|gie|ver|brauch** M energy consumption; **Ener|gie|ver|schwen|dung** F waste of energy; **Ener|gie|ver|sor|gung** F supply of energy; **Ener|gie|ver|sor|gungs|un|ter|neh|men** NT energy supply company; **Ener|gie|wirt|schaft** F *(= Wirtschaftszweig)* energy industry; **ener|gie|wirt|schaft|lich** ADJ relating to the energy industry; **Ener|gie|zu|fuhr** F energy supply

ener|gisch [e'nɛrgɪʃ] ADJ *(= voller Energie)* energetic; *(= entschlossen, streng)* forceful, firm; *Griff, Maßnahmen* vigorous, firm; *Worte* forceful, strong; *Protest* energetic, strong; **einer Sache** *(dat)* **eine ~e Absage erteilen** to forcefully reject sth; **~ werden** to assert oneself *or* one's authority; **wenn das nicht aufhört, werde ich ~!** if this doesn't stop I'll have to put my foot down! ADV *dementieren* strongly, strenuously, emphatically; *sagen* forcefully; *verteidigen* vigorously; **~ durchgreifen** to take vigorous *or* firm action, to act vigorously *or* firmly; **etw ~ betonen** to stress *or* emphasize sth strongly

ener|vie|ren [enɛr'viːrən] *ptp* **enerviert** VT *(old)* to enervate *(form)*

en fa|mille [ã fa'mij] ADV *(geh)* en famille

En|fant ter|ri|ble [ãfã tɛ'ribl] NT **- -, -s -s** *(geh)* enfant terrible

eng [ɛŋ] ADJ **a** *(= schmal) Straße etc* narrow; *(= beengt) Raum* cramped, confined; *(= eng anliegend) Kleidung* tight, close-fitting; *(= ärmlich) Verhältnisse* straitened, reduced; *(= beschränkt) Horizont, Moralbegriff* narrow, limited, restricted; **ein Kleid ~er machen** to take a dress in; **im ~eren Sinne** in the narrow sense; **in die ~ere Wahl kommen** to be put on the short list, to be short-listed; **ein ~erer Ausschuss** a select committee

b *(= nah, dicht, vertraut)* close; **eine Feier im ~sten Kreise** a small party for close friends; **die Hochzeit fand im ~sten Kreise der Familie statt** the wedding was celebrated with just the immediate family present; **die ~ere Heimat** one's home area, the area (where) one comes from

ADV **a** *(= mit wenig Platz)* **~ beieinanderstehen** to stand very close to each other; **~ beisammenstehen** to stand close together; *(Bäume etc)* to be close together; **~ anliegend** tight(-fitting), close-fitting; **~ anliegen** to fit tightly; **~ sitzen** to be tight; **~ begrenzt** restricted, narrow; **~ gebaut sein** *(Anat)* to be narrow-hipped, to have narrow hips; **~ gebaute Frauen** women with narrow hips; **in dem Zimmer standen wir sehr ~** we were very crowded in the room; **~ zusammengedrängt sein** to be crowded together

b *(= dicht) tanzen* close together; **~ bedruckt** densely printed; **~ beschrieben** closely written; **~ nebeneinander** *or* **zusammen** close together

c *(= intim)* **~ liiert** seriously involved; **sich ~ anfreunden** to become close friends; **aufs Engste** *or* **~ste befreundet sein** to be on the closest possible terms; **~ befreundet sein** to be close friends; **mit jdm ~ befreundet sein** to be a close friend of sb; **die ~ befreundeten Mädchen/Männer** the close friends

d *(inf: = verkniffen)* **das darfst du nicht so ~ sehen** *(fig inf)* don't take it so seriously; **solche Dinge sehe ich sehr ~** I'm very particular about that type of thing; **sieh das doch nicht so ~!** don't take it so seriously!, don't make so much of it!; **es wird ~ für ihn** *(fig inf)* he doesn't have much room for manoeuvre *(Brit) or* maneuver *(US)*

En|ga|din ['ɛŋgadiːn] NT **-s das ~** the Engadine

En|ga|ge|ment [ãgaʒə'mãː] NT **-s, -s** **a** *(Theat)* engagement **b** *(geh: = Aktivität)* involvement, engagement; *(= politisches Engagement)* commitment *(für* to)

en|ga|gie|ren [ãga'ʒiːrən] *ptp* **engagiert** VT to engage VR to be/become committed *(für* to); *(in einer Beziehung)* to become involved; **er hat sich sehr dafür engagiert, dass ...** he completely committed himself to ...

en|ga|giert [ãga'ʒiːɐt] ADJ committed; **~e Literatur** (politically/socially) committed literature

En|ga|giert|heit F **-**, *no pl* commitment *(für* to); *(in einer Beziehung)* involvement

eng-: **eng|an|lie|gend** ADJ → **eng ADV a**; **eng|be|druckt** [-bədrʊkt] ADJ → **eng ADV b**; **eng|be|freun|det** ADJ → **eng ADV c**; **eng|be|grenzt** ADJ → **eng ADV a**; **eng|be|schrie|ben** [-bəʃriːbn] ADJ → **eng ADV b**; **eng|brüs|tig** [-brʏstɪç] ADJ narrow-chested

En|ge ['ɛŋə] F **-, -n** **a** *no pl (von Straße etc)* narrowness; *(von Wohnung)* confinement; *(= Gedrängtheit)* crush; *(von Kleid etc)* tightness; *(fig) (= Ärmlichkeit)* straitened circumstances *pl*, poverty; *(= Beschränktheit)* narrowness, limited *or* restricted nature **b** *(= Meerenge)* strait; *(= Engpass)* pass, defile; **jdn in die ~ treiben** *(fig)* to drive sb into a corner

En|gel ['ɛŋl] M **-s, -** *(lit, fig)* angel; **ein rettender ~** *(fig)* a saviour *(Brit) or* savior *(US)*; **ein guter ~** *(fig)* a guardian angel; **ich hörte die ~ im Himmel singen** *(inf)* it hurt like anything *(inf)*, it was agony; **er ist auch nicht gerade ein ~** *(inf)* he's no angel *(inf)*; **wir sind alle keine ~** *(prov)* none of us is perfect

En|gel|chen ['ɛŋlçən] NT **-s, -**, **En|ge|lein** ['ɛŋəlain] NT **-s, -** little angel

En|gel- → *auch* **Engels-**: **en|gel|gleich** ADJ = **engelsgleich**; **En|gel|ma|cher(in)** M(F) *(euph inf)* backstreet abortionist; **En|gel|schar** F host of angels, angelic host

En|gels-: **En|gels|ge|duld** F saintly patience; **sie hat eine ~** she has the patience of a saint; **En|gels|ge|sicht** NT angelic *or* angel('s) face, angelic looks *pl*; **en|gels|gleich** ADJ angelic; **En|gels|haar** NT angel's hair; **en|gels|rein** ADJ pure as the driven snow; **En|gels|trom|pe|te** F *(Bot)* angel's trumpet; **En|gels|zun|gen** PL **(wie) mit ~ reden** to use all one's powers of persuasion

En|gel|wurz [-vʊrts] F **-, -en** *(Bot)* angelica

En|ger|ling ['ɛŋɐlɪŋ] M **-s, -e** *(Zool)* grub *or* larva of the cockchafer *or* May bug

Eng-: **eng|her|zig** ADJ petty, hidebound; **Eng|her|zig|keit** ['ɛŋhɛrtsɪçkait] F **-**, *no pl* pettiness

engl. *abbr von* **englisch**

Eng|land ['ɛŋlant] NT **-s** England

Eng|län|der ['ɛŋlɛndɐ] M **-s, -** **a** Englishman; English boy; **die ~** *pl* the English, the Britishers *(US)*, the Brits *(inf)*; **er ist ~** he's English **b** *(Tech)* adjustable spanner *(Brit)*, monkey wrench

Eng|län|de|rin ['ɛŋlɛndərɪn] F **-, -nen** Englishwoman; English girl

Eng|lein NT **-s, -** little angel

eng|lisch ['ɛŋlɪʃ] ADJ English; *Steak* rare; **die ~e Krankheit** *(dated Med)* rickets *sing*; *(fig)* the English disease *or* sickness; **die Englische Kirche** the Anglican Church, the Church of England; **die Englischen Fräulein** *(Eccl) institute of Catholic nuns for the education of girls*; **~e Broschur** case binding → *auch* **deutsch**

eng|lisch ADJ *(Bibl)* angelic; **der Englische Gruß** the Angelic Salutation, the Ave Maria, the Hail Mary

Eng|lisch(e) ['ɛŋlɪʃ] NT English → *auch* **Deutsch(e)**

Eng|lisch-: **eng|lisch-deutsch/-fran|zö|sisch** *etc* ADJ Anglo-German/-French *etc*; *Wörterbuch* English-German/-French *etc*; **Eng|lisch|horn** NT *(Mus)* cor anglais; **Eng|lisch|kennt|nis|se** PL (a knowledge *sing* of) English, English language skills *pl*; **seine/ihre ~** his/her knowledge of English; **gute ~ Voraussetzung** *(in Annoncen)* English essential; **Eng|lisch|le|der** NT *(Tex)* moleskin; **Eng|lisch|leh|rer(in)** M(F) English teacher; *(Privatlehrer auch)* English tutor; **eng|lisch|spra|chig** ADJ *Gebiet, Minderheit* English-speaking; *Zeitung* English-language *attr*; **Eng|lisch|tra|ben** NT **-s**, *no pl* rising trot; **Eng|lisch|un|ter|richt** M **a** English lessons *pl*, English classes *pl*; *(= einzelne Stunde)* English lesson *or* class **b** *(Unterrichten)* teaching of English; *(Privat-, Einzelunterricht)* English language tuition; **der ~** teaching English, the teaching of English

Eng-: **eng|ma|schig** [-maʃɪç] ADJ close-meshed; *(fig)* close; **ein ~es soziales Netz** a comprehensive social welfare network ADV **~ stricken** to knit to a fine tension; **Eng|pass** M (narrow) pass, defile; *(= Fahrbahnverengung, fig)* bottleneck

En|gramm [ɛn'gram] NT *pl* **-gramme** *(Physiol)* engram

en gros [ã 'gro] ADV wholesale; *(fig)* en masse

En|gros- [ã'gro] *in cpds* = **Großhandels-**

En|gros|sist(in) [ãgrɔ'sɪst(ɪn)] M(F) *(Aus)* wholesale dealer, wholesaler

Eng|stel|le F narrow place, constriction; *(= Fahrbahnverengung, fig)* bottleneck

eng|stir|nig ['ɛŋʃtɪrnɪç] ADJ *(= intolerant)* narrow-minded; *(= mit begrenztem Horizont)* insular; *(im politischen Denken)* parochial

Eng|stir|nig|keit F *(= Intoleranz)* narrow-mindedness; *(= begrenzter Horizont)* insularity; *(im politischen Denken)* parochialism

enig|ma|tisch [enɪ'gmaːtɪʃ] ADJ *(liter)* enigmatic

En|jam|be|ment [ãʒãbə'mãː] NT **-s, -s** *(Poet)* enjambment

En|kel ['ɛŋkl] M **-s, -** *(= Enkelkind)* grandchild; *(= Enkelsohn)* grandson; *(= Nachfahr)* descendant; *(fig)* heir; **er ist ~ eines berühmten Geschlechts** *(geh)* he comes from a famous family *or* line

En|kel M **-s, -** *(dial)* ankle

En|ke|lin ['ɛŋkəlɪn] F **-, -nen** granddaughter

En|kel-: **En|kel|kind** NT grandchild; **En|kel|sohn** M grandson; **En|kel|toch|ter** F granddaughter

En|kla|ve [ɛn'klaːvə] F **-, -n** enclave

en masse [ã 'mas] ADV en masse

en mi|ni|a|ture [ã minja'tyːr] ADV *(geh)* in miniature

enorm [e'nɔrm] ADJ *(= riesig)* enormous; *(inf: = herrlich, kolossal)* tremendous *(inf)*; **~e Hitze/Kälte** tremendous heat/cold ADV *(= riesig)* enormously; *(inf: = herrlich, kolossal)* tremendously; *(= enorm viel)* an enormous amount; **er verdient ~** *(inf)* **er verdient ~ viel (Geld)** *(inf)* he earns an enormous amount (of money)

en pas|sant [ã pa'sã] ADV en passant, in passing

En|que|te [ã'keːt(ə), ã'kɛːt(ə)] F **-, -n** *(form)* survey; *(Aus: = Arbeitstagung)* symposium

En|que|te|kom|mis|si|on [ã'keːt-, ã'kɛːt-] F commission of inquiry, select committee

En|sem|ble [ã'sãːbl] NT **-s, -s** ensemble; *(= Besetzung)* cast

En|sem|ble|spiel [ã'sãːbl-] NT *(Theat)* ensemble

ent|ar|ten [ɛnt'lartn] *ptp* **entartet** VI *aux sein* to degenerate *(zu* into)

ent|ar|tet [ɛnt'lartət] ADJ degenerate

Ent|ar|tung F **-, -en** degeneration

Ent|ar|tungs|er|schei|nung F symptom *or* sign of degeneration

ent|äu|ßern [ɛnt'lɔysɐn] *ptp* **entäußert** VR **sich einer Sache** *(gen)* **~** *(geh)* to relinquish sth, to divest oneself of sth *(form)*; **sich ~** *(Philos)* to be realized

ent|beh|ren [ɛnt'beːrən] *ptp* **entbehrt** VT **a** (= *vermissen*) to miss; (*auch vi*: = *verzichten*) to do *or* manage without; (= *zur Verfügung stellen*) to spare **b** *auch vi* (= *verzichten*) to do *or* manage without; **wir haben jahrelang ~ müssen** for years we had/we have had to do *or* go without; **wir können ihn heute nicht ~** we cannot spare him/it today VI (= *fehlen*) **einer Sache** (*gen*) **~** (*geh*) to lack sth, to be devoid of sth

ent|behr|lich [ɛnt'beːɐlɪç] ADJ dispensable

Ent|behr|lich|keit F -, *no pl* dispensability

Ent|beh|rung F -, -en privation, deprivation, want *no pl*; **~en auf sich** (*acc*) **nehmen** to make sacrifices

ent|beh|rungs|reich, **ent|beh|rungs|voll** ADJ full of privation; **die ~en Kriegsjahre** the deprivation of the war years

ent|bei|nen [ɛnt'bainən] *ptp* **entbeint** VT *Fleisch* to bone

ent|bie|ten [ɛnt'biːtn] *ptp* **entboten** [ɛnt'boːtn] VT *irreg* (*form*) **(jdm) seinen Gruß ~** (*old*) to present one's compliments (to sb) (*form*); **der Vorsitzende entbot der Delegation herzliche Willkommensgrüße** the Chairman *or* the Chair welcomed the delegation cordially

ent|bin|den [ɛnt'bɪndn] *ptp* **entbunden** [ɛnt'bʊndn] *irreg* VT **a** *Frau* to deliver; **sie ist von einem Sohn entbunden worden** she has given birth to a son **b** (= *befreien*: *von Versprechen, Amt etc*) to release (*von* from) VI (*Frau*) to give birth

Ent|bin|dung F delivery, birth; (*von Amt etc*) release

Ent|bin|dungs-: **Ent|bin|dungs|heim** NT maternity home *or* hospital; **Ent|bin|dungs|kli|nik** F maternity clinic; **Ent|bin|dungs|pfle|ger(in)** M(F) obstetric nurse; **Ent|bin|dungs|sta|ti|on** F maternity ward

ent|blät|tern [ɛnt'blɛtɐn] *ptp* **entblättert** VT to strip (of leaves) VR to shed its/their leaves; (*hum inf*) to strip, to shed one's clothes

ent|blö|den [ɛnt'bløːdn] *ptp* **entblödet** VR (*geh*) **sich nicht ~, etw zu tun** to have the effrontery *or* audacity to do sth, to do sth unashamedly

ent|blö|ßen [ɛnt'bløːsn] *ptp* **entblößt** VT **a** *Körperteil* to bare, to expose (*auch Mil*); *Kopf* to bare, to uncover; *Schwert* to draw, to unsheathe; (*fig*) *sein Innenleben* to lay bare, to reveal; **er hat sich entblößt** (*Exhibitionist*) he exposed himself; (*seinen wahren Charakter*) he showed his true colours (*Brit*) *or* colors (*US*) **b** (*liter*: = *des Schutzes berauben*) to divest, to denude (*form*)

ent|blößt [ɛnt'bløːst] ADJ bare

Ent|blö|ßung F -, -en (*von Körperteil etc*) baring, exposure; (*Mil*) exposure; (*von Innenleben*) laying bare, revelation

ent|bren|nen [ɛnt'brɛnən] *ptp* **entbrannt** [ɛnt'brant] VI *irreg aux sein* (*liter*) (*Kampf, Streit, Zorn*) to flare up, to erupt; (*Leidenschaft, Liebe*) to be (a)roused; **in heißer Liebe zu jdm** *or* **für jdn ~** to fall passionately in love with sb; **in** *or* **von Leidenschaft/Wut ~** to become inflamed with passion/anger

ent|bü|ro|kra|ti|sie|ren [ɛntbyrokratiˈziːrən] *ptp* **entbürokratisiert** VT to free of *or* from bureaucracy, to debureaucratize

Ent|bü|ro|kra|ti|sie|rung F -, -en freeing from bureaucracy, debureaucratization

Ent|chen ['ɛntçən] NT -s, - *dim von* **Ente** duckling

ent|de|cken [ɛnt'dɛkn] *ptp* **entdeckt** VT **a** (= *finden*) to discover; *Fehler* to discover, to detect, to spot; (*in der Ferne*) to discern, to spot; (*in einer Menge*) to spot **b** (*old*: = *offenbaren*) **jdm etw ~** to reveal *or* discover (*obs*) sth to sb VR **sich jdm ~** (*old*) to reveal *or* discover (*obs*) oneself to sb (*form*)

Ent|de|cker [ɛnt'dɛkɐ] M -s, -, **Ent|de|cke|rin** [-ərɪn] F -, -nen discoverer

Ent|de|cker|freu|de F joy(s *pl*) *or* thrill of discovery

Ent|de|ckung F discovery; (*von Fehler auch*) detection, spotting; (= *etw Entdecktes auch*) find

Ent|de|ckungs|fahrt F, **Ent|de|ckungs|rei|se** F voyage of discovery; (*zu Lande*) expedition of discovery; **auf ~ gehen** (*hum inf*) to go exploring

ent|dra|ma|ti|sie|ren [ɛntdramatiˈziːrən] *ptp* **entdramatisiert** VT (*lit, fig*) to defuse, to take the heat out of (*inf*)

En|te ['ɛntə] F -, -n duck; (*Press inf*) canard, hoax, false report; (*Aut inf*) Citroën 2CV, deux-chevaux → **lahm**

ent|eh|ren [ɛnt'leːrən] *ptp* **entehrt** VT to dishonour (*Brit*), to dishonor (*US*); (= *entwürdigen*) to degrade; (= *verleumden*) to defame; (= *entjungfern*) to deflower; **~d** degrading; **sich ~** to degrade *or* disgrace oneself

Ent|eh|rung F dishonouring (*Brit*), dishonoring (*US*); (= *Entwürdigung*) degradation; (= *Verleumdung*) defamation; (= *Entjungferung*) defloration

ent|eig|nen [ɛnt'laignən] *ptp* **enteignet** VT to expropriate; *Besitzer* to dispossess

Ent|eig|nung F expropriation; (*von Besitzer*) dispossession

ent|ei|len [ɛnt'lailən] *ptp* **enteilt** VI *aux sein* (*old*) to hasten away (*liter*); (*liter*: *Zeit*) to fly by

ent|ei|sen [ɛnt'laizn] *ptp* **enteist** VT to de-ice; *Kühlschrank* to defrost

ent|ei|sent [ɛnt'laiznt] ADJ *Mineralwasser* iron-reduced

Ent|ei|sung F -, -en de-icing; (*von Kühlschrank*) defrosting

Ent|ei|sungs-: **Ent|ei|sungs|an|la|ge** F de-icing unit; **Ent|ei|sungs|mit|tel** NT de-icer

ent|emo|ti|o|na|li|sie|ren [ɛntlemotsionaliˈziːrən] *ptp* **entemotionalisiert** VT to de-emotionalize

En|ten-: **En|ten|bra|ten** M roast duck; **En|ten|brust** F breast of duck; **En|ten|ei** [-lai] NT duck's egg; **En|ten|flott** NT, **En|ten|grieß** M, **En|ten|grün** NT, **En|ten|grüt|ze** F duckweed; **En|ten|klein** NT -s, *no pl* (*Cook*) duck's giblets *pl* (and trimmings *pl*); **En|ten|kü|ken** NT duckling

En|ten|te [ã'tãːt(ə)] F -, -n (*Pol*) entente

En|ter|beil ['ɛntɐ-] NT boarding axe (*Brit*) *or* ax (*US*)

ent|er|ben [ɛnt'lɛrbn] *ptp* **enterbt** VT to disinherit

En|ter|brü|cke ['ɛntɐ-] F boarding plank

Ent|er|bung F -, -en disinheriting

En|ter|ha|ken ['ɛntɐ-] M grappling iron *or* hook

En|te|rich ['ɛntərɪç] M -s, -e drake

en|tern ['ɛntɐn] VT **a** (= *stürmen*) *Schiff, Haus* to storm **b** (*fig*) (= *betreten*) to enter; (= *erobern*) *Markt, Land* to conquer VI *aux sein* (*Naut*) to board

En|ter|tai|ner [ɛntɐ'teːnɐ] M -s, -, **En|ter|tai|ne|rin** [-ərɪn] F -, -nen entertainer

En|ter-Tas|te ['ɛntɐ-] F (*Comput*) enter key

entf. *abbr von* **entfällt** n/a

ent|fa|chen [ɛnt'faxn] *ptp* **entfacht** VT (*geh*) *Feuer* to kindle; *Leidenschaft, Begierde* to arouse, to kindle (the flames of); *Krieg, Streit* to provoke

ent|fah|ren [ɛnt'faːrən] *ptp* **entfahren** VI *irreg aux sein* **jdm ~** to escape sb's lips; **Blödsinn! entfuhr es ihm** nonsense, he cried inadvertently; **ihr ist ein kleiner Furz ~** (*inf*) she accidentally let off a little fart (*sl*)

ent|fal|len [ɛnt'falən] *ptp* **entfallen** VI *irreg aux sein +dat* **a** (*fig*: *aus dem Gedächtnis*) **jdm ~** to slip sb's mind, to escape sb; **der Name ist mir ~** the name has slipped my mind, the name escapes me **b** (= *nicht in Betracht kommen*) not to apply, to be inapplicable; (= *wegfallen*) to be dropped; (= *erlöschen*) to lapse; **dieser Punkt der Tagesordnung entfällt** this point on the agenda has been dropped **c auf jdn/etw ~** (*Geld, Kosten*) to be allotted *or* apportioned to sb/sth; **auf jeden ~ 100 Euro** (= *erhalten*) each person will receive 100 euros; (= *bezahlen müssen*) each person will pay 100 euros **d** (*form*: = *herunterfallen*) **jds Händen ~** to slip *or* fall *or* drop from sb's hands; **das Glas entfiel ihm** he dropped the glass

ent|fal|ten [ɛnt'faltn] *ptp* **entfaltet** VT **a** (= *auseinanderlegen*) to unfold, to open *or* spread out **b** (*fig*) (= *entwickeln*) *Kräfte, Begabung, Theorie* to develop; (= *beginnen*) *Tätigkeit* to launch into; (= *darlegen*) *Plan, Gedankengänge* to set forth *or* out, to unfold, to expound; **seine Fähigkeiten voll ~** to develop one's abilities to the full **c** (*fig*: = *zeigen*) *Pracht, Prunk* to display, to exhibit VR (*Knospe, Blüte*) to open, to unfold; (*fig*) to develop, to unfold, to blossom (out); **der Garten hat sich zu voller Pracht entfaltet** the garden blossomed (out) into its full magnificence; **hier kann ich mich nicht ~** I can't make full use of my abilities here, I'm held back here

Ent|fal|tung F -, -en unfolding; (*von Blüte auch*) opening; (*fig*) (= *Entwicklung*) development; (*einer Tätigkeit*) launching into; (= *Darstellung*) (*eines Planes, Gedankens*) exposition, setting out, unfolding; (*von Prunk, Tatkraft*) display; **zur ~ kommen** to develop, to blossom

Ent|fal|tungs|mög|lich|kei|ten PL scope *sing or* opportunity for (personal) development

ent|fär|ben [ɛnt'fɛrbn] *ptp* **entfärbt** VT to take the colour (*Brit*) *or* color (*US*) out of, to decolour (*Brit Tech*), to decolor (*US Tech*), to decolorize (*Tech*); (= *bleichen*) to bleach; **das Entfärben** the removal of colour (*Brit*) *or* color (*US*), decolorization (*Tech*) VR (*Stoff, Blätter*) to lose (its/their) colour (*Brit*) *or* color (*US*)

Ent|fär|ber M, **Ent|fär|bungs|mit|tel** NT colour (*Brit*) *or* color (*US*) remover, dye remover, decolorant (*Tech*)

ent|fer|nen [ɛnt'fɛrnən] *ptp* **entfernt** VT to remove (*von, aus* from); **jdn aus der Schule ~** to expel sb from school; **das entfernt uns (weit) vom Thema** that takes us a long way from our subject VR **a sich (von** *or* **aus etw) ~** (= *weggehen*) to go away (from sth), to leave (sth); (= *abfahren, abziehen*) to move off (from sth), to depart (from sth); **sich von seinem Posten/Arbeitsplatz ~** to leave one's post/position; **sich unerlaubt von der Truppe ~** (*Mil*) to go absent without leave; **sich zu weit ~** to go too far away **b** (*fig*) (*von* from) (*von jdm*) to become estranged; (*von Thema*) to depart, to digress; (*von Wahrheit*) to depart, to deviate; **er hat sich sehr weit von seinen früheren Ansichten entfernt** he has come a long way from his earlier views

ent|fernt [ɛnt'fɛrnt] ADJ *Ort, Verwandter* distant; (= *abgelegen*) remote; (= *gering*) *Ähnlichkeit* distant, remote, vague; **10 km ~ von** 10km (away) from; **das Haus liegt 2 km ~** the house is 2km away; **aus den ~esten Ländern** from the furthest corners of the globe; **ich hatte nicht den ~esten Verdacht** I didn't have the slightest *or* remotest suspicion → **weit** ADV remotely, slightly; **nicht einmal ~ (so gut/hübsch** *etc*) not even remotely (as good/pretty *etc*); **~ verwandt** distantly related; **er erinnert mich ~ an meinen Onkel** he reminds me slightly *or* vaguely of my uncle; **das hat nur ~ mit dieser Angelegenheit zu tun** that has only a distant bearing on this matter, that is only vaguely related to this matter; **nicht im Entferntesten!** not in the slightest *or* least!

Ent|fer|nung F -, -en **a** distance; (*Mil*: *bei Waffen*) range; **man hört das Echo auf große ~ (hin)** you can hear the echo from a great distance *or* a long way away; **aus** *or* **in der ~ (hörte er ...)** in the distance (he heard ...); **aus kurzer/großer ~ (schießen)** (to fire) at *or* from close/long range; **aus einiger ~** from a distance; **in einiger ~** at a distance; **etw auf eine ~ von 50 Meter**

treffen to hit sth at a distance of 50 metres; **in acht Kilometer(n)** ~ eight kilometres *(Brit)* or kilometers *(US)* away
b *(= das Entfernen)* removal; *(aus der Schule)* expulsion; **unerlaubte ~ (von der Truppe)** absence without leave; **unerlaubte ~ vom Posten** *etc* absence from one's post *etc* without permission

Ent|fer|nungs|mes|ser M **-s, -** *(Mil, Phot)* rangefinder

Ent|fer|nungs|tas|te F *(Comput)* delete key

ent|fes|seln [ɛnt'fɛsln] *ptp* **entfesselt** VT *(fig)* to unleash

ent|fes|selt [ɛnt'fɛslt] ADJ unleashed; *Leidenschaft, Trieb* unbridled, uncontrolled; *Mensch* wild; *Naturgewalten* raging; **vor Zorn/Begeisterung** ~ wild with rage/enthusiasm; **der ~e Prometheus** Prometheus Unbound

ent|fet|ten [ɛnt'fɛtn] *ptp* **entfettet** VT to remove the grease from, to degrease *(Tech)*; *Wolle* to scour

Ent|fet|tung F **-, -en** **a** *(= das Entfetten)* removal of grease (from), degreasing; *(von Wolle)* scouring **b** *(= Gewichtsabnahme)* losing fat

Ent|fet|tungs|kur F = **Schlankheitskur**

ent|feuch|ten [ɛnt'fɔyçtn] *ptp* **entfeuchtet** [-tət] VT *Luft* to dehumidify; *Mauer* to dry out

ent|flamm|bar ADJ inflammable; *(fig) Hass* easily aroused

Ent|flamm|bar|keit F -, *no pl* inflammability

ent|flam|men [ɛnt'flamən] *ptp* **entflammt** VT *(fig)* to (a)rouse; *Leidenschaft, Hass auch* to inflame; *Begeisterung* to fire VR *(fig)* to be (a)roused *or* fired *or* inflamed VI *aux sein* to burst into flames, to catch fire, to ignite *(Chem etc)*; *(fig) (Zorn, Streit)* to flare up; *(Leidenschaft, Liebe)* to be (a)roused *or* inflamed; **für etw entflammt sein** to be fired with enthusiasm for sth; **in Liebe ~/entflammt sein** to fall/be passionately in love

ent|flech|ten [ɛnt'flɛçtn] *ptp* **entflochten** [ɛnt'flɔxtn] VT *irreg Konzern, Kartell etc* to break up

Ent|flech|tung F **-, -en** *(von Konzern, Kartell)* breaking up

ent|fle|cken [ɛnt'flɛkn] *ptp* **entfleckt** VT to remove the stain(s) from

ent|fleu|chen [ɛnt'flɔyçn] *ptp* **entfleucht** VI *aux sein (obs: = wegfliegen)* to fly away; *(hum: = weggehen)* to be off *(inf)*

ent|flie|gen [ɛnt'fli:gn] *ptp* **entflogen** [ɛnt'flo:gn] VI *irreg aux sein* to fly away, to escape (*+dat or aus* from)

ent|flie|hen [ɛnt'fli:ən] *ptp* **entflohen** [ɛnt'flo:ən] VI *irreg aux sein (geh)* **a** *(= entkommen)* to escape, to flee (*+dat or aus* from); **dem Lärm/der Unrast** *etc* ~ to escape or flee (from) the noise/unrest *etc* **b** (*= vergehen: Zeit, Jugend etc)* to fly past

ent|frem|den [ɛnt'frɛmdn] *ptp* **entfremdet** VT to alienate *(auch Sociol, Philos)*, to estrange; **jdn einem Menschen/einer Sache** *(dat)* ~ to alienate *or* estrange sb from sb/sth; **die lange Trennung hat die Freunde (einander) entfremdet** the long separation made the two friends strangers to each other; **entfremdete Arbeit** *(Sociol)* alienated work; **etw seinem Zweck** ~ to use sth for the wrong purpose, not to use sth for its intended purpose
VR to become alienated *or* estranged (*dat* from); **er hat sich seiner Frau ganz entfremdet** he has become completely alienated from his wife, he has become a complete stranger to his wife; **durch die lange Abwesenheit habe ich mich** *or* **bin ich der Stadt ganz entfremdet** my long absence has made me a stranger to the city

Ent|frem|dung F **-, -en** estrangement; *(Sociol, Philos)* alienation

ent|freun|den [ɛnt'frɔyndn] VT *(Internet)* to unfriend

ent|fros|ten [ɛnt'frɔstn] *ptp* **entfrostet** VT to defrost

Ent|fros|ter [ɛnt'frɔstɐ] M **-s, -** defroster

ent|füh|ren [ɛnt'fy:rən] *ptp* **entführt** VT *jdn* to abduct, to kidnap; *Beute etc* to carry off, to make off with; *LKW, Flugzeug* to hijack; *Mädchen (mit Zustimmung zur Heirat)* to elope with, to run off with; *(hum inf: = wegnehmen)* to borrow *(often hum)*; **sie ließ sich von ihrem Liebhaber ~** she eloped with her lover; **wer hat mir denn meinen Bleistift entführt?** *(inf)* who's made off with my pencil? *(inf)*

Ent|füh|rer(in) M(F) **a** abductor, kidnapper **b** *(von Fahrzeug)* hijacker; *(von Flugzeug)* hijacker, skyjacker *(inf)*

Ent|füh|rung F abduction, kidnapping; *(von Flugzeug, LKW)* hijacking; *(von Mädchen mit Zustimmung zur Heirat)* elopement; **„Die ~ aus dem Serail"** "The Abduction from the Seraglio"

ent|ga|sen [ɛnt'ga:zn] *ptp* **entgast** VT *(Chem)* to degas

ent|ge|gen [ɛnt'ge:gn] ADV *(geh)* **dem Licht/der Zukunft** *etc* **~!** on toward(s) the light/future *etc*!; **neuen Ufern/Abenteuern ~!** on to new shores/adventures! PREP *+dat* contrary to, against; ~ **meiner Bitte** contrary to my request; ~ **allen Erwartungen, allen Erwartungen** ~ contrary to all *or* against all expectation(s)

ent|ge|gen+ar|bei|ten VI *sep +dat* to oppose, to work against

ent|ge|gen+bli|cken VI *sep* = **entgegensehen**

ent|ge|gen+brin|gen VT *sep irreg* **jdm etw** ~ to bring sth to sb; *(fig) Achtung, Freundschaft etc* to show *or* evince sth for sb

ent|ge|gen+ei|len VI *sep aux sein +dat (geh)* to rush toward(s); *(um jdn zu treffen)* to rush to meet

ent|ge|gen+fah|ren VI *sep irreg aux sein +dat* to travel toward(s), to approach; *(um jdn zu treffen)* to travel to meet; *(mit dem Auto)* to drive toward(s)/to meet

ent|ge|gen+fie|bern VI *sep (inf)* **einer Sache** ~ to feverishly await sth; *(ängstlich)* to wait for *or* to await sth with bated breath *or stärker* fear and trembling

ent|ge|gen+ge|hen VI *sep irreg aux sein +dat* to go toward(s), to approach; *(um jdn zu treffen)* to go to meet; *(fig) einer Gefahr, dem Tode, der Zukunft* to face; **dem Ende ~** *(Leben, Krieg)* to draw to a close, to approach its end; **seinem Untergang/Schwierigkeiten** ~ to be heading for disaster/difficulties; **seiner Vollendung** ~ to near *or* approach completion

ent|ge|gen|ge|setzt ADJ *Richtung, Meinung* opposite; *Charakter auch* contrasting; *(fig: = einander widersprechend) Interessen, Meinungen* opposing *attr*, opposed, conflicting *attr*; **einander ~e Interessen/Meinungen** *etc* opposing *or* conflicting interests/views *etc* ADV **genau ~ denken/handeln** *etc* to think/do *etc* exactly the opposite

ent|ge|gen+hal|ten VT *sep irreg +dat* **a** **jdm etw** ~ to hold sth out toward(s) sb **b** *(fig)* **einer Sache ~, dass ...** to object to sth that ...; **dieser Ansicht muss man ~, dass ...** against this view it must be objected that ...

ent|ge|gen+han|deln VI *sep* = **zuwiderhandeln**

ent|ge|gen+kom|men VI *sep irreg aux sein +dat* to come toward(s), to approach; *(um jdn zu treffen)* to (come to) meet; *(fig)* to accommodate; *Wünschen, Bitten* to accommodate, to meet, to comply with; **jdm auf halbem Wege ~** *(lit, fig)* to meet sb halfway; **das kommt unseren Plänen/Vorstellungen** *etc* **sehr entgegen** that fits in very well with our plans/ideas *etc*; **Ihr Vorschlag kommt mir sehr entgegen** I find your suggestion very congenial; **können Sie uns preislich etwas ~?** can you adjust your price a little?

Ent|ge|gen|kom|men NT *(= Gefälligkeit)* kindness, obligingness; *(= Zugeständnis)* concession, accommodation

ent|ge|gen|kom|mend ADJ **a** *Fahrzeug* oncoming **b** *(fig)* obliging, accommodating

ent|ge|gen|kom|men|der|wei|se ADV obligingly, accommodatingly; *(als Zugeständnis)* as a concession

ent|ge|gen+lau|fen VI *sep irreg aux sein +dat* to run toward(s); *(um jdn zu treffen)* to run to meet; *(fig)* to run contrary *or* counter to

Ent|ge|gen|nah|me [-na:mə] F -, *no pl (form) (= Empfang)* receipt; *(= Annahme)* acceptance; **bei** ~ on receipt/acceptance

ent|ge|gen+neh|men VT *sep irreg (= empfangen)* to receive; *(= annehmen)* to accept; **nehmen Sie meinen Dank entgegen** *(form)* please accept my thanks

ent|ge|gen+schau|en VI *sep (esp dial)* = **entgegensehen**

ent|ge|gen+schla|gen VI *sep irreg aux sein +dat (Geruch, Hass)* to confront, to meet; *(Flammen auch)* to leap toward(s); *(Jubel, Begeisterung)* to meet, to greet; **ihm schlug Jubel entgegen** he was greeted with jubilation; **ihm schlug ein widerlicher Geruch entgegen** he was confronted by a nauseating smell

ent|ge|gen+se|hen VI *sep irreg* **a** **jdm** ~ to see sb coming **b** *(fig)* **einer Sache** *(dat)* ~ to await sth; *(freudig)* to look forward to sth; **einer Sache ~ müssen** to have to expect *or* face sth; **Ihrer baldigen Antwort ~d** *(form)* in anticipation of *or* looking forward to your early reply

ent|ge|gen+set|zen VT *sep +dat* **etw einer Sache** ~ to set sth against sth; **wir können diesen Forderungen nichts ~** we have nothing to counter these claims with; **einer Sache Alternativen ~** to put *or* pose alternatives to sth; **dem habe ich entgegenzusetzen, dass ...** against that I'd like to say that ...; **die Gewerkschaften hatten den Regierungsvorschlägen nichts entgegenzusetzen** the unions had nothing to offer in reply to the government's suggestions; **jdm/einer Sache Widerstand ~** to put up *or* offer resistance to sb/sth; **ihren Anklagen konnte er nichts ~** he could find no reply to her accusations → **entgegengesetzt**

ent|ge|gen+ste|hen VI *sep irreg +dat (fig)* to stand in the way of, to be an obstacle to; **dem steht entgegen, dass ...** what stands in the way of that is that ...; **dem steht nichts entgegen** there's no obstacle to that, there's nothing against that; **was steht dem entgegen?** what obstacle is there to that?

ent|ge|gen+stel|len *sep +dat* VT = **entgegensetzen** VR **sich jdm/einer Sache ~** to resist sb/sth, to oppose sb/sth

ent|ge|gen+stem|men VR *sep* **sich jdm/einer Sache ~** to pit oneself against sb/sth, to oppose sb/sth

ent|ge|gen+stre|cken VT *sep* **jdm etw** ~ to hold out sth to sb

ent|ge|gen+stür|zen VI *sep aux sein +dat* to fall upon; *(= zueilen auf)* to rush toward(s)

ent|ge|gen+tre|ten VI *sep irreg aux sein +dat* to step *or* walk up to; *dem Feind* to go into action against; *einer Politik, Forderungen* to oppose; *Behauptungen, Vorurteilen* to counter; *einer Gefahr, Unsitten* to take steps against, to act against

ent|ge|gen+wir|ken VI *sep +dat* to counteract

ent|geg|nen [ɛnt'ge:gnən] *ptp* **entgegnet** VTI to reply; *(kurz, barsch)* to retort (*auf +acc* to); **er entgegnete nichts** he made no reply; **darauf wusste er nichts zu ~** he didn't know what to reply to that

Ent|geg|nung F **-, -en** reply; *(kurz, barsch)* retort

ent|ge|hen [ɛnt'ge:ən] *ptp* **entgangen** [ɛnt'gaŋən] VI *irreg aux sein +dat* **a** *(= entkommen) Verfolgern, dem Feind* to elude, to escape (from); *dem Schicksal, der Gefahr, Strafe* to escape, to avoid
b *(fig: = nicht bemerkt werden)* **dieser Fehler ist mir entgangen** I failed to notice *or* I missed this mistake, this mistake escaped my notice; **mir ist kein Wort entgangen** I didn't miss a word (of it); **es ist meiner Aufmerksamkeit nicht entgangen, dass ...** it has not escaped my attention that ...; **ihr entgeht nichts** she doesn't miss anything *or* a thing; **es ist ihm nicht entgangen, dass ...** he didn't fail to notice that ...,

it didn't escape him that ...; **sich** *(dat)* **etw ~ lassen** to miss sth

ent|geis|tert [ɛnt'gaistɐt] ADJ dumbfounded, thunderstruck, flabbergasted *(inf)*; *Lachen* astonished ADV **er starrte mich ganz ~ an** he stared at me quite dumbfounded *or* thunderstruck *or* flabbergasted *(inf)*; **er reagierte ~** he reacted with complete astonishment

Ent|gelt [ɛnt'gɛlt] NT **-(e)s, -e** *(form)* **a** *(= Bezahlung)* remuneration *(form)*; *(= Entschädigung)* recompense *(form)*, compensation; *(= Anerkennung)* reward **b** *(= Gebühr)* fee, consideration; **gegen ~** for a fee *or* consideration; **jdm etw gegen ~ abgeben** to give sb sth for a consideration

ent|gel|ten [ɛnt'gɛltn] *ptp* **entgolten** [ɛnt'gɔltn] VT *irreg (geh)* **a** *(= büßen)* to pay for; **jdn etw ~ lassen** to make sb pay *or* suffer for sth **b** *(= vergüten)* **jdm etw ~** to repay sb for sth

ent|gif|ten [ɛnt'gɪftn] *ptp* **entgiftet** VT to decontaminate; *(Med)* to detoxicate, to detoxify

Ent|gif|tung F **-, -en** decontamination; *(Med)* detoxication, detoxification

Ent|gif|tungs|sta|ti|on F *(Med)* detox(ification) centre *(Brit)* or center *(US)*

ent|glei|sen [ɛnt'glaizn] *ptp* **entgleist** VI *aux sein* **a** *(Rail)* to be derailed; **einen Zug zum Entgleisen bringen** *or* **~ lassen** to derail a train **b** *(fig: Mensch)* to misbehave; *(= einen Fauxpas begehen)* to commit a faux pas, to drop a clanger *(Brit inf)*, to put one's foot in it

Ent|glei|sung F **-, -en** derailment; *(fig)* faux pas, gaffe, clanger *(Brit inf)*

ent|glei|ten [ɛnt'glaitn] *ptp* **entglitten** [ɛnt'glɪtn] VI *irreg aux sein +dat* to slip; **jdm** *or* **jds Hand ~** to slip from *or* out of sb's grasp; **jdm/einer Sache ~** *(fig)* to slip away from sb/sth

ent|got|ten [ɛnt'gɔtn] *ptp* **entgottet**, **ent|göt|tern** [ɛnt'gœtɐn] *ptp* **entgöttert** VT *(liter)* to remove god(s) from; **die entgötterte Welt** the godless world, the world without god(s)

Ent|göt|te|rung F **-, -en**, **Ent|got|tung** F **-, -en** *(liter)* removal of god(s) (*+gen* from); **die ~ des Olymp** the banishing of the gods from Olympus

ent|grä|ten [ɛnt'grɛ:tn] *ptp* **entgrätet** VT *Fisch* to fillet, to bone

ent|haa|ren [ɛnt'ha:rən] *ptp* **enthaart** VT to remove unwanted hair from, to depilate *(form)*

Ent|haa|rungs-: **Ent|haa|rungs|creme** F depilatory *or* hair removal cream; **Ent|haa|rungs|mit|tel** NT depilatory, hair removal agent

ent|hal|ten [ɛnt'haltn] *ptp* **enthalten** *irreg* VT to contain; **(mit) ~ sein in** *(+dat)* to be included in VR **a** *(geh)* **sich einer Sache** *(gen)* **~** to abstain from sth; **sich nicht ~ können, etw zu tun** to be unable to refrain from doing sth; **sich einer Bemerkung nicht ~ können** to be unable to refrain from making a remark **b** **sich (der Stimme) ~** to abstain

ent|halt|sam [ɛnt'haltza:m] ADJ abstemious; *(sexuell)* chaste; *(= mäßig)* moderate ADV **~ leben** to be abstinent; *(= sexuell)* to be celibate

Ent|halt|sam|keit F **-,** *no pl* abstinence; *(sexuell)* chastity, abstinence; *(= Mäßigkeit)* moderation

Ent|hal|tung F abstinence; *(= Stimmenthaltung)* abstention

ent|här|ten [ɛnt'hɛrtn] *ptp* **enthärtet** VT *Wasser* to soften

Ent|här|ter M (water) softener

Ent|här|tung F *(von Wasser)* softening; *(von Metall)* annealing

Ent|här|tungs|mit|tel NT (water) softener

ent|haup|ten [ɛnt'hauptn] *ptp* **enthauptet** VT to decapitate; *(als Hinrichtung auch)* to behead

Ent|haup|tung F **-, -en** decapitation; *(als Hinrichtung auch)* beheading

ent|häu|ten [ɛnt'hɔytn] *ptp* **enthäutet** VT to skin; *(als Folter etc)* to flay

ent|he|ben [ɛnt'he:bn] *ptp* **enthoben** [ɛnt'ho:bn] VT *irreg* **jdn einer Sache** *(gen)* **~** to relieve sb of sth

ent|hei|li|gen [ɛnt'hailɪgn] *ptp* **entheiligt** VT to desecrate, to profane

Ent|hei|li|gung F **-, -en** desecration, profanation

ent|hem|men [ɛnt'hɛmən] *ptp* **enthemmt** VTI **jdn ~** to make sb lose his inhibitions, to free sb from his inhibitions; **Alkohol wirkt ~d** alcohol has a disinhibiting effect; **(moralisch** *etc***) völlig enthemmt sein** to have no (moral *etc*) inhibitions whatsoever, to have lost one's (moral *etc*) inhibitions

ent|hemmt [ɛnt'hɛmt] *ptp von* **enthemmen** ADJ uninhibited, free of inhibitions → *auch* **enthemmen**

Ent|hemmt|heit [ɛnt'hɛmthait] F **-,** *no pl* loss of inhibitions

ent|hül|len [ɛnt'hʏlən] *ptp* **enthüllt** VT to uncover, to reveal; *Skandal, Lüge auch* to expose; *Denkmal, Gesicht* to unveil; *Geheimnis, Plan, Hintergründe* to reveal VR *(lit, hum)* to reveal oneself; **er hat sich in seiner ganzen Gemeinheit enthüllt** he revealed himself for the villain he was

Ent|hül|lung F **-, -en** uncovering, revealing; *(von Skandal, Lüge auch)* exposure; *(von Denkmal, Gesicht)* unveiling; **noch eine sensationelle ~** another sensational revelation *or* disclosure

Ent|hül|lungs- *in cpds* investigative; **Ent|hül|lungs|au|tor(in)** M(F) investigative author; **Ent|hül|lungs|blatt** NT *(= Zeitung)* scandal sheet; **Ent|hül|lungs|buch** NT exposé; **Ent|hül|lungs|jour|na|lis|mus** M investigative journalism; **Ent|hül|lungs|jour|na|list(in)** M(F) investigative journalist

ent|hül|sen [ɛnt'hʏlzn] *ptp* **enthülst** VT to shell; *Getreide* to husk

En|thu|si|as|mus [ɛntu'ziasmʊs] M **-,** *no pl* enthusiasm

En|thu|si|ast [ɛntu'ziast] M **-en, -en**, **En|thu|si|as|tin** [-'ziastɪn] F **-, -nen** enthusiast

en|thu|si|as|tisch [ɛntu'ziastɪʃ] ADJ enthusiastic ADV enthusiastically

ent|ideo|lo|gi|sie|ren [ɛntlideologi'zi:rən] *ptp* **entideologisiert** VT to free from ideology VR *(Partei)* to dispense with one's ideology

Ent|ideo|lo|gi|sie|rung F freeing from ideology; *(= das Entideologisiertwerden)* decreasing ideological commitment

En|ti|tät [ɛnti'tɛ:t] F **-, -en** *(Philos)* entity

ent|jung|fern [ɛnt'jʊŋfɐn] *ptp* **entjungfert** VT to deflower

Ent|jung|fe|rung F **-, -en** defloration

ent|kal|ken [ɛnt'kalkn] *ptp* **entkalkt** VT to decalcify

ent|kei|men [ɛnt'kaimən] *ptp* **entkeimt** VT *(= keimfrei machen)* to sterilize

ent|ker|nen [ɛnt'kɛrnən] *ptp* **entkernt** VT **a** *Orangen etc* to remove the pips from; *Kernobst* to core; *Steinobst* to stone; *(Biol) Zellen* to denucleate **b** *Gebäude* to gut; *Wohngebiet (= Dichte reduzieren)* to reduce the density of; *(= dezentralisieren)* to decentralize, to disperse

Ent|ker|ner [ɛnt'kɛrnɐ] M **-s, -** *(für Kernobst)* corer; *(für Steinobst)* stoner

ent|klei|den [ɛnt'klaidn] *ptp* **entkleidet** *(geh)* VT to undress; **jdn einer Sache** *(gen)* **~** *(fig)* to strip *or* divest sb of sth VR to undress, to take one's clothes off

ent|kno|ten [ɛnt'kno:tn] *ptp* **entknotet** VT to untie, to undo; *(fig: = entwirren)* to unravel

ent|kof|fe|i|niert [ɛntkɔfei'ni:ɐt] ADJ decaffeinated

ent|ko|lo|ni|a|li|sie|ren [ɛntkoloniali'zi:rən] *ptp* **entkolonialisiert** VT to decolonialize

Ent|ko|lo|ni|a|li|sie|rung F decolonialization

ent|kom|men [ɛnt'kɔmən] *ptp* **entkommen** VI *irreg aux sein* to escape, to get away (*+dat, aus* from)

Ent|kom|men NT escape

Ent|kon|ser|vie|rung F *(von Auto)* de-waxing

ent|kor|ken [ɛnt'kɔrkn] *ptp* **entkorkt** VT *Flasche* to uncork

ent|kör|per|licht [ɛnt'kœrpɐlɪçt] ADJ *(liter)* incorporeal

ent|kräf|ten [ɛnt'krɛftn] *ptp* **entkräftet** VT *(= schwächen)* to weaken, to debilitate, to enfeeble; *(= erschöpfen)* to exhaust, to wear out; *(fig: = widerlegen) Behauptung etc* to refute, to invalidate

Ent|kräf|tung F **-, -en** weakening, debilitation, enfeeblement; *(= Erschöpfung)* exhaustion; *(fig: = Widerlegung)* refutation, invalidation

ent|kramp|fen [ɛnt'krampfn] *ptp* **entkrampft** VT *(fig)* to relax, to ease; *Lage* to ease; **eine entkrampfte Atmosphäre** a relaxed atmosphere

Ent|kramp|fung F **-, -en** *(fig)* relaxation, easing

ent|kri|mi|na|li|sie|ren [ɛntkriminali'zi:rən] *ptp* **entkriminalisiert** VT to decriminalize

Ent|kri|mi|na|li|sie|rung [ɛntkriminali'zi:rʊŋ] F *(von Haschischkonsum etc)* decriminalization

ent|la|den [ɛnt'la:dn] *ptp* **entladen** *irreg* VT to unload; *Batterie etc* to discharge VR *(Gewitter)* to break; *(Schusswaffe)* to go off, to discharge *(form)*; *(elektrische Spannung, Batterie etc)* to discharge; *(langsam)* to run down; *(Sprengladung)* to explode, to go off; *(fig: Emotion)* to vent itself; **sein Zorn entlud sich über mir** he vented his anger on me

Ent|la|dung F **a** *(= das Entladen)* unloading **b** *(von Gewitter)* breaking; *(von Schusswaffe, elektrisch)* discharge; *(von Sprengladung)* explosion; *(von Emotionen)* venting; **etw zur ~ bringen** *(Mil, fig)* to detonate sth

ent|lang [ɛnt'laŋ] PREP *+acc, +dat or (rare) +gen* along; **den** *or (rare)* **dem Fluss ~, ~ dem Fluss** *or (rare)* **des Flusses** along the river ADV along; **am Bach ~** along (by the side of) the stream; **am Haus ~** along (by) the side of the house; **hier ~** this way

ent|lang- PREF along; **ent|lang+ge|hen** VTI *sep irreg aux sein* to walk along, to go along *(auch fig)*; **am Haus ~** to walk along by the side of the house; **ent|lang+schram|men** VI *(fig)* to scrape by; **haarscharf an etw** *(dat)* **~** to escape sth by the skin of one's teeth

ent|lar|ven [ɛnt'larfn] *ptp* **entlarvt** VT *(fig) Spion, Dieb etc* to unmask, to expose; *Pläne, Betrug etc* to uncover, to expose; **sich ~** to reveal one's true colours *(Brit)* or colors *(US)* or character; **sich als Schuft** *etc* **~** to reveal *or* show oneself to be a scoundrel *etc*

Ent|lar|vung F **-, -en** *(von Spion, Dieb)* unmasking, exposure; *(von Plänen, Betrug)* uncovering, exposure

ent|las|sen [ɛnt'lasn] *ptp* **entlassen** VT *irreg (aus* from) *(= gehen lassen, kündigen)* to dismiss; *(nach Streichungen)* to make redundant *(Brit)*, to lay off; *(aus dem Krankenhaus)* to discharge; *Soldaten* to discharge; *(= in den Ruhestand versetzen)* to retire, to pension off *(Brit)*; *(aus dem Gefängnis, aus Verpflichtungen)* to release, to discharge, to free; *(aus der Schule: als Strafe)* to expel, to exclude; **aus der Schule ~ werden** to leave school; *(als Strafe)* to be expelled *or* excluded from school; **jdn mit ein paar freundlichen Worten ~** to dismiss sb *or* send sb away with a few kind words; **jdn in den Ruhestand ~** to retire sb, to pension sb off *(Brit)*; **Soldaten ins Zivilleben ~** to demobilize soldiers; **jdn aus der Verantwortung ~** to free sb from responsibility

Ent|las|sung F **-, -en** dismissal; *(aus dem Krankenhaus, von Soldaten)* discharge; *(aus dem Gefängnis, aus Verpflichtungen)* release, discharge; **um seine ~ einreichen** to tender one's resignation; **es gab 20 ~en** there were 20 redundancies *(esp Brit)* or lay-offs

Ent|las|sungs-: **Ent|las|sungs|fei|er** F *(Sch)* (school-)leaving *(Brit)* or graduation *(US)* ceremony, final prize day (at school) *(Brit)*; **Ent|las|sungs|ge|such** NT (letter of) resignation; *(Jur)* petition for release; **ein ~ stellen** *or* **einreichen** to tender one's resignation; *(Jur)* to petition for one's/sb's release; **Ent|las|sungs|-**

schein M certificate of discharge; *(Mil auch)* discharge papers *pl*; **Ent|las|sungs|wel|le** F (= *Massenentlassungen*) wave of redundancies *(Brit)* or job losses *(US)*; **Ent|las|sungs|zeug|nis** NT *(Sch)* school leaving certificate

ent|las|ten [ɛnt'lastn] *ptp* **entlastet** VT *Achse, Telefonleitungen etc* to relieve the strain *or* load on; *Herz* to relieve the strain on; *Gewissen* to relieve; *(Mil, Rail)* to relieve; *Verkehr* to ease; *Stadtzentrum* to relieve congestion in; *(= Arbeit abnehmen) Chef, Mitarbeiter, Hausfrau* to take some of the load off, to relieve; *(Jur) Angeklagten (völlig)* to exonerate; *(teilweise)* to support the case of; *(Comm: = gutheißen) Vorstand* to approve the activities of; *(von Verpflichtungen, Schulden) jdn* to discharge, to release; **jdn finanziell ~** to ease sb's financial burden; **jds Konto um einen Betrag ~** to credit sb *or* sb's account with a sum, to credit a sum to sb's account

Ent|las|tung F -, -en relief *(auch Mil, Rail etc)*; *(von Achse etc, Herz)* relief of the strain (+*gen* on); *(Jur)* exoneration; *(Comm: von Vorstand)* approval; *(Fin)* credit; *(von Verpflichtungen etc)* release, discharge; **zu jds ~** (in order) to take some of the load off sb; *(Mil)* (in order) to relieve sb; **eine Aussage zur ~ des Angeklagten** a statement supporting the case of the defendant; **zu seiner ~ führte der Angeklagte an, dass ...** in his defence *(Brit)* or defense *(US)* the defendant stated that ...

Ent|las|tungs-: **Ent|las|tungs|ma|te|ri|al** NT *(Jur)* evidence for the defence *(Brit)* or defense *(US)*; **Ent|las|tungs|zeu|ge** M, **Ent|las|tungs|zeu|gin** F *(Jur)* witness for the defence *(Brit)* or defense *(US)*, defence *(Brit)* or defense *(US)* witness; **Ent|las|tungs|zug** M relief train

ent|lau|ben [ɛnt'laubn] *ptp* **entlaubt** VT to strip of leaves; *(Sci)* to defoliate

Ent|lau|bung F -, -en defoliation

Ent|lau|bungs|mit|tel NT defoliant

ent|lau|fen [ɛnt'laufn] *ptp* **entlaufen** VI *irreg aux sein* to run away (+*dat*, *von* from); **ein ~er Sklave/~es Kind** *etc* a runaway slave/child *etc*; **ein ~er Sträfling** an escaped convict; **ein ~er Hund** a lost *or* missing dog; **„Hund ~"** "dog missing"

ent|lau|sen [ɛnt'lauzn] *ptp* **entlaust** VT to delouse

Ent|lau|sung F -, -en delousing

ent|le|di|gen [ɛnt'le:dɪgn] *ptp* **entledigt** *(form)* **VR** **sich einer Person/einer Sache** *(gen)* ~ to rid oneself of sb/sth; **sich einer Pflicht** *(gen)* ~ to discharge a duty; **sich eines Komplizen ~** *(euph)* to dispose of *or* eliminate an accomplice *(euph)*; **sich seiner Schulden ~** to discharge one's debts *(form)*, to pay off one's debts; **sich seiner Kleidung ~** to remove one's clothes **VT** **jdn einer Pflicht** *(gen)* ~ to release sb from a duty

ent|lee|ren [ɛnt'le:rən] *ptp* **entleert** VT to empty; *Darm* to evacuate; *(Sci) Glasglocke* to evacuate

Ent|lee|rung F emptying; *(von Darm, Glasglocke)* evacuation

ent|le|gen [ɛnt'le:gn] ADJ *Ort, Haus (= abgelegen)* remote, out-of-the-way; *(= weit weg)* far away *or* off, remote; *(fig) Gedanke etc* odd, out-of-the-way

Ent|le|gen|heit F -, *no pl* remoteness; *(fig)* oddness

ent|leh|nen [ɛnt'le:nən] *ptp* **entlehnt** VT *(fig)* to borrow (+*dat*, *von* from)

Ent|leh|nung F -, -en *(fig)* borrowing

ent|lei|ben [ɛnt'laibn] *ptp* **entleibt** VR *(obs)* to take one's own life

ent|lei|hen [ɛnt'laiən] *ptp* **entliehen** VT *irreg* to borrow (*von, aus* from)

Ent|lei|her [ɛnt'laiɐ] M -s, -, **Ent|lei|he|rin** [-ərɪn] F -, -nen borrower

Ent|lei|hung F -, -en borrowing

Ent|lein ['ɛntlain] NT -s, - duckling; **das hässliche ~** the Ugly Duckling

ent|lo|ben [ɛnt'lo:bn] *ptp* **entlobt** VR to break off one's engagement

Ent|lo|bung F -, -en breaking off of one's engagement; **eine ~** a broken engagement

ent|lo|cken [ɛnt'lɔkn] *ptp* **entlockt** VT **jdm/einer Sache etw ~** to elicit sth from sb/sth; *(durch Überredung auch)* to coax sth out of sb; *(durch ständige Befragung auch)* to worm sth out of sb

ent|loh|nen [ɛnt'lo:nən] *ptp* **entlohnt**, *(Sw)* **ent|löh|nen** [ɛnt'lø:nən] *ptp* **entlöhnt** VT to pay; *(fig)* to reward

Ent|loh|nung F -, -en, *(Sw)* **Ent|löh|nung** F -, -en pay(-ment); *(fig)* reward; **etw gegen ~ tun** to do sth for payment

ent|lüf|ten [ɛnt'lʏftn] *ptp* **entlüftet** VT to ventilate, to air; *Bremsen, Heizung* to bleed

Ent|lüf|ter M ventilator

Ent|lüf|tung F ventilation, airing; *(von Bremsen, Heizung)* bleeding

Ent|lüf|tungs-: **Ent|lüf|tungs|an|la|ge** F ventilation system; **Ent|lüf|tungs|ven|til** NT *(Tech)* ventilation valve; *(von Motor, Heizung etc)* bleed(er) valve

ent|mach|ten [ɛnt'maxtn] *ptp* **entmachtet** VT to deprive of power

Ent|mach|tung F -, -en deprivation of power

ent|mag|ne|ti|sie|ren [ɛntmagneti'zi:rən] *ptp* **entmagnetisiert** VT to demagnetize

ent|man|nen [ɛnt'manən] *ptp* **entmannt** VT to castrate; *(fig)* to emasculate, to unman

Ent|man|nung F -, -en castration; *(fig)* emasculation

ent|ma|te|ri|a|li|sie|ren [ɛntmateriali'zi:rən] *ptp* **entmaterialisiert** VT to dematerialize

ent|mensch|li|chen [ɛnt'mɛnʃlɪçn] *ptp* **entmenschlicht** VT to dehumanize

ent|menscht [ɛnt'mɛnʃt] ADJ bestial, inhuman

ent|mie|ten [ɛnt'mi:tn] *ptp* **entmietet** VT *(form)* to clear *or* evict tenants from

Ent|mie|tung F -, -en *(form)* clearance

ent|mi|li|ta|ri|sie|ren [ɛntmilitari'zi:rən] *ptp* **entmilitarisiert** VT to demilitarize

Ent|mi|li|ta|ri|sie|rung F -, -en demilitarization

ent|mi|nen [ɛnt'mi:nən] *ptp* **entmint** VT *(Mil)* to clear of mines

ent|mot|ten [ɛnt'mɔtn] *ptp* **entmottet** VT *(fig)* to take out of mothballs

ent|mün|di|gen [ɛnt'mʏndɪgn] *ptp* **entmündigt** VT *(Jur)* to (legally) incapacitate, to declare incapable of managing one's own affairs; *(wegen Geisteskrankheit auch)* to certify; **das Fernsehen entmündigt die Zuschauer, wenn ...** television takes away the viewer's right to form an independent opinion when ...

Ent|mün|di|gung F -, -en (legal) incapacitation; *(wegen Geisteskrankheit auch)* certification

ent|mu|ti|gen [ɛnt'mu:tɪgn] *ptp* **entmutigt** VT to discourage, to dishearten; **sich nicht ~ lassen** not to be discouraged *or* disheartened

Ent|mu|ti|gung F -, -en discouragement

ent|mys|ti|fi|zie|ren [ɛntmʏstifi'zi:rən] *ptp* **entmystifiziert** VT to demystify, to take the mystique out of, to debunk

ent|my|tho|lo|gi|sie|ren [ɛntmytologi'zi:rən] *ptp* **entmythologisiert** VT to demythologize

Ent|nah|me [ɛnt'na:mə] F -, -n *(form)* removal, taking out; *(von Blut)* extraction; *(von Geld)* withdrawal; **vor ~ einer Sache** *(gen)* before removing/extracting/withdrawing sth

ent|na|zi|fi|zie|ren [ɛntnatsifi'tsi:rən] *ptp* **entnazifiziert** VT to denazify

Ent|na|zi|fi|zie|rung -, -en F denazification

ent|neh|men [ɛnt'ne:mən] *ptp* **entnommen** [ɛnt'nɔmən] VT *irreg (aus* +*dat)* to take out (of), to take (from); *(aus Kasse) Geld* to withdraw (from); *(einem Buch etc) Zitat* to take (from); *(fig: = erkennen, folgern)* to infer (from), to gather (from); **wie ich Ihren Worten entnehme, ...** I gather from what you say that ...

ent|ner|ven [ɛnt'nɛrfn] *ptp* **entnervt** VT to unnerve; **~d** unnerving; *(= nervtötend)* nerve-racking

ent|nervt [ɛnt'nɛrft] **PTP** *von* **entnerven** **ADJ** unnerved, nervous, enervated; **ich bin völlig ~** my nerves are shot *(inf)* **ADV** enervated; **er hat ~ aufgegeben** he had reached the end of his tether *(Brit)* or rope *(US)* and give up → *auch* **entnerven**

En|to|derm [ɛnto'dɛrm] NT -s, -e *(Biol)* entoderm, endoderm

ent|ölen [ɛnt'lø:lən] *ptp* **entölt** VT *Kakao* to extract the oil from

En|to|mo|lo|gie [ɛntomolo'gi:] F -, *no pl* entomology

en|to|mo|lo|gisch [ɛntomo'lo:gɪʃ] ADJ entomological

En|tou|ra|ge [ãtu:'ra:ʒ(ə)] F -, *no pl (geh)* entourage

ent|pa|cken [ɛnt'pakn] VT *ptp* **entpackt** *(Comput) Daten* to unpack, to unzip

ent|per|sön|li|chen [ɛntpɛr'zø:nlɪçn] *ptp* **entpersönlicht** VT to depersonalize

ent|pflich|ten [ɛnt'pflɪçtn] *ptp* **entpflichtet** VT *(form) Pfarrer, Professor* to retire

ent|po|li|ti|sie|ren [ɛntpoliti'zi:rən] *ptp* **entpolitisiert** VT to depoliticize

Ent|po|li|ti|sie|rung F depoliticizing, depoliticization

ent|pri|va|ti|sie|ren [ɛntprivati'zi:rən] *ptp* **entprivatisiert** VT to deprivatize, to (re)nationalize

ent|pup|pen [ɛnt'pʊpn] *ptp* **entpuppt** VR *(Schmetterling)* to emerge from its cocoon *or* chrysalis; **sich als Betrüger** *etc* ~ to turn out to be a cheat *etc*; **mal sehen, wie er sich entpuppt** we'll see how he turns out

ent|rah|men [ɛnt'ra:mən] *ptp* **entrahmt** VT *Milch* to remove the cream from, to skim; *(mit Zentrifuge)* to separate; **entrahmte Milch** skimmed milk

Ent|rah|mung F -, -en skimming; *(mit Zentrifuge)* separation

ent|ra|ten [ɛnt'ra:tn] *ptp* **entraten** VI *irreg (geh, old)* **einer Sache** *(gen)* ~ to be devoid of sth; **einer Person/Sache** *(gen)* **~/nicht ~ können** to be able/unable to dispense with sb/sth

ent|rät|seln [ɛnt'rɛ:tsln] *ptp* **enträtselt** VT to solve; *Sinn* to work out; *Schrift* to decipher

ent|rech|ten [ɛnt'rɛçtn] *ptp* **entrechtet** VT **jdn ~** to deprive sb of his rights; **die Entrechteten** those who have lost their rights, those who have been deprived of their rights

Ent|rech|tung F -, -en deprivation of rights; **die ~ des Parlaments** depriving parliament of its rights

Ent|ree [ã'tre:] NT -s, -s *(dated: = Eingang)* entrance; *(obs: = Vorraum)* (entrance) hall; *(= Eintrittsgeld)* entrance *or* admission fee; *(Mus: = Vorspiel)* introduction; *(Cook: = Vorspeise)* entrée; *(Theat: = Auftritt)* solo entrance

ent|rei|ßen [ɛnt'raisn] *ptp* **entrissen** [ɛnt'rɪsn] VT *irreg* **jdm etw ~** *(lit, fig liter)* to snatch sth (away) from sb; **jdn dem Tode ~** *(liter)* to snatch sb from the jaws of death

ent|rich|ten [ɛnt'rɪçtn] *ptp* **entrichtet** VT *(form)* to pay

Ent|rich|tung F *(form)* payment

ent|rie|geln [ɛnt'ri:gln] *ptp* **entriegelt** VT to unbolt, to unlock; *(Comput, Handy etc) Tastatur* to unlock

ent|rin|den [ɛnt'rɪndn] *ptp* **entrindet** VT to remove the bark from, to decorticate *(form)*

ent|rin|gen [ɛnt'rɪŋən] *ptp* **entrungen** [ɛnt'rʊŋən] *irreg* **VT** *(geh)* **jdm etw ~** to wrench *or* wrest sth from sb; **jdm ein Geheimnis** *etc* ~ to wring a secret *etc* out of sb, to wrest a secret *etc* from sb **VR** *(liter)* **sich jds Lippen** *(dat)* ~ to escape from sb's lips; **ein Seufzer entrang sich seiner Brust** he heaved a sigh

ent|rin|nen [ɛnt'rɪnən] *ptp* **entronnen** [ɛnt'rɔnən] VI *irreg aux sein (geh)* **a** +*dat* to escape from; *dem Tod* to escape; **es gibt kein Entrinnen** there is no escape **b** (= *entfliehen: Zeit*) to fly by

ent|rol|len [ɛnt'rɔlən] *ptp* **entrollt** VT *Landkarte etc* to unroll; *Fahne, Segel* to unfurl; **ein Bild des Schreckens ~** *(fig)* to reveal a picture of horror VR to unroll; *(Fahne, Segel)* to unfurl; **ein Bild des Schreckens entrollte sich** *(fig)* a picture of horror unfolded VI *aux sein +dat (rare)* to roll out of

En|tro|pie [ɛntro'pi:] F **-, -n** [-'pi:ən] *(Phys)* entropy

ent|ros|ten [ɛnt'rɔstn] *ptp* **entrostet** VT to derust

Ent|ros|ter [ɛnt'rɔstɐ] M **-s, -, Ent|ros|tungs|mit|tel** NT deruster

ent|rü|cken [ɛnt'rʏkn] *ptp* **entrückt** VT *(geh)* **jdn jdm/einer Sache ~** *(lit, fig)* to carry *or* bear *(liter)* sb away from sb/sth, to transport sb (away) from sb/sth; **jdn (in den Himmel) ~** *(Rel)* to translate sb (into heaven); **der Tod hat sie allen Sorgen entrückt** death has put her beyond all tribulation; **einer Sache** *(dat)* **weit entrückt sein** *(fig)* to be far removed from sth; **jdn jds Blicken ~** to remove sb from sb's sight; **jds Blicken entrückt (sein)** (to be) out of (sb's) sight

ent|rückt [ɛnt'rʏkt] ADJ *(geh) (= verzückt)* enraptured, transported; *(= versunken)* lost in reverie, rapt

Ent|rückt|heit F **-, -en** *(geh)* reverie

Ent|rü|ckung F **-, -en** *(geh)* rapture, ecstasy; *(= Versunkenheit)* rapt absorption; *(Rel: = Versetzung)* translation

ent|rüm|peln [ɛnt'rʏmpln] *ptp* **entrümpelt** VT to clear out; *(fig)* to tidy up

Ent|rüm|pe|lung [ɛnt'rʏmpəlʊŋ] F **-, -en, Ent|rümp|lung** [ɛnt'rʏmplʊŋ] F **-, -en** clear-out; *(= das Entrümpeln)* clearing out; *(fig)* tidying up

ent|rüs|ten [ɛnt'rʏstn] *ptp* **entrüstet** VT *(= empören)* to fill with indignation, to outrage; *(= zornig machen)* to incense, to anger; *(= schockieren)* to outrage, to scandalize VR **sich ~ über** *(+acc) (= sich empören)* to be filled with indignation at, to be outraged at; *(= zornig werden)* to be incensed at; *(= schockiert sein)* to be outraged *or* scandalized at; **das ist unerhört!, entrüstete sich die alte Dame** that is scandalous!, said the old lady incensed

ent|rüs|tet [ɛnt'rʏstət] ADJ *(= empört)* (highly) indignant, outraged; *(= zornig)* incensed; *(= schockiert)* outraged, scandalized ADV indignantly, outraged

Ent|rüs|tung F *(über +acc* at) indignation; *(= Zorn)* anger; **ein Sturm der ~ brach los** a storm of indignation broke out

ent|saf|ten [ɛnt'zaftn] *ptp* **entsaftet** VT to extract the juice from

Ent|saf|ter [ɛnt'zaftɐ] M **-s, -** juice extractor

ent|sa|gen [ɛnt'za:gn] *ptp* **entsagt** VI *+dat (geh)* to renounce; **der Welt ~** to renounce the world; **sie hat vielen Freuden ~ müssen** she had to forgo many pleasures; **dem muss ich ~** I shall have to forgo that

Ent|sa|gung F **-, -en** *(geh: von der Welt etc)* renunciation (of worldly things); **Armut und ~ sind die Grundprinzipien des Klosterlebens** poverty and the renunciation of worldly things are the basic principles of monastic life

ent|sa|gungs|voll ADJ *(geh) Leben* (full) of privation; *Blick, Geste* resigned

ent|sal|zen [ɛnt'zaltsn] *ptp* **entsalzt** VT *irreg* to desalinate

Ent|sal|zung F **-, -en** desalination

Ent|sal|zungs|an|la|ge F desalination plant

Ent|satz [ɛnt'zats] M **-es,** *no pl (Mil)* relief

ent|schä|di|gen [ɛnt'ʃɛ:dɪgn] *ptp* **entschädigt** VT *(für* for) *(lit, fig)* to compensate, to recompense, to indemnify *(form)*; *(für Dienste etc)* to reward; *(esp mit Geld)* to remunerate; *(= Kosten erstatten)* to reimburse, to indemnify *(form)*; **das Theaterstück entschädigte uns für das lange Warten** the play made up for the long wait VR **sich (für etw) ~** to compensate oneself for sth; **ihr Mann ist fremdgegangen, aber sie hat sich reichlich dafür entschädigt** her husband was unfaithful to her but she got her own back with a vengeance

Ent|schä|di|gung F compensation, recompense, indemnification *(form)*; *(für Dienste)* reward; *(mit Geld)* remuneration; *(= Kostenerstattung)* reimbursement; **jdm eine ~ zahlen** to pay sb compensation

Ent|schä|di|gungs-: **Ent|schä|di|gungs|kla|ge** F claim for compensation; **Ent|schä|di|gungs|sum|me** F amount of compensation; **Ent|schä|di|gungs|zah|lung** F *(Zahlen)* compensation payment; *(Betrag)* damages *pl*, compensation

ent|schär|fen [ɛnt'ʃɛrfn] *ptp* **entschärft** VT **a** *Bombe etc* to defuse, to deactivate **b** *(fig) Kurve* to straighten out; *Krise, Lage* to defuse; *Argument* to neutralize; *Buch, Film* to tone down

Ent|scheid [ɛnt'ʃait] M **-(e)s, -e** [-də] *(Sw form)* = **Entscheidung**

ent|schei|den [ɛnt'ʃaidn] ✪ 35.2 *pret* **entschied**, [ɛnt'ʃi:t] *ptp* **entschieden** VT [ɛnt'ʃi:dn] to decide; **das Gericht entschied, dass ...** the court decided *or* ruled that ...; **~ Sie, wie es gemacht werden soll!** you decide how it is to be done; **das Spiel/die Wahl ist entschieden/schon entschieden** the game/election has been decided/is already decided; **den Kampf/Krieg (um etw) für sich ~** to secure victory in the struggle/battle (for sth); **das hat das Spiel zu unseren Gunsten entschieden** that decided the game in our favour *(Brit) or* favor *(US)*; **es ist noch nichts entschieden** nothing has been decided (as) yet → *auch* **entschieden**

VI *(über +acc)* to decide (on); *(Jur auch)* to rule (on); **darüber habe ich nicht zu ~** that is not for me to decide; **der Richter hat für/gegen den Kläger entschieden** the judge decided *or* ruled for/against the plaintiff

VR *(Mensch)* to decide, to make up one's mind, to come to a decision; *(Angelegenheit)* to be decided; **sich für etw ~** to decide in favour *(Brit) or* favor *(US)* of sth, to decide on sth; **sich für jdn ~** to decide in favour *(Brit) or* favor *(US)* of sb; **sich gegen jdn/etw ~** to decide against sb/sth; **jetzt wird es sich ~, wer der Schnellere ist** now we'll see *or* settle who is the quicker

ent|schei|dend ADJ decisive; *Faktor auch* deciding *attr*; *Argument, Aussage auch* conclusive; *Augenblick auch* crucial, critical; *Fehler, Irrtum auch* crucial; **die ~e Stimme** *(bei Wahlen etc)* the deciding *or* casting vote; **für jdn/etw ~ sein** to be decisive *or* crucial for sb/sth; **der alles ~e Augenblick** the all-decisive moment; **das Entscheidende** the decisive *or* deciding factor ADV *schlagen, schwächen* decisively; **~ zu etw beitragen** to be a crucial *or* decisive factor in sth

Ent|schei|der M **-s, -, Ent|schei|de|rin** F **-, -nen** decision-maker

Ent|schei|dung F decision; *(Jur auch)* ruling; *(der Geschworenen auch)* verdict; **um die ~ spielen** *(Sport)* to play the deciding game *or* the decider *(Brit)*; *(bei gleichem Tor-, Punktverhältnis auch)* to play off; **Spiel um die ~** *(Sport)* deciding game, decider *(Brit)*; play-off; **mit den finanziellen ~en habe ich nichts zu tun** I have nothing to do with the financial decision-making *or* decisions; **wie ist die ~ ausgefallen?** which way did the decision go?; **es geht um die ~** it's going to be decisive, it's going to decide things; **die Lage drängt zur ~** the situation is coming to a head; **die Frage kommt heute zur ~** the question will be decided today

Ent|schei|dungs-: **Ent|schei|dungs|be|darf** M need for a decision; **Ent|schei|dungs|be|fug|nis** F decision-making powers *pl*; **Ent|schei|dungs|fin|dung** F **-, -en** decision-making; **Ent|schei|dungs|fra|ge** F *(Gram)* yes-no question; **Ent|schei|dungs|frei|heit** F freedom to decide; **ent|schei|dungs|freu|dig** ADJ able to make decisions, decisive; **Ent|schei|dungs|freu|dig|keit** F **-,** *no pl* decisiveness; **Ent|schei|dungs|gre|mi|um** NT decision-making body; **Ent|schei|dungs|hil|fe** F aid to decision-making; **Ent|schei|dungs|kampf** M decisive encounter, show-down *(inf, auch fig)*; *(Sport)* decider *(Brit)*, deciding round/game *etc*; **Ent|schei|dungs|kri|te|ri|um** NT deciding factor; **Ent|schei|dungs|schlacht** F decisive battle; *(fig)* show-down *(inf)*; **ent|schei|dungs|schwach** ADJ indecisive; **Ent|schei|dungs|schwä|che** F indecisiveness; **Ent|schei|dungs|spiel** NT deciding game, decider *(Brit)*; *(bei gleichem Punkt-, Torverhältnis auch)* play-off; **Ent|schei|dungs|spiel|raum** M room for manoeuvre *(Brit) or* maneuver *(US)* in making a decision; **wir haben hierbei keinen ~** we don't have much choice in this; **Ent|schei|dungs|trä|ger(in)** M(F) decision-maker; **ent|schei|dungs|un|fä|hig** ADJ unable to make decisions; **Ent|schei|dungs|un|fä|hig|keit** F inability to make decisions, indecision

ent|schied *pret von* **entscheiden**

ent|schie|den [ɛnt'ʃi:dn] PTP *von* **entscheiden** ADJ **a** *(= entschlossen)* determined, resolute; *Befürworter* staunch; *Ablehnung* firm **b** *no pred (= eindeutig)* decided, distinct; **er ist ein ~er Könner in seinem Fach** he is unquestionably an expert in his subject ADV **a** *(= strikt) ablehnen* firmly; *bekämpfen* resolutely; *von sich weisen, zurückweisen* staunchly; **das geht ~ zu weit** that's definitely going too far **b** *(= eindeutig)* definitely

Ent|schie|den|heit F **-, -en** *(= Entschlossenheit)* determination, resolution; *(von Befürworter)* staunchness; *(von Ablehnung)* firmness; **etw mit aller ~ dementieren** to deny sth categorically; **etw mit aller ~ ablehnen** to reject sth flatly

ent|schla|cken [ɛnt'ʃlakn] *ptp* **entschlackt** VT *(Metal)* to remove the slag from; *(Med) Körper* to purify

Ent|schla|ckung F **-, -en** *(Metal)* removal of slag (*+gen* from); *(Med)* purification

ent|schla|fen [ɛnt'ʃla:fn] *ptp* **entschlafen** VI *irreg aux sein (geh)* to fall asleep; *(euph auch: = sterben)* to pass away; **der/die Entschlafene** the deceased, the departed

ent|schlei|ern [ɛnt'ʃlaiɐn] *ptp* **entschleiert** VT to unveil; *(fig auch)* to uncover, to reveal VR to unveil (oneself); *(hum)* to strip, to disrobe *(hum, form)*

Ent|schleu|ni|gung [ɛnt'ʃlɔynɪgʊŋ] F **-,** *no pl (hum)* slowing-down (of one's life); **wir brauchen alle dringend eine ~ unseres Lebens** taking things easy and slowing things down is essential for all of us

ent|schlie|ßen [ɛnt'ʃli:sn] *pret* **entschloss** [ɛnt'ʃlɔs], *ptp* **entschlossen** [ɛnt'ʃlɔsn] VR to decide *(für, zu* on); **sich ~, etw zu tun** to decide *or* determine *or* resolve to do sth; **ich entschloss mich zum Kauf dieses Hauses** I decided to buy this house; **ich weiß nicht, wozu ich mich ~ soll** I don't know what to decide; **sich anders ~** to change one's mind; **sich zu nichts ~ können** to be unable to make up one's mind; **zu allem entschlossen sein** to be ready for anything → *auch* **entschlossen**

Ent|schlie|ßung F resolution

Ent|schlie|ßungs|an|trag M *(Pol)* resolution proposal

ent|schloss *pret von* **entschließen**

ent|schlos|sen [ɛnt'ʃlɔsn] ✪ 35.2 PTP *von* **entschließen** ADJ determined, resolute; **ich bin fest ~** I am absolutely determined; **er ist zum Schlimmsten ~** he will stop at nothing, he's prepared to do anything; **kurz ~** straight away, without further ado ADV resolutely; **~ handeln** to act resolutely *or* with determination; **schnell und ~** fast and decisively

Ent|schlos|sen|heit F **-,** *no pl* determination, resolution; **in wilder ~** with fierce determination

ent|schlum|mern [ɛnt'ʃlʊmɐn] *ptp* **entschlummert** VI *aux sein (liter, auch euph: = sterben)* to fall asleep

ent|schlụ̈p|fen [ɛnt'ʃlʏpfn] *ptp* **entschlụ̈pft** VI *aux sein* to escape (*+dat* from), to slip away (*+dat* from); *(Küken)* to be hatched; *(fig: Wort etc)* to slip out (*+dat* from); **mir ist eine unüberlegte Bemerkung entschlüpft** I let slip an ill-considered remark

Ent|schlụss M *(= Entscheidung)* decision; *(= Vorsatz)* resolution, resolve; **zu keinem ~ kommen können** to be unable to make up one's mind *or* to come to a decision; **mein ~ ist gefasst** my decision is made, my mind is made up; **aus eigenem ~ handeln** to act on one's own initiative; **seinen ~ ändern** to change one's mind; **es ist mein fester ~ …** it is my firm intention …, I firmly intend …; **ein Mann von schnellen Entschlüssen sein** to be good at decision-making, to be able to decide quickly

ent|schlụ̈s|seln [ɛnt'ʃlʏsln] *ptp* **entschlụ̈sselt** VT to decipher; *Funkspruch auch* to decode; *(esp Comput)* to decrypt

Ent|schlụ̈s|se|lung F -, -en deciphering; *(von Funkspruch auch)* decoding

Ent|schlụss-: **ent|schlụss|freu|dig** ADJ decisive; **Ent|schlụss|freu|dig|keit** [-frɔydɪçkait] F, *no pl* decisiveness, decision-making zeal; **Ent|schlụss|kraft** F decisiveness, determination; **ent|schlụss|los** ADJ indecisive, irresolute; **Ent|schlụss|lo|sig|keit** F -, -en indecisiveness, irresoluteness

ent|schụld|bar [ɛnt'ʃʊltbaːɐ] ADJ excusable, pardonable

ent|schụl|den [ɛnt'ʃʊldn] *ptp* **entschụldet** VT to free of debts

ent|schụl|di|gen [ɛnt'ʃʊldɪgn] ✪ 45.1 *ptp* **entschụldigt** VT to excuse; **etw mit etw ~** to excuse sth as due to sth; **das ist durch nichts zu ~!, das lässt sich nicht ~!** that is inexcusable!; **der Lehrer entschuldigte das Kind** the teacher excused the child (from attendance); **das entschuldigt nicht, dass er sich so benimmt** that is no excuse for *or* doesn't excuse his behaving like that; **jdn bei jdm/einem Treffen ~** to make *or* present sb's excuses *or* apologies to sb/a meeting; **einen Schüler ~ lassen** *or* **~** to ask for a pupil to be excused; **ich möchte meine Tochter für morgen ~** I would like to have my daughter excused for tomorrow; **ich bitte mich zu ~** I beg *(Brit)* *or* ask to be excused; **bitte entschuldigt die Störung, aber …** please excuse *or* forgive the interruption, but …

VI **entschuldige/~ Sie (bitte)!** (do *or* please) excuse me!, sorry!; *(bei Bitte, Frage etc)* excuse me (please), pardon me *(US)*; **(na) ~ Sie/entschuldige mal!** excuse me!

VR **sich (bei jdm) (wegen** *or* **für etw) ~** *(= um Verzeihung bitten)* to apologize (to sb) (for sth); **sich (bei jdm) ~** *(= sich abmelden, sich rechtfertigen)* to excuse oneself, to make one's excuses (to sb); *(= sich bei Lehrer, Chef abmelden)* to ask (sb) to be excused; **sich (von jdm) ~ lassen** to send *or* convey *(form)* one's excuses *or* apologies (via sb); **sich mit Krankheit ~** to excuse oneself on account of illness

ent|schụl|di|gend ADJ apologetic ADV apologetically

Ent|schụl|di|gung ✪ 45.1, 45.2 F -, -en *(= Grund)* excuse; *(= Bitte um Entschuldigung)* apology; *(Sch: = Brief)* letter of excuse, note; **~!** excuse me!; *(= Verzeihung auch)* sorry!; **als** *or* **zur ~ für …** as an excuse/apology for …, in excuse of … *(form)*; **zu seiner ~ sagte er …** he said in his defence *(Brit)* *or* defense *(US)* that …; **ohne ~ fehlen** to be absent without an excuse; **(jdn) (wegen einer Sache) um ~ bitten** to apologize (to sb) (for sth); **ich bitte vielmals um ~(, dass ich mich verspätet habe)!** I do apologize (for being late)!

Ent|schụl|di|gungs-: **Ent|schụl|di|gungs|brief** M letter of apology; *(Sch)* excuse note; **Ent|schụl|di|gungs|grund** M excuse

ent|schwe̱|ben [ɛnt'ʃveːbn] *ptp* **entschwe̱bt** VI *aux sein* *(geh, hum: = weggehen)* to float *or* waft away (*+dat* from)

ent|schwe̱|feln [ɛnt'ʃveːfln] *ptp* **entschwe̱felt** VT to desulphurize

Ent|schwe̱|fe|lung F -, -en desulphurization

Ent|schwe̱|fe|lungs|an|la|ge F desulphurization plant

ent|schwịn|den [ɛnt'ʃvɪndn] *ptp* **entschwụnden** [ɛnt'ʃvʊndn] VI *irreg aux sein (geh: lit, fig)* to vanish, to disappear (*+dat* from, *in +acc* into); **dem Gedächtnis ~** to fade from one's memory; **die Tage entschwanden wie im Flug** the days flew by *or* raced by

ent|see̱lt [ɛnt'zeːlt] ADJ *(liter)* lifeless, dead

ent|sẹn|den [ɛnt'zɛndn] *ptp* **entsạndt** *or* **entsẹndet** [ɛnt'sant, ɛnt'zɛndət] VT *irreg or reg Abgeordnete etc* to send; *Boten auch* to dispatch

Ent|sẹn|dung F sending; *(von Boten auch)* dispatch

ent|sẹt|zen [ɛnt'zɛtsn] *ptp* **entsẹtzt** VT **a** *(= in Grauen versetzen)* to horrify, to appal *(Brit)*, to appall *(US)* **b** *(Mil) Truppen* to relieve VR **sich über jdn/etw ~** to be horrified *or* appalled at *or* by sb/sth; **sich vor etw** *(dat)* **~** to be horrified *or* appalled at sth → *auch* **entsetzt**

Ent|sẹt|zen [ɛnt'zɛtsn] NT -s, *no pl* horror; *(= Bestürzung auch)* dismay; *(= Erschrecken)* terror; **von ~ erfasst** *or* **ergriffen** *or* **gepackt werden** to be seized with horror/dismay/terror, to be horror-stricken; **zu meinem größten ~ bemerkte ich, dass …** to my horror *or* great dismay I noticed that …; **mit ~ sehen/hören, dass …** to be horrified/dismayed/terrified to see/hear that …

Ent|sẹt|zens|schrei M cry of horror

ent|sẹtz|lich [ɛnt'zɛtslɪç] ADJ dreadful, appalling, hideous; *(inf: = sehr unangenehm auch)* terrible, awful ADV **a** *(= schrecklich) wehtun, schreien* dreadfully, terribly, awfully; **~ aussehen** to look dreadful *or* appalling *or* hideous **b** *(inf: = sehr)* awfully; **~ viel (Geld)** an awful lot (of money) *(inf)*

Ent|sẹtz|lich|keit F -, -e dreadful *or* appalling *or* terrible nature

ent|sẹtzt [ɛnt'zɛtst] ADJ horrified, appalled (*über +acc* at, by); **ein ~er Schrei** a horrified scream, a cry *or* scream of horror ADV in horror; **jdn ~ anstarren** to give sb a horrified look → *auch* **entsetzen**

Ent|sẹt|zung [ɛnt'zɛtsʊŋ] F -, -en *(Mil)* relief

ent|seu̱|chen [ɛnt'zɔyçn] *ptp* **entseu̱cht** VT *(= desinfizieren)* to disinfect; *(= dekontaminieren)* to decontaminate

Ent|seu̱|chung F -, -en decontamination

ent|sị|chern [ɛnt'zɪçɐn] *ptp* **entsịchert** VT **eine Pistole ~** to release the safety catch of a pistol; **eine entsicherte Pistole** a pistol with the safety catch off, a pistol with an unlocked safety catch *(esp US)*

ent|sịn|nen [ɛnt'zɪnən] *ptp* **entsọnnen** [ɛnt'zɔnən] VR *irreg (einer Sache (gen), an etw (acc)* sth) to remember, to recall, to recollect; **wenn ich mich recht entsinne** if my memory serves me correctly *or* right

ent|sọr|gen [ɛnt'zɔrgn] *ptp* **entsọrgt** VT *Abfälle, Schutt, Brennstäbe, Chemikalien, Medikamente* to dispose of; *Ölplattform, Altautos* to break up; **eine Stadt ~** to dispose of a town's refuse and sewage VI to dispose of refuse and sewage

Ent|sọr|gung F -, -en waste disposal; **die ~ von Chemikalien** the disposal of chemicals

Ent|sọr|gungs-: **Ent|sọr|gungs|nach|weis** M proof of disposal; **Ent|sọr|gungs|not|stand** M waste (disposal) emergency; **Ent|sọr|gungs|park** M (nuclear) waste dump

ent|spạn|nen [ɛnt'ʃpanən] *ptp* **entspạnnt** VT *Muskeln, Nerven etc* to relax; *Bogen* to unbend; *Seil* to slacken, to untighten; *Wasser* to reduce the surface tension of; *(fig) Lage, Beziehungen* to ease (up) VR to relax *(auch fig)*; *(= ausruhen)* to rest; *(nach der Arbeit etc)* to unwind, to unbend; *(Lage etc)* to ease; *(Feder etc)* to lose tension

ent|spạnnt [ɛnt'ʃpant] ADJ relaxed; **die Lage ist wieder etwas ~er** the situation is now less tense again

Ent|spạnnt|heit F -, *no pl (der Lage)* lack of tension (*+gen* in); **meine mangelnde ~** the fact that I wasn't relaxed

Ent|spạn|nung F relaxation *(auch fig)*; *(von Lage, Fin: an der Börse)* easing(-up); *(Pol)* easing *or* reduction of tension (*+gen* in), détente; *(des Wassers)* reduction of surface tension; *(von Seil etc)* slackening, untightening; **nach der Arbeit sehe ich zur ~ etwas fern** after work I watch television for a bit to help me unwind

Ent|spạn|nungs-: **Ent|spạn|nungs|be|mü|hun|gen** PL efforts *pl* aimed at easing (political) tension; **Ent|spạn|nungs|po|li|tik** F policy of détente; **Ent|spạn|nungs|tech|nik** F relaxation technique; **Ent|spạn|nungs|übun|gen** PL *(Med etc)* relaxation exercises *pl*

ent|spẹr|ren [ɛnt'ʃpɛrən] *ptp* **entspẹrrt** VT *(Comput) Datensätze* to unlock

ent|spie|gelt [ɛnt'ʃpiːglt] ADJ *Brillengläser, Bildschirm* anti-reflective

ent|spịn|nen [ɛnt'ʃpɪnən] *ptp* **entspọnnen** [ɛnt'ʃpɔnən] VR *irreg (geh)* to develop, to arise

entspr. *abbr von* **entsprechend**

ent|spre̱|chen [ɛnt'ʃprɛçn] ✪ 32.4, 38.1, 53.6 *ptp* **entsprọchen** VI [ɛnt'ʃprɔxn] *irreg +dat* to correspond to; *der Wahrheit* to be in accordance with; *den Tatsachen auch* to fit, to be in accordance with; *(= genügen) Anforderungen, Kriterien* to fulfil *(Brit)*, to fulfill *(US)*, to meet; *einem Anlass* to be in keeping with; *Erwartungen* to come *or* live up to; *einer Beschreibung* to answer, to fit; *einer Bitte, einem Wunsch etc* to meet, to comply with; **sich** *or* **einander ~** to correspond (with each other), to tally; **ihre Ausrüstung entsprach nicht den alpinen Bedingungen** her outfit wasn't suitable for the alpine conditions; **seinem Zweck ~** to fulfil *(Brit)* *or* fulfill *(US)* its purpose

ent|spre̱|chend ADJ corresponding; *(= zuständig)* relevant; *(= angemessen)* appropriate; **der Film war besonders geschmacklos, und die Kritiken waren dann auch ~** the film was particularly tasteless and the reviews of it were correspondingly harsh; **ein der Leistung ~es Gehalt** a salary commensurate with one's performance ADV accordingly; *(= ähnlich, gleich)* correspondingly; **er wurde ~ bestraft** he was suitably *or* appropriately punished; **etw ~ würdigen** to show suitable appreciation for sth PREP *+dat* in accordance with, according to; *(= ähnlich, gleich)* corresponding to; **er wird seiner Leistung ~ bezahlt** he is paid according to output; **er hat sich den Erwartungen ~ entwickelt** he has progressed as we had hoped → **Umstand**

Ent|spre̱|chung F -, -en *(= Äquivalent)* equivalent; *(= Gegenstück)* counterpart; *(= Analogie)* parallel; *(= Übereinstimmung)* correspondence

ent|sprie̱|ßen [ɛnt'ʃpriːsn] *ptp* **entsprọssen** [ɛnt'ʃprɔsn] VI *irreg aux sein (liter: lit, fig)* **einer Sache** *(dat)* *or* **aus etw ~** to spring forth from sth *(liter)*; *(old, hum) aus Ehe, Familie etc* to issue from sth *(old, form)*

ent|sprịn|gen [ɛnt'ʃprɪŋən] *ptp* **entsprụngen** [ɛnt'ʃprʊŋən] VI *irreg aux sein* **a** *(Fluss)* to rise **b** *(= entfliehen)* to escape (*+dat, aus* from) **c** *(= sich herleiten von) +dat* to spring from, to arise from

ent|staat|li|chen [ɛnt'ʃtaːtlɪçn] *ptp* **entstaatlicht** VT to denationalize

Ent|sta|li|ni|sie̱|rung [ɛntʃtalini'ziːrʊŋ] F -, -en destalinization

ent|stạm|men [ɛnt'ʃtamən] *ptp* **entstạmmt** VI *aux sein +dat* to stem *or* come from; *einer Familie auch* to be descended from; *(fig auch)* to originate in *or* from

ent|stau|ben [ɛnt'ʃtaubn] *ptp* **entstaubt** VT to remove the dust from, to free from dust

ent|ste̱|hen [ɛnt'ʃteːən] *ptp* **entstạnden** [ɛnt'ʃtandn] VI *irreg aux sein (= ins Dasein treten)* to come into being; *(= seinen Ursprung haben)* to originate; *(= sich entwickeln)* to arise, to develop *(aus, durch* from); *(= hervorkommen)* to emerge *(aus, durch* from); *(= verursacht werden)* to result *(aus, durch* from); *(Chem: Verbindungen)* to be produced *(aus* from, *durch* through, via); *(Kunstwerk: = geschrieben/gebaut etc werden)* to be written/built *etc*; **das Feuer war durch Nachlässigkeit entstanden** the fire was caused by negligence; **bei Entstehen eines Feuers** in the event of (a) fire; **wir wollen nicht den Eindruck ~ lassen, ...** we don't want to give (rise to) the impression that ..., we don't want to let the impression emerge that ...; **im Entstehen begriffen sein** to be in the process of formation *or* development, to be emerging; **für ~den** *or* **entstandenen Schaden** for damages incurred

Ent|ste|hen NT **-s**, *no pl* → **Entstehung**, → *auch* **entstehen**

Ent|ste|hung F **-, -en** *(= das Werden)* genesis, coming into being; *(= das Hervorkommen)* emergence; *(= Ursprung)* origin; *(= Bildung)* formation

Ent|ste|hungs-: **Ent|ste|hungs|ge|schich|te** F genesis; *(Bibl)* Genesis; **Ent|ste|hungs|ort** M *pl* **-orte** place of origin; **Ent|ste|hungs|ur|sa|che** F original cause; **Ent|ste|hungs|zeit** F time of origin

ent|stei|gen [ɛnt'ʃtaign] *ptp* **entstiegen** [ɛnt'ʃti:gn] VI *irreg aux sein +dat (geh) einem Wagen* to alight from *(form)*; *dem Wasser, dem Bad* to emerge from; *(fig: Dampf etc)* to rise from

ent|stei|nen [ɛnt'ʃtainən] *ptp* **entsteint** VT to stone

ent|stel|len [ɛnt'ʃtɛlən] *ptp* **entstellt** VT *(= verunstalten) Gesicht* to disfigure; *(= verzerren) Gesicht(szüge)* to distort, to contort; *(fig) Bericht, Wahrheit etc* to distort; **etw entstellt wiedergeben** to distort *or* misrepresent sth; **sein von Hass/Schmerz entstelltes Gesicht** his face distorted *or* contorted with hate/pain

ent|stel|lend *prp von* **entstellen** ADJ *Narbe etc* disfiguring

Ent|stel|lung F disfigurement; *(fig)* distortion; *(der Wahrheit)* perversion, distortion

ent|stem|peln [ɛnt'ʃtɛmpln] *ptp* **entstempelt** VT *(Aut)* to cancel the registration of

Ent|sti|ckung [ɛnt'ʃtɪkʊŋ] F **-, -en** denitrification

Ent|sti|ckungs|an|la|ge F denitrification plant

ent|stie|len [ɛnt'ʃti:lən] *ptp* **entstielt** VT *Obst* to remove the stalk(s) from

ent|stoff|li|chen [ɛnt'ʃtɔflɪçn] *ptp* **entstofflicht** VT to dematerialize

ent|stö|ren [ɛnt'ʃtø:rən] *ptp* **entstört** VT *Radio, Telefon* to free from interference; *Auto, Staubsauger* to fit a suppressor to, to suppress

Ent|stö|rer M, **Ent|stör|ge|rät** NT *(für Auto etc)* suppressor; *(für Radio, Telefon)* anti-interference device

Ent|stö|rung F *(von Radio, Telefon)* freeing from interference, suppression of interference; *(von Auto, Staubsauger)* fitting of a suppressor *(+gen* to), suppressing

Ent|stö|rungs|dienst M, **Ent|stö|rungs|stel|le** F telephone maintenance service

ent|strö|men [ɛnt'ʃtrø:mən] *ptp* **entströmt** VI *aux sein* to pour *or* gush out *(+dat, aus* of); *(Gas, Geruch etc)* to issue *or* escape *(+dat, aus* from)

Ent|sub|li|mie|rung F *(Psych, Sociol)* **repressive ~** repressive desublimation

ent|ta|bu|i|sie|ren [ɛnttabui'zi:rən] *ptp* **enttabuisiert** VT to free from taboos, to remove the taboos from

Ent|ta|bu|i|sie|rung F **-, -en** removal of taboos *(+gen* from)

ent|tar|nen [ɛnt'tarnən] *ptp* **enttarnt** VT *Spion* to blow the cover of *(inf)*; *(fig: = entlarven)* to expose; **er wurde enttarnt** *(Spion)* his cover was blown, he was exposed

Ent|tar|nung F exposure

ent|täu|schen [ɛnt'tɔyʃn] *ptp* **enttäuscht** VT to disappoint; *Vertrauen* to betray; **enttäuscht sein über** *(+acc)***/von** to be disappointed at/by *or* in; **er ging enttäuscht nach Hause** he went home disappointed; **sie ist im Leben oft enttäuscht worden** she has had many disappointments in life; **du hast uns sehr enttäuscht** you have really let us down *or* disappointed us; **angenehm enttäuscht sein** *(hum)* to be pleasantly surprised

VI **unsere Mannschaft hat sehr enttäuscht** our team were very disappointing; *(= hat schlecht gespielt)* our team played very disappointingly; **der neue Wagen hat enttäuscht** the new car is a disappointment *or* let-down *(inf)*

Ent|täu|schung F disappointment; **das Theaterstück war eine große ~** the play was a big disappointment *or* let-down *(inf)*; **jdm eine ~ bereiten** to disappoint sb

ent|thro|nen [ɛnt'tro:nən] *ptp* **entthront** VT *(lit, fig)* to dethrone

Ent|thro|nung F **-, -en** *(lit, fig)* dethronement, dethroning

ent|trüm|mern [ɛnt'trʏmɐn] *ptp* **enttrümmert** VT to clear of rubble VI to clear the rubble (away)

ent|völ|kern [ɛnt'fœlkɐn] *ptp* **entvölkert** VT to depopulate

ent|völ|kert [ɛnt'fœlkɐt] PTP *von* **entvölkern** ADJ depopulated; *(= leer)* deserted, unpopulated

Ent|völ|ke|rung F **-, -en** depopulation

entw. *abbr von* **entweder**

ent|wach|sen [ɛnt'vaksn] *ptp* **entwachsen** VI *irreg aux sein +dat* **a** *(geh: = herauswachsen aus)* to spring from **b** *(= zu groß werden für)* to outgrow, to grow out of

ent|waff|nen [ɛnt'vafnən] *ptp* **entwaffnet** VT *(lit, fig)* to disarm

ent|waff|nend ADJ *(fig)* disarming

Ent|waff|nung F **-, -en** disarming; *(eines Landes)* disarmament

ent|wal|den [ɛnt'valdn] *ptp* **entwaldet** VT to deforest

ent|war|nen [ɛnt'varnən] *ptp* **entwarnt** VI to sound *or* give the all-clear

Ent|war|nung F sounding of the all-clear; *(= Signal)* all-clear

ent|wäs|sern [ɛnt'vɛsɐn] *ptp* **entwässert** VT *Grundstück, Moor, Keller* to drain; *Gewebe, Ödem, Körper* to dehydrate

Ent|wäs|se|rung F drainage; *(Chem)* dehydration

Ent|wäs|se|rungs-: **Ent|wäs|se|rungs|an|la|ge** F drainage system; **Ent|wäs|se|rungs|gra|ben** M drainage ditch; **Ent|wäs|se|rungs|ka|nal** M drainage channel

ent|we|der ['ɛntve:dɐ, ɛnt've:dɐ] CONJ **~ ... oder ...** either ... or ...; **~ oder!** make up your mind (one way or the other)!, yes or no; **~ gleich oder gar nicht, ~ jetzt oder nie** it's now or never

Ent|we|der-o|der ['ɛntve:dɐ'lo:dɐ] NT **-, -** **hier gibt es kein ~** there is no alternative; **hier gibt es nur ein ~** there has to be a definite decision one way or the other

ent|wei|chen [ɛnt'vaiçn] *ptp* **entwichen** [ɛnt'vɪçn] VI *irreg aux sein (geh: = fliehen)* to escape *(+dat, aus* from), to run away *(+dat, aus* from); *(= sich verflüchtigen: Gas, Flüssigkeit)* to leak *or* escape *(+dat, aus* from, out of)

ent|wei|hen [ɛnt'vaiən] *ptp* **entweiht** VT to violate *(auch fig)*; *(= entheiligen)* to profane, to desecrate

Ent|wei|hung F **-, -en** violation; *(= Entheiligung)* profanation, desecration

ent|wen|den [ɛnt'vɛndn] *ptp* **entwendet** VT *(form)* **jdm etw/etw aus etw ~** to steal *or* purloin *(hum, form)* sth from sb/sth

Ent|wen|dung F *(form)* theft, stealing, purloining *(hum, form)*

ent|wer|fen [ɛnt'vɛrfn] *ptp* **entworfen** [ɛnt'vɔrfn] VT *irreg* **a** *(= zeichnen, gestalten) Zeichnung etc* to sketch; *Muster, Modell etc* to design **b** *(= ausarbeiten) Gesetz, Vortrag, Schreiben etc* to draft, to draw up; *Plan* to devise, to draw up **c** *(fig) (= darstellen, darlegen) Bild* to depict, to draw; *(= in Umrissen darstellen)* to outline

ent|wer|ten [ɛnt've:ɐtn] *ptp* **entwertet** VT **a** *(= im Wert mindern)* to devalue, to depreciate; *Zeugenaussage, Argument etc auch* to undermine **b** *(= ungültig machen)* to make *or* render invalid; *Münzen* to demonetize; *Briefmarke, Fahrschein* to cancel

Ent|wer|ter [ɛnt've:ɐtɐ] M **-s, -** (ticket-)cancelling *(Brit) or* (ticket-)canceling *(US)* machine

Ent|wer|tung F **a** *(= Wertminderung)* devaluation, depreciation **b** *(von Zeugenaussagen, Argumenten)* undermining **c** *(= Ungültigmachung)* invalidation; *(von Briefmarke, Fahrschein)* cancellation

ent|wi|ckeln [ɛnt'vɪkln] *ptp* **entwickelt** VT to develop *(auch Phot)*; *(Phot) esp Diapositive* to process; *Methode, Verfahren* to develop, to evolve; *(Math) Formel* to expand, to develop; *(Chem) Gas etc* to produce, to generate; *Mut, Energie* to show, to display; **jdm etw ~** to set out *or* expound sth to sb; **etw zu etw ~** to develop sth into sth

VR to develop *(zu* into); *(Chem: Gase etc)* to be produced *or* generated; **das Projekt/der neue Angestellte entwickelt sich gut** the project/the new employee is coming along *or* shaping up nicely; **das Kind entwickelt sich gut** the child is doing well; **er hat sich ganz schön entwickelt** *(inf)* he's turned out really nicely

Ent|wick|ler [ɛnt'vɪklɐ] M **-s, -** *(Phot)* developer

Ent|wick|ler|bad NT *(Phot)* developing bath

Ent|wick|lung F **-, -en** development; *(von Methoden, Verfahren, Gattung auch)* evolution; *(Math: von Formel auch)* expansion; *(= Erzeugung, Chem: von Gasen etc)* production, generation; *(von Mut, Energie)* show, display; *(Phot)* developing; *(esp von Diapositiven)* processing; **das Flugzeug ist noch in der ~** the plane is still being developed, the plane is still in the development stage; **Jugendliche, die noch in der ~ sind** young people who are still in their adolescence or still developing

Ent|wick|lungs-: **Ent|wick|lungs|al|ter** NT adolescence; **Ent|wick|lungs|ar|beit** F development (work); **Ent|wick|lungs|be|schleu|ni|gung** F *(Physiol)* acceleration (in development); **Ent|wick|lungs|bio|lo|gie** F evolutionary biology; **ent|wick|lungs|bio|lo|gisch** ADJ *Prozesse* of evolutionary biology; **Ent|wick|lungs|dienst** M voluntary service overseas *(Brit)*, VSO *(Brit)*, Peace Corps *(US)*; **ent|wick|lungs|fä|hig** ADJ capable of development; **der Plan/die Idee ist durchaus ~** this plan/idea is definitely worth following up *or* expanding; **diese Stelle ist ~** this position has prospects; **Ent|wick|lungs|fä|hig|keit** F capability of development, capacity for development; *(einer Stelle)* prospects *pl*; **Ent|wick|lungs|gang** M *pl* **-gänge** development; **Ent|wick|lungs|ge|biet** NT development area; **Ent|wick|lungs|ge|schich|te** F developmental history, evolution; **ent|wick|lungs|ge|schicht|lich** ADJ evolutionary *attr*, with respect to evolution; **Ent|wick|lungs|hel|fer(in)** M(F) person doing Voluntary Service Overseas *(Brit)*, VSO worker *(Brit)*, Peace Corps worker *(US)*; **ent|wick|lungs|hem|mend** ADJ restricting *or* impeding development; **Ent|wick|lungs|hil|fe** F foreign aid; **Ent|wick|lungs|jah|re** PL adolescent *or* formative *(auch fig)* years, adolescence; **Ent|wick|lungs|kos|ten** PL development costs *pl*; **Ent|wick|lungs|land** NT developing *or* third-world country; **Ent|wick|lungs|mög|lich|keit** F possibility for development; **Ent|wick|lungs|pha|se** F *(Psych)* developmental stage; **Ent|wick|lungs|po|li|tik** F development aid policy; **ent|wick|lungs|po|li|tisch** ADJ development aid policy *attr*; *Sprecher* on development aid policy; **Ent|wick|lungs|psy|cho|lo|gie** F developmental psychology; **Ent|wick-**

lungs|ro|man M *(Liter)* novel showing the development of a character; **Ent|wick|lungs|sta|di|um** NT stage of development; *(der Menschheit etc)* evolutionary stage; **Ent|wick|lungs|stö|rung** F developmental disturbance, disturbance in development; **Ent|wick|lungs|stu|fe** F stage of development; *(der Menschheit etc)* evolutionary stage; **Ent|wick|lungs|zeit** F period of development; *(Biol, Psych)* developmental period; *(Phot)* developing time

ent|win|den [ɛntˈvɪndn] *ptp* **entwunden** [ɛntˈvʊndn] VT *irreg (geh)* **jdm etw ~** to wrest sth from sb

ent|wirr|bar ADJ **schwer ~ sein** *(lit, fig)* to be hard to untangle *or* unravel

ent|wir|ren [ɛntˈvɪrən] *ptp* **entwirrt** VT *(lit, fig)* to untangle, to unravel

ent|wi|schen [ɛntˈvɪʃn] *ptp* **entwischt** VI *aux sein (inf)* to escape, to get away (*+dat, aus* from)

ent|wöh|nen [ɛntˈvøːnən] *ptp* **entwöhnt** VT *Säugling, Jungtier* to wean; **jdn ~** *(einer Gewohnheit, Sucht)* to break sb of the habit (*+dat, von* of), to cure sb (*+dat, von* of), to wean sb (*+dat, von* from); **sich einer Sache** *(gen)* **~** *(geh)* to wean oneself off sth, to disaccustom oneself from sth *(form)*

Ent|wöh|nung F **-, -en** *(von Drogen)* withdrawal; *(von Säugling, Jungtier)* weaning

Ent|wöh|nungs|kur F *(von Drogen)* withdrawal treatment *or* therapy

ent|wöl|ken [ɛntˈvœlkn] *ptp* **entwölkt** VR *(lit, fig liter)* to clear

ent|wür|di|gen [ɛntˈvʏrdɪgn] *ptp* **entwürdigt** VT to degrade; *(= Schande bringen über)* to disgrace VR to degrade *or* abase oneself

ent|wür|di|gend ADJ degrading

Ent|wür|di|gung F degradation, abasement; *(= Entehrung)* disgrace (*+gen* to)

Ent|wurf M **a** *(= Skizze, Abriss)* outline, sketch; *(= Design)* design; *(Archit, fig)* blueprint **b** *(von Plan, Gesetz etc, = Vertragsentwurf, Konzept)* draft (version), framework; *(einer Theorie auch)* outline; *(Parl: = Gesetzentwurf)* bill; *(Comput)* draft; **das Bild ist im ~ fertig** the sketch for the picture is finished; **die Doktorarbeit ist im ~ fertig** the framework for the PhD is finished

Ent|wurfs-: **Ent|wurfs|an|sicht** F *(Comput)* design view; **Ent|wurfs|qua|li|tät** F *(Comput)* draft quality; **Ent|wurfs|sta|di|um** NT **sich im ~ befinden** to be in the planning stage, to be on the drawing board

ent|wur|men [ɛntˈvʊrmən] *ptp* **entwurmt** VT *Katze etc* to worm

ent|wur|zeln [ɛntˈvʊrtsln] *ptp* **entwurzelt** VT *(lit, fig)* to uproot

Ent|wur|ze|lung F **-, -en** *(lit, fig: = das Entwurzeln)* uprooting; *(fig: = das Entwurzeltsein)* rootlessness

ent|zau|bern [ɛntˈtsaubɐn] *ptp* **entzaubert** VT **jdn/etw ~** to break the spell on sb/sth; *(fig auch)* to deprive sb/sth of his/her/its mystique; **ihre romantischen Vorstellungen wurden entzaubert** her romantic illusions were shattered

Ent|zau|be|rung F **-, -en** breaking of the/a spell (*+gen* on); *(fig auch)* deprivation of mystique; *(von Vorstellungen)* shattering, destruction

ent|zer|ren [ɛntˈtsɛrən] *ptp* **entzerrt** VT to correct, to rectify

Ent|zer|rung F correction, rectification; **zeitliche ~** staggering

ent|zie|hen [ɛntˈtsiːən] *ptp* **entzogen** [ɛntˈtsoːgn] *irreg* VT (*+dat* from) to withdraw, to take away; *Gunst etc* to withdraw; *Flüssigkeit* to draw, to extract; *(Chem)* to extract; **jdm Alkohol/Nikotin ~** to deprive sb of alcohol/nicotine; **die Ärzte versuchten ihn zu ~** *(inf)* the doctors tried to cure him of his addiction; **jdm die Erlaubnis** *etc* **~** to withdraw *or* revoke sb's permit *etc*, to take sb's permit *etc* away; **jdm die Rente** *etc* **~** to cut off *or* stop sb's pension *etc*; **jdm sein Vertrauen ~** to withdraw one's confidence *or* trust in sb; **dem Redner das Wort ~** to ask the speaker to stop

VR **sich jdm/einer Sache ~** to evade *or* elude sb/sth; *(= entkommen auch)* to escape (from) sb/sth; **sich seiner Verantwortung ~** to shirk one's responsibilities; **sich jds Verständnis/Kontrolle ~** to be beyond sb's understanding/control; **das entzieht sich meiner Kenntnis/Zuständigkeit** that is beyond my knowledge/authority; **das hat sich meiner Aufmerksamkeit entzogen** that escaped my attention; **sich jds Blicken ~** to be hidden from sight

VI *(inf)* to undergo treatment for (drug) addiction; *(Alkoholiker)* to dry out *(inf)*

Ent|zie|hung F **a** *(von Lizenz etc)* withdrawal, revocation *(form)* **b** *(von Drogen etc) (= Wegnahme)* withdrawal, deprivation; *(= Behandlung)* treatment for drug addiction; *(gegen Alkoholismus)* treatment for alcoholism

Ent|zie|hungs-: **Ent|zie|hungs|an|stalt** F *(für Drogenabhängige)* rehabilitation *or* treatment centre *(Brit) or* center *(US)* for drug addicts, detoxification *or* detox *(inf)* clinic; *(für Alkoholiker)* rehabilitation *or* treatment centre *(Brit) or* center *(US)* for alcoholics, rehab centre *(Brit inf) or* center *(US inf)*, drying-out clinic *(Brit inf)*; **Ent|zie|hungs|kur** F withdrawal treatment; *(für Drogenabhängige auch)* cure for drug addiction; *(für Alkoholiker auch)* cure for alcoholism

ent|zif|fer|bar ADJ decipherable; *Funkspruch etc* decodable

ent|zif|fern [ɛntˈtsɪfɐn] *ptp* **entziffert** VT to decipher; *Geheimschrift, verschlüsselte Botschaft, DNS-Struktur* to decode; **ich kann den Namen nicht ~** I can't make out the name

Ent|zif|fe|rung F **-, -en** deciphering; *(von Funkspruch etc)* decoding

ent|zip|pen *ptp* **entzippt** VT *(Comput) Daten* to unzip

ent|zü|cken [ɛntˈtsʏkn] *ptp* **entzückt** VT to delight; **von jdm/über etw** *(acc)* **entzückt sein** to be delighted by sb/at sth

Ent|zü|cken [ɛntˈtsʏkn] NT **-s**, *no pl* delight, joy; **zu meinem (größten) ~** to my (great) delight *or* joy; **in ~ geraten** to go into raptures; **jdn in (helles) ~ versetzen** to send sb into raptures

ent|zü|ckend ADJ delightful, charming; **das ist ja ~!** how delightful *or* charming!

Ent|zü|ckung F **-, -en** = **Entzücken**

Ent|zug M, *no pl* **a** *(einer Lizenz etc)* withdrawal, revocation *(form)* **b** *(Med) (von Drogen etc)* withdrawal; *(= Entziehungskur) (für Drogenabhängige)* cure for drug addiction; *(für Alkoholiker)* cure for alcoholism; **er ist auf ~** *(Med inf) (Drogenabhängiger)* he is being treated for drug addiction; *(Alkoholiker)* he is being dried out *(inf)*; **kalter ~** *(sl: von Drogen)* cold turkey *(inf)*

Ent|zugs|er|schei|nung F, **Ent|zugs|symp|tom** NT withdrawal symptom

ent|zünd|bar ADJ *(lit, fig)* inflammable; **leicht ~** highly inflammable; *(fig)* easily roused *or* excited

Ent|zünd|bar|keit [ɛntˈtsʏntbaːɐ̯kait] F **-**, *no pl* inflammability

ent|zün|den [ɛntˈtsʏndn] *ptp* **entzündet** VT **a** *Feuer* to light; *Holz etc auch* to set light to, to ignite *(esp Sci, Tech)*; *Streichholz* to light, to strike; *(fig) Streit etc* to start, to spark off; *Hass* to inflame; *Fantasie* to fire; *Begeisterung* to fire, to kindle **b** *(Med)* to inflame VR **a** *(= zu brennen anfangen)* to catch fire, to ignite *(esp Sci, Tech)*; *(fig) (Streit)* to be sparked off; *(Hass)* to be inflamed; *(Fantasie)* to be fired; *(Begeisterung)* to be kindled **b** *(Med)* to become inflamed

ent|zün|det [ɛntˈtsʏndət] PTP *von* **entzünden** ADJ *(Med)* inflamed; *Augen auch* sore

ent|zünd|lich [ɛntˈtsʏntlɪç] ADJ *Gase, Brennstoff* inflammable; *(Med)* inflammatory; **~e Haut** skin which easily becomes inflamed; **ein leicht ~es Temperament** a highly inflammable temper

Ent|zün|dung F **a** *(Med)* inflammation **b** ignition *(esp Sci, Tech)*; **Funken führten zur ~ des Heus** sparks led to the hay catching fire

Ent|zün|dungs- *(Med)*: **ent|zün|dungs|hem|mend** ADJ anti-inflammatory, antiphlogistic *(form)*; **Ent|zün|dungs|hem|mer** M **-s, -** antiphlogistic *(form)*; **Ent|zün|dungs|herd** M focus of inflammation

ent|zwei [ɛntˈtsvai] ADJ *pred* in two (pieces), in half, asunder *(old, poet)*; *(= kaputt)* broken; *(= zerrissen)* torn

ent|zwei+bre|chen VTI *sep irreg (vi: aux sein)* to break in two; *(= zerbrechen)* to break

ent|zwei|en [ɛntˈtsvaiən] *ptp* **entzweit** VT to turn against each other, to divide, to set at variance VR **sich (mit jdm) ~** to fall out (with sb); *(= sich streiten auch)* to quarrel (with sb)

ent|zwei-: **ent|zwei+ge|hen** VI *sep irreg aux sein* to break (in two *or* half), to break asunder *(poet)*; **ent|zwei+rei|ßen** VT *sep irreg* to tear *or* rend in two *or* in half *or* asunder *(poet)*; *(= zerreißen)* to tear to pieces; **ent|zwei+schla|gen** VT *sep irreg* to strike in half *or* in two *or* asunder *(poet)*; *(= zerschlagen)* to smash (to pieces); **ent|zwei+schnei|den** VT *sep irreg* to cut in two *or* half; *(= zerschneiden)* to cut to pieces

Ent|zwei|ung F **-, -en** *(fig) (= Bruch)* split, rupture, break; *(= Streit)* quarrel

en vogue [ã ˈvoːk] ADJ *pred (geh)* in vogue *or* fashion

En|ze|pha|lo|gramm [ɛntsefaloˈgram] NT *pl* **-gramme** *(Med)* encephalogram

En|ze|pha|lo|pa|thie [ɛntsefalopaˈtiː] F **-, -n** [-ˈtiːən] *(Med)* encephalopathy

En|zi|an [ˈɛntsiaːn] M **-s, -e** gentian; *(= Branntwein) spirit distilled from the roots of gentian*

En|zyk|li|ka [ɛnˈtsyːklika] F **-, Enzykliken** [-kn] *(Eccl)* encyclical

En|zyk|lo|pä|die [ɛntsyklopɛˈdiː] F **-, -n** [-ˈdiːən] encyclop(a)edia

en|zyk|lo|pä|disch [ɛntsykloˈpɛːdɪʃ] ADJ encyclop(a)edic

En|zym [ɛnˈtsyːm] NT **-s, -e** enzyme

eo ip|so [ˈeːo ˈɪpso] ADV *(geh)* ipso facto

EP *abbr von* **Europäisches Parlament**

Epau|let|te [epoˈlɛtə] F **-, -n** *usu pl* epaulette; *(US auch)* epaulet

Epen *pl von* **Epos**

Ephe|be [eˈfeːbə] M **-n, -n** *(Hist)* ephebe, ephebus

ephe|mer [efeˈmeːɐ], **ephe|me|risch** [efeˈmeːrɪʃ] ADJ *(geh)* ephemeral

Ephe|ser [ˈeːfezɐ] M **-s, -**, **Ephe|se|rin** [-ərɪn] F **-, -nen** Ephesian

Ephe|ser|brief M Epistle to the Ephesians, Ephesians *sing*

Epi|de|mie [epideˈmiː] F **-, -n** [-ˈmiːən] *(Med, fig)* epidemic

Epi|de|mio|lo|ge [epidemioˈloːgə] M **-n, -n**, **Epi|de|mio|lo|gin** [-ˈloːgɪn] F **-, -nen** epidemiologist

Epi|de|mio|lo|gie [epidemioloˈgiː] F **-**, *no pl* epidemiology

epi|de|mio|lo|gisch [epidemioˈloːgɪʃ] ADJ epidemiological

epi|de|misch [epiˈdeːmɪʃ] ADJ *(Med, fig)* epidemic ADV **sich ~ ausbreiten** *(Med)* to spread as an epidemic; *(fig)* to spread like an epidemic

Epi|der|mis [epiˈdɛrmɪs] F **-, Epidermen** [-ˈdɛrmən] epidermis

Epi|dia|skop [epidiaˈskoːp] NT **-s, -e** epidiascope

Epi|go|ne [epiˈgoːnə] M **-n, -n**, **Epi|go|nin** [-ˈgoːnɪn] F **-, -nen** epigone *(liter)*; *(= Nachahmer)* imitator

epi|go|nen|haft ADJ epigonic *(liter, rare)*; *(= nachahmend)* imitative

Epi|graf [epiˈgraːf] NT **-s, -e** epigraph

Epi|gramm [epiˈgram] NT *pl* **-gramme** epigram

epi|gram|ma|tisch [epigraˈmaːtɪʃ] ADJ epigrammatic

Epi|graph [epiˈgraːf] NT **-s, -e** = **Epigraf**

Epik [ˈeːpɪk] F **-**, *no pl* epic poetry

Epi|ker [ˈeːpikɐ] M **-s, -**, **Epi|ke|rin** [-ərɪn] F **-, -nen** epic poet

Epi|kur [epi'ku:ɐ] M **-s** Epicurus

Epi|ku|re|er [epiku're:ɐ] M **-s, -, Epi|ku|re|e|rin** [-'re:ərɪn] F **-, -nen** *(Philos)* Epicurean; *(fig)* epicure(an)

epi|ku|re|isch [epiku're:ɪʃ] ADJ *(Philos)* Epicurean; *(fig)* epicurean

Epi|la|ti|on waxing, (d)epilation

Epi|lep|sie [epilɛ'psi:] F **-, -n** [-'psi:ən] epilepsy

Epi|lep|ti|ker [epi'lɛptikɐ] M **-s, -, Epi|lep|ti|ke|rin** [-ərɪn] F **-, -nen** epileptic

epi|lep|tisch [epi'lɛptɪʃ] ADJ epileptic

Epi|log [epi'lo:k] M **-s, -e** [-gə] epilogue

episch ['e:pɪʃ] ADJ *(lit, fig)* epic

Epi|skop [epi'sko:p] NT **-s, -e** episcope

Epis|ko|pat [epɪsko'pa:t] M OR NT **-(e)s, -e** episcopacy, episcopate

Epi|so|de [epi'zo:də] F **-, -n** episode

Epi|so|den|film M film in instalments *(Brit)* or installments *(US)*, serial film

epi|so|den|haft, epi|so|disch [epi'zo:dɪʃ] ADJ episodic

Epis|tel [e'pɪstl] F **-, -n** epistle *(auch inf)*; *(old: = Lesung)* lesson; **jdm die ~ lesen** *(old inf)* to read sb the riot act *(inf)*

Epis|te|mo|lo|gie [epɪstemolo'gi:] F **-,** *no pl* epistemology

Epi|taph [epi'ta:f] NT **-s, -e** *(liter)* epitaph

Epi|the|ton [e'pi:tetɔn] NT **-s, Epitheta** [-ta] *(Poet)* epithet

Epi|zent|rum [epi'tsɛntrʊm] NT epicentre *(Brit)*, epicenter *(US)*

epo|chal [epɔ'xa:l] ADJ **a** epochal **b** *(= Epoche machend)* epoch-making, era-making

Epo|che [e'pɔxə] F **-, -n** epoch; **~ machen** to be epoch-making, to mark a new epoch or era; **~ machend** = **epochemachend**

epo|che|ma|chend ADJ epoch-making

Epos ['e:pɔs] NT **-, Epen** ['e:pn] epic (poem), epos

Ep|oxyd|harz [epɔ'ksy:t-] NT epoxy resin

EPROM ['ɛprɔm] NT **-(s), -s** *abbr von* **erasable programmable read-only memory** EPROM

Ep|rou|vet|te [epru'vɛt] F **-, -n** *(Aus Chem)* test tube

Equa|li|zer ['i:kvəlaizɐ] M **-s, -** *(Tech)* equalizer

Equi|pa|ge [ek(v)i'pa:ʒə] F **-, -n** *(old)* equipage

Equipe [e'kɪp] F **-, -n** team

er [e:ɐ] PERS PRON *gen* **seiner**, *dat* **ihm**, *acc* **ihn** he; *(von Dingen)* it; *(von Hund etc)* it, he; *(vom Mond)* it, she *(poet)*; **wenn ich er wäre** if I were him or he *(form)*; **er ist es** it's him, it is he *(form)*; **wer hat das gemacht/ist der Täter? – er/er (ist es)!** who did that/is the person responsible? – he did/is!, him *(inf)*!; **er war es nicht, ich wars** it wasn't him, it was me; **sie ist größer als er** she is taller than he is or him; **Er** *(obs)* you; *(Bibl)* He; **ein Er und eine Sie** *(hum inf)* a he and a she

er|ach|ten [ɛɐ'laxtn] *ptp* **erachtet** VT *(geh)* **jdn/etw für** or **als etw ~** to consider or deem *(form)* sb/sth (to be) sth

Er|ach|ten [ɛɐ'laxtn] NT **-s,** *no pl* **meines ~s, nach meinem ~** in my opinion

er|ah|nen [ɛɐ'la:nən] *ptp* **erahnt** VT = **ahnen**

er|ar|bei|ten [ɛɐ'larbaitn] *ptp* **erarbeitet** VT **a** *(= erwerben) Vermögen etc* to work for; *Wissen etc* to acquire **b** *(= erstellen) Entwurf etc* to work out, to elaborate

Er|ar|bei|tung [ɛɐ'larbaitʊŋ] F **-, -en** *usu sing* **a** *(von Lernstoff etc)* mastering; *(von Wissen)* acquisition **b** *(= Erstellung)* development, creation

Erb-: Erb|adel M hereditary nobility; **Erb|an|la|ge** F *usu pl* hereditary factor(s *pl*); **Erb|an|spruch** M claim to an/the inheritance; **Erb|an|teil** M share or portion of an/the inheritance

er|bar|men [ɛɐ'barmən] *ptp* **erbarmt** VT **jdn ~** to arouse sb's pity, to move sb to pity; **es kann einen ~** it's pitiable; **er sieht zum Erbarmen aus** he's a pitiful sight; **das ist zum Erbarmen** it's pitiful; **sie singt zum Erbarmen** she sings appallingly, she's an appalling singer; **es möchte einen Hund ~** *(inf)* it would melt a heart of stone VR *+gen* to have or take pity (on) *(auch hum inf)*; *(= verzeihen, verschonen)* to have mercy (on); **Herr, erbarme dich (unser)!** Lord, have mercy (upon us)!

Er|bar|men [ɛɐ'barmən] NT **-s,** *no pl (= Mitleid)* pity, compassion *(mit* on); *(= Gnade)* mercy *(mit* on); **aus ~** out of pity; **ohne ~** pitiless(ly), merciless(ly); **er kennt kein ~** he knows no mercy; **kein ~ mit jdm kennen** to be merciless with sb, to show sb no mercy

er|bar|mens|wert ADJ pitiable, wretched, pitiful

er|bärm|lich [ɛɐ'bɛrmlɪç] ADJ *(= erbarmenswert, pej: = dürftig)* pitiful, wretched; *(= gemein, schlecht)* wretched, miserable; *(inf: = furchtbar) Kälte* terrible, hideous ADV *sich verhalten* abominably, wretchedly; *(= sehr schlecht) singen* miserably, appallingly; *(inf: = furchtbar) frieren, wehtun* terribly; **~ aussehen** to look wretched or terrible

Er|bärm|lich|keit F **-, -en** *(= Elend)* wretchedness, misery; *(fig: = Dürftigkeit, Gemeinheit etc)* wretchedness

Er|bar|mungs-: er|bar|mungs|los *(lit, fig)* ADJ pitiless, merciless ADV pitilessly, mercilessly; **Er|bar|mungs|lo|sig|keit** F **-,** *no pl (lit, fig)* pitilessness, mercilessness; **er|bar|mungs|voll** ADJ compassionate, full of pity; **er|bar|mungs|wür|dig** ADJ = **erbarmenswert**

er|bau|en [ɛɐ'bauən] *ptp* **erbaut** VT **a** *(lit, fig: = errichten)* to build **b** *(fig: = seelisch bereichern)* to edify, to uplift; **wir waren von der Nachricht nicht gerade erbaut** *(inf)* we weren't exactly delighted by the news; **der Chef ist von meinem Plan nicht besonders erbaut** *(inf)* the boss isn't particularly enthusiastic about my plan VR **sich ~ an** *(+dat)* to be uplifted or edified by; **abends erbaut er sich an bachschen Kantaten** in the evenings he is uplifted by Bach's cantatas

Er|bau|er [ɛɐ'bauɐ] M **-s, -, Er|bau|e|rin** [-ərɪn] F **-, -nen** builder; *(fig auch)* architect

er|bau|lich [ɛɐ'baulɪç] ADJ edifying *(auch iro)*, uplifting; *(Rel) Buch, Schriften* devotional

Er|bau|lich|keit F **-,** *no pl* edification *no pl*, uplift *no pl*

Er|bau|ung F **-, -en a** building **b** *(fig: seelisch)* edification; **zur ~** for one's edification

Erb-: Erb|bau|er M *pl* **-bauern, Erb|bäu|e|rin** F *farmer with a hereditary right to his/her property*; **Erb|bau|recht** NT *(Jur)* inheritable or hereditary building rights *pl*; **Erb|be|gräb|nis** NT family grave or *(= Gruft)* vault; **erb|be|rech|tigt** ADJ entitled to inherit; **die Erbberechtigten** the legal heirs; **erb|bio|lo|gisch** ADJ genetic; **~es Gutachten** *(Jur)* blood test *(to establish paternity)*

Er|be ['ɛrbə] M **-n, -n** *(lit, fig)* heir *(einer Person (gen)* of or to sb, *einer Sache (gen)* to sth); **gesetzlicher ~** legal heir, heir at law *(Jur)*, heir apparent *(Jur)*; **leiblicher ~** blood-related heir, heir according to bloodright; **direkter ~** direct or lineal heir, heir of the body *(Jur)*; **mutmaßlicher ~** presumptive heir, heir presumptive *(Jur)*; **jdn zum** or **als ~n einsetzen** to appoint sb as or to make sb one's heir

Er|be NT **-s,** *no pl* inheritance; *(fig)* heritage; *(esp Unerwünschtes)* legacy; **das ~ des Faschismus** the legacy of fascism

er|be|ben [ɛɐ'be:bn] *ptp* **erbebt** VI *aux sein (geh: Erde, Mensch etc)* to tremble, to shake, to shudder

erb|ei|gen ['ɛrplaign] ADJ *(= geerbt, vererbt)* inherited; *(= erblich)* hereditary

Erb|ei|gen|schaft F hereditary characteristic

er|ben ['ɛrbn] VT *(lit, fig)* to inherit *(von* from); *Vermögen auch* to come into; *(inf: = geschenkt bekommen)* to get, to be given; **bei ihm ist nichts zu ~** *(inf)* **bei ihm kann man nichts ~** *(inf)* you won't get anything or a sausage *(Brit inf)* out of him VI to inherit

Er|ben|ge|mein|schaft F community of heirs

er|bet|teln [ɛɐ'bɛtln] *ptp* **erbettelt** VT to get by begging; **die Kinder müssen alles auf der Straße ~** the children have to go begging on the streets for everything; **seine Möbel hat er (sich** *dat*) **alle bei seinen Bekannten erbettelt** he cadged *(esp Brit inf)* or mooched *(US inf)* all his furniture off his friends; **die Kinder erbettelten sich die Erlaubnis, ...** the children managed to wheedle permission ...

er|beu|ten [ɛɐ'bɔytn] *ptp* **erbeutet** VT *(Tier) Opfer* to carry off; *(Dieb)* to get away with; *(im Krieg)* to capture, to take

Erb-: erb|fä|hig ADJ *(Jur)* entitled to inherit, heritable *(spec)*; **Erb|fä|hig|keit** F *(Jur)* entitlement to inherit, heritability *(spec)*; **Erb|fak|tor** M *(Biol)* (hereditary) factor, gene; **Erb|fall** M *(Jur)* **im ~** in the case of inheritance; **Erb|feh|ler** M *(lit, fig)* hereditary defect; **Erb|feind(in)** M(F) traditional or arch enemy; **der ~** *(= Teufel)* the Arch-Fiend; **Erb|fol|ge** F (line of) succession; **Erb|fol|ge|krieg** M war of succession

Erb|gut NT **a** *pl* **-güter** *(= Hof)* ancestral estate **b** *no pl (= Nachlass)* estate, inheritance; *(fig)* heritage **c** *no pl (Biol)* genotype, genetic make-up

erb|gut-: erb|gut|schä|di|gend ADJ genetically harmful; **erb|gut|ver|än|dernd** ADJ *Stoff* causing genetic changes; **das hat eine ~e Wirkung** it causes genetic changes

er|bie|ten [ɛɐ'bi:tn] *ptp* **erboten** [ɛɐ'bo:tn] VR *irreg (geh)* **sich ~, etw zu tun** to offer or volunteer to do sth; **sich zu etw ~** to offer one's services for sth

Er|bin ['ɛrbɪn] F **-, -nen** heiress → **Erbe**

Erb|in|for|ma|ti|on ['ɛrp-] F genetic information

er|bit|ten [ɛɐ'bɪtn] *ptp* **erbeten** [ɛɐ'be:tn] VT *irreg* to ask for, to request; **sich ~/nicht ~ lassen** to be/not to be prevailed upon

er|bit|tern [ɛɐ'bɪtɐn] *ptp* **erbittert** VT to enrage, to incense

er|bit|tert [ɛɐ'bɪtɐt] ADJ *Widerstand, Gegner, Diskussion etc* bitter ADV bitterly

Er|bit|te|rung F **-,** *no pl* rage; *(rare: = Heftigkeit)* fierceness, bitterness

Er|bi|um ['ɛrbiʊm] NT **-s,** *no pl (abbr* **Er***)* erbium

Erb|krank|heit ['ɛrp-] F hereditary disease

er|blas|sen [ɛɐ'blasn] *ptp* **erblasst** VI *aux sein* to (go or turn) pale, to blanch; **vor Neid ~** to turn or go *(esp Brit)* green with envy

Erb|las|ser ['ɛrplasɐ] M **-s, -, Erb|las|se|rin** [-ərɪn] F **-, -nen a** person who leaves an inheritance **b** *(= Testator)* testator/testatrix

Erb|last F negative inheritance or heritage, burden from the past; *(= Probleme)* inherited problem(s *pl*)

er|blei|chen [ɛɐ'blaiçn] VI *aux sein* **a** *ptp* **erbleicht** *(geh)* to (go or turn) pale, to blanch **b** *pret* **erblich** [ɛɐ'blɪç], *ptp* **erblichen** [ɛɐ'blɪçn] *(obs, liter: = sterben)* to expire

erb|lich ['ɛrplɪç] ADJ hereditary ADV **er ist ~ belastet, auch sein Vater hatte ...** *(bei Eigenschaft)* it's inherited, his father also had ...; *(bei Krankheit)* it runs in the family, his father also had ...; **er ist ~ schwer (vor)belastet** it runs in the family; **etw ist ~ bedingt** sth is an inherited condition; **etw wird ~ von jdm weitergegeben** sth is passed on as a hereditary trait

Erb|lich|keit F **-,** *no pl* heritability, hereditability

er|bli|cken [ɛɐ'blɪkn] *ptp* **erblickt** VT *(geh)* to see, to perceive; *(= erspähen)* to spot, to catch sight of; **in jdm/etw eine Gefahr** *etc* **~** to see sb/sth as a danger *etc*, to see a danger *etc* in sb/sth → **Licht a**

er|blin|den [ɛɐ'blɪndn] *ptp* **erblindet** VI *aux sein* to go blind, to lose one's sight

Er|blin|dung F **-, -en** loss of sight

er|blon|den [ɛɐ'blɔndn] *ptp* **erblondet** VI *aux sein (hum)* to go blond(e)

er|blü|hen [ɛɐ'bly:ən] *ptp* **erblüht** VI *aux sein (geh)* to bloom, to blossom; **zu voller Schönheit ~** *(fig)* to blossom out

Erb-: **Erb|mas|se** F estate, inheritance; *(Biol)* genotype, genetic make-up; **Erb|on|kel** M *(inf)* rich uncle

er|bo|sen [ɛɐ'bo:zn] *ptp* **erbost** *(geh)* VT to infuriate, to anger; **erbost sein über** *(+acc)* to be furious *or* infuriated at VR **sich ~ über** *(+acc)* to get *or* become furious *or* infuriated about

er|bö|tig [ɛɐ'bø:tɪç] ADJ **~ sein, etw zu tun** *(obs)* to be willing *or* prepared to do sth

Erb-: **Erb|pacht** F hereditary lease(hold); **Erb|päch|ter(in)** M(F) hereditary leaseholder; **Erb|pfle|ge** F eugenics *sing*; **Erb|prinz** M hereditary prince; *(= Thronfolger)* heir to the throne; **Erb|prin|zes|sin** F hereditary princess; *(= Thronfolgerin)* heiress to the throne

er|bre|chen [ɛɐ'brɛçn] *ptp* **erbrochen** [ɛɐ'brɔxn] *irreg* VT **a** *(= ausspucken)* to vomit, to bring up **b** *(liter) Schloss, Siegel* to break open; *Tür auch* to force (open) VIR **(sich) ~** *(Med)* to vomit, to be sick; **etw bis zum Erbrechen tun** *(fig)* to do sth ad nauseam; **etw zum Erbrechen satthaben** *(fig)* to be absolutely sick of sth

Erb|recht ['ɛrp-] NT law of inheritance; *(= Erbanspruch)* right of inheritance *(auf +acc* to)

er|brin|gen [ɛɐ'brɪŋən] *ptp* **erbracht** [ɛɐ'braxt] VT *irreg* to produce, to furnish, to adduce

Er|bro|che|ne(s) [ɛɐ'brɔxənə] NT *decl as adj, no pl* vomit

Erb|scha|den ['ɛrp-] M hereditary defect

Erb|schaft ['ɛrpʃaft] F **-, -en** inheritance; **eine ~ machen** *or* **antreten** to come into an inheritance; **die ~ des Faschismus** the legacy of fascism

Erb|schafts-: **Erb|schafts|aus|ei|nan|der|set|zung** F dispute over an inheritance; **Erb|schafts|kla|ge** F *(Jur)* action for recovery of an/the inheritance; **Erb|schafts|steu|er** F estate *or* death duty *or* duties *pl*; **Erbschafts- und Schenkungssteuer** capital transfer tax

Erb-: **Erb|schein** M certificate of inheritance; **Erb|schlei|cher(in)** M(F) legacy-hunter; **Erb|schlei|che|rei** F legacy-hunting; **Erb|schuld** F inherited debt

Erb|se ['ɛrpsə] F **-, -n** pea; **gelbe** *or* **getrocknete ~n** dried peas

Erb|sen-: **erb|sen|groß** ADJ pea-size, the size of a pea; **Erb|sen|pü|ree** NT ≈ pease pudding *(esp Brit)*; **Erb|sen|sup|pe** F pea soup; **Erb|sen|zäh|ler** M **-s, -**, **Erb|sen|zäh|le|rin** F **-, -nen** *(pej inf)* bean-counter *(pej inf)*; **Erb|sen|zäh|le|rei** [-tsɛ:lə'rai] F **-**, *no pl (pej inf)* bean-counting *(pej inf)*

Erb-: **Erb|strei|tig|keit** F *usu pl* inheritance dispute, quarrel over a will *or* legacy; **Erb|stück** NT heirloom; **Erb|sün|de** F *(Rel)* original sin

Erbs|wurst ['ɛrps-] F *pea meal compressed into the form of a sausage*

Erb-: **Erb|tan|te** F *(inf)* rich aunt; **Erb|teil** NT **a** *(Jur)* AUCH M (portion of an/the) inheritance **b** *(= Veranlagung)* inherited trait; **Erb|tei|lung** F *usu sing* division of an/the estate *(on succession (to the estate))*; **Erb|ver|trag** M testamentary contract, agreement *or* contract of inheritance *(US)*; **Erb|ver|zicht** M renunciation of one's claim to an inheritance; **Erb|wal|ter** ['ɛrpvaltɐ] M **-s, -**, **Erb|wal|te|rin** [-ərɪn] F **-, -nen** *(geh)* trustee

Erd|ach|se ['e:ɐt-] F earth's axis

er|dacht [ɛɐ'daxt] ADJ *Geschichte* made-up → *auch* **erdenken**

Erd-: **Erd|al|ter|tum** NT *(Geol)* Palaeozoic; **Erd|an|zie|hung** F, *no pl* gravitational pull of the earth; **Erd|ap|fel** M *(Aus, S Ger)* potato; **Erd|ar|bei|ten** PL excavation(s *pl*), earthwork *sing*; **Erd|at|mo|sphä|re** F earth's atmosphere; **Erd|bahn** F orbit of the earth, earth's orbit; **Erd|ball** M *(liter)* globe, world

Erd|be|ben NT earthquake, quake

Erd|be|ben-: **Erd|be|ben|ge|biet** NT earthquake area; **erd|be|ben|ge|fähr|det** ADJ at risk from earthquakes; **Erd|be|ben|gür|tel** M earthquake belt *or* zone; **Erd|be|ben|herd** M seismic focus, seismic centre *(Brit) or* center *(US)*; **Erd|be|ben|mes|ser** M **-s, -**, **Erd|be|ben|mess|ge|rät** NT seismograph, seismometer; **Erd|be|ben|op|fer** NT earthquake victim *or* casualty; **Erd|be|ben|schutz** M earthquake protection; **erd|be|ben|si|cher** ADJ *Gebäude etc* earthquake-proof; *Gebiet* not prone to earthquakes; **Erd|be|ben|si|cher|heit** F *(von Gebäude etc)* resistance to earthquakes; **die ~ dieses Gebiets** the fact that this area is not prone to earthquakes; **Erd|be|ben|war|te** F seismological station

Erd-: **Erd|bee|re** F strawberry; **erd|beer|far|ben** [-farbn] ADJ strawberry-colour(ed) *(Brit)*, strawberry-color(ed) *(US)*; **Erd|be|stat|tung** F burial, interment; **Erd|be|völ|ke|rung** F population of the earth, earth's population; **Erd|be|woh|ner(in)** M(F) inhabitant of the earth; *(gegenüber Marsbewohnern etc)* terrestrial, earthling *(hum)*; **Erd|bir|ne** F *(dial)* potato; **Erd|bo|den** M ground, earth; **etw dem ~ gleichmachen** to level sth, to raze sth to the ground; **vom ~ verschwinden** to disappear from *or* off the face of the earth; **als hätte ihn der ~ verschluckt** as if the earth had swallowed him up; **Erd|bro|cken** M clod (of earth)

Er|de ['e:ɐdə] F **-, -n** **a** *(= Welt)* earth, world; **unsere Mutter ~** *(liter)* Mother Earth; **auf ~n** *(old, liter)* on earth; **auf der ganzen ~** all over the world; **niemand auf der ganzen ~** nobody in the whole world **b** *(= Boden)* ground; **in fremder/heimatlicher ~ ruhen** *(liter)* to lie *or* rest in foreign/native soil *(liter)*; **unter der ~** underground, below ground; *(fig)* beneath the soil; **du wirst mich noch unter die ~ bringen** *(inf)* you'll be the death of me yet *(inf)*; **über der ~** above ground; **auf die ~ fallen** to fall to the ground; **auf nackter** *or* **bloßer ~** on the bare ground; **mit beiden Beinen** *or* **Füßen (fest) auf der ~ stehen** *(fig)* to have both feet firmly on the ground → **eben ADJ** **c** *(= Erdreich, Bodenart)* soil, earth *(auch Chem)*; **fette/trockene ~** rich/dry soil; **zu ~ werden** to turn to dust; **~ zu ~** *(Eccl)* dust to dust; **seltene ~n** *(Chem)* rare earths **d** *(Elec: = Erdung)* earth, ground *(US)*

er|den ['e:ɐdn] VT *(Elec)* to earth, to ground *(US)*

Er|den-: **Er|den|bür|ger(in)** M(F) *(geh)* mortal; **ein neuer ~** a new addition to the human race; **er|den|fern** ADJ *(liter)* far from the earth; **Er|den|glück** NT *(liter)* earthly happiness

er|den|ken [ɛɐ'dɛŋkn] *ptp* **erdacht** [ɛɐ'daxt] VT *irreg* to devise, to think up → *auch* **erdacht**

Er|den|kind NT *(geh)* child of the earth *(liter)*

er|denk|lich [ɛɐ'dɛŋklɪç] ADJ *attr* conceivable, imaginable; **alles ~(e) Gute** all the very best; **sich** *(dat)* **alle** *or* **jede ~e Mühe geben** to take the greatest (possible) pains; **alles Erdenkliche tun** to do everything conceivable *or* imaginable

Er|den- *(liter)*: **Er|den|le|ben** NT earthly life, life on earth; **Er|den|rund** [-rʊnt] NT **-s**, *no pl* world

Erd-: **erd|far|ben** [-farbn], **erd|far|big** ADJ earth-coloured *(Brit)*, earth-colored *(US)*; **erd|fern** ADJ *(Astron)* far from the earth; **Erd|fer|ne** F *(Astron)* apogee; **Erd|fern|er|kun|dungs|sa|tel|lit** M long-distance reconnaissance satellite; **Erd|gas** NT natural gas; **Erd|ge|bo|re|ne(r)** ['e:ɐtgəbo:rənə] MF *decl as adj (liter)* mortal; **erd|ge|bun|den** ADJ **a** *(liter)* earthbound **b** *Teleskop, Observatorium* on (the) earth; *Telefonnetz* underground; **Erd|geist** M earth-spirit; **Erd|ge|ruch** M earthy smell; **Erd|ge|schich|te** F geological history, history of the earth; **erd|ge|schicht|lich** ADJ *no pred* geological; **Erd|ge|schoss** NT, **Erd|ge|schoß** NT *(S Ger, Aus)* ground floor, first floor *(US)*; **im ~** on the ground *or* first *(US)* floor; **erd|hal|tig** ADJ containing earth; **Erd|harz** NT bitumen; **Erd|hau|fen** M mound of earth; **Erd|hörn|chen** NT ground squirrel

er|dich|ten [ɛɐ'dɪçtn] *ptp* **erdichtet** VT to invent, to fabricate, to make up; **das ist alles erdichtet und erlogen** it's all pure fabrication

er|dig ['e:ɐdɪç] ADJ earthy

Erd-: **Erd|in|ne|re(s)** ['e:ɐtlɪnərə] NT *decl as adj* interior *or* bowels *pl* of the earth; **Erd|ka|bel** NT underground cable; **Erd|kar|te** F map of the earth; **Erd|käs** ['e:ɐtkɛ:s] M *(Sch sl: = Erdkunde)* geography; **Erd|kern** M earth's core; **Erd|klum|pen** M clod of earth; **Erd|kreis** M globe, world; **auf dem ganzen ~** all over the world; **Erd|krüm|mung** F (the) earth's curvature, curvature of the earth; **Erd|krus|te** F earth's crust; **Erd|ku|gel** F world, earth, globe; **Erd|kun|de** F geography; **erd|kund|lich** ['e:ɐtkʊntlɪç] ADJ geographical; **Erd|lei|tung** F *(Elec)* earth *or* ground *(US)* (connection); *(= Kabel)* underground wire; **Erd|loch** NT *(Mil)* foxhole; **erd|mag|ne|tisch** ADJ geomagnetic; **Erd|mag|ne|tis|mus** M geomagnetism; **Erd|männ|chen** NT *(Zool)* meerkat; **Erd|man|tel** M mantle; **Erd|me|tal|le** PL earth metals *pl*; **Erd|mit|tel|al|ter** NT *(Geol)* Mesozoic; **erd|nah** ADJ *(Astron)* near to the earth; *(fig)* down-to-earth; **Erd|nä|he** F *(Astron)* perigee; **Erd|nuss** F peanut, groundnut; **Erd|nuss|but|ter** F peanut butter; **Erd|ober|flä|che** F surface of the earth, earth's surface

Erd|öl ['e:ɐtlø:l] NT (mineral) oil, petroleum; **~ exportierend** oil-exporting, petroleum-exporting

er|dol|chen [ɛɐ'dɔlçn] *ptp* **erdolcht** VT to stab (to death); **jdn mit Blicken ~** to look daggers at sb

Erd|öl-: **erd|öl|ex|por|tie|rend** ADJ → **Erdöl**; **Erd|öl|feld** NT oil field; **Erd|öl|ge|sell|schaft** F oil company; **Erd|öl|lei|tung** F oil pipeline; **Erd|öl|prei|se** PL oil prices *pl*; **Erd|öl|raf|fi|na|ti|on** F petroleum refining; **Erd|öl|raf|fi|ne|rie** F oil refinery; **Erd|öl|ver|ar|bei|tung** F processing of crude oil

Erd-: **Erd|pech** NT bitumen, asphalt, mineral pitch; **Erd|pol** M *(Geog)* (terrestrial) pole; **Erd|reich** NT soil, earth

er|dreis|ten [ɛɐ'draistn] *ptp* **erdreistet** VR **sich ~, etw zu tun** to have the audacity to do sth; **wie können Sie sich ~!** how dare you!; **er hat sich zu dieser Eigenmächtigkeit erdreistet** he had the audacity to act in this high-handed way

Erd|rin|de ['e:ɐt-] F earth's crust

er|dröh|nen [ɛɐ'drø:nən] *ptp* **erdröhnt** VI *aux sein (geh)* to boom out, to thunder out; *(Kanonen auch)* to roar; *(Luft, Raum)* to resound *(von* with)

er|dros|seln [ɛɐ'drɔsln] *ptp* **erdrosselt** VT to strangle, to throttle

Er|dros|se|lung F strangulation, throttling

er|drü|cken [ɛɐ'drʏkn] *ptp* **erdrückt** VT to crush (to death); *(fig: = überwältigen)* to overwhelm; **ein ~des Gefühl** a stifling feeling; **~de Übermacht** overwhelming superiority; **~des Beweismaterial** overwhelming evidence; **die Schuld erdrückte ihn beinahe** the sense of guilt oppressed him *or* weighed down on him

Erd-: **Erd|rutsch** M landslide, landslip; **politischer ~** political upheaval; *(= überwältigender Wahlsieg)* (political) landslide; **erd|rutsch|ar|tig** ADJ *Sieg* landslide *attr*; *Niederlage* devastating; **Erd|rutsch|sieg** M landslide (victory); **Erd|sa|tel|lit** M earth satellite; **Erd|schat|ten** M shadow of the earth; **Erd|schicht** F layer (of the earth), stratum; **Erd|schluss** M *(Elec)* accidental earth *or* ground *(US)*; **Erd|schol|le** F clod of earth; **Erd|sicht** F *(Aviat)* ground visibility; **Erd|spal|te** F crevice; **Erd|stoß** M (seismic) shock; **Erd|strah|len** PL field lines *pl*; **Erd|strich** M region, area; **Erd|teil** M continent; **Erd|tra|bant** M moon

er|dul|den [ɛɐ'dʊldn] *ptp* **erduldet** VT to endure, to suffer

Erd-: **Erd|um|dre|hung** F rotation *or* revolution of the earth; **Erd|um|fang** M circumference of the earth; **Erd|um|krei|sung** F *(durch Satelliten)* orbit(ing) of the earth; **Erd|um|lauf|bahn** F earth orbit; **Erd|um|run|dung** F *(durch Satelliten)* orbit(ing) of the earth; **Erd|um|se|ge|lung** F voyage around the world, circumnavigation of the globe; **Erd|um|seg|ler(in)** M(F) round-the-world sailor, circumnavigator of the globe

Er|dung ['e:ɐdʊŋ] F -, -en *(Elec)* earth(ing), ground(ing) *(US)*

Erd-: **erd|ver|bun|den**, **erd|ver|wach|sen** ADJ *Mensch, Volksstamm* close to the earth; **Erd|wall** M earthwork, earth bank *or* wall; **Erd|wär|me** F natural heat of the earth; **erd|wärts** ['e:ɐtvɛrts] ADV earthward(s); **Erd|zeit|al|ter** NT geological era

E-Rea|der ['i:ri:dɐ] M -s, - e-reader

er|ei|fern [ɛɐ'laifɐn] *ptp* **ereifert** VR to get excited *or* worked up *(über +acc* over)

er|eig|nen [ɛɐ'laignən] *ptp* **ereignet** VR to occur, to happen

Er|eig|nis [ɛɐ'laignɪs] NT -ses, -se event, occurrence; *(= Vorfall)* incident, event; *(besonderes)* occasion, event → **freudig ADJ b**

er|eig|nis-: **er|eig|nis|los** ADJ uneventful; **Er|eig|nis|lo|sig|keit** F -, *no pl* uneventfulness; **er|eig|nis|reich** ADJ eventful

er|ei|len [ɛɐ'lailən] *ptp* **ereilt** VT *(geh)* to overtake

erek|til [erɛk'ti:l] ADJ *(Physiol)* erectile

Erek|ti|on [erɛk'tsio:n] F -, -en *(Physiol)* erection

Ere|mit [ere'mi:t] M -en, -en, **Ere|mi|tin** [-'mi:tɪn] F -, -nen hermit

Ere|mi|ta|ge [eremi'ta:ʒə] F -, -n hermitage

er|er|ben [ɛɐ'lɛrbn] *ptp* **ererbt** VT to inherit

er|fah|ren[1] [ɛɐ'fa:rən] *ptp* **erfahren** *irreg* VT **a** *Nachricht etc* to learn, to find out; *(= hören)* to hear (*von* about, of); **wenn der Chef das erfährt, wird er wütend** if the boss gets to hear about it *or* finds that out he'll be furious; **etw zu ~ suchen** to try to find out sth; **darf man Ihre Absichten ~?** might one inquire as to your intentions? **b** *(= erleben)* to experience; *(= erleiden auch) Rückschlag* to suffer; *(= empfangen) Liebe, Verständnis* to receive; *Veränderungen etc* to undergo VI to hear (*von* about, of)

er|fah|ren[2] [ɛɐ'fa:rən] ADJ experienced

Er|fah|ren|heit F -, *no pl* experience

Er|fah|rung ✪ 38.1, 46.2 F -, -en experience; *(= Übung auch)* practical knowledge; *(Philos auch)* empirical knowledge; **aus (eigener) ~** from (one's own) experience; **nach meiner ~** in my experience; **~en sammeln** to gain experience; **die ~ hat gezeigt, dass ...** experience has shown that ...; **etw in ~ bringen** to learn *or* to find out sth; **eine ~ machen** to have an experience; **seine ~en machen** to learn (things) the hard way; **jeder muss seine ~en selber machen** everyone has to learn by experience; **ich habe die ~ gemacht, dass ...** I have found that ...; **mit dieser neuen Maschine/Mitarbeiterin haben wir nur gute/schlechte ~en gemacht** we have found this new machine/employee (to be) completely satisfactory/unsatisfactory; **was für ~en haben Sie mit ihm/damit gemacht?** how did you find him/it?; **ich habe mit der Ehe nur schlechte ~en gemacht** I've had a very bad experience of marriage *(esp Brit)*, I've had very bad experience with marriage *(US)*; **durch ~ wird man klug** *(Prov)* one learns by experience

Er|fah|rungs-: **Er|fah|rungs|aus|tausch** M *(Pol)* exchange of experiences; **er|fah|rungs|ge|mäß** ADV **~ ist es ...** experience shows ...; **Er|fah|rungs|me|di|zin** F alternative medicine; **Er|fah|rungs|tat|sa|che** F empirical fact; **Er|fah|rungs|wert** M figure based on experience, empirically established figure; **Er|fah|rungs|wis|sen|schaft** F empirical science

er|fass|bar ADJ recordable; **ein nicht ~es Lebensgefühl** an indefinable feeling of being alive

Er|fass|bar|keit [ɛɐ'fasba:ɐkait] F -, *no pl* ability to be recorded

er|fas|sen [ɛɐ'fasn] *ptp* **erfasst** VT **a** *(= mitreißen: Auto, Strömung)* to catch **b** *(Furcht, Verlangen etc)* to seize; **Angst erfasste sie** she was seized by fear; **Mitleid erfasste sie** she was filled with compassion **c** *(= begreifen)* to grasp, to comprehend, to understand; **er hats endlich erfasst** he's caught on at last **d** *(= einbeziehen)* to include; *(= registrieren)* to record, to register; *Daten* to capture; **alle Fälle werden statistisch erfasst** statistics of all cases are being recorded; **das ist noch nicht statistisch erfasst worden** there are no statistics on it yet **e** *(rare: = ergreifen)* to seize, to catch (hold of)

Er|fas|sung F registration, recording; *(von Daten)* capture; *(= Miteinbeziehung)* inclusion

er|fech|ten [ɛɐ'fɛçtn] *ptp* **erfochten** [ɛɐ'fɔxtn] VT *irreg Sieg* to gain; *Rechte* to fight for and win

er|fin|den [ɛɐ'fɪndn] *ptp* **erfunden** [ɛɐ'fʊndn] VT *irreg* to invent; *(= erdichten auch)* to make up, to fabricate; **das hat sie glatt erfunden** she made it all up; **frei erfunden** completely fictitious; **er hat die Arbeit auch nicht erfunden** *(inf)* he's not exactly crazy about work *(inf)* → **Pulver**

Er|fin|der(in) M(F) inventor

Er|fin|der|geist M inventive genius

er|fin|de|risch [ɛɐ'fɪndərɪʃ] ADJ inventive; *(= fantasievoll auch)* imaginative; *(= findig auch)* ingenious → **Not**

Er|fin|der|schutz M *(Jur)* protection of inventors

Er|fin|dung F -, -en invention; *(= Erdichtung, Lüge auch)* fiction, fabrication; **eine ~ machen** to invent something

Er|fin|dungs-: **Er|fin|dungs|ga|be** F, *no pl*, **Er|fin|dungs|kraft** F, *no pl* inventiveness, inventive talent *or* genius; *(der Menschheit)* power of invention; **er|fin|dungs|reich** ADJ = **erfinderisch**; **Er|fin|dungs|reich|tum** M inventiveness, ingenuity

er|fle|hen [ɛɐ'fle:ən] *ptp* **erfleht** VT *(geh)* to beg for; **etw von jdm ~** to beg *or* beseech *(liter)* sb for sth, to beg sth of sb

Er|folg [ɛɐ'fɔlk] M -(e)s, -e [-gə] success; *(= Ergebnis, Folge)* result, outcome; *(Sport: = Sieg)* victory, success; **mit ~** successfully; **ohne ~** without success, unsuccessfully; **viel ~!** good luck!; **viel ~ dabei!** best of luck with it; **~ haben** to be successful; **keinen ~ haben** to have no success, to be unsuccessful; **ohne ~ bleiben** *or* **sein** to be unsuccessful; **~ versprechend** promising; **ein voller ~** a great success; *(Stück, Roman, Vorschlag etc auch)* a hit; **ein kläglicher ~** not much of a success, a bit of a failure; **~(e) bei Frauen haben** to be successful with women; **sie warnte mich mit dem ~, dass ...** the effect *or* result of her warning me was that ...

er|fol|gen [ɛɐ'fɔlgn] *ptp* **erfolgt** VI *aux sein (form)* *(= folgen)* to follow, to ensue; *(= sich ergeben)* to result; *(= vollzogen werden)* to be effected *(form)* *or* carried out; *(= stattfinden)* to take place, to occur; *(Zahlung)* to be effected *(form)* *or* made; **nach erfolgter Zahlung** after payment has been effected *(form)* *or* made; **es erfolgte keine Antwort** no answer was forthcoming

Er|folg-: **er|folg|ge|krönt** ADJ (ultimately) successful *or* triumphant, successful in the end *pred*; **ihre Stücke waren weltweit ~** her plays enjoyed success around the world; **Er|folg|ha|sche|rei** [-hafə'rai] F -, -en *(pej)* striving or angling for success; **er|folg|los** ADJ unsuccessful, without success ADV unsuccessfully; **~ verlaufen** to be unsuccessful; **Er|folg|lo|sig|keit** F -, *no pl* lack of success; **er|folg|reich** ADJ successful ADV successfully; **~ verlaufen** to be successful; **sich um etw ~ bewerben** to succeed in getting sth

Er|folgs-: **er|folgs|ab|hän|gig** ADJ success-related; *(Econ)* profit-related; **ein ~er Sportler** a sportsman who is depending on victory *or* success; **er|folgs|arm** ADJ short on success; **Er|folgs|aus|sicht** F prospect of success; **Er|folgs|au|tor(in)** M(F) successful author; **Er|folgs|be|tei|li|gung** F *(Comm)* profit-sharing; **Er|folgs|bi|lanz** F record of success; **Er|folgs|buch** NT bestseller, successful book; **Er|folgs|den|ken** NT positive way of thinking; **Er|folgs|druck** M, *no pl* pressure to succeed; **Er|folgs|er|leb|nis** NT feeling of success, sense of achievement; **Er|folgs|film** M successful *or* hit film; **er|folgs|ge|wohnt** ADJ used to success *pred*; **Er|folgs|ho|no|rar** NT performance-related *or* success-related fee; **Er|folgs|kon|zept** NT recipe for success; **Er|folgs|kurs** M success; **auf ~ liegen** to be on course for success; **Er|folgs|kur|ve** F success curve; **Er|folgs|lei|ter** F *(fig)* ladder to success; **die** *or* **auf der ~ nach oben klettern** to climb *or* move up the ladder of success; **Er|folgs|mar|ke** F successful brand; **Er|folgs|mel|dung** F news *sing* of success; **endlich eine ~!** good news at last!; **Er|folgs|mensch** M success, successful person; **als einem ~en widerstrebt ihm so etwas** being used to success *or* succeeding, he reacts against that sort of thing; **er|folgs|ori|en|tiert** [-orienti:ɐt] ADJ achievement-oriented; **Er|folgs|prä|mie** F *(Comm)* efficiency bonus, incentive payment; **Er|folgs|re|zept** NT recipe for success; **Er|folgs|ro|man** M successful novel; **Er|folgs|se|rie** F string of successes; **Er|folgs|sto|ry** *(inf)* success story, tale of success; **Er|folgs|stra|te|gie** F strategy for success; **Er|folgs|wel|le** F wave of success; **Er|folgs|zwang** M **unter ~ stehen** to be under pressure to succeed

er|folg|ver|spre|chend ADJ → **Erfolg**

er|for|der|lich [ɛɐ'fɔrdɐlɪç] ADJ necessary, required, requisite; *(Comput)* required, mandatory; **es ist dringend ~, dass ...** it is a matter of urgent necessity that ...; **etw ~ machen** to make sth necessary, to necessitate sth; **unbedingt ~** (absolutely) essential *or* imperative

er|for|der|li|chen|falls ADV *(form)* if required, if necessary, if need be

er|for|dern [ɛɐ'fɔrdɐn] *ptp* **erfordert** VT to require, to demand, to call for

Er|for|der|nis [ɛɐ'fɔrdɐnɪs] NT -ses, -se requirement; *(= Voraussetzung auch)* prerequisite

er|for|schen [ɛɐ'fɔrʃn] *ptp* **erforscht** VT **a** *Land, Weltraum etc* to explore **b** *Probleme etc* to explore, to investigate, to inquire into; *(in der Wissenschaft auch)* to research into; *Thema etc* to research; *Lage, Meinung, Wahrheit* to ascertain, to find out; **sein Gewissen ~** to search *or* examine one's conscience

Er|for|scher(in) M(F) *(eines Landes)* explorer; *(in Wissenschaft)* investigator, researcher

Er|for|schung F **a** *(von Land, Weltraum etc)* exploration **b** *(von Problemen)* investigation, inquiry (+*gen* into); *(wissenschaftlich)* research (+*gen* into); *(von Thema)* researching; *(von Lage, Meinung, Wahrheit)* ascertaining

er|fra|gen [ɛɐ'fra:gn] *ptp* **erfragt** VT *Weg* to ask, to inquire; *Einzelheiten etc* to obtain, to ascertain; **Einzelheiten zu ~ bei ...** for details apply to ..., details can be obtained from ...

er|fre|chen [ɛɐ'frɛçn] *ptp* **erfrecht** VR **sich ~, etw zu tun** to have the audacity to do sth; **wie können Sie sich zu so einer Behauptung ~?** how dare you (have the audacity to) claim such a thing!

er|freu|en [ɛɐ'frɔyən] *ptp* **erfreut** VT to please, to delight; *Herz* to gladden; **sehr erfreut!** *(dated: bei Vorstellung)* pleased to meet you!, delighted! *(dated)*; **er wollte damit die Menschen ~** he wanted to give people pleasure; **ja, sagte er erfreut** yes, he said delighted(ly); **über jdn/etw erfreut sein** to be pleased *or* delighted about *or* at sb/sth VR **sich einer Sache** *(gen)* **~** *(geh)* to enjoy sth; **sich an etw** *(dat)* ~ to enjoy sth, to take pleasure in sth

er|freu|lich [ɛɐ'frɔylɪç] ADJ pleasant; *Neuerung, Besserung etc* welcome; *(= befriedigend)* gratifying; **es ist wenig ~, dass wir ...** it's not very satisfactory that we ...; **es wäre ~, wenn die Regierung ...** it would be good *or* nice if the government ...; **ich habe diesmal keine Rüge bekommen – das ist ja sehr ~** I didn't get a rebuke this time – that's good to hear *or* I'm so glad; **sehr ~!** very nice! ADV fortunately; **er hat sich ~ wenig beklagt** it was pleasant *or* nice how little he complained

er|freu|li|cher|wei|se ADV happily; **wir haben ~ einmal ein Spiel gewonnen** I'm pleased *or* glad to say that we've won a game at last

er|frie|ren [ɛɐ'fri:rən] *ptp* **erfroren** [ɛɐ'fro:rən] VI *irreg aux sein* to freeze to death, to die of exposure; *(Pflanzen)* to be killed by frost; **erfrorene Glieder** frostbitten limbs VT **sich** *(dat)* **die Füße/Finger ~** to suffer frostbite in one's feet/fingers

Er|frie|rung F -, -en *usu pl* frostbite *no pl*; **Tod durch ~** death from exposure

er|fri|schen [ɛɐ'frɪʃn] *ptp* **erfrischt** VT to refresh VI to be refreshing VR to refresh oneself; *(= sich waschen)* to freshen up

er|fri|schend ADJ *(lit, fig)* refreshing ADV refreshingly; **~ wirken** to be refreshing

Er|fri|schung F -, -en refreshment

Er|fri|schungs-: **Er|fri|schungs|ge|tränk** NT refreshment; **Er|fri|schungs|raum** M refreshment room, cafeteria, snack bar; **Er|fri|schungs|tuch** NT *pl* **-tücher** towelette, refreshing towel

er|fül|len [ɛɐ'fʏlən] *ptp* **erfüllt** VT **a** *Raum etc* to fill; **Hass/Liebe/Ekel** *etc* **erfüllte ihn** he was full of hate/love/disgust *etc*, he was filled with hate/love/disgust *etc*; **Schmerz erfüllte ihn** he was grief-stricken; **Freude erfüllte ihn** his heart was full of *or* filled with joy; **er/sein Leben war von einem starken Pflichtgefühl erfüllt** he/his life was impregnated with a strong sense of duty; **es erfüllt mich mit Genugtuung, dass ...** it gives me great satisfaction to see that ...; **ein erfülltes Leben** a full life

b *(= ausführen, einhalten)* to fulfil *(Brit)*, to fulfill *(US)*; *Bedingungen* to meet, to comply with, to fulfil(l); *Wunsch, Bitte* to fulfi(l), to carry out; *Pflicht, Aufgabe* to fulfil(l), to carry out, to perform; *Erwartungen* to come up to, to fulfil(l); *(Jur) Soll* to achieve; *Plan* to carry through; *Formalitäten* to comply with; *Zweck, Funktion* to serve; **die Fee erfüllte ihm seinen Wunsch** the fairy granted him his wish; **ihr Wunsch nach einem Kind wurde erfüllt** their wish for a child came true *or* was granted; **erfüllst du mir einen Wunsch?** will you do something for me? → **Tatbestand**

VR *(Wunsch, Voraussagung)* to be fulfilled, to come true; **als er diesen Titel bekam, hatte sich sein Leben erfüllt** when he received this title his life had reached fulfilment *(Brit)* or fulfillment *(US)*

VI *(Jur)* to discharge one's debts

Er|fül|lung F fulfilment *(Brit)*, fulfillment *(US)*; *(einer Bitte, eines Wunsches auch)* carrying out; *(einer Pflicht, Aufgabe auch)* performance; *(von Erwartungen)* realization; *(eines Solls)* achievement; *(eines Plans)* execution; *(Jur: = Tilgung)* discharge; **in ~ gehen** to be fulfilled; **in etw** *(dat)* **~ finden** to find fulfil(l)ment in sth

Er|fül|lungs-: **Er|fül|lungs|ge|hil|fe** M, **Er|fül|lungs|ge|hil|fin** F *(Jur)* ≈ agent; *(= Helfershelfer)* henchman *(pej)*; **Er|fül|lungs|ort** M *pl* **-orte** *(Jur) (von Vertrag) place where a contract is to be fulfilled (von Scheck)* place of payment; **Er|fül|lungs|po|li|tik** F *(Hist)* policy of fulfilment *(Brit)* or fulfillment *(US)*; *(pej)* (policy of) appeasement; **Er|fül|lungs|po|li|ti|ker(in)** M(F) *(Hist)* politician supporting the policy of fulfilment *(Brit)* or fulfillment *(US)*; *(pej)* appeaser

Erg [ɛrk] NT **-s, -** *(Sci)* erg

erg. *abbr von* **ergänze** supply, add

er|gän|zen [ɛɐ'gɛntsn] *ptp* **ergänzt** VT to supplement; *(= vervollständigen)* to complete; *Fehlendes* to supply; *Lager, Vorräte* to replenish; *Bericht* to add (sth) to; *Ausführungen* to amplify; *Worte, Summe* to add; *Gesetz, Gesetzentwurf* to amend; **seine Sammlung ~** to add to *or* build up one's collection; **ergänzte Ausgabe** expanded edition; **einander** *or* **sich ~** to complement one another; **um das Team zu ~** to make up the numbers of the team

er|gän|zend [ɛɐ'gɛntsnt] *prp von* **ergänzen** ADJ *(= komplementär)* complementary; *(= nachträglich)* supplementary; *(= zusätzlich)* additional; *(= zum Ganzen gehörig)* integral; **~er Satz** *(Ling)* completive clause ADV **~ hinzufügen** *or* **bemerken** to add *(zu* to); **~ möchte ich noch hinzufügen, dass ...** (as a rider to that) I would like to add that ..., I would amplify that by saying ...; **~ muss noch gesagt werden, dass ...** it should also be added *or* said that ... → *auch* **ergänzen**

Er|gän|zung F -, -en **a** *(= das Ergänzen)* supplementing; *(= Vervollständigung)* completion; *(von Fehlendem)* supply(ing); *(eines Berichts)* addition (+*gen* to); *(von Summe)* addition; *(von Gesetz)* amendment; *(von Lager, Vorräten)* replenishment; **zur ~ meiner Sammlung** to add to *or* build up my collection; **zur ~ des vorher Gesagten möchte ich hinzufügen, dass ...** let me amplify the previous remarks by adding that ...; **zur ~ des Teams** to make up the numbers of the team **b** *(= Zusatz: zu Buch etc)* supplement; *(= Hinzugefügtes, Person)* addition; *(zu einem Gesetz)* amendment; *(Gram)* complement

Er|gän|zungs-: **Er|gän|zungs|ab|ga|be** F supplementary tax; **Er|gän|zungs|an|trag** M *(Parl)* amendment; **Er|gän|zungs|band** [-bant] M *pl* **-bände** supplement(ary volume); **Er|gän|zungs|bin|de|strich** M hyphen; **Er|gän|zungs|men|ge** F *(Math)* complementary set; **Er|gän|zungs|satz** M *(Gram)* complementary clause

er|gat|tern [ɛɐ'gatɐn] *ptp* **ergattert** VT *(inf)* to get hold of

er|gau|nern [ɛɐ'gaunɐn] *ptp* **ergaunert** VT *(inf)* **(sich** *dat)* **etw ~** to get sth by dishonest means

er|ge|ben [ɛɐ'ge:bn] *ptp* **ergeben** *irreg* VT to yield, to produce; *(= zum Ergebnis haben)* to result in; *(= zeigen)* to reveal; *Betrag, Summe* to amount to, to come to

VR **a** *(= kapitulieren)* (+*dat* to) to surrender, to yield, to capitulate; **sich auf Gnade oder Ungnade ~** to surrender unconditionally; **sich in etw** *(acc)* **~** to submit to sth

b sich einer Sache *(dat)* **~** *(= sich hingeben)* to take to sth, to give oneself up to sth; *der Schwermut* to sink into sth; *dem Dienst etc* to devote oneself to sth; **sich dem Suff** *(inf)* **~** to take to drink *(Brit) or* the bottle *(inf)*

c *(= folgen)* to result, to arise, to ensue *(aus* from); **daraus können sich Nachteile ~** this could turn out to be disadvantageous; **das eine ergibt sich aus dem anderen** the one (thing) follows from the other

d *(= sich herausstellen)* to come to light; **es ergab sich, dass unsere Befürchtungen ...** it turned out that our fears ...

er|ge|ben [ɛɐ'ge:bn] ADJ *(= hingegeben, treu)* devoted; *(= demütig)* humble; *(= unterwürfig)* submissive; **einem Laster ~ sein** to be addicted to a vice; **Ihr (sehr) ~er ...** *(old form)* **Ihr ~ster ...** *(old form)* respectfully yours ... *(form)*, your (most) obedient *or* humble servant ... *(old form)* → **treu** ADV

Er|ge|ben|heit F -, *no pl (= Hingabe, Treue)* devotion; *(= Demut)* humility; *(= Unterwürfigkeit)* submissiveness

Er|geb|nis [ɛɐ'ge:pnɪs] NT **-ses, -se** result; *(= Auswirkung auch)* consequence, outcome; **im ~** *(= folglich)* as a result; **die Verhandlungen führten zu keinem ~** the negotiations led nowhere, the negotiations were inconclusive; **die Verhandlungen führten zu dem ~, dass ...** the negotiations led to the conclusion that ...; **zu einem ~ kommen** to come to *or* reach a conclusion; **unsere Anstrengungen blieben ohne ~** our efforts produced no results

er|geb|nis|los ADJ unsuccessful, without result, fruitless; *Verhandlungen auch* inconclusive ADV **~ bleiben/verlaufen** to come to nothing; **Verhandlungen ~ abbrechen** to break off negotiations without having reached any conclusions

Er|geb|nis|lo|sig|keit F -, *no pl* lack of success, fruitlessness; *(von Verhandlungen auch)* inconclusiveness

er|geb|nis|of|fen ADJ *Diskussion* open and unbiased ADV **etw ~ diskutieren** to discuss sth in an open and unbiased way

Er|ge|bung F -, -en *(Mil, fig)* surrender, capitulation; *(fig: = Demut)* humility

er|ge|hen [ɛɐ'ge:ən] *ptp* **ergangen** [ɛɐ'gaŋən] *irreg* VI *aux sein* **a** *(form) (an +acc* to) *(= erteilt, erlassen werden)* to go out, to be issued; *(Einladung)* to go out, to be sent; *(Gesetz)* to be enacted; **~ lassen** to issue; to send; to enact

b etw über sich *(acc)* **~ lassen** to let sth wash over one *(Brit)*, to let sth roll off one's back *(US)*; **sie ließ seine Vorwürfe/alles über sich** *(acc)* **~** she let his reproaches/everything simply wash over her *(Brit)* or roll off her back *(US)*; **sie ließ seine Zärtlichkeiten über sich** *(acc)* **~** she submitted to his intimacies

VI *impers aux sein* **es ist ihm schlecht/gut ergangen** he fared badly/well; **es wird ihm schlecht ~** he will suffer; **wie ist es ihm in der Prüfung ergangen?** how did he fare in *(Brit) or* on *(US)* the exam?

VR **a** *(geh)* to go for a walk *or* stroll, to take the air *(Brit)*

b *(fig)* **sich in etw** *(dat)* **~** to indulge in sth; **er erging sich in Lobreden** he indulged in lavish *or* profuse praise; **er erging sich in Schmähungen** he let out a stream of abuse; **sich (in langen Reden) über ein Thema ~** to hold forth at length on sth, to expatiate on sth

Er|ge|hen [ɛɐ'ge:ən] NT *(geh)* (state of) health

er|gie|big [ɛɐ'gi:bɪç] ADJ *(lit, fig)* productive; *Geschäft* profitable, lucrative; *Thema* productive, fertile; *Kupfervorkommen, Goldmine etc* high-yield *attr*, rich; *Regenfälle* abundant; *(= fruchtbar)* fertile; *(= sparsam im Verbrauch)* economical

Er|gie|big|keit F -, *no pl (lit, fig)* productiveness, productivity; *(von Geschäft)* profitability; *(von Regenfällen)* abundance; *(= Fruchtbarkeit)* fertility; *(= Sparsamkeit im Verbrauch)* economy; **die ~ der Goldmine** the high yield of the gold mine; **die erhöhte ~ dieses Waschmittels** the washing powder's new economical *or* economy formula

er|gie|ßen [ɛɐ'gi:sn] *ptp* **ergossen** [ɛɐ'gɔsn] *irreg* VT *(liter)* to pour (out *or* forth *(liter)*) VR *(geh)* to pour forth *(liter) or* out *(auch fig)*

er|glän|zen [ɛɐ'glɛntsn] *ptp* **erglänzt** VI *aux sein (geh)* to shine, to gleam; *(Licht auch)* to shine out

er|glü|hen [ɛɐ'gly:ən] *ptp* **erglüht** VI *aux sein (liter)* to glow; *(fig) (vor Scham, Zorn)* to burn; *(vor Freude)* to glow; **in Liebe für jdn ~** *(liter)* to fall passionately in love with sb

er|go ['ɛrgo] CONJ therefore, ergo *(liter, hum)*

Er|go|me|ter [ɛrgo'me:tɐ] NT ergometer

Er|go|no|mie [ɛrgono'mi:] F -, *no pl* ergonomics *sing*

er|go|no|misch [ɛrgo'no:mɪʃ] ADJ ergonomic ADV ergonomically

Er|go|the|ra|peut(in) [ɛrgotera'pɔyt(ɪn)] M(F) ergotherapist

Er|go|the|ra|pie [ɛrgotera'pi:] F ergotherapy

er|göt|zen [ɛɐ'gœtsn] *ptp* **ergötzt** VT to delight; **zum Ergötzen aller** to everyone's delight VR **sich an etw** *(dat)* **~** to be amused by sth, to take delight in sth; *(schadenfroh auch, böswillig)* to gloat over sth

er|götz|lich [ɛɐ'gœtslɪç] ADJ delightful

er|grau|en [ɛɐ̯ˈgrauən] *ptp* **ergraut** VI *aux sein* to turn *or* go grey *(Brit) or* gray *(US)* → **Dienst a, Ehre**

er|grei|fen [ɛɐ̯ˈgraifn] *ptp* **ergriffen** [ɛɐ̯ˈgrɪfn] VT *irreg* **a** *(= packen)* to seize; *(= fassen auch)* to grasp, to grip; *Feder, Schwert auch* to take up; *Verbrecher* to seize, to apprehend; *(Krankheit)* to overcome; **das Feuer ergriff den ganzen Wald** the fire engulfed the whole forest → **Besitz a**
b *(fig) Gelegenheit, Macht* to seize; *Beruf* to take up; *Maßnahmen* to take, to resort to; **er ergriff das Wort** he began to speak; *(Parl, bei Versammlung etc)* he took the floor → **Flucht a, Partei c**
c *(fig) jdn (= packen)* to seize, to grip; *(= bewegen)* to move; **von Furcht/Sehnsucht** *etc* **ergriffen werden** to be seized with fear/longing *etc* → *auch* **ergriffen**

er|grei|fend ADJ *(fig)* moving, touching *(auch iro)*

er|grif|fen [ɛɐ̯ˈgrɪfn] ADJ *(fig)* moved → *auch* **ergreifen**

Er|grif|fen|heit F -, *no pl* emotion

er|grim|men [ɛɐ̯ˈgrɪmən] *ptp* **ergrimmt** *(old, liter)* VI *aux sein* to become angry *or* furious VT to incense, to anger

er|grün|den [ɛɐ̯ˈgrʏndn] *ptp* **ergründet** VT *Sinn etc* to fathom; *Geheimnis auch* to penetrate; *Ursache, Motiv* to discover; **ich muss ~, ob …** I have to discover whether …

Er|guss M effusion; *(= Bluterguss)* bruise, contusion *(form)*; *(= Samenerguss)* ejaculation, emission; *(fig)* outpouring, effusion

er|ha|ben [ɛɐ̯ˈha:bn] ADJ **a** *Druck, Muster* raised, embossed
b *(fig) Gedanken, Stil* lofty, elevated, exalted; *Schönheit, Anblick* sublime; *Augenblick* solemn; *Herrscher* illustrious, eminent; **das Erhabene** the sublime; **vom Erhabenen zum Lächerlichen ist nur ein Schritt** it is but a step from the sublime to the ridiculous
c *(= überlegen)* superior; **er dünkt sich über alles/alle ~** he thinks himself to be above it all/superior to everybody; **über etw** *(acc)* **~ (sein)** (to be) above sth; **über jeden Tadel/Verdacht ~ sein** to be above *or* beyond reproach/suspicion
ADV **~ lächeln** to smile in a superior way; **~ tun** to act superior

Er|ha|ben|heit F -, **-en** **a** *(rare: = Erhöhung)* elevation, relief **b** *(fig) (von Gedanken, Stil)* loftiness, elevation; *(von Schönheit, Anblick)* sublimity; *(von Augenblick)* solemnity; *(von Herrscher)* illustriousness, eminence **c** *(= Überlegenheit)* superiority

Er|halt M, *no pl* receipt; *(= das Erhalten)* preservation; **der ~ der Macht** the preservation of power

er|hal|ten [ɛɐ̯ˈhaltn] *ptp* **erhalten** *irreg* VT **a** *(= bekommen)* to get, to receive; *Preis, Orden* to get, to receive, to be awarded; *Strafe, neuen Namen, fünf Jahre Gefängnis* to get, to be given; *Resultat, Produkt, Genehmigung* to obtain, to get; **das Wort ~** to receive permission to speak; **(Betrag) dankend ~** *(form)* received with thanks (the sum of…) → **Besuch a, Kenntnis b**
b *(= bewahren) Gebäude, Natur* to preserve; *Gesundheit etc auch* to maintain; **jdn am Leben/bei guter Laune ~** to keep sb alive/in a good mood; **ich hoffe, dass du uns noch lange ~ bleibst** I hope you'll be with us for a long time yet; *(= nicht sterben)* I hope you'll have many more happy days; **erhalte dir deinen Frohsinn/Optimismus** stay cheerful/optimistic; **er hat sich** *(dat)* **seinen Frohsinn/Optimismus ~** he kept up *or* retained his cheerfulness/optimism; **unser Kind ist uns ~ geblieben** our child was spared; **gut ~** well preserved *(auch hum inf)*, in good condition; **von der Altstadt sind nur noch ein paar Kirchen ~** of the old town only a few churches remain *or* still stand
c *(= unterhalten) Familie* to support, to keep, to maintain
VR *(Brauch etc)* to be preserved, to remain; **sich frisch und gesund ~** to keep *or* stay bright and healthy

er|hal|tens|wert [ɛɐ̯ˈhaltnsve:ɐt] ADJ worth preserving *pred*

Er|hal|ter(in) M(F) preserver, maintainer; *(der Familie)* breadwinner, supporter

er|hält|lich [ɛɐ̯ˈhɛltlɪç] ADJ obtainable, available; **schwer ~** difficult to obtain, hard to come by

Er|hal|tung F -, **-en** *(= Bewahrung)* preservation; *(= Unterhaltung)* support; **die ~ der Energie** *(Phys)* the conservation of energy

er|han|deln [ɛɐ̯ˈhandln] *ptp* **erhandelt** VT to get by bargaining, to bargain for

er|hän|gen [ɛɐ̯ˈhɛŋən] *ptp* **erhängt** VT to hang; **Tod durch Erhängen** death by hanging; **sich ~** to hang oneself

er|här|ten [ɛɐ̯ˈhɛrtn] *ptp* **erhärtet** VT to harden; *(fig) Behauptung etc* to substantiate, to corroborate; *Verdacht* to harden; **etw durch Eid ~** to affirm sth on oath VR *(fig: Verdacht)* to harden

Er|här|tung F *(von Behauptung)* substantiation, corroboration; *(von Verdacht)* hardening

er|ha|schen [ɛɐ̯ˈhaʃn] *ptp* **erhascht** VT to catch *(auch fig)*, to seize, to grab

er|he|ben [ɛɐ̯ˈhe:bn] ✪ 36.2 *ptp* **erhoben** *irreg* [ɛɐ̯ˈho:bn] VT **a** *(= hochheben)* to raise *(auch Math)*, to lift (up); *Glas, Stimme* to raise; **die Hand zum Gruß ~** to raise one's hand in greeting; **seinen** *or* **den Blick ~** to look up; **jdn in den Adelsstand ~** to raise *or* elevate sb to the peerage; **etw zu einem Prinzip/einer Regel** *etc* **~** to make sth into a principle/a rule *etc*, to raise *or* elevate sth to (the level of) a principle/a rule *etc*; **jdn zum Herrscher ~** to install sb as a/the ruler → **Anklage a, Anspruch a, c, Einspruch, Geschrei, Potenz b**
b *Gebühren* to charge, to levy; *Steuern (= einziehen)* to raise, to levy; *(= auferlegen)* to impose
c *Fakten, Daten* to ascertain
d *(liter: = loben)* to laud *(liter)*, to extol *(liter)*
VR **a** *(= aufstehen)* to get up, to rise; *(Flugzeug, Vogel)* to rise
b *(= sich auflehnen)* to rise (up) (in revolt), to revolt
c *(= aufragen)* to rise *(über +dat* above)
d sich über eine Schwierigkeit ~ to rise above *or* overcome a difficulty; **sich über andere ~** to elevate *or* place oneself above others
e *(= aufkommen) (Wind etc, form: Frage etc)* to arise

er|he|bend ADJ elevating, uplifting; *(= beeindruckend)* impressive; *(= erbaulich)* edifying

er|heb|lich [ɛɐ̯ˈhe:plɪç] ADJ *(= beträchtlich)* considerable; *(= wichtig)* important; *(= relevant)* relevant, pertinent; *Verletzung* serious, severe ADV *(= beträchtlich)* considerably; *beschädigen, verletzen* severely

Er|he|bung F **a** *(= Bodenerhebung)* elevation **b** *(= Aufstand)* uprising, revolt; *(= Meuterei)* mutiny **c** *(von Gebühren)* levying, imposition **d** *(= amtliche Ermittlung)* investigation, inquiry; *(= Umfrage)* survey; **~en machen** *or* **anstellen über** *(+acc)* to make inquiries about *or* into **e** *(= das Erheben)* raising; *(in den Adelsstand)* elevation; *(zum Herrscher)* installation *(zu* as); **~ ins Quadrat** squaring; **~ in die dritte Potenz** cubing, raising to the power of three **f** *(fig: = Erbauung)* uplift, elevation

Er|he|bungs|zeit|raum M *(von Umfrage, Daten etc)* survey period

er|hei|schen [ɛɐ̯ˈhaiʃn] *ptp* **erheischt** VT *(old, liter)* to require, to demand; *Achtung* to command

er|hei|tern [ɛɐ̯ˈhaitɐn] *ptp* **erheitert** VT to cheer (up); *(= belustigen)* to entertain, to amuse VR to be amused *(über +acc* by); *(Gesicht)* to brighten, to cheer up

Er|hei|te|rung F -, **-en** amusement; **zur allgemeinen ~** to the general amusement

er|hel|len [ɛɐ̯ˈhɛlən] *ptp* **erhellt** VT to light up *(auch fig)*, to illuminate; *(fig: = klären)* to elucidate, to illuminate; *Geheimnis* to shed light on VR *(lit, fig)* to brighten; *(plötzlich)* to light up VI *(geh: = hervorgehen)* to be evident *or* manifest; **daraus erhellt, dass …** from that it is evident *or* manifest that …

Er|hel|lung F -, **-en** *(fig)* elucidation, illumination

er|hit|zen [ɛɐ̯ˈhɪtsn] *ptp* **erhitzt** VT to heat (up) *(auf +acc* to); **die Gemüter ~** to inflame passions, to whip up feeling VR to get hot, to heat up; *(fig: = sich erregen)* to become heated *(an +dat* over); *(Fantasie etc)* to be inflamed *or* aroused *(an +dat* at); **die Gemüter erhitzten sich** feelings were running high; **erhitzt aussehen** to look hot; *(fig)* to look hot and bothered; **vom Tanzen erhitzt** hot from the dancing

Er|hit|zung F -, **-en** heating up; *(fig) (= Erregung)* excitement; *(der Gemüter, Fantasie)* inflammation

er|hof|fen [ɛɐ̯ˈhɔfn] *ptp* **erhofft** VT to hope for; **sich** *(dat)* **etw ~** to hope for sth *(von* from); **was erhoffst du dir davon?** what do you hope to gain from it?

er|hofft [ɛɐ̯ˈhɔft] PTP *von* **erhoffen** ADJ hoped-for, looked-for *(inf)*

er|hö|hen [ɛɐ̯ˈhø:ən] *ptp* **erhöht** VT to raise; *Preise, Miete etc auch* to increase, to put up; *Zahl auch, Produktion, Kraft* to increase; *Wirkung, Schönheit* to heighten, to enhance; *Spannung* to increase, to heighten; *(Mus) Note* to sharpen; **die Mauern wurden um zwei Meter erhöht** the walls were made two metres *(Brit) or* meters *(US)* higher, the walls were raised (by) two metres *(Brit) or* meters *(US)*; **etw um 10% ~** to raise *or* put up *or* increase sth by 10%; **etw um das Doppelte ~** to increase sth by twice as much again; **erhöhte Temperatur haben** to have a temperature; **erhöhte Wachsamkeit/Anstrengungen** *etc* increased vigilance/efforts *etc*
VR to rise, to increase; *(Spannung etc auch)* to heighten, to intensify; **wer sich selbst erhöht, der wird erniedrigt (werden)** *(Bibl)* whosoever shall exalt himself shall be abased

Er|hö|hung F -, **-en** **a** *(= das Erhöhen)* raising; *(von Preisen, Miete etc)* increase, putting up; *(von Zahl auch, von Produktion, Kraft)* increase; *(von Wirkung)* heightening, enhancement; *(von Spannung)* heightening, intensification **b** *(= Lohnerhöhung)* rise *(Brit)*, raise *(US)*; *(= Preiserhöhung)* increase **c** *(= Hügel)* hill, elevation

Er|hö|hungs|zei|chen NT *(Mus)* sharp (sign)

er|ho|len [ɛɐ̯ˈho:lən] *ptp* **erholt** VR *(von* from) to recover; *(von Krankheit auch)* to recuperate; *(= sich entspannen auch)* to relax, to have a rest; *(fig: Preise, Aktien)* to recover, to rally, to pick up; **er hat sich von dem Schreck(en) noch nicht erholt** he hasn't got over the shock yet; **du siehst sehr erholt aus** you look very rested

er|hol|sam [ɛɐ̯ˈho:lza:m] ADJ restful, refreshing

Er|ho|lung F -, *no pl* recovery; *(von Krankheit auch)* recuperation; *(= Entspannung)* relaxation, rest; *(der Wirtschaft)* recovery, rallying; **der Direktor ist zur ~ in der Schweiz** the director has gone to Switzerland for a holiday *(esp Brit) or* a vacation *(US)* and a rest; *(zur Genesung)* the director is convalescing in Switzerland; **zur ~ an die See fahren** to go to the seaside in order to recover *or* recuperate *or* convalesce; **er braucht dringend ~** he badly needs a holiday *(esp Brit) or* a vacation *(US) or* a break; **Urlaub ist zur ~ da** holidays *(esp Brit) or* vacations *(US)* are for relaxation; **gute ~!** have a good rest

Er|ho|lung|su|chen|de(r) [-zu:xndə] MF *decl as adj* holiday-maker *(esp Brit)*, vacationer *(esp US)*, vacationist *(esp US)*

Er|ho|lungs-: **Er|ho|lungs|auf|ent|halt** M holiday *(esp Brit)*, vacation *(US)*; **er|ho|lungs|be|dürf|tig** ADJ in need of a rest, run-down; **Er|ho|lungs|ge|biet** NT recreation area; **Er|ho|lungs|heim** NT rest home; *(= Ferienheim)* holiday home; *(= Sanatorium)* convalescent home; **Er|ho|lungs|kur** F rest-cure; **Er|ho|lungs|ort** M *pl* **-orte** spa, health resort; **Er|ho|lungs|pau|se** F break; **Er|ho|lungs|rei|se** F holiday *(esp Brit) or* vacation *(US)* trip; **Er|ho|lungs|ur|laub** M holiday *(esp Brit)*, vacation *(US)*; *(nach Krankheit)* convalescent leave; **Er|ho|lungs|wert** M recreational value

er|hö|ren [ɛɐ'hø:rən] *ptp* **erhört** VT *Gebet etc* to hear; *Bitte, Liebhaber* to yield to

Erie|see ['e:ri-] M Lake Erie *no art*

eri|gi|bel [eri'gi:bl] ADJ *(Physiol)* erectile

eri|gie|ren [eri'gi:rən] *ptp* **erigiert** VI to become erect

eri|giert [eri'gi:ɐt] ADJ erect

Eri|ka ['e:rika] F -, **Eriken** [-kn] *(Bot)* heather

er|in|ner|lich [ɛɐ'lɪnɐlɪç] ADJ **soviel mir ~ ist** as far as I (can) remember *or* recall; **die letzte uns ~e Postkarte kam aus Deutschland** the last postcard we (can) remember came from Germany

er|in|nern [ɛɐ'lɪnɐn] *ptp* **erinnert** VT **jdn an etw** *(acc)* ~ to remind sb of sth; **jdn daran ~, etw zu tun/dass ...** to remind sb to do sth/that ...; **etw** ~ *(dial, sl)* to remember *or* recall sth

VR **sich an jdn/etw ~, sich einer Sache** *(gen)* ~ *(old)* to remember *or* recall *or* recollect sb/sth; **sich nur noch dunkel ~ an** *(+acc)* to have only a faint *or* dim recollection *or* memory of; **soweit** *or* **soviel ich mich ~ kann** as far as I remember *etc*, to the best of my recollection; **wenn ich mich recht erinnere, ...** if my memory serves me right *or* correctly ..., if I remember rightly ...

VI **a** ~ **an** *(+acc)* to be reminiscent of, to call to mind, to recall; **sie erinnert sehr an ihre Mutter** she reminds one very much of her mother **b** *(= erwähnen)* **daran ~, dass ...** to point out that ...

Er|in|ne|rung F -, **-en** **a** *(an +acc* of) memory, recollection; *(euph: = Mahnung)* reminder; *(= Andenken)* memento, remembrance, keepsake; **zur ~ an** *(+acc)* in memory of; *(an Ereignis)* in commemoration of; *(als Andenken)* as a memento of; **jdn/etw in guter/schlechter ~ haben** *or* **behalten** to have pleasant/unpleasant memories of sb/sth; **sich** *(dat)* **etw in die ~ zurückrufen** to call sth to mind; **jdm etw in ~ bringen** to remind sb of sth; **ich muss ihm mal schreiben, um mich bei ihm in ~ zu bringen** I'll have to write to him so that he doesn't forget me; **wenn mich meine ~ nicht täuscht** if my memory doesn't deceive me **b** **Erinnerungen** PL *(= Lebenserinnerungen)* reminiscences *pl*; *(Liter)* memoirs *pl*; **~en austauschen** to reminisce

Er|in|ne|rungs-: **Er|in|ne|rungs|bild** NT visual memento *(an +acc* of); **Er|in|ne|rungs|fei|er** F commemoration; **Er|in|ne|rungs|fo|to** NT *(von Urlaub, Ereignis etc)* souvenir photo *or* snapshot; *(von Verstorbenen)* cherished photo(graph); **Er|in|ne|rungs|lü|cke** F gap in one's memory; **Er|in|ne|rungs|schrei|ben** NT *(Comm)* reminder; **Er|in|ne|rungs|stück** NT keepsake *(an +acc* from); **Er|in|ne|rungs|ta|fel** F commemorative plaque; **Er|in|ne|rungs|ver|mö|gen** NT, *no pl* memory, powers *pl* of recollection; **Er|in|ne|rungs|wert** M sentimental value

Erin|ny|en [e'rɪnyən] PL *(Myth)* Furies *pl*, Erin(-n)yes *pl*

Erit|rea [eri'tre:a] NT **-s** Eritrea

Erit|re|er [eri'tre:ɐ] M **-s, -**, **Erit|re|e|rin** [-ərɪn] F **-, -nen** Eritrean

erit|re|isch [eri'tre:ɪʃ] ADJ Eritrean

er|ja|gen [ɛɐ'ja:gn] *ptp* **erjagt** VT to bag, to catch; *(fig: = ergattern)* to get hold of, to hunt down; **um sich dort Reichtum zu ~** to make his fortune

er|kal|ten [ɛɐ'kaltn] *ptp* **erkaltet** VI *aux sein (lit, fig)* to cool (down *or* off), to go cold

er|käl|ten [ɛɐ'kɛltn] *ptp* **erkältet** VR to catch a cold; *(= esp sich verkühlen)* to catch a chill; **sich stark** *or* **sehr/leicht erkältet haben** to have (caught) a bad/slight cold/chill VT **sich** *(dat)* **die Blase ~** to catch a chill in one's bladder *(Brit)*, to get a bladder infection

er|käl|tet [ɛɐ'kɛltət] ADJ with a cold; **(stark) ~ sein** to have a (bad) cold; **wir sind alle ~** we all have colds

Er|käl|tung F **-, -en** cold; *(leicht)* chill; **sich** *(dat)* **eine ~ zuziehen** to catch a cold/chill

Er|käl|tungs|krank|hei|ten PL coughs and sneezes *pl*

er|kämp|fen [ɛɐ'kɛmpfn] *ptp* **erkämpft** VT to win, to secure; **sich** *(dat)* **etw ~** to win sth; **hart erkämpft** hard-won; **er hat sich** *(dat)* **seine Position hart erkämpft** he fought hard for his position *or* to secure his position

er|kau|fen [ɛɐ'kaufn] *ptp* **erkauft** VT to buy; **etw teuer ~** to pay dearly for sth; **den Erfolg mit seiner Gesundheit ~** to pay for one's success with one's health, to buy success at the price of one's health

er|kenn|bar ADJ *(= wiedererkennbar)* recognizable; *(= sichtbar)* visible; *(= wahrnehmbar, ersichtlich)* discernible

Er|kenn|bar|keit [ɛɐ'kɛnba:ɐkait] F -, *no pl (= Wiedererkennbarkeit)* being recognizable; *(= Sichtbarkeit)* visibility; *(= Wahrnehmbarkeit, Ersichtlichkeit)* discernibility

er|ken|nen [ɛɐ'kɛnən] *ptp* **erkannt** [ɛɐ'kant] *irreg* VT **a** *(= wiedererkennen, anerkennen, einsehen)* to recognize *(an +dat* by); *(= wahrnehmen)* to see, to make out, to discern; *Unterschied* to see; *Situation* to see, to understand; **ich erkannte die Lage sofort** I immediately realized what the situation was; **er hat erkannt, dass das nicht stimmte** he realized that it wasn't right; **kannst du ~, ob das da drüben X ist?** can you see *or* tell if that's X over there?; **jdn für schuldig ~** *(Jur)* to find sb guilty; **(jdm) etw zu ~ geben** to indicate sth (to sb); **jdm zu ~ geben, dass ...** to give sb to understand that ...; **sich zu ~ geben** to reveal oneself *(als* to be), to disclose one's identity; **~ lassen** to show, to reveal; **erkenne dich selbst!** know thyself!; **du bist erkannt!** I see what you're after, I know your game **b** *(Bibl, obs)* to know *(Bibl)*

VI **~ auf** *(+acc) (Jur, auf Freispruch)* to grant; *auf Strafe* to impose, to inflict; *(Sport) auf Freistoß etc* to give, to award; **auf drei Jahre Haft ~** to impose a sentence of three years' imprisonment

er|kennt|lich [ɛɐ'kɛntlɪç] ADJ **a** **sich (für etw) ~ zeigen** to show one's gratitude *or* appreciation (for sth) **b** *(rare)* = **erkennbar**

Er|kennt|lich|keit F **-, -en** *(= Dankbarkeit)* gratitude; *(= Gegenleistung)* token of one's gratitude *or* appreciation

Er|kennt|nis [ɛɐ'kɛntnɪs] F *(= Wissen)* knowledge *no pl*; *(= das Erkennen)* recognition, realization; *(Philos, Psych)* cognition *no pl*; *(= Einsicht)* insight, realization; *(= Entdeckung)* finding, discovery; **zur ~ kommen** to see the light; **zu der ~ kommen** *or* **gelangen, dass ...** to come to the realization that ..., to realize that ...

Er|kennt|nis NT **-ses, -se** *(Aus, Sw: Jur)* decision, finding; *(= Urteil)* judg(e)ment; *(der Geschworenen)* verdict

Er|kennt|nis-: **Er|kennt|nis|drang** M thirst for knowledge; **Er|kennt|nis|fä|hig|keit** F cognitive faculty; **Er|kennt|nis|la|ge** F level of knowledge; **Er|kennt|nis|leh|re** F epistemology, theory of knowledge; **Er|kennt|nis|schub** M wealth of new knowledge; **Er|kennt|nis|stand** M level of knowledge; **er|kennt|nis|the|o|re|tisch** ADJ epistemological; **Er|kennt|nis|the|o|rie** F epistemology, theory of knowledge; **Er|kennt|nis|ver|mö|gen** NT cognitive capacity

Er|ken|nung F recognition, identification

Er|ken|nungs-: **Er|ken|nungs|dienst** M police records department; **er|ken|nungs|dienst|lich** ADV **jdn ~ behandeln** to fingerprint and photograph sb; **Er|ken|nungs|mar|ke** F identity disc *(Brit)*, identity *(Brit) or* identification *(US)* tag; **Er|ken|nungs|me|lo|die** F signature tune; **Er|ken|nungs|wort** NT *pl* **-wörter** password; **Er|ken|nungs|zei|chen** NT identification; *(Mil: = Abzeichen)* badge; *(Aviat)* markings *pl*; *(Med)* sign *(für* of); **das ist mein ~** that's what you'll recognize me by

Er|ker ['ɛrkɐ] M **-s, -** bay; *(= kleiner Vorbau)* oriel

Er|ker-: **Er|ker|fens|ter** NT bay window; oriel window; **Er|ker|zim|mer** NT room with a bay *or* oriel window (recess)

er|kie|sen [ɛɐ'ki:zn] *pret* **erkor** [ɛɐ'ko:ɐ], *ptp* **erkoren** [ɛɐ'ko:rən] VT *(obs, liter)* to choose, to elect *(zu* as, to be)

er|klär|bar ADJ explicable, explainable; **leicht ~** easily explained; **schwer ~** hard to explain; **nicht ~** inexplicable

er|klä|ren [ɛɐ'klɛ:rən] *ptp* **erklärt** VT **a** *(= erläutern)* to explain *(jdm etw* sth to sb); *(= begründen)* to account for, to explain; **ich kann mir nicht ~, warum ...** I can't understand why ...; **wie erklärt ihr euch das?** how can *or* do you explain that?, what do you make of that?; **ich erkläre mir die Sache so: ...** the way I see it, ... **b** *(= äußern, bekannt geben)* to declare *(als* to be); *Rücktritt* to announce; *(Politiker, Pressesprecher etc)* to say; **einem Staat den Krieg ~** to declare war on a country; **er erklärte ihr seine Liebe** he declared his love for her; **eine Ausstellung** *etc* **für** *or* **als eröffnet ~** to declare an exhibition *etc* open; **jdn für schuldig/tot/gesund** *etc* **~** to pronounce sb guilty/dead/healthy *etc*

VR **a** *(Sache)* to be explained; **das erklärt sich daraus, dass ...** it can be explained by the fact that ...; **damit hat sich die Sache von selbst erklärt** the affair thereby explained itself; **das erklärt sich (von) selbst** that's self-explanatory **b** *(Mensch)* to declare oneself; *(= Liebe gestehen auch)* to declare one's love; **sich für bankrott** *etc* **~** to declare oneself bankrupt *etc*; **sich für gesund/diensttauglich ~** to pronounce *or* declare oneself healthy/fit for service; **sich für/gegen jdn/etw ~** to declare oneself *or* come out for/against sb/sth → *auch* **erklärt**

VI to explain; **er kann sehr gut ~** he's very good at explaining things

er|klä|rend ADJ explanatory; **einige ~e Worte** a few words of explanation ADV **er fügte ~ hinzu ...** he added in explanation ...

er|klär|lich [ɛɐ'klɛ:ɐlɪç] ADJ **a** = **erklärbar** **b** *(= verständlich)* understandable; **ist Ihnen das ~?** can you find an explanation for that?; **mir ist einfach nicht ~, wie ...** I simply cannot understand how ...

er|klär|li|cher|wei|se ADV understandably

er|klärt [ɛɐ'klɛ:ɐt] ADJ *attr Ziel* professed; *Gegner auch* avowed; *Favorit, Liebling* acknowledged → *auch* **erklären**

er|klär|ter|ma|ßen [ɛɐ'klɛ:ɐtɐ'ma:sn], **er|klär|ter|wei|se** [ɛɐ'klɛ:ɐtɐ'waizə] ADV avowedly

Er|klä|rung F **a** explanation **b** *(= Mitteilung, Bekanntgabe)* declaration; *(eines Politikers, Pressesprechers etc)* statement; **eine ~ (zu etw) abgeben** to make a statement (about *or* concerning sth)

Er|klä|rungs-: **er|klä|rungs|be|dürf|tig** ADJ in need of (an) explanation; **das ist ~** that needs (further) explanation; **Er|klä|rungs|frist** F *period of time granted to sb to explain sth to a commission etc*; **Er|klä|rungs|not|stand** M **im ~ sein** to have a lot of explaining to do; **Er|klä|rungs|ver|such** M **attempt at explanation** *or* **at explaining** *sth*

er|kleck|lich [ɛɐ'klɛklɪç] ADJ considerable

er|klet|tern [ɛɐ'klɛtɐn] *ptp* **erklettert** VT to climb (up); *Berg auch* to scale; *Alpengebiet* to climb

er|klim|men [ɛɐ'klɪmən] *pret* **erklomm** *or* **erklimmte** [ɛɐ'klɔmən], *ptp* **erklommen** *or* **erklimmt** VT *irreg (geh)* to scale; *(fig) Spitze, höchste Stufe* to climb to; *(fig) Leiter* to climb *or* ascend to the top of

er|klin|gen [ɛɐ'klɪŋən] *ptp* **erklungen** [ɛɐ'klʊŋən] VI *irreg (geh) aux sein* to ring out, to resound; **eine Harfe/ein Glöckchen/Stimmchen erklang** (the sound of) a harp/bell/voice was heard, I *etc* heard (the sound of) a harp/bell/voice; **ein**

Lied ~ lassen to burst (forth) into song; **die Gläser ~ lassen** to clink glasses

er|kor *pret von* **erkiesen** *von* **erküren**

er|ko|ren *ptp von* **erkiesen** *von* **erküren**

er|kran|ken [ɛɐ'kraŋkn] *ptp* **erkrankt** VI *aux sein* (= *krank werden*) to be taken ill (*Brit*) *or* sick, to get sick (*esp US*), to fall ill (*an +dat* with); (*Organ, Pflanze, Tier*) to become diseased (*an +dat* with); **erkrankt sein** (= *krank sein*) to be ill/diseased; **die an Krebs erkrankten Menschen** people with *or* suffering from cancer; **die erkrankten Stellen** the diseased *or* affected areas

Er|kran|kung F -, -en illness; (*von Organ, Pflanze, Tier*) disease; **wegen einer plötzlichen ~ des Viehbestandes** because the livestock suddenly became diseased

Er|kran|kungs|fall M case of illness; **im ~** in case of illness

er|küh|nen [ɛɐ'ky:nən] *ptp* **erkühnt** VR (*old, liter*) **sich ~, etw zu tun** to dare to do sth, to make so bold as to do sth

er|kun|den [ɛɐ'kʊndn] *ptp* **erkundet** VT (*esp Mil*) *Gelände, Stellungen* to reconnoitre (*Brit*), to reconnoiter (*US*), to scout; (= *feststellen*) to find out, to establish, to ascertain

er|kun|di|gen [ɛɐ'kʊndɪgn] ✪ 46.1, 48.1 *ptp* **erkundigt** VR **sich (nach etw/über jdn) ~** to ask *or* inquire (about sth/sb); **sich nach jdm ~** to ask after (*Brit*) *or* about sb; **sich bei jdm (nach etw) ~** to ask sb (about sth); **ich werde mich ~** I'll find out

Er|kun|di|gung F -, -en inquiry; (= *Nachforschung auch*) investigation; **~en einholen** *or* **einziehen** to make inquiries

Er|kun|dung F -, -en (*Mil*) reconnaissance

Er|kun|dungs|gang M *pl* **-gänge** (*Mil, fig*) reconnaissance expedition

er|kü|ren [ɛɐ'ky:rən] *pret* **erkor** [ɛɐ'ko:ɐ], *ptp* **erkoren** [ɛɐ'ko:rən] VT (*obs, liter*) to choose, to elect (*zu* as, to be)

Er|lag|schein [ɛɐ'la:k-] M (*Aus*) giro transfer form

er|lah|men [ɛɐ'la:mən] *ptp* **erlahmt** VI *aux sein* to tire, to grow weary; (*Kräfte, fig: Interesse, Eifer*) to flag, to wane

er|lan|gen [ɛɐ'laŋən] *ptp* **erlangt** VT to attain, to achieve; *Alter, Ziel auch* to reach; *Bedeutung auch, Eintritt* to gain

Er|lan|gung F -, *no pl* attainment

Er|lass [ɛɐ'las] M **-es, -e** *or* (*Aus*) **⸚e** [-'lɛsə] **a** (= *Verfügung*) decree, edict; (*der Regierung*) enactment, edict **b** (= *Straferlass, Schuldenerlass, Sündenerlass etc*) remission

er|las|sen [ɛɐ'lasn] *ptp* **erlassen** VT *irreg* **a** *Verfügung* to pass; *Gesetz* to enact; *Embargo etc* to impose; *Dekret* to issue **b** (*von etw entbinden*) *Strafe, Schulden etc* to remit; *Gebühren* to waive; **jdm etw ~** (*Schulden etc*) to release sb from sth; *Gebühren* to waive sth for sb; **bitte ~ Sie es mir, darüber zu sprechen** please don't ask me to talk about that; **jdm die Strafarbeit ~** to let sb off a punishment; **jdm eine Pflicht ~** to release sb from a duty; **ich erlasse ihm den Rest (des Geldes)** I'll waive the rest (of the money), I'll let him off paying the rest (of the money)

er|lau|ben [ɛɐ'laubn] ✪ 36.3 *ptp* **erlaubt** VT **a** (= *gestatten*) to allow, to permit; **jdm etw ~** to allow *or* permit sb (to do) sth; **mein Vater erlaubt mir nicht, dass ich mit Mädchen ausgehe** my father doesn't *or* won't allow me to go out with girls; **es ist mir nicht erlaubt, das zu tun** I am not allowed *or* permitted to do that; **du erlaubst deinem Kind zu viel** you allow your child too much freedom; **~ Sie?** (*form*) **Sie ~?** (*form*) may I?; **~ Sie, dass ich das Fenster öffne?** do you mind if I open the window?; **~ Sie, dass ich mich vorstelle** allow *or* permit me to introduce myself; **~ Sie mal!** do you mind!; **soweit es meine Zeit/das Wetter erlaubt** (*form*) time/weather permitting; **Weiteres wenn es die Zeit erlaubt** more when time permits; **erlaubt ist, was gefällt** (*prov*) a little of what you fancy does you good (*prov*); **erlaubt ist, was sich ziemt** (*prov*) you must only do what is proper

b sich (*dat*) **etw ~** (= *gestatten, sich gönnen*) to allow *or* permit oneself sth; (= *wagen*) *Bemerkung, Vorschlag* to venture sth; (= *sich leisten*) to afford sth; **sich** (*dat*) **~, etw zu tun** (= *so frei sein*) to take the liberty of doing sth; (= *sich leisten*) to afford to do sth; **darf ich mir ~ ...?** might I possibly ...?; **wenn ich mir die folgende Bemerkung ~ darf ...** if I might venture *or* be allowed the following remark ...; **sich** (*dat*) **Frechheiten ~** to take liberties, to be cheeky (*Brit*) *or* fresh (*US*); **sich** (*dat*) **einen Scherz ~** to have a joke; **was die Jugend sich heutzutage alles erlaubt!** the things young people get up to nowadays!; **was ~ Sie sich (eigentlich)!** how dare you!

Er|laub|nis [ɛɐ'laupnɪs] ✪ 36 F -, (*rare*) **-se** permission; (= *Schriftstück*) permit; **mit Ihrer (freundlichen) ~** (*form*) with your (kind) permission, by your leave (*form*); **du brauchst eine elterliche ~** you need your parents' (written) permission; **(jdn) um ~ bitten** to ask (sb) (for) permission, to ask *or* beg leave (of sb) (*form*); **jdm zu etw die ~ geben** *or* **erteilen** (*form*) to give sb permission *or* leave (*form*) for sth

Er|laub|nis|schein M permit

er|laucht [ɛɐ'lauxt] ADJ (*obs, iro*) illustrious; **ein ~er Kreis** a select circle

Er|laucht [ɛɐ'lauxt] F -, -en (*Hist*) Lordship

er|läu|tern [ɛɐ'lɔytɐn] *ptp* **erläutert** VT to explain, to elucidate; (= *klarstellen auch*) to clarify; *Text* to comment on; **~d** explanatory; **~d fügte er hinzu** he added in explanation *or* clarification; **etw anhand von Beispielen ~** to illustrate sth with examples

Er|läu|te|rung F explanation, elucidation; (= *Klarstellung auch*) clarification; (*zu Text*) comment, commentary; **zur ~** in explanation

Er|le ['ɛrlə] F -, -n alder

er|le|ben [ɛɐ'le:bn] *ptp* **erlebt** VT to experience; (= *noch lebend erreichen*) to live to see; (= *durchmachen*) *schwere Zeiten, Sturm* to go through; *Aufstieg, Abenteuer, Enttäuschung* to have; *Erfolg* to have, to enjoy; *Misserfolg, Niederlage* to have, to suffer; *Aufführung* to have, to receive; *Jahrhundertwende, erste Mondlandung* to see; *Schauspieler* to see (perform); *Musik, Gedicht, Fußballspiel, Landschaft* to experience; **im Ausland habe ich viel erlebt** I had an eventful time abroad; **was haben Sie im Ausland erlebt?** what sort of experiences did you have abroad?; **Deutschland, wie ich es erlebt habe, war ...** I remember Germany as being ...; **wir haben wunderschöne Tage in Spanien erlebt** we had a lovely time in Spain; **etwas Angenehmes** *etc* **~** to have a pleasant *etc* experience; **er hat schon viel Schlimmes erlebt** he's had a lot of bad times *or* experiences; **wir haben mit unseren Kindern viel Freude erlebt** our children have given us much pleasure; **ich habe es oft erlebt ...** I've often known *or* seen it happen ...; **so wütend habe ich ihn noch nie erlebt** I've never seen *or* known him so furious; **unser Land hat schon bessere Zeiten erlebt** our country has seen *or* known better times; **ich möchte mal ~, dass du rechtzeitig kommst** I'd like to see you come on time; **er hat gesagt, er möchte helfen – das möchte ich ~!** he said he'd like to help – that I'd like to see!; **das werde ich nicht mehr ~** I won't live to see that; **er möchte mal etwas ~** he wants to have a good time; **er hat viel erlebt** he has been around (*inf*), he has experienced a lot; **das muss man erlebt haben** you've got to have experienced it (for) yourself; **erlebte Rede** (*Liter*) interior monologue; **na, der kann was ~!** (*inf*) he's going to be (in) for it! (*inf*); **hat man so (et)was schon (mal) erlebt!** (*inf*) I've never heard anything like it!; **dass ich das noch ~ darf!** I never thought I'd see the day!; **so was Dummes habe ich noch nie erlebt!** I've never seen/heard anything so stupid in all my life!

Er|le|bens|fall M **im ~** in case of survival; **Versicherung auf den ~** pure endowment insurance

Er|leb|nis [ɛɐ'le:pnɪs] NT **-ses, -se** experience; (= *Abenteuer*) adventure; (= *Liebschaft*) affair; **(jdm) zu einem ~ werden** to be (quite) an experience (for sb)

Er|leb|nis-: **Er|leb|nis|auf|satz** M (*Sch*) essay based on personal experience; **Er|leb|nis|bad** NT adventure pool; **Er|leb|nis|dich|te** F richness of experience; **er|leb|nis|fä|hig** ADJ receptive, able to experience things *pred*; **Er|leb|nis|fä|hig|keit** F receptivity, capacity for experience; **Er|leb|nis|gast|ro|no|mie** F gastronomic experience (*with entertainment or in a theme restaurant*); **er|leb|nis|hung|rig** ADJ thirsty for experience *pred*; (*nach Abenteuer*) thirsty for adventure *pred*; **Er|leb|nis|ly|rik** F poetry based on personal experience; **Er|leb|nis|pä|da|go|gik** F *system of education through practical experience rather than classroom studies*; **Er|leb|nis|park** M adventure park, theme park; **er|leb|nis|reich** ADJ eventful

er|le|di|gen [ɛɐ'le:dɪgn] *ptp* **erledigt** VT **a** *Angelegenheit* to deal with, to take care of; *Akte etc* to process; (= *ausführen*) *Auftrag* to carry out; (= *beenden*) *Arbeit* to finish off, to deal with; *Sache* to settle; **Einkäufe ~** to do the shopping; **ich habe noch einiges in der Stadt zu ~** I've still got a few things to do in town; **ich muss noch schnell was ~** I've just got something to do; **die Sache/er ist für mich erledigt** as far as I'm concerned the matter's closed/I'm finished with him; **erledigt!** (*Stempel*) dealt with, processed; **erledigt, reden wir nicht mehr darüber!** OK, let's say no more about it!; **das ist (damit) erledigt** that's settled, that's taken care of; **wird erledigt!** shall (*Brit*) *or* will do! (*inf*), right-ho! (*Brit inf*), sure thing! (*US inf*); **zu ~** (*Vermerk auf Akten*) for attention; **schon erledigt!** I've already done it; (= *mache ich sofort*) consider it done

b (*inf:* = *ermüden*) to wear *or* knock (*inf*) out; (*inf:* = *ruinieren*) to finish, to ruin; (*inf:* = *töten*) to do in (*inf*); (*inf:* = *k.o. schlagen*) to finish off, to knock out

VR **damit erledigt sich das Problem** that disposes of *or* settles the problem; **das hat sich erledigt** that's all settled; **sich von selbst ~** to take care of itself

er|le|digt [ɛɐ'le:dɪçt] ADJ **a** (*inf*) (= *erschöpft*) shattered (*Brit inf*), done in *pred* (*Brit inf*), all in (*inf*); (= *ruiniert*) finished, ruined; **wenn jetzt die Bullen kommen, sind wir ~** if the cops come now, we've had it (*inf*) **b** (*obs*) *Stelle* vacant

Er|le|di|gung F -, -en (= *Ausführung*) execution, carrying out; (= *Durchführung, Beendung*) completion; (*einer Sache, eines Geschäfts*) settlement; **ich habe noch einige ~en** I still have a few items of business to attend to; **einige ~en in der Stadt** a few things to do in town; **die ~ von Einkäufen** (*form*) shopping; **die ~ meiner Korrespondenz** dealing with my correspondence; **sie betraute ihn mit der ~ ihrer Geschäfte** she entrusted him with (the execution of) her business affairs; **um rasche ~ wird gebeten** please give this your immediate attention; **in ~ Ihres Auftrages** (*form*) in execution of your order (*form*); **in ~ Ihrer Anfrage** (*form*) further to your inquiry

Er|le|di|gungs|ver|merk M actioned stamp

er|le|gen [ɛɐ'le:gn] *ptp* **erlegt** VT **a** *Wild* to shoot, to bag (*Hunt*) **b** (*Aus, Sw:* = *bezahlen*) to pay

er|leich|tern [ɛɐ'laiçtɐn] *ptp* **erleichtert** VT (= *einfacher machen*) to make easier; (*fig*) *Last, Los* to lighten; (= *beruhigen*) to relieve; (= *lindern*) *Not, Schmerz etc* to relieve, to alleviate; **sein Herz/Gewissen** *or* **sich** (*dat*) **das Gewissen ~** to unburden one's heart/conscience; **es würde mein Gewissen ~, wenn ...** it would ease my mind *or* conscience if ...; **jdm etw ~** to make sth easier for sb; **jdn um etw ~** *(hum)* to relieve sb of sth VR *(old)* to relieve oneself

er|leich|tert [ɛɐ'laiçtɐt] PTP *von* **erleichtern** ADJ relieved *(über +acc* about, to hear that) ADV **~ aufatmen** to breathe *or* heave a sigh of relief

Er|leich|te|rung F **-, -en** *(von Last etc)* lightening; *(= Linderung)* relief, alleviation; *(= Beruhigung)* relief; *(= Zahlungserleichterung)* facility; **das trägt zur ~ meiner Aufgabe bei** it makes my work easier; **einem Kranken ~ verschaffen** to give relief to a sick person

er|lei|den [ɛɐ'laidn] *ptp* **erlitten** [ɛɐ'lɪtn] VT *irreg* to suffer; *Verluste, Schaden auch* to sustain, to incur; **den Tod ~** *(old)* to suffer death *(old)* → **Schiffbruch**

Er|len|mei|er|kol|ben ['ɛrlənmaiɐ-] M *(Phys)* Erlenmeyer flask

er|lern|bar ADJ easily learned

er|ler|nen [ɛɐ'lɛrnən] *ptp* **erlernt** VT to learn

er|le|sen [ɛɐ'le:zn] ADJ exquisite; **ein ~er Kreis** a select circle

Er|le|sen|heit F **-,** *no pl* exquisite nature; *(von Kreis)* selectness

er|leuch|ten [ɛɐ'lɔyçtn] *ptp* **erleuchtet** VT to light (up), to illuminate; *(fig)* to enlighten, to inspire; **Herr, erleuchte uns!** Lord, let thy light shine upon us; **hell erleuchtet** brightly lit; *Stadt* brightly illuminated

Er|leuch|tung F **-, -en** *(= Eingebung)* inspiration; *(religiöse auch)* enlightenment *no pl*

er|lie|gen [ɛɐ'li:gn] *ptp* **erlegen** VI *irreg aux sein +dat (lit, fig)* to succumb to; *einem Irrtum* to be the victim of; **zum Erliegen kommen/bringen** to come/bring to a standstill

er|lischt [ɛɐ'lɪʃt] 3. PERS SING *pres von* **erlöschen**

er|lo|gen [ɛɐ'lo:gn] PTP *von* **erlügen** ADJ not true *pred*; *(= erfunden)* made-up *attr*, made up *pred*; **das ist erstunken und ~** that's a rotten lie; **das ist von Anfang bis Ende ~** there's not a word of truth in it, it's a pack of lies *(inf)* → *auch* **erlügen**

Er|lös [ɛɐ'lø:s] M **-es, -e** [-zə] proceeds *pl*

er|lö|schen [ɛɐ'lœʃn] *pres* **erlischt** [ɛɐ'lɪʃt], *pret* **erlosch** [ɛɐ'lɔʃ], *ptp* **erloschen** [ɛɐ'lɔʃn] VI *aux sein (Feuer)* to go out; *(Gefühle, Interesse)* to die; *(Vulkan)* to become extinct; *(Leben)* to come to an end; *(Vertrag, Anspruch etc)* to expire, to lapse; *(Garantie, Mandat)* to expire; *(Hirnfunktionen)* to cease; *(Geschlecht, Name)* to die out; **ein erloschener Vulkan** an extinct volcano; **mit ~der Stimme** *(liter)* in a dying voice; **seine Augen waren erloschen** *(liter)* his eyes were lifeless

er|lö|sen [ɛɐ'lø:zn] *ptp* **erlöst** VT **a** *(= retten)* to save, to rescue *(aus, von* from); *(Rel)* to redeem, to save; *(von Sünden, Qualen)* to deliver *(esp Bibl)*, to release; **erlöse uns von dem Bösen** *(Rel)* deliver us from evil **b** *(Comm: aus Verkauf)* Geld to realize

er|lö|send ADJ relieving, liberating; **sie sprach das ~e Wort** she spoke the word he/she/everybody *etc* was waiting for ADV **~ wirken** to come as a relief; **er empfand es beinahe ~, als ...** it was almost a relief for him when ...

Er|lö|ser [ɛɐ'lø:zɐ] M **-s, -, Er|lö|se|rin** [-ərɪn] F **-, -nen** *(= Befreier)* saviour *(Brit)*, savior *(US)*; **der ~** *(Rel)* the Redeemer

Er|lö|sung F release, deliverance; *(= Erleichterung)* relief; *(Rel)* redemption; **der Tod war für sie eine ~** death was a release for her

er|lü|gen [ɛɐ'ly:gn] *ptp* **erlogen** [ɛɐ'lo:gn] VT *irreg* to fabricate, to make up, to invent; **eine erlogene Geschichte** a fabrication, a fiction

er|mäch|ti|gen [ɛɐ'mɛçtɪgn] *ptp* **ermächtigt** VT to authorize, to empower *(zu etw* to do sth)

er|mäch|tigt [ɛɐ'mɛçtɪçt] ADJ authorized, empowered; **zur Unterschrift ~** authorized to sign

Er|mäch|ti|gung F **-, -en** authorization

Er|mäch|ti|gungs|ge|setz NT *(Pol)* Enabling Act *(esp that of Nazis in 1933)*

er|mah|nen [ɛɐ'ma:nən] *ptp* **ermahnt** VT to exhort *(form)*, to admonish, to urge; *(warnend)* to warn; *(Jur)* to caution; **jdn zum Fleiß/zur Aufmerksamkeit** *etc* **~** to exhort *(form) or* urge sb to work hard/to be attentive *etc*; **muss ich dich immer erst ~?** do I always have to remind *or* tell you first?; **jdn im Guten ~** to give sb a friendly warning

Er|mah|nung F exhortation, admonition, urging; *(warnend)* warning; *(Jur)* caution

er|man|geln [ɛɐ'maŋəln] *ptp* **ermangelt** VI **einer Sache** *(gen)* **~** *(geh)* to lack sth

Er|man|ge|lung [ɛɐ'maŋəlʊŋ] F **-,** *no pl*, **Er|mang|lung** [ɛɐ'maŋlʊŋ] F **-,** *no pl (geh)* **in ~** *+gen* because of the lack of; **in ~ eines Besseren** for lack of something better

er|man|nen [ɛɐ'manən] *ptp* **ermannt** VR to pluck up courage

er|mä|ßi|gen [ɛɐ'mɛsɪgn] *ptp* **ermäßigt** VT to reduce VR to be reduced

er|mä|ßigt [ɛɐ'mɛ:sɪçt] PTP *von* **ermäßigen** ADJ reduced; **zu ~en Preisen** at reduced prices; *(Fahrkarten, Eintritt etc)* at reduced rates

Er|mä|ßi|gung F **-, -en** reduction; *(= Steuerermäßigung)* relief

Er|mä|ßi|gungs|fahr|schein M concessionary *(Brit) or* reduced ticket

er|mat|ten [ɛɐ'matn] *ptp* **ermattet** *(geh)* VT to tire, to exhaust VI *aux sein* to tire, to become exhausted

er|mat|tet [ɛɐ'matət] ADJ *(geh)* exhausted, weary

Er|mat|tung F **-,** *no pl (geh)* exhaustion, weariness, fatigue

er|mes|sen [ɛɐ'mɛsn] *ptp* **ermessen** VT *irreg (= einschätzen) Größe, Weite, Wert* to gauge, to estimate; *(= erfassen, begreifen können)* to appreciate, to realize

Er|mes|sen [ɛɐ'mɛsn] NT **-s,** *no pl (= Urteil)* judgement, estimation; *(= Gutdünken)* discretion; **nach meinem ~** in my estimation; **nach menschlichem ~** as far as anyone can judge; **nach bestem ~ handeln** to act according to one's best judgement; **nach freiem ~** at one's discretion; **nach eigenem ~ handeln** to act on one's own discretion; **etw in jds ~** *(acc)* **stellen, etw jds ~** *(dat)* **anheimstellen** to leave sth to sb's discretion; **in jds ~** *(dat)* **liegen** *or* **stehen** to be within sb's discretion

Er|mes|sens-: Er|mes|sens|ent|schei|dung F *(Jur)* discretionary decision; **Er|mes|sens|fra|ge** F matter of discretion; **Er|mes|sens|frei|heit** F powers *pl* of discretion, discretionary powers *pl*; **Er|mes|sens|miss|brauch** M abuse of (one's powers of) discretion; **Er|mes|sens|spiel|raum** M discretionary powers *pl*

er|mit|teln [ɛɐ'mɪtln] *ptp* **ermittelt** VT to determine *(auch Chem, Math)*, to ascertain; *Person* to trace; *Tatsache, Identität* to establish VI to investigate; **gegen jdn ~** to investigate sb; **in einem Fall ~** to investigate a case

Er|mitt|ler(in) M(F) investigator; **verdeckter ~** undercover investigator

Er|mitt|lung F **-, -en a** *(esp Jur: = Erkundigung)* investigation, inquiry; **~en anstellen** to make inquiries *(über +acc* about) **b** *no pl (= das Ermitteln)* determination, ascertaining; *(von Person)* tracing; *(von Tatsache, Identität)* establishing, establishment

Er|mitt|lungs-: Er|mitt|lungs|aus|schuss M committee of inquiry *(Brit)*, investigative committee *(US)*; **Er|mitt|lungs|rich|ter(in)** M(F) *(Jur)* examining magistrate; **Er|mitt|lungs|stand** M stage of the investigation; **Er|mitt|lungs|ver|fah|ren** NT *(Jur)* preliminary proceedings *pl*

er|mög|li|chen [ɛɐ'mø:klɪçn] *ptp* **ermöglicht** VT to facilitate, to make possible; **jdm etw ~** to make sth possible for sb, to facilitate sth for sb; **es jdm ~, etw zu tun** to make it possible for sb to do sth, to enable sb to do sth; **um uns den freien Austausch von Informationen zu ~** to facilitate the free exchange of information, to make it possible for us *or* to enable us to exchange information freely; **jdm das Studium/eine Reise ~** to make it possible for sb to study/to go on a journey; **(nur) wenn Sie es ~ können** *(form)* (only) if you are able (to); **können Sie es ~, morgen zu kommen?** *(form)* would it be possible for you to *or* are you able to come tomorrow?

er|mor|den [ɛɐ'mɔrdn] *ptp* **ermordet** VT to murder; *(esp aus politischen Gründen)* to assassinate

Er|mor|dung F **-, -en** murder; *(esp politisch)* assassination

er|mü|den [ɛɐ'my:dn] *ptp* **ermüdet** VT to tire VI *aux sein* to tire, to become tired; *(Tech)* to fatigue

er|mü|dend ADJ tiring

Er|mü|dung F **-,** *(rare)* **-en** fatigue *(auch Tech)*, tiredness, weariness

Er|mü|dungs-: Er|mü|dungs|er|schei|nung F sign *or* symptom of fatigue; **Er|mü|dungs|zu|stand** M feeling of tiredness

er|mun|tern [ɛɐ'mʊntɐn] *ptp* **ermuntert** VT *(= ermutigen)* to encourage *(jdn zu etw* sb to do sth); *(= beleben, erfrischen)* to liven up, to stimulate, to invigorate; *(= aufmuntern)* to cheer up; **seine Gegenwart wirkt ~d auf mich** his presence has an enlivening effect on me, his presence stimulates me VR *(rare)* to wake up, to rouse oneself

Er|mun|te|rung F **-, -en** encouragement; *(= Belebung)* enlivening, stimulation; *(= Aufmunterung)* cheering-up

er|mu|ti|gen [ɛɐ'mu:tɪgn] *ptp* **ermutigt** VT *(= ermuntern)* to encourage; *(= Mut geben)* to give courage, to embolden *(form)*; **jdn zu etw ~** to encourage sb to do sth, to give sb the courage *or* embolden sb *(form)* to do sth

Er|mu|ti|gung F **-, -en** encouragement

Ern [e:ɐn] M **-(e)s, -e** *(dial: = Hausflur)* (entrance) hall, hallway

er|näh|ren [ɛɐ'nɛ:rən] *ptp* **ernährt** VT to feed; *(= unterhalten)* to support, to keep, to maintain; **schlecht ernährt** undernourished; **gut ernährt** well-nourished, well-fed; **dieser Beruf ernährt seinen Mann** you can make a good living in this profession VR to eat; **sich gesund ~** to eat healthily, to have a healthy diet; **der Arzt klärte ihn auf, wie er sich ~ sollte** the doctor advised him on his diet; **sich von etw ~** to live *or* subsist on sth; **sich von Übersetzungen ~** to earn one's living by doing translations; **sich selbst ~ müssen** to have to earn one's own living

Er|näh|rer [ɛɐ'nɛ:rɐ] M **-s, -, Er|näh|re|rin** [-ərɪn] F **-, -nen** breadwinner, provider

Er|näh|rung F **-,** *no pl (= das Ernähren)* feeding; *(= Nahrung)* food, nourishment, nutrition *(esp Med)*; *(= Unterhalt)* maintenance; **auf vernünftige ~ achten** to eat sensibly; **die ~ einer großen Familie** feeding a big family; **falsche/richtige/pflanzliche ~** the wrong/a proper/a vegetarian diet

Er|näh|rungs- *in cpds* nutritional; **Er|näh|rungs|be|ra|ter(in)** M(F) nutritional *or* dietary adviser; **Er|näh|rungs|be|ra|tung** F nutritional *or* dietary advice; *(= Beratungsstelle)* nutritional *or* dietary advice centre *(Brit) or* center *(US)*; **er|näh|rungs|be|wusst** ADJ nutrition-conscious; **Er|näh|rungs|feh|ler** M bad *or* unhealthy eating habit; **~ machen** to eat unhealthily *or* an unhealthy diet; **Er|näh|rungs|for|schung** F nutritional research; **Er|näh|rungs|ge|wohn|hei|ten** PL eating habits *pl*; **Er|näh|rungs|krank|heit** F nutritional disease; **Er|näh|rungs|wei|se** F diet, form of nutrition; **Er|näh|rungs|wis|sen|schaft** F dietetics *sing*; **Er|näh|rungs|wis|sen|schaft|ler(in)** M(F) dietician, nutritionist; **Er|näh|rungs|zu|stand** M nutritional state; **in einem guten/schlechten ~ sein** to be well/poorly nourished *or* fed

er|nen|nen [ɛɐ'nɛnən] *ptp* **ernannt** [ɛɐ'nant] VT *irreg* to appoint; **jdn zu etw ~** to make *or* appoint sb sth

Er|nen|nung F appointment *(zu* as)

Er|nen|nungs-: Er|nen|nungs|schrei|ben NT letter of appointment; **Er|nen|nungs|ur|kun|de** F certificate of appointment

er|neu|er|bar ADJ renewable

Er|neu|e|rer [ɛɐ'nɔyərɐ] M **-s, -**, **Er|neu|e|rin** [-ərɪn] F **-, -nen** innovator

er|neu|ern [ɛɐ'nɔyɐn] *ptp* **erneuert** VT to renew; *Forderung, Kritik* to reiterate; *(= renovieren)* to renovate; *(= restaurieren)* to restore; *(= auswechseln) Öl* to change; *Maschinenteile* to replace; *(= wieder beleben)* to revive; **einen Vertrag ~** to renew a contract

Er|neu|e|rung F renewal; *(= Renovierung)* renovation; *(= Restaurierung)* restoration; *(= Auswechslung) (von Öl)* changing; *(von Maschinenteil)* replacement; *(= Wiederbelebung)* revival

Er|neu|e|rungs-: **er|neu|e|rungs|be|dürf|tig** ADJ in need of renewal *or* replacement *pred*; **Er|neu|e|rungs|be|we|gung** F *(in Politik)* reform movement; *(in Religion)* revivalist movement

er|neut [ɛɐ'nɔyt] ADJ *attr* renewed ADV (once) again, once more; **~ Ärger bekommen** to run into fresh trouble

er|nied|ri|gen [ɛɐ'ni:drɪgn] *ptp* **erniedrigt** VT *(= demütigen)* to humiliate; *(= herabsetzen)* to degrade; *(Mus)* to flatten, to flat *(US)* VR to humble oneself; *(pej)* to demean *or* lower oneself

Er|nied|ri|gung F **-, -en** humiliation; *(= Herabsetzung)* degradation; *(Mus)* flattening, flatting *(US)*

Er|nied|ri|gungs|zei|chen NT *(Mus)* flat (sign)

ernst [ɛrnst] ADJ serious; *(= bedenklich, bedrohlich, würdevoll auch)* grave; *(= eifrig, ernsthaft) Mensch, Gesinnung* earnest; *(= feierlich, elegisch)* solemn; **~e Absichten haben** *(inf)* to have honourable *(Brit) or* honorable *(US)* intentions; **es ist nichts Ernstes** it's nothing serious; **~ bleiben** to remain *or* be serious; *(= sich das Lachen verbeißen)* to keep a straight face

ADV *reden, zuhören* earnestly; **es (mit jdm/etw) ~ meinen** to be serious (about sb/sth); **~ gemeint** serious; **jdn/etw ~ nehmen** to take sb/sth seriously; **es steht ~ um ihn** things look bad for him; *(wegen Krankheit)* he's in a bad way; **ich muss mal ganz ~ mit ihr reden** I have to have a serious talk with her

Ernst [ɛrnst] M **-s** *(= Name)* Ernest

Ernst M **-(e)s**, *no pl* seriousness; *(= Bedenklichkeit auch)* gravity; *(= Dringlichkeit, Ernsthaftigkeit von Gesinnung)* earnestness; **feierlicher ~** solemnity; **im ~** seriously; **allen ~es** in all seriousness, quite seriously; **meinen Sie das allen ~es?, ist das Ihr ~?** are you (really) serious?, you're not serious, are you?; **das kann doch nicht dein ~ sein!** you can't mean that seriously!, you can't be serious!; **das ist mein (völliger** *or* **voller) ~** I'm quite serious; **dieses Angebot ist im ~ gemeint** this offer is meant seriously; **es ist mir ~ damit** I'm serious about it, I'm in earnest; **mit etw ~ machen** to put sth into action; **wir sollten endlich ~ machen** let's get down to business; **mit einer Drohung ~ machen** to carry out a threat; **der ~ des Lebens** the serious side of life, the real world; **damit wird es jetzt ~** now it's serious, now it's for real *(inf)*; **mit ~ bei der Sache sein** to do sth seriously

Ernst-: **Ernst|fall** M emergency; **im ~** in case of emergency; **ernst|ge|meint** [-gəmaint] ADJ *attr* → **ernst ADV**; **ernst|haft** ADJ serious; *(= bedenklich, gewichtig auch)* grave; *(= eindringlich, eifrig)* earnest ADV **a** *(= wirklich) annehmen, glauben, wollen, sich verlieben* seriously; *(= mit Ernst) tun* seriously, in earnest **b** *(= schwer) krank, erkranken, sich verschlimmern* seriously **c** *(= eindringlich)* **jdn ~ ermahnen/warnen** to give sb a serious warning; **Ernst|haf|tig|keit** ['ɛrnsthaftɪçkait] F **-**, *no pl* seriousness; *(= Bedenklichkeit, Gewichtigkeit auch)* gravity; *(= Eindringlichkeit, Eifrigkeit)* earnestness; **ernst|lich** ['ɛrnstlɪç] ADJ serious; *(= bedrohlich auch)* grave; *(attr: = eindringlich)* earnest ADV **~ besorgt um** seriously *or* gravely concerned about; **~ böse werden** to get really angry

Ern|te ['ɛrntə] F **-, -n** **a** *(= das Ernten) (von Getreide)* harvest(ing); *(von Kartoffeln)* digging; *(von Äpfeln etc)* picking **b** *(= Ertrag)* harvest *(an +dat* of); *(von Kartoffeln etc auch, von Äpfeln, fig)* crop; **die ~ bergen** *(form) or* **einbringen** to bring in the harvest, to harvest the crop(s); **die ~ seines Fleißes** the fruits of his hard work; **der Tod hielt grausige ~** *(liter)* death took a heavy toll; **du siehst aus, als sei dir die ganze ~ verhagelt** *(fig inf)* you look as though you've lost a shilling and found sixpence

Ern|te-: **Ern|te|ar|bei|ter(in)** M(F) *(von Getreide)* reaper, harvester; *(von Kartoffeln, Obst, Hopfen)* picker; **Ern|te|aus|fall** M crop shortfall *(spec) or* failure; **Ern|te|(dank)|fest** NT harvest festival; **ern|te|frisch** ADJ fresh from the field(s); **Ern|te|ma|schi|ne** F reaper, harvester

ern|ten ['ɛrntn] VT **a** *Getreide* to harvest, to reap; *Kartoffeln* to dig, to get in; *Äpfel, Erbsen* to pick; **ich muss jetzt meinen Apfelbaum ~** it's time I picked my apples **b** *(fig) Früchte, Lohn, Unfrieden* to reap; *Undank, Applaus, Spott* to get

Ern|te|zeit F harvest (time)

er|nüch|tern [ɛɐ'nʏçtɐn] *ptp* **ernüchtert** VT to sober up; *(fig)* to bring down to earth, to sober; **~d** sobering

Er|nüch|te|rung F **-, -en** sobering-up; *(fig)* disillusionment

Er|obe|rer [ɛɐ'lo:bərɐ] M **-s, -**, **Er|obe|rin** [-ərɪn] F **-, -nen** conqueror

er|obern [ɛɐ'lo:bɐn] *ptp* **erobert** VT to conquer; *Festung, Stadt* to take, to capture; *(fig) Sympathie etc* to win, to capture; *neue Märkte* to win, to move into; *Herz, Mädchen* to conquer; *(inf: = ergattern)* to get hold of; **im Sturm ~** *(Mil, fig)* to take by storm

Er|obe|rung F **-, -en** *(lit, fig)* conquest; *(einer Festung, Stadt)* capture, taking; **eine ~ machen** *(fig inf)* to make a conquest; **auf ~en ausgehen** *(fig inf)* to be out to make conquests

Er|obe|rungs-: **Er|obe|rungs|krieg** M war of conquest; **Er|obe|rungs|zug** M campaign of conquest

er|öff|nen [ɛɐ'œfnən] *ptp* **eröffnet** VT **a** *(= beginnen)* to open *(auch Fin, Mil etc)*; *Ausstellung* to open, to inaugurate *(form)*; *Konkursverfahren* to institute, to initiate; *Testament* to open; **etw für eröffnet erklären** to declare sth open **b** *(Med) Geschwür* to lance **c** *(hum, geh)* **jdm etw ~** to disclose *or* reveal sth to sb; **ich habe dir etwas zu ~** I have something to tell you VR **a** *(Aussichten etc)* to open up, to present itself/themselves **b** *(geh)* **sich jdm ~** to open one's heart to sb VI *(Währungskurs)* to open *(mit* at)

Er|öff|nung F **a** *(= Beginn)* opening; *(von Ausstellung)* opening, inauguration; *(von Konkursverfahren)* institution, initiation **b** *(Med: von Geschwür)* lancing **c** *(hum, geh)* disclosure, revelation; **jdm eine ~ machen** to disclose *or* reveal sth to sb; **ich habe dir eine ~ zu machen** I have something to tell you

Er|öff|nungs-: **Er|öff|nungs|an|spra|che** F inaugural *or* opening address; **Er|öff|nungs|fei|er** F, **Er|öff|nungs|fei|er|lich|kei|ten** PL opening ceremony; *(Sportereignisse auch)* opening ceremonies *pl*; **Er|öff|nungs|kurs** M opening price; **Er|öff|nungs|we|hen** PL *(Med)* first stage contractions *pl*

ero|gen [ero'ge:n] ADJ erogenous

er|ör|tern [ɛɐ'lœrtɐn] ✪ 53.1 *ptp* **erörtert** VT to discuss (in detail)

Er|ör|te|rung F **-, -en** discussion; **zur ~ stehen** *(form)* to be under discussion

Eros ['e:rɔs] M **-**, *no pl (esp Philos)* Eros

Eros|cen|ter ['e:rɔssɛntɐ] NT **-s, -** eros centre *(Brit) or* center *(US)*

Ero|si|on [ero'zio:n] F **-, -en** *(Geol, Med)* erosion

Ero|si|ons|schä|den [ero'zio:nsʃɛ:dn] PL *(Geol)* erosion damage, damage *sing* caused by erosion

Ero|ten [e'ro:tn] PL *(Art)* Cupids *pl*

Ero|tik [e'ro:tɪk] F **-**, *no pl* eroticism

Ero|ti|ka [e'ro:tika] PL *(Liter)* erotica *sing*

Ero|ti|ker [e'ro:tikɐ] M **-s, -**, **Ero|ti|ke|rin** [-ərɪn] F **-, -nen** eroticist

ero|tisch [e'ro:tɪʃ] ADJ erotic

Ero|to|ma|ne [eroto'ma:nə] M **-n, -n** sex maniac

Ero|to|ma|nie [erotoma'ni:] F *(Psych)* erotomania *(spec)*

Ero|to|ma|nin [eroto'ma:nɪn] F **-, -nen** nymphomaniac

Er|pel ['ɛrpl] M **-s, -** drake

er|picht [ɛɐ'pɪçt] ADJ **auf etw** *(acc)* **~ sein** to be keen *(Brit) or* bent *(US)* on sth; **er ist nur auf Geld ~** he's only after money

er|press|bar ADJ **~ sein** to be susceptible to blackmail; **~e Politiker** politicians who are susceptible to blackmail; **sich ~ machen** to lay oneself open to blackmail

er|pres|sen [ɛɐ'prɛsn] *ptp* **erpresst** VT *Geld etc* to extort *(von* from); *jdn* to blackmail; **die Kidnapper haben den Vater erpresst** the kidnappers tried to extort money from the father

Er|pres|ser [ɛɐ'prɛsɐ] M **-s, -**, **Er|pres|se|rin** [-ərɪn] F **-, -nen** blackmailer; *(bei Entführung)* kidnapper

Er|pres|ser|brief M blackmail letter

er|pres|se|risch [ɛɐ'prɛsərɪʃ] ADJ blackmailing *attr*; **~er Menschenraub** *(Jur)* kidnapping

Er|pres|ser|me|tho|den PL blackmail *sing*

Er|pres|sung F **-, -en** *(von Geld, Zugeständnissen)* extortion; *(eines Menschen)* blackmail; **die Kidnapper hatten keinen Erfolg mit ihrer ~** the kidnappers failed to get their ransom money, the kidnappers failed in their ransom attempt

Er|pres|sungs|ver|such M blackmail attempt; *(durch Gewaltandrohung)* attempt at obtaining money by menaces; *(bei Entführung)* attempt at getting a ransom

er|pro|ben [ɛɐ'pro:bn] *ptp* **erprobt** VT to test; *(fig)* to (put to the) test

er|probt ADJ tried and tested, proven; *(= zuverlässig)* reliable; *(= erfahren)* experienced

Er|pro|bung [ɛɐ'pro:bʊŋ] F **-, -en** *usu sing* testing, trial(s *pl*)

Er|pro|bungs|pha|se F test phase; **es befindet sich noch in der ~** it is still undergoing tests *or (Maschine, Fahrzeug)* trial runs

er|qui|cken [ɛɐ'kvɪkn] *ptp* **erquickt** VT *(old, liter)* to refresh

er|quick|lich [ɛɐ'kvɪklɪç] ADJ *(= angenehm)* pleasant; *(= anregend)* stimulating

Er|qui|ckung F **-, -en** *(old)* refreshment

Er|ra|ta [ɛ'ra:ta] PL *(Typ)* errata *pl*

er|ra|ten [ɛɐ'ra:tn] *ptp* **erraten** VT *irreg* to guess; *Rätsel* to guess (the answer to); **du hast es ~!** how did you guess?, you guessed!

er|ra|tisch [ɛ'ra:tɪʃ] ADJ *(Geol)* erratic; **ein ~er Block** an erratic

er|rech|nen [ɛɐ'rɛçnən] *ptp* **errechnet** VT to calculate, to work out

er|reg|bar ADJ excitable; *(sexuell)* easily aroused; *(= empfindlich)* sensitive; **schwer ~** not easily aroused

Er|reg|bar|keit [ɛɐ're:kba:ɐkait] F **-**, *no pl* excitability; *(= Empfindlichkeit)* sensitivity

er|re|gen [ɛɐ're:gn] *ptp* **erregt** VT **a** *(= aufregen) jdn, Nerven etc* to excite; *(sexuell auch)* to arouse; *(= erzürnen)* to infuriate, to annoy; **er war vor Wut ganz erregt** he was in a rage *or* fury; **in der Debatte ging es erregt zu** feelings ran high in the debate, the debate was quite heated; **erregte Diskussionen** heated discussions; **erregt lief er hin und her** he paced back and forth in a state of agitation; **freudig erregt** excited → **Gemüt b**

b *(= hervorrufen, erzeugen)* to arouse; *Zorn* to provoke; *Leidenschaften* to arouse, to excite; *Aufsehen, öffentliches Ärgernis, Heiterkeit* to cause, to create; *Aufmerksamkeit* to attract; *Zweifel* to raise VR to get worked up *or* excited *(über +acc* about, over); *(= sich ärgern)* to get annoyed *(über +acc* at)

Er|re|ger [ɛɐ're:gɐ] M **-s, -** *(Med)* cause, causative agent *(spec)*; *(= Bazillus etc)* pathogene *(spec)*

Er|regt|heit [ɛɐ'reːkthait] **F -,** *no pl (esp angenehm)* excitement; *(sexuell auch)* arousal; *(= Beunruhigung)* agitation; *(= Wut)* rage

Er|re|gung **F** **a** *no pl (= das Aufregen)* excitation; *(sexuell auch)* arousal, arousing; *(= das Erzürnen)* infuriation, infuriating
b *no pl (= Erzeugung)* arousal, arousing; *(von Aufsehen, Heiterkeit)* causing, creating; *(von Aufmerksamkeit)* attracting → **Ärgernis a**
c *(= Zustand) (esp angenehm)* excitement; *(sexuell auch)* arousal; *(= Beunruhigung)* agitation; *(= Wut)* rage; *(liter: des Meeres, der Wellen)* turbulence; **in ~ geraten** to get excited/aroused/agitated/into a rage; **jdn in ~ versetzen** to get sb excited/aroused/agitated; to put sb into a rage; **das Meer in ~ versetzen** to make the sea churn

er|reich|bar **ADJ** reachable, able to be reached; *(= nicht weit)* within reach; *(Telec)* obtainable; *Glück, Ziel* attainable; **leicht ~** easily reached; within easy reach; easily attainable; **schwer ~ sein** *(Ort)* not to be very accessible; *(Mensch)* to be difficult to get hold of; *(Gegenstand)* to be difficult to reach; **zu Fuß ~** able to be reached on foot; *(= nicht weit)* within walking distance; **in ~er Nähe** near at hand (*+gen* to); **der Direktor ist nie ~** the director is never available; *(telefonisch)* the director can never be reached; **sind Sie morgen zu Hause ~?** can I get in touch with you at home tomorrow?, are you contactable at home tomorrow? → **telefonisch**

Er|reich|bar|keit [ɛɐ'raiçbaːɐkait] **F -,** *no pl (von Ort, Mensch)* accessibility; *(Telec)* obtainability

er|rei|chen [ɛɐ'raiçn] *ptp* **erreicht** **VT** to reach; *Ort auch* to get to, to arrive at; *Festland, Hafen auch* to make; *Zug* to catch; *Alter, Geschwindigkeit* to reach, to attain; *Absicht, Zweck* to achieve, to attain; *(= einholen)* to catch up with; *(= sich in Verbindung setzen mit) jdn, Büro etc* to contact, to get, to reach; **ein hohes Alter ~** to live to a ripe old age; **vom Bahnhof leicht zu ~** within easy reach of the station; **zu Fuß zu ~** able to be reached on foot; *(= nicht weit)* within walking distance; **wann kann ich Sie morgen ~?** when can I get in touch with you tomorrow?; **du erreichst damit nur, dass …** all you'll achieve is that …; **wir haben nichts erreicht** we achieved nothing; **bei ihm war nichts zu ~** you couldn't get anywhere with him *or* anything out of him

Er|rei|chung **F -,** *no pl (form)* attainment; *(eines Ziels auch)* achievement; **bei ~ des 60. Lebensjahres** on reaching the age of 60

er|ret|ten [ɛɐ'rɛtn] *ptp* **errettet** **VT** *(liter, esp Rel)* to save, to deliver *(liter)*

Er|ret|ter(in) **M(F)** *(liter, esp Rel)* saviour *(Brit esp Rel)*, savior *(US esp Rel)*, deliverer *(liter)*

Er|ret|tung **F** *(liter)* rescue, deliverance *(liter)*; *(Rel)* salvation

er|rich|ten [ɛɐ'rɪçtn] *ptp* **errichtet** **VT** to erect *(auch Math)*, to put up; *(fig: = gründen)* to establish, to set up

Er|rich|tung **F** erection, construction; *(fig: = Gründung)* establishment, setting-up

er|rin|gen [ɛɐ'rɪŋən] *ptp* **errungen** [ɛɐ'rʊŋən] **VT** *irreg* to gain, to win; *den 3. Platz, Erfolg* to gain, to achieve; *Rekord* to set; **ein hart errungener Sieg** a hard-won victory

Er-Ro|man ['eːɐ-] **M** *(Liter)* third-person novel

er|rö|ten [ɛɐ'røːtn] *ptp* **errötet** **VI** *aux sein (über +acc* at) to flush; *(esp aus Verlegenheit, Scham)* to blush; *(Gesicht)* to go *or* turn red, to redden; **jdn zum Erröten bringen** to make sb flush/blush

Er|run|gen|schaft [ɛɐ'rʊŋənʃaft] **F -, -en** achievement; *(inf: = Anschaffung)* acquisition

Er|satz [ɛɐ'zats] **M,** *no pl* substitute *(auch Sport)*; *(für Altes, Zerbrochenes, Mitarbeiter)* replacement; *(inf: = die Ersatzspieler)* substitutes *pl*; *(Mil) (= Ersatztruppen)* replacements *pl*; *(= Reserveheer)* reserves *pl*; *(= das Ersetzen)* replacement, substitution; *(durch Geld)* compensation; *(von Kosten)* reimbursement; **als** *or* **zum ~** as a substitute/replacement; **zum ~ der beschädigten Ware verpflichtet** obliged to replace the damaged item; **als ~ für jdn einspringen** to stand in for sb; **für etw ~ leisten** *(Jur)* to pay *or* provide compensation *or* restitution for sth; **~ schaffen für** to find replacements/a replacement for, to replace

Er|satz-: **Er|satz|an|spruch** **M** *(Jur)* entitlement to compensation; **~ haben** to be entitled to compensation; **Er|satz|bank** **F** *pl* **-bänke** *(Sport)* substitutes' bench; **Er|satz|be|frie|di|gung** **F** *(Psych)* vicarious satisfaction; **das Rauchen ist eine ~** smoking is a substitute; **Er|satz|bril|le** **F** spare (pair of) glasses *pl or* spectacles *pl (Brit)*; **Er|satz|dienst** **M** alternative *or* community service *(for conscientious objectors)*; **Er|satz|dienst|leis|ten|de(r)** [-laistndə] **M** *decl as adj* (civilian) alternative service worker; **Er|satz|droge** **F** substitute drug; **Er|satz|frau** **F** replacement; *(Sport)* substitute; **Er|satz|hand|lung** **F** *(Psych)* substitute (act); **Er|satz|kaf|fee** **M** coffee substitute; **Er|satz|kas|se** **F** state health insurance scheme; **er|satz|los** **ADJ** **~e Streichung** *(von Stelle, Steuer, Regelung)* abolition; *(von Sendung, Veranstaltung)* cancellation **ADV** **etw ~ streichen** *(Stelle, Steuer, Regelung)* to abolish sth; *Sendung, Veranstaltung* to cancel sth; **Er|satz|mann** **M** *pl* **-männer** *or* **-leute** replacement; *(Sport)* substitute; **Er|satz|mi|ne** **F** refill; **Er|satz|ob|jekt** **NT** *(Psych)* substitute, surrogate; **Er|satz|pflicht** **F** liability to pay compensation; **er|satz|pflich|tig** [-pflɪçtɪç] **ADJ** liable to pay compensation; **Er|satz|rad** **NT** *(Aut)* spare wheel; **Er|satz|rei|fen** **M** *(Aut)* spare tyre *(Brit) or* tire *(US)*; **Er|satz|spie|ler(in)** **M(F)** *(Sport)* substitute; **Er|satz|teil** **NT** spare (part); **Er|satz|trup|pen** **PL** replacements *pl*; *(= Reserveheer)* reserve troops *pl*, reserves *pl*; **er|satz|wei|se** **ADV** as an alternative

er|sau|fen [ɛɐ'zaufn] *ptp* **ersoffen** [ɛɐ'zɔfn] **VI** *irreg aux sein (inf)* **a** *(= ertrinken)* to drown, to be drowned **b** *(= überschwemmt werden, Aut)* to be flooded, to flood

er|säu|fen [ɛɐ'zɔyfn] *ptp* **ersäuft** **VT** to drown; **seinen Kummer im Alkohol ~** *(inf)* to drown one's sorrows (in drink *(Brit) or* alcohol) *(inf)*

er|schaf|fen [ɛɐ'ʃafn] *pret* **erschuf** [ɛɐ'ʃuːf], *ptp* **erschaffen** **VT** to create

Er|schaf|fer(in) **M(F)** creator

Er|schaf|fung **F** creation

er|schal|len [ɛɐ'ʃalən] *pret* **erscholl** *or* **erschallte** [ɛɐ'ʃɔl, ɛɐ'ʃaltə], *ptp* **erschollen** *or* **erschallt** [ɛɐ'ʃɔlən, ɛɐ'ʃalt] **VI** *aux sein (geh) (Stimme, Lachen)* to ring out; *(Trompete)* to sound

er|schau|dern [ɛɐ'ʃaudɐn] *ptp* **erschaudert** **VI** *aux sein (geh)* to shudder (*bei* at)

er|schau|en [ɛɐ'ʃauən] *ptp* **erschaut** **VT** *(liter)* to see, to espy *(liter)*

er|schau|ern [ɛɐ'ʃauɐn] *ptp* **erschauert** **VI** *aux sein (geh) (vor Kälte)* to shiver; *(vor Erregung, Ehrfurcht)* to tremble, to shudder

er|schei|nen [ɛɐ'ʃainən] ✪ 53.3 *ptp* **erschienen** **VI** [ɛɐ'ʃiːnən] *irreg aux sein* to appear; *(= vorkommen, wirken wie auch)* to seem (*+dat* to); *(= sich sehen lassen: auf Party etc auch)* to put in an appearance (*auf +dat* at); *(zur Arbeit auch)* to turn up (*zu* for); *(Buch auch)* to come out; **in einem anderen Licht ~** to appear in a different light; **es erscheint (mir) wünschenswert** it seems *or* appears desirable (to me); **das Buch ist in** *or* **bei einem anderen Verlag erschienen** the book was published by *or* brought out by another publisher; **das Buch erscheint nicht mehr** the book is no longer published

Er|schei|nen [ɛɐ'ʃainən] **NT -s,** *no pl* appearance; *(von Geist auch)* apparition; *(von Buch auch)* publication; **um rechtzeitiges ~ wird gebeten** you are kindly requested to attend punctually; **er dankte den Besuchern für ihr (zahlreiches) ~** he thanked his (many) guests for coming; **mit seinem ~ hatte ich nicht mehr gerechnet** I no longer reckoned on his turning up *or* appearing

Er|schei|nung **F -, -en** **a** *no pl (= das Erscheinen)* appearance; **das Fest der ~** *(Eccl)* (the Feast of) the Epiphany; **in ~ treten** *(Merkmale)* to appear, to manifest themselves *(form)*; *(Gefühle)* to show themselves, to become visible *or* obvious; **sie tritt (persönlich) fast nie in ~** she hardly ever appears (in person)
b *(= äußere Erscheinung)* appearance; *(Philos auch: = Naturerscheinung, Vorkommnis)* phenomenon; *(= Krankheitserscheinung, Alterserscheinung)* symptom; *(= Zeichen)* sign, manifestation; **es ist eine bekannte ~, dass …** it is (a) well-known (phenomenon) that …
c *(= Gestalt)* figure; **seiner äußeren ~ nach** judging by his appearance; **er ist eine stattliche ~** he is a fine figure of a man; **eine elegante ~ sein** to cut an elegant figure
d *(= Geistererscheinung)* apparition; *(= Traumbild)* vision

Er|schei|nungs-: **Er|schei|nungs|bild** **NT** *(Biol)* phenotype; *(fig)* image; **sein äußeres ~** his outward appearance; **Er|schei|nungs|da|tum** **NT** *(von Buch, Zeitung)* publication date; *(von Video, Film)* release date; **Er|schei|nungs|form** **F** manifestation; **Er|schei|nungs|jahr** **NT** *(von Buch)* year of publication; **Er|schei|nungs|ort** **M** *pl* **-orte** *(von Buch)* place of publication; **Er|schei|nungs|wei|se** **F** *(von Zeitschrift)* publication dates *pl*; **~: monatlich** appearing monthly

er|schie|ßen [ɛɐ'ʃiːsn] *ptp* **erschossen** [ɛɐ'ʃɔsn] *irreg* **VT** to shoot (dead) **VR** to shoot oneself; **dann kannst du dich ~** you might as well stick your head in a gas oven → *auch* **erschossen**

Er|schie|ßung **F -, -en** shooting; *(Jur: als Todesstrafe)* execution; **die Verurteilten wurden zur ~ abgeführt** the condemned were led off to be shot; **er drohte mit ~ der Geiseln** he threatened to shoot the hostages; **Tod durch ~** *(Jur)* death by firing squad

Er|schie|ßungs|kom|man|do **NT** firing squad

er|schlaf|fen [ɛɐ'ʃlafn] *ptp* **erschlafft** **VI** *aux sein (= ermüden)* to tire, to grow weary; *(= schlaff werden)* to go limp; *(Seil)* to slacken, to go slack; *(Interesse, Eifer)* to wane, to flag **VT** to tire; *(Medikament)* to relax

Er|schlaf|fung **F -,** *no pl* tiredness, weariness; *(= das Schlaffwerden)* limpness; *(von Interesse, Eifer)* waning, flagging

er|schla|gen [ɛɐ'ʃlaːgn] *ptp* **erschlagen** **VT** *irreg* to kill, to strike dead *(liter)*; **vom Blitz ~ werden** to be struck (dead) by lightning

er|schla|gen [ɛɐ'ʃlaːgn] **ADJ** **~ sein** *(inf) (= todmüde)* to be worn out, to be dead beat *(Brit inf)*; *(= erstaunt)* to be flabbergasted *(inf)*

er|schlei|chen [ɛɐ'ʃlaiçn] *ptp* **erschlichen** [ɛɐ'ʃlɪçn] **VT** *irreg* **(sich** *dat*) **etw ~** to obtain sth by devious means *or* in an underhand way; **sich** *(dat)* **jds Gunst/Vertrauen ~** to worm oneself into sb's favour *(Brit) or* favor *(US) or* good graces/into sb's confidence

er|schlie|ßen [ɛɐ'ʃliːsn] *ptp* **erschlossen** [ɛɐ'ʃlɔsn] *irreg* **VT** **a** *Gebiet, Absatzmarkt, Baugelände* to develop, to open up; *Einnahmequelle* to find, to acquire; *Rohstoffquellen, Bodenschätze* to tap; *Wählergruppen* to tap into; **erschlossen** *(Gebiet)* developed **b** *(= folgern)* to deduce, to infer (*aus* from); *Gedicht* to decipher, to work out the meaning of; **daraus ist zu ~, dass …** it can be deduced *or* inferred from this, that … **c** *(Ling, Liter)* to reconstruct **VR** *(liter) (Blüte)* to open (out); **sich jdm ~** *(= verständlich werden)* to disclose itself to sb *(liter)*

Er|schlie|ßungs|kos|ten **PL** development costs *pl*

er|scholl *pret von* **erschallen**

er|schol|len *ptp von* **erschallen**

er|schöpf|bar **ADJ** exhaustible

er|schöp|fen [ɛɐ'ʃœpfn] *ptp* **erschöpft** **VT** *Mittel, Thema, Geduld* to exhaust; *(= ermüden auch)* to tire out; **in erschöpftem Zustand** in a state of exhaustion **VR** **a** *(körperlich)* to exhaust oneself **b** *(fig)* **sich in etw** *(dat)* ~ to amount to nothing more than sth; **darin erschöpft sich seine Bildung** that's the sum total of his education; **ein Schriftsteller, der sich erschöpft hat** an author who has run out of ideas *or* expended his talent

er|schöp|fend ADJ **a** *(= ermüdend)* exhausting **b** *(= ausführlich)* exhaustive ADV exhaustively

er|schöpft [ɛɐˈʃœpft] PTP *von* **erschöpfen** ADJ exhausted; **meine Geduld ist (endgültig) ~** my patience has (finally) run out → **erschöpfen**

Er|schöp|fung F **a** *(= völlige Ermüdung)* exhaustion, fatigue; **bis zur ~ arbeiten** to work to the point of exhaustion **b** *(der Mittel, Vorräte etc)* exhaustion

Er|schöp|fungs|zu|stand M state of exhaustion *no pl*

er|schos|sen [ɛɐˈʃɔsn] ADJ *(inf)* **(völlig) ~ sein** to be whacked *(Brit inf)*, to be dead (beat) *(Brit inf)*, to be exhausted → *auch* **erschießen**

er|schrak *pret von* **erschrecken VIR**

er|schre|cken [ɛɐˈʃrɛkn] *pret* **erschreckte**, *ptp* **erschreckt** VT to frighten, to scare; *(= bestürzen)* to startle, to give a shock *or* a start; *(= zusammenzucken lassen)* to make jump, to give a start, to startle; **es hat mich erschreckt, wie schlecht er aussah** it gave me a shock *or* a start *or* it startled me to see how bad he looked *pret* **erschreckte** *or* **erschrak** [ɛɐˈʃrɛktə, ɛɐˈʃraːk], *ptp* **erschreckt** *or* **erschrocken** [ɛɐˈʃrɛkt, ɛɐˈʃrɔkn] VIR *(vi: aux sein)* to be frightened *(vor +dat* by); *(= bestürzt sein)* to be startled; *(= zusammenzucken)* to jump, to start; **ich bin erschrocken, wie schlecht er aussah** it gave me a shock *or* a start *or* I was shocked *or* startled to see how bad he looked; **sie erschrak bei dem Gedanken, dass ...** the thought that ... gave her a start *or* a scare; **sie erschrak bei dem Knall** the bang made her jump; **~ Sie nicht, ich bins nur** don't be frightened *or* afraid, it's only me; **~ Sie nicht, wenn Sie ihn sehen, er ist sehr alt geworden** don't be alarmed when you see him, he's aged terribly → *auch* **erschrocken**

Er|schre|cken [ɛɐˈʃrɛkn] NT **-s**, *no pl* fright, shock

er|schre|ckend ADJ alarming, frightening ADV **~ aussehen** to look dreadful *or* terrible; **~ wenig Leute** alarmingly few people; **~ viele** an alarmingly large number

er|schrickt [ɛɐˈʃrɪkt] *3. pers sing pres von* **erschrecken**

er|schro|cken [ɛɐˈʃrɔkn] PTP *von* **erschrecken VIR** ADJ frightened, scared; *(= bestürzt)* startled ADV **~ hochspringen/zusammenzucken** to jump, to (give a) start

er|schuf *pret von* **erschaffen**

er|schüt|tern [ɛɐˈʃʏtɐn] *ptp* **erschüttert** VT *Boden, Gebäude, Vertrauen, Glauben etc* to shake; *(fig) Glaubwürdigkeit* to cast doubt upon; *(fig) Gesundheit* to unsettle, to upset; *(= bewegen, Schock versetzen)* to shake severely; **jdn in seinem Glauben ~** to shake *or* shatter sb's faith; **sie war von seinem Tod tief erschüttert** she was severely shaken by his death; **seine Geschichte hat mich erschüttert** I was shattered *(inf)* by his story; **über etw** *(acc)* **erschüttert sein** to be shaken *or* shattered *(inf)* by sth; **mich kann nichts mehr ~** nothing surprises me any more; **er lässt sich durch nichts ~, ihn kann nichts ~** he always keeps his cool *(inf)*

er|schüt|ternd ADJ shattering *(inf)*; *Nachricht auch* distressing; *Verhältnisse auch* shocking

Er|schüt|te|rung F **-, -en** *(des Bodens etc)* tremor, vibration; *(fig) (der Ruhe, Wirtschaftslage)* disruption; *(des Selbstvertrauens)* blow *(+gen* to); *(= seelische Ergriffenheit)* emotion, shock; **bei der ~ des Gebäudes** when the building shook; **die Krise kann zu einer ~ des Staates führen** the crisis could rock the state; **ihr Tod löste allgemeine ~ aus** her death shocked everyone

er|schwe|ren [ɛɐˈʃveːrən] *ptp* **erschwert** VT to make more difficult; *Sachlage auch* to aggravate; *Fortschritt etc auch* to impede, to hinder; **jdm etw ~** to make sth more difficult for sb; **~de Umstände** *(Jur)* aggravating circumstances; **es kommt noch ~d hinzu, dass ...** to compound matters, ...

Er|schwer|nis [ɛɐˈʃveːɐnɪs] F **-, -se** difficulty

Er|schwer|nis|zu|la|ge F hardship allowance

Er|schwe|rung F **-, -en** impediment *(+gen* to), obstruction *(+gen* to); **das bedeutet eine ~ meiner Arbeit** that will make my job more difficult

er|schwin|deln [ɛɐˈʃvɪndln] *ptp* **erschwindelt** VT to obtain by fraud; **sich** *(dat)* **(von jdm) etw ~** to swindle *or* do *(inf)* sb out of sth

er|schwin|gen [ɛɐˈʃvɪŋən] *ptp* **erschwungen** [ɛɐˈʃvʊŋən] VT *irreg* to afford

er|schwing|lich [ɛɐˈʃvɪŋlɪç] ADJ *Preise* within one's means, reasonable; **das Haus ist für uns nicht ~** the house is not within our means

er|se|hen [ɛɐˈzeːən] *ptp* **ersehen** VT *irreg (form)* **etw aus etw ~** to see *or* gather sth from sth

er|seh|nen [ɛɐˈzeːnən] *ptp* **ersehnt** VT *(geh)* to long for

er|sehnt [ɛɐˈzeːnt] ADJ longed-for; **heiß** *or* **lang ~** much-longed-for

er|setz|bar ADJ replaceable; *Schaden* reparable

er|set|zen [ɛɐˈzɛtsn] *ptp* **ersetzt** VT to replace *(auch Comput)*; *(= als Ersatz dienen für, an die Stelle treten von auch)* to take the place of; **niemand kann Kindern die Mutter ~** no-one can take the place of a child's mother, no-one can replace a child's mother; **diese Vase kannst du mir nie ~** you'll never be able to replace that vase

Er|set|zung F **-**, *no pl* replacing; *(von Schaden, Verlust)* compensation, reparation *(+gen* for); *(von Unkosten)* reimbursement, repayment

er|sicht|lich [ɛɐˈzɪçtlɪç] ADJ obvious, clear, apparent; **ohne ~en Grund** for no apparent reason; **hieraus ist klar ~, dass ...** it is obvious *etc* from this that ..., this shows clearly that ...

er|sin|nen [ɛɐˈzɪnən] *ptp* **ersonnen** [ɛɐˈzɔnən] VT *irreg* to devise, to think up; *(= erfinden)* to invent

er|sit|zen [ɛɐˈzɪtsn] *ptp* **ersessen** [ɛɐˈzɛsn] VT *irreg (Jur) Anspruch* to acquire by prescription

er|spä|hen [ɛɐˈʃpɛːən] *ptp* **erspäht** VT to catch sight of, to spot, to espy *(liter)*

er|spa|ren [ɛɐˈʃpaːrən] *ptp* **erspart** VT *Kosten, Zeit, Kummer etc* to save; **jdm/sich etw ~** to spare *or* save sb/oneself sth; **ich kann mir jeglichen Kommentar ~** I don't think I need to comment; **jdm eine Demütigung ~** to spare sb humiliation; **~ Sie sich die Mühe!** save *or* spare yourself the trouble; **Sie können sich alles Weitere ~** you don't need to say any more; **ihr blieb auch nichts erspart** she was spared nothing; **das Ersparte** the savings *pl* VR to be superfluous *or* unnecessary

Er|spar|nis [ɛɐˈʃpaːɐnɪs] F **-, -se** *or (Aus) nt* **-ses, -se** **a** *no pl (an Zeit etc)* saving *(an +dat* of) **b** *usu pl* savings *pl*

er|spie|len [ɛɐˈʃpiːlən] *ptp* **erspielt** VT *(Sport) Punkte, Sieg* to win, to gain; **sich** *(dat)* **etw ~** *(Sympathien, guten Ruf)* to gain sth; *Berühmtheit* to achieve sth; **sich** *(dat)* **Torchancen ~** to create chances (to score)

er|sprieß|lich [ɛɐˈʃpriːslɪç] ADJ *(= förderlich)* beneficial, advantageous; *(= nützlich)* fruitful, profitable; *(= angenehm)* pleasant

erst [eːɐst] ADV **a** first; *(= anfänglich)* at first; **mach ~ (ein)mal die Arbeit fertig** finish your work first; **~ mal ist das gar nicht wahr ...** first *or* for one thing it's just not true ...; **~ einmal musst du an deine Pflicht denken** you should consider your duty first; **wenn du das ~ einmal hinter dir hast** once you've got that behind you; **~ wollte er, dann wieder nicht** first he wanted to, then he didn't → **Arbeit**

b *(= nicht mehr als, bloß)* only; *(= nicht früher als auch)* not until; **eben** *or* **gerade ~** just; **~ gestern** only yesterday; **~ jetzt** *(= gerade eben)* only just; **~ jetzt verstehe ich ...** I have only just understood ...; **~ jetzt wissen wir ...** it is only now that we know ...; **~ morgen** not until *or* before tomorrow; **~ vor Kurzem** only a short time ago; **es ist ~ 6 Uhr** it is only 6 o'clock; **wir fahren ~ übermorgen/~ später** we're not going until the day after tomorrow/until later; **sie war ~ 6 Jahre** she was only 6; **~ als** only when, not until; **~ wenn** only if *or* when, not until

c *(emph: = gar, nun gar)* **da gings ~ richtig los** then it really got going; **was wird Mutter ~ sagen!** whatever will mother say!; **was wird dann ~ passieren?** whatever will happen then?; **sie ist schon ziemlich blöd, aber ~ ihre Schwester!** she is fairly stupid, but you should see her sister!; **da fange ich ~ gar nicht an** I simply won't (bother to) begin; **wie wird er sich ~ ärgern, wenn er das noch erfährt** he really will be annoyed when he finds out about that; **jetzt ~ recht/recht nicht!** that just makes me all the more determined; **da tat er es ~ recht!** so he did it deliberately; **das macht es ~ recht schlimm** that makes it even worse *or* all the worse; **da habe ich mich ~ recht geärgert** then I really did get annoyed

d **wäre er doch ~ zurück!** if only he were back!; **diese Gerüchte darf man gar nicht ~ aufkommen lassen** these rumours *(Brit) or* rumors *(US)* mustn't even be allowed to start

er|star|ken [ɛɐˈʃtarkn] *ptp* **erstarkt** VI *aux sein (geh)* to gain strength, to become stronger

er|star|ren [ɛɐˈʃtarən] *ptp* **erstarrt** VI *aux sein (Finger)* to grow stiff *or* numb; *(Flüssigkeit)* to solidify; *(Gips, Zement etc)* to set, to solidify; *(Blut, Fett etc)* to congeal; *(fig) (Blut)* to freeze, to run cold; *(Lächeln)* to freeze; *(vor Schrecken, Entsetzen etc)* to be paralyzed *or* petrified *(vor +dat* with); *(Haltung, Meinung)* to become rigid *or* fixed; *(Ideen, Kunstform etc)* to ossify, to become rigid; **erstarrte Formen** fossilized forms

Er|star|rung F **-**, *no pl (von Fingern)* stiffness, numbness; *(von Flüssigkeit, Gips, Zement)* solidification; *(von Blut, Fett)* congelation, congealment; *(vor Schrecken, Entsetzen)* paralysis, petrification

er|stat|ten [ɛɐˈʃtatn] *ptp* **erstattet** VT **a** *Unkosten* to refund, to reimburse **b** *(form)* **(Straf)anzeige gegen jdn ~** to report sb; **Meldung ~** to report; **Bericht ~** to (give a) report *(über +acc* on)

Er|stat|tung F **-**, *no pl (von Unkosten)* refund, reimbursement

Erst-: **erst|auf+füh|ren** *ptp* **erstaufgeführt** VT *infin, ptp only (Theat)* to give the first public performance of; **Erst|auf|füh|rung** F *(Theat)* first performance *or* night, première; **Erst|auf|la|ge** F first printing

er|stau|nen [ɛɐˈʃtaunən] *ptp* **erstaunt** VT to astonish, to amaze → *auch* **erstaunt** VI **a** *aux sein (old: = überrascht sein)* to be astonished *or* amazed **b** *(= Erstaunen erregen)* to cause astonishment *or* amazement, to astonish *or* amaze (people); **seine Körperbeherrschung erstaunt immer wieder** his physical control never fails to amaze

Er|stau|nen [ɛɐˈʃtaunən] NT astonishment, amazement; **jdn in ~ (ver)setzen** to astonish *or* amaze sb

er|staun|lich [ɛɐˈʃtaunlɪç] ADJ astonishing, amazing ADV astonishingly, amazingly; **für sein Alter kann er ~ gut lesen** he can read astonishingly *or* amazingly well for his age

er|staunt [ɛɐˈʃtaunt] ADJ astonished, amazed *(über +acc* about) ADV in astonishment, in amazement; **~ blicken** to look astonished → *auch* **erstaunen**

Erst-: **Erst|aus|ga|be** F first edition; **Erst|be|ge|hung** F *(einer Kletterroute)* first conquest *or* ascent; **erst|bes|te(r, s)** [ˈeːɐstˈbɛstə] ADJ *attr* **er hat das ~ Auto gekauft** he bought the first car he saw, he bought any old car *(inf)*; **Erst|be|stei|gung** F *(eines Berges)* first ascent *(+gen* of); **Erst|druck** M *pl* **-drucke** first edition

er|ste|chen [ɛɐˈʃtɛçn] *ptp* **erstochen** [ɛɐˈʃtɔxn] VT *irreg* to stab to death

er|ste|hen [ɛɐ̯ˈʃteːən] *ptp* **erstanden** [ɛɐ̯ˈʃtandn] *irreg* **VT** *(inf: = kaufen)* to buy, to get **VI** *aux sein (form)* to arise; *(Städte)* to rise up; *(Bibl: = auferstehen)* to rise

Ers|te-Hil|fe-: **Ers|te-Hil|fe-Kof|fer** [eːɐ̯stəˈhɪlfə-] **M** first-aid kit; **Ers|te-Hil|fe-Kurs** [eːɐ̯stəˈhɪlfə-] **M** first-aid course; **Ers|te-Hil|fe--Leis|tung** [eːɐ̯stəˈhɪlfə-] **F** administering first aid

er|stei|gen [ɛɐ̯ˈʃtaign] *ptp* **erstiegen** [ɛɐ̯ˈʃtiːgn] **VT** *irreg* to climb; *Felswand auch, Stadtmauer* to scale

er|stei|gern [ɛɐ̯ˈʃtaigɐn] *ptp* **ersteigert** **VT** to buy at an auction

Er|stei|gung **F** ascent; *(von Felswand auch, von Stadtmauer)* scaling

Erst|ein|satz [ˈeːɐ̯st-] **M** ~ **(von Atomwaffen)** first strike

er|stel|len [ɛɐ̯ˈʃtɛlən] *ptp* **erstellt** **VT** **a** *(= bauen)* to construct, to erect **b** *(= anfertigen) Liste etc* to draw up, to make out *(Comput) Datei etc* to create

Er|stel|lung **F** **a** *(= Bau)* construction, erection **b** *(von Liste etc)* drawing up, making out

ers|te|mal △ [ˈeːɐ̯stəmaːl] **ADV** → **erste(r, s)**

ers|ten|mal △ [ˈeːɐ̯stnmaːl] **ADV** → **erste(r, s)**

ers|tens [ˈeːɐ̯stns] **ADV** first(ly), in the first place

Ers|te(r) [ˈeːɐ̯stə(r)] **MF** *decl as adj* first; **die drei ~n** the first three; **der ~ in der Klasse** the top of *or* best in the class; **die ~n werden die Letzten sein** *(Bibl)* the first shall be last; **~r unter Gleichen** first among equals; **der ~ des Monats** the first (day) of the month; **vom nächsten ~n an** as of the first of next month; **er kam als ~r** he was the first to come

ers|te(r, s) [ˈeːɐ̯stə] **ADJ** **a** first; *(fig: = führend auch)* best, foremost; *Seite der Zeitung* front; **~r Stock, ~ Etage** first floor, second floor *(US)*; **die ~ Klasse** *(Rail)* the first class (compartment); **~r Klasse fahren** to travel first class; **das ~ Mal** the first time; **das tue ich das ~ Mal** I'm doing this for the first time, it's the first time I've done this; **zum ~n Mal** for the first time; **der ~ Rang** *(Theat)* the dress circle, the (first) balcony *(US)*; **~ Güte** *or* **Qualität** top quality; **Erste Hilfe** first aid; **die ~n drei** the first three (from each group); **~ Kontakte anknüpfen** to establish preliminary contacts; **am ~n** first; **an ~r Stelle** in the first place; **dieses Thema steht an ~r Stelle unserer Tagesordnung** this subject comes first on our agenda; **in ~r Linie** first and foremost → **Blick, Hand, Mal**, → *auch* **vierte(r, s)** **b** **nimm das ~ Beste!** take anything!; **er hat das ~ beste Auto gekauft** he bought the first car he saw, he bought any old car *(inf)*

er|ster|ben [ɛɐ̯ˈʃtɛrbn] *ptp* **erstorben** [ɛɐ̯ˈʃtɔrbn] **VI** *irreg aux sein (liter)* to die; *(Lärm, Wort)* to die away

ers|te|re(r, s) [ˈeːɐ̯stərə] **ADJ** the former; **der/die/das Erstere** the former

Ers|te(r)-Klas|se- *(Rail)* first class; **Ers|te(r)--Klas|se-Ab|teil** **NT** first class compartment; **Ers|te(r)-Klas|se-Wa|gen** **M** first class carriage *(Brit) or* car *(US)*

Ers|te(s) [ˈeːɐ̯stə(s)] **MF** *decl as adj* **das ~** the first thing; **das ist das ~, was ich höre** that's the first I've heard of it; **als ~s** first of all; **fürs ~** for the time being, for the present; **zum ~n, zum Zweiten, zum Dritten** *(bei Auktionen)* going, going, gone!

Erst-: **Erst|ge|bä|ren|de** [ˈeːɐ̯stgəbɛːrəndə] **F** *decl as adj* primigravida *(spec)*; **erst|ge|bo|ren** [ˈeːɐ̯stgəboːrən] **ADJ** *attr* first-born; **Erst|ge|bo|re|ne(r)** [ˈeːɐ̯stgəboːrənə] **MF** *decl as adj* firstborn (child); **Erst|ge|burt** **F** *(= Kind)* first--born (child); *(= Tier)* first young; *(Hist: auch* **Erstgeburtsrecht**) birthright, right of primogeniture *(Jur)*; **erst|ge|nannt** [-gənant] **ADJ** *attr* first-mentioned; *(= wichtigster)* first to be mentioned

er|sti|cken [ɛɐ̯ˈʃtɪkn] *ptp* **erstickt** **VT** *jdn* to suffocate, to smother; *Feuer* to smother; *Geräusche* to stifle, to smother; *(fig: = unterdrücken) Aufruhr etc* to suppress; **mit erstickter Stimme** in a choked voice **VI** *aux sein* to suffocate; *(Feuer)* to die, to go out; *(Stimme)* to become choked; **an etw** *(dat)* **~** to be suffocated by sth; **an einer Gräte ~** to choke (to death) on a fish bone; **vor Lachen ~** to choke with laughter; **das Kind erstickt förmlich unter der Liebe der Mutter** the child is smothered by motherly love; **unsere Städte ~ im Verkehr** our cities are being choked by traffic; **in der Arbeit ~** *(inf)* to be snowed under with *(Brit) or* in *(US)* work, to be up to one's neck in work *(inf)*; **er erstickt im Geld** *(inf)* he's rolling in money *(inf)*; **die Luft im Zimmer war zum Ersticken** the air in the room was suffocating *or* stifling

Er|sti|ckung **F** **-,** *no pl* suffocation, asphyxiation

Er|sti|ckungs-: **Er|sti|ckungs|ge|fahr** **F** danger of suffocation; **Er|sti|ckungs|tod** **M** death from *or* by suffocation, asphyxia

erst|in|stanz|lich [ˈeːɐ̯stlɪnstantslɪç] **ADJ** *(Jur)* first-instance

erstkl. *abbr von* **erstklassig**

Erst-: **Erst|kläs|ser** [ˈeːɐ̯stklɛsɐ] **M -s, -**, **Erst|kläs|se|rin** [-ərɪn] **F -, -nen** year 1 *or* reception pupil *(Brit)*, first-grader *(US)*; **erst|klas|sig** **ADJ** first-class, first-rate; *(= in erster Spielklasse) Mannschaft* first-division *attr* **ADV** *spielen* excellently; **~ schmecken** *or* **munden** to taste excellent; **~ gekleidet sein** to be perfectly dressed; **das Auto fährt sich ~** that car drives like a dream; **Erst|klas|sig|keit** **F -,** *no pl* excellence; **Erst|kläss|ler** [ˈeːɐ̯stklɛslɐ] **M -s, -**, **Erst|kläss|le|rin** [-ərɪn] **F -, -nen** *(esp S Ger, Sw)* pupil in the first class of primary school, first-grader *(US)*; **Erst|kom|mu|ni|on** **F** first communion; **Erst|la|ge|rung** **F** *(von Atommüll)* initial storage

Erst|li|gist [ˈeːɐ̯stlɪgɪst] **M -s, -en** *(Sport)* first--league *or* first-division team, team in the top division

Erst|ling [ˈeːɐ̯stlɪŋ] **M -s, -e** *(= Kind)* first (child); *(= Tier)* first young; *(= Werk)* first work *or* baby *(inf)*

Erst|lings-: **Erst|lings|film** **M** debut film; **Erst|lings|ro|man** **M** first *or* debut novel; **Erst|lings|werk** **NT** first work

erst|ma|lig [ˈeːɐ̯stmaːlɪç] **ADJ** first **ADV** for the first time

erst|mals [ˈeːɐ̯stmals] **ADV** for the first time

er|strah|len [ɛɐ̯ˈʃtraːlən] *ptp* **erstrahlt** **VI** *aux sein (liter)* to shine; **im Lichterglanz ~** to be aglitter (with lights)

erst|ran|gig [ˈeːɐ̯straŋɪç] **ADJ** **a** *(= sehr bedeutsam)* of top priority, priority *attr*; *(Fin: = ersten Ranges) Gläubiger* preferential; *Schuldner* primary; *Hypothek* first; **von ~er Bedeutung** of paramount importance **b** *(= erstklassig)* first-rate, first-class

er|stre|ben [ɛɐ̯ˈʃtreːbn] *ptp* **erstrebt** **VT** to strive for *or* after, to aspire to

er|stre|bens|wert **ADJ** worthwhile, desirable; *Beruf* desirable

er|stre|cken [ɛɐ̯ˈʃtrɛkn] *ptp* **erstreckt** **VR** to extend *(auf, über +acc* over); *(räumlich auch)* to reach, to stretch *(auf, über +acc* over); *(zeitlich auch)* to carry on, to last *(auf, über +acc* for); **sich auf jdn/etw ~** *(= betreffen)* to apply to sb/sth

Erst-: **Erst|schlag** **M** *(mit Atomwaffen)* first strike; **Erst|schlag|waf|fe** **F** first-strike weapon; **Erst|se|mes|ter** **NT** first-year student, fresher *(Brit inf)*; *(männlich auch)* freshman; **Erst|sen|dung** **F** *(Rad, TV)* first broadcast

Erst-: **Erst|stim|me** **F** first vote; **Erst|stu|di|um** **NT** initial course of studies; *(vor Zweitstudium)* previous course of studies; **Erst|tags|brief** **M** first-day cover; **Erst|tags|stem|pel** **M** date stamp *or* postmark from a first-day cover; **Erst|tä|ter(in)** **M(F)** first offender

> **ERSTSTIMME/ZWEITSTIMME**
>
> For elections to the German **Bundestag** a mixed system of voting operates. Each voter has two votes. The **Erststimme** is used to directly elect a representative in each of the 299 constituencies and this accounts for half of the available seats. The **Zweitstimme** is cast for the **Landesliste** of a party. The number of party candidates sent to the **Bundestag** is in proportion to the result of the poll. The **Erststimme** and the **Zweitstimme** are cast separately. → BUNDESTAG

er|stun|ken [ɛɐ̯ˈʃtʊŋkn] **ADJ** **das ist ~ und erlogen** *(inf)* that's a pack of lies

er|stür|men [ɛɐ̯ˈʃtʏrmən] *ptp* **erstürmt** **VT** *(Mil)* to (take by) storm; *(liter) Gipfel* to conquer

Er|stür|mung **F -, -en** *(Mil)* storming

Erst-: **Erst|ver|öf|fent|li|chung** **F** first publication; **Erst|wäh|ler(in)** **M(F)** first-time voter

er|su|chen [ɛɐ̯ˈzuːxn] *ptp* **ersucht** **VT** *(form)* to request *(jdm um etw* sth of sb)

Er|su|chen [ɛɐ̯ˈzuːxn] **NT -s, -** *(form)* request; **auf ~ von** at the request of; **ein ~ an jdn richten** *or* **stellen** to make a request of sb

er|tap|pen [ɛɐ̯ˈtapn] *ptp* **ertappt** **VT** to catch; **jdn/sich bei etw ~** to catch sb/oneself at *or* doing sth; **ich habe ihn dabei ertappt** I caught him at it *or* doing it

er|tas|ten [ɛɐ̯ˈtastn] *ptp* **ertastet** **VT** to feel, to make out by touch(ing); *(um zu finden)* to feel for

er|tei|len [ɛɐ̯ˈtailən] *ptp* **erteilt** **VT** to give; *Genehmigung auch* to grant; *Auftrag auch* to place *(jdm* with sb); *Lizenz* to issue; **jdm einen Verweis ~** to reproach sb; **Unterricht ~** to teach, to give lessons → **Wort c**

Er|tei|lung **F** giving; *(von Genehmigung auch)* granting; *(von Auftrag auch)* placing; *(von Lizenz)* issuing; **für die ~ von Auskünften zuständig** responsible for giving information

er|tö|nen [ɛɐ̯ˈtøːnən] *ptp* **ertönt** **VI** *aux sein (geh)* to sound, to ring out; **von etw ~** to resound with sth; **~ lassen** to sound; **er ließ seine tiefe Bassstimme ~** his deep bass voice rang out

Er|trag [ɛɐ̯ˈtraːk] **M -(e)s, ⸚e** [-ˈtrɛːgə] *(von Acker)* yield; *(= Ergebnis einer Arbeit)* return; *(= Einnahmen)* proceeds *pl*, return; **~ abwerfen** *or* **bringen** to bring in a return; **vom ~ seiner Bücher/seines Kapitals leben** to live on the proceeds from one's books/the return on one's capital

er|tra|gen [ɛɐ̯ˈtraːgn] ✪ 34.3 *ptp* **ertragen** **VT** *irreg* to bear; *Schmerzen, Leiden, Schicksal auch* to endure; *Ungewissheit, Zweifel auch* to tolerate; *(esp in Frage, Verneinung auch)* to stand; **das ist nicht mehr zu ~** it's unbearable *or* intolerable; **wie erträgst du nur seine Launen?** how do you put up with *or* stand his moods?

er|träg|lich [ɛɐ̯ˈtrɛːklɪç] **ADJ** bearable, endurable; *(= leidlich)* tolerable

er|trag-: **er|trag|los** **ADJ** *Acker* unproductive, infertile; *Geschäft* unprofitable; *Vermögen* providing no return; **er|trag|reich** **ADJ** *Acker* productive, fertile; *Pflanzensorte, Nutztier* productive; *Geschäft, Markt* profitable, lucrative

Er|trags-: **er|trags|arm** **ADJ** *Boden* poor; **Er|trags|aus|schüt|tung** **F** dividend distribution; **Er|trags|kraft** **F**, *no pl* earning power *or* potential; **Er|trags|la|ge** **F**, *no pl* returns *pl*, profits *pl*, profit situation; **Er|trags|min|de|rung** **F** decrease in profit(s) *or* return(s); **Er|trags|schein** **M** dividend coupon; **Er|trags|stei|ge|rung** **F** increase in profit(s) *or* return(s); **Er|trags|steu|er** **F** profit(s) tax, tax on profit(s); **Er|trags|wert** **M** → **Ertrag** capitalized value of potential yield/return(s)

er|trän|ken [ɛɐ̯ˈtrɛŋkn] *ptp* **ertränkt** **VT** to drown; **seinen Kummer** *or* **seine Sorgen im Alkohol ~** to drown one's sorrows **VR** to drown oneself

er|träu|men [ɛɐ̯ˈtrɔymən] *ptp* **erträumt** **VT** to dream of, to imagine; **eine erträumte Welt** an imaginary world; **das war alles nur erträumt** it was all in the mind; **sich** *(dat)* **etw ~** to dream of sth, to imagine sth

er|trin|ken [ɛɐ'trɪŋkn] *ptp* **ertrunken** [ɛɐ'trʊŋkn] VI *irreg aux sein* to drown, to be drowned

Er|trin|ken [ɛɐ'trɪŋkn] NT **-s**, *no pl* drowning

er|trot|zen [ɛɐ'trɔtsn] *ptp* **ertrotzt** VT *(geh)* **(sich** *dat)* **etw ~** to obtain sth by sheer obstinacy *or* defiance

er|tüch|ti|gen [ɛɐ'tʏçtɪgn] *ptp* **ertüchtigt** *(geh)* **VT** to get in (good) trim *(Brit)*, to toughen up, to harden *(US)* **VR** to keep fit, to train

Er|tüch|ti|gung F **-, -en** *(geh)* getting in (good) trim *(Brit)*, toughening up; **körperliche ~** physical training

er|üb|ri|gen [ɛɐ'ly:brɪgn] *ptp* **erübrigt** **VT** *Zeit, Geld* to spare **VR** to be unnecessary *or* superfluous; **jedes weitere Wort erübrigt sich** there's nothing more to be said

eru|ie|ren [eru'i:rən] *ptp* **eruiert** VT *(form) Sachverhalt* to investigate, to find out; *(esp Aus) Person* to trace

Erup|ti|on [erʊp'tsio:n] F **-, -en** *(Geol, Med, fig)* eruption

Erup|tiv|ge|stein [erʊp'ti:f-] NT volcanic rock

erw. *abbr von* **erweitert** extended

er|wa|chen [ɛɐ'vaxn] *ptp* **erwacht** VI *aux sein* to awake, to wake (up); *(aus Ohnmacht etc)* to come to *or* round *(aus* from); *(fig: Gefühle, Verdacht)* to be aroused; *(liter: Tag)* to dawn; **von etw ~** to be awoken *or* woken up by sth; **ein böses Erwachen** *(fig)* a rude awakening

er|wach|sen [ɛɐ'vaksn] *ptp* **erwachsen** **VI** *irreg aux sein (geh)* to arise, to develop; *(Vorteil, Kosten etc)* to result, to accrue; **daraus erwuchsen ihm Unannehmlichkeiten** that caused him some trouble; **daraus wird ihm kein Nutzen ~** no advantage will accrue to him (from this); **mir sind Zweifel ~** I have come to have doubts **ADJ** grown-up, adult; **~ sein** *(Mensch)* to be grown-up *or* an adult

Er|wach|se|nen-: **Er|wach|se|nen|al|ter** NT **im ~** in adulthood, as an adult; **Er|wach|se|nen|bil|dung** F adult education; **Er|wach|se|nen|tau|fe** F adult baptism

Er|wach|se|ne(r) [ɛɐ'vaksənə] MF *decl as adj* adult, grown-up

er|wä|gen [ɛɐ'vɛ:gn] *ptp* **erwogen** [ɛɐ'vo:gn] VT *irreg (= überlegen)* to consider, to deliberate; *(= prüfen)* to consider, to examine; *(= in Betracht ziehen)* to consider, to take into consideration

er|wä|gens|wert ADJ worthy of consideration, worth considering

Er|wä|gung F **-, -en** consideration; **aus folgenden ~en (heraus)** for the following reasons *or* considerations; **etw in ~ ziehen** to consider sth, to take sth into consideration

er|wäh|len [ɛɐ'vɛ:lən] *ptp* **erwählt** VT to choose

er|wäh|nen [ɛɐ'vɛ:nən] ✪ 53.2 *ptp* **erwähnt** VT to mention, to refer to, to make mention of *or* reference to; **ich möchte nur kurz erwähnt haben, dass ...** I would just briefly like to mention that ...; **davon hat er nichts erwähnt, das hat er mit keinem Wort erwähnt** he did not mention it *or* refer to it at all, he made no mention of *or* reference to it; **beiläufig** *or* **nebenbei ~** to mention in passing, to make a passing reference to

er|wäh|nens|wert ADJ worth mentioning

Er|wäh|nung F **-, -en** mention *(+gen* of), reference *(+gen* to); **~ finden** *(form)* to be mentioned, to be referred to

er|wan|dern [ɛɐ'vandɐn] *ptp* **erwandert** VT **er hat sich** *(dat)* **die ganze Insel erwandert** he's walked all over the island and knows it inside out

er|wär|men [ɛɐ'vɛrmən] *ptp* **erwärmt** **VT** to warm, to heat; *(fig)* to warm **VR** to warm up; **sich für jdn/etw ~** *(fig)* to take to sb/sth; **ich kann mich für Goethe/Geometrie nicht ~** Goethe/geometry leaves me cold

Er|wär|mung F **-, -en** warming; **globale ~** global warming; **~ der Erdatmosphäre** warming of the earth's atmosphere

er|war|ten [ɛɐ'vartn] ✪ 35.4, 37.3, 43.2, 47.3 *ptp* **erwartet** VT *Gäste, Ereignis* to expect; **etw von jdm/etw ~** to expect sth from *or* of sb/sth; **ein Kind** *or* **Baby ~** to be expecting a child *or* baby; **das war zu ~** that was to be expected; **etw sehnsüchtig ~** to long for sth; **sie kann den Sommer kaum noch ~** she can hardly wait for the summer, she's really looking forward to the summer; **sie kann es kaum ~, dass Vater heimkommt** she can hardly wait for father to come home, she's really looking forward to father coming home; **was mich da wohl erwartet?** I wonder what awaits me there; **von ihr ist nicht viel Gutes zu ~** no good can come of her; **da hast du (et)was zu ~!** *(iro)* then you'll have something to think about!; **es steht zu ~, dass ...** *(form)* it is to be expected that ...; **über Erwarten** beyond expectation → **wider**

Er|war|tung F expectation; *(= Spannung, Ungeduld)* anticipation; **in ~ einer Sache** *(gen)* in anticipation of sth; **in ~ Ihrer baldigen Antwort** *(form)* in anticipation of *or* looking forward to *or* awaiting your early reply; **zu großen ~en berechtigen** to show great promise; **den ~en entsprechen** *or* **gerecht werden** to come up to expectations; *(= Voraussetzung erfüllen)* to meet the requirements; **hinter den ~en zurückbleiben** not to come up to *or* meet expectations

Er|war|tungs-: **Er|war|tungs|druck** M, *no pl* **unter ~ sein** *or* **stehen** to be under pressure as a result of people's expectations; **er|war|tungs|ge|mäß** ADV as expected; **Er|war|tungs|hal|tung** F expectations *pl*; **Er|war|tungs|ho|ri|zont** M level of expectations; **er|war|tungs|voll** ADJ expectant

er|we|cken [ɛɐ'vɛkn] *ptp* **erweckt** VT **a** *(liter: aus Schlaf, Lethargie)* to wake, to rouse; *(Bibl: vom Tode)* to raise (from the dead); **etw zu neuem Leben ~** to resurrect *or* revive sth **b** *(fig) Freude, Begeisterung etc* to arouse; *Hoffnungen, Zweifel* to raise; *Erinnerungen* to bring back; **(bei jdm) den Eindruck ~, als ob ...** to give (sb) the impression that ...

Er|we|ckung F **-, -en** *(Bibl: vom Tode)* resurrection, raising (from the dead); *(Rel)* revival; *(fig)* arousal, awakening

Er|we|ckungs-: **Er|we|ckungs|be|we|gung** F *(Rel)* revivalist movement, revivalism; **Er|we|ckungs|pre|di|ger(in)** M(F) *(Rel pej)* revivalist preacher

er|weh|ren [ɛɐ've:rən] *ptp* **erwehrt** VR *+gen (geh)* to ward *or* fend off; **er konnte sich kaum der Tränen ~** he could hardly keep *or* hold back his tears → **Eindruck**

er|wei|chen [ɛɐ'vaiçn] *ptp* **erweicht** VT to soften; *(fig: = überreden auch)* to move; **jds Herz ~** to touch sb's heart; **sich (durch Bitten) nicht ~ lassen** to be unmoved (by entreaties), not to give in *or* yield (to entreaties)

Er|weis [ɛɐ'vais] M **-es, -e** [-zə] *(form)* proof

er|wei|sen [ɛɐ'vaizn] *ptp* **erwiesen** [ɛɐ'vi:zn] *irreg* **VT** **a** *(= nachweisen)* to prove; **eine erwiesene Tatsache** a proven fact; **es ist noch nicht erwiesen** it has not been proved *(esp Brit) or* proven yet **b** *(= zuteilwerden lassen)* to show; **jdm einen Gefallen/Dienst ~** to do sb a favour *(Brit) or* favor *(US)*/service; **jdm Achtung ~** to pay respect to sb; **jdm Gutes ~** to be good to sb; **wir danken für die erwiesene Anteilnahme** we thank you for the sympathy you have shown **VR** **sich als etw ~** to prove to be sth, to turn out to be sth; **sich als zuverlässig ~** to prove to be reliable, to prove oneself reliable; **sich jdm gegenüber dankbar ~** to show *or* prove one's gratitude to sb, to show *or* prove oneself grateful to sb; **es hat sich erwiesen, dass ...** it turned out that ...

er|weis|lich [ɛɐ'vaislɪç] *(geh)* **ADJ** provable, demonstrable **ADV** **das ist ~ falsch** that is demonstrably false

er|wei|ter|bar ADJ *(auch Comput)* expandable

Er|wei|ter|bar|keit [ɛɐ'vaitɐba:ɐkait] F **-, -en** *(auch Comput)* expandability

er|wei|tern [ɛɐ'vaitɐn] *ptp* **erweitert** VTR to widen, to enlarge; *Absatzgebiet auch, Geschäft, Abteilung* to expand; *(Comput) Speicher* to expand, to extend; *Kleid* to let out; *(Med)* to dilate; *(Math) Bruch* to make up to the lowest common denominator; *(fig) Interessen, Kenntnisse, Horizont* to broaden; *Macht* to extend; **im erweiterten Sinn** in a broader sense; **erweiterte Einstellungen** *pl (Comput)* advanced settings

Er|wei|te|rung F **-, -en** widening, enlargement; *(von Absatzgebiet auch, von Geschäft, Abteilung)* expansion; *(Med)* dilation; *(Math: von Bruch)* taking to the lowest common denominator; *(fig) (von Interessen, Kenntnissen, Horizont)* broadening; *(von Macht)* extension; **die ~ der EU** the enlargement of the EU

Er|wei|te|rungs-: **Er|wei|te|rungs|bau** M *pl* **-bauten** extension; **Er|wei|te|rungs|kar|te** F *(Comput)* expansion card; **Er|wei|te|rungs|pla|ti|ne** F *(Comput)* expansion board; **Er|wei|te|rungs|spei|cher** M *(Comput)* extended memory (specification), XMS; **Er|wei|te|rungs|steck|platz** M *(Comput)* expansion slot

Er|werb [ɛɐ'vɛrp] M **-(e)s, -e** [-bə] **a** *no pl* acquisition; *(= Kauf)* purchase; **beim ~ eines Autos** when buying a car **b** *(= Broterwerb, Beruf)* living; *(= Verdienst, Lohn)* earnings *pl*, income; **einem ~ nachgehen** to follow a trade *or (akademisch)* profession

er|wer|ben [ɛɐ'vɛrbn] *ptp* **erworben** [ɛɐ'vɔrbn] VT *irreg* to acquire; *Achtung, Ehre, Vertrauen* to earn, to gain, to win; *Pokal* to win; *(Sport) Titel* to win, to gain; *(käuflich)* to purchase; **sich** *(dat)* **etw ~** to acquire *etc* sth; **er hat sich** *(dat)* **große Verdienste um die Firma erworben** he has done great service for the firm → *auch* **erworben**

Er|wer|ber|mo|dell NT *scheme by which tax relief is obtained on investment in property*

Er|werbs-: **Er|werbs|ar|beit** F gainful employment; **er|werbs|be|hin|dert** ADJ *(form)* incapable of gainful employment, partially disabled; **er|werbs|fä|hig** ADJ *(form)* capable of gainful employment; **Er|werbs|fä|hi|ge(r)** [-fɛ:ɪgə] MF *decl as adj (form)* person capable of gainful employment; **Er|werbs|fä|hig|keit** F *(form)* ability to work; **er|werbs|ge|min|dert** [-gəmɪndɐt] ADJ suffering a reduction in (one's) earning capacity; **Er|werbs|kampf** M rat race; **Er|werbs|le|ben** NT working life; **er|werbs|los** ADJ = **arbeitslos**; **Er|werbs|min|de|rung** F reduction in (one's) earning capacity; **Er|werbs|per|son** F *(form)* person capable of gainful employment; **Er|werbs|quel|le** F source of income; **er|werbs|tä|tig** ADJ (gainfully) employed; **Er|werbs|tä|ti|ge(r)** MF *decl as adj* person in gainful employment; **Er|werbs|tä|tig|keit** F gainful employment; **er|werbs|un|fä|hig** ADJ *(form)* incapable of gainful employment, incapacitated; **Er|werbs|un|fä|hi|ge(r)** MF *decl as adj* person incapable of gainful employment; **Er|werbs|un|fä|hig|keit** F inability to work; **Er|werbs|un|fä|hig|keits|ren|te** F disability pension; **Er|werbs|zweig** M line of business

Er|wer|bung F acquisition

er|wi|dern [ɛɐ'vi:dɐn] *ptp* **erwidert** VT **a** *(= antworten)* to reply *(auf +acc* to); *(schroff)* to retort; **darauf konnte er nichts ~** he couldn't answer that, he had no answer to that; **auf meine Frage erwiderte sie, dass ...** in reply *or* answer to my question, she said that ... **b** *(= entgegnen, entgelten) Besuch, Grüße, Komplimente, Gefühle* to return, to reciprocate; *Blick* to return; *(Mil) Feuer* to return

Er|wi|de|rung F **-, -en** **a** *(= Antwort)* reply, answer; *(schroff)* retort, rejoinder; **in ~ Ihres Schreibens vom ...** *(form)* in reply *or* answer to your letter of the ... **b** return, reciprocation; *(von Gefühlen)* reciprocation; *(Mil: des Feuers)* return; **ihre Liebe fand bei ihm keine ~** he did not return her love

er|wie|se|ner|ma|ßen [ɛɐ̯ˈviːznɐˈmaːsn] ADJ as has been proved *(esp Brit)* or proven or shown; **er hat dich ~ betrogen** it has been proved *(esp Brit)* or proven or shown that he has deceived you; **der Angeklagte ist ~ schuldig** the accused has been proved *(esp Brit)* or proven guilty

er|wir|ken [ɛɐ̯ˈvɪrkn] *ptp* **erwirkt** VT *(form)* to obtain

er|wirt|schaf|ten [ɛɐ̯ˈvɪrtʃaftn] *ptp* **erwirtschaftet** VT to make or obtain through good or careful management; **Gewinne ~** to make profits; **seine Frau hat ein kleines Auto erwirtschaftet** his wife has bought a little car with her savings

er|wi|schen [ɛɐ̯ˈvɪʃn] *ptp* **erwischt** VT *(inf) (= erreichen, ertappen)* to catch; *(= ergattern)* to get (hold of); **jdn beim Stehlen ~** to catch sb stealing; **du darfst dich nicht ~ lassen** you mustn't get caught; **ihn hats erwischt!** *(verliebt)* he's got it bad *(inf)*; *(krank)* he's got it, he's caught it; *(gestorben)* he's had it *(inf)*; **die Kugel/der Hund hat ihn am Bein erwischt** the bullet got or caught/the dog got him in the leg

er|wor|ben [ɛɐ̯ˈvɔrbn] ADJ acquired *(auch Med, Jur)* → *auch* **erwerben**

er|wünscht [ɛɐ̯ˈvʏnʃt] ADJ *Wirkung etc* desired; *Eigenschaft, Kenntnisse* desirable; *(= willkommen) Gelegenheit, Anwesenheit* welcome; **persönliche Vorstellung ~** applications should be made in person; **du bist hier nicht ~!** you're not welcome or wanted here!

er|wür|gen [ɛɐ̯ˈvʏrgn] *ptp* **erwürgt** VT to strangle, to throttle

Eryth|ro|zyt [ɛritroˈtsyːt] M **-en, -en** *usu pl (Med)* erythrocyte

Erz [eːɐ̯ts, ɛrts] NT **-es, -e** ore; *(= Bronze)* bronze

erz-, Erz- *in cpds* **a** [eːɐ̯ts, ɛrts] *(Geol)* mineral, ore **b** [ɛrts] *(= ausgemacht)* out-and-out; **ein Erzverbrecher** an out-and-out criminal; **sein Erzrivale** his arch-rival **c** [ɛrts] *(Rang bezeichnend)* arch-

Erz-: **Erz|ab|bau** [eːɐ̯ts-, ɛrts-] M ore extraction; **Erz|ader** [eːɐ̯ts-, ɛrts-] F mineral vein, vein of ore

Er|zähl- *(Liter)*: **Er|zähl|ab|sicht** F narrative intent; **Er|zähl|ebe|ne** F narrative level

er|zäh|len [ɛɐ̯ˈtsɛːlən] *ptp* **erzählt** VT **a** *Geschichte, Witz etc* to tell; *(= berichten) Traum, Vorfall, Erlebnis etc auch* to relate, to recount, to give an account of; **er hat seinen Traum/den Vorfall erzählt** he told (us *etc*) about his dream/the incident; **jdm etw ~** to tell sth to sb; **man erzählt sich, dass ...** people say that ..., it is said that ...; **erzähl mal, was/wie ...** tell me/us what/how ...; **Mutti, erzähl mir was** tell me a story, mummy *(Brit)* or mommy *(US)*; **erzähl mal was** *(inf)* say something; **wem ~ Sie das!** *(inf)* you're telling me!; **das kannst du einem anderen ~** *(inf)* pull the other one *(inf)*, tell that to the marines *(inf)*; **mir kannst du viel** or **nichts ~** *(inf)* don't give or tell me that! *(inf)*; **davon kann ich etwas ~!** *(inf)* I can tell you a thing or two about it; **dem werd ich was ~!** *(inf)* I'll have something to say to him, I'll give him a piece of my mind *(inf)* → **Großmutter**

b *(Liter)* to narrate; **~de Dichtung** narrative fiction; **Grundformen des Erzählens** basic forms of narrative; **erzählte Zeit** narrated time

VI **a** to tell *(von* about, of *(liter))*; **er kann gut ~** he tells good stories, he's a good storyteller; **er hat die ganze Nacht erzählt** he told stories all night

b *(Liter)* to narrate

er|zäh|lens|wert ADJ worth telling

Er|zäh|ler(in) M(F) narrator *(auch Liter)*; *(= Geschichtenerzähler)* storyteller; *(= Schriftsteller)* narrative writer

er|zäh|le|risch [ɛɐ̯ˈtsɛːlərɪʃ] ADJ narrative

Er|zäh|ler|stand|punkt M *(Liter)* point of view of the narrator

Er|zähl-: **Er|zähl|for|men** PL *(Liter)* narrative forms *pl*; **Er|zähl|per|spek|ti|ve** F *(Liter)* narrative perspective

Er|zäh|lung F *(Liter)* story, tale; *(= das Erzählen)* narration, relation; *(= Bericht, Schilderung)* account; **in Form einer ~** in narrative form; **Dialog und ~ wechseln sich ab** dialogue *(Brit)* or dialog *(US)* alternates with narrative

Er|zähl-: **Er|zähl|wei|se** F *(Liter)* narrative style; **Er|zähl|zeit** F *(Liter)* narrative time

Erz-: **Erz|berg|bau** M ore mining; **Erz|berg|werk** NT mineral or ore mine; **Erz|bi|schof** M archbishop; **erz|bi|schöf|lich** ADJ *attr* archiepiscopal; **Erz|bis|tum** NT archbishopric; **Erz|bö|se|wicht** M arrant rogue *(old)*, arch-villain; **Erz|di|a|kon** M archdeacon; **Erz|di|ö|ze|se** F archbishopric; **erz|dumm** ADJ *(inf)* extremely stupid; **Erz|dumm|heit** F *(inf)* extremely stupid thing; **eine ~ sein** to be an extremely stupid thing to do, to be extremely stupid

er|zei|gen [ɛɐ̯ˈtsaign] *ptp* **erzeigt** VR *(geh)* **sich dankbar ~** to show or prove oneself grateful

er|zen [ˈeːɐ̯tsn] ADJ *(liter)* bronze

Erz|en|gel M archangel

er|zeu|gen [ɛɐ̯ˈtsɔygn] *ptp* **erzeugt** VT *(Chem, Elec, Phys)* to generate, to produce; *(Comm) Produkt* to produce, to manufacture; *Wein, Butter etc* to produce; *(fig: = bewirken)* to cause, to engender, to give rise to; *(rare) Kinder* to beget *(old)*; *(fig: = bewirken)* to cause, to engender, to give rise to; **Misstrauen/Angst** *etc* **in** or **bei jdm ~** to give rise to or produce or engender a sense of mistrust/fear *etc* in sb; **der Autor versteht es, Spannung zu ~** the author knows how to create or generate tension

Er|zeu|ger [ɛɐ̯ˈtsɔygɐ] M **-s, -** *(form: = Vater)* begetter *(old)*, progenitor *(form)*

Er|zeu|ger [ɛɐ̯ˈtsɔygɐ] M **-s, -**, **Er|zeu|ge|rin** [-ərɪn] F **-, -nen** *(Comm)* producer, manufacturer; *(von Naturprodukten)* producer

Er|zeu|ger-: **Er|zeu|ger|land** NT country of origin; **Er|zeu|ger|preis** M manufacturer's price

Er|zeug|nis NT product; *(= Industrieprodukt auch)* manufacture *(esp Comm)*; *(Agr)* produce *no indef art, no pl*; *(fig: geistiges, künstlerisches)* creation, product; **deutsches ~** made in Germany; **~ seiner Fantasie** figment of his imagination

Er|zeu|gung F *(Chem, Elec, Phys)* generation, production; *(von Waren)* manufacture, production; *(rare: eines Kindes)* procreation *(form)*; *(geistige, künstlerische)* creation

Er|zeu|gungs|gram|ma|tik F *(Ling)* generative grammar

Erz-: **erz|faul** ADJ bone idle *(Brit inf)*; **Erz|feind(in)** M(F) arch-enemy; *(Theologie auch)* arch-fiend; **Erz|gau|ner(in)** M(F) *(inf)* cunning or sly rascal *(inf)*

Erz-: **Erz|ge|bir|ge** NT Erzgebirge; **Erz|ge|halt** M *usu sing (Min)* ore content; **Erz|gie|ßer(in)** M(F) brass-founder; **Erz|gie|ße|rei** F brass-foundry; **Erz|gru|be** F ore mine; **erz|hal|tig** ADJ ore-bearing, metalliferous *(spec)*

Erz-: **Erz|her|zog** M archduke; **Erz|her|zo|gin** F archduchess; **erz|her|zog|lich** ADJ *attr* archducal; **Erz|her|zog|tum** NT archduchy

Erz|hüt|te [ˈeːɐ̯ts-, ˈɛrts-] F smelting works *sing or pl*

er|zieh|bar ADJ *Kind* educable; *Tier* trainable; **schwer ~** *(Kind)* difficult; *Hund* difficult to train; **das Kind ist schwer ~** he/she is a problem child or a difficult child; **ein Heim für schwer ~e Kinder** a home for problem or difficult children

er|zie|hen [ɛɐ̯ˈtsiːən] *ptp* **erzogen** [ɛɐ̯ˈtsoːgn] VT *irreg Kind* to bring up; *Tier, Körper, Gehör* to train; *(= ausbilden)* to educate; **ein Tier/ein Kind zur Sauberkeit** *etc* **~** to train an animal/to bring up or teach a child to be clean *etc*; **jdn zu einem tüchtigen Menschen ~** to bring sb up to be a fine, upstanding person; **ein gut/schlecht erzogenes Kind** a well-brought-up/badly-brought-up child, a well-bred/an ill-bred child

Er|zie|her [ɛɐ̯ˈtsiːɐ] M **-s, -**, **Er|zie|he|rin** [-ərɪn] F **-, -nen** educator, teacher; *(in Kindergarten)* nursery school teacher; *(= Privatlehrer)* tutor; *(Frau auch, = Gouvernante)* governess; **der Vater war ein strenger ~** the father brought his children up strictly

er|zie|he|risch [ɛɐ̯ˈtsiːərɪʃ] ADJ educational; **ein Vater mit wenig ~em Können** a father with little skill in bringing up children; **~e Maßnahmen ergreifen** to impose discipline; **verschiedene ~e Methoden** different ways of bringing up children ADV **~ wertvoll** educationally valuable; **~ falsch** educationally unsound

Er|zie|hung F, *no pl* upbringing; *(= Ausbildung)* education; *(= das Erziehen)* bringing up; *(von Tieren, Körper, Gehör)* training; *(= Manieren)* upbringing, (good) breeding; **die ~ zu(r) Höflichkeit** teaching (sb) politeness or good manners; *(durch Eltern auch)* bringing (sb) up to be polite or well-mannered

Er|zie|hungs-: **Er|zie|hungs|an|stalt** F approved school *(Brit dated)*, borstal *(Brit dated)*, reformatory *(US)*; **Er|zie|hungs|bei|hil|fe** F *(dated)* → **Ausbildungsbeihilfe**; **Er|zie|hungs|be|ra|tung** F educational guidance or counselling *(Brit)* or counseling *(US)*; **er|zie|hungs|be|rech|tigt** ADJ having parental authority; **Er|zie|hungs|be|rech|tig|te(r)** [-bərɛçtɪçtə] MF *decl as adj* parent or (legal) guardian; **Er|zie|hungs|feh|ler** PL wrong upbringing (*+gen* on the part of); **Er|zie|hungs|geld** NT ≈ child benefit; **Er|zie|hungs|ge|walt** F parental authority; **Er|zie|hungs|heim** NT approved school *(Brit dated)*, borstal *(Brit dated)*, reformatory *(US)*; **Er|zie|hungs|jahr** NT *(nach Geburt)* year off for bringing up one's child/children; *(im Rentenrecht)* year of credited contributions (for each child); **Er|zie|hungs|me|tho|de** F educational method; **Er|zie|hungs|mit|tel** NT educational aid; **Er|zie|hungs|ur|laub** M paid leave for new parent; *(für Mutter auch)* extended maternity leave; *(für Vater auch)* extended paternity leave; **Er|zie|hungs|we|sen** NT, *no pl* educational system; **Er|zie|hungs|wis|sen|schaft** F educational science; **Er|zie|hungs|wis|sen|schaft|ler(in)** M(F) educationalist

er|zie|len [ɛɐ̯ˈtsiːlən] *ptp* **erzielt** VT *Erfolg, Ergebnis* to achieve, to attain, to obtain; *Kompromiss, Einigung* to reach, to arrive at; *Geschwindigkeit* to reach; *Gewinn* to make, to realize; *Preis (Mensch)* to secure; *(Gegenstand)* to fetch; *(Sport) Tor, Punkte* to score; *Rekord* to set; **was willst du damit ~?** what do you hope to achieve by that?

er|zit|tern [ɛɐ̯ˈtsɪtɐn] *ptp* **erzittert** VI *aux sein (liter)* to tremble, to shake, to quake

Erz-: **erz|kon|ser|va|tiv** ADJ ultraconservative; **Erz|kon|ser|va|ti|ve(r)** MF *decl as adj* arch-conservative, dyed-in-the-wool conservative, true blue *(Brit)*; **Erz|la|ger** [ˈeːɐ̯ts-, ˈɛrts-] NT ore deposit; **Erz|lüg|ner(in)** M(F) *(inf)* inveterate or unmitigated liar; **Erz|re|ak|ti|o|när(in)** M(F) ultrareactionary

er|zür|nen [ɛɐ̯ˈtsʏrnən] *ptp* **erzürnt** *(geh)* VT to anger, to incense VR to become or grow angry *(über +acc* about)

Erz|va|ter M *(Bibl)* patriarch; *(fig)* forefather

er|zwin|gen [ɛɐ̯ˈtsvɪŋən] *ptp* **erzwungen** [ɛɐ̯ˈtsvʊŋən] VT *irreg* to force; *(gerichtlich)* to enforce; **etw von jdm ~** to force sth from or out of sb; **sie erzwangen den Zutritt zur Wohnung mit Gewalt** they forced entry into the flat

es [ɛs] PERS PRON *gen* **seiner**, *dat* **ihm**, *acc* **es** **a** *(auf Dinge bezogen)* it; *(auf männliches Wesen bezogen) (nom)* he; *(acc)* him; *(auf weibliches Wesen bezogen) (nom)* she; *(acc)* her

b *(auf vorangehende Substantive, Adjektive bezüglich)* **wer ist da? – ich bin es** who's there? – it's me or I *(form)*; **sie ist klug, er ist es auch** she is clever, so is he; **ich höre jemanden klopfen, es sind die Kinder** I can hear somebody knocking, it's the children; **wer ist die Dame? – es ist meine Frau** who's the lady? – it's *or* she's my wife

c *(auf vorangehenden Satzinhalt bezüglich)* **das Glas wurde zerbrochen, keiner will es getan haben** the glass had been broken, but nobody will admit to doing it; **alle dachten, dass das ungerecht war, aber niemand sagte es** everyone thought it was unjust, but nobody said so

d *(rein formales Subjekt)* **es ist kalt/8 Uhr/Sonntag** it's cold/8 o'clock/Sunday; **es friert mich** I am cold; **es freut mich, dass …** I am pleased *or* glad that …; **es sei denn, dass …** unless …

e *(rein formales Objekt)* **ich halte es für richtig, dass …** I think it (is) right that …; **ich hoffe es** I hope so; **ich habe es satt, zu** *(+infin)*, **ich bin es müde, zu** *(+infin)* I've had enough of *(+prp)*, I'm tired of *(+prp)*

f *(bei unpersönlichem Gebrauch des Verbs)* **es gefällt mir** I like it; **es klopft** there's a knock (at the door); **es regnet** it's raining; **es sich** *(dat)* **schön machen** to have a good time; **bei dem Licht liest es sich gut** this light is good for reading; **es sitzt sich bequem hier** it's comfortable sitting here; **es darf geraucht werden** smoking is permitted; **es wurde gesagt, dass …** it was said that …; **es wurde getanzt** there was dancing; **er lässt es nicht zu, dass ich länger bleibe** he won't allow me to stay any longer

g *(Einleitewort mit folgendem Subjekt)* **es geschah ein Unglück** there was an accident; **es gibt viel Arbeit** there's a lot of work; **es gibt viele Leute, die …** there are a lot of people who …; **es kamen viele Leute** a lot of people came; **es lebe der König!** long live the king!; **es meldete sich niemand** nobody replied; **es war einmal eine Königin** once upon a time there was a queen

es NT -, - *(Mus)* E flat

Es NT -, - **a** *(Mus: Dur)* E flat **b** *(Psych)* id, Id

Es|cape-Tas|te [ɛs'ke:p-] F *(Comput)* escape key

Es|cha|to|lo|gie [ɛʃatolo'gi:] F -, -n [-'gi:ən] *(Rel)* eschatology

Esche ['ɛʃə] F -, -n ash-tree; *(= Holz)* ash

Eschen|holz NT ash

Esel ['e:zl] M -s, - donkey, ass *(old, esp Bibl)*; *(inf: = Dummkopf)* (silly) ass; **du alter ~!** you are an ass *(inf) or* a fool; **ich ~!** I am an ass *(inf) or* a fool!, silly (old) me!; **störrisch wie ein ~** as stubborn as a mule; **der ~ nennt sich selbst zuerst** *(prov)* it's rude to put yourself first; **ein ~ schimpft den andern Langohr** *(prov)* (it's a case of) the pot calling the kettle black *(prov)*; **wenn es dem ~ zu wohl wird, geht er aufs Eis (tanzen)** *(Prov)* complacency makes one *or* you reckless

Ese|lei [e:zə'lai] F -, -en *(inf)* stupidity; *(= Streich)* silly prank

Ese|lin ['e:zəlɪn] F -, -nen she-ass

Esels-: **Esels|brü|cke** F *(= Gedächtnishilfe)* mnemonic, aide-mémoire; *(gereimt)* jingle; **Esels|ohr** NT *(fig)* dog-ear, turned-down corner; **ein Buch mit ~en** a dog-eared book

Es|ka|la|ti|on [ɛskala'tsio:n] F -, -en escalation

es|ka|lie|ren [ɛska'li:rən] *ptp* **eskaliert** VTI *(vi: aux sein)* to escalate

Es|ka|lie|rung F -, -en escalation

Es|ka|mo|ta|ge [ɛskamo'ta:ʒə] F -, -n sleight of hand

es|ka|mo|tie|ren [ɛskamo'ti:rən] *ptp* **eskamotiert** VT to spirit *or* conjure away

Es|ka|pa|de [ɛska'pa:də] F -, -n *(von Pferd)* caper; *(fig)* escapade

Es|ka|pis|mus [ɛska'pɪsmʊs] M -, *no pl (Psych, Sociol)* escapism

Es|ki|mo ['ɛskimo] M -s, -s Eskimo

Es|ki|mo|frau F Eskimo (woman)

es|ki|mo|tie|ren [ɛskimo'ti:rən] *ptp* **eskimotiert** VI *(Sport)* to roll

es|komp|tie|ren [ɛskõ'ti:rən] *ptp* **eskomptiert** VT *(Fin) (= diskontieren)* to discount; *(St Ex)* to preempt

Es|kor|te [ɛs'kɔrtə] F -, -n *(Mil)* escort

es|kor|tie|ren [ɛskɔr'ti:rən] *ptp* **eskortiert** VT to escort

Eso|te|rik [ezo'te:rɪk] F -, *no pl* esotericism

Eso|te|ri|ker [ezo'te:rikɐ] M -s, -, **Eso|te|ri|ke|rin** [-ərɪn] F -, -nen esoteric

eso|te|risch [ezo'te:rɪʃ] ADJ esoteric

Es|pe ['ɛspə] F -, -n aspen; *(Holz auch)* aspen wood

Es|pen|laub NT aspen leaves *pl*; **zittern wie ~** to shake like a leaf

Es|pe|ran|to [ɛspe'ranto] NT -s, *no pl* Esperanto

Es|pres|so [ɛs'prɛso] M -(s), -s *or* **Espressi** [-si] espresso

Es|pres|so NT -(s), -(s), **Es|pres|so|bar** F *(= Café)* coffee *or* espresso bar

Es|pres|so|ma|schi|ne F espresso machine

Esp|rit [ɛs'pri:] M -s, *no pl* wit; **ein Mann von ~** a wit, a witty man

Ess|ap|fel M eating apple, eater

Es|say ['ɛse, ɛ'se:] M OR NT -s, -s *(Liter)* essay

Es|say|ist [ɛse'ɪst] M -en, -en, **Es|say|is|tin** [-'ɪstɪn] F -, -nen *(Liter)* essayist

es|say|is|tisch [ɛse'ɪstɪʃ] ADJ *(Liter) Roman* essayistic; **das ~e Werk Thomas Manns** the essays of Thomas Mann

Ess-: **ess|bar** ADJ edible, eatable; *Pilz* edible; **habt ihr irgend etwas Essbares im Haus?** have you got anything to eat in the house?; **nicht ~** inedible, uneatable; **Ess|be|steck** NT knife, fork and spoon, eating irons *pl (Brit hum)*; **Ess-Brech|sucht** [-'brɛçzʊxt] F -, *no pl* bulimia; **Ess|ecke** F eating area

Es|se ['ɛsə] F -, -n *(dial: = Schornstein)* chimney; *(von Schmiede)* hearth

es|sen ['ɛsn] *pret* **aß** [a:s], *ptp* **gegessen** [gə'gɛsn] VTI to eat; **gut/schlecht ~** *(= Appetit haben)* to have a good/poor appetite; **in dem Restaurant kann man gut ~** that's a good restaurant; **die Franzosen ~ gut** the French eat well, French food is good; **da isst es sich gut** the food is good there, you can eat well there, they do good food there; **warm/kalt ~** to have a hot/cold meal; **tüchtig** *or* **ordentlich ~** to eat well *or* properly; **iss mal tüchtig!** tuck in! *(Brit inf)*, eat up!; **sich satt ~** to eat one's fill; **sich krank ~** to overeat, to overindulge (in food); **jdn arm ~** to eat sb out of house and home; **den Teller leer ~** to eat everything up, to empty one's plate; **~ Sie gern Äpfel?** do you like apples?; **wer hat davon gegessen?** who has been eating that?; **wer hat von meinem Teller gegessen?** who's been eating off my plate?; **gerade ~, beim Essen sein** to be in the middle of eating *or* of a meal; **~ gehen** *(auswärts)* to eat out, to go out to eat; **wann gehst du ~?** when are you going to eat?; *(normalerweise)* when do you eat?; **ich bin ~** *(inf)* I've gone to eat; **nach der Vorstellung gingen wir noch ~** after the performance we went for a meal; **das Thema ist schon lange/noch nicht gegessen** *(fig inf)* the subject is dead and buried/still alive; **selber ~ macht fett** *(prov)* I'm all right, Jack *(Brit prov)*, it's not my problem; **Essen und Trinken hält Leib und Seele zusammen** *(prov)* food and drink keep body and soul together → **heiß ADV a, Tisch**

Es|sen ['ɛsn] NT -s, - *(= Mahlzeit)* meal; *(= Nahrung)* food; *(= Küche)* cooking; *(= Mittagessen)* lunch; *(= Abendessen)* dinner; **bleib doch zum ~** stay for lunch/dinner, stay for a meal; **das ~ kochen** *or* **machen** *(inf)* to cook *or* get the meal; **jdn zum ~ einladen** to invite sb for a meal; **(bitte) zum ~** lunch/dinner is ready; **~ auf Rädern** meals on wheels → **ruhen VI a**

Es|sen(s)-: **Es|sen(s)|aus|ga|be** F serving of meals; *(Stelle)* serving counter; **ab 12.30 Uhr ist in der Kantine ~** meals are served in the canteen from 12.30; **Es|sen(s)|mar|ke** F meal voucher *(Brit) or* ticket *(US)*; **Es|sen(s)|res|te** PL leftovers; **Es|sen(s)|zeit** F mealtime; **bei uns ist um 12.00 Uhr ~** we have lunch at 12; **die Kinder müssen abends zur ~ zu Hause sein** the children have to be at home in time for their evening meal; **Es|sen(s)|zu|schuss** M meal subsidy

Es|sen|tial [ɪ'sɛnʃəl] NT -s, -s essential

es|sen|ti|ell [ɛsɛn'tsiɛl] ADJ = **essenziell**

Es|senz [ɛ'sɛnts] F -, -en **a** *no pl (Philos)* essence **b** *(Cook etc)* essence

es|sen|zi|ell [ɛsɛn'tsiɛl] ADJ *(auch Biol, Chem, Philos)* essential

Es|ser ['ɛsɐ] M -s, -, **Es|se|rin** [-ərɪn] F -, -nen diner; *(pl auch)* people eating; **ein guter** *or* **starker/schlechter ~ sein** to be a good *or* great/poor eater; **auf einen ~ mehr kommt es nicht an** one more person won't make any difference

Es|se|rei [ɛsə'rai] F -, -en *(inf)* guzzling *(inf)*; *(= Mahl)* blowout *(Brit inf)*, nosh-up *(Brit inf)*, feast *(US inf)*; **die ~ im Stehen ist nicht gut** it's not good to eat standing up

Ess-: **Ess|ge|schirr** NT dinner service; *(Mil)* mess tin; **Ess|ge|wohn|hei|ten** PL eating habits *pl*

Es|sig ['ɛsɪç] M -s, -e [-gə] vinegar; **damit ist es ~** *(inf)* it's all off, it's up the spout *(Brit inf)*

Es|sig-: **Es|sig|äther** M ethyl acetate; **Es|sig|es|senz** F vinegar concentrate; **Es|sig|es|ter** M ethyl acetate; **Es|sig|gur|ke** F (pickled) gherkin; **es|sig|sau|er** ADJ *(Chem)* acetic; **essigsaure Tonerde** aluminium acetate; **Es|sig|säu|re** F acetic acid

Ess-: **Ess|kas|ta|nie** F sweet chestnut; **Ess|kul|tur** F gastronomic culture; **Ess|löf|fel** M *(für Suppe)* soup spoon; *(für Nachtisch)* dessert spoon; *(in Rezept)* tablespoon; **ess|löf|fel|wei|se** ADV in tablespoonfuls; *(inf)* by the spoonful; **Ess|lust** F appetite; **Ess|stäb|chen** PL chopsticks *pl*; **Ess|stö|rung** F *usu pl* eating disorder; **Ess|tisch** M dining table; **Ess|un|lust** F loss of appetite; **Ess|wa|ren** PL food *sing*, provisions *pl*; **Ess|zim|mer** NT dining room; **Ess|zwang** M *(Psych)* compulsive eating; **an ~ leiden** to be a compulsive eater

Es|tab|lish|ment [ɪs'tɛblɪʃmənt] NT -s, -s *(Sociol, Press)* establishment

Es|te ['e:stə, 'ɛstə] M -n, -n, **Es|tin** ['e:stɪn, 'ɛstɪn] F -, -nen Est(h)onian

Es|ter ['ɛstɐ] M -s, - *(Chem)* ester

Est|land ['e:stlant, 'ɛst-] NT -s Est(h)onia

est|län|disch ['e:stlɛndɪʃ, 'ɛst-], **est|nisch** ['e:stnɪʃ, 'ɛst-] ADJ Est(h)onian

Est|ni|sch(e) ['e:stnɪʃ, 'ɛst-] NT Est(h)onian → *auch* **Deutsch(e)**

Est|ra|de [ɛs'tra:də] F -, -n **a** podium **b** *(auch* **Estradenkonzert)** *concert of light music etc, especially performed out of doors*

Est|ra|gon ['ɛstragɔn] M -s, *no pl* tarragon

Est|rich ['ɛstrɪç] M -s, -e **a** stone floor **b** *(Sw: = Dachboden)* attic

Es|zett [ɛs'tsɛt] NT -, - eszett, ß

etab|lie|ren [eta'bli:rən] *ptp* **etabliert** VT *(dated)* to establish VR to establish oneself; *(als Geschäftsmann auch)* to set up

etab|liert [eta'bli:ɐt] ADJ established; **er gehört jetzt zu den Etablierten** he is now part of the establishment; **die ~e Oberschicht** the upper echelons of the establishment

Etab|lie|rung [eta'bli:rʊŋ] F -, *no pl* establishment

Etab|lis|se|ment [etablɪsə'mã:] NT -s, -s establishment

Eta|ge [e'ta:ʒə] F -, -n floor; **in** *or* **auf der 2. ~** on the 2nd *or* 3rd *(US)* floor; **er bewohnt im 5. Stock die ganze ~** he lives in *or* occupies the whole of the 5th *or* 6th *(US)* floor

Eta|gen-: **Eta|gen|bad** NT *(im Hotel)* shared bath; **Eta|gen|bett** NT bunk bed; **Eta|gen|du|sche** F *(im Hotel)* shared shower; **Eta|gen|hei|zung** F *heating system which covers one floor of a building*; **Eta|gen|kell|ner(in)** M(F) waiter/waitress on room service; **Eta|gen|woh|nung** F *apartment occupying the whole of one floor of a building*

Eta|ge|re [eta'ʒe:rə] F -, -n *(dated)* étagère

Etap|pe [e'tapə] F -, -n **a** (= *Abschnitt, Stufe, beim Radrennen*) stage; (*einer Strecke auch*) leg **b** (*Mil*) communications zone; **in der ~ liegen** *or* **sein** to be behind the lines

Etap|pen-: **Etap|pen|hengst** M, **Etap|pen|schwein** NT (*Mil sl*) base wallah (*Mil sl*); **Etap|pen|sieg** M (*Sport*) stage win; (*fig*) partial victory; **Etap|pen|sie|ger(in)** M(F) (*Sport*) stage winner; **etap|pen|wei|se** ADJ step-by-step, stage-by-stage ADV step by step, stage by stage

Etat [e'ta:] M -s, -s budget

Etat-: **Etat|jahr** NT financial year; **etat|mä|ßig** ADJ **a** (*Admin*) budgetary **b** *Stürmer, Quarterback etc* regular ADV **das Geld wurde ~ ausgegeben** the money was spent as budgeted; **nicht ~ erfasst** not in the budget, not budgeted for; **Etat|pos|ten** M item in the budget, budgetary item; **Etat|über|schrei|tung** [-y:bɐʃraitʊŋ] F overspending, spending over budget

etc [ɛt'tse:tera] *abbr von* **et cetera** etc, et cetera

etc pp [ɛt'tse:tera'pe:'pe:] ADV (*hum*) and so on and so forth

ete|pe|te|te [e:tape'te:tə] ADJ *pred* (*inf*) fussy, finicky (*inf*), pernickety (*inf*)

Eter|nit® [etɛr'ni:t] M OR NT -s, *no pl* fibre (*Brit*) *or* fiber (*US*) cement

Ethan [e'ta:n] NT -s (*Chem*) ethane

Ethik ['e:tɪk] F -, -en ethics *pl*; (= *Fach*) ethics *sing*; **die ~ Kants** Kantian ethics; **die christliche ~** the Christian ethic, Christian ethics

Ethi|ker ['e:tikɐ] M -s, -, **Ethi|ke|rin** [-ərɪn] F -, -nen moral philosopher

Ethik-: **Ethik|kom|mis|si|on** F ethics committee; **Ethik|un|ter|richt** M (*Sch*) (teaching of) ethics

ethisch ['e:tɪʃ] ADJ ethical

eth|nisch ['ɛtnɪʃ] ADJ ethnic; **~e Säuberung** ethnic cleansing

Eth|no- [ɛtno] *in cpds* ethno-; **Eth|no|graf** [-'gra:f] M -en, -en, **Eth|no|gra|fin** [-'gra:fɪn] F -, -nen ethnographer; **Eth|no|gra|fie** [-gra'fi:] F -, -n [-'fi:ən] ethnography; **eth|no|gra|fisch** [-'gra:fɪʃ] ADJ ethnographic

Eth|no|graph *etc* = **Ethnograf** *etc*

Eth|no|lo|ge [ɛtno'lo:gə] M -n, -n, **Eth|no|lo|gin** [-'lo:gɪn] F -, -nen ethnologist

Eth|no|lo|gie [ɛtnolo'gi:] F -, -n [-'gi:ən] ethnology

Eth|no|rock ['ɛtnorɔk] M, *no pl* (*Mus*) ethnic rock

Etho|lo|ge [ɛto'lo:gə] M -n, -n, **Etho|lo|gin** [-'lo:gɪn] F -, -nen ethologist

Etho|lo|gie [ɛtolo'gi:] F -, *no pl* ethology

Ethos ['e:tɔs] NT -, *no pl* ethos; (= *Berufsethos*) professional ethics *pl*

Eti|kett [eti'kɛt] NT -(e)s, -e (*lit, fig*) label

Eti|ket|te [eti'kɛtə] F -, -n **a** etiquette; **gegen die ~ (bei Hofe) verstoßen** to offend against (court) etiquette, to commit a breach of (court) etiquette **b** (*Aus*: = *Etikett*) label

Eti|ket|ten|schwin|del M (*Pol*) juggling with names; **es ist reinster ~, wenn ...** it is just playing *or* juggling with names if ...

eti|ket|tie|ren [etikɛ'ti:rən] *ptp* **etikettiert** VT (*lit, fig*) to label

Eti|ket|tier|ge|rät NT (*Tech*) labelling (*Brit*) *or* labeling (*US*) machine

et|li|che|mal △ ['ɛtlɪçə'ma:l] ADV → **etliche(r, s)**

et|li|che(r, s) ['ɛtlɪçə] INDEF PRON **a** *sing attr* quite a lot of; **nachdem ~ Zeit verstrichen war** after quite some time; **~ Mal** quite a few times **b** **etliche** PL (*substantivisch*) quite a few, several people/things; (*attr*) several, quite a few **c** **etliches** SING (*substantivisch*) quite a lot; **ich habe ~s daran auszusetzen, aber im Großen und Ganzen ...** I have one or two objections to make but by and large ...; **um ~s älter als ich** quite a lot *or* considerably older than me

Et|ru|ri|en [e'tru:riən] NT -s (*Hist*) Etruria

Et|rus|ker [e'trʊskɐ] M -s, -, **Et|rus|ke|rin** [-ərɪn] F -, -nen Etruscan

et|rus|kisch [e'trʊskɪʃ] ADJ Etruscan

Etsch [ɛtʃ] F - Adige

Etü|de [e'ty:də] F -, -n (*Mus*) étude

Etui [ɛt'vi:, e'tyi:] NT -s, -s case

Etui|kleid [ɛt'vi:-, e'tyi:-] NT box dress

et|wa ['ɛtva] ADV **a** (= *ungefähr, annähernd*) about, approximately; **so ~, ~ so** roughly *or* more or less like this; **wann ~ ...?** about *or* approximately *or* roughly when ...? **b** (= *zum Beispiel*) for instance; **wenn man ~ behauptet, dass ...** for instance if one maintains that ... **c** (*entrüstet, erstaunt*) **hast du ~ schon wieder kein Geld dabei?** don't tell me *or* you don't mean to say you haven't got any money again!; **soll das ~ heißen, dass ...?** is that supposed to mean ...?; **willst du ~ schon gehen?** (surely) you don't want to go already! **d** (*zur Bestätigung*) **Sie kommen doch, oder ~ nicht?** you are coming, aren't you?; **das haben Sie wohl nicht mit Absicht gesagt, oder ~ doch?** surely you didn't say that on purpose, you didn't say that on purpose - or did you?; **sind Sie ~ nicht einverstanden?** do you mean to say that you don't agree?; **ist das ~ wahr?** (surely) it's not true!, (surely) it can't be true!; **ist das ~ nicht wahr?** do you mean to say it's not true? **e** (*in Gegenüberstellung, einschränkend*) **nicht ~, dass ...** (it's) not that ...; **er ist nicht ~ dumm, sondern nur faul** it's not that he's stupid, he's simply lazy; **das hat Fritz getan und nicht ~ sein Bruder** Fritz did it and not his brother; **ich wollte dich nicht ~ beleidigen** I didn't intend to insult you

et|wa|ig ['ɛtvaɪç, ɛt'va:ɪç] ADJ *attr* possible; **~e Einwände/Unkosten** any objections/costs arising *or* which might arise; **bei ~en Beschwerden/Schäden** *etc* in the event of (any) complaints/damage *etc*; **ein Zimmer für ~e Besucher** a room for possible visitors, a room in case there should be visitors

et|was ['ɛtvas] INDEF PRON **a** (*substantivisch*) something; (*fragend, bedingend auch, verneinend*) anything; (*unbestimmter Teil einer Menge*) some; any; **kannst du mir ~ (davon) leihen?** can you lend me some (of it)?; **ohne ~ zu erwähnen** without saying anything; **~ habe ich doch vergessen** there is something I've forgotten; **~ anderes** something else; **das ist ~ (ganz) anderes** that's something (quite) different; **er ist ~** (*inf*) he is somebody; **~ werden** (*inf*) **es zu ~ bringen** (*inf*) to make something of oneself, to get somewhere (*inf*); **aus ihm wird nie ~** (*inf*) he'll never become anything; **er kann ~** he's good; **das ist immerhin ~** at least that's something; **sein Wort gilt ~ beim Chef** what he says counts for something with the boss; **hast du ~?** is (there) something wrong *or* the matter (with you)?; **sie hat ~ mit ihm** (*inf*) she's got something going on with him; **das ist sicher, wie nur ~** (*inf*) that's as sure as (sure) can be (*inf*); **er hat ~ von einem** *or* **vom Schulmeister an sich** he has *or* there is something of the schoolmaster about him; **da ist ~ (Richtiges) dran** there's something in that; **da ist ~ Wahres dran** there is some truth in that **b** (*adjektivisch*) some; (*fragend, bedingend auch*) any; **~ Salz?** some salt?; **~ Petersilie dazugeben** (*Cook*) to add a touch of parsley; **kannst du mir vielleicht ~ Geld leihen?** could you possibly lend me some money?; **~ Nettes** something nice; **~ Schöneres habe ich noch nie gesehen** I have never seen anything more beautiful **c** (*adverbial*) somewhat, a little

Et|was ['ɛtvas] NT -, *no pl* something; **das gewisse ~** that certain something; **ein winziges ~** a tiny little thing

Ety|mo|lo|ge [etymo'lo:gə] M -n, -n, **Ety|mo|lo|gin** [-'lo:gɪn] F -, -nen etymologist

Ety|mo|lo|gie [etymolo'gi:] F -, -n [-'gi:ən] etymology

ety|mo|lo|gisch [etymo'lo:gɪʃ] ADJ etymological

Et-Zei|chen ['ɛt-] NT ampersand

Et|zel ['ɛtsl] M -s Attila the Hun

EU [e:'lu:] F - *abbr von* **Europäische Union** EU

EU-: **EU-Be|am|te(r)** [e:'lu:-] M *decl as adj*, **EU-Be|am|tin** [e:'lu:-] F EU official; **EU-Be|hör|de** [e:'lu:-] F EU institution; **EU-Bei|hil|fe** [e:'lu:-] F EU subsidy; **EU-Be|stim|mung** [e:'lu:-] F EU regulation

euch [ɔyç] PERS PRON *dat, acc von* **ihr** you; (*dat auch*) to/for you; (*refl*) yourselves; **ein Freund von ~** a friend of yours; **wascht ~!** wash yourselves; **setzt ~!** sit (yourselves (*inf*)) down!; **vertragt ~!** stop quarrelling (*Brit*) *or* quarreling (*US*)!

Eu|cha|ris|tie [ɔyçarɪs'ti:] F -, -n [-'ti:ən] (*Eccl*) Eucharist

Eu|cha|ris|tie|fei|er [ɔyçarɪs'ti:-] F (*Eccl*) Eucharist, Eucharistic mass

eu|cha|ris|tisch [ɔyça'rɪstɪʃ] ADJ Eucharistic

EU-ein|heit|lich [e:'lu:-] ADJ standardized within the EU ADV **etw ~ regeln** to regulate sth uniformly throughout the EU

eu|er ['ɔyɐ] POSS PRON **a** (*adjektivisch*) your; **Euer** (*Briefschluss*) yours; **viele Grüße, Euer Hans** best wishes, yours, Hans; **das sind ~e** *or* **eure Bücher** those are your books; **ist das ~ Haus?** is that your house?; **Euer** *or* **Eure Gnaden/Exzellenz/Majestät** your Grace/Excellency/Majesty **b** (*old*: *substantivisch*) yours; **behaltet, was ~ ist** keep what is yours PERS PRON *gen von* **ihr** (*geh*) **wir werden ~ gedenken** we will think of you; **~ beider gemeinsame Zukunft** your common future; **~ aller heimlicher Wunsch** the secret wish of all of you

eu|e|re(r, s) ['ɔyərə] POSS PRON = **eure(r, s)**

eu|ers|glei|chen ['ɔyɐs'glaiçn] PRON *inv* = **euresgleichen**

eu|ert- ['ɔyɐt] *in cpds* = **euret-**

Eu|ge|nik [ɔy'ge:nɪk] F -, *no pl* (*Biol*) eugenics *sing*

eu|ge|nisch [ɔy'ge:nɪʃ] ADJ (*Biol*) eugenic

EU-Gip|fel [e:'lu:-] M (*inf*: = *Gipfelkonferenz*) EU summit

Eu|ka|lyp|tus [ɔyka'lʏptʊs] M -, **Eukalypten** [-tn] (= *Baum*) eucalyptus (tree); (= *Öl*) eucalyptus oil

Eu|ka|lyp|tus|bon|bon M OR NT eucalyptus sweet (*Brit*) *or* candy (*US*)

Euk|lid [ɔy'kli:t] M -s Euclid

euk|li|disch [ɔy'kli:dɪʃ] ADJ Euclidean

EU-Ge|setz NT EU law

EuGH *abbr von* **Europäischer Gerichtshof**

EU-: **EU-Kom|mis|si|on** [e:'lu:-] F EU Commission; **EU-Kon|vent** M European Convention; **EU-Land** [e:'lu:-] NT EU country *or* member

Eu|le ['ɔylə] F -, -n owl; (*pej*: = *hässliche Frau*) crow; **~n nach Athen tragen** (*prov*) to carry coals to Newcastle (*Brit prov*), to do something unnecessary

Eu|len|spie|gel ['ɔylənʃpi:gl] M **Till ~** (*lit*) Till Eulenspiegel; **unser Sohn ist ein richtiger ~** (*fig*) our son is a real scamp (*inf*) *or* rascal (*inf*)

Eu|len|spie|ge|lei [ɔylənʃpi:gə'lai] F -, -en, **Eu|len|spie|gel|streich** M trick, caper

Eu|mel ['ɔyməl] M -s, - **a** (*inf*: = *großes Ding*) whopper (*inf*) **b** *pl* (*sl*: = *großer Busen*) knockers *pl* (*Brit inf*), hooters *pl* (*US inf*)

EU-: **EU-Mi|nis|ter|rat** [e:'lu:-] M Council of Ministers; **EU-Mit|glied** [e:'lu:-] NT, **EU-Mit|glieds|land** [e:'lu:-] NT EU member (state); **EU-Norm** [e:'lu:-] F EU standard

Eu|nuch [ɔy'nu:x] M -en, -en eunuch

Eu|phe|mis|mus [ɔyfe'mɪsmʊs] M -, **Euphemismen** [-mən] euphemism

eu|phe|mis|tisch [ɔyfe'mɪstɪʃ] ADJ euphemistic ADV euphemistically

Eu|pho|rie [ɔyfo'ri:] F -, -n [-'ri:ən] euphoria

eu|pho|risch [ɔy'fo:rɪʃ] ADJ euphoric

Euph|rat ['ɔyfrat] M -(s) Euphrates

Eu|ra|si|en [ɔy'ra:ziən] NT -s Eurasia

Eu|ra|si|er [ɔy'ra:ziɐ] M **-s, -, Eu|ra|si|e|rin** [-iərɪn] F **-, -nen** Eurasian

eu|ra|sisch [ɔy'ra:zɪʃ] ADJ Eurasian

Eu|ra|tom [ɔyra'to:m] *abbr von* **Europäische Atomgemeinschaft** European Atomic Community, Euratom

eu|re(r, s) ['ɔyrə] POSS PRON **a** *(substantivisch)* yours; **der/die/das ~** *or* **Eure** *(geh)* yours; **tut ihr das ~** *or* **Eure** *(geh)* you do your bit *(Brit) or* part *(US)*; **stets** *or* **immer der ~** *or* **Eure** *(form)* yours ever; **die ~n** *or* **Euren** *(geh)* your family, your people; **ihr und die ~n** *or* **Euren** *(geh: = Familie)* you and yours; **der/die ~** *or* **Eure** *(old: = Ehepartner)* your spouse *(old)*; **das ~** *or* **Eure** *(geh: = Besitz)* what is yours **b** *(adjektivisch)* → **euer POSS PRON a**

eu|rer|seits ['ɔyrɐ'zaits] ADV *(= auf eurer Seite)* for your part; *(= von eurer Seite)* from *or* on your part; **den Vorschlag habt ihr ~ gemacht** you made the suggestion yourselves

eu|res|glei|chen ['ɔyrəs'glaiçn] PRON *inv* people like you *or* yourselves; *(pej auch)* the likes of you, your sort

eu|ret|hal|ben ['ɔyrət'halbn] *(dated)* ADV = **euretwegen**

eu|ret|we|gen ['ɔyrət've:gn] ADV *(= wegen euch)* because of you, on account of you, on your account; *(= euch zuliebe auch)* for your sake; *(= um euch)* about you; *(= für euch)* on your behalf

eu|ret|wil|len ['ɔyrət'vɪlən] ADV **um ~** for your sake

Eu|rhyth|mie [ɔyrʏt'mi:] F **-,** *no pl* eurythmics *sing*

eu|ri|ge ['ɔyrɪgə] POSS PRON *(old, geh)* **der/die/das ~** *or* **Eurige** yours; **die Eurigen** your families; **das Eurige** *(= Besitz)* what is yours; **tut ihr das ~** *or* **Eurige** you do your bit *(Brit) or* part *(US)*

Eu|ro ['ɔyro] M **-, -** *(= Währung)* euro; **vier ~ zwanzig** four euros twenty (cents); **das kostet zehn ~** that's ten euros; **mit jedem ~ rechnen, den** *or* **jeden ~ umdrehen** to think twice before spending anything; **mit jedem ~ rechnen müssen** to have to count every penny

eu|ro-, Eu|ro- *in cpds* Euro-; **Eu|ro|cent** M euro cent; **Eu|ro|cent|mün|ze** F euro cent coin; **Eu|ro|cheque** ['ɔyroʃɛk] M **-s, -s** Eurocheque *(Brit)*, Eurocheck *(US)*; **Eu|ro|ci|ty|zug** [-'sɪtɪ-] M European Inter-City train; **Eu|ro|dol|lar** M eurodollar; **Eu|ro|korps** NT *(Mil)* Eurocorps

Eu|ro|krat [ɔyro'kra:t] M **-en, -en, Eu|ro|kra|tin** [-'kra:tɪn] F **-, -nen** Eurocrat

Eu|ro-: **Eu|ro|land** NT **a** *no pl (inf: = Eurozone)* Euroland *(inf)* **b -(e)s, ¨er** *(= Mitgliedsstaat der EU)* euro country; **Eu|ro|mün|ze** F euro coin; **Eu|ro|norm** F European standard

Eu|ro|pa [ɔy'ro:pa] NT **-s** Europe

Eu|ro|pa|ab|ge|ord|ne|te(r) M(F) member of the European Parliament, MEP

Eu|ro|pa|cup [-kap] M European cup

Eu|ro|pä|er [ɔyro'pɛ:ɐ] M **-s, -, Eu|ro|pä|e|rin** [-ərɪn] F **-, -nen** European

eu|ro|pä|isch [ɔyro'pɛ:ɪʃ] ADJ European; **Europäischer Binnenmarkt** European Internal Market; **die Europäische Gemeinschaft** the European Community; **Europäische Freihandelszone** European Free Trade Association; **Europäischer Gerichtshof** European Court of Justice; **Europäische Investitionsbank** European Investment Bank; **Europäische Kommission** European Commission; **Europäische Kulturhauptstadt** European City of Culture; **das Europäische Parlament** the European Parliament; **Europäischer Rat** Council of the European Union; **Europäischer Rechnungshof** European Court of Auditors; **Europäische Union** European Union; **Europäisches Währungsinstitut** European Monetary Institute; **Europäisches Währungssystem** European Monetary System; **Europäische (Wirtschafts- und) Währungsunion** European (Economic and) Monetary Union; **Europäische Wirtschaftsgemeinschaft** European Economic Community, Common Market; **Europäischer Wirtschaftsraum** European Economic Area; **Europäische Zentralbank** European Central Bank

eu|ro|pä|i|sie|ren [ɔyropɛi'zi:rən] *ptp* **europäisiert** VT to Europeanize

Eu|ro|pa-: **Eu|ro|pa|meis|ter(in)** M(F) *(Sport)* European champion; *(= Team, Land)* European champions *pl*; **Eu|ro|pa|meis|ter|schaft** F European championship; **eu|ro|pa|mü|de** ADJ *(Pol)* Euro-fatigued, Euro-weary, tired of Europe *pred*; **Eu|ro|pa|par|la|ment** NT European Parliament; **Eu|ro|pa|pass** M European passport; **Eu|ro|pa|po|kal** M *(Sport)* European cup; **~ der Pokalsieger** (European) Cup-Winners' Cup; **Eu|ro|pa|rat** M Council of Europe; **Eu|ro|pa|stra|ße** F European route; **Eu|ro|pa|wah|len** PL European elections *pl*; **eu|ro|pa|weit** ADJ Europe-wide ADV throughout Europe

eu|ro|pid [ɔyro'pi:t] ADJ *Rasse* Caucasian

Eu|ro|pi|de(r) [ɔyro'pi:də] MF *decl as adj* Caucasian

Eu|ro|pi|um [ɔy'ro:piʊm] NT **-s,** *no pl (abbr* **Eu***)* europium

Eu|ro-: **Eu|ro|pol** ['ɔyropo:l] F **-,** *no pl* Europol; **Eu|ro|scheck** M Eurocheque *(Brit)*, Eurocheck *(US)*; **Eu|ro|scheck|kar|te** F Eurocheque *(Brit) or* Eurocheck *(US)* card; **Eu|ro|ste|cker** M flat two-pinned plug; **Eu|ro|stück** NT (one-)euro coin; **Eu|ro|sym|bol** NT euro symbol; **Eu|ro|tun|nel** M *(= Kanaltunnel)* Eurotunnel; **Eu|ro|vi|si|on** F, *no pl* Eurovision; **Eu|ro|vi|si|ons|sen|dung** F Eurovision broadcast *or* programme *(Brit) or* program *(US)*; **Eu|ro|wäh|rung** F eurocurrency; **Eu|ro|zei|chen** NT, *no pl* euro symbol *or* sign; **Eu|ro|zo|ne** F euro zone

Eu|ryth|mie [ɔyrʏt'mi:] F **-,** *no pl* eurythmics *sing*

EU-Staat [e:'lu:-] M EU country

eus|ta|chi|sche Röh|re [ɔys'taxɪʃə] F *(Anat)* Eustachian tube

Eu|ter ['ɔytɐ] NT **-s, -** udder

Eu|tha|na|sie [ɔytana'zi:] F **-,** *no pl* euthanasia

EU-weit [e:'lu:-] ADJ ADV EU-wide

e. V., E. V. *abbr von* **eingetragener Verein**

ev. *abbr von* **evangelisch**

Eva ['e:fa, 'e:va] F **-s** Eve; **sie ist eine echte ~** *(hum)* she is the archetypal woman

eva|ku|ie|ren [evaku'i:rən] *ptp* **evakuiert** VT to evacuate

Eva|ku|ier|te(r) [evaku'i:ɐtə] MF *decl as adj* evacuee

Eva|ku|ie|rung F **-, -en** evacuation

eva|lu|ie|ren [evalu'i:rən] *ptp* **evaluiert** VT *(geh)* to evaluate

Evan|ge|li|ar [evaŋgeli'a:ɐ] NT **-s, -e, Evan|ge|li|en|buch** [evaŋ'ge:liən-] NT book of the Gospels, Gospel

evan|ge|li|kal [evaŋgeli'ka:l] ADJ evangelical

Evan|ge|li|ka|le(r) [evaŋgeli'ka:lə] MF *decl as adj* evangelical

evan|ge|lisch [evaŋ'ge:lɪʃ] ADJ Protestant ADV **~ denken** to have Protestant beliefs; **~ heiraten** to be married in the Protestant church; **~ beerdigt werden** to be buried as a Protestant; **~ beeinflusst** influenced by Protestantism; **seine Kinder ~ erziehen** to raise one's children as Protestants

Evan|ge|list [evaŋge'lɪst] M **-en, -en, Evan|ge|lis|tin** [-'lɪstin] F **-, -nen** evangelist

Evan|ge|li|um [evaŋ'ge:liʊm] NT **-s, Evangelien** [-liən] Gospel; *(fig)* gospel; **alles, was er sagt, ist für sie (ein) ~** *(fig)* everything he says is gospel to her

eva|po|rie|ren [evapo'ri:rən] *ptp* **evaporiert** VI *aux sein* to evaporate

Eva(s)|kos|tüm NT *(dated hum)* **im ~** in the altogether *(Brit hum)*, in her birthday suit *(hum)*

Evas|toch|ter ['e:fas-, 'e:vas-] F *(dated hum)* coquette

Even|tu|al- [evɛntu'a:l-]: **Even|tu|al|fall** M eventuality; **Even|tu|al|haus|halt** M *(Parl)* emergency *or* contingency budget

Even|tu|a|li|tät [evɛntuali'tɛ:t] F **-, -en** eventuality, contingency

even|tu|ell [evɛn'tuɛl] ADJ *attr* possible ADV possibly, perhaps; **~ rufe ich Sie später an** I may possibly call you later; **ich komme ~ ein bisschen später** I might (possibly) come a little later

Ever|green ['ɛvɐgri:n] M **-s, -s** evergreen

evi|dent [evi'dɛnt] ADJ *(geh: = offenbar)* obvious, clear

Evi|denz [evi'dɛnts] F **-, -en a** *(Philos)* evidence **b** *(Aus)* **etw in ~ halten** to keep a current record of sth, to keep sth up-to-date

Evi|denz|bü|ro NT *(Aus)* registry

ev.-luth. *abbr von* **evangelisch-lutherisch** Lutheran Protestant

Evo|lu|ti|on [evolu'tsio:n] F **-, -en** evolution

evo|lu|ti|o|när [evolutsio'nɛ:ɐ], **evo|lu|ti|o|nis|tisch** [evolutsio'nɪstɪʃ] ADJ evolutionary

Evo|lu|ti|ons|the|o|rie F theory of evolution

evtl. *abbr von* **eventuell**

E-Werk ['e:-] NT *abbr von* **Elektrizitätswerk** generating *or* power station

EWG [e:ve:'ge:] F **-** *abbr von* **Europäische Wirtschaftsgemeinschaft** EEC, Common Market

EWI F **-** *abbr von* **Europäisches Währungsinstitut** EMI

ewig ['e:vɪç] ADJ eternal; *Leben auch* everlasting; *Eis, Schnee* perpetual; *(inf) Nörgelei etc* never-ending; **der Ewige Jude** the Wandering Jew; **das ~e Licht** *(Eccl)* **die ~e Lampe** *(Eccl)* the sanctuary lamp; **in den ~en Frieden** *or* **die ~e Ruhe eingehen** to find eternal peace; **die Ewige Stadt** the Eternal City; **(Gott,) der Ewige** God, the Eternal → **Jagdgründe**

ADV for ever, eternally; **auf ~** for ever; **das dauert ja ~ (und drei Tage** *(hum)***)** it goes on for ever (and a day); **das dauert ja ~, bis …** it'll take ages until … *(inf)*; **er muss sich ~ beklagen** he's eternally *or* for ever complaining; **es ist ~ schade, dass …** *(inf)* it's an enormous pity *or* shame that …; **~ dankbar** eternally grateful; **ich habe Sie ~ lange nicht gesehen** *(inf)* I haven't seen you for absolutely ages *(inf) or* for an eternity

Ewig|gest|ri|ge(r) ['e:vɪç'gɛstrɪgə] MF *decl as adj* person living in the past; *(gegen alles Neue)* stick-in-the-mud *(inf)*

Ewig|keit ['e:vɪçkait] F **-, -en** eternity; *(der Naturgesetze)* immutability; *(inf)* ages; **in die ~ eingehen** to go to eternal rest; **bis in alle ~, amen,** **von ~ zu ~ amen** for ever and ever, amen; **bis in alle ~** for ever, for all eternity *(liter)*; **eine ~** *or* **eine halbe ~** *(hum)* **dauern** *(inf)* to last an age *or* an eternity; **es dauert eine ~** *or* **eine halbe ~** *(hum)*, **bis …** *(inf)* it'll take absolutely ages until … *(inf)*; **ich habe sie seit ~en** *or* **einer ~ nicht gesehen** *(inf)* I haven't seen her for ages

ewig|lich ['e:vɪklɪç] *(liter)* ADJ *attr* eternal, everlasting ADV eternally, for ever, to the end of time *(liter)*

Ewig|weib|li|che(s) ['e:vɪç'vaiplɪçə] NT **-n,** *no pl decl as adj (geh)* eternal feminine

EWR [e:ve:'lɛr] M **-** *abbr von* **Europäischer Wirtschaftsraum** EEA

EWS [e:ve:'lɛs] NT **-** *abbr von* **Europäisches Währungssystem** EMS

EWU [e:ve:'lu:] F **-** *abbr von* **Europäische Währungsunion** EMU

EWWU F **-** *abbr von* **Europäische Wirtschafts- und Währungsunion**

e. Wz. *abbr von* **eingetragenes Warenzeichen**

ex [ɛks] ADV *(inf)* **a** *(= leer)* **(trink) ex!** down the hatch! *(esp Brit inf)*; **etw (auf) ex trinken** to drink sth in one go *or* down in one **b** *(Schluss, vorbei)* (all) over, finished; **ex und hopp** here today, gone tomorrow

Ex- *in cpds* ex-; **ihr Exmann** her ex-husband

ex|akt [ɛ'ksakt] ADJ exact; **eine ~e Wissenschaft** an exact science ADV exactly; **~ arbeiten** to work accurately

Ex|akt|heit F -, *no pl* exactness, precision

ex|al|tiert [ɛksal'tiːɐt] ADJ effusive

Ex|al|tiert|heit F -, **-en** effusiveness

Ex|a|men [ɛ'ksaːmən] NT **-s, -** *or* **Examina** [-mina] exam, examination; *(Univ)* final examinations, finals *pl*; **~ machen** to do *or* take one's exams *or* finals; **das ~ mit Eins machen** to get top marks in an exam *(Brit)*, to get the best grade in an exam *(US)*; *(Univ)* ≈ to get a First *(Brit)*, ≈ to get an A *(US)*; **mündliches/schriftliches ~** oral/written examination

Ex|a|mens-: **Ex|a|mens|angst** F exam nerves *pl*; **Ex|a|mens|ar|beit** F dissertation *(Brit)*, thesis; **Ex|a|mens|kan|di|dat(in)** M(F) candidate (for an examination), examinee

ex|a|mi|nie|ren [ɛksami'niːrən] *ptp* **examiniert** VT *(geh)* to examine; **jdn über etw** *(acc)* **~** *(lit, fig)* to question sb about sth

Ex|e|ge|se [ɛkse'geːzə] F -, **-n** exegesis

Exe|get [ɛkse'geːt] M **-en, -en**, **Exe|ge|tin** [-'geːtɪn] F -, **-nen** exegete

ex|e|ge|tisch [ɛkse'geːtɪʃ] ADJ exegetic(al)

ex|e|ku|tie|ren [ɛkseku'tiːrən] *ptp* **exekutiert** VT *(form)* to execute; **jdn ~** *(Aus: = pfänden)* to seize *or* impound sb's possessions

Ex|e|ku|ti|on [ɛkseku'tsioːn] F -, **-en** execution; *(Aus: = Pfändung)* seizing, impounding

Ex|e|ku|ti|ons|kom|man|do NT firing squad

ex|e|ku|tiv [ɛkseku'tiːf] ADJ executive

Ex|e|ku|tiv|aus|schuss M executive committee

Ex|e|ku|ti|ve [ɛkseku'tiːvə] F -, **-n**, **Ex|e|ku|tiv|ge|walt** F executive; *(Aus)* forces *pl* of law and order

Ex|e|ku|tor [ɛkse'kuːtoːɐ] M **-s, Exekutoren** [-'toːrən], **Ex|e|ku|to|rin** [-'toːrɪn] F -, **-nen** *(Aus)* bailiff

Ex|em|pel [ɛ'ksɛmpl] NT **-s, -** *(geh)* example; *(dated Math: = Rechenexempel)* example *(dated)*; **die Probe aufs ~ machen** to put it to the test → **statuieren**

Ex|emp|lar [ɛksɛm'plaːɐ] NT **-s, -e** specimen; *(= Buchexemplar, Zeitschriftenexemplar)* copy

ex|emp|la|risch [ɛksɛm'plaːrɪʃ] ADJ exemplary; **~es Lehren/Lernen** teaching/learning by example; **das Urteil wurde ~ für alle folgenden Fälle** the verdict set a precedent for all subsequent cases ADV **etw ~ durcharbeiten** to work through sth as an example; **jdm etw ~ zeigen** to give sb a perfect example of sth; **jdn ~ bestrafen** to punish sb as an example (to others)

Ex|emp|li|fi|ka|ti|on [ɛksɛmplifika'tsioːn] F -, **-en** *(geh)* exemplification

ex|emp|li|fi|zie|ren [ɛksɛmplifi'tsiːrən] *ptp* **exemplifiziert** VT *(geh)* to exemplify

ex|er|zie|ren [ɛksɛr'tsiːrən] *ptp* **exerziert** VTI to drill; *(fig)* to practise *(Brit)*, to practice *(US)*

Ex|er|zier|platz M *(Mil)* parade *or* drill ground

Ex|er|zi|ti|en [ɛksɛr'tsiːtsiən] PL *(Eccl)* spiritual exercises *pl*

Ex-: **Ex|frau** F ex-wife, former wife; **Ex|freund** M ex-boyfriend, former boyfriend; **Ex|freun|din** F ex-girlfriend, former girlfriend

Ex|hi|bi|ti|o|nis|mus [ɛkshibitsio'nɪsmʊs] M -, *no pl* exhibitionism

Ex|hi|bi|ti|o|nist [ɛkshibitsio'nɪst] M **-en, -en**, **Ex|hi|bi|ti|o|nis|tin** [-'nɪstɪn] F -, **-nen** exhibitionist

ex|hi|bi|ti|o|nis|tisch [ɛkshibitsio'nɪstɪʃ] ADJ exhibitionist

ex|hu|mie|ren [ɛkshu'miːrən] *ptp* **exhumiert** VT to exhume

Ex|hu|mie|rung F -, **-en** exhumation

Exil [ɛ'ksiːl] NT **-s, -e** exile; **im (amerikanischen) ~ leben** to live in exile (in America); **ins ~ gehen** to go into exile

Exi|lier|te(r) [ɛksi'liːɐtə] MF *decl as adj* exile

Exil-: **Exil|li|te|ra|tur** F literature written in exile *(esp by Germans exiled during the 3rd Reich)*; **Exil|re|gie|rung** F government in exile

exis|tent [ɛksɪs'tɛnt] ADJ *(geh)* existing, existent

Exis|ten|ti|a|lis|mus [ɛksɪstɛntsia'lɪsmʊs] M -, *no pl* = **Existenzialismus**

Exis|ten|ti|a|list [ɛksɪstɛntsia'lɪst] M **-en, -en**, **Exis|ten|ti|a|lis|tin** [-'lɪstɪn] F -, **-nen** = **Existenzialist**

exis|ten|ti|a|lis|tisch [ɛksɪstɛntsia'lɪstɪʃ] ADJ = **existenzialistisch**

Exis|ten|ti|al|phi|lo|so|phie [ɛksɪstɛn'tsiaːl-] F = **Existenzialphilosophie**

exis|ten|ti|ell [ɛksɪstɛn'tsiɛl] ADJ = **existenziell**

Exis|tenz [ɛksɪs'tɛnts] F -, **-en** existence; *(= Lebensgrundlage, Auskommen)* livelihood; *(pej inf: = Person)* character, customer *(inf)*; **eine gescheiterte** *or* **verkrachte ~** *(inf)* a failure; **sich eine (neue) ~ aufbauen** to make a (new) life for oneself; **keine sichere ~ haben** to have no secure livelihood

Exis|tenz-: **Exis|tenz|angst** F *(Philos)* existential fear, angst; *(wirtschaftlich)* fear for one's livelihood *or* existence; **Exis|tenz|be|rech|ti|gung** F right to exist; **hat die UNO noch eine ~?** can the UN still justify its existence?; **exis|tenz|fä|hig** ADJ able to exist; *Firma* viable; **Exis|tenz|fä|hig|keit** F ability to exist; *(von Firma)* viability; **Exis|tenz|grün|der(in)** M(F) *(Econ)* founder of a new business; **Exis|tenz|grund|la|ge** F basis of one's livelihood; **Exis|tenz|grün|dung** F **a** *(= Gründungsvorgang)* establishing a livelihood; *(Econ)* founding of a new business, starting (up) a new *or* one's own business **b** *(Econ: = neu gegründete Firma)* start-up (business); **Exis|tenz|grün|dungs|dar|le|hen** NT, **Exis|tenz|grün|dungs|kre|dit** [-kreːdiːt] M start-up loan, loan to found a new business

Exis|ten|zi|a|lis|mus [ɛksɪstɛntsia'lɪsmʊs] M -, *no pl* existentialism

Exis|ten|zi|a|list [ɛksɪstɛntsia'lɪst] M **-en, -en**, **Exis|ten|zi|a|lis|tin** [-'lɪstɪn] F -, **-nen** existentialist

exis|ten|zi|a|lis|tisch [ɛksɪstɛntsia'lɪstɪʃ] ADJ existential(ist)

Exis|ten|zi|al|phi|lo|so|phie [ɛksɪstɛn'tsiaːl-] F existential(ist) philosophy

exis|ten|zi|ell [ɛksɪstɛn'tsiɛl] ADJ *(geh)* existential; **das Problem der Umweltverschmutzung ist ~** the problem of environmental pollution is of vital significance; **von ~er Bedeutung** of vital significance

Exis|tenz-: **Exis|tenz|kampf** M struggle for survival; **Exis|tenz|mi|ni|mum** NT subsistence level; *(= Lohn)* minimal living wage *or* income; **das Gehalt liegt noch unter dem ~** that salary is not enough to live on, that is not even a living wage; **er verdient nicht einmal das ~** he does not even earn enough to live on, he does not even earn a living wage; **das gibt uns gerade das ~** we just have enough to get by on; **Exis|tenz|phi|lo|so|phie** F existentialism; **Exis|tenz|si|che|rung** F securing one's livelihood

exis|tie|ren [ɛksɪs'tiːrən] *ptp* **existiert** VI to exist; *(Gesetz, Schule etc auch)* to be in existence

Ex|i|tus ['ɛksitʊs] M -, *no pl (Med)* death

exkl. *abbr von* **exklusive**

Ex|kla|ve [ɛks'klaːvə] F -, **-n** *(Pol)* exclave

ex|klu|siv [ɛksklu'ziːf] ADJ exclusive

Ex|klu|siv|be|richt M *(Press)* exclusive (report)

ex|klu|si|ve [ɛksklu'ziːvə] PREP *+gen* exclusive of, excluding ADV **Getränke ~** excluding drinks; **bis zum 20. ~** to the 20th exclusively

Ex|klu|siv|in|ter|view NT *(Press)* exclusive interview

Ex|klu|si|vi|tät [ɛkskluzivi'tɛːt] F -, *no pl* exclusiveness

Ex|klu|siv|recht NT exclusive rights *pl*

Ex|kom|mu|ni|ka|ti|on F *(Eccl)* excommunication

ex|kom|mu|ni|zie|ren [ɛkskɔmuni'tsiːrən] *ptp* **exkommuniziert** VT to excommunicate

Ex|kre|ment [ɛkskre'mɛnt] NT **-(e)s, -e** *usu pl (geh)* excrement *no pl*, excreta *pl*

Ex|kre|ti|on [ɛkskre'tsioːn] F -, **-en** *(Med)* excretion

ex|kul|pie|ren [ɛkskʊl'piːrən] *ptp* **exkulpiert** VT *(Jur) Person* to exculpate; *Verbrechen* to excuse

Ex|kurs [ɛks'kʊrs] M digression

Ex|kur|si|on [ɛkskʊr'zioːn] F -, **-en** (study) trip

Ex|lib|ris [ɛks'liːbriːs] NT -, - ex-libris, bookplate

Ex|mann M ex-husband, former husband

Ex|mat|ri|ku|la|ti|on [ɛksmatrikula'tsioːn] F -, **-en** *(Univ)* being taken off the university register

ex|mat|ri|ku|lie|ren [ɛksmatriku'liːrən] *ptp* **exmatrikuliert** VT *(Univ)* to take off the university register; **sich ~ lassen** to withdraw from the university register

ex|mit|tie|ren [ɛksmɪ'tiːrən] *ptp* **exmittiert** VT *(Admin) Mieter* to evict

Ex|mit|tie|rung F -, **-en** *(Admin)* eviction

Ex|o|dus ['ɛksodʊs] M - *(Bibl, fig)* exodus

exo|gen [ɛkso'geːn] ADJ *(Biol, Geol)* exogenous

ex|or|bi|tant [ɛksɔrbi'tant] ADJ *(geh) Preise* exorbitant; *Alkoholwerte* excessive; **es kam zu einer ~en Überschreitung der Strahlengrenzwerte** radiation levels were greatly exceeded

ex|or|zie|ren [ɛksɔr'tsiːrən] *ptp* **exorziert**, **ex|or|zi|sie|ren** [ɛksɔrtsi'ziːrən] *ptp* **exorzisiert** VT to exorcize

Ex|or|zis|mus [ɛksɔr'tsɪsmʊs] M -, **Exorzismen** [-mən] exorcism

Ex|or|zist [ɛksɔr'tsɪst] M **-en, -en**, **Ex|or|zis|tin** [-'tsɪstɪn] F -, **-nen** exorcist

Exot [ɛ'ksoːt] M **-en, -en**, **Exo|te** [ɛ'ksoːtə] M **-n, -n**, **Exo|tin** [ɛ'ksoːtɪn] F -, **-nen** exotic *or* tropical animal/plant *etc*; *(Mensch)* exotic foreigner

Exo|tik [ɛ'ksoːtɪk] F -, *no pl* exoticism

exo|tisch [ɛ'ksoːtɪʃ] ADJ exotic

Ex|pan|der [ɛks'pandɐ] M **-s, -** *(Sport)* chest expander

ex|pan|die|ren [ɛkspan'diːrən] *ptp* **expandiert** VI to expand *(auch Comput)*

Ex|pan|si|on [ɛkspan'zioːn] F -, **-en** *(Phys, Pol)* expansion

Ex|pan|si|ons-: **Ex|pan|si|ons|kurs** M *(Comm)* expansion(ary) strategy; **auf ~ sein** to be expanding *or* growing; **Ex|pan|si|ons|po|li|tik** F expansionism, expansionist policies *pl*; **Ex|pan|si|ons|spei|cher** M *(Comp)* expanded memory(specification), EMS

ex|pan|siv [ɛkspan'ziːf] ADJ *Politik* expansionist; *Wirtschaftszweige* expanding; *Gase* expansile, expansive

ex|pat|ri|ie|ren [ɛkspatri'iːrən] *ptp* **expatriiert** VT to expatriate

Ex|pe|di|ent [ɛkspe'diɛnt] M **-en, -en**, **Ex|pe|di|en|tin** [-'diɛntɪn] F -, **-nen** *(Comm)* dispatch clerk

ex|pe|die|ren [ɛkspe'diːrən] *ptp* **expediert** VT to dispatch, to send (off)

Ex|pe|di|ti|on [ɛkspedi'tsioːn] F -, **-en** **a** *(= Forschungsexpedition, Mil)* expedition **b** *(= Versendung)* dispatch; *(= Versandabteilung)* dispatch office

Ex|pe|ri|ment [ɛksperi'mɛnt] NT **-(e)s, -e** experiment; **~e machen** *or* **anstellen** to carry out *or* do experiments

Ex|pe|ri|men|tal- *in cpds* experimental; **Ex|pe|ri|men|tal|film** M experimental film

ex|pe|ri|men|tell [ɛksperimɛn'tɛl] ADJ experimental ADV experimentally; **~ vorgehen** to work experimentally, to do experimental work; **etw ~ nachweisen** to prove sth by experiment

ex|pe|ri|men|tie|ren [ɛksperimɛn'tiːrən] *ptp* **experimentiert** VI to experiment (*mit* with)

Ex|pe|ri|men|tier|freu|de [ɛksperi'mɛnt] F, *no pl* eagerness to experiment, love of experimentation, great desire to try out new things

ex|pe|ri|men|tier|freu|dig [ɛksperimɛn'tiːɐ-] ADJ **sie ist sehr ~** she likes *or* loves to experiment, she likes *or* loves to try out new things

Ex|per|te [ɛks'pɛrtə] M **-n, -n**, **Ex|per|tin** [-'pɛrtɪn] F -, **-nen** expert (*für* in)

Ex|per|ten-: **Ex|per|ten|an|hö|rung** F special-ist evidence; **Ex|per|ten|kom|mis|si|on** F think tank; **Ex|per|ten|mei|nung** F expert opinion; **Ex|per|ten|sys|tem** NT *(Comput)* expert system; **Ex|per|ten|team** NT team of experts

Ex|per|tin [-ˈpɛrtɪn] F **-, -nen** expert *(für* in)

Ex|per|ti|se [ɛkspɛrˈtiːzə] F **-, -n** (expert's) report

Expl. *abbr von* **Exemplar**

Ex|pli|ka|ti|on [ɛksplikaˈtsioːn] F **-, -en** *(geh)* explication *(form)*

ex|pli|zie|ren [ɛkspliˈtsiːrən] *ptp* **expliziert** VT *(geh)* to explicate *(form)*

ex|pli|zit [ɛkspliˈtsiːt] *(geh)* ADJ explicit ADV explicitly

ex|pli|zi|te [ɛkspliˈtsiːtə] ADV *(geh)* explicitly

ex|plo|die|ren [ɛksploˈdiːrən] *ptp* **explodiert** VI *aux sein (lit, fig)* to explode

Ex|plo|ra|ti|on [ɛksploraˈtsioːn] F **-, -en** *(eines Landes)* exploration; *(Psych)* examination

Ex|plo|ra|ti|ons|fonds M exploratory investment

ex|plo|rie|ren [ɛksploˈriːrən] *ptp* **exploriert** VT *Gelände* to explore

Ex|plo|si|on [ɛksploˈzioːn] F **-, -en** explosion; **etw zur ~ bringen** to detonate *or* explode sth

Ex|plo|si|ons-: **ex|plo|si|ons|ar|tig** ADJ *Geräusch, Wirkung* explosive; *Wachstum, Zunahme* phenomenal ADV explosively; **das Gerücht verbreitete sich ~** the rumour *(Brit) or* rumor *(US)* spread like wildfire; **Ex|plo|si|ons|ge|fahr** F danger of explosion; **Ex|plo|si|ons|mo|tor** M internal combustion engine; **Ex|plo|si|ons|wel|le** F blast (wave); *(Auswirkung)* impact of the blast

ex|plo|siv [ɛksploˈziːf] ADJ *(lit, fig)* explosive

Ex|plo|siv [ɛksploˈziːf] M **-s, -e** [-və], **Ex|plo|siv|laut** M *(Ling)* plosive

Ex|plo|siv|stoff M explosive

Ex|po|nat [ɛkspoˈnaːt] NT **-(e)s, -e** exhibit

Ex|po|nent [ɛkspoˈnɛnt] M **-en, -en** *(Math)* exponent

Ex|po|nent [ɛkspoˈnɛnt] M **-en, -en**, **Ex|po|nen|tin** [-ˈnɛntɪn] F **-, -nen** *(fig)* exponent, spokesman/-woman

Ex|po|nen|ti|al-: **Ex|po|nen|ti|al|funk|ti|on** F *(Math)* exponential function; **Ex|po|nen|ti|al|glei|chung** F *(Math)* exponential equation

ex|po|nen|ti|ell [ɛksponɛnˈtsiɛl] *(Math)* ADJ exponential ADV exponentially; **~ anwachsen** *(Bevölkerung etc)* to rise at an exponential rate

Ex|po|nen|tin [-ˈnɛntɪn] F **-, -nen** *(fig)* → **Exponent**

ex|po|nie|ren [ɛkspoˈniːrən] *ptp* **exponiert** VT (= *herausheben, dated Phot)* to expose; **jdn zu sehr ~** to overexpose sb VR (= *sich auffällig benehmen)* to behave boisterously; *(in der Politik)* to take a prominent stance; *(in Diskussion)* to make one's presence felt, to come on strong *(inf)*; **die Studenten wollen sich nicht mehr ~** the students are keeping a low profile

ex|po|niert [ɛkspoˈniːɐt] PTP *von* **exponieren** ADJ *Lage etc* exposed → *auch* **exponieren**; **an ~er Stelle stehen** to be in an exposed position

Ex|port [ɛksˈpɔrt] M **-(e)s, -e** export *(an +dat* of); *(= Exportwaren)* exports *pl*

Ex|port- *in cpds* export; **Ex|port|ab|tei|lung** F export department; **Ex|port|an|reiz** M export incentive; **Ex|port|ar|ti|kel** M export; **Ex|port|aus|füh|rung** F export model; **Ex|port|be|schrän|kun|gen** PL export restraints *pl*

Ex|por|teur [ɛkspɔrˈtøːɐ] M **-s, -e**, **Ex|por|teu|rin** [-ˈtøːrɪn] F **-, -nen** exporter

Ex|port-: **Ex|port|ge|schäft** NT **a** (= *Firma)* export business **b** (= *Handel)* export business *or* trade; **Ex|port|han|del** M export business *or* trade

ex|por|tie|ren *ptp* **exportiert** VTI *(auch Comput)* to export

Ex|port-: **Ex|port|kauf|frau** F, **Ex|port|kauf|mann** M exporter; **Ex|port|quo|te** F export ratio; **Ex|port|wa|re** F export

Ex|po|sé [ɛkspoˈzeː] NT **-s, -s**, **Ex|po|see** NT **-s, -s** *(für Film, Buch etc)* outline, plan; (= *Denkschrift)* memo(randum)

Ex|po|si|ti|on F *(Liter, Mus)* exposition; (= *Gliederung eines Aufsatzes)* outline, plan

Ex|po|si|tur F *(Aus)* (= *Zweigstelle)* branch; *(Sch)* annexe *(Brit)*, annex *(US)*

ex|press [ɛksˈprɛs] ADV *(dated)* quickly, expeditiously *(form)*; *(Post)* express

Ex|press [ɛksˈprɛs] M **-es, -e** *(Rail)* express (train)

Ex|press-: **Ex|press|brief** M express letter; **Ex|press|gut** NT express goods *pl*

Ex|pres|si|o|nis|mus [ɛksprɛsioˈnɪsmʊs] M **-**, *no pl* expressionism

Ex|pres|si|o|nist [ɛksprɛsioˈnɪst] M **-en, -en**, **Ex|pres|si|o|nis|tin** [-ˈnɪstɪn] F **-, -nen** expressionist

ex|pres|si|o|nis|tisch [ɛksprɛsioˈnɪstɪʃ] ADJ expressionist *no adv*, expressionistic

ex|pres|sis ver|bis [ɛksˈprɛsiːs ˈvɛrbiːs] ADV *(geh)* explicitly, expressly

ex|pres|siv [ɛksprɛˈsiːf] ADJ expressive

Ex|pres|si|vi|tät [ɛksprɛsiviˈtɛːt] F **-**, *no pl* expressiveness

Ex|press-: **Ex|press|rei|ni|gung** F express dry-cleaning service; **Ex|press|zug** M *(old, Aus)* express (train)

Ex|prop|ri|a|ti|on [ɛkspropriaˈtsioːn] F **-, -en** *(geh)* expropriation

ex|qui|sit [ɛkskviˈziːt] *(geh)* ADJ exquisite ADV exquisitely; **~ schmecken** to taste exquisite

ex|tem|po|rie|ren [ɛkstɛmpoˈriːrən] *ptp* **extemporiert** VTI *(geh)* to improvise, to extemporize, to ad-lib

Ex|ten|sion [ɪksˈtɛnʃn] F *(Comput)* extension

ex|ten|siv [ɛkstɛnˈziːf] ADJ *(auch Agr)* extensive

ex|tern [ɛksˈtɛrn] ADJ external; *Fachleute auch* outside *attr*; **ein ~er Schüler** a day boy ADV **die Prüfung fürs Diplom ~ ablegen** to take an external examination to get one's diploma

Ex|ter|ne(r) [ɛksˈtɛrnə] MF *decl as adj (Sch)* day boy/girl

Ex|ter|nist [ɛkstɛrˈnɪst] M **-en, -en**, **Ex|ter|nis|tin** [-ˈnɪstɪn] F **-, -nen** *(Aus)* **a** (= *Schüler)* day boy/girl **b** *pupil educated by private tuition, not at school*

ex|ter|ri|to|ri|al [ɛkstɛritoˈriaːl] ADJ extraterritorial

Ex|ter|ri|to|ri|a|li|tät [ɛkstɛritorialiˈtɛːt] F **-**, *no pl* extraterritoriality

ex|tra [ˈɛkstra] *inv (inf)* ADJ extra; **etwas Extraes** *(inf)* something special ADV (= *besonders, außerordentlich)* extra, (e)specially; (= *eigens, ausschließlich)* (e)specially, just; (= *gesondert)* separately; (= *zusätzlich)* extra, in addition; *(inf: = absichtlich)* on purpose, deliberately; **etw ~ legen** to put sth in a separate place; **ich gebe Ihnen noch ein Exemplar ~** I'll give you an extra copy; **jetzt tu ichs ~!** *(inf)* just for that I will do it!

Ex|tra [ˈɛkstra] NT **-s, -s** extra; **~s** *pl* bells and whistles *(inf)*; *((Comput: Menüpunkt)* tools

Ex|tra-: **Ex|tra|aus|ga|be** F special edition; **Ex|tra|aus|stat|tung** F extras *pl*; **Ex|tra|blatt** NT special edition; (= *zusätzlich zur Zeitung)* special supplement; **ex|tra|fein** ADJ superfine ADV **~ gemahlener Kaffee** very finely ground coffee

ex|tra|hie|ren [ɛkstraˈhiːrən] *ptp* **extrahiert** VT to extract

Ex|tra|klas|se F **ein Wagen/Film der ~** a top (-of-the-)-line model/a first-rate film *or* movie *(esp US)*; **Service** *etc* **der ~** top-flight service / etc=; **das ist ~** that's brilliant *or* fantastic

Ex|trakt [ɛksˈtrakt] M (MED, PHARM AUCH NT) **-(e)s, -e** extract; *(von Buch etc)* synopsis; **etw im ~ wiedergeben** to summarize sth, to give a summary of sth

Ext|ra|or|di|na|ri|us [ɛkstralɔrdiˈnaːriʊs] M *(Univ)* ≈ reader *(Brit)*, ≈ associate professor *(US)*

Ext|ra|po|la|ti|on [ɛkstrapolaˈtsioːn] F **-, -en** *(Math, fig)* extrapolation

ext|ra|po|lie|ren [ɛktrapoˈliːrən] *ptp* **extrapoliert** VTI *(Math, fig)* to extrapolate

ext|ra|ter|rest|risch ADJ extraterrestrial

Ext|ra|tour F *(fig inf)* special favour *(Brit) or* favor *(US)*; **er will immer eine ~** he always wants something different *or* special

ext|ra|ute|rin [ɛkstraluteˈriːn] ADJ extra-uterine

ext|ra|va|gant [ɛkstravaˈgant] ADJ extravagant; *Kleidung auch* flamboyant ADV extravagantly

Ext|ra|va|ganz [ɛkstravaˈgants] F **-, -en** extravagance; *(von Kleidung auch)* flamboyance

ext|ra|ver|tiert [ɛkstravɛrˈtiːɐt] ADJ *(Psych)* extrovert

Ext|ra|wurst F **a** *(inf: = Sonderwunsch)* special favour *(Brit) or* favor *(US)*; **jdm eine ~ braten** to make an exception of *or* for sb; **er will immer eine ~ (gebraten haben)** he always wants something different *or* special **b** *(Aus: = Lyoner) type of pork or veal sausage*

ext|rem [ɛksˈtreːm] ADJ extreme; *Belastung* excessive; **du bist immer so ~** you always go to extremes; **ist ja ~!** *(sl)* it's way out *(inf)* ADV *kalt, rechts, primitiv* extremely; *sich verbessern, sich verschlechtern, sinken, steigen* radically; **~ schlecht/gut** *etc* extremely badly/well *etc*; **ich habe mich ~ beeilt** I hurried as much as I could

Ext|rem [ɛksˈtreːm] NT **-s, -e** extreme; **von einem ~ ins andere fallen** to go from one extreme to the other

Ext|rem|fall M extreme (case)

Ext|re|mist [ɛkstreˈmɪst] M **-en, -en**, **Ext|re|mis|tin** [-ˈmɪstɪn] F **-, -nen** extremist

ext|re|mis|tisch [ɛkstreˈmɪstɪʃ] ADJ extremist

Ext|re|mi|tät [ɛkstremiˈtɛːt] F **-, -en** *usu pl* extremity *usu pl*

Ext|rem-: **Ext|rem|si|tu|a|ti|on** F extreme situation; **Ext|rem|sport** M, **Ext|rem|sport|art** F extreme sport; **Ext|rem|wert** M extreme (value)

ext|ro|ver|tiert [ɛkstrovɛrˈtiːɐt] ADJ = **extravertiert**

Ex-und-Hopp NT **-**, *no pl (pej)* throwaway mentality

Ex-und-hopp- *in cpds (pej)* throwaway; **~Mentalität** throwaway mentality

ex|zel|lent [ɛkstsɛˈlɛnt] *(geh)* ADJ excellent ADV **~ schmecken** to taste excellent; **~ speisen** to have an excellent meal; **sich ~ fühlen** to feel fantastic

Ex|zel|lenz [ɛkstsɛˈlɛnts] F **-, -en** Excellency

ex|zent|risch [ɛksˈtsɛntrɪʃ] ADJ *(Math, fig)* eccentric

Ex|zent|ri|zi|tät [ɛkstsɛntritsiˈtɛːt] F **-, -en** *(Math, Tech, fig)* eccentricity

ex|zer|pie|ren [ɛkstsɛrˈpiːrən] *ptp* **exzerpiert** VT to select *or* extract *(aus* from)

Ex|zerpt [ɛksˈtsɛrpt] NT **-(e)s, -e** excerpt

Ex|zess [ɛksˈtsɛs] M **-es, -e** **a** excess; **bis zum ~** excessively, to excess; **etw bis zum ~ treiben** to take sth to excess *or* extremes; **bis zum ~ gesteigerter Hass** excessive hate **b** *usu pl (= Ausschreitung)* excess

ex|zes|siv [ɛkstsɛˈsiːf] ADJ excessive

Eye|li|ner [ˈailainɐ] M **-s, -** eyeliner

EZB [eːtsetˈbeː] F *abbr von* **Europäische Zentralbank** ECB

E-Zug [ˈeː-] M *abbr von* **Eilzug**

F

F, f [ɛf] NT -, - F, f; **nach Schema F** *(inf)* in the usual way

F *abbr von* **Fahrenheit, Farad, Fernschnellzug**

f. *abbr von* **und folgende(r, s)**

Fa. *abbr von* **Firma**

fa [fa:] INTERJ *(Mus)* fa(h)

Fa|bel ['fa:bl] F -, -n **a** fable **b** *(inf)* fantastic story **c** *(Liter: = Handlung)* plot

Fa|bel-: **Fa|bel|buch** NT book of fables; **Fa|bel|dich|ter(in)** M(F) writer of fables, fabulist *(form)*

Fa|be|lei [fa:bə'lai] F -, -en **a** *(= das Fabeln)* romancing **b** *(= Geschichte)* fantastic story

Fa|bel-: **Fa|bel|ge|schöpf** NT, **Fa|bel|ge|stalt** F mythical creature; **fa|bel|haft** ADJ splendid, magnificent; *(inf: = unglaublich groß)* fantastic, fabulous ADV splendidly, magnificently; *(inf: = sehr, überaus)* fantastically, fabulously

fa|beln ['fa:bln] VI to romance VT *Unsinn* to concoct, to fabricate

Fa|bel-: **Fa|bel|tier** NT mythical creature; **der Fuchs als ~** the fox (as he appears) in fables; **Fa|bel|welt** F world *or* realm of fantasy; **Fa|bel|we|sen** NT mythical creature

Fab|rik [fa'bri:k] F -, -en factory; *(= Papier-, Baumwollfabrik)* mill; **in die ~ gehen** *(inf)* to work in a factory; **(Preis) ab ~** (price) ex factory *or* works

Fab|rik|an|la|ge F (manufacturing) plant; *(= Fabrikgelände)* factory premises *pl*

Fab|ri|kant [fabri'kant] M -en, -en, **Fab|ri|kan|tin** [-'kantɪn] F -, -nen **a** *(= Fabrikbesitzer)* industrialist **b** *(= Hersteller)* manufacturer

Fab|rik-: **Fab|rik|ar|beit** F, *no pl* factory work; **das ist ~** that is factory-made; **Fab|rik|ar|bei|ter(in)** M(F) factory worker

Fab|ri|kat [fabri'ka:t] NT -(e)s, -e **a** *(= Marke)* make; *(von Nahrungs- und Genussmitteln)* brand **b** *(= Produkt)* product; *(= Ausführung)* model

Fab|ri|ka|ti|on [fabrika'tsio:n] F -, -en manufacture, production

Fab|ri|ka|ti|ons-: **Fab|ri|ka|ti|ons|feh|ler** M manufacturing fault; **Fab|ri|ka|ti|ons|stät|te** F manufacturing *or* production plant

Fab|rik-: **Fab|rik|bau** M *pl* **-bauten** factory (building); **Fab|rik|di|rek|tor(in)** M(F) managing director (of a factory); **fab|rik|frisch** ADJ straight from the factory; **Fab|rik|ge|bäu|de** NT factory building; **Fab|rik|ge|län|de** NT factory site; **Fab|rik|hal|le** F factory building

Fab|rik|ler [fa'bri:klɐ] M -s, -, **Fab|rik|le|rin** [-ərɪn] F -, -nen *(Sw)* factory worker

fab|rik-: **fab|rik|mä|ßig** ADJ **~e Herstellung** mass production; **~er Massenmord** systematic mass murder ADV **~ hergestellt** mass-produced; **fab|rik|neu** ADJ straight from the factory; *(= nagelneu)* brand-new ADV **~ aussehen** to be in mint condition

Fab|riks- *in cpds (Aus)* = **Fabrik-**

Fab|rik-: **Fab|rik|schiff** NT factory ship; **Fab|rik|ver|kauf** M *(= Laden mit Fabrikware)* factory shop *or* outlet; **Fab|rik|wa|re** F *(einzelner Artikel)* manufactured article; *(Gesamtheit von Artikeln)* manufactured goods *pl or* articles *pl*

fab|ri|zie|ren [fabri'tsi:rən] *ptp* **fabriziert** VT **a** *(dated) (= industriell produzieren)* to manufacture, to produce, to fabricate *(dated)* **b** *(inf) Möbelstück etc* to make; *geistiges Produkt* to produce; *Alibi, Lügengeschichte* to concoct, to fabricate **c** *(inf: = anstellen)* to get up to *(inf)*

Fa|bu|lant [fabu'lant] M -en, -en, **Fa|bu|lan|tin** [-'lantɪn] F -, -nen *(geh)* **a** *(pej)* fabulist **b** *(= Erzähler)* romancer, storyteller

fa|bu|lie|ren [fabu'li:rən] *ptp* **fabuliert** VI *(geh)* **a** *(pej: = schwätzen)* to romance **b** *(= fantasievoll erzählen)* to spin a yarn; **er fabulierte, wie ...** he spun some yarns about how ...

Fa|bu|lie|rer [fabu'li:rɐ] M -s, -, **Fa|bu|lie|re|rin** [-ərɪn] F -, -nen *(geh)* romancer, storyteller

fa|bu|lös [fabu'lø:s] ADJ *(geh)* fabulous *(liter)*; *(= unglaubwürdig, hum: = großartig)* fantastic

Face|lif|ting ['fe:sliftɪŋ] NT -s, -s *(lit, fig)* face-lift; **sich einem ~ unterziehen** to have a face-lift

Fa|cet|te [fa'sɛtə] F -, -n facet

Fa|cet|ten-: **fa|cet|ten|ar|tig** ADJ facet(t)ed ADV *schleifen* in facets; **Fa|cet|ten|au|ge** NT compound eye; **Fa|cet|ten|schliff** M facet(t)ing; **ein Amethyst mit ~** a facet(t)ed amethyst

fa|cet|tie|ren [fasɛ'ti:rən] *ptp* **facettiert** VT to facet; **facettiert** *(lit, fig)* facet(t)ed

Fach [fax] NT -(e)s, **=er** ['fɛçɐ] **a** compartment; *(in Tasche, Brieftasche, Portemonnaie etc auch)* pocket; *(in Schrank, Regal etc)* shelf; *(für Briefe etc)* pigeonhole **b** *(= Wissens-, Sachgebiet)* subject; *(= Gebiet)* field; *(= Handwerk)* trade; **ein Mann vom ~** an expert; **sein ~ verstehen** to know one's stuff *(inf) or* one's subject/trade; **das ~ Medizin** *etc* medicine *etc* **c** *(Theat)* mode

-fach [fax] ADJ *suf (= -mal)* times; **dreifach** three times; **für die dreifache Summe** for three times the amount → **vierfach** *etc*

Fach-: **Fach|abi|tur** NT *(Sch) examination entitling the successful candidate to study at a Fachhochschule or certain subjects at a university*; **Fach|ar|bei|ter(in)** M(F) skilled worker; **Fach|ar|bei|ter|brief** M certificate of proficiency; **Fach|arzt** M, **Fach|ärz|tin** F specialist *(für* in); **fach|ärzt|lich** ADJ *Weiterbildung* specialist *attr*; *Untersuchung, Behandlung* by a specialist; **ein ~es Attest** a certificate from *or* signed by a specialist; **ein ~es Gutachten** a specialist's opinion; **Fach|aus|bil|dung** F specialist training; **Fach|aus|druck** M technical *or* specialist term; **Fach|aus|schuss** M committee of experts; **Fach|be|griff** M technical *or* specialist term; **Fach|be|ra|ter(in)** M(F) technical consultant; **Fach|be|reich** M **a** *(= Fachgebiet)* (special) field **b** *(Univ)* school, faculty; **fach|be|zo|gen** ADJ specifically related to one's/the subject; *(= fachlich beschränkt) Job, Weiterbildung, Kenntnisse* specialized; **Fach|bib|li|o|thek** F specialist library; **Fach|blatt** NT (specialist) journal; **ein medizinisches ~** a medical journal; **Fach|buch** NT reference book; **wasserbautechnische Fachbücher** specialist books on hydraulic engineering; **Fach|buch|hand|lung** F specialist bookshop; **~ für Medizin/Mathematik** *etc* bookshop specializing in medical/mathematical *etc* books; **Fach|buch|ver|lag** M specialist publishing company; **~ für Geografie/Fremdsprachen** *etc* publisher of geography/modern language *etc* books; **Fach|chi|ne|sisch** NT, *no pl (inf)* technical jargon *or* mumbo-jumbo *(inf)*

fä|cheln ['fɛçln] *(geh)* VT to fan; *Blätter etc* to stir VI to stir

Fä|cher ['fɛçɐ] M -s, - fan; *(fig)* range, array

Fä|cher-: **fä|cher|ar|tig** ADJ fanlike ADV like a fan; **Fä|cher|be|sen** M *(Hort)* wire rake; **fä|cher|för|mig** ADJ fan-shaped ADV like a fan; **Fä|cher|ge|wöl|be** NT fan vaulting; **ein ~** a fan vault; **Fä|cher|kom|bi|na|ti|on** F *(Sch, Univ)* combination of subjects

fä|chern ['fɛçɐn] VT to fan (out); *(fig)* to diversify; **gefächert** diverse; *Auswahl auch* varied; *Unterricht* diversified VR to fan out

Fä|cher|pal|me F fan palm

fä|cher|über|grei|fend ADJ, ADV = **fachübergreifend**

Fä|che|rung F -, -en variety, range, diversity

Fach-: **Fach|frau** F expert; **fach|fremd** ADJ *Mitarbeiter* with no background in the subject; *Leser auch* uninitiated; *Lektüre, Aufgaben etc* unconnected (with the/one's subject); *Methode* foreign to the subject ADV → **Fach b** outside one's own subject/field, in another subject/field; **Fach|ge|biet** NT (special) field; **fach|ge|bun|den** ADJ → **Fach b** related (to the field/subject); **Fach|ge|lehr|te(r)** MF *decl as adj* specialist; **fach|ge|mäß, fach|ge|recht** ADJ expert; *Ausbildung* specialist *attr* ADV expertly; **nicht ~** incompetently, incorrectly; **Fach|ge|schäft** NT specialist shop, specialty store *(US)*; **~ für Lederwaren** leather shop *or* store *(esp US)*, shop *or* store *(esp US)* specializing in leather goods; **Fach|ge|spräch** NT professional *or* technical discussion; **Fach|grö|ße** F authority; **Fach|grup|pe** F professional group; *(Univ)* study group; *(= Gruppe von Experten)* team of specialists; **Fach|han|del** M specialist shops *pl*, specialty stores *pl (US)*; **Fach|händ|ler(in)** M(F) specialist supplier; **Fach|hoch|schul|ab|schluss** M diploma *(from higher education institution)*; **Fach|hoch|schu|le** F *higher education institution*

> **FACHHOCHSCHULE**
>
> **Fachhochschulen**, or **FH**, are universities of applied sciences. They were set up to teach technology, social and natural sciences, and art.
>
> A **Fachabitur** is the minimum requirement for admission to a **FH**, although many **Fachhochschulen** require students to take an aptitude test as well.
>
> Austria and Switzerland have similar systems.

Fach-: **Fach|idi|ot(in)** M(F) *(inf)* person who can think of nothing but his/her subject, philosophy/chemistry *etc* freak *(inf)*; **Fach|jar|gon** M technical jargon; **Fach|kennt|nis|se** PL specialized knowledge; **Fach|kol|le|ge** M, **Fach|kol|le|gin** F professional colleague; **Fach|kraft** F qualified employee; **Fach|kräf|te|man|gel** M lack of skilled *or* qualified personnel; **Fach|krei|se** PL **in ~n** among experts;

fạch|kun|dig ADJ informed; *(= erfahren)* with a knowledge of the subject; *(= fachmännisch)* proficient ADV **jdn ~ beraten** to give sb informed advice; **~ betreut werden** to receive expert service; **fạch|kund|lich** [-kʊntlɪç] ADJ **~er Unterricht** teaching of technical subjects; **Fạch|leh|rer(in)** M(F) specialist subject teacher; **Fạch|lei|ter(in)** M(F) head of department

fạch|lich [ˈfaxlɪç] ADJ technical; *Ausbildung* specialist *attr*; *Spezialisierung* in one aspect of a/the subject; *(= beruflich)* professional ADV **ein ~ ausgezeichneter Lehrer** a teacher who is academically excellent; **~ hervorragend sein** to be excellent in one's field; **~ hoch qualifizierte Mitarbeiter** staff members who are highly qualified in their field; **sich ~ qualifizieren** to gain qualifications in one's field; **~ auf dem Laufenden bleiben** to keep up to date in one's subject; **das ~ zuständige Ressort** the department responsible for such matters

Fach-: **Fạch|li|te|ra|tur** F specialist *or* technical literature; **Fạch|ma|ga|zin** NT *(= Zeitschrift)* specialist magazine; *(von Berufszweig)* professional magazine; *(gewerblich)* trade magazine; **Fạch|mann** M *pl* **-leute** *or (rare)* **-männer** expert; **fạch|män|nisch** [-mɛnɪʃ] ADJ expert ADV expertly; **~ ausgeführt** expertly done; **Fạch|markt** M specialist shop *(esp Brit)*, specialty store *(US)*; **Fạch|ober|schu|le** F College of Further Education; **Fạch|per|so|nal** NT specialist staff; **Fạch|pres|se** F specialist *or* technical publications *pl*; **die medizinische/philologische** *etc* **~** the medical/philological *etc* publications *pl*; **Fạch|prü|fung** F professional examination; **Fạch|re|dak|teur(in)** M(F) (special) editor; **~ für Sport/Naturwissenschaft** *etc* sports/science *etc* editor; **Fạch|rich|tung** F subject area; **die ~ Mathematik** mathematics; **Fạch|schaft** [ˈfaxʃaft] F **-, -en** *(Univ)* students *pl* of the/a department; **Fạch|schu|le** F technical college; **Fạch|schul|rei|fe** F entrance qualification for a technical college; **Fạch|sim|pe|lei** [faxzɪmpəˈlai] F **-, -en** *(inf)* shoptalk; **fạch|sim|peln** [ˈfaxzɪmpln] VI *insep (inf)* to talk shop; **fạch|spe|zi|fisch** ADJ technical, specialist *attr* ADV *ausbilden* in the field; *arbeiten* in one's own field; **Fạch|spra|che** F technical terminology; **fạch|sprach|lich** ADJ technical ADV in technical terminology; **Fạch|stu|di|um** NT *course of study at a technical college*; **Fạch|ter|mi|nus** M technical term; **Fạch|text** M specialist text; **fạch|über|grei|fend** ADJ *Problematik, Lernziel etc* inter-disciplinary, which extends across the disciplines ADV across the disciplines; **Fạch|ver|band** M *(im Handel)* trade association; *(von Ärzten etc)* association; **Fạch|ver|mitt|lungs|dienst** M professional placement agency; **Fạch|vo|ka|bu|lar** NT technical vocabulary; **Fạch|welt** F experts *pl*; **Fạch|werk** NT, *no pl* half-timbering; **Fạch|werk|bau** M **a** *(= Fachwerkhaus)* half-timbered building *or* house **b** *no pl (auch* **Fachwerkbauweise**) half-timbering; **Fạch|werk|haus** NT half-timbered house; **Fạch|wirt(in)** M(F) business administrator; **Fạch|wis|sen** NT (specialized) knowledge of the/one's subject; **Fạch|wis|sen|schaft|ler(in)** M(F) specialist *or* expert (in a particular subject); **fạch|wis|sen|schaft|lich** ADJ technical; *Publikation, Interesse auch* specialist *attr*; **Fạch|wort** NT *pl* **-wörter** specialist *or* technical term; **Fạch|wör|ter|buch** NT specialist dictionary; *(wissenschaftliches auch)* technical dictionary; **Fạch|wort|schatz** M technical *or* specialized vocabulary; **Fạch|zeit|schrift** F specialist journal; *(technisch)* technical journal; *(naturwissenschaftlich)* scientific journal; *(für Berufe)* trade journal

Fạ|ckel [ˈfakl] F **-, -n** *(lit, fig)* torch; *(der Revolution auch, des Glaubens)* flame

Fạ|ckel|lauf M torch race

fạ|ckeln [ˈfakln] VI *(inf)* to shillyshally *(esp Brit inf)*; **nicht lange gefackelt!** no shillyshallying! *(esp Brit inf)*; **da wird nicht lange gefackelt** there won't be any shillyshallying *(esp Brit inf)*

Fa|ckel-: **Fạ|ckel|schein** M torchlight; **im ~ sah man ...** you could see by the light of the torches ...; **Fạ|ckel|zug** M torchlight procession

Fac|to|ring [ˈfɛktərɪŋ] NT **-s**, *no pl (Fin)* factoring

fad [faːt] ADJ *pred* **a** = **fade ADJ a, b ADV b** *(Aus, S Ger) (= zimperlich)* soft, wet, soppy *(all inf)*

Fäd|chen [ˈfɛːtçən] NT **-s, -** *dim von* **Faden**

fa|de [ˈfaːdə] ADJ **a** *Geschmack* insipid; *Essen auch* tasteless **b** *(fig: = langweilig)* dull **c** *(Aus, S Ger)* = **fad b** ADV **~ schmecken** to have not much of a taste

fä|deln [ˈfɛːdln] VT to thread *(auf etw acc* onto sth) VR **sich durch etw ~** to thread one's way through sth

Fa|den [ˈfaːdn] M **-s, ¨** [ˈfɛːdn] **a** *(lit, fig)* thread; *(an Marionetten)* string; *(Med)* stitch; **der rote ~** *(fig)* the leitmotif, the central theme; **den ~ verlieren** *(fig)* to lose the thread; **alle Fäden laufen hier zusammen** this is the hub of the whole business; **er hält alle Fäden (fest) in der Hand** he holds the reins; **sein Leben hing an einem (dünnen** *or* **seidenen) ~** his life was hanging by a thread; **keinen guten ~ an jdm/etw lassen** *(inf)* to tear sb/sth to shreds *(inf) or* pieces *(inf)*
b *(= Spinnenfaden etc)* thread; *(= Bohnenfaden)* string; **der Klebstoff zieht Fäden** the glue is tacky *(Brit) or* gummy *(US)*; **der Käse zieht Fäden** the cheese has gone stringy; **die Bohnen haben Fäden** the beans are stringy

Fa|den M **-s, -** *(Naut)* fathom

Fa|den-: **fa|den|för|mig** ADJ thread-like; **Fa|den|hef|tung** [-hɛftʊŋ] F **-, -en** *(Typ)* (thread-)stitching; **Fa|den|kreuz** NT crosshair; **jdn/etw im ~ haben** to have sb/sth in one's sights; **ins ~** *(+gen)* **geraten** to come into the firing line of; **Fa|den|nu|deln** PL vermicelli *pl*; **fa|den|schei|nig** [-ʃainɪç] ADJ **a** threadbare **b** *(fig) Argument, Grund* flimsy; *Moral* threadbare *no adv*; *Ausrede* transparent; *Trost* poor; **Fa|den|schlag** M *(Sw Sew)* basted *or* tacked seam; **Fa|den|wurm** M threadworm

Fad|heit F **-, -en** **a** *(von Essen)* tastelessness **b** *(fig: = Langeweile)* dullness

Fa|ding [ˈfeːdɪŋ] NT **-(s)**, *no pl (Rad)* fading

fa|di|sie|ren [fadiˈziːrən] *ptp* **fadisiert** VR *(Aus)* = **langweilen VR**

Fa|gott [faˈgɔt] NT **-(e)s, -e** bassoon

Fa|gott|blä|ser(in) M(F), **Fa|got|tist** [fagɔˈtɪst] M **-en, -en**, **Fa|got|tis|tin** [-ˈtɪstɪn] F **-, -nen** bassoonist

Fä|he [ˈfɛːə] F **-, -n** *(Hunt) (= Füchsin)* vixen; *(= Dächsin)* sow

fä|hig [ˈfɛːɪç] ADJ **a** *(= tüchtig) Mensch, Mitarbeiter etc* capable, competent, able; **sie ist ein ~er Kopf** she has an able mind **b** *pred (= befähigt, bereit)* capable *(zu, +gen* of); **(dazu) ~ sein, etw zu tun** to be capable of doing sth; **bei dem Lärm bin ich keines klaren Gedankens ~** I can't think straight *or* hear myself think with all this noise; **zu allem ~ sein** to be capable of anything

Fä|hig|keit F **-, -en** *(= Begabung)* ability; *(= Tüchtigkeit auch)* capability; *(= Geschicklichkeit auch)* aptitude; *(= praktisches Können)* skill; **die ~ haben, etw zu tun** to be capable of doing sth; **eine Frau von großen ~en** a woman of great ability; **bei deinen ~en ...** with your talents ...

fahl [faːl] ADJ pale; *Mondlicht auch* wan *(liter)*

fahl|gelb ADJ pale yellow

Fahl|heit F **-**, *no pl* paleness; *(von Mondlicht auch)* wanness *(liter)*

Fähn|chen [ˈfɛːnçən] NT **-s, -** **a** *dim von* **Fahne**, → **Wind a** **b** *(= Wimpel)* pennant **c** *(inf, usu pej)* flimsy dress

fahn|den [ˈfaːndn] VI to search *(nach* for)

Fahn|der [ˈfaːndɐ] M **-s, -**, **Fahn|de|rin** [ˈfaːndərɪn] F **-, -nen** investigator

Fahn|dung F **-, -en** search

Fahn|dungs-: **Fahn|dungs|ak|ti|on** F search; **Fahn|dungs|buch** NT wanted (persons) list; **Fahn|dungs|dienst** M CID *(Brit)*, detective branch; **Fahn|dungs|er|folg** M successful result of a/the search; **~e erzielen** to hunt successfully for criminals; **Fahn|dungs|lis|te** F wanted (persons) list

Fah|ne [ˈfaːnə] F **-, -n** **a** flag; *(von Verein etc auch)* banner; *(Mil, von Pfadfinder etc auch)* colours *pl (Brit)*, colors *pl (US)*; **die ~ hochhalten** *(fig)* to keep the flag flying; **die ~ des Glaubens** *etc* **hochhalten** *(fig geh)* to hold aloft the flag *or* banner of faith *etc*; **etw auf seine ~ schreiben** *(fig)* to take up the cause of sth; **mit fliegenden** *or* **wehenden ~n** with beat of drum and flourish of trumpets *(liter)*, with flying colors *(US)*; **mit fliegenden** *or* **wehenden ~n untergehen** to go down with all flags flying; **zu den ~n eilen** *(old, geh)* to join the colours *(Brit) or* colors *(US, old)*; **jdn zu den ~n rufen** *(old, geh)* to call sb up (for military service); **unter der ~ stehen** *(old, geh)*, **der ~ folgen** *(old, geh)* to follow the flag *(old)*, to serve with the colours *(Brit) or* colors *(US, old)*; **unter jds ~n fechten** *or* **kämpfen** *(old, geh)* to fight under sb's flag → **Wind a**
b *(inf)* **eine ~ haben** to reek of alcohol; **man konnte seine ~ schon aus drei Meter Entfernung riechen** you could smell the alcohol on his breath ten feet away
c *(Typ)* galley (proof)

Fah|nen-: **Fah|nen|ab|zug** M *(Typ)* galley (proof); **Fah|nen|eid** M oath of allegiance; **Fah|nen|flucht** F *(Mil, fig)* desertion; **fah|nen|flüch|tig** ADJ **~ sein** *(Mil, fig)* to be a deserter, to have deserted; **~ werden** *(Mil, fig)* to desert; **ein ~er Soldat** a deserter; **Fah|nen|flüch|ti|ge(r)** MF *decl as adj (Mil, fig)* deserter; **fah|nen|ge|schmückt** [-gəʃmʏkt] ADJ beflagged, decorated with flags; **Fah|nen|jun|ker** M **a** *(Mil: = Offiziersanwärter)* officer cadet **b** *(Mil Hist)* colour *(Brit) or* color *(US)* sergeant; **Fah|nen|mast** M flagpole; **Fah|nen|schmuck** M drapery of flags and bunting; **im ~** decked out with flags and bunting; **Fah|nen|stan|ge** F flagpole; **Fah|nen|trä|ger(in)** M(F) standard-bearer, colour-bearer *(Brit)*, color-bearer *(US)*; **Fah|nen|tuch** NT **a** *pl* **-tuche** *(Tex)* bunting **b** *pl* **-tücher** *(= Fahne)* flag; **Fah|nen|wei|he** F consecration of the flag

Fähn|lein [ˈfɛːnlain] NT **-s, -** **a** *dim von* **Fahne** **b** *(= kleine Gruppe)* troop

Fähn|rich [ˈfɛːnrɪç] M **-s, -e** *(Hist)* standard-bearer; *(Mil)* sergeant; **~ zur See** petty officer

Fahr|aus|weis M **a** *(Sw form)* ticket **b** *(Sw)* = **Führerschein**

Fahr|bahn F carriageway *(Brit)*, highway *(US)*, roadway; *(= Fahrspur)* lane; **„Betreten der ~ verboten"** "pedestrians keep off the road"

Fahr|bahn-: **Fahr|bahn|mar|kie|rung** F road marking; **Fahr|bahn|ver|en|gung** F narrowing of the carriageway *(Brit) or* roadway *(US)*; *(= Verkehrsschild)* "road narrows"; **Fahr|bahn|ver|schmut|zung** F dirt on the road

Fahr-: **fahr|bar** ADJ **a** *Liege, Ständer etc* on castors; *Kran, Abschussrampe etc* mobile; **~er Untersatz** *(hum)* wheels *pl (hum)* **b** *(dated)* = **befahrbar**; **fahr|be|reit** ADJ in running order; **etw ~ machen** to get sth in(to) running order; **Fahr|be|reit|schaft** F **a** chauffeur-driven carpool; **~ haben** to be the driver on duty **b** *(eines Fahrzeugs)* good running order

Fähr-: **Fähr|be|trieb** M ferry service; **es herrschte reger ~** there were a lot of ferries running; **Fähr|boot** NT ferry (boat)

Fahr-: **Fahr|bü|che|rei** F mobile library; **Fahr|damm** M *(dial)* carriageway *(Brit)*, highway *(US)*, roadway; *(= Fahrspur)* lane

Fähr|dienst [ˈfɛːɐ-] M ferry service

Fahr-: **Fahr|dienst** M **a ~ haben** to have crew duty **b** *(Rail)* rail service; **Fahr|dienst|lei|ter(in)** M(F) area manager; **Fahr|draht** M *(Rail etc)* overhead contact wire *or* line

Fäh|re [ˈfɛːrə] F **-, -n** ferry

Fahr|ei|gen|schaft F *usu pl* handling characteristic; **die ~en eines Wagens** the handling of a car; **der Wagen hat hervorragende ~en** the car handles excellently

fah|ren ['fa:rən]
pret **fuhr** [fu:ɐ], *ptp* **gefahren** [gə'fa:rən]

1 INTRANSITIVES VERB 3 REFLEXIVES VERB
2 TRANSITIVES VERB

1 – INTRANSITIVES VERB

a = sich fortbewegen *(aux sein) (Fahrzeug, Fahrgast)* to go; *(Autofahrer)* to drive; *(Zweiradfahrer)* to ride; *(Schiff)* to sail; *(Kran, Kamera, Rolltreppe etc)* to move; **mit dem Auto fahren** to go by car; **mit dem Zug fahren** to go by train *or* rail; **mit dem Rad fahren** to cycle, to go by bike; **mit dem Motorrad/Taxi fahren** to go by motorbike/taxi; **mit dem Bus fahren** to go by bus, to ride the bus *(US)*; **mit dem Aufzug fahren** to take the lift, to ride *or* take the elevator *(US)*; **ich fuhr mit dem Fahrrad/Auto in die Stadt** I cycled/drove into town, I went into town on my bike/in the car; **möchtest du lieber mit dem Fahrrad oder mit dem Auto fahren?** would you rather go by bike or by car?; **wir sind mit dem Auto gekommen, und meine Frau ist gefahren** we came by car and my wife drove; **wollen wir fahren oder zu Fuß gehen?** shall we go by car or walk?; **links/rechts fahren** to drive on the left/right; **wie lange fährt man von hier nach Basel?** how long does it take to get to Basle from here?; **ich fahre mit dem Auto nach Schweden** I'm taking the car to Sweden, I'm going to Sweden by car; **mein Chor fährt nächstes Jahr wieder nach Schottland** next year my choir is going to Scotland again; **wie fährt man von hier zum Bahnhof?** how do you get to the station from here?; **wie fährt man am schnellsten zum Bahnhof?** what is the quickest way to the station?; **ich fahre lieber in der Stadt** I prefer driving *or* to drive in town; **zweiter Klasse fahren** to travel *or* go second class; **per Anhalter** *or* **Autostopp fahren** to hitch (-hike); **gegen einen Baum fahren** to drive *or* go into a tree; **über den See fahren** to cross the lake; **die Lok fährt elektrisch/mit Dampf** the engine is powered by electricity/is steam-driven; **der Wagen fährt sehr ruhig** the car is very quiet; **gen Himmel fahren** *(liter)* to ascend into heaven; **zur Hölle fahren** *(liter)* to descend into hell; **fahr zur Hölle** *or* **zum Teufel!** *(old)* the devil take you! *(old)* → **fahrend, Grube** *etc*

b = losfahren *(aux sein) (Verkehrsmittel, Fahrer, Mitfahrer)* to go, to leave; **wann fährt der nächste Bus nach Bamberg?** when does the next bus to Bamberg go *or* leave?; **wann fährst du morgen nach Glasgow? fährst du früh?** when are you leaving for Glasgow tomorrow? are you leaving early in the morning?; **einen fahren lassen** *(inf)* to let off *(inf)*

c = verkehren *(aux sein)* **es fahren täglich zwei Fähren** there are two ferries a day; **fahren da keine Züge?** don't any trains go there?; **fahren Sie bis Walterplatz?** do you go as far as Walterplatz?; **der Bus fährt alle fünf Minuten** there's a bus every five minutes

d = rasen, schießen *(aux sein)* **es fuhr ihm durch den Kopf, dass ...** the thought flashed through his mind that ...; **was ist (denn) in dich gefahren?** what's got into you?; **in die Kleider fahren** to throw on one's clothes; **ich bin hastig in die Kleider gefahren** I hastily pulled on my clothes; **der Blitz fuhr in die Eiche** the lightning struck the oak; **die Katze fuhr ihm ins Gesicht** the cat leapt *or* sprang at his face; **der Hexenschuss fuhr ihm durch den Rücken** a twinge of lumbago shot up his back

e = zurechtkommen *(aux sein)* **(mit jdm) gut fahren** to get on well (with sb); **mit etw gut fahren** to be OK with sth *(inf)*; **mit ihm sind wir gut/schlecht gefahren** we made a good/bad choice when we picked him; **mit diesem teuren Modell fahren Sie immer gut** you'll always be OK with this expensive model *(inf)*; **mit der Billigreise nach Tunesien sind wir schlecht gefahren** the cheap trip to Tunisia turned out badly; **(bei etw) gut/schlecht fahren** to do well/badly (with sth); **du fährst besser, wenn ...** you would do better if ...

f = streichen *(aux sein or haben)* **er fuhr mit der Hand/einem Tuch über den Tisch** he ran his hand/a cloth over the table; **ihre Hand fuhr sanft über sein Haar** she gently ran her hand over his hair; **jdm/sich durchs Haar fahren** to run one's fingers through sb's/one's hair; **sich** *(dat)* **mit der Hand über die Stirn fahren** to pass one's hand over one's brow

g Film *(aux haben) (= eine Kamerafahrt machen)* to track; **die Kamera fuhr auf seine Hand** the camera tracked to his hand

2 – TRANSITIVES VERB

a = lenken *(aux haben) Auto, Bus, Zug etc* to drive; *Fahrrad, Motorrad* to ride; **schrottreif** *or* **zu Schrott fahren** *(durch Unfall)* to write off; *(durch Verschleiß)* to drive into the ground

b = benutzen: Straße, Strecke etc *(aux sein)* to take; **welche Strecke fährt die Linie 59?** which way does the number 59 go?; **einen Umweg fahren** to go a long way round, to go out of one's way; **wir sind die Umleitung gefahren** we followed the diversion *or* detour; **ich fahre lieber Autobahn** I prefer (driving on) motorways *(Brit) or* freeways *(US)*; **diesen steilen Berg musst du im ersten Gang fahren** you have to go up *or* take this steep hill in first gear; **eine so gebirgige Strecke darfst du im Winter nicht ohne Schneeketten fahren** you shouldn't drive such a mountainous route in winter without snow chains → **Eisenbahn, Karussell, Schlitten a**

c = benutzen: Kraftstoff etc *(aux haben)* to use; *Reifen* to drive on

d = befördern *(aux haben)* to take; *(= hierherfahren)* to bring; *Personen* to drive, to take; **Kinder in die Schule fahren** to take children to school; **jemanden ins Krankenhaus fahren** to take sb to hospital; **die Spedition fährt Fisch von der Nordsee nach Nürnberg** the haulage firm transports *or* takes fish from the North Sea to Nuremberg; **wer hat Sie hierher ins Krankenhaus gefahren?** who brought you to the hospital?; **ich fahre dich nach Hause** I'll take *or* drive you home; **jdn in den Tod fahren** *(geh)* to kill sb

e Geschwindigkeit *(aux sein)* to do; **er fuhr über 80 km/h** he did over 80 km/h, he drove at over 80 km/h; **in der Stadt darf man nur Tempo 50 fahren** in town the speed limit is 50 km/h

f Sport *(aux haben or sein) Rennen* to take part in; *Runde etc* to do; *Zeit, Rekord etc* to clock up

g Tech *(aux haben) (= steuern, betreiben)* to run; *(= senden)* to broadcast; *(= durchführen) Überstunden* to do, to work; *Angriff* to launch; **ein Experiment fahren** to run an experiment; **einen Versuch fahren** to run a test; **eine Sonderschicht fahren** to put on an extra shift; **Überstunden fahren** to do overtime; **eine Aufnahme fahren** to do a shot; **einen harten Kurs fahren** *(fig)* to take a hard line

3 – REFLEXIVES VERB

♦ **sich gut fahren mit diesem Wagen fährt es sich gut** it's good driving this car; **bei solchem Wetter/auf dieser Straße fährt es sich gut** it's good driving in that kind of weather/on this road; **der neue Wagen fährt sich gut** the new car is nice to drive; **mit dem neuen Belag fährt sich die Straße gut** the road is good to drive on since it's been resurfaced

---

fah|rend ADJ itinerant; *Musikant auch* travelling *(Brit)*, traveling *(US)*; *Zug, Auto* in motion; **~es Volk** travelling *(Brit) or* traveling *(US)* people; **ein ~er Sänger** a wandering minstrel; **ein unter panamaischer Flagge ~es Schiff** a ship sailing under a Panamanian flag

Fah|ren|heit ['fa:rənhait] *no art* Fahrenheit

Fah|ren|heit|ska|la ['fa:rənhait-] F, *no pl* Fahrenheit scale

fah|ren las|sen *ptp* **fahren lassen** *or (rare)* **fahren gelassen** *irreg*, **fah|ren+las|sen** *ptp* **fahrenlassen** *or (rare)* **fahrengelassen** *sep irreg* VT *(lit)* to let go of, to relinquish one's hold on; *(fig)* to abandon → **fahren 1 b**

Fah|rer ['fa:rɐ] M **-s, -**, **Fah|re|rin** [-ərɪn] F **-, -nen** **a** driver; *(= Chauffeur)* chauffeur/chauffeuse, driver **b** *(Sport inf) (= Radfahrer)* cyclist; *(= Motorradfahrer)* motorcyclist

Fah|rer|air|bag M, **Fah|rer-Air|bag** M *(Aut)* driver airbag

Fah|re|rei [fa:rə'rai] F **-, -en** driving

Fah|rer-: **Fah|rer|flucht** F hit-and-run driving; **~ begehen** to fail to stop after being involved in an accident, to be a hit-and-run driver; **fah|rer|flüch|tig** ADJ *(form)* hit-and-run *attr*; **~ sein** to have failed to stop after being involved in an accident, to be a hit-and-run driver; **Fah|rer|haus** NT (driver's) cab

Fah|re|rin [-ərɪn] F → **Fahrer**

fah|re|risch ['fa:rərɪʃ] ADJ driving *attr* ADV **er ist mir ~ weit überlegen** he is a far better driver than I am; **eine ~ anspruchsvolle Tour** a tour involving a lot of demanding driving

Fah|rer|laub|nis F *(form)* driving licence *(Brit)*, driver's license *(US)*

Fah|rer|sitz M driver's seat

Fahr|gast M passenger

Fahr|gast-: **Fahr|gast|auf|kom|men** NT number *or* volume of passengers; **Fahr|gast|raum** M *(von Auto)* interior; *(Rail etc)* compartment; **Fahr|gast|schiff** NT passenger boat; **Fahr|gast|zel|le** F *(Mot)* passenger cell

Fahr-: **Fahr|ge|fühl** NT **unser neues Modell vermittelt Ihnen ein völlig neues ~** our new model offers you a completely new driving experience; **Fahr|geld** NT fares *pl*; *(für einzelne Fahrt)* fare; **„das ~ bitte passend** *or* **abgezählt bereithalten"** "please tender exact fare" *(form)*, "please have the exact fare ready"; **Fahr|ge|le|gen|heit** F transport *no indef art*, means of transport; **Fahr|ge|mein|schaft** F carpool; **Fahr|ge|schwin|dig|keit** F *(form)* speed; **Fahr|ge|stell** NT **a** *(Aut)* chassis **b** *(Aviat)* undercarriage *(esp Brit)*, landing gear **c** *(hum inf)* legs *pl*; **ein hohes ~** long legs

Fähr- ['fɛ:ɐ-]: **Fähr|ha|fen** M ferry terminal; **Fähr|haus** NT ferry house

fah|rig ['fa:rɪç] ADJ nervous; *(= unkonzentriert)* distracted

Fah|rig|keit F **-,** *no pl* nervousness; *(= Unkonzentriertheit)* distractedness, distraction

Fahr|kar|te F **a** ticket; *(= Zeitfahrkarte, Streckenkarte)* season ticket; *(fig)* passport *(nach* to); **mit diesem Sieg hatten sie die ~ zum Endspiel in der Tasche** this victory was their passport to the final **b** *(Schießsport)* miss

Fahr|kar|ten-: **Fahr|kar|ten|aus|ga|be** F ticket office; **Fahr|kar|ten|au|to|mat** M ticket machine; **Fahr|kar|ten|kon|trol|le** F ticket inspection; **Fahr|kar|ten|kon|trol|leur(in)** M(F) ticket inspector; **Fahr|kar|ten|schal|ter** M ticket office

Fahr-: **Fahr|kom|fort** M (motoring) comfort; **Fahr|kos|ten** PL travelling *(Brit) or* traveling *(US)* expenses *pl*; **Fahr|küns|te** PL driving skills *pl*; **fahr|läs|sig** ['fa:ɐlɛsɪç] ADJ negligent *(auch Jur)* → **Körperverletzung, Tötung** ADV negligently; **~ handeln** to be guilty of negligence, to be negligent; **Fahr|läs|sig|keit** F **-, -en** negligence *(auch Jur)*; **Fahr|leh|rer(in)** M(F) driving instructor; **Fahr|leis|tung** F road performance

Fähr|mann ['fɛ:ɐ-] M *pl* **-männer** *or* **-leute** ferryman

Fahr|nis ['fa:ɐnɪs] F **-, -se** *(Jur)* chattels *pl*, moveables *pl*

Fähr|nis [ˈfɛːɐnɪs] F -, -se *(obs)* peril

Fahr|per|so|nal NT drivers and conductors *pl*; *(Rail)* footplatemen *pl (Brit)*, railroad crews *pl (US)*; *(von Einzelfahrzeug)* bus/tram/train crew

Fahr|plan M timetable, schedule *(US)*; *(fig)* schedule

Fahr|plan-: **Fahr|plan|aus|zug** M *(Rail)* timetable, schedule *(US, for a particular service)*; **fahr|plan|mä|ßig** ADJ scheduled *attr, pred* ADV ~ **verkehren/ankommen** to run/arrive on schedule; **es verlief alles** ~ everything went according to schedule; **Fahr|plan|wech|sel** M *(Rail)* change in (the) timetable *(Brit) or* schedule *(US)*

Fahr-: **Fahr|pra|xis** F, *no pl* driving experience *no indef art*

Fahr|preis M fare

Fahr|preis-: **Fahr|preis|an|zei|ger** M taxi meter; **Fahr|preis|er|mä|ßi|gung** F fare reduction

Fahr|prü|fung F driving test

Fahr|rad NT bicycle, cycle, bike *(inf)*

Fahr|rad-: **Fahr|rad|an|hän|ger** M bicycle trailer; **Fahr|rad|er|go|me|ter** NT bicycle ergometer; **Fahr|rad|fah|rer(in)** M(F) cyclist, bicyclist *(form)*; **Fahr|rad|ge|schäft** NT bicycle *or* cycle shop, bike shop *(inf)*; **Fahr|rad|händ|ler(in)** M(F) bicycle dealer; **gibt es hier einen ~?** is there a cycle shop around here?; **Fahr|rad|helm** M cycle helmet; **Fahr|rad|ku|rier(in)** M(F) cycle courier; **Fahr|rad|rik|scha** F trishaw, pedicab; **Fahr|rad|stän|der** M (bi)cycle stand; **Fahr|rad|ta|xi** NT cycle cab, pedicab; **Fahr|rad|weg** M cycle path, cycleway *(esp Brit)*

Fahr|rin|ne F *(Naut)* shipping channel, fairway

Fahr|schein M ticket

Fahr|schein-: **Fahr|schein|au|to|mat** M ticket machine; **Fahr|schein|block** M *pl* **-blöcke** *or* **-blocks** book of tickets; **Fahr|schein|ent|wer|ter** M automatic ticket stamping machine *(in bus/trams etc)*; **Fahr|schein|heft** NT book of tickets

Fähr|schiff [ˈfɛːɐ-] NT ferry(boat)

Fahr-: **Fahr|schu|le** F driving school; **Fahr|schü|ler(in)** M(F) **a** *(bei Fahrschule)* learner (driver), student (driver) *(US)* **b** *pupil who has to travel some distance to and from school*; **Fahr|schul|leh|rer(in)** M(F) driving instructor; **Fahr|si|cher|heit** F **a** safe driving *or* motoring *(esp Brit) no art*; **erhöhte** ~ safer driving *or* motoring *(esp Brit)* **b** *(von Auto)* driver safety; *(von Skilift, Drahtseilbahn)* operational safety; **Fahr|spur** F lane; **Fahr|steig** M *(auf Flughafen etc)* passenger conveyor, moving walkway *or* pavement *(Brit) or* sidewalk *(US)*; **Fahr|stil** M style of driving; **Fahr|strei|fen** M lane; **Fahr|stuhl** M lift *(Brit)*, elevator *(US)*; **Fahr|stuhl|schacht** M lift *(Brit) or* elevator *(US)* shaft; **Fahr|stun|de** F driving lesson

Fahrt [faːɐt] F -, -en **a** *(= das Fahren)* journey; **„während der ~ nicht hinauslehnen"** "do not lean out of the window while the train/bus *etc* is in motion"; **nach zwei Stunden** ~ after travelling *(Brit) or* traveling *(US)* for two hours; *(mit dem Auto auch)* after two hours' drive → **frei 1 a** **b** *(= Fahrgeschwindigkeit)* speed; **volle/halbe ~ voraus!** *(Naut)* full/half speed ahead!; **30 Knoten ~ machen** to do 30 knots; **~ aufnehmen** to pick up speed; **jdn in ~ bringen** to get sb going; **in ~ kommen** *or* **geraten/sein** to get/have got going

c *(= Reise)* journey; **was kostet eine ~/eine einfache ~ nach London?** how much is it/is a one-way ticket *or* a single *(Brit)* to London?; **gute ~!** bon voyage!, safe journey!; **auf ~ gehen** *(dated)* to take to the road

d *(= Ausflug, Wanderung)* trip; **eine ~ machen** to go on a trip

e *(Naut)* voyage; *(= Überfahrt)* crossing; **für große/kleine ~ zugelassen sein** to be licensed for long/short voyages

f *(Film)* tracking shot

fährt [fɛːɐt] *3. pers sing pres von* **fahren**

Fahrt|an|tritt M start of the journey

Fahr-: **fahr|taug|lich** ADJ fit to drive; *Wagen etc* roadworthy; **Fahr|taug|lich|keit** F fitness to drive; *(von Wagen etc)* roadworthiness; **jdm die ~ bescheinigen** to certify sb fit to drive

Fahrt|dau|er F time for the journey; **bei einer ~ von fünf Stunden** on a five-hour journey; **man muss für diese Strecke mit einer ~ von drei Stunden rechnen** you have to allow three hours for this stretch

Fähr|te [ˈfɛːɐtə] F -, -n tracks *pl*; *(= Witterung)* scent; *(= Spuren)* trail; **auf der richtigen/falschen ~ sein** *(fig)* to be on the right/wrong track; **jdn auf die richtige ~ bringen** *(fig)* to put sb on the right track; **jdn auf eine falsche ~ locken** *(fig)* to put sb off the scent; **eine ~ verfolgen** *(fig)* to follow up (on) a lead; **eine falsche ~ verfolgen** *(fig)* to be on the wrong track

Fahr-: **Fahr|tech|nik** F driving technique; **fahr|tech|nisch** ADJ *Können, Fähigkeiten* driving *attr*; **eine gute ~e Ausbildung bekommen** to learn to drive well ADV **eine ~ schwierige Strecke** a difficult stretch of road (to drive); **~ vollwertige Öko-Autos** environment-friendly cars that drive as well as other cars

Fahr|ten-: **Fahr|ten|buch** NT **a** *(= Kontrollbuch)* driver's log **b** *(= Wandertagebuch)* diary of a trip; **Fahr|ten|mes|ser** NT sheath knife; **Fahr|ten|schrei|ber** M tachograph *(Brit)*, trip recorder; **Fahr|ten|schwim|mer(in)** M(F) *person who has passed an advanced swimming test*; **seinen ~ machen** *(inf)* to do one's advanced swimming test

Fahr|test M road test

Fahrt-: **Fahrt|kos|ten** PL travelling *(Brit) or* traveling *(US)* expenses *pl*; **Fahrt|rich|tung** F direction of travel; *(im Verkehr)* direction of the traffic; **entgegen der ~** *(im Zug)* with one's back to the engine; *(im Bus etc)* facing backwards; **in ~** *(im Zug)* facing the engine; *(im Bus etc)* facing the front; **die Züge in ~ Norden/Süden** *etc* the northbound/southbound *etc* trains; **in ~ Norden sind Stauungen zu erwarten** long delays are affecting northbound traffic; **die Autobahn ist in ~ Norden gesperrt** the northbound carriageway of the motorway is closed *(Brit)*, the northbound lanes of the freeway are closed *(US)*; **Fahrt|rich|tungs|an|zei|ger** M *(Aut)* indicator *(Brit)*, turn signal *(US)*

Fahrt|rou|te F route

Fahrt|schrei|ber M tachograph *(Brit)*, trip recorder

Fahr-: **fahr|tüch|tig** ADJ fit to drive; *Wagen etc* roadworthy; **Fahr|tüch|tig|keit** F fitness to drive; *(von Wagen etc)* roadworthiness

Fahrt-: **Fahrt|un|ter|bre|chung** F break in the journey, stop; **Fahrt|wind** M airstream

Fahr-: **fahr|un|taug|lich** ADJ unfit to drive; *Wagen etc* unroadworthy; **Fahr|un|taug|lich|keit** F unfitness to drive; *(von Wagen etc)* unroadworthiness

Fähr|ver|bin|dung F *(Naut)* ferry service

Fahr-: **Fahr|ver|bot** NT loss of one's licence *(Brit) or* license *(US)*, driving ban; **jdn mit ~ belegen** to ban sb from driving, to take sb's licence *(Brit) or* license *(US)* away; **~ für Privatwagen** ban on private vehicles; **Fahr|ver|hal|ten** NT *(von Fahrer)* behaviour *(Brit) or* behavior *(US)* behind the wheel; *(von Wagen)* road performance

Fähr|ver|kehr [ˈfɛːɐ-] M ferry traffic

Fahr-: **Fahr|was|ser** NT, *no pl* **a** *(Naut)* shipping channel, fairway **b** *(fig)* **in jds ~ geraten** to get in with sb; **in ein gefährliches ~ geraten** to get onto dangerous ground; **in ein politisches/kommunistisches ~ geraten** to get tied up with politics/communism; **in jds ~ segeln** *or* **schwimmen** to follow in sb's wake; **in seinem** *or* **im richtigen ~ sein** to be in one's element; **Fahr|wei|se** F **seine ~** his driving, the way he drives; **Fahr|werk** NT **a** *(Aviat)* undercarriage *(esp Brit)*, landing gear **b** *(Aut)* chassis; **Fahr|wind** M **a** *(Naut)* wind **b** *(= Fahrtwind)* airstream; **Fahr|zeit** F = **Fahrtdauer**

Fahr|zeug NT *pl* **-zeuge** vehicle; *(= Luftfahrzeug)* aircraft; *(= Wasserfahrzeug)* vessel

Fahr|zeug-: **Fahr|zeug|aus|fall** M vehicle breakdown; **Fahr|zeug|aus|stat|tung** F vehicle accessories *pl*; **Fahr|zeug|brief** M (vehicle) title document, log book *(Brit inf)*; **Fahr|zeug|flot|te** F fleet (of vehicles); **Fahr|zeug|füh|rer(in)** M(F) *(form)* driver of a vehicle; **Fahr|zeug|hal|ter(in)** M(F) keeper of the vehicle; **Fahr|zeug|ko|lon|ne** F **a** *(= Schlange)* queue *(Brit) or* line of vehicles *etc* **b** *(auch* **Fahrzeugkonvoi**) convoy; *(bei Staatsbesuchen etc)* motorcade; **Fahr|zeug|len|ker(in)** M(F) *(form)* driver of a vehicle; **Fahr|zeug|pa|pie|re** PL vehicle documents *pl*; **Fahr|zeug|park** M *(form)* fleet; **Fahr|zeug|schein** M (vehicle) registration document, car *or* vehicle license *(Brit) or* licence *(US)*

Faib|le [ˈfɛːbl] NT -s, -s *(geh)* liking; *(= Schwäche auch)* weakness; *(= Vorliebe auch)* penchant

fair [fɛːɐ] ADJ fair *(gegen* to) ADV fairly; **~ spielen** *(Sport)* to play fairly; *(fig)* to play fair

Fair|ness [ˈfɛːɐnɛs] F -, *no pl* fairness

Fair Play [ˈfɛːɐ ˈpleː] NT -, *no pl*, **Fair|play** NT - -, *no pl* fair play

fä|kal [fɛˈkaːl] ADJ *(geh)* faecal *(Brit)*, fecal *(US)*

Fä|kal|dün|ger M natural manure, dung

Fä|ka|li|en [fɛˈkaːliən] PL faeces *pl (Brit)*, feces *pl (US)*

Fä|kal|spra|che F scatological language, scatology

Fa|kir [ˈfaːkiːɐ] M -s, -e fakir

Fak|si|mi|le [fakˈziːmile] NT -s, -s facsimile

Fak|si|mi|le-: **Fak|si|mi|le|aus|ga|be** F facsimile edition; **Fak|si|mi|le|druck** M **a** *pl* **-drucke** printed facsimile **b** *no pl (= Verfahren)* autotype; **Fak|si|mi|le|stem|pel** M signature stamp; **Fak|si|mi|le|un|ter|schrift** F facsimile signature

fak|si|mi|lie|ren [fakzimiˈliːrən] *ptp* **faksimiliert** VT to make a facsimile of, to reproduce in facsimile, to facsimile

Fakt [fakt] NT OR M -(e)s, -en fact; **~ ist, dass ...** the fact is that ...

Fak|ten *pl von* **Fakt, Faktum**

Fak|ten-: **Fak|ten|ma|te|ri|al** NT, *no pl* facts *pl*; **Fak|ten|samm|lung** F collection of facts; **Fak|ten|wis|sen** NT factual knowledge

fak|tisch [ˈfaktɪʃ] ADJ *attr* actual, real ADV **a** in actual fact, actually **b** *(esp Aus inf: = praktisch)* more or less

fak|ti|tiv [faktiˈtiːf, ˈfaktitiːf] ADJ *(Gram)* factitive

Fak|ti|tiv [ˈfaktitiːf] NT -s, -e [-və], **Fak|ti|ti|vum** [faktiˈtiːvʊm] NT -s, **Faktitiva** [-va] *(Gram)* factitive verb

Fak|ti|zi|tät [faktitsiˈtɛːt] F -, -en *(geh)* factuality

Fak|tor [ˈfaktoːɐ] M -s, **Faktoren** [-ˈtoːrən] factor *(auch Math)*

Fak|to|rei [faktoˈrai] F -, -en *(Comm)* trading post

Fak|to|ren|ana|ly|se F factor analysis

Fak|to|tum [fakˈtoːtʊm] NT -s, -s *or* **Faktoten** [-ˈtoːtn] factotum

Fak|tum [ˈfaktʊm] NT -s, **Fakten** [ˈfaktn] fact

Fak|tur [fakˈtuːɐ] F -, -en **a** *(dated)* invoice **b** *(Mus)* structure

Fak|tu|ra [fakˈtuːra] F -, **Fakturen** [-rən] *(Aus dated)* invoice

fak|tu|rie|ren [faktuˈriːrən] *ptp* **fakturiert** VT *(Comm)* to invoice

Fak|tu|rist [faktuˈrɪst] M -en, -en, **Fak|tu|ris|tin** [-ˈrɪstɪn] F -, -nen *(Comm)* **a** book-keeper **b** *(Aus: = Rechnungsprüfer)* invoice clerk

Fa|kul|tas [faˈkʊltas] F -, **Fakultäten** [-ˈtɛːtn] **die ~ für ein Fach haben** to be qualified to teach a subject

Fa|kul|tät [fakʊlˈtɛːt] F -, -en **a** *(Univ: = Fachbereich)* faculty; **(ein Kollege) von der anderen ~ sein** *(hum inf) (= homosexuell sein)* to be one of them (*Brit dated inf*), to be the other way round (*Brit dated inf*), to be queerer than a three dollar bill (*US inf*); (*rare*: = *eine andere Weltanschauung haben*) to be of another school of thought **b** (*obs*: = *Begabung*) faculty **c** (*Math*) factorial

fa|kul|ta|tiv [fakʊlta'ti:f] ADJ (*geh*) optional

Fa|lan|ge [fa'laŋgə] F -, *no pl* (*Pol*) Falange

Fa|lan|gist [falaŋ'gɪst] M **-en, -en**, **Fa|lan|gis|tin** [-'gɪstɪn] F **-, -nen** (*Pol*) Falangist

falb [falp] ADJ (*geh*) *Pferd* dun

Fal|be ['falbə] M **-n, -n** dun

Fal|ke ['falkə] M **-n, -n** falcon; (*fig*) hawk

Fal|ken-: **Fal|ken|au|ge** NT (*Miner*) hawk's-eye; **Fal|ken|bei|ze** F, **Fal|ken|jagd** F falconry

Falk|land-: **Falk|land|in|seln** PL Falkland Islands *pl*; **Falk|land|krieg** M Falklands War

Falk|ner ['falknɐ] M **-s, -**, **Falk|ne|rin** [-ərɪn] F **-, -nen** falconer

Falk|ne|rei [falknə'rai] F **-, -en** **a** falconry **b** (= *Anlage*) falcon house

Fall [fal] M **-(e)s, ⸚e** ['fɛlə] **a** (= *das Hinunterfallen*) fall; **im/beim ~ hat er ...** when/as he fell he ... → **frei 1 a** **b** (= *das Zufallkommen*) fall; (*fig*) (*von Menschen, Regierung*) downfall; (*von Plänen, Gesetz etc*) failure; **zu ~ kommen** (*lit geh*) to fall; **über die Affäre ist er zu ~ gekommen** (*fig*) the affair was *or* caused his downfall; **zu ~ bringen** (*lit geh*) to make fall, to trip up; (*fig*) *Menschen* to cause the downfall of; *Regierung* to bring down; *Gesetz, Plan etc* to thwart; *Tabu* to break down **c** (*fig*: = *Untergang, Sturz*) fall **d** (*von Kurs, Temperatur etc*) drop, fall (+*gen* in) **e** (*von Gardine etc*) hang, drape

Fall ✪ 29, 34.3, 36, 37.4, 39.1, 40.2, 40.3 M **-(e)s, ⸚e** **a** ['fɛlə] (= *Umstand*) **gesetzt den ~** assuming *or* supposing (that); **für den ~, dass ich ...** in case I ...; **für den ~ meines Todes, im ~e meines Todes** in case I die; **für alle Fälle** just in case; **in jedem ~(e)** always; **in keinem ~(e)** never; **auf jeden ~** at any rate, at all events; **auf keinen ~** on no account; **auf alle Fälle** in any case, anyway; **für solche Fälle** for such occasions; **im äußersten ~(e)** if the worst comes to the worst; **im anderen ~(e)** if not, if that is not the case; **im günstigsten/schlimmsten ~(e)** at best/worst; **im ~e eines ~es** if it comes to it; **wenn dieser ~ eintritt** if this should be the case, if this should arise

b (= *gegebener Sachverhalt*) case; **in diesem ~** in this case *or* instance; **ein ~ von ...** a case *or* an instance of ...; **von ~ zu ~** from case to case, from one case to the next; (*hin und wieder*) periodically; **in diesem ~(e) will ich noch einmal von einer Bestrafung absehen, aber ...** I won't punish you on this occasion, but ...; **jds ~ sein** (*inf*) to be sb's cup of tea (*inf*); **klarer ~!** (*inf*) sure thing! (*esp US inf*), you bet! (*inf*)

c (*Jur, Med*: = *Beispiel, Person*) case; **ein hoffnungsloser ~** a hopeless case

d (*Gram*: = *Kasus*) case; **der erste/zweite/dritte/vierte ~** the nominative/genitive/dative/accusative case; **der fünfte ~** (= *Ablativ*) the ablative case; (= *Instrumental*) the instrumental case; **der sechste ~** (= *Vokativ*) the vocative case; (= *Präpositiv*) the prepositional case

Fall NT **-(e)s, -en** (*Naut*) halyard

fäll|bar ADJ (*Chem*) precipitable

Fall-: **Fall|beil** NT guillotine; **Fall|bei|spiel** NT case study; **Fall|be|richt** M case report; **Fall|be|schleu|ni|gung** F gravitational acceleration, acceleration due to gravity; **Fall|bö(e)** F down gust; **Fall|brü|cke** F drawbridge; (= *Enterbrücke*) gangplank

Fal|le ['falə] F **-, -n** **a** (*lit, fig*) trap; **~n legen** *or* **stellen** to set traps; **in eine ~ geraten** *or* **gehen** (*lit*) to get caught in a trap; (*fig*) to fall into a trap; **jdm in die ~ gehen, in jds ~ geraten** to walk *or* fall into sb's trap; **in der ~ sitzen** to be trapped; **jdn in eine ~ locken** (*fig*) to trick sb; **jdm eine ~ stellen** (*fig*) to set a trap for sb **b** (*Tech*) catch, latch **c** (*inf*: = *Bett*) bed; **in der ~ sein** *or* **liegen** to be in bed; **sich in die ~ hauen, in die ~ gehen** to hit the hay (*inf*), to turn in; **ab (mit euch) in die ~!** off to bed!

fal|len ['falən] *pret* **fiel** [fi:l], *ptp* **gefallen** [gə'falən] VI *aux sein* **a** (= *hinabfallen, umfallen*) to fall; (*Gegenstand, Wassermassen*) to drop; (*Theat*: *Vorhang*) to fall, to come down; (*Klappe*) to come down, to drop; **etw ~ lassen** to drop sth; **über etw** (*acc*) **~** to trip over sth; **sich ~ lassen** to drop; (*fig*) to give up; **durch eine Prüfung** *etc* **~** to fail an exam *etc*; **ein gefallener Engel** a fallen angel; **ein gefallenes Mädchen** (*dated*) a fallen woman (*dated*) → *auch* **Groschen b**, **Nase a**

b (= *hängen*: *Vorhang, Kleid etc*) to hang; (= *reichen*) to come down (*bis auf* +*acc* to); **die Haare ~ ihr bis auf die Schultern/über die Augen/ins Gesicht/in die Stirn** her hair comes down to *or* reaches her shoulders/falls into her eyes/face/onto her forehead

c (= *abfallen, sinken*) to drop; (*Wasserstand, Preise, Fieber auch, Thermometer*) to go down; (*Fluss, Kurse, Wert, Aktien auch, Barometer*) to fall; (*Nachfrage, Ansehen*) to fall off, to decrease; **im Preis/Wert ~** to go down *or* drop *or* fall in price/value; **im Kurs ~** to go down, to drop

d (= *im Krieg ums Leben kommen*) to fall, to be killed; **gefallen** killed in action; **er ist gefallen** he was killed in action; **mein Mann ist (im Krieg) gefallen** my husband was killed in the war

e (= *erobert werden*: *Festung, Stadt etc*) to fall

f (*fig*) (*Gesetz, Passus etc*) to be dropped; (*Tabu, Brauch etc*) to disappear

g (*mit schneller Bewegung*) **jdm ins Lenkrad ~** to grab the steering wheel from sb; **einem Pferd in die Zügel ~** to grab a horse's reins; **die Tür fällt ins Schloss** the door clicks shut; **die Tür ins Schloss ~ lassen** to let the door shut; **der Löwe fiel dem Gnu in die Flanke** the lion pounced on (the flank of) the gnu → **Hals a**, **Wort c**

h (= *treffen*: *Wahl, Verdacht*) to fall, to light (*form*) (*auf* +*acc* (up)on); **das Licht fällt durch die Luke** the light comes in through the skylight; **das Los, das zu tun, fiel auf ihn** it fell to his lot to do that

i (= *stattfinden, sich ereignen*: *Weihnachten, Datum etc*) to fall (*auf* +*acc* on); (= *gehören*) to come (*unter* +*acc* under, *in* +*acc* within, under); **in eine Zeit ~** to belong to an era; **unter einen Begriff ~** to be part of a concept; **aus einer Gruppe/Kategorie** *etc* **~** to come outside a group/category *etc*, to be excluded from a group/category *etc*

j (= *zufallen*: *Erbschaft etc*) to go (*an* +*acc* to); **das Elsass fiel an Frankreich** Alsace fell to France; (*nach Verhandlungen*) Alsace went to France

k (= *gemacht, erzielt werden*) (*Entscheidung*) to be made; (*Urteil*) to be passed *or* pronounced; (*Schuss*) to be fired; (*Sport*: *Tor*) to be scored

l (*Wort*) to be uttered *or* spoken; (*Name*) to be mentioned; (*Bemerkung*) to be made

m (= *geraten*) **in Schlaf ~** to fall asleep; **in eine andere Tonart ~** to speak in *or* (*absichtlich*) adopt a different tone (of voice); **in eine andere Sprache ~** to lapse *or* drop into another language; **in eine andere Gangart ~** to change one's pace → **Opfer b**, **Rahmen b**, **Rolle d**

n (= *sein*) → **Last b**, **lästig**, **leichtfallen**, **schwerfallen**

fäl|len ['fɛlən] VT **a** (= *umschlagen*) to fell **b** (*fig*) *Entscheidung* to make, to come to; *Urteil* to pass, to pronounce **c** (= *zum Angriff senken*) *Lanze* to lower, to level; **mit gefälltem Bajonett** with bayonet(s) at the ready **d** (*Chem*) to precipitate **e** (*Math*) **das Lot ~** to drop a perpendicular

fal|len las|sen *ptp* **fallen lassen** *or* (*rare*) **fallen gelassen** *irreg*, **fal|len+las|sen** *ptp* **fallenlassen** *or* (*rare*) **fallengelassen** *sep irreg* VT **a** (= *aufgeben*) *Plan, Mitarbeiter* to drop **b** (= *äußern*) *Bemerkung* to let drop; **hat er irgend etwas darüber ~?** (*inf*) has he let anything drop about it?

Fal|len|stel|ler [-ʃtɛlɐ] M **-s, -**, **Fal|len|stel|le|rin** [-ərɪn] F **-, -nen** (*Hunt*) trapper

Fall-: **Fall|gat|ter** NT portcullis; **Fall|ge|schwin|dig|keit** F (*Phys*) speed of fall; **Fall|ge|setz** NT (*Phys*) law of falling bodies; **Fall|git|ter** NT portcullis; **Fall|gru|be** F (*Hunt*) pit; (*fig rare*) pitfall; **Fall|ham|mer** M pile-driver; **Fall|hö|he** F (*Phys*) (height *or* depth of) drop; (*beim Wasserkraftwerk*) head

fal|lie|ren [fa'li:rən] *ptp* **falliert** VI (*Fin*) to fail, to go bankrupt

fäl|lig ['fɛlɪç] ADJ due *pred*; (*Fin*) *Rechnung, Betrag etc auch* payable; *Wechsel* mature(d); **längst ~** long overdue; **die ~en Zinsen** the interest due; **~ werden** to become *or* fall due; (*Wechsel*) to mature; **am Wochenende ist endlich Rasenmähen ~** the lawn is about due for a cut at the weekend; **am Wochenende ist eine Party ~** a party is about due at the weekend; **der Kerl ist ~** (*inf*) he's for it (*inf*)

Fäl|lig|keit F **-, -en** (*Fin*) settlement date; (*von Wechseln*) maturity; **zahlbar bei ~** payable by settlement date; payable at *or* on maturity

Fäl|lig|keits|tag M, **Fäl|lig|keits|ter|min** M settlement date; (*von Wechsel*) date of maturity

Fall|obst ['fallo:pst] NT windfalls *pl*; **ein Stück ~** a windfall

Fall|out [fɔ:l'aut] M **-s, -s**, **Fall-out** M **-s, -s** fallout

Fall-: **Fall|reep** NT (*Naut*) rope ladder; (= *Treppe*) gangway; **Fall|rohr** NT drainpipe, downpipe (*form*); **Fall|rück|zie|her** M (*Ftbl*) overhead kick, bicycle kick

falls [fals] CONJ (= *wenn*) if; (= *für den Fall, dass*) in case; **~ möglich** if possible; **~ du Lust hast** if you (happen to) want to, if you should (happen to) want to; **gib mir deine Telefonnummer, ~ ich mich verspäten sollte** give me your phone number in case I'm late; **~ ich mich verspäten sollte, rufe ich vorher an** if I'm late *or* in the event of my being late (*form*) I'll phone you first

Fall|schirm M parachute; **mit dem ~ abspringen** to parachute, to make a parachute jump; **mit dem ~ über Frankreich abspringen** to parachute out over France; (*in Kriegszeit*) to parachute into France; **etw mit dem ~ abwerfen** to drop sth by parachute

Fall|schirm-: **Fall|schirm|ab|sprung** M parachute jump; **Fall|schirm|jä|ger(in)** M(F) (*Mil*) paratrooper; **die ~** the paratroop(er)s; **Fall|schirm|sprin|gen** NT parachuting; **Fall|schirm|sprin|ger(in)** M(F) parachutist; **Fall|schirm|trup|pe** F (*Mil*) paratroop(er)s *pl*

Fall-: **Fall|strick** M (*fig*) trap, snare; **jdm ~e** *or* **einen ~ legen** to set a trap *or* snare for sb (to walk into); **Fall|stu|die** F case study; **Fall|sucht** F, *no pl* (*old*) falling sickness (*old*); **fall|süch|tig** ADJ (*old*) epileptic; **Fall|süch|ti|ge(r)** MF *decl as adj* (*old*) epileptic

fällt [fɛlt] *3. pers sing pres von* **fallen**

Fall|tür F trapdoor

Fäl|lung ['fɛlʊŋ] F **-, -en** **a** (*von Bäumen etc*) felling **b** (*Jur*: *eines Urteils*) pronouncement; (*einer Entscheidung*) reaching **c** (*Chem*) precipitation

Fäl|lungs|mit|tel NT (*Chem*) precipitant

Fall-: **fall|wei|se** ADV **a** from case to case **b** (*esp Aus*: = *gelegentlich*) now and again, occasionally ADJ case-by-case *attr*; **Fall|wind** M katabatic (*form*) *or* fall wind; **Fall|wurf** M (*Sport*) diving throw

falsch [falʃ] ADJ **a** (= *verkehrt, fehlerhaft*) wrong; (*in der Logik etc*) false; **richtig oder ~** right or wrong; **wahr oder ~** true or false; **wie mans macht, ist es ~** (*inf*) whatever I/you *etc* do it's bound to be wrong; **mach dir keine ~en Vorstellungen darüber/davon** don't get the wrong idea (*inf*) *or* any misconceptions about it; **du machst dir völlig ~e Vorstellungen** you have *or* you've got quite the wrong idea *or* some misconceptions; **~es Bewusstsein** (*Philos, Sociol*) false consciousness; **~er Alarm** (*lit, fig*) false alarm; **Sie sind hier ~** you're in the wrong place; **bei jdm an den Falschen geraten** *or* **kommen** to pick the wrong person in sb; **am ~en Ort** *or* **Platz sein** to have come to the wrong place; **im ~en Film sein** *(sl)* to be on another planet *(inf)* → **Licht, Pferd**

b *(= unecht, nachgemacht) Zähne etc* false; *Perlen auch* fake; *Würfel* loaded; *(= gefälscht) Pass etc* forged, fake; *Geld* counterfeit; *(= betrügerisch)* bogus, fake; **~er Zopf** hairpiece, switch

c *(= unaufrichtig, unangebracht) Gefühl, Freund, Scham, Pathos etc* false; **ein ~er Hund** *(inf)* **eine ~e Schlange** *(inf)* a snake-in-the-grass; **ein ~es Spiel (mit jdm) treiben** to play (sb) false, to play an underhand game (with sb); **unter ~er Flagge segeln** *(lit, fig)* to sail under false colours *(Brit)* or colors *(US)*; **~er Freund** *(esp Ling)* false friend → **Bescheidenheit**

d *(dial: = tückisch)* nasty

ADV a *(= nicht richtig)* wrongly, incorrectly; **alles ~ machen** to do everything wrong; **etw ~ verstehen** to misunderstand sth, to get sth wrong *(inf)*; **jdn/etw ganz ~ verstehen** to completely misunderstand sb/sth; **~ verstandene Freundschaft** misinterpreted friendship; **etw ~ schreiben/aussprechen** to spell/pronounce sth wrongly *or* incorrectly, to misspell/mispronounce sth; **jdn ~ informieren** to misinform sb; **die Uhr geht ~** the clock is wrong; **Kinder ~ erziehen** to bring children up badly; **~ spielen** *(Mus)* to play the wrong note/notes; *(= unrein)* to play off key, to play out of tune; *(Cards)* to cheat; **~ singen** to sing out of tune, to sing off key; **~ verbunden sein** to have the wrong number

b *(= unaufrichtig)* falsely, insincerely; **~ lachen** to give a false laugh

Falsch [falʃ] M *(old)* **ohne ~ sein** to be without guile *or* artifice

Falsch|aus|sa|ge F *(Jur)* **(uneidliche)** ~ false statement, false evidence

Falsch|eid M *(Jur)* (unintentional) false statement *or* oath

fäl|schen [ˈfɛlʃn] VT to forge, to fake; *Geld, Briefmarken auch* to counterfeit; *(Comm) Bücher* to falsify; *Geschichte, Tatsachen* to falsify → *auch* **gefälscht**

Fäl|scher [ˈfɛlʃɐ] M **-s, -**, **Fäl|sche|rin** [-ərɪn] F **-, -nen** forger; *(von Geld, Briefmarken auch)* counterfeiter

Falsch-: **Falsch|fah|rer(in)** M(F) ghost-driver *(esp US inf)*, *person driving the wrong way on the motorway*; **Falsch|geld** NT counterfeit *or* forged money; **falsch|gläu|big** ADJ *(old Rel)* heterodox; **Falsch|heit** F **-,** *no pl* falsity, falseness; *(von Menschen)* nastiness; **Falsch|in|for|ma|ti|on** F misinformation, piece of false information; *(hum: = Ente)* hoax

fälsch|lich [ˈfɛlʃlɪç] **ADJ** false; *Behauptung auch* erroneous; *Annahme, Glaube auch* mistaken, erroneous **ADV** wrongly, falsely; *behaupten, annehmen, glauben auch* mistakenly, erroneously; *(versehentlich)* by mistake

fälsch|li|cher|wei|se [ˈfɛlʃlɪçɐˈvaizə] ADV wrongly, falsely; *behaupten, annehmen, glauben auch* mistakenly, erroneously

Falsch-: **falsch+lie|gen** *sep irreg (S Ger, Aus, Sw: aux sein)*, **falsch lie|gen** △ *irreg (S Ger, Aus, Sw: aux sein)* VI *(inf)* to be wrong *(bei, in +dat* about, *mit* in); **Falsch|mel|dung** F *(Press)* false report; **Falsch|mün|zer** [-mʏntsɐ] M **-s, -**, **Falsch|mün|ze|rin** [-ərɪn] F **-, -nen** forger, counterfeiter; **Falsch|mün|ze|rei** [-mʏntsəˈrai] F **-, -en** forgery, counterfeiting; **Falsch|par|ken** [-parkn] NT **-s,** *no pl* illegal parking; **Falsch|par|ker** [-parkɐ] M **-s, -**, **Falsch|par|ke|rin** [-ərɪn] M **-, -nen** parking offender; **falsch+spie|len** *sep*, **falsch spie|len** △ VI *(Cards)* to cheat; **Falsch|spie|ler(in)** M(F) *(Cards)* cheat; *(professionell)* cardsharp(er)

Fäl|schung [ˈfɛlʃʊŋ] F **-, -en a** *no pl (= das Fälschen)* forgery, forging, faking; *(von Geld, Briefmarken)* counterfeiting, forgery **b** *(= gefälschter Gegenstand)* forgery, fake

fäl|schungs|si|cher ADJ forgery-proof; *Fahrtenschreiber* tamper-proof

Fäl|schungs|si|cher|heit F forgery-proof nature; *(von Fahrtenschreiber)* tamper-proof nature

Fal|sett [falˈzɛt] NT **-(e)s, -e** falsetto; **~ singen, mit ~stimme singen** to sing falsetto

Fal|si|fi|kat [falzifiˈkaːt] NT **-(e)s, -e** forgery, fake

Fal|si|fi|ka|ti|on [falzifikaˈtsioːn] F **-, -en** falsification

fal|si|fi|zie|ren [falzifiˈtsiːrən] *ptp* **falsifiziert** VT to falsify

Falt-: **falt|bar** ADJ foldable; *(= zusammenklappbar)* collapsible; *Stuhl, Tisch, Fahrrad* folding *attr*, collapsible; **Falt|blatt** NT leaflet; *(in Zeitschrift etc auch)* insert; **Falt|boot** NT collapsible boat

Fält|chen [ˈfɛltçən] NT **-s, -** *dim von* **Falte**

Fal|te [ˈfaltə] F **-, -n a** *(in Stoff, Papier)* fold; *(= Knitterfalte, Bügelfalte)* crease; **in ~n legen** to fold; **~n schlagen** to get creased, to crease; **~n werfen** to fall in folds, to drape **b** *(in Haut)* wrinkle; **strenge ~n** harsh lines; **die Stirn in ~n ziehen** *or* **legen** to knit *or* furrow one's brow **c** *(Geol)* fold

fäl|teln [ˈfɛltln] VT to pleat

fal|ten [ˈfaltn] **VT** to fold; **die Stirn ~** to knit one's brow **VR** to fold

Fal|ten-: **fal|ten|frei** ADJ = **faltenlos**; **Fal|ten|ge|bir|ge** NT fold mountains *pl*; **fal|ten|los** ADJ *Gesicht* unlined; *Haut auch* smooth; *Stoff* uncreased; *Rock* unpleated; **fal|ten|reich** ADJ *Haut* wrinkled; *Gesicht auch* lined; *Kleid, Mantel* tightly pleated; **Fal|ten|rock** M pleated skirt; **Fal|ten|wurf** M fall of the folds

Fal|ter [ˈfaltɐ] M **-s, -** *(= Tagfalter)* butterfly; *(= Nachtfalter)* moth

fal|tig [ˈfaltɪç] **ADJ** *(= zerknittert)* creased; *(= in Falten gelegt)* hanging in folds; *Gesicht, Stirn, Haut* wrinkled **ADV ~ fallen** to hang in folds; **~ gerafft sein** to be gathered into folds

Falt-: **Falt|ka|len|der** M fold-out planner; **Falt|kar|te** F folding *or* fold-up map; **Falt|kar|ton** M collapsible box; **Falt|kin|der|wa|gen** M collapsible pram *(Brit)*, collapsible baby carriage *(US)*; *(= Sportwagen)* baby buggy *(Brit)*, stroller *(US)*; **Falt|pla|ner** M fold-out planner; **Falt|pros|pekt** M leaflet; **Falt|schach|tel** F collapsible box; **Falt|tür** F folding door

Falz [falts] M **-es, -e** *(= Kniff, Faltlinie)* fold; *(zwischen Buchrücken und -deckel)* joint; *(Tech)* rabbet; *(zwischen Blechrändern)* join, lock seam *(spec)*; *(= Briefmarkenfalz)* hinge

fal|zen [ˈfaltsn] VT *Papierbogen* to fold; *Holz* to rabbet; *Blechränder* to join with a lock seam

Fam. *abbr von* **Familie**

fa|mi|li|är [famiˈli̯ɛːɐ] **ADJ a** family *attr* **b** *(= zwanglos)* informal; *(= freundschaftlich)* close; *(pej: = plump-vertraulich)* familiar; **ein ~er Ausdruck** a colloquialism **ADV mit jdm ~ verkehren** to be on close terms with sb; **da geht es so ~ zu** it's so informal there

Fa|mi|li|a|ri|tät [familiariˈtɛːt] F **-, -en** *(= Zwangslosigkeit)* informality; *(= Freundschaftlichkeit)* closeness; *(pej: = plumpe Vertraulichkeit)* familiarity

Fa|mi|lie [faˈmiːli̯ə] F **-, -n** family; **~ Müller** the Müller family; **~ Otto Francke** *(als Anschrift)* Mr & Mrs Otto Francke and family; **eine ~ gründen** to start a family; **~ haben** *(inf)* to have a family; **aus guter ~ sein** to come from a good family; **es liegt in der ~** it runs in the family; **zur ~ gehören** to be one of the family; **es bleibt in der ~** it'll stay in the family → **beste(r, s) ADJ a**

Fa|mi|li|en- *in cpds* family; **Fa|mi|li|en|ähn|lich|keit** F family resemblance; **Fa|mi|li|en|an|ge|hö|ri|ge(r)** MF *decl as adj* family member, relative; **Fa|mi|li|en|an|schluss** M **Unterkunft/Stellung mit ~** *accommodation/job where one is treated as part of the family*; **~ suchen** to wish to be treated as one of the family; **Fa|mi|li|en|an|zei|gen** PL personal announcements *pl*; **Fa|mi|li|en|aus|weis** M family pass; **Fa|mi|li|en|be|ra|tungs|stel|le** F family planning office; **Fa|mi|li|en|be|sitz** M family property; **in ~ sein** to be owned by the family; **Fa|mi|li|en|be|trieb** M family concern *or* business; **Fa|mi|li|en|buch** NT *book of family events with some legal documents*; **Fa|mi|li|en|fei|er** F, **Fa|mi|li|en|fest** NT family party; **Fa|mi|li|en|för|de|rung** F family benefits *pl*; **Fa|mi|li|en|for|schung** F genealogy; **Fa|mi|li|en|fo|to** NT family-photo; **fa|mi|li|en|freund|lich** ADJ *Politik* pro-family *attr*, favourable *(Brit)* or favorable *(US)* to families *pred*; *Hotel etc* family *attr*, that welcomes families *pred*; **Fa|mi|li|en|glück** NT happy family life; **Fa|mi|li|en|grab** NT family grave; **Fa|mi|li|en|gruft** F family vault; **Fa|mi|li|en|klün|gel** M *(inf)* **der ganze ~** the whole tribe *(inf)*; **Fa|mi|li|en|kreis** M family circle; **die Trauung fand im engsten ~ statt** only the immediate family were present at the wedding; **Fa|mi|li|en|le|ben** NT family life; **Fa|mi|li|en|mit|glied** NT member of the family; **Fa|mi|li|en|nach|rich|ten** PL births, marriages and deaths, personal announcements *pl*; **Fa|mi|li|en|na|me** M surname, family name *(US)*; **Fa|mi|li|en|ober|haupt** NT head of the family; **Fa|mi|li|en|pa|ckung** F family (-size) pack; **Fa|mi|li|en|pass** M family passport; **Fa|mi|li|en|pla|nung** F family planning; **Fa|mi|li|en|rat** M family council; **Fa|mi|li|en|recht** NT family law; **Fa|mi|li|en|ro|man** M (family) saga; **Fa|mi|li|en|schmuck** M family jewels *pl*; **Fa|mi|li|en|se|rie** F *(TV)* family series; **Fa|mi|li|en|sinn** M sense of family; **Fa|mi|li|en|stand** M marital status; **Fa|mi|li|en|tra|gö|die** F family tragedy; **Fa|mi|li|en|tref|fen** NT family gathering *or* get-together, family affair *(inf, iro)*; *(= Wiedersehen)* family reunion; **Fa|mi|li|en|un|ter|halt** M family upkeep *or* maintenance; **den ~ verdienen** to support the family; **Fa|mi|li|en|un|ter|neh|men** NT family business *or* company; **Fa|mi|li|en|va|ter** M father (of a family); **Fa|mi|li|en|ver|hält|nis|se** PL family circumstances *pl or* background *sing*; **aus was für ~n kommt sie?** what is her family background?, what kind of family does she come from?; **Fa|mi|li|en|vor|stand** M *(form)* head of the family; **Fa|mi|li|en|wap|pen** NT family arms *pl*; **Fa|mi|li|en|zu|la|ge** F dependants' allowance *(in unemployment benefit)*; **Fa|mi|li|en|zu|sam|men|füh|rung** F *(Pol) principle of allowing families to be united*; **Fa|mi|li|en|zu|wachs** M addition to the family

fa|mos [faˈmoːs] ADJ *(dated inf)* capital *(dated inf)*, splendid

Fa|mu|la [ˈfaːmula] F **-, Famulä** [-lɛ] → **Famulus**

Fa|mu|la|tur [famulaˈtuːɐ] F **-, -en** *period when a medical student does practical work in a hospital*, clinical practice

fa|mu|lie|ren [famuˈliːrən] *ptp* **famuliert** VI *(Med)* to do some practical work

Fa|mu|lus [ˈfaːmulʊs] M **-, Famuli** [-li], **Fa|mu|la** [ˈfaːmula] F **-, Famulä** [-lɛ] **a** *(Med) student doing practical work* **b** *(old)* professor's assistant, student

Fan [fɛn] M **-s, -s** fan; *(Ftbl auch)* supporter

Fa|nal [faˈnaːl] NT **-s, -e** *(liter)* signal (*+gen* for)

Fan|ar|ti|kel [ˈfɛn-] M fan article, piece of fan merchandise

Fa|na|ti|ker [faˈnaːtikɐ] M **-s, -**, **Fa|na|ti|ke|rin** [-ərɪn] F **-, -nen** fanatic

-fa|na|ti|ker(in) M(F) *suf in cpds* fanatic; **ein Fitnessfanatiker** a fitness fanatic *or* freak *(inf)*

fa|na|tisch [faˈnaːtɪʃ] **ADJ** fanatical **ADV** fanatically

fa|na|ti|siert [fanatiˈziːɐt] ADJ *(geh)* rabid

Fa|na|tis|mus [fanaˈtɪsmʊs] M **-,** *no pl* fanaticism

Fan|club [ˈfɛnklʊp] M → **Fanklub**

fand *pret von* **finden**

Fan|fa|re [fan'fa:rə] F -, -n **a** *(Mus)* fanfare **b** *(Aut)* horn

Fan|fa|ren-: **Fan|fa|ren|stoß** M flourish (of trumpets), fanfare; **Fan|fa|ren|zug** M trumpeters *pl*

Fang [faŋ] M -(e)s, ⸚e ['fɛŋə] **a** *no pl (= das Fangen)* hunting; *(mit Fallen)* trapping; *(= Fischen)* fishing; **auf ~ gehen** to go hunting/trapping/fishing; **zum ~ auslaufen** to go fishing **b** *no pl (= Beute) (lit, fig)* catch; *(Wild)* catch, bag; *(fig: Gegenstände)* haul; **einen guten ~ machen** to make a good catch/get a good bag/haul **c** *no pl (Hunt: = Todesstoß)* coup de grâce **d** *usu pl (Hunt) (= Kralle)* talon; *(= Reißzahn)* fang; **in den Fängen** *+gen (fig)* in the clutches of

Fang-: **Fang|arm** M *(Zool)* tentacle; **Fang|ball** M catch; **Fang|ei|sen** NT *(Hunt)* gin trap

Fan|ge|mein|de ['fɛn-] F fan club *or* community; **seine ~** his fan base; **eine treue ~** a faithful band of fans

fan|gen ['faŋən] *pret* **fing** [fɪŋ], *ptp* **gefangen** [gə'faŋən] **VT** *Tier, Fisch, Verbrecher* to catch; *Wild* to catch, to bag; *(mit Fallen)* to trap; *(fig: = überlisten) (durch geschickte Fragen)* to trap; *(durch Versprechungen etc)* to trick; **(sich** *dat***) eine (Ohrfeige** *etc***) ~** *(inf)* to catch it *(Brit inf)*, to get one *(US inf)* → *auch* **gefangen**

VI to catch; **Fangen spielen** to play tag

VR **a** *(in einer Falle)* to get caught; **er hat sich in der eigenen Schlinge** *or* **Falle gefangen** *(fig)* he was hoist with his own petard **b** *(= das Gleichgewicht wiederfinden)* to steady oneself; *(beim Reden etc)* to recover oneself; *(Flugzeug)* to straighten out; *(seelisch)* to get on an even keel again **c** *(= sich verfangen)* to get caught (up); *(Wind)* to get trapped; **ich fing mich mit dem Rock in der Fahrradkette** I got my skirt caught (up) in the bicycle chain

Fän|ger ['fɛŋɐ] M -s, -, **Fän|ge|rin** [-ərɪn] F -, -nen **a** *(= Tierfänger)* hunter; *(mit Fallen)* trapper; *(= Walfänger)* whaler; *(= Robbenfänger)* sealer **b** *(Sport)* catcher

Fang-: **Fang|flot|te** F fishing fleet; **Fang|fra|ge** F catch *or* trick question; **fang|frisch** ADJ *Fisch* freshly caught, fresh-caught, fresh; **Fang|grün|de** PL fishing grounds *pl*; **Fang|korb** M lifeguard, cowcatcher *(inf)*; **Fang|lei|ne** F **a** *(Naut)* hawser **b** *(Aviat)* arresting gear cable **c** *(von Fallschirm)* rigging line; **Fang|mes|ser** NT hunting knife; **Fang|netz** NT **a** *(Hunt, Fishing)* net **b** *(Aviat)* arresting gear

Fan|go ['faŋgo] M -s, *no pl* fango

Fan|go|pa|ckung F fango pack

Fang-: **Fang|quo|te** F (fishing) quota; **Fang|schal|tung** F *(Telec)* interception circuit; **Fang|schiff** NT fishing boat; *(mit Netzen)* trawler; *(= Walfangschiff)* whaler; **Fang|schnur** F *(Mil)* aiguillette; **Fang|schuss** M *(Hunt, fig)* coup de grâce *(with a gun)*; **fang|si|cher** ADJ **ein ~er Torwart** a goalkeeper with a safe pair of hands; **~ sein** to have a safe pair of hands; **Fang|stoß** M coup de grâce *(with a knife)*

fängt [fɛŋt] *3. pers sing pres von* **fangen**

Fang-: **Fang|tuch** NT *pl* **-tücher** life-net *(US)*, jumping-sheet, blanket *(inf)*; **fang|un|si|cher** ADJ butter-fingered; **Fang|ver|bot** NT *(Fishing)* fishing ban; *(von Walen)* whaling ban; **Fang|vor|rich|tung** F arresting device; **Fang|zahn** M canine (tooth), fang; *(von Eber)* tusk

Fan-: **Fan|klub** ['fɛn-] M fan club; *(Ftbl auch)* supporters' club; **Fan|kult** M fan cult; **Fan|post** ['fɛn-] F fan mail; *(einzelner Brief)* fan letter

Fant [fant] M -(e)s, -e *(old pej)* jackanapes *(old)*

Fan|ta|sie [fanta'zi:] F -, -n [-'zi:ən] **a** *no pl (= Einbildung)* imagination; **er hat ~** he's got imagination; **eine schmutzige ~ haben** to have a dirty mind; **in seiner ~** in his mind *or* imagination; **er spielt ohne ~** he plays unimaginatively *or* without any imagination; **seiner ~ freien Lauf lassen** to give free rein to one's imagination **b** *usu pl (= Trugbild, Vorstellung)* fantasy → *auch* **Phantasie**

Fan|ta|sie F -, -n *(Mus)* fantasia

Fan|ta|sie- → *auch* **Phantasie-**: **fan|ta|sie|arm** ADJ unimaginative, lacking in imagination; **fan|ta|sie|be|gabt** ADJ imaginative; **Fan|ta|sie|bild** NT fantasy (picture); **Fan|ta|sie|ge|bil|de** NT **a** *(= fantastische Form)* fantastic form **b** *(= Einbildung)* figment of the *or* one's imagination; **fan|ta|sie|los** ADJ unimaginative, lacking in imagination; **Fan|ta|sie|lo|sig|keit** F -, *no pl* lack of imagination, unimaginativeness; **Fan|ta|sie|preis** M astronomical price *(inf)*; **fan|ta|sie|reich** ADJ ADV = **fantasievoll**

fan|ta|sie|ren [fanta'zi:rən] *ptp* **fantasiert** **VI** to fantasize (*von* about); *(von Schlimmem)* to have visions (*von* of); *(Med)* to be delirious; *(Mus)* to improvise; **er fantasiert von einem großen Haus auf dem Lande** he has fantasies about a big house in the country

VT *Geschichte* to dream up; *(Mus)* to improvise; **was fantasierst du denn da?** *(inf)* what are you (going) on about? *(inf)*; **er hat das alles fantasiert** that's all just (in) his imagination; **er fantasiert, dass die Welt untergeht** he has visions of the world coming to an end; **sie fantasiert, dass sie auswandern will** she fantasizes about emigrating → *auch* **phantasieren**

fan|ta|sie|voll **ADJ** highly imaginative **ADV** highly imaginatively; *reden, antworten* imaginatively

Fan|ta|sie|vor|stel|lung F figment of the imagination

Fan|tast [fan'tast] M -en, -en, **Fan|tas|tin** [-'tastɪn] F -, -nen dreamer, visionary → *auch* **Phantast(in)**

Fan|tas|te|rei [fantastə'rai] F -, -en fantasy → *auch* **Phantasterei**

fan|tas|tisch [fan'tastɪʃ] **ADJ** fantastic; *(= unglaublich auch)* incredible; **~e Literatur** fantasy literature **ADV** fantastically; **~ schmecken/aussehen** to taste/look fantastic; **~ klingen** to sound fantastic; *(unglaublich auch)* to sound incredible; **sie verdient ~** she earns a fantastic amount → *auch* **phantastisch**

Fan|ta|sy|film ['fɛntəzi-] M fantasy film

Fan|zine ['fɛnzi:n] NT -s, -s *(inf)* fanzine

FAQ [fak] PL *abbr von* **frequently asked questions** FAQ

Fa|rad [fa'ra:t] NT -(s), - farad

fa|ra|daysch [fara'de:ʃ] ADJ **~er Käfig** Faraday cage

Farb- *in cpds* colour *(Brit)*, color *(US)*; **Farb|ab|stim|mung** F colo(u)r scheme; *(TV)* colo(u)r adjustment; **Farb|ab|stu|fung** F colo(u)r gradation; **Farb|an|pas|sung** F *(Comput)* colo(u)r matching; **Farb|auf|nah|me** F colo(u)r photo(graph); **Farb|bad** NT dye-bath; **Farb|band** [-bant] NT *pl* **-bänder** *(von Schreibmaschine)* (typewriter) ribbon; **Farb|band** [-bant] M *pl* **-bände** *(= Buch)* book with colo(u)r illustrations; **Farb|band|kas|set|te** F typewriter ribbon cassette

färb|bar ADJ colourable *(Brit)*, colorable *(US)*

Farb-: **Farb|be|richt** M *(Press, TV)* report in colo(u)r; *(in Zeitschriften auch)* colo(u)r feature; **Farb|beu|tel** M paint bomb; **Farb|bild** NT *(Phot)* colo(u)r photo(graph); **Farb|dis|play** NT colour *(Brit)* or color *(US)* display; **Farb|druck** M *pl* **-drucke** colo(u)r print; **Farb|dru|cker** M colo(u)r printer

Far|be ['farbə] F -, -n **a** *(= Farbton, Tönung)* colour *(Brit)*, color *(US)*; **~ bekommen** to get a bit of colo(u)r, to catch the sun *(inf)*; **~ verlieren** to go pale; **in ~** in colo(u)r; **einer Sache** *(dat)* **mehr ~ geben** *(fig)* to give sth more colo(u)r; **etw in den dunkelsten** *or* **schwärzesten ~n schildern** *or* **ausmalen** to paint a black picture of sth; **etw in den glänzendsten ~n schildern** *or* **ausmalen** to paint a rosy picture of sth, to paint sth in glowing colo(u)rs **b** *(= Malerfarbe, Anstrichfarbe)* paint; *(für Farbbad)* dye; *(= Druckfarbe)* ink **c** **Farben** PL *(= Fahne, Univ)* colo(u)rs *pl*; **~n tragende Studenten/Verbindung** *students belonging to a fraternity/student fraternity with traditional heraldic colours* **d** *(Cards)* suit; **~ bedienen** to follow suit; **~ bekennen** *(fig)* to lay one's cards on the table; *(= klaren Standpunkt beziehen)* to nail one's colo(u)rs to the mast

farb|echt ADJ colourfast *(Brit)*, colorfast *(US)*; *(Comput)* true-colour *attr (Brit)*, true-color *attr (US)*

Farb|echt|heit F colourfastness *(Brit)*, colorfastness *(US)*; *(Comput)* true colour *(Brit) or* color *(US)*

Fär|be|mit|tel NT dye

farb|emp|find|lich ADJ *(Phot)* colour-sensitive *(Brit)*, color-sensitive *(US)*

fär|ben ['fɛrbn] **VT** to colour *(Brit)*, to color *(US)*; *Stoff, Haar* to dye → *auch* **gefärbt** **VI** *(= abfärben)* to run *(inf)* **VR** to change colo(u)r; **ihre Wangen färbten sich leicht** she coloured *(Brit) or* blushed slightly; **sich grün/blau** *etc* **~** to turn green/blue *etc*

Far|ben- *in cpds* colour *(Brit)*, color *(US)*; **far|ben|blind** ADJ colo(u)r-blind; **Far|ben|blind|heit** F colo(u)r-blindness; **Far|ben|druck** M, *no pl (Typ)* colo(u)r printing; **far|ben|freu|dig** ADJ colo(u)rful; *Mensch* fond of bright colo(u)rs; **far|ben|froh** ADJ colo(u)rful; **far|ben|kräf|tig** ADJ (very) colo(u)rful, in strong colo(u)rs; **Far|ben|leh|re** F theory of colo(u)r; *(= Fach auch)* chromatics *sing*; **Far|ben|pracht** F blaze of colo(u)r; **in seiner ganzen ~** in all its glory; **far|ben|präch|tig** ADJ gloriously colo(u)rful; **far|ben|reich** ADJ *(auch Mus)* colo(u)rful; **Far|ben|reich|tum** M *(auch Mus)* wealth of colo(u)rs; **Far|ben|sinn** M sense of colo(u)r *(auch Biol)*, colo(u)r sense; **Far|ben|spiel** NT play *or* kaleidoscope of colo(u)rs; **far|ben|tra|gend** ADJ *(Univ)* → **Farbe c**; **Far|ben|zu|sam|men|stel|lung** F colo(u)r combination

Fär|ber ['fɛrbɐ] M -s, -, **Fär|be|rin** [-ərɪn] F -, -nen dyer

Fär|be|rei [fɛrbə'rai] F -, -en **a** *(= Betrieb)* dyeing works *sing or pl* **b** *no pl (= Verfahren)* dyeing

Farb-: **Farb|fern|se|hen** NT colour *(Brit) or* color *(US)* television *or* TV; **Farb|fern|se|her** M, **Farb|fern|seh|ge|rät** NT colo(u)r television (set); **Farb|film** M colo(u)r film; **Farb|fil|ter** M *(Phot)* colo(u)r filter; **Farb|fleck** M paint spot *or* stain; **Farb|fo|to** NT colo(u)r photo(graph); **Farb|fo|to|gra|fie** F *(= Verfahren)* colo(u)r photography; *(= Bild)* colo(u)r photo(graph); **Farb|ge|bung** [-ge:bʊŋ] F -, -en colo(u)ring, coloration

far|big ['farbɪç] **ADJ** **a** coloured *(Brit)*, colored *(US)*; *(fig) Schilderung* vivid, colourful *(Brit)*, colorful *(US)*; **ein ~er Druck** a colo(u)r print; **eine ~e Postkarte** a colo(u)r postcard **b** *attr Hautfarbe* colo(u)red **ADV** *(= in Farbe) anstreichen* in a colo(u)r; *(= anschaulich) schildern* colo(u)rfully, vividly; **~ fotografieren** to take colo(u)r photographs, to photograph in colo(u)r

fär|big ['fɛrbɪç] ADJ *(Aus)* = **farbig ADJ a**

Far|bi|ge(r) ['farbɪgə] MF *decl as adj* coloured *(Brit) or* colored *(US)* man/woman/person *etc*; **die ~n** the colo(u)reds *pl*, colo(u)red people *pl*

Farb-: **Farb|kas|ten** M paintbox; **Farb|kis|sen** NT inkpad; **Farb|klecks** M blob of paint, paint spot; **Farb|kom|bi|na|ti|on** F colo(u)r combination; *(= Farbzusammenstellung)* colo(u)r scheme; **Farb|ko|pie|rer** M colour *(Brit) or* color *(US)* copier; **farb|lich** ['farplɪç] **ADJ** colo(u)r *attr* **ADV** **die Fotokopie ist ~ einwandfrei** the colo(u)rs in this photocopy are excellent; **zwei Sachen ~ aufeinander abstimmen** to match two things up for colo(u)r; **~ harmonisch** in harmonious colo(u)rs; **farb|los** ADJ *(lit, fig)* colo(u)rless; **Farb|lo|sig|keit** F -, *no pl (lit, fig)* colo(u)rlessness; **Farb|mi|ne** F colo(u)red-ink cartridge; **Farb|mi|schung** F (=

gemischte Farbe) mixture of colo(u)rs; *(Comput: bei Druckereigenschaften)* dithering; **Farb|pho|to|gra|phie** F = **Farbfotografie**; **Farb|psy|cho|lo|gie** F psychological implications of colours *(Brit)* or colors *(US)*; **Farb|rol|ler** M paint roller; **Farb|sinn** M sense of colo(u)r *(auch Biol)*, colo(u)r sense; **Farb|stich** M *(Phot, TV)* colo(u)r fault; **Farb|stift** M colo(u)red pen; *(= Buntstift)* crayon, colo(u)red pencil; **Farb|stoff** M *(= Lebensmittelfarbstoff)* (artificial) colo(u)ring; *(= Hautfarbstoff)* pigment; *(für Textilien etc)* dye; **Farb|ta|fel** F colo(u)r plate; *(= Tabelle)* colo(u)r chart; **Farb|ton** M *pl* **-töne** shade, hue; *(= Tönung)* tint; **Farb|tup|fer** M spot of colo(u)r

Fär|bung ['fɛrbʊŋ] F **-, -en** *(= das Färben, Farbgebung)* colouring *(Brit)*, coloring *(US)*; *(= Tönung)* tinge, hue; *(fig)* slant, bias

Farb-: **Farb|wie|der|ga|be** F *(TV etc)* colo(u)r reproduction; **Farb|zu|sam|men|stel|lung** F colo(u)r scheme

Far|ce ['farsə] F **-, -n** **a** *(Theat, fig)* farce **b** *(Cook)* stuffing

far|cie|ren [far'siːrən] *ptp* **farciert** VT *(Cook)* to stuff

Farm [farm] F **-, -en** farm

Far|mer ['farmɐ] M **-s, -**, **Far|me|rin** [-ərɪn] F **-, -nen** farmer

Farm|haus NT farmhouse

Farn [farn] M **-(e)s, -e**, **Farn|kraut** NT fern; *(= Adlerfarn)* bracken

Fä|rö|er [fɛ'røːɐ, 'fɛːrøɐ] PL Faroes *pl*, Faroe Islands *pl*

Fär|se ['fɛrzə] F **-, -n** heifer

Fa|san [fa'zaːn] M **-s, -e** or **-en** pheasant

Fa|sa|ne|rie [fazanə'riː] F **-, -n** [-'riːən] pheasant-house; *(im Freien)* pheasant-run

Fa|sche ['faʃə] F **-, -n** *(Aus)* bandage

fa|schen ['faʃən] VT *(Aus)* to bandage

fa|schie|ren [fa'ʃiːrən] *ptp* **faschiert** VT *(Aus Cook)* to mince; **Faschiertes** mince, minced meat, ground meat *(US)*; **faschiertes Laiberl** or **Laibchen** hamburger

Fa|schi|ne [fa'ʃiːnə] F **-, -n** fascine

Fa|sching ['faʃɪŋ] M **-s, -e** or **-s** *Shrovetide carnival*, Fasching

Fa|schings- *in cpds* carnival; **Fa|schings|diens|tag** M Shrove Tuesday; **Fa|schings|kos|tüm** NT carnival costume, fancy dress *sing or pl*; **Fa|schings|prinz** M carnival prince; **Fa|schings|prin|zes|sin** F carnival princess; **Fa|schings|zeit** F carnival period

Fa|schis|mus [fa'ʃɪsmʊs] M **-**, *no pl* fascism

Fa|schist [fa'ʃɪst] M **-en, -en**, **Fa|schis|tin** [-'ʃɪstɪn] F **-, -nen** fascist

fa|schis|tisch [fa'ʃɪstɪʃ] ADJ fascist

fa|schis|to|id [faʃɪsto'iːt] ADJ fascistic

Fa|scho ['faʃo] M **-s, -s** *(sl)* fascist

Fa|se ['faːzə] F **-, -n** bevel, chamfer

Fa|se|lei [faːzə'lai] F **-, -en** *(pej)* twaddle *(inf)*, drivel *(inf)*

Fa|se|ler ['faːzəlɐ] M **-s, -**, **Fa|se|le|rin** [-ərɪn] F **-, -nen** *(pej)* drivelling *(Brit)* or driveling *(US)* idiot *(pej)*

fa|seln ['faːzln] *(pej)* VI to drivel *(inf)* VT **Blödsinn ~** to talk drivel *(inf)*; **das ist alles gefaselt** that's drivel *(inf)*, that's just (so much) twaddle *(inf)*; **was hat er gefaselt?** what was he drivelling *(Brit)* or driveling *(US)* (on) about? *(inf)*

Fa|se|nacht ['faːzənaxt] M **-**, *no pl (S Ger, Sw)* *Shrovetide carnival*, Fasenacht

Fa|ser ['faːzɐ] F **-, -n** fibre *(Brit)*, fiber *(US)*; **ein Pullover aus synthetischen ~n** a pullover made of synthetic fibre *(Brit)* or fiber *(US)*; **er hat keine trockene ~ am Leib** he's soaked through or drenched; **mit allen ~n des Herzens** *(liter)* with every fibre *(Brit)* or fiber *(US)* of one's being *(liter)*

Fa|ser-: **fa|ser|ar|tig** ADJ fibrous; **Fa|ser|ge|we|be** NT *(Biol)* fibrous tissue

fa|se|rig ['faːzərɪç] ADJ fibrous; *Fleisch, Spargel auch* stringy *(pej)*; *(= zerfasert)* frayed

fa|sern ['faːzɐn] VI to fray

Fa|ser-: **fa|ser|nackt** ADJ = **splitter(faser)nackt**; **Fa|ser|op|tik** F fibre *(Brit)* or fiber *(US)* optics *sing*; **Fa|ser|pflan|ze** F fibre *(Brit)* or fiber *(US)* plant; **Fa|ser|plat|te** F fibreboard *(Brit)*, fiberboard *(US)*; **fa|ser|scho|nend** ADJ gentle *(to fabrics)*; **Fa|ser|schrei|ber** M *(= Schreibstift)* felt-tip pen, fibretip *(Brit)* or fibertip *(US)* pen; **Fa|ser|stoff** M fibrous material

Fas|ler ['faːslɐ] M **-s, -**, **Fas|le|rin** [-ərɪn] F **-, -nen** *(pej)* = **Faseler**

Fas|nacht ['fasnaxt] F, *no pl* = **Fastnacht**

fas|rig ['faːzrɪç] ADJ = **faserig**

Fass [fas] NT **-es, =er** ['fɛsɐ] barrel; *(= kleines Bierfass)* keg; *(zum Gären, Einlegen)* vat; *(zum Buttern)* (barrel) churn; *(für Öl, Benzin, Chemikalien)* drum; **etw in Fässer füllen** to put sth into barrels/drums, to barrel sth; **drei Fässer/~ Bier** three barrels of beer; **vom ~** on tap; *Bier auch* on draught *(Brit)* or draft *(US)*; *Sherry, Wein auch* from the wood *(esp Brit)*; **er trinkt nur Bier vom ~** he only drinks draught *(Brit)* or draft *(US)* beer; **ein ~ ohne Boden** *(fig)* a bottomless pit; **ein ~ aufmachen** *(fig inf)* to kick up a shindy *(Brit inf)* or a storm *(US inf)*; **das schlägt dem ~ den Boden aus** *(inf)* that beats everything!, that takes the biscuit! *(Brit inf)*; **das brachte das ~ zum Überlaufen** *(fig)* that was the last straw *(prov)*, that was the straw that broke the camel's back *(prov)*

Fas|sa|de [fa'saːdə] F **-, -n** *(lit, fig)* façade; *(inf: = Gesicht)* face; **das ist doch nur ~** *(fig)* that's just a façade

Fas|sa|den-: **Fas|sa|den|klet|te|rer** M, **Fas|sa|den|klet|te|rin** F cat burglar; **Fas|sa|den|rei|ni|gung** F exterior cleaning

Fass-: **Fass|band** [-bant] NT *pl* **-bänder** hoop (of a barrel); **fass|bar** ['fasbaːɐ] ADJ comprehensible, understandable; **das ist doch nicht ~!** that's incomprehensible!; **Fass|bar|keit** F **-**, *no pl* comprehensibility; **Fass|bier** NT draught *(Brit)* or draft *(US)* beer; **Fass|bin|der(in)** M(F) *(old, Aus)* cooper

Fäss|chen ['fɛsçən] NT **-s, -** *dim von* **Fass** cask

Fass|dau|be F stave

fas|sen ['fasn] VT **a** *(= ergreifen)* to take hold of; *(hastig, kräftig)* to grab, to seize; *(= festnehmen) Einbrecher etc* to apprehend *(form)*, to seize; *(Mil) Munition* to draw; **jdn beim** or **am Arm ~** to take/grab sb by the arm; **er fasste ihre Hand** he took her hand; **Schauder/Grauen/Entsetzen fasste ihn** he was seized with horror; **fass!** seize!

b *(fig) Beschluss, Entschluss* to make, to take; *Mut* to take; **Vertrauen zu jdm ~** to come to trust sb; **den Gedanken ~, etw zu tun** to form or have the idea of doing sth; **den Vorsatz ~, etw zu tun** to make a resolution to do sth → **Auge a**, **Fuß a**, **Herz e**

c *(= begreifen)* to grasp, to understand; **es ist nicht zu ~** it's unbelievable or incredible; **ich fasse es nicht** I don't believe it

d *(= enthalten)* to hold

e *(= aufnehmen) Essen* to get; *(Rail, Naut) Wasser, Kohlen* to take on; **Essen ~!** come and get it!

f *(= einfassen) Edelsteine* to set; *Bild* to frame; *Quelle* to surround; *(fig: = ausdrücken)* to express; **in Verse/Worte ~** to put into verse/words; **neu ~** *(Manuskript, Rede, Erzählung)* to revise; **etw weit/eng ~** to interpret sth broadly/narrowly

VI **a** *(= nicht abrutschen)* to grip; *(Zahnrad)* to bite

b *(= greifen)* **an/in etw** *(acc)* **~** to feel sth; *(= berühren)* to touch sth; **fass mal unter den Tisch** feel under the table; **sich** *(dat)* **an den Kopf ~** *(fig)* to shake one's head in disbelief; **da fasst man sich** *(dat)* **an den Kopf** *(inf)* you wouldn't believe it, would you?

VR *(= sich beherrschen)* to compose oneself; **fass dich!** pull yourself together!; **sich vor Freude kaum ~ können** to be beside oneself with joy; **sich in Geduld ~** to be patient, to possess one's soul in patience → → *auch* **gefasst**, **kurzfassen**

fäs|ser|wei|se ADV *(= in großen Mengen)* by the gallon; *(= in Fässern)* by the barrel

Fas|set|te etc [fa'sɛtə] F **-, -n** = **Facette** etc

fass|lich ['faslɪç] ADJ comprehensible, understandable

Fass|lich|keit F **-**, *no pl* comprehensibility

Fas|son [fa'sõː] F **-, -s** *(von Kleidung)* style; *(von Frisur)* shape; **aus der ~ geraten** *(lit)* to go out of shape, to lose its shape; *(dated: = dick werden)* to get fat; **jeder soll nach seiner ~ selig werden** *(prov)* everyone has to find his own salvation

fas|so|nie|ren [faso'niːrən] *ptp* **fassoniert** VT *(Aus) Haare* to (cut and) shape

Fas|son|schnitt [fa'sõː-] M *style in which the hair is shaped into the neck (für Herren)* short back and sides

Fass|reif M, **Fass|rei|fen** M hoop

Fas|sung ['fasʊŋ] F **-, -en** **a** *(von Juwelen)* setting; *(von Bild)* frame; *(Elec)* holder

b *(= Bearbeitung, Wortlaut)* version; **ein Film in ungekürzter ~** the uncut version of a film; **ein Buch in ungekürzter ~** the unabridged version of a book; **ein Film in deutscher ~** a film with German dubbing

c *no pl (= Ruhe, Besonnenheit)* composure; **die ~ bewahren** or **behalten** to maintain one's composure; **etw mit ~ tragen** to take sth calmly or with equanimity; **die ~ verlieren** to lose one's composure; **völlig außer ~ geraten** to lose all self-control; **jdn aus der ~ bringen** to disconcert or throw *(inf)* sb; *Redner auch* to put sb off

Fas|sungs-: **Fas|sungs|kraft** F *(liter)* (powers of) comprehension or understanding; **die menschliche ~ übersteigen** to be beyond human understanding; **fas|sungs|los** ADJ stunned, bewildered ADV in bewilderment; **Fas|sungs|lo|sig|keit** F **-**, *no pl* bewilderment; **Fas|sungs|ver|mö|gen** NT *(lit, fig)* capacity; **das übersteigt mein ~** that's beyond me, that's beyond the limits of my comprehension

Fass-: **Fass|wein** M wine from the wood; **fass|wei|se** ADV by the barrel; *(= in Fässern)* in barrels

fast [fast] ADV almost, nearly; **~ nie** hardly ever, almost never; **~ nichts** hardly anything, almost nothing; **ich wäre ~ überfahren worden** I was almost or nearly run over

fas|ten ['fastn] VI to fast

Fas|ten-: **Fas|ten|kur** F diet; **eine ~ machen/anfangen** to be/go on a diet; **Fas|ten|zeit** F period of fasting; *(Eccl)* Lent

Fast|food [faːst'fuːd] NT **-**, *no pl*, **Fast Food** NT **-**, *no pl* fast food

Fast|nacht ['fastnaxt] F, *no pl (= Fasching)* *Shrovetide carnival* *(= Faschingsdienstag)* Shrove Tuesday

FASTNACHT

Fastnacht is another word for **Karneval**. The Rhine **Karneval**, however, is very different from **Fastnacht** in the Swabian-Alemannic region of Germany, and in Switzerland. Here the period of celebration extends beyond Ash Wednesday; indeed **Fastnacht** in Basle only begins after Ash Wednesday. The customs date back over 400 years and have their origin in ancient rites to banish winter. Only traditional costumes and wooden masks are allowed in the processions. Drums and bells are used to drive out the winter, and participants dressed as witches or goblins play tricks on the spectators, sometimes even during the night or at the first light of dawn.
→ KARNEVAL

Fast|nachts-: **Fast|nachts|narr** M, **Fast|nachts|när|rin** F *disguised figure in Shrove Tuesday celebrations*; **Fast|nachts|spiel** NT *(Liter)* Shrovetide play; **Fast|nachts|um|zug** M Shrove Tuesday procession

Fast|tag M day of fasting

Fas|zi|kel [fas'tsiːkl] M **-s, -** *(old, form)* section of manuscript, fascicle *(spec)*

Fas|zi|na|ti|on [fastsinaˈtsioːn] F -, -en fascination; ~ **ausstrahlen** to radiate charm; **jds ~** *(dat)* **erlegen sein** to succumb to sb's fascinating power

fas|zi|nie|ren [fastsiˈniːrən] *ptp* **fasziniert** VTI to fascinate *(an +dat* about); ~**d** fascinating; **mich fasziniert der Gedanke, das zu tun** I'm very attracted by *or* to the idea of doing that

fa|tal [faˈtaːl] ADJ *(geh)* *(= verhängnisvoll)* fatal, fateful, dire; *(= peinlich)* embarrassing, awkward

Fa|ta|lis|mus [fataˈlɪsmʊs] M -, *no pl* fatalism

Fa|ta|list [fataˈlɪst] M -en, -en, **Fa|ta|lis|tin** [-ˈlɪstɪn] F -, -nen fatalist

fa|ta|lis|tisch [fataˈlɪstɪʃ] ADJ fatalistic

Fa|ta|li|tät [fataliˈtɛːt] F -, -en great misfortune

Fa|ta Mor|ga|na [ˈfaːta mɔrˈgaːna] F - -, - -s *or* **Morganen** [mɔrˈgaːnən] *(lit, fig)* Fata Morgana *(liter)*, mirage

Fat|sche [ˈfatʃə] F -, -n *(Aus)* bandage

fat|schen [ˈfatʃn] VT *(Aus)* to bandage

Fatz|ke [ˈfatskə] M -n *or* -s, -n *or* -s *(inf)* stuck-up twit *(Brit inf)* *or* twerp *(inf)*

fau|chen [ˈfauxn] VTI to hiss

faul [faul] ADJ **a** *(= verfault)* bad; *Lebensmittel* off *pred (Brit)*, bad *pred*; *Eier, Obst* rotten, bad; *Holz, Gesellschaftsordnung* rotten; *Geschmack, Geruch* foul, putrid; *Zahn* bad, decayed; *Laub* rotting; *Wasser* foul
b *(= verdächtig)* fishy *(inf)*, suspicious, dubious; *(Comm)* *Wechsel, Scheck* dud *(inf)*; *Kredit* bad; *(= fadenscheinig)* *Ausrede* flimsy, feeble; *Kompromiss* uneasy; *Friede* empty; *(= dumm)* *Witz* bad; **hier ist etwas ~** *(inf)* there's something fishy here *(inf)*; **etwas ist ~ daran** *(inf)* **an der Sache ist etwas ~** *(inf)* there's something fishy about the whole business *(inf)*; **etwas ist ~ im Staate Dänemark** *(prov)* there's something rotten in the State of Denmark *(prov)*
c *(= träge)* lazy, idle; ~ **wie die Sünde** bone idle *(Brit inf)*, very lazy; **nicht ~** *(= reaktionsschnell)* quick as you please; **er hat seinen ~en Tag** *(= müßiger Tag)* he's having a lazy day; *(= faule Stimmung)* he's in a lazy mood → **Haut, Strick**

Fäu|le F -, *no pl* **a** *(Vet)* (liver) rot **b** = **Fäulnis**

fau|len [ˈfaulən] VI *aux sein or haben* to rot; *(Aas auch)* to putrefy; *(Zahn)* to decay; *(Lebensmittel)* to go bad

fau|len|zen [ˈfaulɛntsn] VI to laze *or* loaf *(esp pej inf)* about

Fau|len|zer [ˈfaulɛntsɐ] M -s, - *(Aus: = Linienblatt)* sheet of ruled paper

Fau|len|zer [ˈfaulɛntsɐ] M -s, -, **Fau|len|ze|rin** [-ərɪn] F -, -nen layabout

Fau|len|ze|rei [faulɛntsəˈrai] F -, *(rare)* -en lazing *or* loafing *(esp pej inf)* about

Faul|heit F -, *no pl* laziness, idleness; **er stinkt vor ~** *(inf)* he's bone idle *(Brit inf)* *or* a lazybones *(inf)*

fau|lig [ˈfaulɪç] ADJ going bad; *Lebensmittel* going bad, going off *(Brit)*; *Eier, Obst* going bad, going rotten; *Wasser* stale; *(in Teich, See etc)* stagnating; *Geruch, Geschmack* foul, putrid ADV ~ **schmecken/riechen** to taste/smell bad; *(Wasser)* to taste/smell foul

Fäul|nis [ˈfɔylnɪs] F -, *no pl* rot; *(von Fleisch auch)* putrefaction; *(von Zahn)* decay; *(fig)* decadence, degeneracy; ~ **erregend** putrefactive; **von ~ befallen** rotting, decaying

Fäul|nis|er|re|ger M putrefier

Faul-: **Faul|pelz** M *(inf)* lazybones *sing (inf)*; **Faul|schlamm** M sapropel *(spec)*, sludge; **Faul|tier** NT sloth; *(inf: = Mensch)* lazybones *sing (inf)*

Faun [faun] M -(e)s, -e *(Myth)* faun

Fau|na [ˈfauna] F -, **Faunen** [ˈfaunən] fauna

Faust [faust] F -, **Fäuste** [ˈfɔystə] fist; **die (Hand zur) ~ ballen** to clench one's fist; **jdm eine ~ machen** *(inf)* to shake one's fist at sb; **jdm mit der ~ ins Gesicht schlagen** to punch sb in the face; **jdm die ~ unter die Nase halten** to shake one's fist in sb's face *or* under sb's nose; **mit der ~ auf den Tisch schlagen** *(lit)* to thump on the table (with one's fist); *(fig)* to take a hard line, to put one's foot down; **etw aus der ~ essen** to eat sth with one's hands; **ein Butterbrot auf die ~** a sandwich in one's hand; **die ~/Fäuste in der Tasche ballen** *(fig)* to bottle up *or* choke back one's anger; **mit geballten Fäusten zusehen müssen** *(fig)* to watch in helpless anger; **das passt wie die ~ aufs Auge** *(= passt nicht)* it's all wrong; *(Farbe)* it clashes horribly; *(= ist fehl am Platz)* it's completely out of place; *(= passt gut)* it's just the thing *(inf)* *or* job *(inf)*; **jds ~ im Nacken spüren** *(fig)* to have sb breathing down one's neck; **auf eigene ~** *(fig)* off one's own bat *(Brit inf)*, on one's own initiative; *reisen, fahren* under one's own steam → **eisern ADJ b**

Faust-: **Faust|ab|wehr** F *(Sport)* save using the fists; **herrlich, diese ~ des Torwarts!** the goalkeeper punches the ball clear beautifully!; **Faust|ball** M *form of volleyball*

Fäust|chen [ˈfɔystçən] NT -s, - *dim von* **Faust**; **sich** *(dat)* **ins ~ lachen** to laugh up *(Brit)* *or* in *(US)* one's sleeve; *(bei finanziellem Vorteil)* to laugh all the way to the bank *(inf)*

faust|dick *(inf)* ADJ **eine ~e Lüge** a whopper *(inf)*, a whopping (great) lie *(inf)*; **eine ~e Überraschung** a huge surprise ADV **das ist ~ gelogen** that's a whopping lie *(inf)*, that's a whopper *(inf)*; **er hat es ~ hinter den Ohren** he's a sly *or* crafty one *(inf)*; ~ **auftragen** to lay it on thick *(inf)*

Fäus|tel [ˈfɔystl] M OR NT -s, - sledgehammer

faus|ten [ˈfaustn] VT *Ball* to punch; *(Ftbl auch)* to fist

Faust-: **Faust|feu|er|waf|fe** F handgun; **faust|groß** ADJ as big as a fist, the size of a fist; **Faust|hand|schuh** M mitt(en)

faus|tisch [ˈfaustɪʃ] ADJ Faustian

Faust-: **Faust|kampf** M fist-fight; **Faust|kämp|fer(in)** M(F) *(old)* pugilist *(old)*; **Faust|keil** M hand-axe *(Brit)*, hand-ax *(US)*

Fäust|ling [ˈfɔystlɪŋ] M -s, -e mitt(en)

Faust-: **Faust|pfand** NT security; **Faust|recht** NT, *no pl* law of the jungle; **Faust|re|gel** F rule of thumb; **Faust|schlag** M punch

Fau|teuil [foˈtøːj] M -s, -s *(old, Aus)* leather armchair

Faux|pas [foˈpa] M -, - gaffe, faux pas

fa|vo|ri|sie|ren [favoriˈziːrən] *ptp* **favorisiert** VT to favour *(Brit)*, to favor *(US)*; **die Wettbüros ~ X als Sieger** the betting shops show X as favourite *(Brit)* *or* favorite *(US)*, the betting shops have X to win; **favorisiert werden** to be favourite *(Brit)* *or* favorite *(US)*

Fa|vo|rit [favoˈriːt] M -en, -en, **Fa|vo|ri|tin** [-ˈriːtɪn] F -, -nen favourite *(Brit)*, favorite *(US)*; **„zu ~en hinzufügen"** *(Comput)* "add favo(u)rites"; **„Favoriten verwalten"** *(Comput)* "organize favo(u)rites"

Fa|vo|ri|ten|rol|le [favoˈriːtn-] F role as favourite *(Brit)* *or* favorite *(US)*, favourite *(Brit)* *or* favorite *(US)* tag

Fax [faks] NT -, -e fax

Fax|ab|ruf M fax polling

Fax|an|schluss M *(fax line)*

fa|xen [ˈfaksn] VT to fax, to send by fax

Fa|xen [ˈfaksn] PL **a** *(inf: = Alberei)* fooling about *(Brit)* *or* around; ~ **machen** to fool about *(Brit)* *or* around; **die ~ dicke haben** to be fed up with all the nonsense **b** *(= Grimassen)* ~ **schneiden** to pull faces

Fax-: **Fax|ge|rät** NT fax machine; **Fax|num|mer** F fax number

Fa|yence [faˈjãːs] F -, -n faïence

FAZ [ɛflaːˈtsɛt, fats] F - *abbr von* **Frankfurter Allgemeine Zeitung**

Fa|zit [ˈfaːtsɪt] NT -s, -s *or* -e **das ~ der Untersuchungen war ...** on balance the result of the investigations was ...; **wenn wir aus diesen vier Jahren das ~ ziehen** if we take stock of these four years; **wenn ich das ~ ziehen müsste, würde ich sagen ...** on balance I would say ...

FCKW [ɛftseːkaːˈveː] M -s, -s *abbr von* **Fluorchlorkohlenwasserstoff** CFC

FCKW-frei [ɛftseːkaːˈveː-] ADJ CFC-free

FDGB [ɛfdeːgeːˈbeː] M -(s) *(DDR) abbr von* **Freier Deutscher Gewerkschaftsbund** Free German Trades Union Congress

FDJ [ɛfdeːˈjɔt] F - *(DDR) abbr von* **Freie Deutsche Jugend** Free German Youth

FDJler [ɛfdeːˈjɔtlɐ] M -s, -, **FDJle|rin** [-ərɪn] F -, -nen *(DDR)* member of the Free German Youth

FDP [ɛfdeːˈpeː] F - *abbr von* **Freie Demokratische Partei**

> **FDP**
>
> The **FDP (Freie Demokratische Partei)** was founded in Germany in 1948. It is a central party supporting liberal views. Although relatively small, as a coalition partner of both **CDU** and **SPD** it plays a part in many decisions both at Federal and **Land** level. → CDU, SPD

Fea|ture [ˈfiːtʃɐ] NT -s, -s *(Rad, TV)* feature programme *(Brit)* *or* program *(US)*

Fe|ber [ˈfeːbɐ] M -s, - *(Aus)* February → *auch* **März**

Feb|ru|ar [ˈfeːbruaːɐ] M -(s), -e February → *auch* **März**

Fecht|bahn F *(Sport)* piste

fech|ten [ˈfɛçtn] *pret* **focht** [fɔxt], *ptp* **gefochten** [gəˈfɔxtn] VI *(Sport)* to fence; *(geh: = kämpfen)* to fight; **das Fechten** fencing VT **Degen/Florett ~** to fence with épées/foils; **einen Gang ~** to fence a bout

Fech|ter [ˈfɛçtɐ] M -s, -, **Fech|te|rin** [-ərɪn] F -, -nen fencer

Fech|ter|stel|lung F fencing stance

Fecht-: **Fecht|hand|schuh** M fencing glove; **Fecht|hieb** M (fencing) cut; **Fecht|kunst** F art of fencing; *(= Geschick)* skill in fencing; **Fecht|meis|ter(in)** M(F) fencing master; **Fecht|sport** M fencing

Fe|der [ˈfeːdɐ] F -, -n **a** *(= Vogelfeder)* feather; *(= Gänsefeder etc)* quill; *(= lange Hutfeder)* plume; **leicht wie eine ~** as light as a feather; **~n lassen müssen** *(inf)* not to escape unscathed; **in den ~n stecken** *or* **liegen** *(inf)* to be in one's bed *or* pit *(inf)*; **jdn aus den ~n holen** *(inf)* to drag sb out of bed *(inf)*; **raus aus den ~n!** *(inf)* rise and shine! *(inf)*, show a leg! *(inf)* → **fremd a**
b *(= Schreibfeder)* quill; *(an Federhalter)* nib; **ich greife zur ~ ...** I take up my pen ...; **aus jds ~ fließen** to flow from sb's pen; **dieser Text stammt nicht aus meiner ~** this text was not written by me; **eine scharfe** *or* **spitze ~ führen** to wield a wicked *or* deadly pen; **mit spitzer ~** with a deadly pen, with a pen dipped in vitriol *(liter)*; **ein Mann der ~** *(dated geh)* a man of letters
c *(Tech)* spring
d *(in Holz)* tongue

Fe|der-: **Fe|der|an|trieb** M clockwork; **mit ~** clockwork-driven, driven by clockwork; **Fe|der|ball** M *(= Ball)* shuttlecock, birdie *(US inf)*; *(= Spiel)* badminton; **Fe|der|bein** NT *(Tech)* suspension strut; **Fe|der|be|sen** M feather duster; **Fe|der|bett** NT continental quilt, duvet; **Fe|der|blatt** NT leaf of a spring; **Fe|der|busch** M *(von Vögeln)* crest; *(von Hut, Helm)* plume; **Fe|der|de|cke** F continental quilt, duvet; **Fe|der|fuch|ser** [-fʊksɐ] M -s, -, **Fe|der|fuch|se|rin** [-ərɪn] F -, -nen *(pej)* petty-minded pedant *(pej)*; *(= Schreiberling)* pettifogging penpusher *(pej)* *or* pencilpusher *(US pej)*; **fe|der|füh|rend** ADJ *Behörde etc* in overall charge *(für* of); **Fe|der|füh|rung** F **unter der ~** *+gen* under the overall control of; **die ~ haben** to be in charge, to have overall charge; **Fe|der|ge|wicht** NT *(Sport)* featherweight (class); **Fe|der|ge|wicht|ler** [-gəvɪçtlɐ] M -s, -, **Fe|der|ge|wicht|le|rin** [-ərɪn] F -, -nen *(Sport)* featherweight; **Fe|der|hal|ter** M (dip) pen; *(= Füllfederhalter)* (fountain) pen; *(ohne Feder)* pen

(-holder); **Fe|der|hut** M plumed hat; **Fe|der|kas|ten** M *(Sch)* pencil box; **Fe|der|kern|mat|rat|ze** F interior sprung mattress, inner-spring mattress *(US)*; **Fe|der|kiel** M quill; **Fe|der|kis|sen** NT feather cushion; *(in Bett)* feather pillow; **Fe|der|kleid** NT *(liter)* plumage; **Fe|der|krieg** M *(fig)* war of words; **fe|der|leicht** ADJ light as a feather; *(fig) Musik, Töne* floating; **Fe|der|le|sen** NT **-s**, *no pl* **nicht viel ~s mit jdm/etw machen** to waste no time on sb/sth, to make short work of sb/sth; **ohne langes ~, ohne viel ~s** without ceremony, without any (further) ado; **Fe|der|mäpp|chen** NT, **Fe|der|map|pe** F pencil case; **Fe|der|mes|ser** NT penknife

fe|dern ['fe:dɐn] **VI** **a** *(Eigenschaft)* to be springy **b** *(= hochfedern, zurückfedern)* to spring back; *(Fahrzeug)* to bounce (up and down); *(Springer, Turner: = hochgeschleudert werden)* to bounce; **(in den Knien)** ~ *(Sport)* to bend *or* give at the knees **c** *(Kissen etc)* to shed (feathers); *(Vogel)* to moult *(Brit)*, to molt *(US)*, to shed its feathers **VT** to spring; *Auto, Räder* to fit with suspension; **ein Auto hydraulisch ~** to fit a car with hydraulic suspension → *auch* **gefedert**

fe|dernd ADJ *(Tech)* sprung; *(fig)* jaunty; **~e Radaufhängung** spring suspension; **einen ~en Gang haben** to have a jaunty *or* springy step *or* gait; **mit ~en Schritten** with a spring in one's step

Fe|der-: **Fe|der|pen|nal** ['fe:dɐpɛna:l] NT **-s, -e** *(Aus)* pencil case; **Fe|der|ring** M spring washer; **Fe|der|schmuck** M feather trimming; *(von Indianern etc)* headdress; *(= Federbusch)* plume; *(von Vogel)* plumage; **Fe|der|skiz|ze** F pen-and-ink sketch; **Fe|der|spiel** NT *(Hist)* lure; **Fe|der|strich** M pen-stroke, stroke of the pen; **mit einem** *or* **durch einen ~** with a single stroke of the pen

Fe|de|rung ['fe:dərʊŋ] F **-, -en** springs *pl*, springing; *(Aut auch)* suspension

Fe|der-: **Fe|der|vieh** NT poultry; **Fe|der|waa|ge** F spring balance; **Fe|der|wei|ße(r)** M *decl as adj (dial)* new wine

> **FEDERWEISSER**
>
> **Federweißer** (also known as **Sauser**, **Bitzler** or – in Austria – **Sturm**) is new wine. It is only partially fermented and still contains carbon dioxide and yeast. **Federweißer** is a very popular drink at grape-harvest time and is often enjoyed with a piece of **Zwiebelkuchen**.
> → WEIN

Fe|der-: **Fe|der|wild** NT *(Hunt)* game birds *pl*; **Fe|der|wisch** M *(old)* feather duster; **Fe|der|wölk|chen** NT, **Fe|der|wol|ke** F fleecy cloud; **Fe|der|zeich|nung** F pen-and-ink drawing

Fee [fe:] F **-, -n** ['fe:ən] fairy

Feed|back ['fi:dbɛk] NT **-s, -s**, **Feed-back** NT **-s, -s** feedback

Fee|ling ['fi:lɪŋ] NT *(inf)* **-s, -s** feeling *(für* for)

feen|haft ['fe:ən-] ADJ *(liter)* fairylike

Fe|ge|feu|er ['fe:gə-] NT **das ~** purgatory

fe|gen ['fe:gn] **VT** **a** *(mit Besen)* to sweep; *(= auffegen)* to sweep up; *(Sw) (= wischen)* to wipe; *(mit Bürste)* to scrub; **den Schmutz von etw ~** to sweep sth (clean) **b** *(Hunt) Geweih* to fray **VI** **a** *(= ausfegen)* to sweep (up) **b** *aux sein (inf: = jagen)* to sweep; *(Wind auch)* to race

Fe|ger ['fe:gɐ] M **-s, -** **a** *(inf)* brush **b** *(inf: = Mädchen)* girl

Feh|de ['fe:də] F **-, -n** *(Hist)* feud; **mit jdm eine ~ ausfechten** to feud with sb, to carry on a feud with sb; **mit jdm in ~ liegen** *(lit, fig)* to be feuding with sb, to be in a state of feud with sb

Feh|de|hand|schuh M **jdm den ~ hinwerfen** *(lit, fig)* to throw down the gauntlet to sb; **den ~ aufheben** *(lit, fig)* to take up the gauntlet

fehl [fe:l] ADJ **~ am Platz(e)** out of place

Fehl [fe:l] M *(old, liter)* **ohne ~** without (a) blemish

Fehl-: **Fehl|an|flug** M *(Aviat)* failed approach (to landing); **Fehl|an|pas|sung** F **a** *(Psych)* maladjustment **b** *(Elec)* mismatch; **Fehl|an|zei|ge** F *(inf)* dead loss *(inf)*; **~!** wrong!; **Fehl|auf|schlag** M *(Sport)* fault; **einen ~ machen** to serve a fault; **fehl|bar** ADJ fallible; *(Sw)* guilty; **Fehl|bar|keit** F **-**, *no pl* fallibility; *(Sw)* guilt; **Fehl|be|darf** M uncovered demand; **Fehl|be|die|nung** F *(von Geräten)* operating error; **Fehl|be|le|gung** F *(von Sozialwohnungen)* inappropriate occupation *(of subsidized accommodation)*; **Fehl|be|le|gungs|ab|ga|be** F *tax levied on those inappropriately occupying subsidized accommodation*; **fehl+be|set|zen** *ptp* **fehlbesetzt** VT *sep* to miscast; **Fehl|be|set|zung** F miscasting; **eine ~** a piece *or* bit of miscasting; **Fehl|be|stand** M deficiency; **Fehl|be|trag** M *(form)* deficit, shortfall; **Fehl|bil|dung** F *(Biol)* malformation; *(= Missbildung)* deformity; **Fehl|bit|te** F *(form)* vain request; **Fehl|deu|tung** F misinterpretation; **Fehl|di|ag|no|se** F wrong *or* false diagnosis; **Fehl|dis|po|si|ti|on** F miscalculation; **Fehl|druck** M *pl* **-drucke** *(Typ)* misprint; **Fehl|ein|schät|zung** F false estimation; *(der Lage)* misjudgement

feh|len ['fe:lən] **VI** **a** *(= mangeln)* to be lacking; *(= nicht vorhanden sein)* to be missing; *(in der Schule etc)* to be away *or* absent (*in +dat* from); *(= schmerzlich vermisst werden)* to be missed; **entschuldigt ~** to be absent; **unentschuldigt ~** *(Sch)* to play truant; **das Geld fehlt** *(= ist nicht vorhanden)* there is no money; *(= ist zu wenig vorhanden)* there isn't enough money; **etwas fehlt** there's something missing; **jdm fehlt etw** sb lacks sth, sb doesn't have sth; *(= wird schmerzlich vermisst)* sb misses sth; **mir fehlt Geld** I'm missing some money; **mir ~ 20 Cent am Fahrgeld** I'm 20 cents short for my fare, I'm short of 20 cents for my fare; **mir ~ die Worte** words fail me; **meine Bibliothek fehlt/du fehlst mir sehr** I miss my library/you a lot; **der/das hat mir gerade noch gefehlt!** *(inf)* he/that was all I needed *(iro)*; **das durfte nicht ~** that had to happen

b *(= los sein)* **was fehlt dir?** what's the matter *or* what's up (with you)?; **fehlt dir (et)was?** is something the matter (with you)?; **mir fehlt nichts** there's nothing the matter (with me); **dem Hund scheint etwas zu ~** the dog seems to have something the matter with it, there seems to be something wrong *or* the matter with the dog

c *(old: = etwas falsch machen)* to err

VI *impers* **es fehlt etw** *or* **an etw** *(dat)* there is a lack of sth; *(völlig)* there is no sth, sth is missing; **es ~ drei Messer** there are three knives missing; **es fehlt jdm an etw** *(dat)* sb lacks sth; **es an etw** *(dat)* **~ lassen** to be lacking in sth, to lack sth; **er ließ es uns an nichts ~** *(geh)* he let us want for nothing; **es fehlt hinten und vorn(e), es fehlt an allen Ecken und Enden** *or* **Kanten** we/they *etc* are short of everything; *(bei Kenntnissen)* he/she *etc* has a lot to learn, he/she *etc* has a long way to go; *(bei Klassenarbeit etc)* it's a long way from perfect; **wo fehlt es?** what's the trouble?, what's up? *(inf)*; **es fehlte nicht viel und ich hätte ihn verprügelt** I almost hit him; **es fehlt(e) nur noch, dass wir sonntags arbeiten sollen** working Sundays is all we need *(iro)*

VT *(old Hunt)* to miss; **weit gefehlt!** *(fig)* you're way out! *(inf)*; *(ganz im Gegenteil)* far from it!

Fehl-: **Fehl|ent|schei|dung** F wrong decision; **Fehl|ent|wick|lung** F mistake; **um ~en zu vermeiden** to stop things going off course *or* taking a wrong turn

Feh|ler ['fe:lɐ] ✪ 45.2 M **-s, -** **a** *(= Irrtum, Unrichtigkeit)* mistake, error; *(Sport)* fault; *(Comput)* error; *(= Programmierfehler)* bug; **einen ~ machen** *or* **begehen** to make a mistake *or* error; **ihr ist ein ~ unterlaufen** she's made a mistake; **~!** *(Sport)* fault!; **schwerer** *or* **schwerwiegender ~** *(Comput)* fatal *or* critical error; **voller ~** *(Comput) Programm, Software* bug-ridden

b *(= Mangel)* fault, defect; *(= Charakterfehler auch)* failing; **einen ~ aufweisen** to prove faulty; **jeder hat seine ~** we all have our faults, nobody's perfect; **das ist nicht mein ~** that's not my fault; **einen ~ an sich** *(dat)* **haben** to have a fault; **er hat den ~ an sich, immer dazwischenzureden** *or* **dass er immer dazwischenredet** the trouble with him is that he's always interrupting; **in den ~ verfallen, etw zu tun** to make the mistake of doing sth

Feh|ler-: **Feh|ler|ana|ly|se** F error analysis; **feh|ler|an|fäl|lig** ADJ error-prone; **Feh|ler|an|fäl|lig|keit** F proneness to errors; **Feh|ler|an|zei|ge** F *(Comput)* error message; **Feh|ler|be|he|bung** F *(esp Comput)* troubleshooting; **Feh|ler|be|richt** M *(Comput)* bug report; **Feh|ler|co|de** M error code; **feh|ler|frei** ADJ perfect; *Ware auch* in perfect condition; *Arbeit, Aussprache, Kür etc auch* faultless, flawless; *Messung, Rechnung* correct; *(Comput) Programm* bug-free; **~er Lauf/Sprung** *(Sport)* clear round/jump; **Feh|ler|frei|heit** F *(von Ware)* perfect condition; **Feh|ler|gren|ze** F margin of error; **feh|ler|haft** ADJ *(Mech, Tech)* faulty, defective; *Ware* substandard, imperfect; *Messung, Rechnung, Bescheide* incorrect; *Arbeit, Aussprache* poor; *(Comput) Datei etc* bad, corrupt(ed); **Feh|ler|haf|tig|keit** ['fe:lɐhaftɪçkait] F **-**, *no pl (Mech, Tech)* defectiveness; *(von Ware)* substandard condition; *(von Messung, Rechnung, Bescheiden)* incorrectness; *(von Arbeit, Aussprache)* poorness; **Feh|ler|ko|de** M = **Fehlercode**; **Feh|ler|kor|rek|tur** F **a** *(Sch)* correction of mistakes; *(eines einzelnen Fehlers)* correction **b** *(Comput: = Rechtschreibkorrektur)* spell check; *(für Computerprogramme)* debugging program **c** *(Tech: in CD-Spieler etc)* error correction *or* concealment; **Feh|ler|kor|rek|tur|pro|gramm** NT *(Comput)* **a** *(= Rechtschreibkorrekturprogramm)* spellchecker, spelling checker **b** *(für Computerprogramme)* debugging program; **feh|ler|los** ADJ = **fehlerfrei**; **Feh|ler|mel|dung** F *(Comput)* error message

Fehl|er|näh|rung ['fe:l-] F malnutrition

Feh|ler-: **Feh|ler|quel|le** F cause of the fault; *(in Statistik)* source of error; **Feh|ler|quo|te** F error rate; **Feh|ler|su|che** F troubleshooting; *(Tech)* fault detection; *(= Suche nach möglichen Fehlern)* checking for faults; **feh|ler|to|le|rant** ADJ *(Comput)* fault-tolerant; **Feh|ler|ver|zeich|nis** NT errata *pl*

Fehl-: **Fehl|far|be** F *(Cards)* missing suit; *(= Nicht-Trumpf)* plain *or* side suit; *(= Zigarre)* cigar with a discoloured *(Brit)* *or* discolored *(US)* wrapper; **Fehl|ge|burt** F miscarriage

fehl+ge|hen VI *sep irreg aux sein* **a** *(geh: = sich verirren)* to go wrong, to miss the way; *(Schuss)* to go wide **b** *(= sich irren)* to be wrong *or* mistaken, to err *(form)*; **ich hoffe, ich gehe nicht fehl in der Annahme, dass ...** I trust I am not mistaken in assuming that ...

Fehl-: **fehl|ge|steu|ert** [-gəʃtɔyɐt] ADJ misdirected; *(fig)* mismanaged; **Fehl|griff** M mistake; **einen ~ tun** to make a mistake; **Fehl|in|for|ma|ti|on** F incorrect information *no pl*; **Fehl|in|ter|pre|ta|ti|on** F misinterpretation; **Fehl|in|ves|ti|ti|on** F bad investment; **Fehl|kal|ku|la|ti|on** F miscalculation; **Fehl|kon|struk|ti|on** F bad design; **der Stuhl ist eine ~** this chair is badly designed; **Fehl|lan|dung** F bad landing; **Fehl|leis|tung** F slip, mistake; **freudsche ~** Freudian slip; **fehl+lei|ten** VT *sep* to misdirect; **die Akte wurde fehlgeleitet** the file was sent to the wrong place; **Fehl|lei|tung** F misdirection; **Fehl|pass** M *(Ftbl)* bad pass; **Fehl|pla|nung** F misplanning, bad planning; **eine ~** a piece of misplanning *or* bad planning; **fehl|plat|ziert** [-platsi:ɐt] ADJ *Empörung etc* misplaced; **Fehl|prä|gung** F *(einer Münze)* mis-strike; **Fehl|prog|no|se** F incorrect prognosis; **Fehl|re|ak|ti|on** F incorrect response; **Fehl|schal|tung** F faulty circuit; **fehl+schie|ßen** VI *sep irreg* to shoot wide; **Fehl|schlag** M *(fig)* failure; **fehl+schla|gen** VI *sep irreg aux sein* to go wrong; *(Bemühungen, Versuch)* to fail; *(Hoffnung)* to be misplaced, to come to nothing; *(Comput)* to fail; **Fehl|schluss** M false conclusion; **Fehl|schuss** M miss; **fehl|sich|tig** [-zɪçtɪç] ADJ *(form)* with defective vision; **Fehl|sich|tig|keit** F -, *no pl (form)* defective vision; **Fehl|spe|ku|la|ti|on** F bad speculation; **Fehl|start** M false start; *(Space)* faulty launch; **Fehl|stoß** M *(Ftbl)* miskick; *(Billard)* miscue; **fehl+sto|ßen** VI *sep irreg (Ftbl)* to miskick; *(Billard)* to miscue; **fehl+tre|ten** VI *sep irreg aux sein (geh)* to miss one's footing, to stumble; *(fig)* to err, to lapse; **Fehl|tritt** M *(geh)* false step; *(fig) (= Vergehen)* slip, lapse; *(= Affäre)* indiscretion; **Fehl|ur|teil** NT miscarriage of justice; **Fehl|ver|hal|ten** NT inappropriate behaviour *(Brit)* or behavior *(US)*; *(Psych)* abnormal behaviour *(Brit)* or behavior *(US)*; **Fehl|ver|such** M unsuccessful or abortive attempt; **fehl+ver|wen|den** *ptp* **fehlverwendet** VT *sep* to misappropriate; **Fehl|wurf** M *(Sport)* misthrow, bad throw; *(ungültig)* no-throw; **Fehl|zei|ten** PL working hours *pl* lost; **Fehl|zug** M *(Chess)* bad move; **Fehl|zün|dung** F misfiring *no pl*; **eine ~** a backfire; **das war bei mir eine ~** *(fig inf)* I got hold of the wrong end of the stick *(inf)*

fei|en ['faiən] VT *(old)* to protect *(gegen* from), to make proof *(gegen* against) → *auch* **gefeit**

Fei|er ['faiɐ] F -, -n celebration; *(= Party)* party; *(= Zeremonie)* ceremony; *(= Hochzeitsfeier)* reception; **zur ~ von etw** to celebrate sth; **zur ~ des Tages** in honour *(Brit)* or honor *(US)* of the occasion

Fei|er|abend M **a** *(= Arbeitsschluss)* finishing time; *(= Geschäftsschluss)* closing time; **~ machen** to finish work, to knock off (work) *(inf)*; *(Geschäfte)* to close; **ich mache jetzt ~** I think I'll call it a day *(inf)*, I think I'll knock off now *(inf)*; **um 16.00 Uhr ~ haben** to finish work at 4 o'clock; **~!** *(in Gaststätte)* time, please!; **nach ~** after work; **jetzt ist aber ~!** *(fig inf)* enough is enough; **damit ist jetzt ~** *(fig inf)* that's all over now; **dann ist ~** *(fig inf)* then it's all over, then it's the end of the road; **für mich ist ~** *(fig inf)* I've had enough
b *(= Zeit nach Arbeitsschluss)* evening; **schönen ~!** have a nice evening!

fei|er|lich ['faiɐlɪç] ADJ *(= ernsthaft, würdig)* solemn; *(= festlich)* festive; *(= förmlich)* ceremonial; **das ist ja nicht mehr ~** *(inf)* that's beyond a joke *(inf)* ADV solemnly; **einen Tag ~ begehen** to celebrate a day

Fei|er|lich|keit F -, -en **a** *(= Ernsthaftigkeit, Würde)* solemnity; *(= Festlichkeit)* festiveness; *(= Förmlichkeit)* ceremony **b** *usu pl (= Veranstaltungen)* celebrations *pl*, festivities *pl*

fei|ern ['faiɐn] VT **a** *Ereignis* to celebrate; *Party, Fest, Orgie* to hold; **das muss gefeiert werden!** that calls for a celebration; **Triumphe ~** to achieve a great triumph, to make one's mark **b** *(= umjubeln)* to fête → *auch* **gefeiert** VI **a** *(= eine Feier abhalten)* to celebrate; **die ganze Nacht ~** to make a night of it **b** *(= nicht arbeiten)* to stay off work

Fei|er-: **Fei|er|schicht** F cancelled *(Brit)* or canceled *(US)* shift; **eine ~ fahren/einlegen** to miss/cancel a shift; **Fei|er|stun|de** F ceremony; **Fei|er|tag** M holiday; **fei|er|täg|lich** ADJ holiday *attr (esp Brit)*, vacation *attr (US)*; **~e Stimmung** holiday mood; **das ~e Ruhegebot** *rule discouraging any activity likely to disturb the quietness of Sundays and public holidays* ADV **~ angezogen** in one's Sunday best

fei|er|tags|be|dingt ADJ due to a public holiday/public holidays

Fei|er|tags|stim|mung F holiday mood

feig [faik], **fei|ge** ['faigə] ADJ cowardly; **~ wie er war** like the coward he was ADV in a cowardly way; **er zog sich ~ zurück** he retreated like a coward

Fei|ge ['faigə] F -, -n fig

Fei|gen-: **Fei|gen|baum** M fig tree; **Fei|gen|blatt** NT fig leaf; **ein ~ für etw** *(fig)* a front to hide sth; **als demokratisches ~** *(fig)* to give a veneer of democracy; **Fei|gen|kak|tus** M prickly pear

Feig|heit F -, *no pl* cowardice, cowardliness

Feig|ling ['faiklɪŋ] M -s, -e coward

feil [fail] ADJ *(old, geh)* (up) for sale; **der Ring war ihr um** or **für nichts auf der Welt ~** not for all the world would she have sold the ring

feil+bie|ten VT *sep irreg (old)* to offer for sale

Fei|le ['failə] F -, -n file

fei|len ['failən] VT to file VI to file; *(fig)* to make some improvements; **an etw** *(dat)* **~** *(lit)* to file (away at) sth; *(fig)* to hone sth, to polish sth up

feil+hal|ten VT *sep irreg (old)* to offer for sale → **Maulaffen**

feil|schen ['failʃn] VI *(pej)* to haggle *(um* over)

Feil-: **Feil|span** M filing; **Feil|staub** M (fine) filings *pl*

fein [fain] ADJ **a** *(= nicht grob)* fine; *Humor, Ironie* delicate; *Unterschied* subtle; *(fig: = listig)* cunning
b *(= erlesen)* excellent, choice *attr*; *Geruch, Geschmack* delicate; *Gold, Silber* refined; *Mensch, Charakter* thoroughly nice; *(= prima)* great *(inf)*, splendid, swell *(esp US inf)*; *(iro)* fine; **ein ~er Kerl** a great guy *(inf)*, a splendid person; **~!** great! *(inf)*, marvellous! *(Brit)*, marvelous! *(US)*; *(= in Ordnung)* fine!; **~, dass ...** great that ... *(inf)*, (I'm) so glad that ...; **das ist etwas Feines** that's really something *(inf)* or nice; **das ist nicht die ~e englische Art** that's not the proper way to go about things; **vom Feinsten sein** to be first-rate; **italienisches Design vom Feinsten** Italian design at its finest
c *(= scharf)* sensitive, keen; *Gehör, Gefühl auch* acute
d *(= vornehm)* refined, fine *(esp iro)*, posh *(inf)*; **nicht ~ genug sein** not to be good enough; **dazu ist sie sich** *(dat)* **zu ~** that's beneath her
ADV **a** *(= nicht grob) gemahlen, gesponnen, schleifen, geädert* finely; **ein ~ gestreiftes Hemd** a shirt with very thin stripes; **sie hat ein ~ geschnittenes Gesicht** she has fine features; **~ geschwungene Augenbrauen** finely arched eyebrows
b *(= gut)* **~ säuberlich** (nice and) neat; **etw ~ machen** to do sth beautifully; **das war von dir aber wieder ~ bemerkt** you have such a nice way of putting things; **~ (he)raus sein** to be sitting pretty
c *(= genau)* **etw ~ einstellen** to adjust sth precisely
d *(= elegant)* **er hat sich ~ gemacht** he's dressed to kill *(inf)*; **sie hat sich ~ gemacht** she's all dolled up *(inf)*
e *(baby-talk)* just; **du gehst jetzt ~ nach Hause** now just you go straight home; **sei jetzt mal ~ still** now keep nice and quiet or very very quiet

Fein-: **Fein|ab|stim|mung** F *(Rad, TV)* fine tuning; **Fein|ar|beit** F precision work; **Fein|aus|gleich** M *(Comput)* microspacing; **Fein|bä|cke|rei** F cake shop, patisserie; **Fein|blech** NT thin sheet metal

feind [faint] ADJ *pred* **jdm/einer Sache ~ sein** to be hostile to sb/sth

Feind [faint] M -(e)s, -e [-də], **Fein|din** ['faindɪn] F -, -nen enemy, foe *(liter)*; **jdn zum ~ haben** to have sb as an enemy; **sich** *(dat)* **jdn zum ~ machen** to make an enemy of sb; **sich** *(dat)* **~e schaffen** to make enemies; **er war ein ~ jeden Fortschritts** he was opposed to progress in any shape or form; **ran an den ~** *(inf)* let's get stuck in *(inf)*; **der böse ~** *(Bibl)* the Evil One, the Enemy; **liebet eure ~e** *(Bibl)* love thine enemy *(Bibl)* → *auch* **feind**

-feind M, **-fein|din** F *suf in cpds* -hater; **eine Männerfeindin** a man-hater

Feind- *in cpds* enemy; **Feind|be|rüh|rung** F contact with the enemy; **Feind|bild** NT concept of an/the enemy; **Feind|ein|wir|kung** F *(Mil form)* **durch ~** as a result of enemy action; **er verletzte sich ohne ~** his injury was self-inflicted

Fein|des-: **Fein|des|hand** F *(old, liter)* the hands of the foe *(liter)*; **Fein|des|land** NT *(old, liter)* enemy territory

Fein|din ['faindɪn] F → **Feind**

feind|lich ['faintlɪç] ADJ **a** *(Mil: = gegnerisch)* enemy; **im ~en Lager** *(lit, fig)* in the enemy camp **b** *(= feindselig)* hostile ADV **jdm/einer Sache ~ gegenüberstehen** to be hostile to sb/sth; **einer Sache ausgesprochen ~ gegenüberstehen** to be vehemently opposed to sth, to be extremely hostile to sth

-feind|lich ADJ *suf* anti-; **deutschfeindlich** anti-German

Feind|macht F enemy power; **eine ~ unseres Landes** an enemy of our country

Feind|schaft ['faintʃaft] F -, -en hostility, enmity; **sich** *(dat)* **jds ~ zuziehen** to make an enemy of sb; **mit jdm in ~ leben** or **liegen** to be at daggers drawn with sb, to live in enmity with sb; **eine ~ auf Leben und Tod** mortal enmity

feind|se|lig ADJ hostile ADV hostilely; **jdn ~ ansehen** to give sb a hostile look

Feind|se|lig|keit F -, -en hostility; **~en** hostilities

Fein-: **Fein|ein|stel|lung** F *(Tech)* fine adjustment; *(Radio, Kurzwelle)* fine tuning; **fein|füh|lend**, **fein|füh|lig** [-fy:lɪç] ADJ sensitive; *(= taktvoll)* tactful; **Fein|füh|lig|keit** F -, *no pl* sensitivity; *(= Takt)* tact(fulness); **Fein|ge|bäck** NT cakes and pastries *pl*; **Fein|ge|fühl** NT, *no pl* sensitivity; *(= Takt)* delicacy, tact(fulness); **jds ~ verletzen** to hurt sb's feelings; **fein|ge|mah|len** [-gəma:lən] ADJ → **fein ADV a**; **fein|ge|schnit|ten** ADJ → **fein ADV a**; **fein|ge|schwun|gen** ADJ → **fein ADV a**; **fein|ge|streift** ADJ → **fein ADV a**; **fein|glie|de|rig** [-gli:dərɪç], **fein|glied|rig** [-gli:drɪç] ADJ *Person, Hände* slender; **Fein|gold** NT refined gold

Fein|heit F -, -en **a** *(= Zartheit)* fineness; **die ~ des britischen Humors** the delicate British humour *(Brit)* or humor *(US)* **b** *(= Erlesenheit)* excellence; *(von Gold, Silber)* refinement; **die ~ des Geschmacks** the delicate flavour *(Brit)* or flavor *(US)* **c** *(= Schärfe)* keenness; *(von Gehör, Gefühl auch)* acuteness **d** *(= Vornehmheit)* refinement, poshness *(inf)* **e** **Feinheiten** PL niceties *pl*, finer points *pl*; *(= Nuancen)* subtleties *pl*; **das sind eben die ~en** it's the little things that make the difference

Fein-: **Fein|koh|le** F slack; **fein|kör|nig** ADJ *Film* fine-grain; *Sand, Salz auch* fine; **Fein|kost** F delicacies *pl*; **„Feinkost"** "Delicatessen"; **Fein|kost|ge|schäft** NT delicatessen; **fein+ma|chen** VR *sep* → **fein ADV d**; **fein|ma|schig** [-maʃɪç] ADJ with a fine mesh; *Strickwaren* finely knitted; **Fein|me|cha|nik** F precision engineering; **Fein|me|cha|ni|ker(in)** M(F) precision engineer; **Fein|mess|ge|rät** NT precision instrument; **Fein|mo|to|rik** F *(Med etc)* fine motor skills *pl*; **fein|mo|to|risch** ADJ *(Med etc)* fine-motor; **~e Entwicklung** fine-motor development; **fein|ner|vig** ADJ sensitive; **Fein|po|si|ti|o|nie|rung** F microjustification; **Fein|schliff** M fine finish(ing); **Fein|schme|cker** [-ʃmɛkɐ] M -s, -, **Fein|schme|cke|rin** [-ərɪn] F -, -nen gourmet, epicure; *(fig)* connoisseur; **Fein|schme|cker|lo|kal** NT gourmet restaurant; **fein+schlei|fen** VT *sep irreg* → **fein ADV d**; **Fein|schnitt** M *(= Tabak)* fine cut; *(Film)* final editing; **Fein|sil|ber** NT refined silver; **fein|sin|nig** ADJ sensitive; *Unterscheidung* subtle; **Fein|sin|nig|keit** F -, *no pl* sensitivity; **Fein|staub** M fine dust; **Fein|staub|wert** M fine dust levels *pl*; **Fein|struk|tur** F fine structure; **Fein|un|ze** F troy ounce; **Fein|waa|ge** F precision balance;

Fein|wä|sche F delicates *pl*; **Fein|wasch|mit|tel** NT mild(-action) detergent

Feins|lieb|chen [fainsˈliːpçən] NT **-s, -** *(poet)* lady-love *(poet)*, sweetheart

feist [faist] ADJ fat; *Mensch auch* gross, obese; **ein ~es Lachen** an obscene chuckle

Feist|heit F **-**, *no pl*, **Feis|tig|keit** [ˈfaistıçkait] F **-**, *no pl* fatness; *(von Mensch auch)* grossness, obesity

Fei|tel [ˈfaitl] M **-s, -** *(Aus)* penknife

fei|xen [ˈfaiksn] VI *(inf)* to smirk

Fel|chen [ˈfɛlçn] M **-s, -** whitefish

Feld [fɛlt] NT **-(e)s, -er** [-dɐ] **a** *(= offenes Gelände)* open country; **auf freiem ~** in the open country → **Wald**

b *(= Acker)* field

c *(= Flächenstück: auf Spielbrett)* square; *(an Zielscheibe)* ring; *(Her)* field

d *(Sport: = Spielfeld)* field, pitch; **das ~ beherrschen** to be on top

e *(= Kriegsschauplatz)* (battle)field; **ins ~ ziehen** *or* **rücken** *(old)* to take the field, to march into battle; **auf dem ~e der Ehre fallen** *(euph old)* to fall on the field of honour *(Brit) or* honor *(US)*; **gegen jdn/etw zu ~e ziehen** *(fig)* to crusade against sb/sth; **Argumente ins ~ führen** to bring arguments to bear; **das ~ behaupten** *(fig)* to stand *or* stay one's ground; **jdn aus dem ~ schlagen** *(fig)* to eliminate sb; **das ~ räumen** *(fig)* to quit the field, to bow out; **jdm/einer Sache das ~ überlassen** *or* **räumen** to give way *or* yield to sb/sth; *(freiwillig)* to hand over to sb/sth

f *(fig: = Bereich)* field, area

g *(Ling, Min, Phys, Comput)* field

h *(Sport: = Gruppe)* field; **er ließ das ~ hinter sich** *(dat)* he left the rest of the field behind (him); **das ~ ist geschlossen** the field is bunched (up)

Feld- *in cpds* field; **Feld|ar|beit** F *(Agr)* work in the fields; *(Sci, Sociol)* fieldwork; **Feld|ar|bei|ter(in)** M(F) fieldworker; **Feld|arzt** M *(old Mil)* army doctor; **Feld|be|steck** NT knife, fork and spoon, eating irons *pl* *(Brit hum)*; **Feld|bett** NT campbed, cot *(US)*; **Feld|bin|de** F **a** *(old: = Schärpe)* sash **b** *(Med Mil)* Red Cross armband; **Feld|blu|me** F wild flower; **Feld|dienst** M *(old Mil)* active service; **Feld|elekt|ro|nen** PL *(Elec)* field electrons *pl*; **Feld|ener|gie** F *(Phys)* field energy

Fel|der|wirt|schaft F *(Agr)* crop rotation

Feld-: **Feld|fla|sche** F canteen *(Mil)*, water bottle; **Feld|flug|platz** M (military) airstrip *(near the front)*; **Feld|for|schung** F, *no pl* *(esp Sociol)* field research, fieldwork; **Feld|frucht** F *(Agr)* agricultural crop; **Feld|geist|li|che(r)** M *decl as adj (old Mil)* army chaplain, padre; **Feld|gen|dar|me|rie** F *(old Mil)* military police; **Feld|glei|chung** F *(Math)* field equation; **Feld|got|tes|dienst** M *(Mil)* camp service; **Feld|hand|ball** M European (outdoor) handball; **Feld|ha|se** M European hare; **Feld|hau|bit|ze** F *(Mil)* (field) howitzer; **Feld|heer** NT *(Mil)* army in the field; **Feld|herr(in)** M(F) commander; **Feld|herrn|kunst** F *(old)* strategy; **Feld|herrn|stab** M *(old)* (general's) baton, (general's) swagger stick; **Feld|heu|schre|cke** F grasshopper; *(schädlich)* locust; **Feld|huhn** NT partridge; **Feld|hü|ter** M watchman *(in charge of fields)*; **Feld|jä|ger(in)** M(F) **a** *(old Mil) (= Kurier)* courier; *(= Infanterist)* infantryman **b** ~ *(Mil)* military police; *(bei der Marine)* shore patrol; **Feld|kon|stan|te** F *(Phys)* space constant; **Feld|kraft** F *(Phys)* field intensity *or* strength; **Feld|krä|he** F rook; **Feld|kü|che** F *(Mil)* field kitchen; **Feld|la|ger** NT *(old Mil)* camp, encampment; **Feld|la|za|rett** NT *(Mil)* field hospital; **Feld|ler|che** F skylark; **Feld|li|nie** F *(Phys)* line of force; **Feld|mark** F *pl* **-marken** *(von Gemeinde)* parish land; *(von Gut)* estate; **Feld|mar|schall** M *(old)* field marshal; **Feld|maus** F field mouse, common vole *(spec)*; **Feld|mes|ser** [-mɛsɐ] M **-s, -**, **Feld|mes|se|rin** [-ərın] F **-, -nen** (land) surveyor; **Feld|pflan|ze** F agricultural crop; **Feld|post** F *(Mil)* forces' postal service; **Feld|post|brief** M *(Mil)* forces' letter; **Feld|rain** M edge of the field; **Feld|sa|lat** M lamb's lettuce; **Feld|schlacht** F *(old)* battle; **Feld|schütz** [-ʃʏts] M **-es, -e** *(Mil)* watchman *(in charge of fields)*; **Feld|spat** M *(Geol)* fel(d)spar; **Feld|spie|ler(in)** M(F) *(Sport)* player (on the field); **Feld|stär|ke** F *(Phys)* field strength *or* intensity; *(Rad, TV)* strength of the signal; **Feld|ste|cher** [-ʃtɛçɐ] M **-s, -** (pair of) binoculars, (pair of) field glasses; **Feld|stu|die** F *(esp Sociol)* field study; **Feld|stuhl** M folding stool; **Feld|te|le|fon** NT *(Mil)* field telephone; **Feld|te|le|graf**, **Feld|te|le|graph** M *(Mil)* field telegraph; **Feld|the|o|rie** F *(Ling, Phys, Psych)* field theory; **Feld|ver|such** M field test; **Feld|ver|weis** M = **Platzverweis**; **Feld|wa|che** F *(old Mil)* outpost

Feld-Wald-und-Wie|sen- *in cpds (inf)* common-or-garden *(Brit)*, garden-variety *(esp US)*, run-of-the-mill; **ein ~Arzt** a common-or-garden *(Brit) or* garden-variety *(esp US) or* run-of-the-mill doctor; **ein ~Thema** a run-of-the-mill subject

Feld-: **Feld|we|bel** [ˈfɛltveːbl] M **-s, -**, **Feld|we|be|lin** [-bəlın] F **-, -nen** sergeant; *(fig inf)* sergeant-major (type); **Feld|weg** M track across the fields; **Feld|wei|bel** [ˈfɛltvaibl] M **-s, -**, **Feld|wei|be|lin** [-bəlın] F **-, -nen** *(Sw)* sergeant; **Feld|zei|chen** NT *(old Mil)* standard, ensign; **Feld|zug** M *(old, fig)* campaign

Felg|auf|schwung [ˈfɛlk-] M *(Sport)* upward circle forwards

Fel|ge [ˈfɛlgə] F **-, -n** **a** *(Tech)* (wheel) rim **b** *(Sport)* circle

Fel|gen|brem|se F calliper brake

Felg|um|schwung [ˈfɛlk-] M *(Sport)* circle

Fell [fɛl] NT **-(e)s, -e** **a** fur; *(von Schaf, Lamm)* fleece; *(von toten Tieren)* skin, fell; **ein gesundes ~** a healthy coat; **einem Tier das ~ abziehen** to skin an animal; **ihm sind alle** *or* **die ~e weggeschwommen** *(fig)* all his hopes were dashed **b** *(fig inf: = Menschenhaut)* skin, hide *(inf)*; **ein dickes ~ haben** to be thick-skinned, to have a thick skin; **jdm das ~ gerben** *or* **versohlen** to tan sb's hide *(inf)*; **jdm das ~ über die Ohren ziehen** to dupe sb, to pull the wool over sb's eyes; **ihn** *or* **ihm juckt das ~** he's asking for a good hiding; **das ~ versaufen** to hold the wake **c** *(von Trommel)* skin

Fell- *in cpds* fur; *(Schaffell- etc)* sheepskin *etc*; **eine Fellmütze** a fur/sheepskin hat; **eine Felljacke** a fur/sheepskin jacket

Fel|la|che [fɛˈlaxə] M **-n, -n**, **Fel|la|chin** [-ˈlaxın] F **-, -nen** fellah

Fel|la|tio [fɛˈlaːtsio] F **-, Fellationes** [fɛlaˈtsioːnes] fellatio

Fell-: **Fell|ei|sen** NT *(obs)* knapsack; **Fell|han|del** M trade in skins

Fels [fɛls] M **-en, -en** [ˈfɛlzn] rock; *(= Klippe)* cliff

Fels- *in cpds* → *auch* **Felsen-**: **Fels|bild** NT rock-scape; **Fels|block** M *pl* **-blöcke** boulder; **Fels|bro|cken** M (lump of) rock

Fel|sen [ˈfɛlzn] M **-s, -** rock; *(= Klippe)* cliff

Fel|sen- *in cpds* → *auch* **Fels-**: **Fel|sen|burg** F mountain fortress; **fel|sen|fest** ADJ firm ADV **~ überzeugt sein** to be absolutely *or* firmly convinced; **sich ~ auf jdn verlassen** to put one's complete trust in sb; **Fel|sen|ge|bir|ge** NT **a** rocky mountain range **b** *(Geog)* Rocky Mountains *pl*, Rockies *pl*; **Fel|sen|grab** NT rock tomb; **Fel|sen|grund** M rockbed; *(poet: = Tal)* rocky vale *(poet) or* glen; **Fel|sen|höh|le** F rock cave; **Fel|sen|nest** NT mountain lair *or* hideout; **Fel|sen|riff** NT (rocky) reef; **Fel|sen|schlucht** F rocky valley *or* glen; **Fel|sen|tor** NT arch in the rock

Fels-: **Fels|for|ma|ti|on** F *(Geol)* rock formation; **Fels|ge|stein** NT *(Geol)* (solid) rock; **Fels|glim|mer** M *(Geol)* mica; **Fels|grat** M (rocky) ridge

fel|sig [ˈfɛlzıç] ADJ rocky; *(= steil abfallend) Küste* cliff-lined, cliffy

Fels-: **Fels|kes|sel** M corrie; **Fels|klip|pe** F rocky cliff; *(im Meer)* stack; **Fels|ma|le|rei** F rock painting; **Fels|mas|siv** NT rock massif; **Fels|na|se** F rock overhang *or* shelf; **Fels|spal|te** F crevice; **Fels|vor|sprung** M ledge; **Fels|wand** F rock face; **Fels|wüs|te** F rock desert; **Fels|za|cke** F crag

Fe|lu|ke [feˈluːkə] F **-, -n** felucca

Fe|me [ˈfeːmə] F **-, -n**, **Fe|me|ge|richt** NT *(Hist)* Vehmgericht; *(= Bandengericht)* kangaroo court

Fe|me|mord M *(Hist) killing ordered by a Vehmgericht (fig)* lynch-law killing; *(unter Gangstern)* underworld killing

Fem|ge|richt [ˈfeːm-] NT = **Feme(gericht)**

Fe|mi|nat [femiˈnaːt] NT **-(e)s, -e** female power base

fe|mi|nin [femiˈniːn] ADJ **a** *(Gram)* feminine **b** *(= fraulich)* feminine; *(pej)* effeminate

Fe|mi|ni|num [ˈfeːminiːnʊm] NT **-s, Feminina** [-na] *(Gram)* feminine noun

Fe|mi|nis|mus [femiˈnısmʊs] M **-, Feminismen** [-mən] feminism

Fe|mi|nist [femiˈnıst] M **-en, -en**, **Fe|mi|nis|tin** [-ˈnıstın] F **-, -nen** feminist

fe|mi|nis|tisch [femiˈnıstıʃ] ADJ feminist ADV **~ orientiert sein** to have feminist tendencies

Femme fa|tale [fam faˈtal] F **- -, -s -s** femme fatale

Fem|to|gramm [fɛmtoˈgram] NT femtogram(me)

Fen|chel [ˈfɛnçl] M **-s**, *no pl* fennel

Fen|chel- *in cpds* fennel; **Fen|chel|holz** NT sassafras wood; **Fen|chel|tee** M fennel tea

Fen|der [ˈfɛndɐ] M **-s, -** fender

Fens|ter [ˈfɛnstɐ] NT **-s, -** window *(auch Comput, fig)*; **weg vom ~** *(inf)* out of the game *(inf)*, finished; **~ der Gelegenheit** window of opportunity → **Geld a**

Fens|ter- *in cpds* window; **Fens|ter|aus|schnitt** M *(Comput)* (window) pane; **Fens|ter|bank** F *pl* **-bänke**, **Fens|ter|brett** NT windowsill, window ledge; **Fens|ter|brief|um|schlag** M window envelope; **Fens|ter|ecke** F *(Comput)* window corner; **Fens|ter|flü|gel** M side of a window; **Fens|ter|front** F glass façade; **Fens|ter|glas** NT window glass; *(in Brille)* plain glass; **Fens|ter|griff** M window catch *(Brit) or* knob *(US)*; **Fens|ter|grö|ße** F *(Comput)* window size; **Fens|ter|he|ber** M *(Aut)* window winder *(Brit) or* raiser *(US)*; *(elektronisch)* electric windows *pl*; **Fens|ter|hin|ter|grund** M *(Comput)* window background; **Fens|ter|kitt** M (window) putty; **Fens|ter|klap|pe** F fanlight; **Fens|ter|kreuz** NT mullion and transom *(of a cross window)*; **Fens|ter|kur|bel** F window handle *(for winding car windows)*; **Fens|ter|la|den** M shutter; **Fens|ter|le|der** NT chamois, shammy (leather)

fens|terln [ˈfɛnstɐln] VI *(S Ger, Aus)* to climb through one's sweetheart's bedroom window

Fens|ter-: **fens|ter|los** ADJ windowless; **Fens|ter|pfos|ten** M mullion; **Fens|ter|platz** M seat by the window, window seat; **Fens|ter|put|zer** [-pʊtsɐ] M **-s, -**, **Fens|ter|put|ze|rin** [-ərın] F **-, -nen** window cleaner; **Fens|ter|rah|men** M window frame; **Fens|ter|rand** M *(Comput)* window border; **Fens|ter|re|de** F soapbox speech; **Fens|ter|rei|ni|ger** M **-s, -** *(= Putzmittel)* window *or* glass cleaner; **Fens|ter|rei|ni|ger** M **-s, -**, **Fens|ter|rei|ni|ge|rin** [-gərın] F **-, -nen** window cleaner; **Fens|ter|ro|se** F rose window; **Fens|ter|schei|be** F window pane; **Fens|ter|sims** M window ledge, windowsill; **Fens|ter|stock** M window frame; **Fens|ter|sturz** M **a** *(Build)* window lintel **b** *(Hist)* **der Prager ~** the Prague defenestration; **Fens|ter|tech|nik** F *(Comput)* windowing technique; **Fens|ter|tei|ler** M *(Comput)* split bar; **Fens|ter|um|schlag** M window envelope

Fer|ge ['fɛrgə] M -n, -n *(poet)* ferryman
Fe|ri|al- [fe'ria:l] *in cpds (Aus)* = **Ferien-**
Fe|ri|en ['fe:riən] PL holidays *pl (Brit)*, vacation *sing (US, Univ)*; *(= Ferienreise)* holiday *sing (esp Brit)*, vacation *sing (US)*; *(= Parlamentsferien, Jur)* recess *sing*; **die großen ~** the summer holidays *(esp Brit)*, the long vacation *(US, Univ)*; **~ haben** to be on holiday *(esp Brit) or* vacation *(US)*; **~ machen** to have *or* take a holiday *(esp Brit) or* vacation *(US)*; **~ vom Ich machen** to get away from it all; **in die ~ gehen** *or* **fahren** to go on holiday *(esp Brit) or* vacation *(US)*
Fe|ri|en- *in cpds* holiday *(esp Brit)*, vacation *(US)*; **Fe|ri|en|an|la|ge** F holiday *(esp Brit) or* vacation *(US)* complex; **Fe|ri|en|dorf** NT holiday village; **Fe|ri|en|gast** M holiday-maker *(Brit)*, vacationer *(US)*; *(= Besuch)* person staying on holiday *(esp Brit) or* on vacation *(US)*; **Fe|ri|en|haus** NT holiday home; **Fe|ri|en|kind** NT *child from a town on a state-subsidized holiday*; **Fe|ri|en|ko|lo|nie** F children's holiday *(esp Brit) or* vacation *(US)* camp; **Fe|ri|en|kurs** M vacation course; *(im Sommer auch)* summer course; **Fe|ri|en|la|ger** NT holiday *(esp Brit) or* vacation *(US)* camp; *(für Kinder, im Sommer)* summer camp; **ins ~ fahren** to go to a holiday *(esp Brit) or* vacation *(US)* camp; *(im Sommer)* to go to summer camp; **Fe|ri|en|ord|nung** F holiday dates *pl*; **Fe|ri|en|ort** M *pl* **-orte** holiday *(esp Brit) or* vacation *(US)* resort; **Fe|ri|en|pass** M (school pupil's) holiday *(Brit) or* vacation *(US)* pass *(giving reduced fares etc)*; **Fe|ri|en|rei|se** F holiday *(esp Brit)*, vacation *(US)*; **Fe|ri|en|tag** M day of one's holidays *(Brit) or* vacation *(US)*; **Fe|ri|en|woh|nung** F holiday flat *(Brit)*, vacation apartment *(US)*; **Fe|ri|en|zeit** F holiday *(esp Brit) or* vacation *(US)* period
Fer|kel ['fɛrkl] NT -s, - piglet; *(fig) (unsauber)* pig, mucky pup *(Brit inf)*; *(unanständig)* dirty pig *(inf)*
Fer|ke|lei [fɛrkə'lai] F -, -en *(inf) (= Schmutz)* mess; *(= Witz)* dirty joke; *(= Handlung)* dirty *or* filthy *or* disgusting thing to do
fer|keln ['fɛrkln] VI **a** *(Zool)* to litter **b** *(inf) (= Schmutz verursachen)* to make a mess; *(= schmutzige Witze erzählen)* to tell dirty jokes; *(= sich unanständig benehmen)* to be dirty *or* filthy *or* disgusting
Fer|ma|te [fɛr'ma:tə] F -, -n *(Mus)* fermata, pause
Fer|ment [fɛr'mɛnt] NT -s, -e enzyme
Fer|men|ta|ti|on [fɛrmɛnta'tsio:n] F -, -en fermentation
Fer|men|ter [fɛr'mɛntɐ] M -s, - fermenter
fer|men|tie|ren [fɛrmɛn'ti:rən] *ptp* **fermentiert** VT to ferment
Fer|ment|man|gel M enzyme deficiency
Fer|mi|um ['fɛrmiʊm] NT -s, *no pl (abbr* **Fm**) fermium
fern [fɛrn] ADJ **a** *(räumlich)* distant, far-off, faraway; **~ von hier** a long way (away) from here, far away from here; **von ~(e) betrachtet** seen from a distance; **sich ~ sein** *(fig)* to be not at all close (to one another); **der Ferne Osten** the Far East; **von ~(e) kennen** *(fig)* to know (only) slightly; **das sei ~ von mir** *(fig)* nothing is further from my thoughts, heaven forbid; **von ~ her** *(old)* from afar *(old, liter)*
b *(zeitlich entfernt)* far-off; **~e Vergangenheit** (dim and) distant past; **in nicht (all)zu ~er Zeit** in the not-too-distant future; **der Tag ist nicht mehr ~, wo ...** the day is not far off when ...
PREP *+gen* far (away) from; **~ der Heimat** *(liter)* far from home; **unrasiert und ~ der Heimat** *(hum inf)* down on one's luck and a long way from home
Fern-: **fern|ab** [fɛrn'lap] ADV far away; **~ gelegen** far away; **Fern|ab|fra|ge** F *(Telec)* remote control facility; **Fern|amt** NT (telephone) exchange; **das Gespräch wurde vom ~ vermittelt** the call was connected by the operator; **Fern|auf|nah|me** F *(Phot)* long shot; **Fern|aus|lö|ser** M *(Phot)* cable release; **Fern|bahn** F *(Rail)* main-line service; **Fern|be|ben** NT distant earthquake; **Fern|be|die|nung** F remote control; **fern+blei|ben** VI *sep irreg aux sein* to stay away *(+dat, von* from); **Fern|blei|ben** NT -s, *no pl* absence *(von* from); *(= Nichtteilnahme)* non-attendance; **Fern|blick** M good view; **ein herrlicher ~** a splendid view for miles around
Fer|ne ['fɛrnə] F -, -n **a** *(räumlich)* distance; *(liter. = ferne Länder)* distant lands *pl or* shores *pl (liter)*; **in der ~** in the distance; **aus der ~** from a distance; **in die ~ ziehen** *(liter)* to seek out far-off shores, to seek out distant climes *(liter)*
b *(zeitlich) (= Zukunft)* future; *(= Vergangenheit)* (distant) past; **in weiter ~ liegen** to be a long time off, to be in the distant future
fer|ne ['fɛrnə] ADJ *(poet, geh)* = **fern ADJ**
Fern|emp|fang M *(Rad, TV)* long-distance reception
fer|ner ['fɛrnɐ] ADJ *comp von* **fern** further; **Ihre ~en Aufträge** *(Comm)* your future *or* further orders; **für die ~e Zukunft** for the long term ADV **a** further; **~ liefen ...** *(Sport)* also-rans ...; **unter ~ liefen rangieren** *or* **kommen** *(inf)* to be among the also-rans **b** *(= künftig)* in future; **(auch) ~ etw machen** to continue to do sth; **auch ~ im Amt bleiben** to continue in office
fer|ner|hin ['fɛrnɐhɪn, 'fɛrnɐ'hɪn] ADV = **ferner ADV b**
fer|ner+lie|gen *sep irreg (S Ger, Austr, Sw: aux sein)*, **fer|ner lie|gen** △ *irreg (S Ger, Austr, Sw: aux sein)* VI *(fig)* **nichts läge mir ferner, als ...** nothing could be further from my thoughts *or* mind than ...; **kein Gedanke könnte ~ als ...** nothing could be further from my thoughts than ...
Fern-: **Fern|ex|press** M *(Rail)* long-distance express train; **Fern|fah|rer(in)** M(F) long-distance lorry *(Brit) or* truck driver, trucker *(US)*; **Fern|fah|rer|lo|kal** NT transport café *(Brit)*, truckstop *(US)*; **Fern|flug** M long-distance *or* long-haul flight; **Fern|gas** NT *gas piped over a long distance*; **fern|ge|lenkt** [-gəlɛŋkt] ADJ remote-controlled; *(fig)* manipulated *(von* by); **Fern|ge|schütz** NT *(Mil)* long-range weapon; **Fern|ge|spräch** NT trunk *(Brit) or* long-distance call; **fern|ge|steu|ert** [-gəʃtɔyɐt] ADJ remote-controlled; *(durch Funk auch)* radio-controlled; *(fig)* manipulated *(von* by) → *auch* **fernsteuern**; **Fern|glas** NT (pair of) binoculars *pl*, (pair of) field glasses *pl*; **fern+hal|ten** *sep irreg*, **fern hal|ten** △ *irreg* VT to keep away VR to keep *or* stay away; **Fern|hei|zung** F district heating *(spec)*; **Fern|heiz|werk** NT district heating plant *(spec)*; **fern|her** ['fɛrn'he:ɐ] ADV *(old)* from afar *(old, liter)* → *auch* **fern ADJ a**; **Fern|ko|pie** F *(Telec)* fax; **Fern|ko|pie|rer** M fax (machine); **Fern|kurs** M, **Fern|kur|sus** M correspondence course
Fern|las|ter M long-distance lorry *(Brit) or* truck, juggernaut *(Brit)*
Fern|last-: **Fern|last|fah|rer(in)** M(F) *(inf)* long-distance lorry *(Brit) or* truck driver, trucker *(US)*; **Fern|last|ver|kehr** M long-distance goods traffic; **Fern|last|zug** M long-distance truck-trailer
Fern-: **Fern|lehr|gang** M correspondence course; **Fern|lei|tung** F **a** *(Telec)* trunk *(Brit) or* long-distance line(s) **b** *(= Röhren)* pipeline; **fern+len|ken** VT *sep* to operate by remote control → *auch* **ferngelenkt**; **Fern|len|kung** F remote control; **Fern|lenk|waf|fen** PL *(Mil)* guided missiles; **Fern|licht** NT *(Aut)* full *or* main *or* high *(esp US)* beam; **mit ~ fahren, (das) ~ anhaben** to be *or* drive on full *or* main *or* high *(esp US)* beam; **fern+lie|gen** *sep irreg (S Ger, Austr, Sw: aux sein)*, **fern lie|gen** △ *irreg (S Ger, Austr, Sw: aux sein)* VI *(fig)* **(jdm) ~** to be far from sb's thoughts *or* mind; **es liegt mir fern, das zu tun** far be it from me to do that → **fernerliegen**
Fern|mel|de-: **Fern|mel|de|amt** NT telephone exchange; **Fern|mel|de|dienst** M telecommunications service; *(= Telefondienst)* telephone service; **Fern|mel|de|ge|heim|nis** NT *(Jur)* secrecy of telecommunications
Fern|mel|der M *(form)* telephone
Fern|mel|der(in) M(F) *(Mil inf)* signaller *(Brit)*, signaler *(US)*
Fern|mel|de-: **Fern|mel|de|sa|tel|lit** M communications satellite; **Fern|mel|de|tech|nik** F telecommunications engineering; *(= Telefontechnik)* telephone engineering; **Fern|mel|de|trup|pe** F *(Mil)* signals corps *sing*; **Fern|mel|de|we|sen** NT, *no pl* telecommunications *sing*
Fern-: **Fern|mes|sung** F telemetering; **fern|münd|lich** *(form)* ADJ telephone *attr* ADV by telephone
Fern|ost [fɛrn'lɔst] *no art* **aus/in/nach ~** from/in/to the Far East
Fern|ost|ex|por|te PL exports *pl* to the Far East
Fern|ost|han|del M trade with the Far East
fern|öst|lich [fɛrn'lœstlɪç] ADJ Far Eastern *attr*
Fern|ost|rei|se F journey to the Far East
Fern-: **Fern|ra|ke|te** F long-range missile; **Fern|rei|se** F long-haul journey; **Fern|rohr** NT telescope; **Fern|ruf** M *(form)* telephone number; **~ 68190** Tel. 68190; **Fern|schal|ter** M *(Elec)* remote-control switch; **Fern|schnell|zug** M long-distance express (train); **Fern|schrei|ben** NT telex; **Fern|schrei|ber** M teleprinter; *(Comm)* telex(-machine); **Fern|schrei|ber(in)** M(F) teleprinter operator; *(Comm)* telex operator; **Fern|schreib|netz** NT telex network; **fern|schrift|lich** ADJ, ADV by telex
Fern|seh- *in cpds* television, TV; **Fern|seh|an|sa|ger(in)** M(F) television announcer; **Fern|seh|an|spra|che** F television speech; **Fern|seh|an|stalt** F television company; **Fern|seh|an|ten|ne** F television *or* TV aerial *or* antenna; **Fern|seh|ap|pa|rat** M television *or* TV set; **Fern|seh|de|bat|te** F televised debate; **Fern|seh|emp|fän|ger** M *(form)* television receiver
fern+se|hen VI *sep irreg* to watch television *or* TV *or* telly *(Brit inf)*
Fern|se|hen NT -s, *no pl* television, TV, telly *(Brit inf)*; **~ haben** *(Familie etc)* to have a television; *(Staat etc)* to have television *or* TV; **beim ~ arbeiten** to work *or* be in television; **vom ~ übertragen werden** to be televised; **im** *or (Sw)* **am ~** on television *or* TV *or* (the) telly *(Brit inf)*; **was kommt heute Abend im** *or (Sw)* **am ~?** what's on television *or* TV *or* (the) telly *(Brit inf)* tonight?; **das ~ bringt etw** sth is on television, they're showing sth on television
Fern|se|her M *(inf: = Gerät)* television, TV, telly *(Brit inf)*
Fern|se|her(in) M(F) *(inf: = Zuschauer)* (television) viewer
Fern|seh-: **Fern|seh|film** M television *or* TV film *(Brit)*, television *or* TV movie *(US)*; **Fern|seh|ge|büh|ren** PL television licence *(Brit) or* license *(US)* fee; **Fern|seh|ge|neh|mi|gung** F television licence *(Brit) or* license *(US)*; **Fern|seh|ge|rät** NT television *or* TV set; **fern|seh|ge|recht** ADJ suitable for television ADV **etw ~ aufbereiten** to adapt sth for television; **Fern|seh|jour|na|list(in)** M(F) television *or* TV reporter; **Fern|seh|ka|me|ra** F television *or* TV camera; **wir haben Herrn Schmidt vor die ~ gebeten** we've asked Herr Schmidt to speak to us; **Fern|seh|ka|nal** M (television) channel; **Fern|seh|kon|ser|ve** F (tele)recording; **Fern|seh|norm** F television standard; **Fern|seh|pro|gramm** NT **a** *(= Kanal)* channel, station *(US)* **b** *(= Sendung)* programme *(Brit)*, program *(US)*; *(= Sendefolge)* programmes *pl (Brit)*, programs *pl (US)* **c** *(= Fernsehzeitschrift)* (television) programme *(Brit) or* program *(US)* guide, TV guide; **Fern|seh|pub|li|kum** NT viewers *pl*, viewing public; **Fern|seh|raum** M TV room; **Fern|seh|rech|te** PL television rights *pl*; **Fern|seh|sa|tel|lit** M TV satellite;

Fern|seh|schirm M television *or* TV screen; **Fern|seh|sen|der** M television transmitter; **Fern|seh|sen|dung** F television programme *(Brit) or* program *(US)*; **Fern|seh|spiel** NT television play; **Fern|seh|spot** M **a** *(= Werbespot)* TV ad(vertisement) **b** *(= Kurzfilm)* TV short; **Fern|seh|spre|cher(in)** M(F) television announcer; **Fern|seh|teil|neh|mer(in)** M(F) *(form)* television viewer; **Fern|seh|tru|he** F cabinet TV; **Fern|seh|turm** M television tower; **Fern|seh|über|tra|gung** F television broadcast; *(von außerhalb des Studios)* outside broadcast; **Fern|seh|über|tra|gungs|wa|gen** M outside broadcast vehicle *or* van; **Fern|seh|wer|bung** F, *no pl* **a** *(= Werbung im Fernsehen)* television *or* TV advertising *or* commercials *pl* **b** *(= Werbespot)* television *or* TV commercial *or* ad *(inf)*; **Fern|seh|zeit|schrift** F TV guide; **Fern|seh|zim|mer** NT TV room; **Fern|seh|zu|schau|er(in)** M(F) (television) viewer

Fern|sicht F clear view; **(eine) gute ~ haben** to be able to see a long way

Fern|sprech- *in cpds (form)* telephone → *auch* **Telefon-**; **Fern|sprech|an|schluss** M telephone; **15 Fernsprechanschlüsse haben** to have 15 lines; **Fern|sprech|ap|pa|rat** M telephone; **Fern|sprech|auf|trags|dienst** M telephone services *pl*; **Fern|sprech|buch** NT telephone directory, telephone book

Fern|spre|cher M *(form)* (public) telephone

Fern|sprech-: **Fern|sprech|ge|büh|ren** PL telephone charges *pl*; **Fern|sprech|ge|heim|nis** NT *(Jur)* secrecy of telecommunications; **Fern|sprech|lei|tung** F *(per Draht)* (telephone) line; *(per Radio, Satellit)* telephone link; **Fern|sprech|netz** NT telephone system; **Fern|sprech|teil|neh|mer(in)** M(F) *(form)* telephone subscriber; **Fern|sprech|ver|kehr** M telephone traffic; **Fern|sprech|we|sen** NT, *no pl* telephone system; **Fern|sprech|zel|le** F *(form)* (tele)phone box *or (US)* booth, call box *(Brit)*; **Fern|sprech|zent|ra|le** F telephone exchange

Fern-: **fern+ste|hen** *sep irreg (S Ger, Austr, Sw: aux sein)*, **fern ste|hen** △ *irreg (S Ger, Austr, Sw: aux sein)* VI **jdm/einer Sache ~** to have no connection with sb/sth; **ich stehe ihm ziemlich fern** I'm not on very close terms with him; **fern+steu|ern** VT *sep* to operate by remote control; *(per Funk auch)* to control by radio → *auch* **ferngesteuert**; **Fern|steu|e|rung** F remote control; *(per Funk auch)* radio control; **~ haben** to be remote-controlled/radio-controlled; **Fern|stra|ße** F trunk *or* major road, highway *(US)*; **Fern|stu|di|um** NT correspondence degree course *(with radio, TV etc)*, ≈ Open University course *(Brit)*

> **FERNSTUDIUM**
>
> A **Fernstudium** is a university-level course that does not require the student to attend a particular place of study. The best-known centre for distance learning is the university at Hagen.
>
> The expression **Fernstudium** is also used colloquially for any sort of teaching where the student does not attend regular classes. → GESAMTHOCHSCHULE

Fern-: **Fern|tou|ris|mus** M long-haul tourism; **Fern|trau|ung** F marriage by proxy; **Fern|über|wa|chung** F remote monitoring; **Fern|uni|ver|si|tät** F ≈ Open University *(Brit)*, ≈ correspondence school *(US)*; **Fern|un|ter|richt** M *correspondence course also using radio, TV, multimedia etc*; **Fern|ver|kehr** M **a** *(Transport)* long-distance traffic **b** *(Telec)* trunk *(Brit) or* long-distance traffic; **Fern|ver|kehrs|stra|ße** F trunk *(Brit) or* major road, highway *(US)*; **Fern|ver|mitt|lung(s|stel|le)** F telephone exchange; **Fern|ver|sor|gung** F long-distance supply; **Fern|wär|me** F district heating *(spec)*; **Fern|weh** NT wanderlust; **Fern|wir|kung** F *(Phys)* long-distance effect; **Fern|ziel** NT long-term goal; **Fern|zug** M long-distance train; **Fern|zu|griff** M *(Comput)* remote access; **Fern|zün|dung** F long-range *or* remote ignition

Fer|rat [fɛ'ra:t] NT **-s, -e** *(Chem)* ferrate

Fer|rit [fɛ'ri:t] M **-s, -e** *(Chem)* ferrite

Fer|ro- *in cpds* ferro-; **Fer|ro|mag|ne|tis|mus** [fɛromagne'tɪsmʊs] M ferromagnetism

Fer|se ['fɛrzə] F **-, -n** heel; **jdm (dicht) auf den ~n sein** *or* **folgen/bleiben** to be/stay hard *or* close on sb's heels → **heften VR b**

Fer|sen-: **Fer|sen|au|to|ma|tik** F *(Ski)* automatic heel release; **Fer|sen|bein** NT *(Anat)* heel bone, calcaneus *(spec)*; **Fer|sen|geld** NT **~ geben** to take to one's heels

fer|tig ['fɛrtɪç] ADJ **a** *(= abgeschlossen, vollendet)* finished; *(= ausgebildet)* qualified; *(= reif) Mensch, Charakter* mature; **mit der Ausbildung ~ sein** to have completed one's training; **~ ist die Laube** *(inf) or* **der Lack** *(inf)* (and) there we are!, (and) Bob's your uncle! *(Brit inf)*

b *(= zu Ende)* finished; **mit etw ~ sein, etw ~ haben** to have finished sth; **mit jdm ~ sein** *(fig)* to be finished *or* through with sb; **wird das/werden wir rechtzeitig ~ werden?** will it/we be finished in time?; **mit jdm/etw ~ werden** *(fig)* to cope with sb/sth; **ich werde damit nicht ~** I can't cope with it; **du darfst nicht gehen, ~!** you're not going and that's that *or* and that's the end of it!

c *(= bereit)* ready; **~ zur Abfahrt** ready to go *or* leave; **bist du/ist das Essen ~?** are you/is the meal ready? → **Achtung, Platz**

d *(inf) (= erschöpft)* shattered *(Brit inf)*, all in *(inf)*; *(= ruiniert)* finished; *(= erstaunt)* knocked for six *(Brit inf) or* for a loop *(US inf)*; **mit den Nerven ~ sein** to be at the end of one's tether *(Brit) or* rope *(US)*; **da bin ich ~!** *(= erstaunt)* my God!, well I never! → **fix**

ADV **~ duschen** to finish having a shower; **etw ~ kaufen** to buy sth ready-made; *Essen* to buy sth ready to eat *or* ready-prepared; **~ ausgebildet** fully qualified; **~ essen/lesen** to finish eating/reading

Fer|tig- *in cpds* finished; *(Build)* prefabricated; **Fer|tig|bau** M *(Build) (no pl, = Bauweise)* prefabricated building *pl* **-bauten** *(= Gebäude)* prefabricated building, prefab; **Fer|tig|bau|wei|se** F *(Build)* prefabricated building *or* construction

fer|tig be|kom|men *irreg*, **fer|tig+be|kom|men** *sep irreg* VT to finish, to get finished

Fer|tig|be|ton M *(Build)* ready-mixed concrete

fer|tig+brin|gen *sep irreg*, **fer|tig brin|gen** △ *irreg* VT *(= imstande sein)* to manage; *(iro)* to be capable of; **ich habe es nicht fertiggebracht, ihr die Wahrheit zu sagen** I couldn't bring myself to tell her the truth; **er bringt das fertig** *(iro)* I wouldn't put it past him; **er bringt es fertig und sagt ihr das** he's quite capable of saying that to her

fer|tig brin|gen *irreg*, **fer|tig+brin|gen** *sep irreg* VT *(= vollenden)* to get done

fer|ti|gen ['fɛrtɪgn] VT *(form)* to manufacture

Fer|tig-: **Fer|tig|er|zeug|nis** NT finished product; **Fer|tig|fab|ri|kat** NT finished product; **Fer|tig|ge|richt** NT ready-to-serve meal; **Fer|tig|haus** NT prefabricated house

Fer|tig|keit F **-, -en** skill; **wenig/eine große ~ in etw** *(dat)* **haben** not to be very/to be very skilled at *or* in sth

Fer|tig-: **fer|tig+krie|gen** *sep*, **fer|tig krie|gen** △ VT *(inf)* = **fertigbringen**; **fer|tig krie|gen** , **fer|tig+krie|gen** *sep* VT *(inf)* = **fertig bringen**; **fer|tig+ma|chen** *sep*, **fer|tig ma|chen** △ VT *(inf fig)* **jdn ~** *(= umbringen)* to do sb in; **jdn (fix und) ~** *(= nervös machen)* to drive sb mad *(Brit) or* crazy *(US)*; *(= erschöpfen)* to wear sb out, to take it out of sb *(inf)*; *(= deprimieren)* to get sb down, to shatter sb; *(= abkanzeln)* to tear sb off a strip *(Brit inf)*, to lay into sb *(inf)*; *(in Prüfung, Wettbewerb, Kampf etc)* to give sb a thrashing *(inf)*; *(= ruinieren)* to do for sb *(inf)*; **sich ~** to do oneself in; **fer|tig ma|chen** , **fer|tig+ma|chen** *sep* VT **a** *(= vollenden)* to finish **b** *(= bereit machen)* to get ready; **sich ~** to get ready; **~!** get ready!; *(Sport)* get set!, steady!; **Fer|tig|pro|dukt** NT finished product; **fer|tig+stel|len** *sep*, **fer|tig stel|len** VT to complete; *(Comput)* to finish; **Fer|tig|stel|lung** F completion; **Fer|tig|teil** NT finished part

Fer|ti|gung ['fɛrtɪgʊŋ] F **-, -en** production; **in der ~ arbeiten** to work in production *or* in the production department

Fer|ti|gungs- *in cpds* production; **Fer|ti|gungs|hal|le** F assembly shop; **Fer|ti|gungs|stra|ße** F production *or* assembly line; **Fer|ti|gungs|tech|nik** F production engineering

Fer|tig|wa|re F finished product

fer|tig+wer|den *sep irreg aux sein* VI → **fertig ADJ b**

Fes [fɛs] NT **-, -, fes** NT **-, -** *(Mus)* F flat

Fes [fe:s] M **-(es), -(e)** [-zə] fez

fesch [fɛʃ] ADJ *(S Ger, Aus: inf) (= modisch)* smart; *(= hübsch)* attractive; **das ist ~** that's great *(inf)*; **sei ~!** *(Aus) (= sei brav)* be good; *(= sei kein Frosch)* be a sport *(inf)*

Fes|sel ['fɛsl] F **-, -n** **a** *(= Bande) (lit, fig)* bond, fetter, shackle; *(= Kette)* chain; **sich von den ~n befreien** to free oneself, to loose *(Brit liter) or* loosen *(US liter)* one's bonds; **jdm ~n anlegen, jdn in ~n legen** to fetter *or* shackle sb; *(= anketten)* to put sb in chains; **jdn in ~n schlagen** *(liter, fig)* to put sb in fetters, to enchain sb *(liter)*; **die ~n der Ehe/Liebe** the shackles of marriage/love **b** *(Anat) (von Huftieren)* pastern; *(von Menschen)* ankle

Fes|sel-: **Fes|sel|bal|lon** M captive balloon; **Fes|sel|ge|lenk** NT pastern; *(von Menschen)* ankle joint; **Fes|sel|griff** M lock

fes|seln ['fɛsln] VT **a** *(mit Tau etc)* to tie (up), to bind; *(Hist: mit Handfesseln, Fußschellen)* to fetter, to shackle; *(mit Handschellen)* to handcuff; *(mit Ketten)* to chain (up); **jdn (an Händen und Füßen) ~** to tie/fetter/chain sb (hand and foot); **jdm die Hände auf dem Rücken ~** to tie sb's hands behind his back; **der Gefangene wurde gefesselt vorgeführt** the prisoner was brought in handcuffed/in chains; **jdn ans Bett ~** *(fig)* to confine sb to (his) bed, to keep sb in bed; **jdn ans Haus ~** *(fig)* to tie sb to the house; **jdn an jdn/sich ~** *(fig)* to bind sb to sb/oneself **b** *(= faszinieren)* to grip; *Aufmerksamkeit* to hold; **seine Vorstellung fesselte die Zuschauer** his performance gripped the audience

fes|selnd ADJ gripping

fest [fɛst] ADJ **a** *(= hart)* solid; **~e Nahrung** solid food, solids *pl*; **~e Form** *or* **Gestalt annehmen** *(fig)* to take shape

b *(= stabil)* solid; *Gewebe, Schuhe* tough, sturdy; *(Comm, Fin)* stable; *Zuneigung* strong → **Boden**

c *(= sicher, entschlossen)* firm; *Plan* firm, definite; *Stimme* steady; **eine ~e Meinung von etw haben** to have definite views on sth; **etw ist ~** *(= steht fest)* sth is definite

d *(= kräftig)* firm; *Schlag* hard, heavy

e *(= nicht locker)* tight; *Griff* firm; *(fig) Schlaf* sound

f *(= ständig)* regular; *Freund(in)* steady; *Bindung, Stellung, Mitarbeiter* permanent; *Kosten, Tarif, Einkommen* fixed; *Redewendung* set; **in ~en Händen sein, sich in ~en Händen befinden** *(Besitz)* to be in private hands; *(inf: Mädchen)* to be spoken for; **seinen ~en Platz gewinnen** to establish oneself; **sie hat keinen ~en Platz im Büro** she doesn't have her own desk in the office; **er hat einen ~en Platz in ihrem Herzen** he has a special place in her affections → *auch* **Platz**

ADV **a** *(= kräftig) anpacken, packen* firmly; *drücken, umarmen* tightly; *(inf: = tüchtig, kräftig) helfen, arbeiten* with a will; **~ zuschlagen** to hit hard

b *(= nicht locker) anziehen, zudrehen, verknoten* tight; **~ kochende Kartoffeln** → **festkochend**; **~ verwurzelt** deep-rooted, deep-seated; *Tradition* long-established; **~ umrissen** clear-cut; **die Handbremse ~ anziehen** to put the handbrake on firmly; **die Tür ~ schließen** to shut the door tight; **er hat schon ~ geschlafen** he was sound asleep; **jdn ~ in der Hand haben** to have sb under one's thumb; **etw ~ in der Hand haben** to have sth firmly under control

c *(= sicher) versprechen* faithfully; *zusagen* definitely; **sie sind an den Vertrag ~ gebunden** their contract is binding; **~ verankert** *(lit)* firmly or securely anchored; *(fig)* firmly rooted; **~ entschlossen sein** to be absolutely determined

d *(= dauerhaft)* permanently; **Gehälter sind im Tarifvertrag ~ geregelt** salaries are set in the pay agreement; **~ befreundet sein** to be good friends; *(Freund und Freundin)* to be going steady; **jdn ~ anstellen** to employ sb as a regular member of staff; **~ angestellt** employed on a regular basis; **~ besoldet** on a regular salary; **Geld ~ anlegen** to tie up money

Fest [fɛst] NT **-(e)s, -e** **a** *(= Feier)* celebration; *(= historische Begebenheit)* celebrations *pl*; *(= Party)* party; *(= Hochzeitsfest)* reception; *(= Bankett)* banquet, feast *(old)*; *(= Ballfest)* ball; *(= Kinderfest, Schützenfest)* carnival; **ein ~ zum hundertjährigen Bestehen des Vereins** the club's centenary celebrations, celebrations to mark the club's centenary; **das war ein ~!** *(inf)* it was great fun; **man soll die ~e feiern, wie sie fallen** *(prov)* make hay while the sun shines *(prov)*

b *(= kirchlicher Feiertag)* feast, festival; *(= Weihnachtsfest)* Christmas; **bewegliches/unbewegliches ~** movable/immovable feast; **frohes ~!** Merry or Happy *(esp Brit)* Christmas!

Fest-: **Fest|akt** M ceremony; **fest|an|ge|stellt** ADJ → **fest ADV d**; **Fest|an|ge|stell|te(r)** MF *decl as adj* regular member of staff; **Fest|an|spra|che** F speech; **Fest|an|stel|lung** F permanent post or appointment; **Fest|auf|füh|rung** F festival production; **fest+ba|cken** VI *sep irreg aux sein (dial: = festkleben)* to stick (firmly) *(an +dat* (on)to); **Fest|ban|kett** NT ceremonial banquet; **fest+bei|ßen** VR *sep irreg (Hund etc)* to get a firm hold with its teeth *(an +dat* on); *(Zecke etc)* to attach itself firmly *(an +dat* to); *(fig: = nicht weiterkommen)* to get bogged down *(an +dat* in); **der Hund biss sich an ihrem Bein fest** the dog sank its teeth firmly into her leg; **Fest|be|leuch|tung** F festive lighting or lights *pl*; *(inf: im Haus)* blazing lights *pl*; **was soll denn diese ~?** *(inf)* why is the place lit up like a Christmas tree? *(inf)*; **fest|be|sol|det** [-bəzɔldət] ADJ → **fest ADV d**; **fest+bin|den** VT *sep irreg* to tie up; **jdn/etw an etw** *(dat)* **~** to tie sb/sth to sth; **fest+blei|ben** VI *sep irreg aux sein* to stand firm, to remain resolute; **fest+dre|hen** VT *sep* to screw up tightly; **fest+drü|cken** VT *sep* to press in/down/together firmly

fes|te [ˈfɛstə] ADV *(inf)* = **fest ADV**; **immer ~ druff!** let him/her *etc* have it! *(inf)*, give it to him/her *etc*! *(inf)*

Fes|te [ˈfɛstə] F **-, -n** *(old)* **a** *(= Festung)* fortress; *(= Burgfeste)* castle **b** *(= Erde)* dry land, terra firma; **die ~ des Himmels** *(Bibl)* the firmament

Fest-: **Fest|es|sen** NT banquet, Christmas dinner; **fest+fah|ren** VR *sep irreg (fig)* to get bogged down; *(lit auch)* to get stuck, to stick fast; **fest+fres|sen** VR *sep irreg* to seize up; **fest+frie|ren** VI *sep irreg aux sein* to freeze solid; **Fest|ga|be** F **a** *(= Geschenk)* presentation gift **b** *(= Festschrift)* commemorative paper, festschrift *(esp Brit)*; **Fest|ge|dicht** NT celebratory or occasional poem; **Fest|ge|la|ge** NT banquet; **Fest|ge|läu|te** NT festive peal of bells; **Fest|geld** NT *(Fin)* time deposit; **Fest|ge|wand** NT *(liter)* festive garb *(liter)*; **fest|ge|wur|zelt** [-gəvʊrtslt] ADJ **wie ~** rooted to the spot; **Fest|got|tes|dienst** M festival service; **fest+gur|ten** *sep* VR to strap oneself in VT to strap in; **fest+ha|ken** *sep* VT to hook up *(an +dat* on) VR to get caught (up) *(an +dat* on); **Fest|hal|le** F festival hall

fest+hal|ten *sep irreg* VT **a** *(= nicht loslassen)* to keep a firm hold on, to keep hold of, to hold on to; **jdn am Arm/Rockzipfel ~** to hold on to sb's arm/the hem of sb's coat

b *(= bemerken)* to stress, to emphasize

c *(= inhaftieren)* to hold, to detain

d *(= speichern)* to record; *Atmosphäre etc* to capture; **etw schriftlich ~** to record sth; **etw im Gedächtnis ~** to bear sth firmly in mind; **etw in Wort und Bild ~** to record sth in words and pictures

VI **an etw** *(dat)* **~** to hold or stick *(inf)* to sth; **am Glauben ~** to hold to the faith

VR to hold on *(an +dat* to); **sich irgendwo ~** to hold on to something; **halt dich fest!** *(lit)* hold tight!; **halt dich fest und hör dir das an!** *(inf)* brace yourself and listen to this!

fest+hän|gen VI *sep irreg aux haben or sein (lit, fig)* to be stuck *(an +dat* on, *in +dat* in)

fest+hef|ten VT *sep (mit Nadel)* to pin *(an +dat* (on)to); *(mit Faden)* to tack *(an +dat* (on)to)

fes|ti|gen [ˈfɛstɪgn] VT to strengthen; *Freundschaft, Macht, Ruf auch* to consolidate → *auch* **gefestigt** VR to become stronger; *(Freundschaft, Macht, Ruf auch)* to consolidate

Fes|ti|ger [ˈfɛstɪgɐ] M **-s, -** setting lotion

Fes|tig|keit [ˈfɛstɪçkait] F **-**, *no pl (von Material)* strength; *(fig)* steadfastness; *(von Meinung)* firmness; *(von Stimme)* steadiness; **die ~ seines Charakters** his moral strength, his strength of character

Fes|ti|gung [ˈfɛstɪgʊŋ] F **-, -en** strengthening; *(von Freundschaft, Macht, Ruf auch)* consolidation

Fes|ti|val [ˈfɛstivəl, ˈfɛstival] NT **-s, -s** festival

Fes|ti|vi|tät [fɛstiviˈtɛːt] F **-, -en** *(old, hum inf)* celebration, festivity

Fest-: **fest+kei|len** VT *sep* to wedge; **fest+klam|mern** *sep* VT to clip on *(an +dat* to); **Wäsche an** or **auf der Leine ~** to peg washing on the line VR to cling *(an +dat* to); **fest+kle|ben** VTI *sep (vi: aux sein)* to stick (firmly) *(an +dat* (on)to); **Fest|kleid** NT formal dress; **die Stadt legte ihr ~ an** *(liter)* the town decked itself out in all its finery; **fest+klem|men** *sep* VT to wedge fast; *(mit Klammer, Klemme)* to clip; **festgeklemmt werden** *(aus Versehen)* to get stuck or jammed VIR *(vi: aux sein)* to jam, to stick (fast); **fest+klop|fen** VT *sep* to pack down; **fest+kno|ten** VT *sep* = **festbinden**; **fest|ko|chend** ADJ **~e Kartoffeln** waxy potatoes; **Fest|kom|ma** NT *(auch Comput)* fixed point; **Fest|kör|per** M *(Phys)* solid; **Fest|kör|per|phy|sik** F solid-state physics *sing*; **fest+kral|len** VR *sep (Tier)* to dig one's claws in *(an +dat* -to); *(Mensch)* to dig one's nails in *(an +dat* -to); *(fig)* to cling *(an +dat* to)

Fest|land NT *(nicht Insel)* mainland; *(nicht Meer)* dry land; *(= europäisches Festland)* Continent *(Brit)*, Europe

fest|län|disch [-lɛndɪʃ] ADJ mainland *attr*; Continental, European

Fest|lands-: **Fest|lands|mas|se** F continent; **Fest|lands|so|ckel** M continental shelf

fest+lau|fen *sep irreg* VR *(Schiff)* to run aground; *(fig) (Verhandlungen)* to founder; **die Stürmer liefen sich (an der Verteidigung) immer wieder fest** the forwards kept coming up against a solid line of defence *(Brit)* or defense *(US)* VI *aux sein (Schiff)* to run aground

fest+le|gen *sep* VT **a** *(= festsetzen) Reihenfolge, Termin, Kurs etc* to fix *(auf +acc, bei* for); *Grenze auch* to establish; *Sprachgebrauch* to establish, to lay down; *(= bestimmen) Regelung, Arbeitszeiten* to lay down; *(= feststellen) Geburtsdatum* to determine; *(Comput)* to set, to define; **etw schriftlich/testamentarisch ~** to stipulate or specify sth in writing/in one's will

b **jdn auf etw** *(acc)* **~/darauf ~, etw zu tun** *(= festnageln)* to tie sb (down) to sth/to doing sth; *(= einschränken auch)* to restrict or limit sb to sth/to doing sth; *(= verpflichten)* to commit sb to sth/to doing sth

c *Geld* to put on time deposit, to tie up

VR **a** *(= verbindlich sein)* to tie oneself down *(auf +acc* to); *(= sich verpflichten)* to commit oneself *(auf +acc* to); **ich kann mich darauf nicht ~, ich kann mich auch irren** I can't swear to it, I might be wrong; **sich darauf ~, etw zu tun** to tie oneself down/commit oneself to doing sth

b *(= einen Entschluss fassen)* to decide *(auf +acc* on); **sich darauf ~, etw zu tun** to decide on doing sth or to do sth

Fest|le|gung F **-, -en** *(= Festsetzung)* fixing; *(von Grenze)* establishing; *(von Regelung, Arbeitszeiten)* laying-down

fest|lich [ˈfɛstlɪç] ADJ festive; *(= feierlich)* solemn; *(= prächtig)* splendid, magnificent; **ein ~er Tag** a special or red-letter day ADV *geschmückt* festively; *gekleidet* formally; **etw ~ begehen** to celebrate sth

Fest|lich|keit F **-, -en** celebration; *(= Stimmung)* festiveness

Fest-: **fest+lie|gen** VI *sep irreg* **a** *(= festgesetzt sein)* to have been fixed; *(Sprachgebrauch, Grenze)* to have been established; *(Arbeitszeiten, Regelung)* to have been laid down **b** *(Fin: Geld)* to be on a time deposit, to be tied up **c** *(= nicht weiterkönnen)* to be stuck; *(Naut)* to be aground; **fest+ma|chen** *sep* VT **a** *(= befestigen)* to fix on *(an +dat* -to); *(= festbinden)* to fasten *(an +dat* (on)to); *(Naut)* to moor **b** *(= vereinbaren)* to arrange; **ein Geschäft ~** to clinch a deal **c** *(Hunt: = aufspüren)* to bring to bay **d** *(= beweisen, zeigen)* to demonstrate, to exemplify; **etw an etw/jdm ~** *(fig)* to link sth to sth/sb VI *(Naut)* to moor; **Fest|mahl** NT *(geh)* banquet, feast; **Fest|me|ter** M OR NT cubic metre *(Brit)* or meter *(US)* of solid timber; **fest|na|geln** VT *sep* **a** *Gegenstand* to nail (down/up/on); **etw an/auf etw** *(dat)* **~** to nail sth to sth **b** *(fig inf) jdn* to tie down *(auf +acc* to); **fest+nä|hen** VT *sep* to sew up; *(= annähen)* to sew on; **Fest|nah|me** [-naːmə] F **-, -n** arrest, apprehension; **vorläufige ~** temporary custody; **fest+neh|men** VT *sep irreg* to apprehend, to arrest; **vorläufig ~** to take into custody; **Sie sind festgenommen** you are under arrest; **Fest|netz** NT *(Telec)* landline; **Fest|netz|an|schluss** M *(Telec)* fixed-line or permanent connection; **Fest|of|fer|te** F *(Comm)* firm offer; **Fest|plat|te** F *(Comput)* hard disk; **Fest|plat|ten|lauf|werk** NT hard disk drive; **Fest|platz** M festival ground; *(für Volksfest)* fairground; **Fest|pre|digt** F feast-day sermon; **Fest|preis** M *(Comm)* fixed price; **Fest|pro|gramm** NT festival programme *(Brit)* or program *(US)*; **Fest|punkt** M *(auch Comput)* fixed point; **Fest|re|de** F speech; **eine ~ halten** to make a speech on a special occasion; **fest+re|den** VR *sep* to get involved in a conversation; **Fest|red|ner(in)** M(F) (main) speaker; **fest+ren|nen** VR *sep irreg (inf)* to get bogged down; **unsere Spieler rannten sich (an der gegnerischen Abwehr) fest** our players came up against the solid line of the opponents' defence *(Brit)* or defense *(US)*; **Fest|saal** M hall; *(= Speisesaal)* banqueting hall; *(= Tanzsaal)* ballroom; **fest+sau|fen** VR *sep irreg (inf)* to get stuck in *(inf)*, to make a night of it *(inf)*; **fest+sau|gen** VR *sep* to attach itself firmly *(an +dat* to); **Fest|schmaus** M *(old)* banquet, feast; **Fest|schmuck** M festive decorations *pl*; **im ~** festively decorated; **fest+schnal|len** VTR *sep* = **anschnallen**; **fest+schnü|ren** VT *sep* = **festbinden**; **fest+schrau|ben** VT *sep* to screw (in/on/down/up) tight; **fest+schrei|ben** VT *sep irreg (fig)* to establish; *(Jur)* to enact; **Fest|schrei|bung** F establishment; *(Jur)* enactment; **Fest|schrift** F commemorative publication; *(für Gelehrten)* commemorative paper, festschrift *(esp Brit)*

fest+set|zen *sep* VT **a** *(= bestimmen) Preis, Rente, Grenze* to fix *(bei, auf +acc* at); *Ort, Termin auch* to arrange *(auf +acc, bei* for); *Frist auch* to set; *Arbeitszeiten* to lay down; **der Beginn der Veranstaltung wurde auf zwei Uhr festgesetzt** the event was scheduled to begin at 2 o'clock **b** *(= inhaftieren)* to detain VR *(Staub, Schmutz)* to collect; *(Rost, Ungeziefer, unerwünschte Personen)* to get a foothold; *(Mil)* to take up one's position; *(fig: Gedanke)* to take root, to implant itself

Fest|set|zung F -, -en **a** *(von Preis, Rente, Grenze)* fixing; *(von Ort, Termin)* arrangement; *(von Frist)* setting; *(von Arbeitszeiten)* laying-down **b** *(= Inhaftierung)* detention

fest+sit|zen VI *sep irreg* **a** *(= klemmen, haften)* to be stuck; *(Schmutz)* to cling; *(in Zwischenräumen)* to be trapped **b** *(= stecken geblieben sein)* to be stuck *(bei* on); *(Naut)* to be aground

Fest|spei|cher M *(Comput)* read-only memory, ROM, permanent *or* fixed memory

Fest|spiel NT **a** *(= einzelnes Stück)* festival production **b** **~e** *(= Veranstaltung)* festival *sing*

Fest|spiel-: **Fest|spiel|haus** NT festival theatre *(Brit) or* theater *(US)*; **Fest|spiel|stadt** F festival city

fest-: **fest+stamp|fen** VT *sep* to pound down; *(mit den Füßen auch)* to stamp *or* tread down; **fest+ste|cken** *sep* VT to pin *(an +dat* (on)to, *in +dat* in); *Haare, Rocksaum* to pin up VI *(= stecken geblieben sein)* to be stuck; **fest+ste|hen** VI *sep irreg (= sicher sein)* to be certain; *(= beschlossen sein)* to have been settled *or* fixed; *(= unveränderlich sein)* to be definite; **fest steht** *or* **eines steht fest, dass ...** one thing's (for) certain *or* sure and that is that ...; **so viel steht fest** this *or* so much is certain; **fest|ste|hend** ADJ **a** *(Mech)* fixed **b** *attr (= bestimmt, verbindlich)* definite; *Redewendung, Begriff, Reihenfolge* set; *Brauch* (well-)established; *Terminplan* fixed; **fest|stell|bar** ADJ **a** *(Mech: = arretierbar)* **der Wagen der Schreibmaschine ist ~** the typewriter carriage can be locked in position **b** *(= herauszufinden)* ascertainable; *(= wahrnehmbar, erkennbar)* discernible

fest+stel|len ✪ 53.5, 53.6 VT *sep* **a** *(Mech)* to lock (fast)
b *(= ermitteln)* to ascertain, to find out; *Personalien, Sachverhalt, Datum etc* to establish; *Ursache, Grund* to establish, to determine; *Schaden* to assess; *Krankheit* to diagnose; **einen Totalschaden an einem Wagen ~** to assess a car as a total write-off; **der Arzt konnte nur noch den Tod ~** the doctor found him to be dead
c *(= erkennen)* to tell *(an +dat* from); *Fehler, Unterschied* to find, to detect; *(= bemerken)* to discover; *(= einsehen)* to realize; **wir mussten ~, dass wir uns geirrt hatten** we were forced to realize that we had made a mistake; **ich musste entsetzt/überrascht** *etc* **~, dass ...** I was horrified/surprised *etc* to find that ...
d *(= aussprechen)* to stress, to emphasize

Fest|stell|tas|te F shift *or* caps lock

Fest|stel|lung F **a** *(= Ermittlung)* ascertainment; *(von Personalien, Sachverhalt, Datum, Ursache, Grund)* establishment; *(von Schaden)* assessment; *(von Krankheit)* diagnosis
b *(= Erkenntnis)* conclusion; **zu der ~ kommen** *or* **gelangen, dass ...** to come to the conclusion that ...
c *(= Wahrnehmung)* observation; **die ~ machen** *or* **treffen dass ...** to realize that ...; **wir mussten leider die ~ machen, dass ...** *(form)* it has come to our notice that ...; **ist das eine Frage oder eine ~?** is that a question or a statement (of fact)?
d *(= Bemerkung)* remark, comment, observation; **die abschließende ~** one's closing remarks; **die ~ machen, dass ...** to remark *or* observe that ...

Fest|stel|lungs|kla|ge F action for a declaratory judgement

Fest|stel|lungs|prü|fung F *(esp Aus Sch)* assessment test *(for pupils that were absent for a longer period)*

Fest-: **Fest|stim|mung** F festive atmosphere; *(= Festlaune)* festive mood; **Fest|stoff|ra|ke|te** F solid-fuel rocket; **Fest|ta|fel** F banquet table; *(bei Familienanlässen)* (dinner) table

Fest|tag M **a** *(= Ehrentag)* special *or* red-letter day **b** *(= Feiertag)* holiday, feast (day) *(Eccl)*; **angenehme ~e!** Happy *(esp Brit) or* Merry Christmas/Happy Easter *etc!*

fest|täg|lich ADJ holiday *attr (esp Brit)*, vacation *attr (US)* ADV **~ gestimmt sein** to be in a festive or holiday mood; **~ gekleidet** festively dressed

Fest|tags-: **Fest|tags|klei|dung** F **~ tragen** to be festively dressed; **Fest|tags|lau|ne** F festive mood; **Fest|tags|stim|mung** F festive atmosphere; **in ~** in a festive mood

Fest-: **Fest|treib|stoff|ra|ke|te** F solid-fuel rocket; **fest+tre|ten** *sep irreg* VT to tread down; *(in Teppich etc)* to tread in *(in +acc* -to) VR to get trodden down/in; **das tritt sich fest!** *(hum inf)* don't worry, it's good for the carpet *(hum)*; **fest+trock|nen** VI *sep aux sein* to dry (on); **fest|um|ris|sen** [-ʊmrɪsn] ADJ *attr* → **fest ADV b**; **Fest|um|zug** M procession

Fes|tung ['fɛstʊŋ] F -, -en *(= Befestigung)* fortress; *(= Burgfeste)* castle

Fes|tungs-: **Fes|tungs|gra|ben** M moat; **Fes|tungs|haft** F imprisonment in a fortress; **Fes|tungs|wall** M rampart

Fest-: **Fest|ver|an|stal|tung** F function; **Fest|ver|samm|lung** F assembled company; **fest|ver|wur|zelt** ADJ *attr* → **fest ADV b**; **fest|ver|zins|lich** ADJ fixed-interest *attr*; **Fest|vor|stel|lung** F gala performance; **Fest|vor|trag** M lecture, talk; **fest+wach|sen** VI *sep irreg aux sein* = **anwachsen a**; **Fest|wert|spei|cher** M *(Comput)* read-only memory; **Fest|wie|se** F festival ground; *(für Volksfest)* fairground; **Fest|wo|che** F festival week; **die ~n** the festival *sing*; **fest+wur|zeln** VI *sep aux sein* to take root → **festgewurzelt**; **Fest|zeit** F holiday *(esp Brit) or* vacation *(US)* period; *(= Festspielzeit)* festival (period); **Fest|zelt** NT carnival marquee; **fest+zie|hen** VT *sep irreg* to pull tight; *Schraube* to tighten (up); **Fest|zins** M fixed interest; **Fest|zins|satz** M fixed rate of interest; **Fest|zug** M carnival procession; **fest+zur|ren** VT *sep (Naut)* to lash up; *(fig: = endgültig bestimmen) Entscheidung etc* to finalize

Fe|ta-Kä|se M feta (cheese)

fe|tal [fe'ta:l] ADJ *attr* foetal *(Brit)*, fetal *(US)*

Fe|te ['fe:tə] F -, -n party; **eine ~ feiern** *(als Gastgeber)* to have *or* give *or* throw a party; *(als Gast)* to go to a party

Fe|ten *pl von* **Fetus**

Fe|tisch ['fe:tɪʃ] M -(e)s, -e fetish

fe|ti|schi|sie|ren [fetɪʃi'zi:rən] *ptp* **fetischisiert** VT *(geh)* to make a fetish of

Fe|ti|schis|mus [fetɪ'ʃɪsmʊs] M -, *no pl* fetishism

Fe|ti|schist [fetɪ'ʃɪst] M -en, -en, **Fe|ti|schis|tin** [-'ʃɪstɪn] F -, -nen fetishist

fett [fɛt] ADJ **a** *(= fetthaltig) Speisen, Kost* fatty; *(fig inf: = ölig) Stimme* fat; **ein ~er Bissen** *or* **Brocken** *or* **Happen** *(lit)* a juicy morsel; *(fig)* a lucrative deal
b *(= dick)* fat; *(Typ) Überschrift, Schlagzeilen* bold
c *(= üppig) Boden, Weide, Klee* rich, luxuriant; *(fig inf)* rich; *Beute, Gewinn* fat; *Geschäft* lucrative; **~e Jahre** fat years; **ein ~er Posten** *(inf)* a cushy job *or* number *(inf)* → **sieben**
d *(Aut) Gemisch etc* rich
e *(sl: = toll)* wicked *(sl)*; **das ist voll ~** that's really wicked *(sl)*; **~e Teile** *(= Busen)* tits *pl (sl)*
ADV **a** *(= fetthaltig)* **~ essen** to eat fatty food; **~ kochen** to cook fatty food; *(= viel Fett gebrauchen)* to use a lot of fat
b *(= dick)* **~ gedruckt** *(Typ)* in bold(face); **sich dick und ~ fressen** *(inf)* to stuff oneself *(inf) or* one's face *(inf)*; **~ dasitzen** *(inf)* to sit there like a sack of potatoes *(inf)*; **sich ~ hinsetzen** *(inf)* to plump oneself down like a sack of potatoes *(inf)*

Fett [fɛt] NT -(e)s, -e fat; *(zum Schmieren)* grease; **tierische/pflanzliche ~e** animal/vegetable fats; **~ ansetzen** to put on weight, to get fat; *(Tiere)* to fatten up; **mit heißem ~ übergießen** to baste (with hot fat); **in schwimmendem ~ backen** to deep-fry; **sein ~ bekommen** *(inf) or* **kriegen** *(inf)*/**weghaben** *(inf)* to get/have got what was coming to one *(inf)*, to get/have got one's comeuppance *(inf)*; **ein ~ lösendes Mittel** a grease-cutting agent; **~ schwimmt oben** *(prov hum: Dicke im Wasser)* fat floats → **abschöpfen, schmoren VI a**

Fett-: **fett füt|tern** VT to fatten up; **Fett|ab|sau|gung** [-apzaugʊŋ] F -, -en *(Med)* liposuction; **Fett|ab|la|ge|rung** F deposition of fat; **~en** fatty deposits; **Fett|an|satz** M layer of fat; **zu ~ neigen** to tend to corpulence; **fett|arm** ADJ *Speisen* low-fat, with a low fat content ADV **~ essen** to eat foods with a low fat content *or* which are low in fat; **~ kochen** to cook low-fat meals; **Fett|au|ge** NT globule of fat; **Fett|bauch** M paunch; *(inf: = fetter Mann)* fatso *(inf)*; **fett|bäu|chig** [-bɔyçɪç] ADJ *(inf)* paunchy, fat-bellied *(inf)*; **Fett|be|darf** M fat requirements *pl*; **Fett|creme** F skin cream with oil; **Fett|druck** M, *no pl (Typ)* bold type

Fet|te Hen|ne F *(Bot)* stonecrop

Fett|em|bo|lie F *(Med)* fat-embolism

fet|ten ['fɛtn] VT to grease VI to be greasy; *(= Fett absondern)* to get greasy

Fett-: **Fett|film** M greasy film; **Fett|fleck** M, **Fett|fle|cken** M grease spot, greasy mark; **fett|frei** ADJ fat-free; *Milch* non-fat; *Kost* non-fatty; *Creme* non-greasy ADV **~ kochen** to cook fat-free meals; **~ essen** to eat no fats; **fett|ge|druckt** ADJ *attr* → **fett ADV b**; **Fett|ge|halt** M fat content; **Fett|ge|schwulst** F *(Med)* fatty tumour *(Brit) or* tumor *(US)*; **Fett|ge|we|be** NT *(Anat)* fat(ty) tissue; **fett|glän|zend** ADJ *Hinterkopf* shiny and greasy; **die ~en Ringer** the wrestlers with their oiled bodies glistening; **fett|hal|tig**, *(Aus)* **fett|häl|tig** ADJ fatty; **Fett|haus|halt** M fat balance; **ein gestörter ~** a fat imbalance

Fett|heit F -, *no pl (inf: = Dickheit)* fatness; *(= Fetthaltigkeit)* fattiness

fet|tig ['fɛtɪç] ADJ *Haare, Finger, Speisen* greasy; *Haut auch* oily

Fet|tig|keit F -, *no pl* greasiness; *(von Haut auch)* oiliness

Fett-: **Fett|klops** M *(pej inf)*, **Fett|kloß** M *(pej)* fatty *(inf)*, dumpling *(inf)*; **Fett|klum|pen** M globule of fat; **Fett|le|ber** F fatty liver; **fett|lei|big** [-laibɪç] ADJ *(geh)* obese, corpulent; **Fett|lei|big|keit** F -, *no pl (geh)* obesity, corpulence; **fett|los** ADJ fat-free ADV **völlig ~ essen** to eat no fats at all; **~ kochen** to cook fat-free meals; **fett|lö|send** ADJ → **Fett**; **fett|lös|lich** ADJ fat-soluble; **Fett|mas|sen** PL *(inf)* mass *sing* of fat; **Fett|mops** M *(inf)* roly-poly *(inf)*, dumpling *(inf)*; **Fett|näpf|chen** [-nɛpfçən] NT -s, - *(inf)* **ins ~ treten** to put one's foot in it *(bei jdm* with sb), to drop a clanger *(Brit inf)*; **Fett|pols|ter** NT *(Anat)* (layer of) subcutaneous fat; *(hum inf)* flab *no pl*, padding *no pl*; **~ haben** to be well-padded; **Fett|pöls|ter|chen** NT padding *no pl*; **Fett|pres|se** F grease gun; **fett|reich** ADJ *Speisen* high-fat, with a high fat content; *Haut* oily ADV **~ essen** to eat foods with a high fat content *or* which are high in fat; **~ kochen** to use a lot of fat in cooking; **Fett|sack** M *(inf)* fatso *(inf)*; **Fett|sal|be** F fat-based ointment; **Fett|sau** F *(vulg)* fat slob *(inf)*; **Fett|säu|re** F *(Chem)* fatty acid; **Fett|schicht** F layer of fat; **Fett|schrift** F bold (type *or* face); **Fett|steiß** M *(Anat)* steatopygia *(spec)*; **Fett|stift** M grease pencil, lithographic crayon; *(für Lippen)* lip salve; **Fett|sucht** F, *no pl (Med)* obesity; **fett|süch|tig** ADJ *(Med)* obese; **fett|trie|fend** ADJ greasy, dripping with fat; **Fett|wanst** M *(pej)* potbelly; *(= Mensch)* paunchy man, fatso *(inf)*;

Fett|zel|le F *(Physiol)* fat cell, adipose cell *(spec)*

Fe|tus ['feːtʊs] M - *or* **-sses, -sse** *or* **Feten** ['feːtn] foetus *(Brit)*, fetus *(US)*

fet|zen ['fɛtsn] VI *aux sein (= rasen)* to tear *(inf)*; **gegen jdn/etw ~** to tear into sb/sth VT to rip; **der Sturm fetzte das Dach vom Haus** the storm tore the roof off the house VR *(inf: = sich streiten)* to quarrel viciously; **die beiden ~ sich den ganzen Tag** they are tearing into each other all day long

Fet|zen ['fɛtsn] M **-s, -** **a** *(abgerissen)* shred; *(zerrissen auch)* tatter; *(= Stofffetzen, Papierfetzen, Gesprächsfetzen)* scrap; *(= Kleidung)* rag; *(= Nebelfetzen)* wisp; **in ~ sein, nur noch ~ sein** to be in tatters *or* shreds; **in ~ gekleidet** dressed in rags; **das Kleid ist in ~ gegangen** the dress has fallen to pieces; **etw in ~ (zer)reißen** to tear sth to shreds; **etw in tausend ~ (zer)reißen** to tear sth into a thousand pieces; **..., dass die ~ fliegen** *(inf)* ... like mad *(Brit inf) or* crazy *(inf)* **b** *(Aus: = Scheuertuch)* rag

Fet|zen|ball M *(Aus: = Maskenball)* masked ball

fet|zig ['fɛtsɪç] ADJ *(dated sl)* wild, crazy *(inf)*; *Musik auch* hot; *Rede* rousing

feucht [fɔyçt] ADJ damp; *(= schlüpfrig)* moist; *(= feuchtheiß) Klima* humid; *Jahreszeit* wet, rainy; *Luftmassen* rain-bearing, rain-bringing; *Hände* sweaty; *Tinte, Farbe* wet; **sich ins ~e Element stürzen** *(hum)* to plunge into the water; **sie kriegte/hatte ~e Augen** her eyes moistened/were moist; **ein ~er Abend** *(hum)* a boozy *or* drunken night *(inf)*; **eine ~e Aussprache haben** *(hum inf)* to splutter when one speaks; **das geht dich einen ~en Kehricht an** *(inf)* that's none of your goddamn *(inf) or* bloody *(Brit inf)* business; **~er Traum** *(inf)* wet dream → **Ohr**

Feucht|bio|top NT damp biotope

Feuch|te ['fɔyçtə] F **-,** *no pl* dampness; *(von Luft)* humidity

Feucht-: **feucht|fröh|lich** ADJ *(hum)* merry, convivial; **ein ~er Abend** an evening of convivial drinking; **Feucht|ge|biet** NT marshland; **feucht|heiß** ADJ hot and damp, muggy

Feuch|tig|keit ['fɔyçtɪçkait] F **-,** *no pl* **a** dampness; *(= Schlüpfrigkeit)* moistness; *(von Klima)* humidity; *(von Händen)* sweatiness **b** *(= Flüssigkeit)* moisture; *(= Luftfeuchtigkeit)* humidity

Feuch|tig|keits-: **Feuch|tig|keits|creme** F moisturizer, moisturizing cream; **Feuch|tig|keits|ge|halt** M, **Feuch|tig|keits|grad** M moisture level *or* content; **Feuch|tig|keits|mes|ser** M **-s, -** hygrometer

feucht-: **feucht|kalt** ADJ *Luft, Nacht, Wand* cold and damp; *Höhle, Keller etc auch* dank; **feucht|warm** ADJ *Klima, Luft* muggy, humid; *Boden* warm and damp

feu|dal [fɔy'daːl] ADJ **a** *(Pol, Hist)* feudal **b** *(inf: = prächtig)* plush *(inf)*; *Mahlzeit* slap-up *attr (Brit inf)*, lavish

Feu|dal- *in cpds* feudal; **Feu|dal|herr|schaft** F feudalism

Feu|da|lis|mus [fɔyda'lɪsmʊs] M **-,** *no pl* feudalism

feu|da|lis|tisch [fɔyda'lɪstɪʃ] ADJ feudalistic

Feu|da|li|tät [fɔydali'tɛːt] F **-,** *no pl* **a** *(Hist)* feudality **b** *(inf)* plushness *(inf)*

Feu|dal|sys|tem NT, **Feu|dal|we|sen** NT, *no pl* feudalism, feudal system

Feu|del ['fɔydl] M **-s, -** *(N Ger)* (floor)cloth

feu|deln ['fɔydln] VT *(N Ger)* to wash, to wipe

Feu|er ['fɔyɐ] NT **-s, -** **a** *(= Flamme, Kaminfeuer)* fire; *(= olympisches Feuer)* flame; **am ~** by the fire; **~ machen** to light a/the fire; **~ schlagen** to make fire, to strike a spark; **~ speien** to spew flames *or* fire; **~ speiend, ~ sprühend** *(liter, Drache)* fire-breathing; *Berg* spewing (forth) fire; **~ schnaubend** *(poet)* fire-breathing; **das brennt wie ~** *(fig)* that burns; **~ hinter etw** *(acc)* **machen** *(fig)* to chase sth up; **jdm ~ unterm Hintern** *(inf) or* **Arsch** *(sl)* **machen** to put a bomb under sb; **mit dem ~ spielen** *(fig)* to play with fire; **sie sind wie ~ und Wasser** they're as different as chalk and cheese **b** *(= Funkfeuer)* beacon; *(von Leuchtturm)* light **c** *(= Herd)* fire; **auf offenem ~ kochen** to cook on an open fire; **sie stellte die Kartoffeln aufs ~** she put the potatoes on **d** *(für Zigarette etc)* light; **haben Sie ~?** have you got a light?; **jdm ~ geben** to give sb a light **e** *(= Brand)* fire; **~!** fire!; **~ legen** to start a fire; **an etw** *(acc)***/in etw** *(dat)* **~ legen** to set fire to sth; **~ fangen** to catch fire; **für jdn durchs ~ gehen** to go through fire and water for sb **f** *(= Schwung) (von Frau)* passion; *(von Liebhaber auch)* ardour *(Brit)*, ardor *(US)*; *(von Pferd)* mettle; *(von Wein)* vigour *(Brit)*, vigor *(US)*; **~ haben** to be passionate/ardent/mettlesome/full of vigo(u)r; **~ fangen** to be really taken *(bei* with); **bei jdm ~ fangen** to fall for sb; **~ und Flamme sein** *(inf)* to be dead keen *(Brit inf) (für* on), to be very enthusiastic *(für* about) **g** *(liter: = Glanz)* sparkle, glitter; **das ~ ihrer Augen** her flashing *or* fiery eyes **h** *(= Schießen)* fire; **~!** fire!; **~ frei!** open fire!; **~ geben, das ~ eröffnen** to open fire; **das ~ einstellen** to cease fire *or* firing; **etw unter ~** *(acc)* **nehmen** to open fire on sth; **unter ~** *(dat)* **liegen** to be under fire; **zwischen zwei ~** *(acc)* **geraten** *(fig)* to be caught between the Devil and the deep blue sea *(prov)*

Feu|er- *in cpds* fire; **Feu|er|alarm** M fire alarm; **Feu|er|an|zün|der** M firelighter; **Feu|er|ba|ke** F *(Naut)* light beacon; **Feu|er|ball** M fireball; **Feu|er|be|fehl** M *(Mil)* order to fire; **Feu|er|be|kämp|fung** F fire-fighting; **Feu|er|be|reich** M *(Mil)* firing range; **feu|er|be|reit** ADJ *(Mil) Soldat, Waffe* ready to fire; **feu|er|be|stän|dig** ADJ fire-resistant; **Feu|er|be|stat|tung** F cremation; **Feu|er|ei|fer** M zeal; **mit ~ spielen/diskutieren** to play/discuss with zest; **Feu|er|ei|mer** M fire bucket; **Feu|er|ein|stel|lung** F cessation of fire; *(= Waffenstillstand)* ceasefire; **feu|er|fest** ADJ fireproof; *Geschirr* heat-resistant; **~er Ton** fire clay; **~er Ziegel** firebrick; **Feu|er|fres|ser(in)** M(F) fire-eater; **Feu|er|gar|be** F burst of fire; **Feu|er|gas|se** F fire lane; **Feu|er|ge|fahr** F fire hazard *or* risk; **bei ~** in the event of fire; **feu|er|ge|fähr|lich** ADJ (highly) (in)flammable *or* combustible; **Feu|er|ge|fähr|lich|keit** F (in)flammability, combustibility; **Feu|er|ge|fecht** NT gun fight, shoot-out *(inf)*; **Feu|er|geist** M *(liter)* volatile young genius, fireball; **Feu|er|glo|cke** F fire bell; **Feu|er|gott** M god of fire; **Feu|er|ha|ken** M poker; **Feu|er|holz** NT, *no pl* firewood; **Feu|er|kä|fer** M cardinal beetle; **Feu|er|kopf** M *(fig geh)* hothead; **Feu|er|kult** M *(Rel)* fire cult; **Feu|er|land** ['fɔyɐlant] NT **-s** Tierra del Fuego; **Feu|er|län|der** ['fɔyɐlɛndɐ] M **-s, -**, **Feu|er|län|de|rin** [-ərɪn] F **-, -nen** Fuegian; **Feu|er|lei|ter** F *(am Haus)* fire escape; *(bei Feuerwehrauto)* (fireman's) ladder; *(fahrbar)* turntable ladder; **Feu|er|li|nie** F *(Mil)* firing line

Feu|er|lösch|boot NT fireboat

Feu|er|lö|scher M **-s, -** **a** fire extinguisher **b** *(sl: = Penis)* tool *(sl)*

Feu|er|lösch-: **Feu|er|lösch|ge|rät** NT fire-fighting appliance; **Feu|er|lösch|teich** M emergency water reserve; **Feu|er|lösch|übung** F fire drill; **Feu|er|lösch|zug** M convoy of fire engines, set of appliances *(form)*

Feuer-: **Feu|er|mal** NT *(Med)* port-wine stain; **Feu|er|meer** NT sea of flames, blazing inferno; **Feu|er|mel|der** M fire alarm; **er hat ein Gesicht wie ein ~(, so schön zum Reinschlagen)** *(sl)* he's got the kind of face that just makes you want to hit it

feu|ern ['fɔyɐn] VI **a** *(= heizen)* **mit Öl/Gas ~** to have oil/gas heating; **mit Holz ~** to use wood for one's heating **b** *(Mil)* to fire VT **a** *Ofen* to light; **Öl ~** to have oil heating; **Briketts ~** to use briquettes for one's heating **b** *(inf) (= werfen)* to fling *(inf)*, to sling *(inf)*; *(Ftbl) Ball* to slam *(inf)*; *(ins Tor)* to slam home *(inf) or* in *(inf)* **c** *(inf: = entlassen)* to fire *(inf)*, to sack *(inf)*; **gefeuert werden** to get the sack, to be fired *or* sacked *(all inf)*

Feu|er-: **Feu|er|ofen** M *(Bibl)* fiery furnace; **Feu|er|pat|sche** F fire-beater; **Feu|er|pau|se** F break in the firing; *(vereinbart)* ceasefire; **feu|er|po|li|zei|lich** ADJ *Bestimmungen* laid down by the fire authorities; **~e Notrufleitungen** emergency lines to the fire station ADV **~ verboten** prohibited by order of the fire authorities; **Feu|er|pro|be** F *(Hist: = Gottesurteil)* ordeal by fire; **die ~ bestehen** *(fig)* to pass the (acid) test; **das war seine ~** *(fig)* that was the acid test for him; **Feu|er|qual|le** F stinging jellyfish; **Feu|er|rad** NT fire-wheel; *(= Feuerwerkskörper)* catherine *(Brit) or* pin *(US)* wheel; **feu|er|rot** ADJ fiery red; *Haar auch* flaming; *Kleidung, Auto* scarlet; **~ werden** *(vor Verlegenheit etc)* to turn crimson *or* scarlet; **Feu|er|sa|la|man|der** M fire *or* European salamander; **Feu|er|säu|le** F *(Bibl)* pillar of fire

Feu|ers|brunst F *(geh)* conflagration

Feu|er-: **Feu|er|scha|den** M fire damage *no pl*; **Feu|er|schein** M glow of the fire; **Feu|er|schiff** NT lightship; **Feu|er|schlu|cker** [-ʃlʊkɐ] M **-s, -**, **Feu|er|schlu|cke|rin** [-ərɪn] F **-, -nen** fire-eater; **feu|er|schnau|bend** ADJ → **Feuer a**; **Feu|er|schnei|se** F fire break; **Feu|er|schutz** M **a** *(= Vorbeugung)* fire prevention **b** *(Mil: = Deckung)* covering fire; **Feu|er|schutz|tür** F fire door; **Feu|er|schweif** M fiery tail; **feu|er|si|cher** ADJ = **feuerfest**; **Feu|er|si|re|ne** F fire siren; **feu|er|spei|end** ADJ *attr* → **Feuer a**; **Feu|er|sprit|ze** F fire hose; **Feu|er|stät|te** F *(form)* **a** *(= Koch-, Heizstelle)* fireplace, hearth **b** *(= Brandstelle)* scene of the fire; **Feu|er|stein** M flint; **Feu|er|stel|le** F campfire site; *(= Spuren eines Feuers)* burned spot, remains *pl* of a fire; *(= Herd)* fireplace; **Feu|er|stuhl** M *(inf)* (motor)bike; **Feu|er|sturm** M fire storm; **Feu|er|tau|fe** F baptism of fire; **die ~ bestehen/erhalten** to go through/have one's baptism of fire; **Feu|er|teu|fel** M *(inf)* firebug *(inf)*; **Feu|er|tod** M *(Hist)* (death at) the stake; **den ~ erleiden** to be burned *or* to die at the stake; **Feu|er|trep|pe** F fire escape; **Feu|er|tür** F fire door

Feu|ers|not F *(liter)* fiery peril *(poet)*

Feu|er-: **feu|er|sprü|hend** ADJ *(liter)* → **Feuer a**; **Feu|er|stel|lung** F *(Mil)* firing position; **Feu|er|stoß** M burst of fire; **Feu|er|strahl** M *(geh)* jet of flame *or* fire; *(poet: = Blitz)* thunderbolt; **Feu|er|über|fall** M armed attack

Feu|e|rung ['fɔyərʊŋ] F **-, -en** **a** *(= das Beheizen)* heating **b** *(= Brennstoff)* fuel **c** *(= Heizanlage)* heating system

Feu|er-: **Feu|er|ver|hü|tung** F fire prevention; **Feu|er|ver|si|che|rung** F fire insurance; **feu|er|ver|zinkt** [-fɛɐtsɪŋkt] ADJ (hot-dip) galvanized; **Feu|er|wa|che** F fire station; **Feu|er|waf|fe** F firearm; **Feu|er|wal|ze** F swath of fire; **Feu|er|was|ser** NT, *no pl (inf)* firewater *(inf)*; **Feu|er|wech|sel** M exchange of fire

Feu|er|wehr F fire brigade *(Brit)*, fire department *(US)*; **fahren wie die ~** *(inf)* to drive like the clappers *(Brit inf) or* like a bat out of hell *(US inf)*; **~ spielen** *(fig: = Schlimmes verhindern)* to act as a troubleshooter, to troubleshoot

Feu|er|wehr-: **Feu|er|wehr|au|to** NT fire engine; **Feu|er|wehr|ball** M firemen's ball; **Feu|er|wehr|frau** F firewoman; **Feu|er|wehr|leu|te** PL firemen *pl*, firefighters *pl*; **Feu|er|wehr|mann** M *pl* **-leute** *or* **-männer** fireman; **Feu|er|wehr|schlauch** M fire hose; **Feu|er|wehr|übung** F fire-fighting exercise; **Feu|er|wehr|wa|gen** M fire engine

Feu|er-: **Feu|er|werk** NT fireworks *pl*; *(= Schauspiel auch)* firework display; *(fig)* cavalcade; **Feu|er|wer|ker** [-vɛrkɐ] M **-s, -**, **Feu|er|wer|ke|rin** [-ərɪn] F **-, -nen** firework-maker; **Feu|er|werks|kör|per** M firework; **Feu|er|zan|ge** F fire tongs *pl*; **Feu|er|zan|gen|bow|le** F red wine punch *(containing rum which has been set alight)*

> **FEUERZANGENBOWLE**
> A **Feuerzangenbowle** is wine punch, with rum and sometimes fruit juice added. A piece of sugar loaf, held in tongs over the wine, has rum pored over it, and is then set alight. The sugar slowly melts, caramelizes, and drips into the wine, giving the punch its special taste.

Feu|er-: **Feu|er|zei|chen** NT **a** *(= Signal)* beacon **b** *(Astrol)* fire sign; **Feu|er|zeug** NT *pl* **-zeuge** (cigarette) lighter; **Feu|er|zeug|ben|zin** NT lighter fuel; **Feu|er|zeug|gas** NT lighter gas; **Feu|er|zo|ne** F *(Mil)* firing zone; **Feu|er|zun|ge** F *(Bibl)* tongue of flame

Feuil|le|ton [fœjə'tõ:, 'fœjətõ] NT **-s, -s** *(Press)* **a** *(= Zeitungsteil)* feature pages *pl or* section **b** *(= Artikel)* feature (article)

Feuil|le|to|nis|mus [fœjəto'nɪsmʊs] M **-,** *no pl* *style of writing used in feature articles, often regarded as facile*

Feuil|le|to|nist [fœjəto'nɪst] M **-en, -en**, **Feuil|le|to|nis|tin** [-'nɪstɪn] F **-, -nen** feature writer

feuil|le|to|nis|tisch [fœjəto'nɪstɪʃ] ADJ **dieser Journalist ist ein ~es Talent** this journalist has a natural flair for writing feature articles; **dieser Aufsatz ist zu ~** *(pej)* this essay is too glib *or* facile

Feuil|le|ton-: **Feuil|le|ton|schrei|ber(in)** M(F) feature writer; **Feuil|le|ton|stil** M style used in feature articles; *(pej)* facile *or* glib style

feu|rig ['fɔyrɪç] ADJ *Pferd, Liebhaber, Rede* fiery; *(old: = glühend)* glowing

feu|rio ['fɔyrio] INTERJ *(old)* fire(, fire)!

Fex [fɛks] M **-es** *or* **-en, -e** *or* **-en** *(S Ger, Aus)* enthusiast

Fez [fe:ts, fe:s] M **-(es), -(e)** *(= Hut)* fez

Fez [fe:ts] M **-(e)s,** *no pl (dated inf)* larking about *(Brit inf)*, fooling around *(esp US inf)*; **~ machen** to lark about *(Brit inf)*, to fool around *(esp US inf)*

ff [ɛf'lɛf] ADJ *inv* first-class, top-grade → **Effeff**

ff. *abbr von* **folgende Seiten**

Ffm. *abbr von* **Frankfurt am Main**

FH [ɛf'ha:] F **-, -s** *abbr von* **Fachhochschule**

Fi|a|ker ['fiakɐ] M **-s, -** *(Aus)* **a** *(= Kutsche)* (hackney) cab **b** *(= Kutscher)* cab driver, cabby *(inf)*

Fi|a|le ['fia:lə] F **-, -n** *(Archit)* pinnacle

Fi|as|ko ['fiasko] NT **-s, -s** *(inf)* fiasco; **mit seinem Buch erlebte er ein ~** his book was a complete failure *or* flop *(inf) or* fiasco; **dann gibt es ein ~** it'll be disastrous *or* a fiasco

Fi|bel ['fi:bl] F **-, -n** *(Sch)* primer

Fi|bel F **-, -n** *(Archeol)* fibula *(spec)*, clasp

Fi|ber ['fi:bɐ] F **-, -n** fibre *(Brit)*, fiber *(US)*

Fib|rin [fi'bri:n] NT **-s,** *no pl (Physiol)* fibrin

Fib|rom [fi'bro:m] NT **-s, -e** *(Med)* fibroma *(spec)*

fib|rös [fi'brø:s] ADJ *(Med)* fibrous

Fiche [fi:ʃ] M OR NT **-(s), -s** **a** (micro)fiche **b** *(Sw: = Akte)* file

ficht [fɪçt] *3. pers sing pres von* **fechten**

Fich|te ['fɪçtə] F **-, -n** *(Bot)* spruce; *(Holz auch)* spruce wood

fich|ten ['fɪçtn] ADJ spruce(wood)

Fich|ten- *in cpds* spruce; **Fich|ten|na|del|ex|trakt** M pine essence; **Fich|ten|zap|fen** M spruce cone

Fick [fɪk] M **-s, -s** *(vulg)* fuck *(vulg)*

fi|cken ['fɪkn] VTI *(vulg)* to fuck *(vulg)*; **mit jdm ~** to fuck sb *(vulg)*

fi|cke|rig ['fɪkərɪç], **fick|rig** ['fɪkrɪç] ADJ *(dial)* fidgety

Fick|teu|fel M *(vulg: = Penis)* dick *(sl)*, cock *(sl)*

Fi|cus ['fi:kʊs] M **-, Fici** ['fi:tsi] *(= Zierpflanze)* weeping fig

Fi|dei|kom|miss [fideikɔ'mɪs, 'fi:dei-] NT **-es, -e** *(old Jur)* entail *(form)*, entailed estate

fi|del [fi'de:l] ADJ jolly, merry

Fi|del ['fi:dl] F **-, -n** fiddle

Fi|di|bus ['fi:dibʊs] M **-** *or* **-ses, -** *or* **-se** spill

Fid|schi ['fɪdʒi] NT **-s** Fiji

Fid|schi M **-s, -s** *(pej sl: = Exot)* gook *(pej sl)*

Fid|schi|a|ner [fɪ'dʒia:nɐ] M **-s, -**, **Fid|schi|a|ne|rin** [-ərɪn] F **-, -nen** Fijian

Fid|schi-In|seln ['fɪdʒi-] PL Fiji Islands *pl*

Fie|ber ['fi:bɐ] NT **-s,** *(rare)* **-** **a** temperature; *(sehr hoch, mit Fantasieren)* fever; **~ haben** to have *or* be running a temperature; to be feverish *or* running a fever; **40° ~ haben** to have a temperature of 40; **(jdm) das ~ messen** to take sb's temperature; **im ~ seiner Leidenschaft** in a fever of passion **b** *(= Krankheit)* fever

Fie|ber-: **Fie|ber|an|fall** M attack *or* bout of fever; **Fie|ber|bläs|chen** NT fever blister; **Fie|ber|fan|ta|si|en** PL feverish *or* febrile *(form)* wanderings *pl or* ravings *pl*; **Fie|ber|fle|cken** PL fever spots *pl*; **fie|ber|frei** ADJ free of fever; **Fie|ber|frost** M feverish shivering; **fie|ber|haft** ADJ **a** *(= fieberig)* feverish, febrile *(form)* **b** *(= hektisch)* feverish ADV feverishly

fie|be|rig ['fi:bərɪç] ADJ feverish, febrile *(form)*; **in ~er Eile** with feverish haste

Fie|ber-: **Fie|ber|kur|ve** F temperature curve; **Fie|ber|mes|ser** M **-s, -** *(dated, Sw)* thermometer; **Fie|ber|mit|tel** NT anti-fever drug, antipyretic *(spec)*; **Fie|ber|mü|cke** F malarial mosquito

fie|bern ['fi:bɐn] VI **a** *(Kranker)* to have a fever *or* temperature; *(schwer)* to be feverish *or* febrile *(form)* **b** *(fig)* **nach etw ~** to long feverishly for sth; **vor Ungeduld/Erregung** *(dat)* **~** to be in a fever of impatience/excitement

Fie|ber-: **Fie|ber|phan|ta|si|en** PL = **Fieberfantasien**; **fie|ber|sen|kend** ADJ fever-reducing; **Fie|ber|sen|kung** F reduction of fever; **ein Mittel zur ~** a medicine for reducing fever; **Fie|ber|ta|bel|le** F temperature chart; **Fie|ber|ther|mo|me|ter** NT (clinical) thermometer; **Fie|ber|wahn** M (feverish *or* febrile) delirium; **Fie|ber|zäpf|chen** NT *(Pharm, Med)* fever-reducing *or* antipyretic *(spec)* suppository

fieb|rig ['fi:brɪç] ADJ = **fieberig**

Fie|del ['fi:dl] F **-, -n** fiddle

Fie|del|bo|gen M fiddle bow

fie|deln ['fi:dln] VTI *(hum, pej)* to fiddle; **ein Liedchen ~** to play a song on the fiddle

fie|dern ['fi:dɐn] VR *(Orn)* to acquire its plumage → *auch* **gefiedert**

Fie|de|rung ['fi:dərʊŋ] F **-, -en** **a** *(Orn)* plumage **b** *(Bot)* pinnation *(spec)*

Fied|ler ['fi:dlɐ] M **-s, -**, **Fied|le|rin** [-ərɪn] F **-, -nen** *(hum, pej: = Geiger)* fiddler

fiel *pret von* **fallen**

fie|pen ['fi:pn] VI *(Reh)* to call; *(Hund, Mensch)* to whimper; *(Vogel)* to cheep

Fie|rant [fiə'rant] M **-en, -en**, **Fie|ran|tin** [fiə'rantɪn] F **-, -nen** *(S Ger, Aus)* (street) market trader

fie|ren ['fi:rən] VT *(Naut) Segel, Last* to lower; *Tau* to pay out

fies [fi:s] *(inf)* ADJ *(= abstoßend, unangenehm) Mensch, Gesicht, Geruch, Arbeit* nasty, horrid, horrible; *(= gemein) Charakter, Methoden auch* mean ADV *(= abstoßend, ekelhaft) sich benehmen, lachen* nastily, horribly; *(= gemein) handeln, reagieren* in a nasty way; **~ aussehen** to look horrible; **~ riechen** to smell horrible; **benimm dich nicht so ~!** don't be so horrid!; *(= ordinär)* don't behave so horribly!

Fies|heit F **-, -en** *usu pl (inf)* mean trick

Fies|ling ['fi:slɪŋ] M **-s, -e** *(inf)* *(= abstoßender Mensch)* slob *(inf)*; *(= gemeiner Mensch)* sod *(Brit sl)*, bastard *(sl)*

FI|FA ['fi:fa] F **-**, **Fi|fa** F **-** FIFA

fif|ty-fif|ty ['fɪftɪ'fɪftɪ] ADV *(inf)* fifty-fifty *(inf)*; **~ machen** to go fifty-fifty *(inf)*; **die Sache steht ~** there's a fifty-fifty chance *(inf)*

Fi|ga|ro ['fi:garo] M **-s, -s** *(hum)* hairdresser

Fight [fait] M **-s, -s** fight

figh|ten ['faitn] VI to fight

Figh|ter ['faitɐ] M **-s, -**, **Figh|te|rin** ['faitərɪn] F **-, -nen** fighter

Fi|gur [fi'gu:ɐ] F **-, -en** **a** *(= Bildwerk, Abbildung, Math)* figure; *(gedankenlos hingezeichnet)* doodle **b** *(= Gestalt, Persönlichkeit)* figure; *(= Körperform) (von Frauen)* figure; *(von Männern)* physique; *(inf: = Mensch)* character; **in ganzer ~** *(Phot, Art)* full-figure; **auf seine ~ achten** to watch one's figure; **eine gute/schlechte/traurige ~ machen** *or* **abgeben** to cut a good/poor/sorry figure **c** *(= Romanfigur, Filmfigur etc)* character **d** *(Sport, Mus)* figure; *(= rhetorische Figur)* figure of speech

fi|gu|ral [figu'ra:l] ADJ *(Art)* figured

Fi|gu|ral|mu|sik F figural *or* florid music

Fi|gu|ra|ti|on [figura'tsio:n] F **-, -en** figuration

fi|gu|ra|tiv [figura'ti:f] ADJ figurative ADV figuratively; *(geh: = gegenständlich)* representationally

fi|gur|be|tont ADJ figure-hugging

Fi|gür|chen [fi'gy:ɐçən] NT **-s, -** *dim von* **Figur**

Fi|gu|ren|lau|fen NT **-s,** *no pl* figure skating

fi|gu|rie|ren [figu'ri:rən] *ptp* **figuriert** VI *(geh)* to figure VT *(Mus)* to figure

Fi|gu|ri|ne [figu'ri:nə] F **-, -n** *(Art)* figure; *(= kleine Statue)* figurine; *(Theat)* costume design *or* sketch

fi|gür|lich [fi'gy:ɐlɪç] ADJ **a** *(= übertragen)* figurative **b** *(= figurmäßig)* as regards the/her figure; *(von Männern)* as regards physique **c** *(Art)* figurative ADV *(= figurmäßig)* in terms of the/one's figure; *(= übertragen)* figuratively

Fi|gur|prob|lem NT problem with one's figure, weight problem

Fik|ti|on [fɪk'tsio:n] F **-, -en** fiction

fik|tiv [fɪk'ti:f] ADJ fictitious

File [fail] NT **-s, -s** *(Comput: = Datei)* file

File|ser|ver ['failzœrvɐ] M **-s, -** *(Comput)* file server

File|sha|ring ['failʃeərɪŋ] NT **-,** *no pl (Internet)* file sharing

Fi|let [fi'le:] NT **-s, -s** **a** *(Cook) (= Schweinefilet, Geflügelfilet, Fischfilet)* fillet; *(= Rinderfilet)* fillet steak; *(zum Braten)* piece of sirloin *or* tenderloin *(US)* **b** *(Tex)* netting

Fi|let|ar|beit [fi'le:-] F *(Tex)* netting

fi|le|tie|ren [file'ti:rən] *ptp* **filetiert** VT to fillet

Fi|let-: **Fi|let|steak** NT fillet steak; **Fi|let|stück** NT *(Cook)* piece of sirloin *or* tenderloin *(US)*; *(fig inf: = lohnendes Investitionsobjekt etc)* prime investment choice

Fi|lia ['fi:lia] F **-, Filiae** ['fi:liɛ] *(hum)* daughter, offspring *(hum)*

Fi|li|al|be|trieb [fi'lia:l-] M branch

Fi|li|a|le [fi'lia:lə] F **-, -n** branch

Fi|li|al-: **Fi|li|al|ge|ne|ra|ti|on** F *(Biol)* (first) filial generation; **Fi|li|al|ge|schäft** NT branch; **Fi|li|al|lei|ter(in)** M(F) branch manager/manageress; **Fi|li|al|kir|che** F daughter church; **Fi|li|al|netz** NT network of branches

Fi|li|bus|ter [fili'bʊstɐ] M **-s, -** *(old, fig)* buccaneer

Fi|li|bus|ter [fili'bastɐ] NT **-(s), -** *(Pol)* filibuster

fi|lig|ran [fili'gra:n] ADJ filigree

Fi|lig|ran [fili'gra:n] NT **-s, -e** filigree

Fi|lig|ran|ar|beit F filigree work; *(= Schmuckstück)* piece of filigree work

Fi|li|pi|na [fili'pi:na] F **-, -s** Filipina

Fi|li|pi|no [fili'pi:no] M **-s, -s** Filipino

Fi|li|pi|no [fili'pi:no] NT **-,** *no pl (Ling)* Filipino, Tagalog

Fi|li|us ['fi:liʊs] M **-, -se** *(hum)* son, offspring *(hum)*

Film [fɪlm] M **-(e)s, -e** **a** *(alle Bedeutungen)* film; *(= Spielfilm)* film, movie *(esp US)*, motion picture *(US)*; *(= Dokumentarfilm)* documentary (film); **ein ~ nach dem Roman von E. Marlitt** a film of *or* based on the novel by E. Marlitt; **in einen ~ gehen** to go and see a film, to go to a film; **da ist bei mir der ~ gerissen** *(fig inf)* I had a mental blackout *(inf)* **b** *(= Filmbranche)* films *pl*, movie *(esp US) or* motion-picture *(esp US)* business; **zum ~ gehen/kommen** to go/get *or* break into films *or* movies *(esp US)*; **beim ~ arbeiten** *or* **sein** *(inf)* to work in films *or* in the movie business *(esp US)*

Film- *in cpds* film, movie *(esp US)*; **Film|ama|teur(in)** M(F) home-movie enthusiast *or* buff *(inf)*; **Film|ar|chiv** NT film archives *pl*; **Film|ate|li|er** NT film studio; **Film|auf|nah|me** F **a** *(Einzelszene)* shot, take **b** *(= das Drehen)* **die ~n** *pl* shooting; **Film|auf|roll|spu|le** F, **Film|auf|wi|ckel|spu|le** *(Phot)* take-up spool; **Film|au|tor(in)** M(F) scriptwriter, screen-writer; **Film|ball** M film festival ball; **Film|bau|ten** PL film sets *pl*; **Film|be|ar|bei|tung** F (screen) adaptation; **Film|be|richt** M film report; **Film|be|wer|tungs|stel|le** F ≈ board of film classification; **Film|bio|gra|fie**, **Film|bio|gra|phie** F biopic; **Film|büh|ne** F *(dated)* picture house *(dated)*, movie house *(US)*; **Film|di|va** F *(dated)* screen goddess; **Film|dra|ma** NT film drama

Fil|me|ma|cher(in) M(F) film-maker

Film|emp|find|lich|keit F film speed

fil|men ['fɪlmən] VTI to film

Film-: **Film|ent|wick|ler** M developer; **Film|epos** NT epic film

Fil|mer ['fɪlmɐ] M **-s, -**, **Fil|me|rin** [-ərɪn] F **-, -nen** *(inf)* film *or* movie *(esp US)* director

Fil|me|rei [fɪlmə'rai] F **-, -en** *(inf)* filming

Film-: **Film|er|zäh|lung** F narrative film, screen tale; **Film|fes|ti|val** NT, **Film|fest|spie|le** PL film festival; **Film|för|de|rung** F financial help for the film *or (esp US)* movie industry; **Film|för|de|rungs|ge|setz** NT *law on film subsidies*; **Film|for|mat** NT *(für Fotoapparat)* film size; *(für Filmkamera)* film gauge; **Film|frit|ze** M *(inf)* film *or* movie *(esp US)* guy *(inf)*; **film|ge|recht** ADJ filmable ADV **der Roman muss ~ bearbeitet werden** the novel will have to be adapted for the cinema *or* for film; **Film|ge|schäft** NT film *or* movie *(esp US) or* motion-picture *(esp US)* industry; **Film|ge|schich|te** F history of the cinema; **~ machen** to make film *or* movie *(esp US) or* motion-picture *(esp US)* history; **Film|ge|schich|te** F *(= filmische Erzählung)* screen *or* movie *(esp US)* tale; **Film|grö|ße** F *(= Filmstar)* great star of the screen, great movie star *(esp US)*; **Film|held** M screen *or* movie *(esp US)* hero; **Film|hel|din** F screen *or* movie *(esp US)* heroine

fil|misch ['fɪlmɪʃ] ADJ cinematic; **~es Porträt** film portrait; **eine ~e Dokumentation der Aufführung** a record on film of the production ADV cinematically

Film-: **Film|ka|me|ra** F film *or* movie *(esp US)* camera; *(= Schmalfilmkamera)* cine camera *(Brit)*, movie camera *(esp US)*; **Film|kas|set|te** F film cassette; **Film|kom|po|nist(in)** M(F) composer of film music; **Film|kri|tik** F film *or* movie *(esp US)* criticism *or* reviewing; *(= Artikel)* film *or* movie *(esp US)* review; *(= Kritiker)* film *or* movie *(esp US)* critics *pl*; **Film|ku|lis|se** F setting for a film *or* movie *(esp US)*; **Film|kunst** F cinematic art; **Film|lein|wand** F screen; **Film|ma|te|ri|al** NT film; **Film|mu|sik** F film music, movie soundtrack *(esp US)*; **die originale ~** the original soundtrack

Fil|mo|gra|fie, **Fil|mo|gra|phie** [fɪlmogra'fi:] F **-, -n** [-'fi:ən] filmography

Fil|mo|thek [fɪlmo'te:k] F **-, -en** film *or* movie *(esp US)* library *or* archive

Film-: **Film|pa|last** M picture *or* movie *(esp US)* palace; **Film|part|ner(in)** M(F) film *or* movie *(esp US)* partner *or* co-star; **Film|preis** M film *or* movie *(esp US)* award; **Film|pro|du|zent(in)** M(F) film *or* movie *(esp US)* producer; **Film|pro|jek|tor** M film *or* movie *(esp US)* projector; **Film|prüf|stel|le** F film censorship office; **Film|pub|li|kum** NT filmgoing *or* moviegoing *(esp US)* public; **Film|rech|te** PL film *or* movie *(esp US)* rights *pl*; **Film|re|gie** F direction of a/the film *or* movie *(esp US)*; **Film|re|gis|seur(in)** M(F) film *or* movie *(esp US)* director; **Film|re|por|ta|ge** F film report; **Film|riss** M *(lit)* tear in a film; *(fig inf)* mental blackout *(inf)*; **Film|rol|le** F *(= Spule)* spool of film; *(für Fotoapparat)* roll of film; *(= Part)* film part *or* role, movie role *(esp US)*; **Film|rück|spul|ung** F *(Phot)* film rewind system; **Film|satz** M *(Typ)* = **Lichtsatz**; **Film|schaf|fen|de(r)** MF *decl as adj* film-maker, movie-maker *(esp US)*; **Film|schau|platz** M setting of a film *or* movie *(esp US)*; **Film|schau|spie|ler** M film *or* movie *(esp US)* actor; **Film|schau|spie|le|rin** F film *or* movie *(esp US)* actress; **Film|schön|heit** F screen beauty; **Film|se|rie** F *(esp TV)* film series *sing*; **Film|spu|le** F film spool; **Film|star** M filmstar, movie star *(esp US)*; **Film|stern|chen** NT starlet; **Film|stu|dio** NT film *or* movie *(esp US)* studio; **Film|sze|ne** F scene of a film; **Film|the|a|ter** NT *(form)* cinema, movie theater *(US)*; **Film|trans|port|he|bel** F film advance lever; **Film- und Fern|seh|aka|de|mie** F, **Film- und Fern|seh|hoch|schu|le** F college of film and television technology; **Film|ver|leih** M film *or* movie *(esp US)* distributors *pl*; **Film|vor|füh|rer(in)** M(F) projectionist; **Film|vor|stel|lung** F film *or* movie *(esp US)* show; **Film|welt** F film *or* movie *(esp US)* world; **Film|zen|sur** F film censorship; *(= Zensoren)* film censors *pl*

Fi|lou [fi'lu:] M **-s, -s** *(dated inf)* devil *(inf)*

Fil|ter ['fɪltɐ] NT OR M **-s, -** filter; **eine Zigarette mit/ohne ~** a (filter)tipped/plain cigarette

Fil|ter-: **Fil|ter|an|la|ge** F filter; **Fil|ter|ein|satz** M filter pad; **fil|ter|fein** ADJ finely ground ADV **~ mahlen** to grind finely; **Fil|ter|glas** NT tinted glass; **Fil|ter|kaf|fee** M filter *or* drip *(US)* coffee; **Fil|ter|mund|stück** NT filter-tip

fil|tern ['fɪltɐn] VTI to filter

Fil|ter-: **Fil|ter|pa|pier** NT filter paper; **Fil|ter|rück|stand** M residue *(after filtering)*; **Fil|ter|staub** M filter dust; **Fil|ter|tuch** NT *pl* **-tücher** filter cloth; **Fil|ter|tü|te** F filter bag

Fil|te|rung ['fɪltərʊŋ] F **-, -en** filtering

Fil|ter|zi|ga|ret|te F tipped *or* filter(-tipped) cigarette

Filt|rat [fɪl'tra:t] NT **-(e)s, -e** filtrate

Filt|ra|ti|on [fɪltra'tsio:n] F **-, -en** filtration

filt|rier|bar ADJ filterable

filt|rie|ren [fɪl'tri:rən] *ptp* **filtriert** VT to filter

Filt|rie|rung F **-, -en** filtering

Filz [fɪlts] M **-es, -e** **a** *(Tex)* felt; *(inf: = Filzhut)* felt hat; **grüner ~** green baize **b** *(inf: = Bierdeckel)* beer mat *(esp Brit) or* coaster *(US)* **c** *(inf)* *(= Korruption)* corruption; *(Pol pej)* sleaze *(inf)*

fil|zen ['fɪltsn] VI *(Tex)* to felt, to go felty VT *(inf)* *(= durchsuchen)* **jdn** to frisk, to search; *Gepäck etc* to search, to go through; *(= berauben)* to do over *(inf)*

Filz|hut M felt hat

fil|zig ['fɪltsɪç] ADJ **a** *(= wie Filz)* felty, feltlike **b** *(inf)* *(= korrupt)* corrupt; *(Pol pej)* sleazy *(inf)*

Filz-: **Filz|lat|schen** M *(inf)* carpet slipper; **Filz|laus** F crab louse

Fil|zo|krat [fɪltso'kra:t] M **-en, -en**, **Fil|zo|kra|tin** [-'kra:tɪn] F **-, -nen** *(Pol pej)* corrupt nepotist

Fil|zo|kra|tie [fɪltsokra'ti:] F **-, -n** [-'ti:ən] *(Pol pej)* web of patronage and nepotism, spoils system *(US)*

fil|zo|kra|tisch [fɪltso'kra:tɪʃ] ADJ *(Pol pej)* nepotically corrupt

Filz-: **Filz|pan|tof|fel** M (carpet) slipper; **Filz|schrei|ber** M felt(-tip) pen, felt-tip; **Filz|soh|le** F felt insole; **Filz|stie|fel** M felt boot; **Filz|stift** M felt(-tip) pen, felt-tip

Fim|mel ['fɪml] M **-s, -** *(inf)* **a** *(= Tick)* mania; **er hat diesen ~ mit dem Unkrautjäten** he's got this thing about weeding *(inf)* **b** *(= Spleen)* obsession *(mit* about); **du hast wohl einen ~!** you're crazy *(inf) or* mad *(inf)*!

fi|nal [fi'na:l] ADJ final → **Rettungsschuss**

Fi|na|le [fi'na:lə] NT **-s, -s** *or* **-** *(Mus)* finale; *(Sport)* final, finals *pl*

Fi|nal|geg|ner M *(Sport)* opponent in the final

Fi|na|list [fina'lɪst] M **-en, -en**, **Fi|na|lis|tin** [-'lɪstɪn] F **-, -nen** finalist

Fi|na|li|tät [finali'tɛ:t] F **-, -en** *(Philos)* finality

Fi|na|li|täts|prin|zip NT principle of finality

Fi|nal-: **Fi|nal|satz** M final clause; **Fi|nal|spiel** NT *(Sport)* final

Fi|nan|cier [finã'sie:] M **-s, -s** financier

Fi|nanz [fi'nants] F **-,** *no pl* financial world; **die hohe ~** the world of high finance; **Kreise der ~** financial circles

Fi|nanz- *in cpds* financial; **Fi|nanz|adel** M plutocrats *pl*, plutocracy; **Fi|nanz|ak|ro|bat(in)** M(F) *(pej inf)* financial juggler; **Fi|nanz|amt** NT tax office; **Fi|nanz|aris|to|kra|tie** F plutocrats *pl*, plutocracy; **Fi|nanz|aus|gleich** M *redistribution of income between Bund, Länder and Gemeinden*; **Fi|nanz|aus|schuss** M finance committee; **Fi|nanz|au|to|no|mie** F financial autonomy; **Fi|nanz|be|am|te(r)** M *decl as adj*, **Fi|nanz|be|am|tin** F tax official; **Fi|nanz|be|hör|de** F tax authority; **Fi|nanz|buch|hal|ter(in)** M(F) financial accountant; **Fi|nanz|dienst|leis|ter(in)** M(F) financial service provider; **Fi|nanz|din|ge** PL financial matters *pl*

Fi|nan|zen [fi'nantsn] PL finances *pl*; **das übersteigt meine ~** that's beyond my means

Fi|nan|zer [fi'nantsɐ] M **-s, -**, **Fi|nan|ze|rin** [-ərɪn] F **-, -nen** *(Aus: = Zollbeamter)* customs officer *or* official

Fi|nanz-: **Fi|nanz|fra|ge** F question of finance; **Fi|nanz|ge|ba|ren** NT management of public finances; **Fi|nanz|ge|nie** NT financial genius *or* wizard *(inf)*; **Fi|nanz|ge|richt** NT *tribunal dealing with tax and other financial matters*; **Fi|nanz|hai** M *(pej)* (financial) shark *(inf)*; **Fi|nanz|hil|fe** F financial aid; **Fi|nanz|ho|heit** F financial autonomy

fi|nan|zi|ell [finan'tsiɛl] ADJ financial ADV financially; **sich ~ an etw** *(dat)* **beteiligen** to take a (financial) stake in sth

Fi|nan|zi|er [finan'tsie:] M **-s, -s** financier

fi|nan|zier|bar [finan'tsi:ɐba:ɐ] ADJ financeable; **es ist (nicht) ~** it can(-not) be funded *or* financed, the money can(not) be found

fi|nan|zie|ren [finan'tsi:rən] *ptp* **finanziert** VT to finance, to fund; **frei ~** to finance privately; **ich kann meinen Urlaub nicht ~** I can't afford a holiday *(esp Brit) or* vacation *(US)*

Fi|nan|zie|rung F **-, -en** financing; **zur ~ von etw** to finance sth; **die ~ meines Projekts ist noch nicht gesichert** it isn't certain whether I will have the money for this project

Fi|nan|zie|rungs-: **Fi|nan|zie|rungs|be|darf** M funding *or* borrowing requirement; **Fi|nan|zie|rungs|de|fi|zit** NT budget deficit; **Fi|nan|zie|rungs|ge|sell|schaft** F finance company; **Fi|nan|zie|rungs|loch** NT, **Fi|nan|zie|rungs|lü|cke** F financing gap; **Fi|nan|zie|rungs|plan** M finance plan *or* scheme; **Fi|nan|zie|rungs|zu|sa|ge** F grant of finance

Fi|nanz-: **Fi|nanz|jahr** NT financial year; **Fi|nanz|jong|leur(in)** M(F) *(pej inf)* financial juggler; **Fi|nanz|kraft** F, *no pl* financial strength, financial clout *(inf)*; **fi|nanz|kräf|tig** ADJ financially strong; **Fi|nanz|kri|se** F financial crisis; **Fi|nanz|ma|nage|ment** NT financial management; **Fi|nanz|mi|nis|ter(in)** M(F) ≈ Chancellor of the Exchequer *(Brit)*, ≈ Treasury Secretary *(US)*, finance minister; **Fi|nanz|plan** M financial plan; **Fi|nanz|pla|nung** F financial planning; **Fi|nanz|platz** M financial centre *(Brit) or* center *(US)*; **Fi|nanz|po|li|tik** F financial policy; *(= Wissenschaft, Disziplin)* politics of finance; **fi|nanz|po|li|tisch** ADJ *Fragen, Probleme, Maßnahmen, Entscheidung* relating to financial policy ADV in terms of financial policy; **~ unklug** unwise as regards financial policy; **Fi|nanz|recht** NT financial law; **fi|nanz|schwach** ADJ financially weak; **Fi|nanz|schwä|che** F financial weakness; **Fi|nanz|-**

sprit|ze F injection of capital; **ich brauche eine kleine ~** I need something to boost my cash flow, I could do with a little cash; **fi|nanz|stark** ADJ financially strong; **Fi|nanz|stär|ke** F financial strength; **Fi|nanz|welt** F financial world; **Fi|nanz|we|sen** NT, *no pl* financial system; **ein Ausdruck aus dem ~** a financial term

fi|nas|sie|ren [fina'si:rən] *ptp* **finassiert** VI *(pej)* to machinate, to do some finagling *(inf)*

Fin|del|kind ['fɪndl-] NT *(old)* foundling *(old)*

fin|den ['fɪndn] ✪ 27.1, 34.3, 40.2, 40.3 *pret* **fand**, [fant] *ptp* **gefunden** VT [gə'fʊndn] **a** *(= entdecken)* to find; **ich finde es nicht** I can't find it; **es war nicht/nirgends zu ~** it was not/nowhere to be found; **das muss zu ~ sein** it must be somewhere (to be found); **es ließ sich niemand ~** we/they *etc* couldn't find anybody, there was nobody to be found; **der Grund/die Ursache lässt sich nicht ~** we/they *etc* couldn't find the reason/cause; **etwas an jdm ~** to see something in sb; **nichts dabei ~** to think nothing of it → *auch* **gefunden**

b *(= vorfinden)* to find; **jdn schlafend/bei der Arbeit ~** to find sb asleep/working

c *(in Verbindung mit n siehe auch dort) Trost, Hilfe, Ruhe, Schlaf etc* to find; *Anklang, Zustimmung auch* to meet with; *Beifall* to meet *or* be met with; *Berücksichtigung, Beachtung* to receive; **(den) Mut/(die) Kraft ~, etw zu tun** to find the courage/strength to do sth; **(bei jdm) Anerkennung ~** to find recognition (with sb); **Bestätigung ~** to be confirmed

d *(= ansehen, betrachten)* to think; **es kalt/warm/ganz erträglich** *etc* **~** to find it cold/warm/quite tolerable *etc*; **etw gut/zu teuer/eine Frechheit** *etc* **~** to think (that) sth is good/too expensive/a cheek *etc*; **jdn blöd/nett** *etc* **~** to think (that) sb is stupid/nice *etc*; **wie findest du das?** what do you think?; **wie finde ich denn das?** what do I think (of that)?

VI *(lit, fig: = den Weg finden)* to find one's way; **er findet nicht nach Hause** *(lit)* he can't find his *or* the way home; *(fig)* he can't tear *or* drag himself away *(inf)*; **zu sich selbst ~** to sort oneself out

VTI *(= meinen)* to think; **~ Sie (das)?** do you think so?; **ich finde (das) nicht** I don't think so; **~ Sie (das) nicht auch?** don't you agree?, don't you think so too?; **ich finde, wir sollten/dass wir ...** I think we should/that we ...; **ich kann das** *or* **das kann ich nicht ~** I don't think so; **ich fände es besser, wenn ...** I think it would be better if ...

VR **a** *(= zum Vorschein kommen)* to be found; *(= wiederauftauchen auch)* to turn up; *(= sich befinden auch)* to be; **das wird sich (alles) ~** it will (all) turn up; *(= sich herausstellen)* it'll all come out *(inf)*; **es fand sich niemand, der sich freiwillig gemeldet hätte** there was nobody who volunteered

b *(Angelegenheit etc: = in Ordnung kommen)* to sort itself out; *(Mensch: = zu sich finden)* to sort oneself out; **das wird sich alles ~** it'll all sort itself out

c *(= sich fügen)* **sich in etw** *(acc)* **~** to reconcile oneself to sth, to become reconciled to sth

d *(= sich treffen) (lit)* to find each other; *(fig)* to meet; **da haben sich aber zwei gefunden!** *(iro)* they'll make a fine pair

Fin|der ['fɪndɐ] M **-s, -**, **Fin|de|rin** [-ərɪn] F **-, -nen** finder

Fin|der|lohn M reward for the finder

Fin de Si|è|cle [fɛ̃ d'sjɛkl] NT **- - -**, *no pl* fin de siècle; **die Kunst des ~** fin de siècle art

fin|dig ['fɪndɪç] ADJ resourceful

Fin|dig|keit F **-**, *no pl* resourcefulness

Find|ling ['fɪntlɪŋ] M **-s, -e** **a** *(Geol)* erratic (boulder) **b** *(= Findelkind)* foundling *(old)*

Fine|li|ner ['fainlainɐ] M **-s, -** *(= Stift)* fineliner

Fi|nes|se [fi'nɛsə] F **-, -n** **a** *(= Feinheit)* refinement; *(no pl: = Kunstfertigkeit)* finesse; **mit allen ~n** with every refinement **b** *(= Trick)* trick

fi|nes|sen|reich ADJ artful

fing *pret von* **fangen**

Fin|ger ['fɪŋɐ] M **-s, -** finger; **der kleine ~** one's little finger, one's pinkie *(US, Scot)*; **mit dem ~ auf jdn/etw zeigen** *or* **weisen** *(geh)* to point to sb/sth; **mit ~n auf jdn zeigen** *(fig)* to look askance at sb; **jdm mit dem ~ drohen** to wag one's finger at sb; **jdm eins auf die ~ geben** to give sb a rap across the knuckles; **jdm was auf die ~ geben** to rap sb across the knuckles; **jdm auf die ~ schlagen** *or* **hauen** *or* **klopfen** *(lit, fig)* to rap sb's knuckles, to give sb a rap on the knuckles; **zwei ~ breit** the width of two fingers, two fingers wide **keinen ~ breit nachgeben** *or* **weichen** not to give an inch → *auch* **Fingerbreit**; **(nimm/lass die) ~ weg!** (get/keep your) hands off!; **sich** *(dat)* **nicht die ~ schmutzig machen** *(lit, fig)* not to get one's hands dirty, not to dirty one's hands; **das kann sich jeder an den (fünf** *or* **zehn) ~n abzählen** *(inf)* it sticks out a mile (to anybody) *(inf)*; **das lässt er nicht mehr aus den ~n** he won't let it out of his hands; **jdn/etw in die ~ bekommen** *or* **kriegen** *(inf)* to get one's hands on sb/sth, to get hold of sb/sth; **bei etw die ~ drinhaben** *(inf)* to have a hand in sth; **er hat überall seine ~ drin** *(inf)* he has a finger in every pie *(inf)*; **sich** *(dat)* **die ~ abschreiben** *or* **wund schreiben/wund arbeiten** *etc* to write/work *etc* one's fingers to the bone; **wenn man ihm/dem Teufel den kleinen ~ gibt, (dann) nimmt er (gleich) die ganze Hand** *(prov)* give him an inch and he'll take a mile *(inf)*; **lange ~ machen** *(hum inf)* to be light-fingered; **jdm in** *or* **zwischen die ~ geraten** *or* **fallen** to fall into sb's hands *or* clutches; **die ~ von jdm/etw lassen** *(inf)* to keep away from sb/sth; **sich** *(dat)* **bei** *or* **an etw** *(dat)* **die ~ verbrennen** to burn one's fingers in sth, to get one's fingers burned in sth; **jdm (scharf) auf die ~ sehen** to keep an eye *or* a close eye on sb; **sich** *(dat)* **etw aus den ~n saugen** to conjure sth up *(inf)*, to dream sth up; **sich** *(dat)* **die** *or* **alle ~ nach etw lecken** *(inf)* to be panting *or* dying for sth *(inf)*; **für jdn keinen ~ rühren** not to lift a finger to help sb; **keinen ~ krumm machen** *(inf)* not to lift a finger *(inf)*; **den ~ auf eine/die Wunde legen** to touch on a sore point; **mich** *or* **mir juckt es in den ~n(, etw zu tun)** *(inf)* I'm itching *or* dying to (do sth); **da hast du dich in den ~ geschnitten** *(inf)* you've made a big mistake; **er hat eine** *or* **zehn an jedem ~** he's got a woman for every day of the week; **jdn um den kleinen ~ wickeln** to twist sb round one's little finger; **etw im kleinen ~ haben** *(= perfekt beherrschen)* to have sth at one's fingertips; *(= sicher im Gefühl haben)* to have a feel for sth; **man zeigt nicht mit nacktem ~ auf angezogene Leute** *(inf)* it's rude to point → **spitz ADJ a**

Fin|ger-: **Fin|ger|ab|druck** M fingerprint; **jds Fingerabdrücke nehmen** to take sb's fingerprints, to fingerprint sb; **genetischer ~** genetic fingerprint; **Fin|ger|al|pha|bet** NT manual alphabet; **fin|ger|breit** ADJ the width of a finger; **Fin|ger|breit** M **-, -** finger's breadth, fingerbreadth; *(fig)* inch; **keinen ~ nachgeben** *or* **weichen** not to give an inch → *auch* **Finger**; **fin|ger|dick** ADJ as thick as a finger; **Fin|ger|druck** M *pl* **-drücke** touch of the finger; **Fin|ger|far|be** F finger paint; **fin|ger|fer|tig** ADJ nimble-fingered, dexterous; **Fin|ger|fer|tig|keit** F dexterity; **fin|ger|för|mig** ADJ finger-shaped ADV **die Halbinseln ragen ~ ins Meer hinein** the peninsulas stick out into the sea like fingers; **Fin|ger|ge|lenk** NT finger joint; **Fin|ger|glied** NT phalanx (of the finger) *(form)*; **Fin|ger|ha|keln** NT **-s**, *no pl* finger-wrestling; **Fin|ger|hand|schuh** M glove; **Fin|ger|hut** M **a** *(Sew)* thimble; **ein ~ (voll)** *(fig)* a thimbleful **b** *(Bot)* foxglove; **Fin|ger|kno|chen** M, **Fin|ger|knö|chel** M knucklebone; **Fin|ger|kup|pe** F fingertip; **fin|ger|lang** ADJ *Narbe etc* the length of a finger; **Fin|ger|ling** ['fɪŋəlɪŋ] M **-s, -e** fingerstall

fin|gern ['fɪŋɐn] VI **an** *or* **mit etw** *(dat)* **~** to fiddle with sth; **nach etw ~** to fumble (around) for sth; **... als eine Hand über die Decke fingerte** ... as a hand moved over the bedclothes VT *(= hervorholen)* to fumble around and produce *(inf)*; *(= manipulieren)* to fiddle *(inf)*; *(inf: = bewerkstelligen) Projekt* to wangle *(inf)*

Fin|ger-: **Fin|ger|na|gel** M fingernail; **Fingernägel kauen** to bite one's (finger)nails; **Fin|ger|ring** M ring (for one's finger); **Fin|ger|scha|le** F finger bowl; **Fin|ger|spit|ze** F fingertip, tip of one's finger; **er ist musikalisch bis in die ~n** he's musical right down to his fingertips *or* the tips of his fingers; **das muss man in den ~n haben** you have to have a feel for it; **mir juckt** *or* **kribbelt es in den ~n, das zu tun** I'm itching to do that; **Fin|ger|spit|zen|ge|fühl** NT, *no pl (= Einfühlungsgabe)* instinctive feel *or* feeling; *(im Umgang mit Menschen)* tact and sensitivity, fine feeling; **Fin|ger|spra|che** F manual alphabet, sign language; **Fin|ger|übung** F *(Mus)* finger exercise; *(= Übungsstück)* étude; *(fig) (= erste Arbeit)* first stage of one's apprenticeship; *(= Anfangswerk)* apprentice piece; **Fin|ger|zeig** [-tsaik] M **-s, -e** [-gə] hint; **etw als ~ Gottes/des Schicksals empfinden** to regard sth as a sign from God/as meant

fin|gie|ren [fɪŋ'gi:rən] *ptp* **fingiert** VT *(= vortäuschen)* to fake; *(= erdichten)* to fabricate

fin|giert [fɪŋ'gi:ɐt] ADJ *(= vorgetäuscht)* bogus; *(= erfunden)* fictitious

fi|ni ['fi:ni] ADJ *pred (inf)* **jetzt/dann ist ~** that's it, finito *(inf)*

Fi|nish ['fɪnɪʃ] NT **-s, -s** **a** *(= Endverarbeitung)* finish; *(= Vorgang)* finishing **b** *(Sport: = Endspurt)* final spurt

fi|nit [fi'ni:t] ADJ *(Gram)* finite

Fink [fɪŋk] M **-en, -en** finch

Fin|ken ['fɪŋkn] M **-s, -** *(Sw: = warmer Hausschuh)* (fleece-lined) slipper; **die ~ klopfen** *(inf: = sich davonmachen)* to clear off *(inf)*, to leg it *(inf)*

Fin|ken|schlag M, *no pl* finch's song

Fin|ne ['fɪnə] F **-, -n** **a** *(Zool: = Stadium des Bandwurms)* bladder worm, cysticercus *(form)* **b** *(Med: = Mitesser)* pimple **c** *(= Rückenflosse)* fin **d** *(von Hammer)* peen

Fin|ne M **-n, -n** Finn, Finnish man/boy

Fin|nin ['fɪnɪn] F **-, -nen** Finn, Finnish woman/girl

fin|nisch ['fɪnɪʃ] ADJ Finnish; **der Finnische Meerbusen** the Gulf of Finland

Fin|nisch(e) ['fɪnɪʃ] NT Finnish → *auch* **Deutsch(e)**

fin|nisch-ug|risch ['fɪnɪʃ'lu:grɪʃ] ADJ = **finnougrisch**

Finn|land ['fɪnlant] NT **-s** Finland

Finn|län|der ['fɪnlɛndɐ] M **-s, -**, **Finn|län|de|rin** [-ərɪn] F **-, -nen** Finn

finn|län|disch ['fɪnlɛndɪʃ] ADJ Finnish

finn|lan|di|sie|ren [fɪnlandi'zi:rən] *ptp* **finnlandisiert** VT *(Pol sl)* to Finlandize

Finn|lan|di|sie|rung F **-**, *no pl (Pol sl)* Finlandization

Finn|mark ['fɪnmark] F *pl* **-mark** *(Hist: = Währung)* Finnish mark, markka *(form)*

fin|no|ug|risch [fɪno'lu:grɪʃ] ADJ Finno-Ugric, Finno-Ugrian

Fin|no|ug|ris|tik [fɪnolu'grɪstɪk] F **-**, *no pl* Finno-Ugric studies *pl*

Finn|wal ['fɪnva:l] M finback, finwhale

fins|ter ['fɪnstɐ] ADJ **a** *(= ohne Licht)* dark; *Zimmer, Wald, Nacht* dark (and gloomy); **im Finstern** in the dark; **im Finstern liegen** to be in darkness

b *(= dubios)* shady

c *(= mürrisch, verdrossen, düster)* grim; *Wolken* dark, black

d *(fig: = unaufgeklärt)* dark; **das ~(st)e Mittelalter** the Dark Ages *pl*

e *(= unheimlich) Gestalt, Blick, Gedanken, Drohung, Verschwörung* sinister

ADV **a** *(= mürrisch)* grimly; **es sieht ~ aus** *(fig)*

things look bleak; ~ **entschlossen sein** to be grimly determined; **jdn ~ ansehen** to give sb a black *(Brit) or* dirty *(US)* look **b** *(= unheimlich)* **das alte Haus sah ziemlich ~ aus** the old house looked quite sinister

Fins|ter|ling ['fɪnstɐlɪŋ] **M -s, -e** sinister character; *(= Dunkelmann)* obscurantist

Fins|ter|nis ['fɪnstɐnɪs] **F -, -se a** *(= Dunkelheit, Bibl: = Hölle)* darkness **b** *(Astron)* eclipse

Fin|te ['fɪntə] **F -, -n a** *(Sport)* feint; *(im Rugby)* dummy **b** *(= List)* ruse, subterfuge

fin|ten|reich ADJ artful, crafty; **ein ~er Fuchs** *(inf: = Mensch)* a cunning *or* sly devil *(inf) or* fox

fin|ze|lig ['fɪntsəlɪç], **finz|lig** ['fɪntslɪç] **ADJ** *(N Ger inf)* **a** *(= winzig) Schrift* tiny, weeny *(inf)* **b** *(= knifflig)* fiddly

Fips [fɪps] **M -es, -e** *(dial)* little chap *(Brit inf) or* fellow *(inf)*

fip|sig ['fɪpsɪç] **ADJ** *(dial)* titchy *(inf)*

Fire|wall ['faiɐwɔːl] **F -, -s** *(Comput)* firewall

Fir|le|fanz ['fɪrləfants] **M -es,** *no pl (inf)* **a** *(= Kram)* frippery, trumpery **b** *(= Albernheit)* clowning *or* fooling around; **~ machen** to play the fool, to clown *or* fool around

firm [fɪrm] **ADJ** *pred* **ich bin noch nicht ~** I don't really know it yet; **in einem Fachgebiet ~ sein** to have a sound knowledge of an area

Fir|ma ['fɪrma] **F -, Firmen** ['fɪrmən] **a** company, firm; *(= Kleinbetrieb)* business; **die ~ Wahlster/Lexomat** Wahlster(s)/Lexomat; **die ~ dankt** *(hum)* much obliged (to you) **b** *(= Geschäfts- or Handelsname)* **eine ~ löschen** to strike a company's name/the name of a business from the register; **eine ~ eintragen** to register a company name/ the name of a business; **unter der ~ Smith** under the name of Smith; **unter eigener ~** under one's own name

Fir|ma|ment [fɪrma'mɛnt] **NT -s,** *no pl (liter)* heavens *pl (liter)*, firmament *(Bibl)*

fir|men ['fɪrmən] **VT** *(Rel)* to confirm

Fir|men *pl von* **Firma**

Fir|men-: Fir|men|an|ge|hö|ri|ge(r) MF *decl as adj* member of staff, company employee; **Fir|men|auf|druck M** company stamp; **Fir|men|bü|cher PL** books *pl*, accounts *pl*; **Fir|men|chef(in) M(F)** head of the company, (company) president *(esp US)*; **fir|men|ei|gen ADJ** company *attr*; **~ sein** to belong to the company; **Fir|men|ge|län|de NT** company site; **Fir|men|grün|der(in) M(F)** founder of a/the business, company founder; **Fir|men|grün|dung F** *(= Gründung)* formation *or* founding of a company; *(= neu gegründete Firma)* business start-up; **Fir|men|grup|pe F** group (of companies), conglomerate; **Fir|men|in|ha|ber(in) M(F)** owner of the company; **fir|men|in|tern ADJ** within the company *attr*; *Weiterbildung, Berater auch* in-house *attr*; **~ sein** to be an internal company matter **ADV ~ geregelt** decided within the company; **Fir|men|kopf M** company letterhead; **Fir|men|kun|de M** corporate *or* business customer; *(of bank also)* corporate client; **Fir|men|lo|go NT** company logo; **Fir|men|na|me M** company name; **Fir|men|phi|lo|so|phie F** company philosophy; **Fir|men|re|gis|ter NT** register of companies; **Fir|men|schild NT** company plaque; **Fir|men|schlie|ßung F** closing down (of a firm); **Fir|men|stem|pel M** company stamp; **Fir|men|ver|zeich|nis NT** trade directory; **Fir|men|wa|gen M** company car; **Fir|men|wert M** *(Comm)* goodwill; **Fir|men|zei|chen NT** trademark

fir|mie|ren [fɪr'miːrən] *ptp* **firmiert VI als** *or* **mit ... ~** *(Comm, fig)* to trade under the name of ...

Firm|ling ['fɪrmlɪŋ] **M -s, -e** *(Rel)* candidate for confirmation

Firm|pa|te M, Firm|pa|tin F sponsor

Fir|mung F -, -en *(Rel)* confirmation; **jdm die ~ erteilen** to confirm sb

Firm|ware ['føːɐmwɛːɐ, 'fœrm-] **F** *(Comput)* firmware

firn [fɪrn] **ADJ** *Wein* old

Firn [fɪrn] **M -(e)s, -e** névé, firn

Fir|ne ['fɪrnə] **F -, -n** well-seasoned taste

fir|nig ['fɪrnɪç] **ADJ** *Schnee* névé *attr*

Fir|nis ['fɪrnɪs] **M -ses, -se** *(= Ölfirnis)* oil; *(= Lackfirnis)* varnish

fir|nis|sen ['fɪrnɪsn] **VT** *(mit Ölfirnis)* to oil; *(mit Lackfirnis)* to varnish

Firn|schnee M névé, firn

First [fɪrst] **M -(e)s, -e a** *(= Dachfirst)* (roof) ridge **b** *(geh: = Gebirgskamm)* crest, ridge

First-: First|fei|er F *(Aus)* topping-out ceremony; **First|zie|gel M** ridge tile

Fis [fɪs] **NT -, -, fis** [fɪs] **NT -, -** *(Mus)* F sharp; **in ~** in F sharp major/minor

Fisch [fɪʃ] **M -(e)s, -e a** *(Zool, Cook)* fish; **~e/drei ~e fangen** to catch fish/three fish(es); **~ verarbeitend** fish-processing; **das sind kleine ~e** *(fig inf)* that's child's play *(inf)* *(für* to, for); **ein großer** *or* **dicker ~** *(fig inf)* a big fish; **ein kleiner ~** one of the small fry; **ein paar kleine ~e** some of the small fry; **ein (kalter) ~ sein** *(fig)* to be a cold fish; **munter** *or* **gesund sein wie ein ~ im Wasser** to be in fine fettle; **sich wohlfühlen wie ein ~ im Wasser** to be in one's element; **stumm wie ein ~ sein** *(= sich zu einem Thema nicht äußern)* to keep stumm *(inf)*; **er war den ganzen Abend stumm wie ein ~** he didn't open his mouth all night *(inf)*; **weder ~ noch Fleisch** neither fish nor fowl; **die ~e füttern** *(hum)* to be sick; **~ will schwimmen** *(prov)* fish gives you a thirst; **der ~ stinkt vom Kopf her** the problems are at the top **b** *(Astrol)* Pisces; **die ~e** *(Astron)* Pisces *sing*, the Fish *sing*; **ein ~ sein** to be Pisces *or* a Piscean **c** *(Typ)* character from the wrong fount

Fisch- *in cpds* fish; **Fisch|ad|ler M** osprey; **fisch|ähn|lich ADJ** fish-like; **fisch|arm ADJ** *Gewässer* low in fish; **Fisch|ar|mut F** scarcity of fish; **fisch|ar|tig ADJ** *(Zool)* fish-like; *Geschmack, Geruch* fishy; **Fisch|au|ge NT** *(Phot)* fish-eye lens; **fisch|äu|gig ADJ** fish-eyed; **Fisch|be|cken NT** fishpond; **Fisch|bein NT,** *no pl* whalebone; **Fisch|be|stand M** fish population; **Fisch|be|steck NT** *(einzelnes Set)* fish knife and fork; *(kollektiv)* fish knives and forks *pl*; **Fisch|bla|se F a** *(Zool)* air bladder, swim bladder **b** *(Archit)* foil; **Fisch|blut NT** *(fig)* **~ in den Adern haben** to be a cold fish; **Fisch|bra|te|rei** [-braːtə'rai] **F -, -en, Fisch|brat|kü|che F** fish and chip shop; **Fisch|bröt|chen NT** fish roll *(Brit) or* sandwich *(US)*; **Fisch|brut F** fry *pl*, young fish *pl*; **Fisch|bu|de F** *stand selling fish and various snacks*, ≈ fish and chip stand *(Brit)*; **Fisch|bu|let|te F** fish cake; **Fisch|damp|fer M** trawler

fi|schen ['fɪʃn] **VTI** *(lit, fig)* to fish; **mit (dem) Netz ~** to trawl; **(auf) Heringe ~** to fish for herring → **trüb(e) a**

Fi|scher ['fɪʃɐ] **M -s, -, Fi|sche|rin** [-ərɪn] **F -, -nen** fisherman/-woman

Fi|scher-: Fi|scher|boot NT fishing boat; **Fi|scher|dorf NT** fishing village

Fi|sche|rei [fɪʃə'rai] **F -, -en a** *(= das Fangen)* fishing **b** *(= Fischereigewerbe)* fishing industry, fisheries *pl*

Fi|sche|rei- *in cpds* fishing; **Fi|sche|rei|fre|vel M** *(Jur)* poaching; **Fi|sche|rei|ge|rät NT** fishing tackle; *(= einzelnes Stück)* piece of fishing tackle; **Fi|sche|rei|gren|ze F** fishing limit; **Fi|sche|rei|ha|fen M** fishing port; **Fi|sche|rei|recht NT,** *no pl* **a** fishing rights *pl* **b** *(Jur)* law on fishing; **Fi|sche|rei|schutz|boot NT** fishery protection vessel; **Fi|sche|rei|we|sen NT,** *no pl* fishing *no art*; **Ministerium für ~** ministry of fisheries

Fi|sche|rin [-ərɪn] **F -, -nen** fisherwoman

Fi|scher-: Fi|scher|netz NT fishing net; **Fi|scher|ring M** *(Rel)* Ring of the Fisherman

Fisch|fang M, *no pl* **vom ~ leben** to live by fishing; **zum ~ auslaufen** to set off for the fishing grounds

Fisch|fang-: Fisch|fang|flot|te F fishing fleet; **Fisch|fang|ge|biet NT** fishing grounds *pl*

Fisch-: Fisch|farm F fish farm; **Fisch|fi|let NT** fish fillet; **Fisch|fri|ka|del|le F** fishcake; **Fisch|fut|ter NT** fish food; **Fisch|ge|ruch M** smell of fish, fishy smell; **Fisch|ge|schäft NT** fishmonger's (shop) *(Brit)*, fish shop *(Brit) or* dealer *(US)*; **Fisch|grä|te F** fish bone; **Fisch|grä|ten|mus|ter NT** herringbone (pattern); **Fisch|grün|de PL** fishing grounds *pl*, fisheries *pl*; **Fisch|hal|le F** fish market hall; **Fisch|händ|ler(in) M(F)** fishmonger *(Brit)*, fish dealer *(US)*; *(= Großhändler)* fish merchant; **Fisch|kö|der M** bait; **Fisch|kon|ser|ve F** canned *or* tinned *(Brit)* fish; **Fisch|kopf M,** *(N Ger)* **Fisch|kopp M** *(hum inf)* northerner *(from the German coastal region)*; **Fisch|kut|ter M** fishing cutter; **Fisch|la|den M** fish shop *(Brit) or* dealer *(US)*; **Fisch|le|der NT** shagreen; **Fisch|leim M** isinglass; **Fisch|markt M** fish market; **Fisch|mehl NT** fish meal; **Fisch|milch F** milt, soft roe; **Fisch|ot|ter M** otter; **fisch|reich ADJ** *Gewässer* rich in fish; **Fisch|reich|tum M** wealth of fish; **Fisch|rei|her M** grey heron; **Fisch|reu|se F** fish trap, weir basket; **Fisch|ro|gen M** (hard) roe; **Fisch|schup|pe F** (fish) scale; **Fisch|schup|pen|krank|heit F** ichthyosis *(spec)*; **Fisch|schwarm M** shoal of fish; **Fisch|stäb|chen NT** fish finger *(Brit)*, fish stick *(US)*; **Fisch|ster|ben NT** death of fish; **Fisch|sup|pe F** *(Cook)* fish soup; **Fisch|teich M** fishpond; **Fisch|tran M** train oil; **Fisch|traw|ler** [-trɔːlɐ] **M -s, -** trawler; **fisch|ver|ar|bei|tend ADJ** *attr* → **Fisch a**; **Fisch|ver|ar|bei|tung F** fish processing; **Fisch|wa|ren PL** fish products *pl*; **Fisch|was|ser NT,** *no pl (Cook)* fish stock; **Fisch|wehr NT** fish weir; **Fisch|weib NT** *(dated)* fish seller, fishwoman; *(pej)* fishwife; **Fisch|wil|de|rei F** poaching; **Fisch|wirt|schaft F** fishing industry; **Fisch|zaun M** fish weir; **Fisch|zucht F** fish-farming; *(inf: auch* **Fischzuchtanstalt)** fish farm; **Fisch|zug M a** *(Bibl)* **der ~ des Petrus, Petri ~** the miraculous draught of fishes *(Brit)*, the miraculous catch of fish *(US)* **b** *(fig: = Beutezug)* raid, foray

Fi|si|ma|ten|ten [fizima'tɛntn] **PL** *(inf) (= Ausflüchte)* excuses *pl*; *(= Umstände)* fuss; *(= Albernheiten)* nonsense; **~ machen** to make excuses/a fuss/to get up to some silly things; **mit jdm/etw ~ machen** to mess about with sb/sth *(inf)*

fis|ka|lisch [fɪs'kaːlɪʃ] **ADJ** fiscal

Fis|kal- [fɪs'kaːl-]: **Fis|kal|po|li|tik F,** *no pl* fiscal policy; **fis|kal|po|li|tisch ADJ** politico-economic

Fis|kus ['fɪskʊs] **M -, -se** *or* **Fisken** ['fɪskn] *(= Staatsvermögen)* treasury, exchequer *(Brit)*; *(fig: = Staat)* Treasury

Fi|so|len [fi'zoːlən] **PL** *(Aus)* green beans *pl*

fis|se|lig ['fɪsəlɪç] **ADJ** *(dial)* fine; *(= empfindlich zu handhaben)* fiddly

Fis|sel|re|gen ['fɪsl-] **M** *(dial)* drizzle

Fis|si|on [fɪ'sioːn] **F -, -en** fission

Fis|sur [fɪ'suːɐ] **F -, -en** *(Anat)* fissure; *(Med)* crack

Fis|tel ['fɪstl] **F -, -n** *(Med)* fistula *(spec)*

fis|teln ['fɪstln] **VI** to speak in a falsetto (voice) *or* piping voice

Fis|tel|stim|me F a *(Mus)* falsetto **b** *(= hohes Sprechstimmchen)* falsetto (voice), piping voice

fit [fɪt] **ADJ** fit; **sich ~ halten/machen** to keep/get fit; **jdn/etw wieder ~ machen** to get sb/sth back into shape

Fit|ness ['fɪtnɛs] **F -,** *no pl* physical fitness

Fit|ness-: Fit|ness|cen|ter NT fitness centre *(Brit) or* center *(US)*; **Fit|ness|klub M** gym; **Fit|ness|pro|gramm NT** fitness programme *(Brit)*, training regime *(US)*; **Fit|ness|stu|dio NT** fitness centre *(Brit) or* center *(US)*; **ins ~ gehen** to to to the gym; **Fit|ness|trai|ning NT** fitness training; **~ machen** to work out in the gym

fit|ten ['fɪtn] VT *(Tech)* to fit

Fit|tich ['fɪtɪç] M **-(e)s, -e** *(liter)* wing, pinion *(liter)*; **jdn unter seine ~e nehmen** *(hum)* to take sb under one's wing *(fig)*

Fit|ting ['fɪtɪŋ] NT **-s, -s** *(Tech)* fitting

Fitz|chen ['fɪtsçən] NT **-s, -** *(dial)*, **Fit|zel** ['fɪtsl] M OR NT **-s, -**, **Fit|zel|chen** ['fɪtslçən] NT **-s, -** little bit

fix [fɪks] ADJ **a** *(inf) (= flink)* quick; *(= intelligent)* quick, bright, smart; **in etw** *(dat)* **~ sein** to be quick at sth **b** *(inf)* **~ und fertig sein** *(= nervös)* to be at the end of one's tether *(Brit) or* rope *(US)*; *(= erschöpft)* to be worn out, to be done in *(inf)*, to be all in *(inf)*; *(emotional, seelisch)* to be shattered; *(= ruiniert)* to be done for *(inf)* → *auch* **fertigmachen c** *(= feststehend)* fixed; **~e Idee** obsession, idée fixe ADV *(inf: = schnell)* quickly; **mach ~!** be quick!, look lively! *(inf)*; **das geht ganz ~** that won't take long at all; **geht das nicht ~er?** does it have to take so long?

Fi|xa *pl von* **Fixum**

fi|xen ['fɪksn] VI **a** *(inf: = Drogen spritzen)* to fix *(inf)*, to shoot (up) *(inf)* **b** *(St Ex)* to bear

Fi|xer ['fɪksɐ] M **-s, -**, **Fi|xe|rin** [-ərɪn] F **-, -nen a** *(inf)* fixer *(inf)* **b** *(St Ex)* bear

Fi|xer-: **Fi|xer|be|steck** NT *(inf: = Nadel)* needle; **Fi|xer|stu|be** F *(inf)* junkies' centre *(Brit) or* center *(US, inf)*

Fix|ge|schäft NT *(Comm)* transaction for delivery by a fixed date; *(St Ex)* time bargain

Fi|xier|bad [fɪ'ksiːɐ-] NT fixer

fi|xier|bar ADJ specifiable, definable

fi|xie|ren [fɪ'ksiːrən] *ptp* **fixiert** VT **a** *(= anstarren)* **jdn/etw (mit seinem Blick/seinen Augen) ~** to fix one's gaze/eyes on sb/sth **b** *(= festlegen)* to specify, to define; *Gehälter, Termin etc* to set (*auf +acc* for); *(= schriftlich niederlegen)* to record; **er ist zu stark auf seine Mutter fixiert** *(Psych)* he has a mother fixation; **seine Interessen sind auf Fußball fixiert** he has a fixation about football **c** *(= haltbar machen)* to fix **d** *(Gewichtheben)* to lock; *(Ringen)* to get in a lock

Fi|xier-: **Fi|xier|mit|tel** NT fixer, fixative; **Fi|xier|nat|ron** NT, **Fi|xier|salz** NT hypo

Fi|xie|rung F **-, -en a** *(= Festlegung)* specification, definition; *(von Gehaltern, Terminen)* setting; *(= schriftliche Niederlegung)* recording; *(Psych)* fixation **b** *(= das Anstarren)* fixing of one's gaze (*+gen* on)

Fi|xig|keit ['fɪksɪçkait] F **-**, *no pl (inf)* speed

Fi|xing ['fɪksɪŋ] NT **-s**, *no pl (Fin)* fixing

Fix-: **Fix|kos|ten** PL fixed costs *pl*; **Fix|punkt** M fixed point; **Fix|stern** M fixed star

Fi|xum ['fɪksʊm] NT **-s, Fi̱xa** ['fɪksa] basic salary, basic

Fix|zeit F core time

Fjord [fjɔrt] M **-(e)s, -e** [-də] fiord

FKK [ɛfkaː'kaː] *no art* - *abbr von* **Freikörperkultur**

FKK-An|hän|ger(in) [ɛfkaː'kaː-] M(F) nudist, naturist

FKKler [ɛfkaː'kaːlɐ] M **-s, -**, **FKKle|rin** [ɛfkaː'kaːlərɪn] F *(inf)* **-, -nen** nudist, naturist

FKK-Strand [ɛfkaː'kaː-] M nudist beach

Fla [flaː] F **-**, *no pl (Mil) abbr von* **Flugabwehr**

Flab [flap] F **-**, *no pl (Sw) abbr von* **Fliegerabwehr** anti-aircraft *or* ack-ack unit

flach [flax] ADJ **a** *(= eben, platt, niedrig)* flat; *Gebäude* low; *Abhang* gentle; *Boot* flat-bottomed; **die ~e Klinge/Hand** the flat of the blade/one's hand; **eine ~e Brust** a hollow chest; *(Busen)* a flat chest; **auf dem ~en Land** in the middle of the country **b** *(= untief)* shallow **c** *(= nichtssagend)* flat; *Geschmack* insipid; *(= oberflächlich)* shallow ADV **~ atmen** to take shallow breaths; **sich ~ hinlegen** to lie down; **~ liegen** to lie flat; **~ schlafen** to sleep without a pillow

Flach [flax] NT **-(e)s, -e** *(Naut)* shallows *pl*

Flach-: **Flach|bau** M *pl* **-bauten** low building; **Flach|bau|wei|se** F low style of building; **Flach|bild|schirm** M *(TV)* flat screen; **flach|brüs|tig** [-brʏstɪç] ADJ flat-chested; **Flach|dach** NT flat roof; **Flach|druck** M **a** *no pl (= Verfahren)* planography **b** *pl* **-drucke** *(= Produkt)* planograph; **Flach|dru|cker** M planographic printer

Flä|che ['flɛçə] F **-, -n** *(= Ausdehnung, Flächeninhalt, Math)* area; *(= Oberfläche)* surface; *(von Würfel)* face; *(= Gelände, Landfläche/Wasserfläche)* expanse (of ground/water)

Flach|ei|sen NT flat bar; *(= Werkzeug)* flat-bladed chisel

Flä|chen-: **Flä|chen|aus|deh|nung** F surface area; **Flä|chen|brand** M extensive fire; **sich zu einem ~ ausweiten** *(fig)* to spread to epidemic proportions; **flä|chen|de|ckend** ADJ extensive; **die ~e Versorgung der Bevölkerung mit Gas** a comprehensive *or* extensive gas supply for the population ADV extensively, over a wide area; **wir müssen ~ arbeiten** we need blanket coverage; **Flä|chen|er|trag** M yield per acre/hectare *etc*; **flä|chen|gleich** ADJ *(Math)* equal in area; **flä|chen|haft** ADJ two-dimensional; *(= ausgedehnt)* extensive; **Flä|chen|in|halt** M area; **Flä|chen|land** NT state *(as opposed to city state)*; **Flä|chen|maß** NT unit of square measure; **Flä|chen|nut|zung** F land utilization; **Flä|chen|nut|zungs|plan** M zoning plan, land development plan; **Flä|chen|staat** M state *(as opposed to city state)*; **flä|chen|treu** ADJ *Projektion* equal-area

Flach-: **flach+fal|len** VI *sep irreg aux sein (inf)* not to come off; *(Regelung)* to end; **Flach|fei|le** F flat file; **Flach|glas** NT sheet glass; **Flach|hang** M gentle slope

Flach|heit F **-, -en a** *(= Plattheit)* flatness; *(von Gebäude)* lowness; *(von Abhang)* gentleness **b** *(= mangelnder Tiefgang)* flatness; *(von Geschmack)* insipidity, insipidness; *(= Oberflächlichkeit)* shallowness

flä|chig ['flɛçɪç] ADJ *Gesicht* flat; *Aufforstungen* extensive; *(Art)* two-dimensional

Flä|chig|keit F **-**, *no pl (Art)* two-dimensionality

Flach-: **Flach|kopf** M *(inf)* dunderhead *(inf)*, numskull *(inf)*; **Flach|kopf|schrau|be** F countersunk *(Brit) or* flat-head *(US)* screw; **Flach|küs|te** F flat coast; **Flach|land** NT lowland; *(= Tiefland)* plains *pl*; **Flach|län|der** [-lɛndɐ] M **-s, -**, **Flach|län|de|rin** [-ərɪn] F **-, -nen** lowlander; **Flach|land|ti|ro|ler(in)** M(F) *(inf)* would-be mountain dweller; **flach+le|gen** *sep* VT **a** *(inf: = nicht stellen)* to lay out **b** *(sl) Frau* to lay *(sl)* VR *(inf)* to lie down; **flach+lie|gen** VI *sep irreg (inf)* to be laid up *(inf)*; **Flach|mann** M *pl* **-männer** *(inf)* hip flask; **Flach|mei|ßel** M flat chisel; **Flach|moor** NT fen; **Flach|pass** M *(Ftbl)* low pass; **Flach|re|li|ef** NT bas-relief; **Flach|ren|nen** NT flat (race)

Flachs [flaks] M **-es**, *no pl* **a** *(Bot, Tex)* flax **b** *(inf: = Neckerei, Witzelei)* kidding *(inf)*; *(= Bemerkung)* joke; **~ machen** to kid around *(inf)*; **das war nur ~** I/he *etc* was only kidding *(inf)*; **jetzt mal ganz ohne ~** joking *or* kidding *(inf)* apart

flachs|blond ADJ flaxen

Flach|schuss M *(Ftbl)* low shot

Flach|se ['flaksə] F **-, -n** *(Aus)* tendon

flach|sen ['flaksn] VI *(inf)* to kid around *(inf)*; **mit jdm ~** to kid sb (on) *(inf)*

Flach|se|rei [flaksə'rai] F **-, -en** *(inf)* = **Flachs b**

flachs|far|ben ['flaksfarbn] ADJ flaxen

Flachs|haar NT flaxen hair

Flach|sinn M, *no pl* shallowness

Flachs|kopf ['flaks-] M *(= Kind)* flaxen-haired child; *(= Jugendlicher)* flaxen-haired youth

Flach-: **Flach|was|ser** NT, *no pl* shallow water, shallows *pl*; **Flach|zan|ge** F flat-nosed pliers *pl*

fla|ckern ['flakɐn] VI *(lit, fig)* to flicker

Fla|cker|schein M flicker, flickering light

Fla|den ['flaːdn] M **-s, - a** *(Cook)* round flat dough-cake **b** *(inf: = Kuhfladen)* cowpat *(Brit)*, cow dung

Fla|den|brot NT unleavened bread; **ein ~** an unleavened loaf

fla|dern ['flaːdɐn] VTI *(Aus inf)* to steal, to nick *(Brit inf)*

Fläd|li|sup|pe ['flɛːtli-] F *(Sw)* pancake soup

Fla|gel|lant [flagɛ'lant] M **-en, -en**, **Fla|gel|lan|tin** [-'lantɪn] F **-, -nen** flagellant

Fla|gel|lan|ten|tum [flagɛ'lantntuːm] NT **-s**, *no pl (Rel)* self-flagellation, flagellantism

Fla|gel|lan|tis|mus [flagɛlan'tɪsmʊs] M **-**, *no pl (Psych)* flagellantism

Fla|gel|lat [flagɛ'laːt] M **-en, -en** *(Biol)* flagellate

Fla|gel|la|ti|on [flagɛla'tsioːn] F **-, -en** *(Psych)* flagellation

Fla|geo|lett [flaʒo'lɛt] NT **-s, -s** *or* **-e** *(Mus)* **a** *(Ton)* harmonic **b** *(Instrument)* flageolet

Flag|ge ['flagə] F **-, -n** flag; **die belgische ~ führen** to fly the Belgian flag *or* colours *(Brit) or* colors *(US)*; **unter deutscher ~ fahren** to sail under a German flag; **die ~ streichen** *(lit)* to strike the flag; *(fig)* to capitulate, to show the white flag; **~ zeigen** to nail one's colours *(Brit) or* colors *(US)* to the mast

flag|gen ['flagn] VI to fly flags/a flag; **geflaggt haben** to fly flags/a flag → **halbmast**

Flag|gen-: **Flag|gen|al|pha|bet** NT semaphore *no art*; **Flag|gen|gruß** M dipping of the flag; **Flag|gen|lei|ne** F (flag) halyard; **Flag|gen|mast** M flagpole, flagstaff; **Flag|gen|pa|ra|de** F morning/evening colours *(Brit) or* colors *(US) sing*; **Flag|gen|sig|nal** NT flag signal; **Flag|gen|tuch** NT, *no pl* bunting

Flagg-: **Flagg|lei|ne** F (flag) halyard; **Flagg|of|fi|zier(in)** M(F) flag officer; **Flagg|schiff** NT *(lit, fig)* flagship

flag|rant [fla'grant] ADJ flagrant → **in flagranti**

Flair [flɛːɐ] NT OR (RARE) M **-s**, *no pl (geh)* atmosphere; *(= Nimbus)* aura; *(esp Sw: = Gespür)* flair

Flak [flak] F **-, -(s)** *abbr von* **Flug(zeug)abwehrkanone a** anti-aircraft *or* ack-ack gun **b** *(= Einheit)* anti-aircraft *or* ack-ack unit

Flak-: **Flak|bat|te|rie** F anti-aircraft *or* ack-ack battery; **Flak|hel|fer(in)** M(F) *(Hist)* anti-aircraft auxiliary

Fla|kon [fla'kõː] NT OR M **-s, -s** bottle, flacon

Flak|stel|lung F anti-aircraft *or* ack-ack artillery position

Flam|beau [flã'boː] M **-s, -s** *(geh)* chandelier

flam|bie|ren [flam'biːrən] *ptp* **flambiert** VT *(Cook)* to flambé

flam|biert [flam'biːɐt] *(Cook)* PTP *von* **flambieren** ADJ flambé *(nachgestellt)*; *(bei Plural)* flambés *(nachgestellt)*; **~es Steak** steak flambé

flam|bo|yant [flãboa'jãː] ADJ *(geh, Archit)* flamboyant

Flam|bo|yant|stil [flãboa'jãː-] M flamboyant style

Fla|me ['flaːmə] M **-n, -n** Fleming, Flemish man/boy

Fla|men|co [fla'mɛŋko] M **-(s), -s** flamenco

Fla|min ['flaːmɪn] F **-, -nen**, **Flä|min** ['flɛːmɪn] F **-, -nen** Fleming, Flemish woman/girl

Fla|min|go [fla'mɪŋgo] M **-s, -s** flamingo

flä|misch ['flɛːmɪʃ] ADJ Flemish

Flä|misch(e) ['flɛːmɪʃ] NT Flemish → *auch* **Deutsch(e)**

Flämm|chen ['flɛmçən] NT **-s, -** *dim von* **Flamme**

Flam|me ['flamə] F **-, -n a** *(lit, fig)* flame; **mit ruhiger/flackernder ~ brennen** to burn with a steady/flickering flame; **in ~n aufgehen** to go up in flames; **in (hellen) ~n stehen** to be ablaze, to be in flames; **etw den ~n übergeben** *(liter)* to consign sth to the flames; **etw auf kleiner ~ kochen** *(lit)* to cook sth on a low flame; *(fig)* to let sth just tick over *(Brit)*, to let sth ride; **etw auf großer ~ kochen** to cook sth fast **b** *(= Brennstelle)* flame, burner **c** *(dated inf: = Geliebte)* flame *(inf)*

flam|men ['flamən] VI *(old, fig)* to blaze → *auch* **flammend, geflammt**

flam|mend ADJ fiery; *Zorn* burning; **mit ~em Gesicht** blazing; **~ rot** *(geh)* flame *(Brit) or* flaming red, blazing red

Flam|men-: **Flam|men|meer** NT sea of flames; **Flam|men|tod** M death by burning; **den ~ erleiden** to be burned to death; **jdn zum ~ verurteilen** to sentence sb to be burned to death;

Flam|men|wer|fer M flame-thrower; **Flam|men|zei|chen** NT *(geh)* beacon

Flan|dern ['flandṇ] NT **-s** Flanders *sing*

fland|risch ['flandrɪʃ] ADJ Flemish

Fla|nell [fla'nɛl] M **-s, -e** flannel

fla|nel|len [fla'nɛlən] ADJ *attr* flannel

Fla|nell|hemd NT flannel shirt

Fla|neur [fla'nøːɐ] M **-s, -e, Fla|neu|rin** [-'nøːrɪn] F **-, -nen** *(geh)* stroller

fla|nie|ren [fla'niːrən] *ptp* **flaniert** VI to stroll, to saunter

Flan|ke ['flaŋkə] F **-, -n** **a** *(Anat, Mil, Chess)* flank; *(von Bus, Lastzug etc)* side; **dem Feind in die ~n fallen** to attack the enemy on the flank **b** *(Sport) (Turnen)* flank-vault; *(Ftbl)* cross; *(= Spielfeldseite)* wing

flan|ken ['flaŋkn] VI *(Turnen)* to flank-vault; *(Ftbl)* to centre *(Brit)*, to center *(US)*

Flan|ken-: **Flan|ken|an|griff** M *(Mil, Chess)* flank attack; **Flan|ken|ball** M *(Ftbl)* cross, centre *(Brit)*, center *(US)*; **Flan|ken|de|ckung** F *(Mil)* flank defence *(Brit) or* defense *(US)*; **Flan|ken|schutz** M *(Mil)* protection on the flank; **jdm ~ geben** *(fig)* to give sb added support; **Flan|ken|si|che|rung** F *(Mil)* flank defence *(Brit) or* defense *(US)*

flan|kie|ren [flaŋ'kiːrən] *ptp* **flankiert** VT *(Mil, Chess, fig)* to flank; *(fig: = ergänzen)* to accompany; **~de Maßnahmen** supporting measures

Flansch [flanʃ] M **-(e)s, -e** flange

Flap|pe ['flapə] F **-, -n** *(dial)* pout; **eine ~ ziehen** to look petulant, to pout

flap|pen ['flapn] VI *(N Ger)* to flap

Flaps [flaps] M **-es, -e** *(dial inf: = Flegel)* lout, yob *(Brit inf)*; *(= Kind)* brat *(inf)*

flap|sig ['flapsɪç] ADJ *(inf) Benehmen* cheeky *(Brit)*, fresh *(US)*; *Bemerkung* offhand

Fläsch|chen ['flɛʃçən] NT **-s, -** bottle

Fla|sche ['flaʃə] F **-, -n** **a** bottle; **einem Baby die ~ geben** to give a baby its bottle; **mit der ~ aufziehen** to bottle-feed; **das Kind bekommt die ~** *(momentan)* the child is having its bottle; *(generell)* the child is bottle-fed; **eine ~ Wein/Bier** *etc* a bottle of wine/beer *etc*; **aus der ~ trinken** to drink (straight) from *or* out of the bottle; **zur ~ greifen** *(fig)* to take to the bottle **b** *(inf: = Versager)* dead loss *(Brit inf)*, complete loser *(inf)*; **du ~!** you're a dead loss *(Brit inf) or* complete loser *(inf)*!

Fla|schen-: **Fla|schen|bat|te|rie** F array of bottles; **Fla|schen|bier** NT bottled beer; **Fla|schen|bürs|te** F bottlebrush; **Fla|schen|eti|kett** NT label on a/the bottle; **Fla|schen|gä|rung** F fermentation in the bottle; **Fla|schen|geist** M genie; **Fla|schen|ge|stell** NT wine rack; **fla|schen|grün** ADJ bottle-green; **Fla|schen|hals** M neck of a bottle; *(fig)* bottleneck; **Fla|schen|kind** NT bottle-fed baby; **er ist ein ~** *(hum)* he's a straight-from-the-bottle man *(inf)*, he always drinks straight from the bottle; **Fla|schen|kür|bis** M calabash, bottle gourd; **Fla|schen|milch** F bottled milk; **Fla|schen|nah|rung** F baby milk; **Fla|schen|öff|ner** M bottle opener; **Fla|schen|pfand** NT deposit on a/the bottle; **Fla|schen|post** F message in a/the bottle; **mit der ~** in a bottle; **Fla|schen|re|gal** NT wine rack; **fla|schen|reif** ADJ *Wein* ready for bottling; **Fla|schen|ver|schluss** M bottle top; **Fla|schen|wein** M bottled wine; **fla|schen|wei|se** ADV by the bottle; **Fla|schen|zug** M block and tackle

Flasch|ner ['flaʃnɐ] M **-s, -, Flasch|ne|rin** [-ərɪn] F **-, -nen** *(S Ger)* plumber

Flash [flɛʃ] M **-s, -s** *(Film)* flash, intercut scene *(form)*; *(= Rückblende)* flashback; *(inf)* flash *(inf)*

Flash|lauf|werk ['flɛʃlaufvɛrk] NT *(Comput)* flash drive

Flat|rate F **-, -s** *(Internet, Telec)* flat-rate internet access

Flat|ter-: **Flat|ter|geist** M butterfly; **flat|ter|haft** ADJ butterfly *attr*, fickle; **sie ist ziemlich ~** she's a bit of a butterfly; **Flat|ter|haf|tig|keit** ['flatɐhaftɪçkait] F **-**, *no pl* fickleness

flat|te|rig ['flatərɪç] ADJ fluttery; *Puls* fluttering

Flat|ter|mann M *pl* **-männer** *(inf)* **a** **einen ~ haben** *(= Zittern der Hände)* to have the shakes; *(= Lampenfieber)* to have stage fright **b** *(hum: = Hähnchen)* chicken

flat|tern ['flatɐn] VI *bei Richtungsangabe aux sein (lit, fig)* to flutter; *(= mit den Flügeln schlagen)* to flap its wings; *(Fahne, Segel beim Sturm, Hose)* to flap; *(Haar)* to stream, to fly; *(Blick)* to flicker; *(inf: Mensch)* to be in a flap *(inf)*; *(Lenkung, Auto-rad)* to wobble; **ein Brief flatterte mir auf den Schreibtisch** a letter turned up *or* arrived on my desk

Flat|ter|satz M *(Typ)* unjustified print, ragged right/left

Fla|tu|lenz [flatu'lɛnts] F **-, -en** *(Med)* flatulence

flau [flau] ADJ **a** *Brise, Wind* slack **b** *Geschmack* insipid; *Stimmung* flat; *(Phot inf) Negativ* flat; *Farbe* weak **c** *(= übel)* queasy; *(vor Hunger)* faint; **mir ist ~ (im Magen)** I feel queasy **d** *(Comm) Markt, Börse, Konjunktur* slack; **in meiner Kasse sieht es ~ aus** *(inf)* my finances aren't too healthy *(inf)*

Flau|heit F **-**, *no pl* **a** *(von Farbe)* weakness; *(von Stimmung)* flatness; *(Phot inf: von Negativ)* flatness **b** *(= Übelkeit)* queasiness; *(vor Hunger)* faintness **c** *(Comm: von Markt, Börse, Konjunktur)* slackness

Flaum [flaum] M **-(e)s**, *no pl* **a** *(= Flaumfedern, Härchen, auf Obst)* down **b** *(dial: = Schweinebauchfett)* lard

Flaum-: **Flaum|bart** M downy beard, bum-fluff *no indef art (Brit inf)*, peach fuzz *(US inf)*; **Flaum|fe|der** F down feather, plumule *(spec)*

flau|mig ['flaumɪç] ADJ downy; *Pullover, Schneedecke* fleecy; *(Aus: = flockig)* light and creamy

flaum|weich ADJ *Haut* (as) soft as thistledown; *(fig inf) Mensch* soft; *Haltung* milk-and-water *attr*, lukewarm

Flausch [flauʃ] M **-(e)s, -e** fleece

flau|schig ['flauʃɪç] ADJ fleecy; *(= weich)* soft

Flau|sen ['flauzn] PL *(inf) (= Unsinn)* nonsense; *(= Illusionen)* fancy ideas *pl (inf)*; **macht keine ~!** don't try anything! *(inf)*

Flau|te ['flautə] F **-, -n** **a** *(Met)* calm; **das Schiff geriet in eine ~** the ship was becalmed **b** *(fig) (Comm)* lull, slack period; *(der Stimmung)* fit of the doldrums *(inf)*; *(der Leistung)* period of slackness

Fla|xe ['flaksə] F **-, -n** *(Aus)* tendon

Fläz [flɛːts] M **-es, -e** *(dial inf)* lout, roughneck

flä|zen ['flɛːtsn] VR *(inf)* to sprawl *(in +acc* in)

Flech|se ['flɛksə] F **-, -n** tendon

flech|sig ['flɛksɪç] ADJ *Fleisch* stringy *(inf)*, sinewy

Flecht|ar|beit F wickerwork, basketwork; *(aus Rohr)* canework

Flech|te ['flɛçtə] F **-, -n** **a** *(Bot, Med)* lichen **b** *(geh: = Zopf)* plait, braid

flech|ten ['flɛçtn] *pret* **flocht** [flɔxt], *ptp* **geflochten** [gə'flɔxtn] VT *Haar* to plait, to braid; *Kranz, Korb, Matte* to weave, to make; *Seil* to make; *Stuhl* to cane; **sich/jdm das Haar zu Zöpfen** *or* **in Zöpfe ~** to plait *or* braid one's/sb's hair; **Zitate in eine Rede ~** to punctuate a speech with quotations

Flecht|werk NT **a** *(Art)* interlace **b** = **Geflecht**

Fleck [flɛk] M **-(e)s, -e** *or* **-en** **a** *(= Schmutzfleck)* stain; **dieses Zeug macht ~en** this stuff stains *(in/auf etw (acc)* sth); **einen ~ auf der (weißen) Weste haben** *(fig)* to have blotted one's copybook; **einen ~ auf der Ehre haben** to have a stain on one's honour *(Brit) or* honor *(US)*

b *(= Farbfleck)* splodge *(Brit)*, splotch, blob; *(auf Arm etc)* blotch; *(auf Obst)* blemish; **ein grüner/gelber** *etc* **~** a patch of green/yellow *etc*, a green/yellow *etc* patch; **weißer ~** white patch; *(auf Stirn von Pferd)* star, blaze; *(auf Landkarte)* blank area → **blau a**

c *(= Stelle)* spot, place; **auf demselben ~** in the same place; **sich nicht vom ~ rühren** not to move *or* budge *(inf)*; **nicht vom ~ kommen** not to get any further; **er hat das Herz auf dem rechten ~** *(fig)* his heart is in the right place; **am falschen ~** *(fig)* in the wrong way; *sparen* in the wrong places; **vom ~ weg** on the spot, right away

d *(dial: = Flicken)* patch

e *(Cook dial: = Kaldaune)* entrails *pl*

Fleck|chen ['flɛkçən] NT **-s, -** **a** *dim von* **Fleck** **b** **ein schönes ~ (Erde)** a lovely little spot

fle|cken ['flɛkn] VI *(dial)* to stain → *auch* **gefleckt**

Fle|cken ['flɛkn] M **-s, -** **a** *(old: = Marktflecken)* small town **b** = **Fleck a, b**

Fle|cken-: **Fle|cken|ent|fer|ner** [-lɛntfɛrnɐ] M **-s, -** stain remover; **fle|cken|los** ADJ *(lit, fig)* spotless

Fleck|ent|fer|ner [-lɛntfɛrnɐ] M **-s, -**, **Fleck|ent|fer|nungs|mit|tel** NT stain remover

Fle|cken|was|ser NT *pl* **-wässer** stain remover

Fle|ckerl|tep|pich ['flɛkɐl-] M *(S Ger, Aus)* rag rug

Fleck|fie|ber NT typhus fever

fle|ckig ['flɛkɪç] ADJ marked; *(mit Flüssigkeit auch)* stained; *Obst* blemished; *Tierfell* speckled; *Gesichtshaut* blotchy

Fleck-: **Fleck|ty|phus** M typhus fever; **Fleck|vieh** NT spotted cattle

Fled|de|rer ['flɛdərɐ] M **-s, -, Fled|de|rin** [-ərɪn] F **-, -nen** person who robs dead people; *(fig)* vulture

fled|dern ['flɛdɐn] VT *Leichen* to rob; *(inf: = durchwühlen)* to rummage *or* ferret *(inf)* through

Fle|der-: **Fle|der|maus** F bat; **Fle|der|maus|är|mel** M *(Fashion)* **Mantel mit ~** batwing coat; **Fle|der|wisch** M feather duster

Fleece|shirt NT **-(s), -s** fleece shirt

Fleet [fleːt] NT **-(e)s, -e** *(N Ger)* canal

Fle|gel ['fleːgl] M **-s, -** **a** *(= Lümmel)* lout; *(= Kind)* brat *(inf)* **b** *(= Dreschflegel)* flail

Fle|gel|al|ter NT awkward adolescent phase

Fle|ge|lei [fleːgə'lai] F **-, -en** uncouthness; *(= Benehmen)* uncouth behaviour *(Brit) or* behavior *(US) no pl*; *(= Bemerkung)* uncouth remark; **so eine ~!** how rude *or* uncouth!

Fle|gel-: **fle|gel|haft** ADJ uncouth ADV *sich benehmen* uncouthly; **Fle|gel|haf|tig|keit** ['fleːglhaftɪçkait] F **-, -en** uncouthness; **Fle|gel|jah|re** PL awkward adolescent phase

fle|geln ['fleːgln] VR to loll, to sprawl; **sich in die Bank/den Sessel ~** to loll *or* sprawl all over the bench/in the armchair

fle|hen ['fleːən] VI *(geh)* to plead *(um +acc* for, *zu* with); **..., flehte er zu Gott** ..., he beseeched *or* besought God *(liter, old)*

fle|hent|lich ['fleːəntlɪç] ADJ imploring, pleading, beseeching *(liter, old)*; **eine ~e Bitte** an earnest entreaty *or* plea ADV imploringly, pleadingly, beseechingly *(liter, old)*; **jdn ~ bitten** to plead with sb; **jdn ~ bitten, etw zu tun** to entreat *or* implore sb to do sth

Fleisch [flaiʃ] NT **-(e)s**, *no pl* **a** *(= Gewebe, Muskelfleisch)* flesh; **nacktes ~** *(lit, fig hum)* bare flesh; **vom ~ fallen** to lose (a lot of) weight; **sich** *(dat or acc)* **ins eigene ~ schneiden** to cut off one's nose to spite one's face; **den Weg allen ~es gehen** *(liter)* to go the way of all flesh; **Menschen von ~ und Blut** flesh and blood; **sein eigen ~ und Blut** *(geh)* his own flesh and blood; **jdm in ~ und Blut übergehen** to become second nature to sb; **und das Wort ward ~** *(Bibl)* and the Word was made flesh; **~ geworden** = **fleischgeworden**

b *(= Nahrungsmittel)* meat; *(= Fruchtfleisch)* flesh; **~ fressend** = **fleischfressend**; **~ verarbeitend** meat-processing

Fleisch- *in cpds (Cook)* meat; *(Anat)* flesh; **Fleisch|ab|fäl|le** PL (meat) scraps *pl*; **fleisch|arm** ADJ containing little meat; **~ sein** to contain little meat; **Fleisch|berg** M *(pej inf)* mountain of flesh; **Fleisch|be|schau** F **a** meat inspection **b** *(hum inf)* cattle market *(inf)*; **Fleisch|be|schau|er(in)** M(F) meat inspector; **Fleisch|bro|cken** M lump of meat;

Fleischbrühe F *(= Gericht)* bouillon; *(= Fond)* meat stock; **Fleischbrühwürfel** M (meat) stock cube; **Fleischeinlage** F meat; **Fleischeinwaage** F meat content, weight of meat

Fleischer ['flaiʃɐ] M **-s, -**, **Fleischerin** [-ərɪn] F **-, -nen** butcher; *(pej inf: = Chirurg)* sawbones *sing (inf)*

Fleischerbeil NT meat cleaver

Fleischerei [flaiʃə'rai] F **-, -en** butcher's (shop) *(Brit)*, butcher (shop) *(US)*

Fleischer-: **Fleischerhaken** M meat hook; **Fleischerhandwerk** NT butcher's trade, butchery; **Fleischerhund** M *(lit)* butcher's dog; *(fig)* brute of a dog; **ein Gemüt wie ein ~ haben** *(inf)* to be a callous brute

Fleischerin [-ərɪn] F → **Fleischer**

Fleischer-: **Fleischerinnung** F butchers' guild; **Fleischerladen** M butcher's (shop); **Fleischermesser** NT butcher's knife

Fleischerne(s) NT *decl as adj (S Ger)* meat

Fleischeslust F *(old liter)* carnal lust, lusts *pl* of the flesh

Fleisch-: **Fleischesser(in)** M(F) meat-eater; **Fleischextrakt** M beef extract; **Fleischfarbe** F flesh colour *(Brit)* or color *(US)*; **fleischfarben** [-farbn], **fleischfarbig** ADJ flesh-coloured *(Brit)*, flesh-colored *(US)*; **Fleischfliege** F flesh-fly; **fleischfressend** ADJ **~e Pflanzen** carnivorous plants, carnivores; **~e Tiere** carnivores, carnivorous animals; **Fleischfresser(in)** M(F) *(Zool)* carnivore; **Fleischgenuss** M consumption of meat; **fleischgeworden** ADJ *attr (liter)* incarnate; **der ~e Sohn Gottes** the Son of God incarnate; **Fleischhauer(in)** M(F) *(Aus)* butcher; **Fleischhauerei** F *(Aus)* butcher's (shop) *(Brit)*, butcher (shop) *(US)*

fleischig ['flaiʃɪç] ADJ fleshy

Fleisch-: **Fleischkäse** M meat loaf; **Fleischklopfer** M steak hammer; **Fleischkloß** M, **Fleischklößchen** NT **a** meatball **b** *(pej inf)* mountain of flesh; **Fleischkonserve** F can *or* tin *(Brit)* of meat; *(in Glas)* pot *or* jar of meat; **Fleischkonserven** PL *(als Gattung)* canned *or* tinned *(Brit)* meat *sing*; *(in Glas)* potted *(Brit)* or jarred *(US)* meat *sing*; **Fleischlaiberl** [-laibɐl] NT **-s, -n** *(Aus: = Frikadelle)* meatball

fleischlich ['flaiʃlɪç] ADJ *attr Speisen, Kost* meat; *(liter) Lüste, Genüsse, Begierden* carnal, of the flesh

Fleisch-: **fleischlos** ADJ **a** *(= ohne Fleisch)* meatless; *Kost, Ernährung* vegetarian **b** *(= mager)* thin, lean ADV **~ essen** to eat no meat; **~ kochen** to cook without meat; **Fleischmaschine** F *(Aus, S Ger)* mincer, meat grinder *(esp US)*; **Fleischpastete** F meat vol-au-vent; **Fleischpflanzerl** [-pflantsɐl] NT **-s, -n** *(S Ger: = Frikadelle)* meatball; **Fleischreste** PL left-over meat *sing*; **Fleischsaft** M meat juices *pl*; **Fleischsalat** M diced meat salad with mayonnaise; **Fleischspieß** M *(Cook)* meat skewer; **Fleischstück(chen)** NT piece of meat; **Fleischsuppe** F meat soup; **Fleischtomate** F beef tomato; **Fleischton** M *(Art)* flesh colour *(Brit) or* color *(US)*; **Fleischtopf** M **a** *(Cook)* meat pan **b Fleischtöpfe** *(Bibl)* fleshpots *pl*; *(fig)* good life; **fleischverarbeitend** ADJ *attr* → **Fleisch b**; **Fleischvergiftung** F food poisoning *(from meat)*; **Fleischwaren** PL meat products *pl*; **Fleischwerdung** F **-**, *no pl (Rel, liter)* incarnation; **Fleischwolf** M mincer, meat grinder *(esp US)*; **Rekruten/Prüflinge durch den ~ drehen** *(inf)* to put new recruits/exam candidates through the mill; **Fleischwunde** F flesh wound; **Fleischwurst** F pork sausage

Fleiß [flais] M **-(e)s**, *no pl* diligence; *(= eifriges Tätigsein)* industry; *(= Beharrlichkeit)* application; *(als Charaktereigenschaft)* industriousness; **~ aufwenden** to apply oneself; **ihm fehlt der ~** he lacks application; **mit ~ kann es jeder zu etwas bringen** anybody can succeed if they work hard; **er hat die Prüfung ausschließlich durch ~ geschafft** he passed the exam by sheer hard work *or* simply by working hard; **mit ~ bei der Sache sein** to work hard; **mit ~** *(S Ger)*, **zu ~** *(N Ger) (= absichtlich)* deliberately, on purpose; **ohne ~ kein Preis** *(Prov)* no pain, no gain

Fleiß-: **Fleißarbeit** F industrious piece of work; *(nichts als Fleiß erfordernd)* laborious task; **eine (reine) ~** *(pej)* an industrious but uninspired piece of work; **Fleißaufgabe** F *(Sch)* voluntary extra task

fleißig ['flaisɪç] ADJ **a** *(= arbeitsam)* hard-working *no adv*, industrious, diligent; **~ wie die Bienen sein** to work like beavers; **~e Hände** busy hands; **Fleißiges Lieschen** *(Bot)* busy Lizzie **b** *(= Fleiß zeigend)* diligent, painstaking **c** *(inf: = unverdrossen) Theaterbesucher, Sammler etc* keen *(esp Brit)*, enthusiastic ADV **a** *(= arbeitsam)* industriously, diligently; **~ studieren/arbeiten** to study/work hard **b** *(inf: = unverdrossen) trinken* quite a bit; *trainieren, Diät halten* like a good boy/girl; **~ zulangen** to get stuck in *(inf)*; **wir haben immer ~ bis 12 Uhr getrunken** we were drinking away till 12 o'clock

flektierbar ADJ (in)flectional *(form)*; *Verb* conjugable; *Substantiv, Adjektiv* declinable

flektieren [flɛk'tiːrən] *ptp* **flektiert** VT to inflect *(form)*; *Substantiv, Adjektiv* to decline; *Verb* to conjugate VI to inflect; to be declined; to be conjugated; **„schwimmen" flektiert stark** "schwimmen" is (conjugated as) a strong verb

flennen ['flɛnən] VI *(pej inf)* to blub(ber) *(inf)*

Flennerei [flɛnə'rai] F **-, -en** *(pej inf)* blub(ber)ing *(inf)*

fletschen ['flɛtʃn] VT **die Zähne ~** to bare *or* show one's teeth

fleucht [flɔyçt] *(obs, poet) 3. pers sing pres von* **fliegen** → **kreucht**

Fleurop® ['flɔyrɔp, 'fløːrɔp, flɔy'roːp, flø'roːp] F **-** ≈ Interflora®

Flexi-Bar® ['flɛksibaːɐ] M OR N **-s, -s** *(Sport)* flexi-bar®

flexibel [flɛ'ksiːbl] ADJ *(lit, fig)* flexible; *Holz, Kunststoff auch* pliable ADV flexibly

Flexibilisierung [flɛksibili'ziːrʊŋ] F **-, -en ~ der Arbeitszeit** transition to flexible working hours

Flexibilität [flɛksibili'tɛːt] F **-**, *no pl (lit, fig)* flexibility; *(von Holz, Kunststoff auch)* pliability

Flexion [flɛ'ksioːn] F **-, -en** *(Gram)* inflection

Flexions-: **Flexionsendung** F inflectional ending *or* suffix; **flexionsfähig** ADJ = **flektierbar**; **flexionslos** ADJ uninflected

Flibustier [fli'bʊstiɐ] M **-s, -** *(old, fig)* buccaneer

flicht [flɪçt] *3. pers sing pres von* **flechten**

Flickarbeit ['flɪk-] F *(Sew)* mending

flicken ['flɪkn] VT to mend; *Wäsche (= stopfen auch)* to darn; *(mit Flicken)* to patch → **Zeug d**

Flicken ['flɪkn] M **-s, -** patch; **eine Jacke mit ~** a patched jacket; *(als Schmuck)* a patchwork jacket

Flickenteppich M rag rug

Flick-: **Flickflack** ['flɪkflak] M **-s, -s** *(Sport)* backflip; **Flickschneider(in)** M(F) *(dated)* mender; *(pej)* bungler *(inf)*, bungling tailor; **Flickschuster(in)** M(F) *(old)* cobbler; *(fig pej)* bungler *(inf)*, botcher *(inf)*; **Flickschusterei** F *(old)* cobbler's (shop); **das ist ~** *(fig pej)* that's a patch-up job; **Flickwäsche** F mending; **Flickwerk** NT **die Reform war reinstes ~** the reform had been carried out piecemeal; **Flickwort** NT *pl* **-wörter** filler; **Flickzeug** NT *pl* **-zeuge** *(Sew)* sewing kit; *(für Reifen)* (puncture) repair kit

Flieder ['fliːdɐ] M **-s, - a** lilac; *(dial: = Holunder)* elder **b** *(Aus inf: = Geld)* money

Flieder-: **Fliederbeere** F *(dial)* elderberry; **Fliederbusch** M lilac; **fliederfarben** [-farbn], **fliederfarbig** ADJ lilac; **Fliedertee** M elderflower tea

Fliege ['fliːgə] F **-, -n a** fly; **sie fielen um wie die ~n** they went down like ninepins *(Brit)*, they dropped like flies; **sie starben wie die ~n** they fell like flies; **er tut keiner ~ etwas zuleide** *or* **zu Leide** *(fig)* **er würde keiner ~ ein Bein ausreißen** *(fig)* he wouldn't hurt a fly; **zwei ~n mit einer Klappe schlagen** *(prov)* to kill two birds with one stone *(prov)*; **ihn stört die ~ an der Wand, er ärgert sich über die ~ an der Wand** every little thing irritates him; **die** *or* **'ne ~ machen** *(sl)* to beat it *(inf)* **b** *(= Bärtchen)* imperial **c** *(= Schlips)* bow tie

fliegen ['fliːgn] *pret* **flog** [floːk], *ptp* **geflogen** [gə'floːgn] VI *aux sein* **a** *(durch die Luft, mit Flugzeug)* to fly; *(Raumschiff, Raumfahrer)* to go, to travel *(form)*; **mit General Air ~** to fly (with *or* by) General Air; **in den Urlaub ~** to fly on holiday *(Brit)* or vacation *(US)*; **nach Köln fliegt man zwei Stunden** it takes two hours to fly to Cologne, it's a two-hour flight to Cologne; **ich kann doch nicht ~!** I haven't got wings *(inf)* **b** *(= eilen)* to fly; **jdm/einander in die Arme ~** to fly into sb's/each other's arms; **jdm an den Hals ~** to hurl oneself at sb; **ein Lächeln flog über sein Gesicht** a brief smile lit up his face; **die Zeit fliegt** time flies; **auf jdn/etw ~** *(inf)* to be mad *or* wild about sb/sth *(inf)* **c** *(inf: = fallen)* to fall; **von der Leiter ~** to fall off the ladder; **durchs Examen ~** to fail *or* flunk *(inf)* one's exam **d** *(inf: = hinausgeworfen werden)* to be chucked *or* slung *or* kicked out *(inf)* *(aus, von* of); **aus der Firma ~** to get the sack *or* the boot *(inf)*; **von der Schule ~** to be chucked out of school *(inf)* **e** *(= bewegt werden) (Fahne, Haare)* to fly; *(Puls)* to race **f** *(= geworfen werden)* to be thrown *or* flung *(inf) or* chucked *(inf)*; **geflogen kommen** to come flying; **in den Papierkorb ~** to go into the wastepaper basket, to be immediately consigned to the wastepaper basket; **die Tür flog ins Schloss** the door flew shut; **ein Schuh flog ihm an den Kopf** he had a shoe flung at him; **der Hut flog ihm vom Kopf** his hat flew off his head; **aus der Kurve ~** to skid off the bend → **Luft a**

VT *Flugzeug, Güter, Personen, Route, Einsatz etc* to fly

VR **in dieser Maschine/nachts fliegt es sich angenehm** flying in this plane/at night is pleasant; **das Flugzeug fliegt sich leicht/schwer** this plane is easy/difficult to fly, flying this plane is easy/difficult → *auch* **fliegend**

fliegend ADJ *attr Fische, Untertasse, Start* flying; *Personal* flight; *Würstchenstand, Büchertisch* mobile; **Fliegender Hund** flying fox; **in ~er Eile** *or* **Hast** in a tremendous hurry; **~er Händler** travelling *(Brit) or* traveling *(US)* hawker; *(mit Lieferwagen)* mobile trader; **~er Teppich** flying carpet; **Der Fliegende Holländer** The Flying Dutchman; **~e Hitze** hot flushes *pl (Brit) or* flashes *pl (US)*; **~e Blätter** loose leaves *or* sheets; *(Hist)* broadsheets → **Fahne**

Fliegen-: **Fliegendraht** M wire mesh; **Fliegendreck** M fly droppings *pl*; **Fliegenfänger** M *(= Klebestreifen)* flypaper; **Fliegenfenster** NT wire-mesh window; **Fliegengewicht** NT *(Sport, fig)* flyweight; **Fliegengewichtler** [-gəvɪçtlɐ] M **-s, -**, **Fliegengewichtlerin** [-ərɪn] F **-, -nen** *(Sport)* flyweight; **Fliegengitter** NT fly screen; **Fliegenklatsche** F fly swat; **Fliegenkopf** M *(Typ)* turn; **Fliegennetz** NT fly net; **Fliegenpilz** M fly agaric; **Fliegenrute** F fly rod; **Fliegenschiss** M *(inf)* **sich wegen jedem ~ an der Wand aufregen** to get one's knickers in a twist about nothing *(Brit)*, to get upset about nothing

Flieger ['fliːgɐ] M **-s, - a** *(= Pilot)* airman, aviator *(dated)*, flier *(dated)*; *(Mil: Rang)* aircraftman *(Brit)*, airman basic *(US)*; **er ist bei den ~n** *(dated)* he's in the air force **b** *(inf: = Flug-*

zeug) plane **c** *(= Vogel)* flier **d** *(Radrennen)* sprinter **e** *(Pferderennen)* flier

Flie|ger- *(Mil)*: **Flie|ger|ab|wehr** F air defence *(Brit)* or defense *(US)*; **Flie|ger|ab|zei|chen** NT wings *pl*; **Flie|ger|alarm** M air-raid warning; **Flie|ger|an|griff** M air raid; **Flie|ger|bom|be** F aerial bomb

Flie|ge|rei [fli:gəˈrai] F -, *no pl* flying

Flie|ger|horst M *(Mil)* military airfield *or* aerodrome *(Brit)*

Flie|ge|rin [ˈfli:gərın] F -, **-nen** **a** *(= Pilotin)* airwoman, aviatrix *(dated)*, flier *(dated)* **b** *(Radrennen)* s

flie|ge|risch [ˈfli:gərıʃ] ADJ *attr* aeronautical

Flie|ger-: **Flie|ger|ja|cke** F bomber jacket; **Flie|ger|kar|te** F aviation chart; **Flie|ger|of|fi|zier(in)** M(F) *(Mil, Aviat)* air force officer; **Flie|ger|schu|le** F flying school; **Flie|ger|spra|che** F pilots' jargon; **Flie|ger|staf|fel** F *(Mil)* (air force) squadron; **Flie|ger|trup|pe** F *(Mil)* air corps *sing*

Flieh|burg F refuge

flie|hen [ˈfli:ən] *pret* **floh** [flo:], *ptp* **geflohen** [gəˈflo:ən] **VI** *aux sein* to flee *(vor +dat* from); *(= entkommen)* to escape *(aus* from); **vor jdm/dem Krieg/der Polizei/einem Gewitter ~** to flee from sb/war/the police/before a storm; **aus dem Lande ~** to flee the country → **fliehend** **VT** *(liter)* *(= meiden)* to shun; *(= entkommen)* to flee from; **jds Gegenwart ~** to shun/flee sb's presence

flie|hend ADJ *Kinn* receding; *Stirn* sloping; *Schrift* sloping, slanting

Flie|hen|de(r) [ˈfli:əndə] MF *decl as adj* fugitive

Flieh-: **Flieh|kraft** F centrifugal force; **Flieh|kraft|kupp|lung** F centrifugal clutch

Flie|se [ˈfli:zə] F -, **-n** tile; **~n legen** to lay tiles; **etw mit ~n auslegen** to tile sth

flie|sen [ˈfli:zn] VT to tile

Flie|sen-: **Flie|sen|(fuß)|bo|den** M tiled floor; **Flie|sen|le|ger** [-le:gɐ] M -s, -, **Flie|sen|le|ge|rin** [-ərın] F -, **-nen** tiler

Fließ|band [-bant] NT *pl* **-bänder** conveyor belt; *(als Einrichtung)* assembly *or* production line; **am ~ arbeiten** *or* **stehen** *(inf)* to work on the assembly *or* production line

Fließband-: **Fließ|band|ar|beit** F assembly-line work; **Fließ|band|fer|ti|gung** F belt production

flie|ßen [ˈfli:sn] *pret* **floss** [flɔs], *ptp* **geflossen** [gəˈflɔsn] VI *aux sein* to flow; *(Verkehr, Luftmassen auch)* to move; *(Fluss auch, Tränen)* to run; **es ist genug Blut geflossen** enough blood has been shed *or* spilled; **der Schweiß floss ihm von der Stirn** sweat was pouring off his forehead; **die Steuergelder flossen in dunkle Kanäle** the taxes were diverted along rather dubious channels; **die Mittel für Jugendarbeit ~ immer spärlicher** less and less money is being made available for youth work; **aus der Feder ~** *(geh)* to flow from the pen; **Nachrichten ~ spärlich** the flow of news is minimal; **alles fließt** *(Philos)* all is in a state of flux → **Strom a**

flie|ßend ADJ flowing; *Leitungswasser, Gewässer* running; *Verkehr* moving; *Rede, Vortrag, Sprache* fluent; *Grenze, Übergang* fluid; **sie spricht ein ~es Französisch** she speaks fluent French, she speaks French fluently ADV *sprechen* fluently; **~ warm und kalt Wasser** running hot and cold water

Fließ-: **Fließ|heck** NT fastback; **Fließ|kom|ma** NT *(auch Comput)* floating point; **Fließ|laut** M liquid; **Fließ|punkt** M *(auch Comput)* floating point; **Fließ|satz** M *(Typ)* wordwrap; **Fließ|stra|ße** F *(Tech)* assembly *or* production line; **Fließ|text** M *(Typ)* running text; **Fließ|was|ser** NT, *no pl (esp Aus)* running water

Flim|mer [ˈflımɐ] M -s, - **a** *(Anat)* cilium **b** *no pl (liter. = zitternder Glanz)* shimmer

Flim|mer-: **flim|mer|frei** ADJ *(Opt, Phot)* flicker-free; **Flim|mer|här|chen** NT cilium; **Flim|mer|kas|ten** M, **Flim|mer|kis|te** F *(inf)* TV *(inf)*, (goggle)box *(Brit inf)*, telly *(Brit inf)*, (boob) tube *(US inf)*

flim|mern [ˈflımɐn] VI to shimmer; *(Film, TV)* to flicker; **es flimmert mir vor den Augen** everything is swimming *or* dancing before my eyes; **über den Bildschirm ~** *(inf)* to be on the box *(Brit inf)* or on the tube *(US inf)* or on TV *(inf)* VT *(dial: = blank putzen)* to polish, to shine *(inf)*

Flim|mern [ˈflımɐn] NT **-s**, *no pl (von Luft, Wasser)* shimmering; *(von Bildschirm etc)* flickering; *(von Sternen)* twinkling; *(Med: = Herzflimmern)* fibrillation; **ein ~ vor den Augen** flickering in front of one's eyes

flink [flıŋk] ADJ *(= geschickt)* nimble; *Bewegung, Finger auch* deft; *(= schnell)* quick; *Mundwerk, Zunge* quick, ready; *Augen* sharp ADV *arbeiten, sich bewegen* quickly; *springen* nimbly; **ein bisschen ~!** *(inf)* get a move on!, make it snappy! *(inf)*; **mit etw ~ bei der Hand sein** to be quick (off the mark) with sth

Flink|heit F -, *no pl (= Geschicktheit)* nimbleness; *(von Bewegung, Finger auch)* deftness; *(= Schnelligkeit)* quickness

Flint [flınt] M **-(e)s, -e** *(old)* flint

Flin|te [ˈflıntə] F -, **-n** *(= Schrotflinte)* shotgun; **jdn/etw vor die ~ bekommen** *(fig)* to get hold of sb/sth; **wenn der mir vor die ~ kommt ...** *(fig)* just wait till I get hold of him ...; **die ~ ins Korn werfen** *(fig)* to throw in the sponge *(Brit)* or towel

Flin|ten-: **Flin|ten|lauf** M (shot)gun barrel; **Flin|ten|weib** NT *(pej)* gunwoman

Flint|glas NT flint glass

Flip [flıp] M -s, -s *(Eiskunstlauf)* flip

Flip|chart [ˈflıptʃa:ɐt] F -, -s flip chart

Flip|flop|schal|tung [ˈflıpflɔp-] F flip-flop circuit

Flip|per [ˈflıpɐ] M -s, -, **Flip|per|au|to|mat** M pinball machine

flip|pern [ˈflıpɐn] VT to flip VI to play pinball

flip|pig [ˈflıpıç] *(inf)* ADJ way-out *(inf)*; **er ist ein ~er Typ** he's way-out ADV way-out *(inf)*

flir|ren [ˈflırən] VI to whirr; *(Luft, Hitze)* to shimmer

Flirt [flırt, flø:ɐt, flœrt] M -s, -s **a** *(= Flirten)* flirtation **b** *(dated)* *(= Schwarm)* flame *(dated)*; *(= Mann auch)* beau *(dated)*

flir|ten [ˈflırtn, ˈflø:ɐtn, ˈflœrtn] VI to flirt; **mit einem Gedanken ~** *(inf)* to toy with an idea

Flit|scherl [ˈflıtʃɐl] NT -s, -(n) *(Aus pej inf)* slut

Flitt|chen [ˈflıtçən] NT -s, - *(pej inf)* slut

Flit|ter [ˈflıtɐ] M -s, - **a** *(= Flitterschmuck)* sequins *pl*, spangles *pl* **b** *no pl (pej: = Tand)* trumpery

Flit|ter|gold NT gold foil

flit|tern [ˈflıtɐn] VI *(hum)* to honeymoon

Flit|ter-: **Flit|ter|werk** NT, *no pl (pej: = Tand)* trumpery; **Flit|ter|wo|chen** PL honeymoon *sing*; **in die ~ fahren/in den ~ sein** to go/be on one's honeymoon; **Flit|ter|wöch|ner** [-vœçnɐ] M -s, -, **Flit|ter|wöch|ne|rin** [-ərın] F -, **-nen** *(hum)* honeymooner; **die ~** the honeymoon couple

Flitz|bo|gen [ˈflıts-] M, **Flit|ze|bo|gen** [ˈflıtsə-] M bow and arrow; **ich bin gespannt wie ein ~** *(inf)* the suspense is killing me *(inf)*; **gespannt wie ein ~ sein, ob ...** *(inf)* to be on tenterhooks waiting to see whether ...

Flit|ze [ˈflıtsə] F **die ~ machen** *(sl: = verschwinden)* to bolt *(sl)*

flit|zen [ˈflıtsn] VI *aux sein (inf)* **a** *(= sich schnell bewegen)* to whizz *(inf)*, to dash **b** *(= nackt rennen)* to streak; **(das) Flitzen** streaking

Flit|zer [ˈflıtsɐ] M -s, - *(inf: = Fahrzeug)* sporty little job *(Brit inf)* or number *(US inf)*

Flit|zer [ˈflıtsɐ] M -s, -, **Flit|ze|rin** [-ərın] F -, **-nen** *(inf)* **a** *(= Schnellläufer)* streak of lightning *(inf)* **b** *(= nackter Läufer)* streaker

floa|ten [ˈflo:tn] VTI *(Fin)* to float; **~ (lassen)** to float

Floa|ting [ˈflo:tıŋ] NT -s, -s *(Fin)* floating

F-Loch [ˈɛf-] NT *(Mus)* f-hole

flocht *pret von* **flechten**

Flöck|chen [ˈflœkçən] NT -s, - *dim von* **Flocke**

Flo|cke [ˈflɔkə] F -, **-n** **a** flake; *(= Wollflocke)* piece of wool; *(= Schaumflocke)* blob (of foam); *(= Staubflocke)* ball (of fluff) **b** **Flocken** PL *(inf: = Geld)* dough *(inf)*

flo|ckig [ˈflɔkıç] ADJ *(lit)* fluffy; *(fig)* lively

flog *pret von* **fliegen**

floh *pret von* **fliehen**

Floh [flo:] M **-(e)s, ⸚e** [ˈflø:ə] *(Zool)* flea; **von Flöhen zerbissen** *or* **zerstochen** flea-bitten *attr*, bitten by fleas; **es ist leichter, einen Sack Flöhe zu hüten, als ...** I'd as soon jump in the lake as ...; **jdm einen ~ ins Ohr setzen** *(inf)* to put an idea into sb's head; **die Flöhe husten hören** *(inf)* to imagine things

Floh|biss M fleabite

flö|hen [ˈflø:ən] VT **jdn/sich ~** to get rid of sb's/one's fleas, to debug sb/oneself *(inf)*

Floh-: **Floh|hals|band** NT flea collar; **Floh|hüp|fen** NT -s, *no pl* tiddl(e)ywinks *sing*, *no art*; **Floh|ki|no** NT *(inf)* local fleapit *(inf)*; **Floh|markt** M flea market; **Floh|spiel** NT tiddl(e)ywinks *sing*, *no art*; **Floh|zir|kus** M flea circus

Flo|ka|ti [floˈka:ti] M -s, -s flokati

Flom [flo:m] M -s, *no pl*, **Flo|men** [ˈflo:mən] M -s, *no pl (Cook)* lard

Flop [flɔp] M -s, -s flop *(inf)*

Flop|py Disc [ˈflɔpi-] F -, -s, **Flop|py Disk** F - -, - -s, **Flop|py|disk** △ F - -, - -s floppy disk

Flor [flo:ɐ] M -s, -e *(liter)* array of flowers; **in ~ stehen** to be in full bloom

Flor M -s, -e *or (rare)* ⸚e [ˈflø:rə] **a** *(= dünnes Gewebe)* gauze; *(= Trauerflor)* crêpe **b** *(liter. = Schleier)* veil **c** *(= Teppichflor, Samtflor)* pile

Flo|ra [ˈflo:ra] F -, **Floren** [ˈflo:rən] flora

Flo|ren|ti|ner [florɛnˈti:nɐ] ADJ *attr* Florentine

Flo|ren|ti|ner [florɛnˈti:nɐ] M -s, - **a** *(Cook)* Florentine **b** *(auch* **Florentinerhut***)* picture hat

Flo|ren|ti|ner [florɛnˈti:nɐ] M -s, -, **Flo|ren|ti|ne|rin** [-ərın] F -, **-nen** Florentine

flo|ren|ti|nisch [florɛnˈti:nıʃ] ADJ Florentine

Flo|renz [floˈrɛnts] NT -' *or* **-ens** Florence

Flo|rett [floˈrɛt] NT **-(e)s, -e** **a** *(= Waffe)* foil; **~ fechten** to fence with a foil **b** *(auch* **Florettfechten***)* foil-fencing

Flor|flie|ge F lacewing

flo|rie|ren [floˈri:rən] *ptp* **floriert** VI to flourish, to bloom

Flo|rist [floˈrıst] M **-en, -en**, **Flo|ris|tin** [-ˈrıstın] F -, **-nen** florist

Flos|kel [ˈflɔskl] F -, **-n** set phrase; **eine höfliche/abgedroschene ~** a polite but meaningless/a hackneyed *(Brit)* or clichéd phrase

flos|kel|haft ADJ *Stil, Rede, Brief* cliché-ridden; *Phrasen, Ausdrucksweise* stereotyped

floss *pret von* **fließen**

Floß [flo:s] NT **-es, ⸚e** [ˈflø:sə] raft; *(Fishing)* float

flöß|bar ADJ navigable by raft

Floß|brü|cke F floating bridge

Flos|se [ˈflɔsə] F -, **-n** **a** *(Zool)* *(= Fischflosse)* fin; *(= Walflosse, Robbenflosse)* flipper **b** *(Aviat, Naut: = Leitwerk)* fin **c** *(= Taucherflosse)* flipper **d** *(inf: = Hand)* paw *(inf)*, mauler *(inf)*; **~n hoch!** hands up!

flö|ßen [ˈflø:sn] VTI to raft

Flö|ßer [ˈflø:sɐ] M -s, -, **Flö|ße|rin** [-ərın] F -, **-nen** raftsman/-woman *(Brit)*, rafter *(US)*

Flö|ße|rei [flø:səˈrai] F -, *no pl* rafting

Floß|fahrt F raft trip

Flö|te [ˈflø:tə] F -, **-n** **a** pipe; *(= Querflöte, Orgelflöte, in Zusammensetzungen)* flute; *(= Blockflöte)* recorder; *(= Pikkoloflöte)* piccolo; *(des Pan)* pipes *pl*; *(dial: = Pfeife, Kesselflöte)* whistle; **die ~** *or* **auf der ~ spielen** *or* **blasen** to play the pipe *etc* **b** *(= Kelchglas)* flute glass **c** *(Cards)* flush

flö|ten [ˈflø:tn] VT *(Mus)* to play on the flute; *(auf Blockflöte)* to play on the recorder VI *(Mus)* to play the flute; *(= Blockflöte spielen)* to play the recorder VTI **a** *(Vogel)* to warble; *(dial: = pfei-*

fen) to whistle **b** *(hum inf: = süß sprechen)* to flute, to warble

Flö|ten-: **flö|ten ge|hen** VI *aux sein (inf)* to go west *(esp Brit inf)*, to go for a burton *(dated Brit sl)*, to go to the dogs *(inf)*; **Flö|ten|blä|ser(in)** M(F) = **Flötenspieler(in)**; **Flö|ten|kes|sel** M whistling kettle; **Flö|ten|re|gis|ter** NT flue stop; **Flö|ten|spiel** NT pipe-/flute- *etc* playing; *(= Flötenmusik)* pipe/flute *etc* music; **Flö|ten|spie|ler(in)** M(F) piper; *(von Querflöte)* flautist; *(von Blockflöte)* recorder player; *(von Pikkoloflöte)* piccolo player; **Flö|ten|ton** M *pl* **-tö|ne** **a** *(lit)* sound of flutes/a flute **b** *(inf)* **jdm die Flötentöne beibringen** to teach sb what's what *(inf)*; **Flö|ten|werk** NT flue-work

Flö|tist [flø'tɪst] M **-en, -en**, **Flö|tis|tin** [-'tɪstɪn] F **-, -nen** = **Flötenspieler(in)**

flott [flɔt] ADJ **a** *(= zügig) Fahrt* quick; *Tempo, Geschäft* brisk; *Arbeiter, Bedienung* speedy *(inf)*, quick and efficient; *Tänzer* good; *(= flüssig) Stil, Artikel* racy *(inf)*; *(= schwungvoll) Musik* lively; **den ~en Otto** *or* **Heinrich haben** *(hum inf)* to have the runs *(inf)*
b *(= schick)* smart
c *(= lebenslustig)* fun-loving, fast-living; **~ leben, ein ~es Leben führen** to be a fast liver
d *pred* **~/wieder ~ werden** *(Schiff)* to be floated off/refloated; *(fig inf) (Auto etc)* to be/get back on the road; *(Flugzeug)* to be working/working again; *(Mensch)* to be out of the woods/back on top; *(Unternehmen)* to be/get back on its feet; **wieder ~ sein** *(Schiff)* to be afloat again; *(fig inf) (Auto etc)* to be back on the road; *(Flugzeug)* to be working again; *(Mensch) (gesundheitlich)* to be in the pink again *(inf)*; *(finanziell)* to be in funds *or* in the money again; *(Unternehmen)* to be back on its feet
ADV **a** *(= zügig)* quickly, speedily; **ich komme ~ voran mit meiner Arbeit** I'm making speedy progress with my work; **aber ein bisschen ~!** and look lively!, and make it snappy! *(inf)*
b *(= schick)* stylishly; **~ aussehen** to look stylish; **~ auftreten** to cut a dash *(Brit)*, to look stylish

Flott [flɔt] NT **-(e)s**, *no pl* **a** *(N Ger)* skin of the milk **b** *(= Entenflott)* duckweed

flott+be|kom|men *ptp* **flottbekommen** VT *sep irreg Schiff* to float off; *(fig inf) Auto etc* to get on the road; *Flugzeug* to get working; *Unternehmen* to get on its feet

Flot|te ['flɔtə] F **-, -n** **a** *(Naut, Aviat)* fleet **b** *(Tex) (= Färbebad)* dye (solution); *(= Bleichlösung)* bleach (solution); *(= Einweichlösung)* soaking solution

Flot|ten-: **Flot|ten|ab|kom|men** NT naval treaty; **Flot|ten|ba|sis** F naval base; **Flot|ten|chef(in)** M(F) commander-in-chief of the fleet; **Flot|ten|kom|man|do** NT fleet command; **Flot|ten|pa|ra|de** F naval review; **die ~ abnehmen** to review the fleet; **Flot|ten|stütz|punkt** M naval base; **Flot|ten|ver|band** M naval unit

Flot|til|le [flɔ'tɪl(j)ə] F **-, -n** *(Mil)* flotilla; *(= Fischfangflottille)* fleet

Flot|til|len|ad|mi|ral(in) M(F) *(Mil)* commodore

flott-: **flott+krie|gen** *(inf)*, **flott+ma|chen** VT *sep* = **flottbekommen**; **flott|weg** ['flɔtvɛk] ADV *(inf)* non-stop; **das geht immer ~** there's no hanging about *(inf)*

Flöz [flø:ts] NT **-es, -e** *(Min)* seam

Fluch [flu:x] M **-(e)s, ⸚e** ['fly:çə] curse; *(= Schimpfwort auch)* oath; **ein ~ liegt über** *or* **lastet auf diesem Haus** there is a curse on this house, this house lies under a curse; **~ dem Alkohol!** a curse on alcohol!; **das (eben) ist der ~ der bösen Tat** *(prov)* evil begets evil *(prov)*

fluch|be|la|den [-bəla:dn] ADJ *(liter)* accursed, cursed

flu|chen ['flu:xn] VI *(= Flüche ausstoßen, schimpfen)* to curse (and swear); **auf** *or* **über jdn/etw ~** to curse sb/sth; **jdm/etw ~** *(old)* to curse sb/sth

Flucht [flʊxt] F **-, -en** **a** *(= Fliehen)* flight *(vor +dat* from); *(geglückt)* escape, flight; **die ~ ergreifen** to take flight, to flee; *(erfolgreich auch)* to (make one's) escape; **ihm glückte die ~** he escaped, he succeeded in escaping; **auf der ~ sein** to be fleeing; *(Gesetzesbrecher)* to be on the run; **jdn/etw in die ~ treiben** *or* **jagen** *or* **schlagen** to put sb/sth to flight; **in wilder** *or* **heilloser ~ davonjagen** to stampede; **jdm zur ~ verhelfen** to help sb to escape; **auf der ~ erschossen werden** to be shot while attempting to escape; **sein Heil in der ~ suchen** *(geh)* to take refuge in flight; **die ~ nach vorn antreten** to take the bull by the horns; **die ~ in die Anonymität/die Krankheit antreten** to take refuge in anonymity/illness; **die ~ in den Trotz antreten** to resort to defiance; **die ~ in** *or* **an die Öffentlichkeit antreten** to resort to going public; **die ~ nach Ägypten** *(Bibl)* the flight into Egypt
b *(Hunt)* leap, bound; **eine ~ machen** to make a leap *or* bound
c *(= Häuserflucht)* row; *(= Fluchtlinie)* alignment
d *(= Zimmerflucht)* suite

Flucht-: **flucht|ar|tig** ADJ hasty, hurried, precipitate *(form)*; **in ~er Eile** in great haste ADV hastily, hurriedly; **Flucht|au|to** NT escape car; *(von Gesetzesbrecher)* getaway car; **Flucht|burg** F refuge

fluch|ten ['flʊxtn] *(Archit)* VT to align VI to be aligned

flüch|ten ['flʏçtn] VI **a** *aux sein (= davonlaufen)* to flee *(vor +dat* from); *(erfolgreich)* to escape, to flee; **aus dem Land/Südafrika ~** to flee the country/from South Africa; **vor der Wirklichkeit ~** to escape reality; **sich in (den) Alkohol ~** to take refuge in alcohol; **sich in Ausreden ~** to resort to excuses **b** *auch vr (vi: aux sein) (= Schutz suchen)* to take refuge

Flucht-: **Flucht|fahr|zeug** NT escape vehicle; *(von Gesetzesbrecher)* getaway vehicle; **Flucht|ge|fahr** F risk of escape, risk of an escape attempt; **Flucht|ge|schwin|dig|keit** F *(Phys)* escape velocity; **Flucht|hel|fer(in)** M(F) escape helper; **Flucht|hil|fe** F escape aid; **~ leisten** to aid an escape; **Flucht|hil|fe|or|ga|ni|sa|ti|on** F escape organization

flüch|tig ['flʏçtɪç] ADJ **a** *(= geflüchtet)* fugitive; **~ sein** to be still at large; **ein ~er Verbrecher** a criminal who hasn't been caught; **ein ~er Fahrer** *(nach Unfall)* a hit-and-run driver **b** *(= kurz, schnell vorübergehend)* fleeting, brief; *Gruß* brief **c** *(= oberflächlich)* cursory, sketchy **d** *(Chem)* volatile **e** *(Comput)* **~er Speicher** volatile memory ADV **a** *(= kurz)* fleetingly, briefly; **~ erwähnen** to mention in passing **b** *(= oberflächlich)* cursorily, superficially; **etw ~ lesen** to glance *or* skim through sth; **~ arbeiten** to work hurriedly *or* hastily; **jdn ~ kennen** to have met sb briefly

Flüch|ti|ge(r) ['flʏçtɪgə] MF *decl as adj* fugitive; *(= Ausbrecher)* escaper

Flüch|tig|keit F **-, -en** **a** *(= Kürze)* briefness, brevity **b** *(= Oberflächlichkeit)* hurried nature, sketchiness; *(= Flüchtigkeitsfehler)* careless mistake **c** *(= Vergänglichkeit)* fleeting nature, briefness **d** *(Chem)* volatility

Flüch|tig|keits|feh|ler M careless mistake; *(beim Schreiben auch)* slip of the pen

Flucht|ka|pi|tal NT *(Fin)* flight capital

Flücht|ling ['flʏçtlɪŋ] M **-s, -e** refugee

Flücht|lings- *in cpds* refugee; **Flücht|lings|aus|weis** M refugee's identity card; **Flücht|lings|camp** NT refugee camp; **Flücht|lings|hil|fe** F aid to refugees; *(inf: = Flüchtlingsorganisation)* (refugee) relief agency; **Flücht|lings|la|ger** NT refugee camp; **Flücht|lings|wel|le** F wave *or* tide of refugees

Flucht-: **Flucht|li|nie** F alignment; *(einer Straße)* building line; **Flucht|punkt** M vanishing point; **Flucht|tun|nel** M escape tunnel; **Flucht|ver|dacht** M **bei ~** if an attempt to abscond is thought likely; **es besteht ~** there are grounds for suspecting that he/she *etc* will try to abscond; **flucht|ver|däch|tig** ADJ suspected of planning to abscond; **Flucht|ver|such** M escape attempt *or* bid; **Flucht|weg** M escape route

fluch|wür|dig ADJ *(liter)* dastardly *(old) no adv*, execrable *(liter)*

Flug [flu:k] M **-(e)s, ⸚e** ['fly:gə] *(alle Bedeutungen)* flight; *(= Skiflug)* jump; **im ~(e)** in the air; *(bei Vögeln auch)* in flight, on the wing; **einen ~ antreten** to take off *(nach* for); **einen ~ stornieren** to cancel a booking; **der ~ zum Mond** *(= Fliegen)* travel to the moon; *(= spezifische Fahrt)* the moon flight *or* trip; **wie im ~(e)** *(fig)* in a twinkling *or* flash

Flug|ab|wehr F air defence *(Brit) or* defense *(US)*

Flug|ab|wehr-: **Flug|ab|wehr|ka|no|ne** F anti-aircraft gun; **Flug|ab|wehr|kör|per** M air defence *(Brit) or* defense *(US)* missile; **Flug|ab|wehr|ra|ke|te** F anti-aircraft missile

Flug-: **Flug|an|gel** F fly rod; **Flug|angst** F fear of flying; **Flug|ap|pa|rat** M flying machine; **Flug|asche** F flying ashes *pl*; **Flug|auf|kom|men** NT air traffic; **Flug|bahn** F *(von Vogel, Flugzeug)* flight path; *(von Rakete, Satelliten auch, von Kugel)* trajectory; *(= Kreisbahn)* orbit; **Flug|ball** M *(Sport)* high ball; *(Tennis etc)* volley; **Flug|ba|sis** F *(Mil)* air base; **Flug|be|glei|ter(in)** M(F) flight attendant; **Flug|be|gleit|per|so|nal** NT cabin crew; **Flug|ben|zin** NT aviation fuel; **Flug|be|reich** M operational range *no pl*; **flug|be|reit** ADJ ready for take-off; **Flug|be|reit|schaft** F readiness for take-off; **Flug|be|trieb** M air traffic; **den ~ auf einem Flughafen einstellen** to close an airport; **Flug|be|we|gun|gen** PL aircraft movements *pl*; **Flug|bild** NT *(Zool)* flight silhouette

Flug|blatt NT leaflet; *(= Werbung auch)* handbill

Flug|blatt-: **Flug|blatt|ak|ti|on** F leafleting campaign; **Flug|blatt|ver|tei|ler(in)** M(F) distributor of leaflets *or (für Werbung)* handbills

Flug-: **Flug|boot** NT flying boat; **Flug|buch** NT logbook, flight log; **Flug|da|ten|schrei|ber** M flight recorder; **Flug|dau|er** F flying time; **Flug|deck** NT flight deck; **Flug|dich|te** F density of air traffic; **Flug|dienst** M air traffic services *pl*; *(= Flugverkehr)* air service; **Flug|dra|chen** M hang-glider; **Flug|ech|se** F pterosaur; **die ~n** the Pterosauria; **Flug|ei|gen|schaft** F *usu pl* handling characteristic

Flü|gel ['fly:gl] M **-s, -** **a** *(Anat, Aviat)* wing; **mit den ~n schlagen** to beat *or* flap its wings; **einem Vogel/jdm die ~ stutzen** *or* **beschneiden** to clip a bird's/sb's wings; **die ~ hängen lassen** *(fig inf: = mutlos sein)* to be despondent *or* dejected; **die Hoffnung/der Gedanke verlieh ihm ~** *(liter)* hope/the thought lent him wings *(liter)*
b *(von Hubschrauber, Ventilator)* blade; *(= Propellerflügel auch)* vane; *(= Windmühlenflügel)* sail, vane
c *(= Altarflügel)* sidepiece, wing; *(= Fensterflügel)* casement *(form)*, side; *(= Türflügel)* door *(of double doors)*, leaf *(form)*; *(= Lungenflügel)* lung; *(= Nasenflügel)* nostril
d *(Pol, Mil, Sport)* wing; **der linke/rechte ~** the left/right wing
e *(= Gebäudeflügel)* wing
f *(= Konzertflügel)* grand piano, grand *(inf)*; **auf dem ~ spielen** to play the piano; **am ~: …** at *or* on the piano: …

Flü|gel-: **Flü|gel|ad|ju|tant** M *(Mil, Hist)* aide-de-camp *(often to a general)*; **Flü|gel|al|tar** M winged altar; **Flü|gel|är|mel** M hanging sleeve; **Flü|gel|fens|ter** NT casement window; *(= Verandafenster)* French window *(Brit)*, French door *(US)*; **flü|gel|för|mig** ADJ wing-shaped; **Flü|gel|frau** F *(Ftbl)* wing forward, winger; *(Pol)* person on the wing of a party; **Flü|gel|hau|be** F pinner, cap with upturned lappets; **Flü|gel|horn** NT *(Mus)* flugelhorn; **Flü|gel|kampf** M *(Pol)* factional dispute, party in-fighting; **Flü|gel|klap|pe** F *(Aviat)* wing flap, aileron *(spec)*; **flü|gel|lahm** ADJ with injured wings/an injured wing; *(fig) Industrie etc* ailing; *Mensch* feeble; ~ **sein** *(lit)* to have an injured wing/its wings injured; *(fig: = mutlos)* to be dejected *or* despondent; **einen Vogel ~ schießen** to wing a bird; **eine ~e Ente** *(fig)* a lame duck; **flü|gel|los** ADJ wingless; **Flü|gel|mann** M *pl* **-männer** *or* **-leute** *(Ftbl)* wing forward, winger; *(Mil)* flank man; *(Pol)* person on the wing of a party; **Flü|gel|mut|ter** F *pl* **-muttern** wing *or* butterfly nut; **Flü|gel|ross** NT *(Myth)* winged horse; **Flü|gel|schlag** M *(liter)* beat of its wings; **den ~ der Zeit spüren** *(liter)* to feel the life-pulse of history; **flü|gel|schla|gend** ADJ beating its wings; **Flü|gel|schrau|be** F **a** wing bolt **b** *(= Flügelmutter)* wing *or* butterfly nut; **Flü|gel|span|ne** F, **Flü|gel|spann|wei|te** F wing span; **Flü|gel|spie|ler** M, **Flü|gel|spie|le|rin** F *(Sport)* winger; **Flü|gel|stür|mer** M, **Flü|gel|stür|me|rin** F *(Sport)* wing forward; **Flü|gel|tür** F leaved door *(form)*; *(mit zwei Flügeln)* double door; *(= Verandatür)* French window *(Brit)*, French door *(US)*

Flug-: **Flug|en|te** F *(Cook)* muscovy duck; **Flug|ent|fer|nung** F air *or* flying distance; **Flug|er|fah|rung** F flying experience; **flug|er|probt** [-lɛeproːpt] ADJ flight-tested; **flug|fä|hig** ADJ able to fly; *Flugzeug (= in Ordnung)* airworthy; **Flug|fä|hig|keit** F ability to fly; *(von Flugzeug)* airworthiness; **Flug|feld** NT airfield; **Flug|fre|quenz** F frequency of flights; **Flug|fuchs** M (Indian) flying fox; **Flug|funk** M air radio

Flug|gast M (airline) passenger

Flug|gast-: **Flug|gast|kon|trol|le** F airport security check; **Flug|gast|raum** M passenger cabin

flüg|ge [ˈflʏgə] ADJ fully-fledged; *(fig) Jugendlicher* independent; ~ **werden** *(lit)* to be able to fly; *(fig)* to leave the nest

Flug-: **Flug|ge|län|de** NT airfield; **Flug|ge|päck** NT baggage; **erlaubtes ~ 15 Kilo** baggage allowance 15 kilos; **Flug|ge|rät** NT, *no pl* aircraft; **Flug|ge|schwin|dig|keit** F *(von Vögeln, Insekten)* speed of flight; *(von Flugzeug)* flying speed; *(von Rakete, Geschoss, Ball)* velocity; **Flug|ge|sell|schaft** F airline (company); **Flug|ge|wicht** NT all-up weight

Flug|ha|fen M airport; *(Mil)* aerodrome *(Brit)*, airdrome *(US)*; **der ~ Hamburg** Hamburg airport; **auf dem ~** at the airport

Flug|ha|fen-: **Flug|ha|fen|bus** M airport bus; **Flug|ha|fen|feu|er|wehr** F airport fire fighting service; **Flug|ha|fen|ge|bühr** F airport charges *pl*; **Flug|ha|fen|ge|län|de** NT airport grounds *pl*; **Flug|ha|fen|nä|he** F **in ~** near *or* in the vicinity of the/an airport; **Flug|ha|fen|steu|er** F airport tax

Flug-: **Flug|hö|he** F flying height *(auch Orn)*; *(Aviat)* altitude; **unsere** *or* **die ~ beträgt 10.000 Meter** we are flying at an altitude of 10,000 metres *(Brit)* *or* meters *(US)*; **die ~ erreichen** to reach one's cruising altitude *or* flying height; **Flug|hörn|chen** NT flying squirrel; **Flug|hund** M flying fox; **Flug|in|ge|ni|eur(in)** M(F) flight engineer; **Flug|kan|zel** F cockpit; **Flug|ka|pi|tän(in)** M(F) captain (of an/the aircraft); **Flug|kar|te** F **a** *(= Luftfahrtkarte)* flight *or* aviation chart **b** *(rare: = Flugschein)* plane ticket; **Flug|ki|lo|me|ter** M (air) kilometre *(Brit)* *or* kilometer *(US)*; **Flug|kör|per** M flying object; **Flug|kor|ri|dor** M air corridor; **Flug|kunst** F airmanship, flying skill; **Flug|küns|te** PL flying skills *pl*; *(= Kunststücke)* aerobatic feats *pl*; **Flug|la|ge** F flying position *or* attitude *(spec)*; **Flug|lärm** M aircraft noise; **Flug|leh|rer(in)** M(F) flying instructor; **Flug|leit|sys|tem** NT flight control system; **Flug|lei|tung** F air-traffic *or* flight control; **Flug|li|nie** F **a** *(= Strecke)* airway, air route **b** *(= Fluggesellschaft)* airline (company); **Flug|loch** NT entrance hole; *(bei Bienenstock)* (hive) entrance; **Flug|lot|se** M, **Flug|lot|sin** F air-traffic *or* flight controller; **Flug|ma|nö|ver** NT aerial manoeuvre *(Brit)* *or* maneuver *(US)*; **Flug|mei|le** F air mile; **~n sammeln** to collect air miles; **Flug|mel|de|dienst** M *(Mil)* enemy aircraft warning service; **Flug|me|te|o|ro|lo|gie** F aeronautical meteorology; **Flug|mi|nu|te** F **nach fünf ~n** after flying for five minutes; **dreißig ~n von hier** thirty minutes by air from here; **Flug|mis|si|on** F space mission; **Flug|mo|tor** M aircraft engine; **Flug|netz** NT network of air routes; **Flug|num|mer** F flight number; **Flug|ob|jekt** NT **ein unbekanntes ~** an unidentified flying object, a UFO; **Flug|ord|nung** F flight formation; **Flug|pas|sa|gier(in)** M(F) (airline) passenger; **Flug|per|so|nal** NT flight personnel *pl*; **Flug|plan** M flight schedule; **Flug|platz** M airfield; *(größer)* airport; **Flug|pra|xis** F flying experience; **Flug|preis** M air fare; **Flug|prü|fung** F examination for one's pilot's licence *(Brit)* *or* license *(US)*; **Flug|rei|se** F flight; **eine ~ machen** to travel by air; **Flug|rei|sen|de(r)** MF *decl as adj* (airline) passenger; **Flug|rich|tung** F direction of flight; **die ~ ändern** to change one's flight course; **Flug|rou|te** F air route

flugs [flʊks] ADV without delay, speedily

Flug-: **Flug|sand** M drifting sand; **Flug|sau|ri|er** M pterodactyl; **die ~** the Pterosauria; **Flug|schan|ze** F *(Sport)* ski jump; **Flug|schau** F air *or* flying display; **Flug|schein** M **a** pilot's licence *(Brit)* *or* license *(US)* **b** *(= Flugticket)* plane *or* air ticket; **Flug|schnei|se** F flight path; **Flug|schrei|ber** M flight recorder; **Flug|schrift** F pamphlet; **Flug|schü|ler(in)** M(F) trainee pilot; **Flug|si|cher|heit** F air safety; **Flug|si|cher|heits|be|hör|de** F air safety authority; **Flug|si|che|rung** F air traffic control; **Flug|si|mu|la|tor** M flight simulator; **Flug|sport** M flying, aviation; **Flug|staub** M flue dust; **Flug|steig** M gate; **Flug|stre|cke** F **a** flying distance; **eine große ~ zurücklegen** to fly a long distance **b** *(= Route)* route; **Flug|stun|de** F **a** flying hour; **zehn ~n entfernt** ten hours away by air **b** *(= Unterricht)* flying lesson; **flug|taug|lich** ADJ *Pilot* fit to fly; *Flugzeug* airworthy; **Flug|taug|lich|keit** F *(von Pilot)* fitness to fly; *(von Flugzeug)* airworthiness; **Flug|tech|nik** F **a** aircraft engineering **b** *(= Flugfertigkeit)* flying technique; **flug|tech|nisch** ADJ aeronautical; *Bedeutung, Entwicklung, Prinzipien auch* aerotechnical; *Erfahrung, Fehler* flying *attr*; **eine ~e Ausbildung haben** to have been trained in flying ADV from an aeronautical point of view; **~ ist er perfekt** his flying is perfect; **Flug|ti|cket** NT plane ticket; **Flug|tou|ris|tik** F holiday *(esp Brit)* *or* vacation *(US)* air travel; **flug|tüch|tig** ADJ airworthy; **Flug|tüch|tig|keit** F airworthiness; **flug|un|fä|hig** ADJ unable to fly; *Flugzeug (= nicht in Ordnung)* not airworthy; **flug|un|taug|lich** ADJ *Pilot* unfit to fly; *Flugzeug* not airworthy; **Flug|un|taug|lich|keit** F *(von Pilot)* unfitness to fly; *(von Flugzeug)* lack of airworthiness; **Flug|un|ter|bre|chung** F stop; *(mit Übernachtung auch)* stopover; **flug|un|tüch|tig** ADJ not airworthy; **Flug|ver|an|stal|tung** F air display *or* show; **Flug|ver|bin|dung** F air connection; **es gibt auch eine ~** there are flights there too; **Flug|ver|bot** NT flying ban; **nachts besteht ~ auf dem Flughafen** the airport is closed to air traffic at night; **ein ~ erlassen** to ground; *(über bestimmten Gebieten)* to ban from flying; **Flug|ver|kehr** M air traffic; **Flug|ver|such** M attempt to fly *or* at flight; **Flug|warn|dienst** M *(Mil)* enemy aircraft warning service; **Flug|we|sen** NT, *no pl* aviation *no art*; *(mit Ballons etc)* aeronautics *sing, no art*; **Flug|wet|ter** NT flying weather; **Flug|zeit** F flying time; **Flug|zet|tel** M *(Aus)* leaflet; *(= Werbung auch)* handbill

Flug|zeug NT *pl* **-zeuge** plane, aircraft, aeroplane *(Brit)*, airplane *(US)*; *(= Düsenflugzeug auch)* jet; *(= Segelflugzeug)* glider; **im** *or* **mit dem** *or* **per ~** by air *or* plane; **ein ~ der Lufthansa** a Lufthansa plane/jet

Flug|zeug- *in cpds* aircraft; **Flug|zeug|ab|sturz** M plane *or* air crash; **Flug|zeug|ab|wehr** F *(Mil)* air defence *(Brit)* *or* defense *(US)*; **Flug|zeug|bau** M, *no pl* aircraft construction *no art*; **Flug|zeug|be|sat|zung** F air *or* plane crew; **Flug|zeug|ent|füh|rer(in)** M(F) (aircraft) hijacker, skyjacker; **Flug|zeug|ent|füh|rung** F (aircraft) hijacking, skyjacking; **Flug|zeug|füh|rer(in)** M(F) (aircraft) pilot; **Flug|zeug|hal|le** F (aircraft) hangar; **Flug|zeug|ka|ta|stro|phe** F air disaster; **Flug|zeug|mo|dell** NT model plane; **Flug|zeug|park** M fleet of aircraft; **Flug|zeug|rumpf** M fuselage; **Flug|zeug|schleu|der** F catapult; **Flug|zeug|start** M aeroplane *(Brit)* *or* airplane *(US)* takeoff; **Flug|zeug|trä|ger** M aircraft carrier; **Flug|zeug|typ** M model of aircraft; **Flug|zeug|un|glück** NT plane *or* air crash; **Flug|zeug|ver|band** M *(Mil)* aircraft formation; **Flug|zeug|wrack** NT wreckage of a/the plane

Flug|ziel NT destination

Flu|i|dum [ˈfluːidʊm] NT **-s, Fluida** [-da] **a** *(fig)* aura; *(von Städten, Orten)* atmosphere; **von ihr ging ein geheimnisvolles ~ aus** she was surrounded by an aura of mystery **b** *(Chem)* fluid

Fluk|tu|a|ti|on [flʊktuaˈtsioːn] F **-, -en** fluctuation (+*gen* in)

fluk|tu|ie|ren [flʊktuˈiːrən] *ptp* **fluktuiert** VI to fluctuate

Flun|der [ˈflʊndɐ] F **-, -n** flounder; **da war ich platt wie eine ~** *(inf)* you could have knocked me down with a feather *(inf)*

Flun|ke|rei [flʊŋkəˈrai] F **-, -en** *(inf)* **a** *no pl* (= *Flunkern)* storytelling **b** *(= kleine Lüge)* story

Flun|ke|rer [ˈflʊŋkərɐ] M **-s, -**, **Flun|ke|rin** [-ərɪn] F **-, -nen** *(inf)* storyteller

flun|kern [ˈflʊŋkɐn] *(inf)* VI to tell stories VT to make up

Flunsch [flʊnʃ] M OR F **-(e)s, -e** *(inf)* pout; **eine(n) ~ ziehen** *or* **machen** to pout

Flu|or [ˈfluːoːɐ] NT **-s**, *no pl (abbr* **F***)* fluorine; *(= Fluorverbindung)* fluoride

Flu|or M **-s**, *no pl (Med)* (vaginal) discharge

Flu|or|chlor|koh|len|was|ser|stoff M chlorofluorocarbon

Flu|o|res|zenz [fluorɛsˈtsɛnts] F **-**, *no pl* fluorescence

Flu|o|res|zenz|far|be F luminous paint

flu|o|res|zie|ren [fluorɛsˈtsiːrən] *ptp* **fluoresziert** VI to be luminous, to fluoresce *(form)*

Flu|o|rid [fluoˈriːt] NT **-(e)s, -e** [-də] *(Chem)* fluoride

Flu|o|rit [fluoˈriːt] M **-s, -e** fluorspar, fluorite *(US)*

Flu|or|koh|len|was|ser|stoff M fluorocarbon

Flup|pe [ˈflʊpə] F **-, -en** *(inf)* fag *(Brit)*, ciggy, smoke *(esp US)*

Flur [fluːɐ] M **-(e)s, -e** corridor; *(= Hausflur)* hall

Flur F **-, -en** *(liter)* *(= unbewaldetes Land)* open fields *pl*; *(= Wiese)* meadow, mead *(poet)*; *(Agr) agricultural land of a community* **durch Wald/Feld und ~** through woods/fields and meadows; **allein auf weiter ~ stehen** *(fig)* to be out on a limb

Flur-: **Flur|be|leuch|tung** F corridor light/lights *pl*; *(von Hausflur)* hall light/lights *pl*; **Flur|be|rei|ni|gung** F *reparcelling of the agricultural land of a community*; **Flur|fens|ter** NT corridor window; *(von Hausflur)* hall window; **Flur|form** F *layout of the agricultural land of a community*; **Flur|gar|de|ro|be** F hall stand; **Flur|gren|ze** F boundary of village lands; **Flur|licht** NT corridor light; *(von Hausflur)* hall light; **Flur|na|me** M field-name; **Flur|scha|den** M *damage to an agricultural area* *(fig)* damage; **Flur|to|i|let|te** F toilet on the landing; **Flur|tür** F door to the corridor, hall door

Flu|se [ˈfluːzə] F -, -n bit of fluff; *(= Wollfluse)* bobble; **~n** fluff; bobbles

Fluss [flʊs] M -es, ⸚e [ˈflʏsə] **a** *(= Gewässer)* river; **am ~** by the river; *Stadt* on the river; **unten am ~** down by the river(side); **den ~ aufwärtsfahren/abwärtsfahren** to go upstream *or* upriver/downstream *or* downriver
b *no pl* (*Tech*: *= Schmelzfluss*) molten mass; **im ~ sein** to be molten
c *(= kontinuierlicher Verlauf: von Verkehr, Rede, Strom, Elektronen)* flow; *(von Verhandlungen auch)* continuity; **etw in ~** *(acc)* **bringen** to get sth moving *or* going; **etw kommt** *or* **gerät in ~** sth gets underway *or* going; *(= sich verändern)* sth moves into a state of flux; **im ~ sein** *(= sich verändern)* to be in a state of flux; *(= im Gange sein)* to be in progress, to be going on

Fluss- *in cpds* river; **Fluss|aal** M common eel; **fluss|ab|(wärts)** [flʊsˈlap(vɛrts)] ADV downstream, downriver; **Fluss|arm** M arm of a/the river; **fluss|auf|wärts** [flʊsˈlaufvɛrts] ADV upstream, upriver; **Fluss|bau** M *pl* **-bauten** river control *no art, no pl*; **Fluss|bett** NT riverbed; **Fluss|bie|gung** F bend in the river

Flüss|chen [ˈflʏsçən] NT -s, - little river

Fluss-: **Fluss|dia|gramm** NT flow chart *or* diagram; **Fluss|ebe|ne** F fluvial plain; **Fluss|fisch** M river *or* freshwater fish; **Fluss|ge|biet** NT river basin; **Fluss|ge|fäl|le** NT gradient of a/the river; **Fluss|ge|schie|be** NT silt; **Fluss|ha|fen** M river port

flüs|sig [ˈflʏsɪç] ADJ **a** *(= nicht fest)* liquid; *Honig, Lack* runny; *(= geschmolzen) Glas, Metall* molten; *Butter* melted; **~e Nahrung** liquids *pl*, liquid food; **~ machen** to liquefy; *Glas, Metall, Wachs, Fett* to melt → *auch* **flüssigmachen**; **~ werden** to turn *or* become liquid, to liquefy; *(Lack)* to become runny; *(Glas, Metall)* to become molten; *(Wachs, Fett)* to melt
b *(= fließend) Stil, Spiel* flowing, fluid; **die Polizei meldete ~en Verkehr** the police reported that the traffic was flowing smoothly; **den Verkehr ~ halten** to keep the traffic flowing
c *(= verfügbar) Geld* available; **~es Vermögen** liquid assets *pl*; **ich bin im Moment nicht ~** *(inf)* I'm out of funds at the moment; **wenn ich wieder ~ bin** when I'm in funds again
ADV **a ~ ernährt werden** to be fed on liquids
b *(= fließend)* fluently; **~ lesen/schreiben/sprechen** to read/write/talk fluently

Flüs|sig|gas NT liquid gas

Flüs|sig|keit F -, -en **a** *(= flüssiger Stoff)* liquid **b** *no pl (von Metall, Glas, Wachs etc)* liquidity; *(von Geldern)* availability; *(von Stil)* fluidity

Flüs|sig|keits-: **Flüs|sig|keits|auf|nah|me** F fluid *or* liquid intake; **Flüs|sig|keits|be|darf** M fluid requirement; **Flüs|sig|keits|maß** NT liquid measure; **Flüs|sig|keits|men|ge** F quantity *or* amount of liquid

Flüs|sig-: **Flüs|sig|kris|tall** M liquid crystal; **Flüs|sig|kris|tall|an|zei|ge** F liquid-crystal display, LCD; **flüs|sig+ma|chen** *sep*, **flüs|sig ma|chen** △ VT *(fig)* to realize; *(= in Geld umwandeln auch)* to convert (into cash); **flüs|sig+ma|chen** *sep (= verflüssigen)* → **flüssig** ADJ **a**; **Flüs|sig|spreng|stoff** M liquid explosive

Fluss-: **Fluss|krebs** M crayfish *(Brit)*, crawfish *(US)*; **Fluss|land|schaft** F countryside by a/the river; *(Art)* riverscape; **Fluss|lauf** M course of a/the river; **Fluss|mün|dung** F river mouth; *(von Gezeitenfluss)* estuary; **Fluss|nie|de|rung** F fluvial plain; **Fluss|ni|xe** F river sprite; **Fluss|pferd** NT hippopotamus; **Fluss|re|ge|lung** F, **Fluss|re|gu|lie|rung** F river control *no art, no pl*; **Fluss|re|gu|lie|rung** F river control *no art, no pl*; **Fluss|sand** M river *or* fluvial sand; **Fluss|schiff** NT river boat; **Fluss|schiff|fahrt** F, *no pl* river navigation; *(= Verkehr)* river traffic; **Fluss|spat** M fluorspar, fluorite *(US)*; **Fluss|stahl** M ingot steel; **Fluss|ufer** NT river bank

Flüs|ter-: **Flüs|ter|ga|le|rie** F, **Flüs|ter|ge|wöl|be** NT whispering gallery; **Flüs|ter|kam|pag|ne** F whispering campaign; **Flüs|ter|laut** M whisper

flüs|tern [ˈflʏstɐn] VTI to whisper; *(= etwas lauter tuscheln)* to mutter; **jdm etw ins Ohr ~** to whisper sth in sb's ear; **sich ~d unterhalten** to talk in whispers; **miteinander ~** to whisper together; **wer hat da geflüstert?** who was that whispering?; **das kann ich dir ~** *(inf)* take it from me *(inf)*; *(Zustimmung heischend auch)* I can tell you *(inf)*; **dem werde ich was ~** *(inf)* I'll tell him a thing or two *(inf)*

Flüs|ter-: **Flüs|ter|pa|ro|le** F rumour *(Brit)*, rumor *(US)*, whisper *(inf)*; **Flüs|ter|pro|pa|gan|da** F underground rumours *(Brit) or* rumors *(US) pl*; **Flüs|ter|stim|me** F whisper; **mit ~ sprechen** to talk in a whisper *or* in whispers; **Flüs|ter|ton** M, *no pl* whisper; **sich im ~ unterhalten** to talk in whispers; **Flüs|ter|tü|te** F *(hum inf)* megaphone

Flut [fluːt] F -, -en **a** *(= ansteigender Wasserstand)* incoming *or* flood tide; *(= angestiegener Wasserstand)* high tide; **es ist ~** the tide is coming in; it's high tide, the tide's in; **die ~ kommt** *or* **steigt** *(form)* the tide's coming in *or* rising; **bei ~ baden** to swim when the tide is coming in/at high tide; **bei ~ einlaufen** to come in on the tide/at high tide; **mit der ~** with the tide *or* flood tide *(spec)*; **die ~ tritt um 16.30 Uhr ein** the tide starts to come in *or* turns at 4.30 p.m.; **die ~ geht zurück** the tide has started to go out, the tide has turned → **Ebbe a**
b *usu pl (= Wassermasse)* waters *pl*; **sich in die kühlen ~en stürzen** *(hum)* to plunge into the water
c *(fig: = Menge)* flood; **eine ~ von Tränen** floods of tears

flu|ten [ˈfluːtn] VI *aux sein (geh) (Wasser, Licht)* to flood, to stream, to pour; *(Verkehr)* to stream, to pour; *(Musik)* to flood, to pour; **~des Licht** streaming light VT *(Naut)* to flood

Flut-: **Flut|ha|fen** M tidal harbour *(Brit) or* harbor *(US)*; **Flut|ka|ta|stro|phe** F flood disaster; **Flut|kraft|werk** NT tidal power plant *or* station; **Flut|licht** NT floodlight

Flut|licht-: **Flut|licht|an|la|ge** F floodlights *pl*, floodlighting; **Flut|licht|spiel** NT match played by floodlight, floodlit match

Flut|op|fer NT flood victim

flut|schen [ˈflʊtʃn] VI *(inf)* **a** *aux sein (N Ger: = rutschen)* to slide **b** *(= funktionieren)* to go smoothly *or* well *or* swimmingly *(dated inf)*

Flut-: **Flut|tor** NT floodgate; **Flut|ven|til** NT antiflood valve; **Flut|wel|le** F tidal wave

fl. W. *abbr von* **fließendes Wasser**

focht *pret von* **fechten**

Fock [fɔk] F -, -en *(Naut)* foresail

Fock-: **Fock|mast** M foremast; **Fock|rah** F, **Fock|ra|he** F foreyard; **Fock|se|gel** NT foresail

fö|de|ral [fødeˈraːl] ADJ federal

Fö|de|ra|lis|mus [fødera'lɪsmʊs] M -, *no pl* federalism

Fö|de|ra|list [fødera'lɪst] M -en, -en, **Fö|de|ra|lis|tin** [-ˈlɪstɪn] F -, -nen federalist

fö|de|ra|lis|tisch [fødera'lɪstɪʃ] ADJ federalist

Fö|de|ra|ti|on [føderaˈtsioːn] F -, -en federation

fö|de|ra|tiv [føderaˈtiːf] ADJ federal

fö|de|rie|ren [fødeˈriːrən] *ptp* **föderiert** VR to federate; **föderierte Staaten** federated states

foh|len [ˈfoːlən] VI to foal

Foh|len [ˈfoːlən] NT -s, - foal; *(männliches Pferd auch)* colt; *(weibliches Pferd auch)* filly

Föhn [føːn] M -(e)s, -e **a** *(= Wind)* foehn, föhn; **wir haben ~** the foehn is blowing **b** *(= Haartrockner)* hairdryer

föh|nen [ˈføːnən] VT to dry

Föhn|fri|sur F blow-dried hair

föh|nig [ˈføːnɪç] ADJ foehn *attr*; **es ist ~** there's a foehn (wind)

Föh|re [ˈføːrə] F -, -n Scots pine (tree)

fo|kal [foˈkaːl] ADJ focal

Fo|kus [ˈfoːkʊs] M -, -se focus

fo|kus|sie|ren [fokuˈsiːrən] *ptp* **fokussiert** VTI to focus

Fol|ge [ˈfɔlgə] F -, -n **a** *(= Reihenfolge)* order; *(= Aufeinanderfolge)* succession; *(= zusammengehörige Reihe, Math)* sequence; *(Cards)* run, sequence; *(= Lieferung einer Zeitschrift)* issue; *(= Fortsetzung)* instalment; *(TV, Rad)* episode; *(= Serie)* series; **in chronologischer/zwangloser ~** in chronological/no particular order; **in rascher/dichter ~** in rapid *or* quick/close succession; **Musik in bunter ~** a musical potpourri; **in der** *or* **für die ~** *(form: = in Zukunft)* in future
b *(= Ergebnis)* consequence; *(= unmittelbare Folge)* result; *(= Auswirkung)* effect; **als ~ davon** in consequence, as a result (of that); **dies hatte zur ~, dass ...** the consequence *or* result of this was that ...; **dies hatte seine Entlassung zur ~** this resulted in his dismissal *or* in his being dismissed; **bedenke die ~n!** think of the consequences!; **die ~n werden nicht ausbleiben** there will be repercussions; **die ~n für den Tourismus** the effect on tourism, the consequences for tourism; **für die ~n aufkommen** to take the consequences; **an den ~n eines Unfalls/einer Krankheit sterben** to die as a result of an accident/illness; **das wird ~n haben** that will have serious consequences; **ohne ~n bleiben** to have no consequences; **ihr Verhältnis blieb nicht ohne ~n** *(euph)* their relationship was not exactly unfruitful
c *(form)* **einem Befehl ~ leisten** to comply with *or* obey an order; **einer Einladung** *(dat)* **~ leisten** to accept an invitation

Fol|ge-: **Fol|ge|ein|rich|tung** F facility *or* utility *(US)* for the community; **Fol|ge|er|schei|nung** F result, consequence; **Fol|ge|jahr** NT following year; **Fol|ge|kos|ten** PL subsequent costs *pl*; **Fol|ge|las|ten** PL resultant costs *pl*; **Fol|ge|mo|nat** M following month

fol|gen [ˈfɔlgn] VI *aux sein* **a** *(= kommen nach)* to follow (*jdm/einer Sache* sb/sth); **auf etw** *(acc)* **~** to follow sth, to come after sth; **auf jdn (im Rang) ~** to come *or* rank after sb; **~ Sie mir (bitte/unauffällig)!** come with me please; **es folgt nun** *or* **nun folgt ein Konzert** we now have a concert, a concert now follows; **... dann ~ die Meldungen im Einzelnen** ... followed by the news in detail; **dem** *(liter) or* **auf den Frühling folgt der Sommer** spring is followed by summer; **Fortsetzung folgt** (to be) continued; **wie folgt** as follows → **Tod**
b *(= verstehen)* to follow (*jdm/einer Sache* sb/sth); **können Sie mir ~?** are you with me? *(inf)*, do you follow (me)?
c *(= gehorchen)* to do as *or* what one is told; **einem Befehl/einer Anordnung ~** to follow an order/instruction; **jdm ~** *(inf)* to do what sb tells one
d *+dat (= sich richten nach) einer Mode, einem Vorschlag* to follow; *jdm* to agree with, to go along with *(inf)*
e *(= hervorgehen)* to follow (*aus* from); **was folgt daraus für die Zukunft?** what are the consequences of this for the future?

fol|gend ADJ following; **Folgendes** the following; **er schreibt Folgendes** *or* **das Folgende** he writes (as follows *or* the following); **im Folgenden** in the following; *(schriftlich auch)* below; **es handelt sich um Folgendes** it's like this; *(schriftlich)* it concerns the following

fol|gen|der|ma|ßen [ˈfɔlgndɐˈmaːsn] ADV like this, as follows; **wir werden das ~ machen** we'll do it like this *or* in the following way

Fol|gen-: **fol|gen|los** ADJ without consequences; *(= wirkungslos)* ineffective; **~ bleiben** not to have any consequences; to be ineffective; **das konnte nicht ~ bleiben** that was bound to have serious consequences/could not fail to be effective; **fol|gen|reich** ADJ *(= bedeutsam)* momentous; *(= folgenschwer)* serious; *(= wirkungsvoll)* effective; **fol|gen|schwer** ADJ serious; **die Maßnahme erwies sich als ~** the measure had serious consequences; **Fo̱l|gen|schwe|re** F seriousness

Fo̱l|ge-: **Fo̱l|ge|prob|lem** NT resultant problem; **die ~e einer Sache** *(gen)* the problems arising from *or* out of sth; **fo̱l|ge|recht** *(rare)*, **fo̱l|ge|rich|tig** ADJ (logically) consistent; **das einzig Folgerichtige in dieser Situation** the only logical *or* consistent thing to do in this situation; **fo̱l|ge|rich|tig** ADJ (logically) consistent; **das einzig Folgerichtige in dieser Situation** the only logical *or* consistent thing to do in this situation; **Fo̱l|ge|rich|tig|keit** F logical consistency

fo̱l|gern ['fɔlgɐn] VT to conclude; **aus diesem Brief lässt sich ~, dass ...** it can be concluded *or* we can conclude from this letter that ... VI to draw a/the conclusion; **logisch ~ lernen** to learn to think logically

Fo̱l|ge|rung ['fɔlgərʊŋ] F -, -en conclusion; **daraus ergibt sich die ~, dass ...** from this it can be concluded that ...

Fo̱l|ge-: **Fo̱l|ge|satz** M *(Gram)* consecutive clause; **Fo̱l|ge|ton|horn** NT *(Aus)* = **Martinshorn**; **fo̱l|ge|wid|rig** ADJ *(geh)* logically inconsistent; **Fo̱l|ge|wid|rig|keit** F *(geh)* logical inconsistency; **Fo̱l|ge|wir|kung** F consequence, effect; **eine ~ war ...** one effect *or* result (it had) was ...; **Fo̱l|ge|zeit** F following period, period following

fo̱lg|lich ['fɔlklɪç] ADV CONJ consequently, therefore

fo̱lg|sam ['fɔlkza:m] ADJ obedient

Fo̱lg|sam|keit F -, *no pl* obedience

Fo|li|a̱nt [fo'liant] M -en, -en folio (volume); *(= dicker Band)* tome

Fo̱|lie ['fo:liə] F -, -n **a** *(= Plastikfolie)* film; *(für Projektor)* transparency; *(= Metallfolie, Typ, Cook)* foil; *(= Schicht)* layer of film/foil; **eine ~ aus Kupfer** a thin layer of copper **b** *(fig: = Hintergrund)* background; **etw als ~ benutzen** to use sth as a model

Fo̱|li|en *pl von* **Folie** *von* **Folio**

Fo̱|li|en-: **Fo̱|li|en|kar|tof|fel** F *(Cook)* jacket *(Brit)* or baked *(US)* potato *(baked in foil)*; **Fo̱|li|en|schrei|ber** M marker pen *(for overhead projector transparencies)*; **fo̱|li|en|ver|packt** ADJ wrapped in foil; *(in Alufolie)* aluminium-wrapped *(Brit)*, aluminum-wrapped *(US)*; *(in Plastikfolie)* wrapped in cling film *(Brit)*, plastic-wrapped *(US)*

Fo̱|lio ['fo:lio] NT -s, -s *or* **Folien** [-liən] folio

Folk|lo̱|re [fɔlk'lo:rə, 'fɔlklo:rə] F -, *no pl* folklore; *(= Volksmusik)* folk music

Folk|lo|ri̱st [fɔlklo'rɪst] M -en, -en, **Folk|lo|ri̱s|tin** [-'rɪstɪn] F -, -nen folklorist

folk|lo|ri̱s|tisch [fɔlklo'rɪstɪʃ] ADJ folkloric; *Kleidung* ethnic; **~e Musik** folk music

Folk-: **Folk|sän|ger(in)** M(F) folk singer; **Folk|song** ['fo:k-] M *(Mus)* folk song

Fol|li̱|kel [fɔ'li:kl] M -s, - follicle

Fol|li̱|kel|sprung M ovulation

Fo̱l|säu|re ['fo:l-] F, *no pl (Chem)* folic acid

Fo̱l|ter ['fɔltɐ] F -, -n **a** *(lit, fig)* torture; *(fig auch)* torment; **die ~ anwenden** to use torture **b** *(old: = Folterbank)* rack; **jdn auf die ~ spannen** *(fig)* to keep sb on tenterhooks, to keep sb in an agony of suspense

Fo̱l|ter|bank F *pl* -bänke rack

Fo̱l|te|rer ['fɔltərɐ] M -s, -, **Fo̱l|te|rin** [-ərɪn] F -, -nen torturer

Fo̱l|ter-: **Fo̱l|ter|ge|rät** NT, **Fo̱l|ter|in|stru|ment** NT instrument of torture; **Fo̱l|ter|kam|mer** F, **Fo̱l|ter|kel|ler** M torture chamber; **Fo̱l|ter|knecht** M torturer; **Fo̱l|ter|me|tho|de** F method of torture

fo̱l|tern ['fɔltɐn] VT to torture; *(= quälen auch)* to torment; **jdn ~ lassen** to have sb tortured VI to use torture

Fo̱l|ter|qual F *(lit)* agony of torture; *(fig)* agony of torment

Fo̱l|te|rung ['fɔltərʊŋ] F -, -en torture

Fo̱l|ter|werk|zeug NT instrument of torture

Fon [fo:n] NT -s, -s = **Phon**

Fon [fo:n] *abbr von* **Telefon** Tel

Fö̱n® [fø:n] M -(e)s, -e hairdryer → *auch* **Föhn b**

Fon- = **Phon-**

Fond [fõ:] M -s, -s **a** *(geh: = Wagenfond)* back, rear **b** *(= Hintergrund) (Art)* background; *(Tex)* (back)ground; **im ~ der Bühne** *(Theat)* at the back of the stage **c** *(geh: = Basis)* foundation *(zu* for) **d** *(Cook: = Fleischsaft)* meat juices *pl*

Fon|dant [fõ'dã:] M OR (AUS) NT -s, -s *(Cook)* fondant

Fonds [fõ:] M -, - **a** *(= Geldreserve, fig geh)* fund; **keinen ~ für etw haben** to have no funds for sth **b** *(Fin: = Schuldverschreibung)* government bond

Fonds|bör|se ['fõ:-] F, **Fonds|ge|schäft** NT *(Fin)* market of government bonds

Fon|due [fõ'dy:] NT -s, -s *or* F -, -s fondue

Fo|ne̱m NT -s, -e = **Phonem**

fö̱|nen △ ['fø:nən] VT → **föhnen**

Fo|ne̱|tik *etc* = **Phonetik** *etc*

Fön|fri|sur △ F → **Föhnfrisur**

Fo|no- ['fo:no-, fo:no-] = **Phono-**

Font M -s, -s *(Comput)* font

Fon|tä̱|ne [fɔn'tɛ:nə] F -, -n jet, fount *(poet)*; *(geh: = Springbrunnen)* fountain, fount *(poet)*

Fon|ta|ne̱l|le [fɔnta'nɛlə] F -, -n *(Anat)* fontanelle

fo̱p|pen ['fɔpn] VT *(inf)* **jdn ~** to make a fool of sb; *(= necken)* to pull sb's leg *(inf)*; **er fühlte sich gefoppt** he felt he'd been made a fool of

Fop|pe|re̱i [fɔpə'rai] F -, -en *(inf)* leg-pulling *no pl (inf)*

Fo̱|ra *(Hist) pl von* **Forum**

for|cie̱|ren [fɔr'si:rən] *ptp* **forciert** VT to push; *Entwicklung auch, Tempo* to force; *Konsum, Produktion* to push *or* force up; **seine Anstrengungen ~** to increase one's efforts

for|cie̱rt [fɔr'si:ɐt] ADJ forced

Fö̱r|de ['fœrdə] F -, -n firth *(esp Scot)*, *narrow coastal inlet*

Fö̱r|der-: **Fö̱r|der|an|la|ge** F conveyor; **Fö̱r|der|band** [-bant] NT *pl* -bänder conveyor belt; **Fö̱r|der|be|trag** M *(Univ)* grant; **Fö̱r|der|be|trieb** M *(Min)* production; **den ~ aufnehmen** to start production

Fö̱r|de|rer ['fœrdərɐ] M -s, -, **Fö̱r|de|rin** [-ərɪn] F -, -nen sponsor; *(= Gönner)* patron

Fö̱r|der-: **Fö̱r|der|gel|der** PL grants *pl*, funding *sing*; **Fö̱r|der|klas|se** F *(Sch)* special class; **Fö̱r|der|koh|le** F run of mine (coal), through-and-through coal *(Brit)*; **Fö̱r|der|korb** M mine cage; **Fö̱r|der|kreis** M ~ **für ...** society for the promotion of ...; **Fö̱r|der|kurs** M *(Sch)* special classes *pl*; **Fö̱r|der|kur|sus** M = **Förderkurs**; **Fö̱r|der|land** NT producing country; **Fö̱r|der|leis|tung** F output

fö̱r|der|lich ['fœrdɐlɪç] ADJ beneficial (+*dat* to); **guten Beziehungen ~ sein** to be conducive to good relations; **der Krebsbekämpfung ~ sein** to help in the fight against cancer; **ein der Weiterbildung ~er Kursus** a course which contributes to one's further education

Fö̱r|der-: **Fö̱r|der|ma|schi|ne** F winding engine; **Fö̱r|der|men|ge** F output; **Fö̱r|der|mit|tel** PL aid *sing*; **fo̱r|dern** ['fɔrdɐn] VT **a** *(= verlangen)* to demand; *Preis* to ask; *(in Appell, Aufrufen etc, = erfordern)* to call for; *(= Anspruch erheben auf) Entschädigung, Lohnerhöhung* to claim; **viel/zu viel von jdm ~** to ask *or* demand a lot/too much of sb, to make too many demands on sb → **Rechenschaft b** *(fig: = kosten) Menschenleben, Opfer* to claim **c** *(lit, fig: = herausfordern)* to challenge; **er ist noch nie im Leben richtig gefordert worden** he has never been faced with a real challenge **d** *(Sport)* to make demands on; *(= das Äußerste abverlangen)* to stretch VI to make demands; **er fordert nur, ohne selbst zu geben** he demands everything as a right, without giving anything himself;

fö̱r|dern ['fœrdɐn] VT **a** *(= unterstützen) Handel, Projekt, Entwicklung, Arbeit, Kunst, Wissenschaft* to support; *(= propagieren)* to promote; *(finanziell) bestimmtes Projekt* to sponsor; *Nachwuchs, Künstler* to support, to help; *jds Talent, Kunstverständnis, Neigung* to encourage, to foster; *(= voranbringen) Freundschaft, Frieden* to foster, to promote; *Verdauung* to aid; *Appetit* to stimulate; *Untersuchung, Wahrheitsfindung* to further; **jdn beruflich ~** to help sb in his career **b** *(= steigern) Wachstum* to promote; *Umsatz, Absatz, Produktion, Verbrauch* to boost, to increase **c** *Bodenschätze* to extract; *Kohle, Erz* to mine; **fọr|dernd** ADJ *Verhalten, Ruf* imperious; *Persönlichkeit, Aufgabe* demanding

Fö̱r|der-: **Fö̱r|der|platt|form** F *(Min)* production platform; **Fö̱r|der|quo|te** F *(Min)* production level; **Fö̱r|der|schacht** M *(Min)* winding shaft; **Fö̱r|der|schu|le** F *(Sch)* special school; **Fö̱r|der|seil** NT *(Min)* winding rope; **Fö̱r|der|soh|le** F *(Min)* haulage level; **Fö̱r|der|staa|ten** PL *(Min)* producing countries *pl*; **Fö̱r|der|stu|fe** F *(Sch) mixed ability class(es) intended to foster the particular talents of each pupil*; **Fö̱r|der|turm** M *(Min)* winding tower; *(auf Bohrstelle)* derrick

Fo̱r|de|rung ['fɔrdərʊŋ] F -, -en **a** *(= Verlangen)* demand *(nach* for); *(= Lohnforderung, Entschädigungsforderung etc)* claim *(nach* for); *(in Appell, Aufrufen etc)* call *(nach* for); **~en an jdn stellen** to make demands on sb; **hohe ~en an jdn stellen** to demand a lot of sb; **eine ~ nach etw erheben** to call for sth; **jds ~ erfüllen** to meet sb's demand/claim **b** *(geh: = Erfordernis)* requirement **c** *(Comm: = Anspruch)* claim *(an +acc, gegen* on, against); **eine ~ einklagen** to sue for payment of a debt; **eine ~ eintreiben** *or* **einziehen** to collect a debt **d** *(= Herausforderung)* challenge

Fö̱r|de|rung ['fœrdərʊŋ] F -, -en **a** *(= Unterstützung)* support; *(finanziell)* sponsorship; *(von Nachwuchs, Künstler)* support, help; *(von Talent)* encouragement, fostering; *(von Freundschaft, Frieden)* fostering, promotion; *(von Verdauung)* aid *(gen* to); *(von Appetit)* stimulation; **Maßnahmen zur ~ des Fremdenverkehrs** measures to promote tourism *or* for the promotion of tourism **b** *(inf: = Förderungsbetrag)* grant **c** *(= Gewinnung)* extraction; *(von Kohle, Erz auch)* mining

Fo̱r|de|rungs|ab|tre|tung F *(Jur)* assignment of a claim

Fö̱r|de|rungs-: **Fö̱r|de|rungs|maß|nah|me** F supportive measure; **Fö̱r|de|rungs|maß|nah|men** PL assistance *sing*; **Fö̱r|de|rungs|mit|tel** PL aid *sing*; **Fö̱r|de|rungs|pro|gramm** NT aid programme *(Brit)* or program *(US)*; **fö̱r|de|rungs|wür|dig** ADJ deserving support; **Fö̱r|de|rungs|wür|dig|keit** F **wir waren von der ~ des Projekts nicht überzeugt** we were not convinced that the project deserved support

Fö̱r|der|un|ter|richt M special instruction

Fö̱r|der|wa|gen M *(Min)* tram, mine car

Fo|re̱l|le [fo'rɛlə] F -, -n trout → **blau**

Fo|re̱l|len-: **Fo|re̱l|len|teich** M trout hatchery; **Fo|re̱l|len|zucht** F trout farming; *(= Anlage)* trout farm

Fo̱|ren *pl von* **Forum**

fo|re̱n|sisch [fo'rɛnzɪʃ] ADJ *Medizin, Psychologie, Gutachten* forensic; *(old: = rhetorisch)* oratorical

Fo̱r|ke ['fɔrkə] F -, -n *(N Ger)* pitch fork

Fo̱rm [fɔrm] F -, -en **a** form; *(= Gestalt, Umriss)* shape; **in ~ von Regen/Steuerermäßigungen** in the form of rain/tax reductions; **in ~ von Dragees/Salbe** in pill/cream form, in the form of pills/cream; **in ~ eines Dreiecks** shaped like a triangle, in the shape of a triangle; **eine bestimmte ~ haben** to be in a certain form; to be a certain shape; **seine ~ verlieren, aus der ~ geraten** to lose its shape; *(Kleidung auch)* to go out of shape; **einer Sache** *(dat)* **~ (und Gestalt) geben** *(lit)* to shape sth; *(fig)* to give sth a coherent shape; **Sie müssen Ihr Gesuch in die geeignete ~ kleiden** your application must be in the proper form; **feste ~ annehmen** *(fig)* to take shape; **hässliche/gewalttätige ~en annehmen** *(fig)* to become ugly/violent; **(weibliche) ~en**

feminine figure → **bringen e**
b *(= Gestaltung)* form; **~ und Inhalt** form and content
c Formen PL *(= Umgangsformen)* manners *pl*; **die ~ wahren** to observe the proprieties; **der ~ wegen** *or* **halber, um der ~ zu genügen** for form's sake, as a matter of form; **in aller ~** formally; **ein Mann mit/ohne ~en** a well-mannered/ill-mannered gentleman **d** *(= Kondition)* form; **in bester ~ sein** to be in great form *or* shape; **in ~ bleiben/kommen** to keep/get (oneself) fit *or* in condition; *(Sportler)* to keep/get in form; **hoch in ~** in great form *or* shape; **außer ~** out of condition; **nicht mehr in ~ sein** to be out of shape
e *(= Gießform)* mould *(Brit)*, mold *(US)*; *(= Kuchenform, Backform)* baking tin *(Brit) or* pan *(US)*; *(= Hutform, Schuhform)* block

for|mal [fɔr'maːl] ADJ **a** formal; **~-ästhetisch** formal aesthetic **b** *(= äußerlich) Besitzer, Fehler, Grund* technical ADV **a** formally **b** *(= äußerlich)* technically

For|mal|aus|bil|dung F drill

Form|al|de|hyd ['fɔrmlaldehyːt, fɔrmlalde'hyːt] M -s, *no pl* formaldehyde

For|ma|lie [fɔr'maːliə] F -, -n *usu pl* formality; *(= Äußerlichkeit)* technicality

For|ma|lin® [fɔrma'liːn] NT -s, *no pl* formalin

for|ma|li|sie|ren [fɔrmali'ziːrən] *ptp* **formalisiert** VT to formalize

For|ma|lis|mus [fɔrma'lɪsmʊs] M -, *no pl* formalism *no pl*

For|ma|list [fɔrma'lɪst] M -en, -en, **For|ma|lis|tin** [-'lɪstɪn] F -, -nen formalist

for|ma|lis|tisch [fɔrma'lɪstɪʃ] ADJ formalistic

For|ma|li|tät [fɔrmali'tɛːt] F -, -en formality; *(= Äußerlichkeit)* technicality; **alle ~en erledigen** to go through all the formalities

for|ma|li|ter [fɔr'maːlitɐ] ADV *(geh)* in form; *(= äußerlich)* technically

for|mal|ju|ris|tisch, for|mal|recht|lich ADJ technical

For|mans ['fɔrmans] NT -, **Formanzien** [fɔr'mantsiən] *or* **Formantia** [fɔr'mantsia] *(Ling)* formative (element)

For|mat [fɔr'maːt] NT -(e)s, -e **a** *(= Größenverhältnis)* size; *(von Zeitung, Papierbogen, Fotografie, Film)* format; *(von Buch)* trim size, trim *(inf)*; **im ~ DIN A4** in A4 (format) **b** *(= Rang, Persönlichkeit)* stature **c** *(fig: = Niveau)* class *(inf)*, quality; **internationales ~ haben** to be of international quality

for|ma|tie|ren [fɔrma'tiːrən] *ptp* **formatiert** VTI *(Comput)* to format; **neu ~** to reformat

For|ma|tie|rung F -, -en *(Comput)* formatting

For|ma|ti|on [fɔrma'tsioːn] F -, -en formation; *(= Gruppe)* group

For|ma|tions|flug M *(Mil)* formation flying

for|ma|tiv [fɔrma'tiːf] ADJ formative

For|ma|tiv [fɔrma'tiːf] NT -s, -e [-və] *(Ling)* syntactic morpheme; *(= Formans)* formative (element)

For|mat|vor|la|ge F *(Comput)* style (sheet)

Form-: form|bar ADJ *(lit, fig)* malleable; **Form|bar|keit** ['fɔrmbaːɐkait] F -, *no pl (lit, fig)* malleability; **form|be|stän|dig** ADJ **a ~ sein** to hold *or* retain its shape **b** *(Sport)* consistent in form; **Form|blatt** NT form; **Form|brief** M form letter

Förm|chen ['fœrmçən] NT -s, - *(im Sandkasten)* (plastic) mould *(Brit) or* mold *(US)*; *(Cook)* baking dish

Form|ei|sen NT structural steel

For|mel ['fɔrml] F -, -n formula; *(von Eid etc)* wording; *(= Floskel)* set phrase; **etw auf eine ~ bringen** to reduce sth to a formula

For|mel-1-Ren|nen [fɔrml'lains-] NT Formula-1 race

Form|ele|ment NT *(esp Art)* formal element, element of form

for|mel|haft ADJ **a** *(= floskelhaft) Sprache, Stil* stereotyped; **~e Wendung** set phrase **b** *(= als Formel)* formulistic ADV *(= floskelhaft) sich ausdrücken, schreiben* in clichés; **~ klingen** to sound clichéd; **~ reden** to talk in set phrases

For|mel|haf|tig|keit ['fɔrmlhaftɪçkait] F -, *no pl (= formelhafte Art)* stereotyped nature; *(einer Wendung)* setness

for|mell [fɔr'mɛl] ADJ formal ADV *(= offiziell)* formally, officially; **als Bürgermeister musste er den Vorfall ~ verurteilen** as mayor he had to deplore the incident as a matter of form

For|mel-: For|mel|samm|lung F *(Math)* formulary; **For|mel|spra|che** F system of notation

for|men ['fɔrmən] VT to form, to shape; *Charakter auch, Eisen* to mould *(Brit)*, to mold *(US)*; *Wörter* to articulate; **schön geformte Glieder** beautifully shaped limbs; **der Krieg hat ihn geformt** the war shaped him *or* his character; **~de Kraft** formative power VR *(lit)* to form *or* shape itself; *(fig)* to mature

For|men-: For|men|fül|le F wealth of forms; **For|men|leh|re** F morphology; *(Mus)* theory of musical form; **for|men|reich** ADJ with a great variety *or* wealth of forms; **~ sein** to have a great variety *or* wealth of forms; **For|men|reich|tum** M wealth of forms; **For|men|sinn** M sense of form, feeling for form; **For|men|spra|che** F *(geh)* use of forms

For|mer ['fɔrmɐ] M -s, -, **For|me|rin** [-ərɪn] F -, -nen moulder *(Brit)*, molder *(US)*

For|me|rei [fɔrmə'rai] F -, -en moulding *(Brit) or* molding *(US)* shop

Form-: Form|feh|ler M irregularity; *(gesellschaftlich)* breach of etiquette; **Form|fleisch** NT pressed meat; **Form|ge|bung** [-geːbʊŋ] F -, -en *(geh)* design; **Form|ge|fühl** NT sense of form; **form|ge|recht** ADJ *(lit, fig)* correct, proper; **Form|ge|stal|ter(in)** M(F) *(geh)* designer; **Form|ge|stal|tung** F design; **form|ge|wandt** ADJ urbane, suave

for|mi|da|bel [fɔrmi'daːbl] ADJ *(dated)* formidable

for|mie|ren [fɔr'miːrən] *ptp* **formiert** VT *Truppen* to draw up; *Kolonne, Zug* to form (into), to fall into; *(= bilden)* to form VR to form up

For|mie|rung F -, -en formation; *(Mil: von Truppen)* drawing-up

-för|mig [fœrmɪç] ADJ *suf* -shaped; **sternförmig** star-shaped

Form|kri|se F *(esp Sport)* loss of form

förm|lich ['fœrmlɪç] ADJ **a** *(= formell)* formal **b** *(= regelrecht)* positive ADV **a** *(= formell)* formally **b** *(= regelrecht)* positively; **ich hätte ~ weinen können** I really could have cried

Förm|lich|keit F -, -en **a** *no pl (von Benehmen)* formality **b** *usu pl (= Äußerlichkeit)* social convention; **bitte keine ~en!** please don't stand on ceremony

form|los ADJ **a** *(= ohne Form)* shapeless; *Vortrag, Aufsatz, Roman* unstructured **b** *(= zwanglos)* informal, casual **c** *(Admin) Antrag* unaccompanied by a form/any forms

Form|lo|sig|keit F -, *no pl* **a** *(= Gestaltlosigkeit)* shapelessness, lack of shape; *(von Vortrag, Aufsatz, Roman)* lack of structure **b** *(= Zwanglosigkeit)* informality, casualness

Form-: Form|sa|che F matter of form, formality; **form|schön** ADJ elegant, elegantly proportioned; **Form|schön|heit** F elegant proportions *pl*, elegance; **Form|schwä|che** F poor form; **~n zeigen** to be in *or* on poor form; **Form|stren|ge** F strict observance of form; **Form|tief** NT loss of form; **sich in einem ~ befinden** to be badly off form; **form|treu** ADJ = **formbeständig**

For|mu|lar [fɔrmu'laːɐ] NT -s, -e form

For|mu|lar|vor|schub M *(Comput)* form feed

for|mu|lie|ren [fɔrmu'liːrən] *ptp* **formuliert** VT to word, to phrase, to formulate; **... wenn ich es mal so ~ darf** ... if I might put it like that VI to use words skilfully *(Brit) or* skillfully *(US)*; **..., wie der Kanzler formulierte** ... as the chancellor put it; **wenn ich mal so ~ darf** if I might put it like that

For|mu|lie|rung F -, -en wording, phrasing *no pl*, formulation

For|mung ['fɔrmʊŋ] F -, -en **a** *no pl (= Formen)* forming, shaping; *(von Eisen)* moulding *(Brit)*, molding *(US)*; *(von Charakter)* moulding *(Brit)*, molding *(US)*, shaping, formation; *(von Wörtern)* articulation; **zur ~ muss das Eisen erhitzt werden** the iron has to be heated before it can be moulded *(Brit) or* molded *(US)* **b** *(= Form)* shape; *(von Felsen, Dünen etc auch)* formation

Form-: Form|ver|än|de|rung F change in the form; *(einer Sprache)* change in the forms; *(= Gestaltveränderung)* change in the shape; **eine kleine ~ vornehmen** to make a small modification; **Form|ver|stoß** M breach of form; **form|voll|en|det** ADJ perfect; *Vase etc* perfectly shaped; *Gedicht, Musikstück* perfectly structured ADV **er verabschiedete/verneigte sich ~** he took his leave/bowed with perfect elegance; **Form|vor|schrift** F formal requirement; **form|wid|rig** ADJ incorrect; *(Admin, Jur)* irregular; *Urkunde* incorrectly drawn up; **Form|wil|le** M *(geh)* striving for form

forsch [fɔrʃ] ADJ brash; *(dated: = schneidig)* dashing *(dated)* ADV brashly; **eine Sache ~ anpacken** to attack sth energetically *or* with vigour *(Brit) or* vigor *(US)*

for|schen [fɔrʃn] VI **a** *(= suchen)* to search (*nach* for), to seek *(liter)* (*nach jdm/etw* sb/sth); **in alten Papieren ~** to search in old papers; **nach der Wahrheit ~** to seek *or* search after truth **b** *(= Forschung betreiben)* to research; **über etw** *(acc)* **~** to research on *or* into sth VT *(Sw)* = **erforschen b**

for|schend ADJ *Blick* searching ADV searchingly; **etw ~ betrachten** to look at sth very closely; **jdn ~ ansehen** to look at sb searchingly, to give sb a searching look

For|scher ['fɔrʃɐ] M -s, -, **For|sche|rin** [-ərɪn] F -, -nen **a** *(= Wissenschaftler)* researcher; *(in Medizin, Naturwissenschaften)* research scientist **b** *(= Forschungsreisender)* explorer

For|scher-: For|scher|ar|beit F research; **For|scher|blick** M, *no pl (geh)* scientific eye; **For|scher|drang** M, *no pl (geh)* intellectual curiosity; *(als Entdecker)* urge to explore; **For|scher|geist** M *(geh)* inquiring mind; *(= Entdeckungsreisender)* explorer; *(= Entdeckergeist)* exploratory spirit; **der Mensch in seinem angeborenen ~ ist bestrebt, ...** man, with his inquiring mind, strives ...

For|sche|rin [-ərɪn] F → **Forscher**

for|sche|risch ['fɔrʃərɪʃ] ADJ research *attr*; *Begeisterung* for research; *Ehrgeiz* in the field of research; **eine ~e Höchstleistung** a triumph for research

Forsch|heit F -, -en brashness

For|schung ['fɔrʃʊŋ] F -, -en **a** research *no pl*; **eingehende ~en** intensive research; **ältere/verschiedene ~en** older/various studies; **~en betreiben** to research, to be engaged in research **b** *no pl (= Wissenschaft)* research *no art*; **~ und Lehre** research and teaching; **~ und Entwicklung** research and development, R&D

For|schungs- *in cpds* research; **For|schungs|ar|beit** F research; **For|schungs|auf|ga|be** F research assignment; *(= Forschungsauftrag eines Wissenschaftlers)* research duty; **For|schungs|auf|trag** M research assignment *or* contract; **For|schungs|bal|lon** M observation balloon; **For|schungs|be|reich** M = **Forschungsgebiet**; **For|schungs|be|richt** M research report; **For|schungs|drang** M exploratory urge; **For|schungs|er|geb|nis** NT result of the research; **neueste ~se** results of the latest research; **For|schungs|ge|biet** NT field of research; **ein/das ~ der Medizin** a/the field of medical research; **For|schungs|ge|gen|stand** M object of research; **For|schungs|ge|mein|schaft** F research council; **For|schungs|me|tho|de** F method of research; **For|schungs|mi|nis|ter(in)** M(F) minister of science; **For|schungs|mi|nis|te|ri|um** NT ministry of research and development; **For|schungs|ob|jekt** NT object of research; **For|schungs|rei|se** F expedition; **For|schungs|rei|sen|de(r)** MF *decl as adj* explorer; **For|schungs|sa|tel|lit** M research satellite; **For|schungs|schiff** NT research vessel; **For|schungs|se|mes|ter** NT sabbatical term; **For|schungs|sta|ti|on** F research station; **For|schungs|sti|pen|di|um** NT research fellowship; **For|schungs|tä|tig|keit** F research *no indef art*; **For|schungs|vor|ha|ben** NT research project; **For|schungs|zent|rum** NT research centre *(Brit) or* center *(US)*; **For|schungs|zweck** M purpose of the *or* our *etc* research; **für ~e** *pl*, **zu ~en** *pl* for research purposes *pl*; **For|schungs|zweig** M branch of research

Forst [fɔrst] M **-(e)s, -e(n)** forest

Forst-: **Forst|aka|de|mie** F school of forestry; **Forst|amt** NT forestry office; **Forst|as|ses|sor(in)** M(F) *graduate forestry official who has completed the probationary period*; **Forst|be|am|te(r)** M *decl as adj*, **Forst|be|am|tin** F forestry official

fors|ten ['fɔrstn] VT *(form)* to forest

Förs|ter ['fœrstɐ] M **-s, -**, **Förs|te|rin** [-ərın] F **-, -nen** forest warden *or* ranger *(US)*

Förs|te|rei [fœrstə'rai] F **-, -en** forest warden's *or* ranger's *(US)* lodge

Forst-: **Forst|fre|vel** M *(Jur)* offence *(Brit) or* offense *(US)* against the forest laws; **Forst|haus** NT forester's lodge; **Forst|meis|ter(in)** M(F) forestry commissioner, chief (forest) ranger *(US)*; **Forst|recht** NT forest law; **Forst|re|vier** NT forestry district; **Forst|scha|den** M forest damage *no pl*; **Forst|schäd|ling** M forest pest; **Forst|schu|le** F school of forestry; **Forst|ver|wal|tung** F forestry commission; **Forst|we|sen** NT, *no pl* forestry *no art*; **Forst|wirt(in)** M(F) graduate in forestry; **Forst|wirt|schaft** F forestry; **forst|wirt|schaft|lich** ADJ forestry *attr*; **nach ~en Gesichtspunkten** from the point of view of good forestry management; **Forst|wis|sen|schaft** F forestry

For|sy|thie [fɔr'zy:tsiə, *(Aus)* fɔr'zy:tiə] F **-, -n** forsythia

fort [fɔrt] ADV **a** *(= weg)* away; *(= verschwunden)* gone; **~ mit ihm/damit!** away with him/it!, take him/it away!; **etw ist ~** sth has gone *or* disappeared; **es war plötzlich ~** it suddenly disappeared; **die Katze ist schon seit gestern ~** the cat has been missing since yesterday; **er ist ~** he has left *or* gone; *(dial: = ist nicht zu Hause)* he isn't here; **weit ~** far away, a long way away; **von zu Hause ~** away from home; **wann sind Sie von zu Hause ~?** *(dial)* when did you leave home?; **nur ~ von hier!** *(geh)* let us begone *(old)*; **~ von hier!** *(geh)* begone! *(old)*, hence! *(old)*
b *(= weiter)* on; **und so ~** and so on, and so forth; **das ging immer so weiter und so ~ und so ~** *(inf)* that went on and on and on; **in einem ~** incessantly, continually

Fort [fo:ɐ] NT **-s, -s** fort

fort- PREF *in cpd vbs (= weg)* away → *auch* **weg-**

Fort-: **fort|ab** [fɔrt'lap] *(rare)*, **fort|an** [fɔrt'lan] *(geh)* ADV from this time on, henceforth *(old, liter)*, henceforward *(old)*; **fort+be|ge|ben** *ptp* **fortbegeben** VR *sep irreg (geh)* to depart, to leave; **sich aus dem Schloss** *etc* **~** to depart from *(form) or* to leave the castle *etc*; **Fort|be|stand** M, *no pl* continuance; *(von Staat, Institution)* continued existence; *(von Gattung etc)* survival; **fort+be|ste|hen** *ptp* **fortbestanden** VI *sep irreg* to continue; *(Staat, Institution)* to continue in existence; *(Zustand)* to continue (to exist); **fort+be|we|gen** *ptp* **fortbewegt** *sep* VT to move away VR to move; **Fort|be|we|gung** F, *no pl* locomotion; **Fort|be|we|gungs|mit|tel** NT means *sing* of locomotion; **fort+bil|den** VT *sep* **jdn/sich ~** to continue sb's/one's education; **Fort|bil|dung** F, *no pl* further education; **berufliche ~** further vocational training

Fort|bil|dungs-: **Fort|bil|dungs|kurs** M in-service training course; **Fort|bil|dungs|maß|nah|me** F continuing *or* further education *(esp Brit)* provision

Fort-: **fort+blei|ben** VI *sep irreg aux sein* to stay away; **Fort|blei|ben** NT **-s**, *no pl* absence; **fort+brin|gen** VT *sep irreg* to take away; *(zur Reparatur, Reinigung etc)* to take in; *Brief, Paket etc* to post *(Brit)*, to mail *(esp US)*; *(= zurückbringen)* to take back; *(= bewegen)* to move; **Fort|dau|er** F continuance, continuation; **fort+dau|ern** VI *sep* to continue; **fort|dau|ernd** ADJ continuing; *(in der Vergangenheit)* continued ADV constantly, continuously

for|te ['fɔrtə] ADV *(Mus, Pharm)* forte

For|te ['fɔrtə] NT **-s, -s** *or* **Forti** [-ti] forte

Fort-: **fort+ei|len** VI *sep (geh)* to hurry *or* hasten away; **fort+ent|wi|ckeln** *ptp* **fortentwickelt** *sep* VT to develop VR to develop; **Fort|ent|wick|lung** F, *no pl* development; **fort+exis|tie|ren** *ptp* **fortexistiert** VI *sep* = **fortbestehen**; **fort+fah|ren** *sep* VI **a** *aux sein (= wegfahren)* to go away; *(= abfahren)* to leave, to go; *(= einen Ausflug machen)* to go out **b** *aux haben or sein (= weitermachen)* to continue; **~, etw zu tun** to continue doing sth *or* to do sth; **in einer Tätigkeit ~** to continue with an activity; **ich fahre fort…** as I was about to say … VT *(= wegbringen)* to take away; *Wagen* to drive away; **Fort|fall** M discontinuance; **fort+fal|len** VI *sep irreg aux sein* to cease to exist; *(= nicht mehr zutreffend sein)* to cease to apply; *(Zuschuss etc)* to be discontinued *or* stopped; *(= abgeschafft werden)* to be abolished; **fort+flie|gen** VI *sep aux sein* to fly away *or* off; **fort+füh|ren** *sep* VT **a** *(= fortsetzen)* to continue, to carry on **b** *(= wegführen)* to take away; *(zu Fuß, fig)* to lead away VI *(fig)* to lead away; **Fort|füh|rung** F continuation; **Fort|gang** M, *no pl* **a** *(= Weggang)* departure *(aus* from*)*; **bei seinem ~** when he left, on his departure; **nach seinem ~** after he had left, after his departure **b** *(= Verlauf)* progress; **seinen ~ nehmen** to progress; **fort+ge|hen** VI *sep aux sein* **a** *(= weggehen)* to leave; **von zu Hause ~** to leave home; **geh fort!** go away!; **geh nicht fort!** don't go (away)! **b** *(= weitergehen)* to go on; **fort|ge|schrit|ten** ADJ advanced; **zu ~er Stunde wurden sie fröhlich** as the night wore on they got quite merry; **er kam zu ~er Stunde** he came at a late hour → *auch* **fortschreiten**; **Fort|ge|schrit|te|nen|kurs** M advanced course; **Fort|ge|schrit|te|ne(r)** ['fɔrtgəʃrıtnə] MF *decl as adj* advanced student; **fort|ge|setzt** ADJ continual, constant, incessant; *Betrug, Steuerhinterziehung, Handlung* repeated → *auch* **fortsetzen**; **fort|hin** [fɔrt'hın] ADV *(dated)* from this time on, henceforth *(old, liter)*, henceforward *(old)*

For|ti *pl von* **Forte**

For|ti|fi|ka|ti|on [fɔrtifika'tsio:n] F **-, -en** *(old Mil)* fortification

For|tis|si|mo [fɔr'tısimo] NT **-s, -s** *or* **Fortissimi** [-mi] fortissimo; **im ~ spielen** to play fortissimo

Fort-: **fort+ja|gen** *sep* VT *Menschen* to throw out *(aus, von* of*)*; *Tier, Kinder* to chase out *(aus, von* of*)* VI *aux sein* to race *or* career off; **fort+kom|men** VI *aux sein* **a** *(= wegkommen)* to get away; *(= weggebracht werden)* to be taken away; **mach, dass du fortkommst!** begone! *(old)*, be off! **b** *(= abhandenkommen)* to disappear, to vanish **c** *(= vorankommen)* to get on well; **im Leben ~** to get on in life *or* in the world; **Fort|kom|men** NT **a** *(lit, fig: = Weiterkommen)* progress; **jdn am ~ hindern** to hold sb back, to hinder sb's progress **b** *(= Auskommen)* **sein ~ finden** to find a means of earning one's living; **fort+kön|nen** VI *sep irreg* to be able to get away; **fort+las|sen** VT *sep irreg* **a** *(= weggehen lassen)* **jdn ~** to let sb go, to allow sb to go **b** *(= auslassen)* to leave out, to omit; **fort+lau|fen** VI *sep irreg aux sein* to run away; **der Hund ist mir fortgelaufen** the dog has run away from me; **meine Freundin ist mir fortgelaufen** my girlfriend has (gone off and) left me; **fort|lau|fend** ADJ *Handlung* ongoing; *Erscheinen* serial *attr*; *Zahlungen* regular; *(= andauernd)* continual ADV *(= andauernd)* continually; **die Handlung geht ~ weiter** the storyline unfolds steadily; **~ nummeriert** *(Geldscheine, Motoren)* serially numbered; *Blätter, Seiten* consecutively numbered; **fort+le|ben** VI *sep (liter)* to live on; **fort+lo|ben** VT **jdn auf einen Posten ~** to kick sb upstairs; **fort+lo|cken** VT *sep* to lure away; **fort+ma|chen** VR *sep (inf)* to clear out *or* off *(inf)*; **fort+müs|sen** VI *sep irreg* to have to go *or* leave; *(= ausgehen müssen)* to have to go out; *(Brief)* to have to go (off); **fort+neh|men** VT *sep irreg* to take away *(jdm* from sb*)*; **fort+pflan|zen** VR *sep (Mensch, Tier)* to reproduce; *(Pflanzen auch)* to propagate (itself); *(Schall, Wellen, Licht)* to travel, to be transmitted; *(Gerücht)* to spread

Fort|pflan|zung F, *no pl* reproduction; *(von Pflanzen)* propagation

Fort|pflan|zungs-: **fort|pflan|zungs|fä|hig** ADJ capable of reproduction; *Pflanze* capable of propagation; **Fort|pflan|zungs|fä|hig|keit** F reproductive capacity; *(von Pflanze)* capacity for propagation; **Fort|pflan|zungs|ge|schwin|dig|keit** F *(Phys)* speed of propagation; **Fort|pflan|zungs|me|di|zin** F reproductive medicine; **Fort|pflan|zungs|or|gan** NT reproductive organ; **Fort|pflan|zungs|trieb** M reproductive instinct; **fort|pflan|zungs|un|fä|hig** ADJ incapable of reproduction; *Pflanze* incapable of propagation

Fort-: **fort+räu|men** VT *sep (lit, fig)* to clear away; **fort+rei|sen** VI *sep aux sein* to go away; **fort+rei|ßen** VT *sep irreg* to snatch *or* tear away; *(Menge, Flut, Strom)* to sweep *or* carry away; *(fig)* to carry away; **jdn/etw mit sich ~** *(lit)* to carry *or* sweep sb/sth along; **fort+ren|nen** VI *sep irreg aux sein* to race *or* tear *(inf)* off *or* away; **fort+rü|cken** *sep* VT to move away VI *aux sein* to move away; **Fort|satz** M *(Anat)* process; **fort+schaf|fen** VT *sep* to remove; **fort+sche|ren** VR *sep (inf)* to clear off *(inf) (aus* out of*)*, to clear out *(inf) (aus* of*)*; **fort+schi|cken** VT *sep* to send away; *Brief etc* to send off; **fort+schlei|chen** VIR *sep irreg (inf)* to slink *or* creep away; **fort+schlep|pen** *sep* VT to drag away; *(fig) Fehler, Traditionen* to perpetuate VR to drag oneself along; *(fig) (Fehler, Traditionen)* to be perpetuated; *(Beziehung, Unterhaltung)* to limp along; **fort+schrei|ben** VT *sep irreg* **a** *Statistik etc* to extrapolate **b** *(= weiterführend aktualisieren) Programm etc* to continue; **Fort|schrei|bung** F *(von Statistik)* extrapolation; *(von Programm)* continuation; **fort+schrei|ten** VI *sep irreg aux sein (= vorwärtsschreiten)* to progress; *(= weitergehen)* to continue; *(Entwicklung, Sprache)* to develop; *(Wissenschaft)* to advance; *(Zeit)* to go *or* march *(liter)* on; **die Ausbreitung der Epidemie schreitet weiter fort** the epidemic is continuing to spread → *auch* **fortgeschritten**; **fort|schrei|tend** ADJ progressive; *Alter, Wissenschaft* advancing

Fort|schritt M advance; *(esp Pol)* progress *no pl*; **gute ~e machen** to make good progress, to get on *(inf) or* progress well; **~e erzielen** to make progress; **~e in der Medizin** advances in medicine; **das ist ein wesentlicher ~** that's a considerable step forward; **dem ~ dienen** to further progress

fort|schritt|lich ['fɔrtʃrıtlıç] ADJ progressive *(auch Pol)*; *Mensch, Ideen auch* forward-looking ADV progressively; **~ eingestellt sein** *or* **denken** to be progressive *or* forward-looking

Fort|schritt|lich|keit F **-**, *no pl* progressiveness

Fort|schritts-: **Fort|schritts|fa|na|ti|ker(in)** M(F) fanatical progressive; **fort|schritts|feind|lich** ADJ anti-progressive; **Fort|schritts|feind|lich|keit** F anti-progressiveness; **Fort|schritts|glau|be** M belief in progress; **fort|schritts|gläu|big** ADJ ~ **sein** to believe in progress; **das ~e 19. Jahrhundert** the 19th century with its belief in progress; **Fort|schritts|gläu|big|keit** F naïve belief in progress; **Fort|schritts|op|ti|mis|mus** M belief in progress

fort-: **fort+seh|nen** VR *sep* to long *or* yearn to be away (*aus* from); **fort+set|zen** *sep* VT to continue; *(nach Unterbrechung auch)* to resume; **den Weg zu Fuß ~** to continue on foot; **„wird fortgesetzt"** "to be continued" → *auch* **fortgesetzt** VR *(zeitlich)* to continue; *(räumlich)* to extend

Fort|set|zung ['fɔrtzɛtsʊŋ] F **-, -en** a *no pl (= das Fortsetzen)* continuation; *(esp nach Unterbrechung)* resumption b *(= folgender Teil) (Rad, TV)* episode; *(eines Romans)* instalment *(Brit)*, installment *(US)*; **ein Film in drei ~en** a film in three parts; **„Fortsetzung folgt"** "to be continued" c *(= Anschlussstück)* continuation

Fort|set|zungs-: **Fort|set|zungs|ge|schich|te** F serial; **Fort|set|zungs|ro|man** M serialized novel; **Fort|set|zungs|se|rie** F series

fort-: **fort+steh|len** VR *sep irreg (geh)* to steal *or* slip away; **sich aus etw ~** to steal *or* slip out of sth; **fort+stre|ben** VI *sep (geh)* to attempt *or* try to get away (*aus* from); **fort+stür|zen** VI *sep aux sein (geh)* to rush off *or* away; *(Pferd)* to bolt; **fort+trei|ben** *sep irreg* VT a *(= verjagen)* to drive away b *(= weitertragen)* to carry away c *(fig: = weitermachen)* to go *or* keep *or* carry on with; **wenn er es weiter so forttreibt wie bisher ...** if he goes *or* keeps *or* carries on as he has been (doing) ... VI *aux sein* to be carried away

For|tu|na [fɔr'tu:na] F - *(Myth)* Fortuna; *(fig)* Fortune

For|tune [fɔr'ty:n] F -, *no pl (geh)*, **For|tü|ne** [fɔr'ty:nə] F -, *no pl* good fortune; **politische ~ haben** to have good fortune in politics; **keine ~ haben** to have no luck

fort-: **fort+wäh|ren** VI *sep (geh)* to continue, to persist; **fort|wäh|rend** ADJ *no pred* constant, continual, incessant ADV constantly, continually, incessantly; **fort+wäl|zen** VT *sep* to roll away; **mit sich ~** to carry away (with it); **fort|weg** ['fɔrtvɛk] ADV *(rare)* the whole time, all the time; **er hat ~ geschwatzt** he was chattering the whole time *or* all the time; **fort+wir|ken** VI *sep* to continue to have an effect; **das wirkt noch bis heute fort** that still has an effect today; **das Gesehene wirkte noch lange in ihm fort** what he had seen affected him *or* went on having an effect on him for a long time; **das Fortwirken klassischer Ideale** the continued effect of classical ideals; **fort+wol|len** VI *sep* to want to get away (*aus* from); **Fort|zah|lung** F *(von Lohn, Gehalt)* continued payment; **fort+zeu|gen** VI *sep (liter)* to continue to have an effect; **fort+zie|hen** *sep irreg* VT to pull away; *(mit großer Anstrengung)* to drag away; *(Strom, Strudel)* to carry away VI *aux sein* a *(= weiterziehen)* to move on; *(Vögel)* to migrate b *(von einem Ort)* to move away (*aus* from); *(aus einer Wohnung)* to move out (*aus* of)

Fo|rum ['fo:rʊm] NT **-s, Foren** *or (Hist)* **Fora** ['fo:rən, 'fo:ra] forum; **etw vor das ~ der Öffentlichkeit bringen** to bring sth before the forum of public opinion

Fo|rums|dis|kus|si|on F, **Fo|rums|ge|spräch** NT forum (discussion)

For|ward ['fɔ:wəd, 'fo:ɐvart] M **-(s), -s** *(esp Aus Ftbl)* forward

Forz [fɔrts] M **-es, -e** *(dial inf)* = **Furz**

Fos|bu|ry|flop ['fɔsbərıflɔp] M Fosbury flop

fos|sil [fɔ'si:l] ADJ *attr* fossil *attr*, fossilized; *Brennstoff, Energie* fossil *attr*; **~ beheizte** *or* **~e Kraftwerke** fossil-fuelled *(Brit) or* fossil-fueled *(US)* power stations

Fos|sil [fɔ'si:l] NT **-s, -ien** [-liən] *(lit, fig)* fossil

fö|tal [fø'ta:l] ADJ foetal *(Brit)*, fetal *(US)*

Fö|ten *pl von* **Fötus**

Fo|to ['fo:to] NT **-s, -s** photo(graph), snap(-shot) *(inf)*; **ein ~ machen** to take a photo(-graph)

Fo|to M **-s, -s** *(dial inf)* camera

Fo|to- *in cpds (Sci)* photo → *auch* **Photo-**; **Fo|to|al|bum** NT photograph album; **Fo|to|ama|teur(in)** M(F) amateur photographer; **Fo|to|ap|pa|rat** M camera; **Fo|to|ar|bei|ten** PL photographic work *sing*; **Fo|to|ar|chiv** NT photo archives *pl*; **Fo|to|ar|ti|kel** PL photographic equipment *sing*; **Fo|to|ate|li|er** NT (photographic) studio; **Fo|to|aus|rüs|tung** F photographic equipment *sing*; **Fo|to|au|to|mat** M *(für Passfotos)* photo booth; **Fo|to-CD** [-tse:de:] F Photo CD®; **Fo|to|che|mie** F photochemistry; **fo|to|che|misch** ADJ photochemical; **Fo|to|ecke** F corner; **fo|to|elekt|risch** ADJ photoelectric; **Fo|to|fi|nish** NT *(Sport)* photo finish

fo|to|gen [foto'ge:n] ADJ photogenic

Fo|to|ge|schäft NT photographic shop

Fo|to|graf [foto'gra:f] M **-en, -en**, **Fo|to|gra|fin** [-'gra:fın] F **-, -nen** photographer

Fo|to|gra|fie [fotogra'fi:] F **-, -n** [-'fi:ən] a photography b *(= Bild)* photo(-graph)

fo|to|gra|fie|ren [fotogra'fi:rən] *ptp* **fotografiert** VT to photograph, to take a photo(graph) of; **sich ~ lassen** to have one's photo(graph) *or* picture taken; **sie lässt sich gut ~** she photographs well, she comes out well in photos VI to take photos *or* photographs

Fo|to|gra|fie|ren [fotogra'fi:rən] **-s**, *no pl (= Fotografie)* photography; *(als Handlung)* taking (of) photographs *or* pictures *(inf)*

fo|to|gra|fisch [foto'gra:fıʃ] ADJ photographic ADV photographically

Fo|to-: **Fo|to|in|dust|rie** F photographic industry; **Fo|to|jour|na|list(in)** M(F) photojournalist; **Fo|to|ko|pie** F photocopy; **fo|to|ko|pie|ren** [fotoko'pi:rən] *ptp* **fotokopiert** VT *insep* to photocopy, to make a photocopy of; **Fo|to|ko|pie|rer** M, **Fo|to|ko|pier|ge|rät** NT photocopier; **Fo|to|la|bor** NT photo lab; **Fo|to|la|bo|rant(in)** M(F) photographic lab(-oratory) assistant; **Fo|to|ma|te|ri|al** NT photographic materials *pl*; **fo|to|me|cha|nisch** ADJ photomechanical; **Fo|to|mo|dell** NT photographic model; **Fo|to|mon|ta|ge** F photomontage

Fo|ton ['fo:tɔn, fo'to:n] NT **-s, -en** [-'to:nən] photon

Fo|to-: **Fo|to|pa|pier** NT photographic paper; **Fo|to|re|por|ta|ge** F photo reportage *or* feature; **Fo|to|re|por|ter(in)** M(F) press photographer; **Fo|to|ro|man** M photo book; **Fo|to|satz** M *(Typ)* = **Lichtsatz**; **Fo|to|syn|the|se** [fotozʏn'te:zə, 'fo:tozʏnte:zə] F photosynthesis; **Fo|to|ta|sche** F camera bag; *(größer)* camera holdall; **Fo|to|ter|min** M photo call; **Fo|to|thek** [foto'te:k] F **-, -en** photographic collection; **fo|to|trop** [foto'tro:p] ADJ phototropic; **Fo|to|vol|ta|ik** [fotovɔl'ta:ık] F **-**, *no pl (Phys)* photovoltaics *sing*; **fo|to|vol|ta|isch** [-vɔl'ta:ıʃ] ADJ photovoltaic; **Fo|to|zeit|schrift** F photographic magazine; **Fo|to|zel|le** F photoelectric cell

Fö|tus ['fø:tʊs] M **-** *or* **-ses, Föten** *or* **-se** foetus *(Brit)*, fetus *(US)*

Fot|ze ['fɔtsə] F **-, -n** *(vulg)* cunt *(vulg)*

Föt|zel ['fœtsl] M **-s, -** *(Sw)* scoundrel, rogue

foul [faul] ADJ *(Sport)* **das war aber ~** *(inf)* that was a foul ADV **~ spielen** to foul

Foul [faul] NT **-s, -s** *(Sport)* foul

Foul|elf|me|ter ['faul-] M *(Ftbl)* penalty (kick)

fou|len ['faulən] VTI *(Sport)* to foul; **es wurde viel gefoult** there was a lot of fouling

Foul|spiel ['faul-] NT *(Sport)* foul play

Fou|ra|ge [fu'ra:ʒə] F **-**, *no pl (Mil old)* forage

Fox [fɔks] M **-(es), -e**, **Fox|ter|ri|er** M fox terrier

Fox|trott ['fɔkstrɔt] M **-s, -e** *or* **-s** foxtrot

Fo|yer [foa'je:] NT **-s, -s** foyer; *(in Hotel auch)* lobby, entrance hall

FPÖ [ɛfpe:'ø:] F - *abbr von* **Freiheitliche Partei Österreichs**

Fr. *abbr von* **Frau**

Fracht [fraxt] F **-, -en** a *(= Ladung)* freight *no pl*; *(von Flugzeug, Schiff auch)* cargo; *(= Güter auch)* payload; **etw per ~ schicken** to send sth freight, to freight sth b *(= Frachtpreis)* freight *no pl*, freightage *no pl*; *(bei Lastwagen)* carriage *no pl*; *(= Frachttarif)* freight/carriage rate

Fracht|brief M consignment note, waybill

Fracht|damp|fer M *(dated)* cargo *or* freight steamer

Frach|ten|bahn|hof M *(Aus)* freight *or* goods *(esp Brit)* depot

Frach|ter ['fraxtɐ] M **-s, -** freighter

Fracht-: **Fracht|flug|zeug** NT cargo *or* freight plane, (air) freighter; **fracht|frei** ADJ, ADV carriage paid *or* free; **Fracht|füh|rer(in)** M(F) *(form)* carrier; **Fracht|geld** NT freight, freightage; *(bei Lastwagen)* carriage; **Fracht|gut** NT (ordinary) freight *no pl*; **etw als ~ schicken** to send sth freight *or* as ordinary freight; **Fracht|kos|ten** PL freight charges *pl*; **Fracht|ma|schi|ne** F *(Aviat)* cargo *or* freight plane, (air) freighter; **Fracht|post|zent|rum** NT parcel depot; **Fracht|raum** M hold; *(= Ladefähigkeit)* cargo space; **Fracht|schiff** NT cargo ship, freighter; **Fracht|schiff|fahrt** F cargo shipping; **Fracht|sen|dung** F freight load; *(Aviat, Naut)* cargo of freight; **als ~** (as) freight; **Fracht|ta|rif** M freight rate *or* charge; **Fracht|ver|kehr** M goods traffic; **Fracht|zent|rum** NT *(für Gütertransport)* freight *or* goods *(esp Brit)* depot; *(von Post®)* parcel depot; **Fracht|zet|tel** M consignment note, waybill

Frack [frak] M **-(e)s, -s** *(inf) or* **=e** ['frɛkə] tails *pl*, tail coat; **im ~** in tails

Frack-: **Frack|hemd** NT dress shirt; **Frack|ho|se** F dress trousers *pl (esp Brit) or* pants *pl (esp US)*; **Frack|ja|cke** F tails *pl*, tail coat; **Frack|sau|sen** NT **~ haben** *(inf)* to be in a funk *(inf)*; **Frack|schoß** M coat-tail; **Frack|ver|leih** M dress hire (service); **Frack|wes|te** F waistcoat *or* vest *(US, worn with tails)*; **Frack|zwang** M requirement to wear tails; **(es herrscht) ~** tails are obligatory, you have to wear tails, it is white tie; **„Frackzwang"** "tails", "white tie"

Fra|ge ['fra:gə] ✪ 39.3, 42.1, 43.3, 53.1, 53.2, 53.5, 53.6 F **-, -n** question; *(= Rückfrage, Zwischenfrage auch)* query; *(= Problem auch)* problem; *(= Angelegenheit auch)* matter, issue *(esp Pol)*; **eine ~ zu etw** a question on sth; **jdm eine ~ stellen, an jdn eine ~ stellen** *or* **richten** to ask sb a question; **an jdn eine ~ haben** to have a question for sb; **gestatten Sie mir eine ~?** *(form)* might I ask a question?; *(in Diskussionen auch)* permit me to ask you a question *(form)*; **auf eine ~ mit Ja oder Nein antworten** to answer a question with a straight yes or no; **sind noch ~n?, hat jemand noch eine ~?** does anyone have any further questions?, are there any more *or* any further questions?; **auf eine dumme ~ (bekommt man) eine dumme Antwort** *(prov)* ask a silly question (get a silly answer) *(prov)*; **die deutsche ~** the German question *or* issue; **das ist (doch sehr) die ~** that's (just *or* precisely) the question/problem, that's the whole question/problem; **das ist die große ~** that's the big *or* sixty-four thousand dollar *(inf)* question; **das ist gar keine ~, natürlich dürfen Sie heute freinehmen** you don't even need to ask, of course you can take today off; **das ist gar keine ~, das steht** *or* **ist außer ~** there's no question *or* doubt about it; **dass ..., steht** *or* **ist außer ~** that ... is beyond question, ..., there's no question *or* doubt about it; **ohne ~** without question *or* doubt; **in ~ kommen** to be possible; *Bewerber* to be worth considering; **sollte er für diese Stelle in ~ kommen, ...** if he should be considered for this position ...; **in ~ kommende Möglichkeiten** possible opportunities; **für jdn/etw nicht in ~ kommen** to be out of the question for sb/sth; **das kommt (überhaupt) nicht in ~!** that's (quite) out of the question; **etw in ~ stellen** to question sth, to query sth, to call sth into question; **eine ~ der Zeit/des Geldes** a question *or* matter of time/money → *auch* **infrage**

-fra|ge F *suf in cpds* question of; *(= Problem auch)* problem of; **die Arbeitslosenfrage** the unemployment issue; **eine Zeit- und Kostenfrage** a question of time and money

Fra|ge-: **Fra|ge|bo|gen** M questionnaire; *(= Formular)* form; **Fra|ge|bo|gen|ak|ti|on** F poll; **Fra|ge|für|wort** NT interrogative pronoun

fra|gen ['fra:gn] ✪ 28.1, 29, 33.2 VTI to ask; **nach** *or* **wegen** *(inf)* **jdm ~** to ask after sb; *(in Hotel etc)* to ask for sb; **ich fragte sie nach den Kindern** I asked her how the children were doing; **nach jds Namen/Alter/dem Weg ~** to ask sb's name/age/the way; **nach Arbeit/Post ~** to ask whether there is/was any work/mail; **nach den Ursachen ~** to inquire as to the causes; **ich fragte sie nach ihren Wünschen** I asked her what she wanted; **ich habe nicht nach Einzelheiten gefragt** I didn't ask any details; **nach den Folgen ~** to bother *or* care about the consequences; **er fragte nicht danach, ob ...** he didn't bother *or* care whether ...; **wegen etw ~** to ask about sth; **frag (mich/ihn) lieber nicht** you'd better not ask (me/him) that; **das frage ich dich!** I could ask you the same; **da fragst du noch?** you still have to ask?, you still don't know?; **frag nicht so dumm!** don't ask silly questions; **du fragst zu viel** you ask too many questions; **da fragst du mich zu viel** *(inf)* I really couldn't say; **man wird ja wohl noch ~ dürfen** *(inf)* I was only asking *(inf)*, there's no law against asking, is there? *(inf)*; **wenn ich (mal) ~ darf** if I may *or* might ask; **ohne lange zu ~** without asking a lot of questions → *auch* **gefragt**

VR to wonder; **das/da frage ich mich** I wonder; **das frage ich mich auch** that's just what I was wondering; **ja, das fragt man sich** yes, that's the question; **es fragt sich, ob ...** it's debatable *or* questionable whether *or* if ...; **man fragt sich, ob ...** one wonders whether *or* if ...; **da muss man sich ~, ob ...** you *or* one can't help wondering whether *or* if ...; **ich frage mich, wie/wo ...** I'd like to know how/where ..., I really wonder how/where ...

fra|gend ADJ *Blick* questioning, inquiring; *(Gram)* interrogative ADV **jdn ~ ansehen** to give sb a questioning look

Fra|gen-: **Fra|gen|ka|ta|log** M package *or* slew *(US inf)* of questions; **ein ganzer ~** a long list of questions; **Fra|gen|kom|plex** M, **Fra|gen|kreis** M set of questions

Fra|ger ['fra:gɐ] M **-s, -**, **Fra|ge|rin** [-ərɪn] F **-, -nen** questioner; **wer ist denn der lästige ~?** who is this wretched person who keeps asking questions?

Fra|ge|rei [fra:gə'rai] F **-, -en** questions *pl*

Fra|ge-: **Fra|ge|satz** M *(Gram)* interrogative sentence; *(= Nebensatz)* interrogative clause; **Fra|ge|stel|ler** [-ʃtɛlɐ] M **-s, -**, **Fra|ge|stel|le|rin** [-ərɪn] F **-, -nen** questioner; *(= Interviewer)* interviewer; **Fra|ge|stel|lung** F **a** formulation of a question; **das ist eine falsche ~** the question is wrongly put *or* stated *or* formulated **b** *(= Frage)* question; **Fra|ge|stun|de** F *(Parl)* question time *no art (Brit)*; **Fra|ge-und-Ant|wort-Spiel** NT question and answer game; **Fra|ge|wort** NT *pl* **-wörter** interrogative (particle); **Fra|ge|zei|chen** NT question mark *(auch fig)*, interrogation mark *or* point *(form)*; **hinter diese Behauptung muss man ein dickes** *or* **großes ~ setzen** *(fig)* this statement should be taken with a large pinch of salt; **dastehen/dasitzen wie ein ~** to slouch

fra|gil [fra'gi:l] ADJ *(geh)* fragile

Fra|gi|li|tät [fragili'tɛ:t] F **-**, *no pl (geh)* fragility

frag|lich ['fra:klɪç] ✪ 53.6 ADJ **a** *(= zweifelhaft)* uncertain; *(= fragwürdig)* doubtful, questionable; **eine ~e Sache** a moot point **b** *attr (= betreffend)* in question; *Angelegenheit* under discussion; **zu der ~en Zeit** at the time in question

Frag|lich|keit F **-**, *no pl (= Zweifelhaftigkeit)* uncertainty; *(= Fragwürdigkeit)* doubtfulness

frag|los ADV undoubtedly, unquestionably

Frag|ment [frag'mɛnt] NT **-(e)s, -e** fragment; **~ bleiben** to remain a fragment

frag|men|ta|risch [fragmɛn'ta:rɪʃ] ADJ fragmentary ADV **die Manuskripte sind nur ~ erhalten** only fragments of the manuscript have been preserved; **~ überlieferte Texte** fragmentary texts

frag|wür|dig ADJ **a** doubtful, dubious **b** *(pej) Lokal, Mensch, Kreise, Geschäfte* dubious

Frag|wür|dig|keit F **-, -en a** doubtful *or* dubious nature, doubtfulness **b** *(pej: von Lokal, Mensch, Kreisen, Geschäften)* dubious nature

frais ['frɛ:z], **frai|se** ['frɛ:zə] ADJ *inv (Aus Fashion)* strawberry(-coloured) *(Brit)*, strawberry(-colored) *(US)*

Frai|sen ['fraizn] PL *(Aus Med)* **die ~** (infant) spasms *pl*

Frak|tal [frak'ta:l] NT **-s, -e** fractal

Frak|ti|on [frak'tsio:n] F **-, -en a** *(Pol)* ≈ parliamentary *or* congressional *(US)* party; *(von mehreren Parteien)* ≈ coalition party; *(= Sondergruppe)* group, faction **b** *(Aus: = Ortsteil)* area **c** *(Chem)* fraction

frak|ti|o|nell [fraktsio'nɛl] *(Pol)* ADJ **~e Gruppen** factions within the parliamentary *etc* party ADV **~ entschieden** decided by the parliamentary *etc* party

frak|ti|o|nie|ren [fraktsio'ni:rən] *ptp* **fraktioniert** VT *(Chem)* to fractionate

Frak|ti|ons- *in cpds (Pol)* party; **Frak|ti|ons|bil|dung** F formation of factions/a faction; **Frak|ti|ons|füh|rer(in)** M(F) party whip, floor leader *(US)*; **frak|ti|ons|los** ADJ *Abgeordneter* independent; **Frak|ti|ons|mit|glied** NT member of a parliamentary *etc* party; **Frak|ti|ons|sit|zung** F party meeting; **Frak|ti|ons|spal|tung** F party split; *(auf Dauer)* split into two parties; **Frak|ti|ons|spre|cher(in)** M(F) party spokesperson; **Frak|ti|ons|stär|ke** F **a** numerical strength of a/the parliamentary *etc* party **b** *(= erforderliche Mitgliederzahl) numerical strength required for recognition of a parliamentary party*; **Frak|ti|ons|sta|tus** M party status; **Frak|ti|ons|vor|sit|zen|de(r)** MF *decl as adj* party whip, floor leader *(US)*; **Frak|ti|ons|vor|stand** M ≈ party executive; **Frak|ti|ons|zwang** M requirement to vote in accordance with party policy; **unter ~ stehen** to be under the whip

Frak|tur [frak'tu:ɐ] F **-, -en a** *(Typ)* Gothic print, Fraktur; **(mit jdm) ~ reden** *(inf)* to be blunt (with sb) **b** *(Med)* fracture

Frak|tur|schrift F Gothic script

Frame [fre:m] NT **-, -s** *(Comput: von Browser)* frame

Franc [frã:] M **-s, -s** *(Hist)* franc

Fran|chise ['frɛntʃaiz] M **-**, *no pl* franchise

Fran|chise-: **Fran|chise-Ge|ber(in)** M(F) franchisor; **Fran|chise-Neh|mer(in)** M(F) franchisee

Fran|chi|sing ['frɛntʃaizɪŋ] NT **-s**, *no pl* franchising

Fran|ci|um ['frantsiʊm] NT **-s**, *no pl (abbr* **Fr**) francium

frank [fraŋk] ADV **~ und frei** frankly, openly

Fran|ke ['fraŋkə] M **-n, -n** *(Geog)* Franconian; *(Hist)* Frank

Fran|ken ['fraŋkn] NT **-s** Franconia

Fran|ken M **-s, - (Schweizer) ~** (Swiss) franc

Fran|ken|wein M Franconian wine

Frank|furt ['fraŋkfʊrt] NT **-s ~ (am Main)** Frankfurt (on the Main); **~ (Oder)** Frankfurt on the Oder

Frank|fur|ter ['fraŋkfʊrtɐ] ADJ Frankfurt *attr*; **~ Buchmesse** Frankfurt book fair

Frank|fur|ter ['fraŋkfʊrtɐ] M **-s, -** *(inf: = Würstchen)* frankfurter

Frank|fur|ter ['fraŋkfʊrtɐ] M **-s, -**, **Frank|fur|te|rin** [-ərɪn] F **-, -nen** *(= Einwohner Frankfurts)* Frankfurter

frank|fur|te|risch ['fraŋkfʊrtərɪʃ] *(inf)*, **frank|fur|tisch** ['fraŋkfʊrtɪʃ] ADJ Frankfurt *attr*; **er spricht Frankfurterisch** *or* **Frankfurtisch** he speaks the Frankfurt dialect

fran|kie|ren [fraŋ'ki:rən] *ptp* **frankiert** VT to stamp; *(mit Maschine)* to frank

Fran|kier|ma|schi|ne F franking machine

Fran|kie|rung F **-, -en** franking; *(= Porto auch)* postage

Frän|kin ['frɛŋkɪn] F **-, -nen** Franconian (woman)

frän|kisch ['frɛŋkɪʃ] ADJ Franconian

Fränk|ler ['frɛŋklɐ] M **-s, -**, **Fränk|li** ['frɛŋkli] NT **-s, -** *(inf) (Sw)* franc (piece)

fran|ko ['fraŋko] ADV *(Comm)* carriage paid; *(von Postsendungen)* post-free *(Brit)*, postpaid

Fran|ko-: **Fran|ko|ka|na|dier(in)** M(F) French-Canadian; **fran|ko|ka|na|disch** ADJ French-Canadian; **Fran|ko|ma|nie** F *(geh)* Francomania; **fran|ko|phil** [fraŋko'fi:l] ADJ *(geh)* Francophile; **Fran|ko|phi|le(r)** [fraŋko'fi:lə] MF *decl as adj* Francophile; **Fran|ko|phi|lie** [fraŋkofi'li:] F **-**, *no pl (geh)* Francophilia; **fran|ko|phob** [fraŋko'fo:p] ADJ *(geh)* Francophobe; **Fran|ko|pho|bie** [fraŋkofo'bi:] F, *no pl (geh)* Francophobia; **fran|ko|fon** [fraŋko'fo:n] ADJ francophone; **Fran|ko|fo|nie** [fraŋkofo'ni:] F **-**, *no pl* francophonia; **fran|ko|phon** *etc* = **frankofon** *etc*

Frank|reich ['fraŋkraiç] NT **-s** France

Fräns|chen ['frɛnsçən] NT **-s, -** *dim von* **Franse**

Fran|se ['franzə] F **-, -n** *(lose)* (loose) thread; *(von Haar)* strand of hair; **~n** *(= Pony)* fringe *(Brit)*, bangs *pl (US)*; **ein mit ~n besetzter Schal** a shawl with a fringe, a fringed shawl

fran|sen ['franzn] VI to fray (out)

fran|sig ['franzɪç] ADJ *(Sew)* fringed *no adv*; *Haar* straggly *no adv*; *(= ausgefasert)* frayed *no adv*

Franz [frants] M **-'** *or* **-ens** Francis; *(bei Deutschen)* Franz

Franz [frants] NT **-**, *no pl (Sch inf: = Französisch)* French

Franz-: **Franz|band** [-bant] M *pl* **-bände** leather binding; **ein ~-Buchrücken** a leather spine; **Franz|brannt|wein** M alcoholic liniment

Fran|zis|ka|ner [frantsɪs'ka:nɐ] M **-s, -** *(Eccl)* Franciscan (friar)

Fran|zis|ka|ne|rin [frantsɪs'ka:nərɪn] F **-, -nen** *(Eccl)* Franciscan (nun)

Fran|zis|ka|ner|or|den M *(Eccl)* Franciscan Order, Order of St. Francis

Franz|mann ['frants-] M *pl* **-männer** *(dated sl)* Frenchie *(inf)*, frog *(pej inf)*

Fran|zo|se [fran'tso:zə] M **-n, -n a** Frenchman/French boy; **er ist ~** he's French; **die ~n** the French **b** *(= Werkzeug)* adjustable spanner, monkey wrench

Fran|zo|sen-: **fran|zo|sen|feind|lich** ADJ anti-French; **Fran|zo|sen|krank|heit** F *(old)* French disease *(old)*, syphilis

Fran|zö|sin [fran'tsø:zɪn] F **-, -nen** Frenchwoman/French girl; **sie ist ~** she's French

fran|zö|sisch [fran'tsø:zɪʃ] ADJ French; **die ~e Schweiz** French-speaking Switzerland; **die Französische Revolution** the French Revolution; **die ~e Krankheit** *(old)* the French disease *(old)*, syphilis; **~es Bett** double bed; **~e Spielkarten** ordinary playing cards; **~ kochen** to do French cooking; **(auf) ~ Abschied nehmen** to leave without saying goodbye; **sich (auf) ~ empfehlen** to leave without saying goodbye; *(= ohne zu zahlen)* to leave without paying; *(= sich unerlaubt entfernen)* to take French leave; **es auf Französisch** *or* **~ machen** *(inf)* to have oral sex → *auch* **deutsch**

Fran|zö|sisch(e) [fran'tsø:zɪʃ] NT French → *auch* **Deutsch(e)**

fran|zö|sisch|spra|chig [-ʃpra:xɪç] ADJ French-speaking, francophone → *auch* **deutschsprachig**

frap|pant [fra'pant] *(geh)* ADJ *Schnelligkeit, Entdeckung* remarkable, astounding; *Verbesserung, Wirkung, Ähnlichkeit, Beispiele auch* striking ADV remarkably; **auf jdn ~ wirken** to astound sb

frap|pie|ren [fra'pi:rən] *ptp* **frappiert** VT *(= verblüffen)* to astound, to astonish, to amaze VI *(Sache)* to be astounding *or* astonishing

frap|pie|rend ADJ astonishing, astounding

Frä|se ['frɛ:zə] F -, -n **a** *(= Werkzeug)* milling cutter; *(für Holz)* moulding *(Brit) or* molding *(US)* cutter; *(= Bodenfräse)* rotary hoe **b** *(= Bart)* chinstrap (beard)

frä|sen ['frɛ:zn] VT to mill, to mill-cut; *Holz* to mould *(Brit)*, to mold *(US)*

Frä|ser ['frɛ:zɐ] M **-s, -** milling cutter; *(für Holz)* moulding *(Brit) or* molding *(US)* cutter

Frä|ser ['frɛ:zɐ] M **-s, -**, **Frä|se|rin** [-ərɪn] F **-, -nen** milling cutter

Fräs|ma|schi|ne F milling machine

fraß *pret von* **fressen**

Fraß [fra:s] M **-es, -e** **a** food; *(pej inf)* muck *(inf) no indef art*; **etw einem Tier zum ~ vorwerfen** to feed sth to an animal; **jdn den Kritikern zum ~ vorwerfen** to throw sb to the critics **b** *(= Abfressen)* **vom ~ befallen** eaten away

Fra|ter ['fra:tɐ] M **-s, Fratres** ['fra:tre:s] *(Eccl)* Brother

fra|ter|ni|sie|ren [fratɛrni'zi:rən] *ptp* **fraternisiert** VI to fraternize

Fra|ter|ni|sie|rung F **-, -nen** fraternization

Fratz [frats] M **-es, -e** *or (Aus)* **-en, -en** **a** *(pej)* brat **b** *(= schelmisches Mädchen)* rascal, scallywag *(inf)*

Frätz|chen ['frɛtsçən] NT **-s, -** *dim von* **Fratz** *von* **Fratze**

Frat|ze ['fratsə] F **-, -n** **a** grotesque face **b** *(= Grimasse)* grimace; *(inf: = Gesicht)* face, phiz *(Brit dated inf)*; *(fig: = Zerrbild)* caricature; **jdm eine ~ schneiden** to pull *or* make a face at sb; **eine ~ ziehen, das Gesicht zu einer ~ verziehen** to pull *or* make a face, to grimace

frat|zen|haft ADJ grotesque

frau [frau] INDEF PRON *proposed feminist alternative to "man"* → **man**

Frau [frau] F **-, -en** **a** *(= weiblicher Mensch)* woman; **zur ~ werden** to become a woman; **von ~ zu ~** woman to woman; **Unsere Liebe ~** *(Eccl)* our blessed Lady, the blessed Virgin **b** *(= Ehefrau)* wife; **sich** *(dat)* **eine ~ nehmen** *(dated)* to marry, to take a wife *(old)*; **willst du meine ~ werden?** will you marry me?, will you be my wife?; **jdn zur ~ haben** to be married to sb; **seine zukünftige ~** his bride-to-be; **seine geschiedene ~** his ex-wife **c** *(= Anrede)* madam; *(mit Namen)* Mrs; *(für eine unverheiratete Frau)* Miss, Ms; **liebe ~!** *(dated)* my dear lady!; **~ Doktor** doctor; **Ihre (liebe) ~ Mutter/Schwester** *(form)* your good mother/sister; **~ Nachbarin** *(old)* neighbour *(Brit old) or* neighbor *(US old)*

Frau|chen ['frauçən] NT **-s, -** *dim von* **Frau** *(inf: von Hund)* mistress; **geh zum ~** go to your mistress

Frau|en- *in cpds* women's; *(einer bestimmten Frau)* woman's; *(Sport)* ladies', women's; **Frau|en|an|teil** M percentage *or* proportion of women; **Frau|en|ar|beit** F **a** *(= Arbeit für Frauen, von Frauen)* female *or* women's labour *(Brit) or* labor *(US)*; **das ist keine ~** that's no job for a woman; **niedrig bezahlte ~** badly paid jobs for women **b** *(= Arbeit zugunsten der Frau)* work among women; **in der ~ tätig sein** to be involved in work among women; **Frau|en|art** F **nach ~** *(dated)* as women do; **Frau|en|arzt** M, **Frau|en|ärz|tin** F gynaecologist *(Brit)*, gynecologist *(US)*; **Frau|en|be|auf|trag|te(r)** MF *decl as adj (in Gewerkschaft etc)* women's representative; *(= Beamter)* officer for women's issues; **Frau|en|be|ruf** M career for women; **frau|en|be|wegt** ADJ feminist; **Frau|en|be|weg|te(r)** [-bəve:ktə] MF *decl as adj* feminist; **Frau|en|be|we|gung** F women's *(auch Hist) or* feminist movement; **Frau|en|blatt** NT women's magazine; **Frau|en|buch** NT women's book; **Frau|en|chor** M ladies' *or* female choir; **Frau|en|eman|zi|pa|ti|on** F female emancipation *no art*, emancipation of women; *(in der heutigen Zeit auch)* women's lib(eration); **Frau|en|fach|schu|le** F domestic science college; **Frau|en|feind** M misogynist; **frau|en|feind|lich** ADJ anti-women *pred*; *Mensch, Verhalten auch* misogynous; **Frau|en|feind|lich|keit** F misogyny; *(im Berufsleben)* discrimination against women; **Frau|en|fra|ge** F question of women's rights; **frau|en|freund|lich** ADJ pro-women *pred*; **Frau|en|freund|lich|keit** F positive attitude toward(s) women; **Frau|en|front** F women's front; **Frau|en|funk** M woman's radio, ≈ Woman's Hour *(Brit)*; **Frau|en|ge|fäng|nis** NT women's prison; **Frau|en|ge|schich|te** F affair with a woman; **~n** *(= Affären)* womanizing; *(= Erlebnisse)* sexploits *pl (hum inf)*, experiences with women *pl*; **Frau|en|ge|stalt** F female figure; *(Liter, Art)* female character; **Frau|en|grup|pe** F women's group; **Frau|en|haar** NT **a** woman's hair **b** *(Bot)* maidenhair (fern); **frau|en|haft** ADJ womanly *no adv*; **Frau|en|hand** F **von (zarter) ~** by a woman's fair hand; **Frau|en|has|ser** [-hasɐ] M **-s, -** misogynist, woman-hater; **Frau|en|haus** NT **a** women's refuge **b** *(Ethnologie)* women's house; **Frau|en|heil|kun|de** F gynaecology *(Brit)*, gynecology *(US)*; **Frau|en|held** M lady-killer; **Frau|en|ken|ner** M connoisseur of women; **Frau|en|klei|der** PL women's clothes *pl or* clothing *sing*; **Frau|en|kli|nik** F gynaecological *(Brit) or* gynecological *(US)* hospital *or* clinic; **Frau|en|klos|ter** NT convent, nunnery *(old)*; **Frau|en|krank|heit** F, **Frau|en|lei|den** NT gynaecological *(Brit) or* gynecological *(US)* disorder; **Facharzt für ~en und Geburtshilfe** gynaecologist *(Brit) or* gynecologist *(US)* and obstetrician; **Frau|en|li|te|ra|tur** F women's literature; *(emanzipatorisch)* feminist writings *pl or* literature; **Frau|en|man|tel** M *(Bot)* lady's mantle; **Frau|en|mord** M murder of a woman; **Frau|en|mör|der(in)** M(F) murderer *(of women/a woman)*; **Frau|en|or|den** M *(Eccl)* women's order; **Frau|en|po|li|tik** F feminist politics *sing or pl*; **Frau|en|quo|te** F quota for women; **Frau|en|recht|ler** [-rɛçtlɐ] M **-s, -**, **Frau|en|recht|le|rin** [-ərɪn] F **-, -nen** feminist; *(in der heutigen Zeit auch)* Women's Libber *(inf)*; **frau|en|recht|le|risch** [-rɛçtlərɪʃ] ADJ feminist ADV **sich ~ betätigen** to be involved in women's rights *or (in der heutigen Zeit auch)* Women's Lib; **Frau|en|re|fe|rat** NT women's department; **Frau|en|re|fe|rent(in)** M(F) consultant on women's issues; **Frau|en|sa|che** F **a** *(= Frauenangelegenheit)* women's affair; **das ist ~** that's women's business **b** *(euph: = Menstruation)* women's curse; **Frau|en|schän|der** [-ʃɛndɐ] M **-s, -** rapist; **Frau|en|schuh** M, *no pl (Bot)* lady's slipper *no pl*; **Frau|en|sport** M women's sport; **Frau|en|sta|ti|on** F women's ward; **Frau|en|stim|me** F woman's voice; *(Parl)* woman's vote; **~n** women's voices/votes; **Frau|en|stimm|recht** NT vote for women, female suffrage *no art*; **Frau|en|tausch** M wife-swapping; *(Anthropologie)* exchange of partners; **Frau|en|treff** M *(inf)* women's meeting place *or* haunt *(inf) or* hangout *(inf)*; **Frau|en|typ** M **a** feminine type (of woman); **mütterlicher ~** motherly type of woman **b** *(inf)* ladies' man; **Frau|en|über|schuss** M surplus of women; **Frau|en|ver|band** M, **Frau|en|ver|ein** M women's association *or* society; **Frau|en|wahl|recht** NT vote for women, female suffrage *no art*; **Frau|en|zeit|schrift** F women's magazine; **Frau|en|zent|rum** NT women's advice centre *(Brit) or* center *(US)*; **Frau|en|zim|mer** NT *(old, dated)* woman; *(hum)* woman, female *(inf)*, broad *(US inf)*

Frau|ens- ['frauəns-]: **Frau|ens|leu|te** PL *(hum inf)* womenfolk *pl*; **Frau|ens|per|son** F female person; *(hum inf)* female *(inf)*, broad *(US inf)*

Fräu|lein ['frɔylain] NT **-s, -** *or (inf)* **-s** *(dated)* **a** *(= unverheiratete weibliche Person)* young lady; **ein altes** *or* **älteres ~** an elderly spinster **b** *(= Anrede)* Miss; **Ihr ~ Tochter/Braut** your daughter/bride **c** *(= weibliche Angestellte)* young lady; *(= Verkäuferin)* assistant; *(= Kellnerin)* waitress; *(= Lehrerin)* teacher, mistress; **~!** Miss!; *(= Kellnerin auch)* waitress!; **das ~ vom Amt** the operator, the switchboard girl

Fräu|lein|wun|der NT girl wonder

frau|lich ['fraulɪç] ADJ feminine; *(= reif)* womanly *no adv*

Frau|lich|keit F **-**, *no pl* femininity; *(= frauliche Reife)* womanliness

Freak [fri:k] M **-s, -s** *(inf)* freak *(inf)*

frea|kig ['fri:kɪg] ADJ *(inf)* freaky *(inf)*

frech [frɛç] ADJ **a** *(= unverschämt)* cheeky *(esp Brit)*, fresh *pred (esp US)*, impudent; *Lüge* brazen, bare-faced *no adv*; **~ werden** to get cheeky *etc*; **halt deinen ~en Mund!** (you) shut up and stop being cheeky *etc*; **~ wie Oskar** *(inf) or* **wie ein Spatz sein** *(inf)* to be a cheeky little devil *(Brit inf)*, to be a little monkey **b** *(= herausfordernd) Kleidung, Texte etc* saucy *(inf)* ADV *lachen* impudently; *anlügen* brazenly; **jdm ~ kommen** to get cheeky *etc* with sb; **sich ~ benehmen** to be cheeky *etc*

Frech|dachs M *(inf)* cheeky monkey *(Brit inf) or* devil *(Brit inf)*, monkey, smart aleck *(US)*

Frech|heit F **-, -en** **a** *no pl (= Verhalten)* impudence; *(esp von Kindern)* cheekiness *(esp Brit)*, impudence; **das ist der Gipfel der ~** that's the height of impudence; **die ~ haben** *or* **besitzen, ... zu ...** to have the cheek *(esp Brit) or* nerve *(inf) or* impudence to ... **b** *(= Äußerung, Handlung)* piece *or* bit of cheek *(esp Brit) or* impudence; **sich** *(dat)* **einige ~en erlauben** *or* **herausnehmen** to be a bit cheeky *(esp Brit) or* fresh *(esp US)*; **solche ~en** what cheek *(esp Brit) or* impudence

Free|mail F *(Internet)* freemail, free web-based e-mail

Free|sie ['fre:ziə] F **-, -n** freesia

Free|ware ['fri:wɛ:ɐ] F **-, -s** *(Comput)* freeware

Fre|gat|te [fre'gatə] F **-, -n** frigate

Fre|gat|ten|ka|pi|tän(in) M(F) commander

Fre|gatt|vo|gel [fre'gat-] M frigate bird

frei [frai]

1 ADJEKTIV 2 ADVERB

1 – ADJEKTIV

a = unbehindert free; **frei von etw** free of sth; **sich von etw frei halten** to avoid sth; *von Vorurteilen etc* to be free of sth; *von Verpflichtungen* to keep oneself free of sth; **sich von etw frei machen** to free oneself from sth; **die Straße frei geben/machen** to open/clear the road; **jdm den Weg frei geben** to let sb past *or* by; **sie hatte einen freien Blick aufs Meer** she had a clear view of the sea; **der Film ist frei (für Jugendliche) ab 16 (Jahren)** this film is suitable for persons aged 16 years and over; **frei sein** *(Sport)* to be free *or* not marked; **ich bin so frei** *(form)* may I?

♦ **frei + Substantiv**

Siehe auch unter dem Eintrag für das jeweilige Substantiv.

freier Durchgang thoroughfare; **von Kiel nach Hamburg hatten wir freie Fahrt** we had a clear run from Kiel to Hamburg; **einem Zug freie Fahrt geben** to give a train the "go" signal; **der Polizist gab uns freie Fahrt** the policeman signalled *(Brit) or* signaled *(US)* us on; **für etw freie Fahrt geben** *(fig)* to give sth the go-ahead; **der freie Fall** *(Phys)* free fall; **auf freiem Fuß sein** to be free; **freie Hand haben** to have a free hand; **jdm freie Hand lassen** to give sb free rein, to give sb a free hand; **das Recht der freien Rede** *or* **auf freie Rede** the right of free speech, the right to freedom of speech; **freie Rhythmen** free verse; **aus freien Stücken** of one's own free will; **jdm zur freien Verfügung stehen** to be completely at sb's disposal; **aus freiem Willen** of one's own free will; **freier Zugang** unlimited *or* unrestricted access; **freier Zutritt** unrestricted access → **Lauf**

b [= unabhängig] free; *Schriftsteller, Journalist etc* freelance; *(= nicht staatlich)* private

♦ **frei + Substantiv**

Siehe auch unter dem Eintrag für das jeweilige Substantiv.

freier Beruf independent profession; **Freie Demokratische Partei** Free Democratic Party; **Freie Deutsche Jugend** *(DDR) youth wing of the former East German Socialist Unity Party;* **Freier Deutscher Gewerkschaftsbund** *(DDR) Trades Union Congress of the former East Germany;* **Freie Hansestadt Bremen** Free Hansa Town of Bremen; **Freie und Hansestadt Hamburg** Free Hansa Town of Hamburg; **freier Markt** free market; **freie Marktwirtschaft** free-market economy; **freier Mitarbeiter** freelance, freelancer; **freier Mitarbeiter sein** to be freelance; **als freier Mitarbeiter arbeiten** to work freelance; **freie Reichsstadt** *(Hist)* free city of the Empire; **freie Tankstelle** independent petrol *(Brit) or* gas *(US)* station; **die freie Wirtschaft** private enterprise; **in die freie Wirtschaft gehen** to go into the private sector

c [= verfügbar] *Mittel, Geld* available; *Zeit* free; **Herr Mayer ist jetzt frei** Mr Mayer is free now; **ich bin jetzt frei für ihn** I can see him now; *(am Telefon)* I can speak to him now

d [= arbeitsfrei] **morgen/Mittwoch ist frei** tomorrow/Wednesday is a holiday; **sich frei machen** *(= freie Zeit einplanen)* to arrange to be free → *auch* **freibekommen, freigeben, freihaben, freinehmen**

e [= ohne Hilfsmittel] **etw aus freier Hand zeichnen** to draw sth freehand; **ein Vortrag in freier Rede** an extemporary talk

f [= unbesetzt] *Zimmer, Toilette* vacant; *Taxi* for hire; **ist hier noch frei?, ist dieser Platz noch frei?** is anyone sitting here?, is this seat free?; **im Kino/Flugzeug waren noch zehn freie Plätze** in the cinema/plane there were still ten seats free; **„frei"** *(an Taxi)* "for hire"; *(an Toilettentür)* "vacant"; **„Zimmer frei"** "vacancies"; **frei stehen** *(= leer stehen)* to stand empty; **haben Sie noch etwas frei?** *(in Hotel)* do you have any vacancies?; **bei HarperCollins sind einige Stellen frei** there are some vacancies at HarperCollins; **etw frei halten** *(= nicht besetzen)* to keep sth free *or* clear; *(= reservieren)* to keep sth, to save sth; **„Ausfahrt/Einfahrt frei halten"** "keep clear"; **einen Platz frei machen** *(= aufstehen)* to vacate a seat; *(= leer räumen)* to clear a seat; **einen Platz für jdn frei lassen** to keep a seat for sb; **für etw Platz frei lassen/machen** to leave/make room for sth; **eine Wohnung frei machen** to vacate a flat → *auch* **Bahn, Ring**

g [= offen] **unter freiem Himmel** in the open air; **im freien Raum** *(Astron)* in (outer) space; **auf freier Strecke** *(Rail)* between stations; **eine Frage/Aussage im freien Raum stehen lassen** to leave a question/statement hanging in mid-air → **Freie(s), Feld**

h [= kostenlos] free; **Eintritt frei** admission free; **frei Schiff** free on board → **Haus**

i [= unkonventionell] *Sitten, Erziehung* liberal; **freie Liebe** free love

j [= unbekleidet] bare; **mit freiem Oberkörper** stripped to the waist; **sich frei machen** *(= sich entkleiden)* to take one's clothes off, to strip

k [= ungeschützt] *Autor* out of copyright; **seit die Rechte an Karl May frei geworden sind** since Karl May's books have been out of copyright

2 – ADVERB

a [= ungehindert] freely; *sprechen* openly; **frei beweglich** free-moving; **frei hängend** suspended; **frei erfunden** purely fictional; **er hat das frei erfunden** he made it up; **frei schalten und walten** to do what one wants; **das ist frei wählbar** you can choose as you please, it's completely optional; **frei definierbare Zeichen** *(Comput)* user-definable characters

♦ **frei (herum)laufen frei laufend** *(Hunde, Katzen)* feral; *Huhn* free-range; **Eier von frei laufenden Hühnern** free-range eggs; **frei herumlaufen** *(inf)* to be free, to be running around free *(inf)*; **der Verbrecher läuft immer noch frei herum** the criminal is still at large

♦ **frei lebend** *Wölfe, Mustangherden etc* living in the wild; *Katzen, Stadttauben* feral; *Mikroorganismen* free-living

♦ **frei stehen** *(Haus)* to stand by itself; *(Sport)* to be free *or* not marked; **ein frei stehendes Gebäude** a free-standing building → *auch* **c**

♦ **frei nach** based on; **frei nach Goethe** *(Zitat)* as Goethe didn't say

b [= ungezwungen] **sich frei und ungezwungen verhalten, frei und locker auftreten** to have a relaxed manner, to be easy-going; **sie benimmt sich etwas zu frei** she's rather free in her behaviour *(Brit) or* behavior *(US)*; **frei atmen können** *(= erleichtert sein)* to be able to breathe easy

c [= ohne Hilfsmittel] unaided, without help; **das Kind kann frei stehen** the child can stand on its own *or* without any help; **frei schwimmen** to swim unaided; **frei in der Luft schweben** to hang in mid-air; **frei sprechen** to speak without notes; **frei finanziert** *(Wohnungsbau)* privately financed

Frei-: **Frei|an|la|ge** F *(im Zoo)* outdoor *or* open-air enclosure; *(Sport)* sports ground, playing fields *pl*; *(= Park)* park grounds *pl*; **Frei|bad** NT open-air (swimming) pool, lido; **Frei|bal|lon** M free balloon; **Frei|bank** F *(rare) pl* **-bänke** *stall or shop selling substandard meat*; **frei+be|kom|men** *ptp* **freibekommen** *sep irreg*, **frei be|kom|men** *ptp* **frei bekommen** *irreg* VT **a** *(= befreien)* **jdn ~** to get sb freed *or* released; **etw ~** to get sth free, to free sth **b einen Tag/eine Woche ~** to get a day/a week off; **Frei|be|ruf|ler** [-bəru:flɐ] M **-s, -**, **Frei|be|ruf|le|rin** [-ərın] F **-, -nen** freelance, freelancer; **frei|be|ruf|lich** ADJ freelance ADV **~ arbeiten** to work freelance; **~ tätig sein** to do freelance work, to freelance; **Frei|be|trag** M tax allowance; **Frei|beu|ter** [-bɔytɐ] M **-s, -**, **Frei|beu|te|rin** [-ərın] F **-, -nen** pirate, buccaneer, freebooter *(old)*; *(fig)* exploiter; **Frei|beu|te|rei** [-bɔytə'rai] F **-, -en** piracy, buccaneering, freebooting *(old)*; *(fig)* exploitation; **frei|be|weg|lich** △ ADJ → **frei 2 a**; **Frei|bier** NT free beer; **frei|blei|bend** ADJ subject to alteration; **Frei|bord** M *(Naut)* freeboard; **Frei|brief** M **a** *(Hist)* *(= Privileg)* royal charter; *(= Freilassung)* letter of manumission **b** *(fig)* licence *(Brit)*, license *(US)*

Frei|burg ['fraibʊrk] NT **-s a** *(in Deutschland)* Freiburg **b** *(in der Schweiz: Kanton, Stadt)* Fribourg

Frei-: **Frei|deck** NT uncovered level *(of multi-storey car park)*; **Frei|den|ker(in)** M(F) freethinker; **frei|den|ke|risch** ADJ freethinking

frei|en ['fraiən] *(old)* VT to wed *(old, liter)* VI **um ein Mädchen ~** to woo *(old) or* court *(dated)* a girl; **jung gefreit hat nie gereut** *(Prov)* marry young and you'll never regret it

Freie(r) ['fraiə] MF *decl as adj (Hist)* freeman

Frei|er ['fraiɐ] M **-s, - a** *(dated, hum)* suitor **b** *(inf: von Dirne)* (prostitute's) client, john *(US inf)*

Frei|ers|fü|ße PL **auf ~n gehen** *(hum)* to be courting *(dated)*

Freie(s) ['fraiə] NT *decl as adj* **das ~** the open (air); **im ~n** in the open (air); **ins ~ gehen** to go outside *or* into the open (air); **ins ~ gelangen** to get out; **im ~n übernachten** to sleep out in the open

Frei-: **Frei|ex|emp|lar** NT free copy; **Frei|fahr|schein** M free ticket; **Frei|fahrt** F free journey; **~ haben** to travel free; **frei|fi|nan|ziert** △ [-finantsi:ɐt] → **frei 2 c**; **Frei|flä|che** F open space; **Frei|flug** M free flight; **Frei|frau** F baroness *(by marriage)*; **Frei|fräu|lein** NT baroness *(in her own right)*; **Frei|ga|be** F release; *(von Preisen, Wechselkursen)* decontrol, lifting of control (*+gen* on); *(von Straße, Strecke, Flugbahn)* opening; *(von Film)* passing; *(Ftbl: von Ball)* putting back into play; **Frei|gang** M *(von Strafgefangenen)* day release; **~ bekommen** to be let out on parole; **während des ~s** while on parole; **Frei|gän|ger** [-gɛŋɐ] M **-s, -**, **Frei|gän|ge|rin** [-ərın] F **-, -nen** day release prisoner; **frei+ge|ben** *sep irreg*, **frei ge|ben** *irreg* VT to release *(an +acc* to); *Gefangene, Ehepartner auch* to set free; *Preise, Wechselkurse* to decontrol, to lift controls on; *Film* to pass; *(Ftbl) Ball* to put back into play; *Spieler* to release; *(Comput) Dateien im Netzwerk* to share; **etw zum Verkauf ~** to allow sth to be sold on the open market → *auch* **frei 1 a** VI **jdm ~** to give sb a holiday *(Brit)*, to give sb vacation *(US)*; **jdm zwei Tage ~** to give sb two days off; **frei|ge|big** ['fraigeːbɪç] ADJ generous; **Frei|ge|big|keit** F **-,** *no pl* generosity; **Frei|ge|he|ge** NT open-air *or* outdoor enclosure; **Frei|geist** M freethinker; **frei|geis|tig** ADJ freethinking; **Frei|ge|län|de** NT open-air exhibition ground; **Frei|ge|las|se|ne(r)** [-gəlasnə] MF *decl as adj (Hist)* freedman/-woman; *(= ex-Gefangener)* released prisoner; **Frei|ge|päck** NT baggage allowance; **Frei|ge|richt** NT *(Hist)* Vehmgericht; **frei|ge|stellt** PTP *von* **freistellen** ADJ **a** *(wahlweise)* optional **b** *(= befreit)* **~ sein von** to be exempt from → *auch* **freistellen**; **frei|gie|big** ['fraigiːbɪç] ADJ generous; **Frei|graf** M *(Hist)* Vehmic judge; **Frei|gren|ze** F *(bei Steuer)* tax exemption limit; **frei+ha|ben** *sep irreg*, **frei ha|ben** *irreg* VI to have a holiday *(Brit)*, to have vacation *(US)*; **ich habe heute/zwei Tage frei** I have today/two days off; **eine Stunde ~** *(Sch)* to have a free period; **die sechste Stunde ~** *(Sch)* to have the sixth period free; **er hat mittags eine Stunde frei** he has an hour free at midday; **fünf Minuten ~** to have five minutes (free); **Frei|ha|fen** M free port; **frei+hal|ten** *sep irreg* VT *(= jds Zeche begleichen)* to pay for; **sich von jdm ~ lassen** to let sb pay for one → **frei 1 f**; **Frei|hand|bü|che|rei** F open-shelf library; **Frei|han|del** M free trade; **Frei|han|dels|zo|ne** F free trade area; **die kleine ~** EFTA, the European Free Trade Area; **frei|hän|dig** ADJ, ADV *Zeichnung* freehand; *Radfahren* without hands, (with) no hands; *Schießen* offhand *(spec)*, without support; *Vergabe von Aufträgen* private; **Frei|hand|zeich|nung** F freehand drawing; **frei|hän|gend** ADJ → **frei 2a**

Frei|heit ['fraihait] F **-, -en a** *no pl* freedom; **die ~** freedom; *(= persönliche Freiheit als politisches Ideal)* liberty; **~, Gleichheit, Brüderlichkeit** liberty, equality, fraternity; **persönliche ~** personal freedom; **in ~** *(dat)* **sein** to be free; *(Tier)* to be in the wild; **in ~ leben** *(Tier)* to live in the wild; **in ~ geboren** born free; **jdn/etw in ~** *(acc)* **setzen** to set sb/sth free; **jdm die ~ schenken** to give sb his/her *etc* freedom, to free sb; **der Weg in die ~** the path to freedom **b** *(= Vorrecht)* freedom *no pl*; **dichterische ~** poetic licence *(Brit) or* license *(US)*; **alle ~en haben** to have all the freedom possible; **die ~ haben** *or* **genießen** *(geh)*, **etw zu tun** to be free *or* at liberty to do sth, to have *or* enjoy the freedom to do sth; **sich** *(dat)* **die ~ nehmen, etw zu tun** to take the liberty of doing sth; **sich** *(dat)* **zu viele ~en erlauben** to take too many liberties

frei|heit|lich ['fraihaitlɪç] ADJ liberal; *Verfassung* based on the principle of liberty; *Demokratie* free; **die ~-demokratische Grundordnung** the free democratic constitutional structure ADV erziehen liberally; ~ **gesinnt** or **eingestellt** liberal

Frei|heit|li|che(r) ['fraihaitlıçə] MF decl as adj (Aus Pol) member of the (Austrian) Freedom Party; **die ~n** pl the (Austrian) Freedom Party

Frei|heits-: **Frei|heits|be|griff** M concept of freedom; **Frei|heits|be|rau|bung** F (Jur) wrongful deprivation of personal liberty; **Frei|heits|be|we|gung** F liberation movement; **Frei|heits|de|likt** NT (Jur) offence (Brit) or offense (US) against personal liberty; **Frei|heits|drang** M, no pl urge or desire for freedom; **Frei|heits|ent|zug** M imprisonment; **frei|heits|feind|lich** ADJ operating against freedom; Kräfte auch anti-freedom attr; **Frei|heits|kampf** M fight for freedom; **Frei|heits|kämp|fer(in)** M(F) freedom fighter; **Frei|heits|krieg** M war of liberation; **Frei|heits|lie|be** F love of liberty; **frei|heits|lie|bend** ADJ freedom-loving; **Frei|heits|rech|te** PL civil rights and liberties pl; **Frei|heits|sta|tue** F Statue of Liberty; **Frei|heits|stra|fe** F prison sentence; **er erhielt eine ~ von zwei Jahren** he was given a two-year prison sentence, he was sentenced to two years' imprisonment

Frei-: **frei|he|raus** [fraihe'raus] ADV candidly, frankly; **Frei|herr** M baron; **frei|herr|lich** ADJ attr baronial

Frei|in ['fraiın] F -, -nen baroness (in her own right)

Frei-: **frei+kämp|fen** sep VT to get free; (durch Gewaltanwendung) to free by force VR to get free; to free oneself by force; **Frei|kar|te** F free or complimentary ticket; **frei+kau|fen** VT sep **jdn/sich ~** to buy sb's/one's freedom; **Frei|kir|che** F Free Church; **Frei|klet|tern** NT free climbing; **frei+kom|men** VI sep irreg aux sein **a** (= entkommen) to get out (aus of); (= befreit werden) to be released or freed (aus, von from) **b** (= sich bewegen lassen: Boot) to come free; **Frei|kon|zert** NT (Sw) open-air concert; **Frei|kör|per|kul|tur** F, no pl nudism, naturism; **Frei|korps** NT (Mil) volunteer corps sing

Frei|land NT, no pl (Hort) open beds pl; **auf/im ~** outdoors

Frei|land-: **Frei|land|an|bau** M outdoor cultivation; **Frei|land|ge|mü|se** NT outdoor vegetables pl; **Frei|land|hal|tung** F, no pl free-range husbandry; **Eier/Hühner aus ~** free-range eggs/chickens; **Frei|land|kul|tur** F outdoor cultivation; **Frei|land|ver|such** M outdoor trial

Frei-: **frei+las|sen** sep irreg, **frei las|sen** irreg VT to set free, to free; (aus Haft, Gefangenschaft auch) to release; Hund to let off the lead or leash → auch **frei 1 f**; **Frei|las|sung** F -, -en release; (von Sklaven) setting free; **Frei|lauf** M (Aut) neutral; (bei Fahrrad) freewheel; **im ~ fahren** to coast (in neutral); to freewheel; **frei+lau|fen** VR sep irreg (Sport) to get free; **frei|lau|fend** ADJ → **frei 2 a**; **frei|le|bend** ADJ → **frei 2 a**; **frei+le|gen** sep, **frei le|gen** VT to expose; Ruinen, Trümmer to uncover; (fig) to lay bare, to expose; **Frei|le|gung** F -, -en (lit, fig) exposure; (von Ruinen, Trümmern) uncovering; **Frei|lei|tung** F overhead cable

frei|lich ['frailıç] ADV **a** (= allerdings) admittedly; **es scheint ~ nicht leicht zu sein** admittedly or certainly it doesn't seem easy **b** (esp S Ger: = natürlich) of course, certainly, sure (esp US); **aber ~!** of course!; **ja ~** yes of course

Frei|licht- in cpds open-air; **Frei|licht|büh|ne** F open-air theatre (Brit) or theater (US); **Frei|licht|ki|no** NT open-air cinema; (= Autokino) drive-in cinema; **Frei|licht|mu|se|um** NT open-air museum

Frei-: **Frei|los** NT free lottery ticket; (Sport) bye; **frei+ma|chen** sep VT **a** (fig) to stamp; (mit Frankiermaschine) to frank; **einen Brief mit 55 Cent ~** to put stamps to the value of 55 cents on a letter **b** → auch **frei 1 a,f** VR → auch **frei 1 a, d, j**; **Frei|ma|chung** [-maxʊŋ] F -, no pl (von Brief etc) stamping; (mit Frankiermaschine) franking; **Frei|mar|ke** F (postage) stamp; **Frei|mau|rer** M Mason, Freemason; **Frei|mau|re|rei** [-maurə'rai] F -, no pl Freemasonry; **frei|mau|re|risch** [-maurərıʃ] ADJ Masonic; **Frei|mau|rer|lo|ge** F Masonic Lodge

Frei|mut M, no pl frankness, honesty, openness; **mit allem ~** perfectly frankly or honestly or openly

frei|mü|tig ['fraimy:tıç] ADJ frank, honest, open ADV frankly, honestly, openly

Frei|mü|tig|keit F -, no pl frankness, honesty, openness

Frei-: **frei|neh|men** sep irreg, **frei neh|men** irreg VT **einen Tag ~** to take a day off; **Frei|platz** M **a** free or complimentary seat **b** (Univ) scholarship; (Sch auch) free place **c** (Sport) outdoor court; **frei+pres|sen** VT sep **jdn ~** to obtain sb's release, to get sb set free; **versuchen, jdn freizupressen** to demand sb's release; **Frei|raum** M (fig) freedom no art, no pl (zu for); **~ brauchen, in dem man sich entwickeln kann** to need freedom to develop or in which to develop; **die Universität ist kein gesellschaftlicher ~** university isn't a social vacuum; **frei|re|li|gi|ös** ADJ non-denominational; **Frei|sass** ['fraizas] M -en, -en, **Frei|sas|se** ['fraizasə] M -n, -n (Hist) yeoman; **frei|schaf|fend** ADJ attr freelance; **Frei|schaf|fen|de(r)** [-ʃafndə] MF decl as adj freelance, freelancer; **frei+schal|ten** VT sep (Telec) Leitung to clear; Handy to connect, to enable; **Frei|schar** F (Hist) (irregular) volunteer corps sing; **Frei|schär|ler** [-ʃɛ:ɐlɐ] M -s, -, **Frei|schär|le|rin** [-ərın] F -, -nen guerrilla; (Hist) irregular (volunteer); **frei+schau|feln** sep, **frei schau|feln** VT to clear, to dig clear; **frei+schie|ßen** sep irreg, **frei schie|ßen** irreg VT **sich** (dat) **den Weg ~** to shoot one's way out; **jdn ~** to shoot sb free; **Frei|schuss** M free shot; **frei+schwim|men** VR sep irreg (Sport) to pass a test by swimming for 15 minutes (fig) to learn to stand on one's own two feet; **Frei|schwim|men** NT 15-minute swimming test

> **FREISCHWIMMER**
>
> The **Freischwimmer** badge is awarded to people who can swim for 15 minutes without holding onto the side of the pool, and who can dive from the lower diving board. Children without the **Freischwimmer** badge on their swimsuit are not allowed to use the deep end of a public swimming pool unless supervised. The next level up is the **Fahrtenschwimmer**, which entails a 30-minute swimming test, beginning with a dive from the higher diving board.

Frei-: **Frei|schwin|ger** [-ʃvıŋɐ] M -s, - **a** (= Sessel) cantilevered chair **b** (= Uhr) caseless pendulum clock; **frei+set|zen** VT sep to release; (euph) Arbeitskräfte to make redundant; (vorübergehend) to lay off; **Frei|set|zung** F -, -en release; (euph) dismissal; (vorübergehend) laying off; **Frei|sinn** M, no pl (dated) liberalism; **frei|sin|nig** ADJ (dated) liberal; **Freisinnige Partei** (Sw) Swiss Liberal Party; **Frei|spiel** NT free game; **frei+spie|len** sep VR **a** (Sport) to get into space **b** (Theat, Film) to get over one's stage fright VT (Sport) **jdn ~** to play sb clear, to create space for sb; **Frei|sprech|an|la|ge** F hands-free (headset); (im Auto) hands-free (car kit); **frei+spre|chen** VT sep irreg **a** Angeklagten, Beschuldigten to acquit; **jdn von einer Schuld ~** (Jur) to find sb not guilty; **jdn von einem Verdacht ~** to clear sb of suspicion; **jdn wegen erwiesener Unschuld ~** to prove sb not guilty **b** (Handwerk) Auszubildende to qualify; **Frei|spruch** M acquittal; **es ergeht ~** the verdict is "not guilty"; **auf ~ plädieren** to plead not guilty; **Frei|staat** M free state; **der ~ Bayern/Sachsen** the Free State of Bavaria/Saxony

> **FREISTAAT**
>
> During the Weimar Republic most **Länder** were called **Freistaat**; after the Second World War the majority chose other ways of describing themselves. Prior to re-unification only Bavaria kept the name **Freistaat**, as a sign of its independence within the federation. Two of the new **Länder**, Saxony and Thuringia, now also use this title.

Frei-: **Frei|statt** [-ʃtat] F -, ≃en, **Frei|stät|te** F (liter) sanctuary; **frei+ste|hen** VI sep irreg (= überlassen sein) **es steht jdm frei, etw zu tun** sb is free or at liberty to do sth; **das steht Ihnen völlig frei** that is completely up to you; **es steht Ihnen frei, ob ...** it is up to you whether ... → auch **frei 1 f**; **frei+stel|len** VT sep **a** (= anheimstellen) **jdm etw ~** to leave sth (up) to sb **b** (= zur Verfügung stellen) Mittel to make available; Personal to release **c** (= befreien) to exempt; **einen Schüler vom Unterricht ~** to excuse a pupil from a lesson/his lessons; **Frei|stel|lungs|auf|trag** M (Fin: an Bank) application for exemption from taxation of income from capital; **Frei|stem|pel** M frank

Frei|stil- in cpds freestyle; **Frei|stil|rin|gen** NT all-in or freestyle wrestling

Frei-: **Frei|stoß** M (Ftbl) free kick (für to, for); **Frei|stoß|tor** NT (Ftbl) goal from a free kick ; **Frei|stück** NT free copy; **Frei|stun|de** F free hour; (Sch) free period

Frei|tag ['fraita:k] M Friday; **der Schwarze ~** the day of the Wall Street crash; **ein schwarzer ~** a black day → auch **Dienstag**

frei|täg|lich ADJ attr Friday

frei|tags ['fraita:ks] ADV on Fridays, on a Friday

Frei-: **Frei|tisch** M free meals pl; **Frei|tod** M suicide; **den ~ wählen** or **suchen** to decide to put an end to one's life; **frei|tra|gend** ADJ self-supporting; Konstruktion, Brücke, Flügel cantilever attr; Treppe hanging, cantilever attr; **Frei|trep|pe** F (flight of) steps (+gen leading up to); **Frei|übung** F exercise; **~en machen** to do one's exercises; **Frei|um|schlag** M stamped addressed envelope, s.a.e.

frei|weg [frai'vɛk] ADV openly; (= freiheraus) straight out, frankly; **er fing an, ~ zu erzählen** he started talking away

Frei-: **Frei|wild** NT (fig) fair game; **frei|wil|lig** ADJ voluntary; (Jur) Gerichtsbarkeit auch non-contentious; (= freigestellt) Versicherung, Unterricht optional; **~e Feuerwehr** voluntary fire brigade (Brit) or fire department (US) ADV voluntarily; **sich ~ melden** to volunteer (zu, für for); **etw ~ machen** to do sth voluntarily, to do sth of one's own free will; **~ in den Tod gehen** to take one's own life; **sich ~ verpflichten** (bei Militär) to enlist; **Frei|wil|li|ge(r)** [-vılıgə] MF decl as adj volunteer; **~ vor!** volunteers, one pace forwards!; **Frei|wil|li|gen|ar|mee** F volunteer army; **Frei|wil|lig|keit** F voluntary nature, voluntariness; **Frei|wurf** M free throw; **Frei|zei|chen** NT (Telec) dial tone; **Frei|zeich|nungs|klau|sel** F (Jur, Comm) exemption from liability clause

Frei|zeit F **a** (= arbeitsfreie Zeit) free or spare or leisure time **b** (= Zusammenkunft) weekend/holiday course; (Eccl) retreat

Frei|zeit-: **Frei|zeit|an|ge|bot** NT leisure activity; **ein breites ~ bereitstellen** to offer a wide range of leisure activities; **Frei|zeit|an|zug** M jogging suit; **Frei|zeit|aus|gleich** M time off in lieu (Brit), time off instead of pay (US); **Frei|zeit|be|klei|dung** F casual clothes pl; (als Warengattung) leisurewear no pl; **Frei|zeit|be|schäf|ti|gung** F leisure pursuit or activity; **Frei|zeit|dro|ge** F recreational drug; **Frei|zeit|ein|rich|tung** F recreational facility; **Frei|zeit|for|scher(in)** M(F) researcher in leisure activities; **Frei|zeit|ge|stal|tung** F organization of one's leisure time; **das Problem der ~** the leisure problem; **Frei|zeit|heim** NT *(für Jugendliche) hostel for groups of young people with organized leisure activities*; **Frei|zeit|hemd** NT sports shirt; **Frei|zeit|in|dust|rie** F leisure industry; **Frei|zeit|klei|dung** F casual clothes *pl*; *(= Warengattung)* leisurewear *no pl*; **Frei|zeit|park** M amusement park; **Frei|zeit|prob|lem** NT problem of leisure, leisure problem; **Frei|zeit|sek|tor** M leisure sector; **Frei|zeit|ver|hal|ten** NT recreational behaviour *(Brit)* or behavior *(US)*, recreational patterns *pl*; **Frei|zeit|wert** M **München hat einen hohen ~** Munich has a lot to offer in the way of recreational and leisure facilities

Frei-: **frei|zü|gig** ADJ **a** *(= reichlich) Gebrauch, Anwendung* liberal **b** *(in moralischer Hinsicht)* permissive **c** *(= den Wohnort frei wählen könnend)* free to move ADV **a** *(= reichlich)* freely, liberally; **~ Geld ausgeben** to spend money freely or liberally **b** *(= moralisch locker)* **sich ~ benehmen** to be loose; **~ gekleidet** provocatively dressed; **Frei|zü|gig|keit** [-tsy:gɪçkait] F -, *no pl* **a** *(= Großzügigkeit)* liberality **b** *(in moralischer Hinsicht)* permissiveness **c** *(= Beweglichkeit: von Waren, freie Wahl des Wohnorts etc)* freedom of movement

fremd [frɛmt] ADJ **a** *(= andern gehörig)* someone else's; *Bank, Bibliothek, Firma* different; *(Comm, Fin, Pol)* outside *attr*; **ohne ~e Hilfe** without anyone else's/outside help, without help from anyone else/outside; **ich schlafe nicht gern in ~en Betten** I don't like sleeping in strange beds; **~es Eigentum** someone else's property, property not one's own *(form)*; **das ist nicht für ~e Ohren** that is not for other people to hear; **etw geht in ~e Hände über** sth passes into the hands of strangers or into strange hands; **sich mit ~en Federn schmücken** to claim all the glory for oneself
b *(= fremdländisch)* foreign, alien *(esp Admin, Pol)*
c *(= andersartig)* strange; *Planeten* other; *Welt* different
d *(= unvertraut)* strange; **jdm ~ sein** *(= unbekannt)* to be unknown to sb; *(= unverständlich)* to be foreign or alien to sb; *(= nicht in jds Art)* to be foreign or alien to sb or to sb's nature; **es ist mir ~, wie ...** I don't understand how ...; **das ist eine mir ~e Seite seines Wesens** that is a side of his character which I haven't seen before; **ich bin hier/in London ~** I'm a stranger here/to London; **meine Heimat ist mir ~ geworden** I've become a stranger in my own country, my own country has become quite foreign or alien to me; **sich** or **einander** *(dat)* **~ werden** to grow apart, to become strangers (to one another); **sich ~ fühlen** to feel alien, to feel like a stranger; **~ tun** to be reserved

Fremd-: **Fremd|ar|bei|ter(in)** M(F) *(neg!)* foreign worker; **fremd|ar|tig** ADJ strange; *(= exotisch)* exotic ADV **~ aussehen/klingen/anmuten** to look/sound/seem strange or exotic; **Fremd|ar|tig|keit** F, *no pl* strangeness; *(= Exotik)* exoticism; **Fremd|be|stäu|bung** F cross-fertilization; **fremd|be|stimmt** ADJ heteronomous ADV **~ handeln** to act under orders; **Fremd|be|stim|mung** F heteronomy

Frem|de ['frɛmdə] F -, *no pl (liter)* **die ~** foreign parts *pl*; **in die ~ gehen** to go to foreign parts, to go abroad; **in der ~ sein** to be in foreign parts, to be abroad

frem|de(l)n ['frɛmd(l)n] VI *(S Ger, Sw)* to be scared of strangers

Frem|den-: **Frem|den|bett** NT spare or guest bed; *(in Hotel)* hotel bed; **frem|den|feind|lich** ADJ hostile to strangers; *(= ausländerfeindlich)* hostile to foreigners, xenophobic; **Frem|den|feind|lich|keit** F xenophobia; **Frem|den|füh|rer** M guide(book); **Frem|den|füh|rer(in)** M(F) (tourist) guide; **Frem|den|hass** M xenophobia; **Frem|den|has|ser** [-hasɐ] M -s, -, **Frem|den|has|se|rin** [-hasərɪn] F -, -nen xenophobe *(form)*; **er ist ein ~** he hates foreigners; **Frem|den|le|gi|on** F Foreign Legion; **Frem|den|le|gi|o|när** M Foreign Legionnaire; **Frem|den|pass** M alien's passport; **Frem|den|po|li|zei** F aliens branch (of the police); *(Aviat)* aliens office

Frem|den|ver|kehr M tourism *no def art*

Frem|den|ver|kehrs-: **Frem|den|ver|kehrs|amt** NT tourist office; **Frem|den|ver|kehrs|ort** M *pl* **-orte** tourist resort, tourist centre *(Brit)* or center *(US)*; **Frem|den|ver|kehrs|ver|ein** M tourist association

Frem|den|zim|mer NT guest room

Frem|de(r) ['frɛmdə] MF *decl as adj (= Unbekannter, Ortsfremder)* stranger; *(= Ausländer)* foreigner; *(Admin, Pol)* alien; *(= Tourist)* visitor

Fremd-: **Fremd|fi|nan|zie|rung** F outside financing; **fremd+ge|hen** VI *sep irreg aux sein (inf)* to be unfaithful; **Fremd|heit** F -, *(rare)* **-en** *(= ausländische Natur)* foreignness; *(= Unvertrautheit)* strangeness; *(= Entfremdung)* alienation; *(zwischen Menschen)* reserve; **Fremd|herr|schaft** F, *no pl* foreign rule; **Fremd|ka|pi|tal** NT outside capital; **Fremd|kör|per** M foreign body; *(fig)* alien element; **sich als ~ fühlen** to feel out of place; **fremd|län|disch** [-lɛndɪʃ] ADJ foreign *no adv*; *(= exotisch)* exotic; **Fremd|ling** ['frɛmtlɪŋ] M -s, -e *(liter)* stranger

Fremd|spra|che F foreign language; **eine Begabung für ~n** a gift for languages

Fremd|spra|chen-: **Fremd|spra|chen|kor|res|pon|dent(in)** M(F), **Fremd|spra|chen|sek|re|tär(in)** M(F) bilingual secretary; **Fremd|spra|chen|un|ter|richt** M language teaching; **~ haben/erteilen** to have/give language classes

Fremd-: **fremd|spra|chig** ADJ in a foreign language; *Fähigkeiten* (foreign) language; **die ~e Bevölkerung** non-English/non-German *etc* speakers; **fremd|sprach|lich** ADJ foreign; **~er Unterricht** language teaching; **Fremd|stoff** M foreign matter *no pl* or substance; **Fremd|ver|schul|den** NT third-party responsibility; **Fremd|wäh|rung** F foreign currency; **Fremd|wort** NT *pl* **-wörter** borrowed or foreign word, borrowing; **Rücksichtnahme ist für ihn ein ~** *(fig)* he's never heard of the word consideration; **Fremd|wör|ter|buch** NT dictionary of borrowed or foreign words

fre|ne|tisch [fre'ne:tɪʃ] ADJ frenetic, frenzied; *Beifall auch* wild ADV wildly

fre|quen|tie|ren [frekvɛn'ti:rən] *ptp* **frequentiert** VT *(geh)* to frequent

Fre|quenz [fre'kvɛnts] F -, -en **a** *(= Häufigkeit)* frequency *(auch Phys)*; *(Med)* (pulse) rate **b** *(= Stärke)* numbers *pl*; *(= Verkehrsdichte)* volume of traffic

Fre|quenz- *in cpds* frequency; **Fre|quenz|be|reich** M *(Rad)* frequency range

Fres|ke ['frɛskə] F -, -n *(rare)*, **Fres|ko** ['frɛsko] NT -s, **Fresken** [-kn] fresco

Fres|sa|li|en [frɛ'sa:liən] PL *(inf)* grub *sing (sl)*, eats *pl (inf)*

Fress|beu|tel M *(für Pferd)* nosebag

Fres|se ['frɛsə] F -, -n *(vulg) (= Mund)* trap *(inf)*, gob *(Brit inf)*, cakehole *(Brit inf)*; *(= Gesicht)* mug *(inf)*; **die ~ halten** to shut one's trap or gob or face *(all inf)*; **eine große ~ haben** *(sl)* to be a loud-mouth *(inf)*; **jdn** or **jdm in die ~ hauen, jdm die ~ polieren** to smash sb's face in *(inf)*; **ach du meine ~!** *(sl)* bloody hell! *(Brit inf)*, Jesus Christ! *(sl)*

fres|sen ['frɛsn] *pret* **fraß** [fra:s], *ptp* **gefressen** [gə'frɛsn] VI **a** *(= essen)* to feed, to eat; *(sl: Menschen)* to eat, to nosh *(Brit inf)*; *(gierig)* to guzzle *(inf)*; **jdm aus der Hand ~** *(lit, fig inf)* to eat out of sb's hand; **für drei ~** to eat enough for a whole army *(inf)*; **er isst nicht, er frisst (wie ein Schwein)** he eats like a pig → **Vogel, Scheunendrescher**
b *(= zerstören)* to eat away *(an etw (dat)* sth)
VT **a** *(= verzehren) (Tier, sl: Mensch)* to eat; *(= sich ernähren von)* to feed or live on; *(sl: = gierig essen)* to guzzle *(inf)*, to scoff *(Brit inf)*, to scarf down *(US inf)*; **etwas zu ~** something to eat; **den Napf leer ~** *(Tiere)* to lick the bowl clean; *(Menschen)* to polish everything off *(inf)*; **jdn arm ~, jdm die Haare vom Kopf ~** to eat sb out of house and home → **Bauer a, Not a**
b *(in Wendungen)* **Kilometer ~** to burn up the kilometres *(Brit)* or kilometers *(US)*; **Löcher in etw** *(acc)* **~** *(lit)* to eat holes in sth; **ein Loch in den Geldbeutel ~** to make a big hole in one's pocket; **ich habe dich zum Fressen gern** *(inf)* you're good enough to eat *(inf)*; **ich könnte dich ~** *(inf)* I could eat you *(inf)*; **ich will dich doch nicht ~** *(inf)* I'm not going to eat you *(inf)*; **ich fresse einen Besen** or **meinen Hut, wenn ...** *(inf)* I'll eat my hat if ...; **jdn/etw gefressen haben** *(inf)* to have had one's fill or as much as one can take of sb/sth; **jetzt hat er es endlich gefressen** *(inf)* he's got it or got there at last *(inf)*, at last the penny's dropped; **einen Narren** or **Affen an jdm/etw gefressen haben** to dote on sb/sth → **Weisheit a**
c *(= verbrauchen) Benzin, Ersparnisse* to eat or gobble up; *Zeit* to take up
d *(geh: Neid, Hass)* to eat up
VR **a** *(= sich bohren)* to eat one's way *(in +acc* into, *durch* through)
b **sich satt ~** *(Tier)* to gorge itself; *(sl: Mensch)* to stuff oneself or one's face *(inf)*; **sich voll ~** → **vollfressen**; **von diesem Futter wird sich Ihr Hund krank ~** this food will make your dog sick

Fres|sen NT -s, *no pl* food; *(sl)* grub *(sl)*; *(sl: = Schmaus)* blow-out *(inf)* → **gefunden ADJ**

Fres|ser ['frɛsɐ] M -s, -, **Fres|se|rin** [-ərɪn] F -, -nen *(Tier)* eater

-fres|ser(in) M(F) *suf in cpds* **a** *(= Esser von etw)* eater **b** *(= Bekämpfer von jdm)* -basher *(inf)*

Fres|se|rei [frɛsə'rai] F -, -en *(inf)* **a** *no pl (= übermäßiges Essen)* guzzling *(inf)*; *(= Gefräßigkeit)* piggishness *(inf)*, gluttony **b** *(= Schmaus)* blow-out *(inf)*, nosh-up *(Brit inf)*

Fress-: **Fress|feind** M *(Zool)* predator; **Fress|gier** F voraciousness; *(pej: von Menschen)* gluttony, piggishness *(inf)*; **Fress|korb** M *(inf) (für Picknick)* picnic hamper or basket; *(= Geschenkkorb)* food hamper or basket; **Fress|lust** F **a** *(Zool)* appetite **b** → **Fressgier**; **Fress|napf** M feeding bowl; **Fress|pa|ket** NT *(inf)* food parcel *(Brit)* or package; **Fress|sack** M *(sl)* greedy guts *(Brit inf)*, glutton; **Fress|sucht** F *(inf)* gluttony; *(krankhaft)* craving for food; **Fress|wel|le** F *(hum inf)* wave of gluttony; **Fress|werk|zeu|ge** PL feeding equipment *no pl* or organs *pl*; *(von Insekten)* mouthpart; **Fress|zel|le** F *(Med)* = **Makrophage**

Frett|chen ['frɛtçən] NT -s, - ferret

Freu|de ['frɔydə] F -, -n **a** *no pl* pleasure; *(innig)* joy *(über +acc* at); *(= Erfreutheit)* delight *(über +acc* at); **~ an etw** *(dat)* **haben** to get or derive pleasure from sth; **er hat ~ an seinen Kindern** his children give him pleasure; **~ am Leben haben** to enjoy life; **wenn man an der Arbeit keine ~ hat** if you don't get any pleasure out of your work, if you don't enjoy your work; **vor ~** with joy; **die ~ an der Natur** the joy one gets from nature; **der Garten ist seine ganze ~** the garden is his pride and joy; **daran hat er seine ~** that gives him pleasure; *(iro)* he thinks that's fun; **es ist eine (wahre** or **reine) ~, zu ...** it's a (real) joy or pleasure to ...; **es war eine reine ~, das mit anzusehen** it was a joy to see; **es ist keine (reine) ~, das zu tun** *(iro)* it's not exactly fun doing that; **es ist mir eine ~, zu ...** it's a real pleasure for me to ...; **jdm ~ machen** to give sb pleasure; **das Kind macht seinen Eltern viel/nur ~** the child gives his parents a lot of/nothing but joy; **er macht ihnen keine/wenig ~** he's no joy/not much of a joy to them; **es macht ihnen keine/wenig ~** they don't enjoy it (at all)/much; **jdm eine ~ machen** or **bereiten** to make sb happy; **jdm eine ~ machen wollen** to want to do something to please sb; **zu meiner großen ~** to my great delight; **zu unserer größten ~ können wir Ihnen mitteilen ...** we are pleased to be able to inform you ...; **Sie hätten seine ~ sehen sollen** you should have seen how happy he was; **aus ~ an der Sache** for the love of it *or* the thing; **aus Spaß an der ~** *(inf)* for the fun *or* hell *(inf)* of it *or* the thing; **in Freud und Leid zu jdm halten** *(dated)* to stand by sb come rain, come shine

b *(= Vergnügung)* joy; **die kleinen ~n des Lebens** the pleasures of life; **herrlich und in ~n leben** to live a life of ease; **mit ~n** with pleasure; **da kommt ~ auf** this is where the fun starts

Freu|den-: **Freu|den|bot|schaft** F good news *sing*, glad tidings *pl (old, Bibl)*; **Freu|den|fest** NT celebration; **Freu|den|feu|er** NT bonfire; **Freu|den|ge|heul** NT, **Freu|den|ge|schrei** NT shrieks *pl* of joy; **Freu|den|haus** NT *(dated, hum)* house of pleasure *or* ill-repute; **Freu|den|jun|ge** M *(hum)* male prostitute; **Freu|den|mäd|chen** NT *(dated, hum)* lady of easy virtue *(euph)*, prostitute; **Freu|den|mahl** NT celebration meal, banquet *(old)*, feast; **freu|den|reich** ADJ *(geh)* joyful, joyous; **Freu|den|ruf** M, **Freu|den|schrei** M joyful cry, cry of joy; **Freu|den|sprung** M joyful leap; **einen ~ machen** to jump for joy; **Freu|den|tag** M happy *or* joyful *(esp liter)* day; **Freu|den|tanz** M dance of joy; **einen ~ aufführen** *or* **vollführen** to dance with joy; **Freu|den|tau|mel** M ecstasy (of joy); **Freu|den|trä|nen** PL tears *pl* of joy; **freu|den|voll** ADJ = **freudvoll**

freu|de-: **freu|de|strah|lend** ADJ *no pred* beaming with delight; *Gesicht auch* beaming ADV beaming with delight; **freu|de|trun|ken** ADJ *(liter)* delirious with joy

Freu|di|a|ner [frɔyˈdiaːnɐ] M **-s, -**, **Freu|di|a|ne|rin** F [-ərɪn] **-, -nen** Freudian

freu|dig [ˈfrɔydɪç] ADJ **a** *(= froh gestimmt)* joyful; *(= gern bereit)* willing; *(= begeistert)* enthusiastic; **jdn ~ stimmen** to raise sb's spirits **b** *(= beglückend)* happy, joyful *(liter)*; **eine ~e Nachricht** some good *or* joyful *(liter)* news, some glad tidings *pl (old, Bibl)*; **ein ~es Ereignis** *(euph)* a happy *or* blessed event *(euph)* ADV happily, joyfully; **einen Vorschlag ~ begrüßen** to greet a suggestion with delight; **etw ~ erwarten** to look forward to sth with great pleasure; **~ überrascht sein** to be pleasantly surprised

Freud-: **freud|los** ADJ joyless, cheerless ADV **~ dahinleben** to lead a joyless *or* cheerless existence; **Freud|lo|sig|keit** F **-,** *no pl* joylessness, cheerlessness

freudsch [frɔytʃ] ADJ *attr* Freudian → **Fehlleistung**

freud|voll ADJ *(geh)* joyful, joyous *(liter)*; *Tage, Leben* filled with joy

freu|en [ˈfrɔyən] ✪ 31, 38.3, 46.4, 47.5, 48.1, 48.2, 51.1, 51.2, 52.2, 52.3 VR **a** *(= froh sein)* to be glad *or* pleased *(über +acc, (geh) +gen* about); **sich über ein Geschenk ~** to be pleased with a present; **sich sehr** *or* **riesig** *(inf)* **~** to be delighted *or* ever so pleased *(inf) (über +acc* about); **ich habe es bekommen, freute sie sich** I've got it, she said happily *or (stärker)* joyfully; **sich an etw** *(dat)* **~** to get *or* derive a lot of pleasure from sth; **er freut sich sehr an seinen Kindern** his children give him a lot of pleasure; **sich für jdn ~** to be glad *or* pleased *or* happy for sb; **sich mit jdm ~** to share sb's happiness; **sich seines Lebens ~** to enjoy life; **ich freue mich, Ihnen mitteilen zu können, ...** I'm pleased to be able to tell you ... → **Kind**

b sich auf jdn/etw ~ to look forward to seeing sb/to sth; **sich auf das Kind ~** to look forward to the child being born *or* to the child's birth; **sich zu früh ~** to get one's hopes up too soon

VT *impers* to please; **es freut mich/ihn, dass ...** I'm/he's pleased *or* glad that ...; **es freut mich/ihn sehr, dass ...** I'm/he's delighted *or* very pleased *or* very glad that ...; **das freut mich** I'm really pleased; **es freut mich sehr/es hat mich sehr gefreut, Ihre Bekanntschaft zu machen** *(form)* (I'm) pleased to meet/have met you

Freund [frɔynt] M **-(e)s, -e** [-də] **a** *(= Kamerad)* friend; **wir sind schon seit 1954 ~e** we've been friends since 1954; **mit jdm gut ~ sein** to be good friends with sb; **das habe ich ihm unter ~en gesagt** that was just between ourselves; **10 Euro unter ~en** 10 euros to a friend; **~ und Feind** friend and foe; **dein/Ihr ~ und Helfer** your friend and helper; **ein schöner ~** *(iro inf)* a fine friend; **jdn zum ~ haben** to have sb for *or* as a friend; **guter ~!** *(liter)* my dear man → **alt a**

b *(= Liebhaber)* boyfriend; *(esp älter)* gentleman-friend

c *(fig) (= Anhänger)* lover; *(= Förderer)* friend; **ein ~ der Kunst** an art lover; **ich bin kein ~ von Hunden** I'm no lover of dogs; **er ist kein ~ von vielen Worten** he's not one for talking much, he's a man of few words; **ich bin kein ~ von so etwas** I'm not keep on that sort of thing; **ein ~ des Alkohols sein** to like one's drink

freund ADJ *inv (old)* **jdm ~ sein/bleiben/werden** to be/remain/become sb's friend

Freun|des-: **Freun|des|hand** F *(geh)* **jdm die ~ reichen** to extend the hand *or* arm of friendship to sb; **von ~** by the hand of a friend

-freund(in) M(F) *suf in cpds* **a** *(= Kamerad)* friend; **ein Schulfreund von mir** a school friend of mine **b** *(fig: = Liebhaber)* lover of; **eine Musikfreundin** a music-lover, a lover of music

Freund|chen [ˈfrɔyntçən] NT **-s, -** *(inf)* my friend *(iro)*; **~, ~!** watch it, mate *(Brit inf) or* my friend!

Freun|des|kreis M circle of friends; **etw im engsten ~ feiern** to celebrate sth with one's closest friends

Freund-Feind-Den|ken NT *attitude that if you're not for us you're against us*

Freun|din [ˈfrɔyndɪn] F **-, -nen a** friend; *(= Liebhaberin)* girlfriend; *(esp älter)* lady-friend **b** *(fig: = Anhängerin, Förderin)* → **Freund c**

-freundin F *suf in cpds* = **-freund(in)**

freund|lich [ˈfrɔyntlɪç] ADJ **a** *(= wohlgesinnt)* friendly *no adv*; **bitte recht ~!** say cheese! *(inf)*, smile please!; **mit ~en Grüßen, mit ~em Gruß** (with) best wishes

b *(= liebenswürdig)* kind *(zu* to); **würden Sie bitte so ~ sein und das tun?** would you be so kind *or* good as to do that?, would you be kind *or* good enough to do that?; **das ist sehr ~ von Ihnen** that's very kind *or* good of you

c *(= ansprechend) Aussehen, Landschaft, Wetter etc* pleasant; *Zimmer, Einrichtung, Farben* cheerful; *Atmosphäre* friendly, congenial; *(Fin, Comm: = günstig)* favourable *(Brit)*, favorable *(US)*

ADV *(= wohlwollend) bitten, fragen* nicely; **jdn ~ anschauen** to give sb a friendly look; **jdn ~ behandeln** to be friendly toward(s) sb; **einem Vorschlag ~ gegenüberstehen** to be in favour *(Brit) or* favor *(US)* of a suggestion, to be well-disposed to a suggestion

-freund|lich ADJ *suf* **a** *(= wohlgesinnt)* pro-; **eine israelfreundliche Politik** a pro-Israel policy **b** *(= liebend)* fond of; **er ist sehr kinderfreundlich** he is very fond of children **c** *(= geeignet)* -friendly; **umweltfreundlich** eco-friendly **d** *(= schonend)* kind to; **ein magenfreundlicher Kaffee** a coffee which is kind to *or* gentle on the stomach

freund|li|cher|wei|se [ˈfrɔyntlɪçɐˈvaizə] ADV kindly; **er trug uns ~ die Koffer** he was kind enough to carry our cases for us, he kindly carried our cases (for us)

Freund|lich|keit F **-, -en a** *no pl (= Wohlgesonnenheit)* friendliness; *(= Liebenswürdigkeit)* kindness; *(von Aussehen, Landschaft, Wetter etc)* pleasantness; *(von Zimmer, Einrichtung, Farben)* cheerfulness; *(von Atmosphäre)* friendliness, congeniality; **würden Sie (wohl) die ~ haben, das zu tun?** would you be so kind *or* good as to do that?, would you be kind *or* good enough to do that?; **die ~ des Investitionsklimas** the favourable *(Brit) or* favorable *(US)* climate for investment

b *(= freundliche Handlung, Gefälligkeit)* kindness, favour *(Brit)*, favor *(US)*; *(= freundliche Bemerkung)* kind remark; **jdm ~en erweisen** to be kind to sb; **jdm ein paar ~en sagen** to say a few kind words to sb; *(iro)* to say a few choice words to sb

Freund|schaft [ˈfrɔyntʃaft] F **-, -en a** *(= freundschaftliches Verhältnis)* friendship; **mit jdm ~ schließen** to make *or* become friends with sb, to form a friendship with sb; **jdm die ~ anbieten** to offer sb one's friendship; **in aller ~** in all friendliness; **da hört die ~ auf** *(inf)* friendship doesn't go that far; **in Geldsachen hört die ~ auf** friendship doesn't extend to money matters → **kündigen VT, Geschenk b** *no pl (dial: = Verwandtschaft)* relatives *pl*, relations *pl* **c** *(DDR)* *the Pioneer groups in one school*

freund|schaft|lich [ˈfrɔyntʃaftlɪç] ADJ friendly *no adv*; **~e Gefühle** feelings of friendship ADV **jdm ~ verbunden sein** to be friends with sb; **mit jdm ~ verkehren** to be on friendly terms with sb; **jdm ~ gesinnt sein** to feel friendly toward(s) sb; **jdm ~ auf die Schulter klopfen** to give sb a friendly slap on the back

Freund|schafts-: **Freund|schafts|ban|de** PL *(liter)* ties *pl* of friendship; **Freund|schafts|be|such** M *(Pol)* goodwill visit; **Freund|schafts|bund** M *pl* **-bünde** friendly alliance; **Freund|schafts|dienst** M favour *(Brit) or* favor *(US)* to a friend; **jdm einen ~ erweisen** to do sb a favo(u)r; **Freund|schafts|preis** M (special) price for a friend; **er überließ mir sein Auto zu einem ~/einem ~ von 800 Euro** he let me have his car cheaply/for 800 euros because we're friends; **ich mache dir einen ~** *(inf)* seeing we're friends I'll let you have it for a special price; **Freund|schafts|spiel** NT *(Sport)* friendly game *or* match, friendly *(inf)*; **Freund|schafts|ver|trag** M *(Pol)* treaty of friendship

Fre|vel [ˈfreːfl] M **-s, -** *(geh)* sin *(gegen* against); *(= Tat auch)* heinous deed *(liter)*; *(fig)* crime *(an +dat* against)

fre|vel|haft ADJ *(geh) (= verwerflich)* sinful; *Leichtsinn, Verschwendung* wanton

Fre|vel|haf|tig|keit [ˈfreːflhaftɪçkait] F **-,** *no pl (geh) (= Verwerflichkeit)* sinfulness; *(von Leichtsinn, Verschwendung)* wantonness

fre|veln [ˈfreːfln] VI *(liter)* to sin *(gegen, an +dat* against)

Fre|vel|tat F *(liter)* heinous deed *(liter)*

Frev|ler [ˈfreːflɐ] M **-s, -**, **Frev|le|rin** [-ərɪn] F **-, -nen** *(liter)* sinner; **die Strafe für den ~ an der Natur/gegen Gott** the punishment for someone who sins against nature/God

frev|le|risch [ˈfreːflərɪʃ] ADJ *(liter)* = **frevelhaft**

fri|de|ri|zi|a|nisch [frideriˈtsiaːnɪʃ] ADJ of Frederick the Great

Frie|de [ˈfriːdə] M **-ns, -n** *(old)* peace; **der ~ der Natur** the tranquillity of nature; **~ auf Erden** peace on earth; **~ sei mit euch** peace be with you; **~ seiner Asche** God rest his soul; **~, Freude, Eierkuchen** *(inf)* everything is rosy

Frie|den [ˈfriːdn] M **-s, - a** peace; **ein langer, ungestörter ~** a long period of uninterrupted peace; **im ~** in peacetime, in time of peace; **in ~ und Freiheit leben** to live at peace and in freedom; **im tiefsten ~** (living) in perfect tranquillity; **seit letztem Jahr herrscht in dieser Gegend ~** this region has been at peace since last year; **~ schließen** to make one's peace; *(Pol)* to conclude *(form) or* make peace; **seinen ~ mit jdm/etw machen** to make one's peace with sb/sth; **~ stiften** to make peace *(zwischen +dat* between)

b *(= Friedensschluss)* peace; *(= Vertrag)* peace treaty; **der Westfälische ~** *(Hist)* the Peace of Westphalia; **den ~ diktieren** to dictate the peace terms; **über den ~ verhandeln** to hold peace negotiations; **den ~ einhalten** to keep the peace, to keep to the peace agreement

c *(= Harmonie)* peace, tranquillity; **sozialer ~** social harmony; **der häusliche ~** domestic harmony; **in ~ und Freundschaft** *or* **Eintracht leben**

to live in peace and harmony *or* tranquillity **d** *(= Ruhe)* peace; **jdn in ~ lassen** to leave sb in peace; **um des lieben ~s willen** *(inf)* for the sake of peace and quiet; **sein schlechtes Gewissen ließ ihn keinen ~ mehr finden** his guilty conscience gave him no peace; **ich traue dem ~ nicht** *(inf)* something (fishy) is going on *(inf)*; **(er) ruhe in ~** rest in peace

Frie|dens- *in cpds* peace; **Frie|dens|ab|kom|men** NT peace agreement; **Frie|dens|ak|ti|vist(in)** M(F) peace activist; **Frie|dens|ap|pell** M call for peace; **Frie|dens|be|din|gun|gen** PL peace terms *pl*; **Frie|dens|be|mü|hung** F *usu pl* peace effort; *(= Friedensangebot)* peace move; **frie|dens|be|wegt** ADJ *Gruppen* campaigning for peace; *Aktivitäten* peace *attr*; **Frie|dens|be|weg|te(r)** [-bəveːktə] MF *decl as adj* peace activist; **Frie|dens|be|we|gung** F peace movement; **Frie|dens|bruch** M violation of the peace; **Frie|dens|en|gel** M *(lit, fig)* angel of peace; **Frie|dens|fahrt** F *international cycling race through eastern Europe*; **Frie|dens|for|scher(in)** M(F) peace researcher; **Frie|dens|for|schung** F peace studies *sing*; **Frie|dens|füh|ler** PL **die ~ ausstrecken** *(inf)* to make a tentative move toward(s) peace *(in Richtung* with); **Frie|dens|ini|ti|a|ti|ve** F peace initiative; **Frie|dens|kämp|fer(in)** M(F) pacifist; **Frie|dens|kon|fe|renz** F peace conference; **Frie|dens|kuss** M *(Eccl)* pax, kiss of peace; **Frie|dens|la|ger** NT *(Hist) nations of the Socialist bloc*; **Frie|dens|lie|be** F love of peace; **Frie|dens|marsch** M peace march; **Frie|dens|no|bel|preis** M Nobel peace prize; **Frie|dens|ord|nung** F *(Pol)* peace framework; **Frie|dens|pfei|fe** F peace pipe; **mit jdm die ~ rauchen** *(lit)* to smoke a peace pipe with sb; *(fig)* to make (one's) peace *or* to bury the hatchet with sb; **miteinander die ~ rauchen** *(fig)* to bury the hatchet; **Frie|dens|pflicht** F *(Ind) obligation binding on employers and unions to avoid industrial action during wage negotiations*; **Frie|dens|plan** M peace plan; **Frie|dens|po|li|tik** F policy of peace; **Frie|dens|preis** F peace prize *or* award; **der ~ des deutschen Buchhandels** the peace prize of the German book trade; **Frie|dens|pro|duk|ti|on** F peacetime production; **Frie|dens|pro|zess** M peace process; **Frie|dens|rich|ter(in)** M(F) justice of the peace, JP; **Frie|dens|schluss** M peace agreement; **frie|dens|si|chernd** ADJ *Streitkräfte* peacekeeping; **~e Maßnahmen** measures to ensure peace; **Frie|dens|si|che|rung** F maintenance of peace; **Maßnahmen zur ~** measures to ensure peace; **Frie|dens|stär|ke** F *(Mil)* peacetime strength; **frie|dens|stif|tend** ADJ peacemaking; **Frie|dens|stif|ter(in)** M(F) peacemaker; **Frie|dens|tau|be** F dove of peace; **Frie|dens|trup|pen** PL peacekeeping forces *pl*; **Frie|dens|ver|hand|lun|gen** PL peace negotiations *pl*; **Frie|dens|ver|trag** M peace treaty; **Frie|dens|vor|schlag** M peace proposal; **Frie|dens|wil|le** M desire *or* wish for peace; **Frie|dens|wirt|schaft** F peacetime economy; **Frie|dens|zeit** F period of peace; **in ~en** in peacetime, in times of peace; **Frie|dens|zu|stand** M state of peace; **im ~** at peace

fried|fer|tig ['friːtfɛrtɪç] ADJ *Mensch* peaceable; *Miteinander* peaceful; *Hund* placid; **selig sind die Friedfertigen** *(Bibl)* blessed are the peacemakers

Fried|fer|tig|keit F, *no pl* peaceable nature; *(von Hund)* placidness; **in seiner ~ hat er ...** peaceable as he is, he ...; **aus reiner ~ hat er ...** because of his peaceable nature, he ...; **sie wurden von den Polizeibeamten zur ~ ermahnt** they were warned by the police officers to keep the peace

Fried|hof ['friːthoːf] M *(= Kirchhof)* graveyard; *(= Stadtfriedhof etc)* cemetery; **auf dem ~** in the graveyard/cemetery

Fried|hofs-: **Fried|hofs|at|mos|phä|re** F gloomy atmosphere; **im Haus herrscht eine ~** the house is like a graveyard; **Fried|hofs|gärt|ne|rei** F cemetery flower shop; **Fried|hofs|ka|pel|le** F cemetery chapel; **Fried|hofs|ru|he** F *(lit)* → **Friedhof** peace of the graveyard/cemetery; *(fig)* deathly quiet

fried|lich ['friːtlɪç] ADJ **a** *(= nicht kriegerisch, gewaltlos) Lösung, Demonstration* peaceful; *(= friedfertig) Mensch* peaceable; *(= sanftmütig) Tier* placid; **etw auf ~em Wege lösen** to find a peaceful solution to sth, to solve sth peacefully *or* by peaceful means; **damit er endlich ~ ist** *(inf)* to keep him happy; **nun sei doch endlich ~!** *(fig inf)* give it a rest! *(inf)*; **sei ~, ich will keinen Streit** take it easy *or* calm down, I don't want any trouble; **die ~e Nutzung der Kernenergie** the use of nuclear power for peaceful purposes **b** *(= friedvoll)* peaceful
ADV **a** *(= in Frieden)* peacefully **b ~ sterben** *or* **einschlafen** *(euph)* to die peacefully; **jetzt kann ich ~ sterben** now I can die in peace

Fried|lich|keit F -, *no pl* **a** (= *Gewaltfreiheit: von Demonstration, Volk, Zeiten)* peacefulness; (= *Friedfertigkeit: von Mensch)* peaceable nature; (= *Sanftmut)* placidity **b** *(= friedvolle Atmosphäre)* peacefulness

fried-: **fried|lie|bend** ADJ peace-loving; **fried|los** ADJ **a** *(liter: = ruhelos) Leben, Europa* without peace; *Mensch* unable to find peace **b** *(Hist) Person* outlawed; **fried|sam** ['friːtzaːm] ADJ *(old)* = **friedlich**

Fried|rich ['friːdrɪç] M **-s** Frederick; **~ der Große** Frederick the Great; **seinen ~ Wilhelm unter etw** *(acc)* **setzen** *(inf)* to put one's signature *or* monicker *(Brit inf)* to sth, to put one's John Hancock on sth *(US inf)*

frie|ren ['friːrən] *pret* **fror** [froːɐ], *ptp* **gefroren** [gə'froːrən] VI **a** *auch vt impers (= sich kalt fühlen)* to be cold; **ich friere, mich friert, es friert mich** *(geh)* I'm cold; **wie ein Schneider ~** *(inf)* to be frozen to the bone *(inf)*; **mir** *or* **mich ~ die Zehen, mich friert es** *or* **ich friere an den Zehen** my toes are cold **b** *aux sein (= gefrieren)* to freeze; *(Fluss auch)* to freeze over VI *impers* to freeze; **heute Nacht hat es gefroren** it was below freezing last night

Fries [friːs] M **-es, -e** [-zə] *(Archit, Tex)* frieze

Frie|se ['friːzə] M **-n, -n**, **Frie|sin** ['friːzɪn] F **-, -nen** Fri(e)sian

Frie|sen|nerz ['friːzn-] M *(inf hum)* oilskin jacket

frie|sisch ['friːzɪʃ] ADJ Fri(e)sian → *auch* **deutsch**

Frie|sisch(e) ['friːzɪʃ] NT Fri(e)sian → *auch* **Deutsch(e)**

Fries|land ['friːslant] NT **-s** Friesland

fri|gid [fri'giːt], **fri|gi|de** [fri'giːdə] ADJ frigid

Fri|gi|di|tät [frigidi'tɛːt] F -, *no pl* frigidity

Fri|ka(n)|del|le [frika(n)'dɛlə] F **-, -n** *(Cook)* rissole

Fri|kas|see [frika'seː] NT **-s, -s** *(Cook)* fricassee

fri|kas|sie|ren [frika'siːrən] *ptp* **frikassiert** VT *(Cook)* to fricassee

Fri|ka|tiv [frika'tiːf] M **-s, -e** [-və], **Fri|ka|tiv|laut** M *(Ling)* fricative

Frik|ti|on [frɪk'tsioːn] F **-, -en** *(Tech, fig geh)* friction *no pl*

Fris|bee® ['frisbi] NT **-, -s** Frisbee®; **~® spielen** to play (with a) Frisbee®

Fris|bee|schei|be ['frisbi-] F Frisbee®

frisch [frɪʃ] ADJ **a** fresh; *Wäsche, Kleidung* clean; *(= feucht) Farbe, Fleck* wet; **~es Obst** fresh fruit; **~e Eier** new-laid *(Brit)* or freshly-laid eggs; **sich ~ machen** to freshen up; **mit ~en Kräften** with renewed vigour *(Brit)* or vigor *(US)* or strength; **~en Mut fassen** to gain new courage; **~e Luft schöpfen** to get some fresh air; **jdn an die ~e Luft setzen** *(inf)* to show sb the door; **jdn auf ~er Tat ertappen** to catch sb in the act, to catch sb red-handed **b** *(= munter) Wesen, Art* bright, cheery; *Erzählung, Farbe* cheerful; *(= gesund) Aussehen, Gesichtsfarbe* fresh; *Mädchen* fresh-looking; **~ und munter sein** *(inf)* to be bright and lively; **~, fromm, fröhlich, frei** *(prov) motto of a 19th century gymnastic movement (iro)* cheerfully, gaily **c** *(= kühl)* cool, chilly; *Luft, Wind auch* fresh; **es weht ein ~er Wind** *(lit)* there's a fresh wind; *(fig)* the wind of change is blowing
ADV **a** *(= neu)* freshly; **~ von** *or* **aus etw** fresh from sth; **Bier ~ vom Fass** beer (straight) from the tap; **~ gestrichen** newly *or* freshly painted; *(auf Schild)* wet paint; **~ geschlachtet** fresh(ly) slaughtered; *Geflügel* fresh(ly) killed; **~ gefallener Schnee** freshly *or* newly fallen snow; **~ gebacken** *Brot etc* fresh from the oven → *auch* **frischgebacken**; **~ gewaschen** *Kind* clean; *Hemd etc auch* freshly washed *or* laundered; **das Bett ~ beziehen** to change the bed, to make the bed up with fresh sheets; **das ist mir noch ~ in Erinnerung** that is still fresh in my mind *or* memory **b** *(= munter)* **immer ~ drauflos!** don't hold back!; **er geht immer ~ drauflos** he doesn't hang about; **er redet/schreibt immer ~ drauflos** he just talks/writes away; **~ begonnen, halb gewonnen** *(prov)* **~ gewagt ist halb gewonnen** *(Prov)* a good start is half the battle

frisch|auf [frɪʃ'lauf] INTERJ *(old)* let us away *(old)*

Fri|sche ['frɪʃə] F -, *no pl* **a** freshness; **wegen der ~ der Farbe** because the paint is/was still wet **b** *(von Wesen)* brightness; *(von Erzählung, Farbe)* cheerfulness; *(= gesundes Aussehen)* freshness; **in voller körperlicher und geistiger ~** in perfect health both physically and mentally; **in alter ~** *(inf)* as always **c** *(= Kühle)* coolness, chilliness; *(von Luft, Wind)* freshness, chilliness

Fri|sche|da|tum NT sell-by date

Frisch-: **Frisch|ei** ['frɪʃlai] NT new-laid *(Brit)* or freshly-laid egg; **Frisch|fisch** M fresh fish; **Frisch|fleisch** NT fresh meat; **frisch-fröh|lich** ADJ bright and cheerful; **frisch|ge|ba|cken** [-gəbakn] ADJ **a** *(inf, fig, Ehepaar, Ehemann, Ehefrau)* newly-wed; *Diplom-Ingenieur etc* newly-qualified; *Minister, Pressesprecher etc* newly-appointed **b** *Brot etc* → **frisch** ADV **a**; **frisch|ge|fal|len** ADJ → **frisch** ADV **a**; **Frisch|ge|mü|se** NT fresh vegetables *pl*; **frisch|ge|schlach|tet** *etc* ADJ → **frisch** ADV **a**

fri|schen ['frɪʃn] VT *Metall* to refine VI *(Wildschwein)* to farrow

Frisch|hal|te-: **Frisch|hal|te|beu|tel** M airtight bag; **Frisch|hal|te|box** F air-tight container; **Frisch|hal|te|da|tum** NT sell-by date; **Frisch|hal|te|fo|lie** F clingfilm; **Frisch|hal|te|pa|ckung** F airtight pack

Frisch-: **Frisch|kä|se** M cream cheese; **Frisch|ling** ['frɪʃlɪŋ] M **-s, -e** **a** *(Hunt) young wild boar* **b** *(hum: = Neuling)* complete beginner

Frisch|luft F fresh air

Frisch|luft-: **Frisch|luft|fa|na|ti|ker(in)** M(F) fresh air fiend *or* fanatic; **Frisch|luft|zu|fuhr** F fresh air supply

Frisch-: **Frisch|milch** F fresh milk; **Frisch|was|ser** NT, *no pl* fresh water; **frisch|weg** [frɪʃ'vɛk] ADV *(= ohne Hemmungen)* straight out *(inf)*; **die Kinder fingen ~ an zu singen** the children started to sing right off *(inf)*; **Frisch|wurst** F sausage *(unsmoked, undried etc)*; **Frisch|zel|le** F *(Med)* live cell; **Frisch|zel|len|kur** F, **Frisch|zel|len|the|ra|pie** F *(Med)* live-cell *or* cellular therapy

Fri|seur [fri'zøːɐ] M **-s, -e** hairdresser; *(= Herrenfriseur auch)* barber; *(= Geschäft)* hairdresser's, barber's

Fri|seu|rin [fri'zøːrɪn] F **-, -nen** (female) hairdresser

Fri|seur|sa|lon [fri'zøːɐ-] M hairdresser's, hairdressing salon

Fri|seu|se [fri'zøːzə] F **-, -n** (female) hairdresser

Fri|sier|creme F hair cream

fri|sie|ren [fri'zi:rən] *ptp* **frisiert** VT **a** *(= kämmen)* **jdn ~, jdm das Haar ~** to do sb's hair; *(nach dem Legen)* to comb sb's hair out; **ihr elegant frisierter Kopf** her elegant hairdo; **sie ist stets gut frisiert** her hair is always beautifully done; **eine modisch frisierte Dame** a lady with a fashionable hairstyle *or* hairdo **b** *(inf: = abändern) Abrechnung* to fiddle; *Bericht, Meldung* to doctor *(inf)*; **die Bilanzen ~** to cook the books *(inf)* **c** *(inf) Auto, Motorrad, Motor* to soup up *(inf)* VR to do one's hair

Fri|sier-: **Fri|sier|hau|be** F *(= Trockner)* hairdryer hood; *(beim Friseur)* hairdryer; **Fri|sier|kom|mo|de** F dressing table; **Fri|sier|sa|lon** M hairdressing salon; *(für Herren)* barber's shop; **Fri|sier|spie|gel** M dressing (table) mirror; **Fri|sier|stab** M styling brush; **Fri|sier|tisch** M dressing table; **Fri|sier|um|hang** M hairdressing cape

Fri|sör [fri'zø:ɐ] M **-s, -e**, **Fri|sö|se** [-'zø:zə] F **-, -n** = **Friseur, Friseuse**

frisst [frɪst] *3. pers sing pres von* **fressen**

Frist [frɪst] F **-, -en** **a** *(= Zeitraum)* period; *(= Kündigungsfrist)* period of notice; **eine ~ von vier Tagen/Wochen** *etc* four days/weeks *etc*; **eine ~ einhalten** to meet a deadline; *(bei Rechnung)* to pay within the period stipulated; **jds ~ verlängern, jdm die ~ verlängern** to give sb more time; **jds ~** *or* **jdm die ~ um zwei Tage verlängern** to give sb two more days; **die Bibliothek hat mir die ~ für die Rückgabe der Bücher verlängert** the library extended the loan-period on my books; **eine ~ verstreichen lassen** to let a deadline pass; *(bei Rechnung)* not to pay within the period stipulated; **innerhalb kürzester ~** without delay **b** *(= Zeitpunkt)* deadline (*zu* for); *(bei Rechnung)* last date for payment; **eine ~ versäumen** *or* **verpassen** to miss a deadline/the last date for payment **c** *(= Aufschub)* extension, period of grace; **jdm eine ~ von vier Tagen/Wochen geben** to give sb four days'/weeks' grace

Frist|ab|lauf M **nach ~** after the deadline has/had expired; *(bei Rechnung)* after expiry of the stipulated period

fris|ten ['frɪstn] VT **sein Leben** *or* **Dasein ~/mit etw ~** to eke out an existence/one's existence with sth; **ein kümmerliches Dasein ~** to eke out a miserable existence; *(Partei, Institution)* to exist on the fringes; **die Bauern mussten in Armut ihr Leben ~** the peasants barely managed to scrape a living

Fris|ten|lö|sung F, **Fris|ten|re|ge|lung** F *law allowing the termination of a pregnancy within the first three months*

Frist-: **frist|ge|mäß**, **frist|ge|recht** ADJ, ADV within the stated period; **jdm fristgerecht kündigen** to fire sb with (proper) notice *(inf)*; **fristgerecht kündigen** to give proper notice; **frist|los** ADJ instant, without notice ADV *entlassen, kündigen* without notice; **Frist|ver|län|ge|rung** F extension

Fri|sur [fri'zu:ɐ] F **-, -en** hairstyle

Fri|teu|se △ [fri'tø:zə] F **-, -n** → **Fritteuse**

fri|tie|ren △ [fri'ti:rən] *ptp* **fritiert** VT → **frittieren**

Frit|ta|ten [frɪ'ta:tn] PL *(Aus)* pancake strips *pl*, strips *pl* of pancake

Frit|ten ['frɪtn] PL *(inf)* chips *pl (Brit)*, fries *pl (esp US inf)*

Frit|ten|bu|de F *(inf)* chip shop *(Brit)*, chippie *(Brit inf)*, ≈ hotdog stand

Frit|teu|se [fri'tø:zə] F **-, -n** chip pan *(Brit)*, deep-fat fryer

frit|tie|ren [fri'ti:rən] *ptp* **frittiert** VT to (deep) fry

frit|tiert ADJ deep-fried

Frit|tü|re [fri'ty:rə] F **-, -n** **a** *(= Fritteuse)* chip pan *(Brit)*, deep-fat fryer **b** *(= Fett)* fat **c** *(= Speise)* fried food

-frit|ze [frɪtsə] M *suf in cpds* **-n, -n** *(inf)* chap *(Brit inf)*, guy *(inf)*; **Computerfritze** computer chap *(Brit inf)* or guy *(inf)*

fri|vol [fri'vo:l] ADJ *(= leichtfertig)* frivolous; *(= anzüglich) Witz, Bemerkung* risqué, suggestive; *(= verantwortungslos)* irresponsible

Fri|vo|li|tät [frivoli'tɛ:t] F **-, -en** **a** *no pl (= Leichtfertigkeit)* frivolity; *(= Anzüglichkeit: von Witz, Bemerkung)* suggestiveness; *(= Verantwortungslosigkeit)* irresponsibility **b** *(= Bemerkung)* risqué remark

Fri|vo|li|tä|ten|ar|beit F *(Sew)* tatting

Frl. *abbr von* **Fräulein**

froh [fro:] ADJ **a** *(= heiter)* happy; *(= dankbar)* glad, happy; *(= erfreut)* glad, pleased, happy; **über etw** *(acc)* **~ sein** to be pleased with sth; **(darüber) ~ sein, dass ...** to be glad *or* pleased that ...; **um etw ~ sein** to be grateful for sth; **~ gelaunt** joyful *(liter)*, cheerful, happy; **~ gestimmt** *(geh)* happy, joyful *(liter)*; **~en Mutes** *or* **Sinnes sein** *(old, geh)* to be cheerful, to be of good cheer *(old)*; **~en Mutes machte sie sich an die Arbeit** *(old, geh)* cheerfully *or* with a light heart she set herself to work; **seines Lebens nicht (mehr) ~ werden** not to enjoy life any more; **da wird man seines Lebens nicht mehr ~!** it makes your life a misery **b** *(= erfreulich)* happy, joyful; *Nachricht* good, happy; **~e Ostern!** Happy Easter!; **~e Weihnachten!** Happy *(esp Brit)* or Merry Christmas!; **die Frohe Botschaft** the Gospel

froh-: **froh|ge|launt** ADJ → **froh a**; **froh|ge|mut** [-gəmu:t] ADJ *(old)* with a cheerful heart; **froh|ge|stimmt** ADJ → **froh a**

fröh|lich ['frø:lɪç] ADJ happy, cheerful, merry; *Lieder, Lachen, Stimme auch* gay *(dated)*; **~e Weihnachten!** Happy *(esp Brit)* or Merry Christmas!; **~es Treiben** gaiety ADV *(= unbekümmert)* merrily, blithely, gaily; **er kam einfach so ~ ins Zimmer marschiert** he came waltzing into the room *(inf)*

Fröh|lich|keit F **-,** *no pl* happiness; *(= fröhliches Wesen)* happy *or* cheerful nature; *(= gesellige Stimmung)* merriment, gaiety

froh|lo|cken [fro'lɔkn] *ptp* **frohlockt** VI *(geh)* to rejoice (*über +acc* over, at); *(vor Schadenfreude auch)* to gloat (*über +acc* over, *bei* at)

Froh-: **Froh|na|tur** F *(geh)* **a** *(= Mensch)* happy *or* cheerful soul *or* person **b** *(= Wesensart)* happy *or* cheerful nature; **Froh|sinn** M, *no pl* cheerfulness; *(= fröhliches Wesen)* cheerful nature; **froh|sin|nig** ADJ cheerful

fromm [frɔm] ADJ *comp* **=er** *or* **-er** ['frœmɐ], *superl* **=ste(r, s)** ['frœmstə] **a** *(= gläubig)* religious; *Christ* devout; *Werke* good; *Leben, Tun* godly, pious; *(= scheinheilig)* pious, sanctimonious; **~ werden** to become religious, to turn to *or* get *(inf)* religion; **mit ~em Augenaufschlag** *or* **Blick** looking as if butter wouldn't melt in his/her *etc* mouth; **~e Sprüche** pious words **b** *(old: = rechtschaffen) Bürger, Leute, Denkart* god-fearing, upright; **es kann der Frömmste nicht in Frieden leben, wenn es dem bösen Nachbarn nicht gefällt** *(Prov)* you can't be on good terms with a bad neighbour *(Brit)* or neighbor *(US)* , however hard you try **c** *(old: = gehorsam)* meek, docile; *Tier* quiet, docile; **~ wie ein Lamm sein** to be as meek *or* *(Tier)* gentle as a lamb **d** *(fig)* **eine ~e Lüge, ein ~er Betrug** self-deception; **das ist ja wohl nur ein ~er Wunsch** that's just a pipe dream

Fröm|me|lei [frœmə'lai] F **-, -en** *(pej)* false piety

fröm|meln ['frœmln] VI *(pej)* to act piously, to affect piety

from|men ['frɔmən] VI *(old)* **jdm ~** to avail sb *(form)*; **jdm nichts ~** to avail sb naught *(old)*; **was frommt ihm das Geld?** of what avail is the money to him? *(form)*

Fröm|mig|keit ['frœmɪçkait] F **-,** *no pl (= Gläubigkeit)* religiousness; *(von Christ)* devoutness; *(von Leben, Tun, Schriften, Werken)* godliness, piousness; *(old: = Rechtschaffenheit)* uprightness

Frömm|ler ['frœmlɐ] M **-s, -**, **Frömm|le|rin** [-ərɪn] F **-, -nen** *(pej)* sanctimonious hypocrite

frömm|le|risch ['frœmlərɪʃ] ADJ *(pej)* pious, sanctimonious

Fron [fro:n] F **-, -en**, **Fron|ar|beit** F *(Hist)* socage *no pl*; *(fig)* drudgery *no pl*; *(= Sklavenarbeit)* slavery

Fron|de ['frõ:də] F **-, -n** *(Pol)* faction

Fron|deur [frõ'dø:ɐ] M **-s, -e**, **Fron|deu|rin** [-'dø:rɪn] F **-, -nen** factionist

Fron|dienst M *(Hist)* socage *no pl*; **jdm ~e leisten** to do socage (work) for sb

fro|nen ['fro:nən] VI *(Hist)* to labour *(Brit)* or labor *(US)* for one's feudal lord; *(fig geh)* to labour *(Brit)*, to labor *(US)*

frö|nen ['frø:nən] VI *+dat (geh)* to indulge in; *seiner Eitelkeit* to indulge

Fron|leich|nam [fro:n'laiçna:m] *no art* **-(e)s**, *no pl* (the Feast of) Corpus Christi; **zu** *or* **an ~** at the Feast of Corpus Christi, on Corpus Christi

Fron|leich|nams-: **Fron|leich|nams|fest** NT Feast of Corpus Christi; **Fron|leich|nams|pro|zes|si|on** F, **Fron|leich|nams|zug** M Corpus Christi procession

Front [frɔnt] F **-, -en** **a** *(= Vorderseite)* front; *(= Vorderansicht)* frontage; **die hintere ~** the back; **der General schritt die ~ der wartenden Truppen ab** the general inspected the waiting troops **b** *(= Kampflinie, -gebiet)* front; **in vorderster ~ stehen** to be in the front line; **auf breiter ~** along a wide front; **an der ~** at the front; **klare ~en schaffen** *(fig)* to clarify the/one's position **c** *(Met)* front **d** *(= Einheit)* ranks *pl*; *(in Namen)* front; **sich einer geschlossenen ~ gegenübersehen** to be faced with a united front; **~ gegen jdn/etw machen** to make a stand against sb/sth **e** *(Sport: = Führung)* **in ~ liegen** to be in the lead; **in ~ gehen** to go into *or* take the lead

Front|ab|schnitt M section of the front

fron|tal [frɔn'ta:l] ADJ *no pred Angriff* frontal; *Zusammenstoß* head-on; *Position* at the front ADV *angreifen (Mil)* from the front; *(fig)* head-on; *zusammenstoßen* head-on; *darstellen* front-on

Fron|tal-: **Fron|tal|an|griff** M frontal attack; **Fron|tal|un|ter|richt** M *(Sch)* didactic teaching, chalk and talk *(inf)*; **Fron|tal|zu|sam|men|stoß** M head-on collision

Front-: **Front|an|sicht** F front(al) view; **Front|an|trieb** M *(Aut)* front-wheel drive; **Front|be|gra|di|gung** F straightening of the front; *(fig)* streamlining operation; **Front|be|richt** M report from the front; **Front|dienst** M, **Front|ein|satz** M service at the front; **er wurde zum ~ nach Rumänien abkommandiert** he was posted to serve on the Romanian front; **Front|en|de** NT *(Comput)* front end

Fron|ten|sys|tem NT *(Met)* frontal system

Fron|tis|piz [frɔnti'spi:ts] NT **-es, -e** *(Archit, Typ)* frontispiece

Front-: **Front|kämp|fer(in)** M(F) frontline soldier; **Front|la|der** [-la:dɐ] M **-s, -** front loader; **Front|mo|tor** M front-mounted engine; **Front|schei|be** F *(Mot)* (front) windscreen *(Brit)*, (front) windshield *(US)*; **Front|schwein** NT *(sl)*, **Front|sol|dat(in)** M(F) frontline soldier; **Front|spoi|ler** M *(Aut)* front spoiler; **Front|stadt** F frontier town; **Front|ur|laub** M leave from the front; **Front|wand** F frontage; **Front|wech|sel** M *(fig)* about-turn; **Front|zu|la|ge** F supplement for service at the front

Fron|vogt M *(Hist)* (socage) overseer

fror *pret von* **frieren**

Frosch [frɔʃ] M **-(e)s, =e** ['frœʃə] frog; *(= Feuerwerkskörper)* (fire)cracker, jumping jack *(Brit)*; **einen ~ in der Kehle** *or* **im Hals haben** *(inf)* to have a frog in one's throat; **sei kein ~!** *(inf)* be a sport!

Frosch-: **Frosch|au|ge** NT *(fig inf)* pop eye; **er hat ~n** he has pop eyes, he is pop-eyed; **Frosch|biss** M *(Bot)* frogbit; **Frosch|hüp|fen**

NT **-s**, *no pl* leapfrog; **Frosch|kö|nig** M Frog Prince; **Frosch|kon|zert** NT *(hum)* frog chorus; **Frosch|laich** M frogspawn; **Frosch|lurch** M salientian *(form)*, member of the frog family; **Frosch|mann** M *pl* **-männer** frogman; **Frosch|maul** NT *(fig inf)* pout; **Frosch|per|spek|ti|ve** F worm's-eye view; *(fig)* blinkered view; **etw aus der ~ fotografieren/sehen** to take/get a worm's-eye view of sth; **etw aus der ~ betrachten** *(fig)* to have a blinkered view of sth; **Frosch|schen|kel** M frog's leg; **Frosch|test** M *(Med)* Bickenbach (pregnancy) test

Frost [frɔst] M **-(e)s, ⸗e** ['frœstə] **a** frost; **es herrscht strenger/klirrender ~** there's a hard *or* heavy/crisp frost; **bei eisigem ~** in heavy frost; **~ (ab)bekommen** *(Hände, Ohren)* to get frostbitten; **~ vertragen (können)** to be able to stand (the) frost **b** *(Med: = Schüttelfrost)* fit of shivering *or* the shivers *(inf)*; **er wurde von einem heftigen ~ geschüttelt** he shivered violently

Frost-: **frost|an|fäl|lig** ADJ susceptible to frost; **Frost|an|fäl|lig|keit** F susceptibility to frost; **Frost|auf|bruch** M frost damage; **frost|be|stän|dig** ADJ frost-resistant; **Frost|beu|le** F chilblain; **Frost|bo|den** M frozen ground; *(ständig gefroren)* permafrost; **Frost|ein|bruch** M sudden frost

frös|te|lig ['frœstəlɪç] ADJ *(inf)* chilly; **er ist ein ~er Mensch** he's a chilly mortal *(inf)*, he feels the cold

frös|teln ['frœstln] VI to shiver; *(vor Angst auch)* to tremble; *(vor Entsetzen auch)* to shudder; **im Fieber ~** to shiver feverishly VT *impers* **es fröstelte mich** I shivered/trembled/shuddered

frost|emp|find|lich ADJ *Pflanzen etc* frost-sensitive *attr*, sensitive to frost *pred*, delicate, not hardy *pred*

fros|ten ['frɔstn] VT to freeze → *auch* **gefrostet**

Fros|ter ['frɔstɐ] M **-s, -** *(im Kühlschrank)* icebox *(Brit)*, freezer compartment; *(= Gefriertruhe)* freezer, deep-freeze

Frost-: **frost|frei** ADJ frost-free, free from *or* of frost; **die Nacht war ~** there was no frost overnight; **Frost|ge|fahr** F danger of frost; **Frost|gren|ze** F *(Met)* frost line

fros|tig ['frɔstɪç] ADJ *(lit, fig)* frosty; **ein ~er Hauch** an icy draught *(Brit) or* draft *(US)* ADV **jdn ~ begrüßen** to give sb a frosty greeting; **~ klingen** to sound frosty; **jdn ~ empfangen** to give sb a frosty reception, to receive sb frostily; **jdn ~ abfertigen** to be very frosty to sb

Fros|tig|keit F **-,** *no pl (lit, fig)* frostiness

Frost-: **frost|klar** ADJ clear and frosty; **frost|klir|rend** ADJ *attr (liter)* crisp and frosty

fröst|lig ['frœstlɪç] ADJ = **fröstelig**

Frost-: **Frost|scha|den** M frost damage; **Frost|schutz** M protection against frost; **Frost|schutz|mit|tel** NT *(Aut)* antifreeze; **frost|si|cher** ADJ frostproof; *Ort* free of frost; **Frost|war|nung** F frost warning; **Frost|wet|ter** NT frosty weather

Frot|tee [frɔ'te:] NT OR M **-s, -s** terry towelling *(Brit)*, terry-cloth toweling *(US)*; **ein Kleid aus ~** a towelling *(Brit) or* terry-cloth *(US)* dress

Frot|tee-: **Frot|tee|hand|tuch** NT (terry) towel *(Brit)*, terry-cloth towel *(US)*; **Frot|tee|kleid** NT towelling *(Brit) or* terry-cloth *(US)* dress; **Frot|tee|tuch** NT *pl* **-tücher** (terry) towel *(Brit)*, terry-cloth towel *(US)*

frot|tie|ren [frɔ'ti:rən] *ptp* **frottiert** VT *Haut* to rub; *jdn, sich* to rub down

Frot|tier-: **Frot|tier|hand|tuch** NT (terry) towel *(Brit)*, terry-cloth towel *(US)*; **Frot|tier|tuch** NT *pl* **-tücher** (terry) towel *(Brit)*, terry-cloth towel *(US)*

Frot|ze|lei [frɔtsə'lai] F **-, -en** *(inf)* teasing; *(= Bemerkung)* teasing remark

frot|zeln ['frɔtsln] VTI *(inf)* to tease; **über jdn/etw ~** to make fun of sb/sth

Frucht [frʊxt] F **-, ⸗e** ['frʏçtə] *(Bot, fig)* fruit; *(= Embryo)* foetus *(Brit)*, fetus *(US)*; *(no pl: = Getreide)* crops *pl*; **Früchte** *(= Obst)* fruit *sing*; **Früchte tragen** *(lit, fig)* to bear fruit; **~ tragend** = **fruchttragend**; **~ bringend** = **fruchtbringend**; **die Früchte des Feldes** *(liter)* the fruits of the earth *(liter)*; **verbotene Früchte** forbidden fruits; **eine ~ der Liebe** *(old euph)* a love child; **an ihren Früchten sollt ihr sie erkennen** *(Bibl)* by their fruits ye shall know them *(Bibl)*

Frucht|an|satz M *(Bot)* fruit buds *pl*

frucht|bar ADJ **a** *(lit, fig: = zeugungsfähig, reiche Frucht bringend)* fertile → **Boden a** **b** *(lit, fig: = viele Nachkommen zeugend, viel schaffend)* prolific; *(Bibl)* fruitful **c** *(fig: = nutzbringend)* fruitful, productive; **etw für jdn/etw ~ machen** to use sth for the good of sb/sth, to use sth to benefit sb/sth

Frucht|bar|keit ['frʊxtba:ɐkait] F **-,** *no pl* **a** *(lit, fig: = Zeugungsfähigkeit, Ergiebigkeit)* fertility **b** *(lit, fig: = viele Nachkommen zeugend, Schaffensreichtum)* prolificness **c** *(fig: = Nutzen)* fruitfulness, productiveness

Frucht|bar|keits-: **Frucht|bar|keits|göt|tin** F fertility goddess; **Frucht|bar|keits|kult** M fertility cult; **Frucht|bar|keits|sym|bol** NT fertility symbol; **Frucht|bar|keits|zau|ber** M fertility rite

Frucht|bar|ma|chung [-maxʊŋ] F **-, -en** *(von Wüste)* reclamation

Frucht-: **Frucht|be|cher** M fruit sundae; *(Bot)* cupule *(spec)*, cup; **Frucht|bla|se** F amniotic sac; **Frucht|bon|bon** M OR NT fruit drop; **frucht|brin|gend** ADJ *(geh)* fruitful, productive

Frücht|chen ['frʏçtçən] NT **-s, -** *dim von* **Frucht** *(inf) (= Tunichtgut)* good-for-nothing; *(= Kind)* rascal *(inf)*; **du bist mir ein sauberes** *or* **nettes ~** *(iro)* you're a right one *(inf)*

Früch|te|brot NT fruit loaf

Frucht|ein|waa|ge F net weight of fruit

fruch|ten ['frʊxtn] VI to bear fruit; **nichts ~** to be fruitless

Früch|te|tee M fruit tea *or* infusion

Frucht-: **Frucht|fleisch** NT flesh *(of a fruit)*; **Frucht|flie|ge** F fruit fly; **Frucht|fol|ge** F *(Agr)* rotation of crops

fruch|tig ['frʊxtɪç] ADJ fruity

Fruch|tig|keit F **-,** *no pl* fruitiness

Frucht-: **Frucht|kap|sel** F *(Bot)* capsule; **Frucht|kno|ten** M *(Bot)* ovary; **frucht|los** ADJ *(fig)* fruitless; **Frucht|lo|sig|keit** F **-,** *no pl (fig)* fruitlessness; **Frucht|mark** NT *(Cook)* fruit pulp; **Frucht|pres|se** F fruit press *or* squeezer; **Frucht|saft** M fruit juice; **Frucht|säu|re** F fruit acid; **Frucht|stand** M *(Bot)* multiple fruit; **frucht|tra|gend** ADJ *attr* fruit-bearing; **Frucht|was|ser** NT, *no pl (Physiol)* amniotic fluid; **das ~ ist vorzeitig abgegangen** her waters broke early; **Frucht|was|ser|un|ter|su|chung** F *(Med)* amniocentesis; **Frucht|wech|sel** M crop rotation; **Frucht|zu|cker** M fructose

fru|gal [fru'ga:l] *(geh)* ADJ frugal ADV frugally

früh [fry:] ADJ early; **am ~en Morgen** early in the morning, in the early morning; **in ~er Jugend** in one's early youth; **in ~er Kindheit** in one's early childhood; **in ~ester Kindheit** very early in one's childhood; **der ~e Goethe** the young Goethe; **ein Werk des ~en Picasso** an early work by Picasso; **ein ~er Picasso** an early Picasso

ADV **a** early; *(= in jungen Jahren)* young, at an early age; *(in Entwicklung)* early on; **von ~ auf** from an early age; **es ist noch ~ am Tag/im Jahr** it is still early in the day/year; **von ~ bis spät** from morning till night, from dawn to dusk; **er hat schon ~ erkannt, dass ...** he recognized early on that ...; **du hast dich nicht ~ genug angemeldet** you didn't apply early *or* soon enough; **zu ~ starten** to start too soon; **ein ~ vollendeter Maler/Dichter** *etc (liter)* a young artist/poet *etc* whose genius reached its climax early; **~ übt sich, was ein Meister werden will** *(Prov)* there's nothing like starting young

b **Freitag/morgen ~** Friday/tomorrow morning; **heute ~** this morning

Früh- *in cpds* early; **Früh|an|ti|ke** F early classical period; **früh|auf** △ ['fry:lauf] ADV → **früh** ADV **a**; **Früh|auf|ste|her** [-laufʃte:ɐ] M **-s, -**, **Früh|auf|ste|he|rin** [-ərɪn] F **-, -nen** early riser, early bird *(inf)*; **Früh|beet** NT cold frame; **Früh|be|hand|lung** F early *or* prompt treatment *no indef art*

Früh|chen ['fry:çən] NT **-s, -** *(inf)* premature baby, prem *(inf)*, pre(e)mie *(US inf)*

Früh-: **früh|christ|lich** ADJ early Christian; **Früh|di|ag|no|se** F early diagnosis; **Früh|dienst** M early duty; **~ haben** to be on early duty

Frü|he ['fry:ə] F **-,** *no pl* **a** *(liter: = Frühzeit)* dawn; **in der ~ des Tages** in the early morning **b** *(= Morgen)* **in der ~** early in the morning; **in aller ~, gleich in der ~** at (the) crack of dawn

Früh-: **Früh|ehe** F young marriage; **Früh|ent|wick|ler(in)** M(F) early developer

frü|her ['fry:ɐ] *comp von* **früh** ADJ **a** earlier; **in ~en Jahren/Zeiten** in the past; **in ~en Zeitaltern** in past ages

b *(= ehemalig)* former; *(= vorherig) Besitzer, Wohnsitz* previous; **der Kontakt zu seinen ~en Freunden ist abgebrochen** he lost contact with his old friends

ADV **a** earlier; **~ als 6 Uhr/Freitag kann ich nicht kommen** I can't come earlier than 6 o'clock/earlier *or* sooner than Friday; **~ geht's nicht** *(= kann nicht früher gemacht werden)* it can't be done any earlier *or* sooner; *(= ich kann nicht früher kommen)* I can't make it any earlier *or* sooner; **~ am Abend hat er gesagt ...** earlier (on) in the evening he said ...; **alle, die sich ~ angemeldet haben, werden zuerst berücksichtigt** the first to apply will be the first to be considered; **das hättest du ~ sagen müssen/wissen sollen** you should have said that before *or* sooner/known that before; **~ oder später** sooner or later

b *(= in jüngeren Jahren, in vergangenen Zeiten)* **Herr X, ~ Direktor eines Industriebetriebs** Herr X, formerly director of an industrial concern; **ich habe ihn ~ mal gekannt** I used to know him; **~ habe ich so etwas nie gemacht** I never used to do that kind of thing; **~ stand hier eine Kirche** there used to be a church here; **~ war alles besser/war das alles anders** things were better/different in the old days, things used to be better/different; **genau wie ~** just as it/he *etc* used to be; **Erzählungen von/Erinnerungen an ~** stories/memories of times gone by *or* of bygone days *(liter)*; **das habe ich noch von ~** I had it before; **ich kannte ihn von ~** I knew him before; **ich kenne ihn von ~** I've known him some time; **wir kennen uns noch von ~** we got to know each other some time ago; **meine Freunde von ~** my old friends

Früh|er|ken|nung F *(Med)* early diagnosis

frü|hes|tens ['fry:əstns] ADV at the earliest; **~ am Sonntag** on Sunday at the earliest; **wann kann das ~ fertig sein?** what is the earliest that can be ready?

frü|hes|te(r, s) ['fry:əstə] ADJ *superl von* **früh**

frü|hest|mög|lich ['fry:əst'mø:klɪç] ADJ *attr* earliest possible

Früh-: **Früh|ge|bo|re|ne(s)** [-gəbo:rənə] NT *decl as adj* premature baby *or* infant *(form)*; **Früh|ge|burt** F premature birth; *(= Kind)* premature baby; **sie hatte/meine Tochter war eine ~** her baby/my daughter was premature *or* born prematurely; **Früh|ge|mü|se** NT early vegetables *pl*; **Früh|ge|schich|te** F early history; **Früh|got|tes|dienst** M early service; **Früh|herbst** M early autumn *or* fall *(US)*; **früh|herbst|lich** ADJ early autumn *or* fall *(US) attr*; **Früh|in|va|li|de(r)** MF *decl as adj* premature invalid; **Früh|in|va|li|di|tät** F early retirement due to ill health

Früh|jahr NT spring

Früh|jahrs-: **Früh|jahrs|bo|te** M *(liter)* harbinger of spring *(liter)*; **Früh|jahrs|mü|dig|keit** F springtime lethargy; **Früh|jahrs|putz** M spring-cleaning

Früh-: **Früh|ka|pi|ta|lis|mus** M early capitalism; **Früh|kar|tof|feln** PL early potatoes *pl*; **früh|kind|lich** ADJ *(Psych)* of early childhood; *Sexualität, Entwicklung* in early childhood; *Trauma, Erlebnisse* from early childhood; **Früh|konzert** NT early morning concert; *(von Vögeln)* dawn chorus; **Früh|kul|tur** F **a** early culture **b** *(Hort)* propagated seedlings *pl*

Früh|ling ['fry:lɪŋ] M **-s, -e** spring; **es wird ~, der ~ kommt** spring is coming; **im ~** in spring; **die Stadt des ewigen ~s** *(poet)* the springtime city *(liter)*; **im ~ des Lebens stehen** *(poet)* to be in the springtime of one's life *(liter)*; **einem neuen ~ entgegengehen** *(fig)* to start to flourish again; **seinen zweiten ~ erleben** to go through one's second adolescence

Früh|lings- *in cpds* spring; **Früh|lings|an|fang** M first day of spring; **Früh|lings|bo|te** M *(liter)* harbinger of spring *(liter)*; **Früh|lings|fest** NT spring festival; **Früh|lings|ge|füh|le** PL *(hum inf)* **~ haben/bekommen** to be/get frisky *(hum inf)*; **wenn sich ~ (bei ihm) regen** when he starts to feel frisky *(hum inf)*, when the sap starts to rise *(hum)*; **früh|lings|haft** ADJ springlike ADV **sich ~ kleiden** to dress in spring clothes; **es ist schon ~ warm** it's as warm as it is in spring; **Früh|lings|rol|le** F *(Cook)* spring roll; **Früh|lings|sup|pe** F spring vegetable soup; **Früh|lings|zeit** F springtime, springtide *(liter)*; **Früh|lings|zwie|bel** F spring *(Brit)* or green *(US)* onion

Früh-: **Früh|mes|se** F early mass; **früh|mor|gend|lich** ADJ early morning; **früh|mor|gens** ADV early in the morning; **Früh|ne|bel** M early morning mist; **Früh|neu|hoch|deutsch** NT Early New High German; **früh|pen|si|o|nie|ren** *ptp* **frühpensioniert** VT *insep* **jdn ~** to give sb early retirement; **Früh|pen|si|o|nie|rung** F early retirement; **früh|reif** ADJ precocious; *(körperlich)* mature at an early age; **Früh|rei|fe** F precociousness; *(von Körper)* early maturity; **Früh|rent|ner(in)** M(F) person who has retired early; **Früh|schicht** F early shift; **ich gehöre zur ~** *(inf)* I'm on the early shift; **Früh|schop|pen** M morning *or (mittags)* lunchtime drinking; **zum ~ gehen** to go for a morning/lunchtime drink

> **FRÜHSCHOPPEN**
>
> A **Frühschoppen** is a morning get-together, when friends meet over a **Schoppen**. Depending on the region, this may be a glass of wine or a beer and schnapps. The custom of enjoying a **Frühschoppen** on Sundays between church and the midday meal is still popular, particularly in rural areas.

Früh-: **Früh|som|mer** M early summer; **früh|som|mer|lich** ADJ early summer *attr*; **das Wetter ist schon ~** the weather is already quite summery; **Früh|sport** M early morning exercise; **~ treiben** to get some early morning exercise; **Früh|sta|di|um** NT early stage; **im ~** in the early stages; **Früh|start** M false start

Früh|stück NT **-s, -e** breakfast; *(= Frühstückspause)* morning or coffee break; **zweites ~** ≈ elevenses *(Brit inf)*, ≈ midmorning snack; **um 9 Uhr ist ~** breakfast is at 9 o'clock; **was isst du zum ~?** what do you have for breakfast?; **die ganze Familie saß beim ~** the whole family were having breakfast

früh|stü|cken ['fry:ʃtʏkn] *insep* VI to have breakfast, to breakfast VT to breakfast on

Früh|stücks-: **Früh|stücks|brett** NT wooden platter; **Früh|stücks|brot** NT sandwich *(for one's morning snack)*; **Früh|stücks|bü|fett** NT, **Früh|stücks|büf|fet** NT *(esp Aus)* breakfast buffet; **Früh|stücks|di|rek|tor(in)** M(F) *(pej)* figurehead; **Früh|stücks|fern|se|hen** NT breakfast television; **Früh|stücks|fleisch** NT luncheon meat; **Früh|stücks|pau|se** F morning or coffee break; **~ machen** to have one's morning or coffee break; **Früh|stücks|tel|ler** M dessert plate; **Früh|stücks|zim|mer** NT breakfast room

Früh-: **früh|ver|ren|ten** [-fɛerɛntn] *ptp* **frühverrentet** VT *insep* **jdn ~** to give sb early retirement; **Früh|ver|ren|tung** F early retirement; **früh|voll|en|det** ADJ *attr (liter)* → **früh** ADV **a**; **Früh|voll|en|de|te(r)** MF *decl as adj* **ein ~r** a young artist/poet *etc* whose genius reached its climax early; **Früh|warn|sys|tem** NT early warning system; **Früh|werk** NT early work; **Früh|zeit** F early days *pl*; **die ~ des Christentums** early Christian times; **die ~ der Menschheit** the early days of mankind; **früh|zei|tig** ADJ early; *(= vorzeitig auch)* premature; *Tod auch* premature, untimely ADV early; *(= vorzeitig)* prematurely; *(= früh genug)* in good time, early; *(= ziemlich am Anfang)* early on; **es kann ~ erkannt werden** it can be spotted in advance; **Früh|zug** M early train; **Früh|zün|dung** F *(Aut)* pre-ignition

Frust [frʊst] M **-(e)s**, *no pl (inf)* frustration *no art*; **das ist der totale ~, wenn ...** it's totally frustrating when ...

frus|ten ['frʊstn] VTI *(inf)* **von etw gefrustet sein** to be frustrated by sth; **das frustet** it's frustrating

Frust|es|sen NT comfort *or* stress eating

Frust|kauf M *(inf)* retail therapy *no pl*, comfort shopping *no pl*

Frust|ra|ti|on [frʊstra'tsio:n] F **-, -en** frustration

frust|rie|ren [frʊs'tri:rən] *ptp* **frustriert** VT to frustrate; *(inf: = enttäuschen)* to upset

frz. *abbr von* **französisch**

F-Schlüs|sel ['ɛf-] M *(Mus)* F *or* bass clef

FTP [ɛfti:'pi:] **nt -s, -s** *(Comput) abbr von* **file transfer protocol** FTP

FU [ɛf'lu:] F - *abbr von* **Freie Universität (Berlin)**

Fuchs [fʊks] M **-es, ¨-e** ['fʏksə] **a** *(= Tier)* fox; *(fig auch)* cunning devil *(inf)*; **er ist ein alter** *or* **schlauer ~** *(inf)* he's a cunning old devil *(inf)* or fox *(inf)*; **schlau wie ein ~** as cunning as a fox; **wo sich ~ und Hase** *or* **die Füchse gute Nacht sagen** *(hum)* in the back of beyond *(esp Brit)*, in the middle of nowhere **b** *(= Fuchspelz)* fox (fur) **c** *(= Pferd)* chestnut; *(mit hellerem Schwanz und Mähne)* sorrel; *(inf: = Mensch)* redhead **d** *(Univ)* new member of a student fraternity

Fuchs-: **Fuchs|band|wurm** M fox tapeworm; **Fuchs|bau** M *pl* **-baue** fox's den; **Fuchs|ei|sen** NT *(Hunt)* fox trap

fuch|sen ['fʊksn] *(inf)* VT to vex, to annoy VR to be annoyed *or* cross

Fuch|sie ['fʊksiə] F **-, -n** *(Bot)* fuchsia

fuch|sig ['fʊksɪç] ADJ *(inf)* **a** *(= rotblond) Haar* ginger, carroty *(inf)* **b** *(= wütend)* mad *(inf)*

Füch|sin ['fʏksɪn] F **-, -nen** vixen

Fuchs-: **Fuchs|jagd** F fox-hunting; *(= einzelne Jagd)* fox hunt; **Fuchs|loch** NT foxhole; **Fuchs|pelz** M fox fur; **fuchs|rot** ADJ *Fell* red; *Pferd* chestnut; *Haar* ginger, carroty *(inf)*; **Fuchs|schwanz** M **a** fox's tail; *(Hunt)* (fox's) brush **b** *(Bot)* love-lies-bleeding, amaranth **c** *(Tech: = Säge)* handsaw; **fuchs|teu|fels|wild** ADJ *(inf)* hopping mad *(inf)*

Fuch|tel ['fʊxtl] F **-, -n** **a** *(Hist: = Degen)* broadsword; *(fig inf: = Knute)* control; **unter jds ~** under sb's thumb; **er ist unter ihre ~ gekommen** *or* **geraten** she's got *or* gotten *(US)* him under her thumb; **er steht unter der ~** he's not his own master **b** *(Aus, S Ger inf: = zänkische Frau)* shrew, vixen

fuch|teln ['fʊxtln] VI *(inf)* **(mit den Händen) ~** to wave one's hands about *(inf)*; **mit etw ~** to wave sth about *or* around; *(drohend)* to brandish sth

fuch|tig ['fʊxtɪç] ADJ *(inf)* (hopping) mad *(inf)*

Fu|der ['fu:dɐ] NT **-s, -** **a** *(= Wagenladung)* cartload **b** *(= Hohlmaß für Wein)* tun

fu|der|wei|se ADV by the cartload; **~ Salat essen** *(hum)* to eat tons of salad *(inf)*

Fud|schi|ja|ma [fudʒi'ja:ma] M **-s** Fujiyama

Fuf|fi ['fʊfi] M **-s, -s** *(hum inf: = Fünfzigeuroschein)* fifty *(inf)* (big ones *pl*)

fuff|zehn ['fʊftse:n] NUM *(dial)* fifteen

Fuff|zi|ger ['fʊftsɪgɐ] M **-s, -** *(dial) (= Fünfzigeuroschein)* fifty-euro note *(Brit)* or bill *(US)*; *(= Fünfzigcentstück)* fifty-cent piece; **er ist ein falscher ~** *(inf)* he's a real crook *(inf)*

Fug [fu:k] M *(geh)* **mit ~ und Recht** with complete justification; **etw mit ~ und Recht tun** to be completely justified in doing sth

Fu|ge ['fu:gə] F **-, -n** **a** joint; *(= Ritze)* gap, crack; **in allen ~n krachen** to creak at the joints; **aus den ~n gehen** *or* **geraten** *(Auto etc)* to come apart at the seams; **die Welt ist/die Zeiten sind aus den ~n geraten** *(geh)* the world is/the times are out of joint *(liter)* **b** *(Mus)* fugue

fu|gen ['fu:gn] VT to joint

fü|gen ['fy:gn] VT **a** *(= setzen, einfügen)* to put, to place; *(geh) Worte, Satz* to formulate; **Wort an Wort ~** to string words together **b** *(geh: = bewirken)* to ordain; *(Schicksal)* to ordain, to decree; **der Zufall fügte es, dass ...** fate decreed that ... VR **a** *(= sich unterordnen)* to be obedient, to obey; **sich jdm/einer Sache** *or* **in etw** *(acc) (geh)* **~** to bow to sb/sth; *Anordnungen etc* to obey sth; **sich dem** *or* **in das Schicksal ~** to accept one's fate, to bow to one's fate **b** *impers (geh: = geschehen)* **es hat sich so gefügt** it was decreed by fate; **es fügte sich, dass ...** it so happened that ...

Fu|gen-: **fu|gen|los** ADJ *Übergang* smooth; **Fu|gen-s** [-lɛs] NT *(Ling)* linking "s"; **Fu|gen|zei|chen** NT *(Ling)* linking letter

füg|lich ['fy:klɪç] ADV *(liter)* justifiably, reasonably

füg|sam ['fy:kza:m] ADJ *Mensch, Tier* obedient; *Haar* manageable

Füg|sam|keit F **-**, *no pl (von Mensch, Tier)* obedience

Fü|gung ['fy:gʊŋ] F **-, -en** **a** *(= Bestimmung)* chance, stroke of fate; **eine glückliche ~** a stroke of good fortune, a happy chance *(Brit)*; **göttliche ~** divine providence; **eine ~ Gottes/des Schicksals** an act of divine providence/of fate; **eine seltsame ~ wollte es, dass er ...** by some *or* a strange chance he ... **b** *(Ling: = Wortgruppe)* construction

fühl|bar ADJ *(= spürbar)* perceptible; *(= beträchtlich auch)* marked; **bald wird die Krise auch bei uns ~** the crisis will soon be felt here too

füh|len ['fy:lən] VT **a** *(= spüren, empfinden)* to feel; **Mitleid mit jdm ~** to feel sympathy for sb **b** *(= ertasten) Beule, Erhebung* to feel; *Puls* to feel, to take VI **a** *(geh: = empfinden)* to feel **b** **nach etw ~** to feel for sth VR **a** *(= empfinden, sich halten für)* to feel; **sich krank/beleidigt/verantwortlich ~** to feel ill *(Brit)* or sick *(esp US)*/insulted/responsible; **wie ~ Sie sich?** how are you feeling?, how do you feel?; **er fühlte sich als Held** he felt (like) a hero **b** *(inf: = stolz sein)* to think one is so great *(inf)*

Füh|ler ['fy:lɐ] M **-s, -** *(Zool)* feeler, antenna; *(von Schnecke)* horn; **seine ~ ausstrecken** *(fig inf)* to put out feelers (*nach* towards)

Füh|ler|leh|re F feeler gauge

fühl|los ADJ *(geh)* = **gefühllos**

Fühl|lo|sig|keit F **-**, *no pl (geh)* = **Gefühllosigkeit**

Füh|lung ['fy:lʊŋ] F **-, -en** contact; **mit jdm in ~ bleiben/stehen** to remain *or* stay/be in contact *or* touch with sb

Füh|lung|nah|me [-na:mə] F **-, -n** **die erste ~ der beiden Parteien** the initial contact between the two parties

fuhr *pret von* **fahren**

Fuhr-: **Fuhr|amt** NT *(form)* cleansing department; **Fuhr|be|trieb** M haulage business

Fuh|re ['fu:rə] F **-, -n** *(= Ladung)* load; *(= Taxieinsatz)* fare; **eine ~ Stroh** a (cart- *or* wagon-)load of straw; **wir müssen die Leute in zwei ~n zum Bahnhof bringen** we'll have to take the people to the station in two loads

füh|ren ['fy:rən] VT **a** *(= geleiten)* to take; *(= vorangehen, -fahren)* to lead; **eine alte Dame über die Straße ~** to help an old lady over the road; **sie hat uns den richtigen Weg geführt** she showed us the right way; **er führte uns durch das Schloss** he showed us (a)round the castle; **er führte uns durch Italien** he was our guide in Italy; **eine Klasse zum Abitur ~** ≈ to see a class through to A-levels *(Brit)* or to their high school diploma *(US)*; **jdn zum (Trau)altar ~** to lead sb to the altar
b *(= leiten) Geschäft, Betrieb etc* to run; *Gruppe, Expedition etc* to lead, to head; *Schiff* to captain; *Armee etc* to command
c *(= in eine Situation bringen)* to get *(inf)*, to lead; *(= veranlassen zu kommen/gehen)* to bring/take; **der Hinweis führte die Polizei auf die Spur des Diebes** that tip put the police on the trail of the thief; **das führt uns auf das Thema ...** that brings *or* leads us (on)to the subject ...; **was führt Sie zu mir?** *(form)* what brings you to me?; **ein Land ins Chaos ~** to reduce a country to chaos
d *(= registriert haben)* to have a record of; **wir ~ keinen Meier in unserer Kartei** we have no (record of a) Meier on our files
e *(= handhaben) Pinsel, Bogen, Kamera etc* to wield; **den Löffel zum Mund/das Glas an die Lippen ~** to raise one's spoon to one's mouth/one's glass to one's lips; **die Hand an die Mütze ~** to touch one's cap
f *(= entlangführen) Leitung, Draht* to carry
g *(form: = steuern) Kraftfahrzeug* to drive; *Flugzeug* to fly, to pilot; *Kran, Fahrstuhl* to operate; *Schiff* to sail
h *(= transportieren)* to carry; *(= haben) Autokennzeichen, Wappen, Namen* to have, to bear; *Titel* to have; *(= selbst gebrauchen)* to use; **Geld/seine Papiere bei sich ~** *(form)* to carry money/one's papers on one's person; **der Fluss führt Hochwasser** the river is running high
i *(= im Angebot haben)* to stock, to carry *(spec)*, to keep; **etw ständig im Munde ~** to be always talking about sth; **er führt diesen Spruch ständig im Munde** he is always using that phrase
VI **a** *(= in Führung liegen)* to lead; *(bei Wettkämpfen)* to be in the lead, to lead; **die Mannschaft führt mit 10 Punkten Vorsprung** the team has a lead of 10 points, the team is in the lead *or* is leading by 10 points; **die Firma XY führt in Videorekordern** XY is the leading firm for video recorders
b *(= verlaufen) (Straße)* to go; *(Kabel, Pipeline etc)* to run; *(Spur)* to lead; **das Rennen führt über 10 Runden/durch ganz Frankreich** the race takes place over 10 laps/covers France; **die Straße führt nach Kiel/am Rhein entlang** the road goes to Kiel/runs *or* goes along the Rhine; **die Brücke führt über die Elbe** the bridge crosses *or* spans the Elbe; **der Waldweg führt zu einem Gasthof** the forest path leads *or* goes to an inn
c *(= als Ergebnis haben)* **zu etw ~** to lead to sth, to result in sth; **das führt zu nichts** that will come to nothing; **es führte zu dem Ergebnis, dass er entlassen wurde** it resulted in *or* led to his being dismissed; **das führt dazu, dass noch mehr Stellen abgebaut werden** it'll lead to *or* end in further staff reductions *or* job cuts; **wohin soll das alles nur ~?** where is it all leading (us)?
VR *(form: = sich benehmen)* to conduct oneself, to deport oneself *(form)*

füh|rend ADJ leading *attr*; *Rolle, Persönlichkeit auch* prominent; **diese Firma ist im Stahlbau ~** that is one of the leading firms in steel construction; **die Amerikaner sind in der Leichtathletik ~** the Americans lead the world *or* are the world leaders in athletics

Füh|rer ['fy:rɐ] M **-s, -** *(= Buch)* guide; **~ durch England** guide to England

Füh|rer ['fy:rɐ] M **-s, -, Füh|re|rin** [-ərɪn] F **-, -nen a** *(= Leiter)* leader; *(= Oberhaupt)* head; **der ~** *(Hist)* the Führer *or* Fuehrer **b** *(= Fremdenführer, Bergführer)* guide **c** *(form: = Lenker)* driver; *(von Flugzeug)* pilot; *(von Kran, Fahrstuhl)* operator; *(von Schiff)* person in charge

Füh|rer-: **Füh|rer|haus** NT cab; *(von Kran auch)* cabin; **füh|rer|los** ADJ *Gruppe, Partei* leaderless *no adv*, without a leader; *Wagen* driverless *no adv*, without a driver; *Flugzeug* pilotless *no adv*, without a pilot; *Schiff* with no-one at the helm; **Füh|rer|na|tur** F *(fig)* born *or* natural leader; **Füh|rer|rol|le** F role of a/the leader, leadership role

Füh|rer|schein M *(für Auto)* driving licence *(Brit)*, driver's license *(US)*; *(für Motorboot)* motorboat licence *(Brit)* or license *(US)*; **den ~ machen** *(Aut)* to learn to drive; *(= die Prüfung ablegen)* to take one's (driving) test; **jdm den ~ entziehen** to take away sb's driving licence *(Brit)* or driver's license *(US)*, to disqualify sb from driving; **ihm ist der ~ abgenommen worden** he's lost his licence *(Brit)* or license *(US)*; **~ auf Probe** probationary driving licence *(Brit)* or driver's license *(US)*

Füh|rer|schein-: **Füh|rer|schein|ent|zug** M disqualification from driving; **Füh|rer|schein|prü|fung** F driving test; **praktische ~** practical (part of the) driving test; **theoretische ~** theoretical (part of the) driving test, driving theory test

Füh|rer|stand M *(von Zug)* cab; *(von Kran auch)* cabin

Fuhr-: **Fuhr|geld** NT delivery charge; **Fuhr|ge|schäft** NT haulage business

füh|rig ['fy:rɪç] ADJ *Schnee* good (for skiing)

Fuhr-: **Fuhr|knecht** M *(old)* carter; *(= Kutscher)* coachman; **Fuhr|leu|te** *pl von* **Fuhrmann**; **Fuhr|lohn** M delivery charge; **Fuhr|mann** M *pl* **-leute** carter *(Brit)*, carrier; *(= Kutscher)* coachman; **der ~** *(Astron)* Auriga, the Charioteer; **Fuhr|park** M fleet (of vehicles)

Füh|rung ['fy:rʊŋ] F **-, -en a** *no pl* guidance, direction; *(von Partei, Expedition etc)* leadership; *(Mil)* command; *(eines Unternehmens etc)* management; **unter der ~** *(+gen)* under the direction/leadership/command/management of, directed/led *or* headed/commanded/managed by; **wer hat hier die ~?** *(Mil)* who is in command here?
b *no pl (= die Führer)* leaders *pl*, leadership *sing*; *(Mil)* commanders *pl*; *(eines Unternehmens etc)* directors *pl*
c *(= Besichtigung)* guided tour (*durch* of)
d *no pl (= Vorsprung)* lead; **die klare ~ haben** *(bei Wettkämpfen)* to have a clear lead; **die Firma hat eine klare ~ auf diesem Gebiet** the firm clearly leads the field in this area; **in ~ gehen/liegen** to go into/be in the lead
e *no pl (= Betragen)* conduct; **wegen guter ~ vorzeitig aus der Haft entlassen werden** to be released from prison early for good behaviour *(Brit)* or behavior *(US)*
f *no pl (= Handhabung)* touch
g *(Mech)* guide, guideway
h *(form: = Lenken)* **zur ~ eines Kraftfahrzeugs/Wasserfahrzeugs/Flugzeugs berechtigt sein** to be licensed to drive a motor vehicle/be in charge of a vessel/fly *or* pilot an aircraft
i *no pl (= Betreuung)* running; **die ~ der Akten/Bücher** keeping the files/books

Füh|rungs-: **Füh|rungs|an|spruch** M claims *pl* to leadership; **seinen ~ anmelden** to make a bid for the leadership; **Füh|rungs|auf|ga|be** F executive duty; **Füh|rungs|eta|ge** F *(von Partei, Verband)* leadership; *(von Unternehmen)* management; **Füh|rungs|kraft** F *(Person)* executive; **Füh|rungs|kri|se** F leadership crisis; *(Comm)* management crisis; **Füh|rungs|of|fi|zier(in)** M(F) *(DDR)* commanding officer; **Füh|rungs|qua|li|tät** F *usu pl* leadership qualities *pl*; **Füh|rungs|rie|ge** F leadership; *(in company)* management team; **Füh|rungs|rol|le** F role of leader; **Füh|rungs|schicht** F ruling classes *pl*; **Füh|rungs|schie|ne** F guide rail; **füh|rungs|schwach** ADJ *Partei, Chef* weak; **Füh|rungs|schwä|che** F weak leadership; **Füh|rungs|spit|ze** F highest echelon of the leadership; *(eines Unternehmens etc)* top management; **Füh|rungs|stab** M *(Mil)* command *no pl*; *(Comm)* top management; **Füh|rungs|stär|ke** F strong leadership; **~ zeigen** to be a strong leader, to show distinctive leadership qualities; **Füh|rungs|stil** M style of leadership; *(Comm auch)* management style; **Füh|rungs|tor** NT *(Ftbl)* goal which gives/gave a/the team the lead; **Füh|rungs|wech|sel** M change of leadership; **Füh|rungs|zeug|nis** NT → **polizeilich**

Fuhr-: **Fuhr|un|ter|neh|men** NT haulage business; **Fuhr|un|ter|neh|mer(in)** M(F) haulier *(Brit)*, haulage contractor, carrier, trucking operator *(US)*; **Fuhr|werk** NT wagon; *(= Pferdefuhrwerk)* horse and cart; *(= Ochsenfuhrwerk)* oxcart; **fuhr|wer|ken** ['fu:ɐvɛrkn] VI *insep* **a** *(inf)* **in der Küche ~** to bustle around in the kitchen; **mit den Armen ~** to wave one's arms about **b** *(S Ger, Aus)* to drive a cart; **Fuhr|we|sen** NT, *no pl* cartage business

Fül|le ['fʏlə] F **-,** *no pl* **a** *(= Körpermasse)* corpulence, portliness **b** *(= Stärke)* fullness; *(von Stimme, Klang auch)* richness; *(von Wein auch)* full-bodiedness; *(von Haar)* body **c** *(= Menge)* wealth; **eine ~ von Fragen/Eindrücken** *etc* a whole host of questions/impressions *etc*; **in ~** in abundance → **Hülle e**

fül|len ['fʏlən] VT **a** *(= mit Inhalt füllen)* to fill; *(Cook)* to stuff; **etw in Flaschen ~** to bottle sth; **etw in Säcke ~** to put sth into sacks → *auch* **gefüllt b** *(= in Anspruch nehmen)* to fill, to occupy; *Regal* to fill, to take up VR *(Theater, Badewanne)* to fill up; **ihre Augen füllten sich mit Tränen** her eyes filled with tears

Fül|len ['fʏlən] NT **-s, -** = **Fohlen**

Fül|ler ['fʏlɐ] M **-s, - a** *(= Füllfederhalter)* fountain pen **b** *(Press)* filler

Füll-: **Füll|fe|der|hal|ter** M fountain pen; **Füll|ge|wicht** NT **a** *(Comm)* weight at time of packing; *(auf Dosen)* net weight **b** *(von Waschmaschine)* maximum load, capacity; **Füll|horn** NT *(liter)* cornucopia; *(fig auch)* horn of plenty

fül|lig ['fʏlɪç] ADJ *Mensch* corpulent, portly; *Figur, Busen* generous, ample; *Frisur* bouffant *attr*

Füll-: **Füll|mas|se** F filler, filling material; *(= Zahnfüllmasse)* filling compound; **Füll|ma|te|ri|al** NT filler, filling material

Füll|sel ['fʏlzl] NT **-s, -** *(in Paket etc)* packing; *(in Geschriebenem) (= Wort)* filler; *(= Floskel)* padding

Full|time-Job, **Full|time|job** ['fʊltaimdʒɔp] M full-time job

Fül|lung ['fʏlʊŋ] F **-, -en** filling; *(= Geflügelfüllung, Fleischfüllung, Stofftierfüllung, Polsterfüllung)* stuffing; *(= Türfüllung)* panel; *(von Pralinen)* centre *(Brit)*, center *(US)*

Füll-: **Füll|wort** NT *pl* **-wörter** filler (word); **Füll|zei|chen** NT *(Comput)* leader

ful|mi|nant [fʊlmi'nant] ADJ *(geh)* brilliant

Fum|mel ['fʊml] M **-s, -** *(inf)* rag; **im ~** *(sl: = in Frauenkleidung)* in drag *(inf)*

Fum|me|lei [fʊmə'lai] F **-, -en** *(inf)* fidgeting, fiddling; *(= Petting)* petting, groping *(inf)*

Fum|mel|kram M *(inf)* fiddle *(inf)*, fiddly job *(inf)*

fum|meln ['fʊmln] VI *(inf)* to fiddle; *(= hantieren)* to fumble; *(erotisch)* to pet, to grope *(inf)*; **an etw** *(dat)* or **mit etw ~** to fiddle (about)/fumble around with sth

Fund [fʊnt] M **-(e)s, -e** [-də] find; *(= das Entdecken)* discovery, finding; **einen ~ machen** to make a find

Fun|da|ment [fʊnda'mɛnt] NT **-(e)s, -e** *(lit, fig)* foundation *(usu pl)*; **das ~ zu etw legen** *(fig)* **das ~ für etw schaffen** *(fig)* to lay the foundations for sth

fun|da|men|tal [fʊndamɛn'ta:l] ADJ fundamental ADV fundamentally

Fun|da|men|ta|lis|mus [fʊndamɛnta'lɪsmʊs] M **-,** *no pl* fundamentalism

Fun|da|men|ta|list [fʊndamɛnta'lɪst] M **-en, -en**, **Fun|da|men|ta|lis|tin** [-'lɪstɪn] F **-, -nen** fundamentalist

fun|da|men|ta|lis|tisch [fʊndamɛnta'lɪstɪʃ] ADJ fundamentalist

fun|da|men|tie|ren [fʊndamɛn'tiːrən] *ptp* **fundamentiert** VI to lay the foundations

Fund-: **Fund|amt** NT, **Fund|bü|ro** NT lost property office *(Brit)*, lost and found *(US)*; **Fund|gru|be** F *(fig)* treasure trove; **eine ~ des Wissens** a treasury of knowledge

Fun|di ['fʊndi] M **-s, -s** *or f* **-, -s** *(Pol inf)* fundamentalist *(of the Green party)*

fun|die|ren [fʊn'diːrən] *ptp* **fundiert** VT *(fig)* to back up

fun|diert [fʊn'diːɐt] ADJ sound; **schlecht ~** unsound

fün|dig ['fʏndɪç] ADJ *(Min) Sohle* rich; **~ werden** to make a strike; *(fig)* to strike it lucky; **~e Mitbürger sollen ...** anyone who finds it/them should ...

Fund-: **Fund|ort** M *pl* **-orte der ~ von etw** (the place) where sth is/was found; **Fund|sa|chen** PL lost property *sing*; **Fund|stät|te** F, **Fund|stel|le** F *(in Suchmaschine etc)* hit; **die ~ von etw** (the place) where sth is/was found

Fun|dus ['fʊndʊs] M **-, -** *(lit, fig)* fund; *(Theat)* basic equipment; **der ~ seines reichen Wissens** his rich fund of knowledge

fünf [fʏnf] NUM five; **es ist ~ Minuten vor zwölf** *(lit)* it's five to twelve; *(fig)* it's almost too late; **sie warteten bis ~ Minuten vor zwölf** *(fig)* they waited till the eleventh hour; **seine ~ Sinne beieinanderhaben** *or* **beisammenhaben** to have all one's wits about one; **seine ~ Sinne zusammennehmen** to gather one's wits together; **man musste seine ~ Sinne zusammennehmen** you had to have your wits about you; **~(e) gerade sein lassen** *(inf)* to turn a blind eye, to look the other way → *auch* **Finger, vier**

Fünf [fʏnf] F **-, -en** five → *auch* **Vier**

Fünf- *in cpds* five; **Fünf|cent|stück** [fʏnf'(t)sɛnt-] NT five-cent piece; **Fünf|eck** NT pentagon; **fünf|eckig** ADJ pentagonal, five-cornered

Fün|fer ['fʏnfɐ] M **-s, -** *(inf) (= Fünfcentmünze)* five-cent piece; *(= Fünfeuroschein)* five-euro note *(Brit)* or bill *(US)* → *auch* **Vierer**

Fünf-: **Fünf|eu|ro|schein** [fʏnf'ɔyro-] M five-euro note *(Brit)* or bill *(US)*; **fünf|fach** ['fʏnffax] ADJ fivefold → *auch* **vierfach**; **fünf|fü|ßig** ADJ *(Poet)* pentametrical; **~er Jambus** iambic pentameter; **Fünf|gang|ge|trie|be** NT five-speed gearbox; **Fünf|gang|schal|tung** F five-speed gears *pl*; **fünf|hun|dert** ['fʏnf'hʊndɐt] NUM five hundred; **Fünf|jah|res|plan** M five-year plan; **fünf|jäh|rig** ADJ *Frist, Plan, Amtszeit etc* five-year, quinquennial *(form)*; *Kind* five-year-old; **eine ~e Zeitspanne** a period of five years, a quinquennium *(form)* → *auch* **vierjährig**; **Fünf|kampf** M *(Sport)* pentathlon

Fünf|ling ['fʏnflɪŋ] M **-s, -e** quintuplet

Fünf-: **fünf|mal** ['fʏnfmaːl] ADV five times → *auch* **viermal**; **Fünf|mark|schein** [fʏnf'mark-] M *(Hist)* five-mark note *(Brit)* or bill *(US)*; **Fünf|mark|stück** NT *(Hist)* five-mark piece; **Fünf|me|ter|raum** M *(Ftbl)* six-yard box; **Fünf|pfen|nig|stück** [fʏnf'pfɛnɪç-] NT *(Hist)* five-pfennig piece

Fünf|pro|zent-: **Fünf|pro|zent|gren|ze** F *(Parl)* five-percent barrier; **Fünf|pro|zent|hür|de** F *(Parl)* five-percent hurdle; **Fünf|pro|zent|klau|sel** F five-percent rule

> **FÜNFPROZENTKLAUSEL**
>
> Electoral law in Germany contains a **Fünfprozentklausel,** which permits only parties that poll at least 5% of the votes over an entire electoral area to have a stake in the allocation of seats. This rule was introduced after the Second World War to guard against the fragmentation of parties, which was seen as one of the causes of the collapse of the Weimar Republic.

Fünf-: **fünf|sei|tig** [-zaitɪç] ADJ *(Geometrie)* five-sided; *Brief* five-page *attr*; **Fünf|strom|land** [fʏnf'ʃtroːm-] NT, *no pl (Geog)* Punjab; **Fünf|ta|ge|wo|che** [fʏnf'taːgə-] F, *no pl* five-day week; **fünf|tä|gig** ADJ five-day *attr*; **fünf|tau|send** ['fʏnf'tauznt] NUM five thousand; **Fünf|tau|send|me|ter|lauf, 5000-m-Lauf** [fʏnftauznd'meːtɐ-] M five thousand metres *(Brit)* or meters *(US)*

Fünf|tel ['fʏnftl] NT **-s, -** fifth → *auch* **Viertel**

fünf|tens ['fʏnftns] ADV fifth(ly), in the fifth place

fünf|te(r, s) ['fʏnftə] ADJ fifth; **die ~ Kolonne** the fifth column → *auch* **vierte(r, s), Rad**

Fünf-: **Fünf|uhr|tee** M afternoon tea; **Fünf|und|drei|ßig|stun|den|wo|che** F thirty-five-hour week; **fünf|und|zwan|zig** NUM twenty-five; **fünf|zehn** ['fʏnftseːn] NUM fifteen

fünf|zig ['fʏnftsɪç] NUM fifty → *auch* **vierzig**

Fünf|zig ['fʏnftsɪç] F **-, -en** fifty → *auch* **Vierzig**

Fünf|zig|cent|stück [fʏnftsɪç'(t)sɛnt-] NT fifty-cent piece

Fünf|zi|ger ['fʏnftsɪgɐ] M **-s, -** *(inf) (= Fünfzigeuroschein)* fifty-euro note *(Brit)* or bill *(US)*; *(= Fünfzigcentstück)* fifty-cent piece → *auch* **Fuffziger**

Fünf|zi|ger ['fʏnftsɪgɐ] M **-s, -**, **Fünf|zi|ge|rin** [-ərɪn] F **-, -nen** *(inf: = Fünfzigjähriger)* fifty-year-old → *auch* **Vierziger**

Fünf|zi|ger|jah|re , fünf|zi|ger Jah|re ['fʏnftsɪgɐ-] PL fifties *pl*

Fünf|zig-: **Fünf|zig|eu|ro|schein** [fʏnftsɪç'ɔyro-] M fifty-euro note *(Brit)* or bill *(US)*; **fünf|zig|jäh|rig** ADJ *Person* fifty-year-old *attr*; *Zeitspanne* fifty-year; **er ist ~ verstorben** he died at (the age of) fifty; **Fünf|zig|mark|schein** [fʏnftsɪç'mark-] M *(Hist)* fifty-mark note *(Brit)* or bill *(US)*; **Fünf|zig|pfen|nig|stück** [fʏnftsɪç'pfɛnɪç-] NT *(Hist)* fifty-pfennig piece

fun|gie|ren [fʊŋ'giːrən] *ptp* **fungiert** VI to function *(als* as a)

Fun|gi|zid [fʊŋgi'tsiːt] NT **-(e)s, -e** [-də] fungicide

Funk [fʊŋk] M **-s,** *no pl* radio, wireless *(dated)*; **über** *or* **per ~** by radio; **er arbeitet beim ~** he works in radio *or* broadcasting

Funk [faŋk] M **-s,** *no pl* funk

-funk *suf in cpds* broadcasts *pl*, programmes *pl (Brit)*, programs *pl (US)*; **Hausfrauenfunk** housewives' broadcasts *pl*, programmes *pl (Brit)* or programs *pl (US)* for housewives

Funk-: **Funk|ama|teur(in)** M(F) radio ham, amateur radio enthusiast; **Funk|an|la|ge** F radio set *or* transceiver; **Funk|auf|klä|rung** F *(Mil)* radio intelligence; **Funk|aus|stel|lung** F radio and television exhibition; **Funk|ba|ke** F radio beacon; **Funk|bild** NT telephotograph *(spec)*, radio picture; **Funk|brü|cke** F radio bridge

Fünk|chen ['fʏŋkçən] NT **-s, -** *dim von* **Funke**; **ein ~ Wahrheit** a grain of truth; **kein ~ Wahrheit** not a grain of truth

Funk|dienst M radio communication service

Fun|ke ['fʊŋkə] M **-ns, -n** **a** *(lit, fig)* spark; **~n sprühen** to spark, to send out *or* emit sparks; **~n sprühend** giving off *or* emitting sparks; *(fig) Diskussion* lively; *Augen* flashing *attr*, fiery; **ihre Augen sprühten ~n** her eyes flashed; **der zündende ~** *(fig)* the vital spark; **der ~ der Begeisterung sprang auf die Zuschauer über** the audience was infected by his/her *etc* enthusiasm; **arbeiten, dass die ~n fliegen** *or* **sprühen** *(inf)* to work like mad *(inf)* or crazy *(inf)*; **zwischen den beiden sprang der ~ über** *(inf)* something clicked between them *(inf)*
b *(= ein bisschen)* scrap; *(von Hoffnung auch)* gleam, ray, glimmer; *(von Anstand)* scrap, spark

Funk|ein|rich|tung F radio (equipment); **mit ~ versehen** radio-equipped, equipped with radio

fun|keln ['fʊŋkln] VI to sparkle; *(Sterne auch)* to twinkle; *(Edelsteine auch)* to glitter; *(Edelmetall)* to gleam; *(Augen) (vor Freude)* to gleam, to twinkle; *(vor Zorn)* to glitter, to flash

fun|kel|na|gel|neu ['fʊŋkl'naːgl'nɔy] ADJ *(inf)* brand-new

fun|ken ['fʊŋkn] **VT** *Signal* to radio; **SOS ~** to send out *or* radio an SOS **VI** **a** *(= senden)* to radio **b** *(= Funken sprühen)* to give off *or* emit sparks, to spark; *(fig inf: = funktionieren)* to work **VI** *impers* **endlich hat es bei ihm gefunkt** *(inf)* it finally clicked (with him) *(inf)*, the light finally dawned (on him)

Fun|ken ['fʊŋkn] M **-s, -** = **Funke**

Fun|ken-: **Fun|ken|ent|la|dung** F spark discharge; **Fun|ken|flug** M **der Brand wurde durch ~ von einer Lokomotive verursacht** the fire was caused by sparks from a locomotive; **Fun|ken|git|ter** NT fireguard; **fun|ken|sprü|hend** ADJ → **Funke a**

Funk|ent|stö|rung ['fʊŋklɛnt-] F suppression of interference

funk|ent|stört ['fʊŋklɛntʃtøːɐt] ADJ (radio noise-)suppressed

Fun|ker ['fʊŋkɐ] M **-s, -**, **Fun|ke|rin** [-ərɪn] F **-, -nen** radio *or* wireless operator

Funk-: **Funk|fern|steu|e|rung** F radio control; *(= Anlage)* radio-control equipment *no pl*; **Funk|feu|er** NT radio beacon; **Funk|ge|rät** NT **a** *no pl* radio equipment **b** *(= Sprechfunkgerät)* radio set, walkie-talkie; **Funk|haus** NT broadcasting centre *(Brit)* or center *(US)*, studios *pl*

fun|kig ['faŋkɪç] ADJ *(inf)* funky *(inf)*; **~er Rock** *(Mus)* funk rock

Funk-: **Funk|kol|leg** NT educational radio broadcasts *pl*; **Funk|kon|takt** M radio contact; **Funk|loch** NT *(Telec)* dead spot, area with no reception; **Funk|mess|ge|rät** NT radar (equipment) *no pl*; **Funk|na|vi|ga|ti|on** F radio navigation; **Funk|netz** NT radio network; *(= Funktelefonnetz)* radio telephone network; **Funk|or|tung** F radiolocation; **Funk|pei|lung** F radio direction finding; **Funk|ruf** M **a** radio call **b** *(Telec)* (radio) paging; **Funk|ruf|dienst** M *(Telec)* (radio) paging service; **Funk|ruf|emp|fän|ger** M (radio) pager; **Funk|ruf|netz** NT *(Telec)* (radio) paging network; **Funk|sig|nal** NT radio signal; **Funk|sprech|ge|rät** NT radio telephone; *(tragbar)* walkie-talkie; **Funk|sprech|ver|kehr** M radiotelephony; **Funk|spruch** M radio signal; *(= Mitteilung)* radio message; **Funk|sta|ti|on** F radio station; **funk|still** ADJ non-transmitting; **Funk|stil|le** F radio silence; *(fig)* silence; **Funk|strei|fe** F police radio patrol; **Funk|strei|fen|wa|gen** M police radio patrol *or* squad car; **Funk|ta|xi** NT radio taxi *or* cab; **Funk|tech|nik** F radio technology; **Funk|te|le|fon** NT radio telephone; **Funk|te|le|fon|netz** NT *(Telec)* radio telephone network

Funk|ti|on [fʊŋk'tsioːn] F **-, -en** *(= Zweck, Aufgabe, Math)* function; *(no pl: = Tätigkeit)* functioning; *(= Amt)* office; *(= Stellung)* position; **in ~ treten** to come into operation; *(Organ, Maschine etc)* to start to function; **in ~ sein** to be in operation; *(Organ, Maschine etc)* to be functioning; **etw außer ~ setzen** to stop sth functioning; **dieser Bolzen hat die ~, den Apparat senkrecht zu halten** the function of this bolt is to hold the machine upright

funk|ti|o|nal [fʊŋktsio'naːl] ADJ = **funktionell**

Funk|ti|o|na|lis|mus [fʊŋktsiona'lɪsmʊs] M **-,** *no pl* functionalism

funk|ti|o|na|li|sie|ren [fʊŋktsionali'ziːrən] *ptp* **funktionalisiert** VT to make functional, to give a functional design *(etw* to sth)

funk|ti|o|na|lis|tisch [fʊŋktsiona'lɪstɪsch] ADJ functionalist

Funk|ti|o|na|li|tät [fʊŋktsionali'tɛːt] F **-, -en** practicality

Funk|ti|o|när [fʊŋktsio'nɛːɐ] M **-s, -e**, **Funk|ti|o|nä|rin** [-'nɛːrɪn] F **-, -nen** functionary, official

funk|ti|o|nell [fʊŋktsio'nɛl] ADJ functional *(auch Med)*, practical

funk|ti|o|nie|ren [fʊŋktsio'niːrən] *ptp* **funktioniert** VI to work; *(Maschine etc auch)* to function, to operate; *(inf: = gehorchen)* to obey

Funk|ti|ons-: **Funk|ti|ons|bild** NT, *no pl* job profile; **funk|ti|ons|fä|hig** ADJ able to work; *Maschine etc auch* in working order; **Funk|ti|ons|fä|hig|keit** F ability to work; **die ~ einer Maschine überprüfen** to check if a machine is in working order; **Funk|ti|ons|leis|te** F *(Comput)* toolbar; **Funk|ti|ons|prü|fung** F *(Med)* function test; **Funk|ti|ons|stö|rung** F *(Med)* malfunction, functional disorder; **Funk|ti|ons|tas|te** F *(Comput)* function key; **funk|ti|ons|tüch|tig** ADJ in working order; *Organ* sound; **Funk|ti|ons|tüch|tig|keit** F ability to operate; *(von Organ)* soundness; **Funk|ti|ons|verb** NT *(Ling)* empty verb; **Funk|ti|ons|wei|se** F -, -n mode of operation

Funk-: **Funk|turm** M radio tower; **Funk|uhr** F radio-controlled clock; **Funk|uni|ver|si|tät** F educational radio broadcasts *pl*; **Funk|ver|bin|dung** F radio contact; **Funk|ver|kehr** M radio communication *or* traffic; **Funk|wa|gen** M radio car; **Funk|weg** M **auf dem ~** by radio; **Funk|wer|bung** F radio advertising; **Funk|we|sen** NT, *no pl* radio; *(= Sendesystem)* broadcasting system; **Funk|zent|ra|le** F (radio) call centre *(Brit) or* center *(US)*

Fun|sel ['fʊnzl] F -, -n, **Fun|zel** ['fʊntsl] F -, -n *(inf)* dim light, gloom

für [fyːɐ] PREP +*acc* **a** for; **~ was ist denn dieses Werkzeug?** *(inf)* what is this tool (used) for?; **kann ich sonst noch etwas ~ Sie tun?** will there be anything else?; **~ mich** for me; *(= meiner Ansicht nach)* in my opinion *or* view; **diese Frage muss jeder ~ sich (alleine) entscheiden** everyone has to decide this question for *or* by themselves; **das ist gut ~ Migräne** that's good for migraine; **~ zwei arbeiten** *(fig)* to do the work of two people; **~ einen Deutschen ...** for a German ...; **~s Erste** for the moment; **~s nächste Mal** next time
b *(Zustimmung)* for, in favour *(Brit) or* favor *(US)* of; **sich ~ etw entscheiden** to decide in favo(u)r; **was Sie da sagen, hat etwas ~ sich** there's something in what you're saying; **er hat was ~ sich** he's not a bad person; **das hat was ~ sich** it's not a bad thing
c *(Gegenleistung)* (in exchange) for; **das hat er ~ zehn Pfund gekauft** he bought it for ten pounds
d *(Ersatz)* for, instead of, in place of; **~ jdn einspringen** to stand in for sb
e *(Aufeinanderfolge)* **Tag ~ Tag** day after day; **Schritt ~ Schritt** step by step
f *(in Verbindung mit vb, adj siehe auch dort)* **etw ~ sich behalten** to keep sth to oneself; **~ etw bekannt sein** to be famous *or* known for sth; **ich halte sie ~ intelligent** I think she is intelligent
g **was ~** → **was**
ADV *(old poet)* **~ und ~** for ever and ever

Für ['fyːɐ] NT **das ~ und Wider** the pros and cons *pl*

Fu|ra|ge [fu'raːʒə] F -, *no pl (Mil old)* forage

für|bass [fyːɐ'bas] ADV *(obs)* onwards; **~ gehen** *or* **schreiten** to continue on one's way

Für|bit|te F *(Eccl, fig)* intercession; **er legte beim Kaiser ~ für die Gefangenen ein** he interceded with the Emperor on behalf of the prisoners

Für|bit|ten NT -s, *no pl (Eccl)* prayers *pl*; *(fig)* pleading

Fur|che ['fʊrçə] F -, -n *(= Ackerfurche, Gesichtsfalte)* furrow; *(= Wagenspur)* rut; **ein von ~n durchzogenes Gesicht** a deeply furrowed *or* lined face

fur|chen ['fʊrçn] VT to furrow; *(Zeit, Sorge etc) Gesicht etc auch* to line; **die Spuren des Traktors furchten den Weg** the tractor made ruts *or* furrows in the road → *auch* **gefurcht**

fur|chig ['fʊrçɪç] ADJ *Stirn* furrowed; *(durch Wagenspuren etc auch)* rutted

Furcht [fʊrçt] F -, *no pl* fear; **aus ~ vor jdm/etw** for fear of sb/sth; **ohne ~ sein** to be fearless, to be without fear; **~ vor jdm/etw haben** *or* **empfinden** to be afraid of sb/sth, to fear sb/sth; **~ ergriff** *or* **packte ihn** fear seized him, he was seized with fear; **jdn in ~ versetzen, jdm ~ einflößen** to frighten *or* scare sb; **~ einflößend** terrifying, fearful; **~ erregend** = **furchterregend**; **ohne ~ und Tadel** without fear or reproach

furcht|bar ADJ terrible, awful, dreadful; **ich habe einen ~en Hunger** I'm ever so hungry *(inf)*, I'm terribly hungry *(inf)* ADV terribly *(inf)*, awfully *(inf)*; **wir haben ~ gelacht** we laughed ourselves silly *(inf)*

Furcht|bar|keit F -, -en **a** *no pl (= Furchtbarsein, von Zorn)* awesomeness; **die ~ der Armut/Zustände in diesem Land** the dreadful poverty/conditions in this country **b** *usu pl (= furchtbare Geschehnisse)* terrible *or* awful *or* dreadful things *pl*

furcht|ein|flö|ßend ADJ → **Furcht**

fürch|ten ['fʏrçtn] VT **jdn/etw ~** to be afraid of sb/sth, to fear sb/sth; **das Schlimmste ~** to fear the worst; **~, dass ...** to be afraid *or* to fear that ...; **es war schlimmer, als ich gefürchtet hatte** it was worse than I had feared; **Gott ~** to fear God → *auch* **gefürchtet** VR to be afraid *(vor +dat* of); **sich im Dunkeln ~** to be afraid *or* scared of the dark VI **für** *or* **um jdn/jds Leben/etw ~** to fear for sb/sb's life/sth; **zum Fürchten aussehen** to look frightening *or* terrifying; **da kannst du das Fürchten lernen** that will scare you stiff; **jdn das Fürchten lehren** to put the fear of God into sb

fürch|ter|lich ['fʏrçtɐlɪç] ADJ ADV = **furchtbar**

Furcht-: **furcht|er|re|gend** ADJ terrifying, fearful; **furcht|los** ADJ *Person* fearless, intrepid; *Entschlossenheit* fearless; **Furcht|lo|sig|keit** F -, *no pl* fearlessness, intrepidity; **furcht|sam** ['fʊrçtzaːm] ADJ timid, timorous; **Furcht|sam|keit** F -, *(rare)* **-en** timidity, timorousness

Fur|chung ['fʊrçʊŋ] F -, -en *(Biol)* cleavage

für|der(hin) ['fʏrdɐ(hɪn)] ADV *(obs)* hereafter *(old)*, in future

für|ei|nan|der [fyːɐlai'nandɐ] ADV for each other, for one another

Fu|rie ['fuːriə] F -, -n *(Myth)* fury; *(fig)* hellcat *(esp Brit)*, termagant; **wie von ~n gejagt** *or* **gehetzt** *(liter)* as though the devil himself were after him/them *etc*; **sie gingen wie ~n aufeinander los** they went for each other like cats *or* wild things

fu|ri|os [fu'rioːs] ADJ high-energy, dynamic

Fur|nier [fʊr'niːɐ] NT -s, -e veneer

fur|nie|ren [fʊr'niːrən] *ptp* **furniert** VT to veneer; **mit Mahagoni furniert** with a mahogany veneer

Fu|ro|re [fu'roːrə] F - *or nt* -s, *no pl* sensation; **~ machen** *(inf)* to cause a sensation

Für|sor|ge F, *no pl* **a** *(= Betreuung)* care; *(= Sozialfürsorge)* welfare **b** *(inf: = Sozialamt)* welfare *(inf)*, welfare services; **der ~ zur Last fallen** to be a burden on the state **c** *(inf: = Sozialunterstützung)* social security *(Brit)*, welfare *(US)*; **von der ~ leben** to live on social security *(Brit) or* welfare *(US)*

Für|sor|ge-: **Für|sor|ge|amt** NT (church) welfare office; **Für|sor|ge|be|ruf** M job in one of the welfare services; **Für|sor|ge|er|zie|hung** F education in a special school; **Für|sor|ge|pflicht** F *(Jur) employer's obligation to provide for the welfare of his employees*

Für|sor|ger ['fyːɐzɔrgɐ] M -s, -, **Für|sor|ge|rin** [-ərɪn] F -, -nen welfare worker

für|sor|ge|risch ['fyːɐzɔrgərɪʃ] ADJ welfare *attr* ADV **alte Menschen ~ betreuen** to look after the welfare of old people

Für|sor|ge-: **Für|sor|ge|satz** M rate of social security (benefit) *(Brit)*, rate of welfare *(US)*; **Für|sor|ge|staat** M welfare state; **Für|sor|ge|un|ter|stüt|zung** F social security benefit *(Brit)*, welfare *(US)*

für|sorg|lich ['fyːɐzɔrklɪç] ADJ caring; *Mensch auch* solicitous; **~e Pflege** attentive care ADV **jdn sehr ~ behandeln** to lavish care on sb

Für|sorg|lich|keit F -, *no pl* **die ~, mit der er sie pflegte** how caringly he looked after her; **gerührt von der ~ meines Chefs** touched by how caring my boss was

Für|spra|che F recommendation; **für jdn ~ einlegen** to recommend sb *(bei* to), to put in a word for sb *(inf) (bei* with); **auf ~ von jdm** on sb's recommendation

Für|sprech ['fyːɐʃprɛç] M -s, -e **a** *(old: = Rechtsbeistand)* counsel **b** *(Sw: = Rechtsanwalt)* barrister *(Brit)*, lawyer

Für|spre|cher(in) M(F) **a** advocate **b** *(Sw: = Rechtsanwalt)* barrister *(Brit)*, lawyer

Fürst [fʏrst] M -en, -en prince; *(= Herrscher)* ruler; **geistlicher ~** prince bishop; **wie ein ~ leben** to live like a lord *or* king; **der ~ der Finsternis** *or* **dieser Welt** *(liter)* the Prince of Darkness *or* of this world *(Bibl)*

Fürst|bi|schof M *(Hist)* prince bishop

Fürs|ten-: **Fürs|ten|ge|schlecht** NT, **Fürs|ten|haus** NT royal house; **Fürs|ten|stand** M royal rank; **jdn in den ~ erheben** to create sb prince

Fürs|ten|tum ['fʏrstntuːm] NT -s, **Fürstentümer** [-tyːmɐ] principality, princedom *(old)*; **das ~ Monaco/Liechtenstein** the principality of Monaco/Liechtenstein

Fürs|tin ['fʏrstɪn] F -, -nen princess; *(= Herrscherin)* ruler

fürst|lich ['fʏrstlɪç] ADJ *(lit)* princely *no adv*; *(fig auch)* handsome, lavish ADV **jdn ~ bewirten** to entertain sb right royally; **jdn ~ belohnen** to reward sb handsomely; **~ leben** to live like a king *or* lord

Fürst|lich|keit F -, **a** *no pl* princeliness **b** *(form: = fürstliche Persönlichkeit)* royal personage *(form)*

Furt [fʊrt] F -, -en ford

Fu|run|kel [fu'rʊŋkl] NT OR M -s, - boil

für|wahr [fyːɐ'vaːɐ] ADV *(old)* forsooth *(old)*, in truth *(old)*

Für|wort NT *pl* **-wörter** *(Gram)* pronoun

Furz [fʊrts] M -(e)s, ⸗e ['fʏrtsə] *(inf)* fart *(inf)*; **einen ~ (fahren) lassen** to let off (a fart) *(inf)*

fur|zen ['fʊrtsn] VI *(inf)* to fart *(inf)*

Fu|sel ['fuːzl] M -s, - *(pej)* rotgut *(inf)*, hooch *(esp US inf)*

Fu|sel|öl NT fusel oil

Fü|si|lier [fyzi'liːɐ] M -s, -e *(old Mil, Sw)* fusilier

fü|si|lie|ren [fyzi'liːrən] *ptp* **füsiliert** VT *(old Mil)* to execute by firing squad

Fu|si|on [fu'zioːn] F -, -en amalgamation; *(von Unternehmen auch)* merger; *(von Atomkernen, Zellen)* fusion

fu|si|o|nie|ren [fuzio'niːrən] *ptp* **fusioniert** VTI to amalgamate; *(Unternehmen auch)* to merge

Fu|si|o|ni|tis [fuzio'niːtɪs] F -, *no pl (hum pej: = Comm)* merger mania

Fu|si|ons|re|ak|tor M fusion reactor

Fuß [fuːs] M -es, ⸗e ['fyːsə] **a** *(= Körperteil)* foot; *(S Ger, Aus: = Bein)* leg; **zu ~** on foot; **zu ~ gehen/kommen** to walk, to go/come on foot; **er ist gut/schlecht zu ~** he is steady/not so steady on his feet; **sich jdm zu Füßen werfen** to prostrate oneself before sb; **jdm zu Füßen fallen/liegen/sitzen** to fall/lie/sit at sb's feet; **jdm zu Füßen sinken** to sink to the ground at sb's feet; **jdm zu Füßen fallen** *or* **sinken** *(fig: Bittsteller)* to go down on one's knees to *or* before sb; **das Publikum lag/sank ihm zu Füßen** he had the audience at his feet; **den ~ in** *or* **zwischen die Tür stellen** to get *or* put one's foot in the door; **den ~ auf die Erde/den Mond setzen** to set foot on the earth/the moon; **über seine eigenen Füße stolpern** to trip over one's own feet; *(fig)* to get tied up in knots; **kalte Füße bekommen** *(lit, fig)* **sich** *(dat)* **kalte Füße holen** *(lit, fig)* to get cold feet; **so schnell/weit ihn seine Füße trugen** as fast/far as his legs would carry him; **bei ~!** heel!; **jdm zwischen die Füße geraten** *or* **kommen** to get under sb's feet; **jdm etw vor die Füße werfen** *or* **schmeißen** *(inf) (lit)* to throw sth at sb; *(fig)* to tell sb to keep *or* stuff *(inf)* sth; **jdn mit Füßen treten** *(fig)* to walk all over sb; **etw mit Füßen treten** *(fig)* to treat sth with contempt; **(festen) ~ fassen** *(lit, fig)* to gain a foothold; *(= sich niederlassen)* to settle down; **auf eigenen Füßen stehen** *(lit)* to stand by oneself; *(fig)* to stand on one's own two feet; **jdn auf freien ~ setzen** to release sb, to set sb free; **jdn auf dem falschen ~ erwischen** *(fig)* to catch sb on the wrong foot; **auf großem ~ leben** to live the high life; **mit jdm auf gutem ~ stehen** to be on good terms with sb; **jdm/einer Sache auf dem ~e folgen** *(lit)* to be hot on the heels of sb/sth; *(fig)* to follow hard on sb/sth; **mit einem ~ im Grab stehen** to have one foot in the grave → **Boden a**, **Hand e**, **Gewehr**, **frei 1 a** **b** *(von Gegenstand)* base; *(= Tisch-, Stuhlbein)* leg; *(von Schrank, Gebirge)* foot; **auf schwachen** *or* **tönernen Füßen stehen** to be built on sand **c** *(Poet)* foot **d** *(von Strumpf)* foot **e** *pl* - *(Längenmaß)* foot; **~ breit** = **Fußbreit**; **12 ~ lang** 12 foot *or* feet long

Fuß-: **Fuß|ab|druck** M footprint; **Fuß|ab|strei|fer** [-lapʃtraifɐ] M **-s, -** footscraper; *(= Matte)* doormat; **Fuß|ab|tre|ter** M doormat; **Fuß|an|gel** F *(lit)* mantrap; *(fig)* catch, trap; **Fuß|ar|beit** F, *no pl (Sport)* footwork; **Fuß|bad** NT foot bath

Fuß|ball M **a** *(no pl: = Fußballspiel)* football *(esp Brit)*, soccer **b** *(= Ball)* football *(esp Brit)*, soccer ball

Fuß|bal|ler [-balɐ] M **-s, -**, **Fuß|bal|le|rin** [-ərɪn] F **-, -nen** *(inf)* footballer *(esp Brit)*, soccer player

fuß|bal|le|risch ['fu:sbalərɪʃ] **ADJ** *Leistungen etc* footballing *(esp Brit)*, soccer-playing *(US)* **ADV** **~ überlegen sein** to have superior football(ing) *(esp Brit)* *or* soccer(-playing) *(US)* skills

Fuß|ball-: **Fuß|ball|mann|schaft** F football *(esp Brit)* *or* soccer team; **Fuß|ball|match** NT *(Aus)* football *(esp Brit)* *or* soccer match; **Fuß|ball|meis|ter|schaft** F football *(esp Brit)* *or* soccer league championship; **Fuß|ball|platz** M football pitch *(esp Brit)*, soccer field *(US)*; **Fuß|ball|row|dy** M football *(esp Brit)* *or* soccer hooligan; **Fuß|ball|schuh** M football boot *(esp Brit)*, soccer shoe *(US)*; **Fuß|ball|spiel** NT football *(esp Brit)* *or* soccer match; *(= Sportart)* football *(esp Brit)*, soccer; **Fuß|ball|spie|ler(in)** M(F) football *(esp Brit)* *or* soccer player; **Fuß|ball|sta|di|on** NT football *(esp Brit)* *or* soccer *(US)* stadium; **Fuß|ball|to|to** M OR NT football *(esp Brit)* *or* soccer *(US)* pools *pl*; **Fuß|ball|ver|ein** M football *(esp Brit)* *or* soccer club

Fuß|bank F *pl* **-bänke** footstool

Fuß|bo|den M floor

Fuß|bo|den-: **Fuß|bo|den|be|lag** M floor covering; **Fuß|bo|den|hei|zung** F (under)-floor heating

Fuß-: **fuß|breit** ADJ a foot wide; **Fuß|breit** M **-**, *no pl* foot; **keinen ~ weichen** *(lit, fig)* not to budge an inch *(inf)*; **Fuß|brem|se** F foot brake; **Fuß|ei|sen** NT mantrap

Fus|sel ['fʊsl] F **-, -n** *or m* **-s, -** fluff *no pl*; **ein(e) ~** some fluff, a bit of fluff

fus|se|lig ['fʊsəlɪç] ADJ *(= von Fusseln bedeckt)* covered with fluff; *(= fusselnd)* giving off fluff; *(= ausgefranst)* frayed; **sich** *(dat)* **den Mund ~ reden** *(inf)* to talk till one is blue in the face

fus|seln ['fʊsln] VI to give off fluff

fü|ßeln ['fy:sln] VI to play footsie *(inf)* *(mit* with)

fu|ßen ['fu:sn] VI to rest, to be based *(auf +dat* on)

Fuß-: **Fuß|en|de** NT *(von Bett)* foot; **Fuß|fall** M = **Kniefall**; **fuß|fäl|lig** ADJ, ADV = **kniefällig**; **Fuß|fes|sel** F **a** **~n** *pl (= Knebel)* shackles *pl* **b** **elektronische ~** electronic tag

Fuß|gän|ger [-gɛŋɐ] M **-s, -**, **Fuß|gän|ge|rin** [-ərɪn] F **-, -nen** pedestrian

Fuß|gän|ger-: **Fuß|gän|ger|am|pel** F pedestrian lights *pl*; **Fuß|gän|ger|brü|cke** F footbridge; **Fuß|gän|ger|in|sel** F traffic island; **Fuß|gän|ger|über|gang** M pedestrian crossing; **Fuß|gän|ger|über|weg** M pedestrian crossing *(Brit)*, crosswalk *(US)*; *(auch* **Fußgängerüberführung**) pedestrian bridge; **Fuß|gän|ger|un|ter|füh|rung** F underpass, pedestrian subway *(Brit)*; **Fuß|gän|ger|zo|ne** F pedestrian precinct *or* zone

Fuß-: **Fuß|ge|her(in)** M(F) *(Aus)* pedestrian; **Fuß|ge|lenk** NT ankle; **fuß|hoch** **ADJ** ankle-deep **ADV** up to one's ankles

-fü|ßig [fy:sɪç] ADJ *suf* **a** -legged; **ein dreifüßiger Tisch** a three-legged table **b** *(Poet)* -foot; **fünffüßiger Jambus** iambic pentameter

Fuß-: **fuß|kalt** ADJ **das Haus ist immer ~** the floor in that house is always cold; **Fuß|kett|chen** NT ankle bracelet; **fuß|krank** ADJ **~ sein** to have bad feet *or* trouble with one's feet; *(fig)* to be lagging behind; **Fuß|kran|ke(r)** MF *decl as adj* person with bad feet; *(fig)* laggard; **Fuß|lap|pen** M footcloth; **Fuß|lei|den** NT foot complaint; **Fuß|leis|te** F skirting (board) *(Brit)*, baseboard *(US)*

fuss|lig ADJ = **fusselig**

Füß|ling ['fy:slɪŋ] M **-s, -e** *(von Strumpf)* foot; *(= Socke)* sockette *(dated Brit)*

Fuß-: **Fuß|marsch** M walk; *(Mil)* march; **Fuß|mat|te** F doormat; **Fuß|no|te** F footnote; **Fuß|pfad** M footpath; **Fuß|pfle|ge** F chiropody; **zur ~ gehen** to go to the chiropodist; **Fuß|pfle|ger(in)** M(F) chiropodist; **Fuß|pilz** M *(Med)* athlete's foot; **Fuß|pu|der** M foot powder; **Fuß|punkt** M **a** *(Astron)* nadir **b** *(Math)* foot *(of a perpendicular)*; **Fuß|re|flex|zo|nen|mas|sa|ge** F = **Reflexzonenmassage**; **Fuß|schweiß** M foot perspiration; **Fuß|soh|le** F sole of the foot; **Fuß|sol|dat** M *(Mil old)* foot soldier; **Fuß|spit|ze** F toes *pl*; **sich auf die ~n stellen** to stand on tiptoe; **Fuß|sprung** M **einen ~ machen** to jump feet-first; **Fuß|spur** F footprint; **Fuß|stap|fe** F, **Fuß|stap|fen** M footprint; **in jds ~n** *(pl)* **treten** *(fig)* to follow in sb's footsteps; **Fuß|steig** M **a** *(= Weg)* footpath **b** *(S Ger: = Bürgersteig)* pavement *(Brit)*, sidewalk *(US)*; **Fuß|stüt|ze** F footrest; **fuß|tief** ADJ, ADV ankle-deep; **Fuß|tritt** M *(= Geräusch)* footstep; *(= Spur auch)* footprint; *(= Stoß)* kick; **jdm einen ~ geben** *or* **versetzen** to kick sb, to give sb a kick; **jdn mit einem ~ hinausbefördern** to kick sb out; **einen ~ bekommen** *(fig)* to be kicked out; **Fuß|trup|pe** F infantry *no pl*; **Fuß|volk** NT, *no pl* **a** *(Mil old)* footmen *pl* **b** *(fig)* **das ~** the rank and file; **Fuß|wan|de|rung** F walk; **Fuß|wa|schung** F foot-washing; **die ~ Christi** the washing of Christ's feet; **Fuß|weg** M **a** *(= Pfad)* footpath **b** *(= Entfernung)* **es sind nur 15 Minuten ~** it's only 15 minutes' walk; **Fuß|wur|zel** F *(Anat)* tarsus; **Fuß|zei|le** F *(Comput)* footer

Fu|ton ['fu:tɔn] M **-s, -s** futon

Fu|ton|mat|rat|ze F futon

futsch [fʊtʃ] ADJ *pred (inf) (= weg)* gone, vanished; *(S Ger: = kaputt)* bust *(inf)*, broken

Fut|ter ['fʊtɐ] NT **-s, -** **a** *no pl* (animal) food *or* feed; *(esp für Kühe, Pferde etc)* fodder; **gut im ~ sein** to be well-fed **b** *(= Auskleidung, Kleiderfutter, Briefumschlagfutter)* lining; *(= Türfutter)* casing **c** *(= Spannfutter)* chuck

Fut|te|ral [fʊtə'ra:l] NT **-s, -e** case

Fut|ter-: **Fut|ter|ge|trei|de** NT forage cereal; **Fut|ter|häus|chen** [-hɔysçən] NT birdhouse; **Fut|ter|krip|pe** F manger; **an der ~ sitzen** *(inf)* to be well-placed; **Fut|ter|mit|tel** NT animal feed *no pl*; **Fut|ter|mit|tel|ad|di|ti|ve** PL feed additives *pl*; **Fut|ter|mit|tel|in|dus|trie** F (animal) feed industry

fut|tern ['fʊtɐn] *(hum inf)* **VI** to stuff oneself *(inf)* **VT** to scoff *(Brit inf)*, to scarf *or* chow *(US inf)*

füt|tern ['fʏtɐn] VT **a** *Tier, Kind, Kranke* to feed; **„Füttern verboten"** "do not feed the animals" **b** *Kleidungsstück* to line

Fut|ter-: **Fut|ter|napf** M bowl; **Fut|ter|neid** M *(fig)* green-eyed monster *(hum)*, jealousy; **Fut|ter|pflan|ze** F forage plant; **Fut|ter|rü|be** F *root vegetable used to feed animals*; **Fut|ter|sack** M nosebag; **Fut|ter|stoff** M lining (material); **Fut|ter|su|che** F search for food; **auf ~ sein** to be searching for food; **Fut|ter|trog** M feeding trough

Füt|te|rung ['fʏtərʊŋ] F **-, -en** feeding; **die ~ der Nilpferde findet um 17.00 Uhr statt** feeding time for the hippos is 5 pm

Fut|ter|ver|wer|ter [-fɛɐve:ɐtɐ] M **-s, -**, **Fut|ter|ver|wer|te|rin** F [-ərɪn] **-, -nen** *(inf: Mensch)* **er ist ein guter ~** he looks like he can really pack it away *(inf)*

Fu|tur [fu'tu:ɐ] NT **-(e)s, -e** *(Gram)* future (tense)

Fu|tu|ra *pl von* **Futurum**

fu|tu|risch [fu'tu:rɪʃ] ADJ *(Gram)* future

Fu|tu|ris|mus [futu'rɪsmʊs] M **-**, *no pl* futurism

fu|tu|ris|tisch [futu'rɪstɪʃ] ADJ **a** *(= zukunftsweisend)* futuristic **b** *(= den Futurismus betreffend)* futurist

Fu|tu|ro|lo|ge [futuro'lo:gə] M **-n, -n**, **Fu|tu|ro|lo|gin** [-'lo:gɪn] F **-, -nen** futurologist

Fu|tu|ro|lo|gie [futurolo'gi:] F **-**, *no pl* futurology

fu|tu|ro|lo|gisch [futuro'lo:gɪʃ] ADJ futurological

Fu|tu|rum [fu'tu:rʊm] NT **-s, Futura** [-ra] *(Gram)* future (tense)

Fux [fʊks] M **-es, ⸚e** ['fʏksə] *(Univ) new member of a student fraternity*

Fux|ma|jor M *(Univ) student in charge of the new members of a fraternity*

fu|zeln ['fu:tsln] VI *(Aus)* to write small

Fuz|zi ['fʊtsi] M **-s, -s** *(inf)* freak *(inf)*

Fuz|zi-Lo|gik ['fazi,lo:gɪk] F **-**, *no pl (Comput)* fuzzy logic

G

G, g [geː] NT -, - G, g
g [geː] *abbr von* **Gramm**
gab *pret von* **geben**
Ga|bar|di|ne ['gabardiːn, gabar'diːn(ə)] M -s *or* f -, *no pl* gaberdine, gabardine
Ga|be ['gaːbə] F -, -n **a** (*dated*: = *Geschenk*) gift, present (+*gen* of, from); (= *Schenkung*) donation (+*gen* from); (*Eccl*: = *Opfer*) offering → **mild(e)** ADJ b **b** (= *Begabung*) gift; **die ~ haben, etw zu tun** to have a natural *or* (*auch iro*) (great) gift for doing sth **c** (*Med*) (= *das Verabreichen*) administering; (= *Dosis*) dose
Ga|bel ['gaːbl] F -, -n fork; (= *Heugabel, Mistgabel*) pitchfork; (= *Deichsel*) shafts *pl*; (*Telec*) rest, cradle; (*Hunt*: = *Geweih mit zwei Enden*) two-pointed antler; (= *zwei Enden des Geweihs*) branch, fork
Ga|bel-: **Ga|bel|bis|sen** M canapé; **Ga|bel|bock** M (*Hunt*: = *Rehbock*) two-pointer; (= *Gabelantilope*) pronghorn (antelope); **Ga|bel|deich|sel** F shafts *pl*; **ga|bel|för|mig** ADJ forked *no adv* ADV **sich ~ teilen** to fork; **Ga|bel|früh|stück** NT ≈ mid-morning snack; **Ga|bel|hirsch** M (*Hunt*: = *Rothirsch*) two-pointer; (= *Andenhirsch*) guemal
ga|be|lig ['gaːbəlɪç] ADJ, ADV = **gabelförmig**
ga|beln ['gaːbln] VR to fork → *auch* **gegabelt**
Ga|bel|stap|ler [-ʃtaːplɐ] M -s, - fork-lift truck
Ga|be|lung F -, -en fork
Ga|ben|tisch M *table for Christmas or birthday presents*
Ga|bun [ga'buːn] NT -s Gabon
G8, G-8 [geː'laxt] F - G8
G8-Staat, G-8-Staat M G8 nation
ga|ckern ['gakɐn] VI (*lit, fig*) to cackle
Ga|do|li|ni|um [gado'liːniʊm] NT -s, *no pl* (*abbr* **Gd**) gadolinium
Gaf|fel ['gafl] F -, -n (*Naut*) gaff
Gaf|fel-: **Gaf|fel|scho|ner** M (*Naut*) fore-and-aft schooner; **Gaf|fel|se|gel** NT (*Naut*) gaff-sail
gaf|fen ['gafn] VI to gape, to gawp (*inf*), to stare (*nach* at), to rubberneck (*esp US inf*); **gaff nicht, hilf mir lieber!** don't just stand there staring, come and help!
Gaf|fer ['gafɐ] M -s, -, **Gaf|fe|rin** [-ərɪn] F -, -nen gaper, gawper (*inf*), starer, rubbernecker (*esp US inf*); **die neugierigen ~ bei einem Unfall** the nosy people standing staring at an accident, the rubbernecks at an accident (*esp US inf*)
Gaf|fe|rei [gafə'rai] F -, *no pl* gaping, gawping (*inf*), staring, rubbernecking (*esp US inf*)
Gag [gɛ(ː)k] M -s, -s (= *Filmgag*) gag; (= *Werbegag*) gimmick; (= *Witz*) joke; (*inf*: = *Spaß*) laugh
ga|ga ['gaga] ADJ *pred inv* (*inf*) gaga (*inf*)
Ga|gat [ga'gaːt] M -(e)s, -e, **Ga|gat|koh|le** F jet
Ga|ge ['gaːʒə] F -, -n (*esp Theat*) fee; (= *regelmäßige Gage*) salary
gäh|nen ['gɛːnən] VI (*lit, fig*) to yawn; **~de Leere** total emptiness; **im Kino herrschte ~de Leere** the cinema was (totally) deserted; **ein ~der Abgrund** a yawning abyss; **ein ~des Loch** a gaping hole; **ein Gähnen** a yawn; **das Gähnen unterdrücken** to stop oneself (from) yawning; **das Gähnen der Schüler** the pupils' yawning; **das war zum Gähnen (langweilig)** it was one big yawn (*inf*)
GAL [geːlaː'lɛl] F - *abbr von* **Grün-Alternative Liste** *electoral pact of Greens and alternative parties*
Ga|la ['gala, 'gaːla] F -, -s formal *or* evening *or* gala dress; (*Mil*) full *or* ceremonial *or* gala dress; **sich in ~ werfen** to get all dressed up (to the nines (*esp Brit inf*)), to put on one's best bib and tucker (*Brit inf*)
Ga|la- *in cpds* formal, evening; (*Mil*) full ceremonial, gala; (*Theat*) gala; **Ga|la|abend** M gala evening; **Ga|la|an|zug** M formal *or* evening dress; (*Mil*) full *or* ceremonial *or* gala dress; **Ga|la|di|ner** NT formal dinner; **Ga|la|emp|fang** M formal reception
ga|lak|tisch [ga'laktɪʃ] ADJ galactic
Ga|lan [ga'laːn] M -s, -e (*old*) gallant; (*hum auch*) beau
ga|lant [ga'lant] (*dated*) ADJ gallant; **die ~e Dichtung** galant poetry; **~es Abenteuer** affair of the heart, amatory adventure ADV gallantly
Ga|lan|te|rie [galantə'riː] F -, -n [-'riːən] (*dated*) gallantry
Ga|lan|te|rie|wa|ren PL (*old*) fashion accessories *pl*
Ga|la-: **Ga|la|uni|form** F (*Mil*) full dress *or* ceremonial *or* gala uniform; **Ga|la|vor|stel|lung** F (*Theat*) gala performance
Gä|le ['gɛːlə] M -n, -n, **Gä|lin** ['gɛːlɪn] F ['gɛːlɪn] -, -nen Gael
Ga|lee|re [ga'leːrə] F -, -n galley
Ga|lee|ren|skla|ve M, **Ga|lee|ren|sträf|ling** M galley slave
Ga|le|o|ne [gale'oːnə] F -, -n (*Hist*) galleon
Ga|le|rie [galə'riː] F -, -n [-'riːən] **a** (= *Empore, Gang, Kunstgalerie, Mil, Naut*) gallery; **auf der ~** in the gallery **b** (= *Geschäftspassage*) arcade
Ga|le|rist [galə'rɪst] M -en, -en, **Ga|le|ris|tin** [-'rɪstɪn] F -, -nen gallery owner
Gal|gen ['galgn] M -s, - gallows *pl*, gibbet; (*Film*) boom; (*Tech*) crossbeam; (= *Spiel*) hangman; **jdn an den ~ bringen** to bring sb to the gallows; **an den ~ mit ihm!** let him swing!, to the gallows with him!; **jdn am ~ hinrichten** to hang sb (from the gallows)
Gal|gen-: **Gal|gen|frist** F (*inf*) reprieve; **jdm eine ~ geben** to give sb a reprieve, to reprieve sb; **Gal|gen|hu|mor** M gallows humour (*Brit*) *or* humor (*US*); **sagte er mit ~** he said with a macabre sense of humo(u)r; **Gal|gen|strick** M, **Gal|gen|vo|gel** M (*inf*) gallows bird (*inf*)
Ga|li|ci|en [ga'liːtsiən] NT -s, *no pl* Galicia
Ga|li|läa [gali'lɛːa] NT -s, *no pl* Galilee
Ga|li|lä|er [gali'lɛːɐ] M -s, -, **Ga|li|lä|e|rin** [-ərɪn] F -, -nen Galilean
ga|li|lä|isch [gali'lɛːɪʃ] ADJ Galilean
Gä|lin ['gɛːlɪn] F ['gɛːlɪn] -, -nen Gael
Ga|li|on [ga'lioːn] NT -s, -s (*Hist*) cutwater
Ga|li|ons|fi|gur F figurehead
gä|lisch ['gɛːlɪʃ] ADJ Gaelic
Gall|ap|fel ['gal-] M gallnut; (*an Eichen*) oak apple, oak gall
Gal|le ['galə] F -, -n (*Anat*) (= *Organ*) gall bladder; (= *Flüssigkeit*) bile, gall; (*Bot, Vet*) gall; (*fig*: = *Bosheit*) gall, virulence; **bitter wie ~** bitter as gall; **seine ~ verspritzen** (*fig*) to pour out one's venom; **jdm kommt die ~ hoch** sb's blood begins to boil; **die ~ läuft ihm über** (*inf*) he's seething *or* livid → **Gift**
gal|le|bit|ter ADJ very bitter; *Wein, Geschmack auch* acid, acrid; *Bemerkung* caustic
Gal|len- *in cpds* gall; **gal|len|bit|ter** ADJ = **gallebitter**; **Gal|len|bla|se** F gall bladder; **Gal|len|gang** M *pl* **-gänge** bile duct; **Gal|len|grieß** M small gallstones *pl*; **Gal|len|ko|lik** F gallstone colic; **Gal|len|lei|den** NT trouble with one's gall bladder; **Gal|len|stein** M gallstone
Gal|lert [ga'lɛrt, 'galɐt] NT -(e)s, -e jelly (*Brit*), Jell-O® (*US*)
gal|lert|ar|tig ADJ jelly-like (*Brit*), Jell-O-like® (*US*), gelatinous
Gal|ler|te [ga'lɛrtə, 'galɐtə] F -, -n jelly (*Brit*), Jell-O® (*US*)
Gal|li|en ['galiən] NT -s Gaul
Gal|li|er ['galiɐ] M -s, -, **Gal|li|e|rin** [-iərɪn] F -, -nen Gaul
gal|lig ['galɪç] ADJ gall-like *attr*; (*fig*) *Mensch, Bemerkung, Humor* caustic, acerbic ADV (*fig*) caustically
gal|lisch ['galɪʃ] ADJ Gallic
Gal|li|um ['galiʊm] NT -s, *no pl* (*abbr* **Ga**) gallium
Gal|li|zis|mus [gali'tsɪsmʊs] M -, **Gallizismen** [-mən] (*Ling*) Gallicism
Gal|lo|ne [ga'loːnə] F -, -n gallon
Gall|sei|fe ['gal-] F ox-gall soap
Ga|lopp [ga'lɔp] M -s, -s *or* -e gallop; (= *Tanz*) galop; **im ~** (*lit*) at a gallop; (*fig*) at top *or* high speed; **langsamer ~** canter; **gestreckter/kurzer ~** full/checked gallop; **in den ~ verfallen** to break into a gallop; **das Pferd sprang in fliegendem ~ über die Mauer** the horse flew *or* soared over the wall in mid-gallop
ga|lop|pie|ren [galɔ'piːrən] *ptp* **galoppiert** VI *aux haben or sein* to gallop; **~de Inflation** galloping inflation
Ga|lopp-: **Ga|lopp|renn|bahn** F racecourse, racetrack; **Ga|lopp|ren|nen** NT horse race (*on the flat*); **zum ~ gehen** to go to the races
Ga|lo|sche [ga'lɔʃə] F -, -n galosh *usu pl*, overshoe
galt *pret von* **gelten**
gal|va|nisch [gal'vaːnɪʃ] ADJ galvanic
Gal|va|ni|seur [galvani'zøːɐ] M -s, -e, **Gal|va|ni|seu|rin** [-'zøːrɪn] F -, -nen electroplater
Gal|va|ni|sier|an|stalt F electroplating works *sing or pl*
gal|va|ni|sie|ren [galvani'ziːrən] *ptp* **galvanisiert** VT to electroplate; (*mit Zink auch*) to galvanize
Gal|va|ni|sie|rung F -, -en electroplating; (*mit Zink auch*) galvanizing
Gal|va|nis|mus [galva'nɪsmʊs] M -, *no pl* galvanism
Gal|va|no [gal'vaːno] NT -s, -s (*Typ*) electrotype, electro (*inf*)
Gal|va|no-: **Gal|va|no|me|ter** NT -s, - galvanometer; **Gal|va|no|plas|tik** F (*Tech*) electroforming, galvanoplasty (*form*); (*Typ*) electrotype
Ga|ma|sche [ga'maʃə] F -, -n gaiter; (= *kurze Gamasche*) spat; (= *Wickelgamasche*) puttee; **sie hat**

~n vor ihm/davor *(dated inf)* he/it makes her shake in her shoes *(inf)*

Ga|ma|schen|ho|se F (pair of) leggings *pl*

Gam|be ['gambə] F -, -n viola da gamba

Gam|bia ['gambia] NT -s (the) Gambia

Game|boy® ['ge:mbɔy] M -(s), -s *(Comput)* Gameboy®

Game|con|trol|ler ['ge:mkɔn,tro:lɐ] M -(s), - *(Comput)* game controller

Game|port ['ge:mpɔrt] M -(s), -s *(Comput)* game port

Game|show ['ge:mʃo:] F game show

Gam|ma ['gama] NT -(s), -s gamma

Gam|ma|strah|len ['gama-] PL gamma rays *pl*

Gam|ma|strah|lung F gamma radiation

Gam|mel ['gaml] M -s, *no pl (dial)* junk *(inf)*, rubbish

Gam|mel-: **Gam|mel|dienst** M *(Mil sl)* lazy spell of duty; **Gam|mel|fleisch** NT *(inf)* rotten meat

gam|me|lig ['gaməlɪç] ADJ *(inf) Lebensmittel* old, ancient *(inf)*; *Kleidung* tatty *(inf)*; *Auto* decrepit; **das Fleisch ist ja schon ganz ~** the meat has already gone off *(Brit)* or bad

Gam|mel|le|ben NT *(inf)* loafing or bumming around *no art (inf)*

gam|meln ['gamln] VI *(inf)* to laze about, to loaf about *(Brit)* or around *(inf)*, to bum around *(inf)*

Gamm|ler ['gamlɐ] M -s, -, **Gamm|le|rin** [-ərɪn] F -, -nen long-haired layabout *(Brit)* or bum *(inf)*

Gams [gams] F -, -(en) [-zn] *(Aus, S Ger Hunt)* chamois

Gäms|bart △ M, **Gams|bart** M *tuft of hair from a chamois worn as a hat decoration*, shaving brush *(hum inf)*

Gäms|bock △ M, **Gams|bock** M chamois buck

Gäm|se ['gɛmzə] F -, -n chamois

Gäms|le|der △ NT, **Gams|le|der** NT chamois (leather)

gang [gaŋ] ADJ ~ **und gäbe sein** to be the usual thing, to be quite usual

Gang [gaŋ] M -(e)s, ⸚e ['gɛŋə] **a** *(no pl: = Gangart)* walk, way of walking, gait; *(eines Pferdes)* gait, pace; **einen leichten ~ haben** to be light on one's feet, to walk lightly; **einen schnellen ~ haben** to be a fast walker; **jdn an seinem** or **am ~ erkennen** to recognize sb's walk or sb by the way he walks; **jdn am aufrechten ~ erkennen** to recognize sb from his upright carriage; **in aufrechtem ~** *(fig)* with one's head held high; **seinen ~ verlangsamen** to slow down; **seinen ~ beschleunigen** to speed up

b *(= Besorgung)* errand; *(= Spaziergang)* walk; **einen ~ machen** or **tun** to go on an errand/for a walk; **einen ~ zum Anwalt/zur Bank machen** to go to one's lawyer/the bank, to pay a visit to one's lawyer/the bank; **einen schweren ~ tun** to do something difficult; **das war für ihn immer ein schwerer ~** it was always hard for him; **ich muss einen schweren ~ tun** I have a difficult thing to do; **sein erster ~ war ...** the first thing he did was ...; **den ~ nach Canossa** or **Kanossa antreten** *(fig)* to eat humble pie; **der ~ nach Canossa** or **Kanossa** *(Hist)* the pilgrimage to Canossa; **der ~ an die Börse** flotation (on the stock exchange)

c *(no pl) (Bewegung eines Motors)* running; *(einer Maschine)* running, operation; *(= Ablauf)* course; *(eines Dramas)* development; **der Motor hat einen leisen ~** the engine runs quietly; **der ~ der Ereignisse/der Dinge** the course of events/things; **seinen (gewohnten) ~ gehen** *(fig)* to run its usual course; **etw in ~ bringen** or **setzen** to get or set sth going; *(fig auch)* to get sth off the ground or under way; **etw in ~ halten** *(lit, fig)* to keep sth going; *Maschine, Motor auch* to keep sth running; **in ~ kommen** to get going; *(fig auch)* to get off the ground or under way; **in ~ sein** to be going; *(Maschine auch)* to be in operation, to be running; *(Motor auch)* to be running; *(fig)* to be off the ground or under way; *(= los sein)* to be going on or happening; **in vollem ~** in full swing; **es ist etwas im ~(e)** *(inf)* something's up *(inf)* → **tot c**

d *(= Arbeitsgang)* operation; *(eines Essens)* course; *(Fechten, im Zweikampf)* bout; *(beim Rennen)* heat; **ein Essen von** or **mit vier Gängen** a four-course meal

e *(= Verbindungsgang)* passage(way); *(Rail, in Gebäuden)* corridor; *(= Hausflur) (offen)* passage (-way), close *(Scot)*; *(hinter Eingangstür)* hallway; *(im oberen Stock)* landing; *(zwischen Sitzreihen, in Geschäft)* aisle; *(= Tunnel: in Stadion, zu Flugzeug)* gangway; *(= Säulengang)* colonnade, passage; *(= Bogengang)* arcade, passage; *(= Wandelgang)* walk; *(in einem Bergwerk)* tunnel, gallery; *(= Durchgang zwischen Häusern)* passage(-way); *(Anat)* duct; *(= Gehörgang)* meatus; *(Min: = Erzgang)* vein; *(Tech: eines Gewindes)* thread

f *(Mech)* gear; *(bei Fahrrad)* gear, speed; **den ersten ~ einschalten** or **einlegen** to engage first (gear); **auf** or **in den dritten ~ schalten** to change *(Brit)* or shift *(US)* into third (gear); **in die Gänge kommen** *(fig)* to get started or going

Gang [gɛŋ] F -, -s gang

Gang|art F **a** walk, way of walking, gait; *(von Pferd)* gait, pace; *(= Haltung)* carriage, bearing; *(fig)* stance; **Menschen haben eine aufrechte ~** humans walk upright; **eine leicht nach vorne gebeugte ~ haben** to walk with one's body bent slightly forward; **eine schnellere ~ vorlegen** to walk faster; **eine harte ~** *(fig)* a tough stance or line **b** *(Min)* gangue, matrix

gang|bar ADJ *(lit) Weg, Brücke etc* passable; *(fig) Lösung, Weg* practicable; **nicht ~** impassable; impracticable

Gän|gel|band [-bant] NT *pl* **-bänder jdn am ~ führen** *(fig) (Lehrer etc)* to spoon-feed sb; *(Ehefrau, Mutter)* to keep sb tied to one's apron strings

Gän|ge|lei [gɛŋə'lai] F -, -en spoon-feeding; **warum wehrt er sich nicht gegen die ~ seiner Mutter/Frau?** why doesn't he fight against being tied to his mother's/wife's apron strings?

gän|geln ['gɛŋln] VT *(fig)* **jdn ~** to spoon-feed sb, to treat sb like a child; *(Mutter, Ehefrau)* to keep sb tied to one's apron strings

Gang|he|bel M *(Tech)* gear lever

gän|gig ['gɛŋɪç] ADJ **a** *(= üblich)* common; *(= aktuell)* current; *Münze* current; *(= vertretbar)* possible; **~e Praxis sein** to be common practice **b** *(= gut gehend) Waren* popular, in demand; **die ~ste Ausführung** the best-selling model **c** *(rare: = gut laufend)* **~ sein** *(Pferd)* to be a good goer; *(Hund)* to be well-trained; **ein ~es/schlecht ~es Gespann** a fast/slow team; **einen Hund ~ machen** *(Hunt)* to train a dog

Gang|li|en ['gaŋ(g)liən] PL *(Anat)* ganglia *pl*

Gang|li|en-: **Gang|li|en|sys|tem** NT gangliar or ganglionic system; **Gang|li|en|zel|le** F gangliocyte, ganglion cell

Gang|platz M *(Aviat, Rail etc)* aisle seat

Gan|grän [gaŋ'grɛ:n] NT -s, -e, **Gan|grä|ne** [gaŋ'grɛ:nə] F -, -n *(Med)* gangrene

Gang|schal|tung F gears *pl*

Gangs|ter ['gɛŋstɐ, 'gaŋstɐ] M -s, - gangster

Gangs|ter-: **Gangs|ter|boss** △ M gang boss; **Gangs|ter|braut** F *(inf)* (gangster's) moll *(inf)*; **Gangs|ter|film** M gangster film or movie *(esp US)*; **Gangs|ter|me|tho|den** PL strong-arm tactics *pl*

Gang|way ['gɛŋwe:] F -, -s *(Naut)* gangway; *(Aviat)* steps *pl*

Ga|no|ve [ga'no:və] M -n, -n *(inf)* crook; *(hum: = listiger Kerl)* sly old fox → *auch* **Ganovin**

Ga|no|ven-: **Ga|no|ven|eh|re** F honour *(Brit)* or honor *(US)* among(st) thieves; **das verbietet mir meine ~** even crooks have some honour *(Brit)* or honor *(US)*; **Ga|no|ven|spra|che** F underworld slang

Ga|no|vin [ga'no:vɪn] F -, -nen *(inf)* crook

Gans [gans] F -, ⸚e ['gɛnzə] goose; **wie die Gänse schnattern** to cackle away, to cackle like a bunch of old hens *(inf)*

Gans- *in cpds (Aus)* = **Gänse-**

Gäns|chen ['gɛnsçən] NT -s, - gosling; *(fig inf)* little goose *(inf)*

Gän|se- *in cpds* goose; **Gän|se|blüm|chen** NT, **Gän|se|blu|me** F daisy; **Gän|se|bra|ten** M roast goose; **Gän|se|brust** F *(Cook)* breast of goose; **Gän|se|fe|der** F (goose-)quill; **Gän|se|fett** NT goose-fat; **Gän|se|füß|chen** PL *(inf)* inverted commas *pl*, quotation marks *pl*, sixty-sixes and ninety-nines *pl (inf)*; **Gän|se|haut** F *(fig)* goose pimples *pl (Brit)*, goose flesh *(Brit)*, goose bumps *pl*; **eine ~ bekommen** or **kriegen** *(inf)* to get goose pimples *(Brit)* or goose flesh *(Brit)* or goose bumps, to go all goose-pimply *(Brit inf)*; **Gän|se|kiel** M (goose-)quill; **Gän|se|klein** NT -s, *no pl* goose pieces *pl*; *(= Innereien)* goose giblets *pl*; **Gän|se|le|ber|pas|te|te** F pâté de foie gras, goose-liver pâté; **Gän|se|marsch** M **im ~** in single or Indian file

Gän|se|rich ['gɛnzərɪç] M -s, -e, *(Aus)* **Gan|ser** ['ganzɐ] M -s, - gander

Gän|se-: **Gän|se|schmalz** NT goose dripping; **Gän|se|wein** M *(hum)* Adam's ale *(hum)*, water

Gan|ter ['gantɐ] M -s, - *(N Ger)* gander

ganz [gants] ADJ **a** whole, entire; *(= vollständig)* complete; *Wahrheit* whole; **eine ~e Zahl** a whole number, an integer; **eine ~e Note** *(Mus)* a semibreve *(Brit)*, a whole note *(US)*; **eine ~e Pause** *(Mus)* a semibreve *(Brit)* or whole note *(US)* rest; **die ~e Mannschaft war ...** the whole or entire team was ..., all the team were ...; **die ~en Tassen/Kinder** *(inf)* all the cups/children; **~ England/London** the whole of England/London *(Brit)*, all (of) England/London; **in ~ Großbritannien** throughout Great Britain; **wir fuhren durch ~ England** we travelled *(Brit)* or traveled *(US)* all over England; **in ~ England/London** in the whole of *(Brit)* or in all England/London; **die ~e Zeit** all the time, the whole time; **der ~e Kram** the whole lot *(Brit)*, all the stuff *(US)*; **eine ~e Menge** quite a lot; **sein ~es Geld/Vermögen** all his money/fortune, his entire or whole fortune; **seine ~en Sachen** all his things; **seine ~e Kraft** all his strength; **sie ist seine ~e Freude** *(inf)* she's the apple of his eye *(inf)*; **du bist ja mein ~es Leben** you're my whole life; **du hast mir den ~en Spaß verdorben** you've spoiled all my fun; **ein ~er Mann** a real or proper man → **Arbeit**

b **Käse/eine Sammlung ~** or **im Ganzen kaufen** to buy a whole cheese/a collection as a whole; **im (Großen und) Ganzen (genommen)** on the whole, by and large, (taken) all in all

c *(inf: = unbeschädigt)* intact; **etw wieder ~ machen** to mend sth; **wieder ~ sein** to be mended

d *(inf: = nicht mehr als)* all of; **ich verdiene im Monat ~e 1000 EUR** I earn all of 1000 euros a month; **noch ~e zehn Minuten** all of ten minutes

ADV *(= völlig)* quite; *(= vollständig, ausnahmslos)* completely; *(= ziemlich, leidlich)* quite; *(= sehr)* really; *(= genau)* exactly, just; **~ hinten/vorn** right at the back/front; **nicht ~** not quite; **~ gewiss!** most certainly, absolutely; **ein ~ gutes Buch** *(= ziemlich)* quite a good book; *(= sehr gut)* a very or really good book; **ich habe mich ~ riesig gefreut** *(inf)* I was really pleased; **du hast ihn ~ fürchterlich beleidigt** you've really insulted him very badly; **ein ~ billiger Trick/böser Kerl** a really cheap trick/evil character; **du bist ein ~ Schlauer** you're really a crafty one; **das war ~ lieb von dir** that was really nice of you; **das ist mir ~ gleich** it's all the same or all one to me; **er hat ~ recht** he's quite or absolutely right; **~ mit Ruß bedeckt** all or completely covered with soot; **~ allein** all alone; **du bist ja ~ nass** you're all wet; **so ~ vergnügt/traurig** *etc* so very happy/sad *etc*; **~ Aufmerksamkeit/Demut** *etc*

sein to be all attention/humility *etc*; **etwas ~ Intelligentes/Verrücktes** *etc* something really clever/mad *etc*; **es ist ~ aus** it's all over; **~ wie Sie meinen** just as you think (best); **~ gleich wer** it doesn't matter who, no matter who; **eine Zeitschrift ~ lesen** to read a magazine right through, to read a magazine from cover to cover; **das habe ich nicht ~ gelesen** I haven't read it all yet, I haven't finished reading it yet; **ein ~ ~ hoher Berg** a very very *or* really really high mountain; **~ und gar** completely, utterly; **~ und gar nicht** not at all, not in the least; **noch nicht ~ zwei Uhr** not quite two o'clock yet; **ich habe ~ den Eindruck, dass ...** I've rather got the impression that ...; **ein ~ klein wenig** just a little *or* tiny bit; **das mag ich ~ besonders gerne** I'm particularly *or* especially fond of that; **sie ist ~ die Mutter** she's just *or* exactly like her mother; **etw ~ oder gar nicht machen** to do sth properly or not at all

Ganz|auf|nah|me F *(Phot)* full-length photo (-graph)

Gän|ze ['gɛntsə] F **-,** *no pl (form, Aus)* entirety; **zur ~** completely, fully, in its entirety

Gan|ze(s) ['gantsə] NT *decl as adj* whole; *(= alle Sachen zusammen)* lot; *(= ganzer Satz, ganze Ausrüstung)* complete set; **etw als ~s sehen** to see sth as a whole; **das ~ kostet ...** altogether it costs ...; **das ~ alleine machen** to do the whole thing *or* it all on one's own; **das ~ halt!** *(Mil)* parade, halt!; **das ist nichts ~s und nichts Halbes** that's neither one thing nor the other; **das ~ gefällt mir gar nicht** I don't like it at all, I don't like anything about it; **aufs ~ gehen** *(inf)* to go all out; **es geht ums ~** everything's at stake

Ganz|heit F **-,** *(rare)* **-en** *(= Einheit)* unity; *(= Vollständigkeit)* entirety; **als ~** as an integral whole; **in seiner ~** in its entirety

ganz|heit|lich ['gantshaitlɪç] ADJ *(= umfassend einheitlich)* integral; *Lernen* integrated; *Medizin* holistic ADV **ein Problem ~ betrachten/darstellen** to view/present a problem in its entirety

Ganz|heits-: **Ganz|heits|me|di|zin** F holistic medicine; **Ganz|heits|me|tho|de** F look-and-say method; **Ganz|heits|psy|cho|lo|gie** F holism

Ganz-: **Ganz|jah|res|rei|fen** ['gantsja:rəs-] M *(Mot)* all-season tyre *(Brit) or* tire *(US)*; **ganz|jäh|rig** ADJ ADV all (the) year round; **Ganz|le|der** NT **ein Buch in ~** a leather-bound book, a book with a leather binding; **Ganz|le|der|band** M leather-bound volume; **ganz|le|dern** ADJ leather-bound, bound in leather; **Ganz|lei|nen** NT **a** *(= Stoff)* pure linen **b** *(= Ganzeinband)* **ein Buch in ~** a cloth-bound book, a book with a cloth binding; **Ganz|lei|nen|band** M cloth-bound volume

gänz|lich ['gɛntslɪç] ADV completely, totally ADJ *(rare)* complete, total

Ganz-: **ganz+ma|chen** VT *sep* → **ganz ADJ c**; **ganz|sei|den** ADJ pure silk; **ganz|sei|tig** [-zaitɪç] ADJ *Anzeige etc* full-page; **ganz|tä|gig** ADJ all-day; *Arbeit, Stelle* full-time; **ein ~er Ausflug** a day trip ADV **~ arbeiten** to work full-time; **sie ist jetzt ~ zu Hause** she's at home all day now; **das Schwimmbad ist ~ geöffnet** the swimming pool is open all day

ganz|tags ['gantsta:ks] ADV *arbeiten* full-time

Ganz|tags-: **Ganz|tags|be|schäf|ti|gung** F full-time occupation; **Ganz|tags|be|treu|ung** F all-day *or* full-day care; **Ganz|tags|schu|le** F all-day schooling *no pl or* schools *pl*; *(= Gebäude)* all-day school; **Ganz|tags|stel|le** F full-time job

Ganz-: **Ganz|ton** M *pl* **-töne** *(Mus)* (whole) tone; **ganz|wol|len** ADJ all-wool

gar [ga:ɐ] ADV **a** *(= überhaupt)* at all; **~ keines** none whatsoever, none at all; **~ kein Grund** no reason whatsoever, no reason at all; **~ niemand** not a soul, nobody at all *or* whatsoever; **~ nichts** nothing at all *or* whatsoever; **~ nicht schlecht** *or* **übel** not bad at all, not at all bad **b** *(old, S Ger, Aus: zur Verstärkung)* **es war ~ so kalt/warm** it was really *or* so cold/warm; **er wäre ~ zu gern noch länger geblieben** he would really *or* so have liked to stay longer; **es ist ~ zu dumm, dass er nicht gekommen ist** *(S Ger, Aus)* it's really *or* so *or* too stupid that he didn't come → **ganz ADV**

c *(geh, S Ger, Aus: = sogar)* even; **er wird doch nicht ~ verunglückt sein?** he hasn't had an accident, has he?; **du hast das doch nicht ~ meinem Mann erzählt?** you haven't told my husband, have you?; **warum nicht ~?** (and) why not?, why not indeed?; **und nun will sie ~ ...** and now she even wants ...; **hast du eine Wohnung, oder ~ ein eigenes Haus?** do you have a flat *(Brit) or* apartment, or perhaps even a house of your own?

d *(obs, Aus, S Ger: = sehr)* really, indeed; **ein ~ feiner Mensch** a really splendid person, a splendid person indeed; **~ schön** passing fair *(obs)*; **er kommt ~ oft** he comes really frequently *or* very frequently indeed; **~ mancher** many a person; **~ manchmal** many a time, many a time and oft *(old)*

ADJ **a** *Speise* done *pred*, cooked; **das Steak ist ja nur halb ~** this steak is only half-cooked → **gar kochen**

b *(form) Leder* tanned, dressed; *(Agr) Boden* well-prepared

c *(S Ger, Aus) (= verbraucht)* used up, finished; *(= zu Ende)* at an end, over; **das Öl wird ja nie ~** we'll never use all this oil

Ga|ra|ge [ga'ra:ʒə] F **-, -n** garage; *(= Hochgarage, Tiefgarage)* car park *(Brit)*, parking garage *(US)*; **das Auto in einer ~ unterstellen** to garage one's car *(Brit)*, to park one's car in a garage *(esp US)*

Ga|ra|gen|tor [ga'ra:ʒn-] NT garage door

ga|ra|gie|ren [gara'ʒi:rən] *ptp* **garagiert** VT *(Aus, Sw)* to park

Ga|rant [ga'rant] M **-en, -en**, **Ga|ran|tin** [-'rantɪn] F [ga'rantɪn] **-, -nen** guarantor

Ga|ran|tie [garan'ti:] F **-, -n** [-'ti:ən] *(lit, fig)* guarantee; *(auf Auto)* warranty; **die Uhr hat ein Jahr ~** the watch is guaranteed for a year *or* has a year's guarantee; **drei Jahre ~ auf etw gewähren** *or* **geben** to give a three-year guarantee/warranty on sth; **das fällt noch unter die ~, das geht noch auf ~** that comes under *or* is covered by the guarantee/warranty; **ich gebe dir meine ~ darauf** *(fig inf)* I guarantee (you) that; **unter ~** under guarantee/warranty; *(fig: = garantiert)* guaranteed

Ga|ran|tie-: **Ga|ran|tie|an|spruch** M → **Garantie** right to claim under guarantee/warranty; **Ga|ran|tie|frist** F → **Garantie** guarantee/warranty period; **Ga|ran|tie|lohn** M guaranteed minimum wage

ga|ran|tie|ren [garan'ti:rən] *ptp* **garantiert** VT to guarantee *(jdm etw* sb sth); **der Name dieser Firma garantiert Qualität** the name of this firm is a guarantee of good quality *or* guarantees good quality; **er konnte mir nicht ~, dass ...** he couldn't give me any guarantee that ... VI to give a guarantee; **für etw ~** to guarantee sth; **er konnte für nichts ~** he couldn't guarantee anything

ga|ran|tiert [garan'ti:ɐt] ADV guaranteed; *(inf)* I bet *(inf)*; **er kommt ~ nicht** I bet he won't come *(inf)*, he's bound not to come

Ga|ran|tie|schein M guarantee, certificate of guarantee *(form)*; *(für Auto)* warranty

Ga|ran|tin [-'rantɪn] F [ga'rantɪn] **-, -nen** guarantor

Gar|aus ['ga:ɐlaus] M *(inf)* **jdm den ~ machen** to do sb in *(inf)*, to bump sb off *(inf)*; **einer Sache** *(dat)* **den ~ machen** to put an end *or* a stop to sth

Gar|be ['garbə] F **-, -n** *(= Korngarbe)* sheaf; *(= Lichtgarbe)* beam; *(Mil: = Schussgarbe)* burst of fire; *(Metal)* faggot; **das Getreide wurde in** *or* **zu ~n gebunden** the corn was bound into sheaves

Gar|ben|bin|de|ma|schi|ne F *(Agr)* sheaf-binder, sheaf-binding machine

Gär|bot|tich ['gɛ:ɐ-] M fermenting vat

Gar|çon|ni|ère [garsɔ'niɛ:rə] F **-, -n** *(Aus)* one-room flat *(Brit) or* apartment, efficiency *(US)*

Gar|de ['gardə] F **-, -n** guard; **~ zu Fuß** *(Hist)* Foot Guards *pl*; **bei der ~** in the Guards; **die alte/junge ~** *(fig)* the old/young guard

Gar|de-: **Gar|de|maß** NT *height required for eligibility for the Guards*; **~ haben** *(inf)* to be as tall as a tree; **Gar|de|of|fi|zier(in)** M(F) Guards officer; **Gar|de|re|gi|ment** NT Guards regiment

Gar|de|ro|be [gardə'ro:bə] F **-, -n** **a** *(= Kleiderbestand)* wardrobe *(Brit)*; **eine umfangreiche ~ haben** to have a large wardrobe, to have a great many clothes **b** *(= Kleiderablage)* hall stand; *(im Theater, Kino etc)* cloakroom *(Brit)*, checkroom *(US)*; **seinen Mantel an der ~ abgeben** to leave one's coat in the cloakroom *(Brit) or checkroom (US)* **c** *(Theat: = Umkleideraum)* dressing room

Gar|de|ro|ben-: **Gar|de|ro|ben|frau** F cloakroom *(Brit) or* checkroom *(US)* attendant; **Gar|de|ro|ben|ha|ken** M coat hook; **Gar|de|ro|ben|mann** M *pl* **-männer** cloakroom *(Brit) or* checkroom *(US)* attendant; **Gar|de|ro|ben|mar|ke** F, **Gar|de|ro|ben|schein** M cloakroom *(Brit) or* checkroom *(US)* ticket; **Gar|de|ro|ben|schrank** M hall cupboard; **Gar|de|ro|ben|stän|der** M hat stand *(Brit)*, hat tree *(US)*

Gar|de|ro|bi|er [gardəro'bie:] M **-s, -s** **a** *(Theat: für Kostüme)* wardrobe master; *(im Umkleideraum)* dresser **b** *(an der Abgabe)* cloakroom *(Brit) or* checkroom *(US)* attendant

Gar|de|ro|bi|e|re [gardəro'bie:rə] F **-, -n** **a** *(Theat: für Kostüme)* wardrobe mistress; *(im Umkleideraum)* dresser **b** *(an der Abgabe)* cloakroom *(Brit) or* checkroom *(US)* attendant

gar|dez [gar'de:] INTERJ *(Chess)* gardez

Gar|di|ne [gar'di:nə] F **-, -n** curtain *(Brit)*, drape *(US)*; *(= Scheibengardine)* net *(Brit) or* café *(US)* curtain, curtain → **schwedisch**

Gar|di|nen-: **Gar|di|nen|band** [-bant] NT *pl* **-bänder** curtain tape; **Gar|di|nen|blen|de** F pelmet *(Brit)*, valance *(esp US)*; **Gar|di|nen|pre|digt** F *(inf)* dressing-down *(Brit)*, talking-to; **jdm eine ~ halten** to give sb a dressing-down *(Brit) or* a talking-to; **Gar|di|nen|rol|le** F, **Gar|di|nen|röll|chen** NT curtain runner; **Gar|di|nen|stan|ge** F curtain rail; *(zum Ziehen)* curtain rod

Gar|dist [gar'dɪst] M **-en, -en** *(Mil)* guardsman

Gar|dis|tin [gar'dɪstɪn] F **-, -nen** *(Mil)* guardswoman

ga|ren ['ga:rən] *(Cook)* VTI to cook; *(auf kleiner Flamme)* to simmer

gä|ren ['gɛ:rən] *pret* **gor** *or* **gärte**, *ptp* **gegoren** *or* **gegärt** VI *aux haben or sein* to ferment; *(Hefe)* to work; *(fig: Gefühle etc)* to seethe; **die Wut/das Unrecht gärte in ihm** he was seething with anger/a sense of injustice; **in ihm gärt es** he is in a state of inner turmoil VT to ferment

Gä|ren NT **-s,** *no pl* fermentation; **ins ~ kommen** to start fermenting

Ga|ret|te [ga'rɛtə] F **-, -n** *(Sw: = Schubkarren)* barrow

Gar-: **gar ko|chen**, **gar+ko|chen** *sep* VT **etw ~** to cook sth through; **Gar|kü|che** F hot food stall

Gär|fut|ter ['gɛ:ɐ-] NT *(Agr)* silage *no pl*

Gär|mit|tel ['gɛ:ɐ-] NT ferment

Garn [garn] NT **-(e)s, -e** **a** thread; *(= Baumwollgarn)* thread, cotton; *(= Häkelgarn, fig: = Seemannsgarn)* yarn; **ein ~ spinnen** *(fig)* to spin a yarn **b** *(= Netz)* net; **jdm ins ~ gehen** *(fig)* to fall into sb's snare, to fall *or* walk into sb's trap

Gar|ne|le [gar'ne:lə] F **-, -n** *(Zool)* prawn; *(= Granat)* shrimp

gar|ni [gar'ni] ADJ → **Hotel garni**

gar|nie|ren [gar'ni:rən] *ptp* **garniert** VT *Kuchen, Kleid* to decorate; *Gericht* to garnish; *(fig) Reden etc* to garnish

Gar|nie|rung F -, -en **a** *(= das Garnieren)* decoration; *(von Gericht, fig: von Rede)* garnishing **b** *(= Material zur Garnierung)* decoration; *(von Gericht)* garnish; **Zitate als ~ einer Rede** quotations to garnish a speech

Gar|ni|son [garni'zo:n] F -, -en *(Mil)* garrison; **mit ~ belegen** to garrison; **in ~ liegen** to be garrisoned

Gar|ni|son(s)- *in cpds* garrison; **Gar|ni|son(s)|kir|che** F garrison church; **Gar|ni|son(s)|stadt** F garrison town

Gar|ni|tur [garni'tu:ɐ] F -, -en **a** *(= Satz)* set; *(= Unterwäsche)* set of (matching) underwear; **die erste ~** *(fig)* the pick of the bunch, the top-notches *pl (inf)*; **erste/zweite ~ sein, zur ersten/zweiten ~ gehören** to be first-rate *or* first-class/second-rate **b** *(= Besatz)* trimming **c** *(Mil: = Uniform)* uniform; **erste ~** number one uniform *or* dress

Garn-: **Garn|knäu|el** M OR NT ball of thread *or* yarn; **Garn|rol|le** F spool; *(von Baumwolle, Nähgarn)* cotton reel; **Garn|spin|ne|rei** F spinning mill

Ga|rot|te [ga'rɔtə] F -, -n garrotte

ga|rot|tie|ren [garɔ'ti:rən] *ptp* **garottiert** VT to garrotte

gars|tig ['garstɪç] ADJ *(dated)* nasty, horrible

Gars|tig|keit F -, -en *(dated)* **a** *no pl* nastiness **b** ~en *pl (= garstige Äußerungen)* nasty *or* horrible remarks *pl*

Gär|stoff ['gɛ:ɐ-] M ferment

Gar|ten ['gartn] M -s, ⸚ ['gɛrtn] garden; *(= Obstgarten)* orchard; **öffentlicher/botanischer/zoologischer ~** public/botanic(al)/zoological gardens *pl*; **im ~ arbeiten** to work in the garden, to do some gardening

Gar|ten- *in cpds* garden; **Gar|ten|ab|fäl|le** PL garden waste *sing*; **Gar|ten|ar|beit** F gardening *no pl*; **Gar|ten|ar|chi|tekt(in)** M(F) landscape gardener; **Gar|ten|bau** M, *no pl* horticulture

Gar|ten|bau-: **Gar|ten|bau|aus|stel|lung** F horticultural exhibition; **Gar|ten|bau|be|trieb** M market garden, truck farm *(US)*

Gar|ten-: **Gar|ten|beet** NT flower *or* vegetable bed; **Gar|ten|blu|me** F garden *or* cultivated flower; **Gar|ten|ge|rät** NT gardening tool *or* implement; **Gar|ten|haus** NT summer house; *(für Geräte)* garden shed; *(= Hinterhaus)* back *or* rear building; **Gar|ten|ko|lo|nie** F allotments *pl*; **Gar|ten|lau|be** F *(= Gartenhäuschen)* summer house; *(aus Blattwerk)* arbour *(Brit)*, arbor *(US)*, bower; *(für Geräte)* garden shed; **Gar|ten|lo|kal** NT beer garden; *(= Restaurant)* garden café; **Gar|ten|mö|bel** PL garden furniture; **Gar|ten|sche|re** F secateurs *pl (Brit)*, pruning shears *pl*; *(= Heckenschere)* shears *pl*; **Gar|ten|schlauch** M garden hose; **Gar|ten|tür** F garden gate; **Gar|ten|zaun** M garden fence; *(Typ, Comput inf)* number sign, hash (sign); **Gar|ten|zwerg** M garden gnome; *(pej inf)* squirt *(inf)*

Gärt|ner ['gɛrtnɐ] M -s, -, **Gärt|ne|rin** [-ərɪn] F -, -nen gardener → **Bock a**

Gärt|ne|rei [gɛrtnə'rai] F -, -en **a** *(= Baumschule, für Setzlinge)* nursery; *(für Obst, Gemüse, Schnittblumen)* market garden *(Brit)*, truck farm *(US)* **b** *no pl (= Gartenarbeit)* gardening; *(= Gartenbau)* horticulture

gärt|ne|risch ['gɛrtnərɪʃ] ADJ *attr* gardening; *Betrieb, Erzeugnisse auch, Ausbildung* horticultural; **~e Gestaltung** landscaping; **die ~en Kosten** the cost of the landscaping ADV **einen Park ~ gestalten** to landscape a park; **~ ausgebildet** trained in horticulture

gärt|nern ['gɛrtnɐn] VI to garden

Gä|rung ['gɛ:rʊŋ] F -, -en fermentation; *(fig)* ferment, turmoil; **in ~ kommen** to start fermenting; **in ~ sein** *(fig)* to be in ferment *or* in a turmoil

Gä|rungs-: **Gä|rungs|er|re|ger** M ferment; **Gä|rungs|pro|zess** M process of fermentation

Gar|zeit ['ga:ɐ-] F cooking time

Gas [ga:s] NT -es, -e [-zə] gas; *(Aut: = Gaspedal)* accelerator, gas pedal *(esp US)*; **~ geben** *(Aut)* to accelerate, to put one's foot down *(inf)*, to step on the gas *(inf)*; *(auf höhere Touren bringen)* to rev up; **~ wegnehmen** *(Aut)* to decelerate, to ease one's foot off the accelerator *or* gas *(inf)*, to throttle back *(US)*; **mit ~ vergiften** to gas

Gas- *in cpds* gas; **Gas|an|griff** M *(Mil)* gas attack; **Gas|ba|de|ofen** M gas(-fired) water heater; **Gas|be|häl|ter** M gas holder, gasometer; **gas|be|heizt** [-bəhaitst] ADJ gas-heated; **gas|be|trie|ben** [-bətri:bn] ADJ *(Tech)* gas-driven, gas-powered; **Gas|dich|te** F *(Phys)* density of a/the gas; **Gas|er|zeu|gung** F generation of gas; *(Ind)* gas production; **Gas|ex|plo|si|on** F gas explosion; **Gas|fern|ver|sor|gung** F *(= System)* long-distance gas supply; **Gas|feu|er|zeug** NT gas lighter; **Gas|fla|sche** F bottle of gas, gas canister; **gas|för|mig** ADJ gaseous, gasiform; **Gas|ge|ruch** M smell of gas; **Gas|grill** M, **Gas|grill|ge|rät** NT gas grill, gas barbecue; **Gas|hahn** M gas tap; **den ~ aufdrehen** *(fig)* to put one's head in the gas oven; **Gas|he|bel** M *(Aut)* accelerator (pedal), gas pedal *(esp US)*; *(= Handgashebel)* (hand) throttle; **Gas|hei|zung** F gas (central) heating; **Gas|herd** M gas cooker; **Gas|hül|le** F atmosphere; **Gas|in|stal|la|teur(in)** M(F) gas fitter; **Gas|kam|mer** F gas chamber; **Gas|ko|cher** M camping stove; **Gas|kraft|werk** NT gas-fired power station; **Gas|krieg** M chemical *or* gas warfare; **Gas|la|ter|ne** F gas (street)lamp; **Gas|lei|tung** F *(= Rohr)* gas pipe; *(= Hauptrohr)* gas main; **Gas|licht** NT gaslight; *(= Beleuchtung)* gas lighting; **Gas|mann** M *pl* **-männer** gasman; **Gas|mas|ke** F gas mask; **Gas|ofen** M *(= Heizofen)* gas fire *or* heater; *(= Heizungsofen)* gas(-fired) boiler; *(= Backofen)* gas oven; *(= Herd)* gas cooker *or* stove

Ga|so|lin [gazo'li:n] NT -s, *no pl* petroleum ether

Ga|so|me|ter [gazo'me:tɐ] M gasometer

Gas-: **Gas|pe|dal** NT *(Aut)* accelerator (pedal), gas pedal *(esp US)*; **Gas|pis|to|le** F tear gas gun; **Gas|plas|ma** NT gas plasma; **Gas|rohr** NT gas pipe; *(= Hauptrohr)* gas main

Gäss|chen ['gɛsçən] NT -s, - alley(way)

Gas|se ['gasə] F -, -n lane; *(= Durchgang)* alley (-way); *(S Ger, Aus: = Stadtstraße)* street; *(Rugby)* line-out; **die schmalen ~n der Altstadt** the narrow streets and alleys of the old town; **eine ~ bilden** to clear a passage; *(Rugby)* to form a line-out; **eine ~ für jdn bilden** to make way *or* clear a path for sb; **sich** *(dat)* **eine ~ bahnen** to force one's way; **auf der ~** *(S Ger, Aus)* on the street; **etw über die ~ verkaufen** *(Aus)* to sell sth to take away

Gas|sen-: **Gas|sen|hau|er** M *(old, inf)* popular melody; **Gas|sen|jar|gon** M gutter language; **Gas|sen|jun|ge** M, **Gas|sen|mäd|chen** NT *(pej)* street urchin, street Arab *(Brit)*, street kid *(inf)*; **Gas|sen|schän|ke** F, **Gas|sen|schen|ke** F *(S Ger)* off-sales *(Brit)*, package store *(US)*

Gas|si ['gasi] ADV *(inf)* **~ gehen** to go walkies *(Brit inf)*, to go for a walk; **mit einem Hund ~ gehen** to take a dog (for) walkies *(Brit inf)*, to take a dog out for a walk

Gast [gast] M -es, ⸚e ['gɛstə] guest; *(= Besucher auch, Tourist)* visitor; *(in einer Gaststätte)* customer; *(Theat)* guest (star); *(Univ: = Gasthörer)* observer, auditor *(US)*; **Vorstellung vor geladenen Gästen** performance before an invited audience; **ungeladener ~** uninvited guest; *(bei einer Party auch)* gatecrasher *(esp Brit)*, party-crasher *(US)*; **jdn zu ~ bitten** *(form)* to request the pleasure of sb's company *(form)*; **wir haben heute Abend Gäste** we're having people round *(Brit) or* around *or* we're having company this evening; **bei jdm zu ~ sein** to be sb's guest(s); **in einem anderen Ort zu ~ sein** to visit another place

Gast M -(e)s, -en *(Naut)* *(= Signalgast)* signalman; *(= Radiogast)* operator

Gast-: **Gast|ar|bei|ter(in)** M(F) *(neg!)* immigrant *or* foreign worker; **Gast|do|zent(in)** M(F) visiting *or* guest lecturer

Gäs|te-: **Gäs|te|bett** NT spare *or* guest bed; **Gäs|te|buch** NT visitors' book

Gas|tech|nik F gas engineering

Gäs|te-: **Gäs|te|hand|tuch** NT guest towel; **Gäs|te|haus** NT guest house; **Gäs|te|heim** NT *(dated)* guest house, boarding house; **Gäs|te|lis|te** F guest list; **Gäs|te-WC** NT guest toilet; **Gäs|te|zim|mer** NT guest *or* spare room

Gast-: **Gast|fa|mi|lie** F host family; **gast|frei**, **gast|freund|lich** ADJ hospitable ADV hospitably; **Gast|freund|lich|keit** F -, *no pl*, **Gast|freund|schaft** F -, *no pl* hospitality; **gast|ge|bend** ADJ *attr Land, Theater* host *attr*; *Mannschaft* home *attr*; **Gast|ge|ber** M host; **Gast|ge|be|rin** F hostess; **Gast|ge|schenk** NT present *(brought by a guest)*; **Gast|haus** NT, **Gast|hof** M inn; **Gast|hö|rer(in)** M(F) *(Univ)* observer, auditor *(US)*

gas|tie|ren [gas'ti:rən] *ptp* **gastiert** VI to guest, to make a guest appearance

Gast-: **Gast|land** NT host country; **gast|lich** ['gastlɪç] ADJ hospitable ADV hospitably; **Gast|lich|keit** F -, *no pl* hospitality; **Gast|mahl** NT *(old)* banquet; **Platos „Gastmahl"** Plato's "Symposium"

Gas|tod M death by gassing; **den ~ sterben** to be gassed

Gast-: **Gast|pro|fes|sor(in)** M(F) visiting professor; **Gast|recht** NT right to hospitality; **Gast|red|ner(in)** M(F) guest speaker

gast|risch ['gastrɪʃ] ADJ *(Med)* gastric

Gast|ri|tis [gas'tri:tɪs] F -, **Gastritiden** [-'ti:dn] gastritis

Gast|rol|le F *(Theat)* guest role; **eine ~ geben** *or* **spielen** *(lit)* to make a guest appearance; *(fig)* to put in *or* make a fleeting *or* brief appearance

Gast|ro|nom [gastro'no:m] M -en, -en, **Gast|ro|no|min** [-'no:mɪn] F -, -nen *(= Gastwirt)* restaurateur; *(= Koch)* cuisinier, cordon bleu cook *(esp Brit)*

Gast|ro|no|mie [gastrono'mi:] F -, *no pl (form: = Gaststättengewerbe)* catering trade; *(geh: = Kochkunst)* gastronomy

gast|ro|no|misch [gastro'no:mɪʃ] ADJ gastronomic

Gast|ro|sko|pie [gastrosko'pi:] F -, -n [-'pi:ən] *(Med)* gastroscopy

Gast-: **Gast|spiel** NT *(Theat)* guest performance; *(Sport)* away match; **ein ~ geben** *(lit)* to give a guest performance; *(fig inf)* to put in *or* make a fleeting *or* brief appearance; **Gast|spiel|rei|se** F *(Theat)* tour; **auf ~** on tour; **Gast|stät|te** F *(= Restaurant)* restaurant; *(= Trinklokal)* pub *(Brit)*, bar; **Gast|stät|ten|ge|wer|be** NT catering trade; **Gast|stu|be** F lounge

Gas|tur|bi|ne F gas turbine

Gast-: **Gast|vor|le|sung** F *(Univ)* guest lecture; **Gast|vor|stel|lung** F *(Theat)* guest performance; **eine ~ geben** to give a guest performance; **Gast|vor|trag** M guest lecture; **Gast|wirt** M *(Besitzer)* restaurant owner *or* proprietor; *(Pächter)* restaurant manager; *(von Kneipe)* landlord; **Gast|wir|tin** F *(Besitzerin)* restaurant owner *or* proprietress; *(Pächterin)* restaurant manageress; *(von Kneipe)* landlady; **Gast|wirt|schaft** F = **Gaststätte**; **Gast|zim|mer** NT guest room

Gas-: **Gas|uhr** F gas meter; **Gas|ver|brauch** M gas consumption; **Gas|ver|gif|tung** F gas poisoning; **Gas|ver|sor|gung** F *(= System)* gas supply (+*gen* to); **Gas|werk** NT gasworks *sing or pl*; *(= Gasverwaltung)* gas board; **Gas|wol|ke**

F gas cloud; **Gas|zäh|ler** M gas meter; **Gas|zent|ral|hei|zung** F gas central heating

Gate|way ['ge:twe:] NT -s, -s *(Comput)* gateway

Gatt [gat] NT -(e)s, -en *or* -s *(Naut)* (= *Speigatt*) scupper; (= *Heckform*) stern; (= *kleiner Raum*) locker; (= *Loch*) clew; (= *enge Durchfahrt*) strait

GATT [gat] NT -s GATT

Gat|te ['gatə] M -n, -n *(form)* husband, spouse *(form)*; **die (beiden) ~n** both partners, husband and wife

Gat|ten-: **Gat|ten|lie|be** F *(form)* married *or* conjugal *(form)* love; **Gat|ten|mord** M *(form)* murder of one's husband/wife; **Gat|ten|wahl** F *(Biol)* choice of mate; **das Ritual der ~** the complicated ritual of choosing a mate

Gat|ter ['gatɐ] NT -s, - **a** (= *Tür*) gate; (= *Zaun*) fence; (= *Rost*) grating, grid **b** *(Tech: auch* **Gat|ter|säge**) gangsaw, framesaw

Gat|tin ['gatın] F -, -nen *(form)* wife, spouse *(form)*

Gat|tung ['gatʊŋ] F -, -en *(Biol)* genus; *(Liter, Mus, Art)* genre, form; *(fig:* = *Sorte)* type, kind

Gat|tungs-: **Gat|tungs|be|griff** M generic concept; **Gat|tungs|na|me** M generic term

Gau [gau] M OR NT -(e)s, -e **a** *(Hist)* gau, *a tribal district, later an administrative district under the Nazis* **b** (= *Bezirk*) district, region, area

GAU [gau] M -(s) *abbr von* **größter anzunehmender Unfall** MCA, maximum credible accident; *(fig inf)* worst-case scenario

Gau|be ['gaubə] F -, -n dormer window

Gau|dee [gau'de:] F -, -n [-'de:ən] *(Aus)* fun *no pl*; **auf der ~ sein** to be out gallivanting *(inf)*

Gau|di ['gaudi] NT -s *or (S Ger, Aus)* f -, *no pl (inf)* fun; **das war eine ~** that was great fun; **das war eine ~ auf der Party** the party was great fun

Gau|di|um ['gaudiʊm] NT -s, *no pl (old)* amusement, entertainment

Gau|ke|lei [gaukə'lai] F -, -en trickery *no pl*; **~en** tricks *pl*, trickery

gau|keln ['gaukln] VI *(liter) (Schmetterling)* to flutter; *(fig)* to flit

Gau|kel|spiel NT *(liter)* illusion; **ein ~ mit jdm treiben** to play sb false *(liter)*, to deceive sb

Gauk|ler ['gauklɐ] M -s, - *(Orn)* bateleur eagle

Gauk|ler ['gauklɐ] M -s, -, **Gauk|le|rin** [-ərın] F -, -nen *(liter)* travelling *(Brit) or* traveling *(US)* entertainer; *(fig)* storyteller

Gaul [gaul] M -(e)s, **Gäu|le** ['gɔylə] *(pej)* nag, hack; *(rare:* = *Arbeitspferd)* workhorse → **Schwanz a**, **schenken VT a**, **scheu**

Gau|lei|ter(in) M(F) *(Pol)* Gauleiter, *head of a Nazi administrative district*

Gaul|lis|mus [go'lısmʊs] M -, *no pl* Gaullism

Gaul|list [go'lıst] M -en, -en, **Gaul|lis|tin** [-'lıstın] F -, -nen Gaullist

gaul|lis|tisch [go'lıstıʃ] ADJ Gaullist *no adv*

Gau|men ['gaumən] M -s, - palate *(auch fig)*, roof of the/one's mouth; **die Zunge klebte ihm vor Durst am ~** his tongue was hanging out (with thirst); **einen feinen ~ haben** *(fig)* to be (something of) a gourmet, to enjoy good food; **das kitzelt mir den ~** *(fig)* that tickles my taste buds *or* my palate

Gau|men-: **Gau|men|freu|den** PL culinary delights *pl*; **Gau|men|kit|zel** M *(inf)* delight for the taste buds; **Gau|men|laut** M palatal (sound); **Gau|men|man|del** F *(Anat)* (palatine) tonsil; **Gau|men|plat|te** F (dental) plate; **Gau|men|se|gel** NT soft palate, velum *(spec)*; **Gau|men|zäpf|chen** NT uvula

Gau|ner ['gaunɐ] M -s, - rogue, rascal, scoundrel; (= *Betrüger*) crook; *(hum inf:* = *Schelm auch)* scamp, scallywag *(Brit inf)*; *(inf:* = *gerissener Kerl)* cunning devil *(inf)*, sly customer *(inf)*; **kleine ~** (= *Kriminelle*) small-time crooks → *auch* **Gaunerin**

Gau|ner|ban|de F → **Gauner** bunch of rogues *or* rascals *or* scoundrels/crooks; *(hum: Kinder auch)* bunch of scamps *or* scallywags *(Brit inf) or* rascals

Gau|ne|rei [gaunə'rai] F -, -en swindling *no pl*, cheating *no pl*

gau|ner|haft ADJ rascally *no adv*

Gau|ne|rin ['gaunərın] F -, -nen rascal; (= *Betrügerin*) crook → *auch* **Gauner**

gau|nern ['gaunɐn] VI *(inf)* (= *betrügen*) to swindle, to cheat; (= *stehlen*) to thieve; **er hat sich durchs Leben gegaunert** he cheated his way through life

Gau|ner-: **Gau|ner|spra|che** F underworld jargon; **Gau|ner|zin|ken** M *tramp's or gypsy's sign written on wall etc*

Ga|vot|te [ga'vɔt(ə)] F -, -n *(Mus)* gavotte

Ga|za|strei|fen ['ga:za:-] M Gaza Strip

Ga|ze ['ga:zə] F -, -n gauze; (= *Drahtgaze auch*) (wire) mesh

Ga|ze|bin|de ['ga:zə-] F gauze bandage

Ga|zel|le [ga'tsɛlə] F -, -n gazelle

Ga|zet|te [ga'tsɛtə, ga'zɛtə] F -, -n *(old, pej)* gazette *(old)*, (news)paper, rag *(pej inf)*

GB NT *abbr* **a** *von* **Gigabyte** Gb **b** *von* **Großbritannien** GB

g-Druck ['ge:-] M *pl* **-drücke** *(Aviat)* g-force

Ge|äch|te|te(r) [gə'lɛçtətə] MF *decl as adj* outlaw; *(fig)* outcast

Ge|äch|ze [gə'lɛçtsə] NT -s, *no pl* groaning *no pl*, groans *pl*

ge|ädert [gə'lɛ:dɐt] ADJ veined

ge|ar|tet [gə'la:ɐtət] ADJ **gutmütig ~ sein** to be good-natured; **freundlich ~ sein** to have a friendly nature; **er ist (eben) so ~(, dass ...)** it's (just) his nature (to ...); **sie ist ganz anders ~** she has a completely different nature, she's quite different; **so ~e Probleme** problems of this nature; **das Problem ist so ~, dass ...** the nature of the problem is such that ...; **eine wie auch immer ~e Erklärung** a statement of any kind whatsoever

Ge|äst [gə'lɛst] NT -(e)s, *no pl* branches *pl*, boughs *pl (liter)*; *(von Adern etc)* branches *pl*

geb. *abbr von* **geboren**

Ge|bab|bel [gə'babl] NT -s, *no pl (inf)* babbling

Ge|bäck [gə'bɛk] NT -(e)s, -e (= *Kekse*) biscuits *pl (Brit)*, cookies *pl (US)*; (= *süße Teilchen*) pastries *pl*; (= *rundes Hefegebäck*) buns *pl*; (= *Törtchen*) tarts *pl*, tartlets *pl*; **allerlei (Kuchen und) ~** all kinds of cakes and pastries

ge|ba|cken *ptp von* **backen**

Ge|bälk [gə'bɛlk] NT -(e)s, -e timberwork *no pl*, timbers *pl*; *(Archit:* = *Verbindung zu Säulen)* entablature; **ein Partisan im ~** *(inf)* a nigger in the woodpile *(Brit pej)* → **knistern**

ge|ballt [gə'balt] **ADJ** (= *konzentriert*) *Energie, Kraft, Ladung* concentrated *(auch fig)*; *Stil, Berichterstattung* concise; *Banalität, Naivität* undiluted, unmitigated; *Beschuss* massed; **eine ~e Ladung Salz** a pile of salt **ADV es kommt alles ~ auf einmal** everything happens at once; **die Probleme treten jetzt ~ auf** the problems are piling up now → *auch* **ballen**

ge|bannt [gə'bant] ADJ spellbound; **vor Schreck ~** rigid with fear; **(wie) ~** fascinated, in fascination; *(stärker)* spellbound → *auch* **bannen**

ge|bar *pret von* **gebären**

Ge|bär|de [gə'bɛ:ɐdə] F -, -n gesture; *(lebhafte auch)* gesticulation

ge|bär|den [gə'bɛ:ɐdn] *ptp* **gebärdet** VR to behave, to conduct oneself *(form)*

Ge|bär|den-: **Ge|bär|den|dol|met|scher(in)** M(F) sign-language interpreter; **Ge|bär|den|spiel** NT, *no pl* gestures *pl*, gesticulation(s *pl*); **das ~ der Sänger** the singers' use of gesture; **Ge|bär|den|spra|che** F gestures *pl*; (= *Zeichensprache*) sign language; *(in Stummfilmen etc)* gesturing; (= *unbewusste Gebärdensprache*) body language

ge|ba|ren [gə'ba:rən] *ptp* **gebart** VR *(rare)* to behave, to conduct oneself *(form)*

Ge|ba|ren [gə'ba:rən] NT -s, *no pl* **a** behaviour *(Brit)*, behavior *(US)* **b** *(Comm:* = *Geschäftsgebaren)* conduct

ge|bä|ren [gə'bɛ:rən] *pres* **gebärt** *or (geh)* **gebiert** [gə'bi:ɐt], *pret* **gebar** [gə'ba:ɐ], *ptp* **geboren** [gə'bo:rən] **VT** to give birth to; *Kind auch* to bear *(old, form)*, to be delivered of *(old)*; *(fig liter:* = *erzeugen)* to breed; **jdm ein Kind ~** to bear *or* give sb a child; **geboren werden** to be born; **wo sind Sie geboren?** where were you born?; **aus der Not geborene Ideen** ideas springing *or* stemming from necessity → *auch* **geboren VI** to give birth

ge|bär-: **ge|bär|fä|hig** ADJ *Alter* child-bearing; *Frau* capable of bearing children; **ge|bär|freu|dig** ADJ *Frau* who has/had given birth many times; *Tier* prolific; **ein ~es Becken haben** to have child-bearing hips

Ge|bär|mut|ter F *pl* **-mütter** *(Anat)* womb, uterus

Ge|bär|mut|ter-: **Ge|bär|mut|ter|hals** M neck of the womb *or* uterus, cervix; **Ge|bär|mut|ter|hals|krebs** M cancer of the cervix; **Ge|bär|mut|ter|krebs** M cancer of the uterus; **Ge|bär|mut|ter|mund** M mouth of the uterus

Ge|ba|rung F -, -en *(Aus Comm:* = *Geschäftsgebaren)* conduct

Ge|ba|rungs- *(Aus Comm)*: **Ge|ba|rungs|be|richt** M financial report; **Ge|ba|rungs|jahr** NT financial year; **Ge|ba|rungs|kon|trol|le** F audit

ge|bauch|pin|selt [gə'bauxpınzlt] ADJ *(hum inf)* **sich ~ fühlen** to feel flattered

Ge|bäu|de [gə'bɔydə] NT -s, - building; (= *Prachtgebäude*) edifice; *(fig:* = *Gefüge)* structure; *(von Ideen)* edifice; *(von Lügen)* web

Ge|bäu|de-: **Ge|bäu|de|kom|plex** M building complex; **Ge|bäu|de|rei|ni|ger(in)** M(F) cleaner; (= *Fensterputzer*) window cleaner; (= *Fassadenreiniger*) building cleaner; **Ge|bäu|de|rei|ni|gung** F (= *das Reinigen*) commercial cleaning; (= *Firma*) cleaning contractors *pl*; **Ge|bäu|de|scha|den** M damage to a/the building; **Ge|bäu|de|teil** M part of the building; **Ge|bäu|de|trakt** M part of the building; **einen neuen ~ errichten** to add an extension to the/a building; **Ge|bäu|de|ver|si|che|rung** F buildings insurance

ge|baut [gə'baut] ADJ built; **gut ~ sein** to be well-built; **stark ~ sein** to have a broad frame; **... so, wie du ~ bist** *(inf)* ... a big man/woman like you; **ein gut ~es Stück** a well-constructed play → *auch* **bauen**

ge|be|freu|dig ADJ generous, open-handed

Ge|be|freu|dig|keit ['ge:bəfrɔydıçkait] F -, *no pl* generosity, open-handedness

Ge|bein [gə'bain] NT **a** skeleton; **der Schreck fuhr ihm ins ~** *(old)* his whole body trembled with fear **b Gebeine** PL *(geh)* bones *pl*, mortal remains *pl (liter)*; *(esp von Heiligen etc)* relics *pl*

Ge|bell [gə'bɛll] NT -s, *no pl*, **Ge|bel|le** [gə'bɛlə] NT -s, *no pl* barking; *(von Jagdhunden)* baying; *(fig inf:* = *Geschimpfe)* bawling *(inf)*

ge|ben ['ge:bn]

pret **gab** [ga:p], *ptp* **gegeben** [gə'ge:bn]

1 TRANSITIVES VERB	3 UNPERSÖNLICHES VERB
2 INTRANSITIVES VERB	4 REFLEXIVES VERB

1 – TRANSITIVES VERB

a to give; (= *reichen*) to give, to pass; *Schatten, Kühle* to provide; **wer hat dir das gegeben?** who gave you that?; **gibs mir!** give it to me!, give me it!; **was darf ich Ihnen geben?** what can I get you?; **könnten Sie mir die Butter/den Korkenzieher geben?** could you pass me the butter/the corkscrew?; **geben Sie mir bitte zwei Flaschen Bier** I'd like two bottles of beer, please; **ich gebe dir das Auto für 500 Euro** (= *verkaufen*) I'll let you have the car for 500 euros; **ich gebe dir das Auto für zwei Tage** (= *überlassen*) I'll let you have the car for two days; **sich** *(dat)* **(von jdm) etw geben lassen** to ask (sb) for sth; **geben Sie mir bitte Herrn**

Braun *(Telec)* can I speak to Mr Braun please?; **man kann nicht für alles geben** *(= spenden)* you can't give to everything; **geben** *or* **Geben ist seliger denn nehmen** *or* **Nehmen** *(Bibl)* it is more blessed to give than to receive; **ich gäbe viel darum, zu …** I'd give a lot to …; **sie würde ihr Leben für ihre Kinder geben** she'd give her life for her children; **sie gaben ihr Leben fürs Vaterland** they gave *or* laid down their lives for their country; **jdm einen Tritt geben** to give sb a kick; *(fig inf)* to give sb the boot *(inf)*; **gibs ihm (tüchtig)!** *(inf)* let him have it! *(inf)*; **ein gutes Beispiel geben** to set a good example; **jdm etw zu verstehen geben** to make sth known to sb; **jdn/etw verloren geben** to give sb/sth up for lost; **das Buch hat mir viel gegeben** I got a lot out of the book → *auch* **gegeben**

b = Cards to deal; **er hat mir drei Asse und zwei Buben gegeben** he dealt me three aces and two jacks; **da hast du mir aber ein lausiges Blatt gegeben** you've given *or* dealt me a lousy hand

c = gewähren, verleihen to give; *Thema, Aufgabe, Problem* to set; **jdm einen Preis geben** to give sb a prize; **einen Elfmeter/einen Freistoß geben** to give a penalty kick/a free kick; **gebe Gott, dass …** God grant that …; **Taktgefühl ist ihm nicht gegeben** he's not over-endowed with tact; **es war ihm nicht gegeben, seine Eltern lebend wiederzusehen** he was not to see his parents alive again

d = schicken, übergeben to send; *(dial: = tun)* to put; **in die Post geben** to post *(Brit)*, to mail *(esp US)*; **ein Auto in Reparatur geben** to have a car repaired; **ein Kind in Pflege geben** to put a child in care; **Zucker über etw** *(acc)* **geben** *(dial)* to sprinkle sugar over sth; **Milch an den Teig geben** *(dial)* to add milk to the dough → **Bescheid a, Nachricht**

e = ergeben, erzeugen to produce; **die Kuh gibt Milch** the cow produces milk; **die Kuh gibt 25 Liter** the cow produces *or* gives 25 litres *(Brit)* *or* liters *(US)*; **2 + 2 gibt 4** 2 + 2 makes 4; **fünf Manuskriptseiten geben eine Druckseite** five pages of manuscript equal *or* make one page of print; **ein Pfund gibt fünf Klöße** a pound will make five dumplings; **Rotwein gibt Flecken** red wine leaves stains; **das gibt Ärger/Probleme** that will cause trouble/problems; **was wird das noch geben?** where will it end?

f = veranstalten *Konzert, Fest* to give; *Theaterstück etc* to do; **am Schillertheater geben sie wieder „Maria Stuart"** they are doing "Maria Stuart" at the Schillertheater again; **was wird heute im Theater gegeben?** what's on at the theatre *(Brit)* *or* theater *(US)* today?

g = unterrichten to teach; **Englisch/Deutsch geben** to teach English/German; **er gibt Nachhilfeunterricht/Tanzstunden** he gives private tuition/dancing lessons *(Brit)*, he does tutoring/gives dancing lessons

h andere Wendungen

♦ **viel/nicht viel auf etw** *(acc)* **geben** to set great/little store by sth; **auf die Meinung der Lehrer brauchst du nichts zu geben** you needn't bother about what the teachers think; **ich gebe nicht viel auf seinen Rat** I don't think much of his advice

♦ **etw von sich geben** *Laut, Worte, Flüche* to utter; *Meinung* to express; **was er gestern von sich gegeben hat, war wieder einmal völlig unverständlich** what he was going on about yesterday was, as ever, completely incomprehensible

2 – INTRANSITIVES VERB

a Cards to deal; **der links von mir Sitzende gibt** the person sitting on my left deals; **wer gibt?** whose deal is it?, whose turn is it to deal?

b Sport = *Aufschlag haben* to serve; **wer gibt?** whose serve is it?

3 – UNPERSÖNLICHES VERB

♦ **es gibt** *(+sing)* there is; *(+pl)* there are; **es gibt da noch ein Problem** there's still one problem; **es gibt dieses Jahr viele Äpfel** there are a lot of apples this year; **gibt es einen Gott?** is there a God?; **gibt es den Osterhasen?** is there really an Easter Bunny?; **heute gibts noch Regen** it's going to rain today; **es wird noch Ärger geben** there'll be trouble (yet); **darauf gibt es 10% Rabatt** you get 10% discount on it; **was gibts zum Mittagessen?** what's for lunch?; **freitags gibt es bei uns immer Fisch** we always have fish on Fridays; **wann gibts was zu essen? – es gibt gleich was** when are we going to get something to eat? – it's on its way; **es gibt gleich Mittagessen!** it's nearly time for lunch!; **jetzt gibt es keine Süßigkeiten mehr** (you're getting) no more sweets now; **was gibts?** what's the matter?, what is it?; **ein Mensch mit zwei Köpfen? das gibts nicht!** a two-headed person? there's no such thing!; **das gibts nicht, dass ein Vegetarier Metzger wird** it's impossible, a vegetarian wouldn't become a butcher, it's inconceivable that a vegetarian would become a butcher; **so was gibts also!** *(inf)* who'd have thought it! *(inf)*; **das gibts doch nicht!** I don't believe it!; **das darf es doch nicht geben!** I don't believe it!; **das hat es ja noch nie gegeben!** it's unbelievable!; **so was gibts bei uns nicht!** *(inf)* that's just not on! *(inf)*; **da gibts nichts** *(inf)* there's no two ways about it *(inf)*; **was es nicht alles gibt!** it's a funny old world!; **hat es sonst noch etwas gegeben?** was there anything else?; **gleich gibts was!** *(inf)* there's going to be trouble!

4 – REFLEXIVES VERB

♦ **sich geben**

a = nachlassen *Regen* to ease off; *(Schmerzen)* to ease, to lessen; *(Leidenschaft, Begeisterung)* to lessen, to cool; *(freches Benehmen)* to lessen

b = aufgeben, ergeben **sich gefangen geben** to give oneself up; **sich verloren geben** to give oneself up for lost → **schlagen VT a, erkennen VT a**

c = sich erledigen to sort itself out; *(= aufhören)* to stop; **das wird sich schon geben** it'll all work out; **machen Sie erst mal die dringensten Sachen, der Rest wird sich (von alleine) geben** do the most urgent things first, the rest will sort itself out; **gibt sich das bald!** *(inf)* cut it out! *(inf)*

d = sich benehmen to behave; **sich als etw geben** to play sth; **sich freundlich geben** to behave in a friendly way, to be friendly; **sich als große Dame geben** to play the great lady; **sich von oben herab geben** to behave condescendingly, to be condescending; **sich von der besten Seite geben** to show one's best side; **nach außen gab er sich heiter** outwardly he seemed quite cheerful; **sie gibt sich, wie sie ist** she's completely genuine, there's no pretence *(Brit)* *or* pretense *(US)* with her

---

Ge|be|ne|dei|te [gəbeneˈdaitə] F *decl as adj no pl (Eccl)* **die ~** the Blessed Virgin

Ge|ber [ˈgeːbɐ] M **-s, -**, **Ge|be|rin** [-ərɪn] F **-, -nen** giver; *(Cards)* dealer

Ge|ber-: **Ge|ber|kon|fe|renz** F *(Pol)* donor conference; **Ge|ber|land** NT donor country; **Ge|ber|lau|ne** F generous mood; **in ~ sein** to be feeling generous, to be in a generous mood

Ge|bet [gəˈbeːt] NT **-(e)s, -e** prayer; **ein ~ sprechen** to say a prayer; **sein ~ sprechen** *or* **verrichten** to say one's prayers; **das ~ des Herrn** the Lord's Prayer; **die Hände zum ~ falten** to join one's hands in prayer; **jdn ins ~ nehmen** *(fig)* to take sb to task; *(iro: bei Polizeiverhör etc)* to put the pressure on sb

Ge|bet|buch NT prayer book, missal *(US)*

ge|be|ten *ptp von* **bitten**

Ge|bet|läu|ten NT **-s**, *no pl (Aus)* angelus

Ge|bets-: **Ge|bets|man|tel** M prayer shawl, tallith; **Ge|bets|müh|le** F prayer wheel; **ge|bets|müh|len|haft** ADJ constant, continual ADV constantly, continually; **Ge|bets|rie|men** M phylactery; **Ge|bets|stät|te** F place of prayer; **Ge|bets|tep|pich** M prayer mat *or* rug

Ge|bet|tel [gəˈbɛtl] NT **-s**, *no pl* begging

ge|beugt [gəˈbɔykt] ADJ **a** *Haltung* stooped; *Kopf* bowed; *Beine* bent; *Schultern* sloping **b** *(Gram) Verb, Substantiv* inflected ADV **~ sitzen/stehen** to sit/stand hunched over → *auch* **beugen**

ge|biert [gəˈbiːɐt] *(geh) 3. pers sing pres von* **gebären**

Ge|biet [gəˈbiːt] NT **-(e)s, -e a** area, region; *(= Fläche, Stadtgebiet)* area; *(= Staatsgebiet)* territory **b** *(fig: = Fach)* field; *(= Teilgebiet)* branch; **auf diesem ~** in this field

ge|bie|ten [gəˈbiːtn] *pret* **gebot** [gəˈboːt], *ptp* **geboten** [gəˈboːtn] *(geh)* VT *(= verlangen)* to demand; *(= befehlen)* to command; **jdm etw ~** to command sb to do sth; **der Ernst der Lage gebietet sofortiges Handeln** the seriousness of the situation demands immediate action → **Einhalt, Ehrfurcht** VI **a** *(liter: = herrschen)* to have command *(über +acc* over); **über ein Land/Volk ~** to have dominion over a country/nation **b** *(geh: = verfügen)* **über etw** *(acc)* **~** *(über Geld etc)* to have sth at one's disposal; *über Wissen etc* to have sth at one's command → *auch* **geboten**

Ge|bie|ter [gəˈbiːtɐ] M **-s, -** *(liter)* master, lord; *(über Heer)* commander *(über +acc* of); **(mein) Herr und ~** *(old)* (my) lord and master

Ge|bie|te|rin [gəˈbiːtərɪn] F **-, -nen** *(liter, old)* mistress, lady; *(über Heer)* commander

ge|bie|te|risch [gəˈbiːtərɪʃ] *(geh)* ADJ imperious; *(= herrisch)* domineering; *Ton* peremptory ADV imperiously; *(= unbedingt)* absolutely

Ge|biets-: **Ge|biets|ab|tre|tung** F *(form)* cession of territory; **Ge|biets|an|spruch** M territorial claim; **Ge|biets|er|wei|te|rung** F territorial expansion; **ge|biets|fremd** ADJ *(= aus anderem Fachgebiet)* from a different specialist field; **Ge|biets|ho|heit** F territorial sovereignty; **Ge|biets|kör|per|schaft** F regional administrative body; **Ge|biets|lei|ter(in)** M(F) *(Comm)* regional manager; **Ge|biets|re|form** F local government reform; **Ge|biets|teil** M area (of territory); **ge|biets|wei|se** ADV *(= nach Gebieten)* locally; *(= in einzelnen Gebieten)* in some areas

Ge|bil|de [gəˈbɪldə] NT **-s, -** *(= Ding)* thing; *(= Gegenstand)* object; *(= Bauwerk)* construction; *(= Schöpfung)* creation; *(= Muster)* pattern; *(= Form)* shape; *(= Einrichtung)* organization; *(der Fantasie)* figment

ge|bil|det [gəˈbɪldət] ADJ educated; *(= gelehrt)* learned, erudite; *(= wohlerzogen)* well-bred; *(= kultiviert)* cultured, cultivated; *(= belesen)* well-read; *Manieren* refined ADV **sich ~ unterhalten** to have a cultured conversation → *auch* **bilden**

Ge|bil|de|te(r) [gəˈbɪldətə] MF *decl as adj* educated person; **die ~n** the intellectuals

Ge|bim|mel [gəˈbɪml] NT **-s**, *no pl (inf)* ting-a-ling *(inf)*

Ge|bin|de [gəˈbɪndə] NT **-s, - a** *(= Blumengebinde)* arrangement; *(= Sträußchen)* posy; *(= Blumenkranz)* wreath; *(= Getreidegarbe)* sheaf **b** *(von Garn)* skein

Ge|bir|ge [gəˈbɪrgə] NT **-s, - a** mountains *pl*, mountain range; **im/ins ~** in/into the mountains **b** *(Min)* rock

ge|bir|gig [gəˈbɪrgɪç] ADJ mountainous

Ge|birg|ler [gəˈbɪrklɐ] M **-s, -**, **Ge|birg|le|rin** [-ərɪn] F **-, -nen** mountain-dweller, highlander

Ge|birgs- *in cpds* mountain; **Ge|birgs|bach** M mountain stream; **Ge|birgs|bahn** F mountain railway *(Brit)* *or* railroad *(US)* *(crossing a mountain range)*; *(in Alpen)* transalpine railway *(Brit)* *or* railroad *(US)*; **Ge|birgs|blu|me** F mountain flower, flower growing in the mountains; **Ge|birgs|jä|ger(in)** M(F) *(Mil)* mountain soldier; *(pl auch)* mountain troops *pl*; **Ge|birgs|land|schaft** F *(= Gegend)* mountainous region; (= *Gemälde*) mountainscape; (= *Ausblick*) mountain scenery; **Ge|birgs|mas|siv** NT massif; **Ge|birgs|rü|cken** M mountain ridge; **Ge|birgs|stock** M massif; **Ge|birgs|stra|ße** F mountain road; **Ge|birgs|trup|pen** PL mountain troops *pl*; **Ge|birgs|wand** F mountain face; **Ge|birgs|zug** M mountain range

Ge|biss [gə'bɪs] NT **-es, -e** **a** (= *die Zähne*) (set of) teeth *pl*; (= *künstliches Gebiss*) dentures *pl*; **ich habe noch mein ganzes ~** I still have all my teeth **b** (*am Pferdezaum*) bit

Ge|biss-: **Ge|biss|ab|druck** M impression; **Ge|biss|ano|ma|lie** F deformity of the teeth

ge|bis|sen *ptp von* **beißen**

Ge|blä|se [gə'blɛːzə] NT **-s, -** fan, blower; (= *Motorgebläse*) supercharger; (= *Verdichter*) compressor

Ge|blä|se-: **Ge|blä|se|luft** F air from a blower; **Ge|blä|se|mo|tor** M supercharger (engine)

ge|bla|sen *ptp von* **blasen**

ge|bli|chen *ptp von* **bleichen**

ge|blie|ben *ptp von* **bleiben**

Ge|blö|del [gə'bløːdl] NT **-s**, *no pl* (*inf*) nonsense; (= *blödes Gerede auch*) twaddle (*inf*), baloney (*inf*); (*von Komiker*) patter; **die Unterhaltung artete in allgemeines ~ aus** the conversation degenerated into silliness

Ge|blök [gə'bløːk] NT **-(e)s**, *no pl*, **Ge|blö|ke** [gə'bløːkə] NT **-s**, *no pl* (*von Schaf, Kalb*) bleating; (*von Kuh*) lowing; (*inf*: *von Mensch*) bawling (*inf*)

ge|blümt [gə'blyːmt], (*Aus*) **ge|blumt** [gə'bluːmt] ADJ flowered; (*Liter, fig*) *Stil* flowery

Ge|blüt [gə'blyːt] NT **-(e)s**, *no pl* (*geh*) (= *Abstammung*) descent, lineage; (*fig*: = *Blut*) blood; (*liter*: = *Geschlecht*) family; **von edlem ~** of noble blood

ge|bo|gen [gə'boːgn] *ptp von* **biegen** ADJ *Nase* curved

ge|bo|ren [gə'boːrən] *ptp von* **gebären** ADJ born; **blind ~ sein** to have been born blind; **er ist blind ~** he was born blind; **~er Engländer/Londoner sein** to be English/a Londoner by birth; **er ist der ~e Erfinder** he's a born inventor; **Hanna Schmidt ~e** *or* **geb. Müller** Hanna Schmidt, née Müller; **sie ist eine ~e Müller** she was born Müller, her maiden name was Müller

Ge|bo|ren|zei|chen NT *asterisk used to denote "date of birth"*

ge|bor|gen [gə'bɔrgn] *ptp von* **bergen** ADJ **sich ~ fühlen** to feel secure *or* safe; **~ sein** to be secure *or* safe

Ge|bor|gen|heit F **-**, *no pl* security

ge|bors|ten *ptp von* **bersten**

ge|bot *pret von* **gebieten**

Ge|bot [gə'boːt] NT **-(e)s, -e** **a** (= *Gesetz*) law; (= *Regel, Vorschrift*) rule; (*Bibl*) commandment; (= *Grundsatz*) precept; (*old*: = *Verordnung*) decree; (*old*: = *Befehl*) command **b** (*geh*: = *Erfordernis*) requirement; **das ~ der Stunde** the needs of the moment; **Besonnenheit ist das ~ der Stunde** what is called for now is calm; **das ~ der Vernunft** the dictates of reason; **das ~ der Vernunft verlangt, dass ...** reason dictates that ... **c** (= *Verfügung*) command; **jdm zu ~e stehen** to be at sb's command *or* (*Geld etc*) disposal **d** (*Comm*: *bei Auktionen*) bid

ge|bo|ten [gə'boːtn] *ptp von* **gebieten, bieten** ADJ (*geh*) (= *ratsam, angebracht*) advisable; (= *notwendig*) necessary; (= *dringend geboten*) imperative; **bei aller ~en Achtung** with all due respect

Ge|bots|schild NT *pl* **-schilder**, **Ge|bots|zei|chen** NT mandatory sign; (*Mot auch*) traffic sign (giving an instruction)

Gebr. *abbr von* **Gebrüder** Bros

Ge|brab|bel [gə'brabl] NT **-s**, *no pl* (*inf*) jabbering (*inf*), prattling (*inf*)

ge|bracht *ptp von* **bringen**

ge|brannt [gə'brant] *ptp von* **brennen** ADJ **~er Kalk** quicklime; **~e Mandeln** *pl* burnt (*Brit*) *or* baked (*US*) almonds *pl*; **~er Ton** fired clay; **~es Kind scheut das Feuer** (*Prov*) once bitten, twice shy (*Prov*)

ge|bra|ten *ptp von* **braten**

Ge|bra|te|ne(s) [gə'braːtnə] NT *decl as adj* fried food

Ge|bräu [gə'brɔy] NT **-(e)s, -e** brew; (*pej*) strange concoction; (*fig*) concoction (*aus* of)

Ge|brauch [gə'braux] M **-(e)s, Gebräuche** [gə'brɔyçə] (= *Benutzung*) use; (*eines Wortes*) usage; (= *Anwendung*) application; (= *Brauch, Gepflogenheit*) custom; **falscher ~** misuse; (= *falsche Anwendung*) misapplication; **von etw ~ machen** to make use of sth; **in ~ sein** to be used, to be in use; **etw in ~** (*dat*) **haben** to use sth; *Auto etc* to run sth; **allgemein in ~** (*dat*) in general use; **etw in ~ nehmen** (*form*) to put sth into use; **zum äußeren/inneren ~** to be taken externally/internally; **vor ~ (gut) schütteln** shake (well) before use

ge|brau|chen [gə'brauxn] *ptp* **gebraucht** VT (= *benutzen*) to use; (= *anwenden*) to apply; **sich zu etw ~ lassen** to be useful for sth; (= *missbrauchen*) to be used as sth; **nicht mehr zu ~ sein** to be no longer any use, to be useless; **er/das ist zu nichts zu ~** he's/that's (of) no use to anybody, he's/that's absolutely useless; **das kann ich gut ~** I can make good use of that, I can really use that; **ich könnte ein neues Kleid/einen Whisky ~** I could use a new dress/a whisky; **Geld kann ich immer ~** money's always useful → **gebraucht**

ge|bräuch|lich [gə'brɔyçlɪç] ADJ (= *verbreitet*) common; (= *gewöhnlich*) usual, customary; (= *herkömmlich*) conventional; **nicht mehr ~** (*Ausdruck etc*) no longer used

Ge|bräuch|lich|keit F **-**, *no pl* (= *Herkömmlichkeit*) conventionality; **die ~ dieses Wortes/Verfahrens** how common this word/procedure is

Ge|brauchs-: **Ge|brauchs|an|lei|tung** F (*form*), **Ge|brauchs|an|wei|sung** F (*für Arznei*) directions *pl*; (*für Geräte etc*) instructions *pl* (for use); **Ge|brauchs|ar|ti|kel** M article for everyday use; (*pl*: *esp Comm*) basic consumer goods *pl*; **ge|brauchs|fä|hig** ADJ in working order, usable; **etw ~ machen** to put sth into working order; **ge|brauchs|fer|tig** ADJ ready for use; *Nahrungsmittel auch* instant; **Ge|brauchs|ge|gen|stand** M commodity; (= *Werkzeug, Küchengerät*) utensil; **Ge|brauchs|gra|fik**, **Ge|brauchs|gra|phik** F commercial art; **Ge|brauchs|gra|fi|ker(in)**, **Ge|brauchs|gra|phi|ker(in)** M(F) commercial artist; **Ge|brauchs|gut** NT *usu pl* consumer item; **Konsum- und Gebrauchsgüter** consumer and utility goods; **Ge|brauchs|li|te|ra|tur** F functional writing; **Ge|brauchs|ly|rik** F everyday poetry; **Ge|brauchs|mö|bel** PL utility furniture *no pl*; **Ge|brauchs|mu|sik** F functional music; **Ge|brauchs|mus|ter** NT (*Jur*) utility model; **Ge|brauchs|mus|ter|schutz** M protection of utility models; **Ge|brauchs|wert** M utility value

ge|braucht [gə'brauxt] ADJ *Auto* second-hand, used; *Kleidung, Computer etc* second-hand; *Verpackung* used ADV **etw ~ kaufen** to buy sth second-hand → *auch* **brauchen**

Ge|braucht|wa|gen M used *or* second-hand car

Ge|braucht|wa|gen-: **Ge|braucht|wa|gen|händ|ler(in)** M(F) used *or* second-hand car dealer; **Ge|braucht|wa|gen|markt** M used *or* second-hand car market

Ge|braucht|wa|ren PL second-hand goods *pl*

Ge|braucht|wa|ren-: **Ge|braucht|wa|ren|händ|ler(in)** M(F) dealer in second-hand goods; **Ge|braucht|wa|ren|hand|lung** F second-hand shop

ge|bräunt [gə'brɔynt] ADJ (= *braun gebrannt*) (sun-)tanned → *auch* **bräunen**

ge|bre|chen [gə'brɛçn] *ptp* **gebrochen** VI *irreg* (*old liter*) **es gebricht an etw** (*dat*) sth is lacking; **es gebricht ihm an Mut** he lacks courage

Ge|bre|chen [gə'brɛçn] NT **-s, -** (*geh*) affliction; (*fig*) weakness; **die ~ des Alters** the afflictions *or* infirmities of old age

ge|brech|lich [gə'brɛçlɪç] ADJ frail; (= *altersschwach*) infirm; (*fig*: = *unvollkommen*) weak

Ge|brech|lich|keit F **-**, *no pl* frailty; (= *Altersschwäche*) infirmity; (*fig*: = *Unvollkommenheit*) weakness

ge|brieft ADJ briefed

ge|bro|chen [gə'brɔxn] *ptp von* **brechen** ADJ broken; *Mensch auch* crushed; **~e Zahl** (*Math*) fraction; **mit ~em Herzen, ~en Herzens** broken-hearted; **an ~em Herzen** of a broken heart ADV **~ Deutsch sprechen** to speak broken German

Ge|brü|der [gə'bryːdɐ] PL (*Comm*) Brothers *pl*; **~ Müller** Müller Brothers

Ge|brüll [gə'brʏl] NT **-(e)s**, *no pl* (*von Rind*) bellowing; (*von Esel*) braying; (*von Löwe*) roar; (*in Todesangst*) screaming; (*von Mensch*) yelling; **auf ihn mit ~!** (*inf*) go for him!, at him!

Ge|brumm [gə'brʊm] NT **-(e)s**, *no pl*, **Ge|brum|me** [gə'brʊmə] NT **-s**, *no pl* buzzing; (*von Motor, von Bass, Singen*) droning; (*inf*: = *Gebrummel*) grumping (*inf*)

Ge|brum|mel [gə'brʊml] NT **-s**, *no pl* grumping

ge|bückt [gə'bʏkt] ADJ **eine ~e Haltung** a stoop ADV **~ gehen** to stoop; **~ stehen** to stand stooped → *auch* **bücken**

ge|bü|gelt [gə'byːglt] ADJ (*inf*: = *perplex*) knocked flat (*inf*) → *auch* **bügeln**, → **geschniegelt**

Ge|bühr [gə'byːɐ] F **-, -en** **a** charge; (= *Postgebühr*) postage *no pl*; (= *Honorar, Beitrag*) fee; (= *Schulgebühr, Studiengebühr*) fees *pl*; (= *Vermittlungsgebühr*) commission; (= *Straßenbenutzungsgebühr*) toll; **~en erheben** to make *or* levy (*form*) a charge, to charge postage/a fee *etc*; **zu ermäßigter ~** at a reduced rate; **eine ~ von 50 Euro bezahlen, 50 Euro ~(en) bezahlen** to pay a fee/charge *etc* of 50 euros; **~ (be)zahlt Empfänger** postage to be paid by addressee; **die ~en für Rundfunk/Fernsehen werden erhöht** radio/television licences (*Brit*) are going up **b** (= *Angemessenheit*) **nach ~** suitably, properly; **über ~** excessively

ge|büh|ren [gə'byːrən] *ptp* **gebührt** (*geh*) VI to be due (+*dat* to); **ihm gebührt Anerkennung/Achtung** he deserves *or* is due recognition/respect; **das gebührt ihm** (= *steht ihm zu*) it is his (just) due; (= *gehört sich für ihn*) it befits him VR to be proper *or* seemly *or* fitting; **wie es sich gebührt** as is proper

Ge|büh|ren-: **Ge|büh|ren|an|he|bung** F increase in charges; **Ge|büh|ren|an|zei|ger** M call-fee indicator (*Brit*), tollcharge meter (*US*); **Ge|büh|ren|be|frei|ung** F exemption from charges *or* costs

ge|büh|rend ADJ (= *verdient*) due; (= *angemessen*) suitable; (= *geziemend*) proper; **das ihm ~e Gehalt** the salary he deserves; **jdm die ~e Achtung erweisen/verweigern** to pay/deny sb the respect due to him ADV duly, appropriately, suitably; **etw ~ feiern** to celebrate sth in a fitting manner; **etw ~ zu schätzen/würdigen wissen** to appreciate sth; **jdn ~ loben** to give sb due credit

Ge|büh|ren-: **Ge|büh|ren|ein|heit** F (*Telec*) (tariff) unit; **Ge|büh|ren|er|hö|hung** F increase in charges; **Ge|büh|ren|er|lass** M remission of charges; **Ge|büh|ren|er|mä|ßi|gung** F reduction in charges; **ge|büh|ren|frei** ADJ free of charge; *Brief, Paket* post-free (*Brit*), postpaid; *Telefonnummer* Freefone® (*Brit*), toll-free (*US*) ADV free of charge; **Ge|büh|ren|frei|heit** F exemption from charges; **Ge|büh|ren|mar|ke** F revenue stamp; **Ge|büh|ren|ord|nung** F scale of charges, tariff; **ge|büh|ren|pflich|tig** [-pflɪçtɪç] ADJ subject *or* liable to a charge, chargeable; *Autobahnbenutzung* subject to a toll; **~e Verwarnung** (*Jur*) fine; **~e Autobahn** toll road (*Brit*), turnpike (*US*) ADV **jdn ~ verwarnen** to fine sb; **Ge|-**

bühren|satz M rate (of charge); **Ge|büh|ren|zäh|ler** M meter

ge|bühr|lich [gəˈbyːɐlɪç] ADJ, ADV = **gebührend**

Ge|bums [gəˈbʊms] NT **-es**, *no pl*, **Ge|bum|se** [gəˈbʊmzə] NT **-s**, *no pl* (*inf*: = *Gepolter*) thumping, thudding

ge|bün|delt [gəˈbʏndlt] ADJ *Strahlen* bundled; (*fig*) joint → *auch* **bündeln**

ge|bun|den [gəˈbʊndn] *ptp von* **binden** ADJ tied (*an +acc* to); (*durch Verpflichtungen etc*) tied down; *Kapital* tied up; *Preise* controlled; (*Ling, Phys, Chem*) bound; *Buch* cased, hardback; *Wärme* latent; (*Mus*) legato; **in ~er Rede** in verse; **sozial ~e Mietwohnungen** fixed-rent flats (*Brit*) *or* apartments; **zeitlich ~ sein** to be restricted as regards time; **vertraglich ~ sein** to be bound by contract; **anderweitig ~ sein** to be otherwise engaged

Ge|bun|den|heit F **-**, *no pl* (*von Kapital, Preisen etc*) restriction; **auf Grund der ~ unseres Kapitals** because our capital is tied up; **ein Gefühl der ~** a feeling of being tied down; **die ~ an jdn/etw/einen Ort** being tied to sb/sth/a place

Ge|burt [gəˈbuːɐt] ✪ 51.1 F **-, -en** (*lit, fig*) birth; (*fig*: = *Produkt*) fruit, product; **von ~** by birth; **von ~ an** from birth; **von hoher/adliger ~** of good/noble birth; **bei der ~ sterben** (*Mutter*) to die in childbirth; (*Kind*) to die at birth; **das war eine schwere ~!** (*fig inf*) that took some doing (*inf*); **die Gnade der späten ~** the good fortune of being born too late (*and so free from association with the Nazi era*)

Ge|bur|ten-: **Ge|bur|ten|be|schrän|kung** F population control; **Ge|bur|ten|buch** NT register of births; **Ge|bur|ten|de|fi|zit** NT birth deficit; **Ge|bur|ten|kon|trol|le** F, **Ge|bur|ten|re|ge|lung** F birth control; **Ge|bur|ten|ra|te** F birthrate; **Ge|bur|ten|rück|gang** M drop in the birthrate; **ge|bur|ten|schwach** ADJ *Jahrgang* with a low birthrate; **ge|bur|ten|stark** ADJ *Jahrgang* with a high birthrate; **Ge|bur|ten|sta|tis|tik** F birth statistics *pl*; **Ge|bur|ten|über|schuss** M excess of births over deaths; **Ge|bur|ten|zah|len** PL, **Ge|bur|ten|zif|fer** F number of births, birthrate; **Ge|bur|ten|zu|wachs** M increase in the birthrate

ge|bür|tig [gəˈbʏrtɪç] ADJ **~er Londoner sein, aus London ~ sein** to have been born in London, to be London-born, to be a native Londoner

Ge|burts-: **Ge|burts|adel** M hereditary nobility; **er stammt aus altem ~** he comes from a long line of nobility; **Ge|burts|an|zei|ge** F birth announcement; **Ge|burts|da|tum** NT date of birth; **Ge|burts|feh|ler** M congenital defect; **Ge|burts|haus** NT **das ~ Kleists** the house where Kleist was born; **Ge|burts|hel|fer(in)** M(F) (*Med*) (= *Arzt*) obstetrician; (= *Hebamme*) midwife; (*fig*) midwife; **Ge|burts|hil|fe** F **a** assistance at a birth; **~ leisten** to assist at a birth; **bei etw ~ leisten** (*fig*) to help sth see the light of day **b** (*als Fach*) obstetrics *sing*; (*von Hebamme auch*) midwifery; **Ge|burts|jahr** NT year of birth; **Ge|burts|la|ge** F presentation; **Ge|burts|land** NT native country; **Ge|burts|na|me** M birth name, name at birth; (*einer Frau auch*) maiden name; **Ge|burts|ort** M *pl* **-orte** birthplace; **Ge|burts|stadt** F native town; **Ge|burts|stät|te** F (*geh*) birthplace

Ge|burts|tag ✪ 50.3 M birthday; (*auf Formularen*) date of birth; **herzlichen Glückwunsch zum ~!** happy birthday!, many happy returns (of the day)!; **jdm zum ~ gratulieren** to wish sb (a) happy birthday, to wish sb many happy returns (of the day); **heute habe ich ~** it's my birthday today; **~ feiern** to celebrate one's/sb's birthday; **jdm etw zum ~ schenken** to give sb sth for his/her birthday

Ge|burts|tags- *in cpds* birthday; **Ge|burts|tags|fei|er** F birthday party; **Ge|burts|tags|gruß** M birthday greeting; **Ge|burts|tags|kind** NT birthday boy/girl

Ge|burts-: **Ge|burts|ur|kun|de** F birth certificate; **Ge|burts|we|hen** PL labour (*Brit*) *or* labor (*US*) pains *pl*; (*fig auch*) birth pangs *pl*; **Ge|burts|zan|ge** F (pair of) forceps *pl*

Ge|büsch [gəˈbʏʃ] NT **-(e)s, -e** bushes *pl*; (= *Unterholz*) undergrowth, brush

ge|checkt ADJ (= *überprüft*) checked

Geck [gɛk] M **-en, -en** (*pej*) fop (*dated esp Brit*), dandy, dude

ge|cken|haft ADJ (*pej*) foppish (*dated esp Brit*), dandyish

Ge|cko [ˈgɛko] M **-s, -s** (*Zool*) gecko

ge|dacht [gəˈdaxt] *ptp von* **denken, gedenken** ADJ *Linie, Größe, Fall* imaginary; **als Kapitalanlage ~e Lebensversicherung** life assurance intended *or* meant as a capital investment

Ge|dächt|nis [gəˈdɛçtnɪs] NT **-ses, -se** memory; (= *Andenken auch*) remembrance; **etw aus dem ~ hersagen** to recite sth from memory; **das ist seinem ~ entfallen** it went out of his mind; **jdm im ~ bleiben** to stick in sb's mind; **im ~ bleiben** to be remembered; **etw im ~ behalten** to remember sth; **sich** (*dat*) **etw ins ~ zurückrufen** to recall sth, to call sth to mind; **wenn mich mein ~ nicht trügt** if my memory serves me right; **noch frisch in jds ~** (*dat*) **sein** to be still fresh in sb's mind; **zum ~ der** *or* **an die Toten** in memory *or* remembrance of the dead

Ge|dächt|nis-: **Ge|dächt|nis|feh|ler** M lapse of memory; **Ge|dächt|nis|fei|er** F commemoration; (*kirchliche*) memorial *or* commemorative service; **Ge|dächt|nis|hil|fe** F memory aid, mnemonic; **er machte sich ein paar Notizen als ~** he made a few notes to aid his memory; **Ge|dächt|nis|kon|zert** NT memorial concert; **Ge|dächt|nis|lü|cke** F gap in one's memory; (*Psych*) localized amnesia; **da habe ich eine ~** I just don't remember anything about it; **Ge|dächt|nis|pro|to|koll** NT minutes *pl* written from memory; **Ge|dächt|nis|ren|nen** NT memorial race; **Ge|dächt|nis|schu|lung** F memory training; **Ge|dächt|nis|schwund** M amnesia, loss of memory; **Ge|dächt|nis|stö|rung** F partial *or* (*vorübergehend*) temporary amnesia; **Ge|dächt|nis|stüt|ze** F memory aid, mnemonic; **Ge|dächt|nis|übung** F memory training exercise; **Ge|dächt|nis|ver|lust** M loss of memory; **Ge|dächt|nis|zel|le** F (*Med*) memory cell

ge|dämpft [gəˈdɛmpft] ADJ **a** (= *vermindert*) *Geräusch* muffled; *Farben, Musikinstrument, Stimmung* muted; *Optimismus* cautious; *Licht, Freude* subdued; *Wut* suppressed; *Entwicklung, Wachstum* restrained; (*Tech*) *Schwingung* damped; **mit ~er Stimme** in a low voice **b** (*Cook*) steamed → *auch* **dämpfen**

Ge|dan|ke [gəˈdaŋkə] ✪ 35.2, 39.2 M **-ns, -n** thought (*über +acc* on, about); (= *Idee, Plan, Einfall*) idea; (= *Konzept*) concept; (= *Betrachtung*) reflection (*über +acc* on); **der bloße ~ an ...** the mere thought of ...; **da kam mir ein ~** then I had an idea, then something occurred to me; **einen ~n fassen** to formulate an idea; **bei diesem Lärm kann man ja keinen ~n fassen** you can't hear yourself think in this noise; **seine ~n beisammenhaben** to have one's mind *or* thoughts concentrated; **in ~n vertieft** *or* **versunken/verloren sein** to be deep *or* sunk/lost in thought; **in ~n, Worten und Werken sündigen** to sin in thought, word and deed; **in ~n bin ich bei dir** in thought I am with you, my thoughts are with you; **jdn auf andere ~n bringen** to take sb's mind off things; **schwarzen ~n nachhängen** to think gloomy *or* dismal thoughts; **wo hat er nur seine ~n?** whatever is he thinking about?; **sich** (*dat*) **über etw** (*acc*) **~n machen** to think about sth; (= *sich sorgen*) to worry *or* be worried about sth; **mach dir keine ~n (darüber)!** don't worry about it!; **man macht sich** (*dat*) **so seine ~n** (*inf*) I've got my ideas; **daran würde ich keinen ~n verschwenden** I wouldn't even give it a thought; **kein ~ (daran)!** (= *stimmt nicht*) not a bit of it! (*inf*); (= *kommt nicht infrage*) (that's) out of the question; **etw ganz in ~n** (*dat*) **tun** to do sth (quite) without thinking; **jds ~n lesen** to read sb's mind *or* thoughts; **ich kann doch nicht ~n lesen!** I'm not a mind-reader!; **auf einen ~n kommen** to have *or* get an idea; **wie kommen Sie auf den ~n?** what gives you that idea?, what makes you think that?; **auf dumme ~n kommen** (*inf*) to get up to mischief; **jdn auf den ~n bringen, etw zu tun** to give sb the idea of doing sth; **sich mit dem ~n tragen, etw zu tun** (*geh*) **mit dem ~n spielen, etw zu tun** to toy with *or* consider the idea of doing sth; **der europäische/olympische ~** the European/Olympic idea

Ge|dan|ken-: **Ge|dan|ken|ar|mut** F lack of thought; (= *Ideenarmut*) lack of originality; **Ge|dan|ken|aus|tausch** M (*Pol*) exchange of ideas; **Ge|dan|ken|blitz** M (*inf*) sudden inspiration, brainwave (*inf*); **Ge|dan|ken|flug** M (*geh*) flight(s *pl*) of thought; **Ge|dan|ken|fol|ge** F reasoning; **Ge|dan|ken|frei|heit** F freedom of thought; **Ge|dan|ken|fül|le** F wealth of ideas; **Ge|dan|ken|gang** M *pl* **-gänge** train of thought; **Ge|dan|ken|ge|bäu|de** NT edifice *or* construct of ideas; **Ge|dan|ken|gut** NT, *no pl* body of thought; **Ge|dan|ken|ket|te** F chain of thought; **Ge|dan|ken|le|sen** NT **-s**, *no pl* mind-reading; **ge|dan|ken|los** ADJ (= *unüberlegt*) unthinking; (= *zerstreut*) absent-minded; (= *rücksichtslos*) thoughtless ADV (= *unüberlegt*) unthinkingly; (= *rücksichtslos*) thoughtlessly; **etw ~ tun** to do sth without thinking; **Ge|dan|ken|lo|sig|keit** F **-, -en** (= *Unüberlegtheit*) lack of thought; (= *Zerstreutheit*) absent-mindedness; (= *Rücksichtslosigkeit*) thoughtlessness; **Ge|dan|ken|ly|rik** F reflective poetry; **ge|dan|ken|reich** ADJ full of ideas; **Ge|dan|ken|reich|tum** M wealth of ideas; **Ge|dan|ken|rei|he** F chain of thought; **ge|dan|ken|schwer** ADJ *Buch, Lektüre etc* deep, heavy; *Person* weighed down with his *or* her thoughts *pred*; **Ge|dan|ken|spiel** NT intellectual game; (*fantasierend*) game of make-believe; (*als psychologische Taktik*) mind game; **Ge|dan|ken|split|ter** M aphorism; **Ge|dan|ken|sprung** M mental leap, jump from one idea to another; **Ge|dan|ken|strich** M dash; **Ge|dan|ken|tie|fe** F depth of thought; **Ge|dan|ken|über|tra|gung** F telepathy (*auch fig*), thought transference; **Ge|dan|ken|ver|bin|dung** F, **Ge|dan|ken|ver|knüp|fung** F association of ideas; **ge|dan|ken|ver|lo|ren** ADJ, ADV lost in thought; **ge|dan|ken|voll** ADJ (= *nachdenklich*) thoughtful, pensive; **Ge|dan|ken|welt** F world of thought *or* ideas; **die römische ~** (= *Ideenwelt*) (the world of) Roman thought; **er lebt in seiner eigenen ~** he lives in a world of his own

ge|dank|lich [gəˈdaŋklɪç] ADJ intellectual; (= *vorgestellt*) imaginary; **sich** (*dat*) **~** *or* **in ~er Hinsicht näherkommen** to find a common way of thinking; **in ~er Hinsicht übereinstimmen** to have an affinity of mind; **die große ~e Klarheit in seinem Werk** the great clarity of thought in his work ADV intellectually; **sie leben ~ in einer anderen Welt** in their minds *or* imagination they live in another world

Ge|därm [gəˈdɛrm] NT **-(e)s, -e**, **Ge|där|me** [gəˈdɛrmə] NT **-s, -** (*old, liter*) **a** bowels *pl*, entrails *pl* **b Gedärme** PL intestines *pl*; **da drehen sich einem ja die ~e um!** it's enough to make your insides *or* stomach turn over!

Ge|deck [gəˈdɛk] NT **-(e)s, -e** **a** (= *Tischgedeck*) cover; **ein ~ auflegen** to lay (*Brit*) *or* set a place; **ein ~ für drei Personen** places *or* covers for three people; **eine Tafel mit zehn ~en** a table laid (*Brit*) *or* set for ten (people) **b** (= *Menü*) set meal, table d'hôte **c** (*im Nachtklub*) cover charge

ge|deckt [gəˈdɛkt] ADJ *Farben* muted; *Basar, Gang, Dach* covered; *Tisch* set *or* laid *(Brit)* for a meal → *auch* **decken**

Ge|deih [gəˈdai] M **auf ~ und Verderb** for better or (for) worse; **jdm auf ~ und Verderb ausgeliefert sein** to be completely and utterly at sb's mercy

ge|dei|hen [gəˈdaiən] *pret* **gedieh** [gəˈdi:], *ptp* **gediehen** [gəˈdi:ən] VI *aux sein* to thrive; *(wirtschaftlich auch)* to prosper, to flourish; *(geh: = sich entwickeln)* to develop; *(fig: = vorankommen)* to make progress *or* headway, to progress; **die Sache ist so weit gediehen, dass ...** the matter has reached the point *or* stage where ...

Ge|dei|hen [gəˈdaiən] NT **-s,** *no pl* thriving; *(wirtschaftlich auch)* prospering, flourishing; *(= Gelingen)* success; **zum ~ dieses Vorhabens braucht es Geduld und Glück** if this plan is to succeed patience and luck will be called for

ge|deih|lich [gəˈdailɪç] ADJ *(geh) (= vorteilhaft)* beneficial, advantageous; *(= erfolgreich)* successful

Ge|denk|aus|stel|lung F commemorative exhibition

ge|den|ken [gəˈdɛŋkn] ✪ 35.3 *pret* **gedachte,** [gəˈdaxtə] *ptp* **gedacht** VI [gəˈdaxt] *irreg +gen* **a** *(geh) (= denken an)* to remember, to think of; *(= erwähnen)* to recall; **in seiner Rede gedachte er der Toten** in his speech he remembered the dead **b** *(= feiern)* to commemorate, to remember **c ~, etw zu tun** to propose to do sth

Ge|den|ken [gəˈdɛŋkn] NT **-s,** *no pl* memory *(an +acc* of); **zum** *or* **im ~ an jdn** in memory *or* remembrance of sb; **etw in gutem ~ behalten** to treasure the memory of sth; **jdm ein ehrendes ~ bewahren** to remember sb with honour *(Brit) or* honor *(US)*

Ge|denk-: Ge|denk|fei|er F commemoration; **Ge|denk|got|tes|dienst** M memorial *or* commemorative service; **Ge|denk|mar|ke** F commemorative stamp; **Ge|denk|mi|nu|te** F minute's silence; **Ge|denk|mün|ze** F commemorative coin; **Ge|denk|re|de** F commemorative speech; **Ge|denk|stät|te** F memorial; **Ge|denk|stein** M commemorative *or* memorial stone; **Ge|denk|stun|de** F hour of commemoration; **Ge|denk|ta|fel** F plaque; **Ge|denk|tag** M commemoration day; **Ge|denk|ver|an|stal|tung** F commemoration (ceremony)

Ge|dicht [gəˈdɪçt] NT **-(e)s, -e** poem; **die ~e Enzensbergers** Enzensberger's poetry *or* poems; **dieses Kleid/der Nachtisch ist ein ~** *(fig inf)* this dress/the dessert is sheer poetry

Ge|dicht-: Ge|dicht|band *pl* **-bände** M book of poems *or* poetry; **Ge|dicht|form** F poetic form; **in ~** in verse; **Ge|dicht|samm|lung** F collection of poems; *(von mehreren Dichtern auch)* anthology; **Ge|dicht|zyk|lus** M cycle of poems, poem cycle

ge|die|gen [gəˈdi:gn] ADJ **a** *Metall* pure, native *(Min)* **b** *(von guter Qualität)* high-quality; *(= geschmackvoll)* tasteful; *(= rechtschaffen)* upright; *Verarbeitung* solid; *Kenntnisse* sound **c** *(inf: = wunderlich)* peculiar

Ge|die|gen|heit F **-,** *no pl* **a** *(von Metall)* purity **b** *(= gute Qualität)* high quality; *(= geschmackvolle Atmosphäre)* tastefulness; *(= Rechtschaffenheit)* uprightness; *(von Verarbeitung)* solidity; *(von Kenntnissen)* soundness

ge|dieh *pret von* **gedeihen**

ge|die|hen *ptp von* **gedeihen**

ge|dient [gəˈdi:nt] ADJ **ein ~er Soldat sein** to have completed one's (military) service → *auch* **dienen**

Ge|din|ge [gəˈdɪŋə] NT **-s, -** *(Miner)* **im ~ arbeiten** to work on a piece-rate basis

Ge|döns [gəˈdø:ns] NT **-es** [-zəs], *no pl (dial inf)* fuss, hullabaloo *(inf)*

ge|dopt [gəˈdo:pt] PTP *von* **dopen** ADJ **sie war ~** she had taken drugs; **die ~en Schwimmer wurden disqualifiziert** the swimmers who had taken drugs were disqualified → *auch* **dopen**

gedr. *abbr von* **gedruckt**

Ge|drän|ge [gəˈdrɛŋə] NT **-s,** *no pl (= Menschenmenge)* crowd, crush; *(= Drängeln)* jostling; *(Sport)* bunching; *(Rugby)* scrum(-mage); **vor der Theaterkasse herrschte ~** there was a big crowd at the ticket office; **ein offenes ~** *(Rugby)* a loose scrum; **ins ~ kommen** *or* **geraten** *(fig)* to get into a fix *(inf)*

Ge|drän|gel [gəˈdrɛŋl] NT **-s,** *no pl (inf) (= Menschenmenge)* crush; *(= Drängeln)* shoving *(inf)*

ge|drängt [gəˈdrɛŋt] ADJ packed; *(fig) Stil* terse; **~e Übersicht** synopsis ADV **~ voll** packed full, jam-packed *(inf)*; **~ stehen** to be crowded together → *auch* **drängen**

Ge|drängt|heit F **-,** *no pl (von Stil)* terseness; *(von Übersicht)* conciseness

ge|drech|selt [gəˈdrɛkslt] ADJ *(pej) Rede, Sätze, Stil* stilted; **wie ~ reden** to speak stiltedly; **kunstvoll ~e Sätze** nicely turned phrases → *auch* **drechseln**

Ge|dröhn [gəˈdrø:n] NT **-(e)s,** *no pl,* **Ge|dröh|ne** [gəˈdrø:nə] NT **-s,** *no pl (von Motoren)* droning; *(von Kanonen, Lautsprecher, Hämmern etc)* booming

ge|dro|schen *ptp von* **dreschen**

ge|druckt [gəˈdrʊkt] ADJ printed; **~e Schaltung** printed circuit board, PCB; **lügen wie ~** *(inf)* to lie right, left and centre *(Brit inf) or* center *(US inf)* → *auch* **drucken**

ge|drückt [gəˈdrʏkt] ADJ *Stimmung* depressed, dejected; *Schweigen* gloomy; *Konjunktur, Preise* depressed; **~er Stimmung sein** to be in low spirits, to feel depressed → *auch* **drücken**

Ge|drückt|heit F **-,** *no pl* depression, dejection

ge|drun|gen [gəˈdrʊŋən] *ptp von* **dringen** ADJ *Person, Gestalt* stocky; *Gebäude, Form* squat

Ge|drun|gen|heit F **-,** *no pl* stockiness; *(von Gebäude, Form)* squatness

ge|duckt [gəˈdʊkt] ADJ *Haltung, Mensch* crouching; *Kopf* lowered; *Haus* low; **hinter einer Hecke ~** crouching down behind a hedge ADV **~ sitzen** to sit hunched up *(Brit) or* over *(US)* → *auch* **ducken**

Ge|du|del [gəˈdu:dl] NT **-s,** *no pl (inf) (von Klarinette etc)* tootling; *(von Dudelsack)* droning, whining; *(von Radio)* noise

Ge|duld [gəˈdʊlt] F **-,** *no pl* patience; **mit jdm/etw ~ haben** to be patient *or* have patience with sb/sth; **sich mit ~ wappnen** to possess one's soul in patience; **mir geht die ~ aus, mir reißt die ~, ich verliere die ~** my patience is wearing thin, I'm losing my patience; **meine ~ mit dir ist erschöpft** you've exhausted my patience; **jds ~ auf eine harte Probe stellen** to try sb's patience

ge|dul|den [gəˈdʊldn] *ptp* **geduldet** VR to be patient

ge|dul|dig [gəˈdʊldɪç] ADJ patient; **~ wie ein Lamm** meek as a lamb → **Papier a** ADV patiently

Ge|dulds-: Ge|dulds|ar|beit F job calling for patience; **Ge|dulds|fa|den** M **jetzt reißt mir aber der ~!** *(inf)* I'm just about losing my patience; **einen langen ~ haben** to have a lot of patience, to have the patience of Job; **Ge|dulds|pro|be** F trial of (one's) patience; **das war eine harte ~** it was enough to try anyone's patience *or* to try the patience of a saint; **Ge|dulds|spiel** NT puzzle

ge|dun|gen *ptp von* **dingen**

ge|dun|sen [gəˈdʊnzn] ADJ bloated

ge|durft *ptp von* **dürfen**

ge|ehrt [gəˈle:ɐt] ADJ honoured *(Brit)*, honored *(US)*, esteemed; **sehr ~e Damen und Herren!** Ladies and Gentlemen!; **sehr ~er Herr Kurz!** dear Mr Kurz; **Sehr ~e Damen und Herren** *(in Briefen)* Dear Sir or Madam → *auch* **ehren**

ge|eig|net [gəˈlaignət] ADJ *(= passend)* suitable; *(= richtig)* right; **sie ist für diesen Posten nicht ~** she's not the right person for this job; **er ist nicht der ~e Mann für meine Tochter** he's not the right *or* a suitable man for my daughter; **im ~en Augenblick** at the right moment; **er ist zu dieser Arbeit nicht ~** he's not suited to this work; **er wäre zum Lehrer gut/schlecht ~** he would/wouldn't make a good teacher → *auch* **eignen**

ge|eig|ne|ten|orts [gəˈlaignətnˈlɔrts] ADV *(form)* in an appropriate place

Ge|eig|net|heit F **-,** *no pl (= Passen)* suitability; *(= Richtigkeit)* rightness

ge|eist [gəˈlaist] ADJ *Früchte, Getränke, Suppe* iced

Geest [ge:st] F **-, -en, Geest|land** NT *coastal sandy moorlands of N.W. Germany*

Ge|fahr [gəˈfa:ɐ] F **-, -en a** danger *(für* to, for); *(= Bedrohung)* threat *(für* to, for); **die ~en des Dschungels/Verkehrs/dieses Berufs** the dangers *or* perils *or* hazards of the jungle/traffic/this job; **~ bringend** dangerous; **in ~ sein** *or* **schweben** to be in danger *or* jeopardy; *(= bedroht)* to be threatened; **in ~ geraten** to be under threat; **außer ~** *(= nicht gefährdet)* not in danger; *(= nicht mehr gefährdet)* out of danger; *Patient* out of danger, off the danger list; **sich ~en** *or* **einer ~ aussetzen** to expose oneself to danger, to put oneself in danger; **es besteht die ~, dass ...** there's a risk *or* the danger that ...; **er liebt die ~** he likes living dangerously; **(nur) bei ~ (bedienen)!** (to be used only) in case of emergency!; **wer sich in ~ begibt, kommt darin um** *(Prov)* if you play with fire, you must expect to get your fingers burned **b** *(= Wagnis, Risiko)* risk *(für* to, for); **auf eigene ~** at one's own risk *or (stärker)* peril; **auf die ~ hin, etw zu tun/dass jd etw tut** at the risk of doing sth/of sb doing sth; **~ laufen, etw zu tun** to run the risk of doing sth; **unter ~ seines eigenen Lebens** at the risk of one's own life; **auf eigene Rechnung und ~** *(Comm)* at one's own account and risk

ge|fahr|brin|gend ADJ → **Gefahr a**

ge|fähr|den [gəˈfɛ:ɐdn] *ptp* **gefährdet** VT to endanger; *Position, Wirtschaft, Chancen etc auch* to jeopardize; *(= bedrohen)* to threaten; *(= aufs Spiel setzen)* to put at risk; **Versetzung** *or* **Vorrücken gefährdet** *(Sch) comment on a school report indicating that the pupil may have to repeat a year*

ge|fähr|det [gəˈfɛ:ɐdət] ADJ *Tierart* endangered; *Ehe, Jugend, Bevölkerungsgruppe, Unternehmen, Gebiet* at risk *pred*; **von Erdbeben ~** at risk from earthquakes; **Gefährdete** people at risk

Ge|fähr|dung F **-, -en a** *(= das Gefährden)* endangering; *(von Position, Wirtschaft, Chancen)* endangering, jeopardizing; *(= das Riskieren)* risking **b** *(= Gefahr)* danger *(+gen* to)

Ge|fähr|dungs|haf|tung F risk liability

ge|fah|ren *ptp von* **fahren**

Ge|fah|ren-: Ge|fah|ren|be|reich M danger zone; **Ge|fah|ren|herd** M danger area; **Ge|fah|ren|mo|ment** NT potential danger; **Ge|fah|ren|mo|ment** M *(= Schrecksekunde)* moment of danger; **Ge|fah|ren|quel|le** F source of danger; **Ge|fah|ren|stel|le** F danger spot; **Ge|fah|ren|zo|ne** F danger zone *or* area; **Ge|fah|ren|zu|la|ge** F danger money; **eine ~ von 200 Euro** 200 euros' danger money

Ge|fahr-: Ge|fahr|gut NT hazardous materials *pl*; **Ge|fahr|gut|trans|port** M transport of hazardous materials

ge|fähr|lich [gəˈfɛ:ɐlɪç] ADJ dangerous; *(= gewagt auch)* risky; *(= lebensgefährlich auch)* perilous; **das ~e Alter** *(fig)* the dangerous age ADV dangerously; *(= gewagt auch)* recklessly

Ge|fähr|lich|keit F **-,** *no pl* dangerousness; *(= Gewagtheit auch)* riskiness; *(= Lebensgefahr auch)* perilousness

Ge|fahr-: ge|fahr|los ADJ safe; *(= harmlos)* harmless ADV safely; *(= harmlos)* harmlessly; **Ge|fahr|lo|sig|keit** F **-,** *no pl* safety; *(= Harmlosigkeit)* harmlessness; **Ge|fahr|stel|le** F danger spot

Ge|fährt [gəˈfɛ:ɐt] NT **-(e)s, -e** *(dated)* wagon, carriage; *(hum)* jalopy *(inf)*

Ge|fähr|te [gəˈfɛːɐtə] M **-n, -n**, **Ge|fähr|tin** [gəˈfɛːɐtɪn] F **-, -nen** *(geh) (lit, fig)* companion; *(= Lebensgefährte auch)* partner (through life)

Ge|fahr-: **ge|fahr|voll** ADJ dangerous, full of danger; **Ge|fahr|zei|chen** NT danger sign

Ge|fäl|le [gəˈfɛlə] NT **-s, -** **a** *(= Neigung) (von Fluss)* drop, fall; *(von Land, Straße)* slope; *(= Neigungsgrad)* gradient; **das Gelände hat ein starkes ~** the land slopes down steeply; **der Fluss hat ein starkes ~** the river drops suddenly; **ein ~ von 10%** a gradient of 10%; **starkes ~!** steep hill **b** *(fig: = Unterschied)* difference; **das Nord-Süd-~** the North-South divide

ge|fal|len [gəˈfalən] ✪ 34.3, 34.4, 40.2 *pret* **gefiel**, [gəˈfiːl] *ptp* **gefallen** VI [gəˈfalən] to please *(jdm* sb); **es gefällt mir (gut)** I like it (very much *or* a lot); **es gefällt ihm, wie sie spricht** he likes the way she talks; **das gefällt mir gar nicht, das will mir gar nicht ~** *(dated)* I don't like it at all *or* one little bit; **das könnte dir so ~!** *(inf)* no way! *(inf)*; **das Stück hat ~** *(geh)* the play was well received; **das gefällt mir schon besser** *(inf)* that's more like it *(inf)*; **er gefällt mir gar nicht** *(inf: gesundheitlich)* I don't like the look of him *(inf)*; **sich** *(dat)* **in einer Rolle ~** to fancy oneself in a role; **er gefällt sich in der Rolle des Leidenden** he likes playing the martyr; **sich** *(dat)* **etw ~ lassen** *(= dulden)* to put up with sth, to tolerate sth; **er lässt sich alles ~** he'll put up with anything; **das lasse ich mir (von Ihnen/denen) nicht ~!** I won't stand for *or* put up with that (from you/them)!; **das lasse ich mir ~!** that's just the job *(inf) or* thing *(inf)*, there's nothing I'd like better

ge|fal|len [gəˈfalən] *ptp von* **fallen, gefallen**

Ge|fal|len [gəˈfalən] NT **-s**, *no pl (geh)* pleasure; **an etw** *(dat)* **~ finden** to derive *or* get pleasure from sth, to delight in sth; **an jdm/aneinander (großes) ~ finden** to take a (great) fancy to sb/each other; **bei jdm ~ finden** to appeal to sb

Ge|fal|len M **-s, -** favour *(Brit)*, favor *(US)*; **jdn um einen ~ bitten** to ask sb a favo(u)r; **jdm einen ~ erweisen, jdm einen ~ tun** to do sb a favo(u)r; **tun Sie mir den ~ und schreiben Sie** would you do me a favo(u)r and write, would you do me the favo(u)r of writing; **Sie würden mir einen ~ tun, wenn ...** you'd be doing me a favo(u)r if ...; **jdm etw zu ~ tun** *(geh)* to do sth to please sb; **ihm zu ~** to please him

Ge|fal|le|nen|denk|mal NT war memorial

Ge|fal|le|ne(r) [gəˈfalənə] MF *decl as adj* soldier killed in action; **die ~n und die Toten des Krieges** the soldiers and civilians who died in the war; **ein Denkmal für die ~n des Krieges** a memorial to those killed in the war

Ge|fäl|le|stre|cke F incline

ge|fäl|lig [gəˈfɛlɪç] ADJ **a** *(= hilfsbereit)* helpful, obliging; **sich ~ zeigen** to show oneself willing to oblige; **jdm ~ sein** to oblige *or* help sb **b** *(= ansprechend)* pleasing; *(= freundlich)* pleasant **c** **Zigarette ~?** *(form)* would you care for a cigarette? → **gefälligst**

Ge|fäl|lig|keit F **a** *(= Gefallen)* favour *(Brit)*, favor *(US)*; **jdm eine ~ erweisen** to do sb a favo(u)r **b** *no pl (= gefälliges Wesen)* pleasantness; *(= Entgegenkommen)* helpfulness; **etw aus ~ tun** to do sth out of the kindness of one's heart

Ge|fäl|lig|keits|ak|zept NT, **Ge|fäl|lig|keits|wech|sel** M *(Fin)* accommodation bill *or* paper

ge|fäl|ligst [gəˈfɛlɪçst] ADV *(inf)* kindly; **sei ~ still!** kindly keep your mouth shut! *(inf)*

Ge|fäll|stre|cke F incline

Ge|fall-: **Ge|fall|sucht** F craving for admiration; **ge|fall|süch|tig** ADJ desperate to be admired

ge|fällt [gəˈfɛlt] *3. pers sing pres von* **gefallen**

ge|fälscht [gəˈfɛlʃt] ADJ forged

ge|fan|gen [gəˈfaŋən] *ptp von* **fangen** ADJ *(= gefangen genommen)* captured; *(fig)* captivated; **sich ~ geben** to give oneself up, to surrender

Ge|fan|ge|nen-: **Ge|fan|ge|nen|auf|se|her(in)** M(F) guard; **Ge|fan|ge|nen|aus|tausch** M exchange of prisoners; **Ge|fan|ge|nen|be|frei|ung** F rescue of a prisoner/prisoners; *(als Delikt)* aiding and abetting the escape of a prisoner; **Ge|fan|ge|nen|für|sor|ge** F prison welfare; *(inf: = Dienst)* prison welfare service; **Ge|fan|ge|nen|haus** NT *(Aus)* prison; **Ge|fan|ge|nen|hilfs|or|ga|ni|sa|ti|on** F prisoners' rights organization; **Ge|fan|ge|nen|la|ger** NT prison camp; **Ge|fan|gen|en|miss|hand|lung** F mistreatment of prisoners; **Ge|fan|ge|nen|wär|ter(in)** M(F) prison officer *or* guard, (prison) warder *(Brit)*, jailer *(old inf)*

Ge|fan|ge|ne(r) [gəˈfaŋənə] MF *decl as adj* captive; *(= Sträfling, Kriegsgefangene, fig)* prisoner; **500 ~ machen** *(Mil)* to take 500 prisoners; **keine ~n machen** *(Mil)* to take no prisoners (alive)

Ge|fan|gen-: **ge|fan|gen hal|ten** VT *irreg* to hold prisoner; *Geiseln* to hold; *Tiere* to keep in captivity; *(fig)* to captivate; **Ge|fan|gen|haus** NT *(form, Aus)* prison; **Ge|fan|gen|nah|me** [-naːmə] F **-, -n** capture; *(= Verhaftung)* arrest; **bei der ~** on one's capture/arrest; **ge|fan|gen neh|men** VT *irreg Mensch* to take captive; *(= verhaften)* to arrest; *(Mil)* to take prisoner; *(fig)* to captivate; **Ge|fan|gen|schaft** [gəˈfaŋənʃaft] F **-, -en** captivity; **in ~ geraten** to be taken prisoner; **ge|fan|gen set|zen** VT to take into captivity; *(= verhaften)* to imprison

Ge|fäng|nis [gəˈfɛŋnɪs] NT **-ses, -se** prison, jail, gaol *(Brit)*; *(= Gefängnisstrafe)* imprisonment; **im ~ sein** *or* **sitzen** *(inf)* to be in prison; **ins ~ kommen** to be sent to prison; **zwei Jahre ~ bekommen** to get two years' imprisonment, to get two years in prison; **auf Meineid steht ~** perjury is punishable by imprisonment *or* by a prison sentence

Ge|fäng|nis- *in cpds* prison; **Ge|fäng|nis|auf|ent|halt** M prison term, time in prison; **Ge|fäng|nis|auf|se|her(in)** M(F) warder *(Brit)*, prison officer *or* guard, jailer *(old inf)*; **Ge|fäng|nis|di|rek|tor(in)** M(F) prison governor, prison warden *(esp US)*; **Ge|fäng|nis|ge|bäu|de** NT prison; **Ge|fäng|nis|geist|li|che(r)** MF *decl as adj* prison chaplain; **Ge|fäng|nis|haft** F imprisonment; **Ge|fäng|nis|hof** M prison yard; **Ge|fäng|nis|in|sas|se** M, **Ge|fäng|nis|in|sas|sin** F inmate; **Ge|fäng|nis|re|vol|te** F prison riot(s *pl*); **Ge|fäng|nis|stra|fe** F prison sentence; **eine ~ von zehn Jahren** ten years' imprisonment; **er wurde zu einer ~ verurteilt** he was sent to prison, he was given a prison sentence; **Ge|fäng|nis|tor** NT prison gate *usu pl*; **für ihn öffneten sich die ~e** the prison gates were opened for him; **Ge|fäng|nis|wär|ter(in)** M(F) warder *(Brit)*, prison officer *or* guard, jailer *(old inf)*; **Ge|fäng|nis|zel|le** F prison cell

ge|färbt [gəˈfɛrpt] ADJ dyed; *Lebensmittel* artificially coloured *(Brit) or* colored *(US)*; *(fig) Aussprache* tinged; *Bericht* biased; **ihre Sprache ist schottisch ~** her accent has a Scottish tinge *or* ring to it; **konservativ ~ sein** to have a conservative bias; **rot ~es Haar** dyed red hair, hair dyed red → *auch* **färben**

Ge|fa|sel [gəˈfaːzl] NT **-s**, *no pl (pej)* twaddle *(inf)*, drivel *(inf)*

Ge|fäß [gəˈfɛːs] NT **-es, -e** vessel *(auch Anat, Bot)*; *(= Behälter)* receptacle; *(= Degenkorb)* coquille

Ge|fäß|chi|rur|gie F *(Med)* vascular surgery

ge|fäß|er|wei|ternd ADJ vasodilatory

Ge|fäß|er|wei|te|rung F vasodilation, vascular dilatation

Ge|fäß|lei|den NT angiopathy, vascular disease

ge|fasst [gəˈfast] ADJ *(= ruhig)* composed, calm; *Stimme* calm; *Lächeln* composed; **einen sehr ~en Eindruck machen** to appear cool, calm and collected; **auf etw** *(acc)* **~ sein** to be prepared *or* ready for sth; **sich auf etw** *(acc)* **~ machen** to prepare oneself for sth; **er kann sich auf etwas ~ machen** *(inf)* I'll give him something to think about *(inf)* ADV *(= beherrscht)* calmly → *auch* **fassen**

Ge|fasst|heit F **-**, *no pl* composure, calm(-ness)

Ge|fäß-: **ge|fäß|ver|en|gend** ADJ vasoconstrictive; **Ge|fäß|ver|en|gung** F vasoconstriction, vascular constriction; **Ge|fäß|ver|schluss** M, **Ge|fäß|ver|stop|fung** F embolism; **Ge|fäß|wand** F vascular wall

Ge|fecht [gəˈfɛçt] NT **-(e)s, -e** *(lit, fig)* battle; *(Mil)* encounter, engagement; *(= Scharmützel)* skirmish; **ein hartes ~** fierce fighting; **das ~ abbrechen/einleiten** to cease/open combat; **jdn/etw außer ~ setzen** *(lit, fig)* to put sb/sth out of action; **mit diesen Argumenten setzte er seinen Gegner außer ~** he shot down his opponents with these arguments; **Argumente ins ~ führen** to advance arguments; **im Eifer** *or* **in der Hitze des ~s** *(fig)* in the heat of the moment; **klar zum ~!** *(Naut)* clear for action!; *(fig)* clear the decks!

Ge|fechts-: **Ge|fechts|ab|schnitt** M battle zone; **Ge|fechts|auf|klä|rung** F tactical reconnaissance; **Ge|fechts|aus|bil|dung** F combat training; **ge|fechts|be|reit** ADJ ready for action *or* battle; *(= einsatzfähig)* (fully) operational; **Ge|fechts|be|reit|schaft** F readiness for action *or* battle; **in ~** fully operational; **Ge|fechts|feld** NT battleground; **Ge|fechts|feld|waf|fe** F battleground weapon; **ge|fechts|klar** ADJ *(Naut)* cleared for action; **ein Schiff ~ machen** to clear a ship for action; **Ge|fechts|kopf** M warhead; **Ge|fechts|lärm** M noise of battle; **ge|fechts|mä|ßig** ADJ combat *attr*, under combat conditions; **Ge|fechts|pau|se** F break in the fighting; **Ge|fechts|stand** M command post; **Ge|fechts|stär|ke** F fighting strength; **Ge|fechts|übung** F field exercise, manoeuvres *pl (Brit)*, maneuvers *pl (US)*

ge|fe|dert [gəˈfeːdɐt] ADJ *Matratze* sprung; *Karosserie* spring-suspended; *Sohlen* cushion *attr*; **ein gut ~es Auto** a car with good suspension; **eine gut ~e Kutsche** a well-sprung carriage → *auch* **federn**

ge|fei|ert [gəˈfaiɐt] ADJ celebrated → *auch* **feiern**

Ge|feil|sche [gəˈfailʃə] NT **-s**, *no pl (inf)* haggling

ge|feit [gəˈfait] ADJ **gegen etw ~ sein** to be immune to sth; **niemand ist gegen den Tod ~** nobody is immortal; **dagegen ist keiner ~** that could happen to anyone

ge|fes|tigt [gəˈfɛstɪçt] ADJ *Tradition, Verhältnisse* established; *Charakter* steady; *Bindungen* firm; **sittlich ~ sein** to have a sense of moral responsibility → *auch* **festigen**

Ge|fie|del [gəˈfiːdl] NT **-s**, *no pl (inf)* fiddling *(inf)*, scraping *(pej)*

Ge|fie|der [gəˈfiːdɐ] NT **-s, -** plumage, feathers *pl*; *(old: von Pfeil)* flight

ge|fie|dert [gəˈfiːdɐt] ADJ feathered; *Blatt* pinnate; **die ~en Sänger** *(poet)* the feathered songsters *(poet)*; **unsere ~en Freunde** *(geh)* our feathered friends → *auch* **fiedern**

ge|fiel *pret von* **gefallen**

Ge|fil|de [gəˈfɪldə] NT **-s, -** *(old, liter)* realm; **die ~ der Seligen** the Elysian fields; **die heimatlichen ~** *(hum)* home pastures

ge|fin|kelt [gəˈfɪŋklt] ADJ *(esp Aus)* cunning, crafty

Ge|fla|cker [gəˈflakɐ] NT **-s**, *no pl* flickering

ge|flammt [gəˈflamt] ADJ *Marmor* waved, rippled; *Holz* wavy-grained; *Stoff* watered

Ge|flat|ter [gəˈflatɐ] NT **-s**, *no pl* fluttering; *(von Fahne etc: bei starkem Wind)* flapping

Ge|flecht [gəˈflɛçt] NT **-(e)s, -e** *(lit, fig)* network; *(= Gewebe)* weave; *(= Rohrgeflecht)* wickerwork, basketwork; *(von Haaren)* plaiting *(Brit)*, braiding *(US)*

ge|fleckt [gəˈflɛkt] ADJ spotted; *Blume, Vogel* speckled; *Haut* blotchy

Ge|flenn [gəˈflɛn] NT **-(e)s**, *no pl*, **Ge|flen|ne** [gəˈflɛnə] NT **-s**, *no pl (pej inf)* blubbering *(inf)*

Ge|flim|mer [gəˈflɪmɐ] NT **-s**, *no pl* shimmering; *(Film, TV)* flicker(ing); *(durch heiße Luft)* heat haze; *(von Stern)* twinkling

Ge|flis|sen|heit [gəˈflɪsnhait] F **-**, *no pl (geh)* = **Beflissenheit**

ge|flis|sent|lich [gəˈflɪsntlɪç] *(geh)* ADJ deliberate, intentional; **zur ~en Beachtung** *(form)* for your attention ADV deliberately, intentionally

ge|floch|ten *ptp von* **flechten**

ge|flo|gen *ptp von* **fliegen**

ge|flo|hen *ptp von* **fliehen**

ge|flos|sen *ptp von* **fließen**

Ge|flü|gel [gəˈflyːgl] NT **-s**, *no pl (Zool, Cook)* poultry *no pl*; *(= Vögel auch)* fowl

Ge|flü|gel- *in cpds (Cook)* chicken/turkey *etc*; *(allgemein)* poultry; **Ge|flü|gel|creme|sup|pe** F cream of chicken/turkey *etc* soup; **Ge|flü|gel|farm** F poultry farm, chicken *or* turkey *etc* farm; **Ge|flü|gel|fleisch** NT poultry; **Ge|flü|gel|händ|ler(in)** M(F) poulterer, poultry dealer; **Ge|flü|gel|hand|lung** F poulterer's; **Ge|flü|gel|klein** NT **-s**, *no pl* giblets *pl*; **Ge|flü|gel|le|ber** F chicken/turkey *etc* liver; **Ge|flü|gel|pest** F bird flu, avian influenza *or* flu; **Ge|flü|gel|sa|lat** M chicken/turkey *etc* salad; **Ge|flü|gel|sche|re** F poultry shears *pl*

ge|flü|gelt [gəˈflyːglt] ADJ winged; **~e Worte** familiar *or* standard quotations; **er spricht immer in ~en Worten** he always speaks in quotations

Ge|flü|gel|zucht F poultry farming

Ge|flun|ker [gəˈflʊŋkɐ] NT **-s**, *no pl (inf)* fibbing *(inf)*; **das ist alles ~** it's all lies *or* fibs *(inf)*

Ge|flüs|ter [gəˈflʏstɐ] NT **-s**, *no pl* whispering; *(von Bäumen, Blättern auch)* rustling

ge|foch|ten *ptp von* **fechten**

Ge|fol|ge [gəˈfɔlgə] NT **-s, -** retinue, entourage; *(= Trauergefolge)* cortege; *(fig)* wake; **im ~** in the wake *(+gen* of); **etw im ~ haben** *(fig)* to result in sth, to bring sth in its wake

Ge|folg|schaft [gəˈfɔlkʃaft] F **-, -en** **a** *(= die Anhänger)* following; *(NS: = Betriebsgefolgschaft)* workforce; *(Hist: = Gefolge)* retinue, entourage **b** *(= Treue)* fealty *(Hist)*, allegiance *(auch Hist)*, loyalty

Ge|folg|schafts|treue F fealty *(Hist)*, allegiance *(auch Hist)*, loyalty

Ge|folgs|mann M *pl* **-leute** *or* **-männer**, **Ge|folgs|frau** F follower; *(Hist)* liegeman/-woman

Ge|fra|ge [gəˈfraːgə] NT **-s**, *no pl (inf)* questions *pl*; **hör auf mit deinem ~!** stop pestering me with (your) questions!

ge|fragt [gəˈfraːkt] ADJ *Waren, Sänger etc* in demand *pred* → *auch* **fragen**

ge|frä|ßig [gəˈfrɛːsɪç] ADJ gluttonous; *(fig geh)* voracious; *Flammen, Feuer* all-enveloping; **~e Stille** *(hum)* the silence of people who enjoy their food

Ge|frä|ßig|keit F **-**, *no pl* gluttony; *(fig geh)* voracity

Ge|frei|te(r) [gəˈfraitə] MF *decl as adj (Mil)* lance corporal *(Brit)*, private first class *(US)*; *(Naut)* able seaman *(Brit)*, seaman apprentice *(US)*; *(Aviat)* leading aircraftman *(Brit)*, airman first class *(US)*

ge|fres|sen [gəˈfrɛsn] *ptp von* **fressen**

Ge|frett [gəˈfrɛt] NT **-s**, *no pl (Aus)* worry

Ge|frier-: **Ge|frier|beu|tel** M *(Cook)* freezer bag; **Ge|frier|box** F freezer box; **Ge|frier|brand** M *(Cook)* freezer burn; **Ge|frier|chi|rur|gie** F cryosurgery

ge|frie|ren *ptp* **gefroren** VI *irreg aux sein (lit, fig)* to freeze → **Blut**

Ge|frier-: **Ge|frier|fach** NT freezer *or* ice compartment, icebox *(esp US)*; **Ge|frier|fleisch** NT frozen meat; **Ge|frier|ge|mü|se** NT frozen vegetables *pl*; **ge|frier|ge|trock|net** [-gətrɔknət] ADJ freeze-dried; **Ge|frier|kost** F frozen food; **Ge|frier|punkt** M freezing point; *(von Thermometer)* zero; **auf dem ~ stehen** to be at freezing point/zero; **Temperaturen unter dem ~** temperatures below zero, temperatures below freezing (point); **Ge|frier|raum** M deepfreeze room; **Ge|frier|schrank** M (upright) freezer; **Ge|frier|schutz|mit|tel** NT *(Aut)* antifreeze; **Ge|frier|tem|pe|ra|tur** F freezing temperature; **Ge|frier|trock|nung** F **-**, *no pl* freeze-drying; **Ge|frier|tru|he** F freezer, deepfreeze; **Ge|frier|ver|fah|ren** NT freezing process

ge|fro|ren *ptp von* **frieren, gefrieren**

ge|fros|tet ADJ *Glas* frosted → *auch* **frosten**

ge|frus|tet ADJ *(inf)* frustrated; **ich bin total ~** I'm totally frustrated, I'm at my wits' end

Ge|fuch|tel [gəˈfʊxtl] NT **-s**, *no pl* gesticulating

Ge|fü|ge [gəˈfyːgə] NT **-s, -** *(lit, fig)* structure; *(= Baugefüge auch)* construction; *(= Aufbau)* structure, make-up

ge|fü|gig [gəˈfyːgɪç] ADJ *(= willfährig)* submissive; *(= gehorsam)* obedient; **jdn ~ machen** to make sb bend to one's will

Ge|fü|gig|keit F **-**, *no pl (= Willfährigkeit)* submissiveness; *(= Gehorsamkeit)* obedience

Ge|fühl [gəˈfyːl] NT **-(e)s, -e** **a** *(= Sinneswahrnehmung)* feeling; **etw im ~ haben** to have a feel for sth; **sie hat mehr ~ in den Fingern als ich** she has a better sense of touch than I do; **er hat kein ~ für heiß und kalt** he can't tell *or* feel the difference between hot and cold

b *(= seelische Empfindung, Ahnung)* feeling; *(= Emotionalität)* sentiment; **ich habe das ~, dass ...** I have the feeling that ...; **ich habe ein ~, als ob ...** I feel as though ...; **es geht gegen mein ~ ...** I don't like ...; **mein ~ täuscht mich nie** my instinct is never wrong; **jds ~e erwidern** to return sb's affection; **jds ~e verletzen** to hurt sb's feelings; **ein Mensch ohne ~** *(= hartherzig)* a person without any feelings; *(= gefühlskalt)* a person without any emotions; **er ist zu keinem menschlichen ~ fähig** he is incapable of (feeling) any human emotion; **~ und Verstand** emotion and reason, sense and sensibility; **die Romantik war das Zeitalter des ~s** romanticism was the age of sensibility; **das höchste der ~e** *(inf)* the ultimate

c *(= Verständnis)* feeling; *(= Sinn)* sense; **ein ~ für Zahlen/Musik** a feeling for figures/music; **ein ~ für Gerechtigkeit/Anstand/Proportionen/Rhythmus** a sense of justice/decency/proportion/rhythm; **Tiere haben ein ~ dafür, wer sie mag** animals can sense who likes them; **einen Apparat mit ~ behandeln** to treat an appliance sensitively

ge|füh|lig [gəˈfyːlɪç] ADJ *(pej geh)* mawkish

Ge|füh|lig|keit F **-**, *no pl (pej geh)* mawkishness

ge|fühl|los ADJ *(= unempfindlich, hartherzig)* insensitive; *(= mitleidlos)* callous, unfeeling; *Glieder* numb, dead *pred*; **ich habe ganz ~e Finger** my fingers are completely numb, my fingers have gone dead ADV coldly, callously; **sich ~ verhalten** to be cold

Ge|fühl|lo|sig|keit F **-, -en** *(= Unempfindlichkeit, Hartherzigkeit)* insensitivity; *(= Mitleidlosigkeit)* callousness; *(von Gliedern)* numbness, deadness

Ge|fühls-: **Ge|fühls|an|wand|lung** F (fit of) emotion; **ge|fühls|arm** ADJ unemotional; **Ge|fühls|ar|mut** F lack of emotion *or* feeling; **Ge|fühls|auf|wal|lung** F, **Ge|fühls|aus|bruch** M emotional outburst; **Ge|fühls|aus|bruch** M emotional outburst; **Ge|fühls|aus|druck** M, **Ge|fühls|äu|ße|rung** F expression of one's emotions; **ge|fühls|be|dingt**, **ge|fühls|be|stimmt** ADJ emotional; **ge|fühls|be|tont** ADJ emotional; *Rede, Äußerung auch* emotive; **Ge|fühls|din|ge** PL emotional matters *pl*; **Ge|fühls|du|se|lei** [-duːzəˈlai] F **-, -en** *(pej)* mawkishness; **ge|fühls|echt** ADJ *Lied, Gedicht* emotionally honest; *Kondom* ultrasensitive; **ge|fühls|ge|la|den** ADJ (very) emotional, emotionally charged; *Wort etc auch* emotive; **ge|fühls|kalt** ADJ cold; **Ge|fühls|käl|te** F coldness; **Ge|fühls|krüp|pel** M *(pej)* emotional cripple; **Ge|fühls|la|ge** F emotional state; **Ge|fühls|le|ben** NT emotional life; **ge|fühls|mä|ßig** ADJ *(= gefühlsgesteuert)* instinctive; *(= gefühlsbetont)* emotional ADV instinctively, emotionally; **Ge|fühls|mensch** M emotional person; **Ge|fühls|nerv** M sensory nerve; **Ge|fühls|re|gung** F stir of emotion; *(= seelische Empfindung)* feeling; **ge|fühls|roh** ADJ hard-hearted; **Ge|fühls|sa|che** F matter of feeling; **Kochen ist zum großen Teil ~** cooking is largely something you have a feel for; **Ge|fühls|schwel|ge|rei** F wallowing *no pl* in one's emotions; **ge|fühls|se|lig** ADJ sentimental; **Ge|fühls|se|lig|keit** F sentimentality; **ge|fühls|tief** ADJ intense; **Ge|fühls|tie|fe** F emotional depth, depth of feeling; **Ge|fühls|über|schwang** M flood of emotions; **Ge|fühls|wal|lung** F emotional outburst; **Ge|fühls|welt** F emotions *pl*

ge|fühl|voll ADJ **a** *(= empfindsam)* sensitive; *(= ausdrucksvoll)* expressive; *Volleystopp etc* delicate **b** *(= liebevoll)* loving ADV with (so much) feeling; *(= ausdrucksvoll)* expressively; **sehr ~ singen** to sing with feeling

ge|füllt [gəˈfʏlt] ADJ *Paprikaschoten etc* stuffed; *Brieftasche* full; **~e Pralinen** chocolates with soft centres *(Brit)*, candies with soft centers *(US)* → *auch* **füllen**

Ge|fum|mel [gəˈfʊml] NT **-s**, *no pl (inf)* fiddling *(inf)*; *(= Hantieren)* fumbling *(inf)*; *(erotisch)* groping *(inf)*; **diese Arbeit ist ein furchtbares ~** this work is a terrible fiddle *(Brit inf)*, this work is very tricky

ge|fun|den [gəˈfʊndn] *ptp von* **finden** ADJ **das war ein ~es Fressen für ihn** that was handing it to him on a plate

Ge|fun|kel [gəˈfʊŋkl] NT **-s**, *no pl (von Sonne, Glas, Wein etc)* sparkling; *(von Sternen auch)* twinkling; *(von Augen) (vor Freude)* gleaming, twinkling; *(vor Zorn)* flashing; *(von Edelsteinen)* glittering; *(von Edelmetall)* gleaming

ge|furcht [gəˈfʊrçt] ADJ *Stirn, Sand, Acker* furrowed; **eine von Sorgen ~e Stirn** a careworn brow → *auch* **furchen**

ge|fürch|tet [gəˈfʏrçtət] ADJ dreaded *usu attr*; **~ sein** to be feared → *auch* **fürchten**

ge|ga|belt [gəˈgaːblt] ADJ forked, bifurcate *(spec)*; *Zunge* forked → *auch* **gabeln**

Ge|ga|cker [gəˈgakɐ] NT **-s**, *no pl (lit, fig)* cackle, cackling

ge|gan|gen *ptp von* **gehen**

ge|ge|ben [gəˈgeːbn] *ptp von* **geben** ADJ **a** *(= bekannt)* given **b** *(= vorhanden)* given *attr*; *(Philos: = real)* factual; *Bedingung, Voraussetzung* fulfilled *pred*; **im ~en Fall ...** should the situation arise ...; **bei den ~en Tatsachen/der ~en Situation** given these facts/this situation; **etw als ~ voraussetzen** to assume sth **c** *(= günstig)* **zu ~er Zeit** in due course

ge|ge|be|nen|falls [gəˈgeːbnənˈfals] ADV should the situation arise; *(= wenn nötig)* if need be, if necessary; *(= eventuell)* possibly; *(Admin)* if applicable

Ge|ge|ben|heit [gəˈgeːbnhait] F **-, -en** *usu pl* (actual) fact; *(= Realität)* actuality; *(= Zustand)* condition; **sich mit den ~en abfinden** to come to terms with the facts as they are

ge|gen [ˈgeːgn] PREP *+acc* **a** *(= wider)* against; **X ~ Y** *(Sport, Jur)* X versus Y; **für oder ~** for or against; **~ seinen Befehl** contrary to *or* against his orders; **haben Sie ein Mittel ~ Schnupfen?** do you have anything for colds?; **etwas/nichts ~ jdn/etw haben** to have something/nothing against sb/sth; **~ etw sein** to be against sth, to be opposed to sth; **10 ~ 1 wetten** to bet 10 to 1

b *(= in Richtung auf)* towards, toward *(US)*; *(= nach)* to; *(= an)* against; **~ einen Baum rennen/prallen** to run/crash into a tree; **er pochte ~ das Tor** he hammered on the gate; **etw ~ das Licht halten** to hold sth to *or* against the light; **~ Osten** *etc* **fahren** to travel eastwards *(Brit) or*

eastward *(US) etc,* to travel to(wards) the east *etc;* **es wird ~ Abend kühler** it grows cooler toward(s) evening
c *(= ungefähr)* round about, around; *(= nicht mehr als)* getting on for; *(= nicht später als)* towards; **~ 5 Uhr** around 5 o'clock
d *(= gegenüber)* towards, to; **sie ist immer fair ~ mich gewesen** she's always been fair to me
e *(= im Austausch für)* for; **~ bar** for cash; **~ Bezahlung/Quittung** against payment/a receipt
f *(= verglichen mit)* compared with, in comparison with

Ge|gen-: **Ge|gen|ak|ti|on** F counteraction; **Ge|gen|an|ge|bot** NT counteroffer; **Ge|gen|an|griff** M *(Mil, fig)* counterattack; **Ge|gen|an|sicht** F opposite opinion; **Ge|gen|an|trag** M countermotion; *(Jur)* counterclaim; **Ge|gen|an|zei|ge** F *(Med)* contraindication; **Ge|gen|ar|gu|ment** NT counterargument; **Ge|gen|aus|sa|ge** F counterstatement; **Ge|gen|be|din|gung** F countercondition, counterstipulation; **Ge|gen|be|fehl** M *(Mil)* countermand, countercommand; **Ge|gen|be|haup|tung** F counterclaim; **Ge|gen|bei|spiel** NT counterexample; **Ge|gen|be|such** M return visit; **jdm einen ~ machen** to return sb's visit; **Ge|gen|be|we|gung** F *(Tech, fig)* countermovement; *(Mus)* contramotion; **Ge|gen|be|weis** M counterevidence *no indef art, no pl;* **den ~ zu etw erbringen** *or* **antreten** to produce evidence to counter sth; **bis zum ~ müssen wir ...** until we have evidence to the contrary we must ...; **Ge|gen|bu|chung** F cross entry

Ge|gend ['ge:gnt] F **-, -en** [-dn] area; *(= Wohngegend auch)* neighbourhood *(Brit),* neighborhood *(US),* district; *(= geografisches Gebiet, Körpergegend)* region; *(= Richtung)* direction; *(inf: = Nähe)* area; **die ~ von London, die Londoner ~** the London area; **er wohnt in der ~ des Bahnhofs** he lives in the area near the station; **Neuwied liegt in einer schönen ~** Neuwied is in a beautiful area; **eine schöne ~ Deutschlands** a beautiful part of Germany; **hier in der ~** (a)round here, in this area, hereabouts; **ungefähr in dieser ~** somewhere in this area; **die ganze ~ spricht davon** it's the talk of the neighbourhood *(Brit) or* neighborhood *(US);* **ein bisschen durch die ~ laufen** *(inf)* to have a stroll (a)round; **sie warfen die leeren Bierflaschen einfach in die ~** *(inf)* they just threw the empty beer bottles around anywhere; **brüll nicht so durch die ~** *(inf)* don't scream your head off *(inf)*

Ge|gen-: **Ge|gen|dar|stel|lung** F reply; **Ge|gen|de|monst|ra|ti|on** F counterdemonstration; **Ge|gen|dienst** M favour *(Brit) or* favor *(US)* in return; **jdm einen ~ leisten** *or* **erweisen** to return the favo(u)r, to do sb a favo(u)r in return; **Ge|gen|drei|er** M *(Sport)* bracket; **Ge|gen|druck** M, *no pl (Tech)* counterpressure; *(fig)* resistance → **Druck a**

ge|gen|ei|nan|der [ge:gnlai'nandɐ] ADV against each other *or* one another; *(= zueinander)* to(wards) each other *or* one another; *(= im Austausch)* for each other *or* one another; **sich ~ aufheben** to cancel each other *or* one another out; **sie haben etwas ~** they've got something against each other

Ge|gen|ei|nan|der [ge:gnlai'nandɐ] NT **-s,** *no pl* conflict

ge|gen|ei|nan|der-: **ge|gen|ei|nan|der+hal|ten** *sep irreg,* **ge|gen|ei|nan|der hal|ten** △ *irreg* VT *(lit)* to hold together; *(fig)* to compare; **ge|gen|ei|nan|der+pral|len** *sep,* **ge|gen|ei|nan|der pral|len** △ *aux sein* VI to collide; **ge|gen|ei|nan|der+ste|hen** *sep irreg (S Ger, Aus, Sw: aux sein),* **ge|gen|ei|nan|der ste|hen** △ *irreg (S Ger, Aus, Sw: aux sein)* VI *(fig)* to be on opposite sides; **im Wettbewerb ~** to be opponents; **ge|gen|ei|nan|der+stel|len** *sep,* **ge|gen|ei|nan|der stel|len** △ VT *(lit)* to put together; *(fig)* to compare; **ge|gen|ei|nan|der+sto|ßen** *sep irreg aux sein,* **ge|gen|ei|nan|der sto|ßen** △ *irreg aux sein* VI to bump into each other; *(= kollidieren)* to collide

Ge|gen-: **Ge|gen|ent|wurf** M alternative plan; **Ge|gen|er|klä|rung** F counterstatement; *(= Dementi)* denial, disclaimer; **Ge|gen|fahr|bahn** F oncoming carriageway *(Brit) or* highway *(US) or (= Spur)* lane; **Ge|gen|feu|er** NT backfire; **Ge|gen|fi|nan|zie|rung** F *(Pol) financing of state expenditure by means of cuts, tax increases etc;* **Ge|gen|for|de|rung** F counterdemand; *(Comm)* counterclaim; **Ge|gen|fra|ge** F counterquestion; **darf ich mit einer ~ antworten?** may I answer your question with another (of my own)?; **jdm eine ~ stellen** to ask sb a question in reply (to his); **Ge|gen|ga|be** F *(geh)* = **Gegengeschenk**; **Ge|gen|ge|ra|de** F *(Sport)* back straight, backstretch *(US);* **Ge|gen|ge|schenk** NT present *or* gift in return; **jdm etw als ~ überreichen** to give sb sth in return; **Ge|gen|ge|walt** F counterviolence; **Gewalt mit ~ beantworten** to counter violence with violence; **Ge|gen|ge|wicht** NT counterbalance *(auch fig),* counterweight, counterpoise; **als (ausgleichendes) ~ zu etw wirken** *(lit, fig)* to counterbalance sth; **Ge|gen|gift** NT antidote *(gegen* to); **Ge|gen|gleis** NT opposite track; **Ge|gen|grund** M reason against; **Gründe und Gegengründe (für etw)** reasons for and against (sth); **Ge|gen|gut|ach|ten** NT opposing opinion, counter-opinion; **ge|gen+hal|ten** VI *sep (= sich wehren)* to counter; *(= standhalten)* to stand one's ground; **Ge|gen|kai|ser** M *(Hist)* anti-emperor; **Ge|gen|kan|di|dat(in)** M(F) rival candidate; **als ~ zu jdm aufgestellt werden** to be put up as a candidate against sb; **Ge|gen|kla|ge** F *(Jur)* countercharge; **~ gegen jdn erheben** to put in a countercharge against sb, to countercharge sb; **Ge|gen|klä|ger(in)** M(F) *(Jur)* bringer of a countercharge; **Ge|gen|kö|nig** M *(Hist)* anti-king; **Ge|gen|kraft** F *(lit, fig)* counterforce; **Ge|gen|kul|tur** F alternative culture; **Ge|gen|kurs** M *(lit, fig)* opposite course; **einen ~ steuern** to take an opposing course of action; **ge|gen|läu|fig** ADJ *(Tech) Bewegung* contrarotating; *(fig) Tendenz, Entwicklung, Meinung* contrary, opposite; **Ge|gen|leis|tung** F service in return; **als ~ für etw** in return for sth; **ich erwarte keine ~** I don't expect anything in return; **ge|gen+len|ken** VI *sep (Aut)* to steer in the opposite direction; **ge|gen+le|sen** VTI *sep irreg* to countercheck; **Ge|gen|licht** NT **bei ~ Auto fahren** to drive with the light in one's eyes; **etw bei** *or* **im ~ aufnehmen** *(Phot)* to take a backlit *or* contre-jour photo(graph) of sth

Ge|gen|licht- *(Phot)*: **Ge|gen|licht|auf|nah|me** F backlit *or* contre-jour photo(graph) *or* shot; **Ge|gen|licht|blen|de** F lens hood

Ge|gen-: **Ge|gen|lie|be** F requited love; *(fig: = Zustimmung)* approval; **sie fand keine ~** *(lit)* her love was not returned *or* reciprocated; *(fig)* she met with no approval; **auf ~/wenig ~ stoßen** *(fig)* to be welcomed/hardly welcomed with open arms; **Ge|gen|macht** F hostile power; **Ge|gen|maß|nah|me** F countermeasure; **~n zur Bekämpfung der Inflation** measures to counter inflation; **Ge|gen|mei|nung** F opposite view *or* opinion; **Ge|gen|mit|tel** NT *(Med)* antidote *(gegen* to); **Ge|gen|mut|ter** F *pl* **-muttern** *(Tech)* locknut; **Ge|gen|of|fen|si|ve** F *(lit, fig)* counteroffensive; **Ge|gen|papst** M *(Hist)* antipope; **Ge|gen|part** M *(= Theat, Mus)* opposite number; **Ge|gen|par|tei** F other side; *(Sport)* opposing side; *(Jur)* opposing party; **Ge|gen|pol** M counterpole; *(fig)* antithesis *(zu* of, to); **Ge|gen|po|si|ti|on** F opposite standpoint; **Ge|gen|pro|be** F crosscheck; **die ~ zu etw machen** to carry out a crosscheck on sth, to crosscheck sth; **Ge|gen|pro|pa|gan|da** F counterpropaganda; **Ge|gen|re|ak|ti|on** F counter-reaction; **Ge|gen|rech|nung** F **a** *(Math: = Gegenprobe)* crosscheck **b** *(Comm)* set-off; *(= Gegenschuld)* offset; **die ~ aufmachen** *(fig)* to present one's own reckoning; **Ge|gen|re|de** F *(= Antwort)* reply; *(= Widerrede)* contradiction; **eine ~ zu jds Rede halten** to reply to sb's speech; **keine ~!** no contradiction!; **Rede und ~** dialogue *(Brit),* dialog *(US);* **eine Diskussion, in der Rede und ~ einander abwechseln** a discussion with a lively exchange between the speakers; **Ge|gen|re|for|ma|ti|on** F *(Hist)* Counter-Reformation; **Ge|gen|re|gie|rung** F rival government; **Ge|gen|re|vo|lu|ti|on** F counter-revolution; **Ge|gen|rich|tung** F opposite direction; **Ge|gen|ru|der** NT opposed control surfaces *pl*

Ge|gen|satz ✪ 32.1 M *(= konträrer Gegensatz)* contrast; *(= kontradiktorischer Gegensatz, Gegenteil)* opposite; *(= Unvereinbarkeit)* conflict; *(= Unterschied)* difference; *(Philos)* antithesis; *(Mus)* countersubject; **Gegensätze** *(= Meinungsverschiedenheiten)* differences *pl;* **im ~ zu** unlike, in contrast to; **Marx, im ~ zu ...** Marx, as against ...; **er, im ~ zu mir, ...** unlike me, he ...; **einen krassen ~ zu etw bilden** to contrast sharply with sth; **Gegensätze ziehen einander** *or* **sich an** *(prov)* opposites attract; **im ~ zu etw stehen** to conflict with sth; **Gegensätze ausgleichen** to even out differences; **unüberbrückbare Gegensätze** irreconcilable differences

ge|gen|sätz|lich ['ge:gnzɛtslɪç] ADJ *(= konträr)* contrasting; *(= widersprüchlich)* opposing; *(= unterschiedlich)* different; *(= unvereinbar)* conflicting; **Schwarz und Weiß sind ~e Begriffe** black and white are opposites; **eine ~e Meinung** a conflicting view ADV **sie verhalten sich völlig ~** they behave in totally different ways; **~ veranlagt sein** to have contradictory characteristics

Ge|gen|sätz|lich|keit F **-, -en** (+*gen* between) *(= Kontrast)* contrast; *(= Widersprüchlichkeit)* opposition; *(= Unterschiedlichkeit)* difference; *(= Unvereinbarkeit)* conflict; **die ~ dieser beiden Systeme** the contrast between *or* contrasting nature of these two systems; **bei aller ~ ...** in spite of all (the) differences ...

Ge|gen|satz|paar NT pair of opposites

Ge|gen-: **Ge|gen|schlag** M *(Mil)* reprisal; *(fig)* retaliation *no pl;* **einen ~ (gegen jdn) führen** to strike back (at sb); **zum ~ ausholen** to prepare to retaliate; **Ge|gen|sei|te** F *(lit, fig)* other side; *(= gegenüberliegende Seite auch)* opposite side; **ge|gen|sei|tig** ['ge:gnzaitɪç] ADJ mutual; *(= wechselseitig auch)* reciprocal; **in ~em Einverständnis** by mutual agreement ADV each other, one another; **sie beschuldigten sich ~** they (each) accused one another *or* each other; **sich ~ bedingen** to be contingent (up)on one another *or* each other; **sich ~ ausschließen** to be mutually exclusive, to exclude one another; **Ge|gen|sei|tig|keit** F **-,** *no pl* mutuality; *(= Wechselseitigkeit auch)* reciprocity; **ein Abkommen/Vertrag auf ~** a reciprocal agreement/treaty; **Versicherung auf ~** mutual insurance; **das beruht auf ~** the feeling is mutual; **Ge|gen|sei|tig|keits|prin|zip** NT, *no pl (Pol etc)* principle of reciprocity, reciprocity principle; **Ge|gen|sinn** M, *no pl* **im ~** in the opposite direction; **ge|gen|sin|nig** ADJ *(Tech)* in the opposite direction; *(= widersprüchlich)* contradictory; **Ge|gen|spie|ler(in)** M(F) opponent; *(bei Mannschaftsspielen auch)* opposite number; *(Liter)* antagonist; **Ge|gen|spi|o|na|ge** F counterespionage, counterintelligence; **Ge|gen|sprech|an|la|ge** F (two-way) intercom; *(Telec)* duplex (system); **Ge|gen|sprech|ver|kehr** M two-way communication

Ge|gen|stand M *(= Ding)* object, thing; *(Econ: = Artikel)* article; *(= Thema, Angelegenheit, Stoff)* subject; *(von Gespräch, Diskussion)* subject, topic; *(der Neugier, des Hasses etc, Philos)* object; *(Aus: = Schulfach)* subject; **ein harter ~ fiel ihm auf den Kopf** something hard *or* a hard object fell on his head; **sie wurde mit einem stumpfen ~ erschlagen** she was killed by a blow from a blunt instrument; **~ des Gespötts** laughing stock, object of ridicule; *(Mensch auch)* figure of fun

ge|gen|ständ|lich [ˈgeːgnʃtɛntlɪç] ADJ concrete; *(Philos)* objective; *(Art)* representational; *(= anschaulich)* graphic(al); **die ~e Welt** the world of objects

Ge|gen|ständ|lich|keit F -, *no pl* concreteness; *(Philos)* objectivity; *(Art)* representationalism; *(= Anschaulichkeit)* graphic(al)ness

Ge|gen|stand|punkt M opposite point of view

Ge|gen|stands-: **ge|gen|stands|los** ADJ *(= überflüssig)* redundant, unnecessary; *(= grundlos)* unfounded, groundless; *(= hinfällig)* irrelevant; *(Art)* non-representational, abstract; **bitte betrachten Sie dieses Schreiben als ~, falls ...** please disregard this notice if ...; **Ge|gen|stands|lo|sig|keit** F -, *no pl (Art)* abstraction; **Ge|gen|stands|wort** NT *pl* **-wörter** concrete noun

Ge|gen-: **ge|gen+steu|ern** VI *sep (Aut)* to steer in the opposite direction; *(fig)* to take countermeasures; **Ge|gen|stim|me** F *(Parl)* vote against; **der Antrag wurde mit 250 Stimmen bei** *or* **und 30 ~n angenommen** the motion was carried by 250 votes to 30; **der Antrag wurde ohne ~n angenommen** the motion was carried unanimously; **Ge|gen|stoß** M *(Mil, Sport)* counterattack; **Ge|gen|stra|te|gie** F *(Mil, Pol, Sport)* counterstrategy; **Ge|gen|strö|mung** F *(lit, fig)* countercurrent; **Ge|gen|stück** NT opposite; *(= passendes Gegenstück)* counterpart

Ge|gen|teil NT, *no pl* opposite *(von* of); *(= Umkehrung)* reverse *(von* of); **im ~!** on the contrary!; **ganz im ~** quite the reverse; **das ~ bewirken** to have the opposite effect; *(Mensch)* to achieve the exact opposite; **ins ~ umschlagen** to swing to the other extreme; **eine Äußerung ins ~ umkehren** *or* **verkehren** to twist a statement to mean just the opposite

ge|gen|tei|lig ADJ *Ansicht, Wirkung, Erfahrung* opposite, contrary; **eine ~e Meinung** a contrary opinion; **~e Aussagen** contradictory statements; **~e Behauptungen** statements to the contrary; **ich habe nichts Gegenteiliges gehört** I've heard nothing to the contrary ADV **sich ~ entscheiden** to come to a different decision

Ge|gen|teils|be|weis M *(Jur)* evidence to the contrary

Ge|gen|tor NT *(esp Ftbl, Sport)* **sie konnten ein ~ verhindern** they managed to stop any goals being scored against them; **ein ~ hinnehmen müssen** to concede a goal; **ein ~ erzielen** to score

Ge|gen|tref|fer M *(Sport)* = **Gegentor**

ge|gen|über [geːgnˈlyːbɐ] PREP +*dat* **a** *(örtlich)* opposite; **er wohnt mir ~** he lives opposite me, he lives across from me; **er saß mir genau/schräg ~** he sat directly opposite *or* facing me/diagonally across from me **b** *(= zu)* to; *(= in Bezug auf)* with regard *or* respect to, as regards; *(= angesichts, vor)* in the face of; *(= im Vergleich zu)* in comparison with, compared with; **mir ~ hat er das nicht geäußert** he didn't say that to me; **allem Politischen ~ ist er misstrauisch** he's distrustful of anything political, he's distrustful as far as anything political is concerned; **er ist allem Neuen ~ wenig aufgeschlossen** he's not very open-minded about anything new *or* where anything new is concerned ADV opposite; **der Park ~** the park opposite; **die Leute von ~** *(inf)* the people opposite

Ge|gen|über [geːgnˈlyːbɐ] NT **-s, -** *(bei Kampf)* opponent; *(bei Diskussion)* opposite number; **mein ~ im Zug/am Tisch** the person (sitting) opposite me in the train/at (the) table; **wir haben einen freien Ausblick und kein ~** we've an open view with no building opposite

ge|gen|über-: **ge|gen|über+lie|gen** VI *sep irreg +dat* to be opposite, to face; **sich** *(dat)* **~** to face each other; **ge|gen|über|lie|gend** ADJ *attr* opposite; **das ~e Grundstück** the plot of land opposite; **der der Hypotenuse ~e Winkel** the angle opposite *or* facing the hypotenuse; **ge|gen|über+se|hen** VR *sep irreg +dat* **sich einer Aufgabe ~** to be faced *or* confronted with a task; **ge|gen|über+sit|zen** VI *sep irreg +dat* to sit opposite *or* facing; **ge|gen|über+ste|hen** VI *sep irreg +dat* to be opposite, to face; *jdm* to stand opposite *or* facing; **jdm feindlich/freundlich/desinteressiert ~** to have a hostile/friendly/disinterested attitude toward(s) sb; **einem Plan freundlich ~** to be favourably *(Brit)* *or* favorably *(US)* disposed to a plan; **einer Gefahr ~** to be faced with a danger; **ge|gen|über+stel|len** VT *sep (= konfrontieren mit)* to confront (+*dat* with); *(fig: = vergleichen)* to compare (+*dat* with); **sich einer Sache** *(dat)* **gegenübergestellt sehen** to be faced *or* confronted with sth; **Ge|gen|über|stel|lung** F confrontation; *(fig: = Vergleich)* comparison; **ge|gen|über|+tre|ten** VI *sep irreg aux sein* **jdm ~** to face sb

Ge|gen-: **Ge|gen|ver|kehr** M oncoming traffic; **Ge|gen|vor|schlag** M counterproposal

Ge|gen|wart [ˈgeːgnvart] F -, *no pl* **a** *(= jetziger Augenblick)* present; *(= heutiges Zeitalter)* present (time *or* day); *(Gram)* present (tense); **in der ~ leben** to live in the present; *(= den Augenblick genießen)* to live for the present *or* for today; **die Literatur/Musik der ~** contemporary literature/music; **die Probleme der ~** the problems of today, today's problems; **in der ~ stehen** *(Gram)* to be in the present (tense) **b** *(= Anwesenheit)* presence; **in ~** +*gen* in the presence of

ge|gen|wär|tig [ˈgeːgnvɛrtɪç, geːgnˈvɛrtɪç] ADJ **a** *attr (= jetzig)* present; *(= heutig)* present, current, present-day; **der ~e Minister** the present minister; **der ~e Preis** the current price **b** *(geh: = anwesend)* present *pred*; **es ist mir im Moment nicht ~** I can't recall it at the moment ADV **a** *(= augenblicklich)* at present, at the moment; *(= heutzutage)* at present, currently **b sich** *(dat)* **etw ~ halten** *(geh)* to bear sth in mind

Ge|gen|wär|tig|keit F -, *no pl* **a** *(= Anwesenheit)* presence **b** *(mit Bezug zur Gegenwart)* present-day relevance

Ge|gen|warts-: **ge|gen|warts|be|zo|gen** [-bətsoːgn] ADJ relevant to present times; **ein sehr ~er Mensch** a person whose life revolves very much (a)round the present; **Ge|gen|warts|be|zug** M relevance (to present times); **Ge|gen|warts|deutsch** NT modern German; **Ge|gen|warts|form** F *(Gram)* present (tense); **ge|gen|warts|fremd** ADJ out-of-touch (with reality); **Ge|gen|warts|kunst** F contemporary art; **ge|gen|warts|nah, ge|gen|warts|na|he** ADJ relevant (to the present); **Ge|gen|warts|nä|he** F relevance (to the present); **Ge|gen|warts|prob|lem** NT current *or* topical problem; **Ge|gen|warts|ro|man** M contemporary novel; **Ge|gen|warts|schaf|fen** NT contemporary scene; **Ge|gen|warts|spra|che** F present-day language; **die englische ~** modern English

Ge|gen-: **Ge|gen|wehr** F resistance; **Ge|gen|wert** M equivalent; **es wurden Waren im ~ von 8.000 Euro entwendet** goods to the value of *or* worth 8,000 euros were taken; **Ge|gen|wind** M headwind; **wir hatten starken ~** there was a strong headwind; **Ge|gen|win|kel** M *(Geom)* opposite angle; *(korrespondierend)* corresponding angle; **Ge|gen|wir|kung** F reaction, counteraction; **diese Tabletten können eine ~ haben** these tablets can have the opposite effect; **ge|gen+zeich|nen** VT *sep* to countersign; **Ge|gen|zeich|nung** F *(= Unterschrift)* countersignature; *(= das Unterschreiben)* countersigning; **Ge|gen|zeu|ge** M, **Ge|gen|zeu|gin** F witness for the other side; **Ge|gen|zug** M **a** countermove; **im ~ zu etw** as a countermove to sth **b** *(= Luftzug)* cross-draught *(Brit)*, cross-draft *(US)* **c** *(Rail)* corresponding train in the other direction; *(= entgegenkommender Zug)* oncoming train

ge|ges|sen *ptp von* **essen**

ge|gli|chen *ptp von* **gleichen**

ge|glie|dert [gəˈgliːdɐt] ADJ jointed; *(fig)* structured; *(= organisiert)* organized; **das ~e Schulwesen** the tiered school system → *auch* **gliedern**

ge|glit|ten *ptp von* **gleiten**

Ge|glit|zer [gəˈglɪtsɐ] NT **-s,** *no pl* glitter(ing)

ge|glom|men *ptp von* **glimmen**

Geg|ner [ˈgeːgnɐ] M **-s, -**, **Geg|ne|rin** [-ərɪn] F **-, -nen** opponent *(auch Sport)*, adversary; *(= Rivale)* rival; *(= Feind)* enemy; **ein ~ der Todesstrafe sein** to be against *or* opposed to capital punishment

geg|ne|risch [ˈgeːgnərɪʃ] ADJ *attr* opposing; *(Mil: = feindlich)* enemy *attr*, hostile; *Übermacht* of the enemy; **das ~e Tor** the opponents' goal

Geg|ner|schaft [ˈgeːgnɐʃaft] F **-, -en** opposition

ge|gol|ten *ptp von* **gelten**

ge|go|ren *ptp von* **gären**

ge|gos|sen *ptp von* **gießen**

gegr. *abbr von* **gegründet** established, est.

ge|gra|ben *ptp von* **graben**

ge|grif|fen *ptp von* **greifen**

Ge|grin|se [gəˈgrɪnzə] NT **-s,** *no pl (inf)* grin(-ning)

Ge|grö|le [gəˈgrøːlə] NT **-s,** *no pl (inf)* raucous bawling *(inf)*

Ge|grü|bel [gəˈgryːbl] NT **-s,** *no pl (inf)* worrying

Ge|grun|ze [gəˈgrʊntsə] NT **-s,** *no pl* grunting

Ge|ha|be [gəˈhaːbə] NT **-s,** *no pl (inf)* affected behaviour *(Brit)* *or* behavior *(US)*

ge|ha|ben [gəˈhaːbn] *ptp* **gehabt** VR *(old, Aus)* to behave, to deport oneself *(old, form)*; **gehab dich wohl!** *(old, dial)* farewell! *(old)*

ge|habt [gəˈhaːpt] *ptp von* **haben**

Ge|hack|te(s) [gəˈhaktə] NT *decl as adj* mince *(Brit)*, minced *(Brit)* *or* ground *(US)* meat

Ge|halt [gəˈhalt] M **-(e)s, -e a** *(= Anteil)* content; **der ~ an Eiweiß/Kohlenhydraten** the protein/carbohydrate content; **ein hoher ~ an Kohlenmonoxid** a high carbon monoxide content **b** *(fig) (= Inhalt)* content; *(= Substanz)* substance; **~ und Gestalt** *(Liter)* form and content

Ge|halt NT OR (AUS) M **-(e)s, ⸚er** [gəˈhɛltɐ] salary; *(esp Eccl)* stipend

ge|hal|ten [gəˈhaltn] *ptp von* **halten** ADJ **~ sein, etw zu tun** *(form)* to be required to do sth

Ge|halt-: **ge|halt|los** ADJ *Nahrung* non-nutritious; *(fig)* empty; *(= oberflächlich)* shallow, empty; **dieses Brot ist ziemlich ~** there's not much nourishment in this bread; **ge|halt|reich** ADJ **a** *Erz* high-yield **b** = **gehaltvoll**

Ge|halts-: **Ge|halts|ab|rech|nung** F salary statement; **die ~ ist abgeschlossen** the salaries have been worked out; **Ge|halts|ab|zug** M salary deduction; **Ge|halts|an|glei|chung** F salary adjustment; **Ge|halts|an|spruch** M salary claim; **Ge|halts|auf|bes|se|rung** F salary increase; **Ge|halts|be|schei|ni|gung** F salary declaration; **Ge|halts|emp|fän|ger(in)** M(F) salary-earner; **~ sein** to receive a salary, to be salaried; **die Firma hat 500 ~** the firm has 500 employees *or* salaried staff; **Ge|halts|er|hö|hung** F salary increase, rise *(Brit)* *or* raise *(esp US)* in salary; *(regelmäßig)* increment; **Ge|halts|for|de|rung** F salary claim; **Ge|halts|fort|zah|lung** F continued payment of salary; **Ge|halts|grup|pe** F, **Ge|halts|klas|se** F salary bracket; **er ist in der ~ 6** he's on grade 6 on the salary scale; **Ge|halts|kon|to** NT current account *(Brit)*, checking account *(US)*; **Ge|halts|kür|zung** F cut in salary; **Ge|halts|mit|tei|lung** F salary statement; **Ge|halts|nach|zah|lung** F back payment; **Ge|halts|pfän|dung** F deduction of salary (at source); **Ge|halts|stei|ge|rung** F increase in salary; **Ge|halts|strei|fen** M salary slip; **Ge|halts|stufe** F = **Gehaltsgruppe**; **Ge|halts|ver|hand|lung** F salary negotiations *pl*; **Ge|halts|vor|rü|ckung** F **-, -en** *(Aus)* = **Gehaltserhöhung**; **Ge|halts|vor|stel|lung** F, **Ge|halts|wunsch** M salary requirement; **Ge|halts|zah|lung** F salary payment; **der Tag der ~ ist**

der 28. salaries are paid on the 28th; **Ge|halts|zet|tel** M *(inf)* pay slip; **Ge|halts|zu|la|ge** F *(= Gehaltserhöhung)* salary increase, rise *(Brit) or* raise *(esp US)* in salary; *(regelmäßige)* increment; *(= Extrazulage)* salary bonus

ge|halt|voll ADJ *Speise* nutritious, nourishing; *Wein* full-bodied; *(fig)* rich in content; **ein ~es Buch** a book which says a great deal

Ge|häm|mer [gəˈhɛmɐ] NT **-s,** *no pl* hammering

ge|han|di|capt, ge|han|di|kapt [gəˈhɛndikɛpt] ADJ handicapped *(durch* by) → *auch* **handicapen**

Ge|hän|ge [gəˈhɛŋə] NT **-s, -** **a** garland; *(= Ohrgehänge)* drop, pendant **b** *(= Wehrgehänge)* ammunition belt **c** *(Min: = Abhang)* declivity, incline **d** *(Build)* system of fascines **e** *(sl: = Geschlechtsorgane)* goolies *pl (Brit inf)*, balls *pl (inf)*

ge|han|gen *ptp von* **hängen**

Ge|häng|te(r) [gəˈhɛŋtə] MF *decl as adj* hanged man/woman; **die ~n** the hanged

Ge|hän|sel [gəˈhɛnzl] NT **-s,** *no pl (inf)* mocking; **hört auf mit dem ~!** stop making fun of me/him *etc!*

ge|har|nischt [gəˈharnɪʃt] ADJ *(Hist: = gepanzert)* armour-clad *(Brit)*, armor-clad *(US)*; *(fig) Brief, Abfuhr etc* strong; *Antwort* sharp, sharply-worded; **ein ~er Ritter** a knight in armour *(Brit) or* armor *(US)*

ge|häs|sig [gəˈhɛsɪç] ADJ spiteful ADV spitefully; **~ von jdm reden** to say nasty things about sb

Ge|häs|sig|keit F **-, -en** spite, spitefulness; **~en** spiteful things; **jdm ~en sagen** to be spiteful to sb

Ge|haue [gəˈhauə] NT **-s,** *no pl (inf)* fisticuffs *(inf)*; **Schluss mit dem ewigen ~!** stop fighting all the time!

ge|hau|en *ptp von* **hauen**

ge|häuft [gəˈhɔyft] ADJ *Löffel* heaped; **ein ~er Teelöffel Salz** a heaped teaspoonful of salt; **das ~e Auftreten bestimmter Krankheiten** the frequent occurrence of certain diseases ADV in large numbers; **dieser Fehler tritt ~ auf** this error occurs more and more frequently → *auch* **häufen**

Ge|häu|se [gəˈhɔyzə] NT **-s, -** **a** case; *(= Radiogehäuse, Kameragehäuse, Uhrgehäuse, Kompassgehäuse)* case, casing; *(= Lautsprechergehäuse)* box; *(= großes Lautsprechergehäuse, Radiogehäuse)* cabinet **b** *(= Schneckengehäuse)* shell **c** *(= Obstgehäuse)* core

geh|be|hin|dert [ˈgeːbəhɪndɐt] ADJ unable to walk properly

Geh|be|hin|der|te(r) [ˈgeːbəhɪndɐtə] MF *decl as adj* person with walking difficulties, physically challenged person *(esp US)*

Geh|bock M *pl* **-böcke** *(= Laufhilfe)* walker, walking frame

Ge|he|ge [gəˈheːgə] NT **-s, -** reserve; *(im Zoo)* enclosure, compound; *(= Wildgehege)* preserve; **jdm ins ~ kommen** *(fig inf)* to get under sb's feet *(inf)*; *(= ein Recht streitig machen)* to poach on sb's preserves

ge|hei|ligt [gəˈhailɪçt] ADJ *Brauch, Tradition, Recht, Prinzip, Symbol* sacred; *Räume* sacrosanct; **sein ~es Mittagsschläfchen** *(inf)* his precious afternoon nap → *auch* **heiligen**

ge|heim [gəˈhaim] ADJ secret; **seine ~sten Gefühle/Wünsche/Gedanken** his innermost *or* most private feelings/wishes/thoughts; **streng ~** top secret; **die ~en Verführer** the hidden persuaders; **Geheimer Rat** privy council; *(Mitglied)* privy councillor; **~ bleiben** to remain (a) secret; **im Geheimen** in secret, secretly ADV secretly; **~ abstimmen** to vote by secret ballot → *auch* **geheimtun**

Ge|heim- *in cpds* secret; **Ge|heim|agent(in)** M(F) secret agent; **Ge|heim|bund** M *pl* **-bünde** secret society; **Ge|heim|dienst** M secret service; **Ge|heim|dienst|ler** [-diːnstlɐ] M **-s, -**, **Ge|heim|dienst|le|rin** [-ərɪn] F **-, -nen** *(inf)* man/woman from the secret service; **Ge|heim|fach** NT secret compartment; *(= Schublade)* secret drawer; **Ge|heim|fa|vo|rit** M personal favourite *(Brit) or* favorite *(US)*; **ge|heim hal|ten** VT *irreg* **etw (vor jdm) ~** to keep sth a secret (from sb)

Ge|heim|hal|tung F, *no pl* secrecy; **zur ~ von etw verpflichtet sein** to be sworn to secrecy about sth

Ge|heim|hal|tungs-: Ge|heim|hal|tungs|pflicht F obligation to maintain secrecy; **Ge|heim|hal|tungs|stu|fe** F security classification

Ge|heim-: Ge|heim|kon|to NT private *or* secret account; **Ge|heim|leh|re** F esoteric doctrine

Ge|heim|nis [gəˈhaimnɪs] NT **-ses, -se** secret; *(= rätselhaftes Geheimnis)* mystery; **das ~ der Schönheit/des Erfolgs** the secret of beauty/success; **das ~ der Auferstehung/des Lebens** the mystery of the Resurrection/of life; **ein offenes** *or* **öffentliches** *(rare)* **~** an open secret; **das ist das ganze ~** *(inf)* that's all there is to it; **aus etw ein/kein ~ machen** to make a big secret about sth/no secret of sth; **sie hat ein süßes ~** *(inf)* she's expecting a happy event

Ge|heim|nis-: Ge|heim|nis|krä|mer(in) M(F) *(inf)* secretive person; **Ge|heim|nis|krä|me|rei** [-krɛːməˈrai] F **-, -en** *(inf)* secretiveness; **Ge|heim|nis|trä|ger(in)** M(F) bearer of secrets; **Ge|heim|nis|tu|er** [-tuːɐ] M **-s, -**, **Ge|heim|nis|tu|e|rin** [-ərɪn] F **-, -nen** secretive person; **Ge|heim|nis|tu|e|rei** F secretiveness; **ge|heim|nis|tu|e|risch** [-tuːərɪʃ] ADJ secretive; **ge|heim|nis|um|wit|tert** ADJ *(geh)* shrouded in mystery *(liter)*; **Ge|heim|nis|ver|rat** M ≈ offence under the Official Secrets Act *(Brit)*, ≈ treason against the State *(US)*; **ge|heim|nis|voll** ADJ mysterious; **~ tun** to be mysterious; **mit etw ~ tun** to make a big mystery of sth

Ge|heim-: Ge|heim|num|mer F secret number *(auch Telec)*; *(= Geheimzahl, PIN)* PIN (number), personal identification number; **Ge|heim|po|li|zei** F secret police; **Ge|heim|po|li|zist(in)** M(F) member of the secret police; **Ge|heim|rat** M, **Ge|heim|rä|tin** F privy councillor; **Ge|heim|rats|ecken** PL *(inf)* receding hairline *sing*; **er hat ~** he has a receding hairline; **Ge|heim|re|zept** NT secret recipe; **Ge|heim|schloss** NT combination lock; **Ge|heim|schrift** F code, secret writing; **Ge|heim|tin|te** F invisible ink; **Ge|heim|tipp** M (personal) tip; **Ge|heim|trep|pe** F secret staircase; **ge|heim+tun** *sep irreg*, **ge|heim tun** *irreg* VI to be secretive; **mit etw ~** to be secretive about sth; **Ge|heim|tür** F secret door; **Ge|heim|waf|fe** F secret weapon; **Ge|heim|wis|sen|schaft** F secret *or* esoteric lore; **Ge|heim|zahl** F PIN (number), personal identification number; **Ge|heim|zei|chen** NT secret sign; *(= Chiffre)* cipher

Ge|heiß [gəˈhais] NT **-es,** *no pl (geh)* behest *(old, form) no pl*; **auf jds ~** *(acc)* at sb's behest *or* bidding

ge|hei|ßen *ptp von* **heißen**

ge|hemmt [gəˈhɛmt] ADJ *Mensch* inhibited; *Benehmen* self-conscious ADV *sich benehmen* in an inhibited way, self-consciously; **~ sprechen** to have inhibitions in speaking → *auch* **hemmen**

ge|hen [ˈgeːən] *aux sein*
pret **ging** [gɪŋ], *ptp* **gegangen** [gəˈgaŋən]
✪ 43.4, 53.1

1 INTRANSITIVES VERB	3 UNPERSÖNLICHES VERB
2 TRANSITIVES VERB	4 REFLEXIVES VERB

1 – INTRANSITIVES VERB

a to go; **wo er geht und steht, singt er** everywhere he goes, he sings; **gehen wir!** let's go!; **ich muss gehen** I must go *or* be off; **bitte gehen Sie!** *(= verlassen Sie das Zimmer)* please leave!; *(Vortritt gewährend)* after you!; **geh doch!** go on (then)!; **geh schon!** go on!; **wie geht man dorthin?** how do you get there?; **er ist gegangen worden** *(hum inf)* he was given the push *(hum inf)*; **er ist von uns gegangen** *(euph)* he has passed away; **der Schmerz ging sehr tief** the pain went very deep

♦ **gehen + Infinitiv schwimmen/tanzen gehen** to go swimming/dancing; **spielen gehen** to go and play; **schlafen gehen** to go to bed

b = zu Fuß gehen to go, to walk; **das Kind lernt gehen** the baby is learning to walk; **am Stock** *(dat)* **gehen** to walk with a stick; **an Krücken** *(dat)* **gehen** to walk with *or* on crutches; **auf Stelzen** *(dat)* **gehen** to walk on stilts; **wie lange geht man bis zum Bus?** how long a walk is it to the bus?; **er ging im Zimmer auf und ab** he walked up and down the room; **das Pferd geht (im Schritt)** the horse is walking; **das Pferd geht Trab** the horse is trotting

c mit Präposition

In Verbindung mit Präpositionen siehe auch unter dem Eintrag für die Präposition.

♦ **gehen + als** *(= sich verkleiden)* to go as sth; **als Schreiner gehen** *(dial: = arbeiten)* to work as a carpenter

♦ **gehen + an er ging an den Tisch** he went to the table; **gehen Sie (mir) nicht an meine Sachen!** don't touch my things!; **er ist an meine Geldbörse gegangen** he went into my purse; **das Erbe ging an ihn** the inheritance went to him → *auch* **b**

♦ **gehen + auf sie gingen auf den Berg** they went up the mountain; **sie ging auf die Straße** she went out into the street; **auf die andere Seite gehen** to cross to the other side, to go over to the other side; **das Fenster geht auf den Hof** the window overlooks the yard; **diese Tür geht auf den Balkon** this door leads onto the balcony; **das geht auf sein Konto** *or* **auf ihn** he's responsible for that; **das ging auf Sie!** that was aimed at you!; **das Bier geht auf mich** *(inf)* the beer's on me; **auf wen geht das Bier?** *(inf)* who's paying for the beer? → *auch* **b**

♦ **gehen + aus sie ging aus dem Zimmer** she went out of *or* left the room; **er ist wieder ohne Schirm aus dem Haus gegangen** he's gone out without his umbrella again; **jdm aus dem Licht/Weg gehen** to get out of sb's light/way

♦ **gehen + bis er ging bis zum Zaun** he went up to the fence; **er ging bis zur Straße** he went as far as the street; **das Wasser ging ihm bis zum Bauch** the water went up to his waist; **der Rock ging ihr bis zum Knöchel** the skirt went down to her ankles

♦ **gehen + durch wir gingen durch den Wald** we went through the wood; **das Klavier geht nicht durch die Tür** the piano won't go *or* fit through the door

♦ **gehen + gegen das geht gegen meine Prinzipien** *or* **meine Überzeugung** it's against my principles

♦ **gehen + in geh mal in die Küche** go into the kitchen; **du kannst unmöglich in einem roten Mantel zu einer Beerdigung gehen** you can't possibly go to a funeral in a red coat, you can't possibly wear a red coat to a funeral; **ins Kloster gehen** *(Mann)* to enter a monastery; *(Frau)* to enter a convent; **in die Industrie/Politik gehen** to go into industry/politics; **in die Gewerkschaft/Partei gehen** to join the union/party; **wie viele Leute gehen in deinen Wagen?** how many people can you get in your car?; **in diesen Saal gehen 300 Leute** this hall holds 300 people; **in diesen Krug geht ein ganzer Liter** this jug holds a whole litre *(Brit) or* liter *(US)*; **3 geht in 9 dreimal** 3 into 9 goes 3; **das will mir nicht in den Kopf gehen** I just can't understand it; **in die tausende** *or* **Tausende gehen** to run into (the) thousands; **er geht ins siebzigste Jahr** he's getting on for seventy; **in sich** *(acc)* **gehen** to stop and think

♦ **gehen + mit** mit jdm gehen to go with sb; (= *befreundet sein*) to go out with sb, to be with sb; mit der Zeit gehen to move with the times; mit der Mode gehen to follow fashion

♦ **gehen + nach** er ging nach München he went to Munich; diese Straße geht nach Hannover this road goes to Hanover; diese Tür geht nach draußen/nach nebenan this door leads to the outside/into the next room; das Schiff geht nach Harwich the boat is going to Harwich; nach einer Regel gehen to follow a rule; wenn man nach seiner Aussage gehen kann (= *urteilen*) if his statement is anything to go by; man darf nicht nur nach dem Äußeren gehen (= *urteilen*) you shouldn't judge *or* go just by appearances

♦ **gehen + über** über die Straße gehen to cross the road; über die Brücke gehen to cross the bridge, to go over the bridge; die Brücke geht dort über den Fluss the bridge crosses the river there; die Reise geht über Dresden we/they *etc* are going via Dresden; das geht über meine Kräfte that's more than I can manage; (*seelisch*) that's more than I can handle; sein Garten geht ihm über alles his garden is the thing that means most to him; nichts geht über (+*acc*) ... there's nothing to beat ...

♦ **gehen + unter** unter Menschen gehen to mix with people; jetzt ist er unter die Dichter gegangen he's now joined the poetic fraternity

♦ **gehen + zu** zur Post® gehen to go to the post office; zum Metzger gehen to go to the butcher's; zur Schule gehen to go to school; zu jdm gehen to go to see sb; geh mal zu deiner Oma in die Küche go to your granny in the kitchen, go and see granny in the kitchen; zur See gehen to go to sea; zum Militär gehen to join the army; zum Theater gehen to go on the stage; zur Universität gehen to go to university

d [= sich bewegen] ich hörte, wie die Tür ging I heard the door (go); diese Tür/Schublade geht schwer this door/drawer is very stiff; mein Rasenmäher geht schwer my lawnmower is hard to push; heute geht ein scharfer Wind there's a bitter wind today; die See geht hoch the sea is running high

e [= ertönen] *Klingel, Glocke, Telefon* to ring, to go; ständig geht bei ihr das Telefon the phone is constantly going *or* ringing in her house; wie geht das Lied/Gedicht? how does the song/poem go?

f [= funktionieren] to work; (*Auto, Uhr*) to go; mein Computer geht schon wieder nicht my computer's not working again; dieses Programm geht nur, wenn man dieses Betriebssystem hat this program only works if you've got this operating system; mein Auto geht mal, mal nicht my car sometimes goes and sometimes doesn't; die Uhr geht gut the clock keeps good time; die Uhr geht falsch/richtig the clock is wrong/right; so geht das, das geht so this is the way to do it; wir bauen uns aus Pappkartons ein Haus, und das geht so: ... we're making a house out of cardboard boxes, and this is how: ...

g [= florieren] *Geschäft* to do well; (= *verkauft werden*) to sell; das Milchgeschäft an der Lessingstraße geht gut, seit dort eine Schule eröffnet wurde the dairy on Lessingstraße has been doing well since a school opened there; mein Geschäft geht gut, aber ich könnte noch mehr Umsatz brauchen my business is doing well, but I could do with a bigger turnover; wie gehen die Geschäfte? how's business?; seit es im Fernsehen diskutiert wurde, geht das Buch besser the book is selling better since it was discussed on TV; das geht wie warme Semmeln it's selling like hot cakes

h [= dauern] to go on; wie lange geht das denn noch? how much longer is it going to go on?; es geht schon eine halbe Stunde it's been going (on) for half an hour; mein Kurs geht vom 2. bis 28. Juni my course is from the 2nd to the 28th of June

i [= aufgehen] *Hefeteig* to rise; Hefeteig muss zwei- bis dreimal gehen yeast dough has to rise two or three times

j [= sich kleiden] ohne Hut gehen not to wear a hat; an einem Tag wie heute geht man einfach nicht ohne Hut/Schirm on a day like this you simply can't go out without a hat/umbrella; sorgfältig gekleidet gehen to be carefully dressed

k [= betreffen] der Artikel ging gegen ... the article criticized ...; das Buch ging um ... the book was about ...; die Wette geht um 50 Euro the bet is for 50 euros; mein Vorschlag geht dahin, dass ... my suggestion is that ...

l [= möglich, gut sein] to be all right, to be OK (*inf*); Montag geht Monday's all right; Montag, das geht gut Monday's fine; geht morgen? – ja, morgen geht gut is tomorrow all right? – yes, tomorrow's fine; das geht doch nicht that's not on (*Brit*) *or* not OK; Dienstag geht auch nicht (*inf*) Tuesday's no good either

m [andere Redewendungen] (ach) geh (doch), das darf doch nicht wahr sein! (*inf*) get away with you (*Brit*) *or* come on, that can't be true! (*inf*); (ach) geh, so schlimm ist das nicht! (*inf*) (oh) come on, it's not that bad!; gehen Sie (mir) doch mit Ihren Ausreden! (*inf*) I don't want any of your excuses!; geh! (*Aus inf: erstaunt*) get away! (*Brit inf*), get out of here! (*US inf*)

♦ **vor sich gehen** was geht hier vor sich? what's going on here?; ich weiß nicht, wie das vor sich geht I don't know the procedure

♦ **so/zu weit gehen** to go so/too far; er ging so weit, ihr eine Gehaltserhöhung zu versprechen he went so far as to promise her a rise (*Brit*) *or* raise (*esp US*); das geht einfach zu weit this is just going too far

2 – TRANSITIVES VERB

er ging eine Meile he walked a mile; ich gehe immer diesen Weg/diese Straße I always go this way/along this road

3 – UNPERSÖNLICHES VERB

a [= ergehen] wie geht es Ihnen? how are you?; (*zu Patient*) how are you feeling?; wie gehts? how are things?; (*bei Arbeit etc*) how's it going?; wie gehts sonst? (*inf*) how are things otherwise?; wie gehts denn (so)? – es geht (*inf*) how are things? – all right *or* not too bad (*inf*); danke, es geht (*inf*) all right, thanks, not too bad, thanks (*inf*); es geht ihm gut/schlecht he's fine/not well; es geht mir (wieder) besser I'm better now; nach einem Bad gings mir gleich besser once I'd had a bath I felt better; sonst gehts dir gut? (*iro*) are you sure you're feeling all right? (*iro*); wie war denn die Prüfung? – ach, es ging ganz gut how was the exam? – oh, it went quite well; mir ist es genauso gegangen (= *ich habe dasselbe erlebt*) it was just the same *or* just like that for me; (= *ich habe dasselbe empfunden*) I felt the same way; lass es dir gut gehen look after yourself, take care of yourself; so geht es (eben) (= *so ist das Leben*) that's how it goes, that's the way things go

b [= sich machen lassen, möglich sein] es geht it is possible; (= *funktioniert*) it works; solange es geht as long as possible; geht es? (*ohne Hilfe*) can you manage?; es geht nicht (= *ist nicht möglich*) it's impossible; (= *kommt nicht in Frage*) it's not on; es wird schon gehen I'll/he'll *etc* manage; (= *wird sich machen lassen*) it'll be all right; wir müssen uns damit abfinden, es geht eben nicht anders we'll just have to put up with it, there's no other way; so geht es nicht that's not the way to do it; (*entrüstet*) it just won't do; morgen geht es nicht tomorrow's no good

c [= führen] dann geht es immer geradeaus then it's straight on (*Brit*) *or* ahead; Sie nehmen die erste rechts, und dann geht es immer geradeaus bis zur Ampel you take the first right and then it's straight on (*Brit*) *or* ahead till you get to the traffic lights; dann ging es nach Süden/ins Gebirge (= *gingen wir/sie etc*) then we/they *etc* set off for the south/the mountains; wohin geht es diesmal in Urlaub? where are you going on holiday (*Brit*) *or* vacation (*US*) this time?

d [andere Wendungen] es geht ein starker Wind there's a strong wind (blowing); es geht das Gerücht, dass er kündigen will the rumour (*Brit*) *or* rumor (*US*) is going (a)round that he's going to hand in his notice; es geht auf 9 Uhr it is approaching 9 o'clock; es ging schon auf den Winter (*geh*) winter was approaching

♦ **es geht um** (= *betrifft*) es geht um seinen Vertrag it's about his contract; worum gehts denn? what's it about?; ich weiß nicht, worum es geht I don't know what this is about; worum geht es in diesem Film/bei eurem Streit? what is this film/your argument about?; es geht um Leben und Tod it's a matter of life and death; es geht um meinen Ruf my reputation is at stake; es geht ihm nur um eins he's only interested in one thing; darum geht es mir nicht (= *habe ich nicht gemeint*) that's not my point; (= *spielt keine Rolle für mich*) that doesn't matter to me; es geht bei diesem Geschäft um 5 Millionen (= *sind im Spiel*) the deal involves 5 million; (= *stehen auf dem Spiel*) 5 million are at stake in the deal; wenn es ums Schauspielern geht, reicht ihm so schnell keiner das Wasser when it comes to acting, there's nobody to touch him; wenn es an die Kleinigkeiten geht, fängt der Ärger erst an when it comes to the details the trouble starts

♦ **es geht nach jdm** it's up to sb; wenn es nach mir ginge ... if it were *or* was up to me ...; es kann nicht immer alles nach dir gehen you can't expect to have your own way all the time

4 – REFLEXIVES VERB

♦ **sich gehen** es geht sich schlecht hier it's not nice walking here; mit den hochhackigen Schuhen geht es sich auf diesem steinigen Weg schlecht it's not nice walking on this stony path in high heels; in diesen Schuhen geht es sich bequem these shoes are comfortable to walk in

---

Ge|hen NT -s, *no pl* (= *Zu-Fuß-Gehen*) walking; (= *Abschied*) leaving; (*Sport*) (= *Disziplin*) walking; (= *Wettbewerb*) walk

Ge|henk [gəˈhɛŋk] NT -(e)s, -e (*Hist*) (*für Schwert*) sword belt; (*für Degen*) knife belt; (*für Pistolen*) gun belt

Ge|henk|te(r) [gəˈhɛŋktə] MF *decl as adj* hanged man/woman; die ~n the hanged

ge|hen las|sen *ptp* gehen lassen *or* (*rare*) gehen gelassen *irreg*, **ge|hen+las|sen** *ptp* gehenlassen *or* (*rare*) gehengelassen *sep irreg* VT (*inf:* = *in Ruhe lassen*) to leave alone VR **a** (= *sich nicht beherrschen*) to lose one's self-control, to lose control of oneself **b** (= *nachlässig sein*) to let oneself go

Ge|her [ˈgeːɐ] M -s, -, **Ge|he|rin** [-ərɪn] F -, -nen (*Sport*) walker; er ist Weltmeister der ~ he's the world champion in walking

Ge|het|ze [gəˈhɛtsə] NT -s, *no pl* (*inf*) **a** (= *Eile*) mad rush *or* dash **b** (*pej:* = *das Aufhetzen*) backbiting (*pej inf*)

ge|hetzt [gəˈhɛtst] ADJ harassed → *auch* hetzen

ge|heu|er [gəˈhɔyɐ] ADJ nicht ~ (= *beängstigend*) scary (*inf*); (= *spukhaft*) eerie, creepy (*inf*), spooky; (= *verdächtig*) dubious, fishy; (= *unwohl*) uneasy; es ist mir nicht ganz ~ it is scary (*inf*); it is eerie *etc or* gives me the creeps (*inf*); it seems a bit dubious *or* fishy to me; I feel uneasy about it; mir ist es hier nicht ~ (= *mir ist unheimlich*) this place gives me the creeps (*inf*);

(= mir ist unwohl) I have got an uneasy feeling about this place

Ge|heul [gəˈhɔyl] NT **-(e)s,** *no pl,* **Ge|heu|le** [gəˈhɔylə] NT **-s,** *no pl* howling

Geh|ge|rät NT Zimmer® *(Brit),* walker *(US)*

Geh|hil|fe M **-, -n** *(Gestell etc)* walking aid

Ge|hil|fe [gəˈhɪlfə] M **-n, -n, Ge|hil|fin** [-ˈhɪlfɪn] F **-, -nen** **a** *(dated: = Helfer)* assistant, helper **b** *(= kaufmännischer Gehilfe)* trainee **c** *(Jur)* accomplice

Ge|hil|fen|brief M diploma

Ge|hil|fen|schaft [gəˈhɪlfnʃaft] F **-,** *no pl (Sw)* aiding and abetting

Ge|hil|fin [-ˈhɪlfɪn] F → **Gehilfe**

Ge|hirn [gəˈhɪrn] NT **-(e)s, -e** brain; *(= Geist)* mind; **das ist nicht seinem ~ entsprungen** *(inf)* he didn't think of that himself; **hast du denn kein ~ im Kopf?** *(inf)* haven't you got any brains *or* a brain in your head? *(inf)*

Ge|hirn- *in cpds* → *auch* **Hirn-**: **Ge|hirn|ak|ro|ba|tik** F *(inf)* mental acrobatics *pl;* **ge|hirn|am|pu|tiert** [-lamputiːɐt] ADJ *(pej sl)* dead from the neck up *(inf);* **Ge|hirn|blu|tung** F brain *or* cerebral haemorrhage *(Brit) or* hemorrhage *(US);* **Ge|hirn|chi|rurg(in)** M(F) brain surgeon; **Ge|hirn|chi|rur|gie** F brain surgery; **Ge|hirn|er|schüt|te|rung** F concussion; **Ge|hirn|er|wei|chung** [-lɛɐvaiçʊŋ] F **-, -en** *(lit, fig inf)* softening of the brain; **Ge|hirn|haut|ent|zün|dung** F *(Med)* meningitis; **Ge|hirn|kas|ten** M *(inf)* thick skull; **Ge|hirn|lap|pen** M *(Anat)* lobe of the brain, brain lobe; **Ge|hirn|nerv** M cranial nerve; **Ge|hirn|rin|de** F cerebral cortex; **Ge|hirn|schlag** M stroke; **Ge|hirn|schwund** M atrophy of the brain; **Ge|hirn|sub|stanz** F brain matter; **graue ~** grey *(Brit) or* gray *(US)* matter; **Ge|hirn|tod** M *(Med)* brain death; **ge|hirn|tot** ADJ = **hirntot**; **Ge|hirn|tu|mor** M *(Med)* brain tumour *(Brit) or* tumor *(US);* **Ge|hirn|wä|sche** F brainwashing *no pl;* **jdn einer ~ unterziehen** to brainwash sb; **Ge|hirn|zel|le** F brain cell

gehl [geːl] ADJ *(dial)* yellow

gehn [geːn] = **gehen**

ge|ho|ben [gəˈhoːbn] *ptp von* **heben** ADJ *Sprache, Ausdrucksweise* elevated, lofty; *(= anspruchsvoll) Ausstattung, Unterhaltungsprogramm* sophisticated; *Stellung* senior, high; *Stimmung* elated; *Ansprüche* high; *Mittelschicht* upper; **ein Hotel der ~en Kategorie** a luxury hotel; **Güter des ~en Bedarfs** semi-luxuries; **~er Dienst** professional and executive levels of the civil service ADV **sich ~ ausdrücken** to use elevated language

Ge|höft [gəˈhœft, gəˈhøːft] NT **-(e)s, -e** farm(-stead)

ge|hol|fen *ptp von* **helfen**

Ge|hol|per [gəˈhɔlpɐ] NT **-s,** *no pl,* **Ge|hol|pe|re** [gəˈhɔlpərə] NT **-s,** *no pl* bumping

Ge|hölz [gəˈhœlts] NT **-es, -e** *(geh)* copse, coppice, spinney; *(= Dickicht)* undergrowth

Ge|hol|ze [gəˈhɔltsə] NT **-s,** *no pl (Sport inf)* bad play; *(unfair)* rough play

Ge|hop|pel [gəˈhɔpl] NT **-s,** *no pl,* **Ge|hop|pe|le** [gəˈhɔplə] NT **-s,** *no pl* hopping

Ge|hör [gəˈhøːɐ] NT **-(e)s** *(rare)* **-e** **a** *(= Hörvermögen)* hearing; *(Mus)* ear; **kein musikalisches ~ haben** to have no ear for music; **ein schlechtes ~ haben** to be hard of hearing, to have bad hearing; *(Mus)* to have a bad ear (for music); **nach dem ~ singen/spielen** to sing/play by ear; **absolutes ~** perfect pitch; **das ~ verlieren** to go *or* become deaf

b *(geh: = Anhörung)* **ein Musikstück zu ~ bringen** to perform a piece of music; **~ finden** to gain a hearing; **jdm ~/kein ~ schenken** to listen/not to listen to sb; **schenkt mir ~!** *(old)* lend me your ears *(old);* **um ~ bitten** to request a hearing; **sich** *(dat)* **~ verschaffen** to obtain a hearing; *(= Aufmerksamkeit)* to gain attention

Ge|hör|bil|dung F aural training

ge|hor|chen [gəˈhɔrçn] *ptp* **gehorcht** VI to obey *(jdm* sb); *(Wagen, Maschine etc)* to respond *(jdm/einer Sache* to sb/sth); **seine Stimme gehorchte ihm nicht mehr** he lost control over his voice; **der Junge gehorcht überhaupt nicht** the boy is always disobedient, the boy is never obedient → **Wort f**

ge|hö|ren [gəˈhøːrən] *ptp* **gehört** VI **a** **jdm ~** *(= jds Eigentum sein)* to belong to sb, to be sb's; **das Haus gehört ihm** he owns the house, the house belongs to him; **ihm gehört meine ganze Liebe** he is the only one I love, he has all my love; **ihr Herz gehört einem anderen** her heart belongs to another

b *(= den richtigen Platz haben)* to go; *(Mensch)* to belong; *(= gebühren)* to deserve; **das gehört nicht hierher** *(Gegenstand)* it doesn't go here; *(Vorschlag)* it is irrelevant here; **das Buch gehört ins Regal** the book belongs in *or* goes on the bookshelves; **das gehört nicht zur Sache/zum Thema** that is off the point, that is irrelevant; **dieser Betrag gehört unter die Rubrik „Einnahmen"** this sum comes *or* belongs under the heading "credits"; **er gehört ins Bett** he should be in bed; **er gehört verprügelt** *(dial)* he needs a thrashing, he ought to be thrashed

c **~ zu** *(= zählen zu)* to be amongst, to be one of; *(= Bestandteil sein von)* to be part of; *(= Mitglied sein von)* to belong to; **es gehört zu seiner Arbeit/zu seinen Pflichten** it's part of his work/one of his duties; **zur Familie ~** to be one of the family; **zu diesem Kleid gehört ein blauer Hut** *(= ist Bestandteil von)* a blue hat goes with *or* belongs to this dress; *(= würde dazu passen)* a blue hat would go with this dress; **zum Wild gehört einfach Rotwein** red wine is a must with venison

d **~ zu** *(= Voraussetzung sein, nötig sein)* to be called for by; **zu dieser Arbeit gehört viel Konzentration** this work calls for *or* takes a lot of concentration; **dazu gehört Mut** that takes courage; **dazu gehört nicht viel** it doesn't take much; **dazu gehört (schon) einiges** *or* **etwas** that takes some doing *(inf);* **dazu gehört mehr** there's more to it than that

VR to be (right and) proper; **das gehört sich einfach nicht** that's just not done; **wie es sich gehört** *(= wie es sich schickt)* as is (right and) proper; *(= wie es zünftig ist)* comme il faut; **benimm dich, wie es sich gehört!** behave yourself properly

Ge|hör-: **Ge|hör|feh|ler** M **ein ~** a hearing defect, defective hearing; **Ge|hör|gang** M *pl* **-gänge** auditory canal

ge|hör|ge|schä|digt ADJ hearing-impaired

ge|hö|rig [gəˈhøːrɪç] ADJ **a** *(geh)* **jdm/zu etw ~** belonging to sb/sth; **zu etw ~ sein** to belong to sth; **nicht zur Sache ~** irrelevant; **alle nicht zum Thema ~en Vorschläge** all suggestions not pertaining to *or* relevant to the topic

b *attr (= gebührend)* proper; *(= notwendig auch)* necessary, requisite; **er behandelt seinen Vater nicht mit dem ~en Respekt** he doesn't treat his father with proper respect *or* with the respect due to him

c *(inf: = beträchtlich, groß)* good *attr,* good and proper *(inf),* well and truly; **eine ~e Achtung vor jdm haben** to have a healthy respect for sb; **eine ~e Tracht Prügel** a good *or* proper thrashing

ADV *(inf: = ordentlich) ausschimpfen* severely; *verwarnen* sharply; **ich habs ihm ~ gegeben** *(inf)* I showed him what's what *(inf),* I gave him what for *(inf); (mit Worten)* I gave him a piece of my mind *(inf);* **jdm ~ Bescheid stoßen** to give sb a piece of one's mind; **jdn ~ verprügeln** to give sb a good beating; **ich habe mich in ihm ~ getäuscht** I was totally wrong about him; **da hast du dich ~ getäuscht!** you're badly *or* terribly mistaken; **sich ~ verspäten** to be terribly late

ge|hör|los ADJ *(form)* deaf; **~ sein** to have no hearing

Ge|hör|lo|sen|schu|le F *(form)* school for the deaf

Ge|hör|lo|se(r) [gəˈhøːɐloːzə] MF *decl as adj (form)* deaf person

Ge|hörn [gəˈhœrn] NT **-(e)s, -e** *(Hunt)* antlers *pl,* set of antlers

Ge|hör|nerv M auditory nerve

ge|hörnt [gəˈhœrnt] ADJ horned; *(= mit Geweih)* antlered; **ein ~er Ehemann** *(hum inf)* a cuckold; **der Gehörnte** Satan

ge|hor|sam [gəˈhoːɐzaːm] ADJ obedient; **Ihr ~ster Diener** *(old)* your most obedient servant *(old),* yours obediently *(old)* ADV obediently; **melde ~st** reporting, sir; **ich bitte ~st** *(old)* I respectfully beg

Ge|hor|sam [gəˈhoːɐzaːm] M **-s,** *no pl* obedience; **jdm den ~ verweigern** to refuse to obey sb

Ge|hor|sam|keit F **-,** *no pl* obedience

Ge|hor|sams-: **Ge|hor|sams|pflicht** F duty to obey; **Ge|hor|sams|ver|wei|ge|rung** F *(Mil)* insubordination, refusal to obey orders

Ge|hör-: **Ge|hör|schutz** M ear protectors *pl,* earmuffs *pl;* **Ge|hör|sinn** M sense of hearing; **Ge|hör|sturz** M (temporary) loss of hearing

geh|ren [ˈgeːrən] VTI *(Tech)* to mitre *(Brit),* to miter *(US)*

Geh|rock M frock coat

Geh|rung [ˈgeːrʊŋ] F **-, -en** *(Tech) (= das Gehren)* mitring; *(= Eckfuge)* mitre *(Brit) or* miter *(US)* joint

Geh|steig M pavement *(Brit),* sidewalk *(US)*

Geh|stö|rung F problem (with) walking, impaired walking

Geht|nicht|mehr [ˈgeːtnɪçtmeːɐ] NT **trinken/tanzen bis zum ~** to drink/dance till one drops *(inf);* **sich bis zum ~ verschulden** to get up to one's ears in debt *(inf)*

Ge|hu|pe [gəˈhuːpə] NT **-s,** *no pl (inf)* hooting, honking

Ge|hus|te [gəˈhuːstə] NT **-s,** *no pl (inf)* coughing

Geh-: **Geh|ver|band** M *(Med)* walking cast; **Geh|ver|such** M **a** *(von Kind, nach Unfall, Verletzung)* attempt at walking; **erste ~e** first attempts at walking **b** *(fig)* tentative step; **Geh|wa|gen** M *(= Laufhilfe)* walker, walking frame, ≈ Zimmer® frame *(Brit);* **Geh|weg** M footpath

Gei [gai] F **-, -en** *(Naut)* stay

Gei|er [ˈgaiɐ] M **-s, -** *(lit, fig)* vulture; **weiß der ~!** *(inf)* God knows!

Gei|fer [ˈgaifɐ] M **-s,** *no pl* slaver; *(= Schaum vor dem Mund)* froth, foam; *(fig pej)* venom; **seinen ~ (gegen etw) verspritzen** to pour out one's venom (on sth)

gei|fern [ˈgaifɐn] VI to slaver; *(= Schaum vor dem Mund haben)* to foam at the mouth; *(fig pej)* to be full of spite; **vor Wut ~** to be spitting with rage; **vor Neid ~** to be drooling with envy; **gegen jdn/etw ~** to revile sb/sth

Gei|ge [ˈgaigə] F **-, -n** violin, fiddle *(inf);* **die erste/zweite ~ spielen** *(lit)* to play first/second violin; *(fig)* to call the tune/play second fiddle; **nach jds ~ tanzen** *(fig)* to dance to sb's tune

gei|gen [ˈgaign] VI to play the violin, to (play the) fiddle *(inf)* VT *Lied* to play on a/the violin *or* fiddle *(inf);* **jdm die Meinung ~** *(inf)* to give sb a piece of one's mind *(inf)*

Gei|gen-: **Gei|gen|bau** M, *no pl* violin-making; **Gei|gen|bau|er(in)** M(F) *pl* **-bauer(innen)** violin-maker; **Gei|gen|bo|gen** M violin bow; **Gei|gen|harz** NT rosin; **Gei|gen|kas|ten** M **a** violin case **b** **Geigenkästen** PL *(hum inf)* clodhoppers *pl (inf);* **Gei|gen|sai|te** F violin string; **Gei|gen|strich** M stroke of the violin bow

Gei|ger [ˈgaigɐ] M **-s, -, Gei|ge|rin** [-ərɪn] F **-, -nen** violinist, fiddler *(inf);* **erster ~** first violin

Gei|ger|zäh|ler M Geiger counter

geil [gail] ADJ **a** randy *(Brit),* horny; *(pej: = lüstern)* lecherous; **auf jdn ~ sein** to be lusting after sb **b** *(Agr) Boden* rich, fertile; *(= üppig)* luxuriant; *Vegetation* rank **c** *(sl: = prima)* brilliant *(inf),* wicked *(inf);* **der Typ ist ~** he's a cool guy *(inf)* ADV **a** *(= lüstern)* lecherously; **jdn ~**

ansehen to give sb a lecherous look **b** *(sl: = prima) spielen, tanzen* brilliantly; **~ aussehen** to look cool *(inf)*

Geil|heit F -, *no pl* **a** randiness *(Brit)*, horniness; *(pej: = Lüsternheit)* lecherousness **b** *(Agr) (von Boden)* richness, fertility; *(= Üppigkeit)* luxuriance; *(von Vegetation)* rankness

Gei|sel ['gaizl] F -, -n hostage; **jdn als ~ nehmen** to take sb hostage; **~n stellen** to produce hostages

Gei|sel-: **Gei|sel|be|frei|ung** F *(= Befreiungsaktion)* freeing of the hostages; *(= Freilassung)* release of the hostages; **Gei|sel|dra|ma** NT hostage crisis; **Gei|sel|gangs|ter** M *(Press sl)* hostage taker; **Gei|sel|haft** F captivity (as a hostage); **Gei|sel|nah|me** [-na:mə] F -, -n hostage-taking; **mit ~ der Besatzung** with the crew taken hostage; **Gei|sel|neh|mer(in)** M(F) hostage-taker

Gei|ser ['gaizɐ] M -s, - geyser

Gei|sha ['ge:ʃa] F -, -s geisha (girl)

Geiß [gais] F -, -en **a** *(S Ger, Aus, Sw: = Ziege)* (nanny-)goat **b** *(von Rehwild etc)* doe

Geiß-: **Geiß|bart** M *(Bot)* goatsbeard; *(esp S Ger inf: = Spitzbart)* goatee (beard); **Geiß|blatt** NT honeysuckle, woodbine; **Geiß|bock** M billy goat

Gei|ßel ['gaisl] F -, -n **a** *(lit, fig)* scourge; *(dial: = Peitsche)* whip **b** *(Biol)* flagellum

Gei|ßel|bru|der M *(Eccl)* flagellator

gei|ßeln ['gaisln] VT **a** *(= peitschen)* to whip, to flagellate *(esp Rel)* **b** *(fig) (= kasteien)* to chastise; *(= anprangern)* to castigate; *(= heimsuchen)* to scourge

Gei|ßel|tier|chen NT flagellate

Gei|ße|lung F -, -en **a** *(= das Peitschen)* whipping, flagellation *(esp Rel)* **b** *(= Kasteiung)* chastisement; *(= Anprangerung)* castigation

Geiß-: **Geiß|fuß** M *(= Gehreisen)* parting tool; *(= Brechstange)* crowbar; **Geiß|hirt(in)** M(F) goatherd; **Geiß|kitz** NT (female) kid; **Geiß|lein** ['gaislain] NT -s, - kid

Geiß|ler ['gaislɐ] M -s, - *(Rel)* flagellator

Geiß|lung ['gaislʊŋ] F -, -en = **Geißelung**

Geist [gaist] M -(e)s, -er **a** *no pl (= Denken, Vernunft)* mind; **der menschliche ~, der ~ des Menschen** the human mind; **~ und Materie** mind and matter; **mit ~ begabt** endowed with a mind; **„Phänomenologie des ~es"** "Phenomenology of the Spirit"

b *(Rel: = Seele, außerirdisches Wesen)* spirit; *(= Gespenst)* ghost; **~ und Körper** mind and body; **seinen ~ aufgeben** *or* **aushauchen** *(liter, iro)* to give up the ghost; **der ~ ist willig, aber das Fleisch ist schwach** *(prov)* the spirit is willing, but the flesh is weak; **der Heilige ~** the Holy Ghost *or* Spirit; **der ~ Gottes** the Spirit of God; **der böse ~** the Evil One; **der ~ der Finsternis** the Prince of Darkness; **gute/böse ~er** good/evil spirits; **die Stunde der ~er** the witching hour; **der gute ~ des Hauses** *(geh)* the moving spirit in the household; **von allen guten ~ern verlassen sein** *(inf)* to have taken leave of one's senses *(inf)*; **jdm auf den ~ gehen** *(inf)* to get on sb's nerves; **in dem Schloss gehen ~er um** the castle is haunted, the castle is walked by ghosts *(liter)*

c *(no pl: = Intellekt)* intellect, mind; *(fig: = Denker, Genie)* mind; **~ haben** to have a good mind *or* intellect; *(Witz)* to show wit; **einen regen/lebhaften ~ haben** to have an active/lively mind; **ein Mann von großem ~** a man of great intellect, a man with a great mind; **die Rede zeugte nicht von großem ~** the speech was not particularly brilliant; **das geht über meinen ~** *(inf)* that's way over my head *(inf)*, that's beyond me *(inf)*; **hier scheiden sich die ~er** this is the parting of the ways; **seinen ~ anstrengen** *(inf)* to use one's brains *(inf)*; **sie sind verwandte ~er** they are kindred spirits; **kleine ~er** *(iro: ungebildet)* people of limited intellect; *(kleinmütig)* small-minded *or* petty-minded people → **unruhig**

d *no pl (= Wesen, Sinn, Gesinnung)* spirit; **in kameradschaftlichem ~** in a spirit of comradeship; **in diesem Büro herrscht ein kollegialer ~** this office has a friendly atmosphere; **in seinem/ihrem ~** in his/her spirit; **in jds ~ handeln** to act in the spirit of sb; **der ~ der Zeit/der russischen Sprache** the spirit *or* genius *(liter)* of the times/of the Russian language; **nach dem ~ des Gesetzes, nicht nach seinem Buchstaben gehen** to go by the spirit rather than the letter of the law; **daran zeigt sich, wes ~es Kind er ist** that (just) shows what kind of person he is

e *no pl (= Vorstellung)* mind; **etw im ~(e) vor sich sehen** to see sth in one's mind's eye; **sich im ~(e) als etw/als jd/an einem Ort sehen** to see *or* picture oneself as sth/as sb/in a place; **im ~e bin ich bei euch** I am with you in spirit, my thoughts are with you

Geis|ter-: **Geis|ter|bahn** F ghost train; **Geis|ter|be|schwö|rer** [-bəʃvø:rɐ] M -s, -, **Geis|ter|be|schwö|re|rin** [-ərɪn] F -, -nen **a** *(der Geister herbeiruft)* necromancer **b** *(der Geister austreibt)* exorcist; **Geis|ter|be|schwö|rung** F **a** *(= Herbeirufung)* necromancy **b** *(= Austreibung)* exorcism; **Geis|ter|bild** NT *(TV)* ghost image; **~er** ghosting *no pl*; **Geis|ter|er|schei|nung** F (ghostly) apparition; *(im Traum etc)* vision; **eine ~ haben** to see a ghost *or* an apparition; *(im Traum etc)* to have a vision; **Geis|ter|fah|rer(in)** M(F) *(inf)* ghost-driver *(US inf)*, *person driving the wrong way on the motorway*; **Geis|ter|ge|schich|te** F ghost story; **Geis|ter|glau|be** M belief in the supernatural; **geis|ter|haft** ADJ ghostly *no adv*, unearthly *no adv*; *(= übernatürlich)* supernatural; **Geis|ter|hand** F **wie von** *or* **durch ~** as if by magic; **Geis|ter|haus** NT **a** *(= Spukhaus)* haunted house **b** *(Rel: = Sitz von Geistern)* spirit house

geis|tern ['gaistɐn] VI *aux sein* to wander like a ghost; **der Gedanke geisterte in seinem Hirn** *or* **durch sein Hirn** the thought haunted him *or* his mind; **Lichter geisterten hinter den Fenstern** ghostly lights shone through the windows; **Schatten geisterten an der Wand** ghostly *or* ghostlike shadows played on the wall

Geis|ter-: **Geis|ter|se|her(in)** M(F) visionary; **Geis|ter|stadt** F ghost town; **Geis|ter|stim|me** F ghostly voice; **Geis|ter|stun|de** F witching hour; **Geis|ter|welt** F spirit world; **Geis|ter|zug** M empty train (speeding along)

Geis|tes-: **geis|tes|ab|we|send** ADJ absent-minded ADV absent-mindedly; **~ blicken** to have an absent-minded look on one's face; **jdn ~ ansehen** to give sb an absent-minded look; **Geis|tes|ab|we|sen|heit** F absent-mindedness; **Geis|tes|an|stren|gung** F mental effort; **Geis|tes|ar|beit** F brainwork *(inf)*; **Geis|tes|ar|bei|ter(in)** M(F) brain-worker *(inf)*; **Geis|tes|ar|mut** F dullness, intellectual poverty; *(von Mensch auch)* poverty of mind; **Geis|tes|art** F disposition; **Geis|tes|blitz** M brainwave *(Brit)*, brainstorm *(US)*, flash of inspiration; **Geis|tes|ga|be** F intellectual gift; **Geis|tes|ge|gen|wart** F presence of mind; **geis|tes|ge|gen|wär|tig** ADJ quick-witted ADV quick-wittedly; **~ duckte er sich unter das Steuer** with great presence of mind he ducked below the steering wheel; **Geis|tes|ge|schich|te** F, *no pl* history of ideas; **die ~ der Goethezeit** the intellectual history of Goethe's time; **geis|tes|ge|schicht|lich** ADJ relating to the history of ideas *pred (nachgestellt)*; **geis|tes|ge|stört** ADJ mentally disturbed *or (stärker)* deranged; **du bist wohl ~!** *(inf)* are you out of your mind? *(inf)*; **Geis|tes|ge|stör|te(r)** MF *decl as adj* a mentally disturbed/deranged person; **Geis|tes|ge|stört|heit** F -, *no pl* mental instability *or (stärker)* derangement; **Geis|tes|grö|ße** F **a** *no pl (= Genialität)* greatness of mind **b** *(= genialer Mensch)* great mind, genius; **Geis|tes|hal|tung** F attitude of mind; **geis|tes|krank** ADJ mentally ill; **Geis|tes|kran|ke(r)** MF *decl as adj* mentally ill person; **die ~n** the mentally ill; **Geis|tes|krank|heit** F mental illness; *(= Wahnsinn)* insanity; **geis|tes|schwach** ADJ feebleminded; **Geis|tes|stö|rung** F mental disturbance *or (stärker)* derangement; **Geis|tes|ver|fas|sung** F frame *or* state of mind; **geis|tes|ver|wandt** ADJ spiritually akin *(mit* to); **die beiden sind ~** they are kindred spirits; **Geis|tes|ver|wand|te(r)** MF *decl as adj* kindred spirit; **Geis|tes|ver|wandt|schaft** F spiritual affinity *(mit* to); **Geis|tes|ver|wir|rung** F mental confusion; **Geis|tes|welt** F *(liter)* world of thought; **Geis|tes|wis|sen|schaft** F arts subject; **die ~en** the arts; *(als Studium)* the humanities; **Geis|tes|wis|sen|schaft|ler(in)** M(F) arts scholar; *(= Student)* arts student; **geis|tes|wis|sen|schaft|lich** ADJ *Fach, Studium, Fakultät* arts *attr*; **~e Psychologie** humanistic psychology ADV **er ist mehr ~ orientiert** he is more orientated toward(s) the arts; **Geis|tes|zu|stand** M mental condition; **jdn auf seinen ~ untersuchen** to give sb a psychiatric examination; **du musst dich mal auf deinen ~ untersuchen lassen** *(inf)* you need your head examined *(inf)*

Geist-: **geist|feind|lich** ADJ anti-intellectual; **Geist|feind|lich|keit** F anti-intellectualism; **Geist|hei|ler(in)** M(F) faith healer

geis|tig ['gaistɪç] ADJ **a** *(= unkörperlich) Wesen, Liebe, Existenz* spiritual; **ein ~es Band** a spiritual bond; **~-moralisch** spiritual and moral; **~-moralische Erneuerung** spiritual and moral renewal; **~-seelisch** mental and spiritual

b *(= intellektuell)* intellectual; *(Psych)* mental; **~e Arbeit** intellectual work, brainwork *(inf)*; **~e Nahrung** intellectual nourishment; **~er Diebstahl** plagiarism *no pl*; **~es Eigentum** intellectual property; **der ~e Vater** the spiritual father

c *(= imaginär)* **jds ~es Auge** sb's mind's eye; **etw vor seinem ~en Auge sehen** to see sth in one's mind's eye

d *attr (= alkoholisch)* spirituous

ADV *(= intellektuell)* intellectually; *(Med)* mentally; **~ anspruchsvoll/anspruchslos** intellectually demanding/undemanding, highbrow/lowbrow *(inf)*; **~ nicht mehr folgen können** to be unable to understand *or* follow any more; **~ behindert/zurückgeblieben** mentally handicapped *or* deficient *or* disabled/retarded

Geis|tig|keit F -, *no pl* intellectuality

geis|tig-see|lisch ADJ mental and spiritual ADV mentally and spiritually

geist|lich ['gaistlɪç] ADJ *Angelegenheit, Einstellung, Führer, Beistand* spiritual; *(= religiös) Drama, Dichtung, Schrift* religious; *Musik* religious, sacred; *(= kirchlich)* ecclesiastical; *Gewand* ecclesiastical, clerical; **~es Amt** religious office; **~er Orden** religious order; **~es Recht** canon law; **der ~e Stand** the clergy; **die ~en Weihen empfangen** to take holy orders

Geist|li|che ['gaistlɪçə] F *decl as adj* woman priest; *(von Freikirchen)* woman minister

Geist|li|che(r) ['gaistlɪçə] M *decl as adj* clergyman; *(= Priester)* priest; *(= Pastor, von Freikirchen)* minister; *(= Gefängnisgeistliche, Militärgeistliche etc)* chaplain

Geist|lich|keit F -, *no pl* clergy; *(= Priester)* priesthood; *(= Pastoren; von Freikirchen)* ministry

Geist-: **geist|los** ADJ *(= dumm)* stupid; *(= langweilig)* dull; *(= einfallslos)* unimaginative; *(= trivial)* inane; **Geist|lo|sig|keit** F -, -en **a** *no pl (= Dummheit)* stupidity; *(= Langweiligkeit)* dullness; *(= Einfallslosigkeit)* unimaginativeness; *(= Trivialität)* inanity **b** *(= geistlose Äußerung)* inane remark; **geist|reich** ADJ *(= witzig)* witty; *(= klug)* intelligent; *(= einfallsreich)* ingenious; *Beschäftigung, Gespräch, Unterhaltung* intellectually stimulating; *(= schlagfertig)* quick-witted; **das war sehr ~** *(iro)* that was bright *(iro)*; **geist|sprü|hend** ADJ *attr (geh)* scintillatingly *or* brilliantly witty; **geist|tö|tend** ADJ soul-destroying; **geist|voll** ADJ *Mensch, Äußerung* wise, sage; *Buch, Gespräch, Beschäftigung* intellectual

Gei|tau [ˈgaitau] NT *(Naut)* stay
Geiz [gaits] M **-es,** *no pl* meanness *(esp Brit)*, stinginess *(inf)*; *(= Sparsamkeit, Knauserei auch)* miserliness
gei|zen [ˈgaitsn] VI to be mean *(esp Brit) or* stingy *(inf)*; *(= sparsam, knausrig sein auch)* to be miserly; *(mit Worten, Zeit)* to be sparing; **mit etw ~** to be mean *etc* with sth; **sie geizt nicht mit ihren Reizen** she doesn't mind showing what she's got; **nach etw ~** *(old)* to crave (for) sth
Geiz|hals M miser
gei|zig [ˈgaitsɪç] ADJ mean *(esp Brit)*, stingy *(inf)*; *(= sparsam, knausrig auch)* miserly; *(mit Geld auch)* tight-fisted; **„Der Geizige"** "The Miser"
Geiz|kra|gen M *(inf)* skinflint
Ge|jam|mer [gəˈjamɐ] NT **-s,** *no pl* moaning (and groaning); *(inf: = Klagen auch)* bellyaching *(inf)*, griping *(inf)*
Ge|jauch|ze [gəˈjauxtsə] NT **-s,** *no pl* jubilation, exultation *(liter)*, rejoicing
Ge|jau|le [gəˈjaulə] NT **-s,** *no pl* howling; *(von Tieren auch)* yowling
Ge|joh|le [gəˈjoːlə] NT **-s,** *no pl* howling; *(von Betrunkenen etc)* caterwauling
gek. *abbr von* **gekürzt** abbreviated
ge|kannt *ptp von* **kennen**
Ge|kei|fe [gəˈkaifə] NT **-s,** *no pl* carping, nagging
Ge|ki|cher [gəˈkɪçɐ] NT **-s,** *no pl* giggling, tittering; *(spöttisch)* sniggering, snickering
Ge|kläff [gəˈklɛf] NT **-(e)s,** *no pl* yapping *(auch fig pej)*, yelping
Ge|klap|per [gəˈklapɐ] NT **-s,** *no pl* clatter(ing)
Ge|klat|sche [gəˈklatʃə] NT **-s,** *no pl (inf)* **a** *(von Händen)* clapping **b** *(pej: = Tratscherei)* gossiping, tittle-tattling *(Brit inf)*
ge|klei|det [gəˈklaidət] PTP *von* **kleiden** ADJ **a** *(= angezogen)* **gut/schlecht ~** well/badly dressed; **korrekt ~** correctly dressed; **weiß/schwarz ~ sein** to be dressed in white/black; **in Lumpen ~** dressed in rags **b** *(fig)* **eine in freundliche Worte ~e Kränkung** an insult cloaked in friendly words *(form)*, a backhanded compliment → *auch* **kleiden**
Ge|klim|per [gəˈklɪmpɐ] NT **-s,** *no pl (inf) (= Klaviergeklimper)* tinkling; *(stümperhaft)* plonking *(inf)*; *(= Banjogeklimper etc)* twanging; *(von Geld)* jingling; *(von Wimpern)* fluttering
Ge|klin|gel [gəˈklɪŋl] NT **-s,** *no pl* ringing; *(von Motor)* pinking, knocking
Ge|klirr [gəˈklɪr] NT **-(e)s,** *no pl,* **Ge|klir|re** [gəˈklɪrə] NT **-s,** *no pl* clinking; *(von Gläsern auch)* tinkling; *(von Fensterscheiben)* rattling; *(von Ketten etc)* clanging, clanking; *(von Waffen)* clashing; *(von Lautsprecher, Mikrofon)* crackling; *(von Eis)* crunching
ge|klom|men *ptp von* **klimmen**
Ge|klön [gəˈkløːn] NT **-(e)s,** *no pl,* **Ge|klö|ne** [gəˈkløːnə] NT **-s,** *no pl (inf)* natter *(inf)*
Ge|klop|fe [gəˈklɔpfə] NT **-s,** *no pl* knocking; *(von Fleisch, Teppich)* beating; *(des Spechts)* tapping, hammering; *(des Motors)* knocking, pinking
ge|klun|gen *ptp von* **klingen**
Ge|knall [gəˈknal] NT **-(e)s,** *no pl,* **Ge|knal|le** [gəˈknalə] NT **-s,** *no pl* banging; *(von Tür auch)* slamming; *(bei Feuerwerk)* banging; *(von Pfropfen)* popping; *(von Peitsche)* cracking; **das ununterbrochene ~ von Schüssen** the constant sound of shots being fired
Ge|knarr [gəˈknar] NT **-(e)s,** *no pl,* **Ge|knar|re** [gəˈknarə] NT **-s,** *no pl* creaking; *(von Stimme)* rasping, grating
Ge|knat|ter [gəˈknatɐ] NT **-s,** *no pl (von Motorrad)* roaring; *(von Presslufthammer)* hammering; *(von Maschinengewehr)* rattling, chattering; *(von Schüssen)* rattling (out)
ge|knickt [gəˈknɪkt] ADJ *(inf)* glum, dejected → *auch* **knicken**
Ge|knickt|heit F **-,** *no pl (inf)* dejection
ge|knif|fen *ptp von* **kneifen**
Ge|knip|se [gəˈknɪpsə] NT **-s,** *no pl (inf)* snap-taking *(inf)*
Ge|knis|ter [gəˈknɪstɐ] NT **-s,** *no pl* crackling, crackle; *(von Papier, Seide)* rustling
ge|knüp|pelt [gəˈknʏplt] ADV **~ voll** *(inf)* packed (out), chock-a-block *(inf)* → *auch* **knüppeln**
ge|kom|men *ptp von* **kommen**
ge|konnt [gəˈkɔnt] *ptp von* **können** ADJ masterly ADV in a masterly fashion
Ge|krächz [gəˈkrɛçts] NT **-es,** *no pl,* **Ge|kräch|ze** [gəˈkrɛçtsə] NT **-s,** *no pl* croaking
Ge|kra|kel [gəˈkraːkl] NT **-s,** *no pl (inf)* scrawl, scribble; *(= Krakeln)* scrawling, scribbling
ge|kränkt [gəˈkrɛŋkt] PTP *von* **kränken** ADJ hurt, offended *(über +acc* at, by); *Stolz* injured → *auch* **kränken**
Ge|krat|ze [gəˈkratsə] NT **-s,** *no pl* scratching
Ge|kreisch [gəˈkraiʃ] NT **-(e)s,** *no pl,* **Ge|krei|sche** [gəˈkraiʃə] NT **-s,** *no pl* screeching; *(von Vogel auch)* squawking; *(von Reifen, Bremsen auch)* squealing; *(von Mensch auch)* shrieking, squealing
Ge|kreu|zig|te(r) [gəˈkrɔytsɪçtə] MF *decl as adj* crucified (person); **Jesus der ~** Jesus the Crucified
Ge|krie|che [gəˈkriːçə] NT **-s,** *no pl (inf)* crawling, creeping
ge|kri|schen *(old, hum) ptp von* **kreischen**
Ge|krit|zel [gəˈkrɪtsl] NT **-s,** *no pl* **a** scribbling, scrawling; *(= Männchenmalen)* doodling **b** *(= Gekritzeltes)* scribble, scrawl; doodle
ge|kro|chen *ptp von* **kriechen**
Ge|krö|se [gəˈkrøːzə] NT **-s, -** *(Anat)* mesentery; *(= Kutteln)* tripe; *(= essbare Eingeweide)* chitterlings *pl*; *(von Geflügel)* giblets *pl*
ge|krümmt [gəˈkrʏmt] PTP *von* **krümmen** ADJ curved; *(= hakenartig)* hooked; *(= gebogen, gebeugt)* bent; *(= verzogen, verworfen)* warped → *auch* **krümmen**
ge|kühlt [gəˈkyːlt] ADJ *Getränke* chilled; *Räume* air-conditioned ADV **etw ~ servieren** to serve sth chilled → *auch* **kühlen**
ge|küns|telt [gəˈkʏnstlt] ADJ artificial; *Sprache, Benehmen auch* affected ADV affectedly; **er spricht sehr ~** his speech is very affected; **~ lachen** to give an affected laugh, to laugh affectedly
Gel [geːl] NT **-s, -e** gel
Ge|la|ber [gəˈlaːbɐ] NT **-s,** *no pl,* **Ge|la|be|re** [gəˈlaːbərə] NT **-s,** *no pl (inf)* jabbering *(inf)*, prattling *(inf)*
Ge|läch|ter [gəˈlɛçtɐ] NT **-s, -** laughter; **in ~ ausbrechen** to burst into laughter, to burst out laughing; **sich dem ~ aussetzen** to make oneself a laughing stock, to expose oneself to ridicule; **jdn dem ~ preisgeben** *(geh)* to make sb a laughing stock
ge|lack|mei|ert [gəˈlakmaiɐt] ADJ *(inf)* duped, conned *(inf)*; **~ sein, der Gelackmeierte sein** *(= hintergangen worden sein)* to have been duped *or* conned *(inf)*; *(= dumm dastehen)* to look a right fool *(Brit inf)*, to look like a complete fool
ge|la|den [gəˈlaːdn] *ptp von* **laden**, *von* **laden** ADJ **a** loaded; *(Phys, fig) Atmosphäre* charged; *(inf: = wütend)* (hopping *(inf)*) mad; **der Chef war mächtig ~** *(inf)* the boss was absolutely hopping mad *(inf)*; **mit Spannung ~** charged with tension **b ~ haben** *(inf)* to be tanked up *(inf)*
Ge|la|ge [gəˈlaːgə] NT **-s, -** feast, banquet; *(= Zechgelage)* carouse
ge|la|gert [gəˈlaːgɐt] ADJ **ähnlich ~** similar; **in anders/ähnlich/besonders ~en Fällen** in different/similar/exceptional cases; **anders ~ sein** to be different → *auch* **lagern**
ge|lähmt [gəˈlɛːmt] ADJ *(lit, fig)* paralysed; **er ist seit seinem Unfall ~** his accident left him paralysed, he's been paralysed since his accident; **er hat ~e Beine** his legs are paralysed, he's paralysed in the legs; **er ist an beiden Beinen ~** he is paralysed in both legs; **er ist von der Hüfte abwärts ~** he is paralysed from the waist down; **vor Angst wie ~ sein** to be petrified, to be paralysed with fear → *auch* **lähmen**
Ge|län|de [gəˈlɛndə] NT **-s, - a** *(= Land)* open country; *(Mil: = Gebiet, Terrain)* ground; **offenes ~** open country; **schwieriges ~** difficult terrain or country; **das ~ erkunden** *(Mil)* to reconnoitre *(Brit)*, to reconnoiter *(US)* **b** *(= Gebiet)* area **c** *(= Grundstück) (= Fabrikgelände, Schulgelände etc)* grounds *pl*; *(= Baugelände)* site; *(= Ausstellungsgelände)* exhibition centre *(Brit) or* center *(US)*
Ge|län|de-: **Ge|län|de|fahrt** F cross-country drive; **für ~en gut geeignet** well-suited to cross-country driving *or* to driving cross-country; **Ge|län|de|fahr|zeug** NT cross-country *or* all-terrain vehicle; **ge|län|de|gän|gig** ADJ *Fahrzeug* suitable for cross-country driving; **Ge|län|de|gän|gig|keit** [-gɛŋɪçkait] F **-,** *no pl* suitability for cross-country driving; **Ge|län|de|lauf** M cross-country run; *(= Wettbewerb)* cross-country race; **er macht gerne ~** he enjoys cross-country running; **Ge|län|de|marsch** M cross-country march; **einen ~ machen** to march cross-country
Ge|län|der [gəˈlɛndɐ] NT **-s, -** railing(s *pl*); *(= Treppengeländer)* banister(s *pl*)
Ge|län|de-: **Ge|län|de|rad** NT all-terrain bike, mountain bike; **Ge|län|de|rei|fen** M *(Mot)* off-road *or* cross-country tyre *(Brit) or* tire *(US)*; **Ge|län|de|ren|nen** NT cross-country race; **Ge|län|de|ritt** M cross-country riding; **ein ~** a cross-country ride; **für ~e ungeeignet** unsuitable for cross-country riding; **Ge|län|de|spiel** NT scouting game; *(Mil)* field exercise; **Ge|län|de|übung** F field exercise; **Ge|län|de|wa|gen** M cross-country *or* general-purpose vehicle
ge|lang *pret von* **gelingen**
ge|lan|gen [gəˈlaŋən] *ptp* **gelangt** VI *aux sein* **an/auf** *etc* **etw** *(acc)***/zu etw ~** *(lit, fig)* to reach sth; *(fig: mit Mühe)* to attain sth; *(= erwerben)* to acquire sth; **zum Ziel ~** to reach one's goal; *(fig auch)* to attain one's end *or* goal; **in jds Besitz ~** to come into sb's possession; **in die richtigen/falschen Hände ~** to fall into the right/wrong hands; **zu Reichtum ~** to come into a fortune; *(durch Arbeit)* to make a *or* one's fortune; **zu Ruhm ~** to achieve *or* acquire fame; **zur Reife ~** to reach *or* attain *(form)* maturity; **zu einer Überzeugung ~** to become convinced; **zum Abschluss ~** *(form)* to reach a conclusion; **zur Abstimmung ~** *(form)* to be put to the vote; **zur Durchführung/Aufführung ~** *(form)* to be carried out/performed; **zur Auszahlung ~** *(form)* to be paid out; **an die Macht ~** to come to power
ge|lang|weilt [gəˈlaŋvailt] ADJ bored ADV **die Zuschauer saßen ~ da** the audience sat there looking bored; **er hörte ihr ~ zu** he was bored listening to her → *auch* **langweilen**
ge|lappt [gəˈlapt] ADJ *Blatt* lobate, lobed
Ge|lär|me [gəˈlɛrmə] NT **-s,** *no pl (inf)* = **Lärm**
ge|las|sen [gəˈlasn] *ptp von* **lassen** ADJ *(= ruhig)* calm; *(= gefasst auch)* cool, composed *no adv*; **~ bleiben** to keep calm *or* cool ADV calmly; **etw ~ hinnehmen** to take sth calmly *or* with composure; **~ blicken** to have a calm look on one's face; **sie blickte mich ~ an** she looked at me calmly
Ge|las|sen|heit F **-,** *no pl (= Ruhe)* calmness; *(= Gefasstheit auch)* coolness, composure
Ge|la|ti|ne [ʒelaˈtiːnə] F **-,** *no pl* gelatine
ge|la|ti|nie|ren [ʒelatiˈniːrən] *ptp* **gelatiniert** VTI to gelatinize
Ge|läuf [gəˈlɔyf] NT **-(e)s, -e a** *(Hunt)* tracks *pl (of game birds)* **b** *(von Pferderennbahn)* turf
Ge|lau|fe [gəˈlaufə] NT **-s,** *no pl (inf)* running about; **das war ein ~** that was a real run-around *(inf)*
ge|lau|fen *ptp von* **laufen**
ge|läu|fig [gəˈlɔyfɪç] ADJ *(= üblich)* common; *(= vertraut)* familiar; *(dated: = redegewandt)* fluent; **eine ~e Redensart** a common saying; **das ist**

mir nicht ~ I'm not familiar with that, that isn't familiar to me

Ge|läu|fig|keit F -, *no pl (= Häufigkeit)* frequency; *(= Leichtigkeit)* ease; *(dated: = Redegewandtheit)* fluency

ge|launt [gə'launt] ADJ *pred* **gut ~** good-tempered, good-humoured *(Brit)*, good-humored *(US)*; *(vorübergehend)* in a good mood; **schlecht ~** bad-tempered, ill-humoured *(Brit)*, ill-humored *(US)*; *(vorübergehend)* in a bad mood; **wie ist er ~?** what sort of mood is he in?

Ge|läut [gə'lɔyt] NT **-(e)s,** *no pl*, **Ge|läu|te** [gə'lɔytə] NT **-s,** *no pl* **a** *(= Glockenläuten)* ringing; *(harmonisch auch)* chiming; *(= Läutwerk)* chime **b** *(Hunt)* baying

gelb [gɛlp] ADJ yellow; *(bei Verkehrsampel)* amber; **die Blätter werden ~** the leaves are turning (yellow); **~er Fleck** *(Anat)* yellow spot; **Gelbe Rübe** carrot; **die ~e Rasse** the yellow race, the Orientals *pl*; **die ~e Gefahr** *(Pol pej)* the yellow peril; **der Gelbe Fluss** the Yellow River; **das Gelbe Meer** the Yellow Sea; **Gelbe Karte** *(Ftbl)* yellow card; **die Gelben Seiten®** the Yellow Pages®; **die ~e Post®** the postal service *(excluding telecommunications and banking services)*; **~er Sack** yellow bag *(for the collection of recyclable packaging material)*; **~ vor Neid** green with envy; **Löwenzahn blüht ~** the dandelion has a yellow flower → *auch* **gelbärgern, gelbschlagen**

Gelb [gɛlp] NT **-s, -** *or (inf)* **-s** yellow; *(von Verkehrsampel)* amber; **die Ampel stand auf ~** the lights were amber, the lights had turned amber; **bei ~ stehen bleiben** to stop on amber

gelb+är|gern VR *sep* **sich grün- und ~** *(inf)* to be furious

Gel|be(r) ['gɛlbə] MF *decl as adj* Oriental

Gel|be(s) ['gɛlbə] NT *decl as adj (vom Ei)* yolk; **das ist nicht gerade das ~ vom Ei** *(inf)* it's not exactly brilliant

Gelb-: **Gelb|fie|ber** NT yellow fever; **Gelb|fil|ter** M *(Phot)* yellow filter; **gelb|grün** ADJ yellowish-green; **Gelb|kör|per|hor|mon** NT gestagen; **Gelb|kreuz** NT *(Chem)* mustard gas

gelb|lich ['gɛlplɪç] ADJ yellowish, yellowy; *Gesichtsfarbe* sallow

Gelb|ling ['gɛlplɪŋ] M **-s, -e** *(Bot)* chanterelle

Gelb-: **gelb+schla|gen** VT *sep irreg* **jdn grün- und ~** *(inf)* to beat sb black and blue; **Gelb|sucht** F jaundice; **gelb|süch|tig** ADJ jaundiced; **er ist ~** he has jaundice; **Gelb|wurz** [-vʊrts] F -, *no pl* turmeric

Geld [gɛlt] NT **-(e)s, -er** [-dɐ] **a** *no pl (= Zahlungsmittel)* money; **bares ~** cash; **großes ~** notes *pl (Brit)*, bills *pl (US)*; **kleines ~** change; **~ und Gut** wealth and possessions; **alles für unser ~!** and we're paying for it!; **~ aufnehmen** to raise money; **aus etw ~ machen** to make money out of sth; **zu ~ machen** to sell off; *Aktien* to cash in; **(mit etw) ~ machen** *(inf)* to make money (from sth); **um ~ spielen** to play for money; **ins ~ gehen** *(inf) or* **laufen** *(inf)* to cost a pretty penny *(inf)*; **das kostet ein (wahnsinniges) ~** *(inf)* that costs a fortune *or* a packet *(Brit inf) or* a bunch *(US inf)*; **etw für teures ~ kaufen** to pay a lot for sth; **das habe ich für billiges ~ gekauft** I got it cheaply, I didn't pay much for it; **ich stand ohne ~ da** I was left penniless *or* without a penny; **in** *or* **im ~ schwimmen** *(inf)* to be rolling in it *(inf)*, to be loaded *(inf)*; **er hat ~ wie Heu** *(inf)* he's got stacks of money *(inf)*, he's filthy *or* stinking rich *(inf)*; **das ~ auf die Straße werfen** *(inf) or* **zum Fenster hinauswerfen** *(inf)* to spend money like water *(inf) or* like it was going out of fashion *(inf)*; **da hast du das ~ zum Fenster hinausgeworfen** *(inf)* that's money down the drain *(inf)*; **mit ~ um sich werfen** *or* **schmeißen** *(inf)* to chuck one's money around *(inf)*; **gutes ~ dem schlechten hinterherwerfen** *or* **nachwerfen** *(inf)* to throw good money after bad; **jdm das ~ aus der Tasche ziehen** *or* **lotsen** *(inf)* to get *or* squeeze money out of sb; **am ~ hängen** *or* **kleben** to be tight with money; **hinterm ~ her sein** *(inf)* to be a money-grubber *(Brit inf)*, to be money-crazy *(US inf)*; **das ist nicht für ~ zu haben** *(inf)* that can't be bought; **sie/das ist nicht mit ~ zu bezahlen** *(inf)* she/that is priceless; **nicht für ~ und gute Worte** *(inf)* not for love nor money; **~ allein macht nicht glücklich(, aber es beruhigt)** *(prov)* money isn't everything(, but it helps) *(prov)*; **~ oder Leben!** your money or your life!; **~ stinkt nicht** *(Prov)* there's nothing wrong with money; **~ regiert die Welt** *(Prov)* money makes the world go round *(prov)* **b** **Gelder** PL *(= Geldsummen)* money; **tägliche ~er** day-to-day money *or* loans *pl*; **staatliche/öffentliche ~er** state/public funds *pl or* money **c** *(St Ex: = Geldkurs)* buying rate, bid price

Geld-: **Geld|ab|wer|tung** F currency devaluation; **Geld|adel** M **der ~** the money aristocracy; *(hum: = die Reichen)* the rich *pl*; **Geld|an|ge|le|gen|heit** F financial matter; **jds ~en** sb's financial affairs; **Geld|an|la|ge** F (financial) investment; **Geld|an|le|ger(in)** M(F) (financial) investor; **Geld|an|wei|sung** F money order; **Geld|aris|to|kra|tie** F **die ~** the money aristocracy; **Geld|auf|wer|tung** F currency revaluation; **Geld|aus|ga|be** F (financial) expenditure; **Geld|aus|ga|be|au|to|mat** M cash machine *or* dispenser *(Brit)*, money machine, ATM; **Geld|au|to|mat** M *(zum Geldabheben)* cash machine *or* dispenser *(Brit)*, money machine, ATM; *(zum Geldwechseln)* change machine; **Geld|be|trag** M amount (of money), sum (of money); **Geld|beu|tel** M wallet, billfold *(US)*; *(für Münzen)* purse *(Brit)*, wallet *(US)*; **tief in den ~ greifen** *(inf)* to dig deep (into one's pocket) *(inf)*; **Geld|bom|be** F strongbox; **Geld|bör|se** F wallet, billfold *(US)*; *(für Münzen)* purse *(Brit)*, wallet *(US)*; **Geld|bo|te** M, **Geld|bo|tin** F security guard; **Geld|brief** M registered letter *(containing money)*; **Geld|brief|trä|ger(in)** M(F) *postman/-woman who delivers money orders*; **Geld|bu|ße** F *(Jur)* fine; **eine hohe ~** a heavy fine; **Geld|din|ge** PL financial matters *pl*; **Geld|ein|la|ge** F capital invested *no pl*; **Geld|ein|wurf** M slot; **beim ~ müssen Sie …** when inserting the money you should …; **Geld|ent|wer|tung** F *(= Inflation)* currency depreciation; *(= Abwertung)* currency devaluation; **Geld|er|werb** M **zum ~ arbeiten** to work to earn money; **etw zum ~ machen** to make money out of sth; **Geld|fäl|schung** F counterfeiting; **Geld|ge|ber(in)** M(F) financial backer; *(esp Rad, TV)* sponsor; *(hum: = Arbeitgeber)* employer; **Geld|ge|schäft** NT financial transaction; **Geld|ge|schenk** NT gift of money; **Geld|gier** F avarice; **geld|gie|rig** ADJ avaricious; **Geld|hahn** M **(jdm) den ~ zudrehen** *or* **abdrehen** to cut off sb's money supply; **den ~ öffnen** to loosen the purse strings; **Geld|hei|rat** F **das war eine reine ~** she/he *etc* just got married for the money; **Geld|herr|schaft** F plutocracy

gel|dig ['gɛldɪç] ADJ *(esp Aus)* moneyed, monied

Geld-: **Geld|in|sti|tut** NT financial institution; **Geld|kar|te** F *(aufladbar)* charge card; **Geld|kas|set|te** F cash box; **Geld|kat|ze** F *(Hist)* money pouch; *(= Gürtel)* money belt; **Geld|knapp|heit** F shortage of money; **Geld|kurs** M *(St Ex)* buying rate, bid price

geld|lich ['gɛltlɪç] ADJ financial ADV financially

Geld-: **Geld|man|gel** M lack of money; **Geld|markt** M money market; **Geld|men|ge** F money supply; **Geld|mit|tel** PL funds *pl*; **Geld|not** F *(= Geldmangel)* lack of money; *(= Geldschwierigkeiten)* financial difficulties *pl*; **Geld|po|li|tik** F financial policy; **etwas von ~ verstehen** to know something about the politics of finance; **Geld|prä|mie** F bonus; *(als Auszeichnung)* (financial) award; *(als Belohnung)* (financial) reward; **Geld|preis** M cash prize; **Geld|quel|le** F source of income; **Geld|rol|le** F roll of money *or* coins; **Geld|rück|ga|be** F **a** *(als Handlung)* returning the money **b** *(Aufschrift auf Automaten)* coin return; **keine ~** no change given; **Geld|sa|che** F money *or* financial matter; **in ~n hört die Gemütlichkeit auf** *(prov)* business is business *(prov)*; **Geld|sack** M money bag; *(pej inf: = reicher Mann)* moneybags *sing*; **auf dem ~ sitzen** *(inf)* to be sitting on a pile of money *(inf)*; **Geld|sä|ckel** M *(dial)* money bag; *(fig: von Kanton, Staat etc)* coffers *pl*; **Geld|schein** M banknote *(esp Brit)*, bill *(US)*; **Geld|schöp|fung** F *(Fin)* money creation; **Geld|schrank** M safe; **Geld|schrank|kna|cker(in)** M(F) *(inf)* safe-blower; **Geld|schuld** F (financial) debt; **Geld|schwie|rig|kei|ten** PL financial difficulties *pl*; **Geld|se|gen** M *(fig)* windfall, bonanza, financial godsend; **Geld|sen|dung** F cash remittance; **Geld|sor|gen** PL financial worries *pl*, money troubles *pl*; **~ haben, in ~ sein** to have financial worries, to have money troubles; **Geld|sor|te** F *(Fin)* (type of) currency; **Geld|spen|de** F donation, gift of money; **Geld|spiel|au|to|mat** M slot machine; **Geld|sprit|ze** F *(inf)* injection of money; **Geld|stra|fe** F fine; **jdn zu einer ~ verurteilen, jdn mit einer ~ belegen** to fine sb, to impose a fine on sb; **Geld|stück** NT coin; **Geld|sum|me** F sum of money; **Geld|ta|sche** F purse *(Brit)*, wallet *(US)*; *(für Herren)* wallet, billfold *(US)*; *(sackartig)* money bag; **Geld|trans|port** M transport of money; **einen ~ sichern** to safeguard an armoured *(Brit) or* armored *(US)* car *(carrying money)*; **Geld|trans|por|ter** M armoured *(Brit) or* armored *(US)* car *(for transporting money)*; **Geld|um|lauf** M circulation of money; **Geld|um|tausch** M = **Geldwechsel**; **Geld|ver|die|ner(in)** M(F) *(inf)* moneymaker *(inf)*; **Geld|ver|kehr** M money transactions *pl*; **Geld|ver|knap|pung** F financial restraint; **Geld|ver|le|gen|heit** F financial embarrassment *no pl*; **in ~ sein** to be short of money; **jdm aus einer ~ helfen** to help sb out of his financial difficulties; **Geld|ver|lei|her(in)** M(F) moneylender; **Geld|ver|schwen|dung** F waste of money; **Geld|vo|lu|men** NT *(Fin)* money supply; **Geld|wasch|an|la|ge** F money-laundering outfit; **Geld|wä|sche** F money laundering; **Geld|wech|sel** M exchange of money; **beim ~ muss man eine Gebühr bezahlen** there is a charge for changing money; **„Geldwechsel"** "bureau de change" *(Brit)*, exchange counter *(US)*; **Geld|wech|sel|au|to|mat** M change machine; **Geld|wechs|ler** M *(= Automat)* change machine; **Geld|wechs|ler(in)** M(F) money-changer; **geld|wert** ADJ **~er Vorteil** perk, payment in kind; **~e Leistung** payment in kind; **Geld|wert** M cash value; *(Fin: = Kaufkraft)* (currency) value; **innerer/äußerer ~** internal/external value of currency; **Geld|wert|sta|bi|li|tät** F stability of a/the currency; **Geld|we|sen** NT, *no pl* monetary system; **Geld|wirt|schaft** F money economy; **Geld|zu|wen|dun|gen** PL money *sing*; *(= Geldgeschenk)* gifts *pl* of money; *(= regelmäßiges Geldgeschenk)* allowance *sing*; **private ~ erhalten** to receive a private income

ge|least ADJ *Fahrzeug etc* leased

ge|leckt [gə'lɛkt] ADJ slick; **wie ~ aussehen** *(Mann)* to be spruced up; *(Zimmer, Boden etc)* to be spick and span → *auch* **lecken**

Ge|lee [ʒe'le:] M OR NT **-s, -s** jelly

Ge|le|ge [gə'le:gə] NT **-s, -** *(= Vogelgelege)* clutch (of eggs); *(= Froschgelege)* spawn *no pl*; *(von Reptilien)* eggs *pl*

ge|le|gen [gə'le:gn] *ptp von* **liegen** ADJ **a** *(= befindlich, liegend) Haus, Ort* situated; *Grundstück auch* located; **ein herrlich ~er Ort** a place in a magnificent area **b** *(= passend)* opportune; **zu ~er Zeit** at a convenient time **c** *pred (= wichtig)* **mir ist viel/nichts daran ~** it matters a great deal/doesn't matter to me ADV **wenn ich nicht ~ komme, gehe ich gleich wieder** if it's not convenient, I'll go immediately; **du kommst mir gerade ~** you've come at just the right time; *(iro)* you do pick your time well; **es kommt mir sehr/nicht sehr ~** it comes just at the right/wrong time

Ge|le|gen|heit [gəˈle:gnhait] F -, -en **a** *(= günstiger Umstand, Zeitpunkt)* opportunity; **bei ~** some time (or other); **bei passender ~** when the opportunity arises; **bei passender ~ werde ich ...** when I get the opportunity *or* chance I'll ...; **bei der ersten (besten) ~** at the first opportunity; **(die) ~ haben** to get an *or* the opportunity *or* a *or* the chance *(etw zu tun* to do sth); **jdm (die) ~ geben** *or* **bieten** to give sb an *or* the opportunity *or* a *or* the chance *(etw zu tun* to do sth); **~ macht Diebe** *(Prov)* opportunity makes a thief

b *(= Anlass)* occasion; **bei dieser ~** on this occasion; **ein Kleid für alle ~en** a dress suitable for all occasions → **Schopf**

c *(Comm)* bargain

Ge|le|gen|heits-: **Ge|le|gen|heits|ar|beit** F **a** casual work *no pl* **b** *(eines Autors)* minor work; **Ge|le|gen|heits|ar|bei|ter(in)** M(F) casual labourer *(Brit) or* laborer *(US)*; **Ge|le|gen|heits|dich|ter(in)** M(F) occasional poet; **Ge|le|gen|heits|dieb(in)** M(F) opportunistic *or* sneak thief; **Ge|le|gen|heits|ge|dicht** NT occasional poem; **Ge|le|gen|heits|job** M *(inf)* occasional job *or* work, casual job; **Ge|le|gen|heits|kauf** M bargain; **Ge|le|gen|heits|rau|cher(in)** M(F) occasional smoker; **Ge|le|gen|heits|trin|ker(in)** M(F) occasional drinker

ge|le|gent|lich [gəˈle:gntlɪç] ADJ *attr* occasional; **von ~en Ausnahmen abgesehen** except for the odd occasion ADV *(= manchmal)* occasionally, now and again; *(= bei Gelegenheit)* some time (or other); **wenn Sie ~ dort sind** if you happen to be there; **lassen Sie ~ etwas von sich hören!** keep in touch PREP *+gen (geh)* **~ seines 60. Geburtstags** on the occasion of his 60th birthday

ge|leh|rig [gəˈle:rɪç] ADJ *Schüler, Tier* quick and eager to learn ADV **sich bei etw ~ anstellen** to be quick to grasp sth

Ge|leh|rig|keit F -, *no pl* quickness and eagerness to learn

ge|lehr|sam [gəˈle:ɐza:m] ADJ **a** *(old)* = **gelehrt** ADJ **b** *(rare)* = **gelehrig**

Ge|lehr|sam|keit F -, *no pl (geh)* learning, erudition

ge|lehrt [gəˈle:ɐt] ADJ *Mensch* learned, erudite; *(= wissenschaftlich) Mensch, Literatur, Anmerkungen* scholarly; **~e Gesellschaft** *(old)* learned society → *auch* **lehren**

Ge|lehr|ten-: **Ge|lehr|ten|fa|mi|lie** F family of scholars; **Ge|lehr|ten|kopf** M scholarly profile; **Ge|lehr|ten|streit** M dispute amongst the scholars; **Ge|lehr|ten|welt** F world of learning

Ge|lehr|te(r) [gəˈle:ɐtə] MF *decl as adj* scholar; **darüber sind sich die ~n noch nicht einig, darüber streiten sich die ~n** that's a moot point

Ge|lehrt|heit F -, *no pl* learning, erudition

Ge|lei|er [gəˈlaiɐ] NT **-s**, *no pl* droning

Ge|lei|se [gəˈlaizə] NT **-s, -** *(geh, Aus)* = **Gleis**

Ge|leit [gəˈlait] NT **-(e)s, -e** *(Hist: = Gefolge)* retinue, entourage; *(= Begleitung, Mil)* escort; *(Naut)* convoy, escort; *(= Leichenzug)* cortege; **freies** *or* **sicheres ~** safe-conduct; **jdm das ~ geben** to escort *or* accompany sb; **„zum ~"** "preface" → **letzte(r, s) a**

Ge|leit-: **Ge|leit|boot** NT escort *or* convoy ship; **Ge|leit|brief** M *(Hist)* letter of safe-conduct

ge|lei|ten [gəˈlaitn] *ptp* **geleitet** VT *(geh)* to escort; *(= begleiten auch)* to accompany; *(Naut)* to convoy, to escort

Ge|leit-: **Ge|leit|fahr|zeug** NT escort vehicle; *(Naut)* escort vessel; **Ge|leit|schiff** NT escort *or* convoy ship; **Ge|leit|schutz** M escort; *(Naut auch)* convoy; **jdm ~ gewähren** *or* **geben** to give sb an escort/a convoy; *(persönlich)* to escort/convoy sb; **im ~ (von Polizeifahrzeugen)** under (police) escort; **Ge|leit|wort** NT *pl* **-worte** *(geh)* preface; **Ge|leit|zug** M *(Mil, Naut)* convoy; **im ~ fahren** to drive in convoy; *(Naut)* to sail under convoy

ge|lenk [gəˈlɛŋk] ADJ *(old)* = **gelenkig**

Ge|lenk [gəˈlɛŋk] NT **-(e)s, -e** joint; *(= Handgelenk)* wrist; *(= Fußgelenk)* ankle; *(= Kettengelenk)* link; *(= Scharniergelenk)* hinge

Ge|lenk-: **Ge|lenk|bus** M articulated bus; **Ge|lenk|ent|zün|dung** F arthritis; **Ge|lenk|fahr|zeug** NT articulated vehicle

ge|len|kig [gəˈlɛŋkɪç] ADJ agile; *(= geschmeidig)* supple ADV **~ verbunden sein** *(Tech)* to be jointed; *(zusammengefügt)* to be articulated; *(mit Kettengelenk)* to be linked; *(mit Scharniergelenk)* to be hinged

Ge|len|kig|keit F -, *no pl* agility; *(= Geschmeidigkeit)* suppleness

Ge|lenk-: **Ge|lenk|kopf** M, **Ge|lenk|ku|gel** F *(Anat)* head of a bone, condyle *(spec)*; **Ge|lenk|leuch|te** F Anglepoise® (lamp); **Ge|lenk|om|ni|bus** M articulated bus; **Ge|lenk|pfan|ne** F *(Anat)* glenoid cavity; **Ge|lenk|plas|tik** F *(Med)* arthroplasty; **Ge|lenk|pup|pe** F jointed doll; **Ge|lenk|rheu|ma|tis|mus** M rheumatic fever

Ge|lenks- *in cpds (Aus)* = **Gelenk-**

Ge|lenk-: **Ge|lenk|schmie|re** F *(Anat)* synovial fluid; **Ge|lenk|stan|ge** F *(Tech)* toggle link; **Ge|lenk|wel|le** F *(Tech)* cardan shaft; **Ge|lenk|zug** M articulated train

ge|lernt [gəˈlɛrnt] ADJ trained; *Arbeiter* skilled → *auch* **lernen**

ge|le|sen *ptp von* **lesen**

ge|liebt ADJ dear, beloved *(liter, Eccl)* → *auch* **lieben**

Ge|lieb|te [gəˈli:ptə] F *decl as adj* sweetheart; *(= Mätresse)* mistress; *(liter: als Anrede)* beloved *(liter)*

Ge|lieb|te(r) [gəˈli:ptə] M *decl as adj* sweetheart, lover *(old)*; *(= Liebhaber)* lover; *(liter: als Anrede)* beloved *(liter)*

ge|lie|fert [gəˈli:fɐt] ADJ **~ sein** *(inf)* to have had it *(inf)*; **jetzt sind wir ~** that's the end *(inf)* → *auch* **liefern**

ge|lie|hen *ptp von* **leihen**

ge|lie|ren [ʒeˈli:rən] *ptp* **geliert** VI to gel

Ge|lier-: **Ge|lier|mit|tel** NT gelling agent; **Ge|lier|zu|cker** M preserving sugar

ge|lin|de [gəˈlɪndə], **ge|lind** [gəˈlɪnt] ADJ **a** *(geh) (= mäßig, mild)* mild; *(= schonend, vorsichtig)* gentle; *Wind, Frost, Regen* light; *Klima, Anhöhe* gentle **b** *(inf: = heftig)* awful *(inf)*; **da packte mich ~ Wut** I got pretty angry ADV **~ gesagt** putting it mildly, to put it mildly

ge|lin|gen [gəˈlɪŋən] *pret* **gelang** [gəˈlaŋ], *ptp* **gelungen** [gəˈlʊŋən] VI *aux sein (= glücken)* to succeed; *(= erfolgreich sein)* to be successful; **es gelang ihm, das zu tun** he succeeded in doing it; **es gelang ihm nicht, das zu tun** he failed to do it, he didn't succeed in doing it; **dem Häftling gelang die Flucht** the prisoner managed to escape, the prisoner succeeded in escaping; **dein Plan wird dir nicht ~** you won't succeed with your plan; **es will mir nicht ~** I can't seem to manage it; **es will mir nicht ~ ... zu ...** I can't seem to manage to ...; **das Bild ist ihr gut/schlecht gelungen** her picture turned out well/badly → *auch* **gelungen**

Ge|lin|gen [gəˈlɪŋən] NT **-s**, *no pl (geh) (= Glück)* success; *(= erfolgreiches Ergebnis)* successful outcome; **gutes ~ für Ihren Plan!** good luck with your plan!; **auf gutes ~!** to success!

Ge|lis|pel [gəˈlɪspl] NT **-s**, *no pl (= das Lispeln)* lisping; *(= Geflüster)* whispering

ge|lit|ten *ptp von* **leiden**

gell [gɛl] ADJ shrill, piercing

gell, **gel|le** [ˈgɛlə] INTERJ *(S Ger, Sw)* = **gelt**

gel|len [ˈgɛlən] VI to shrill; *(= von lauten Tönen erfüllt sein)* to ring; **der Lärm gellt mir in den Ohren** the noise makes my ears ring; **ein schriller Schrei gellte durch die Nacht** a shrill scream pierced the night

gel|lend ADJ shrill, piercing; **ein ~es Pfeifkonzert** a shrill barrage of catcalls ADV **~ um Hilfe schreien** to scream for help

ge|lo|ben [gəˈlo:bn] *ptp* **gelobt** VT *(geh)* to vow, to swear; **die Fürsten gelobten dem König Treue** the princes pledged their loyalty *or* vowed loyalty to the king; **ich habe mir gelobt, das Rauchen aufzugeben** I've vowed *or* made a pledge *or* sworn to give up smoking; **das Gelobte Land** *(Bibl)* the Promised Land; **ich schwöre und gelobe, ...** I (do) solemnly swear and promise ...

Ge|löb|nis [gəˈlø:pnɪs] NT **-ses, -se** *(geh)* vow; **ein** *or* **das ~ ablegen** to take a vow

Ge|löb|nis|fei|er F swearing-in ceremony

Ge|lo|der [gəˈlo:dɐ] NT **-s**, *no pl (geh)* blaze

ge|lo|gen *ptp von* **lügen**

ge|löst [gəˈlø:st] ADJ relaxed; **danach war sie ~ und entspannt** afterwards she felt calm and relaxed → *auch* **lösen**

Ge|löst|heit F -, *no pl* relaxed feeling; *(= gelöste Stimmung)* relaxed mood

Gel|se [ˈgɛlzə] F **-, -n** *(Aus)* gnat, mosquito

gelt [gɛlt] INTERJ *(S Ger)* right; **morgen kommst du wieder, ~?** you'll be back tomorrow, won't you *or* right?; **~, du leihst mir 5 Euro?** you'll lend me 5 euros, won't you *or* right?; **ich werde es mal versuchen, ~?** well, I'll give it a try; **es ist schön heute – ~?** it's nice today – isn't it just?

gel|ten [ˈgɛltn] *pret* **galt** [galt], *ptp* **gegolten** [gəˈgɔltn] VI **a** *(= gültig sein)* to be valid; *(Gesetz)* to be in force; *(Preise)* to be effective; *(Münze)* to be legal tender; *(= erlaubt sein)* to be allowed *or* permitted; *(= zählen)* to count; **die Wette gilt!** the bet's on!, it's a bet!; **was ich sage, gilt!** what I say goes!; **das gilt nicht!** that doesn't count!; *(= ist nicht erlaubt)* that's not allowed!; **das Gesetz gilt für alle** the law applies to everyone; **diese Karte gilt nur für eine Person** this ticket only admits one → **geltend**

b *+dat (= bestimmt sein für)* to be meant for *or* aimed at

c *+dat (geh: = sich beziehen auf)* to be for; **seine ganze Liebe galt der Musik** music was his only love; **sein letzter Gedanke galt seinem Volk** his last thought was for his people

d *(= zutreffen)* **für jdn/etw ~** to hold (good) for sb/sth, to go for sb/sth; **das gleiche gilt auch für ihn/von ihm** the same goes for him too/is true of him too

e ~ als *or* **für** *(rare)* to be regarded as; **es gilt als sicher, dass ...** it seems certain that ...

f ~ lassen to accept; **das lasse ich ~!** I'll agree to that!, I accept that!; **für diesmal lasse ich es ~** I'll let it go this time; **etw als etw ~ lassen** to accept sth as sth; **er lässt nur seine eigene Meinung ~** he won't accept anybody's opinion but his own

VTI *impers (geh)* **es gilt, ... zu ...** it is necessary to ...; **jetzt gilt es, Mut zu zeigen/zusammenzuhalten** it is now a question of courage/of sticking together; **jetzt gilts!** this is it!; **was gilts?** *(bei Wette)* what do you bet?; **es gilt!** done!, you're on!, it's a deal!

VT *(= wert sein)* to be worth; *(= zählen)* to count for; **was gilt die Wette?** what do you bet?

gel|tend ADJ *attr Preise, Tarife* current; *Gesetz, Regelung* in force; *(= vorherrschend) Meinung etc* currently accepted, prevailing; **~ machen** *(form)* to assert; **einen Einwand ~ machen** to raise an objection; **~es Recht sein** to be the law of the land

Gel|tend|ma|chung [-maxʊŋ] F -, *no pl (form)* enforcement

Gel|tung [ˈgɛltʊŋ] F **-, -en** *(= Gültigkeit)* validity; *(von Münzen)* currency; *(= Wert)* value, worth; *(= Einfluss)* influence; *(= Ansehen)* prestige; **~ haben** to have validity; *(Münzen)* to be legal tender, to have currency; *(Gesetz)* to be in force; *(Preise)* to be effective; *(Auffassung etc)* to be prevalent; *(=*

Einfluss haben) to carry weight; *(= angesehen sein)* to be recognized; **an ~ verlieren** to lose prestige; **einer Sache** *(dat)* **~ verschaffen** to enforce sth; **sich** *(dat)* **~ verschaffen** to establish one's position; **etw zur ~ bringen** to show sth (off) to advantage; *(durch Kontrast)* to set sth off; **zur ~ kommen** to show to advantage; *(durch Kontrast)* to be set off; **in diesem Konzertsaal kommt die Musik voll zur ~** the music can be heard to its best advantage in this concert hall

Gel|tungs-: **Gel|tungs|be|dürf|nis** NT, *no pl* need for admiration; **gel|tungs|be|dürf|tig** ADJ desperate for admiration; **Gel|tungs|be|dürf|tig|keit** F need for admiration; **Gel|tungs|be|reich** M **der ~ einer Fahrkarte/eines Gesetzes** the area within which a ticket is valid/a law is operative; **Gel|tungs|dau|er** F *(einer Fahrkarte etc)* period of validity; **die ~ eines Vertrages/einer Genehmigung** the period during which a contract is in force/a licence *(Brit)* or license *(US)* is valid; **Gel|tungs|drang** M, **Gel|tungs|stre|ben** NT need for admiration; **Gel|tungs|sucht** F craving for admiration; **gel|tungs|süch|tig** ADJ craving admiration; **Gel|tungs|trieb** M *(= Geltungsbedürfnis)* need for admiration; *(= Geltungssucht)* craving for admiration

Ge|lüb|de [gəˈlʏpdə] NT **-s, -** *(Rel, geh)* vow; **ein/das ~ ablegen** *or* **tun** to take a vow

Ge|lump [gəˈlʊmp] NT **-(e)s,** *no pl,* **Ge|lum|pe** [gəˈlʊmpə] NT **-s,** *no pl (inf: = Plunder, Sachen)* junk, trash; *(pej: = Gesindel)* trash

ge|lun|gen [gəˈlʊŋən] *ptp von* **gelingen** ADJ *attr* **a** *(= geglückt)* successful; **ein gut ~er Abend** a very successful evening; **ein gut ~er Braten** a roast that turned out very well; **eine nicht so recht ~e Überraschung** a surprise that didn't quite come off **b** *(inf: = drollig)* priceless *(inf)*; **du bist mir ein ~er Bursche** you're priceless *(inf)*, you ARE a funny chap *(Brit)*

Ge|lüst [gəˈlʏst] NT **-(e)s, -e, Ge|lüs|te** [gəˈlʏstə] NT **-s, -** *(geh)* desire; *(= Sucht)* craving *(auf +acc, nach* for)

ge|lüs|ten [gəˈlʏstn] *ptp* **gelüstet** VT *impers (liter, iro)* **es gelüstet mich** *or* **mich gelüstet nach ...** I am overcome by desire for ...; *(= süchtig sein nach)* I have a craving for ...; **es gelüstet mich, das zu tun** I'm more than tempted to do that, I'm sorely tempted to do that

Ge|lüs|ten [gəˈlʏstn] NT **-s,** *no pl* desire; *(= Sucht)* craving *(nach* for)

GEMA [ˈgeːma] F **-,** *no pl abbr von* **Gesellschaft für musikalische Aufführungs- und mechanische Vervielfältigungsrechte** *musical copyright watchdog body*

ge|mach [gəˈmaːx] ADV *(old)* slowly; **~!** not so fast!; *(= nichts übereilen)* one mustn't rush things!

Ge|mach [gəˈmaːx] NT **-(e)s, ¨er** [gəˈmɛːçɐ] *(geh)* chamber *(old, form)*; **sich in seine Gemächer zurückziehen** to repair to one's chamber *(old, hum)*

ge|mäch|lich [gəˈmɛːçlɪç] ADJ leisurely; *Mensch* unhurried; **ein ~es Leben führen** to lead a quiet life ADV *erledigen, frühstücken* leisurely; **er wanderte ~ durch die Wiesen** he strolled through the meadows, he took a leisurely stroll through the meadows; **ein ~ fließender Strom** a gently flowing river

Ge|mäch|lich|keit F **-,** *no pl* leisureliness; *(= Ruhe)* peace

ge|macht [gəˈmaxt] ADJ **a** made; **für etw ~ sein** to be made for sth; **ein ~er Mann sein** to be made, to be a made man → **Bett b** *(= gewollt, gekünstelt)* false, contrived **c (ist) ~!** *(inf)* done! *(inf)* → *auch* **machen**

Ge|mäch|te [gəˈmɛçtə] NT **-s, -** *(old, hum)* private parts *pl*, privates *pl (inf)*

GEMA-Ge|büh|ren [ˈgeːma-] PL royalties *pl (payable to the GEMA)*

Ge|mahl [gəˈmaːl] M **-s, -e** *(geh, form)* spouse *(old, form)*, husband; *(= Prinzgemahl)* consort; **bitte grüßen Sie Ihren Herrn ~** please give my regards to your husband

Ge|mahl NT **-** *or* **-(e)s, -e** *(obs)* spouse *(old, form)*, wife

Ge|mah|lin [gəˈmaːlɪn] F **-, -nen** *(geh, form)* spouse *(old, form)*, wife; *(von König auch)* consort; **bitte empfehlen Sie mich Ihrer Frau ~** please give my regards to your wife *(form)* or to your good lady *(Brit)*

ge|mah|nen [gəˈmaːnən] *ptp* **gemahnt** VT *(geh)* **jdn an jdn/etw ~** to remind sb of sb/sth, to put sb in mind of sb/sth

Ge|mäl|de [gəˈmɛːldə] NT **-s, -** painting; *(fig: = Schilderung)* portrayal

Ge|mäl|de-: **Ge|mäl|de|aus|stel|lung** F exhibition of paintings; **Ge|mäl|de|ga|le|rie** F picture gallery; **Ge|mäl|de|samm|lung** F collection of paintings; *(= Gemäldegalerie)* art collection

Ge|man|sche [gəˈmanʃə] NT **-s,** *no pl (dial)* mush; **hör auf mit dem ~!** stop messing around with it!

Ge|mar|kung [gəˈmarkʊŋ] F **-, -en** *(dated, form)* *(= Feldmark)* bounds *pl*; *(= Gemeindegebiet)* district

ge|ma|sert [gəˈmazɐt] ADJ *Holz* grained → *auch* **masern**

ge|mäß [gəˈmɛːs] PREP *+dat* in accordance with; **Ihren Anordnungen ~** as per your instructions, in accordance with your instructions; **~ den Bestimmungen** under the regulations; **~ § 209** under § 209 ADJ appropriate (*+dat* to); **dieser Umgang ist seiner sozialen Stellung nicht ~** the company he is keeping ill befits *or* does not befit his social position; **eine ihren Fähigkeiten ~e Arbeit** a job suited to her abilities; **das einzig Gemäße** the only fitting thing

ge|mä|ßigt [gəˈmɛːsɪçt] ADJ moderate; *Klima, Zone* temperate; *Optimismus etc* qualified → *auch* **mäßigen**

Ge|mäu|er [gəˈmɔyɐ] NT **-s, -** *(geh)* masonry, walls *pl*; *(= Ruine)* ruins *pl*

Ge|mau|schel [gəˈmaufl] NT **-s,** *no pl (pej inf)* scheming

Ge|me|cker [gəˈmɛkɐ] NT **-s,** *no pl,* **Ge|me|cke|re** [gəˈmɛkərə] NT **-s,** *no pl,* **Ge|meck|re** [gəˈmɛkrə] NT **-s,** *no pl (von Ziegen)* bleating; *(inf: = Nörgelei)* moaning, bellyaching *(inf)*; *(= meckerndes Lachen)* cackling

ge|mein [gəˈmain] ✪ 32.5 ADJ **a** *pred no comp* *(= gemeinsam)* **etw ~ mit jdm/etw haben** to have sth in common with sb/sth; **jdm/einer Sache** *(dat)* **~ sein** *(geh)* to be common to sb/sth; **nichts mit jdm ~ haben wollen** to want nothing to do with sb; **das ist beiden ~** it is common to both of them **b** *attr no comp (Biol, old: = üblich, verbreitet, öffentlich)* common; **~er Bruch** *(Math)* vulgar fraction; **~es Recht** common law; **ein ~er Soldat** a common soldier, a private *(US)*; **das ~e Volk/Wohl** the common people/good *or* weal *(old)*; **der ~e Mann** the ordinary man **c** *(= niederträchtig)* mean; *(= roh, unverschämt)* mean, nasty; *Verräter, Lüge* contemptible; **das war ~ von dir!** that was mean *or* nasty of you; **ein ~er Streich** a dirty *or* rotten trick; **alles ins Gemeine ziehen** to cheapen *or* debase everything **d** *(= ordinär)* vulgar; *Bemerkung, Witz* vulgar, dirty, coarse **e** *(inf: = unangenehm)* horrible, awful ADV **a** *(= niederträchtig) behandeln* meanly; *betrügen, hintergehen* despicably; **er hat sie ~ im Stich gelassen** he abandoned her in a despicable way **b** *(inf: = unangenehm)* horribly, awfully; **die Prüfung war ~ schwer** the exam was horribly *or* awfully difficult; **das hat ~ wehgetan** it hurt terribly

Ge|mein|be|sitz M common property

Ge|mein|de [gəˈmaində] F **-, -n a** *(= Kommune)* municipality; *(= Gemeindebewohner auch)* community; *(inf: = Gemeindeamt)* local authority; **die ~ Burg** the municipality of Burg **b** *(= Pfarrgemeinde)* parish; *(= Gläubige auch)* parishioners *pl*; *(beim Gottesdienst)* congregation **c** *(= Anhängerschaft) (von Theater etc)* patrons *pl*; *(von Schriftsteller etc)* following

Ge|mein|de-: **Ge|mein|de|ab|ga|ben** PL local taxes *pl*; **Ge|mein|de|am|mann** M *(Sw)* **a** = **Gemeindevorsteher(in) b** *(= Gerichtsvollzieher)* bailiff; **Ge|mein|de|amt** NT local authority; *(= Gebäude)* local administrative office; **Ge|mein|de|bau** M *pl* **-bauten** *(Aus)* subsidized housing; **Ge|mein|de|be|am|te(r)** M *decl as adj*, **Ge|mein|de|be|am|tin** F local government officer; **Ge|mein|de|be|hör|de** F local authority; **Ge|mein|de|be|schluss** M local government decision; **Ge|mein|de|be|zirk** M district; *(Aus)* ward; **im ~ Dumfries** in the district of Dumfries; **Ge|mein|de|bü|che|rei** F public *or* local *(Brit)* library; **Ge|mein|de|die|ner(in)** M(F) *(dated)* beadle; **ge|mein|de|ei|gen** ADJ local authority *attr*; *(esp städtisch)* municipal; **Ge|mein|de|ei|gen|tum** NT communal property; **Ge|mein|de|glied** NT *(Eccl)* parishioner; **Ge|mein|de|haus** NT *(Eccl)* parish rooms *pl*; *(von Freikirchen)* church rooms *pl*; *(katholisch)* parish house; **Ge|mein|de|hel|fer(in)** M(F) *(Eccl)* parish worker; **Ge|mein|de|mit|glied** NT *(Eccl)* parishioner; **Ge|mein|de|ord|nung** F bylaws *pl*, ordinances *pl (US)*; **Ge|mein|de|prä|si|dent(in)** M(F) *(Sw)* mayor; **Ge|mein|de|rat** M local council; **Ge|mein|de|rat** M, **Ge|mein|de|rä|tin** F local councillor *(Brit)*, councilman/-woman *(US)*; **Ge|mein|de|rats|wahl** F local elections *pl*, elections *pl* for the local council; **Ge|mein|de|saal** M *(Eccl)* church hall; **Ge|mein|de|schwes|ter** F district nurse; *(Eccl) nun working in a parish as a nurse or social worker*; **Ge|mein|de|spi|tal** NT *(Aus)* local hospital; **Ge|mein|de|steu|er** F local tax

ge|mein|deutsch ADJ standard German

Ge|mein|de-: **Ge|mein|de|vä|ter** PL *(hum)* venerable councillors *(Brit)* or councilors *(US) pl (hum)*; **Ge|mein|de|ver|tre|tung** F district council; **Ge|mein|de|ver|wal|tung** F local administration *or* government; **Ge|mein|de|vor|stand** M ≈ aldermen *pl*; **Ge|mein|de|vor|ste|her(in)** M(F) head of the local council; *(= Bürgermeister)* mayor; **Ge|mein|de|wahl** F local election; **Ge|mein|de|zent|rum** NT community centre *(Brit)* or center *(US)*; *(Eccl)* parish rooms *pl*; *(von Freikirchen)* church rooms *pl*; *(katholisch)* parish house

Ge|mein|ei|gen|tum NT common property

Ge|mei|ne(r) [gəˈmainə] M *decl as adj* **a** *(dated: = Soldat)* common soldier, private *(US)*; **die ~n** the ranks **b** *(Typ)* lower-case letter; **in ~n** in lower case

Ge|mein-: **ge|mein|ge|fähr|lich** ADJ dangerous to the public, constituting a public danger; **ein ~er Verbrecher** a dangerous criminal ADV **~ handeln** to endanger public safety; **Ge|mein|ge|fähr|lich|keit** F danger to the public; **Ge|mein|geist** M public spirit; **ge|mein|gül|tig** ADJ = **allgemein ADV**; **Ge|mein|gut** NT, *no pl (lit, fig)* common property; **Schumanns Lieder gehören zum ~ der Deutschen** Schumann's Lieder are part of the German heritage

Ge|mein|heit F **-, -en a** *no pl (= Niedertracht)* meanness; *(= Rohheit, Unverschämtheit auch)* nastiness **b** *no pl (= Vulgarität)* vulgarity; *(von Bemerkung, Witz)* vulgarity, coarseness **c** *(= Tat)* mean *or* dirty trick; *(= Behandlung)* nasty treatment *no pl*; *(= Worte)* mean thing; **das war eine ~** *(= Handlung)* that was a mean thing to do; *(= Bemerkung)* that was a mean thing to say **d** *(inf: = ärgerlicher Umstand)* (blasted *(Brit inf)*) nuisance

Ge|mein-: **ge|mein|hin** [gəˈmainhɪn] ADV generally; **Ge|mein|kos|ten** PL overheads *pl*, overhead costs *pl*; **Ge|mein|nutz** [-nʊts] **M -es,** *no pl* public *or* common good; **~ geht vor Eigennutz** (*dated prov*) service before self (*Prov*); **ge|mein|nüt|zig** ADJ of benefit to the public *pred*; (*= wohltätig*) charitable; **~er Verein** charitable *or* non-profit-making organization; **~e Einrichtung** charitable *or* non-profit-making institution; **er wurde zu 80 Stunden ~er Arbeit verurteilt** he was sentenced to 80 hours' community service; **Ge|mein|nüt|zig|keit** [-nʏtsɪçkait] **F -,** *no pl* benefit to the public; **die ~ einer Organisation** the charitable status of an organization; **Ge|mein|platz M** commonplace

ge|mein|sam [gə'mainza:m] ADJ (*= mehreren gehörend*) *Eigenschaft, Interesse, Zwecke, Politik* common; *Konto* joint; *Freund* mutual; (*= von mehreren unternommen*) *Aktion, Ausflug, Nutzung* joint; **sie haben vieles ~, ihnen ist vieles ~** they have a great deal in common; **die Firma ist ~es Eigentum** *or* **das ~e Eigentum der beiden Brüder** the firm belongs jointly to *or* is the joint property of the two brothers; **unser ~es Leben** our life together; **der Gemeinsame Markt** the Common Market; **die ~e (europäische) Währung** the single (European) currency; **mit jdm ~e Sache machen** to make common cause with sb; **er betonte das Gemeinsame** he stressed all that we/they had in common
ADV together; **etw ~ haben** to have sth in common; **es gehört den beiden ~** it belongs jointly to the two of them; **~ genutzt** (*Comput*) shared

Ge|mein|sam|keit F -, -en a (*= gemeinsame Interessen, Eigenschaft etc*) common ground *no pl*; **die ~en zwischen ihnen sind sehr groß** they have a great deal in common **b** *no pl* (*= gemeinsames Besitzen*) joint possession; (*von Freunden, Interessen*) mutuality; **uns verbindet die ~ unserer Interessen** we are united by common interests

Ge|mein|schaft [gə'mainʃaft] **F -, -en** community; (*= Gruppe*) group; (*= Zusammensein*) company; (*= Zusammengehörigkeitsgefühl*) sense of community; **die ~ Unabhängiger Staaten** the Commonwealth of Independent States; **in ~ mit** jointly with, together with; **in ~ mit jdm leben** to live in close companionship with sb; **die ~ der Heiligen/der Gläubigen** the communion of saints/of the faithful; **eheliche ~** (*Jur*) matrimony

ge|mein|schaft|lich [gə'mainʃaftlɪç] ADJ **a** = **gemeinsam b** (*Jur*) **~e Straftat** joint offence (*Brit*) *or* offense (*US*)

Ge|mein|schafts-: **Ge|mein|schafts|ak|ti|on F** cooperative *or* joint action; **Ge|mein|schafts|an|schluss M** (*Telec*) party line; **Ge|mein|schafts|an|ten|ne F** block *or* party aerial *or* antenna (*esp US*); **Ge|mein|schafts|ar|beit F** teamwork; **das Buch ist eine ~** the book is a team effort; (*von zwei Personen*) the book is a joint effort; **Ge|mein|schafts|auf|ga|be F** joint task; (*= Aufgabe des Bundes*) federal project; **Ge|mein|schafts|beich|te F** (*Eccl*) general confession; **Ge|mein|schafts|be|sitz M** (*= Besitzrechte*) joint ownership; (*= konkretes Objekt*) joint property; **in ~** jointly owned; **ge|mein|schafts|bil|dend** ADJ community-building; (*= einigend*) unifying; **Ge|mein|schafts|de|pot NT** (*Fin*) joint security deposit; **Ge|mein|schafts|ehe F** group *or* communal marriage; **Ge|mein|schafts|er|zie|hung F** coeducation; (*= soziale Erziehung*) social education; **ge|mein|schafts|fä|hig** ADJ capable of living in a community; **Ge|mein|schafts|ge|fühl NT** sense of community; (*= Uneigennützigkeit*) public-spiritedness; **Ge|mein|schafts|geist M** community spirit, esprit de corps; **Ge|mein|schafts|grab NT** communal grave; **Ge|mein|schafts|haft F** group confinement; **Ge|mein|schafts|hil|fe F a** community welfare services *pl* **b** (*in EU*) Community aid; **Ge|mein|schafts|kü|che F** (*= Kantine*) canteen; (*= gemeinsame Kochgelegenheit*) communal *or* (*kleiner*) shared kitchen; **Ge|mein|schafts|kun|de F** social studies *pl*; **Ge|mein|schafts|le|ben NT** community life; **Ge|mein|schafts|leis|tung F** collective achievement; **Ge|mein|schafts|pra|xis F** joint practice; **Ge|mein|schafts|pro|duk|ti|on F a** (*= Gemeinschaftsarbeit*) teamwork **b** (*Rad, TV, Film*) co-production; **Ge|mein|schafts|raum M** common room; **ge|mein|schafts|schä|di|gend, ge|mein|schafts|schäd|lich** ADJ *Verhalten* antisocial; **Ge|mein|schafts|schu|le F** interdenominational school; **Ge|mein|schafts|sen|dung F** simultaneous broadcast; **Ge|mein|schafts|sinn M** community spirit, esprit de corps; **ge|mein|schafts|stif|tend** ADJ promoting a sense of community; **Ge|mein|schafts|un|ter|neh|men NT** (*Econ*) joint venture; **Ge|mein|schafts|wäh|rung F** common *or* single currency; (*in EU*) single European currency; **Ge|mein|schafts|wer|bung F** joint advertising *no pl*; **~ machen** to advertise jointly, to run a joint advertisement; **Ge|mein|schafts|woh|nung F** shared flat (*Brit*) *or* apartment; **Ge|mein|schafts|zel|le F** communal cell

Ge|mein-: **Ge|mein|schuld|ner(in) M(F)** (*Jur*) bankrupt; **Ge|mein|sinn M,** *no pl* public spirit; **Ge|mein|spra|che F** standard language; **ge|mein|sprach|lich** ADJ standard language *attr*; **ge|mein|ver|ständ|lich** ADJ generally comprehensible ADV **sich ~ ausdrücken** to make oneself generally understood; **wissenschaftliche Probleme ~ darstellen** to present scientific problems in such a way that they can be generally understood; **Ge|mein|werk NT** (*Sw*) voluntary work; **Ge|mein|we|sen NT** community; (*= Staat*) polity; **Ge|mein|wil|le M** collective will; **Ge|mein|wirt|schaft F** cooperative economy; **ge|mein|wirt|schaft|lich** ADJ cooperative; **Ge|mein|wohl NT** public welfare; **das dient dem ~** it is in the public interest

Ge|men|ge [gə'mɛŋə] **NT -s, - a** (*= Mischung*) mixture (*aus of*); (*Agr*) mixed crop; (*fig*) mixture; (*= wirres Durcheinander*) jumble (*aus of*) **b** (*= Gewühl*) bustle; (*= Handgemenge*) scuffle; **mit jdm ins ~ kommen** to come to blows with sb

ge|mes|sen [gə'mɛsn] *ptp von* **messen** ADJ **a** (*= würdevoll*) measured, studied; **~en Schrittes** with measured tread **b** (*dated: = zurückhaltend*) reticent **c** *attr* (*= angemessen*) *Abstand, Entfernung* respectful

Ge|mes|sen|heit F -, *no pl* **a** (*= Würde*) measuredness, studiedness **b** (*dated: = Zurückhaltung*) reticence

Ge|met|zel [gə'mɛtsl] **NT -s, -** bloodbath; (*= Massaker auch*) slaughter, massacre

ge|mie|den *ptp von* **meiden**

Ge|misch [gə'mɪʃ] **NT -(e)s, -e a** (*lit, fig*) mixture (*aus of*) **b** *no pl* (*= Durcheinander*) jumble (*aus of*)

ge|mischt [gə'mɪʃt] ADJ mixed; (*inf: = nicht sehr gut auch*) patchy; **mit ~en Gefühlen** with mixed feelings; **~er Teller** (*mit verschiedenen Speisen*) mixed platter *or* plate; **~es Eis** assorted ice cream; (*mit selbstgewählten Sorten auch*) your choice of ice cream; **~es Doppel** (*Sport*) mixed doubles *pl* → *auch* **mischen**

Ge|mischt-: **Ge|mischt|bau|wei|se F** composite construction; **ge|mischt|ras|sig** ADJ of mixed race; *Ehe* mixed-race; (*mit mehreren Rassen*) multi-racial; **ge|mischt|spra|chig** ADJ multilingual; **Ge|mischt|wa|ren|hand|lung F** (*dated*) grocery and general store

ge|mit|telt [gə'mɪtlt] ADJ average

Gem|me ['gɛmə] **F -, -n** (*erhaben*) cameo; (*vertieft*) intaglio

ge|mocht *ptp von* **mögen**

ge|mol|ken *ptp von* **melken**

ge|mop|pelt [gə'mɔplt] ADJ → **doppelt**

Ge|mot|ze [gə'mɔtsə] **NT -s,** *no pl* (*inf*) moaning, fault-finding

Gems-: **Gems|bart** △ **M** → **Gamsbart, Gämsbart**; **Gems|bock** △ **M** → **Gämsbock**

Gem|se △ ['gɛmzə] **F -, -n** → **Gämse**

Gems|le|der △ **NT** → **Gämsleder**

Ge|mun|kel [gə'mʊŋkl] **NT -s,** *no pl* rumours *pl* (*Brit*), rumors *pl* (*US*); (*= Klatsch*) gossip

Ge|murk|se [gə'mʊrksə] **NT -s,** *no pl* (*inf pej*) **a** (*als Tätigkeit*) messing around **b** (*= Ergebnis von Pfuscharbeit*) mess

Ge|mur|mel [gə'mʊrml] **NT -s,** *no pl* murmuring; (*= unverständliches Reden auch*) mumbling; **zustimmendes ~ ging durch den Saal** a murmur of approval ran through the hall

Ge|mur|re [gə'mʊrə] **NT -s,** *no pl* (*inf*) grumbling (*inf*)

Ge|mü|se [gə'my:zə] **NT -s,** (*rare*) **-** vegetables *pl*; **frisches ~** fresh vegetables; **ein ~** a vegetable; **junges ~** (*hum inf*) whippersnappers *pl* (*inf*), green young things *pl* (*inf*)

Ge|mü|se-: **Ge|mü|se|(an)|bau M,** *no pl* vegetable-growing; (*für den Handel*) market gardening (*Brit*), truck farming (*US*); **Ge|mü|se|beet NT** vegetable bed *or* patch; **Ge|mü|se|bei|la|ge F** vegetables *pl*; **~ nach Wunsch** a choice of vegetables; **Ge|mü|se|brü|he F a** (*= Gemüsesuppe*) vegetable soup **b** (*= Gemüsepulver, -brühwürfel*) vegetable stock; **Ge|mü|se|ein|topf M** vegetable stew; **Ge|mü|se|fach NT** vegetable compartment; **Ge|mü|se|frau F** (*inf*) vegetable woman (*inf*); **Ge|mü|se|frit|ze M** (*inf*) vegetable seller; **Ge|mü|se|gar|ten M** vegetable *or* kitchen garden; **quer durch den ~** (*hum inf*) a real assortment; **in dem Geschäft dort gibt es alles quer durch den ~** they have everything but the kitchen sink in that shop there (*esp Brit inf*); **Ge|mü|se|händ|ler(in) M(F)** greengrocer (*esp Brit*), vegetable salesman/saleswoman (*US*); (*= Großhändler*) vegetable supplier; **Ge|mü|se|hand|lung F** greengrocer's (shop) (*esp Brit*), produce shop (*US*); **Ge|mü|se|kon|ser|ve F** tinned (*Brit*) *or* canned vegetables *pl*; (*in Gläsern*) preserved vegetables *pl*; **Ge|mü|se|la|den M** greengrocer's (shop) (*esp Brit*), produce shop (*US*); **Ge|mü|se|markt M** vegetable market; **Ge|mü|se|pflan|ze F** vegetable; **Ge|mü|se|plat|te F** (*Cook*) **eine ~** assorted vegetables *pl*; **Ge|mü|se|saft M** vegetable juice; **Ge|mü|se|sor|te F** kind *or* type of vegetable; **Ge|mü|se|stand M** (*= Marktstand*) vegetable stall *or* stand; **Ge|mü|se|sup|pe F** vegetable soup; **Ge|mü|se|zwie|bel F** Spanish onion

ge|mü|ßigt [gə'my:sɪçt] ADV = **bemüßigt**

ge|musst *ptp von* **müssen**

ge|mus|tert [gə'mʊstɐt] ADJ patterned → *auch* **mustern**

Ge|müt [gə'my:t] **NT -(e)s, -er a** (*= Geist*) mind; (*= Charakter*) nature, disposition; (*= Seele*) soul; (*= Gefühl*) feeling; (*= Gutmütigkeit*) warm-heartedness; **viel ~ haben** to be very warm-hearted; **die Menschen hatten damals mehr ~** people had more soul in those days; **das denkst du (dir) so einfach in deinem kindlichen ~!** that's what you think in your innocence; **etwas fürs ~** (*hum*) something for the soul; (*Film, Buch etc*) something sentimental; **jds ~ bewegen** (*liter*) to stir sb's heart *or* emotions; **sich** (*dat*) **etw zu ~e führen** (*= beherzigen*) to take sth to heart; (*hum inf*) *Glas Wein, Speise, Buch etc* to indulge in sth; **das ist ihr aufs ~ geschlagen** that made her worry herself sick (*inf*) **b** (*fig: = Mensch*) person; (*pl*) people; **sie ist ein ängstliches ~** she's a nervous soul, she has a nervous disposition; **die ~er erregen** to cause a stir; **wir müssen warten, bis sich die ~er beruhigt haben** we must wait until feelings have cooled down

ge|müt|lich [gə'my:tlɪç] ADJ **a** (*= bequem, behaglich*) comfortable, comfy (*inf*); (*= freundlich*) friendly *no adv*; (*= zwanglos*) informal; (*= klein und intim*) cosy (*Brit*), cozy (*US*), snug; *Schwatz, Beisammensein etc* cosy (*Brit*), cozy (*US*); **wir verbrachten einen ~en Abend** we spent a very

pleasant evening
b *Mensch* good-natured, pleasant; *(= leutselig)* approachable, friendly; *(= gelassen)* easy-going *no adv*, relaxed *no adv*
c *(= gemächlich)* unhurried, leisurely; **in ~em Tempo** at a comfortable *or* leisurely speed
ADV **a** *(= behaglich)* leisurely; *einrichten* comfortably; **wir wollen das Wochenende ~ gestalten** we plan to have a leisurely weekend; **es sich/jdm ~ machen** to make oneself/sb comfortable
b *(= gemächlich)* leisurely; **er arbeitete ~ vor sich hin** he worked away at a leisurely pace, he worked away unhurriedly

Ge|müt|lich|keit F -, *no pl* **a** *(= Bequemlichkeit, Behaglichkeit)* comfort; *(von Lokal, Wohnung)* comfortable ambience; *(= Freundlichkeit)* friendliness; *(= Zwanglosigkeit)* informality; *(= Intimität)* cosiness *(Brit)*, coziness *(US)*, snugness
b *(von Mensch)* good nature, pleasantness; *(= Leutseligkeit)* approachability, friendliness; *(= Gelassenheit)* easy-going nature; **da hört doch die ~ auf!** *(inf)* that's going too far; **da hört bei mir die ~ auf** I won't stand for that; **ein Prosit der ~!** happy days!
c *(= Gemächlichkeit)* unhurriedness, leisureliness; **in aller ~** at one's leisure; **ihr sitzt da in aller ~, und ich arbeite wie ein Verrückter** you sit there as though there were all the time in the world and I'm working like mad

Ge|müts-: **ge|müts|arm** ADJ emotionally impoverished; **Ge|müts|ar|mut** F emotional impoverishment; **Ge|müts|art** F disposition, nature; **ein Mensch von heiterer ~** a person of cheerful disposition *or* nature; **Ge|müts|be|we|gung** F emotion; **bist du zu keiner ~ fähig?** can't you show some emotion?; **ge|müts|kalt** ADJ cold; **ge|müts|krank** ADJ emotionally disturbed; **Ge|müts|kran|ke(r)** MF *decl as adj* emotionally disturbed person; **Ge|müts|krank|heit** F emotional disorder *or* disturbance; **Ge|müts|krüp|pel** M *(inf)* emotional cripple; **Ge|müts|la|ge** F mood; **je nach ~** as the mood takes me/him *etc*; **Ge|müts|le|ben** NT emotional life; **Ge|müts|lei|den** NT emotional disorder *or* disturbance; **Ge|müts|mensch** M good-natured, phlegmatic person; **du bist vielleicht ein ~!** *(iro inf)* you're a fine one! *(inf)*; *(= das ist unmöglich)* you'll be lucky! *(inf)*; **Ge|müts|re|gung** F = **Gemütsbewegung**; **Ge|müts|ru|he** F calmness; *(= Kaltblütigkeit)* sang-froid, composure, coolness; *(= Phlegma)* placidness; **in aller ~** *(inf)* (as) cool as a cucumber *(inf) or* as you please *(inf)*; *(= gemächlich)* at a leisurely pace; *(= aufreizend langsam)* as if there were all the time in the world; **du hast eine ~!** you take everything so calmly; **deine ~ möchte ich haben!** *(iro)* I like your cool! *(Brit inf)*, I'd like to have your composure; **Ge|müts|ver|fas|sung** F, **Ge|müts|zu|stand** M frame *or* state of mind

ge|müt|voll ADJ sentimental; *(= warmherzig)* warm-hearted

gen [gɛn] PREP *+acc (old, liter)* towards, toward; **~ Norden/Osten** *etc* northwards/eastwards *etc*; **~ Himmel blicken** to look up to the sky, to look heavenwards

Gen [geːn] NT **-s, -e** gene

Gen- *in cpds* genetic; *(= genmanipuliert)* genetically modified *or* engineered

ge|nannt *ptp von* **nennen**

ge|nant [ʒe'nant] ADJ *(dated) (= schüchtern)* bashful, shy; *(= peinlich)* embarrassing

ge|narbt [gə'narpt] ADJ *Leder* grained

ge|nas *pret von* **genesen**

Ge|nä|sel [gə'nɛːzl] NT **-s**, *no pl* nasal voice

ge|nau [gə'nau] ✪ 28.2, 40.2, 43.1, 43.1, 52.5, 53.1, 53.3, 53.6 **ADJ** exact; *(= richtig auch)* accurate; *(= präzis auch)* precise; *(= sorgfältig auch)* meticulous; *(= förmlich genau auch)* punctilious; **haben Sie die ~e Zeit?** have you got *(esp Brit) or* do you have the right *or* exact time?; **Genaueres** further details *pl or* particulars *pl*; **Genaueres weiß ich nicht** I don't know any more than that; **man weiß nichts Genaues über ihn** no-one knows anything definite about him
ADV **~!** *(inf)* exactly!, precisely!, quite!; **~ dasselbe** just *or* exactly the same; **~ das Gegenteil** just *or* exactly the opposite; **~ in der Mitte** right in the middle; **~ das wollte ich sagen** that's just *or* exactly what I wanted to say; **ich kenne ihn ~** I know just *or* exactly what he's like; **etw ~ wissen** to know sth for certain *or* for sure; **etw ~ nehmen** to take sth seriously; **~ genommen** strictly speaking; **er nimmt es sehr/nicht sehr ~** he's very/not very particular *(mit etw* about sth); **einen Entschluss ~ überlegen** to think a decision over very carefully; **meine Uhr geht ~** my watch keeps accurate time; **es stimmt auf den Millimeter ~** it's right to the millimetre *(Brit) or* millimeter *(US)*; **die Schuhe passten mir ~** the shoes fitted me perfectly; **das reicht ~** that's just enough; **~estens, aufs ~este** *or* **Genaueste** (right) down to the last (little) detail; **~ entgegengesetzt** diametrically opposed; **~ auf die Minute** dead *(inf) or* exactly on time; **so ~ wollte ich es (nun auch wieder) nicht wissen!** *(iro)* you can spare me the details → **Wahrheit**

ge|nau|ge|nom|men △ ADV → **genau ADV**

Ge|nau|ig|keit F -, *no pl (= Exaktheit)* exactness; *(= Richtigkeit)* accuracy; *(= Präzision)* precision; *(= Sorgfalt)* meticulousness

ge|nau|so [gə'nauzoː] ADV *(vor Adjektiv)* just as; *(alleinstehend)* just *or* exactly the same

Gen|bank F *pl* **-banken** gene bank

Gen|darm [ʒan'darm, ʒã'darm] M **-en, -en** *(old, Aus)* gendarme

Gen|dar|me|rie [ʒandarmə'riː, ʒã-] F **-, -n** [-'riːən] *(old, Aus)* gendarmerie

Gen|da|tei F *(Jur, Polizei)* DNA profile

Ge|nea|lo|ge [genea'loːgə] M **-n, -n**, **Ge|nea|lo|gin** [-'loːgɪn] F **-, -nen** genealogist

Ge|nea|lo|gie [genealo'giː] F **-, -n** [-'giːən] genealogy

ge|nea|lo|gisch [genea'loːgɪʃ] ADJ genealogical

ge|nehm [gə'neːm] ADJ *(geh)* acceptable; **eine ihm ~e Antwort** an answer acceptable to him; **jdm ~ sein** to be acceptable to sb; **ist es so ~?** is that agreeable *or* acceptable to you?; **wenn es ~ ist** if you are agreeable

ge|neh|mi|gen [gə'neːmɪgn] *ptp* **genehmigt** VT *Baupläne, Antrag, Veränderungen* to approve; *(= erlauben)* to sanction; *(= Lizenz erteilen)* to license; *Durchreise, Aufenthalt* to authorize; *(= zugestehen)* to grant; *Bitte* to agree to, to assent to, to grant; **wer kann mir die Teilnahme ~?** from whom do I get permission to take part?; **„genehmigt"** "approved"; *(inf)* permission granted *(hum)*; **sich** *(dat)* **etw ~** to indulge in sth; *(= kaufen)* to lash *or* splash out on sth; **sich** *(dat)* **einen ~** *(hum inf)* to have a little drink

Ge|neh|mi|gung F **-, -en** **a** *(von Bauplan, Antrag, Veränderungen)* approval; *(= Lizenzerteilung)* licensing; *(von Durchreise, Aufenthalt)* authorization; *(= das Zugestehen)* granting **b** *(= Erlaubnis)* approval; *(= Lizenz)* licence *(Brit)*, license *(US)*; *(für Durchreise, Aufenthalt) (= Berechtigungsschein)* permit; **mit freundlicher ~ von** by kind permission of

Ge|neh|mi|gungs-: **Ge|neh|mi|gungs|pflicht** F *(form)* licence *(Brit) or* license *(US)* requirement; **ge|neh|mi|gungs|pflich|tig** [-pflɪçtɪç] ADJ *(form)* requiring official approval; *(mit Visum, Stempel, Marke)* requiring official authorization; *(mit schriftlicher Genehmigung)* requiring a licence *(Brit) or* license *(US)*; **Radiosender sind ~** a licence *(Brit) or* license *(US)* is required for radio transmitters

ge|neigt [gə'naikt] ADJ *(geh) Zuhörer, Publikum* willing; *Aufmerksamkeit* kind; *(obs: = huldvoll)* gracious; **~er Leser!** gentle reader; **jdm/einer Sache ~ sein** to be well-disposed *or* favourably *(Brit) or* favorably *(US)* disposed to sb/sth; **~ sein, etw zu tun** to be inclined to do sth; **nicht ~ sein, etw zu tun** not to be inclined to do sth → *auch* **neigen, Ohr**

Ge|neigt|heit F -, *no pl (geh) (= Bereitwilligkeit)* inclination; *(= Wohlwollen)* goodwill *(gegenüber* towards); *(= Huld)* favour *(Brit)*, favor *(US) (gegenüber* to)

Ge|ne|ra *pl von* **Genus**

Ge|ne|ral [genə'raːl] M **-(e)s, -e** *or* **¨-e** [-'rɛːlə], **Ge|ne|ra|lin** [-'raːlɪn] F **-, -nen** **a** *(Mil, Eccl)* general; **Herr ~** General **b** *(inf: = Generaldirektor)* head

Ge|ne|ral-: **Ge|ne|ral|ab|so|lu|ti|on** F general absolution; **Ge|ne|ral|agent(in)** M(F) general agent; **Ge|ne|ral|agen|tur** F general agency; **Ge|ne|ral|am|nes|tie** F general amnesty; **Ge|ne|ral|an|griff** M *(Mil, fig)* general attack; **Ge|ne|ral|an|walt** M, **Ge|ne|ral|an|wäl|tin** F *(Jur: des Europäischen Gerichtshofs)* advocate general; **Ge|ne|ral|bass** M (basso) continuo; **Ge|ne|ral|beich|te** F general confession; **Ge|ne|ral|be|voll|mäch|tig|te(r)** MF *decl as adj* plenipotentiary; *(Comm)* general representative; **Ge|ne|ral|bun|des|an|walt** M, **Ge|ne|ral|bun|des|an|wäl|tin** F Chief Federal Prosecutor; **Ge|ne|ral|di|rek|ti|on** F head office; **Ge|ne|ral|di|rek|tor(in)** M(F) chairman/-woman, president *(US)*, CEO; **Ge|ne|ral|feld|mar|schall(in)** M(F) field marshal, general of the army *(US)*; **Ge|ne|ral|gou|ver|neur(in)** M(F) governor general

Ge|ne|ra|lin [-'raːlɪn] F **-, -nen** → **General**

Ge|ne|ral-: **Ge|ne|ral|in|spek|teur(in)** M(F) inspector general; **Ge|ne|ral|in|ten|dant(in)** M(F) *(Theat, Mus)* director

ge|ne|ra|li|sie|ren [genərali'ziːrən] *ptp* **generalisiert** VI to generalize

Ge|ne|ra|li|sie|rung F **-, -en** generalization

Ge|ne|ra|lis|si|mus [genəra'lɪsimʊs] M **-, Generalissimi** *or* **-se** generalissimo

Ge|ne|ra|list [genəra'lɪst] M **-en, -en**, **Ge|ne|ra|lis|tin** [-'lɪstɪn] F **-, -nen** generalist

Ge|ne|ra|li|tät [genərali'tɛːt] F **-,** *(rare)* **-en** *(Mil)* generals *pl*

Ge|ne|ral-: **Ge|ne|ral|klau|sel** F general *or* blanket clause; **Ge|ne|ral|kon|sul(in)** M(F) consul general; **Ge|ne|ral|kon|su|lat** NT consulate general; **Ge|ne|ral|leut|nant** M lieutenant general *(Brit)*, major general *(US)*; *(Brit Aviat)* air marshal; **Ge|ne|ral|ma|jor(in)** M(F) major general *(Brit)*, brigadier general *(US)*; *(Brit Aviat)* air vice-marshal; **Ge|ne|ral|mu|sik|di|rek|tor(in)** M(F) (chief) musical director; **Ge|ne|ral|nen|ner** M *(Math, fig)* common denominator; **Ge|ne|ral|obe|re(r)** [-loːbərə] M *decl as adj (Eccl)* general *(of a religious order)*; **Ge|ne|ral|obe|rin** F *(Eccl)* general *(of a women's order)*; **Ge|ne|ral|oberst** M *(Hist)* senior general; **Ge|ne|ral|pau|se** F *(Mus)* general rest; **Ge|ne|ral|prä|ven|ti|on** F *(Jur)* general deterrence; **Ge|ne|ral|pro|be** F *(Theat, fig)* dress rehearsal; *(Mus)* final rehearsal; **Ge|ne|ral|re|prä|sen|tanz** F *(esp Aus)* sole *or* exclusive agency *or* distribution; **Ge|ne|ral|sek|re|tär(in)** M(F) secretary-general; **Ge|ne|ral|staats|an|walt** M, **Ge|ne|ral|staats|an|wäl|tin** F *public prosecutor for a provincial court*, ≈ district attorney *(US)*; **Ge|ne|ral|stab** M general staff; **Ge|ne|ral|stabs|kar|te** F ≈ Ordnance Survey map *(Brit)*, detailed map *(on the scale 1:100 000)*; **ge|ne|ral|stabs|mä|ßig** **ADJ** *Aktion* planned with military precision **ADV** *planen, organisieren* with military precision; **Ge|ne|ral|stabs|of|fi|zier(in)** M(F) general staff officer; **Ge|ne|ral|streik** M general strike; **Ge|ne|ral|sy|no|de** F general synod; **ge|ne|ral|über|ho|len** *ptp* **generalüberholt** VT *infin, ptp only* **etw ~ lassen** to give sth a general overhaul; **etw ~ lassen** to have sth generally overhauled; **Ge|ne|ral|über|ho|lung** F **-, -en** complete overhaul; **Ge|ne|ral|ver|samm|lung** F general meeting; **Ge|ne|ral|ver|tre|ter(in)** M(F) general representative; **Ge|ne|ral|ver|tre|tung** F sole agency; **Ge|ne|ral|vi|kar** M vicar general;

Ge|ne|ral|voll|macht F general *or* full power of attorney

Ge|ne|ra|ti|on [genəra'tsio:n] F -, -en generation; **ein technisches Gerät der ersten ~** a piece of first-generation technology; **~ X/@** generation X/@

Ge|ne|ra|ti|o|nen-: **Ge|ne|ra|ti|o|nen|kon|flikt** M generation gap; **ge|ne|ra|ti|o|nen|lang** ADJ age-long ADV for generations; **Ge|ne|ra|ti|o|nen|ver|trag** M *(Econ)* *system whereby old people receive a pension from contributions being made by current working population*

Ge|ne|ra|ti|ons-: **ge|ne|ra|ti|ons|be|dingt** ADJ due to the difference in generation(s); **Ge|ne|ra|ti|ons|kon|flikt** M generation gap; **Ge|ne|ra|ti|ons|prob|lem** NT problem of one generation; **ein ~ der Jugend** a problem of the younger generation; **Ge|ne|ra|ti|ons|wech|sel** M *(Biol)* alternation of generations; **wir brauchen einen ~ in der Regierung** we need a new generation in government

ge|ne|ra|tiv [genəra'ti:f] ADJ generative; **~e Zellen** reproductive cells; **~e (Transformations)grammatik** (transformational) generative grammar

Ge|ne|ra|tor [genə'ra:to:ɐ] M -s, **Generatoren** generator; *(= Gasgenerator auch)* producer

Ge|ne|ra|tor|gas NT producer gas

ge|ne|rell [genə'rɛl] ADJ general ADV in general; *(= normalerweise)* normally; **~ kann man sagen, dass ...** generally *or* in general one can say that ...

ge|ne|rie|ren [genə'ri:rən] *ptp* **generiert** VT *(Ling, geh)* to generate

Ge|ne|ri|kum [ge'ne:rikʊm] NT -s, **Generika** [-ka] generic drug

ge|ne|rös [genə'rø:s] ADJ *(geh)* generous; *(= freigebig auch)* munificent *(liter)*

Ge|ne|ro|si|tät [genərozi'tɛ:t] F -, *(rare)* **-en** *(geh)* generosity; *(= Freigebigkeit auch)* munificence *(liter)*

Ge|ne|se [ge'ne:zə] F -, **-n** *(Biol, fig)* genesis

ge|ne|sen [gə'ne:zn] *pret* **genas** [gə'na:s], *ptp* **genesen** [gə'ne:zn] VI *aux sein (geh)* to convalesce; *(fig)* to recuperate

Ge|ne|sen|de(r) [gə'ne:zndə] MF *decl as adj* convalescent

Ge|ne|sis ['ge:nezɪs, 'gɛnezɪs] F -, *no pl* genesis; **die ~** *(Bibl)* (the Book of) Genesis

Ge|ne|sung [gə'ne:zʊŋ] ✪ 50.4 F -, *(rare)* **-en** convalescence, recovery *(auch fig)*; **auf dem Wege der ~** on the road to recovery; **ich wünsche baldige ~** I wish you a speedy recovery; **er fuhr zur ~ ins Sanatorium** he went into a sanatorium *(esp Brit)* or sanitarium *(US)* to convalesce

Ge|ne|sungs-: **Ge|ne|sungs|heim** NT *(dated)* convalescent home; **Ge|ne|sungs|pro|zess** M convalescence; **der ~ hat sich verzögert** his *etc* convalescence was protracted; **Ge|ne|sungs|ur|laub** M convalescent leave

Ge|ne|tik [ge'ne:tɪk] F -, *no pl* genetics *sing*

Ge|ne|ti|ker [ge'ne:tikɐ] M -s, -, **Ge|ne|ti|ke|rin** [-ərɪn] F -, **-nen** geneticist

ge|ne|tisch [ge'ne:tɪʃ] ADJ genetic; *Vater* biological ADV genetically

Ge|ne|za|reth [ge'ne:tsarɛt] **der See ~** the Sea of Galilee

Genf [gɛnf] NT -s Geneva

Gen|fer ['gɛnfɐ] ADJ *attr* Genevan; **der ~ See** Lake Geneva; **~ Konvention** Geneva Convention

Gen|fer ['gɛnfɐ] M -s, -, **Gen|fe|rin** [-ərɪn] F -, **-nen** Genevan, native *or (= Einwohner)* inhabitant of Geneva

Gen-: **Gen|for|scher(in)** M(F) genetic researcher; **Gen|for|schung** F genetic research

ge|ni|al [ge'nia:l] ADJ *Entdeckung, Einfall, Mensch* brilliant; *Künstler, Stil auch* inspired; *(= erfinderisch)* ingenious; **ein ~er Mensch, ein Genialer** a genius; **ein ~es Werk** a work of genius; **das war eine ~e Idee** that idea was *or* showed a stroke of genius

ge|ni|a|lisch [ge'nia:lɪʃ] ADJ *(geh)* brilliant; *(= unkonventionell)* eccentric

Ge|ni|a|li|tät [geniali'tɛ:t] F -, *no pl (von Künstler, Musiker etc)* genius; *(von Idee, Lösung etc)* brilliance; *(= Erfindungsreichtum)* ingenuity

Ge|nick [gə'nɪk] NT **-(e)s, -e** neck; **jdn am ~ packen** to grab sb by the scruff of the neck; **ein Schlag ins ~** a blow on the back of the neck; **seinen Hut ins ~ schieben** to push one's hat back (on one's head); **sich** *(dat)* **das ~ brechen** to break one's neck; *(fig)* to kill oneself; **jdm/einer Sache das ~ brechen** *(fig)* to finish sb/sth

Ge|nick-: **Ge|nick|schuss** M shot in the neck; **Ge|nick|star|re** F stiffness of the neck; *(Med)* (cerebral) meningitis; **~ haben** *(inf)* to have a stiff neck

Ge|nie [ʒe'ni:] NT -s, -s genius; **er ist ein ~** he's a (man of) genius; **er ist ein ~ im Taktieren** he's a genius when it comes to tactics, he has a genius for tactics

Ge|nie F -, -s *(Sw Mil)* engineer corps

Ge|ni|en *pl von* **Genius**

ge|nie|ren [ʒe'ni:rən] *ptp* **geniert** VR to be embarrassed; **sich vor Fremden ~** to be shy of *or* with strangers; **~ Sie sich nicht!** don't be shy!; **dabei geniere ich mich** I get embarrassed doing it; **ich geniere mich, das zu sagen** I don't like to say it; **er genierte sich (gar) nicht, das zu tun** it didn't bother him (at all) to do that → *auch* **geniert** VT **jdn ~** *(= peinlich berühren)* to embarrass sb; *(old, dial: = stören)* to bother *or* disturb sb; **das geniert mich wenig!** that doesn't bother *or* worry me

ge|nier|lich [ʒe'ni:ɐlɪç] ADJ **a** *(inf: = lästig)* bothersome; *(= genant)* embarrassing **b** *(dated: = schüchtern)* shy, bashful

ge|niert [ʒe'ni:ɐt] ADJ embarrassed ADV with embarrassment → *auch* **genieren**

ge|nieß|bar ADJ *(= essbar)* edible; *(= trinkbar)* drinkable; *(fig: = annehmbar)* acceptable; **er ist heute nicht ~** *(fig inf)* he is unbearable today

Ge|nieß|bar|keit [gə'ni:sba:ɐkait] F -, *no pl (= Essbarkeit)* edibility; *(= Trinkbarkeit)* drinkability; *(fig)* acceptability

ge|nie|ßen [gə'ni:sn] *pret* **genoss** [gə'nɔs] *ptp* **genossen** [gə'nɔsn] VT **a** *(lit, fig: = sich erfreuen an)* to enjoy; **den Wein muss man ~** this is a wine to be savoured *(Brit)* or savored *(US)*; **er ist heute nicht zu ~** *(inf)* he is unbearable today **b** *(= essen)* to eat; *(= trinken)* to drink; **das Essen ist kaum zu ~** the meal is scarcely edible; **der Wein ist kaum zu ~** the wine is scarcely drinkable → **Vorsicht, Kavalier**

Ge|nie|ßer [gə'ni:sɐ] M -s, -, **Ge|nie|ße|rin** [-ərɪn] F -, **-nen** connoisseur; *(des Lebens)* pleasure-lover; *(= Feinschmecker)* gourmet, epicure; **er ist ein stiller ~** he really knows how to enjoy life in his quiet way

ge|nie|ße|risch [gə'ni:sərɪʃ] ADJ appreciative; **sein ~er Ausdruck** his expression of pleasure ADV appreciatively; *(= mit Behagen)* pleasurably; **~ schmatzte er mit den Lippen** he smacked his lips with relish; **~ zog er an seiner Zigarre** he puffed at his cigar with relish

Ge|nie-: **Ge|nie|streich** M stroke of genius; **Ge|nie|trup|pe** F *(Sw Mil)* engineer corps

ge|ni|tal [geni'ta:l] ADJ genital

Ge|ni|tal- *in cpds* genital; **Ge|ni|tal|be|reich** M genital area

Ge|ni|ta|le [geni'ta:lə] NT -s, **Genitalien** [-liən] genital; **die Genitalien** the genitals *or* genitalia *(form)*

Ge|ni|tiv ['ge:niti:f] M -s, -e [-və] *(= Fall)* genitive (case); *(= Form)* genitive (form); **im ~** in the genitive

Ge|ni|tiv|ob|jekt NT genitive object

Ge|ni|us ['ge:niʊs] M -, **Genien** ['ge:niən] **a** *(Myth)* genius, guardian spirit **b** *(= Genie)* genius; **~ loci** *(geh)* genius loci **c** *(Art)* genius

Gen-: **Gen|la|bor** NT genetics laboratory; **Gen|ma|ni|pu|la|ti|on** F genetic manipulation; **gen|ma|ni|pu|liert** [-manipuli:ɐt] ADJ genetically engineered *or* modified; **~e Lebensmittel** genetically modified food, frankenfood *(inf)*; **~es Hühnchen** genetically modified chicken, frankenchicken *(inf)*; **Gen|mu|ta|ti|on** F gene mutation

Ge|nom [ge'no:m] NT -s, -e genome

Ge|nom|ana|ly|se F genome analysis

ge|nom|men *ptp von* **nehmen**

ge|noppt [gə'nɔpt] ADJ *Teppich, Stoff, Wolle* nubbly; *Gummi* pimpled

Ge|nör|gel [gə'nœrgl] NT -s, *no pl (inf)* moaning, grumbling, carping

ge|noss *pret von* **genießen**

Ge|nos|se [gə'nɔsə] M -n, -n, **Ge|nos|sin** [-'nɔsɪn] F -, **-nen** comrade; *(dated: = Gefährte auch)* companion; *(= Mitglied einer Genossenschaft)* member of a cooperative; *(pej: = Kumpan)* mate *(Brit inf)*, buddy *(US inf)*, pal *(inf)*; **X und ~n** *(Jur)* X and others; *(pej)* X and co *(inf)*

ge|nos|sen *ptp von* **genießen**

Ge|nos|sen-: **Ge|nos|sen|schaft** [gə'nɔsnʃaft] F -, **-en** cooperative; **Ge|nos|sen|schaf|ter** [-ʃaftɐ] M -s, -, **Ge|nos|sen|schaf|te|rin** [-ərɪn] F -, **-nen**, **Ge|nos|sen|schaft|ler** [-ʃaftlɐ] M -s, -, **Ge|nos|sen|schaft|le|rin** [-ərɪn] F -, **-nen** member of a cooperative; **ge|nos|sen|schaft|lich** [-ʃaftlɪç] ADJ cooperative ADV **~ organisiert** organized as a cooperative

Ge|nos|sen|schafts-: **Ge|nos|sen|schafts|bank** F *pl* **-banken** cooperative bank; **Ge|nos|sen|schafts|bau|er** M, **Ge|nos|sen|schafts|bäu|e|rin** F cooperative farmer; **Ge|nos|sen|schafts|be|trieb** M cooperative; **Ge|nos|sen|schafts|we|sen** NT, *no pl* cooperative system

Ge|nos|sin [-'nɔsɪn] F → **Genosse**

ge|nö|tigt [gə'nø:tɪçt] ADJ **~ sein, etw zu tun** to be forced *or* obliged to do sth; **sich ~ sehen, etw zu tun** to feel (oneself) obliged to do sth

Ge|no|typ [geno'ty:p] M, **Ge|no|ty|pus** [geno'ty:pʊs] M genotype

ge|no|ty|pisch [geno'ty:pɪʃ] ADJ genotypic

Ge|no|zid [geno'tsi:t] M OR NT **-(e)s, -e** *or* **-ien** [-də, -diən] *(geh)* genocide

Gen|raps M GM rapeseed

Gen|re ['ʒã:rə] NT -s, -s genre

Gen|re-: **Gen|re|bild** NT genre picture; **Gen|re|ma|ler(in)** M(F) genre painter; **Gen|re|ma|le|rei** F, *no pl* genre painting

Gent [gɛnt] NT -s Ghent

Gen-: **Gen|tech|nik** F genetic engineering; **Gen|tech|ni|ker(in)** M(F) genetic engineer; **gen|tech|nik|frei** ADJ *Lebensmittel etc* GM-free, not genetically modified *pred*; **gen|tech|nisch** ADJ *Fortschritte etc* in genetic engineering ADV *manipulieren* genetically; *produzieren, herstellen* by means of genetic engineering; **~ vermehren** to reproduce through genetic engineering; **~ verändert** genetically modified *or* manipulated; **~ veränderte Organismen/Lebensmittel** genetically manipulated organisms/food; **~ verändertes Getreide** GM crops *pl*; **Gen|tech|no|lo|gie** F genetic engineering; **gen|tech|no|lo|gisch** ADJ *Verfahren, Zeitalter* of genetic engineering ADV **~ hergestellte Arzneimittel** drugs produced by means of genetic engineering; **Gen|test** M *(Med)* DNA test; **Gen|the|ra|pie** F gene therapy; **Gen|trans|fer** M genetic transfer

Ge|nua ['ge:nua] NT -s Genoa

Ge|nu|e|se [genu'e:zə] M -n, -n, **Ge|nu|e|sin** [-'e:zɪn] F -, **-nen**, **Ge|nu|e|ser** [genu'e:zɐ] M -s, -, **Ge|nu|e|se|rin** [-ərɪn] F -, **-nen** Genoese

ge|nu|e|sisch [genu'e:zɪʃ] ADJ Genoese

ge|nug [gə'nu:k] ADV enough; **~ Platz, Platz ~** enough *or* sufficient room; **groß/alt/reich ~** big/old/rich enough; **~ davon** enough of that; **~ der vielen Worte!** enough of words!; **danke, das ist ~** that's enough, thank you; **das ist wenig ~** that's precious little; **und damit noch nicht ~** and that's not all; **sie sind jetzt ~, um ...** there are enough of them now to ...;

sag, wenns ~ ist! *(beim Einschenken etc)* say when!; **jetzt ist(s) aber ~!** that's enough, that does it!; **(von etw) ~ haben** to have (got) enough (of sth); *(= einer Sache überdrüssig sein)* to have had enough (of sth); **er kann nicht ~ bekommen** *or* **kriegen** he can't get enough; **nicht ~, dass er sein ganzes Geld verspielt, außerdem ... er ...** not only does he gamble away all his money, he also ...; **er konnte sich nicht ~ darin tun, ihre Gastfreundschaft zu loben** *(geh)* he could not praise her hospitality enough *or* sufficiently; **sich** *(dat)* **selbst ~ sein** to be sufficient unto oneself; *(= gern allein sein)* to be content with one's own company; **Manns ~ sein, um zu ...** to be man enough to ...

Ge|nü|ge [gəˈnyːgə] F **-,** *no pl* **zur ~** enough; **das habe ich zur ~ getan/gehört/gesehen** I have done/heard/seen it often enough *or (stärker, abwertend)* quite often enough; **etw zur ~ kennen** to know sth well enough; *(abwertender)* to know sth only too well, to be only too familiar with sth; **jdm ~ tun** *(geh)* to satisfy sb; **jds Forderungen** *(dat)* **~ tun** *(geh)* to satisfy *or* meet sb's demands; **jds Erwartungen** *(dat)* **~ tun** *(geh)* to fulfil *(Brit) or* fulfill *(US)* sb's expectations

ge|nü|gen [gəˈnyːgn] *ptp* **genügt** VI **a** *(= ausreichen)* to be enough *or* sufficient (*+dat* for); **das genügt (mir)** that's enough *or* sufficient (for me), that will do (for me); **dieses Haus genügt uns** we're happy with this house; **dieses Haus genügt für uns** this house is enough for us **b** *+dat (= befriedigen, gerecht werden) den Anforderungen* to satisfy; *jds Wünschen, Erwartungen* to fulfil *(Brit)*, to fulfill *(US)*

ge|nü|gend ADJ **a** *inv (= ausreichend)* enough, sufficient **b** *(= befriedigend)* satisfactory ADV *(= reichlich)* enough, sufficiently; **ich habe ~ oft versucht, zu ...** I have tried often enough *or* sufficiently often to ...

ge|nug|sam [gəˈnuːkzaːm] ADV *(geh)* enough; **es ist ~ bekannt** it is sufficiently well-known

ge|nüg|sam [gəˈnyːkzaːm] ADJ *(= anspruchslos) Tier, Pflanze* undemanding; *Mensch auch* modest; **ein ~es Leben führen** to live modestly ADV *leben* modestly; **sich ~ ernähren** to live on *or* to have a simple diet

Ge|nüg|sam|keit F **-,** *no pl (von Mensch)* undemanding nature; **die ~ einer Pflanze/eines Tieres** the modest requirements of a plant/an animal; **seine bewundernswerte ~** his admirably undemanding nature

ge|nug|tun VI *sep irreg +dat (dated)* to satisfy; **er konnte sich** *(dat)* **nicht ~, ihre Schönheit zu preisen** he couldn't praise her beauty enough, he never tired of praising her beauty

Ge|nug|tu|ung [gəˈnuːktuːʊŋ] F **-,** *(rare)* **-en** satisfaction *(über +acc* at); **für etw ~ leisten** to make amends for sth; **~ verlangen** *or* **fordern** to demand satisfaction; **ich hörte mit ~, dass ...** it gave me great satisfaction to hear that ...; **das hat mir ~ verschafft** that gave me a sense of satisfaction

ge|nu|in [genuˈiːn] ADJ *(geh)* genuine

Ge|nus [ˈgeːnʊs, ˈgɛnʊs] NT **-, Ge|nera** [ˈgeːnera, ˈgɛnera] **a** *(Biol)* genus **b** *(Gram)* gender; **~ verbi** voice of the verb

Ge|nuss [gəˈnʊs] M **-es, ⸚e** [gəˈnʏsə] **a** *no pl (= das Zusichnehmen)* consumption; *(von Drogen)* taking, use; *(von Tabak)* smoking; **der ~ von Alkohol ist Kindern verboten** children are forbidden to drink *or* consume *(form)* alcohol; **der übermäßige ~ von Tabak ist gesundheitsschädlich** excessive smoking is injurious to one's health; **nach dem ~ der Pilze** after eating the mushrooms **b** *(= Vergnügen)* pleasure; **die Genüsse des Lebens** the pleasures *or* joys of life; **etw mit ~ essen** to eat sth with relish; **den Wein hat er mit ~ getrunken** he really enjoyed the wine **c** *no pl (= Nutznießung)* **in den ~ von etw kommen** *(von Vergünstigungen)* to enjoy sth; *(von Renten, Prämie etc)* to be in receipt of sth

Ge|nuss-: **ge|nuss|freu|dig** ADJ *(geh)* pleasure-loving *no adv*; **Ge|nuss|gift** NT *(form)* social drug

ge|nüss|lich [gəˈnʏslɪç] ADJ pleasurable ADV with pleasure; **er grunzte ~** he grunted with obvious enjoyment; **er schmatzte ~** he smacked his lips with relish

Ge|nuss-: **Ge|nuss|mensch** M hedonist; *(auf Essen und Trinken bezogen)* bon vivant; **Ge|nuss|mit|tel** NT *semi-luxury foods and tobacco*; **ge|nuss|reich** ADJ enjoyable; **Ge|nuss|schein** M *(Fin)* profit-participation certificate; **Ge|nuss|sucht** F pursuit of pleasure; **ge|nuss|süch|tig** ADJ pleasure-seeking; **ge|nuss|voll** ADJ *Aufenthalt, Urlaub, Erlebnis, Abend* delightful; *Schmatzen* appreciative; *Lächeln* gratified ADV with obvious enjoyment

Geo|dä|sie [geodɛˈziː] F **-,** *no pl* geodesy, geodetics *sing*

Geo|dät [geoˈdɛːt] M **-en, -en, Geo|dä|tin** [-ˈdɛːtɪn] F **-, -nen** geodesist

Geo|drei|eck® [ˈgeo-] NT *(inf)* set square

Geo|graf [geoˈgraːf] M **-en, -en, Geo|gra|fin** [-ˈgraːfɪn] F **-, -nen** geographer

Geo|gra|fie [geograˈfiː] F **-,** *no pl* geography

geo|gra|fisch [geoˈgraːfɪʃ] ADJ *no pred* geographic(al)

Geo|graph *etc* = **Geograf** *etc*

Geo|lo|ge [geoˈloːgə] M **-n, -n, Geo|lo|gin** [-ˈloːgɪn] F **-, -nen** geologist

Geo|lo|gie [geoloˈgiː] F **-,** *no pl* geology

geo|lo|gisch [geoˈloːgɪʃ] ADJ *no pred* geological

Geo|me|ter [geoˈmeːtɐ] M **-s, -, Geo|me|te|rin** [-ərɪn] F **-, -nen** **a** surveyor **b** *(old)* geometrician

Geo|met|rie [geomeˈtriː] F **-,** *no pl* geometry

geo|met|risch [geoˈmeːtrɪʃ] ADJ geometric; **~er Ort** locus

Geo|mor|pho|lo|gie F geomorphology

Geo|phy|sik F geophysics *sing*

Geo|po|li|tik F geopolitics *pl or (als Fachgebiet) sing*

geo|po|li|tisch ADJ *no pred* geopolitical

ge|ord|net [gəˈɔrdnət] ADJ *Leben, Zustände* well-ordered; **in ~en Verhältnissen leben** to live a well-ordered life; **Kinder aus ~en Verhältnissen** children from well-ordered backgrounds; **~e Verhältnisse schaffen** to put things on an orderly basis → *auch* **ordnen**

Geor|gette [ʒɔrˈʒɛt] F **-, -s,** *or nt* **-s, -s** georgette

Ge|or|gi|en [geˈɔrgiən] NT **-s** Georgia *(in Caucasia)*

Ge|or|gi|er [geˈɔrgiɐ] M **-s, -, Ge|or|gi|e|rin** [-iərɪn] F **-, -nen** Georgian

ge|or|gisch ADJ Georgian

Geo-: **geo|sta|ti|o|när** ADJ geostationary; **geo|stra|te|gisch** ADJ geostrategic; **Geo|wis|sen|schaft** F earth science; **geo|zent|risch** ADJ geocentric

ge|paart [gəˈpaːɐt] PTP *von* **paaren** ADJ *(fig)* **Bosheit ~ mit Dummheit** maliciousness coupled *or* combined with stupidity → *auch* **paaren**

Ge|päck [gəˈpɛk] NT **-(e)s,** *no pl* luggage *no pl (Brit)*, baggage *no pl*; *(Mil: = Marschgepäck)* baggage; *(von Soldat, Pfadfinder etc)* kit; *(von Bergsteiger)* pack; **mit leichtem ~ reisen** to travel light

Ge|päck-: **Ge|päck|ab|fer|ti|gung** F *(= Vorgang) (am Bahnhof)* luggage *(Brit) or* baggage processing; *(am Flughafen)* checking-in of luggage *(Brit) or* baggage; *(= Stelle) (am Bahnhof)* luggage *(Brit) or* baggage office; *(am Flughafen)* luggage *(Brit) or* baggage check-in; **Ge|päck|ab|la|ge** F luggage *(Brit) or* baggage rack; **Ge|päck|an|nah|me** F *(= Vorgang)* checking-in of luggage *(Brit) or* baggage; *(auch* **Gepäckannahmestelle**) *(am Bahnhof) (zur Beförderung)* luggage *(Brit) or* baggage office; *(zur Aufbewahrung)* left-luggage office *(Brit)*, baggage checkroom *(US)*; *(am Flughafen)* luggage *(Brit) or* baggage check-in; **Ge|päck|auf|be|wah|rung** F *(= das Aufbewahren)* looking after left luggage *no art (Brit) or* baggage *no art*; *(auch* **Gepäckaufbewahrungsstelle**) left-luggage office *(Brit)*, baggage checkroom *(US)*; **Ge|päck|auf|be|wah|rungs|schein** M left-luggage ticket *(Brit)*, check number *(US)*; **Ge|päck|auf|kle|ber** M luggage *(Brit) or* baggage sticker; **Ge|päck|aus|ga|be** F *(auch* **Gepäckausgabestelle**) *(am Bahnhof) (zur Beförderung)* (out-counter of the) luggage *(Brit) or* baggage office; *(zur Aufbewahrung)* (out-counter of the) left-luggage office *(Brit) or* baggage checkroom *(US)*; *(am Flughafen)* luggage *(Brit) or* baggage reclaim; **wir müssen noch zur ~** we still have to collect our luggage *(Brit) or* baggage; **Ge|päck|band** [-bant] NT *pl* **-bänder** luggage *(Brit) or* baggage conveyor belt; **Ge|päck|er|mitt|lung** F luggage *(Brit) or* baggage tracing; **Ge|päck|fach** NT luggage *(Brit) or* baggage compartment; *(im Flugzeug)* overhead compartment; **Ge|päck|iden|ti|fi|zie|rung** F luggage *(Brit) or* baggage identification; **Ge|päck|kar|ren** M luggage *(Brit) or* baggage trolley, cart *(US)*; **Ge|päck|kon|trol|le** F luggage *(Brit) or* baggage control *or* check; **Ge|päck|marsch** M *(Mil)* pack march; **Ge|päck|netz** NT luggage *(Brit) or* baggage rack; **Ge|päck|raum** M *(Aut)* boot *(Brit)*, trunk *(US)*

Ge|päcks- *(Aus) in cpds* = **Gepäck-**

Ge|päck-: **Ge|päck|schal|ter** M = **Gepäckannahme**; **Ge|päck|schein** M luggage *(Brit) or* baggage ticket; **Ge|päck|schließ|fach** NT luggage *(Brit) or* baggage locker; **Ge|päck|stück** NT piece *or* item of luggage *(Brit) or* baggage; **Ge|päck|trä|ger** M *(am Fahrrad)* carrier; **Ge|päck|trä|ger(in)** M(F) porter *(Brit)*, baggage handler *(Brit) or* carrier; **Ge|päck|ver|si|che|rung** F luggage *(Brit) or* baggage insurance; **Ge|päck|wa|gen** M luggage van *(Brit)*, baggage car *(US)*

ge|pan|zert [gəˈpantsɐt] PTP *von* **panzern** ADJ *Fahrzeug* armoured *(Brit)*, armored *(US)*; *Tier* mailed; *(mit Hornhaut)* sclerodermic *(spec)* → *auch* **panzern**

Ge|pard [ˈgeːpart] M **-s, -e** [-də] cheetah

ge|pfef|fert [gəˈpfɛfɐt] ADJ *(inf) (= hoch) Preise, Mieten* steep; *(= schwierig) Fragen, Prüfung* tough; *(= hart) Kritik* biting; *Strafpredigt* tough; *(= anzüglich) Witz, Geschichte* spicy; **jdm eine ~e Ohrfeige geben** to give sb a clout *(inf)*, to clout sb one *(inf)* → *auch* **pfeffern**

Ge|pfei|fe [gəˈpfaifə] NT **-s,** *no pl* whistling

ge|pfif|fen *ptp von* **pfeifen**

ge|pflegt [gəˈpfleːkt] ADJ **a** *(= nicht vernachlässigt)* well looked after; *Garten auch* well-tended; *Parkanlagen auch* well-kept; *Mensch, Äußeres, Hund* well-groomed; *Aussehen* well-groomed, soigné *(liter)* → *auch* **pflegen** **b** *(= kultiviert, niveauvoll)* civilized; *Atmosphäre, Restaurant* sophisticated; *Ausdrucksweise, Gespräche* cultured; *Sprache, Stil* cultured, refined; *Umgangsformen* refined; *(= angenehm) Abend* pleasant; **ein ganz ~es Bad nehmen** to have a nice long bath **c** *(= erstklassig) Speisen, Weine* excellent; *(inf: = von guter Qualität)* decent; **„gepflegte Küche"** "excellent cuisine" ADV **a** *(= kultiviert)* **sich ~ unterhalten** to have a civilized conversation; **sich ~ ausdrücken** to have a cultured way of speaking; **drück dich gefälligst ein bisschen ~er aus** don't be so crude; **sehr ~ wohnen** to live in style; **so richtig ~ essen gehen** *(inf)* to go to a really nice restaurant **b** *(inf: = gut, gründlich)* **sich ganz ~ ausruhen** to have a good long rest

Ge|pflegt|heit F **-,** *no pl* **a die ~ des Gartens/Rasens** the well-tended garden/well-kept lawn; **die ~ ihrer Hände erstaunte mich** I was amazed at how beautifully looked-after her hands were; **die ~ seines Aussehens** his well-groomed appearance **b die ~ ihrer Aussprache/ihres Stils** her refined *or* cultured accent/style

ge|pflo|gen *(old) ptp von* **pflegen**

Ge|pflo|gen|heit [gə'pflo:gnhait] F -, -en (geh) (= Gewohnheit) habit; (= Verfahrensweise) practice; (= Brauch) custom, tradition

Ge|plän|kel [gə'plɛŋkl] NT -s, - skirmish; (fig) squabble

Ge|plap|per [gə'plapɐ] NT -s, no pl babbling; (fig: = Geschwätz auch) chatter(ing)

Ge|plärr [gə'plɛr] NT -(e)s, no pl, **Ge|plär|re** [gə'plɛrə] NT -s, no pl bawling; (von Radio) blaring

Ge|plät|scher [gə'plɛtʃɐ] NT -s, no pl splashing; (pej inf: = Unterhaltung) babbling

ge|plät|tet [gə'plɛtət] ADJ pred (inf) floored (inf); **ich bin ganz ~** (inf) I'm flabbergasted (inf) → auch **plätten**

Ge|plau|der [gə'plaudɐ] NT -s, no pl (geh) chatting

ge|pols|tert [gə'pɔlstɐt] PTP von **polstern** ADJ Möbel etc upholstered; Kleidung etc padded; **sie ist gut ~** (inf, euph) she's well-padded → auch **polstern**

Ge|pol|ter [gə'pɔltɐ] NT -s, no pl (= Krach) din; (an Tür etc) banging, thudding; (von Kutsche etc) clattering; (inf: = Geschimpfe) ranting; **die Fässer fielen mit ~ die Treppe hinunter** the barrels went thudding down the stairs

gepr. abbr von **geprüft**

Ge|prä|ge [gə'prɛ:gə] NT -s, no pl (auf Münzen) strike; (fig) (= Eigentümlichkeit) character; (= Aura) aura; **das hat den 60er Jahren ihr ~ gegeben** or **verliehen** it has left its mark or stamp on the sixties

Ge|prah|le [gə'pra:lə] NT -s, no pl (inf) boasting, bragging

Ge|prän|ge [gə'prɛŋə] NT -s, no pl (geh) splendour (Brit), splendor (US), magnificence

Ge|pras|sel [gə'prasl] NT -s, no pl clatter(ing), rattle, rattling; (von Regen, Hagel) drumming; (von Feuer) crackle, crackling

ge|prie|sen ptp von **preisen**

ge|puf|fert [gə'pʊfɐt] ADJ (Chem, Comput) buffered

ge|punk|tet [gə'pʊŋktət] ADJ Linie dotted; Stoff, Kleid spotted; (regelmäßig) polka-dot → auch **punkten**

Ge|qua|ke [gə'kva:kə] NT -s, no pl croaking; (pej inf: = Geschwätz) chatter

Ge|quä|ke [gə'kvɛ:kə] NT -s, no pl (inf) (von Kind) whining; (von Radio) blaring

ge|quält [gə'kvɛ:lt] ADJ Lächeln forced; Miene, Ausdruck pained; Gesang, Stimme strained → auch **quälen**

Ge|quas|sel [gə'kvasl] NT -s, no pl (pej inf) chattering

Ge|quat|sche [gə'kvatʃə] NT -s, no pl (pej inf) gabbing (inf); (= Blödsinn) twaddle (inf)

Ge|quen|gel [gə'kvɛŋl] NT -s, no pl, **Ge|quen|ge|le** [gə'kvɛŋələ] NT -s, no pl, **Ge|queng|le** [gə'kvɛŋlə] NT -s, no pl whining

Ge|quie|ke [gə'kvi:kə] NT -s, no pl squealing

Ge|quiet|sche [gə'kvi:tʃə] NT -s, no pl squeaking; (von Reifen, Mensch) squealing

ge|quol|len ptp von **quellen**

Ger [ge:ɐ] M -(e)s, -e (old) javelin (used by the ancient Germanic peoples)

ge|ra|de [gə'ra:də] ADJ straight; Zahl even; (= aufrecht) Haltung upright; (fig: = aufrichtig) Charakter honest; Mensch upright, upstanding; **eine ~ Körperhaltung haben** to hold oneself up straight; **in ~r Linie von jdm abstammen** to be directly descended from sb; **seinen ~n Weg gehen** (fig) to maintain one's integrity; **jdn mit ~m und offenem Blick ansehen** to look sb straight in the face; **das ~ Gegenteil** the exact or very opposite, exactly or just the opposite → **fünf**

ADV **a** (= nicht krumm) straight; **~ gewachsen sein** (Mensch) to be clean-limbed; (Baum) to be straight; **~ sitzen/stehen** to sit up/stand up straight

b (= im Augenblick, soeben) just; **wenn Sie ~ Zeit haben** if you have time just now; **wo Sie ~ da sind** just while you're here; **er wollte ~ aufstehen** he was just about to get up; **der Zug war ~ weg** the train had just gone; **~ erst** only just; **da wir ~ von Geld sprechen, …** talking of money …; **es macht uns ~ so viel Spaß** we're just enjoying it so much

c (= knapp) just; **~ so viel, dass er davon leben kann** just enough for him to live on; **sie hat die Prüfung ~ so bestanden** she just about passed the exam; **~ noch** only just; **~ noch zur rechten Zeit** just in time; **das hat ~ noch gefehlt!** (iro) that's all we wanted!

d (= genau) just; (= direkt) right; **es ist ~ 8 Uhr** it's just 8 o'clock; **~ zur rechten Zeit** at just or exactly the right time, just at the right time; **~ heute hab ich an dich gedacht** I was thinking of you just or only today; **jdm ~ in die Augen sehen** to look sb straight or right in the eyes; **~ deshalb** that's just or exactly why; **~ umgekehrt, ~ das Gegenteil** exactly or just the opposite; **das ist es ja ~!** that's just or exactly it!; **so ist es ~ richtig** that's just or exactly right

e (= speziell, besonders) especially; **~, weil …** just because …; **~ du solltest dafür Verständnis haben** you should be particularly understanding; **sie ist nicht ~ eine Schönheit** she's not exactly a beauty; **das war nicht ~ schön/interessant** that wasn't particularly or exactly nice/interesting; **du kannst dich ~ beklagen** (iro) what are you complaining about?, you've got a lot to complain about (iro)

f (= ausgerechnet) **warum ~ das?** why that of all things?; **warum ~ heute?** why today of all days?; **warum ~ ich?** why me of all people?; **warum ~ im Winter?** why in winter of all times?; **warum ~ in Venedig?** why in Venice of all places?; **~ diesem Trottel musste ich begegnen** of all people I would have to meet that idiot

g (inf: = erst recht) **nun ~!** you try and stop me now! (inf); **jetzt** or **nun ~ nicht!** I'll be damned if I will! (inf)

Ge|ra|de [gə'ra:də] F -n, -n **a** (Math) straight line **b** (Sport) (von Renn-, Laufbahn) straight; (Boxen) straight left/right; **seine rechte ~ traf ihn genau am Kinn** he hit him with a straight right to the chin

ge|ra|de-: **ge|ra|de|aus** [gəra:də'laus] ADV straight ahead; gehen, fahren straight on (Brit) or ahead; **ge|ra|de+bie|gen** VT sep irreg (fig inf) to straighten out, to put straight, to sort out; **ge|ra|de bie|gen** irreg, **ge|ra|de+bie|gen** sep irreg VT Stange etc to straighten out; **ge|ra|de hal|ten** irreg VT to hold straight VR to hold oneself (up) straight; **ge|ra|de|he|raus** [gəra:dəhe'raus] (inf) ADJ pred forthright, frank, plain-spoken ADV frankly; **~ gesagt** quite frankly; **ge|ra|de le|gen** VT to put straight; **ge|ra|de ma|chen**, **ge|ra|de+ma|chen** sep VT to straighten (out)

ge|ra|den|wegs [gə'ra:dnve:ks] ADV = **gerade(s)wegs**

ge|ra|de rich|ten, **ge|ra|de+rich|ten** sep VT to straighten up; (horizontal) to straighten out

ge|rä|dert [gə'rɛ:dɐt] ADJ (inf) **wie ~ sein, sich wie ~ fühlen** to be or feel (absolutely) whacked (inf)

ge|ra|de-: **ge|ra|de sit|zen** VI irreg (S Ger, Aus, Sw: aux sein) to sit up straight; **ge|ra|de|so** [gə'ra:dəzo:] ADV = **ebenso**; **ge|ra|de|so|gut** △ ADV → **ebenso**; **ge|ra|de|so|viel** △ ADV → **ebenso**; **ge|ra|de+ste|hen** VI sep irreg (S Ger, Aus, Sw: aux sein) **für jdn/etw ~** (fig) to be answerable or to answer for sb/sth; **ge|ra|de ste|hen** VI irreg (S Ger, Aus, Sw: aux sein) (= aufrecht stehen) to stand up straight; **ge|ra|de(s)|wegs** [gə'ra:də(s)ve:ks] ADV straight; **~ auf etw** (acc) **losgehen** (fig) to get straight down to sth; **ge|ra|de|zu** [gə'ra:dətsu:, gəra:də'tsu:] ADV **a** (= beinahe) virtually, almost; (= wirklich, durchaus) really; **das ist doch ~ Selbstmord** that's nothing short of suicide, that's absolute suicide; **das ist ja ~ verblüffend/lächerlich!** that is absolutely amazing/ridiculous! **b** (= ohne Umschweife) frankly; **er sagte mir ~, dass …** he told me straight out or frankly that …; **~ aufs Ziel zusteuern** (fig) to go straight to the point ADJ pred (inf) (= ehrlich) frank, candid; (= unverblümt) blunt

Ge|rad-: **Ge|rad|füh|rung** F (Tech) guide; **Ge|rad|heit** F -, no pl (fig) (= Aufrichtigkeit) rectitude; (= Freimut) frankness, candour (Brit), candor (US); **ge|rad|li|nig** [-li:nɪç] ADJ straight; Abkomme, Abstammung direct; Entwicklung etc linear; (fig: = aufrichtig) straight ADV **~ denken/handeln** to be straight; **~ verlaufen** to run in a straight line; **die Straße verläuft ~ durch die Wiesen** the road runs in a straight line through the meadows; **Ge|rad|li|nig|keit** F -, no pl straightness; **sie ist für ihre ~ bekannt** she is known for coming straight to the point; **ge|rad|sin|nig** ADJ (geh) upright

Ge|raf|fel [gə'rafl] NT -s, no pl (Aus, S Ger) junk

ge|ram|melt [gə'ramlt] ADV **~ voll** (inf) (jam) packed (inf), chock-a-block (inf) → auch **rammeln**

Ge|ran|gel [gə'raŋl] NT -s, no pl (= Balgerei) scrapping; (fig: = zäher Kampf) wrangling; **ein kurzes ~ der beiden Spieler** a short scrap between the two players; **das ~ um die Sonderangebote** the tussle over the bargains

Ge|ra|nie [ge'ra:niə] F -, -n geranium

ge|rann pret von **gerinnen**

ge|rannt ptp von **rennen**

Ge|rant [ʒe'rant] M -en, -en, **Ge|ran|tin** [-'rantɪn] F -, -nen (Sw) manager/manageress

Ge|ra|schel [gə'raʃl] NT -s, no pl rustle, rustling

Ge|ras|sel [gə'rasl] NT -s, no pl rattle, rattling

ge|rät [gə'rɛ:t] 3. pers sing pres von **geraten**

Ge|rät [gə'rɛ:t] NT -(e)s, -e **a** piece of equipment; (= Vorrichtung) device; (= Apparat) gadget; (= landwirtschaftliches Gerät) implement; (= elektrisches Gerät) appliance; (= Radiogerät, Fernsehgerät, Telefon) set; (= Messgerät) instrument; (= Küchengerät) utensil; (= Werkzeug, Gartengerät) tool; (= Turngerät) piece of apparatus; (inf: = Penis) tool (sl) **b** no pl (= Ausrüstung) equipment no pl; (von Handwerker) tools pl

Ge|rä|te-: **Ge|rä|te|an|bie|ter(in)** M(F) (= Leasinggeber) lessor (of the equipment); **Ge|rä|te|me|di|zin** F (usu pej) high-tech(nology) medicine

ge|ra|ten [gə'ra:tn] pret **geriet** [gə'ri:t], ptp **geraten** [gə'ra:tn] VI aux sein **a** (= zufällig gelangen) to get (in +acc into); **an jdn ~** (= jdn kennenlernen) to come across sb; (= jdn bekommen) to find sb, to dig sb up (pej); **an etw** (acc) **~** to get sth, to come by sth; **an einen Ort ~** to come to a place; **an den Richtigen/Falschen ~** to come to the right/wrong person; **unter ein Fahrzeug ~** to fall under a vehicle; **mit der Hand in eine Maschine ~** to get one's hand caught in a machine; **in Gefangenschaft ~** to be taken prisoner; **das Schiff ist in einen Sturm ~** the boat got caught in a storm; **in Bewegung ~** to begin to move; **ins Stocken ~** to come to a halt; **ins Schleudern ~** to go into a skid; **in Brand ~** to catch fire; **in Angst/Begeisterung/Schwierigkeiten ~** to get scared/enthusiastic/into difficulties; **in Vergessenheit ~** to fall into oblivion; **aus der Bahn ~** (lit) to come off or leave the track; (fig) to go off the rails; **auf krumme Wege** or **die schiefe Bahn ~** to stray from the straight and narrow; **aus der Fassung/der Form ~** to lose one's composure/one's shape; **außer sich ~** (**vor etw** dat) to be beside oneself (with sth); **unter schlechten Einfluss ~** to come under a bad influence → **Abweg, Haar**

b (= sich entwickeln, gelingen, ausfallen) to turn out; **ihm gerät einfach alles** everything he does turns out well or is a success, everything always goes right for him; **mein Aufsatz ist mir zu lang ~** my essay turned out too long; **der Junge/Kaktus ist gut ~** the boy/cactus turned out well; **nach jdm ~** to take after sb

ge|ra|ten *ptp von* **raten, geraten** ADJ *(geh: = ratsam)* advisable; **ich halte es für ~** I think it would be advisable

Ge|rä|te-: **Ge|rä|te|raum** M equipment room; **Ge|rä|te|schup|pen** M tool shed; **Ge|rä|te|trei|ber** M *(Comput)* device driver; **Ge|rä|te|tur|nen** NT apparatus gymnastics *no pl*

Ge|ra|te|wohl NT **aufs ~** on the off-chance; *(aussuchen, auswählen etc)* at random; **er hat die Prüfung einfach aufs ~ versucht** he decided to have a go at the exam just on the off chance of passing; **er ist aufs ~ nach Amerika ausgewandert** he emigrated to America just like that; **wir schlugen aufs ~ diesen Weg ein** we decided to trust to luck and come this way

Ge|rät|schaf|ten PL *(= Ausrüstung)* equipment *sing*; *(= Werkzeug)* tools *pl*

Ge|rat|ter [gəˈratɐ] NT **-s**, *no pl* clatter(ing), rattle, rattling; *(von Maschinengewehr)* chatter(ing)

Ge|räu|cher|te(s) [gəˈrɔyçɐtə] NT, *no pl decl as adj* smoked meat *(especially bacon and ham)*

ge|raum [gəˈraum] ADJ *attr* **vor ~er Zeit** some time ago; **seit ~er Zeit** for some time; **es dauerte eine ~e Weile** it took some time; **in/aus ~er Entfernung** at/from some distance; **ein ~es Maß an Arbeit/Zeit** a good deal of work/time

ge|räu|mig [gəˈrɔymɪç] ADJ *Haus, Zimmer, Auto* spacious, roomy; *Schrank, Koffer, Kofferraum auch* capacious

Ge|räu|mig|keit F **-**, *no pl (von Haus, Zimmer, Auto)* spaciousness, roominess; *(von Schrank, Koffer, Kofferraum auch)* capaciousness

Ge|rau|ne [gəˈraunə] NT **-s**, *no pl (liter)* whispering

Ge|raun|ze [gəˈrauntsə] NT **-s**, *no pl (S Ger, Aus: inf)* grousing *(esp Brit inf)*, grouching *(inf)*

Ge|räusch [gəˈrɔyʃ] NT **-(e)s, -e** sound; *(esp unangenehm)* noise; **der Arzt horchte meine Brust auf ~e ab** the doctor listened to my chest for any unusual sounds; **die ~e des Verkehrs** the noise of the traffic; **aus dem Keller hörte man verdächtige ~e** suspicious noises came from the cellar; **mit einem dumpfen ~** with a dull thud

Ge|räusch-: **ge|räusch|arm** ADJ quiet; **Ge|räusch|ar|mut** F quietness; **ge|räusch|däm|mend** [-dɛmənt], **ge|räusch|dämp|fend** [-dɛmpfənt] ADJ noise-reducing, noise--insulating; **Ge|räusch|dämp|fung** F sound damping; *(stärker)* deadening of sound; **ge|räusch|emp|find|lich** ADJ sensitive to noise; *(Tech)* sound-sensitive; **Ge|räusch|ku|lis|se** F background noise; *(Film, Rad, TV)* sound effects *pl*; **ge|räusch|los** ADJ silent ADV silently, without a sound; **sie fanden eine ~e Lösung des Problems** *(fig)* they found out how to solve the problem quietly *or* without a lot of fuss; *(fig)* quietly, without a lot of fuss; **Ge|räusch|lo|sig|keit** F **-**, *no pl* quietness, noiselessness; *(fig)* lack of fuss; **Ge|räusch|mes|ser** M **-s, -** sound level recorder; **Ge|räusch|pe|gel** M sound level; **ge|räusch|voll** ADJ *(= laut)* loud; *(= lärmend)* noisy ADV *(= laut)* loudly; *(= lärmend)* noisily; **weniger ~** with less noise

Ge|räus|per [gəˈrɔyspɐ] NT **-s**, *no pl* throat-clearing

ger|ben [ˈgɛrbn] VT to tan; **vom Wetter gegerbte Haut** weather-beaten skin → **Fell**

Ger|ber [ˈgɛrbɐ] M **-s, -**, **Ger|be|rin** [ˈgɛrbərɪn] [-ərɪn] F **-, -nen** tanner

Ger|be|ra [ˈgɛrbera] F **-, -(s)** *(Bot)* gerbera

Ger|be|rei [gɛrbəˈrai] F **-, -en** **a** *no pl (= Gerben)* tanning **b** *(= Werkstatt)* tannery

Ger|be|rin [ˈgɛrbərɪn] [-ərɪn] F **-, -nen** tanner

Ger|ber|lo|he F tanbark

Gerb|säu|re F tannic acid

Gerb|stoff M tanning agent

Ger|bung F **-, -en** tanning

ge|recht [gəˈrɛçt] ADJ **a** *(= rechtgemäß, verdient)* just; *(= unparteiisch auch)* fair; *(= rechtschaffen)* upright; **~ gegen jdn sein** to be fair *or* just to sb; **~er Lohn für alle Arbeiter!** fair wages for all workers!; **seinen ~en Lohn bekommen** *(fig)* to get one's just deserts *or* reward; **das ist nur ~** that's only fair *or* right *or* just; **~er Gott** *or* **Himmel!** *(inf)* good heavens (above)!; **die Gerechten** the just; **Gott, der Gerechte** God the righteous; **der Gerechte muss viel leiden** *(prov)* no rest for the wicked *(iro prov)*; **den Schlaf des Gerechten schlafen** *(usu hum)* to sleep the sleep of the just
b *(= berechtigt)* just, legitimate; **~er Zorn** righteous anger; **sich für eine ~e Sache einsetzen** to fight for a just cause
c **jdm/einer Sache ~ werden** to do justice to sb/sth; **den Bedingungen ~ werden** to fulfil *(Brit) or* fulfill *(US)* the conditions; **jds Erwartungen** *(dat)* **~ werden** to come up to *or* fulfil *(Brit) or* fulfill *(US)* sb's expectations → **Sattel**
ADV fairly; *(= rechtgemäß)* justly

-ge|recht ADJ *suf* suitable for; **behindertengerecht** suitable for disabled people

ge|rech|ter|wei|se [gəˈrɛçtɐˈvaizə] ADV to be fair

ge|recht|fer|tigt [gəˈrɛçtfɛrtɪçt] ADJ justified

Ge|rech|tig|keit [gəˈrɛçtɪçkait] F **-**, *no pl* **a** justice; *(= das Gerechtsein)* justness; *(= Unparteilichkeit)* fairness; *(= Rechtschaffenheit)* righteousness; **die ~ nahm ihren Lauf** justice took its course; **jdm/einer Sache ~ widerfahren lassen** to be just to sb/sth; *(fig)* to do justice to sb/sth **b** *(geh: = Gerichtsbarkeit)* justice; **jdn (den Händen) der ~ ausliefern** to bring sb to justice

Ge|rech|tig|keits-: **Ge|rech|tig|keits|fim|mel** M *(pej inf)* thing about justice *(inf)*; **Ge|rech|tig|keits|ge|fühl** NT sense of justice; **Ge|rech|tig|keits|lie|be** F love of justice; **ge|rech|tig|keits|lie|bend** ADJ **ein ~er Mensch** a lover of justice, a person with a love of justice; **~ sein** to have a love of justice; **Ge|rech|tig|keits|sinn** M, *no pl* sense of justice

Ge|recht|sa|me [gəˈrɛçtza:mə] F **-, -n** *(Hist)* rights *pl*

Ge|re|de [gəˈre:də] NT **-s**, *no pl* talk; *(= Klatsch)* gossip(ing); **ins ~ kommen** *or* **geraten** to get oneself talked about; **jdn ins ~ bringen** to get sb talked about; **kümmere dich nicht um das ~ der Leute** don't worry about what people say

ge|re|gelt [gəˈre:gl̩t] ADJ *Arbeit(szeiten), Mahlzeiten* regular; *Leben* well-ordered; **~er Katalysator** computer-controlled *or* feedback catalytic converter; **~er Markt** *(St Ex)* over-the-counter *or* official market → *auch* **regeln**

ge|rei|chen [gəˈraiçn] *ptp* **gereicht** VI *(geh)* **jdm zur Ehre ~** to do sb honour *(Brit) or* honor *(US)*, to redound to sb's honour *(Brit form) or* honor *(US form)*; **jdm zum Schaden/Nutzen ~** to be damaging/beneficial to sb, to redound to sb's benefit *(form)*; **jdm/einer Sache zum Vorteil ~** to be an advantage to sb/sth, to redound to sb's advantage *(form)*; *(= vorteilhaft erscheinen lassen)* to be advantageous for sb/sth

ge|reift [gəˈraift] ADJ *(fig)* mature; *Produkt, Technologie* fully developed → *auch* **reifen**

Ge|reift|heit F **-**, *no pl (fig)* maturity

ge|reizt [gəˈraitst] ADJ *(= verärgert)* irritated; *(= reizbar)* irritable, touchy; *(= nervös)* tetchy *(esp Brit inf)*, edgy; **im Zimmer herrschte ~e Stimmung** there was a strained atmosphere in the room ADV *(= verärgert)* irritably → *auch* **reizen**

Ge|reizt|heit F **-**, *no pl (= Verärgertheit)* irritation; *(= Reizbarkeit)* irritability, touchiness; *(= Nervosität)* tetchiness *(esp Brit inf)*, edginess; **die ~ der Atmosphäre** the strained atmosphere

Ge|ren|ne [gəˈrɛnə] NT **-s**, *no pl (inf)* running, racing; *(= das Umherlaufen)* running *or* racing about *(Brit) or* around

ge|reu|en [gəˈrɔyən] *ptp* **gereut** *(old, geh)* VT *impers* **es gereut mich, dass ...** I regret that ..., I am sorry that ...; **es wird Sie nicht ~** you will not regret it VT **meine Tat gereut mich** I regret my action

Ger|fal|ke [ˈge:ɐ-] M gyrfalcon, gerfalcon

Ge|ri|a|ter [geˈria:tɐ] M **-s, -**, **Ge|ri|a|te|rin** [-ərɪn] F **-, -nen** geriatrician

Ge|ri|at|rie [geriaˈtri:] F **-**, *no pl* geriatrics *sing*

ge|ri|at|risch [geˈria:trɪʃ] ADJ geriatric

Ge|richt [gəˈrɪçt] NT **-(e)s, -e** *(= Speise)* dish; **leckere ~e** delicious meals

Ge|richt NT **-(e)s, -e** **a** *(= Behörde)* court (of justice); *(= Gebäude)* court(house), law courts *pl*; *(= die Richter)* court, bench; **Hohes ~!** My Lord! *(Brit)*, Your Honor! *(US)*; **vor ~ erscheinen/aussagen** to appear/testify in court; **vor ~ kommen** *(Fall)* to come to court; *(Mensch)* to come *or* appear before a/the court; **vor ~ stehen** to stand trial; **jdn vor ~ laden** to summon *or* call sb to appear in court; **jdn/einen Fall vor ~ bringen** to take sb/a case to court; **mit etw vor ~ gehen** to go to court about sth, to take legal action about sth; **jdn bei ~ verklagen** to take sb to court; **jdn/einen Fall vor ~ vertreten** to represent sb/a case in court; **das ~ zieht sich zur Beratung zurück** the court will adjourn
b **das Jüngste** *or* **Letzte ~** the Last Judgement; **über jdn/etw ~ halten** to pronounce judgement on sb/sth; **über jdn zu ~ sitzen** *(fig)* to sit in judgement on sb; **mit jdm (scharf) ins ~ gehen** *(fig)* to judge sb harshly

ge|richt|lich [gəˈrɪçtlɪç] ADJ *attr* judicial; *Bestimmung, Entscheidung etc* court; *Medizin, Psychologie* forensic; *Verhandlung* legal; **~e Schritte gegen jdn einleiten** to initiate legal proceedings against sb; **laut ~em Beschluss** according to the decision of a/the court, according to a/the court decision; **ein ~es Nachspiel** a court sequel; **ein ~es Nachspiel haben** to finish up in court; **eine Sache ~** *or* **auf ~em Weg klären** to settle a matter in court *or* by litigation
ADV *anerkannt* by a court; *durchsetzbar* legally, by the court; *klären* in court; **jdn ~ belangen** *(= strafrechtlich)* to prosecute sb; *(= zivilrechtlich)* to bring legal proceedings against sb; **~ gegen jdn vorgehen** to take legal action against sb, to litigate against sb; **jdn ~ vertreten** to represent sb in and out of court; **Schulden ~ beitreiben** to enforce the payment of debts; **jdm etw ~ untersagen lassen** to get an injunction against sb doing sth; **jdn ~ für tot erklären lassen** to have sb declared legally dead; **~ vereidigter Dolmetscher** court-appointed interpreter; **~ angeordnet** ordered by the courts

Ge|richts-: **Ge|richts|ak|ten** PL court records *pl*; **Ge|richts|arzt** M, **Ge|richts|ärz|tin** F court doctor; **Ge|richts|as|ses|sor(in)** M(F) ≈ junior barrister *or* lawyer *(Brit)*, assistant judge *(US)*

Ge|richts|bar|keit [gəˈrɪçtsba:ɐkait] F **-, -en** jurisdiction

Ge|richts-: **Ge|richts|be|richt|er|stat|ter(in)** M(F) legal correspondent; **Ge|richts|be|schluss** M decision of a/the court, court decision; **Ge|richts|be|zirk** M juridical district; **Ge|richts|die|ner(in)** M(F) *(old)* court usher; **Ge|richts|ent|scheid** M, **Ge|richts|ent|schei|dung** F court decision; **Ge|richts|fe|ri|en** PL court vacation, recess; **Ge|richts|ge|bäu|de** NT law court(s *pl*), courthouse *(US)*; **Ge|richts|ge|büh|ren** PL = **Gerichtskosten**; **Ge|richts|herr** M *(Hist)* lord of the manor; **Ge|richts|hof** M court (of justice), law court; **Oberster ~** Supreme Court (of Justice); **der hohe ~** the high court; **Ge|richts|ho|heit** F jurisdiction; **Ge|richts|kas|se** F **den Betrag von 200 Euro an die ~ zahlen** to pay the court 200 euros; **Ge|richts|kos|ten** PL court costs *pl*; **jdn zum Tragen der ~ verurteilen** *(form)* **jdm die ~ auferlegen** *(form)* to order sb to pay costs; **ge|richts|kun|dig** ADJ = **gerichtsnotorisch**; **Ge|richts|me|di|zin** F forensic medicine, medical jurisprudence; **Ge|richts|me|di|zi|ner(in)** M(F) forensic doctor; **ge|richts|me|di|zi|nisch** ADJ forensic medical *attr* ADV **die Leiche wurde ~ untersucht** the body was examined by an expert in forensic medicine; **ge|richts|no|to|risch** ADJ known to the court; **Ge|richts|ord|nung** F rules *pl* of the court; **Ge|richts|ort** M *pl* **-orte** town etc with a court; ~ **ist Stuttgart** *(Vertragsbedingung)* any legal case arising from this contract shall be heard in Stuttgart; **Ge|richts|prä|si|dent(in)** M(F) president of the court; **Ge|richts|re|fe|ren|dar(in)** M(F) *law student who has passed the first State Examination,* ≈ articled barrister *(Brit),* ≈ law graduate *(US);* **Ge|richts|re|por|ter(in)** M(F) legal correspondent; **Ge|richts|saal** M courtroom; **Ge|richts|schrei|ber(in)** M(F) clerk of the court *(Brit),* registrar *(US);* **Ge|richts|spra|che** F language of the courts; **Ge|richts|stand** M *(form)* court of jurisdiction; **Ge|richts|ta|fel** F court notice board; *(für öffentliche Bekanntmachungen)* ≈ public notice board; **Ge|richts|tag** M court day; **Montag ist** ~ the court sits on Mondays, the court is in session on Mondays; **Ge|richts|ter|min** M date of a/the trial; *(für Zivilsachen)* date of a/the hearing; **einen ~ ansetzen** to fix a date for a/the trial/hearing; **Ge|richts|ver|fah|ren** NT court *or* legal proceedings *pl*; **ein ~ gegen jdn einleiten** to institute legal proceedings against sb; *(zivil auch)* to litigate against sb; **er wurde ohne ordentliches ~ verurteilt** he was sentenced without a proper trial; **Ge|richts|ver|fas|sung** F legal constitution; **Ge|richts|ver|hand|lung** F trial; *(zivil)* hearing; **Ge|richts|voll|zie|her** [-fɔltsiːɐ] M **-s, -, Ge|richts|voll|zie|he|rin** [-ərɪn] F **-, -nen** bailiff; **Ge|richts|weg** M **auf dem** ~ through the courts; **Ge|richts|we|sen** NT, *no pl* judiciary, judicial system

ge|rie|ben [gəˈriːbn] *ptp von* **reiben** ADJ *(fig inf)* smart, sharp; *(= verschlagen auch)* tricky, sly, fly *(Brit inf)*; **der ist verdammt** ~ *(inf)* there are no flies on him *(Brit inf)*, you can't pull the wool over his eyes

ge|rie|ren [geˈriːrən] *ptp* **geriert** VR *(geh)* to project an image

Ge|rie|sel [gəˈriːzl] NT **-s**, *no pl (von Sand)* trickling; *(von Schnee)* floating down

ge|riet *pret von* **geraten**

ge|rif|felt [gəˈrɪflt] *ptp von* **riffeln** ADJ *Glas, Säule etc* grooved, fluted; *(= gerippt)* ribbed; *(= eng gewellt)* corrugated → *auch* **riffeln**

ge|ring [gəˈrɪŋ] ADJ **a** *(= nicht sehr groß, niedrig) Temperatur, Luftdruck, Leistung, Produktion* low; *Gehalt, Preis* low, modest; *Menge, Vorrat, Betrag, Entfernung* small; *Wert* little *attr*; *(= kurz) Zeit, Entfernung* short; **mit ~en Ausnahmen** with few exceptions; **Berge von ~er Höhe** low hills; **etw in ~er Höhe anbringen** to fix sth fairly low down; **seine Leistung erhielt eine zu ~e Bewertung** his achievement wasn't rated highly enough

b *(= unbedeutend, unerheblich)* slight; *Chance auch* small, slim; *Bedeutung, Rolle* minor; **die ~ste Kleinigkeit** the least *or* smallest *or* slightest little thing; **das ist meine ~ste Sorge** that's the least of my worries; **die Kosten sind nicht ~** the costs are not inconsiderable; **nicht das Geringste** nothing at all; **nicht im Geringsten** not in the least *or* slightest; **das Geringste** the least thing; **nichts Geringeres als ...** nothing less than ...

c *(= unzulänglich) Qualität, Kenntnisse* poor; *(= abschätzig) Meinung* low, poor

d *attr (fig geh) Familie, Herkunft* humble; **(auch) der Geringste** even the most humble person; **kein Geringerer als Freud ...** no less a person than Freud

ADV **a** *(= wenig)* ~ **gerechnet** at a conservative estimate

b *(= abschätzig)* ~ **von jdm sprechen** to speak badly of sb; ~ **von jdm denken** to have a low opinion of sb

ge|ring ach|ten △, **ge|ring+ach|ten** *sep* VT = **gering schätzen**

ge|rin|gelt [gəˈrɪŋlt] ADJ **a** *Muster* ringed; *Socken* hooped **b** *(= lockig) Haare* curly

Ge|ring-: **ge|ring|fü|gig** [-fyːgɪç] ADJ *(= unwichtig)* insignificant; *Verbesserung, Unterschied* slight; *Vergehen, Verletzung* minor; *Einzelheiten* minor, trivial; *Betrag* small; **~e Beschäftigung** part-time employment ADV slightly; **sein Zustand hat sich ~ gebessert** his condition is marginally *or* slightly improved; **Ge|ring|fü|gig|keit** F **-, -en a** *(Jur)* **ein Verfahren wegen ~ einstellen** to dismiss a case because of the trifling nature of the offence *(Brit) or* offense *(US)* **b** *(von Betrag)* insignificance **c** *(= Kleinigkeit)* little *or* small thing, trifle; **Ge|ring|fü|gig|keits|gren|ze** F lower earnings limit; **ge|ring schät|zen** △, **ge|ring+schät|zen** *sep* VT *(= verachten) Menschen, Leistung* to think little of, to have a poor *or* low opinion of; *Erfolg, Reichtum* to set little store by *(Brit) or* in *(US)*, to place little value on; *menschliches Leben* to have scant regard for, to place little value on; *(= missachten) Gefahr, Folgen* to disregard; **eine Tugend, die man nicht ~ sollte** a virtue not to be despised; **ge|ring|schät|zig** [-ʃɛtsɪç] ADJ contemptuous; *Bemerkung auch* disparaging ADV contemptuously; **Ge|ring|schät|zig|keit** F **-**, *no pl* contemptuousness; **Ge|ring|schät|zung** F, *no pl (= Ablehnung)* disdain; *(von Bemerkung)* disparagement *(für, +gen* of); *(= schlechte Meinung)* poor *or* low opinion *(für, +gen* of); *(für Erfolg, Reichtum, menschliches Leben)* low regard *(für, +gen* for)

ge|rings|ten|falls ADV *(geh)* at (the very) least

ge|ring|wer|tig ADJ *(rare)* inferior; *Nahrung* low-value

ge|rinn|bar ADJ = **gerinnungsfähig**

ge|rin|nen [gəˈrɪnən] *pret* **gerann** [gəˈran], *ptp* **geronnen** [gəˈrɔnən] VI *aux sein* to coagulate; *(Blut auch)* to clot; *(Milch auch)* to curdle; **mir gerann (vor Schreck) das Blut in den Adern** *(fig)* my blood ran cold; **zu etw ~** *(fig geh)* to develop into sth

Ge|rinn|sel [gəˈrɪnzl] NT **-s, - a** *(= Blutgerinnsel)* clot, coagulum *(spec)* **b** *(geh: = Rinnsal)* rivulet, trickle

Ge|rin|nung F **-, -en** coagulation; *(von Blut auch)* clotting; *(von Milch auch)* curdling

Ge|rin|nungs-: **ge|rin|nungs|fä|hig** ADJ coagulable; **Ge|rin|nungs|fä|hig|keit** F coagulability; **ge|rin|nungs|hem|mend** ADJ *(Med)* anticoagulant; **Ge|rin|nungs|hem|mer** M **-s, -** *(Med)* anticoagulant

Ge|rip|pe [gəˈrɪpə] NT **-s, -** skeleton; *(von Schiff, Flugzeug auch, von Schirm, Gebäude)* frame; *(von Blatt auch)* ribbing; *(fig: = Grundplan)* framework; **er ist nur noch ein ~** he's nothing but skin and bones

ge|rippt [gəˈrɪpt] ADJ ribbed *no adv*; *Säule* fluted *no adv*; **~e Sohlen** grip soles → *auch* **rippen**

Ge|riss [gəˈrɪs] NT **-es**, *no pl (Aus inf)* crush

ge|ris|sen [gəˈrɪsn] *ptp von* **reißen** ADJ crafty, cunning

Ge|ris|sen|heit F **-**, *no pl* cunning

ge|rit|ten *ptp von* **reiten**

ge|ritzt [gəˈrɪtst] ADJ *pred (inf)* **die Sache ist ~** everything's fixed up *or* settled → *auch* **ritzen**

Germ [gɛrm] M OR F **-**, *no pl (Aus)* baker's yeast

Ger|ma|ne [gɛrˈmaːnə] M **-n, -n, Ger|ma|nin** [-ˈmaːnɪn] F **-, -nen** Teuton; **die alten ~n** the Teutons

Ger|ma|nen|tum [gɛrˈmaːnəntuːm] NT **-s**, *no pl* Teutonicism; *(= Kultur)* Teutonism; *(= Gesamtheit der Germanen)* Teutonic world, Teutons *pl*

ger|ma|nisch [gɛrˈmaːnɪʃ] ADJ Germanic; **~es Seminar** Institute of Germanic Studies

ger|ma|ni|sie|ren [gɛrmaniˈziːrən] *ptp* **germanisiert** VT to Germanize

Ger|ma|ni|sie|rung F **-, -en** Germanization

Ger|ma|nis|mus [gɛrmaˈnɪsmʊs] M **-, Germanismen** [-mən] *(Ling)* Germanism

Ger|ma|nist [gɛrmaˈnɪst] M **-en, -en, Ger|ma|nis|tin** [-ˈnɪstɪn] F **-, -nen** Germanist; *(= Student auch)* German student; *(= Wissenschaftler auch)* German specialist

Ger|ma|nis|tik [gɛrmaˈnɪstɪk] F **-**, *no pl* German (studies *pl*); **~ studieren** to do German studies, to study German; **Professor der ~** professor of German studies *or* German

ger|ma|nis|tisch [gɛrmaˈnɪstɪʃ] ADJ German; *Zeitschrift* on German studies

Ger|ma|ni|um [gɛrˈmaːniʊm] NT **-s**, *no pl (abbr* **Ge**) germanium

ger|ma|no|phil [gɛrmanoˈfiːl] ADJ Germanophile

Ger|ma|no|phi|lie [gɛrmanofiˈliː] F **-**, *no pl* Germanophilia

ger|ma|no|phob [gɛrmanoˈfoːp] ADJ Germanophobe

Ger|ma|no|pho|bie [gɛrmanofoˈbiː] F Germanophobia

gern [gɛrn], **ger|ne** [ˈgɛrnə] ADV *comp* **lieber**, *superl* **am liebsten a** *(= freudig)* with pleasure; *(= bereitwillig)* with pleasure, willingly, readily; **(aber) ~!** of course!; **ja, ~!** (yes) please; **kommst du mit? – ja, ~** are you coming too? – oh yes, I'd like to; **darf ich das? – ja, ~** can I do that? – (yes,) of course; **~ geschehen!** you're welcome!; *(esp US)*, not at all!, my pleasure!; **„Witwer, 61, sucht Partnerin, ~ älter/mit Kindern"** "widower, aged 61, seeks partner, age not important/children not a problem"; **von mir aus kann er ja ~ älter sein** I don't mind if he's older; **etw ~ tun** to like doing sth *or* to do sth *(esp US)*; **etw ~ essen/trinken** to like sth; **sie isst am liebsten Spargel** asparagus is her favourite *(Brit) or* favorite *(US)* food; **~ ins Kino gehen** to like *or* enjoy going to the cinema; **das tue ich für mein Leben ~** I adore doing that; **etw ~ sehen** to like sth; **das sähe ich ~** I would welcome it; **das wird nicht ~ gesehen** that's frowned (up)on; **er sieht es nicht ~, wenn wir zu spät kommen** he doesn't like us arriving late; **ein ~ gesehener Gast** a welcome visitor; **das glaube ich ~** I can quite *or* well believe it, I'm quite willing to believe it; **das würde ich zu ~ tun** I'd really love to do that; **er macht seine Arbeit ~ und mit Freude** he does his work willingly and gets a lot of pleasure out of it; **ich stehe ~ zu Ihren Diensten** *(old form)* I am happy *or* pleased to be of service to you; **ich bin ~ dazu bereit** I'm quite willing *or* happy to do it; **jdn/etw ~ mögen** to like sb/sth, to be fond of sb/sth; **jdn/etw ~ haben** → **gernhaben**; **das kannst du ~ haben** you're welcome to it, you can have it with pleasure; **er hat es ~, wenn man ihm schmeichelt** he likes being flattered, he likes it when you flatter him; **ich hätte** *or* **möchte ~ ...** I would like ...; **ich hätte ~ Herrn Kurtz gesprochen** could I speak to Mr Kurtz?, I would like to speak to Mr Kurtz, please; **wie hätten Sies (denn) ~?** how would you like it? → **gut ADV, lieber**

b *(= gewöhnlich, oft)* **etw ~ tun** to tend to do sth; **Weiden wachsen ~ an Flüssen** willows tend to grow by rivers; **morgens lässt er sich ~ viel Zeit** he likes to leave himself a lot of time in the mornings

Ger|ne|groß [ˈgɛrnəgroːs] M **-, -e** *(hum)* **er war schon immer ein kleiner ~** he always did like to act big *(inf)*

gern|ge|se|hen △ ADJ → **gern a**

gern+ha|ben VT *sep irreg* to like sb/sth, to be fond of sb/sth; **du kannst/er kann mich mal ~!** *(inf)* (you can)/(he can) go to hell! *(inf)*, stuff you/him! *(Brit inf)*, screw you/him *(sl)* → *auch* **fressen, Herz**

Ge|rö|chel [gəˈrœçl] NT **-s**, *no pl* groans *pl*; *(von Sterbenden)* (death) rattle

ge|ro|chen *ptp von* **riechen**

Ge|röll [gəˈrœl] NT **-(e)s, -e** detritus *no pl*; *(im Gebirge auch)* scree *no pl*; *(größeres)* boulders *pl*

Ge|röl|le [gəˈrœlə] NT **-s, -** *(rare)* = **Geröll**

Ge|röll-: **Ge|röll|hal|de** F scree (slope); **Ge|röll|la|wi|ne** F scree avalanche; **Ge|röll|schutt** M rock debris

ge|ron|nen *ptp von* **rinnen, gerinnen**

Ge|ron|to|kra|tie [gerɔntokraˈtiː] F **-, -n** [-tiːən] *(Pol)* gerontocracy

Ge|ron|to|lo|ge [gerɔntoˈloːgə] M **-n, -n, Ge|ron|to|lo|gin** [-ˈloːgɪn] F **-, -nen** *(Med)* gerontologist

Ge|ron|to|lo|gie [gerɔntoloˈgiː] F **-**, *no pl (Med)* gerontology

ge|ron|to|lo|gisch [gerɔnto'lo:gɪʃ] ADJ *(Med)* gerontological

Ge|rös|te|te [gə'rœstətə, gə'rø:stətə] PL *decl as adj (S Ger, Aus: Cook)* sauté potatoes *pl*

Gers|te ['gɛrstə] F -, -n barley

Gers|ten- *in cpds* barley; **Gers|ten|grau|pen** PL pearl barley *sing*; **Gers|ten|grüt|ze** F barley groats *pl*; *(= Brei)* barley porridge; **Gers|ten|korn** NT *pl* **-körner** **a** barleycorn **b** *(Med)* stye; **Gers|ten|saft** M *(hum)* beer; **Gers|ten|zu|cker** M barley sugar

Ger|te ['gɛrtə] F -, -n switch; *(= Reitgerte auch)* crop; **sie ist schlank wie eine ~** she is slim and willowy, she is as slender as a reed

ger|ten|schlank ADJ slim and willowy

Ge|ruch [gə'rʊx] M **-(e)s, ⸚e** [gə'rʏçə] **a** smell, odour *(Brit)*, odor *(US)* *(nach* of); *(= Duft)* fragrance, scent, perfume *(nach* of); *(von Kuchen etc)* aroma *(nach* of); *(unangenehm)* stench *(nach* of); **der starke ~ nach Alkohol/Knoblauch** the reek of alcohol/garlic **b** *no pl (= Geruchssinn)* sense of smell **c** *no pl (fig: = Ruf)* reputation; **in den ~ von etw kommen** to get a reputation for sth

Ge|ruch-: **ge|ruch|los** ADJ odourless *(Brit)*, odorless *(US)*; *(= duftlos)* scentless; **~ sein** not to have a smell, to be odourless *(Brit)* or odorless *(US)*; *(Blumen)* not to smell, to have no scent; **Ge|ruch|lo|sig|keit** F -, *no pl* lack of smell

Ge|ruchs-: **Ge|ruchs|be|läs|ti|gung** F **das ist eine ~** the smell is a real nuisance; **ge|ruchs|bin|dend** ADJ deodorizing *no adv*; **ge|ruchs|emp|find|lich** ADJ sensitive to smell; **~ sein** to have a sensitive nose; **Ge|ruchs|emp|fin|dung** F **a** *(= Riechempfindung)* smell **b** *(= Geruchssinn)* sense of smell; **Ge|ruchs|nerv** M olfactory nerve; **ge|ruchs|neut|ral** ADJ = **geruchlos**; **Ge|ruchs|or|gan** NT organ of smell, olfactory organ; **Ge|ruchs|sinn** M, *no pl* sense of smell; **Ge|ruchs|ver|schluss** M *(Tech)* odour *(Brit)* or odor *(US)* trap; **Ge|ruchs|werk|zeu|ge** PL olfactory organs *pl*

Ge|rücht [gə'rʏçt] NT **-(e)s, -e** rumour *(Brit)*, rumor *(US)*; **es geht das ~, dass ...** there's a rumo(u)r (going (a)round) that ..., it's rumo(u)red that ...; **das halte ich für ein ~** *(inf)* I have my doubts about that

Ge|rüch|te-: **Ge|rüch|te|kü|che** F *(inf)* gossip factory *(inf)*; **die Pressestelle ist eine wahre ~** the press office is filled with rumour-mongers *(Brit)* or rumor-mongers *(US)*; **Ge|rüch|te|ma|cher(in)** M(F) rumour-monger *(Brit)*, rumor-monger *(US)*; **ge|rüch|te|wei|se** ADV **etw ~ hören** to hear sth rumoured *(Brit)* or rumored *(US)*; **~ ist bekannt geworden, dass ...** rumour *(Brit)* or rumor *(US)* has it that ...; **ich habe ~ erfahren, dass ...** I've heard a rumour *(Brit)* or rumor *(US)* that ...; **das ist mir ~ zu Ohren gekommen** I've heard it rumoured *(Brit)* or rumored *(US)*

ge|ruch|til|gend ADJ deodorizing *no adv*, deodorant *attr*

ge|rücht|wei|se ADV = **gerüchteweise**

Ge|ru|ckel [gə'rʊkl] NT **-s**, *no pl* jerking, jolting

Ge|ru|fe [gə'ru:fə] NT **-s**, *no pl* calling

ge|ru|fen *ptp von* **rufen**

ge|ru|hen [gə'ru:ən] *ptp* **geruht** VT **~, etw zu tun** *(dated form)* to deign or condescend to do sth *(auch iro)*, to be pleased to do sth

ge|ru|hig [gə'ru:ɪç] ADJ, ADV *(old)* = **ruhig**

ge|ruh|sam [gə'ru:za:m] ADJ peaceful; *Spaziergang etc* leisurely ADV leisurely; **~ essen** to eat in peace (and quiet)

Ge|ruh|sam|keit F -, *no pl* peacefulness; *(von Spaziergang etc)* leisureliness

Ge|rum|pel [gə'rʊmpl] NT **-s**, *no pl* rumbling, rumble

Ge|rüm|pel [gə'rʏmpl] NT **-s**, *no pl* junk

Ge|run|di|um [ge'rʊndiʊm] NT **-s, Gerundien** [-di:ən] gerund

ge|run|div [gerʊn'di:f] ADJ gerundival

Ge|run|div [gerʊn'di:f] NT **-s, -e** [-və] gerundive

ge|run|di|visch [gerʊn'di:vɪʃ] ADJ = **gerundiv**

Ge|run|di|vum [gerʊn'di:vʊm] NT **-s, Gerundiva** [-va] gerundive

ge|run|gen *ptp von* **ringen**

Ge|rüst [gə'rʏst] NT **-(e)s, -e** scaffolding *no pl*; *(= Gestell)* trestle; *(= Brückengerüst, Dachgerüst)* truss; *(= Hängegerüst)* cradle; *(fig: = Gerippe)* framework *(zu* of); **ein ~ aufstellen** to put up or erect scaffolding

Ge|rüst-: **Ge|rüst|bau** M, *no pl* erection of scaffolding; **„W. Friedrich GmbH, ~"** "W. Friedrich Ltd, Scaffolders"; **Ge|rüst|bau|er(in)** M(F) *pl* **-bauer(innen)** scaffolder; **Ge|rüst|stan|ge** F scaffolding pole

Ge|rüt|tel [gə'rʏtl] NT **-s**, *no pl* shaking (about); *(im Zug, Wagen etc)* jolting (about)

ge|rüt|telt [gə'rʏtlt] ADJ **ein ~es Maß von** or **an etw** *(dat)* a fair amount of sth; **er besitzt ein ~es Maß (an) Unverschämtheit** he has more than his fair share of impudence ADV **~ voll** chock-a-block *(esp Brit inf)*, jam-packed *(inf)*, chock-full → *auch* **rütteln**

ges [gɛs] NT **-, -, Ges** NT **-, -** *(Mus)* G flat

Ge|salb|te(r) [gə'zalptə] M *decl as adj (Rel)* **der ~** the Lord's Anointed

ge|sal|zen [gə'zaltsn] *ptp von* **salzen** ADJ *(fig inf) Witz* spicy; *Preis, Rechnung* steep, fancy *(inf)*, stiff

Ge|sal|ze|ne(s) [gə'zaltsnə] NT *decl as adj (Cook)* salted meat

ge|sam|melt [gə'zamlt] ADJ *Aufmerksamkeit, Kraft* collective; *Werke* collected → *auch* **sammeln**

ge|samt [gə'zamt] ADJ *attr* whole, entire; **die ~e Familie** all the family, the whole or entire family; **die ~en Lehrkräfte** all the teachers; **im ~en** in all; **die ~en Kosten** the total costs

Ge|samt [gə'zamt] NT **-s**, *no pl (liter)* = **Gesamtheit**

Ge|samt-: **Ge|samt|an|sicht** F general or overall view; **Ge|samt|auf|la|ge** F *(von Zeitung etc)* total circulation; *(von Buch)* total edition; **bisherige ~ 300.000 Stück** sales totalling *(Brit)* or totaling *(US)* 300,000; **Ge|samt|aus|fuhr** F total exports *pl*; **Ge|samt|aus|ga|be** F complete edition; **Ge|samt|be|darf** M complete needs *pl*; **Ge|samt|be|stand** M *(an Tieren, Pflanzen etc)* total stock; **Ge|samt|be|trag** M total (amount); **Ge|samt|bild** NT general or overall picture; **ge|samt|deutsch** ADJ all-German; **Ministerium für ~e Fragen** *(Hist)* Ministry for all-German Affairs; **Ge|samt|deutsch|land** NT all Germany; **ein ~ hat auch schon von 1871 bis 1945 bestanden** there was also a united Germany from 1871 to 1945; **Ge|samt|ein|druck** M general or overall impression; **Ge|samt|ein|fuhr** F total imports *pl*; **Ge|samt|ein|kom|men** NT total income; **Ge|samt|er|geb|nis** NT overall result; **Ge|samt|er|lös** M total proceeds *pl*; **Ge|samt|er|trag** M total yield; **Ge|samt|flä|che** F total area; **Ge|samt|ge|sell|schaft** F *(Sociol)* society as a whole; **ge|samt|ge|sell|schaft|lich** ADJ *(Sociol) Problem, Kosten* relating to society as a whole; *Produktion, Solidarität* by society as a whole; **Ge|samt|ge|wicht** NT total weight; *(eines LKWs etc auch)* laden weight; **Ge|samt|gläu|bi|ger** PL *(Jur)* joint creditors *pl*; **ge|samt|haft** *(esp Sw)* ADJ = **gesamt** ADV = **insgesamt**; **Ge|samt|haf|tung** F *(Jur)* joint liability

Ge|samt|heit F -, *no pl* totality; **die ~ der ...** all the ...; *(= die Summe)* the totality of ...; **die ~ (der Bevölkerung)** the population (as a whole); **die ~ der Studenten/Arbeiter** the entire student population/workforce, all the students/workers; **die ~ der Delegierten** all the delegates; **in seiner ~** in its entirety; **das Volk in seiner ~** the nation as a whole

ge|samt|heit|lich ADJ overall ADV as a whole

Ge|samt-: **Ge|samt|hoch|schu|le** F ≈ polytechnic *(Brit)*, ≈ college; **Ge|samt|in|te|res|se** NT general interest; **Ge|samt|ka|pi|tal** NT total capital; **Ge|samt|ka|ta|log** M central catalogue *(Brit)* or catalog *(US)*; **Ge|samt|klas|se|ment** NT *(Sport)* overall placings *pl*; **Ge|samt|kon|zept** NT overall plan or idea or design, master plan; **Ge|samt|kos|ten** PL total or overall costs *pl*; **Ge|samt|kunst|werk** NT *(bei Wagner)* synthesis of the arts; *(= Show, Happening)* multi-media performance or show; **Ge|samt|la|ge** F general situation; **Ge|samt|mas|se** F *(Comm)* total assets *pl*; **Ge|samt|no|te** F *(Sch)* overall mark *(Brit)* or grade *(US)*; **Ge|samt|nut|zungs|dau|er** F useful life; **Ge|samt|pla|nung** F overall planning; **Ge|samt|preis** M total price, all-in price *(inf)*; **Ge|samt|scha|den** M total damage; **ein ~ von 5.000 Euro** damage totalling *(Brit)* or totaling *(US)* 5,000 euros; **Ge|samt|schau** F synopsis *(über +acc* of); **Ge|samt|schuld|ner** PL *(Jur)* (joint) debtors *pl*; **Ge|samt|schu|le** F comprehensive school

> **GESAMTSCHULE**
>
> The **Gesamtschulen**, created during the educational reforms of the 1970s, were intended to replace the traditional division of schools into **Hauptschule, Realschule** and **Gymnasium**. They enable students to learn a subject at a level appropriate to them: for example, if their week mathematics has prevented them going to a **Gymnasium**, they can still study, say, languages to a high level at the **Gesamtschule**. They also make it possible for students who might not have been considered capable of taking the **Abitur** to do so. → ABITUR, GYMNASIUM, HAUPTSCHULE, REALSCHULE

Ge|samt-: **Ge|samt|sie|ger(in)** M(F) *(Sport)* overall winner; **Ge|samt|stär|ke** F total strength; **Ge|samt|stim|men|zahl** F total number of votes cast; **Ge|samt|stra|fe** F *(Jur)* overall sentence *(for a series of offences, longer than the maximum sentence for the most serious one but less than the total sentences taken consecutively)*; **Ge|samt|sum|me** F total amount; **Ge|samt|über|sicht** F general survey *(über +acc* of); **Ge|samt|um|satz** M total turnover; **Ge|samt|ver|mö|gen** NT total assets *pl*; **Ge|samt|werk** NT complete works *pl*; **Ge|samt|wert** M total value; **im ~ von ...** totalling *(Brit)* or totaling *(US)* ... in value; **Ge|samt|wer|tung** F *(Sport)* overall placings *pl*; **er liegt in der ~ vorn** he's leading overall, he has the overall lead; **Ge|samt|wir|kung** F general or overall effect; **Ge|samt|wirt|schaft** F national economy; **ge|samt|wirt|schaft|lich** ADJ national economic *attr* ADV **~ nicht vertretbar** not justifiable from the point of view of the national economy; **Ge|samt|zahl** F total number; **eine ~ von 8.000 Punkten** a total of 8,000 points; **Ge|samt|zu|sam|men|hang** M general view

ge|sandt *ptp von* **senden**

Ge|sand|te(r) [gə'zantə] M *decl as adj*, **Ge|sand|tin** [gə'zantɪn] F **-, -nen** envoy, legate; *(inf: = Botschafter)* ambassador; **päpstlicher ~r** (papal) nuncio

Ge|sandt|schaft [gə'zantʃaft] F **-, -en** legation; *(inf: = Botschaft)* embassy; *(= päpstliche Gesandtschaft)* nunciature

Ge|sang [gə'zaŋ] M **-(e)s, ⸚e** [gə'zɛŋə] **a** *(= Lied, Vogelgesang)* song; *(= Preislied)* hymn; *(= gregorianischer Gesang etc)* chant; **erster ~ der Ilias** first book of the Iliad; **erster ~ von Dantes Inferno** first canto of Dante's Inferno; **geistliche Gesänge** religious hymns and chants **b** *no pl (= das Singen)* singing; *(von Mönchen etc)* chanting

Ge|sang-: **Ge|sang|buch** NT *(Eccl)* hymnbook; **das richtige/falsche ~ haben** *(inf)* to belong to the right/wrong denomination; **Ge|sang|leh|rer(in)** M(F) singing teacher

ge|sang|lich [gə'zaŋlɪç] ADJ vocal; *Begabung* for singing

Ge|sangs- *in cpds (Aus)* = **Gesang-**

Ge|sangs|ein|la|ge F vocal number

Ge|sangs|kunst F singing technique

Ge|sang-: **Ge|sang|stun|de** F singing lesson; **Ge|sang(s)|un|ter|richt** M singing lessons *pl*; **Ge|sang(s)|ver|ein** M choral society *(Brit)*, glee club *(US)*; **mein lieber Herr Gesangverein!** *(hum)* ye gods and little fishes! *(hum)*

Ge|säß [gəˈzɛːs] NT **-es, -e** seat, bottom, posterior *(hum)*

Ge|säß-: **Ge|säß|ba|cke** F buttock, cheek; **Ge|säß|mus|kel** M gluteal muscle *(spec)*; **Ge|säß|spal|te** F *(form)* cleft between the buttocks; **Ge|säß|ta|sche** F back pocket

ge|sät|tigt [gəˈzɛtɪçt] ADJ *(Chem)* saturated → *auch* **sättigen**

Ge|säu|sel [gəˈzɔyzl] NT **-s**, *no pl* *(von Blättern)* rustling, rustle, whisper; *(vom Wind)* murmur (-ing), whisper(ing), sigh(ing); *(fig iro: von Menschen)* purring

gesch. *abbr von* **geschieden** divorced

Ge|scha|cher [gəˈʃaxɐ] NT **-s**, *no pl* *(pej)* haggling *(um* about)

Ge|schä|dig|te(r) [gəˈʃɛːdɪçtə] MF *decl as adj* victim

ge|schaf|fen *ptp von* **schaffen**

ge|schafft *ptp von* **schaffen** ADJ *(inf: = erschöpft)* shattered, whacked *(inf)*; **ich bin ~** I've had it *(inf)* → *auch* **schaffen**

Ge|schäft [gəˈʃɛft] NT **-(e)s, -e** **a** *(= Gewerbe, Handel)* business *no pl*; *(= Geschäftsabschluss)* (business) deal *or* transaction; **~ ist ~** business is business; **wie geht das ~?, wie gehen die ~e?** how's business?; **mit jdm ins ~ kommen** to do business with sb; **mit jdm ~e machen** to do business with sb, to have business dealings with sb; **im ~ sein** to be in business; **für jdn die ~e führen** to act for sb; *(im Gewerbe, Handel)* to run the business for sb; **ein ~ tätigen** to do a deal, to make a transaction, to carry out a transaction; **dunkle ~e treiben** to be involved in some shady dealings *or* business; **ein gutes/schlechtes ~ machen** to make a good/bad deal; **dabei hat er ein ~ gemacht** he made a profit by it; **~e mit etw machen** to make money out of sth; **das ~ mit der Lust** the sex industry; **Boulevardzeitungen leben von dem ~ mit der Angst** the popular press make their living by trading on people's fears
b *(= Aufgabe)* duty; **das gehört zu den ~en des Ministers** that is one of the minister's duties, that is part of the minister's work; **seinen ~en nachgehen** to go about one's business
c *(= Firma)* business; *(= Laden)* shop *(Brit)*, store; *(inf: = Büro)* office; **die ~e schließen um 17.30 Uhr** the shops *(esp Brit) or* stores close at 5.30; **ich gehe um 8 Uhr ins ~** I go to work *or* to the office at 8.00; **im ~** at work, in the office; *(= im Laden)* in the shop
d *(baby-talk: = Notdurft)* **kleines/großes ~** little/big job *(baby-talk)*, number one/two *(baby-talk)*; **ein ~ machen** to do a job *(baby-talk)*; **sein ~ verrichten** to do one's business *(euph)*

Ge|schäf|te-: **ge|schäf|te|hal|ber** ADV *(= in Geschäften)* on business; *(= wegen Geschäften)* because of business; **Ge|schäf|te|ma|cher(in)** M(F) *(pej)* profiteer; **Ge|schäf|te|ma|che|rei** [-maxəˈrai] F **-, -en** *(pej)* profiteering *no indef art*

ge|schäf|tig [gəˈʃɛftɪç] ADJ *(= betriebsam)* busy; *Stadt auch* bustling; **~es Treiben, ~es Hin und Her** hustle and bustle, bustling activity ADV busily; **~ hin und her laufen** to bustle (a)round (busily); **~ tun, sich ~ geben** to try to look busy

Ge|schäf|tig|keit F **-**, *no pl* busyness; *(= geschäftiges Treiben)* (hustle and) bustle; **eine enorme ~ entfalten** *or* **an den Tag legen** to get incredibly busy

Ge|schaftl|hu|ber [gəˈʃaftlhuːbɐ] M **-s, -**, **Ge|schaftl|hu|be|rin** [-ərɪn] F **-, -nen** *(S Ger)* busybody

ge|schäft|lich [gəˈʃɛftlɪç] ADJ *(= das Geschäft betreffend)* business *attr*; *(= sachlich) Ton* businesslike; **ich habe mit ihm etwas Geschäftliches zu besprechen** I have some business *or* business matters to discuss with him ADV *(= in Geschäften)* on business; *(= wegen Geschäften)* because of business; *(= geschäftlich gesehen)* from a business point of view; **er hat morgen ~ in Berlin zu tun** he has business in Berlin tomorrow, he has to be in Berlin on business tomorrow; **~ verhindert** prevented by business; **~ verreist** away on business; **~ mit jdm verkehren** to have business dealings with sb

Ge|schäfts-: **Ge|schäfts|ab|lauf** M course of business; **Ge|schäfts|ab|schluss** M business deal *or* transaction; **Ge|schäfts|adres|se** F business address; **Ge|schäfts|an|ge|le|gen|heit** F business matter *or* affair; **Ge|schäfts|an|teil** M share of a/the business; **Ge|schäfts|auf|ga|be** F, **Ge|schäfts|auf|lö|sung** F closure of a/the business; **Räumungsverkauf wegen ~** closing-down sale; **Ge|schäfts|aus|la|ge** F window display; **Ge|schäfts|au|to** NT company car; **Ge|schäfts|bank** F *pl* **-banken** commercial bank; **Ge|schäfts|be|din|gun|gen** PL terms *pl* of business; **Ge|schäfts|be|reich** M *(Parl)* responsibilities *pl*; **Minister ohne ~** minister without portfolio; **Ge|schäfts|be|richt** M report; *(einer Gesellschaft)* company report; **Ge|schäfts|be|sit|zer(in)** M(F) = **Geschäftsinhaber(in)**; **Ge|schäfts|be|zie|hun|gen** PL business connections *pl* *(zu* with); **Ge|schäfts|brief** M business letter; **Ge|schäfts|bü|cher** PL books *pl*, accounts *pl*; **Ge|schäfts|er|öff|nung** F opening of a shop *(Brit) or* store; **Ge|schäfts|es|sen** NT business lunch *etc*; **ge|schäfts|fä|hig** ADJ **a** *(Jur)* capable of contracting *(form)*, competent *(form)*; **voll/beschränkt ~ sein** to have complete/limited competence **b** *Firma, System* able to function; **Ge|schäfts|fä|hig|keit** F **a** *(Jur)* (legal) competence **b** *(von Firma, System)* ability to function; **Ge|schäfts|frau** F businesswoman; **Ge|schäfts|freund(in)** M(F) business associate; **ge|schäfts|füh|rend** ADJ *attr* executive; *(= stellvertretend)* acting; *Regierung* caretaker; **Ge|schäfts|füh|rer(in)** M(F) *(von Laden)* manager/manageress; *(von Unternehmen)* managing director, CEO; *(von Verein)* secretary; *(von Partei)* whip; **Ge|schäfts|füh|rung** F management; **mit der ~ beauftragt** *(abbr* **m.d.G.b.**) in charge of administration; **Ge|schäfts|gang** M **a** *no pl* business *no art* **b** *pl* **-gänge** *(= Besorgung)* errand; **Ge|schäfts|ge|ba|ren** NT business methods *pl or* practices *pl*; **Ge|schäfts|ge|heim|nis** NT business secret; **Ge|schäfts|geist** M business sense *or* acumen; **Ge|schäfts|haus** NT **a** *(= Gebäude)* business premises *pl*; *(mit Büros)* office block **b** *(= Firma)* house, firm; **Ge|schäfts|herr(in)** M(F) *(Sw)* owner (of a business); **Ge|schäfts|idee** F business idea; **Ge|schäfts|in|ha|ber(in)** M(F) owner (of a business); *(von Laden, Restaurant)* proprietor/proprietress, owner; **Ge|schäfts|in|te|res|se** NT business interest; **Ge|schäfts|jahr** NT financial year; **Ge|schäfts|ju|bi|lä|um** NT company anniversary; *(kleineres Geschäft)* business anniversary; **Ge|schäfts|ka|pi|tal** NT working capital; **Ge|schäfts|kos|ten** PL business expenses *pl*; **das geht alles auf ~** it's all on expenses; **Ge|schäfts|la|ge** F **a** *(= Wirtschaftslage)* business situation **b** **in erstklassiger ~** in a good business location; **Ge|schäfts|le|ben** NT business life; **er steht noch im ~** he's still active in the world of business; **Ge|schäfts|lei|tung** F management; **Ge|schäfts|lis|te** F *(Sw)* = **Tagesordnung**; **Ge|schäfts|mann** M *pl* **-leute** businessman; **ge|schäfts|mä|ßig** ADJ businesslike ADV *klingen* businesslike; *erledigen, gekleidet sein* in a businesslike manner; **Ge|schäfts|mä|ßig|keit** F businesslike manner; **Ge|schäfts|me|tho|den** PL business methods *pl*; **Ge|schäfts|mo|dell** NT *(Comm)* business model; **Ge|schäfts|ord|nung** F standing orders *pl*; **zur ~!** point of order!; **eine Frage zur ~** a question on a point of order; **Ge|schäfts|pa|pie|re** PL business papers *pl*; **Ge|schäfts|part|ner(in)** M(F) business partner; *(= Geschäftsfreund)* business associate; **Ge|schäfts|räu|me** PL (business) premises *pl*; *(= Büroräume)* offices *pl*; **in den ~n** on the premises; in the offices; **Ge|schäfts|rei|se** F business trip; **auf ~ sein** to be on a business trip; **Ge|schäfts|rück|gang** M decline in business; **Ge|schäfts|sa|che** F business matter *or* affair; **ge|schäfts|schä|di|gend** ADJ bad for business; **~es Verhalten** = **Geschäftsschädigung**; **Ge|schäfts|schä|di|gung** F conduct *no art* injurious to the interests of the company *(form)*; **Ge|schäfts|schluss** M close of business; *(von Läden)* closing time; **nach ~** out of office *or* working hours/after closing time; **Ge|schäfts|sinn** M, *no pl* business sense *or* acumen; **Ge|schäfts|sitz** M place of business; **Ge|schäfts|stel|le** F offices *pl*; *(von Gericht)* administrative office; **Ge|schäfts|stra|ße** F shopping street; **Ge|schäfts|stun|den** PL office *or* working hours *pl*; *(von Läden)* (shop *(esp Brit) or* store) opening hours *pl*; **„Geschäftsstunden"** "hours of opening"; **Ge|schäfts|tä|tig|keit** F business activity; **Ge|schäfts|trä|ger(in)** M(F) *(Pol)* chargé d'affaires, representative *(US)*; **ge|schäfts|tüch|tig** ADJ business-minded; **Ge|schäfts|tüch|tig|keit** F business sense; **Ge|schäfts|über|nah|me** F takeover of a/the business; *(eines Ladens)* takeover of a/the shop *(esp Brit) or* store; **ge|schäfts|un|fä|hig** ADJ *(Jur)* not capable of contracting *(form)*, (legally) incompetent *(form)*; **Ge|schäfts|un|fä|hig|keit** F *(Jur)* (legal) incompetence; **Ge|schäfts|ver|bin|dung** F business connection; **in ~ mit jdm stehen** to have business connections with sb; **Ge|schäfts|ver|kehr** M **a** business *no art*; **in regem ~ mit einer Firma stehen** to do a considerable amount of business with a firm **b** *(= Straßenverkehr)* business traffic; **Ge|schäfts|vier|tel** NT **a** *(= Geschäftsgegend)* shopping area **b** *(= Banken- und Versicherungsviertel)* business *or* commercial district; **Ge|schäfts|vo|lu|men** NT volume of trade; **Ge|schäfts|wa|gen** M company car; **Ge|schäfts|welt** F world of business, business world; **Ge|schäfts|wert** M value of a/the business; **Ge|schäfts|zeit** F business *or* office hours *pl*; *(von Läden)* (shop *(esp Brit) or* store) opening hours *pl*; **Ge|schäfts|zim|mer** NT office; **Ge|schäfts|zweig** M branch of a/the business

ge|schah *pret von* **geschehen**

Ge|schä|ker [gəˈʃɛːkɐ] NT **-s**, *no pl (inf)* flirting

ge|scha|mig [gəˈʃaːmɪç] ADJ *(esp Aus inf)* = **gschamig**

ge|schätzt *ptp von* **schätzen** ADJ *(fig: = angesehen)* respected, esteemed *(form)*; *Freund etc* valued; *(= beliebt)* well-liked

Ge|schau|kel [gəˈʃaukl] NT **-s**, *no pl* *(im Schaukelstuhl)* swinging; *(in Bus, Wagen)* lurching; *(in Boot)* pitching, rolling

ge|scheckt [gəˈʃɛkt] ADJ spotted; *Pferd* skewbald, pinto *(US)*

ge|sche|hen [gəˈʃeːən] *pret* **geschah** [gəˈʃaː], *ptp* **geschehen** [gəˈʃeːən] VI *aux sein* to happen *(jdm* to sb); *(= vorkommen auch)* to occur; *(= stattfinden auch)* to take place; *(= ausgeführt werden)* to be done; *(Verbrechen)* to be committed; **ihr Selbstmord geschah aus Verzweiflung** her despair led her to commit suicide; **es ist nun einmal ~** what's done is done; **Dein Wille geschehe** *(Bibl)* Thy *or* Your will be done; **es wird ihm nichts ~** nothing will happen to him; **das geschieht ihm (ganz) recht** it serves him right; **ihm ist ein Unrecht ~** he has been wronged; **ihm ist ein Missgeschick ~** he had a mishap; **er wusste nicht, wie ihm geschah** he didn't know what was going on *or* happening; **was soll mit ihm/damit ~?** what is to be done with him/it?; **als er sie sah, war es um ihn ~** he was lost the moment he set eyes on her; **da war es um mei-**

ne Seelenruhe ~ that was an end to my peace of mind; **es kann ~, dass ...** it could happen that ...; **und so geschah es, dass ...** and so it happened *or* came about that ...; **es muss etwas ~** something must be done; **so ~ am ...** such was the case on ...; **Geschehenes ruhen lassen** *(geh)* to let bygones be bygones → **gern a**

Ge|sche|hen [gəˈʃeːən] NT **-s,** *(rare)* **-** events *pl,* happenings *pl*

Ge|scheh|nis [gəˈʃeːnɪs] NT **-ses, -se** *(geh)* event; *(= Vorfall auch)* incident

ge|scheit [gəˈʃait] ADJ **a** clever; *Mensch, Idee* clever, bright; *(= vernünftig)* sensible; **du bist wohl nicht recht ~?** you must be out of your mind *or* off your head; **sei ~!** be sensible; **es wäre ~er ...** it would be wiser *or* more sensible ...; **jetzt bin ich so ~ wie vorher** I'm none the wiser now **b** *(S Ger: = tüchtig, ordentlich)* proper, good; **ich habe ihm ~ die Meinung gesagt** *(S Ger)* I really gave him a piece of my mind; **wie ~** *(Aus inf)* like mad *or* crazy *(inf)*

Ge|schenk [gəˈʃɛŋk] NT **-(e)s, -e** present, gift; *(= Schenkung)* gift; **jdm ein ~ machen** to give sb a present; **jdm etw zum ~ machen** to make sb a present of sth, to give sb sth (as a present); **ein ~ seiner Mutter** a present *or* gift from his mother; **ein ~ Gottes** a gift from *or* of God; **das war ein ~ des Himmels** it was a godsend; **kleine ~e erhalten die Freundschaft** *(prov)* little presents keep a friendship alive

Ge|schenk- *in cpds* gift; **Ge|schenk|ar|ti|kel** M gift; **Ge|schenk|gut|schein** M gift voucher; **Ge|schenk|idee** F gift idea; **Ge|schenk|korb** M (gift) hamper, gift basket; **Ge|schenk|pa|ckung** F gift pack *or* box; *(von Pralinen)* gift box; **Ge|schenk|pa|pier** NT wrapping paper, giftwrap; **etw in ~ einwickeln** to giftwrap sth

Ge|schenks- [gəˈʃɛŋks] *(Aus) in cpds* = **Geschenk-**

Ge|schenk|sen|dung F gift parcel *(esp Brit) or* package

Ge|scher|te(r) [gəˈʃeːɐtə] MF *decl as adj (Aus inf)* idiot

Ge|schicht|chen [gəˈʃɪçtçən] NT **-s, -** little story

Ge|schich|te [gəˈʃɪçtə] F **-, -n a** *no pl (= Historie)* history; **~ des Altertums/der Neuzeit, Alte/Neue ~** ancient/modern history; **die ~ Spaniens/der Menschheit** the history of Spain/mankind; **~ machen** to make history; **das ist längst ~** that's past history **b** *(= Erzählung, Lügengeschichte)* story; *(= Märchen, Fabel etc)* tale, story; *(= Kurzgeschichte)* short story; **das sind alles bloß ~n** that's all just made up, that's just a story; **~n erzählen** to tell stories **c** *(inf: = Angelegenheit, Sache)* affair, business *no pl;* **das sind alte ~n** that's old hat *(inf);* **das ist (wieder) die alte ~** it's the same old *or* the old old story (all over again); **alte ~n wieder aufwärmen** to rake up the past; **die ganze ~** the whole business; **eine schöne ~!** *(iro)* a fine how-do-you-do! *(inf);* **das sind ja nette ~n!** *(iro)* this is a fine thing; **die ~ mit seinem Magen** the trouble *or* business with his stomach; **als er damals diese ~ mit der Tänzerin hatte** when he was having that affair with the dancer; **mach keine ~n!** don't be silly! *(inf);* *(= Dummheiten)* don't do anything silly!

Ge|schich|ten-: **Ge|schich|ten|buch** NT storybook; **Ge|schich|ten|er|zäh|ler(in)** M(F) *(lit, fig)* storyteller

ge|schicht|lich [gəˈʃɪçtlɪç] ADJ *(= historisch)* historical; *(= bedeutungsvoll)* historic ADV historically; **~ bedeutsam** historic; **~ denken** to think in terms of history; **etw ~ betrachten** to consider sth from the historical point of view; **~ belegt** *or* **nachgewiesen sein** to be a historical fact; **~ bewandert sein** to be well-versed in history, to be familiar with history

Ge|schichts-: **Ge|schichts|at|las** M historical atlas; **Ge|schichts|auf|fas|sung** F, **Ge|schichts|be|trach|tung** F conception of history; **Ge|schichts|be|wäl|ti|gung** F, *no pl* coming to terms with the past; **Ge|schichts|be|wusst|sein** NT awareness of history, historical awareness; **Ge|schichts|buch** NT history book; **Ge|schichts|deu|tung** F interpretation of history; **Ge|schichts|dra|ma** NT historical drama; **Ge|schichts|epo|che** F period of history; **Ge|schichts|fäl|schung** F falsification of history; **Ge|schichts|for|scher(in)** M(F) historian; **Ge|schichts|for|schung** F historical research; **Ge|schichts|kennt|nis** F knowledge of history *no pl,* historical knowledge *no pl;* **Ge|schichts|klit|te|rung** F historical misrepresentation; **Ge|schichts|leh|rer(in)** M(F) history teacher; **ge|schichts|los** ADJ *Land, Stadt* with no history; *Zeit* with no historical records; *Volk* with no sense of history, ahistorical; *Politik, Weltanschauung* ahistorical; **Ge|schichts|lo|sig|keit** F **-,** *no pl (von Land, Stadt)* lack of history; *(von Zeit)* absence of historical records (+*gen* for); *(von Volk)* historical unawareness; *(von Politik, Weltanschauung)* ahistoricity *(form);* **Ge|schichts|phi|lo|soph(in)** M(F) philosopher of history; **Ge|schichts|phi|lo|so|phie** F philosophy of history; **ge|schichts|phi|lo|so|phisch** ADJ *Schrift etc* on the philosophy of history; *Interesse, Studien* in the philosophy of history; **Ge|schichts|schrei|ber(in)** M(F) historian, historiographer; **Ge|schichts|schrei|bung** F historiography; **Ge|schichts|ver|ständ|nis** NT, *no pl* conception *or* reading of history; **Ge|schichts|werk** NT historical work; **Ge|schichts|wis|sen|schaft** F (science of) history; **Ge|schichts|wis|sen|schaft|ler(in)** M(F) historian; **Ge|schichts|zahl** F (historical) date

Ge|schick [gəˈʃɪk] NT **-(e)s, -e** *(geh) (= Schicksal)* fate; *(= politische etc Entwicklung, Situation)* fortune; **ein gütiges ~** good fortune, providence; **ein schlimmes/schweres/trauriges ~** a sad fate

Ge|schick NT **-s,** *no pl* skill

Ge|schick|lich|keit [gəˈʃɪklɪçkait] F **-,** *no pl* skill, skilfulness *(Brit),* skillfulness *(US);* *(= Taktik auch)* cleverness, adroitness; *(= Fingerfertigkeit auch)* dexterity; *(= Beweglichkeit)* agility; **für** *or* **zu etw ~ haben** *or* **zeigen** to be clever at sth

Ge|schick|lich|keits-: **Ge|schick|lich|keits|fah|ren** NT **-s,** *no pl (Sport)* skill tests *pl;* *(Aut)* manoeuvring *(Brit) or* maneuvering *(US)* tests *pl;* **Ge|schick|lich|keits|spiel** NT game of skill; **Ge|schick|lich|keits|übung** F exercise in skill; *(= Beweglichkeitsübung)* exercise in agility

ge|schickt [gəˈʃɪkt] ADJ **a** skilful *(Brit),* skillful *(US);* *(= taktisch auch)* clever, adroit; *(= fingerfertig auch)* dexterous; *(= beweglich)* agile **b** *(S Ger)* = **praktisch ADJ** ADV *(= clever)* cleverly; **~ agieren** to be clever

Ge|schickt|heit F **-,** *no pl* = **Geschicklichkeit**

Ge|schie|be [gəˈʃiːbə] NT **-s,** *no pl* **a** *(Geol)* debris; *(in Flüssen)* deposit **b** *(= Gedränge)* pushing and shoving *(inf)*

ge|schie|den [gəˈʃiːdn] *ptp von* **scheiden** ADJ divorced; **eine ~e Frau** a divorced woman, a divorcee; **Uta Schwarz, ~e Böhme** Uta Schwarz, former married name Böhme; **von dem Moment an waren wir (zwei) ~e Leute** *(inf)* after that it was the parting of the ways for us *(inf)*

Ge|schie|de|ne F *decl as adj* divorcee, divorced woman; **seine ~** *(inf)* his ex *(inf)*

Ge|schie|de|ne(r) [gəˈʃiːdnə] M *decl as adj* divorced man, divorcé; **ihr ~r** *(inf)* her ex *(inf)*

ge|schie|nen *ptp von* **scheinen**

Ge|schimp|fe [gəˈʃɪmpfə] NT **-s,** *no pl (inf)* cursing; *(tadelnd)* scolding

Ge|schirr [gəˈʃɪr] NT **-(e)s, -e a** *no pl (= Haushaltsgefäße)* crockery *(Brit),* tableware; *(= Küchengeschirr)* pots and pans *pl,* kitchenware; *(= Teller etc)* china; *(zu einer Mahlzeit benutzt)* dishes *pl;* **(das) ~ (ab)spülen** to wash *or* do the dishes *(Brit),* to wash up; **feuerfestes ~** ovenware **b** *(= Service)* (dinner/tea *etc*) service; *(= Glasgeschirr)* set of glasses; *(= feuerfestes Geschirr)* set of ovenware; **das gute ~** the best china **c** *(old) (= Gefäß)* vessel, pot; *(= Nachtgeschirr)* chamber pot **d** *(von Zugtieren)* harness; **einem Pferd das ~ anlegen** to harness (up) a horse; **sich ins ~ legen** *or* **werfen** *(Pferde, Ochsen)* to pull hard; *(fig)* to put one's shoulder to the wheel, to put one's back into it

Ge|schirr-: **Ge|schirr|auf|zug** M dumb waiter; **Ge|schirr|hand|tuch** NT tea towel *(Brit),* dishtowel *(US);* **Ge|schirr|ma|cher(in)** M(F) harness-maker; **Ge|schirr|schrank** M china cupboard *(Brit) or* cabinet *(US);* **Ge|schirr|spü|len** NT **-s,** *no pl* washing-up; **Ge|schirr|spü|ler** M, **Ge|schirr|spül|ma|schi|ne** F dishwasher; **Ge|schirr|spül|mit|tel** NT washing-up liquid *(Brit),* dishwashing liquid *(US);* **Ge|schirr|tuch** NT *pl* **-tücher** tea towel *(Brit),* dishtowel *(US)*

Ge|schiss [gəˈʃɪs] NT **-es,** *no pl (inf)* fuss and bother

ge|schis|sen *ptp von* **scheißen**

Ge|schlab|ber [gəˈʃlabɐ] NT **-s,** *no pl (inf)* slurping

ge|schla|fen *ptp von* **schlafen**

ge|schla|gen *ptp von* **schlagen**

ge|schlaucht *ptp von* **schlauchen** ADJ *(inf)* whacked *(inf),* dead beat *(inf)* → *auch* **schlauchen**

Ge|schlecht [gəˈʃlɛçt] NT **-(e)s, -er a** sex; *(Gram)* gender; **Jugendliche beiderlei ~s** young people of both sexes; **das andere ~** the opposite sex; **das schwache/schöne/starke ~** the weaker/fair/stronger sex; **das dritte ~** transvestites *pl;* *(= Homosexuelle)* homosexuals *pl* **b** *(geh: = Geschlechtsteil)* sex *(liter)* **c** *(liter) (= Gattung)* race; *(= Generation)* generation; *(= Sippe)* house; *(= Abstammung)* lineage; **das menschliche ~, das ~ der Menschen** the human race; **das ~ der Götter** the gods; **er ist vornehmen ~s** he is of noble lineage

Ge|schlech|ter-: **Ge|schlech|ter|fol|ge** F line; **Ge|schlech|ter|kampf** M battle of the sexes; **Ge|schlech|ter|kun|de** F genealogy; **Ge|schlech|ter|tren|nung** F segregation of the sexes

ge|schlecht|lich [gəˈʃlɛçtlɪç] ADJ sexual; **~e Erziehung** sex education ADV **mit jdm ~ verkehren** to have sexual intercourse with sb; **sich ~ vermehren** *(Biol)* to reproduce sexually

Ge|schlecht|lich|keit F **-,** *no pl* sexuality

Ge|schlechts-: **ge|schlechts|ab|hän|gig** ADJ sexually determined; **Ge|schlechts|akt** M sex(ual) act; **Ge|schlechts|be|stim|mung** F sex determination; **Ge|schlechts|chro|mo|som** NT sex chromosome; **Ge|schlechts|drang** M sex(ual) urge; **Ge|schlechts|drü|se** F sex gland; **Ge|schlechts|er|zie|hung** F sex(ual) education; **ge|schlechts|ge|bun|den** ADJ = **geschlechtsabhängig**; **Ge|schlechts|ge|nos|se** M, **Ge|schlechts|ge|nos|sin** F person of the same sex; **jds ~n** those *or* people of the same sex as sb; **Ge|schlechts|hor|mon** NT sex hormone; **ge|schlechts|krank** ADJ suffering from a sexually transmitted disease, suffering from VD *(dated) or* a venereal disease *(dated);* **ein Geschlechtskranker** a person with VD *(dated) or* with a sexually transmitted disease; **Ge|schlechts|krank|heit** F sexually transmitted disease, venereal disease *(dated);* **eine ~ haben** to have a sexually transmitted disease, to have VD *(dated);* **Ge|schlechts|le|ben** NT sex life; **Ge|schlechts|lei|den** NT sexually transmitted disease, venereal disease *(dated);* **ge|schlechts|los** ADJ asexual *(auch Biol),* sexless; **Ge|schlechts|lo|sig|keit** F **-,** *no pl* asexuality *(auch Biol),* sexlessness; **Ge|schlechts|lust** F *(geh)* lust; **Ge|schlechts|merk|mal** NT sex(ual) characteristic; **Ge|-**

schlechts|or|gan NT sex(ual) organ; **Ge|schlechts|reif** ADJ sexually mature; **Ge|schlechts|rei|fe** F sexual maturity; **Ge|schlechts|rol|le** F *(Sociol)* sex role; **ge|schlechts|spe|zi|fisch** ADJ *(Sociol)* sex-specific; **Ge|schlechts|teil** NT genitals *pl*; **Ge|schlechts|trieb** M sex(ual) urge; sex(ual) drive; **Ge|schlechts|um|wand|lung** F sex change; **Ge|schlechts|un|ter|schied** M difference between the sexes; **Ge|schlechts|ver|ir|rung** F sexual perversion; **Ge|schlechts|ver|kehr** M sexual intercourse; **Ge|schlechts|wort** NT *pl* **-wörter** *(Gram)* article; **Ge|schlechts|zel|le** F sexual cell

ge|schli|chen *ptp von* **schleichen**

ge|schlif|fen [gəˈʃlɪfn] *ptp von* **schleifen** ADJ *Manieren, Ausdrucksweise* polished, refined; *Sätze* polished; *Edelstein* facetted

Ge|schlif|fen|heit F -, *(rare)* **-en** *(= Feinheit)* refinement; *(= Schliff)* polish

ge|schlos|sen [gəˈʃlɔsn] *ptp von* **schließen** ADJ closed; *(= vereint)* united, unified; **in sich** *(dat)* ~ self-contained; *Mensch, Charakter* well-rounded; *Buch, Handlung* well-knit; *Systeme, Produktionskreisläufe* closed; **es war eine ~e Wolkendecke vorhanden** the sky was completely overcast; **ein ~es Ganzes** a unified whole; **~e Gesellschaft** closed society; *(= Fest)* private party; **in ~er Sitzung** in closed session; *(Jur)* in camera; **ein ~er Wagen** a saloon car *(Brit)*, a sedan *(US)*; **~e Ortschaft** built-up area; **in ~er Formation** *(Aviat)* in close formation
ADV ~ **für etw sein/stimmen** to be/vote unanimously in favour *(Brit)* or favor *(US)* of sth; **wir protestierten ~ gegen das neue Gesetz** we were unanimous in our protest against the new law; **~ hinter jdm stehen** to stand solidly behind sb; **wir gingen ~ mit der ganzen Klasse ins Kino** the whole class went to the cinema en masse *or* as a body; **dieses zwölfbändige Lexikon wird nur ~ abgegeben** this twelve-volume encyclopedia is only sold as a complete set; **dieser Vokal wird ~ ausgesprochen** this vowel has closed articulation

Ge|schlos|sen|heit F -, *no pl* unity

Ge|schluch|ze [gəˈʃlʊxtsə] NT **-s**, *no pl* sobbing

ge|schlun|gen *ptp von* **schlingen** , *von* **schlingen**

Ge|schlür|fe [gəˈʃlʏrfə] NT **-s**, *no pl (inf)* slurping

Ge|schmack [gəˈʃmak] M **-(e)s, ⸚e** *or (hum, inf)* **⸚er** [gəˈʃmɛkə, gəˈʃmɛkɐ] *(lit, fig)* taste; *(= Aroma auch)* flavour *(Brit)*, flavor *(US)*; *(S Ger: = Geruch)* smell; *(no pl: = Geschmackssinn)* sense of taste; **je nach ~** to one's own taste; **Salz (je) nach ~ hinzufügen** add salt to taste; **seinen ~ bilden** *or* **entwickeln** *(lit)* to develop one's sense of taste; *(fig)* to acquire a sense of the aesthetic; **an etw** *(dat)* **~ finden** to acquire a taste for sth; **auf den ~ kommen** to acquire a taste for it; **einen guten ~ haben** *(Essen)* to taste good; **er hat einen guten ~** *(fig)* he has good taste; **für meinen ~** for my taste; **das ist nicht mein/nach meinem ~** that's not my/to my taste; **die Geschmäcker sind verschieden** tastes differ; **über ~ lässt sich (nicht) streiten** *(prov)* there's no accounting for taste(s) *(prov)*

ge|schmäck|le|risch [gəˈʃmɛklərɪʃ] ADJ highly elaborate

ge|schmack|lich [gəˈʃmaklɪç] ADJ *(lit, fig)* as regards taste; **ausgezeichnete ~e Qualitäten** *(form)* exquisite flavour *(Brit)* or flavor *(US)*, exquisite taste ADV **~ besser/hervorragend/Spitzenklasse sein** to taste better/fantastic/excellent; **etw ~ verbessern** to improve the taste of sth

ge|schmack|los ADJ *(lit, fig)* tasteless; *(= taktlos auch)* in bad taste

Ge|schmack|lo|sig|keit F -, **-en** a *no pl (lit, fig)* tastelessness, lack of taste; *(= Taktlosigkeit auch)* bad taste b *(= Beispiel der Geschmacklosigkeit)* example of bad taste; *(= Bemerkung)* remark in bad taste; **das ist eine ~!** that is the most appalling bad taste!

Ge|schmacks-: **ge|schmacks|bil|dend** ADJ aesthetically formative; **Ge|schmacks|bil|dung** F formation of good taste; **Ge|schmacks|emp|fin|dung** F sense of taste; **keine ~ haben** to be unable to taste anything; **Ge|schmacks|fra|ge** F matter *or* question of (good) taste; **Ge|schmacks|knos|pen** PL taste buds *pl*; **Ge|schmacks|mus|ter** NT *(Jur)* registered design; **Ge|schmacks|nerv** M taste bud; **ge|schmacks|neut|ral** ADJ tasteless; **Ge|schmacks|rich|tung** F taste; **in sieben neuen ~en** in seven new flavours *(Brit)* or flavors *(US)*; **Ge|schmacks|sa|che** F matter of taste; **das ist ~** it's (all) a matter of taste; **Ge|schmacks|sinn** M, *no pl* sense of taste; **Ge|schmacks|trä|ger** M *(Cook)* flavour *(Brit)* or flavor *(US)* carrier; **Ge|schmacks|ver|ir|rung** F **unter ~ leiden** *(iro)* to have no taste; **der Hut ist eine ~** that hat is an aberration; **Ge|schmacks|ver|stär|ker** M *(Chem, Cook)* flavour *(Brit)* or flavor *(US)* enhancer

ge|schmack|voll ADJ tasteful; **~e Kleider tragen** to dress tastefully; **das war eine nicht sehr ~e Bemerkung** that remark was not in very good taste ADV tastefully

Ge|schmat|ze [gəˈʃmatsə] NT **-s**, *no pl (inf)* noisy eating

Ge|schmei|de [gəˈʃmaidə] NT **-s, -** *(geh)* jewellery *no pl (Brit)*, jewelry *no pl (US)*; **ein ~** a piece of jewel(le)ry

ge|schmei|dig [gəˈʃmaidɪç] ADJ a *Leder, Haut* supple; *Körper, Bewegung auch* lithe, lissom(e); *Fell* sleek; *(= weich) Handtuch, Haar* soft; *Teig* workable; *Wachs* malleable; *(= anschmiegsam)* soft and clinging; **er hat einen ~en Gang** he moves with supple grace b *(fig) (= anpassungsfähig)* adaptable, flexible; *(= wendig)* adroit; *Zunge, Worte* glib, smooth ADV *(= wendig)* smoothly, supply; *(in Bezug auf Tanzen)* lithely; **~ glitt die Katze vom Stuhl** the cat slid off the chair with feline grace

Ge|schmei|dig|keit F -, *no pl* a *(von Leder, Haut)* suppleness; *(von Körper, Bewegung auch)* litheness; *(von Fell)* sleekness; *(= Weichheit) (von Handtuch, Haar)* softness; *(von Wachs)* malleability; *(= Anschmiegsamkeit)* clinging softness b *(fig) (= Anpassungsfähigkeit)* flexibility; *(= Wendigkeit)* adroitness; *(von Zunge, Worten)* glibness

Ge|schmeiß [gəˈʃmais] NT **-es**, *no pl* a *(old lit, fig)* vermin *pl* b *(Hunt)* droppings *pl*

Ge|schmet|ter [gəˈʃmɛtɐ] NT **-s**, *no pl* flourish

Ge|schmier [gəˈʃmiːɐ] NT **-(e)s**, *no pl*, **Ge|schmie|re** [gəˈʃmiːrə] NT **-s**, *no pl (inf)* mess; *(= Handschrift)* scrawl; *(= Geschriebenes)* scribble; *(= schlechtes Bild)* daub

ge|schmis|sen *ptp von* **schmeißen**

ge|schmol|zen *ptp von* **schmelzen**

Ge|schmor|te(s) [gəˈʃmoːɐtə] NT *decl as adj (Cook)* braised meat

Ge|schmun|zel [gəˈʃmʊntsl] NT **-s**, *no pl* smiling

Ge|schmus [gəˈʃmuːs] NT **-es**, *no pl*, **Ge|schmu|se** [gəˈʃmuːzə] NT **-s**, *no pl (inf)* cuddling; *(von Pärchen)* cuddling, canoodling *(Brit inf)*

Ge|schnä|bel [gəˈʃnɛːbl] NT **-s**, *no pl* billing; *(hum: = Küsserei)* billing and cooing

Ge|schnat|ter [gəˈʃnatɐ] NT **-s**, *no pl (lit)* cackle, cackling; *(fig)* jabber, jabbering

Ge|schnet|zel|te(s) [gəˈʃnɛtsltə] NT *decl as adj (esp Sw Cook) meat cut into strips stewed to produce a thick sauce*

ge|schnie|gelt [gəˈʃniːglt] ADJ *(pej)* flashy; **~ und gebügelt** *or* **gestriegelt** spruced up

ge|schnit|ten *ptp von* **schneiden**

ge|schno|ben *ptp von* **schnauben**

Ge|schnüf|fel [gəˈʃnʏfl] NT **-s**, *no pl* sniffing; *(fig)* nosing *or* sniffing about *(Brit)* or around

ge|scho|ben *ptp von* **schieben**

ge|schol|len *(old) ptp von* **schallen**

ge|schol|ten *ptp von* **schelten**

Ge|schöpf [gəˈʃœpf] NT **-(e)s, -e** *(= Geschaffenes)* creation; *(= Lebewesen)* creature; **wir sind alle ~e Gottes** we are all God's creatures; **sie ist sein ~** *(geh)* she is his creature

ge|scho|ren *ptp von* **scheren**

Ge|schoss [gəˈʃɔs] NT **-es, -e**, △**Ge|schoß** [gəˈʃoːs] *(Aus, S Ger)* NT **-es, -e** projectile *(form)*; *(= Wurfgeschoss, Rakete etc auch)* missile; *(= Kugel auch)* bullet; *(fig inf: = scharf geschossener Ball)* shot; **ferngelenktes ~** guided missile

Ge|schoss NT **-es, -e**, **Ge|schoß** *(Aus, S Ger)* NT **-es, -e** *(= Stockwerk)* floor, storey *(Brit)*, story *(US)*; **im ersten ~** on the first *(Brit)* or second *(US)* floor; **das Haus hat vier ~e** the house has four storeys *(Brit)* or storys *(US)*; **das Kaufhaus hat vier ~e** the department store has four floors

Ge|schoss|bahn F trajectory; *(einer Rakete auch)* flight path

ge|schos|sen *ptp von* **schießen**

Ge|schoss-: **Ge|schoss|gar|be** F burst of fire; **Ge|schoss|ha|gel** M hail of bullets

-ge|schos|sig [gəʃɔsɪç], *(Aus, S Ger)* **-ge|scho|ßig** [gəʃoːsɪç] ADJ *suf* -storey *attr (Brit)*, -story *attr (US)*, -storeyed *(Brit)*, -storied *(US)*; **mehrgeschossig** multistorey *etc*

ge|schraubt [gəˈʃraupt] ADJ *(pej) Stil, Redeweise* pretentious → *auch* **schrauben**

Ge|schrei [gəˈʃrai] NT **-s**, *no pl* shouts *pl*, shouting; *(von Kindern, Fußballfans, Streitenden auch)* yells *pl*, yelling; *(von Verletzten, Babys, Popfans)* screams *pl*, screaming; *(= schrilles Geschrei)* shrieks *pl*, shrieking; *(fig: = Aufhebens)* fuss, to-do *(inf)*; **viel ~ um etw machen** to kick up *(inf)* or make a big fuss about sth; **ein großes ~ erheben** to set up a cry; *(fig)* to raise an outcry

Ge|schreib|sel [gəˈʃraipsl] NT **-s**, *no pl (inf)* scribble; *(fig: = Schreiberei)* scribblings *pl*

ge|schrie|ben *ptp von* **schreiben**

ge|schrie|en, **ge|schrien** *ptp von* **schreien**

ge|schrit|ten *ptp von* **schreiten**

ge|schult *ptp von* **schulen** ADJ **hervorragend ~e Mitarbeiter** outstandingly trained employees; **ein ~es Auge/Ohr haben** to have a practised *(Brit)* or practiced *(US)* or an expert eye/ear → *auch* **schulen**

ge|schun|den *ptp von* **schinden** ADJ *Land, Volk* ravaged, devastated; **der ~e Leib Christi** the broken body of Christ

Ge|schütz [gəˈʃʏts] NT **-es, -e** gun; **schweres ~** heavy artillery; **eine Kanone ist ein ~** a cannon is a piece of artillery; **ein ~ auffahren** to bring up a gun; **schweres** *or* **grobes ~ auffahren** *(fig)* to bring up one's big guns

Ge|schütz-: **Ge|schütz|be|die|nung** F gunnery; *(= Personal)* gun crew; **Ge|schütz|don|ner** M roar *or* booming of (the) guns; **Ge|schütz|feu|er** NT shell fire; **Ge|schütz|rohr** NT gun barrel; **Ge|schütz|stand** M, **Ge|schütz|stel|lung** F gun emplacement

ge|schützt [gəˈʃʏtst] ADJ *Winkel, Ecke* sheltered; *Pflanze, Tier, Kennwort, Datei* protected; **ein ~er Platz** a sheltered spot *or* place; **~er Feiertag** unpaid statutory holiday *(Brit)* or vacation *(US)*; **~er Trennstrich** *(Comput)* nonbreaking hyphen; **~es Leerzeichen** *(Comput)* nonbreaking space → *auch* **schützen**

Ge|schütz|turm M gun turret

Geschw. *abbr von* **Geschwister**

Ge|schwa|der [gəˈʃvaːdɐ] NT **-s, -** squadron

Ge|schwa|der-: **Ge|schwa|der|kom|man|deur(in)** M(F) *(Naut)* commodore; **Ge|schwa|der|kom|mo|do|re** M *(Aviat)* squadron leader *(Brit)*, major *(US)*

Ge|schwa|fel [gəˈʃvaːfl] NT **-s**, *no pl (inf)* waffle *(Brit inf)*, blather *(inf)*

Ge|schwal|le [gəˈʃvalə] NT **-s**, *no pl (pej inf)* waffle *(Brit inf)*, blather *(inf)*

ge|schwänzt [gəˈʃvɛntst] ADJ *Peitsche* with tails; *Haar* in a ponytail

Ge|schwätz [gəˈʃvɛts] NT **-es**, *no pl (pej)* prattle; *(= Klatsch)* tittle-tattle *(Brit inf)*, gossip

Ge|schwat|ze [gəˈʃvatsə] NT -s, *no pl, (S Ger)* **Ge|schwät|ze** [gəˈʃvɛtsə] NT -s, *no pl (inf)* chattering, nattering *(inf)*

ge|schwät|zig [gəˈʃvɛtsɪç] ADJ talkative, garrulous; *(= klatschsüchtig)* gossipy

Ge|schwät|zig|keit F -, *no pl* talkativeness, garrulousness; *(= Klatschsucht)* constant gossiping; **das haben wir deiner ~ zu verdanken** we've you and your eternal chattering/gossiping to thank for that

ge|schweift [gəˈʃvaift] ADJ **a** curved; **~e Klammer** *(Typ)* curly bracket, brace → *auch* **schweifen** **b** *Stern* with a tail

ge|schwei|ge [gəˈʃvaigə] CONJ **~ (denn)** let *or* leave alone, never mind

ge|schwie|gen *ptp von* **schweigen**

ge|schwind [gəˈʃvɪnt] ADJ *(old, S Ger)* swift, quick, fast *no adv*; **~!** quick(ly)!, hurry!; **~en Schrittes** *(geh)* with rapid steps; **~ wie der Wind** *(geh)* as swift as the wind

Ge|schwin|dig|keit [gəˈʃvɪndɪçkait] F -, -en speed; *(= Schnelligkeit auch)* swiftness, quickness; *(Phys: von Masse)* velocity; **mit einer ~ von ...** at a speed of ...; **mit höchster ~** at top speed; **mit rasender ~ fahren** to belt *or* tear along *(inf)*; **eine zu große ~ draufhaben** *(inf)* to be going too fast; **an ~ zunehmen** to gather *or* pick up speed; *(Phys: Masse)* to gain momentum; **die ~ steigern/verringern** to increase/decrease one's speed, to speed up/slow down

Ge|schwin|dig|keits-: **Ge|schwin|dig|keits|ab|fall** M *(Phys)* loss of speed; **Ge|schwin|dig|keits|be|gren|zung** F, **Ge|schwin|dig|keits|be|schrän|kung** F speed limit; **gegen die ~ verstoßen** to exceed the speed limit; **Ge|schwin|dig|keits|kon|trol|le** F speed check; **Ge|schwin|dig|keits|mes|ser** M -s, - tachometer; *(Aut auch)* speedometer, speedo *(Brit inf)*; **Ge|schwin|dig|keits|über|schrei|tung** [-ly:bɐʃraitʊŋ] F -, -en, **Ge|schwin|dig|keits|über|tre|tung** F exceeding the speed limit, speeding; **Ge|schwin|dig|keits|zu|nah|me** F *(Phys)* increase in velocity

Ge|schwirr [gəˈʃvɪr] NT -s, *no pl (von Insekten)* buzzing; *(von Pfeilen)* whizzing

Ge|schwis|ter [gəˈʃvɪstɐ] PL brothers and sisters *pl*, siblings *pl*; **wir sind drei ~** there are three of us in my *or* our family; **haben Sie noch ~?** do you have any brothers or sisters?

Ge|schwis|ter NT -s, - *(form, Sw)* sibling *(form)*; *(= Bruder)* brother; *(= Schwester)* sister

Ge|schwis|ter|chen [gəˈʃvɪstɐçən] NT -s, - little brother/sister

ge|schwis|ter|lich [gəˈʃvɪstɐlɪç] ADJ brotherly/sisterly ADV in a brotherly/sisterly way; **sie leben ~ zusammen** they live together as brother and sister

Ge|schwis|ter-: **Ge|schwis|ter|lie|be** F brotherly/sisterly love; *(gegenseitig)* love between a brother and a sister; **ge|schwis|ter|los** ADJ who have no brothers or sisters ADV **~ aufwachsen** to grow up as an only child; **Ge|schwis|ter|paar** NT brother and sister *pl*; **die beiden sind ein reizendes ~** the children are a lovely pair

ge|schwol|len [gəˈʃvɔlən] *ptp von* **schwellen** ADJ *(pej)* turgid, pompous, bombastic ADV *(pej)* turgidly, pompously, bombastically

ge|schwom|men *ptp von* **schwimmen**

ge|schwo|ren [gəˈʃvo:rən] *ptp von* **schwören**

Ge|schwo|re|nen-: **Ge|schwo|re|nen|bank** F *pl* **-bänke** jury box; *(= die Geschworenen)* jury; **Ge|schwo|re|nen|ge|richt** NT = **Schwurgericht**; **Ge|schwo|re|nen|lis|te** F panel

Ge|schwo|re|ne(r) [gəˈʃvo:rənə] MF *decl as adj* juror; **die ~n** the jury *sing or pl*

Ge|schwor|ne(r) [gəˈʃvo:ɐnə] MF *decl as adj (Aus)* = **Geschworene(r)**

Ge|schwulst [gəˈʃvʊlst] F -, ¨-e [gəˈʃvʏlstə] growth; *(= Hirngeschwulst, Krebsgeschwulst etc auch)* tumour *(Brit)*, tumor *(US)*

ge|schwulst|ar|tig ADJ growth-like; tumorous

Ge|schwulst|kno|ten M growth

ge|schwun|den *ptp von* **schwinden**

ge|schwun|gen *ptp von* **schwingen** ADJ curved; **eine leicht ~e Nase** a slightly curved nose; **eine kühn ~e Nase** an aquiline nose; **~e Klammer** *(Typ)* curly bracket, brace

Ge|schwür [gəˈʃvy:ɐ] NT -s, -e ulcer; *(= Hautgeschwür auch)* sore; *(= Furunkel)* boil; *(fig)* running sore, ulcer

ge|schwür|ar|tig ADJ ulcerous ADV **sich ~ verändern** to become ulcerous, to ulcerate; **~ wachsen** *(fig)* to spread like a cancer

ge|seg|net [gəˈze:gnət] ADJ *(geh)* **mit etw ~ sein** to be blessed with sth; **~en Leibes sein** *(old, Bibl)* to be great with child *(old, Bibl)*; **~es neues Jahr!** Happy New Year; **~e Mahlzeit!** for what we are about to receive may the Lord make us truly thankful; **im ~en Alter von 84 Jahren** at the ripe old age of 84; **einen ~en Schlaf haben** to be a sound sleeper; **einen ~en Appetit haben** to have a healthy appetite → *auch* **segnen**

ge|se|hen *ptp von* **sehen**

Ge|seich [gəˈzaiç] NT -s, *no pl (sl)* claptrap *(inf)*

Ge|sei|er [gəˈzaiɐ] NT -s, *no pl*, **Ge|sei|re** [gəˈzairə] NT -s, *no pl (pej inf)* **a** *(= Gejammer)* moaning, bellyaching *(inf)* **b** *(= Geschwafel)* claptrap *(inf)*

Ge|selch|te(s) [gəˈzɛlçtə] NT *decl as adj (S Ger, Aus)* salted and smoked meat

Ge|sel|le [gəˈzɛlə] M -n, -n **a** *(= Handwerksgeselle)* journeyman **b** *(old inf: = Bursche)* fellow **c** *(dated: = Kamerad)* companion

ge|sel|len [gəˈzɛlən] *ptp* **gesellt** VR **sich zu jdm ~** to join sb; **dazu gesellte sich noch, dass ...** *(geh)* in addition to this was the fact that ..., this was accompanied by the fact that ... → **gleich 1**

Ge|sel|len-: **Ge|sel|len|brief** M journeyman's certificate; **Ge|sel|len|jah|re** PL years *pl* as a journeyman; **Ge|sel|len|prü|fung** F examination to become a journeyman; **Ge|sel|len|stück** NT journeyman's piece; **Ge|sel|len|zeit** F period as a journeyman

ge|sel|lig [gəˈzɛlɪç] ADJ sociable, convivial; *Tier* gregarious; *Verkehr* social; **der Mensch ist ein ~es Tier** man is a social creature *or* animal; **~es Beisammensein** social gathering, get-together *(inf)*; **sie genehmigten sich in ~er Runde ein paar Bierchen** they had a friendly little get-together over a couple of beers ADV **sie saßen ~ bei einer Flasche Wein zusammen** they were sitting together over a friendly bottle of wine

Ge|sel|lig|keit F -, -en **a** *no pl* sociability, conviviality; *(von Tieren)* gregariousness; *(= geselliges Leben)* social intercourse; **die ~ lieben** to be sociable, to enjoy company **b** *(= Veranstaltung)* social gathering

Ge|sel|lin [gəˈzɛlɪn] F -, -nen *(= Handwerksgesellin)* journeyman

Ge|sell|schaft [gəˈzɛlʃaft] F -, -en **a** *(Sociol, fig: = Oberschicht)* society; **die ~ verändern** to change society; **eine Dame der ~** a society lady; **die ~ der Stadt** the high society of the town; **jdn in die ~ einführen** to introduce sb into society **b** *(= Vereinigung)* society; *(Comm)* company; **die ~ der Freunde** the Society of Friends; **~ des bürgerlichen Rechts** private company *or* corporation *(US)*; **~ mit beschränkter Haftung** limited company *(Brit)* or corporation *(US)* **c** *(= Abendgesellschaft)* reception, party; *(= Gäste)* guests *pl*, party; **geschlossene ~** private party; **eine erlesene ~ hatte sich eingefunden** a select group of people had gathered **d** *(in Restaurant etc)* function **e** *(= Umgang, Begleitung)* company, society *(old, form)*; **zur ~** to be sociable; **in schlechte ~ geraten** to get into bad company; **da befindest du dich in guter ~** then you're in good company; **jdm ~ leisten** to keep sb company **f** *(= Kreis von Menschen)* group of people; *(pej)* pack, bunch, crowd *(all inf)*; **diese Familie/Abteilung ist eine komische ~** that family/department are an odd bunch *(inf)*; **wir waren eine bunte ~** we were a mixed bunch

Ge|sell|schaf|ter [gəˈzɛlʃaftɐ] M -s, -, **Ge|sell|schaf|te|rin** [-ərɪn] F -, -nen **a** *(= Unterhalter)* companion; *(euph: = Prostituierte)* escort; **ein guter ~ sein** to be good company; **er ist nicht der Typ des ~s** he's not good company; **mit einem so anregenden ~ ...** with somebody who is such good company ... **b** *(Comm) (= Teilhaber)* shareholder; *(= Partner)* partner; **stiller ~** sleeping *(Brit)* or silent *(US)* partner

ge|sell|schaft|lich [gəˈzɛlʃaftlɪç] ADJ social; *(Sociol auch)* societal; **~e Produktion** production by society ADV **er ist ~ erledigt** he's ruined socially; **sich ~ unmöglich machen** *or* **danebenbenehmen** to disgrace oneself socially

Ge|sell|schafts-: **Ge|sell|schafts|abend** M social evening; **Ge|sell|schafts|an|teil** M *(Comm)* share of the business; **Ge|sell|schafts|an|zug** M formal dress; **Ge|sell|schafts|auf|bau** M, *no pl* structure of society; **Ge|sell|schafts|bild** NT *(Sociol)* view of society; **Ge|sell|schafts|da|me** F *(old)* (lady's) companion; **ge|sell|schafts|fä|hig** ADJ *Verhalten, Gedankengut, Kunstrichtung* socially acceptable; *Mensch, Aussehen auch* presentable; **ge|sell|schafts|feind|lich** ADJ hostile to society; **Ge|sell|schafts|form** F social system; **Ge|sell|schafts|for|ma|ti|on** F *(Sociol)* development of society; **Ge|sell|schafts|ka|pi|tal** NT *(Comm)* company's capital; **Ge|sell|schafts|klas|se** F *(Sociol)* social class; **Ge|sell|schafts|klatsch** M society gossip; **Ge|sell|schafts|klei|dung** F formal dress; **Ge|sell|schafts|kri|tik** F social criticism, criticism of society; **Ge|sell|schafts|kri|ti|ker(in)** M(F) social critic; **ge|sell|schafts|kri|tisch** ADJ critical of society; **die ~e Funktion einer Zeitung** the function of a newspaper as a critic of society *or* social critic ADV **sich ~ äußern** to be critical of society; **~ denken** to have a critical attitude toward(s) society; **Ge|sell|schafts|leh|re** F *(dated)* sociology; *(Sch)* social studies *pl*; **Ge|sell|schafts|ord|nung** F social system; **Ge|sell|schafts|po|li|tik** F social politics *sing*; **Ge|sell|schafts|raum** M function room; **Ge|sell|schafts|ro|man** M social novel; **Ge|sell|schafts|schicht** F stratum of society, social stratum; **Ge|sell|schafts|spiel** NT party game, parlour *(Brit)* or parlor *(US)* game; **Ge|sell|schafts|struk|tur** F structure of society; *(bestimmte auch)* social structure; **Ge|sell|schafts|stück** NT *(Theat)* comedy of manners; *(Art)* genre painting; **Ge|sell|schafts|sys|tem** NT social system; **Ge|sell|schafts|tanz** M ballroom dance; **Ge|sell|schafts|ver|än|de|rung** F social change; **Ge|sell|schafts|ver|trag** M *(Philos)* social contract; *(Comm)* articles *pl* of partnership, partnership agreement; **Ge|sell|schafts|wis|sen|schaf|ten** PL social sciences *pl*; **ge|sell|schafts|wis|sen|schaft|lich** ADJ sociological

Ge|senk [gəˈzɛŋk] NT -(e)s, -e **a** *(Tech)* die **b** *(Min)* blind shaft, winze

Ge|senk|schmie|de F *(Tech)* drop forge

ge|ses|sen *ptp von* **sitzen**

Ge|setz [gəˈzɛts] NT -es, -e *(Jur: = Naturgesetz, Prinzip)* law; *(= Gesetzbuch)* statute book; *(Parl: = Vorlage)* bill; *(nach Verabschiedung)* act; *(= Satzung, Regel)* rule; **das Copyrightgesetz** the Copyright Act; **(zum) ~ werden** to become law, to pass into law; **aufgrund des ~es, nach dem ~** under the law *(über +acc* on); **vor dem ~** in (the eyes of the) law; **im Sinne des ~es** within the meaning of the act; **steht etwas davon im ~?** is there any law about it?; **ich kann nichts im ~ finden, wonach das verboten wäre** I can't find any law forbidding it; **das ~ der Schwerkraft** the law of gravity; **das ~ des Dschungels** the law of the jungle; **das erste** *or* **oberste ~** **(der Wirtschaft** *etc***)** the golden rule (of industry *etc*); **das ~ Mose** *(Bibl)* the Law of Moses, the Mosaic Law; **ein ungeschriebenes ~** an unwritten rule; **wenn uns das ~ des Handelns aufgezwungen wird** if we are forced to take the initiative *or* the first step

Ge|setz-: Ge|setz|blatt NT law gazette; **Ge|setz|buch** NT statute book; **Bürgerliches ~** Civil Code; **Ge|setz|ent|wurf** M (draft) bill

Ge|set|zes-: Ge|set|zes|än|de|rung F change in the law; **Ge|set|zes|bre|cher(in)** M(F) law-breaker; **Ge|set|zes|hü|ter(in)** M(F) *(iro)* guardian of the law; **Ge|set|zes|ini|ti|a|ti|ve** F legislative initiative; *(Sw: = Volksbegehren)* petition for a referendum; **Ge|set|zes|kraft** F the force of law; **~ erlangen** to become law; **~ haben** to be law; **ge|set|zes|kun|dig** ADJ (well-)versed in the law; **Ge|set|zes|la|ge** F **wie ist die ~?** what is the legal position?; **Ge|set|zes|lü|cke** F legal loophole; **Ge|set|zes|no|vel|le** F amendment; **Ge|set|zes|samm|lung** F compendium of laws *(zu on)*; **Ge|set|zes|ta|feln** PL *(Bibl)* tablets *pl (on which the Ten Commandments were written)*; **Ge|set|zes|text** M wording of a/the law; **ge|set|zes|treu** ADJ *Person* law-abiding; *Verhalten* in accordance with the law; **Ge|set|zes|treue** F **seine ~ wurde angezweifelt** it was questioned how law-abiding he was; **Ge|set|zes|über|tre|tung** F infringement of a/the law; **Ge|set|zes|vor|la|ge** F (draft) bill; **Ge|set|zes|werk** NT corpus of laws; **ge|set|zes|wid|rig** ADJ illegal; *(unrechtmäßig)* unlawful ADV illegally; *(= unrechtmäßig)* unlawfully; **Ge|set|zes|wid|rig|keit** F **a** *no pl* illegality; *(= Unrechtmäßigkeit)* unlawfulness **b** *pl (= gesetzwidrige Handlungen)* illegal acts *pl*

Ge|setz-: ge|setz|ge|bend ADJ *attr* legislative, law-making; **die ~e Gewalt** the legislature; **Ge|setz|ge|ber** M legislature, legislative body; **Ge|setz|ge|ber(in)** M(F) legislator, law-maker; **ge|setz|ge|be|risch** [-ge:bərɪʃ] ADJ *attr* legislative; **Ge|setz|ge|bung** [-ge:bʊŋ] F **-, -en** legislation *no pl*

Ge|setz|ge|bungs-: Ge|setz|ge|bungs|ho|heit F legislative sovereignty; **Ge|setz|ge|bungs|not|stand** M legislative state of emergency

ge|setz|kun|dig ADJ = **gesetzeskundig**

ge|setz|lich [gəˈzɛtslɪç] ADJ *Verpflichtung, Bestimmungen, Vertreter, Zahlungsmittel* legal; *Feiertag, Rücklage, Zinsen, Regelungen* statutory; *(= rechtmäßig)* lawful, legitimate; **~e Krankenversicherung** statutory health insurance; **auf ~em Wege zur Macht gelangen** to come to power by legal means ADV legally; *(= durch Gesetze auch)* by law; *(= rechtmäßig)* lawfully, legitimately; **~ zu etw verpflichtet sein** to be required by law to do sth, to be legally required to do sth → **schützen**

Ge|setz|lich|keit F **-,** *no pl* **a** *(= Regel)* law **b** *(= das Gesetzlichsein)* legality; *(= Rechtmäßigkeit)* lawfulness, legitimacy; *(= Rechtsordnung)* law

Ge|setz-: ge|setz|los ADJ *Gruppe, Staat, Zeit* lawless; **Ge|setz|lo|sig|keit** F **-, -en** lawlessness; **ge|setz|mä|ßig** ADJ **a** *(= gesetzlich)* legal; *(= rechtmäßig)* lawful, legitimate **b** *(= einem Naturgesetz folgend)* following a set pattern; *(rare: = regelmäßig)* regular ADV **a** *(= dem Gesetz entsprechend)* legally **b** *(= regelmäßig)* **~ ablaufen** to follow a set pattern; **Ge|setz|mä|ßig|keit** [gəˈzɛtsmɛːsɪçkait] F **-, -en a** *(= Regel)* law; **unser Seelenleben folgt vielleicht uns unbekannten ~en** perhaps the life of the mind runs in accordance with laws which are unknown to us **b** *no pl (= Gesetzlichkeit)* legality; *(= Rechtmäßigkeit)* lawfulness, legitimacy; *(= Regelmäßigkeit)* regularity

ge|setzt [gəˈzɛtst] ADJ *(= reif)* sedate, sober; **ein Herr im ~en Alter** a man of mature years → *auch* **setzen** CONJ **~ den Fall, ...** assuming (that) ...

Ge|setzt|heit F **-,** *no pl (= Reife)* sedateness

ge|setz|wid|rig ADJ ADV = **gesetzeswidrig**

Ge|setz|wid|rig|keit F = **Gesetzeswidrigkeit**

Ge|seuf|ze [gəˈzɔyftsə] NT **-s,** *no pl* sighing

ges. gesch. *abbr von* **gesetzlich geschützt** reg'd

ge|si|chert [gəˈzɪçɐt] ADJ *Einkommen, Existenz* secure; *Fakten, Erkenntnisse* definite, solid; **~es Gewehr** gun with the safety catch on → *auch* **sichern**

Ge|sicht [gəˈzɪçt] NT **-(e)s, -er a** face; **ein ~ machen** *or* **ziehen** *(inf)* to make *or* pull a face; **ein intelligentes/trauriges/böses/wütendes ~ machen** to look intelligent/sad/cross/angry; **ein langes ~ machen** to make *or* pull a long face; **was machst du denn heute für ein ~?** what's up with you today?; **jdm ein ~ schneiden** *(inf)* to make *or* pull a face at sb; **jdm ins ~ spucken** to spit in sb's face; **jdm ins ~ lachen** to laugh in sb's face; **jdm ins ~ lügen** to lie to sb's face; **jdm ins ~ sehen** to look sb in the face; **den Tatsachen ins ~ sehen** to face facts; **jdm etw ins ~ sagen** to tell sb sth to his face; **mir schien die Sonne ins ~** the sun was (shining) in my eyes; **es stand ihm im** *or* **ins ~ geschrieben** it was written all over his face; **jdm ins ~ springen** *(fig inf)* to go for sb; **aufs ~ fallen** to fall on one's face; *(fig inf: Brot etc)* to fall sticky side down; **sein wahres ~ zeigen** to show (oneself in) one's true colours *(Brit) or* colors *(US)*; **neue ~er sehen** to see some new faces; **das sieht man ihm am ~ an** you can see *or* tell (that) from his face; **sich** *(dat)* **eine (Zigarette) ins ~ stecken** *(inf)* to stick a cigarette in one's face *(inf) or* mouth; **jdm wie aus dem ~ geschnitten sein** to be the spitting image of sb; **der Hut steht ihr gut zu ~** *(dated)* her hat is very becoming, her hat becomes her; **dieses Verhalten steht dir nicht zu ~** *(dated)* such behaviour *(Brit) or* behavior *(US)* ill becomes you, it ill becomes you to behave like that; **das** *or* **sein ~ verlieren** to lose face; **das ~ wahren** *or* **retten** to save face → **Schlag a**

b *(fig) (= Aussehen)* look, appearance; *(einer Stadt, Landschaft etc)* face, appearance; *(geh: = Charakter)* character; **ein anderes/freundlicheres ~ bekommen** to look quite different/more friendly; **die Sache bekommt ein anderes ~** the matter takes on a different complexion; **das gibt der Sache ein neues ~** that puts a different complexion on the matter *or* on things

c *no pl (old: = Sehvermögen)* sight; **das Zweite ~** second sight; **jdn aus dem ~ verlieren** *(lit)* to lose sight of sb; *(fig)* to lose touch with sb; **etw aus dem ~ verlieren** *(lit, fig)* to lose sight of sth; **jdn/etw zu ~ bekommen** to set eyes on sb/sth, to see sb/sth; **jdm zu ~ kommen** *(geh)* to be seen by sb

Ge|sicht NT **-(e)s, -e ~e haben** to have visions

Ge|sichts-: Ge|sichts|aus|druck M (facial) expression; *(= Mienenspiel auch)* face; **einen ängstlichen ~ haben** to look scared, to have a scared look *or* expression on one's face; **Ge|sichts|bil|dung** F *(geh)* features *pl*; **Ge|sichts|creme** F face cream; **Ge|sichts|far|be** F complexion; **Ge|sichts|feld** NT field of vision, visual field; **Ge|sichts|hälf|te** F side *or* half of the face; **seine linke ~** the left side *or* half of his face; **Ge|sichts|haut** F facial skin; **Ge|sichts|kon|trol|le** F face check *(carried out by bouncers)*; **Ge|sichts|kreis** M **a** *(dated) (= Umkreis)* field of vision; *(= Horizont)* horizon; **jds ~** *(dat)* **entschwinden** to disappear from (sb's) sight, to be lost to sight; **jdn aus dem** *or* **seinem ~ verlieren** to lose sight of sb **b** *(fig)* horizons *pl*, outlook; **Ge|sichts|läh|mung** F facial paralysis; **ge|sichts|los** ADJ *(fig)* faceless; **Ge|sichts|lo|sig|keit** F **-,** *no pl* facelessness; **Ge|sichts|mas|ke** F face mask; *(eines Chirurgen)* mask; **Ge|sichts|mas|sa|ge** F facial massage, facial; **Ge|sichts|milch** F face lotion; **Ge|sichts|mus|kel** M facial muscle; **Ge|sichts|nerv** M facial nerve; **Ge|sichts|ope|ra|ti|on** F operation to one's face; **sich einer ~ unterziehen** to undergo facial surgery; **Ge|sichts|pa|ckung** F face pack; **Ge|sichts|par|tie** F part of the/one's face; **Ge|sichts|pfle|ge** F care of one's face; **Ge|sichts|plas|tik** F facial *or* cosmetic surgery; **Ge|sichts|pu|der** M face powder; **Ge|sichts|punkt** M *(= Betrachtungsweise)* point of view, standpoint; *(= Einzelheit)* point; **unter diesem ~ betrachtet** looked at from this point of view *or* standpoint; **Ge|sichts|ro|se** F *(Med)* facial erysipelas *(spec)*; **Ge|sichts|schä|del** M *(Anat)* facial bones *pl*; **Ge|sichts|schnitt** M features *pl*; **ein ovaler ~** an oval face; **ein feiner ~** delicate features *pl*; **Ge|sichts|sinn** *no pl (spec)* M sense of sight *or* vision; **Ge|sichts|straf|fung** [-ʃtrafʊŋ] F facelift; **Ge|sichts|ver|lust** M loss of face; **Ge|sichts|was|ser** NT *pl* **-wässer** face lotion; **Ge|sichts|win|kel** M visual angle; *(fig)* angle, point of view; **Ge|sichts|zü|ge** PL features *pl*

Ge|sims [gəˈzɪms] NT **-es, -e** [-zə] ledge

Ge|sin|de [gəˈzɪndə] NT **-s, -** *(old)* servants *pl*; *(= Bauerngesinde)* (farm)hands *pl*

Ge|sin|del [gəˈzɪndl] NT **-s,** *no pl (pej)* riffraff *pl*

Ge|sin|de-: Ge|sin|de|ord|nung F *(Hist) rules governing relations between servant and master*; **Ge|sin|de|stu|be** F *(old)* servants' room

Ge|sin|ge [gəˈzɪŋə] NT **-s,** *no pl (inf)* singing

ge|sinnt [gəˈzɪnt] ADJ *usu pred* **jdm günstig/übel ~ sein** to be well/favourably *(Brit) or* favorably *(US)*/ill disposed to(wards) sb; **jdm freundlich/feindlich ~ sein** to be friendly/hostile to(wards) sb; **sozial/fortschrittlich ~ sein** to be socially/progressively minded; **er ist anders ~ als wir** his views are different from ours, he holds different views from us; **die so ~en Mitglieder** the members holding *or* taking this view

Ge|sin|nung [gəˈzɪnʊŋ] F **-, -en** *(= Charakter)* cast of mind; *(= Ansichten)* views *pl*, basic convictions *pl*; *(= Einstellung)* fundamental attitude; *(= Denkart)* way of thinking; *(einer Gruppe)* ethos; **eine liberale ~** liberal-mindedness; **eine edle ~** noble-mindedness; **anständige ~** decency; **seiner ~ treu bleiben** to remain loyal to one's basic convictions; **wegen seiner ~ verfolgt werden** to be persecuted because of one's views *or* basic convictions *or* way of thinking; **seine wahre ~ zeigen** to show (oneself in) one's true colours *(Brit) or* colors *(US)*

Ge|sin|nungs-: Ge|sin|nungs|freund(in) M(F), **Ge|sin|nungs|ge|nos|se** M, **Ge|sin|nungs|ge|nos|sin** F like-minded person; **Herr Klein und seine Gesinnungsgenossen von der Opposition** Mr Klein and people from the Opposition who think as he does *or* who share his views; **ge|sin|nungs|los** *(pej)* ADJ unprincipled ADV **sich ~ verhalten** to behave in an unprincipled manner, to show a total lack of principle; **Ge|sin|nungs|lo|sig|keit** F **-,** *no pl* lack of principles; **Ge|sin|nungs|lump** M *(pej)* timeserver *(pej inf)*; **Ge|sin|nungs|schnüf|fe|lei** F *(pej)* **~ betreiben** to snoop around and find out people's political convictions; **Ge|sin|nungs|tä|ter(in)** M(F) person motivated by moral convictions; *(aus politischen Gründen)* person motivated by political convictions; **ge|sin|nungs|treu** ADJ true to one's convictions; **Ge|sin|nungs|treue** F loyalty to one's convictions; **Ge|sin|nungs|wan|del** M, **Ge|sin|nungs|wech|sel** M conversion

ge|sit|tet [gəˈzɪtət] ADJ **a** *(= wohlerzogen)* well-mannered, well-behaved **b** *(= zivilisiert, kultiviert)* civilized ADV **die Kinder benahmen sich sehr ~** the children were very well-behaved *or* well-mannered; **die Demonstration lief ~ ab** it was an orderly demonstration

Ge|sit|tung [gəˈzɪtʊŋ] F **-,** *no pl (geh) (= zivilisiertes Verhalten)* civilized (mode of) behaviour *(Brit) or* behavior *(US)*; *(= Gesinnung)* ethos

Ge|socks [gəˈzɔks] NT **-es,** *no pl (pej inf)* riffraff *pl*

Ge|söff [gəˈzœf] NT **-(e)s, -e** *(inf)* muck *(inf)*, swill *(inf)*

ge|sof|fen *ptp von* **saufen**

ge|so|gen *ptp von* **saugen**

ge|son|dert [gəˈzɔndɐt] ADJ separate ADV separately; **dieses Thema wird ~ behandelt** this subject will be dealt with separately; **~ berücksichtigt werden** to receive special consideration

ge|son|nen [gəˈzɔnən] *ptp von* **sinnen** ADJ **a ~ sein, etw zu tun** to be of a mind to do sth **b** *(incorrect)* = **gesinnt**

ge|sot|ten [gəˈzɔtn] *ptp von* **sieden** ADJ *(dial)* boiled; **Gesottenes** boiled meat

ge|spal|ten [gəˈʃpaltn] *ptp von* **spalten** ADJ *Bewusstsein* split; *Lippe, Rachen* cleft; *Huf* cloven; *Zunge* forked; *Gesellschaft, Nation, Konjunktur* divided; **mit ~er Zunge reden** *(old, liter)* to talk falsely; *(esp in Indianergeschichten)* to talk with forked tongue; **bei dieser Frage sind die Meinungen ~** opinions are divided on this question

Ge|spann [gəˈʃpan] NT **-(e)s, -e** **a** *(= Zugtiere)* team; *(= zwei Ochsen)* yoke **b** *(= Wagen und Zugtier) (= Ochsengespann)* oxcart, ox-drawn cart; *(= Pferdegespann)* horse and cart; *(zur Personenbeförderung)* horse and carriage; *(fig inf: = Paar)* pair; **ein gutes ~ abgeben** to make a good team

ge|spannt [gəˈʃpant] ADJ **a** *Seil, Schnur* taut **b** *(fig) Lage* tense; *Beziehungen auch* strained; **seine Nerven waren aufs Äußerste** *or* **äußerste ~** his nerves were at breaking point **c** *(= neugierig)* curious; *(= begierig)* eager; *Aufmerksamkeit* close; **in ~er Erwartung** in eager *or* keen anticipation; **ich bin ~, wie er darauf reagiert** I wonder how he'll react to that, I'd like to see how he reacts to that; **ich bin sehr ~, was ich zu Weihnachten bekomme** I'm longing *or* dying to know what I'm getting for Christmas; **ich bin schon sehr auf diesen Film ~** I'm dying to see this film; **ich bin auf seine Reaktion sehr ~** I'm longing *or* dying to see how he reacts; **ich bin ~ wie ein Regenschirm** *(hum inf)* *or* **Flitzbogen** *(hum inf)* I'm dying to know/see/find out, I'm on tenterhooks *(esp Brit) or* on pins and needles *(US)*; **da bin ich aber ~!** I'm looking forward to that; *(iro)* (oh really?) that I'd like to see!
ADV intently; **~ zuhören/zusehen** to be engrossed with what's going on; **~ in seinem Buch lesen** to be engrossed in one's book → *auch* **spannen**

Ge|spannt|heit F **-,** *no pl* **a** *(von Seil, Schnur)* tension **b** *(fig) (von Lage)* tension; *(von Beziehungen auch)* strain **c** *(= Neugierde)* eager anticipation; **es herrscht große ~** everyone is on tenterhooks *(esp Brit) or* on pins and needles *(US)*

ge|spa|ßig [gəˈʃpaːsɪç] ADJ *(S Ger, Aus)* = **spaßig**

Ge|spenst [gəˈʃpɛnst] NT **-(e)s, -er** ghost, spectre *(Brit liter)*, specter *(US liter)*; *(fig: = Gefahr)* spectre *(Brit)*, specter *(US)*; **~er sehen** *(fig inf)* to imagine things; **er sieht wie ein ~ aus** *(inf)* he looks like a ghost

Ge|spens|ter-: **Ge|spens|ter|ge|schich|te** F ghost story; **Ge|spens|ter|glau|be** M belief in ghosts; **ge|spens|ter|haft** ADJ ghostly *no adv*; *(fig)* eerie, eery ADV eerily; **er sah ~ bleich aus** he was deadly *or* deathly pale, he looked like a ghost; **~ wirken/aussehen** to seem/look ghostly *or* eerie; **Ge|spens|ter|schiff** NT phantom ship; **Ge|spens|ter|stun|de** F witching hour

ge|spens|tern [gəˈʃpɛnstɐn] *ptp* **gespenstert** VI *aux sein (rare)* = **geistern**

ge|spens|tig [gəˈʃpɛnstɪç] *(rare)* ADJ, ADV = **gespenstisch**

ge|spens|tisch [gəˈʃpɛnstɪʃ] ADJ, ADV **a** = **gespensterhaft** **b** *(fig: = bizarr, unheimlich)* eerie, eery; **es ist ~ ruhig** there is an eerie calm

ge|spickt [gəˈʃpɪkt] *ptp von* **spicken** ADJ *(inf)* **mit Fehlern ~** riddled with mistakes; **seine Brieftasche war ~ (voll)** his wallet was bulging, he was loaded *(inf)* → *auch* **spicken**

ge|spie|en *ptp von* **speien**

Ge|spie|le [gəˈʃpiːlə] M **-n, -n** *(old liter, hum)*, **Ge|spie|lin** [gəˈʃpiːlɪn] F **-, -nen** *(old liter, hum)* playmate

ge|spielt [gəˈʃpiːlt] ADJ feigned; **mit ~em Interesse** with a pretence *(Brit) or* pretense *(US)* of being interested → *auch* **spielen**

ge|spien *ptp von* **speien**

ge|spie|sen *(hum) ptp von* **speisen**

Ge|spinst [gəˈʃpɪnst] NT **-(e)s, -e** **a** *(Tex)* weave; *(= gedrehtes Garn)* thread, spun yarn; *(von Spinne)* gossamer; *(von Raupe)* cocoon **b** *(fig geh)* web; *(von Lügen)* tissue, web; *(der Fantasie)* product, fabrication

Ge|spinst|fa|ser F *(Tex)* spinning fibre *(Brit) or* fiber *(US)*

ge|splis|sen *ptp*

ge|spon|nen *ptp von* **spinnen**

Ge|spons [gəˈʃpɔns] M **-es, -e** [-zə] *(old, hum)* spouse *(hum, form)*

ge|spon|sert ADJ sponsored

ge|spornt [gəˈʃpɔrnt] ADJ → **gestiefelt**

Ge|spött [gəˈʃpœt] NT **-(e)s,** *no pl* mockery; *(höhnisch auch)* derision, ridicule; *(= Gegenstand des Spotts)* laughing stock; **jdn/sich zum ~ der Leute machen** to make sb/oneself a laughing stock *or* an object of ridicule; **zum ~ werden** to become a laughing stock; **zum ~ der ganzen Welt werden** to become the laughing stock of the whole world; **mit jdm sein ~ treiben** to poke fun at sb

Ge|spräch [gəˈʃprɛːç] ✪ 27 NT **-(e)s, -e** **a** *(= Unterhaltung)* conversation; *(= Diskussion)* discussion; *(= Dialog)* dialogue *(Brit)*, dialog *(US)*; **~e** *(Pol)* talks; **ich habe ein sehr interessantes ~ mit ihm geführt** I had a very interesting conversation *or* talk with him; **ein ~ unter vier Augen** a confidential *or* private talk; **ein ~ unter Freunden** a conversation between friends; **mit jdm ein ~ anknüpfen** to start a conversation with sb; **das ~ auf etw** *(acc)* **bringen** to bring *or* steer the conversation *etc* (a)round to sth; **im ~ sein** *(lit)* to be being discussed, to be being talked about; *(in der Schwebe)* to be under discussion; **mit jdm ins ~ kommen** to get into conversation with sb; *(fig)* to establish a dialogue *(Brit) or* dialog *(US)* with sb
b *(= Gesprächsstoff)* **das ~ des Tages** the topic of the hour; **das ~ der Stadt** the talk of the town; **zum ~ werden** to become a talking point
c *(Telec: = Anruf)* (telephone) call; **wir haben in unserem gestrigen ~ vereinbart, dass ...** we agreed in our telephone conversation yesterday that ...; **ein ~ für dich** a call for you; **stundenlange ~e führen** to be on the telephone for hours

ge|sprä|chig [gəˈʃprɛːçɪç] ADJ talkative, chatty *(inf)*; *(= mitteilsam)* communicative; **jdn ~ machen** to make sb talk, to loosen sb's tongue ADV **~ von etw erzählen** to talk volubly *or* expansively about sth

Ge|sprä|chig|keit F **-,** *no pl* talkativeness, chattiness *(inf)*; *(= Mitteilsamkeit)* communicativeness; **von unglaublicher ~ sein** to be incredibly talkative *or* chatty *(inf)*

Ge|sprächs-: **ge|sprächs|be|reit** ADJ *(esp Pol)* ready to talk; **Ge|sprächs|be|reit|schaft** F *(esp Pol)* readiness to talk; **Ge|sprächs|dau|er** F **a** *(Telec)* call time **b nach vierstündiger ~** after four hours of talks; **Ge|sprächs|ein|heit** F *(Telec)* unit; **Ge|sprächs|fa|den** M line of communication *(zu* with); **den ~ weiterspinnen** to pursue the line of conversation; **Ge|sprächs|fet|zen** M scrap *or* snippet of conversation; **Ge|sprächs|form** F **in ~** in dialogue *(Brit) or* dialog *(US)* form; **Ge|sprächs|ge|bühr** F *(Telec)* charge for a/the call; **Ge|sprächs|ge|gen|stand** M topic; **der Skandal ist ~ Nummer eins** the scandal is the number one topic; **damit die Leute endlich einen ~ haben** so that people at last have something to talk about; **Ge|sprächs|gut|ha|ben** NT *(bei Prepaidhandy)* free calling credit, credit minutes *pl*; **Ge|sprächs|kli|ma** NT mood of the discussion *or* conversation; *(Pol)* atmosphere of the talks; **Ge|sprächs|part|ner(in)** M(F) interlocutor *(form)*; **~ bei der Diskussion sind die Herren X, Y und Z** taking part in the discussion are Mr X, Mr Y and Mr Z; **mein ~ bei den Verhandlungen** my opposite number at the talks; **er ist nicht gerade ein anregender ~** he's not exactly an exciting conversationalist; **wer war dein ~?** who did you talk with?; **mein ~ heute Abend ist ...** with me this evening is ...; **Ge|sprächs|pau|se** F break in a/the conversation; *(bei Verhandlungen)* break in the talks; **eine ~ einlegen** to have a break, to break off (for a while); **Ge|sprächs|run|de** F discussion(s *pl*); *(Pol)* round of talks; **Ge|sprächs|stoff** M topics *pl*; *(= Diskussionsstoff)* topics to discuss; **Ge|sprächs|teil|neh|mer(in)** M(F) participant in a/the discussion; *(bei Fernsehserien etc)* panellist *(Brit)*, panelist *(US)*; **Ge|sprächs|the|ma** NT = **Gesprächsgegenstand**; **Ge|sprächs|the|ra|pie** F *(Psych)* counselling *(Brit)*, counseling *(US)*; **Ge|sprächs|um|lei|tung** F *(Telec)* call routing system; **ge|sprächs|wei|se** ADV in conversation

ge|spreizt [gəˈʃpraitst] *(fig)* ADJ affected, unnatural ADV *reden, sich ausdrücken* affectedly, unnaturally → *auch* **spreizen**

Ge|spreizt|heit F **-,** *no pl* affectation; **von unerträglicher ~** unbearably affected

ge|spren|kelt [gəˈʃprɛŋklt] ADJ speckled; **schwarz ~** speckled with black → *auch* **sprenkeln**

Ge|spritz|te(r) [gəˈʃprɪtstə] M *decl as adj (S Ger, Aus)* spritzer, wine with soda water

ge|spro|chen *ptp von* **sprechen**

ge|spros|sen *ptp von* **sprießen**

ge|sprun|gen *ptp von* **springen**

Ge|spür [gəˈʃpyːɐ] NT **-s,** *no pl* feel(ing)

gest. *abbr von* **gestorben**

Ge|sta|de [gəˈʃtaːdə] NT **-s, -** *(liter)* strand *(poet)*

Ge|sta|gen [gɛstaˈgeːn] NT **-s, -e** *(Med)* gestagen

Ge|stalt [gəˈʃtalt] F **-, -en** **a** *(lit, fig)* form; *(= Umriss auch)* shape; **in ~ von** *(fig)* in the form of; **(feste) ~ annehmen** *or* **gewinnen** to take shape; **einer Sache** *(dat)* **~ geben** *or* **verleihen** to shape sth; **das Abendmahl in beiderlei ~** *(Eccl)* Communion under both kinds; **sich in seiner wahren ~ zeigen** *(fig)* to show (oneself in) one's true colours *(Brit) or* colors *(US)*; **~ geworden** *(liter)* made flesh *pred* → **Ritter a** **b** *(= Wuchs)* build **c** *(= Person, Persönlichkeit, Traumgestalt)* figure; *(in Literaturwerken auch, pej: = Mensch)* character

ge|stal|ten [gəˈʃtaltn] *ptp* **gestaltet** VT *Text, Wohnung* to lay out; *Programm, Abend, Layout* to arrange; *Arbeitsplatz, Benutzeroberfläche* to organize; *Arbeitszeit, Freizeit, Abend* to organize, to structure; *Schaufenster* to dress; *Zukunft, Beziehung, Gesellschaft, Politik* to shape; **etw rationeller/effizienter/flexibler ~** to make sth more rational/efficient/flexible; **ich gestalte mein Leben so, wie ich will** I live *or* organize my life the way I want to; **etw interessanter/moderner** *etc* **~** to make sth more interesting/modern *etc*; **der Umbau wurde nach den ursprünglichen Plänen gestaltet** the conversion was carried out in accordance with the original plans; **die Gastgeber haben den Abend sehr lebendig gestaltet** our hosts laid on a very lively evening; **etw künstlerisch ~** to give artistic form to sth; **schöpferisches Gestalten** creative expression; **einen historischen Stoff zu einem Roman ~** to fashion *or* mould *(Brit) or* mold *(US)* a historical subject into a novel; **einen Stoff literarisch ~** to give literary form to one's material
VR *(= werden)* to become; *(= sich entwickeln)* to turn *or* develop *(zu* into); **sich schwierig ~** *(Verhandlungen etc)* to run into difficulties; **sich zu einem Erfolg ~** to turn out to be a success

Ge|stal|ter [gəˈʃtaltɐ] M **-s, -**, **Ge|stal|te|rin** [-ərɪn] F **-, -nen** creator; *(Tech: rare)* designer

ge|stal|te|risch [gəˈʃtaltərɪʃ] ADJ creative

Ge|stalt-: **Ge|stalt|leh|re** F *(dated)* morphology; **ge|stalt|los** ADJ formless, shapeless, amorphous; **Ge|stalt|psy|cho|lo|gie** F gestalt psychology; **Ge|stalt|the|ra|pie** F *(spec)* gestalt therapy

Ge|stal|tung F -, -en **a** *(= das Gestalten)* shaping, forming, fashioning *(zu* into); *(von Wohnung)* layout; *(von Abend, Programm)* arrangement; *(von Schaufenster)* dressing; *(von Freizeit)* structuring; **wir bemühen uns um eine möglichst interessante ~ des Sprachunterrichts** we are trying to structure our language-teaching as interestingly as possible **b** *(liter. = Gestaltetes)* creation

Ge|stal|tungs-: **Ge|stal|tungs|form** F form; **Ge|stal|tungs|kraft** F creative power; **Ge|stal|tungs|mit|tel** NT artistic means *sing*; **verschiedene ~** different artistic methods; **Ge|stal|tungs|prin|zip** NT formal principle

Ge|stam|mel [gəˈʃtaml] NT -s, *no pl* stammering, stuttering

ge|stand *pret von* **gestehen**

ge|stan|den *ptp von* **stehen, gestehen** ADJ *attr Seefahrer, Fachmann etc* experienced; **ein ~er Mann, ein ~es Mannsbild** a mature and experienced man

ge|stän|dig [gəˈʃtɛndɪç] ADJ **~ sein** to have confessed; **ein ~er Mörder** a murderer who confessed

Ge|stän|dig|keit F **die ~ des Angeklagten** the fact that the accused confesses/has confessed *etc*

Ge|ständ|nis [gəˈʃtɛntnɪs] NT -ses, -se confession; **ein ~ ablegen** to make a confession; **jdm ein ~ machen** to make a confession to sb; **jdn zu einem ~ zwingen** to force sb to make a confession

Ge|stän|ge [gəˈʃtɛŋə] NT -s, - *(von Gerüst)* bars *pl*, struts *pl*; *(von Maschine)* linkage; *(Min: = Bohrgestänge)* drill stem

Ge|stank [gəˈʃtaŋk] M -(e)s, *no pl* stink, stench

Ge|stän|ker [gəˈʃtɛŋkɐ] NT -s, *no pl (inf)* troublemaking, stirring *(inf)*

Ge|sta|po [geˈstaːpo, gəˈʃtaːpo] F -, *no pl* Gestapo

ge|stat|ten [gəˈʃtatn] ✪ 30, 36, 37.4 *ptp* **gestattet** VT to allow, to permit; *(= einwilligen in)* to agree *or* consent to; **jdm etw ~** to allow sb sth; **jdm ~, etw zu tun** to allow *or* permit sb to do sth; **~ Sie eine Frage?** may I ask you something *or* a question?; **sich** *(dat)* **~, etw zu tun** *(geh)* to take the liberty of doing sth, to be *or* make so bold as to do sth *(dated, hum)*; **sich** *(dat)* **etw ~** to permit *or* allow oneself sth; **wenn ich mir eine Frage/Bemerkung ~ darf ...** *(geh)* if I might be permitted a question/comment, if I may make *or* be so bold *or* free as to ask a question/make a remark ...; **mein Gehalt gestattet mir das nicht** *(geh)* my salary won't permit it; **wenn es die Umstände ~ ...** *(geh)* circumstances permitting ...

VI **~ Sie?(, darf ich ...), ~ Sie, dass ich ...?** may I ...?, would you mind if I ...?; **wenn Sie ~ ...** with your permission ...

Ges|te [ˈgɛstə, ˈgeːstə] F -, -n *(lit, fig)* gesture

Ge|steck [gəˈʃtɛk] NT -(e)s, -e flower arrangement

ge|steckt [gəˈʃtɛkt] ADV **~ voll** *(dial)* chock-a-block *(esp Brit inf)*, jam-packed *(inf)* → *auch* **stecken**

ge|ste|hen [gəˈʃteːən] *pret* **gestand** [gəˈʃtant], *ptp* **gestanden** [gəˈʃtandn] VTI to confess *(jdm etw* sth to sb); **offen gestanden ...** to be frank ..., quite frankly ...

Ge|ste|hungs|kos|ten [gəˈʃteːʊŋs-] PL, **Ge|ste|hungs|preis** M *(Comm)* production costs *pl*

Ge|stein [gəˈʃtain] NT -(e)s, -e rock(s *pl*); *(= Schicht)* rock stratum

Ge|steins-: **Ge|steins|ader** F vein of rock; **Ge|steins|art** F type of rock; **Ge|steins|boh|rer** M, **Ge|steins|bohr|ma|schi|ne** F rock drill; **Ge|steins|bro|cken** M rock; **Ge|steins|kun|de** F petrography; **Ge|steins|mas|se** F mass of rock; **Ge|steins|mehl** NT mineral powder; **Ge|steins|pro|be** F rock sample; **Ge|steins|schicht** F rock layer *or* stratum

Ge|stell [gəˈʃtɛl] NT -(e)s, -e **a** stand; *(= Regal)* shelf; *(= Ablage)* rack; *(= Rahmen, Bettgestell, Brillengestell, Tischgestell)* frame; *(auf Böcken)* trestle; *(= Wäschegestell)* clothes dryer; *(aus Holz)* clotheshorse; *(= Fahrgestell)* chassis; *(= Flugzeuggestell)* undercarriage *(esp Brit)*, landing gear; *(Tech: von Hochofen)* hearth **b** *(fig, inf: = Beine)* pins *pl (inf)*; **langes ~** beanpole *(inf)*

Ge|stel|lung F **a** *(old, Mil)* muster **b** *(form)* furnishing *(form)*, making available; **ich bitte um ~ von zwei Fahrzeugen** I request that two vehicles be made available

Ge|stel|lungs|be|fehl M *(Mil)* call-up *(Brit)*, draft papers *pl (US)*

ge|stelzt [gəˈʃtɛltst] ADJ stilted ADV *reden, sich ausdrücken* stiltedly → *auch* **stelzen**

Ge|stelzt|heit F -, *no pl* stiltedness *no pl*

ges|tern [ˈgɛstɐn] ADV yesterday; **~ Abend** *(früh)* yesterday evening; *(spät)* last night; **die Zeitung von ~** yesterday's paper; **Ansichten von ~** outdated views, opinions of yesteryear *(liter)*; **er ist nicht von ~** *(inf)* he wasn't born yesterday; **~ vor acht Tagen** a week (ago) yesterday, yesterday week; **~ in acht Tagen** a week (from) yesterday

Ges|tern [ˈgɛstɐn] NT -, *no pl* yesterday; **das ~** yesterday, yesteryear *(liter)*; **im ~** in the past

Ge|sti|chel [gəˈʃtɪçl] NT -s, *no pl* snide remarks *pl*

ge|stie|felt [gəˈʃtiːflt] ADJ **a** wearing boots, in boots; **der Gestiefelte Kater** Puss-in-Boots **b ~ und gespornt** *(fig inf)* ready and waiting, ready for the off *(Brit inf)*

ge|stie|gen *ptp von* **steigen**

ge|stielt [gəˈʃtiːlt] ADJ stemmed *(auch Bot)*

Ges|tik [ˈgɛstɪk, ˈgeːstɪk] F -, *no pl* gestures *pl*

Ges|ti|ku|la|ti|on [gɛstikulaˈtsioːn] F -, -en gesticulation(s *pl*)

ges|ti|ku|lie|ren [gɛstikuˈliːrən] *ptp* **gestikuliert** VI to gesticulate

Ges|ti|ku|lie|ren NT -s, *no pl* gesticulation(s *pl*), gesticulating

ge|stimmt [gəˈʃtɪmt] ADJ **froh/düster ~** in a cheerful/sombre *(Brit) or* somber *(US)* mood → *auch* **stimmen**

Ge|stimmt|heit F -, -en mood

Ge|stirn [gəˈʃtɪrn] NT -(e)s, -e star, heavenly body

ge|stirnt [gəˈʃtɪrnt] ADJ *attr (geh)* starry, star-studded *(liter)*

ges|tisch [ˈgɛstɪʃ, ˈgeːstɪʃ] ADJ gestural ADV **etw ~ und mimisch zum Ausdruck bringen** to express sth using gestures and mime; **all seine Worte waren ~ untermalt** everything he said was underlined by gesture

ge|sto|ben *ptp von* **stieben**

Ge|stö|ber [gəˈʃtøːbɐ] NT -s, - *(leicht)* snow flurry; *(stark)* snowstorm

ge|sto|chen [gəˈʃtɔxn] *ptp von* **stechen** ADJ *Handschrift, Zeichnung* clear, neat ADV **~ scharfe Fotos** needle-sharp photographs; **wie ~ schreiben** to write clearly *or* in a neat hand

ge|stockt [gəˈʃtɔkt] ADJ *(S Ger) Milch* soured

ge|stoh|len [gəˈʃtoːlən] *ptp von* **stehlen** ADJ **der/das kann mir ~ bleiben** *(inf)* he/it can go hang *(inf)*

Ge|stöhn [gəˈʃtøːn] NT -(e)s, *no pl*, **Ge|stöh|ne** [gəˈʃtøːnə] NT -s, *no pl* moaning, groaning

ge|stopft [gəˈʃtɔpft] ADV **~ voll** *(inf)* jam-packed *(inf)* → *auch* **stopfen**

ge|stor|ben *ptp von* **sterben**

ge|stört [gəˈʃtøːɐt] ADJ disturbed; *Schlaf auch* broken; *Verhältnis auch* troubled; *Rundfunkempfang* poor, with a lot of interference; *Einverständnis* troubled, disrupted; **seelisch/geistig ~ sein** to be (psychologically/mentally) unbalanced *or* disturbed; **~er Kreislauf** circulation problems; **Kinder aus ~en Familien** children from problem families → *auch* **stören**

ge|sto|ßen *ptp von* **stoßen**

Ge|stot|ter [gəˈʃtɔtɐ] NT -s, *no pl* stuttering, stammering

Ge|stram|pel [gəˈʃtrampl] NT -s, *no pl* kicking about *(Brit) or* around; *(beim Radfahren)* pedalling *(Brit)*, pedaling *(US)*

Ge|sträuch [gəˈʃtrɔyç] NT -(e)s, -e shrubbery, bushes *pl*; *(= Dickicht)* thicket

ge|streckt [gəˈʃtrɛkt] ADJ *Galopp* full; *Winkel, Flugbahn* elongated → *auch* **strecken**

ge|streift [gəˈʃtraift] ADJ striped; **eine rot-grün ~e Bluse** a red and green striped blouse → *auch* **streifen**

Ge|strei|te [gəˈʃtraitə] NT -s, *no pl (inf)* bickering *(inf)*, quarrelling *(Brit)*, quarreling *(US)*

ge|streng [gəˈʃtrɛŋ] ADJ *(old)* strict, stern; **~er Herr!** gracious master *or* Lord; **die Gestrengen Herren** → **Eisheiligen**

ge|stresst [gəˈʃtrɛst] PTP *von* **stressen** ADJ stressed (out), under stress; **~ sein** to be under stress, to be suffering from stress → *auch* **stressen**

ge|stri|chen [gəˈʃtrɪçn] *ptp von* **streichen** ADJ *(= genau voll)* **ein ~es Maß** a level measure; **ein ~er Teelöffel voll** a level teaspoon(ful) ADV **~ voll** level; *(= sehr voll)* full to the brim; **er hat die Hosen ~ voll** *(inf)* he's wetting *(inf) or* shitting *(sl)* himself; **ich habe die Nase ~ voll** *(inf)* I'm fed up (to the back teeth with it) *(inf)*

ge|strie|gelt [gəˈʃtriːglt] ADJ **~ und gebügelt** dressed up to the nines → *auch* **striegeln**

gest|rig [ˈgɛstrɪç] ADJ *attr* yesterday's; **unser ~es Gespräch** our conversation (of) yesterday; **unser ~es Schreiben** our letter of yesterday; **am ~en Abend** *(geh) (früh)* yesterday evening; *(spät)* last night; **am ~en Tage** *(geh)* yesterday

ge|strit|ten *ptp von* **streiten**

Ge|strüpp [gəˈʃtrʏp] NT -(e)s, -e undergrowth, brushwood; *(fig)* jungle

ge|stuft [gəˈʃtuːft] ADJ *(= in Stufen)* terraced; *Haarschnitt* layered; *(fig) (= abgestuft)* graded; *(zeitlich)* staggered → *auch* **stufen**

Ge|stühl [gəˈʃtyːl] NT -(e)s, -e seating

Ge|stüm|per [gəˈʃtʏmpɐ] NT -s, *no pl (pej inf)* bungling; **sein erbärmliches ~ auf dem Klavier** his pathetic plonking away on the piano *(inf)*

ge|stun|ken *ptp von* **stinken**

Ges|tus [ˈgɛstʊs] M -, *no pl (geh)* **a** *(= Gestik)* gestures *pl* **b** *(fig: = Ausdruck)* air

Ge|stüt [gəˈʃtyːt] NT -(e)s, -e stud; *(= Anlage auch)* stud farm

Ge|stüt|buch NT stud book

Ge|stüts-: **Ge|stüts|brand** M stud brand; **Ge|stüts|hengst** M stud (horse); **Ge|stüts|pferd** NT horse at stud; **Ge|stüts|zei|chen** NT stud brand

Ge|such [gəˈzuːx] NT -(e)s, -e petition *(auf +acc, um* for); *(= Antrag)* application *(auf +acc, um* for); **ein ~ einreichen** *or* **stellen** to make *or* lodge a petition/an application

Ge|such|stel|ler [-ʃtɛlɐ] M -s, -, **Ge|such|stel|le|rin** [-ərɪn] F -, -nen *(dated)* petitioner; *(= Antragsteller)* applicant

ge|sucht [gəˈzuːxt] ADJ *(= begehrt)* sought after; **sehr ~** (very) much sought after; **Ingenieure sind ~e Arbeitskräfte** engineers are much sought after → *auch* **suchen**

Ge|su|del [gəˈzuːdl] NT -s, *no pl (pej)* = **Sudelei**

Ge|sül|ze [gəˈzʏltsə] NT -s, *no pl (inf)* claptrap *(inf)*

Ge|summ [gəˈzʊm] NT -(e)s, *no pl* humming, droning

Ge|sums [gəˈzʊms] NT -es [-zəs], *no pl (inf)* fuss

ge|sund [gəˈzʊnt] ADJ *comp* **-er** *or* **=er** [gəˈzʏndɐ], *superl* **-este(r, s)** *or* **=este(r, s)** [gəˈzʏndəstə] *(allgemein)* healthy; *(= arbeits-, leistungsfähig)* fit; *Unternehmen, Politik* sound; *(= heilsam) Lehre* salutary; **frisch und ~, ~ und munter, ~ wie ein Fisch (im Wasser)** in the pink *(Brit)*, hale and hearty *(esp Brit)*, (as) sound as a bell; **ich fühle mich nicht ganz ~** I don't feel very *or* too well; **sonst**

bist du ~? *(iro inf)* are you feeling all right? *(iro)*, you need your head examined *(inf)*; wieder ~ werden to get better, to get well again, to recover; Äpfel sind ~ apples are good for you, apples are good for your health; bleib (schön) ~! look after yourself
ADV *comp* ¨er or -er, *superl* am ¨esten or -esten ~ leben to have a healthy lifestyle; sich ~ ernähren to have a healthy diet; ~ essen to eat healthily; jdn ~ pflegen to nurse sb back to health → gesundschreiben

Ge|sund-: **ge|sund+be|ten** VT *sep* to heal through prayer; **Ge|sund|be|ten** NT -s, *no pl* faith healing; **Ge|sund|be|ter** [-be:tɐ] M -s, -, **Ge|sund|be|te|rin** [-ərɪn] F -, -nen faith healer; **Ge|sund|be|te|rei** [-be:təˈrai] F -, *no pl (pej inf)* praying; **Ge|sund|brun|nen** M *(fig)* das ist ein wahrer ~ it's like a fountain of youth

ge|sun|den [gəˈzʊndn] *ptp* gesundet VI *aux sein (geh)* to recover *(auch fig)*, to regain one's health

Ge|sun|de(r) [gəˈzʊndə] MF *decl as adj* healthy person

Ge|sund|heit F -, *no pl (= seelisches, körperliches Wohlbefinden)* health; *(= gesunder Zustand)* healthiness; *(= Arbeits-, Leistungsfähigkeit)* fitness; *(von Unternehmen, Politik)* healthiness, soundness; *(von Klima, Lebensweise etc)* healthiness; bei guter ~ in good health; bei bester ~ in the best of health; mit meiner ~ steht es nicht zum Besten I'm not in the best of health, my health is not all (that) it might be; ~! bless you; auf Ihre ~! your (very good) health; eine robuste/eiserne/zarte ~ haben to have a robust/an iron/a delicate constitution

ge|sund|heit|lich [gəˈzʊnthaitlɪç] ADJ ~e Schäden damage to one's health; sein ~er Zustand (the state of) his health; aus ~en Gründen for health reasons ADV ~ geht es mir nicht besonders my health is not particularly good; in ~ schlechtem Zustand in a poor state of health; wie geht es Ihnen ~? how is your health?; sie ist ~ angeschlagen she is in poor health; sich ~ wohlfühlen to feel physically well

Ge|sund|heits-: **Ge|sund|heits|amt** NT public health department; **Ge|sund|heits|apos|tel** M *(iro)* health freak *(inf)* or nut *(inf)*; **Ge|sund|heits|at|test** NT health certificate; **Ge|sund|heits|be|hör|de** F health authorities *pl*; **ge|sund|heits|be|wusst** ADJ health-conscious; **Ge|sund|heits|dienst** M health service; **Ge|sund|heits|fa|na|ti|ker(in)** M(F) health freak *(inf)* or nut *(inf)*; **ge|sund|heits|för|dernd** ADJ healthy, good for the health; **Ge|sund|heits|för|de|rung** F promotion of good health; **Ge|sund|heits|für|sor|ge** F health care; **ge|sund|heits|ge|fähr|dend** [-gəfɛɐdnt] ADJ unhealthy, bad for one's health; ~ sein *(auch)* to be a health hazard; **ge|sund|heits|hal|ber** ADV for health reasons; **Ge|sund|heits|pfle|ge** F hygiene; Ratschläge zur ~ health advice; öffentliche ~ public health (care); **ge|sund|heits|po|li|tisch** ADJ health policy *attr*, relating to health policy; die ~e Sprecherin der Partei the party's spokeswoman on health; **Ge|sund|heits|scha|den** M health defect; Gesundheitsschäden damage to one's health; viele Arbeiter haben dabei einen ~ davongetragen the health of many workers has suffered as a result; **ge|sund|heits|schä|di|gend**, **ge|sund|heits|schäd|lich** ADJ unhealthy, damaging to (one's) health; **Ge|sund|heits|schäd|lich|keit** F unhealthiness; **Ge|sund|heits|sys|tem** NT public health system; **Ge|sund|heits|tee** M herbal tea; **Ge|sund|heits|vor|sor|ge** F health care, healthcare *(US)*; **Ge|sund|heits|we|sen** NT, *no pl* health service; **Ge|sund|heits|zeug|nis** NT certificate of health, health certificate; **Ge|sund|heits|zu|stand** M, *no pl* state of health

ge|sund-: **ge|sund+ma|chen** VR *sep (fig inf)* to grow fat *(an +dat* on) → *auch* machen 2 b; **ge|sund+pfle|gen** VT *sep* → gesund ADV; **ge|sund+schrei|ben** VT *sep irreg* jdn ~ to certify sb (as) fit; **ge|sund+schrump|fen** *sep* VT *(fig)* to trim down, to streamline VR to be trimmed down or streamlined; **Ge|sund|schrump|fung** F trimming down, streamlining; **ge|sund+sto|ßen** VR *sep irreg (sl)* to line one's pockets *(inf)*

Ge|sun|dung [gəˈzʊndʊŋ] F -, *no pl (lit, fig)* recovery; *(= Genesung)* convalescence, recuperation; seine ~ macht Fortschritte he's progressing well

ge|sun|gen *ptp von* singen

ge|sun|ken *ptp von* sinken

Ge|surr [gəˈzʊr] NT -(e)s, *no pl*, **Ge|sur|re** [gəˈzʊrə] NT -s, *no pl* humming

Ge|tä|fel [gəˈtɛːfl] NT -s, *no pl*, *(Sw)* **Ge|tä|fer** [gəˈtɛːfɐ] NT -s, *no pl* panelling *(Brit)*, paneling *(US)*

ge|tan [gəˈtaːn] *ptp von* tun ADJ nach ~er Arbeit when the day's work is done

Ge|tän|del [gəˈtɛndl] NT -s, *no pl (dated, geh)* dalliance *(old, liter)*

Ge|tier [gəˈtiːɐ] NT -s, *no pl* a *(= Tiere, esp Insekten)* creatures *pl* b *(einzelnes)* creature

ge|ti|gert [gəˈtiːgɐt] ADJ *(mit Streifen)* striped; *(mit Flecken)* piebald; ~e Katze tabby (cat)

Ge|to|be [gəˈtoːbə] NT -s, *no pl (inf)* chasing about

ge|tönt [geˈtøːnt] ADJ *Glas, Scheibe, Brille* tinted → *auch* tönen

Ge|to|se [gəˈtoːzə] NT -s, *no pl* raging

Ge|tö|se [gəˈtøːzə] NT -s, *no pl* din, racket, row; *(von Auto, Beifall etc)* roar; mit ~ with a din *etc*

ge|tra|gen [gəˈtraːgn] *ptp von* tragen ADJ *(fig) Melodie, Tempo etc* stately *no adv*

Ge|tra|gen|heit F -, *no pl* stateliness

Ge|träl|ler [gəˈtrɛlɐ] NT -s, *no pl* trilling

Ge|tram|pel [gəˈtrampl] NT -s, *no pl* trampling; *(= Beifallsgetrampel, Protestgetrampel)* stamping

Ge|tränk [gəˈtrɛŋk] NT -(e)s, -e drink, beverage *(form)*; er gibt viel für ~e aus he spends a lot on drink

Ge|trän|ke-: **Ge|trän|ke|au|to|mat** M drinks machine or dispenser *(Brit)*, beverage machine or dispenser *(US)*; **Ge|trän|ke|do|se** F drinks can *(Brit)*, beverage can *(US)*; **Ge|trän|ke|kar|te** F *(in Café)* list of beverages; *(in Restaurant)* wine list; **Ge|trän|ke|ki|osk** M drinks *(Brit)* or beverage *(US)* stand; **Ge|trän|ke|markt** M drinks cash-and-carry *(Brit)*, beverage store *(US)*; **Ge|trän|ke|stand** M drinks *(Brit)* or beverage *(US)* stand; **Ge|trän|ke|steu|er** F alcohol tax

Ge|trap|pel [gəˈtrapl] NT -s, *no pl* patter; *(= Hufgetrappel)* clop

Ge|tratsch [gəˈtraːtʃ] NT -(e)s, *no pl*, **Ge|trat|sche** [gəˈtraːtʃə] NT -s, *no pl (pej)* gossip, gossiping

ge|trau|en [gəˈtrauən] *ptp* getraut VR to dare; getraust du dich or dir *(inf)* das? do you dare do that?; ich getraue mich nicht dorthin I don't dare (to) go there, I daren't go there; ich getraue mich zu behaupten, dass ... *(geh)* ich getraue mir die Behauptung, dass ... *(geh)* I would venture to say that ...

Ge|trei|de [gəˈtraidə] NT -s *(form)* - grain, cereal; in diesem Klima wächst kein ~ grain doesn't or cereals don't grow in this climate; das ~ steht gut the grain or cereal crop is doing well

Ge|trei|de-: **Ge|trei|de(an)|bau** M, *no pl* cultivation of grain or cereals; **Ge|trei|de|art** F cereal; **Ge|trei|de|bör|se** F grain or corn *(Brit)* exchange; **Ge|trei|de|ern|te** F grain harvest; **Ge|trei|de|feld** NT grain field, cornfield *(Brit)*; **Ge|trei|de|flo|cke** F *usu pl* cereal; **Ge|trei|de|gar|be** F sheaf of grain; **Ge|trei|de|han|del** M grain trade; **Ge|trei|de|händ|ler(in)** M(F) grain or corn *(Brit)* merchant; **Ge|trei|de|kam|mer** F granary; **Ge|trei|de|korn** NT *pl* -körner grain; **Ge|trei|de|land** NT a grain-growing land, cornland *(Brit)* b *no pl (= Getreidefelder)* grain fields *pl*, cornfields *pl (Brit)*; **Ge|trei|de|lie|fe|run|gen** PL grain supply *sing* or supplies *pl (an +dat* to); **Ge|trei|de|müh|le** F *(= Müllereibetrieb, Gerät)* flour mill; **Ge|trei|de|pflan|ze** F cereal (plant); **Ge|trei|de|pro|dukt** NT cereal product; **Ge|trei|de|si|lo** NT OR M, **Ge|trei|de|spei|cher** M silo; **Ge|trei|de|wirt|schaft** F grain cultivation; Indiens ~ ist fast autark India is almost self-supporting in terms of grain cultivation

ge|trennt [gəˈtrɛnt] ADJ separate; *(Telec, Comput) Verbindung* disconnected; sie führten ~e Kasse they each paid for themselves → Tisch ADV ~ wohnen not to live together, to live separately; ~ leben to be separated, to live apart; ~ schlafen not to sleep together, to sleep in different rooms → *auch* trennen, marschieren

ge|trennt|ge|schlech|tig [-gəʃlɛçtɪç] ADJ *(Bot)* di(o)ecious

Ge|trennt|schrei|bung F writing as two/three *etc* words; zu beachten ist die ~ von „wie viel" remember that "wie viel" is written as two (separate) words

ge|tre|ten *ptp von* treten

ge|treu [gəˈtrɔy] ADJ a *(= genau, entsprechend)* faithful, true *no adv* b *(liter, dated)* faithful, loyal, trusty *(old)* PREP *+dat* true to; ~ dem Motto ... true to the motto ...

Ge|treu|e(r) [gəˈtrɔyə] MF *decl as adj* (faithful or trusty) follower

ge|treu|lich [gəˈtrɔylɪç] ADJ = getreu

Ge|trie|be [gəˈtriːbə] NT -s, - a *(Tech)* gears *pl*; *(= Getriebekasten)* gearbox; *(= Antrieb)* drive; *(von Uhr)* movement, works *pl* → Sand b *(= lebhaftes Treiben)* bustle, hurly-burly

Ge|trie|be- *in cpds (Tech)* gear

ge|trie|ben *ptp von* treiben

Ge|trie|be-: **Ge|trie|be|öl** NT gear(box) oil; **Ge|trie|be|scha|den** M gearbox trouble *no indef art*

Ge|tril|ler [gəˈtrɪlɐ] NT -s, *no pl* warbling

Ge|trip|pel [gəˈtrɪpl] NT -s, *no pl* tripping along; *(affektiert)* mincing

ge|trof|fen *ptp von* treffen

ge|tro|gen *ptp von* trügen

Ge|trom|mel [gəˈtrɔml] NT -s, *no pl* drumming

ge|trost [gəˈtroːst] ADJ confident; du kannst ~ sein, sei ~ rest assured, never fear; er war ~en Mutes *(old)* his mind was reassured ADV a *(= vertrauensvoll)* confidently; ~ sterben to die in peace b *(= bedenkenlos)* wenn er frech ist, darfst du ihm ~ eine runterhauen if he's naughty, feel free to or don't hesitate to hit him; du kannst dich ~ auf ihn verlassen you need have no fears about relying on him; man kann ~ behaupten/annehmen, dass ... one need have no hesitation in or about asserting/assuming that ...

ge|trübt [gəˈtryːpt] ADJ ein ~es Verhältnis zu jdm haben to have an unhappy relationship with sb; er hat ein ~es Verhältnis zur Wirklichkeit he doesn't have a very good grip on reality → auch trüben

ge|trun|ken *ptp von* trinken

Get|to [ˈgɛto] NT -s, -s ghetto

Get|to|blas|ter [-blaːstɐ] M -s, - *(inf)* ghetto blaster *(inf)*, boom box *(esp US inf)*

get|to|i|sie|ren [gɛtoiˈziːrən] *ptp* gettoisiert VT to ghettoize

Ge|tue [gəˈtuːə] NT -s, *no pl (pej)* to-do *(inf)*, fuss; *(= geheuchelte Höflichkeit)* affectation; ein ~ machen to make a to-do *(inf)* or fuss; *(= überhöflich sein, sich wichtigmachen)* to put on airs

Ge|tüm|mel [gəˈtʏml] NT -s, *no pl* turmoil; das ~ des Kampfes the tumult of battle; sich ins ~ stürzen to plunge into the tumult or hurly-burly

ge|tüp|felt [gəˈtʏpfəlt] ADJ *Kleid etc* spotted; *(= mit kleinen Tupfen)* dotted → *auch* tüpfeln

Ge|tu|schel [gəˈtʊʃl] NT -s, *no pl* whispering

ge|übt [gəˈyːpt] ADJ *Auge, Ohr, Griff* practised *(Brit)*, practiced *(US)*; *Fahrer, Segler etc* proficient; mit ~em Auge with a practised *(Brit)* or practiced *(US)* eye; ~ **sein** to be experienced; **im Schreiben/Reden ~ sein** to be a proficient writer/talker → *auch* **üben**

Ge|vat|ter [gəˈfatɐ] **M -s** *or* **-n, -n** *(obs) (= Pate)* godfather; *(fig)* brother; ~ **Tod** (Death) the Reaper *(liter)*

Ge|vat|te|rin [gəˈfatərɪn] **F -, -nen** *(obs)* godmother; *(fig)* sister *(old)*

Ge|viert [gəˈfiːɐt] **NT -s, -e** *(old: = Quadrat)* square; *(Min)* crib; *(Typ)* quad(rat); **5 Meter im ~** *(old)* 5 metres *(Brit) or* meters *(US)* square

GEW [geːleːˈveː] **F -** *abbr von* **Gewerkschaft Erziehung und Wissenschaft** ≈ NUT *(Brit)*, teachers' union

Ge|wächs [gəˈvɛks] **NT -es, -e** **a** *(= Pflanze)* plant; **er ist ein seltsames ~** *(dated)* he is an odd specimen *(inf)* **b** *(= Weinjahrgang)* wine **c** *(Med)* growth

ge|wach|sen [gəˈvaksn] *ptp von* **wachsen** **ADJ** **a** *(= von allein entstanden)* evolved; **diese in Jahrtausenden ~en Traditionen** these traditions which have evolved over the millennia **b** **jdm ~ sein** to be a match for sb; **einer Sache** *(dat)* **~ sein** to be up to sth; **er ist seinem Bruder (an Stärke/Intelligenz) durchaus ~** he is his brother's equal in strength/intelligence

Ge|wächs|haus **NT** greenhouse; *(= Treibhaus)* hothouse

Ge|wa|ckel [gəˈvakl] **NT -s,** *no pl (inf) (von Tisch, Stuhl etc)* wobbling; **~ mit den Hüften** wiggling one's hips

ge|wagt [gəˈvaːkt] **ADJ** **a** *(= kühn)* daring; *(= gefährlich)* risky **b** *(= moralisch bedenklich)* risqué → *auch* **wagen**

Ge|wagt|heit **F -, -en** **a** *no pl (= Kühnheit)* daring; *(= Gefährlichkeit)* riskiness; *(= moralische Bedenklichkeit)* risqué nature **b** *(= gewagte Äußerung)* daring remark

ge|wählt [gəˈvɛːlt] **ADJ** *Sprache* refined, elegant **ADV** **sich ~ ausdrücken** to express oneself elegantly, to express oneself in a refined manner → *auch* **wählen**

Ge|wählt|heit **F -,** *no pl* elegance

ge|wahr [gəˈvaːɐ] **ADJ** *pred* **etw** *or* **einer Sache** *(gen)* **~ werden** *(geh)* to become aware of sth

Ge|währ [gəˈvɛːɐ] **F -,** *no pl* guarantee; **jdm ~ dafür geben, dass ...** to guarantee (sb *or* to sb) that ...; **dadurch ist die ~ gegeben, dass ...** that guarantees that ...; **(die) ~ für etw bieten** to offer a guarantee for sth; **keine ~ für etw bieten** to offer no guarantee for sth; **die ~ für jds Zahlungsfähigkeit übernehmen** to guarantee sb's ability to pay; **die Angabe erfolgt ohne ~** this information is supplied without liability; **„ohne ~"** *(auf Fahrplan, Preisliste)* "subject to change"; *(bei Lottozahlen, statistischen Angaben)* "no liability assumed"; **für etw ~ leisten** to guarantee sth

ge|wah|ren [gəˈvaːrən] *ptp* **gewahrt** **VT** *(liter)* to become aware of

ge|wäh|ren [gəˈvɛːrən] *ptp* **gewährt** **VT** to grant; *Rabatt, Vorteile* to give; *Sicherheit, Trost, Schutz* to afford, to give; **jdm Unterstützung ~** to provide sb with support, to support sb; **jdn ~ lassen** *(geh)* not to stop sb

ge|währ|leis|ten [gəˈvɛːɐlaistn] *ptp* **gewährleistet** **VT** *insep (= sicherstellen)* to ensure *(jdm etw* sb sth); *(= garantieren)* to guarantee *(jdm etw* sb sth)

Ge|währ|leis|tung **F** guarantee; **zur ~ der Sicherheit** to ensure safety

Ge|wahr|sam [gəˈvaːɐzaːm] **M -s,** *no pl* **a** *(= Verwahrung)* safekeeping; **etw in ~ nehmen/haben** to take sth into/have sth in safekeeping; **etw (bei jdm) in ~ geben** to hand sth over (to sb) for safekeeping **b** *(= Haft)* custody; **jdn in ~ nehmen** to take sb into custody; **in ~ sein, sich in ~ befinden** to be in custody

Ge|währs-: **Ge|währs|frau** **F**, **Ge|währs|mann** **M** *pl* **-männer** *or* **-leute** source; **Ge|währs|trä|ger(in)** **M(F)** *(Fin)* guarantor

Ge|wäh|rung **F,** *no pl* granting; *(von Rabatt, Vorteilen)* giving; *(von Sicherheit, Schutz)* affording

Ge|walt [gəˈvalt] **F -, -en** **a** *(= Machtbefugnis, Macht, Herrschaft)* power; **die drei ~en** *(Pol)* the three powers; **die ausübende** *or* **vollziehende/gesetzgebende/richterliche ~** the executive/legislature/judiciary; **elterliche ~** parental authority; **jdn/etw in seine ~ bringen** to bring sb/sth under one's control; **jdn in seiner ~ haben** to have sb in one's power; **~ über jdn haben** *or* **besitzen** to have power over sb; **etw in der ~ haben** *(= übersehen)* to have control of sth; *(= steuern können)* to have sth under control; *(= entscheiden können)* to have sth in one's power; **sich in der ~ haben** to have oneself under control; **in jds ~** *(dat)* **sein** *or* **stehen** to be in sb's power; **unter jds ~** *(dat)* **sein** *or* **stehen** to be under sb's control; **die ~ über etw** *(acc)* **verlieren** to lose control of sth; **~ über Leben und Tod (haben)** (to have) power over life and death

b *no pl (= Zwang)* force; *(= Gewalttätigkeit)* violence; **~ anwenden** to use force; **höhere ~** acts/an act of God; **nackte ~** brute force; **mit ~** by force; **mit aller ~** *(inf)* for all one is worth; **jdm/einer Sache ~ antun** to do violence to sb/sth; **einer Frau ~ antun** to violate a woman; **sich** *(dat)* **~ antun** *(fig: = sich überwinden)* to force oneself; **~ geht vor Recht** *(Prov)* might is right *(Prov)*

c *no pl (= Heftigkeit, Wucht)* force; *(= elementare Kraft auch)* power; **die ~ der Explosion/des Sturmes** the force of the explosion/storm; **er warf sich mit ~ gegen die Tür** he hurled himself violently against the door

Ge|walt-: **Ge|walt|akt** **M** act of violence; **Ge|walt|an|dro|hung** **F** threat of violence; **unter ~** under threat of violence; **Ge|walt|an|wen|dung** **F** use of force *or* violence; **ge|walt|be|ja|hend** **ADJ** condoning violence; **ge|walt|be|reit** **ADJ** ready to use violence, violent; **Ge|walt|be|reit|schaft** **F** propensity to violence; **Ge|walt|ein|wir|kung** **F** violence

Ge|wal|ten|tei|lung **F**, **Ge|wal|ten|tren|nung** **F** separation of powers

Ge|walt-: **ge|walt|frei** **ADJ, ADV** = **gewaltlos**; **Ge|walt|frei|heit** **F** non-violence; **Ge|walt|frie|de(n)** **M** dictated peace; **ge|walt|ge|neigt** **ADJ** inclined toward(s) violence, violent; **Ge|walt|herr|schaft** **F**, *no pl* tyranny; **Ge|walt|herr|scher(in)** **M(F)** tyrant

ge|wal|tig [gəˈvaltɪç] **ADJ** **a** *(= heftig) Sturm etc* violent **b** *(= groß, riesig)* colossal, immense; *(= wuchtig auch)* massive; *Anblick* tremendous; *Stimme, Töne* powerful; *(inf: = sehr groß) Unterschied, Hitze etc* tremendous, colossal *(inf)*; *Summe* huge **c** *(geh: = mächtig)* powerful; **die Gewaltigen der Erde** the mighty rulers of the world **ADV** *(inf: = sehr)* enormously; **sich ~ irren** to be very much mistaken, to be very wrong, to be way out *(inf)*; **du musst dich ~ ändern** you'll have to change one hell of a lot *(inf)*; **er hat sich ~ in meine Schwester verknallt** he's really got it bad for my sister *(inf)*

Ge|wal|tig|keit **F -,** *no pl* **a** *(= Heftigkeit)* violence **b** *(= gewaltige Größe)* colossal *or* immense size; *(= Wuchtigkeit)* massiveness

Ge|walt-: **Ge|walt|kri|mi|na|li|tät** **F** violent crime(s *pl*); **Ge|walt|kur** **F** drastic measures *pl*; *(= Hungerdiät)* crash diet; **Ge|walt|leis|tung** **F** feat of strength, tour de force; **ge|walt|los** **ADJ** non-violent **ADV** *(= ohne Zwang)* without force; *(= ohne Gewaltanwendung)* without violence; **Ge|walt|lo|sig|keit** **F -,** *no pl* non-violence; **Ge|walt|marsch** **M** forced march; **im ~** at a cracking pace *(inf)*; **Ge|walt|maß|nah|me** **F** *(fig)* drastic measure; **jdm mit ~n drohen** to threaten to use force against sb; *(fig)* to threaten sb with drastic action; **Ge|walt|mensch** **M** pusher *(inf)*; *(= brutaler Mensch)* brute; **Ge|walt|mo|no|pol** **NT** monopoly on the use of force; **Ge|walt|or|gie** **F** orgy of violence; **ge|walt|sam** [gəˈvaltzaːm] **ADJ** forcible; *Tod, Auseinandersetzung, Aufstand* violent **ADV** forcibly, by force; **Ge|walt|sam|keit** **F -, -en** **a** *no pl* violence **b** *(= gewaltsame Handlung)* act of violence; **Ge|walt|spi|ra|le** **F** spiral of violence (and counter-violence); **Ge|walt|streich** **M** *(Mil)* storm; *(fig)* coup (de force); **Ge|walt|tat** **F** act of violence; **Ge|walt|tä|ter(in)** **M(F)** violent criminal; **ge|walt|tä|tig** **ADJ** violent; **Ge|walt|tä|tig|keit** **F** *(no pl: = Brutalität)* violence; *(= Handlung)* act of violence; **Ge|walt|ver|bre|chen** **NT** crime of violence; **Ge|walt|ver|bre|cher(in)** **M(F)** violent criminal; **ge|walt|ver|herr|li|chend** **ADJ** glorifying violence *pred*; **Ge|walt|ver|herr|li|chung** **F** glorification of violence

Ge|walt|ver|zicht **M** non-aggression

Ge|walt|ver|zichts-: **Ge|walt|ver|zichts|ab|kom|men** **NT** non-aggression treaty; **Ge|walt|ver|zichts|er|klä|rung** **F** declaration renouncing the use of force, non-aggression declaration

Ge|walt|vi|deo **NT** violent video, video nasty *(Brit)*

Ge|wand [gəˈvant] **NT -(e)s, ⸗er** [gəˈvɛndɐ] *(geh: = Kleidungsstück)* garment; *(weites, langes)* robe, gown; *(Eccl)* vestment, robe; *(old: = Kleidung)* garb, garments *pl*, apparel *(old)*;; *(fig: = Maske)* guise; **ein altes Buch in neuem ~** an old book with a new look *or* appearance *or* livery, an old book dressed up

ge|wan|det [gəˈvandət] **ADJ** *(old, hum)* clad, apparelled *(Brit old)*, appareled *(US old)*; **blau/gelb ~** clad in blue/yellow

ge|wandt [gəˈvant] *ptp von* **wenden** **ADJ** skilful *(Brit)*, skillful *(US)*; *(körperlich)* nimble; *(= geschickt)* deft, dexterous; *Auftreten, Redner, Stil* elegant **ADV** elegantly

Ge|wandt|heit **F -,** *no pl* skilfulness *(Brit)*, skillfulness *(US)*; *(von Körper)* nimbleness; *(= Geschicktheit)* deftness, dexterity; *(von Stil)* elegance

ge|wann *pret von* **gewinnen**

ge|wapp|net [gəˈvapnət] **ADJ** armed *(gegen* against), prepared *(gegen* for) → *auch* **wappnen**

ge|wär|tig [gəˈvɛrtɪç] **ADJ** *pred (geh)* prepared *(+gen* for); **~ sein, dass ...** to be prepared for the possibility that ...

ge|wär|ti|gen [gəˈvɛrtɪgn] *ptp* **gewärtigt** **VTR** *(geh)* to expect; *(= sich einstellen auf auch)* to be prepared for; **~, dass ...** to expect that ...; to be prepared for the possibility that ...; **etw ~ müssen** to have to be prepared for sth, to have to expect sth

Ge|wäsch [gəˈvɛʃ] **NT -(e)s,** *no pl (pej inf)* twaddle *(inf)*, claptrap *(inf)*

ge|wa|schen *ptp von* **waschen**

Ge|wäs|ser [gəˈvɛsɐ] **NT -s, -** stretch of water; **~** *pl* inshore waters *pl*, lakes, rivers and canals *pl*; **ein fließendes/stehendes ~** a stretch of running/standing water

Ge|wäs|ser-: **Ge|wäs|ser|kun|de** **F** hydrography; **Ge|wäs|ser|schutz** **M** prevention of water pollution

Ge|we|be [gəˈveːbə] **NT -s, -** *(= Stoff)* fabric, material; *(= Gewebeart)* weave; *(Biol)* tissue; *(fig)* web

Ge|we|be- *in cpds:* **Ge|we|be|flüs|sig|keit** **F** *(Physiol)* tissue *or* lymph fluid; **Ge|we|be|pro|be** **F** *(Med)* tissue sample; **ge|we|be|scho|nend** **ADJ** *(Comm)* kind to fabrics; *(Med)* tissue-conserving

Ge|webs-: **Ge|webs|flüs|sig|keit** **F** *(Med)* lymph; **Ge|webs|trans|plan|ta|ti|on** **F** *(Med)* tissue graft

Ge|wehr [gəˈveːɐ] **NT -(e)s, -e** *(= Flinte)* rifle; *(= Schrotbüchse)* shotgun; **~ ab!** *(Mil)* order arms!; **das ~ über!** *(Mil)* shoulder arms!; **an die ~e!** *(Mil)* to arms!; *(dated inf)* let's get cracking *(inf) or* started; **präsentiert das ~!** *(Mil)* present arms!; **das ~** *or* **mit dem ~ (auf jdn) anlegen** to aim (at sb); *(Mil)* to train a gun (on sb); **~ bei Fuß stehen** *(Mil)* to stand at order arms; *(fig inf)* to be at the ready

Ge|wehr-: **Ge|wehr|griff** **M** rifle position; **~e üben** to do rifle drill; **Ge|wehr|kol|ben** **M**

(von Flinte) rifle butt; *(von Schrotbüchse)* butt of a shotgun; **Ge|wehr|ku|gel** F rifle bullet; **Ge|wehr|lauf** M *(von Flinte)* rifle barrel; *(von Schrotbüchse)* barrel of a shotgun; **Ge|wehr|mün|dung** F *(von Flinte/Schrotbüchse)* muzzle (of a rifle/shotgun); **Ge|wehr|rie|men** M *(von Flinte)* rifle sling; *(von Schrotbüchse)* gunsling; **Ge|wehr|sal|ve** F volley of gunfire

Ge|weih [gəˈvai] NT **-(e)s, -e** antlers *pl*; **das ~** the antlers; **ein ~** a set of antlers

Ge|weih-: **Ge|weih|en|de** [-lɛndə] NT point *or* tine *(spec)* of an antler; **Ge|weih|schau|fel** F palm (of an antler)

Ge|wei|ne [gəˈvainə] NT **-s**, *no pl (inf)* crying

Ge|wer|be [gəˈvɛrbə] NT **-s, -** **a** trade; **Handel und ~** trade and industry; **das älteste ~ der Welt** *(hum)* the oldest profession in the world *(hum)*; **ein dunkles ~** a shady business; **einem dunklen ~ nachgehen** to be in a shady trade, to have a shady occupation; **seinem ~ nachgehen** to carry on *or* practise *(Brit) or* practice *(US)* one's trade; **ein ~ (be)treiben** *or* **ausüben** to practise *(Brit) or* practice *(US)* a trade **b** *(Sw: = Bauerngehöft)* farm

Ge|wer|be-: **Ge|wer|be|amt** NT ≈ factory inspectorate; **Ge|wer|be|auf|sicht** F ≈ health and safety control; **Ge|wer|be|auf|sichts|amt** NT ≈ factory inspectorate *(Brit)*; **Ge|wer|be|be|trieb** M commercial enterprise; **Ge|wer|be|flä|che** F commercial space; **Ge|wer|be|frei|heit** F freedom of trade; **Ge|wer|be|ge|biet** NT industrial area; *(eigens angelegt)* trading estate *(esp Brit)*; **Ge|wer|be|leh|rer(in)** M(F) teacher in a trade school; **Ge|wer|be|müll** M commercial waste; **Ge|wer|be|ord|nung** F trading regulations *pl*; **Ge|wer|be|schein** M trading licence *(Brit) or* license *(US)*; **Ge|wer|be|schu|le** F trade school; **Ge|wer|be|steu|er** F trade tax; **Ge|wer|be|tä|tig|keit** F commercial activity; **ge|wer|be|trei|bend** ADJ [-traibnd] trading, engaged in a trade *pred*; **Ge|wer|be|trei|ben|de(r)** [-traibndə] MF *decl as adj* trader; **Ge|wer|be|ver|ein** M *(old)* trade association; **Ge|wer|be|zweig** M branch of a/the trade

ge|werb|lich [gəˈvɛrplɪç] ADJ commercial; *Lehrling, Genossenschaft* trade *attr*; *(= industriell)* industrial; **~e Arbeiter** industrial workers; **die ~e Wirtschaft** industry; **~er Rechtsschutz** legal protection of industrial property; **die ~en Berufe** the trades ADV **diese Räume dürfen nicht ~ genutzt werden** these rooms are not to be used for commercial purposes

ge|werbs|mä|ßig ADJ professional; **der ~e Vertrieb von etw** selling sth as a business; **~e Unzucht** *(form)* prostitution ADV professionally, for gain

Ge|werk|schaft [gəˈvɛrkʃaft] F **-, -en** (trade *or* trades *or* labor *(US)*) union

Ge|werk|schaf|ter [gəˈvɛrkʃaftɐ] M **-s, -**, **Ge|werk|schaf|te|rin** [-ərɪn] F **-, -nen**, **Ge|werk|schaft|ler** [gəˈvɛrkʃaftlɐ] M **-s, -**, **Ge|werk|schaft|le|rin** [-ərɪn] F **-, -nen** trade *or* labor *(US)* unionist

ge|werk|schaft|lich [gəˈvɛrkʃaftlɪç] ADJ (trade *or* labor *(US)*) union *attr*; **~er Vertrauensmann** *(im Betrieb)* shop steward *(esp Brit)* ADV **wir haben uns ~ organisiert** we organized ourselves into a union; **~ organisierter Arbeiter** union member; **~ engagiert** involved in the (trade *or* labor *(US)*) union movement; **~ tätig sein** to be active in the union

Ge|werk|schafts- *in cpds* (trade *or* labor *(US)*) union; **Ge|werk|schafts|bank** F *pl* **-banken** trade *or* labor *(US)* union bank; **Ge|werk|schafts|be|we|gung** F (trade *or* labor *(US)*) union movement; **Ge|werk|schafts|boss** M *(usu pej)* (trade *or* labor *(US)*) union boss; **Ge|werk|schafts|bund** M *pl* **-bünde** federation of trade *or* labor *(US)* unions, ≈ Trades Union Congress *(Brit)*, ≈ Federation of Labor *(US)*; **ge|werk|schafts|ei|gen** ADJ owned by a (trade *or* labor *(US)*) union; **ge|werk|schafts|feind|lich** ADJ anti-(trade) union *attr*; **Ge|werk|schafts|füh|rer(in)** M(F) (trade *or* labor *(US)*) union leader; **Ge|werk|schafts|kon|gress** M trade *or* labor *(US)* union conference; **Ge|werk|schafts|mit|glied** NT member of a/the (trade *or* labor *(US)*) union; **Ge|werk|schafts|tag** M trade *or* labor *(US)* union conference; **Ge|werk|schafts|ver|band** M federation of trade *or* labor *(US)* unions; **Ge|werk|schafts|ver|samm|lung** F (trade) union meeting; **Ge|werk|schafts|vor|sit|zen|de(r)** MF *decl as adj* (trade *or* labor *(US)*) union president; **Ge|werk|schafts|we|sen** NT, *no pl* (trade *or* labor *(US)*) union movement

ge|we|sen [gəˈveːzn] *ptp von* **sein** ADJ *attr* former

ge|wi|chen *ptp von* **weichen**

ge|wichst [gəˈvɪkst] ADJ *(inf)* fly *(Brit inf)*, crafty → *auch* **wichsen**

Ge|wicht [gəˈvɪçt] NT **-(e)s, -e** **a** *no pl (lit, fig)* weight; **dieser Stein hat ein großes ~** this rock is very heavy; **dieser Stein hat ein ~ von 100 kg** this rock weighs 100 kg; **er hat sein ~ gehalten** he has stayed the same weight; **er brachte zu viel ~ auf die Waage** he weighed in too heavy; **spezifisches ~** specific gravity; **das hat ein ~!** *(inf)* it isn't half heavy! *(Brit inf)*, it's very heavy!; **etw nach ~ verkaufen** to sell sth by weight; **~ haben** *(lit)* to be heavy; *(fig)* to carry weight; **ins ~ fallen** to be crucial; **nicht ins ~ fallen** to be of no consequence; **auf etw** *(acc)* **~ legen, einer Sache** *(dat)* **~ beilegen** *or* **beimessen** to set (great) store by sth, to lay stress on sth → **Waagschale**

b *(Metallstück zum Beschweren etc, Sport)* weight

ge|wich|ten [gəˈvɪçtn] *ptp* **gewichtet** VT *(Statistik)* to weight; *(fig)* to evaluate

Ge|wicht-: **Ge|wicht|he|ben** NT **-s**, *no pl (Sport)* weightlifting; **Ge|wicht|he|ber(in)** M(F) weightlifter

ge|wich|tig [gəˈvɪçtɪç] ADJ **a** *(dated: = schwer)* heavy, hefty *(inf)*; **eine ~e Persönlichkeit** *(hum inf)* a personage of some weight **b** *(fig) (= wichtig)* weighty; *(= wichtigtuerisch)* self-important; *(= einflussreich)* influential

Ge|wich|tig|keit F **-**, *no pl (fig) (= Wichtigkeit)* weightiness; *(= Wichtigtuerei)* self-importance; *(= Einflussreichtum)* influence

Ge|wichts-: **Ge|wichts|ab|nah|me** F loss of weight; **Ge|wichts|ana|ly|se** F *(Chem)* gravimetric analysis; **Ge|wichts|an|ga|be** F indication of weight; **die Hersteller von Fleischwaren sind zur ~ verpflichtet** the manufacturers of meat products are obliged to show the weight; **Ge|wichts|ein|heit** F unit of weight; **Ge|wichts|klas|se** F *(Sport)* weight (category); **Ge|wichts|kon|trol|le** F weight check; **ge|wichts|los** ADJ weightless; *(fig)* lacking substance; **Ge|wichts|prob|le|me** PL weight problems *pl*; **Ge|wichts|satz** M set of weights; **Ge|wichts|ver|la|ge|rung** F shifting of weight; *(fig)* shift of *or* in emphasis; **Ge|wichts|ver|lust** M loss of weight, weight loss; **Ge|wichts|ver|schie|bung** F shifting of weight; *(fig)* shift of *or* in emphasis; **Ge|wichts|zu|nah|me** F increase in weight

Ge|wich|tung [gəˈvɪçtʊŋ] F **-, -en** *(Statistik)* weighting; *(fig)* evaluation

ge|wieft [gəˈviːft] ADJ *(inf)* fly *(inf)*, crafty (*in* +*dat* at)

ge|wiegt [gəˈviːkt] ADJ shrewd, slick *(inf)*, canny *(esp Scot inf)* → *auch* **wiegen**

Ge|wie|her [gəˈviːɐ] NT **-s**, *no pl* whinnying; *(fig)* guffawing, braying

ge|wie|sen *ptp von* **weisen**

ge|willt [gəˈvɪlt] ADJ **~ sein, etw zu tun** to be willing to do sth; *(= entschlossen)* to be determined to do sth

Ge|wim|mel [gəˈvɪml] NT **-s**, *no pl* swarm, milling mass; *(= Menge)* crush, throng

Ge|wim|mer [gəˈvɪmɐ] NT **-s**, *no pl* whimpering

Ge|win|de [gəˈvɪndə] NT **-s, -** *(Tech)* thread

Ge|win|de- *(Tech)*: **Ge|win|de|boh|rer** M (screw) tap; **Ge|win|de|bol|zen** M threaded bolt; **Ge|win|de|frä|sen** NT **-s**, *no pl* thread milling; **Ge|win|de|gang** M *pl* **-gänge** pitch (of screw thread); **Ge|win|de|schnei|den** NT **-s**, *no pl* thread cutting; *(für Innengewinde)* tapping

ge|win|kelt [gəˈvɪŋklt] ADJ angled

Ge|winn [gəˈvɪn] M **-(e)s, -e** **a** *(= Ertrag)* profit; **~ abwerfen** *or* **bringen** to make a profit; **~ bringend** = **gewinnbringend**; **~ erzielen** to make a profit; **aus etw ~ schlagen** *(inf)* to make a profit out of sth; **etw mit ~ verkaufen** to sell sth at a profit

b *(= Preis, Treffer)* prize; *(bei Wetten, Glücksspiel)* winnings *pl*; **einen großen ~ machen** to win a lot; **jedes Los ist ein ~** every ticket a winner; **er hat im Lotto einen ~ gehabt** he had a win on the lottery

c *no pl (fig: = Vorteil)* gain; **das ist ein großer ~ (für mich)** I have gained a lot from this, that is of great benefit (to me); **ein ~ für die Abteilung** a valuable addition to the department

Ge|winn-: **Ge|winn|an|teil** M **a** *(Comm)* dividend **b** *(beim Wetten etc)* share; **Ge|winn|aus|schüt|tung** F prize draw; **Ge|winn|be|tei|li|gung** F **a** *(Ind) (= Prinzip)* profit-sharing; *(= Summe)* (profit-sharing) bonus **b** *(= Dividende)* dividend; **ge|winn|brin|gend** ADJ *(lit, fig)* profitable ADV profitably; **~ wirtschaften** to make a profit; **Ge|winn|chan|ce** F chance of winning; **~n** *(beim Wetten)* odds; **Ge|winn|ein|bruch** M slump in profits, (big) drop in profits **die Firma hat einen ~ erlitten** the firm's profits slumped, the firm experienced a slump in (its) profits

ge|win|nen [gəˈvɪnən] *pret* **gewann** [gəˈvan], *ptp* **gewonnen** [gəˈvɔnən] VT **a** *(= siegen in)* to win; *(= erwerben, bekommen)* to gain, to win; *Preis, jds Herz* to win; **jdn (für etw) ~** to win sb over (to sth); **jdn für sich ~** to win sb over (to one's side); **jdn zum Freund ~** to win sb as a friend; **es gewinnt den Anschein, als ob …** *(form)* it would appear that …; **das Ufer ~** *(liter)* to reach *or* gain *(liter)* the bank; **Zeit ~** to gain time; **was ist damit gewonnen?** what good is that?; **was ist damit gewonnen, wenn du das tust?** what is the good *or* use of you *or* your doing that?; **wie gewonnen, so zerronnen** *(Prov)* easy come easy go *(prov)*

b *(als Profit)* to make (a profit of)

c *(= erzeugen)* to produce, to obtain; *Erze etc* to mine, to extract, to win *(liter)*; *(aus Altmaterial)* to reclaim, to recover

VI **a** *(= Sieger sein)* to win (*bei, in* +*dat* at)

b *(= profitieren)* to gain; *(= sich verbessern)* to gain something; **an Bedeutung ~** to gain (in) importance; **an Boden ~** *(fig)* to gain ground; **an Höhe ~** to gain height; **an Geschwindigkeit ~** to pick up *or* gain speed; **an Klarheit ~** to gain in clarity; **sie gewinnt durch ihre neue Frisur** her new hairstyle does something for her; **sie gewinnt bei näherer Bekanntschaft** she improves on closer acquaintance → **wagen VT**

ge|win|nend ADJ *(fig)* winning, winsome

Ge|win|ner [gəˈvɪnɐ] M **-s, -**, **Ge|win|ne|rin** [-ərɪn] F **-, -nen** winner

Ge|win|ner|stra|ße F *(inf)* **auf der ~ sein** to be headed for a win, to be on the way to victory

Ge|winn-: **Ge|winn|er|war|tung** F anticipated profit; **Ge|winn|er|zie|lungs|ab|sicht** F *(Comm)* profit motive; **Ge|winn|ge|mein|schaft** F *(Comm)* profit pool; **Ge|winn|klas|se** F prize category; **Ge|winn|lis|te** F list of winners, winners list; **Ge|winn|los** NT winning ticket; **Ge|winn|ma|xi|mie|rung** F maximization of profit(s); **Ge|winn|mit|nah|me** F *(Fin)* profit taking; **Ge|winn|num|mer** F winning number; **Ge|winn|satz** M *(Tennis etc)* **mit drei Gewinnsätzen spielen** to play the best of five sets; **der dritte Satz war sein ~** the third set was the winning set for him; **Ge|winn|schuld|ver|schrei|bung** F *(Fin)* income bond;

Ge|winn|schwel|le F *(Econ)* breakeven point; **Ge|winn|span|ne** F profit margin; **Ge|winn|spiel** NT competition; *(TV)* game show; **Ge|winn|stre|ben** NT pursuit of profit; **Ge|winn|sucht** F profit-seeking; **aus ~** for motives of (material) gain; *(finanziell)* for motives of (financial) gain; **ge|winn|süch|tig** ADJ profit-seeking *attr*; **ge|winn|träch|tig** ADJ profitable

Gewinnummer △ F → **Gewinnnummer**

Ge|winn- und Ver|lust|rech|nung F *(Fin)* profit-and-loss account

Ge|win|nung [gəˈvɪnʊŋ] F -, *(rare)* **-en** *(von Kohle, Öl)* extraction; *(von Energie, Plutonium)* production

Ge|winn-: **Ge|winn|warnung** F *(Comm euph)* profit warning; **Ge|winn|zahl** F winning number; **Ge|winn|zo|ne** F **die ~ erreichen** to move into profit; **in der ~ sein** to be in profit

Ge|win|sel [gəˈvɪnzl] NT **-s**, *no pl (lit, fig)* whining

Ge|winst [gəˈvɪnst] M **-(e)s, -e** *(old)* = **Gewinn**

Ge|wir|bel [gəˈvɪrbl] NT **-s**, *no pl* whirl(ing)

Ge|wirr [gəˈvɪr] NT **-(e)s**, *no pl* tangle; *(fig: = Durcheinander)* jumble; *(von Paragrafen, Klauseln etc)* maze, confusion; *(von Gassen)* maze; *(von Stimmen)* confusion, babble

Ge|wis|per [gəˈvɪspɐ] NT **-s**, *no pl* whispering

ge|wiss [gəˈvɪs] ADJ **a** *(= sicher)* certain, sure (+*gen* of); **ich bin dessen ~** *(geh)* I'm certain *or* sure of it; **das ist so ~, wie die Nacht dem Tag folgt** *(geh)* as sure as night follows day; **darüber weiß man noch nichts Gewisses** nothing certain is known as yet

b *attr* certain; **ein ~er Herr Müller** a certain Herr Müller; **in ~em Maße** to some *or* a certain extent; **in ~em Sinne** in a (certain) sense → **Etwas**

ADV *(geh)* certainly; **Sie denken ~, dass ...** no doubt you think that ...; **ich weiß es ganz ~** I'm certain *or* sure of it; **eins ist (ganz) ~** one thing is certain *or* sure; **eins weiß ich (ganz) ~** there's one thing I know for certain *or* sure; **(ja) ~!** certainly, sure *(esp US)*; **(aber) ~ (doch)!** (but) of course; **darf ich ...? – (aber) ~ (doch)!** may I ...? – but, of course, may I ...? – by all means

Ge|wis|sen [gəˈvɪsn] NT **-s**, *no pl* conscience; **ein schlechtes ~** a guilty *or* bad conscience; **jdn/etw auf dem ~ haben** to have sb/sth on one's conscience; **das hast du auf dem ~** it's your fault; **jdm ins ~ reden** to have a serious talk with sb; **jdm ins ~ reden, etw zu tun** to get *or* persuade sb to do sth; **das musst du vor deinem ~ verantworten** you'll have to answer to your own conscience for that; **ein gutes ~ ist ein sanftes Ruhekissen** *(Prov)* I *etc* just want to have a clear conscience, I *etc* just want to be able to sleep nights *(esp US)* → **Ehre, Wissen**

Ge|wis|sen-: **ge|wis|sen|haft** ADJ *Mensch, Arbeit, Politik* conscientious ADV conscientiously; **Ge|wis|sen|haf|tig|keit** [gəˈvɪsnhaftɪçkait] F -, *no pl* conscientiousness; **ge|wis|sen|los** ADJ unprincipled, without conscience, unscrupulous; *(= verantwortungslos)* irresponsible; **~ sein** to have no conscience; **wie kann man so ~ sein und ...** how could anybody be so unscrupulous/irresponsible as to ... ADV unscrupulously; **sich unmenschlich und ~ verhalten** to behave inhumanly and immorally; **Ge|wis|sen|lo|sig|keit** F -, *no pl* unscrupulousness; *(= Verantwortungslosigkeit)* irresponsibility

Ge|wis|sens-: **Ge|wis|sens|angst** F pangs *pl* of conscience; **Ge|wis|sens|bis|se** PL pangs *pl* of conscience; **mach dir deswegen keine ~!** there's nothing for you to feel guilty about; **~ bekommen** to get a guilty conscience; **ohne ~** without compunction, without feeling guilty; **Ge|wis|sens|ent|schei|dung** F question of conscience, matter for one's conscience to decide; **Ge|wis|sens|er|for|schung** F examination of one's conscience; **Ge|wis|sens|fra|ge** F matter of conscience; **Ge|wis|sens|frei|heit** F freedom of conscience; **Ge|wis|sens|grün|de** PL conscientious reasons *pl*; **Ge|wis|sens|kon|flikt** M moral conflict; **Ge|wis|sens|not** F moral dilemma; **Ge|wis|sens|qual** F *(geh)* pangs *pl* of conscience; **Ge|wis|sens|sa|che** F matter of conscience; **Ge|wis|sens|zwang** M, *no pl* moral constraint(s *pl*); **Ge|wis|sens|zwei|fel** M moral doubt

ge|wis|ser|ma|ßen [gəˈvɪsɐˈmaːsn] ADV *(= sozusagen)* so to speak, as it were; *(= auf gewisse Weise)* in a way, to an extent

Ge|wiss|heit ✪ 43.1 F -, **-en** certainty; **mit ~** with certainty; *wissen* for certain *or* sure; **~ erlangen** to achieve certain knowledge; **(zur) ~ werden** to become a certainty → **verschaffen b**

ge|wiss|lich [gəˈvɪslɪç] ADV *(old, geh)* = **gewiss** ADV

Ge|wit|ter [gəˈvɪtɐ] NT **-s, -** thunderstorm; *(fig)* storm

Ge|wit|ter-: **Ge|wit|ter|flie|ge** F thunder fly; **Ge|wit|ter|front** F *(Met)* storm front; **Ge|wit|ter|him|mel** M stormy sky, thunderclouds *pl*

ge|wit|te|rig [gəˈvɪtərɪç] ADJ thundery; **~e Schwüle** thundery (and oppressive) air ADV **~ schwül** thundery (and oppressive)

Ge|wit|ter|luft F thundery atmosphere; **es ist ~** there's thunder in the air *or* about

ge|wit|tern [gəˈvɪtɐn] *ptp* **gewittert** VI *impers* **es gewittert** it's thundering

Ge|wit|ter-: **Ge|wit|ter|nei|gung** F *(Met)* likelihood of thunderstorms; **Ge|wit|ter|re|gen** M, **Ge|wit|ter|schau|er** M thundery shower; **ge|wit|ter|schwül** ADJ = **gewitterig**; **Ge|wit|ter|schwü|le** F thundery (and oppressive) atmosphere; **Ge|wit|ter|stim|mung** F *(fig)* stormy atmosphere; **Ge|wit|ter|sturm** M thunderstorm; **Ge|wit|ter|wand** F wall *or* mass of thunderclouds; **Ge|wit|ter|wol|ke** F thundercloud; *(fig inf)* storm cloud; **Vater hatte ~n auf der Stirn** Father's face was as black as thunder; **Ge|wit|ter|zie|ge** F *(pej inf)* sour old hag

ge|witt|rig [gəˈvɪtrɪç] ADJ, ADV = **gewitterig**

Ge|wit|zel [gəˈvɪtsl] NT **-s**, *no pl* joking, jokes *pl*

ge|witzt [gəˈvɪtst] ADJ crafty, cunning

Ge|witzt|heit F -, *no pl* craftiness, cunning

ge|wo|ben *ptp von* **weben**

Ge|wo|ge [gəˈvoːgə] NT **-s**, *no pl* surging; *(von Kornfeld)* waving; *(hum: von Busen)* surging

ge|wo|gen [gəˈvoːgn] *ptp von* **wiegen**

ge|wo|gen ADJ *(geh)* well-disposed, favourably *(Brit) or* favorably *(US)* disposed (+*dat* towards)

Ge|wo|gen|heit F -, *no pl (geh)* favourable *(Brit) or* favorable *(US)* attitude

ge|wöh|nen [gəˈvøːnən] *ptp* **gewöhnt** VT **jdn an etw** *(acc)* **~** to make sb used *or* accustomed to sth, to accustom sb to sth; **einen Hund an Sauberkeit ~** to house-train a dog; **Sie werden sich noch daran ~ müssen, dass ...** you'll have to get used to *or* have to accept the fact that ...; **an jdn/etw gewöhnt sein, jdn/etw gewöhnt sein** *(inf)* to be used to sb/sth; **daran gewöhnt sein, etw zu tun** to be used to doing sth

VR **sich an jdn/etw ~** to get *or* become used to sb/sth, to accustom oneself to sb/sth; **du musst dich an Ordnung/Pünktlichkeit ~** you must get used to being orderly/punctual, you must get into the habit of being orderly/punctual; **sich daran ~, etw zu tun** to get used *or* accustomed to doing sth; **das bin ich gewöhnt** I'm used to it

Ge|wohn|heit [gəˈvoːnhait] F -, **-en** habit; **aus (lauter) ~** from (sheer) force of habit; **die ~ haben, etw zu tun** to have a habit of doing sth; **wie es seine ~ war, nach alter ~** as was his wont *or* custom; **das ist ihm zur ~ geworden** it's become a habit with him; **sich** *(dat)* **etw zur ~ machen** to make a habit of sth

Ge|wohn|heits-: **ge|wohn|heits|ge|mäß, ge|wohn|heits|mä|ßig** ADJ habitual ADV *(= ohne nachzudenken)* automatically; **Ge|wohn|heits|mensch** M creature of habit; **Ge|wohn|heits|recht** NT *(Jur)* **a** *(im Einzelfall)* established *or* customary right **b** *(als Rechtssystem)* common law; **ge|wohn|heits|recht|lich** ADJ *Recht* unwritten; **Ge|wohn|heits|sa|che** F question of habit; **Ge|wohn|heits|tä|ter(in)** M(F) habitual *or* persistent offender; **Ge|wohn|heits|tier** NT **der Mensch ist ein ~** *(inf)* man is a creature of habit; **Ge|wohn|heits|trin|ker(in)** M(F) habitual drinker; **Ge|wohn|heits|ver|bre|cher(in)** M(F) habitual criminal

ge|wöhn|lich [gəˈvøːnlɪç] ADJ **a** *attr (= allgemein, üblich)* usual, customary; *(= normal)* normal; *(= durchschnittlich)* ordinary; *(= alltäglich)* everyday; **ein ~er Sterblicher** an ordinary mortal; **~er Bruch** *(Math)* vulgar fraction **b** *(pej: = ordinär)* common ADV normally, usually; **wie ~** as usual, as per usual *(Brit inf)*; **sie zieht sich immer so ~ an** she always wears such plain clothes

Ge|wöhn|lich|keit F -, *no pl (pej)* commonness

ge|wohnt [gəˈvoːnt] ADJ usual; **etw** *(acc)* **~ sein** to be used to sth; **ich bin es ~, früh aufzustehen** I am used to getting up early

ge|wohn|ter|ma|ßen [gəˈvoːntɐˈmaːsn] ADV usually

Ge|wöh|nung [gəˈvøːnʊŋ] F -, *no pl (= das Sichgewöhnen)* habituation *(an +acc* to); *(= das Angewöhnen)* training *(an +acc* in); *(= Sucht)* habit, addiction; **die ~ an den Kindergarten kann bei einigen Kindern ziemlich lange dauern** it can take a fairly long time for some children to get used to kindergarten

ge|wöh|nungs|be|dürf|tig ADJ ... that takes (some) time to get used to; **die neue Software ist ~** the new software takes some time to get used to *or* takes some getting used to

Ge|wöl|be [gəˈvœlbə] NT **-s, -** *(= Deckengewölbe)* vault; *(= Kellergewölbe auch)* vaults *pl*

Ge|wöl|be-: **Ge|wöl|be|bo|gen** M arch (of a vault); **Ge|wöl|be|pfei|ler** M pier (of a vault)

ge|wölbt [gəˈvœlpt] ADJ *Stirn* domed; *Himmel, Decke, Dach* vaulted; *Brust* bulging; *Nase* aquiline → *auch* **wölben**

ge|wölkt [gəˈvœlkt] ADJ *(liter) Stirn* o'erclouded *(poet)*

Ge|wöl|le [gəˈvœlə] NT **-s, -** *(Zool)* cast, pellet

ge|wollt [gəˈvɔlt] ADJ **a** *(= gekünstelt)* forced, artificial **b** *(= erwünscht)* desired → *auch* **wollen**

ge|won|nen *ptp von* **gewinnen**

ge|wor|ben *ptp von* **werben**

ge|wor|den *ptp von* **werden**

ge|wor|fen *ptp von* **werfen**

ge|wrun|gen *ptp von* **wringen**

Ge|wühl [gəˈvyːl] NT **-(e)s**, *no pl* **a** *(pej: = das Wühlen) (in Kisten, Schubladen etc)* rummaging around; *(im Schlamm etc)* wallowing (about) **b** *(= Gedränge)* crowd, throng; *(= Verkehrsgewühl)* chaos, snarl-up *(Brit inf)*

ge|wun|den [gəˈvʊndn] *ptp von* **winden** ADJ *Weg, Fluss etc* winding; *Erklärung* roundabout *no adv*, tortuous

ge|wun|ken *(dial) ptp von* **winken**

ge|wür|felt [gəˈvʏrflt] ADJ *Stoff, Kleidungsstück etc* check(ed) → *auch* **würfeln**

Ge|wür|ge [gəˈvʏrgə] NT **-s**, *no pl (vor dem Erbrechen)* retching

Ge|würm [gəˈvʏrm] NT **-(e)s**, *no pl* worms *pl*; *(= Kriechtiere)* creeping animals *pl*, creepy-crawlies *pl (inf)*; *(fig)* vermin

Ge|würz [gəˈvʏrts] NT **-es, -e** spice; *(= Kräutersorte)* herb; *(= Pfeffer, Salz)* condiment

Ge|würz-: **Ge|würz|bord** NT spice rack; **Ge|würz|es|sig** M spiced vinegar; *(= Kräuteressig)* herb vinegar; **Ge|würz|gur|ke** F pickled gherkin; **Ge|würz|kraut** NT potherb; **Ge|würz|ku|chen** M spice cake; **Ge|würz|mi|schung** F mixed herbs *pl*; *(= Gewürzsalz)* herbal salt; **Ge|würz|nel|ke** F clove; **Ge|würz|pap|ri|ka** M paprika; **Ge|würz|pflan|ze** F spice plant;

(= Kräuterpflanze) herb; **Ge|würz|re|gal** NT spice rack; **Ge|würz|stän|der** M cruet (set)

Ge|wu|sel [gəˈvuːzl] NT **-s,** *no pl (dial)* = **Gewimmel**

ge|wusst *ptp von* **wissen**

Gey|sir [ˈgaizɪr] M **-s, -e** geyser

gez. *abbr von* **gezeichnet**

ge|zackt [gəˈtsakt] ADJ *Fels* jagged; *Hahnenkamm* toothed; *Blatt* serrated, dentate *(spec)* → *auch* **zacken**

ge|zahnt [gəˈtsaːnt], **ge|zähnt** [gəˈtsɛːnt] ADJ serrated; *(Bot)* serrated, dentate *(spec)*; *(Tech)* cogged; *Briefmarke* perforated

Ge|zänk [gəˈtsɛŋk] NT **-(e)s,** *no pl,* **Ge|zan|ke** [gəˈtsaŋkə] NT **-s,** *no pl (inf)* quarrelling *(Brit)*, quarreling *(US)*

Ge|zap|pel [gəˈtsapl] NT **-s,** *no pl (inf)* wriggling

ge|zeich|net [gəˈtsaiçnət] ADJ marked; *(als Straffälliger auch)* branded; **vom Tode ~ sein, ein vom Tode Gezeichneter sein** to have the mark of death on one; **sein Gesicht war von Krankheit ~** one could see from his face how ill he was → *auch* **zeichnen**

Ge|zei|ten [gəˈtsaitn] PL tides *pl*

Ge|zei|ten-: **Ge|zei|ten|ener|gie** F tidal energy; **Ge|zei|ten|kraft|werk** NT tidal power plant *or* station; **Ge|zei|ten|strom** M, **Ge|zei|ten|strö|mung** F tidal current; **Ge|zei|ten|ta|fel** F table of (the) tides; **Ge|zei|ten|wech|sel** M turn of the tide

Ge|zer|re [gəˈtsɛrə] NT **-s,** *no pl* tugging

Ge|ze|ter [gəˈtseːtɐ] NT **-s,** *no pl (inf) (lit)* nagging; *(fig)* clamour *(Brit)*, clamor *(US)*; **in ~** *(acc)* **ausbrechen** *(fig)* to set up *or* raise a clamour *(Brit) or* clamor *(US)*

Ge|zie|fer [gəˈtsiːfɐ] NT **-s,** *no pl (obs)* vermin

ge|zie|hen *ptp von* **zeihen**

ge|zielt [gəˈtsiːlt] ADJ purposeful; *Schuss* well-aimed; *Frage, Maßnahme, Forschung etc* specific; *Werbung* selective, targeted; *Hilfe* well-directed; *Indiskretion* deliberate ADV *vorgehen, ansetzen* directly; *forschen, planen, helfen* specifically; *werben* selectively; **~ schießen** to shoot to kill; **er hat sehr ~ gefragt** he asked very specific questions → *auch* **zielen**

ge|zie|men [gəˈtsiːmən] *ptp* **geziemt** *(old, geh)* VI +*dat* to befit; **dieses Verhalten geziemt ihm nicht** such behaviour *(Brit) or* behavior *(US)* ill befits him VR to be proper; **wie es sich geziemt** as is proper; **wie es sich für ein artiges Kind geziemt** as befits a well-behaved child

ge|zie|mend ADJ proper

ge|ziert [gəˈtsiːɐt] ADJ affected ADV affectedly → *auch* **zieren**

Ge|zirp [gəˈtsɪrp] NT **-(e)s,** *no pl,* **Ge|zir|pe** [gəˈtsɪrpə] NT **-s,** *no pl* chirruping, chirping

Ge|zisch [gəˈtsɪʃ] NT **-es,** *no pl,* **Ge|zi|sche** [gəˈtsɪʃə] NT **-s,** *no pl* hiss(ing)

Ge|zi|schel [gəˈtsɪʃl] NT **-s,** *no pl (fig: = Klatsch)* gossip, tittle-tattle *(Brit inf)*

ge|zo|gen [gəˈtsoːgn] *ptp von* **ziehen** ADJ *Gewehrlauf etc* rifled; *Soldat* conscript(ed); **ein Gezogener** *(Mil inf)* a conscript

Ge|zücht [gəˈtsʏçt] NT **-(e)s, -e** *(obs) (pej: = Brut)* brood; *(inf: = Gesindel)* riffraff *pl*, rabble *pl*

ge|zu|ckert [gəˈtsʊkɐt] ADJ sugared; **zu stark ~ sein** to have too much sugar in it → *auch* **zuckern**

Ge|zün|gel [gəˈtsʏŋl] NT **-s,** *no pl (geh) (von Schlange)* darting *or* flicking of its tongue; *(von Flamme)* flickering

Ge|zweig [gəˈtsvaik] NT **-(e)s** [-gəs] *no pl (geh)* branches *pl*

Ge|zwin|ker [gəˈtsvɪŋkɐ] NT **-s,** *no pl* winking

Ge|zwit|scher [gəˈtsvɪtʃɐ] NT **-s,** *no pl* chirruping, twitter(ing)

ge|zwun|gen [gəˈtsvʊŋən] *ptp von* **zwingen** ADJ *(= nicht entspannt)* forced; *Atmosphäre* strained; *Stil, Benehmen* stiff ADV stiffly; **~ lachen** to give a forced *or* strained laugh; **~ wirken** to seem stiff *or* strained

ge|zwun|ge|ner|ma|ßen [gəˈtsvʊŋənɐˈmaːsn] ADV of necessity; **etw ~ tun** to be forced to do sth, to do sth of necessity

Ge|zwun|gen|heit F **-,** *no pl* artificiality; *(von Atmosphäre)* constraint; *(von Stil, Benehmen)* stiffness

Gfrett [kfrɛt] NT **-s,** *no pl (Aus)* = **Gefrett**

ggf. *abbr von* **gegebenenfalls**

Gha|na [ˈgaːna] NT **-s** Ghana

Gha|na|er [ˈgaːnaɐ] M **-s, -, Gha|na|e|rin** [-ərɪn] F **-, -nen** Ghanaian

gha|na|isch [ˈgaːnaɪʃ] ADJ Ghanaian

Ghet|to [ˈgɛto] *etc* = **Getto** *etc*

Ghost|wri|ter [ˈgoːstraitɐ] M **-s, -, Ghost|wri|te|rin** [-ərɪn] F **-, -nen** ghostwriter; **er ist der ~ des Premiers** he ghosts *or* ghostwrites for the PM

gib [giːp] IMPER *sing von* **geben**

Gib|bon [ˈgɪbɔn] M **-s, -s** gibbon

gibt [giːpt] *3. pers sing pres von* **geben**

Gicht [gɪçt] F **-, -en** **a** *no pl (Med, Bot)* gout **b** *(Metal)* throat (of a/the furnace)

Gicht-: **Gicht|an|fall** M attack of gout; **Gicht|gas** NT *(Metal)* top gas; **Gicht|kno|ten** M gouty deposit, tophus *(form)*; **gicht|krank** ADJ gouty; **Gicht|kran|ke(r)** MF *decl as adj* gout sufferer

Gi|ckel [ˈgɪkl] M **-s, -** *(dial)* cock; *(jünger)* cockerel

Gie|bel [ˈgiːbl] M **-s, -** gable; *(= Türgiebel, Fenstergiebel)* pediment

Gie|bel-: **Gie|bel|dach** NT gabled roof; **Gie|bel|feld** NT tympanum *(spec)*; **Gie|bel|fens|ter** NT gable window; **Gie|bel|haus** NT gabled house

gie|be|lig [ˈgiːbəlɪç] ADJ gabled

Gie|bel-: **Gie|bel|sei|te** F gable end; **Gie|bel|wand** F gable end *or* wall; **Gie|bel|zim|mer** NT attic room

gieb|lig [ˈgiːblɪç] ADJ gabled

Gie|per [ˈgiːpɐ] M **-s,** *no pl (dial)* craving *(auf* +*acc* for)

Gier [giːɐ] F **-,** *no pl (nach* for) greed; *(nach Geld auch)* avarice, lust; *(nach Macht, Ruhm auch)* craving, lust; *(= Lüsternheit)* lust

gie|ren [ˈgiːrən] VI *(pej)* to lust *(nach* for)

gie|ren VI *(Naut)* to yaw

gie|ren VI *(Sw: = quietschen) (Tür, Scharnier etc)* to creak

gie|rig [ˈgiːrɪç] ADJ greedy; *(nach Geld)* avaricious; *(= lüstern)* lustful; **~ nach etw sein** to be greedy for sth; *nach Vergnügen auch* to crave sth; *nach Wissen auch* to be avid for sth; *(sexuell)* to lust for sth ADV greedily; **etw ~ verschlingen** *(lit, fig)* to devour sth greedily

Gieß|bach M (mountain) torrent

gie|ßen [ˈgiːsn] *pret* **goss** [gɔs] *ptp* **gegossen** [gəˈgɔsn] VT **a** *Flüssigkeit* to pour; *(= verschütten)* to spill; *Pflanzen, Garten etc* to water; *(liter) Licht* to shed; **gieß das Glas nicht so voll!** don't fill the glass so full! **b** *Glas* to found *(zu* (in)-to); *Metall auch* to cast *(zu* into) VI *impers* to pour; **es gießt in Strömen** *or* **wie aus Eimern** it's pouring down, it's bucketing down *(Brit inf)*, it's coming down in buckets *(US inf)*

Gie|ßer [ˈgiːsɐ] M **-s, -** *(an Kanne)* pourer

Gie|ßer [ˈgiːsɐ] M **-s, -, Gie|ße|rin** [-ərɪn] F **-, -nen** *(Metal)* caster, founder

Gie|ße|rei [giːsəˈrai] F **-, -en** **a** *no pl (= Gießen)* casting, founding **b** *(= Werkstatt)* foundry

Gie|ße|rei-: **Gie|ße|rei|ar|bei|ter(in)** M(F) foundry worker; **Gie|ße|rei|be|trieb** M foundry; **Gie|ße|rei|tech|nik** F foundry practice

Gie|ße|rin [-ərɪn] F **-, -nen** *(Metal)* caster, founder

Gieß-: **Gieß|form** F mould *(Brit)*, mold *(US)*; **Gieß|gru|be** F foundry pit; **Gieß|kan|ne** F watering can; **Gieß|kan|nen|prin|zip** NT *(inf)* principle of indiscriminate all-round *(Brit) or* all-around *(US)* distribution; **Gieß|kel|le** F, **Gieß|löf|fel** M casting ladle; **Gieß|ofen** M foundry furnace; **Gieß|pfan|ne** F casting ladle

giet|zig [ˈgiːtsɪç] ADJ *(Sw)* = **geizig**

GIF [dʒɪf] NT **-** *(Comput) abbr von* **graphics interchange format** GIF

Gift [gɪft] NT **-(e)s, -e** *(lit, fig)* poison; *(= Bakteriengift)* toxin; *(= Schlangengift, fig: = Bosheit)* venom; **~ nehmen** to poison oneself; **das ist (wie) ~ für ihn** *(inf)* that is very bad for him; **darauf kannst du ~ nehmen** *(inf)* you can bet your bottom dollar *or* your life on that *(inf)*; **sein ~ verspritzen** to be venomous; **~ und Galle spucken** *(inf) or* **speien** to be fuming, to be in a rage

Gift-: **Gift|am|pul|le** F poison capsule; **Gift|be|cher** M cup of poison; **Gift|cock|tail** M *(fig)* toxic *or* poisonous cocktail; **Gift|drü|se** F venom gland

gif|ten [ˈgɪftn] VI *(inf)* to be nasty *(gegen* about)

Gift-: **Gift|fass** NT toxic waste drum; **Gift|fracht** F, *no pl* toxic cargo; **gift|frei** ADJ non-toxic, non-poisonous; **Gift|gas** NT poison gas; **Gift|gas|wol|ke** F cloud of poison gas, poison gas cloud; **gift|grün** ADJ bilious green; **gift|hal|tig,** *(Aus)* **gift|häl|tig** ADJ containing poison, poisonous, toxic; **Gift|hauch** M *(liter)* miasma *(liter)*

gif|tig [ˈgɪftɪç] ADJ **a** *(= Gift enthaltend)* poisonous; *Stoff, Chemikalien etc auch* toxic **b** *(fig) (= boshaft, hasserfüllt)* venomous; *(= zornig)* vitriolic → **Zunge** **c** *(= grell)* bilious ADV **a** *(= böse)* venomously **b** *(= grell)* **etw ist ~ grün/gelb** sth is a bilious green/yellow

Gif|tig|keit F **-,** *no pl* **a** poisonous nature; *(von Stoff, Chemikalien etc auch)* toxicity **b** *(fig) (= Boshaftigkeit)* venom; *(= Zornigkeit)* vitriol

Gift-: **Gift|kü|che** F devil's workshop; **Gift|ler** [ˈgɪftlɐ] M **-s, -, Gift|le|rin** [-lərɪn] F **-, -nen** *(Aus inf)* drug-user, junkie *(inf)*; **Gift|mi|scher** [-mɪʃɐ] M **-s, -, Gift|mi|sche|rin** [-ərɪn] F **-, -nen** preparer of poison; *(fig)* troublemaker, stirrer *(inf)*; *(hum: = Apotheker)* chemist; **Gift|mord** M poisoning; **Gift|mör|der(in)** M(F) poisoner; **Gift|müll** M toxic waste; **Gift|müll|de|po|nie** F toxic waste dump; **Gift|not|ruf|zent|ra|le** F poison information *or* control centre *(Brit) or* center *(US)*; **Gift|nu|del** F **a** *(= Zigarre, Zigarette)* cancer tube *(hum inf)* **b** *(= gehässige Frau)* vixen, shrew; **Gift|pfeil** M poisoned arrow; **Gift|pflan|ze** F poisonous plant; **Gift|pilz** M poisonous toadstool; **Gift|schlan|ge** F poisonous snake; **Gift|schrank** M poison cabinet; **Gift|stoff** M poisonous *or* toxic substance; **Gift|wir|kung** F effect of (the) poison; **die ~ machte sich nach ein paar Sekunden bemerkbar** the poison took effect after a few seconds; **Gift|zahn** M fang; **jdm die Giftzähne ausbrechen** *(fig inf)* to draw sb's fangs; **Gift|zwerg** M *(inf)* spiteful little devil *(inf)*

Gi|ga|byte [ˈgiga-] NT *(Comput)* gigabyte

gi|gamp|fen [ˈgiːgampfn] *ptp* **gigampft** VI *(Sw)* to swing

Gi|gant [giˈgant] M **-en, -en, Gi|gan|tin** [-ˈgantɪn] F **-, -en** giant; *(Myth)* Titan; *(fig auch)* colossus

gi|gan|tisch [giˈgantɪʃ] ADJ gigantic, colossal

Gi|gan|tis|mus [giganˈtɪsmʊs] M **-,** *no pl (Med)* gigantism; *(fig)* giantism

Gi|gan|to|ma|nie [gigantomaˈniː] F, *no pl (geh)* love of things big

Gi|ga|watt [ˈgiga-] NT *(Elec)* gigawatt

Gi|gerl [ˈgiːgɐl] M OR NT **-s, -(n)** *(Aus inf)* dandy, peacock *(inf)*

Gi|go|lo [ˈʒiːgolo, ˈʒigolo] M **-s, -s** gigolo

gil|ben [ˈgɪlbn] VI *aux sein (liter)* to yellow

Gil|de [ˈgɪldə] F **-, -n** guild

Gil|de|haus NT guildhall

Gi|let [ʒiˈleː] NT **-s, -s** *(Aus, Sw)* waistcoat *(Brit)*, vest *(US)*

gilt [gɪlt] *3. pers sing pres von* **gelten**

Gim|pel [ˈgɪmpl] M **-s, -** *(Orn)* bullfinch; *(inf: = Einfaltspinsel)* ninny *(inf)*

Gin [dʒɪn] M **-s, -s** gin; **~ Tonic** gin and tonic

Gin|fizz ['dʒɪnfɪs] **M -, -, Gin-Fizz M -, -** gin-fizz

ging *pret von* **gehen**

Gin|seng ['gɪnzɛŋ, 'ʒɪnzɛŋ] **M -s, -s** *(Bot)* ginseng

Gin|seng|wur|zel ['gɪnzɛŋ-, 'ʒɪnzɛŋ-] **F** *(Bot)* ginseng root

Gins|ter ['gɪnstɐ] **M -s, -** *(Bot)* broom; *(= Stechginster)* gorse

Gip|fel ['gɪpfl] **M -s, - a** *(= Bergspitze)* peak; *(= höchster Punkt eines Berges)* summit **b** *(fig: = Höhepunkt)* height; *(des Ruhms, der Karriere)* height, peak; *(der Vollkommenheit)* epitome; **den ~ erreichen** to reach the summit; **er hat den ~ seiner Wünsche/Träume erreicht** all his wishes/dreams have been fulfilled *or* have come true; **das ist der ~!** *(inf)* that's the limit, that takes the biscuit *(Brit) or* cake *(inf)* **c** *(= Gipfelkonferenz)* summit **d** *(Sw: = Croissant)* croissant

Gip|fel|ge|spräch NT *(Pol)* summit talks *pl*

Gip|fe|li ['gɪpfəli] **NT -s, -** *(Sw: = Croissant)* croissant

Gip|fel-: **Gip|fel|kon|fe|renz F** *(Pol)* summit conference; **Gip|fel|kreuz NT** cross on the summit of a/the mountain; **Gip|fel|leis|tung F** crowning achievement

gip|feln ['gɪpfln] **VI** to culminate *(in +dat* in)

Gip|fel-: **Gip|fel|punkt M** *(lit)* zenith; *(fig)* high point; **Gip|fel|stür|mer(in) M(F)** conqueror of a/the peak; **Gip|fel|teil|neh|mer(in) M(F)** *(Pol inf)* summiteer; **Gip|fel|tref|fen NT** *(Pol)* summit (meeting)

Gips [gɪps] **M -es, -e a** plaster; *(= gebrannter Gips, Art)* plaster (of Paris); *(Chem)* gypsum **b** *(= Gipsverband)* plaster; **einen Arm in ~ legen** to put an arm in plaster *(Brit) or* in a cast; **er lag sechs Wochen in ~** he was in plaster *(Brit) or* in a cast for six weeks

Gips- *in cpds* plaster; **Gips|ab|druck M, Gips|ab|guss M** plaster cast; **Gips|be|cher M** plaster mixing cup; **Gips|bein NT** *(inf)* leg in plaster *(Brit) or* in a cast

gip|sen ['gɪpsn] **VT** to plaster; *Arm, Bein* to put in plaster *(Brit) or* in a cast

Gip|ser ['gɪpsɐ] **M -s, -, Gip|se|rin** [-ərɪn] **F -, -nen** plasterer

gip|sern ['gɪpsɐn] **ADJ** *attr* plaster

Gips-: **Gips|fi|gur F** plaster (of Paris) figure; **Gips|form F** plaster (of Paris) mould *(Brit) or* mold *(US)*; **Gips|kopf M** *(inf)* blockhead, dimwit, num(b)skull *(all inf)*; **Gips|kor|sett NT** *(Med)* plaster jacket; **Gips|kra|wat|te F** *(Med)* plaster collar; **Gips|mo|dell NT** *(Art, Archit etc)* plaster model; **Gips|ver|band M** *(Med)* plaster cast *or* bandage *(form)*; **er trug den Arm im ~** he had his arm in plaster *(esp Brit) or* in a plaster cast, he had his arm in a cast

Gi|raf|fe [gi'rafə] **F -, -n** giraffe

Gi|ri ['ʒi:ri] *(Aus) pl von* **Giro**

Girl [gø:ɐl, gœrl] **NT -s, -s** *(inf)* girl; *(= Revuegirl etc)* chorus girl

Gir|lan|de [gɪr'landə] **F -, -n** garland *(aus* of); **etw mit ~n schmücken** to garland sth, to decorate sth with garlands

Gir|lie ['gø:ɐli, 'gœrli] **NT -s, -s** *(inf)* girlie *(inf)*

Gir|litz ['gɪrlɪts] **M -es, -e** *(Orn)* serin (finch)

Gi|ro ['ʒi:ro] **NT -s, -s** *or (Aus)* **Giri** ['ʒi:ri] *(Fin)* (bank) giro; *(= Indossament)* endorsement; **durch ~** by giro

Gi|ro-: **Gi|ro|bank F** *pl* **-banken** clearing bank; **Gi|ro|ge|schäft NT** (bank) giro transfer; **Gi|ro|kon|to NT** current account; **Gi|ro|über|wei|sung F** giro transfer; **Gi|ro|ver|kehr M** giro system; *(= Girogeschäft)* giro transfer (business); **Gi|ro|zent|ra|le F** clearing house

gir|ren ['gɪrən] **VI** *(lit, fig)* to coo

gis [gɪs] **NT -, -, Gis NT -, -** *(Mus)* G sharp; **Gis-Dur** G sharp major; **~-Moll** G sharp minor

Gischt [gɪʃt] **M -(e)s, -e** *or f* **-, -en** spray

Gi|tar|re [gi'tarə] **F -, -n** guitar

Gi|tar|re(n)-: **Gi|tar|re(n)|spiel NT** guitar-playing; **Gi|tar|re(n)|spie|ler(in) M(F)** guitarist, guitar-player

Gi|tar|rist [gita'rɪst] **M -en, -en, Gi|tar|ris|tin** [-'rɪstɪn] **F -, -nen** guitarist

Git|ter ['gɪtɐ] **NT -s, -** bars *pl*; *(engstäbig, vor Türen, Schaufenstern)* grille; *(in Fußboden, Straßendecke)* grid, grating; *(für Gewächse etc)* lattice, trellis; *(= feines Drahtgitter)* (wire-)mesh; *(= Kamingitter)* fireguard; *(= Geländer)* railing *usu pl*; *(Phys, Chem: = Kristallgitter)* lattice; *(Elec, Geog)* grid; **hinter ~n** *(fig inf)* behind bars

Git|ter-: **Git|ter|bett NT** cot *(Brit)*, crib *(US)*; **Git|ter|elekt|ro|de F** *(Elec)* grid (electrode); **Git|ter|fens|ter NT** barred window; **Git|ter|mast M** *(Elec)* (lattice) pylon; **Git|ter|netz NT** *(Geog)* grid; *(in Tabelle)* grid lines *pl*; **Git|ter|rost M** grid, grating; **Git|ter|span|nung F** *(Elec)* grid voltage; **Git|ter|stab M** bar; **Git|ter|struk|tur F** *(Chem)* lattice structure; **Git|ter|tor NT** (paled) gate; **Git|ter|tüll M** latticework tulle; **Git|ter|tür F** (paled) gate; **Git|ter|ver|schlag M** crate; **Git|ter|zaun M** paling; *(mit gekreuzten Stäben)* lattice fence

Gk F -, *no pl abbr von* **Gemeinschaftskunde** *(Sch inf)* social studies *pl*

Glace ['gla:sə] **F -, -n** *(Sw)* ice (cream)

Gla|cee- = **Gla|cé-**

Gla|cé-: **Gla|cé|hand|schuh M** kid glove; **jdn mit ~en anfassen** *(fig)* to handle sb with kid gloves; **Gla|cé|le|der NT** glacé leather

gla|cie|ren [gla'si:rən] *ptp* **glaciert VT** *(Cook)* to glaze

Gla|cis [gla'si:] **NT -, -** [-'si:s, -'si:s] *(Mil)* glacis

Gla|di|a|tor [gla'dia:to:ɐ] **M -s, Gladiatoren** *ptp* gladiator

Gla|di|o|le [gla'dio:lə] **F -, -n** *(Bot)* gladiolus

Gla|mour ['glɛmɐ] **M OR NT -s,** *no pl (Press sl)* glamour *(Brit)*, glamor *(US)*

Gla|mour|girl ['glɛmɐ-] **NT** glamour *(Brit) or* glamor *(US)* girl

gla|mou|rös [glamu'rø:s] **ADJ** glamorous

Glanz [glants] **M -es,** *no pl* gleam; *(von Oberfläche auch)* shine; *(= Funkeln)* sparkle, glitter; *(von Augen)* sparkle; *(von Haaren)* sheen, shine; *(von Seide, Perlen)* sheen, lustre *(Brit)*, luster *(US)*; *(von Farbe)* gloss; *(blendender: von Sonne, Scheinwerfer etc)* glare; *(fig) (der Schönheit, Jugend)* radiance; *(von Ruhm, Erfolg)* glory; *(= Gepränge, Pracht)* splendour *(Brit)*, splendor *(US)*; **mit ~ und Gloria** *(iro inf)* in grand style; **eine Prüfung mit ~ bestehen** *(inf)* to pass an exam with flying colours *(Brit) or* colors *(US)*; **den ~ verlieren** *or* **einbüßen** *(Metall, Leder, Möbel)* to lose its shine; *(Diamanten, Augen, fig)* to lose its/one's/their sparkle; **welch ~ in dieser Hütte!** *(iro)* to what do I owe the honour *(Brit) or* honor *(US)* (of this visit)? *(iro)*

Glanz|ab|zug M *(Phot)* glossy *or* gloss print

glän|zen ['glɛntsn] **VI** *(lit, fig)* to shine; *(polierte Oberfläche auch)* to gleam; *(= glitzern)* to glisten; *(= funkeln)* to sparkle; *(= blenden)* to glare; *(Hosenboden, Ellbogen, Nase)* to be shiny; **vor jdm ~ wollen** to want to shine in front of sb; **ihr Gesicht glänzte vor Freude** her face shone with joy, her face was radiant with joy; **~des Haar** glossy hair → **Gold**

glän|zend ADJ shining; *Haar, Seide auch* lustrous; *Metall, Leder, Holz auch* gleaming; *(= strahlend)* radiant; *(= blendend)* dazzling; *(= glitzernd)* glistening; *(= funkelnd)* sparkling, glittering; *Papier* glossy, shiny; *Stoff, Nase, Hosenboden, Ellbogen* shiny; *(fig)* brilliant; *Erfolg* brilliant, dazzling; *Aussehen, Fest* dazzling; *Zukunft* brilliant, glittering; *Gesellschaft* glittering; *(= erstklassig)* marvellous *(Brit)*, marvelous *(US)*, splendid; **~ in Form** *(inf)* in splendid form; **ein ~er Reinfall** *(iro)* a glorious failure

ADV *(= sehr gut)* brilliantly; **wir haben uns ~ amüsiert** we had a marvellous *(Brit) or* marvelous *(US) or* great *(inf)* time; **mir geht es ~** I'm just fine; **~ miteinander auskommen** to get along fantastically *or* brilliantly

Glanz-: **Glanz|form F,** *no pl (inf)* brilliant form; **Glanz|gras NT** canary grass; **Glanz|idee F** *(inf)* brilliant idea; **Glanz|koh|le F** glance coal; **Glanz|lack M** gloss (paint); **Glanz|le|der NT** patent leather; **Glanz|lein|wand F** *(Tex)* glazed taffeta; **Glanz|leis|tung F** brilliant achievement; **eine wissenschaftliche ~** a brilliant scientific achievement; **Glanz|licht NT a** *(Art, fig)* highlight **b** *(Phys)* reflected light; **glanz|los ADJ** *(lit, fig)* dull; *Augen, Haar, Vorstellung auch, Sieg* lacklustre *(Brit)*, lackluster *(US)*; *Lack, Oberfläche* matt; **Glanz|num|mer F** big number, pièce de résistance; **Glanz|pa|pier NT** glossy paper; **Glanz|pa|ra|de F** *(Sport)* brilliant save; **Glanz|pe|ri|o|de F** heyday; **Glanz|po|li|tur F** gloss polish; **Glanz|punkt M** *(fig)* highlight, high spot; **Glanz|rol|le F** star role; **Glanz|stück NT** pièce de résistance; **glanz|voll ADJ** *(fig)* brilliant; *Zukunft auch* glittering; *Darstellung, Unterhaltung auch* sparkling; *Sieg auch* dazzling; *(= prachtvoll)* glittering; **Glanz|zeit F** heyday; **seine ~ ist vorüber** he has had his day

Gla|rus ['gla:rʊs] **NT -** Glarus

Glas [gla:s] **NT -es, ¨-er** *or (als Maßangabe)* **-** ['glɛ:zɐ] **a** *(= Stoff, Gefäß)* glass; *(= Konservenglas)* jar; **buntes** *or* **farbiges** *or* **gefärbtes ~** coloured *(Brit) or* colored *(US)* glass; *(von Fenstern)* stained glass; **„Vorsicht ~!"** "glass – handle with care"; **ein ~ Milch** a glass of milk; **ein ~ Marmelade** a pot *(Brit) or* jar of jam; **ein ~ Gurken** a jar of gherkins; **zwei ~ Wein** two glasses of wine; **zu tief ins ~ gucken** *(inf) or* **schauen** *(inf)* **ein ~ über den Durst trinken** *(inf)* to have one too many, to have one over the eight *(Brit inf)*; **unter ~** behind glass; *(Gewächs)* under glass

b *(= Brillenglas)* lens *sing*; *(= Fernglas)* binoculars *pl*, (field) glasses *pl*; *(= Opernglas)* opera glasses *pl*; **Gläser** *(old: = Brille)* spectacles *pl*, glasses *pl*

Glas [gla:s] **NT -es, -en** ['gla:zn] *(Naut: = halbe Stunde)* bell; **es schlägt acht ~en** it's eight bells

Glas- *in cpds* glass; **Glas|bal|lon M** carboy; **Glas|bau M** *pl* **-bauten** glass structure; **Glas|bau|stein M** glass block; **glas+bla|sen VI** *sep irreg* to blow glass; **Glas|blä|ser(in) M(F)** glass-blower; **Glas|blä|se|rei** [-blɛ:zə'rai] **F -, -en a** *no pl (= Handwerk)* glass-blowing **b** *(= Werkstatt)* glassworks *sing or pl*; **Glas|bruch M** broken glass

Gläs|chen ['glɛ:sçən] **NT -s, -** *dim von* **Glas** *(= Getränk)* little drink; **darauf müssen wir ein ~ trinken** we must drink to that, that calls for a little drink

Glas-: **Glas|con|tai|ner M** bottle bank; **Glas|dach NT** glass roof

Gla|ser ['gla:zɐ] **M -s, -, Gla|se|rin** [-ərɪn] **F -, -nen** glazier

Gla|se|rei [gla:zə'rai] **F -, -en a** *no pl (= Handwerk)* glazing **b** *(= Werkstatt)* glazier's workshop

Gla|ser-: **Gla|ser|hand|werk NT** glazing; **Gla|ser|kitt M** glazier's putty; **Glä|ser|klang M** *(dated)* the clink of glasses

Gla|ser|meis|ter(in) M(F) master glazier

glä|sern ['glɛ:zɐn] **ADJ** glass; *(liter: = starr)* glassy; *(fig: = durchschaubar)* transparent; *Verwaltung* open; **der ~e Bürger** the citizen under the eye of Big Brother **ADV sich ~ anfühlen** to feel like glass

Glä|ser-: **Glä|ser|tuch NT** *pl* **-tücher** glass-cloth; **glä|ser|wei|se ADV** by the glassful

Glas|fab|rik F glassworks *sing or pl*

Glas|fa|ser F glass fibre *(Brit) or* fiber *(US)*, fibreglass *(Brit)*, fiberglass *(US)*

Glas|fa|ser-: **Glas|fa|ser|ka|bel NT** optical fibre *(Brit) or* fiber *(US)* cable; **Glas|fa|ser|op|tik F** fibre optics *sing (Brit)*, fiber optics *sing (US)*; **Glas|fa|ser|pa|pier NT** fibreglass *(Brit) or* fiberglass *(US)* paper; **glas|fa|ser|ver|stärkt** [-fɛɐʃtɛrkt] **ADJ** fibreglass-reinforced *(Brit)*, fiberglass-reinforced *(US)*

Glas-: **Glas|fi|ber F** glass fibre *(Brit) or* fiber *(US)*, fibreglass *(Brit)*, fiberglass *(US)*; **Glas|fi|ber|stab M** *(Sport)* glass fibre *(Brit) or* fiber

(US) pole; **Glas|flüg|ler** [-fly:glɐ] M -s, - (Zool) clearwing; **Glas|ge|schirr** NT glassware; **Glas|glo|cke** F glass cover or dome; (als Lampenschirm) glass ball; **Glas|har|fe** F musical glasses pl; **Glas|har|mo|ni|ka** F musical glasses pl, glass harmonica; **glas|hart** ADJ brittle; Stimme steely; Nein definite; wirtschaftliche Positionen unequivocal; Koalitionsfrage clear-cut ADV verhandeln without compromise; **diese Frage stellt sich ~** this issue is clear-cut; **Glas|haus** NT greenhouse; (in botanischen Gärten etc) glasshouse; **wer (selbst) im ~ sitzt, soll nicht mit Steinen werfen** (Prov) people who live in glass houses shouldn't throw stones (Prov); **Glas|hüt|te** F glassworks sing or pl

gla|sie|ren [gla'zi:rən] ptp **glasiert** VT to glaze; Kuchen to ice (Brit), to frost (esp US)

gla|sig ['gla:zɪç] ADJ Blick glassy; (Cook) Kartoffeln waxy; Speck, Zwiebeln transparent

Glas-: **Glas|in|dust|rie** F glass industry; **Glas|kas|ten** M glass case; (in Fabrik, Büro) glass box; (Hort) cold frame; **glas|klar** ADJ (lit) clear as glass; (fig) crystal-clear; **Glas|kol|ben** M glass flask; (von Glühlampe, Radioröhre etc) glass bulb; **Glas|ku|gel** F glass ball; (= Murmel) marble; **Glas|ma|le|rei** F glass painting; **Glas|mas|se** F molten glass

Glas|nost ['glasnɔst] F -, no pl (Pol) glasnost

Glas-: **Glas|nu|del** F fine Chinese noodle; **Glas|pa|pier** NT glasspaper; **Glas|per|le** F glass bead; **Glas|plat|te** F glass top; **Glas|rei|ni|ger** M **a** (= Glasreinigungsmittel) glass cleaner **b** (Beruf) window cleaner; **Glas|röhr|chen** NT small glass tube; **Glas|röh|re** F glass tube; **Glas|schei|be** F sheet of glass; (von Fenster) pane of glass; **Glas|scher|be** F fragment of glass, piece of broken glass; **~n** broken glass; **Glas|schlei|fer(in)** M(F) (Opt) glass grinder; (Art) glass cutter; **Glas|schliff** M (Opt) glass grinding; (Art) glass cutting; **Glas|schmel|ze** F glass melt; **Glas|schnei|der** M (Gerät) glass cutter; **Glas|schrank** M glass-fronted cupboard; **Glas|split|ter** M splinter of glass

Glast [glast] M -(e)s, no pl (poet) = **Glanz**

Gla|sur [gla'zu:ɐ] F -, -en glaze; (Metal) enamel; (= Zuckerguss) icing (Brit), frosting (esp US)

Glas-: **Glas|ve|ran|da** F glass veranda, sun room or parlor (US); **Glas|ver|si|che|rung** F glass insurance; **Glas|wa|ren** PL glassware sing; **glas|wei|se** ADJ ADV by the glass; **Glas|wol|le** F glass wool; **Glas|zie|gel** M (für Wand) glass brick; (für Dach) glass tile; **Glas|zy|lin|der** M glass cylinder; (von Petrolelumlampe) (glass) chimney

glatt [glat] ADJ comp **-er** or **=er** ['glɛtɐ], superl **-es|te(r, s)** or **=es|te(r, s)** ['glɛtəstə] **a** (= eben) smooth; Meer auch unruffled; Haar straight; (Med) Bruch clean; Stoff (= faltenlos) uncreased; (= ungemustert) plain; (Aus) Mehl finely ground **b** (= schlüpfrig) slippery; **auf dem ~en Parkett der Außenpolitik ausrutschen** to come a cropper (Brit inf) or to blunder in the tricky area of foreign policy **c** (fig) Landung, Ablauf smooth; **eine ~e Eins** (Sch) a straight A **d** attr (inf: = klar, eindeutig) outright; Lüge, Unsinn etc downright, outright; Absage auch flat; **das kostet ~e 1.000 Euro** it costs a good 1,000 euros **e** (pej: = allzu gewandt) smooth, slick
ADV comp **-er** or **=er**, superl **am -esten** or **=esten** **a** (= eben) bügeln, hobeln, walzen (till) smooth; polieren highly; rühren till smooth; schneiden straight; **~ rasieren** to shave; **~ rasiert** (Mann, Kinn) clean-shaven; Beine shaved; **~ stricken** to knit garter stitch → auch **glatt kämmen, glatt legen** etc **b** (= problemlos) smoothly; **er hat sich ~ aus der Affäre gezogen** he wriggled his way neatly out of the whole affair → auch **glattgehen** **c** (inf: = einfach) completely; leugnen, ablehnen flatly; vergessen clean; **jdm etw ~ ins Gesicht sagen** to tell sb sth to his/her face; **das ist doch ~ gelogen** that's a downright lie; **die Rechnung ist ~ aufgegangen** the sum works out exactly; **es kostete ~ EUR 10.000** it cost a good 10,000 euros

Glät|te ['glɛtə] F -, no pl **a** (= Ebenheit) smoothness; (von Haar) sleekness **b** (= Schlüpfrigkeit) slipperiness **c** (= Politur) polish **d** (fig) (des Auftretens) smoothness, slickness; (des Stils) polish

Glatt|eis NT ice; **„Vorsicht ~!"** "danger, black ice"; **sich auf ~ begeben** (fig) **aufs ~ geraten** (fig) to skate on thin ice; **jdn aufs ~ führen** (fig) to take sb for a ride

Glatt|eis|bil|dung F formation of black ice

Glät|tei|sen ['glɛt-] NT (Sw) iron, smoothing iron (old)

Glatt|eis|ge|fahr F danger of black ice

glät|ten ['glɛtn] VT (= glatt machen) to smooth out; (= glatt streichen) Haar, Tuch to smooth; (esp Sw: = bügeln) to iron; (fig: = stilistisch glätten) to polish up VR to smooth out; (Wellen, Meer, fig) to subside

Glät|ter ['glɛtɐ] M -s, -, **Glät|te|rin** [-ərɪn] F -, -nen (esp Sw) presser

glatt-: **glatt+ge|hen** sep irreg aux sein, **glatt ge|hen** △ irreg aux sein VI to go smoothly or OK (inf); **glatt ho|beln**, **glatt+ho|beln** sep VT to plane smooth; **glatt käm|men**, **glatt+käm|men** sep VT to comb straight; (mit Haarpomade) to sleek down; **glatt le|gen**, **glatt+le|gen** sep VT to fold up carefully; **glatt+ma|chen** VT sep (inf: = begleichen) to settle; **glatt ma|chen**, **glatt+ma|chen** sep VT (= glatt streichen) to smooth out; Haare to smooth (down); (mit Kamm) to comb straight; **glatt po|lie|ren**, **glatt+po|lie|ren** sep VT to polish highly; **glatt ra|sie|ren**, **glatt+ra|sie|ren** sep VT to shave; **glatt|ra|siert** [-razi:ɐt] ADJ → **glatt ADV a**; **glatt rüh|ren**, **glatt+rüh|ren** sep VT to stir till smooth; **glatt schlei|fen** irreg, **glatt+schlei|fen** sep irreg VT to rub smooth; Linsen, Diamanten etc to grind smooth; Felsen etc to wear smooth; **glatt strei|chen** irreg, **glatt+strei|chen** sep irreg VT to smooth out; Haare to smooth (down); **glatt wal|zen**, **glatt+wal|zen** sep VT to roll smooth; **glatt|weg** ['glatvɛk] ADV (inf) simply, just, just like that (inf); **er hat meinen Vorschlag ~ abgelehnt** he simply turned my suggestion down, he turned my suggestion down just like that (inf); **das ist ~ erlogen** that's a blatant lie; **glatt|zün|gig** [-tsʏŋɪç] ADJ (pej geh) glib, smooth-tongued

Glat|ze ['glatsə] F -, -n **a** bald head; (rare: = kahle Stelle) bald patch or spot; **eine ~ bekommen/haben** to go/be bald; **er zeigt Ansätze zu einer ~** he shows signs of going bald; **ein Mann mit ~** a bald(-headed) man, a man with a bald head; **sich** (dat) **eine ~ schneiden lassen** to have one's head shaved **b** (inf: = Skinhead) skin (inf)

Glatz-: **Glatz|kopf** M bald head; (inf: = Mann mit Glatze) baldie (inf); **glatz|köp|fig** ADJ bald(-headed); **Glatz|köp|fig|keit** [-kœpfɪkkait] F -, no pl baldness

Glau|be ['glaubə] M -ns, no pl (= Vertrauen, religiöse Überzeugung, Konfession) faith (an +acc in); (= Überzeugung, Meinung) belief (an +acc in); **~, Liebe, Hoffnung** faith, hope and charity; **im guten** or **in gutem ~n** in good faith; **(bei jdm) ~n finden** to be believed (by sb); (Bericht, Aussage etc auch) to find credence (with sb); **den ~n an jdn/etw verlieren** to lose faith in sb/sth; **jdm ~n schenken** to believe sb, to give credence to sb; **jdn in dem ~n (be)lassen, dass ...** to let sb believe that ...; **lass ihn bei seinem ~n!** let him keep his illusions; **er ist katholischen ~ns** he is of the Catholic faith → **Treue**

glau|ben ['glaubn] ✪ 33.2, 39.1, 53.5, 53.6 VTI (= Glauben schenken, überzeugt sein, vertrauen) to believe (an +acc in); (= meinen, annehmen, vermuten) to think; **jdm ~** to believe sb; **das glaube ich dir gerne/nicht** I quite/don't believe you; **glaube es mir** believe me; **diese Geschichte/das soll ich dir ~?** do you expect me to believe that story/that?; **er glaubte mir jedes Wort** he believed every word I said; **ich glaube kein Wort davon** I don't believe a word of it; **jdm (etw) aufs Wort ~** to take sb's word (for sth); **ich glaube dir jedes Wort (einzeln)** (iro) pull the other one (inf); **d(a)ran ~ müssen** (inf: = sterben) to cop it (Brit inf), to bite the dust (US inf), to buy it (inf); **das glaubst du doch selbst nicht!** you can't be serious; **das will ich ~!** (dated: als Antwort) I'm sure!, I can well believe it; **jdn etw ~ machen wollen** to try to make sb believe sth; **das glaube ich nicht von ihm** I can't believe that of him; **ob du es glaubst oder nicht, ...** believe it or not ...; **wers glaubt, wird selig** (iro) a likely story (iro); **wer hätte das je geglaubt!** who would have thought it?; **ich glaubte ihn zu kennen, doch ...** I thought I knew him, but ...; **ich glaubte ihn in Berlin** I thought he was in Berlin; **ich glaubte ihn tot/in Sicherheit** I thought he was dead/safe; **er glaubte sich unbeobachtet** he thought nobody was watching him; **man glaubte ihm den Fachmann** one could well believe him to be an expert; **es ist nicht** or **kaum zu ~** it's incredible or unbelievable; **ich glaube, ja** I think so; **ich glaube, nein** I don't think so, I think not

Glau|ben ['glaubn] M -s, no pl = **Glaube**

Glau|bens-: **Glau|bens|ar|ti|kel** M article of faith; **Glau|bens|be|kennt|nis** NT creed; **Glau|bens|be|we|gung** F religious movement; **Glau|bens|bru|der** M co-religionist (form), brother in faith, fellow Buddhist/Christian/Jew etc → auch **Glaubensschwester**; **Glau|bens|din|ge** PL matters pl of faith; **Glau|bens|ei|fer** M religious zeal; **Glau|bens|fra|ge** F question of faith; **Glau|bens|frei|heit** F freedom of worship, religious freedom; **Glau|bens|ge|mein|schaft** F religious sect; (christliche auch) denomination; **Glau|bens|ge|nos|se** M, **Glau|bens|ge|nos|sin** F co-religionist (form); **Glau|bens|kampf** M religious battle; **Glau|bens|krieg** M religious war; **Glau|bens|leh|re** F dogmatics sing; (pej: = Doktrin) doctrine, dogma; **Glau|bens|rich|tung** F (religious) persuasion, religious orientation; **Glau|bens|sa|che** F matter of faith; **Glau|bens|satz** M dogma, doctrine; **Glau|bens|schwes|ter** F co-religionist (form), fellow Buddhist/Christian/Jew etc → auch **Glaubensbruder**; **Glau|bens|spal|tung** F schism; **glau|bens|stark** ADJ deeply religious; **Glau|bens|streit** M religious controversy; **glau|bens|ver|wandt** ADJ **jdm ~ sein** to be of a similar faith to sb; **Glau|bens|wech|sel** M change of faith or religion; **zum ~ bereit sein** to be prepared to change one's faith or religion; **Glau|bens|zwei|fel** M usu pl religious doubt; **Glau|bens|zwist** M religious controversy

Glau|ber|salz ['glaubɐ-] NT (Chem) Glauber('s) salt

glaub|haft ADJ credible, believable; (= einleuchtend) plausible; **(jdm) etw (überzeugend) ~ machen** to substantiate sth (to sb), to satisfy sb of sth ADV believably, credibly

Glaub|haf|tig|keit ['glauphaftɪçkait] F -, no pl credibility; (= Evidenz) plausibility

Glaub|haft|ma|chung ['glauphaftmaxʊŋ] F -, no pl (Jur) substantiation

gläu|big ['glɔybɪç] ADJ Katholik etc devout; (= vertrauensvoll) trusting ADV **~ hörten sie meiner Geschichte zu** they listened to and believed my story

Gläu|bi|ge(r) ['glɔybɪgə] MF decl as adj believer; **die ~n** the faithful

Gläu|bi|ger ['glɔybɪgɐ] M -s, -, **Gläu|bi|ge|rin** ['glɔybɪgərɪn] F -, -nen (Comm) creditor

Gläu|bi|ger-: **Gläu|bi|ger|an|sprü|che** PL creditors' claims pl; **Gläu|bi|ger|aus|schuss** M committee or board of creditors; **Gläu|bi|ger|bank** F pl **-banken** creditor bank

Gläu|bi|ge|rin ['glɔybɪgərɪn] F -, -nen *(Comm)* creditor

Gläu|bi|ger-: **Gläu|bi|ger|land** NT, **Gläu|bi|ger|staat** M creditor nation *or* state; **Gläu|bi|ger|ver|samm|lung** F meeting of creditors

Gläu|big|keit F -, *no pl* devoutness; *(= Vertrauen)* trust

glaub|lich ['glauplɪç] ADJ **kaum ~** scarcely credible

glaub|wür|dig ADJ *Mensch, Beweise* credible; **~e Quellen** reliable sources ADV credibly; **sich ~ verhalten** to be reliable *or* credible

Glaub|wür|dig|keit F -, *no pl* credibility

Glau|kom [glau'ko:m] NT **-s, -e** *(Med)* glaucoma

gla|zi|al [gla'tsia:l] ADJ *(Geol)* glacial

Gla|zi|al [gla'tsia:l] NT **-s, -e** *(Geol)* glacial epoch *or* episode

gleich [glaiç]

1 ADJEKTIV	3 PRÄPOSITION
2 ADVERB	4 BINDEWORT

1 – ADJEKTIV

a [= identisch, ähnlich] same; **das gleiche, aber nicht dasselbe Auto** a similar car, but not the same one; **der/die/das gleiche ... wie** the same ... as; **in gleicher Weise** in the same way; **die beiden Briefe kamen mit der gleichen Post** the two letters arrived in the same post *(Brit)* or mail; **zur gleichen Zeit** at the same time; **die beiden haben gleiches Gewicht** they are both the same weight, they both weigh the same; **ich fahre den gleichen Wagen wie Sie** I drive the same car as you; **das kommt** *or* **läuft aufs Gleiche hinaus** it amounts to the same thing; **wir wollten alle das Gleiche** we all wanted the same thing; **es ist genau das Gleiche** it's exactly the same; **es waren die Gleichen, die ...** it was the same ones who ...; **ihr Männer seid doch alle gleich!** you men are all the same!; **es ist mir (alles** *or* **ganz) gleich** it's all the same to me; **Gleich und Gleich gesellt sich gern** *(Prov)* birds of a feather flock together *(Prov)*; **Gleiches mit Gleichem vergelten** to pay someone back in the same coin *(Brit)*, to pay sb back in kind; **ganz gleich wer/was** *etc* no matter who/what *etc* → **Boot, Münze, Strang**

b [= gleichwertig, gleichberechtigt] equal; **in gleichem Abstand** at an equal distance; **zu gleichen Teilen** in equal parts; **zwei mal zwei (ist) gleich vier** two twos are four, two times two is four; **vier plus/durch/minus zwei ist gleich ...** four plus/divided by/minus two is ...; **jdm (an etw** *dat***) gleich sein** to be sb's equal (in sth); **gleicher Lohn für gleiche Arbeit** equal pay for equal work; **gleiche Rechte, gleiche Pflichten** equal rights, equal responsibilities; **mit jdm in einem Ton von gleich zu gleich reden** *(geh)* to talk to sb as an equal; **alle Menschen sind gleich, nur einige sind gleicher** *(hum)* all men are equal, but some are more equal than others; **wir sind in gleicher Weise daran schuld** we are equally to blame

2 – ADVERB

a [= ohne Unterschied] equally; *(= auf gleiche Weise)* alike, the same; **der Lehrer behandelt alle Kinder gleich** the teacher treats all the children equally; **gleich gekleidet** dressed alike *or* the same; **sie sind gleich groß/alt/schwer** they are the same size/age/weight

♦ **gleich bleibend** = **gleichbleibend**

♦ **gleich geartet** = **gleichgeartet**

♦ **gleich gesinnt** *or* **denkend** like-minded

♦ **gleich lautend** = **gleichlautend**

b [räumlich] right, just; **das Wohnzimmer ist gleich neben der Küche** the living room is right *or* just next to the kitchen; **gleich hinter dem Haus ist ein großer Garten** there's a big garden just behind the house

c [zeitlich] *= sofort* immediately; *(= bald)* in a minute; **ich komme gleich** I'm just coming; **ich komme gleich wieder** I'll be right back; **du kriegst gleich eine Ohrfeige** you'll get a slap in a minute; **es muss nicht gleich sein** there's no hurry; **es ist gleich drei Uhr** it's almost *or* very nearly three o'clock; **das mache ich gleich heute** I'll do that today; **gleich zu** *or* **am Anfang** right at the beginning, at the very beginning; **gleich danach** straight *or* right afterwards; **ich werde ihn gleich morgen besuchen** I'll go and see him tomorrow; **gleich zu Beginn der Vorstellung** right at the beginning of the performance; **habe ich es nicht gleich gesagt!** what did I tell you?; **das habe ich mir gleich gedacht** I thought that straight away; **warum nicht gleich so?** why didn't you say/do that in the first place?; **na komm schon! – gleich!** come along! – I'm just coming! *or* – I'll be right there; **wann machst du das? – gleich!** when are you going to do it? – right away *or* in just a moment; **gleich als** *or* **nachdem er ...** as soon as he ...; **so wirkt das Bild gleich ganz anders** suddenly, the picture has changed completely; **wenn das stimmt, kann ichs ja gleich aufgeben** if that's true I might as well give up right now; **deswegen brauchst du nicht gleich zu weinen** there's no need to start crying because of that; **er ging gleich in die Küche/vor Gericht** he went straight to the kitchen/to court; **sie hat sich gleich zwei Hüte gekauft** she went and bought TWO hats; **bis gleich!** see you later!

d [in Fragesätzen] again; **wie war doch gleich die Nummer/Ihr Name?** what was the number/your name again?

3 – PRÄPOSITION *(+dat)*

(liter) like; **einer Epidemie gleich, gleich einer Epidemie** like an epidemic

4 – BINDEWORT

(old, liter) **ob er gleich ...** although he ...; **wenn er gleich ...** even if he ...

Gleich-: **gleich|alt|rig** ADJ (of) the same age; **die beiden sind ~** they are both the same age; **Gleichaltrige** people/children (of) the same age; **gleich|ar|mig** ADJ *(Phys) Hebel* equal-armed; **gleich|ar|tig** ADJ of the same kind (*+dat* as); *(= ähnlich)* similar (*+dat* to); *(= homogen)* homogeneous (*+dat* with) ADV in the same way; similarly; homogeneously; **Gleich|ar|tig|keit** F similarity; *(= Homogenität)* homogeneity; **gleich|auf** ['glaiç'lauf] ADV *(esp Sport)* equal; **~ liegen** to be lying equal, to be equal, to be level-pegging *(Brit)*; **gleich|be|deu|tend** ADJ synonymous *(mit* with); *(= so gut wie)* tantamount *(mit* to); **Gleich|be|hand|lung** F equal treatment; **Gleich|be|hand|lungs|grund|satz** M principle of equal treatment; **gleich|be|rech|tigt** ADJ with equal *or* the same rights; *Partner, Möglichkeiten, Dialog* equal; *Amtssprache* equally recognized *or* valid; **~ sein** to have equal rights; **Gleich|be|rech|ti|gung** F equal rights *sing or pl*, equality (*+gen* for); **gleich blei|ben** VI *irreg aux sein* to stay *or* remain the same; *(Temperaturen, Geschwindigkeit, Kurs auch)* to remain constant; **sich** *(dat)* **~** *(Mensch)* to stay *or* remain the same; **das bleibt sich gleich** it doesn't matter; **gleich|blei|bend** ADJ *Kurs* constant, steady; *Temperatur (von Wetter)* steady; *(in Brutkasten etc)* constant; **~ sein** to remain the same; *(Temperatur) (von Wetter)* to remain steady; *(in Brutkasten etc)* to remain constant; **mehr Urlaub bei ~em Gehalt** more holidays *(esp Brit)* or vacation *(US)* with the same pay; **in ~em Abstand** always at the same distance; **unter ~en Umständen** if things remain as they are ADV **~ gute Qualität** consistent(ly) good quality; **er ist immer ~ zuvorkommend** he is always equally helpful; **gleichden|kend** ADJ like-minded

glei|chen ['glaiçn] *pret* **glich** [glɪç], *ptp* **geglichen** [gə'glɪçn] VI **jdm/einer Sache ~** to be like sb/sth; **sich ~** to be alike *or* similar; **jdm an Erfahrung/Schönheit ~** to be sb's equal *or* to equal sb in experience/beauty

glei|chen|tags ['glaiçnta:ks] ADV *(esp Sw)* (on) the same day

glei|cher|ma|ßen ['glaiçɐ'ma:sn] ✪ 53.5 ADV, **glei|cher|wei|se** ['glaiçɐ'vaizə] ADV equally; **~ ... und ...** both ... and ...

Gleich-: **gleich|falls** ADV *(= ebenfalls)* likewise; *(= auch)* also; *(= zur gleichen Zeit)* at the same time; **danke ~!** thank you, (and) the same to you; **gleich|far|big** ADJ (of) the same colour *(Brit)* or color *(US)*; **gleich|för|mig** ADJ of the same shape; *(= einheitlich, fig: = eintönig)* uniform *(auch Phys)*; *(= ähnlich)* similar; **Gleich|för|mig|keit** ['glaiçfœrmɪçkait] F -, *no pl* similarity of shape; *(= Einheitlichkeit, fig: = Eintönigkeit)* uniformity *(auch Phys)*; *(= Ähnlichkeit)* similarity; **gleich|ge|ar|tet** ADJ of the same kind; *(= ähnlich)* similar; **gleich|ge|schlech|tig** [-gəʃlɛçtɪç] ADJ *(Biol, Zool)* of the same sex, same-sex *attr*; *(Bot)* homogamous; **gleich|ge|schlecht|lich** ADJ **a** homosexual **b** = **gleichgeschlechtig**; **Gleich|ge|schlecht|lich|keit** F homosexuality *no def art*; **gleich|ge|sinnt** ADJ → **gleich 2 a**; **Gleich|ge|sinnt|heit** [-gəzɪnthait] F -, *no pl* like-mindedness; **gleich|ge|stellt** ADJ equal (*+dat* to, with), on a par (*+dat* with); **er spricht nur mit Gleichgestellten** he only speaks to his equals; **rechtlich ~** equal in law → *auch* **gleichstellen**; **gleich|ge|stimmt** ADJ → **gleich 2 a**

Gleich|ge|wicht NT, *no pl (lit)* balance, equilibrium *(auch Phys, Chem)*; *(fig) (= Stabilität)* balance; *(= seelisches Gleichgewicht)* equilibrium; **im ~** *(lit)* balanced, in equilibrium; **(wieder) ins ~ kommen** *(fig)* to become more balanced again; to regain one's equilibrium; **das ~ verlieren, aus dem ~ kommen** to lose one's balance *or* equilibrium *(auch fig)*; **das ~ behalten** *(lit)* to keep one's balance *or* equilibrium; *(fig)* to retain one's equilibrium; **jdn aus dem ~ bringen** to throw sb off balance; *(fig auch)* to disturb sb's equilibrium; **das ~ einer Sache wiederherstellen** to get sth back into balance *or* equilibrium; **das ~ zwischen ...** *(dat)* **und ... halten** to maintain a proper balance between ... and ...; **diese Dinge müssen sich** *(dat)* **das ~ halten** *(fig)* these things should balance each other out; **das ~ der Kräfte** the balance of power

gleich|ge|wich|tig ADJ *(= ausgeglichen) Verhältnis* balanced; *(= gleich wichtig)* equal in weight ADV **die Kommission ist nicht ~ zusammengesetzt** the commission is not properly balanced

Gleich|ge|wichts-: **Gleich|ge|wichts|emp|fin|den** NT, **Gleich|ge|wichts|ge|fühl** NT sense of balance; **Gleich|ge|wichts|la|ge** F *(fig)* equilibrium; **Gleich|ge|wichts|or|gan** NT organ of equilibrium; **Gleich|ge|wichts|sinn** M sense of balance; **Gleich|ge|wichts|stö|rung** F impaired balance, disturbance of the sense of balance; **Gleich|ge|wichts|übung** F *(Sport)* balancing exercise; **Gleich|ge|wichts|zu|stand** M equilibrium

gleich|gül|tig ADJ indifferent *(gegenüber, gegen* to, towards); *(= uninteressiert)* apathetic *(gegenüber, gegen* towards); *(= unwesentlich)* trivial, immaterial, unimportant; **das ist mir ~** it's a matter of (complete) indifference to me; **Politik ist ihm ~** he doesn't care about politics; **~, was er tut** no matter what he does, irrespective of what he does; **es ist mir ~, was er tut** I don't care what he does; **er war ihr nicht ~ geblieben** she had not remained indifferent to him

Gleich|gül|tig|keit F indifference *(gegenüber, gegen* to, towards); *(= Desinteresse)* apathy *(gegenüber, gegen* towards)

Gleich|heit F -, -en **a** *no pl (= gleiche Stellung)* equality; *(= Identität)* identity; *(= Übereinstimmung)* correspondence; *(Ind)* parity **b** *(= Ähnlichkeit)* similarity

Gleich|heits-: **Gleich|heits|grund|satz** M, **Gleich|heits|prin|zip** NT principle of equality; **Gleich|heits|zei|chen** NT *(Math)* equals sign

Gleich-: **Gleich|klang** M *(fig)* harmony, accord; **gleich+kom|men** VI *sep irreg aux sein +dat* **a** *(= die gleiche Leistung etc erreichen)* to equal *(an +dat* for), to match *(an +dat* for, in); **niemand kommt ihm an Dummheit gleich** no-one can equal *or* match him for stupidity **b** *(= gleichbedeutend sein mit)* to be tantamount *or* equivalent to, to amount to; **Gleich|lauf** M, *no pl (Tech)* synchronization; **gleich|lau|fend** ADJ parallel *(mit* to); *(Tech)* synchronized; **gleich|lau|tend** ADJ identical; **~e Abschrift** duplicate (copy); **~e Wörter** homophones; *(= gleich buchstabiert)* homonyms; **gleich+ma|chen** VT *sep* to make the same, to level out → **Erdboden**; **Gleich|ma|cher(in)** M(F) *(pej)* leveller *(Brit pej)*, leveler *(US pej)*, egalitarian; **Gleich|ma|che|rei** [-maxəˈrai] F -, -en *(pej)* levelling down *(Brit pej)*, leveling down *(US pej)*, egalitarianism; **gleich|ma|che|risch** [-maxərɪʃ] ADJ levelling *(Brit pej)*, leveling *(US pej)*, egalitarian; **Gleich|maß** NT, *no pl* **a** *(= Ebenmaß)* evenness; *(von Proportionen auch)* symmetry **b** *(geh: = Regelhaftigkeit)* monotony *(pej)*, regularity; **gleich|mä|ßig** ADJ even, regular; *Puls* steady, regular; *Abstände* regular; *Proportionen* symmetrical ADV **a** *(= regelmäßig)* regularly; **er ist immer ~ freundlich** he is always consistently friendly **b** *(= in gleicher Stärke, Größe, Anzahl)* evenly; **sie hat die Äpfel ~ unter die Kinder verteilt** she distributed the apples evenly among the children; **die Farbe ~ auftragen** apply the paint evenly; **Gleich|mä|ßig|keit** F evenness, regularity; *(von Puls)* steadiness, regularity; *(von Abständen)* regularity; *(von Proportionen)* symmetry; **mit** *or* **in schöner ~** *(iro)* with monotonous regularity; **Gleich|mut** M equanimity, serenity, composure; **gleich|mü|tig** [-myːtɪç] ADJ serene, composed; *Stimme* calm ADV **etw ~ sagen** to say sth calmly; **Gleich|mü|tig|keit** F -, *no pl* equanimity, composure; **gleich|na|mig** [-naːmɪç] ADJ of the same name; *(Math)* with a common denominator; **Brüche ~ machen** to reduce fractions to a common denominator

Gleich|nis [ˈglaiçnɪs] NT -ses, -se **a** *(Liter)* simile **b** *(= Allegorie)* allegory; *(Bibl)* parable

gleich|nis|haft ADJ *(Liter)* as a simile; *(= allegorisch)* allegorical; *(= biblisch)* parabolic ADV *(Liter)* in a simile; *(= allegorisch)* allegorically; *(= biblisch)* in a parable

Gleich-: **gleich|ran|gig** [-raŋɪç] ADJ *Beamte etc* equal in rank *or* status *(mit* to), at the same level *(mit* as); *Straßen etc* of the same grade *(mit* as), equally graded; *Probleme, Regelungen etc* equally important, of equal status; **Gleich|ran|gig|keit** F -, *no pl* equal status; *(von Straßen)* equal grading; **gleich+rich|ten** VT *sep (Elec)* to rectify; **Gleich|rich|ter** M *(Elec)* rectifier; **Gleich|rich|ter|röh|re** F *(Elec)* rectifier tube *(esp US)* or valve; **Gleich|rich|tung** F *(Elec)* rectification

gleich|sam [ˈglaiçzaːm] ADV *(geh)* as it were, so to speak; **~, als ob** just as if

Gleich-: **gleich+schal|ten** *sep (Pol, NS: pej)* VT to bring *or* force into line VR to conform, to step into line; **Gleich|schal|tung** F *(Pol, NS: pej)* bringing *or* forcing into line; *(unter Hitler auch)* gleichschaltung; **er wehrte sich gegen eine ~** he refused to be brought *or* forced into line; **gleich|schen|ke|lig** [-ʃɛŋkəlɪç], **gleich|schenk|lig** [-ʃɛŋklɪç] ADJ *Dreieck* isosceles; **Gleich|schritt** M, *no pl (Mil)* marching in step; **im ~** *(lit, fig)* in step; **im ~, marsch!** forward march!; **im ~ marschieren** to march in step; **~ halten** *(lit, fig)* to keep in step; **gleich+se|hen** VI *sep irreg* **jdm/einer Sache ~** to look like sb/sth; **gleich|sei|tig** [-zaitɪç] ADJ *Dreieck* equilateral; **gleich+set|zen** VT *sep (= als dasselbe ansehen)* to equate *(mit* with); *(= als gleichwertig ansehen)* to treat as equivalent *(mit* to); **nichts ist mit echter Wolle gleichzusetzen** there's nothing to compare with pure wool; **Gleich|set|zung** F -, -en **die ~ der Arbeiter mit den Angestellten** treating workers as equivalent to office employees; **gleich|sil|big** ADJ with the same number of syllables; **Gleich|stand** M, *no pl* **a** *(Sport)* **den ~ erzielen** to draw level; **beim ~ von 1:1** with the scores level *(Brit)* or equal at 1 all **b** *(Pol)* equal stage of development; **gleich+ste|hen** VI *sep irreg* to be equal *(+dat* to *or* with), to be on a par *(+dat* with); *(Sport)* to be level *(Brit)* or equal *(+dat* with); **er steht im Rang einem Hauptmann gleich** he is equal in rank to a captain; **Gleichstehende** equals, people on an equal footing; **gleich+stel|len** VT *sep* **a** *(rechtlich etc)* to treat as equal, to give parity of treatment (to); **dass Frauen und Männer arbeitsrechtlich gleichzustellen sind** that men and women should be treated as equals *or* equally *or* given parity of treatment as far as work is concerned → *auch* **gleichgestellt** **b** = **gleichsetzen**; **Gleich|stel|lung** F **a** *(rechtlich etc)* equality *(+gen* of, for), equal status *(+gen* of, for), parity **b** = **Gleichsetzung**; **Gleich|stel|lungs|be|auf|trag|te(r)** MF *decl as adj* equal rights representative; **Gleich|strom** M *(Elec)* direct current, DC; **Gleich|tritt** M = **Gleichschritt**; **gleich+tun** VT *impers sep irreg* **es jdm ~** to equal *or* match sb; **es jdm im Laufen** *etc* **~** to equal *or* match sb at *or* in running *etc*

Glei|chung [ˈglaiçʊŋ] F -, -en equation; **eine ~ ersten/zweiten Grades** a simple *or* linear/quadratic equation, an equation of the first/second degree *(form)*

Gleich-: **gleich|viel** ADV *(geh)* nonetheless; **~ ob** no matter whether; **~ wie** however; **~ wohin** no matter where; **gleich|wer|tig** ADJ of the same value; *(= gleich zu bewerten) Leistung, Qualität* equal *(+dat* to); *Gegner* equally *or* evenly matched; *Partner* equal; *(Chem)* equivalent; **Gleich|wer|tig|keit** F, *no pl* equal value; *(= von gleich zu bewertender Leistung, Qualität)* equality; *(Chem)* equivalence, equivalency; **gleich|wie** ADV *(old)* (just) as; **gleich|win|ke|lig**, **gleich|wink|lig** ADJ *(Geometrie)* equiangular *(form)*, with (all) angles equal; **gleich|wohl** ADV *(geh)* nevertheless, nonetheless; **gleich|zei|tig** ADJ simultaneous ADV simultaneously, at the same time; *(= ebenso, sowohl)* at the same time; **ihr sollt nicht alle ~ reden** you mustn't all speak at the same time; **Gleich|zei|tig|keit** [ˈglaiçtsaitɪçkait] F -, *no pl* simultaneity; **gleich+zie|hen** VI *sep irreg (inf)* to catch up *(mit* with)

Gleis [glais] NT -es, -e [-zə] *(Rail)* line, track, rails *pl*; *(= einzelne Schiene)* rail; *(= Bahnsteig)* platform; *(fig)* rut; **~ 6** platform *or* track *(US)* 6; **„Überschreiten der ~e verboten"** "passengers must not cross the line *(Brit)* or tracks"; **ein totes ~** *(lit)* a siding; *(fig)* a dead end; **jdn/etw aufs tote ~ schieben** to put sb/sth on ice *(inf)*; **aus dem ~ springen** to jump the rails; **aus dem ~ kommen** *(fig)* to go off the rails *(Brit inf)*, to get off the track *(US inf)*; **etw ins (rechte) ~ bringen** *(fig)* to straighten *or* sort sth out; **jdn aus dem ~ bringen** *(fig)* to put sb off his stroke *(Brit)*, to throw sb off track *(US)*; **wieder im richtigen ~ sein** *(fig)* to be back on track *or* on the rails *(Brit inf)* or on the right lines *(Brit inf)*; **wieder ins richtige ~ kommen** *(fig)* to get back on track *or* on the rails *(Brit inf)* or on the right lines *(Brit inf)*

Gleis-: **Gleis|an|la|gen** PL railway *(Brit)* or railroad *(US)* lines *pl*; **Gleis|an|schluss** M works siding; **Gleis|ar|bei|ten** PL work on the line, line *or* track repairs *pl*; **Gleis|bau** M, *no pl* railway *(Brit)* or railroad *(US)* construction; **Gleis|bau|stel|le** F place where work is being done on the line; **überall auf der Strecke waren ~n** work was being done all along the line; **Gleis|bett** NT ballast; **Gleis|brem|se** F rail brake; **Gleis|drei|eck** NT triangular junction

-glei|sig [glaizɪç] ADJ *suf (lit, fig)* -track; **eingleisig** single-track; **mehrgleisig** multi-track; **eine eingleisige Denkweise** a narrow-minded way of thinking

Gleis-: **Gleis|ket|te** F caterpillar® track; **Gleis|ket|ten|fahr|zeug** NT caterpillar® vehicle; **Gleis|kör|per** M railway *(Brit)* or railroad *(US)* embankment

Gleis|ner [ˈglaisnɐ] M -s, -, **Gleis|ne|rin** [-ərɪn] F -, -nen *(old)* hypocrite, dissembler *(liter)*

gleis|ne|risch [ˈglaisnərɪʃ] ADJ *(old)* dissembling *(liter)*, hypocritical

glei|ßen [ˈglaisn] VI *(liter)* to gleam, to glisten

Gleit-: **Gleit|boot** NT hydroplane; **Gleit|bü|gel** M *(Elec)* pantograph, current collector

glei|ten [ˈglaitn] *pret* **glitt** [glɪt], *ptp* **geglitten** [gəˈglɪtn] VI **a** *aux sein (Vogel, Flugzeug, Tänzer, Boot, Skier, Schlange)* to glide; *(Blick)* to pass, to range; *(Hand)* to slide, to glide; **ein Lächeln glitt über ihr Gesicht** a smile flickered across her face; **sein Auge über etw** *(acc)* **~ lassen** to cast an eye over sth; **die Finger über etw** *(acc)* **~ lassen** to glide *or* slide one's fingers over *or* across sth **b** *aux sein (= rutschen)* to slide; *(Auto)* to skid; *(= entgleiten: Gegenstand)* to slip; *(geh: = ausrutschen)* to slip; **zu Boden ~** to slip to the ground; *(auf den Fußboden)* to slip to the floor; **ins Wasser ~** to slide *or* slip into the water; **ins Gleiten kommen** to start to slide *or* slip **c** *(Ind inf: = gleitende Arbeitszeit haben)* to have flex(i)time

glei|tend ADJ **~e Löhne** *or* **Lohnskala** sliding wage scale; **~e Arbeitszeit** flexible working hours *pl*, flex(i)time; **~er Übergang** gradual transition; **~er Ruhestand** gradual retirement

Glei|ter [ˈglaitɐ] M -s, - *(Aviat)* glider

Gleit-: **Gleit|flug** M glide; **im ~ niedergehen** to glide *or* plane down; **Gleit|flug|zeug** NT glider; **Gleit|klau|sel** F *(Comm)* escalator clause; **Gleit|kom|ma** NT floating point; **Gleit|ku|fe** F *(Aviat)* landing skid; **Gleit|mit|tel** NT *(Med)* lubricant; **Gleit|schirm** M paraglider; **Gleit|schirm|flie|gen** NT -s, *no pl* paragliding; **Gleit|schirm|flie|ger(in)** M(F) paraglider; **Gleit|schutz** M *(Aut)* anti-skid(-ding) device; **Gleit|se|geln** NT, *no pl* hang-gliding; **Gleit|segler** M *(Fluggerät)* hang-glider; **Gleit|segler(in)** M(F) hang-glider; **Gleit|sicht|bril|le** F, **Gleit|sicht|glä|ser** PL multifocals *pl*, varifocals *pl*; **Gleit|tag** M flexiday; **Gleit|wachs** NT *(für Skier)* wax; **Gleit|win|kel** M gliding angle; **Gleit|zeit** F flex(i)time; **~ haben** to be on flexitime

Glen|check [ˈglɛntʃɛk] M -(s), -s glencheck

Glet|scher [ˈglɛtʃɐ] M -s, - glacier

Glet|scher-: **glet|scher|ar|tig** ADJ glacial; **Glet|scher|bach** M glacial stream; **Glet|scher|brand** M glacial sunburn; **Glet|scher|bril|le** F sunglasses *pl*; **Glet|scher|eis** NT glacial ice; **Glet|scher|feld** NT glacier; **Glet|scher|for|schung** F glaciology; **Glet|scher|kun|de** F glaciology; **Glet|scher|müh|le** F *(Geol)* moulin; **Glet|scher|ski|fah|ren** NT glacier skiing; **Glet|scher|spal|te** F crevasse; **Glet|scher|tor** NT mouth (of glacier); **Glet|scher|was|ser** NT, *no pl* glacier water; **Glet|scher|zun|ge** F glacier snout

Glib|ber [ˈglɪbɐ] M -s, *no pl (inf)* slime

glib|be|rig [ˈglɪbərɪç] ADJ *(inf)* slimy

glich *pret von* **gleichen**

Glied [gliːt] NT -(e)s, -er [-dɐ] **a** *(= Körperteil)* limb, member *(form)*; *(= Fingerglied, Zehenglied)* joint; **seine ~er recken** to stretch (oneself); **an allen ~ern zittern** to be shaking all over; **der Schreck fuhr ihm in alle ~er** the shock made him shake all over; **der Schreck sitzt** *or* **steckt ihr noch in den ~ern** she is still shaking with *(Brit)* or from *(esp US)* the shock; **sich** *(dat)* **alle ~er brechen** to break every bone in one's body **b** *(= Penis)* penis, organ, member *(form)* **c** *(= Kettenglied, fig)* link

d (*= Teil*) section, part; (*von Grashalm*) segment **e** (*= Mitglied*) member; (*Mil etc*) rank; (*Bibl*) generation; (*Math*) term; **aus dem ~ treten** (*Mil*) to step forward (out of the ranks); **ins ~ zurücktreten** (*Mil*) to step back into the ranks

Glie|der-: **Glie|der|arm|band** NT (*von Uhr*) expanding bracelet; **Glie|der|bau** M, *no pl* limb structure; (*= Körperbau*) build; **Glie|der|fü|ßer** [-fy:sɐ] M **-s, -** *usu pl* (*Zool*) arthropod; **glie|der|lahm** ADJ heavy-limbed, weary; **ich bin ganz ~** my limbs are so stiff

glie|dern [ˈgli:dɐn] VT **a** (*= ordnen*) to structure, to order, to organize **b** (*= unterteilen*) to (sub)divide (*in +acc* into) → *auch* **gegliedert** VR (*= zerfallen in*) **sich ~ in** (*+acc*) to (sub)divide into; (*= bestehen aus*) to consist of

Glie|der-: **Glie|der|pup|pe** F jointed doll; (*= Marionette*) (string) puppet, marionette; (*Art*) lay figure; **Glie|der|rei|ßen** NT rheumatic pains *pl*; **Glie|der|satz** M (*Ling*) period; **Glie|der|schmer|zen** PL painful limbs *pl* (and joints *pl*); **Glie|der|schwe|re** F heaviness in one's limbs; **Glie|der|tier** NT articulate

Glie|de|rung [ˈgli:dərʊŋ] F **-, -en a** (*= das Gliedern*) structuring, organization; (*= das Unterteilen*) subdivision **b** (*= Aufbau*) structure; (*= Unterteilung, von Organisation*) subdivision **c** (*= Aufstellung in Reihe etc*) formation

Glie|de|rungs-: **Glie|de|rungs|an|sicht** F (*Comput*) outline view; **Glie|de|rungs|punkt** M **a** (*von Vortrag etc*) (subordinate) point **b** (*Comput: = Zeichen*) bullet

Glie|der-: **Glie|der|zu|cken** NT **-s**, *no pl* twitching of the limbs; **Glie|der|zug** M articulated train

Glied-: **Glied|kir|che** F member church; **Glied|ma|ßen** PL limbs *pl*; **Glied|satz** M (*Ling*) subordinate clause; **Glied|staat** M member *or* constituent state; **glied|wei|se** ADV (*Mil*) in ranks

glim|men [ˈglɪmən] *pret* **glomm** *or* (*rare*) **glimmte** [glɔm, ˈglɪmtə], *ptp* **geglommen** *or* (*rare*) **geglimmt** [gəˈglɔmən, gəˈglɪmt] VI to glow; (*Feuer, Asche auch*) to smoulder (*Brit*), to smolder (*US*); **~der Hass** (*geh*) smouldering (*Brit*) *or* smoldering (*US*) hatred; **noch glomm ein Funken Hoffnung in ihm** (*geh*) a ray of hope still glimmered within him

Glim|mer [ˈglɪmɐ] M **-s, - a** (*Min*) mica **b** (*rare: = Schimmer*) gleam, glint

glim|mern [ˈglɪmɐn] VI to glimmer

Glim|mer|schie|fer M (*Min*) mica schist

Glimm-: **Glimm|lam|pe** F glow lamp; **Glimm|stän|gel** M (*dated inf*) fag (*esp Brit inf*), cigarette, butt (*US inf*)

glimpf|lich [ˈglɪmpflɪç] ADJ (*= mild*) mild, light, lenient; *Unfall* minor; *Verletzungen* slight, light; *Folgen* negligible; **wegen des ~en Ausgangs des Unfalls** because the accident wasn't too serious; **einen ~en Ausgang nehmen** to pass off without serious consequences
ADV *bestrafen* mildly; **~ bestraft werden** to receive a mild punishment; **~ davonkommen** to get off lightly; **mit jdm ~ umgehen** *or* **verfahren** to treat sb mildly *or* leniently; *mit Gefangenem* to treat sb humanely; **~ abgehen** *or* **ablaufen** *or* **verlaufen** to pass (off) without serious consequences; **die Sache ist für sie ~ abgegangen** *or* **verlaufen** they got off lightly

Glitsch|bahn F (*dial*) slide

glit|schen [ˈglɪtʃn] VI *aux sein* (*inf*) to slip (*aus* out of)

glit|schig [ˈglɪtʃɪç] ADJ (*inf*) slippery, slippy (*inf*)

glitt *pret von* **gleiten**

Glit|zer- [ˈglɪtsɐ] *in cpds* glitzy (*inf*)

Glit|zer|gel NT (*Fashion*) glitter gel, body glitter

glit|zern [ˈglɪtsɐn] VI to glitter; (*Stern auch*) to twinkle

Glit|zer|welt [ˈglɪtsɐ-] F (*usu pej*) glitzy world, glitz; (*der Schickeria*) (world of the) glitterati; (*des Films etc*) wonder world

glo|bal [gloˈba:l] ADJ **a** (*= weltweit*) global, world-wide; **~e Erwärmung** global warming **b** (*= ungefähr, pauschal*) general ADV **a** (*= weltweit*) world-wide; **~ verbreitet** global, worldwide **b** (*= pauschal*) **sich** (*dat*) **etw ~ vorstellen** to have a general idea of sth; **jdm etw ~ erläutern** to give sb a general idea of sth; **~ gerechnet** in round figures

glo|ba|li|sie|ren [globaliˈzi:rən] *ptp* **globalisiert** VT to globalize

Glo|ba|li|sie|rung F **-**, *no pl* globalization

Glo|ba|li|sie|rungs|geg|ner(in) M(F) anti-globalization protester, antiglobalist

Glo|bal-: **Glo|bal|steu|e|rung** F overall control; **Glo|bal|stra|te|gie** F (*Pol*) global *or* worldwide strategy

Glo|ben *pl von* **Globus**

Glo|be|trot|ter [ˈglo:bətrɔtɐ, ˈglo:ptrɔtɐ] M **-s, -**, **Glo|be|trot|te|rin** [-ərɪn] F **-, -nen** globetrotter

Glo|bu|li [ˈglo:buli] PL (*Pharm*) globules *pl*

Glo|bus [ˈglo:bʊs] M **-** *or* **-ses, Globen** *or* **-se** globe; (*inf: = Kopf*) nut (*inf*)

Glöck|chen [ˈglœkçən] NT **-s, -** (little) bell

Glo|cke [ˈglɔkə] F **-, -n a** (*auch Blüte*) bell; (*= Käseglocke etc*) cover; (*= Florettglocke*) coquille; (*in Labor*) bell jar; (*= Taucherglocke*) (diving) bell; (*= Damenhut*) cloche; (*inf: = Herrenhut*) bowler; **nach den ~n von Big Ben** after the chimes from Big Ben, after Big Ben strikes; **etw an die große ~ hängen** (*inf*) to shout sth from the rooftops; **wissen, was die ~ geschlagen hat** (*inf*) to know what one is in for (*inf*), to know what's in store for one; **über der Stadt wölbte sich eine dichte ~ von Rauch** a thick pall of smoke hung over the city **b** (*sl: = Hoden*) **Glocken** PL balls *pl*

Glo|cken-: **Glo|cken|bal|ken** M (bell) yoke; **Glo|cken|blu|me** F bellflower, campanula; **Glo|cken|bron|ze** F bell metal; **glo|cken|för|mig** ADJ bell-shaped; **Glo|cken|ge|läut** NT, **Glo|cken|ge|läu|te** NT (peal of) bells *pl*; **Glo|cken|gie|ßer(in)** M(F) bellfounder; **Glo|cken|gie|ße|rei** F bellfoundry; **Glo|cken|guss** M bell-founding; **glo|cken|hell** ADJ (*geh*) bell-like; *Stimme auch* as clear as a bell; **Glo|cken|helm** M top of a/the bell; **Glo|cken|klang** M ringing *or* (*esp hell auch*) pealing (of bells); **Glo|cken|klöp|pel** M clapper, tongue (of a/the bell); **Glo|cken|läu|ten** NT **-s**, *no pl* (peal of) bells *pl*; **Glo|cken|man|tel** M cope (*for founding bell*); **glo|cken|rein** ADJ (*geh*) bell-like; *Stimme auch* as clear as a bell; **Glo|cken|rock** M flared skirt; **Glo|cken|schlag** M stroke (of a/the bell); (*von Uhr auch*) chime; **es ist mit dem ~ 6 Uhr** on the stroke it will be 6 o'clock; **auf den** *or* **mit dem ~** on the stroke of eight/nine *etc*; (*= genau pünktlich*) on the dot; **Glo|cken|spei|se** F bell metal; **Glo|cken|spiel** NT (*in Turm*) carillon; (*automatisch auch*) chimes *pl*; (*= Instrument*) glockenspiel; **Glo|cken|strang** M bell rope; **Glo|cken|stu|be** F belfry; **Glo|cken|stuhl** M bell cage; **Glo|cken|ton** M *pl* **-töne** sound of a/the bell; **Glo|cken|turm** M belltower, belfry; **Glo|cken|wei|he** F consecration of a/the bell; **Glo|cken|zei|chen** NT ring of a/the bell; **auf ein ~ erschien der Butler** a ring on the bell summoned the butler; **Glo|cken|zug** M (*= Glockenstrang*) bell rope; (*= Klingelschnur*) bell pull, bell cord

glo|ckig [ˈglɔkɪç] ADJ bell-shaped; *Kleid, Rock* flared

Glöck|ner [ˈglœknɐ] M **-s, -**, **Glöck|ne|rin** [-ərɪn] F **-, -nen** bell-ringer; **„Der ~ von Notre-Dame"** "The Hunchback of Notre Dame"

glomm *pret von* **glimmen**

Glo|ria [ˈglo:ria] NT **-s, -s** (*Eccl*) gloria, Gloria → **Glanz**

Glo|ria F **-** *or nt* **-s**, *no pl* (*usu iro*) glory

Glo|rie [ˈglo:riə] F **-, -n a** *no pl* (*= Ruhm*) glory, splendour (*Brit*), splendor (*US*) **b** (*= Heiligenschein*) halo

Glo|ri|en|schein M halo; (*fig*) aura

glo|ri|fi|zie|ren [glorifiˈtsi:rən] *ptp* **glorifiziert** VT to glorify

Glo|ri|fi|zie|rung F **-, -en** glorification

Glo|ri|o|le [gloˈrio:lə] F **-, -n** halo; (*fig*) aura

glo|ri|os [gloˈrio:s] ADJ (*oft iro*) glorious, magnificent

glor|reich [ˈglo:ɐ-] ADJ glorious; **der ~e Rosenkranz** (*Eccl*) the Glorious Mysteries *pl* ADV *zurückkehren, herrschen* victoriously; **~ siegen** to have *or* achieve a glorious victory; **seine Laufbahn ~ beenden** to bring one's career to a glorious conclusion

Gloss [glɔs] NT **-, -** gloss

Glos|sar [glɔˈsa:ɐ] NT **-s, -e** glossary

Glos|se [ˈglɔsə] F **-, -n a** (*Liter*) gloss (*zu* on) **b** (*Press, Rad etc*) commentary **c** **Glossen** PL (*inf*) snide *or* sneering comments; **seine ~n über jdn/etw machen** (*inf*) to make snide comments about sb/sth

Glos|sen|schrei|ber(in) M(F) (*Press*) commentator

glos|sie|ren [glɔˈsi:rən] *ptp* **glossiert** VT **a** (*Liter*) to gloss, to write a gloss/glosses on **b** (*= bespötteln*) to sneer at **c** (*Press, Rad etc*) to do a commentary on, to commentate on

Glotz-: **Glotz|au|ge** NT **a** (*usu pl: inf*) staring *or* goggle (*inf*) eye; **~n machen** to stare (goggle-eyed), to gawp **b** (*Med*) exophthalmia (*spec*); **glotz|äu|gig** ADJ ADV (*inf*) goggle-eyed (*inf*)

Glot|ze [ˈglɔtsə] F **-, -n** (*inf*) **a** (*= Fernseher*) goggle-box (*Brit inf*), one-eyed monster (*Brit pej inf*), boob tube (*US inf*) **b** (*= Bildschirm*) screen

glot|zen [ˈglɔtsn] VI (*pej inf*) (*auf, in +acc* at) to stare, to gawp, to gape

Glo|xi|nie [glɔˈksi:niə] F **-, -n** (*Bot*) gloxinia

Glubsch|au|ge [ˈglʊpʃ-] NT (*inf*) = **Glotzauge a**

gluck [glʊk] INTERJ **a** (*von Huhn*) cluck **b** (*von Flüssigkeit*) glug; **~ ~, weg war er** (*inf*) glug glug, and he'd gone

Glück [glʏk] ✪ 50.5 NT **-(e)s**, (*rare*) **-e a** luck; **ein seltenes ~** a funny stroke *or* piece of luck; **~/kein ~ haben** to be lucky/unlucky; **er hat das ~ gehabt, zu ...** he was lucky enough to ..., he had the good fortune to ...; **~ gehabt!** that was lucky; **auf gut ~** (*= aufs Geratewohl*) on the off chance; (*= unvorbereitet*) trusting to luck; (*= wahllos*) at random; **ein ~!** how lucky!, what a stroke *or* piece of luck!; **ein ~, dass ...** it is/was lucky that ...; **es ist ein wahres ~, dass ...** it's really lucky that ...; **du hast ~ im Unglück gehabt** it could have been a great deal worse (for you); **in ~ und Unglück** in good times and in bad, through thick and thin; **viel ~ (bei ...)!** good luck (with ...)!, the best of luck (with ...)!; **~ bei Frauen haben** to be successful with women; **jdm ~ für etw wünschen** to wish sb luck for sth; **jdm ~ wünschen zu ...** to congratulate sb on ...; **er wünscht dir ~ bei deiner Prüfung** he wishes you (good) luck in (*Brit*) *or* on (*US*) your exam; **ich wünsche dir ~ bei deiner Prüfung** good luck in (*Brit*) *or* on (*US*) your exam; **jdm zum neuen Jahr/zum Geburtstag ~ wünschen** to wish sb (a) Happy New Year/happy birthday; **zum ~** luckily, fortunately; **zu seinem ~** luckily *or* fortunately for him; **das ist dein ~!** that's lucky for you!; **~ auf!** (*Min*) good luck!; **mehr ~ als Verstand haben** to have more luck than brains; **sie weiß noch nichts von ihrem ~** (*iro*) she doesn't know anything about it yet; **damit wirst du bei ihr kein ~ haben** you won't have any joy with her (with that) (*inf*), that won't work with her; **~ bringend** lucky; **~ verheißend** (*liter, Religion, Gesichtsausdruck*) which holds out a promise of happiness; *Zeichen etc* propitious (*form*), auspicious; **sein ~ machen** to make one's fortune; **sein ~ probieren** *or* **versuchen** to try one's luck; **er kann von ~ reden** *or* **sagen, dass ...** he can count himself lucky that ..., he can thank his lucky stars that ... (*inf*); **sein ~ mit Füßen treten** to turn one's back on fortune; **~ muss der Mensch haben** (*inf*) my/your *etc* luck is in; **das war das ~ des Tüchtigen** he/she deserved the break (*inf*),

he/she deserved his/her good luck; **das hat mir gerade noch zu meinem ~ gefehlt!** *(iro)* that was all I wanted; **man kann niemanden zu seinem ~ zwingen** *(prov)* you can lead a horse to water but you can't make him drink *(Prov)*; **ein Kind des ~s sein** *(geh)* to have been born under a lucky star; **ein Stiefkind des ~s sein** *(geh)* to be a born loser; **jeder ist seines ~es Schmied** *(Prov)* life is what you make it *(prov)*, everyone is the architect of his own future
b *(= Freude)* happiness; **eheliches ~** wedded *or* marital bliss; **er ist ihr ganzes ~** he is her whole life; **das Streben nach ~** the pursuit of happiness; **~ und Glas, wie leicht bricht das!** *(Prov)* happiness is such a fragile thing

Glück-: **Glück|auf** [glʏk'lauf] NT **-s**, *no pl* (cry of) "good luck"; **glück|brin|gend** ADJ lucky

Glu|cke ['glʊkə] F **-, -n** *(= Bruthenne)* broody *or* sitting hen; *(mit Jungen)* mother hen; **wie eine ~ ist sie ständig um ihre Kinder herum** she fusses (a)round her children like a mother hen

glu|cken ['glʊkn] VI **a** *(= brüten)* to brood; *(= brüten wollen)* to go broody; *(fig inf)* to sit around **b** *(= Küken rufen)* to cluck

glü|cken ['glʏkn] VI *aux sein* to be a success, to be successful; **nicht ~** to be a failure, not to be a success; *(Plan auch)* to miscarry; **ihm glückt alles/nichts** everything/nothing he does is a success, he succeeds/fails at whatever he does; **geglückt** *(Feier, Experiment, Aktion)* successful; *Wahl* lucky; *Überraschung* real; **dieses Bild/die Torte ist dir gut geglückt** your picture/cake has turned out very well; **endlich ist es ihm geglückt** at last he managed it; **es wollte nicht ~** it wouldn't go right

glu|ckern ['glʊkɐn] VI to glug

glück|haft ADJ *(geh) Erinnerung, Ergebnis, Augenblick* happy

Gluck|hen|ne ['glʊk-] F = **Glucke**

glück|lich ['glʏklɪç] ✪ 41, 50.2 ADJ **a** *(= erfolgreich, vom Glück begünstigt)* lucky, fortunate; *(= vorteilhaft, treffend, erfreulich)* happy; **~e Reise!** bon voyage!, pleasant journey!; **er kann sich ~ schätzen(, dass ...)** he can count *or* consider himself lucky (that ...); **wer ist der/die Glückliche?** who is the lucky man/woman/girl *etc*? → **Hand c**
b *(= froh, selig)* happy; **ein ~es Ende, ein ~er Ausgang** a happy ending; **~ machen** to bring happiness; **jdn ~ machen** to make sb happy, to bring sb happiness
ADV **a** *(= mit Glück)* by *or* through luck; *(= vorteilhaft, treffend, erfreulich)* happily; **~ zurückkommen** *(= in Sicherheit)* to come back safely
b *(= froh, selig)* happily; **die ~-heiteren Tage der Kindheit** the bright and happy days of childhood

glück|li|cher|wei|se ['glʏklɪçɐ'vaizə] ADV luckily, fortunately

Glück-: **glück|los** ADJ hapless, luckless; **Glück|sa|che** F = **Glückssache**

Glücks-: **Glücks|au|to|mat** M *(fig)* gaming machine; **Glücks|bo|te** M, **Glücks|bo|tin** F bearer of (the) glad *or* good tidings; **Glücks|bot|schaft** F glad *or* good tidings *pl*; **Glücks|brin|ger** [-brɪŋɐ] M **-s, -** *(= Talisman)* lucky charm; **Glücks|brin|ger** [-brɪŋɐ] M **-s, -**, **Glücks|brin|ge|rin** [-ərɪn] F **-, -nen** bearer of (the) glad tidings; **Glücks|bu|de** F try-your-luck stall

glück|se|lig [glʏk'ze:lɪç] ADJ blissfully happy, blissful; *Lächeln, Gesichtsausdruck auch* rapturous

Glück|se|lig|keit F bliss, rapture *(liter)*

gluck|sen ['glʊksn] VI **a** *(= lachen) (Kleinkind)* to gurgle; *(Erwachsener)* to chortle **b** *(= gluckern)* to glug

Glücks-: **Glücks|fall** M piece *or* stroke of luck; **durch einen ~** by a lucky chance; **im ~ kannst du mit einer Geldstrafe rechnen** if you're lucky you'll get away with a fine; **Glücks|fee** F *(fig hum)* good fairy, fairy godmother; **Glücks|ge|fühl** NT feeling of happiness; **Glücks|göt|tin** F goddess of luck; **die ~ ist mir nicht hold** *(hum, geh)* (Dame) Fortune has deserted me; **Glücks|ha|fen** M *(S Ger, Aus)* try-your-luck stall; **Glücks|kind** NT child of Fortune; **Glücks|klee** M four-leaf(ed) clover; **Glücks|li|nie** F line of fortune *or* luck; **Glücks|pfen|nig** M *(fig)* lucky penny, *(shiny) coin supposed to bring luck*; **Glücks|pil|le** F *(inf)* (get-)happy pill; **Glücks|pilz** M lucky beggar *(Brit inf) or* devil *(inf)*; **Glücks|rad** NT wheel of fortune; **Glücks|rit|ter** M adventurer; **Glücks|sa|che** F **das ist ~** it's a matter of luck; **ich hab gedacht ... – Denken ist ~** *(inf)* I thought ... – you thought?; **Glücks|schwein|(chen)** NT *pig as a symbol of good luck*; **Glücks|spiel** NT game of chance; **Glücks|spie|ler(in)** M(F) gambler; **Glücks|stern** M lucky star; **Glücks|sträh|ne** F lucky streak; **eine ~ haben** to be on a lucky streak; **Glücks|tag** M lucky day

glück|strah|lend ADJ beaming with happiness; *Kind, Frau auch* radiant (with happiness)

Glücks-: **Glücks|tref|fer** M stroke of luck; *(beim Schießen, Ftbl)* lucky shot, fluke *(inf)*; **Glücks|um|stand** M fortunate circumstance; **Glücks|zahl** F lucky number

glück|ver|hei|ßend ADJ → **Glück**

Glück|wunsch ✪ 50.6, 51.1, 51.2, 51.3 M congratulations *pl* (*zu* on); **herzlichen ~** congratulations; **herzlichen ~ zum Geburtstag!** happy birthday, many happy returns of the day; **Glückwünsche zur Verlobung/zur bestandenen Prüfung** congratulations on your engagement/on passing your examination

Glück|wunsch-: **Glück|wunsch|ad|res|se** F message of congratulations, congratulatory message; **Glück|wunsch|kar|te** F greetings card; **Glück|wunsch|schrei|ben** NT letter of congratulations; **Glück|wunsch|te|le|gramm** NT greetings telegram

Glüh- *(Elec)*: **Glüh|bir|ne** F (electric) light bulb; **Glüh|draht** M filament

glü|hen ['gly:ən] VI to glow; *(fig auch)* to be aglow; **der Ofen/die Sonne glüht, dass man es nicht aushalten kann** the fire/sun is too hot to bear; **vor Fieber/Scham ~** to be flushed with fever/shame; **vor Verlangen** *etc* **~** *(liter)* to burn with desire *etc* VT to heat until red-hot

glü|hend ADJ glowing; *(= heiß glühend) Metall* red-hot; *Hitze* blazing; *(fig: = leidenschaftlich)* ardent; *Hass* burning; *Wangen* flushed, burning ADV *lieben* madly, passionately; **~ heiß** scorching; *Sonne auch* blazing hot; **jdn ~ beneiden** to be consumed by envy for sb; **jdn ~ verehren** to worship sb; **sich ~ hassen** to have a burning hatred for one another

Glüh-: **Glüh|fa|den** M *(Elec)* filament; **Glüh|ker|ze** F *(Aut)* heater *or* incandescent plug; **Glüh|lam|pe** F *(form)* electric light bulb; **Glüh|ofen** M *(Metal)* annealing furnace; **Glüh|strumpf** M (gas) mantle; **Glüh|wein** M glühwein, mulled wine, glogg *(US)*; **Glüh|würm|chen** NT glow-worm; *(fliegend)* firefly

Glu|ko|se [glu'ko:zə] F **-, -n** glucose

Glupsch|au|ge ['glʊpʃ-] NT *(N Ger inf)* = **Glotzauge a**

glup|schen ['glʊpʃn] VI *(N Ger inf)* (*auf, in +acc* at) to gawp, to gape

Glut [glu:t] F **-, -en a** *(= glühende Masse, Kohle)* embers *pl*; *(= Tabaksglut)* burning ash; *(= Hitze)* heat **b** *(fig liter) (= glühende Farbe, Hitze)* glow; *(auf Gesicht)* flush, redness; *(= Leidenschaft)* ardour *(Brit)*, ardor *(US)*

Glu|ta|mat [gluta'ma:t] NT **-(e)s, -e** glutamate

Glu|ta|min [gluta'mi:n] NT **-s, -e** glutamine

Glu|ta|min|säu|re F glutamic acid

Glut-: **glut|äu|gig** ADJ *(geh)* with smouldering *(Brit) or* smoldering *(US)* eyes; **Glut|ball** M *(poet)* fiery orb *(poet)*; **Glu|ten** [glu'te:n] NT **-s**, *no pl (Chem, Physiol)* gluten

Glu|ten-: **glu|ten|frei** ADJ *Lebensmittel* gluten-free; **glu|ten|hal|tig** ADJ *Lebensmittel* gluten-containing, containing gluten *pred*

Glut-: **Glut|hauch** M *(liter)* torrid *or* sweltering heat; **glut|heiß** ADJ *(geh) Tag* swelteringly hot; *Sand, Gesicht* red-hot; **Glut|hit|ze** F sweltering heat; **glut|rot** ADJ *(liter)* fiery red; **Glut|rö|te** F *(liter)* fiery red; **glut|voll** ADJ passionate; **Glut|wind** M *(liter)* torrid wind

Gly|ce|rin [glytse'ri:n] NT = **Glyzerin**

Gly|kol [gly'ko:l] NT **-s, -e** glycol

Gly|ze|rin [glytse'ri:n] NT **-s**, *no pl (Chem)* glycerin(e)

Gly|zi|nie [gly'tsi:niə] F **-, -n** wisteria

GmbH [ge:lɛmbe:'ha:] F **-, -s** *abbr von* **Gesellschaft mit beschränkter Haftung** limited company, Ltd

Gna|de ['gna:də] F **-, -n** *(= Barmherzigkeit)* mercy; *(= heilig machende Gnade)* grace; *(= Gunst)* favour *(Brit)*, favor *(US)*; *(= Verzeihung)* pardon; **um ~ bitten** to ask for *or* crave *(liter)* mercy; **jdn um ~ für seine Sünden bitten** to ask sb to pardon (one for) one's sins; **jds ~ finden, bei jdm** *or* **vor jdm** *or* **vor jds Augen** *(dat)* **~ finden** to find favo(u)r with sb *or* in sb's eyes; **~ vor** *or* **für Recht ergehen lassen** to temper justice with mercy; **etw aus ~ und Barmherzigkeit tun** to do sth out of the kindness of one's heart; **ohne ~** without mercy; **~!** mercy!; **bei jdm in (hohen) ~n stehen** *(old)* to stand high in sb's favo(u)r; **von jds ~n** by the grace of sb; **Fürst von Gottes ~n** *(Hist)* by the Grace of God, Prince; **jdn in ~n entlassen** to allow sb to go unpunished; **jdn in ~n wieder aufnehmen** to restore sb to favo(u)r; **sich** *(dat)* **eine ~ erbitten** *(geh)* to ask *or* crave *(liter)* a favo(u)r; **jdm eine ~ gewähren** *(geh)* to grant sb a favo(u)r; **Euer ~n!** *(Hist)* Your Grace; **die Jungfrau der ~n** *(Eccl)* Our Lady of Mercy; **die ~ haben, etw zu tun** *(iro)* to graciously consent to do sth

gna|den ['gna:dn] VI **(dann) gnade dir Gott!** (then) God help you, (then) heaven have mercy on you

Gna|den-: **Gna|den|akt** M act of mercy; **Gna|den|bild** NT *(Eccl)* picture *or (= Figur)* statue with miraculous powers; **Gna|den|brot** NT, *no pl* **jdm das ~ geben** to keep sb in his/her old age; **einem Pferd das ~ geben** to put a horse out to grass; **das ~ bei jdm essen** to be provided for by sb (in one's old age); **Gna|den|er|lass** M *(Jur)* general pardon; **Gna|den|frist** F (temporary) reprieve; **eine ~ von 24 Stunden** a 24 hour(s') reprieve, 24 hours' grace; **Gna|den|ge|such** NT plea for clemency; **Gna|den|kraut** NT hedge hyssop; **gna|den|los** ADJ merciless ADV mercilessly; **Gna|den|lo|sig|keit** F **-**, *no pl* mercilessness; **Gna|den|mit|tel** PL *(Eccl)* means *pl* of grace; **gna|den|reich** ADJ *(old, Eccl)* gracious; **Maria, die Gnadenreiche** Our Gracious Lady; **Gna|den|schuss** M coup de grâce *(by shooting)*; **Gna|den|stoß** M coup de grâce *(with sword etc) (auch fig)*; **Gna|den|tod** M *(geh)* mercy killing, euthanasia; **Gna|den|ver|hei|ßung** F promise of grace; **gna|den|voll** ADJ *(old, Eccl)* gracious; **Gna|den|weg** M, *no pl* **auf dem ~** by a pardon; **jedem Häftling steht der ~ offen** every prisoner is at liberty to ask for a pardon

gnä|dig ['gnɛ:dɪç] ADJ *(= barmherzig)* merciful; *(= gunstvoll, herablassend)* gracious; *Strafe* lenient; *(= freundlich)* kind; **das ~e Fräulein** *(form)* the young lady; **die ~e Frau** *(form)* the mistress, madam; **der ~e Herr** *(old)* the master; **darf ich das ~e Fräulein zum Tanz bitten?** *(dated)* may I have the pleasure of this dance? *(form)*; **~es Fräulein** *(dated)* madam; *(= jüngere Dame)* miss; **~e Frau** *(form)* madam, ma'am; **~er Herr** *(old)* sir; **meine Gnädige** *(dated) or* **Gnädigste** *(dated)* my dear madam; **~er Gott!** *(inf)* merciful heavens! *(inf)*; **Gott sei uns ~!** *(geh)* (may the good) Lord preserve us; **sei doch so ~ und mach mal Platz!** *(iro)* would you be so good as to make some room?
ADV *(= milde) urteilen* leniently; *zensieren* generously; *(= herablassend) lächeln, nicken* graciously; **~ davonkommen** to get off lightly; **es ~ machen**

to be lenient, to show leniency; **machen wirs ~ mit dem Hausputz** let's take it easy with the cleaning

gnat|zig ['gnatsıç] ADJ *(dial)* bearish *(inf)*, bad-tempered

Gnat|zig|keit F -, *no pl (dial)* bearishness *(inf)*, bad temper

Gneis [gnais] M **-es, -e** [-zə] *(Geol)* gneiss

Gnom [gno:m] M **-en, -en** gnome

gno|men|haft ADJ gnomish

Gno|sis ['gno:zıs] F -, *no pl (Rel)* gnosis

Gnos|tik ['gnɔstık] F -, *no pl (Rel)* gnosticism

Gnos|ti|ker ['gnɔstikɐ] M **-s, -**, **Gnos|ti|ke|rin** [-ərın] F **-, -nen** *(Rel)* gnostic

gnos|tisch ['gnɔstıʃ] ADJ *(Rel)* gnostic

Gnos|ti|zis|mus [gnɔsti'tsısmʊs] M -, *no pl (Rel)* Gnosticism

Gnu [gnu:] NT **-s, -s** *(Zool)* gnu, wildebeest

Go [go:] NT -, *no pl* go *(Japanese board game)*

Goal [go:l] NT **-s, -s** *(Aus, Sw: Sport)* goal

Goal- *(Aus, Sw)*: **Goal|get|ter** [-gɛtɐ] M **-s, -**, **Goal|get|te|rin** [-ərın] F **-, -nen** (prolific) striker; **Goal|kee|per** [-ki:pɐ] M **-s, -**, **Goal|kee|pe|rin** [-ərın] F **-, -nen**, **Goal|mann** M *pl* **-männer** goalkeeper, goalie *(inf)*; **Goal|stan|ge** F crossbar

Go|be|lin [gobə'lɛ̃:] M **-s, -s** tapestry, Gobelin; *(= Webart)* tapestry weave

Go|ckel ['gɔkl] M **-s, -** *(esp S Ger baby-talk)* cock; *(fig)* old goat *(inf)*

Gode|mi|ché [go:dmi'ʃe:] M **-, -s** dildo

Go|derl ['go:dɐl] NT **-s, -n jdm das ~ kratzen** *(Aus inf)* to butter sb up *(inf)*

Goe|the ['gø:tə] M **-s** Goethe

goe|thesch ['gø:təʃ], **goe|thisch** ['gø:tıʃ] ADJ Goethean

Go-go-Girl ['go:go-] NT go-go dancer *or* girl

Goi ['go:i] M **-(s), Gojim** ['go:ji:m, go'ji:m] goy, Gentile

Go-in [go:'ın] NT **-(s), -s die Versammlung wurde durch ein ~ gestört** the meeting was disrupted (by demonstrators); **ein ~ veranstalten** to disrupt a/the meeting

Go|kart ['go:ka:ɐt] M **-(s), -s** kart, go-cart

Go|lan [go'la:n] M **-s der ~** the Golan

Go|lan|hö|hen PL, **Go|lan-Hö|hen** PL Golan Heights *pl*

Gold [gɔlt] NT **-(e)s** [-dəs], *no pl (abbr* **Au**) *(lit, fig)* gold; **nicht mit ~ zu bezahlen** *or* **aufzuwiegen sein** to be worth one's weight in gold; **nicht für alles ~ der Welt** *(liter)* not for all the money in the world; **er hat ein Herz aus ~** he has a heart of gold; **er hat ~ in der Kehle** he has a golden voice; **zehnmal olympisches ~ holen** to win ten golds in the Olympics; **es ist nicht alles ~, was glänzt** *(Prov)* all that glitters *or* glisters is not gold *(Prov)* → **Morgenstunde, treu ADJ**

Gold- *in cpds* gold; *(von Farbe, Zool)* golden; **Gold|ader** F vein of gold; **Gold|am|mer** F yellowhammer; **Gold|am|sel** F golden oriole; **Gold|ar|beit** F goldwork; **Gold|bar|ren** M gold ingot; **Gold|barsch** M *(= Rotbarsch)* redfish; *(= Kaulbarsch)* ruff; **Gold|ba|sis** F gold basis; **eine Währung auf ~** a gold-based currency; **gold|be|stickt** [-bəʃtıkt] ADJ embroidered with gold (thread); **gold|be|tresst** [-bətrɛst] ADJ trimmed with gold braid; **Gold|blech** NT gold foil; **gold|blond** ADJ golden blond; **Gold|bor|te** F gold edging *no pl*; **Gold|broi|ler** M *(dial Cook)* roast chicken; **Gold|de|ckung** F *(Fin)* gold backing; **Gold|doub|lé** NT, **Gold|dub|lee** NT gold-plated metal; **Gold|druck** M **a** *pl* **-drucke** gold print **b** *no pl (= Schrift)* gold lettering; **gold|durch|wirkt** [-dʊrçvırkt] ADJ shot with gold thread

gol|den ['gɔldn] ADJ *attr (lit, fig)* golden; *(= aus Gold)* gold, golden *(liter)*; **Goldene Schallplatte** gold disc; **~er Humor** irrepressible sense of humour *(Brit) or* humor *(US)*; **~e Worte** wise words, words of wisdom; **ein ~es Herz haben** to have a heart of gold; **~e Berge versprechen** to promise the moon (and the stars); **die ~e Mitte** *or* **den ~en Mittelweg wählen** to strike a happy medium; **sich** *(dat)* **eine ~e Nase verdienen** to make a mint; **~e Hochzeit** golden wedding (anniversary); **Goldener Schnitt** *(Math, Art)* golden section; **das Goldene Buch** the visitors' book; **die Goldene Stadt** *(geh)* Prague; **das Goldene Horn** *(Geog)* the Golden Horn; **die Goldene Horde** *(Hist)* the Golden Horde; **das Goldene Zeitalter** *(Myth, fig)* the golden age; **das Goldene Vlies** *(Myth)* the Golden Fleece; **das Goldene Kalb** *(Bibl)* the golden calf; **der Tanz ums Goldene Kalb** *(fig)* the worship of Mammon *(fig)* → **Brücke**

ADV like gold; **~ schimmern** to shimmer like gold

Gold-: **Gold|esel** M *(Liter)* gold-ass; **leider habe ich keinen ~** *(fig)* money doesn't grow on trees, I'm afraid; **Gold|fa|den** M gold thread; **gold|far|ben** [-farbn], **gold|far|big** ADJ golden, gold-coloured *(Brit)*, gold-colored *(US)*; **Gold|fe|der** F gold nib; **Gold|fie|ber** NT *(fig)* gold fever; **Gold|fisch** M goldfish; **sich** *(dat)* **einen ~ angeln** *(hum inf)* to make a rich catch, to marry money; **Gold|fuchs** M **a** *(= Pferd)* golden chestnut (horse) **b** *(old inf)* gold piece; **Gold|fül|lung** F *(Med)* gold filling; **gold|ge|fasst** ADJ *Brille* gold-rimmed; *Edelstein* set in gold; **gold|gelb** ADJ golden brown, old gold; **gold|ge|lockt** ADJ *(dated)* with golden locks; **gold|ge|rän|dert** [-gərɛndɐt] ADJ edged with gold; *Brille* gold-rimmed; **~e Bilanzen** highly profitable results; **Gold|ge|wicht** NT gold weight, ≈ troy weight; **Gold|glanz** M *(liter)* golden gleam; **gold|glän|zend** ADJ *(liter)* gleaming gold; **Gold|grä|ber** [-grɛ:bɐ] M **-s, -**, **Gold|grä|be|rin** [-ərın] F **-, -nen** gold-digger; **Gold|grä|ber|stim|mung** F gold-rush mood; **Gold|gru|be** F *(lit, fig)* gold mine; **Gold|grund** M, *no pl (Art)* gold ground; **gold|hal|tig**, *(Aus)* **gold|häl|tig** ADJ gold-bearing, auriferous *(spec)*; **Gold|hams|ter** M (golden) hamster

gol|dig ['gɔldıç] ADJ **a** *(fig inf: = allerliebst)* sweet, cute; **du bist vielleicht ~!** *(iro)* the ideas you get! **b** *(poet: = golden)* golden; **~e Zeiten** golden days

Gold-: **Gold|jun|ge** M *(inf)* blue-eyed boy *(Brit inf)*, golden boy *(inf)*; *(Sport)* gold medallist *(Brit) or* medalist *(US)*; **Gold|kä|fer** M *(inf: = reiches Mädchen)* rich girl; **Gold|kehl|chen** [-ke:lçən] NT **-s, -** *(inf)* singer with a/the golden voice; **Gold|kind** NT *(inf)* little treasure *(inf)*, dear child; **mein ~** *(als Anrede)* (my) pet *or* precious; **Gold|klum|pen** M gold nugget; **Gold|küs|te** F *(Geog)* Gold Coast; **Gold|lack** M **a** *(Bot)* wallflower **b** *(= Glanzlack)* gold lacquer; **Gold|mäd|chen** NT *(inf)* blue-eyed girl *(Brit inf)*, golden girl *(inf)*; *(Sport)* gold medallist *(Brit) or* medalist *(US)*; **Gold|mark** F *pl* **-mark** *(Hist)* gold mark

Gold|me|dail|le F gold medal

Gold|me|dail|len|ge|win|ner(in) M(F) gold medallist *(Brit) or* medalist *(US)*

Gold-: **Gold|mi|ne** F gold mine; **Gold|mund|stück** NT gold tip; **Gold|mün|ze** F gold coin; **Gold|pa|pier** NT gold foil; **Gold|pa|ri|tät** F *(Fin)* gold parity; **Gold|preis** M gold price, price of gold; **Gold|pro|be** F assay (for gold); **Gold|rah|men** M gilt frame; **Gold|rand** M gold edge; **mit ~** with a gold edge; **Gold|rausch** M gold fever; **Gold|re|gen** M *(Bot)* laburnum; *(= Feuerwerkskörper)* Roman candle; *(fig)* riches *pl*; **gold|reich** ADJ rich in gold; **Gold|reif** M *(geh)* circlet of gold; *(= Ring)* gold ring; *(= Armband)* gold bracelet; **Gold|re|ser|ve** F *(Fin)* gold reserves *pl*; **gold|rich|tig** *(inf)* ADJ absolutely *or* dead *(inf)* right; *Mensch* all right *(inf)* ADV exactly right; *sich verhalten, machen, tun* perfectly; **du liegst (damit) ~** you're absolutely *or* dead *(inf)* right (there); **sie hat ~ gehandelt** what she did was absolutely right; **Gold|schatz** M golden treasure; *(von Geld)* hoard of gold; *(Kosewort)* treasure

Gold|schmied(in) M(F) goldsmith

Gold|schmie|de-: **Gold|schmie|de|ar|beit** F *(= Handwerk)* gold work; *(= Gegenstand)* worked gold article; **Gold|schmie|de|hand|werk** NT, **Gold|schmie|de|kunst** F gold work

Gold-: **Gold|schmuck** M gold jewellery *(Brit) or* jewelry *(US)*; **Gold|schnitt** M, *no pl* gilt edging; **Gold|schnitt|aus|ga|be** F gilt-edged edition; **Gold|schrift** F gold lettering; **Gold|stück** NT piece of gold; *(= Münze)* gold coin *or* piece, piece of gold *(old)*; *(fig inf)* jewel, treasure; **Gold|su|che** F search for gold; **Gold|su|cher(in)** M(F) gold-hunter; **Gold|ton** M *pl* **-töne** golden colour *(Brit) or* color *(US)*; **Gold|to|pas** M yellow topaz; **Gold|tres|se** F gold braid; **Gold|über|zug** M layer of gold plate; **Gold|uhr** F gold watch; **gold|um|rän|dert, gold|um|ran|det** [-ʊmrandət] ADJ = **goldgerändert**; **Gold|vor|kom|men** NT gold deposit; **Gold|vor|rat** M *(Fin)* gold reserves *pl*; **Gold|waa|ge** F gold *or* bullion balance; **jedes Wort** *or* **alles auf die ~ legen** *(= sich vorsichtig ausdrücken)* to weigh one's words; *(= überempfindlich sein)* to be hypersensitive; **Gold|wäh|rung** F gold standard; **eine ~** a currency on the gold standard; **Gold|wa|ren** PL gold articles *pl*; **Gold|wä|scher(in)** M(F) gold panner; **Gold|wert** M, *no pl* value in gold; *(= Wert des Goldes)* value of gold; **Gold|zahn** M gold tooth

Go|lem ['go:lɛm] M **-s**, *no pl* golem

Golf [gɔlf] M **-(e)s, -e** *(= Meerbusen)* gulf; **der ~ von Biskaya** the Bay of Biscay; **der (Persische) ~** the (Persian) Gulf

Golf NT **-s**, *no pl (Sport)* golf

Golf- *in cpds (Sport)* golf; *(Geog, Pol)* Gulf

Golf|ball M golf ball

Gol|fer ['gɔlfɐ] M **-s, -**, **Gol|fe|rin** [-ərın] F **-, -nen** *(inf)* golfer

Golf-: **Golf|klub** M golf club; **Golf|krieg** M Gulf War; **Golf|platz** M golf course; **Golf|pro|fi** M *(inf)* golf pro; *(inf)*; **Golf|rat** M *(Pol)* Gulf Council; **Golf|schlä|ger** M golf club; **Golf|spiel** NT **das ~** golf; **Golf|spie|ler(in)** M(F) golfer; **Golf|staa|ten** PL **die ~** the Gulf States *pl*; **Golf|strom** M, *no pl (Geog)* Gulf Stream; **Golf|ta|sche** F golf bag, caddie; **Golf|wa|gen** M *(Golf)* caddie cart

Gol|ga|tha ['gɔlgata] NT **-s** *(Bibl)* Golgotha

Go|li|ath ['go:liat] M **-s, -s** *(Bibl, fig)* Goliath

Go|na|de [go'na:də] F **-, -n** *(Biol)* gonad

Gon|del ['gɔndl] F **-, -n** gondola; *(von Sessellift etc auch)* (cable) car

Gon|del-: **Gon|del|bahn** F cable railway; **Gon|del|fahrt** F trip in a gondola; **Gon|del|füh|rer(in)** M(F) gondolier

gon|deln ['gɔndln] VI *aux sein (inf) (= reisen)* to travel (a)round; *(= herumfahren)* to drive (a)round; **nach Schönefeld und zurück ~** to travel to Schönefeld and back; **durch die Welt ~** to go globetrotting *(inf)*

Gon|do|li|e|re [gɔndo'lie:rə] M **-, Gondolieri** [-ri] gondolier

Gong [gɔŋ] M **-s, -s** gong; *(bei Boxkampf etc)* bell; **der ~ zur dritten Runde** the bell for the third round

gon|gen ['gɔŋən] VI *impers* **es hat gegongt** the gong has gone *or* sounded; **es gongte zum Essen** the gong went *or* sounded for dinner *etc* VI to ring *or* sound a/the gong

Gong|schlag M stroke of the gong

gön|nen ['gœnən] VT **jdm etw ~** not to (be)grudge sb sth; *(= zuteilwerden lassen)* to grant *or* allow sb sth; **jdm etw nicht ~** to (be)grudge sb sth; not to grant *or* allow sb sth; **sich** *(dat)* **etw ~** to allow oneself sth; **jdm ~, dass ...** not to (be)grudge sb the fact that ...; **er gönnte mir keinen Blick** he didn't spare me a single glance; **er gönnt ihr nicht die Luft zum Atmen** he (be)grudges her the very air she breathes; **ich gönne ihm diesen Erfolg/seine Frau von ganzem Herzen** I'm delighted for him that he's had this success/that he has such a nice wife; **das sei ihm gegönnt** I don't (be)grudge him that; **man gönnt sich ja sonst nichts** *(hum inf)* you've got to spoil yourself sometimes

Gön|ner ['gœnɐ] M **-s, -, Gön|ne|rin** [-ərɪn] F **-, -nen** patron; *(Frau auch)* patroness

Gön|ner-: **gön|ner|haft** *(pej)* ADJ patronizing ADV patronizingly; **~ tun, sich ~ geben** to play the big benefactor; **Gön|ner|haf|tig|keit** ['gœnɐhaftɪçkait] F **-,** *no pl (pej)* patronizing; **Gön|ner|mie|ne** F *(pej)* patronizing air; **Gön|ner|schaft** ['gœnɐʃaft] F **-,** *no pl (= Förderung)* patronage

Go|no|kok|kus [gono'kɔkʊs] M **-, Gonokokken** [-'kɔkn] *(Med)* gonococcus

Go|nor|rhö [gonɔ'røː] F **-, -en** [-'røːən], **Go|nor|rhöe** [gonɔ'røː] F **-, -n** [-'røːən] *(Med)* gonorrhoea *(Brit)*, gonorrhea *(US)*; **er hat die ~** he has gonorrh(o)ea

Good|will ['gʊdwɪl] M **-s,** *no pl (auch Econ)* goodwill, good will

Good|will-: **Good|will|be|such** ['gʊdwɪl-] M goodwill visit; **Good|will|rei|se** ['gʊdwɪl-] F, **Good|will|tour** ['gʊdwɪl-] F goodwill journey *or* trip

Go|pher ['goːfɐ] NT **-(s),** *no pl (Comp, Internet)* gopher, Gopher

gor *pret von* **gären**

Gör [gøːɐ] NT **-(e)s, -en** *(inf)* **a** *(= kleines Kind)* brat *(pej inf)*, kid *(inf)* **b** *(= Mädchen)* (cheeky *(Brit) or* fresh *(US) or* saucy) little miss

gor|disch ['gɔrdɪʃ] ADJ **der Gordische Knoten** *(Myth)* the Gordian knot; **ein ~er Knoten** *(fig)* a Gordian knot

Gö|re ['gøːrə] F **-, -n a** *(= kleines Mädchen)* (cheeky *(Brit) or* fresh *(US)*) little miss **b** *(= kleines Kind)* brat *(pej inf)*, kid *(inf)*

Gore|tex® ['goːrə'tɛks] NT **-,** *no pl* Gore-Tex®

Gor|gon|zo|la [gɔrgɔn'tsoːla] M **-s, -s** gorgonzola (cheese)

Go|ril|la [go'rɪla] M **-s, -s** gorilla; *(inf: = Leibwächter)* heavy *(Brit inf)*, goon *(US inf)*; *(sl: = Türsteher)* bouncer *(inf)*

Go|sche ['gɔʃə] F **-, -n** *(S Ger inf)* gob *(inf)*, mouth; **eine freche ~ haben** to have the cheek of the devil *(Brit inf)*, to be fresh *(US)*; **halt die ~!** shut your mouth *or* gob *(inf) or* trap *(inf)*

Go|schen ['gɔʃn] F **-, -** *(S Ger, Aus: pej)* = **Gosche**

Gos|pel ['gɔspl] NT OR M **-s, -s, Gos|pel|song** M gospel song

goss *pret von* **gießen**

Gos|se ['gɔsə] F **-, -n a** *(= Rinnstein)* gutter **b** *(fig)* gutter; *(rare: = Abfluss, Gully)* drain; **in der ~ enden** *or* **landen** to end up in the gutter; **jdn aus der ~ holen** *or* **ziehen** to take sb from the gutter, to pull sb out of the gutter; **jdn** *or* **jds Namen durch die ~ ziehen** *or* **schleifen** to drag sb's name through the mud

Gos|sen-: **Gos|sen|aus|druck** M *pl* **-ausdrücke** vulgarity; **Gos|sen|jar|gon** M, **Gos|sen|spra|che** F gutter language, language of the gutter

Go|te ['goːtə] M **-n, -n, Go|tin** ['goːtɪn] F **-, -nen** Goth

Gö|te|borg ['gøːtəbɔrk] NT **-s** Gothenburg

Go|tha ['goːta] M **-s, -s** *directory of the German nobility,* ≈ Debrett's (Peerage) *(Brit)*

Go|tik ['goːtɪk] F **-,** *no pl (Art)* Gothic (style); *(= gotische Epoche)* Gothic period; **ein Meisterwerk der ~** a masterpiece of Gothic architecture *etc*; **typisch für die ~** typical of Gothic

Go|tin ['goːtɪn] F **-, -nen** Goth

go|tisch ['goːtɪʃ] ADJ Gothic; **~e Schrift** *(Typ)* Gothic (script)

Gott [gɔt] M **-es, =er** ['gœtɐ] **a** god; *(als Name)* God; **~ der Herr** the Lord God; **~ (der) Vater** God the Father; **~ der Allmächtige** Almighty God, God (the) Almighty; **der liebe ~** the good *or* dear Lord; **an ~ glauben** to believe in God; **zu ~ beten** *or* **flehen** *(liter)* to pray to God; **er ist ihr ~** she worships him like a god; **bei ~ schwören** to swear by Almighty God **b in ~ entschlafen** *(liter)* to pass away *or* on; **dein Schicksal liegt in ~es Hand** you are *or* your fate is in God's hands; **dich hat ~ im Zorn erschaffen!** God left something out when he put you together! *(hum)*; **dem lieben ~ den Tag stehlen** to laze the day(s) away; **den lieben ~ einen guten** *or* **frommen Mann sein lassen** *(inf)* to take things as they come; **er ist wohl (ganz und gar) von ~** *or* **von den Göttern verlassen** *(inf)* he's (quite) taken leave of his senses; **~ ist mein Zeuge** *(liter)* as God is my witness; **wie ~ ihn geschaffen hat** *(hum inf)* as naked as the day (that) he was born; **ein Anblick** *or* **Bild für die Götter** *(hum inf)* a sight for sore eyes; **das wissen die Götter** *(inf)* heaven *or* God (only) knows; **~ weiß** *(inf)* heaven knows *(inf)*, God knows *(inf)*; **er hat ~ weiß was erzählt** *(inf)* he said God knows what *(inf)*; **ich bin weiß ~ nicht prüde, aber ...** heaven *or* God knows I'm no prude but ...; **so ~ will** *(geh)* God willing, DV *(esp Brit)*; **vor ~ und der Welt** before the whole world; **~ und die Welt** *(fig)* everybody; **über ~ und die Welt reden** *(fig)* to talk about everything under the sun, to talk about anything and everything; **im Namen ~es** in the name of God; **dann mach es eben in ~es Namen** just do it then; **warum in ~es Namen ...?** why in God's name ...?; **leider ~es** unfortunately, alas; **was ~ tut, das ist wohlgetan** God does all things well; **~es Mühlen mahlen langsam** *(hum)* the mills of God grind slowly (but they grind exceeding fine); **ein Leben wie ~ in Frankreich führen, wie ~ in Frankreich leben** *(inf)* to be in clover *(esp Brit)*, to be in the lap of luxury, to live the life of Riley *(Brit inf)*; **was ~ zusammengefügt hat, soll der Mensch nicht scheiden** what God has joined together let no man put asunder

c *(in Ausrufen)* **grüß ~!** *(esp S Ger, Aus)* hello, good morning/afternoon/evening; **~ zum Gruß!** *(old)* God be with you *(old)*; **~ sei mit dir!** *(old)* God be with you *(old)*; **~ mit dir!** *(old)* God bless you; **vergelts ~!** *(dated)* God bless you, may you be rewarded; **wollte** *or* **gebe ~, dass ...** *(old)* (may) God grant that ...; **~ soll mich strafen, wenn ...** *(old)* may God strike me dumb if ...; **~ steh mir bei!** God help me!; **~ hab ihn selig!** God have mercy on his soul; **in ~es Namen!** for heaven's *or* goodness sake!; **ach (du lieber) ~!** *(inf)* oh Lord! *(inf)*, oh heavens! *(inf)*; **mein ~!, ach ~!** (my) God!; *(als Leerformel in Antworten)* (oh) well, (oh) you know; **großer ~!** good Lord *or* God!; **~ im Himmel!** *(dated)* heavens above!; **bei ~!** by God!; **~ behüte** *or* **bewahre!, da sei ~ vor!** God *or* Heaven forbid!; **um ~es willen!** for heaven's *or* God's sake!; **~ sei Dank!** thank God!

Gott-: **gott|ähn|lich** ADJ godlike ADV *verehren* as a god; **gott|be|gna|det** [-bəgnaːdət] ADJ divinely gifted; **gott|be|hü|te** [gɔtbə'hyːtə] *(esp Aus)*, **gott|be|wah|re** [gɔtbə'vaːrə] ADV heaven *or* God forbid

Gott|chen ['gɔtçən] NT **(ach) ~!** *(inf)* gosh! *(inf)*, golly! *(inf)*

Gott|er|bar|men NT **zum ~** *(inf)* pitiful(ly), pathetic(ally) *(inf)*

Göt|ter-: **Göt|ter|bild** NT idol; **Göt|ter|bo|te** M *(Myth)* messenger of the gods; **Göt|ter|däm|me|rung** F götterdämmerung, twilight of the gods; **Göt|ter|epos** NT epic of the gods; **Göt|ter|gat|te** M *(dated hum)* lord and master *(hum)*, better half *(inf)*

Gott-: **gott|er|ge|ben** ADJ *(= demütig)* meek; *(= fromm)* pious ADV meekly; **Gott|er|ge|ben|heit** F meekness

Göt|ter-: **Göt|ter|ge|stalt** F god; **göt|ter|gleich** ADJ godlike; **Göt|ter|sa|ge** F myth about the gods/a god; *(als Literaturform)* mythology of the gods; **Göt|ter|spei|se** F *(Myth)* food of the gods; *(Cook)* jelly *(Brit)*, Jell-O® *(US)*; **Göt|ter|trank** M *(Myth)* drink of the gods; **Göt|ter|va|ter** M *(Myth)* father of the gods; **Göt|ter|welt** F *(Myth)* realm of the gods; *(= alle Götter zusammen)* the gods *pl*

Got|tes-: **Got|tes|acker** M *(old)* God's acre; **Got|tes|an|be|te|rin** F *(Zool)* praying mantis; **Got|tes|be|griff** M conception of God; **Got|tes|be|weis** M proof of the existence of God; **der ontologische** *etc* **~** the ontological *etc* argument

Got|tes|dienst M **a** *(= Gottesverehrung)* worship **b** *(Eccl)* service; **zum ~ gehen** to go to church; **dem ~ beiwohnen** *(form)* to attend church

Got|tes|dienst|be|such M church attendance

Got|tes-: **Got|tes|frau** F *(old, iro)* woman of God; **Got|tes|frie|de** M *(Hist)* *(= Pax Dei)* Peace of God; *(= Treuga Dei)* Truce of God; **Got|tes|furcht** F *(geh)* fear of God; **jdn zur ~ erziehen** to teach sb to fear God; **got|tes|fürch|tig** [-fʏrçtɪç] ADJ God-fearing; **Got|tes|ga|be** F gift of *or* from God; **Got|tes|ge|richt** NT **a** punishment of God **b** *(Hist: = Gottesurteil)* trial by ordeal; **Got|tes|ge|schenk** NT gift of *or* from God; **Got|tes|gna|den|tum** NT, *no pl (Hist)* doctrine of divine right; **Got|tes|haus** NT place of worship; **Got|tes|lamm** NT *(Rel)* Lamb of God; **Got|tes|läs|te|rer** M, **Got|tes|läs|te|rin** F blasphemer; **got|tes|läs|ter|lich** ADJ blasphemous ADV blasphemously; **Got|tes|läs|te|rung** F blasphemy; **Got|tes|leug|ner** [-lɔygnɐ] M **-s, -, Got|tes|leug|ne|rin** [-ərɪn] F **-, -nen** *(dated)* unbeliever; **Got|tes|lohn** M, *no pl (old)* reward from God; **etw für einen ~ tun** to do sth for love; **Got|tes|mann** M *pl* **-männer** *(old, iro)* man of God; **Got|tes|mut|ter** F, *no pl (Rel)* Mother of God; **Maria, die ~** Mary (the) Mother of God; **Got|tes|sohn** M *(Rel)* Son of God; **Got|tes|staat** M theocracy; **Augustins „Gottesstaat"** Augustine's "City of God"; **Got|tes|ur|teil** NT *(Hist)* trial by ordeal

Gott-: **gott|froh** ADJ *(esp Sw)* = **heilfroh**; **gott|ge|fäl|lig** *(old)* ADJ godly, pleasing in the sight of God *(form)* ADV **~ leben** to live in a manner pleasing in the sight of God; **gott|ge|ge|ben** ADJ god-given; **etw als ~ hinnehmen** to take *or* accept sth as god-given; **gott|ge|sandt** [-gəzant] ADJ *(old, liter)* sent from God; **gott|ge|weiht** [-gəvait] ADJ *(liter)* dedicated to God; **gott|ge|wollt** ADJ willed by God; **gott|gläu|big** ADJ religious; *(NS)* non-denominational

Gott|hard|chi|ne|se ['gɔthart-] M *(Sw pej)* Eyetie *(Brit pej sl)*, Italian

Gott|heit ['gɔthait] F **-, -en a** *no pl (= Göttlichkeit)* divinity, godhood, godship; **die ~** *(= Gott)* the Godhead **b** *(= esp heidnische Göttergestalt)* deity; **jdn wie eine ~ verehren** to worship sb like a god

Göt|tin ['gœtɪn] F **-, -nen** goddess

Gott|kö|nig M god-king

gött|lich ['gœtlɪç] ADJ *(lit, fig)* divine; **du bist ja ~!** *(dated)* you (really) are a one *(dated Brit inf)*, you're a little dickens *(dated US inf)*; **das Göttliche im Menschen** the divine in Man ADV **wir haben uns ~ amüsiert** *(= lustig gemacht)* we were terribly amused; *(= gut unterhalten)* we had a wonderful time

Gött|lich|keit F **-,** *no pl* divinity

Gott-: **gott|lob** [gɔt'loːp] INTERJ thank God *or* heavens *or* goodness; **er ist ~ wieder gesund** he has recovered now, thank God *or* heavens *or* goodness; **gott|los** ADJ godless; *(= verwerflich)* ungodly; **Gott|lo|sig|keit** F **-,** *no pl* godlessness; **Gott|sei|bei|uns** [gɔtzai'bailʊns, gɔt'zai-] M **-,** *no pl (euph)* **der ~** the Evil One, the Tempter

Gotts-: **gotts|er|bärm|lich** *(inf)* ADJ dreadful, godawful *(inf)* ADV dreadfully; **Gotts|öbers|te(r)** ['gɔtsløːbɐstə] M *decl as adj (Aus iro)* his lordship *(iro)*, my noble lord *(iro)*; **die ~n** the noble lords

Gott-: **Gott|su|cher(in)** M(F) seeker after God; **Gott|va|ter** M, *no pl* God the Father; **gott|ver|dam|mich** [gɔtfɛɐ'damɪç] INTERJ *(inf)*

bloody hell (*Brit inf*), God Almighty (*inf*); **gott|ver|dammt**, **gott|ver|flucht** ADJ *attr* (*inf*) goddamn(ed) (*inf*), damn(ed) (*inf*), bloody (*Brit inf*); **gott|ver|ges|sen** ADJ **a** godless **b** = **gottverlassen**; **gott|ver|las|sen** ADJ god-forsaken ADV ~ **allein** utterly alone; **Gott|ver|trau|en** NT trust *or* faith in God; **dein ~ möchte ich haben!** I wish I had your faith; **gott|voll** ADJ (*fig inf*) divine; **du bist ja ~!** you're a right one! (*dated Brit inf*), you're a little dickens (*dated US inf*); **Gott|we|sen** NT (*liter*) god(head)

Göt|ze ['gœtsə] M **-n, -n** (*lit, fig*) idol

Göt|zen-: **Göt|zen|an|be|ter(in)** M(F) idolater; (*fig*) worshipper; **Göt|zen|bild** NT idol, graven image (*Bibl*); **Göt|zen|die|ner(in)** M(F) idolater/idolatress; (*fig*) worshipper; **Göt|zen|dienst** M, **Göt|zen|glau|be** M, **Göt|zen|ver|eh|rung** F idolatry

Götz von Ber|li|chin|gen [gœts fɔn 'bɛrlɪçɪŋən] M (*euph*) **er beschimpfte ihn mit ~** he used a few four-letter words to (*Brit*) *or* with (*US*) him

Götz|zi|tat NT **das ~** ≈ the V-sign (*Brit*), ≈ the finger (*US*)

Gou|ache [gu'a(:)ʃ] F **-, -n** (*Art*) gouache

Gour|mand [gʊr'mã:] M **-s, -s** glutton, gourmand

Gour|met [gʊr'mɛ, -'me:] M **-s, -s** gourmet

gou|tie|ren [gu'ti:rən] *ptp* **goutiert** VT **a** (*fig*) (*= Gefallen finden an*) to appreciate; (*= gutheißen*) to approve (of) **b** (*rare*: *= kosten, genießen*) to taste, to partake of (*liter*)

Gou|ver|nan|te [guvɛr'nantə] F **-, -n** governess; (*pej*) schoolmarm

gou|ver|nan|ten|haft ADJ schoolmarmish

Gou|ver|ne|ment [guvɛrnə'mã:] NT **-s, -s** **a** (*Hist*) (*= Regierung*) government; (*= Verwaltung*) administration **b** province

Gou|ver|neur [guvɛr'nø:ɐ] M **-s, -e**, **Gou|ver|neu|rin** [-'nø:rɪn] F **-, -nen** governor

Grab [gra:p] NT **-(e)s, =er** ['grɛ:bɐ] grave; (*= Gruft*) tomb, sepulchre (*Brit*), sepulcher (*US*); (*fig*: *= Untergang*) end, ruination; **das Heilige ~** the Holy Sepulchre (*Brit*) *or* Sepulcher (*US*); **jdn zu ~e tragen** to bear sb to his grave; **ins ~ sinken** (*old liter*) to be laid in the earth (*liter*); **ein frühes ~ finden** (*geh*) to go to an early grave; **ein ~ in fremder Erde finden** (*geh*) to be buried in foreign soil; **ein feuchtes** *or* **nasses ~ finden** (*liter*), **sein ~ in den Wellen finden** (*liter*) to go to a watery grave, to meet a watery end; **ein Geheimnis mit ins ~ nehmen** to take a secret with one to the grave; **treu bis ans ~** faithful to the end, faithful unto death (*liter*); **(bis) über das ~ hinaus** in death, beyond the grave; **verschwiegen wie ein** *or* **das ~** (as) silent as the grave; **er würde sich im ~e umdrehen, wenn ...** he would turn in his grave if ...; **du bringst mich noch ins ~** *or* **an den Rand des ~es!** you'll be the death of me yet (*inf*), you'll send me to an early grave; **mit einem Bein** *or* **Fuß im ~e stehen** (*fig*) to have one foot in the grave; **sich** (*dat*) **selbst sein** *or* **sich** (*dat*) **sein eigenes ~ graben** *or* **schaufeln** (*fig*) to dig one's own grave; **seine Hoffnungen** *etc* **zu ~e tragen** (*geh*) to abandon *or* bury one's hopes *etc* → *auch* **Grabmal**

Grab|bei|ga|be F (*Archeol*) burial object

Grab|be|lei [grabə'lai] F **-, -en** (*inf*) groping *or* rummaging (around) (*inf*)

grab|beln ['grabln] VI (*inf*) to grope about (*Brit*) *or* around, to rummage (around)

Grab|bel|tisch M (*inf*) cheap goods table *or* counter

Gräb|chen ['grɛ:pçən] NT **-s, -** *dim von* **Grab**

Grab|denk|mal NT monument

gra|ben ['gra:bn] *pret* **grub** [gru:p], *ptp* **gegraben** [gə'gra:bn] VT (*in Erde etc*) to dig; **seine Zähne/Nägel in etw** (*acc*) **~** to sink one's teeth/nails into sth VI (*auch Archeol*) to dig; **nach Gold/Erz ~** to dig for gold/ore; **in etw** (*dat*) **~** (*fig*: *in Archiven, Quellen, jds Vergangenheit*) to dig around in VR **sich in etw** (*acc*) **~** (*Zähne, Krallen*) to sink into sth; **der Fluss hat sich in den Fels gegraben** the river has eaten its way into the rock; **das hat sich mir tief ins Gedächtnis gegraben** (*geh*) it has imprinted itself firmly on my memory; **sich durch etw ~** to dig one's way through sth → **Grube**

Gra|ben ['gra:bn] M **-s, =** ['grɛ:bn] ditch; (*= trockener Graben, Mil*) trench; (*Sport*) ditch; (*Sport*: *= Wassergraben*) water jump; (*= Burggraben*) moat; (*Geol*) rift (valley), graben (*spec*); **im ~ liegen** (*Mil*) to be in the trenches

Gra|ben-: **Gra|ben|bruch** M (*Geol*) (rift) valley, graben (*spec*); **Gra|ben|kampf** M, **Gra|ben|krieg** M (*Mil*) trench warfare *no pl, no indef art*; **Gra|ben|sen|ke** F (*Geol*) (rift) valley, graben (*spec*)

Grä|ber *pl von* **Grab**

Grä|ber-: **Grä|ber|feld** NT cemetery, burial ground; **Grä|ber|fund** M grave find

Gra|bes- (*liter*): **Gra|bes|dun|kel** NT sepulchral darkness; **Gra|bes|käl|te** F grave-like cold; **Gra|bes|luft** F grave-like air; **Gra|bes|rand** M **am ~** on the very brink of the grave; **Gra|bes|ru|he** F, **Gra|bes|stil|le** F deathly hush *or* silence; **Gra|bes|stim|me** F sepulchral voice

Grab-: **Grab|fund** M grave find; **Grab|ge|läu|te** NT **a** (death) knell **b** = **Grabgesang b**; **Grab|ge|leit** NT (*geh*) **jdm das ~ geben** to accompany *or* follow sb's coffin; **Grab|ge|sang** M **a** funeral hymn, dirge **b** (*fig*) **der ~ einer Sache** (*gen*) **sein** to sound the death knell for sth; **Grab|ge|wöl|be** NT vault; (*von Kirche, Dom*) crypt; **Grab|hü|gel** M mound (*over a grave*); (*Archeol*) barrow, tumulus (*form*); **Grab|in|schrift** F epitaph, inscription (*on gravestone etc*); **Grab|kam|mer** F burial chamber; **Grab|kreuz** NT (cross-shaped) gravestone, cross; **Grab|le|gung** [-le:gʊŋ] F **-, -en** burial, interment

Gräb|lein ['grɛ:plain] NT **-s, -** *dim von* **Grab**

Grab-: **Grab|licht** NT candle (on a grave); **Grab|mal** NT *pl* **-mäler** *or* (*geh*) **-male** monument; (*= Grabstein*) gravestone; **das ~ des Unbekannten Soldaten** the tomb of the Unknown Warrior *or* Soldier; **Grab|ni|sche** F burial niche; **Grab|pfle|ge** F care of the grave(s)/of graves; **Grab|plat|te** F memorial slab; **Grab|re|de** F funeral oration; **Grab|schän|der** [-ʃɛndɐ] M **-s, -**, **Grab|schän|de|rin** [-ərɪn] F **-, -nen** defiler of the grave(s)/of graves; **Grab|schän|dung** F defilement of graves

grab|schen ['grapʃn] VTI = **grapschen**

Grab-: **Grab|schmuck** M plants *pl* (*on a grave*); (*= Kränze*) wreaths *pl* (*on a grave*); **Grab|schrift** F epitaph, inscription (*on gravestone etc*); **Grab|spruch** M epitaph, inscription (*on gravestone etc*); **Grab|stät|te** F grave; (*= Gruft*) tomb, sepulchre (*Brit*), sepulcher (*US*); **Grab|stein** M gravestone, tombstone; **Grab|stel|le** F (burial) plot; **Grab|sti|chel** M (*Art*) burin

gräbt [grɛ:pt] *3. pers sing pres von* **graben**

Gra|bung F **-, -en** (*Archeol*) excavation

Gra|bungs-: **Gra|bungs|ar|bei|ten** PL (*Archeol*) (archaeological (*Brit*) *or* archeological (*US*)) excavations *pl or* dig *sing*; **Gra|bungs|fund** M (*Archeol*) (arch[a]eological) find; **Gra|bungs|stät|te** F (*Archeol*) arch(a)eological site

Grab-: **Grab|ur|ne** F funeral urn; **Grab|werk|zeug** NT (*Zool*) claw

Grac|chen ['graxn] PL **die ~** (*Hist*) the Gracchi

Gracht [graxt] F **-, -en** canal

grad [gra:t] (*inf*) = **gerade**

Grad [gra:t] M **-(e)s, -e** [-də] (*Sci, Univ, fig*) degree; (*Mil*) rank; (*Typ*: *= Schriftgrad*) size; **ein Winkel von 45 ~** an angle of 45 degrees, a 45-degree angle; **unterm 32. ~ nördlicher Breite** latitude 32 degrees north; **4 ~ Kälte** 4 degrees below freezing point *or* zero, 4 degrees below; **4 ~ Wärme** 4 degrees above freezing point *or* zero; **20 ~ Fahrenheit/Celsius** 20 (degrees) Fahrenheit/centigrade *or* Celsius; **um 5 ~ wärmer sein** to be 5 degrees warmer; **null ~** zero; **Wasser auf 80 ~ erhitzen** to heat water to 80 degrees; **es kocht bei 100 ~** boiling occurs at 100 degrees; **in ~e einteilen** to calibrate, to graduate; **ein Verwandter zweiten/dritten ~es** a relative once/twice removed; **Vetter zweiten ~es** second cousin; **Verbrennungen ersten/zweiten ~es** (*Med*) first-/second-degree burns; **in einem** *or* **bis zu einem gewissen ~(e)** up to a certain point, to a certain degree; **in hohem ~(e)** to a great *or* large extent; **im höchsten ~(e)** extremely → **Gleichung**

grad- = **gerade-**

Gra|da|ti|on [grada'tsio:n] F **-, -en** gradation

Grad|bo|gen M (*Surv, Mil*) quadrant

gra|de ['gra:də] (*inf*) = **gerade**

Grad|ein|tei|lung F calibration, graduation

Gra|di|ent [gra'diɛnt] M **-en, -en** (*Sci*) gradient

gra|die|ren [gra'di:rən] *ptp* **gradiert** VT **a** (*= in Grade einteilen*) to calibrate, to graduate **b** (*= abstufen*) to grade

Grad-: **Grad|kreis** M (*Math*) graduated circle; **grad|mä|ßig** ADJ = **graduell ADJ**; **Grad|mes|ser** M **-s, -** (*fig*) gauge (*+gen, für* of); **Grad|netz** NT (*Geog*) latitude and longitude grid; **Grad|ska|la** F scale (of degrees)

gra|du|ell [gra'duɛl] ADJ (*= allmählich*) gradual; (*= gering*) slight ADV (*= geringfügig*) slightly; (*= allmählich*) gradually

gra|du|ie|ren [gradu'i:rən] *ptp* **graduiert** VT **a** (*= in Grade einteilen*) to calibrate, to graduate **b** (*Univ*) to confer a degree upon, to graduate; **graduierter Ingenieur** *engineer with the diploma of a School of Engineering*, engineering graduate VI (*Univ*) to graduate

Gra|du|ier|te(r) [gradu'i:ɐtə] MF *decl as adj* graduate

Gra|du|ie|rung F **-, -en** (*Univ*) graduation

Grad-: **Grad|un|ter|schied** M difference of degree; **grad|wei|se** ADJ, ADV by degrees

Grae|cum ['grɛ:kʊm] NT **-s**, *no pl* (*Univ, Sch*) examination in Greek

Graf [gra:f] M **-en, -en** count; (*als Titel*) Count; (*britischer Graf*) earl; (*als Titel*) Earl; **~ Koks** *or* **Rotz** (*inf*) Lord Muck (*Brit hum inf*), His Highness (*hum inf*)

Graf [gra:f] M **-en, -en** (*Sci*) graph

Graf NT **-s, -e** (*Ling*) graph

Gra|fem [gra'fe:m] NT **-s, -e** (*Ling*) = **Graphem**

Gra|fen-: **Gra|fen|fa|mi|lie** F, **Gra|fen|ge|schlecht** NT → **Graf** family of counts/earls; **Gra|fen|kro|ne** F → **Graf** (count's/earl's) coronet; **Gra|fen|stand** M → **Graf** (*Hist*) (*= Rang*) rank of count; earldom; (*= Gesamtheit der Grafen*) counts *pl*/earls *pl*; **jdn in den ~ erheben** to confer the rank of count/earl upon sb

Graf|fel ['grafl] NT **-s**, *no pl* (*Aus, S Ger inf*) junk

Graf|fi|ti [gra'fi:ti] NT **-s, -s** graffiti

Graf|fi|ti-Spra|yer(in) M(F) graffiti sprayer

Graf|fi|to [gra'fi:to] M OR NT **-(s)**, **Graffiti** [-'fi:ti] (*Art*) graffito

Gra|fie [gra'fi:] F **-, -n** [-fi:ən] (*Ling*) written form

Gra|fik ['gra:fɪk] F **-, -en** **a** *no pl* (*Art*) graphic arts *pl*; (*= Technik*) graphics *sing*; (*= Entwurf*) design **b** (*Art*: *= Darstellung*) graphic; (*= Druck*) print; (*= Schaubild*) illustration; (*= technisches Schaubild*) diagram

Gra|fik-: **Gra|fik|be|schleu|ni|ger** M (*Comput*) graphics accelerator; **Gra|fik|bild|schirm** M (*Comput*) graphics screen; **Gra|fik|de|sign** NT, *no pl* (*Fach*) graphic design; **Gra|fik|dru|cker** M graphics printer

Gra|fi|ker ['gra:fikɐ] M **-s, -**, **Gra|fi|ke|rin** [-ərɪn] F **-, -nen** graphic artist; (*= Illustrator*) illustrator; (*= Gestalter*) (graphic) designer

Gra|fik- (*Comput*): **gra|fik|fä|hig** ADJ **~ sein** to be able to do graphics; **Gra|fik|fä|hig|keit** F graphics capability; **Gra|fik|kar|te** F graphics card; **Gra|fik|mo|dus** M graphics mode; **Gra|fik|mög|lich|keit** F graphics facility; **gra|fik|ori|en|tiert** [-orienti:ɐt] ADJ graphics-orientated, graphics-oriented; **Gra|fik|pro|gramm** NT graphics program

Gräfin ['grɛ:fɪn] F -, -nen countess

gra|fisch ['gra:fɪʃ] ADJ graphic; (= *schematisch*) diagrammatic, schematic; **~es Gewerbe** graphic trades *pl* ADV graphically, with a graph/graphs; **eine Funktion ~ darstellen** *(Math)* to show a function on a graph

Gra|fit [gra'fi:t] M -s, -e graphite

Gra|fit- : **gra|fit|grau** ADJ dark grey *(Brit)* or gray *(US)*; **Gra|fit|stab** NT *(Tech)* graphite rod; **Gra|fit|stift** M lead pencil

gräf|lich ['grɛ:flɪç] ADJ count's/earl's; **das ~e Schloss** the count's/earl's castle; **ein ~er Diener** one of the count's/earl's servants

Gra|fo|lo|ge [grafo'lo:gə] M -n, -n, **Gra|fo|lo|gin** [-'lo:gɪn] F -, -nen graphologist

Gra|fo|lo|gie [grafolo'gi:] F -, *no pl* graphology

Graf|schaft ['gra:fʃaft] F -, -en land of a count; earldom; *(Admin)* county

Gra|ham|brot ['gra:ham-] NT (type of) wholemeal bread

grä|ko- ['grɛ:ko], **Grä|ko-** PREF graeco-, greco- *(esp US)*, Graeco-, Greco- *(esp US)*; **~romanisch** Graeco-Roman, Greco-Roman *(esp US)*

Gral [gra:l] M -s, *no pl* *(Liter)* **der (Heilige) ~** the (Holy) Grail

Grals- *in cpds* of the (Holy) Grail; **Grals|hü|ter(in)** M(F) *(lit)* keeper of the (Holy) Grail; *(fig)* guardian; **Grals|su|che** F quest for the (Holy) Grail

gram [gra:m] ADJ *pred (geh)* **jdm ~ sein** to bear sb ill will

Gram [gra:m] M -(e)s, *no pl (geh)* grief, sorrow; **vom** *or* **von ~ gebeugt** bowed down with grief *or* sorrow

grä|men ['grɛ:mən] VR **sich über jdn/etw ~** to grieve over sb/sth; **sich zu Tode ~** to die of grief *or* sorrow VT to grieve

gram|er|füllt [-lɛɐfʏlt] ADJ *(geh)* grief-stricken, woebegone

Gram|fär|bung ['gram-] F *(Med)* Gram's method

gram|ge|beugt ADJ *(geh)* bowed down with grief *or* sorrow

gräm|lich ['grɛ:mlɪç] ADJ morose, sullen; *Gedanken* morose

Gramm [gram] NT -s, -e *or (nach Zahlenangabe)* - gram(me); **100 ~ Mehl** 100 gram(me)s of flour

Gram|ma|tik [gra'matɪk] F -, -en grammar; (= *Grammatikbuch)* grammar (book)

gram|ma|ti|ka|lisch [gramati'ka:lɪʃ] ADJ grammatical ADV grammatically

Gram|ma|ti|ker [gra'matikɐ] M -s, -, **Gram|ma|ti|ke|rin** [-ərɪn] F -, -nen grammarian

Gram|ma|tik|re|gel F grammatical rule

gram|ma|tisch [gra'matɪʃ] ADJ grammatical ADV grammatically

Gramm|atom ['gramlato:m] NT gram(me) atom

Gram|mel ['graml] F -, -n *(S Ger, Aus: Cook)* ≈ crackling *no indef art, no pl (Brit)*, ≈ cracklings *pl (US)*, ≈ greaves *pl*

Gramm|mo|le|kül NT gram(me) molecule

Gram|mo|fon [gramo'fo:n] NT -s, -e, **Gram|mo|phon®** NT -s, -e *(dated)* gramophone *(dated)*, phonograph *(dated)*

gram- *(Med)*: **gram|ne|ga|tiv** [-'ne:gati:f] ADJ Gram-negative; **gram|po|si|tiv** [-'po:ziti:f] ADJ Gram-positive

gram|voll ADJ *(geh)* grief-stricken, sorrowful

Gran [gra:n] NT -(e)s, -e *or (nach Zahlenangabe)* - *(old)* **a** (= *Apothekergewicht)* grain **b** (= *Edelmetallgewicht)* grain

Grän [grɛ:n] NT -(e)s, -e (= *Edelmetallgewicht)* grain

Gra|nat [gra'na:t] M -(e)s, -e *or (Aus)* -en **a** *(Miner)* garnet **b** *(N Ger: = Garnele)* shrimp

Gra|nat|ap|fel M pomegranate

Gra|na|te [gra'na:tə] F -, -n *(Mil)* (= *Geschoss)* shell; (= *Handgranate)* grenade

Gr|anat-: **Gra|nat|feu|er** NT shelling, shellfire; **unter heftigem ~ liegen** to be under heavy shellfire *or* shelling; **Gra|nat|split|ter** M → **Granate** shell/grenade splinter; **Gra|nat|trich|ter** M shell crater; **Gra|nat|wer|fer** M mortar

Grand [grã:] M -s, -s *(Cards)* grand; **~ ouvert** open grand; **~ Hand** grand solo

Gran|de ['grandə] M -n, -n grandee

Gran|deur [grã'dø:ɐ] F -, *no pl (geh)* grandeur

Gran|dez|za [gran'dɛtsa] F -, *no pl* grandeur

Grand|ho|tel ['grã:hotɛl] NT luxury hotel

gran|di|os [gran'dio:s] ADJ magnificent, superb; *(hum)* fantastic *(inf)*, terrific *(inf)* ADV (= *hervorragend)* magnificently, superbly, fantastically; **sich ~ amüsieren** to have a magnificent *or* fantastic time; **sich ~ erholen** to make a splendid recovery

Gran|di|o|si|tät [grandiozi'tɛ:t] F -, *no pl* magnificence

Grand Prix [grã 'pri:] M - -, - - Grand Prix

Grand|seig|neur [grãsɛn'jø:ɐ] M -s, -s *or* -e *(geh)* nobleman

Grand-Tou|ris|me-Wa|gen [grãtu'rism-] M, **GT-Wa|gen** [ge:'te:-] M *(Aut)* GT (model)

Gra|nit [gra'ni:t] M -s, -e granite; **auf ~ beißen (bei ...)** to bang one's head against a brick wall (with ...)

gra|ni|ten [gra'ni:tn] ADJ *attr* granite, granitic *(spec)*; *(fig)* rigid

Gran|ne ['granə] F -, -n **a** (= *Ährenborste)* awn, beard **b** *(bei Tieren)* long coarse hair

Grant [grant] M -s, *no pl (inf: S Ger, Aus)* **einen ~ haben** to be mad *(inf)* or cross (*wegen* about, *auf jdn* at sb)

gran|teln ['grantln] VI *(inf: S Ger, Aus)* **a** (= *schlechte Laune haben)* to be in a bad mood, to be grumpy, to have the hump *(Brit inf)* **b** (= *meckern, herumnörgeln)* to grumble, to be cross *(inf)*

gran|tig ['grantɪç] *(inf: S Ger, Aus)* ADJ grumpy ADV grumpily

Grant|ler ['grantlɐ] M -s, -, **Grant|le|rin** ['grantlərɪn] F -, -nen *(inf: S Ger, Aus)* crosspatch, (old) grouch

Grantl|hu|ber ['grantlhu:bɐ] M -s, - *(inf: S Ger, Aus)* crosspatch, (old) grouch

Gra|nu|lat [granu'la:t] NT -(e)s, -e granules *pl*

gra|nu|lie|ren [granu'li:rən] *ptp* **granuliert** VTI to granulate

Grape|fruit ['gre:pfru:t] F -, -s grapefruit

Grape|fruit|saft ['gre:pfru:tzaft] NT grapefruit juice

Graph [gra:f] M -en, -en *(Sci)* graph

Graph NT -s, -e *(Ling)* graph

Gra|phem [gra'fe:m] NT -s, -e *(Ling)* grapheme

Gra|phie [gra'fi:] F -, -n [-fi:ən] = **Grafie**

Gra|phik ['gra:fɪk] F -, -en = **Grafik**

gra|phisch ['gra:fɪʃ] ADJ, ADV = **grafisch**

Gra|phit [gra'fi:t] *etc* = **Grafit** *etc*

Gra|pho|lo|ge [grafo'lo:gə] *etc* = **Grafologe** *etc*

Grap|pa ['grapa] M -s, -s *or f* -, -s grappa

grap|schen ['grapʃn], **grap|sen** ['grapsn] *(inf)* VT **sich** *(dat)* **etw ~** to grab sth; *(S Ger, Aus: hum: = stehlen)* to pinch *(inf)* or swipe *(inf)* sth VI **a nach etw ~** to make a grab at sth **b** (= *fummeln)* to grope *(inf)*

Grap|scher ['grapʃɐ] M -s, - *(inf)* **a** (= *Person)* groper *(inf)* **b** (= *Griff)* grab

Gras [gra:s] NT -es, =er ['grɛ:zɐ] grass; **ins ~ beißen** *(inf)* to bite the dust *(inf)*; **das ~ wachsen hören** to be highly perceptive, to have a sixth sense; (= *zu viel hineindeuten)* to read too much into things; **über etw** *(acc)* **~ wachsen lassen** *(fig)* to let the dust settle on sth; **darüber ist viel ~ gewachsen** *(fig)* that's dead and buried; **wo er zuschlägt, wächst kein ~ mehr** *(inf)* he packs quite a punch; **wo er hinlangt, da wächst kein ~ mehr** once he gets his hands on something you'll never recognize it any more

Gras- *in cpds* grass; **gras|be|deckt, gras|be|wach|sen** ADJ grassy, grass-covered; **Gras|bü|schel** NT tuft of grass

Gräs|chen ['grɛ:sçən] NT -s, - *dim von* **Gras**

gra|sen ['gra:zn] VI to graze

Gras-: **Gras|flä|che** F grassland; (= *Rasen)* piece *or* patch of grass; **Gras|fleck** M **a** grassy spot **b** *(auf Kleidern etc)* grass stain; **Gras|fres|ser** M herbivore; **Gras|frosch** M grass frog; **gras|grün** ADJ grass-green; **Gras|halm** M blade of grass; **Gras|hüp|fer** M *(inf)* grasshopper

gra|sig ['gra:zɪç] ADJ grassy

Gras-: **Gras|land** NT, *no pl* grassland; **Gras|mäh|ma|schi|ne** F mower; **Gras|mü|cke** F *(Orn)* warbler; **Gras|nar|be** F turf; **Gras|nel|ke** F *(Bot)* thrift; **Gras|pflan|ze** F grass *or* graminaceous *(form)* plant

Grass [gras] NT -, *no pl (sl)* grass *(inf)*

Gras|sa|men M grass seed

gras|sie|ren [gra'si:rən] *ptp* **grassiert** VI to be rife; *(Krankheit auch)* to be rampant, to rage

gräss|lich ['grɛslɪç] ADJ **a** hideous; *Verbrechen auch* heinous, abominable **b** (= *intensiv, unangenehm)* terrible, dreadful, awful; *Mensch* horrible, awful ADV **a** (= *schrecklich)* horribly **b** (*inf*: = *äußerst)* terribly, dreadfully, awfully; **~ müde** terribly *or* dreadfully *or* awfully tired

Gräss|lich|keit F -, -en **a** hideousness; *(von Verbrechen auch)* heinousness **b** (= *grässliche Tat etc)* atrocity

Gras-: **Gras|so|de** F *(esp N Ger)* turf, sod; **Gras|step|pe** F savanna(h); **Gras|strei|fen** M strip of grass, grassy strip; **Gras|tep|pich** M *(geh)* sward *no indef art, no pl (liter)*; **gras|über|wach|sen** [-ly:bɐvaksn], **gras|über|wu|chert** [-ly:bɐvu:xɐt] ADJ overgrown with grass; **Gras|wuchs** M grass

Grat [gra:t] M -(e)s, -e (= *Berggrat)* ridge; *(Tech)* burr; *(Archit)* hip *(of roof)*; *(fig)* (dividing) line, border

Grä|te ['grɛ:tə] F -, -n (fish) bone

Gra|ti|fi|ka|ti|on [gratifika'tsio:n] F -, -en bonus

gra|ti|nie|ren [grati'ni:rən] *ptp* **gratiniert** VT *(Cook)* to brown (the top of); **gratinierte Zwiebelsuppe** onion soup au gratin

gra|tis ['gra:tɪs] ADV free; *(Comm)* free (of charge); **~ und franko** *(dated)* free of charge

Gra|tis- *in cpds* free; **Gra|tis|ak|tie** F bonus share; **Gra|tis|ex|emp|lar** NT free *or* complimentary copy; **Gra|tis|pro|be** F free sample

Grät|sche ['grɛ:tʃə] F -, -n *(Sport)* straddle

grät|schen ['grɛ:tʃn] VI *aux sein* to do a straddle (vault) VT *Beine* to straddle, to put apart

Grätsch-: **Grätsch|sitz** M straddle position; **Grätsch|sprung** M straddle vault; **Grätsch|stel|lung** F straddle (position); **in ~ gehen** to take up a straddle position

Gra|tu|lant [gratu'lant] M -en, -en, **Gra|tu|lan|tin** [-'lantɪn] F -, -nen well-wisher; **er war der erste ~** he was the first to offer his congratulations

Gra|tu|la|ti|on [gratula'tsio:n] F -, -en congratulations *pl*; **zur ~ bei jdm erscheinen** to call on sb to congratulate him/her

Gra|tu|la|ti|ons-: **Gra|tu|la|ti|ons|be|such** M congratulatory visit; **Gra|tu|la|ti|ons|cour** [-ku:ɐ] F -, -en congratulatory reception; **Gra|tu|la|ti|ons|kar|te** F congratulations card; **Gra|tu|la|ti|ons|schrei|ben** NT letter of congratulation

gra|tu|lie|ren [gratu'li:rən] ✪ 40.4, 50.6 *ptp* **gratuliert** VI **jdm (zu einer Sache) ~** to congratulate sb (on sth); **jdm zum Geburtstag ~** to wish sb many happy returns (of the day); **(ich) gratuliere!** congratulations!; **Sie können sich** *(dat)* **~, dass alles gut gegangen ist** you can count yourself lucky that everything went off all right

Grat|wan|de|rung F *(lit)* ridge walk; *(fig)* balancing act, tightrope walk

grau [grau] ADJ grey *(Brit)*, gray *(US)*; *Gesicht(sfarbe) auch* ashen; (= *trostlos)* gloomy, dark, bleak; **~e Haare bekommen, ~ werden** *(inf)* to go grey *(Brit)* or gray *(US)*; **der Himmel** *or* **es sieht ~ in ~ aus** the sky *or* it is looking very grey *(Brit)* or gray *(US)*; **er malte die Lage ~ in**

~ *(fig)* he painted a gloomy *or* dark *or* bleak picture of the situation; **~e Eminenz** éminence grise; **der ~e Markt** *(Comm)* the grey *(Brit) or* gray *(US)* market; **die (kleinen) ~en Zellen** *(hum)* the little grey *(Brit) or* gray *(US)* cells; **die ~e Substanz** *(Anat)* the grey *(Brit) or* gray *(US)* matter; **der ~e Alltag** dull *or* drab reality, the daily round *or* grind; **in ~er Vorzeit** *(fig)* in the dim and distant past; **das liegt in ~er Ferne** *(fig)* it's in the dim and distant future; **~ ist alle Theorie** *(prov)* theory is no use without practice; **das ist bloß ~e Theorie** that's all very well in theory; **Graue Panther** Gray Panthers *(US)*, old people's action group
ADV *(= mit grauer Farbe) anstreichen, färben* grey *(Brit)*, gray *(US)*; *tapezieren auch, einrichten, sich kleiden* in grey *(Brit) or* gray *(US)*; **~ gestreift** grey-striped *(Brit)*, gray-striped *(US)*; **~ meliert** flecked with grey *(Brit) or* gray *(US)*; *Haar auch* greying *(Brit)*, graying *(US)*

Grau [grau] NT **-s, -(s)** grey *(Brit)*, gray *(US)*; *(fig)* dullness, drabness

Grau-: **grau|äu|gig** ADJ grey-eyed *(Brit)*, gray-eyed *(US)*; **grau|blau** ADJ grey-blue *(Brit)*, gray-blue *(US)*; **grau|braun** ADJ greyish-brown *(Brit)*, grayish-brown *(US)*; **Grau|brot** NT *bread made from more than one kind of flour*

Grau|bün|den [grau'bʏndn] NT **-s** *(Geog)* the Grisons

Grau|bünd|ner [grau'bʏndnɐ] M **-s, -**, **Grau|bünd|ne|rin** [-ərın] F **-, -nen** inhabitant of the Grisons

Gräu|el ['grɔyəl] M **-s, -** **a** *no pl (= Grauen, Abscheu)* horror; **~ vor etw** *(dat)* **haben** to have a horror of sth **b** *(= Gräueltat)* atrocity **c** *(= Gegenstand des Abscheus)* abomination; **sie/er/es ist mir ein ~** I loathe *or* detest her/him/it; **die Prüfung ist mir ein ~** I'm really dreading the exam; **es ist mir ein ~, das zu tun** I loathe *or* detest *or* cannot bear doing that

Gräu|el-: **Gräu|el|ge|schich|te** F, **Gräu|el|mär|chen** NT horror story; **Gräu|el|mel|dung** F, **Gräu|el|nach|richt** F report of an atrocity/atrocities; **Gräu|el|pro|pa|gan|da** F atrocity propaganda, horror stories *pl*; **Gräu|el|tat** F atrocity

grau|en ['grauən] VI *(geh: Tag)* to dawn; **es begann zu ~** dawn began to break

grau|en VI *impers* **mir graut vor etw** *(dat)*, **es graut mir vor etw** *(dat)* I dread sth; **mir graut vor ihm** I'm terrified of him

Grau|en ['grauən] NT **-s,** *no pl* **a** horror *(vor* of); **mich überlief ein ~** I shuddered with horror; **~ erregend** = **grauenerregend** **b** *(= grauenhaftes Ereignis)* horror

grau|en|er|re|gend ADJ terrible, atrocious

grau|en|haft, grau|en|voll ADJ terrible, atrocious; *Schmerz* terrible; *(inf) Durcheinander* appalling, horrendous ADV *sich benehmen* atrociously, horrendously, appallingly; *wehtun* horrendously, atrociously; **~ aussehen** to look ghastly; **die Wohnung war ~ durcheinander** the apartment was in an appalling *or* horrendous mess

Grau-: **Grau|fuchs** M grey *(Brit) or* gray *(US)* fox; **Grau|gans** F grey(lag) *(Brit) or* gray(lag) *(US)* goose; **grau|ge|streift** ADJ → **grau ADV**; **grau|grün** ADJ grey-green *(Brit)*, gray-green *(US)*; **Grau|guss** M *(Tech)* grey *(Brit) or* gray *(US)* iron; **grau|haa|rig** ADJ grey-haired *(Brit)*, gray-haired *(US)*; **Grau|hörn|chen** NT *(Zool)* grey *(Brit) or* gray *(US)* squirrel; **Grau|kopf** M *(fig)* grey-haired *(Brit) or* gray-haired *(US)* man/woman; **grau|köp|fig** ADJ grey-haired *(Brit)*, gray-haired *(US)*

grau|len ['graulən] *(inf)* VI *impers* **davor grault mir** I dread it; **mir grault vor ihm** I'm scared *or* frightened of him VR **sich vor jdm/etw ~** to be scared *or* frightened of sb/sth VT to drive out *(aus* of)

grau|lich ['graulıç] ADJ = **gräulich**

gräu|lich ['grɔylıç] ADJ = **grässlich**

gräu|lich ADJ *(= Farbe)* greyish *(Brit)*, grayish *(US)*

Grau|markt M grey *(Brit) or* gray *(US)* market

Grau|markt|ti|cket NT *(Aviat)* bucket shop ticket

grau|me|liert ADJ *attr* → **grau ADV**

Grau|pe ['graupə] F **-, -n** grain of pearl barley; **~n** pearl barley *sing*

Grau|pel ['graupl] F **-, -n** (small) hailstone; **~n** soft hail *sing*, graupel *sing (spec)*

grau|pe|lig ['graupəlıç] ADJ *Schauer* of soft hail; **~er Schnee** snow mixed with fine hail; **~er Hagel** soft hail

grau|peln ['graupln] VI *impers* **es graupelt** a soft hail is falling

Grau|pel-: **Grau|pel|re|gen** M, **Grau|pel|schau|er** M sleet; **Grau|pel|wet|ter** NT soft hail

Grau|pen|sup|pe F barley broth *or* soup

graup|lig ['grauplıç] ADJ = **graupelig**

Grau|rei|her M *(Zool)* grey *(Brit) or* gray *(US)* heron

graus [graus] ADJ *(old)* afeared *(old, liter)*

Graus [graus] M **-es** [-zəs], *no pl* horror; **es war ein ~ zu sehen, wie ...** it was terrible to see how ...; **es ist ein ~ mit ihm!** he's impossible!, he's the limit!, will he never learn!; **o ~!** *(old, hum)* oh horror! *(old, hum)*, (alack and) alas! *(old, iro)*

grau|sam ['grauza:m] ADJ **a** *(= gefühllos, roh)* cruel *(gegen, zu* to) **b** *(inf)* terrible, awful, dreadful ADV **a** *(= auf schreckliche Weise)* cruelly; **~ ums Leben kommen** to die a cruel death; **sich ~ für etw rächen** to take (a) cruel revenge for sth **b** *(inf: = furchtbar)* terribly, horrendously, dreadfully

Grau|sam|keit F **-, -en** **a** *no pl* cruelty **b** *(= grausame Tat)* (act of) cruelty; *(stärker)* atrocity

Grau-: **Grau|schim|mel** M **a** *(= Pferd)* grey *(Brit) or* gray *(US)* (horse) **b** *(= Pilz)* grey mould *(Brit)*, gray mold *(US)*; **Grau|schlei|er** M *(von Wäsche)* grey(ness) *(Brit)*, gray(ness) *(US)*; *(fig)* veil; **grau|schwarz** ADJ greyish-black *(Brit)*, grayish-black *(US)*

grau|sen ['grauzn] VI *impers* **mir graust vor** *or* **es graust mir vor der Prüfung** I am dreading the exam

Grau|sen ['grauzn] NT **-s,** *no pl* **a** = **Grauen a** **b** *(inf)* **da kann man das große** *or* **kalte ~ kriegen** it's enough to give you the creeps *(inf) or* willies *(Brit inf)*

grau|sig ['grauzıç] ADJ, ADV = **grauenhaft**

graus|lich ['grauslıç] ADJ, ADV *(dial)* = **grässlich**

Grau-: **Grau|specht** M grey-headed *(Brit) or* gray-headed *(US)* woodpecker; **Grau|stu|fe** F shade of grey *(Brit) or* gray *(US)*; **~en** *pl (Comput)* grayscale *sing*; **Grau|tier** NT *(hum inf)* (jack)ass, donkey, mule; **Grau|ton** M *pl* **-töne** grey colour *(Brit)*, gray color *(US)*; **Grau|wal** M grey *(Brit) or* gray *(US)* whale; **grau|weiß** ADJ greyish *(Brit) or* grayish *(US)* white; **Grau|zo|ne** F *(fig)* grey *(Brit) or* gray *(US)* area

Gra|veur [gra'vøːɐ] M **-s, -e**, **Gra|veu|rin** [-'vøːrın] F **-, -nen** engraver

Gra|vier-: **Gra|vier|an|stalt** F engraving establishment; **Gra|vier|ar|beit** F engraving

gra|vie|ren [gra'viːrən] *ptp* **graviert** VT to engrave

gra|vie|rend ADJ serious, grave

Gra|vier-: **Gra|vier|ma|schi|ne** F engraving machine; **Gra|vier|na|del** F graver, burin

Gra|vie|rung [gra'viːrʊŋ] F **-, -en** engraving

Gra|vi|met|rie [gravime'triː] F **-,** *no pl* gravimetry

gra|vi|met|risch [gravi'meːtrıʃ] ADJ gravimetric

Gra|vis ['graːvıs] M **-, -** *(Gram)* grave accent

Gra|vi|ta|ti|on [gravita'tsioːn] F **-,** *no pl* gravitation, gravitational pull

Gra|vi|ta|ti|ons-: **Gra|vi|ta|ti|ons|feld** NT gravitational field; **Gra|vi|ta|ti|ons|ge|setz** NT law of gravity; **Gra|vi|ta|ti|ons|kraft** F gravitational force

gra|vi|tä|tisch [gravi'tɛːtıʃ] ADJ grave, solemn

gra|vi|tie|ren [gravi'tiːrən] *ptp* **gravitiert** VI *(Phys, fig)* to gravitate *(zu* towards)

Gra|vur [gra'vuːɐ] F **-, -en**, **Gra|vü|re** [gra'vyːrə] F **-, -n** engraving

Gra|zie ['graːtsiə] F **-, -n** **a** *(Myth)* Grace; *(hum)* beauty, belle **b** *no pl (= Liebreiz)* grace(fulness)

gra|zil [gra'tsiːl] ADJ delicate; *(rare: = geschmeidig)* nimble ADV **~ gebaut sein** to have a delicate figure

gra|zi|ös [gra'tsiøːs] ADJ graceful; *(= lieblich)* charming ADV gracefully

Grä|zis|mus [grɛ'tsısmʊs] M **-, Gräzismen** [-mən] *(Ling)* Graecism, Grecism *(esp US)*

Grä|zist [grɛ'tsıst] M **-en, -en**, **Grä|zis|tin** [-'tsıstın] F **-, -nen** Greek scholar, Hellenist

Grä|zis|tik [grɛ'tsıstık] F **-,** *no pl* Greek studies *pl*

Green|horn ['griːnhɔːɐn] NT **-s, -s** *(inf)* greenhorn *(inf)*

Green|peace ['griːnpiːs] NT *no art* Greenpeace

Green|pea|cer ['griːnpiːsɐ] M **-s, -**, **Green|pea|ce|rin** [-ərın] F **-, -nen** *(inf)* member of Greenpeace

Green|wich-Zeit ['grınıdʒ-, -ıtʃ-] F, **Green|wi|cher Zeit** ['grınıdʒɐ-] F **(die) ~** GMT, Greenwich Mean Time

Gre|gor ['greːgoːɐ] M **-s** Gregory

Gre|go|ri|a|nik [grego'riaːnık] F **-,** *no pl* Gregorian music

gre|go|ri|a|nisch [grego'riaːnıʃ] ADJ Gregorian; **~er Gesang** Gregorian chant, plainsong

Greif [graif] M **-(e)s** *or* **-en, -e(n)** *(Myth)* **(Vogel) ~** griffin, griffon, gryphon

Greif-: **Greif|arm** M claw arm; **Greif|bag|ger** M grab dredger; **greif|bar** ADJ *(= konkret)* tangible, concrete; *(= erreichbar)* available; *Ware* available, in stock *pred*; **~e Gestalt** *or* **~e Formen annehmen** to take on (a) concrete *or* tangible form; **~ nahe, in ~er Nähe** within reach; **Greif|be|we|gung** F grasping movement

grei|fen ['graifn] *pret* **griff** [grıf], *ptp* **gegriffen** [gə'grıfn] VT **a** *(= nehmen, packen)* to take hold of, to grasp; *(= grapschen)* to seize, to grab; *Saite* to stop, to hold down; *Akkord* to strike; **eine Oktave ~** to stretch *or* reach an octave; **diese Zahl ist zu hoch/zu niedrig gegriffen** *(fig)* this figure is too high/low; **zum Greifen nahe sein** *(Sieg)* to be within reach; *(Folgerung)* to be obvious (to anyone); **die Gipfel waren zum Greifen nahe** you could almost touch the peaks; **aus dem Leben gegriffen** taken from life
b *(= fangen)* to catch; **Greifen spielen** to play catch *or* tag; **sich** *(dat)* **jdn/etw ~** to grab sb/sth; **den werde ich mir mal ~** *(inf)* I'm going to tell him a thing or two *(inf) or* a few home truths *(Brit)*
VI **a** **hinter sich** *(acc)* **~** to reach behind one; **um sich ~** *(fig)* to spread, to gain ground; **unter etw** *(acc)* **~** to reach under sth; **in etw** *(acc)* **~** to put one's hand into sth, to reach into sth; **nach einer Sache ~** to reach for sth; *(um zu halten)* to clutch *or (hastig)* grab at sth; **an etw** *(acc)* **~** *(= fassen)* to take hold of sth, to grasp sth; *(= berühren)* to touch sth; **zu etw ~** *(zu Pistole)* to reach for sth; *(fig) zu Methoden, Mitteln* to turn *or* resort to sth; **zur Flasche ~** to take *or* turn to the bottle; **er greift gern nach einem guten Buch** he likes to settle down with a good book; **tief in die Tasche ~** *(fig)* to dig deep in one's pocket(s); **in die Saiten/Tasten ~** to strike up a tune; **nach den Sternen ~** to reach for the stars; **nach dem rettenden Strohhalm ~** to clutch at a straw; **zum Äußersten ~** to resort to extremes; **nach der Macht ~** to try to seize power; **die Geschichte greift ans Herz** the story really tears *or* tugs at one's heartstrings
b *(= nicht rutschen, einrasten)* to grip; *(fig) (= wirksam werden)* to take effect; *(= zum Ziel/Erfolg führen)* to achieve its ends; *(= zutreffen) (Gesetz, Vorschrift)* to apply; *(Vergleich, Unterscheidung)* to hold; **zu kurz ~** to fall short

Grei|fer ['graifɐ] M **-s, -** *(Tech)* grab

Greif-: **Greif|fuß** M prehensile foot; **Greif|re|flex** M gripping reflex *or* response; **Greif|trupp** M riot squad; **Greif|vo|gel** M bird of prey, raptor *(spec)*; **Greif|werk|zeug** NT prehensile organ; **Greif|zan|ge** F (pair of) tongs *pl*; **Greif|zir|kel** M (outside) callipers *pl (Brit) or* calipers *pl (US)*

grei|nen ['grainən] VI *(pej)* to whine, to whimper

greis [grais] ADJ aged; *(= ehrwürdig)* venerable; *(= altersgrau)* grey *(Brit)*, gray *(US)*, hoary *(liter, hum)*; **sein ~es Haupt schütteln** *(usu iro)* to shake one's wise old head

Greis [grais] M **-es, -e** [-zə] old man; **ein neunzigjähriger ~** an old man of ninety, a ninety-year-old man

Grei|sen-: **Grei|sen|al|ter** NT extreme old age; **grei|sen|haft** ADJ very old, aged *attr*; *(von jüngerem Menschen) Gesicht, Ansicht, Aussehen* aged *attr*; **das ~e Verhalten dieser Kinder** the way these children behave like old people; **Grei|sen|haf|tig|keit** ['graiznhaftıçkait] F -, *no pl* **sie zeigt keine Anzeichen von ~** she shows no signs of old age; **verfrühte ~** premature ageing; **die ~ dieser Kindergesichter** the little old men's faces of these children; **Grei|sen|haupt** NT *(geh)* hoary head; *(iro)* wise old head

Grei|sin ['graizın] F **-, -nen** old lady; **eine neunzigjährige ~** an old lady of ninety, a ninety-year-old lady

grell [grɛl] ADJ *Stimme, Schrei, Ton* shrill, piercing; *Licht, Sonne* glaring, dazzling; *Farbe* garish, gaudy, loud; *Kleidung, Mode* loud, flashy; *Gegensatz* sharp; *(stärker)* glaring; *(fig) Inszenierung, Szene* lurid ADV *(= sehr hell) scheinen* brightly; *(= schrill)* shrilly; *(= auffallend)* garishly; **~ beleuchtet** *or* **erleuchtet** dazzlingly bright; **~ leuchten** to be garish; **~ klingen/tönen** to sound shrill; **ihre Stimme klang ~** her voice sounded shrill; **~ gegen etw** *(acc)* **abstechen** to contrast very sharply with sth

grell-: **grell|be|leuch|tet** [-bəlɔyçtət], **grell|er|leuch|tet** [-lɛɐlɔyçtət] ADJ *attr* → **grell ADV**; **grell|bunt** ADJ gaudily coloured *(Brit) or* colored *(US)*; *Farbe* gaudy

Grel|le ['grɛlə] F -, *no pl*, **Grell|heit** F -, *no pl (von Stimme, Schrei, Ton)* shrillness; *(von Licht, Sonne)* glare; *(von Farbe)* garishness, gaudiness

grell|rot ADJ garish *or* gaudy red ADV **~ geschminkt** painted a garish *or* gaudy red

Gre|mi|um ['gre:mium] NT **-s, Gremien** ['gre:miən] body; *(= Ausschuss)* committee

Gre|na|dier [grena'di:ɐ] M **-s, -e** *(Mil)* **a** *(Hist)* grenadier **b** *(= Infanterist)* infantryman

Grenz- *in cpds* border, frontier; **Grenz|ab|fer|ti|gung** F border *or* frontier clearance; **Grenz|ab|schnitt** M sector of the/a border *or* frontier; **Grenz|an|la|gen** PL border installations *pl*; **Grenz|baum** M *(= Schlagbaum)* frontier barrier; **Grenz|be|gra|di|gung** F straightening of the border/a border/borders; **Grenz|be|reich** M frontier *or* border zone *or* area; *(fig)* limits *pl*; **im ~ liegen** *(fig)* to lie at the limits; **Grenz|be|völ|ke|rung** F inhabitants *pl* of the/a border zone; *(esp in unwegsamen Gebieten)* frontiersmen *pl*; **Grenz|be|woh|ner(in)** M(F) inhabitant of the/a border zone; *(esp in unwegsamen Gebieten)* frontiersman/-woman; **Grenz|be|zirk** M border district; **Grenz|durch|bruch** M breaking through the/a border *or* frontier

Gren|ze ['grɛntsə] F **-, -n** border; *(= Landesgrenze auch)* frontier; *(= Stadtgrenze, zwischen Grundstücken)* boundary; *(fig: zwischen Begriffen)* dividing line, boundary; *(fig: = äußerstes Maß, Schranke)* limits *pl*, bounds *pl*; **die ~ zwischen Spanien und Frankreich** the Spanish-French border *or* frontier; **die ~ zu Österreich** the border with Austria, the Austrian border; **über die ~ gehen/fahren** to cross the border; **(bis) zur äußersten ~ gehen** *(fig)* to go as far as one can; **jdm ~n setzen** to lay down limits for sb; **einer Sache** *(dat)* **~n setzen** *or* **stecken** to set a limit *or* limits to sth; **keine ~n kennen** *(fig)* to know no bounds; **seine ~n kennen** to know one's limitations; **seiner Großzügigkeit sind keine ~n gesetzt** there is no limit to his generosity; **hart an der ~ des Möglichen** bordering *or* verging on the limits of what is possible; **innerhalb seiner ~n bleiben** *(fig)* to stay within one's limits; *(finanziell)* to live within one's means; **jdn in seine ~n verweisen** *(fig)* to put sb in his place; **die ~n einhalten** to stay within the limits; **sich in ~n halten** *(fig)* to be limited; **die ~n des Möglichen** the bounds of possibility; **die oberste/unterste ~** *(fig)* the upper/lower limit; **die ~n seines Amtes überschreiten** to exceed one's office; **über die ~(n)** *(+gen)* **... hinaus** *(fig)* beyond the bounds of ...; **an ~n stoßen** *(fig)* to come up against limiting factors; **alles hat seine ~n** there is a limit *or* there are limits to everything

gren|zen ['grɛntsn] VI **an etw** *(acc)* **~** *(lit)* to border (on) sth; *(fig)* to border *or* verge on sth

Gren|zen-: **gren|zen|los** ADJ *(lit, fig)* boundless; **sich ins Grenzenlose verlieren** to disappear into the distance; *(fig)* to go too far ADV boundlessly; *(fig)* immensely; **Gren|zen|lo|sig|keit** F -, *no pl* boundlessness; *(fig)* immensity

Gren|zer ['grɛntsɐ] M **-s, -**, **Gren|ze|rin** [-ərın] F **-, -nen** *(inf)* **a** *(= Zöllner)* customs man/woman; *(= Grenzsoldat)* border *or* frontier guard **b** = **Grenzbewohner(in)**

Grenz-: **Grenz|fall** M borderline case; **Grenz|fluss** M river forming a/the border *or* frontier; **Grenz|for|ma|li|tä|ten** PL border formalities *pl*; **Grenz|gän|ger** [-gɛŋɐ] M **-s, -**, **Grenz|gän|ge|rin** [-ərın] F **-, -nen** *(= Arbeiter)* international commuter *(across a local border)*; *(= heimlicher Grenzgänger)* illegal border *or* frontier crosser; *(= Schmuggler)* smuggler; **Grenz|ge|biet** NT border *or* frontier area *or* zone; *(fig)* border(ing) area; **Grenz|kon|flikt** M border *or* frontier dispute; **Grenz|kon|trol|le** F border *or* frontier control; **Grenz|land** NT border *or* frontier area *or* zone

Grenz|ler ['grɛntslɐ] M **-s, -**, **Grenz|le|rin** [-ərın] F **-, -nen** *(inf)* = **Grenzbewohner(in)**

Grenz-: **Grenz|li|nie** F border; *(Sport)* line; **Grenz|mark** F *pl* **-marken** *(Hist)* border *or* frontier area *or* zone; **grenz|nah** ADJ close to the border *or* frontier; **Grenz|nä|he** F closeness to the border *or* frontier; **in ~ zur Ukraine** close to the border *or* frontier with the Ukraine; **Grenz|nut|zen** M *(Econ)* marginal utility; **Grenz|pfahl** M boundary post; **Grenz|pos|ten** M border guard; **Grenz|schutz** M **a** *no pl* protection of the border(s) *or* frontier(s) **b** *(= Truppen)* border *or* frontier guard(s); **Grenz|si|che|rungs|an|la|gen** PL border *or* frontier protection *sing*; **Grenz|si|tu|a|ti|on** F borderline situation; **Grenz|sol|dat(in)** M(F) border *or* frontier guard; **Grenz|sper|re** F border *or* frontier barrier; *(fig: des Grenzverkehrs)* ban on border traffic; **Grenz|stadt** F border town; **Grenz|stein** M boundary stone; **Grenz|strei|tig|keit** F boundary dispute; *(Pol)* border *or* frontier dispute; **Grenz|über|gang** M **a** *(= Stelle)* border *or* frontier crossing(-point) **b** *(= Grenzübertritt)* crossing of the border; **grenz|über|schrei|tend** ADJ *attr (Comm, Jur)* across the border *or* frontier/(the) borders *or* frontiers, cross-border; **Grenz|über|schrei|tung** F **-, -en** *(lit)* crossing (of) a/the border; *(fig)* boundary crossing, crossing boundaries; **Grenz|ver|kehr** M border *or* frontier traffic; **kleiner ~** regular border traffic; **Grenz|ver|lauf** M boundary line *(between countries)*; **Grenz|ver|let|zer** [-fɛɐlɛtsɐ] M **-s, -**, **Grenz|ver|let|ze|rin** [-ərın] F **-, -nen** border *or* frontier violator; **Grenz|ver|let|zung** F violation of the/a border *or* frontier; **Grenz|wa|che** F border guard; **Grenz|wacht** F *(Sw)* border *or* frontier guard; **Grenz|wall** M border rampart; **Grenz|wert** M limit; **Grenz|zei|chen** NT boundary marker; **Grenz|zie|hung** F drawing up of the/a border *or* frontier; **Grenz|zwis|chen|fall** M border incident *or* clash

Gret|chen|fra|ge ['gre:tçən-] F *(fig)* crunch question *(inf)*, sixty-four-thousand-dollar question *(inf)*

Greu|el △ ['grɔyəl] M **-s, -** → **Gräuel**

Greu|el- △ → **Gräuel-**

greu|lich △ ['grɔylıç] ADJ, ADV → **gräulich**

Grey|er|zer ['graiɐtsɐ] M **-s, - ~ (Käse)** Gruyère

Grie|be ['gri:bə] F **-, -n** ≈ crackling *no indef art, no pl (Brit)*, ≈ cracklings *pl (US)*, ≈ greaves *pl*

Grie|ben|schmalz NT ≈ dripping with crackling *etc*

Griebs(ch) [gri:ps, gri:pʃ] M **-es, -e** *(dial)* **a** *(= Apfelgriebs(ch), Birnengriebs(ch))* core **b** *(= Gurgel)* throat, gullet

Grie|che ['gri:çə] M **-n, -n**, **Grie|chin** ['gri:çın] F **-, -nen** Greek; **zum ~n gehen** to go to a *or* the Greek restaurant

Grie|chen|land ['gri:çnlant] NT **-s** Greece

Grie|chen|tum ['gri:çntu:m] NT **-s**, *no pl* **das ~** **a** *(= Volkstum)* Greekness, Hellenism **b** *(= Zivilisation)* Hellenism, (the) Greek civilization; *(= Kultur)* Greek culture, things *pl* Greek **c** *(= Gesamtheit der Griechen)* the Greeks *pl*

Grie|chin ['gri:çın] F **-, -nen** Greek (woman/girl)

grie|chisch ['gri:çıʃ] ADJ Greek; *Kleidung, Architektur, Vase, Stil, Profil auch* Grecian; **die ~e Tragödie** Greek tragedy; **~es Feuer** Greek fire; **~-orthodox** Greek Orthodox; **~-römisch** Graeco-Roman, Greco-Roman *(esp US)* → *auch* **deutsch**

Grie|chi|sch(e) ['gri:çıʃ] NT Greek → *auch* **Deutsch(e)**

grie|nen ['gri:nən] VI *(N Ger inf)* to smirk *(inf)*

Gries|gram ['gri:sgra:m] M **-(e)s, -e** grouch *(inf)*, misery

gries|grä|mig ['gri:sgrɛ:mıç] ADJ grumpy, grouchy *(inf)* ADV grumpily, grouchily *(inf)*; **~ aussehen** to look grumpy *or* grouchy *(inf)*; **er guckte ~ in die Gegend** he looked around with a grumpy expression on his face

Grieß [gri:s] M **-es, -e** **a** semolina; *(= Reisgrieß)* ground rice **b** *(= Kies)* gravel *(auch Med)*; *(= Sand)* grit

Grieß-: **Grieß|brei** M semolina; **Grieß|kloß** M, **Grieß|klöß|chen** NT semolina dumpling; **Grieß|no|ckerl** NT **-s, -(n)** *(S Ger, Aus Cook)* semolina dumpling; **Grieß|pud|ding** M semolina pudding

griff *pret von* **greifen**

Griff [grıf] M **-(e)s, -e** **a** *(= das Greifen)* **der ~ an etw** *(acc)* taking hold of sth, grasping sth; *(= Berührung)* touching sth; **der ~ nach etw** reaching for sth; **einen ~ in die Kasse tun** to put one's hand in the till; **einen tiefen ~ in den Geldbeutel tun** *(fig)* to dig deep in one's pocket; **der ~ nach der Droge/der Flasche** turning *or* taking to drugs/the bottle; **der ~ nach der Macht** the bid for power; **das ist ein ~ nach den Sternen** that's just reaching for the stars

b *(= Handgriff)* grip, grasp; *(beim Ringen, Judo, Bergsteigen)* hold; *(beim Turnen)* grip; (*Mus*: *= Fingerstellung*) fingering; (*inf*: *= Akkord*) chord; (*vom Tuch*: *= Anfühlen*) feel, texture; **mit festem ~** firmly; **einen ~ ansetzen** *(Ringen)* to put on *or* apply a hold; **jdn/etw im ~ haben** *(fig)* to have the upper hand of sb/sth, to have sb/sth under control, to have the upper hand of sb/sth; *(geistig)* to have a good grasp of sth; **ein falscher ~** *(fig)* a false move; **jdn/etw in den ~ bekommen** *(fig)* to get the upper hand of sb/sth, to gain control of sb/sth; *(geistig)* to get a grasp of sth; **(mit jdm/etw) einen guten** *or* **glücklichen ~ tun** to make a wise choice (with sb/sth), to get on to a good thing (with sb/sth) *(inf)*; **etw mit einem ~ tun** *(fig)* to do sth in a flash

c *(= Stiel, Knauf)* handle; *(= Pistolengriff)* butt; *(= Schwertgriff)* hilt; *(an Saiteninstrumenten)* neck

d *usu pl (Hunt: = Kralle)* talon

e **Griffe** PL *(Mil)* rifle positions *pl*; **~e üben** *or* **kloppen** *(inf)* to do rifle drill

Griff-: **griff|be|reit** ADJ ready to hand, handy; **etw ~ halten** to keep sth handy, to keep sth to *(Brit)* or on hand; **Griff|brett** NT *(Mus)* fingerboard
Grif|fel ['grɪfl] M **-s, -** slate pencil; *(Bot)* style
Grif|fel|kas|ten M pencil case *or* box
grif|fig ['grɪfɪç] ADJ *Boden, Fahrbahn etc* that has a good grip; *Rad, Sohle, Profil* that grips well; *Gewebe* firm; *(fig) Ausdruck* useful, handy; *Slogan* pithy; *Formulierung, Theorie* concise; *(Aus) Mehl* coarse-grained; **etw auf eine ~e Formel bringen** to break sth down into a simple phrase ADV *(= eingängig) darstellen, formulieren* pithily, concisely
Grif|fig|keit F **-**, *no pl* grip; *(von Slogan)* pithiness
Griff|loch NT finger hole
Grill [grɪl] M **-s, -s** grill; *(Aut: = Kühlergrill)* grille
Grill|abend M (evening) barbecue, barbecue *or* BBQ night
Gril|la|de [gri'ja:də] F **-, -n** *(Cook)* grill
Grill|an|zün|der M barbecue lighter
Gril|le ['grɪlə] F **-, -n** **a** *(Zool)* cricket **b** *(dated inf: = Laune)* silly notion *or* idea; **~n im Kopf haben** to be full of big ideas; **~n fangen** to be moody
gril|len ['grɪlən] VT to grill VR **sich ~ (lassen)** *(inf)* to roast *(inf)*
gril|len|haft ADJ *(dated) (= trübsinnig)* moody; *(= sonderbar)* strange, extraordinary
Grill- *(Cook)*: **Grill|fest** NT barbecue party; **Grill|ge|richt** NT grill; **Grill|koh|le** F charcoal; **Grill|par|ty** F barbecue, barbie *(inf)*; **Grill|plat|te** F mixed grill; **Grill|platz** M barbecue area; **Grill|res|tau|rant** NT, **Grill|room** [-ru:m] M **-s, -s**, **Grill|stu|be** F grillroom, grill and griddle
Gri|mas|se [gri'masə] F **-, -n** grimace; **~n schneiden** *or* **ziehen** *or* **machen** to grimace, to make *or* pull faces; **sein Gesicht zu einer ~ verziehen** to twist one's face into a grimace
Gri|mas|sen|schnei|der(in) M(F) face-puller
grimm [grɪm] ADJ *(old)* = **grimmig**
Grimm [grɪm] M **-(e)s**, *no pl (old)* fury, wrath *(old, liter)*, ire *(old, liter)* *(auf +acc* against)
Grimm|darm M colon
Grim|men ['grɪmən] NT **-s**, *no pl (S Ger)* griping pains *pl*
grim|mig ['grɪmɪç] ADJ **a** *(= zornig)* furious, wrathful *(liter)*; *Gegner* fierce; *Miene* grim; **~er Humor** grim *or* morbid humour *(Brit) or* humor *(US)* **b** *(= sehr groß, heftig) Kälte, Spott etc* severe, harsh ADV furiously, grimly; **~ lächeln** to smile grimly
Grind [grɪnt] M **-(e)s, -e** [-də] scab; *(inf: Sw, S Ger: = Kopf)* bonce *(Brit inf)*, head
Grind|wal M pilot whale
grin|sen ['grɪnzn] VI to grin; *(vor Schadenfreude, Dreistigkeit, höhnisch auch)* to smirk; **er grinste über beide Ohren** his grin was ear to ear
Grin|sen NT **-s**, *no pl* grin; *(schadenfroh, dreist, höhnisch auch)* smirk
grip|pal [grɪ'pa:l] ADJ *(Med)* influenzal; **~er Infekt** influenza infection
Grip|pe ['grɪpə] F **-, -n** 'flu, influenza; *(= Erkältung)* cold
Grip|pe- *in cpds* 'flu, influenza; **Grip|pe|kran|ke(r)** MF *decl as adj* 'flu sufferer, person with (the) 'flu; **Grip|pe|(schutz)|imp|fung** F influenza vaccination; **Grip|pe|vi|rus** NT OR M 'flu virus; **Grip|pe|wel|le** F wave of 'flu *or* influenza
grip|pös [grɪ'pø:s] ADJ *attr* influenzal
Grips [grɪps] M **-es, -e** *(inf)* nous *(Brit inf)*, brains *pl (inf)*, sense; **nun strengt mal euren ~ an** use your nous *(Brit inf)*, use your common sense; **~ zu etw haben** to have the nous *(Brit inf) or* brains *(inf) or* common sense to do sth
Gris|li|bär M = **Grizzlybär**
Griss [grɪs] NT **-es**, *no pl (Aus inf)* crush
Grizz|ly|bär M ['grɪsli-] M grizzly (bear)
grob [gro:p] ADJ *comp* **=er** ['grø:bɐ], *superl* **=ste(r, s)** ['grø:pstə] **a** *(= nicht fein) Material, Oberfläche etc* coarse; *Arbeit* dirty *attr* **b** *(= ungefähr)* rough; **in ~en Umrissen** roughly **c** *(= schlimm, groß)* gross *(auch Jur)*; **den gröbsten Schmutz habe ich schon weggeputzt** I have already cleaned off the worst of the dirt; **ein ~er Fehler** a bad mistake, a gross error; **wir sind aus dem Gröbsten heraus** we're out of the woods (now), we can see the light at the end of the tunnel (now); **~e Fahrlässigkeit** gross negligence **d** *(= brutal, derb)* rough; *(fig: = derb)* coarse; *Antwort* rude; *(= unhöflich)* ill-mannered; **~ gegen jdn werden** to become offensive (towards sb); **auf einen ~en Klotz gehört ein ~er Keil** *(Prov)* one must answer rudeness with rudeness → **Geschütz**
ADV *comp* **=er**, *superl* **am =sten** **a** *(= nicht fein)* **~ zerkleinern/hacken** to chop coarsely; **etw ~ schneiden** to cut sth in large pieces; *Käse* to cut sth in thick slices; **~ gemahlen** coarsely ground; **~ mahlen** to grind coarsely **b** *(= ungefähr)* **~ geschätzt/gemessen/gerechnet** approximately, roughly, at a rough estimate; **etw ~ umreißen/skizzieren** to give a rough idea of sth; **etw ~ wiedergeben** to give a superficial *or* an approximate account of sth **c** *(= schlimm)* **~ fahrlässig handeln** to commit an act of gross negligence **d** *(= brutal) anfassen, behandeln* roughly; *massieren* hard, roughly; *(= unhöflich)* rudely; *(= barsch)* curtly; **~ mit jdm umspringen** to rough sb up; **jdm ~ kommen** *(inf)* to get coarse with sb
grob-, Grob- *in cpds* coarse
Gro|be(s) ['gro:bə] NT *decl as adj (fig)* dirty work; **ein Mann fürs ~** *(inf)* a man who does the dirty work
grob-: **grob|fa|se|rig, grob|fas|rig** ADJ coarse-fibred *(Brit)*, coarse-fibered *(US)*; **grob|ge|mah|len** [-gəma:lən] ADJ *attr* → **grob ADV a**; **grob+ha|cken** VT *sep* → **grob ADV a**
Grob|heit F **-, -en** **a** *(= Beschimpfung, Ausdrucksweise)* foul language *no pl* **b** *(= Manieren)* bad manners *pl* **c** *(von Material)* coarseness; *(von Gerät)* crudeness
Gro|bi|an ['gro:bia:n] M **-(e)s, -e** brute
grob-: **grob|klot|zig** ADJ *(pej) Benehmen, Kerl etc* clumsy, hamfisted; **grob|kno|chig** ADJ big-boned; **grob|kör|nig** ADJ coarse-grained
gröb|lich ['grø:plɪç] ADJ **a** *(form: = schlimm)* gross **b** *(geh: = heftig, derb)* gross ADV **a** *(form: = schwerwiegend)* grossly; *missachten* grossly, largely **b** *(geh: = derb)* badly; *beleidigen, kränken* deeply, badly; **jdn ~ beschimpfen** to call sb rude names
Grob-: **grob+mah|len** VT *sep irreg* → **grob ADV a**; **grob|ma|schig** [-maʃɪç] ADJ large-meshed; *(= grob gestrickt)* loose-knit *attr* ADV coarsely; **grob|mo|to|risch** ADJ gross-motor *attr*; **~e Entwicklung** gross-motor development; **Grob|mo|to|rik** F **-**, *no pl (Med etc)* gross motor skills *pl*; **grob|schläch|tig** [-ʃlɛçtɪç] ADJ coarse; *Mensch* big-built, heavily built; *(fig)* unrefined; **Grob|schläch|tig|keit** F **-**, *no pl* coarseness; *(von Mensch)* heavy *or* big build; *(fig)* lack of refinement; **grob+schnei|den** VT *sep irreg* → **grob ADV a**; **Grob|schnitt** M *(= Tabak)* coarse cut; **Grob|strick** M coarse knit
Grö|faz ['grø:fats] M **-'** *(iro)* **der ~** the Big Chief *(hum)*, the great General *(iro)*
Grog [grɔk] M **-s, -s** grog
grog|gy ['grɔgi] ADJ *pred (Boxen)* groggy; *(inf: = erschöpft)* all-in *(inf)*
grö|len ['grø:lən] VTI *(pej)* to bawl; **~de Stimme/Menge** raucous voice/crowd; **~d durch die Straßen ziehen** to roam rowdily through the streets
Grö|le|rei [grø:lə'rai] F **-, -en** *(pej)* bawling *no pl*
Groll [grɔl] M **-(e)s**, *no pl (= Zorn)* anger, wrath *(liter)*; *(= Erbitterung)* resentment; **einen ~ gegen jdn hegen** to harbour *(Brit) or* harbor *(US)* a grudge against sb
grol|len ['grɔlən] VI *(geh)* **a** *(= dröhnen)* to rumble; *(Donner auch)* to roll, to peal *(liter)* **b** *(= böse sein)* **(jdm) ~** to be annoyed (with sb); **(mit) seinem Schicksal ~** to bemoan one's fate
Grön|land ['grø:nlant] NT **-s** Greenland
Grön|län|der ['grø:nlɛndɐ] M **-s, -**, **Grön|län|de|rin** [-ərɪn] F **-, -nen** Greenlander
grön|län|disch ['grø:nlɛndɪʃ] ADJ Greenland *attr*
Grön|land|wal M bowhead (whale)
groo|ven ['gru:vn] VI *(Mus sl)* **das groovt** it's grooving
Gros [gro:] NT **-, -** [gro:s] *(= Mehrzahl)* major *or* greater part, majority, bulk → **en gros**
Gros [grɔs] NT **-ses, -se** *or (bei Zahlenangaben)* **-** *(Measure)* gross
Gro|schen ['grɔʃn] M **-s, -** **a** *(Aus: Hist)* groschen; *(in Polen)* grosz; *(Hist)* groschen **b** *(Hist inf)* 10-pfennig piece; *(fig)* penny, cent *(US)*; **seine paar ~ zusammenhalten** to scrape together a few pence *or* pennies/cents *(US)*; **sich (dat) ein paar ~ verdienen** to earn (oneself) a few pence *or* pennies/cents *(US)*, to earn (oneself) a bit of pocket money; **der ~ ist gefallen** *(hum inf)* the penny has dropped *(inf)*; **bei ihm fällt der ~ pfennigweise** he's pretty slow on the uptake, it takes him a while to catch on
Gro|schen-: **Gro|schen|blatt** NT *(pej)* (cheap) rag *(inf)*, sensational (news)paper; **die Groschenblätter** the gutter press *(Brit pej)*, the yellow press *(US)*; **Gro|schen|grab** NT *(hum: = Spielautomat)* one-armed bandit; **diese Parkuhr ist ein richtiges ~** this parking meter just swallows *or* eats up your money; **Gro|schen|heft** NT *(pej)* pulp magazine; *(= Krimi auch)* penny dreadful *(dated)*; **Gro|schen|ro|man** M *(pej)* cheap *or* dime-store *(US)* novel

groß [gro:s]

1 ADJEKTIV 2 ADVERB

1 – ADJEKTIV

comp **=er** ['grø:sɐ], *superl* **=te(r, s)** ['grø:stə]

a big; *Fläche, Raum, Haus, Hände* big, large; *Höhe, Breite* great; *Größe, Tube, Dose, Packung etc* large; *(Typ) Buchstabe* capital; **ein ganz großes Haus/Buch** a great big house/book; **der große (Uhr)zeiger** the big *or* minute hand; **x ist größer als 10** *(Math)* x is greater than 10; **die Wiese ist 10 Hektar groß** the field measures 10 hectares; **ein 2 Hektar großes Grundstück** a 2-hectare plot of land; **ein Loch größer machen** to make a hole bigger; **ein großes Bier, ein Großes** *(inf)* ≈ a pint (of beer) *(Brit)*, a large beer; **großes Geld** notes *pl (Brit)*, bills *pl (US)*; **ich habe nur großes Geld** I haven't got any change on me; **die große Masse** *(fig)* the vast majority; **im Großen und Ganzen (gesehen)** by and large; **im Großen einkaufen** to buy in bulk *or* quantity → **Glocke**

b = hoch, hochgewachsen tall; **ein großer Mann** a tall man; **wie groß bist du?** how tall are you?; **er ist 1,80 Meter groß** he's one metre *(Brit) or* meter *(US)* eighty (tall); **du bist groß geworden** you've grown

c = älter *Bruder, Schwester* big; **unsere Große** our eldest *or* oldest (daughter); *(von zweien)* our elder daughter; **unser Großer** our eldest *or* oldest (son); *(von zweien)* our elder son; **Groß und Klein** young and old (alike); **mit etw groß geworden sein** to have grown up with sth; **die Großen** *(= Erwachsene)* the grown-ups; *(= ältere Kinder)* the older children; **zu groß für etw sein** to be too big for sth; **er ist ein großes Kind** he's a big *or* a great big *(inf)* baby

d zeitlich *Verzögerung, Rede* big, long; **die große Pause** *(Sch)* the long *or* lunch break; **die großen Ferien** the summer holidays *(Brit) or* holiday *(US)*

e = beträchtlich, wichtig, bedeutend great; *Erfolg, Enttäuschung, Hoffnung, Eile* great, big; *Gewinn, Ereignis* big; *Katastrophe, Schreck* terrible; *Summe* large; *Geschwindigkeit* high; **er hat Großes geleistet** he has achieved great things; **die größ-**

ten Erfindungen unseres Jahrhunderts the greatest inventions of our century; **ein großer Dichter wie Goethe** a great poet like Goethe; **eine große Dummheit machen** to do something very *or* really stupid; **großen Durst haben** to be very thirsty; **er ist kein großer Esser** *(inf)* he's not a big eater; **eine der größeren Firmen** one of the major companies; **die großen Fragen unserer Zeit** the great *or* big questions of our time; **das große Ganze** the broader *or* wider view; **große Gefühle** strong feelings; **vor meinem Haus war** *or* **herrschte ein großer Lärm** there was a lot of noise outside my house; **großen Hunger haben** to be very hungry; **ich habe große Lust zu verreisen** I'd really like to go away (on holiday *(Brit)* or vacation *(US)*); **sie hatte große Lust, sich zu verkleiden** she really wanted to get dressed up; **ich habe keine große Lust** I don't particularly want to; **große Mode sein** to be all the rage *(inf)*; **einen großen Namen haben** to be a big name; **die große Nummer** *(im Zirkus)* the big number, the star turn *(esp Brit)*; **ich bin kein großer Redner** *(inf)* I'm no great speaker; **ich bin kein großer Opernfreund** *(inf)* I'm not a great opera fan; **im größten Regen/Schneesturm** in the middle of a downpour/snowstorm; **jds große Stunde** sb's big moment; **eine größere Summe** a biggish *or* largish sum; **er ist kein großer Trinker** *(inf)* he's not a big drinker; **die große Welt** *(= die Fremde)* the big wide world; *(= die oberen zehntausend)* high society, the upper crust; **große Worte** big words; **große Worte machen** to use grand words

f [= großartig, bewundernswert] *iro* great; **das ist** *or* **finde ich ganz groß** *(inf)* that's really great *(inf)*

g [in Eigennamen] Great; **die Großen Seen** the Great Lakes; **der Große Ozean** the Pacific; **Karl der Große** Charlemagne; **Alfred/Friedrich der Große** Alfred/Frederick the Great

h [Mus] **große Sexte** major sixth

2 – ADVERB
comp **=er**, *superl* **am =ten**

a [= nicht klein] **groß gewachsen** tall; **groß gemustert** large-print, with a large print; **groß kariert** large-check(ed); **groß machen** *(baby-talk)* to do number two *(baby-talk)*, to do a poo *(Brit baby-talk)*; **groß daherreden** *(inf)* to talk big *(inf)* → **großschreiben**

b [= in großem Ausmaß] **groß einkaufen gehen** to go on a spending spree, to splash out *(Brit inf)*; **groß ausgehen** to go out somewhere expensive; **groß feiern** to have a big celebration; **groß aufgemacht** dressed up to the nines; **groß angelegt** large-scale; **groß und breit** *(fig inf)* at great length

c [= besonders] **jdn groß anblicken** to give sb a hard stare; **groß in Mode sein** to be all the rage *(inf)*; **was ist das schon groß?** *(inf)* big deal! *(inf)*, so what? *(inf)*; **was soll man da schon groß machen/sagen?** *(inf)* what can you do/say?; **er hat sich nicht gerade groß für unsere Belange eingesetzt** *(inf)* he didn't exactly put up a big fight for us; **ich habe mich nie groß um Politik gekümmert** *(inf)* I've never been a great one for politics *(inf)*; **ich kümmere mich nicht groß darum** *(inf)* I don't take much notice; **ganz groß rauskommen** *(inf)* to make the big time *(inf)*

Groß- PREF *(vor Namen von Ballungsräumen)* Greater; **~Berlin** Greater Berlin

Groß-: **Groß|ab|neh|mer(in)** M(F) *(Comm)* bulk purchaser *or* buyer; **Groß|ad|mi|ral** M *(Naut Hist)* Grand Admiral, ≈ Admiral of the Fleet; **Groß|ak|ti|o|när(in)** M(F) major *or* principal shareholder; **Groß|alarm** M red alert; **~ geben** to give a red alert; **groß|an|ge|legt** ADJ → **groß 2 b**; **Groß|an|griff** M large-scale *or* major attack; **Groß|an|lass** M *(Sw)* = **Großveranstaltung**; **groß|ar|tig** ADJ wonderful, superb, splendid; *Erfolg* tremendous; *(= prächtig) Bauwerk etc* magnificent, splendid; **er hat Großartiges geleistet** he has achieved great things; **eine ~e Frau** a wonderful *or* fine woman ADV wonderfully, splendidly, magnificently; **ha, ~** *(iro)* wonderful!, that's just great *or* wonderful; **~ tun** *(pej)* to show off, to give oneself airs; **Groß|ar|tig|keit** F magnificence, splendour *(Brit)*, splendor *(US)*; **Groß|auf|ge|bot** NT large number *or* contingent (*an* +*dat* of); **ein ~ an Polizisten** a large police contingent; **Groß|auf|nah|me** F *(Phot, Film)* close-up; **Groß|auf|trag** M *(Comm)* large-scale *or* major order; **Groß|bank** F *pl* **-banken** major *or* big bank; **Groß|bau|er** M *pl* **-bauern**, **Groß|bäu|e|rin** F big farmer; **groß|bäu|er|lich** ADJ of a big farmer/big farmers; **Groß|bau|stel|le** F construction site; **Groß|be|ben** NT *(Geol)* major earthquake; **Groß|be|häl|ter** M tank; *(= Container)* container; **Groß|be|trieb** M large concern; *(Agr)* big farm; **Groß|be|zü|ger** [-bətsyːgɐ] M **-s, -, Groß|be|zü|ge|rin** [-ərɪn] F **-, -nen** *(Sw)* bulk purchaser *or* buyer; **Groß|bild** NT blow-up; **Groß|bild|ka|me|ra** F plate camera; **Groß|bild|schirm** M large screen; **Groß|bour|geoi|sie** F *(Sociol, Pol)* upper classes *pl*, upper bourgeoisie; **Groß|brand** M enormous blaze, major *or* big fire; **Groß|bri|tan|ni|en** [groːsbri'taniən] NT (Great) Britain; **groß|bri|tan|nisch** [groːsbri'tanɪʃ] ADJ (Great) British, Britannic *(rare)*; **Groß|buch|sta|be** M capital (letter), uppercase letter *(Typ)*; **Groß|bür|ger(in)** M(F) *(Sociol)* member of the upper classes; **groß|bür|ger|lich** ADJ *(Sociol)* upper-class; **Groß|bür|ger|tum** NT *(Sociol)* upper classes *pl*; **Groß|com|pu|ter** M mainframe (computer); **Groß|de|monst|ra|ti|on** F mass demonstration; **groß|deutsch** ADJ *(Hist)* Pan-German; **das Großdeutsche Reich** *(NS)* the Reich; **Groß|deutsch|land** NT *(NS)* Greater Germany; **Groß|druck** M, *no pl* large print; **ein Buch im ~** a large-print book

Grö|ße [grøːsə] F **-, -n** **a** *(= Format, Maßeinheit)* size; **nach der ~** according to size; **er trägt** *or* **hat ~ 48** he takes *or* is size 48 **b** *no pl (= Höhe, Körpergröße)* height; *(= Flächeninhalt)* size, area, dimensions *pl*; *(= Dimension)* size, dimensions *pl*; *(Math, Phys)* quantity; *(Astron)* magnitude; **nach der ~** according to height/size; **eine unbekannte ~** *(lit, fig)* an unknown quantity; **ein Stern erster ~** a star of the first magnitude **c** *no pl (= Ausmaß)* extent; *(= Bedeutsamkeit)* significance **d** *no pl (= Erhabenheit)* greatness **e** *(= bedeutender Mensch)* leading light, important figure

Groß-: **Groß|ein|kauf** M bulk purchase, bulk purchasing *no indef art, no pl*; **Groß|ein|satz** M **~ der Feuerwehr/Polizei** *etc* large-scale operation by the fire brigade/police *etc*; **der ~ von Truppen** the large-scale use *or* deployment of troops; **groß|el|ter|lich** ADJ *attr* of one's grandparents; **im ~en Haus wohnen** to live in one's grandparents' house; **Groß|el|tern** PL grandparents *pl*

Grö|ßen|an|ga|be F (indication *or* specification of) size

Groß-: **Groß|en|kel** M great-grandchild; *(= Junge)* great-grandson; **Groß|en|ke|lin** F great-granddaughter

Grö|ßen-: **Grö|ßen|klas|se** F *(Astron)* magnitude; *(Comm)* (size) class; **Grö|ßen|ord|nung** F scale; *(= Größe)* magnitude; *(Math)* order (of magnitude); **ich denke in anderen ~en** I think on a different scale

gro|ßen|teils ['groːsn'tails] ADV mostly, for the most part; **er macht seine Arbeit ~ selbstständig** he does his work mostly on his own, he does his work on his own for the most part

Grö|ßen-: **Grö|ßen|un|ter|schied** M *(im Format)* difference in size; *(in der Höhe, im Wuchs)* difference in height; *(in der Bedeutung)* difference in importance; **Grö|ßen|ver|hält|nis** NT proportions *pl* (+*gen* between); *(= Maßstab)* scale; **im ~ 1:100** on the scale 1:100; **etw im richtigen ~ sehen** to see sth in perspective; **Grö|ßen|wahn|(sinn)** M megalomania, delusions *pl* of grandeur; **grö|ßen|wahn|sin|nig** ADJ *Mensch, Bauten etc* megalomaniac(al); **er ist ~** he is a megalomaniac; **Grö|ßen|wahn|sin|ni|ge(r)** MF *decl as adj* megalomaniac

grö|ßer *comp von* **groß**

grö|ße|ren|teils ['grøːsərən'tails] ADV = **großenteils**

Groß-: **Groß|fahn|dung** F large-scale manhunt; **Groß|fa|mi|lie** F extended family; **Groß|feu|er** NT major fire, enormous blaze; **groß|flä|chig** ADJ extensive; *Gemälde, Muster etc* covering a large area; *Gesicht* flat-featured; **Groß|flug|ha|fen** M major airport; **Groß|flug|zeug** NT large-capacity aircraft; **Groß|for|mat** NT large size; *(bei Büchern, Fotos auch)* large format; **ein ... im ~** a large-size .../large-format ...; **groß|for|ma|tig** [-fɔrmaːtɪç] ADJ large-size; *Bücher, Fotos auch* large-format; **Groß|fo|to** NT giant photo(graph); **Groß|fürst** M *(Hist)* grand prince; **Groß|fürs|ten|tum** NT *(Hist)* grand principality; **Groß|fürs|tin** F *(Hist)* grand princess; **groß+füt|tern** VT *sep* to raise, to rear; **Groß|ga|ra|ge** F large (underground) car park *(Brit)* or parking garage *(US)*; **Groß|ge|mein|de** F *municipality with several villages or districts*; **groß|ge|mus|tert** ADJ → **groß 2 c**; **groß|ge|wach|sen** ADJ → **groß 2 c**; **Groß|grund|be|sitz** M **a** large-scale land-holding **b** *(= die Großgrundbesitzer)* big landowners *pl*; **Groß|grund|be|sit|zer(in)** M(F) big landowner

Groß|han|del M wholesale trade, wholesaling *no art*; **etw im ~ kaufen** to buy sth wholesale

Groß|han|dels- *in cpds* wholesale; **Groß|han|dels|kauf|frau** F, **Groß|han|dels|kauf|mann** M wholesaler; **Groß|han|dels|preis** M wholesale price; **Groß|han|dels|ra|batt** M bulk discount

Groß-: **Groß|händ|ler(in)** M(F) wholesaler; *(inf: = Großhandlung)* wholesaler's; **Groß|hand|lung** F wholesale business; **groß|her|zig** ADJ *Mensch, Geschenk, Angebot* generous, magnanimous; **~e Motive** the best of motives; **Groß|her|zig|keit** [-hɛrtsɪçkait] F **-**, *no pl* generosity, magnanimity; **Groß|her|zog** M grand duke; **(der) ~ Roland** Grand Duke Roland; **Groß|her|zo|gin** F grand duchess; **groß|her|zog|lich** ADJ grand ducal; **Groß|her|zog|tum** NT grand duchy; **das ~ Luxemburg** the Grand Duchy of Luxembourg; **Groß|hirn** NT cerebrum; **Groß|hirn|rin|de** F cerebral cortex; **Groß|in|dust|rie** F major *or* big industry; **groß|in|dust|ri|ell** ADJ major industrial *attr*; **Groß|in|dust|ri|el|le(r)** MF *decl as adj* major *or* big industrialist; **die französischen ~n** the major *or* big French industrialists; **Groß|in|qui|si|tor** M *(Hist)* Grand Inquisitor

Gros|sist [grɔ'sɪst] M **-en, -en**, **Gros|sis|tin** [-'sɪstɪn] F **-, -nen** wholesaler; *(inf: = Großhandlung)* wholesaler's

Groß-: **groß|jäh|rig** ADJ *(dated)* of age, major *(form)*; **~ werden** to come of age, to reach the age of majority; **groß|ka|li|be|rig** [-kaliːbərɪç], **groß|ka|lib|rig** [-kaliːbrɪç] ADJ large-calibre *(Brit)*, large-caliber *(US)*

Groß|kampf-: **Groß|kampf|schiff** NT capital ship; **Groß|kampf|tag** M *(Mil)* day of a/the great battle; **Montag ist bei uns im Büro meist ~** *(hum)* it's usually all systems go on Monday in the office *(inf)*

Groß-: **Groß|ka|pi|tal** NT **das ~** big business; **Groß|ka|pi|ta|list(in)** M(F) big capitalist; **was, du willst 50 Euro? ich bin doch kein ~!** what - you want 50 euros? I'm not made of money! *(inf)*; **groß|ka|riert** ADJ → **groß 2 c**; **Groß|kat|ze** F big cat; **Groß|kind** NT *(Sw)* grandchild; **Groß|ki|no** NT multiplex cinema; **Groß|kli|ma** NT macroclimate; **Groß|knecht** M *(old)* chief (farm)hand; **Groß|-**

kon|zern M big *or* large combine; **Groß|kop|fe(r)|te(r)** ['gro:skɔpfətə, -kɔpftətə] MF *decl as adj (Aus, S Ger. pej)* bigwig *(inf)*, bigshot *(inf)*; **Groß|kotz** ['gro:skɔts] M **-es, -e** *(pej inf)* swank *(inf)*; **groß|kot|zig** ['gro:skɔtsɪç] *(pej inf)* ADJ swanky *(inf)* ADV swankily *(inf)*, pretentiously; ~ **auftreten** to act swankily *or* pretentiously, to be swanky *(inf) or* pretentious; **Groß|kot|zig|keit** F **-, -en** *(pej inf)* swank *(inf) no pl*; **Groß|kraft|werk** NT large power plant; **Groß|kreuz** NT Grand Cross; **Groß|kü|che** F canteen kitchen; **Groß|kun|de** M, **Groß|kun|din** F *(Comm)* major client; **Groß|kund|ge|bung** F mass rally; **Groß|lein|wand** F *(Film)* big screen; **Groß|macht** F *(Pol)* big *or* great power

Groß|macht-: **Groß|macht|po|li|tik** F (big) power politics; **Groß|macht|stel|lung** F great-power *or* big-power status

Groß-: **Groß|ma|ma** [-mama:] F grandmama *(dated)*, grandma; **Groß|manns|sucht** F, *no pl (pej)* craving for status; **Groß|markt** M hypermarket *(Brit)*, large supermarket; **groß|ma|schig** [-maʃɪç] ADJ, ADV = **grobmaschig**; **Groß|mast** M mainmast; **Groß|maul** NT *(pej inf)* bigmouth *(inf)*, loudmouth *(inf)*; **groß|mäu|lig** [-mɔylɪç] *(pej inf)* ADJ big-mouthed *attr (inf)*, loudmouthed *(inf)*; *Erklärungen, Worte* boastful ADV boastfully; ~ **verkünden, dass ...** to brag *or* boast that ...; **Groß|mäu|lig|keit** F **-,** *no pl (pej inf)* big mouth *(inf)*; **Groß|meis|ter** M Grand Master; **Groß|mo|gul** M *(Hist)* Great Mogul; **Groß|muf|ti** M *(Hist)* grand mufti; **Groß|mut** F **-,** *no pl* magnanimity; **groß|mü|tig** [-my:tɪç] ADJ magnanimous ADV magnanimously; **Groß|mü|tig|keit** F **-,** *no pl* magnanimity; **Groß|mut|ter** F grandmother; **das kannst du deiner ~ erzählen!** *(inf)* you can tell that one to the marines *(Brit inf)*, pull the other one *(inf)*; **groß|müt|ter|lich** ADJ *attr* **a** *(= von der Großmutter)* of one's grandmother; **im ~en Haus wohnen** to live in one's grandmother's house; **das ~e Erbe** one's inheritance from one's grandmother **b** *(= in der Art einer Großmutter)* grandmotherly; **groß|müt|ter|li|cher|seits** ADV on one's grandmother's side; **Groß|nef|fe** M great-nephew; **Groß|nich|te** F great-niece; **Groß|of|fen|si|ve** F *(Mil)* major offensive; **Groß|ok|tav** [-ɔkta:f] NT **-s,** *no pl* large octavo; **Groß|on|kel** M great-uncle; **Groß|pa|ckung** F large *or* economy pack; **Groß|pa|pa** [-papa:] M grandpapa *(dated)*, grandpa; **Groß|plas|tik** F large sculpture; **groß|po|rig** ADJ large-pored; **Groß|pro|duk|ti|on** F large-scale production; **Groß|pro|du|zent(in)** M(F) large-scale producer; **Groß|pro|jekt** NT large-scale project; **Groß|putz** M **-es, -e** thorough cleaning, ≈ spring cleaning; **Groß|quart** NT large quarto; **Groß|rat** M, **Groß|rä|tin** F *(Sw)* member of a/the Cantonal parliament

Groß|raum M *(einer Stadt)* **der ~ München** the Munich area *or* conurbation, Greater Munich

Groß|raum-: **Groß|raum|ab|teil** NT *(Rail)* open-plan carriage *(Brit) or* car *(US)*; **Groß|raum|bü|ro** NT open-plan office; **Groß|raum|flug|zeug** NT large-capacity aircraft

Groß-: **groß|räu|mig** [-rɔymɪç] ADJ **a** *(= mit großen Räumen)* with large rooms; ~ **sein** to have large rooms **b** *(= mit viel Platz, geräumig)* roomy, spacious **c** *(= über große Flächen)* extensive **d** *(= im großen Umkreis)* **~es Umfahren eines Gebietes** making a large detour (a)round an area ADV **ein Gebiet ~ absperren** to cordon off a large area; **Ortskundige sollten den Bereich ~ umfahren** local drivers should find an alternative route well away from the area; **Groß|raum|wa|gen** M *(von Straßenbahn)* articulated tram *(esp Brit) or* streetcar *(US)*; *(Rail)* open-plan carriage *(Brit) or* car *(US)*; **Groß|raz|zia** F large-scale raid; **Groß|rech|ner** M mainframe (computer); **Groß|rei|ne|ma|chen** NT thorough cleaning, ≈ spring-cleaning; **Groß|schiff|fahrts|weg** M major waterway *(for seagoing ships)*; **groß+schrei|ben** VT *sep irreg* **a ein Wort ~** to write a word with a capital/in capitals; **b großgeschrieben werden** *(fig inf)* to be stressed, to be given pride of place, to be writ large; **groß schrei|ben** △ VT *irreg* → **großschreiben b**; **Groß|schrei|bung** F capitalization; *(Typ, Comput)* upper-case; **Groß-/Kleinschreibung** *(Comput)* case-sensitive; **Groß-/Kleinschreibung beachten** *(Comput)* match case; **Groß|se|gel** NT *(Naut)* mainsail; **groß|spre|che|risch** [-ʃprɛçərɪʃ] ADJ *(pej)* boastful, boasting *attr*, bragging *attr*; **groß|spu|rig** [-ʃpu:rɪç] *(pej)* ADJ flashy *(inf)*, showy *(inf)* ADV **etw ~ erklären** to make a show of saying sth; ~ **reden** to speak flamboyantly; **sich ~ benehmen** to be flashy; **Groß|spu|rig|keit** F **-, -en** *(pej)* flashiness *(inf) no pl*, showiness *(inf) no pl*

Groß|stadt F city

Groß|stadt|be|völ|ke|rung F city population

Groß|städ|ter(in) M(F) city dweller

groß|städ|tisch ADJ big-city *attr* ADV **München wirkt ~er als Bonn** Munich has more of a big-city feel to it than Bonn

Groß|stadt- *in cpds* city; **Groß|stadt|kind** NT city child, city kid *(inf)*; **Groß|stadt|mensch** M city dweller; **der** ~ urban man, city dwellers *pl*

Groß-: **Groß|tan|te** F great-aunt; **Groß|tat** F great feat; **eine medizinische ~** a great medical feat; **groß|tech|nisch** ADJ *Projekt, Anlage, Produktion, Nutzung* large-scale ADV **Kernkraft ~ erzeugen** to produce nuclear power on a large scale

Groß|teil M large part; **zum ~** in the main, for the most part; **zu einem ~** for the most part

groß|teils ['gro:stails], **größ|ten|teils** ['grø:stn'tails] ADV in the main, for the most part

größ|te(r, s) *superl von* **groß**

Größt-: **Größt|maß** NT *(fig)* maximum amount *(an +dat* of); **größt|mög|lich** ADJ *attr* greatest possible

Groß-: **Groß|tuer** [-tu:ɐ] M **-s, -**, **Groß|tu|e|rin** [-ərɪn] F **-, -nen** *(pej)* boaster, bragger, show-off; **Groß|tu|e|rei** [-tu:ə'rai] F *(pej)* **a** *no pl* boasting, bragging, showing off **b** *(= großtuerische Äußerung etc)* boast; **groß|tu|e|risch** [-tu:ərɪʃ] ADJ *(pej)* boastful, bragging; **groß+tun** *sep irreg (pej)* VI to boast, to brag, to show off VR **sich mit etw ~** to show off *or* boast *or* brag about sth; **Groß|un|ter|neh|men** NT large concern; **Groß|un|ter|neh|mer(in)** M(F) big businessman/-woman *or* entrepreneur

Groß|va|ter M grandfather

groß|vä|ter|lich ADJ **a** *(= vom Großvater)* of one's grandfather; **er hat den ~en Betrieb übernommen** he has taken over his grandfather's business; **das ~e Erbe** one's inheritance from one's grandfather **b** *(= in der Art eines Großvaters)* grandfatherly

groß|vä|ter|li|cher|seits ADV on one's grandfather's side

Groß|va|ter-: **Groß|va|ter|ses|sel** M, **Groß|va|ter|stuhl** M *(inf)* fireside armchair; **Groß|va|ter|uhr** F *(inf)* grandfather clock

Groß-: **Groß|ver|an|stal|tung** F big event; *(= Großkundgebung)* mass rally; **eine sportliche ~** a big sporting event; **Groß|ver|brau|cher(in)** M(F) large consumer; **Groß|ver|die|ner(in)** M(F) big earner; **Groß|ver|such** M *(esp Psych)* large-scale experiment; **Groß|vieh** NT cattle and horses *pl*; **Groß|vieh|ein|heit** *(Agr)* livestock unit; **Groß|we|sir** M *(Hist)* grand vizier; **Groß|wet|ter|la|ge** F general weather situation; **die politische ~** the general political climate

Groß|wild NT big game

Groß|wild-: **Groß|wild|jagd** F big-game hunting; **eine ~** a big-game hunt; **auf ~ gehen** to go big-game hunting; **Groß|wild|jä|ger(in)** M(F) big-game hunter

Groß-: **Groß|wör|ter|buch** NT large *or* comprehensive dictionary; **groß|wüch|sig** [-vy:ksɪç] ADJ *(form)* tall; **groß+zie|hen** VT *sep irreg* to raise; *Tier* to rear; **groß|zü|gig** ADJ generous; *(= weiträumig)* spacious; *Plan* large-scale, ambitious; *(inf: = ungenau)* generous, liberal ADV generously; *(= spendabel)* magnanimously; *(= weiträumig)* spaciously; ~ **gerechnet** at a liberal *or* generous estimate; **Groß|zü|gig|keit** [-tsy:gɪçkait] F **-,** *no pl* generosity; *(= Weiträumigkeit)* spaciousness; *(von Plan)* (large) scale, ambitiousness; *(inf: = Ungenauigkeit)* generousness, liberality

gro|tesk [gro'tɛsk] ADJ grotesque ADV grotesquely; **~ wirken/aussehen** to look grotesque

Gro|tesk [gro'tɛsk] F **-,** *no pl (Typ)* grotesque, sans serif

Gro|tes|ke [gro'tɛskə] F **-, -n** *(Art)* grotesque(rie); *(Liter)* grotesquerie

gro|tes|ker|wei|se [gro'tɛskɐ'vaizə] ADV ironically enough

Grot|te ['grɔtə] F **-, -n** **a** *(= Höhle)* grotto **b** *(sl: = Vagina)* pussy *(sl)*

Grot|ten|olm [-ɔlm] M **-s, -e** *(Zool)* olm *(spec)*

Grou|pie ['gru:pi] NT **-s, -s** groupie

Group|ware ['gru:pwɛ:ɐ] F **-, -s** *(Comput: = Gruppen-Software)* groupware

grub *pret von* **graben**

Grub|ber ['grubɐ] M **-s, -** *(Agr)* grubber

Grüb|chen ['gry:pçən] NT **-s, -** dimple

Gru|be ['gru:bə] F **-, -n** pit; *(klein)* hole, hollow; *(Min)* mine, pit; *(dated: = Gruft, Grab)* grave; **wer andern eine ~ gräbt(, fällt selbst hinein)** *(Prov)* you can easily fall into your own trap; **in die ~ (ein)fahren** to go down the pit; **in die** *or* **zur ~ fahren** *(old)* to give up the ghost

Grü|be|lei [gry:bə'lai] F **-, -en** brooding *no pl*

grü|beln ['gry:bln] VI to brood *(über +acc* about, over)

Gru|ben- *in cpds* pit *(Brit)*, mine; **Gru|ben|ar|bei|ter(in)** M(F) pit *(Brit) or* mine worker; *(Mann auch)* miner, pitman *(Brit)*; **Gru|ben|gas** NT firedamp; **Gru|ben|un|glück** NT mining accident *or* disaster, pit disaster; **Gru|ben|wa|gen** M mine car

Grüb|ler ['gry:blɐ] M **-s, -**, **Grüb|le|rin** [-ərɪn] F **-, -nen** brooder, brooding type

grüb|le|risch ['gry:blərɪʃ] ADJ pensive, brooding

grü|e|zi ['gry:ɛtsi] INTERJ *(Sw)* hello, hi *(inf)*, good morning/afternoon/evening

Gruft [gruft] F **-, =e** ['grʏftə] tomb, vault; *(in Kirchen)* crypt; *(= offenes Grab)* grave

Gruf|ti ['grufti] M **-s, -s** **a** *(inf: = älterer Mensch)* old fogey *(inf)* **b** *(sl: = Okkultist)* ≈ goth

gruf|tig ['gruftɪç] ADJ *(inf: = altmodisch) Musik, Mode* square *(inf)*, old hat *(inf)*; *(= moderig) Keller etc* musty

grum|meln ['grumln] VI to rumble; *(inf: = brummeln)* to mumble

Grum|met ['grumət] NT **-s,** *no pl*, **Grumt** [grumt] NT **-s,** *no pl (Agr)* aftermath, rowen *(dial, US)*

grün [gry:n] ADJ *(alle Bedeutungen)* green; *(Pol auch)* ecological; **~e Heringe** fresh herrings; **Aal ~** *(Cook)* (dish of) fresh eel *(with parsley sauce)*; **~er Salat** lettuce; **die Grüne Insel** the Emerald Isle; **ein ~er Junge** *(inf)* a greenhorn *(inf)*; **~es Licht (für etw) geben/haben** *(fig)* to give/have got the go-ahead *or* green light (for sth); **(noch) im ~en Bereich** *(fig)* (still) all clear; **komm an meine ~e Seite!** *(inf)* come and sit up close to me; **am ~en Tisch, vom ~en Tisch aus** from a bureaucratic ivory tower; **über die ~e Grenze fahren/kommen** *(inf)* to cross the border illegally *(in a wood etc)*; **die ~e Hölle** *(fig)* the green hell of the jungle; **die ~en Lungen der Großstadt** *(fig)* the breathing spaces of the city; **~e Minna** *(inf)* Black Maria *(Brit inf)*, paddy wagon *(US inf)*; **der Grüne Plan** *(Pol)* Agricultural Aid Plan; **die ~e Tonne** container for re-

cyclable waste; **wir haben ~e Weihnachten gehabt** we didn't have a white Christmas; **~e Welle** phased traffic lights; **~e Welle bei 60 km/h** traffic lights phased for 60 kmph; **~ im Gesicht werden** to go green (about the gills *(inf)*); **~e Witwe** *(inf)* lonely suburban housewife; **auf keinen ~en Zweig kommen** *(fig inf)* to get nowhere; **die beiden sind sich gar nicht ~** *(inf)* there's no love lost between them; **er ist dir nicht ~** *(inf)* you're not in his good books *(inf)*
ADV *(= in grüner Farbe) gekleidet* (in) green; *(= mit grüner Farbe) streichen, anmalen* green; *umranden, unterstreichen* in green → **blauärgern, blauschlagen**

GRÜNER PUNKT

The **Grüner Punkt** is a symbol used on packaging materials which are suitable for recycling and which should therefore be put in the **gelbe Tonne** or **gelber Sack**, separate from other waste. Manufacturers wishing to use the symbol on their products must obtain a permit from **DSD (Duales System Deutschland GmbH)**. → DUALES SYSTEM

GRÜNE WOCHE

The International **Grüne Woche**, which takes place every year in Berlin, is a food fair focusing on food science, agriculture and horticulture. It is particularly popular with the general public, since delicacies and specialities from all over the world are on offer.

Grün [gry:n] NT **-s, -** *or (inf)* **-s** green; *(= Grünflächen)* green spaces *pl*; *(Golf)* green; *(Cards: = Pik)* spades *pl*; **die Ampel steht auf ~** the light is (at *(Brit)*) green; **das ist dasselbe in ~** *(inf)* it's (one and) the same (thing)

Grün- *in cpds* green; **Grün|al|ge** F green alga; **grün|al|ter|na|tiv** ADJ *(Pol)* green alternative; **Grün|an|la|ge** F green space *or* area; **grün|äu|gig** ADJ green-eyed; **grün|blau** ADJ green-ish-blue, greeny-blue; **grün|blind** ADJ suffering from red-green colour-blindness *(Brit) or* color-blindness *(US)*; **Grün|blind|heit** F red--green colour-blindness *(Brit) or* color-blindness *(US)*

Grund [grʊnt] ✪ 42.2, 44.1, 44.2, 53.2 M **-(e)s, ⸚e** **a** ['grʏndə] *no pl (= Erdboden)* ground; *(old, dial: = Erdreich)* soil, ground; **~ und Boden** land; **in ~ und Boden** *(fig, sich blamieren, schämen)* utterly; *verdammen* outright; **jdn in ~ und Boden reden** not to leave sb a leg to stand on, to shoot sb's arguments to pieces; **bis auf den ~ zerstören/abtragen** to raze to the ground
b *(Aus) (= Bauplatz)* (building) plot; *(= Grundstück)* grounds *pl*, land *no indef art, no pl*
c *no pl (esp Art)* ground; *(Her)* field
d *no pl (von Gefäßen, Becken etc)* bottom; *(= Meeresgrund)* (sea)bed; *(liter: = Talgrund)* bottom of the/a valley; **~ suchen** *(im Wasser)* to look for a foothold, to try to find the bottom; **auf ~ stoßen** *(Naut)* to (run to) ground; **ein Schiff auf ~ setzen** to scuttle a ship; **das Glas/den Becher bis auf den ~ leeren** to drain the glass/tumbler
e *no pl (lit, fig: = Fundament)* foundation(s *pl*); *(= das Innerste)* depths *pl*; **von ~ auf** *or* **aus** entirely, completely; **etw von ~ auf ändern** to change sth fundamentally *or* from top to bottom; **von ~ auf neu gebaut/geplant** rebuilt/re--planned from scratch; **ein von ~ auf aufrechter Mensch** a thoroughly honest fellow; **den ~ zu etw legen** *(lit, fig)* to lay the foundations of *or* for sth; **einer Sache** *(dat)* **auf den ~ gehen** *(fig)* to get to the bottom of sth; **im ~e seines Herzens** in one's heart of hearts; **im ~e (genommen)** basically, fundamentally
f *(= Ursache, Veranlassung, Ausrede)* reason; *(= Beweggrund)* grounds *pl*, reason; **aus gesundheitlichen** *etc* **Gründen** for health *etc* reasons, on health *etc* grounds; **aus dem einfachen ~e, dass ...** for the simple reason that ...; **ohne ~** without reason; **auf ~** *or* **aufgrund von Zeugenaussagen** on the basis *or* strength of the witnesses' testimonies; **auf ~** *or* **aufgrund einer Verwechslung/seiner Eifersucht** owing to *or* because of a mistake/his jealousy; **ich habe ~ zu der Annahme, dass ...** I have reason to believe *or* grounds for believing that ...; **Gründe und Gegengründe** pros and cons, arguments for and against; **einen ~ zum Feiern haben** to have good cause for (a) celebration; **du hast keinen ~ zum Klagen** you have no cause to complain *or* for complaint; **die Gründe für und wider** the cases for and against; **jdm ~ (zu etw) geben** to give sb good reason *or* cause (for sth); **jdm allen ~ geben, etw zu glauben** to give sb every reason to believe *etc* sth; **aus diesem ~** for this reason; **aus guten Gründen, mit gutem ~** with good reason; **aus welchem ~(e)?** for what reason?; **aus Gründen** for reasons of; **zu ~e = zugrunde**

Grund-: **Grund|ak|kord** M *(Mus)* chord in root position; **Grund|an|schau|ung** F, **Grund|an|sicht** F fundamental philosophy; **grund|an|stän|dig** ADJ thoroughly decent; **Grund|an|strich** M first coat; *(= erstes Anstreichen)* application of the first coat; **Grund|aus|bil|dung** F *(Mil)* basic training; **Grund|aus|stat|tung** F basic equipment; **Grund|bau** M **a** *pl* **-bauten** *(Archit)* foundation(s *pl*) **b** *no pl (= Grundarbeiten)* laying of the foundations **c** *no pl (Univ: = Fach)* civil engineering; **Grund|be|deu|tung** F *(Ling)* primary *or* basic meaning; **Grund|be|griff** M basic concept; **Grund|be|sitz** M land, property; *(= das Besitzen)* ownership of land *or* property; **Grund|be|sit|zer(in)** M(F) landowner; **Grund|buch** NT land register; **Grund|buch|amt** NT land registry *or* office; **grund|ehr|lich** ADJ thoroughly honest; **Grund|ei|gen|tum** NT land, property; *(= das Besitzen)* ownership of land *or* property; **Grund|ei|gen|tü|mer(in)** M(F) landowner; **Grund|ein|stel|lung** F fundamental philosophy; **Grund|eis** NT ground ice, anchor-ice → **Arsch a**

grün|den ['grʏndn] VT to found; *Argument etc* to base (*auf +acc* on); *Heim, Geschäft* to set up; **gegründet 1857** established *or* founded in 1857; **eine Familie ~** to get married (and have a family) VI to be based *or* founded (*in +dat* on) VR **sich auf etw** *(acc)* **~** to be based *or* founded on sth

Grün|der ['grʏndɐ] M **-s, -**, **Grün|de|rin** [-ərɪn] F **-, -nen** founder

Grün|der|fi|gur F founder

Grün|der|jah|re PL **a** *(Hist)* years of rapid industrial expansion in Germany (from 1871) **b** *(fig: von Atomzeitalter etc)* early days *pl*

Grund-: **Grund|er|werb** M acquisition of land; **Grund|er|werbs|steu|er** F tax on land acquisition, land transfer tax

Grün|der|zeit F, *no pl (Hist)* = **Gründerjahre**

Grund-: **grund|falsch** ADJ utterly wrong; **Grund|far|be** F primary colour *(Brit) or* color *(US)*; *(= Grundierfarbe)* ground colour *(Brit) or* color *(US)*; **Grund|fes|ten** PL *(fig)* foundations *pl*; **etw bis in die ~** *or* **in seinen ~ erschüttern** to shake sth to the *or* its very foundations; **an den ~ von etw rütteln** to shake the (very) foundations of sth; **Grund|flä|che** F *(Math)* base; **Grund|form** F basic form *(auch Gram)*; **Grund|frei|be|trag** M tax-free allowance; **Grund|ge|bühr** F basic *or* standing charge; **Grund|ge|dan|ke** M basic idea; **Grund|ge|halt** NT *(= Entlohnung ohne Zulagen)* basic salary; **grund|ge|scheit** ADJ extremely bright

Grund|ge|setz NT **a** *(= Grundprinzip)* basic law **b das ~** the (German) Constitution

GRUNDGESETZ

The **"Grundgesetz** of the Federal Republic of Germany" is the German Constitution, which came into force in 1949. It was actually intended as a temporary measure until Germany could be re-united, but upon re-unification in 1990 the **Grundgesetz** was retained, since it enjoyed a high level of trust. For changes to be made to the **Grundgesetz** a two-thirds majority is needed both in the **Bundestag** and in the **Bundesrat**. If citizens consider that their basic rights, as laid down in the **Grundgesetz**, have been violated by the state authorities, they can ask for independent arbitration from the **Bundesverfassungsgericht**, which is binding on all parties. → BUNDESRAT, BUNDESTAG

Grund|ge|setz-: **Grund|ge|setz|än|de|rung** F amendment of the (German) Constitution; **grund|ge|setz|wid|rig** ADJ unconstitutional

Grund-: **Grund|hal|tung** F basic position; **grund|häss|lich** ADJ extremely *or* dreadfully ugly; **Grund|herr** M *(Hist)* lord of the manor; **Grund|herr|schaft** F *(Hist)* manorial system; **Grund|idee** F basic idea

grun|die|ren [grʊn'di:rən] *ptp* **grundiert** VT to undercoat; *(Art)* to ground

Grun|dier|far|be F, **Grun|dier|schicht** F undercoat

Grun|die|rung F **-, -en** **a** *no pl (= das Grundieren)* undercoating; *(Art)* grounding **b** *(= Farbe, Fläche)* undercoat; *(Art)* ground

Grund-: **Grund|irr|tum** M fundamental error; **Grund|ka|pi|tal** NT share capital; *(= Anfangskapital)* initial capital; **Grund|kennt|nis|se** PL basic knowledge (*in +dat* of), basics *pl*; **Grund|kurs** M *(Sch, Univ)* basic *or* base course; **Grund|la|ge** F basis; *(Mus)* root position; **als ~ für etw dienen** to serve as a basis for sth; **auf der ~ von** *or* **+gen** on the basis of; **die ~n einer Wissenschaft** the fundamental principles of a science; **die ~n eines Lehrfachs** the rudiments of a subject; **etw auf eine neue ~ stellen** *(Beziehungen)* to put sth on a different footing *or* basis; *Organisation etc* to change the basic structure(s) of sth; **jeder ~ entbehren** to be completely unfounded *or* without foundation; **Grund|la|gen|for|schung** F pure research; **Grund|last** F *(Tech)* constant load; **Grund|last|ka|pa|zi|tät** F *(Tech)* constant load capacity; **grund|le|gend** ADJ fundamental, basic (*für* to); *Werk, Textbuch* standard ADV fundamentally; **das muss sich ~ verändern** that has to change fundamentally; **sich zu etw ~ äußern** to make a statement of fundamental importance on sth; **Grund|le|gung** [-le:gʊŋ] F **-, -en** *(lit, fig)* laying of the foundations; *(fig: = Grundriss)* outline

gründ|lich ['grʏntlɪç] ADJ thorough; *Vorbereitung auch* careful; *Arbeit* painstaking, careful ADV thoroughly; *(inf: = sehr auch)* really; **jdm ~ die Meinung sagen** to give sb a real piece of one's mind; **da haben Sie sich ~ getäuscht** you're completely mistaken there

Gründ|lich|keit F **-,** *no pl* thoroughness; *(von Vorbereitung auch)* carefulness

Grund-: **Grund|li|nie** F *(Math, Sport)* baseline; **Grund|li|ni|en|spiel** NT baseline game; **Grund|lohn** M basic pay *or* wage(s *pl*); **grund|los** ADJ **a** *Tiefe etc* bottomless **b** *(fig: = unbegründet)* groundless, unfounded; **~es Lachen** laughter for no reason (at all) ADV *(fig)* without reason, for no reason (at all); **Grund|mau|er** F foundation wall; **bis auf die ~n niederbrennen** to be gutted; **Grund|men|ge** F *(Math)* fundamental *or* universal set; **Grund|mo|rä|ne** F *(Geol)* ground moraine; **Grund|nah|rungs|mit|tel** NT basic food(stuff)

Grün|don|ners|tag [gry:n'dɔnɐsta:k] M Maundy Thursday

Grund-: **Grund|ord|nung** F basic order; **Grund|pfand|recht** NT encumbrance on property; **Grund|pfei|ler** M *(Archit)* supporting pier; *(fig)* cornerstone, keystone; **Grund|prin|zip** NT basic *or* key principle; **Grund|re|chen|art** F, **Grund|rech|nungs|art** F basic arithmetical operation; **Grund|recht** NT basic *or* fundamental right; **Grund|re|gel** F basic rule; *(fürs Leben etc)* maxim; **Grund|ren|te** F *(Econ)* ground rent; *(Insur)* basic pension; **Grund|rich|tung** F general tendency *or* direction; **Grund|riss** M *(von Gebäude)* ground *or* floor plan; *(Math)* base; *(= Abriss)* outline, sketch; **„Grundriss der chinesischen Grammatik"** "Outlines of Chinese Grammar"

Grund|satz M principle; **aus ~** on principle; **ein Mann mit** *or* **von Grundsätzen** a man of principle; **an seinen Grundsätzen festhalten, bei seinen Grundsätzen bleiben** to stand by *or* keep to one's principles; **es sich** *(dat)* **zum ~ machen, etw zu tun** to make a principle of doing sth, to make it a matter of principle to do sth

Grund|satz-: **Grund|satz|de|bat|te** F, **Grund|satz|dis|kus|si|on** F debate on (general) principles; **Grund|satz|ent|schei|dung** F decision of general principle; **Grund|satz|er|klä|rung** F declaration of principle; **Grund|satz|fra|ge** F basic issue; *(= Schlüsselfrage)* key question

grund|sätz|lich ['grʊntzɛtslɪç] **ADJ** fundamental; *Verbot* absolute; *Möglichkeit* in principle; *Frage* of principle **ADV** *(= allgemein, im Prinzip)* in principle; *(= aus Prinzip)* on principle; *(= immer)* always; *(= völlig)* absolutely; **sich zu etw ~ äußern** to make a statement of principle on sth; **er ist ~ anderer Meinung als sie** he always disagrees with her, he disagrees with her on principle; **ihre Meinungen sind ~ verschieden** their views are fundamentally different; **das erlaube ich Ihnen ~ nicht** I will most definitely not permit that; **das ist ~ verboten** it is absolutely forbidden; **das ist ~ möglich** it is possible in principle; **er hat ~ kein Interesse für so etwas** he has absolutely no interest in that sort of thing

Grund|sätz|lich|keit F -, *no pl* fundamental nature

Grund|satz-: **Grund|satz|pa|pier** NT *(Pol)* (written) statement of principles; **Grund|satz|re|fe|rat** NT speech *or (schriftlich)* paper setting out a basic principle; **Grund|satz|ur|teil** NT judgement that establishes a principle; **Grund|satz|ver|ein|ba|rung** F *(Jur)* agreement in principle

Grund-: **grund|schlecht** ADJ thoroughly bad; **Grund|schrift** F *(Typ)* base type; **Grund|schuld** F mortgage; **Grund|schu|le** F primary *(Brit) or* elementary school; **Grund|schü|ler(in)** M(F) primary *(Brit) or* elementary (-school) pupil; **Grund|schul|leh|rer(in)** M(F) primary *(Brit) or* elementary(-school) teacher

> **GRUNDSCHULE**
>
> In Germany, children begin school at the age of six and attend **Grundschule** for four years. After the fourth year they take an aptitude test, which helps pupils and parents decide whether they should attend a **Gymnasium**, a **Realschule** or a **Hauptschule**.
>
> In Austria the corresponding school is called a **Volksschule**. In Switzerland children attend a **Primarschule** for the first three to six years (depending on canton) as part of the **Volksschule**. → GYMNASIUM, HAUPTSCHULE, REALSCHULE

Grund-: **grund|so|li|de** ADJ very respectable; **grund|stän|dig** ADJ **a** *(= bodenständig)* indigenous **b** *Schule* primary *attr (Brit)*, elementary *attr* **c** *(Bot)* basal, basilar; **Grund|stein** M *(lit, fig)* foundation stone; **der ~ zu etw sein** to form the foundation(s) of *or* for sth; **den ~ zu etw legen** *(lit)* to lay the foundation stone of sth; *(fig)* to lay the foundations of *or* for sth; **Grund|stein|le|gung** [-le:gʊŋ] F -, **-en** laying of the foundation stone; **Grund|stel|lung** F *(Turnen)* starting position; *(Boxen)* on-guard position; *(Chess)* initial *or* starting position; *(Mus)* root position; **Grund|steu|er** F (local) property tax, ≈ rates *pl (Brit dated)*; **Grund|stim|me** F bass; **Grund|stim|mung** F prevailing mood; **Grund|stock** M basis, foundation; **Grund|stoff** M basic material; *(= Rohstoff)* raw material; *(Chem)* element; **Grund|stoff|in|dust|rie** F primary industry

Grund|stück NT plot (of land); *(= Baugrundstück auch)* site; *(bebaut)* property; *(= Anwesen)* estate; **in ~en spekulieren** to speculate in property *or* in real estate

Grund|stücks-: **Grund|stücks|haf|tung** F real estate collateral; **Grund|stücks|mak|ler(in)** M(F) estate agent *(Brit)*, real estate agent, realtor *(US)*; **Grund|stücks|markt** M property market; **Grund|stücks|preis** M land price; **Grund|stücks|spe|ku|lant(in)** M(F) property speculator; **Grund|stücks|spe|ku|la|ti|on** F property speculation

Grund-: **Grund|stu|di|um** NT *(Univ)* basic course; **Grund|stu|fe** F **a** first stage; *(Sch)* ≈ junior *(Brit) or* grade *(US)* school **b** *(Gram)* positive (degree); **Grund|ten|denz** F, **Grund|te|nor** M basic trend; *(verborgen)* underlying trend; **Grund|ton** M *pl* **-töne** *(Mus) (eines Akkords)* root; *(einer Tonleiter)* tonic keynote; *(= Grundfarbe)* ground colour *(Brit) or* color *(US)*; **Grund|übel** NT basic *or* fundamental evil; *(= Nachteil)* basic problem; **Grund|um|satz** M *(Physiol)* basal metabolism

Grün|dung F -, **-en** founding, foundation; *(Archit: = Fundament)* foundation(s *pl*); *(= das Anlegen des Fundaments)* laying of the foundations; *(von Heim, Geschäft)* setting up; **die ~ einer Familie** getting married (and having a family)

Grün|dün|ger M *(Agr)* green manure

Grün|dungs-: **Grün|dungs|jahr** NT year of the foundation; **Grün|dungs|ka|pi|tal** NT initial capital; **Grün|dungs|rek|tor(in)** M(F) *(Univ)* first vice chancellor *(Brit)*, first university president *(US)*; **Grün|dungs|ver|samm|lung** F inaugural meeting *(of a new company)*

Grün|dün|gung F *(Agr)* green manuring

Grund-: **grund|ver|kehrt** ADJ completely wrong; **Grund|ver|mö|gen** NT landed property, real estate; **grund|ver|schie|den** ADJ totally *or* entirely different; **Grund|was|ser** NT, *no pl* ground water; **Grund|was|ser|spie|gel** M, **Grund|was|ser|stand** M water table, ground-water level; **Grund|wehr|dienst** M national *(Brit) or* selective *(US)* service; **den ~ absolvieren** *or* **leisten** to do one's national *(Brit) or* selective *(US)* service; **Grund|wert** M *(Philos)* fundamental value; **Grund|wer|te|ka|ta|log** M *(Philos)* index of fundamental values; **Grund|wis|sen** NT basic knowledge *(in +dat* of); **Grund|wort** NT *pl* **-wörter** *(Gram)* root; **Grund|zahl** F *(Math)* base (number); *(= Kardinalzahl)* cardinal number; **Grund|zins** M *(Hist)* feudal dues *pl (Hist)*; **Grund|zug** M essential feature *or* trait; **„Grundzüge der Geometrie"** "Basic Geometry", "(The) Rudiments of Geometry"; **etw in seinen Grundzügen darstellen** to outline (the essentials of) sth; **dieses Werk entstand in seinen Grundzügen schon ...** the essential features *or* the essentials of this work appeared as early as ...

grü|nen ['gry:nən] VI *(geh)* to turn green; *(fig: Liebe, Hoffnung)* to blossom (forth)

Grü|nen-: **Grü|nen|ab|ge|ord|ne|te(r)** MF *decl as adj* Green MP *or* representative; **Grü|nen|frak|ti|on** F Green Party *(in Parliament/on council)*

Grü|ne(r) ['gry:nə] MF *decl as adj* **a** *(Pol)* Green **b** *(dated inf: = Polizist)* cop *(inf)*, copper *(Brit inf)*, bluebottle *(dated Brit inf)*

> **DIE GRÜNEN**
>
> The political party **Die Grünen**, which is now part of **Bündnis 90/Die Grünen**, was founded in 1980. It grew out of numerous citizens' action groups operating at the time, together with the women's and peace movements. It focuses on environmental policy, the need for Germany's economic and social orders to create a more equal society for men and women, the subordination of executive bodies to grass-roots decisions, and an active peace policy with the ultimate aim of multilateral disarmament. → BÜNDNIS 90/DIE GRÜNEN

Grü|ne(s) ['gry:nə] NT *decl as adj (= Farbe)* green; *(als Ausschmückung)* greenery; *(= Gemüse)* greens *pl*, green vegetables *pl*; *(= Grünfutter)* green stuff; **ins ~ fahren** to go to the country; **wir essen viel ~s** *(inf)* we eat a lot of greens; **~s in die Suppe tun** *(inf)* to put green vegetables in the soup

Grün-: **Grün|fink** M greenfinch; **Grün|flä|che** F green space *or* area; **Grün|fut|ter** NT green fodder, greenstuff; *(inf: = Salat)* salad; *(inf: = Gemüse)* green vegetables *pl*, greens *pl (inf)*; **grün|gelb** ADJ greenish yellow, greeny-yellow; **Grün|gür|tel** M green belt; **Grün|kern** M *(= unreifer Dinkel)* (dried) unripe spelt grain; **Grün|kohl** M (curly) kale; **Grün|land** NT, *no pl* meadowland *no indef art*, grassland *no indef art*; **grün|lich** ['gry:nlɪç] ADJ greenish; **Grün|pflan|ze** F non-flowering *or* foliage plant; **Grün|pha|se** F *(Mot)* green phase; **Grün|rock** M *(hum)* gamekeeper; *(= Jäger)* huntsman *(esp Brit)*, hunter; **Grün|schna|bel** M *(inf)* (little) whippersnapper *(inf)*; *(= Neuling)* greenhorn *(inf)*; **sei still, du ~!** be quiet, you little know-all! *(Brit inf) or* know-it-all *(US inf)*; **Grün|span** M, *no pl* verdigris; **~ ansetzen** *or* **bilden** to form verdigris; *(fig)* to grow hoary; **Grün|specht** M green woodpecker; **Grün|stich** M *(Phot)* green cast; **grün|sti|chig** [-ʃtɪçɪç] ADJ with a green cast; **Grün|strei|fen** M central reservation *(Brit)*, median (strip) *(US, Austral)*; *(am Straßenrand)* grass verge; **Grün|tee** M green tea

grun|zen ['grʊntsn] VTI to grunt

Grün|zeug NT, *no pl* greens *pl*, green vegetables *pl*; *(= Kräuter)* herbs *pl*

Grunz|laut M grunt

Grüpp|chen ['grʏpçən] NT **-s, -** *(usu pej)* little group

Grup|pe ['grʊpə] F **-, -n** group *(auch Math)*; *(von Mitarbeitern auch)* team; *(Mil)* ≈ squad; *(Aviat)* ≈ squadron *(Brit)*, ≈ group *(US)*; *(von Pfadfindern)* section; *(= Klasse, Kategorie)* class, group; **eine ~ Zuschauer** *or* **von Zuschauern** a group of onlookers; **eine ~ von Beispielen** a list *or* series of examples; **~n (zu je fünf/sechs) bilden** to form (into) *or* to make groups (of five/six)

Grup|pen- *in cpds* group; **Grup|pen|ar|beit** F teamwork; **Grup|pen|bild** NT group portrait; **Grup|pen|bil|dung** F group formation, formation of groups; **Grup|pen|dy|na|mik** F *(Psych)* group dynamics; **grup|pen|dy|na|misch** ADJ *(Psych)* group-dynamic; **Grup|pen|ego|is|mus** M self-interest of the/a group; **Grup|pen|füh|rer(in)** M(F) group leader; *(Mil)* squad leader; **Grup|pen|le|ben** NT group living; **Grup|pen|lei|ter(in)** M(F) group manager; **Grup|pen|mit|glied** NT member of a/the group, group member; **Grup|pen|pä|da|go|gik** F group teaching; **Grup|pen|psy|cho|lo|gie** F group psychology; **Grup|pen|rei|se** F group travel *no pl*; **Grup|pen|sex** M group sex; **Grup|pen|sieg** M *(Sport)* **den ~ erringen** to win in one's group; **Grup|pen|sie|ger(in)** M(F) *(Sport)* group winner, winner in *or* of a/the group; **grup|pen|spe|zi|fisch** ADJ group-specific; **Grup|pen|sta|tus** M *(Pol)* interest-group status; **Grup|pen|the|ra|pie** F group therapy; **Grup|pen|un|ter|richt** M group learning; **Grup|pen|ver|ge|wal|ti|gung** F multiple rape, gang bang *(inf)*; **grup|pen|wei|se** ADV in groups; *(Ind, Comm, Sport auch)* in teams; *(Mil)* in squads; *(Aviat)* in squadrons; **Grup|pen|zwang** M, *no pl (Psych)* (peer) group pressure

grup|pie|ren [grʊ'pi:rən] *ptp* **gruppiert** **VT** to group **VR** to form a group/groups, to group

Grup|pie|rung F -, -en **a** *no pl* grouping **b** (= *Konstellation)* grouping; (= *Gruppe)* group; *(Pol)* faction

Grus [gru:s] M -es, -e [-zə] (= *Gesteinsschutt)* rubble; (= *Kohlengrus)* slack

Gru|sel-: **Gru|sel|ef|fekt** M horror effect; **Gru|sel|film** M horror *or* gothic film; **Gru|sel|ge|schich|te** F tale of horror, horror *or* gothic story

gru|se|lig ['gru:zəlıç] ADJ horrifying, gruesome; *Geschichte, Film* creepy, spine-chilling

Gru|sel|mär|chen NT tale of horror, horror story

gru|seln ['gru:zln] VTI *impers* **mich** *or* **mir gruselt auf Friedhöfen** cemeteries give me an eerie feeling, cemeteries give me the creeps; **hier kann man das Gruseln lernen** this will teach you the meaning of fear VR **hier würde ich mich ~** a place like this would give me the creeps; **sie gruselt sich vor Schlangen** snakes give her the creeps

Gru|si|cal ['gru:zikl] NT -s, -s *(hum)* comic horror *or* gothic film *or* (= *Theaterstück)* play

grus|lig ['gru:slıç] ADJ = **gruselig**

Gruß [gru:s] ✪ 48.2 M -es, ⸚e **a** ['gry:sə] greeting; (= *Grußgeste, Mil)* salute; **zum ~** in greeting; **der deutsche ~** *(NS)* the Nazi salute; **er ging ohne ~ an mir vorbei** he walked past me without saying hello

b *(als Zeichen der Verbundenheit)* **viele Grüße** best wishes *(an +acc* to); **bestell Renate bitte viele Grüße von mir** please give Renate my best wishes *or* my regards, remember me to Renate *(Brit)*; **schick mir einen ~ aus Paris** drop me a line from Paris; **sag ihm einen schönen ~** say hello to him (from me); **einen (schönen) ~ an Ihre Gattin!** my regards to your wife

c *(als Briefformel)* **mit bestem ~, mit besten Grüßen** yours; **mit brüderlichem/sozialistischem ~** *(Pol)* yours fraternally; **mit freundlichen Grüßen** *or* **freundlichem ~** *(bei Anrede Mr/Mrs/Miss X)* Yours sincerely, Yours truly *(esp US)*; *(bei Anrede Sir(s)/Madam)* Yours faithfully, Yours truly *(esp US)*

Gruß|adres|se F, **Gruß|an|spra|che** F, **Gruß|bot|schaft** F *(Pol)* message of greeting

grü|ßen ['gry:sn] ✪ 48.2, 50.1 VT **a** (= *guten Tag sagen zu)* to greet; *(Mil)* to salute; **grüßt er dich auch nicht?** doesn't he say hello to you either?; **sei gegrüßt** *(old, geh, iro)* greetings; **grüß dich!** *(inf)* hello there!, hi! *(inf)*

b (= *Grüße übermitteln)* **Otto lässt dich (schön) ~** Otto sends his regards *or* best wishes, Otto asked to be remembered to you *(Brit)*; **ich soll Sie von ihm ~** he sends his regards *etc*; **grüß mir deine Mutter!, grüß deine Mutter von mir!** remember me to your mother *(Brit)*, give my regards to your mother; **und grüß mir Wien/den Goldenen Löwen** and say hello to Vienna/the Golden Lion for me; **grüß Gott!** *(S Ger, Aus)* hello

VI to say hello, to give a greeting *(form)*; *(Mil)* to salute; **Otto lässt ~** Otto sends his regards; **die Berge grüßten aus der Ferne** *(liter)* the mountains greeted us in the distance

VR **ich grüße mich nicht mehr mit ihm** I don't say hello to him any more

Gruß-: **Gruß|for|mel** F form of greeting; *(am Briefanfang)* salutation; *(am Briefende)* complimentary close, ending; **gruß|los** ADV without a word of greeting, without saying hello; *(beim Abschied)* without saying goodbye; **Gruß|ord|nung** F *(Mil)* saluting hierarchy; **Gruß|pflicht** F *(Mil)* obligation to salute; **Gruß|schrei|ben** NT greeting; *(Pol)* letter of greeting; **Gruß|te|le|gramm** NT greetings telegram; *(Pol)* goodwill telegram; **Gruß|wort** NT *pl* **-worte** greeting

Grütz-: **Grütz|beu|tel** M *(Med)* wen; **Grütz|brei** M gruel

Grüt|ze ['grytsə] F -, -n **a** groats *pl*; (= *Brei)* gruel; **rote ~** *type of red fruit jelly* **b** *no pl (inf:* = *Verstand)* brains *pl (inf)*; **der hat ~ im Kopf** *(inf)* he's got brains *(inf)*

Grütz|kopf M *(inf)* **a** (= *Dummkopf)* thickhead *(inf)*, thickie *(inf)* **b** (= *Verstand)* thick head

Gschaftl|hu|ber ['kʃaftlhu:bɐ] M -s, -, **Gschaftl|hu|be|rin** [-ərın] F -, -nen *(S Ger, Aus: inf)* busybody

gscha|mig ['kʃa:mıç] ADJ *(Aus inf)* bashful

Gscher|te(r) ['kʃe:ɐtə] MF *decl as adj (Aus inf)* idiot

Gschnas [kʃna:s] NT -, *no pl (Aus inf)* fancy-dress *or* costume *(US)* party

G7, G-7 [ge:'zi:bn] F - G7

G7-Staat, G-7-Staat [ge:'zi:bn-] M G7 nation

GSM-Mo|dem M *(Comput, Telec)* GSM modem

Gspu|si ['kʃpu:zi] NT -s, -s *(S Ger, Aus: inf)* **a** (= *Liebschaft)* affair, carry-on *(inf)* **b** (= *Liebste(r))* darling, sweetheart

Gstan|zel [kʃ'tantsl] NT -s, -n, **Gstanzl** [kʃ-'tantsl] NT -s, -n *(S Ger, Aus inf)* (rude) song *(containing humour, innuendo or criticism)*

Gstät|ten ['kʃtɛtn] F -, - *(Aus inf)* grassy patch of land on a hillside

GTI-Mo|dell [ge:te:'li:-] NT *(Aut)* GTI model

Gu|a|no ['gua:no] M -s, *no pl* (= *Dünger aus Vogelmist)* guano

Gu|a|te|ma|la [guate'ma:la] NT -s Guatemala

Gu|a|te|mal|te|ke [guatemal'te:kə] M -n, -n, **Gu|a|te|mal|te|kin** [-'te:kın] F -, -nen Guatemalan

gu|a|te|mal|te|kisch [guatemal'te:kıʃ] ADJ Guatemalan

Gu|a|ve ['gua:və] F -, -en guava

Gu|a|ya|na [gua'ja:na] NT -s Guiana; (= *ehem. Brit.-Guayana)* Guyana

Gu|a|ya|ner [gua'ja:nɐ] M -s, -, **Gu|a|ya|ne|rin** [-ərın] F -, -nen → **Guayana** Guianese/Guyanese

gu|a|ya|nisch [gua'ja:nıʃ] ADJ → **Guayana** Guianese/Guyanese

gu|cken ['gʊkn] VI (= *sehen)* to look *(zu* at); *(heimlich auch)* to peep, to peek; (= *hervorschauen)* to peep *(aus* out of); **lass mal ~!** let's have a look, give us a look *(inf)*; **jdm in die Karten ~** to look *or* have a look at sb's cards VT *(inf)* **Fernsehen ~** to watch telly *(Brit inf) or* television

Gu|cker ['gʊkɐ] M -s, - *(inf)* **a** (= *Fernglas)* telescope; (= *Opernglas)* opera glass(es *pl)* **b** PL (= *Augen)* peepers *(inf)*, eyes *pl*

Guck-: **Guck|fens|ter** NT small window; *(in Tür)* peephole, judas window; **Guck|in|die|luft** ['gʊkındi:lʊft] M → **Hans**; **Guck|kas|ten** M *(inf:* = *Fernseher)* telly *(Brit inf)*, gogglebox *(Brit inf)*, tube *(US inf)*; **Guck|kas|ten|büh|ne** F proscenium *or* fourth-wall stage; **Guck|loch** NT peephole

Gue|ril|la [ge'rılja] F -, -s **a** (= *Guerillakrieg)* guerilla war **b** (= *Guerillaeinheit)* guerilla unit

Gue|ril|la M -(s), -s (= *Guerillakämpfer)* guerilla

Gue|ril|la- *in cpds* guerilla; **Gue|ril|la|krieg** M guerilla war

Gue|ril|le|ro [gerıl'je:ro] M -s, -s, **Gue|ril|le|ra** [gerıl'je:ra] F -, -s guerilla fighter

Guern|sey [gø:enzi] NT -s Guernsey

Gu|gel|hupf ['gu:glhʊpf] M -s, -e *(S Ger, Aus)*, **Gu|gel|hopf** ['gu:glhɔpf] M -s, -e *(Sw) (Cook)* gugelhupf

Güg|ge|li ['gygəli] NT -s, - *(Sw Cook)* roast chicken

GUI [gui] NT -s, -s *(Comput:* = *grafische Benutzeroberfläche) abbr von* **graphical user interface** GUI

Guil|lo|ti|ne [gıljo'ti:nə, gijo'ti:nə] F -, -n guillotine

guil|lo|ti|nie|ren [gıljoti'ni:rən, gijo-] *ptp* **guillotiniert** VT to guillotine

Gui|nea [gi'ne:a] NT -s *(Geog)* Guinea

Gui|ne|er [gi'ne:ɐ] M -s, -, **Gui|ne|e|rin** [-ərın] F -, -nen Guinean

gui|ne|isch [gi'ne:ıʃ] ADJ Guinean

Gu|lag ['gu:lak] M -(s), -s gulag

Gu|lasch ['gu:laʃ, 'gʊlaʃ] NT OR M -(e)s, -e *or* -s goulash; **ich mache aus dir ~!** *(inf)* I'll beat the living daylights out of you *(inf)*

Gu|lasch-: **Gu|lasch|ka|no|ne** F *(Mil sl)* field kitchen; **Gu|lasch|kom|mu|nis|mus** M *(pej) communism which is concerned only with material well-being*; **Gu|lasch|sup|pe** F goulash soup

Gul|den ['gʊldn] M -s, - *(Hist)* (= *Münze)* florin; (= *niederländischer Gulden)* g(u)ilder, gulden

gül|den ['gʏldn] ADJ *(poet)* golden

Gül|le ['gʏlə] F -, *no pl (S Ger, Sw)* liquid manure

Gul|ly ['gʊli] M OR NT -s, -s drain

gül|tig ['gʏltıç] ADJ valid; **nach den ~en Bestimmungen** according to current regulations; **nach dem bis Mai noch ~en Gesetz** according to the law in force until May; **ab wann ist der Fahrplan ~?** when does the timetable come into effect *or* force?; **~ für zehn Fahrten** valid *or* good for ten trips; **~ werden** to become valid; *(Gesetz, Vertrag)* to come into force *or* effect; *(Münze)* to become legal tender

Gül|tig|keit F -, *no pl* validity; *(von Gesetz)* legal force; **die alten Geldscheine verlieren im Herbst ihre ~** the old notes *(Brit) or* bills *(US)* cease to be legal tender in the autumn

Gül|tig|keits-: **Gül|tig|keits|be|reich** M range of validity; *(eines Gesetzes etc)* scope; **Gül|tig|keits|dau|er** F period of validity; *(eines Gesetzes)* period in force; **Gül|tig|keits|prü|fung** F *(Comput)* validation

Gu|lyás ['gʊlaʃ] NT OR M -, -e *(esp Aus)* goulash

Gum|mi ['gʊmi] NT OR M -s, -s (= *Material)* rubber; (= *Gummiarabikum)* gum; (= *Radiergummi)* rubber *(Brit)*, eraser; (= *Gummiband)* rubber *or* elastic *(esp Brit)* band; *(in Kleidung etc)* elastic; *(inf:* = *Kondom)* rubber *(esp US inf)*, Durex®

Gum|mi- *in cpds* rubber; **Gum|mi|an|zug** M wetsuit; **Gum|mi|ara|bi|kum** NT -s, *no pl* gum arabic; **gum|mi|ar|tig** ADJ rubbery ADV like rubber; **Gum|mi|band** [-bant] NT *pl* **-bänder** rubber *or* elastic *(esp Brit)* band; *(in Kleidung)* elastic; **Gum|mi|bär|chen** [-bɛ:ɐçən] NT -s, - ≈ jelly baby *(Brit)*, gummi bear; **Gum|mi|baum** M rubber plant; **Gum|mi|be|griff** M *(inf)* elastic concept; **Gum|mi|boot** NT inflatable boat, rubber dinghy

gum|mie|ren [gʊ'mi:rən] *ptp* **gummiert** VT to gum; **gummiert** *(Briefmarke, Kuvert)* gummed; *(Tech)* rubberized

Gum|mie|rung F -, -en **a** (= *Verfahren)* gumming **b** (= *gummierte Fläche)* gum

Gum|mi-: **Gum|mi|ge|schoss** NT rubber bullet; **Gum|mi|hand|schuh** M rubber glove; **Gum|mi|harz** NT gum resin; **Gum|mi|ho|se** F, **Gum|mi|hös|chen** [-hø:sçən] NT plastic pants *pl*; **Gum|mi|kis|sen** NT inflatable rubber cushion; **Gum|mi|knüp|pel** M rubber truncheon; **Gum|mi|lin|se** F *(Phot)* zoom lens; **Gum|mi|man|tel** M plastic raincoat, plastic mac *(Brit)*; **Gum|mi|muf|fe** F *(Comput: für Akustikkoppler)* rubber cups *pl*; **Gum|mi|pa|ra|graf**, **Gum|mi|pa|ra|graph** M *(inf)* ambiguous clause; **Gum|mi|rei|fen** M rubber tyre *(Brit) or* tire *(US)*; **Gum|mi|sau|ger** M rubber teat *(Brit) or* nipple *(US)*; **Gum|mi|schlauch** M rubber hose; *(bei Fahrrad etc)* inner tube; **Gum|mi|schutz** M *(dated)* sheath; **Gum|mi|soh|le** F rubber sole; **Gum|mi|stie|fel** M rubber boot, gumboot, wellington (boot) *(Brit)*, wellie *(Brit inf)*; *(bis zu den Oberschenkeln)* wader; **Gum|mi|strumpf** M rubber *or* elastic stocking; **Gum|mi|tier** NT rubber animal; *(aufblasbar)* inflatable animal; **Gum|mi|un|ter|la|ge** F rubber sheet; **Gum|mi|wa|ren** PL rubber goods *pl*; **Gum|mi|wucht|ge|schoss** NT rubber bullet; **Gum|mi|zel|le** F padded cell; **Gum|mi|zug** M (piece of) elastic

Gunst [gʊnst] F -, *no pl* favour *(Brit)*, favor *(US)*; (= *Wohlwollen auch)* goodwill; (= *Gönnerschaft auch)* patronage; *(des Schicksals etc)* benevolence; **zu meinen/deinen ~en** in my/your favo(u)r; **jdm eine ~ erweisen** *(geh)* to do sb a kindness; **jdm die ~ erweisen, etw zu tun** *(geh)* to be so gracious as to do sth for sb; **jds ~ besitzen** *or* **genießen, in jds** *(dat)* **~ stehen** to have *or* enjoy sb's favo(u)r, to be in favo(u)r with sb; **zu ~en** = **zugunsten**

Gunst-: **Gunst|be|weis** M, **Gunst|be|zei|gung** [-bətsaigʊŋ] F -, -en mark of favour *(Brit)* or favor *(US)*; **Gunst|ge|wer|be** NT *(hum)* the oldest profession in the world *(hum)*, prostitution; **Gunst|ge|werb|le|rin** F *(hum)* lady of easy virtue, prostitute

güns|tig ['gʏnstɪç] ADJ favourable *(Brit)*, favorable *(US)*; *(zeitlich, bei Reisen etc)* convenient; *Angebot, Preis etc* reasonable, good; **bei ~er Witterung** weather permitting; **die Fähre um 3 Uhr ist ~er** the 3 o'clock ferry is more convenient *or* better; **im ~sten Fall(e)** with luck; **im ~sten Licht** *(lit, fig)* in the most favo(u)rable light; **mit Geschäften und Erholungsmöglichkeiten in ~er Lage** convenient for shops and recreational facilities

ADV *kaufen, verkaufen* for a good price; *einkaufen, beziehen* at a good price; **jdm etw ~er geben** to give sb sth at a discount *or* for less; **jdm/einer Sache ~ gesinnt sein** *(geh)* to be favourably *(Brit) or* favorably *(US)* disposed toward(s) sb/sth; **es trifft sich ~, dass ...** it's very lucky that ...; **~ bei etw abschneiden** to do well in sth, to come out of sth very well; **die Stadt liegt ~ (für)** the town is well situated (for); **wie komme ich am ~sten nach ...?** what's the best *or* easiest way to get to ...?; **„Fernseher ~ abzugeben"** "television for sale: bargain price"

güns|ti|gen|falls ADV at best; *(bei Geldbeträgen auch)* at (the) most

Güns|tig|keits|prin|zip NT principle of advantage

güns|tigs|ten|falls ADV at the very best; *(bei Geldbeträgen auch)* at (the) most

Günst|ling ['gʏnstlɪŋ] M -s, -e *(pej)* favourite *(Brit)*, favorite *(US)*

Günst|lings|wirt|schaft F *(pej)* (system of) favouritism *(Brit) or* favoritism *(US)*

Gupf [gʊpf] M -(e)s, -e *(Aus)* head

Gup|py ['gʊpi] M -s, -s *(Zool)* guppy

Gur|gel ['gʊrgl] F -, -n throat; *(= Schlund)* gullet; **jdm die ~ zudrücken** *or* **abdrücken** *or* **abschnüren** *or* **zuschnüren** *(lit, fig)* to strangle sb; **dann springt** *or* **geht sie mir an die ~!** *(inf)* she'll kill me *(inf)*; **sein Geld durch die ~ jagen** *(inf)* to pour all one's money down one's throat *or* gullet *(inf)*; **sich** *(dat)* **die ~ schmieren** *(hum)* to oil one's throat *or* gullet *(inf)*

Gur|gel|mit|tel NT gargle

gur|geln ['gʊrgln] VI **a** *(= den Rachen spülen)* to gargle **b** *(Wasser, Laut)* to gurgle

Gur|gel|was|ser NT *pl* **-wässer** gargle

Gürk|chen ['gʏrkçən] NT -s, - midget gherkin *(Brit)*, baby gherkin pickle *(US)*

Gur|ke ['gʊrkə] F -, -n **a** cucumber; *(= Essiggurke)* gherkin; **saure ~n** pickled gherkins **b** *(hum inf: = Nase)* hooter *(inf)*, conk *(Brit inf)*, nose **c** *(sl: = Schrottauto)* banger *(Brit inf)*, jalopy *(inf)*

gur|ken ['gʊrkn] VI *aux sein (sl)* to drive

Gur|ken-: **Gur|ken|ho|bel** M slicer; **Gur|ken|sa|lat** M cucumber salad

gur|ren ['gʊrən] VI *(lit, fig)* to coo

Gurt [gʊrt] M -(e)s, -e *(= Gürtel, Sicherheitsgurt, Ladestreifen)* belt; *(= Riemen)* strap; *(= Sattelgurt)* girth; *(Archit)* girder

Gurt|band [-bant] NT *pl* **-bänder** waistband

Gür|tel ['gʏrtl] M -s, - *(= Gurt, Zone)* belt; *(= Absperrkette)* cordon; **den ~ enger schnallen** *(lit, fig)* to tighten one's belt

Gür|tel-: **Gür|tel|li|nie** F waist; **ein Schlag unter die ~** *(lit)* a blow below the belt; **das war ein Schlag unter die ~** *(fig)* that really was (hitting) below the belt; **Gür|tel|rei|fen** M radial (tyre *(Brit)* or tire *(US)*); **Gür|tel|ro|se** F *(Med)* shingles *sing or pl*; **Gür|tel|schnal|le** F belt buckle; **Gür|tel|ta|sche** F belt bag, pouch; **Gür|tel|tier** NT armadillo

gür|ten ['gʏrtn] *(geh)* VT to gird *(old)*; *Pferd* to girth VR to gird oneself

Gurt-: **Gurt|muf|fel** M *(inf)* person who refuses to wear a seat belt; **Gurt|pflicht** F, *no pl* **es besteht ~** the wearing of seat belts is compulsory; **Gurt|straf|fer** [-ʃtrafɐ] M -s, - *(Aut)* seat-belt tensioner; **Gurt|zwang** M, *no pl* = **Gurtpflicht**

Gu|ru ['gu:ru] M -s, -s *(lit, fig)* guru

GUS [gʊs] F - *abbr von* **Gemeinschaft Unabhängiger Staaten** CIS

Gu|sche ['gʊʃə] F -, -n *(dial)* = **Gosche**

Guss [gʊs] M -es, ¨-e ['gʏsə] **a** *(Metal)* *(no pl: = das Gießen)* casting, founding; *(= Gussstück)* cast; **(wie) aus einem ~** *(fig)* a unified whole **b** *(= Strahl)* stream, gush; *(inf: = Regenguss)* cloudburst, downpour; **kalte Güsse** *(Med)* cold affusions **c** *(= Zuckerguss)* icing, frosting *(esp US)*; *(durchsichtig)* glaze; **einen Kuchen mit einem ~ überziehen** to ice *or* frost *(US)* a cake

Guss-: **Guss|as|phalt** M poured asphalt; **Guss|be|ton** M cast concrete; **Guss|ei|sen** NT cast iron; **guss|ei|sern** ADJ cast-iron; **Guss|form** F mould *(Brit)*, mold *(US)*; **Guss|naht** F seam; **Guss|stahl** M cast steel

GUS-Staat ['gʊs-] M CIS state

gus|tie|ren [gʊs'ti:rən] *ptp* **gustiert** VT **a** = **goutieren** **b** *(Aus)* to taste, to try

gus|ti|ös [gʊs'tiø:s] ADJ *(Aus)* appetizing

Gus|to ['gʊsto] M -s *(rare)* -s *(geh, Aus)* **a** *(= Appetit)* **~ auf etw** *(acc)* **haben** to feel like sth **b** *(fig: = Geschmack)* taste; **nach jds ~** to sb's taste; **mit ~** with gusto; **nach eigenem ~** just as one/he *etc* likes

Gus|to|stü|ckerl NT -s, -(n) *(Aus inf)* delicacy

gut [gu:t] ADJ *comp* **besser** ['bɛsɐ], *superl* **beste(r, s)** ['bɛstə] good; **probieren Sie unsere ~en Weine/Speisen!** try our fine wines/food; **er ist in der Schule/in Spanisch sehr ~** he's very good at school/Spanish; **~e Frau!** *(dated)* my dear lady; **er macht sich** *(dat)* **einen ~en Tag** *(= faulenzt)* he's taking things easy for a day; *(= amüsiert sich)* he's having a good day of it; **die ~e Stube** the best *or* good room; **das ist ~ gegen** *or* **für** *(inf)* **Husten** it's good for coughs; **wozu ist das ~?** *(inf)* what's that for?; **er ist immer für eine Überraschung ~** *(inf)* he's always good for a surprise; **das war Pech, aber wer weiß, wozu es ~ ist** it was bad luck, but it's an ill wind (that blows nobody any good) *(Brit prov)*, it was bad luck, but every cloud has a silver lining *(prov)*; **sei so ~ (und) gib mir das** would you mind giving me that; **würden Sie so ~ sein und ...** would you be good enough to ...; **jdm ~ sein** *(old)* to love sb; **sie ist ihm von Herzen ~** *(old)* her heart is his *(liter)*; **bist du mir wieder ~?** *(dated)* are you friends with me again?; **dafür ist er sich zu ~** he wouldn't stoop to that sort of thing; **sind die Bilder/die Brötchen ~ geworden?** did the pictures/rolls turn out all right?; **ist dein Magen wieder ~?** is your stomach better *or* all right again?; **es wird alles wieder ~!** everything will be all right; **es ist ganz ~, dass ...** it's good that ...; **wie ~, dass ...** it's good that ..., how fortunate that ...; **~, dass du das endlich einsiehst** it's a good thing *or* job (that) you realize it at last; **so was ist immer ~** that's always useful; **ich will es damit ~ sein lassen** I'll leave it at that; **lass das ~ sein!** don't worry; **lass mal ~ sein!** *(= ist genug)* that's enough, that'll do; *(= ist erledigt)* just leave it; **jetzt ist aber ~!** *(inf)* that's enough; **das ist ja alles ~ und schön, aber ...** that's all very well but ..., that's all well and good but ...; **ein ~es Stück Weg(s)** *(dated)* a good way; **ein ~es Pfund Reis** a good pound of rice; **~e Besserung!** get well soon; **auf ~e Freundschaft!** here's to us!; **auf ~es Gelingen!** here's to success!; **~!** good; *(= in Ordnung)* (all) right, OK; **schon ~!** (it's) all right *or* OK; **~, ~!** all right; **also ~!** all right *or* OK then; **nun ~!** fair enough, all right then; **~ und schön** *(inf)* fair enough, that's all well and good; **du bist ~!** *(inf)* you're a fine one! → **drei, Ding a, Dienst c, Ende, Geist b, Gesellschaft e, Miene, Riecher**

ADV *comp* **besser**, *superl* **am besten** well; **~ aussehend** good-looking; **~ schmecken/riechen** to taste/smell good; **sie spricht ~ Schwedisch** she speaks Swedish well, she speaks good Swedish; **es ~ haben** to have a good time of it, to have it good *(esp US)*; **unser Volk hat es noch nie so ~ gehabt** our people have never had it so good; **er hat es in seiner Jugend nicht ~ gehabt** he had a hard time (of it) when he was young; **du hast es ~!** you've got it made; **~ wohnen** to have a nice home; **das kann ~ sein** that may well be; **so ~ wie nichts** next to nothing; **so ~ wie nicht** hardly, scarcely; **so ~ wie verloren** as good as lost; **so ~ ich kann** as best I can, as well as I can; **es dauert ~(e) drei Stunden** it lasts a good three hours; **nehmen Sie ~ ein Pfund Mehl** take a good pound of flour; **~ betucht** *(inf)* well-heeled *(Brit inf)*, well-off *(inf)*; **~ bezahlt** *(Person, Job)* highly-paid; **~ dotiert** *(Job)* well-paid; *Vertrag* lucrative; **~ gehend** flourishing, thriving; **~ gelaunt** cheerful, in a good mood; **~ gelungen** very successful; *Überraschung* wonderful; **~ gemeint** well-meaning, well-meant; **~ gesinnt** → **gutgesinnt**; **~ sitzend** well-fitting; **~ verdienend** with a good salary, high-income; **das ist aber ~ gewogen/eingeschenkt!** that's a generous measure; **~ und gern** easily; **das lässt sich nicht ~ machen** that wouldn't be easy; **(das hast du) ~ gemacht!** well done!; **o, wie gut das tut!** oh, that's good → *auch* **guttun**; **darauf kann man ~ verzichten** you can easily *or* well do without that; **machs ~!** *(inf)* cheers! *(Brit)*, cheerio! *(Brit)*, bye!; *(stärker)* look after yourself, take care; **pass ~ auf!** be very careful; **ich kann ihn jetzt nicht ~ im Stich lassen** I can't very well let him down now → **Gute(s), lachen VI, reden VI, beraten VT a, Besen a**

Gut [gu:t] NT -(e)s, ¨-er ['gy:tɐ] **a** *(= Eigentum)* property; *(lit, fig: = Besitztum)* possession; **irdische Güter** worldly goods; **geistige Güter** intellectual wealth; **nicht um alle Güter der Welt** *(geh)* not for all the world; **bewegliche Güter** movables; **unbewegliche Güter** immovables **b** *no pl (= das Gute)* good, Good; **~ und Böse** good and evil, Good and Evil; **das höchste ~** *(Philos)* the greatest good; *(= Gesundheit etc)* one's most valuable possession **c** *(= Ware, Frachtgut)* item; **Güter** goods; *(= Frachtgut)* freight *sing*, goods *(esp Brit)* **d** *no pl (dated: = Material)* material (to be treated) **e** *(= Landgut)* estate **f** *no pl (Naut)* rigging, gear; **laufendes/stehendes ~** running/standing rigging *or* gear

-gut NT -(e)s, *no pl suf in cpds* **a** *(denotes material intended for or having undergone a process)* **Saatgut** seed; **Mahlgut** *(zum Mahlen bestimmt)* substance(s) to be ground; *(gemahlen)* ground substance(s) **b** *(often not translated in English: denotes the totality of an abstract possession)* **das deutsche Musikgut/Gedankengut** (the body of) German music/thought

Gut-: **gut|ach|ten** ['gu:tlaxtn] VI *insep (usu infin, no ptp) (esp Jur)* to act as an expert witness; **Gut|ach|ten** ['gu:tlaxtn] NT -s, - report; **Gut|ach|ter** ['gu:tlaxtɐ] M -s, -, **Gut|ach|te|rin** [-ərɪn] F -, -nen expert; *(= Schätzer auch)* valuator; *(Jur: in Prozess)* expert witness; **gut|acht|lich** *(form)* ADJ expert ADV **etw ~ feststellen** to ascertain sth in an expert's report; **gut|ar|tig** ADJ *Kind, Hund etc* good-natured; *Geschwulst, Geschwür* benign; **Gut|ar|tig|keit** F, *no pl (von Kind, Tier etc)* good nature; *(von Geschwulst)* benignity; **gut|aus|se|hend** ADJ → **gut ADV**; **gut|be|tucht** ADJ → **gut ADV**; **gut|be|zahlt** ADJ → **gut ADV**; **gut|bür|ger|lich** ADJ solid middle-class; *Küche* homely *(Brit)*, good plain; **gut|do|tiert** [-doti:ɐt] ADJ → **gut ADV**; **Gut|dün|ken** ['gu:tdʏŋkn] NT -s, *no pl* discretion;

nach (eigenem) ~ at one's own discretion, as one sees fit, as one thinks fit *or* best

Gü|te ['gy:tə] **F -,** *no pl* **a** *(= Herzensgüte, Freundlichkeit)* goodness, kindness; *(Gottes auch)* loving kindness; **würden Sie die ~ haben, zu ...** *(form)* would you have the goodness *or* kindness to ... *(form)*; **ein Vorschlag zur ~** a suggestion; **in ~** amicably; **meine ~, ist der dumm!** *(inf)* my goodness, is he stupid! *(inf)*; **ach du liebe** *or* **meine ~!** *(inf)* oh my goodness!, goodness me! **b** *(einer Ware)* quality; **ein Reinfall erster ~** *(inf)* a first-class flop, a flop of the first order *or* water *(inf)*

Gü|te|grad M, **Gü|te|klas|se** F *(Comm)* grade

Gu|te|nacht-: **Gu|te|nacht|ge|schich|te** [gu:tə'naxt-] **F** bedtime story; **Gu|te|nacht|kuss** [gu:tə'naxt-] **M** goodnight kiss

Gu|te(r) ['gu:tə] **MF** *decl as adj* **mein ~r** *(dated)* my dear friend; *(= Ehemann)* my dear husband; **meine ~** *(old)* my dear; *(= Ehefrau)* my dear wife; **der/die ~** the dear kind soul; *(mitleidig)* the poor soul; **die ~n und die Bösen** the good and the bad; *(inf: in Westernfilmen etc)* the goodies and the baddies *(inf)*

Gü|ter-: **Gü|ter|ab|fer|ti|gung** F **a** *no pl* dispatch of freight *or* goods *(esp Brit)* **b** *(= Abfertigungsstelle)* freight *or* goods *(esp Brit)* office; **Gü|ter|ab|wä|gung** F choice between conflicting rights; **Gü|ter|an|ge|bot** NT range of goods for sale; **Gü|ter|bahn|hof** M freight *or* goods *(esp Brit)* depot; **Gü|ter|fern|ver|kehr** M long-distance haulage; **Gü|ter|ge|mein|schaft** F *(Jur)* community of property; **in ~ leben** to have community of property; **Gü|ter|nah|ver|kehr** M short-distance haulage *(up to 50 km)*; **Gü|ter|schup|pen** M freight depot, goods shed *(Brit)*; **Gü|ter|tren|nung** F *(Jur)* separation of property; **in ~ leben** to have separation of property; **Gü|ter|ver|kehr** M freight *or* goods *(esp Brit)* traffic; **Gü|ter|wa|gen** M *(Rail)* freight car *(US)*, goods truck *(Brit)*; **Gü|ter|zug** M freight *or* goods *(esp Brit)* train

Gu|te(s) ['gu:tə] **NT** *decl as adj* **~s tun** to do good; **es hat alles sein ~s** *(prov)* every cloud has a silver lining *(Prov)*, it's an ill wind (that blows nobody any good) *(Brit Prov)*; **alles ~!** all the best!, good luck!; **man hört über sie nur ~s** you hear so many good things about her; **das führt zu nichts ~m** it'll lead to no good; **jdm (viel) ~s tun** to be (very) good to sb; **des ~n zu viel tun** to overdo things; **das ist des ~n zu viel** that is too much of a good thing; **das ~ daran** the good thing about it; **das ~ siegt** Good *or* good shall triumph; **das ~ im Menschen** the good in man; **im ~n wie im Bösen** for better or for worse; **im ~n** *(sich trennen)* amicably; **ich sage es dir im ~n** I want to give you a friendly piece of advice

Gü|te-: **Gü|te|sie|gel** NT *(Comm)* stamp of quality; **Gü|te|ter|min** M, **Gü|te|ver|hand|lung** F *(Jur)* conciliation proceedings *pl*; **Gü|te|zei|chen** NT mark of quality; *(fig auch)* hallmark

Gut-: **gut ge|hen** *irreg aux sein*, **gut+ge|hen** *sep irreg aux sein* **VI** **a** *impers* **es geht ihm gut** he is doing well *or* nicely; *(= er ist gesund)* he is well; **sonst gehts dir gut!** *(iro)* are you feeling all right?, are you in your right mind? **VI** to go (off) well; **das ist noch einmal gut gegangen** it turned out all right; **wenn es gut geht** with luck; **das konnte ja nicht ~** it was bound to go wrong; **wenn das man gut geht!** *(N Ger)* that's asking for trouble; **hoffentlich geht es mit den beiden gut!** *(inf)* I hope things will work out for the two of them → *auch* **gehen 3 a** **a** *Geschäft, Ware, Uhr* → **gehen 1 f, g**; **gut|ge|hend** ADJ → **gut** ADV; **gut|ge|klei|det** ADJ → **gekleidet a**; **gut|ge|launt** ADJ → **gut** ADV; **gut|ge|lun|gen** ADJ → **gut** ADV; **gut|ge|meint** [-gəmaint] ADJ → **gut** ADV; **gut|ge|sinnt** ADJ well-disposed (*dat* towards); *(= von edler Gesinnung)* right-thinking; **gut|ge|stellt** ADJ well-off; **~ sein** to be well off; **gut|gläu|big** ADJ trusting; *(= vertrauensselig auch)* credulous; **Gut|gläu|big|keit** F trusting nature; *(= Vertrauensseligkeit auch)* credulity

Guth. *abbr von* **Guthaben**

Gut-: **gut+ha|ben** ['gu:tha:bn] VT *sep irreg* **etw ~** to be owed sth (*bei* by), to have sth coming (to one) (*bei* from) *(inf)*; **Gut|ha|ben** ['gu:tha:bn] NT **-s, -** *(Fin: = Bankguthaben)* credit; **auf meinem Konto ist** *or* **habe ich ein ~ von 500 Euro** my account is 500 euros in credit; **gut+hei|ßen** ['gu:thaisn] VT *sep irreg* to approve of; *(= genehmigen)* to approve; **Gut|hei|ßung** F **-, -en** approval; **gut|her|zig** ADJ kind-hearted, kindly; **Gut|her|zig|keit** F **-,** *no pl* kind-heartedness, kindliness

gü|tig ['gy:tɪç] ADJ kind; *(= edelmütig)* generous, gracious; **mit Ihrer ~en Erlaubnis** *(dated form)* with your kind permission; **würden Sie so ~ sein, zu ...** *(dated form)* would you be so kind as to ...

güt|lich ['gy:tlɪç] ADJ amicable ADV amicably; **sich ~ einigen** to come to an amicable agreement; **wir haben uns ~ auf 10 000 Euro geeinigt** we reached an amicable settlement of 10,000 euros; **etw ~ schlichten** to settle sth amicably; **sich an etw** *(dat)* **~ tun** to make free with sth *(Brit)*, to use sth freely

Gut-: **gut+ma|chen** VT *sep* **a** *(= in Ordnung bringen) Fehler* to put right, to correct; *Schaden* to make good; **du hast viel an ihm gutzumachen** you've a lot to make up to him (for) → *auch* **wiedergutmachen** **b** *(= gewinnen)* to make (*bei* out of, on); **gut|mü|tig** ['gu:tmy:tɪç] ADJ *Mensch, Tier* good-natured; **Gut|mü|tig|keit** F **-,** *no pl* good nature; **jds ~ ausnützen** to presume upon sb's good nature; **gut|nach|bar|lich** ADJ neighbourly *(Brit)*, neighborly *(US)* ADV in a neighbourly *(Brit)* *or* neighborly *(US)* fashion, as good neighbours *(Brit)* *or* neighbors *(US)*; **gut+sa|gen** ['gu:tzagn] VI *sep (dated)* to vouch (*für* for)

Guts|be|sit|zer(in) M(F) lord/lady of the manor; *(als Klasse)* landowner

Gut-: **Gut|schein** M voucher, coupon; *(für Umtausch)* credit note; **Gut|schein|heft** NT book of vouchers *(Brit)* *or* coupons *(US)*; **gut+schrei|ben** ['gu:tʃraibn] VT *sep irreg* to credit (*+dat* to); **Gut|schrift** F **a** *no pl (= Vorgang)* crediting **b** *(= Bescheinigung)* credit note; *(= Betrag)* credit (item)

Guts-: **Guts|haus** NT manor (house); **Guts|herr** M squire, lord of the manor; **Guts|her|rin** F lady of the manor; **Guts|herr|schaft** F squire and his family; **Guts|hof** M estate

gut-: **gut|si|tu|iert** ADJ → **situiert a**; **gut|sit|zend** ADJ → **gut** ADV; **gut+ste|hen** *sep irreg (S Ger, Aus, Sw: aux sein)*, **gut ste|hen** △*irreg (S Ger, Aus, Sw: aux sein)* VR **a** *(= wohlhabend sein)* to be well off; **sich bei** *or* **mit jdm/etw ~** to be well off with sb/sth **b** *(= sich verstehen)* **sich mit jdm ~** to get on well with sb → *auch* **stehen 4**; **gut+stel|len** VR *sep* **a** *(= wohlhabend sein)* to be well off **b** **sich mit jdm ~** to put oneself on good terms with sb

Guts|ver|wal|ter(in) M(F) steward

Gut-: **Gut|temp|ler** ['gu:ttɛmplɐ] M **-s, -**, **Gut|temp|le|rin** [-ərɪn] F **-, -nen** Good Templar; **gut+tun** *sep irreg*, **gut tun** △ *irreg* VI **jdm ~** to do sb good; **das tut gut** that's good → *auch* **gut** ADV

gut|tu|ral [gʊtu'ra:l] ADJ guttural

Gut|tu|ral [gʊtu'ra:l] M **-s, -e**, **Gut|tu|ral|laut** M *(Ling)* guttural (sound)

Gut-: **gut|un|ter|rich|tet** ADJ → **unterrichtet**; **gut|ver|die|nend** ADJ → **gut** ADV; **gut|wil|lig** ADJ willing; *(= entgegenkommend)* obliging; *(= wohlwollend)* well-meaning; **Gut|wil|lig|keit** ['gu:tvɪlɪçkait] F **-,** *no pl* willingness; *(= Entgegenkommen)* obliging ways *pl*; *(= Wohlwollen)* well-meaningness

Gu|ya|na [gu'ja:na] NT **-s** Guiana; *(= ehem. Brit.-Guyana)* Guyana

Gu|ya|ner [gu'ja:nɐ] M **-s, -**, **Gu|ya|ne|rin** [-ərɪn] F **-, -nen** → **Guyana** Guianese/Guyanese

gu|ya|nisch [gu'ja:nɪʃ] ADJ → **Guyana** Guianese/Guyanese

GVO *abbr von* **genetisch veränderte Organismen** GMO

gym|na|si|al [gymna'zia:l] ADJ *attr* ≈ at grammar schools *(Brit)*, ≈ at high schools *(US)*; **die ~e Oberstufe** ≈ the sixth form *(Brit)*, ≈ the twelfth grade *(US)*

Gym|na|si|al-: **Gym|na|si|al|bil|dung** F ≈ grammar school education *(Brit)*, ≈ high school education *(US)*; **Gym|na|si|al|leh|rer(in)** M(F), **Gym|na|si|al|pro|fes|sor(in)** *(Aus)* M(F) ≈ grammar school teacher *(Brit)*, ≈ high school teacher *(US)*

Gym|na|si|ast [gymna'ziast] M **-en, -en**, **Gym|na|si|as|tin** [-'ziastɪn] F **-, -nen** ≈ grammar school pupil *(Brit)*, ≈ high school student *(US)*

Gym|na|si|um [gym'na:ziʊm] NT **-s, Gymnasien** [-ziən] **a** *(Sch)* ≈ grammar school *(Brit)*, ≈ high school *(US)* **b** *(Hist)* gymnasium

> **GYMNASIUM**
>
> A **Gymnasium** is a secondary school which students attend for nine or, in some federal states, eight years and which leads to the **Abitur**. The final two years at a **Gymnasium** (two and a half in some **Länder**) are known as the **Kollegstufe**. The curriculum varies according to the type of school: in a **humanistisches Gymnasium** Latin and Greek are taught; in a **neusprachliches Gymnasium** English, Latin and French or other lingua franca are taught; and in a **mathematisch-naturwissenschaftliches Gymnasium** the emphasis is on the sciences. A **Gymnasium** may offer several of these curricula, which pupils choose from when they reach a certain class, usually the seventh or ninth.
> Since nowadays many students who have taken their **Abitur** do not necessarily continue studying but undertake a period of training instead, new types of **Gymnasien** (for example **Wirtschaftsgymnasien**) have been created with an emphasis on practical work. → ABITUR, KOLLEGSTUFE

Gym|nas|tik [gym'nastɪk] F **-,** *no pl* keep-fit exercises *pl*; *(= Turnen)* gymnastics *sing*; **~ machen** to do keep-fit (exercises)/gymnastics

Gym|nas|tik|an|zug M leotard

Gym|nas|ti|ker [gym'nastikɐ] M **-s, -**, **Gym|nas|ti|ke|rin** [-ərɪn] F **-, -nen** gymnast

Gym|nas|tik-: **Gym|nas|tik|leh|rer(in)** M(F) PE *or* physical education teacher; **Gym|nas|tik|saal** M gymnasium; **Gym|nas|tik|un|ter|richt** M gymnastics *sing*

gym|nas|tisch [gym'nastɪʃ] ADJ gymnastic

Gy|nä|ko|lo|ge [gynɛko'lo:gə] M **-n, -n**, **Gy|nä|ko|lo|gin** [-'lo:gɪn] F **-, -nen** gynaecologist *(Brit)*, gynecologist *(US)*, gyno *(esp US inf)*

Gy|nä|ko|lo|gie [gynɛkolo'gi:] F **-,** *no pl* gynaecology *(Brit)*, gynecology *(US)*

gy|nä|ko|lo|gisch [gynɛko'lo:gɪʃ] ADJ gynaecological *(Brit)*, gynecological *(US)* ADV **sich ~ untersuchen lassen** to have a gyn(a)ecological examination; **~ betreuen/behandeln** to give/administer gyn(a)ecological treatment

Gy|ros ['gy:rɔs] NT **-,** *no pl* ≈ doner kebab

Gy|ro|skop [gyro'sko:p] NT **-s, -e** gyroscope

H

H, h [haː] NT -, - H, h; *(Mus)* B

h [haː] *abbr von* **hora(e)** *(= Stunde)* hr; **120 km/h** 120 km/h *or* kmph

ha *abbr von* **Hektar** hectare

ha [haː] INTERJ ha; *(triumphierend)* aha; *(überrascht, erstaunt, verärgert)* oh; *(verächtlich)* huh; **ha no** *(S Ger inf, Selbstverständliches betonend)* why not; *(ungläubig)* well, well; *(aufmunternd)* come on; *(resignierend)* oh well

hä [hɛ, hɛː] INTERJ what

Haag [haːk] M **-s der ~, Den ~** The Hague; **in** *or* **im ~, in Den ~** in The Hague

Haa|ger [ˈhaːgɐ] ADJ *attr* Hague; **~ Konventionen** Hague Conventions; **~ Schiedshof** International Court of Justice in The Hague

Haar [haːɐ] NT **-(e)s, -e** **a** *(= Menschenhaar)* hair; **sie hat schönes ~** *or* **schöne ~e** she has nice hair; **sich** *(dat)* **die ~e** *or* **das ~ schneiden lassen** to have *or* get one's hair cut, to have a haircut; **sich** *(dat)* **durch die ~e fahren** to run one's fingers through one's hair
b *(Bot, Zool: = Material)* hair
c *(in Wendungen)* **~e auf den Zähnen haben** to be a tough customer *(Brit) or* cookie *(esp US)*; **~e lassen (müssen)** to suffer badly, to come off badly; **jdm kein ~ krümmen** not to harm a hair on sb's head; **sich** *(dat)* **die ~e wachsen lassen** to grow one's hair; **darüber lass dir keine grauen ~e wachsen** don't worry your head about it, don't lose any sleep over it; **er findet immer ein ~ in der Suppe** he always finds something to quibble about; **jdm aufs ~ gleichen** to be the spitting image of sb; **sie gleichen sich** *(dat)* **aufs ~** they are the spitting image of each other, they're as alike as two peas in a pod; **das ist an den ~en herbeigezogen** that's rather far-fetched; **sich** *(dat)* **die ~e raufen** to tear one's hair out; **an jdm/etw kein** *or* **nicht ein gutes ~ lassen** to pick *or* pull sb/sth to pieces; **sich** *(dat)* **in die ~e geraten** *or* **kriegen** *(inf)* to quarrel, to squabble; **sich** *(dat)* **in den ~en liegen** to be at loggerheads *(Brit)*, to be at daggers drawn; **jdm die ~e vom Kopf fressen** *(inf)* to eat sb out of house and home; **er hat mehr Schulden als ~e auf dem Kopf** he's up to his ears in debt; **um kein ~ besser** no better, not a bit *or* whit better; **um ein** *or* **ums ~** very nearly, almost; **er hat mich um ein ~ getroffen** he just missed (hitting) me by a hair's breadth; **um kein** *or* **nicht ein ~ breit** not an inch → **Berg a**

Haar-: **Haar|ana|ly|se** F genetic analysis of hair; **Haar|an|satz** M hairline; **Haar|aus|fall** M hair loss; **Haar|balg** M *(Anat)* hair follicle; **Haar|band** [-bant] NT *pl* **-bänder** hairband; *(= Schleife)* hair ribbon; **Haar|bo|den** M scalp; **Haar|breit** NT **nicht ein ~, um kein ~** not an inch; **Haar|bürs|te** F hairbrush; **Haar|bü|schel** NT tuft of hair

haa|ren [ˈhaːrən] VI *(Tier)* to moult *(Brit)*, to molt *(US)*, to lose its coat *or* hair; *(Pelz etc)* to shed (hair); *(Teppich)* to shed VR *(Tier)* to moult *(Brit)*, to molt *(US)*

Haar-: **Haar|ent|fer|ner** [-lɛntfɛrnɐ] M **-s, -**, **Haar|ent|fer|nungs|mit|tel** NT hair remover, depilatory; **Haar|er|satz** M *(form)* hairpiece; *(= Perücke)* wig; *(= Toupet)* toupee

Haa|res|brei|te [ˈhaːrəsbraitə] F *inv* **(nur) um ~** almost, very nearly; *verfehlen* by a hair's breadth; **er wich nicht um ~ von seiner Meinung ab** he did not change his opinion one iota

Haa|re|wa|schen NT, *no pl* hair-washing, shampoo(ing); *(beim Friseur)* shampoo, wash; **bei jedem ~** every time you wash your hair

Haar-: **Haar|far|be** F hair colour *(Brit) or* color *(US)*; **haar|fein** ADJ **ein ~er Riss** a hairline crack; **Haar|fes|ti|ger** M (hair) setting lotion; **Haar|flech|te** F *(old, geh)* plait *(Brit)*, braid *(US)*; **Haar|garn** NT yarn made from hair; **Haar|ge|fäß** NT *(Anat)* capillary; **haar|ge|nau** ADJ exact; *Übereinstimmung* total ADV exactly; **die Beschreibung trifft ~ auf ihn zu** the description fits him exactly *or* to a T *(esp Brit inf)*; **jdm etw ~ erklären** to explain sth to sb in great detail; **das trifft ~ zu** that is absolutely right

haa|rig [ˈhaːrɪç] ADJ hairy; *(inf) (= heikel, gefährlich)* hairy *(inf)*; *(= schwierig)* nasty

Haar-: **Haar|klam|mer** F *(= Klemme)* hairgrip *(Brit)*, bobby pin *(US)*; *(= Spange)* hair slide *(Brit)*, barrette *(US)*; **Haar|kleid** NT *(geh)* coat; **haar|klein** ADJ *(inf) Beschreibung* detailed ADV in great *or* minute detail; **er hat mir alles ~ berechnet** he charged me for absolutely everything; **Haar|klem|me** F hairgrip *(Brit)*, bobby pin *(US)*; **Haar|kranz** M *(von Männern)* fringe (of hair) *(Brit)*, bangs *pl (US)*; *(= Frauenfrisur) plaits fixed around one's head*; **Haar|künst|ler(in)** M(F) *(usu hum)* hair artiste; **Haar|lack** M hair lacquer; **haar|los** ADJ hairless; *(= glatzköpfig)* bald; **Haar|mo|de** F hairstyle; **Haar|na|del** F hairpin; **Haar|na|del|kur|ve** F hairpin bend; **Haar|netz** NT hairnet; **Haar|öl** NT hair oil; **Haar|pfle|ge** F hair care; **zur ~** (for caring) for one's hair; **Haar|pfle|ge|mit|tel** NT hair care product; **Haar|pracht** F superb head of hair; **Haar|riss** M *(Tech) (in Metall, Pflaster etc)* hairline crack; **haar|scharf** ADJ *Beschreibung, Wiedergabe* exact; *Gedächtnis* very sharp, very clear; *Unterschied* very fine; *Beobachtung* very close ADV *treffen* exactly; *danebentreffen, vorbeitreffen* barely; *folgern, schließen* precisely; **die Kugel ging ~ daneben** the bullet missed by a hair's breadth; **~ an jdm vorbeizielen** to aim to just miss sb; **~ an jdm vorbeischießen** to shoot just past sb; **der Glassplitter traf ihn ~ über dem Auge** the splinter of glass only just missed his eye; **Haar|schlei|fe** F hair ribbon; **Haar|schmuck** M ornaments *pl* for one's hair; **Haar|schnei|de|ma|schi|ne** F, **Haar|schnei|der** M **-s, -** *(= Gerät)* electric clippers *pl*; **Haar|schnei|der(in)** M(F) *(inf: = Friseur)* barber; **Haar|schnitt** M **a** *(= Frisur)* haircut, hairstyle **b** *(= das Haarschneiden)* haircut; **Haar|schopf** M mop *or* shock of hair; **ihr roter ~** her mop *or* shock of red hair; **Haar|sei|te** F *(von Fell)* fleece side; *(von Pelz)* fur side; *(von Teppich)* pile side; **Haar|sieb** NT fine sieve; **Haar|spal|ter** [-ʃpaltɐ] M **-s, -**, **Haar|spal|te|rin** [-ərɪn] F **-, -nen** pedant, hairsplitter; **Haar|spal|te|rei** [-ʃpaltəˈrai] F **-, -en** splitting hairs *no indef art, no pl*; **eine solche ~** hairsplitting like that; **haar|spal|te|risch** [-ʃpaltərɪʃ] ADJ hairsplitting; *Unterschied* minute; **Haar|span|ge** F hair slide *(Brit)*, barrette *(US)*; **Haar|spit|ze** F end (of a hair); **gespaltene ~n** split ends; **Haar|spray** NT OR M hairspray; **Haar|sträh|ne** F strand *or (dünner)* wisp of hair; **haar|sträu|bend** [-ʃtrɔybnt] ADJ hair-raising; *(= empörend)* shocking, terrible; *(= unglaublich) Frechheit* incredible ADV *brutal* hair-raisingly; *schlecht* painfully; *obszön* terribly, shockingly; *frech* incredibly; *sich benehmen* shockingly; **Haar|strich** M *(= dünner Strich)* hairline, hair stroke; *(von Tierfell)* growth of the hair; **Haar|stu|dio** NT hair stylist's; **Haar|teil** NT hairpiece; **Haar|tol|le** F quiff; *(= Hahnenkamm)* cockscomb; **Haar|tö|ner** [-tøːnɐ] M **-s, -** hair-tinting lotion; **Haar|tö|nung** F tinting; **Haar|tracht** F *(dated, geh: = Frisur)* hairstyle; **Haar|trans|plan|ta|ti|on** F hair transplant; *(= Vorgang)* hair transplantation; **Haar|trock|ner** [-trɔknɐ] M **-s, -** hairdryer; **Haar|wä|sche** F washing one's hair *no art*; **eine regelmäßige ~** washing one's hair regularly; **Haar|wasch|mit|tel** NT shampoo; **Haar|was|ser** NT *pl* **-wässer** hair lotion; **Haar|wech|sel** M change of coat; **Haar|wild** NT *(Hunt)* game animals *pl*; **Haar|wir|bel** M cowlick; *(am Hinterkopf)* crown; **Haar|wuchs** M growth of hair; **einen kräftigen ~ haben** to have a lot of hair *or* a full head of hair; **einen spärlichen ~ haben** to have little hair *or* a thin head of hair; **Haar|wuchs|mit|tel** NT hair restorer; **Haar|wur|zel** F root of a/the hair

Hab [haːp] NT **~ und Gut** possessions, belongings, worldly goods *all pl*

Hab|acht|stel|lung [haːpˈlaxtʃtɛlʊŋ] F = **Habtachtstellung**

Ha|be [ˈhaːbə] F **-**, *no pl (geh)* possessions *pl*, belongings *pl*

Ha|be|as|kor|pus|ak|te [haːbeasˈkɔrpʊs-] F *(Jur)* Act of Habeas Corpus

Ha|be|dank [ˈhaːbədaŋk, -ˈdaŋk] NT **-s**, *no pl (poet)* thanks *pl*; **ein herzliches ~** heartfelt thanks

ha|ben [ˈhaːbn]
pres **hat** [hat], *pret* **hatte** [ˈhatə], *ptp* **gehabt** [gəˈhaːpt]

1 HILFSVERB	3 UNPERSÖNLICHES VERB
2 TRANSITIVES VERB	4 REFLEXIVES VERB

1 – HILFSVERB

ich habe/hatte gerufen I have/had called, I've/I'd called; **er will ihn gesehen haben** he says (that) he saw him; **du hättest den Brief früher schreiben können** you could have written the letter earlier; **wenn er mich angerufen hätte, wäre ich gleich gekommen** if he had phoned me, I would have come at once

2 – TRANSITIVES VERB

In Verbindung mit Substantiv siehe auch Eintrag für das jeweilige Substantiv.

Im Präsens wird im britischen Englisch oft *have got* verwendet.

a = besitzen to have; **wir haben ein Haus/Auto** we've got a house/car; **ich hatte viele Bücher** I had a lot of books; **er hat eine Brille** he's got *or* wears glasses; **eine böse Schwiegermutter haben** to have an awful mother-in-law; **er hat noch nie eine Frau gehabt** he's never had a woman; **was man hat, das hat man** *(inf)* what you've got, you've got; **wer hat, der hat** some people have everything; **die habens (ja)** *(inf)* they can afford it

b = als Eigenschaft aufweisen **sie hatte blaue Augen/lange Beine** she had blue eyes/long legs; **er hat eine große Nase/abstehende Ohren** he's got a big nose/sticking-out ears; **man hat wieder lange Haare** long hair is in fashion again

c = bekommen, erhalten to have; *Note* to get; *(= studieren) Fach* to do; **kann ich mal das Handtuch haben?** can I have the towel?; **dürfte ich die Butter haben?** could I have the butter?; **kann ich noch etwas Brot haben?** could I have some more bread?; **was möchten Sie haben?** what would you like?; **da hast du 10 Euro/das Buch** there's 10 euros/the book; **wie hätten Sie es gern?** how would you like it?; **woher hast du denn das?** where did you get that from?; **Schule/Unterricht haben** to have school/lessons; **in der ersten Stunde haben wir Englisch** *(inf)* we have English first lesson; **an unserer Schule haben wir ab dem ersten Schuljahr Französisch und Englisch** *(inf)* at our school we have *or* do French and English in the first year; **was hast du diesmal in Englisch?** what did you get in English this time?; **gute Schulnoten haben** to get good marks *(Brit) or* grades *(US)*; **gutes/schlechtes Wetter haben** to have good/bad weather; **morgen werden wir Nebel haben** we'll have fog tomorrow; **was haben wir heute für ein Wetter?** what's the weather like today?; **heute haben wir 10°** it's 10° today; **in Australien haben sie jetzt Winter** it's winter in Australia now; **wie viel Uhr haben wir?** what's the time?; **was für ein Datum haben wir heute?, den Wievielten haben wir heute?** what's the date today?, what's today's date?

d = verfügen über *Zeit, Muße, Beziehungen, Erfahrung* to have; **Zeit haben, etw zu tun** to have the time to do sth; **er hat immer Zeit für seine Kinder** he always has time for his children; **ich habe jetzt keine Zeit** I haven't got time now; **wenn ich nur Zeit hätte!** if only I had time!; **die Sache hat Zeit** it's not urgent; **in diesem Job muss man Beziehungen haben** in this job you need to have connections; **mit Computern habe ich keine Erfahrung** I've got no experience of computers

e = zeitweise ergriffen, bedrückt sein von to have; **Durst haben** to be thirsty; **Hunger haben** to be hungry; **eine Krankheit haben** to have an illness; **Grippe/Masern/eine schreckliche Erkältung haben** to have flu/measles/a terrible cold; **Husten haben** to have a cough; **Fieber haben** to have a temperature; **ich kann heute nicht kommen, ich habe Fieber** I can't come today, I've got a temperature; **Peter hat Windpocken** Peter's got chicken pox; **Angst haben** to be afraid; **gute/schlechte Laune haben** to be in a good/bad mood; **Sorgen haben** to be worried; **erhebliche Zweifel haben** to have grave doubts; **die Hoffnung haben, dass etw geschieht** to have hopes that sth will happen; **was hat er denn?** what's the matter with him?; **hast du was?** are you all right?, is something the matter?; **ich habe nichts** I'm all right

f = sich zusammensetzen aus **ein Meter hat 100 cm** there are 100 cm in a metre *(Brit) or* meter *(US)*; **ein Euro hat 100 Cent** there are 100 cents in a euro; **unser Haus hat 4 Etagen** our house has 4 storeys *(Brit) or* stories *(US)*

g mit Präposition

Für *haben* in Verbindung mit Präpositionen siehe auch unter dem Eintrag für die Präposition.

♦ **haben + an sie hat eine große Hilfe an ihren Kindern** her children are a great help to her, she gets a lot of help from her children; **sie werden schon merken, was sie an ihm haben** they'll see what an asset he is; **jd/etw hat eine nette Art an sich** *(dat)* there is something nice about sb/sth; **das hat er/sie/es so an sich** *(dat)* that's just the way he/she/it is; **es am Herzen/Magen/an der Leber haben** *(inf)* to have heart/stomach/liver trouble

♦ **haben + für sich das hat etwas für sich** there's something to be said for that

♦ **haben + gegen etw gegen jdn/etw haben** to have sth against sb/sth; **jdn/etw gegen sich haben** to have sb/sth against one

♦ **haben + in es in den Beinen haben** *(inf: = leiden)* to have trouble with one's legs

♦ **haben + in sich das hat es in sich** *(inf) (= schwierig)* that's a tough one; *(= alkoholreich)* that's strong; *(= reichhaltig)* that's rich

♦ **haben + mit etwas mit jdm haben** *(euph)* to have a thing with sb *(inf)*; **sie hat etwas mit einem verheirateten Mann** she's involved with a married man; **er hat es mit dem Malen/Bergsteigen** *(inf)* he has a passion for painting/mountaineering; **was hat es mit seiner Frage auf sich?** what is his question actually about?

♦ **haben + von etwas von etw haben** *(inf)* to get something out of sth; **das hast du jetzt davon!** now see what's happened!; **das hat er von seinem Leichtsinn** that's what comes of his foolishness; **die blonden Haare hat sie von ihrem Vater** she gets her blonde hair from her father; **er hat etwas von einem Hochstapler an sich** he's a bit of a con man; **sie hat etwas von einer Aristokratin an sich** there's something aristocratic about her; **mehr/weniger von etw haben** *(inf)* to get more/less out of *or* from sth; **da habe ich dann mehr davon** that way I get more out of it; **nichts davon/von etw haben** to get nothing out of it/sth; **sie hat viel von ihrem Vater/wenig von ihrer Mutter** she's very like her father/not at all like her mother; **dieses Werk von Braque hat viel von Picasso** this work by Braque owes a lot to Picasso; **Kinder haben nicht viel von ihren Eltern, wenn Mutter und Vater arbeiten** children don't see much of their parents if both the mother and the father work

♦ **haben + vor sich ich hatte gar keine Ahnung, wen ich da vor mir hatte** I had no idea who I was talking to; **wissen Sie eigentlich, wen Sie vor sich haben?** do you actually realize who you're talking to?

♦ **haben + zu er wollte sie zur Frau haben** he wanted to make her his wife → *auch* **h**

h in anderen Verbindungen

♦ **es haben + Adjektiv es gut/schön/bequem haben** to have it good/nice/easy; **sie hat es warm in ihrem Zimmer** it's warm in her room; **wir haben es noch weit bis nach Hause** it's still a long way home; **es schlecht haben** to have a bad time; **er hat es nicht leicht mit ihr** he has a hard time with her; **du hast es gut, du darfst schon nach Hause** it's all right for you, you can go home

♦ **haben + zu + Infinitiv** *(= verfügen über, müssen)* to have to; **nichts mehr zu essen haben** to have nothing left to eat; **ich habe zu tun** I'm busy; **ich habe nichts zu tun** I have nothing to do; **du hast zu gehorchen** you have to obey; **ich habe nicht zu fragen** I'm not to ask questions

♦ **zu haben sein etw ist zu haben** *(= erhältlich)* sth is to be had; **jd ist zu haben** *(= nicht verheiratet)* sb is single; *(sexuell)* sb is available; **für etw zu haben sein** to be ready for sth; **für Whisky ist er immer zu haben** he's always ready for a whisky; **der ist doch für jeden Ulk zu haben** he's always ready for a lark *(inf)*; **er ist nicht dafür zu haben** *(= nicht interessiert)* he's not keen on it *(Brit)*, he's not interested in it; *(= möchte nicht beteiligt sein)* he won't have anything to do with it

i andere Wendungen **ich habs!** *(inf)* I've got it!, I know!; **da hast dus/haben wirs!** *(inf)* there you/we are!; **wie gehabt** as before; **ich kann das nicht haben!** *(inf)* I can't stand it!; **ich kann es nicht haben, wenn du immer den Teller ableckst** I can't stand the way you lick your plate

3 – UNPERSÖNLICHES VERB

♦ **es hat** *(dial: = es gibt) (bei Objekt im Singular)* there is; *(bei Objekt im Plural)* there are; **es hat noch Kaffee** there's still some coffee left; **hier hat es noch viele schöne alte Bauernhäuser** there are still a lot of beautiful old farmhouses here; **damit hat es noch Zeit** it's not urgent, it can wait

♦ **es hat sich** *(inf)* **und damit hat es sich** and that's that; **es hat sich was mit der Liebe!** so much for love!; **es hat sich was mit der Hoffnung!** so much for my hopes!; **hat sich was!** some hopes!

4 – REFLEXIVES VERB

♦ **sich haben**

a = sich anstellen *inf* to make a fuss; **was hast du dich denn so?** what are you making such a fuss about?; **hab dich nicht so** stop making such a fuss

b = erledigt sein **die Sache hat sich** that's done

Ha|ben ['ha:bn] NT **-s,** *no pl* credit; **im ~ stehen** to be on the credit side

Ha|be|nichts ['ha:bənɪçts] M **-(es), -e** have-not

Ha|ben-: **Ha|ben|sei|te** F credit side; **Ha|ben|zin|sen** PL interest *sing* on credit

Ha|be|rer ['ha:bərɐ] M **-s, -** *(Aus inf)* bloke *(Brit inf)*, chap *(Brit inf)*, guy *(inf)*

Ha|ber|sack ['ha:bɐzak] M *(old)* knapsack, haversack

Hab-: **Hab|gier** F greed, acquisitiveness; **hab|gie|rig** ADJ greedy, acquisitive; **hab|haft** ['ha:phaft] ADJ **jds/einer Sache ~ werden** *(geh)* to get hold of sb/sth

Ha|bicht ['ha:bɪçt] M **-s, -e** hawk; *(= Hühnerhabicht)* goshawk

Ha|bichts|na|se F hooked nose

ha|bil [ha'bi:l] ADJ *(dated, geh)* skilful *(Brit)*, skillful *(US)*, clever

ha|bil. *abbr von* **habilitatus**; **Dr. ~** *doctor with postdoctoral university teaching qualification*

Ha|bi|li|tand [habili'tant] M **-en, -en** [-dn], **Ha|bi|li|tan|din** [-'tandɪn] F **-, -nen** *person writing postdoctoral thesis to qualify as a professor*

Ha|bi|li|ta|ti|on [habilita'tsio:n] F **-, -en** **a** *(= Festakt) ceremony at which sb receives his/her qualification as a professor* **b** *(= Lehrberechtigung)* postdoctoral lecturing qualification

Ha|bi|li|ta|ti|ons|schrift F *postdoctoral thesis required for qualification as a professor*

ha|bi|li|tie|ren [habili'ti:rən] *ptp* **habilitiert** VR to qualify as a professor VT to confer qualification as a professor on

ha|bi|li|tiert [habili'ti:ɐt] ADJ qualified to assume a professorship

Ha|bit [ha'bi:t, 'ha:bɪt] NT OR M **-s, -e** *(= Ordenskleid)* habit; *(geh: = Aufzug)* attire

Ha|bit ['hɛbɪt] NT OR M **-s, -s** *(Psych)* habit

Ha|bi|tat [habi'ta:t] NT **-s, -e** *(Zool)* habitat

ha|bi|tu|ell [habi'tuɛl] ADJ *(geh)* habitual

Ha|bi|tus ['ha:bitʊs] M **-,** *no pl (geh, Med)* disposition

Habs|burg ['ha:psbʊrk] NT **-s** Hapsburg, Habsburg

Habs|bur|ger ['ha:psbʊrgɐ] ADJ *attr* = **habsburgisch**

Habs|bur|ger ['ha:psbʊrgɐ] M **-s, -**, **Habs|bur|ge|rin** [-ərɪn] F **-, -nen** Hapsburg, Habsburg

habs|bur|gisch ['ha:psbʊrgɪʃ] ADJ Hapsburg *attr*, Habsburg *attr*, of the Hapsburgs *or* Habsburgs

Hab-: **Hab|schaft** ['ha:pʃaft] F **-, -en**, **Hab|se|lig|kei|ten** ['ha:pze:lɪçkaitn] PL possessions, belongings, effects *(form)* all *pl*; **Hab|se|lig|-**

kei|ten ['ha:pze:lıçkaitn] PL possessions, belongings, effects *(form)* *all pl*; **Hab|sucht** ['ha:pzʊxt] F greed, acquisitiveness; **hab|-süch|tig** ['ha:pzʏçtıç] ADJ greedy, acquisitive

Habt|acht|stel|lung [ha:pt'laxtʃtɛlʊŋ] F *(Mil, fig)* attention; **in ~ stehen** *or* **sein** to stand to *or* be at attention

hach [hax] INTERJ oh; *(verächtlich)* huh

Ha|chel ['haxl] F **-, -n** *(Aus)* slicer

ha|cheln ['haxln] VTI *(Aus)* to chop, to slice

Hach|se ['haksə] F **-, -n** *(dial)* = **Haxe**

Hack-: **Hack|bank** F *pl* **-bänke** butcher's chopping *(Brit)* *or* cutting *(US)* board; **Hack|bau** M, *no pl (Agr)* hoe-farming; **Hack|beil** NT chopper, cleaver; **Hack|block** M *pl* **-blöcke** chopping block; **Hack|bra|ten** M meat loaf; **Hack|brett** NT **a** chopping board *(Brit)*, cutting board *(US)* **b** *(Mus)* dulcimer

ha|cke ['hakə] ADJ *(sl: = betrunken)* pissed *(Brit inf)*, plastered *(inf)*

Ha|cke ['hakə] F **-, -n** **a** *(dial: = Ferse, am Strumpf)* heel **b** *(dial, Mil: = Absatz)* heel; **die ~n zusammenschlagen** *or* **zusammenklappen** *(Mil)* to click one's heels; **einen im** *or* **am ~n haben** *(N Ger inf)* to be pickled *(inf)* → **ablaufen VT a**

Ha|cke F **-, -n** **a** *(= Pickel)* pickaxe *(Brit)*, pickax *(US)*, pick; *(= Gartenhacke)* hoe **b** *(Aus)* hatchet, axe *(Brit)*, ax *(US)*

Ha|cke|beil NT chopper, cleaver

ha|cke|dicht ADJ *(sl: = betrunken)* pissed *(Brit inf)*, plastered *(inf)*

ha|ckeln ['hakln] VI *(Aus)* to have a job, to work *(bei* for); *(= schwer arbeiten)* to graft *(inf)*

ha|cken ['hakn] **VT** **a** *(= zerkleinern)* to chop; *(im Fleischwolf)* to mince *(Brit)*, to grind *(US)* **b** *Garten, Erdreich* to hoe **c** *(mit spitzem Gegenstand) Loch* to hack, to chop; *(Vogel)* to peck **VI** **a** *(mit dem Schnabel)* to peck; *(mit spitzem Gegenstand)* to hack, to chop; **ich habe mich** *or* **mir in den Finger gehackt** I've cut my finger; **nach jdm/etw ~** to peck at sth/sb **b** *(im Garten etc)* to hoe **c** *(Comput)* to hack *(in +acc* into) **VR** *(= sich verletzen)* to cut (oneself)

Ha|cken ['hakn] M **-s, -** *(= Ferse)* heel

Ha|cken|trick M *(Sport)* backheel

Ha|cke|pe|ter ['hakəpe:tɐ] M **-s, -** **a** *(N Ger)* mince *(Brit)*, minced *(Brit)* *or* ground *(US)* meat **b** *(S Ger)* seasoned raw meat loaf

Ha|cker ['hakɐ] M **-s, -**, **Ha|cke|rin** [-ərın] F **-, -nen** *(Comput)* hacker

ha|cke|voll ADJ *(inf)*, **ha|cke|zu** ADJ *(sl)* *(= betrunken)* pissed *(Brit inf)*, plastered *(inf)*

Hack-: **Hack|fleisch** NT mince *(Brit)*, minced *(Brit)* *or* ground *(US)* meat; **jdn zu** *or* **aus jdm ~ machen** *(inf)* to make mincemeat of sb *(inf)*; *(= verprügeln)* to beat sb up; **Hack|frucht** F root crop; **Hack|klotz** M chopping block

Hack|ler ['haklɐ] M **-s, -**, **Hack|le|rin** [-lərın] F **-, -nen** *(Aus)* worker, person having a job; *(= Schwerarbeiter)* grafter *(inf)*

Hack|ler|re|ge|lung ['haklɐ-] F *(Aus)* *official regulation entitling people that have been employed for a long time to start drawing their pension prematurely without any deductions*

Hack|ord|nung F *(lit, fig)* pecking order

Häck|sel ['hɛksl] NT OR M **-s**, *no pl* chaff

Häck|sel|ma|schi|ne F chaffcutter

Hack-: **Hack|steak** NT hamburger; **Hack|-stock** M *(Aus)* chopping block

Ha|der ['ha:dɐ] M **-s**, *no pl (geh)* *(= Zwist)* discord; *(= Unzufriedenheit)* discontentment; **in ~ mit sich und der Welt leben** to be at odds with oneself and the world

Ha|de|rer ['ha:dərɐ] M **-s, -**, **Ha|de|rin** [-ərın] F **-, -nen** *(geh: = unzufriedener Mensch)* grumbler

Ha|der|lump M *(Aus, S Ger)* good-for-nothing

ha|dern ['ha:dɐn] VI *(dated, geh)* *(= streiten)* to quarrel, to wrangle *(mit* with); *(= unzufrieden sein)* to be at odds *(mit* with); **hadere nicht mit deinem Schicksal** you must accept your fate

Ha|dern ['ha:dɐn] PL *(S Ger, Aus)* rags *pl* *(for making paper)*

Ha|dern|pa|pier NT rag paper

Ha|des ['ha:dɛs] M **-**, *no pl (Myth)* Hades

Had|ri|an ['ha:dria:n] M **-s** Hadrian

Had|schi ['ha:dʃi] M **-s, -s** hajji

Ha|fen ['ha:fn] M **-s, ¨** ['hɛ:fn] **a** harbour *(Brit)*, harbor *(US)*; *(= Handelshafen, für große Schiffe)* port; *(= Jachthafen)* marina; *(= Hafenanlagen)* docks *pl*; **in den ~ einlaufen** to put into harbo(u)r/port **b** *(fig)* haven; **im ~ der Ehe landen** to get married; **in den ~ der Ehe einlaufen** to enter the state of matrimony

Ha|fen M **-s, ¨** *or* **-** *(dial)* **a** *(= Kochtopf)* pot, pan; *(= Schüssel)* dish, bowl; *(= Krug)* jug **b** *(= Nachttopf)* chamber pot

Hä|fen ['hɛ:fn] M **-s, -** *(Aus)* **a** (sauce)pan **b** *(inf: = Gefängnis)* jug *(inf)*, clink *(inf)*

Ha|fen- *in cpds* harbour *(Brit)*, harbor *(US)*; *(bei Handelshafen, für große Schiffe)* port; **Ha|fen|amt** NT harbo(u)r/port authority; **Ha|fen|an|la|gen** PL docks *pl*; **Ha|fen|ar|bei|ter(in)** M(F) dockworker, docker; **Ha|fen|arzt** M, **Ha|fen|-ärz|tin** F port doctor; **Ha|fen|be|cken** NT harbour *(Brit)* *or* harbor *(US)* basin, (wet) dock; **Ha|fen|be|hör|den** PL harbo(u)r/port authorities *pl*; **Ha|fen|blo|cka|de** F blockade of a harbo(u)r/port

Hä|fen|bru|der ['hɛ:fn-] M *(Aus inf)* jailbird *(inf)*

Ha|fen-: **Ha|fen|ein|fahrt** F harbo(u)r/port entrance; **die ~ von Dover** the entrance to Dover Harbour; **Ha|fen|ge|bühr** F *usu pl* harbo(u)r/port dues *pl*; **Ha|fen|knei|pe** F *(inf)* dockland pub *(Brit)* *or* bar; **Ha|fen|meis|ter(in)** M(F) harbourmaster/-mistress *(Brit)*, harbormaster/-mistress *(US)*; **Ha|fen|meis|te|rei** F harbourmaster's *(Brit)* *or* harbormaster's *(US)* office; **Ha|fen|po|li|zei** F port *or* dock police; **Ha|fen|rund|fahrt** F (boat-)trip round the harbo(u)r; **Ha|fen|stadt** F port; *(am Meer auch)* seaport; **Ha|fen|vier|tel** NT dock area

Ha|fer ['ha:fɐ] M **-s, -** oats *pl*; **ihn sticht der ~** *(inf)* he's feeling his oats *(inf)*

Ha|fer-: **Ha|fer|brei** M porridge; **Ha|fer|flo|-cken** PL rolled oats *pl*; **Ha|fer|grüt|ze** F porridge; **Ha|fer|kleie** F oat bran; **Ha|fer|korn** NT *pl* **-körner** (oat) grain

Ha|ferl ['ha:fɐl] NT **-s, -n**, **Hä|ferl** ['hɛ:fɐl] NT **-s, -n** *(S Ger, Aus inf)* *(= große Tasse, Becher)* mug; *(= Schüssel)* bowl; *(= Topf)* pot

Ha|ferl|schuh ['ha:fɐl-] M *type of brogue*

Ha|fer-: **Ha|fer|mehl** NT oatmeal; **Ha|fer|sack** M fodder bag; **Ha|fer|schleim** M gruel

Haff [haf] NT **-(e)s, -s** *or* **-e** lagoon

Haf|lin|ger ['ha:flıŋɐ] M **-s, -** Haflinger (horse)

Haf|ner ['ha:fnɐ] M **-s, -**, **Haf|ne|rin** [-ərın] F **-, -nen**, **Häf|ner** ['hɛ:fnɐ] M **-s, -**, **Häf|ne|rin** [-ərın] F **-, -nen** *(S Ger)* *(= Töpfer)* potter; *(= Ofensetzer)* stove-fitter

Haf|ne|rei [ha:fnə'rai] F **-, -en** *(S Ger)* *(= Töpferei)* pottery; *(= Ofensetzerbetrieb)* stove-fitter's works *sing or pl*

Haf|ni|um ['ha:fniʊm, 'hafniʊm] NT **-s**, *no pl* *(abbr* **Hf**) hafnium

Haft [haft] F **-**, *no pl (vor dem Prozess)* custody; *(= Haftstrafe)* imprisonment; *(= Haftzeit)* prison sentence, term of imprisonment; *(politisch)* detention; **sich in ~ befinden** to be in custody/prison/detention; **eine schwere/leichte ~ verhängen** to impose a long/short term of imprisonment; **jdn aus der ~ entlassen** to release sb from custody/prison/detention; **eine ~ absitzen** *(inf)* to do time *(inf)*; **in ~ sitzen** to be held in custody/prison/detention; **in ~ nehmen** to take into custody, to detain

-haft ADJ *suf* **a** *(= -artig)* -like; -ish; -ly; **kindhaft** childlike; **jungenhaft** boyish; **frauenhaft** womanly; **riesenhaft** gigantic **b** *(auf Eigenschaft bezüglich)* -ly; -ive; **lebhaft** lively; **schwatzhaft** talkative **c** *(in Verbableitungen)* -ing; **wohnhaft** residing, resident **d** *(Möglichkeit bezeichnend)* -ible, -able; **glaubhaft** credible, believable

Haft-: **Haft|an|stalt** F detention centre *(Brit)* *or* center *(US)*; **Haft|aus|schlie|ßungs|grund** M grounds *pl* for not imposing a prison sentence; **Haft|aus|set|zung** F suspended prison sentence; *(= Unterbrechung)* parole; **haft|bar** ADJ *(für jdn)* legally responsible; *(für etw)* (legally) liable; **jdn für etw ~ machen** to make *or* hold sb liable for sth; **Haft|bar|keit** ['haftba:ɐkait] F **-**, *no pl (für jdn)* (legal) responsibility; *(für etw)* (legal) liability; **Haft|be|fehl** M warrant; **einen ~ gegen jdn ausstellen** to issue a warrant for sb's arrest; **Haft|be|schwer|de** F appeal against a remand in custody; **Haft|dau|er** F term of imprisonment

Haf|tel ['haftl] NT **-s, -** *(Aus)* hook and eye *sing*

Haf|tel|ma|cher M *(Aus)* **aufpassen wie ein ~** to watch like a hawk

haf|ten ['haftn] VI *(Jur)* **für jdn ~** to be (legally) responsible for sb; **für etw ~** to be (legally) liable for sth; **(jdm) für jdn/etw ~** *(= verantwortlich sein)* to be responsible (to sb) for sb/sth; **die Versicherung hat für den Schaden nicht gehaftet** the insurance company did not accept liability (for the damage); **für Garderobe kann nicht gehaftet werden** the management can accept no responsibility for articles deposited, all articles are left at owner's risk

haf|ten VI **a** *(= kleben)* to stick *(an +dat* to); *(Klebstoff auch, Reifen, Phys)* to adhere; *(= sich festsetzen: Rauch, Schmutz, Geruch)* to cling *(an +dat* to); **an jdm ~** *(fig: Makel etc)* to hang over sb, to stick to sb **b** *(Eindruck, Erinnerung)* to stick (in one's mind); *(Blick)* to become fixed; **an etw** *(dat)* **~** *(= hängen)* to be fixed on sth; **bei den Schülern haftet nichts** nothing sinks in with these pupils; **~de Eindrücke** lasting impressions

haf|ten blei|ben *irreg aux sein*, **haf|ten+blei|-ben** *sep irreg aux sein* VI to stick; *(an or auf +dat* to) *(= sich festsetzen: Rauch, Schmutz, Geruch)* to cling; *(Klebstoff)* to cling, to adhere; *(Phys)* to adhere; *(Eindruck, Gelerntes)* to stick

Haft-: **Haft|ent|las|se|ne(r)** [-ɛntlasənə] MF *decl as adj* released prisoner; **Haft|ent|las|-sung** F → **Haft** release from custody/prison/detention; **Haft|ent|schä|di|gung** F compensation for wrongful imprisonment; **Haft|eti|-kett** NT adhesive label; **haft|fä|hig** ADJ **a** *Material* adhesive; *Reifen* with good road-holding; **auf etw** *(dat)* **~ sein** to stick to sth **b** *(Jur)* fit to be kept in prison; **Haft|fä|hig|keit** F, *no pl* **a** *(von Material)* adhesive strength; *(von Reifen)* road-holding **b** *(Jur)* fitness to be kept in prison; **Haft|grund** M **a** *(Jur)* grounds *pl* for detaining sb (in custody) **b** *(Tech)* base

Häft|ling ['hɛftlıŋ] M **-s, -e** prisoner; *(politisch auch)* detainee

Häft|lings-: **Häft|lings|klei|dung** F prison uniform *or* clothes *pl*; **Häft|lings|re|vol|te** F prison *or* prisoners' revolt

Haft-: **Haft|no|tiz** F Post-it®; **Haft|or|gan** NT suction pad; **Haft|pflicht** F **a** *(= Schadenersatzpflicht)* (legal) liability; *(für Personen)* (legal) responsibility; **die ~ der Versicherung erstreckt sich nicht auf Glas und Silber** the insurance does not cover glass and silver **b** *(inf: = Haftpflichtversicherung)* personal *or* public *(US)* liability insurance; *(für Auto)* ≈ third party insurance; **ich bin in keiner ~** I don't have any personal liability insurance *etc*; **haft|pflich|tig** [-pflıçtıç] ADJ liable; **haft|pflicht|ver|si|chert** [-fɛɐzıçɐt] ADJ **~ sein** to have personal *or* public *(US)* liability insurance; *(Autofahrer)* ≈ to have third-party insurance; **Haft|pflicht|ver|-si|che|rung** F personal *or* public *(US)* liability insurance *no indef art*; *(von Autofahrer)* ≈ third-party insurance; **Haft|prü|fung** F review of remand in custody; **Haft|psy|cho|se** F prison psychosis *no indef art*; **Haft|pul|ver** NT *(für Gebiss)* denture fixative *or* adhesive; **Haft|rei|-bung** F *(Phys)* static friction; **Haft|rich|ter(in)** M(F) magistrate; **Haft|scha|len** PL contact lenses *pl*; **Haft|stra|fe** F prison sentence; **haft|un|fä|hig** ADJ *(Jur)* unfit to be kept in prison; **Haft|un|fä|hig|keit** F, *no pl (Jur)* unfitness to be kept in prison *(because of illness etc)*

Haf|tung ['haftʊŋ] ✪ 47.3 F -, -en **a** *(Jur)* (legal) liability; *(für Personen)* (legal) responsibility; **für Ihre Garderobe übernehmen wir keine ~** articles are left at owner's risk, the management accepts no responsibility for articles deposited **b** *(Tech, Phys, von Reifen)* adhesion

Haf|tungs- *(Jur)*: **Haf|tungs|be|schrän|kung** F limitation of liability; **Haf|tungs|kla|ge** F action to establish liability

Haft-: **Haft|ur|laub** M parole; **Haft|ver|kür|zung** F shortened sentence; **Haft|ver|scho|nung** F exemption from imprisonment; **Haft|zeit** F prison sentence

Hag [ha:k] M -(e)s, -e [-gə] *(poet, old)* *(= Hain)* grove; *(= Hecke)* hedge

Ha|ge-: **Ha|ge|bu|che** ['ha:gəbu:xə] F hornbeam; **Ha|ge|but|te** ['ha:gəbʊtə] F -, -n rose hip; *(inf: = Heckenrose)* dog rose; **Ha|ge|but|ten|tee** M rose-hip tea; **Ha|ge|dorn** M *pl* -dorne hawthorn

Ha|gel ['ha:gl] M -s, *no pl* **a** hail; *(= Hagelschauer)* hailstorm **b** *(= große Menge)* *(von Steinen, Geschossen)* hail; *(von Vorwürfen, Drohungen, Anschuldigungen)* stream; *(von Schimpfworten)* stream, torrent

Ha|gel|korn NT *pl* -körner hailstone

ha|geln ['ha:gln] **VI** *impers* **es hagelt** it's hailing **VI** **etw hagelt auf jdn/etw** *(Schläge, Geschosse, Steine)* sth rains down on sb/sth; *(Vorwürfe, Schimpfworte)* sb is showered with sth **VT** *impers* *(lit)* to hail (down); **es hagelte etw** *(fig)* sth rained down; *Vorwürfe, Schimpfworte* there was a shower of sth

Ha|gel-: **Ha|gel|scha|den** M damage caused by hail; **Ha|gel|schau|er** M (short) hailstorm; **Ha|gel|schlag** M **a** *(Met)* hail; *(= Hagelschauer)* hailstorm **b** *(Cook)* sugar crystals *pl*; **Ha|gel|schlo|ße** [-ʃlo:sə] F -, -n *(dial)* hailstone; **Ha|gel|sturm** M hailstorm; **Ha|gel|wet|ter** NT *(lit)* hailstorm

ha|ger ['ha:gɐ] ADJ gaunt, thin; *Mensch auch* lean

Ha|ge|stolz ['ha:gəʃtɔlts] M -es, -e *(old, hum)* confirmed bachelor

Ha|gio- [hagio-]: **Ha|gio|graf** [-'gra:f] M -en, -en, **Ha|gio|gra|fin** [-'gra:fɪn] F -, -nen *(form)* hagiographer; **Ha|gio|gra|fen** [-'gra:fn] PL *(Bibl)* Hagiographa; **Ha|gio|gra|fie** [-gra'fi:] F -, -n [-'fi:ən] *(form)* hagiography; **Ha|gio|graph** *etc* → **Hagiograf** *etc*

ha|ha [ha'ha:, ha'ha], **ha|ha|ha** [haha'ha:, haha'ha] INTERJ haha, ha, ha, ha

Hä|her ['hɛ:ɐ] M -s, - jay

Hahn [ha:n] M -(e)s, ¨-e ['hɛ:nə] **a** *(= männlicher Vogel)* cock; *(= männliches Haushuhn auch)* rooster; *(jünger)* cockerel; *(= Wetterhahn)* weathercock; **der gallische ~** the French cockerel; **~ im Korb sein** *(= Mann unter Frauen)* to be cock of the walk; **danach kräht kein ~ mehr** *(inf)* no one cares two hoots about that any more *(inf)*; **jdm den (roten) ~ aufs Dach setzen** to set sb's house on fire **b** *pl auch* -en *(Tech)* tap, faucet *(US)*; *(= Zapfhahn auch)* spigot; *(= Schwimmerhahn)* ball cock **c** *(= Abzug)* trigger

Hähn|chen ['hɛ:nçən] NT -s, - chicken; *(= junger Hahn)* cockerel

Hah|nen-: **Hah|nen|bal|ken** M *(Build)* ridge beam; **Hah|nen|fe|der** F cock's plume; **Hah|nen|fuß** M *(Bot)* buttercup; **Hah|nen|fuß|ge|wächs** NT buttercup; **Hah|nen|kamm** M *(auch Frisur)* cockscomb; **Hah|nen|kampf** M **a** cockfight; *(Sport)* cockfighting **b** *(= Spiel)* children's hopping game; **Hah|nen|schrei** M cockcrow; **beim ersten ~** *(fig)* at cockcrow; **Hah|nen|sporn** M *pl* -sporen cock's spur; **Hah|nen|tritt** M, **Hah|nen|tritt|mus|ter** NT dogtooth check

Hah|ni|um ['ha:niʊm] NT -s, *no pl* *(abbr* **Ha)** hahnium

Hahn|rei ['ha:nrai] M -s, -e *(dated)* cuckold; **jdn zum ~ machen** to cuckold sb

Hai [hai] M -(e)s, -e, **Hai|fisch** M *(lit, fig)* shark

Hai|fisch|flos|sen|sup|pe F shark's-fin soup

Hain [hain] M -(e)s, -e *(poet, geh)* grove

Hain|bu|che F hornbeam

Ha|i|ti [ha'i:ti] NT -s Haiti

Ha|i|ti|a|ner [hai'tia:nɐ] M -s, -, **Ha|i|ti|a|ne|rin** [-ərɪn] F -, -nen Haitian

ha|i|ti|a|nisch [hai'tia:nɪʃ] ADJ Haitian

Ha|i|ti|er [ha'i:tiɐ] M -s, -, **Ha|i|ti|e|rin** [-iərɪn] F -, -nen Haitian

ha|i|tisch [ha'i:tɪʃ] ADJ Haitian

Häk|chen ['hɛ:kçən] NT -s, - **a** *(Sew)* (small) hook; **was ein ~ werden will, krümmt sich beizeiten** *(Prov)* there's nothing like starting young **b** *(= Zeichen)* tick *(Brit)*, check *(US)*; *(auf Buchstaben)* diacritic *(spec)*, accent **c** *(= Instrument)* dental probe

Hä|kel|ar|beit F crochet (work) *no indef art*; *(= das Häkeln auch)* crocheting; *(= Gegenstand)* piece of crochet (work)

Hä|ke|lei [hɛ:kə'lai] F -, -en crocheting, crochet work

Hä|kel|garn NT crochet thread

ha|keln ['ha:kln] **VI** *(= Fingerhakeln machen)* to finger-wrestle **VTI** **a** *(Ftbl, Hockey etc)* to trip up **b** *(Rugby)* to heel **c** *(beim Ringen)* Gegner to get in a foot-lock

hä|keln ['hɛ:kln] VTI to crochet

Hä|kel|na|del F crochet hook

ha|ken ['ha:kn] **VI** *(= klemmen)* to stick; **es hakt** *(fig)* there's some delay, there are sticking points; **es hakt bei jdm** *(inf: = versteht nicht)* sb is stuck **VT** **a** *(= befestigen)* to hook *(an +acc* to) **b** *(= einhängen, um etw legen)* to hook *(in +acc* in, *um* around) **VTI** *(Sport)* to trip up

Ha|ken ['ha:kn] M -s, - **a** hook; *(aus Holz auch)* peg; **~ und Öse** hook and eye; **mit ~ und Ösen spielen** *(Ftbl inf)* to foul **b** *(inf: = Schwierigkeit)* snag, catch; **die Sache hat einen ~** there's a snag *or* a catch; **die Sache ist ganz ohne ~ und Ösen** there's no catch; **ein Angebot ohne ~ und Ösen** an offer with no strings attached; **wo ist der ~?** what's the catch? *(inf)* **c** *(= plötzlicher Richtungswechsel)* **einen ~ schlagen** to dart sideways; **~ *pl* schlagen** to dart from side to side **d** *(Boxen)* hook **e** = **Häkchen b**

Ha|ken-: **ha|ken|för|mig** ADJ hooked, hook-shaped; *Nase* hooked; **Ha|ken|kral|le** F pinch hook; **Ha|ken|kreuz** NT swastika; **Ha|ken|kreuz|fah|ne** F swastika flag; **Ha|ken|na|se** F hooked nose, hooknose

ha|kig ['ha:kɪç] ADJ = **hakenförmig**

Ha|la|li [hala'li:] NT -s, -(s) *(Hunt)* mort

halb [halp] **ADJ** **a** *(Bruchteil)* half; *Lehrauftrag etc* part-time; **ein ~er Kuchen/Meter** *etc* half a cake/metre *(Brit)* or meter *(US)* *etc*; **der ~e Kuchen/Tag** *etc* half the cake/day *etc*; **eine ~e Stunde** half an hour; **alle ~e Stunde** every half hour; **ein ~es Jahr** six months *pl*, half a year; **ein ~es Dutzend** half a dozen; **auf ~er Höhe** at half the normal height; *(zum Gipfel)* halfway up; **auf ~em Wege, auf ~er Strecke** *(lit)* halfway; *(fig)* halfway through; **jdm auf ~em Weg entgegenkommen** *(fig)* to meet sb halfway; **das ~e Hundert** fifty, half a hundred *(old)*; **zum ~en Preis** (at) half price; **den Apfel nur ~ essen** to eat only half the apple; **Kleid mit ~em Arm** dress with half-length sleeves **b** *(Mus)* **eine ~e Note** a minim *(Brit)*, a half-note *(US)*; **ein ~er Ton** a semitone; **~e Pause** minim *(Brit)* or half-note *(US)* rest **c** *inv (Uhrzeit)* **~ zehn** half past nine; **fünf Minuten vor/nach ~ zwei** twenty-five (minutes) past one/to two; **es schlägt ~** it's striking the half hour; **um drei Minuten nach ~** at three minutes past the half hour; **um fünf Minuten nach ~** at twenty-five to **d** *inv, no art (bei geografischen Namen)* **~ Deutschland/London** half of Germany/London **e** *(= teilweise, stückhaft) Maßnahmen* half; *Reformen* partial; *(= vermindert) Tempo* half; *Lächeln* slight; *Licht* poor; **~e Arbeit leisten** to do a bad job; **die ~e Freude** half the pleasure; **die ~e Wahrheit** half of *or* part of the truth; **nichts Halbes und nichts Ganzes** neither one thing nor the other; **mit ~em Ohr** with half an ear; **ein ~er Mensch/eine ~e Frau sein, sich nur wie ein ~er Mensch/eine ~e Frau fühlen** not to feel like a complete person/woman; *(= energielos)* to feel half dead; **eine ~e Sache machen** not to do it properly; **keine ~en Sachen machen** not to do things by halves **f** *(inf)* *(= große Anzahl, großer Teil)* **die ~e Stadt/Welt/Arbeit** half the town/world/work; **sie ist schon eine ~e Schottin** she is already half Scottish; **ein ~er Elektriker/Mechaniker** something of an electrician/mechanic; **(noch) ein ~es Kind sein** to be hardly *or* scarcely more than a child

ADV **a** *(= zur Hälfte)* half; **~ gar** half-cooked, half-done; *(fig) Idee* half-baked; **~ links** *(Sport, spielen)* (at) inside left; *(im Theater) sitzen* left of centre *(Brit)* or center *(US)*; **~ links abbiegen** to fork left; **die Straße ~ links** the left fork; **das Auto kam von ~ links** the car came from a/the left fork; **~ linke(r, s)** *(Sport)* inside left; **die ~ linke Abzweigung/Straße** the left fork; **~ rechte(r, s)** *(Sport)* inside right; **die ~ rechte Abzweigung/Straße** the right fork; **~ rechts** *(Sport, spielen)* (at) inside right; *(im Theater) sitzen* right of centre *(Brit)* or center *(US)*; **~ rechts abbiegen** to fork right; **die Straße ~ rechts** the right fork; **das Auto kam von ~ rechts** the car came from a/the right fork; **~ rechts/links abzweigen** *(Straße, Fahrer)* to fork (off) to the right/left, to turn half right/left; **~ voll** half-filled; *Behälter auch* half-full; **die Zeit ist ~ vorbei** half the time has already gone **b** *(= nicht ganz, teilweise)* half; **~ automatisch** semi-automatic; **~ erwachsen** half grown (up); **~ fest** → **halbfest**; **~ offen** half-open; *Gefängnis* open; **~ offener Vollzug** daytime release *(for prisoners)*; **~ reif** half-ripe; **~ verdaut** *(lit, fig)* half-digested; **~ wach** half awake; **in ~ wachem Zustand** half awake; **~ zivilisiert** half-civilized; **~ so gut** half as good; **etw nur ~ verstehen** to only half understand sth; **ich hörte nur ~ zu** I was only half listening; **das ist ~ so schlimm** it's not as bad as all that; *(Zukünftiges)* that won't be too bad; **er weiß alles nur ~** he only knows about things superficially; **etw nur ~ machen** to only half-do sth *(inf)* **c** *(= fast vollständig)* almost, nearly; *blind, roh* half; **~ fertig** half-finished; *(Ind)* semi-finished; *(fig)* immature; **ich war schon ~ fertig** I was almost *or* nearly finished; **~ nackt** half-naked; *Arm* half-covered; **~ tot** *(lit)* half dead; **wir haben uns ~ totgelacht** we almost died laughing; **ich hätte mich ~ totärgern können** I could have kicked myself *(inf)* → **frisch ADV b** **d** **~ lachend, ~ weinend** half laughing, half crying; **~ Mensch, ~ Pferd** half *or* part man, half *or* part horse; **Wein oder Sprudel? – ~ und ~** wine or mineral water? – half and half **e** **mit jdm ~e-~e machen** *(inf)* to go halves with sb *(Brit)*, to go 50/50 with sb; **~ und ~** *(inf: = beinahe)* more or less; **gefällt es dir? – ~ und ~** do you like it? – sort of *(inf)* *or* so-so *(inf)*

Halb-: **Halb|af|fe** M prosimian; **halb|amt|lich** ADJ semi-official; **halb|au|to|ma|tisch** ADJ → **halb ADV b**; **Halb|band** [-bant] M *pl* -bände half-binding; **Halb|bil|dung** F smattering of knowledge *or* *(in Bezug auf Ausbildung)* education; **halb|bit|ter** ADJ *Schokolade* semi-sweet; **Halb|blut** NT **a** *(= Mensch)* half-caste **b** *(= Tier)* crossbreed; **Halb|blü|ter** [-bly:tɐ] M -s, - crossbreed; **Halb|blü|ti|ge(r)** [-bly:tɪgə] MF *decl as adj* half-caste; **Halb|bru|der** M half-brother; **Halb|de|ckung** F *(Fin)* partial cover; **halb|dun|kel** ADJ half-dark, dim; **Halb|dun|kel** NT semi-darkness, half-dark; *(= Dämmerung)* dusk, twilight

Hal|be ['halbə] F *decl as adj (esp S Ger)* = **Halbe(r)**

Halb|edel|stein M semi-precious stone

Hal|be(r) ['halbə] M *decl as adj* half a litre *(Brit)* or liter *(US)* (of beer); **trinken Sie noch einen ~n!** ≈ have another pint! *(Brit)*, ≈ have another beer!

hal|ber ['halbɐ] PREP +*gen (nachgestellt) (dated, geh) (= wegen)* on account of; *(= um ... willen)* for the sake of

hal|ber ADJ, ADV *(S Ger)* → **halb ADJ c ADV b, c**

-hal|ber ADV *suf (= wegen)* on account of; *(= um ... willen)* for the sake of; **gesundheitshalber** for reasons of health, for medical reasons; **vorsichtshalber** to be on the safe side, as a precaution; **sicherheitshalber** *(= aus Sicherheitsgründen)* for safety reasons; *(= um sicher zu sein)* to be on the safe side

Halb-: **halb|er|wach|sen** ADJ → **halb ADV b**; **Halb|er|zeug|nis** NT *(Comm)* semi-finished product

Hal|be(s) ['halbə] NT *decl as adj* = **Halbe(r)**

Halb-: **Halb|fab|ri|kat** NT semi-finished product; **halb|fer|tig** ADJ → **halb ADV c**; **halb|fest** ADJ *(Zustand, Materie)* semi-solid; *Gelee* half-set; **halb|fett** ADJ **a** *(Typ)* secondary bold **b** *Lebensmittel* medium-fat ADV *(Typ)* in secondary bold; **Halb|fi|na|le** NT semi-final; **Halb|fin|ger|hand|schuh** M fingerless glove; **halb|gar** ADJ → **halb ADV a**; **halb|ge|bil|det** ADJ half-educated; **Halb|ge|schoss** NT *(Archit)* mezzanine floor; **Halb|ge|schwis|ter** PL half brothers and sisters *pl*; **Halb|glat|ze** F receding hairline; **Halb|gott** M *(Myth, fig)* demigod; **Halbgötter in Weiß** *(iro)* doctors

Halb|heit F -, -en *(pej)* half measure; **er ist nicht für ~en** he is not one for half measures, he doesn't do things by halves; **mach keine ~en** *(inf)* don't do things by halves

Halb-: **halb|her|zig** ADJ half-hearted ADV half-heartedly; **na, dieses Ja kam aber sehr ~** well, that yes sounded very half-hearted; **Halb|her|zig|keit** [-hɛrtsɪçkait] F -, *no pl* half-heartedness *no pl*; **halb|hoch** ADJ *Baum* half-grown; *Stern* halfway up the sky; *(Comput) Laufwerkschacht* half-height ADV **den Ball ~ abspielen** to pass the ball at shoulder height; **~ fliegen** to fly at half (its/one's *etc* normal) height

hal|bie|ren [hal'biːrən] *ptp* **halbiert** VT to halve, to divide in half *or* two; *(Geometrie)* to bisect; *(= in zwei schneiden)* to cut in half; **eine Zahl ~** to divide a number by two

Hal|bie|rung F -, -en halving, dividing in half *or* two; *(Geometrie)* bisection

Halb-: **Halb|in|sel** F peninsula; **Halb|in|va|li|de** M, **Halb|in|va|li|din** F semi-invalid, partially disabled

Halb|jahr NT half-year *(auch Comm)*, six months; **im ersten/zweiten ~** in the first/last six months of the year

Halb|jah|res-: **Halb|jah|res|be|richt** M half-yearly report; **Halb|jah|res|bi|lanz** F half-yearly figures *pl*; **Halb|jah|res|kurs** M six-month course; **Halb|jah|res|zeug|nis** NT *(Sch)* half-yearly report

Halb-: **halb|jäh|rig** ADJ *attr Kind* six-month-old; *Lehrgang etc* six-month; *Kündigung* six months; **halb|jähr|lich** ADJ half-yearly *(auch Comm)*, six-monthly; **in ~em Wechsel** changing every six months ADV every six months, twice a year, twice yearly; **Halb|jahrs|aus|weis** M *(Aus Sch)* half-yearly report; **Halb|jahrs|kurs** M six-month course; **Halb|ju|de** M, **Halb|jü|din** F half Jew; **~ sein** to be half Jewish; **Halb|kan|ton** M sub-canton; **Halb|kon|so|nant** M semi-consonant; **Halb|kreis** M semicircle; **halb|kreis|för|mig** ADJ semicircular ADV in a semicircle; **Halb|ku|gel** F hemisphere; **nördliche/südliche ~** northern/southern hemisphere; **halb|ku|gel|för|mig** ADJ hemispherical; **halb|lang** ADJ *Kleid, Rock* mid-calf length; *Haar* chin-length; **nun mach mal ~!** *(inf)* now wait a minute!; **halb|laut** ADJ low ADV in a low voice, in an undertone; **Halb|le|der** NT *(= Verfahren)* half-binding; **in ~ binden** to bind in half-leather, to half-bind; **Halb|le|der|band** M *(= Buch)* half-bound volume; *(= Ausgabe)* half-bound edition; **halb|lei|nen** ADJ *attr Stoff* made of a fifty per cent linen mixture; *Bucheinband* half-cloth; **Halb|lei|nen** NT *Stoff* fifty per cent linen material; *(= Bucheinband)* half-cloth; **Halb|lei|nen|band** M *(= Buch)* volume bound in half-cloth; *(= Ausgabe)* edition bound in half-cloth; **Halb|lei|ter** M *(Phys)* semiconductor; **halb|lin|ke(r, s)** ADJ *attr* → **halb ADV a**; **Halb|lin|ke(r)** MF *decl as adj*, **Halb|links** M -, - *(Sport)* inside left; **halb|links** ADV → **halb ADV a**; **Halb|li|ter|fla|sche** F half-litre *(Brit)* or half-liter *(US)* bottle; **halb|mast** ['halpmast] ADV at half-mast; **(eine Flagge) ~ hissen** to hoist a flag to half-mast; **~ flaggen** to fly flags/a flag at half-mast; **auf ~ stehen** to fly *or* be at half-mast; **seine Socken hängen auf ~** *(hum: = sind verrutscht)* his socks are at half-mast; **halb|matt** ADJ *(Phot)* semi-matt; **Halb|mes|ser** M -s, - radius; **Halb|me|tall** NT semi-metal; **Halb|mo|nats|schrift** F fortnightly periodical; **Halb|mond** M *(Astron)* half-moon; *(= Symbol)* crescent; *(an Fingernägeln)* half-moon; **bei ~** when there is a half-moon; **wir haben ~** there's a half-moon; **halb|mo|nat|lich** ADJ half-monthly ADV half-monthly, fortnightly, biweekly *(US)*; **halb|mond|för|mig** ADJ crescent-shaped; **halb|nackt** ADJ → **halb ADV c**; **halb|of|fen** ADJ → **halb ADV b**; **halb|part** ['halppart] ADV **~ machen** *(bei einer Unternehmung)* to go halves; *(bei Gewinn)* to split it fifty-fifty; **Halb|pen|si|on** F half-board; **in ~ wohnen** to have half-board; **Halb|pro|dukt** NT semi-finished product; **halb|rech|te(r, s)** ADJ → **halb ADV a**; **Halb|rech|te(r)** MF *decl as adj*, **Halb|rechts** M -, - *(Sport)* inside right; **halb|rechts** ADV → **halb ADV a**; **halb|reif** ADJ → **halb ADV b**; **Halb|re|li|ef** NT half-relief, mezzo-relievo; **halb|rund** ADJ *attr Tisch etc* semicircular; *Ecke* half-rounded; **Halb|rund** ['halprʊnt] NT -(e)s, *(rare)* -e [-də] semicircle, half-circle; **im ~** in a semicircle; **Halb|schat|ten** M half shadow; *(Astron)* penumbra; **Halb|schlaf** M light sleep; **im ~ sein** to be half asleep; **Halb|schritt|tas|te** F condensed key, half-space key; **Halb|schuh** M shoe; **Halb|schwer|ge|wicht** NT **a** *no pl (= Klasse)* light-heavyweight division; **ein Boxkampf im ~** a light-heavyweight contest **b** *(= Boxer)* light-heavyweight; **Halb|schwer|ge|wicht|ler(in)** M(F) light-heavyweight; **Halb|schwes|ter** F half-sister; **Halb|sei|de** F fifty per cent *(Brit)* or percent *(US)* silk mixture; **halb|sei|den** ADJ *(lit)* fifty per cent *(Brit)* or percent *(US)* silk; *(fig) Dame* fast; *Aussehen* flashy; *(= schwul)* gay; *(= zweifelhaft, undurchsichtig)* dubious; **~es Milieu, ~e Kreise** the demimonde; **halb|sei|tig** [-zaitɪç] ADJ *Anzeige etc* half-page; *(Med) Kopfschmerzen* in one side of one's head; **~e Lähmung** one-sided paralysis, hemiplegia ADV **~ gelähmt** paralyzed on one side, hemiplegic; **halb|staat|lich** ADJ *attr* partly state-run *or* state-controlled; **halb|stark** ADJ *attr Sprache, Manieren, Jugendliche* rowdy; **Halb|star|ke(r)** M *decl as adj* young hooligan, young rowdy *(Brit)*; **halb|stün|dig** ADJ *attr* half-hour *attr*, lasting half an hour; **halb|stünd|lich** ADJ half-hourly ADV every half an hour, half-hourly; **Halb|stür|mer(in)** M(F) *(Ftbl)* half-back

halb|tä|gig ADJ *attr* half-day *attr*; *Fahrt, Ausflug, Urlaub, Arbeit etc* half a day's *attr* ADV → **halbtags**

halb|tags ['halptaːks] ADV *(= morgens)* in the mornings; *(= nachmittags)* in the afternoons; *(in Bezug auf Angestellte auch)* part-time

Halb|tags-: **Halb|tags|ar|beit** F *(= Arbeitsverhältnis)* half-day job; *(morgens auch)* morning job; *(nachmittags auch)* afternoon job; *(von Angestellten auch)* part-time job; **Halb|tags|be|schäf|tig|te(r)** MF *decl as adj* = **Halbtagskraft**; **Halb|tags|be|schäf|ti|gung** F = **Halbtagsarbeit**; **Halb|tags|kraft** F worker employed for half-days only; **Halb|tags|schu|le** F half-day school

Halb-: **Halb|ton** M *pl* **-töne** *(Mus)* semitone; *(Art, Phot)* halftone; **Halb|ton|schritt** M semitone; **halb|tot** ADJ → **halb ADV c**; **Halb|to|ta|le** F *(Film)* medium shot; **Halb|trau|er** F half-mourning; **halb|tro|cken** ADJ *Wein* medium-dry; **halb|ver|daut** [-fɛɐdaut] ADJ → **halb ADV b**; **Halb|vers** M half-line, hemistich; **Halb|vo|kal** M semivowel; **halb|voll** ADJ → **halb ADV a**; **halb|wach** ADJ → **halb ADV b**; **Halb|wahr|heit** F half-truth; **Halb|wai|se** F *person who has lost one parent*; **er/sie ist ~** he/she has lost one of his/her parents; **halb|wegs** ['halp'veːks] ADV **a** partly; *gut, adäquat* reasonably; *annehmbar* halfway; **wenn es dir wieder ~ gut geht** when you're feeling a bit better; **wenn Sie ~ eine Vorstellung haben, ...** if you have the least idea ... **b** *(dated: = auf halber Strecke)* halfway; **Halb|welt** F demimonde; **Halb|welt|da|me** F demimondaine; **Halb|wel|ter|ge|wicht** NT *(= Klasse)* light-welterweight *no def art*; *(= Sportler)* light-welterweight; **Halb|wert(s)|zeit** F *(Phys)* half-life; **halb|wild** ADJ *attr Mensch* uncivilized; *Tier* half wild; **wie die Halbwilden** *(inf)* like (a bunch of) savages; **Halb|wis|sen** NT *(pej)* superficial knowledge; **halb|wö|chent|lich** ADJ twice-weekly ADV twice weekly; **halb|wüch|sig** [-vyːksɪç] ADJ adolescent; **Halb|wüch|si|ge(r)** [-vyːksɪgə] MF *decl as adj* adolescent; **Halb|wüs|te** F semi-desert; **Halb|zei|le** F *(Poet)* half-line; **Halb|zeit** F *(Sport) (= Hälfte)* half; *(= Pause)* half-time

Halb|zeit-: **Halb|zeit|pfiff** M half-time whistle; **Halb|zeit|stand** M half-time score

halb|zi|vi|li|siert ADJ → **halb ADV b**

Hal|de ['haldə] F -, -n **a** *(= Abfallhalde)* mound, heap; *(Min: = Abbauhalde)* slag heap; *(fig)* mountain; **etw auf ~ legen** *(Ware, Vorräte)* to stockpile sth; *Pläne etc* to shelve sth **b** *(geh: = Abhang)* slope

half *pret von* **helfen**

Half|back ['haːfbɛk] M -s, -s *(Sw)* half-back

Half|pipe ['haːfpaip] F -, -s *(Sport)* half-pipe

Hälf|te ['hɛlftə] F -, -n **a** half; **die ~ der Kinder war abwesend** half the children were absent; **die ~ einer Sache** *(gen)* or **von etw** half (of) sth; **eine ~ des Apfels** half of the apple; **wir haben schon die ~ (des Vorrats) verbraucht** we have already used up half (the stocks); **die ~ ist gelogen** half of it is lies; **Rentner zahlen die ~** pensioners pay half price; **um die ~ mehr** half as much again; **um die ~ zu viel** too much by half; **um die ~ steigen** to increase by half *or* by fifty per cent; **um die ~ kleiner** half as small *or* big; **um die ~ größer** half as big again; **es ist zur ~ fertig/voll** it is half finished/full; **die Beiträge werden je zur ~ vom Arbeitgeber und Arbeitnehmer bezahlt** the employer and employee each pay half (of) the contribution; **das werde ich zur ~ bezahlen** I will pay half (of it); **meine bessere ~** *(hum inf)* my better half *(hum inf)*
b *(= Mitte: einer Fläche)* middle; **auf der ~ des Weges** halfway

hälf|ten ['hɛlftn] VT *(rare)* = **halbieren**

Half|ter ['halftɐ] M OR NT -s, - *(für Tiere)* halter

Half|ter F -, -n *or nt* -s, - *(= Pistolenhalfter)* holster

half|tern ['halftɐn] VT to halter, to put a halter on

hal|ky|o|nisch [hal'kyoːnɪʃ] ADJ *(liter)* **~e Tage** halcyon days

Hall [hal] M -(e)s, -e **a** reverberation, echo **b** *(= Nachhall)* echo

Hal|le ['halə] F -, -n hall; *(= Hotelhalle)* lobby, vestibule; *(= Werkshalle, Fabrikhalle)* shed; *(= Sporthalle)* (sports) hall, gym(nasium); *(= Tennishalle)* covered tennis court(s *pl*); *(= Schwimmhalle)* indoor swimming pool; *(= Flugzeughalle)* hangar; **in der ~** *(im Gegensatz zu draußen)* inside, indoors; **Fußball in der ~** indoor football *(esp Brit)* or soccer; **in der ~ des Postamts** in the post office; **in diesen heiligen ~n** *(iro)* in these august surroundings *(iro)*

hal|le|lu|ja [hale'lu:ja] INTERJ halleluja(h)

Hal|le|lu|ja [hale'lu:ja] NT **-s, -s** *(Rel, Mus)* halleluja(h); **das ~ aus Händels „Messias"** the Hallelujah Chorus from Handel's "Messiah"

hal|len ['halən] VI to reverberate, to echo *(auch fig)*, to resound

Hal|len- *in cpds (Sport)* indoor; **Hal|len|bad** NT indoor swimming pool; **Hal|len|fuß|ball** M indoor football *(esp Brit)* or soccer; **Hal|len|kir|che** F hall church; **Hal|len|meis|ter|schaft** F *(Sport)* indoor championship(s *pl*); **Hal|len|schwimm|bad** NT indoor swimming pool; **Hal|len|sport** M indoor sport(s *pl*); **Hal|len|ten|nis** NT indoor tennis; **Hal|len|tur|nier** NT *(Sport)* indoor tournament; *(Leichtathletik auch)* indoor meeting

hal|leysch ['haleʃ] ADJ **der Halleysche Komet** Halley's comet

Hal|lig ['halıç] F **-, -en** [-gn] *a small island off the west coast of Schleswig-Holstein*

Hal|li|masch ['halimaʃ] M **-(e)s, -e** *(Bot)* honey agaric

hal|lo [ha'lo:, 'halo] INTERJ **a** hello; *(zur Begrüßung)* hi *(inf)*, hello **b** *(überrascht)* hello

Hal|lo [ha'lo:, 'halo] NT **-s, -s** cheer *usu pl*; (= *Gruß*) hello

Hal|lod|ri [ha'lo:dri] M **-s, -(s)** *(Aus, S Ger. inf)* rogue

Hall|statt|zeit ['halʃtat-] F, *no pl (Archeol)* Hallstatt period

Hal|lu|zi|na|ti|on [halutsina'tsio:n] F **-, -en** hallucination; **ich leide wohl an ~en** *(fig)* I must be seeing things

hal|lu|zi|na|to|risch [halutsina'to:rıʃ] ADJ hallucinatory

hal|lu|zi|nie|ren [halutsi'ni:rən] *ptp* **halluziniert** VI to hallucinate

hal|lu|zi|no|gen [halutsino'ge:n] ADJ *(Med)* hallucinogenic

Hal|lu|zi|no|gen [halutsino'ge:n] NT **-s, -e** *(Med)* hallucinogen

Halm [halm] M **-(e)s, -e** stalk, stem; (= *Grashalm*) blade of grass; (= *Strohhalm, zum Trinken*) straw; **Getreide auf dem ~** standing grain

Hal|ma ['halma] NT **-s,** *no pl* halma, Chinese chequers *sing (Brit)*, Chinese checkers *sing (US)*

Hälm|chen ['hɛlmçən] NT **-s, -** *dim von* **Halm**

Ha|lo ['ha:lo] M **-(s), -s** or **-nen** [-'lo:nən] *(Astron, Met)* halo; *(TV)* shadow

ha|lo|gen [halo'ge:n] ADJ halogenous

Ha|lo|gen [halo'ge:n] NT **-s, -e** halogen

Ha|lo|gen-: **Ha|lo|gen|bir|ne** F halogen bulb; **Ha|lo|gen(glüh)|lam|pe** F halogen lamp; **Ha|lo|gen|leuch|te** F halogen lamp; **Ha|lo|gen|licht** NT halogen light; **Ha|lo|gen|schein|wer|fer** M halogen headlamp

Hals [hals] M **-es, =e** ['hɛlzə] **a** *(von außen gesehen)* neck; **einen langen ~ machen, den ~ recken** to crane one's neck; **sich** *(dat)* **nach jdm/etw den ~ verrenken** *(inf)* to crane one's neck to see sb/sth; **jdm um den ~ fallen** to fling one's arms (a)round sb's neck; **sich jdm an den ~ werfen** *(fig inf)* to throw oneself at sb; **sich** *(dat)* **den ~ brechen** *(inf)* to break one's neck; **etw kostet jdn** or **jdm den ~** *(inf)* **etw bricht jdm den ~** *(inf)* sth will cost sb his/her neck; **sich um den** or **seinen ~ reden** *(inf)* to put one's head in the noose; **~ über Kopf abreisen/den Koffer packen** to leave/pack one's case in a rush or hurry; **sich ~ über Kopf in jdn verlieben** to fall head over heals for sb; **ihm steht das Wasser bis zum ~** *(fig)* he is up to his neck in it *(inf)*; **bis über den ~** *(fig inf)* up to one's ears; **jdn auf dem** or **am ~ haben** *(inf)* to be lumbered *(Brit)* or saddled with sb *(inf)*; **jdm/sich etw auf den ~ laden** *(inf)* to lumber *(Brit)* or saddle sb/oneself with sth *(inf)*; **jdn jdm auf den ~ schicken** or **hetzen** *(inf)* to put sb onto sb; **jdm etw an den ~ wünschen** to wish sth on sb; **jdm mit etw vom ~(e) bleiben** *(inf)* not to bother sb with sth *(inf)*; **sich** *(dat)* **jdn/etw vom ~e schaffen** *(inf)* to get sb/sth off one's back *(inf)*; **jdm jdn/etw vom ~e schaffen** *(inf)* to get sb/sth off sb's back *(inf)*
b (= *Kehle, Rachen*) throat; **sie hat es am** or **im ~** *(inf)* she has a sore throat; **aus vollem ~(e)** at the top of one's voice; **aus vollem ~(e) lachen** to roar with laughter; **es hängt** or **wächst mir zum ~ heraus** *(inf)* I'm sick and tired of it, I've had it up to here *(inf)*; **sie hat es in den falschen** or **verkehrten ~ bekommen** *(inf)* (= *sich verschlucken*) it went down the wrong way; (= *falsch verstehen*) she took it wrongly; **etw bleibt jdm im ~ stecken** *(lit, fig)* sth sticks in sb's throat; **er kann den ~ nicht vollkriegen** or **voll genug kriegen** *(fig inf)* he is never satisfied
c (= *Flaschenhals, Geigenhals, Säulenhals*) neck; (= *Notenhals*) stem → **brechen VT a**
d *(von Knochen)* neck; (= *Gebärmutterhals*) cervix, neck of the womb

Hals [hals] M **-es, -en** [-zn] *(Naut)* tack

Hals-: **Hals|ab|schnei|der(in)** M(F) *(pej inf)* shark *(inf)*; **hals|ab|schnei|de|risch** ['halsl-apʃnaidərıʃ] ADJ *(pej inf) Preise, Maßnahme* extortionate, exorbitant; *Mensch* cutthroat *(inf)*; **Hals|an|satz** M base of the neck; **Hals|aus|schnitt** M neck(line); **Hals|band** [-bant] NT *pl* **-bänder** (= *Hundehalsband*) collar; (= *Schmuck*) necklace; *(eng anliegend)* choker; **hals|bre|che|risch** ['halsbrɛçərıʃ] ADJ dangerous, risky; *Tempo* breakneck; *Fahrt* hair-raising; *Weg* treacherous ADV *herumturnen, klettern* recklessly; **~ schnell/rasant/wild** at breakneck pace; *fahren* at breakneck speed; **Hals|bund** M *pl* **-bünde**, **Hals|bünd|chen** NT neckband

Häls|chen ['hɛlsçən] NT **-s, -** *dim von* **Hals**

hal|sen ['halzn] VT *(rare)* to embrace

hal|sen VI *(Naut)* to wear

Hals-: **Hals|ent|zün|dung** F sore throat; **Hals|grat** M *(esp S Ger, Cook)* neck (of pork); **Hals|ket|te** F (= *Schmuck*) necklace; *(für Hund)* chain; **Hals|krau|se** F *(Fashion, Zool)* ruff; *(Med)* cervical or neck collar; **Hals|län|ge** F neck; **(um) eine ~** by a neck; **um zwei ~n** by half a length; **hals|los** ADJ without a neck; **Hals|man|schet|te** F orthopaedic *(Brit)* or orthopedic *(US)* collar

Hals-Na|sen-Oh|ren-: **Hals-Na|sen-Oh|ren-Arzt** M, **Hals-Na|sen-Oh|ren-Ärz|tin** F ear, nose and throat specialist; **Hals-Na|sen-Oh|ren-Heil|kun|de** F ear, nose and throat medicine; **Hals-Na|sen-Oh|ren-Krank|heit** F disease of the ear, nose and throat

Hals-: **Hals|par|tie** F *(außen)* neck area, area or region of the neck; *(innen)* throat area, area or region of the throat; **Hals|schlag|ader** F carotid (artery); **Hals|schmer|zen** PL sore throat *sing*; **Hals|schmuck** M necklace; *(Sammelbegriff)* necklaces *pl*; **hals|star|rig** [-ʃtarıç] ADJ obstinate, stubborn; **Hals|star|rig|keit** F **-,** *no pl* obstinacy, stubbornness; **Hals|stück** NT *(Cook)* neck; **Hals|tuch** NT *pl* **-tücher** scarf; **Hals- und Bein|bruch** INTERJ good luck; **Hals|weh** NT sore throat; **Hals|wei|te** F neck size; **Hals|wi|ckel** M *(Med)* throat compress; **Hals|wir|bel** M cervical vertebra; **Hals|wir|bel|säu|le** F *(Anat)* cervical vertebrae *pl*

halt [halt] INTERJ stop; *(Mil)* halt

halt ADV *(dial)* **a** → **eben ADV d b** *(Aus)* **und so ~** and so on or forth

Halt [halt] M **-(e)s, -e a** *(für Füße, Hände, Festigkeit)* hold; *(lit, fig:* = *Stütze)* support; *(fig:* = *innerer Halt)* security *no art*; **~ haben** *(Ding)* to hold; **jdm/einer Sache ~ geben** to support sb/sth; **dem Haar ~ geben** to give hold to one's hair; **keinen ~ haben** to have no hold/support; to be insecure; **~ suchen/finden** to look for/find a hold/a support/security; **auf dem Eis den ~ verlieren** to lose one's footing on the ice; **ohne inneren ~** insecure **b** *(geh:* = *Anhalten)* stop; **ohne ~** non-stop, without stopping; **~ machen** = **haltmachen**

hält [hɛlt] *3. pers sing pres von* **halten**

halt|bar ✪ 53.3 ADJ **a** (= *nicht leicht verderblich*) **~ sein** *(Lebensmittel)* to keep (well); **~e Lebensmittel** food which keeps (well); **das ist sechs Monate ~** that will keep for six months; **etw ~ machen** to preserve sth; **~ bis 6.11.** use by 6 Nov; **nur begrenzt ~** perishable; **schlecht ~** highly perishable; **~ gemacht** artificially preserved
b (= *widerstandsfähig*) durable; *Stoff, Kleider* hard-wearing; *Beziehung, Ehe* long-lasting
c *Behauptung, Theorie, Annahme* tenable
d *pred Festung* defensible; **die Stadt ist nicht mehr ~** the town can't be held any longer
e *Position, Rang, Platz* tenable; *Zustand, Lage* tolerable; **diese Position ist nicht mehr ~** this position can't be maintained any longer
f *(Sport) Ball, Wurf* stoppable; *Schuss auch* savable

halt|bar|ge|macht △ ADJ *attr* → **haltbar a**

Halt|bar|keit ['haltba:ɐkait] F **-,** *no pl* **a** *(von Lebensmitteln)* **eine längere ~ haben** to keep longer; **Lebensmittel von kurzer ~** perishable food; **die begrenzte ~ von Fleisch** the perishability of meat **b** (= *Widerstandsfähigkeit*) durability **c** *(von Behauptung, Theorie, Annahme)* tenability

Halt|bar|keits-: **Halt|bar|keits|da|tum** NT eat-by date *(Brit)*, best-before date, use-by date; **Halt|bar|keits|dau|er** F *length of time for which food may be kept*; **eine kurze/lange ~ haben** to be/not to be perishable

Hal|te-: **Hal|te|bo|gen** M *(Mus)* tie; **Hal|te|bucht** F *(Mot)* lay-by, rest stop *(US)*; **Hal|te|griff** M **a** grip, handle; *(in Bus)* strap; *(an Badewanne)* handrail **b** *(Sport)* hold; **Hal|te|gurt** M seat or safety belt; *(an Kinderwagen)* safety harness

hal|ten ['haltn]
pret **hielt** [hi:lt], *ptp* **gehalten** [gə'haltn]
✪ 28.1, 30, 33.1, 34.1, 39.2, 41

1 TRANSITIVES VERB
2 INTRANSITIVES VERB
3 REFLEXIVES VERB

1 – TRANSITIVES VERB

a [= festhalten] to hold; **jdm etw halten** to hold sth for sb; **jdm den Mantel halten** to hold sb's coat (for him/her); **kannst du mir bitte die Leiter halten?** could you please hold the ladder for me?; **sich** *(dat)* **den Kopf/Bauch halten** to hold one's head/stomach

b [= in eine bestimmte Position bringen] **etw gegen das Licht halten** to hold sth up to the light; **den Arm in die Höhe halten** to hold one's arm up; **einen Fuß/einen Zeh ins Wasser halten** to put a foot/a toe in the water

c [= tragen] **die drei Pfeiler halten die Brücke** the three piers support the bridge; **meinst du, der kleine Nagel hält das schwere Ölbild?** do you think this small nail will take the weight of the heavy oil painting?; **nur zwei morsche Bretter hielten den Balkon noch** there were only two rotten boards holding the balcony up; **zwei Schlaufen halten den Vorhang an der Seite** two loops hold back the curtain

d [= zurückhalten, aufhalten] to hold; *(Sport)* to save; **die Wärme/Feuchtigkeit halten** to retain heat/moisture; **er kann den Urin** or **das Wasser nicht halten** he's incontinent; **einen Elfmeter** or **Strafstoß halten** to save a penalty; **das ist ein toller Torwart, der hält jeden Ball!** he's a great goalkeeper, he makes great saves!; **ich konnte ihn/es gerade noch halten** I just managed to grab hold of him/it; **haltet den Dieb!** stop thief!; **sie lässt sich nicht halten, sie ist nicht zu halten** *(fig)* there's no holding her back; **es hält mich hier nichts mehr** there's nothing to keep me here any more; **es hält dich niemand** nobody's stopping you

e = behalten *Festung, Rekord* to hold; *Position* to hold (on to); **den Schnabel** *or* **Mund halten** *(inf)* to keep one's mouth shut *(inf)*

f = unterhalten, besitzen *Chauffeur, Lehrer* to employ; *Haustier* to keep; *Auto* to run; **sich** *(dat)* **eine Geliebte halten** to keep a mistress; **sich** *(dat)* **eine Perserkatze/einen Hausfreund halten** to have a Persian cat/a live-in lover; **wir können uns kein Auto halten** we can't afford (to run) a car; **(sich** *dat***) eine Zeitung/Zeitschrift halten** to get a paper/magazine

g = einhalten, erfüllen to keep; **ein Versprechen halten** to keep a promise; **man muss halten, was man verspricht** a promise is a promise; **der Film hält nicht, was er/der Titel verspricht** the film doesn't live up to expectations/its title

h = beibehalten, aufrechterhalten *Niveau* to keep up, to maintain; *Tempo, Disziplin, Temperatur* to maintain; *Kurs* to keep to, to hold; **Ruhe halten** to keep quiet; **die Balance** *or* **das Gleichgewicht halten** to keep one's balance; **den Ton halten** to stay in tune *or* in key; **die These lässt sich nicht länger halten** *or* **ist nicht länger zu halten** this hypothesis is no longer tenable; **Kontakt halten** to keep in touch; **(mit jdm) Verbindung halten** to keep in touch (with sb); **Abstand halten!** keep your distance!; **etw sauber halten** to keep sth clean; **das Essen warm halten** to keep the food warm; **viel Sport hält jung/schlank** doing a lot of sport keeps you young/slim; **er hält sein Haus immer tadellos** he keeps his house immaculate; **halten Sie die Erklärungen einfach** keep the explanations simple; **wenn es neblig ist, sollten Sie den Abstand immer so groß wie möglich halten** if it's foggy you should always stay as far as possible from the car in front; **ein Land besetzt halten** to keep a country under occupation

i = behandeln to treat; **die Gefangenen werden in diesen Gefängnissen wie Tiere gehalten** the prisoners are treated like animals in these prisons; **er hält seine Kinder sehr streng** he's very strict with his children

j = handhaben, verfahren mit **das kannst du (so) halten, wie du willst** that's entirely up to you

♦ **es mit etw/jdm halten wie halten Sie es mit Ihrer Steuererklärung?** how do you deal with your tax return?; **wie hältst dus mit der Religion?** what's your attitude toward(s) religion?; **wir halten es mit den Abrechnungen anders** we deal with invoices in a different way; **er hält es nicht so sehr mit der Sauberkeit** he's not over-concerned about cleanliness; **es mehr** *or* **lieber mit jdm/etw halten** to prefer sb/sth

k = gestalten **ein in Brauntönen gehaltener Raum** a room done in different shades of brown; **sie beschloss das Zimmer in Grün zu halten** she decided to do the room in green; **das Kleid ist in dunklen Tönen gehalten** it is a dark-coloured *(Brit)* or dark-colored *(US)* dress; **das Mobiliar ist in einem hellen Holz gehalten** the furniture is made of a light wood

l = veranstalten, abhalten *Fest, Pressekonferenz* to give; *Rede* to make; *Gottesdienst, Zwiesprache* to hold; *Wache* to keep; **Selbstgespräche halten** to talk to oneself; **Unterricht halten** to teach; **Mittagsschlaf halten** to have an afternoon nap; **Winterschlaf halten** to hibernate

m = einschätzen, denken

♦ **jdn/etw für etw halten** to think sb/sth sth; **ich habe das Bild für ein Original gehalten** I thought the picture was an original; **etw für angebracht/schön halten** to think *or* consider sth appropriate/beautiful; **jdn für ehrlich halten** to think *or* consider sb honest; **ich habe ihn (irrtümlich) für seinen Bruder gehalten** I (mis)took him for his brother; **wofür halten Sie mich?** what do you take me for?; **das halte ich nicht für möglich** I don't think that is possible; **ich halte es für Unsinn, alles noch einmal abzuschreiben** I think it's silly to copy everything out again

♦ **etw von jdm/etw halten** to think sth of sb/sth; **nicht viel von jdm/etw halten** not to think much of sb/sth; **nicht viel vom Beten/Sparen halten** not to be a great one for praying/saving *(inf)*; **ich halte nichts davon, das zu tun** I'm not in favour *(Brit)* or favor *(US)* of (doing) that

♦ **etwas/viel auf etw** *(acc)* **halten** to consider sth important/very important; **er hält etwas auf gute Manieren** he considers good manners important; **der Chef hält viel auf Pünktlichkeit** the boss attaches a lot of importance to punctuality → **Stück c**

n → **gehalten**

2 – INTRANSITIVES VERB

a = festhalten to hold; *(= haften bleiben)* to stick; *(Sport)* to make a save; **kannst du mal einen Moment halten?** can you just hold that (for) a moment?; **unser Tormann hat heute wieder großartig gehalten** our goalkeeper made some good saves again today; **kann der denn (gut) halten?** is he a good goalkeeper?

b = bestehen bleiben, haltbar sein to last; *(Konserven)* to keep; *(Wetter)* to last, to hold; *(Frisur, Comm: Preise)* to hold; *(Stoff)* to be hard-wearing; **der Waffenstillstand hält nun schon drei Wochen** the truce has now held for three weeks; **Rosen halten länger, wenn man ein Aspirin ins Wasser tut** roses last longer if you put an aspirin in the water; **dieser Stoff hält lange** this material is hard-wearing

c = stehen bleiben, anhalten to stop; **zum Halten bringen** to bring to a standstill; **halten lassen** *(Mil)* to call a halt

♦ **halt mal** *(= Moment mal)* hang on *(inf)*, hold on; **halt mal, stop!** *(hum)* hang on *(inf)* or hold on a minute! → **halt**

d andere Redewendungen

♦ **auf etw** *(acc)* **halten** *(= zielen)* to aim at sth; *(= steuern)* to head for sth; *(= Wert legen auf)* to attach importance to sth; **sehr auf etw halten** to attach great importance to sth

♦ **auf sich** *(acc)* **halten** *(= auf sein Äußeres achten)* to take a pride in oneself; *(= selbstbewusst sein)* to be self-confident

♦ **an sich** *(acc)* **halten** *(= sich beherrschen)* to control oneself; **ich musste an mich halten, um nicht in schallendes Gelächter auszubrechen** I had to control myself so as not to burst into fits of laughter

♦ **zu jdm halten** *(= beistehen, treu sein)* to stand by sb; *(= favorisieren)* to support sb

3 – REFLEXIVES VERB

♦ **sich halten**

a = sich festhalten to hold on *(an +dat* to); **er konnte sich gerade noch an dem Griff halten, als der Zug mit einem scharfen Ruck anfuhr** he just managed to grab hold of the strap when the train suddenly jolted forward; **sie konnte sich auf dem glatten Abhang nicht halten** she couldn't keep her footing on the slippery slope; **er konnte sich auf dem wilden Mustang nur drei Sekunden halten** he could only stay on the wild mustang three seconds

b = eine bestimmte Körperhaltung haben to carry *or* hold oneself; **er hält sich sehr aufrecht** he holds *or* carries himself very erect; **sich (im Gleichgewicht) halten** to keep one's balance; **sich auf den Beinen halten** to stay on one's feet; **sich (nach) links halten** to keep (to the) left; **sich nach Westen halten** to keep going westwards; **der Autofahrer hielt sich ganz rechts** the driver kept to the right; **ich halte mich an die alte Methode** I'll stick to *or* with the old method; **sich an ein Versprechen halten** to keep a promise; **sich an die Tatsachen/den Text halten** to keep *or* stick to the facts/text → **Vorschrift**

c = sich nicht verändern *Lebensmittel, Blumen* to keep; *(Wetter)* to last, to hold; *(Geruch, Rauch)* to linger; *(Preise)* to hold; *(Brauch, Sitte)* to continue; **der Geruch von Knoblauch hält sich ewig** the smell of garlic lingers for ages *(inf)*

d = seine Position behaupten to hold on; *(in Kampf)* to hold out; **er hat sich in der Spitzenposition gehalten** he held on to the lead; **er hat sich im erbarmungslosen Wettbewerb prächtig gehalten** he held on amazingly in the cut-throat competition; **das Geschäft kann sich in dieser Straße nicht halten** the shop can't continue to stay open in this street

♦ **sich gut halten** *(in Prüfung, Spiel etc)* to do well; **er hat sich ziemlich gut gehalten** *(körperlich)* he is quite well-preserved; **sie hat sich in der schweren Prüfung unerwartet gut gehalten** she did unexpectedly well in the difficult exam

e = sich beherrschen to control oneself; **sich nicht halten können** to be unable to control oneself

f andere Wendungen

♦ **sich halten an** *(+acc)* **sich an jdn halten** *(= sich wenden an)* to ask sb; *(= sich richten nach)* to follow sb; *(= sich gutstellen mit)* to keep in with sb; **ich halte mich lieber an den Wein** I'd rather keep *or* stick to wine

♦ **sich halten für er hält sich für einen Spezialisten/für besonders klug** he thinks he's a specialist/very clever

---

Hal|te-: Hal|te|platz M *(= Taxihalteplatz)* taxi rank *(Brit)* or stand; **Hal|te|punkt** M *(Rail)* stop

Hal|ter ['haltɐ] M **-s, -** **a** *(= Halterung)* holder **b** *(= Sockenhalter)* garter; *(= Strumpfhalter, Hüfthalter)* suspender *(Brit)* or garter *(US)* belt **c** *(rare: = Griff)* handle

Hal|ter ['haltɐ] M **-s, -, Hal|te|rin** [-ərɪn] F **-, -nen** *(Jur: von Kraftfahrzeug, Tier)* owner

Hal|te|rie|men M strap

hal|ter|los ADJ **~e Strümpfe** hold-ups *(Brit)*, stockings not requiring a garter belt *(US)*

Hal|te|rung ['haltərʊŋ] F **-, -en** mounting; *(für Regal etc)* support

Hal|te-: Hal|te|schild NT *pl* **-schilder** stop sign; **Hal|te|schlau|fe** F *(in Bus etc)* strap; **Hal|te|seil** NT safety rope; **Hal|te|sig|nal** NT *(Rail)* stop signal; **Hal|te|stel|le** F stop; **Hal|te|ver|bot** NT **(absolutes** *or* **uneingeschränktes) ~** no stopping; *(= Stelle)* no-stopping zone; **eingeschränktes ~** no waiting; *(= Stelle)* no-waiting zone; **hier ist ~** there's no stopping here; **im ~ stehen** to have parked in a no-stopping zone; **Hal|te|ver|bot(s)|schild** NT *pl* **-schilder** no-stopping sign; **Hal|te|vor|rich|tung** F mounting; *(für Regal etc)* support

-hal|tig [haltɪç], *(Aus)* **-häl|tig** [hɛltɪç] ADJ *suf* containing; **stark alkoholhaltig** containing a lot of alcohol, with a high alcohol content

Halt-: halt|los ADJ *(= schwach)* insecure; *(= hemmungslos)* unrestrained; *(= unbegründet)* groundless, unfounded; **Halt|lo|sig|keit** F **-,** *no pl* *(= Schwäche)* lack of security; *(= Hemmungslosigkeit)* lack of inhibitions; *(= Unbegründetheit)* groundlessness; **halt+ma|chen** VI *sep* to stop, to call a halt; **vor nichts ~** *(fig)* to stop at nothing; **vor niemandem ~** *(fig)* to spare no-one; **Halt|sig|nal** NT *(Rail)* stop signal; **Halt|tas|te** F pause button

Hal|tung ['haltʊŋ] F **-, -en** **a** *(= Körperhaltung)* posture; *(= Stellung)* position; *(esp Sport)* *(= typische Stellung)* stance; *(bei der Ausführung)* style; **~ annehmen** *(esp Mil)* to stand to attention **b** *(fig)* *(= Auftreten)* manner; *(= Einstellung)* attitude; **in majestätischer/würdiger ~** with majestic/dignified bearing **c** *no pl* *(= Beherrschtheit)* composure; **~ bewahren** to keep one's composure **d** *no pl (von Tieren, Fahrzeugen)* keeping

Hal|tungs-: Hal|tungs|feh|ler M **a** *(Med)* bad posture *no indef art, no pl* **b** *(Sport)* style fault; **Hal|tungs|män|gel** PL bad posture *sing*; **Hal|tungs|scha|den** M damaged posture *no pl*; **zu Haltungsschäden führen** to damage one's posture

Halt|zei|chen NT *(Rail)* stop signal

Ha|lun|ke [ha'lʊŋkə] M **-n, -n** **a** scoundrel **b** *(hum)* rascal, scamp

Hä|ma|tit [hɛma'tiːt] M **-s, -e** haematite *(Brit)*, hematite *(US)*

Hä|ma|to|lo|ge [hɛmato'loːgə] M **-n, -n**, **Hä|ma|to|lo|gin** [-'loːgɪn] F **-, -nen** haematologist *(Brit)*, hematologist *(US)*

Hä|ma|to|lo|gie [hɛmatolo'giː] F **-,** *no pl* haematology *(Brit)*, hematology *(US)*

hä|ma|to|lo|gisch [hɛmato'loːgɪʃ] ADJ haematological *(Brit)*, hematological *(US)*

Hä|ma|tom [hɛma'toːm] NT **-s, -e** haematoma *(Brit)*, hematoma *(US)*

Ham|burg ['hambʊrk] NT **-s** Hamburg

Ham|bur|ger ['hambʊrgɐ] ADJ *attr* Hamburg

Ham|bur|ger ['hambʊrgɐ] M **-s, -** *(Cook)* hamburger

Ham|bur|ger ['hambʊrgɐ] M **-s, -**, **Ham|bur|ge|rin** [-ərɪn] F **-, -nen** native *or* (= *Einwohner*) inhabitant of Hamburg

Ham|bur|ger|bröt|chen NT roll *or* bun (for hamburger)

ham|bur|gern ['hambʊrgɐn] VI to speak with a Hamburg dialect

ham|bur|gisch ['hambʊrgɪʃ] ADJ Hamburg *attr*

Hä|me ['hɛːmə] F **-,** *no pl (rare)* malice

hä|misch ['hɛːmɪʃ] ADJ *Lächeln* malicious; *Bemerkung auch* spiteful ADV maliciously; *bemerken auch* spitefully; **er hat sich ~ gefreut** he gloated; **~ grinsen** to grin maliciously, to smirk

Ha|mit [ha'miːt] M **-en, -en**, **Ha|mi|tin** [-'miːtɪn] F **-, -nen** Hamite

ha|mi|tisch [ha'miːtɪʃ] ADJ Hamitic

Ham|mel ['haml] M **-s, -** *or (rare)* **¨** ['hɛml] **a** *(Zool)* wether, castrated ram **b** *no pl (Cook)* mutton **c** *(fig pej)* ass, donkey

Ham|mel-: **Ham|mel|bei|ne** PL **jdm die ~ lang ziehen** *(hum inf)* to give sb a dressing-down; **jdn bei den ~n nehmen** *or* **kriegen** *(inf: = zur Verantwortung ziehen)* to take sb to task; **Ham|mel|bra|ten** M roast mutton; **Ham|mel|fleisch** NT mutton; **Ham|mel|her|de** F herd *or* flock of wethers *or* rams; *(pej inf)* flock of sheep; **Ham|mel|keu|le** F *(Cook)* leg of mutton; **Ham|mel|sprung** M *(Parl)* division

Ham|mer ['hamɐ] M **-s, ¨** ['hɛmɐ] **a** (= *Werkzeug, von Auktionator*) hammer; (= *Holzhammer*) mallet; **~ und Sichel** hammer and sickle; **unter den ~ kommen** to come under the hammer; **zwischen ~ und Amboss geraten** *(fig)* to come under attack from both sides; **das ist ein ~!** *(inf)* (= *unerhört*) that's absurd! **b** (= *Sportgerät*) hammer **c** *(Anat)* hammer, malleus **d** (= *Klavierhammer, Glockenhammer*) hammer

häm|mer|bar ADJ malleable

Häm|mer|chen ['hɛmɐçən] NT **-s, -** *dim von* **Hammer**

Ham|mer-: **ham|mer|för|mig** ADJ hammer-shaped; **Ham|mer|hai** M hammerhead (shark); **Ham|mer|kla|vier** NT *(Mus Hist)* pianoforte; **Ham|mer|kopf** M hammerhead; *(Sport: auch* **Ham|mer|ku|gel***)* hammerhead

häm|mern ['hɛmɐn] VI **a** *(mit Hammer, Gegenstand)* to hammer; *(mit den Fäusten etc)* to pound; *(inf: beim Klavierspielen etc)* to pound, to thump **b** (= *hämmerndes Geräusch verursachen: Maschine, Motor*) to make a hammering sound **c** *(Puls, Herz, Blut)* to pound VT **a** (= *bearbeiten*) to hammer; *Blech, Metallgefäße, Schmuck etc* to beat **b** *(inf) Melodie, Rhythmus etc* to hammer *or* pound out **c** *(fig inf: = einprägen)* **jdm etw ins Bewusstsein ~** to hammer *or* knock sth into sb's head *(inf)* VI *impers* **es hämmert** there's a sound of hammering

Ham|mer-: **Ham|mer|schlag** M **a** hammer blow; *(fig)* bolt from the blue **b** *(Sport) (Boxen)* rabbit punch; *(Faustball)* smash **c** *(Schmiederei)* hammer *or* mill scale; **Ham|mer|schmied** M *(old)* person working in a hammer mill; **Ham|mer|schmie|de** F *(old)* hammer mill; **Ham|mer|stiel** M handle *or* shaft of a/the hammer; **Ham|mer|wer|fen** NT **-s,** *no pl (Sport)* hammer(-throwing); **Ham|mer|wer|fer(in)** M(F) *(Sport)* hammer-thrower; **Ham|mer|werk** NT *(old)* hammer mill; **Ham|mer|wurf** M *(Sport)* **a** hammer throw **b** (= *Hammerwerfen*) hammer(-throwing); **Ham|mer|ze|he** F *(Med)* hammertoe

Ham|mond|or|gel ['hɛmənd-] F electric organ

Hä|mo|glo|bin [hɛmoglo'biːn] NT **-s,** *no pl* haemoglobin *(Brit)*, hemoglobin *(US)*

Hä|mo|phi|le(r) [hɛmo'fiːlə] MF *decl as adj* haemophiliac *(Brit)*, hemophiliac *(US)*

Hä|mo|phi|lie [hɛmofi'liː] F **-, -n** [-'liːən] haemophilia *(Brit)*, hemophilia *(US)*

Hä|mor|rho|i|den [hɛmɔro'iːdən] PL, **Hä|mor|ri|den** [hɛmɔ'riːdən] PL piles *pl*, haemorrhoids *pl (Brit)*, hemorrhoids *pl (US)*

Hä|mor|rho|i|den|schau|kel F, **Hä|mor|ri|den|schau|kel** F *(hum)* boneshaker *(inf)*

Ham|pe|lei [hampə'lai] F **-, -en** *(pej inf)* (continual) fidgeting *no pl*

Ham|pel|mann M *pl* **-männer** **a** jumping jack **b** *(inf)* (= *zappeliger Mensch*) fidget; **er ist nur ein ~** he just lets people walk all over him; **jdn zu einem ~ machen** to walk all over sb

ham|peln ['hampln] VI to jump about; (= *zappeln*) to fidget

Hams|ter ['hamstɐ] M **-s, -** hamster

Hams|ter|ba|cken PL *(fig inf)* chubby cheeks *pl*

Hams|te|rer ['hamstərɐ] M **-s, -**, **Hams|te|rin** [-ərɪn] F **-, -nen** *(fig inf)* hoarder

Hams|ter-: **Hams|ter|fahrt** F foraging trip; **auf ~ gehen** to go foraging; **Hams|ter|kauf** M panic buying *no pl*; **Hamsterkäufe machen** to buy in order to hoard; *(bei Knappheit)* to panic-buy

hams|tern ['hamstɐn] VTI (= *speichern*) to hoard; *(bei Hamsterfahrt)* to forage; (= *Hamsterkäufe machen*) to panic-buy

Hams|ter-: **Hams|ter|ta|sche** F large shopping bag; **Hams|ter|wa|re** F → **hamstern** hoarded/foraged/panic-bought goods

Hand [hant] -, ¨e ['hɛndə]

SUBSTANTIV (F)

a allgemein hand *(auch Mus, Cards)*; **jdm die Hand drücken/schütteln/küssen** to press/shake/kiss sb's hand; **jdm die Hand geben** *or* **reichen** *(geh)* to give sb one's hand; **die Arbeit seiner Hände** his handiwork, the work of his own hands; **sie leben von der Arbeit ihrer Hände** they make a living by working with their hands; **in die Hände klatschen** to clap one's hands; **ich hatte eine schreckliche Hand** *(Cards)* I had a terrible hand; **Hände hoch!** (put your) hands up!; **Hand aufs Herz** hand on heart; **Hand aufs Herz, ich wars nicht** it wasn't me, cross my heart *or* I swear it; **eine Hand breit** ≈ six inches wide → *auch* **Handbreit**; **zwei Hände breit** ≈ a foot wide; **eine Hand voll** = **Handvoll**

b Sport *no pl (inf: = Handspiel)* handball; **das war ganz klar Hand** it was a blatant handball; **Hand machen** to handle the ball

c mit Adjektiv

Siehe auch unter dem Eintrag für das jeweilige Adjektiv.

ein Auto aus erster Hand a car which has had one previous owner; **etw aus erster Hand wissen** to have first-hand knowledge of sth; **der Chef zeigt** *or* **hat mit seinen Mitarbeitern eine feste Hand** the boss takes a firm hand with his employees; **in festen Händen sein** *(fig)* to be spoken for; **mit der flachen Hand** with the flat *or* palm of one's hand; **bei etw eine glückliche Hand haben** to be lucky with sth; **in guten Händen sein** to be in good hands; **besser als in die hohle Hand gespuckt** *(inf)* better than a slap in the face with a wet fish *(Brit inf)*, could be worse; **mit leeren Händen** empty-handed; **mit leeren Händen dastehen** to stand there empty-handed; **ihm fehlt die leitende** *or* **lenkende Hand** he lacks a guiding hand; **letzte Hand an etw** *(acc)* **legen** to put the finishing touches to sth; **linker Hand, zur linken Hand** on the left-hand side; **eine lockere** *or* **lose Hand haben** *(hum inf)* to lash out at the slightest provocation; **aus** *or* **von privater Hand** privately; **„aus privater Hand abzugeben"** "private sale"; **rechter Hand, zur rechten Hand** on *or* to the right(-hand side); **eine ruhige Hand** a steady hand; **der Hund ist dort in schlechten Händen** that's not a good home for the dog; **eine sichere Hand** *(lit)* a steady hand; *(fig)* a sure hand; **in sicheren Händen sein** to be in safe hands; **eine starke Hand** *(fig)* a firm hand; **das Geld mit vollen Händen ausgeben** to spend money hand over fist *(inf)*; **hinter vorgehaltener Hand** on the quiet; **aus zweiter Hand** second hand; **Kleider aus zweiter Hand** second-hand clothes → **rechte(r, s) a**, **linke(r, s) a**

d mit Präposition

Siehe auch unter dem Eintrag für die jeweilige Präposition.

♦ **an + Hand** **er hatte seine kleine Tochter an der Hand** he had his little daughter by the hand; **er hat jemanden an der Hand, der mir meine Küche streichen könnte** he knows of somebody who could paint my kitchen for me; **jdn an der Hand fassen** to grab sb by the hand; **jdn an die Hand nehmen** to take sb by the hand; **jdm an die Hand gehen** to lend sb a (helping) hand; **an Hand von** *or* *+gen* → **anhand**

♦ **auf + Hand/Händen** **auf der Hand** *(Cards)* in one's hand; **das liegt auf der Hand** *(inf)* that's obvious; **jdn auf Händen tragen** to cherish sb

♦ **aus + Hand** **aus der Hand** *(zeichnen, entwerfen etc)* freehand; **jdm etw aus der Hand nehmen** to take sth from *or* off sb *(auch fig)*, to take sth out of sb's hand; **etw aus der Hand essen** to eat sth with one's fingers; **jdm aus der Hand fressen** *(lit, fig)* to eat out of sb's hand; **etw aus der Hand geben** to let sth out of one's hands; **etw aus der Hand legen** to put sth aside

♦ **bei + Hand** **jdn bei der Hand nehmen** to take sb by the hand; **etw bei der Hand haben** to have sth to hand; *Ausrede, Erklärung* to have sth ready; **mit etw schnell** *or* **gleich bei der Hand sein** *(inf)* to be ready with sth

♦ **durch + Hand/Hände** **durch jds Hände** *or* **Hand gehen** to pass *or* go through sb's hands

♦ **für + Hand** **Klaviersonate für vier Hände** piano sonata for four hands

♦ **in + Hand/Hände(n)** **er nimmt niemals ein Buch in die Hand** he never picks up a book; **Hand in Hand** hand in hand; **jdm/einer Sache in die Hände arbeiten** to play into sb's hands/the hands of sth; **jdm in die Hand** *or* **Hände fallen** *or* **geraten** *or* **kommen** to fall into sb's hands; **jdn/etw in die Hand** *or* **Hände kriegen** *or* **bekommen** to get one's hands on sb/sth; **jdn (fest) in der Hand haben** to have sb (well) in hand; **etw in der Hand haben** to have sth; **ich habe diese Entscheidung nicht in der Hand** the decision is out of my hands; **etw gegen jdn in der Hand haben** to have sth on sb; **diese Gebiete sind zurzeit in serbischer Hand** these areas are in Serbian hands at the moment; **dieser Laden ist schon seit Jahren in türkischer Hand** this shop has been owned by Turks for years; **in welcher Hand ist dieses Hotel im Augenblick?** who currently owns this hotel?; **der Badestrand ist im Juli immer fest in deutscher Hand** in July this beach is always taken over by Germans; **in jds Hände** *(acc)* **übergehen** to pass to sb *or* into sb's hands; **sich in der Hand haben** to have a grip on oneself; **etw in Händen halten** *(geh)* to hold *or* have sth in one's hands; **etw in jds Hand** *or* **Hände legen** to put sth in sb's hands; **etw liegt** *or* **ist in jds Hand** sth is in sb's hands; **in jds Hand sein** to be in sb's hands; **etw in die Hand nehmen** to pick sth up; *(fig)* to take sth in hand; **jdm etw in die Hand versprechen** to promise sb sth *or* sth to sb; **jdm etw in die Hand** *or* **Hände spielen** to pass sth on to sb

♦ **mit + Hand/Händen mit der Hand** *(= in Handarbeit)* by hand; **(bei etw) mit Hand anlegen** to lend a hand (with sth); **das ist mit Händen zu greifen** *(fig)* that's obvious; **sich mit Händen und Füßen gegen etw wehren** to fight sth tooth and nail

♦ **um + Hand um jds Hand bitten** *or* **anhalten** to ask for sb's hand (in marriage)

♦ **unter + Hand/Händen unter der Hand** *(fig)* on the quiet; **Geld schmilzt** *or* **zerrinnt ihm unter den Händen** money runs through his fingers like water; **jdm unter der Hand** *or* **den Händen wegsterben** to die while under sb's care

♦ **von + Hand von Hand geschrieben** handwritten; **von Hand genäht** hand-sewn; **Vermittlung von Hand** *(Telec)* operator-connected calls *pl;* **von Hand zu Hand gehen** to pass from hand to hand; **von jds Hand sterben** to die at sb's hands; **die Arbeit ging ihr leicht von der Hand** she found the work easy; **die Arbeit ging ihr flott** *or* **schnell von der Hand** she sailed through the work; **etw lässt sich nicht von der Hand weisen, etw ist nicht von der Hand zu weisen** sth is undeniable; **von der Hand in den Mund leben** to live from hand to mouth

♦ **zu + Hand/Händen zur Hand sein** to be at hand; **etw zur Hand haben** to have sth to hand; *Ausrede, Erklärung* to have sth ready; **etw zur Hand nehmen** to pick sth up; **jdm zur Hand gehen** to lend sb a (helping) hand; **zu jds Händen, zu Händen von jdm** for the attention of sb; **Klaviersonate zu vier Händen** piano sonata for four hands; **zu vier Händen spielen** *(Mus)* to play a (piano) duet → **treu ADJ**

e mit Verb

Siehe auch unter dem Eintrag für das jeweilige Verb.

sich *(dat)* **für jdn/etw die Hand abhacken lassen** *(inf)* to stake one's life on sb/sth; **die** *or* **seine Hand aufhalten** *or* **hinhalten** *(fig inf)* to hold out one's hand (for money); **darauf gaben sie sich die Hand** they shook hands on it; **man konnte die Hand nicht vor (den) Augen sehen** you couldn't see your hand in front of your face; **eine Hand wäscht die andere** you scratch my back, I'll scratch yours; **ich wasche meine Hände in Unschuld** I wash my hands of it *or* of the matter; **die Hände überm Kopf zusammenschlagen** to throw up one's hands in horror

♦ **Hand + haben die Hand auf etw** *(dat)* **haben** to keep a tight rein on sth; **alle Hände voll zu tun haben** to have one's hands full; **bei etw die** *or* **seine Hand im Spiel haben** to have a hand in sth; **dabei hatte Eifersucht die Hand im Spiel** jealousy had a part to play in this; **er hat überall seine Hand im Spiel** he has a finger in every pie; **Hand und Fuß haben** to make sense; **was er macht, hat weder Hand noch Fuß** what he's doing doesn't make any sense at all; **die Geschichte, die du mir erzählt hast, hat Hand und Fuß** the story you told me hangs together perfectly; **diese Ausrede hat weder Hand noch Fuß** this excuse doesn't stand up

♦ **Hand + halten die Hand auf etw** *(dat)* **halten** to keep a tight rein on sth; **die Hand auf der Tasche halten** *(inf)* to control the purse strings; **die** *or* **seine Hand über jdn halten** to protect *or* shield sb

♦ **Hand/Hände + legen Hand an jdn legen** *(geh)* to assault sb; **Hand an sich legen** *(geh)* to kill oneself; **seine** *or* **die Hand auf etw** *(acc)* **legen** *(geh)* to lay (one's) hands on sth; **die Hände in den Schoß legen** *(fig)* to sit back and do nothing; **seine** *or* **die Hand für jdn ins Feuer legen** to vouch for sb

♦ **Hand + reichen sich** *or* **einander die Hand fürs Leben reichen** to tie the knot; **sich** *or* **einander** *(geh)* **die Hand reichen können** *(fig)* to be tarred with the same brush; **da können wir uns die Hand reichen** snap! *(inf)*

Hand-: **Hand|ab|wehr** F *(Sport)* save; **durch ~ klären** to save, to clear; **Hand|ab|zug** M *(Typ)* proof pulled by hand; *(Phot)* print made by hand; **Hand|an|trieb** M hand-driven mechanism; **mit ~** hand-driven; **Hand|ap|pa|rat** M **a** reference books *pl (on open shelves)* **b** *(Telec)* handset

Hand|ar|beit F **a** work done by hand; *(Gegenstand)* article made by hand, handmade article; **etw in ~ herstellen** to produce *or* make sth by hand; **der Tisch ist ~** the table is handmade *or* made by hand **b** *(= körperliche Arbeit)* manual work **c** *(= Nähen, Sticken etc, als Schulfach)* needlework *no pl; (= Stricken)* knitting *no pl; (= Häkeln)* crochet(ing) *no pl;* **diese Tischdecke ist ~** this tablecloth is handmade; **eine ~ aus dem 18. Jahrhundert** a piece of needlework *etc* from the 18th century **d** *(kunsthandwerklich)* handicraft *no pl;* **eine ~** a piece of handicraft work

hand|ar|bei|ten VI *insep* → **Handarbeit c** to do needlework/knitting/crocheting

Hand|ar|bei|ten NT **-s,** *no pl (Sch)* needlework

Hand|ar|bei|ter(in) M(F) manual worker

Hand|ar|beits-: **Hand|ar|beits|ge|schäft** NT needlework and wool shop; **Hand|ar|beits|heft** NT sewing, knitting and crocheting manual; **Hand|ar|beits|korb** M workbasket

Hand-: **Hand|auf|he|ben** NT **-s,** *no pl (bei Wahl)* show of hands; **sich durch ~ zu Wort melden** to ask for permission to speak by raising one's hand; **Hand|auf|le|gen** NT **-s,** *no pl,* **Hand|auf|le|gung** [-laufle:gʊŋ] F **-, -en** laying on of hands; **Hand|aus|ga|be** F *(= Buch)* concise edition; **Hand|ball** M **a** *(= Ball)* handball **b** *no pl (inf auch nt) (= Spiel)* handball; **Hand|bal|len** M *(Anat)* ball of the thumb; **Hand|bal|ler** [-balɐ] M **-s, -, Hand|bal|le|rin** [-ərɪn] F **-, -nen** handball player; **Hand|ball|spiel** NT **a** *(= Spiel)* game of handball **b** *(= Disziplin)* handball *no def art;* **Hand|ball|spie|ler(in)** M(F) handball player; **hand|be|dient** [-bədi:nt] ADJ manually operated, hand-operated; **Hand|be|die|nung** F hand *or* manual operation *or* control; **mit** *or* **für ~** hand-operated; **Hand|beil** NT hatchet; **Hand|be|sen** M hand brush; **Hand|be|trieb** M hand *or* manual operation; **für** *or* **mit ~** hand-operated; **hand|be|trie|ben** [-bətri:bn] ADJ hand-operated; **Hand|be|we|gung** F sweep of the hand; *(= Geste, Zeichen)* gesture; **Hand|bib|li|o|thek** F reference library *or* books *pl (on open shelves);* **Hand|boh|rer** M gimlet, auger; **Hand|bohr|ma|schi|ne** F (hand) drill; **Hand|brau|se** F shower attachment; **hand|breit** ['hantbrait] ADJ ≈ six inches wide ADV ≈ six inches; **Hand|breit** ['hantbrait] F **-, -** hand's width; **Hand|brem|se** F handbrake *(Brit),* parking brake *(US);* **Hand|buch** NT handbook; *(technisch)* manual; **Hand|bü|che|rei** F reference library *or* books *pl (on open shelves)*

Händ|chen ['hɛntçən] NT **-s, -** *dim von* **Hand** little hand; **~ halten** *(inf)* to hold hands; **~ haltend** holding hands; **~ haltend gehen/sitzen** to walk/sit hand in hand; **für etw ein ~ haben** *(inf)* to have a knack for sth; *(= gut können)* to be good at sth; **~ geben** to shake hands

Händ|chen|hal|ten NT **-s,** *no pl* holding hands *no def art*

händ|chen|hal|tend → **Händchen**

Hand-: **Hand|creme** F hand cream; **Hand|deu|tung** F palmistry; **Hand|druck** M *(Typ, Tex)* **a** *pl* **-drucke** block print **b** *no pl (= Verfahren)* block printing; **Hand|du|sche** F shower attachment

Hän|de-: **Hän|de|druck** M *pl* **-drücke** handshake; **Hän|de|hand|tuch** NT hand towel

Hand|ein|stel|lung F *(Tech)* manual *or* hand-operated setting

Hän|de|klat|schen NT applause *no pl*

Han|del ['handl] M **-s,** *no pl* **a** *(= das Handeln)* trade; *(esp mit illegaler Ware)* traffic; **~ mit etw/einem Land** trade in sth/with a country **b** *(= Warenverkehr)* trade; *(= Warenmarkt)* market; **im ~ sein** to be on the market; **etw in den ~ bringen** to put sth on the market; **etw aus dem ~ ziehen** to take sth off the market; **(mit jdm) ~ (be)treiben** to trade (with sb); **~ treibend** trading **c** *(= Abmachung, Geschäft)* deal, transaction; *(inf)* deal **d** *(= Wirtschaftszweig)* commerce, trade; *(= die Handel Treibenden)* trade **e** *(dial: = Handelsunternehmen)* business; **er betreibt/hat einen ~ in** *or* **mit Kohlen und Heizöl** he runs/has a coal and fuel oil business

Han|del ['handl] M **-s,** ⸚ ['hɛndl] *usu pl* quarrel, argument

han|del|bar [-ba:ɐ] ADJ *(St Ex)* **an der Börse ~** negotiable on the stock exchange; **frei ~** freely negotiable

Hand|elf|me|ter M penalty for a handball

han|deln ['handln] VI **a** *(= Handel treiben)* to trade; **er handelt mit Gemüse** he trades *or* deals in vegetables, he's in the vegetable trade; **er handelt mit Drogen** he traffics in drugs; **er handelt in Gebrauchtwagen** he's in the second-hand car trade, he sells second-hand cars **b** *(= feilschen)* to bargain, to haggle *(um* about, over); *(fig: = verhandeln)* to negotiate *(um* about); **ich lasse schon mit mir ~** I'm open to persuasion; *(in Bezug auf Preis)* I'm open to offers **c** *(= tätig werden, agieren)* to act; **er ist ein schnell ~der Mensch** he's a quick-acting person **d** *(= sich verhalten)* to act, to behave; **gegen jdn** *or* **an jdm gut/als Freund ~** *(geh)* to act *or* behave well/as *or* like a friend toward(s) sb **e** *(= zum Thema haben)* **von etw ~, über etw** *(acc)* **~** to deal with sth; *(Aufsatz etc auch)* to be about sth

VR *impers* **a es handelt sich bei diesen sogenannten UFOs um optische Täuschungen** these so-called UFOs are optical illusions; **es handelt sich hier/dabei um ein Verbrechen** it's a crime we are dealing with here/there; **bei dem Festgenommenen handelt es sich um X** the person arrested is X **b** *(= betreffen)* **sich um etw ~** to be about sth, to concern sth; **worum handelt es sich, bitte?** what's it about, please?; **es handelt sich darum, dass ich einen Kredit beantragen möchte** it is about *or* concerns a loan which I wish to apply for **c** *(= um etw gehen, auf etw ankommen)* **sich um etw ~** to be a question *or* matter of sth; **es handelt sich nur ums Überleben** it's simply a question of survival

VT **a** *(= verkaufen)* to sell *(für* at, for); *(an der Börse)* to quote *(mit* at) **b** *Preis etc (= hinaufhandeln)* to push up, to raise; *(= herunterhandeln)* to bring down **c** *(fig)* **er wird als der neue Außenminister gehandelt** *(= ist im Gespräch)* he is being talked about for the position of foreign minister

Han|deln NT **-s,** *no pl* **a** *(= Feilschen)* bargaining, haggling **b** *(= das Handeltreiben)* trading; **das ~ mit Antiquitäten** trading *or* dealing in antiques **c** *(= Verhalten)* behaviour *(Brit),* behavior *(US)* **d** *(= das Tätigwerden)* action

han|delnd ADJ **die ~en Personen in einem Drama** the characters in a drama, the dramatis personae *pl;* **das ~e Subjekt** the active subject

Han|dels-: **Han|dels|ab|kom|men** NT trade agreement; **Han|dels|aka|de|mie** F *(Aus)* commercial college, business school; **Han|dels|aka|de|mi|ker(in)** M(F) *(Aus)* graduate of a commercial college, business school graduate; **Han|dels|ar|ti|kel** M commodity; **Han|dels|at|ta|ché** M commercial attaché; **Han|dels|bank** F *pl* **-banken** merchant bank; **Han|dels|be|schrän|kung** F trading restriction, restriction on trade; **Han|dels|be|trieb**

M trading *or* business concern; **Han|dels|be|zeich|nung** F trade name; **Han|dels|be|zie|hun|gen** PL trade relations *pl*; **Han|dels|bi|lanz** F balance of trade; **aktive/passive** ~ balance of trade surplus/deficit; **Han|dels|brauch** M trade *or* commercial practice; **Han|dels|de|fi|zit** NT trade deficit; **han|dels|ei|nig** ADJ *pred* ~ **werden/sein** to agree terms, to come to an agreement; **Han|dels|em|bar|go** NT trade embargo; **han|dels|fä|hig** ADJ *Güter etc* marketable, merchantable; **Han|dels|fir|ma** F (commercial *or* business) firm; **Han|dels|flag|ge** F *(Naut)* merchant flag; **Han|dels|flot|te** F merchant fleet; **Han|dels|frei|heit** F **a** *(Comm)* freedom of trade *no pl* **b** *(rare: = Handlungsfreiheit)* freedom of action; **Han|dels|ge|sell|schaft** F commercial company; **Han|dels|ge|setz** NT commercial law; **Han|dels|ge|setz|buch** NT code of commercial law; **Han|dels|ge|wer|be** NT commerce *no art*; **Han|dels|gut** NT commodity; **Han|dels|ha|fen** M trading port; **Han|dels|haus** NT business house, firm; **Han|dels|hemm|nis** NT trade barrier; **Han|dels|kam|mer** F chamber of commerce; **Han|dels|ket|te** F **a** chain of retail shops **b** *(= Weg der Ware)* sales route *(from manufacturer to buyer)*; **Han|dels|klas|se** F grade; **Heringe der ~ 1** grade 1 herring; **Han|dels|krieg** M trade war; **Han|dels|kri|se** F commercial crisis; **Han|dels|leh|rer(in)** M(F) teacher of commercial subjects; **Han|dels|macht** F trading nation *or* power; **Han|dels|mak|ler(in)** M(F) broker; **Han|dels|ma|ri|ne** F merchant navy, mercantile marine *(form)*; **Han|dels|mar|ke** F trade name; **Han|dels|met|ro|po|le** F commercial metropolis; **Han|dels|mi|nis|ter(in)** M(F) ≈ Trade Secretary *(Brit)*, ≈ Secretary of Commerce *(US)*; **Han|dels|mi|nis|te|ri|um** NT ≈ Board of Trade *(Brit)*, ≈ Department of Commerce *(US)*; **Han|dels|mis|si|on** F trade mission; **Han|dels|na|me** M trade name; **Han|dels|na|ti|on** F trading nation; **Han|dels|nie|der|las|sung** F branch (of a trading organization); **Han|dels|ob|jekt** NT commodity; **Han|dels|or|ga|ni|sa|ti|on** F trading organization; **Han|dels|part|ner(in)** M(F) trading partner; **Han|dels|platz** M trading centre *(Brit) or* center *(US)*; **Han|dels|po|li|tik** F trade *or* commercial policy; **han|dels|po|li|tisch** ADJ relating to trade *or* commercial policy ADV as far as trade *or* commercial policy is concerned; **Han|dels|re|al|schu|le** F *(esp Sw)* commercial school *or* college; **Han|dels|recht** NT commercial law *no def art, no pl*; **han|dels|recht|lich** ADJ of commercial law ADV according to commercial law; **Han|dels|re|gis|ter** NT register of companies; **Han|dels|rei|sen|de(r)** MF *decl as adj* commercial traveller *(Brit) or* traveler *(US)*; **Han|dels|schiff** NT trading ship *or* vessel, merchantman *(old)*; **Han|dels|schiff|fahrt** F merchant shipping *no def art*; **Han|dels|schluss** M *(St Ex)* close of trade; *(an New Yorker Börse)* closing bell; **Han|dels|schran|ke** F *usu pl* trade barrier; **Han|dels|schu|le** F commercial school *or* college; **Han|dels|schü|ler(in)** M(F) student at a commercial school *or* college; **Han|dels|span|ne** F profit margin; **Han|dels|sper|re** F trade embargo *(gegen* on); **Han|dels|spra|che** F commercial language; **Han|dels|stadt** F trading city *or* centre *(Brit) or* center *(US)*; **Han|dels|stand** M *(Sociol)* merchant class; **Han|dels|stra|ße** F *(Hist)* trade route; **Han|dels|stütz|punkt** M trading base; **han|dels|üb|lich** ADJ usual *or* customary (in the trade *or* in commerce); *Produkt, Ware* standard; **etw zu den ~en Preisen kaufen** to buy sth at normal (trade) prices; **Han|dels|un|ter|neh|men** NT commercial enterprise; **Han|dels|ver|kehr** M trade; **Han|dels|ver|trag** M trade agreement; **Han|dels|ver|tre|ter(in)** M(F) commercial traveller *(Brit) or* traveler *(US)*; **Han|dels|ver|tre|tung** F trade mission; **Han|dels|volk** NT trading nation; **Han|dels|wa|re** F commodity; **keine ~** no commercial value; **Han|dels|wa|ren** PL commodities *pl*, merchandise *sing*; **Han|dels|weg** M **a** sales route **b** *(Hist: = Handelsstraße)* trade route; **Han|dels|we|sen** NT, *no pl* commerce, trade *no def art*; **Han|dels|zent|rum** NT trading *or* commercial centre *(Brit) or* center *(US)*; **Han|dels|zweig** M branch

hän|del|süch|tig ADJ *(geh, old)* quarrelsome

Han|dels|wert M market value

han|del|trei|bend ADJ *attr* → **Handel a**

Han|del|trei|ben|de(r) [-traibndə] MF *decl as adj* trader, tradesman/-woman

Hän|de-: **Hän|de|rin|gen** NT **-s,** *no pl (fig)* wringing of one's hands; **hän|de|rin|gend** [ˈhɛndərɪŋənt] ADV wringing one's hands; *(fig) um etw bitten* imploringly; **~ nach etw suchen** to search desperately for sth; **Hän|de|schüt|teln** NT **-s,** *no pl* handshaking; **Hän|de|trock|ner** [-trɔknɐ] M **-s, -** hand drier; **Hän|de|wa|schen** NT **-s,** *no pl* washing one's hands; **jdn zum ~ schicken** to send sb to wash his/her hands

Hand-: **Hand|fe|ger** M hand brush; **wie ein wild gewordener ~** *(inf)* like a wild thing; **Hand|fer|tig|keit** F dexterity; **Hand|fes|sel** F **a** manacle; **etw als ~ benutzen** to tie sb's hands together with sth **b** *(= Handschelle)* handcuff; **hand|fest** ADJ **a** *(= kräftig) Mensch* sturdy, robust; *Essen* solid, substantial **b** *(fig) Schlägerei* violent; *Skandal* huge; *Vorschlag, Argument* well-founded, solid; *Beweis* solid, tangible; *Interesse* strong; *Lüge, Betrug* flagrant, blatant; **Hand|feu|er|lö|scher** M hand fire extinguisher; **Hand|feu|er|waf|fe** F handgun; **Hand|flä|che** F palm *or* flat (of the/one's hand); **Hand|funk|ge|rät** NT walkie-talkie; **Hand|gas** NT, *no pl (Aut: = Vorrichtung)* hand throttle; **~ haben/geben** to have a/pull out the hand throttle; **mit ~ fahren** to use the hand throttle; **hand|ge|ar|bei|tet** ADJ handmade; *Stickerei etc* handworked; **hand|ge|bun|den** ADJ hand-bound; **hand|ge|fer|tigt** [-gəfɛrtɪçt] ADJ = **handgearbeitet**; **hand|ge|knüpft** [-gəknʏpft] ADJ *Teppich* hand-knotted; **Hand|geld** NT *(Sport)* transfer fee; *(Hist)* earnest money; *(Mil Hist)* bounty; **Hand|ge|lenk** NT wrist; **aus dem ~** *(fig inf) (= ohne Mühe)* with the greatest of ease, effortlessly; *(= improvisiert)* off the cuff; **etw aus dem ~ schütteln** *(fig inf)* to do sth effortlessly *or* with no trouble at all; **ein lockeres** *or* **loses ~ haben** *(inf)* to let fly at the slightest provocation; **Hand|ge|lenk|schüt|zer** M wrist pad; **hand|ge|macht** ADJ handmade; **hand|ge|malt** [-gəma:lt] ADJ hand-painted; **hand|ge|mein** ADJ **(mit jdm) ~ werden** to come to blows (with sb); **Hand|ge|men|ge** NT scuffle, fight; **hand|ge|näht** [-gənɛ:t] ADJ hand-sewn; **Hand|ge|päck** NT hand luggage *no pl or* baggage *no pl*; **Hand|ge|rät** NT *(Sport)* hand apparatus; **hand|ge|recht** ADJ, ADV handy; **hand|ge|schlif|fen** ADJ *Edelstein, Glas* hand-cut; *Linse* hand-ground; **hand|ge|schmie|det** [-gəʃmi:dət] ADJ hand-forged; **hand|ge|schöpft** [-gəʃœpft] ADJ *Papier* handmade; **hand|ge|schrie|ben** ADJ handwritten; **hand|ge|setzt** ADJ *(Typ)* hand-set, set by hand; **hand|ge|spon|nen** ADJ hand-spun; **hand|ge|steu|ert** [-gəʃtɔyɐt] ADJ *(Tech)* hand-operated; **hand|ge|strickt** [-gəʃtrɪkt] ADJ hand-knitted; *(fig)* homespun; *Lösung* homegrown; **Hand|ge|strick|te(s)** [-gəʃtrɪktə] NT *decl as adj* hand-knitted goods *pl*; **hand|ge|webt** [-gəve:pt] ADJ hand-woven; **Hand|gra|na|te** F hand grenade; **hand|greif|lich** [ˈhantgraiflɪç] ADJ **a** *Streit, Auseinandersetzung* violent; **~ werden** to become violent **b** *(fig) (= offensichtlich)* clear; *Lüge* blatant, flagrant ADV **etw ~ vor Augen führen** to demonstrate sth clearly; **Hand|greif|lich|keit** F **-, -en a** *usu pl* violence *no pl* **b** *(fig: = Offensichtlichkeit)* clarity; *(von Lüge)* blatancy; **Hand|griff** M **a** *(= Bewegung)* movement; *(im Haushalt)* chore; **keinen ~ tun** not to lift a finger; **mit einem ~** *(öffnen)* with one flick of the wrist; *(= schnell)* in no time; **mit ein paar ~en** in next to no time **b** *(= Gegenstand)* handle; **hand|groß** ADJ hand-sized; **hand|hab|bar** ADJ manageable; **leicht/schwer ~** easy/difficult to manage; **Hand|hab|bar|keit** F **-,** *no pl* manageability; **Hand|ha|be** [ˈhantha:bə] F *(fig)* **ich habe gegen ihn keine ~** I have no hold on him; **etw als ~ (gegen jdn) benutzen** to use sth as a lever (against sb); **hand|ha|ben** VT *insep* to handle; *Maschine auch* to operate, to work; *Gesetz* to implement, to administer; **Hand|ha|bung** [ˈhantha:bʊŋ] F **-, -en** handling; *(von Maschine auch)* operation, working; *(von Gesetz)* implementation, administration; **Hand|har|mo|ni|ka** F concertina; **Hand|he|bel** M manually operated *or* hand-operated lever

Han|di|cap [ˈhɛndikɛp] NT **-s, -s** *(Sport, fig)* handicap

han|di|ca|pen [ˈhɛndikɛpn] VT *insep* to handicap → *auch* **gehandicapt**

-hän|dig [hɛndɪç] ADJ *suf* -handed; **linkshändig** left-handed

Han|di|kap [ˈhɛndikɛp] *etc* NT → **Handicap** *etc*

Han|di|kap- [ˈhɛndikɛp-]: **Han|di|kap|ren|nen** NT handicap (race); **Han|di|kap|spiel** NT handicap game

Hand-in-Hand-Ar|bei|ten NT **-s,** *no pl* cooperation

hän|disch [ˈhɛndɪʃ] ADJ *(Aus)* manual

Hand-: **Hand|ka|me|ra** F hand-held camera; **Hand|kan|te** F side of the/one's hand; **Hand|kan|ten|schlag** M karate chop; **Hand|kar|re** F, **Hand|kar|ren** M handcart; **Hand|kä|se** M *strong-smelling round German cheese*; **Hand|ka|ta|log** M ready-reference catalogue *(Brit) or* catalog *(US)*; **Hand|kof|fer** M (small) suitcase; **hand|ko|lo|riert** [-kolori:ɐt] ADJ hand-coloured *(Brit)*, hand-colored *(US)*; **Hand|korb** M (small) basket; **Hand|kreis|sä|ge** F hand-held circular saw; **Hand|kur|bel** F hand crank; *(Aut)* starting handle; **Hand|kuss** M kiss on the hand; *(Eccl)* kiss *(on the ring of a bishop etc)*; **mit ~** *(fig inf)* with pleasure, gladly; **zum ~ kommen** *(Aus fig)* to come off worse; **Hand|lam|pe** F inspection lamp; **Hand|lan|ger** [ˈhantlaŋɐ] M **-s, -** odd-job man, handyman; *(fig) (= Untergeordneter)* dogsbody *(Brit inf)*, drudge *(US)*; *(pej: = Gehilfe)* henchman; **Hand|lan|ger|ar|beit** F *(pej)* donkey-work *no pl*; **Hand|lan|ger|dienst** M dirty work *no pl*; **Hand|lan|ge|rin** [ˈhantlaŋərɪn] F **-, -nen** *(lit)* odd-job woman; *(fig) (= Untergeordnete)* dogsbody *(Brit inf)*, drudge *(US)*; *(pej: = Gehilfin)* henchman; **Hand|lauf** M *(an Treppen)* handrail

Händ|ler [ˈhɛndlɐ] M **-s, -**, **Händ|le|rin** [-ərɪn] F **-, -nen** trader, dealer; *(= Autohändler)* dealer; *(= Ladenbesitzer)* shopkeeper *(Brit)*, store owner *(US)*; *(= Fischhändler)* fishmonger *(Brit)*, fish dealer *(US)*; *(= Fleischhändler)* butcher; *(= Gemüsehändler)* greengrocer *(Brit)*, produce dealer *(US)*; **ambulanter** *or* **fliegender ~** street trader

Händ|ler-: **Händ|ler|preis** M trade price; **Händ|ler|ra|batt** M trade discount

Hand-: **Hand|le|se|kunst** F **(die) ~** palmistry, (the art of) reading palms; **Hand|le|ser(in)** M(F) palm reader, palmist; **Hand|leuch|te** F inspection lamp

hand|lich [ˈhantlɪç] ADJ **a** *Gerät, Format, Form* handy; *Gepäckstück* manageable, easy to manage; *Auto* manoeuvrable *(Brit)*, maneuverable *(US)* **b** *(Sw: = behände)* handy, dexterous **c** *(Sw: = mit der Hand)* with one's hand(s)

Hand|lich|keit F **-,** *no pl (von Gerät, Format, Form)* handiness; *(von Gepäckstück)* manageability; *(von Auto)* manoeuvrability *(Brit)*, maneuverability *(US)*

Hand|ling NT *(= Handhabung)* handling

Hand-: **Hand|li|nie** F line (in the palm of the hand); **Hand|li|ni|en|deu|tung** F **(die)** ~ palmistry; **Hand|lö|scher** [-lœʃɐ] M, **Hand|lösch|ge|rät** NT fire extinguisher *(hand-held)*

Hand|lung ['handlʊŋ] F **-, -en** **a** *(= Vorgehen, Handeln)* action, deed; *(= Tat, Akt)* act **b** *(= Geschehen)* action; *(= Handlungsablauf)* plot; **der Ort der ~** the scene of the action **c** *(dated) (mit Waren)* business; *(= Laden)* shop *(esp Brit)*, store

Hand|lungs-: **Hand|lungs|ab|lauf** M plot; **hand|lungs|arm** ADJ thin on plot; **Hand|lungs|ar|mut** F lack of plot *or* action; **Hand|lungs|be|darf** M need for action; **Hand|lungs|be|voll|mäch|tig|te(r)** MF *decl as adj* authorized agent, proxy; **hand|lungs|fä|hig** ADJ *Regierung, Bündnis* capable of acting, able to act; *(Jur)* empowered *or* authorized to act; **eine ~e Mehrheit** a working majority; **Hand|lungs|fä|hig|keit** F *(von Regierung, Bündnis)* ability to act; *(Jur)* power to act; **Hand|lungs|frei|heit** F freedom of action; **Hand|lungs|ge|rüst** NT *(Liter)* framework; **hand|lungs|reich** ADJ action-packed, full of action; **Hand|lungs|reich|tum** M abundance of action; **Hand|lungs|rei|sen|de(r)** MF *decl as adj (Comm)* commercial traveller *(Brit) pr* traveler *(US)*, rep, representative *(dated)*; **Hand|lungs|spiel|raum** M scope (of action); **Hand|lungs|strang** M *(Liter, Theat)* strand (of the plot); **Hand|lungs|the|o|rie** F *(Sociol)* theory of action; **hand|lungs|un|fä|hig** ADJ *Regierung, Bündnis* incapable of acting, unable to act; *(Jur)* without power to act; **Hand|lungs|un|fä|hig|keit** F *(von Regierung, Bündnis)* inability to act; *(Jur)* lack of power to act; **Hand|lungs|verb** NT transitive verb; **Hand|lungs|ver|lauf** M plot; **Hand|lungs|voll|macht** F proxy; **Hand|lungs|wei|se** F way of behaving, behaviour *no pl (Brit)*, behavior *no pl (US)*, conduct *no pl*; **eine selbstlose ~** unselfish behaviour *(Brit) or* behavior *(US) or* conduct; **eine edelmütige ~** noble conduct

Hand-: **Hand|mehr** ['hantmeːɐ] NT **-s**, *no pl (Sw)* show of hands; **Hand|müh|le** F hand-mill

Hand|out, **Hand-out** ['hɛntaut] NT **-s, -s** handout

Hand-: **Hand|pfle|ge** F care of one's hands; **Hand|pres|se** F *(Typ)* hand-press; **Hand|pum|pe** F hand-pump; **Hand|pup|pe** F glove *(Brit) or* hand *(US)* puppet; **Hand|pup|pen|spiel** NT *(= Technik)* glove *(Brit) or* hand *(US)* puppetry; *(= Stück)* glove *(Brit) or* hand *(US)* puppet show; **Hand|rei|chung** ['hantraiçʊŋ] F **-, -en** **a** helping hand *no pl* **b** *(= Instruktion, Empfehlung)* recommendation **c** *(= Handzettel)* handout; **Hand|rü|cken** M back of the/one's hand; **auf beiden ~** on the back of both hands; **Hand|sä|ge** F hand saw; **Hand|satz** M *(Typ)* hand-setting, hand-composition; **Hand|schal|ter** M manual switch; **Hand|schal|tung** F *(Aut)* manual controls *pl*; **Hand|schel|le** F *usu pl* handcuff; **jdm ~n anlegen** to handcuff sb, to put handcuffs on sb; **in ~n** in handcuffs, handcuffed; **Hand|schlag** M **a** *(= Händedruck)* handshake; **mit** *or* **durch** *or* **per ~** with a handshake; **ein Geschäft durch ~ abschließen** to shake on a deal; **goldener ~** *(fig inf)* golden handshake *(inf)* **b** **keinen ~ tun** not to do a stroke (of work); **Hand|schrei|ben** NT handwritten letter; **Hand|schrift** F **a** handwriting; *(fig)* (trade)mark; **er hat eine gute/leserliche ~** he has a good/legible hand, he has good/legible handwriting; **etw trägt/verrät jds ~** *(fig)* sth bears *or* has sb's (trade)mark; *(Kunstwerk auch)* sth shows the hand of sb; **eine kräftige/gute ~ haben** *or* **schreiben** *(fig inf)* to be a hard/good hitter **b** *(= Text)* manuscript; **Hand|schrif|ten|deu|tung** F **(die)** ~ the study of handwriting, graphology; **hand|schrift|lich** ADJ handwritten ADV *korrigieren, einfügen* by hand; *sich bewerben* in writing; **einen Brief ~ beantworten** to answer a letter by hand

Hand|schuh M *(= Fingerhandschuh)* glove; *(= Fausthandschuh)* mitten, mitt *(inf)*

Hand|schuh-: **Hand|schuh|fach** NT, **Hand|schuh|kas|ten** M *(Aut)* glove compartment; **Hand|schuh|ma|cher(in)** M(F) glove maker

Hand-: **Hand|schutz** M protection *no pl* for the hands; *(= Handschuhe)* hand protection *no pl*; *(an Maschine)* hand guard; **Hand|set|zer(in)** M(F) *(Typ)* hand compositor; **hand|sig|niert** [-zɪgniːɐt] ADJ signed, autographed; **Hand|skiz|ze** F rough sketch; **Hand|spie|gel** M hand mirror *or* glass; **Hand|spiel** NT, *no pl* **a** *(Sport)* handball **b** *(Cards)* (finishing a game by) playing all one's hand at once; **Hand|stand** M *(Sport)* handstand; **Hand|stand|über|schlag** M *(Sport)* handspring; **Hand|steu|e|rung** F manual control; **Hand|streich** M **in** *or* **durch einen ~** in a surprise coup; *(Mil)* by surprise; **in einem** *or* **durch einen kühnen/detailliert geplanten ~** in a bold/minutely planned coup; **hand|streich|ar|tig** ADJ sudden and unexpected ADV suddenly and unexpectedly; **Hand|ta|sche** F handbag *(Brit)*, purse *(US)*; **Hand|ta|schen|raub** M bag-snatching; **Hand|tel|ler** M palm (of the/one's hand); **Hand|trom|mel** F hand drum

Hand|tuch NT *pl* **-tücher** towel; *(= Geschirrhandtuch)* tea towel, tea cloth; *(= Papierhandtuch)* paper towel; **das ~ werfen** *(lit)* to throw in the towel; *(fig inf)* to throw in the sponge *(Brit) or* towel

Hand|tuch- *in cpds* towel; **Hand|tuch|au|to|mat** M towel dispenser; **Hand|tuch|hal|ter** M towel rail *(Brit) or* rack *(US)*; **Hand|tuch|spen|der** M towel dispenser

Hand-: **Hand|um|dre|hen** NT *(fig)* **im ~** in the twinkling of an eye; **hand|ver|le|sen** ADJ *Obst etc* hand-graded; *(fig) Gesellschaft etc* hand-picked; **hand|ver|mit|telt** [-fɛɐmɪtlt] ADJ *Telefongespräch* connected through *or* by the operator; **Hand|ver|mitt|lung** F connection by the operator; **eine durch ~ hergestellte Telefonverbindung** a call connected through *or* by the operator; **Hand|voll** ['hantfɔl] F **-, -** *(lit, fig)* a handful; **werfen Sie drei ~ Badesalz in die Wanne** sprinkle three handfuls of bath salts into the tub; **es war nur eine ~ Leute im Publikum** there were only a handful of people in the audience; **Hand|waf|fe** F hand weapon; **Hand|wa|gen** M handcart; **hand|warm** ADJ hand-hot *(Brit)*, warm ADV **etw ~ waschen** to wash sth in hand-hot *(Brit) or* warm water; **Hand|wasch|be|cken** NT wash-hand basin; **Hand|wä|sche** F washing by hand; *(= Wäschestücke)* hand wash; **Hand|web|stuhl** M hand loom

Hand|werk NT **a** *(= Beruf)* trade; *(= Kunsthandwerk)* craft; *(fig: = Tätigkeit)* business; **das Leder verarbeitende ~** the leather worker's trade; **das ~ des Bäckers** the baking trade; **das ~ des Schneiders/Schreiners** the trade of tailor/joiner; **das ~ des Töpfers** the potter's craft; **der Krieg ist das einzige ~, das er versteht** *or* **beherrscht** war is the only business he knows anything about; **sein ~ verstehen** *or* **beherrschen** *(fig)* to know one's job; **jdm ins ~ pfuschen** *(fig)* to tread on sb's toes; **jdm das ~ legen** *(fig)* to put a stop to sb's game *(inf) or* to sb **b** *no pl (= Wirtschaftsbereich)* trade

hand|wer|keln ['hantvɛrkln] VI *insep (hum)* to potter *(Brit) or* putter *(US)* around (making things)

Hand|wer|ker ['hantvɛrkɐ] M **-s, -** tradesman, (skilled) manual worker; *(= Kunsthandwerker)* craftsman; **wir haben seit Wochen die ~ im Haus** we've had workmen *or* tradesmen in the house for weeks

Hand|wer|ke|rin ['hantvɛrkərɪn] F **-, -nen** tradeswoman, (skilled) manual worker; *(= Kunsthandwerkerin)* craftswoman

Hand|wer|ker|schaft ['hantvɛrkɐʃaft] F **-**, *no pl* trade *sing or pl*

hand|werk|lich ['hantvɛrklɪç] ADJ → **Handwerker** *Ausbildung* as a manual worker/craftsman/craftswoman; *(fig)* technical; **~er Beruf** skilled trade; **die ~e Ausführung des Möbelstücks** the workmanship *or* craftsmanship of the piece of furniture; **~es Können** craftsmanship; **~e Fähigkeiten** manual skills; **~er Betrieb** workshop; **~es Produkt** product *(made by craftsmen/craftswomen)*; **~e Tätigkeit** skilled manual job ADV **das ist ~ eine Katastrophe** this is a disgraceful *or* an incredibly slipshod piece of work; **~ begabt sein** to be good with one's hands; **eine ~ ausgezeichnete Leistung** a masterpiece of craftsmanship; **~ ist der Fotograf perfekt** technically the photographer is perfect

Hand|werks-: **Hand|werks|be|ruf** M skilled trade; **Hand|werks|be|trieb** M workshop; **Hand|werks|bur|sche** M *(old)* travelling *(Brit) or* traveling *(US)* journeyman; **Hand|werks|ge|sel|le** M; **Hand|werks|ge|sel|lin** F journeyman (apprentice); **Hand|werks|kam|mer** F trade corporation; **Hand|werks|mann** M *pl* **-leute** *(obs)* (skilled) manual worker; **Hand|werks|meis|ter(in)** M(F) master craftsman/-woman; **Hand|werks|rol|le** F register of master craftspeople; **Hand|werks|zeug** NT, *no pl* tools *pl*; *(fig)* tools of the trade *pl*, equipment

Hand-: **Hand|werk|zeug** NT hand tools *pl*; **Hand|win|de** F hand-winch; **Hand|wör|ter|buch** NT concise dictionary; **Hand|wur|zel** F *(Anat)* carpus; **Hand|wur|zel|kno|chen** M *(Anat)* carpal bone

Han|dy ['hɛndi] NT **-s, -s** *(Telec)* mobile (phone), cell(ular) phone *(US)*

Handy-: **Han|dy|num|mer** F mobile *(Brit) or* cell phone *(US)* number; **Han|dy|ver|bot** NT mobile phone ban *(Brit)*, cell phone ban *(US)*

Hand-: **hand|zahm** ADJ *Tier* tame enough to be handled; *(fig inf) Mensch, Frage* tame; **Hand|zei|chen** NT signal; *(= Geste auch)* sign; *(bei Abstimmung)* show of hands; **durch ~** by a show of hands; **er gab mir durch ein ~ zu verstehen, dass ich still sein sollte** he signalled *(Brit) or* signaled *(US)* to me to be quiet, he gave me a sign to be quiet; **Hand|zeich|nung** F **a** *(= Skizze)* sketch **b** *(Art)* drawing; **Hand|zet|tel** M handout, leaflet, handbill

ha|ne|bü|chen ['haːnəbyːçn] ADJ *(geh)* outrageous, scandalous

Hanf [hanf] M **-(e)s**, *no pl (= Pflanze, Faser)* hemp; *(= Samen)* hemp seed

Hänf|ling ['hɛnflɪŋ] M **-s, -e** *(Orn)* linnet

Hanf|seil NT, **Hanf|strick** M hemp-rope

Hang [haŋ] M **-(e)s, ⸚e** ['hɛŋə] **a** *(= Abhang)* slope **b** *no pl (= Neigung)* tendency; **er hat einen (deutlichen) ~ zur Kriminalität** he has a (marked) tendency toward(s) criminality

hang|ab|wärts ADV downhill

Han|gar ['haŋgaːɐ, haŋ'gaːɐ] M **-s, -s** hangar, shed

Hän|ge-: **Hän|ge|ba|cken** PL flabby cheeks *pl*; **Hän|ge|bauch** M drooping belly *(inf)*; **Hän|ge|brü|cke** F suspension bridge; **Hän|ge|brust** F, **Hän|ge|bu|sen** M *(pej)* sagging *or* droopy *(inf)* breasts *pl or* bosom *no pl*; **Hän|ge|dach** NT suspended roof; **Hän|ge|glei|ten** NT *(Sport)* hang-gliding; **Hän|ge|glei|ter** M *(Sport)* hang-glider; **Hän|ge|kleid** NT loose dress, smock; **Hän|ge|lam|pe** F droplight

han|geln ['haŋln] VIR *(vi: aux sein or haben)* **er hangelte sich an einem Tau über den Fluss** he moved hand over hand along a rope over the river; **er hangelte sich am Fels hinunter** he let himself down the cliff hand over hand; **er hangelte sich über den Abgrund** he crossed the chasm hand over hand

Hän|ge-: **Hän|ge|map|pe** F suspension file; **Hän|ge|mat|te** F hammock

han|gen ['haŋən] VI *(obs, dial) (dial:) aux sein* = **hängen 1**

Han|gen ['haŋən] NT **mit ~ und Bangen** with fear and trembling

hän|gen ['hɛŋən]

1 INTRANSITIVES VERB 3 REFLEXIVES VERB
2 TRANSITIVES VERB

1 – INTRANSITIVES VERB

pret **hing** [hɪŋ], *ptp* **gehangen** [gə'haŋən]

a = herunterhängen to hang; **die Vorhänge hängen schief** the curtains don't hang straight; **die Gardinen hängen schon** the curtains are already up; **ihre Haare hängen bis auf die Schultern** her hair comes down to her shoulders; **die Haare hängen ihr ins Gesicht** her hair falls over her face; **mit hängenden Schultern** with drooping shoulders; **die Blumen ließen die Köpfe hängen** the flowers drooped; **den Kopf hängen lassen** *(fig)* to be downcast; **die Kleider hingen ihr in Fetzen am Leib** her clothes hung (on her) in tatters; **es sieht sehr schick aus, wenn dieses Kleid ein wenig lose hängt** this dress looks very elegant if it's a bit loose; **sie hängt den ganzen Tag aus dem Fenster** she leans *or* hangs out of the window all day

b = gehenkt werden to hang; **dafür wirst du hängen, Schurke!** you'll hang for this, villain!

c = befestigt, angeschlossen sein to hang; *(Wohnwagen etc, Lautsprecher, Telefonapparat etc)* to be connected (up) (*an +dat* to), to be attached (*an +dat* to); **der Wohnwagen hängt am Auto** the caravan is attached to the car, the caravan is on the car; **die Tür hängt in den Angeln** the door hangs on its hinges; **das Bild hängt an der Wand/am Nagel** the picture is hanging on the wall/from a nail; **die Wäsche hängt auf der Leine** the washing is hanging on the line; **das Bild hängt schief** the picture is (hanging) crooked; **der Knopf hängt nur noch an einem Faden** the button is only hanging by a thread; **der Patient hängt an der künstlichen Niere/am Tropf** the patient is on the kidney machine/on the drip; **das Kalb hing am Euter der Mutter** the calf hung on to its mother's udder; **sie hing ihm am Hals** she hung (a)round his neck; **sie hing ihm an der Schulter** she clung to his shoulder

d = festhängen to be caught (*an +dat* on); *(= kleben)* to be stuck (*an +dat* to); **mit einer Masche im Stacheldraht hängen** to be caught on barbed wire by a thread; **mit dem Ärmel an einem Dorn hängen** to have one's sleeve caught on a thorn; **ihre Blicke** *or* **Augen hingen an dem Sänger** her eyes were fixed on the singer; **sie hing am Mund** *or* **an den Lippen des Redners** she hung on the speaker's every word; **Ihnen hängt da eine Fluse am Kragen** there's a bit of fluff *(Brit)* or fuzz *(US)* on your collar; **manchmal hängt wegen der statischen Elektrizität noch Staub an den CDs** sometimes static electricity makes dust stick to CDs; **daran hängt viel Arbeit** there's a lot of work involved in that

e = sich aufhalten *inf* to hang around *(inf)*; **sie hängt ständig in Discos** she hangs around discos; **er hängt den ganzen Tag vor dem Fernseher** he sits in front of the television all day

f = behangen sein
♦ **hängen voller** *or* **voll** to be full of; **der Schrank hängt voll(er) Kleider** the cupboard is full of clothes; **der Baum hängt voller Früchte** the tree is laden down with fruit

g = sich neigen to lean; **in der Kurve hängen** *(Motorradfahrer)* to lean into the bend; **der Wagen hängt (stark) nach rechts** the car leans (badly) to the right; **häng nicht so auf dem Stuhl, setz dich gerade hin!** *(inf)* don't slouch on your chair like that, sit up straight!

h = schweben to hang; **eine Wolke hing im Tal** a cloud hung over the valley; **eine Gefahr/ein Fluch hängt über uns** danger/a curse is hanging over us; **eine unerträgliche Spannung hing im Raum** there was unbearable tension in the room → **Luft a**

i = nicht vorankommen to be behind schedule; *(Sch inf)* to be behind; **der Prozeß hängt** the trial is behind schedule; **meine Examensarbeit hängt** I'm behind (schedule) with my dissertation; **er hängt in Chemie** *(inf)* he's behind in chemistry

j Chess **die Partie hängt** the game has been held over *or* adjourned; **der Springer hängt** the knight is vulnerable

k gefühlsmäßig
♦ **an jdm/etw hängen** *(= lieben)* to love sb/sth; *(inf: = abhängen von)* to depend on sb/sth; **ich hänge am Leben/an meinem Beruf** I love life/ my job; **er geht nicht auf die Expedition mit, er hängt nämlich am Leben** he's not going on the expedition because he values his life; **es hängt an ihm/an unserer Abstimmung, ob wir Truppen schicken** it depends on him/on our vote whether we send troops

2 – TRANSITIVES VERB

pret **hängte** *or* **hing**, *ptp* **gehängt** *or* **gehangen**

a = aufhängen, henken to hang; **am nächsten Tag wurde er gehängt** they hanged him the next day; **wir müssen noch die Gardinen hängen** we still have to put up *or* hang the curtains; **dieses Bild sollten wir etwas höher hängen** we should hang this picture a bit higher up; **und hierher hängen wir noch einen Spiegel** and we'll hang *or* put a mirror here; **er hängt sich all sein Geld** *or* **alles auf den Leib** *(inf)* he spends all his money on clothes; **er hängte den Telefonhörer in die Gabel** he replaced the receiver; **er hängte die Wand voll Bilder** he hung pictures all over the wall → **Nagel, Brotkorb, Glocke**
♦ **hängen an** *(+acc) (= anschließen)* to connect to; *(= befestigen) Wohnwagen etc* to hitch up to; **das Bild an die Wand hängen** to hang the picture on the wall; **eine Notiz ans Schwarze Brett hängen** to put a note on the notice board *(Brit) or* bulletin board *(US)*; **das Telefon an die neue Anlage hängen** to connect the phone to the new system

b = hängen lassen to dangle; **die Füße ins Wasser hängen** to dangle one's feet in the water; **seine Nase in etw** *(acc)* **hängen** *(inf)* to stick one's nose into sth *(inf)*

3 – REFLEXIVES VERB

♦ **sich hängen** *pret* **hängte**, *ptp* **gehängt**
♦ **sich an etw** *(acc)* **hängen** *(= sich festhalten)* to hang on to sth; *(= sich festsetzen)* to stick to sth; *(= sich gefühlsmäßig binden)* to be fixated on sth; **er hängte sich an den untersten Ast** he hung onto the lowest branch; **er hängte sich ihr an den Hals/Arm/Rockzipfel** he hung on to *or* clung to her neck/arm/coat-tails; **man sollte sich nicht an Äußerlichkeiten hängen** you shouldn't be too concerned with outward appearances; **er hängte sich ans Telefon** *or* **an die Strippe** *(inf)* he got on the phone; **sich an den Wasserhahn hängen** *(inf)* to have a drink straight from the tap; **sich an die Flasche hängen** *(inf)* to hit the bottle *(inf)*; **sich an ein Fahrzeug hängen** *(= dicht verfolgen)* to be in hot pursuit of a vehicle
♦ **sich an jdn hängen** *(= anschließen)* to tag on to sb *(inf)*, to latch on to sb *(inf)*; *(= gefühlsmäßig binden)* to become attached to sb; *(= verfolgen)* to go after sb, to pursue sb
♦ **sich in etw** *(acc)* **hängen** *(sl) (= sich engagieren)* to be involved in sth

---

Hän|gen NT **-s**, *no pl* **a Tod durch ~** death by hanging **b mit ~ und Würgen** *(inf)* by the skin of one's teeth

hän|gen blei|ben *irreg aux sein*, **hän|gen+blei|ben** *sep irreg aux sein* VI **a** *(= sich verfangen)* to get caught (*an +dat* on) **b** *(Sport) (= zurückbleiben)* to get left behind; *(= nicht durch-, weiterkommen)* not to get through; **der Aufschlag blieb im Netz hängen** the ball didn't get past the net; **der Angriff blieb vor dem Strafraum hängen** the attack didn't get past the front of the penalty area; **die Mannschaft blieb schon in der ersten Runde hängen** the team didn't get past *or* through the first round **c** *(Sch inf: = nicht versetzt werden)* to stay down **d** *(= sich aufhalten)* to stay on; **bei einer Nebensächlichkeit ~** to get bogged down with a secondary issue, to get sidetracked **e** *(= sich festsetzen, haften bleiben)* to get stuck *or* caught (*in, an +dat* on); *(Blick, Augen)* to rest (*an +dat* on); **es bleibt ja doch alles an mir hängen** *(fig inf)* in the end it's all down to me anyhow *(inf)*; **der Verdacht ist an ihm hängen geblieben** suspicion rested on him; **vom Lateinunterricht ist bei ihm nicht viel hängen geblieben** *(fig inf)* not much of his Latin stuck *(inf)*

hän|gend ADJ hanging; **~e Gärten** hanging gardens; **mit ~er Zunge kam er angelaufen** *(fig)* he came running up panting; **mit ~em Kopf** *(fig)* in low spirits, crestfallen; **~ befestigt sein** to be hung up; **~e Ventile** *(Tech)* overhead valves

hän|gen las|sen *ptp* **hängen lassen** *or (rare)* **gelassen** *irreg*, **hän|gen+las|sen** *ptp* **hängenlassen** *or (rare)* **hängengelassen** *sep irreg* VT **a** *(= vergessen)* to leave behind **b** *(inf: = im Stich lassen)* to let down **c** *(Sch: = nicht versetzen)* to keep down VR to let oneself go; **lass dich nicht so hängen!** don't let yourself go like this!, pull yourself together!; **er lässt sich furchtbar hängen** he has really let himself go

Hän|ge-: **Hän|ge|ohr** NT lop ear; **Hän|ge|par|tie** F *(Chess)* adjourned game; *(fig)* stalemate; **Hän|ge|pflan|ze** F trailing plant

Hä|nger ['hɛŋɐ] M **-s, - a** *(= Anhänger)* trailer **b** *(= Hängekleid)* loose dress, smock **c** *(= Mantel)* loose(-fitting) coat **d** *(inf: im Text)* **einen ~ haben** to go blank **e** *(inf)* = **Durchhänger**

Han|gerl ['haŋɐl] NT **-s, -(n)** *(Aus)* **a** *(= Lätzchen)* bib **b** *(= Geschirrhandtuch)* tea towel

Hän|ge-: **Hän|ge|schloss** NT padlock; **Hän|ge|schrank** M wall cupboard; **Hän|ge|schul|tern** PL drooping shoulders *pl*

hän|gig ['hɛŋɪç] ADJ **a** *(Sw Jur)* = **anhängig b** *(form)* sloping, inclined

Hang|la|ge F sloping site; **in ~** situated on a slope

hängt [hɛŋt] *3. pers sing pres von* **hängen**

Hang|tä|ter(in) M(F) *(Jur) person with criminal tendencies*

Han|ne|mann ['hanəman] M **~ geh du voran** *(inf)* you go first

Han|ni|bal ['hanibal] M **-s** Hannibal

Han|no|ver [ha'no:fɐ] NT **-s** Hanover

Han|no|ve|ra|ner [hanovə'ra:nɐ] M **-s, -** *(= Pferd)* Hanoverian (horse)

Han|no|ve|ra|ner [hanovə'ra:nɐ] M **-s, -**, **Han|no|ve|ra|ne|rin** [-ərɪn] F **-, -nen** Hanoverian

han|no|ve|risch [ha'no:fərɪʃ] *(rare)*, **han|no|versch**, **han|nö|versch** *(old)* ADJ Hanoverian

Hans [hans] M **-'** *or* **-ens** [-zns] **~ Guckindieluft** Johnny Head-in-the-Air; **~ im Glück** *(fig)* lucky dog *(inf) or* devil *(inf)*

Han|sa ['hanza] F **-**, *no pl (Hist)* Hanseatic League, Hansa, Hanse

Han|sa|plast® [hanza'plast, 'hanza-] NT **-(e)s**, *no pl* ≈ Elastoplast® *(Brit)*, ≈ Band-Aid® *(esp US)*

Häns|chen ['hɛnsçən] NT **-s, -** *dim von* **Hans**; **was ~ nicht lernt, lernt Hans nimmermehr** *(Prov)* ≈ you can't teach an old dog new tricks *(Prov)*

Hans|dampf [hans'dampf, 'hans-] M **-(e)s, -e** Jack-of-all-trades (and master of none); **er ist ein ~ in allen Gassen** he knows everybody and everything

Han|se ['hanzə] F **-**, *no pl (Hist)* Hanseatic League, Hansa, Hanse

Han|se|at [hanze'a:t] M **-en, -en**, **Han|se|a|tin** [hanze'a:tɪn] F **-, -nen** citizen of a Hansa town; *(Hist)* Hanseatic merchant, merchant belonging to the Hanseatic League

Han|se|a|ten|geist M Hanseatic spirit
han|se|a|tisch [hanze'a:tɪʃ] ADJ **a** *(Hist)* Hanseatic **b** *(= hansestädtisch)* Hanseatic; ~ **zurückhaltend** cool and reserved
Han|se|bund M, *no pl (Hist)* Hanseatic League
Han|sel ['hanzl] M **-s, -**, **Hän|sel** ['hɛnzl] M **-s, -** *dim von* **Hans** *(dial: = Trottel)* dolt, ninny *(inf)*; **Hänsel und Gretel** Hansel and Gretel; **ein paar** ~ *(dial: = wenige)* a few
Hän|se|lei [hɛnzə'lai] F **-, -en** teasing *no pl*
hän|seln ['hɛnzln] VT to tease
Han|se-: **Han|se|stadt** F Hansa *or* Hanseatic *or* Hanse town; **han|se|städ|tisch** ADJ Hanseatic

HANSESTADT

In the Middle Ages the **Hanse** (Hanseatic League) was a powerful alliance of independent trading centres on the Baltic and North Sea coasts. Its aim was to represent and protect the common commercial interests of its members. From the time of the Thirty Years' War up to the present the Hanseatic tradition has been continued by Lübeck, Hamburg and Bremen in particular. Bremen and Hamburg are both independent **Länder** with the titles **Freie Hansestadt Bremen** and **Freie Hansestadt Hamburg** respectively. Since re-unification other cities – Stralsund, Wismar, Greifswald and Rostock – have re-adopted the title of **Hansestadt**.

han|sisch ['hanzɪʃ] ADJ *(Hist)* Hanseatic
Hans|wurst [hans'vʊrst, 'hans-] M **-(e)s, -e** *or (hum)* **⸚e** **a** buffoon, clown **b** *(Theat)* fool, clown
Hans- [hans-]: **Hans|wurs|ti|a|de** [hansvʊrs'tia:də] F **-, -n** **a** clowning, buffoonery **b** *(Theat)* ≈ harlequinade
Han|tel ['hantl] F **-, -n** *(Sport)* dumbbell
han|teln ['hantln] VI *(Sport)* to exercise with dumbbells
Han|tel|trai|ning NT *(Sport)* dumbbells training
han|tie|ren [han'ti:rən] *ptp* **hantiert** VI **a** *(= arbeiten)* to be busy **b** *(= umgehen mit)* **mit etw** ~ to handle sth; **seine Geschicklichkeit im Hantieren mit Begriffen** *(fig)* his skill in handling ideas **c** *(= herumhantieren)* to tinker *or* fiddle about *(an +dat* with, on)
han|tig ['hantɪç] ADJ *(Aus, S Ger)* **a** *(= bitter)* bitter **b** *(= barsch)* brusque, abrupt
ha|pe|rig ['ha:pərɪç] ADJ, ADV *(N Ger)* = **stockend**
ha|pern ['ha:pɐn] VI *impers (inf)* **es hapert an etw** *(dat) (= fehlt)* there is a shortage *or* lack of sth; **es hapert bei jdm mit etw** *(= fehlt)* sb is short of sth, sb is badly off for sth; **es hapert (bei jdm) mit etw** *(= klappt nicht)* sb has a problem with sth; **mit der Grammatik hapert es bei ihm** he's weak in *or* poor at grammar
Häpp|chen ['hɛpçən] NT **-s, -** *dim von* **Happen** morsel, bit; *(= Appetithappen)* titbit *(Brit)*, tidbit *(US)*
häpp|chen|wei|se ADV *(inf: lit, fig)* bit by bit
Hap|pen ['hapn] M **-s, -** *(inf)* mouthful, morsel; *(= kleine Mahlzeit)* bite, snack; **ein fetter** ~ *(fig)* a good catch; **nach dem Theater aßen wir noch einen** ~ after the theatre *(Brit) or* theater *(US)* we had a bite to eat *(inf) or* a snack; **ich habe heute noch keinen** ~ **gegessen** I haven't had a bite to eat all day
Hap|pe|ning ['hɛpənɪŋ] NT **-s, -s** *(Theat)* happening; *(Art)* action painting
hap|pig ['hapɪç] ADJ *(inf) Preis, Zuwachs etc* steep *(inf)*
hap|py ['hɛpi] ADJ *inv (inf)* happy
Hap|py End ['hɛpi'lɛnt] NT **-s, -s**, **Hap|py|end** NT **-s, -s** happy ending; **ein Film/Buch/eine Geschichte mit Happy-End** a film/book/story with a happy ending
Ha|ra|ki|ri [hara'ki:ri] NT **-(s), -s** hara-kiri
Ha|rald ['ha:ralt] M **-s** Harold

Ha|rass ['haras] M **-es, -e**, **Ha|ras|se** ['harasə] F **-, -n** *(Aus, Sw: = Kasten, Kiste)* crate
Här|chen ['hɛ:rçən] NT **-s, -** *dim von* **Haar** little *or* tiny hair
Hard|core- *in cpds* hard-core; **Hard|core|por|no** M *(= Film)* hard-core porn film
Hard|co|ver ['ha:ɐdkavɐ] NT **-s, -s** hardcover
Hard|co|ver|aus|ga|be F *(von Buch)* hardcover edition
Hard|li|ner ['ha:ɐdlaɪnɐ] M **-s, -**, **Hard|li|ne|rin** [-ərɪn] F **-, -nen** *(Pol)* hardliner
Hard|rock ['ha:ɐdrɔk] M **-s**, *no pl* hard rock
Hardt|hö|he F Hardthöhe *(German Ministry of Defence)*
Hard|top ['ha:ɐdtɔp] NT OR M **-s, -s** *(Aut: = Wagen, Dach)* hardtop; **ein Kabrio mit** ~ a convertible with a hardtop
Hard|ware ['ha:ɐdwɛ:ɐ] F **-, -s** *(Comput)* hardware
Hard|ware- ['ha:ɐdwɛ:ɐ-]: **Hard|ware|an|for|de|run|gen** PL *(Comput)* system requirements; **Hard|ware|er|ken|nung** F *(Comput)* hardware detection
Ha|rem ['ha:rɛm] M **-s, -s** *(auch hum inf)* harem
Ha|rems-: **Ha|rems|da|me** F lady of the/a harem; **Ha|rems|wäch|ter** M harem guard
hä|ren ['hɛ:rən] ADJ *(rare)* **~es Gewand** hair shirt
Hä|re|sie [hɛre'zi:] F **-, -n** [-'zi:ən] *(lit, fig)* heresy
Hä|re|ti|ker [hɛ're:tikɐ] M **-s, -**, **Hä|re|ti|ke|rin** [-ərɪn] F **-, -nen** *(lit, fig)* heretic
hä|re|tisch [hɛ're:tɪʃ] ADJ *(lit, fig)* heretical
Har|fe ['harfə] F **-, -n** harp
Har|fe|nist [harfə'nɪst] M **-en, -en**, **Har|fe|nis|tin** [-'nɪstɪn] F **-, -nen** harpist
Har|fen-: **Har|fen|klang** M sound of the/a harp; **Har|fen|spiel** NT, *no pl* harp-playing; **Har|fen|spie|ler(in)** M(F) harp-player, harpist
Harf|ner ['harfnɐ] M **-s, -** *(old)*, **Harf|ne|rin** [-ərɪn] F **-, -nen** *(old)* harp-player, harpist
Har|ke ['harkə] F **-, -n** *(esp N Ger)* rake; **jdm zeigen, was eine** ~ **ist** *(fig inf)* to show sb what's what *(inf)*
har|ken ['harkn] VTI *(esp N Ger)* to rake
Har|le|kin ['harleki:n] M **-s, -e** Harlequin
Har|le|ki|na|de [harleki'na:də] F **-, -n** = **Hanswurstiade**
Harm [harm] M **-(e)s**, *no pl (poet, obs)* sore affliction *(liter)*, grief
här|men ['hɛrmən] VTR *(old)* = **grämen**
harm|los ADJ **a** *(= ungefährlich)* harmless; *Berg, Piste, Kurve* easy **b** *(= unschuldig, gutartig, naiv)* innocent; *(= unbedenklich)* harmless, innocuous; **er ist ein ~er Mensch** he's harmless (enough), he's an innocuous type ADV **a** *(= ungefährlich)* harmlessly **b** *(= unschuldig)* innocently, innocuously
Harm|lo|sig|keit F **-**, *no pl* **a** *(= Ungefährlichkeit)* harmlessness **b** *(= Unschuld, Naivität)* innocence; *(= Unbedenklichkeit)* harmlessness, innocuousness; **in aller** ~ in all innocence
Har|mo|nie [harmo'ni:] F **-, -n** [-'ni:ən] *(Mus, fig)* harmony
Har|mo|nie-: **Har|mo|nie|be|dürf|nis** NT, *no pl* need for peace and harmony; **Har|mo|nie|ge|setz** NT *usu pl* rule of harmony; **Har|mo|nie|leh|re** F *(= Gebiet)* harmony; *(= Theorie)* harmonic theory; **Har|mo|nie|mu|sik** F music for wind instruments
har|mo|nie|ren [harmo'ni:rən] *ptp* **harmoniert** VI *(Mus, fig)* to harmonize; *(farblich auch)* to go together, to match
Har|mo|nik [har'mo:nɪk] F **-**, *no pl* harmony
Har|mo|ni|ka [har'mo:nika] F **-, -s** *or* **Harmoniken** harmonica; *(= Mundharmonika auch)* mouth organ; *(= Ziehharmonika)* accordion
Har|mo|ni|ka|tür F folding *or* accordion door
har|mo|nisch [har'mo:nɪʃ] ADJ *(Mus, Math)* harmonic; *(= wohlklingend, fig)* harmonious ADV harmoniously; ~ **klingende Akkorde** harmonious chords; **etw** ~ **mischen** to make a harmonious mixture out of sth; ~ **komponiert sein** to be a harmonious composition; **das klingt nicht sehr** ~ that's not a very harmonious sound; ~ **verlaufen** to be harmonious; **sie leben** ~ **zusammen** they live together in harmony
har|mo|ni|sie|ren [harmoni'zi:rən] *ptp* **harmonisiert** VT *Musik, Steuern* to harmonize; *(fig)* to coordinate
Har|mo|ni|sie|rung F **-, -en** *(von Musik, Steuern)* harmonization; *(fig)* coordination
Har|mo|ni|um [har'mo:niʊm] NT **-s, Harmonien** [-'ni:ən] harmonium
Harn [harn] M **-(e)s, -e** urine; ~ **lassen** to pass water, to urinate
Harn-: **Harn|bla|se** F bladder; **Harn|bla|sen|ent|zün|dung** F cystitis; **Harn|drang** M *(form)* urge *or* need to pass water *or* to urinate
har|nen ['harnən] VI *(form)* to urinate, to pass water, to micturate *(form)*
Harn-: **Harn|ent|lee|rung** F urination, passing of water, micturition *(form)*; **Harn|fla|sche** F urinal
Har|nisch ['harnɪʃ] M **-(e)s, -e** armour *(Brit)*, armor *(US)*; **in** ~ **sein** *(fig)* to be up in arms, to have one's hackles up; **jdn in** ~ **bringen** *(fig)* to get sb up in arms, to get sb's hackles up
Harn-: **Harn|las|sen** NT **-s**, *no pl (form)* urination, passing of water, micturition *(form)*; **Harn|lei|ter** M ureter; **Harn|or|gan** NT urinary organ; **Harn|pro|be** F urine sample *or* specimen; **Harn|röh|re** F urethra; **Harn|säu|re** F *(Chem)* uric acid; **Harn|stein** M *(Med)* urinary calculus; **Harn|stoff** M *(Chem)* urea, carbamide; **harn|trei|bend** ADJ *(form)* diuretic; **Harn|un|ter|su|chung** F urine analysis, urinalysis; **Harn|ver|gif|tung** F uraemia *(Brit)*, uremia *(US)*; **Harn|we|ge** PL *(Anat)* urinary tract *sing*; **Harn|zu|cker** M sugar in the urine
Harp|si|chord [harpsi'kɔrt] NT **-(e)s, -e** [-də] *(old)* harpsichord, cembalo
Har|pu|ne [har'pu:nə] F **-, -n** harpoon
Har|pu|nen|ge|schütz NT, **Har|pu|nen|ka|no|ne** F, **Har|pu|nen|wer|fer** M harpoon gun
Har|pu|nier [harpu'ni:ɐ] M **-s, -e**, **Har|pu|nie|rin** [-'ni:rɪn] F **-, -nen** harpooner
har|pu|nie|ren [harpu'ni:rən] *ptp* **harpuniert** VTI to harpoon
Har|py|ie [har'py:jə] F **-, -n** *usu pl (Myth)* Harpy
har|ren ['harən] VI *(geh)* **jds/einer Sache ~, auf jdn/etw** ~ to await sb/sth, to wait for sb/sth → **Ding b**
harsch [harʃ] ADJ **a** *(= barsch) Worte, Kritik, Ton, Reaktion* harsh **b** *(= verharscht) Schnee* frozen
Harsch [harʃ] M **-(e)s**, *no pl* frozen snow
har|schen ['harʃn] VI to freeze over
har|schig ['harʃɪç] ADJ *Schnee* frozen
Harsch|schnee M frozen snow
hart [hart] ADJ *comp* **⸚er** ['hɛrtɐ], *superl* **⸚este(r, s)** ['hɛrtəstə] **a** *(= nicht weich, nicht sanft)* hard; *Matratze, Bett, Federung, Apfelschale* hard, firm; *Aufprall, Ruck* violent, hard; *Wind* strong; *Ei* hard-boiled; ~ **werden** to get hard, to harden; **Eier ~ kochen** to hard-boil eggs; **er hat einen ~en Leib** *(Med old)* he is constipated; **er hat einen ~en Schädel** *or* **Kopf** *(fig)* he's pig-headed *or* obstinate; **ein ~es Herz haben** *(fig)* to have a hard heart, to be hard-hearted; ~ **wie Stahl/Stein** as hard as steel/stone
b *(= scharf) Konturen, Kontrast, Formen* sharp; *(Phot) Negativ* sharp; *(Gesichts)züge, Konsonant* hard; *Licht* harsh, hard; *Klang, Ton, Aussprache, Akzent* harsh
c *(= rau) Spiel, Gegner* rough; *(fig) Getränke* strong; *Droge* hard; *Porno* hard-core; *Kriminalfilm etc, Western* tough
d *(= widerstandsfähig, robust)* tough; **gelobt sei, was ~ macht** *(prov, usu iro)* treat 'em rough, make 'em tough! *(inf)*; **er ist ~ im Nehmen** he's tough
e *(= stabil, sicher) Währung, Devisen* stable; **in ~en Dollars** in hard dollars
f *(= streng, gnadenlos, kompromisslos) Mensch, Kampf* hard; *Wort* strong, harsh; *Winter, Frost, Ver-*

tragsbedingung hard, severe; *Strafe, Urteil, Kritik* severe, harsh; *Maßnahmen, Gesetze, Politik, Kurs* tough; *Auseinandersetzung* violent; **der ~e Kern einer Vereinigung** the hard core of an organization; **er ist durch eine ~e Schule gegangen** *(fig)* he has been through a hard school; **~ bleiben** to stand *or* remain firm; **~ mit jdm sein** to be hard on sb, to be harsh with sb; **es fielen ~e Worte** hard *or* strong *or* harsh words were used; **es geht ~ auf ~** it's a tough fight, it's a real battle

g *(= schwer zu ertragen) Los, Schicksal, Tatsache* hard, cruel; *Verlust* cruel; *Wirklichkeit, Wahrheit* harsh; **es war sehr ~ für ihn, dass er ...** it was very hard for him to ...; **oh, das war ~!** *(inf: Witz etc)* oh, that was painful!; **das Härteste** *(sl: = Zumutung)* a real bummer *(inf)* or pisser *(Brit sl)*

h *(= mühevoll, anstrengend) Arbeit, Leben, Zeiten* hard, tough

i *(Phys) Strahlen* hard

j *(Comput) Trennung, Zeilenumbruch* hard

ADV *comp* **=er**, *superl* **am =esten** **a** *(= nicht weich)* hard; **er schläft gerne ~** he likes sleeping on a hard surface/bed; **~ gebrannt** *(Ziegel, Keramik)* hard-baked; **~ gefroren** frozen, frozen stiff *pred*, frozen solid *pred*; **der Boden ist ~ gefroren** the ground is frozen hard *or* solid; **~ gekocht** *or* **gesotten** *(Aus) (Ei)* hard-boiled; *Mensch* hard-baked *(inf)*, hard-boiled; **~ geworden** hard

b *(= scharf) kontrastiert* sharply; **~ klingen** *(Sprache)* to sound hard; *(Bemerkung)* to sound harsh; **er spricht manche Laute zu ~ aus** he pronounces some sounds too hard

c *(= heftig, rau)* roughly; *fallen, aufprallen, zuschlagen* hard; **er lässt die Kupplung immer so ~ kommen** he always lets the clutch out so roughly *or* violently; **~ bedrängt** hard-pressed; **~ bedrängt sein** to be put under pressure; **~ aneinandergeraten** *(= sich prügeln)* to come to blows, to have a (real) set-to *(inf)*; *(= sich streiten)* to get into a fierce argument, to have a (real) set-to *(inf)*; **~ einsteigen** *(Sport)* to go hard at it; **jdn ~ anfahren** to bite sb's head off *(inf)*; **jdm ~ zusetzen** to give sb a hard time; **etw trifft jdn ~** *(lit, fig)* sth hits sb hard; **~ diskutieren** to have a vigorous discussion; **~ spielen** *(Sport)* to play rough

d *(= streng)* severely, harshly; **~ durchgreifen** to take tough *or* rigorous action; **jdn ~ anfassen** to be hard on sb, to treat sb harshly; **man muss sie ~ anfassen** you have to keep them in line

e *(= mühevoll)* hard; **~ arbeiten** to work hard; **es kommt mich ~ an** *(geh)* I find it hard

f *(= nahe)* close *(an +dat* to); **das ist ~ an der Grenze der Legalität/des Zumutbaren** that's pushing legality/reasonableness to its (very) limit(s), that's on the very limits of legality/of what's reasonable; **das ist ~ an der Grenze zum Kriminellen/zum Kitsch** that's very close to being criminal/kitsch; **wir fuhren ~ am Abgrund vorbei** *(fig)* we were (very) close to disaster, we were on the (very) brink of disaster; **~ am Wind (segeln)** *(Naut)* (to sail) close to the wind; **~ auf ein Ziel zuhalten** *(Naut)* to head straight for a destination

Hart-: **Hart|bahn** F *(Sport)* hard track; **hart|be|drängt** [-bədrɛŋt] ADJ → **hart ADV c**; **Hart|be|ton** M (especially) hard concrete; **hart|blät|te|rig**, **hart|blätt|rig** ADJ *(Bot)* hard-leaved

Här|te ['hɛrtə] F **-, -n** **a** hardness; *(von Matratze)* firmness; *(von Aufprall, Ruck)* violence, hardness; *(= Härtegrad)* degree *or* grade (of hardness)

b *no pl (= Schärfe) (von Konturen, Kontrast, Formen)* sharpness; *(von Gesichtszügen)* hardness; *(von Licht, Klang, Akzent)* harshness

c *(= Rauheit: von Spiel, Gegner)* roughness *no pl*; **sie spielten mit größter ~** they played very rough

d *no pl (= Robustheit)* toughness

e *no pl (= Stabilität: von Währung, Devisen)* stability

f *no pl (= Strenge) (von Mensch, Kampf)* hardness; *(von Worten)* harshness; *(von Winter, Frost, Vertragsbedingungen)* hardness, severity; *(von Strafe, Urteil, Kritik)* severity; *(von Maßnahmen, Gesetz, Politik)* toughness; *(von Auseinandersetzung)* violence; **eine Auseinandersetzung in großer ~ führen** to have a violent argument; **mit großer ~ diskutieren** to have a very heated discussion

g *(= Belastung) (von Schicksal, Verlust)* cruelty; *(von Wahrheit)* harshness; **der Schicksalsschlag traf ihn in seiner ganzen ~** this blow of fate struck him with all its force *or* cruelty; **soziale ~n** social hardships; *(= Fälle)* cases of social hardship; **das ist die ~** *(sl: = Zumutung)* that's a bit much *or* a real killer *(inf)*

h *(Phys, von Strahlen)* degree of penetration

Här|te-: **Här|te|aus|gleich** M *(Admin)* compensation for (social) hardship; **Här|te|fall** M case of hardship; *(inf: = Mensch)* hardship case; **Här|te|fall|re|ge|lung** F hardship provision (ruling); **Här|te|fonds** M hardship fund; **Här|te|grad** M degree *or* grade of hardness; **Här|te|klau|sel** F hardship clause; **Här|te|mit|tel** NT *(Metal)* hardening agent

här|ten ['hɛrtn] **VT** to harden; *Stahl auch* to temper **VI** to harden **VR** *(Stoff)* to harden

Här|te-: **Här|te|ofen** M *(Metal)* tempering oven *or* furnace; **Här|te|pa|ra|graf**, **Här|te|pa|ra|graph** M paragraph dealing with cases of hardship

här|ter *comp von* **hart**

Här|ter ['hɛrtɐ] M **-s, -** *(Tech)* hardener, hardening agent

Här|te|ska|la F scale of hardness, Mohs scale

här|tes|te(r, s) *superl von* **hart**

Här|te-: **Här|te|stu|fe** F *(von Material, Wasser)* hardness grade; **Här|te|test** M endurance test; *(fig)* acid test; **Här|te|zu|stand** M hard state; **im ~ lässt sich das Material wie Metall bearbeiten** in the hard state *or* when it is hard this material can be worked like metal

Hart-: **Hart|fa|ser|plat|te** F hardboard, fiberboard *(US)*; **hart|ge|brannt** ADJ → **hart ADV a**; **hart|ge|fro|ren** ADJ → **hart ADV a**; **hart|ge|kocht** [-gəkɔxt] ADJ → **hart ADV a**; **Hart|geld** NT hard cash; **hart|ge|sot|ten** ADJ **a** *(fig)* hard-baked *(inf)*, hard-boiled **b** *(Aus)* → **hart ADV a**; **hart|ge|wor|den** ADJ → **hart ADV a**; **Hart|gum|mi** M OR NT hard rubber; **hart|her|zig** ADJ hard-hearted; **Hart|her|zig|keit** [-hɛrtsɪçkait] F **-**, *no pl* hard-heartedness; **Hart|holz** NT hardwood; **hart|hö|rig** ADJ **a** *(= nicht reagierend)* unresponsive **b** *(dated: = schwerhörig)* hard of hearing; **Hart|kä|se** M hard cheese; **hart+ko|chen** VT *sep* → **hart ADJ a**; **Hart|laub|ge|wächs** NT *(Bot)* sclerophyllous evergreen *(spec)*; **hart|lei|big** ['hartlaibɪç] ADJ *(Med old)* constipated; *(fig) (= stur)* unyielding, intransigent; *(= hartnäckig)* obdurate; **Hart|lei|big|keit** F **-**, *no pl (Med old)* constipation; *(fig) (= Sturheit)* intransigence; *(= Hartnäckigkeit)* obduracy; **hart+lö|ten** VTI *sep* to hard-solder; **Hart|me|tall** NT hard metal; **hart|nä|ckig** ['hartnɛkɪç] **ADJ** *(= stur) Mensch, Haltung* obstinate, stubborn; *(= ausdauernd) Widerstand, Gerücht* stubborn; *Lügner, Husten* persistent; *(= beharrlich)* dogged, persistent; *(= langwierig) Erkältung, Fleck* stubborn **ADV** *(= beharrlich)* persistently; *(= stur)* stubbornly; **das Gerücht hielt sich ~** the rumour *(Brit)* *or* rumor *(US)* persisted stubbornly; **Hart|nä|ckig|keit** F **-**, *no pl (= Sturheit)* obstinacy, stubbornness; *(= Beharrlichkeit)* doggedness; **ein Fleck von besonderer ~** a particularly stubborn *or* persistent stain; **Hart|pa|ckung** F hard pack; **Hart|pap|pe** F cardboard; **Hart|platz** M *(Sport)* hard sports area; *(für Ballspiele)* hard pitch; *(Tennis)* hard court; **Hart|scha|len|kof|fer** M hard-sided case; **hart|scha|lig** [-ʃa:lɪç] ADJ *Frucht* hard-shelled, testaceous *(spec)*; *Apfel, Traube* having a tough skin, tough-skinned; *Koffer* hard-sided; **Hart|spi|ri|tus** [-ʃpi:ritʊs] M methylated spirits in solid form

Har|tung ['hartʊŋ] M **-s, -e** *(obs)* January

Här|tung ['hɛrtʊŋ] F **-, -en** *(Tech)* hardening; *(von Stahl auch)* tempering

Hart-: **Hart|wa|re** F hardware *no pl*; **Hart|wei|zen** M durum wheat; **Hart|wei|zen|grieß** M semolina; **Hart|wurst** F salami-type sausage

Harz [ha:ɐts] NT **-es, -e** resin

Harz M **-es** *(Geog)* Harz Mountains *pl*

harz|ar|tig ADJ resin-like, resinous, resinoid

har|zen ['ha:ɐtsn] **VT** *Wein* to treat with resin, to resinate **VI** *(Baum, Holz)* to secrete *or* exude resin

Har|zer ['ha:ɐtsɐ] ADJ *(Geog)* Harz; **~ Roller** *(Zool)* roller canary; *(Cook)* (roll-shaped) Harz cheese; **~ Käse** *(Cook)* (roll-shaped) Harz cheese

Har|zer ['ha:ɐtsɐ] M **-s, -** *(Cook)* Harz cheese

Har|zer ['ha:ɐtsɐ] M **-s, -**, **Har|ze|rin** [-ərɪn] F **-, -nen** native *or* (= *Einwohner*) inhabitant of the Harz Mountains

harz|hal|tig ADJ *Holz* resinous, containing resin

har|zig ['ha:ɐtsɪç] ADJ **a** *Holz, Geruch, Geschmack, Wein* resinous, resiny **b** *(Sw fig: = zähflüssig)* slow-moving

Ha|sard [ha'zart] NT **-s**, *no pl* = **Hasardspiel**; **(mit etw) ~ spielen** *(fig geh)* to gamble (with sth)

Ha|sar|deur [hazar'dø:ɐ] M **-s, -e**, **Ha|sar|deu|se** [-'dø:zə] F **-, -n** *(geh)* gambler

Ha|sard|spiel [ha'zart-] NT game of chance; *(fig geh)* gamble; **glatte Fahrbahnen machen das Autofahren zum ~** slippery roads make driving hazardous

Hasch [haʃ] NT **-(s)**, *no pl (inf)* hash *(inf)*

Ha|schee [ha'ʃe:] NT **-s, -s** *(Cook)* hash

ha|schen ['haʃn] *(dated, geh)* **VT** to catch; **hasch mich, ich bin der Frühling** *(hum inf)* come and get me, boys! *(hum)* **VI** **nach etw ~** to make a grab at sth; **nach Beifall/Lob** *etc* **~** to fish *or* angle *(Brit)* for applause/praise *etc*

ha|schen VI *(inf)* to smoke (hash) *(inf)*

Ha|schen NT **-s**, *no pl* catch, tag

Häs|chen ['hɛ:sçən] NT **-s, -** **a** *dim von* **Hase** young hare, leveret **b** *(inf: = Kaninchen, Playboyhäschen)* bunny *(inf)* **c** *(= Kosename)* sweetheart, sweetie(-pie)

Ha|scher ['haʃɐ] M **-s, -** *(inf)*, **Ha|sche|rin** [-ərɪn] F **-, -nen** *(inf)* hash smoker

Hä|scher ['hɛʃɐ] M **-s, -** *(old, geh)* henchman

Ha|scherl ['haʃɐl] NT **-s, -(n)** *(Aus inf)* poor soul *or* thing *or* creature

ha|schie|ren [ha'ʃi:rən] *ptp* **haschiert** VT *(Cook) Fleisch* to mince *(Brit)*, to grind *(US)*

Ha|schisch ['haʃɪʃ] NT OR M **-(s)**, *no pl* hashish

Ha|schisch|rausch M state of euphoria produced by hashish; **im ~** under the effects of hashish

Hasch|mich ['haʃmɪç] M **-s**, *no pl (inf)* **einen ~ haben** to have a screw loose *(inf)*, to be off one's rocker *(inf)*

Ha|se ['ha:zə] M **-n, -n** hare; *(männlich auch)* buck; *(dial: = Kaninchen, Osterhase, in Märchen)* rabbit; **falscher ~** *(Cook)* meat loaf; **wissen/sehen, wie der ~ läuft** *(fig inf)* to know/see which way the wind blows; **alter ~** *(fig inf)* old hand; **da liegt der ~ im Pfeffer** *(inf)* that's the crux of the matter; **mein Name ist ~(, ich weiß von nichts)** I don't know anything about anything

Ha|sel ['ha:zl] F **-, -n** *(Bot)* hazel

Ha|sel-: **Ha|sel|huhn** NT hazel grouse; **Ha|sel|kätz|chen** NT *(Bot)* (hazel) catkin, lamb's tail *(inf)*; **Ha|sel|maus** F dormouse; **Ha|sel|nuss** F hazelnut, cobnut; **ha|sel|nuss|braun** ADJ hazel; **ha|sel|nuss|groß** ADJ hazelnut-sized, the size of a hazelnut *pred*; **Ha|sel|ru|te** F hazel rod *or* switch; **Ha|sel|strauch** M hazel-bush

Ha|sen-: **Ha|sen|bra|ten** M roast hare; **Ha|sen|fuß** M **a** hare's foot **b** *(dated inf: = Feigling)* milksop *(dated)*; **ha|sen|fü|ßig** ADJ *(dated inf: = feige)* chicken-hearted *(inf)*, lily-livered *(inf)*; **Ha|sen|herz** NT **a** hare's heart **b** *(dated inf: = Feigling)* milksop *(dated)*; **Ha|sen|jagd** F hare-hunt; **auf (die) ~ gehen** to go hunting hares, to go on a hare-hunt; **Ha|sen|klein** [-klain] NT **-s**, *no pl (Cook)* jointed hare; **Ha|sen|pa|nier** NT **das ~ ergreifen** *(dated inf)* to turn tail (and run); **Ha|sen|pfef|fer** M *(Cook)* ≈ jugged hare; **ha|sen|rein** ADJ *(Hunt) Hund* trained to chase hares only on command; **jd/etw ist nicht (ganz) ~** *(inf)* sb/sth is not (quite) above board, there's something fishy about sb/sth *(inf)*; **das ist alles ~** *(inf)* everything's above board; **Ha|sen|rü|cken** M *(Cook)* saddle of hare; **Ha|sen|schar|te** F *(Med)* hare-lip

Hash|tag ['hɛʃtɛk] M *(Internet)* hashtag

Hä|sin ['hɛːzɪn] F **-, -nen** doe, female hare

Has|pel ['haspl] F **-, -n a** *(= Förderwinde)* windlass **b** *(= Garnhaspel)* reel

has|peln ['haspln] VT **a** *(inf: = hastig sprechen)* to splutter, to sputter; *Gebete, Entschuldigung* to sp(l)utter out **b** *(= wickeln)* to wind up, to reel up; *(= abwickeln)* to unwind, to reel off VI *(inf)* to splutter, to sputter

Hass [has] M **-es**, *no pl* **a** hatred, hate *(auf +acc, gegen* of); **Liebe und ~** love and hate *or* hatred; **sich** *(dat)* **jds ~ zuziehen, jds ~ auf sich** *(acc)* **ziehen** to incur sb's hatred **b** *(inf: = Wut, Ärger)* **wenn ich so etwas sehe, könnt ich einen ~ kriegen** *(inf)* when I see something like that I could get really angry; **einen ~ (auf jdn) schieben** *(inf) or* **haben** *(inf)* to be really sore (with sb) *(inf)*

Hass- : **Hass|aus|bruch** M burst of hatred; **Hass|brief** N hate letter; **~e** *pl (als Sammelbegriff)* hatemail *no pl*

has|sen ['hasn] ✪ 34.3 VT to hate, to detest, to loathe; **etw ~ wie die Pest** *(inf)* to detest sth VI to hate

has|sens|wert ADJ hateful, odious, detestable

Hass-: **hass|er|füllt** [-lɛɐfʏlt] ADJ, ADV full of hate *or* hatred; **Hass|ge|fühl** NT feeling of hatred

häss|lich ['hɛslɪç] ADJ **a** *(= scheußlich)* ugly; **~ wie die Nacht** *or* **die Sünde** (as) ugly as sin **b** *(= gemein)* nasty, mean; **das war ~ von ihm** that was nasty *or* mean of him **c** *(= unerfreulich)* nasty; *Vorfall, Streit* nasty, ugly ADV **a** *(= gemein)* **sich ~ benehmen** to be mean *or* nasty; **~ über jdn sprechen** to say nasty *or* mean things about sb **b** *(= nicht schön)* hideously; **~ zugerichtet sein** to be in a hideous state *or* condition; **~ grün/braun/gelb** a hideous green/brown/yellow

Häss|lich|keit F **-, -en a** *no pl (= Scheußlichkeit)* ugliness **b** *(= Gemeinheit, Unfreundlichkeit)* nastiness **c** *(Bemerkung)* nasty *or* mean remark

Hass-: **Hass|lie|be** F love-hate relationship *(für* with); **~ für jdn empfinden** to have a love-hate relationship with sb; **Hass|ob|jekt** NT (object of) hate; **sein bevorzugtes ~** his pet hate; **Hass|pre|di|ger** M, **Hass|pre|di|ge|rin** F preacher of hatred; **Hass|ti|ra|de** F tirade of hatred; **hass|ver|zerrt** [-fɛɐtsɛrt] ADJ *Gesicht* twisted (up) with hatred

hast [hast] *2. pers sing pres von* **haben**

Hast [hast] F **-,** *no pl* haste; **voller ~** in great haste, in a great hurry *or* rush; **ohne ~** without haste, without hurrying *or* rushing; **mit fliegender/rasender ~** in a tearing/frantic hurry; **mit einer solchen ~** in such a hurry *or* rush, in such haste; **nur keine (jüdische) ~!** not so fast!, hold your horses! *(inf)*

has|te ['hastə] *(inf) contr von* **hast du; (was) ~ was kannste** as quick *or* fast as possible; **~ was, biste was** *(prov)* money brings status

has|ten ['hastn] VI *aux sein (geh)* to hasten *(form)*, to hurry

has|tig ['hastɪç] ADJ hasty; *Essen auch, Worte* hurried, rushed; **sein ~es Rauchen** his hasty way of smoking ADV hastily; **etw ~ tun** to do sth hastily; **nicht so ~!** not so fast!; **er schlang sein Essen ~ hinunter** he gobbled down his food

Has|tig|keit F **-,** *no pl* hurriedness; **sie isst/schwimmt** *etc* **mit einer solchen ~** she eats/swims *etc* in such a hasty manner

hat [hat] *3. pers sing pres von* **haben**

Ha|tha-Yo|ga ['haːta-] NT hatha yoga

Hät|sche|lei [hɛtʃə'lai] F **-, -en** *(pej)* pampering, mollycoddling

Hät|schel|kind NT *(pej) (= Kind)* pampered child; *(fig: = Liebling)* blue-eyed boy/girl *(Brit inf)*, golden-haired boy/girl *(US inf)*, darling

hät|scheln ['hɛtʃln] VT *(= zu weich behandeln)* to pamper, to mollycoddle; *(= bevorzugen)* to pamper, to indulge; *Industrie, Firma* to give preferential treatment to

hat|schen ['haːtʃn] VI *aux sein (Aus, S Ger: inf) (= schlendern)* to amble along; *(= mühsam gehen)* to trudge along; *(= hinken)* to hobble; **durch die Berge ~** to trudge through the mountains

hat|schert ['haːtʃɐt] ADJ *(Aus inf)* hobbling; **er geht ~** he hobbles (along)

hat|schi [ha'tʃiː, 'hatʃi] INTERJ atishoo *(Brit)*, achoo; **~ machen** *(baby-talk)* to sneeze

hat|te *pret von* **haben**

Hat|trick ['hɛtrɪk] M *(Sport)* hat-trick; *(fig)* masterstroke

Hatz [hats] F **-, -en a** *(Hunt, fig)* hunt **b** *(fig: esp S Ger, Aus)* rush

Hau [hau] M **-s, -e** *(inf)* bash *(inf)*, clout *(inf)*; **einen ~ haben** to be thick *(inf)*

Häub|chen ['hɔypçən] NT **-s, -** *dim von* **Haube**

Hau|be ['haubə] F **-, -n a** bonnet; *(Aus, S Ger: = Mütze)* (woollen) cap; *(von Krankenschwester etc)* cap; **jdn unter die ~ bringen** *(hum)* to marry sb off; **unter der ~ sein** *(hum)* to be married; **unter die ~ kommen** *(hum)* to get married **b** *(bei Vögeln)* crest **c** *(allgemein: = Bedeckung)* cover; *(= Trockenhaube)* (hair) dryer, drying hood *(US)*; *(für Kaffee-, Teekanne)* cosy *(Brit)*, cozy *(US)*; *(= Motorhaube)* bonnet, hood *(US)*; **der hat einiges unter der ~** *(inf: Wagen)* it's got quite some engine *(inf)*

Hau|ben-: **Hau|ben|ler|che** F crested lark; **Hau|ben|mei|se** F crested tit; **Hau|ben|tau|cher** M *(Zool)* great crested grebe

Hau|bit|ze [hau'bɪtsə] F **-, -n** howitzer

Hauch [haux] M **-(e)s, -e a** *(geh: = Atem)* breath; *(= Luftzug)* breath of air, breeze **b** *(= Duft)* smell; *(von Parfüm)* smell, waft; **ein ~ von Frühling** *(poet)* a breath of spring **c** *(= Flair)* aura, air; **ihr Haus hat den ~ des Exotischen** their house has an exotic air (about it) *or* an aura of exoticism **d** *(= Andeutung, Anflug)* hint, touch; *(von Lächeln)* hint, ghost

hauch|dünn ADJ extremely thin; *Scheiben, Schokoladentäfelchen* wafer-thin; *Strümpfe, Strumpfhose* sheer; *(fig) Mehrheit* extremely narrow; *Sieg* extremely close ADV **das Make-up ~ auftragen** to apply a thin layer of foundation; **etw ~ schneiden** to cut sth paper-thin *or* wafer-thin

hau|chen ['hauxn] VI to breathe; **gegen/auf etw** *(acc)* **~** to breathe on sth VT *(lit, fig)* to breathe; **jdn einen Kuss auf die Wange ~** *(liter)* to brush sb's cheek with one's lips; **das Jawort ~** *(liter)* to breathe "I will"; **jdm etw** *(acc)* **ins Ohr ~** *(liter)* to whisper sth in sb's ear; **er hauchte mir den Zigarettenrauch ins Gesicht** he blew cigarette smoke in(to) my face

Hauch-: **hauch|fein** ADJ extremely fine; **Hauch|laut** M *(Phon)* aspirate; **hauch|zart** ADJ very delicate; *Schokoladentäfelchen* wafer-thin

Hau|de|gen M *(fig)* old campaigner, (old) war-horse

Haue ['hauə] F **-, -n a** *(S Ger, Sw, Aus) (= Pickel)* pickaxe *(Brit)*, pickax *(US)*, pick; *(= Gartenhacke)* hoe **b** *no pl (inf: = Prügel)* (good) hiding *(inf) or* spanking; **~ kriegen** to get a good hiding *(inf) or* spanking

hau|en ['hauən] *pret* **haute** ['hautə], *ptp* **gehauen** *or (dial)* **gehaut** [gə'hauən, gə'haut] VT **a** *pret auch* **hieb** [hiːp] *(inf: = schlagen)* to hit, to clout *(inf)*, to clobber *(inf)*; **er haute den Stein in zwei Teile** he smashed the stone in two; **er haute ihr das Heft um die Ohren** he hit *or* clouted *(inf) or* clobbered *(inf)* her round *(Brit) or* around the head with the exercise book

b *(inf: = verprügeln)* to hit, to belt *(inf)*, to thump *(inf)*; **hau(t) ihn!** let him have it! *(inf)*, belt *or* thump him (one) *(inf)*

c *(= meißeln) Statue, Figur* to carve; *Stufen* to cut, to hew *(form)*; *Loch* to cut, to knock

d *pret* **hieb** [hiːp] *(geh: = mit Waffe schlagen)* to make a thrust at sb; **jdn aus dem Sattel/vom Pferd ~** to knock sb out of the saddle/from his horse

e *(inf* [hiːp]*: = stoßen) jdn, Gegenstand* to shove *(inf)*; *Körperteil* to bang, to knock *(an +acc* on, against); **das haut einen vom Stuhl** *or* **aus den Latschen** *or* **aus dem Anzug** it really knocks you sideways *(inf)*

f *(inf) (= werfen)* to chuck *(inf)*, to fling; *Farbe* to slap *(inf) (auf +acc* on); **er hat ihm eine 6 ins Zeugnis gehauen** he slammed a 6 on his report *(Brit) or* report card *(US) (inf)*

g *(dial) (= fällen) Baum* to chop (down), to hew (down); *(= zerhacken) Holz, Fleisch* to chop (up)

h *(Min) Erz* to cut; *Kohle* to break

VI **a** *pret auch* **hieb** *(inf: = schlagen)* to hit; **jdm ins Gesicht ~** to hit *or* clout *(inf) or* clobber *(inf)* [hiːp] sb in the face; **jdm auf die Schulter ~** to clap *or* slap sb on the shoulder; **hau doch nicht so (auf die Tasten)** don't thump like that; **er haute und haute** he banged *or* thumped away

b *(inf: = prügeln)* **nicht ~, Papi!** don't hit *or* thump *(inf)* me, daddy!; **er haut immer gleich** he's quick to lash out

c *pret* **hieb** *(geh: mit Waffe)* to lash out; **er hieb mit dem Degen (auf seinen Gegner)** he made a thrust (at his opponent) with his dagger; **es geht auf Hauen und Stechen** *(fig)* [hiːp] there's a tough battle

d *aux sein (inf: = stoßen)* to bang, to hit; **er ist mit dem Fuß gegen einen spitzen Stein gehauen** he banged *or* hit his foot against a sharp stone

VR *(inf)* **a** *(= sich prügeln)* to scrap, to fight; **sich mit jdm ~** to scrap *or* fight with sb

b *(= sich setzen, legen)* to fling oneself

Hau|er¹ ['hauɐ] M **-s, -** *(Zool)* tusk; *(hum: = großer Zahn)* fang

Hau|er² ['hauɐ] M **-s, -**, **Hau|e|rin** [-ərɪn] F **-, -nen a** *(Min)* face worker *(Brit)*, miner **b** *(Aus: = Winzer)* wine-grower

Häu|er ['hɔyɐ] M **-s, -**, **Häu|e|rin** [-ərɪn] F **-, -nen** *(Aus Min)* face worker *(Brit)*, miner

Hau|e|rei [hauə'rai] F **-, -en** *(inf)* scrap, fight

Häuf|chen ['hɔyfçən] NT **-s, -** *dim von* **Haufen** small heap *or* pile; **ein ~ Unglück** a picture of misery → **Elend**

Hau|fe ['haufə] M **-ns, -n** *(rare)* = **Haufen**

häu|feln ['hɔyfln] VT **a** *Kartoffeln, Spargel* to hill up **b** *(= Haufen machen aus)* to heap *or* pile up

Hau|fen ['haufn] M **-s, - a** heap, pile; **jdn/ein Tier über den ~ rennen/fahren** *etc (inf)* to knock *or* run sb/an animal down, to run over sb/an animal; **jdn/ein Tier über den ~ schießen** *(inf) or* **knallen** *(inf)* to shoot sb/an animal down; **etw** *(acc)* **über den ~ werfen** *(inf) or* **schmeißen** *(inf) (= verwerfen)* to throw *or* chuck *(inf)* sth out; *(= durchkreuzen)* to mess sth up *(inf)*; **der Hund hat da einen ~ gemacht** the dog has made a mess there *(inf)*; **so viele Dummköpfe/so viel Idiotie/so viel Geld habe ich noch nie auf einem ~ gesehen** *(inf)* I've never seen so many fools/so much idiocy/so much money in one place before

b *(inf: = große Menge)* load *(inf)*, heap *(inf)*; **ein ~ Arbeit/Geld/Bücher** a load *or* heap of work/money/books *(all inf)*, piles *or* loads *or* heaps of work/money/books *(all inf)*; **ein ~ Unsinn** a load of (old) rubbish *(inf)*, a load of nonsense *(inf)*; **ein ~ Zeit** loads *or* heaps of time *(both inf)*; **ich hab noch einen ~ zu tun** I still have loads *or* piles *or* heaps *or* a load to do

(all inf); **in ~** by the ton *(inf)*; **er hat einen ganzen ~ Freunde** he has a whole load of friends *(inf)*, he has loads *or* heaps of friends *(both inf)*
c *(= Schar)* crowd; *(von Vögeln)* flock; *(= Sternenhaufen)* cluster of stars; **ein ~ Schaulustige(r)** a crowd of onlookers; **dichte ~ von Reisenden** dense crowds of travellers *(Brit) or* travelers *(US)*; **dem ~ folgen** *(pej)* to follow the crowd; **der große ~** *(pej)* the common herd, the masses *pl*
d *(= Gruppe, Gemeinschaft)* crowd *(inf)*, bunch *(inf)*; *(Mil)* troop

häu|fen [ˈhɔyfn] VT to pile up, to heap up; *(= sammeln)* to accumulate; **Bücher auf den Tisch ~** to pile books onto the table; **Lob auf jdn ~** *(fig)* to heap praise(s) (up)on sb → *auch* **gehäuft** VR *(lit, fig: = sich ansammeln)* to mount up; *(= zahlreicher werden: Unfälle, Fehler, Fachausdrücke etc)* to occur increasingly often; **das kann schon mal vorkommen, es darf sich nur nicht ~** these things happen, just as long as they don't happen too often

Hau|fen-: **Hau|fen|dorf** NT scattered village; **hau|fen|wei|se** ADV **a** *(= in Haufen)* in heaps *or* piles **b** *(inf: = in großer Zahl, Menge)* piles *or* heaps *or* loads of *(all inf)*; **etw ~ haben** to have piles *or* heaps *or* loads of sth *(all inf)*; **Hau|fen|wol|ke** F cumulus (cloud)

häu|fig [ˈhɔyfɪç] ADJ frequent; *(= weitverbreitet auch)* common, widespread; **seine Anfälle werden ~er** his attacks are becoming more frequent ADV often, frequently

Häu|fig|keit F -, -en frequency; *(= räumliche Verbreitung)* commonness

Häu|fig|keits- *in cpds* frequency-; **Häu|fig|keits|grad** M frequency rank; **Häu|fig|keits|wör|ter|buch** NT frequency dictionary; **Häu|fig|keits|zahl** F, **Häu|fig|keits|zif|fer** F frequency

Häu|fung [ˈhɔyfʊŋ] F -, -en **a** *(fig: = das Anhäufen)* accumulation, amassment **b** *(= das Sichhäufen)* increasing number; **in ähnlicher ~** in similar numbers *pl*

Haupt [haupt] NT -(e)s, **Häupter** [ˈhɔyptɐ] **a** *(geh: = Kopf)* head; **entblößten ~es** bareheaded; **gesenkten/erhobenen ~es** with one's head bowed/raised; **zu jds Häupten** at sb's head; **jdn aufs ~ schlagen** *(fig: = besiegen)* to vanquish sb;; **eine Reform an ~ und Gliedern** a total *or* wide-reaching reform **b** *(= zentrale Figur)* head **c** *(poet: von Berg)* peak

Haupt- *in cpds* main, principal, chief; **Haupt|ab|neh|mer(in)** M(F) *(Comm)* biggest *or* main buyer; **Haupt|ach|se** F main *or* principal axis; *(von Fahrzeug)* main axle; **Haupt|ak|teur(in)** M(F) *(lit, fig)* leading light; *(pej)* kingpin; **Haupt|ak|ti|on** F → **Haupt- und Staatsaktion**; **Haupt|ak|ti|o|när(in)** M(F) principal *or* main shareholder; **Haupt|ak|zent** M **a** *(Ling)* main *or* primary accent *or* stress **b** *(fig)* main emphasis; **auf etw** *(acc)* **den ~ legen** to put *or* place the main emphasis on sth; **Haupt|al|tar** M high altar; **haupt|amt|lich** ADJ full-time; **~e Tätigkeit** full-time office ADV (on a) full-time (basis); **~ tätig sein** to work full-time; **Haupt|an|ge|klag|te(r)** MF *decl as adj* main *or* principal defendant; **Haupt|an|schluss** M *(Telec)* main extension; **nur einen ~ haben** to have a phone without extensions; **Haupt|an|teil** M main *or* principal part *or* share; **Haupt|ar|beit** F main (part of the) work; **Haupt|at|trak|ti|on** F main *or* chief attraction; *(bei Veranstaltung etc)* big draw *(inf)*; **Haupt|aus|gang** M main exit; **Haupt|bahn|hof** M main *or* central station; **Haupt|be|las|tungs|zeu|ge** M, **Haupt|be|las|tungs|zeu|gin** F main *or* principal witness for the prosecution; **Haupt|be|ruf** M chief *or* main occupation *or* profession; **er ist Lehrer im ~** his main *or* chief occupation *or* profession is that of teacher; **haupt|be|ruf|lich** ADJ *Lehrer, Gärtner etc* full-time; **~e Tätigkeit** main *or* chief occupation ADV full-time; **~ tätig sein** to be employed full-time, to be in full-time employment; **er ist ~ bei dieser Firma tätig** *(= voll angestellt)* he is employed full-time by this firm; *(im Gegensatz zu Nebenerwerb)* his main employment is at this firm; **Haupt|be|schäf|ti|gung** F **a** main *or* chief occupation *or* pursuit **b** *(= Hauptberuf)* main *or* chief occupation *or* job; **Haupt|be|stand|teil** M main constituent; *(Tech)* main component; **Haupt|be|trieb** M **a** *(= Zentralbetrieb)* headquarters *sing or pl* **b** *(= geschäftigste Zeit)* peak period; *(= Hauptverkehrszeit)* rush hour; **Haupt|buch** NT *(Comm)* ledger; **Haupt|bü|ro** NT head office; **Haupt|dar|stel|ler** M principal actor, leading man; **Haupt|dar|stel|le|rin** F principal actress, leading lady; **Haupt|da|ten** PL main facts *pl*; **Haupt|deck** NT main deck; **Haupt|do|ku|ment** NT *(Comput)* main document; **Haupt|ein|gang** M main entrance; **Haupt|ein|kaufs|zeit** F main shopping hours *pl*; **Haupt|ein|nah|me|quel|le** F main *or* chief source of income; **Haupt|ein|wand** M main *or* chief *or* principal objection (*gegen* to)

Häup|tel [ˈhɔyptl] NT -s, - *(Aus)* head (of lettuce etc)

Häup|tel|sa|lat M *(Aus)* lettuce

Haupt-: **Haupt|ent|las|tungs|zeu|ge** M, **Haupt|ent|las|tungs|zeu|gin** F main *or* principal witness for the defence *(Brit) or* defense *(US)*; **Haupt|er|be** M principal heir; **Haupt|er|be** NT principal inheritance; **Haupt|er|bin** F principal heir(ess); **Haupt|er|eig|nis** NT main *or* principal event

Haup|tes|län|ge F **jdn um ~ überragen** *(lit, fig)* to be head and shoulders above sb

Haupt-: **Haupt|fach** NT *(Sch, Univ)* main *or* principal subject, major *(US)*; **etw im ~ studieren** to study sth as one's main *or* principal subject, to major in sth *(US)*; **Haupt|feh|ler** M main *or* chief *or* principal fault; **Haupt|feind(in)** M(F) main *or* chief enemy; **Haupt|feld** [ˈhauptfelt] NT *(bei Rennen)* (main) pack; **Haupt|feld** [ˈhauptfelt] M -s, -s *(sl)*, **Haupt|feld|we|bel(in)** M(F) (company) sergeant major; **Haupt|fi|gur** F *(Liter)* central *or* main *or* principal character *or* figure; *(fig)* leading *or* central figure; **Haupt|film** M main film; **Haupt|for|de|rung** F main *or* chief *or* principal demand; **Haupt|fra|ge** F main *or* principal question *or* issue; **Haupt|gang** M *pl* **-gänge** **a** *(Archit etc)* main corridor; *(in Kirche, Theater, Kino)* central aisle **b** *(Cook)* main course; **Haupt|ge|bäu|de** NT main building; **Haupt|ge|dan|ke** M main idea; **Haupt|ge|frei|te(r)** MF *decl as adj* ≈ lance corporal *(Brit)*, ≈ private first class *(US)*; **Haupt|ge|gen|stand** M **a** main *or* chief topic, main subject **b** *(Aus Sch)* = **Hauptfach**; **Haupt|ge|richt** NT main course

Haupt|ge|schäft NT **a** *(= Zentrale)* head office, headquarters *sing or pl* **b** *(= Hauptverdienst)* main business, major part of one's business

Haupt|ge|schäfts-: **Haupt|ge|schäfts|stel|le** F head office, headquarters *sing or pl*; **Haupt|ge|schäfts|stra|ße** F main shopping street; **Haupt|ge|schäfts|zeit** F peak (shopping) period *or* hours *pl*

Haupt-: **Haupt|ge|sichts|punkt** M main *or* major consideration; **Haupt|ge|sprächs|the|ma** NT main topic of conversation, conversation topic number one; **Haupt|ge|wicht** NT *(lit)* major part of the weight, bulk of the weight; *(fig)* main emphasis; **Haupt|ge|winn** M first prize; **Haupt|grund** M main *or* principal *or* chief reason; **Haupt|haar** NT *(geh)* hair (of the/one's head); **Haupt|hahn** M mains cock *or* tap *(Brit)*; **Haupt|hand|lung** F *(Liter etc)* main plot; **Haupt|in|te|res|se** NT main *or* chief interest; **Haupt|kampf|li|nie** F main front; **Haupt|kenn|zei|chen** NT main feature, chief *or* principal characteristic; **Haupt|klä|ger(in)** M(F) principal plaintiff; **Haupt|last** F main load, major part of the load; *(fig)* main *or* major burden; **Haupt|leid|tra|gen|de(r)** MF *decl as adj* main victim; **die ~n** *pl* the ones to suffer most, the ones who suffer/suffered *etc* most; **Haupt|lei|tung** F mains *pl*; **Haupt|leu|te** *pl von* **Hauptmann a**; **Haupt|lie|fe|rant(in)** M(F) main *or* principal *or* chief supplier

Häupt|ling [ˈhɔyptlɪŋ] M -s, -e chief(tain); *(esp von Dorf)* headman; *(fig, inf: = Boss)* chief *(inf)*

häupt|lings [ˈhɔyptlɪŋs] ADV *(old, geh)* = **kopfüber**

Haupt-: **Haupt|macht** F *(Mil)* bulk *or* main body of its/the forces; **Haupt|mahl|zeit** F main meal; **Haupt|man|gel** M main deficiency, main *or* principal defect; **Haupt|mann** M *pl* **-leute** **a** *(Mil)* captain **b** *(Hist: = Führer)* leader; **Haupt|mas|se** F bulk, main body; **Haupt|me|nü** NT *(Comput)* main menu; **Haupt|merk|mal** NT main feature, chief *or* principal characteristic; **Haupt|mie|ter(in)** M(F) main tenant; **Haupt|mo|tiv** NT **a** *(= Beweggrund)* primary *or* main motive **b** *(Art, Liter, Mus)* main *or* principal motif; **Haupt|nah|rung** F staple *or* principal food, staple diet; **Haupt|nah|rungs|mit|tel** NT staple *or* principal food; **Haupt|nen|ner** M *(Math, fig)* common denominator; **Haupt|nie|der|las|sung** F head office, headquarters *sing or pl*; **Haupt|ord|ner** M *(Comput)* top-level folder; **Haupt|per|son** F *(lit, fig)* central figure; **Haupt|pla|ti|ne** F *(Comput)* motherboard; **Haupt|por|tal** NT main portal *or* doorway; **Haupt|post** F *(inf)*, **Haupt|post|amt** NT main post office; **Haupt|pro|be** F final rehearsal; *(= Kostümprobe)* dress rehearsal; **Haupt|prob|lem** NT main *or* chief *or* principal problem; **Haupt|pro|dukt** NT main product; *(esp im Gegensatz zu Nebenprodukt)* primary product; **Haupt|pro|zes|sor** M *(Comput)* main processor; **Haupt|quar|tier** NT *(Mil, fig)* headquarters *sing or pl*; **Haupt|quel|le** F *(lit, fig)* main *or* primary source; **Haupt|rech|ner** M *(Comput)* mainframe (computer); **Haupt|rech|nungs|art** F *(Math)* basic arithmetical operation; **Haupt|red|ner(in)** M(F) main *or* principal speaker; **Haupt|re|fe|rent(in)** M(F) main *or* principal speaker; **Haupt|rei|se|zeit** F peak travelling *(Brit) or* traveling *(US)* time(s *pl*); **Haupt|rohr** NT main pipe; *(von Gas-/Wasserleitung)* main, mains pipe; **Haupt|rol|le** F *(Film, Theat)* leading *or* main role *or* part, lead; **die ~ spielen** *(fig)* to be all-important; *(= wichtigste Person sein)* to play the main role *or* part; **Haupt|run|de** F *(Sport)* main round; **Haupt|sa|che** F main thing; *(in Brief, Rede etc)* main point; **in der ~** in the main, mainly; **~, es klappt/du bist glücklich** the main thing is that it comes off/you're happy; **haupt|säch|lich** ADV mainly, chiefly, principally ADJ main, chief, principal; **Haupt|sai|son** F peak *or* high season; **~ haben** to have its/their peak season; **Haupt|satz** M **a** *(Gram) (übergeordnet)* main clause; *(alleinstehend)* sentence **b** *(Mus)* first *or* main subject **c** *(Philos)* main proposition; **Haupt|schal|ter** M *(Elec)* main *or* master switch; **Haupt|schiff** NT *(Archit)* nave; **Haupt|schlag|ader** F aorta; **Haupt|schlüs|sel** M master key; **Haupt|schul|ab|schluss** M **den ~ haben** ≈ to have completed secondary school *or* junior high (school) *(US)*; **Haupt|schuld** F main blame, principal fault *(esp Jur)*; **Haupt|schul|di|ge(r)** MF *decl as adj* person mainly to blame *or* at fault, main offender *(esp Jur)*; **er ist der ~** he is mainly to blame *or* at fault, he is the main offender *(esp Jur)*; **Haupt|schu|le** F ≈ secondary school, ≈ junior high (school) *(US)*; **Haupt|schü|ler(in)** M(F) ≈ secondary school *or* junior high (school) *(US)* pupil; **Haupt|schul|leh|rer(in)** M(F) ≈ secondary school *or* junior high (school) *(US)* teacher

HAUPTSCHULE

A **Hauptschule** caters for the last five years of the compulsory nine years at school in Germany. Students can then stay on for another year and, if their marks are good enough, obtain a **qualifizierter Hauptschulabschluss**, known colloquially as a **Quali**, which gives them a better chance in the job market and also entitles them to attend a **Fachoberschule**.

In Austria a **Hauptschule** covers school years five to eight and also offers opportunities for young people who wish to go on to higher education. In Switzerland compulsory schooling is provided by a **Volksschule**. → ORIENTIERUNGSSTUFE

Haupt-: **Haupt|schwie|rig|keit** F main or chief or principal difficulty; **Haupt|se|gel** NT mainsail; **Haupt|se|mi|nar** NT *(Univ)* seminar for advanced students; **Haupt|sen|de|zeit** F *(TV)* peak viewing hours *pl*, prime time; **Haupt|si|che|rung** F *(Elec)* main fuse; **Haupt|sitz** M head office, headquarters *sing or pl*; **seinen ~ in X haben** to be based in X; **Haupt|sor|ge** F main or chief worry; **Haupt|spei|cher** M *(Comput)* random access memory, RAM, main memory; **Haupt|stadt** F capital (city); **Haupt|städ|ter(in)** M(F) citizen of the capital, metropolitan; **haupt|städ|tisch** ADJ metropolitan, of the capital (city); **Haupt|stoß|rich|tung** F *(Mil, fig)* main object of one's/the attack (*gegen* on); **Haupt|stra|ße** F *(= Durchgangsstraße)* main or major road; *(im Stadtzentrum etc)* main street; **Haupt|stre|cke** F *(Rail)* main line; *(= Straße)* main or primary *(Admin)* route; **Haupt|streit|punkt** M *(fig)* main issue or point of contention; **Haupt|strö|mung** F *(lit, fig)* main current; **Haupt|stu|di|um** NT *(Univ)* main course (of studies); **Haupt|stüt|ze** F *(fig)* mainstay, main support or prop; **Haupt|sün|de** F *(Rel)* cardinal sin; **Haupt|tä|ter(in)** M(F) main or chief or principal culprit; **Haupt|tä|tig|keit** F main or principal or chief activity; *(beruflich)* main occupation; **Haupt|teil** M main part; *(= größter Teil auch)* major part; **Haupt|the|ma** NT main or principal topic; *(Mus, Liter)* main or principal theme; **Haupt|ton** M *pl* **-töne** *(Ling)* main or primary stress; *(Mus)* principal note; **Haupt|tref|fer** M top prize, jackpot *(inf)*; **den ~ machen** *(inf)* to win the top prize, to hit the jackpot *(inf)*; **Haupt|trep|pe** F main staircase or stairs *pl*; **Haupt|tri|bü|ne** F main stand; *(Sport auch)* grandstand; **Haupt|tu|gend** F cardinal virtue; **Haupt- und Staats|ak|ti|on** F **aus etw eine ~ machen** to make a great issue of sth, to make a song and dance about sth *(inf)*, to make a Federal case out of sth *(US inf)*; **Haupt|un|ter|schied** M main or principal difference; **Haupt|ur|sa|che** F main or chief or principal cause; **Haupt|ver|ant|wort|li|che(r)** MF *decl as adj* person mainly or chiefly responsible; **Haupt|ver|ant|wor|tung** F main responsibility; **Haupt|ver|die|ner(in)** M(F) main or principal earner; **Haupt|ver|dienst** M main income; **Haupt|ver|dienst** NT chief merit; **Haupt|ver|fah|ren** NT *(Jur)* main proceedings *pl*; **Haupt|ver|hand|lung** F *(Jur)* main hearing

Haupt|ver|kehr M peak(-hour) traffic; *(= Verkehrsteilnehmer)* main traffic, bulk of the traffic

Haupt|ver|kehrs-: **Haupt|ver|kehrs|ader** F main highway *(US)*, arterial route; **Haupt|ver|kehrs|stra|ße** F *(in Stadt)* main street; *(= Durchgangsstraße)* main thoroughfare; *(zwischen Städten)* main highway, trunk road *(Brit)*; **Haupt|ver|kehrs|zeit** F peak traffic times *pl*; *(in Stadt, bei Pendlern auch)* rush hour

Haupt-: **Haupt|ver|le|sen** NT **-s, -** *(Sw Mil)* roll call; **Haupt|ver|samm|lung** F general meeting; **Haupt|ver|wal|tung** F head office, headquarters *sing or pl*; **Haupt|ver|zeich|nis** NT *(Comput)* root directory; **Haupt|wa|che** F main police station; **Haupt|wä|sche** F, **Haupt|wasch|gang** M main wash; **Haupt|werk** NT **a** *(Art etc)* main or principal work **b** *(= Fabrik)* main factory or works *sing or pl*; **Haupt|wohn|sitz** M main place of residence, main domicile *(form)*; **Haupt|wort** NT *pl* **-wörter** *(Gram)* noun; **haupt|wört|lich** ADJ *(Gram)* nominal; **Haupt|zeit** F *(= Hauptsaison)* peak times *pl*; *(in Bezug auf Obst etc)* main season; **Haupt|zeu|ge** M, **Haupt|zeu|gin** F principal or main or chief witness; **Haupt|ziel** NT main or principal aim or goal; **Haupt|zoll|amt** NT main customs office; **Haupt|zug** M **a** *(Rail)* scheduled train **b** *usu pl (= Charakteristikum)* main or principal feature, chief characteristic; **Haupt|zweck** M main or chief purpose or object

hau ruck [ˈhau ˈrʊk] INTERJ heave-ho

Hau|ruck [hauˈrʊk] NT **-s, -s** heave

Hau|ruck|ver|fah|ren NT **etw im ~ tun** to do sth in a great hurry

Haus [haus] -es, Häuser [ˈhɔyzɐ]

SUBSTANTIV (NT)

a [= Gebäude] house; **er war nicht im Haus, sondern im Garten** he wasn't indoors or in the house but in the garden; **Tomaten kann man im Haus ziehen** tomatoes can be grown indoors or in the house; **lass uns ins Haus gehen** let's go inside or into the house; **der Klavierlehrer kommt ins Haus** the piano teacher comes to the house; **aus dem Haus gehen** to leave the house; **mit jdm Haus an Haus wohnen** to live next door to sb; **wir wohnen Haus an Haus** we live next door to each other; **von Haus zu Haus gehen** to go from door to door or from house to house; **das Haus Gottes** or **des Herrn** *(geh)* the House of God or of the Lord; **Haus der Jugend** youth centre *(Brit)* or center *(US)*; **das (gemeinsame) europäische Haus** the (common) European house

b [= Zuhause, Heim] home; **Haus und Hof** or **Herd verlassen** to leave one's home (behind), to leave house and home; **Haus und Hof verspielen** to gamble away the roof over one's head; **Haus und Hof verlieren** to lose the roof over one's head; **etw ins Haus liefern** to deliver sth to the door; **wir liefern frei Haus** we offer free delivery; **ein großes Haus führen** *(fig)* to entertain lavishly or in style; **jdm das Haus führen** to keep house for sb; **jdm das Haus verbieten** not to allow sb in the house; **aus dem Haus sein** to be away from home; **außer Haus essen** to eat out; **im Hause meiner Schwester** at my sister's (house); **er hat nichts zu essen im Haus** he has no food in the house; **jdn ins Haus nehmen** to take sb in(to one's home); **ein Fernsehgerät kommt mir nicht ins Haus!** I won't have a television set in the house!; **ins Haus stehen** *(fig)* to be on the way; **jdm steht etw ins Haus** *(fig)* sb is facing sth; **Grüße von Haus zu Haus** *(form)* regards from ourselves to you all; **Haus halten** = **haushalten**

♦ **nach Hause** or **nachhause** *(lit, fig)* home; **jdn nach Hause bringen** to take or see sb home; **jdn nach Hause schicken** *(lit)* to send sb home; *(fig inf)* to send sb packing *(inf)*

♦ **zu Hause** or **zuhause** at home; **Borussia hat zu Hause 3:1 gewonnen** Borussia have won 3-1 at home; **bei jdm zu Hause** in sb's house; **bei uns zu Hause** at home; **wie gehts zu Hause?** how are things at home?; **von zu Hause aus** from home; **heute bin ich für niemanden zu Hause** I'm not at home to anybody today; **irgendwo zu Hause sein** *(Mensch, Tier)* to live somewhere; *(= sich heimisch fühlen)* to feel at home somewhere; **dieser Brauch ist in Polen zu Hause** this custom comes from Poland; **in etw** *(dat)* **zu Hause sein** *(fig)* to be at home in sth; **sich wie zu Hause fühlen** to feel at home; **fühl dich wie zu Hause!** make yourself at home!; **damit kannst du zu Hause bleiben** *(fig inf)*, **bleib doch damit zu Hause** *(fig inf)* you can keep it/them *etc (inf)*

c [= Unternehmen] House *(form)*; **das Haus Siemens** *(geh)* the House of Siemens; **„Haus Talblick"** "Talblick (House)"; **das erste Haus am Platze** *(geh) (= Hotel)* the best hotel in town; *(= Kaufhaus)* the best store in town; **ein gut geführtes Haus** *(geh: = Restaurant etc)* a well-run house; **er ist nicht im Hause** *(= in der Firma)* he's not in the building, he's not in; **in unserem Hause dulden wir keine Drogen/keinen Alkohol** *(= in unserer Firma)* we do not allow drugs/alcohol on the premises

d [= Bewohnerschaft eines Hauses] household; **der Herr des Hauses** *(form)* the head of the household; **ein Freund des Hauses** a friend of the family; **die Dame/Tochter** *etc* **des Hauses** *(form)* the lady/daughter *etc* of the house

e [= Herkunft] *geh* **aus gutem/bürgerlichem Haus(e)** from a good/middle-class family; **aus adligem Haus(e)** of noble birth, of or from a noble house *(form)*; **von Hause aus** *(= ursprünglich)* originally; *(= von Natur aus)* naturally

f [= Dynastie] House; **das Haus Windsor** the House of Windsor; **das Haus Habsburg** the Hapsburg dynasty; **aus dem Haus Davids** of the House of David

g [= Theater] theatre *(Brit)*, theater *(US)*; *(= Saal, Publikum)* house; **das große/kleine Haus** the large or main/small theatre *(Brit)* or theater *(US)*; **vor vollem Haus spielen** to play to a full house

h [Parl] House; **Hohes Haus!** *(form)* ≈ honourable *(Brit)* or honorable *(US)* members (of the House)!; **dieses hohe Haus ...** the or this House ...

i [von Schnecke] shell, house *(inf)*

j [Astrol] house

k [= Kerl] *(dated) inf* chap *(Brit inf)*, fellow; **grüß dich Hans, (du) altes Haus!** *(inf)* hello Hans, old chap *(Brit inf)* or buddy *(esp US inf)*

Haus-: **Haus|al|tar** M family or house altar; **Haus|an|dacht** F family worship; **Haus|an|ge|stell|te(r)** MF *decl as adj* domestic servant; *(esp Frau)* domestic; **Haus|an|ten|ne** F roof aerial *(Brit)* or antenna *(US)*; **Haus|an|zug** M leisure suit; **Haus|apo|the|ke** F medicine cupboard or chest; **Haus|ar|beit** F **a** housework *no pl* **b** *(Sch)* homework *no indef art, no pl*, piece of homework, assignment *(esp US)*; **Haus|ar|rest** M *(im Internat)* detention; *(Jur)* house arrest; **~ haben** to be in detention/under house arrest; **Fritz kann nicht zum Spielen rauskommen, er hat ~** Fritz can't come out to play - he's grounded or being kept in; **Haus|arzt** M, **Haus|ärz|tin** F family doctor, GP; *(von Heim, Anstalt)* resident doctor; **Haus|auf|ga|be** F *(Sch)* homework *sing, no indef art*; **seine ~n machen** *(auch fig)* to do one's homework; **Haus|auf|ga|ben|be|treu|ung** F, **Haus|auf|ga|ben|über|wa|chung** F *(Sch)* homework supervision; **Haus|auf|satz** M *(Sch)* homework essay, essay for homework; **haus|ba|cken** [ˈhausbakn] ADJ *(fig)* homespun, drab, homely *(US)*; *Kleidung* unadventurous; **Haus|ball** M (private) ball or dance; **Haus|bank** F *pl* **-banken** bank; **Haus|bar** F home bar; *(= Möbelstück)* cocktail or drinks cabinet; **Haus|bau** M **a** *pl* **-bauten** house building or construction **b** *no pl (= das Bauen)* building of a/the house; **Haus|berg** M *(einer Stadt)* local mountain; *(= beliebtester Berg)* favourite *(Brit)* or favorite *(US)* mountain; *(eines Sportlers)* home slopes *pl*; **Haus|be|set|zer(in)** M(F) squatter; **Haus|be|set|zung** F squatting; *(Einzug)* moving into a squat; **Haus|be|sitz** M house ownership; **~ haben** to own a house/houses; **Haus|be|sit|zer** M homeowner, house-owner; *(= Hauswirt)* landlord; **Haus|be|-**

sit|ze|rin F homeowner, house-owner; (= *Hauswirtin*) landlady; **Haus|be|sor|ger(in)** M(F) (*Aus*) caretaker, janitor; **Haus|be|such** M home visit; **Haus|be|woh|ner(in)** M(F) (house) occupant *or* occupier; **Haus|bib|li|o|thek** F library; **Haus|bock** M (*Zool*) house longhorn; **Haus|boot** NT houseboat; **Haus|brand** M **a** house fire **b** (= *Brennstoff*) domestic *or* heating fuel; **Haus|brief|kas|ten** M letter box (*Brit*), mailbox (*US*); **Haus|bur|sche** M pageboy, bellboy (*US*), bellhop (*US*)

Häus|chen ['hɔysçən] NT -s, - **a** *dim von* **Haus** **b** (*fig inf*) **ganz aus dem ~ sein vor ...** to be out of one's mind with ... (*inf*); **ganz aus dem ~ geraten** to go berserk (*inf*); **jdn (ganz) aus dem ~ bringen** to make sb go berserk (*inf*) **c** (*inf*: = *Karo*) square, block **d** (*euph inf*: = *Toilette*) loo (*Brit inf*), bathroom (*US*), smallest room (*Brit hum inf*); (*außerhalb des Gebäudes*) privy, outside loo (*Brit inf*), outhouse (*US*)

Haus-: **Haus|da|me** F housekeeper; **Haus|de|tek|tiv(in)** M(F) house detective; (*von Kaufhaus*) store detective; **Haus|die|ner(in)** M(F) (*in Hotel*) hotel servant; (= *Gepäckträger*) (hotel) porter; **Haus|dra|chen** M (*inf*) dragon (*inf*), battle-axe (*Brit inf*), battle-ax (*US inf*); **Haus|durch|su|chung** F (*Aus*) = **Haussuchung**; **haus|ei|gen** ADJ belonging to a/the hotel/firm *etc*; **Haus|ei|gen|tü|mer(in)** M(F) homeowner; **Haus|ein|fahrt** F (*Aus*), **Haus|ein|gang** M (house) entrance

Häu|sel ['hɔyzl] NT -s, - (*Aus dial*) = **Häuschen a, c**

hau|sen ['hauzn] VI **a** (= *wohnen*) to live **b** (= *wüten*) **(übel** *or* **schlimm) ~** to wreak *or* create havoc; **schrecklich ~** to wreak the most dreadful havoc; **wie die Vandalen ~** to act like vandals **c** (*Sw, S Ger*: = *sparsam sein*) to be economical

Hau|sen ['hauzn] M -s, - (*Zool*) sturgeon

Häu|ser ['hɔyzɐ] M -s, -, **Häu|se|rin** [-ərɪn] F -, -nen (*Aus, S Ger*: = *Haushälter*) housekeeper

Häu|ser-: **Häu|ser|block** M *pl* **-blocks** *or* (*rare*) **-blöcke** block (of houses); **Häu|ser|flucht** F row of houses; **Häu|ser|front** F front of a terrace, front of a row of houses

Häu|se|rin F -, -nen (*Aus, S Ger*: = *Haushälterin*) housekeeper

Häu|ser-: **Häu|ser|kampf** M (*Mil*) house-to-house fighting; (*Pol*) squatting actions *pl*; (= *einzelner Fall*) squat(ting action); **Häu|ser|mak|ler(in)** M(F) estate agent (*Brit*), realtor (*US*); **Häu|ser|meer** NT mass of houses; **Häu|ser|rei|he** F row of houses; (*aneinandergebaut*) terrace; **Häu|ser|schlucht** F **die ~en New Yorks** the urban jungle of New York; **Häu|ser|zei|le** F = **Häuserreihe**

Haus-: **Haus|flag|ge** F (*Naut*) house flag; **Haus|flur** M (entrance) hall, hallway

Haus|frau F **a** housewife; (= *Gastgeberin*) hostess **b** (*Aus, S Ger*: = *Hauswirtin*) landlady

Haus|frau|en-: **Haus|frau|en|art** F **Wurst** *etc* **nach ~** home-made-style sausage *etc*; **Haus|frau|en|bri|ga|de** F (*DDR*) housewives' brigade; **Haus|frau|en|da|sein** NT life of a housewife; **das ~ satthaben** to be fed up of being (just) a housewife; **Haus|frau|en|pflicht** F housewifely duty

Haus-: **haus|frau|lich** ADJ housewifely; **Haus|freund** M **a** (= *Freund der Familie*) friend of the family **b** (*euph inf*) man friend; **Haus|freun|din** F (= *Freundin der Familie*) friend of the family; **Haus|frie|de(n)** M domestic peace; **Haus|frie|dens|bruch** M (*Jur*) trespass (*in sb's house*); **Haus|gans** F (domestic) goose; **Haus|gast** M (*von Pension etc*) resident, guest; **Haus|ge|brauch** M **für den ~** (*Gerät*) for domestic *or* household use; *Obst-, Gemüseanbau* for one's own consumption; **sein Französisch reicht für den ~** (*inf*) his French is (good) enough to get by (on); **Haus|ge|burt** F home birth; **Haus|ge|hil|fe** M, **Haus|ge|hil|fin** F home help; **Haus|geist** M **a** household spirit; (= *Gespenst*) household ghost **b** (*hum*: = *Hausangestellter*) faithful retainer (*old, hum*); **haus|ge|macht** ADJ home-made; (*fig*) *Problem etc* of one's own making; **Haus|ge|mein|schaft** F household (community); **mit jdm in ~ leben** to live together with sb (in the same household); **Haus|ge|nos|se** M, **Haus|ge|nos|sin** F fellow tenant; **Haus|göt|ter** PL (*Myth*) household gods *pl*

Haus|halt ['haushalt] M -(e)s, -e **a** (= *Hausgemeinschaft*) household; (= *Haushaltsführung*) housekeeping; **Geräte für den ~** household utensils; **den ~ führen** to run the household; **jdm den ~ führen** to keep house for sb **b** (*fig: Biol etc*) balance **c** (= *Etat*) budget

Haus|halt- *in cpds* = **Haushalts-**

haus+hal|ten ['haushaltn] VI *sep irreg* **a** (= *sparsam wirtschaften*) to be economical; **mit etw ~** (*mit Geld, Zeit*) to be economical with sth, to use sth economically; *mit Kräften, Vorräten auch* to conserve sth **b** (= *den Haushalt führen*) to keep house

Haus|häl|ter ['haushɛltɐ] M -s, -, **Haus|häl|te|rin** [-ərɪn] F -, -nen, **Haus|hal|ter(in)** M(F) housekeeper

haus|häl|te|risch ['haushɛltərɪʃ] ADJ thrifty, economical ADV thriftily, economically; **mit etw ~ umgehen** = **haushalten a**

Haus|halts- *in cpds* household; (*Pol*) budget; **Haus|halts|ar|ti|kel** M household item *or* article; **Haus|halts|buch** NT housekeeping book; **(ein) ~ führen** to keep a housekeeping book; **Haus|halts|de|bat|te** F (*Parl*) budget debate; **Haus|halts|de|fi|zit** NT (*Pol*) budget deficit; **Haus|halts|ent|wurf** M (*Pol*) draft budget, budget proposals *pl*; **Haus|halts|fra|gen** PL (*Pol*) budgetary questions *pl*; **Haus|halts|füh|rung** F housekeeping; **doppelte ~** running two homes; **Haus|halts|geld** NT housekeeping money; **Haus|halts|ge|rät** NT household appliance; **Haus|halts|hil|fe** F domestic *or* home help; **Haus|halts|jahr** NT (*Pol, Econ*) financial *or* fiscal year; **Haus|halts|kas|se** F household *or* family budget; **Haus|halts|loch** NT budget deficit; **das ~ stopfen** to cure current budget shortfalls; **Haus|halts|mit|tel** PL (*Pol*) budgetary funds *pl*; **Haus|halts|pa|ckung** F family pack; **Haus|halts|plan** M (*Pol*) budget; **Haus|halts|pla|nung** F (*Pol*) budgetary planning, planning of a budget; **Haus|halts|po|li|tik** F (*Pol*) budgetary policy; **haus|halts|po|li|tisch** ADJ concerning budgetary policy; *Sprecher, Ausschuss* on budgetary policy ADV **die Regierung hat ~ versagt** the government has failed in its budgetary policy; **Haus|halts|vor|stand** M (*form*: = *Verantwortlicher in einem privaten Haushalt*) head of a/the household; **Haus|halts|waa|ge** F kitchen scales *pl*; **Haus|halts|wa|ren** PL household goods *pl*

Haus|hal|tung F **a** (= *das Haushaltführen*) housekeeping, household management; (= *das Sparsamsein*) economizing (*mit* with) **b** (*form*: = *Haushalt*) household

Haus|hal|tungs-: **Haus|hal|tungs|buch** NT housekeeping book; **Haus|hal|tungs|kos|ten** PL household *or* housekeeping expenses *pl*; **Haus|hal|tungs|vor|stand** M (*form*) head of the household

Haus-: **Haus|herr** M **a** head of the household; (= *Gastgeber, Sport*) host **b** (*Jur*) householder **c** (*Aus, S Ger*) (= *Hausbesitzer*) homeowner, house-owner; (= *Hauswirt*) landlord; **Haus|her|rin** F **a** lady of the house; (= *Gastgeberin*) hostess **b** (*Aus, S Ger*: = *Hausbesitzerin*) homeowner, house-owner; (= *Hauswirtin*) landlady; **haus|hoch** ADJ (as) high as a house/houses; (*fig*) *Sieg* crushing; **der haushohe Favorit** the hot favourite (*Brit inf*) *or* favorite (*US inf*) ADV high (in the sky); **jdn ~ schlagen** to give sb a hammering (*inf*) *or* thrashing (*inf*); **~ gewinnen** to win hands down, to win by miles (*inf*); **jdm ~ überlegen sein** to be head and shoulders above sb; **Haus|huhn** NT domestic fowl

hau|sie|ren [hau'ziːrən] *ptp* **hausiert** VI to hawk, to peddle (*mit etw* sth); **mit etw ~ gehen** (*fig, mit Plänen etc*) to hawk sth about; *mit Gerüchten* to peddle sth; **„Hausieren verboten"** "no hawkers *or* peddlers"

Hau|sie|rer [hau'ziːrɐ] M -s, -, **Hau|sie|re|rin** [-ərɪn] F -, -nen hawker, peddler, pedlar (*Brit*)

haus|in|tern ADJ = **firmenintern**

Hau|sis ['haʊziz] PL (*inf*: = *Hausaufgaben*) homework

Haus-: **Haus|ja|cke** F house jacket; **Haus|ju|rist(in)** M(F) company lawyer; **Haus|ka|nin|chen** NT domestic rabbit; **Haus|ka|pel|le** F **a** (*Rel*) private chapel **b** (= *Musikkapelle*) resident band; (*an Fürstenhof*) resident *or* private orchestra; **Haus|kat|ze** F domestic cat; **Haus|kauf** M house-buying *no art*, house purchase; **Haus|kleid** NT housecoat; **Haus|kon|zert** NT family concert; **Haus|kor|rek|tur** F (*Typ*) proofreading (*carried out by the publishers*)

Häus|le|bau|er ['hɔysləbauɐ] M -s, - *sing rare* (*inf*) private developer

Haus-: **Haus|leh|rer(in)** M(F) (private) tutor; **Haus|leu|te** PL **a** (*dial inf*: = *Wirtsleute*) landlord and landlady **b** (*S Ger, Sw*: = *Bewohner*) tenants *pl*

häus|lich ['hɔyslɪç] ADJ *Angelegenheiten, Pflichten, Friede, Umfeld* domestic; *Pflege* home *attr*; (= *der Familie gehörend*) family *attr*; (= *an häuslichen Dingen interessiert*) domesticated; (= *das Zuhause liebend*) home-loving; **der ~e Herd** the family home ADV **sich ~ niederlassen** to make oneself at home; **sich ~ einrichten** to settle in

Häus|lich|keit F -, *no pl* domesticity

Haus|ma|cher-: **Haus|ma|cher|art** F **Wurst** *etc* **nach ~** home-made-style sausage *etc*; **Haus|ma|cher|kost** F home cooking; **Haus|ma|cher|wurst** F home-made sausage

Haus-: **Haus|macht** F (*Hist*) allodium; (*fig*) power base; **Haus|mäd|chen** NT (house)maid; **Haus|mann** M *pl* **-männer** (= *den Haushalt versorgender Mann*) househusband; **Haus|manns|kost** F plain cooking *or* fare; (*fig*) plain fare; **Haus|man|tel** M housecoat; **Haus|mär|chen** NT folk tale; **„Haus- und Kindermärchen"** "Fairy Tales"; **Haus|mar|ke** F (= *eigene Marke*) own brand *or* label; (= *bevorzugte Marke*) favourite (*Brit*) *or* favorite (*US*) brand; **Haus|maus** F house mouse; **Haus|meis|ter** M **a** caretaker, janitor **b** (*dated Sw*: = *Hausbesitzer*) house-owner; **Haus|mit|tei|lung** F internal memo; **Haus|mit|tel** NT household remedy; **Haus|müll** M domestic rubbish (*Brit*) *or* garbage (*US*), domestic refuse; **Haus|mu|sik** F music at home, family music; **Haus|mut|ter** F *pl* **-mütter** (*von Herberge etc*) housemother; **Haus|müt|ter|chen** NT (*hum*) little mother; (*pej*) housewife, wife and mother; **Haus|num|mer** F street *or* house number; **Haus|ord|nung** F house rules *pl* *or* regulations *pl*; **Haus|par|tei** F tenant; (*Aus*) household; **Haus|post** F internal *or* in-house mail; **Haus|pos|til|le** [-pɔstɪlə] F -, -n (*old*) collection of instructional reading for the family; (*fig*) manual;; **Haus|putz** M house cleaning; **Haus|rat** M, *no pl* household equipment *or* goods *pl*; **Haus|rat|ver|si|che|rung** F (household) contents insurance; **Haus|recht** NT right(s *pl*) as a householder (*to forbid sb entrance*); **von seinem ~ Gebrauch machen** to show sb the door, to tell sb to leave; **Haus|rind** NT domestic cattle *pl*; **Haus|samm|lung** F house-to-house *or* door-to-door collection; **Haus|schlach|ten** NT -s, *no pl*, **Haus|schlach|tung** F home slaughtering; **Haus|schlüs|sel** M front-door key, house key; **Haus|schuh** M slipper; **Haus|schwamm** M dry rot; **Haus|schwein** NT domestic pig

Hausse ['(h)oːs(ə)] F -, -n (*Econ*: = *Aufschwung*) boom (*an +dat* in); (*St Ex*: = *Kurssteigerung*) bull market; **~ haben** (*St Ex*) to rise on the Stock

Exchange; **wenn man ~ hat, …** *(St Ex)* when there's a bull market …; **auf ~ spekulieren** *(St Ex)* to bull

Haus|se|gen M house blessing *or* benediction; **bei ihnen hängt der ~ schief** *(hum)* they're a bit short on domestic bliss *(inf)*

Hausse|spe|ku|la|ti|on ['(h)oːsə-] F *(St Ex)* bull speculation

Haus|si|er [(h)o'sieː] M **-s, -s** *(St Ex)* bull

Haus-: **Haus|stand** M household, home; **einen ~ gründen** to set up house *or* home; **Haus|su|chung** [-zuːxʊŋ] F **-, -en** *(in einem Haus)* house search; *(in mehreren Häusern)* house-to-house search; **Haus|su|chungs|be|fehl** M search warrant; **Haus|te|le|fon** NT internal telephone; **Haus|tier** NT domestic animal; *(aus Liebhaberei gehalten)* pet; **Haus|toch|ter** F lady's help; **Haus|trau|ung** F wedding at home; **Haus|tür** F front door; **gleich vor der ~** *(fig inf)* on one's doorstep; **Haus|tür|ge|schäft** NT door-to-door sales *pl*; **Haus|ty|rann(in)** M(F) *(inf)* domestic *or* household tyrant; **Haus|übung** F *(Aus Sch)* home exercise; **Haus|va|ter** M *(von Herberge etc)* housefather; **Haus|ver|bot** NT ban on entering the house; **jdm ~ erteilen** to bar *or* ban sb from the house, to forbid sb to enter the house; **in einem Lokal/bei jdm ~ haben** to be barred *or* banned from a pub *(Brit) or* bar/sb's house; **Haus|ver|samm|lung** F house meeting; **Haus|ver|wal|ter(in)** M(F) (house) supervisor; **Haus|ver|wal|tung** F property *or* house management; **Haus|wap|pen** NT family coat of arms; **Haus|wart** [-vart] M **-(e)s, -e**, **Haus|war|tin** F **-, -nen** caretaker, janitor; **Haus|wirt** M landlord; **Haus|wir|tin** F landlady

Haus|wirt|schaft F **a** (= *Haushaltsführung)* housekeeping **b** *(Sch)* home economics *sing*, domestic science *(esp Brit old)*

haus|wirt|schaft|lich ADJ domestic; **ein ~er Kurs** a course on home economics *or* domestic science *(esp Brit old)*; **die ~e Versorgung von Patienten** taking care of the housework in patients' homes ADV **~ interessiert** interested in domestic matters

Haus|wirt|schafts-: **Haus|wirt|schafts|leh|re** F *(Sch)* home economics *sing*, domestic science *(esp Brit old)*; **Haus|wirt|schafts|leh|rer(in)** M(F) home economics teacher, domestic science teacher *(esp Brit old)*; **Haus|wirt|schafts|schu|le** F school of home economics *or* domestic science *(esp Brit old)*

Haus-: **Haus|wurf|sen|dung** F mailshot, direct mail advertisement *(US)*; **Haus|zei|tung** F, **Haus|zeit|schrift** F company magazine; **Haus|zelt** NT frame tent; **Haus|zent|ra|le** F *(Telec)* (internal) switchboard

Haus-zu-Haus-: **Haus-zu-Haus-Trans|port** M, **Haus-zu-Haus-Ver|kehr** M *(Rail etc)* door-to-door service

Haut [haut] F **-, Häute** ['hɔytə] skin; *(dick, esp von größerem Tier)* hide; (= *geschälte Schale von Obst etc)* peel; *(inf: = Mensch)* sort *(inf)*; **nass bis auf die ~** soaked to the skin; **nur ~ und Knochen sein** to be only *or* nothing but skin and bones; **viel ~ zeigen** *(hum)* to show all one's got *(hum)*, to show a lot (of bare skin); **mit ~ und Haar(en)** *(inf)* completely, totally; **er ist ihr mit ~ und Haar(en) verfallen** *(inf)* he's head over heels in love with her, he's fallen for her hook, line and sinker *(inf)*; **das geht** *or* **dringt unter die ~** that gets under one's skin; **in seiner ~ möchte ich nicht stecken** I wouldn't like to be in his shoes; **er fühlt sich nicht wohl in seiner ~** *(inf)* **ihm ist nicht wohl in seiner ~** *(inf)* (= *unglücklich, unzufrieden)* he's (feeling) rather unsettled; (= *unbehaglich)* he feels uneasy *or* uncomfortable; **er kann nicht aus seiner ~ heraus** *(inf)* he can't change the way he is, a leopard can't change its spots *(prov)*; **aus der ~ fahren** *(inf) (aus Ungeduld)* to work oneself up into a sweat *(inf)*; *(aus Wut)* to go through the roof *(inf)*, to hit the ceiling *(inf)*; **das ist zum Aus-der-~-Fahren!** it's enough to drive you up the wall *(inf) or* round the bend *(Brit inf)*; **auf der faulen ~ liegen** *(inf)* **sich auf die faule ~ legen** *(inf)* to sit back and do nothing, not to lift a finger *(inf)*; **seine ~ zu Markte tragen** (= *sich in Gefahr begeben)* to risk one's neck *or* hide *(inf)*; *(euph: Frau)* to sell one's charms; **seine eigene ~ retten** to save one's (own) skin; *(esp vor Prügel)* to save one's (own) hide *(inf)*; **sich seiner ~ wehren** to defend oneself vigorously; **seine ~ so teuer wie möglich verkaufen** *(inf)* to sell oneself as dearly as possible → **ehrlich ADJ**

Haut- *in cpds* skin; **Haut|ab|schür|fung** F graze; **Haut|arzt** M, **Haut|ärz|tin** F skin specialist, dermatologist; **Haut|at|mung** F cutaneous respiration; **die ~ verhindern** to stop the skin from breathing; **Haut|aus|schlag** M (skin) rash *or* eruption *(form)*

Häut|chen ['hɔytçən] NT **-s, -** *dim von* **Haut** *(auf Flüssigkeit)* skin; *(Anat, Bot)* membrane; *(an Fingernägeln)* cuticle

hau|te *pret von* **hauen**

Haute Cou|ture [(h)oːt ku'tyːɐ] F **- -,** *no pl* haute couture

häu|ten ['hɔytn] VT *Tiere* to skin VR *(Tier)* to shed its skin; *(Schlange auch)* to slough (its skin); *(hum: Mensch)* to peel

haut|eng ADJ skintight

Haute|vo|lee [(h)oːtvo'leː] F **-,** *no pl* upper crust

Haut-: **Haut|fal|te** F skin fold; **Haut|far|be** F skin colour *(Brit) or* color *(US)*; **nur, weil er eine andere ~ hat** just because his skin is a different colo(u)r; **haut|far|ben** [-farbn] ADJ flesh-coloured *(Brit)*, flesh-colored *(US)*; **Haut|flüg|ler** [-flyːglɐ] M **-s, -** hymenopter (-on); **haut|freund|lich** ADJ *Stoff, Kleidung* kind to one's *or* the skin; **~es Heftpflaster** micropore tape

-häu|tig [hɔytɪç] ADJ *suf* -skinned; **dunkelhäutig** dark-skinned

Haut-: **Haut|ju|cken** NT **-s,** *no pl* itching; **eine Creme gegen ~** a cream for skin irritations; **Haut|kli|nik** F dermatology clinic, skin clinic; **Haut|kon|takt** M skin contact; **Haut|krank|heit** F skin disease; **Haut|krebs** M *(Med)* skin cancer; **haut|nah** ADJ **a** *(Anat)* close to the skin **b** (= *sehr eng, Sport)* (very) close **c** *(fig inf: = wirklichkeitsnah) Kontakt* (very) close; *Problem* that affects us/him *etc* directly; *Darstellung, Schilderung* deeply affecting ADV **a** (= *eng)* **~ tanzen** to dance very close(ly); **~ in Kontakt mit jdm/etw kommen** to come into (very) close contact with sb/sth **b** *(inf: = direkt) darstellen, schildern* realistically; **etw ~ erleben** to experience sth at close quarters; **Haut|pfle|ge** F skin care; **Haut|pfle|ge|mit|tel** NT skin-care product; **Haut|pilz** M *(Med)* fungal skin infection, dermatophyte *(spec)*; **haut|scho|nend** ADJ kind to the skin; *Spülmittel auch* kind to the hands; **Haut|spe|zi|a|list(in)** M(F) skin specialist, dermatologist; **Haut|trans|plan|ta|ti|on** F (= *Operation)* skin graft; (= *Verfahren)* skin grafting; **Haut|typ** M skin type; **was für ein ~ ist sie?** what's her skin type?

Häu|tung ['hɔytʊŋ] F **-, -en** skinning; *(von Schlange)* sloughing; **verschiedene ~en durchmachen** to slough several skins

Haut-: **haut|ver|träg|lich** ADJ non-irritating, hypoallergenic, kind to the skin *pred*; **Haut|wun|de** F superficial *or* skin wound

Ha|van|na(zi|gar|re) [ha'vana-] F **-, -s** Havana (cigar)

Ha|va|rie [hava'riː] F **-, -n** [-'riːən] **a** *(Naut, Aviat)* (= *Unfall)* accident; (= *Schaden)* average *(spec)*, damage *no indef art, no pl* **b** *(Aus)* (= *Kraftfahrzeugunfall)* accident; (= *Kraftfahrzeugschaden)* damage *no indef art, no pl*

ha|va|rie|ren [hava'riːrən] *ptp* **havariert** VI **a** *(Schiff)* to be damaged **b** *(Aus: Fahrzeug)* to crash

ha|va|riert [hava'riːɐt] ADJ *Schiff, Kraftwerk* damaged

Ha|va|rist [hava'rɪst] M **-en, -en** (= *Schiff)* damaged ship

Ha|va|rist [hava'rɪst] M **-en, -en**, **Ha|va|ris|tin** [-'rɪstɪn] F **-, -nen** (= *Reeder)* owner of a/the damaged ship

Ha|waii [ha'vaii, ha'vai] NT **-s** Hawaii

Ha|wai|ia|ner [havai'iaːnɐ] M **-s, -**, **Ha|wai|ia|ne|rin** [-ərɪn] F **-, -nen** Hawaiian

Ha|waii|gi|tar|re [ha'vaii-, ha'vai-] F Hawaiian guitar

ha|wai|isch [ha'vaiɪʃ] ADJ Hawaiian

Ha|xe ['haksə] F **-, -n** *(Cook)* leg (joint); *(S Ger inf)* (= *Fuß)* foot, plate of meat *(Brit inf)*; (= *Bein)* leg; **„Haxen abkratzen!"** *(hum inf)* "wipe your feet!"

Hbf *abbr von* **Hauptbahnhof**

H-Bom|be ['haː-] F H-bomb

h. c. [haː'tseː] *abbr von* **honoris causa**

HD [haː'deː] *abbr* **a** *(Comput) von* **High Density** **b** *(Sw) von* **Hilfsdienst**

HD-Dis|ket|te [haː'deː-] F *(Comput)* HD diskette

he [heː] INTERJ hey; *(fragend)* eh

Hea|der ['hɛdɐ] M **-s, -** *(Comput)* header

Head|hun|ter ['hɛdhantɐ] M **-s, -**, **Head|hun|te|rin** [-ərɪn] F **-, -nen** head-hunter

Hea|ring ['hiːərɪŋ] NT **-(s), -s** hearing

hea|vy ['hɛvi] ADJ *pred (sl)* **a** (= *schwierig)* heavy *(inf)*; **das war einfach zu ~ für sie** *(Erlebnis etc)* it was simply too much for her to take **b** (= *unerhört)* beyond belief

Hea|vy|me|tal ['hɛvi'mɛtl] NT **-,** *no pl (Mus)* heavy metal

Heb|am|me ['heːplamə, 'heːbamə] F **-, -n** midwife

He|be-: **He|be|bal|ken** M, **He|be|baum** M lever; **He|be|bock** M (hydraulic) jack; **He|be|büh|ne** F hydraulic ramp

He|bel ['heːbl] M **-s, - a** *(Phys: = Griff)* lever; *(an Maschinen)* handle, lever; *(fig)* leverage; **den ~ ansetzen** to position the lever; *(fig)* to tackle it, to set about it; **den ~ an der richtigen Stelle ansetzen** *(fig)* to set about *or* tackle it in the right way; **alle ~ in Bewegung setzen** *(inf)* to move heaven and earth; **am längeren ~ sitzen** *(inf)* to have the whip hand **b** *(Sport: = Hebelgriff)* lever hold

He|bel-: **He|bel|arm** M (lever) arm; **He|bel|griff** M *(Sport)* lever hold; **He|bel|kraft** F, **He|bel|wir|kung** F leverage

he|ben ['heːbn] *pret* **hob** [hoːp], *ptp* **gehoben** [gə'hoːbn] VT **a** (= *nach oben bewegen)* to lift, to raise; *Augenbraue, Kamera, Fernglas* to raise; **die Stimme ~** (= *lauter sprechen)* to raise one's voice, to speak up; (= *höher sprechen)* to raise one's/the pitch; **die Hand gegen jdn ~** *(geh)* to raise one's hand against sb; **die Faust gegen jdn ~** *(geh)* to shake one's fist at sb; **einen ~ gehen** *(inf)* to go for a drink; **er hebt gern einen** *(inf)* he likes *or* enjoys a drink → *auch* **gehoben**

b (= *nach oben befördern, hochheben)* to lift; *Wrack* to raise, to bring up; *Schatz* to dig up; *(Sport) Gewicht* to lift; **er hob das Kind auf die Mauer/vom Baum** he lifted the child (up) onto the wall/ (down) from the tree; **jdn auf die Schultern ~** to hoist *or* lift sb onto one's shoulders; **den Ball in den Strafraum/ins Tor ~** to lob the ball into the penalty area/goal; **heb deine Füße!** pick your feet up!

c (= *verbessern) Farbe* to bring out, to enhance; *Selbstbewusstsein, Effekt* to heighten; *Ertrag* to increase; *Geschäft* to increase, to boost; *Stimmung, Wohlstand* to improve; *Niveau* to raise, to increase; *jds Ansehen* to boost, to enhance; **jds Stimmung ~** to cheer sb up; **das hebt den Mut** that boosts *or* raises one's morale

d *(S Ger: = halten)* to hold

VR **a** (= *sich nach oben bewegen)* to rise; *(Vorhang)* to go up, to rise; *(Nebel, Deckel)* to lift; **sich ~ und senken** *(Schiff)* to rise and fall; *(Busen)* to heave

b *(geh: = emporragen)* to tower up, to rise up **c** *(= sich bessern) (Stimmung, Konjunktur, Handel)* to improve; **da hob sich seine Stimmung** that cheered him up **d** *(S Ger: = sich halten)* to hold on *(an +dat* to) **VT** *impers* **es hebt jdn** *(inf)* **es hebt jdm den Magen** *(inf)* sb feels sick; **es hebt mich** *or* **es hebt mir den Magen, wenn ich das sehe** *(inf)* seeing that makes me feel sick *or* turns my stomach *(inf)*
VI **a** *(Sport)* to do weightlifting **b** *(S Ger: = haltbar sein)* to hold; *(Nahrungsmittel)* to keep

He|ber ['he:bɐ] **M -s, -** **a** *(Chem)* pipette **b** *(Tech)* (hydraulic) jack

He|ber **M -s, -** *(Ftbl: inf)* lob

He|ber ['he:bɐ] **M -s, -, He|be|rin** [-ərɪn] **F -, -nen** *(Sport: = Gewichtheber)* weightlifter

He|be|satz **M** *(Fin)* rate of assessment

Heb|rä|er [he'brɛ:ɐ] **M -s, -, Heb|rä|e|rin** [-ərɪn] **F -, -nen** Hebrew

heb|rä|isch [he'brɛ:ɪʃ] **ADJ** Hebrew

Heb|rä|isch(e) [he'brɛ:ɪʃ] **NT** Hebrew → *auch* **Deutsch(e)**

Heb|ri|den [he'bri:dn] **PL die ~** the Hebrides *pl*

He|bung ['he:bʊŋ] **F -, -en** **a** *(von Schatz, Wrack etc)* recovery, raising **b** *(Geol)* elevation, rise (in the ground) **c** *no pl (fig: = Verbesserung)* improvement; *(von Effekt, Selbstbewusstsein)* heightening; *(von Lebensstandard, Niveau)* rise; **seine Fröhlichkeit trug zur ~ der gedrückten Stimmung bei** his cheerfulness helped to relieve the subdued mood **d** *(Poet)* stressed *or* accented syllable

he|cheln ['hɛçln] **VT** *Flachs, Hanf* to hatchel, to heckle **VI** **a** *(inf: = lästern)* to gossip **b** *(= keuchen)* to pant

Hecht [hɛçt] **M -(e)s, -e** *(Zool)* pike; *(inf: = Bursche)* chap *(inf)*, bloke *(Brit inf)*, guy *(inf)*; **das ist ein ~** *(inf)* he's some guy *(inf)*, he's quite a guy *(inf)*; **er ist (wie) ein ~ im Karpfenteich** *(fig)* *(= sehr aktiv)* he certainly shakes people up; *(= sorgt für Unruhe)* he's a stirrer *(inf)*

hech|ten ['hɛçtn] **VI** *aux sein (inf)* to dive, to make a (headlong) dive; *(beim Schwimmen)* to do a racing dive; *(beim Turnen)* to do a forward dive

Hecht-: **Hecht|rol|le** **F** *(Sport)* dive roll; **Hecht|sprung** **M** *(beim Schwimmen)* racing dive; *(beim Turnen)* forward dive; *(Ftbl inf)* (headlong *or* full-length) dive; **Hecht|sup|pe** **F es zieht wie ~** *(inf)* it's blowing a gale (in here) *(inf)*, there's a terrible draught *(Brit)* *or* draft *(US)*

Heck [hɛk] **NT -(e)s, -e** *pl auch* **-s** **a** *pl auch* **-s** *(Naut)* stern; *(Aviat)* tail, rear; *(Aut)* rear, back **b** *(N Ger: = Gatter)* gate

Heck|an|trieb **M** *(Aut)* rear-wheel drive

He|cke ['hɛkə] **F -, -n** hedge; *(am Wegrand)* hedgerow

He|cken-: **He|cken|ro|se** **F** dog rose, wild rose; **He|cken|sche|re** **F** hedge clippers *pl*; *(elektrisch)* hedge trimmer; **He|cken|schüt|ze** **M**, **He|cken|schüt|zin** **F** sniper

Heck-: **Heck|fens|ter** **NT** *(Aut)* rear window *or* windscreen *(Brit)* *or* windshield *(US)*; **Heck|flos|se** **F** *(Aut)* tail fin; **Heck|klap|pe** **F** *(Aut)* tailgate; **heck|las|tig** [-lastɪç] **ADJ** tail-heavy; **Heck|licht** **NT** *(Aviat)* tail-light

Heck|meck ['hɛkmɛk] **M -s,** *no pl (inf) (= dummes Gerede)* nonsense, rubbish *(Brit)*; *(= dumme Streiche)* stupid *or* daft *(Brit inf)* things *pl*; *(= Umstände)* fuss, palaver *(inf)*; *(= unnötiges Zeug)* rubbish; **mach doch keinen ~** don't be so stupid *or* daft *(Brit inf)*

Heck|mo|tor **M** *(Aut)* rear engine; **mit ~** rear-engined

Heck|schei|be **F** *(Aut)* rear windscreen *(Brit)* *or* windshield *(US)*

Heck|schei|ben-: **Heck|schei|ben|hei|zung** **F** rear windscreen *(Brit)* *or* windshield *(US)* heater; **Heck|schei|ben|wi|scher** **M** rear windscreen *(Brit)* *or* windshield *(US)* wiper

Heck-: **Heck|schüt|ze** **M**, **Heck|schüt|zin** **F** rear gunner; **Heck|spoi|ler** **M** rear spoiler; **Heck|tür** **F** *(Aut)* tailgate; *(von Lieferwagen)* rear doors *pl*; **Heck|tür|mo|dell** **NT** hatchback (car); **Heck|wel|le** **F** *(Naut)* wash *no pl*

he|da ['he:da] **INTERJ** hey there

He|de|rich ['he:dərɪç] **M -s,** *no pl (Bot)* wild radish

Hedge|fonds ['hɛdʒfõ:] **M** *(Fin)* hedge fund

Hedge|ge|schäft ['hɛdʒ-] **NT** *(Fin)* hedge transaction

He|do|nis|mus [hedo'nɪsmʊs] **M -,** *no pl* hedonism

he|do|nis|tisch [hedo'nɪstɪʃ] **ADJ** hedonistic

Heer [he:ɐ] **NT -(e)s, -e** *(lit, fig)* army; **beim ~** in the army; **in das ~ eintreten** to join the army, to enlist in the army

Heer|bann **M** *(Hist)* levy

Hee|res-: **Hee|res|be|richt** **M** military communiqué *or* despatch; **Hee|res|be|stän|de** **PL** army stores *pl* *or* supplies *pl*; **Hee|res|dienst** **M,** *no pl (Hist)* military service; **Hee|res|dienst|vor|schrift** **F** army regulations *pl*; **Hee|res|grup|pe** **F** army group; **Hee|res|lei|tung** **F** command; **Hee|res|zug** **M** *(Hist)* campaign

Heer-: **Heer|füh|rer(in)** **M(F)** *(Hist)* army commander; **Heer|la|ger** **NT** army camp; **der Flughafen glich einem ~** the airport was like a refugee camp; **Heer|schar** **F** *(liter)* legion, troop; *(fig: = große Menge)* host; **die himmlischen ~en** the heavenly hosts; **Heer|schau** **F** *(old)* military parade; **Heer|stra|ße** **F** military road; **Heer|we|sen** **NT,** *no pl* army

He|fe ['he:fə] **F -, -n** yeast; **die ~ des Volkes** *(geh: = treibende Kraft)* the (driving) force behind the people; *(pej: = Abschaum)* the scum of the earth

He|fe-: **He|fe|ge|bäck** **NT** yeast-risen pastry; **He|fe|kranz** **M** ≈ savarin; **He|fe|ku|chen** **M** yeast cake; **He|fe|pilz** **M** yeast plant; **He|fe|stück|(chen)** **NT** *small fruit tart,* ≈ Danish pastry; **He|fe|teig** **M** yeast dough; **wie ein ~ auseinandergehen** *(fig inf)* to put on mounds of fat; **He|fe|teil|chen** **NT** *small fruit tart,* ≈ Danish pastry; **He|fe|zopf** **M** plaited *or* braided *(US)* yeast bun

Heft [hɛft] **NT -(e)s, -e** *(von Werkzeug, Messer)* handle; *(von Säge, Feile auch)* grip; *(von Dolch, Schwert)* hilt; **das ~ in der Hand haben** *(fig)* to hold the reins, to be at the helm; **das ~ in der Hand behalten** *(fig)* to remain in control *or* at the helm; **das ~ aus der Hand geben** *(fig)* to hand over control *or* the reins; **jdm das ~ aus der Hand nehmen** *(fig)* to seize control from sb; **ich lasse mir nicht das ~ aus der Hand nehmen** nobody's going to take over from me

Heft **NT -(e)s, -e** **a** *(= Schreibheft)* exercise book **b** *(= Zeitschrift)* magazine; *(= Comicheft)* comic; *(= Nummer)* number, issue; **„National Geographic 1998, ~ 3"** "National Geographic 1998, No 3" **c** *(= geheftetes Büchlein)* booklet

Heft|chen ['hɛftçən] **NT -s, -** **a** *dim von* **Heft** **b** *(pej) (= billiger Roman)* rubbishy *(Brit)* *or* cheap *or* pulp novel *(pej)*; *(= schlechte Zeitschrift, Comicheftchen)* rag *(pej inf)* **c** *(= Fahrkartenheftchen, Eintrittskartenheftchen)* book(let) of tickets; *(= Briefmarkenheftchen)* book of stamps

hef|ten ['hɛftn] **VT** **a** *(= nähen) Saum, Naht* to tack (up), to baste; *Buch* to sew, to stitch; *(= klammern)* to clip *(an +acc* to); *(mit Heftmaschine)* to staple *(an +acc* to) **b** *(= befestigen)* to pin, to fix; **er heftete mit Reißzwecken eine Landkarte an die Wand** he pinned a map on the wall; **jdm ein Abzeichen an die Brust ~** to pin a decoration to sb's chest; **den Blick** *or* **die Augen auf jdn/etw ~** to gaze at sb/sth, to fix one's eyes on sb/sth, to stare fixedly at sb/sth
VR **a** *(Blick, Augen)* **sich auf jdn/etw ~** to fix onto sb/sth **b** **sich an jdn ~** to latch on to sb; **sich an jds Spur** *or* **Fährte ~** to follow sb's trail; **sich an jds Fersen** *or* **Sohlen ~** *(fig) (= jdn verfolgen)* to dog sb's heels; *(bei Rennen etc)* to stick to sb's heels

Hef|ter ['hɛftɐ] **M -s, -** **a** (loose-leaf) file **b** *(= Heftapparat)* stapler

Heft|fa|den **M**, **Heft|garn** **NT** tacking thread

hef|tig ['hɛftɪç] **ADJ** **a** *(= stark, gewaltig)* violent; *Kopfschmerzen* severe; *Schmerz* intense, acute; *Erkältung* severe; *Fieber* raging, severe; *Zorn, Ärger, Hass* violent, burning *no adv*, intense; *Liebe, Sehnsucht* ardent, burning *no adv*, intense; *Leidenschaft* violent; *Abneigung* intense; *Widerstand* vehement; *Weinen* bitter; *Lachen* uproarious; *Atmen* heavy; *Kontroverse, Kampf, Wind* fierce; *Regen* lashing *no adv*, driving *no adv*, heavy; *Frost* severe, heavy; **ein ~er Regenguss** a downpour **b** *(= jähzornig, ungehalten) Mensch* violent(-tempered); *Ton* fierce, vehement; *Worte* violent; **~ werden** to fly into a passion **c** *(sl: = sehr gut)* wicked *(sl)*; **das ist ganz schön ~** *(sl: = unangenehm)* that's a bummer *(sl)* *or* a pisser *(Brit sl)*
ADV *regnen, schneien, zuschlagen* hard; *verprügeln* severely; *aufprallen* with great force, hard; *schütteln, rühren* vigorously; *nicken* emphatically; *zittern* badly; *dementieren, schimpfen* vehemently; *verliebt* passionately, madly *(inf)*; **es stürmt/gewittert ~** there is a violent storm/thunderstorm; **sich ~ streiten** to have a violent argument; **der Regen schlug ~ gegen die Scheiben** the rain pounded *or* beat against the windows; **sie knallte die Tür ~ ins Schloss** she slammed *or* banged the door (shut); **er hat ~ dagegen gewettert** he raged vehemently against it

Hef|tig|keit **F,** *no pl (= Stärke, Gewalt)* violence; *(von Kopfschmerzen)* severity; *(von Schmerz)* intensity, acuteness; *(von Widerstand)* vehemence; *(von Liebe, Abneigung)* intensity; *(von Kampf, Wind)* ferocity, fierceness; *(von Regen)* heaviness; *(von Frost)* severity, heaviness

Heft-: **Heft|klam|mer** **F** staple; **Heft|ma|schi|ne** **F** stapler; **Heft|naht** **F** *(Sew)* basted *or* tacked seam; *(Tech)* tack weld; **Heft|pflas|ter** **NT** (sticking) plaster, adhesive tape *(US)*; **Heft|ro|man** **M** cheap paperback novel, dime novel *(US)*; **Heft|stich** **M** tacking stitch; **Heft|zwe|cke** **F** drawing pin *(Brit)*, thumb tack *(US)*

He|ge|li|a|ner [he:gə'lia:nɐ] **M -s, -, He|ge|li|a|ne|rin** [-ərɪn] **F -, -nen** Hegelian

he|ge|li|a|nisch [he:gə'lia:nɪʃ], **he|gelsch** ['he:glʃ] **ADJ** Hegelian

He|ge|mo|nie [hegemo'ni:] **F -, -n** [-'ni:ən] hegemony

he|gen ['he:gn] **VT** **a** *(= pflegen) Wild, Pflanzen* to care for, to tend; *(geh: = umsorgen) jdn* to care for, to look after; **jdn ~ und pflegen** to lavish care and attention on sb **b** *(= empfinden, haben) Hass, Groll, Verdacht* to harbour *(Brit)*, to harbor *(US)*; *Misstrauen, Achtung, Abneigung* to feel; *Zweifel* to entertain; *Hoffnung, Wunsch* to cherish; *Plan, Unternehmen* to foster; **ich hege den starken Verdacht, dass ...** I have a strong suspicion that ...; **ich hege schon lange den Plan auszuwandern** for a long time I've been contemplating emigrating

He|ger ['he:gɐ] **M -s, -, He|ge|rin** [-ərɪn] **F -, -nen** gamekeeper

Hehl [he:l] **NT OR M kein** *or* **keinen ~ aus etw machen** to make no secret of sth

Heh|ler ['he:lɐ] **M -s, -, Heh|le|rin** [-ərɪn] **F -, -nen** receiver (of stolen goods), fence *(inf)*; **der ~ ist schlimmer als der Stehler** *(Prov)* it is worse to condone a crime than to commit it

Heh|le|rei [he:lə'rai] **F -, -en** receiving (stolen goods)

hehr [he:ɐ] **ADJ** *(liter)* noble, sublime

hei [hai] **INTERJ** wow

Heia ['haia] **F -,** *no pl (baby-talk)* bye-byes *(Brit baby-talk)*, bye-bye *(US baby-talk)*, beddy-byes *(Brit baby-talk)*, beddy-bye *(US baby-talk)*; **ab in die ~** off to bye-byes *etc*; **in die ~ gehen** to go bye-byes *etc*; **heia machen** to have a little nap *or* sleep

Heia|bett NT *(baby-talk)* beddy-byes *(Brit baby-talk)*, beddy-bye *(US baby-talk)*

Hei|de ['haidə] F -, -n **a** moor, heath; *(= Heideland)* moorland, heathland **b** *(= Heidekraut)* heather

Hei|de ['haidə] M -n, -n, **Hei|din** ['haidɪn] F -, -nen heathen, pagan; *(= Nichtjude)* Gentile

Hei|de-: **Hei|de|kraut** NT heather; **Hei|de|land** NT moorland, heathland

Hei|del|bee|re F bilberry, blueberry *(esp US)*

Hei|del|beer|kraut NT, **Hei|del|beer|strauch** M bilberry *or* blueberry *(esp US)* bush

Hei|den-: **Hei|den|angst** F **eine ~ vor etw** *(dat)* **haben** *(inf)* to be scared stiff of sth *(inf)*; **Hei|den|ar|beit** F *(inf)* real slog *(inf)*; **Hei|den|geld** NT *(inf)* packet *(Brit inf)*, bundle *(US inf)*; **Hei|den|krach** M *(inf)*, **Hei|den|lärm** M *(inf)* unholy din *(inf)*; **hei|den|mä|ßig** *(inf)* ADJ huge, massive ADV incredibly; **~ Geld verdienen** to earn a (real) packet *(Brit inf)* *or* bundle *(US inf)*; **Hei|den|mis|si|on** F missionary work among the heathen; **Hei|den|res|pekt** M *(inf)* healthy respect; **Hei|den|spaß** M *(inf)* terrific fun; **einen ~ haben** to have a whale of a time *(inf)*; **das macht ihm einen ~** he finds it terrific fun; **Hei|den|spek|ta|kel** M *(inf)* awful row; *(= Schimpfen)* awful fuss

Hei|den|tum ['haidntu:m] NT **-s**, *no pl* heathenism, heathendom, paganism; **das ~** *(= Menschen)* the heathen *pl*, the pagans *pl*

hei|di [hai'di:, 'haidi] INTERJ **~ ging es den Berg hinab** down the hill they/we *etc* went; **~ (, dann gehts los)** here they/we *etc* go

Hei|din ['haidɪn] F → **Heide**

heid|nisch ['haidnɪʃ] ADJ heathen; *(auf Götterkult bezüglich)* pagan ADV like a heathen *or* pagan; **~ denken** to have heathen *or* pagan beliefs; **~ geprägt** characterized by heathen *or* pagan customs; **~ leben** to live a heathen *or* pagan life

Heid|schnu|cke ['haitʃnʊkə] F -, -n *German moorland sheep*

hei|kel ['haikl] ADJ **a** *(= schwierig, gefährlich)* *Angelegenheit, Situation, Thema* tricky, delicate; *Frage* awkward, tricky **b** *(dial)* *Mensch* particular, pernickety *(inf)*, persnickety *(US inf)* *(in Bezug auf +acc* about); *(= wählerisch)* fussy, particular; *(in Bezug aufs Essen)* fussy, choosy **c** *(dial)* *Stoff, Farbe* difficult; **der Stoff ist mir zu ~** that material is too much of a nuisance

heil [hail] ADJ **a** *(= unverletzt)* *Mensch* unhurt, uninjured; *Glieder* unbroken; *Haut* undamaged; **wieder ~ sein/werden** *(= wieder gesund)* to be/get better again; *(Wunde)* to have healed/to heal up; *(Knochen)* to have mended/to mend; **~ machen** *(inf)* *(= heilen)* to make better; *(= reparieren)* to fix, to mend; **Gott sei Dank sind die Glieder noch ~** thank goodness there are no broken bones; **mit ~en Gliedern** *or* **~ am Ziel ankommen** to reach the finish without breaking any bones; **mit ~er Haut davonkommen** to escape unscathed *or (lit auch)* in one piece **b** *(inf: = ganz)* intact; *Kleidungsstück* decent *(inf)*; **die Uhr ist wieder ~** the clock's back in working order; **die ~e Welt** an ideal world *(without problems, uncertainties etc)* ADV *(= unverletzt)* all in one piece, safe and sound; *(= unbeschädigt)* in good shape, all in one piece; **~ nach Hause kommen** to get home safe and sound; **etw ~ überstehen** *(Unfall)* to come through sth without a scratch; *Prüfung* to get through sth

Heil [hail] NT **-s**, *no pl* **a** *(= Wohlergehen)* well-being, good; **sein ~ bei jdm versuchen** *(inf)* to try one's luck with sb; **jdm ~ und Segen wünschen** to wish sb every blessing **b** *(Eccl, fig)* salvation; **sein ~ in etw** *(dat)* **suchen** to seek one's salvation in sth; **sein ~ in der Flucht suchen** to flee for one's life; **~ bringend** *(Rel)* redeeming; *Wirkung, Kur* beneficial; *Kräuter* medicinal; **sie warteten auf den ~ bringenden Regen** they were waiting for the vitally needed rain; **zu jds ~(e) gereichen** *(geh)* to be sb's salvation; **im Jahr des ~s 1848** *(old)* in the year of grace 1848 *(old)* INTERJ **~!** hail! *(old)*; **~ dem König!** long live *or* God save the King!; **~ Hitler!** *(NS)* heil Hitler!; **Berg/Ski/Petri ~!** good climbing/skiing/fishing!

Hei|land ['hailant] M **-(e)s, -e** [-də] *(Rel)* Saviour *(Brit)*, Savior *(US)*, Redeemer; *(fig geh: = Retter)* saviour *(Brit)*, savior *(US)*

Heil-: **Heil|an|stalt** F nursing home; *(für Suchtoder Geisteskranke)* home; **~ für Geisteskranke** mental home; **Heil|bad** NT *(= Bad)* medicinal bath; *(= Ort)* spa, watering-place *(old)*; **heil|bar** ADJ curable; **Heil|bar|keit** ['hailba:ɐkait] F -, *no pl* curability; **heil|brin|gend** ADJ → **Heil b**

Heil|butt M halibut

hei|len ['hailən] VI *aux sein (Wunde, Bruch)* to heal (up); *(Entzündung)* to clear up VT *Kranke, Krankheiten* to cure; *Wunde* to heal; *(Rel)* to heal; **als geheilt entlassen werden** to be discharged with a clean bill of health; **Jesus heilt uns von unseren Sünden** Jesus redeems us from our sins; **jdn von etw ~** *(lit, fig)* to cure sb of sth; **von jdm/etw geheilt sein** *(fig)* to have got over sb/sth; **die Zeit heilt alle Wunden** *(Prov)* time heals all wounds *(prov)*

heil|lend ADJ healing

Hei|ler ['haile] M **-s, -**, **Hei|le|rin** [-ərɪn] F **-, -nen** *(geh)* healer

Heil-: **Heil|er|de** F healing earth; **Heil|er|folg** M success; **zum ~ führen** to lead to a successful cure; **Heil|fas|ten** NT **-s**, *no pl* therapeutic fasting; **Heil|fleisch** NT **ich habe gutes ~** I heal quickly *or* easily; **heil|froh** ADJ *pred (inf)* ecstatic; **Heil|gym|nas|tik** F physiotherapy; **Heil|haut** F **eine gute/schlechte ~ haben** to have skin that heals quickly/doesn't heal quickly

hei|lig ['hailɪç] ADJ **a** holy; *(= geweiht, geheiligt)* sacred, holy; *(bei Namen von Heiligen)* Saint; *(old: = fromm)* devout, saintly; *(pej)* holier-than-thou; **jdm ~ sein** *(lit, fig)* to be sacred to sb; **bei allem, was ~ ist** by all that is sacred, by all that I hold sacred; **die ~e Veronika** Saint Veronica; **der ~e Augustinus** Saint Augustine; **Heiliger Abend** Christmas Eve; **das ~e Abendmahl, die ~e Kommunion** Holy Communion; **die Heilige Dreifaltigkeit/Familie/Stadt** the Holy Trinity/Family/City; **die Heilige Jungfrau** the Blessed Virgin; **Heilige Maria** Holy Mary; **der Heilige Geist/Vater/Stuhl** the Holy Spirit/Father/See; **die Heiligen Drei Könige** the Three Kings *or* Wise Men, the Magi; **das Heilige Land** the Holy Land; **die Heilige Schrift** the Holy Scriptures *pl*; **das Heilige Römische Reich** the Holy Roman Empire; **die Heilige Allianz** the Holy Alliance; **das Heiligste** *(lit, fig)* the holy of holies **b** *(fig: = ernst)* *Eid, Pflicht* sacred, solemn; *Recht* sacred; *Eifer, Zorn* righteous; *(von Ehrfurcht erfüllt)* *Stille, Schauer* awed; *(= unantastbar)* *Würde, Gefühl, Gewohnheit* sacred; **~e Kuh** sacred cow; **es ist mein ~er Ernst** I am deadly serious *(Brit)*, I am in dead earnest **c** *(inf: = groß)* incredible *(inf)*; *Respekt* healthy, incredible *(inf)*; **mit jdm/etw seine ~e Not haben** to have a hard time with sb/sth; **von einer ~en Angst gepackt werden** to be scared out of one's wits **d** *(inf: in Ausrufen)* **(ach du) ~er Bimbam** *or* **Strohsack!, ~es Kanonenrohr!** holy smoke! *(inf)*, hell's bell's! *(inf)*

Hei|lig|abend [hailɪç'la:bnt] M Christmas Eve

> **HEILIGABEND**
>
> **Heiligabend** is the evening of December 24th and is the time for **Bescherung**, when people exchange presents. According to tradition, the presents are brought – especially in Protestant areas – by the **Christkind**, who is rather like an angel and the baby Jesus combined. Around midnight candle-lit **Christmetten** take place. These are festive Christmas services in celebration of Jesus' birth. A traditional meal – usually goose, turkey or carp – is eaten on Christmas Day.

hei|li|gen ['hailɪgn] VT *(= weihen)* to hallow, to sanctify; *(= heilig halten)* to hallow, to keep holy; *Sonntag etc* to keep holy, to observe; **der Zweck heiligt die Mittel** the end justifies the means; **durch die Zeit geheiligt** time-honoured *(Brit)*, time-honored *(US)* → *auch* **geheiligt**

Hei|li|gen-: **Hei|li|gen|bild** NT holy picture; **Hei|li|gen|fi|gur** F figure *or* statue of a saint; **Hei|li|gen|le|gen|de** F life *or* story of the saints; **Hei|li|gen|schein** M halo; **jdn mit einem ~ umgeben** *(fig)* to put sb on a pedestal; **sich mit einem ~ umgeben** *(fig)* to be holier-than-thou; **Hei|li|gen|ver|eh|rung** F veneration of the saints

Hei|li|ge(r) ['hailɪgə] MF *decl as adj (lit, fig)* saint; **ein sonderbarer** *or* **wunderlicher ~r** *(inf)* a queer fish *(Brit inf)*, an odd bird *(US inf)*

Hei|lig-: **hei|lig+hal|ten** *sep irreg*, **hei|lig hal|ten** △ *irreg* VT to keep holy; *Andenken auch* to keep sacred; *Sonntag auch* to observe; **Hei|lig|keit** F -, *no pl* holiness; *(= Geweihtheit, Geheiligtheit auch, von Eigentum)* sacredness; *(von Zorn)* righteousness; **Eure/Seine ~** your/his Holiness; **im Geruch der ~ stehen** to be surrounded by an aura of sanctity; **hei|lig+spre|chen** *sep irreg*, **hei|lig spre|chen** △ *irreg* VT to canonize; **Hei|lig|spre|chung** [-ʃprɛçʊŋ] F **-, -en** canonization; **Hei|lig|tum** ['hailɪçtu:m] NT **-s, -tümer** [-ty:mɐ] *(= Stätte)* shrine; *(= Gegenstand)* (holy) relic; **Schändung eines ~s** sacrilege; **jds ~ sein** *(inf)* *(Zimmer)* to be sb's sanctum; *(Gegenstand etc)* to be sacrosanct (to sb)

Hei|li|gung F, *no pl* **die ~ des Sonntags** Lord's day *or* Sunday observance; **die ~ des Sabbats** the observance of the Sabbath

Heil-: **Heil|kli|ma** NT healthy climate; **heil|kli|ma|tisch** ADJ *Kurort* with a curative climate *(nachgestellt)*; **Heil|kraft** F healing power; **heil|kräf|tig** ADJ *Pflanze, Tee* medicinal; *Wirkung* curative; **ein ~es Mittel** a curative; **Heil|kraut** NT *usu pl* medicinal herb; **Heil|kun|de** F medicine; **heil|kun|dig** ADJ skilled in the art of healing, skilled in medicine; **Heil|kun|di|ge(r)** [-kʊndɪgə] MF *decl as adj* person skilled in medicine *or* in the art of healing, healer; **heil|los** ADJ unholy *(inf)*; *Durcheinander, Verwirrung auch* hopeless; *Schreck* terrible, frightful ADV **sich ~ verirren** to get hopelessly lost; **~ verschuldet sein** to be up to one's ears in debt; **die Partei war ~ zerstritten** the party was hopelessly divided; **Heil|me|tho|de** F cure; **Heil|mit|tel** NT *(lit, fig)* remedy, cure; *(= Medikament)* medicine; **Heil|pä|da|go|gik** F remedial education; **Heil|pflan|ze** F medicinal plant; **Heil|prak|ti|ker(in)** M(F) non-medical practitioner; **Heil|quel|le** F medicinal spring; **Heil|sal|be** F (medicated) ointment; **heil|sam** ['hailza:m] ADJ **a** *(dated: = heilend)* *Wirkung* healing; *Arznei* curative, healing; *Klima* salutary, beneficial **b** *(fig: = förderlich)* *Erfahrung, Strafe, Einfluss, Schock* salutary

Heils-: **Heils|ar|mee** F Salvation Army; **Heils|bot|schaft** F message of salvation, gospel

Heil|schlaf M healing sleep *(induced for therapeutic ends)*

Heils-: **Heils|ge|schich|te** F heilsgeschichte, *interpretation of history stressing God's saving grace*; **Heils|leh|re** F *(Rel, fig)* doctrine of salvation; **Heils|ord|nung** F order of salvation

Heil|stät|te F *(form)* sanatorium *(Brit)*, sanitarium *(US)*, clinic

Hei|lung ['hailʊŋ] F -, *(rare)* **-en** *(= das Heilen)* *(von Wunde)* healing; *(von Krankheit, Kranken)* curing; *(Rel)* healing; *(= das Gesundwerden)* cure; **~ in etw** *(dat)* **finden** to find relief in sth

Hei|lungs-: **Hei|lungs|chan|cen** PL chances *pl* of recovery; **Hei|lungs|pro|zess** M healing process

Heil-: **Heil|ver|fah|ren** NT (course of) treatment; **Heil|was|ser** NT *(aus Heilquelle)* healing water(s *pl*); *(in Flaschen)* healing water; **Heil|zweck** M **zu ~en** for medicinal purposes

heim [haim] ADV home; **~, bitte** let's go home; **~ ins Reich** *(NS)* back to the Reich *(referring to formerly German areas and their inhabitants)*

Heim [haim] NT **-(e)s, -e** *(= Zuhause, Anstalt)* home; *(= Obdachlosenheim, für Lehrlinge)* hostel; *(= Studentenwohnheim)* hall of residence, hostel, dormitory *(US)*; *(von Sportverein)* clubhouse; *(= Freizeitheim)* recreation centre *(Brit)* or center *(US)*; **~ und Herd** *(liter)* house and home

Heim- *in cpds* home; **Heim|abend** M social evening; **Heim|ar|beit** F *(Ind)* homework *no indef art*, outwork *no indef art*; **etw in ~ herstellen lassen** to have sth produced by homeworkers; **Heim|ar|bei|ter(in)** M(F) *(Ind)* homeworker; **Heim|ar|beits|platz** M **die Zahl der Heimarbeitsplätze nimmt zu** more and more people work from home

Hei|mat ['haima:t] F **-, -en** home; *(= Heimatort auch)* home town *(Brit)*, hometown *(US)*; *(= Heimatland auch)* native country; *(Bot, Zool auch)* natural habitat; **die ~ verlassen** to leave one's home; **jdm zur ~ werden** to become sb's home; **politische ~** political home

Hei|mat- *in cpds* home; **Hei|mat|an|schrift** F home address; **Hei|mat|dich|ter(in)** M(F) regional writer; **Hei|mat|dich|tung** F regional literature; **Hei|mat|er|de** F native soil; **Hei|mat|film** M *sentimental film in idealized regional setting*; **Hei|mat|flug|ha|fen** M home airport; **Hei|mat|for|scher(in)** M(F) local historian; **Hei|mat|for|schung** F research into local history; **Hei|mat|ha|fen** M home port; **Hei|mat|kun|de** F *(Sch)* local history; **hei|mat|kund|lich** [-kʊntlɪç] ADJ local history *attr*; **er hat ~e Interessen** he is interested in local history; **Hei|mat|kunst** F regional art; **Hei|mat|land** NT native country *or* land; **hei|mat|lich** ['haima:tlɪç] ADJ *(= zur Heimat gehörend)* native; *Bräuche, Dialekt* local; *(= an die Heimat erinnernd) Gefühle, Wehmut* nostalgic; *Klänge* of home; **die ~en Berge** the mountains of (one's) home; **~er Boden** native soil ADV **das mutet mich ~ an, das kommt mir ~ vor, das berührt mich ~** that reminds me of home; **Hei|mat|lie|be** F love of one's native country *or* land; **hei|mat|los** ADJ homeless; **Hei|mat|lo|se(r)** ['haima:tlo:zə] MF *decl as adj* homeless person; **die ~n** the homeless; **Hei|mat|lo|sig|keit** F **-**, *no pl* homelessness; **Hei|mat|mu|se|um** NT museum of local history; **Hei|mat|ort** M *pl* **-orte** a home town *(Brit)*, hometown *(US)*; *(= Dorf)* home village b *(= Heimathafen)* home port; **Hei|mat|recht** NT right of domicile; **Hei|mat|schrift|stel|ler(in)** M(F) regional writer; **Hei|mat|spra|che** F native dialect; *(Baskisch etc)* native language; **hei|mat|ver|trie|ben** ADJ displaced; **Hei|mat|ver|trie|be|ne(r)** MF *decl as adj* displaced person, expellee *(esp from eastern regions of the German Empire at the end of World War II)*

Heim-: **heim+be|ge|ben** *ptp* **heimbegeben** VR *sep irreg (geh)* to make one's way home; **heim+be|glei|ten** *ptp* **heimbegleitet** VT *sep* **jdn ~** to take *or* see sb home; **Heim|be|woh|ner(in)** M(F) resident (of a/the home); **heim+brin|gen** VT *sep irreg (= nach Hause bringen)* to bring home; *(= heimbegleiten)* to take *or* see home; **Heim|büg|ler** M rotary iron

Heim|chen ['haimçən] NT **-s, -** *(Zool)* house cricket; **~ (am Herd)** *(pej: = Hausfrau)* housewife

Heim-: **Heim|com|pu|ter** M home computer; **heim+dür|fen** VI *sep irreg* **darf ich/sie heim?** may I/she go home?; **heim+ei|len** VI *sep aux sein (geh)* to hurry home

hei|me|lig ['haiməlɪç] ADJ cosy *(Brit)*, cozy *(US)*; *Atmosphäre auch* homely

Hei|me|lig|keit F **-**, *no pl* cosiness *(Brit)*, coziness *(US)*

Heim-: **heim+fah|ren** VTI *sep irreg (vi: aux sein)* to drive home; **Heim|fahrt** F journey home, return journey; *(Naut)* return voyage, voyage home; **heim+fin|den** VI *sep irreg* to find one's way home; **heim+füh|ren** VT *sep* to take home; **ein Mädchen ~** *(dated)* to take a girl as one's wife *(dated)*; **Heim|gang** M *pl* **-gänge** *(euph geh: = Tod)* passing away; **beim ~ meiner Mutter** when my mother was called to her Lord *or* Maker *(euph)*; **Heim|ge|gan|ge|ne(r)** [-gəgaŋənə] MF *decl as adj (euph geh)* deceased; **unser lieber ~r** our dear departed friend/father *etc*; **heim+ge|hen** *sep irreg aux sein* VI to go home; *(euph geh)* to pass away *or* on VI *impers* **es geht heim** we're going home; **heim+ho|len** VT *sep* to fetch home; **Gott hat ihn heimgeholt** he has been called to his Maker; **Heim|in|dust|rie** F cottage industry

hei|misch ['haimɪʃ] ADJ a *(= einheimisch) (Zool, Bot)* indigenous, native *(in +acc* to); *Rohstoffe* native; *(= national) Wirtschaft, Markt, Industrie* domestic, home; *(= ortsansässig)* local; *(= regional)* regional; *Gewässer, Landschaft* native; **etw ~ machen** to introduce sth *(in +dat* to); **vor ~em Publikum** *or* **vor ~er Kulisse spielen** *(Sport)* to play in front of a home crowd b *(= vertraut)* familiar; **an einem Ort ~ sein** to feel at home in a place; **sich ~ fühlen** to feel at home; **vom ~en Herd weg sein** to be away from house and home; **in einer Sprache** *etc* **~ sein** to be *or* feel at home in a language *etc*; **sich ~ machen** to make oneself at home; **~ werden** to become acclimatized *(an, in +dat* to), to settle in *(an, in +dat* to)

Heim-: **Heim|kampf** M *(Sport)* home match *or* game; *(Boxen)* home fight; **Heim|kehr** ['haimke:ɐ] F **-**, *no pl* homecoming, return; **heim+keh|ren** VI *sep aux sein* to return home *(aus* from); **Heim|keh|rer** ['haimke:rɐ] M **-s, -**, **Heim|keh|re|rin** [-ərɪn] F **-, -nen** homecomer; **Heim|kind** NT institution child, child brought up in a home; **Heim|ki|no** NT home movies *pl*; *(= Ausrüstung)* home movie kit; *(inf: = TV)* gogglebox *(Brit inf)*, tube *(US inf)*; **heim+kom|men** VI *sep irreg aux sein* to come *or* return home; **heim+kön|nen** VI *sep irreg* to be able to go home; **Heim|kunft** ['haimkʊnft] F **-**, *no pl (geh)* homecoming, return; **Heim|lei|ter(in)** M(F) → **Heim** head *or* warden of a/the home/hostel; **Heim|lei|tung** F → **Heim** person(s) in charge of a/the home/hostel; **ihr wurde die ~ übertragen** she was put in charge of the home/hostel; **heim+leuch|ten** VI *sep (fig inf)* **jdm ~** to give sb a piece of one's mind

heim|lich ['haimlɪç] ADJ *(= geheim, verborgen)* secret; *Treffen auch* clandestine; *Benehmen* secretive; *Bewegungen* furtive ADV secretly; *treffen, tun auch* in secret; *lachen* inwardly; **er blickte sie ~ an** he stole a glance at her; **sich ~ entfernen** to steal *or* sneak away; **~, still und leise** *(inf)* quietly, on the quiet

Heim|lich|keit F **-, -en** secrecy; *(= Geheimnis)* secret; **in aller ~** secretly, in secret; **nur keine ~en!** *(inf)* stop being (so) secretive, no secrets now!

Heim|lich-: **Heim|lich|tu|er** [-tu:ɐ] M **-s, -**, **Heim|lich|tu|e|rin** [-ərɪn] F **-, -nen** secretive person; **Heim|lich|tu|e|rei** F secrecy, secretiveness; **heim|lich+tun** *sep irreg*, **heim|lich tun** △ *irreg* VI to be secretive *(mit* about)

Heim-: **heim+müs|sen** VI *sep irreg* to have to go home; **Heim|mut|ter** F *pl* **-mütter** warden of a/the home; *(von Jugendherberge)* hostel warden; **Heim|nie|der|la|ge** F *(Sport)* home defeat; **Heim|ord|nung** F → **Heim** rules *pl* and regulations *pl* of a/the home/hostel; **Heim|or|gel** F home organ; **Heim|rei|se** F journey home, homeward journey; *(Naut)* voyage home, homeward voyage; **heim+rei|sen** VI *sep aux sein* to travel home; **Heim|sau|na** F home sauna; **heim+schi|cken** VT *sep* to send home; **Heim|ser|vice** M home-delivery service; **Heim|sieg** M *(Sport)* home win *or* victory; **Heim|spiel** NT *(Sport)* home match *or* game; **Heim|statt** F *(liter)* home; **ohne ~** without a home; **Heim|stät|te** F a *(= Zuhause)* home b *(Jur)* homestead

heim+su|chen ['haimzu:xn] VT *sep* to strike; *(für längere Zeit)* to plague; *(Feind)* to attack; *(Gespenst)* to haunt; *(Krankheit)* to afflict; *(Albträume, Vorstellungen)* to afflict, to haunt; *(Schicksal)* to overtake, to afflict; *(inf: = besuchen)* to descend on *(inf)*; **von Dürre heimgesucht** drought-stricken; **vom Streik heimgesucht** strike-torn; **von Krieg heimgesucht** war-torn, war-ravaged; **Gott suchte die Ägypter mit schweren Plagen heim** God visited terrible plagues on the Egyptians

Heim|su|chung F **-, -en** a *(= Schicksalsschlag)* affliction; *(= Katastrophe)* disaster; *(= Plage)* plague b **Mariä ~** the visitation of Mary

Heim|trai|ner M exercise machine; *(= Trimmrad)* exercise bike

Heim|trai|ner(in) M(F) personal trainer

heim+trau|en VR *sep* to dare to go home

Heim|tü|cke F, *no pl (= Hinterlist)* insidiousness; *(= Boshaftigkeit)* maliciousness; *(von Mensch)* treachery; *(von Krankheit)* insidiousness; *(Jur)* malice; *(= Gefährlichkeit)* treacherous nature

heim|tü|ckisch ADJ *(= hinterlistig)* insidious; *(= boshaft)* malicious; *Krankheit* insidious; *(= gefährlich) Glatteis, Maschine* treacherous ADV *überfallen, verraten* insidiously, treacherously

Heim-: **Heim|un|ter|brin|gung** F accommodation in a home; **Heim|va|ter** M warden of a/the home; *(von Jugendherberge)* hostel warden; **Heim|vor|teil** M *(Sport, fig)* home advantage; **heim|wärts** ['haimvɛrts] ADV *(= nach Hause zu)* home; *(= auf dem Heimweg)* on the way home; **~ ziehen/gehen** to go homewards; **Heim|weg** M way home; **sich auf den ~ machen** to set out *or* head for home; **Heim|weh** M homesickness *no art*; **~ haben/bekommen** to be/become homesick *(nach* for); **krank vor ~ sein** to be pining for home, to be very homesick; **heim|weh|krank** ADJ homesick; **Heim|wer|ken** [-vɛrkn] NT do-it-yourself *(inf)*, DIY; **Heim|wer|ker** [-vɛrkɐ] M **-s, -**, **Heim|wer|ke|rin** [-ərɪn] F **-, -nen** do-it-yourself *or* DIY enthusiast, do-it-yourselfer *(inf)*; **Heim|wer|ker|be|darf** M do-it-yourself *or* DIY products *pl*; **heim+wol|len** VI *sep* to want to go home; **heim+zah|len** VT *sep* **jdm etw ~** to pay sb back for sth; **heim+zie|hen** *sep irreg* VI *aux sein* to return home VT *impers* **es zog ihn heim** he felt he wanted to go home

Hein [hain] M **Freund ~** *(old)* Death

Hei|ni ['haini] M **-s, -s** *(inf)* bloke *(Brit inf)*, guy *(inf)*; *(= Dummkopf)* idiot, fool

Hein|zel|männ|chen ['haintslmɛnçən] NT brownie

Hei|rat ['haira:t] F **-, -en** marriage; *(= Feier)* wedding; *(= Partie)* match

hei|ra|ten ['haira:tn] ✪ 51.3 VT to marry VR to get married VI to get married, to marry; **aufs Land/in die Stadt/nach Berlin ~** to marry *or* get married and settle in the country/in town/in Berlin; **in eine reiche/alte Familie ~** to marry into a rich/old family; **~ müssen** *(euph)* to have to get married; **„wir ~"** "we are getting married"; **„geheiratet haben ..."** ≈ "marriages", ≈ "marriage announcements"

Hei|ra|ten NT **-s**, *no pl* marriage, getting married *no def art*

Hei|rats-: **Hei|rats|ab|sich|ten** PL marriage plans *pl*; **Hei|rats|al|ter** NT marriageable *or* marrying age; *(Jur) minimum legal age for marriage*; **Hei|rats|an|non|ce** F advertisement for a marriage partner; **Hei|rats|an|trag** M proposal (of marriage); **jdm einen ~ machen** to propose to sb; **Hei|rats|an|zei|ge** F a (=

Bekanntgabe) announcement of a forthcoming marriage **b** *(= Annonce für Partnersuche)* advertisement for a marriage partner; **Hei|rats|bü|ro** NT marriage bureau; **Hei|rats|er|laub|nis** F consent (to a marriage); **hei|rats|fä|hig** ADJ **eine Frau/ein Mann im ~en Alter** a woman/man of marriageable age; **Hei|rats|in|sti|tut** NT marriage bureau; **Hei|rats|kan|di|dat** M *(= Bräutigam)* husband-to-be; *(= Ehewilliger)* eligible bachelor; **Hei|rats|kan|di|da|tin** F *(= Braut)* bride-to-be; *(= Ehewillige)* eligible woman; **hei|rats|lus|tig** ADJ eager to get married; **Hei|rats|markt** M **a** *(in Zeitung)* marriage ads *pl* **b** *(= Treff für Heiratswillige)* marriage market, cattle market *(pej inf)*; **hei|rats|mü|de** ADJ *(inf)* unwilling to marry; **Hei|rats|schwin|del** M marriage proposal made under false pretences *(Brit)* or pretenses *(US)*; **Hei|rats|schwind|ler(in)** M(F) person who makes a marriage proposal under false pretences *(Brit)* or pretenses *(US)*; **Hei|rats|ur|kun|de** F marriage certificate; **Hei|rats|ur|laub** M leave to get married; **Hei|rats|ver|mitt|ler(in)** M(F) marriage broker; **Hei|rats|ver|mitt|lung** F *(= Büro)* marriage bureau; **diskrete ~** marriages arranged discreetly; **Hei|rats|ver|spre|chen** NT *(Jur)* promise of marriage; **Bruch des ~s** breach of promise (of marriage); **hei|rats|wil|lig** ADJ ready to get married

hei|sa INTERJ hey

hei|schen VT *(geh)* **a** *Beifall, Hochachtung, Aufmerksamkeit etc* to demand **b** *(dated: = erbitten)* to beg or ask for

hei|ser ADJ hoarse; *(= dunkel klingend)* husky; *Laut* croaky ADV **~ reden** to talk hoarsely, to talk in a hoarse voice; **sich ~ schreien/reden** to shout/talk oneself hoarse

Hei|ser|keit F -, *no pl* hoarseness

heiß ADJ **a** hot; *Zone* torrid; **brennend/siedend/glühend ~** burning/boiling/scorching hot; **drückend ~** oppressively hot; **jdm ist/wird ~** sb is/is getting hot; **sie hat einen ~en Kopf** *(wegen Fieber)* she has a burning forehead; *(vom Denken)* her head is spinning; **etw ~ machen** to heat sth up; **~e Tränen weinen** to cry one's heart out; **mit der ~en Nadel genäht** thrown together; **ein Paar Heiße** *(dial)* a couple of hot sausages; **~!** *(inf: = fast gefunden)* you're hot → **baden**

b *(= heftig) Diskussion, Kampf, Auseinandersetzung* heated, fierce; *Zorn* impassioned; *Begierde* passionate, burning; *(= innig) Liebe, Wunsch* burning, fervent; **~en Dank** very many thanks

c *(= aufreizend) Musik, Sachen, Bilder* hot; *(inf: = sexuell erregt)* hot, randy *(Brit inf)*, horny *(inf)*; **~e Höschen** hot pants

d *(= gefährlich) Ware, Geld* hot; *(= radioaktiv) Teilchen etc* hot; *Gegend, Thema* hotly-disputed; **das wird ein ~er Winter** things are going to be pretty hot this winter *(inf)*; **ein ~es Eisen** a hot potato; **ein ~es Eisen anfassen** *(inf)* to grasp the nettle

e *attr (inf) Favorit, Tip, Maschine* hot; **ein ~er Ofen** a motorbike; **~er Draht** hotline; **~e Spur** firm lead

f *pred (inf: = brünstig)* **~ sein** to be on heat

ADV **a** *(= nicht kalt)* **~ waschen** to wash with hot water; **etw ~ trinken** to drink sth hot; **~ baden** to have a hot bath; **~ duschen** to take a hot shower; **es überläuft mich ~ und kalt** I feel hot and cold all over; **es wird nichts so ~ gegessen, wie es gekocht wird** *(prov)* things are never as bad as they seem

b *(= heftig)* **sich** *(dat)* **etw ~ wünschen** to be dying to have sth; **~ ersehnt** much longed for; **~ geliebt** dearly beloved; **eine ~ geführte Diskussion** a passionate discussion; **es ging ~ her** things got heated; **das Gebiet/die Stadt ist ~ umkämpft** the area/town is being hotly or fiercely fought over; **ein ~ umkämpfter Markt** a fiercely contested market; **~ umstritten** *(Frage)* hotly debated; *Künstler etc* highly controversial; **jdn/etw ~ und innig lieben** to love sb/sth madly → **heiß laufen, heißmachen, heißreden**

hei|ßa [ˈhaisa] INTERJ hey

heiß|blü|tig ADJ *(= erregbar)* hot-tempered; *(= leidenschaftlich)* hot-blooded; *Affäre, Tanz* passionate

hei|ßen [ˈhaisn] *pret* **hieß** [hiːs], *ptp* **geheißen** [gəˈhaisn] VT **a** *(= nennen)* to call; *(old: = Namen geben) jdn, Ort* to name; **das heiße ich klug vorgehen!** that's what I call being clever; **jdn einen Lügner** *etc* **~** to call sb a liar *etc*; **oder wie heißt man das?** *(inf)* ... or what do you call it?; **... oder wie man das heißt** ... or whatever it's called

b *(geh: = auffordern)* to tell, to bid *(form)*; **jdn etw tun ~** to tell sb to do sth, to bid sb do sth; **jdn willkommen ~** to bid sb welcome

VI **a** *(= den Namen haben, bezeichnet werden)* to be called *(Brit)* or named; *(= als Titel haben)* to be titled; **wie ~ Sie/heißt die Straße?** what are you/is the street called?, what's your name/the name of the street?; **ich heiße Müller** I'm called or my name is Müller; **sie heißt jetzt anders** her name is different now, she has changed her name; **nach jdm ~** to be called after *(Brit)* or for *(US)* sb; **wie kann man nur Gotthelf/so ~?** how can anyone have a name like Gotthelf/like that?; **wie heißt das?** what is that called?; **eigentlich heißt es richtig X** actually the correct word is X; **... und wie sie alle ~** ... and the rest of them; **... so wahr ich Franz-Josef heiße** *(als Bekräftigung)* ... as sure as I'm standing here; **... dann will ich Fridolin ~** ... then I'm a Dutchman *(Brit)* or a monkey's uncle

b *(= bestimmte Bedeutung haben)* to mean; **was heißt „gut" auf Englisch?** what is the English (word) for "gut"?; **„gut" heißt auf Englisch „good"** the English (word) for "gut" is "good"; **soll** or **will ~** *(am Satzanfang)* in other words; **ich weiß, was es heißt, allein zu sein** I know what it means to be alone

c *(= lauten)* to be; *(Spruch, Gedicht etc)* to go

d das heißt that is; *(= in anderen Worten)* that is to say

VI *impers* **a es heißt, dass ...** *(= es geht die Rede)* they say that ...; **es soll nicht ~, dass ...** never let it be said that ...

b *(= zu lesen sein)* **in der Bibel/im Gesetz/in seinem Brief heißt es, dass ...** the Bible/the law/his letter says that ..., in the Bible *etc* it says that ...; **bei Hegel/Goethe** *etc* **heißt es ...** Hegel/Goethe says ...; **es heißt hier ...** it says here ...

c *(= es ist nötig)* **es heißt, etw zu tun** you/we/he *etc* must do sth; **nun heißt es handeln** now it's time to act; **da heißt es aufgepasst** or **aufpassen** you'd better watch out

Heiß-: **heiß|er|sehnt** ADJ → **heiß ADV b**; **heiß|ge|liebt** ADJ → **heiß ADV b**; **Heiß|hun|ger** M ravenous or voracious appetite; **etw mit ~ essen** to eat sth ravenously or voraciously; **etw mit wahrem ~ verschlingen** *(fig)* to really devour sth; **heiß|hung|rig** ADJ ravenous, voracious ADV ravenously, voraciously; **heiß lau|fen** *irreg aux sein*, **heiß+lau|fen** △ *sep irreg aux sein* VI *(Motor, Auto, Maschinenteil)* to overheat; *(Diskussionsteilnehmer etc)* to become heated; *(Telefonleitungen, -drähte)* to buzz

Heiß|luft F hot air; **Kochen mit ~** fan-assisted cooking

Heiß|luft-: **Heiß|luft|bal|lon** M hot-air balloon; **Heiß|luft|hei|zung** F hot-air heating; **Heiß|luft|herd** M fan-assisted oven; **Heiß|luft|mo|tor** M hot-air or Stirling® engine; **Heiß|luft|trock|ner** [-trɔknɐ] M **-s, -** hot-air dryer

Heiß-: **heiß+ma|chen** VT *sep* **a** *(inf, fig)* **jdn ~** to turn sb on *(inf)* → *auch* **Hölle b** *(= erhitzen)* → **heiß ADJ a**; **Heiß|man|gel** F *(= Gerät)* rotary iron; *(= Ort)* laundry specializing in ironing sheets etc; **heiß+re|den** VT *sep* **sich** *(die Köpfe)* **~** to talk till one is blue in the face; **Heiß|sporn** M *pl* **-sporne** hothead; **heiß|um|kämpft** [-ʊmkɛmpft] ADJ → **heiß ADV b**; **heiß|um|strit|ten** ADJ → **heiß ADV b**; **Heiß|was|ser|be|rei|ter** [-bəraitɐ] M **-s, -** geyser, water heater; **Heiß|was|ser|spei|cher** M hot (water) tank

hei|ter [ˈhaitɐ] ADJ *(= fröhlich)* cheerful; *(= ausgeglichen)* serene; *(= amüsant) Geschichte* amusing, funny; *(= leicht betrunken)* merry; *(= hell, klar) Farbe, Raum* bright; *Himmel, Tag* bright, clear; *Wetter* clear, fine; *(Met)* fair; **~ werden** to become cheerful; *(Gesicht)* to brighten; *(Wetter)* to brighten or clear up; **~er werden** to cheer up; *(Wetter)* to brighten up, to become brighter; **das kann ja ~ werden!** *(iro)* that sounds great *(iro)*; **aus ~em Himmel** *(fig)* out of the blue

Hei|ter|keit F -, *no pl (= Fröhlichkeit)* cheerfulness; *(von Mensch, Wesen auch)* happiness; *(= Ausgeglichenheit)* serenity; *(= Helligkeit, Klarheit, von Himmel, Tag)* clearness; *(= heitere Stimmung)* merriment; *(= Belustigung)* amusement; **allgemeine ~ hervorrufen** to cause general merriment or amusement

Hei|ter|keits-: **Hei|ter|keits|aus|bruch** M fit of merriment; **Hei|ter|keits|er|folg** M **einen ~ haben** to raise a laugh

Heiz-: **Heiz|an|la|ge** F heating system; **Heiz|ap|pa|rat** M heater; **heiz|bar** ADJ *Heckscheibe etc* heated; *Zimmer auch* with heating; **der Saal ist schwer ~** the hall is difficult to heat → *auch* **beheizbar**; **Heiz|(bett)|de|cke** F electric blanket; **Heiz|ele|ment** NT heating element

hei|zen [ˈhaitsn] VI *(= die Heizung anhaben)* to have the/one's heating on; *(= Wärme abgeben)* to give off heat; **der Ofen heizt gut** the stove gives (off) a good heat; **mit Holz/Strom** *etc* **~** to use wood/electricity *etc* for heating; **ab November wird geheizt** the heating is put on in November VT *(= warm machen)* to heat; *(= verbrennen)* to burn; *(= beheizen) Lokomotive* to stoke; **den Ofen heize ich nur mit Holz** I only burn wood in the stove VR **sich gut/schlecht ~** to be easily/not easily heated, to be easy/hard to heat

Hei|zer [ˈhaitsɐ] M **-s, -**, **Hei|ze|rin** [-ərɪn] F **-, -nen** boilerman; *(von Lokomotive, Schiff)* stoker

Heiz-: **Heiz|flä|che** F heating surface; **Heiz|gas** NT fuel gas; **Heiz|ge|rät** NT heater; **Heiz|kes|sel** M boiler; **Heiz|kis|sen** NT electric heat pad; **Heiz|kör|per** M *(= Gerät)* heater; *(von Zentralheizung)* radiator; *(= Element)* heating element; **Heiz|kör|per|ver|klei|dung** F radiator cover; **Heiz|kos|ten** PL heating costs *pl*

Heiz|kos|ten-: **Heiz|kos|ten|ab|rech|nung** F heating bill; **Heiz|kos|ten|pau|scha|le** F fixed heating cost

Heiz|kraft F calorific or heating power

Heiz|kraft|werk NT thermal power station

Heiz|lüf|ter M fan heater

Heiz|ma|te|ri|al NT fuel *(for heating)*

Heiz|ofen M heater

Heiz|öl NT heating or fuel oil

Heiz|plat|te F hotplate

Heiz|son|ne F electric fire

Heiz|strah|ler M electric (wall) heater

Hei|zung [ˈhaitsʊŋ] F **-, -en** heating; *(= Heizkörper)* heater; *(von Zentralheizung)* radiator

Hei|zungs-: **Hei|zungs|an|la|ge** F heating system; **Hei|zungs|bau|er** M **-s, -**, **Hei|zungs|bau|e|rin** [-bauərɪn] F **-, -nen** heating engineer; **Hei|zungs|kel|ler** M boiler room; **Hei|zungs|mon|teur(in)** M(F) heating engineer; **Hei|zungs|rohr** NT heating pipe; **Hei|zungs|tech|nik** F heating engineering

Heiz|wert M calorific value

Hek|tar [hɛkˈtaːɐ, ˈhɛktaːɐ] NT OR M **-s, -e** hectare

Hek|tik [ˈhɛktɪk] F **-,** *no pl (= Hast)* hectic rush; *(von Großstadt etc)* hustle and bustle; *(von Leben etc)* hectic pace; **sie isst/arbeitet mit einer solchen ~** she eats/works at such a hectic pace; **nur keine ~** take it easy

hek|tisch ['hɛktɪʃ] ADJ (*auch dated Med*) hectic; *Mensch auch* frantic; *Arbeiten* frantic, furious ADV hectically; **es geht ~ zu** things are hectic; **ich lebe zurzeit ~** my life is very hectic just now; **nur mal nicht so ~** take it easy

Hek|to-: **Hek|to|gra|fie** [hɛktogra'fi:] F -, -n [-'fi:ən] (= *Verfahren*) hectography; (= *Abzug*) hectograph (copy); **hek|to|gra|fie|ren** [hɛktogra'fi:rən] *ptp* **hektografiert** VT *insep* to hectograph, to copy; **Hek|to|gra|phie** *etc* → **Hektografie** *etc*; **Hek|to|li|ter** [hɛkto'li:tɐ, 'hɛkto-] M OR NT hectolitre (*Brit*), hectoliter (*US*); **Hek|to|watt** [hɛkto'vat, 'hɛkto-] NT hectowatt

He|lan|ca® [he'laŋka] NT -, *no pl* stretch fabric

he|lau [he'lau] INTERJ *greeting used at Carnival time*

Held [hɛlt] M -en, -en [-dn] hero; **der ~ des Tages** the hero of the hour; **kein ~ in etw** (*dat*) **sein** not to be very brave about sth; (*in Schulfach etc*) to be no great shakes at sth (*inf*); **du bist mir ein (rechter** *or* **schöner) ~!** (*iro*) some hero you are!; **den ~en spielen** (*inf*) to come *or* play the (great) hero

Hel|den-: **Hel|den|brust** F (*hum*) manly chest; **Hel|den|dar|stel|ler** M (*Theat*) heroic leading man; **Hel|den|dich|tung** F epic *or* heroic poetry; **Hel|den|epos** NT heroic epic; **Hel|den|fried|hof** M military cemetery; **Hel|den|ge|denk|tag** M (*old*) ≈ Remembrance Day, ≈ Memorial Day (*US*); **Hel|den|ge|stalt** F hero; **hel|den|haft** ADJ heroic, valiant ADV heroically, valiantly; **Hel|den|lied** NT (*Liter*) epic song *or* lay; **Hel|den|mut** M heroic courage; **hel|den|mü|tig** [-my:tɪç] ADJ, ADV = **heldenhaft**; **Hel|den|po|se** F heroic pose; **Hel|den|rol|le** F (*Theat*) hero's part *or* role; **Hel|den|sa|ge** F heroic saga; **Hel|den|stück** NT **das war kein ~** (*inf*) that didn't exactly cover you/him *etc* in glory; **Hel|den|tat** F heroic deed *or* feat; **Hel|den|te|nor** M heroic tenor; **Hel|den|tod** M heroic death, hero's death; **den ~ sterben** to die a hero's death; (*Mil*) to be killed in action; **Hel|den|tum** ['hɛldntu:m] NT -s, *no pl* heroism

Hel|din ['hɛldɪn] F -, -nen heroine → *auch* **Held**

hel|fen ['hɛlfn] *pret* **half** [half], *ptp* **geholfen** [gə'hɔlfn] VI **a** (= *Beistand geben*) to help (*jdm* sb); (= *mit anfassen*) to lend a hand, to help; **jdm bei etw ~** to help sb with sth, to lend sb a hand with sth; **jdm etw tun ~** to help sb do sth; **er half ihr aus dem Mantel/einer Verlegenheit** he helped her out of her coat *or* off with her coat/out of a difficulty; **ihm/dir ist nicht zu ~** (*fig*) he is/you are beyond help; **dem Kranken ist nicht mehr zu ~** the patient is beyond help; **ich kann mir nicht ~** I can't help it; **ich kann mir nicht ~, ich muss es tun** I can't help doing it; **ich werd dir/ihm (schon) ~!** I'll give you/him what for (*inf*); **ich werde dir ~, die Tapeten zu beschmieren** I'll teach you to mess up the wallpaper (*inf*); **er weiß sich** (*dat*) **zu ~** he is very resourceful; **man muss sich** (*dat*) **nur zu ~ wissen** (*prov*) you just have to use your head; **er weiß sich** (*dat*) **nicht mehr zu ~** he is at his wits' end; **hilf dir selbst, dann** *or* **so hilft dir Gott** (*Prov*) God helps those who help themselves (*Prov*)

b *auch vi impers* (= *dienen, nützen*) to help; **es hilft nichts** it's no use *or* no good; **da ist nicht zu ~** there's no help for it; **da hilft alles nichts ...** there's nothing for it ...; **da hilft kein Jammern und kein Klagen** it's no use moaning; **es hilft ihm nichts, dass ...** it's no use to him that ...; **das hilft mir wenig, damit ist mir nicht geholfen** that's not much help to me; **das hat mir schon viel geholfen** that has been a great help to me; **was hilfts?** what's the use?; **was hülfe es dem Menschen, wenn ...** (*Bibl*) what does it profit a man if ... (*Bibl*)

c (= *heilsam sein*) to help; (= *heilen: auch Arzt*) to cure; **diese Arznei hilft gegen** *or* **bei Kopfweh** this medicine is good for headaches, this medicine helps to relieve headaches; **jetzt kann nur noch eine Operation ~** only an operation will help now *or* do any good now

Hel|fer ['hɛlfɐ] M -s, -, **Hel|fe|rin** [-ərɪn] F -, -nen helper; (= *Mitarbeiter*) assistant; (*von Verbrecher*) accomplice; (*inf*: = *Gerät*) help; **~ in Steuersachen** tax adviser; **ein ~ in der Not** a friend in need

Hel|fers|hel|fer(in) M(F) accomplice; (*Jur: vor/nach begangener Tat*) accessory before/after the fact

Hel|fer-: **Hel|fer|syn|drom** NT (*Psych*) (helpless) helper syndrome; **Hel|fer|zel|le** F (*Med*) helper cell

Hel|go|land ['hɛlgolant] NT -s Heligoland

He|li ['he:li] M -s, - (*Sw inf*) helicopter

He|li|kop|ter [heli'kɔptɐ] M -s, - helicopter

He|li|kop|ter-Ski|ing [-ski:ɪŋ] NT -s, *no pl*, **He|li|kop|ter|ski|ing** NT -s, *no pl* helicopter skiing

He|li|port [heli'pɔrt] M -s, -s heliport

He|li|ski|ing [-ski:ɪŋ] NT -s, *no pl* helicopter skiing

He|li|um ['he:liʊm] NT -s, *no pl* (*abbr* **He**) helium

hell [hɛl] ADJ **a** (*optisch*) light; *Licht, Beleuchtung, Himmel* bright; *Farbe* light, pale; *Kleidungsstück* light-coloured (*Brit*), light-colored (*US*); *Haar, Teint* fair; *Hautfarbe (von Rasse)* fair, pale; (*fig*) *Zukunft* bright; **es wird ~** it's getting light; **~ bleiben** to stay light; **am ~en Tage** in broad daylight; **bis in den ~en Morgen schlafen** to sleep late; **in ~en Flammen** in flames, ablaze; **~es Bier** ≈ lager

b (*akustisch*) *Laut, Ton, Stimme* high(-pitched); *Gelächter* ringing

c (*inf*: = *klug*) *Junge* bright, intelligent; (= *geistig klar*) *Augenblicke* lucid; **er ist ein ~er Kopf, er hat einen ~en Kopf** he has brains → **helle**

d *attr* (= *stark, groß*) great; *Verwunderung etc* utter; *Verzweiflung, Unsinn* sheer, utter; *Neid* pure; **in ~en Scharen** in great numbers; **seine ~e Freude an etw** (*dat*) **haben** to find great joy *or* pleasure in sth

ADV **a** (= *licht*) brightly; **~ leuchtend** brightly shining; *Farbe* bright; *Kleid* brightly coloured (*Brit*) *or* colored (*US*); **~ lodernd** blazing; **~ strahlend** brilliant, brightly shining

b (= *hoch*) **~ klingen** to sound high(-pitched); **~ tönen** to have a high-pitched ring

c (= *sehr*) absolutely; **von etw ~ begeistert/entzückt sein** to be very enthusiastic/quite delighted about sth

hell- *in cpds (esp auf Farben bezüglich)* light

Hel|las ['hɛlas] NT -' Hellas

hell-: **hell|auf** ['hɛl'lauf] ADV completely, utterly; **~ lachen** to laugh out loud; **~ begeistert sein** to be wildly enthusiastic; **hell|blau** ADJ light blue; **hell|blond** ADJ very fair, blonde; **hell|braun** ADJ light brown; **Hell|dun|kel** NT (*Art*) chiaroscuro

hel|le ['hɛlə] ADJ *pred* (*inf*) bright, clever; **Mensch, sei ~!** use your loaf, mate! (*Brit inf*), use your brain, buddy! (*US inf*)

Hel|le ['hɛlə] F -, *no pl* = **Helligkeit**

Hel|le|bar|de [hɛlə'bardə] F -, -n (*Hist*) halberd

Hel|le|ne [hɛ'le:nə] M -n, -n, **Hel|le|nin** [-'le:nɪn] F -, -nen (ancient) Greek, Hellene

hel|le|nisch [hɛ'le:nɪʃ] ADJ Hellenic

hel|le|ni|sie|ren [hɛleni'zi:rən] *ptp* **hellenisiert** VT to hellenize

Hel|le|nis|mus [hɛle'nɪsmʊs] M -, *no pl* Hellenism

Hel|le|nist [hɛle'nɪst] M -en, -en, **Hel|le|nis|tin** [-'nɪstɪn] F -, -nen Hellenist

Hel|le|nis|tik [hɛle'nɪstɪk] F -, *no pl* classical Greek studies *pl*

hel|le|nis|tisch [hɛle'nɪstɪʃ] ADJ Hellenistic; **die ~e Staatenwelt** the Hellenistic World

Hel|ler ['hɛlɐ] M -s, - (*Hist*) heller; **das ist keinen (roten** *or* **lumpigen)** *or* **nicht einen ~ wert** that isn't worth a brass farthing (*Brit*), that's worth nothing; **er besitzt keinen (roten** *or* **lumpigen)** ~ he doesn't have a penny to his name (*esp Brit*), he doesn't have two pennies to rub together (*esp Brit*); **darauf geb ich keinen (roten) ~** I wouldn't give you tuppence (*Brit*) *or* a dime (*US*) for it; **auf ~ und Pfennig, bis auf den letzten ~** (down) to the last farthing (*Brit*) *or* penny (*esp Brit*); *stimmen* down to the last detail

Hel|le(s) ['hɛlə] NT *decl as adj* (= *Bier*) ≈ lager; **zwei ~, bitte** two lagers, please

helleuchtend △ ADJ *attr* → **hell ADV a**

hell-: **hell|haa|rig** ADJ fair-haired; **hell|häu|tig** ADJ fair-skinned; (*von Rasse auch*) pale-skinned; **hell|hö|rig** ADJ keen (*Brit*) *or* quick (*US*) of hearing; (*Archit*) poorly soundproofed; **~ sein** (*fig: Mensch*) to have sharp ears; **als er das sagte, wurde ich ~** when he said that I pricked up my ears; **jdn ~ machen** to make sb prick up their ears

hellicht ADJ → **helllicht**

Hel|lig|keit F -, *no pl* lightness; (*von Licht, Beleuchtung, Himmel*) brightness; (*von Farbe*) lightness, paleness; (*von Haar, Teint, Haut*) fairness; (= *helles Licht*) light; (*Phys, Astron*) luminosity

Hel|lig|keits-: **Hel|lig|keits|reg|ler** M brightness control; **Hel|lig|keits|stu|fe** F brightness level

Hel|ling ['hɛlɪŋ] M -s, -e *or f* -, -en *or* **Hellingen** ['hɛlɪgn] (*Naut*) slipway

Hell-: **hell|leuch|tend** ADJ → **hell ADV a**; **hell|licht** ['hɛllɪçt] ADJ **am ~en Tage** in broad daylight; **es ist ~er Tag** it is broad daylight; **hell|lo|dernd**, **hellodernd** △ ADJ → **hell ADV a**; **Hell|raum|pro|jek|tor** M (*Sw*) overhead projector; **hell|rot** ADJ bright red; **hell|se|hen** VI *infin only* **~ können** to have second sight, to be clairvoyant; **du kannst wohl ~!** you must be clairvoyant; **Hell|se|hen** NT clairvoyance; **Hell|se|her(in)** M(F) (*lit, fig*) clairvoyant; **hell|se|he|risch** ADJ *attr* clairvoyant; **hell|sich|tig** ['hɛlzɪçtɪç] ADJ shrewd; **Hell|sich|tig|keit** F -, *no pl* shrewdness; **hell|strah|lend** ADJ *attr* → **hell ADV a**; **hell|wach** ADJ (*lit*) wide-awake; (*fig*) alert; **Hell|wer|den** NT daybreak

Helm [hɛlm] M -(e)s, -e helmet; (*Archit*) helm roof

Helm-: **Helm|busch** M plume; **Helm|pflicht** F **es besteht ~** the wearing of crash helmets is compulsory; **Helm|schmuck** M crest; **Helm|zwang** M = **Helmpflicht**

He|lot [he'lo:t] M -en, -en Helot

He|lo|ten|tum [he'lo:tntu:m] NT -s, *no pl* (= *Sklaverei*) helotism, helotage; (= *alle Heloten*) helotry

Hel|sin|ki ['hɛlzɪŋki] NT -s Helsinki

Hel|ve|tis|mus [hɛlve'tɪsmʊs] M -, **Helvetismen** [-'tɪsmən] (*Ling*) Helveticism

hem [həm, hm] INTERJ hem

Hemd [hɛmt] NT -(e)s, -en [-dn] (= *Oberhemd*) shirt; (= *Unterhemd*) vest (*Brit*), undershirt (*US*); **etw wie das** *or* **sein ~ wechseln** (*fig*) to change sth with monotonous regularity; **für dich gebe ich auch das letzte** *or* **mein letztes ~ her** (*inf*) I'd give you the shirt off my back (*inf*); **nass bis aufs ~** wet through, soaked to the skin; **jdn bis aufs ~ ausziehen** (*fig inf*) to have the shirt off sb's back (*inf*), to fleece sb (*inf*); **sich** (*dat*) **(wegen etw) ins ~ machen** (*sl*) to get one's knickers in a twist (over sth) (*Brit inf*), to get all worked up (about sth) (*inf*); **das ~ ist mir näher als der Rock** (*prov*) charity begins at home (*Prov*)

Hemd-: **Hemd|är|mel** M shirtsleeve; **in ~n** in one's shirtsleeves; **Hemd|blu|se** F shirt (-blouse), shirtwaist (*US*); **Hemd|blu|sen|kleid** NT shirtwaister (*Brit*) *or* shirtwaist (*US*) (dress); **Hemd|brust** F dickey

Hem|den-: **Hem|den|matz** M (*inf*) *small child dressed only in a vest*, ≈ Wee Willie Winkie; **Hem|den|stoff** M shirting

Hẹmd-: **Hẹmd|ho|se** F combinations *pl*, combs *pl (inf)*; **Hẹmd|knopf** M shirt button; **Hẹmd|kra|gen** M shirt collar

Hẹmds-: **Hẹmds|är|mel** M shirtsleeve; **in ~n** in one's shirtsleeves; **hẹmds|är|me|lig** ADJ shirt-sleeved; *(fig inf)* down-to-earth; *Ausdrucksweise, Empfang, Einstellung* casual

He|mi|sphä|re [hemi'sfɛ:rə] F hemisphere

he|mi|sphä|risch [hemi'sfɛ:rɪʃ] ADJ hemispheric(al)

hẹm|men ['hɛmən] VT *Entwicklung, Fortschritt* to hinder, to hamper; *Lauf der Geschehnisse etc* to check; *(= verlangsamen)* to slow down; *Maschine, Rad* to check; *Wasserlauf* to stem; *(Med) Blut* to staunch; *(Psych)* to inhibit; *Leidenschaften* to restrain, to check; **jdn in seiner Entwicklung ~** to hinder *or* hamper sb's development → *auch* **gehemmt**

Hẹmm|nis ['hɛmnɪs] NT **-ses, -se** hindrance, impediment *(für* to)

Hẹmm-: **Hẹmm|rad** NT *(von Uhr)* escapement; **Hẹmm|schuh** M brake shoe; *(fig)* hindrance, impediment *(für* to); **jdm einen ~ in den Weg legen** *(fig)* to obstruct sb; **Hẹmm|schwel|le** F inhibition level *or* threshold; **eine ~ überwinden** to overcome one's inhibitions; **Hẹmm|stoff** M *(Chem)* inhibitor

Hẹm|mung ['hɛmʊŋ] F **-, -en** **a** *(Psych)* inhibition; *(= Bedenken)* scruple; **da habe ich ~en** I've got scruples about that; **an ~en leiden** to suffer from inhibitions; **keine ~en kennen** to have no inhibitions, not to feel inhibited; **nur keine ~en** don't feel inhibited **b** *(von Entwicklung, Fortschritt)* hindering, hampering; *(= Verlangsamung)* slowing down **c** *(von Gewehr)* **bei einer ~ des Gewehrs** when the gun is jammed **d** *(von Uhr)* escapement

Hẹm|mungs-: **hẹm|mungs|los** ADJ *(= rückhaltlos)* unrestrained; *(= skrupellos)* unscrupulous ADV *brüllen, schreien, jubeln, weinen* without restraint; *sich hingeben, genießen* wantonly; *foltern, töten* without conscience; **jdn ~ machen** to remove sb's inhibitions; **Hẹm|mungs|lo|sig|keit** F **-, -en** *(= Rückhaltlosigkeit)* lack *no pl* of restraint; *(= Skrupellosigkeit)* unscrupulousness *no pl*; **Hẹm|mungs|nerv** M inhibitor (nerve)

Hẹndl ['hɛndl] NT **-s, -(n)** *(S Ger, Aus)* chicken

Hẹndl|bra|te|rei [-bra:tərai] F **-, -en** *(S Ger, Aus)* grilled chicken place

Hẹngst [hɛŋst] M **-(e)s, -e** stallion; *(= Kamelhengst, Eselhengst)* male; *(sl: = Mann)* stud *(inf)*

Hẹngst|foh|len NT, **Hẹngst|fül|len** NT (male) foal, colt

Hẹn|kel ['hɛŋkl] M **-s, -** handle

Hẹn|kel-: **Hẹn|kel|glas** NT glass with a handle; **Hẹn|kel|korb** M basket with a handle; **Hẹn|kel|krug** M jug (with a handle); **Hẹn|kel|mann** M *pl* **-männer** *(inf) set of containers for reheating lunch at work*; **Hẹn|kel|oh|ren** PL *(inf)* big, sticking-out ears *pl (inf)*; **Hẹn|kel|topf** M pot *or* pan with a handle/handles

hẹn|ken ['hɛŋkn] VT *(old)* to hang

Hẹn|ker ['hɛŋkɐ] M **-s, -** hangman; *(= Scharfrichter)* executioner; **zum ~** *(old inf)* hang it all *(inf)*, zounds *(obs inf)*; **was zum ~!** *(old inf)* what the devil *(inf)*; **hols der ~!** *(old inf)* the devil take it! *(old inf)*; **hol mich der ~** *(old inf)* zounds *(obs inf)*; **scher dich** *or* **geh zum ~!** *(old inf)* go to the devil! *(inf)*; **wie der ~ fahren** *(inf)* to drive like a maniac *(inf)*

Hẹn|ker(s)|beil NT executioner's axe *(Brit) or* ax *(US)*

Hẹn|kers-: **Hẹn|kers|hand** F **durch** *or* **von ~ sterben** to be executed; **Hẹn|kers|knecht** M *(Hist)* hangman's *or (von Scharfrichter)* executioner's assistant; *(fig)* torturer; *(= Handlanger)* henchman; **Hẹn|kers|mahl** NT, **Hẹn|kers|mahl|zeit** F last meal before execution; *(hum inf)* last slap-up meal *(Brit)*, final feast *(esp US, before examination etc)*

Hẹn|na ['hɛna] F **-** *or nt* **-(s)**, *no pl* henna; **mit ~ färben** to dye with henna, to henna

Hẹn|ne ['hɛnə] F **-, -n** hen

He|pa|ti|tis [hepa'ti:tɪs] F **-, Hepatitiden** [-ti-'ti:dn] hepatitis

her [he:ɐ] ADV → *auch* **herkommen, hermüssen, her sein** *etc* **a** *(räumlich)* **von der Kirche/Frankreich/dem Meer ~** from the church/France/the sea; **er winkte vom Nachbarhaus ~** he waved from the house next door; **~ zu mir!** come here (to me); **um mich ~** (all) around me; **von weit ~** from a long way off *or* away, from afar *(liter)* → *auch* **hin**

b *(in Aufforderung)* **Bier/Essen ~!** bring (me/us) some beer/food (here); **~ mit dem Geld!** hand over your money!, give me your money!; **(wieder) ~ mit den alten Bräuchen** give me/us the old way of doing things, bring back the old customs, I say; **~ damit!** give me that, give that here *(inf)*; **immer ~ damit!** let's have it/them (then)

c *(von etwas aus gesehen)* **von der Idee/Form ~** as for the idea/form, as far as the idea/form is concerned *or* goes; **vom finanziellen Standpunkt ~** from the financial point of view; **von den Eltern ~ gute Anlagen haben** to have inherited good qualities from one's parents

d *(zeitlich)* **ich kenne ihn von früher ~** I know him from before *or* from earlier times, I used to know him (before); **von der Schule/meiner Kindheit ~** since school/my childhood; **von der letzten Saison ~** from last season → **her sein**

he|rab [hɛ'rap] ADV down; **den Hügel/die Treppe ~** down the hill/stairs; **von oben ~** (down) from above → **oben**

he|rab- PREF → *auch* **herunter-, runter-** down; **he|rab+bli|cken** VI *sep (lit, fig)* to look down *(auf +acc* on); **he|rab+fle|hen** VT *sep (liter)* to call down; **he|rab+flie|ßen** VI *sep irreg aux sein* to flow down; **he|rab+hän|gen** VI *sep irreg* to hang down; **langes ~des Haar** long, flowing hair; **he|rab+kom|men** VI *sep irreg aux sein (geh)* to come down, to descend *(liter, form)*; **he|rab+las|sen** *sep irreg* VT to let down, to lower VR **a** *(lit)* to let oneself down, to lower oneself **b** *(fig)* to lower oneself; **sich zu etw ~** to condescend *or* deign to do sth; **sich auf jds Ebene** *(acc)* **~** to descend to sb's level; **wenn du dich ~ könntest, mir dabei zu helfen** if you would condescend *or* deign to help me with it; **he|rab|las|send** ADJ condescending; *Verachtung* haughty ADV condescendingly; **sich ~ benehmen** to be condescending; **He|rab|las|sung** [-lasʊŋ] F **-**, *no pl* condescension; **he|rab+min|dern** VT *sep (= schlechtmachen) Leistung, Qualitäten* to belittle, to disparage; *(= bagatellisieren) Gefahr, Problem* to minimize, to make little of; *(= reduzieren) Geschwindigkeit, Länge, Niveau* to reduce; **he|rab+rie|seln** VI *sep aux sein* to trickle down; *(Schneeflocken, Staub, Musik)* to float *or* waft down; **he|rab+se|hen** VI *sep irreg (lit, fig)* to look down *(auf +acc* on); **he|rab+sen|ken** VR *sep (geh: Nebel, Dunkelheit, Abend)* to fall; **he|rab+set|zen** VT *sep Ware* to reduce; *Preise, Kosten auch* to lower; *Geschwindigkeit auch* to slacken off; *Niveau* to lower, to debase; *(= schlechtmachen) Leistungen, Fähigkeiten, jdn* to belittle, to disparage; **zu stark herabgesetzten Preisen** at greatly reduced prices; **he|rab|set|zend** ADJ disparaging ADV disparagingly; **sich ~ über jdn äußern** to speak disparagingly of sb; **He|rab|set|zung** [-zɛtsʊŋ] F **-, -en** *(von Ware)* reduction; *(von Preisen, Kosten auch)* lowering; *(von Niveau)* debasement, lowering; *(von Leistungen, Fähigkeiten)* belittling, disparagement; *(= Kränkung)* slight, snub; **he|rab+sin|ken** VI *sep irreg aux sein* to sink (down); *(liter: Nacht)* to fall, to descend *(liter)*; **he|rab+stei|gen** VI *sep irreg aux sein* to get down, to descend; *(von Pferd)* to dismount; *(von Berg)* to climb down, to descend; **he|rab+sto|ßen** VI *sep irreg aux sein* to swoop (down); **he|rab+stür|zen** *sep* VT to push off *(von etw* sth) VI *aux sein* to fall off *(von etw* sth); *(Felsbrocken)* to fall down *(von* from); *(geh: Wasserfall)* to cascade *or* plunge down, to come rushing down VR to jump off *(von etw* sth); **er stürzte sich vom Turm herab** he threw himself off *or* from the tower, he jumped off *or* from the tower; **he|rab+wür|di|gen** *sep* VT to belittle, to disparage VR to degrade *or* lower oneself; **He|rab|wür|di|gung** F belittling, disparagement; **he|rab+zie|hen** VT *sep irreg (lit)* to pull down; *Mundwinkel* to turn down; *(fig) jdn* to drag down

He|ral|dik [he'raldɪk] F **-**, *no pl* heraldry

he|ral|disch [he'raldɪʃ] ADJ heraldic

he|ran [hɛ'ran] ADV **rechts/links ~!** over to the right/left; **immer** *or* **nur ~!** come on *or* along (then)!; **bis an etw** *(acc)* **~** close *or* near to sth, right by *or* beside sth; *(mit Bewegungsverb)* right up to sth

he|ran- PREF → *auch* **ran-:** **he|ran+ar|bei|ten** VR *sep (= sich nähern)* to work one's way along; **sich an jdn/etw ~** to work one's way (along *or* over) toward(s) sb/sth; **he|ran+bil|den** VT *sep* to train (up); *(in der Schule)* to educate; **he|ran+brin|gen** VT *sep irreg (= herbringen)* to bring over; **sein Spurt brachte ihn näher an den führenden Läufer heran** his spurt brought him up toward(s) the leader *or* brought him nearer to the leader; **die Schüler bedächtig an diese schwierigen Probleme ~** to introduce the pupils slowly to these difficult problems; **he|ran+ei|len** VI *sep aux sein (geh)* to rush *or* hurry over; **he|ran+fah|ren** VTI *sep irreg aux sein* to drive *or (mit Fahrrad)* ride up *(an +acc* to); **he|ran+füh|ren** *sep* VT *jdn* to lead up; *Truppen* to bring up; **jdn an etw** *(acc)* **~** *(lit)* to lead/bring sb up to sth; *(fig) (Frage, Problem)* to lead *or* bring sb to sth; *(Lehrer etc)* to introduce sb to sth VI **an etw** *(acc)* **~** *(lit, fig)* to lead to sth; **he|ran+ge|hen** VI *sep irreg aux sein* to go up *(an +acc* to); **ich würde nicht näher ~** I wouldn't go any nearer *or* closer; **an jdn/etw ~** *(lit)* to go up to sb/sth; *(fig: = angreifen) an Problem, Aufgabe* to tackle *or* approach sth; *an Gegner* to set about sb; **he|ran+kom|men** VI *sep irreg aux sein* **a** *(räumlich)* to come *or* draw near *(an +acc* to), to approach *(an etw (acc)* sth); *(zeitlich)* to draw near *(an +acc* to), to approach *(an etw (acc)* sth); **das lasse ich mal an mich ~** *(fig inf)* I'll cross that bridge when I come to it *(prov)*; **die Verfolger kamen dicht an den führenden Läufer heran** those behind were almost catching up with the leader; **unsere Verfolger kamen immer näher heran** our pursuers were gaining on us; **auf 1:3 ~** to pull up *or* back to 1-3; **er lässt alle Probleme an sich ~** he always adopts a wait-and-see attitude **b** *(= erreichen, bekommen)* **an den Chef/Motor kommt man nicht heran** you can't get hold of the boss/get at *or* to the engine; **wie komme ich nur an das Kapital heran?** how do I get hold of *or (wenn festgelegt)* get at the capital? **c** *(= sich messen können mit)* **an jdn ~** to be up to the standard of sb; **an etw** *(acc)* **~** to be up to (the standard of) sth; **an diesen Wissenschaftler kommt keiner heran** there's no-one who is a patch on *(Brit) or* a match for *(US)* this scientist; **er kommt nicht an seinen Vater heran** he's not a patch on *(Brit) or* a match for *(US)* his father **d** **an etw** *(acc)* **~** *(= grenzen an)* to verge on sth; **he|ran+ma|chen** VR *sep (inf)* **sich an etw** *(acc)* **~** to get down to sth, to get going on sth *(inf)*; **sich an jdn ~** to approach sb, to have a go at sb *(inf)*; *an Mädchen* to make up to sb, to chat sb up *(esp Brit inf)*; **he|ran+na|hen** VI *sep aux sein (geh)* to approach; *(Katastrophe, Unwetter auch)* to be imminent; **He|ran|na|hen** NT **-s**, *no pl (geh)* approach; **he|ran+pir|schen** VR *sep* **sich an jdn/etw ~** to stalk up on sb/sth; **he|ran+rei|chen** ✪ 32.3 VI *sep* **an jdn/etw ~** *(lit) (Mensch)* to reach sb/sth; *(Weg, Gelände etc)* to reach (up to) sth; *(fig: = sich messen können mit)* to come up to (the standard of) sb/sth, to come near sb/sth; **er reicht bei Weitem nicht an mich heran** *(fig)* he is nowhere near as good as me, he can't touch me *(inf)*; **he|ran+rei|fen** VI *sep aux sein (geh) (Obst)* to ripen; *(fig) (Jugend-*

liche) to mature; *(Plan, Entschluss, Idee)* to mature, to ripen; **zur Frau/zum Mann/zum Erwachsenen ~** to mature into a woman/a man/an adult; **he|ran+rü|cken** *sep* VI *aux sein (= sich nähern)* to approach *(an etw (acc)* sth); *(Truppen auch)* to advance *(an +acc* upon, towards); *(= dicht aufrücken)* to move nearer *or* closer *(an +acc* to); **er rückte mit seinem Stuhl heran** he brought *or* drew his chair up *or* nearer VT to move over *or* up *(an +acc* to); **rück deinen Stuhl heran** bring *or* draw up your chair; **he|ran+schaf|fen** VT *sep* to bring (along); **he|ran+schlei|chen** VIR *sep irreg (vi: aux sein)* to creep up *(an etw (acc)* to sth, *an jdn* on sb); **he|ran+tas|ten** VR *sep (lit)* to feel *or* grope one's way over *(an +acc* to); *(fig)* to feel one's way; **sich an eine Frage ~** to approach a matter cautiously; **he|ran+tra|gen** VT *sep irreg* to bring (over), to carry over; **etw an jdn ~** *(fig)* to take sth to sb, to go to sb with sth; **he|ran+tre|ten** VI *sep irreg aux sein (lit)* to move up *(an +acc* to); **näher ~** to move nearer; **bitte treten Sie näher heran!** this way!, come along!; **an jdn ~** *(fig) (= konfrontieren: Probleme, Zweifel, Versuchung)* to confront *or* face sb; **mit etw an jdn ~** *(= sich wenden an)* to go to *or* approach sb with sth; **he|ran+wach|sen** VI *sep irreg aux sein (geh)* to grow; *(Kind)* to grow up; *(fig: Probleme, Konkurrenz)* to grow up *(jdm* around sb); **zu einer schönen jungen Frau ~** to grow (up) into *or* to be a lovely young woman; **die ~de Generation** the rising generation, the up-and-coming generation; **He|ran|wach|sen|de(r)** MF *decl as adj (Jur)* adolescent; **he|ran+wa|gen** VR *sep* to venture near, to dare to go near; **sich an etw (acc) ~** *(lit)* to venture near sth, to dare to go near sth; *(fig)* to venture to tackle sth; **er wagte sich nicht an sie heran** he did not dare to approach her; **he|ran+win|ken** VT *sep* to beckon *or* wave over; *Taxi* to hail; **einen Polizisten ~** to call a policeman over

he|ran+zie|hen *sep irreg* VT **a** *(= näher bringen)* to pull over, to draw near *(an +acc* to)
b *(= zu Hilfe holen)* to call in; *Literatur* to consult; **jdn zur Hilfe/Unterstützung ~** to enlist sb's aid *or* help/support
c *(= einsetzen) Arbeitskräfte, Kapital* to bring in; **jdn zu einer Aufgabe ~** to enlist sb to do a task
d *(= geltend machen) Recht, Paragrafen, Quelle, Zitat* to call *or* bring into play; **etw zum Vergleich ~** to use sth by way of comparison
e *(= aufziehen) Tier, Kind* to raise; *Pflanze* to cultivate; **jdn zu etw ~** to bring sb up to be sth; **sich** *(dat)* **Revolutionäre/Jasager ~** *(pej)* to make revolutionaries/yes men for oneself
VI *aux sein* to approach; *(Mil)* to advance

He|ran|zie|hungs|be|scheid M *(Admin)* final notice

he|rauf [hɛˈrauf] ADV up; **vom Tal ~** up from the valley; **von unten ~** up from below; **vom Süden ~** *(inf)* up from the south PREP *+acc* up; **den Fluss/den Berg/die Treppe ~** up the river/mountain/stairs

he|rauf- *pref → auch* **rauf-** up; **he|rauf+ar|bei|ten** VR *sep (lit, fig)* to work one's way up; **he|rauf+bli|cken** VI *sep (geh)* to look up *(zu* to); **he|rauf+däm|mern** VI *sep aux sein (liter)* to dawn; **he|rauf+füh|ren** *sep* VT *Pferd etc* to lead up; *jdn* to show up VI *(Weg etc)* to lead up

he|rauf- PREF → *auch* **rauf-** up; **he|rauf+be|mü|hen** *ptp* **heraufbemüht** *sep (geh)* VT to trouble to come up, to ask (to come) up VR to take the trouble to come up; **he|rauf+be|schwö|ren** *ptp* **heraufbeschworen** VT *sep irreg* **a** *(= wachrufen) Erinnerung, Vergangenheit* to evoke **b** *(= herbeiführen) Unglück, Streit, Krise* to cause, to give rise to; **he|rauf+bit|ten** VT *sep irreg* to ask (to come) up; **he|rauf+brin|gen** VT *sep irreg* to bring up; **he|rauf+drin|gen** VI *sep irreg aux sein* to rise (up) from below; *(Geruch)* to waft up; **ein Geräusch drang zu ihm herauf** a noise from below reached him *or* his ears; **he|rauf+dür|fen** VI *sep irreg (inf)* to be allowed up; **he|rauf+kom|men** VI *sep irreg aux sein* to come up; *(in oberes Stockwerk)* to come up(stairs); *(auf Boot, Kutsche)* to climb *or* come *or* get aboard; *(Mond, Geräusch, Nebel, Wolke)* to rise; *(Gewitter)* to approach; **he|rauf+la|den** VT *sep irreg (Comput)* to upload; **he|rauf+las|sen** VT *sep irreg* to allow (to come) up; **er wollte mich nicht in den 2. Stock ~** he wouldn't let me come up to the 2nd *(Brit) or* 3rd *(US)* floor; **he|rauf+rei|chen** *sep* VT to hand *or* pass up VI to reach; **der Baum reicht bis zum Fenster herauf** the tree reaches (up to) *or* comes up to the window; **he|rauf+set|zen** *sep* VT *Preise etc* to increase, to raise VR **komm setz dich zu mir herauf** come up here and sit with me, come and sit up here with me;; **he|rauf+stei|gen** VI *sep irreg aux sein* **a** *(= heraufklettern)* to climb up; *(Dampf, Rauch)* to rise; *(Erinnerungen)* to well up *(in jdm* in sb) **b** *(liter: = anbrechen) (Tag, neue Zeit)* to dawn; *(Dämmerung)* to break; **he|rauf+tra|gen** *sep irreg* VT to carry up; **he|rauf+zie|hen** *sep irreg* VT to pull up; **er zog ihn zu sich herauf** *(lit)* he pulled him up to him; *(fig)* he raised him to his own level VI *aux sein* **a** *(Gewitter, Unheil etc)* to approach; *(liter, Nacht, Tag, Zeitalter)* to draw nigh *(liter) or* near **b** *(= nach oben umziehen)* to move up

he|raus [hɛˈraus] ADV → *auch* **herauskommen, heraus sein** *etc* out; **~ da!** *(inf)* get *or* come out of there!; **da ~?** out of there?; **~ aus den Federn!** *(inf)* rise and shine! *(inf)*; **~ mit ihm** *(inf)* get him out!; **~ damit!** *(inf) (= gib her)* hand it over!; *(= heraus mit der Sprache!)* out with it! *(inf)*; **zum Fenster ~** out of the window; **nach vorn ~ wohnen** to live facing *or* at the front; **von innen ~** to the core, through and through; **das rostet von innen ~ durch** it's rusting through from the inside; **mir ist von innen ~ kalt** I'm cold inside; **etw von innen ~ heilen** to cure sth from inside; **aus einem Gefühl der Verlassenheit ~** out of a feeling of forlornness → **freiheraus**

he|raus- PREF → *auch* **raus-** out; **he|raus+ar|bei|ten** *sep* VT *(aus Stein, Holz)* to carve *(aus* out of); *(fig)* to bring out VR to work one's way out *(aus* of); **he|raus+be|kom|men** *ptp* **herausbekommen** VT *sep irreg* **a** *Fleck, Nagel etc* to get out *(aus* of) **b** *(= ermitteln, herausfinden) Täter, Ursache, Geheimnis* to find out *(aus jdm* from sb); *Lösung, Aufgabe* to work *or* figure out **c** *Wechselgeld* to get back; **Sie bekommen noch 1 Euro heraus** you still have 1 euro change to come; **he|raus+bil|den** VR *sep* to form, to develop *(aus* out of); **he|raus+bo|xen** VT *sep (aus* of) *Ball* to punch out; *(inf) jdn* to bail out *(inf)*; **he|raus+brin|gen** VT *sep irreg* **a** *(lit)* to bring out *(aus* of) **b** *(inf: = entfernen, ermitteln)* = **herausbekommen a, b c** *(auf den Markt bringen)* to bring out; *neues Modell* to bring out, to launch; **jdn/etw ganz groß ~** to launch sb/sth in a big way, to give sb/sth a big build-up; **die Affäre wurde in allen Zeitungen groß herausgebracht** the affair made a big splash in the papers, they made a big splash of the affair in the papers **d** *(= hervorbringen) Worte* to utter, to say; **er brachte kein Wort/keinen Ton heraus** he couldn't utter a word/sound; **aus ihm war kein Wort herauszubringen** they couldn't get a (single) word out of him; **he|raus+dre|hen** VT *sep Birne, Schraube* to unscrew *(aus* from); **he|raus+drin|gen** VI *sep irreg aux sein* to come out *(aus* of); *(Wasser, Information auch)* to leak out *(aus* from); **he|raus+drü|cken** VT *sep* to squeeze out *(aus* of); **die Brust ~** to stick one's chest out; **he|raus+fah|ren** *sep irreg* VI *aux sein* **a** *(aus* of) to come out; *(Auto, Fahrer)* to come *or* drive out; *(Zug)* to pull *or* draw out; *(Radfahrer)* to ride out; **aufs Land/zu Besuch herausgefahren kommen** to drive *or* come out to the country/for a visit **b** *(= schnell herauskommen)* to leap out; *(= entweichen)* to come out; *(Wort etc)* to slip out, to come out; **das Wort ist mir nur so herausgefahren** that word just came *or* slipped out somehow VT **a** *(aus* of) *Zug, Auto* to drive out; *Fahrrad* to ride out **b** *(Sport)* **eine gute** *or* **schnelle Zeit/den Vorsprung ~** to make good time/the lead; **einen Sieg ~** to drive to victory; *(bei Rad-/Motorradrennen)* to ride to victory; **verlorene Minuten ~** to make up for lost time; **he|raus+fil|tern** VT *sep (aus* of) to filter out; *(fig auch)* to sift out; **he|raus+fin|den** *sep irreg* VT *Fehler, Fakten, Täter etc* to find out; *(= herauslesen) Gesuchtes* to pick out *(aus* from (among)), to find *(aus* (from) among); **er hat herausgefunden, dass …** he has found out *or* discovered that …; *(= erkannt)* he has found *or* discovered that … VIR to find one's way out *(aus* of); **he|raus+fi|schen** VT *sep (inf)* to fish out *(inf) (aus* of); **sich** *(dat)* **etw ~** to pick sth out (for oneself); **sich immer das Beste aus allem ~** always to take the best of everything; **he|raus+flie|gen** *sep irreg* VI *aux sein (aus* of) *(lit)* to fly out; *(inf: = herausfallen)* to come flying out VT to fly out *(aus* of)

He|raus|for|de|rer [hɛˈrausfɔrdərɐ] M **-s, -**, **He|raus|for|de|rin** [-ərɪn] F **-, -nen** challenger

he|raus+for|dern [hɛˈrausfɔrdɐn] *sep* VT *(esp Sport)* to challenge *(zu* to); *(= provozieren)* to provoke *(zu etw* to do sth); *Kritik, Protest* to invite; *(= heraufbeschwören) Gefahr* to court; *Unglück* to court, to invite; **das Schicksal ~** to tempt fate *or* providence VI **zu etw ~** *(= provozieren)* to invite sth

he|raus|for|dernd ADJ provocative; *(= lockend auch)* inviting; *Blick auch* come-hither *attr*; *(= Auseinandersetzung suchend) Reden, Haltung, Blick* challenging ADV *(= aggressiv, sexuell)* provocatively; *(= lockend)* invitingly; **jdn ~ ansehen** to give sb a provocative look

He|raus|for|de|rung F challenge; *(= Provokation)* provocation

he|raus+füh|len VT *sep (fig)* to sense *(aus* from)

he|raus+füh|ren VTI *sep (lit, fig)* to lead out *(aus* of)

He|raus|ga|be F **a** *(= Rückgabe)* return, handing back; *(von Personen)* handing over, surrender, delivery; **Klage auf ~** action for restitution *or* return *(für* of) **b** *(von Buch etc)* publication

he|raus+ge|ben *sep irreg* VT **a** *(= zurückgeben)* to return, to hand *or* give back; *Gefangene etc* to hand over, to surrender, to deliver
b *(= veröffentlichen, erlassen)* to issue; *Buch, Zeitung* to publish; *(= bearbeiten)* to edit
c *(= Wechselgeld geben) Betrag* to give in *or* as change; **wie viel hat er dir herausgegeben?** how much change *or* what change did he give you (back)?; **2 EUR/zu wenig ~** to give 2 euros change/too little change
d *(= herausreichen)* to hand *or* pass out *(aus* of)
VI *(= Wechselgeld geben)* to give change *(auf +acc* for); **er hat vergessen, mir herauszugeben** he's forgotten to give me my change; **können Sie (mir) ~?** can you give me change?, have you got the *or* enough change?; **falsch ~** to give the wrong change

He|raus|ge|ber(in) M(F) *(= Verleger)* publisher; *(= Redakteur)* editor

he|raus-: **he|raus+ge|hen** VI *sep irreg aux sein (aus* of) to go out; *(Fleck, Korken etc)* to come out; **aus sich ~** *(fig)* to come out of one's shell *(fig)*; **he|raus+grei|fen** VT *sep irreg* to pick *or* single out *(aus* of); *Beispiel* to take; **sich** *(dat)* **einzelne Demonstranten ~** to pick on *or* single out individual demonstrators; **he|raus+ha|ben** VT *sep irreg (inf)* **a** *(= entfernt haben)* to have got out *(aus* of); **ich will ihn aus der Firma ~** I want him out of the firm **b** *(= begriffen haben)* to have got *(inf)*; *(= gelöst haben) Problem, Rätsel, Aufgabe* to have solved; *Geheimnis* to have found out; **ich habe es jetzt heraus, wie man das am besten macht** I've got it - I know the best way to do it now; **jetzt hat er die Handhabung der Maschine heraus** he's got the knack or hang of the machine now (inf) → Dreh **a** **c** (= zurückbekommen haben) to have got back; **he|raus+hal|ten** sep irreg VT **a** (lit) Hand, Gegenstand to put or stick out (aus of) **b** (= fernhalten) Tiere, Eindringlinge to keep out (aus of) **c** (fig: = nicht verwickeln) to keep out (aus of) VR to keep out of it; sich aus etw ~ to keep out of sth; halt du dich mal heraus! you keep or stay out of it or this; **he|raus+hän|gen** sep VT to hang out (aus of); den Intellektuellen ~ (inf) to show off about being an intellectual (inf) VI irreg to hang out (aus of); **he|raus+hau|en** ptp herausgehauen VT sep **a** (inf: aus misslicher Lage) jdn ~ to get sb off the hook (inf) **b** (aus Stein) Stufe, Figur, Relief to carve, to cut (aus out of); **he|raus+he|ben** sep irreg VT to lift out (aus of); (fig: = betonen) to bring out VR to stand out; er hebt sich durch seine Begabung heraus he stands out on account of his talent; **he|raus+hel|fen** VI sep irreg jdm ~ (lit, fig) to help sb out (aus of); jdm aus dem Zug ~ to help sb off the train; **he|raus+ho|len** VT sep **a** (lit) to get out (aus of) **b** Bedingungen, Vorteil to gain; günstiges Ergebnis, hohe Umsätze, Vorsprung, gute Zeit, Sieg to achieve; Gewinn to make; Herstellungskosten to recoup; etw aus etw ~ to get sth from sth; alles aus sich ~ to get the best from oneself; das Letzte aus sich ~ to give one's all **c** (= herauspauken) to get off the hook (inf); mein Anwalt wird mich da ~ my solicitor will get me off (the hook (inf)); **he|raus+hö|ren** VT sep (= wahrnehmen) to hear; (= fühlen) to detect, to sense (aus in); **he|raus+keh|ren** VT sep (lit) to sweep out (aus of); (fig: = betonen) Bildung, Überlegenheit to parade; Strenge ~ to show one's sterner or stricter side; den reichen Mann/Vorgesetzten ~ to parade the fact that one is rich/the boss; **he|raus+kit|zeln** VT sep (inf) etw aus jdm ~ to worm sth out of sb (inf); **he|raus+klin|gen** VI sep irreg to ring out (aus from); (= zum Ausdruck kommen) to ring through (aus etw sth)

he|raus+kom|men VI sep irreg aux sein **a** (= nicht innen bleiben) to come out (aus of); ich bin schon seit Tagen aus den Kleidern/dem Haus nicht herausgekommen I haven't had these clothes off/I haven't been out of the house in days; er ist nie aus seinem Land/Dorf herausgekommen he has never been out of or has never left his country/village; sie kommt zu wenig heraus (inf) she doesn't go or get out enough; aus sich ~ to come out of one's shell; er kam aus dem Staunen/der Verwunderung nicht heraus he couldn't get over his astonishment/amazement; er kam aus dem Lachen nicht heraus he couldn't stop laughing; wie kommen wir bloß hier heraus? how do or shall we get out of here?

b (aus bestimmter Lage) to get out (aus of); aus seinen Schwierigkeiten/Sorgen ~ to get over one's difficulties/worries; aus den Schulden ~ to get out of debt; mit einem Gewinn ~ to get or win a prize

c (= auf den Markt kommen) to come out; (neues Modell) to come out, to be launched; mit einem neuen Modell ~ to bring out a new model, to come out with a new model

d (= bekannt gegeben werden) to come out; (Gesetz) to come into force; (= bekannt werden: Schwindel, Betrug etc) to come to light, to come out; es wird bald ~, dass du das Auto gestohlen hast they'll soon find out or it will soon come out that you stole the car

e (= sichtbar werden) to come out; (Fleck) to appear; (= zur Geltung kommen, hörbar werden) to come over; ganz groß ~ (inf) to make a big splash (inf), to have a big impact

f (= geäußert werden) to come out; mit etw ~ to come out with sth; mit der Sprache ~ to come out with it (inf)

g (= Resultat haben) bei etw ~ to come of sth, to emerge from sth; und was soll dabei ~? and what is that supposed to achieve?, and where is that supposed to get us?; bei dieser Rechenaufgabe kommt 10 heraus this sum comes to 10, the answer to this sum is 10; es kommt nichts dabei heraus, da kommt nichts bei heraus (inf) it doesn't get us anywhere, it doesn't achieve anything; dabei wird nichts Gutes ~ no good will come of it; es kommt auf eins or auf dasselbe or aufs Gleiche heraus it comes (down) to or boils down to the same thing

h (Sw: = ausgehen) to turn out

i (inf: = aus der Übung kommen) to get out of practice

j (Cards) to lead; wer kommt heraus? whose lead is it?, who leads?

he|raus-: **he|raus+krie|gen** VT sep (inf) = herausbekommen; **he|raus+kris|tal|li|sie|ren** ptp herauskristallisiert sep VT (Chem) to crystallize (aus out of); (fig) Fakten, Essenz, Punkte to extract (aus from) VR (Chem) to crystallize (out); (fig) to crystallize, to take shape; **he|raus+las|sen** VT sep irreg to let out (aus of); **he|raus+lau|fen** sep irreg VI aux sein to run out (aus of) VT (Sport) Vorsprung, Zeit, Sekunden to gain; Sieg, zweiten Platz auch to win; **he|raus+le|sen** VT sep irreg (= erkennen) to gather (aus from); aus seinem Brief/seiner Miene las ich Kummer heraus from his letter/expression I could tell or I gathered that he was worried; was die Kritiker aus seinem Roman alles ~ wollen the things the critics try to read into his novel; **he|raus+lo|cken** VT sep (aus of) to entice out; Gegner, Tier auch to lure out; etw aus jdm ~ (= ablisten) to get or worm (inf) sth out of sb; jdn aus seiner Reserve ~ to draw sb out of his shell; **he|raus+ma|chen** sep (inf) VT (aus of) to take out; Fleck to get out VR (= sich gut entwickeln) to come on (well); (finanziell) to do well; (nach Krankheit) to pick up; sie hat sich prächtig herausgemacht she has really blossomed or bloomed; **he|raus+müs|sen** VI sep irreg (inf) **a** (= entfernt werden müssen) to have to come out **b** (= aufstehen müssen) to have to get up **c** (= gesagt werden müssen) to have to come out; **he|raus|nehm|bar** ADJ removable; **he|raus+neh|men** VT sep irreg **a** (= entfernen) to take out (aus of); (inf) Zahn to pull out; Kind (aus der Schule etc) to take away, to remove (aus from); sich (dat) die Mandeln ~ lassen to have one's tonsils out; den Gang ~ (Aut) to put the car into neutral **b** (inf: = sich erlauben) es sich (dat) ~, etw zu tun to have the nerve to do sth (inf); sich (dat) Freiheiten ~ to take liberties; Sie nehmen sich zu viel heraus you're going too far; **he|raus+pi|cken** VT sep (aus of) (Vögel) to peck out; (fig) das Beste to pick out; **he|raus+plat|zen** VI sep aux sein (inf) (= spontan sagen) to blurt it out; (= lachen) to burst out laughing; mit etw ~ to blurt sth out; **he|raus+pres|sen** VT sep (aus of) to squeeze out; Saft etc auch to press out; Geld, Geständnis auch to wring out; **he|raus+put|zen** VT sep jdn to dress up; (= schmücken) Stadt, Weihnachtsbaum, Wohnung etc to deck out; sich prächtig ~ to get dressed up, to do oneself up (inf); (Stadt) to be decked out magnificently; **he|raus+quet|schen** VT sep (lit, fig) to squeeze out (inf); etw aus jdm ~ to squeeze sth out of sb (inf); **he|raus+ra|gen** VI sep = hervorragen; **he|raus|ra|gend** ADJ **a** (lit: = vorstehend) projecting **b** (fig: = ausgezeichnet) excellent, outstanding; **he|raus+re|den** VR sep to talk one's way out of it (inf); **he|raus+rei|ßen** VT sep irreg **a** (lit) (aus of) to tear or rip out; Zahn to pull out; Baum to pull out or up **b** jdn aus etw ~ (aus Umgebung) to tear sb away from sth; aus Arbeit, Spiel, Unterhaltung to drag sb away from sth; aus Schlaf, Träumerei to startle sb out of sth; aus Lethargie, Sorgen to shake sb out of sth; jdn aus seinem Kummer ~ to take sb out of himself **c** (inf: aus Schwierigkeiten) jdn ~ to get sb out of it (inf) **d** (inf: = wiedergutmachen) to save; **he|raus+rü|cken** sep VT to push out (aus of); (inf: = hergeben) Geld to cough up (inf); Beute, Gegenstand to hand over VI aux sein **a** (lit) to move out **b** (inf: = hergeben) mit etw ~ (mit Geld) to cough sth up (inf); mit Beute to hand sth over **c** (inf: = aussprechen) mit etw ~ to come out with sth; rück schon mit deinem Problem heraus! come on (now), out with it, out with it now, what's the problem?; mit der Sprache ~ to come out with it; **he|raus+ru|fen** sep irreg VT to call or shout out (aus of); das Publikum rief den Schauspieler noch dreimal heraus the audience called the actor back another three times VI to call or shout out (aus of); **he|raus+rut|schen** VI sep aux sein (lit) to slip out (aus of); (fig inf: Bemerkung) to slip out; das ist mir nur so herausgerutscht it just slipped out somehow, I just let it slip (out) somehow; **he|raus+sau|gen** VT sep to suck out (aus of); **he|raus+schä|len** sep VT das Essbare etc (aus of) to get out, to dig out (inf); (= ausschneiden) schlechte Stelle auch to scrape out; (fig: = absondern) Fakten, Elemente to single out; sich aus seinen Sachen ~ (inf) to peel off one's clothes VR (fig: = deutlich werden) to become evident or apparent; **he|raus+schau|en** VI sep (dial) **a** (Mensch) to look out (aus, zu of) **b** (= zu sehen sein) to show **c** (inf) = herausspringen c; **he|raus+schin|den** VT sep irreg (inf) = herausschlagen VT b; **he|raus+schla|gen** sep irreg VT **a** (lit) to knock out (aus of); aus einem Stein Funken ~ to strike sparks from or off a stone **b** (inf: = erreichen) Geld to make; Erlaubnis, Verzögerung, Gewinn, Vorteil to get; Zeit to gain; seine Kosten ~ to cover one's costs VI aux sein (Flammen) to leap or shoot out; die Flammen schlugen zum Dach heraus the flames were leaping through the roof; **he|raus+schleu|dern** VT sep (= werfen) to hurl out (aus of); Piloten to eject; (fig) Fragen, Vorwürfe, wütende Worte to burst out with; **he|raus+schlüp|fen** VI sep aux sein (lit, fig) to slip out (aus of); **he|raus+schme|cken** sep VT to taste VI to be prominent (over the other flavours (Brit) or flavors (US)); **he|raus+schmei|ßen** VT sep irreg (inf: lit, fig) to throw or chuck (inf) or sling (inf) out (aus of); **he|raus+schnei|den** VT sep irreg to cut out (aus of); **he|raus+schrei|ben** VT sep irreg Stellen, Zitat etc to copy out (aus of); **he|raus+schrei|en** VT sep irreg Hass, Gefühle to shout out

he|raus sein VI irreg aux sein (inf) **a** (= entfernt sein) to be out

b (= hervorgekommen sein: Sterne, Blumen etc) to be out

c (= herausgekommen sein) (Buch, Programm etc) to be out; (Gesetz) to be in force

d (= bekannt sein) to be known; (= entschieden sein) to have been or to be settled or decided

e (= hinter sich haben) (aus of) to be out, to have got out; aus der Schule ~ to have left school; aus dem Gröbsten or Ärgsten or Schlimmsten ~ to have got past the worst (part); (bei Krise, Krankheit) to be over the worst; wenn ich nur erst aus dieser Stadt heraus wäre if only I were out of this town → fein ADV b

f (= gesagt worden sein) (Wahrheit) to be out; (Worte) to have come out

he|raus-: **he|raus+lü|gen** VR sep irreg to lie one's way out of it; sich aus etw ~ to lie one's way out of sth; **he|raus+pau|ken** VT sep (inf) jdn (aus etw) ~ to bail sb out (of sth) (inf); **he|raus+schie|ßen** sep irreg VI **a** (lit) aus einem Gebäude ~ to shoot from a building **b** aux sein (auch herausgeschossen kommen) (aus of) to shoot out VT to shoot out

he|rau|ßen [hɛ'rausn] ADV (S Ger, Aus) out here

he|raus-: **he|raus+sprin|gen** VI sep irreg aux sein (aus of) **a** (lit) to jump or leap out **b** (= sich lösen) to come out; aus dem Gleis ~ to jump the rails **c** (inf) dabei springt ein fetter Gewinn heraus there is a handsome profit in it; dabei springt nichts heraus there's nothing to be got out of it; **was springt für mich dabei heraus?** what's in it for me?; **he|raus+spru|deln** *sep* VI *aux sein* to bubble out (*aus* of) VT *Worte, Sätze* to come gushing out with; **he|raus+ste|hen** VI *sep irreg* (*S Ger: aux sein*) to stand *or* stick out, to protrude; **he|raus+stel|len** *sep* VT **a** (*lit*) to put outside; (*Sport*) to send off **b** (*fig: = hervorheben*) to emphasize, to underline; *jdn* to give prominence to VR (*Unschuld, Wahrheit*) to come to light; **sich als falsch/wahr/richtig/begründet ~** to show itself to be *or* to prove (to be) wrong/true/correct/well-founded; **es stellte sich heraus, dass ...** it turned out *or* emerged that ...; **es wird sich ~, wer recht hat/was getan werden muss** we shall see who is right/what must be done; **das muss sich erst ~** that remains to be seen; **he|raus+stre|cken** VT *sep* to stick out (*zu, aus* of); **he|raus+strei|chen** VT *sep irreg* **a** *Fehler etc* to cross out, to delete (*aus* in) **b** (*= betonen*) *Verdienste etc* to stress, to lay great stress upon; **he|raus+strö|men** VI *sep aux sein* (*aus* of) (*Flüssigkeit*) to stream *or* pour out; (*Gas*) to come out; (*geh: Menschenmenge*) to pour out; **he|raus+stür|zen** VI *sep aux sein* **a** (*auch herausgestürzt kommen*) (*= eilen*) to rush out (*aus* of) **b** (*= fallen*) to fall out; **zum Fenster ~** to fall out of the window; **he|raus+su|chen** VT *sep* to pick out; **he|raus+tre|ten** VI *sep irreg aux sein* to step *or* come out (*aus* of), to emerge (*aus* from); (*Adern etc*) to stand out, to protrude; **he|raus+trom|meln** VT *sep* (*inf*) to get out; **he|raus+wach|sen** VI *sep irreg aux sein* to grow out (*aus* of); **he|raus+wa|gen** VR *sep* to dare to come out (*aus* of), to venture out (*aus* of) *or* forth (*liter*) (*aus* from); **he|raus+win|den** VR *sep irreg* (*fig*) to wriggle out of it; **sich aus etw ~** to wriggle out of sth; **he|raus+wirt|schaf|ten** VT *sep* to make (*aus* out of); **he|raus+wol|len** VI *sep* to want to get out (*aus* of); **nicht mit etw ~** (*inf: = sagen wollen*) not to want to come out with sth (*inf*); **er wollte nicht mit der Sprache heraus** (*inf*) he didn't want to come out with it (*inf*); **he|raus+zie|hen** *sep irreg* VT to pull out (*aus* of); (*= herausschleppen*) to drag out (*aus* of); (*Chem, Med*) to extract (*aus* from); **die Essenz aus einem Buch ~** to extract the main substance from a book; **muss ich dir die Antworten einzeln ~?** (*inf*) do I have to drag answers out of you one by one? VR to pull oneself out (*aus* of)

herb [hɛrp] ADJ **a** *Geruch* sharp; *Geschmack* sharp, tangy; *Parfüm* tangy; *Wein* dry **b** *Enttäuschung, Verlust, Niederlage* bitter; *Erwachen* rude; *Erkenntnis, Wahrheit* cruel **c** (*= streng*) *Züge, Gesicht* severe, harsh; *Art, Wesen, Charakter, Mensch* dour; *Schönheit* severe, austere **d** (*= unfreundlich*) *Worte, Kritik* harsh ADV **~ riechen** *or* **duften** to smell tangy; **~ schmecken** to taste tangy; *Wein* to taste dry

Her|ba|ri|um [hɛrˈbaːriʊm] NT **-s, Herbarien** herbarium, herbary

her|bei [hɛɐ̯ˈbai] ADV (*geh*) come (here); **(alle Mann) ~!** come here(, everybody)!

her|bei-: **her|bei+brin|gen** VT *sep irreg jdn, Gegenstand* to bring over; *Indizien, Beweise* to provide; *Sachverständige* to bring in; **her|bei+ei|len** VI *sep aux sein* (*geh*) to hurry *or* rush over; **her|bei+füh|ren** VT *sep* **a** (*= bewirken*) *Entscheidung, Konfrontation etc* to bring about; (*= verursachen*) to cause; **den Tod** *etc* **~** (*Med*) to cause death *etc* (*form*) **b** (*an einen Ort*) to bring; *Schaulustige* to draw; **her|bei+ho|len** VT *sep* to bring; *Verstärkung* to bring in; *Arzt, Taxi, Polizisten* to fetch; **einen Arzt ~ lassen** to send for a doctor; **her|bei+kom|men** VI *sep irreg aux sein* to come *or* draw near, to approach; **her|bei+las|sen** VR *sep irreg* **sich zu etw ~, sich ~, etw zu tun** to condescend *or* deign to do sth; **her|bei+lau|fen** VI *sep irreg aux sein* to come running up; **her|bei+re|den** VT *sep* **etw ~** to bring sth about by talking about it; **Probleme ~** to create problems by talking about them; **her|bei+ru|fen** VT *sep irreg* to call over; *Verstärkung* to call in; *Arzt, Polizei, Taxi* to call; **her|bei+schaf|fen** VT *sep* to bring; *Geld* to get, to get hold of (*inf*); *Beweise* to produce; **her|bei+seh|nen** VT *sep* to long for; **her|bei+strö|men** VI *sep aux sein* (*geh*) to come flocking, to come in (their) crowds; **her|bei+win|ken** VT *sep* = **heranwinken**; **her|bei+wün|schen** VT *sep* **(sich** *dat*) **etw ~** to long for sth; **(sich** *dat*) **jdn ~** to wish sb were *or* was here; **her|bei+zau|bern** VT *sep* to conjure up; **her|bei+zie|hen** *sep irreg* VT → **Haar c** VI *aux sein* to approach; **her|bei+zi|tie|ren** *ptp* **herbeizitiert** VT *sep* (*inf*) to send for

her-: **her+be|kom|men** *ptp* **herbekommen** VT *sep irreg* (*inf*) to get; **her+be|mü|hen** *ptp* **herbemüht** *sep* (*geh*) VT **jdn ~** to trouble sb to come here VR to take the trouble to come here; **her+be|or|dern** *ptp* **herbeordert** VT *sep* to summon, to send for

Her|ber|ge [ˈhɛrbɛrgə] F **-, -n a** *no pl* (*= Unterkunft*) lodging *no indef art*, accommodation *no indef art*; (*fig*) refuge **b** (*old: = Gasthaus*) inn; (*= Jugendherberge*) (youth) hostel

Her|bergs-: **Her|bergs|el|tern** PL (youth hostel) wardens *pl*; **Her|bergs|mut|ter** F *pl* **-mütter**, **Her|bergs|va|ter** M (youth hostel) warden

her-: **her+be|stel|len** *ptp* **herbestellt** VT *sep* to ask to come; **her+be|ten** VT *sep* (*pej*) to rattle off

Herb|heit F **-,** *no pl* **a** (*von Geruch*) sharpness; (*von Parfüm*) tanginess; (*von Geschmack*) sharpness, tanginess; (*von Wein*) dryness **b** (*von Enttäuschung, Verlust*) bitterness; (*von Erwachen*) rudeness **c** (*= Strenge*) (*von Gesicht, Zügen*) severity, harshness; (*von Art, Wesen, Charakter, Mensch*) dourness; **die ~ dieser Wahrheit/Erkenntnis** the cruel truth/realization; **ihre Schönheit ist von einer gewissen ~** she has a certain severe beauty **d** (*= Unfreundlichkeit: von Worten, Kritik*) harshness

her+bit|ten VT *sep irreg* to ask to come

Her|bi|zid [hɛrbiˈtsiːt] NT **-(e)s, -e** [-də] herbicide

her+brin|gen VT *sep irreg* to bring (here); **bring mir das Buch her** bring me the book (over) → *auch* **hergebracht**

Herbst [hɛrpst] M **-(e)s, -e** autumn, fall (*US*); **im ~** in autumn, in the fall (*US*); **der ~ des Lebens** (*liter*) the autumn of (one's) life (*liter*); **auch der ~ hat noch schöne Tage** (*prov*) you're never too old

Herbst- *in cpds* autumn, fall (*US*); **Herbst|an|fang** M beginning of autumn *or* fall (*US*); **Herbst|as|ter** F Michaelmas daisy

herbs|ten [ˈhɛrpstn] VI *impers* **es herbstet** (*liter*) autumn *or* fall (*US*) is nigh (*liter*) VT (*dial*) *Wein* to harvest

Herbs|tes- (*poet*) *in cpds* = **Herbst-**

Herbst-: **Herbst|far|ben** PL autumn *or* autumnal colours *pl* (*Brit*), fall colors *pl* (*US*); **Herbst|fe|ri|en** PL autumn holiday(s *pl*) (*esp Brit*) *or* vacation (*US*); (*Sch*) autumn half-term holiday(s *pl*) (*esp Brit*) *or* vacation (*US*); **Herbst|laub** NT autumn *or* fall (*US*) leaves *pl*

herbst|lich [ˈhɛrpstlɪç] ADJ autumn *attr*; (*= wie im Herbst auch*) autumnal; **das Wetter wird schon ~** autumn *or* fall (*US*) is in the air; **das Wetter ist schon ~** it's already autumn *or* fall (*US*) weather ADV **~ kühles Wetter** cool autumn *or* fall (*US*) weather; **~ gefärbtes Laub** leaves in autumnal colours (*Brit*) *or* fall colors (*US*); **sich ~ kleiden** to dress for the autumn *or* fall (*US*)

Herbst-: **Herbst|mo|nat** M autumn month; **der ~** (*old*) September; **Herbst|ne|bel** M autumn mist; **Herbst|sturm** M autumn *or* fall (*US*) storm; **Herbst-Tag|und|nacht|glei|che** F *decl as adj* autumnal equinox; **Herbst|zeit|lo|se** [ˈhɛrpsttsaitloːzə] F *decl as adj* meadow saffron

Herd [heːɐ̯t] M **-(e)s, -e** [-də] **a** (*= Küchenherd*) cooker, stove; (*= Kohleherd*) range; (*fig: = Heim*) home; **eigener ~ ist Goldes wert** (*Prov*) there's no place like home (*Prov*); **den ganzen Tag am ~ stehen** (*fig*) to slave over a hot stove all day **b** (*Med: = Krankheitsherd*) focus; (*Geol: von Erdbeben*) epicentre (*Brit*), epicenter (*US*); (*fig: von Rebellion etc*) seat **c** (*Tech*) hearth

Herd|ab|deck|plat|te F electric ring cover

Her|de [ˈheːɐ̯də] F **-, -n** (*lit*) herd; (*von Schafen, fig geh: = Gemeinde*) flock; **mit der ~ laufen** (*pej*) **der ~ folgen** (*pej*) to follow the herd

Her|den-: **Her|den|ins|tinkt** M (*lit, fig pej*) herd instinct; **Her|den|mensch** M (*pej*) sheep (*pej*), herd-follower (*pej*); **Her|den|tier** NT gregarious animal; **Her|den|trieb** M (*lit, fig pej*) herd instinct; **her|den|wei|se** ADV in herds; (*Schafe*) in flocks; (*fig*) in crowds *or* herds

Herd|plat|te F (*von Kohleherd*) (top) plate; (*von Elektroherd*) hotplate

he|rein [hɛˈrain] ADV in; **~!** come in!, come! (*form*); **nur ~!** do come in!; **immer ~!** come along in!; **hier ~!** in here!; **von (dr)außen ~** from outside; **auf dem Wege von draußen ~** on the way in

he|rein- PREF → *auch* **rein-** in; **he|rein+be|kom|men** *ptp* **hereinbekommen** VT *sep irreg* (*inf*) *Waren* to get in; *Radiosender* to get; *Unkosten etc* to recover; **he|rein+be|mü|hen** *ptp* **hereinbemüht** *sep* (*geh*) VT to trouble to come in VR to take the trouble to come in; **he|rein+bit|ten** VT *sep irreg* to ask (to come) in; **he|rein+bre|chen** VI *sep irreg aux sein* **a** (*= eindringen: Wasser, Flut, Wellen*) to gush in; **über jdn/etw ~** (*lit, fig*) to descend upon sb/sth **b** (*Gewitter*) to break; (*Krieg, Pest*) to break out; **das Unglück brach über ihn herein** misfortune overtook him **c** (*liter: = anbrechen*) (*Nacht, Abend*) to fall, to close in; (*Winter*) to set in **d** (*lit: = nach innen stürzen*) to fall in; **he|rein+brin|gen** VT *sep irreg* **a** (*= nach innen bringen*) to bring in **b** (*inf: = wettmachen*) *Geldverlust* to make good; *Zeit-, Produktionsverluste* to make up for; *Unkosten* to get back; **he|rein+drän|gen** VIR *sep* to push one's way in; **he|rein+drin|gen** VI *sep irreg aux sein* (*Licht, Wasser*) to come in (*in +acc* -to); **ein Geräusch/Geruch drang ins Zimmer herein** a sound/smell reached the room; **he|rein+dür|fen** VI *sep irreg* (*inf*) to be allowed in; **darf ich herein?** may *or* can I come in?; **he|rein+fah|ren** VTI *sep irreg* (*vi: aux sein*) to drive in; (*mit Fahrrad*) to ride in; **he|rein+fal|len** VI *sep irreg aux sein* **a** (*= nach innen fallen*) to fall in (*in +acc* -to) **b** (*inf*) (*= sich täuschen lassen*) to fall for it (*inf*); (*= betrogen werden*) to be had (*inf*); **auf jdn/etw ~** to be taken in by sb/sth, to be taken for a ride (by sb) (*inf*)/to fall for sth; **mit jdm/etw ~** to have a bad deal with sb/sth; **he|rein+füh|ren** VT *sep* to show in; **he|rein+ho|len** VT *sep* to bring in (*in +acc* -to); **he|rein+kom|men** VI *sep irreg aux sein* to come in (*in +acc* -to); **wie ist er hereingekommen?** how did he get in?; **ins Haus ~** to come in *or* inside; **he|rein+krie|gen** VT *sep* (*inf*) = **hereinbekommen**; **he|rein+las|sen** VT *sep irreg* to let in (*in +acc* -to); **he|rein+le|gen** VT *sep* **a** (*= nach innen legen*) to lay (down) **b** (*inf*) **jdn ~** (*= betrügen*) to take sb for a ride (*inf*); (*= anführen*) to take sb in; **he|rein+neh|men** VT *sep irreg* to bring in (*in +acc* -to); (*= in Liste, Kollektion etc aufnehmen*) to put in, to include; (*Comm*) *Aufträge* to accept; **he|rein+nö|ti|gen** VT *sep* to urge to come in; **sie hat mich förmlich hereingenötigt** she insisted that I come in; **he|rein+plat|zen** VI *sep aux sein* (*inf*) to burst *or* come bursting in (*in +acc* to); **bei jdm ~** to burst in on sb; **he|rein+reg|nen** VI *impers sep* **es regnet herein** the rain is coming in; **he|rein+rei|ten** *sep irreg* VTI (*vi: aux sein*) to ride in (*in +acc* -to) VR (*inf*) to land oneself in it *or* in the soup (*inf*); **he|rein+ru|fen** VT *sep irreg* to call in; **he|rein+schau|en** VI *sep (dial)* to look in (*in +acc* -to); **(bei jdm) ~** *(inf)* to look in on sb *(inf)*, to look sb up *(inf)*; **he|rein+schlei|chen** VIR *sep irreg (vi: aux sein)* (*in +acc* to) to creep *or* slip in; *(heimlich)* to sneak in; **he|rein+schmug|geln** VT *sep* (*in +acc* -to) to smuggle in; **he|rein+schnei|en** *sep* VI *impers* **es schneit herein** the snow's coming in VI *aux sein (inf)* to drop in *(inf)*; **he|rein+se|hen** VI *sep irreg* to look in (*in +acc* -to); **he|rein+spa|zie|ren** *ptp* **hereinspaziert** VI *sep aux sein* to breeze in (*in +acc* -to); **hereinspaziert!** come right in!; **he|rein+ste|cken** VT *sep* (*in +acc* -to) to put in; *Kopf, Hand auch* to stick in; **he|rein+strö|men** VI *sep aux sein* (*in +acc* -to) to stream *or* pour in; *(geh: Menschenmassen)* to pour in; (*in +acc* -to); **he|rein+stür|men** VI *sep aux sein* to storm *or* come storming in (*in +acc* -to); **he|rein+stür|zen** VI *sep aux sein* to rush in (*in +acc* -to); **he|rein+wa|gen** VR *sep* (*in +acc* -to) to dare to come in, to venture in; **he|rein+wol|len** VI *sep (inf)* to want to come in

Her-: **her+fah|ren** *sep irreg* VI *aux sein* to come *or* get here; **hinter/vor jdm/etw ~** to drive *or* *(mit Rad)* ride (along) behind/in front of *or* ahead of sb/sth; **der Detektiv fuhr hinter dem Auto her** the detective followed *or* trailed the car VT to drive *or* bring here; **Her|fahrt** F journey here; **auf der ~** on the journey *or* way here; **her+fal|len** VI *sep irreg aux sein* **über jdn ~** to attack sb, to fall upon sb; *(mit Fragen)* to attack sb, to pitch into sb *(esp Brit)*; *(= kritisieren)* to pull sb to pieces; **über etw** *(acc)* **~** to descend upon sth; *über Geschenke, Essbares etc* to pounce upon sth; **her+fin|den** VI *sep irreg* to find one's way here

herg. *abbr von* **hergestellt** manufactured, mfd

Her|gang M *pl (rare)* **-gänge** *(von Schlacht)* course; **schildern Sie mir genau den ~ dieses Vorfalls** tell me exactly what happened; **der ~ des Unfalls** the way the accident happened, the details of the accident

her-: **her+ge|ben** *sep irreg* VT *(= weggeben)* to give away; *(= überreichen, aushändigen)* to hand over; *(= zurückgeben)* to give back; **gib das her!** give me that, let me have that; **viel/einiges ~** *(inf: = erbringen)* to be a lot of use/of some use; **wenig ~** *(inf)* not to be much use; **das Buch gibt nicht viel her** the book doesn't tell me/you (very) much; **das Thema gibt viel/nichts her** there's a lot/nothing to this topic; **ein Essen, das was hergibt** a fine spread; **was die Beine hergaben** as fast as one's legs would carry one; **was die Lunge/Stimme hergab** at the top of one's voice; **seinen Namen für etw ~** to lend one's name to sth VR **sich zu** *or* **für etw ~** to be (a) party to sth; **dazu gebe ich mich nicht her** I won't have anything to do with it; **eine Schauspielerin, die sich für solche Filme hergibt** an actress who allows herself to be involved in such films; **her|ge|bracht** ADJ *(= traditionell)* traditional; **in ~er Weise** as is/was traditional → *auch* **herbringen**; **her+ge|hen** *sep irreg aux sein* VI **a hinter/vor/neben jdm ~** to walk (along) behind/in front of *or* ahead of/beside sb **b** *(S Ger, Aus)* = **herkommen** **c ~ und etw tun** *(= einfach tun)* just *or* simply to (go and) do sth VI *impers (inf) (= zugehen)* **so geht es her** that's the way it goes *or* is; **es ging heiß her** things got heated *(inf)*, (the) sparks flew; **hier geht es hoch her** there's plenty going on here; **her+ge|hö|ren** *ptp* **hergehört** VI *sep* to belong here; *(fig auch)* to be relevant; **her|ge|lau|fen** ADJ *attr (pej)* = **dahergelaufen**; **her+ha|ben** VT *sep irreg (inf)* **wo hat er das her?** where did he get that from?; **her+hal|ten** *sep irreg* VT to hold out VI to suffer (for it), to pay for it; **für etw ~** to pay for sth; **er muss als Sündenbock ~** he is the scapegoat; **als Entschuldigung für etw ~** to serve *or* be used as an excuse for sth; **her+ho|len** VT *sep (inf)* to fetch; **~ lassen** to send for; **weit hergeholt sein** *(fig)* to be far-fetched; **her+hö|ren** VI *sep (inf)* to listen; **alle** *or* **alles mal ~!** listen (to me) *or* listen here *(inf)* *or* pay attention everybody, everybody listen (to me)

He|ring ['he:rɪŋ] M **-s, -e** **a** herring; **ein gedörrter ~** a kipper; **wie die ~e zusammengedrängt** packed in like sardines (in a tin); **dünn wie ein ~** as thin as a rake *(Brit)* or rail *(US)* **b** *(= Zeltpflock)* (tent) peg **c** *(fig inf: = schwächlicher Mensch)* weakling

He|rings-: **He|rings|fän|ger** M *(= Heringsfangschiff)* herring boat; **He|rings|fi|let** NT *(Cook)* herring fillet; **He|rings|topf** M pickled herring with sour cream

he|rin|nen [he'rɪnən] ADV *(S Ger, Aus)* = **drinnen, innen**

her-: **her+ja|gen** *sep* VT *(auf jdn zu)* to drive *or* chase over *or* across; **jdn vor sich** *(dat)* **~** to drive sb along in front of one VI *aux sein* **hinter jdm ~** to chase after sb; **hinter etw** *(dat)* **~** to be after sth; **her+kom|men** VI *sep irreg aux sein* to come here; *(= sich nähern)* to come, to approach; *(= herstammen)* to come from; **komm her!** come here!; **von jdm/etw ~** *(= stammen)* to come from sb/sth; **ich weiß nicht, wo das herkommt** *(was der Grund ist)* I don't know why it is, I don't know what the reason is; **her|kömm|lich** ['he:ɐkœmlɪç] ADJ conventional; **nach ~em Brauch** according to convention; **her+krie|gen** VT *sep (inf)* to get; **ich kriege ihn einfach nicht her** I simply can't get him to come (here)

Her|ku|les ['hɛrkulɛs] M **-', -se** *(Myth, fig)* Hercules

Her|ku|les|ar|beit F *(fig)* Herculean task

her|ku|lisch [hɛr'ku:lɪʃ] ADJ Herculean

Her|kunft ['he:ɐkʊnft] F **-, ⸚e** [-kʏnftə] origin; *(soziale)* background, origins *pl*; **er ist britischer ~** *(gen)*, **er ist seiner ~ nach Brite** he is of British extraction *or* descent *or* origin; **er ist aristokratischer ~** *(gen)* he comes from an aristocratic family, he is of aristocratic descent

Her|kunfts-: **Her|kunfts|be|zeich|nung** F *(Comm)* designation of origin; **Her|kunfts|land** NT *(Comm)* country of origin; **Her|kunfts|ort** M *pl* **-orte** place of origin

her-: **her+lau|fen** VI *sep irreg aux sein* to come running; **lauf doch mal her zu mir!** come over here to me; **hinter** *(lit, fig)***/vor/neben jdm ~** to run after/ahead of/beside sb; **her+lei|ern** ['he:ɐlaiɐn] VT *sep (inf)* to spout *(inf)*; **her+lei|hen** VT *sep irreg (Aus, S Ger)* to lend (out); **her+lei|ten** *sep* VT **a** *(= ableiten, folgern)* to derive (*aus* from) **b** *(= an bestimmten Ort leiten)* to bring VR **sich von etw ~** to come from sth, to be derived from sth; **Her|lei|tung** F *(von Wort etc)* derivation; **her+lo|cken** VT *sep* to entice, to lure

her+ma|chen *sep (inf)* VR **sich über etw** *(acc)* **~** *(= in Angriff nehmen, über Arbeit, Buch, Essen)* to get stuck into sth *(inf)*; *(= Besitz ergreifen) über Eigentum, Gegenstände* to pounce (up)on sth; **sich über jdn ~** to lay into sb *(inf)* VT **viel ~** to look impressive; **wenig ~** not to look very impressive; **nichts ~** not to be up to much *(inf)*; **von jdm/etw viel ~** to crack sb/sth up to be quite fantastic *(inf)*, to make a big thing of sb/sth *(inf)*; **von jdm/etw wenig** *or* **nicht viel ~** not to make a big thing of sb/sth *(inf)*; **viel von sich ~** to be full of oneself; **er macht wenig** *or* **nicht viel von sich her** he's pretty modest

Her|maph|ro|dit [hɛrmafro'di:t] M **-en, -en** hermaphrodite

Her|me|lin [hɛrmə'li:n] NT **-s, -e** *(Zool)* ermine

Her|me|lin M **-s, -e** *(= Pelz)* ermine

Her|me|neu|tik [hɛrme'nɔytɪk] F **-,** *no pl* hermeneutics *sing*

her|me|neu|tisch [hɛrme'nɔytɪʃ] ADJ hermeneutic(al)

Her|mes|bürg|schaft ['hɛrmɛs-] F government export credit guarantee

her|me|tisch [hɛr'me:tɪʃ] ADJ *(lit, fig)* hermetic ADV **die Häftlinge sind ~ von der Außenwelt abgeschlossen** the prisoners are completely shut off from the outside world; **~ abgeriegelt** completely sealed off

her+müs|sen VI *sep irreg (inf)* **a das muss her** I/we have to have it **b** *(= kommen müssen)* to have to come (here); **hinter jdm ~** to have to go after sb

her|nach [hɛɐ'na:x] ADV *(dated, dial)* afterwards

her+neh|men VT *sep irreg* **a** *(= beschaffen)* to get, to find; **wo soll ich das ~?** where am I supposed to get that from? **b** *(dial inf)* **jdn ~** *(= stark fordern, belasten)* to make sb sweat *(inf)*; *(= mitnehmen: Krankheit, Schock, Nachricht, Anstrengung)* to take it out of sb *(inf)* **c (sich** *dat*) **jdn ~** *(dial: = tadeln, verprügeln)* to give it to sb *(inf)*, to let sb have it *(inf)* **d** *(dial: = nehmen)* to take

her|nie|der [hɛɐ'ni:dɐ] ADV *(liter)* down

he|ro|ben [he'ro:bn] ADV *(Aus, S Ger)* up here

He|roe [he'ro:ə] M **-n, -n** *(geh)* hero

He|ro|en|kult [he'ro:ən-] M *(geh)* hero worship

He|ro|in [hero'i:n] NT **-s,** *no pl* heroin

He|ro|in-: **he|ro|in|ab|hän|gig** ADJ addicted to heroin; **He|ro|in|ab|hän|gi|ge(r)** MF *decl as adj* heroin addict

He|ro|i|ne [hero'i:nə] F **-, -n** *(dated Theat)* heroine

He|ro|in-: **He|ro|in|han|del** M *(auf der Straße)* heroin dealing; *(international)* heroin trafficking; **He|ro|in|op|fer** NT *(= Herointote(r))* heroin victim; **he|ro|in|süch|tig** ADJ addicted to heroin; **He|ro|in|süch|ti|ge(r)** MF *decl as adj* heroin addict; **He|ro|in|to|te(r)** MF *decl as adj* heroin victim

he|ro|isch [he'ro:ɪʃ] *(geh)* ADJ heroic ADV heroically

he|ro|i|sie|ren [heroi'zi:rən] *ptp* **heroisiert** VT *(geh) jdn* to make a hero of; *Tat* to glorify

He|ro|is|mus [hero'ɪsmʊs] M **-,** *no pl (geh)* heroism

He|rold ['he:rɔlt] M **-(e)s, -e** [-də] *(Hist: = Bote)* herald; *(fig: = Vorbote auch)* harbinger

He|ros ['he:rɔs] M **-, Heroen** [he'ro:ən] hero

Her|pes ['hɛrpɛs] M **-,** *no pl (Med)* herpes

Her|pes-: **Her|pes|bläs|chen** NT herpes blister; **Her|pes|vi|rus** NT OR M herpes virus

Herr [hɛr] M **-(e)n, -en** **a** *(= Gebieter)* lord, master; *(= Herrscher)* lord, ruler (*über +acc* of); *(von Hund)* master; **mein ~ und Gebieter** my lord and master; **der junge ~** *(form)* the young master; **die ~en der Schöpfung** *(hum: = Männer)* the gentlemen; **sein eigener ~ sein** to be one's own master *or* boss; **~ im eigenen Haus sein** to be master in one's own house; **~ einer Sache** *(gen)* **sein/werden** *(= in der Hand haben)* to have/get sth under control; **~ der Lage** *or* **Situation sein/bleiben** to be/remain master of the situation, to have/keep the situation under control; **nicht mehr ~ seiner Sinne sein** not to be in control of oneself any more; **~ über Leben und Tod sein** to have the power of life and death *(gen* over); **über jdn/etw ~ werden** to master sb/sth; **man kann nicht** *or* **niemand kann zwei ~en dienen** *(prov)* no man can serve two masters *(prov)*; **wie der ~, sos Gescherr!** *(Prov)* like master, like man! *(prov)* → **Land c**

b *(= Gott, Christus)* Lord; **Gott, der ~** the Lord God; **der ~ Jesus** the Lord Jesus; **der ~ der Heerscharen** the Lord of Hosts; **~, du meine Güte!** good(ness) gracious (me)!; **~ des Himmels!** good Lord!; **er ist ein großer Schwindler/Esser** *etc* **vor dem ~n** *(hum inf)* what a great fibber/eater *etc* he is

c *(= feiner Herr, Mann)* gentleman; **ein geistlicher ~** a clergyman; **ein adliger ~, ein ~ von Adel** a nobleman; **„Herren"** *(= Toilette)* "gentlemen", "gents", "men"; **den (großen) ~n spielen** *or* **markieren** *(inf)* to give oneself airs, to put on airs → **alt**

d *(vor Eigennamen)* Mr; *(vor Titeln) usu not translated (in Anrede ohne Namen)* sir; **(mein) ~!**

sir!; **bitte, der ~** *(beim Servieren)* there you are, sir; **der ~ wünscht?** what can I do for you, sir?; **Ihr ~ Vater** *(form)* your father; **~ Nachbar** *(old)* excuse me, sir; **~ Dr./Doktor/Professor Schmidt** Dr/Doctor/Professor Schmidt; **~ Doktor** doctor; **~ Professor** professor; **~ Präsident/Vorsitzender** Mr President/Chairman; **der ~ Präsident/Vorsitzende** the President/Chairman; **lieber** *or* **werter** *(dated) or* **sehr geehrter** *or* **sehr verehrter** *(form)* **~ Bell** *(in Brief)* Dear Mr Bell; **an den ~n Abgeordneten C. Schmidt** C. Schmidt, MP; **werte ~en, sehr geehrte ~en** *(in Brief)* Dear Sirs *(Brit)*, to whom it may concern *(US)* **e** *(allgemein gesehen: = Tanzpartner, Begleiter)* gentleman; *(auf eine bestimmte Dame bezogen)* partner; *(bei Cocktailparty, Theaterbesuch etc)* (gentleman) companion **f** *(Sport)* **4x100m-Staffel der ~en** men's 4 x 100m relay

Her|rchen ['hɛrçən] NT **-s, -** *dim von* **Herr** *(inf: von Hund)* master; **geh zum ~** go to your master

Her-: **her+rei|chen** VT *sep* to hand, to pass; **Her|rei|se** F journey here; **auf der ~ von Köln** on the journey from Cologne

Her|ren- *in cpds* men's; *(auf Kleidung bezüglich auch)* gents' *(dated)*; *(auf einzelnes Exemplar bezüglich)* man's, gent's; **Her|ren|abend** M stag night; **seinen/einen ~ haben** to have one's/a night out with the boys *(inf)*; **Her|ren|ar|ti|kel** PL gentlemen's requisites *pl (dated)*; **Her|ren|aus|stat|ter** [-lausʃtatɐ] M **-s, -**, **Her|ren|aus|stat|te|rin** [-ərɪn] F **-, -nen** gents' *or* men's outfitter; **Her|ren|be|glei|tung** F **~ erwünscht** please bring a gentleman *or (bei Ball)* partner; **in ~** in the company of a gentleman; **Her|ren|be|kannt|schaft** F gentleman acquaintance; **eine ~ machen** to make the acquaintance of a gentleman; **Her|ren|be|klei|dung** F menswear; **Her|ren|be|such** M (gentle)man visitor/visitors; **Her|ren|dop|pel** NT *(Tennis etc)* men's doubles *sing*; **Her|ren|ein|zel** NT *(Tennis etc)* men's singles *sing*; **Her|ren|fahr|rad** NT man's bicycle *or* bike *(inf)*; **Her|ren|fri|seur(in)** M(F) men's hairdresser, barber; **Her|ren|ge|sell|schaft** F **a** *(= gesellige Runde)* stag party **b** *no pl (= Begleitung von Herrn)* **in ~ sein** to be in the company of gentlemen/a gentleman; **Her|ren|haus** NT **a** manor house **b** *(Hist)* upper chamber; **Her|ren|jah|re** PL → **Lehrjahr**; **Her|ren|kon|fek|ti|on** F men's ready-to-wear clothes *pl*; *(= Abteilung)* menswear department; **Her|ren|le|ben** NT life of luxury and ease; **her|ren|los** ADJ abandoned; *Hund etc* stray; **Her|ren|ma|ga|zin** NT *(Zeitschrift für Männer)* men's magazine; **Her|ren|man|gel** M shortage of men; **Her|ren|mensch** M member of the master race; **Her|ren|mo|de** F men's fashion; **Her|ren|par|tie** F *(= Ausflug)* men-only outing; *(= Gesellschaft)* stag party; **Her|ren|pilz** M *(Bot: = Steinpilz)* cep, porcini *(esp US)*; **Her|ren|rad** NT man's bicycle *or* bike *(inf)*; **Her|ren|ras|se** F master race; **Her|ren|rei|ten** NT **-s**, *no pl* amateur racing; **Her|ren|rei|ter** M **a** *(Sport)* amateur jockey **b** *(iro)* stuffed shirt *(inf)*; **Her|ren|sa|lon** M barber's; **Her|ren|sat|tel** M (man's) saddle; **im ~ reiten** to ride astride; **Her|ren|sau|na** M *(euph)* massage parlour *(Brit) or* parlor *(US)*; **Her|ren|schnei|der(in)** M(F) gentlemen's tailor; **Her|ren|schnitt** M *(= Frisur)* haircut like a man's; **Her|ren|sitz** M **a** *(= Gutshof)* manor house **b** **im ~ reiten** to ride astride; **Her|ren|tie|re** PL primates *pl*; **Her|ren|to|i|let|te** F men's toilet *or* restroom *(US)*, gents *sing*; **Her|ren|volk** NT master race; **Her|ren|welt** F, *no pl (dated hum)* gentlemen *pl*; **Her|ren|win|ker** M *(hum)* kiss curl *(Brit)*, spit curl *(US)*; **Her|ren|witz** M dirty joke; **Her|ren|zim|mer** NT study; *(= Rauchzimmer)* smoking room

Herr|gott M *(dated inf) (Anrede)* God, Lord; **der ~** God, the Lord (God); *(S Ger, Aus: = Figur)* figure of the Lord; **~ (Sakrament)!** *(inf)* good God *or* Lord!; **~ noch mal!** *(inf)* damn it all! *(inf)*

Herr|gotts-: **Herr|gotts|frü|he** F **in aller ~** *(inf)* at the crack of dawn; **Herr|gotts|schnit|zer(in)** M(F) *(S Ger, Aus)* carver of crucifixes; **Herr|gotts|win|kel** M *(S Ger, Aus) corner of a room with a crucifix*

her+rich|ten *sep* VT **a** *(= vorbereiten)* to get ready *(+dat, für* for); *Bett* to make; *Tisch* to set **b** *(= instand setzen, ausbessern)* to do up *(inf)* VR *(dial)* to get dressed up

Her|rin ['hɛrɪn] F **-, -nen** *(Hist: = Herrscherin)* female ruler; *(von Hund, old: = Hausherrin)* mistress; **die ~** *(Anrede)* my lady

her|risch ['hɛrɪʃ] ADJ overbearing, imperious; *Ton auch* peremptory ADV imperiously, overbearingly; *auffordern* peremptorily

herr|je(h) [hɛr'je:], **herr|je|mi|ne** [hɛr'je:mine] INTERJ goodness gracious

herr|lich ['hɛrlɪç] ADJ marvellous *(Brit)*, marvelous *(US)*; *Anblick, Tag, Wetter auch* magnificent, glorious, lovely; *Kleid* gorgeous, lovely; *Essen, Witz, Geschichte* marvel(l)ous, wonderful, lovely; **das ist ja ~** *(iro)* that's great ADV **du bist so ~ doof/naiv** *(iro)* you are so wonderfully stupid/naïve; **wir haben uns ~ amüsiert** we had marvel(l)ous fun *or* a marvel(l)ous time; **~ feiern** to have a marvellous time; **~ schmecken** *or* **munden** to taste absolutely delicious

Herr|lich|keit F **-, -en a** *no pl (= Schönheit, Pracht)* glory, magnificence, splendour *(Brit)*, splendor *(US)*; **die ~ Gottes** the glory of God; **Pracht und ~** pomp and circumstance; *(von Natur)* glory; **die ~ wird nicht lange dauern** *(iro inf)* this is too good to last; **ist das die ganze ~?** is that all there is to it?; **aus und vorbei mit der ~** here we go again **b** *usu pl (= prächtiger Gegenstand)* treasure **c** *(obs: Anrede)* lordship

Herr|schaft ['hɛrʃaft] F **-, -en a** *no pl (= Macht)* power; *(= Staatsgewalt)* rule; **zur ~ gelangen** *or* **kommen** to come to power; **sich der ~ bemächtigen** to seize power; **unter der ~** under the rule *(+gen, von* of); **unter jds ~** *(acc)* **fallen** to come under sb's rule; **während der ~** *(+gen)* in the reign of **b** *no pl (= Gewalt, Kontrolle)* control; **er verlor die ~ über sich** he lost his self-control; **er verlor die ~ über sein Auto** he lost control of his car, his car went out of control **c** *(old: = Dienstherrschaft)* master and mistress *pl*; **die ~en** *(= Damen und Herren)* the ladies and gentlemen; **hohe ~en** *(dated)* persons of high rank *or* standing; **meine alten ~en** *(dated inf: = Eltern)* my old man and old woman; **ältere ~en** *(iro: = alte Leute)* old folks; **würden die ~en bitte ...** ladies and gentlemen, would you please ...; **was wünschen die ~en?** what can I get you?; *(von Butler)* you rang?; **(meine) ~en!** ladies and gentlemen! **d** *(inf: Ausruf)* **~ (noch mal)** hang it (all) *(inf)* **e** *(Hist: = Landgut)* domain, estate, lands *pl*

herr|schaft|lich ['hɛrʃaftlɪç] ADJ of a person of high standing; *(= vornehm)* grand; **die ~e Kutsche** his lordship's coach

Herr|schafts-: **Herr|schafts|an|spruch** M claim to power; *(von Thronfolger)* claim to the throne; **Herr|schafts|be|reich** M territory; **Herr|schafts|form** F form *or* type of rule; **Herr|schafts|ge|walt** F authority, power; **herr|schafts|los** ADJ without rule *or* government; **Herr|schafts|lo|sig|keit** F **-**, *no pl* state of being without rule *or* government; **Herr|schafts|struk|tur** F power structure; **Herr|schafts|sys|tem** NT system of rule

herr|schen ['hɛrʃn] VI **a** *(= Macht, Gewalt haben)* to rule; *(König)* to reign; *(fig) (Mensch)* to dominate; *(Geld)* to hold sway; *(Tod, Terror)* to rule, to hold sway **b** *(= vorherrschen) (Angst, Ungewissheit, Zweifel)* to prevail; *(Verkehr, Ruhe, Betriebsamkeit)* to be prevalent; *(Nebel, Regen, Kälte)* to be predominant; *(Krankheit, Not)* to be rampant, to rage; *(Meinung, Ansicht)* to predominate; **überall herrschte Freude/Terror** there was joy/terror everywhere; **im Zimmer herrschte bedrückende Stille** it was oppressively quiet in the room; **hier herrscht Ordnung** things are orderly (a)round here; **hier herrscht ein anderer Ton** the atmosphere is different here; **hier ~ ja Zustände!** things are in a pretty state around here! **c** *(= in herrischem Ton reden)* to snap, to bark VI *impers* **es herrscht schlechtes Wetter** the weather is bad, we're having bad weather; **es herrschte Schweigen** silence reigned; **es herrscht Ungewissheit darüber, ob ...** there is uncertainty about whether ...

herr|schend ADJ *Partei, Klasse* ruling; *König* reigning; *Bedingungen, Verhältnisse, Meinungen* prevailing; *Mode* current; **die Herrschenden** the rulers, those in power

Herr|scher ['hɛrʃɐ] M **-s, -**, **Herr|sche|rin** [-ərɪn] F **-, -nen** *(über +acc* of) ruler; *(= König/Königin auch)* sovereign

Herr|scher-: **Herr|scher|blick** M imperious look; **mit ~** with an imperious look; **Herr|scher|fa|mi|lie** F ruling family; **Herr|scher|ge|schlecht** NT ruling dynasty; **Herr|scher|haus** NT ruling house *or* dynasty

Herr|sche|rin [-ərɪn] F → **Herrscher**

Herr|scher-: **Herr|scher|kult** M ruler cult; **Herr|scher|mie|ne** F imperious *or* commanding air; **Herr|scher|na|tur** F **a** *(= Mensch)* domineering person **b** *(= Wesensart)* domineering character; **Herr|scher|paar** NT ruler *or* sovereign and his *or* her consort

Herrsch|sucht F, *no pl* domineeringness

herrsch|süch|tig ADJ domineering

her-: **her+rü|cken** *sep* VT to move nearer *or* closer VI *aux sein* to move *or* come nearer *or* closer; **her+ru|fen** VT *sep irreg* to call (over); *Tier* to call; **her+rüh|ren** VI *sep* **von etw ~** to be due to sth, to stem from sth; **her+sa|gen** VT *sep* to recite; **her+schaf|fen** VT *sep (inf)* = **herbeischaffen**; **her+schau|en** VI *sep (dial)* to look here *or* this way; **zu jdm ~** to look in sb's direction; **da schau her!** *(Aus inf)* well, I never! *(inf)*; **her+schen|ken** VT *sep (inf: = verschenken)* to give away; **her+schi|cken** VT *sep* to send; **jdn hinter jdm ~** to send sb after sb; **her+schlei|chen** VIR *sep irreg (vi: aux sein)* **a** *(an bestimmten Ort)* to creep up **b** **(sich) hinter jdm ~** to creep along behind sb; **her+se|hen** VI *sep irreg* **a** *(= hierher sehen)* to look here *or* this way; **zu jdm ~** to look in sb's direction **b** **hinter jdm/etw ~** to follow sb/sth with one's eyes; **her sein** VI *irreg aux sein* **a** *(zeitlich)* **das ist schon 5 Jahre her** that was 5 years ago; **es ist schon 5 Jahre her, dass ...** it was 5 years ago that ...; **es ist kaum ein Jahr her, dass ...** it's hardly a year since ...; **wie lange ist es her?** how long ago was it? **b** *(= herstammen)* to come from; **mit jdm/etw ist es nicht weit her** *(inf)* sb/sth is not up to much *(inf)* **c** **hinter jdm/etw ~** to be after sb/sth; **dahinter ~, dass jd etw tut** to be on to sb to do sth; **her+spi|o|nie|ren** *ptp* **herspioniert** VI *sep* **hinter jdm ~** to spy on sb; **her+stam|men** VI *sep* **a** *(= abstammen)* to come from; **wo stammst du her?** where do you come from originally? **b** *(= herrühren)* **von etw ~** to stem from sth **c** *(= herkommen)* **von jdm/etw ~** to come from sb/sth

her|stell|bar ADJ capable of being produced *or* manufactured; **schwer ~e Waren** goods which are difficult to produce *or* manufacture

her+stel|len VT *sep* **a** *(= erzeugen)* to produce; *(esp industriell)* to manufacture; **von Hand ~** to make *or* produce by hand; **in Deutschland hergestellt** made in Germany **b** *(= zustande bringen)* to establish; *Kontakt* to establish, to make; *(Telec) Verbindung* to make; *Stromkreis* to complete **c** *(gesundheitlich) jdn* to restore to health; *Gesundheit* to restore; **er ist wieder ganz hergestellt** he has quite recovered **d** *(an bestimmten Platz)* to put *or* place here; **sich (zu jdm) ~** to come over (to sb); **etw zu jdm ~** to put sth by sb

Her|stel|ler [ˈheːɐ̯ʃtɛlɐ] **M -s, -**, **Her|stel|le|rin** [-ərɪn] **F -, -nen** *(= Produzent)* manufacturer; *(in Verlag)* production manager

Her|stel|ler-: **Her|stel|ler|an|ga|be F** a *(= Nennung der Herstellerfirma)* manufacturer's details *pl* b *(= Produktinformation)* **~n** *pl* product information *sing*; **Her|stel|ler|be|trieb M**, **Her|stel|ler|fir|ma F** manufacturing firm, manufacturer

Her|stel|lung F a *(= Erzeugung)* production; *(esp industriell)* manufacture b *(= das Zustandebringen)* establishment c *(von Gesundheit)* restoration d *(= Abteilung in Verlag)* production department

Her|stel|lungs-: **Her|stel|lungs|feh|ler M** manufacturing defect *or* fault; **Her|stel|lungs|kos|ten PL** manufacturing *or* production costs *pl*; **Her|stel|lungs|land NT** country of manufacture; **Her|stel|lungs|preis M** cost of manufacture; **Her|stel|lungs|ver|fah|ren NT** manufacturing *or* production method

her-: **her+stür|zen** *sep* VI *aux sein* a *(auch* **hergestürzt kommen***)* to come rushing up b **hinter jdm/etw ~** to rush after sb/sth VR **sich hinter jdm ~** to throw oneself after sb; **her+tra|gen** VT *sep irreg* a *(an bestimmten Ort)* to carry here b **etw vor/hinter jdm/etw ~** to carry sth in front of/behind sb/sth; **her+trau|en** VR *sep* to dare to come here; **her+trei|ben** *sep irreg* VT a *(an bestimmten Ort)* to drive here; *(Wind)* to blow here; *(Strömung)* to wash here; **etw zu uns ~** to drive/blow/wash sth over to us b **jdn/etw vor jdm/etw ~** to drive *or (Wind)* blow sb/sth in front of *or* before sb/sth; **jdn/etw hinter jdm/etw ~** to drive *or (Wind)* blow sb/sth behind sb/sth; **was treibt dich her?** what brings you here? VI *aux sein* to be driven *(vor +dat* in front of, before); *(Wolken)* to blow; *(in der Strömung)* to be washed; **her+tre|ten** VI *sep irreg aux sein* to step up

Hertz [hɛrts] **NT -, -** *(Phys, Rad)* hertz

he|rü|ben [hɛˈryːbn] **ADV** *(S Ger, Aus)* over here

he|rü|ber [hɛˈryːbɐ] **ADV** over here; *(über Fluss, Straße, Grenze etc)* across; **~ und hinüber** to and fro, back and forth; **da ~** over/across there

he|rü|ber- PREF → *auch* **rüber-** over; *(über Fluss, Straße, Grenze etc)* across; **he|rü|ber+bit|ten** VT *sep irreg* to ask (to come) over; **he|rü|ber+brin|gen** VT *sep irreg* → **herüber** to bring over/across *(über etw (acc)* sth); **he|rü|ber+dür|fen** VI *sep irreg* → **herüber** to be allowed (to come) over/across; **he|rü|ber+fah|ren** *sep irreg* → **herüber** VI *aux sein* to come *or (mit Auto auch)* drive over/across *(über etw (acc)* sth) VT *(über etw (acc)* sth) *Auto etc* to drive over/across; *Fahrgast, Güter* to take over/across; **he|rü|ber+flie|gen** VTI *sep irreg (vi: aux sein)* → **herüber** to fly over/across *(über etw (acc)* sth); **he|rü|ber+ge|ben** VT *sep irreg* to pass *(über +acc* over); **he|rü|ber+ho|len** VT *sep* to fetch; *jdn* to fetch over; **he|rü|ber+kom|men** VI *sep irreg aux sein* → **herüber** to come over/across *(über etw (acc)* sth); *(inf: zu Nachbarn)* to pop round *(Brit inf)*, to call round; **wie sind die Leute (über die Mauer/den Fluss) herübergekommen?** how did the people get over (the wall)/across (the river)?; **he|rü|ber+las|sen** VT *sep irreg* → **herüber** to allow (to come) over/across *(über etw (acc)* sth); *(aus Land)* to allow (to come) out; **he|rü|ber+lau|fen** VI *sep irreg aux sein* → **herüber** to run over/across *(über etw (acc)* sth); **he|rü|ber+rei|chen** *sep* VT to pass *(über +acc* over) VI to reach across *(über etw (acc)* sth); **he|rü|ber+ret|ten** VT *sep* **etw in die Gegenwart ~** to preserve sth; **he|rü|ber+schi|cken** VT *sep* → **herüber** to send over/across; **he|rü|ber+schwim|men** VI *sep irreg aux sein* to swim across *(über etw (acc)* sth); **he|rü|ber+se|hen** VI *sep irreg* → **herüber** to look over *(über etw (acc)* sth); **zu jdm ~** to look over/across to sb; **he|rü|ber+wech|seln** VI *sep aux sein or haben (Tiere)* to cross *(über etw (acc)* sth); **in unsere Partei/unseren Verein ~** to join our party/club, to swap parties/clubs (and join ours); **he|rü|ber+we|hen** *sep* → **herüber** *(über etw (acc)* sth) VI a *(Wind)* to blow over/across b *aux sein (Klang)* to be blown over/across; *(Duft)* to waft over/across VT to blow over/across; **he|rü|ber+wer|fen** VT *sep irreg* → **herüber** to throw over/across *(über etw (acc)* sth); **he|rü|ber+wol|len** VI *sep* → **herüber** to want to come over/across *(über etw (acc)* sth); **he|rü|ber+zie|hen** *sep irreg* → **herüber** *(über etw (acc)* sth) VT to pull over/across; *(fig)* to win over VI *aux sein (Truppen, Wolken)* to move over/across; *(= umziehen)* to move

he|rum [hɛˈrʊm] **ADV** a *(örtlich richtungsangebend)* **um ... ~** (a)round; **links/rechts ~** (a)round to the left/right; **hier/dort ~** (a)round here/there; **oben ~** *(über Gegenstand, Berg)* over the top; *(in Bezug auf Körper)* (a)round the top; **sie ist oben ~ ziemlich füllig** she's quite well endowed *(hum)*; **unten ~** *(unter Gegenstand)* underneath; *(um Berg, in Bezug auf Körper)* (a)round the bottom; **oben/unten ~ fahren** to take the top/lower road; **wasch dich auch unten ~** *(euph)* don't forget to wash down below; **verkehrt ~** the wrong way (a)round; *(= hinten nach vorn)* back to front; *(= links nach außen)* inside out; *(= oben nach unten)* upside down; **immer um etw ~** round and round sth *(esp Brit)*, around and around sth

b *(= kreisförmig angeordnet, in der Nähe)* **um ... ~** around; **hier ~** (a)round here; *(= in der Nähe auch)* hereabouts; **alle um mich ~ wussten, dass ...** everyone (a)round me knew that ...

c **um ... ~** *(ungefähre Mengenangabe)* about, around; *(Zeitangabe)* (at) about *or* around → *auch* **herum sein**

he|rum- PREF → *auch* **umher-, rum-** (a)round; **he|rum+al|bern** VI *sep (inf)* to fool *or* lark *(inf)* around; **he|rum+är|gern** VR *sep (inf)* **sich mit jdm/etw ~** to keep struggling with sb/sth; **he|rum+bal|gen** VR *sep (inf)* to romp about; **he|rum+bal|lern** VI *sep* to fire in all directions *or* all over the place; **he|rum+bas|teln** VI *sep (inf)* to tinker *or* mess *(inf)* about *(an +dat* with); **he|rum+be|kom|men** *ptp* **herumbekommen** VT *sep irreg (inf) jdn* to talk round *(esp Brit) or* around *(esp US)*; **etw ~** to (manage to) get sth round *(um etw* sth); **he|rum+bes|sern** VI *sep* **an etw** *(dat)* **~** to fiddle around correcting sth; **he|rum+blät|tern** VI *sep* **(in einem Buch) ~** to leaf *or* browse through a book; **he|rum+boh|ren** VI *sep (mit Stock, Finger etc)* to poke around; *(mit Bohrer)* to drill; **in der Nase ~** to pick one's nose; **he|rum+brin|gen** VT *sep irreg (inf)* a *(= überreden)* to talk round *(esp Brit) or* around *(esp US)* b *Zeit* to get through;; **he|rum+brül|len** VI *sep* to yell; **he|rum+bum|meln** VI *sep (inf)* a *(= trödeln)* to mess about *(inf)* b *aux sein (= spazieren)* to stroll (a)round *(in etw (dat)* sth); **he|rum+deu|teln** VI *sep (inf)* **an etw** *(+dat)* **~** to quibble *or* to split hairs over sth; **daran ist nichts herumzudeuteln** it's perfectly plain; **he|rum+dok|tern** [hɛˈrʊmdɔktɐn] VI *sep (inf)* **an jdm/einer Krankheit/einer Wunde ~** to try to cure sb/an illness/to heal a wound *(unsuccessfully, using many different treatments)*; **an etw** *(dat)* **~** *(fig)* to fiddle *or* tinker about with sth; **he|rum+dre|hen** *sep* VT *Schlüssel* to turn; *(= wenden) Decke, Tuch, Braten etc* to turn (over) → **Wort** VR to turn (a)round; *(im Liegen)* to turn over VI *(inf)* **an etw** *(dat)* **~** to fiddle *or* tinker about with sth; **he|rum+drü|cken** *sep* VR *(inf)* a *(= sich aufhalten)* to hang around *(inf) (um etw* sth) b *(= vermeiden)* **sich um etw ~** to dodge sth VI **an etw** *(dat)* **~** to squeeze sth VT *Hebel* to turn; **he|rum+druck|sen** VI *sep (inf)* to hum and haw *(inf)*; **he|rum+er|zäh|len** *ptp* **herumerzählt** VT *sep* **etw bei jdm ~** to tell sb about sth; **erzähl das nicht herum** don't spread that (a)round; **he|rum+ex|pe|ri|men|tie|ren** *ptp* **herumexperimentiert** VI *sep* to experiment; **he|rum+fah|ren** *sep irreg* VI *aux sein* a *(= umherfahren)* to go *or* travel *or (mit Auto)* drive (a)round; **in der Stadt ~** to go/drive (a)round the town b *(= um etw herumfahren)* to go *or (mit Auto)* drive *or (mit Schiff)* sail (a)round c *(= sich rasch umdrehen)* to turn (a)round quickly, to spin (a)round d *auch aux haben* **sich** *(dat)* **(mit den Händen) in den Haaren ~** to run one's fingers through one's hair VT to drive (a)round; **he|rum+fin|gern** VI *sep (inf)* **an etw** *(dat)* **~** to fiddle about with sth; *an Körperteil* to finger sth; **he|rum+flat|tern** VI *sep aux sein (= umherflattern)* to flutter about; **um etw ~** to flutter around sth; **he|rum+fle|geln** VI *sep* to loll about *or* around; **he|rum+flie|gen** *sep irreg* VI *aux sein* to fly around *(um jdn/etw* sb/sth); *(inf: = herumliegen)* to be kicking around *(inf)* VT *jdn* to fly about *or* around; **he|rum+fra|gen** VI *sep (inf)* to ask around *(bei* among); **he|rum+fuch|teln** VI *sep (inf)* **(mit den Händen) ~** to wave one's hands about *(Brit) or* around; **mit einer Pistole ~** to wave a pistol around, to brandish a pistol; **he|rum+füh|ren** *sep* VT a *jdn, Tier* to lead (a)round *(um etw* sth); *(bei Besichtigung)* to take *or* show (a)round; **jdn in einer Stadt/im Haus ~** to take *or* show sb (a)round a town/the house b *(= leiten, dirigieren)* **jdn/etw um etw ~** to direct sb/sth around sth c *(= bauen)* **etw um etw ~** to build *or* take sth (a)round sth VI **um etw ~** to go (a)round sth; **he|rum+fuhr|wer|ken** VI *sep (inf)* to bustle about, to busy oneself; **he|rum+fum|meln** VI *sep (inf) (an +dat* with) to fiddle *or* fumble about; *(an Auto)* to mess about; *(= basteln)* to tinker (about); **he|rum+ge|ben** VT *sep irreg* to hand *or* pass (a)round; **he|rum+ge|hen** VI *sep irreg aux sein (inf)* a *(= um etw herumgehen)* to walk *or* go (a)round *(um etw* sth) b *(= ziellos umhergehen)* to go *or* wander (a)round *(in etw (dat)* sth); **es ging ihm im Kopf herum** it went round and round in his head c *(= von einem zum andern gehen: Mensch)* to go (a)round; *(= herumgereicht werden)* to be passed *or* handed (a)round; *(= weitererzählt werden)* to go (a)round *(in etw (dat)* sth); **etw ~ lassen** to circulate sth d *(zeitlich: = vorbeigehen)* to pass; **he|rum+geis|tern** VI *sep aux sein (inf) (Gespenster etc)* to haunt *(in etw (dat)* sth); *(Mensch)* to wander (a)round; **in jds Kopf ~** *(Idee)* to possess sb; **he|rum+gon|deln** VI *sep aux sein (inf)* to drive around; **he|rum+gur|ken** [hɛˈrʊmgʊrkən] VI *sep aux sein (inf)* to cruise; **in der Gegend ~** to cruise the area; **he|rum+ha|ben** VT *sep irreg (inf)* a *Zeit* to have finished b *(= überredet haben)* to have talked round *(esp Brit) or* around *(esp US)*; **he|rum+ha|cken** VI *sep (fig inf)* **auf jdm ~** to pick on sb *(inf)*; **he|rum+hän|gen** VI *sep irreg* a *(inf: = unordentlich aufgehängt sein)* to hang around b *(inf: = sich lümmeln)* to loll about c *(inf: = ständig zu finden sein)* to hang out *(inf)*; **he|rum+han|tie|ren** *ptp* **herumhantiert** VI *sep (inf)* to fiddle (about) *(an +dat* with); **he|rum+het|zen** VI *sep aux sein* to rush around; **he|rum+hor|chen** VI *sep (inf)* to keep one's ears open; **he|rum+hu|ren** VI *sep (inf)* to whore around *(inf)*; **he|rum+ir|ren** VI *sep aux sein* to wander (a)round; **he|rum+kno|beln** VI *sep (inf)* **an etw** *(dat)* **~** to rack one's brains about sth; **he|rum+kom|man|die|ren** *ptp* **herumkommandiert** *sep (inf)* VT to order about, to boss around *or* about *(Brit, inf)* VI to give orders; **he|rum+kom|men** VI *sep irreg aux sein (inf)* a *(um eine Ecke etc)* to come round *(Brit) or* around *(um etw* sth) b *(= herumgehen, herumfahren etc können)* to get (a)round *(um etw* sth); **mit den Armen um etw ~** to be able to get one's arms (a)round sth c *(= vermeiden können)* **um etw ~** to get out of sth, to avoid sth; **darum ~, etw zu machen** to get out of *or* avoid doing sth; **wir kommen um die Tatsache nicht herum, dass ...** we cannot get away from *or* overlook the fact that ... **d** *(= reisen)* to get about *(Brit) or* around *(in etw (dat)* sth); **er ist viel** *or* **weit herumgekommen** he has got around a great deal, he has seen a lot of the world; **he|rum+krab|beln** VI *sep aux sein (inf)* to crawl around *or* about; **he|rum+kra|men** VI *sep (inf)* to rummage about *or* around; **he|rum+kreb|sen** VI *sep (inf)* **a** *(= sich verzweifelt bemühen)* to struggle **b** *(= sich unwohl fühlen)* to drag oneself about *(Brit) or* around *(inf)* **c** *aux sein (= langsam or schwerfällig gehen)* to trudge (a)round; **he|rum+krie|chen** VI *sep irreg aux sein (inf)* to crawl about *or* around *(um etw* sth); **he|rum+krie|gen** VT *sep (inf)* = **herumbekommen**; **he|rum+kri|ti|sie|ren** *ptp* **herumkritisiert**, **he|rum+krit|teln** *ptp* VI *sep* to find fault *(an +dat* with), to pick holes *(an +dat* in); **he|rum+ku|rie|ren** *ptp* **herumkuriert** VI *sep* = **herumdoktern**; **he|rum+kur|ven** VI *sep aux sein (inf)* cruise around *(in +dat* sth); **he|rum+kut|schie|ren** *ptp* **herumkutschiert** VTI *sep (vi: aux sein)* to drive around; **he|rum+la|bo|rie|ren** *ptp* **herumlaboriert** VI *sep (inf)* **an etw** *(dat)* ~ to try to get rid of sth; **he|rum+lau|fen** VI *sep irreg aux sein (inf) (= um etw herumlaufen)* to run round *(Brit) or* around *(um etw* sth); *(= umherlaufen)* to run *or* go about *(Brit) or* around; **so kannst du doch nicht ~** *(fig inf)* you can't run *or* go (a)round (looking) like that; **he|rum+lie|gen** VI *sep irreg (inf)* to lie about *(Brit) or* around *(um etw* sth); **he|rum+lüm|meln** VIR *sep (inf)* to loll around; **he|rum+lun|gern** VI *sep (inf)* to hang about *(Brit) or* (a)round; **he|rum+ma|chen** *sep (inf)* VI **a** *(= sich überlegen)* to consider; **da braucht man doch nicht so lange herumzumachen** you don't need to think about it for so long **b** *(= sich beschäftigen)* **an jdm ~** to fuss about sb; **an etw** *(dat)* ~ to mess about with sth; **mit jdm ~** to mess around with sb **c** *(= herumfingern)* **an etw** *(dat)* ~ to pick at sth; *an den Haaren* to fiddle with sth **d** *(= herumnörgeln)* **an jdm/etw ~** to go on at sb/about sth *(inf)* VT to put (a)round *(um etw* sth); **he|rum+mä|keln** VI *sep* to find fault *(an +dat* with); **he|rum+nör|geln** VI *sep* **an jdm/etw ~** to find fault with sb/sth; **he|rum+pfu|schen** VI *sep (inf)* to mess about *(inf) (an +dat* with); **he|rum+pus|seln** VI *sep (inf)* to fiddle about *(an +dat* with); **he|rum+quä|len** VR *sep (inf)* to struggle; *(mit Problemen)* to worry oneself sick *(mit* over) *(inf)*; **sich mit Rheuma ~** to be plagued by rheumatism; **he|rum+ra|ten** VI *sep irreg (inf)* to guess; **he|rum+rät|seln** VI *sep* **an etw** *(dat)* ~ to (try to) figure sth out; **er rätselte herum** he tried to figure it out; **he|rum+re|den** VI *sep (inf) (= belangloses Zeug reden)* to talk *or* chat away; **um etw ~** *(ausweichend)* to talk around sth; **he|rum+reichen** VT *sep* **a** *(= herumgeben)* to pass (a)round; *(fig inf) Besucher* to show off **b** *(= lang genug sein)* to reach round *(Brit) or* around *(um etw* sth); **he|rum+rei|sen** VI *sep aux sein* to travel about *(Brit) or* around; **he|rum+rei|ßen** VT *sep irreg* to pull *or* swing (a)round (hard); **das Steuer ~** *(fig)* to change *or* alter course; **he|rum+rei|ten** VI *sep irreg* **a** *aux sein (= umherreiten)* to ride about *(Brit) or* (a)round; *(= um etw herumreiten)* to ride (a)round *(um etw* sth) **b** *(fig inf)* **auf jdm/etw ~** to keep on at sb/about sth; **he|rum+ren|nen** VI *sep irreg aux sein (inf) (= um etw herumrennen)* to run (a)round *(um etw* sth); *(= umherrennen)* to run about *(Brit) or* (a)round; **he|rum+rut|schen** VI *sep aux sein (inf)* to fidget about; **he|rum+schar|wen|zeln** *ptp* **herumscharwenzelt** VI *sep aux sein (inf)* to dance attendance *(um* on); **he|rum+schi|cken** VT *sep (inf) jdn* to send round *(bei* to); *Brief etc* to circulate; **he|rum+schla|gen** *sep irreg* VT *Papier, Tuch etc* to wrap (a)round *(um etw* sth) VR *(inf)* **sich mit jdm ~** *(lit)* to fight *or* scuffle with sb; *(fig)* to fight a running battle with sb; **sich mit etw ~** *(fig)* to keep struggling with sth; **he|rum+schlei|chen** VI *sep irreg aux sein* to creep (a)round *(um etw* sth); **he|rum+schlei|fen** VI *sep (dial inf)* to drag around; **he|rum+schlen|dern** VI *sep aux sein* to stroll *or* saunter about *(in der Stadt* (in) the town); **he|rum+schlep|pen** VT *sep (inf) Sachen* to lug (a)round *(inf)*; *jdn* to drag (a)round; **etw mit sich ~** *(Kummer, Sorge, Problem)* to be troubled *or* worried by sth; *Krankheit, Infektion* to be going (a)round with sth; **he|rum+schnüf|feln** VI *sep (inf)* to sniff (a)round *(in etw (dat)* sth); *(fig)* to snoop (a)round *(in +dat* in); **he|rum+schrei|en** VI *sep irreg (inf)* to shout out loud; **he|rum+schwän|zeln** VI *sep aux sein (inf)* to dance attendance *(um* on); **he|rum+schwir|ren** VI *sep aux sein (inf)* **sie muss hier irgendwo ~** she must be floating (a)round here somewhere *(inf)*; **he|rum sein** VI *irreg aux sein (inf)* **a** *(= vorüber sein)* to be past *or* over **b** *(= verbreitet worden sein: Gerücht, Neuigkeit, Nachricht)* to have got (a)round **c** *(= in jds Nähe sein)* **um jdn ~** to be around sb **d** *(= um etw gelaufen, gefahren sein)* to be around *(um etw* sth); **he|rum+sit|zen** VI *sep irreg aux haben or sein* to sit around *(um jdn/etw* sb/sth); **he|rum+spa|zie|ren** VI *sep aux sein (inf)* to walk *or* stroll around *(in +dat* sth, *um* sth); **he|rum+spie|len** VI *sep (inf)* **mit etw ~** to play about *(Brit) or* around with sth; **an etw** *(dat)* ~ to fiddle about *(Brit) or* around with sth; **auf etw** *(dat)* ~ to play around on sth; **he|rum+spre|chen** VR *sep irreg* to get about *(Brit) or* around; **es dürfte sich herumgesprochen haben, dass ...** it has probably got out that ...; **he|rum+spu|ken** VI *sep* to haunt; **die Idee spukt jdm im Kopf** *or* **in jds Kopf herum** sb has the idea; **he|rum+stän|kern** VI *sep (inf)* to moan, to gripe *(inf)*, to bellyache *(inf)*; **he|rum+ste|hen** VI *sep irreg aux haben or sein* **a** *(Sachen)* to be lying around; **der Sessel steht blöd herum** the chair is in a stupid place **b** *(Menschen)* to stand (a)round *(um jdn/etw* sb/sth); **he|rum+stö|bern** VI *sep (inf)* **a** *(= suchen)* to rummage about *(Brit) or* around **b** *(= herumschnüffeln)* to snoop (a)round; **he|rum+sto|chern** VI *sep (inf)* to poke about *(Brit) or* around; **im Essen ~** to pick at one's food; **in den Zähnen ~** to pick one's teeth; **he|rum+sto|ßen** VT *sep irreg jdn* to shove (a)round; **he|rum+strei|chen** VI *sep irreg aux sein (um jdn/etw* sb/sth) to creep (a)round; *(Verbrecher, Katze)* to prowl (a)round; **he|rum+strei|fen** VI *sep aux sein* to roam around; **he|rum+strei|ten** VR *sep irreg* to squabble; **he|rum+streu|nen, he|rum+strol|chen** VI *sep aux sein (inf)* to prowl (a)round; **he|rum+stro|mern** VI *sep aux sein (inf)* to wander *or* roam about *or* around; **he|rum+tan|zen** VI *sep aux sein (inf) (= umhertanzen)* to dance (a)round; **um jdn/etw ~** to dance (a)round sb/sth; **sie tanzt ihm auf der Nase herum** she does as she pleases *or* likes with him; **he|rum+tap|pen** VI *sep aux sein (inf)* to grope around *or* about; **he|rum+tas|ten** VI *sep* **a** *(= tastend fühlen)* to grope about *(Brit) or* around **b** *aux sein (inf: = tastend gehen)* to grope about *(Brit) or* around; **he|rum+to|ben** VI *sep (inf)* **a** *auch aux sein (= umherlaufen)* to romp about *(Brit) or* (a)round **b** *(= schimpfen)* to shout and scream; **he|rum+tol|len** VI *sep aux sein (inf)* to romp about *or* around; **he|rum+tra|gen** VT *sep irreg (inf)* **a** *(= mit sich tragen)* to carry about *(Brit) or* (a)round; **um etw ~** to carry (a)round sth; **Sorgen mit sich ~** to have worries; **eine Idee mit sich ~** to be contemplating an idea, to be thinking about an idea **b** *(= weitererzählen)* to spread (a)round; **he|rum+tram|peln** VI *sep aux sein (inf)* to trample *(auf +dat* on); **jdm auf den Nerven ~, auf jds Nerven ~** to get on sb's nerves; **auf jdm ~** *(fig)* to get at sb; **he|rum+trei|ben** VR *sep irreg (inf) (= herumziehen in)* to hang about *(Brit) or* (a)round *(in +dat* in) *(inf)*; *(in schlechter Gesellschaft)* to hang about *(Brit) or* (a)round in bad company; **die treibt sich mal wieder irgendwo in Spanien herum** she's off gadding about *(Brit) or* roaming around in Spain again *(inf)*; **sich mit jdm ~** to hang *or* knock *(Brit)* around with sb *(inf)*

He|rum|trei|ber(in) M(F) *(pej)* **a** *(= Mensch ohne feste Arbeit, Wohnsitz)* tramp **b** *(inf) (= Streuner)* vagabond; *(liederlich)* good-for-nothing; *(= Frau)* tramp *(inf)*

he|rum-: he|rum+tre|ten VI *sep irreg (inf)* to trample *(auf +dat* on); **he|rum+trö|deln** VI *sep (inf)* to dawdle *(mit* over); **he|rum+tur|nen** VI *sep aux sein (inf)* to clamber *or* scramble about; **he|rum+va|ga|bun|die|ren** *ptp* **herumvagabundiert** VI *sep aux sein (pej)* to roam about; **he|rum+wäl|zen** *sep* VT *Stein* to turn over VR to roll around; **sich (schlaflos) im Bett ~** to toss and turn in bed; **he|rum+wan|dern** VI *sep aux sein (= umhergehen)* to wander about; **um etw ~** to wander (a)round sth; **he|rum+wer|fen** *sep irreg* VT **a** *(= achtlos werfen)* to throw around *(in etw (dat)* sth) **b** *(= heftig bewegen) Kopf* to turn (quickly); *Steuer, Hebel* to throw around VR to roll over; **sich (im Bett) ~** to toss and turn (in bed) VI *(inf)* **mit Bemerkungen/Geld** *etc* **~** to fling *or* throw remarks/one's money *etc* around; **he|rum+wi|ckeln** VT *sep (um etw* sth) to wrap (a)round; *Schnur, Faden etc* to wind (a)round; **he|rum+wir|beln** VTI *sep (vi: aux sein)* **jdn ~, mit jdm ~** to whirl *or* spin sb (a)round; **he|rum+wirt|schaf|ten** VI *sep (inf)* to potter *(Brit) or* putter *(US)* about; **he|rum+wüh|len** VI *sep (inf)* to rummage about *or* around; *(Schwein)* to root around; *(= herumschnüffeln)* to nose *or* snoop about *or* around; **he|rum+wursch|teln** [-vʊrʃtln] VI *sep (inf)* → **herumwursteln**; **he|rum+wurs|teln** VI *sep (inf)* to fiddle *or* mess *(inf)* about *(Brit) or* (a)round *(an +dat* with); **he|rum+zan|ken** VR *sep* to squabble; **he|rum+zap|pen** VI *sep (TV inf)* to zap around *(inf)*; **he|rum+zei|gen** VT *sep* to show (a)round; **he|rum+zie|hen** *sep irreg* VI *aux sein* **a** *(= von Ort zu Ort ziehen)* to move around; *(inf: = sich herumtreiben in)* to go around *(in etw (dat)* sth); **in der Welt ~** to roam the world; **mit jdm ~** *(inf)* to go *or* hang around with sb **b** *(= um etw herumziehen)* to move (a)round *(um etw* sth) VR **sich um etw ~** *(Hecke etc)* to run (a)round sth; **he|rum|zie|hend** ADJ *attr Händler* itinerant; *Musikant, Schauspieler* wandering, strolling; **he|rum+zi|geu|nern** *ptp* **herumzigeunert** VI *sep aux sein (pej, neg!)* to roam *or* wander (a)round *(in etw (dat)* sth)

he|run|ten [hɛˈrʊntn] ADV *(S Ger, Aus)* down here

he|run|ter [hɛˈrʊntɐ] ADV down; **~!** get down!; **~ mit euch** get down; **~ mit ihm** get him down; **~ damit** get *or* bring it down; *(in Bezug auf Kleider)* get *or* take it off; **da/hier ~** down there/here; **den Hut ~, ~ mit dem Hut** get *or* take your hat off; **vom Berg ~** down the mountain; **vom Himmel ~** down from heaven; **bis ins Tal ~** down into the valley → *auch* **herunter sein** *etc* PREP *+acc (nachgestellt)* down

he|run|ter- PREF → *auch* **runter-, herab-** down; **he|run|ter+be|kom|men** *ptp* **herunterbekommen** VT *sep irreg* = **herunterkriegen**; **he|run|ter+be|mü|hen** *ptp* **herunterbemüht** *(geh) sep* VT **jdn ~** to ask sb to come down VR to trouble to come down, to take the trouble to come down; **he|run|ter+bit|ten** VT *sep irreg* **jdn ~** to ask sb to come down; **he|run|ter+bren|nen** VI *sep irreg* **a** *(Sonne)* to burn *or* scorch down **b** *aux sein (Haus, Feuer, Kerze etc)* to burn down; **he|run|ter+brin|gen** VT *sep irreg* **a** *(= nach unten bringen)* to bring down **b** *(= zugrunde richten)* to ruin **c** *(inf)* = **herunterkriegen**; **he|run|ter+drü|cken** VT *sep Hebel, Pedal* to press down; *Preise* to force *or* bring down; *Niveau* to lower; **he|run|ter+fah|ren** *sep irreg* VI *aux sein* to go down; **heruntergefahren kommen** to come down VT to bring down; *Reaktor, Server (= völlig abschalten)* to shut down; *(= Leistung ver-*

ringern) to scale down; *(= verringern, nach unten drücken)* to cut down; **die Zahl ...** *(gen)* ~ to cut down the number of ...; **he|run|ter+fal|len** VI *sep irreg aux sein* to fall down; **von etw** ~ to fall off sth; **ihm fiel die Kinnlade herunter** his jaw dropped; **he|run|ter+flie|gen** VI *sep irreg aux sein* to fly down; *(inf)* to fall down; **he|run|ter+ge|ben** VT *sep irreg* to hand down; **he|run|ter+ge|hen** VI *sep irreg aux sein* to go down; *(Fieber, Temperatur auch)* to drop; *(Preise auch)* to come down, to drop; *(Flugzeug)* to descend; **von etw** ~ *(inf)* to get down from sth, to get off sth; **auf etw** *(acc)* ~ *(Preise)* to go down to sth; *(Geschwindigkeit)* to slow down to sth; **mit den Preisen** ~ to lower *or* cut one's prices; **he|run|ter|ge|kom|men** ADJ *Haus* dilapidated; *Stadt* run-down; *Mensch* down-at-heel; **he|run|ter+ha|ben** VT *sep irreg (inf) (= heruntergeholt haben)* to have got down; *(= abgenommen haben)* to have lost; **he|run|ter+han|deln** VT *sep (inf) Preis, Gebühren* to beat down; **etw um 20 Euro** ~ to get 20 euros knocked off sth; **jdn (auf etw** *acc)* ~ to knock sb down (to sth); **he|run|ter+hän|gen** VI *sep irreg* to hang down; *(Haare)* to hang; **he|run|ter+hau|en** VT *sep irreg (inf)* **a** **jdm eine** ~ to give sb a clip round the ear (*Brit inf*), to slap sb on the side of the head **b** *(= schnell machen)* to dash *or* knock off *(inf)*; **he|run|ter+he|ben** VT *sep irreg* to lift down; **he|run|ter+hel|fen** VI *sep irreg* **jdm** ~ to help sb down; **he|run|ter+ho|len** VT *sep* to fetch down; *(inf) Vogel* to bring down, to bag; *Flugzeug* to bring down; **he|run|ter+klap|pen** VT *sep* to turn down; *Sitz* to fold down; *Deckel* to close; **he|run|ter+klet|tern** VI *sep aux sein* to climb down; **he|run|ter+kom|men** VI *sep irreg aux sein* **a** *(= nach unten kommen)* to come down; *(inf: = herunterkönnen)* to get down **b** *(fig inf: = verfallen) (Stadt, Firma)* to go downhill; *(Wirtschaft)* to go to rack and ruin; *(gesundheitlich)* to become run-down; **er ist so weit heruntergekommen, dass ...** *(sittlich)* he has sunk so low that ... → **heruntergekommen** **c** *(fig inf: = wegkommen: von schlechten Noten etc)* to get over (*von etw* sth); **von Drogen/vom Alkohol** ~ to kick the habit *(inf)*; **he|run|ter+kön|nen** VI *sep irreg* to be able to get down; **he|run|ter+krie|gen** VT *sep (inf)* **a** *(= herunterholen, schlucken können)* to get down; *(= abmachen können)* to get off **b** *(= abnehmen)* to lose; **he|run|ter+kur|beln** VT *sep Fensterscheibe* to wind down; **he|run|ter+la|den** VT *sep irreg (Comput)* to download (*auf +acc* onto); **etw aus dem Internet** ~ to download sth from the Internet; **he|run|ter+las|sen** *sep irreg* VT *(= abseilen) Gegenstand* to let down, to lower; *Hose* to take down; *jdn* to lower; **sie lässt mich nicht herunter** *(inf)* she won't let me down VR *(am Seil)* to lower oneself; **he|run|ter+lei|ern** [hɛ'rʊntɐlaiɐn] VT *sep (inf)* to reel off; **he|run|ter+le|sen** VT *sep irreg (pej)* to read off; **he|run|ter+ma|chen** VT *sep (inf)* **a** *(= schlechtmachen)* to run down, to knock *(inf)* **b** *(= zurechtweisen)* to tell off **c** *(= abmachen)* to take down; *Schminke, Farbe, Dreck* to take off; **he|run|ter+neh|men** VT *sep irreg* to take down; *(inf: von Schule)* to take away; **etw vom Tisch** *etc* ~ to take sth off the table *etc*; **he|run|ter+put|zen** VT *sep (inf)* **jdn** ~ to tear sb off a strip (*Brit inf*), to give sb an earful *(inf)*; **he|run|ter+ras|seln** VT *sep (inf)* to rattle *or* reel off; **he|run|ter+rei|chen** *sep* VT to pass *or* hand down VI to reach down; **he|run|ter+rei|ßen** VT *sep irreg (inf)* **a** *(von oben nach unten)* to pull *or* tear down **b** *(= abreißen) Pflaster, Tapete etc* to pull off; **he|run|ter+rut|schen** VI *sep aux sein* to slide down → **Buckel a**; **he|run|ter+schal|ten** VI *sep (Aut)* to change *or* shift (*US*) down (*in +acc* into); **he|run|ter+schie|ßen** *sep irreg* VT *(mit Geschoss)* to shoot down VI *aux sein (inf: = sich schnell bewegen)* to shoot down; **he|run|ter+schla|gen** VT *sep irreg* **a** **jdm den Hut** *etc* ~ to knock sb's hat *etc* off; **etw vom Baum** ~ to knock sth off the tree **b** *Kragen, Hutkrempe* to turn down; **he|run|ter+schlin|gen** VT *sep irreg (inf) Essen* to gobble down, to wolf down; *Getränk* to gulp down; **he|run|ter+schlu|cken** VT *sep* to swallow; **he|run|ter+schrau|ben** VT *sep (lit) Deckel etc* to screw off; *Petroleumlampe* to turn down; *(fig) Ansprüche, Niveau* to lower; **he|run|ter+se|hen** VI *sep irreg* **a** *(von oben)* to look down **b** *(fig: = mustern)* **an jdm** ~ to look sb up and down **c** *(fig: = geringschätzig behandeln)* **auf jdn** ~ to look down on sb; **he|run|ter sein** VI *sep irreg aux sein (inf)* **a** *(von oben)* to be down **b** *(= heruntergelassen sein)* to be down **c** *(= abgeschnitten sein)* to be (cut) off **d** *(Fieber, Preise)* to be lower *or* down; **wenn die 5 Kilo Übergewicht herunter sind** when I/you *etc* have lost those 5 kilos excess weight **e** *(inf)* **mit den Nerven** ~ to be at the end of one's tether (*Brit*) *or* rope (*US*); **mit der Gesundheit** ~ to be run-down **f** *(= abgewirtschaftet haben)* to be in a bad way; **he|run|ter+set|zen** VT *sep (inf)* = **herabsetzen**; **he|run|ter+spie|len** VT *sep (inf) Stück* to run through; *(= verharmlosen) Problem, Vorfall* to play down; **he|run|ter+sprin|gen** VI *sep irreg aux sein* to jump down; **he|run|ter+stei|gen** VI *sep irreg aux sein* to climb down; **he|run|ter+stür|zen** *sep* VI *aux sein (= herunterfallen)* to fall *or* tumble down; *(inf: = heruntereilen)* to rush down VT **a** **jdn** ~ to throw sb down **b** *(inf: = schnell trinken)* to gulp down VR to throw oneself down; **he|run|ter+wer|fen** VT *sep irreg* to throw down; *(unabsichtlich)* to drop; **he|run|ter+wirt|schaf|ten** VT *sep (inf)* to bring to the brink of ruin; **he|run|ter+wol|len** VI *sep (inf)* to want to get down; **he|run|ter+zie|hen** *sep irreg* VT **a** *(= nach unten ziehen)* to pull down; *Pullover etc* to pull off; **etw von etw** ~ to pull sth off sth **b** *(fig)* **jdn auf sein Niveau** *or* **seine Ebene** *or* **zu sich** ~ to pull sb down to one's own level VI *aux sein* to go *or* move down; *(= umziehen)* to move down

her|vor [hɛɐ'foːɐ] ADV **aus etw** ~ out of sth; **hinter dem Tisch** ~ out from behind the table; ~ **mit euch** *(geh)* out you come

her|vor-: **her|vor+bre|chen** VI *sep irreg aux sein (geh)* to burst *or* break out; *(Sonne, fig: Gefühl)* to break through; *(Quelle, Flüssigkeit)* to gush out *or* forth *(liter)*; **her|vor+brin|gen** VT *sep irreg* **a** *(= entstehen lassen)* to produce; *Worte* to utter **b** *(= verursachen) Unheil, Böses* to create; **her|vor+drin|gen** VI *sep irreg aux sein (geh)* to issue forth *(liter)*; **her|vor+ge|hen** ✪ 53.4 VI *sep irreg aux sein* **a** *(geh: = entstammen)* to come (*aus* from); **aus der Ehe gingen zwei Kinder hervor** the marriage produced two children **b** *(= sich ergeben, zu folgern sein)* to follow; **daraus geht hervor, dass ...** from this it follows that ... **c** *(= etwas überstehen)* to emerge; **als Sieger** ~ to emerge victorious; **aus etw** ~ to come out of sth; **her|vor+gu|cken** VI *sep (inf)* to peep out (*unter +dat* (from) under); **her|vor+he|ben** VT *sep irreg* to emphasize, to stress; **her|vor+ho|len** VT *sep* to bring out; **her|vor+keh|ren** VT *sep (geh)* to emphasize; **er kehrt immer den feinen Mann hervor** he always emphasizes what a gentleman he is; **her|vor+kom|men** VI *sep irreg aux sein* to come out (*hinter +dat* from behind); **her|vor+kra|men** VT *sep (inf)* **a** *Fotos, Besteck etc* to dig out **b** *(fig) Erinnerungen etc* to dredge up; **her|vor+lo|cken** VT *sep* to entice *or* lure out (*aus* from, *hinter +dat* from behind); **dein Gejammer lockt bei mir keine Träne hervor** your moaning is not going to move me; **her|vor+quel|len** VI *sep irreg aux sein (Wasser)* to gush forth (*aus* from) *(liter)*; *(Tränen)* to well up (*aus* in); *(Blut)* to spurt out (*aus* of); *(Körperfülle)* to bulge *or* protrude (*aus* from, *unter +dat* from under); **her|vor+ra|gen** VI *sep* **a** *(Felsen, Stein etc)* to jut out, to project; *(Nase)* to protrude **b** *(fig: = sich auszeichnen)* to stand out; **er ragt unter den anderen/durch seine Intelligenz hervor** he stands out from the others/because of his intelligence; **her|vor|ra|gend** ADJ **a** *(lit: = vorstehend)* projecting; *esp Körperteil* protruding **b** *(fig: = ausgezeichnet)* excellent; *Mensch, Leistung etc* excellent, outstanding; **er hat Hervorragendes geleistet** his achievement was outstanding ADV *(= ausgezeichnet)* very well; **etw ~ beschreiben/interpretieren** to give an excellent description/interpretation of sth; ~ **kochen** to be an excellent cook; ~ **schmecken** to taste exquisite; **her|vor+ru|fen** ✪ 44.2 VT *sep irreg* **a** *(= rufen)* **jdn** ~ to call (to) sb to come out; *(Theat etc)* to call for sb **b** *(= bewirken)* to cause, to give rise to; *Bewunderung* to arouse; *Reaktion, Krankheit* to cause; *Eindruck* to create; **her|vor+se|hen** VI *sep irreg (Unterrock)* to show; *(Mensch)* to look out; **hinter etw** *(dat)* ~ *(Mensch)* to look out from behind sth; *(Mond, Sterne)* to shine out from behind sth; **her|vor+sprin|gen** VI *sep irreg aux sein* **a** *(Mensch, Tier)* to jump *or* leap out (*hinter +dat* from behind) **b** *(Felsen)* to project, to jut out; *(Nase)* to protrude, to stick out; **her|vor+spru|deln** VI *sep aux sein* to bubble *or* gush out; *(Worte)* to gush (out); **her|vor+ste|chen** VI *sep irreg aux sein (lit, fig)* to stand out; **her|vor|ste|chend** ADJ striking; **her|vor+ste|hen** VI *sep irreg aux sein (Spitze)* to project, to jut out; *(Nase, Ohren etc)* to stick out; **her|vor+sto|ßen** VT *sep irreg (fig) Worte* to gasp (out); **her|vor+stür|zen** VI *sep aux sein* to rush *or* hurtle out (*hinter +dat* from behind); **her|vor+su|chen** VT *sep (= heraussuchen)* to look out; **her|vor+trau|en** VR *sep (inf)* to dare to come out; **her|vor+tre|ten** VI *sep irreg aux sein* **a** *(= heraustreten)* to step out, to emerge (*hinter +dat* from behind); *(Backenknochen)* to protrude; *(Adern)* to bulge; *(Sonne, Mond)* to emerge (*hinter +dat, aus* from behind) **b** *(= sichtbar werden)* to stand out; *(fig)* to become evident **c** *(= an die Öffentlichkeit treten)* to come to the fore; **her|vor+tun** VR *sep irreg* to distinguish oneself; *(inf: = sich wichtigtun)* to show off (*mit etw* sth); **her|vor+wa|gen** VR *sep* to dare to come out; **her|vor+zau|bern** VT *sep (lit, fig)* to conjure up; **her|vor+zie|hen** VT *sep irreg* to pull out (*unter +dat* from under); **etw aus/zwischen etw** *(dat)* ~ to pull sth out of/from among sth

Her-: **her+wa|gen** VR *sep* to dare to come; **her|wärts** ['heːɐvɛrts] ADV on the way here; **Her|weg** M, *no pl* way here; **auf dem** ~ on the way here

Herz [hɛrts] -ens, -en

SUBSTANTIV (NT)

a [= Organ] heart; **ein gesundes/schwaches Herz haben** to have a healthy/weak heart; **Operation/Eingriff am offenen Herzen** open-heart surgery; **sein Herz schlägt sehr schnell** he has a very high heart rate; **mir schlug das Herz bis zum Hals** my heart was thumping *or* pounding; **sein Herz schlug höher** his heart leapt *or* beat faster; **die Herzen höherschlagen lassen** to touch people's hearts; **er drückte sie an sein Herz** he clasped her to his breast; **sie drückte den Teddybär ans Herz** she clutched her teddy to her heart, she held her teddy tight; **komm an mein Herz** come into my arms

b [= Herzform] heart; **Herzen aus Teig ausstechen** to cut hearts out of pastry; **ein Herz auf das i malen** to draw a heart on (top of) the i

c [Kosewort] *(old)* **du, mein liebes Herz** you, my love

d [Cards] = *Karte* heart; *(no pl: = Farbe)* hearts *pl*; **Herz (aus)spielen** to play hearts; *(einzelne Karte)* to play a heart; **Herz ist Trumpf** hearts are trumps; **hast du noch Herz?** do you have any hearts left?

e [= Inneres] heart; **das Herz des Salats hat sehr zarte Blätter** the leaves of the lettuce heart are very tender; **das Parlament befindet sich im Herzen der Stadt** the parliament is in the heart of the city; **das Herz der Sache** the heart of the matter

f = Gemüt heart; **im Grund seines/meines Herzens** in his/my heart of hearts; **die Dame seines Herzens** the woman he has given his heart to; **ein Herz und eine Seele sein** to be the best of friends

♦ **Adjektiv + Herz** **mit ganzem Herzen** wholeheartedly; **er ist mit ganzem Herzen bei der Arbeit** he is putting his heart and soul into his work; **jdm von ganzem Herzen danken** to thank sb with all one's heart; **ein goldenes Herz** a heart of gold; **ein gutes Herz haben** *(fig)* to be good-hearted, to have a good heart; **sie konnte nicht leichten Herzens darauf verzichten** she couldn't easily do without it; **schweren Herzens** with a heavy heart; **mir ist das Herz schwer** I have a heavy heart; **jdm das Herz schwermachen** to grieve sb; **aus tiefstem Herzen** from the bottom of one's heart; **traurigen Herzens** with a sad heart

♦ **Präposition + Herz**

Die in Verbindung mit *Herz* verwendeten Präpositionen sind alphabetisch angeordnet.

dieser Hund ist mir ans Herz gewachsen I have grown fond of *or* become attached to this dog; **es liegt mir am Herzen** I am very concerned about it; **es liegt mir sehr am Herzen, dass der Spielplatz gebaut wird** it's very important to me that the playground be built; **jdm etw ans Herz legen** to entrust sth to sb's care; **ich lege es dir ans Herz, das zu tun** I would ask you particularly to do that; **etw auf dem Herzen haben** to have sth on one's mind; **jdn auf Herz und Nieren prüfen** to examine sb very thoroughly; **du sprichst mir aus dem Herzen** that's just what I feel; **er hat sie in sein Herz geschlossen** he has grown fond of her; **es ging mir bis ins Herz** it cut me to the quick; *(= traurig stimmen)* it saddened me very much; **es gab mir einen Stich ins Herz** it hurt me; *(= traurig stimmen)* it saddened me; **ein Mann nach meinem Herzen** a man after my own heart; **ohne Herz** heartless; **es wurde ihr leichter ums Herz** she felt relieved; **ich weiß, wie es dir ums Herz ist** I know how you feel; **ein Kind unter dem Herzen tragen** *(Bibl, old)* to be with child *(old)*; **von Herzen** with all one's heart; **etw von Herzen gern tun** to love doing sth; **jdn von Herzen gern haben** to love sb dearly; **von Herzen kommend** heartfelt; **der Applaus kam von Herzen** the applause was heartfelt; **eine schwere Last** *or* **eine Zentnerlast fiel ihr vom Herzen** she felt a weight lifted from her mind; **sich** *(dat)* **etw vom Herzen reden** to get sth off one's chest; **den Weg in die** *or* **zu den Herzen finden** to find one's way into people's hearts; **es ging mir zu Herzen** it touched me deeply; **sich** *(dat)* **etw zu Herzen nehmen** to take sth to heart

♦ **Verb + Herz**

Die in Verbindung mit *Herz* verwendeten Verben sind alphabetisch angeordnet (siehe auch *Präposition + Herz*).

alles, was das Herz begehrt everything one's heart desires; **mir blutet das Herz, mein Herz blutet** *(auch iro)* my heart bleeds; **jds Herz brechen** to break sb's heart; **dabei dreht sich mir das Herz im Leib um** it makes me feel sick at heart; **sein Herz für etw entdecken** to start liking sth; **alle Herzen im Sturm erobern** to capture people's hearts; **sich** *(dat)* **ein Herz fassen** to take heart; **gib deinem Herzen einen Stoß!** go on!; **mein Herz gehört dir** my heart belongs to you; **mein Herz gehört der Musik** music is the love of my life; **jds Herz gewinnen** to win sb's heart; **hast du denn (gar) kein Herz?** how can you be so heartless?; **haben Sie doch ein Herz!** have a heart!; **ein Herz für jdn/etw haben** to be fond of sb/sth; **habt ein Herz für die Armen** spare a thought for the poor; **er hat das Herz auf dem** *or* **am rechten Fleck** his heart is in the right place; **sein Herz an jdn/etw hängen** to commit oneself heart and soul to sb/sth; **jds Herz hängt an jdm/etw** sb is committed heart and soul to sb/sth; *an Geld* sb is preoccupied with sth; **mir lacht das Herz im Leibe** my heart is leaping with joy; **seinem Herzen Luft machen** to give vent to one's feelings; **sich** *(dat)* **ein Herz nehmen** to take heart; **sein Herz in beide Hände nehmen** to take one's courage in both hands; **der Anblick rührte ihr das Herz** the sight touched her heart; **jdm sein Herz schenken** to give sb one's heart; **jds Herz stehlen** to steal sb's heart; **das Herz auf der Zunge tragen** to speak one's mind; **ihr tat das Herz im Leibe weh** she felt terribly saddened; **es zerreißt mir das Herz** it breaks my heart → auch **Hose**

her+zäh|len VT *sep* to count

Herz-: **herz|al|ler|liebst** ADJ *(old, hum)* most charming; **Herz|al|ler|liebs|te(r)** [hɛrtsˈalɐˈliːpstə] MF *decl as adj (old, hum)* darling, dearest; **Herz|an|fall** M heart attack; **Herz|ass** NT ace of hearts; **Herz|at|ta|cke** F heart attack

her+zau|bern VT *sep* to produce out of thin air

Herz-: **herz|be|klem|mend** ADJ oppressive; **Herz|be|klem|mung** F **~en bekommen** to feel as if one cannot breathe; **Herz|be|schwer|den** PL heart trouble *sing*; **Herz|beu|tel** M pericardium; **Herz|beu|tel|ent|zün|dung** F pericarditis; **herz|be|we|gend** ADJ heart-rending; **Herz|blatt** NT **a** *(Bot)* grass of Parnassus **b** *(dated inf)* darling; **herz|blätt|rig** ADJ heart-shaped; **Herz|blut** NT *(poet)* lifeblood; **mit ~** *(= leidenschaftlich)* passionately; **Herz|bu|be** M jack *or* knave of hearts

Herz|chen [ˈhɛrtsçən] NT **-s, -** little heart; *(inf: Kosewort)* (little) darling

Herz-: **Herz|chi|rurg(in)** M(F) heart *or* cardiac surgeon; **Herz|chi|rur|gie** F heart *or* cardiac surgery; **Herz|da|me** F **a** *(Cards)* queen of hearts **b** *(old, hum: = Angebetete)* beloved

Her|ze|go|wi|na [hɛrtseˈgoːvina] F **- die ~** Herzegovina, Hercegovina

her+zei|gen VT *sep* to show; **zeig (mal) her!** let me see, let's see; **das kann man ~** that's worth showing off

Her|ze|leid [ˈhɛrtsəlait] NT *(old)* heartache

her|zen [ˈhɛrtsn] VT *(dated)* to hug

Her|zens-: **Her|zens|an|ge|le|gen|heit** F *(dated: = Liebesangelegenheit)* affair of the heart; **es ist ihm eine ~** it is a matter close to his heart; **Her|zens|be|dürf|nis** NT *(dated)* **es ist mir ein ~** it is a matter dear to my heart; **Her|zens|bil|dung** F, *no pl (geh)* nobleness of heart; **Her|zens|bre|cher(in)** M(F) *(fig inf)* heartbreaker; **Her|zens|er|gie|ßung** [-lɛɐgiːsʊŋ] F **-, -en**, **Her|zens|er|guss** M *(dated, hum)* emotional outpourings *pl*; **Her|zens|freu|de** F *(dated)* **es ist mir eine ~** it warms my heart; **Her|zens|grund** M, *no pl (dated)* **aus tiefstem ~** from the very bottom of one's heart; **her|zens|gut** ADJ good-hearted; **Her|zens|gü|te** F good-heartedness; **Her|zens|lust** F **nach ~** to one's heart's content; **Her|zens|qual** F *(old) usu pl* great emotional torment *pl rare*; **Her|zens|wunsch** M dearest wish

Herz-: **herz|er|freu|end** ADJ heart-warming; **herz|er|fri|schend** ADJ refreshing; **herz|er|grei|fend** ADJ heart-rending; **herz|er|qui|ckend** ADJ refreshing; **herz|er|wär|mend** ADJ heart-warming; **herz|er|wei|chend** ADJ heart-rending ADV heart-rendingly; **Herz|er|wei|te|rung** F cardiectasis *(spec)*, dilation of the heart; **Herz|feh|ler** M cardiac *or* heart defect; **Herz|flat|tern** NT **-s**, *no pl* palpitations *pl* (of the heart); **Herz|flim|mern** NT **-s**, *no pl* heart flutter; *(= Kammerflimmern)* (ventricular) fibrillation; **ich habe ~** *(fig)* my heart misses *or* skips a beat; **herz|för|mig** ADJ heart-shaped; **Herz|ge|gend** F, *no pl* cardiac region, area of the heart *(auch fig)*; **Herz|ge|räu|sche** PL heartbeats *pl*

herz|haft ADJ **a** *(dated: = mutig)* brave **b** *(= kräftig)* hearty; *Händedruck, Griff* firm; *Geschmack* strong **c** *(= nahrhaft) Essen* substantial ADV **~ gähnen** to yawn loudly; **alle packten ~ an** everyone pitched in and helped; **alle griffen ~ zu** everyone got stuck in *(inf)*; **das schmeckt ~** that's good honest fare; **jdn ~ küssen** to give sb a big fat kiss; **~ lachen** to laugh hard

her+zie|hen *sep irreg* VT to draw *or* pull closer *or* nearer; **jdn/etw hinter sich** *(dat)* **~** to pull *or* drag sb/sth (along) behind one VI **a** *aux sein (= herankommen)* to approach; **hinter/neben/vor jdm ~** to march along behind/beside/in front of sb **b** *aux sein (= umziehen)* to move here **c** *aux sein* **über jdn/etw ~** *(inf)* to knock sb/sth *(inf)*, to pull sb/sth to pieces *(inf)*

her|zig [ˈhɛrtsɪç] ADJ delightful, sweet

Herz-: **Herz|in|farkt** M heart attack, cardiac infarction *(spec)*; **Herz|in|suf|fi|zi|enz** F cardiac insufficiency; **Herz|ja|gen** NT **-s**, *no pl* palpitations *pl*; **Herz-Je|su-Bild** NT Sacred Heart painting; **Herz|kam|mer** F ventricle; **Herz|kir|sche** F (bigarreau) cherry; **Herz|klap|pe** F cardiac *or* heart valve; **Herz|klap|pen|ent|zün|dung** F endocarditis; **Herz|klap|pen|feh|ler** M valvular heart defect; **Herz|klop|fen** NT **-s**, *no pl* **ich hatte/bekam ~** my heart was/started pounding; *(durch Kaffee)* I had/got palpitations; **mit ~** with a pounding heart, with one's heart in one's mouth; **Herz|krampf** M heart spasm; **herz|krank** ADJ suffering from a heart condition; **~ sein/werden** to have/get a heart condition; **Herz|krank|heit** F heart condition; **Herz|kranz|ge|fäß** NT *usu pl* coronary (blood) vessel; **Herz-Kreis|lauf-Er|kran|kung** F cardiovascular disease *or* condition; **Herz|lei|den** NT heart condition; **herz|lei|dend** ADJ with a heart condition

herz|lich [ˈhɛrtslɪç] ✪ 48.2, 49, 50.6, 51.1, 51.2, 51.3, 52 ADJ *Empfang, Freundschaft, Atmosphäre* warm; *Wesen, Mensch* warm(-hearted); *Lachen* hearty; *Bitte* sincere; **~e Grüße an Ihre Frau** kind(est) regards to your wife, remember me to your wife; **mit ~en Grüßen** kind regards; **~en Dank!** many thanks, thank you very much indeed; **~es Beileid!** you have my sincere *or* heartfelt sympathy *or* condolences *pl*; **zu jdm ~ sein** to be kind to sb; **eine ~e Bitte an jdn richten** to make a cordial request to sb → **Glückwunsch**

ADV *(= freundlich)* warmly; *sich bedanken, Glück wünschen* sincerely; *(= ziemlich) langweilig, uninteressant* totally; **jdm ~ gratulieren** to congratulate and wish sb all the best; **~ schlecht** pretty awful; **~ wenig** precious little; **verbleibe ich als Ihr ~ grüßender...** I remain with best regards your...; **~ gern!** with the greatest of pleasure!; **ich würde ~ gern einmal wieder die Stätten meiner Kindheit besuchen** I should so much like to visit my childhood haunts again; **ich habe es ~ satt** I am thoroughly *or* utterly sick of it, I'm sick and tired of it

Herz|lich|keit F **-**, *no pl (von Empfang, Freundschaft)* warmth; *(von Wesen, Mensch)* warm(hearted)ness

Herz-: **Herz|lieb|chen** NT *(old)* sweetheart, dearest; **Herz|liebs|te(r)** [hɛrtsˈliːpstə] MF *decl as adj (old)* darling, dearest; **Herz|li|nie** F heart line; **herz|los** ADJ heartless, unfeeling; **Herz|lo|sig|keit** F **-**, *no pl* heartlessness *no pl*; **Herz-Lun|gen-Ma|schi|ne** F heart-lung machine; **Herz|mas|sa|ge** F heart massage; **Herz|mit|tel** NT cardiac drug; **Herz|mu|schel** F *(Zool)* cockle; **Herz|mus|kel** M heart *or* cardiac muscle

Her|zog [ˈhɛrtsoːk] M **-s, ⸚e** *or (rare)* **-e** [ˈhɛrtsøːgə, -tsoːgə] duke; **Otto ~ von Stein** Otto Duke of Stein, Duke Otto of Stein

Her|zo|gin [ˈhɛrtsoːgɪn] F **-, -nen** duchess

her|zog|lich [ˈhɛrtsoːklɪç] ADJ *attr* ducal

Her|zogs|wür|de F *(= Rang)* dignity *or* rank of a duke; *(= Titel)* dukedom; **der König verlieh ihm die ~** the king bestowed a dukedom *or* the rank of duke upon him
Her|zog|tum ['hɛrtsoːktuːm] NT **-s, Herzogtümer** [-tyːmɐ] dukedom, duchy
Herz-: **Herz|pa|ti|ent(in)** M(F) heart *or* cardiac patient; **Herz|rhyth|mus** M heart *or* cardiac rhythm; **Herz|rhyth|mus|stö|rung** F palpitations *pl*, cardiac disrhythmia *(spec)*; **Herz|schei|de|wand** F *(Anat)* heart septum, septum of the heart; **Herz|schlag** M **a** *(einzelner)* heartbeat; **einen ~ lang** *(liter)* for one fleeting second; **mit jedem ~** *(liter)* with every beat of my/his *etc* heart **b** *(= Herztätigkeit)* heart *or* pulse rate; *(fig liter)* throbbing *or* pulsating life **c** *(= Herzstillstand)* heart attack, heart failure *no indef art, no pl*; **Herz|schmerz** M stabbing pain in the chest
Herz-Schmerz- *in cpds (inf)* schmaltzy *(inf)*; **Herz-Schmerz-Ro|man** M *(inf)* schmaltzy novel *(inf)*
Herz-: **Herz|schritt|ma|cher** M pacemaker; **Herz|schwä|che** F a weak heart; **wegen einer vorübergehenden ~** because my/his *etc* heart faltered for a moment; **an ~ leiden** to have a weak heart; **herz|stär|kend** ADJ cardiotonic *(spec)*; **ein ~es Mittel** a cardiac stimulant, a cardiotonic *(spec)* ADV **~ wirken** to stimulate the heart; **Herz|stich** M *usu pl* stabbing pain in the chest; **Herz|still|stand** M cardiac arrest; **Herz|stol|pern** NT **-s,** *no pl* irregular heartbeat; **Herz|stück** NT *(fig geh)* heart, core; **Herz|tä|tig|keit** F heart *or* cardiac activity; **Herz|tod** M death from heart disease; **Herz|tö|ne** PL *(Med)* cardiac sounds
her|zu- [hɛɐ'tsu] *in cpds* = **herbei-**
Her|zug M *(inf)* **a** *(Rail)* down train **b** *no pl (= Umzug)* **seit meinem ~** since I came here, since coming here
Herz-: **Herz|ver|fet|tung** F fatty degeneration of the heart; **Herz|ver|sa|gen** NT heart failure; **Herz|vier** F **die ~** the four of hearts; **Herz|zen|trum** NT *(= Klinik)* heart centre *(Brit) or* center *(US)*; **herz|zer|rei|ßend** ADJ heartbreaking, heart-rending ADV **~ weinen** to weep distressingly
He|se|ki|el [he'zeːkieːl, -kiel] M **-'** Ezekiel
Hes|se ['hɛsə] M **-n, -n, Hes|sin** ['hɛsɪn] F **-, -nen** Hessian
Hes|sen ['hɛsn] NT **-s** Hesse
hes|sisch ['hɛsɪʃ] ADJ Hessian
He|tä|re [he'tɛːrə] F **-, -n** *(Hist)* hetaira; *(fig geh: = Dirne)* courtesan
He|te ['heːtə] F **-, -n** *(sl: = Heterosexuelle(r))* hetero; **er ist eine ~** he's straight *(inf)*
He|te|ra ['heːtera, 'hɛtera, he'teːra] F **-, -s** *(inf)* heterosexual female
he|te|ro ['heːtero, 'hɛtero, he'teːro] ADJ *pred (inf)* hetero *(inf)*, straight *(inf)*
He|te|ro ['heːtero, 'hɛtero, he'teːro] M **-s, -s** *(inf)* hetero *(inf)*
He|te|ro-: **he|te|ro|dox** [hetero'dɔks] ADJ *(geh)* heterodox; **He|te|ro|do|xie** [heterodɔ'ksiː] F **-, -n** [-'ksiːən] *(geh)* heterodoxy; **he|te|ro|gen** [hetero'geːn] ADJ *(geh)* heterogeneous; **He|te|ro|ge|ni|tät** [heterogeni'tɛːt] F **-,** *no pl (geh)* heterogeneity; **he|te|ro|nom** [hetero'noːm] ADJ *(geh)* heteronomous; **He|te|ro|no|mie** [heterono'miː] F **-,** *no pl (geh)* heteronomy; **He|te|ro|se|xu|a|li|tät** [hetero-] F heterosexuality; **he|te|ro|se|xu|ell** [hetero-] ADJ heterosexual; **He|te|ro|se|xu|el|le(r)** [heteroze'ksuɛlə] MF *decl as adj* heterosexual
He|thi|ter [he'tiːtɐ] M **-s, -, He|thi|te|rin** [-ərɪn] F **-, -nen** Hittite
he|thi|tisch [he'tiːtɪʃ] ADJ Hittite
Hetz [hɛts] F **-,** *(rare)* **-en** *(Aus inf)* laugh *(inf)*; **aus** *or* **zur ~** for a laugh
Hetz- *(pej) in cpds* inflammatory, rabble-rousing *(pej)*; **Hetz|ar|ti|kel** M *(pej; Press)* inflammatory article; **Hetz|blatt** NT *(pej; Press)* smear-sheet, scandal rag

Het|ze ['hɛtsə] F **-, -n** **a** *no pl (= Hast)* (mad) rush, hurry; *(= Getriebensein)* hustle and bustle, (mad) rush **b** *no pl (pej: = Aufreizung)* rabble-rousing propaganda **c** *(Hunt)* hounding *(auf +acc* of)
het|zen ['hɛtsn] VT **a** *(lit, fig: = jagen)* to hound; **die Hunde auf jdn/etw ~** to set the dogs on(to) sb/sth → **Hund a**
b *(inf: = antreiben)* to rush, to hurry
VR to hurry oneself, to rush oneself
VI **a** *(= sich beeilen)* to rush; **hetz nicht so** don't be in such a rush
b *aux sein (= eilen)* to tear, to race, to dash; **ich bin ganz schön gehetzt, um ...** I rushed like mad to ... *(inf)*, I had an awful rush to ...; **hetz nicht so** don't go so fast
c *(pej: = Hass schüren)* to agitate, to stir up hatred; *(inf: = lästern)* to say malicious things; **gegen jdn/etw ~** to stir up hatred against sb/sth; **er hetzt immer gegen seinen Onkel** he's always running his uncle down, he's always saying malicious things about his uncle; **sie hat so lange gehetzt, bis er ...** she kept on being nasty until he finally ...; **zum Krieg ~** to agitate for war; **gegen Minderheiten ~** to stir up hatred against minorities; **bei jdm gegen jdn ~** to try to turn *or* set sb against sb → *auch* **gehetzt**
Het|zer ['hɛtsɐ] M **-s, -, Het|ze|rin** [-ərɪn] F **-, -nen** rabble-rouser, malicious agitator
Het|ze|rei [hɛtsə'rai] F **-, -en** **a** *no pl (= Hast)* (mad) rush, hurry **b** *(= das Hassschüren)* rabble-rousing, malicious agitation, mischief-making; **~ zum Krieg** warmongering **c** *(= hetzerische Äußerung)* rabble-rousing attack *(gegen* on)
het|ze|risch ['hɛtsərɪʃ] ADJ rabble-rousing *attr*, virulent
Hetz-: **hetz|hal|ber** ADV *(Aus inf)* for a laugh *(inf)*; **Hetz|hund** M hound, hunting dog; **Hetz|jagd** F **a** *(lit, fig)* hounding *(auf +acc* of) **b** *(fig: = Hast)* rush, hurry; **es war die reinste ~** it was one mad rush; **Hetz|kam|pag|ne** F malicious campaign; **Hetz|re|de** F inflammatory speech
Heu [hɔy] NT **-(e)s,** *no pl* hay; **Geld wie ~ haben** *(inf)* to have pots *or* oodles of money *(inf)*
Heu-: **Heu|bo|den** M, *(Sw)* **Heu|büh|ne** F hayloft; **Heu|bün|del** NT bundle *or* bale of hay
Heu|che|lei [hɔyçə'lai] F **-, -en** hypocrisy; **spar dir deine ~en** cut out the hypocrisy *or* cant
heu|cheln ['hɔyçln] VI to be a hypocrite VT *Zuneigung, Mitleid etc* to feign, to simulate
Heuch|ler ['hɔyçlɐ] M **-s, -, Heuch|le|rin** [-ərɪn] F **-, -nen** hypocrite
heuch|le|risch ['hɔyçlərɪʃ] ADJ hypocritical; **~es Gerede** hypocritical talk, cant
heu|en ['hɔyən] VI *(dial)* to make hay; **das Heuen** haymaking
heu|er ['hɔyɐ] ADV *(S Ger, Aus, Sw)* this year
Heu|er ['hɔyɐ] F **-, -n** *(Naut)* pay
Heu|er-: **Heu|er|bü|ro** NT (seamen's) employment office; **Heu|er|lohn** M pay
heu|ern ['hɔyɐn] VT to sign on, to engage, to hire
Heu|ern|te F hay harvest; *(= Ertrag)* hay crop
Heu|er|ver|trag M contract of employment *(of seaman)*
Heu-: **Heu|fie|ber** NT hay fever; **Heu|for|ke** F *(N Ger)*, **Heu|ga|bel** F pitchfork, hayfork; **Heu|hau|fen** M haystack, hayrick
Heul|bo|je F *(Naut)* whistling buoy
heu|len ['hɔylən] VI **a** *(inf: = weinen)* to howl, to bawl *(inf)*, to wail; *(vor Schmerz)* to scream; *(vor Wut)* to howl; **ich hätte ~ können** I could have cried; **es ist einfach zum Heulen** it's enough to make you weep → **Elend b** *(Flugzeug, Motor)* to roar; *(Wind, Tiere)* to howl; *(Sirene)* to wail
Heu|len NT **-s,** *no pl* **a** *(= das Weinen)* howling, bawling, wailing; **~ und Zähneklappern** *(Bibl)* wailing and gnashing of teeth **b** *(von Flugzeug, Motor)* roaring; *(von Wind, Tier)* howling; *(von Sirene)* wailing

Heu|ler ['hɔylɐ] M **-s, -** **a** *(von Motor)* roar **b** *(= Feuerwerkskörper)* screamer **c** *(= Seehundbaby)* seal pup
Heu|le|rei [hɔylə'rai] F **-, -en** *(inf)* constant bawling *(inf)*
Heul- *(inf)*: **Heul|krampf** M fit of blubbering *(inf)*; **Heul|pe|ter** ['hɔylpeːtɐ] M **-s, -, Heul|su|se** ['hɔylzuːzə] F **-, -n** crybaby *(inf)*; **Heul|ton** M *pl* **-töne** *(von Sirene)* wail
Heu-: **Heu|ma|chen** NT **-s,** *no pl*, **Heu|mahd** F haymaking; **Heu|mond** M *(old liter)*, **Heu|mo|nat** M *(old)* July; **Heu|rei|ter** M, **Heu|reu|ter** [-rɔytɐ] M **-s, -** rickstand
heu|rig ['hɔyrɪç] ADJ *attr (S Ger, Aus)* this year's; **der ~e Wein** this year's wine
Heu|ri|ge ['hɔyrɪgə] PL *decl as adj (esp Aus)* early potatoes *pl*
Heu|ri|ge(r) ['hɔyrɪgə] M *decl as adj (Aus)* **a** *(= wine)* new wine **b** *(= restaurant)* wine tavern

> **HEURIGER**
>
> **Heuriger** is the name given in Austria to wine from the most recent harvest, drunk from Martinmas (November 11th) onwards. Bars where the wine is drunk are also called **Heurige**. The **Heurige** bars in the area around Vienna are especially well known.

Heu|ris|tik [hɔy'rɪstɪk] F **-,** *no pl* heuristics *sing*
heu|ris|tisch [hɔy'rɪstɪʃ] ADJ heuristic
Heu-: **Heu|schnup|fen** M hay fever; **Heu|scho|ber** M barn; **Heu|schre|cke** ['hɔyʃrɛkə] F **-, -n** grasshopper; *(in heißen Ländern)* locust; **Heu|schre|cken|pla|ge** F plague of locusts; **Heu|spei|cher** M *(S Ger)*, **Heu|sta|del** M *(Aus, Sw)* barn
heu|te ['hɔytə], **heut** [hɔyt] *(inf)* ADV **a** *(= an diesem Tag)* today; **~ Morgen** this morning; **~ Abend** this evening, tonight; **~ früh** this morning; **~ Nacht** tonight; **„heute geschlossen"** "closed today"; **~ noch** *(= heutzutage)* still ... today, even today; **ich muss ~ noch zur Bank** I must go to the bank today; **bis ~** *(= bisher, heute immer noch)* to this day; **bis ~ nicht** *(= noch nicht)* not ... to this day; **von ~ ab** *or* **an, ab ~** from today (on), from this day (forth) *(liter)*; **~ in einer Woche** a week today *or* from now, today week; **~ vor acht Tagen** a week ago today; **~ in einem Jahr** a year from today *or* now, a year hence *(geh)*; **Milch/die Zeitung von ~** today's milk/paper; **~ mir, morgen dir** *(Prov)* (it's my turn today,) your turn may come tomorrow; **lieber ~ als morgen** the sooner the better; **etw von ~ auf morgen verschieben** to put sth off until tomorrow; **von ~ auf morgen** *(fig: = rasch, plötzlich)* overnight, from one day to the next
b *(= in der gegenwärtigen Zeit)* nowadays, these days, today; **das Heute** the present, today; **das Italien/der Mensch von ~** present-day *or* contemporary *or* modern Italy/man; **der Bauer/die Frau/die Stadt von ~** the farmer/woman/town of today, today's farmers/women/towns; **die Jugend von ~** the young people of today, modern youth
heu|tig ['hɔytɪç] ADJ *attr* today's; *(= von heute auch)* the day's; *(= gegenwärtig)* modern, contemporary; **der ~e Tag** today; **am ~en Abend** this evening; **anlässlich Ihres ~en Geburtstags** to mark your birthday today; **unser ~es Schreiben** *(Comm)* our letter of today('s date); **die ~e Zeitung** today's paper; **bis zum ~en Tage** to date, to this day; **aus ~er Sicht** from today's standpoint, from a modern *or* contemporary point of view; **wir Heutigen** *(geh)* we people of today, we modern men and women
heu|ti|gen|tags ['hɔytɪgn'taːks, 'hɔytɪgntaːks] ADV *(dated)* = **heute b**
heut|zu|ta|ge ['hɔyttsutaːgə] ADV nowadays, these days, today
Heu-: **Heu|wa|gen** M haycart, haywagon; **Heu|wen|der** [-vɛndɐ] M **-s, -** tedder

He|xa- *in cpds* hexa-; **he|xa|de|zi|mal** [hɛksadetsi'ma:l] ADJ *(Comput)* hexadecimal, hex; **He|xa|de|zi|mal|codem** *(Comput)* hex code; **He|xa|de|zi|mal|zahl** F *(Comput)* hexadecimal number; **He|xa|eder** [hɛksa'le:dɐ] NT **-s, -** hexahedron; **He|xa|gon** [hɛksa'go:n] NT **-s, -e** hexagon; **he|xa|go|nal** [hɛksago'na:l] ADJ hexagonal; **He|xa|gramm** [hɛksa'gram] NT *pl* **-gramme** hexagram; **He|xa|me|ter** [hɛ'ksa:metɐ] M hexameter

He|xe ['hɛksə] F **-, -n** witch; *(inf: = altes Weib)* old hag *or* crone; **diese kleine ~!** that little minx *or* hussy!

he|xen ['hɛksn] VI to practise *(Brit) or* practice *(US)* witchcraft; **er kann ~** he knows (how to work) black magic; **ich kann doch nicht ~** *(inf)* I can't work miracles, I'm not a magician VT to conjure up; **~, dass ...** to cast a (magic) spell so that ...

He|xen-: **He|xen|ein|mal|eins** NT magic square; **He|xen|glau|be** M belief in witches; **He|xen|haus** NT enchanted house; **He|xen|häus|chen** [-hɔysçən] NT gingerbread house; **He|xen|jagd** F *(Hist, fig)* witch-hunt; **He|xen|kes|sel** M *(fig)* pandemonium *no art*, bedlam *no art*; **ein wahrer ~** absolute pandemonium *or* bedlam; **He|xen|kü|che** F *(fig)* witches' kitchen; **He|xen|kunst** F witchcraft, sorcery, witchery; **He|xen|meis|ter** M sorcerer; **He|xen|pro|be** F *(Hist)* witches' ordeal; **He|xen|pro|zess** M witch trial; **He|xen|ring** M fairy ring; **He|xen|sab|bat** M witches' sabbath; *(fig)* bedlam *no art*, pandemonium *no art*; **es war ein wahrer ~** it was sheer pandemonium; **He|xen|schuss** M *(Med)* lumbago; **He|xen|ver|bren|nung** F burning of a witch/witches; **He|xen|ver|fol|gung** F witch-hunt; **He|xen|wahn** M obsessive belief in witches; **He|xen|werk** NT sorcery, witchcraft, witchery

He|xer ['hɛksɐ] M **-s, -** sorcerer

He|xe|rei [hɛksə'rai] F **-, -en** witchcraft *no pl*, sorcery, witchery *no pl*; *(von Zaubertricks)* magic *no pl*

hey INTERJ wow

HG F - *abbr von* **Handelsgesellschaft**

hg. *abbr von* **herausgegeben** ed.

Hi|a|tus ['hia:tʊs] M **-, -** ['hia:tu:s] hiatus

hib|be|lig ['hɪbəlɪç] ADJ *(dial)* jittery

Hi|bis|kus [hi'bɪskʊs] M **-, Hibisken** [-kn] hibiscus

hick [hɪk] INTERJ hic

Hick|hack ['hɪkhak] M OR NT **-s, -s** squabbling *no pl*

hie [hi:] ADV *(old)* here; **~ und da** *(= manchmal)* (every) now and then, every so often, (every) once in a while; *(= stellenweise)* here and there; **~ ... ~** *or* **da** on the one side ... on the other (side)

hieb *(geh) pret von* **hauen**

Hieb [hi:p] M **-(e)s, -e** [-bə] **a** *(= Schlag)* stroke, blow; *(= Fausthieb)* blow; *(= Peitschenhieb)* lash, crack; *(Fechten)* cut; **auf den ersten ~ fällt kein Baum** *(prov)* Rome wasn't built in a day *(Prov)*; **auf einen ~** *(inf)* in one go; **ein Glas auf einen ~ leer trinken** *(inf)* to down a glass in one *(inf)* **b** *(= Hiebwunde)* gash, slash **c Hiebe** PL *(dated: = Prügel)* hiding, thrashing, beating; **~e bekommen** to get a hiding *or* thrashing *or* beating; **gleich gibt es** *or* **setzt es ~e!** you'll get a (good) hiding in a minute **d** *(fig)* dig, cutting remark; **der ~ saß** that (dig) went *or* struck home; **~e bekommen** to be on the receiving end of some cutting remarks

Hieb-: **hieb|fest** ADJ **hieb- und stichfest** *(fig)* watertight; **Hieb|waf|fe** F cutting weapon; **Hieb|wun|de** F gash, slash

hielt *pret von* **halten**

hie|nie|den ['hi:'ni:dn, hi'ni:dn, *(emph)* 'hi:ni:dn] ADV *(old liter)* here below

hier [hi:ɐ] ADV **a** *(räumlich)* here; *(= in diesem Land)* here, (here) in this country; *(= hier am Ort)* here, locally; **~ zu Lande = hierzulande**; **das Haus ~** this house; **dieser ~** this one (here); **~!** *(beim Appell)* present!, here!; **~ und da** here and there; **Herr Direktor ~, Herr Direktor da** *(iro)* yes sir, yes sir, three bags full, sir; **~ draußen/drinnen** out/in here; **~ entlang** along here; **~ herum** hereabouts, (a)round here; **~ hinein** in here; **~ oben/unten** up/down here; **~ vorn/hinten** in front/at the back here, here in front/at the back; **er ist von ~** he's a local (man), he comes from (a)round here; **er ist nicht von ~** he's a stranger here, he's not a local; **Tag Klaus, ~ (spricht) Hans** *(Telec)* hello, Klaus, Hans here; **~ spricht Dr. Müller** *(Telec)* this is Dr Müller (speaking); **von ~ ab** from here (on *or* onwards); **von ~ aus** from here; **~ sehen Sie ...** here you (can) see ...; **~ und heute** *(geh)* here and now; **das Hier und Heute** *(geh)* the here and now; **er ist ein bisschen ~ oben** *(inf)* he's got a screw loose *(inf)*

b *(zeitlich)* now; **~ und da** (every) now and then, every so often; **von ~ ab** *or* **an** from now on, henceforth *(form)*

c *(fig)* here; **das steht mir bis ~** *(inf)* I'm fed up to here *(inf) or* to the back teeth *(inf)* (with it), I've had it up to here *(inf)*; **~ versagte ihm die Stimme** here *or* at this point *or* at this juncture his voice failed him

hie|ran ['hi:ran, hi:'ran, *(emph)* 'hi:ran] ADV **a** *(lit)* here **b** *(fig)* **wenn ich ~ denke** when I think of *or* about this; **er erinnert sich ~** he remembers this; **~ erkenne ich es** I recognize it by this; **~ kann es keinen Zweifel geben** there can be no doubt about that

Hie|rarch [hie'rarç] M **-en, -en a** *(Hist)* high priest *(in ancient Greece)* **b** *(fig: = Machthaber)* top man

Hie|rar|chie [hierar'çi:] F **-, -n** [-'çi:ən] hierarchy

hie|rar|chisch [hie'rarçɪʃ] ADJ hierarchic(al) ADV hierarchically; *aufbauen, gliedern* with a hierarchical structure

hier-: **hie|rauf** ['hi:rauf, hi:'rauf, *(emph)* 'hi:rauf] ADV **a** *(lit)* (on) here, on this **b** *(fig)* on this; *(= daraufhin)* hereupon; **er setzte sich, und ~ ...** he sat down and then ...; **hie|rauf|hin** ['hi:rauf'hɪn, hi:rauf'hɪn, *(emph)* 'hi:raufhɪn] ADV hereupon; **und ~ ...** and then ...; **hie|raus** ['hi:'raus, hi:'raus, *(emph)* 'hi:raus] ADV **a** *(lit)* out of this, from here; **~ ist das Geld gestohlen worden** the money was stolen from here **b** *(fig)* from this; **~ folgt, dass ..., ~ geht hervor, dass ...** from this it follows that ..., hence (it follows that) ...; **hier+be|hal|ten** *sep irreg*, **hier be|hal|ten** △ *irreg* VT **jdn/etw ~** to keep sb/sth here; **hier|bei** ['hi:ɐ'bai, hi:ɐ'bai, *(emph)* 'hi:ɐbai] ADV **a** *(lit: = währenddessen)* doing this **b** *(fig) (= bei dieser Gelegenheit)* on this occasion; *(= in diesem Zusammenhang)* in this connection; **hier+blei|ben** *sep irreg aux sein*, **hier blei|ben** △ *irreg aux sein* VI to stay here; **hiergeblieben!** stop!; **hier|durch** ['hi:ɐ'dʊrç, hi:ɐ'dʊrç, *(emph)* 'hi:ɐdʊrç] ADV **a** *(lit)* through here **b** *(fig)* through this; **ich lasse mich ~ nicht ärgern** I won't let this annoy me; **~ teilen wir Ihnen mit, dass ...** we hereby inform you that ...; **hie|rein** ['hi:'rain, hi:'rain, *(emph)* 'hi:rain] ADV *(lit)* in(to) this, in here; **hier|für** ['hi:ɐ'fy:ɐ, hi:ɐ'fy:ɐ, *(emph)* 'hi:ɐfy:ɐ] ADV for this; **hier|ge|gen** ['hi:ɐ'ge:gn, hi:ɐ'ge:gn, *(emph)* 'hi:ɐge:gn] ADV *(lit, fig)* against this; **hier|her** ['hi:ɐ'he:ɐ, hi:ɐ'he:ɐ, *(emph)* 'hi:ɐhe:ɐ] ADV here; **(komm) ~!** come here *or* hither *(liter, old)*; **bis ~** *(örtlich)* up to here; *(zeitlich)* up to now, so far; **mir stehts bis ~** *(inf)* I'm fed up to here *or* to the back teeth *(inf)* → **bis**; **hier|he|rauf** ['hi:ɐhɛ'rauf, hi:ɐhɛ'rauf, *(emph)* 'hi:ɐhɛrauf] ADV up here; **bis ~** up to here

hier|her: **hier|her+be|mü|hen** *sep*, **hier|her be|mü|hen** △ *(geh)* VT **jdn** to ask *or* trouble to come (here) VR to take the trouble to come (here); **hier|her+bit|ten** *sep irreg*, **hier|her bit|ten** △ *irreg* VT to ask to come (here); **hier|her+bli|cken** *sep*, **hier|her bli|cken** △ VI to look this way, to look over here; **hier|her+brin|gen** *sep irreg*, **hier|her brin|gen** △ *irreg* VT to bring (over) here; **hier|her+fah|ren** *sep irreg*, **hier|her fah|ren** △ *irreg* VI *aux sein* to come here VT *etw* to drive here; *jdn* to drive (here), to give a lift *or* ride (here); **hier|her+füh|ren** *sep*, **hier|her füh|ren** △ VT to lead here VI *(Weg etc)* to lead here, to come this way; **hier|her ge|hören , hier|her+ge|hören** *sep* VI to belong here; *(fig: = relevant sein)* to be relevant; **nicht ~de Bemerkungen** irrelevant remarks; **hier|her+ho|len** *sep*, **hier|her ho|len** △ VT to bring here; **hier|her+kom|men** *sep irreg aux sein*, **hier|her kom|men** △ *irreg aux sein* VI to come here; **hier|her+lau|fen** *sep irreg aux sein*, **hier|her lau|fen** △ *irreg aux sein* VI to run here; **hierhergelaufen kommen** to come running up; **hier|her+le|gen** *sep*, **hier|her le|gen** △ VT to lay (down) here VR to lie (down) here, to lay oneself (down) here; **hier|her+lo|cken** *sep*, **hier|her lo|cken** △ VT to entice *or* lure here; **hier|her+schaf|fen** *sep*, **hier|her schaf|fen** △ VT to bring here; **hier|her+schi|cken** *sep*, **hier|her schi|cken** △ VT to send here; **hier|her+set|zen** *sep*, **hier|her set|zen** △ VT to put here VR to sit (down) here; **hier|her+stel|len** *sep*, **hier|her stel|len** △ VT to put here VR to stand here; **hier|her+tra|gen** *sep irreg*, **hier|her tra|gen** △ *irreg* VT to carry here

hier|he|rum ['hi:ɐhɛ'rʊm, hi:ɐhɛ'rʊm, *(emph)* 'hi:ɐhɛrʊm] ADV (a)round here; *(= in diese Richtung)* this way (a)round; *(inf: = ungefähr hier)* hereabouts, (a)round here (somewhere)

hier|her: **hier|her+wa|gen** *sep*, **hier|her wa|gen** △ VR to dare to come here; **hier|her+zie|hen** *sep irreg*, **hier|her zie|hen** △ *irreg* VT *(fig)* to bring here VI *aux sein* to come here; *(= umziehen)* to move here

hier-: **hier|hin** ['hi:ɐ'hɪn, hi:ɐ'hɪn, *(emph)* 'hi:ɐhɪn] ADV here; **~ und dorthin** here and there; **bis ~** up to here; **hier|hi|nab** ['hi:ɐhɪ'nap, hi:ɐhɪ'nap, *(emph)* 'hi:ɐhɪnap] ADV down here; **hier|hi|nauf** ['hi:ɐhɪ'nauf, hi:ɐhɪ'nauf, *(emph)* 'hi:ɐhɪnauf] ADV up here; **hier|hi|naus** ['hi:ɐhɪ'naus, hi:ɐhɪ'naus, *(emph)* 'hi:ɐhɪnaus] ADV out here; **hier|hi|nein** ['hi:ɐhɪ'nain, hi:ɐhɪ'nain, *(emph)* 'hi:ɐhɪnain] ADV in here; **hier|hin|ter** ['hi:ɐ'hɪntɐ, hi:ɐ'hɪntɐ, *(emph)* 'hi:ɐhɪntɐ] ADV behind here; **hier|hi|nun|ter** ['hi:ɐhɪ'nʊntɐ, hi:ɐhɪ'nʊntɐ, *(emph)* 'hi:ɐhɪnʊntɐ] ADV down here; **hie|rin** ['hi:'rɪn, hi:'rɪn, *(emph)* 'hi:rɪn] ADV *(lit, fig)* in this; **hier+las|sen** *sep irreg*, **hier las|sen** △ *irreg* VT to leave here; **hier|mit** ['hi:ɐ'mɪt, hi:ɐ'mɪt, *(emph)* 'hi:ɐmɪt] ADV with this, herewith *(obs, form)*; **~ ist der Fall erledigt** this settles the matter; **~ bin ich einverstanden** I agree to this; **~ erkläre ich ...** *(form)* I hereby declare ... *(form)*; **~ bestätigen wir den Eingang Ihres Briefes** we herewith *or* hereby acknowledge receipt of your letter; **~ wird bescheinigt, dass ...** this is to certify that ...; **hier|nach** ['hi:ɐ'na:x, hi:ɐ'na:x, *(emph)* 'hi:ɐna:x] ADV after this, afterwards; *(= daraus folgend)* according to this; **hier|ne|ben** ['hi:ɐ'ne:bn, hi:ɐ'ne:bn, *(emph)* 'hi:ɐne:bn] ADV beside this, next to this

Hie|ro|gly|phe [hiero'gly:fə] F **-, -n** hieroglyph(ic); *(fig hum)* hieroglyphic

Hie|ro|gly|phen|schrift F hieroglyphic script *or* writing

hier-: **hier|orts** ['hi:ɐ'ɔrts, hi:ɐ'ɔrts, *(emph)* 'hi:ɐɔrts] ADV *(geh)* here; **hier sein** VI *irreg aux sein* to be here; **Hier|sein** NT **während meines ~s** during my stay; **was ist der Zweck seines ~s?** what is the purpose of his being here *or* of his presence?; **hier|selbst** ['hi:ɐ'zɛlpst, hi:ɐ'zɛlpst, *(emph)* 'hi:ɐzɛlpst] ADV *(old)* in this very place, even here *(old)*; **hie|rü|ber** ['hi:'ry:bɐ, hi:'ry:bɐ, *(emph)* 'hi:ry:bɐ] ADV **a** *(lit)* over this *or* here; *(= oberhalb dieser Stelle)* over it **b** *(fig)* about this; *(geh: = währenddessen)* in the midst of it; **~ ärgere ich mich** this makes me angry; **hie|rum** ['hi:'rʊm, hi:'rʊm, *(emph)*

ˈhiːrʊm] ADV **a** *(lit)* (a)round this *or* here **b** *(fig)* about *or* concerning this; **~ handelt es sich nicht** this isn't the issue; **hie|run|ter** [hiːˈrʊntɐ, hiːˈrʊntɐ, *(emph)* ˈhiːrʊntɐ] ADV **a** *(lit)* under *or* beneath this *or* here **b** *(fig)* by this *or* that; *(= in dieser Kategorie)* among these; **~ fallen auch die Sonntage** this includes Sundays; **hier|von** [ˈhiːɐˈfɔn, hiːɐˈfɔn, *(emph)* ˈhiːɐfɔn] ADV **a** *(lit) (örtlich)* from here *or* this; *(= von diesem etc)* from this; *(= aus diesem Material)* out of this **b** **~ habe ich nichts gewusst** I knew nothing of *or* about this; **~ abgesehen** apart from this; **~ kannst du nichts haben** you can't have any of this; **hier|vor** [ˈhiːɐˈfoːɐ, hiːɐˈfoːɐ, *(emph)* ˈhiːɐfoːɐ] ADV **a** *(lit)* in front of this *or* here **b** *(fig)* **~ ekele/fürchte ich mich** it revolts/frightens me; **~ möge uns Gott bewahren** may God preserve us from this; **~ hat er großen Respekt** he has a great respect for this; **hier|zu** [ˈhiːɐˈtsuː, hiːɐˈtsuː, *(emph)* ˈhiːɐtsuː] ADV **a** *(= dafür)* for this; *(= dazu)* with this **b** *(= außerdem)* in addition to this, moreover **c** *(= zu diesem Punkt)* about this; **~ gehören auch die Katzen** this also includes the cats; **~ habe ich etwas Wichtiges zu sagen** I have something important to say on *or* about *or* to this; **~ wünsche ich Ihnen viel Glück** I wish you luck in this; **vgl. ~ S.370** cf p 370; **hier|zu|lan|de** [ˈhiːɐtsuˈlandə, *(emph)* ˈhiːɐtsulandə] ADV in these parts; **hier|zwi|schen** [ˈhiːɐˈtsvɪʃn, hiːɐˈtsvɪʃn, *(emph)* ˈhiːɐtsvɪʃn] ADV between these

hie|sig [ˈhiːzɪç] ADJ *attr* local; **die ~en Verhältnisse** local conditions, conditions here; **meine ~en Verwandten** my relatives here; **er ist kein Hiesiger** he is not a local (man), he's not from these parts

hieß *pret von* **heißen**

hie|ven [ˈhiːfn, ˈhiːvn] VT *(esp Naut)* to heave

Hi-Fi-An|la|ge [ˈhaifi-] F hi-fi set *or* system

Hift|horn [ˈhɪfthɔrn] NT *(Hunt)* hunting horn

high [hai] ADJ *pred (inf)* high *(inf)*

high|ja|cken [ˈhaidʒɛkn] VT *insep* to hi(gh)jack

High|ja|cker [ˈhaidʒɛkɐ] M **-s, -**, **High|ja|cke|rin** [-ərɪn] F **-, -nen** hi(gh)jacker

High|life [ˈhailaif] NT **-s**, *no pl* high life; **~ machen** *(inf)* to live it up *(inf)*

High|light [ˈhailait] NT **-s, -s** highlight

high|lighten [ˈhailaitn] VT *insep (Comput) Textpassagen etc* to highlight

High Sno|bi|e|ty [ˈhaisnoˈbaiiti] F **-**, *no pl (hum)* snob class, snobby social circles *pl*

High So|ci|e|ty [ˈhaisoˈsaiiti] F **-**, *no pl* high society

High|tech [haiˈtɛk] NT **-**, *no pl* high tech, hi tech

High|tech- *in cpds* high-tech; **High|tech|in|dus|trie** F high-tech industry; **High|tech|pro|dukt** NT high-tech product; **High|tech|un|ter|neh|men** NT high-tech company

hi|hi [hiˈhiː] INTERJ heehee, teehee

hi|ja|cken [ˈhaidʒɛkn] VT *insep* to hi(gh)jack

Hi|ja|cker [ˈhaidʒɛkɐ] M **-s, -**, **Hi|ja|cke|rin** [-ərɪn] F **-, -nen** hi(gh)jacker

hilb [hɪlp] ADJ *(Sw)* sheltered, protected from the wind

Hil|de|brands|lied [ˈhɪldəbrants-] NT, *no pl (Liter)* Lay of Hildebrand

hilf [hɪlf] *imper sing von* **helfen**

Hil|fe [ˈhɪlfə] F **-, -n** **a** *no pl* help; *(finanzielle)* aid, assistance, help; *(für Notleidende)* aid, relief; **zu ~!** help!; **um ~ rufen/schreien** to call/shout for help; **jdm zu ~ kommen** to come to sb's aid *or* assistance *or* rescue; **jdn um ~ bitten** to ask sb for help *or* assistance; **jdm ~ leisten** to help sb; **bei jdm ~ suchen** to seek sb's help *or* assistance; **~ suchend** *(Mensch)* seeking help; *Blick* imploring, beseeching; **sich ~ suchend umsehen** *or* **umblicken** to look (a)round for help; **täglich wenden sich Hunderte** *or* **hunderte ~ suchend an diese Organisation** hundreds turn every day to this organization seeking help; **~ Suchende(r)** = **Hilfesuchende(r)**; **mit ~** with the help *or* aid (*gen* of); **ohne ~** without help *or* assistance; *(= selbständig)* unaided; **etw zu ~ nehmen** to use sth; **ohne fremde ~ gehen** to walk unaided; **jds Gedächtnis** *(dat)* **zu ~ kommen** to jog sb's memory → **erste(r, s), mithilfe**

b *(= Hilfsmittel, Hilfestellung)* aid; *(= Haushaltshilfe)* (domestic) help; **~n geben** *(beim Turnen)* to give support; *(beim Reiten)* to give aids; **du bist mir eine schöne ~!** *(iro)* a fine help YOU are (to me)! *(iro)*

c *(Comput)* help

Hil|fe-: **hil|fe|be|dürf|tig** ADJ = **hilfsbedürftig**; **Hil|fe|be|dürf|tig|keit** F = **Hilfsbedürftigkeit**; **hil|fe|fle|hend** ADJ imploring, beseeching; **Hil|fe|funk|ti|on** F *(Comput; in Software)* help function; **Hil|fe|ge|such** NT request for help; **Hil|fe|leis|tung** F aid, assistance; **unterlassene ~** *(Jur)* denial of assistance; **Hil|fe|me|nü** NT *(Comput; in Software)* help menu; **Hil|fe|ruf** M call for help; **Hil|fe|schrei** M cry *or* shout for help, cry of "help"; **Hil|fe|stel|lung** F *(Sport, fig)* support; **jdm ~ geben** to give sb support; *(fig auch)* to back sb up; **hil|fe|su|chend** ADJ, ADV → **Hilfe a**; **Hil|fe|su|chen|de(r)** MF *decl as adj* person seeking help, person in need of help; **die ~n** *pl* those seeking help, those in need of help; **Hil|fe|tas|te** F *(Comput)* help key

Hilf-: **hilf|los** ADJ helpless; *(= schutzlos auch)* defenceless *(Brit)*, defenseless *(US)*; *(= ratlos auch)* clueless *(inf)* ADV helplessly; *meinen, stammeln* uncertainly; **einer Sache** *(dat)* **~ ausgeliefert sein** to be completely at the mercy of sth; **Hilf|lo|sig|keit** F **-**, *no pl* helplessness; *(= Schutzlosigkeit auch)* defencelessness *(Brit)*, defenselessness *(US)*; *(= Ratlosigkeit)* cluelessness *(inf)*; **hilf|reich** ADJ helpful; *(= nützlich auch)* useful; **eine ~e Hand** a helping hand; **er reichte ihr ~ seine Hand** he held out a helping hand to her

Hilfs-: **Hilfs|ak|ti|on** F relief action; **Hilfs|ar|bei|ter(in)** M(F) labourer *(Brit)*, laborer *(US)*; *(in Fabrik)* unskilled worker; **Hilfs|as|sis|tent(in)** M(F) *(Univ)* ≈ tutorial assistant; **hilfs|be|dürf|tig** ADJ in need of help; *(= Not leidend)* needy, in need *pred*; **die Hilfsbedürftigen** the needy, those in need; **Hilfs|be|dürf|tig|keit** F need(iness); **hilfs|be|reit** ADJ helpful, ready to help *pred*; **Hilfs|be|reit|schaft** F helpfulness, readiness to help; **Hilfs|dienst** M emergency service; *(bei Katastrophenfall)* (emergency) relief service; *(= Kfz-Hilfsdienst)* (emergency) breakdown service; **Hilfs|feu|er|wehr** F auxiliary fire service; **Hilfs|fonds** M relief fund; **Hilfs|geist|li|che(r)** MF *decl as adj* curate; **Hilfs|gel|der** PL back-up funds *pl*; **Hilfs|gü|ter** PL relief aid *sing*; **Hilfs|ko|mi|tee** NT relief action committee; **Hilfs|kon|struk|ti|on** F *(Math)* rough diagram; *(fig)* temporary measure; **Hilfs|kraft** F assistant, helper; *(= Aushilfe)* temporary worker; **wissenschaftliche/fachliche ~** research/technical assistant; **Hilfs|leh|rer(in)** M(F) supply teacher; **Hilfs|li|nie** F *(Math)* auxiliary line; **Hilfs|maß|nah|me** F relief action *no pl*; *(zur Rettung)* rescue action *no pl*; **Hilfs|me|nü** NT *(Comput; in Software)* help menu; **Hilfs|mit|tel** NT aid; **Hilfs|mo|tor** M *(Aut)* auxiliary engine; **Fahrrad mit ~** moped, motor-assisted bicycle; **Hilfs|or|ga|ni|sa|ti|on** F relief organization; **Hilfs|pa|ket** NT aid package; **Hilfs|per|so|nal** NT auxiliary staff; *(= Aushilfspersonal)* temporary staff *or* help; **Hilfs|po|li|zei** F auxiliary police; **Hilfs|po|li|zist(in)** M(F) auxiliary policeman/-woman; **Hilfs|pre|di|ger(in)** M(F), **Hilfs|pries|ter** M curate; **Hilfs|pro|gramm** NT **a** *(zur Hungerhilfe etc)* relief *or* aid programme *(Brit) or* program *(US)* **b** *(Comput)* utility program; **Hilfs|quel|le** F **a** *(= Geldquelle)* source of money, pecuniary *or* financial (re)sources *pl* **b** *(für wissenschaftliche Arbeit)* source; **Hilfs|ru|der** NT *(Aviat)* auxiliary rudder; **Hilfs|schiff** NT auxiliary vessel; **Hilfs|schu|le** F *(dated)* special school; **Hilfs|schü|ler(in)** M(F) *(dated)* pupil at/from a special school; **Hilfs|schul|leh|rer(in)** M(F) *(dated)* teacher at a special school; **Hilfs|schwes|ter** F auxiliary (nurse); **Hilfs|she|riff** M assistant *or* deputy sheriff; **Hilfs|spra|che** F auxiliary language; **Hilfs|trans|port** M transport of relief aid; **Hilfs|trieb|werk** NT auxiliary engine; **Hilfs|trupp** M group of helpers; **Hilfs|trup|pe** F *(Mil)* auxiliary troops *pl*; *(= Verstärkung)* reinforcements *pl*; *(Pol pej)* back-up army *or* boys *pl*; **Hilfs|verb** NT auxiliary *or* helping *(US)* verb; **Hilfs|werk** NT relief organization; **hilfs|wil|lig** ADJ willing to help *pred*; **Hilfs|wil|li|ge(r)** [-vɪlɪgə] MF *decl as adj* voluntary helper; **Hilfs|wis|sen|schaft** F *(+gen* to) complementary science; *(= Geisteswissenschaft)* complementary subject; **Hilfs|zeit|wort** NT auxiliary *or* helping *(US)* verb

hilft [hɪlft] *3. pers sing pres von* **helfen**

Hi|ma|la|ja [hiˈmaːlaja, himaˈlaːja] M **-(s) der ~** the Himalayas *pl*

Him|bee|re [ˈhɪmbeːrə] F raspberry

Him|beer-: **Him|beer|eis** NT raspberry ice (cream); **Him|beer|geist** M, *no pl* (white) raspberry brandy; **him|beer|rot** ADJ raspberry-coloured *(Brit)*, raspberry-colored *(US)*; **Him|beer|saft** M raspberry juice; **Him|beer|strauch** M raspberry bush

Him|mel [ˈhɪml] M **-s**, *(poet)* **-** **a** sky; **am ~** in the sky; **unter dem ~ Spaniens, unter spanischem ~** under *or* beneath a Spanish sky; **zwischen ~ und Erde** in midair; **~ und Erde** *(Cook) mashed potato and apple with black pudding and fried liver sausage*; **in den ~ ragen** to tower (up) into the sky; **jdn/etw in den ~ (er)heben** *or* **loben** *or* **rühmen** to praise sb/sth to the skies; **jdm hängt der ~ voller Geigen** everything in the garden is lovely for sb; **gute Lehrer fallen nicht vom ~** good teachers don't grow on trees; **der Frieden fällt nicht einfach vom ~, sondern ...** peace doesn't just fall out of the blue, but ...; **eher stürzt der ~ ein, als dass ...** *(geh)* the skies will fall before ... *(liter)*

b *(Rel: = Himmelreich)* heaven; **im ~** in heaven; **den Blick gen ~ richten** *(liter)* to look heavenward(s), to raise one's eyes toward(s) heaven; **in den ~ kommen** to go to heaven; **zum** *or* **in den ~ auffahren, gen ~ fahren** to ascend into heaven; **der Sohn des ~s** *(= Kaiser von China)* the Celestial Emperor; **der ~ auf Erden** heaven on earth; **dem ~ sei Dank** *(old)* thank God *or* Heaven(s); **der ~ ist** *or* **sei mein Zeuge** *(old)* as Heaven *or* God is my witness; **(das) weiß der ~!** *(inf)* God *or* Heaven (only) knows; **der ~ bewahre mich davor!** *(old)* may Heaven *or* God preserve me; **das schreit zum ~** it's a scandal; **es stinkt zum ~** *(inf)* it stinks to high heaven *(inf)*; **der ~ verhüte** *(old)* Heaven *or* God forbid; **(ach) du lieber ~!** *(inf)* good Heavens!, good (-ness) gracious!; **~ (noch mal)!** *(inf)* good God!, hang it all! *(inf)*; **um(s) ~s willen** *(inf)* for Heaven's *or* goodness' sake *(inf)*; **~, Arsch und Zwirn** *(dated inf) or* **Wolkenbruch** *(dated inf)* bloody hell! *(Brit inf)*, Christ Almighty! *(inf)*; **~ und Hölle** *(= Kinderspiel)* hopscotch; **~ und Hölle** *or* **Erde in Bewegung setzen** to move heaven and earth

c *(= Betthimmel etc)* canopy; *(im Auto)* roof

Him|mel-: **him|mel|an** [hɪmlˈlan] ADV *(poet)* heavenward(s); **him|mel|angst** [ˈhɪmlˈlaŋst] ADJ *pred* **mir wurde ~** I was scared to death; **Him|mel|bett** NT four-poster (bed); **him|mel|blau** ADJ sky-blue, azure *(liter)*; **Him|mel|don|ner|wet|ter** [ˈhɪmlˈdɔnɐˈvɛtɐ] INTERJ *(inf)* damn it *(inf)*; **~ noch (ein)mal!** damn and blast it! *(inf)*

Him|mel|fahrt F **a** *(Rel)* **Christi ~** the Ascension of Christ; **Mariä ~** the Assumption of the Virgin Mary **b** *(no art: = Feiertag)* Ascension Day

HIMMELFAHRT

Himmelfahrt (Ascension Day) is a public holiday in Germany and celebrates the Ascension of Christ into heaven forty days after Easter. It is also called **Vatertag** (Father's Day) or **Männertag**, and fathers get presents from their children. Men tend to leave their wives and children at home on this day and go out drinking with their friends.

Him|mel|fahrts-: **Him|mel|fahrts|kom|man|do** NT (*Mil inf*) suicide squad *or* (= *Unternehmung*) mission; **Him|mel|fahrts|na|se** F (*hum inf*) turned-up *or* snub nose; **Him|mel|fahrts|tag** M **der ~** Ascension Day; **am ~** on Ascension Day

Him|mel-: **Him|mel|herr|gott** ['hɪml'hɛrgɔt] INTERJ (*inf*) damn (it) (*inf*), bloody hell (*Brit inf*); **~ noch (ein)mal!** damn and blast! (*inf*); **Him|mel|herr|gott|sak|ra** ['hɪml'hɛrgɔt'za:kra] INTERJ (*S Ger, Aus*) damn (it) (*inf*), bloody hell (*Brit inf*); **him|mel|hoch** ADJ sky-high ADV high into the sky; **~ jauchzend, zu Tode betrübt** up one minute and down the next; **Him|mel|reich** NT, *no pl* (*Rel*) Kingdom of Heaven; **ins ~ eingehen** *or* **kommen** to enter the Kingdom of Heaven; **ein ~ für ...** I'd give anything *or* my right arm for ...; **Him|mel|schlüs|sel** M OR NT (*Bot*) cowslip; **him|mel|schrei|end** ADJ *Unrecht* outrageous, scandalous; *Unkenntnis, Verhältnisse* appalling; *Unsinn* utter *attr*; *Schande* crying *attr*

Him|mels-: **Him|mels|ach|se** F celestial axis; **Him|mels|äqua|tor** M celestial equator, equinoctial line *or* circle; **Him|mels|bahn** F (*liter*) celestial path *or* orbit; **Him|mels|blau** NT (*liter*) sky blue; **Him|mels|braut** F (*liter*) bride of Christ (*liter*); **Him|mels|er|schei|nung** F celestial phenomenon; **Him|mels|fes|te** F (*liter*) firmament (*liter*);; **Him|mels|fürst** M (*Rel, liter*) King of Heaven; **Him|mels|ga|be** F (*geh*) gift from heaven; **Him|mels|ge|wöl|be** NT (*liter*) vault of heaven (*liter*), firmament (*liter*); **Him|mels|kar|te** F star map *or* chart; **Him|mels|kö|ni|gin** F (*Rel*) Queen of Heaven; **Him|mels|kör|per** M heavenly *or* celestial body; **Him|mels|ku|gel** F (*liter*) celestial globe (*liter*) *or* sphere (*liter*); **Him|mels|kun|de** F astronomy; **Him|mels|kup|pel** F (*liter*) vault of heaven (*liter*), firmament (*liter*); **Him|mels|lei|ter** F (*Bot*) Jacob's Ladder; **Him|mels|macht** F **die Liebe ist eine ~** love is a power of heaven; **Him|mels|pfor|te** F (*liter*) gate of heaven; **Him|mels|pol** M celestial pole; **Him|mels|rich|tung** F direction; **die vier ~en** the four points of the compass; **Him|mels|schlüs|sel** M OR NT (*Bot*) cowslip; **Him|mels|schrift** F skywriting; **Him|mels|spi|on** M (*inf*) spy satellite; **Him|mels|stür|mer(in)** M(F) (*liter*) (romantic) idealist; **Him|mels|tor** NT, **Him|mels|tür** F (*geh*) gate of heaven

him|mel|stür|mend ADJ *attr* (*liter*) boundless; *Projekt, Vision* highly ambitious

Him|mels-: **Him|mels|wa|gen** M (*Astron*) Great Bear; **Him|mels|zelt** NT (*poet*) canopy of heaven (*poet*), firmament (*liter*)

him|mel-: **him|mel|wärts** ['hɪmlvɛrts] ADV (*liter*) heavenward(s); **him|mel|weit** (*fig inf*) ADJ tremendous, fantastic (*inf*); **zwischen uns besteht ein ~er Unterschied** there's a world of difference between us ADV **~ voneinander entfernt** (*fig*) **~ verschieden** (*fig*) poles apart; **sich ~ unterscheiden** to be worlds apart from each other, to be totally different from each other; **wir sind noch ~ davon entfernt** we're still nowhere near it

himm|lisch ['hɪmlɪʃ] ADJ **a** *attr* (= *göttlich*) heavenly, celestial (*liter*); **eine ~e Fügung** divine providence; **der ~e Vater** our Heavenly Father; **die Himmlischen** (*old poet*) the gods; **das ~e Jerusalem** the new Jerusalem **b** (*fig*) (= *wunderbar*) heavenly, divine; (= *unerschöpflich*) *Geduld* infinite ADV (= *wunderbar*) *schmecken* heavenly; **~ passen** to fit perfectly; **~ singen** to sing exquisitely *or* divinely; **~ schön** just heavenly, perfectly beautiful; **~ warm** wonderfully warm; **~ bequem** beautifully *or* wonderfully comfortable

hin [hɪn] ADV **a** (*räumlich*) **bis zum Haus ~** up to the house, as far as the house; **geh doch ~ zu ihr!** go to her; (= *besuche sie auch*) go and see her; **nach Süden/Stuttgart ~** towards (*Brit*) *or* toward (*US*) the south/Stuttgart; **über die ganze Welt ~** all over the world, throughout the world; **die Wüste erstreckt sich über 2000 km ~** the desert stretches for 2000 km; **nach außen ~** (*fig*) outwardly; **das Boot glitt über die Wellen ~** the boat glided along over the waves; **~ fahre ich mit dem Zug, zurück ...** on the way out I'll take the train, coming back ...; **die Fähre geht heute Abend nur noch (zur Insel) ~** the ferry's only making the outward trip *or* is only going out (to the island) this evening; **zur anderen Seite ~ sind es 2 km** it's 2 kms to the other side; **bis zu diesem Punkt ~** up to this point; **die Straße verläuft nach rechts ~** the road goes off to the right; **dreht euch/seht mal alle zur Tafel ~** face the/look at the blackboard **b** (*als Teil eines Wortpaares*) **~ und her** (*räumlich*) to and fro, back and forth; (= *hin und zurück*) there and back; **~ und her fahren** to travel to and fro, to travel back and forth; **jdn/etw ~ und her fahren** to drive sb/sth to and fro, to drive sb/sth back and forth; **etw ~ und her überlegen** to weigh sth up; **etw ~ und her diskutieren** to discuss sth over and over, to discuss sth a lot; **das Hin und Her** the comings and goings *pl*, the to-ings and fro-ings *pl*; **nach langem Hin und Her** eventually; **das reicht nicht ~ und nicht her** (*inf*) that won't go very far at all, that's nothing like enough (*inf*); **Regen/Skandal ~, Regen/Skandal her** rain/scandal or no rain/scandal, whether it rains/whether it's a scandal or not; **Mörder/Sohn ~, Mörder/Sohn her** murderer/son or not, I don't care whether he is a murderer/his *etc* son; **~ und zurück** there and back; **eine Fahrkarte ~ und zurück** a return (ticket), a round trip ticket (*esp US*); **einmal London ~ und zurück** a return *or* round trip ticket (*esp US*) to London; **~ und zurück? – nein, nur ~ bitte** return *or* round trip ticket (*esp US*) ? – no, just a single (*Brit*) *or* one way please; **der Flug von X nach Y ~ und zurück kostet ...** the return flight *or* round trip ticket (*esp US*) from X to Y costs ...; **~ und wieder** (every) now and then, (every) now and again **c** (*zeitlich*) **es sind nur noch drei Tage ~** it's only three days (from) now; **bis zu den Wahlen sind es noch drei Wochen ~** it's (still) three weeks till *or* until the elections; **noch weit ~** a long way off *or* away; **lange Zeit ~** for a long time, over a long period; **zum Sommer ~** toward(s) summer, as summer draws nearer *or* approaches; **gegen Mittag ~** toward(s) midday; **über die Jahre ~** over the years, as (the) years go by; **die Kälte zog sich bis in den Juni ~** the cold lasted up until (and during) June **d** (*fig*) **auf meine Bitte/meinen Vorschlag ~** at my request/suggestion; **auf meinen Brief/Anruf ~** on account of my letter/phone call; **auf die Gefahr ~, ... zu werden** at the risk of being ...; **auf sein Versprechen ~** on the basis of his promise; **auf seinen Rat ~** on his advice; **etw auf etw** (*acc*) **~ untersuchen/prüfen** to inspect/check sth for sth; **etw auf etw** (*acc*) **~ planen/anlegen** to plan/design sth with sth in mind; **vor sich ~ sprechen** *etc* to talk *etc* to oneself; **vor sich ~ stieren** to stare straight ahead, to stare into space; **vor sich ~ dösen** to doze **e** (*inf: als trennbarer Bestandteil von Adverbien*) **da will ich nicht ~** I don't want to go (there); **wo geht ihr ~?** where are you going? **f** (*elliptisch*) **nichts wie ~** (*inf*) let's go (then)!, what are we waiting for? (*inf*); **wo ist es/sie ~?** where has it/she gone? → **hin sein, nach, zu** *etc*

hi|nab [hɪ'nap] ADV PREF = **hinunter**

hi|nan [hɪ'nan] ADV (*liter*) upwards

hi|nan- PREF (*liter*) = **hinauf-**

hin+ar|bei|ten VI *sep* **auf etw** (*acc*) **~** (*auf ein Ziel*) to work toward(s) sth, to aim at sth; *auf eine Prüfung* to work for sth

hi|nauf [hɪ'nauf] ADV up; **den Berg/die Straße ~** up the mountain/street; **den Fluss ~** up the river; **die Treppe ~** up the stairs, upstairs; **dort ~** up there; **bis ~ zu** up to

hi|nauf- PREF → *auch* **herauf-, rauf-** up; **hi|nauf+ar|bei|ten** VR *sep* (*lit, fig*) to work one's way up; **hi|nauf+be|ge|ben** *ptp* **hinaufbegeben** VR *sep irreg* (*geh*) to go up(stairs); **hi|nauf+be|glei|ten** *ptp* **hinaufbegleitet** VT *sep* to take up(stairs); **hi|nauf+be|mü|hen** *ptp* **hinaufbemüht** *sep* (*geh*) VT to trouble to go/come up(stairs) VR to take the trouble *or* to trouble to go/come up(stairs); **hi|nauf+bit|ten** VT *sep irreg* to ask to come up(stairs); **hi|nauf+bli|cken** VI *sep* to look up; **hi|nauf+brin|gen** VT *sep irreg* to take up; **hi|nauf+fah|ren** *sep irreg* VI *aux sein* to go up; (*in Auto auch*) to drive up VT *jdn* to take up; (*in Auto auch*) to drive up; *Aufzug* to take up; **hi|nauf+fal|len** VI *sep irreg aux sein* **die Treppe ~** (*hum*) to fall up the stairs; **hi|nauf+füh|ren** VTI *sep* to lead up; **hi|nauf+ge|hen** VI *sep irreg aux sein* to go up; (*Preise, Fieber auch*) to rise; **die Treppe ~** to go *or* walk up the stairs; **einen Berg ~** to climb *or* go up a mountain; **mit dem Preis ~** to put up the price; **hi|nauf+ge|lan|gen** *ptp* **hinaufgelangt** VI *sep aux sein* (*geh*) to (manage to) get up; **hi|nauf+klet|tern** VI *sep aux sein* to climb up; **auf einen Baum ~** to climb up a tree; **hi|nauf+kom|men** VI *sep irreg aux sein* to come up; (= *schaffen*) to (manage to) get up; **hi|nauf+lau|fen** VI *sep irreg aux sein* to run up; **die Treppe ~** to run up the stairs; (*im Haus auch*) to run upstairs; **hi|nauf+rei|chen** *sep* VI to reach up VT to hand *or* pass up; **hi|nauf+schau|en** VI *sep* (*dial*) to look up; **hi|nauf+schi|cken** VT *sep* to send up; **hi|nauf+schie|ben** VT *sep irreg* to push up; **hi|nauf+schrau|ben** VT *sep* to screw up; (*fig*) *Preise* to put *or* push (*esp US*) up; *Produktion, Forderungen* to step up; **hi|nauf+se|hen** VI *sep irreg* to look up; **hi|nauf+set|zen** VT *sep* (*fig*) *Preis etc* to raise, to increase, to put *or* push (*esp US*) up; **hi|nauf+stei|gen** VI *sep irreg aux sein* to climb up; **hi|nauf+tra|gen** VT *sep irreg* to carry *or* take up; **hi|nauf+trei|ben** VT *sep irreg* **a** *Vieh etc* to drive up; **das Vieh den Berg ~** to drive the cattle up the mountain **b** (*fig*) *Kurs, Preis* to push up, to force up; **hi|nauf+zie|hen** *sep irreg* VT to pull up VI *aux sein* to move up VR to pull oneself up; **sich an einem Seil ~** to pull oneself up with a rope

hi|naus [hɪ'naus] ADV **a** (*räumlich*) out; **~ (mit dir)!** (get) out!, out you go!; **über** (*+acc*) **~** beyond, over; **aus dem** *or* **zum Fenster ~** out of the window; **hier/dort ~** this/that way out; **hinten/vorn ~** at the back *or* rear/front; **nach hinten/vorn ~ wohnen** to live towards (*Brit*) *or* toward (*US*) *or* facing the back/the front; **zur Straße ~** facing the street; **durch die Tür ~** out of *or* out through the door **b** (*zeitlich*) **auf Jahre/Monate ~** for years/months to come; **bis weit über die siebzig ~** until well over *or* after *or* past seventy; **wir werden damit über Mittwoch ~ beschäftigt sein** we'll be busy with that until after Wednesday **c** (*fig*) **über** (*+acc*) **~** over and above; (*über Gehalt, Summe auch*) on top of; **über das Grab ~** beyond the grave; **darüber ~** over and above this, on top of this, in addition to this → **hinaus sein, hinauswollen** *etc*

hi|naus- PREF → *auch* **heraus-, raus-**: **hi|naus+be|för|dern** *ptp* **hinausbefördert** VT *sep jdn* to kick out (*inf*), to chuck out (*inf*) (*aus* of); **hi|naus|be|ge|ben** *ptp* **hinausbegeben** VR *sep irreg* (*geh*) to go out (*aus* of); **hi|naus+be|glei|ten** *ptp* **hinausbegleitet** VT *sep* to see out (*aus* of); **hi|naus+beu|gen** VR *sep* to lean out (*aus* of); **sich zum Fenster ~** to lean out of the window; **hi|naus+bli|cken** VI *sep* to look out (*aus* of); **zum Fenster ~** to look out of the window; **hi|naus+brin|gen** VT *sep irreg* to take out (*aus* of); **hi|naus+bug|sie|ren** *ptp* **hinausbugsiert** VT *sep (inf) jdn* to steer *or* hustle out (*aus* of); **hi|naus+drän|gen** *sep* VT to force out (*aus* of); *(eilig)* to hustle out (*aus* of); *(fig)* to oust (*aus* from), to force out (*aus* of) VI *aux sein* to push *or* force one's way out (*aus* of); **hi|naus+dür|fen** VI *sep irreg* to be allowed (to go) out (*aus* of); **darf ich hinaus?** may I go out?; **über einen Punkt nicht ~** not to be allowed (to go) beyond a point; **hi|naus+ei|len** VI *sep aux sein (geh)* to hurry out (*aus* of); **hi|naus+ekeln** VT *sep (inf)* to drive out (*aus* of); **hi|naus+fah|ren** *sep irreg* VI *aux sein* **a aus etw ~** to go out of sth, to leave sth; *(in Fahrzeug auch)* to drive out of sth **b** *(= reisen)* to go out; **aufs Meer ~** to sail out across the sea **c über etw** *(acc)* **~** to go beyond sth VT *Wagen* to drive out (*aus* of); **hi|naus+fal|len** VI *sep irreg aux sein* (*aus* of) to fall out; *(Licht)* to come out; **hi|naus+fin|den** VI *sep irreg* to find one's *or* the way out (*aus* of); **ich finde schon allein hinaus** I can find my own way out, I can see myself out; **hi|naus+flie|gen** *sep irreg* VI *aux sein* (*aus* of) **a** *(= fortfliegen)* to fly out; *(inf: = hinausfallen)* to go flying out *(inf)*; **über ein Ziel ~** to fly past *or* go flying past a target **b** *(inf: = hinausgeworfen werden)* to get kicked *or* chucked out *(inf)* VT to fly out (*aus* of); **hi|naus+füh|ren** *sep* VI **a** *(= nach draußen führen)* to lead out (*aus* of) **b** *(= weiter führen als)* **über etw** *(acc)* **~** *(lit, fig)* to go beyond sth VT to lead out (*aus* of); *(Weg, Reise)* to take (*über +acc* beyond); **hi|naus+ge|hen** *sep irreg aux sein* VI **a** *(= nach draußen gehen)* to go out(side); **aus dem Zimmer/auf die Straße ~** to go *or* walk out of the room/out onto the street **b** *(= gesandt werden)* to go (out), to be sent out **c auf etw** *(acc)* **~** *(Tür, Zimmer)* to open onto sth; *(Fenster)* to look (out) onto sth, to open onto sth; **das Fenster geht nach Osten hinaus** the window looks *or* faces east; **das Fenster geht zum Hof hinaus** the window looks out onto the courtyard; **zu** *or* **nach etw ~** *(Straße, Weg)* to go out to **d** *(fig: = überschreiten)* **über etw** *(acc)* **~** to go beyond sth; **das geht über meine Kräfte hinaus** it's too much for me to bear, I (just) can't take any more; **über seine Befugnisse ~** to overstep one's authority, to exceed one's powers VI *impers* **wo geht es hinaus?** where's the way out?; **hi|naus+ge|lan|gen** *ptp* **hinausgelangt** VI *sep aux sein (geh) (lit)* to get out; **über etw** *(acc)* **~** *(fig)* to get beyond sth; **hi|naus+ge|lei|ten** *ptp* **hinausgeleitet** VT *sep (geh)* to show out (*aus* of); **hi|naus+grau|len** VT *sep (inf)* to drive out (*aus* of); **hi|naus+grei|fen** VI *sep irreg (fig)* **über etw** *(acc)* **~** to reach beyond sth; **hi|naus+gu|cken** VI *sep* to look out (*aus* of); **hi|naus+hal|ten** VT *sep irreg* to hold out; **den Kopf zum Fenster ~** to stick *or* put one's head out of the window; **hi|naus+hän|gen** VTI *sep irreg* to hang out; **eine Fahne zum Fenster ~** to hang a flag out of the window; **hi|naus+he|ben** VT *sep irreg* **etw über etw** *(acc)* **~** to raise *or* lift sth above sth, to put sth on a higher *or* different level from sth; **hi|naus+ja|gen** *sep* (*aus* of) VT *(lit: aus dem Zimmer, nach draußen)* to drive *or* chase out; *(fig: aus dem Haus)* to turn *or* drive out VI *aux sein* to bolt *or* dive out; **hi|naus+ka|ta|pul|tie|ren** *ptp* **hinauskatapultiert** VT *sep (Pol sl)* to throw out, to chuck out *(inf)* (*aus* of); **hi|naus+klet|tern** VI *sep aux sein* to climb out (*aus* of); **hi|naus+kom|men** VI *sep irreg aux sein* **a** *(= nach außen kommen)* to come out(side); **ich bin den ganzen Tag noch nicht hinausgekommen** I haven't been out(-side) yet today; **zu jdm aufs Land ~** to come out to see sb in the country **b über etw** *(acc)* **~** to go beyond sth; *(fig)* to get beyond sth **c** *(fig: = hinauslaufen)* **das kommt auf dasselbe** *or* **auf eins** *or* **aufs Gleiche hinaus** it boils *or* comes down to the same thing, it amounts *or* comes to the same thing; **hi|naus+kom|pli|men|tie|ren** [hɪˈnauskɔmplimɛntiːrən] *ptp* **hinauskomplimentiert** VT *sep (hum)* to usher out (*aus* of); **hi|naus+kön|nen** VI *sep irreg (inf)* to be able to get out; **hi|naus+las|sen** VT *sep irreg* (*aus* of) to leave out; *(= hinausbegleiten)* to show out; **hi|naus+lau|fen** VI *sep irreg aux sein* (*aus* of) **a** *(lit)* to run out **b** *(fig)* **auf etw** *(acc)* **~** to amount to sth; **es läuft auf dasselbe** *or* **auf eins** *or* **aufs Gleiche hinaus** it boils *or* comes down to the same thing, it amounts *or* comes to the same thing; **wo(rauf) soll das ~?** how's it all going to end?, what are things coming to?; **hi|naus+leh|nen** VR *sep* to lean out (*aus* of); **sich zum Fenster ~** to lean out of the window; **hi|naus+ma|növ|rie|ren** *ptp* **hinausmanövriert** VT *sep* **sich/jdn aus etw ~** to manoeuvre *(Brit)* *or* maneuver *(US)* oneself/sb out of sth; **hi|naus+müs|sen** VI *sep irreg* to have to go out (*aus* of); **hi|naus+neh|men** VT *sep irreg* to take out (*aus* of); **hi|naus+po|sau|nen** *ptp* **hinausposaunt** VT *sep (inf)* to broadcast *(inf)*; **hi|naus+ra|gen** VI *sep aux sein* **a** *(horizontal)* to project, to jut out (*über +acc* beyond); *(vertikal)* to tower up (*über +acc* above, over) **b** *(fig)* **über jdn/etw ~** to tower above sb/sth; **hi|naus+re|den** VR *sep (dial)* to talk one's way out of it *(inf)*; **hi|naus+rei|chen** *sep* VT to hand *or* pass out (*aus* of); **jdm etw zum Fenster ~** to hand *or* pass sb sth out of the window VI **a** *(= bis nach draußen reichen)* to reach, to stretch (*bis* as far as) **b über etw** *(acc)* **~** *(lit)* to stretch beyond sth; *(fig)* to go beyond sth; **hi|naus+ren|nen** VI *sep irreg aux sein* to run out (*aus* of); **hi|naus+rü|cken** VI *sep aux sein (lit)* to move out (*aus* of); **die Soldaten rückten zur Stadt hinaus** the soldiers marched *or* moved out of (the) town; **hi|naus+schaf|fen** VT *sep* to take out (*aus* of); **hi|naus+schau|en** VI *sep (dial)* = **hinausblicken**; **hi|naus+sche|ren** VR *sep* to get out (*aus* of); **hi|naus+schi|cken** VT *sep* to send out (*aus* of); **hi|naus+schie|ben** VT *sep irreg* **a** *Gegenstand* to push out (*aus* of) **b** *(fig)* to put off, to postpone; **hi|naus+schie|ßen** VI *sep irreg* **a er hat zum Fenster hinausgeschossen** he fired out of the window **b** *aux sein (= hinausrennen)* to shoot *or* dart out (*aus* of); **hi|naus+schmei|ßen** VT *sep irreg (inf)* to kick *or* chuck out *(inf)* (*aus* of); **Hi|naus|schmiss** M *(inf)* **man drohte ihm mit ~ (aus dem Restaurant)** they threatened to kick *or* chuck him out (of the restaurant) *(inf)*; **das war ein regelrechter ~** he was simply kicked *or* chucked out *(inf)*; **hi|naus+schmug|geln** VT *sep* to smuggle out (*aus* of); **hi|naus+schrei|en** *sep irreg* VI to shout out (*aus* of); **zum Fenster ~** to shout out of the window VT *(geh) Schmerz, Hass* to proclaim *(geh)*; **hi|naus+schwim|men** VI *sep irreg aux sein* (*aus* of) (*über +acc* beyond, past) to swim out; *(Gegenstände)* to float out; **hi|naus+se|hen** VI *sep irreg* = **hinausblicken**; **hi|naus sein** VI *irreg aux sein* **a** *(lit inf: = hinausgegangen sein)* to be out, to have gone out **b** *(fig: = hinter sich haben)* **über etw** *(acc)* **~** *(über Kindereien, Dummheiten)* to be past *or* beyond sth; *über ein Alter* to be past sth; **hi|naus+set|zen** *sep* VT to put out(-side); **jdn ~** *(inf)* to chuck *or* kick sb out *(inf)* VR to (go and) sit outside; **hi|naus+sprin|gen** VI *sep irreg aux sein* to jump out (*aus, zu* of); **hi|naus+steh|len** VR *sep irreg (geh)* to steal out *(geh)* (*aus* of); **hi|naus+stei|gen** VI *sep irreg aux sein* to climb out (*aus* of); **zum Fenster ~** to climb out of the window; **hi|naus+stel|len** VT *sep* to put *or* take out(side); *Sportler* to send off; **hi|naus+stre|cken** VT *sep* to stick *or* put out (*aus* of); **hi|naus+strö|men** VI *sep aux sein* to pour out (*aus* of); *(geh: Menschenmassen auch)* to come milling out (*aus* of); **hi|naus+stür|men** VI *sep aux sein* to storm out (*aus* of); **hi|naus+stür|zen** *sep* (*aus* of) VI *aux sein* **a** *(= hinausfallen)* to fall out **b** *(= hinauseilen)* to rush *or* dash out VR to throw oneself out, to dive out VT to throw out; **hi|naus+tra|gen** VT *sep irreg* **a** *(= nach außen tragen)* to carry out (*aus* of) **b** *(geh)* **etw in alle Welt ~** to spread sth abroad **c** *(= weiter tragen als)* **etw über etw** *(acc)* **~** to carry sth over *or* beyond sth; **hi|naus+trei|ben** VT *sep irreg* to drive out (*aus* of); **hi|naus+tre|ten** VI *sep irreg aux sein* to step out(side); **ins Leben ~** *(geh)* to go out into the world; **hi|naus+trom|pe|ten** *ptp* **hinaustrompetet** VT *sep (inf)* to broadcast *(inf)*; **hi|naus+wach|sen** VI *sep irreg aux sein* **über etw** *(acc)* **~** *(lit)* to grow taller than sth; *(fig: durch zunehmende Reife, Fortschritte etc)* to outgrow sth; **er wuchs über sich selbst hinaus** he surpassed himself; **hi|naus+wa|gen** VR *sep* to venture out (*aus* of); **hi|naus+wei|sen** *sep irreg* VT **jdn ~** to show sb the door, to ask sb to leave VI to point out(wards); **über eine Frage/Sache ~** *(fig)* to reach *or* point beyond a question/matter; **hi|naus+wer|fen** VT *sep irreg* (*aus* of) **a** *(= nach außen werfen, wegwerfen)* to throw *or* cast *(liter)* out; **einen Blick ~** to glance *or* look out(side), to take a glance *or* look out(side); **das ist hinausgeworfenes Geld** it's money down the drain; **Geld zum Fenster ~** to throw money out of the window *or* down the drain **b** *(inf) (= entfernen)* to chuck *or* kick out *(inf)*; **hi|naus+wol|len** VI *sep* to want to go *or* get out (*aus* of); **worauf willst du hinaus?** *(fig)* what are you getting *or* driving at?; **hoch ~** to aim high, to set one's sights high

Hi|naus|wurf M *(inf)* **einen ~ riskieren** to risk getting thrown *or* kicked out; **jdm mit dem ~ drohen** to threaten to throw *or* kick sb out

hi|naus- PREF → *auch* **heraus-, raus-**: **hi|naus+zie|hen** *sep irreg* VT **a** *(= nach draußen ziehen)* to pull out (*aus* of) **b** *(fig) Verhandlungen etc* to protract, to drag out; *Urlaub etc* to prolong VI *aux sein* to go out (*aus* of); **in die Welt ~** to go out into the world; **aufs Land/vor die Stadt ~** to move out into the country/out of town; **den Dampf/Rauch ~ lassen** to let the steam/smoke out VR *(Verhandlungen etc)* to drag on; *(Abfahrt etc)* to be delayed, to be put off VT *impers* **es zog ihn hinaus in die weite Welt** he felt the urge to go out into the big wide world; **mich ziehts wieder hinaus in die Ferne** I feel the urge to travel again; **bei diesem schönen Wetter ziehts mich hinaus** I want to be out-of-doors with the weather like this; **hi|naus+zö|gern** *sep* VT to delay, to put off VR to be delayed, to be put off

hin-: **hin+be|ge|ben** *ptp* **hinbegeben** VR *sep irreg (geh)* **sich zu jdm ~** *(form)* to go to sb, to betake oneself to sb *(old, form)*; **hin+be|kom|men** *ptp* **hinbekommen** VT *sep irreg (inf)* = **hinkriegen**; **hin+be|mü|hen** *ptp* **hinbemüht** *sep (geh)* VT **jdn ~** to trouble sb to go, to give sb the trouble of going VR to take the trouble to go; **hin+be|or|dern** *ptp* **hinbeordert** VT *sep* to summon, to send for; **hin+be|stel|len** *ptp* **hinbestellt** VT *sep* to tell to go/come; **hin+bie|gen** VT *sep irreg (fig inf) (= in Ordnung bringen)* to arrange, to sort out; *(= deichseln)* to wangle *(inf)*; *(= interpretieren) Text, Wortlaut* to twist; **die Sache** *or* **das werden wir schon ~** we'll sort it out somehow; **hin+blät|tern** VT *sep (inf)* to fork *or* shell out *(inf)*, to cough up *(inf)*; **Hin|blick** M **im** *or* **in ~ auf** *(+acc) (= angesichts)* in view of; *(= mit Bezug auf)* with regard to; **im ~ darauf, dass ...** in view of the fact that ...; **hin+bli|cken** VI *sep* to look *or* glance (*auf +acc, nach* at, towards); **hin+brin|gen** VT *sep irreg* **a** *etw* to take there; *(= begleiten) jdn* to take there; *(in Auto)* to drive *or* take there **b** *(fig) Zeit* to spend, to pass; *(in Muße)* to idle *or* while away; **sein Leben kümmerlich ~** to eke out an existence **c** = **hinkriegen**; **hin+deich|seln** VT *sep (inf) etw* to arrange, to sort out;

hin+den|ken VI *sep irreg* **wo denkst du hin?** whatever are you thinking of!

hin|der|lich ['hɪndəlɪç] ADJ ~ **sein** to be in the way, to be a nuisance; *(Kleidungsstück auch)* to be restricting; **ein ~er Gipsverband** a restricting (plaster) cast, a (plaster) cast that gets in the way *or* that is a nuisance; **einer Sache** *(dat)* ~ **sein** to be a hindrance *or* obstacle to sth; **eher ~ als nützlich sein** to be more of a hindrance than a help; **jdm ~ sein** to get in sb's way ADV **sich ~ auswirken** to prove to be a hindrance

hin|dern ['hɪndən] VT **a** *Fortschritte, Wachstum* to impede, to hamper; *jdn* to hinder (*bei* in) **b** (= *abhalten von*) to prevent (*an +dat* from), to stop; **ja bitte, ich will Sie nicht ~** please do, I won't stand in your way; **machen Sie, was Sie wollen, ich kann Sie nicht ~** do what you like, I can't stop *or* prevent you; **was hindert dich (daran), hinzugehen?** what prevents *or* keeps you from going (there)?, what stops you going (there)? VI (= *stören*) to be a hindrance (*bei* to)

Hin|der|nis ['hɪndənɪs] NT **-ses, -se a** *(lit, fig)* obstacle; (= *Erschwernis, Behinderung*) hindrance; *(beim Sprechen)* handicap, impediment; **sie empfand das Kind als ~/als ~ für ihre Karriere** she saw the child as a hindrance/as a hindrance to *or* an obstacle for her career; **gesetzliches ~** *(form)* legal impediment *or* obstacle; **jdm ~se in den Weg legen** *(fig)* to put obstacles in sb's path *or* way; **eine Reise mit ~sen** a journey full of hitches **b** (*Sport*: = *Hürde*) hurdle; *(beim Pferderennen)* fence, jump; *(Golf)* hazard

Hin|der|nis-: **Hin|der|nis|lauf** M steeplechase *(in athletics)*; **Hin|der|nis|läu|fer(in)** M(F) steeplechaser *(in athletics)*; **Hin|der|nis|ren|nen** NT steeplechase

Hin|de|rung F **-, -en a** (= *Behinderung*) hindrance; **ohne ~** without let or hindrance *(Jur)* **b** (= *Störung*) obstruction

Hin|de|rungs|grund M obstacle; **etw als ~ angeben** to give sth as an excuse

hin+deu|ten VI *sep* to point (*auf +acc, zu* at); **es deutet alles darauf hin, dass ...** everything indicates that ..., everything points to the fact that ...

Hin|di ['hɪndi] NT **-** Hindi

Hin|din ['hɪndɪn] F **-, -nen** *(old, liter)* hind

hin-: **hin+drän|gen** *sep* VT **jdn zum Ausgang ~** to push sb toward(s) the exit VR **sich zu etw ~** to push one's way toward(s) sth VI **zum Ausgang ~** to push one's way toward(s) the exit; **auf eine Änderung ~** to agitate for a change; **alles in ihrem Innern drängte zum Künstlerberuf hin** everything within her urged her toward(s) an artistic profession; **hin+dre|hen** VT *sep (fig inf)* to arrange

Hin|du ['hɪndu] M **-(s), -(s)** Hindu

Hin|du|is|mus [hɪndu'ɪsmʊs] M **-,** *no pl* Hinduism

hin|du|is|tisch [hɪndu'ɪstɪʃ] ADJ Hindu ADV ~ **denken** to have Hindu beliefs; ~ **beeinflusst** influenced by Hinduism; ~ **erzogen werden** to be brought up (as) a Hindu

hin|durch [hɪn'dʊrç] ADV **a** *(räumlich)* through; **dort ~** through there; **mitten ~** straight through; **quer ~** straight across; **durch den Wald ~** through the wood **b** *(zeitlich)* through(out); **das ganze Jahr ~** throughout the year, all (the) year round; **die ganze Nacht ~** all (through the) night, throughout the night, all night long; **die ganze Zeit ~** all the time; **Jahre ~** for years (and years); **den ganzen Tag ~** all day (long); **durch etw ~** through sth

hin|durch+ge|hen VI *sep irreg aux sein (lit, fig)* to go through (*durch etw* sth)

hin+dür|fen VI *sep irreg* to be allowed to go (*zu* to); **da darfst du nicht mehr hin** you are not to go *or* you mustn't go there any more

Hin|dus|tan ['hɪndʊsta:n, -tan] NT **-s** Hindustan

Hin|dus|ta|ni [hɪndʊs'ta:ni] NT **-(s),** *no pl* Hindustani

hin+ei|len VI *sep aux sein (geh)* to rush *or* hurry (*zu* to); **ich eilte sofort hin** I rushed there at once

hi|nein [hɪ'nain] ADV **a** *(räumlich)* in; **da ~** in there; **nur ~!** *(inf)* go right in!; **~ mit dir!** *(inf)* in you go!; **in etw** *(acc)* ~ into sth; **bis in etw** *(acc)* ~ right inside sth; **mitten ~ in etw** *(acc)* right into the middle of sth; **leg es oben/unten ~** put it in the top/bottom → **Blaue(s) b** *(zeitlich)* into; **bis tief in die Nacht ~** well *or* far into the night

hi|nein- PREF → *auch* **ein-, herein-, rein-** in; **hi|nein+be|ge|ben** *ptp* **hineinbegeben** VR *sep irreg (geh)* to enter (*in etw (acc)* sth); **hi|nein+bei|ßen** VI *sep irreg* ~ **in** *(+acc)* to bite into, to take a bite of; **hi|nein+be|kom|men** *ptp* **hineinbekommen** VT *sep irreg (inf)* to get in (*in +acc* -to); **hi|nein+be|mü|hen** *ptp* **hineinbemüht** *sep (geh)* VT to trouble to go in VR to take the trouble *or* to trouble to go in (*in +acc* -to); **hi|nein+bli|cken** VI *sep* = **hineinsehen**; **hi|nein+boh|ren** *sep* (*in +acc* -to) VT to dig in VR to bore one's way in; **hi|nein+brin|gen** VT *sep irreg* **a** (= *hineintragen*) to take in (*in +acc* -to) **b** (*inf*: = *hineinbekommen*) to get in (*in +acc* -to); **hi|nein+bug|sie|ren** *ptp* **hineinbugsiert** VT *sep (inf)* to manoeuvre *(Brit) or* maneuver *(US)* in (*in +acc* -to); **hi|nein+den|ken** VR *sep irreg* **sich in ein Problem ~** to think oneself into a problem; **sich in jdn ~** to put oneself in sb's position; **hi|nein+deu|ten** VT *sep* **etw in einen Satz ~** to read sth into a sentence; **etw in die Natur ~** to attribute nature with sth; **hi|nein+drän|gen** *sep* (*in +acc* -to) VT to push in VIR *(vi: aux sein)* to push one's way in; **hi|nein+dür|fen** VI *sep irreg (inf)* to be allowed in (*in +acc* -to); **Kinder dürfen in den Film nicht hinein** children are not allowed to see the film *or* movie *(US)*; **hi|nein+fal|len** VI *sep irreg aux sein* to fall in (*in +acc* -to); **hi|nein+fin|den** VR *sep irreg (fig)* (= *sich vertraut machen*) to find one's feet; (= *sich abfinden*) to come to terms with it; **sich ~ in etw** *(acc)* to get familiar with sth; to come to terms with sth; **hi|nein+fres|sen** VT *sep irreg (inf)* **etw in sich** *(acc)* ~ *(lit)* to wolf sth (down) *(inf)*, to gobble sth down *or* up; *(fig) Kummer etc* to suppress sth; **hi|nein+ge|heim|nis|sen** [hɪ'naingəhaimnɪsn] *ptp* **hineingeheimnisst** VT *sep (inf)* **etw in etw** *(acc)* ~ to read sth into sth; **hi|nein+ge|hen** VI *sep irreg aux sein* **a** (= *betreten*) to go in; **in etw** *(acc)* ~ to go into sth, to enter sth **b** (= *hineinpassen*) to go in (*in +acc* -to); **in den Bus gehen 50 Leute hinein** the bus holds 50 people, there is room for 50 people in the bus; **hi|nein+ge|lan|gen** *ptp* **hineingelangt** VI *sep aux sein (geh)* to get in (*in +acc* -to); **hi|nein+ge|ra|ten** *ptp* **hineingeraten** VI *sep irreg aux sein* **in etw** *(acc)* ~ to get involved in sth, to get into sth; **in ein Unwetter ~** to be caught in a thunderstorm; **in eine Schlägerei ~** to get into a brawl, to get involved in a brawl; **hi|nein+gie|ßen** VT *sep irreg* to pour in (*in +acc* -to); **etw in sich ~** *(inf)* to pour sth down one's throat *(inf)*, to down sth; **hi|nein+grei|fen** VI *sep irreg* to reach inside; **in etw** *(acc)* ~ to reach into sth; **hi|nein+gu|cken** VI *sep (inf, in Zimmer, Kiste)* to look *or* take a look in (*in +acc* -to); *(in Buch)* to take a look in (*in etw (acc)* sth); **hi|nein+hal|ten** *sep irreg* VT to put in (*in etw (acc)* sth) VI (*inf*: *mit Gewehr etc*) to aim (*in +acc* at); **mitten in die Menge ~** to aim into the crowd; **hi|nein+hei|ra|ten** VI *sep* = **einheiraten**; **hi|nein+in|ter|pre|tie|ren** *ptp* **hineininterpretiert** VT *sep* = **hineindeuten**; **hi|nein+klet|tern** VI *sep aux sein* to climb in (*in +acc* -to); **hi|nein+knien** VR *sep (fig inf)* **sich in etw** *(acc)* ~ to get into sth *(inf)*; **hi|nein+kom|men** VI *sep irreg aux sein* (*in +acc* -to) **a** (= *betreten*) to come in **b** (*lit, fig*: = *hineingelangen können*) to get in; **nach 21 Uhr kommt man nicht (mehr) hinein** you can't get in after 9 o'clock **c** = **hineingeraten**; **hi|nein+kom|pli|men|tie|ren** [hɪ'nainkɔmplimɛnti:rən] *ptp* **hineinkomplimentiert** VT *sep* to usher in (*in +acc* -to); **hi|nein+krie|chen** VI *sep irreg aux sein* to creep *or* slip in (*in +acc* -to); **hi|nein+krie|gen** VT *sep (inf)* to get in (*in +acc* -to); **hi|nein+la|chen** VI *sep* **in sich ~** to laugh to oneself; **hi|nein+las|sen** VT *sep irreg* to let in (*in +acc* -to); **hi|nein+lau|fen** VI *sep irreg aux sein* to run in (*in +acc* -to); **in sein eigenes Unglück ~** to be heading for misfortune; **etw in sich ~ lassen** *(inf)* to knock sth back *(inf)*; **hi|nein+le|gen** VT *sep* **a** *(lit, fig) Gefühl etc* to put in (*in +acc* -to) **b** (= *hineindeuten*) **etw in jds Worte ~** to put sth in sb's mouth; **hi|nein+le|sen** VT *sep irreg* **etw in etw** *(acc)* ~ to read sth into sth; **hi|nein+leuch|ten** VI *sep* to shine in (*in +acc* -to); **mit einer Lampe in eine Höhle ~** to shine a light into a cave; **hi|nein+ma|növ|rie|ren** *ptp* **hineinmanövriert** VT *sep* to manoeuvre *(Brit) or* maneuver *(US)* in (*in +acc* -to); **hi|nein+pas|sen** *sep* VI **in etw** *(acc)* ~ to fit into sth; *(fig)* to fit in with sth VT to fit in (*in +acc* -to); **hi|nein+pfu|schen** VI *sep (inf)* **jdm in seine Arbeit/Angelegenheiten ~** to meddle *or* interfere in sb's work/affairs; **hi|nein+plat|zen** VI *sep aux sein (fig inf)* to burst in (*in +acc* -to); **hi|nein+pres|sen** VT *sep* **a** *Gegenstand* to press in (*in +acc* -to) **b** *(fig)* **etw in ein Schema ~** to force sth into a mould *(Brit) or* mold *(US)*; **er lässt sich in kein Schema ~** he won't be pigeonholed *(inf)*; **hi|nein+pro|ji|zie|ren** *ptp* **hineinprojiziert** VT *sep* to project (*in +acc* into); **sich in jdn ~** to project one's ideas/feelings *etc* into *or* onto sb; **hi|nein+pum|pen** VT *sep* to pump in (*in +acc* -to); *Geld auch* to pour in; **hi|nein+quet|schen** VT *sep Gegenstand* to squeeze *or* press in (*in +acc* -to); **sich in etw** *(+acc)* ~ to squeeze into sth; **sie konnte sich gerade noch ~** *(in Bus etc)* she just about managed to squeeze in; **hi|nein+ra|gen** VI *sep aux sein (lit, fig)* to project (*in +acc* into); **hi|nein+re|den** VI *sep* **a** (*lit*: = *unterbrechen*) to interrupt (*jdm* sb); **jdm ~** (*fig*: = *sich einmischen*) to meddle *or* interfere in sb's affairs; **jdm in seine Angelegenheiten/Entscheidungen/in alles ~** to meddle *or* interfere in sb's affairs/decision-making/in all sb's affairs **b ins Leere ~** to talk into a vacuum, to talk to oneself VR **sich in (seine) Wut ~** to work oneself up into a rage; **hi|nein+reg|nen** VI *impers sep* **es regnet (ins Zimmer) hinein** (the) rain is coming in(to) the room; **hi|nein+rei|chen** *sep* VT to hand *or* pass in; **(jdm) etw zum** *or* **durchs Fenster ~** to hand *or* pass sth in (to sb) through the window VI (= *lang genug sein*) to reach in (*in +acc* -to); (= *sich erstrecken*) to extend (*in +acc* as far as); **in etw** *(acc)* ~ *(zeitlich)* to go over into sth; **Bräuche, die bis ins 21. Jahrhundert ~** customs that persist into the 21st century; **hi|nein+rei|ßen** VT *sep irreg (fig inf)* to drag in (*in +acc* -to); **hi|nein+rei|ten** *sep irreg* VI *aux sein* to ride in (*in +acc* -to) VT *(inf)* = **reinreiten**; **hi|nein+ren|nen** VI *sep irreg aux sein* to run in (*in +acc* -to); **in sein Unglück/Verderben ~** to be heading for misfortune/disaster; **hi|nein+ru|fen** VT *sep irreg* to call *or* shout in (*in +acc* -to); **hi|nein+rut|schen** VI *sep aux sein* **a** *(lit)* to slide (*in +acc* into) **b** *(fig)* → **hineinschliddern**; **hi|nein+schaf|fen** VT *sep* to bring/take in (*in +acc* -to); **hi|nein+schau|en** VI *sep (dial)* = **hineinsehen**; **hi|nein+schau|feln** VT *sep* to shovel in (*in +acc* -to); **Essen in sich ~** *(inf)* to shovel food into oneself *or* down one's gullet *(inf)*; **hi|nein+schie|ßen** VI *sep irreg* **a** *aux sein* (*inf*: *Wasser etc*) to rush *or* gush in (*in +acc* -to); **hineingeschossen kommen** *(Wasser)* to come gushing *or* rushing in; (*inf*: *Mensch*) to shoot in *(inf)*, to come shooting in *(inf)* **b in eine Menschenmenge ~** to shoot into a crowd; **hi|nein+schla|gen** VT *sep irreg* (*in +acc* -to) *Nagel* to knock in; *Eier* to break in; *Krallen* to sink in; **ein Loch ins Eis ~** to knock a hole in the ice; **hi|nein+schlei|chen** VIR *sep irreg (vi: aux sein)* to creep *or* sneak in *(in +acc* -to); **hi|nein+schlid|dern** VI *sep aux sein (inf)* **in etw** *(acc)* ~ to get involved in sth, to get mixed up with sth; **hi|nein+schlin|gen** VT *sep irreg* **etw (gierig) in sich** *(acc)* ~ to devour sth (greedily); **hi|nein+schlit|tern** VI *sep aux sein (inf)* = **hineinschliddern**; **hi|nein+schlüp|fen** VI *sep aux sein* to slip in *(in +acc* -to); **hi|nein+schmug|geln** VT *sep* to smuggle in *(in +acc* -to); **hi|nein+schnei|en** *sep* VI *impers* **es schneit (ins Zimmer) hinein** the snow is coming in(to the room) VI *aux sein (inf)* to drop in *(inf)*; **hi|nein+schnup|pern** VI *sep (fig inf)* **in etw** *(+acc)* ~ *(= ausprobieren)* to give sth a try; *(in Firma etc)* to take a look at sth; *(in eine Arbeit)* to have a go at sth, to get a taste of sth; *(in Buch)* to dip into sth; **hi|nein+schrei|ben** VT *sep irreg* to write in *(in etw (acc)* sth); **hi|nein+schüt|ten** VT *sep* to pour in *(in +acc* -to); **etw in sich** ~ *(inf)* to knock sth back *(inf)*; **hi|nein+se|hen** VI *sep irreg* to look in; **ins Zimmer/Fenster** ~ to look into the room/in at the window; **eben mal** ~ *(inf)* to look *or* pop in *(inf)*; **sich** *(dat)* **in etw** *(acc)* **nicht** ~ **lassen** to keep sth to oneself; **hi|nein+set|zen** *sep* VT to put in *(in +acc* -to) VR *(in Fahrzeug)* to get into *(in etw (acc)* sth); *(in Sessel)* to sit (oneself) down *(in +acc* in(to)); *(in Sessellift, Kettenkarussell etc)* to sit oneself in *(in etw (acc)* sth); **sich wieder ~/ins Zimmer** ~ to go back and sit inside/in the room; **hi|nein+spa|zie|ren** *ptp* **hineinspaziert** VI *sep aux sein* to walk in *(in +acc* -to); **nur hineinspaziert!** please go in; **hi|nein+spie|len** *sep* VI *(= beeinflussen)* to have a part to play *(in +acc* in); **in etw** *(acc)* ~ *(= grenzen an)* to verge on sth; **da spielen noch andere Gesichtspunkte hinein** other factors enter into it VT *(Sport)* **den Ball in den Strafraum** *etc* ~ to play the ball into the penalty area *etc*; **hi|nein+spre|chen** VI *sep irreg* **ins Mikrofon** ~ to speak *or* talk into the microphone; **hi|nein+sprin|gen** VI *sep irreg aux sein (in +acc* -to) **a** *(= hineinhüpfen)* to jump *or* leap *or* spring in **b** *(inf: = hineinlaufen)* to pop in *(inf)*; **hi|nein+ste|cken** VT *sep (in +acc* -to) to put in; *Nadel etc auch* to stick in; **den Kopf zum Fenster** ~ to put *or* stick one's head in at *or* in through the window; **Geld/Arbeit** *etc* **in etw** *(acc)* ~ to put money/some work *etc* into sth; **viel Mühe in etw** *(acc)* ~ to put a lot of effort into sth; **hi|nein+stei|gern** VR *sep* to get into a state, to work oneself up into a state, to get worked up; **sich in seine Wut/Hysterie/seinen Ärger** ~ to work oneself up into a rage/hysterics/a temper; **sich in seinen Kummer** ~ to let oneself be completely taken up with one's worries; **sich in seinen Schmerz** ~ to let the pain take one over completely; **sie hat sich in die Vorstellung hineingesteigert, dass ...** she has managed to convince herself that ..., she has talked herself into believing that ...; **sich in eine Rolle** ~ to become completely caught up in a role; **hi|nein+stop|fen** VT *sep* to stuff *or* cram in *(in +acc* -to); **Essen in sich** *(acc)* ~ to stuff oneself (with food) *(inf)*; **hi|nein+sto|ßen** *sep irreg* VT *Schwert etc* to thrust in *(in +acc* -to); **jdn in etw** ~ *(lit)* to push sb into sth; *(fig)* to plunge sb into sth VI *aux sein* **in eine Lücke** ~ to steer into a space; **in ein Gebiet** ~ to enter a district; **hi|nein+strö|men** VI *sep aux sein* to stream *or* flood in *(in +acc* -to); *(geh: Menschenmassen)* to pour in *(in +acc* -to); **hi|nein+stür|men** VI *sep aux sein* to storm in *(in +acc* -to), to come storming in; **hi|nein+stür|zen** *sep* VI *aux sein* to plunge in *(in +acc* -to); *(= hineineilen)* to rush in *(in +acc* -to); **zur Tür** ~ to rush in through the door VT to throw *or* hurl in *(in +acc* -to); **jdn ins Elend** ~ to plunge sb into misery VR *(in +acc* -to) to throw *or* hurl oneself in, to plunge in; **sich in die Arbeit** ~ to throw oneself into one's work; **sich ins Vergnügen** ~ to plunge in and start enjoying oneself, to let it all hang out *(inf)*; **hi|nein+tap|pen** VI *sep aux sein (fig inf)* to walk right into it *(inf)*; **in eine Falle** ~ to walk into a trap; **hi|nein+tra|gen** VT *sep irreg (in +acc* -to) to carry in; *(fig)* to bring in; **hi|nein+trei|ben** VT *sep irreg* to drive in *(in +acc* -to); **jdn in etw** *(acc)* ~ *(fig)* to force sb into sth; **hi|nein+tun** VT *sep irreg* to put in *(in +acc* -to); **einen Blick in etw** *(acc)* ~ to take a look in sth; *(ins Buch etc)* to take a look at sth; **hi|nein+ver|set|zen** *ptp* **hineinversetzt** VR *sep* **sich in jdn** *or* **in jds Lage** ~ to put oneself in sb's position; **sich in etw** *(acc)* **hineinversetzt fühlen** to imagine oneself in sth; **sich in eine Rolle** ~ to empathize with a part; **hi|nein+wach|sen** VI *sep irreg aux sein* **in etw** *(acc)* ~ *(lit, fig)* to grow into sth; **hi|nein+wa|gen** VR *sep* to venture in *(in +acc* -to); **hi|nein+we|hen** VI *sep* **in etw** *(acc)* ~ *(Wind, fig)* to blow into sth; *Brise* to waft into sth; **hi|nein+wer|fen** VT *sep irreg (in +acc* -to) to throw in; *Truppen* to send in; **den Ball durchs Fenster** ~ to throw the ball in through the window; **hi|nein+wol|len** VI *sep (inf)* to want to go *or* get in *(in +acc* -to); **das will mir nicht in den Kopf hinein** I just can't understand it; **hi|nein+zer|ren** VT *sep (lit, fig)* to drag in *(in +acc* -to); **hi|nein+zie|hen** *sep irreg* VT to pull *or* drag in *(in +acc* -to); **jdn in eine Angelegenheit/einen Streit** ~ to drag sb into an affair/a quarrel VI *aux sein (in +acc* -to) to go in; *(in ein Haus)* to move in; **hi|nein+zwän|gen** *sep (in +acc* -to) VT to force *or* squeeze in VR to squeeze (oneself) in; **hi|nein+zwin|gen** VT *sep irreg* to force in *(in +acc* -to)

hin-: **hin+fah|ren** *sep irreg* VI *aux sein* to go there; *(mit Fahrzeug auch)* to drive there; *(mit Schiff auch)* to sail there; **mit der Hand über etw** *(acc)* ~ *(fig)* to run one's hand over sth; **fahre hin!** *(old, poet)* farewell! *(old)*, fare-thee-well! *(old, poet)* VT to drive *or* take there; **Hin|fahrt** F journey there; *(Naut)* voyage out; *(Rail)* outward journey; **auf der** ~ on the journey *or* way there *etc*; **hin+fal|len** VI *sep irreg aux sein* to fall (down)

hin|fäl|lig ADJ **a** *Mensch* frail **b** *(fig: = ungültig)* invalid; *Argument* untenable, invalid; **etw ~ machen** to render sth invalid, to invalidate sth

Hin|fäl|lig|keit F, *no pl* frailness; *(von Argument)* invalidity

hin-: **hin+fin|den** VIR *sep irreg (inf)* to find one's way there; **hin+flä|zen**, **hin+fle|geln** VR *sep (inf)* to loll about *(Brit) or* around; **hin+flie|gen** VI *sep irreg aux sein* to fly there; *(inf: = hinfallen)* to come a cropper *(Brit inf)*, to fall flat on one's face *(inf)*; **der Ball flog über die Köpfe hin** the ball flew over their heads; **Hin|flug** M outward flight; **hin|füh|ren** *sep* VT to lead there; **jdn zu etw** ~ *(fig)* to lead sb to sth VI to lead *or* go there; **zu/zwischen etw** *(dat)* ~ to lead to/between sth; **wo soll das ~?** *(fig)* where is this leading to?

hin|fort [hɪnˈfɔrt] ADV *(old)* henceforth *(old)*

hing *pret von* **hängen**

Hin|ga|be F, *no pl (fig) (= Begeisterung)* dedication; *(= Selbstlosigkeit)* devotion; *(= völliges Aufgehen)* (self-)abandon; **mit ~ tanzen/singen** *etc* to dance/sing *etc* with abandon; **unter ~ seines Lebens** *(geh)* by laying down one's life

hin|ga|be|fä|hig ADJ *(= begeisterungsfähig)* capable of dedication; *(= selbstlos)* capable of devotion

Hin|gang M, *no pl (old, form)* decease, demise *(form)*

hin+ge|ben *sep irreg* VT to give up; *Ruf, Zeit, Geld auch* to sacrifice; *Leben* to lay down, to sacrifice VR **a** **sich einer Sache** *(dat)* ~ *(der Arbeit)* to devote *or* dedicate oneself to sth; *dem Laster, Genuss, der Verzweiflung* to abandon oneself to sth; **sich Hoffnungen** ~ to cherish hopes; **sich einer Illusion** ~ to labour *(Brit) or* labor *(US)* under an illusion **b** **sie gab sich ihm hin** she gave herself *or* surrendered to him; **sich Gott** ~ to give oneself to God

hin|ge|bend ADJ devoted

Hin|ge|bung [ˈhɪnge:bʊŋ] F -, *no pl* = **Hingabe**

hin|ge|bungs|voll ADJ *(= selbstlos)* devoted; *(= begeistert)* abandoned ADV *(= selbstlos)* devotedly; *(= begeistert)* with abandon; *lauschen* raptly

hin|ge|gen [hɪnˈge:gn] CONJ *(geh)* however; *(= andererseits auch)* on the other hand

hin-: **hin|ge|gos|sen** [ˈhɪngəgɔsn] ADJ *(fig inf)* **sie lag/saß wie ~ auf dem Bett** she had draped herself artistically on the bed; **hin+ge|hen** VI *sep irreg aux sein* **a** *(= dorthin gehen)* to go (there); **gehst du auch hin?** are you going too?; **wo gehst du hin?** where are you going?; **wo geht es hier hin?** where does this go? **b** *(Zeit)* to pass, to go by **c** *(fig: = tragbar sein)* **das geht gerade noch hin** that will just about do *or* pass; **diesmal mag es noch ~** I'll let it go *or* pass this once; **(jdm) etw ~ lassen** to let sth pass, to let sb get away with sth; **hin+ge|hö|ren** *ptp* **hingehört** VI *sep* to belong; **wo gehört das hin?** where does this belong *or* go?; **wo gehören die Gabeln hin?** where do the forks live *(Brit inf) or* belong?; **hin+ge|lan|gen** *ptp* **hingelangt** VI *sep aux sein (geh)* to get there; **hin+ge|ra|ten** *ptp* **hingeraten** VI *sep irreg aux sein* **irgendwo** ~ to get somewhere; **wo bin ich denn hier ~?** *(inf)* what kind of place is this then?; **hin|ge|ris|sen** ADJ enraptured, enchanted; **hin- und hergerissen sein** to be torn *(zwischen* between); **ich bin ganz hin- und hergerissen** *(iro)* absolutely great *or* fantastic! *(iro)* ADV with rapt attention; **~ lauschen** to listen with rapt attention → *auch* **hinreißen**; **Hin|ge|schie|de|ne(r)** MF *decl as adj (geh euph)* **der/die** ~ the deceased *auch pl*, the departed *auch pl*; **hin+glei|ten** VI *sep irreg aux sein* to glide; *(geh: Zeit)* to slip away; **Hin|gu|cker** M *(inf) (= Mensch)* looker *(inf)*; *(= Sache)* eye-catcher *(inf)*; **hin+ha|ben** VT *sep irreg (inf)* **wo willst du dies ~?** where do you want this (to go)?; **hin+hal|ten** VT *sep irreg* **a** *(= entgegenstrecken)* to hold out *(jdm* to sb) **b** *(fig)* *jdn* to put off, to stall; *(Mil)* to stave off

Hin|hal|te-: **Hin|hal|te|po|li|tik** F stalling *or* delaying policy; **Hin|hal|te|tak|tik** F stalling *or* delaying tactics *pl*

hin-: **hin+hän|gen** *sep irreg (inf)* VT **a** *(= aufhängen)* to hang up **b** *(fig inf: = melden, verpetzen, verleumden)* **jdn (bei jdm)** ~ to blacken somebody's name (with sb); **hin+hau|en** *sep irreg (inf)* VT **a** *(= nachlässig machen)* to knock off *(inf)* **b** *(= hinwerfen)* to slam *or* plonk *(inf) or* bang down; *(fig: = aufgeben) Arbeit, Studium, Ausbildung* to chuck in *(inf)* VI **a** *(= zuschlagen)* to hit hard; **(mit der Faust)** ~ to thump *or* clobber *(inf)* it/sth (with one's fist) **b** *(= gut gehen)* **es hat hingehauen** I/we *etc* just managed it; **das wird schon ~** it will be OK *(inf) or* all right **c** *(= klappen, in Ordnung sein)* to work; **ich habe das so lange geübt, bis es hinhaute** I practised *(Brit) or* practiced *(US)* it till I could do it VR *(inf: = sich schlafen legen)* to crash out *(inf)* VT *impers* **es hat ihn hingehauen** he fell over; **hin+ho|cken** VR *sep* to squat (down); **hock dich hin!** *(inf)* plonk yourself down; **hin+hö|ren** VI *sep* to listen; **hin+kau|ern** VR *sep* to cower (down)

Hin|ke|bein [ˈhɪŋkəbain] NT, **Hin|ke|fuß** [ˈhɪŋkəfu:s] M *(inf: = verletztes Bein)* gammy leg *(inf)*

Hin|kel|stein [ˈhɪŋkl-] M *(inf)* menhir

hin|ken [ˈhɪŋkn] VI **a** *(= gehbehindert sein)* to limp, to walk with a limp; **mit** *or* **auf dem rechten Bein** ~ to have a limp in one's right leg **b** *aux sein (= sich fortbewegen)* to limp **c** *(fig) (Beispiel)* to be inappropriate; *(Vergleich)* to be misleading; *(Vers, Reim)* to be clumsy

hin-: **hin+klot|zen** VT *sep (inf) Hochhäuser etc* to throw up; **hin+knal|len** *sep (inf)* VT to slam *or* bang down VI *aux sein* to fall flat; **hin+knien** VIR *sep (vi: aux sein)* to kneel (down); **hin+kom|men** VI *sep irreg aux sein* **a** *(= an ei-*

nen Ort hinkommen) **(da)** ~ to get there; **nach X** ~ to get to X; **kommst du mit hin?** are you coming too?; **wie komme ich zu dir hin?** how do I get to your place?; **könnt ihr alle zu ihm ~?** can you all go to his place? **b** *(= an bestimmten Platz gehören)* to go; **wo ist das Buch hingekommen?** where has the book got to *(Brit)* or gone?; **wo kämen wir denn hin, wenn ...** *(inf)* where would we be if ...; **wo kämen wir denn da hin?** *(inf)* where would we be then? **c** *(inf: = in Ordnung kommen)* **das kommt schon noch hin** that will turn out OK *(inf)* **d** *(inf: = auskommen)* to manage; **wir kommen (damit) hin** we will manage **e** *(inf: = ausreichen, stimmen)* to be right; **hin+krie|gen** VT *sep (inf)* **a** *(= fertigbringen)* to do, to manage; **wie er es nur immer hinkriegt, dass die anderen alles für ihn machen** I don't know how he manages to get the others to do everything for him; **das hast du gut hingekriegt** you've made a nice job of it; **wie kriegt sie das bloß immer hin?** I don't know how she does it **b** *(= in Ordnung bringen)* to mend, to fix; *(gesundheitlich)* to cure; **hin+krit|zeln** VT *sep* to scribble down; **hastig hingekritzelte Zeilen** hastily scribbled lines

Hin|kunft F *(Aus)* **in ~** in (the) future

hin|künf|tig *(Aus)* ADJ future ADV in (the) future

hin+lan|gen VI *sep (inf)* **a** *(= zupacken)* to grab him/her/it *etc*; *(= ziehen/schieben)* to pull/push hard; *(dial: = anfassen)* to touch; *(= zuschlagen)* to take a (good) swipe *(inf)*; *(= foulen)* to play rough → **Gras b** *(= sich bedienen)* to help oneself to a lot; *(= viel Geld verlangen)* to overcharge **c** *(= ausreichen)* to do; *(Geld)* to stretch; **mein Geld langt dafür nicht hin** my money won't stretch to that *(esp Brit)* or that far **d** *(= auskommen)* to manage

hin|läng|lich [ˈhɪnlɛŋlɪç] ADJ *(= ausreichend)* adequate; **keine ~e Anzahl** an insufficient number ADV *(= ausreichend)* adequately; *(= zu Genüge)* sufficiently; **~ bekannt sein** to be common knowledge

hin+las|sen VT *sep irreg* **jdn (da) ~** to let sb go (there)

hin+lau|fen VI *sep irreg aux sein* **a** *(= zu bestimmter Stelle laufen)* to run there; *(= vorbei-, entlang-, dahinlaufen)* to run; *(inf: zu Veranstaltung, Amt, Rechtsanwalt etc)* to rush **b** *(dial inf: = nicht fahren)* to walk **c** *(= verlaufen: mit Ortsangabe, in bestimmte Richtung)* to run

hin+le|gen *sep* VT **a** *(= hintun)* to put down; *Zettel* to leave *(jdm* for sb); *(= flach legen) Verletzten etc* to lay down; *(ins Bett, zum Schlafen)* to put to bed; *(inf: = bezahlen müssen)* to fork out *(inf)* **b** *(inf: = glänzend darbieten)* to perform; *Rede, Vortrag* to give effortlessly and brilliantly; **er hat einen tollen Stepptanz hingelegt** he did a neat bit of tap-dancing VR to lie down; **~!** *(Mil)* down!; **sich lang ~, sich der Länge nach ~** *(inf)* to fall flat; **da legst du dich (lang) hin!** *(inf)* it's unbelievable

hin+len|ken VT *sep* **etw auf etw** *(acc)* **~** *(Fahrzeug, Pferd)* to steer sth toward(s) sth; *Fluss, Wasser, Blicke, jds Aufmerksamkeit* to direct sth to sth; *Schritte, Gespräch* to turn sth to sth

hin+lüm|meln VR *sep (inf)* to loll or lounge about *(Brit)* or around *(auf +acc* on)

hin+ma|chen *sep* VT *(inf)* **a** *(= anbringen)* to put on; *Bild* to put up **b** *(= kaputt machen)* to wreck, to ruin VI **a** *(inf: = Notdurft verrichten)* to do one's/its *etc* business *(euph)* **b** *(dial: = sich beeilen)* to get a move on *(inf)* **c** *aux sein (dial inf: = an bestimmten Ort gehen)* to go there

Hin-: **Hin|marsch** M way or *(Mil)* march there; **hin+mor|den** VT *sep (geh)* to massacre; **hin+müs|sen** VI *sep irreg* to have to go; **Hin|nah|me** [ˈhɪnnaːmə] F -, *no pl* acceptance; **hin+neh|men** VT *sep irreg* **a** *(= ertragen)* to take, to accept; *Beleidigung* to swallow; **etw als selbstverständlich ~** to take sth for granted **b** *(inf: = mitnehmen)* to take; **hin+nei|gen** *sep* VT *Kopf, Körper* to incline VR *(zu* towards) *(Mensch)* to lean; *(fig)* to incline, to have leanings; *(Zweige, Baum)* to lean; *(Landschaft)* to incline VI *(fig)* **zu etw ~** to incline toward(s) sth; *zu Vorbild* to tend to follow sth

hin|nen [ˈhɪnən] ADV *(old, liter)* **von ~** hence; **von ~ gehen** or **scheiden** *(fig)* to depart (from) this life *(form)*, to pass on

Hin-: **hin+pas|sen** VI *sep (= Platz haben)* to fit (in); *(= gut aussehen)* to go (well); *(Mensch: = am Platz sein)* to fit in; **hin+pfef|fern** VT *sep (inf) Gegenstand* to bang or slam down *(inf)*; *(fig) Antwort, Kritik (mündlich)* to rap out; *(schriftlich)* to scribble down; **hin+pfu|schen** VT *sep (inf)* to dash off; **hin+plap|pern** VT *sep* to say; *Unsinn* to talk; **das hat sie nur so hingeplappert** she said that without thinking; **hin+plump|sen** VI *sep aux sein (inf)* to fall down (with a thud); **etw ~ lassen** to dump or plump *(inf)* sth down; **sich ~ lassen** to plump oneself down *(inf)*, to flop down; **hin+raf|fen** VT *sep (liter)* to carry off; **hin+rei|chen** *sep* VT **jdm etw ~** to hand or pass sb sth or sth to sb; *Hand* to hold out sth to sb VI **a** *(= ausreichen)* to be enough, to suffice *(form)* **b** *(= sich erstrecken)* **bis zu etw ~** to stretch to sth; **hin|rei|chend** ADJ *(= ausreichend)* adequate; *(= genug)* sufficient; *(= reichlich)* ample; **keine ~en Beweise** insufficient evidence; **gegen ihn besteht ~er Tatverdacht** there is sufficient suspicion against him ADV *lange, oft* enough; *aufklären, informieren* adequately; **es ist noch ~ Zeit** there is ample time; **hin+rei|ben** VT *sep (S Ger inf)* **jdm etw ~** to rub sb's nose in sth; **Hin|rei|se** F journey there or out, outward journey; *(mit Schiff)* voyage out, outward voyage; **Hin- und Rückreise** journey there and back; **die ~ nach London** the journey to London; **auf der ~** on the way there; **hin+rei|ßen** VT *sep irreg (fig)* **a** *(= begeistern)* to thrill, to enrapture → *auch* **hingerissen b** *(= überwältigen)* **jdn zu etw ~** to force sb into sth; **die Zuschauer zu Beifallsstürmen ~** to elicit thunderous applause from the audience; **sich ~ lassen** to let oneself be or get carried away; **sich zu einer Entscheidung ~ lassen** to let oneself be carried away into making a decision; **hin|rei|ßend** ADJ fantastic; *Landschaft, Anblick* enchanting; *Schönheit, Mensch* captivating; *Redner* thrilling, fantastic ADV **~ (schön) aussehen** to look quite enchanting; **~ (schön) Klavier spielen** to play the piano quite enchantingly or delightfully; **~ tanzen** to dance enchantingly or delightfully; **hin+ren|nen** VI *sep irreg aux sein* = **hinlaufen a**; **hin+rich|ten** VT *sep* to execute; **jdn durch den Strang ~** to hang sb; **jdn durch den elektrischen Stuhl ~** to execute sb on the electric chair

Hin|rich|tung F execution

Hin|rich|tungs-: **Hin|rich|tungs|kom|man|do** NT execution or *(bei Erschießen)* firing squad; **Hin|rich|tungs|stät|te** F place of execution

Hin-: **hin+rot|zen** VT *sep (inf)* to spew out *(inf)*; **hin+rü|cken** VT *sep Gegenstand* to push over; **Hin|run|de** F *(Sport)* first half of the season; *(= Hinspiel)* ≈ corresponding match *(Brit)* or game *(US)* in the first half of the season; **hin+sa|gen** VT *sep* to say without thinking; **hin+schaf|fen** VT *sep* to get there; **hin+schau|en** VI *sep (dial)* = **hinsehen**; **hin+schei|ßen** VI *sep irreg (vulg)* to crap *(sl)*; **hin+schi|cken** VT *sep* to send; **hin+schie|ben** VT *sep irreg* to push over; **hin+schei|den** VI *sep irreg aux sein (liter)* to pass away, to depart (from) this life *(form)*; **der Hingeschiedene** the deceased, the (dear *(Brit)* or dearly) departed; **Hin|schei|den** NT **-s**, *no pl (liter)* demise; **Hin|schied** [ˈhɪnʃiːt] M **-(e)s** [-dəs], *no pl (Sw liter)* demise; **hin+schie|len** VI *sep* to glance *(zu* at); **hin+schlach|ten** VT *sep* to slaughter, to butcher; **hin+schla|gen** VI *sep irreg* **a** *(= dageschlagen)* to strike, to hit **b** *aux sein (= hinfallen)* to fall over; **der Länge nach** or **längelang** or **lang ~** *(inf)* to fall flat (on one's face); **hin+schlei|chen** VIR *sep irreg (vi: aux sein)* to creep or steal or sneak up; **hin+schlep|pen** *sep* VT to carry, to lug *(inf)*; *(inf: = mitnehmen)* to drag along VR *(Mensch)* to drag oneself along; *(fig)* to drag on; **hin+schlu|dern** VT *sep (inf) Arbeit* to dash off; **hin+schmei|ßen** VT *sep irreg (inf) (= hinwerfen)* to fling or chuck down *(inf)*; *(fig: = aufgeben) Arbeit etc* to chuck or pack in *(inf)*; **hin+schmel|zen** VI *sep irreg aux sein (hum, inf) (Mensch)* to swoon; *(Wut)* to melt away; **hin+schmie|ren** VT *sep (inf) Schmutz* to spread, to smear; *(pej) (= malen)* to daub; *(= flüchtig schreiben)* to scribble; **hin+schrei|ben** *sep irreg* VT to write; *(= flüchtig niederschreiben)* to scribble down *(inf)*; *Aufsatz* to dash off VI *(inf)* to write (there); **hin+schwin|den** VI *sep irreg aux sein* = **dahinschwinden**; **hin+se|hen** VI *sep irreg* to look; **ich kann (gar) nicht ~** I can't bear to look; **ohne hinzusehen** without looking; **bei genauerem Hinsehen** on looking more carefully; **vor sich ~** to look or stare straight ahead

hin sein VI *irreg aux sein (inf)* **a** *(= kaputt sein)* to have had it; **hin ist hin** what's done is done **b** *(= erschöpft sein)* to be shattered *(Brit inf)* or exhausted **c** *(= verloren sein)* to be lost; *(Ruhe)* to have disappeared; *(= ruiniert sein)* to be in ruins **d** *(= tot sein)* to have kicked the bucket *(inf)* **e** *(= begeistert sein)* **(von etw) hin (und weg) sein** to be mad about sth **f bis dahin ist es noch lange hin** it's a long time till then

hin+set|zen *sep* VT to put or set down; *jdn* to seat, to put; *Kind* to sit down VR **a** *(lit)* to sit down; **sich gerade ~** to sit up straight **b** *(inf: = sich bemühen)* to buckle down to it, to set to

Hin|sicht ✪ 32.3 F, *no pl* **in dieser ~** in this respect or regard; **in mancher** or **gewisser ~** in some or many respects or ways; **in jeder ~** in every respect; **in finanzieller ~** financially; **in wirtschaftlicher ~** economically; **in beruflicher ~** with regard to my/his *etc* job; **in ~ auf** *(+acc) (= bezüglich)* with regard to; *(= in Anbetracht)* in view of

hin|sicht|lich [ˈhɪnzɪçtlɪç] PREP *+gen (= bezüglich)* with regard to; *(= in Anbetracht)* in view of

hin-: **hin+sie|chen** VI *sep aux sein (geh)* = **dahinsiechen**; **hin+sin|ken** VI *sep irreg aux sein (geh)* to sink (down); *(= ohnmächtig werden)* to faint, to swoon; *(tot)* to drop down dead; **hin+sol|len** VI *sep (inf)* **wo soll ich/das Buch hin?** where do I/does the book go?; **wo soll ich mit dem Brief hin?** what should I do with this letter?; **eigentlich sollte ich ja zu der Party hin** I really ought to go to the party; **Hin|spiel** NT *(Sport)* first leg; **hin+star|ren** VI *sep* to stare; **hin+stel|len** *sep* VT **a** *(= niederstellen)* to put down; *(an bestimmte Stelle)* to put; *(inf) Gebäude* to put up; *(= abstellen) Fahrzeug* to put, to park; **er tut seine Pflicht, wo man ihn auch hinstellt** he does his duty wherever he is **b** *(= auslegen) Vorfall, Angelegenheit, Sachlage* to describe; **jdn/etw als jdn/etw ~** *(= bezeichnen)* to make sb/sth out to be sb/sth VR to stand; *(Fahrer)* to park; **sich gerade ~** to stand up straight; **sich vor jdn** or **jdm ~** to stand in front of sb; **sie hat sich vor mich/ihn hingestellt** she came and stood in front of me/went and stood in front of him; **sich als etw ~** *(fig)* to make oneself out to be sth; **hin+steu|ern** *sep* VI **a** *aux sein* to steer; **wo steuert sie hin?** where is she going? **b** *(fig)* **in der Diskussion auf etw** *(acc)* **~** to steer the discussion toward(s) sth; **auf ein Ziel ~** *(fig)* to aim at a goal VT to steer; **hin+stre|cken** *sep* VT **a** *Hand, Gegenstand* to hold out **b** *(liter) jdn* to fell VR to stretch (oneself) out, to lie down; **hin+strö|men** VI *sep aux sein (Fluss, Wasser)* to flow; *(geh: Menschen)* to flock there; **sie strömten zur Ausstellung hin** they flocked to the exhibition; **hin+stür|zen** VI *sep aux sein* **a** *(= hinfallen)* to fall down heavily **b** *(= hineilen)* **zu jdm/etw ~** to rush or dash toward(s) sb/sth

Hint|an-: **hint|an+set|zen** [hɪnt'lan-] VT *sep (= zurückstellen)* to put last; *(= vernachlässigen)* to neglect; **Hint|an|set|zung** [hɪnt'lanzɛtsʊŋ] F -, *no pl* disregard; *(= Vernachlässigung)* neglect; **unter ~ einer Sache** *(gen) (form)* regardless of sth, without regard for sth; **hint|an+stel|len** [hɪnt-'lan-] VT *sep (= zurückstellen)* to put last; *(= vernachlässigen)* to neglect

hin|ten ['hɪntn] ADV **a** behind; **von ~** from the back; *(bei Menschen auch)* from behind; **nach ~** to the back; **von weit ~** from the very back; **~ im Buch/in der Schlange** at the back of the book/queue *(Brit) or* line *(US)*; **~ auf der Liste** at the end of the list; **sich ~ anstellen** to join the end of the queue *(Brit) or* line *(US)*; **~ im Bild** in the back of the picture; **nach ~ abgehen** *(Theat)* to exit at the back of the stage; **nach ~ laufen** to run to the back; **von ~ anfangen** to begin from the end; **das Alphabet von ~ aufsagen** to say the alphabet backwards; **etw ~ anfügen** to add sth at the end; **~ bleiben** *(lit)* to stay behind, to stay at the back; *(fig)* to lag behind
b *(= am rückwärtigen Ende)* at the back; *(Naut)* aft; *(= am Gesäß)* on one's behind; **von ~** from behind; *jdn erkennen auch* from the back; **~ im Auto/Bus** in the back of the car/bus; **der Blinker ~** the rear indicator *(esp Brit) or* blinker *(US)*; **~ und vorn nichts haben** *(inf)* to be as flat as a pancake *(esp Brit inf) or* board *(US inf)*; **nach ~** to the back; *fallen, ziehen* backwards; **jdn am liebsten von ~ sehen** *(inf)* to be glad to see the back of sb; **nach ~ ausschlagen** *(Pferd)* to kick out → **Auge**
c *(= auf der Rückseite)* at the back; *(von Gebäude)* at the back *or* rear; **das Buch ist ~ schmutzig** the back (cover) of the book is dirty; **~ auf der Medaille** on the back *or* the reverse side of the medal; **ein nach ~ gelegenes Zimmer** a room facing the back; **ein Blick nach ~** a look behind; **etw von ~ und vorn betrachten** *(fig)* to consider sth from all angles
d *(= weit entfernt)* **das Auto da ~** the car back there; **sie waren ziemlich weit ~** they were quite far back; **~ im Walde** deep in the forest; **~ in der Mongolei** far away in Mongolia
e *(fig)* **~ und vorn** *(betrügen)* left, right and centre *(Brit) or* center *(US)*; *bedienen* hand and foot; *verwöhnen* rotten *(inf)*; *egal sein* absolutely, utterly; **das stimmt ~ und vorn nicht, das stimmt weder ~ noch vorn** that is absolutely untrue; **das reicht** *or* **langt ~ und vorn nicht** *or* **weder ~ noch vorn** that's nowhere near enough; **dann heißt es Frau Schmidt ~ und Frau Schmidt vorn** then it's Mrs Schmidt this and Mrs Schmidt that; **ich weiß nicht mehr, wo ~ und vorn ist** I don't know whether I'm coming or going

hin|ten-: **hin|ten|dran** ['hɪntn'dran] ADV *(inf) (= am hinteren Ende)* at the back; *(fig: = im Hintertreffen)* behind; **hin|ten|drauf** ['hɪntn'drauf] ADV *(inf)* on the back; *(von LKW)* in the back; *(= auf Gesäß)* on one's behind; **hin|ten|drein** ['hɪntn'drain] ADV = **hinterher**; **hin|ten|he|rum** ['hɪntnhɛ'rʊm] ADV **a** *(= von der hinteren Seite)* from the back; **kommen Sie ~** come (a)round the back **b** *(fig inf) (= auf Umwegen)* in a roundabout way; *(= illegal)* under the counter; **er hat mir ~ erzählt, dass sie ...** he told me behind her back that she ...; **hin|ten|nach** ['hɪntn'na:x] ADV *(Aus, S Ger)* = **hinterher**; **hin|ten|rum** ['hɪntn'rʊm] ADV *(inf)* = **hintenherum**; **hin|ten|über** ['hɪntn'ly:bɐ] ADV backwards; **er fiel/kippte ~** he fell over backwards; **hin|ten|über|kip|pen** VI *sep aux sein* to topple *or* fall over backwards

hin|ter ['hɪntɐ] PREP *+dat or (mit Bewegungsverben) +acc* **a** *(räumlich)* behind; **~ dem Haus** behind the house, at the back *or* rear of the house; **~ jdm/etw her** behind sb/sth; **~ etw** *(acc)* **kommen** *(fig: = herausfinden)* to get to the bottom of sth; **~ die Wahrheit kommen** to get to the truth; **sich ~ jdn stellen** *(lit)* to stand behind sb; *(fig)* to support sb, to get behind sb; **~ jdm/etw stehen** *(lit, fig)* to be behind sb/sth; **jdn ~ sich** *(dat)* **haben** *(lit, fig)* to have sb behind one; **~ dem Hügel/der Tür hervor** (out) from behind the hill/door; **jdn weit ~ sich** *(dat)* **lassen** to leave sb far behind; *(im Rennen auch)* to outdistance sb; **~ etw** *(dat)* **stecken, sich ~ etw** *(dat)* **verbergen** to be *or* lie behind sth; **~ seinen Reden steckt nicht viel** there's not much in his speeches
b *+dat (= nach)* after; **vier Kilometer ~ Glasgow/~ der Grenze** four kilometres *(Brit) or* kilometers *(US)* outside Glasgow/beyond the border; **~ diesem Satz steht ein Fragezeichen** there is a question mark at the end of this sentence; **er ist ~ mir dran** it's his turn after me
c *+dat (in Rangfolge)* after; *(in Bedeutung)* behind; **an Talent nicht ~ jdm zurückstehen** to be just as talented as sb; **sie stand nicht ~ ihm zurück** she did not lag behind him; **ich stelle das Privatleben ~ der Arbeit zurück** I put my work before my private life
d **etw ~ sich** *(dat)* **haben** *(= zurückgelegt haben)* to have got through sth; *Strecke* to have covered sth; *Land* to have left sth; *(= überstanden haben)* to have got sth over (and done) with; *Krankheit, Zeit* to have been through sth; *anstrengende Tage* to have had sth; *Studium* to have completed *or* finished sth; **sie hat viel ~ sich** she has been through a lot; **das Schlimmste haben wir ~ uns** we're past the worst, we are over the worst; **etw ~ sich** *(acc)* **bringen** to get sth over (and done) with; *Strecke* to cover sth; *Arbeit* to get sth done; **das liegt ~ ihr** that is behind her; **sich ~ etw** *(acc)* **machen** to get down to sth → **her sein c**
e *(inf)* = **dahinter**

Hin|ter-: **Hin|ter|achs|an|trieb** M *(Mot)* rear wheel drive; **Hin|ter|ach|se** F rear *or* back axle; **Hin|ter|an|sicht** F rear *or* back view; **Hin|ter|aus|gang** M back *or* rear exit; **Hin|ter|ba|cke** F *usu pl* buttock; *(von Tier)* hindquarter; **sich auf die ~n setzen** *(fig inf)* to get down to it; **Hin|ter|bänk|ler** [-bɛŋklɐ] M **-s, -**, **Hin|ter|bänk|le|rin** [-ərɪn] F **-, -nen** *(Pol pej)* backbencher; **Hin|ter|bein** NT hind leg; **sich auf die ~e stellen** *or* **setzen** *(lit)* to rear up (on one's hind legs); *(fig inf) (= sich widersetzen)* to kick up a fuss *(inf)*; *(= sich anstrengen)* to pull one's socks up *(inf)*

Hin|ter|blie|be|nen-: **Hin|ter|blie|be|nen|für|sor|ge** F *welfare service for surviving dependents*; **Hin|ter|blie|be|nen|ren|te** F surviving dependents' pension

Hin|ter|blie|be|ne(r) [hɪntɐ'bli:b(ə)nə] MF *decl as adj* surviving dependent; **die ~n** the bereaved family

hin|ter-: **hin|ter|brin|gen** *ptp* **hinterbracht** VT *insep irreg* **jdm etw ~** to mention sth to sb; **Hin|ter|deck** NT *(Naut)* afterdeck; **hin|ter|drein** [hɪntɐ'drain] ADV = **hinterher**

hin|te|re ADJ = **hintere(r, s)**

hin|ter|ei|nan|der [hɪntɐlai'nandɐ] ADV *(räumlich)* one behind the other, behind each other; *(= in einer Reihe nebeneinander)* next to one another; *(= in Reihenfolge, nicht gleichzeitig, ohne Unterbrechung)* one after the other; **~ hereinkommen** to come in one by one, to come in one at a time; **dicht ~** *(räumlich)* close behind one another; *(zeitlich)* close on one another; **zwei Tage ~** two days running; **dreimal ~** three times in a row; **es hat monatelang ~ geregnet** it has rained for months on end; **etw ~ tun** *(= nicht gleichzeitig)* to do sth one after the other; *(= der Reihe nach)* to do sth in turn; *(= ohne Unterbrechung)* to do sth in one go

hin|ter|ei|nan|der-: **hin|ter|ei|nan|der+fah|ren** *sep irreg aux sein*, **hin|ter|ei|nan|der fah|ren** △ *irreg aux sein* VI *(mit Auto/Fahrrad)* to drive/ride one behind the other; **hin|ter|ei|nan|der+ge|hen** *sep irreg aux sein*, **hin|ter|ei|nan|der ge|hen** △ *irreg aux sein* VI to walk one behind the other; **hin|ter|ei|nan|der|her** ADV behind one another; **hin|ter|ei|nan|der+schal|ten** *sep*, **hin|ter|ei|nan|der schal|ten** △ VT *(Elec)* to connect in series; **Hin|ter|ei|nan|der|schal|tung** F *(Elec)* series connection; **hin|ter|ei|nan|der+ste|hen** *sep irreg (S Ger, Austr, Sw: aux sein)*, **hin|ter|ei|nan|der ste|hen** △ *irreg (S Ger, Austr, Sw: aux sein)* VI to stand one behind the other; **hin|ter|ei|nan|der|weg** [hɪntɐlainandɐ'vɛk] ADV *(zeitlich)* running, in a row; *(= nacheinander)* one after the other

Hin|ter|ein|gang M rear entrance

Hin|te|re(r) ['hɪntərə] MF *decl as adj* person/man/woman *etc* at the back

hin|te|re(r, s) ['hɪntərə] ADJ back; *(von Tier, Gebäude, Zug auch)* rear; **der/die/das Hintere** the one at the back; **das ~ Ende des Saals** the back *or* rear of the room; **die Hinteren** those at the back, those behind; **am ~n Ende** at the far end → **hinterste(r, s)**

Hin|ter-: **hin|ter|fot|zig** ['hɪntɐfɔtsɪç] ADJ *(dial inf)* underhand(ed); **Hin|ter|fot|zig|keit** F **-, -en** *(dial inf)* underhandedness; *(= Bemerkung)* underhand(ed) remark; **hin|ter|fra|gen** *ptp* **hinterfragt** VT *insep* to question; **etw kritisch ~** to examine sth critically; **Hin|ter|fuß** M hind foot; **Hin|ter|gau|men|laut** M velar (sound); **Hin|ter|ge|bäu|de** NT = **Hinterhaus**; **Hin|ter|ge|dan|ke** M ulterior motive; **ohne ~n** without any ulterior motive(s); **hin|ter|ge|hen** *ptp* **hintergangen** VT *insep irreg (= betrügen)* to deceive; *Ehepartner etc auch* to be unfaithful to; *(= umgehen) Verordnung, Gesetze, Prinzip* to circumvent; **hin|ter+ge|hen** VI *sep irreg aux sein (dial inf)* to go to the back *or* rear *(in +acc* of); **Hin|ter|ge|stell** NT *(hum inf) (= Beine)* hind legs *pl (inf)*, pins *pl (inf)*; *(= Po)* rump *(inf)*, backside *(inf)*; **Hin|ter|glas|ma|le|rei** F *(= Bild)* verre églomisé picture; *(= Technik)* verre églomisé technique

Hin|ter|grund M *(von Bild, Raum)* background; *(von Bühne, Saal)* back; (*Theat*: *= Kulisse*) backdrop, backcloth; (*fig*: *= verborgene Zusammenhänge*) background *no pl* (*+gen* to); **im ~** in the background; **im ~ der Bühne** at the back of the stage; **vor dem ~** *(lit, fig)* against the background; **der musikalische/akustische ~** the background music/sounds *pl*; **im ~ bleiben/stehen** *(lit, fig)* to stay/be in the background; **in den ~ treten** *or* **rücken** *(fig)* to be pushed into the background; **jdn/etw in den ~ drängen** to push sb/sth into the background

Hin|ter|grund-: **Hin|ter|grund|be|richt** M background report; **Hin|ter|grund|ge|spräch** NT *(Pol)* briefing; **Hin|ter|grund|gra|fik** F *(Comput)* background image

hin|ter|grün|dig ['hɪntɐgrʏndɪç] ADJ cryptic, enigmatic ADV cryptically, enigmatically

Hin|ter|grün|dig|keit F **-, -en** crypticness, enigmaticness; *(= Bemerkung)* cryptic *or* enigmatic remark

Hin|ter|grund-: **Hin|ter|grund|in|for|ma|ti|on** F background information *no pl* *(über +acc* about, on); **eine ~** (a piece of *or* some) background information; **Hin|ter|grund|mu|sik** F background music; **Hin|ter|grund|pro|gramm** NT *(Comput)* background program

Hin|ter-: **hin|ter+ha|ken** VI *sep (inf)* to follow that/it *etc* up; **Hin|ter|halt** M **a** ambush; **jdn aus dem ~ überfallen** to ambush *or* waylay sb; **jdn/etw aus dem ~ angreifen** *(esp Mil)* to ambush sb/sth; *(Sport, fig)* to make a surprise attack on sb/sth; **im ~ lauern** *or* **liegen** to lie in wait *or (esp Mil)* ambush **b** *(inf)* **etw im ~ haben** to have sth in reserve; **ohne ~** unreservedly; **hin|ter|häl|tig** ['hɪntɐhɛltɪç] ADJ underhand(ed), devious; *Lächeln* devious ADV in an underhand way, deviously; **Hin|ter|häl|tig|keit** F **-, -en** underhandedness, deviousness; *(= Handlung)* underhand(ed) *or* devious act; **Hin|ter|hand** F *(von Pferd, Hund)* hindquarters *pl*; **etw in der ~ haben** (*fig*: *= in Reserve*) to have sth up one's sleeve; **Hin|ter|haupt** NT back of one's/the head; **Hin|ter|haus** NT *part of a* *tenement house accessible only through a courtyard and thus considered inferior*

hin|ter|her [hɪntɐ'heːɐ, 'hɪntɐheːɐ] ADV *(räumlich)* behind, after; *(zeitlich)* afterwards

hin|ter|her-: **hin|ter|her+fah|ren** VI *sep irreg aux sein* to drive behind *(jdm* sb); **hin|ter|her+ge|hen** VI *sep irreg aux sein* to follow *(jdm* sb); **hin|ter|her+hin|ken** VI *sep aux sein* to limp behind *(jdm* sb); *(fig)* to lag behind *(hinter etw (dat)* sth, *mit* with, in); **hin|ter|her+kom|men** VI *sep irreg aux sein* **a** *(= danach kommen) (räumlich)* to follow (behind *or* after); *(zeitlich)* to come after **b** *(= als Letzter kommen)* to bring up the rear; **hin|ter|her+lau|fen** VI *sep irreg aux sein* to run behind *(jdm* sb); **jdm ~** *(fig inf: = sich bemühen um)* to run after sb, to run (a)round after sb; **einem Mädchen ~** *(inf)* to run after a girl; **hin|ter|her+ru|fen** VI *sep irreg* **jdm (etw) ~** to call (sth) after sb; **hin|ter|her+schi|cken** VT *sep* to send on *(jdm* to sb); *jdn* to send after *(jdm* sb); **hin|ter|her sein** VI *irreg aux sein (inf) (lit: = verfolgen)* to be after *(jdm* sb); *(fig: = zurückgeblieben sein)* to lag behind; **~, dass ...** to see to it that ...

Hin|ter-: **Hin|ter|hof** M back yard; *(zwischen Vorder- und Hinterhaus)* courtyard; **Hin|ter|in|di|en** NT South-East Asia; **Hin|ter|kan|te** F rear edge; *(Aerodynamics)* trailing edge; **Hin|ter|kopf** M back of one's head; **etw im ~ haben/behalten** *(inf)* to have/keep sth in the back of one's mind; **Hin|ter|la|der** ['hɪntɐlaːdɐ] M **-s, -** breech-loader; *(inf: = Homosexueller)* fag *(pej)*;; **Hin|ter|la|ge** F *(Sw)* security; **Hin|ter|land** NT hinterland; *(Ind)* back-up area; **hin|ter|las|sen** *ptp* **hinterlassen** VT *insep irreg* to leave; *(testamentarisch auch)* to bequeath *(jdm etw* sb sth, sth to sb); **~e Werke/Schriften** posthumous works; **hin|ter+las|sen** VT *sep irreg (dial inf)* **jdn ~** to let sb go behind, to allow sb to go behind; **Hin|ter|las|sen|schaft** [hɪntɐ'lasnʃaft] F **-, -en** estate; *(literarisch, fig)* legacy; **die ~ seines Vorgängers aufarbeiten** to finish (off) somebody else's (unfinished) work; **jds ~ antreten** *(= beerben)* to inherit sb's estate; *(= jdm nachfolgen)* to follow sb; **Hin|ter|las|sung** [hɪntɐ'lasʊŋ] F **-**, *no pl (form)* **unter ~ von Schulden** leaving (unsettled *or* unpaid) debts; **hin|ter|las|tig** [-lastɪç] ADJ *(Aviat)* tail-heavy; *(Naut)* stern-heavy; **Hin|ter|lauf** M *(Hunt)* hind leg; **hin|ter|le|gen** *ptp* **hinterlegt** VT *insep* **a** *(= verwahren lassen)* to deposit **b** *(= als Pfand hinterlegen)* to leave; **Hin|ter|le|gung** [hɪntɐ'leːgʊŋ] F **-, -en** deposit

Hin|ter|le|gungs-: **Hin|ter|le|gungs|schein** M deposit receipt; **Hin|ter|le|gungs|sum|me** F sum deposited

Hin|ter|leib M *(Zool)* hindquarters *pl*; *(von Insekten)* abdomen

Hin|ter|list F **a** *(= Tücke)* craftiness, cunning; *(= Verrat)* treachery; *(= Betrug)* deceitfulness **b** *(= Trick, List)* ruse, trick

hin|ter|lis|tig ADJ *(= tückisch)* crafty, cunning; *(= verräterisch)* treacherous; *(= betrügerisch)* deceitful ADV *(= tückisch)* cunningly; *(= betrügerisch)* deceitfully

hin|term ['hɪntɐm] = **hinter dem**

Hin|ter|mann M *pl* **-männer** **a** person behind; *(= Auto)* car behind; **mein ~** the person/car behind me; **(vorsicht,) Hintermann!** *(Ftbl)* man on! **b** *(inf) (= Gewährsmann)* contact; **die Hintermänner des Skandals** the men behind the scandal **c** *(Fin: von Wechsel)* subsequent endorser

Hin|ter|mann|schaft F *(Sport)* defence *(Brit)*, defense *(US)*

hin|tern ['hɪntɐn] = **hinter den**

Hin|tern ['hɪntɐn] M **-s, -** *(inf)* bottom *(inf)*, backside *(inf)*, behind; **ein Tritt in den ~** a kick up the backside *(inf)*, a kick in the pants *(inf)*; **jdm den ~ versohlen** to tan sb's hide; **ein paar auf den ~ bekommen, den ~ vollbekommen** to get one's bottom smacked *(inf)*; **sich auf den ~ setzen** *(= hinfallen)* to fall on one's bottom *etc*; *(= eifrig arbeiten)* to buckle down to work; **jdm in den ~ kriechen** to lick sb's boots, to suck up to sb; **mit dem Zeugnis kann er sich** *(dat)* **den ~ (ab)wischen** he might as well use that certificate for toilet paper; **ich könnte mir** *or* **mich in den ~ beißen** I could kick myself

Hin|ter-: **Hin|ter|pfo|te** F hind paw; **Hin|ter|pfui|teu|fel** [hɪntɐpfui'tɔyfl] NT **-s**, *no pl (pej inf)* the back of beyond *(esp Brit)*, the middle of nowhere

Hin|ter|rad NT rear *or* back wheel

Hin|ter|rad-: **Hin|ter|rad|an|trieb** M rear wheel drive; **Hin|ter|rad|brem|se** F rear (wheel) brake

hin|ter|rücks ['hɪntɐrʏks] ADV from behind; *(fig: = heimtückisch)* behind sb's back; **jdn ~ ermorden** to murder sb treacherously

hin|ters ['hɪntɐs] = **hinter das**

Hin|ter-: **Hin|ter|schiff** NT stern; **Hin|ter|sei|te** F back; *(von Münze)* reverse side; *(inf: = Hintern)* backside *(inf)*; **Hin|ter|sinn** M, *no pl* underlying *or* deeper meaning *(+gen* behind); **hin|ter|sin|nig** ADJ cryptic

hin|ters|te(r, s) ['hɪntɐstə] ADJ *superl von* **hintere(r, s)** very back, backmost; *(= entlegenste)* remotest; **die Hintersten** those at the very back; **das ~ Ende** the very end *or (von Saal)* back; **in der ~n Reihe** in the very back row; **das Hinterste zuvorderst kehren** *(inf)* to turn everything upside down

Hin|ters|te(r) ['hɪntɐstɐ] M *decl as adj (inf)* bottom *(inf)*, backside *(inf)*, behind

Hin|ter-: **Hin|ter|ste|ven** M *(Naut)* sternpost; *(hum inf: = Gesäß)* backside *(inf)*; **Hin|ter|stüb|chen** NT **etw im ~ haben** *(fig)* to have sth at the back of one's mind; **Hin|ter|teil** NT **a** *(inf)* backside *(inf)*; *(von Tier)* hindquarters *pl* **b** AUCH M back *or* rear part; **Hin|ter|tref|fen** NT **im ~ sein** to be at a disadvantage; **ins ~ geraten** *or* **kommen** to fall behind; **hin|ter|trei|ben** *ptp* **hintertrieben** VT *insep irreg (fig)* to foil, to thwart; *Gesetz* to block; **Hin|ter|trei|bung** [-'traibʊŋ] F **-, -en** foiling, thwarting; *(von Gesetz)* blocking; **Hin|ter|trep|pe** F back stairs *pl*; **Hin|ter|trep|pen|ro|man** M *(pej)* cheap *or* trashy novel, penny dreadful *(dated Brit)*, dime novel *(US)*; **Hin|ter|tup|fin|gen** [hɪntɐ'tʊpfɪŋən] NT **-s**, *no pl (inf)* the back of beyond *(esp Brit)*, the middle of nowhere; **Hin|ter|tür** F, *(Aus)* **Hin|ter|türl** [-tyːɐl] NT **-s, -n** back door; *(fig inf: = Ausweg, Umweg)* loophole; **durch die ~** *(fig)* through the back door; **sich** *(dat)* **eine ~** *or* **ein ~chen offenhalten** *or* **offenlassen** *(fig)* to leave oneself a way out *or* a loophole; **Hin|ter|wäld|ler** [-vɛltlɐ] M **-s, -**, **Hin|ter|wäld|le|rin** [-ərɪn] F **-, -nen** *(inf)* backwoodsman, hillbilly *(esp US)*; **hin|ter|wäld|le|risch** [-vɛltlərɪʃ] ADJ *(inf)* backwoods *attr*; *Ansichten, Benehmen, Methoden auch* hick *attr*; **ein ~er Mensch** a backwoodsman, a hillbilly *(esp US)*; **hin|ter|zie|hen** *ptp* **hinterzogen** VT *insep irreg Steuern* to evade; *Material* to appropriate; **Hin|ter|zie|hung** F *(von Steuern)* evasion; *(von Material)* appropriation; **Hin|ter|zim|mer** NT back room

hin-: **hin+tra|gen** VT *sep irreg* to take *or* carry there; **hin+trei|ben** *sep irreg* VT *(Wind)* to blow; *(Strömung)* to wash VT *impers* **es trieb ihn immer wieder hin** something always drove him back there; **hin+tre|ten** VI *sep irreg* **a** *aux sein* **vor jdn ~** to go up to sb; *vor Gott* to step before sb; **zu jdm/etw ~** to step over to sb/sth **b** *(= mit Fuß stoßen)* to kick; **hin+tun** VT *sep irreg (inf)* to put; **ich weiß nicht, wo ich ihn ~ soll** *(fig)* I can't (quite) place him

hi|nü|ber [hɪ'nyːbɐ] ADV over; *(über Grenze, Straße, Fluss auch)* across; **da ~** over there; **~ und herüber** back and forth; **quer ~** right across; **bis zum anderen Ufer ~** over *or* across to the other bank → **hinüber sein**

hi|nü|ber- PREF → *auch* **herüber-, rüber-**: **hi|nü|ber+be|för|dern** *ptp* **hinüberbefördert** VT *sep* to transport across *(über etw (acc)* sth); **hi|nü|ber+bli|cken** VI *sep* to look across *(zu jdm* to sb); **hi|nü|ber+brin|gen** VT *sep irreg* to take across *(über etw (acc)* sth); **hi|nü|ber+däm|mern** VI *sep aux sein (= einschlafen)* to doze off; *(= sterben)* to pass away in one's sleep; **hi|nü|ber+fah|ren** *sep irreg* VT *(über etw (acc)* sth) *jdn* to take across; *Gepäck etc auch* to carry across; *Auto* to drive across VI *aux sein* to travel *or* go across; **nach Frankreich ~** to cross *or* go across to France; **über den Fluss ~** to cross the river; **hi|nü|ber+füh|ren** *sep* VT **jdn (über die Straße/dort/in das andere Zimmer) ~** to take sb across (the street)/over (there)/over (into the other room) VI *(= verlaufen: Straße, Brücke)* to go across *(über etw (acc)* sth); **hi|nü|ber+ge|hen** VI *sep irreg aux sein* **a** *(= hingehen)* to go *or* walk across; *(zu anderem Haus, zu jdm)* to go *or* walk over *(über etw (acc)* sth) **b** *(euph: = sterben)* to pass away; **hi|nü|ber+ge|lan|gen** *ptp* **hinübergelangt** VI *sep aux sein (geh)* to get across *(über etw (acc)* sth); **hi|nü|ber+hel|fen** VI *sep irreg* **jdm ~** to help sb across *(über etw (acc)* sth); *(fig: über Schwierigkeiten)* to help sb out *(über +acc* of); **jdm (ins Jenseits) ~** *(= leichten Tod verschaffen)* to help sb to die; *(= töten)* to bump sb off *(inf)*; **hi|nü|ber+kom|men** VI *sep irreg aux sein (über etw (acc)* sth) to come across; *(über Brücke, Fluss auch, über Hindernis, zu Besuch)* to come over; *(= hinüberkönnen)* to get across/over; **hi|nü|ber+las|sen** VT *sep irreg* to let *or* allow across; *(über Kreuzung, Brücke auch, zu Besuch)* to let *or* allow over *(über etw (acc)* sth); **hi|nü|ber+rei|chen** *sep* VT to pass across; *(über Zaun etc)* to pass over *(jdm* to sb, *über etw (acc)* sth) VI to reach across *(über etw (acc)* sth); *(fig)* to extend *(in +acc* into); **hi|nü|ber+ret|ten** *sep* VT to bring to safety; *(fig) Humor, Tradition* to keep alive; **etw in die Gegenwart ~** to keep sth alive VR *(über Grenze)* to reach safety; *(fig: Brauch)* to be kept alive; **hi|nü|ber+ru|fen** *sep irreg* VT to call out VI to call over *(über etw (acc)* sth); **hi|nü|ber+schaf|fen** VT *sep* to get across *(über etw (acc)* sth); **hi|nü|ber+schi|cken** VT *sep* to send across *or (zu Besuch)* over *(über etw (acc)* sth); **hi|nü|ber+schlum|mern** VI *sep aux sein (euph: = sterben)* to pass away; **hi|nü|ber+schwim|men** VI *sep irreg aux sein* to swim across *(über etw (acc)* sth); **hi|nü|ber sein** VI *irreg aux sein (inf)* **a** *(= verdorben sein)* to be off *or* bad; *(= kaputt, unbrauchbar, tot sein)* to have had it *(inf)*; *(= ruiniert sein: Firma, Politiker)* to be done for *(inf)* **b** *(= betrunken sein)* to be well away *(inf)*; *(= betäubt sein)* to be (knocked) out *(inf)*; **hi|nü|ber+spie|len** *sep* VI *(geh)* **dieses Rot spielt leicht ins Violett hinüber** this red has a slight purple tinge *or* tinge of purple VT *Ball* to pass *(jdm* to sb); **hi|nü|ber+stei|gen** VI *sep irreg aux sein* to climb over *(über etw (acc)* sth); **hi|nü|ber+tra|gen** VT *sep irreg* to carry across *(über etw (acc)* sth); **hi|nü|ber+wech|seln** VI *sep aux haben or sein* to change over *(zu, in +acc* to); **zu einer anderen Partei ~** to go over to another party; **hi|nü|ber+wer|fen** VT *sep irreg* to throw over *(über etw (acc)* sth); **einen Blick ~** to glance over; **hi|nü|ber+zie|hen** *sep irreg* VT to pull across *(über etw (acc)* sth); *(fig: = umstimmen)* to win over *(auf +acc* to) VI *aux sein* **a** *(= marschieren)* to move *or* march across **b** *(= sich bewegen: Rauch, Wolken)* to move across *(über etw (acc)* sth) VR *(= sich erstrecken)* to stretch over *(nach, zu* to)

hin und her → **hin**

hin- und her+be|we|gen VTR *sep* to move back and forward *or* forth

Hin|und|her|ge|re|de NT *(inf)* **das ewige ~** this continual argy-bargy *(Brit inf) or* carrying-on *(inf)*

hin- und her+ge|ris|sen ADJ *pred* **~ sein** to be in a terrible dilemma, to be torn *(zwischen +dat* between)

Hin- und Rück-: **Hin- und Rück|fahrt** F return journey, round trip *(US)*; **Hin- und**

Rück|flug M return flight; **Hin- und Rück|rei|se** F journey *or* trip *(esp US)* there and back, round trip; **Hin- und Rück|weg** M round trip

hi|nun|ter [hɪ'nʊntɐ] ADV down; **bis ~ zu** down to; **ins Tal ~** down into the valley; **am Hügel ~** down the hill; **dort** *or* **da ~** down there; **~ mit ihm!** down with him; **~ mit der Arznei** get this medicine down PREP *+acc (nachgestellt)* down

hi|nun|ter- PREF → *auch* **herunter-, runter-** down; **hi|nun|ter+bli|cken** VI *sep* to look down; **hi|nun|ter+brin|gen** VT *sep irreg* to take down; *(inf: = schlucken können)* to be able to get down; **hi|nun|ter+fah|ren** *sep irreg* VI *aux sein* to go down; *(Fahrstuhl, Bergbahn auch)* to descend; **in etw** *(acc)***/nach etw ~** to go down into sth/to sth VT *jdn* to take down; *Fahrzeug* to drive down; **hi|nun|ter+fal|len** VI *sep irreg aux sein* to fall down; **hi|nun|ter+flie|ßen** VI *sep irreg aux sein* to flow down; **hi|nun|ter+ge|hen** VI *sep irreg aux sein* to go down; *(zu Fuß auch)* to walk down; *(Flugzeug)* to descend *(auf +acc* to); **hi|nun|ter+gie|ßen** VT *sep irreg* to pour down; *Getränke* to knock back *(inf)*; **hi|nun|ter+kip|pen** VT *sep* to tip down; *(inf) Getränke* to knock back *(inf)*; **hi|nun|ter+klet|tern** VI *sep aux sein* to climb down; **hi|nun|ter+las|sen** VT *sep irreg* to lower, to let down; **er lässt mich nicht hinunter** *(inf)* he won't let me get down; **hi|nun|ter+lau|fen** VI *sep irreg aux sein* to run down; **es lief ihm eiskalt den Rücken hinunter** a shiver ran down his spine; **hi|nun|ter+rei|chen** *sep* VT to hand *or* pass down VI to reach down; *(fig: in Rangfolge)* to apply *(bis zu* down to); **hi|nun|ter+rei|ßen** VT *sep irreg* to pull *or* drag down; **hi|nun|ter+schal|ten** VI *sep (Aut)* to change *or* shift *(US)* down; **hi|nun|ter+schau|en** VI *sep (dial)* to look down; **hi|nun|ter+schlin|gen** VT *sep irreg (inf)* to gulp down; *Essen* to gobble down; **hi|nun|ter+schlu|cken** VT *sep* to swallow (down); *(fig) Beleidigung* to swallow; *Kritik* to take; *Ärger, Tränen* to choke back; **hi|nun|ter+schmei|ßen** VT *sep irreg (inf)* to throw *or* chuck *(inf)* down; **hi|nun|ter+schüt|ten** VT *sep* = **hinuntergießen**; **hi|nun|ter+se|hen** VI *sep irreg* to look down; **hi|nun|ter+spü|len** VT *sep* **a** *(in Toilette, Ausguss)* to flush away; **etw die Toilette/den Ausguss ~** to flush sth down the toilet/drain **b** *Essen, Tablette* to wash down; *(fig) Ärger* to soothe; **hi|nun|ter+stür|zen** *sep* VI *aux sein* **a** *(= hinunterfallen)* to tumble *or* fall down **b** *(= eilig hinunterlaufen)* to rush *or* dash down VT *jdn* to throw *or* hurl down; *Getränk* to gulp down VR to throw *or* fling oneself down; **hi|nun|ter+wer|fen** VT *sep irreg* to throw down; *(inf: = fallen lassen)* to drop; **einen Blick ~** to glance down; **hi|nun|ter+wür|gen** VT *sep Essen etc* to choke down; *(fig) Wut, Tränen* to choke back; **hi|nun|ter+zie|hen** *sep irreg* VT to pull down VI *aux sein* to move down

hin+wa|gen VR *sep* to dare to go there

hin|wärts ['hɪnvɛrts] ADV on the way there; **die Strecke ~** the way there

hin|weg [hɪn'vɛk] ADV **a** *(old: = fort)* away; **~ mit der Unterdrückung** down with oppression **b über jdn/etw ~** over sb *or* sb's head/sth; **über alle Hindernisse** *etc* **~** *(fig)* despite all the difficulties *etc* **c** *(zeitlich)* **über eine Zeit ~** over a period of time; **über zwei Jahre ~** over (a period of) two years

Hin|weg M way there; **auf dem ~** on the way there

hin|weg- PREF → *auch* **weg-** away; **hin|weg+brin|gen** VT *sep irreg (fig)* **jdn über etw** *(acc)* **~** to help sb get over sth; **hin|weg+ge|hen** VI *sep irreg aux sein* **über etw** *(acc)* **~** to pass over *or* across sth; *(= nicht beachten)* to pass over *or* disregard sth; **hin|weg+hel|fen** VI *sep irreg (fig)* **jdm über etw** *(acc)* **~** to help sb get over sth; **hin|weg+kom|men** VI *sep irreg aux sein (fig)* **über etw** *(acc)* **~** *(= überstehen, verwinden)* to get over sth; *(= sich hinwegsetzen können)* to dismiss sth; **ich komme nicht darüber hinweg, dass ...** *(inf)* I can't get over the fact that ...; **hin|weg+raf|fen** VT *sep (geh)* to carry off; **hin|weg+se|hen** VI *sep irreg* **über jdn/etw ~** *(lit)* to see over sb *or* sb's head/sth; *(fig) (= ignorieren)* to ignore sb/sth; *(= unbeachtet lassen)* to overlook sb/sth; **darüber ~, dass ...** to overlook the fact that ...; **hin|weg+set|zen** *sep* VI *aux haben or sein* **über etw** *(acc)* **~** to jump *or* leap over sth VR *(fig)* **sich über etw** *(acc)* **~** *(= nicht beachten)* to disregard *or* dismiss sth; *(= überwinden)* to overcome sth; **hin|weg+täu|schen** VT *sep* **jdn über etw** *(acc)* **~** to mislead *or* deceive sb about sth; **darüber ~, dass ...** to hide the fact that ...; **sich nicht darüber ~ lassen, dass ...** not to blind oneself to the fact that ...; **hin|weg+trös|ten** VT *sep* **jdn über etw** *(acc)* **~** to console sb about sth; **deine Entschuldigung tröstet mich nicht darüber hinweg, dass ...** your apology does not make up for the fact that ...

Hin|weis ['hɪnvais] M **-es, -e** [-zə] **a** *(= Rat)* tip, piece of advice; *(= Bemerkung)* comment; *(amtlich)* notice; *(Comput)* note; **darf ich mir den ~ erlauben, dass ...** may I point out that ..., may I draw your attention to the fact that ...; **~e für den Benutzer** notes for the user **b** *(= Verweis)* reference; **unter ~ auf** *(+acc)* with reference to **c** *(= Anhaltspunkt, Anzeichen)* indication; *(esp von Polizei)* clue **d** *(= Anspielung)* allusion *(auf +acc* to)

hin+wei|sen *sep irreg* VT **jdn auf etw** *(acc)* **~** to point sth out to sb VI **auf jdn/etw ~** to point to sb/sth; *(= verweisen)* to refer to sb/sth; **darauf ~, dass ...** to point out that ...; *(nachdrücklich)* to stress *or* emphasize that ...; *(= anzeigen)* to indicate that ...

hin|wei|send ADJ *(Gram)* demonstrative

Hin|weis|schild NT *pl* **-schilder, Hin|weis|ta|fel** F sign

hin-: **hin+wen|den** *sep irreg* VT to turn *(zu, nach* towards) VR *(lit)* to turn *(zu, nach* towards, to); *(fig: Mensch)* to turn *(zu* to); **Hin|wen|dung** F *(fig)* turning *(zu* to); **eine ~ zum Besseren** a turn for the better

hin+wer|fen *sep irreg* VT **a** *(= wegwerfen, zu Boden werfen)* to throw down; *(= fallen lassen)* to drop; **jdm etw ~** to throw sth to sb **b** *(= flüchtig machen) Bemerkung* to drop casually; *Wort* to say casually; *Zeilen, Roman, Zeichnung* to dash off; **einen Blick ~** to glance at it/them; **eine hingeworfene Bemerkung** a casual remark **c** *(inf: = aufgeben) Arbeit, Stelle* to give up, to chuck (in) *(inf)* VR to throw *or* fling oneself down; *(auf die Knie)* to go down *or* throw oneself down on one's knees

hin|wie|der [hɪn'vi:dɐ] ADV *(= dagegen)* on the other hand; *(= dann wieder)* in turn

hin-: **hin+wirk|en** VI *sep* **auf etw** *(acc)* **~** to work toward(s) sth; **kannst du (nicht) (bei ihm) darauf ~, dass er mich empfängt?** couldn't you use your influence to get him to see me *or* to make him see me?; **hin+wol|len** VI *sep (inf)* to want to go

Hinz [hɪnts] M **~ und Kunz** *(inf)* every Tom, Dick and Harry; **von ~ zu Kunz** from pillar to post *(Brit)*, from one place to another

hin-: **hin+zäh|len** VT *sep* to count out *(jdm* to sb); **hin+zau|bern** VT *sep (fig)* to rustle *or* whip up *(inf)*; **hin+zie|hen** *sep irreg* VT **a** *(= zu sich ziehen)* to draw *or* pull *(zu* towards); *(fig: = anziehen)* to attract *(zu* to); **es zieht sie zur Kunst hin** she feels attracted to art **b** *(fig: = in die Länge ziehen)* to draw *or* drag out VI *aux sein* **a** *(= sich in bestimmte Richtung bewegen)* to move *(über +acc* across, *zu* towards); *(= weggehen, -marschieren)* to move *or* go away **b** *(liter: Wolken, Rauch etc)* to drift, to move *(an +dat* across) **c** *(= umziehen)* to move there VR **a** *(= lange dauern)* to drag on; *(= sich verzögern)* to be delayed **b** *(= sich erstrecken)* to stretch, to extend; **hin+zie|len** VI *sep* **auf etw** *(acc)* **~** to aim at sth; *(Pläne etc)* to be aimed at sth; *(Bemerkung)* to refer to sth

hin|zu [hɪn'tsu:] ADV *(räumlich)* there, thither *(obs)*; *(= überdies, obendrein)* besides, in addition; **~ kommt noch, dass ich ...** moreover I ...

hin|zu-: **hin|zu+be|kom|men** *ptp* **hinzubekommen** VT *sep irreg* to get in addition; **hin|zu+den|ken** VT *sep irreg* to add in one's mind *or* imagination; **hin|zu+dich|ten** VT *sep* = **hinzuerfinden**; **hin|zu+er|fin|den** *ptp* **hinzuerfunden** VT *sep irreg* **etw ~** to make up and add sth *(zu* to); **hin|zu+fü|gen** VT *sep* to add *(+dat* to); *(= beilegen)* to enclose; **Hin|zu|fü|gung** F addition; **unter ~ von etw** *(form)* by adding sth; *(als Beilage)* enclosing sth; **hin|zu+ge|sel|len** *ptp* **hinzugesellt** VR *sep (geh)* to join *(jdm* sb); **hin|zu+ge|win|nen** *ptp* **hinzugewonnen** VT *sep irreg* to get in addition; *neue Mitglieder* to gain; **hin|zu+kau|fen** VTI *sep* to buy in addition *(zu* to); **Karten ~** to buy more *or* additional tickets; **hin|zu+kom|men** VI *sep irreg aux sein* **a** *(= hinkommen, eintreffen)* to arrive; **sie kam gerade hinzu, als ...** she happened to come on the scene when ...; **es werden später noch mehrere ~** more people will join us later *or* will come along later; **(zu etw) ~** *(= sich anschließen)* to join sth **b** *(= zusätzlich eintreten)* to supervene, to ensue; *(= beigefügt werden)* to be added; **zu etw ~** to be added to sth; **es kommt noch hinzu, dass ...** there is also the fact that ...; **kommt sonst noch etwas hinzu?** will there be anything else?; **hin|zu+neh|men** VT *sep irreg* to include; **etw zu etw ~** to add sth to sth; **hin|zu+rech|nen** VT *sep* to add on; **hin|zu+set|zen** VT *sep* to add; **hin|zu+sto|ßen** VI *sep irreg aux sein (geh: = hinzukommen)* to arrive, to join up with; **hin|zu+tre|ten** VI *sep irreg aux sein* **a** *(= herantreten)* to come up; **zu den anderen ~** to join the others **b** *(zusätzlich)* = **hinzukommen b**; **hin|zu+tun** VT *sep irreg (inf)* to add; **Hin|zu|tun** NT = **Dazutun**; **hin|zu+ver|die|nen** VT *sep* **etw ~** to have additional earnings; **hin|zu+zäh|len** VT *sep* to add; **hin|zu+zie|hen** VT *sep irreg* to consult; **Hin|zu|zie|hung** F, *no pl* consultation *(+gen* with); **unter ~ eines Lexikons** by consulting an encyclop(a)edia

Hiob ['hi:ɔp] M **-s** Job; **das Buch ~** the Book of Job

Hiobs|bot|schaft F bad news *no pl or* tidings *pl*

Hiobs|post F *(old)* = **Hiobsbotschaft**

hip [hɪp] ADJ *(sl)* hip *(inf)*

Hip-Hop ['hɪphɔp] M **-(s)**, *no pl*, **Hip|hop** M **-(s)**, *no pl (Mus)* hip-hop

Hip|pe ['hɪpə] F **-, -n** *(= Messer)* pruning knife; *(= Sense des Todes)* scythe

hipp, hipp, hur|ra ['hɪp 'hɪp hʊ'ra:] INTERJ hip, hip, hurrah *or* hurray

Hipp|hipp|hur|ra ['hɪp'hɪphʊ'ra:] NT **-s, -s** cheer; **ein dreifaches ~** three cheers

Hip|pie ['hɪpi] M **-s, -s** hippie

Hip|po|drom [hɪpo'dro:m] NT OR M **-s, -e** hippodrome

hip|po|kra|tisch [hɪpo'kra:tɪʃ] ADJ Hippocratic; **~er Eid** Hippocratic oath

Hirn [hɪrn] NT **-(e)s, -e** **a** *(Anat)* brain **b** *(inf) (= Kopf)* head; *(= Verstand)* brains *pl*, mind; **sich** *(dat)* **das ~ zermartern** to rack one's brain(s); **diese Idee ist doch nicht deinem ~ entsprungen?** that's not your own idea *or* your brainwave, is it? **c** *(Cook)* brains *pl*

Hirn- → *auch* **Gehirn-**: **Hirn|an|hang** M, **Hirn|an|hang(s)|drü|se** F *(Anat)* pituitary gland; **Hirn|funk|ti|on** F *(= Funktion)* brain function, function of the brain; *(= Funktionieren)* functioning of the brain; **hirn|ge|schä|digt** ADJ brain-damaged; **Hirn|ge|spinst** NT fantasy; **Hirn|haut** F *(Anat)* meninges *pl*; **Hirn|haut|ent|zün|dung** F *(Med)* meningitis; **hirn|los** ADJ brainless; **Hirn|lo|sig|keit** F *(fig pej)* brainlessness; *(Handlung)* crazy thing to do; **Hirn|mas|se** F cerebral matter; **Hirn|rin|de** F *(Anat)* cerebral cortex; **hirn|ris|sig** ADJ hare-brained; **Hirn|scha|den** M brain damage; **Hirn|scha|le** F *(Anat)* cranium; **Hirn|stamm** M *(Anat)* brainstem; **Hirn|sub|stanz** F *(Anat)* cerebral matter; **Hirn|tod** M *(Med)* brain death; **hirn|tot** ADJ braindead; **Hirn|to|te(r)** MF *decl as adj* braindead person/man/woman; **die ~n** the braindead; **Hirn|tu|mor** M brain tumour *(Brit) or* tumor *(US)*; **hirn|ver|brannt** ADJ hare-brained; **Hirn|win|dung** F *(Anat)* convolution of the brain; **Hirn|zent|rum** NT brain centre *(Brit) or* center *(US)*

Hirsch [hɪrʃ] M **-es, -e** **a** *(= Paarhufer)* deer; *(= Rothirsch)* red deer; *(= männlicher Rothirsch)* stag; *(Cook)* venison **b** *(inf: Schimpfwort)* clot *(Brit inf)*, clod *(US inf)*

Hirsch-: **Hirsch|art** F kind *or* species *sing* of deer; **Hirsch|bock** M stag; **Hirsch|bra|ten** M *(Cook)* roast of venison; *(= Gericht)* roast venison; **Hirsch|brunft** F, **Hirsch|brunst** F rut; **zur Zeit der ~** during the rutting season; **Hirsch|fän|ger** M hunting knife; **Hirsch|ge|weih** NT antlers *pl*

Hirsch|horn NT horn

Hirsch|horn-: **Hirsch|horn|knopf** M horn button; **Hirsch|horn|salz** NT *(Chem)* ammonium carbonate

Hirsch-: **Hirsch|jagd** F stag hunt; **Hirsch|kä|fer** M stag beetle; **Hirsch|kalb** NT (male) fawn, (male) deer calf; **Hirsch|keu|le** F haunch of venison; **Hirsch|kuh** F hind; **Hirsch|le|der** NT buckskin, deerskin; **hirsch|le|dern** ADJ buckskin, deerskin; **Hirsch|le|der|ne** [-leːdɐnə] F *decl as adj (esp Aus)* buckskin breeches *pl*, buckskins *pl (US)*

Hir|se [ˈhɪrzə] F **-, -n** millet

Hir|se-: **Hir|se|brei** M millet gruel; **Hir|se|korn** NT *pl* **-körner** millet seed

Hirt [hɪrt] M **-en, -en** *(dated)* herdsman; *(= Schafhirt)* shepherd; **wie der ~, so die Herde** *(Prov)* like master, like man *(prov)* → *auch* **Hirtin**

Hir|te [ˈhɪrtə] M **-n, -n** **a** = **Hirt** **b** *(Eccl: = Seelsorger)* shepherd; **der Gute ~** the Good Shepherd

Hir|ten-: **Hir|ten|amt** NT *(Eccl)* pastorate, pastorship; **Hir|ten|brief** M *(Eccl)* pastoral; **Hir|ten|dich|tung** F *(Liter)* pastoral poetry; **Hir|ten|flö|te** F shepherd's pipe; **Hir|ten|ge|dicht** NT pastoral; **Hir|ten|gott** M god of shepherds; **Hir|ten|hund** M sheepdog; **Hir|ten|jun|ge** M, **Hir|ten|kna|be** M *(liter)* shepherd boy; **Hir|ten|lied** NT shepherd's song; **hir|ten|los** ADJ *(lit, fig)* shepherdless; **Hir|ten|mäd|chen** NT young shepherdess; **Hir|ten|spiel** NT pastoral (play); **Hir|ten|stab** M shepherd's crook; *(Eccl)* crosier; **Hir|ten|tä|schel(kraut)** [ˈhɪrtntɛʃl-] NT **-s, -** shepherd's-purse; **Hir|ten|volk** NT pastoral people

Hir|tin [ˈhɪrtɪn] F **-, -nen** herdswoman; *(= Schafhirtin)* shepherdess → *auch* **Hirt**

His [hɪs] NT **-, -**, **his** NT **-, -** *(Mus)* B sharp

His|bol|lah [hɪsˈbɔlaː] F **-,** *no pl* Hizbollah

His|pa|nis|mus [hɪspaˈnɪsmʊs] M **-, Hispanismen** [-mən] *(Ling)* Hispanicism

His|pa|nist [hɪspaˈnɪst] M **-en, -en**, **His|pa|nis|tin** [-ˈnɪstɪn] F **-, -nen** Spanish specialist, Hispanist; *(= Student)* Spanish student; *(= Professor etc)* Spanish lecturer/professor

His|pa|nis|tik [hɪspaˈnɪstɪk] F **-,** *no pl* Spanish (language and literature)

his|sen [ˈhɪsn] VT to hoist

His|ta|min [hɪstaˈmiːn] NT **-s,** *no pl* histamine

His|to|lo|ge [hɪstoˈloːgə] M **-n, -n**, **His|to|lo|gin** [-ˈloːgɪn] F **-, -nen** histologist

His|to|lo|gie [hɪstoloˈgiː] F **-,** *no pl* histology

his|to|lo|gisch [hɪstoˈloːgɪʃ] ADJ histological

His|tör|chen [hɪsˈtøːɐçən] NT **-s, -** anecdote; *(= Klatschgeschichte)* little tale *or* story

His|to|rie [hɪsˈtoːriə] F **-, -n** **a** *no pl (old: = Weltgeschichte)* history **b** *(= Erzählung)* story, tale; **Shakespeares ~n** Shakespeare's history plays *or* histories

His|to|ri|en-: **His|to|ri|en|ma|ler(in)** M(F) historical painter; **His|to|ri|en|ma|le|rei** F historical painting

His|to|rik [hɪsˈtoːrɪk] F **-,** *no pl* history

His|to|ri|ker [hɪsˈtoːrikɐ] M **-s, -**, **His|to|ri|ke|rin** [-ərɪn] F **-, -nen** historian

His|to|rio|graf [hɪstorioˈgraːf] M **-en, -en**, **His|to|rio|gra|fin** [-ˈgraːfɪn] F **-, -nen** historiographer

His|to|rio|graph *etc* = **Historiograf** *etc*

his|to|risch [hɪsˈtoːrɪʃ] ADJ historical; *Verständnis, Kenntnisse auch* of history; *(= geschichtlich bedeutsam) Gestalt, Ereignis, Gebäude* historic ADV historically; **das ist ~ belegt** there is historical evidence for this, that is historically documented; **~ denken** to think in historical terms; **~ betrachtet** seen in the light of history, looked at *or* considered from a historical perspective

his|to|risch-kri|tisch ADJ *Ausgabe* historico-critical

His|to|ris|mus [hɪstoˈrɪsmʊs] M **-,** *no pl* historicism

Hit [hɪt] M **-s, -s** *(Mus, fig inf)* hit

Hit|ler [ˈhɪtlɐ] M **-s** Hitler

Hit|ler|bärt|chen M Hitler *or* toothbrush moustache

Hit|le|rei [hɪtləˈrai] F **-,** *no pl (pej inf) (= Hitlerfaschismus)* Hitlerite fascism; *(= Hitlerkult)* Hitlerite cult

Hit|ler-: **Hit|ler|gruß** M Hitler salute; **Hit|ler|ju|gend** F Hitler Youth (organization); **Hit|ler|jun|ge** M member of the Hitler Youth; **Hit|ler|reich** NT, *no pl* (Third) Reich; **Hit|ler|zeit** F Hitler era

Hit-: **Hit|lis|te** F *(Mus)* charts *pl* → *auch* **Hitparade**; **Hit|pa|ra|de** F hit parade; **in der ~** *(Mus)* in the charts *pl*; **hit|ver|däch|tig** ADJ **ein ~es Lied** a potential hit; **der Song ist ~** the song could hit the charts

Hit|ze [ˈhɪtsə] F **-, -n** **a** heat; *(= Hitzewelle)* heat wave; **~ abweisend** heat-repellent; **vor ~ umkommen** to be sweltering (in the heat); **eine ~ ist das!** the heat (is incredible)!; **die fliegende ~ bekommen** *(Med)* to get hot flushes *(Brit) or* flashes *(US)*; *(inf)* to get all hot and bothered; **bei starker/mittlerer/mäßiger ~ backen** *(Cook)* bake in a hot/medium/moderate oven **b** *(fig)* passion; **in ~ geraten** to get heated; **leicht in ~ geraten** to get worked up easily; **jdn in ~ bringen** to get sb all worked up; **sich in ~ reden** to get oneself all worked up; **in der ~ des Gefecht(e)s** *(fig)* in the heat of the moment **c** *(Zool)* heat

Hit|ze-: **hit|ze|ab|wei|send** ADJ → **Hitze a**; **Hit|ze|aus|schlag** M heat rash, prickly heat *no art*; **hit|ze|be|stän|dig** ADJ heat-resistant; **Hit|ze|be|stän|dig|keit** F heat resistance; **Hit|ze|bläs|chen** [-blɛːsçən] PL heat spots *pl (Brit)*, heat rash *sing*; **Hit|ze|ein|wir|kung** F effect of (the) heat; **hit|ze|emp|find|lich** ADJ sensitive to heat; **Hit|ze|fe|ri|en** PL *(Sch) time off from school on account of excessively hot weather*; **hit|ze|fest** ADJ heat-resistant, heat-proof; **hit|ze|frei** ADJ **~ haben** *to have time off from school on account of excessively hot weather*

> **HITZEFREI**
>
> Since German school holidays are spread out through the year, lessons take place in July and August when it can be very hot. If at noon the temperature is above 30°C in the shade, the day is declared **hitzefrei** and pupils and teachers are sent home.

Hit|ze-: **Hit|ze|pe|ri|o|de** F hot spell; **Hit|ze|pi|ckel** PL *(inf)* heat spots *pl (Brit)*, heat rash *sing*; **Hit|ze(schutz)|schild** M heat shield; **Hit|ze|stau** M heat accumulation, accumulation of heat, build-up of heat; **Hit|ze|wal|lung** F *usu pl (Med)* hot flush *(Brit) or* flash *(US)*; **Hit|ze|wel|le** F heat wave

hit|zig [ˈhɪtsɪç] ADJ **a** *(= aufbrausend) Mensch* hot-headed; *Antwort, Reaktion, Atmosphäre, Debatte* heated; *(= leidenschaftlich) Temperament, Typ, Diskussionsteilnehmer* passionate; *Blut* hot; **~ werden** *(Mensch)* to flare up; *(Debatte)* to grow heated; **nicht so ~!** don't get so excited!, hold your horses! *(inf)*; **ein ~er Kopf** *(geh)* a hothead **b** *(dated Med: = fiebrig) Kopf, Gesichtsfarbe* fevered; *Fieber* high **c** *(Zool)* on *(esp Brit) or* in heat ADV *(= heftig)* heatedly; **eine Debatte ~ führen** to lead a heated debate; **es ging ~ zu** things got heated

Hit|zig|keit F **-,** *no pl (von Mensch)* hot-headedness; *(von Antwort, Reaktion, Debatte)* heatedness; *(von Temperament, Typ, Diskussionsteilnehmer)* passion

Hitz-: **Hitz|kopf** M hothead; **hitz|köp|fig** ADJ hot-headed; **Hitz|schlag** M *(Med)* heatstroke

HIV [haːliːˈfau] NT **-(s),** *(rare)* **-(s)** *abbr von* **Human Immunodeficiency Virus** HIV

HIV- *in cpds* HIV-; **HIV-in|fi|ziert** [haːliːˈfau-] ADJ HIV-infected; **HIV-ne|ga|tiv** [-ˈneːgatiːv] ADJ HIV-negative; **HIV-Ne|ga|ti|ve(r)** [-ˈneːgatiːvə] MF *decl as adj person who is HIV-negative*; **HIV-po|si|tiv** [-ˈpoːzitiːv] ADJ HIV-positive; **HIV-Po|si|ti|ve(r)** [-ˈpoːzitiːvə] MF *decl as adj person who is HIV-positive*; **HIV-Test** M HIV test; **HIV-Vi|rus** NT HIV-virus

Hi|wi [ˈhiːvi] M **-s, -s** **a** *abbr von* **Hilfswillige(r)** **b** *(Univ sl)* helper **c** *(pej inf: = Hilfskraft)* dogsbody *(Brit inf)*, drudge *(US)*

hj. *abbr von* **halbjährlich**

Hj. *abbr von* **Halbjahr**

hl. *abbr von* **heilig**

Hl. *abbr von* **Heilige(r)** St

hm [hm] INTERJ hm

H-Milch [ˈhaː-] F long-life milk

h-Moll [ˈhaː-] NT **-,** *no pl* B-minor

HNO-Arzt [haːlɛnˈloː-] M, **HNO-Ärz|tin** F ENT specialist

Hoax M **-, -es** *(Internet)* hoax; *(= E-Mail auch)* hoax e-mail; *(= Virenwarnung auch)* hoax virus warning

hob *pret von* **heben**

Hob|by [ˈhɔbi] NT **-s, -s** hobby

Hob|by-: **Hob|by|fe|ri|en** PL activity holiday *sing (Brit)*, golfing/climbing/painting *etc* vacation *(US)*; **Hob|by|fo|to|graf(in)** M(F) amateur photographer; **Hob|by|gärt|ner(in)** M(F) amateur *or* keen gardener; **sie ist ~in** gardening is her hobby; **Hob|by|koch** M, **Hob|by|kö|chin** F **er ist ~** cooking is his hobby; **Hob|by|pho|to|graph(in)** M(F) amateur photographer; **Hob|by|raum** M hobby room, workroom

Ho|bel [ˈhoːbl] M **-s, -** *(Tech)* plane; *(Cook)* slicer

Ho|bel-: **Ho|bel|bank** F *pl* **-bänke** carpenter's or joiner's bench; **Ho|bel|ei|sen** NT plane iron; **Ho|bel|ma|schi|ne** F planer, planing machine; **Ho|bel|mes|ser** NT plane iron

ho|beln [ˈhoːbln] VT **a** *auch vi (Tech)* to plane *(an etw (dat)* sth); *(= glätten) Brett* to plane down; **wo gehobelt wird, da fallen Späne** *(Prov)* you can't make an omelette without breaking eggs *(Prov)* **b** *(Cook)* to slice

Ho|bel|span M, *(Aus)* **Ho|bel|schar|te** F shaving

Ho|boe [hoˈboːə] F **-, -n** *(old)* oboe

hoch [hoːx]

1 ADJEKTIV	2 ADVERB

1 – ADJEKTIV

attr **hohe(r, s)** [ˈhoːə], *comp* **höher** [ˈhøːɐ], *superl* **≈ste(r, s)** [ˈhøːçstə]

a längenmäßig high; *Wuchs, Baum, Mast* tall; *Leiter* tall, long; **ein hohes, geräumiges Zimmer** a spacious room with a high ceiling, a spacious, high-ceilinged room; **der Schnee lag/das Wasser stand zwei Meter hoch** the snow/water was two metres *(Brit) or* meters *(US)* deep;

der Eiffelturm ist 321 m hoch the Eiffel tower is 321 metres *(Brit)* or meters *(US)* high; **das ist mir zu hoch** *(fig inf)* that's (well) above *(esp Brit)* or over my head

b [mengenmäßig] *Preis, Verdienst, Temperatur, Druck etc* high; *Betrag, Summe* large; *Strafe, Gewicht* heavy; *Schaden* extensive; *Lotteriegewinn* big; *Profit* high, big; **die britische Armee musste hohe Verluste hinnehmen** the British Army suffered heavy losses; **in hohem Maße verdächtig** highly suspicious; **in hohem Maße gefährdet** in grave danger; **das ist in hohem Maße abhängig von …** this is heavily dependent on …; **mit hoher Wahrscheinlichkeit** in all probability

c [Alter] great, advanced; **ein hohes Alter erreichen** to live to a great *or* an advanced age; **er ist hoch an Jahren** he has reached a great *or* an advanced age

d [Mus] high; **das hohe C** top C

e [= bedeutend] *Stellung, Position, Rang, Amt, Adel, Meinung, Lebensstandard, Ansprüche* high; *Geburt* high, noble; *Ehre, Bedeutung, Genuss, Gut, Glück* great; *Fest, Besuch, Feiertag, Jubiläum* important; *Offizier* high-ranking; **er/sie ist hoher** *or* **der hohe Favorit** he/she is the hot favourite *(Brit)* or favorite *(US)*; **ein hohes Tier** *(fig inf)* a big fish *(inf)*; **hohe Herrschaften** *(form: als Anrede)* ladies and gentlemen; **hohe Persönlichkeiten aus Politik und Wirtschaft** important *or* top *(inf)* politicians and businesspeople; **ein Mann von hohem Ansehen/hoher Bildung** a man of high standing/of great culture; **das hohe Haus** *(Parl)* the House → **Gewalt**

f [feste Wendungen] **in hoher Blüte stehen** to be in full bloom; *(Mensch)* to be in one's prime; *(Kultur)* to be at its zenith; **hohe Flut** spring tide; **die hohe Jagd** deer hunting; **das Hohe Lied** = **Hohelied**; **ein hohes Lied auf jdn/etw singen** to sing sb's/sth's praises; **der hohe Norden** the far North; **die Hohe Schule** *(beim Reiten)* haute école; **die hohe Schule des Lebens** the school of life; **im hohen Sommer** at the height of summer; **es ist hohe Zeit** *(geh)* it's high time → **höchste(r, s), bestimmen, Welle a, Kopf a, Tasse, Bogen a, Kante**

2 – ADVERB

comp **höher**, *superl* **am ⸗sten**

a [= oben] high; **hoch oben** high up; **ein hoch gelegener Ort in den Alpen** a place situated high up in the Alps; **hoch am Himmel** high in the sky; *(Flugzeug, Vogel)* high up in the sky; **die Sonne steht hoch** the sun is high in the sky; **10.000 Fuß hoch fliegen** to fly at a height of 10,000 feet; **zwei Treppen hoch wohnen** to live two floors up; **hoch sitzen** to sit up high; **die See geht hoch** the sea is running high; **wie hoch steht das Thermometer?** what's the temperature?; **der Alkoholgehalt liegt sehr hoch** the alcohol level is very high; **wie hoch kalkulieren Sie seine Chancen?** how high would you put *or* how would you rate his chances?

b [= nach oben] up; **komm zu mir, hier ~!** come to me, up here!; **hoch emporragend** towering (up); **hoch werfen** to throw high; **hoch gewachsen** → **hochgewachsen**; **ein hoch aufgeschossener Mann** a very tall man; **den Kopf hoch tragen** to hold one's head high; **die Nase hoch tragen** *(inf)* to be stuck-up *(inf)* or toffee-nosed *(Brit inf)*; **nach Hamburg hoch** up to Hamburg

c [Mus] high; **die Sopranistin sang etwas zu hoch** the soprano sang a bit sharp

d [Math] **3 hoch 2** 3 squared, 3 (raised) to the power (of) 2; **7 hoch 3** 7 cubed, 7 to the power of 3; **3 hoch 4/5** 3 to the power of 4/5

e [im übertragenen Sinn]

♦ **hoch + Adjektiv hoch begabt** = **hochbegabt**; **hoch empfindlich** → **hochempfindlich**; **hoch kompliziert** highly complicated *or* complex; **hoch konzentriert** *Mensch* very focused; *Gesichtsausdruck* of great concentration → *auch* **hochkonzentriert**

♦ **hoch + Verb**

Die in Verbindung mit *hoch* verwendeten Verben sind alphabetisch angeordnet.

das rechne ich ihm hoch an (I think) that is very much to his credit; **hoch angesehen** highly regarded; **hoch beansprucht** *(Tech)* highly stressed; **hoch beglückt** = **hochbeglückt**; **ein hoch beladener Lastwagen** a lorry with a high load; **hoch besteuert** heavily taxed; **hoch bezahlt** highly paid; **hoch dotiert** *(Mensch)* highly remunerated; *Arbeit* highly remunerative; **hoch geehrt** = **hochgeehrt**; **hoch geehrter Herr** *(old: im Brief)* esteemed Sir *(old)*; **hoch einschätzen** to estimate generously; **zu hoch einschätzen** to overestimate; **hoch entwickelt** *(Kultur, Volk, Land)* highly developed; *(= verfeinert) Geräte, Maschinen, Methoden* highly sophisticated; **hoch favorisiert sein** to be the hot favourite *(Brit)* or favorite *(US)*; **hoch gewinnen** to win handsomely; **es ging hoch her** *(inf)* there were lively goings-on *(inf)*; **hoch hinauswollen** to be ambitious; **hoch industrialisiert** highly industrialized; **wie hoch kommt das?** how much is that?; **wenn es hoch kommt** *(inf)* at (the) most, at the outside; **hoch lebe der König!** long live the King!; **hoch qualifiziert** highly qualified; *Arbeitsplätze* for the highly qualified; **hoch schätzen** to estimate generously; **zu hoch schätzen** to overestimate; **hoch geschätzt** *(Mensch)* highly esteemed; *Organisation, Preis* highly prestigious; **in Japan ist dieses Gericht eine hoch geschätzte Delikatesse** in Japan, this dish is considered a great delicacy; **hoch gespannt** *(fig) Erwartungen* extreme; **hoch motiviert** highly motivated; **hoch setzen** *or* **spielen** to play for high stakes; **hoch spezialisiert** highly specialized; **hoch gesteckt** → **hochgesteckt**; **hoch stehend** → **hochstehend**; **hoch gestellte** → **hochgestellt**; **in der Rangordnung sehr hoch stehen** to be very high up in the hierarchy; **hoch verlieren** to lose heavily; **hoch verschuldet** deep in debt; **dieses Gemälde ist hoch versichert** this picture is heavily insured, this picture is insured for a large sum; **hoch wetten** to place high bets → **Kurs b, hochleben**

f [andere Wendungen] **die Polizei rückte an, 50 Mann hoch** *(inf)* the police arrived, 50 strong; **hoch!** cheers!; **die Menge rief hoch!** the crowd cheered

♦ **hoch in hoch in den Bergen** high in the mountains; **hoch in der Luft** high in the air; **hoch in den Siebzigern** in one's late seventies; **bis hoch ins 13. Jahrhundert** until well into the 13th century

♦ **hoch und heilig hoch und heilig versprechen** to promise faithfully; **hoch und heilig schwören** *(inf)* to swear blind *(inf)*

Hoch [hoːx] NT **-s, -s a** *(= Ruf)* **ein (dreifaches) ~ für** *or* **auf jdn ausbringen** to give three cheers for sb; **ein ~ dem Brautpaar** a toast to the bride and groom **b** *(Met, fig)* high

Hoch-: **hoch|acht|bar** ADJ *attr (dated)* highly respectable; **hoch ach|ten, hoch+ach|ten** VT to respect highly; **Hoch|ach|tung** F deep respect; **jdm seine ~ für seine Leistung zollen** to be full of admiration for sb's achievement; **bei aller ~ vor jdm/etw** with (the greatest) respect for sb/sth; **meine ~!** well done!; **mit vorzüglicher ~** *(form: Briefschluss)* yours faithfully; **hoch|ach|tungs|voll** ADV *(Briefschluss) (bei Anrede mit Sir/Madam)* yours faithfully *(Brit)*, sincerely yours *(US)*; *(bei Anrede mit Namen)* yours sincerely *(Brit)*, sincerely yours *(US)*; **Hoch|adel** M high nobility; **hoch|ak|tiv** ADJ *Atommüll etc* high-level; **hoch|ak|tu|ell** ADJ highly topical; **hoch|al|pin** ADJ (high) alpine; *Ausrüstung* high-altitude; **Hoch|al|pi|nist(in)** M(F) high-altitude climber; **Hoch|al|tar** M high altar; **Hoch|amt** NT *(Eccl)* High Mass; **hoch|an|ge|se|hen** ADJ → **hoch 2 e**; **hoch|an|stän|dig** ADJ very decent; **Hoch|an|ten|ne** F roof aerial *(Brit)* or antenna *(US)*; **hoch+ar|bei|ten** VR *sep* to work one's way up; **hoch|auf|ge|schos|sen** ADJ → **hoch 2 b**; **hoch|auf|lö|send** ADJ *(Comput, TV)* high-resolution; **Hoch|bahn** F elevated railway *(Brit)* or railroad *(US)*, el *(US inf)*; **Hoch|ba|rock** M OR NT high baroque; **Hoch|bau** M, *no pl* structural engineering → **Hoch- und Tiefbau**; **hoch+bäu|men** [-bɔymən] VR *sep (Tier)* to rear; **hoch|be|an|sprucht** [-bəlanʃprʊxt] ADJ → **hoch 2 e**; **hoch|be|gabt** ADJ highly gifted *or* talented; **Hoch|be|gab|ten|för|de|rung** F *(= Beihilfe)* bursary *(Brit)* or scholarship for highly gifted students; *(= System)* scholarship system for highly gifted students; *(= Unterricht)* extra *or* specialized tuition for highly gifted students; **Hoch|be|gab|te(r)** MF *decl as adj* gifted person *or* child; **hoch|be|glückt** [-bəglʏkt] ADJ supremely *or* blissfully happy, highly delighted; **hoch|bei|nig** ADJ long-legged; *Auto* high on the road; **hoch+be|kom|men** *ptp* **hochbekommen** VT *sep irreg Stein, Motorhaube etc* to (manage to) lift *or* get up; *Reißverschluss* to (manage to) get *or* do up; **er bekommt keinen hoch** *(inf: Erektion)* he can't get it up *(inf)*; **hoch|be|la|den** ADJ → **hoch 2 e**; **hoch|be|rühmt** ADJ very famous; **hoch|be|steu|ert** ADJ → **hoch 2 e**; **hoch|be|tagt** ADJ aged *attr*, advanced in years; **er ist ~** he has reached a great *or* an advanced age; **Hoch|be|trieb** M *(in Geschäft, Fabrik etc)* peak period; *(im Verkehr)* rush hour; *(= Hochsaison)* high season; **~ haben** to be at one's/its busiest; **hoch|be|zahlt** ADJ → **hoch 2 e**; **hoch+bie|gen** VTR *sep irreg* to bend up *or* upward(s); **hoch+bin|den** VT *sep irreg Haare, Pflanze* to tie up; **hoch+bli|cken** VI *sep* to look up; **Hoch|blü|te** F *(fig) (von Geschichte, Literatur)* golden age; **seine ~ haben** to be at its zenith; **hoch+bo|cken** VT *sep* to jack up; **hoch+brin|gen** VT *sep irreg (inf)* **a** *(= nach oben bringen)* to bring *or* take up **b** *(inf: = hochheben, hochdrücken können)* to (manage to) get up; **einen/keinen ~** *(inf)* to be able/not to be able to get it up *(inf)* **c** *(fig) (= leistungsfähig machen)* to get going; *Kranken* to get back on his *etc* feet; *Schüler* to get up to scratch **d** *(fig inf: = ärgern)* **jdn ~** to get sb's back up *(inf)*; **Hoch|burg** F *(fig)* stronghold; **Hoch|de|cker** [-dɛkɐ] M **-s, -** *(Aviat)* high-wing monoplane; **hoch|deutsch** ADJ standard *or* High German; **die ~e Lautverschiebung** the High German sound shift; **Hoch|deutsch(e)** NT standard *or* High German, the standard *or* High German language → *auch* **Deutsch(e)**; **hoch+die|nen** VR *sep* to work one's way up; **hoch|do|tiert** [-dotiːɐt] ADJ *attr* → **hoch 2 e**; **hoch+dre|hen** VT *sep Fenster* to wind up; *Motor* to rev

Hoch|druck M **a** *no pl (Met)* high pressure **b** *no pl (Typ: = Verfahren)* surface *or* relief printing **c** *pl* **-drucke** *(Typ: = Gedrucktes)* relief print **d** *no pl (Phys)* high pressure **e** *no pl (Med: = Blutdruck)* high blood pressure **f** *no pl (fig)* **mit ~ arbeiten** to work at full stretch

Hoch|druck-: **Hoch|druck|ge|biet** NT *(Met)* high-pressure area, anticyclone; **Hoch|druck|ver|fah|ren** NT *(Typ)* relief printing method

Hoch|druck|zo|ne F *(Met)* high-pressure area, anticyclone

Hoch-: **Hoch|ebe|ne** F plateau; **hoch|emp|find|lich** ADJ *(Tech, Material, Gerät, Instrumente)* highly sensitive; *Film* fast; *Stoff* very delicate; **diese Farbe/dieser Teppich ist ~** this colour *(Brit)* or color *(US)*/carpet shows up everything; **Hoch|ener|gie|la|ser** M high-energy laser; **hoch|ent|wi|ckelt** [-lɛntvɪklt] ADJ → **hoch 2 e**; **hoch|er|freut** [-ɛɐˈfrɔyt] ADJ delighted *(über +acc* at), very pleased *(über +acc* about); **hoch|er|ho|ben** [-lɛɐhoːbn] ADJ raised high; **~en Hauptes** *(fig)* with (one's) head held high; **hoch|ex|plo|siv** ADJ *(lit, fig)* highly explosive; **hoch+fah|ren** *sep irreg* **VI** *aux sein* **a** *(= nach oben fahren)* to go up; *(in Auto)* to drive *or* go up **b** *(erschreckt)* to start (up); **aus dem Schlaf ~** to wake up with a start **c** *(= auf-*

brausen) to flare up VT to take up; (in Auto auch) to drive up; (fig) Produktion to raise, to increase; Reaktor (= in Betrieb nehmen) to start up; (= Leistung erhöhen) to ramp up; Computer to boot up, to start; **hoch|fah|rend** ADJ a (= überheblich) arrogant b = **hochfliegend**; **hoch|fa|vo|ri|siert** ADJ → **hoch 2 e**; **hoch|fein** ADJ (= qualitativ hochwertig) high quality; (= auserlesen) highly select; **hoch|fest** ADJ Kunststoff reinforced; **Hoch|fi|nanz** F high finance; **Hoch|flä|che** F plateau; **hoch+flie|gen** VI sep irreg aux sein to fly up; (Vogel auch) to soar; (= in die Luft geschleudert werden) to be thrown up; **hoch|flie|gend** ADJ Pläne, Ideen etc ambitious; (= übertrieben) high-flown; **hoch|flo|rig** [-floːrɪç] ADJ Samt, Teppich deep-pile attr; **Hoch|form** F top form; **Hoch|for|mat** NT vertical format; (Comput) portrait (format); **hoch|fre|quent** ADJ high frequency; **Hoch|fre|quenz** F (Elec) high frequency, radio frequency

Hoch|fre|quenz-: **Hoch|fre|quenz|strom** M high-frequency current; **Hoch|fre|quenz|tech|nik** F radio-frequency engineering

Hoch-: **Hoch|fri|sur** F upswept hairstyle; **sie hat eine ~** she wears her hair up; **Hoch|ga|ra|ge** F multistorey car park (Brit), multistory parking garage (US); **hoch|ge|be|ne|deit** [-gəbenedait] ADJ (old, Eccl) most blessed; **Hoch|ge|bir|ge** NT high mountains pl, high mountain region or area; **Hoch|ge|birgs|pflan|ze** F alpine plant; **hoch|ge|bo|ren** ADJ (dated) high-born; **(Eure or Euer) Hochgeboren** (Anrede) your Honour (Brit) or Honor (US); **seine Hochgeboren** his Honour (Brit) or Honor (US); **hoch|ge|ehrt** highly honoured (Brit) or honored (US); **Hoch|ge|fühl** NT elation; **ein ~ haben** to have a feeling of elation, to feel elated; **im ~ des Sieges** elated by the victory; **hoch+ge|hen** VI sep irreg aux sein a (= sich nach oben bewegen) to rise; (Preise) to go up, to rise; (Ballon) to ascend, to rise; (Wellen) to surge b (inf: = hinaufgehen) to go up c (inf: = explodieren) to blow up; (Bombe) to go off; **etw ~ lassen** to blow sth up d (inf: = wütend werden) to go through the roof; **da geht einem der Hut hoch** (fig inf) it's enough to make you blow your top (inf) e (inf: = gefasst werden) to get nabbed (inf); **jdn ~ lassen** to bust sb (inf); **hoch|geis|tig** ADJ highly intellectual; Lektüre, Mensch auch highbrow no adv; **hoch|ge|le|gen** ADJ → **hoch 2 a**; **hoch|ge|lehrt** ADJ erudite, very learned; **hoch|ge|mut** [-gəmuːt] ADJ (geh) cheerful, in good spirits; **Hoch|ge|nuss** M great or special treat; (= großes Vergnügen) great pleasure; **jdm ein ~ sein** to be a real treat for sb; **Hoch|ge|richt** NT (Hist) (= Gericht) criminal court; (= Richtstätte) scaffold; **hoch|ge|rüs|tet** [-gərʏstət] ADJ Land with a full military arsenal; Technik, System highly sophisticated; **eine ~e Supermacht** a military superpower; **hoch|ge|schätzt** ADJ → **hoch 2 e**; **hoch|ge|schlos|sen** ADJ Kleid etc high-necked

Hoch|ge|schwin|dig|keits- in cpds high-speed; **Hoch|ge|schwin|dig|keits|ka|me|ra** F high-speed camera; **Hoch|ge|schwin|dig|keits|stre|cke** F (Rail) high-speed rail link; **Hoch|ge|schwin|dig|keits|zug** M a (Rail) high-speed train b (= Rennstrecke) high-speed track; (Abschnitt) high-speed section

hoch-: **hoch|ge|spannt** ADJ → **hoch 2 e**; **hoch|ge|steckt** [-gəʃtɛkt] ADJ (fig, Ziele) ambitious; Ansprüche, Erwartungen considerable; **hoch|ge|stellt** [-gəʃtɛlt] ADJ a Ziffer superscript, superior; **~es Zeichen** superscript; **ein ~es r** a superscript r b **~e Persönlichkeiten aus Politik und Wirtschaft** important or top (inf) politicians and businesspeople; **hoch|ge|sto|chen** ADJ (pej inf) highbrow; Reden highfaluting; Stil pompous; (= eingebildet) stuck-up (inf); **hoch|ge|wach|sen** ADJ tall; **hoch|ge|züch|tet** [-gətsʏçtət] ADJ (usu pej) Motor souped-up (inf); Geräte fancy (inf); Tiere, Pflanzen overbred; System, Wohlfahrtsstaat etc over-developed

Hoch|glanz M high polish or shine; (Phot) gloss; **etw auf ~ polieren or bringen** to polish sth until it gleams; (fig) to make sth spick and span

Hoch|glanz- in cpds glossy; **Hoch|glanz|ab|zug** M (Phot) glossy print; **Hoch|glanz|blatt** NT (Press) glossy (inf)

hoch|glän|zend ADJ Stoff, Oberfläche very shiny; Papier, Fotoabzug very glossy; Möbel highly polished

Hoch|glanz-: **Hoch|glanz|ma|ga|zin** NT (Press) glossy magazine, glossy (inf); **Hoch|glanz|pa|pier** NT high gloss paper; **Hoch|glanz|po|li|tur** F (= Oberfläche) mirror polish or finish; (= Poliermittel) (furniture) polish

Hoch-: **Hoch|go|tik** F high gothic period; **hoch|gra|dig** [-graːdɪç] ADJ no pred extreme; (inf) Unsinn etc absolute, utter ADV extremely; **hoch+gu|cken** VI sep to look up; **hoch|ha|ckig** [-hakɪç] ADJ Schuhe high-heeled; **hoch+hal|ten** VT sep irreg a (= in die Höhe halten) to hold up b (= in Ehren halten) to uphold; **Hoch|haus** NT high-rise building, multistorey (Brit) or multistory (US) building; (= Wolkenkratzer) sky-scraper; **hoch+he|ben** VT sep irreg Hand, Arm to lift, to raise, to hold up; Kind, Last to lift up; **durch Hochheben der Hände abstimmen** to vote by (a) show of hands; **hoch|herr|schaft|lich** ADJ very elegant or grand; Wohnung auch palatial; **hoch|her|zig** ADJ generous, magnanimous; Mensch auch big-hearted; **Hoch|her|zig|keit** [-hɛrtsɪçkait] F -, no pl generosity, magnanimity; (von Mensch auch) big-heartedness; **hoch|in|dust|ri|a|li|siert** [-ɪndʊstrializiːɐt] ADJ → **hoch 2 e**; **hoch|in|tel|li|gent** ADJ highly intelligent; **hoch|in|te|res|sant** ADJ very or most interesting; **hoch+ja|gen** VT sep (inf) a (= aufscheuchen) Vögel to scare up; Menschen to get up b (= sprengen) to blow up c Motor to rev up; **hoch+ju|beln** VT sep (inf) Künstler, Film, Politiker etc to build up, to hype (inf); **hoch+käm|men** VT sep Haar to put up; **hoch|kant** [ˈhoːxkant] ADV a (lit) on end; **~ stellen** to up-end, to put on end b (fig inf: auch **hochkantig**) **~ hinauswerfen/hinausfliegen** to chuck/be chucked out (inf); **hoch|ka|rä|tig** ADJ a Diamanten, Gold high-carat b (fig) top-class ADV **ein ~ besetzter Film** a film with a top-class cast; **Hoch|kir|che** F High Church; **hoch|klapp|bar** ADJ Tisch, Stuhl folding; Sitz tip-up; **hoch+klap|pen** sep VT Tisch, Stuhl to fold up; Sitz to tip up; Kühlerhaube, Deckel to raise, to lift up; Mantelkragen to turn up VI aux sein (Tisch, Stuhl) to fold up; (Sitz) to tip up; **hoch+klet|tern** VI sep aux sein (lit, fig) to climb up; **hoch+ko|chen** sep VT Thema to stir up VI aux sein (Emotionen) to run high; Gerüchte to spread; **hoch+kom|men** VI sep irreg aux sein a (inf: = hinauf-, heraufkommen) to come up b (inf) **das Essen ist ihm hochgekommen** he threw up (his meal) (inf); **es kommt mir hoch** it makes me sick c (= aufstehen können) to (manage to) get up; (fig: = sich aufraffen, gesund werden) to get back on one's feet d (inf: beruflich, gesellschaftlich) to come up in the world; **niemanden (neben sich** dat**) ~ lassen** not to tolerate competition; **hoch|kom|pli|ziert** ADJ → **hoch 2 e**; **Hoch|kon|junk|tur** F boom; **hoch+kön|nen** VI sep irreg (inf) (= aufstehen können) to be able to get up; (= hinaufsteigen können) to be able to get up (auf etw (acc) onto sth, auf Berg the mountain); **hinten nicht mehr ~** (inf) to be more dead than alive; **hoch|kon|zent|riert** ADJ a (Chem) highly concentrated b Mensch → **hoch 2 e**; **hoch+krem|peln** VT sep Ärmel, Hosenbeine to roll up; **hoch+krie|gen** VT sep (inf) = **hochbekommen**; **hoch|kul|ti|viert** ADJ highly sophisticated; Lebensart highly civilized; **Hoch|kul|tur** F (very) advanced civilization; **hoch+kur|beln** VT sep Fenster to wind up; **hoch+la|den** VT sep irreg (Comput) to upload; **Hoch|land** NT highland; **das schottische ~** the Scottish Highlands pl; **Hoch|län|der** [ˈhoːxlɛndɐ] M -s, -, **Hoch|län|de|rin** [-ərɪn] F -, -nen highlander; **Hoch|land|kaf|fee** M high-grown coffee; **Hoch|lau|tung** F (Ling) Standard German pronunciation; **hoch+le|ben** VI sep **jdn ~ lassen** to give three cheers for sb; **er lebe hoch!** three cheers (for him)!; **hoch lebe der König!** long live the King!; **hoch+le|gen** VT sep a Beine etc to put up b (inf: = nach oben legen) to put high up

Hoch|leis|tung F first-class performance

Hoch|leis|tungs- in cpds high-performance; **Hoch|leis|tungs|mo|tor** M high-performance engine; **Hoch|leis|tungs|öl** NT heavy-duty oil; **Hoch|leis|tungs|sor|te** F (Agr) high-yield variety; **Hoch|leis|tungs|sport** M top-class sport; **Hoch|leis|tungs|sport|ler(in)** M(F) top athlete; **Hoch|leis|tungs|trai|ning** NT intensive training

höch|lich(st) [ˈhøːçlɪçst] ADV (dated) highly, greatly, most

Hoch-: **hoch|löb|lich** ADJ (dated) very or highly praiseworthy; (iro) most appreciated; **Hoch|lohn|land** NT country with high wage costs; **Hoch|mit|tel|al|ter** NT high Middle Ages pl; **hoch|mo|dern** [-modɛrn] ADJ very modern, ultra-modern ADV in a very modern way, in an ultra-modern way; **hoch|mo|disch** ADJ highly or very fashionable, the height of fashion pred; **hoch|mö|gend** ADJ influential; **Hoch|moor** NT moor; **Hoch|mut** M arrogance; **~ kommt vor dem Fall** (Prov) pride comes before a fall (Prov); **hoch|mo|ti|viert** ADJ highly motivated → auch **hoch 2 e**; **hoch|mü|tig** [ˈhoːxmyːtɪç] ADJ arrogant; **Hoch|mü|tig|keit** F -, no pl arrogance; **hoch|nä|sig** [ˈhoːxnɛːzɪç] (inf) ADJ snooty (inf) ADV snootily (inf), haughtily, snobbishly; **Hoch|nä|sig|keit** F -, no pl (inf) snootiness (inf); **Hoch|ne|bel** M (low) stratus; **hoch+neh|men** VT sep irreg a (= heben) to lift; Kind, Hund to pick or lift up b (dial: in oberes Stockwerk) to take up c (inf: = necken) **jdn ~** to pull sb's leg d (inf: = verhaften) to pick up (inf); **Hoch|ofen** M blast furnace; **hoch|of|fi|zi|ell** ADJ highly or extremely formal; **hoch+päp|peln** VT sep (inf) Tier, Kind, Kranken to feed up; (fig) to nurse back to health; **Hoch|par|ter|re** NT raised ground floor; **Hoch|pla|teau** NT plateau; **hoch|po|ly|mer** [-polymeːɐ] ADJ (Chem) high-polymeric; **hoch|prei|sig** [-praizɪç] ADJ high-priced; **Hoch|preis|po|li|tik** F policy of high pricing; **hoch|pro|zen|tig** ADJ alkoholische Getränke high-proof; Lösung highly concentrated; Gewinnzuwächse, Rabatte high-percentage; Wertpapiere high-interest; **hoch+pu|schen** VT sep Problem to play up, to make a lot of; **er wurde zur literarischen Sensation hochgepuscht** he was built up to be a literary sensation; **hoch|qua|li|fi|ziert** ADJ → **hoch 2 e**; **Hoch|rad** NT penny-farthing (Brit) or ordinary (US) (bicycle); **hoch|räd|rig** ADJ with high wheels; **hoch+ra|gen** VI sep aux sein or haben (Bäume) to rise (up); (Berge, Türme, Häuser) to tower (up), to rise up; **hoch+ran|ken** VIR sep (vi: aux sein) to creep (up), to climb (up); **hoch+rech|nen** sep VT to project VI to make a projection; **Hoch|rech|nung** F projection; **Hoch|reck** NT high or horizontal bar; **hoch+re|cken** sep VT Arme, Hände to raise or stretch up; **den Hals or Kopf ~** to crane one's neck VR to draw oneself up; **hoch|rein** ADJ high-purity; **hoch+rei|ßen** VT sep irreg Arme to bring up; Kamera, Waffe to lift quickly; (Aviat) to put into a steep climb, to hoick (spec); **Hoch|re|li|ef** NT high relief; **Hoch|re|nais|sance** F high renaissance; **hoch|rot** ADJ bright red; **mit ~em Gesicht** with one's face as red as a beetroot *(Brit)* or beet *(US)*; **Hoch|ruf** M cheer; **hoch+rüs|ten** VT *sep* **ein Land ~** to increase the weaponry of a country; **Hoch|rüs|tung** F, *no pl* arms build-up; **hoch+rut|schen** VI *sep aux sein (Kleidungsstück)* to ride up; *(inf: = aufrücken)* to move up; **Hoch|sai|son** F high season; **hoch schät|zen** △, **hoch+schät|zen** *sep* VT to respect highly; **hoch+schau|keln** *sep* VT *Problem, Angelegenheit* to blow up VR to work oneself up; **hoch+scheu|chen** VT *sep (inf)* = **aufscheuchen**; **hoch+schie|ßen** *sep irreg* VI *aux sein* to shoot up VT *Feuerwerksrakete, Leuchtkugel* to send up; **hoch+schla|gen** *sep irreg* VT *Kragen* to turn up VI *aux sein (Wellen)* to surge up; *(Flammen)* to leap up; **hoch+schnel|len** VI *sep aux sein (Lachse)* to leap up; *(Feder, Mensch, Preise auch)* to shoot up; **Hoch|schrank** M tall cupboard; **hoch+schrau|ben** *sep*, **hoch schrau|ben** △ VT **a** *(lit)* to raise; **b** *(fig) Preise* to force up; *Erwartungen* to raise; *Forderungen, Ansprüche* to increase; **hoch+schre|cken** VTI *sep (vi: irreg aux sein)* = **aufschrecken**

Hoch|schul-: **Hoch|schul|ab|schluss** M degree; **mit ~** with a degree; **Hoch|schul|ab|sol|vent(in)** M(F) graduate; **Hoch|schul|(aus)|bil|dung** F *(= Ausbildung)* college training; *(an Universität)* university training; *(= Bildung)* university education

Hoch|schu|le F college; *(= Universität)* university; **Technische ~** technical college, college of technology

Hoch|schü|ler(in) M(F) student; *(Univ auch)* undergraduate

Hoch|schul-: **Hoch|schul|leh|rer(in)** M(F) → **Hochschule** college/university teacher, lecturer *(Brit)*; **Hoch|schul|po|li|tik** F higher education policy; **Hoch|schul|re|form** F university reform; **Hoch|schul|rei|fe** F *academic standard required for university entrance*; **er hat (die) ~** ≈ he's got his A-levels *(Brit)*, ≈ he's graduated from high school *(US)*; **Hoch|schul|stu|di|um** NT higher education, university education; **Hoch|schul|we|sen** NT, *no pl* system of higher education, university system; **Hoch|schul|zu|gang** M university entrance or admission

hoch|schwan|ger ADJ well advanced in pregnancy, very pregnant

Hoch|see F high sea; **auf ~** on the high seas or open sea

Hoch|see-: **Hoch|see|fi|sche|rei** F deep-sea fishing; **Hoch|see|jacht** F ocean(-going) yacht; **Hoch|see|kut|ter** M deep-sea cutter; **Hoch|see|schiff|fahrt** F deep-sea shipping; **hoch|see|tüch|tig** ADJ ocean-going

Hoch-: **hoch+se|hen** VI *sep irreg* to look up **er sah zu uns hoch** he looked up to us; **Hoch|seil** NT high wire, tightrope; **Hoch|seil|akt** M *(von Artisten)* high-wire or tightrope act; *(fig)* tightrope walk; **hoch|sen|si|bel** ADJ *Apparat, Angelegenheit, Gespräch, Daten, Patient* highly sensitive; **Hoch|si|cher|heits|ge|fäng|nis** NT high-security prison; **Hoch|si|cher|heits|trakt** M high-security wing; **Hoch|sitz** M *(Hunt)* (raised) hide; **Hoch|som|mer** M height of the summer; *(= Zeitabschnitt)* midsummer *no art*; **hoch|som|mer|lich** ADJ very summery

Hoch|span|nung F *(Elec)* high voltage, high tension; *(fig)* high tension; **„Vorsicht ~"** "danger - high voltage"

Hoch|span|nungs-: **Hoch|span|nungs|lei|tung** F high-tension line, power line; **Hoch|span|nungs|mast** M pylon; **Hoch|span|nungs|tech|nik** F high-voltage engineering

hoch|spe|zi|a|li|siert [-ʃpetsiali'siːɐt] ADJ → **hoch 2 e**

Hoch-: **hoch+spie|len** VT *sep (fig)* to blow up, to play up; **etw (künstlich) ~** to blow sth (up) out of all proportion; **Hoch|spra|che** F standard language; **hoch|sprach|lich** ADJ standard; **~e Prosa** prose in standard German/English *etc* ADV **~ heißt es ...** in standard German/English *etc* that's ...; **hoch+sprin|gen** VI *sep irreg aux sein* **a** *(inf: = aufspringen)* to jump up *(an jdm* on sb); **auf etw** *(acc)* **~** to jump (up) on sth **b** *(inf: = schnell hinauflaufen)* to run up **c** *infin, ptp only (Sport)* to do the high jump; **Hoch|sprin|ger(in)** M(F) high jumper; **Hoch|sprung** M *(= Disziplin)* high jump; *(= Sprung)* jump

höchst [hø:çst] ADJ → **höchste(r, s)** ADV *(= überaus)* highly, extremely, most

Höchst|al|ter [hø:çst-] NT maximum age

Hoch-: **hoch|stäm|mig** ADJ *Baum* tall; *Rosen* long-stemmed; **Hoch|stand** M *(Hunt)* (raised) hide; **Hoch|sta|pe|lei** [hoːxʃtaːpə'lai] F **-, -en** *(Jur)* fraud; *(einzelner Fall)* swindle, con trick; *(fig: = Aufschneiderei)* boasting *no pl*; **hoch+sta|peln** ['hoːxʃtaːpln] VI *sep* to be fraudulent, to practise fraud *(form)*; *(fig)* to put one over *(inf)*; **Hoch|stap|ler** ['hoːxʃtaːplɐ] M **-s, -**, **Hoch|stap|le|rin** [-ərɪn] F **-, -nen** confidence trickster; *(Mann auch)* con man *(inf)*; *(fig)* fraud; **Hoch|start** M *(Sport)* standing start

Höchst-: **Höchst|be|trag** ['hø:çst-] M maximum amount; **Höchst|bie|ten|de(r)** ['hø:çstbi:tndə] MF *decl as adj* highest bidder

höchs|te ADJ = **höchste(r, s)**

Höchs|te = **Höchste(r), Höchste(s)**

hoch-: **hoch+ste|cken** VT *sep* to pin up; *Haare auch* to put up; **hoch|ste|hend** ADJ **a** *(gesellschaftlich)* of high standing; *(kulturell)* highly advanced; *(geistig)* highly intellectual; *(entwicklungsmäßig, qualitativ)* superior **b** *Kragen* turned-up; **hoch+stei|gen** ['hoːxʃtaign] VI *sep irreg aux sein* = **hinaufsteigen, heraufsteigen a, aufsteigen a**; **hoch+stel|len** VT *sep* **a** *(an höhere Stelle) Stühle etc* to put up; *(außer Reichweite)* to put or place high up; **hochgestellte Zahlen** superior numbers **b** *(inf: = höher einstellen) Heizung, Ventilator etc* to turn up **c** *Kragen* to turn up; **Hoch|stell|tas|te** F *(Comput)* shift key; **hoch+stem|men** *sep* VT to lift or raise up (with great effort) VR to raise oneself up

höchst|ei|gen [hø:çstl'aign] ADJ, ADV *(dated, hum)* in person; **in ~er Person** *(dated, hum)* in person; **in ~em Interesse** in one's own interest

höchs|ten|falls ['hø:çstnfals] ADV at (the) most, at the outside

höchs|tens ['hø:çstns] ADV **a** *(= nicht mehr, länger als)* not more than; *(= bestenfalls)* at the most, at best **b** *(= außer)* except

höchs|te(r, s) ['hø:çstə] ADJ *superl von* **hoch** **a** *(räumliche Ausdehnung)* highest; *Wuchs, Zimmer, Baum, Mast* tallest; *Leiter* tallest, longest

b *Preis, Verdienst, Temperatur, Druck etc* highest; *Betrag, Summe* largest; *Strafe, Gewicht* heaviest; *Profit* highest, biggest; *Lotteriegewinn* biggest; *Verlust* most severe; *Schaden* most expensive; *(= maximal) Verdienst, Temperatur, Geschwindigkeit etc* maximum *attr*; **im ~n Grade/Maße** extremely; **im ~n Fall(e)** at the most

c *(im Rang)* highest; *Ehre* greatest; *Fest* most important; *Offizier* highest-ranking; **das ~ Wesen** the Supreme Being; **die ~ Instanz** the supreme court of appeal; **sich an ~r Stelle beschweren** to complain to the highest authority

d *attr (qualitativ, äußerst) Lebensstandard, Ansprüche* highest; *Bedeutung, Genuss, Glück* greatest, supreme; *Gut, Freude* greatest; *Not, Gefahr, Wichtigkeit* utmost, greatest; *Konzentration* extreme; **zu meiner ~n Zufriedenheit** to my great satisfaction

e *Alter* greatest; *(Mus)* highest

f *(in Wendungen)* **~ Zeit** or **Eisenbahn** *(inf)* high time; **der ~ Norden** the extreme North; **das ist das ~ der Gefühle** that is the highest or most sublime feeling or of feelings; **aufs Höchste** or **~ erfreut** *etc* highly or greatly or tremendously *(inf)* pleased *etc*; **das ist das Höchste, was ich bezahlen/tun kann** that is the most I can pay/do

ADV **am ~n** **a** *(= in größter Höhe)* highest; **mittags steht die Sonne am ~n** the sun is highest at noon

b *(= in größtem Ausmaß) verehren, schätzen* most (of all); *versichern, begabt* most; *besteuert, verlieren* (the) most heavily; *verschuldet* (the) most deeply; **in der Rangordnung am ~n stehen** to be the highest up in the hierarchy; **er ist am ~n qualifiziert** he is the most (highly) qualified; **am ~n stehen** *(Kurse, Temperatur)* to be at its highest

Höchs|te(r) ['hø:çstə] M *decl as adj* **der ~** the Lord, the Supreme Being

Höchs|te(s) ['hø:çstə] NT *decl as adj (fig)* highest good; **nach dem ~n streben** to aspire to the ideal or to perfection

Höchst-: **Höchst|fall** M **im ~** *(= nicht mehr, länger als)* not more than; *(= bestenfalls)* at the most, at best; **Höchst|form** F *(Sport)* top form; **Höchst|fre|quenz|wel|le** F microwave; **Höchst|ge|bot** NT highest bid; **Höchst|ge|schwin|dig|keit** F top or maximum speed; **zulässige ~** speed limit; **Höchst|gren|ze** F upper limit

Hoch-: **hoch|stie|lig** [-ʃtiːlɪç] ADJ long-stemmed; **hoch+sti|li|sie|ren** *ptp* **hochstilisiert** VT *sep* to build up *(zu* into); **Hoch|stim|mung** F high spirits *pl*

Höchst-: **Höchst|leis|tung** F best performance; *(bei Produktion)* maximum output; **Höchst|mar|ke** F *(von Wasserstand etc)* highest level or mark; **Höchst|maß** NT maximum amount *(an +dat* of); **höchst|per|sön|lich** ['hø:çstpɛr'zøːnlɪç] ADV personally; **es ist der Prinz ~** it's the prince in person; **Höchst|preis** M top or maximum price

Hoch-: **Hoch|stra|ße** F fly-over; **hoch+stre|ben** VI *sep aux sein (geh)* **a** *(= aufragen)* to soar, to tower **b** *(fig: = nach Höherem streben)* to aspire *(nach* to, after); **hoch+strei|fen** VT *sep Ärmel* to push up

Höchst-: **höchst|rich|ter|lich** ['hø:çst'rɪçtɐlɪç] ADJ of the supreme court; **Höchst|satz** M *(beim Glücksspiel)* maximum stake; *(bei Versicherungen)* maximum rate; **Höchst|stand** M highest level; **Höchst|stra|fe** F maximum penalty; **höchst|wahr|schein|lich** ['hø:çstvaːɐ'ʃainlɪç] ✪ 42.2 ADV in all probability, most probably or likely; **Höchst|wert** M maximum value

hoch+sty|len VT *sep* to give style to; *(pej) Person* to hype *(inf)*; *Auto* to soup up *(inf)*; *Laden etc* to tart up *(Brit inf)*, to dress up *(esp US)*; **ein hochgestyltes Produkt** a stylish product

höchst|zu|läs|sig ADJ *attr* maximum (permissible)

Hoch-: **Hoch|tal** NT high-lying valley; **Hoch|tech|no|lo|gie** F high technology; **Hoch|tem|pe|ra|tur|re|ak|tor** M high temperature reactor; **hoch|tö|nend** ADJ *Worte, Reden* high-sounding; **Hoch|tö|ner** M *(= Hochtonlautsprecher)* tweeter; **Hoch|tour** F **auf ~en laufen/arbeiten** *(Maschinen)* to run at full speed; *(fig: Mensch, Fabrik etc)* to run/work at full steam; **etw auf ~en bringen** *(Motor)* to rev sth up to full speed; *Maschine, Produktion, Kampagne* to get sth into full swing; **jdn auf ~en bringen** *(inf)* to get sb really going *(inf)*; **hoch|tou|rig** [-tuːrɪç] ADJ *Motor* high-revving ADV **~ fahren** to drive at high revs; **hoch|tra|bend** *(pej)* ADJ pompous, turgid ADV pompously; **hoch+trei|ben** *sep irreg*, **hoch trei|ben** △ *irreg* VT **a** *(= hinauftreiben)* to drive up **b** *(fig) Preise, Löhne, Kosten* to force up; **Hoch- und Tief|bau** M, *no pl* structural and civil engineering; **hoch|ver|dient** ADJ *attr Mensch* of great merit; *Lob, Sieg* much-deserved; **hoch|ver|ehrt** ADJ *attr* highly respected or esteemed; *(in Brief)* esteemed *(old)*; **~er Herr Vorsitzender ...** Mr Chairman ...; **~er Herr Präsident!** Mr President, Sir!; *(in Brief)* Dear Sir; **Hoch|ver|rat** M high treason; **Hoch|ver|rä|ter(in)** M(F) person guilty of high treason, traitor; **hoch|ver|rä|te|risch** ADJ treasonable; **hoch|ver|schul|det** [-fɛɐʃʊldət] ADJ → **hoch 2 e**; **hoch|ver|zins|lich**

ADJ high interest-bearing; **Hoch|wald** M timber forest

Hoch|was|ser NT *pl* **-wasser** **a** *(= Höchststand von Flut)* high tide **b** *(= überhoher Wasserstand in Flüssen, Seen)* high water; *(= Überschwemmung)* flood; **~ haben** *(Fluss)* to be in flood; **er hat ~** *(hum inf)* his trousers are at half-mast *(esp Brit inf)*, he has (on) floods *(US inf)*

Hoch|was|ser-: **Hoch|was|ser|ge|fahr** F danger of flooding; **Hoch|was|ser|ho|sen** PL *(hum inf)* trousers *pl* at half-mast *(Brit inf)*, floods *pl (US inf)*; **Hoch|was|ser|ka|ta|stro|phe** F flood disaster; **Hoch|was|ser|mar|ke** F high-water mark; **Hoch|was|ser|scha|den** M flood damage; **Hoch|was|ser|schutz** M flood protection; **Hoch|was|ser|stand** M high-water level

Hoch-: **hoch+wer|fen** VT *sep irreg* to throw up; **hoch|wer|tig** ADJ high-quality *attr*, of high quality; *Nahrungsmittel* highly nutritious; *Stahl* high-grade; *(Chem)* high-valency *attr*, of high valency; **Hoch|wild** NT big game *(including bigger game birds)*; **hoch|will|kom|men** ADJ most *or* very welcome; **sie sind uns als Gäste ~** we are delighted to welcome them as our guests; **hoch|wirk|sam** ADJ highly effective; **hoch+wöl|ben** *sep* VT **etw ~** to make sth bulge up VR to bulge up; **hoch+wol|len** VI *sep (inf)* to want up *(inf)*; *(= aufstehen wollen auch)* to want to get up; *(= in die Höhe wollen auch, nach Norden wollen)* to want to go up; **Hoch|wür|den** M **-s**, *no pl (dated: Anrede)* Reverend Father; **hoch|wür|dig** ADJ *(dated)* Reverend; **Hoch|zahl** F exponent

Hoch|zeit ['hɔxtsait] ✪ 51.3, 52.1 F **-, -en** wedding; *(= Eheschließung auch)* marriage; **~ machen** *or* **haben** to get married; **~ halten** *or* **feiern** to have a wedding; **etw zur ~ geschenkt bekommen/schenken** to get/give sth as a wedding present; **grüne ~** wedding day; **silberne/goldene/diamantene ~** silver/golden/diamond wedding (anniversary); **man kann nicht auf zwei ~en tanzen** *(prov)* you can't have your cake and eat it *(prov)*

Hoch|zeit ['ho:xtsait] F **-, -en** *(= Blütezeit)* golden age

hoch|zei|ten ['hɔxtsaitn] VI *insep (dated, Aus, S Ger)* to marry

Hoch|zei|ter ['hɔxtsaitɐ] M **-s, -** *(dated, Aus, Sw, S Ger)* bridegroom; **die ~** the bride and groom

Hoch|zei|te|rin ['hɔxtsaitərın] F **-, -nen** *(dated, Aus, Sw, S Ger)* bride

hoch|zeit|lich ['hɔxtsaitlıç] ADJ bridal *attr*, wedding *attr* ADV **die Braut war ~ gekleidet** the bride was in her wedding dress; **der Bräutigam war ~ gekleidet** the groom was in his wedding attire; **~ geschmückt** decorated for a/the wedding

Hoch|zeits- *in cpds* wedding; **Hoch|zeits|an|zei|ge** F wedding announcement; **Hoch|zeits|fei|er** F wedding celebration; *(= Empfang)* reception, wedding breakfast; **Hoch|zeits|fest** NT wedding celebration; **Hoch|zeits|flug** M *(Zool)* nuptial flight; **Hoch|zeits|gast** M wedding guest; **Hoch|zeits|ge|sell|schaft** F wedding party; **Hoch|zeits|kleid** NT wedding dress, bridal dress *or* gown; **Hoch|zeits|nacht** F wedding night; **Hoch|zeits|rei|se** F honeymoon; **wohin geht die ~?** where are you going on (your) honeymoon?; **Hoch|zeits|rei|sen|de** PL *decl as adj* honeymoon couple, honeymooners *pl*; **Hoch|zeits|tag** M wedding day; *(= Jahrestag)* wedding anniversary; **Hoch|zeits|vi|deo** NT wedding video; **Hoch|zeits|zug** M wedding procession

hoch+zie|hen *sep irreg* VT **a** *Gegenstand* to pull up; *Hosen etc auch* to hitch up; *Fahne* to run up; *Augenbrauen* to raise, to lift; **die Maschine ~** *(Aviat)* to put the aircraft into a steep climb; **er zog die Knie bis unters Kinn hoch** he drew his knees up toward(s) his chin **b** *(inf: = bauen)* to throw up *(inf)* VR to pull oneself up; **sich an etw** *(dat)* **~** to climb up sth; *(fig inf)* to get a kick out of sth *(inf)*

Hoch-: **Hoch|ziel** NT *(geh)* ultimate goal

Hoch|zins-: **Hoch|zins|pha|se** F *(Fin)* period of high interest rates, high interest rate policy; **Hoch|zins|po|li|tik** F *(Fin)* high interest rate policy

hoch|zu|frie|den ADJ very satisfied

Hock [hɔk] M **-s, ¨-e** ['hœkə] *(Sw, dial)* get-together

Ho|cke ['hɔkə] F **-, -n** squatting position; *(= Übung)* squat; *(beim Turnen)* squat vault; *(beim Skilaufen)* crouch; *(beim Ringen)* mat position; **in die ~ gehen** to squat (down); **in der ~ sitzen** to squat

Ho|cke F **-, -n** stook, shock

ho|cken ['hɔkn] VI *(S Ger: aux sein)* **a** *(= in der Hocke sitzen)* to squat, to crouch **b** *(inf: = sitzen)* to sit; *(auf Hocker)* to perch **c** *(pej inf)* to sit around **d** *(Sport)* **übers Pferd ~** to squat-vault over the horse VR **a** *(= in Hockstellung gehen)* to squat **b** *(inf: = sich setzen)* to sit down, to plonk oneself down *(inf)*

ho|cken blei|ben, *(fig auch)* **ho|cken+blei|ben** *sep* VI *irreg aux sein (dial inf)* = **sitzen bleiben**

Ho|cker ['hɔkɐ] M **-s, -** **a** *(= Stuhl)* stool; **jdn vom ~ reißen** *or* **hauen** *(fig inf)* to bowl sb over *(inf)* **b** *(Archeol)* seated burial

Hö|cker ['hœkɐ] M **-s, -** **a** *(von Kamel, inf: = Buckel)* hump; *(auf Schnabel)* knob **b** *(= Erhebung)* bump; *(in Gelände)* hump; *(= kleiner Hügel)* hummock, hump

Ho|cker|grab NT seated burial

hö|cke|rig ['hœkərıç] ADJ *(= uneben)* bumpy; *(= buckelig)* hunch-backed; *Nase* with a bump; *Schnabel* with a knob

Ho|ckey ['hɔki, 'hɔke] NT **-s**, *no pl* hockey *(Brit)*, field hockey *(US)*

Ho|ckey-: **Ho|ckey|ball** M (field *(US)*) hockey ball; **Ho|ckey|schlä|ger** M (field *(US)*) hockey stick; **Ho|ckey|spie|ler(in)** M(F) (field *(US)*) hockey player; **Ho|ckey|stock** M (field *(US)*) hockey stick

höck|rig ['hœkrıç] ADJ = **höckerig**

Hock-: **Hock|sitz** M squat; **Hock|sprung** M *(Sport)* *(über Gerät)* squat vault; *(beim Bodenturnen)* crouch jump; **Hock|stel|lung** F crouched *or* squatting position; *(Archeol)* seated position

Ho|de ['ho:də] M **-n, -n** *or f* **-, -n**, **Ho|den** ['ho:dn] M **-s, -** testicle

Ho|den-: **Ho|den|bruch** M scrotal hernia; **Ho|den|ent|zün|dung** F inflammation of the testicles, orchitis *(spec)*; **Ho|den|sack** M scrotum

Hof [ho:f] M **-(e)s, ¨-e** ['hø:fə] **a** *(= Platz)* yard; *(= Innenhof)* courtyard; *(= Schulhof)* schoolyard, playground; *(= Kasernenhof)* square **b** *(= Bauernhof)* farm; *(= Gebäudekomplex)* farm(yard) **c** *(= Fürstenhof)* court; **bei** *or* **am ~e** at court; **am ~e Ludwig XIV.** at the court of Louis XIV; **~ halten** *(lit, fig)* to hold court **d** **einem Mädchen den ~ machen** *(dated, hum)* to court a girl *(dated)*, to pay court to a girl *(form)* **e** *(um Sonne, Mond)* halo **f** *(in Namen: = Gasthof, Hotel)* hotel, inn

Hof-: **Hof|amt** NT court appointment; **Hof|arzt** M, **Hof|ärz|tin** F court physician; **Hof|ball** M court ball; **Hof|da|me** F lady-in-waiting; **Hof|dich|ter(in)** M(F) court poet; *(in GB)* poet laureate; **Hof|ein|fahrt** F courtyard entrance

hö|feln ['hø:fln] VI *(Sw)* to flatter *(jdm* sb)

Hof-: **Hof|er|be** M, **Hof|er|bin** F heir to a/the farm; **Hof|eti|ket|te** F court etiquette; **hof|fä|hig** ['ho:ffε:ıç] ADJ acceptable at court; *(= gesellschaftsfähig)* presentable; **jdn/etw ~ machen** *(fig)* to make sb/sth (socially) acceptable; **Hof|fä|hig|keit** F *(fig)* (social) acceptability

Hof|fart ['hɔfart] F **-**, *no pl (dated)* pride, arrogance, haughtiness

hof|fär|tig ['hɔfεrtıç] ADJ *(dated)* proud, arrogant, haughty

hof|fen ['hɔfn] ✪ 30, 31, 48.2 VI **a** *(= von Hoffnung erfüllt sein)* to hope; **auf Gott ~** to trust in God; **auf jdn ~** to set one's hopes on sb; **auf etw ~** *(acc)* to hope for sth; **da bleibt nur zu ~** one can only hope; **sie hofften auf ihre Verbündeten** *(auf Erscheinen)* they were waiting for their allies; *(auf Hilfe)* they set their hopes on their allies; **der Mensch hofft, solange er lebt** *(Prov)* hope springs eternal *(prov)*; **Hoffen und Harren macht manchen zum Narren** *(Prov)* some people never give up hoping **b** *(= wünschen und erwarten)* to hope; **~, dass ...** to hope that ...; **ich will nicht ~, dass er das macht** I hope he doesn't do that; **ich will/wir wollen ~, dass ...** I/we can only hope that ..., it is to be hoped that ...
VT to hope for; **~ wir das Beste!** let's hope for the best!; **es ist zu ~** it is to be hoped; **ich hoffe es** I hope so; **das will ich (doch wohl) ~** I should (jolly well *(Brit inf)*) hope so; **das wollen wir ~** let's hope so; **ich will es nicht ~** I hope not; **sie hatten nichts mehr zu ~** they had nothing left to hope for

hof|fent|lich ['hɔfntlıç] ADV hopefully; **~!** I hope so, let us hope so; **~ nicht** I/we hope not; **~ ist das bald vorbei** I/we *etc* hope that it will be over soon, hopefully it will be over soon; **du bist mir doch ~ nicht böse** I (do) hope (that) you're not angry with me

-höf|fig [hœfıç] ADJ *suf (Min)* promising a rich yield of; **ein erdölhöffiges Gebiet** an area which promises a rich yield of oil

höff|lich ['hœflıç] ADJ *(Min)* promising a rich yield

Hoff|nung ['hɔfnʊŋ] F **-, -en** hope; *(auf Gott)* trust *(auf +acc* in); **sich** *(dat)* **~en machen** to have hopes; **sich** *(dat)* **keine ~en machen** not to hold out any hopes; **er macht sich ~en bei ihr** *(inf)* he fancies his chances with her *(Brit inf)*, he thinks his chances with her are quite good *(esp US)*; **mach dir keine ~(en)!** I wouldn't even think about it; **jdm ~en machen** to raise sb's hopes; **jdm ~en machen, dass ...** to lead sb to hope that ...; **jdm auf etw** *(acc)* **~en machen** to lead sb to expect sth; **jdm keine ~en machen** not to hold out any hopes for sb; **seine ~en auf jdn/etw setzen** to place one's hopes in sb/sth, to pin one's hopes on sb/sth; **die ~ aufgeben/verlieren** to abandon/lose hope; **eine ~ begraben** *or* **zu Grabe tragen** to abandon a hope; **eine ~ zerstören/enttäuschen** to dash/disappoint sb's hopes; **in der ~, bald von Ihnen zu hören** hoping to hear from you soon, in the hope of hearing from you soon; **sich einer ~/unbegründeten/falschen ~en hingeben** to cherish hopes/unfounded hopes/false hopes; **zu schönen** *or* **zu den schönsten ~en berechtigen** to give rise to great hopes; **~ auf etw** *(acc)* **haben** to have hopes of getting sth; **guter ~ sein** *(euph: = schwanger)* to be expecting

Hoff|nungs-: **hoff|nungs|freu|dig**, **hoff|nungs|froh** ADJ hopeful ADV in happy anticipation; **Hoff|nungs|fun|ke(n)** M glimmer of hope; **Hoff|nungs|lauf** M *(Sport)* repechage; **hoff|nungs|los** ADJ hopeless; **ein ~er Romantiker** an eternal romantic ADV hopelessly; **Hoff|nungs|lo|sig|keit** F **-**, *no pl* hopelessness; *(= Verzweiflung)* despair; **Hoff|nungs|schim|mer** M glimmer of hope; **Hoff|nungs|strahl** M ray of hope; **Hoff|nungs|trä|ger(in)** M(F) person on whom hopes are pinned; **er war der ~ der Partei** he carried the hopes of the party; **hoff|nungs|voll** ADJ hopeful; *(= vielversprechend)* promising ADV full of hope

Hof-: **Hof|gang** M *pl* **-gänge** yard exercise; **Hof|geist|li|che(r)** MF *decl as adj* court chaplain; **Hof|ge|sell|schaft** F court society; **Hof|ge|sin|de** NT **a** *(auf Bauernhof)* farm workers *pl* **b** *(am Fürstenhof)* servants *pl* at (the/a) court; **hof+hal|ten** △ VI *sep irreg* →

Hof c; **Hof|hal|tung** F (holding of) court; **Hof|herr(in)** M(F) *(= Gutsherr)* estate owner; *(in England)* squire; **Hof|hund** M watchdog

ho|fie|ren [ho'fi:rən] *ptp* **hofiert** VT *(dated)* to court

hö|fisch ['hø:fɪʃ] ADJ **a** *(= eines Fürstenhofs) Leben, Sitten, Vergnügen* courtly *no adv* **b** *(Liter) Dichtung etc* courtly *no adv* **c** *(old: = kultiviert) Benehmen, Kleidung* sophisticated

Hof-: **Hof|ka|pel|le** F **a** *(= Kirche am Hof)* court chapel **b** *(Mus)* court orchestra; **Hof|knicks** M court *or* formal curtsey *(Brit) or* curtsy *(US)*; **Hof|la|ger** NT temporary residence; **~ halten** to hold court; **Hof|le|ben** NT court life

höf|lich ['hø:flɪç] ADJ polite; *(= zuvorkommend)* courteous ADV politely; **ich bitte Sie ~** I (would) respectfully ask you; **wir teilen Ihnen ~(st) mit** we would inform you, we would like to inform you

Höf|lich|keit F **-, -en** **a** *no pl* politeness; *(= Zuvorkommenheit)* courteousness; **jdm etw mit aller ~ sagen** to tell sb sth very politely, to tell sb sth with the utmost politeness **b** *(= höfliche Bemerkung)* compliment; **jdm ~en sagen** to compliment sb

Höf|lich|keits-: **Höf|lich|keits|be|such** M courtesy visit; **Höf|lich|keits|be|zei|gung** [-bətsaigʊŋ] F **-, -en** act *or* mark of courtesy; **Höf|lich|keits|flos|kel** F *(pej)*, **Höf|lich|keits|for|mel** F polite phrase; **höf|lich|keits|hal|ber** ADV out of courtesy

Hof|lie|fe|rant(in) M(F) purveyor to the court

Höf|ling ['hø:flɪŋ] M **-s, -e** courtier; *(pej: = Schmeichler)* sycophant

Hof-: **Hof|mar|schall** M *(Hist)* major-domo; *(in GB)* Lord Chamberlain; **Hof|meis|ter** M *(Hist)* **a** *(= Gutsverwalter)* steward, bailiff **b** *(= Erzieher)* (private) tutor; **Hof|narr** M *(Hist)* court jester; **Hof|pre|di|ger** M *(Hist)* court chaplain; **Hof|rat** M *(Hist)* Court Counsellor *(Brit) or* Counselor *(US)*; **Hof|rat** M, **Hof|rä|tin** F **a** *(in GB)* Privy Councillor *(Brit) or* Councilor *(US)* **b** *(Aus: Ehrentitel)* Hofrat, ≈ Councillor *(Brit)*, ≈ Councilor *(US)*; **Hof|sän|ger** M *(Hist)* minstrel; **Hof|schran|ze** [-ʃrantsə] F **-, -n** *or (rare) m* **-n, -n** *(Hist pej)* fawning courtier; **Hof|sei|te** F courtyard side *(of building)*; **Hof|staat** ['ho:fʃta:t] M *(Hist)* (royal *etc*) household; **Hof|statt** ['ho:fʃtat] F **-, -en** *or* **Hofstätten** [-ʃtɛtn] farmstead; **Hof|the|a|ter** NT *(Hist)* court *or* royal theatre *(Brit) or* theater *(US)*; **Hof|tor** NT yard gate; **Hof|trau|er** F court mourning; **Hof|tür** F yard gate

HO-Ge|schäft [ha:'lo:-] NT *(DDR)* state retail shop

ho|he ADJ → **hoch**

Hö|he ['hø:ə] F **-, -n** **a** *(= Ausdehnung nach oben)* height; *(= Flughöhe, Berghöhe, über Meeresspiegel)* height, altitude; *(Astron, Math)* altitude; *(von Schnee, Wasser)* depth; **in die/der ~** (up) into/in the air; **aus der ~** from above; **Ehre sei Gott in der ~** glory to God in the highest *or* on high; **an ~ gewinnen** *(Aviat)* to gain height, to climb; **in einer ~ von** at a height/an altitude of; **in die ~ gehen/treiben** *(fig: Preise etc)* to go up/force up; **einen Betrieb wieder in die ~ bringen** to put a business back on its feet again; **in die ~ gehen** *(fig inf)* to hit the roof *(inf)*

b *(= Anhöhe)* hill; *(= Gipfel)* top, summit; *(fig: = Höhepunkt, Blütezeit etc)* height; **auf der ~ sein** *(fig inf) (leistungsfähig)* to be at one's best; *(gesund)* to be fighting fit *(Brit inf)*, to be (as) fit as a fiddle; **die sanften ~n** the gentle slopes; **sich nicht auf der ~ fühlen, nicht auf der ~ sein** *(leistungsfähig)* to feel below par; *(gesundheitlich)* not to be up to scratch; **auf der ~ des Lebens** in the prime of (one's) life; **die ~n und Tiefen des Lebens** the ups and downs of life; **auf der ~ der Zeit** up-to-date; **das ist doch die ~!** *(fig inf)* that's the limit!

c *(= Ausmaß, Größe) (von Mieten, Preisen, Unkosten, Temperatur, Geschwindigkeit, Strafe, Phys: von Stromspannung)* level; *(von Summe, Gewinn, Verlust, Gewicht, Geldstrafe)* size, amount; *(von Wert, Druck)* amount; *(von Einkommen)* size; *(von Schaden)* extent; **ein Zuwachs/Betrag in ~ von** an increase/amount of; **Zinsen in ~ von** interest at the rate of; **bis zu einer ~ von** up to a maximum of

d *(fig: = Größe: von Lebensstandard, Ansprüchen etc)* level

e *(= Tonhöhe) (Mus: von Stimme)* pitch; *(Rad)* treble *no pl*; **die ~n einstellen** *(Rad)* to adjust the treble

f *(Naut, Geog: = Breitenlage)* latitude; **auf der ~ von** at the level of; **auf der ~ von Dover** *(Naut)* off Dover; **auf gleicher ~** level with each other

Ho|heit ['ho:hait] F **-, -en** **a** *no pl (= Staatshoheit)* sovereignty *(über +acc* over) **b** *(= Mitglied einer fürstlichen Familie)* member of a/the royal family; *(als Anrede)* Highness; **Seine/Ihre Königliche ~** His/Her Royal Highness

ho|heit|lich ['ho:haitlɪç] ADJ *(von Staatsgewalt ausgehend) Befehl, Handlung, Aufgabe, Behörde* sovereign; *(von einem Fürsten) Gemächer* royal; *Auftreten, Geste* majestic

Ho|heits-: **Ho|heits|ab|zei|chen** NT nationality marking; **Ho|heits|akt** M act of sovereignty; **Ho|heits|be|reich** M **a** *(= Hoheitsgebiet)* sovereign territory **b** *(= Rechtsbereich)* jurisdiction; **Ho|heits|ge|biet** NT sovereign territory; **Ho|heits|ge|walt** F (national) jurisdiction; **Ho|heits|ge|wäs|ser** PL territorial waters *pl*; **Ho|heits|recht** NT *usu pl* sovereign jurisdiction *or* rights *pl*; **ho|heits|voll** ADJ majestic; **Ho|heits|zei|chen** NT national emblem

Ho|he|lied [ho:ə'li:t] NT **-(e)s** *od* **Hohen Liedes** [ho:ən 'li:dəs], *no pl* Song of Songs; *(fig geh)* song → *auch* **hoch 1 f**

Hö|hen-: **Hö|hen|an|ga|be** F altitude reading; *(auf Karte)* altitude mark; **Hö|hen|angst** F fear of heights; **Hö|hen|flos|se** F *(Aviat)* tailplane; **Hö|hen|flug** M high-altitude flight; **geistiger/künstlerischer ~** intellectual/artistic flight (of fancy); **hö|hen|gleich** ADJ level ADV on a level; **Hö|hen|kli|ma** NT mountain climate; **Hö|hen|krank|heit** F *(Med)* altitude sickness; *(im Gebirge auch)* mountain sickness; *(beim Fliegen auch)* aeroembolism *(spec)*; **Hö|hen|kur|ort** M mountain (health) resort; **Hö|hen|la|ge** F altitude; **Hö|hen|leit|werk** NT *(Aviat)* elevators *pl*; **Hö|hen|li|nie** F contour (line); **Hö|hen|luft** F mountain air; **Hö|hen|mar|ke** F benchmark; **Hö|hen|mes|ser** M **-s, -** *(Aviat)* altimeter, altitude meter; **Hö|hen|mes|sung** F **a** *(Aviat)* measuring altitude **b** *(Tech)* levelling *(Brit)*, leveling *(US)*; **Hö|hen|me|ter** M *(nach oben)* elevation gain; *(nach unten)* elevation descent; **die letzten 50 ~** the last 50 metres *(Brit) or* meters *(US)* in height; **Hö|hen|re|kord** M *(Aviat)* altitude record; **Hö|hen|rü|cken** M (mountain) crest *or* ridge; **Hö|hen|ru|der** NT *(Aviat)* elevator; **Hö|hen|schicht** F contour level; **Hö|hen|schrei|ber** M *(Aviat)* altigraph; **Hö|hen|son|ne** F *(im Gebirge)* mountain sun; *(= Lampe der eingetragenen Marke Höhensonne)* ≈ sunray lamp; *(= Behandlung)* sunray treatment; **Hö|hen|steu|er** NT *(Aviat)* elevator; **Hö|hen|strah|lung** F cosmic radiation; **Hö|hen|trai|ning** NT *(Sport)* (high-)altitude training; **Hö|hen|un|ter|schied** M difference in altitude; **Hö|hen|ver|lust** M loss of height *or* altitude; **hö|hen|ver|stell|bar** ADJ height-adjustable; **Hö|hen|weg** M *(am Gebirgskamm)* ridgeway, ridge path; *(an Höhenzug entlang)* path running along a/the mountain range; **Hö|hen|wind** M high-altitude wind; **Hö|hen|zahl** F *(auf Landkarten)* height above sea level; **Hö|hen|zug** M range of hills, mountain range

Ho|he|pries|ter [ho:ə'pri:stɐ] M **-s** *or* **Hohen Priesters, -** high priest

ho|he|pries|ter|lich [ho:ə'pri:stɐlɪç] ADJ *Gewänder, Amt* high priest's *attr*

Hö|he|punkt M highest point; *(von Abend, Tag, Leben)* high point, high spot; *(von Veranstaltung)* high spot, highlight; *(von Karriere, des Ruhms, der Macht)* pinnacle, peak, height; *(des Glücks etc)* height, peak; *(von Entwicklung)* peak, summit, apex; *(von Kurve)* vertex; *(eines Stücks, = Orgasmus)* climax; **auf den ~ bringen** to bring to a climax; **den ~ erreichen** to reach a *or* its/one's climax; *(Krankheit)* to reach *or* come to a crisis; **den ~ überschreiten** to pass the peak

hö|her ['hø:ɐ] ADJ *comp von* **hoch** *(lit, fig)* higher; *Macht* superior; *Klasse* upper; *Auflage* bigger; *(Comput) Programmiersprache* high-level; **~e Berufsstände** the professions; **~e Bildung** higher education; **~es Lehramt** ≈ graduate teachership; **~e Schule** secondary school, high school *(esp US)*; **~e Töchterschule** *(old, hum)* school for young ladies; **~e Tochter** *(dated, hum)* young lady; **~e Gewalt** an act of God; **in ~em Maße** to a greater extent; **~er Blödsinn** *(iro)* utter nonsense; **in ~en Regionen** *or* **Sphären schweben** to have one's head in the clouds; **sich zu Höherem berufen fühlen** to feel (oneself) called to higher *or* greater things

ADV **a** *(= weiter nach oben) wachsen, steigen, fliegen* higher; **~ liegen** to be higher up; **~ liegend** higher → **Herz, höherschlagen**

b *(= mit höherem Wert) bewertet, versichert* more highly; **etw ~ bewerten** to rate sth higher *or* more highly; **sich ~ versichern** to increase one's insurance (cover) → **höhergestellt, höherstehend**

ho|he(r, s) ADJ → **hoch**

hö|her-: **hö|her|ge|stellt** ADJ higher, more senior; **hö|her|klas|sig** ADJ *(Sport) Verein, Mannschaft, Fußball* higher-division *attr*; **hö|her|lie|gend** ADJ → **höher ADV a**; **hö|her+schla|gen** VI *sep irreg (fig)* **das lässt Kinderherzen ~** that makes children's hearts beat faster → *auch* **Herz**; **hö|her+schrau|ben** *sep*, **hö|her schrau|ben** △ VT *(fig) Anforderungen* to increase, to step up; *Ansprüche* to increase; *Preise* to force *or* push up; **hö|her|ste|hend** ADJ higher; **hö|her+stu|fen** *sep*, **hö|her stu|fen** △ VT *Person* to upgrade; **hö|her|wer|tig** ADJ of higher quality; *Qualität* higher; *(Chem)* of higher valency

hohl [ho:l] ADJ **a** *(lit, fig: = leer)* hollow; *Geschwätz etc* empty, shallow; *Blick* empty, vacant **b** *(= konkav)* hollow; *Augen, Wangen* hollow, sunken; **ein ~es Kreuz** a hollow back; **in der ~en Hand** in the hollow of one's hand; **aus der ~en Hand trinken** to drink with cupped hands; **eine ~e Hand machen** *(lit)* to cup one's hand; *(fig inf)* to hold one's hand out *(for money, a tip etc)*; **~e Gasse** narrow pass *or* defile **c** *Klang, Stimme, Husten* hollow ADV **~ klingen** to sound hollow; **~ scheinen** to appear *or* seem hollow

Hohl-: **hohl|äu|gig** ADJ hollow-eyed, sunken-eyed; **Hohl|block** M *pl* **-blöcke**, **Hohl|block|stein** M, **Hohl|block|zie|gel** M cavity block

Höh|le ['hø:lə] F **-, -n** cave, cavern; *(in Baum)* hole, hollow bit; *(= Tierbehausung)* cave, den; *(= Augenhöhle)* socket; *(fig: = schlechte Wohnung)* hovel, hole *(inf)*

Höh|len- *in cpds* cave; **Höh|len|bär** M cave-bear; **Höh|len|be|woh|ner(in)** M(F) cave dweller, troglodyte; *(männlich auch)* caveman; **Höh|len|for|scher(in)** M(F) cave explorer; *(unter der Erde auch)* potholer; **Höh|len|for|schung** F, **Höh|len|kun|de** F speleology; **Höh|len|gleich|nis** NT *(Philos)* Allegory of the Cave; **Höh|len|ma|le|rei** F cave painting; **Höh|len|mensch** M caveman; **Höh|len|tier** NT cave-animal; **Höh|len|zeich|nung** F *(Hist)* cave drawing

Hohl-: **Hohl|heit** F **-**, *no pl (lit, fig: = Leere)* hollowness; *(von Geschwätz)* emptiness, shallowness; **Hohl|kopf** M *(pej)* blockhead *(inf)*, numskull *(inf)*, dunce; **hohl|köp|fig** ADJ *(pej)* empty-headed, brainless, foolish; **Hohl|kör|per** M hollow body; **Hohl|kreuz** NT *(Med)* hollow back; **Hohl|ku|gel** F hollow sphere;

Hohl|maß NT measure of capacity; *(für Getreide etc auch)* dry measure; **Hohl|na|del** F *(Med)* cannula

Hohl|raum M hollow space; *(Build auch)* cavity

Hohl|raum-: **Hohl|raum|ver|sie|ge|lung** F *(Aut)* cavity seal; **Hohl|raum|zie|gel** M cavity block

Hohl-: **Hohl|saum** M *(Sew)* hemstitch; **Hohl|saum|ar|beit** F drawn-thread work; **Hohl|schliff** M hollow grinding; **ein Messer mit ~** a hollow-ground knife; **Hohl|spie|gel** M concave mirror; **Hohl|tie|re** PL coelenterata *(spec)*

Höh|lung ['hø:lʊŋ] F **-, -en** hollow

Hohl-: **hohl|wan|gig** [-vaŋɪç] ADJ hollow-cheeked; **Hohl|weg** M narrow pass *or* defile; **Hohl|wür|mer** PL aschelminthes *pl (spec)*; **Hohl|zie|gel** M **a** *(= Hohlstein)* cavity brick **b** *(= Dachziegel)* hollow tile

Hohn [ho:n] M **-(e)s**, *no pl* scorn, derision, mockery; **jdn mit ~ und Spott überschütten** to heap *or* pour scorn on sb; **nur ~ und Spott ernten** to get nothing but scorn and derision; **das hat er mir zum ~ getan** he did it just to show his contempt for me; **ein ~ auf etw** *(acc)* a mockery of sth; **das ist der reine** *or* **reinste ~** it's a sheer *or* utter mockery; **den Tatsachen zum ~** in defiance of the facts; **~ lachen** to laugh scornfully *or* derisively; **ich höre ihn schon ~ lachen** I can hear his sneers already; **~ sprechen** to make a mockery (*+dat* of); **jdm ~ sprechen** to mock (at) sb, to deride sb; **das spricht jeder Vernunft ~** that flies right in the face of all reason

höh|nen ['hø:nən] VT *(geh)* jdn to mock VI to jeer, to scoff, to sneer *(über +acc* at)

Hohn|ge|läch|ter NT scornful *or* derisive *or* sneering laughter

höh|nisch ['hø:nɪʃ] ADJ scornful, mocking, sneering ADV scornfully, mockingly; **~ grinsen** to sneer, to smirk, to grin scornfully; **jdn ~ verspotten** to jeer at sb, to deride sb

Hohn-: **hohn+la|chen** VI *sep* → **Hohn**; **Hohn|la|chen** NT scornful *or* derisive *or* sneering laughter; **hohn+spre|chen** VI *sep irreg* → **Hohn**

ho|ho [ho'ho:] INTERJ oho

hoi [hɔy] INTERJ *(Sw)* hello

Hö|ker ['hø:kɐ] M **-s, -**, **Hö|ke|rin** [-ərɪn] F **-, -nen**, **Hö|ker|weib** NT *(old, pej)* street trader, pedlar *(Brit)*, peddler *(US)*

hö|kern ['hø:kɐn] VI *(old)* to peddle; **mit etw ~** to peddle sth

Ho|kus|po|kus [ho:kʊs'po:kʊs] M **-**, *no pl (= Zauberformel)* hey presto; *(= Zauberstück)* (conjuring) trick(s *pl*); *(fig) (= Täuschung)* hocus-pocus *(inf)*, jiggery-pokery *(Brit inf)*; *(= Drumherum)* palaver *(esp Brit inf)*, fuss; **die veranstalten immer einen ~, wenn Besuch kommt** they always make such a palaver *(esp Brit inf) or* fuss when they have visitors

hold [hɔlt] ADJ **a** *(poet, dated)* fair, sweet; *(hum)* dear, beloved, fair; **~er Friede** sweet *or* blessed peace; **die ~e Weiblichkeit** *(hum)* the fair sex; **mein ~er Gatte** *(hum)* my dear *or* beloved husband *(hum)*; **meine Holde** my sweet **b** *pred (geh: = gewogen)* **jdm ~ sein** to be fond of *or* well-disposed to(wards) sb; **das Glück war ihm ~** fortune smiled upon him

Hol|der ['hɔldɐ] M **-s, -** *(dial)* elder; *(= Früchte)* elderberries *pl*

Hol|ding ['ho:ldɪŋ] F **-, -s**, **Hol|ding|ge|sell|schaft** F *(Comm)* holding company

Hol|drio ['hɔldrio] NT **-s, -s** (shout of) halloo

hold|se|lig ADJ *(liter)* sweet, lovely, fair

ho|len ['ho:lən] VT **a** *(= holen gehen)* to fetch, to get; *(= herunternehmen)* to get *or* take *or* fetch down; *(= herausnehmen)* to get *or* take out; **Luft** *or* **Atem ~** to draw breath; **jdn aus dem Bett ~** to get *or* drag *(inf)* sb out of bed; **das Kind musste geholt werden** the baby had to be pulled out → **Teufel b**

b *(= abholen)* to fetch, to pick up; *Verbrecher, Patienten* to take away

c *(= kaufen)* to get, to pick up *(inf)*

d *(= herbeirufen, holen lassen) Polizei, Hilfe* to fetch, to get; **jdn ~ lassen** to send for sb; **einen Moment, ich lasse ihn schnell ans Telefon ~** just a moment, I'll have someone fetch *or* get him to the phone; **der Professor hat seinen Assistenten an die neue Uni geholt** the professor brought his assistant to the new university

e *(= erringen, gewinnen) Sieg, Preis* to win, to get

f *(= sich zuziehen) Krankheit* to catch, to get; *elektrischen Schlag* to get; **sich** *(dat)* **Schläge ~** to get a beating; **sonst wirst du dir etwas ~** or you'll catch something; **sich** *(dat)* **eine Erkältung/den Tod** *(inf)* **~** to catch a cold/one's death *(inf)*

g *(= bekommen, erwerben)* to get; **sich** *(dat)* **etw ~** to get (oneself) sth; **dabei ist nichts zu ~** *(inf)* there's nothing in it; **bei ihm ist nichts zu ~** *(inf)* you *etc* won't get anything out of him

h *(Naut) Anker* to raise, to hoist; *Segel, Taue* to take in

ho|lis|tisch [ho'lɪstɪʃ] ADJ holistic ADV holistically

hol|la ['hɔla] INTERJ hullo, hallo, hello, hey; *(überrascht)* hey; *(= hoppla)* whoops

Hol|land ['hɔlant] NT **-s** Holland, the Netherlands *pl*

Hol|län|der ['hɔlɛndɐ] M **-s**, *no pl (= Käse)* Dutch cheese

Hol|län|der ['hɔlɛndɐ] M **-s, -** *(bei Papierherstellung)* hollander

Hol|län|der ['hɔlɛndɐ] M **-s, -** *(= Mensch)* Dutchman; **die ~** the Dutch (people); **er ist ~** he is Dutch *or* a Dutchman → **fliegend**

Hol|län|de|rin ['hɔlɛndərɪn] F **-, -nen** Dutchwoman, Dutch girl → *auch* **Holländer**

hol|län|disch ['hɔlɛndɪʃ] ADJ Dutch

Hol|län|disch(e) ['hɔlɛndɪʃ] NT Dutch, the Dutch language → *auch* **Deutsch(e)**

Hol|le ['hɔlə] F **- Frau ~ schüttelt die Betten aus** it is snowing

Höl|le ['hœlə] F **-**, *(rare)* **-n** hell; **in der ~** in hell; **die ~ auf Erden** hell on earth; **fahr zur ~!** *(liter)* go to the devil!; **zur ~ mit ...** to hell with ... *(inf)*; **in die ~ kommen** to go to hell; **ich werde ihm die ~ heißmachen** *(inf)* I'll give him hell *(inf)*; **sie machte ihm das Leben zur ~** she made his life (a) hell *(inf)*; **es war die (reinste) ~** *(inf)* it was (pure) hell *(inf)*; **die ~ ist los** *(inf)* all hell has broken loose *(inf)*

Höl|len- *in cpds (= der Hölle)* of hell, infernal; *(inf: = groß)* hellish *(inf)*, infernal *(inf)*; **Höl|len|angst** F *(inf)* terrible fear; **eine ~ haben** to be scared stiff *(inf)*; **Höl|len|brand** M *(liter)* hellfire; **Höl|len|brut** F *(pej liter)* diabolical *or* fiendish mob *or* rabble; **Höl|len|fahrt** F Descent into Hell; **Höl|len|fürst** M *(liter)* Prince of Darkness; **Höl|len|ge|stank** M *(inf)* diabolical smell *or* stench; **Höl|len|hund** M *(Myth)* hound of hell, hellhound; **Höl|len|lärm** M *(inf)* hellish *or* infernal noise *(inf)*; **Höl|len|mäch|te** PL *(liter)* powers of darkness *pl*; **Höl|len|ma|schi|ne** F *(dated)* infernal machine *(dated)*, time bomb; **Höl|len|pein** F *(liter)*, **Höl|len|qual** F *(liter)* torments *pl* of hell; *(fig inf)* agony; **eine Höllenqual/Höllenqualen ausstehen** to suffer agony; **Höl|len|ra|chen** M *(liter)*, **Höl|len|schlund** M *(liter)* jaws *pl* of hell; **Höl|len|spek|ta|kel** M *(inf)* hellish *or* infernal noise *(inf)*; **Höl|len|stein** M *(Chem)* silver nitrate, lunar caustic

Hol|ler ['hɔlɐ] M **-s, -** *(dial)* elder; *(= Früchte)* elderberries *pl*

Hol|le|rith|ma|schi|ne [hɔlə'rɪt-, 'hɔlərɪt-] F Hollerith machine

höl|lisch ['hœlɪʃ] ADJ **a** *attr (= die Hölle betreffend)* infernal, of hell **b** *(inf: = außerordentlich)* dreadful, frightful, hellish *(inf)*; **eine ~e Angst haben** to be scared stiff *(inf)* ADV *(inf)* like hell *(inf)*, hellishly *(inf)*; **~ fluchen** to swear like a trooper; **es tut ~ weh** it hurts like hell *(inf)*, it's hellish(ly) painful *(inf)*; **die Prüfung war ~ schwer** the exam was hellish(ly) difficult *(inf)*

Hol|ly|wood|schau|kel ['hɔliwʊd-] F swing hammock

Holm [hɔlm] M **-(e)s, -e a** *(von Barren)* bar; *(von Geländer)* rail; *(von Leiter)* side rail **b** *(Aviat) (längs)* longeron; *(quer)* spar **c** *(= Stiel, Griff) (= Axtholm)* shaft, handle; *(= Ruderholm)* shaft

Holm M **-(e)s, -e** islet, small island

Hol|mi|um ['hɔlmiʊm] NT **-s**, *no pl (abbr* **Ho**) holmium

Ho|lo|caust ['ho:lokaust, holo'kaust, 'hɔləkɔ:st] M **-(s), -(s)** holocaust

Ho|lo|caust- *in cpds* holocaust; **Ho|lo|caust|ge|denk|stät|te** F holocaust memorial

Ho|lo|gra|fie, **Holographie** [hologra'fi:] F **-, -n** [-'fi:ən] holography

Ho|lo|gramm [holo'gram] NT *pl* **-gramme** hologram

hol|pe|rig ['hɔlpərɪç] ADJ **a** *Weg, Pflaster* bumpy **b** *(= schwerfällig) Rede, Verse* clumsy, jerky ADV **~ lesen** to read jerkily *or* haltingly

hol|pern ['hɔlpɐn] VI to bump, to jolt; **beim Lesen holpert er noch** he still stumbles (over his words) when reading, he still reads haltingly; **~de Verse** rough *or* stumbling *or* halting verse

Hol|per|schwel|le ['hɔlpɐ-] F *(Mot)* speed bump *or* hump, sleeping policeman *(inf Brit)*

holp|rig ['hɔlprɪç] ADJ = **holperig**

Hol|schuld ['ho:l-] F *(Comm) debt to be collected from the debtor at his residence*

hol|ter|die|pol|ter [hɔltɐdi'pɔltɐ] ADV helter-skelter; **der Wagen fuhr ~ den Berg hinunter** the cart went careering down the mountainside; **die Blechdose fiel ~ die Treppe hinunter** the tin went crash bang wallop down the stairs *(inf)*

hol|über [ho:l'ly:bɐ] INTERJ *(old)* **Fährmann ~!** ahoy there, ferryman *or* boatman!

Ho|lun|der [ho'lʊndɐ] M **-s, -** elder; *(= Früchte)* elderberries *pl*; **Spanischer** *or* **Blauer ~** lilac

Ho|lun|der- *in cpds* elder; **Ho|lun|der|bee|re** F elderberry; **Ho|lun|der|busch** M, **Ho|lun|der|strauch** M elder bush; **Ho|lun|der|wein** M elderberry wine

Holz [hɔlts] NT **-es, ¨-er** ['hœltsɐ] **a** wood; *(esp zum Bauen, Schreinern)* timber, lumber *(esp US)*; *(= Streichholz)* match; **ein ~** a piece of wood *or* timber *or* lumber *(esp US)*; *(= Holzart)* a wood; **lange Hölzer** long, untrimmed logs *or* timbers; **runde Hölzer** short, untrimmed logs *or* timbers; **flüssiges ~** *(Tech)* plastic wood; **aus ~** made of wood, wooden; **~ fällen** to fell trees, to cut down trees; **~ sägen** *(lit)* to saw wood; *(inf: = schnarchen)* to snore, to saw wood *(US inf)*; **~ verarbeitend** wood-processing; **aus einem anderen ~ (geschnitzt) sein** *(fig)* to be cast in a different mould *(Brit) or* mold *(US)*; **aus grobem ~ geschnitzt sein** *(fig)* to be insensitive; **aus hartem** *or* **härterem ~ geschnitzt sein** *(fig)* to be made of stern *or* sterner stuff; **aus demselben ~ geschnitzt sein** *(fig)* to be cast in the same mould *(Brit) or* mold *(US)*; **er saß da wie ein Stück ~** he sat there like a block of wood; **ich bin nicht aus ~!** I'm not made of stone, I am made of flesh and blood; **~ vor der Hütte** *or* **Tür haben** *(inf)* to be well-endowed *or* well-stacked *(inf)*, to have big boobs *(inf)*; **~!** *(Tennis etc)* wood!; **Dummheit und Stolz wachsen auf einem ~** *(Prov)* stupidity and pride grow on the same tree *(prov)*

b *(= Kegel)* skittle, ninepin; **~ schieben** to play skittles *or* ninepins; **gut ~!** have a good game!

c *(dated: = Wald, Gehölz)* wood, woods *pl*

Holz- *in cpds* wood; *(= aus Holz auch)* wooden; *(Build, Comm etc)* timber, lumber *(esp US)*; **Holz|ap|fel** M crab apple; **Holz|ar|bei|ter(in)** M(F) woodworker; *(im Wald)* woodcutter, lumberjack *(esp US)*; **holz|arm** ADJ *Gegend* sparsely wooded *or* timbered; *Papier* with (a) low wood content; **Holz|art** F kind of wood *or* timber; **holz|ar|tig** ADJ woody, wood-like; **Holz|asche** F wood ashes *pl*;

Holz|au|ge NT ~ **sei wachsam** *(inf)* be careful; **Holz|bau** M **a** *no pl* wood-frame *or* timber-frame construction **b** *pl* **-bauten** wooden building; **Holz|bau|wei|se** F, *no pl* timber *or* wood-frame construction; **Holz|be|ar|bei|tung** F woodworking; *(im Sägewerk)* timber processing; **Holz|bein** NT wooden leg; **Holz|be|stand** M stock of wood *or* timber, wood *or* timber stock; *(im Wald)* stand of timber; **Holz|bild|hau|er(in)** M(F) wood carver; **Holz|blä|ser(in)** M(F) woodwind player; **wo sitzen die ~?** where do the woodwind sit?, where does the woodwind section sit?; **Holz|blas|in|stru|ment** NT woodwind instrument; **Holz|block** M *pl* **-blöcke** block of wood; **Holz|bock** M **a** *(= Stützgestell)* wooden stand *or* trestle **b** *(= Insekt)* wood tick, dog tick; **Holz|bo|den** M **a** *(= Fußboden)* wooden floor **b** *(für Holz)* wood loft, timber loft **c** *(von Truhe etc)* wooden bottom **d** *(Forest)* wooded *or* timbered ground; **Holz|boh|rer** M **a** *(Tech)* wood drill **b** *(Zool)* goat moth, leopard moth; **Holz|brand|ma|le|rei** F *(Art)* pokerwork, pyrography *(form)*; **Holz|brei** M wood pulp; **Holz|bün|del** NT bundle of wood, faggot

Hölz|chen ['hœltsçən] NT **-s, -** small piece of wood; *(= Streichholz)* match

Holz-: Holz|druck M *pl* **-drucke** *(Art)* wood engraving; **Holz|dü|bel** M wooden dowel; **Holz|ein|schlag** M tree-felling, cutting-down of trees, timber harvesting *(US)*

hol|zen ['hɔltsn] VI **a** *(= Bäume fällen)* to cut down *or* fell timber, to lumber *(esp US)*; *(fig inf: = abbauen, reduzieren)* to cut back **b** *(esp Ftbl)* to hack; *(inf: = sich schlagen)* to fight; *(Mus)* to play badly **c** *(inf: = schimpfen)* to moan *or* grumble *(gegen* about) VT *(rare) Wald* to clear

Hol|zer ['hɔltsɐ] M **-s, -**, **Hol|ze|rin** [-ərɪn] F **-, -nen** *(esp Ftbl)* hacker, rough player

Hol|ze|rei [hɔltsə'rai] F **-, -en** *(inf) (= Rauferei)* roughhouse *(inf)*; *(Ftbl auch)* rough game *or* match; *(Mus)* third- *or* fourth-rate playing

höl|zern ['hœltsɐn] ADJ *(lit, fig)* wooden; **so ein ~er Kerl** such a wooden sort of chap ADV *(fig)* woodenly, stiffly

Holz-: Holz|fäl|len NT **-s**, *no pl* tree-felling, lumbering; **Holz|fäl|ler** [-fɛlɐ] M **-s, -**, **Holz|fäl|le|rin** [-fɛlərɪn] F **-, -nen** woodcutter, lumberjack *(esp US)*; **Holz|fa|ser** F wood fibre *(Brit)* or fiber *(US)*; **Holz|fa|ser|plat|te** F (wood) fibreboard *(Brit)* or fiberboard *(US)*; **Holz|fäu|le** F wood rot; **holz|frei** ADJ *Papier* wood-free; **Holz|fre|vel** M *(Jur)* offence *(Brit)* or offense *(US)* against forest laws, infringement of forest regulations; **Holz|ha|cken** NT **-s**, *no pl* cutting *or* chopping wood; **Holz|ha|cker(in)** M(F) *(Aus old)* woodcutter; **holz|hal|tig** ADJ *Papier* woody; **Holz|ham|mer** M mallet; **jdm etw mit dem ~ beibringen** to hammer sth into sb *(inf)*; **Holz|ham|mer|me|tho|de** F *(inf)* sledgehammer method *(inf)*; **Holz|han|del** M timber *or* lumber *(esp US)* trade; **Holz|hau|fen** M woodpile, pile *or* stack of wood; **Holz|haus** NT wooden *or* timber house

hol|zig ['hɔltsɪç] ADJ woody; *Spargel, Rettich auch* stringy, tough

Holz-: Holz|kitt M plastic wood; **Holz|klas|se** F *((Aviat hum))* coach class; **Holz|klotz** M wood block, block of wood, log; *(= Spielzeug)* wooden brick; **er saß da wie ein ~** *(inf)* he sat there like a block *or* lump of wood; **Holz|koh|le** F charcoal; **Holz|kopf** M *(fig inf)* blockhead *(inf)*; **Holz|la|ger** NT timberyard; **Holz|na|gel** M wooden nail *or* peg; **Holz|ofen** M wood-burning oven; **Holz|pan|ti|ne** F, **Holz|pan|tof|fel** M clog; **Holz|pflas|ter** NT wood-block paving; **Holz|pflock** M (wooden) peg; **holz|reich** ADJ well-wooded; **ein ~es Land** a country rich in timber; **Holz|reich|tum** M abundance of timber; **Holz|schäd|ling** M wood pest; **Holz|scheit** NT piece of (fire)wood, log; **Holz|schlag** M *(= Vorgang)* tree-felling, lumbering; *(= Ort)* felling or lumbering area; **Holz|schliff** M mechanical wood pulp; **Holz|schnei|der(in)** M(F) wood engraver; **Holz|schnitt** M *(Art)* **a** *no pl (= Kunst)* (art of) wood engraving **b** *(= Gegenstand)* wood engraving, woodcut; **holz|schnitt|ar|tig** *(fig)* ADJ simplistic ADV simplistically; **Holz|schnit|zer(in)** M(F) wood carver; **Holz|schnit|ze|rei** F (art *or* craft of) wood carving; **Holz|schuh** M wooden shoe, clog, sabot; **Holz|schuh|tanz** M clog dance; **Holz|schutz|mit|tel** NT wood preservative; **Holz|schwamm** M wood fungus, dry rot; **Holz|span** M chip (of wood); *(beim Hobeln)* wood shaving; **Holz|split|ter** M splinter *or* sliver of wood; **Holz|sta|pel** M pile of wood, woodpile; **Holz|stich** M wood engraving; **Holz|stift** M small wooden nail *or* pin; **Holz|stock** M (engraved) wood block; **Holz|stoß** M pile of wood, woodpile; **Holz|ta|fel** F wooden panel; *(Sch)* wooden blackboard; **Holz|tä|fe|lung** F wood(en) panelling *(Brit)* or paneling *(US)*; **Holz|tau|be** F wood pigeon; **holz|ver|ar|bei|tend** ADJ *attr* → **Holz a**; **Holz|ver|ar|bei|tung** F woodworking; *(= Holzveredelung)* wood processing; **Holz|ver|ede|lung** F wood processing; **Holz|ver|koh|lung** F carbonization, wood distillation; **Holz|ver|schlag** M **a** *(= Schuppen)* wooden shed **b** *(= Verpackung)* wooden crate; **Holz|wa|ren** PL wooden articles, articles made of wood; **Holz|weg** M logging-path; **auf dem ~ sein** *(fig inf)* to be on the wrong track *(inf)*; **wenn du meinst, ich gebe dir das, dann bist du auf dem ~** if you think I'm going to give it to you, you've got another think *(Brit)* or thought *(US)* coming *(inf)*; **Holz|wirt|schaft** F timber *or* lumber *(esp US)* industry; **Holz|wol|le** F wood-wool; **Holz|wurm** M woodworm

Home-: Home|ban|king ['ho:mbɛŋkɪŋ] NT **-**, *no pl* home banking; **Home|page** ['ho:mpe:dʒ] F **-, -s** *(Comput, im Internet)* home page

ho|me|risch [ho'me:rɪʃ] ADJ Homeric

Home-: Home|sit|ter ['ho:mzɪtɐ] M **-s, -**, **Home|sit|te|rin** [-ərɪn] F **-, -nen** housesitter; **Home|trai|ner** ['ho:mtre:nɐ] M = **Heimtrainer**; **Home|shop|ping** NT home shopping; **Home-Tas|te** F *(Comput: = Pos-1-Taste)* home key

Hom|mage [ɔ'ma:ʒ] F **-, -n** homage

Ho|mo ['ho:mo] M **-s, -s** *(dated inf)* homo *(dated inf)*, queer *(inf)*

ho|mo-, Ho|mo- *in cpds* homo; **Ho|mo-Ehe** F gay *or* same-sex marriage; **ho|mo|fon** ADJ *(Mus)* homophonic; *(Ling)* homophonous; **Ho|mo|fon** NT **-s, -e** *(Ling)* homophone; **Ho|mo|fo|nie** F **-** *(Mus, Ling)* homophony; **ho|mo|gen** [homo'ge:n] ADJ homogeneous; **ho|mo|ge|ni|sie|ren** [homogeni'zi:rən] *ptp* **homogenisiert** VT to homogenize; **Ho|mo|ge|ni|tät** [homogeni'tɛ:t] F **-**, *no pl* homogeneity; **Ho|mo|graf** [homo'gra:f] NT **-s, -e** *(Ling)* homograph; **Ho|mo|gra|fie** [homogra'fi:] F **-**, *no pl (Ling)* homography; **Ho|mo|graph** *etc* = **Homograf** *etc*; **ho|mo|nym** [homo'ny:m] ADJ homonymous; **Ho|mo|nym** [homo'ny:m] NT **-(e)s, -e** homonym; **Ho|mo|ny|mie** [homony'mi:] F **-**, *no pl* homonymy

Ho|möo|path [homøo'pa:t] M **-en, -en**, **Ho|möo|pa|thin** [-'pa:tɪn] F **-, -nen** homoeopath

Ho|möo|pa|thie [homøopa'ti:] F **-**, *no pl* homoeopathy

ho|möo|pa|thisch [homøo'pa:tɪʃ] ADJ homoeopathic

Ho|mo-: ho|mo|phil [homo'fi:l] ADJ *(geh)* homophile; **ho|mo|phob** [homo'fo:p] ADJ *(geh)* homophobic; **Ho|mo|pho|bie** F *(geh)* homophobia; **ho|mo|phon** [homo'fo:n] *etc* = **homofon** *etc*; **Ho|mo|se|xu|a|li|tät** [homozɛksuali'tɛ:t] F homosexuality; **ho|mo|se|xu|ell** [homozɛ'ksuɛl] ADJ homosexual; **Ho|mo|se|xu|el|le(r)** [homozɛ'ksuɛlə] MF *decl as adj* homosexual

Ho|mun|ku|lus [ho'mʊŋkulʊs] M **-, -se** *or* **Homunkuli** [-li] homunculus

Hon|du|ras [hɔn'du:ras] NT **-** Honduras

ho|nett [hɔ'nɛt] ADJ *(dated, geh)* honest, upright, respectable

Hong|kong ['hɔŋkɔŋ] NT **-s** Hong Kong

Ho|nig ['ho:nɪç] M **-s**, *no pl* honey; **türkischer ~** halva(h), ≈ nougat; **sie schmierte ihm ~ ums Maul** *or* **um den Bart** *or* **um den Mund** *(fig inf)* she buttered him up *(inf)*; **~ aus etw saugen** *(fig inf)* to capitalize on sth

Ho|nig-: Ho|nig|bie|ne F honeybee; **Ho|nig|brot** NT **a** *(= Kuchen)* honey cake **b** *(= Brot mit Honig)* bread and honey; **ho|nig|far|ben** ADJ honey-coloured *(Brit)*, honey-colored *(US)*; **ho|nig|gelb** ADJ honey-yellow; **Ho|nig|klee** M *(Bot)* melitot; **Ho|nig|ku|chen** M honey cake; **Ho|nig|ku|chen|pferd** NT *(fig inf)* simpleton; **grinsen wie ein ~** to grin like a Cheshire cat; **Ho|nig|le|cken** NT **-s**, *no pl (fig)* **das ist kein ~** it's no picnic; **Ho|nig|me|lo|ne** F honeydew melon; **Ho|nig|mond** M *(rare)* honeymoon; **Ho|nig|schle|cken** NT **-s**, *no pl* **das ist kein ~** it's no picnic; **Ho|nig|schleu|der** F honey extractor; **ho|nig|süß** ADJ as sweet as honey; *(fig) Worte, Ton* honeyed; *Lächeln* sickly sweet ADV **er lächelte ~** he smiled a sickly sweet smile; **Ho|nig|tau** M *(pflanzlich, tierisch)* honeydew; **Ho|nig|wa|be** F honeycomb; **Ho|nig|wein** M mead; **Ho|nig|zel|le** F honeycomb cell

Hon|neurs [(h)ɔ'nø:ɐs] PL **die ~ machen** *(geh, iro)* to do the honours *(Brit)* or honors *(US)*, to welcome the guests

Ho|no|rar [hono'ra:ɐ] NT **-s, -e** fee; *(= Autorenhonorar)* royalty

Ho|no|rar-: Ho|no|rar|ab|rech|nung F statement of account; *(von Schriftsteller)* royalties account; **Ho|no|rar|ba|sis** F **auf ~** on a fee-paying basis; **ho|no|rar|frei** ADJ free of charge; **Ho|no|rar|kon|sul(in)** M(F) honorary consul; **Ho|no|rar|pro|fes|sor(in)** M(F) honorary professor *(with no say in faculty matters)*

Ho|no|ra|ti|o|ren [honora'tsio:rən] PL dignitaries *pl*, notabilities *pl*

ho|no|rie|ren [hono'ri:rən] *ptp* **honoriert** VT **a** *(= bezahlen)* to pay; *(Fin) Wechsel, Scheck* to honour *(Brit)*, to honor *(US)*, to meet; **jdm etw ~** to pay sb (a fee) for sth, to remunerate sb for sth; **meine Arbeit wird schlecht honoriert** my work is poorly remunerated **b** *(= zu würdigen wissen) Vorschläge* to acknowledge; *(= belohnen) Bemühungen* to reward

Ho|no|rie|rung F **-, -en** *(einer Rechnung)* payment (of a fee); *(= Bezahlung)* remuneration; *(Comm: von Wechsel, Scheck)* acceptance

ho|no|rig [ho'no:rɪç] ADJ *(dated) (= ehrenhaft)* honourable *(Brit)*, honorable *(US)*; *(= anständig)* decent

Ho|no|rig|keit F **-**, *no pl (dated) (= Ehrenhaftigkeit)* honourableness *(Brit)*, honorableness *(US)*; *(= Anständigkeit)* decency

ho|no|ris cau|sa [ho'no:rɪs 'kauza] ADV **Dr. ~** honorary doctor

hop|fen ['hɔpfn] VT *Bier* to hop

Hop|fen ['hɔpfn] M **-s, -** *(Bot)* hop; *(beim Brauen)* hops *pl*; **bei** *or* **an ihm ist ~ und Malz verloren** *(inf)* he's a hopeless case, he's a dead loss *(Brit inf)*

Hop|fen- *in cpds* hop; **Hop|fen|(an)|bau** M, *no pl* hop cultivation, hop-growing; **Hop|fen|dar|re** F hop drier *or* kiln; **Hop|fen|stan|ge** F hop-pole

Hop|lit [hɔ'pli:t] M **-en, -en** *(Hist)* hoplite

hopp [hɔp] INTERJ quick; **bei ihr muss alles ~ ~ gehen** she insists on doing everything double-quick *or* at the double *(inf)*; **mach mal ein bisschen ~!** *(inf)* chop, chop! *(inf)*; **~e ~e Reiter machen** *(baby-talk)* to ride a cock-horse *(on sb's knee, Brit)*, to ride the horsy *(US)*

hop|peln ['hɔpln] VI *aux sein (Hase)* to lollop

Hop|pel|pop|pel ['hɔpl'pɔpl] NT **-s, -** *(dial)* **a** *breakfast made from scrambled egg with ham and fried potatoes* **b** *(= Getränk)* eggnog

hopp|la ['hɔpla] INTERJ *(beim Stolpern, Zusammenstoßen, Fangen etc)* whoops, oops; *(beim Zuwerfen)* catch; **~, jetzt habe ich die richtige Idee!** aha *or* Eureka, now I've got it!; **~, wer kommt denn da?** oh look, who's that coming there?; **~, jetzt komm ich!** look out, here I come!

hopp+neh|men VT *sep (inf: = verhaften)* to catch, to nick *(inf)*

hops [hɔps] INTERJ jump; **~ waren sie über den Graben weg** with a jump they were over the ditch

hops ADJ *pred (inf)* **~ sein** *(= verloren)* to be lost; *(Geld)* to be down the drain *(inf)*; *(= entzwei)* to be broken *or* kaputt *(inf)* → **hopsgehen, hopsnehmen**

Hops [hɔps] M **-es, -e** *(inf)* hop, jump; **einen ~ über etw** *(acc)* **machen** to hop *or* jump over sth

hop|sa ['hɔpsa] INTERJ = **hoppla**

hop|sa|la ['hɔpsala] INTERJ upsadaisy

hop|sa|sa ['hɔpsasa] INTERJ up we go

hop|sen ['hɔpsn] VI *aux sein (inf) (= hüpfen)* to hop; *(= springen)* to jump

Hop|ser ['hɔpsɐ] M **-s, -** **a** *(inf: = kleiner Sprung)* (little) jump *or* leap; **sein Herz tat vor Freude einen ~** his heart gave a little leap for joy **b** *(= Tanz)* ecossaise

Hop|se|rei [hɔpsə'rai] F **-, -en** *(inf) (= Hüpferei)* jumping about, jumping up and down; *(pej: = Tanzen)* hopping about *(Brit) or* around

hops+ge|hen VI *sep irreg aux sein (inf: = verloren gehen)* to get lost; *(inf: = entzweigehen)* to get broken; *(inf: = sterben)* to kick the bucket *(inf)*, to croak *(inf)*

hops+neh|men VT *sep irreg* **jdn ~** *(inf: = verhaften)* to nab sb *(inf)*

Hör-: **Hör|ap|pa|rat** M hearing aid; **hör|bar** ADJ audible; **sich ~ machen** *(inf)* to speak up; **hör|be|hin|dert** ADJ hard of hearing *pred*, partially deaf, with impaired hearing *pred*; **Hör|be|hin|der|te(r)** MF *decl as adj* person who is hard of hearing, hearing-impaired person; **Hör|be|reich** M *(des Ohrs)* hearing range; *(eines Senders)* transmission area; **Hör|bild** NT *(Rad)* feature broadcast, radio feature; **Hör|bril|le** F hearing-aid glasses *pl or* spectacles *pl*; **Hör|buch** NT talking book

hor|chen ['hɔrçn] VI to listen *(+dat, auf +acc* to); *(heimlich)* to eavesdrop; **horch!** *(liter)* hark! *(old, liter)*

Hor|cher ['hɔrçɐ] M **-s, -**, **Hor|che|rin** [-ərɪn] F **-, -nen** eavesdropper; **der ~ an der Wand hört seine eigne Schand** *(Prov)* eavesdroppers never hear any good about themselves

Horch-: **Horch|ge|rät** NT *(Mil)* sound detector *or* locator; *(Naut)* hydrophone; **Horch|pos|ten** M *(Mil)* listening post; **auf ~ sein** to be listening out for sth

Hor|de ['hɔrdə] F **-, -n** *(lit, fig)* horde

Hor|de F **-, -n** rack

hor|den|wei|se ['hɔrdnvaizə] ADV in hordes

hö|ren ['hø:rən] VTI **a** *(= wahrnehmen)* to hear; **ich höre dich nicht** I can't hear you; **ich hörte ihn kommen** I heard him coming; **sei mal still, ich will das ~** be quiet, I want to hear this *or* listen to this; **er hat an der Wand gehört** he was listening at the wall; **gut/schlecht ~** to have good/bad hearing, to hear/not to hear well; **schwer ~** to be hard of hearing; **du hörst wohl schwer** *or* **schlecht!** *(inf)* you must be deaf!, are you hard of hearing?; **hört, hört!** *(Zustimmung)* hear! hear!; *(Missfallen)* come, come!; **etw an etw** *(dat)* **~** to hear sth from sth; **das lässt sich ~** *(fig)* that doesn't sound bad; **das lässt sich schon eher ~** *(inf)* that sounds (a bit) more like it; **das werde ich noch lange ~ müssen** *or* **zu ~ bekommen** I shall never hear the end *or* last of it; **ich will gar nichts ~!** I don't want to hear it; **ich habe sagen ~** I've heard said *or* tell; **ich habe es sagen ~** I've heard it said; **er hört sich gern reden** he likes the sound of his own voice; **hör mal!, ~ Sie mal!** listen; **na hör mal!, na ~ Sie mal!** wait a minute!, look here!, listen here!

b *(= anhören) Hörspiel, Vortrag, Radio* to listen to; *Berichte, Sänger* to hear; *(= zu Wort kommen lassen)* to listen to, to hear; *(Rad: = empfangen)* to get; **ich will auch gehört werden** I want to be heard too; **bei wem ~ Sie in diesem Semester?** whose lectures are you going to this term?; **eine französische Vorlesung bei Professor X ~** to go to a French lecture by Professor X

c *(= sich nach etw richten)* to listen, to pay attention; *(dial: = gehorchen)* to obey, to listen; **auf jdn/etw ~** to listen to *or* heed sb/sth; **wer nicht ~ will, muss fühlen** *(Prov)* what did I tell you?; **der Hund hört auf den Namen Tobias** the dog answers to the name of Tobias

d *(= erfahren)* to hear; **von etw ~** to hear about *or* of sth; **von jdm gehört haben** to have heard of sb; **von jdm ~** *(= Nachricht bekommen)* to hear from sb; **Sie werden noch von mir ~** *or* **zu ~ kriegen** *(inf: = Drohung)* you'll be hearing from me, you haven't heard the last of this; **man hörte nie mehr etwas von ihm** he was never heard of again; **nie gehört!** *(inf)* never heard of him/it *etc*; **etwas/nichts von sich ~ lassen** to get/not to get in touch; **lassen Sie von sich ~** keep in touch; **ich lasse von mir ~** I'll be in touch; **er ließ nichts von sich ~** I *etc* haven't heard from him; **nach allem, was ich (über ihn/darüber) höre** from what I've heard *or* I hear (about him/it); **soviel man hört** from what I hear/one hears; **er kommt, wie ich höre** I hear he's coming; **man höre und staune!** would you believe it!; **so etwas** *or* **das habe ich ja noch nie gehört!** I've never heard anything like it (in all my life)!; **er wollte nichts** *or* **von nichts gehört haben** he pretended not to have heard anything about it; **ich will davon** *or* **von der Sache nichts gehört haben** I don't want to know anything about it; **ich will mal nichts gehört haben** *(inf)* I haven't heard a thing, right? *(inf)*

Hö|ren NT **-s**, *no pl* hearing; *(= Radiohören)* listening; **das ~ von Musik** listening to music; **es verging ihm ~ und Sehen** he didn't know whether he was coming or going *(inf)*; **er fuhr so schnell, dass mir ~ und Sehen verging** he drove so fast I almost passed out

Hö|ren|sa|gen NT **vom ~** from *or* by hearsay

hö|rens|wert ADJ **~ sein** to be worth hearing, to be worth listening to

Hö|rer ['hø:rɐ] M **-s, -** *(Telec)* receiver; *(= Kopfhörer)* headphone, earphone

Hö|rer ['hø:rɐ] M **-s, -**, **Hö|re|rin** [-ərɪn] F **-, -nen** *(Rad)* listener; *(Univ)* student (attending lectures); **sich als ~ einschreiben** to enrol *(Brit) or* enroll *(US)* for a lecture course

Hö|rer|brief M listener's letter

Hö|rer|schaft ['hø:rɐʃaft] F **-**, *(rare)* **-en** *(Rad)* listeners *pl*, audience; *(Univ)* number of students (attending a lecture)

Hör-: **Hör|feh|ler** M *(Med)* hearing defect; **diese falsche Information beruht auf einem ~** the wrong information was relayed because something was misheard; **das war ein ~** I/he *etc* misheard it; **Hör|fol|ge** F *(Rad)* radio series; *(= Geschichte in Fortsetzungen)* radio serial; **Hör|funk** M sound radio; **Hör|ge|rät** NT, **Hör|hil|fe** F hearing aid; **hör|ge|schä|digt** ADJ hard of hearing *pred*, partially deaf, with impaired hearing *pred*; **Hör|gren|ze** F auditory threshold, limit of hearing

hö|rig ['hø:rɪç] ADJ dependent *(+dat* on); *(Hist)* in bondage; **jdm (sexuell) ~ sein** to be (sexually) dependent on sb; **sich** *(dat)* **jdn ~ machen** to make sb sexually dependent on one; **er ist ihr ~** she has sexual power over him

Hö|ri|ge(r) ['hø:rɪgə] MF *decl as adj (Hist)* bondsman/-woman, serf; *(fig: = sexuell Hörige)* person who is sexually dependent on sb

Hö|rig|keit F **-**, *no pl* dependence; *(Hist)* bondage, serfdom; *(sexuell)* sexual dependence

Ho|ri|zont [hori'tsɔnt] M **-(e)s, -e** *(lit, fig)* horizon; *(Geol auch)* zone; **am ~** on the horizon; **das geht über meinen ~** *(fig)* that is beyond me *or* my comprehension; **er hat einen begrenzten** *or* **beschränkten ~** he has limited horizons; **künstlicher ~** *(Aviat)* artificial horizon

ho|ri|zon|tal [horitsɔn'ta:l] ADJ horizontal; **das ~e Gewerbe** *(inf)* the oldest profession in the world *(inf)* ADV horizontally

Ho|ri|zon|ta|le [horitsɔn'ta:lə] F **-(n), -n** *(Math)* horizontal (line); **er befindet sich in der ~n** *(inf)* he is lying down (in bed); **sich in die ~ begeben** *(inf)* to adopt the horizontal *(hum)*

Hor|mon [hɔr'mo:n] NT **-s, -e** hormone

hor|mo|nal [hɔrmo'na:l], **hor|mo|nell** [hɔrmo'nɛl] ADJ hormone *attr*, hormonal ADV *behandeln, beeinflussen* with hormones; *beeinflusst, gesteuert* by hormones; **~ bedingt sein** to be caused by hormones; *(Störung)* to be caused by a hormonal imbalance; **jdn/etw ~ behandeln** to treat sb/sth with hormones, to give sb hormone treatment

Hor|mon-: **Hor|mon|be|hand|lung** F hormone treatment; **Hor|mon|cock|tail** M hormone cocktail; **Hor|mon|drü|se** F endocrine gland; **Hor|mon|haus|halt** M hormone *or* hormonal balance; **Hor|mon|prä|pa|rat** NT hormone preparation; **Hor|mon|skan|dal** M (growth) hormone scandal; **Hor|mon|spie|gel** M hormone level; **Hor|mon|sprit|ze** F hormone injection, shot of hormones *(inf)*

Hör|mu|schel F *(Telec)* earpiece

Horn [hɔrn] NT **-(e)s, ¨er** ['hœrnɐ] **a** *(von Tieren, = Trinkhorn)* horn; *(fig inf: = Beule)* bump, lump; **jdn mit den Hörnern aufspießen** to gore sb; **sich** *(dat)* **die Hörner ablaufen** *or* **abschleifen** *or* **abstoßen** *(inf)* to sow one's wild oats; **jdm Hörner aufsetzen** *(inf)* to cuckold sb, to give sb horns *(old)*; **Hörner tragen** *(fig)* to be a cuckold; **das ~ von Afrika** *(Geog)* the Horn of Africa → **Stier**

b *(Mus)* horn; *(Mil)* bugle; *(von Auto etc)* horn, hooter; **die Hörner** *(im Orchester)* the horns *pl*, the horn section; **ins ~ stoßen** to blow *or* sound the horn; **ins gleiche ~ blasen** *or* **stoßen** *or* **tuten** to chime in; **kräftig ins ~ stoßen** *(fig inf: = angeben)* to blow one's own trumpet

c *(bei Schnecke)* horn, feeler

Horn-: **horn|ar|tig** ADJ horn-like; **Horn|ber|ger Schie|ßen** ['hɔrnbɛrgɐ] NT **wie das ~ ausgehen** *or* **enden** to come to nothing; **Horn|blä|ser(in)** M(F) *(Mus)* horn player; **Horn|blen|de** F *(Geol)* hornblende; **Horn|bril|le** F horn-rimmed glasses *pl or* spectacles *pl*

Hörn|chen ['hœrnçən] NT **-s, -** **a** *(= kleines Horn)* little horn **b** *(= Gebäck)* croissant **c** *(Zool)* squirrel; *(= Backenhörnchen)* chipmunk, ground squirrel; *(= Flughörnchen)* flying squirrel

Hör|ner|klang M sound of horns *or* bugles

hör|nern ['hœrnɐn] ADJ (made of) horn

Hör|nerv M auditory nerve

Horn-: **horn|för|mig** ADJ horn-shaped; **Horn|ge|stell** NT **eine Brille mit ~** horn-rimmed glasses *pl*; **Horn|haut** F (patch of) hard *or* horny skin, callous; *(des Auges)* cornea; **Horn|haut|ent|zün|dung** F *(Med)* inflammation of the cornea, keratitis *(spec)*; **Horn|haut|trü|bung** F *(Med)* corneal opacity

hor|nig ['hɔrnɪç] ADJ horny, like horn

Hor|nis|se [hɔr'nɪsə] F **-, -n** hornet

Hor|nis|sen|nest NT hornet's nest

Hor|nist [hɔr'nɪst] M **-en, -en**, **Hor|nis|tin** [-'nɪstɪn] F **-, -nen** horn player; *(Mil)* bugler

Horn-: **Horn|kamm** M horn comb; **Horn|ochs** M, **Horn|och|se** M *(fig inf)* blockhead *(inf)*, idiot; **Horn|sig|nal** NT *(Mil)* bugle call; *(Rail)* horn signal; *(von Auto)* honk, hoot

Hor|nung ['hɔrnʊŋ] M **-s, -e** *(obs)* February

Horn|vieh NT horned cattle *pl*; *(fig inf: = Idiot)* blockhead *(inf)*, idiot

Hör|or|gan NT organ of hearing

Ho|ro|skop [horo'sko:p] NT **-s, -e** horoscope; **jdm das ~ stellen** to cast sb's horoscope

Hör|pro|be F **jetzt eine ~ aus seiner letzten CD** now here's a sample from his latest CD
hor|rend [hɔ'rɛnt] ADJ horrendous ADV *teuer* horrendously
hor|ri|bi|le dic|tu [hɔ'ri:bile 'dɪktu] ADV *(geh)* terrible to relate
hor|ri|do [hɔri'do:] INTERJ *(Hunt)* halloo
Hor|ri|do [hɔri'do:] NT **-s, -s** halloo(ing)
Hör|rohr NT **a** ear trumpet **b** *(Med)* stethoscope
Hor|ror ['hɔro:ɐ] M **-s,** *no pl* horror (*vor +dat* of); **ein unbeschreiblicher ~ überfiel mich** I was seized by an indescribable feeling of horror
Hor|ror- *in cpds* horror; **Hor|ror|film** M horror film; **Hor|ror|scho|cker** M *(Press sl)* (*= Film*) horror film; (*= Roman*) horror novel; (*= Buch*) horror book; **Hor|ror|sze|na|rio** NT nightmare scenario; **Hor|ror|sze|ne** F scene of horror, horrific scene; **Hor|ror|trip** M *(inf)* horror trip *(inf)*; **Hor|ror|vi|si|on** M nightmare vision
Hör-: **Hör|saal** M *(Univ)* lecture room *or* hall, lecture theatre *(Brit) or* theater *(US)*; **Hör|schwel|le** F auditory threshold
Hors|d'oeuv|re [(h)ɔr'dœ:vrə, ˌh̯o:ɐ'dœ:vrə] NT **-s, -s** hors d'oeuvre
Hör|spiel NT *(Rad)* radio play
Horst [hɔrst] M **-(e)s, -e** **a** (*= Nest*) nest; (*= Adlerhorst*) eyrie **b** (*= Gehölz*) thicket, shrubbery **c** *(Bot)* (*von Blumen*) cluster; (*von Bambus, Gras*) tuft **d** *(Geol)* horst **e** (*= Fliegerhorst*) military airfield, military aerodrome *(Brit)*
Hör|sturz M hearing loss
Hort [hɔrt] M **-(e)s, -e** **a** *(old, poet: = Schatz)* hoard, treasure **b** *(geh: = Zufluchtsstätte)* refuge, shelter; **ein ~ der Freiheit** a stronghold of liberty; **der Herr sei mein ~** *(Bibl)* the Lord be my refuge *(Bibl)* **c** (*= Kinderhort*) ≈ after-school care club *(Brit)*, ≈ after-school daycare *(US)*
hor|ten ['hɔrtn] VT *Geld, Vorräte etc* to hoard; *Rohstoffe etc* to stockpile
Hor|ten|sie [hɔr'tɛnziə] F **-, -n** hydrangea
Hort|platz M (*= Platz in Kinderhort*) place in an after-school care club *or* centre *(Brit) or* center *(US)*
Hor|tung F **-, -en** hoarding; (*von Rohstoffen*) stockpiling
Hör-: **Hör|ver|mö|gen** NT hearing (capacity); **Hör|wei|te** F hearing range; **in/außer ~** within/out of hearing *or* earshot; **Hör|zent|rum** NT *(Anat)* auditory *or* acoustic centre *(Brit) or* center *(US)*
Hös|chen ['hø:sçən] NT **-s, -** **a** (*= Kinderhose*) (pair of) trousers *pl (esp Brit) or* pants *pl (esp US)*; (*= Strampelhöschen*) (pair of) rompers *pl*; **kurze(s) ~** (pair of) shorts *pl* **b** (*= Unterhose*) (pair of) panties *pl or* knickers *pl (Brit)*; (*für Kinder*) (pair of) underpants *pl or* pants *pl (Brit)* **c** *(Zool: einer Biene)* pollen load *or* pellet
Hös|chen|win|del F disposable nappy *(Brit) or* diaper *(US)*
Ho|se ['ho:zə] F **-, -n** trousers *pl (esp Brit)*, pants *pl (esp US)*; (*= Damenhose auch*) slacks *pl*; (*= Bundhose*) breeches *pl*; (*= Reithose*) jodhpurs *pl*, (riding) breeches *pl*; (*= Badehose*) swimming trunks *pl*; (*= Unterhose*) underpants *pl*, pants *pl (Brit)*; (*von Vogel*) leg feathers *pl*; **ich brauche eine neue ~** I need a new pair of trousers *etc*, I need some new trousers *etc*; **zwei ~n** two pairs of trousers *etc*; **die ~n anhaben** *(fig inf)* to wear the trousers *(Brit) or* pants *(inf)*; **das Herz fiel** *or* **rutschte ihm in die ~** *(inf)* his heart was in his mouth; **die ~n voll haben** *(lit)* to have dirtied oneself, to have made a mess in one's pants *(Brit)*; *(fig inf)* to be scared shitless *(sl)*, to be wetting oneself *(inf)*; **sich** *(dat)* **in die ~n machen** *(lit)* to dirty oneself, to make a mess in one's pants *(Brit)*; *(fig inf)* to shit *(sl) or* wet *(inf)* oneself; **in die ~ gehen** *(inf)* to be a complete flop *(inf)*; **tote ~** *(inf)* nothing doing *(inf)*; **der Film war tote ~** *(inf)* the film was a dead loss *(Brit inf) or* a waste of time

Ho|sen-: **Ho|sen|an|zug** M trouser suit *(Brit)*, pantsuit *(US)*; **Ho|sen|auf|schlag** M turn-up *(Brit)*, cuff *(US)*; **Ho|sen|band** [-bant] NT *pl* **-bänder** knee-band; **Ho|sen|band|or|den** M Order of the Garter; **Ho|sen|bein** NT trouser *(esp Brit) or* pant *(esp US)* leg; **Ho|sen|bo|den** M seat (of trousers *(esp Brit) or* pants *(esp US)*); **den ~ vollkriegen** *(inf)* to get a smacked bottom; **sich auf den ~ setzen** *(inf)* (*= arbeiten*) to get stuck in *(inf)*, to knuckle down; (*= stillsitzen*) to sit down and stay sitting down; **Ho|sen|bo|je** F *(Naut)* breeches buoy; **Ho|sen|bü|gel** M trouser *(esp Brit) or* pant *(esp US)* hanger; **Ho|sen|bund** M *pl* **-bünde** waistband; **Ho|sen|klam|mer** F trouser clip *(esp Brit)*, cycle clip; **Ho|sen|klap|pe** F flap; **Ho|sen|knopf** M trouser *(esp Brit) or* pant *(esp US)* button; **Ho|sen|latz** M (*= Verschluss*) flies *pl*, fly; (*von Latzhose*) bib; **Ho|sen|matz** M *(inf)* (*= kleines Kind*) **du (kleiner) ~** my little darling; **Ho|sen|naht** F trouser *(esp Brit) or* pant *(esp US)* seam; **mit den Händen an der ~** *(Mil)* (stand to attention,) thumbs on (your) trouser *(esp Brit) or* pant *(esp US)* seams; **Ho|sen|rock** M divided skirt, culottes *pl*; **Ho|sen|schei|ßer(in)** M(F) **a** *(inf: = Kind)* mucky pup *(Brit inf)*, pig *(inf)*; **du kleiner ~** you mucky little pup *(Brit inf)*, you little pig *(inf)* **b** *(sl: = Feigling)* chicken *(inf)*; (*= Junge*) scaredy-pants *(inf)*; **Ho|sen|schlitz** M flies *pl*, fly; **Ho|sen|span|ner** M trouser *(esp Brit) or* pant *(esp US)* hanger; **Ho|sen|stall** M *(inf: = Schlitz)* flies *pl*, fly; **Ho|sen|ta|sche** F trouser pocket *(Brit)*, pant(s) *or* trousers pocket *(US)*; **Ho|sen|trä|ger** PL (pair of) braces *pl (Brit) or* suspenders *pl (US)*
ho|si|an|na [ho'ziana] INTERJ hosanna
Ho|si|an|na [ho'ziana] NT **-s, -s** hosanna
Hos|pi|tal [hɔspi'ta:l] NT **-s, -e** *or* **Hospitäler** [-'tɛ:lɐ] *(dated)* **a** (*= Krankenhaus*) hospital **b** (*= Pflegeheim*) (old people's) home
Hos|pi|ta|lis|mus [hɔspita'lɪsmʊs] M **-,** *no pl (Med)* hospitalism
Hos|pi|tant [hɔspi'tant] M **-en, -en**, **Hos|pi|tan|tin** [-'tantɪn] F **-, -nen** *(Univ)* someone sitting in on lectures *or (Sch)* classes, auditor *(US)*
Hos|pi|ta|ti|on [hɔspita'tsio:n] F **-, -en** *(Univ)* sitting in on lectures *or (Sch)* classes (*bei jdm* with sb)
hos|pi|tie|ren [hɔspi'ti:rən] *ptp* **hospitiert** VI *(Univ)* to sit in on lectures *or (Sch)* classes (*bei jdm* with sb)
Hos|piz [hɔs'pi:ts] NT **-es, -e** hospice; (*= christliches Hospiz*) *private hotel under religious management*
Host [ho:st] M **-s, -s** *(Comput)* host
Host|com|pu|ter [ho:st-] M *(Comput)* host (computer)
Hos|tess ['hɔstɛs, hɔs'tɛs] F **-, -en** hostess
Hos|tie ['hɔstiə] F **-, -n** *(Eccl)* host, consecrated wafer
Hos|ti|en-: **Hos|ti|en|ge|fäß** NT pyx, ciborium; **Hos|ti|en|kelch** M chalice; **Hos|ti|en|schach|tel** F box for communion wafers; **Hos|ti|en|schrein** M tabernacle; **Hos|ti|en|tel|ler** M paten
Host|lauf|werk [ho:st-] NT *(Comput)* host drive
Hot|dog ['hɔt'dɔk] NT OR M **-s, -s**, **Hot Dog** NT OR M **-s, -s** *(Cook)* hot dog
Ho|tel [ho'tɛl] NT **-s, -s** hotel
Ho|tel|boy M page (boy), bellboy *(US)*, bellhop *(US)*
Ho|tel|fach NT, *no pl* hotel management
Ho|tel|fach-: **Ho|tel|fach|frau** F hotel manageress; **Ho|tel|fach|mann** M hotel manager; **Ho|tel|fach|schu|le** F college of hotel management
Ho|tel|füh|rer M hotel guide
Ho|tel gar|ni [ho'tɛl gar'ni:] NT **- -, -s -s** bed and breakfast hotel
Ho|tel-: **Ho|tel|ge|wer|be** NT hotel business; **Ho|tel|hal|le** F (hotel) lobby

Ho|te|li|er [hotɛ'lie:] M **-s, -s** hotelier
Ho|tel|le|rie [hotɛlə'ri:] F **-,** *no pl (Sw)* hotel business
Ho|tel-: **Ho|tel|nach|weis** M hotel register; **Ho|tel|pa|ge** M page (boy), bellboy *(US)*, bellhop *(US)*; **Ho|tel|per|so|nal** NT hotel staff; **Ho|tel|por|ti|er** M hotel *or* hall porter; **Ho|tel|rech|nung** F hotel bill *(Brit) or* check *(US)*; **Ho|tel|sil|ber** NT hotel cutlery; **Ho|tel- und Gast|stät|ten|ge|wer|be** NT hotel and restaurant trade, catering industry; **Ho|tel|ver|zeich|nis** NT hotel register; **Ho|tel|zim|mer** NT hotel room
Hot|key ['hɔtki:] M **-s, -s** *(Comput)* hot key
Hot|line ['hɔtlain] F **-, -s** *(Telec: = Informationsdienst, Sorgentelefon)* helpline; **eine ~ einrichten** to set up a helpline
Hot|spot ['hɔtspɔt] M **-s, -s** *(Geol, Comput)* hot spot
hott [hɔt] INTERJ (*= vorwärts*) gee up; (*= nach rechts*) gee
Hot|ten|tot|te [hɔtn'tɔtə] M **-n, -n**, **Hot|ten|tot|tin** [-'tɔtɪn] F **-, -nen** Hottentot; **sie benehmen sich wie die ~n** *(inf)* they behave like savages
hpts. *abbr von* **hauptsächlich**
Hptst. *abbr von* **Hauptstadt**
Hr. *abbr von* **Herr** Mr
Hrn. *abbr von* **Herrn**
hrsg. *abbr von* **herausgegeben** edited, ed.
Hrsg. *abbr von* **Herausgeber** ed.
HTML [ha:te:lɛm'lɛl] *abbr (Comput, Internet) von* **Hypertext Markup Language** HTML
HTML- *(Comput, Internet)*: **HTML-Datei** F HTML file; **HTML-Dokument** NT HTML document; **HTML-Format** NT HTML format
http [ha:te:te:'pe:] *abbr (Comput, Internet) von* **hypertext transfer** *or* **transport protocol** http
hu [hu:] INTERJ *(Schaudern)* ugh; *(Schrecken, Kälte etc)* whew
hü [hy:] INTERJ (*= vorwärts*) gee up; (*= nach links*) wo hi; **einmal sagt er hü, einmal hott** *(inf)* first he says one thing and then another, he's always chopping and changing *(Brit inf)*
Hub [hu:p] M **-(e)s, ⸚e** ['hy:bə] *(Tech)* **a** (*bei Maschinen: = Kolbenhub*) (piston) stroke **b** (*bei Kränen: = Leistung*) lifting *or* hoisting capacity, lift
Hub|bel ['hʊbl] M **-s, -** *(inf)* bump
hub|be|lig ['hʊbəlɪç] ADJ *(inf)* bumpy
Hub|ble|te|le|skop ['habl-] NT, **Hub|ble-Te|le|skop** NT Hubble telescope
hubb|lig ['hʊblɪç] ADJ *(inf)* bumpy
Hub|brü|cke F lift bridge
Hu|bel ['hu:bl] M **-s, -** *(inf)* bump
hü|ben ['hy:bn] ADV over here, (on) this side; **~ und** *or* **wie drüben** on both sides
Hu|ber|tus|jagd [hu'bɛrtʊs-] F St Hubert's Day hunt
Hub-: **Hub|in|sel** F drilling rig *or* platform; **Hub|kar|ren** M lift(ing) truck; **Hub|kraft** F lifting *or* hoisting capacity; **Hub|mag|net** M solenoid; **Hub|raum** M *(Aut)* cubic capacity
hübsch [hʏpʃ] ADJ **a** (*= gut aussehend*) pretty; (*= reizvoll*) *Ausflug, Geschenk* lovely, delightful, nice; *(inf: = nett)* lovely, nice; **sich ~ machen** to make oneself look pretty; **das wäre doch ~, wenn …** it would be lovely if …; **ihr (beiden) Hübschen** *(inf)* you two
b *(iro inf: = unangenehm)* fine, pretty, nice; **eine ~e Geschichte/Bescherung** a pretty kettle of fish, a fine how-d'ye-do; **das kann ja ~ werden** that'll be just great; **da hast du dir etwas Hübsches eingebrockt!** now you've got yourself into a fine *or* pretty mess!
c *(inf: = beträchtlich)* tidy, pretty, nice; **ein ~es Vermögen** a pretty penny *(inf)*; **ein ~es Sümmchen** a tidy sum
ADV **a** (*= nett*) *einrichten, dekorieren, gestalten, sich kleiden* nicely; **~ aussehen** to look pretty; **er macht das schon ganz ~** he's doing it very nicely *or* well
b (*= ziemlich*) pretty; *fluchen, dazulernen, reinlegen* really; **da musste ich aber ganz ~ arbeiten** I

really had to work pretty hard; **ganz ~ viel bezahlen** to pay quite a bit
c *(inf: = wie es sein soll)* **~ artig/leise** nice and good/quiet; **das werde ich ~ bleiben lassen** I'm going to leave well alone; **das wirst du ~ bleiben lassen!** don't you dare; **das wirst du ~ sein lassen** you're going to do nothing of the kind; **sei ~ artig!** be a good boy/girl; **immer ~ langsam!** nice and easy does it, (take it) nice and slowly

Hub|schrau|ber ['hu:pʃraubɐ] M **-s, -** helicopter

Hub|schrau|ber-: **Hub|schrau|ber|dienst** M helicopter service; **Hub|schrau|ber|flug|platz** M, **Hub|schrau|ber|lan|de|platz** M heliport; **Hub|schrau|ber|trä|ger** M *(Naut)* helicopter-carrier

Hub-: **Hub|stap|ler** [-ʃta:plɐ] M **-s, -** stacking truck; **Hub|vo|lu|men** NT *(Tech)* cubic capacity

huch [hʊx] INTERJ ooh

Hu|cke ['hʊkə] F **-, -n** *(obs) (= Last)* load; *(= Korb)* pannier; **jdm die ~ vollhauen** *(inf)* to give sb a good thrashing *(inf)* or hiding; **die ~ vollkriegen** *(inf)* to get a thrashing *(inf)* or hiding; **jdm die ~ vollügen** *(inf)* to tell sb a pack of lies; **sich** *(dat)* **die ~ vollsaufen** *(inf)* to have a skinful *(Brit inf)*, to have a few (too many)

hu|cke|pack ['hʊkəpak] ADV piggy-back *(auch Comput)*, pick-a-back; **ein Kind ~ nehmen/tragen** to give a child a piggy-back (ride), to carry a child piggy-back or pick-a-back

Hu|cke|pack-: **Hu|cke|pack|ver|fah|ren** NT *(Space, Rail)* piggy-back system; *(Chem)* piggy-back process; **Hu|cke|pack|ver|kehr** M *(Rail)* piggy-back transport *(US)*, motorail service; **im ~** by motorail

Hu|de|lei [hu:də'lai] F **-, -en** *(esp S Ger, Aus: inf)* slipshod or sloppy *(inf)* work

hu|deln ['hu:dln] VI *(esp S Ger, Aus: inf)* to work sloppily, to do slipshod work

Hud|ler ['hu:dlɐ] M **-s, -**, **Hud|le|rin** [-ərɪn] F **-, -nen** *(esp S Ger, Aus: inf)* slipshod or sloppy worker, bungler *(inf)*

hud|lig ['hu:dlɪç] *(esp S Ger, Aus: inf)* ADJ slipshod, sloppy *(inf)* ADV sloppily, carelessly; **~ arbeiten** to work sloppily, to do sloppy or slipshod work

Hud|ri|wud|ri ['hu:dri'vu:dri] M **-s, -s**, **Hud|ri-Wud|ri** M **-s, -s** *(Aus inf: = unruhiger Mensch)* bag or bundle of nerves

Huf [hu:f] M **-(e)s, -e** hoof; **einem Pferd die ~e beschlagen** to shoe a horse

Huf|be|schlag M (horse)shoeing

Huf|ei|sen NT horseshoe

Huf|ei|sen-: **huf|ei|sen|för|mig** ADJ horseshoe-shaped, (in) the shape of a horseshoe ADV in the shape of a horseshoe; **Huf|ei|sen|mag|net** M horseshoe magnet

Hu|fen|dorf NT *village arranged in a straight line with strips of farmland extending behind each house*

Huf-: **Huf|lat|tich** M *(Bot)* coltsfoot; **Huf|na|gel** M horseshoe nail; **Huf|schlag** M *(= Getrappel)* hoofbeats *pl*; *(= Stoß)* kick (from a horse); **dabei hat er einen ~ abbekommen** the horse kicked him; **Huf|schmied(in)** M(F) blacksmith, farrier; **Huf|schmie|de** F smithy, blacksmith's or farrier's (workshop)

Hüft-: **Hüft|bein** NT hipbone; **hüft|be|tont** ADJ **ein ~es Kleid** a dress that emphasizes the hips; **Hüft|bruch** M fractured hip, hip fracture

Hüf|te ['hʏftə] F **-, -n** hip; *(von Tieren)* haunch; **bis an die ~n reichen** to come up to the waist; **wir standen bis an die ~n in Brennnesseln/im Wasser** we stood waist-high or up to the waist in (stinging) nettles/waist-deep or up to the waist in water; **aus der ~ schießen** to shoot from the hip; **mit wiegenden ~n** with hips swaying; **die Arme in die ~n stützen** to put one's hands on one's hips; **er stand mit den Armen in die ~n gestützt da** he stood there hands on hips, he stood there with arms akimbo

Hüft-: **Hüft|ge|gend** F hip region; **Hüft|ge|lenk** NT hip joint; **Hüft|gür|tel** M, **Hüft|hal|ter** M girdle; **hüft|hoch** ADJ *Pflanzen etc* waist-high; *Wasser etc* waist-deep; **hüfthohe Gummistiefel** rubber waders ADV **wir standen ~ im Farnkraut/Schlamm** we stood waist-high or up to the waist in ferns/waist-deep or up to the waist in mud

Huf|tier NT hoofed animal, ungulate *(form)*

Hüft-: **Hüft|kno|chen** M hipbone; **Hüft|lei|den** NT hip trouble; **Hüft|schmerz** M pain in the hip; **Hüft|um|fang** M hip measurement; **Hüft|ver|ren|kung** F dislocation of the hip

Hü|gel ['hy:gl] M **-s, -** hill; *(= Grab-, Erdhaufen)* mound; **ein kleiner ~** a hillock

Hü|gel-: **hü|gel|ab** [hy:gl'lap] ADV downhill; **hü|gel|an** [hy:gl'lan], **hü|gel|auf** [hy:gl'lauf] ADV uphill; **Hü|gel|beet** NT raised bed; **Hü|gel|grab** NT *(Archeol)* barrow, tumulus

hü|ge|lig ['hy:gəlɪç] ADJ hilly, undulating, rolling *attr*

Hü|gel-: **Hü|gel|ket|te** F range or chain of hills; **Hü|gel|land** NT hilly country

Hu|ge|not|te [hugə'nɔtə] M **-n, -n**, **Hu|ge|not|tin** [-'nɔtɪn] F **-, -nen** Huguenot

hüg|lig ['hy:glɪç] ADJ = **hügelig**

huh [hu:] INTERJ = **hu**

hüh [hy:] INTERJ = **hü**

Huhn [hu:n] NT **-(e)s, ¨er** ['hy:nɐ] **a** chicken *(auch Cook)*; *(= Henne)* hen, chicken; *(Gattung)* fowl, gallinaceous bird *(form)*; **mit den Hühnern aufstehen** *(inf)* to get up with the lark; **mit den Hühnern zu Bett gehen** *(inf)* to go to bed early; **da lachen ja die Hühner** *(inf)* what a joke, it's enough to make a cat laugh *(inf)*; **ich sehe aus wie ein gerupftes ~** *(inf)* my hair looks like a haystack *(Brit inf)* or a rat's nest *(US inf)* → **blind ADJ a**
b *(fig inf)* **du krankes ~** you poor old thing; **ein verrücktes** or **komisches** or **ulkiges ~** a queer bird or fish *(Brit inf)*, a strange or odd character; **ein dummes ~** a silly goose; **ein versoffenes ~** a tippler *(inf)*

Hühn|chen ['hy:nçən] NT **-s, -** (young) chicken, pullet; *(= Brathühnchen)* (roast) chicken; **mit jdm ein ~ zu rupfen haben** *(inf)* to have a bone to pick with sb *(inf)*

Hüh|ner-: **Hüh|ner|au|ge** NT *(Med)* corn; **jdm auf die ~n treten** *(hum)* to tread on sb's corns *(Brit inf)* or feet *(US inf)*; **Hüh|ner|au|gen|pflas|ter** NT corn plaster; **Hüh|ner|bouil|lon** F, **Hüh|ner|brü|he** F (clear) chicken broth; **Hüh|ner|brust** F *(Cook)* chicken breast; *(Med inf)* pigeon breast *(Brit)*, chicken breast *(US)*; *(sl: = flacher Busen)* **eine ~ haben** to be as flat as a pancake *(esp Brit inf)* or a board *(US inf)*; **Hüh|ner|dieb(in)** M(F) chicken thief; **er musste sich wie ein ~ wegschleichen** he had to slink off with his tail between his legs; **Hüh|ner|draht** M chicken wire; **Hüh|ner|ei** [-lai] NT hen's egg; **Hüh|ner|farm** F chicken farm; **Hüh|ner|fleisch** NT chicken (meat); **Hüh|ner|fri|kas|see** NT chicken fricassee; **Hüh|ner|fut|ter** NT chicken feed; **Hüh|ner|gott** M *(Miner)* holystone; **Hüh|ner|ha|bicht** M goshawk; **Hüh|ner|haus** NT henhouse, chicken coop; **Hüh|ner|hof** M chicken run; **Hüh|ner|hund** M pointer; **Hüh|ner|klein** [-klain] NT **-s**, *no pl (Cook)* chicken trimmings *pl*; **Hüh|ner|le|ber|pas|te|te** F chicken liver pâté; **Hüh|ner|lei|ter** F chicken ladder; **Hüh|ner|mist** M chicken droppings *pl*; *(zum Düngen)* chicken manure; **Hüh|ner|pas|te|te** F chicken pie; **Hüh|ner|pest** F *(Vet)* fowl pest; **Hüh|ner|stall** M henhouse, chicken coop; **Hüh|ner|stan|ge** F perch, (chicken) roost; **Hüh|ner|sup|pe** F chicken soup; **Hüh|ner|vö|gel** PL *(Orn)* gallinaceans *pl (form)*, gallinaceous birds *pl (form)*; **Hüh|ner|zucht** F chicken breeding or farming

hui [hui] INTERJ whoosh; **~, das war aber schnell!** wow, that was quick!; **außen ~, innen pfui** *(prov inf)* he/she/it is fine on the outside, but inside it's a different story *(inf)*

Hu|la-Hoop [hu:la'hʊp] M OR NT **-s**, *no pl* Hula Hoop®

Hu|la-Hoop-Rei|fen [hu:la'hʊp-] M Hula Hoop®

Huld [hʊlt] F **-**, *no pl (old liter) (= Güte)* grace, graciousness; *(= Gunst)* favour *(Brit)*, favor *(US)*; **jdm seine ~ schenken** to bestow one's favour *(Brit)* or favor *(US)* upon sb *(liter)*; **sie stand in seiner ~** she was in his good graces

hul|di|gen ['hʊldɪgn] VI *+dat (liter)* **a** *einem König, Papst etc* to render or do or pay homage to; *einem Künstler, Lehrmeister etc* to pay homage to; *einer Dame* to pay one's attentions or addresses to *(liter)* **b** *einer Ansicht* to subscribe to; *einer Sitte, einem Glauben etc* to embrace; *einem Laster* to indulge in

Hul|di|gung F **-, -en** *(old, liter)* **a** *(Hist: = Treueid)* homage, oath of allegiance **b** *(= Verehrung)* homage; *(einer Dame)* attentions *pl (liter)*, addresses *pl (liter)*; *(= Beifall)* homage; **jdm seine ~ darbringen** to pay homage to sb

huld|reich, **huld|voll** ADJ *(old, liter)* gracious ADV *(geh)* graciously; **~ lächelnd** with a gracious smile; **~ tun** *(iro)* to act gallantly

Hül|fe ['hʏlfə] F **-, -n** *(obs)* = **Hilfe a**

Hül|le ['hʏlə] F **-, -n** **a** cover; *(für Ausweiskarten etc)* holder, case; *(= Cellophanhülle)* wrapping; *(liter, hum: = Kleidung)* clothes *pl*, piece of clothing; *(liter: eines Menschen)* exterior; *(= abgestreifte Schlangenhaut)* skin; **die ~n fallen lassen** to peel or strip off; **die letzten ~n fallen lassen** to shed the last layer; **der Körper als ~ der Seele** the body as the temple of the soul; **die sterbliche ~** the mortal remains *pl*
b *(Anat)* integument
c *(Bot)* involucre *(form)*
d *(Phys: = Atomhülle)* shell
e **in ~ und Fülle** in abundance; **Äpfel/Whisky/Frauen/Sorgen** *etc* **in ~ und Fülle** apples/whisky/women/worries *etc* galore; **es gab alles in ~ und Fülle** there was plenty or an abundance of everything

hül|len ['hʏlən] VT *(geh)* to wrap; **in Dunkel gehüllt** shrouded in darkness; **in Flammen gehüllt** enveloped in flames; **in Wolken gehüllt** covered or enveloped or veiled *(liter)* in clouds; **sich fest in seinen Mantel ~** to wrap oneself up tight in one's coat; **sich (über etw** *acc***) in Schweigen ~** to remain silent (on or about sth)

hül|len|los ADJ unclothed

Hüll|wort NT *pl* **-wörter** *(Ling)* euphemism

Hül|se ['hʏlzə] F **-, -n** **a** *(= Schale)* hull, husk; *(= Schote)* pod; *(Bot: = Frucht)* involucre *(form)* **b** *(= Etui, Kapsel)* case; *(für Film)* cartridge; *(Phys: für gefährliche Stoffe)* capsule; *(von Geschoss)* case; *(von Patronen)* (cartridge) case; **er ist nur noch eine leere ~** he is now just an empty shell

Hül|sen|frucht F *usu pl* peas and beans *pl*, pulse *(form)*

hu|man [hu'ma:n] ADJ humane; *(= verständnisvoll auch)* considerate ADV *(= menschenfreundlich)* humanely; **die Abschiebung ~er gestalten** to carry out deportations in a more humane way

Hu|man-: **Hu|man|ge|ne|tik** F human genetics *sing*; **Hu|man|ge|ne|ti|ker(in)** M(F) human geneticist; **hu|man|ge|ne|tisch** ADJ human genetic *attr*

Hu|ma|ni|sie|rung [humani'zi:rʊŋ] F **-**, *no pl* humanization

Hu|ma|nis|mus [huma'nɪsmʊs] M **-**, *no pl* humanism; *(Hist)* Humanism

Hu|ma|nist [huma'nɪst] M **-en, -en**, **Hu|ma|nis|tin** [-'nɪstɪn] F **-, -nen** humanist; *(Hist)* Humanist; *(= Altsprachler)* classicist

hu|ma|nis|tisch [huma'nɪstɪʃ] ADJ humanist(ic); *(Hist)* Humanist; *(= altsprachlich)* classical; **~e Bildung** classical education, education in the classics or the humanities; **~es Gymnasium** *secondary school with bias on Latin and*

Greek, ≈ grammar school *(Brit)* ADV **jdn ~ bilden** to provide sb with a humanistic *or* classical education; **~ gebildet** educated in the classics *or* humanities; **~ erzogen werden** to receive a classical *or* humanistic education

hu|ma|ni|tär [humaniˈtɛːɐ] ADJ humanitarian

Hu|ma|ni|tät [humaniˈtɛːt] F -, *no pl* humaneness, humanity; *(als Bildungsideal)* humanitarianism

Hu|ma|ni|täts|du|se|lei [-duzəlai] F -, -en *(pej)* sentimental humanitarianism

Hu|man-: **Hu|man|ka|pi|tal** NT human resources *pl*, human capital; **Hu|man|me|di|zin** F (human) medicine; **Hu|man|me|di|zi|ner(in)** M(F) *(= Student)* medical student; *(= Arzt)* doctor of medicine; **hu|man|me|di|zi|nisch** ADJ human medicine *attr*; **hu|man|öko|lo|gisch** ADJ human ecological *attr*

Hum|bug [ˈhʊmbʊk] M -s, *no pl (inf) (= Schwindel)* humbug *(inf)*; *(= Unsinn auch)* stuff and nonsense *(inf)*

Hum|mel [ˈhʊml] F -, -n bumblebee; **~n im** *or* **unterm Hintern haben** *(dated inf)* to have ants in one's pants *(inf)*

Hum|mer [ˈhʊmɐ] M -s, - lobster

Hum|mer-: **Hum|mer|cock|tail** M lobster cocktail; **Hum|mer|fleisch** NT lobster (meat); **Hum|mer|krab|ben** PL king prawns *pl*; **Hum|mer|reu|se** F lobster pot; **Hum|mer|sche|re** F lobster claw

Hu|mor [huˈmoːɐ] M -s, *(rare)* -e humour *(Brit)*, humor *(US)*; *(= Sinn für Humor)* sense of humo(u)r; **er hat keinen (Sinn für) ~** he has no sense of humo(u)r; **etw mit ~ nehmen/tragen** to take/bear sth cheerfully *or* with a sense of humo(u)r; **er nahm die Bemerkung mit ~ auf** he took the remark good-humo(u)redly *or* in good humo(u)r; **er hat einen eigenartigen ~** he has a strange sense of humo(u)r; **er verliert nie den ~** he never loses his sense of humo(u)r; **langsam verliere ich den ~** it's getting beyond a joke; **da hat selbst er den ~ verloren** it was going too far even for him, even he didn't think it funny any more; **~ ist, wenn man trotzdem lacht** *(prov)* having a sense of humo(u)r means looking on the bright side

Hu|mo|res|ke [humoˈrɛskə] F -, -n *(Liter)* humorous story; *(= Sketch)* humorous sketch; *(Mus)* humoresque

hu|mo|rig [huˈmoːrɪç] ADJ *(geh)* humorous, genial

Hu|mo|rist [humoˈrɪst] M -en, -en, **Hu|mo|ris|tin** [-ˈrɪstɪn] F -, -nen **a** humorist **b** *(= Komiker)* comedian; *(Frau auch)* comedienne

hu|mo|ris|tisch [humoˈrɪstɪʃ] ADJ humorous; **er ist** *or* **hat ein großes ~es Talent** he is a very funny *or* amusing person

Hu|mor-: **hu|mor|los** ADJ humourless *(Brit)*, humorless *(US)*; *Buch etc auch* lacking in *or* devoid of humour *(Brit) or* humor *(US)*; *Mensch auch* lacking a sense of humour *(Brit) or* humor *(US)* ADV humourlessly *(Brit)*, humorlessly *(US)*; **sich ~ verhalten** to have no sense of humour *(Brit) or* humor *(US)*; **er hat recht ~ auf unsere Scherze reagiert** he didn't find our jokes funny at all; **Hu|mor|lo|sig|keit** F -, *no pl* humourlessness *(Brit)*, humorlessness *(US)*; *(von Mensch auch)* lack of humour *(Brit) or* humor *(US)*; **mit der für ihn typischen ~** with his usual lack of humour *(Brit) or* humor *(US)*; **hu|mor|voll** ADJ humorous, amusing ADV humorously, amusingly, wittily; **~ über etw** *(acc)* **hinweggehen** to make light of sth; **er kann sehr ~ erzählen** he is a very amusing *or* humorous talker

hu|mos [huˈmoːs] ADJ *Boden* humus *attr*

Hum|pe|lei [hʊmpəˈlai] F -, *no pl (inf)* hobbling

hum|peln [ˈhʊmpln] VI **a** *aux sein* to hobble **b** *(inf: = ständig hinken)* to limp, to walk with a limp, to have a limp

Hum|pen [ˈhʊmpn] M -s, - tankard, mug; *(aus Ton)* stein

Hu|mus [ˈhuːmʊs] M -, *no pl* humus

Hu|mus|bo|den M, **Hu|mus|er|de** F humus soil

Hund [hʊnt] M -(e)s, -e [-də] **a** dog; *(esp Jagdhund)* hound; *(inf: = Schurke)* swine *(inf)*, bastard *(sl)*; **der Große/Kleine ~** *(Astron)* Great(er)/Little *or* Lesser Dog; **junger ~** puppy, pup; **die Familie der ~e** the dog *or* canine family; **~e, die (viel) bellen, beißen nicht** *(Prov)* empty vessels make most noise *(Prov)*; **getroffene ~e bellen** *(inf)* if the cap fits, wear it; **viele ~e sind des Hasen Tod** *(Prov)* there is not much one person can do against many; **wie ~ und Katze leben** to live like cat and dog, to lead a cat-and-dog life; **ich würde bei diesem Wetter keinen ~ auf die Straße jagen** I wouldn't send a dog out in this weather; **damit kann man keinen ~ hinterm Ofen hervorlocken** *(inf)* that's not going to tempt anybody; **müde wie ein ~ sein** *(inf)* to be dog-tired; **er ist bekannt wie ein bunter ~** *(inf)* everybody knows him; **kein ~ nimmt ein Stück Brot von ihm** everyone avoids him like the plague; **das ist (ja) zum Junge-~e-Kriegen** *(inf)* it's enough to give you kittens; **da wird der ~ in der Pfanne verrückt** *(inf)* it's enough to drive you crazy *(inf) or* round the twist *(Brit inf)*; **da liegt der ~ begraben** *(inf)* (so) that's what is/was behind it all; *(Haken, Problem etc)* that's the problem; **er ist mit allen ~en gehetzt** *(inf)* he knows all the tricks, there are no flies on him *(Brit inf)*; **er ist ein armer ~** he's a poor soul *or* devil *(inf)*; **er ist völlig auf dem ~** *(inf)* he's really gone to the dogs *(inf)*; **auf den ~ kommen** *(inf)* to go to the dogs *(inf)*; **jdn auf den ~ bringen** *(inf)* to ruin sb; *(gesundheitlich)* to ruin sb's health; **die Weiber haben/der Suff hat ihn auf den ~ gebracht** *(inf)* women have/drink has been his ruin *or* downfall; **vor die ~e gehen** *(inf)* to go to the dogs *(inf)*; *(= sterben)* to die, to perish; *(= getötet werden)* to cop it *(Brit inf)*, to be killed; **du blöder ~** *(inf)* you silly *or* stupid bastard *(sl)*; **du gemeiner ~** *(inf)* you rotten bastard *(sl)*; **du schlauer** *or* **gerissener ~** *(inf)* you sly *or* crafty devil *or* old fox; **schlafende ~e soll man nicht wecken** *(prov)* let sleeping dogs lie *(Prov)*
b *(Min: = Förderwagen)* truck, tub

Hünd|chen [ˈhʏntçən] NT -s, - *dim von* **Hund** doggy *(baby-talk)*, little dog; *(= kleiner Hund)* small *or* little dog; *(= junger Hund)* puppy, pup, puppy dog *(inf)*

Hun|de-: **Hun|de|ar|beit** F *(fig inf)* **eine ~** an awful job, the devil's own job *(inf)*; **Hun|de|art** F breed (of dog); **Hun|de|biss** M dog bite; **er hat einen ~ abbekommen** he has been bitten by a dog; **Hun|de|blick** M **jdn mit ~ ansehen** to give sb a hangdog look; **Hun|de|dreck** M dog dirt *(Brit) or* mess *(inf)*; **hun|de|elend** ADJ *(inf)* **mir ist ~** I feel lousy *(inf)*; **Hun|de|fän|ger(in)** M(F) dog-catcher; **Hun|de|floh** M dog flea; **Hun|de|fraß** M *(pej inf)* (pig)swill *(pej inf)*; **Hun|de|füh|rer(in)** M(F) dog handler; **Hun|de|fut|ter** NT dog food; **Hun|de|ge|bell** NT barking (of dogs); **Hun|de|ge|kläff** NT *(pej)* yapping (of dogs); **Hun|de|ge|spann** NT team of dogs; **Hun|de|hals|band** NT dog collar; **Hun|de|hal|ter(in)** M(F) *(form)* dog owner; **Hun|de|hal|tung** F owning dogs; **Hun|de|hüt|te** F *(lit, fig)* (dog) kennel; **hun|de|kalt** ADJ *(inf)* freezing cold; **Hun|de|käl|te** F *(inf)* freezing cold; **Hun|de|kot** M dog dirt *(Brit) or* mess *(inf)*; **Hun|de|köt|tel** [-kœtl] M -s, - *(inf)* dog dirt *(Brit) or* mess *(inf)*; **Hun|de|ku|chen** M dog biscuit; **Hun|de|le|ben** NT *(inf)* dog's life *(inf)*; **Hun|de|lei|ne** F dog lead *(Brit) or* leash; **Hun|de|lieb|ha|ber(in)** M(F) dog lover; **Hun|de|lohn** M *(pej inf)* miserable *or* rotten *(inf)* wage(s *pl*); **Hun|de|mar|ke** F dog licence *(Brit) or* license *(US)* disc, dog tag *(US)*; *(hum inf: = Erkennungsmarke)* identity disc, dog tag *(US inf)*; **hun|de|mü|de** ADJ *pred* ADV *(inf)* dog-tired; **Hun|de|nah|rung** F dog food; **Hun|de|narr** M, **Hun|de|när|rin** F *(inf)* fanatical dog lover, dog freak *(inf)*; **Hun|de|ras|se** F breed (of dog); **Hun|de|ren|nen** NT greyhound *or* dog racing *no art*, dogs *(inf)*; *(= Wettkampf)* greyhound race

hun|dert [ˈhʊndɐt] NUM a *or* one hundred; **einige ~** *or* **Hundert Menschen** a few hundred people; **einer unter ~** one in a hundred; **in ~ Jahren** in a hundred years (from now); **ich wette ~ gegen eins** *(inf)* I'll bet *or* lay a hundred to one, I'll bet you anything *(inf)*

Hun|dert [ˈhʊndɐt] F -, -en *(= Zahl)* hundred

Hun|dert NT -s, -e hundred; **es geht in die ~e** *or* **hunderte** it runs into the hundreds; **~e** *or* **hunderte von Menschen** hundreds of people; **einer unter ~en** *or* **hunderten** one out of hundreds; **zehn vom ~** ten per cent *(Brit) or* percent *(US)*; **zu ~en** *or* **hunderten** by the hundred, in (their) hundreds; **einige ~** *or* **hundert (Stecknadeln)** a few hundred (pins)

hun|dert|eins [ˈhʊndɐtˈlains] NUM a *or* one hundred and one

Hun|der|ter [ˈhʊndɐtɐ] M -s, - **a** *(von Zahl)* (the) hundred **b** *(= Geldschein)* hundred(-euro/-pound/-dollar *etc* note *(Brit) or* bill *(US)*)

hun|der|ter|lei [ˈhʊndɐtɐˈlai] ADJ *inv* a hundred and one

Hun|dert-: **Hun|dert|eu|ro|schein** M (one) hundred euro note *(Brit) or* bill *(US)*; **hun|dert|fach** ADJ hundredfold; **die ~e Menge** a hundred times the amount ADV a hundred times; **jdm etw ~ zurückgeben** *(fig)* to repay sb a hundredfold for sth, to repay sb a hundred times over for sth; **hun|dert|fünf|zig|pro|zen|tig** *(iro)* ADJ fanatical; **er ist ein Hundertfünfzigprozentiger** he's a fanatic ADV **sich/etw ~ beweisen** to prove oneself/sth twice over; **Hun|dert|jahr|fei|er** F centenary, centennial *(US)*; *(= Festlichkeiten auch)* centenary *or* centennial celebrations *pl*; **hun|dert|jäh|rig** ADJ *attr* (one-)hundred-year-old; **der Hundertjährige Kalender** the Hundred Years' Calendar *(for weather prediction)*; **der Hundertjährige Krieg** *(Hist)* the Hundred Years' War; **das Ergebnis einer ~en Entwicklung/Arbeit** the result of a hundred years of development/work; **Hun|dert|jäh|ri|ge(r)** [-jɛːrɪgə] MF *decl as adj* centenarian; **hun|dert|jähr|lich** ADJ every hundred years; **hun|dert|mal** ADV a hundred times; **ich hab dir schon ~ gesagt …** if I've told you once I've told you a hundred times …; **Hun|dert|me|ter|lauf** M *(Sport)* **der/ein ~** the/a 100 metres *(Brit) or* meters *(US) sing*; **hun|dert|pro** ADV *(inf: = hundertprozentig, absolut)* absolutely; **bist du dir sicher? – ~** are you sure? – I'm positive; **hun|dert|pro|zen|tig** ADJ (a *or* one) hundred per cent *(Brit) or* percent *(US)*; *Alkohol* pure; **ein ~er Konservativer** *etc* an out-and-out conservative *etc* ADV *sicher sein, einer Meinung sein* one hundred per cent *(Brit) or* percent *(US)*; **er ist ~ Amerikaner** *etc* he's one hundred per cent *(Brit) or* percent *(US)* American *etc*; **Sie haben ~ recht** you're absolutely right; **das weiß ich ~** that's a fact; **ich werde ihn ~ im Krankenhaus besuchen** I'll definitely visit him in hospital; **~?** *(inf)* are you absolutely sure?; **Hun|dert|satz** M *(form)* percentage; **Hun|dert|schaft** [ˈhʊndɐtʃaft] F -, -en *(Mil)* group of a *or* one hundred; *(Hist: bei den Römern)* century

hun|derts|te(r, s) [ˈhʊndɐtstə] ADJ hundredth; **vom Hundertsten ins Tausendste kommen** *(fig)* to get carried away

hun|derts|tel [ˈhʊndɐtstl] ADJ hundredth; **eine ~ Sekunde** a hundredth of a second

Hun|derts|tel [ˈhʊndɐtstl] NT -s, - hundredth; **sie hat zwei ~ Vorsprung** *(Sport)* she leads by two hundredths of a second

Hun|derts|tel|se|kun|de F hundredth of a second

Hun|dert-: **hun|dert|tau|send** NUM a *or* one hundred thousand; **~e** *or* **Hunderttausende von Menschen** hundreds of thousands of people; **Hun|dert|tau|sends|tel** NT hundred thousandth; **hun|dert|und|eins** ['hʊndɐt|ʊnt'lains] NUM a *or* one hundred and one; **hun|dert|wei|se** ADV by the hundred, in hundreds

Hun|de-: **Hun|de|sa|lon** M dog parlour *(Brit) or* parlor *(US)*; **Hun|de|schei|ße** F *(inf)* dog shit *(sl)*, dog mess *(inf)*; **Hun|de|schlit|ten** M dog sled(ge) *or* sleigh; **Hun|de|schnau|ze** F nose, snout; **kalt wie eine ~** *(fig inf)* cold (-blooded); **Hun|de|sohn** M *(pej liter)* cur; **Hun|de|sper|re** F ban on (bringing in) dogs; **Hun|de|staf|fel** F dog branch; **Hun|de|stau|pe** F *(Vet)* distemper; **Hun|de|steu|er** F dog licence *(Brit) or* license *(US)* fee; **Hun|de|wa|che** F *(Naut)* middle watch; **Hun|de|wet|ter** NT *(inf)* foul *or* filthy weather; **Hun|de|zucht** F dog breeding; **Hun|de|züch|ter(in)** M(F) dog breeder; **Hun|de|zwin|ger** M (dog) compound; *(städtisch)* dog pound

Hün|din ['hʏndɪn] F -, -nen bitch

hün|disch ['hʏndɪʃ] ADJ *(fig)* fawning *attr*, sycophantic; **~e Ergebenheit** dog-like devotion

Hünd|lein ['hʏntlain] NT -s, - *dim von* **Hund** doggy *(baby-talk)*, little dog; *(= kleiner Hund)* little *or* small dog

Hunds-: **Hunds|fott** ['hʊntsfɔt] M -s, **Hunds|föt|ter** [-fœtɐ] *(obs, dial)* (miserable) cur; **hunds|föt|tisch** ['hʊntsfœtɪʃ] ADJ *(obs, dial)* dastardly *(old)*; **hunds|ge|mein** ['hʊntsgə'main] *(inf)* ADJ shabby, mean; *(= schwierig)* fiendishly difficult; *Schmerz etc* terrible; **er kann ~ werden** he can get really nasty ADV **es tut ~ weh** it hurts like hell *(inf)*; **hunds|mi|se|ra|bel** ['hʊntsmizə'ra:bl] *(inf)* ADJ abominable, abysmal *(inf)*, lousy *(inf)* ADV abominably; **~ arbeiten** to do abysmal *or* pitiful work; **mir geht es ~, ich fühle mich ~** I feel rotten *(inf) or* lousy *(inf)*; **Hunds|stern** ['hʊnts-] M Dog Star; **Hunds|ta|ge** ['hʊnts-] PL dog days *pl*; **Hunds|veil|chen** ['hʊnts-] NT (heath) dog violet

Hü|ne ['hy:nə] M -n, -n giant, colossus; **ein ~ von Mensch** *(geh)* a giant of a man

Hü|nen-: **Hü|nen|ge|stalt** F *(geh)* Titanic *or* colossal figure *or* frame; **Hü|nen|grab** NT megalithic grave; **hü|nen|haft** ADJ *(geh)* gigantic, colossal

Hun|ger ['hʊŋɐ] M -s, *no pl (lit, fig)* hunger *(nach* for); *(= Hungersnot)* famine; *(nach Bildung)* thirst, hunger; *(nach fernen Ländern, Sonne etc)* yearning; *(nach Literatur)* appetite; **~ bekommen/haben** to get/be hungry; **ich habe keinen richtigen ~** I'm not really hungry; **~ auf etw** *(acc)* **haben** to feel like (eating) sth; **den ~ bekämpfen** to combat hunger; **~ leiden** *(geh)* to go hungry, to starve; **ich habe ~ wie ein Wolf** *or* **Bär** *(inf)* I could eat a horse *(inf)*; **~s** *(liter) or* **vor ~ sterben** to die of hunger *or* starvation, to starve to death; **ich sterbe vor ~** *(inf)* I'm starving *(inf)*, I'm dying of hunger *(inf)*; **~ ist der beste Koch** *(Prov)* hunger is the best cook *(Prov)*

Hun|ger-: **Hun|ger|blo|cka|de** F hunger *or* starvation blockade; **Hun|ger|da|sein** NT existence at starvation level; **Hun|ger|ge|fühl** NT hungry feeling; **Hun|ger|jahr** NT hungry year, year of hunger; **Hun|ger|künst|ler(in)** M(F) (professional) faster, *person who, for pay, goes without nourishment for prolonged periods*; **ich bin doch kein ~** I'm not on a starvation diet; **Hun|ger|kur** F starvation diet; **Hun|ger|land** NT famine-stricken country; **Hun|ger|le|ben** NT existence at starvation level; **Hun|ger|lei|der** [-laidɐ] M -s, -, **Hun|ger|lei|de|rin** [-ərɪn] F -, -nen *(dated)* starving wretch, starveling; **Hun|ger|lohn** M starvation wages *pl*; *(fig auch)* pittance

hun|gern ['hʊŋɐn] VI **a** *(= Hunger leiden)* to go hungry, to starve; **jdn ~ lassen** to let sb go hungry; *(zur Strafe auch)* to make sb starve; **ich hungere schon seit fünf Tagen** I haven't eaten a thing for five days **b** *(= fasten)* to go without food **c** *(fig geh: = verlangen)* to hunger *(nach* for) VT *impers (geh)* **mich hungert** I am *or* feel hungry; **ihn hungert nach Macht** he hungers *or* is hungry for power VR **sich zu Tode ~** to starve oneself to death; **sich schlank ~** to go on a starvation diet; **er hat sich durch die Studentenzeit gehungert** he starved his way through university

hun|gernd ADJ *no comp* hungry, starving

Hun|ger|ödem NT *(Med)* famine oedema *(spec)*

Hun|gers|not F famine

Hun|ger-: **Hun|ger|streik** M hunger strike; **Hun|ger|tag** M *(inf)* fast day; **Hun|ger|tod** M death from starvation; **den ~ erleiden** *or* **sterben** to die of hunger *or* starvation; **Hun|ger|tuch** NT *pl* **-tücher** *(Eccl)* Lenten veil; **am ~ nagen** *(fig)* to be starving, to be on the breadline *(inf)*; **Hun|ger|turm** M *(Hist)* dungeon, oubliette

hung|rig ['hʊŋrɪç] ADJ *(lit, fig)* hungry *(nach* for); **Arbeit macht ~** work makes you hungry, work gives you an appetite; **Gartenarbeit macht ~** gardening is hungry work; **ich bin ~ wie ein Wolf** (I'm so hungry) I could eat a horse; **~ nach etw** *or* **auf etw** *(acc)* **sein** to feel like (eating) sth; **~ nach Luft** gasping for air; **~ nach Literatur** hungry for good literature

Hun|ne ['hʊnə] M -n -n, **Hun|nin** ['hʊnɪn] F -, -nen *(Hist)* Hun

Hun|ni ['hʊnɪ] M -s, -s *(hum inf: = Hunderteuroschein)* hundred *(inf)*

Hu|pe ['hu:pə] F -, -n horn; **auf die ~ drücken** to sound the horn

hu|pen ['hu:pn] VI to sound *or* hoot *or* honk *(Aut inf)* the horn, to hoot; **„hupen"** "sound your horn"

Hüpf|burg ['hʏpf-] F bouncy castle®

hup|fen ['hʊpfn] VI *(esp S Ger) aux sein* = **hüpfen**; **das ist gehupft wie gesprungen** *(inf)* it doesn't make any difference, it's six of one and half a dozen of the other *(inf)*

hüp|fen ['hʏpfn] VI *aux sein* to hop; *(Lämmer, Zicklein etc)* to frisk, to gambol; *(Ball)* to bounce; **vor Freude ~** to jump for joy; **die Kinder hüpften vor Freude im Zimmer herum** the children went skipping round the room in sheer delight; **sein Herz hüpfte vor Freude** his heart leapt for joy; **Hüpfen spielen** to play (at) hopscotch

Hüp|fer ['hʏpfɐ] M -s, -, *(esp S Ger)* **Hup|fer** ['hʊpfɐ] M -s, - hop, skip, bounce; **mein Herz machte einen ~** my heart leapt

Hüpf|spiel NT hopscotch

Hup-: **Hup|kon|zert** NT *(inf)* chorus of hooting *or* horns; **Hup|sig|nal** NT *(Aut)* hoot; **„Hupsignal geben"** "sound your horn"; **Hup|ton** M *pl* **-töne** sound of a horn; **Hup|ver|bot** NT *(Hinweis)* no horns to be sounded; **Hup|zei|chen** NT *(Aut)* hoot; **„Hupzeichen geben"** "sound your horn"

Hür|de ['hʏrdə] F -, -n **a** *(Sport, fig)* hurdle; **eine ~ nehmen** to take *or* clear a hurdle **b** *(= Viehzaun)* fold, pen

Hür|den-: **Hür|den|lauf** M *(= Sportart)* hurdling; *(= Wettkampf)* hurdles *pl or sing*; **Hür|den|läu|fer(in)** M(F) hurdler; **Hür|den|ren|nen** NT *(Pferdesport)* steeplechase

Hu|re ['hu:rə] F -, -n whore

hu|ren ['hu:rən] VI *(inf)* to whore, to go whoring

Hu|ren-: **Hu|ren|bock** M *(vulg)* whoremonger; **hu|ren|haft** ADJ *(pej)* whorish; **Hu|ren|haus** NT *(dated)* whorehouse *(inf)*, brothel; **Hu|ren|kind** NT *(old)* child of a whore; *(Typ)* widow; **Hu|ren|sohn** M *(vulg)* bastard *(sl)*, son of a bitch *(sl)*

Hu|re|rei [hu:rə'rai] F -, *no pl (inf)* whoring

hur|ra [hʊ'ra:, 'hʊra] INTERJ hurray, hurrah

Hur|ra [hʊ'ra:, 'hʊra] NT -s, -s cheers *pl*; **ein dreifaches ~** three cheers

Hur|ra-: **Hur|ra|ge|schrei** NT cheering; **Hur|ra|pat|ri|ot(in)** M(F) flag-waving patriot, jingoist, chauvinist; **Hur|ra|pat|ri|o|tis|mus** M flag-waving, jingoism, chauvinism; **Hur|ra|ruf** M cheer

Hur|ri|kan ['hʊrikan, 'harɪkən] M -s, -e *or (bei engl. Aussprache)* -s hurricane

hur|tig ['hʊrtɪç] ADJ *(old, dial)* nimble; *(= schnell)* quick

Hur|tig|keit F -, *no pl (old, dial)* nimbleness; *(= Schnelligkeit)* quickness, speed

Hu|sar [hu'za:ɐ] M -en, -en *(Hist)* hussar

Hu|sa|ren|streich M, **Hu|sa|ren|stück** NT *(fig)* (daring) escapade *or* exploit

husch [hʊʃ] INTERJ **a** *(aufscheuchend)* shoo **b** *(antreibend)* come on **c** *(= schnell)* quick, quickly now; **er macht seine Arbeit immer ~ ~** *(inf)* he always whizzes through his work *(inf)*; **und ~, weg war er** and whoosh! he was gone

Husch [hʊʃ] M -(e)s, -e *(inf)* **im ~** in a flash *(inf) or* jiffy *(inf)*; **er kam auf einen ~ vorbei** he dropped in on me *or* dropped by for a minute

hu|schen ['hʊʃn] VI *aux sein* to dart, to flit; *(Mäuse etc auch)* to scurry; *(Lächeln)* to flash, to flit; *(Licht)* to flash

Hus|ky ['haski] M -s, -s husky

hus|sa(sa) ['hʊsa(sa)] INTERJ *(old liter)* tally-ho; *(= hü)* gee up

hüs|teln ['hy:stln] VI to give a slight cough, to cough slightly; **er hüstelt noch** he still has a slight cough; **anstatt zu antworten, hüstelte er nur spöttisch** instead of answering he just cleared his throat sarcastically

hus|ten ['hu:stn] VI to cough; **auf etw** *(acc)* **~** *(inf)* not to give a damn for sth *(inf)*; **der Motor hustet** *(inf)* the engine is coughing (and spluttering) VT to cough; *Blut* to cough (up); **denen werde ich was** *or* **eins ~** *(inf)* I'll tell them where they can get off *(inf)*

Hus|ten ['hu:stn] M -s, *no pl* cough; **~ haben** to have a cough

Hus|ten-: **Hus|ten|an|fall** M coughing fit; **Hus|ten|bon|bon** M OR NT cough drop, cough sweet *(Brit)*; **Hus|ten|mit|tel** NT cough medicine; *(= Bonbon)* cough drop, cough sweet *(Brit)*; **Hus|ten|reiz** M tickle in *or* irritation of the throat; **seinen ~ unterdrücken** to suppress the need *or* urge to cough; **Hus|ten|saft** M cough syrup *or* mixture; **hus|ten|stil|lend** ADJ cough-relieving ADV **das wirkt ~** it relieves coughing *or* one's cough; **Hus|ten|tee** M *tea which is good for coughs*; **Hus|ten|trop|fen** PL cough drops *pl*

Hut [hu:t] M -(e)s, =e ['hy:tə] hat; *(von Pilz)* cap; **den ~ aufsetzen/abnehmen/lüften** *(geh)* to put on/take off/raise one's hat; **den** *or* **mit dem ~ in der Hand** with one's hat in one's hand; **vor jdm den ~ abnehmen** *or* **ziehen** *(fig)* to take off one's hat to sb; **vor etw** *(dat)* **den ~ ziehen** *(fig)* to take off one's hat to sth; **~ ab!** I take my hat off to him/you *etc*; **~ ab vor solcher Leistung!** I take my hat off to you/that; **mit dem ~e in der Hand kommt man durch das ganze Land** *(Prov)* politeness will serve you well in life; **das kannst du dir an den ~ stecken!** *(inf)* you can stick *(inf) or* keep *(inf)* it; **unter einen ~ bringen** *or* **kriegen** *(inf)* to reconcile, to accommodate, to cater for; *Verpflichtungen, Termine* to fit in; **da geht einem der ~ hoch** *(inf, vor Zorn)* it's enough to make you blow your top *(inf)*; *(vor Spaß, Überraschung)* it is amazing, it beats everything; **den** *or* **seinen ~ nehmen (müssen)** *(inf)* to (have to) go, to (have to) pack one's bags *(inf)*; **das ist doch ein alter ~!** *(inf)* that's old hat! *(inf)*; **jdm eine auf den ~ geben** *(inf)* to give sb a rocket *(Brit inf)*, to give sb an earful *(inf)*; **eins auf den ~ kriegen** *(inf)* to get a rocket *(Brit inf)*, to get an earful *(inf)*; **damit/mit ihm habe ich nichts am ~** *(inf)* I don't want to have anything to do with that/him

Hut F -, *no pl* **a** *(geh)* protection, keeping; **unter** *or* **in meiner ~** in my keeping; *(Kinder)* in my care; **in guter** *or* **sicherer ~** in safe keeping, in good *or* safe hands **b auf der ~ sein** to be on one's guard *(vor +dat* against)

Hut-: **Hut|ab|la|ge** F hat rack; **Hut|band** [-bant] NT *pl* **-bänder** hatband; *(von Damenhut)* hat ribbon

Hüt|chen ['hy:tçən] NT **-s, -** *dim von* **Hut** little hat
Hüt|chen|spiel NT thimblerig
Hüt|chen|spie|ler(in) M(F) thimblerigger
Hü|te|jun|ge M *(liter)* shepherd boy
hü|ten ['hy:tn] ✪ 28.1, 29.2 VT to look after, to mind; *Vieh etc auch* to tend, to keep watch over *(liter)*; *(geh) Geheimnisse* to guard, to keep; *(geh) Briefe, Gegenstände* to keep; **das Bett/Haus ~** to stay in bed/indoors; **hüte deine Zunge!** *(liter)* guard your tongue! *(liter)*
VR to guard (*vor +dat* against), to be on one's guard (*vor +dat* against), to beware (*vor +dat* of); **ich werde mich ~!** no fear!, not likely!, I'll do nothing of the kind!; **du wirst dich schwer ~!** you'll do nothing of the kind!; **ich werde mich ~, ihm das zu erzählen** there's no chance of me telling him that; **sich ~, etw zu tun** to take care not to do sth; **hüte dich, etwas zu verraten** take care not to give anything away, mind you don't give anything away; **~ Sie sich vor ihm** be on your guard against him
Hü|ter ['hy:tɐ] M **-s, -, Hü|te|rin** [-ərın] F **-, -nen** guardian, keeper, custodian; *(= Viehhüter)* herdsman; **die ~ der Ordnung** *(hum)* the custodians of the law; **soll ich meines Bruders ~ sein?** *(Bibl)* am I my brother's keeper?
Hut-: **Hut|fe|der** F (hat) feather; *(größere, bei Tracht)* plume; **Hut|filz** M (hat) felt; **Hut|ge|schäft** NT hat shop, hatter's (shop); *(für Damen auch)* milliner's (shop); **Hut|grö|ße** F hat size, size of hat; **Hut|krem|pe** F brim (of a hat); **Hut|la|den** M = **Hutgeschäft**; **Hut|ma|cher(in)** M(F) hatter, hat maker; *(von Damenhüten auch)* milliner; **Hut|na|del** F hatpin; **Hut|schach|tel** F hatbox
Hut|sche ['hʊtʃə] F **-, -n** *(Aus)* swing
hut|schen ['hʊtʃn] *(Aus)* VI = **schaukeln** VR *(inf)* to go away
Hut-: **Hut|schlei|fe** F hat bow; **Hut|schnur** F hat string *or* cord; **das geht mir über die ~** *(inf)* that's going too far
Hutsch|pferd ['hʊtʃ-] NT *(Aus)* rocking horse
Hut|stän|der M hat stand
Hüt|te ['hʏtə] F **-, -n** a hut; *(= schäbiges Häuschen)* shack, hut; (*hum:* = *Haus*) humble abode; *(= Jagdhütte)* (hunting) lodge; *(= Holzhütte, Blockhütte)* cabin; *(= Wochenendhäuschen)* cottage; *(= Schutzhütte)* hut, bothy *(Scot)*; *(= Hundehütte)* kennel; *(Bibl)* Tabernacle; *(Naut)* poop; **hier lasst uns eine ~ bauen** let's stay here → **Glanz** b (*Tech:* = *Hüttenwerk*) iron and steel works *pl or sing*; *(= Glashütte)* glassworks *pl or sing*; *(= Ziegelhütte)* brickworks *pl or sing*
Hüt|ten-: **Hüt|ten|ar|bei|ter(in)** M(F) worker in an iron and steel works; **Hüt|ten|in|dust|rie** F iron and steel industry; **Hüt|ten|kä|se** M cottage cheese; **Hüt|ten|kom|bi|nat** NT *(DDR)* iron and steel combine; **Hüt|ten|kun|de** F metallurgy; **Hüt|ten|rauch** M *(Chem)* flaky arsenic; *(Metal)* waste gases *pl*; **Hüt|ten|ru|he** F **um zehn ist ~** lights out at ten; **Hüt|ten|schuh** M slipper-sock; **Hüt|ten|tech|nik** F metallurgical engineering; **Hüt|ten|werk** NT = **Hütte b**; **Hüt|ten|we|sen** NT, *no pl* iron and steel industry; **Hüt|ten|zau|ber** M après-ski party
Hut|zel ['hʊtsl] F **-, -n** *(S Ger)* a dried pear b *(inf)* wizened *or* wrinkled old woman
Hut|zel|brot NT *(S Ger)* fruit bread; **ein ~** a fruit loaf
hut|ze|lig ['hʊtsəlıç] ADJ *Obst* dried; *Mensch* wizened
Hut|zel-: **Hut|zel|männ|chen** NT, **Hut|zel|männ|lein** NT gnome; **Hut|zel|weib|lein** NT *(inf)* wizened *or* wrinkled old woman
hutz|lig ['hʊtslıç] ADJ = **hutzelig**
HwG [ha:ve:'ge:] *(Admin sl) abbr von* **häufig wechselnder Geschlechtsverkehr** frequent changing of sexual partners
HwG-Mäd|chen [ha:ve:'ge:-] NT *(Admin sl) girl listed by police or medical authorities as being promiscuous*
Hy|ä|ne [hy'ɛ:nə] F **-, -n** hyena; *(fig)* wildcat
Hy|a|zin|the [hya'tsıntə] F **-, -n** hyacinth
hyb|rid [hy'bri:t] ADJ a *(Biol, Ling)* hybrid b *(liter. = hochmütig)* arrogant, hubristic *(liter)*
Hyb|rid|an|trieb [hy'bri:t-] M hybrid drive
Hyb|ri|de [hy'bri:də] F **-, -n** *or* M **-n, -n** *(Biol)* hybrid
Hyb|rid- [hy'bri:t-]: **Hyb|rid|spra|che** F *(Comput)* hybrid language; **Hyb|rid|ver|si|on** F *(Comput)* hybrid version
Hyb|ris ['hy:brıs] F **-,** *no pl (liter)* hubris *(liter)*
Hyd|ra ['hy:dra] F **-** *(Zool, Myth, fig liter)* hydra
Hyd|rant [hy'drant] M **-en, -en** hydrant
Hyd|rat [hy'dra:t] NT **-(e)s, -e** hydrate
Hyd|rau|lik [hy'draulık] F **-,** *no pl* hydraulics *sing*; *(= Antrieb, Anlage)* hydraulic system, hydraulics *pl*
hyd|rau|lisch [hy'draulıʃ] ADJ hydraulic ADV hydraulically
Hyd|rid [hy'dri:t] NT **-(e)s, -e** [-də] hydride
hyd|rie|ren [hy'dri:rən] *ptp* **hydriert** VT *(Chem)* to hydrogenate
Hyd|ro-: **Hyd|ro|bio|lo|gie** F hydrobiology; **Hyd|ro|dy|na|mik** F hydrodynamics *sing*; **hyd|ro|dy|na|misch** ADJ hydrodynamic; **hyd|ro|geo|lo|gisch** ADJ hydrogeological; **Hyd|ro|gra|fie** F **-,** *no pl* hydrography; **hyd|ro|gra|fisch** [hydro'gra:fıʃ] ADJ hydrographic(al); **Hyd|ro|gra|phie** [hydrogra'fi:] *etc* = **Hydrografie** *etc*; **Hyd|ro|kul|tur** [hydro-, 'hy:dro-] F *(Bot)* hydroponics *sing*; **Hyd|ro|ly|se** [hydro'ly:zə] F **-, -n** *(Chem)* hydrolysis; **hyd|ro|nuk|le|ar** ADJ hydronuclear; **hyd|ro|phil** [hydro'fi:l] ADJ hydrophilic; **hyd|ro|phob** [hydro'fo:p] ADJ hydrophobic; **Hyd|ro|sta|tik** F *(Phys)* hydrostatics *sing*; **Hyd|ro|the|ra|pie** F *(Med)* hydrotherapy
Hy|gi|e|ne [hy'gie:nə] F **-,** *no pl* hygiene; **politische ~** political expediency
Hy|gi|e|ne-: **Hy|gi|e|ne|ar|ti|kel** PL toiletries *pl*; **Hy|gi|e|ne|pa|pier** NT (toilet) tissue
hy|gi|e|nisch [hy'gie:nıʃ] ADJ hygienic ADV hygienically; **das ist ~ nicht zu vertreten** that's not at all hygienic
Hyg|ro-: **Hyg|ro|me|ter** [hygro'me:tɐ] NT *(Met)* hygrometer; **Hyg|ro|skop** [hygro'sko:p] NT **-s, -e** *(Met)* hygroscope
Hy|men ['hy:mən] NT **-s, -** *(Anat)* hymen, maidenhead
Hym|ne ['hʏmnə] F **-, -n** hymn; *(= Nationalhymne)* (national) anthem
hym|nisch ['hʏmnıʃ] ADJ hymnal; **~e Worte** *(liter)* paean *(liter)*; **jdn/etw in ~en Worten loben** *(liter)* to sing paeans to sb/sth *(liter)*
Hym|nus ['hʏmnʊs] M **-, Hymnen** [-nən] *(liter)* hymn
Hype M *(inf)* hype *(inf)*
hy|per|ak|tiv [hypɐlak'ti:f] ADJ hyperactive
Hy|per|ak|ti|vi|tät F hyperactivity
Hy|per|bel [hy'pɛrbl] F **-, -n** *(Math)* hyperbola; *(Rhetorik)* hyperbole
hy|per|bo|lisch [hypɐ'bo:lıʃ] ADJ hyperbolic
hy|per|kor|rekt [hy:pɐ-] ADJ hypercorrect
hy|per|kri|tisch [hypɐ-, 'hy:pɐ-] ADJ hypercritical
Hy|per|link ['haipɐlıŋk] M OR NT **-s, -s** *(Comput)* hyperlink
Hy|per|me|dia [hy:pɐ-] NT *no art (Comput)* hypermedia *sing*
Hy|per|me|di|um [hy:pɐ-] NT **-s, -medien** [-diən] *(Comput)* hypermedium
hy|per|mo|dern [hy:pɐ-] *(inf)* ADJ ultramodern ADV in an ultramodern way
hy|per|schick ADJ *(inf)* hyper-trendy *(inf)*
hy|per|sen|si|bel [hypɐ-] ADJ hypersensitive
hy|per|sen|si|bi|li|sie|ren [hypɐzɛnzibili'zi:rən] *ptp* **hypersensibilisiert** VT *insep (esp Phot)* to hypersensitize
Hy|per|text ['haipɐ-] M, *no pl (Comput)* hypertext
Hy|per|to|nie [hypɐto'ni:] F **-, -n** [-'ni:ən] *(Med)* hypertonia
hy|per|troph [hypɐ'tro:f] ADJ *(Med)* hypertrophic; *(fig liter)* hypertrophied *(liter)*
Hy|per|tro|phie [hypɐtro'fi:] F **-, -n** *(Med)* hypertrophy
Hy|per|ven|ti|la|ti|on [hypɐ-] F *(Med)* hyperventilation
Hyp|no|se [hʏp'no:zə] F **-, -n** hypnosis; **unter ~ stehen** to be under hypnosis; **jdn in ~ versetzen** to put sb under hypnosis
Hyp|no|se|be|hand|lung F hypnotherapy
Hyp|no|ti|kum [hʏp'no:tikʊm] NT **-s, Hypnotika** [-ka] *(Pharm)* hypnotic
hyp|no|tisch [hʏp'no:tıʃ] ADJ hypnotic
Hyp|no|ti|seur [hʏpnoti'zø:ɐ] M **-s, -e, Hyp|no|ti|seu|rin** [-'zø:rın] F **-, -nen** hypnotist
hyp|no|ti|sier|bar ADJ hypnotizable
hyp|no|ti|sie|ren [hʏpnoti'zi:rən] *ptp* **hypnotisiert** VT to hypnotize
Hyp|no|tis|mus [hʏpno'tısmʊs] M **-,** *no pl* hypnotism
Hy|po|chon|der [hypo'xɔndɐ, hypɔ-] M **-s, -** hypochondriac
Hy|po|chond|rie [hypoxɔn'dri:, hypɔ-] F **-,** *(rare)* **-n** [-'dri:ən] hypochondria
hy|po|chond|risch [hypo'xɔndrıʃ, hypɔ-] ADJ hypochondriac(al)
Hy|po|krit [hypo'kri:t] M **-en, -en, Hy|po|kri|tin** [-'kri:tın] F **-, -nen** *(liter)* hypocrite
hy|po|kri|tisch [hypo'kri:tıʃ] ADJ *(liter)* hypocritical
Hy|po|phy|se [hypo'fy:zə] F **-, -n** *(Anat)* hypophysis *(spec)*, pituitary gland
Hy|po|sen|si|bi|li|sie|rung [hypozɛnzibili'zi:rʊŋ] F *(Med)* hyposensitization, desensitization
Hy|pos|ta|se [hypo'sta:zə] F **-, -n** *(liter, Philos)* hypostasis
hy|pos|ta|sie|ren [hyposta'zi:rən] *ptp* **hypostasiert** VTI *(liter, Philos)* to hypostatize
Hy|pos|ta|sie|rung F **-, -en** *(liter, Philos)* hypostatization
hy|po|tak|tisch [hypo'taktıʃ] ADJ *(Gram)* hypotactic
Hy|po|ta|xe [hypo'taksə] F *(Gram)* hypotaxis
Hy|po|te|nu|se [hypote'nu:zə] F **-, -n** *(Math)* hypotenuse
Hy|po|thek [hypo'te:k] F **-, -en** mortgage; *(fig) (= Belastung)* burden of guilt; *(= Handikap)* handicap; **eine ~ aufnehmen** to raise a mortgage; **etw mit einer ~ belasten** to mortgage sth
hy|po|the|ka|risch [hypote'ka:rıʃ] ADJ **~er Gläubiger** mortgagee; **~er Kredit** mortgage credit; **~e Sicherheit** mortgage security ADV **das Haus ist ~ belastet** the house is mortgaged
Hy|po|the|ken-: **Hy|po|the|ken|bank** F *pl* **-banken** *bank specializing in mortgages*; **Hy|po|the|ken|brief** M mortgage deed *or* certificate; **Hy|po|the|ken|dar|le|hen** NT mortgage (loan); **hy|po|the|ken|frei** ADJ unmortgaged; **Hy|po|the|ken|gläu|bi|ger(in)** M(F) mortgagee; **Hy|po|the|ken|pfand|brief** M mortgage bond; **Hy|po|the|ken|schuld** F mortgage debt; **Hy|po|the|ken|schuld|ner(in)** M(F) mortgagor, mortgager; **Hy|po|the|ken|ur|kun|de** F mortgage deed *or* certificate; **Hy|po|the|ken|zin|sen** PL mortgage interest
Hy|po|the|se [hypo'te:zə] F hypothesis
hy|po|the|tisch [hypo'te:tıʃ] ADJ hypothetical ADV hypothetically
Hys|te|rek|to|mie [hʏsterɛkto'mi:] F **-, -n** [-'mi:ən] hysterectomy
Hys|te|rie [hʏste'ri:] F **-, -n** [-'ri:ən] hysteria
Hys|te|ri|ker [hʏs'te:rikɐ] M **-s, -, Hys|te|ri|ke|rin** [-ərın] F **-, -nen** hysteric, hysterical person
hys|te|risch [hʏs'te:rıʃ] ADJ hysterical; **einen ~en Anfall bekommen** *(fig)* to go into *or* have hysterics ADV hysterically

I

I, i [iː] [iː] NT I, i; **der Punkt** *or* **das Tüpfelchen auf dem i** *(lit)* the dot on the i; *(fig)* the final touch

i [iː] [iː] INTERJ *(inf)* ugh *(inf)*; **i bewahre!** *(dated)* not on your life! *(inf)*; **i wo!** not a bit of it! *(inf)*, (good) heavens no!

i. A. *abbr von* **im Auftrag** pp

IAA [iːlaːˈlaː] F -, -s *abbr von* **Internationale Automobil-Ausstellung** International Car Show

IAEA [iːlaːleːˈlaː] F - *abbr von* **Internationale Atomenergie-Agentur** IAEA

iah [ˈiːˈaː, iˈaː] INTERJ heehaw

ia|hen [ˈiːˈaːən, iˈaːən] *ptp* **iaht** VI to heehaw *(inf)*, to bray

i. Allg. *abbr von* **im Allgemeinen**

Iam|bus [ˈiambʊs] M -, **Iamben** [-bn] *(Poet)* iamb(us), iambic foot

Ibe|rer [iˈbeːrɐ] M -s, -, **Ibe|re|rin** [-ərɪn] F -, -nen Iberian

ibe|risch [iˈbeːrɪʃ] ADJ Iberian; **die Iberische Halbinsel** the Iberian Peninsula

Ibe|ro|ame|ri|ka [iˈbeːrolameːrika] NT Ibero-America

ibe|ro|ame|ri|ka|nisch [iˈbeːrolamerikaːnɪʃ] ADJ Ibero-American

IBFG [iːbeːlɛfˈgeː] M -s *abbr von* **Internationaler Bund Freier Gewerkschaften** ICFTU

ibi|dem [iˈbiːdɛm,ˈiːbidɛm] ADV ibid

Ibi|za [iˈbɪtsa] NT -s Ibiza

IC® [iːˈtseː] M -(s), -s *abbr von* **Intercityzug**

IC- *in cpds* intercity; **IC-Be|treu|er(in)** M(F) intercity steward

ICE® [iːtseːˈleː] M -(s), -s *abbr von* **Intercity-Expresszug**

> **ICE®**
>
> The **ICE** – or **Intercityexpresszug** – is a high-speed train running every two hours on certain routes in Germany. As well as greatly reduced journey times, the **ICE** offers greater comfort, with telephone, laptop points and video screens for first-class passengers. Fares for the **ICE** are considerably higher than for other trains.

ich [ɪç] PERS PRON *gen* **meiner**, *dat* **mir**, *acc* **mich** I; **immer ~!** (it's) always me!; **immer ~ soll an allem schuld sein** it's always my fault; **~ Idiot!** what an idiot I am!; **und ~ Idiot habe es gemacht** and I, like a fool, did it, and idiot that I am, I did it; **~ nicht!** not me!, not I!; **ihr könnt ja hingehen, aber ~ nicht!** you're welcome to go, but I won't; **wer hat den Schlüssel? – ~ nicht!** who's got the key? – not me!; **~ selbst** I myself; **könnte ~ bitte den Chef sprechen? – das bin ~ (selbst)** could I speak to the boss? – I am the boss *or* that's me; **~ (selbst) war es** it was me *or* I *(form)*; **wer hat gerufen? – ~!** who called? – (it was) me, I did!; **kennst du mich nicht mehr? - ~ bins!** don't you remember me? it's me!; **~, der immer so gutmütig ist, ~, der ~ immer so gutmütig bin** I, who am always so good-natured

Ich [ɪç] NT -(s), -(s) self; *(Psych)* ego; **das eigene ~** one's (own) self/ego; **das eigene ~ verleugnen** to deny the self; **mein anderes** *or* **zweites ~** *(= selbst)* my other self; *(= andere Person)* my alter ego

Ich-: **Ich|be|wusst|sein** NT awareness of the self; **ich|be|zo|gen** ADJ self-centred *(Brit)*, self-centered *(US)*, egocentric; **Ich|be|zo|gen|heit** F -, *no pl* self-centredness *(Brit)*, self-centeredness *(US)*, egocentricity; **Ich|er|zäh|ler(in)** M(F) first-person narrator; **Ich|er|zäh|lung** F story in the first person, first-person narrative; **Ich|form** F first person; **Ich|ge|fühl** NT *(Psych)* consciousness *or* perception of the self; **Ich|laut** M *(Phon)* ch *sound as in ich*; **Ich|ro|man** M novel in the first person, first-person novel; **Ich|stär|ke** F *(Psych)* ego strength; **Ich|sucht** F, *no pl* egoism; **ich|süch|tig** ADJ egoistic(al)

Icon [ˈaikn, ˈaikɔn] NT -s, -s *(Comput)* icon

IC-Zu|schlag [iːˈtseː-] M intercity supplement

ide|al [ideˈaːl] ADJ ideal ADV ideally; **da wohnt ihr ~** where you live is ideally located

Ide|al [ideˈaːl] NT -s, -e ideal; **sie ist das ~ einer Lehrerin** she's the ideal *or* perfect teacher

Ide|al- *in cpds* ideal; **Ide|al|be|set|zung** F *(von Rolle)* ideal casting; *(von Team, Firma etc)* ideal person, perfect choice; *(zwei oder mehr Personen)* dream team, ideal line-up; **Ide|al|bild** NT ideal

ide|a|ler|wei|se [ideˈaləˈvaizə] ADV ideally

Ide|al-: **Ide|al|fall** M ideal case; **im ~** ideally; **Ide|al|fi|gur** F ideal figure; **Ide|al|ge|wicht** NT ideal *or* optimum weight

ide|a|li|sie|ren [idealiˈziːrən] *ptp* **idealisiert** VT to idealize

Ide|a|li|sie|rung F -, -en idealization

Ide|a|lis|mus [ideaˈlɪsmʊs] M -, *no pl* idealism

Ide|a|list [ideaˈlɪst] M -en, -en, **Ide|a|lis|tin** [-ˈlɪstɪn] F -, -nen idealist

ide|a|lis|tisch [ideaˈlɪstɪʃ] ADJ idealistic

Ide|al-: **Ide|al|kon|kur|renz** F *(Jur) commission of two or more crimes in one and the same act*; **Ide|al|li|nie** F *(Sport)* ideal *or* racing line; **Ide|al|ty|pus** M *(Sociol)* ideal type; **Ide|al|vor|stel|lung** F ideal; **Ide|al|zu|stand** M ideal state of affairs

Idee [iˈdeː] ✪ 38.1, 38.2, 40.3, 53.1, 53.3 F -, -n **a** [iˈdeːən] (= *Einfall, Philos*) idea; **die ~ zu etw** the idea for sth; **überhaupt keine ~n haben** to have not a single idea in one's head, to have no ideas at all; **wie kommst du denn auf DIE ~?** whatever gave you that idea?; **ich kam auf die ~, sie zu fragen** I hit on the idea of asking her; **jdn auf die ~ bringen, etw zu tun** to give sb the idea of doing sth; **jdn auf andere ~n bringen** to make sb think about something else; **es war nur so eine ~** it was just a fantasy; **~n müsste man haben!** what it is to have ideas!
b *(= ein wenig)* shade, trifle; **eine ~ Salz** a touch *or* hint of salt; **keine ~ besser** not a whit better

ide|ell [ideˈɛl] ADJ ideational *(form, Philos)*; *Wert, Anteil, Gesichtspunkt, Ziele* non-material; *Bedürfnisse, Unterstützung* spiritual

Ide|en-: **ide|en|arm** ADJ *(= einfallsarm)* lacking in ideas; *(= fantasiearm)* unimaginative, lacking in imagination; **Ide|en|ar|mut** F *(= Einfallsarmut)* lack of ideas; *(= Fantasiearmut)* unimaginativeness, lack of imagination; **Ide|en|aus|tausch** M exchange of ideas; **Ide|en|gut** NT, *no pl* ideas *pl*, intellectual goods *pl*; **ide|en|los** ADJ *(= einfallslos)* devoid of ideas; *(= fantasielos)* unimaginative, devoid of imagination; **Ide|en|lo|sig|keit** F -, *no pl* lack of ideas; *(= Fantasielosigkeit)* unimaginativeness, lack of imagination; **ide|en|reich** ADJ *(= einfallsreich)* full of ideas; *(= fantasiereich)* imaginative, full of imagination; **Ide|en|reich|tum** M inventiveness; *(= Fantasie)* imaginativeness; **Ide|en|welt** F world of ideas *or* forms

Iden [ˈiːdn] PL **die ~ des März** the Ides of March

Iden|ti|fi|ka|ti|on [idɛntifikaˈtsioːn] F -, -en identification

Iden|ti|fi|ka|ti|ons|fi|gur F role model

iden|ti|fi|zie|ren [idɛntifiˈtsiːrən] *ptp* **identifiziert** VT to identify VR **sich ~ mit** to identify (oneself) with

Iden|ti|fi|zie|rung F -, -en identification

iden|tisch [iˈdɛntɪʃ] ADJ identical (*mit* with)

Iden|ti|tät [idɛntiˈtɛːt] F -, -en identity

Iden|ti|täts-: **Iden|ti|täts|kar|te** F *(Sw)* identity *or* ID card, ID *(inf)*; **Iden|ti|täts|kri|se** F identity crisis; **Iden|ti|täts|nach|weis** M proof of identity

Ideo|gramm [ideoˈgram] NT *pl* **-gramme** *(Ling)* ideogram

Ideo|lo|ge [ideoˈloːgə] M -n, -n, **Ideo|lo|gin** [-ˈloːgɪn] F -, -nen ideologist

Ideo|lo|gie [ideoloˈgiː] F -, -n [-ˈgiːən] ideology

ideo|lo|gie|frei ADJ free from ideology *pred*, ideologically unencumbered *or* unbiased

ideo|lo|gisch [ideoˈloːgɪʃ] ADJ ideological ADV ideologically

ideo|lo|gi|sie|ren [ideologiˈziːrən] *ptp* **ideologisiert** VT to ideologize

Ideo|lo|gi|sie|rung F -, -en ideologization

Idi|om [iˈdioːm] NT -s, -e idiom

Idio|ma|tik [idioˈmaːtɪk] F -, *no pl* idiomaticalness; *(= Redewendungen)* idioms *pl*

idio|ma|tisch [idioˈmaːtɪʃ] ADJ idiomatic ADV idiomatically; **~ völlig einwandfreie/richtige Übersetzungen** perfect/correct idiomatic translations

Idio|plas|ma [idioˈplasma] NT *(Biol)* germ plasm, idioplasm

Idi|ot [iˈdioːt] M -en, -en, **Idi|o|tin** [iˈdioːtɪn] F -, -nen idiot; *(auch inf)* fool

Idi|o|ten-: **Idi|o|ten|ar|beit** F *(pej inf)* donkeywork *(inf)*, drudgery, mindless work *or* job; **Idi|o|ten|hü|gel** M *(hum inf)* nursery *or* beginners' slope; **idi|o|ten|si|cher** *(inf)* ADJ foolproof *no adv* ADV **etw ~ erklären** to explain sth so that even a fool *or* an idiot could understand it; **~ gestaltet** *or* **konzipiert sein** to be designed to be foolproof; **~ zu bedienen** extremely easy *or* simple to operate

Idi|o|tie [idioˈtiː] F -, -n [-ˈtiːən] idiocy; *(inf)* lunacy, madness, craziness

Idi|o|tin [iˈdioːtɪn] F -, -nen idiot; *(auch inf)* fool

idi|o|tisch [iˈdioːtɪʃ] ADJ idiotic

Idi|o|tis|mus [idioˈtɪsmʊs] M -, **Idiotismen** [-mən] idiotism; *(inf)* lunacy, madness, craziness

Idol [iˈdoːl] NT -s, -e idol

Idyll [iˈdʏl] NT -s, -e idyll; *(= Gegend)* idyllic place *or* spot

Idyl|le [i'dʏlə] F -, -n idyll

idyl|lisch [i'dʏlɪʃ] ADJ idyllic ADV idyllically; **hier wohnt ihr wirklich ~** it is really idyllic where you live

IG [iː'geː] F -, -s *abbr von* **Industriegewerkschaft** ≈ TU *(Brit)*

Igel ['iːgl] M -s, - **a** *(Zool)* hedgehog; *(= Blumenigel)* pin holder **b** *(Mil: = Igelstellung)* position of all-round defence *(Brit) or* defense *(US)*

igitt(igitt) [i'gɪt(i'gɪt)] INTERJ *(inf)* ugh! *(inf)*

Ig|lu ['iːglu] M OR NT -s, -s igloo

ig|no|rant [ɪgno'rant] ADJ ignorant

Ig|no|rant [ɪgno'rant] M -en, -en, **Ig|no|ran|tin** [-'rantɪn] F -, -nen ignoramus

Ig|no|ranz [ɪgno'rants] F -, *no pl* ignorance

ig|no|rie|ren [ɪgno'riːrən] *ptp* **ignoriert** VT to ignore

IHK [iːhaː'kaː] F -, -s *abbr von* **Industrie- und Handelskammer**

ihm [iːm] PERS PRON *dat von* **er, es** *(bei Personen)* to him; *(bei Tieren und Dingen)* to it; *(nach Präpositionen)* him/it; **ich gab es ~** I gave it (to) him; **ich gab ~ den Brief** I gave him the letter, I gave the letter to him; **ich sagte ~, dass …** I told him that …, I said to him that …; **ich werde es ~ sagen** I'll tell him; **es war ~, als ob er träumte** he felt as though he were dreaming; **es ist ~ nicht gut** he doesn't feel well; **sie schnitt ~ die Haare** she cut his hair (for him); **ein Freund von ~** a friend of his, one of his friends; **wir gingen zu ~** *(= haben ihn aufgesucht)* we went to see him; *(= mit zu ihm nach Hause)* we went to his place; **ich habe ~ das gemacht** I did it for him; **sie hat ~ einen Pulli gestrickt** she knitted him a sweater, she knitted a sweater for him

ihn [iːn] PERS PRON *acc von* **er** him; *(bei Tieren und Dingen)* it

ih|nen ['iːnən] PERS PRON *dat von* **sie b** to them; *(nach Präpositionen)* them → *auch* **ihm**

Ih|nen ['iːnən] PERS PRON *dat von* **Sie** to you; *(nach Präpositionen)* you → *auch* **ihm**

ihr [iːɐ] PERS PRON **a** *gen* **euer**, *dat* **euch**, *acc* **euch** *2. pers pl nom* you; **Ihr** *(obs, dial: als Anrede eines Erwachsenen)* thou *(obs, dial)* **b** *dat von* **sie a** *(bei Personen)* to her; *(bei Tieren und Dingen)* to it; *(nach Präpositionen)* her/it; **Ihr** *(obs: in der Anrede eines weiblichen Wesens)* (to) thee *(obs, dial)* → *auch* **ihm** POSS PRON **a** *(einer Person)* her; *(eines Tiers, Dinges, Abstraktum)* its **b** *(von mehreren)* their

Ihr [iːɐ] PERS PRON → **ihr PERS PRON a, b** POSS PRON *sing and pl* your; **~ Franz Müller** *(Briefschluss)* yours, Franz Müller

ih|rer ['iːrɐ] PERS PRON *(geh)* **a** *gen von* **sie a** *(bei Personen)* of her; **wir werden ~ gedenken** we will remember her **b** *gen von* **sie b** of them; **es waren ~ zehn** there were ten of them, they were ten; **wir werden ~ gedenken** we will remember them

Ih|rer ['iːrɐ] PERS PRON *gen von* **Sie** *(geh)* of you; **wir werden ~ gedenken** we will remember you

ih|re(r, s) ['iːrə] POSS PRON *(substantivisch)* **a** *(einer Person)* hers; *(eines Tiers)* its; **der/die/das ~** *or* **Ihre** *(geh)* hers/its; **sie tat das ~** *or* **Ihre** *(geh)* she did her part; **Ihre Majestät** Her Majesty; **sie und die ~n** *or* **Ihren** *(geh: = Familie)* she and hers; **das ~** *or* **Ihre** *(geh: = Besitz)* what is hers **b** *(von mehreren)* theirs; **der/die/das ~** *or* **Ihre** *(geh)* theirs; **sie taten das ~** *or* **Ihre** *(geh)* they did their part

Ih|re(r, s) ['iːrə] POSS PRON *sing and pl (substantivisch)* yours; **der/die/das ~** *(geh)* yours; **stets** *or* **ganz der ~** *(old)* yours ever; **schöne Grüße an Sie und die ~n** *(geh)* best wishes to you and your family; **tun Sie das ~** *(geh)* you do your bit

ih|rer|seits ['iːrɐ'zaits] ADV *(bei einer Person)* for her part; *(bei mehreren)* for their part; *(von ihrer Seite)* on her/their part

Ih|rer|seits ['iːrɐ'zaits] ADV for your part; *(von Ihrer Seite)* on your part

ih|res|glei|chen ['iːrəs'glaiçn] PRON *inv (von einer Person)* people like her; *(von mehreren)* people like them; *(von Dingen)* others like it, similar ones; *(pej)* people like her/them, her/their sort, the likes of her/them; **sie fühlt sich unter ~ am wohlsten** she feels most at home among her own kind *or* among people like her(self); **eine Frechheit, die ~ sucht!** incredible impudence!

Ih|res|glei|chen ['iːrəs'glaiçn] PRON *inv* people like you; *(pej auch)* your sort, the likes of you; **Sie sollten Kontakt mit ~ pflegen** you should keep in contact with your own kind (of people) *or* with people like yourself *or* you

ih|ret|hal|ben ['iːrət'halbn] *(dated)* ADV = **ihretwegen**

Ih|ret|hal|ben ['iːrət'halbn] *(dated)* ADV = **Ihretwegen**

ih|ret|we|gen ['iːrət'veːgn], **ih|ret|wil|len** ['iːrət'vɪlən] ADV *(bei Personen) (= wegen ihr/ihnen) (sing)* because of her; *(pl)* because of them; *(= ihr/ihnen zuliebe auch)* for her sake/their sake(s); *(= um sie)* about her/them; *(= für sie)* on her/their behalf; *(bei Dingen und Tieren) (sing)* because of it; *(pl)* because of them; **sie sagte, ~ könnten wir gehen** she said that, as far as she was concerned, we could go

Ih|ret|we|gen ['iːrət'veːgn], **Ih|ret|wil|len** ['iːrət'vɪlən] ADV because of you; *(= Ihnen zuliebe) (sing auch)* for your sake; *(pl auch)* for your sake(s); *(= um Sie)* about you; *(= für Sie)* on your behalf

ih|ri|ge ['iːrɪgə] POSS PRON *(old, geh)* **der/die/das ~** *or* **Ihrige** *(von einer Person)* hers; *(von mehreren)* theirs → *auch* **ihre(r, s)**

Ih|ri|ge ['iːrɪgə] POSS PRON **der/die/das ~** yours → *auch* **Ihre(r, s)**

Ih|ro ['iːro] POSS PRON *(obs)* your

i. J. *abbr von* **im Jahre**

Ike|ba|na [ike'baːna] NT -s, *no pl* ikebana

Iko|ne [i'koːnə] F -, -n *(auch fig)* icon

Iko|nen|ma|le|rei F icon painting; *(Bild)* icon

Ilex ['iːlɛks] F OR M -, - holly

Ili|as ['iːlias] F - Iliad

ill. *abbr von* **illustriert**

il|le|gal [ɪle'gaːl, 'ɪl-] ADJ illegal ADV illegally; **sich ~ betätigen** to engage in illegal activities

Il|le|ga|li|tät [ɪlegali'tɛːt, 'ɪl-] F -, -en illegality

il|le|gi|tim [ɪlegi'tiːm, 'ɪl-] ADJ illegitimate

Il|le|gi|ti|mi|tät [ɪlegitimi'tɛːt, 'ɪl-] F -, *no pl* illegitimacy

il|li|quid [ɪli'kviːt, 'ɪl-] ADJ *(Comm)* illiquid

Il|li|qui|di|tät [ɪlikvidi'tɛːt, 'ɪl-] F -, *no pl (Comm)* illiquidity

il|lo|yal [ɪloa'jaːl, 'ɪl-] ADJ disloyal ADV *sich verhalten* disloyally

Il|lo|ya|li|tät [ɪloajali'tɛːt, 'ɪl-] F -, *no pl* disloyalty

Il|lu|mi|na|ti|on [ɪlumina'tsioːn] F -, -en illumination

il|lu|mi|nie|ren [ɪlumi'niːrən] *ptp* **illuminiert** VT to illuminate

Il|lu|si|on [ɪlu'zioːn] F -, -en illusion; **jdm alle ~en nehmen** *or* **rauben** to rob sb of all his/her *etc* illusions; **sich** *(dat)* **~en machen** to delude oneself; **darüber macht er sich keine ~en** he doesn't have any illusions about it; **sich der ~ hingeben, dass …** to be under the illusion that …, to labour *(Brit) or* labor *(US)* under the misapprehension that …

il|lu|si|o|när [ɪluzio'nɛːɐ] ADJ illusionary

Il|lu|si|o|nis|mus [ɪluzio'nɪsmʊs] M -, *no pl* illusionism

Il|lu|si|o|nist [ɪluzio'nɪst] M -en, -en, **Il|lu|si|o|nis|tin** [-'nɪstɪn] F -, -nen illusionist

il|lu|si|o|nis|tisch [ɪluzio'nɪstɪʃ] ADJ *(Art)* illusionistic

il|lu|si|ons|los ADJ **ein ~er Mensch** a person with no illusions; **~ sein** to have no illusions; **~ werden** to lose one's illusions

Il|lu|si|ons|lo|sig|keit F -, *no pl* lack of illusions

il|lu|so|risch [ɪlu'zoːrɪʃ] ADJ illusory; **es ist völlig ~, zu glauben …** it's a complete illusion to believe …

il|lus|ter [ɪ'lʊstɐ] ADJ *(geh)* illustrious

Il|lust|ra|ti|on [ɪlʊstra'tsioːn] F -, -en illustration; **zur ~ von etw** to illustrate sth, as an illustration of sth

il|lust|ra|tiv [ɪlʊstra'tiːf] ADJ **a** *(mit Anschauungsmaterial)* illustrated **b** *(= anschaulich)* illustrative ADV **a** *(= mit Anschauungsmaterial)* with illustrations; **etw ~ aufzeigen** to show sth with illustrations **b** *(= anschaulich)* vividly; **er hat sehr ~ geschildert, wie …** he described very vividly how …

Il|lust|ra|tor [ɪlʊs'traːtoːɐ] M -s, **Illustratoren**, **Il|lust|ra|to|rin** [-'toːrɪn] F -, -nen illustrator

il|lust|rie|ren [ɪlʊs'triːrən] *ptp* **illustriert** VT to illustrate *(jdm etw* sth for sb)

Il|lust|rier|te [ɪlʊs'triːɐtə] F *decl as adj* magazine, mag *(inf)*

Il|lust|rie|rung F -, -en illustration

Il|tis ['ɪltɪs] M -ses, -se polecat

im [ɪm] PREP *contr von* **in dem a** *(räumlich)* in the; **im zweiten Stock** on the second floor; **im Theater** at the theatre *(Brit) or* theater *(US)*; **die Beleuchtung im Theater** the lighting in the theatre *(Brit) or* theater *(US)*; **Freiburg im Breisgau** Freiburg in Breisgau; **im Bett** in bed; **im „Faust"** in "Faust"

b *(zeitlich)* in the; **im Mai** in May; **im Jahre 1866** in (the year) 1866; **im Alter von 91 Jahren** at the age of 91; **im letzten/nächsten Jahr** last/next year; **im letzten Jahr des Krieges** in the last year of the war; **im nächsten Jahr ging er** (in) the next year he went

c *+superl* **nicht im Geringsten** not in the slightest

d *(als Verlaufsform)* **im Kommen/Gehen** *etc* **sein** to be coming/going *etc*; **etw im Liegen/Stehen** *etc* **tun** to do sth lying down/standing up *etc*

e **im Trab/Laufschritt** *etc* at a trot/run *etc*

IM [iː'lɛm] *abbr von* **inoffizieller Mitarbeiter** (**der Stasi**) (Stasi) collaborator

> **IM**
>
> **IM** stands for **inoffizieller Mitarbeiter**, an unofficial collaborator of the **Stasi** in the former East Germany. These were members of the public who – sometimes voluntarily, to gain financial and other perks, sometimes because of external pressures – spied on their colleagues and friends and even their own families for the **Stasi**. The number of **IMs** is estimated at 500,000. → STASI

Image ['ɪmɪtʃ] NT -(s), -s image

Image-: **Image|bil|dend** ADJ image-building; **Image|bro|schü|re** F *(esp Comm)* promotional pamphlet *or* brochure; **Image|kam|pag|ne** F *(Pol, Comm)* image-building *or* image-rebuilding campaign; **Image|pfle|ge** F image building; **Image|ver|fall** M loss of prestige; **Image|ver|lust** M damage to one's image; **Image|wer|bung** F image promotion; **~ (für sich) betreiben** to promote one's image

ima|gi|när [imagi'nɛːɐ] ADJ imaginary

Ima|gi|na|ti|on [imagina'tsioːn] F -, -en *(geh)* imagination

Imag|ing ['ɪmɪdʒɪŋ] NT -, *no pl (Comput)* imaging

Ima|go [i'maːgo] F -, **Imagines** [i'maːgineːs] *(Biol, Psych)* imago; *(Art)* image

Imam [i'maːm] M -s, -s *or* -e imam

IMAP ['aimɛp] *(Comput, Internet) abbr of* **Internet Message Access Protocol** IMAP

Im|biss ['ɪmbɪs] M -es, -e snack

Im|biss-: **Im|biss|bu|de** F = **Imbissstand**; **Im|biss|hal|le** F snack bar; **Im|biss|stand** M ≈ hot-dog stall *or* stand; **Im|biss|stu|be** F café; *(in Kaufhaus etc)* cafeteria

Imi|ta|ti|on [imita'tsioːn] F -, -en imitation

Imi|ta|tor [imi'taːtoːɐ] M -s, **Imitatoren**, **Imi|ta|to|rin** [-'toːrɪn] F -, -nen imitator; *(von Schmuck, einem Bild)* copyist

imi|tie|ren [imi'tiːrən] *ptp* **imitiert** VT to imitate; **imitierter Schmuck** imitation jewellery *(Brit) or* jewelry *(US)*

Im|ker ['ɪmkɐ] M **-s, -, Im|ke|rin** [-ərɪn] F **-, -nen** beekeeper, apiarist *(form)*

Im|ke|rei [ɪmkə'rai] F **-,** *no pl* beekeeping, apiculture *(form)*

im|kern ['ɪmkɐn] VI to keep bees

im|ma|nent [ɪma'nɛnt] ADJ inherent, intrinsic; *Kriterien* internal; *(Philos)* immanent; **einer Sache** *(dat)* **~ sein** to be inherent in sth; **~e Wiederholung** incorporative repetition

Im|ma|nenz [ɪma'nɛnts] F **-,** *no pl (Philos)* immanence

im|ma|te|ri|ell [ɪmate'riɛl, 'ɪm-] ADJ *Vermögenswerte* incorporeal, immaterial; **~es Vermögen** immaterial *or* tangible assets *pl*

Im|mat|ri|ku|la|ti|on [ɪmatrikula'tsio:n] F **-, -en** matriculation *(form)*, registration *(at university)*

im|mat|ri|ku|lie|ren [ɪmatriku'li:rən] *ptp* **immatrikuliert** VT to register *(at university)* (*an +dat* at) VR to matriculate *(form)*, to register *(at university)*

Im|me ['ɪmə] F **-, -n** *(poet)* bee

im|mens [ɪ'mɛns] ADJ immense, huge, enormous ADV immensely, enormously; **~ groß sein** to be huge

im|mer ['ɪmɐ] ADV **a** *(= häufig, ständig)* always; **schon ~** always; **auf** *or* **für ~** for ever, for always; **~ diese Aufregung/Nörgelei** this continual excitement/grumbling; **~ diese Probleme!** all these problems!; **~ diese Studenten** these wretched students *(inf)*; **~ das Telefon** that wretched phone *(inf)*; **~, wenn ...** whenever ..., every time that ...; **~ mal** *(inf)* from time to time, now and again; **~ geradeaus gehen** to keep going straight on; **~ während = immerwährend**; **~ und ewig** *(liter)* for ever and ever; **~ langsam voran!** *(inf)* **(nur) ~ schön langsam!** *(inf)* take your time (about it), take it slowly; **~ (schön) mit der Ruhe** *(inf)* take it easy; **(nur) ~ her damit!** *(inf)* (just) hand it over!; **noch ~, ~ noch** still; **~ noch nicht** still not (yet); **bist du denn ~ noch nicht fertig?** are you still not ready?, aren't you ready yet?; **nur ~ zu!** keep it up!, keep up the good work!; **~ wieder** again and again, time after time, time and (time) again; **etw ~ wieder tun** to keep on doing sth; **wie ~** as usual, as always → **Sprung a, Nase a**
b *+comp* **~ besser** better and better; **~ häufiger** more and more often; **~ mehr** more and more; **es nimmt ~ mehr zu** it increases all the time, it increases continually, it keeps on increasing; **~ größer werdende Schulden** constantly increasing debts; **sein Verhältnis zu ihr wird ~ schlechter** his relationship with her gets worse and worse, his relationship with her goes from bad to worse; **nicht ~, aber ~ öfter** not always, but more and more often
c wer (auch) ~ whoever; **wie (auch) ~** however; **wann (auch) ~** whenever; **wo (auch) ~** wherever; **was (auch) ~** whatever
d *(inf: = jeweils)* **gib mir ~ drei Bücher auf einmal** give me three books at a time; **stellt euch in einer Reihe auf, ~ zwei zusammen** line up in twos; **~ am dritten Tag** every third day

im|mer-: **im|mer|dar** ['ɪmɐda:ɐ] ADV *(liter)* forever, evermore; **im|mer|fort** ['ɪmɐ'fɔrt] ADV = **immerzu**; **im|mer|grün** ['ɪmɐgry:n] ADJ *attr (lit, fig)* evergreen; **Im|mer|grün** ['ɪmɐgry:n] NT evergreen; **im|mer|hin** ['ɪmɐ'hɪn] ADV all the same, anyhow, at any rate; *(= wenigstens)* at least; *(= schließlich)* after all; **im|mer|wäh|rend** ['ɪmɐ'vɛ:rənt] ADJ perpetual, eternal; *Kalender* perpetual; **im|mer|zu** ['ɪmɐ'tsu:] ADV all the time, the whole time, constantly

Im|mig|rant [ɪmi'grant] M **-en, -en, Im|mig|ran|tin** [-'grantɪn] F **-, -nen** immigrant

Im|mig|ra|ti|on [ɪmigra'tsio:n] F **-, -en** immigration

im|mig|rie|ren [ɪmi'gri:rən] *ptp* **immigriert** VI *aux sein* to immigrate

Im|mis|si|on [ɪmɪ'sio:n] F *(Jur) effect on nearby property of gases, smoke, noise, smells etc*

Im|mis|si|ons-: **Im|mis|si|ons|scha|den** M pollution damage; **Im|mis|si|ons|schutz** M air pollution control; **Im|mis|si|ons|schutz|ge|setz** NT air pollution laws *pl*

im|mo|bil [ɪmo'bi:l, 'ɪm-] ADJ immobile, immoveable; *Vermögen, Besitz* real, immoveable

Im|mo|bi|lie [ɪmo'bi:liə] F **-, -n a eine ~** a property **b Immobilien** PL real estate *sing*, real *or* immoveable property *sing (form)*, immoveables *pl (form)*; *(in Zeitungsannoncen)* property *sing*

Im|mo|bi|li|en-: **Im|mo|bi|li|en|fonds** M *(Fin)* real estate fund; **Im|mo|bi|li|en|händ|ler(in)** M(F), **Im|mo|bi|li|en|mak|ler(in)** M(F) (real) estate agent *(Brit)*, realtor *(US)*; **Im|mo|bi|li|en|markt** M *(Comm)* property market

Im|mo|ra|li|tät [ɪmorali'tɛ:t, 'ɪm-] F immorality

Im|mor|ta|li|tät [ɪmortali'tɛ:t, 'ɪm-] F immortality

Im|mor|tel|le [ɪmɔr'tɛlə] F **-, -n** *(Bot)* everlasting (flower), immortelle

im|mun [ɪ'mu:n] ADJ immune (*gegen* to)

Im|mun- *in cpds (Med)* immune; **Im|mun|ab|wehr** [ɪ'mu:n-] F *(Med)* immune defence *(Brit) or* defense *(US)*; **Im|mun|glo|bu|lin** [ɪ'mu:nglobuli:n] NT **-s, -e** *(Med)* immunoglobulin

im|mu|ni|sie|ren [ɪmuni'zi:rən] *ptp* **immunisiert** VT *(form)* to immunize (*gegen* against)

Im|mu|ni|sie|rung F **-, -en** *(form)* immunization (*gegen* against)

Im|mu|ni|tät [ɪmuni'tɛ:t] F **-,** *(rare)* **-en** immunity

im|mu|no|gen ADJ immunogenic

Im|mu|no|ge|ni|tät [ɪmunogeni'tɛ:t] F **-,** *no pl* immunogenicity

Im|mu|no|lo|ge [ɪmuno'lo:gə] M **-n, -n, Im|mu|no|lo|gin** [-'lo:gɪn] F **-, -nen** immunologist

Im|mu|no|lo|gie [ɪmunolo'gi:] F **-,** *no pl* immunology

im|mu|no|lo|gisch [ɪmuno'lo:gɪʃ] ADJ immunological

Im|mun-: **Im|mun|re|ak|ti|on** F *(Med)* immunological reaction, immunoreaction; **Im|mun|schwä|che|krank|heit** F immune deficiency disease *or* syndrome; **Im|mun|sys|tem** NT immune system; **Im|mun|the|ra|pie** F *(Med)* immunotherapy

Im|pe|danz F **-, -en** *(Phys, Elec: = Scheinwiderstand)* impedance

Im|pe|ra|tiv ['ɪmperati:f] M **-s, -e** [-və] *(Gram)* imperative (form); *(Philos)* imperative

im|pe|ra|ti|visch [ɪmpera'ti:vɪʃ] ADJ *(Gram)* imperative

Im|pe|ra|tor [ɪmpe'ra:to:ɐ] M **-s, Imperatoren** *(Hist)* emperor; *(Mil)* general

im|pe|ra|to|risch [ɪmpera'to:rɪʃ] ADJ imperial; *(fig)* imperious

Im|per|fekt ['ɪmpɛrfɛkt] NT, **Im|per|fek|tum** [ɪmpɛr'fɛktʊm, 'ɪm-] NT *(Gram)* imperfect (tense)

Im|pe|ri|a|lis|mus [ɪmperia'lɪsmʊs] M **-,** *no pl* imperialism

Im|pe|ri|a|list [ɪmperia'lɪst] M **-en, -en, Im|pe|ri|a|lis|tin** [-'lɪstɪn] F **-, -nen** imperialist

im|pe|ri|a|lis|tisch [ɪmperia'lɪstɪʃ] ADJ imperialistic

Im|pe|ri|um [ɪm'pe:riʊm] NT **-s, Imperien** [-riən] *(= Gebiet)* empire; *(= Herrschaft)* imperium

im|per|ti|nent [ɪmpɛrti'nɛnt] ADJ *(geh)* impertinent, impudent

Im|per|ti|nenz [ɪmpɛrti'nɛnts] F **-, -en** *(geh)* impertinence, impudence

Im|pe|tus ['ɪmpetʊs] M **-,** *no pl (geh)* impetus, momentum; *(= Tatkraft)* drive

Impf-: **Impf|ak|ti|on** F vaccination *or* inoculation programme *(Brit) or* program *(US)*; **Impf|arzt** M, **Impf|ärz|tin** F vaccinator, inoculator; **Impf|aus|weis** M vaccination card

imp|fen ['ɪmpfn] VT to vaccinate, to inoculate

Impf|ling ['ɪmpflɪŋ] M **-s, -e** *person who has just been or is to be vaccinated*

Impf-: **Impf|pass** M vaccination card, *record of the vaccinations one has been given*; **Impf|pflicht** F compulsory vaccination *or* inoculation, requirement to be vaccinated *or* inoculated; **Impf|pis|to|le** F vaccination gun; **Impf|scha|den** M vaccine damage; **Impf|schein** M certificate of vaccination *or* inoculation; **Impf|schutz** M protection given by vaccination; **Impf|stoff** M vaccine, serum

Imp|fung F **-, -en** vaccination, inoculation

Impf|zwang M = **Impfpflicht**

Im|plan|tat [ɪmplan'ta:t] NT **-(e)s, -e** implant

Im|plan|ta|ti|on [ɪmplanta'tsio:n] F **-, -en** *(Med)* implantation

im|ple|men|tie|ren [ɪmplemɛn'ti:rən] *ptp* **implementiert** VT to implement

im|pli|zie|ren [ɪmpli'tsi:rən] *ptp* **impliziert** VT to imply

im|pli|zit [ɪmpli'tsi:t], **im|pli|zi|te** [ɪm'pli:tsite] *(geh)* ADV by implication, implicitly; **etw ~ sagen** to imply sth, to say sth by implication

im|plo|die|ren [ɪmplo'di:rən] *ptp* **implodiert** VI *aux sein* to implode

Im|plo|si|on [ɪmplo'zio:n] F **-, -en** implosion

Im|pon|de|ra|bi|li|en [ɪmpɔndera'bi:liən] PL *(geh)* imponderables *pl*

im|po|nie|ren [ɪmpo'ni:rən] *ptp* **imponiert** VI to make an impression (*jdm* on sb), to impress (*jdm* sb); **dadurch hat er imponiert** he made an impression by that; **es imponiert mir, wie sie das schafft** it impresses me how she manages it, I'm impressed by the way she manages it

im|po|nie|rend ADJ impressive; *Gebäude auch* imposing

Im|po|nier|ge|ha|be NT *(Zool)* display pattern; *(fig pej)* exhibitionism

Im|port [ɪm'pɔrt] M **-(e)s, -e a** *(= Handel)* import; **der ~ sollte den Export nicht übersteigen** imports should not exceed exports; **der ~ von Obst und Gemüse ist gestiegen** the import *or* importation of fruit and vegetables has increased, fruit and vegetable imports have increased **b** *(= Importware)* import; **der Salat ist holländischer ~** the lettuce was imported from Holland

Im|port- *in cpds* import

Im|por|te [ɪm'pɔrtə] F **-, -n** *usu pl* imported cigar

Im|por|teur [ɪmpɔr'tø:ɐ] M **-s, -e, Im|por|teu|rin** [-'tø:rɪn] F **-, -nen** importer

Im|port|fir|ma F import business, importer(s *pl*)

Im|port|ge|schäft NT *(= Handel)* import trade; *(= Firma)* import business

im|por|tie|ren [ɪmpɔr'ti:rən] *ptp* **importiert** VT *(auch Comput)* to import

Im|port|land NT importing country

im|po|sant [ɪmpo'zant] ADJ *Gebäude, Kunstwerk, Figur* imposing; *Leistung* impressive; *Stimme* commanding

im|po|tent ['ɪmpotɛnt, ɪmpo'tɛnt] ADJ impotent

Im|po|tenz ['ɪmpotɛnts, ɪmpo'tɛnts] F **-,** *no pl* impotence

im|präg|nie|ren [ɪmprɛ'gni:rən] *ptp* **imprägniert** VT to impregnate; *(= wasserdicht machen)* to (water)proof

Im|präg|nie|rung F **-, -en** impregnation; *(von Geweben)* (water)proofing; *(nach der Reinigung)* reproofing

im|prak|ti|ka|bel ['ɪmpraktika:bl, ɪmprakti'ka:bl] ADJ impracticable

Im|pre|sa|rio [ɪmpre'za:rio] M **-s, -s** *or* **Impresari** [-ri] impresario

Im|pres|si|on [ɪmprɛ'sio:n] F impression (*über +acc* of)

Im|pres|si|o|nis|mus [ɪmprɛsio'nɪsmʊs] M **-,** *no pl* impressionism

Im|pres|si|o|nist [ɪmprɛsio'nɪst] M **-en, -en, Im|pres|si|o|nis|tin** [-'nɪstɪn] F **-, -nen** impressionist

im|pres|si|o|nis|tisch [ɪmprɛsio'nɪstɪʃ] ADJ impressionistic

Im|pres|sum [ɪm'prɛsʊm] NT **-s, Impressen** [-sn] imprint; *(von Zeitung)* masthead

Im|pri|ma|tur [ɪmpri'maːtʊr] NT **-s,** *no pl (Typ)* imprimatur

Im|pro|vi|sa|ti|on [ɪmprovizaˈtsioːn] F **-, -en** improvisation; *(von Rede, Gedicht, Musik auch)* extemporization

Im|pro|vi|sa|ti|ons|ta|lent NT talent for improvisation; *(= Mensch)* (great) improviser

im|pro|vi|sie|ren [ɪmproviˈziːrən] *ptp* **improvisiert** VTI to improvise; *(Mus auch)* to extemporize; *eine Rede auch* to ad-lib *(inf)*, to extemporize

Im|puls [ɪmˈpʊls] M **-es, -e** impulse; **etw aus einem ~ heraus tun** to do sth on the spur of the moment, to do sth on impulse; **einer Sache** *(dat)* **neue ~e geben** to give sth new impetus *or* momentum; **äußere ~e veranlassten ihn dazu** external factors made him do it

Im|puls|bild NT *(Sch, Ausgangsbasis für Aufsatz etc)* inspirational picture

im|pul|siv [ɪmpʊlˈziːf] ADJ impulsive; **~e Äußerungen/Entschlüsse** spur of the moment *or* impulsive remarks/decisions ADV impulsively; **~ handeln** to act impulsively *or* on impulse

Im|pul|si|vi|tät [ɪmpʊlziviˈtɛːt] F **-,** *no pl* impulsiveness

Im|puls|text M *(Sch, Ausgangsbasis für Aufsatz etc)* inspirational short text

im|stan|de [ɪmˈʃtandə] ✪ 43.4 ADJ *pred* **~ sein, etw zu tun** *(= fähig)* to be able to do sth, to be capable of doing sth; *(= in der Lage)* to be in a position to do sth; **er ist zu allem ~** he's capable of anything; **er ist ~ und erzählt es meiner Mutter** he's (quite) capable of telling my mother

in [ɪn] PREP → *auch* **im, ins** **a** *(räumlich) (wo? +dat)* in; *(innen)* in(side); *(wohin? +acc)* in, into; **sind Sie schon in Deutschland gewesen?** have you ever been to Germany?; **in der Schweiz** in Switzerland; **in die Schweiz** to Switzerland; **er ist Professor in St. Andrews** he is a professor at St. Andrews (University); **in die Schule/Kirche gehen** to go to school/church; **er ist in der Schule/Kirche** he's at *or* in school/church; **die Heizung in der Schule/Kirche** the heating in the school/church; **er ging ins Konzert** he went to the concert

b *(zeitlich: wann? +dat)* in; **in diesem Jahr** *(laufendes Jahr)* this year; *(jenes Jahr)* (in) that year; **heute/morgen in acht Tagen/zwei Wochen** a week/two weeks today/tomorrow; **bis ins 18. Jahrhundert** into *or* up to the 18th century; **vom 16. bis ins 18. Jahrhundert** from the 16th to the 18th century; **bis ins 18. Jahrhundert zurück** back to the 18th century

c **in Englisch steht er sehr schwach** he's very weak in *or* at English; **das ist in Englisch** it's in English; **ins Englische übersetzen** to translate into English; **in Geschichte haben wir einen neuen Lehrer** we've a new teacher in *or* for history; **in die hunderte** *or* **Hunderte gehen** to run into (the) hundreds; **er macht jetzt in Gebrauchtwagen** *(inf)* he's in the second-hand car business now; **sie hat es in sich** *(dat) (inf)* she's quite a girl; **der Text/die Rechenarbeit hat es in sich** *(dat) (inf)* the text/the arithmetic test is a tough one; **dieser Whisky hat es in sich** *(dat) (inf)* this whisky packs quite a punch *(inf)*, this whisky has quite a kick *(inf)*

ADJ *pred (inf)* **in sein** to be in *(inf)*

in|adä|quat ADJ inadequate

in|ak|ku|rat ADJ inaccurate

in|ak|tiv ADJ inactive; *Mitglied* non-active; *(Mil)* inactive, on the reserve list

In|ak|ti|vi|tät F inactivity; *(von Mitglied)* non-activity

in|ak|zep|ta|bel ADJ unacceptable

In|an|griff|nah|me [ɪnˈlangrɪfnaːmə] F **-, -n** *(form)* starting, commencement *(form)*

In|an|spruch|nah|me [ɪnˈlanʃprʊxnaːmə] F **-, -n** *(form)* **a** *(= Beanspruchung)* demands *pl*, claims *pl* (+*gen* on); **seine ~ durch diese Nebenbeschäftigung** the demands *or* claims made on him by this second job; **im Falle einer ~ von Arbeitslosenunterstützung** where unemployment benefit has been sought *(form)*; **bei ~ des Versicherungsschutzes entfällt der Rabatt** the discount is forfeited should an insurance claim be submitted **b** *(= Auslastung: von Einrichtungen, Verkehrssystem etc)* utilization; **wegen zu geringer ~ der Cafeteria** as a result of under-utilization of the cafeteria

in|ar|ti|ku|liert [ˈɪnlartikuliːɐt, ɪnlartikuˈliːɐt] ADJ inarticulate

In|au|gen|schein|nah|me [ɪnˈlaugnʃainnaːmə] F **-, -n** *(form)* inspection

inbegr. *abbr von* **inbegriffen**

In|be|griff [ˈɪnbəgrɪf] M, *no pl* perfect example; *(der Schönheit, Güte, des Bösen etc)* epitome, embodiment; **sie war der ~ der Schönheit/Tugend** she was beauty/virtue personified *or* incarnate; **diese neue Kirche ist der ~ der modernen Architektur** this new church epitomizes modern architecture

in|be|grif|fen [ˈɪnbəgrɪfn] ADJ *pred* included; **die Mehrwertsteuer ist im Preis ~** the price includes VAT, the price is inclusive of VAT, VAT is included in the price

In|be|sitz|nah|me [ɪnbəˈzɪtsnaːmə] F **-, -n** *(form)* taking possession

In|be|trieb|nah|me [ɪnbəˈtriːpnaːmə] F **-, -n** commissioning; *(von Gebäude, U-Bahn etc)* inauguration; **die ~ des Geräts erfolgt in zwei Wochen** the appliance will be put into operation in two weeks

In|brunst [ˈɪnbrʊnst] F, *no pl* fervour *(Brit)*, fervor *(US)*, ardour *(Brit)*, ardor *(US)*

in|brüns|tig [ˈɪnbrʏnstɪç] ADJ fervent, ardent ADV fervently, ardently

In|bus|schlüs|sel® [ˈɪnbʊs-] M *(Tech)* ≈ Allen key®

In|cen|tive|rei|se [ɪnˈsɛntɪv-] F incentive holiday

In|danth|ren® [ɪndanˈtreːn] NT **-s, -e** *colourfast dye*

In|de|fi|nit|pro|no|men [ɪndefiˈniːt-, ˈɪndefiniːt-] NT indefinite pronoun

in|de|kli|na|bel [ˈɪndeklinaːbl] ADJ *(Ling)* indeclinable

in|dem [ɪnˈdeːm] CONJ **a** *(= während der ganzen Zeit)* while, whilst *(Brit liter)*; *(= in dem Augenblick)* as; **~ er sich hinsetzte, sagte er ...** sitting down, he said ..., as he sat down he said ... **b** *(= dadurch, dass)* **~ man etw macht** by doing sth ADV *(old)* meanwhile, (in the) meantime

In|der [ˈɪndɐ] M **-s, -, In|de|rin** [-ərɪn] F **-, -nen** Indian; **zum ~ gehen** to go to a/the Indian restaurant

in|des [ɪnˈdɛs], **in|des|sen** [ɪnˈdɛsn] ADV **a** *(zeitlich)* meanwhile, (in the) meantime **b** *(adversativ)* however CONJ **a** *(geh) (zeitlich)* while **b** *(adversativ)* **~** *(liter)* however; *(= andererseits)* whereas

In|dex [ˈɪndɛks] M **-(es), -e** *or* **Indizes** [ˈɪnditseːs] index *(auch Comput)*; *(Eccl)* Index

In|dex|an|lei|he F *(Fin)* index-linked loan, index loan

in|de|xie|ren [ɪndɛˈksiːrən] *ptp* **indexiert** VTI *(Comput)* to index

in|de|zent [ˈɪndetsɛnt] ADJ *(geh)* indecent

In|di|a|ner [ɪnˈdiaːnɐ] M **-s, -, In|di|a|ne|rin** [-ərɪn] F **-, -nen** Native American, American Indian; *(in Western)* (Red) Indian

In|di|a|ner|re|ser|vat NT Native American reservation, Indian reservation

in|di|a|nisch [ɪnˈdiaːnɪʃ] ADJ Native American, American Indian; *(in Western)* (Red) Indian

In|di|a|nis|tik [ɪndiaˈnɪstɪk] F **-,** *no pl* Native American studies *pl*, American Indian studies *pl*

In|di|en [ˈɪndiən] NT **-s** India

In|dienst|nah|me [ɪnˈdiːnstnaːmə] F *(geh)* commissioning, taking into service

in|dif|fe|rent [ˈɪndɪfərɛnt, ɪndɪfəˈrɛnt] ADJ **a** *(geh)* indifferent *(gegenüber* to) **b** *(Chem, Phys)* inert; *Gas* inert, rare, inactive

In|dif|fe|renz [ˈɪndɪfərɛnts, ɪndɪfəˈrɛnts] F *(geh)* indifference *(gegenüber* to, towards)

In|dig|na|ti|on [ɪndɪgnaˈtsioːn] F **-,** *no pl (geh)* indignation *(über +acc* at)

in|dig|niert [ɪndiˈgniːɐt] ADJ *(geh)* indignant

In|dig|ni|tät [ɪndigniˈtɛːt] F **-,** *no pl (Jur)* incapability of inheriting

In|di|go [ˈɪndiːgo] NT OR M **-s, -s** indigo

in|di|go|blau ADJ indigo-blue

In|di|ka|ti|on [ɪndikaˈtsioːn] F **-, -en** *(Med)* indication; **ethische/eugenische/medizinische/soziale ~** ethical/eugenic/medical/social grounds for the termination of pregnancy

In|di|ka|tiv [ˈɪndikatiːf] M **-s, -e** [-və] *(Gram)* indicative

in|di|ka|ti|visch [ɪndikaˈtiːvɪʃ, ˈɪn-] ADJ *(Gram)* indicative

In|di|ka|tor [ɪndiˈkaːtoːɐ] M **-s, Indikatoren** indicator

In|dio [ˈɪndio] M **-s, -s** (Central/South American) Indian

in|di|rekt [ˈɪndirɛkt, ɪndiˈrɛkt] ADJ indirect; **~e Rede** indirect *or* reported speech ADV indirectly; **~ beleuchtet sein** to have indirect lighting

in|disch [ˈɪndɪʃ] ADJ Indian; **der Indische Ozean** the Indian Ocean

in|dis|kret [ɪndɪsˈkreːt, ˈɪn-] ADJ indiscreet ADV indiscreetly

In|dis|kre|ti|on [ɪndɪskreˈtsioːn, ˈɪn-] F indiscretion

in|dis|ku|ta|bel [ɪndɪskuˈtaːbl, ˈɪn-] ADJ out of the question; *(= sehr schlecht)* indescribably bad

in|dis|po|niert [ɪndɪspoˈniːɐt, ˈɪn-] ADJ *(geh)* indisposed

In|dis|po|si|ti|on [ɪndɪspoziˈtsioːn, ˈɪn-] F *(geh)* indisposition

In|di|um [ˈɪndiʊm] NT **-s,** *no pl (abbr* **In**) indium

in|di|vi|du|a|li|sie|ren [ɪndividualiˈziːrən] *ptp* **individualisiert** VT to individualize

In|di|vi|du|a|li|sie|rung F **-, -en** individualization

In|di|vi|du|a|lis|mus [ɪndividuaˈlɪsmʊs] M **-,** *no pl* individualism

In|di|vi|du|a|list [ɪndividuaˈlɪst] M **-en, -en, In|di|vi|du|a|lis|tin** [-ˈlɪstɪn] F **-, -nen** individualist

in|di|vi|du|a|lis|tisch [ɪndividuaˈlɪstɪʃ] ADJ individualistic

In|di|vi|du|a|li|tät [ɪndividualiˈtɛːt] F **-, -en** **a** *no pl* individuality **b** *(= Charakterzüge)* individual characteristic

In|di|vi|du|al|ver|kehr [ɪndiviˈduaːl-] M *(Mot)* private transport

in|di|vi|du|ell [ɪndiviˈduɛl] ADJ individual ADV individually; **etw ~ gestalten** to give sth a personal note; **es ist ~ verschieden** it differs from person to person *or* from case to case, it's different for each person

In|di|vi|du|um [ɪndiˈviːduʊm] NT **-s, Individuen** [-duən] individual

In|diz [ɪnˈdiːts] NT **-es, -ien** [-tsiən] **a** *(Jur)* clue; *(als Beweismittel)* piece of circumstantial evidence; **alles beruht nur auf ~ien** everything rests only on circumstantial evidence **b** *(= Anzeichen)* sign, indication *(für* of)

In|di|zes *pl von* **Index**

In|di|zi|en|be|weis M circumstantial evidence *no pl*, piece of circumstantial evidence

in|di|zie|ren [ɪndiˈtsiːrən] *ptp* **indiziert** VT *(Med)* to indicate; *(Eccl)* to put on the Index; *(Comput)* to index

In|do|chi|na [ˈɪndoˈçiːna] NT Indochina

In|do|eu|ro|pä|er(in) [ˈɪndolɔyroˈpɛːɐ] M(F) Indo-European

in|do|eu|ro|pä|isch [ˈɪndolɔyroˈpɛːɪʃ] ADJ Indo-European

in|do|ger|ma|nisch [ˈɪndogɛrˈmaːnɪʃ] ADJ Indo-Germanic, Indo-European

In|dok|tri|na|ti|on [ɪndɔktrinaˈtsioːn] F **-, -en** indoctrination

in|dok|tri|nie|ren [ɪndɔktriˈniːrən] *ptp* **indoktriniert** VT to indoctrinate

In|do|ne|si|en [ɪndo'neːziən] NT **-s** Indonesia

In|do|ne|si|er [ɪndo'neːziɐ] M **-s, -, In|do|ne|si|e|rin** [-iərɪn] F **-, -nen** Indonesian

in|do|ne|sisch [ɪndo'neːzɪʃ] ADJ Indonesian

In|dos|sa|ment [ɪndɔsa'mɛnt] NT **-(e)s, -e** *(Comm)* endorsement

In|dos|sant [ɪndɔ'sant] M **-en, -en, In|dos|san|tin** [-'santɪn] F **-, -nen** *(Comm)* endorser

In|dos|sat [ɪndɔ'saːt] M **-en, -en, In|dos|sa|tin** [-'saːtɪn] F **-, -nen** *(Comm)* endorsee

in|dos|sie|ren [ɪndɔ'siːrən] *ptp* **indossiert** VT *(Comm)* to endorse

In|duk|ti|on [ɪndʊk'tsioːn] F **-, -en** induction

In|duk|ti|ons-: **in|duk|ti|ons|ge|här|tet** [-gəhɛrtət] ADJ induction-hardened; **In|duk|ti|ons|schlei|fe** F induction loop; **In|duk|ti|ons|strom** M induced current

in|duk|tiv [ɪndʊk'tiːf, 'ɪn-] ADJ inductive

in|dust|ri|a|li|sie|ren [ɪndʊstriali'ziːrən] *ptp* **industrialisiert** VT to industrialize

in|dust|ri|a|li|siert [ɪndʊstriali'ziːɐt] PTP *von* **industrialisieren** ADJ industrialized

In|dust|ri|a|li|sie|rung F **-, -en** industrialization

In|dust|rie [ɪndʊs'triː] F **-, -n** [-'triːən] industry; **in der ~ arbeiten** to be *or* work in industry

In|dust|rie- *in cpds* industrial; **In|dust|rie|ab|fäl|le** PL industrial waste; **In|dust|rie|ab|wäs|ser** PL industrial sewage *sing or* wastewater *sing*, industrial effluents *pl*; **In|dust|rie|an|la|ge** F industrial plant *or* works *pl*; **In|dust|rie|be|trieb** M industrial firm *or* company; **In|dust|rie|bra|che** F industrial wasteland, brownfield site; **In|dust|rie|er|zeug|nis** NT industrial product; **In|dust|rie|ge|biet** NT, **In|dust|rie|ge|län|de** NT industrial area; *(= Gewerbegebiet)* industrial estate; **In|dust|rie|ge|werk|schaft** F industrial (trade) union; **~ Druck und Papier** printers' union; **In|dust|rie|ka|pi|tän(in)** M(F) *(inf)* captain of industry; **In|dust|rie|kauf|mann** M, **In|dust|rie|kauf|frau** F industrial clerk; **In|dust|rie|kom|bi|nat** NT *(DDR)* industrial combine; **In|dust|rie|land** NT industrialized country; **In|dust|rie|land|schaft** F industrial landscape

in|dust|ri|ell [ɪndʊstri'ɛl] ADJ industrial ADV industrially; **Japan hat nach dem zweiten Weltkrieg ~ enorm expandiert** Japan experienced a period of enormous industrial expansion *or* development after World War II

In|dust|ri|el|le(r) [ɪndʊstri'ɛlə] MF *decl as adj* industrialist

In|dust|rie-: **In|dust|rie|müll** M industrial waste; **In|dust|rie|na|ti|on** F industrial nation; **In|dust|rie|park** M industrial estate *(Brit) or* park *(US)*; **In|dust|rie|ro|bo|ter** M industrial robot; **In|dust|rie|spi|o|na|ge** F industrial espionage; **In|dust|rie|staat** M industrial nation; **In|dust|rie|stand|ort** M site of major industries, (heavily) industrialized area; **In|dust|rie|stadt** F industrial town; **In|dust|rie- und Han|dels|kam|mer** F chamber of commerce; **In|dust|rie|zweig** M branch of industry

in|du|zie|ren [ɪndu'tsiːrən] *ptp* **induziert** VT *(Phys)* to induce

in|ef|fek|tiv [ɪnlɛfɛk'tiːf, 'ɪn-] ADJ ineffective, ineffectual; *(= unproduktiv auch)* inefficient ADV ineffectively; *(= unproduktiv auch)* inefficiently

In|ef|fek|ti|vi|tät [ɪnlɛfɛktivi'tɛːt, 'ɪn-] F ineffectiveness, ineffectualness; *(= Unproduktivität auch)* inefficiency

in|ei|nan|der [ɪnlai'nandɐ] ADV *sein* in(side) one another *or* each other; *verkeilen, verschachteln etc* into one another *or* each other; **~ übergehen** to merge (into one another *or* each other); **die Fäden haben sich alle ~ verwickelt** the threads have got all tangled up in each other *or* in one another; **sich ~ verlieben** to fall in love with each other

in|ei|nan|der-: **in|ei|nan|der+flie|ßen** *sep irreg aux sein*, **in|ei|nan|der flie|ßen** △ *irreg aux sein* VI to merge; *(Farben, Flüsse auch)* to flow into each other *or* one another; **in|ei|nan|der+fü|gen** *sep*, **in|ei|nan|der fü|gen** △ VT to fit into each other *or* one another; **in|ei|nan|der+grei|fen** *sep irreg*, **in|ei|nan|der grei|fen** △ *irreg* VI *(lit)* to interlock; *(Zahnräder, Zinken auch)* to mesh *or* engage (with each other *or* one another); *(fig: Ereignisse, Ressorts etc)* to overlap; **in|ei|nan|der+le|gen** *sep*, **in|ei|nan|der le|gen** △ VT to put into each other *or* one another; **in|ei|nan|der+pas|sen** *sep*, **in|ei|nan|der pas|sen** △ VI to fit into each other *or* one another, to fit together; **in|ei|nan|der+schie|ben** *sep irreg*, **in|ei|nan|der schie|ben** △ *irreg* VTR to telescope; **sich ~ lassen** to be telescopic

in|fam [ɪn'faːm] ADJ infamous

In|fa|mie [ɪnfa'miː] F **-, -n** [-'miːən] *(geh)* infamy; **das ist eine ~** that's infamous *or* outrageous

In|fan|te|rie [ɪnfantə'riː, 'ɪn-] F **-, -n** [-'riːən] infantry

In|fan|te|rie|re|gi|ment NT infantry *or* foot regiment

In|fan|te|rist [ɪnfantə'rɪst, 'ɪn-] M **-en, -en, In|fan|te|ris|tin** [-'rɪstɪn] F **-, -nen** infantryman/-woman, foot soldier

in|fan|til [ɪnfan'tiːl] ADJ infantile

In|fan|ti|lis|mus [ɪnfanti'lɪsmʊs] M **-, Infantilismen** infantilism

In|fan|ti|li|tät [ɪnfantili'tɛːt] F **-,** *no pl* childishness, puerility *(pej)*

In|farkt [ɪn'farkt] M **-(e)s, -e** *(Med)* infarct *(spec)*; *(= Herzinfarkt)* coronary (thrombosis)

in|farkt|ge|fähr|det ADJ *Patient* coronary-risk *attr*

In|fekt [ɪn'fɛkt] M **-(e)s, -e, In|fek|ti|on** [ɪnfɛk'tsioːn] F **-, -en** infection

In|fek|ti|ons-: **In|fek|ti|ons|ge|fahr** F danger of infection; **In|fek|ti|ons|herd** M focus of infection; **In|fek|ti|ons|ket|te** F chain of infection; **In|fek|ti|ons|krank|heit** F infectious disease; **In|fek|ti|ons|ri|si|ko** NT risk of infection, infection risk

in|fek|ti|ös [ɪnfɛk'tsiøːs] ADJ infectious

in|fer|na|lisch [ɪnfɛr'naːlɪʃ] ADJ *(geh)* infernal

In|fer|no [ɪn'fɛrno] NT **-s,** *no pl (lit, fig)* inferno

In|filt|ra|ti|on F infiltration

in|filt|rie|ren [ɪnfɪl'triːrən] *ptp* **infiltriert** VT to infiltrate

in|fi|nit [ɪnfi'niːt, 'ɪn-] ADJ *(Gram)* non-finite

in|fi|ni|te|si|mal [ɪnfinitezi'maːl] ADJ *(Math)* infinitesimal

In|fi|ni|tiv ['ɪnfinitiːf] M **-s, -e** [-və] infinitive

In|fi|ni|tiv-: **In|fi|ni|tiv|kon|struk|ti|on** F infinitive construction; **In|fi|ni|tiv|satz** M infinitive clause

in|fi|zie|ren [ɪnfi'tsiːrən] *ptp* **infiziert** VT to infect; **mit einem Virus infiziert** *(Comput)* virus-infected VR to be *or* get infected *(bei* by)

in fla|gran|ti [ɪn fla'granti] ADV in the act, red-handed, in flagrante delicto *(form)*

In|fla|ti|on [ɪnfla'tsioːn] F **-, -en** inflation

in|fla|ti|o|när [ɪnflatsio'nɛːɐ] ADJ inflationary; *(fig)* over-extensive ADV **sich ~ entwickeln** to develop in an inflationary way

in|fla|ti|o|nis|tisch [ɪnflatsio'nɪstɪʃ] ADJ inflationary

In|fla|ti|ons-: **In|fla|ti|ons|angst** F fear of inflation; **in|fla|ti|ons|hem|mend** ADJ anti-inflationary ADV **~ wirken** to be anti-inflationary; **In|fla|ti|ons|ra|te** F rate of inflation; **in|fla|ti|ons|si|cher** ADJ inflation-proof ADV **Geld ~ anlegen** to put money into inflation-proof investments

in|fla|to|risch [ɪnfla'toːrɪʃ] ADJ inflationary

in|fle|xi|bel [ɪnflɛ'ksiːbl, 'ɪn-] ADJ *(lit, fig)* inflexible

In|fle|xi|bi|li|tät [ɪnflɛksibili'tɛːt, 'ɪn-] F *(lit, fig)* inflexibility

In|flu|enz [ɪnflu'ɛnts] F **-, -en** *(Phys)* electrostatic induction

In|fo ['ɪnfo] NT **-, -s** *(inf)* **a** *(= Information)* info *(inf)* **b** *(Sch inf: = Informatik)* computer studies *pl*

In|fo|da|tei F *(Comput)* readme file

In|fo|dienst M *(inf)* information service

in|fol|ge [ɪn'fɔlgə] ✪ 44.1 PREP *+gen or von* as a result of, owing to, because of

in|fol|ge|des|sen [ɪnfɔlgə'dɛsn] ADV consequently, as a result (of that), because of that

In|fo|ma|te|ri|al NT *(inf)* info *(inf)*, bumf *(Brit inf)*

In|for|mant [ɪnfɔr'mant] M **-en, -en, In|for|man|tin** [-tɪn] F **-, -nen** **a** *(= Informationsquelle)* source (of information); *(in Forschung, für Regierung)* informant **b** *(= Denunziant)* informer

In|for|ma|tik [ɪnfɔr'maːtɪk] F **-,** *no pl* information technology, informatics *sing*; *(= Schulfach)* computer studies *pl*

In|for|ma|ti|ker [ɪnfɔr'maːtikɐ] M **-s, -, In|for|ma|ti|ke|rin** [-ərɪn] F **-, -nen** computer *or* information scientist

In|for|ma|ti|on [ɪnfɔrma'tsioːn] ✪ 46.1, 46.4, 47.1, 48.3 F **a** information *no pl (über +acc* about, on); **eine ~** (a piece of) information; **~en weitergeben** to pass on information; **zu Ihrer ~** for your information **b** *(= Stelle)* information desk

in|for|ma|ti|o|nell [ɪnfɔrmatsio'nɛl] ADJ informational; **~e Selbstbestimmung** control over one's personal data

In|for|ma|ti|ons-: **In|for|ma|ti|ons|aus|tausch** M exchange of information; **In|for|ma|ti|ons|blatt** NT information leaflet; **In|for|ma|ti|ons|bü|ro** NT information bureau; **In|for|ma|ti|ons|de|fi|zit** NT information lag, lack of information; **In|for|ma|ti|ons|fluss** M flow of information; **In|for|ma|ti|ons|ge|halt** M information content; **In|for|ma|ti|ons|ge|sell|schaft** F information society; **In|for|ma|ti|ons|ge|win|nung** F information gathering; **In|for|ma|ti|ons|lü|cke** F information gap; **In|for|ma|ti|ons|ma|te|ri|al** NT information (material); *(= Prospekte etc)* literature; **In|for|ma|ti|ons|quel|le** F source of information; **In|for|ma|ti|ons|schal|ter** M information desk; **In|for|ma|ti|ons|stand** M **a** information stand **b** *no pl (= Wissensstand)* level of information; **In|for|ma|ti|ons|tech|nik** F, **In|for|ma|ti|ons|tech|no|lo|gie** F information technology; **In|for|ma|ti|ons|the|o|rie** F information theory; **In|for|ma|ti|ons|trä|ger** M *(Comput)* (data) storage medium; **In|for|ma|ti|ons|ver|an|stal|tung** F briefing; **In|for|ma|ti|ons|ver|ar|bei|tung** F information processing; **In|for|ma|ti|ons|vor|sprung** M **einen ~ haben** to be better informed; **In|for|ma|ti|ons|wis|sen|schaft** F information science; **In|for|ma|ti|ons|zent|rum** NT information centre *(Brit) or* center *(US)*

in|for|ma|tiv [ɪnfɔrma'tiːf] ADJ informative ADV informatively; **~ beschreiben** to describe informatively *or* in great detail; **~ berichten** to give an informative report

in|for|ma|to|risch [ɪnfɔrma'toːrɪʃ] ADJ informational

in|for|mell [ɪnfɔr'mɛl, 'ɪn-] ADJ informal ADV informally; **die EU-Minister trafen sich ~** EU ministers met informally

in|for|mie|ren [ɪnfɔr'miːrən] *ptp* **informiert** VT to inform *(über +acc, von* about, of); **jdn von** *or* **über etw** *(acc)* **~** to inform sb of sth, to fill sb in on sth *(inf)*; **da bist du falsch** *or* **nicht richtig informiert** you've been misinformed, you've been wrongly informed; **jdn nur unvollständig/einseitig ~** to give sb only part of/one side of the information; **informierte Kreise** informed circles VR to find out, to inform oneself *(über +acc* about); **sich ständig über den neuesten Stand der Medizin ~** to keep oneself informed about the latest developments in medicine

In|for|miert|heit F **-,** *no pl* knowledge; **wegen der zunehmenden ~ der Jugendlichen** since young people are becoming increasingly well-informed; **die mangelnde ~ der Bevölkerung** the population's lack of information

In|fo|stand ['ɪnfo-] M *(inf)* information stand

In|fo|tain|ment [ɪnfo'te:nmənt] NT **-s,** *no pl* infotainment

In|fo|tel|e|fon ['ɪnfo-] NT information line

in|fra|ge [ɪn'fra:gə], **in Fra|ge** ADV **~ kommen** to be possible; **~ kommend** possible; *Bewerber* worth considering; **sollte er für diese Stelle ~ kommen, …** if he should be considered for this position …; **für jdn/etw nicht ~ kommen** to be out of the question for sb/sth; **das kommt (überhaupt) nicht ~!** that's (quite) out of the question!; **etw ~ stellen** to question sth, to query sth, to call sth into question

In|fra-: **in|fra|rot** ADJ infrared; **In|fra|rot|strah|ler** M infrared lamp; **In|fra|rot|strah|lung** F infrared radiation; **In|fra|schall** M infrasonic *or* subsonic waves *pl*; **In|fra|struk|tur** F infrastructure

In|fu|si|on [ɪnfu'zio:n] F infusion

In|fu|si|ons|schlauch M drip tube, IV *or* intravenous tube

Ing. *abbr von* **Ingenieur**

In|ge|ni|eur [ɪnʒe'niø:ɐ] M **-s -e, In|ge|ni|eu|rin** [-'niø:rɪn] F **-, -nen** engineer

In|ge|ni|eur-: **In|ge|ni|eur|bü|ro** [ɪnʒe'niø:ɐ-] NT engineer's office; **In|ge|ni|eur|schu|le** [ɪnʒe'niø:ɐ-] F school of engineering

In|gre|di|enz [ɪngre'diɛnts] F **-, -en** *(= Zutat, Bestandteil)* **a** *(Cook)* ingredient **b** *(Pharm etc)* constituent (part), component

In|grimm M *(liter)* wrath, ire *(liter)*

in|grim|mig ADJ *(liter)* wrathful *(liter)*, ireful *(liter)*

Ing|wer ['ɪŋvɐ] M **-s, -** ginger

Inh. **a** *abbr von* **Inhaber** prop. **b** *abbr von* **Inhalt**

In|ha|ber ['ɪnha:bɐ] M **-s, -, In|ha|be|rin** [-ərɪn] F **-, -nen** *(von Geschäft, Firma)* owner; *(von Hotel, Restaurant auch)* proprietor/proprietress; *(von Konto, Aktie, Lizenz, Patent, Rekord, Orden)* holder; *(von Scheck, Pass)* bearer

In|ha|ber|pa|pier NT *(Fin)* bearer security

In|ha|ber|schuld|ver|schrei|bung F *(Fin)* bearer bond

in|haf|tie|ren [ɪnhaf'ti:rən] *ptp* **inhaftiert** VT *insep* to take into custody

In|haf|tie|rung F **-, -en** *(= das Inhaftieren)* arrest; *(= Haft)* imprisonment

In|ha|la|ti|on [ɪnhala'tsio:n] F **-, -en** *(Med)* inhalation

in|ha|lie|ren [ɪnha'li:rən] *ptp* **inhaliert** VTI *insep (Med, inf)* to inhale

In|halt M **a** *(von Behälter, Paket)* contents *pl* **b** *(von Buch, Brief, Begriff)* content, contents *pl*; *(des Lebens)* meaning; **welchen ~ hatte der Film/das Gespräch?, was hatte der Film/das Gespräch zum ~?** what was the subject matter *or* content of the film/discussion?; **über ~e diskutieren** to discuss the real issues; **ein Brief des ~s, dass …** *(form)* a letter to the effect that … **c** *(Math) (= Flächeninhalt)* area; *(= Rauminhalt)* volume; **der ~ der Flasche beträgt zwei Liter** the bottle has a volume of two litres *(Brit)* or liters *(US)*, the bottle holds two litres *(Brit)* or liters *(US)*

in|halt|lich ['ɪnhaltlɪç] ADJ, ADV as regards content

In|halts-: **In|halts|an|ga|be** F summary, précis *(esp Sch)*; **in|halts|arm** ADJ *(geh)* lacking (in) content; *Leben* meaningless; **in|halts|be|zo|gen** ADJ *(Ling)* content-oriented; **in|halts|gleich** ADJ **a** *(Math)* equal **b** *Buch etc* **… ist ~ mit …** … has the same content(s) as …, … is identical in content to …; **in|halts|leer** ADJ = **inhaltsarm**; **in|halts|los** ADJ empty; *Leben auch* meaningless; *Buch, Vortrag* lacking in content; **in|halts|reich** ADJ *Leben, Tag* full; *Ausstellung, Text* substantial; *Beziehung* meaningful; **in|halts|schwer** ADJ *(geh: = bedeutungsvoll)* significant, of consequence; **In|halts|stoff** M constituent, ingredient; **In|halts|über|sicht** F summary of the contents; **In|halts|ver|zeich|nis** NT list *or* table of contents; *(Comput)* directory; **„Inhaltsverzeichnis"** "contents"

in|hä|rent [ɪnhe'rɛnt] ADJ *(geh)* inherent

in|hu|man [ɪnhu'ma:n, 'ɪn-] ADJ *(= unmenschlich, brutal)* inhuman; *(= unbarmherzig)* inhumane ADV inhumanly

In|hu|ma|ni|tät [ɪnhumani'tɛ:t, 'ɪn-] F inhumanity

Ini|ti|a|le [ini'tsia:lə] F **-, -n** *(geh)* initial

ini|ti|a|li|sie|ren [initsiali'zi:rən] *ptp* **initialisiert** VT *(Comput)* to initialize

Ini|ti|a|li|sie|rung [initsiali'zi:rʊŋ] F **-, -en** *(Comput)* initialization

Ini|ti|a|ti|on [initsia'tsio:n] F **-, -en** initiation

Ini|ti|a|ti|ons|ri|tus M initiation rite

ini|ti|a|tiv [initsia'ti:f] ADJ **~ werden** to take the initiative

Ini|ti|a|tiv|be|wer|bung F speculative application

Ini|ti|a|ti|ve [initsia'ti:və] F **-, -n** **a** initiative; **aus eigener ~** on one's own initiative; **die ~ ergreifen** to take the initiative; **auf jds ~** *(acc)* **hin** on sb's initiative **b** *(Sw Pol)* petition for a referendum

Ini|ti|a|tor [ini'tsia:to:ɐ] M **-s, Initiatoren, Ini|ti|a|to|rin** [-'to:rɪn] F **-, -nen** *(geh)* initiator

ini|ti|ie|ren [initsi'i:rən] *ptp* **initiiert** VT *(geh)* initiate

In|jek|ti|on [ɪnjɛk'tsio:n] F **-, -en** injection

In|jek|ti|ons|sprit|ze F hypodermic (syringe)

in|ji|zie|ren [ɪnji'tsi:rən] *ptp* **injiziert** VT *(form)* to inject *(jdm etw* sb with sth)

In|ka ['ɪŋka] M **-(s), -s** Inca

In|kar|na|ti|on [ɪnkarna'tsio:n] F **-, -en** incarnation

In|kas|so [ɪn'kaso] NT **-s, -s** *or (Aus)* **Inkassi** [-si] *(Fin)* collection

In|kas|so-: **In|kas|so|bü|ro** NT, **In|kas|so|fir|ma** F *(Fin)* collection agency; **In|kas|so|stel|le** F *(Fin)* collection point

In|kauf|nah|me [ɪn'kaufna:mə] F **-,** *no pl (form)* acceptance; **unter ~ finanzieller Verluste** accepting the inevitable financial losses

inkl. *abbr von* **inklusive**

in|klu|si|ve [ɪnklu'zi:və] PREP *+gen* inclusive of; **~ Heizung** heating included, inclusive of *or* including heating ADV inclusive

in|ko|gni|to [ɪn'kɔgnito] ADV incognito

In|ko|gni|to [ɪn'kɔgnito] NT **-s, -s** incognito

in|kom|pa|ti|bel [ɪnkɔmpa'ti:bl, 'ɪn-] ADJ incompatible

In|kom|pa|ti|bi|li|tät F incompatibility

in|kom|pe|tent [ɪnkɔmpe'tɛnt, 'ɪn-] ADJ incompetent

In|kom|pe|tenz [ɪnkɔmpe'tɛnts, 'ɪn-] F incompetence

in|kon|gru|ent [ɪnkɔŋgru'ɛnt, 'ɪn-] ADJ *(Math)* non-congruent

In|kon|gru|enz [ɪnkɔŋgru'ɛnts, 'ɪn-] F *(Math)* non-congruence

in|kon|se|quent [ɪnkɔnze'kvɛnt, 'ɪn-] ADJ inconsistent ADV inconsistently

In|kon|se|quenz [ɪnkɔnze'kvɛnts, 'ɪn-] F inconsistency

in|kons|tant [ɪnkɔn'stant, 'ɪn-] ADJ inconstant

In|kons|tanz [ɪnkɔn'stants, 'ɪn-] F inconstancy

in|kon|ti|nent ['ɪnkɔntinɛnt] ADJ *(Med)* incontinent

In|kon|ti|nenz ['ɪnkɔntinɛnts] F **-, -en** *(Med)* incontinence

In|kor|po|ra|ti|on F *(geh)* incorporation

in|kor|po|rie|ren [ɪnkɔrpo'ri:rən] *ptp* **inkorporiert** VT *(geh)* to incorporate *(in +acc* in, into)

in|kor|rekt [ɪnkɔ'rɛkt, 'ɪn-] ADJ incorrect ADV incorrectly; *gekleidet* inappropriately

In|kor|rekt|heit F **a** *no pl (des Benehmens)* incorrectness, impropriety; *(der Arbeit etc)* incorrectness, inaccuracy **b** *(= Formfehler)* impropriety, breach of propriety; *(= Ungenauigkeit)* inaccuracy

In|kraft|tre|ten, In-Kraft-Tre|ten △ [ɪn'krafttre:tn] NT **-s,** *no pl* coming into effect *or* force; **das ~ von etw verhindern** to prevent sth from coming into effect *or* force; **bei ~ von etw** when sth comes/came *etc* into effect *or* force

in|kre|men|tell ADJ incremental; **~e Suche** *(Comput)* incremental search

in|kri|mi|nie|ren [ɪnkrimi'ni:rən] *ptp* **inkriminiert** VT to incriminate

In|ku|ba|ti|on [ɪnkuba'tsio:n] F **-, -en** incubation

In|ku|ba|ti|ons|zeit F incubation period

In|ku|ba|tor [ɪnku'ba:to:ɐ] M **-s, Inkubatoren** incubator

In|ku|bus ['ɪnkubʊs] M **-, Inkuben** [-bn] incubus

In|ku|lanz [ɪnku'lants, 'ɪn-] F disobligingness

In|ku|na|bel [ɪnku'na:bl] F **-, -n** incunabulum

In|land NT, *no pl* **a** *(als Staatsgebiet)* home; **im ~ hergestellte Waren** home-produced goods, goods produced at home; **im In- und Ausland** at home and abroad; **die Gebühren für einen Brief im ~** inland *or* domestic letter rates **b** *(= Inneres eines Landes)* inland; **im ~** inland; **ins ~ ziehen** to move inland

In|land- *in cpds (Comm)* home, domestic; *(Geog)* inland; **In|land|be|darf** M home *or* domestic requirements *pl*; **In|land|eis** NT ice sheet; **In|land|flug** M domestic *or* internal flight

in|län|disch ['ɪnlɛndɪʃ] ADJ domestic; *(Geog)* inland

In|lands-: **In|lands|ge|schäft** NT *(Comm)* domestic trade; **In|lands|ge|spräch** NT *(Telec)* inland call; **In|lands|markt** M home *or* domestic market; **In|lands|por|to** NT inland postage; **In|lands|ver|kehr** M domestic traffic; *(= Handel)* home trade; **Briefe im ~** letters within the country, inland *or* domestic letters; **er ist Fernfahrer, aber nur im ~** he's a long-distance driver, but only on inland *or* domestic routes

In|laut M **im ~ vorkommen** to occur (word) medially, to occur in (word) medial position

In|lett ['ɪnlɛt] NT **-(e)s, -e** *(= Hülle)* cambric case; *(= Inlettstoff)* cambric

in|lie|gend ADJ, ADV *(form, Aus)* enclosed

In|li|ner ['ɪnlainɐ] M **-s, -** *(= Rollschuh)* in-line skate

in|line|ska|ten ['ɪnlainske:tn] VI *only infinitive* to go *or* to be in-line skating *or* roller-blading, to blade *(inf)*

In|line|ska|ter ['ɪnlainske:tɐ] M **-s, -** *(= Rollschuh)* in-line skate

In|line|ska|ter ['ɪnlainske:tɐ] M **-s, -, In|line|ska|te|rin** ['ɪnlainske:tərɪn] F **-, -nen** roller-blader

In|line|skates ['ɪnlainske:ts] *pl* in-line skates

in|mit|ten [ɪn'mɪtn] PREP *+gen* in the middle *or* midst of ADV **~ von** amongst, surrounded by

in|ne+ha|ben ['ɪnəha:bn] VT *sep irreg (form)* to hold

in|ne+hal|ten ['ɪnəhaltn] *sep irreg* VI to pause, to stop; **er hielt im Satz inne** he paused in mid-sentence; **er hielt im Sprechen inne** he stopped speaking in mid-flow; **mit der Rede ~** to pause, to stop speaking; **mit der Rede ~, um Luft zu holen** to pause for breath VT *(old)* = **einhalten**

in|nen ['ɪnən] ADV **a** inside; *(= auf der Innenseite)* on the inside; *(= im Haus)* indoors, inside; **~ und außen** inside and out(side); **der Mantel hat ~ Pelz und außen Leder** the coat has fur (on the) inside and leather (on the) outside; **nach ~** inwards; **tief ~ tut es doch weh** deep down inside it really hurts; **die Tür geht nach ~ auf** the door opens inwards; **die Truppen drangen nach ~ vor** the troops pushed inland; **die Haare nach ~ tragen** to have one's hair curled under; **nach ~ laufen** to be pigeon-toed; **von ~** from (the) inside; **wie sieht das Haus von ~ aus?** what does the house look like inside?, what does the inside of the house look like?; **sich von ~ her aufwärmen** to warm oneself from (the) inside, to get warm inside **b** *(esp Aus)* = **drinnen**

In|nen-: **In|nen|an|ten|ne** F indoor aerial *(Brit)* or antenna *(US)*; **In|nen|ar|bei|ten** PL work on the interior; **In|nen|ar|chi|tekt(in)**

M(F) interior designer; **In|nen|ar|chi|tek|tur** F interior design; **In|nen|auf|nah|me** F indoor photo(graph); *(Film)* indoor shot *or* take; **In|nen|aus|stat|tung** F interior décor *no pl*; *(= das Ausstatten)* interior decoration and furnishing; *(von Auto)* interior fittings *pl (Brit) or* fixtures *pl*; **In|nen|bahn** F *(Sport)* inside lane; **In|nen|be|leuch|tung** F interior lighting; **In|nen|de|ko|ra|ti|on** F interior decoration; **In|nen|dienst** M office duty; **im ~ sein** to work in the office; **~ machen** *or* **haben** to work in the office, to be on office duty; **in|nen|drin** [ˈɪnən-ˈdrɪn] ADV *(inf)* inside; **In|nen|ein|rich|tung** F (interior) furnishings *pl*; *(= das Einrichten)* interior furnishing *no pl*; **In|nen|flä|che** F **a** *(= innere Fläche)* inside, inside *or* interior surface; *(der Hand)* palm **b** *(= Flächeninhalt)* internal surface area; **In|nen|hof** M inner courtyard; *(bei Universitäten, Klöstern)* quadrangle, quad *(inf)*; **In|nen|kur|ve** F inside bend; **In|nen|le|ben** NT, *no pl* **a** *(inf: seelisch)* inner *or* emotional life; **sein ~ offenbaren** to reveal one's innermost thoughts *or* feelings **b** *(inf: körperlich)* insides *pl*; **In|nen|leuch|te** F *(Aut)* courtesy *or* interior light; **In|nen|mi|nis|ter(in)** M(F) minister of the interior; *(in GB)* Home Secretary; *(in den USA)* Secretary of the Interior; **In|nen|mi|nis|te|ri|um** NT ministry of the interior; *(in GB)* Home Office; *(in den USA)* Department of the Interior; **In|nen|po|li|tik** F domestic policy; *(= innere Angelegenheiten)* home *or* domestic affairs *pl*; **In|nen|po|li|ti|ker(in)** M(F) domestic politician; **in|nen|po|li|tisch** ADJ domestic, internal; *Sprecher* on domestic policy; **auf ~em Gebiet** in the field of home affairs; **aus ~er Sicht** (seen) from the point of view of domestic policy ADV **~ gesehen** from the point of view of domestic policy; **~ bewandert sein** to be well-versed in *or* familiar with domestic policy; **~ unverantwortlich/bedenklich** irresponsible/questionable as far as domestic policy is concerned; **~ hat die Regierung versagt** the government has failed with its domestic policy; **In|nen|raum** M **a Innenräume** inner rooms *pl*; **die prächtigen Innenräume des alten Schlosses** the magnificent interior *or* rooms of the old castle **b** *no pl* room inside; *(von Wagen)* interior; **einen kleinen ~ haben** to be small inside, not to have much room inside; *(Wagen auch)* to have a small interior; **mit großem ~** with a lot of room inside; *(Wagen auch)* with a large interior; **In|nen|rol|le** F, *no pl* **eine ~ tragen** to have one's hair turned *or* curled under at the ends; **In|nen|sei|te** F inside; **die ~ von etw nach außen kehren** to turn sth inside out; **In|nen|spie|gel** M *(Aut)* interior mirror; **In|nen|stadt** F town centre *(Brit) or* center *(US)*, centre *(Brit) or* center *(US)* of the town; *(einer Großstadt)* city centre *(Brit) or* center *(US)*, centre *(Brit) or* center *(US)* of the city; **In|nen|ta|sche** F inside pocket; **In|nen|tem|pe|ra|tur** F inside temperature; *(in einem Gebäude)* indoor temperature; **wir haben 20° ~** the temperature indoors is 20°; **bei 20° ~** when the temperature indoors *or* the indoor temperature is 20°, when it's 20° indoors; **In|nen|to|i|let|te** F inside toilet; **In|nen|welt** F, *no pl* inner world; **er hat sich völlig in seine ~ zurückgezogen** he has withdrawn completely into his own private world; **In|nen|ver|tei|di|ger** M, **In|nen|ver|tei|di|ge|rin** F *(Ftbl)* central defender; **In|nen|win|kel** M *(Math)* interior angle

in|ner-: **in|ner|be|trieb|lich** ADJ in-house ADV in-house, within the company *or* corporation; **das wird ~ geregelt werden** that will be settled in-house; **in|ner|deutsch** ADJ **der ~e Handel** the domestic German trade; **die ~e Grenze** *(Hist)* the inner-German border; **Ministerium für ~e Beziehungen** *(Hist)* Ministry *(Brit) or* Department of Intra-German Relations; **in|ner|dienst|lich** ADJ internal, in-house

In|ne|rei|en [ɪnəˈraiən] PL innards *pl*; *(von Geflügel auch)* giblets *pl*

in|ne|re(r, s) [ˈɪnərə] ADJ **a** *(örtlich)* inner; *(= im Körper befindlich, inländisch)* internal; **Facharzt für ~ Krankheiten** internist; **das ~ Ohr** the inner ear; **die ~n Angelegenheiten eines Landes** the internal *or* home *or* domestic affairs of a country; **der Whisky sorgte für die ~ Wärme** *(hum)* the whisky warmed our/their *etc* insides *(inf)*; **Innere Mission** Home Mission; *(= Diakonisches Werk)* church social welfare programme *(Brit) or* program *(US)*; **~r Monolog** *(Liter)* interior monologue; **im innersten Herzen** deep in one's heart, in one's heart of hearts; **eine ~ Uhr** *(inf)* an internal *or* a biological clock; **~ Emigration** inner emigration, *withdrawal into private life of artists and intellectuals who remained in Germany through the Nazi period but did not support the Third Reich; any similar withdrawal*
b *(= geistig, seelisch)* inner; **~ Werte** *pl* inner worth *no pl*; **eine ~ Stimme** an inner voice, a voice within; **vor meinem ~n Auge** in my mind's eye; **~ Führung** *(Mil)* moral leadership

In|ne|re(s) [ˈɪnərə] NT *decl as adj* **a** inside; *(von Kirche, Wagen, Schloss)* interior, inside; *(= Mitte)* middle, centre *(Brit)*, center *(US)*; **Minister des Inner(e)n** minister of the interior; *(in GB)* Home Secretary; *(in den USA)* Secretary of the Interior; **das ~ nach außen kehren** to turn something inside out; **ins ~ des Landes** into the heart of the country **b** *(fig: = Gemüt, Geist)* heart; **ich wusste, was in seinem ~n vorging** I knew what was going on inside him; **sein ~s rebellierte dagegen** his inner self rebelled against it; **im tiefsten ~n** (deep) in one's heart, in one's heart of hearts

in|ner|halb [ˈɪnɐhalp] PREP +*gen* **a** *(örtlich)* inside, within; **~ dieser Regelung** within this ruling **b** *(zeitlich)* within; **~ (von) zehn Minuten** within ten minutes, in ten minutes, inside (of) ten minutes ADV inside; *(eines Landes)* inland; **weiter ~** further in; **weiter ~ im Lande** further inland

in|ner|lich [ˈɪnɐlɪç] ADJ **a** *(= körperlich)* internal **b** *(= geistig, seelisch)* inward, inner *no adv*; *Gedicht, Mensch* inward; *Hemmung* inner ADV **a** *(= im Körper)* internally; **dieses Medikament ist ~ anzuwenden** this medicine is to be taken internally **b** *(= gemütsmäßig)* inwardly, inside; **~ gefestigt sein** to have inner strength; **jdm ~ verbunden sein** to have very deep feelings for sb; **ein ~ gefestigter Mensch** a person of inner strength; **~ schäumte er vor Wut** inwardly *or* inside he was boiling with rage; **~ lachen** to laugh inwardly *or* to oneself

In|ner|lich|keit F -, *no pl (liter)* inwardness

in|ner-: **in|ner|par|tei|lich** ADJ within the party; **~e Schwierigkeiten** internal difficulties in the party, difficulties within the party; **eine ~e Diskussion** a party discussion; **~e Demokratie** democracy (with)in the party structure ADV (with)in the party; **in|ner|staat|lich** ADJ domestic, internal

in|ners|te(r, s) [ˈɪnɐstə] ADJ *superl von* **innere(r, s)** innermost, inmost; *(fig auch)* deepest

In|ners|te(s) [ˈɪnɐstə] NT *decl as adj (lit)* innermost part, heart; *(fig)* heart; **tief im ~n liebte sie ihn** in her heart of hearts she loved him, deep in her heart she loved him; **bis ins ~ getroffen** hurt to the quick, deeply *or* profoundly hurt

in|nert [ˈɪnɐt] PREP +*gen or dat (Aus, Sw)* within, in, inside (of); **~ nützlicher Frist** *(= in der vorgeschriebenen Zeit)* within the allotted time, within the time allowed; *(= in absehbarer Zeit)* in the foreseeable future

in|ne+wer|den [ˈɪnə-] VI *sep irreg aux sein* (**sich** *dat*) **einer Sache** *(gen)* **~** to become aware *or* cognizant *(form)* of sth

in|ne+woh|nen [ˈɪnə-] VI *sep +dat* to be inherent in

in|nig [ˈɪnɪç] ADJ **a** *Glückwünsche, Grüße* heartfelt *no adv*, hearty; *Beileid* heartfelt, deep, profound; *Vergnügen* deep, profound; *Freundschaft, Kontakte* close, intimate; *Beziehung* intimate; **mein ~ster Wunsch** my dearest wish **b** *(Chem) Verbindung* intimate ADV deeply, profoundly; **etw aufs ~ste** *or* **Innigste erhoffen/wünschen** to hope/wish for sth most fervently *or* ardently; **jdn ~ lieben** to love sb dearly *or* deeply, to love sb with all one's heart

In|nig|keit F -, *no pl (von Glückwünschen, Grüßen)* warmth, sincerity; *(von Empfindung)* depth; *(von Liebe)* intensity; *(von Freundschaft, Kontakten, Beziehung)* closeness; **mit ~ beten/hoffen** to pray/hope fervently

in|nig|lich [ˈɪnɪklɪç] ADV *(poet) (= herzlich)* sincerely, warmly; *(= tief)* deeply, profoundly; *lieben* deeply, dearly; *(= eng)* intimately, closely

In|no|va|ti|on [inovaˈtsio:n] F -, **-en** innovation

in|no|va|ti|ons-: **in|no|va|ti|ons|feind|lich** ADJ hostile to (any form of) innovation, unwilling to adapt (to the times), Luddite; **in|no|va|ti|ons|freu|dig** ADJ innovative

In|nung [ˈɪnʊŋ] F -, **-en** (trade) guild; **du blamierst die ganze ~** *(hum inf)* you're letting the (whole) side down *(inf)*

in|of|fi|zi|ell [ɪnɔfiˈtsiɛl, ˈɪn-] ADJ unofficial ADV unofficially; **jdm etw ~ mitteilen** to tell sb sth unofficially *or* off the record

In|oku|la|ti|on [ɪnlokulaˈtsio:n] F -, **-en** inoculation

in|oku|lie|ren [ɪnlokuˈli:rən] *ptp* **inokuliert** VT to inoculate

in|ope|ra|bel [ɪnloperˈra:bl, ˈɪn-] ADJ *(Med)* inoperable

in|op|por|tun [ɪnɔpɔrˈtu:n, ˈɪn-] ADJ inopportune

in pet|to [ɪn ˈpɛto] → **petto**

in punc|to [ɪn ˈpʊŋkto] → **punkto**

In|put [ˈɪnpʊt] M OR NT **-s, -s** input

In|qui|si|ti|on [ɪnkviziˈtsio:n] F -, **-en** Inquisition

In|qui|si|ti|ons-: **In|qui|si|ti|ons|ge|richt** NT Court of the Inquisition, inquisitional court; **In|qui|si|ti|ons|me|tho|de** F inquisitional method

In|qui|si|tor [ɪnkviˈzi:to:ɐ] M **-s, Inquisitoren** inquisitor

in|qui|si|to|risch [ɪnkviziˈto:rɪʃ] ADJ inquisitorial ADV inquisitorially

ins [ɪns] *contr von* **in das**; **~ Rollen/Rutschen geraten** *or* **kommen** to start rolling/sliding

In|sas|se [ˈɪnzasə] M **-n, -n**, **In|sas|sin** [ˈɪnsasɪn] F -, **-nen** *(von Fahrzeug)* passenger; *(von Auto auch)* occupant; *(von Anstalt)* inmate

In|sas|sen|ver|si|che|rung F passenger insurance

ins|be|son|de|re [ɪnsbəˈzɔndərə] ADV particularly, (e)specially, in particular

In|schrift F inscription, legend *(form)*

In|sekt [ɪnˈzɛkt] NT **-(e)s, -en** insect; **~en fressend** = **insektenfressend**

In|sek|ten-: **In|sek|ten|be|kämp|fung** F insect control; **In|sek|ten|be|kämp|fungs|mit|tel** NT insecticide; **in|sek|ten|fres|send** ADJ insect-eating, insectivorous *(form)*; **In|sek|ten|fres|ser** M insect eater, insectivore *(form)*; **In|sek|ten|gift** NT insecticide; **In|sek|ten|kun|de** F entomology; **In|sek|ten|pla|ge** F plague of insects; **In|sek|ten|pul|ver** NT insect powder, (powder) insecticide; **In|sek|ten|schutz|mit|tel** NT insect repellent; **In|sek|ten|spray** NT insect spray, bug *(US inf)* spray; **In|sek|ten|stich** M *(von Ameisen, Mücken, Flöhen)* insect bite; *(von Bienen, Wespen)* (insect) sting; **In|sek|ten|ver|til|gungs|mit|tel** NT insecticide

In|sek|ti|zid [ɪnzɛktiˈtsi:t] NT **-s, -e** [-də] *(form)* insecticide

In|sel [ˈɪnzl] F -, **-n** *(lit, fig)* island, isle *(poet)*; **die Britischen ~n** the British Isles; **die ~ Man** the Isle of Man; **reif für die ~ sein** *(inf)* to be ready to get away from it all

In|sel|be|woh|ner(in) M(F) islander, inhabitant of an/the island
In|sel|chen ['ɪnzlçən] NT -s, - little island, islet *(poet)*
In|sel-: **In|sel|grup|pe** F archipelago, group of islands; **In|sel|ket|te** F chain *or* string of islands, island chain; **In|sel|la|ge** F island position; **Großbritannien, infolge seiner ~ …** Great Britain, because it is an island …; **In|sel|men|ta|li|tät** F insular mentality; **in|sel|reich** ADJ with a lot of islands; **In|sel|reich** NT island kingdom; **In|sel|staat** M island state; **In|sel|volk** NT island nation *or* race *or* people; **In|sel|welt** F island world; **die ~ Mittelamerikas** the world of the Central American islands
In|se|rat [ɪnze'ra:t] NT -(e)s, -e advert *(inf)*, ad *(inf)*, advertisement
In|se|ra|ten|teil M advertisement section, adverts *pl (inf)*, ads *pl (inf)*
In|se|rent [ɪnze'rɛnt] M -en, -en, **In|se|ren|tin** [-'rɛntɪn] F -, -nen advertiser
in|se|rie|ren [ɪnze'ri:rən] *ptp* **inseriert** VTI to advertise; **etw in der Zeitung ~** to advertise sth in the paper, to insert *or* put an advertisement in the paper for sth
ins|ge|heim [ɪnsgə'haim, 'ɪns-] ADV secretly, in secret
ins|ge|mein [ɪnsgə'main, 'ɪns-] ADV *(old)* in general, on the whole, by and large
ins|ge|samt [ɪnsgə'zamt, 'ɪns-] ADV *(= alles zusammen)* altogether; *(= im Großen und Ganzen)* all in all, on the whole, by and large; **die Kosten belaufen sich auf ~ 1.000 EUR** the costs amount to a total of EUR 1,000; **ein Verdienst von ~ 2.000 EUR** earnings totalling *(Brit) or* totaling *(US)* EUR 2,000
In|si|der ['ɪnsaidɐ] M -s, -, **In|si|de|rin** [-ərɪn] F -, -nen insider; **der Witz war nur für ~ verständlich** that was an in-joke *(Brit)* or inside joke *(esp US)*, that joke was just for the in-crowd; **~ der Jazzszene** those in on the jazz scene, those in the know about the jazz scene
In|si|der-: **In|si|der|ge|schäft** NT insider deal; **In|si|der|han|del** M insider trading *or* dealing; **In|si|der|in|for|ma|ti|on** F inside information; **In|si|der|krei|se** PL insider circles *pl*, (the) inner circle *sing (iro)*; **In|si|der|wis|sen** NT inside knowledge
In|sig|ni|en [ɪn'zɪgniən] PL insignia *pl*
in|sig|ni|fi|kant [ɪnzɪgnifi'kant, 'ɪn-] ADJ *(geh)* insignificant, of no consequence
in|sis|tie|ren [ɪnzɪs'ti:rən] *ptp* **insistiert** VI *(geh)* to insist *(auf +dat* on)
In|skrip|ti|on [ɪnskrɪp'tsio:n] F -, -en inscription
ins|künf|tig ['ɪnskʏnftɪç] ADJ, ADV *(Sw)* = **zukünftig**
in|so|fern [ɪnzo'fɛrn, ɪn'zo:fɛrn, 'ɪn-] ADV in this respect; **~ als** in so far as, inasmuch as, in that; **er hat ~ recht, als …** he's right in so far as *or* inasmuch as *or* in that … CONJ [ɪnzo'fɛrn, ɪn'zo:fɛrn, 'ɪn-] *(= wenn)* if
in|sol|vent [ɪnzɔl'vɛnt, 'ɪn-] ADJ *(Comm)* insolvent
In|sol|venz [ɪnzɔl'vɛnts, 'ɪn-] F -, -en *(Comm)* insolvency
in|so|weit [ɪn'zo:vait, ɪnzo:'vait, 'ɪn-] ADV, CONJ = **insofern**
Insp. *abbr von* **Inspektor**
in spe [ɪn 'spe:] ADJ *(inf)* to be, future; **unser Schwiegersohn ~** our son-in-law-to-be, our future son-in-law
In|spek|teur [ɪnspɛk'tø:ɐ] M -s, -e, **In|spek|teu|rin** [-'tø:rɪn] F -, -nen *(Mil)* Chief of Staff
In|spek|ti|on [ɪnspɛk'tsio:n] F -, -en **a** inspection; *(Aut)* service; **ich habe mein Auto zur ~ gebracht** I've taken my car in for a service *or* to be serviced **b** *(= Behörde)* inspectorate
In|spek|ti|ons|rei|se F tour of inspection
In|spek|tor [ɪn'spɛkto:ɐ] M -s, **Inspektoren**, **In|spek|to|rin** [-'to:rɪn] F -, -nen inspector; *(= Verwalter, Aufseher)* superintendent

In|spi|ra|ti|on [ɪnspira'tsio:n] F -, -en inspiration
in|spi|rie|ren [ɪnspi'ri:rən] *ptp* **inspiriert** VT to inspire; **sich von etw ~ lassen** to get one's inspiration from sth
In|spi|zi|ent [ɪnspi'tsiɛnt] M -en, -en, **In|spi|zi|en|tin** [-'tsiɛntɪn] F -, -nen *(Theat)* stage manager; *(= Aufseher)* inspector
in|spi|zie|ren [ɪnspi'tsi:rən] *ptp* **inspiziert** VT to inspect
In|spi|zie|rung F -, -en inspection
in|sta|bil [ɪnsta'bi:l, 'ɪn-] ADJ unstable
In|sta|bi|li|tät F instability
In|stal|la|teur [ɪnstala'tø:ɐ] M -s, -e, **In|stal|la|teu|rin** [-'tø:rɪn] F -, -nen plumber; *(= Elektroinstallateur)* electrician, electrical fitter; *(= Gasinstallateur)* gas fitter
In|stal|la|ti|on [ɪnstala'tsio:n] F -, -en **a** *(no pl: = das Installieren)* installation; *(Tech)* installation, fitting **b** *(= Anlage)* installation; *(in Bauten)* fittings *pl*, installations *pl*; *(= Wasserinstallation)* plumbing *no pl* **c** *(old, Sw: = Amtseinsetzung)* installation
In|stal|la|ti|ons-: **In|stal|la|ti|ons|an|wei|sun|gen** PL *(Comput)* installation instructions; **In|stal|la|ti|ons|as|sis|tent** M *(Comput)* installation assistant; **In|stal|la|ti|ons|da|tei** F *(Comput)* installation file; **In|stal|la|ti|ons|pro|gramm** NT *(Comput)* installation program
in|stal|lie|ren [ɪnsta'li:rən] *ptp* **installiert** VT to install *(auch fig, Comput)*, to put in VR to install oneself
in|stand [ɪn'ʃtant], **in Stand** ADJ in good condition *or* repair; *(= funktionsfähig)* in working order, working; **etw ~ halten** to maintain sth, to keep sth in good condition *or* repair/in working order; **etw ~ setzen** to get sth into good condition *or* repair/into working order; *(= reparieren auch)* to repair sth; **ein Haus ~ besetzen** to squat in a house (and do it up)
In|stand-: **In|stand|hal|tung** F *(von Gerät)* maintenance, servicing; *(von Gebäude)* maintenance, upkeep; **In|stand|hal|tungs|kos|ten** PL maintenance costs *pl*; *(von Gebäude auch)* upkeep costs *pl*
in|stän|dig ['ɪnʃtɛndɪç] ADJ urgent ADV **~ bitten** to beg, to implore, to beseech; **~ hoffen** to hope fervently
In|stand-: **In|stand|set|zung** [ɪn'ʃtantzɛtsʊŋ] F -, -en *(von Gerät)* overhaul; *(von Gebäude)* restoration; *(= Reparatur)* repair; **In|stand|set|zungs|ar|bei|ten** PL repairs *pl*, repair work
In|stanz [ɪn'stants] F -, -en **a** *(= Behörde)* authority; **er ging von einer ~ zur nächsten** he went from one office *or* department to the next **b** *(Jur)* court; *(= Verhandlungsstadium)* (court) case; **Verhandlung in erster/letzter ~** first/final court case; **Verhandlung in zweiter ~** second court case, hearing at the court of second instance *(form)*; **Berufung in erster/zweiter ~** first/second appeal; **ein Urteil letzter ~** *(lit, fig)* a final judgement; **er ging durch alle ~en** he went through all the courts
In|stan|zen|weg M, **In|stan|zen|zug** M *(Aus)* official *or* prescribed channels *pl*; *(Jur)* stages *pl* of appeal; **auf dem ~** through (the official *or* prescribed) channels/the various stages of appeal
Ins|tinkt [ɪn'stɪŋkt] M -(e)s, -e *(lit, fig)* instinct; **aus ~** instinctively, by instinct
ins|tinkt|haft ADJ instinctive
Ins|tinkt|hand|lung F instinctive act; **das ist eine reine ~** it's purely instinctive (behaviour *(Brit) or* behavior *(US)*)
ins|tink|tiv [ɪnstɪŋk'ti:f] ADJ instinctive ADV instinctively; **etw ~ genau wissen** to know sth at gut level
ins|tinkt|los ADJ *Art, Bemerkung* insensitive
ins|tinkt|mä|ßig ADJ instinctive ADV instinctively, by instinct; *(= Instinkte betreffend)* as far as instinct is concerned

ins|tinkt|si|cher ADJ **~ sein** to have a good *or* unerring instinct, to have a good nose *(inf)* ADV **~ handeln** to rely on one's instincts; **er hat wieder einmal ~ gehandelt** his instinct proved him right again
In|sti|tut [ɪnsti'tu:t] NT -(e)s, -e institute; *(Jur. = Institution)* institution
In|sti|tu|ti|on [ɪnstitu'tsio:n] F -, -en institution
in|sti|tu|ti|o|na|li|sie|ren [ɪnstitutsionali'zi:rən] *ptp* **institutionalisiert** VT to institutionalize
in|sti|tu|ti|o|nell [ɪnstitutsio'nɛl] ADJ institutional
In|sti|tuts|lei|ter(in) M(F) director of an/the institute
in|stru|ie|ren [ɪnstru'i:rən] *ptp* **instruiert** VT to instruct; *(über Unternehmen, Plan etc)* to brief; *Anwalt* to brief
In|struk|teur [ɪnstrʊk'tø:ɐ] M -s, -e, **In|struk|teu|rin** [-'tø:rɪn] F -, -nen instructor
In|struk|ti|on [ɪnstrʊk'tsio:n] F -, -en instruction; **laut ~** according to instructions
in|struk|tiv [ɪnstrʊk'ti:f] ADJ instructive
In|stru|ment [ɪnstru'mɛnt] NT -(e)s, -e instrument; *(= Hammer etc auch)* tool, implement; **er ist ~ des …** he is the instrument of …
in|stru|men|tal [ɪnstrumɛn'ta:l] *(Mus)* ADJ instrumental ADV **jdn ~ begleiten** to provide the instrumental accompaniment for sb; **~ musizieren** to play musical instruments
In|stru|men|tal- *in cpds* instrumental; **In|stru|men|tal|be|glei|tung** F instrumental accompaniment; **ohne ~ singen** to sing unaccompanied
in|stru|men|ta|li|sie|ren [ɪnstrumɛntali'zi:rən] *ptp* **instrumentalisiert** VT **a** *(Mus)* to arrange for instruments **b** *(fig)* instrumentalize; *Theorie, Plan etc* to harness; *(= ausnutzen)* to exploit
In|stru|men|ta|li|sie|rung F *(Mus)* instrumental arrangement; *(fig)* instrumentalization
In|stru|men|tal-: **In|stru|men|tal|satz** M *(Gram)* instrumental clause; *(Mus) (= Bearbeitung)* instrumental version; *(= Teilstück)* instrumental section; **In|stru|men|tal|stück** NT instrumental piece
In|stru|men|ta|ri|um [ɪnstrumɛn'ta:riʊm] NT -s, **Instrumentarien** *(lit)* equipment, instruments *pl*; *(Mus)* instruments *pl*; *(fig)* apparatus
in|stru|men|tell [ɪnstrumɛn'tɛl] ADJ **a** *(= mit Instrumenten)* with instruments; *Analytik* instrumental **b** *(= als Mittel dienend) Vernunft, Intelligenz* used as an instrument
In|stru|men|ten-: **In|stru|men|ten|brett** NT instrument panel; **In|stru|men|ten|flug** M instrument flight; *(= das Fliegen auch)* instrument flying, flying on instruments; **In|stru|men|ten|ta|fel** F control *or* instrument panel
in|stru|men|tie|ren [ɪnstrʊmɛn'ti:rən] *ptp* **instrumentiert** VT *(Mus)* to arrange for instruments; *(für Orchester)* to orchestrate; *(Tech)* to fit out *or* equip with instruments
In|stru|men|tie|rung F -, -en instrumentation
In|suf|fi|zi|enz ['ɪnzʊfitsiɛnts] F -, -en *(Med, geh)* insufficiency
In|su|la|ner [ɪnzu'la:nɐ] M -s, -, **In|su|la|ne|rin** [-ərɪn] F -, -en *(usu hum)* islander
in|su|lar [ɪnzu'la:ɐ] ADJ insular
In|su|lin [ɪnzu'li:n] NT -s, *no pl* insulin
In|su|lin- *in cpds* insulin; **In|su|lin|schock** M insulin *or* hypoglycaemic *(Brit spec) or* hypoglycemic *(US spec)* shock; **In|su|lin|sprit|ze** F insulin injection *or* jab *(inf)*, insulin shot *(US)*; **In|su|lin|stoß** M insulin boost
In|sze|na|tor [ɪnstse'na:to:ɐ] M -s, **Inszenatoren**, **In|sze|na|to|rin** [-'to:rɪn] F -, -nen *(Theat)* director; *(fig)* stage manager
in|sze|na|to|risch [ɪnstsena'to:rɪʃ] ADJ directing *attr*, directorial; *Anforderungen* directorial; **eine ~e Glanzleistung** a brilliant piece of directing *or (fig)* stage management
in|sze|nie|ren [ɪnstse'ni:rən] *ptp* **inszeniert** VT **a** *(Theat)* to direct; *(Rad, TV)* to produce **b**

(fig) to stage-manage; **einen Streit ~** to start an argument; **ein Theater ~** to kick up a fuss *(inf)*

In|sze|nie|rung F -, -en production; **ein Stück in neuer ~ aufführen** to put on a new production of a play

in|takt [ɪn'takt] ADJ intact; **ich bin nach meiner Grippe noch nicht ganz ~** *(inf)* I'm still feeling a bit fragile after my flu

In|takt|heit F -, *no pl* intactness

In|tar|sia [ɪn'tarzia] F -, **Intarsien** [-ziən], **In|tar|sie** [ɪn'tarziə] F -, -n *usu pl* marquetry *no pl*, inlay, inlaid work *no pl*

in|te|ger [ɪn'te:gɐ] *(geh)* ADJ **~ sein** to be full of integrity; **ein integrer Mensch** a person of integrity ADV **sich ~ verhalten** to behave with integrity

in|teg|ral [ɪnte'gra:l] ADJ *attr* integral

In|teg|ral [ɪnte'gra:l] NT -s, -e integral

In|teg|ral-: **In|teg|ral|helm** M full-face helmet; **In|teg|ral|rech|nung** F integral calculus

In|teg|ra|ti|on [ɪntegra'tsio:n] F -, -en integration *(auch Comput)*

In|teg|ra|ti|ons-: **In|teg|ra|ti|ons|fi|gur** F unifying figure; **In|teg|ra|ti|ons|klas|se** F *(Sch)* integrated class; **In|teg|ra|ti|ons|kraft** F unifying force

> **INTEGRATIONSKLASSEN**
>
> **Integrationsklassen** are classes designed to enable children and young people with physical disabilities and learning difficulties to attend mainstream schools.

in|teg|ra|tiv [ɪntegra'ti:f] ADJ *Erziehung, Zusammenarbeit etc* integrated; *Weltanschauung etc* holistic

in|teg|rier|bar ADJ integrable *(auch Math)*

in|teg|rie|ren [ɪnte'gri:rən] *ptp* **integriert** VT to integrate *(auch Math)*

in|teg|riert [ɪnte'gri:ɐt] ADJ integrated *(in* into); *Sicherheitsvorrichtung auch* integral, in-built; **~e Schaltung** integrated circuit; **~e Gesamtschule** ≈ comprehensive (school) *(Brit)*, ≈ high school *(US)*

In|teg|rie|rung F -, -en integration *no pl*

In|teg|ri|tät [ɪntegri'tɛ:t] F -, *no pl (geh)* integrity

In|tel|lekt [ɪnte'lɛkt] M -(e)s, *no pl* intellect

In|tel|lek|tu|a|lis|mus [ɪntɛlɛktua'lɪsmʊs] M -, *no pl* intellectualism

in|tel|lek|tu|ell [ɪntɛlɛk'tuɛl] ADJ intellectual

In|tel|lek|tu|el|le(r) [ɪntɛlɛk'tuɛlə] MF *decl as adj* intellectual

In|tel|lel|le(r) [ɪnte'lɛlə] MF *decl as adj (hum inf)* intellectual, egghead *(inf)*

in|tel|li|gent [ɪnteli'gɛnt] ADJ intelligent; *Chipkarte, Waffe etc* smart ADV cleverly, ingeniously; *sich verhalten* intelligently; **~ ausgedacht** well thought out

In|tel|li|genz [ɪnteli'gɛnts] F -, -en intelligence; *(= Personengruppe)* intelligentsia *pl*; **Elefanten haben eine hoch entwickelte ~** elephants are highly intelligent; **künstliche ~** artificial intelligence

In|tel|li|genz-: **In|tel|li|genz|bes|tie** F *(pej inf)* egghead *(inf)*; **In|tel|li|genz|grad** M intelligence level, level of intelligence

In|tel|li|gen|zi|ja [ɪnteli'gɛntsija] F -, *no pl* intelligentsia *pl*

In|tel|li|genz|leis|tung F display of intelligence; **eine ~ von jdm** a display of sb's intelligence; **das war wieder eine ~ von dir!** *(iro)* that was intelligent *or* bright of you *(iro)*

In|tel|li|genz|ler [ɪnteli'gɛntslɐ] M -s, -, **In|tel|li|genz|le|rin** [-ərɪn] F -, -nen *(inf)* egghead *(inf)*

In|tel|li|genz-: **In|tel|li|genz|quo|ti|ent** M intelligence quotient, IQ; **In|tel|li|genz|test** M intelligence test; **einen ~ mit jdm machen** to give sb an intelligence test, to test sb's IQ

In|ten|dant [ɪntɛn'dant] M -en, -en, **In|ten|dan|tin** [-'dantɪn] F -, -nen director; *(Theat)* theatre *(Brit) or* theater *(US)* manager

In|ten|dan|tur [ɪntɛndan'tu:ɐ] F -, -en *(= Amtszeit)* period of directorship; *(= Amtssitz)* director's office; *(Theat)* theatre *(Brit) or* theater *(US)* manager's office; **während seiner ~** while he was director/theatre *(Brit) or* theater *(US)* manager, during his directorship

In|ten|danz [ɪntɛn'dants] F -, -en *(= Amt)* directorship; *(= Büro)* director's office; *(Theat)* theatre *(Brit) or* theater *(US)* manager's office

in|ten|die|ren [ɪntɛn'di:rən] *ptp* **intendiert** VT *(geh)* to intend; **eine Beleidigung hatte ich damit nicht intendiert** I didn't intend that as an insult

In|ten|si|tät [ɪntɛnzi'tɛ:t] F -, *(rare)* -en intensity

in|ten|siv [ɪntɛn'zi:f] ADJ *Arbeit, Forschung, Diskussion, Kontakte, Landwirtschaft* intensive; *Beziehungen* deep, very close; *Farbe, Gefühl, Geschmack* intense; *Geruch* intense, powerful, strong; *Blick* intent, intense ADV **jdn ~ beobachten** to watch sb intently; *(Polizei)* to put sb under close surveillance; **sich ~ bemühen** to try hard; **~ bestrebt sein** to make an intense effort; **~ duftend** with an intense *or* powerful scent; **~ nach etw schmecken** to taste strongly of sth

in|ten|si|vie|ren [ɪntɛnzi'vi:rən] *ptp* **intensiviert** VT to intensify

In|ten|si|vie|rung F -, -en intensification

In|ten|siv-: **In|ten|siv|kurs** M intensive course; **In|ten|siv|me|di|zin** F intensive care (medicine); **In|ten|siv|sta|ti|on** F intensive care unit, ICU, critical care unit *(US)*, CCU *(US)*

In|ten|ti|on [ɪntɛn'tsio:n] F -, -en intention, intent

in|ten|ti|o|nal [ɪntɛntsio'na:l] ADJ *(auch Philos)* intentional

in|ter-, In|ter- *in cpds* inter-; **in|ter|agie|ren** *ptp* **interagiert** VI to interact; **In|ter|ak|ti|on** F interaction; **in|ter|ak|tiv** ADJ interactive; **eine ~e Anwendung** *(Comput)* an interactive application; **~e Tafel** whiteboard ADV interactively; **~ gestaltet** designed for interactive use

In|ter|ci|ty [ɪntɐ'sɪti] M -(s), -s intercity (train)

In|ter|ci|ty-: **In|ter|ci|ty|ex|press** M high-speed intercity (train); **In|ter|ci|ty|ver|kehr** M *(Rail)* intercity traffic, express traffic; **In|ter|ci|ty|zug** M intercity (train)

In|ter-: **In|ter|den|tal|bürs|te** F *(zur Zahnpflege)* interdental *or* ID brush; **in|ter|de|pen|dent** [ɪntɐdepɛn'dɛnt] ADJ interdependent; **In|ter|de|pen|denz** F interdependence; **in|ter|dis|zip|li|när** [ɪntɐdɪstsipli'nɛ:ɐ] ADJ interdisciplinary ADV **diese Probleme müssen ~ gelöst werden** interdisciplinary solutions are required here; **~ ausgerichtet/angelegt/zusammengesetzt** interdisciplinary

in|te|res|sant [ɪntərɛ'sant] ADJ interesting; **zu diesem Preis ist das nicht ~ für uns** *(Comm)* we are not interested at that price; **das ist ja ~!** (that's) very interesting!; **sich ~ machen** to attract attention (to oneself); **sich bei jdm ~ machen** to attract sb's attention ADV **sich ~ anhören, ~ klingen** to sound interesting; **sich ~ lesen** to be interesting; **diese Autorin schreibt sehr ~** this author's writing is very interesting; **~ erzählen** to tell interesting stories; **~ erzählen können** to be a good storyteller

in|te|res|san|ter|wei|se [ɪntərɛ'santɐ'vaizə] ADV interestingly enough

In|te|res|se [ɪntə'rɛsə] ✪ 28.1, 29.2, 47.1 NT -s, -n interest; **~ an jdm/etw** *or* **für jdn/etw haben** to be interested in sb/sth; **aus ~** out of interest, for interest; **mit (großem) ~** with (great) interest; **im ~** +*gen* in the interests of; **es liegt in Ihrem eigenen ~** it's in your own interest(s); **die ~n eines Staates wahrnehmen** to look after the interests of a state; **sein ~ gilt …** his interest is *or* lies in …, he's interested in …; **das ist für uns nicht von ~** that's of no interest to us, we're not interested in that; **er tat es** *or* **handelte in meinem ~** he did it for my good *or* in my interest

In|te|res|se-: **in|te|res|se|hal|ber** ADV for *or* out of interest; **in|te|res|se|los** ADJ indifferent; **In|te|res|se|lo|sig|keit** F -, *no pl* indifference

In|te|res|sen-: **In|te|res|sen|be|reich** M, **In|te|res|sen|ge|biet** NT field of interest; **das gehört nicht zu meinem ~** that isn't one of my interests, that's outside my field of interests; **In|te|res|sen|ge|gen|satz** M clash of interests; **In|te|res|sen|ge|mein|schaft** F **a** community of interests; *(= Menschen)* group of people sharing interests **b** *(Econ)* syndicate; **In|te|res|sen|grup|pe** F interest group; *(= Lobby)* lobby; **In|te|res|sen|kol|li|si|on** F conflict of interests; **In|te|res|sen|schwer|punkt** M focus of interest; **In|te|res|sen|sphä|re** F *(Pol)* sphere of influence

In|te|res|sent [ɪntərɛ'sɛnt] M -en, -en, **In|te|res|sen|tin** [-'sɛntɪn] F -, -nen interested person *or* party *(form)*; *(= Bewerber auch)* applicant; *(Comm: = Kauflustiger auch)* prospective customer; **~en werden gebeten …** those interested are requested …; **es haben sich mehrere ~en gemeldet** several people have shown interest

In|te|res|sen|ten|kreis M market

In|te|res|sen-: **In|te|res|sen|ver|band** M syndicate; *(= Lobby)* lobby; **In|te|res|sen|ver|tre|tung** F representation of interests; *(= Personen)* group representing one's interests

in|te|res|sie|ren [ɪntərɛ'si:rən] *ptp* **interessiert** VT to interest *(für, an +dat* in); **es würde mich doch sehr ~, was du damit machen willst** it would interest me very much to know *or* I'd be very interested to know what you want to do with it; **das interessiert mich (gar) nicht!** I'm not (the least *or* slightest bit) interested; **ich liege hier im Sterben, aber das interessiert dich gar nicht** here I am on my deathbed, but you don't care; **das hat dich nicht zu ~!** that's none of your business!, don't be so nosey! *(inf)* VR to be interested *(für* in); *(= mit Interesse verfolgen auch)* to take an interest *(für* in); **er begann schon mit acht Jahren, sich für Musik zu ~** he started to be interested in music when he was eight, he started to take *or* show an interest in music when he was eight

in|te|res|siert [ɪntərɛ'si:ɐt] ADJ interested *(an +dat* in); **vielseitig ~ sein** to have a wide range of interests; **politisch ~** interested in politics; **ein ~er Mensch** a person with a number of interests ADV with interest; **sich ~ zeigen** to act interested; **sich an etw** *(dat)* **~ zeigen** to show an interest in sth; **~ zuhören** *etc* to listen *etc* with interest

In|ter|face ['ɪntɐfe:s] NT -, -s *(Comput)* interface

In|ter|fe|renz [ɪntɐfe'rɛnts] F -, -en *(Phys, Ling)* interference *no pl*

In|ter|fe|ron [ɪntɐfe'ro:n] NT -s, -e interferon

In|ter|ho|tel ['ɪntɐ-] NT *(DDR)* international hotel

In|te|ri|eur [ɛ̃te'riø:ɐ] NT -s, -s *or* -e *(geh)* interior

In|te|rim ['ɪnterɪm] NT -s, -s interim

In|te|rims- *in cpds* interim; **In|te|rims|ab|kom|men** NT interim agreement; **In|te|rims|lö|sung** F interim *or* stopgap solution; **In|te|rims|re|gie|rung** F caretaker *or* provisional government; **In|te|rims|schein** M *(Fin)* scrip

In|ter|jek|ti|on [ɪntɐjɛk'tsio:n] F -, -en interjection

In|ter-: **in|ter|kon|fes|si|o|nell** [ɪntɐkɔnfɛsio'nɛl] ADJ interdenominational; **in|ter|kon|ti|nen|tal** [ɪntɐkɔntinɛn'ta:l] ADJ intercontinental; **In|ter|kon|ti|nen|tal|ra|ke|te** [ɪntɐkɔntinɛn'ta:l-] F intercontinental missile; **in|ter|kul|tu|rell** ADJ intercultural, between (different) cultures; **In|ter|leu|kin** [ɪntɐlɔy'ki:n] NT -s, -e interleukin; **in|ter|li|ne|ar** [ɪntɐline'a:ɐ] ADJ interlinear

In|ter|mez|zo [ɪntɐ'mɛtso] NT -s, -s *or* **Intermezzi** [-tsi] *(Mus)* intermezzo; *(fig auch)* interlude; *(ärgerlich)* contretemps *sing*

in|ter|mit|tie|rend [ɪntɐmɪ'ti:rənt] ADJ intermittent

in|tern [ɪn'tɛrn] ADJ internal; **~er Schüler** boarder; **diese Maßnahmen müssen vorläufig ~ bleiben** for the time being these measures must be kept private; **die ~en Schwierigkeiten des Landes** the country's internal *or* domestic difficulties ADV internally

-in|tern ADJ *suf* **schulinterne/ausschussinterne Angelegenheiten** internal school/committee matters; **etw schulintern regeln** to settle sth internally within the school/schools

in|ter|na|li|sie|ren [ɪntɐrnali'zi:rən] *ptp* **internalisiert** VT *(spec)* to internalize

In|ter|nat [ɪntɐ'na:t] NT **-(e)s, -e** boarding school

in|ter|na|ti|o|nal [ɪntɐnatsio'na:l] ADJ international ADV internationally; **~ von Interesse** of international interest; **~ operierende Organisationen** international organizations; **~ kochen** to cook foreign dishes

In|ter|na|ti|o|na|le [ɪntɐnatsio'na:lə] F **-, -n** Internationale

in|ter|na|ti|o|na|li|sie|ren [ɪntɐnatsionali'zi:rən] *ptp* **internationalisiert** VT to internationalize

In|ter|na|ti|o|na|lis|mus [ɪntɐnatsiona'lɪsmʊs] M **-**, *no pl* internationalism

In|ter|nats|schu|le F boarding school

In|ter|nats|schü|ler(in) M(F) boarder, boarding (school) pupil

In|ter|net ['ɪntɐnɛt] NT **-**, *no pl (Comput)* Internet; **Anschluss ans ~ haben** to be connected to the Internet; **im ~ surfen** to surf the Internet

In|ter|net-: **In|ter|net|adres|se** F Internet address; **In|ter|net|an|schluss** M Internet connection *or* access *or* account; **In|ter|net|auf|tritt** M web presence; *(= Homepage)* website; **In|ter|net|auk|ti|on** F online auction; **in|ter|net|ba|siert** ADJ Internet-based; **~e Anwendung** Internet-based application; **In|ter|net|be|nut|zer(in)** M(F) Internet user; **In|ter|net|brow|ser** M Internet browser; **In|ter|net|ca|fé** NT Internet café; **In|ter|net|dienst** M Internet service; **In|ter|net|dienst|an|bie|ter** M Internet service provider, ISP; **In|ter|net-Ein|zel|händ|ler(in)** M(F) e-tailer; **in|ter|net|fä|hig** ADJ *Kabelnetz, Gerät* Internet-enabled; **eine Stadt ~ machen** to supply a town/city with a cable network for Internet use; **In|ter|net|han|del** M Internet commerce, e-commerce; **In|ter|net|händ|ler(in)** M(F) online trader *or* dealer; **In|ter|net|kno|ten** M point of presence, pop; **In|ter|net|nut|zer(in)** M(F) Internet user; **In|ter|net|pro|vi|der** M Internet provider; **In|ter|net|sei|te** F Internet site, Web page; **In|ter|net|user(in)** M(F) Internet user; **In|ter|net|ver|bin|dung** F Internet connection; **In|ter|net|zu|gang** M, **In|ter|net|zu|griff** M Internet access

In|tern|ge|spräch NT *(Telec)* internal call

in|ter|nie|ren [ɪntɐ'ni:rən] *ptp* **interniert** VT to intern

In|ter|nier|te(r) [ɪntɐ'ni:ɐtə] MF *decl as adj* internee

In|ter|nie|rung F **-, -en** internment

In|ter|nie|rungs|la|ger NT internment camp

In|ter|nist [ɪntɐ'nɪst] M **-en, -en**, **In|ter|nis|tin** [-'nɪstɪn] F **-, -nen** internist

In|tern|spei|cher [ɪn'tɛrn-] M *(Comput)* memory

In|ter|num [ɪn'tɛrnʊm] NT **-s, Interna** [-na] *usu pl (geh)* internal matter; *(geheim)* restricted information

In|ter|ope|ra|bi|li|tät [ˌɪntɐopərabili'tɛ:t] F **-**, *no pl (Comput)* interoperability

in|ter|par|la|men|ta|risch [ɪntɐparlamɛn'ta:rɪʃ] ADJ interparliamentary

In|ter|pel|la|ti|on [ɪntɐpɛla'tsio:n] F **-, -en** (parliamentary) question

in|ter|pel|lie|ren [ɪntɐpɛ'li:rən] *ptp* **interpelliert** VI to ask a (parliamentary) question

in|ter|pla|ne|tar [ɪntɐplane'ta:ɐ], **in|ter|pla|ne|ta|risch** [ɪntɐplane'ta:rɪʃ] ADJ interplanetary *no adv*

In|ter|pol ['ɪntɐpo:l] F **-** Interpol

In|ter|po|la|ti|on [ɪntɐpola'tsio:n] F **-, -en** interpolation

in|ter|po|lie|ren [ɪntɐpo'li:rən] *ptp* **interpoliert** VT to interpolate

In|ter|pret [ɪntɐ'pre:t] M **-en, -en**, **In|ter|pre|tin** [-'pre:tɪn] F **-, -nen** interpreter *(of music, art etc)*; **Lieder verschiedener ~en** songs by various singers

In|ter|pre|ta|ti|on [ɪntɐpreta'tsio:n] F **-, -en** interpretation; *(eines Liedes auch)* version

In|ter|pre|ter [ɪn'tø:ɐprete, ɪn'tœr-] M **-s, -** *(Comput)* interpreter

in|ter|pre|tie|ren [ɪntɐpre'ti:rən] *ptp* **interpretiert** VT to interpret; **etw falsch ~** to misinterpret sth

In|ter|pre|tin [-'pre:tɪn] F → **Interpret**

in|ter|punk|tie|ren [ɪntɐpʊŋk'ti:rən] *ptp* **interpunktiert** VT to punctuate

In|ter|punk|ti|on F punctuation

In|ter|punk|ti|ons-: **In|ter|punk|ti|ons|re|gel** F rule of punctuation, punctuation rule; **In|ter|punk|ti|ons|zei|chen** NT punctuation mark

In|ter|rail|kar|te ['ɪntɐre:l-] F inter-rail ticket

In|ter|re|gio [ɪntɐ're:gio] M **-s, -s**, **In|ter|re|gio|zug** M *fast train running at regular intervals*

In|ter|reg|num [ɪntɐ'rɛgnʊm] NT **-s, Interregnen** *or* **Interregna** [-nən, -na] interregnum

in|ter|ro|ga|tiv [ɪntɐroga'ti:f, 'ɪntɐ-] ADJ interrogative

In|ter|ro|ga|tiv-: **In|ter|ro|ga|tiv|pro|no|men** [ɪntɐroga'ti:f-] NT interrogative pronoun; **In|ter|ro|ga|tiv|satz** [ɪntɐroga'ti:f-] M interrogative clause

In|ter|rupt [ɪntɐ'rʊpt] M **-s, -s** *(Comput)* interrupt

In|ter|rup|tus [ɪntɐ'rʊptʊs] M **-**, *no pl (inf)* coitus interruptus

In|ter|shop ['ɪntɐʃɔp] M **-s, -s** *(DDR)* international shop

in|ter|stel|lar [ɪntɐstɛ'la:ɐ] ADJ interstellar

In|ter|vall [ɪntɐ'val] NT **-s, -e** interval *(auch Mus)*; **sich in längeren ~en sehen** to see each other at infrequent intervals

In|ter|vall-: **In|ter|vall|schal|tung** F interval switch; **In|ter|vall|trai|ning** NT interval training

in|ter|ve|nie|ren [ɪntɐve'ni:rən] *ptp* **interveniert** VI to intervene

In|ter|ven|ti|on [ɪntɐvɛn'tsio:n] F **-, -en** intervention

In|ter|view ['ɪntɐvju:, ɪntɐ'vju:] NT **-s, -s** interview

in|ter|vie|wen [ɪntɐ'vju:ən, 'ɪntɐ-] *ptp* **interviewt** VT to interview *(jdn zu etw* sb on *or* about sth)

In|ter|view|er [ɪntɐ'vju:ɐ, 'ɪntɐ-] M **-s, -**, **In|ter|view|e|rin** [-ərɪn] F **-, -nen** interviewer

In|ter|vi|si|on [ɪntɐvi'zio:n] F Intervision

In|ter|zo|nen- *in cpds (Hist)* interzonal; **In|ter|zo|nen|zug** [ɪntɐ'tso:nən-] M *(Hist) train for traffic between West Germany and the GDR*

In|thro|ni|sa|ti|on [ɪntroniza'tsio:n] F **-, -en** enthronement

in|thro|ni|sie|ren [ɪntroni'zi:rən] *ptp* **inthronisiert** VT to enthrone

In|ti|fa|da [ɪnti'fa:da] F **-**, *no pl* intifada

in|tim [ɪn'ti:m] ADJ intimate; **ein ~er Kenner von etw sein** to have an intimate knowledge of sth; **etw im ~en Kreis feiern** to celebrate sth with one's closest *or* most intimate friends; **meine ~en Angelegenheiten** my intimate personal affairs

In|tim-: **In|tim|be|reich** M **a** *(Anat)* genital area **b** *(fig)* = **Intimsphäre**; **In|tim|feind(in)** M(F) favourite *(Brit) or* favorite *(US)* enemy; **In|tim|hy|gi|e|ne** F personal hygiene

In|ti|mi|tät [ɪntimi'tɛ:t] F **-, -en** intimacy; **jdm allerlei ~en erzählen** to tell sb all kinds of intimate details *or* intimacies; **bitte keine ~en!** please don't go into intimate details; **zwischen den beiden kam es zu ~en** they became intimate with each other; **~en austauschen** to kiss and pet; **bitte keine ~en in meinem Haus!** I'll have none of that sort of thing going on in my house!; **er hat sich einige ~en erlaubt** he became rather familiar

In|tim-: **In|tim|ken|ner(in)** M(F) *(form)* expert *(von, +gen* on *or* in), authority *(von, +gen* on), connoisseur *(von, +gen* of); **er ist ein ~ von ...** he has an intimate knowledge of ...; **In|tim|kon|takt** M *(form)* intimate contact; **In|tim|le|ben** NT sex *or* love life; **In|tim|lo|ti|on** F vaginal lotion; **In|tim|part|ner(in)** M(F) *(form)* sexual partner; **In|tim|pfle|ge** F intimate hygiene; *(von Frauen meist)* feminine hygiene; **In|tim|schmuck** M body jewellery *(Brit) or* jewelry *(US)*; **In|tim|sphä|re** F private life; **jds ~ verletzen** to invade sb's privacy; **diese Frage greift in die ~ ein** that question is an invasion of my/your *etc* privacy; **In|tim|spray** NT intimate deodorant spray

In|ti|mus ['ɪntimʊs] M **-, Intimi** [-mi] *(hum)* confidant

In|tim|ver|kehr M intimacy; **~ mit jdm haben** to be intimate with sb

in|to|le|rant [ɪntole'rant, 'ɪn-] ADJ intolerant *(einer Sache gegenüber* of sth, *jdm gegenüber* of *or* towards sb) ADV intolerantly; **in solchen Dingen zeigt er sich absolut ~** he is completely intolerant about such things

In|to|le|ranz [ɪntole'rants, 'ɪn-] F intolerance

In|to|na|ti|on [ɪntona'tsio:n] F **-, -en** intonation

in|to|nie|ren [ɪnto'ni:rən] *ptp* **intoniert** VT **a einen Satz falsch/anders ~** to give a sentence the wrong/a different intonation **b** *(Mus) Melodie* to sing; *(Kapelle)* to play; *Ton* to give; **wer kann das Lied ~?** who can start the song off?, who can show us how the song goes?

In|tra|net ['ɪntranɛt] NT **-s, -s** *(Comput)* Intranet

in|tran|si|gent [ɪntranzi'gɛnt] ADJ *(liter)* intransigent

in|tran|si|tiv ADJ intransitive ADV intransitively

in|tra|ve|nös [ɪntrave'nø:s] ADJ intravenous ADV intravenously

in|tri|gant [ɪntri'gant] ADJ *(geh)* scheming, designing

In|tri|gant [ɪntri'gant] M **-en, -en**, **In|tri|gan|tin** [-'gantɪn] F **-, -nen** schemer, intriguer

In|tri|ge [ɪn'tri:gə] F **-, -n** intrigue, conspiracy, scheme

In|tri|gen-: **In|tri|gen|spiel** NT intriguing, plotting; **In|tri|gen|wirt|schaft** F, *no pl* hive of intrigue

in|tri|gie|ren [ɪntri'gi:rən] *ptp* **intrigiert** VI to intrigue, to scheme, to plot

In|tro|i|tus [ɪn'tro:itʊs] M **-, -** *(= Gesang)* introit; *(Anat)* introitus

in|tro|ver|tiert [ɪntrovɛr'ti:ɐt] ADJ introverted

In|tro|ver|tiert|heit F **-**, *no pl* introversion

in|tu|bie|ren [ɪntu'bi:rən] *ptp* **intubiert** VT *(Med)* to intubate

In|tu|i|ti|on [ɪntui'tsio:n] F **-, -en** intuition

in|tu|i|tiv [ɪntui'ti:f] ADJ intuitive ADV intuitively

in|tus ['ɪntʊs] ADJ *(inf)* **etw ~ haben** *(= wissen)* to get *or* have got *(Brit)* sth into one's head *(inf)*; *Essen, Alkohol* to have sth down *(inf) or* inside one *(inf)*; **er hat schon etwas** *or* **einiges ~** he's had a few

in|va|lid [ɪnva'li:t], **in|va|li|de** [ɪnva'li:də] ADJ *(rare)* disabled, invalid *attr*

In|va|li|de [ɪnva'li:də] M **-n, -n**, **In|va|li|din** [-'li:dɪn] F **-, -nen** disabled person, invalid; **er ist ~** he's disabled, he's an invalid; **der Krieg hat ihn zum ~n gemacht** he was disabled in the war; **ich mache dich zum ~n!** *(inf)* I'll cripple you! *(Brit inf)*, I'll kill you! *(inf)*

In|va|li|den-: **In|va|li|den|heim** NT home for disabled persons *or* people, home for the disabled; **In|va|li|den|ren|te** F disability pension;

In|va|li|den|ver|si|che|rung F disability insurance

In|va|li|din [-'li:dɪn] F → **Invalide**

In|va|li|di|tät [ɪnvalidi'tɛ:t] F -, *no pl* disability

in|va|ri|a|bel [ɪnva'ria:bl, 'ɪn-] ADJ invariable

in|va|ri|ant [ɪnva'riant, 'ɪn-] ADJ invariant

In|va|ri|an|te F -, -n *(Math)* invariant, invariable

In|va|ri|anz [ɪnva'rianz, 'ɪn-] F -, -en invariance

In|va|si|on [ɪnva:'zio:n] F -, -en *(lit, fig)* invasion

In|va|sor [ɪn'va:zo:ɐ] M -s, **Invasoren**, **In|va|so|rin** [-'zo:rɪn] F -, -nen *usu pl* invader

In|vek|ti|ve [ɪnvɛk'ti:və] F -, -n *(geh)* invective *no pl*

In|ven|tar [ɪnvɛn'ta:ɐ] NT -s, -e **a** *(= Verzeichnis)* inventory; *(Comm)* assets and liabilities *pl*; **das ~ aufnehmen** to do the inventory; **etw ins ~ aufnehmen** to put sth on the inventory **b** *(= Einrichtung)* fittings *pl (Brit)*, equipment; *(= Maschinen)* equipment *no pl*, plant *no pl*; **lebendes ~** livestock; **totes ~** fixtures and fittings *pl (Brit)*, fixtures and equipment *(US)*; **er gehört schon zum ~** *(fig)* he's part of the furniture

In|ven|ta|ri|sa|ti|on [ɪnvɛntariza'tsio:n] F -, -en compilation of an inventory

in|ven|ta|ri|sie|ren [ɪnvɛntari'zi:rən] *ptp* **inventarisiert** VT to take *or* make an inventory of

In|ven|ta|ri|sie|rung F -, -en compilation of an inventory

In|ven|tur [ɪnvɛn'tu:ɐ] F -, -en stocktaking; **~ machen** to stocktake

In|ver|si|on [ɪnvɛr'zio:n] F -, -en *(Gram)* inversion

In|ver|si|ons-: **In|ver|si|ons|la|ge** F *(Met)* temperature inversion, inverted atmospheric conditions *pl*; **In|ver|si|ons|tem|pe|ra|tur** F temperature inversion; **In|ver|si|ons|wet|ter|la|ge** F *(Met)* inverted atmospheric conditions *pl*, temperature inversion

in|ver|tiert [ɪnvɛr'ti:ɐt] ADJ inverted; **~e Darstellung** *(Comput)* reverse image

in|ves|tie|ren [ɪnvɛs'ti:rən] *ptp* **investiert** VT *(Comm)* to invest; *(fig auch)* to put; **Geld in seine Freundin ~** *(inf)* to invest money in one's girlfriend *(hum)*; **Gefühle in jdn ~** *(inf)* to become (emotionally) involved with sb VI to invest

In|ves|tie|rung F -, -en, **In|ves|ti|ti|on** [ɪnvɛsti'tsio:n] F -, -en investment

In|ves|ti|ti|ons- *in cpds* investment; **In|ves|ti|ti|ons|an|reiz** M investment incentive; **In|ves|ti|ti|ons|gut** NT *usu pl* item of capital expenditure; **In|ves|ti|ti|ons|hil|fe** F investment aid; **In|ves|ti|ti|ons|kos|ten** PL investment costs *pl*, cost *(sing)* of investment

In|ves|ti|tur [ɪnvɛsti'tu:ɐ] F -, -en *(Eccl)* investiture

in|ves|tiv [ɪnvɛs'ti:f] ADJ investment *attr*

In|vest|ment [ɪn'vɛstmənt] NT -s, -s investment

In|vest|ment-: **In|vest|ment|ban|ker(in)** M(F) investment banker; **In|vest|ment|ban|king** NT -s, *no pl* investment banking; **In|vest|ment|fonds** M investment fund; **In|vest|ment|ge|sell|schaft** F investment trust; **In|vest|ment|pa|pier** NT, **In|vest|ment|zer|ti|fi|kat** NT investment fund certificate; **In|vest|ment|spa|ren** NT saving through an investment trust

In|ves|tor [ɪn'vɛsto:ɐ] M -s, -en [ɪnvɛs'to:rən], **In|ves|to|rin** [ɪnvɛs'to:rɪn] -, -nen *(Econ)* investor

In-vi|tro-Fer|ti|li|sa|ti|on [ɪn'vi:trofɛrtilizatsio:n] F -, -en in vitro fertilization

in|wärts ['ɪnvɛrts] ADV = **einwärts**

in|wen|dig ['ɪnvɛndɪç] ADJ *(rare)* inside ADV **a** *(inf)* **jdn/etw in- und auswendig kennen** to know sb/sth inside out **b** *(= innen)* inside; **die Pflaume war ~ schlecht** the plum was rotten inside

in|wie|fern [ɪnvi'fɛrn], **in|wie|weit** [ɪnvi'vait] ADV *(im Satz)* to what extent, how far; *(alleinstehend)* in what way

In|zah|lung|nah|me [ɪn'tsa:lʊŋna:mə] F -, -n *(Comm)* **die ~ von etw** the acceptance of sth in part payment *or* as a trade-in; **bei ~ des alten Wagens** when the old car is traded in *or* is taken as a trade-in

In|zest ['ɪntsɛst] M -(e)s, -e incest *no pl*

in|zes|tu|ös [ɪntsɛstu'ø:s] ADJ incestuous ADV **er lebte jahrelang ~ mit seiner Tochter** he lived for years in an incestuous relationship with his daughter

In|zucht F inbreeding

inzw. *abbr von* **inzwischen**

in|zwi|schen [ɪn'tsvɪʃn] ADV (in the) meantime, meanwhile; **ich gehe ~ zur Bank** I'll go to the bank in the meantime; **sie hatte ~ davon erfahren** meanwhile *or* in the meantime she'd learned of this; **er hat sich ~ verändert** he's changed since (then); **er ist ~ 18 geworden** he's now 18

IOK [i:lo:'ka:] NT -s *abbr von* **Internationales Olympisches Komitee** IOC

Ion [io:n, 'i:ɔn] NT -s, -en ['io:nən] ion

Io|nen|(aus)|tau|scher [-(laus)tauʃɐ] M -s, - ion exchanger

Io|ni|sa|ti|on [ioniza'tsio:n] F -, -en ionization

io|nisch ['io:nɪʃ] ADJ *(Archit, Poet)* ionic; *(Mus)* ionian; **Ionisches Meer** Ionian Sea; **die Ionischen Inseln** the Ionian Islands

io|ni|sie|ren [ioni'zi:rən] *ptp* **ionisiert** VT to ionize

Io|no|sphä|re [iono'sfɛ:rə] F ionosphere

IP-Adresse [i'pe:-] F *(Comput, Internet)* IP address

I-Punkt ['i:-] M dot on the i; **~e setzen** *or* **machen** to dot one's *or* the i's, to put the dots on the i's

IQ [i:'ku:] M -s, -s *abbr von* **Intelligenzquotient** IQ

IR [i:'lɛr] M -(s), -s *abbr (Rail) von* **Interregiozug** ≈ fast train running at regular intervals

i. R. [i:'lɛr] *abbr von* **im Ruhestand** retd

IRA [i:lɛr'la:] *abbr* -, *no pl von* **Irisch-Republikanische Armee** IRA

Irak [i'ra:k, 'i:rak] M -s **(der)** ~ Iraq

Ira|ker [i'ra:kɐ] M -s, -, **Ira|ke|rin** [-ərɪn] F -, -nen Iraqi

ira|kisch [i'ra:kɪʃ] ADJ Iraqi

Iran [i'ra:n] M -s **(der)** ~ Iran

Ira|ner [i'ra:nɐ] M -s, -, **Ira|ne|rin** [-ərɪn] F -, -nen Iranian

ira|nisch [i'ra:nɪʃ] ADJ Iranian

IRC *abbr von* **Internet Relay Chat** IRC

ir|den ['ɪrdn] ADJ earthenware, earthen; **~e Waren** earthenware

ir|disch ['ɪrdɪʃ] ADJ earthly *no adv*; **den Weg alles Irdischen gehen** to go the way of all flesh

Ire ['i:rə] M -n, -n Irishman; Irish boy; **die ~n** the Irish; **er ist ~** he is Irish → *auch* **Irin**

ir|gend ['ɪrgnt] ADV at all; **wenn ~ möglich, wenn es ~ geht** if it's at all possible; **was ich ~ kann ...** whatever I can ...; **wer (es) ~ kann, wer ~ es kann** whoever can; **so sanft wie ~ möglich** as gently as possible, as gently as I/you *etc* possibly can; **so lange ich ~ kann** as long as I possibly can; **wo es ~ geht, wo ~ es geht** where it's at all possible, wherever (it's) possible *mit indef pron* **~ so ein Tier** some animal; **ein Fuchs oder ~ so ein Tier** a fox or some such animal → **irgendetwas, irgendjemand**

ir|gend|ein ['ɪrgnt'lain] INDEF PRON some; *(fragend, verneinend, bedingend)* any; **er hat so ~ Schimpfwort verwendet** he used some swearword or other; **ich will nicht ~ Buch** I don't want just any (old *(inf)*) book; **haben Sie noch ~en Wunsch?** is there anything else you would like?; **das kann ~ anderer machen** somebody *or* someone else can do it

ir|gend|ei|ne(r, s) ['ɪrgnt'lainə] INDEF PRON *(nominal) (bei Personen)* somebody, someone; *(bei Dingen)* something; *(fragend, verneinend, bedingend)* anybody, anyone; anything; **welchen wollen Sie? – ~n** which one do you want? – any one *or* any old one *(inf)*

ir|gend|ein|mal ['ɪrgntlain'ma:l] ADV some time or other, sometime; *(fragend, bedingend)* ever

ir|gend|et|was ['ɪrgnt'lɛtvas] INDEF PRON something; *(fragend, verneinend, bedingend)* anything; **was zieh ich an? – ~** what shall I wear? – anything *or* any old thing *(inf)*

ir|gend|je|mand ['ɪrgnt'je:mant] INDEF PRON somebody; *(fragend, verneinend, bedingend)* anybody; **ich bin nicht ~** I'm not just anybody

ir|gend|wann ['ɪrgnt'van] ADV some time; **~ werde ich wohl kommen** I'll come some time; **~ einmal** some time; *(fragend, bedingend)* ever

ir|gend|was ['ɪrgnt'vas] INDEF PRON *(inf)* something; *(fragend, verneinend, bedingend)* anything; **er murmelte so ~** he murmured something or other; **was soll ich sagen? – ~** what shall I say? – anything *or* any old thing *(inf)*

ir|gend|wel|che(r, s) ['ɪrgnt'vɛlçə] INDEF PRON some; *(fragend, verneinend, bedingend, = jede beliebige)* any; **sind noch ~ Reste da?** is there still something left?, is there anything left?

ir|gend|wer ['ɪrgnt've:ɐ] INDEF PRON *(inf)* somebody; *(fragend, verneinend, bedingend)* anybody; **ich bin nicht ~** I'm not just anybody

ir|gend|wie ['ɪrgnt'vi:] ADV somehow (or other); **ist es ~ möglich?** is it at all possible?; **kannst du dir das ~ vorstellen?** can you possibly imagine it?; **ich hab das ~ schon mal gesehen** I've just got a feeling I've seen it before

ir|gend|wo ['ɪrgnt'vo:] ADV somewhere (or other), someplace *(esp US inf)*; *(fragend, verneinend, bedingend)* anywhere, any place *(esp US inf)*

ir|gend|wo|her ['ɪrgntvo'he:ɐ] ADV from somewhere (or other), from someplace *(esp US inf)*; *(fragend, verneinend, bedingend)* from anywhere or any place *(esp US inf)*

ir|gend|wo|hin ['ɪrgntvo'hɪn] ADV somewhere (or other), someplace *(esp US inf)*; *(fragend, verneinend, bedingend)* anywhere, any place *(esp US inf)*

Iri|di|um [i'ri:diʊm] NT -s, *no pl (abbr* **Ir***)* iridium

Irin ['i:rɪn] F -, -nen Irishwoman; Irish girl; **sie ist ~** she is Irish → *auch* **Ire**

Iris ['i:rɪs] F -, - *or (Opt auch)* **Iriden** [i'ri:dn] iris

irisch ['i:rɪʃ] ADJ Irish; **~-römisches Bad** Turkish bath; **Irische See** Irish Sea

Iris-: **Iris|di|ag|nos|tik** F iridology; **Iris|di|ag|nos|ti|ker(in)** M(F) iridologist

iri|sie|ren [iri'zi:rən] *ptp* **irisiert** VI to iridesce; **~d** iridescent

IRK [i:lɛr'ka:] *abbr* -(s), *no pl von* **Internationales Rotes Kreuz** IRC

Ir|land ['ɪrlant] NT -s Ireland; *(= Republik Irland)* Eire

ir|län|disch ['ɪrlɛndɪʃ] ADJ Irish; **Irländisches Moos** Irish moss

Iro|ke|sen|(haar)|schnitt [iro'ke:zn-] M mohican (haircut) *(Brit)*, mohawk *(US)*

Iro|nie [iro'ni:] F -, *(rare)* -n [-'ni:ən] irony

iro|nisch [i'ro:nɪʃ] ADJ ironic, ironical ADV ironically

iro|ni|sie|ren [ironi'zi:rən] *ptp* **ironisiert** VT to treat ironically

irr [ɪr] ADJ, ADV = **irre**

ir|ra|ti|o|nal [ɪratsio'na:l, 'ɪr-] ADJ irrational *(auch Math)* ADV irrationally

Ir|ra|ti|o|na|lis|mus M irrationalism

Ir|ra|ti|o|na|li|tät [ɪratsionali'tɛ:t, 'ɪr-] F irrationality

ir|re ['ɪrə] ADJ **a** *(= geistesgestört)* mad, crazy, insane; **das macht mich ganz ~** it's driving me mad *or* crazy *or* insane; **jdn für ~ halten** *(inf)* to think sb is mad *or* crazy; **jdn für ~ erklären** *(inf)* to tell sb he/she *etc* is mad *or* crazy; **~s Zeug reden** *(fig)* to say crazy things, to babble away **b** *pred (= verwirrt, unsicher)* muddled, confused **c** *(dated inf) Party, Hut* wild *(inf)*, crazy *(inf)* ADV **a** *(= verrückt)* insanely, in a mad *or* insane way; **wie ~** *(fig inf)* like mad *(inf) or* crazy *(inf)* **b** *(dated inf)* **er war ~ angezogen** he was wearing outrageous *or* wild *(inf)* clothes

c *(dated inf: = sehr)* incredibly *(inf)*; ~ **gut** brilliant *(inf)*; ~ **hübsch** *(sl)* dead *(Brit inf)* or real *(esp US inf)* pretty

Ir|re [ˈɪrə] F -, *no pl* **jdn in die ~ führen** *(lit, fig)* to lead sb astray; **sich in die ~ führen lassen** *(lit, fig)* to be led astray, to be misled

ir|re|al [ˈɪrea:l, ɪreˈa:l] ADJ unreal

Ir|re|a|li|tät [ɪrealiˈtɛ:t, ˈɪr-] F unreality

Ir|re-: **ir|re+füh|ren** VT *sep* to mislead; *(lit auch)* to lead astray; **sich ~ lassen** to be misled, to be led astray; **ir|re|füh|rend** ADJ misleading ADV **sie hat sich ~ ausgedrückt** the way she said it was very misleading; **die Strecke ist ~ ausgeschildert** the signs are very misleading; **Ir|re|füh|rung** F misleading; **durch bewusste ~ der Öffentlichkeit** by deliberately misleading the public; **ir|re+ge|hen** VI *sep irreg aux sein* **a** *(lit geh)* *(= sich verirren)* to go astray, to lose one's way; *(= umherirren)* to wander astray **b** *(fig)* to be mistaken

ir|re|gu|lär [ɪreguˈlɛ:ɐ, ˈɪr-] ADJ *(auch Mil)* irregular

Ir|re|gu|la|ri|tät [ɪregulariˈtɛ:t, ˈɪr-] F -, -en irregularity

ir|re+lei|ten VT *sep* to mislead, to lead astray; **irregeleitete Jugendliche** misguided youth; **~de Informationen** misleading information

ir|re|le|vant [ɪreleˈvant, ˈɪr-] ADJ irrelevant *(für* for, to)

Ir|re|le|vanz [ɪreleˈvants, ˈɪr-] F irrelevance *(für* for, to)

ir|re|li|gi|ös [ɪreliˈgiø:s, ˈɪr-] ADJ irreligious

Ir|re|li|gi|o|si|tät [ɪreligioziˈtɛ:t, ˈɪr-] F irreligion

ir|re+ma|chen VT *sep* to confuse, to muddle

ir|ren [ˈɪrən] ✪ 39.1 VI **a** *(= sich täuschen)* to be mistaken *or* wrong; **Irren ist menschlich** *(Prov)* to err is human *(Prov)* **b** *aux sein (= ziellos umherschweifen)* to wander, to stray, to roam VR to be mistaken *or* wrong; **jeder kann sich mal ~** anyone can make a mistake, everyone makes mistakes; **sich in jdm/etw ~** to be mistaken in *or* about sb/about sth, to be wrong about sb/sth; **wenn ich mich nicht irre ...** if I'm not mistaken ..., unless I'm very much mistaken ...; **ich irre mich nie!** I'm never wrong *or* mistaken!, I never make mistakes!

Ir|ren-: **Ir|ren|an|stalt** F *(dated)* lunatic asylum *(dated)*, loony bin *(inf)*; **Ir|ren|arzt** M, **Ir|ren|ärz|tin** F *(old, pej)* psychiatrist; **Ir|ren|haus** NT *(dated, pej)* lunatic asylum *(dated)*, loony bin *(inf)*; **hier geht es zu wie im ~** *(inf)* this place is an absolute madhouse; **ir|ren|haus|reif** ADJ *(inf)* **~ sein** to be cracking up *(inf)*

ir|re|pa|ra|bel [ɪrepaˈra:bl, ˈɪr-] ADJ irreparable ADV *beschädigen* irreparably; **das Organ/Gewebe ist ~ geschädigt** the organ/tissue has suffered irreversible damage

Ir|re(r) [ˈɪrə] MF *decl as adj* lunatic; *(fig auch)* madman/-woman; **ein armer ~r** *(hum inf)* a poor fool *or* idiot

ir|re+re|den VI *sep* to rave, to rant, to talk dementedly

Ir|re|sein NT insanity; **manisch-depressives ~** manic depression, manic-depressive psychosis

ir|re|ver|si|bel [ɪrevɛrˈzi:bl, ˈɪr-] ADJ *(Phys, Biol)* irreversible

Ir|re|ver|si|bi|li|tät [ɪrevɛrzibiliˈtɛ:t, ˈɪr-] F -, *no pl (Phys, Biol)* irreversibility

ir|re+wer|den VI *sep irreg aux sein* **an jdm/etw ~** *(liter)* to lose (one's) faith in sb/sth

Irr-: **Irr|fahrt** F wandering, odyssey *(liter)*; **nach langer ~** after a long period of wandering *(auch fig)*; **Irr|gang** M *pl* **-gänge** *(lit)* blind alley *(in maze, pyramid)*; *(fig: usu pl)* maze, labyrinth; **die Irrgänge des Gebäudes** the maze *or* labyrinth of corridors in the building; **Irr|gar|ten** M maze, labyrinth; **Irr|glau|be(n)** M *(Rel)* heretical belief, heresy *(auch fig)*; *(= irrige Ansicht)* mistaken belief; **irr|gläu|big** ADJ heretical; **die Irrgläubigen** the heretics

ir|rig [ˈɪrɪç] ADJ incorrect, wrong, false

ir|ri|ger|wei|se [ˈɪrɪgɐˈvaizə] ADV wrongly, incorrectly; **etw ~ glauben** to believe sth mistakenly *or* wrongly

Ir|ri|ta|ti|on [ɪritaˈtsio:n] F -, -en irritation

ir|ri|tie|ren [ɪriˈti:rən] *ptp* **irritiert** VT *(= verwirren)* to confuse, to muddle; *(= ärgern)* to irritate

Irr-: **Irr|läu|fer** M **a** *stray letter, document etc delivered to the wrong address* **b** *(Mil)* stray bullet/grenade *etc*; **Irr|leh|re** F heresy, heretical *or* false doctrine; **Irr|licht** NT jack-o'-lantern, will-o'-the-wisp; **irr|lich|tern** [ˈɪrlɪçtɐn] VI *insep* to flit about; **der ~de Künstler** the erratic artist

Irr|sinn M, *no pl* madness, insanity; **das ist ja ~!** *(inf)* that's (sheer *or* absolute) madness *or* lunacy!; **auf den ~ verfallen, etw zu tun** to have the mad *or* crazy idea of doing sth

irr|sin|nig ADJ mad, crazy, insane; *(inf: = stark)* terrific, tremendous; **wie ein Irrsinniger** like a madman; **ein ~er Verkehr** *(inf)* a terrific *or* crazy *(inf)* amount of traffic ADV like crazy; *(= äußerst)* terribly, dreadfully, incredibly; *sich freuen* so much; **das Kind schrie wie ~** the child yelled like mad *(inf)* or like crazy *(inf)*; **~ viel** an insane amount, an incredible amount, a hell of a lot *(inf)*; **~ viele Leute** *(inf)* a tremendous *or* terrific number of people

Irr|sin|nig|keit [ˈɪrzɪnɪçkait] F -, *no pl* madness, craziness, insanity

Irr|sinns- *in cpds (inf)* terrific, tremendous; **Irr|sinns|hit|ze** F *(inf)* **da ist eine ~** the heat there is absolutely incredible; **Irr|sinns|tat** F insanity; **Irr|sinns|ver|kehr** M *(inf)* **da ist ein ~** there's a crazy *(inf)* or terrific amount of traffic there

Irr|tum [ˈɪrtu:m] M -s, ¨er mistake, error; **ein ~ von ihm** a mistake on his part; **im ~ sein, sich im ~ befinden** to be wrong *or* mistaken, to be in error; **~!** wrong!, you're wrong there!; **~, ich war es gar nicht!** that's where you're wrong *or* you're wrong there, it wasn't me!; **~ vorbehalten!** *(Comm)* errors excepted; **einen ~ zugeben** to admit to (having made) a mistake *or* an error; **jdm einen ~ nachweisen** to show that sb has made a mistake

irr|tüm|lich [ˈɪrty:mlɪç] ADJ *attr* incorrect, erroneous ADV incorrectly, erroneously; *(= aus Versehen)* by mistake

irr|tüm|li|cher|wei|se [ˈɪrty:mlɪçɐˈvaizə] ADV mistakenly, erroneously; *(= aus Versehen)* by mistake

Ir|rung [ˈɪrʊŋ] F -, -en *(liter)* **die ~en und Wirrungen meines Lebens** the aberrations of my life → **Irrtum**

Irr-: **Irr|weg** M **a** wandering *or* tortuous path; *(= Irrfahrt)* wandering **b** *(fig)* **auf dem ~ sein** to be on the wrong track; **zu studieren erwies sich für ihn als ~** going to university turned out to be a mistake for him; **auf ~e geraten** to go astray, to leave the straight and narrow; **irr+wer|den** VI *sep irreg aux sein* **an jdm/etw ~** *(liter)* to lose (one's) faith in sb/sth; **Irr|wisch** [ˈɪrvɪʃ] M -es, -e **a** *(= Irrlicht)* jack-o'-lantern, will-o'-the-wisp **b** *(= lebhafter Mensch)* imp; **Irr|witz** M madness; **irr|wit|zig** ADJ mad

ISBN [i:ɛsbe:ˈɛn] F -, -s *abbr von* **Internationale Standard-Buchnummer** ISBN **b** *(Comput) von* **Industrial Standard Business Network** ISBN

ISBN-Num|mer [i:ɛsbe:ˈɛn-] F *(von Büchern)* ISBN (number)

Is|chi|as [ˈɪʃias, ˈɪsçias] M OR NT -, *no pl* sciatica

Is|chi|as|nerv M sciatic nerve

ISDN [i:ɛsde:ˈɛn] *abbr von* **Integrated Services Digital Network** *(Telec)* ISDN

ISDN-: **ISDN-Ad|res|se** F *(Telec)* ISDN address; **ISDN-An|la|ge** F *(Telec)* ISDN connection; **ISDN-An|schluss** [i:ɛsde:ˈɛn-] M *(Telec)* ISDN connection; **ISDN-Kar|te** F *(Telec)* ISDN card; **ISDN-Netz** [i:ɛsde:ˈɛn-] NT *(Telec)* ISDN network; **ISDN-Teil|neh|mer(in)** M(F) *(Telec)* ISDN user

Ise|grim [ˈi:zəgrɪm] M -s, -e *(Liter)* the big bad wolf

Is|lam [ɪsˈla:m, ˈɪslam] M -s, *no pl* Islam

is|la|misch [ɪsˈla:mɪʃ] ADJ Islamic ADV **~ denken** to have Islamic beliefs; **~ heiraten** to have a Muslim wedding; **~ beeinflusst** influenced by Islam; **seine Kinder ~ erziehen** to raise one's children as Muslims

Is|la|mi|sie|rung [ɪslamiˈzi:rʊŋ] F -, -en Islamization

Is|land [ˈi:slant] NT -s Iceland

Is|län|der [ˈi:slɛndɐ] M -s, -, **Is|län|de|rin** [-ərɪn] F -, -nen Icelander

is|län|disch [ˈi:slɛndɪʃ] ADJ Icelandic; **Isländisches Moos** Iceland moss

Is|län|disch(e) [ˈi:slɛndɪʃ] NT Icelandic → *auch* **Deutsch(e)**

Is|mus [ˈɪsmʊs] M -, **Ismen** [-mən] *(pej)* ism

Iso|ba|re [izoˈba:rə] F -, -n isobar

iso|chron [izoˈkro:n] ADJ isochronous, isochronal

Iso|chro|nis|mus [izokroˈnɪsmʊs] M -, *no pl* isochronism

Iso|drink [ˈi:zo-] M -s, -s isotonic drink

Iso|la|ti|on [izolaˈtsio:n] F -, -en **a** *(= das Absondern, Isolieren)* isolation *(auch Med, Biol)*; *(von Häftlingen)* isolation, putting in solitary confinement; *(= das Isoliertsein)* isolation *(auch Med, Biol)*; *(von Häftlingen)* solitary confinement; **die Studenten protestierten gegen die ~ politischer Häftlinge** the students protested against political prisoners' being put in solitary confinement **b** *(Elec, gegen Lärm, Kälte etc)* insulation

Iso|la|ti|o|nis|mus [izolatsioˈnɪsmʊs] M -, *no pl* isolationism

iso|la|ti|o|nis|tisch [izolatsioˈnɪstɪʃ] ADJ isolationist

Iso|la|ti|ons|fol|ter F *(pej)*, **Iso|la|ti|ons|haft** F solitary confinement

Iso|la|tor [izoˈla:to:ɐ] M -s, **Isolatoren** insulator

Iso|lier-: **Iso|lier|band** [-bant] NT *pl* **-bänder** insulating tape, friction tape *(US)*; **iso|lier|bar** ADJ isolable; *(Tech)* insulable; **Iso|lier|box** F *(für Imbiss, Getränke etc)* cooler (box)

iso|lie|ren [izoˈli:rən] *ptp* **isoliert** VT **a** *(= absondern)* to isolate *(auch Med, Biol)*; *Häftlinge* to isolate, to put in(to) solitary confinement; **jdn isoliert halten** to keep sb in isolation *or* isolated/in solitary confinement; **völlig isoliert leben** to live in complete isolation, to live isolated from the world; **ein Problem isoliert betrachten** to look at a problem in isolation **b** *elektrische Leitungen, Häuser, Fenster* to insulate VR to isolate oneself *or* to cut oneself off (from the world)

I|so|lier-: **Iso|lier|fens|ter** NT double-glazed window; **so|lier|haft** F solitary confinement; **Iso|lier|kan|ne** F Thermos® flask, vacuum flask; **Iso|lier|mas|se** F insulating compound; **Iso|lier|ma|te|ri|al** NT insulating material; **Iso|lier|schicht** F insulating layer; **Iso|lier|sta|ti|on** F isolation ward

Iso|liert|heit [izoˈli:ɐthait] F -, -en isolatedness

Iso|lie|rung F -, -en = **Isolation**

Iso|mat|te [ˈi:zo-] F foam mattress, Karrimat®

Iso|mer [izoˈme:ɐ] NT -s, -e *(Chem)* isomer

Iso|me|rie [izomeˈri:] F -, *no pl* isomerism

Iso|met|rie [izomeˈtri:] F -, *no pl* isometry

iso|met|risch [izoˈme:trɪʃ] ADJ isometric

iso|morph [izoˈmɔrf] ADJ isomorphic; *Kristalle auch* isomorphous

Iso|ther|me [izoˈtɛrmə] F isotherm

iso|to|nisch ADJ isotonic

Iso|top [izoˈto:p] NT -s, -e isotope

ISP [ailɛsˈpi:] M -s, -s *abbr von* **Internet Service Provider** ISP

Is|ra|el [ˈɪsrae:l, ˈɪsraɛl] NT -s Israel; **das Volk ~** the people of Israel

Is|ra|e|li [ɪsraˈe:li] M -(s), -(s) Israeli

Is|ra|e|li [ɪsraˈe:li] F -, -(s), **Is|ra|e|lin** [ɪsraˈe:lɪn] F -, -nen Israeli

is|ra|e|lisch [ɪsraˈe:lɪʃ] ADJ Israeli

Is|ra|e|lit [ɪsraeˈli:t] M -en, -en, **Is|ra|e|li|tin** [-ˈli:tɪn] F -, -nen Israelite

is|ra|e|li|tisch [israe'li:tɪʃ] ADJ Israelite
isst [ɪst] *3. pers sing pres von* **essen**
ist [ɪst] *3. pers sing pres von* **sein**
Is|tan|bul ['istambu:l] NT **-s** Istanbul
Ist|be|stand ['ɪst-] M *(= Geld)* cash in hand; *(= Waren)* actual stock
Ist|gleich|zei|chen [ɪst'glaiç-] NT equals sign
Isth|mus ['ɪstmʊs] M **-, Isthmen** [-mən] isthmus
Ist|leis|tung F actual output
Is|tri|en ['ɪstriən] NT **-s** Istria
Ist-: **Ist|si|tu|a|ti|on** F actual state *or* situation; **Ist|stär|ke** F *(Mil)* actual *or* effective strength; **Ist|wert** M actual value; **Ist|zu|stand** M actual state *or* status
IT *abbr von* **Informationstechnologie** IT
Ita|ker ['i:takɐ] M **-s, -, Ita|ke|rin** [-ərɪn] F **-, -nen** *(pej dated inf)* dago *(pej)*, Eyetie *(Brit pej)*
Ita|li|en [i'ta:liən] NT **-s** Italy
Ita|li|e|ner [ita'lie:nɐ] M **-s, -, Ita|li|e|ne|rin** [-ərɪn] F **-, -nen** Italian; **zum ~ gehen** to go to an/the Italian restaurant
ita|li|e|nisch [ita'lie:nɪʃ] ADJ Italian; **die ~e Schweiz** Italian-speaking Switzerland
Ita|li|e|nisch(e) [ita'lie:nɪʃ] NT Italian → *auch* **Deutsch(e)**
Ita|lo|wes|tern ['i:talo-, i'ta:lo-] M spaghetti western
ITB [i:te:'be:] F *abbr von* **Internationale Tourismusbörse** *travel and tourism fair in Berlin*
ite|ra|tiv [itera'ti:f, 'i:t-] ADJ *(Gram)* iterative
IT-Spe|zi|a|list(in) M(F) IT specialist
i-Tüp|fel|chen ['i:-] NT dot (on the/an i); **bis aufs ~** *(fig)* (right) down to the last (little) detail
i. V. [i:'fau] *abbr von* **in Vertretung, im Vorjahre, in Vorbereitung**
It|zig ['ɪtsɪç] M **-(e)s, -e** [-gə] *(dated pej)* Yid *(pej)*, Jewboy *(pej)*
Iwan ['i:va:n] M **-s**, *no pl (inf)* **der ~** *(= Volk)* the Russkies *pl (inf)*; *(= Mensch)* the Russky *(inf)*
IWF [i:ve:'ɛf] M **-** *abbr von* **Internationaler Währungsfonds** IMF

J

J, j [jɔt, *(Aus)* jeː] **NT** J, j

ja [jaː] **ADV** **a** *(zustimmend)* yes; *(bei Trauung)* I do; **kommst du morgen? – ja** are you coming tomorrow? – yes(, I am); **haben Sie das gesehen? – ja** did you see it? – yes(, I did); **ich glaube ja** (yes,) I think so; **sagen Sie doch Ja** *or* **ja** please say yes; **zu etw Ja** *or* **ja sagen** to say yes to sth; **Ja und Amen** *or* **ja und amen zu etw sagen** *(inf)* to agree (slavishly) with sth; **wenn ja** if so; **ja! ja!, riefen die Zuschauer** go on! go on!, shouted the crowd
b *(fragend)* really?; **er war gestern da – ja?** he was there yesterday – really? *or* was he?; **ich habe gekündigt – ja?** I've quit – really? *or* have you?; **ja, bitte?** yes?, hello?
c *(feststellend)* **aber ja!** yes, of course, but of course; **ach ja!** oh yes; **nun ja** oh well; **kann ich reinkommen? – ja bitte** can I come in? – yes, do; **ja doch** *or* **freilich** *or* **gewiss** yes, of course; **ja so!** I see
d *(zweifelnd, ungläubig)* really?; **ich esse gern rohen Fisch – ja?** I like raw fish – really? *or* do you?; **er braucht keinen Urlaub, er arbeitet lieber – ja?** he doesn't need a holiday *(esp Brit)* *or* vacation *(US)*, he'd rather work – really? *or* would he?
e *(unbedingt)* **komm ja pünktlich!** be punctual; **sei ja vorsichtig!** be careful; **vergessen Sie es JA nicht!** don't forget, whatever you do!; **tu das JA nicht, ich warne dich!** just don't do that, I'm warning you
f *(einräumend, schließlich)* **es ist ja noch früh** it's still early (after all); **sie ist ja erst fünf** (after all) she's only five; **es ist ja nicht so schlimm** it's not really as bad as all that, (after all) it's not that bad; **das ist ja richtig, aber ...** that's (certainly) right, but ...; **ich kann es ja mal versuchen, aber ...** I could always try it, but ...
g *(als Steigerung)* even, nay *(liter)*; **das ist gut, ja sogar sehr gut** it's good, in fact it's very good
h *(feststellend)* **da hat mans ja, da haben wirs ja** there you are (then); **da kommt er ja** there *or* here he is; **das ist es ja** that's just it; **hier IST ja Herr Meier** here's Mr Meier himself; **ja, was haben wir denn hier?** well, what have we here?; **das sag ich ja!** that's just what I say; **das wissen wir ja alle** we all know that (anyway); **Sie wissen ja, dass ...** you (already) know that ..., as you know ...; **Sie wissen ja, wie das so ist** you know how it is(, don't you?)
i *(verstärkend, = wirklich)* just; **das ist ja fürchterlich** that's (just) terrible, terrible, that's what it is!; **das weiß man ja eben nie vorher** you just never know in advance
j *(= aber)* **ja, sagen Sie mal** now look here; **ja, was du nicht sagst!** you don't say!
k *(vergewissernd)* right?, OK?; **du kommst doch morgen, ja?** you're coming tomorrow, right? *or* aren't you?; **du rufst mich doch an, ja?** you'll give me a call, OK? *or* won't you?; **das ist also abgemacht, ja?** that's agreed then, right? *or* OK?

Ja [jaː] **NT -s, -(s)** yes; **mit Ja antworten/stimmen** to answer/vote yes; **ein Ja zum Kind/Frieden** a vote in favour *(Brit)* *or* favor *(US)* of children/peace; **das Ja vor dem Traualtar sprechen** to say "I do" at the altar

Ja|bo [ˈjaːbo] **M -s, -s** *abbr von* **Jagdbomber**

Jacht [jaxt] **F -, -en** yacht

Jacht-: **Jacht|club** **M** yacht club; **Jacht|ha|fen** **M** marina; **Jacht|klub** **M** yacht club; **Jacht|sport** **M** yachting, sailing

jäck [jɛk] **ADJ** *(dial)* crazy

Jäck|chen [ˈjɛkçən] **NT -s, -** **a** *dim von* **Jacke** little jacket **b** *(= Babyjäckchen)* matinée jacket *(Brit)*, knitted cardigan

Ja|cke [ˈjakə] **F -, -n** jacket, coat *(esp US)*; *(= Wolljacke)* cardigan; *(Comm: = Unterhemd)* vest *(Brit)*, undershirt *(US)*; **das ist ~ wie Hose** *(inf)* it doesn't make any difference (either way), it's six of one and half a dozen of the other *(inf)*; **jdm die ~ vollhauen** *(inf)* to give sb a thrashing; **wem die ~ passt ...** *(fig inf)* if the cap *(Brit)* *or* shoe *(US)* fits ...

Ja|cken-: **Ja|cken|kleid** **NT** *(= Kostüm)* costume, suit, two-piece; *(= Kleid und Jacke)* two-piece, dress and jacket; **Ja|cken|ta|sche** **F** jacket *or* coat *(esp US)* pocket

Ja|cket|kro|ne [ˈdʒɛkɪt-] **F** *(Zahnmedizin)* jacket crown

Ja|ckett [ʒaˈkɛt] **NT -s, -s** jacket, coat *(esp US)*

Ja|ckett|ta|sche **F** jacket *or* coat *(esp US)* pocket

Jack|pot [ˈdʒɛkpɔt] **M -s, -s** *(im Lotto etc)* rollover jackpot; **den ~ knacken** to hit the jackpot

Jac|quard|mus|ter [ʒaˈkaːr-] **NT** Jacquard weave

Ja|de [ˈjaːdə] **M** OR **F -,** *no pl* jade

ja|de|grün **ADJ** jade green

Jagd [jaːkt] **F -, -en** [-dn] **a** hunt; *(= das Jagen)* hunting; *(fig: = Verfolgung)* chase *(nach* after); *(= Wettlauf)* race; **die ~ auf Rotwild/Fasanen** deer-hunting/pheasant-hunting; **hohe/niedere ~** big/small game-hunting; **auf der ~ (nach etw) sein** *(lit)* to be hunting (for sth); *(fig auch)* to be on the hunt (for sth); **auf die ~ (nach etw) gehen** *(lit, fig)* to go hunting (for sth); **auf jdn/etw ~ machen** *(lit, fig)* to hunt for sb/sth; **von der ~ leben** to live by hunting; **ein Buch über die ~** a book about hunting; **die ~ nach Geld/Glück** the pursuit of *or* quest for money/fortune; **in wilder ~ sprengten sie über die Brücke** in their wild chase they charged over the bridge
b *(= Jagdrevier)* preserve, shoot
c *(= Wildbestand)* game
d *(= Jagdgesellschaft)* hunt, hunting *or* shooting party

Jagd-: **Jagd|auf|se|her(in)** **M(F)** *(= Angestellter)* gamekeeper; *(= Beamter)* game warden; **jagd|bar** **ADJ ... sind ~** ... may be hunted; **Jagd|beu|te** **F** bag; **Jagd|bom|ber** **M** *(Mil)* fighter-bomber; **Jagd|fie|ber** **NT** hunting fever; **Jagd|flin|te** **F** hunting rifle, sporting gun *or* rifle, shotgun; **Jagd|flug|zeug** **NT** *(Mil)* fighter plane *or* aircraft; **Jagd|fre|vel** **M** *(form)* poaching; **Jagd|frev|ler(in)** **M(F)** *(form)* poacher; **Jagd|ge|biet** **NT** hunting ground; **Jagd|ge|schwa|der** **NT** *(Mil)* fighter squadron; **Jagd|ge|sell|schaft** **F** hunt, hunting *or* shooting party; **Jagd|ge|wehr** **NT** hunting rifle, sporting gun *or* rifle, shotgun; **Jagd|glück** **NT** good luck *or* fortune in hunting; **wir hatten kein ~** we didn't bag anything; **Jagd|göt|tin** **F** goddess of hunting *or* the hunt *or* the chase *(liter)*; **Jagd|grün|de** **PL in die ewigen ~ eingehen** to go to the happy hunting grounds; **Jagd|haus** **NT** hunting lodge; **Jagd|herr(in)** **M(F)** owner of a/the hunting ground; **Jagd|horn** **NT** hunting horn; **Jagd|hund** **M** hunting dog; **Jagd|hüt|te** **F** hunting lodge; **Jagd|mes|ser** **NT** hunting knife; **Jagd|päch|ter(in)** **M(F)** game tenant; **Jagd|recht** **NT** **a** hunting *or* shooting rights *pl* **b** *(= Jagdbestimmungen)* game laws *pl*; **Jagd|ren|nen** **NT** steeplechase; **Jagd|re|vier** **NT** shoot; *(von Indianern etc)* preserve; **Jagd|scha|den** **M** damage caused by hunting; **Jagd|schein** **M** hunting licence *(Brit)* *or* license *(US)*; *(für Jagd mit Gewehr auch)* shooting licence *(Brit)* *or* license *(US)*; **einen ~ haben** *(hum)* to be certified *(inf)*; **Jagd|schloss** **NT** hunting lodge; **Jagd|schutz** **M** **a** *(Hunt)* game protection **b** *(Mil)* fighter cover; **Jagd|staf|fel** **F** *(Mil)* fighter squadron; **Jagd|sze|ne** **F** *(Art)* hunting scene; **Jagd|ta|sche** **F** game bag; **Jagd|ver|bot** **NT** ban on hunting; *(als Strafe)* ban from hunting; **Jagd|we|sen** **NT,** *no pl* hunting; **Jagd|wild** **NT** game; **Jagd|wurst** **F** smoked sausage; **Jagd|zeit** **F** hunting *or* shooting season

ja|gen [ˈjaːgn] **VT** **a** *Tier, Menschen* to hunt
b *(= hetzen)* to chase, to drive; *(= treiben) Wild* to drive; **jdn in die Flucht ~** to put sb to flight; **jdn zu Tode ~** to hound sb to death; **jdn aus dem Bett ~** *(inf)* to chase sb out of bed; **jdn aus dem Haus ~** to drive *or* chase sb out of the house; **jdm eine Spritze in den Arm ~** *(inf)* to stick a needle in sb's arm; **ein Unglück jagte das andere** one misfortune followed hard on (the heels of) the other; **Geld/Benzin durch den Auspuff ~** *(inf)* to burn money/a lot of juice *(inf)*; **sein ganzes Geld durch die Kehle ~** to booze *(esp Brit inf)* *or* drink all one's money away; **mit diesem Essen kannst du mich ~** *(inf)* I wouldn't eat this if you paid me
c *(= erlegen)* to bag
VI **a** *(= auf die Jagd gehen)* to hunt, to go hunting
b *aux sein (= rasen)* to race; **nach etw ~** to chase after sth; **in ~der Eile** in great haste
VR *(Geschehnisse etc)* to follow one on the heels of the other

Jä|ger [ˈjɛːgɐ] **M -s, -** **a** hunter, huntsman; **~ und Sammler** hunters and gatherers **b** *(Mil)* *(= Gebirgsjäger)* rifleman; *(= Jagdflieger)* fighter pilot **c** *(= Jagdflugzeug)* fighter (plane)

Jä|ger|ba|tail|lon **NT** rifle battalion

Jä|ge|rei [jɛgəˈrai] **F -,** *no pl* hunting

Jä|ger|hut **M** Tyrolean hat

Jä|ge|rin [ˈjɛːgərɪn] **F -, -nen** huntress, huntswoman → *auch* **Jäger a, b**

Jä|ger-: **Jä|ger|la|tein** **NT** *(inf)* hunters' yarns *pl*; **jdm ~ auftischen** to tell sb tall stories about one's hunting exploits; **Jä|ger|schnit|zel** **NT** *veal or pork cutlet with mushrooms and peppers*

Jä|gers|mann **M** *pl* **-leute** *(dated, liter)* hunter, huntsman

Jä|ger-: **Jä|ger|spra|che** **F** hunter's jargon; **Jä|ger|zaun** **M** rustic fence

Ja|gu|ar [ˈjaːguaːɐ] **M -s, -e** jaguar

jäh [jɛː], **jä|he** ['jɛːə] *(geh)* ADJ **a** *(= plötzlich)* sudden; *Schmerz* sudden, sharp; *(= unvermittelt) Wechsel, Ende, Bewegung* sudden, abrupt; *Flucht* sudden, headlong, precipitous **b** *(= steil)* sheer ADV **a** *(= plötzlich)* suddenly, just; *enden, wechseln, sich bewegen* abruptly; **eine grandiose Idee schoss ihr ~ durch den Kopf** a grandiose idea just popped (right) into her head **b** *(= steil)* steeply, sharply; **der Abhang steigt ~ an/fällt ~ ab** the slope rises/falls sharply *or* steeply

jäh|lings ['jɛːlɪŋs] ADV *(liter)* **a** *(= plötzlich)* suddenly; *aufhören, abbrechen* suddenly, abruptly; *fliehen* headlong **b** *(= steil)* steeply, precipitously; *hinabfallen* headlong

Jahr [jaːɐ] NT **-(e)s, -e a** year; **ein halbes ~** six months *sing or pl*; **ein drei viertel ~** nine months *sing or pl*; **anderthalb ~e** one and a half years *sing*, eighteen months *sing or pl*; **zwei ~e Garantie** a two-year guarantee; **im ~(e) 1066** in (the year) 1066; **die sechziger ~e** the sixties *sing or pl*; **alle ~e** every year; **alle zehn ~e** every ten years; **alle ~e wieder** year after year; **ein ~ ums andere** year after year; **auf ~e hinaus** for years ahead; **auf ~ und Tag** to the very day; **einmal im ~(e)** once a year; **das ganze ~ über** all year (round *or* through); **pro ~** a year, per annum; **das Buch des ~es** the book of the year; **noch nach ~en** years later; **nach ~ und Tag** after (many) years; **vor ~ und Tag** (many) years ago; **seit ~ und Tag** for years; **mit den ~en** as (the) years go by, over the years; **zwischen den ~en** *(inf)* between Christmas and New Year; **(freiwilliges) soziales/ökologisches ~** year of voluntary work in the social services/environmental sector

b *(= Alter, Lebensjahr)* **er ist zehn ~e (alt)** he is ten years old; **mit dreißig ~en** at the age of thirty; **Personen über 18 ~e/unter 18 ~en** people over/under (the age of) 18; **in die ~e kommen** *(inf)* to be getting on (in years); **man sieht ihm seine ~e nicht an** his age doesn't show; **in den besten ~en sein** *or* **stehen** to be in the prime of one's life; **mit den ~en** as one gets older

jahr|aus [jaːɐ'laus] ADV **~, jahrein** year in, year out

Jahr|buch NT yearbook; *(= Ausgabe einer Sammlung etc)* annual; *(= Kalender)* almanac

Jähr|chen ['jɛːɐçən] NT **-s, -** *(hum inf)* year

jah|re|lang ['jaːrəlaŋ] ADJ *attr* years of; **~es Warten** years of waiting; **~e Planung/Forschung** years of planning/research ADV for years; **und dann dauerte es noch ~, bevor …** and then it took years until …; **schon ~ verspricht man uns …** they've been promising us … for years

jäh|ren ['jɛːrən] VR **heute jährt sich der Tag, dass …** *or* **an dem …** it's a year ago today that …; **der Tag jährt sich zum dritten Mal, dass …** *or* **an dem …** it's three years ago that …

Jah|res- *in cpds* annual, yearly; **Jah|res|ab|rech|nung** F *(Comm)* → **Jahresabschluss a**; **Jah|res|ab|schluss** M **a** *(Comm)* annual accounts *pl*; **den ~ prüfen** to audit accounts **b** *(= Jahresende)* end of the year; **Jah|res|an|fang** M beginning of the year; **Jah|res|ar|beits|zeit** F working year; **meine ~ beträgt 1500 Stunden** my working year consists of 1500 hours, I work 1500 hours per year; **Jah|res|aus|gleich** M *(Fin)* = **Lohnsteuerjahresausgleich**; **Jah|res|aus|klang** M *(geh)* **zum ~** to see the old year out; **Jah|res|be|ginn** M beginning of the year; **Jah|res|bei|trag** M annual *or* yearly subscription; **Jah|res|be|richt** M annual *or* yearly report; *(Sch)* annual (activity) report; **Jah|res|best|leis|tung** F *(Sport)* year's best performance *or* time *(in races)*, best performance of *or* for the year; **Jah|res|best|zeit** F *(Sport)* best time of *or* for the year; **Jah|res|bi|lanz** F *(Comm)* annual balance sheet; **Jah|res|durch|schnitt** M annual *or* yearly average; **Jah|res|ein|kom|men** NT annual income; **Jah|res|en|de** NT end of the year; **Jah|res|fei|er** F anniversary; *(= Feierlichkeiten)* anniversary celebrations *pl*; **Jah|res|frist** F **binnen/nach ~** within/after (a period of) one year; **Jah|res|ge|halt** NT annual salary; **Jah|res|haupt|ver|samm|lung** F *(Comm)* annual general meeting, AGM; **Jah|res|kar|te** F annual season ticket; **Jah|res|mit|te** F middle of the year; **Jah|res|mit|tel** NT *(Met)* average annual temperature; **Jah|res|netz|kar|te** F annual season ticket; **Jah|res|prü|fung** F *(Aus Sch)* end-of-year test *or* exam; **Jah|res|ring** M *(eines Baumes)* annual ring; **Jah|res|rück|blick** M review of *or* (a) look back at the year's events; **Jah|res|tag** M anniversary; **Jah|res|um|satz** M *(Comm)* annual *or* yearly turnover; **Jah|res|ur|laub** M annual holiday *(esp Brit) or* vacation *(US)*, annual leave; **Jah|res|ver|dienst** M annual income, annual earnings *pl*; **Jah|res|wa|gen** M one-year-old car; **Jah|res|wech|sel** M, **Jah|res|wen|de** F new year; **jdm zum ~ Glück wünschen** to wish sb a happy New Year; **Jah|res|zahl** F date, year; **Jah|res|zeit** F season; **für die ~ zu kalt** cold for the time of year; **Jah|res|zeug|nis** NT *(Sch)* annual (school) report, annual (school) report card *(US)*; **Jah|res|zins** M annual interest; **effektiver ~** annual percentage rate, APR

Jahr|fünft [jaːɐ'fʏnft] NT **-(e)s, -e** five years *pl*, quinquennium *(form)*

Jahr|gang M *pl* **-gänge a** *(Sch, Univ)* year; **er ist ~ 1980** he was born in 1980; **die Jahrgänge 1980-83** the 1980-83 age group; **er ist mein ~, wir sind ein ~** we were born in the same year; *(als Schulabgänger etc)* we were in the same year **b** *(= alle Zeitschriften etc von einem Jahr)* year's issues *pl*; *(einer Fachzeitschrift)* volume; **Nr. 20, ~ 31** No. 20, 31st year; **Spiegel, ~ 1980** Spiegel of the year 1980 *or* for 1980 **c** *(von Wein)* vintage, year

Jahr|hun|dert [jaːɐ'hʊndɐt] NT century; **das ~ der Aufklärung** the Age of Enlightenment; **~e haben die Menschen …** for centuries men have …

jahr|hun|der|te-: **jahr|hun|der|te|alt** ADJ centuries-old; **jahr|hun|der|te|lang** ADJ centuries of; **eine ~e Entwicklung** a development lasting centuries ADV for centuries

Jahr|hun|dert-: **Jahr|hun|dert|fei|er** F centenary; *(= Feierlichkeiten)* centenary celebrations *pl*; **Jahr|hun|dert|hoch|was|ser** NT *(dieses Jahrhunderts)* flood of the century; *(nur alle hundert Jahre vorkommend)* once-in-a-century flood; **Jahr|hun|dert|wein** M *(der ganze Jahrgang)* vintage of the century; *(einzelne Sorte)* rare vintage; **Jahr|hun|dert|wen|de** F turn of the century; **Jahr|hun|dert|werk** NT **a** once-in-a-century work; *(in der Planung auch)* once-in-a-century project; *(nach Fertigstellung auch)* once-in-a-century achievement **b** *(= Jahrhunderte dauerndes Werk)* work of centuries

-jäh|rig [jɛːrɪç] ADJ *suf* **a** *(= … Jahre alt)* -year-old; **ein Fünfjähriger** a five-year-old **b** *(= Jahre dauernd)* years of; **nach elfjährigen Verhandlungen** after eleven years of negotiations; **nach dreijähriger Verspätung** after a three-year delay **c** *(Ordinalzahl)* **das 70-jährige Jubiläum** the 70th anniversary; **das zehnjährige Bestehen von etw** the tenth anniversary of sth

jähr|lich ['jɛːɐlɪç] ADJ annual, yearly ADV every year, annually, yearly; *(Comm)* per annum; **einmal/zweimal ~** once/twice a year *or* yearly

Jähr|ling ['jɛːɐlɪŋ] M **-s, -e** yearling

Jahr|markt M (fun-)fair; **~ der Eitelkeiten** *(liter)* vanity fair

Jahr|markts-: **Jahr|markts|bu|de** F booth *or* stall (at a fairground); *(= Schaubude)* sideshow; **Jahr|markts|künst|ler(in)** M(F) fairground artiste

Jahr-: **Jahr|mil|li|o|nen** [jaːɐmɪ'lioːnən] PL millions of years; **jahr|mil|li|o|nen|lang** [jaːɐmɪ'lioːnən-] ADJ millions of years of; **eine ~e Entwicklung** a development lasting millions of years ADV for millions of years; **Jahr|tau|send** [jaːɐ'tauznt] NT millennium, a thousand years; **in unserem ~** in our millennium; **~e** thousands of years; **jahr|tau|sen|de|lang** [jaːɐ'tauzndə-] ADJ thousands of years of; **eine ~e Entwicklung** a development lasting thousands of years ADV for millennia *or* thousands of years; **Jahr|tau|send|fei|er** [jaːɐ'tauznt-] F millennium; *(= Feierlichkeiten)* millennium celebrations *pl*; **Jahr|tau|send|wen|de** F millennium; **Jahr|zehnt** [jaːɐ'tseːnt] NT **-(e)s, -e** decade; **jahr|zehn|te|lang** [jaːɐ'tseːntə-] ADJ decades of; **eine ~e Entwicklung** a development lasting decades ADV for decades

Jah|ve ['jaːvə] M **-s**, **Jah|we** ['jaːvə] M **-s** Jehovah, Yahweh *(rare)*

Jäh|zorn M violent temper; *(plötzlicher Ausbruch)* outburst of temper *or* rage, violent outburst; **im ~** in a violent temper *or* rage; **zum ~ neigen** to be prone to violent outbursts (of temper)

jäh|zor|nig ADJ violent-tempered, irascible; *(= erregt)* furious, in a violent temper; **er ist manchmal so ~, dass …** he sometimes becomes so furious that …, he sometimes gets into such a violent temper that …

Jak [jak] M **-s, -s** yak

Ja|kob ['jaːkɔp] M **-s** James; *(Bibl)* Jacob → **wahr**

Ja|ko|bi|ner [jako'biːnɐ] M **-s, -**, **Ja|ko|bi|ne|rin** [-ərɪn] F **-, -nen** *(Hist)* Jacobin; *(Rel auch)* Dominican

Ja|ko|bi|ner|müt|ze F liberty cap

Ja|kobs|lei|ter F *(Bibl, Bot)* Jacob's ladder; *(Naut auch)* rope ladder

Ja|kobs|mu|schel F scallop

Ja|ko|bus [ja'koːbʊs] M **-'** James

Ja|lou|sie [ʒalu'ziː] F **-, -n** [-'ziːən] venetian blind

Ja|mai|ka [ja'maika] NT **-s** Jamaica

Ja|mai|ka|ner [jamai'kaːnɐ] M **-s, -**, **Ja|mai|ka|ne|rin** [-ərɪn] F **-, -nen** Jamaican

ja|mai|ka|nisch [jamai'kaːnɪʃ] ADJ Jamaican

Jam|ben|dich|tung F iambic poetry

jam|bisch ['jambɪʃ] ADJ *(Poet)* iambic

Jam|bus ['jambʊs] M **-, Jamben** [-bn] *(Poet)* iamb(us), iambic foot

Jam|mer ['jamɐ] M **-s,** *no pl* **a** *(= Elend)* misery, wretchedness; **ein Bild des ~s bieten** *or* **sein** to be the picture of misery; **der ~ überkam ihn** a feeling of misery came over him; **es ist ein ~, diesen Verfall mit ansehen zu müssen** it is a wretched thing *or* it is heartbreaking to have to watch this decay; **es wäre ein ~, wenn …** *(inf)* it would be a crying shame if … *(inf)* **b** *(= Klage)* wailing

Jam|mer-: **Jam|mer|bild** NT *(geh)* picture of misery, piteous *or* wretched sight; **Jam|mer|ge|schrei** NT *(inf)* wailing; **Jam|mer|ge|stalt** F wretched figure; **Jam|mer|lap|pen** M *(sl)* wet *(inf)*, sissy *(inf)*

jäm|mer|lich ['jɛmɐlɪç] ADJ wretched, pitiful; *(= beklagenswert auch)* lamentable, deplorable; *(inf) Erklärung, Bericht, Entschuldigung etc* pitiful, pathetic *(inf)*; *Feigling* appalling, terrible ADV *sterben etc* pitifully, miserably; *versagen* miserably; *(inf: = sehr)* terribly *(inf)*; *(inf: = schlecht)* pathetically

Jäm|mer|lich|keit F **-,** *no pl* wretchedness

jam|mern ['jamɐn] VI to wail *(über +acc* over); *(= sich beklagen auch)* to moan, to yammer *(inf)*; **nach jdm/etw ~** to whine *or* yammer *(inf)* for sb/sth; **der Gefangene jammerte um Wasser** the prisoner begged pitifully *or* moaned for water VT *(old)* to move to pity; **er jammert mich** I feel sorry for him, I pity him

Jam|mer-: **jam|mer|scha|de** ADJ **es ist ~** *(inf)* it's a terrible pity, it's a crying shame *(inf)*; **Jam|mer|tal** NT *(Bibl, liter)* vale of tears *(liter)*; **jam|mer|voll** ADJ, ADV = **jämmerlich**

Jan|ker ['jaŋkɐ] M **-s, -** *(S Ger, Aus)* Tyrolean jacket; *(= Strickjacke)* cardigan

Jän|ner ['jɛnɐ] M **-s, -** *(Aus, Sw, S Ger)* January

Ja|nu|ar ['januaːɐ] M **-(s), -e** January → *auch* **März**

Ja|nus- *(Myth, liter)*: **Ja|nus|ge|sicht** NT, **Ja|nus|kopf** M Janus face; **ja|nus|ge|sich|tig, ja|nus|köp|fig** ADJ Janus-faced; **Ja|nus|köp|fig|keit** F -, *no pl* Janus-faced character

Ja|pan ['ja:pan] NT **-s** Japan

Ja|pa|ner [ja'pa:nɐ] M **-s, -, Ja|pa|ne|rin** [-ərɪn] F **-, -nen** Japanese

ja|pa|nisch [ja'pa:nɪʃ] ADJ Japanese

Ja|pa|nisch(e) [ja'pa:nɪʃ] NT Japanese → *auch* **Deutsch(e)**

Ja|pa|no|lo|ge [japano'lo:gə] M **-n, -n, Ja|pa|no|lo|gin** [-'lo:gɪn] F **-, -nen** Japanese specialist; *(= Student)* student of Japanese (studies)

Ja|pa|no|lo|gie [japanolo'gi:] F **-,** *no pl* Japanese studies

jap|pen ['japn] VI *(N Ger inf: = japsen)* to pant

Japs [japs] M **-es, -e** *(pej inf: = Japaner)* Jap *(pej inf)*

jap|sen VI *(inf)* to pant

Jar|gon [ʒar'gõ:] M **-s, -s** jargon, slang, lingo *(inf)*

Ja|sa|ger ['ja:za:gɐ] M **-s, -** yes man

Ja|sa|ge|rin ['ja:za:gərɪn] F **-, -nen** yes woman

Jas|min [jas'mi:n] M **-s, -e** jasmine

Jas|pis ['jaspɪs] M **-(ses), -se** jasper

Ja|stim|me ['ja:-] F vote in favour *(Brit)* or favor *(US)* (of), vote for; *(Parl auch)* aye *(Brit)*, yea *(US)*

jä|ten ['jɛ:tn] VTI to weed

Jau|che ['jauxə] F **-,** *no pl* liquid manure; *(Med)* sanies *(form)*, ichor *(form)*; *(= Abwasser)* sewage; **das stinkt wie ~** it stinks like nobody's business *(inf)*, it stinks to high heaven

Jau|che|gru|be F cesspool, cesspit; *(Agr)* liquid manure pit

jau|chen ['jauxn] VI to manure; *(Med)* to discharge (sanies *(form)* or ichor *(form)*) VT to manure

Jau|chen|gru|be F = **Jauchegrube**

Jau|che|wa|gen M liquid manure transporter or *(= Karren)* cart

jauch|zen ['jauxtsn] VI *(geh)* to rejoice *(liter)*, to exult *(liter)*; *(Publikum)* to cheer; *(Kinder)* to shout and cheer; *(Säugling)* to chuckle, to laugh

Jauch|zer ['jauxtsɐ] M **-s, -** jubilant cheer or shout; **sie stieß einen lauten, begeisterten ~ aus** she gave a loud yippee *(inf)*, she cheered

jau|len ['jaulən] VI *(lit, fig)* to howl; *(lit)* to yowl

Jau|se ['jauzə] F **-, -n** *(Aus)* break (for a snack); *(= Proviant)* snack; **eine ~ halten** or **machen** to stop for a snack

jau|sen ['jauzn] VI *(Aus)* = **jausnen**

Jau|sen|sta|ti|on F *(Aus)* snack bar

jaus|nen ['jauznən] VI *(Aus)* to stop for a bite to eat or a snack; *(auf Arbeit)* to have a tea *(Brit)* or coffee *(esp US)* break

Ja|va ['ja:va] NT **-s** Java

Ja|va® ['dʒa:va] NT **-** *(Programmiersprache)* Java®

Ja|va|ner [ja'va:nɐ] M **-s, -, Ja|va|ne|rin** [-ərɪn] F **-, -nen** Javanese

ja|va|nisch [ja'va:nɪʃ] ADJ Javanese

ja|wohl [ja'vo:l] ADV, **ja|woll** [ja'vɔl] *(hum, inf)* ADV yes; *(Mil)* yes, sir; *(Naut)* aye, aye, sir; **stimmt das wirklich? – ~** is that really right? – yes, it is or yes, indeed; **haben Sie 50 euro gesagt? – ~** did you say 50 euros? – right or correct or I did or I did indeed

Ja|wort ['ja:-] NT *pl* **-worte jdm das ~ geben** to consent to marry sb, to say yes to sb; *(bei Trauung)* to say "I do"; **sich** or **einander das ~ geben** to get married

Jazz [dʒɛs, jats] M **-,** *no pl* jazz

Jazz- *in cpds* jazz; **Jazz|band** ['dʒɛs-, 'jats-] F jazz band

Jaz|zer ['dʒɛsɐ, 'jatsɐ] M **-s, -, Jaz|ze|rin** [-ərɪn] F **-, -nen** *(inf)* jazz musician; *(Mann auch)* jazzman *(inf)*

Jazz-: **Jazz|gym|nas|tik** ['dʒɛs-, 'jats-] F jazz gymnastics *sing*, popmobility, jazzercise *(US)*; **Jazz|kel|ler** ['dʒɛs-, 'jats-] M jazz club

je [je:] ADV **a** *(= jemals)* ever **b** *(= jeweils)* every, each; **für je drei Stück zahlst du einen Euro** you pay one euro for (every) three; **je zwei Schüler aus jeder Klasse** two children from each class; **ich gebe euch je zwei Äpfel** I'll give you two apples each, I'll give each of you two apples; **sie zahlten je einen Euro** they paid one euro each, each (of them) paid one euro

PREP *+acc (= pro)* per; **je Person zwei Stück** two per person; **je zehn Exemplare ein Freiexemplar** one free copy for every ten copies

CONJ **a je eher, desto** or **umso besser** the sooner the better; **je länger, je lieber** the longer the better

b je nach according to, depending on; **je nach Wunsch** just as one wishes; **je nachdem** it all depends; **je nachdem, wie gut man arbeitet ...** depending on how well you work ...

je INTERJ **ach** or **o je!** oh dear!; **o je!** *(old)* alas! *(old)*; **je nun** *(dated)* oh, well

Jeans [dʒi:nz] PL jeans *pl*

Jeans- *in cpds* denim; **Jeans|an|zug** ['dʒi:nz-] M denim suit; **jeans|far|ben** ['dʒi:nz-] ADJ denim-coloured *(Brit)*, denim-colored *(US)*; **Jeans|ho|se** ['dʒi:nz-] F = **Jeans**; **Jeans|ja|cke** ['dʒi:nz-] F denim jacket; **Jeans|stoff** ['dʒi:nz-] M denim

Jeck [jɛk] M **-en, -en** *(dial)* fool; *(zu Fasching)* carnival reveller *(Brit)* or reveler *(US)*

je|den|falls ['je:dn'fals] ADV anyhow, in any case; *(= zumindest)* at least, at any rate; **~ ist es schon zu spät** it's too late now anyhow or in any case; **er ist nicht gekommen, aber er hat sich ~ entschuldigt** he didn't come but at least he apologized or he did at least apologize; **ob er krank ist, weiß ich nicht, ~ ist er nicht gekommen** I don't know whether he's ill or not, at any rate or in any case or anyhow he didn't come; **er sagte nichts über den Mord, ~ nichts Neues** he said nothing about the murder, or at any rate or at least nothing new; **er ist nicht reif zum Studieren, ~ jetzt noch nicht** he's not mature enough to study, at least or at any rate not yet; **ich weiß nicht, ob das nötig ist, ~ ist es hier so üblich** I don't know if it's necessary, but it's what we do here (anyhow or at any rate)

je|de(r, s) ['je:də] INDEF PRON **a** *(adjektivisch)* *(= einzeln)* each; *(esp von zweien)* either; *(= jeder von allen)* every; *(= jeder beliebige)* any; **~ von beiden kann sich verspäten** either of them could be late; **ohne ~ Anstrengung/Vorstellung** *etc* without any effort/idea *etc*, with no effort/idea *etc*; **~s Mal** every or each time; **~s Mal, wenn sie ...** each or every time she ..., whenever she ...; **~s Mal ist es so(, dass ...)** it happens every or each time (that ...); **zu ~r Stunde** at all times; **es kann ~n Augenblick passieren** it might happen any minute or at any moment; **fern von ~r Kultur** far from all civilization → **Kind**

b *(substantivisch) (= einzeln)* each (one); *(= jeder von allen)* everyone, everybody; *(= jeder Beliebige)* anyone, anybody; **~r von uns** each (one)/every one/any one of us; **ein ~r** *(liter)* each (one); **~r von uns beiden** each (one) of us; **er gab ~m von beiden ein Buch** he gave each or both of them a book; **~r Zweite** every other or second one; **~r für sich** everyone for himself; **~r/~/~s für sich ist ganz nett, aber beide zusammen ...** each one by himself/herself/itself or each one alone is quite nice, but together ...; **geht jetzt ~r in sein Bett!** go to bed now, both/all of you; **das kann ~r** anyone or anybody can do that; **das kann nicht ~r** not everyone or everybody can do that; **er spricht nicht mit ~m** he doesn't speak to just anybody or anyone

je|der|mann ['je:dɐman] INDEF PRON everyone, everybody; *(= jeder Beliebige auch)* anyone, anybody; **Jedermann** *(Theat)* Everyman; **das ist nicht ~s Sache** it's not everyone's cup of tea *(inf)*; **Herr/Frau Jedermann** Mr/Mrs Average (Citizen)

je|der|zeit ['je:dɐ'tsait] ADV at any time; **du kannst ~ kommen** you can come any time (you like); **ja, ~** sure, any time

je|des|mal △ ['je:dəs'ma:l] ADV → **jede(r, s) a**

je|doch [je'dɔx] CONJ ADV however; **er verlor ~ die Nerven** he lost his nerve however or though

jed|we|de(r, s) ['je:t've:də] INDEF PRON *(old)* = **jede(r, s)**

Jeep® [dʒi:p] M **-s, -s** Jeep®

jeg|li|che(r, s) ['je:klɪçə] INDEF PRON *(adjektivisch)* any; *(substantivisch: old, liter: auch* **ein jeglicher)** each (one)

je|her ['je:he:ɐ, 'je:'he:ɐ] ADV **von** or **seit ~** always; **das ist schon seit ~ so** it has always been like that

Je|ho|va [je'ho:va] M **-s** Jehovah; **die Zeugen ~s** Jehovah's Witnesses

jein [jain] ADV *(hum)* yes and no

Je|län|ger|je|lie|ber [je'lɛŋɐje'li:bɐ] NT **-s, -** honeysuckle

je|mals ['je:ma:ls] ADV ever

je|mand ['je:mant] INDEF PRON somebody, someone; *(bei Fragen, bedingenden Sätzen auch, Negation)* anybody, anyone; **ist da ~?** is anybody or somebody there?; **du lachst so, hat dir ~ ein Kompliment gemacht?** why are you smiling? has somebody or someone paid you a compliment?; **ohne ~en zu fragen** without asking anybody or anyone; **ich brauche ~en, der mir den Fernseher repariert** I need somebody or someone to repair my television set; **~ Fremdes** a stranger; **~ Neues** somebody or someone new; **~ anders** somebody or someone else

Je|men ['je:mən] M **-s der ~** Yemen

je|mi|ne ['je:mine] INTERJ *(old)* = **ojemine, herrjemine**

Je|na|er Glas® ['je:naɐ] NT ≈ Pyrex®, heat-proof glass

je|ne(r, s) ['je:nə] DEM PRON *(geh)* **a** *(adjektivisch)* that; *(pl)* those; *(= der Vorherige, die Vorherigen)* the former; **in ~m Leben, in ~r Welt** in the next life or world; **in ~n Tagen** in those days; *(zukünftig)* in those days ahead, in those days to come; **in ~r Zeit** at that time, in those times **b** *(substantivisch)* that one; *(pl)* those (ones); *(= der Vorherige, die Vorherigen)* the former; **bald dieser, bald ~r** first one then the other; **von diesem und ~m sprechen** to talk about this and that

jen|sei|tig ['je:nzaitɪç, 'jɛn-] ADJ *attr* opposite, other; **die ~en Vororte** the suburbs on the other side; **das ~e Leben** the life hereafter, the life after death

jen|seits ['je:nzaits, 'jɛn-] PREP *+gen* on the other side of; **2 km ~ der Grenze** 2 kms beyond the border, 2 kms the other side of the border ADV **~ von** on the other side of; **~ von Gut und Böse** beyond good and evil, over and above good and evil; *(hum inf)* past it *(inf)*

Jen|seits ['je:nzaits, 'jɛn-] NT **-,** *no pl* hereafter, next world; **jdn ins ~ befördern** *(inf)* to send sb to kingdom come *(inf)*

Jen|seits|glau|be M belief in life after death, belief in the afterlife

Je|re|mi|as [jere'mi:as] M **-'** *(Bibl)* Jeremiah

Jer|sey ['dʒø:ɐzi] NT **-s** *(Geog)* Jersey

Je|sa|ja [je'za:ja] M **-s** *(Bibl)* Isaiah

Jes|ses ['jɛsəs] INTERJ *(inf)* Jesus *(inf)*

Je|su|it [je'zui:t] M **-en, -en** Jesuit

Je|su|i|ten-: **Je|su|i|ten|or|den** M Jesuit Order; **Je|su|i|ten|schu|le** F Jesuit school

je|su|i|tisch [je'zui:tɪʃ] ADJ Jesuit

Je|sus ['je:zʊs] M *gen* **Jesu**, *dat* **-** or **Jesu** ['je:zu], *acc* **-** or **Jesum** ['je:zʊm] Jesus; **~ Christus** Jesus Christ; **~, Maria (und Josef)!** *(dial inf)* holy Mary mother of God! *(dial inf)*

Je|sus-: **Je|sus|kind** NT **das ~** the Infant Jesus, the Christ Child; **Je|sus|kna|be** M **der ~** the Infant Jesus, the boy Jesus; **Je|sus|lat|schen** PL *(inf)* Jesus sandals *pl*

Jet [dʒɛt] **M -(s), -s** *(inf)* jet

Jet|lag ['jʒɛtlɛg] **M -s, -s** jetlag; **unter ~ leiden** to suffer from jetlag, to be jetlagged

Je|ton [ʒə'tõ:] **M -s, -s** chip

Jet|set ['dʒɛtsɛt] **M -s,** *(rare)* **-s** *(inf)* jet set

jet|ten ['dʒɛtn] **VI** *aux sein (inf)* to jet *(inf)*, to fly

Jet|zeit|al|ter **NT** *(inf)* jet age

jet|zig ['jɛtsɪç] **ADJ** *attr* present *attr*, current; **in der ~en Zeit** in our *or* present times; **im ~en Augenblick** at the present moment (in time)

jet|zo ['jɛtso] **ADV** *(obs)* = **jetzt**

jetzt [jɛtst] **ADV** now; *(= heutzutage auch)* nowadays; **sie ist ~ in der Schweiz** she's in Switzerland now, she's now in Switzerland; **bis ~** so far; **ich bin ~ (schon) fünf Tage hier** I have been here five days now; **für ~** for now, for the present; **gleich ~, ~ gleich** right now, straight away; **schon ~** already; **~ schon?** already?; **~ noch?** (what) now?; **das ist noch ~ der Fall** it's still the case today; **~ oder nie!** (it's) now or never!; **habe ich ~ das Bügeleisen herausgezogen?** now did I unplug the iron?, did I unplug the iron now?

Jetzt [jɛtst] **NT -,** *no pl (geh)* present

Jetzt|zeit **F,** *no pl (geh)* present (time), modern times *pl or* age

jew. *abbr von* **jeweils**

je|wei|lig ['je:vailɪç] **ADJ** *attr* respective; *(= vorherrschend) Verhältnisse, Bedingungen* prevailing; **die ~e Regierung** the government of the day

je|weils ['je:vails] **ADV** at a time, at any one time; *(= jedes Mal)* each time; *(= jeder Einzelne)* each; **~ am Monatsletzten** on the last day of each month; **die ~ betroffenen Landesregierungen müssen ...** each of the governments concerned must ...; **die ~ durch Schiebetüren abgetrennten Räume** the rooms, each (of which are) separated (off) by sliding doors; **die ~ Größten aus einer Gruppe** the biggest from each group

Jg. *abbr von* **Jahrgang**

JH *abbr von* **Jugendherberge** YH

Jh. *abbr von* **Jahrhundert**

jhrl. *abbr von* **jährlich**

jid|disch ['jɪdɪʃ] **ADJ** Yiddish

Jid|disch(e) ['jɪdɪʃ] **NT** Yiddish → *auch* **Deutsch(e)**

Jin|gle **M -(s), -(s)** *(= kurze, einprägsame Melodie)* jingle

Jiu-Jit|su ['dʒi:u'dʒɪtsu] **NT -s,** *no pl* j(i)u-jitsu

Job [dʒɔp] **M -s, -s** *(inf)* job *(auch Comput)*

job|ben ['dʒɔbn] **VI** *(inf)* to work, to have a job

Job|ber ['dʒɔbɐ] **M -s, -, Job|be|rin** [-ərɪn] **F -, -nen** *(inf)* jobber

Job- [dʒɔp]

Job|cen|ter, Job-Cen|ter **NT** job centre *(Brit) or* center *(US)*

Job|kil|ler ['dʒɔpkɪlɐ] **M** *(inf)* job killer

Job|sha|ring ['dʒɔpʃɛ:rɪŋ] **NT -s,** *no pl* job sharing

Job|su|che ['dʒɔp-] **F,** *no pl* job hunting; **auf ~ sein** to be looking for a job

Job|ver|mitt|lung **F** **a** *(= das Vermitteln)* job finding **b** *(= Stelle)* employment agency

Joch [jɔx] **NT -(e)s, -e** **a** *(lit, fig)* yoke; **Ochsen ins ~ spannen** to yoke *or* harness oxen; **sich einem ~** *or* **unter ein ~ beugen** *(fig)* to submit to *or* bend under the yoke; **das ~ abwerfen** *or* **abschütteln** *(fig)* to shake *or* throw off the yoke **b** *(dated: = Gespann Ochsen)* yoke **c** *(Archit)* truss; *(= Kirchenjoch)* bay; *(= Brückenjoch)* span **d** *(= Bergjoch)* ridge **e** *(old: = Feldmaß)* acre

Joch-: **Joch|bein** **NT** cheekbone, malar bone *(form)*; **Joch|bo|gen** **M** **a** *(Anat)* zygomatic arch *(spec)*, zygoma *(spec)* **b** *(Archit)* bay

Jo|ckei ['dʒɔke, 'dʒɔkai] **M -s, -s** = **Jockey**

Jo|ckey ['dʒɔki] **M -s, -s** jockey

Jo|ckey|müt|ze **F** jockey cap

Jod [jo:t] **NT -(e)s** [-dəs], *no pl (abbr* **J***)* iodine

jo|deln ['jo:dln] **VTI** to yodel

jod|hal|tig **ADJ** containing iodine, iodic *(form)*

jo|diert [jo'di:ɐt] **ADJ** **~es Speisesalz** iodized table salt

Jod|ler ['jo:dlɐ] **M -s, -** *(= Ruf)* yodel

Jod|ler ['jo:dlɐ] **M -s, -, Jod|le|rin** [-ərɪn] **F -, -nen** yodeller *(Brit)*, yodeler *(US)*

Jod-: **Jod|man|gel** **M** iodine deficiency; **Jod|prä|pa|rat** **NT** iodine preparation; **Jod|quel|le** **F** iodine(-containing) spring; **Jod|sal|be** **F** iodine ointment; **Jod|salz** **NT** iodized salt; **Jod|tink|tur** **F** iodine tincture

Jo|ga ['jo:ga] **M OR NT -(s),** *no pl* yoga

Jo|ga|sitz **M,** *no pl* lotus position

jog|gen ['dʒɔgn] **VI** to jog

Jog|ger ['dʒɔgɐ] **M -s, -, Jog|ge|rin** [-ərɪn] **F -, -nen** jogger

Jog|ging ['dʒɔgɪŋ] **NT -,** *no pl* jogging

Jog|ging- *in cpds* jogging; **Jog|ging|an|zug** **M** jogging suit, tracksuit

Jo|ghurt ['jo:gʊrt] **M OR NT -(s), -(s)** yog(h)urt

Jo|ghurt-: **Jo|ghurt|be|rei|ter** [-bəraitɐ] **M -s, -s** yog(h)urt maker; **Jo|ghurt|drink** [-drɪŋk] **M -s, -s** yog(h)urt drink

Jo|gi ['jo:gi] **M -s, -s** yogi

Jo|gurt ['jo:gʊrt] **M OR NT -(s), -(s)** = **Joghurt**

Jo|gurt|be|rei|ter [-bəraitɐ] **M -s, -s** = **Joghurtbereiter**

Jo|hann [jo'han, 'jo:han] **M -s** John

Jo|han|na [jo'hana] **F -s** Joanna; **(die heilige) ~ von Orléans** (Saint) Joan of Arc

Jo|han|nes [jo'hanəs, jo'hanɛs] **M -'** *or (ohne Artikel)* **Johannis** [-nɪs] **a** *(Bibl)* John **b** *(sl: = Penis)* John Thomas *(Brit hum inf)*, Johnnie *(US hum inf)*

Jo|han|nes|evan|ge|li|um **NT** St John's Gospel, Gospel according to St. John

Jo|han|ni(s) [jo'hani, jo'hanɪs] **NT -** Midsummer's Day

Jo|han|nis-: **Jo|han|nis|bee|re** **F** **Rote ~** redcurrant; **Schwarze ~** blackcurrant; **Jo|han|nis|beer|strauch** **M** *(roter)* redcurrant bush; *(schwarzer)* blackcurrant bush; **Jo|han|nis|brot** **NT** *(Bot)* carob; **Jo|han|nis|brot|baum** **M** carob tree; **Jo|han|nis|fest** **NT** Midsummer's Day; **Jo|han|nis|feu|er** **NT** Midsummer's Eve bonfire; **Jo|han|nis|kä|fer** **M** *(= Glühwürmchen)* glow-worm; *(= Junikäfer)* summer chafer; **Jo|han|nis|kraut** **NT,** *no pl* St. John's wort; **Jo|han|nis|nacht** **F** Midsummer's Eve; **Jo|han|nis|tag** **M** Midsummer's Day; **Jo|han|nis|trieb** **M** *(Bot)* lammas shoot; *(fig)* late romantic stirrings *pl*; **Jo|han|nis|würm|chen** **NT** = **Johanniskäfer**

Jo|han|ni|ter [joha'ni:tɐ] **M -s, -** Knight of St. John of Jerusalem; **~ Unfallhilfe** St. John's Ambulance (Brigade)

Jo|han|ni|ter|or|den **M** Order of St. John of Jerusalem

joh|len ['jo:lən] **VI** to howl

Joint [dʒɔynt] **M -s, -s** *(inf)* joint *(inf)*

Joint Ven|ture [dʒɔynt 'vɛntʃə] **NT -s, -s, Joint|ven|ture** △ **NT - -s, - -s** *(Comm)* joint venture

Jo-Jo [jo'jo, 'jo:'jo:] **NT -s, -s** yo-yo

Jo-Jo-Ef|fekt **M** yo-yo effect

Jo|ker ['jo:kɐ, 'dʒo:kɐ] **M -s, -** *(Cards)* joker; *(fig)* trump card

Jo|kus ['jo:kʊs] **M -, -se** *(dated, inf)* jape *(dated)*, joke, prank; **da hat sich jemand einen ~ gemacht** someone's been playing a prank

Jol|le ['jɔlə] **F -, -n** *(Naut)* jolly boat, dinghy

Jol|len|kreu|zer **M** cabin yacht

Jo|na ['jo:na] **M -s, Jo|nas** ['jo:nas] **M -'** *(Bibl)* Jonah

Jong|leur [ʒõ'glø:ɐ, ʒɔŋ'lø:ɐ] **M -s, -e, Jong|leu|rin** [-'glø:rɪn, -'lø:rɪn] **F -, -nen** juggler

jong|lie|ren [ʒõ'gli:rən, ʒɔŋ'li:rən] *ptp* **jongliert** **VI** *(lit, fig)* to juggle

Jop|pe ['jɔpə] **F -, -n** *(dial)* jacket

Jor|dan ['jɔrdan] **M -s** Jordan; **über den ~ gehen** *(inf)* to cross the great divide *(inf)*

Jor|da|ni|en [jɔr'da:niən] **NT -s** Jordan

Jor|da|ni|er [jɔr'da:niɐ] **M -s, -, Jor|da|ni|e|rin** [-iərɪn] **F -, -nen** Jordanian

jor|da|nisch [jɔr'da:nɪʃ] **ADJ** Jordanian

Jo|sef ['jo:zɛf] **M -s, Jo|seph** **M -s** Joseph

Jot [jɔt] **NT -, -** (the letter) J/j

Jo|ta ['jo:ta] **NT -(s), -s** iota; **kein ~, nicht ein ~** not a jot, not one iota

Joule [dʒu:l] **NT -(s), -** *(abbr* **J***)* joule

Jour fixe [ʒu:r'fɪks] **M -s -, -s -** regular meeting

Jour|nail|le [ʒʊr'naljə, ʒʊr'na:jə] **F -,** *no pl (pej)* yellow press; *(= Presse im Allgemeinen)* press; *(= Journalisten)* hacks *pl (pej)*

Jour|nal [ʒʊr'na:l] **NT -s, -e** **a** *(dated: = Tagebuch)* journal *(old)*, diary; *(Comm)* daybook; *(Naut)* log(book) **b** *(dated: = Zeitschrift)* magazine, periodical; *(old: = Zeitung)* journal *(old)*; *(= Fachjournal)* journal

Jour|nal|dienst **M** *(Aus)* = **Bereitschaftsdienst**

Jour|na|lis|mus [ʒʊrna'lɪsmʊs] **M -,** *no pl* journalism

Jour|na|list [ʒʊrna'lɪst] **M -en, -en, Jour|na|lis|tin** [-'lɪstɪn] **F -, -nen** journalist

Jour|na|lis|tik [ʒʊrna'lɪstɪk] **F -,** *no pl* journalism

jour|na|lis|tisch [ʒʊrna'lɪstɪʃ] **ADJ** journalistic **ADV** **~ arbeiten** to work as a journalist; **jdn ~ ausbilden** to train sb to be a journalist; **etw ~ aufbereiten** to edit sth for journalistic purposes; **~ geschrieben** written in a journalistic style

jo|vi|al [jo'via:l] **ADJ** jovial **ADV** jovially

Jo|vi|a|li|tät [joviali'tɛ:t] **F -,** *no pl* joviality

Joy|stick ['dʒɔystɪk] **M -s, -s** *(Comput)* joystick

JPEG ['dʒe:pɛk] **NT -** *(Comput) abbr von* **Joint Photographic Experts Group** JPEG

jr. *abbr von* **junior** jnr, jr

Ju|bel ['ju:bl] **M -s,** *no pl (von Volk, Menge etc)* jubilation; *(= Jubelrufe auch)* cheering; **~, Trubel, Heiterkeit** laughter and merriment

Ju|bel-: **Ju|bel|fei|er** **F, Ju|bel|fest** **NT** jubilee; *(= Feierlichkeiten)* jubilee celebration; **Ju|bel|ge|schrei** **NT** *(pej)* shouting and cheering; **Ju|bel|greis(in)** **M(F)** *old person celebrating a jubilee or anniversary (fig inf)* cheerful old soul *(inf)*; **Ju|bel|hoch|zeit** **F** special wedding anniversary *(silver, golden etc anniversary)*; **Ju|bel|jahr** **NT** jubilee year; **nur alle ~e (einmal)** *(inf)* once in a blue moon *(inf)*

ju|beln ['ju:bln] **VI** to cheer, to shout with joy, to rejoice *(liter)*; **jubelt nicht zu früh** don't start celebrating too early

Ju|bel-: **Ju|bel|paar** **NT** happy couple *(celebrating a special e.g. silver or golden wedding anniversary)*; **Ju|bel|ruf** **M** (triumphant) cheer; **Ju|bel|tag** **M** (silver, golden *etc*) wedding anniversary

Ju|bi|lar [jubi'la:ɐ] **M -s, -e, Ju|bi|la|rin** [-'la:rɪn] **F -, -nen** *person celebrating an anniversary*

Ju|bi|la|te [jubi'la:tə] *no art (Eccl)* Jubilate (Sunday)

Ju|bi|lä|um [jubi'lɛ:ʊm] **NT -s, Jubiläen** [-'lɛ:ən] jubilee; *(= Jahrestag)* anniversary

Ju|bi|lä|ums- *in cpds* jubilee; **Ju|bi|lä|ums|jahr** **NT** jubilee year

ju|bi|lie|ren [jubi'li:rən] *ptp* **jubiliert** **VI** *(liter)* to rejoice *(liter)*; *(Vögel)* to sing joyfully

juch|he(i) [jʊx'he:, jʊx'hai], **juch|hei|ßa, juch|hu** *(inf)* **INTERJ** hurrah, hooray

Juch|ten ['jʊxtn] **NT OR M -s,** *no pl* **a** *(= Juchtenleder)* Russia leather *or* calf, Russia **b** *(= Parfüm)* Russian leather

Juch|ten|le|der **NT** Russia leather *or* calf, Russia

juch|zen ['jʊxtsn] **VI** to shriek with delight

ju|ckeln ['jʊkln] **VI** *aux sein (inf: Auto, Zug)* to jog *or* chug along; **er ist durch die Stadt/über Land gejuckelt** he's been jogging around town/across country

ju|cken ['jʊkn] **VTI** to itch; **es juckt mich am Rücken, der Rücken juckt mir** *or* **mich** my back itches; **der Stoff juckt mich** this material makes me itch; **es juckt mich, das zu tun** *(inf)* I'm itching to do it *(inf)*; **ihn juckt das Geld dabei** *(inf)* he finds the money attractive; **das juckt mich doch nicht** *(inf)* I don't care; **lass ~** *(sl)* let your hair down *(inf)*; **ihn** *or* **ihm juckt das Fell** *(inf) or* **der Buckel** *(inf)* he's asking for a good hiding; **wens juckt, der kratze sich** *(prov)* if you don't like it you know what you can do *(inf)* VT *(= kratzen)* to scratch

Juck-: **Juck|pul|ver** NT itching powder; **Juck|reiz** M itching; **einen ~ in der Nase haben** to have an itch in one's nose

Ju|däa [ju'dɛːa] NT **-s** Jud(a)ea

Ju|da|is|mus [juda'ɪsmʊs] M **-,** *no pl* Judaism

Ju|das ['juːdas] M **-'** *(Bibl)* Judas

Ju|das M **-', -se** *(fig liter)* Judas

Ju|das-: **Ju|das|kuss** M *(liter)* Judas kiss; **der ~** *(Bibl)* the Betrayal; **Ju|das|lohn** M *(liter)* blood money, thirty pieces *pl* of silver

Ju|de ['juːdə] M **-n, -n** Jew; **er ist ~** he is a Jew → *auch* **Jüdin**

Ju|den-: **Ju|den|christ(in)** M(F) Judaeo-Christian; **Ju|den|feind(in)** M(F) anti-Semite; **ju|den|feind|lich** ADJ anti-Semitic ADV **sich ~ verhalten** to be anti-Semitic; **sich ~ äußern** to make anti-Semitic remarks; **Ju|den|geg|ner(in)** M(F) anti-Semite; **Ju|den|hass** M anti-Semitism; **Ju|den|heit** F **-,** *no pl* Jewry; **Ju|den|stern** M *symbol of the star of David usually made of yellow cloth that Jews had to display on their clothing in Nazi Germany from 1941*; **Ju|den|tum** ['juːdntuːm] NT **-s,** *no pl* **a** *(= Judaismus)* Judaism **b** *(= Gesamtheit der Juden)* Jews *pl*, Jewry **c** *(= jüdisches Wesen)* Jewishness; **Ju|den|ver|fol|gung** F persecution of (the) Jews; **Ju|den|vier|tel** NT Jewish quarter

Jü|din ['jyːdɪn] F **-, -nen** Jew, Jewish woman

jü|disch ['jyːdɪʃ] ADJ Jewish ADV **~ denken** to have Jewish beliefs; **~ heiraten** to have a Jewish wedding; **~ beeinflusst** influenced by Judaism; **seine Kinder ~ erziehen** to raise one's children as Jews

ju|di|zie|ren [judi'tsiːrən] *ptp* **judiziert** VI *(old, Jur)* = **urteilen**

Ju|do ['juːdo] M **-s, -s** *(Pol inf)* Young Democrat

Ju|do NT **-s,** *no pl* judo

Ju|do|an|zug M judo outfit *or* uniform

Ju|do|ka [ju'doːka] M **-(s), -(s)** judoka

Ju|gend ['juːgnt] F **-,** *no pl* **a** *(= Jugendzeit)* youth; *(= das Jungsein, Jugendlichkeit)* youth, youthfulness; **frühe ~** early youth, adolescence; **früheste ~** early adolescence; **in ihrer ~ waren sie ...** in their youth they were ...; **von ~ an** *or* **auf** from one's youth **b** *(= junge Menschen)* youth, young people *pl*; **die heutige ~, die ~ von heute** young people *or* the youth of today, modern youth; **die weibliche/männliche ~** young women/men; **die studentische ~** student youth; **~ hat keine Tugend** *(Prov)* young people are all the same; **Haus der ~** youth centre *(Brit) or* center *(US)* **c** *(Sport)* youth team

Ju|gend-: **Ju|gend|al|ter** NT adolescence; **Ju|gend|amt** NT youth welfare department; **Ju|gend|ar|beit** F, *no pl* **a** *(= Arbeit Jugendlicher)* youth employment **b** *(= Jugendfürsorge)* youth work; **Ju|gend|ar|beits|lo|sig|keit** F youth unemployment; **Ju|gend|ar|rest** M *(Jur)* detention; **Ju|gend|ban|de** F gang of youths; **Ju|gend|be|kannt|schaft** F friend of one's youth; **Ju|gend|be|treu|er(in)** M(F) youth leader, ≈ adult supervisor who looks after young people; **Ju|gend|be|we|gung** F **a** youth movement **b** *(Hist)* German Youth Movement *(of the early 1920s)*; **Ju|gend|bild** NT picture *or* photo taken when one was young; **~er Churchills** pictures of the young Churchill; **Ju|gend|bild|nis** NT *(Art, fig)* **~ von X** portrait of X as a young man/woman; **Ju|gend|bri|ga|de** F *(DDR)* youth brigade *(work team consisting of young people)*; **Ju|gend|buch** NT book for the younger reader *or* for young people; **Ju|gend|bü|che|rei** F library for the younger reader; **Ju|gend|buch|ver|lag** M publishing house specializing in literature for young people; **Ju|gend|club** M youth club; **Ju|gend|elf** F youth team; **Ju|gend|er|in|ne|rung** F youthful memory; **meine ~en** memories of my youth; **ju|gend|frei** ADJ suitable for young people; *Film* U(-certificate) *(Brit)*, G *(US)*; **Ju|gend|freund(in)** M(F) friend of one's youth; **Ju|gend|funk** M *(Rad)* broadcasting *or* radio for young people; *(= Sendung)* broadcast *or* programme *(Brit) or* program *(US)* for young people; **Ju|gend|für|sor|ge** F youth welfare; *(für Schulkinder)* child guidance; **Ju|gend|ge|dicht** NT youthful poem; **ju|gend|ge|fähr|dend** ADJ liable to corrupt the young; **Ju|gend|ge|richt** NT juvenile court; **Ju|gend|ge|spiele** M, **Ju|gend|ge|spie|lin** F *(hum)* young playmate; **Ju|gend|grup|pe** F youth group; **Ju|gend|heim** NT **a** youth club **b** *(= Wohnheim)* young people's home

Ju|gend|her|ber|ge® F youth hostel®

Ju|gend|her|bergs-: **Ju|gend|her|bergs|aus|weis** M youth hostelling card *(Brit)*, youth hostel ID *(US)*, YHA card *(Brit)*; **Ju|gend|her|bergs|mut|ter** F, **Ju|gend|her|bergs|va|ter** M youth hostel warden; **Ju|gend|her|bergs|ver|band** M ≈ Youth Hostel Association *(Brit)*, youth hostelling association

Ju|gend-: **Ju|gend|hil|fe** F *(Admin)* help for young people; **Ju|gend|ir|re|sein** NT *(Med)* juvenile schizophrenia; **Ju|gend|jah|re** PL days *pl* of one's youth; **Ju|gend|klub** M youth club; **Ju|gend|kri|mi|na|li|tät** F juvenile delinquency

ju|gend|lich ['juːgntlɪç] ADJ *(= jung)* young; *(= von Jugend, jung wirkend)* youthful; **eine ~e Erscheinung** a young-looking *or* youthful-looking person; **~e Banden** gangs of youths; **ein ~er Täter** a young offender, a juvenile delinquent; **~er Leichtsinn** youthful frivolity; **das sagst du so in deinem ~en Leichtsinn** *(hum)* I admire your confidence ADV youthfully; **sich ~ geben** to appear youthful; **~ wirken** to seem youthful; **er kleidet sich immer sehr ~** he always wears very youthful *or* young-looking clothes

Ju|gend|li|che(r) ['juːgntlɪçə] MF *decl as adj* young person; *(männlich auch)* youth

Ju|gend|lich|keit F **-,** *no pl* youthfulness

Ju|gend-: **Ju|gend|lie|be** F **a** young love **b** *(= Geliebter)* love *or* sweetheart of one's youth; **Ju|gend|li|te|ra|tur** F literature for younger readers *or* young people; **Ju|gend|mann|schaft** F youth team; **Ju|gend|meis|ter(in)** M(F) *(Sport)* youth champion; **Ju|gend|meis|ter|schaft** F *(Sport)* youth championships *pl*; **Ju|gend|or|ga|ni|sa|ti|on** F youth organization; **Ju|gend|pfle|ge** F youth welfare; **Ju|gend|pfle|ger(in)** M(F) youth (welfare) worker; **Ju|gend|psy|cho|lo|gie** F adolescent psychology; **Ju|gend|recht** NT law relating to young persons; **Ju|gend|rich|ter(in)** M(F) *(Jur)* magistrate *(in a juvenile court)*; **Ju|gend|schrif|ten** PL publications *pl* for young people; *(eines Autors)* youthful writings *pl*; **Ju|gend|schrift|stel|ler(in)** M(F) writer of books for young people; **Ju|gend|schutz** M protection of children and young people; **Ju|gend|sek|te** F youth sect; **Ju|gend|sen|dung** F *(Rad)* programme *(Brit) or* program *(US)* for younger listeners; *(TV)* programme *(Brit) or* program *(US)* for younger viewers; **Ju|gend|spie|le** PL youth games *pl*; **Ju|gend|stil** M, *no pl (Art)* Art Nouveau; **Ju|gend|straf|an|stalt** F *(form)* young offenders' institution *(Brit)*, juvenile correction institution *or* facility *(US)*; **Ju|gend|stra|fe** F detention *no art* in a young offenders' *(Brit) or* juvenile correction *(US)* institution; **Ju|gend|streich** M youthful exploit *or* escapade; **Ju|gend|sün|de** F youthful misdeed; **Ju|gend|the|a|ter** NT youth theatre *(Brit) or* theater *(US)*; **Ju|gend|tor|heit** F youthful folly, folly of one's youth; **Ju|gend|traum** M youthful dream; **Ju|gend|ver|band** M youth organization; **Ju|gend|ver|bot** NT **für einen Film ~ aussprechen** to ban a film for young people; **Ju|gend|ver|tre|tung** F youth representatives *pl*; **Ju|gend|vor|stel|lung** F performance for young people; **Ju|gend|wei|he** F *(Rel)* initiation; *(in Eastern Germany) ceremony in which 14-year-olds are given adult social status*; **Ju|gend|zeit** F youth, younger days *pl*; **Ju|gend|zen|trum** NT youth centre *(Brit) or* center *(US)*

Ju|go|sla|we [jugo'slaːvə] M **-n, -n** *(Hist)*, **Ju|go|sla|win** [-'slaːvɪn] F **-, -nen** *(Hist)* Yugoslav *(Hist)*

Ju|go|sla|wi|en [jugo'slaːviən] NT **-s** *(Hist)* Yugoslavia *(Hist)*

ju|go|sla|wisch [jugo'slaːvɪʃ] ADJ *(Hist)* Yugoslav(ian) *(Hist)*

Ju|li [ju'lai, 'juːlai] M **-(s), -s** *(esp Comm)* July

Ju|li ['juːli] M **-(s), -s** July → *auch* **März**

Ju|li M **-s, -s** *(Pol inf)* Young Liberal

ju|li|a|nisch [ju'liaːnɪʃ] ADJ **der ~e Kalender** the Julian calendar

Jum|bo ['jʊmbo] M **-s, -s**, **Jum|bo|jet** ['jʊmbodʒɛt] M **-s, -s** jumbo (jet)

Jum|per ['jʊmpɐ, 'dʒampɐ] M **-s, -** **a** jumper *(Brit)*, sweater **b** *(Comput)* jumper

Jum|per|kleid ['jʊmpɐ, 'dʒampɐ] NT jumper dress

jun. *abbr von* **junior** jun

jung [jʊŋ] ADJ *comp* **=er** ['jʏŋɐ], *superl* **=ste(r, s)** ['jʏŋstə] *(lit, fig)* young; *Aktien* new; **Jung und Alt** (both) young and old; **von ~ auf** from one's youth; **der ~e Meyer** young Meyer; *(= Sohn)* Meyer junior; **sie ist 18 Jahre ~** *(hum)* she's 18 years young *(hum)*; **sich** *(dat)* **ein ~es Herz bewahren** to stay young at heart; **wie ein ~er Gott** divinely; **er sieht aus wie ein ~er Gott** he looks divine *(inf)* → **jünger, jüngste(r, s), Gemüse, Pferd**

ADV *comp* **=er**, *superl* **am =sten ~ aussehen** to look young; **~ heiraten/sterben** to marry/die young; **jünger heiraten** to marry earlier; **sie starb jünger als ihr Mann** she died before her husband; **~ gefreit, nie gereut** *(Prov)* if you marry young you won't regret it; **so ~ kommen wir nicht mehr zusammen** *(hum)* you're only young once

Jung- *in cpds* young; **Jung|aka|de|mi|ker(in)** M(F) graduate; **Jung|ar|bei|ter(in)** M(F) juvenile employee *or* worker; **Jung|bau|er** M *pl* **-bäuer**, **Jung|bäu|e|rin** F young farmer; **Jung|brun|nen** M fountain of youth; **Jung|bür|ger(in)** M(F) junior citizen

Jung|chen ['jʊŋçən] NT **-s, -** *(inf)* lad *(inf)*, laddie *(Scot inf)*

Jung|de|mo|krat(in) M(F) Young Democrat

Jun|ge ['jʊŋə] M **-n, -n** *or (dated inf)* **-ns** *or (inf)* **Jungs** [jʊŋs] boy; *(= Laufjunge)* errand boy; *(Cards)* jack, knave; **~, ~!** *(inf)* boy oh boy *(inf)*; **sie ist ein richtiger ~** she's a real tomboy; **alter ~** *(inf)* my old mate *(Brit inf) or* pal *(inf)*; **mein lieber ~!** my dear boy; *(in Brief)* my dear son; **ein schwerer ~** *(inf)* a (big-time) crook *(inf)*; **unsere Jungs haben gewonnen** our boys *or* lads *(Brit inf)* won

Jün|gel|chen ['jʏŋlçən] NT **-s, -** *(pej)* young lad *(Brit inf) or* boy

jun|gen ['jʊŋən] VI to have young; *(Hündin auch)* to have pups; *(Katze auch)* to have kittens

Jun|gen-: **Jun|gen|ge|sicht** NT boy's *or* boyish face; **jun|gen|haft** ADJ boyish; **sie ist ein ~es Mädchen** she's a bit of a tomboy; **Jun|gen|klas|se** F *(Sch)* boys' class; **Jun|gen|schu|le** F boys' school; **Jun|gen|streich** M boyish prank *or* trick

Jun|ge(r) MF *decl as adj (inf)* **der/die ~** Mr/Miss X junior, the young Mr/Miss X; **die ~n** the young ones

jün|ger ['jʏŋɐ] ADJ **a** *comp von* **jung** younger; **Holbein der Jüngere** Holbein the Younger, the younger Holbein **b** *Geschichte, Entwicklung etc* recent; **die ~e Steinzeit** the later *or* New Stone Age ADV **sie sieht ~ aus, als sie ist** she looks younger than she is, she doesn't look her age → *auch* **jung**

Jün|ger ['jʏŋɐ] M **-s, -** *(Bibl, fig)* disciple

Jün|ge|rin ['jʏŋərɪn] F **-, -nen** *(fig)* disciple

Jün|ger|schaft ['jʏŋɐʃaft] F -, *no pl* disciples *pl*; *(= Jüngertum)* discipleship

Jun|ge(s) ['jʊŋə] NT *decl as adj (Zool)* young one; *(von Hund)* pup(py); *(von Katze)* kitten; *(von Wolf, Löwe, Bär)* cub; *(von Vogel)* young bird, nestling; **die ~n** the young

Jung|fer ['jʊŋfɐ] F -, -n **a** *(old, hum) (= ledige Frau)* spinster; **eine alte ~** an old maid **b** *(old: = Jungfrau)* virgin, maiden *(old)*; *(als Anrede)* mistress *(old)* **c** *(= Kammerjungfer)* maid

jüng|fer|lich ['jʏŋfɐlɪç] ADJ old-maidish

Jung|fern-: **Jung|fern|fahrt** F maiden voyage; **Jung|fern|flug** M maiden flight; **Jung|fern|-häut|chen** NT *(Anat)* hymen *(Anat)*, maidenhead; **Jung|fern|in|seln** PL Virgin Islands *pl*; **Jung|fern|kranz** M *(old)* (bridal) bouquet; **Jung|fern|re|de** F *(Parl)* maiden speech; **Jung|fern|rei|se** F maiden voyage; **Jung|-fern|schaft** ['jʊŋfɐnʃaft] F -, *no pl* virginity; **Jung|fern|stand** M *(old)* spinsterhood; **Jung|-fern|zeu|gung** F *(Biol)* parthenogenesis

Jung|fil|mer(in) M(F) young film maker; **die deutschen ~** the young German film makers

Jung|frau F virgin; *(Astron, Astrol)* Virgo *no art*; **ich bin ~** I am a virgin; *(Astrol)* I am (a) Virgo; **die ~ Maria** the Virgin Mary; **die Heilige ~** the Blessed *or* Holy Virgin; **die ~ von Orléans** Joan of Arc, the Maid of Orleans; **dazu bin ich gekommen wie die ~ zum Kind(e)** it just fell into my hands

jung|fräu|lich ['jʊŋfrɔylɪç] ADJ *Mädchen, Schnee* virgin; *(liter) Seele* pure, innocent

Jung|fräu|lich|keit F -, *no pl (von Mädchen, Schnee)* virginity; *(liter: von Seele)* purity, innocence

Jung|ge|sel|le M bachelor

Jung|ge|sel|len-: **Jung|ge|sel|len|bu|de** F *(inf)* bachelor pad *(inf)*; **Jung|ge|sel|len|da|-sein** NT bachelor's life; **Jung|ge|sel|len|-haus|halt** M bachelor('s) household *or* pad; **Jung|ge|sel|len|le|ben** NT bachelor's life; **Jung|ge|sel|len|tum** ['jʊŋgəzɛləntu:m] NT -s, *no pl* bachelorhood, bachelordom; **Jung|ge|-sel|len|wirt|schaft** F, *no pl (inf)* bachelor squalor; **Jung|ge|sel|len|woh|nung** F bachelor flat *(Brit)* *or* apartment; **Jung|ge|sel|len|-zeit** F bachelor days *pl*

Jung|ge|sel|lin F single woman

Jung|leh|rer(in) M(F) student teacher

Jüng|ling ['jʏŋlɪŋ] M -s, -e *(liter, hum)* youth

Jüng|lings-: **Jüng|lings|al|ter** NT *(liter)* youth; **jüng|lings|haft** ADJ *(geh)* youthful, boyish

Jung-: **jung+machen** VT *sep* → **machen 1 g**; **Jung|mä|del** NT *(dated)* young girl; **Jung|-mann** M *pl* **-männer** *(dated)* young man; **Jung|-pflan|ze** F young plant, seedling; **Jung|so|-zi|a|list(in)** M(F) Young Socialist

jüngst [jʏŋst] ADV *(geh)* recently, lately; **der ~ verstorbene ...** the late ...; **der ~ erlassene Befehl** the recent decree

Jung|stein|zeit F Neolithic age, New Stone Age

jüngs|tens ['jʏŋstns] ADV *(old, liter)* = **jüngst**

jüngs|te(r, s) ['jʏŋstə] ADJ **a** *superl von* **jung** youngest **b** *Werk, Schöpfung, Ereignis* latest, (most) recent; *Zeit, Vergangenheit* recent; **in der ~n Zeit** recently; **ein Ausdruck aus der ~n Zeit** a recent expression; **das Jüngste Gericht** the Last Judgement; **der Jüngste Tag** Doomsday, the Day of Judgement; **man merkt, dass er/sie nicht mehr der/die Jüngste ist** you can tell that he/she is not as young as he/she used to be; **sie ist auch nicht mehr die Jüngste** she's no (spring) chicken *(inf)*

Jung-: **Jung|stier** M young steer; **Jung|tier** NT young animal; **Jung|un|ter|neh|mer(in)** M(F) young entrepreneur, young businessman/-woman; **Jung|ver|hei|ra|te|te(r)** [-fɛɐhairatətə] MF *decl as adj* newly-wed; **jung|ver|-mählt** [-fɛɐmɛ:lt] ADJ *(geh)* newly-wed, recently married; **Jung|ver|mähl|te(r)** MF *decl as adj (form)* **die (beiden) ~n** the newly-weds *pl*, the young couple *sing*; **Jung|vieh** NT young cattle *pl*; **Jung|wäh|ler(in)** M(F) young voter; **Jung|wild** NT young game

Ju|ni ['ju:ni] M -(s), -s June → *auch* **März**

Ju|ni|kä|fer M chafer

ju|ni|or ['ju:niɔɐ] ADJ **Franz Schulz ~** Franz Schulz, Junior

Ju|ni|or ['ju:niɔɐ] M -s, **Junioren** [ju'nio:rən] **a** *(usu hum: = Sohn)* junior; **wie gehts dem ~?** how's junior? **b** *(auch* **Juniorchef***)* son of the boss; *(= Sohn des Vorsitzenden)* son of the chair(man); **kann ich mal den ~(chef) sprechen?** can I speak to Mr X junior? **c** *usu pl (Sport)* junior

Ju|ni|or|chef M boss's son, son of the boss

Ju|ni|or|che|fin F boss's daughter, daughter of the boss

Ju|ni|o|rin [ju'nio:rɪn] F -, -nen → **Junior c**

Ju|ni|or-: **Ju|ni|or|part|ner(in)** M(F) junior partner; **Ju|ni|or|pass** M *(Rail)* ≈ young person's railcard *(Brit)*, ≈ youth railroad pass *(US)*

Junk|bond ['dʒaŋkbɔnd] M -s, -s, **Junk-Bond** M -s, -s *(Fin)* junk bond

Jun|ker ['jʊŋkɐ] M -s, - *(Hist)* squire; *(preußisch)* Junker

Jun|ker|tum ['jʊŋkɐtu:m] NT -s, *no pl* squirarchy; *(in Preußen)* Junkerdom

Junk|food ['dʒaŋkfu:d] NT -s, -s, **Junk-Food** NT -s, -s *(inf)* junk food

Jun|kie ['dʒaŋki] M -s, -s *(inf)* junkie *(inf)*

Junk|mail F *(Comput, Internet)* junk mail, spam *(inf)*

Junk|tim ['jʊŋktɪm] NT -s, -s *(Pol: = Paket)* package (deal); **zwischen X und Y besteht ein ~** X is dependent on Y

Ju|no ['ju:no] M -(s), -s *(esp Comm)* June

Jun|ta ['xʊnta, 'jʊnta] F -, **Junten** [-tn] *(Pol)* junta

Jupe [ʒy:p] M -s, -s *(Sw)* skirt

Ju|pi|ter ['ju:pitɐ] M -s Jupiter

Ju|pi|ter|lam|pe® F ≈ klieg light

jur. *abbr von* **juristisch**

Ju|ra ['ju:ra] M -s, *no pl (Geol, Geog)* Jura (Mountains) *pl*

Ju|ra *no art (Univ)* law

Ju|ras|si|er [ju'rasiɐ] M -s, -, **Ju|ras|si|e|rin** [-iərɪn] F -, -nen person from the Canton of Jura

ju|ras|sisch [ju'rasɪʃ] ADJ *(Geol)* Jurassic; *(= aus Kanton Jura)* of the Canton of Jura

Ju|ra|stu|di|um NT study of law; **das ~ dauert acht Semester** the law degree (course) takes four years

ju|ri|disch [ju'ri:dɪʃ] ADJ, ADV *(old, Aus)* = **juristisch**

Ju|ris|dik|ti|on [jurɪsdɪk'tsio:n] F -, *no pl (geh)* administration of justice; *(rare: = Gerichtshoheit)* jurisdiction

Ju|ris|pru|denz [jurɪspru'dɛnts] F -, *no pl (geh)* jurisprudence

Ju|rist [ju'rɪst] M -en, -en, **Ju|ris|tin** [-'rɪstɪn] F -, -nen jurist, legal eagle *(hum inf)*; *(= Student)* law student

Ju|ris|ten|deutsch NT, **Ju|ris|ten|spra|che** F, *no pl* legalese *(pej)*, legal jargon *or* language

Ju|ris|te|rei [jurɪstə'rai] F -, *no pl (inf)* law

ju|ris|tisch [ju'rɪstɪʃ] ADJ legal; *Problem etc auch* juridical *(form)*; *Studium auch* law *attr*; **die ~e Fakultät** the Faculty of Law; **eine ~e Person** a legal entity, a corporation, a corporate body ADV legally; **~ denken** to think in legal terms; **etw ~ betrachten** to consider the legal aspects of sth; **etw ~ bewerten** to assess sth from a legal point of view

Ju|ror ['ju:ro:ɐ] M -s, **Juroren** [-'ro:rən], **Ju|ro|rin** [-'ro:rɪn] F -, -nen juror, member of the jury; *(bei Wettbewerb)* member of the jury, judge, adjudicator

Jur|te ['jʊrtə] F -, -n yurt

Ju|ry [ʒy'ri:, 'ʒy:ri] F -, -s jury *sing or pl*; *(bei Wettbewerb auch)* judges *pl*, adjudicators *pl*

Jus [ʒy:] F OR M OR NT -, *no pl* **a** *(= Bratensaft)* gravy; *(geliert)* dripping **b** *(Sw: = Fruchtsaft)* juice

Jus [ju:s] NT -, **Jura** ['ju:ra] *(Aus, Sw: = Univ)* law

just [jʊst] ADV *(old)* precisely, exactly, just; **~ gekommen** just come

jus|tier|bar [jʊs'ti:ɐba:ɐ] ADJ *(Tech)* adjustable

jus|tie|ren [jʊs'ti:rən] *ptp* **justiert** VT to adjust; *Gewehr, Zielfernrohr etc auch* to collimate *(form)*; *Münzen auch* to weight; *(Typ, Comput)* to justify

Jus|tier|schrau|be F *(Tech)* adjusting screw

Jus|tie|rung F -, -en adjustment; *(von Gewehr, Zielfernrohr auch)* collimation *(form)*; *(von Münzen auch)* weighting; *(Typ, Comput)* justification

Jus|tier|waa|ge F adjusting balance

Jus|ti|tia [jʊs'ti:tsia] F -s Justice; *(fig)* the law

jus|ti|ti|a|bel [jʊsti'tsia:bl] ADJ = **justiziabel**

Jus|ti|ti|ar [jʊsti'tsia:ɐ] M -s, -e, **Jus|ti|ti|a|rin** [-'tsia:rɪn] F -, -nen = **Justiziar(in)**

Jus|tiz [jʊs'ti:ts] F -, *no pl (als Prinzip)* justice; *(als Institution)* judiciary; *(= die Gerichte)* courts *pl*

jus|ti|zi|a|bel [jʊsti'tsia:bl] ADJ *(geh)* litigable

Jus|ti|zi|ar [jʊsti'tsia:ɐ] M -s, -e, **Jus|ti|zi|a|rin** [-'tsia:rɪn] F -, -nen lawyer, legal adviser

Jus|tiz-: **Jus|tiz|be|am|te(r)** M *decl as adj*, **Jus|tiz|be|am|tin** F judicial officer; **Jus|tiz|-be|hör|de** F legal *or* judicial authority; **Jus|-tiz|ge|walt** F judiciary (power); **Jus|tiz|ho|-heit** F legal sovereignty; **Jus|tiz|irr|tum** M miscarriage of justice, judicial error *(esp US)*; **Jus|tiz|mi|nis|ter(in)** M(F) minister of justice, justice minister; **Jus|tiz|mi|nis|te|ri|um** NT ministry of justice, ≈ Department of Justice *(US)*; **Jus|tiz|mord** M judicial murder; **Jus|-tiz|pa|last** M palace of justice; **Jus|tiz|ver|-wal|tung** F administration of justice; **Jus|-tiz|voll|zugs|an|stalt** F *(form)* place of detention

Ju|te ['ju:tə] F -, *no pl* jute

Ju|te|ta|sche ['ju:tə-] F jute *or* burlap bag

Jüt|land ['jy:tlant] NT -s *(Geog)* Jutland

ju|ve|nil [juve'ni:l] ADJ *(geh)* juvenile

Ju|wel [ju've:l] M OR NT -s, -en jewel, gem; **~en** *(= Schmuck)* jewellery *(Brit)*, jewelry *(US)*

Ju|wel NT -s, -e *(fig)* jewel, gem

Ju|we|lier [juve'li:ɐ] M -s, -e, **Ju|we|lie|rin** [-'li:rɪn] F -, -nen jeweller *(Brit)*, jeweler *(US)*; *(= Geschäft)* jewel(l)er's (shop)

Ju|we|lier-: **Ju|we|lier|ge|schäft** NT jeweller's *(Brit)* *or* jeweler's *(US)* (shop); **Ju|we|-lier|wa|ren** PL jewellery *(Brit)*, jewelry *(US)*

Jux [jʊks] M -es, -e *(inf)* **etw aus ~ tun/sagen** to do/say sth as a joke *or* in fun; **etw aus lauter ~ und Tollerei tun** to do sth out of sheer high spirits *or* for sheer fun; **sich** *(dat)* **einen ~ aus etw machen** to make a joke (out) of sth

ju|xen ['jʊksn] VI *(inf)* to joke

ju|xig ['jʊksɪç] ADJ *(inf)* funny

jwd [jɔtve:'de:] ADV *(hum)* in the back of beyond *(Brit)*, in the middle of nowhere; *(= weit entfernt)* miles out *(inf)*

K

K, k [ka:] NT -, - K, k
Ka|a|ba ['ka:aba] F -, *no pl* Kaaba, Caaba
Ka|ba|le [ka'ba:lə] F -, -n *(old)* cabal *(old)*
Ka|ba|rett [kaba'rɛt, 'kabarɛt, -re] NT -s, -e *or* -s **a** cabaret; *(= Darbietung)* cabaret (show); **ein politisches ~** a satirical political revue, a political satire **b** *(= Servierplatte)* serving dish *(divided into sections)*
Ka|ba|ret|tist [kabare'tɪst] M -en, -en, **Ka|ba|ret|tis|tin** [-'tɪstɪn] F -, -nen cabaret artist
ka|ba|ret|tis|tisch [kabarɛ'tɪstɪʃ] ADJ cabaret *attr*; *(politisch-satirisch)* political revue *attr*
Ka|bäus|chen [ka'bɔysçən] NT -s, - *(inf) (= Zimmer)* cubbyhole *(inf)*; *(= Laube)* hut, cabin
Kab|ba|la ['kabala] F - *(Rel)* cabbala
Kab|be|lei [kabə'lai] F -, -en *(inf)* bickering, squabbling
kab|be|lig ['kabəlɪç] ADJ *Meer* choppy
kab|beln ['kabln] VIR *(inf)* to bicker, to squabble
Ka|bel ['ka:bl] NT -s, - **a** *(Elec)* wire; *(von Elektrogeräten)* wire, flex *(Brit)*; *(= Telefonkabel)* flex *(Brit)*, cord; *(= Strom- oder Telegrafenleitung)* cable **b** *(old Naut: = Tau)* rope; *(= Drahtseil)* cable **c** *(old: = Telegramm)* cable(gram)
Ka|bel-: **Ka|bel|an|schluss** M *(TV)* cable connection; **~ bekommen** to get cable (TV); **Ka|bel|baum** M *(Elec)* harness; **Ka|bel|be|richt** M cabled report; **Ka|bel|fern|se|hen** NT cable television
Ka|bel|jau ['ka:bljau] M -s, -e *or* -s cod
Ka|bel-: **Ka|bel|klem|me** F *(Tech)* cable clip *or* clamp; **Ka|bel|län|ge** F *(Naut)* cable, cable's length; **Ka|bel|le|ger** [-le:gɐ] M -s, - *(Naut)* cable layer; **Ka|bel|man|tel** M cable covering
ka|beln ['ka:bln] VTI to cable
Ka|bel-: **Ka|bel|netz** NT *(TV)* cable network; **Ka|bel|trom|mel** F cable drum *or* reel; **Ka|bel|tu|ner** M *(TV)* cable decoder *or* tuner
Ka|bi|ne [ka'bi:nə] F -, -n *(= Umkleidekabine, Anprobierkabine, Duschkabine)* cubicle; *(Naut, Aviat, von Kran)* cabin; *(= Vorführkabine)* projection room; *(= Seilbahnkabine)* car
Ka|bi|nen-: **Ka|bi|nen|bahn** F cable railway; **Ka|bi|nen|kof|fer** M cabin trunk; **Ka|bi|nen|per|so|nal** NT *(Aviat)* cabin crew; **Ka|bi|nen|rol|ler** M bubble car
Ka|bi|nett [kabi'nɛt] NT -s, -e **a** *(Pol)* cabinet **b** *(für Kunstsammlungen) (= Raum)* gallery; *(= Schrank)* cabinet **c** *(Aus: = kleines Zimmer)* closet
Ka|bi|nett M -s, -e *(= Wein) high-quality German white wine*
Ka|bi|netts-: **Ka|bi|netts|be|schluss** M cabinet decision; **Ka|bi|netts|bil|dung** F formation of a/the cabinet; **Ka|bi|netts|chef(in)** M(F) head of the cabinet; **Ka|bi|netts|fra|ge** F *(rare)* = **Vertrauensfrage**; **Ka|bi|netts|jus|tiz** F *interference in the course of justice by a sovereign*; **Ka|bi|netts|mit|glied** NT cabinet member, member of the cabinet
Ka|bi|nett|stück NT **a** *(old: einer Sammlung)* showpiece, pièce de résistance **b** *(fig)* masterstroke
Ka|bi|netts|um|bil|dung F cabinet reshuffle
Ka|bi|nett|wein M *high-quality German white wine*
Ka|bis ['ka:bɪs] M -, *no pl (Sw, S Ger)* = **Weißkohl**
Kab|rio ['ka:brio] NT -(s), -s *(inf)* convertible
Kab|ri|o|lett [kabrio'lɛt, *(Aus, S Ger)* kabrio'le:] NT -s, -s **a** *(Aut)* convertible **b** *(Hist)* cabriolet
Ka|buff [ka'bʊf] NT -s, -e *or* -s *(inf)* (poky) little corner
Ka|chel ['kaxl] F -, -n (glazed) tile; **etw mit ~n auslegen** to tile sth, to cover sth with *or* in tiles
ka|cheln ['kaxln] VT to tile
Ka|chel|ofen M tiled stove
kack|braun ADJ *(sl)* dirty brown
Ka|cke ['kakə] F -, *no pl* **a** *(vulg)* crap *(sl)*, shit *(sl)*; **dann ist aber die ~ am Dampfen** *(sl)* then the shit really will hit the fan *(sl)* **b** *(sl: = Mist)* crap *(inf)*; **so 'ne ~** shit *(sl)*
ka|cken ['kakn] VI *(vulg)* to crap *(sl)*, to shit *(sl)*
ka|ckig ['kakɪç] ADJ *(sl) Farbe* shitty *(inf)*
Ka|da|ver [ka'da:vɐ] M -s, - carcass
Ka|da|ver|ge|hor|sam M *(pej)* blind *or* slavish obedience
Ka|denz [ka'dɛnts] F -, -en cadence; *(= Improvisation)* cadenza
Ka|der ['ka:dɐ] M -s, - *(Mil, Pol)* cadre; *(Sport)* squad; *(= Fachleute)* group of specialists; *(= Fachmann)* specialist; *(Sw: = Vorgesetzte)* management
Ka|der-: **Ka|der|lei|ter(in)** M(F) *(Hist)* personnel officer; **Ka|der|schmie|de** F, *no pl (pej)* élite school
Ka|dett [ka'dɛt] M -en, -en, **Ka|det|tin** [-'dɛtɪn] F -, -nen *(Mil)* cadet
Ka|det|ten-: **Ka|det|ten|an|stalt** F cadet school; **Ka|det|ten|schul|schiff** NT naval (cadet) training ship
Ka|di ['ka:di] M -s, -s *(dated inf)* beak *(inf)*; **jdn vor den ~ schleppen** to take sb to court; **zum ~ laufen** to go to court
Kad|mi|um ['katmiʊm] NT -s, *no pl* cadmium
Kä|fer ['kɛ:fɐ] M -s, - **a** beetle (*auch inf: VW*) **b** *(dated inf: = Mädchen)* bird *(esp Brit inf)*, chick *(esp US inf)*, babe *(inf)*; **ein flotter ~** a nice bit of skirt *(Brit inf)*, a real babe *(inf)*
Kaff [kaf] NT -s, -s *or* -e *(inf)* dump *(inf)*, hole *(inf)*
Kaf|fee ['kafe, ka'fe:] M -s, -s **a** coffee; **zwei ~, bitte!** two coffees, please; **~ mit Milch** white coffee *(Brit)*, coffee with milk; **schwarzer ~** black coffee; **~ verkehrt** *(dated)* white coffee *(Brit) (made with hot milk)*, coffee with hot milk; **~ kochen** to make coffee; **das ist kalter ~** *(inf)* that's old hat *(inf)* **b** *no pl (= Nachmittagskaffee)* ≈ (afternoon) tea *(Brit)*, (afternoon) coffee and cake; **~ und Kuchen** coffee and cakes, ≈ afternoon tea *(Brit)*; **jdn zu ~ und Kuchen einladen** to invite sb for *or* to coffee and cakes *or* (afternoon) tea *(Brit)*
Kaf|fee NT -s, -s *(old: = Café)* café
Kaf|fee-: **Kaf|fee|au|to|mat** M coffee machine *or* dispenser; **Kaf|fee|boh|ne** F coffee bean; **kaf|fee|braun** ADJ coffee-coloured *(Brit)*, coffee-colored *(US)*; **Kaf|fee-Er|satz** M coffee substitute; **Kaf|fee-Ex|trakt** M coffee essence; **Kaf|fee|fahrt** F day trip; *(= Verkaufsfahrt)* promotional trip *(during which passengers are served coffee and offered goods to buy)*; **Kaf|fee|fil|ter** M coffee filter; *(inf: = Filterpapier)* filter (paper); **Kaf|fee|ge|schirr** NT coffee set; **Kaf|fee|haus** NT café; **Kaf|fee|haus|mu|sik** F *(pej)* palm court music; **Kaf|fee|kan|ne** F coffeepot; **Kaf|fee|klatsch** M, *no pl (inf)*, **Kaf|fee|kränz|chen** NT coffee klatsch *(US)*, ≈ coffee morning *(Brit)*; **ich treffe mich mit meinen Freundinnen zu einem ~** I'm meeting some friends for a chat over (a cup of) coffee *or* tea; **Kaf|fee|löf|fel** M coffee spoon; **Kaf|fee|ma|schi|ne** F coffee machine; **Kaf|fee|mi|schung** F blended coffee; **Kaf|fee|müh|le** F coffee grinder; **Kaf|fee|müt|ze** F cosy *(Brit) or* cozy *(US, for coffeepot)*; **Kaf|fee|pau|se** F coffee break; **Kaf|fee|rös|ter** [-rø:stɐ, -rœstɐ] M -s, - coffee roaster; **Kaf|fee|sah|ne** F (coffee) cream; **Kaf|fee|satz** M coffee grounds *pl*; **aus dem ~ wahrsagen** *or* **lesen** to read (the) tea leaves; **Kaf|fee|ser|vice** [-zɛrvi:s] NT coffee set; **Kaf|fee|sor|te** F type *or* sort of coffee; **Kaf|fee|strauch** M coffee tree; **Kaf|fee|stu|be** F coffee shop; **Kaf|fee|tan|te** F *(hum)* coffee addict; *(in Café)* old biddy; **Kaf|fee|tas|se** F coffee cup; **Kaf|fee|tisch** M *(= Frühstückstisch)* breakfast table; *(nachmittags)* (afternoon) tea table *(Brit)*, serving table *(US)*; **Kaf|fee|wär|mer** [-vɛrmɐ] M -s, - cosy *(Brit) or* cozy *(US, for coffeepot)*; **Kaf|fee|was|ser** NT, *no pl* water for coffee, coffee water; **ich habe das ~ schon aufgesetzt** I've just put the kettle on; **Kaf|fee|wei|ßer** [-vaisɐ] M, *no pl* coffee whitener *(Brit) or* creamer *(US)*
Kaf|fer ['kafɐ] M -s, - *(pej inf: = dummer Kerl)* thickhead *(inf)*, duffer *(inf)*
Kaf|fer ['kafɐ] M -n, -n, **Kaf|fe|rin** [-ərɪn] F -, -nen kaffir; *(pej inf)* nigger *(pej)*
Kä|fig ['kɛ:fɪç] M -s, -e [-gə] cage; **sie sitzt in einem goldenen ~** *(fig)* she is just a bird in a gilded cage
Kä|fig-: **Kä|fig|hal|tung** F caging; **Kä|fig|vo|gel** M cage bird
kaf|ka|esk [kafka'ɛsk] ADJ Kafkaesque
Kaf|tan ['kaftan] M -s, -e caftan
kahl [ka:l] ADJ *Mensch, Kopf* bald; *(= kahl geschoren)* shaved, shorn; *Vogel* bald, featherless; *Wand, Raum* bare; *Pflanze, Baum* bare, leafless; *Landschaft, Berge* barren, bleak; **eine ~e Stelle** a bald patch; **~ werden** *(Mensch)* to go bald; *(Baum)* to lose its leaves; **~ geschoren** *(Kopf)* shaven, shorn
Kahl-: **Kahl|fraß** M defoliation; **kahl fres|sen** *irreg*, **kahl+fres|sen** *sep irreg* VT to strip bare; *Ernte* to destroy completely; **Kahl|frost** M black frost; **kahl|ge|scho|ren** ADJ → **kahl**; **Kahl|heit** F -, *no pl (von Mensch, Kopf, Vogel)* baldness; *(von Wand, Raum)* bareness; *(von Pflanze, Baum)* bareness, leaflessness; *(von Landschaft, Berg)* barrenness; **Kahl|kopf** M bald head; *(= Mensch)* bald person; **ein ~ sein** to be bald; **kahl|köp|fig** ADJ baldheaded; **Kahl|köp|fig|keit** [-kœpfɪçkait] F -, *no pl* baldness; **kahl sche|ren** *irreg*, **kahl+sche|ren** *sep irreg* VT *Schafe* to shear; *Hecken* to cut right back; **jdn ~** to shave sb's head; **Kahl|schlag** M **a** *(= abgeholzte Fläche)* clearing **b** *(= Tätigkeit)* deforestation **c** *(inf)* **(Aktion)** ~ *(= Entlassungen)* axing; *(= Abriss)* demolition; **kahl schla|gen** *irreg*, **kahl+schla|gen** *sep irreg* VT to deforest, to clear; **Kahl|wild** NT *(= geweihlose, weibliche Tiere)* does *pl*; *(= geweihlose Kälber)* fawns *pl*

Kahm [ka:m] M -(e)s, *no pl* mould *(Brit)*, mold *(US)*

kah|mig ['ka:mɪç] ADJ mouldy *(Brit)*, moldy *(US)*

Kahn [ka:n] M -(e)s, ¨-e ['kɛ:nə] **a** (small) boat; *(= Stechkahn)* punt; ~ **fahren** to go boating/punting **b** *(= Lastschiff)* barge; **ein alter** ~ *(inf)* an old tub *(inf)* **c** *(inf) (= Bett)* bed, pit *(inf)*; *(dated: = Gefängnis)* jug *(dated inf)*; *(Ftbl: = Tor)* net **d Kähne** PL *(= große Schuhe)* clodhoppers *pl (inf)*

Kahn|fahrt F row; *(in Stechkahn)* punt

Kai [kai] M -s, -e *or* -s quay; *(= Uferdamm auch)* waterfront

Kai|an|la|ge F quayside

Kai|man ['kaiman] M -s, -e *(Zool)* cayman

Kai|mau|er F quay wall

Kains|mal ['kains-] NT *pl* **-male**, **Kains|zei|chen** NT *(= Stigma)* mark of Cain

Kai|ro ['kairo] NT -s Cairo

Kai|ser ['kaizɐ] M -s, - emperor; **der deutsche** ~ the German Emperor, the Kaiser; **des ~s neue Kleider** *(fig)* the emperor's new clothes; **wo nichts ist, hat der ~ sein Recht verloren** *(Prov)* you can't get blood from a stone; **gebt dem ~, was des ~s ist!** *(Bibl)* render unto Caesar the things which are Caesar's; **(da,) wo selbst der ~ zu Fuß hingeht** *(dated hum)* the smallest room (in the house) *(hum)*; **das ist ein Streit um des ~s Bart** that's just splitting hairs; **er kommt sich vor wie der ~ von China** *(inf)* he thinks he's the king of the castle, he thinks he's God → *auch* **Kaiserin**

Kai|ser-: **Kai|ser|ad|ler** M imperial eagle; **Kai|ser|haus** NT imperial family

Kai|se|rin ['kaizərɪn] F -, -nen empress → *auch* **Kaiser**

Kai|se|rin|mut|ter F *pl* **-mütter** dowager empress

Kai|ser|kro|ne F **a** imperial crown **b** *(Bot)* crown imperial

kai|ser|lich ['kaizɐlɪç] ADJ imperial; **diese Besitzungen waren früher** ~ these possessions used to belong to the Emperor; **Seine Kaiserliche Majestät/Hoheit** His Imperial Majesty/Highness ADV ~ **gesinnt** monarchistic, imperialistic

Kai|ser|li|che(r) ['kaizɐlɪçə] MF *decl as adj* Imperialist

kai|ser|lich-kö|nig|lich ['kaizɐlɪç'kø:nɪklɪç] ADJ imperial and royal *(pertaining to the Dual Monarchy of Austro-Hungary)*

Kai|ser-: **Kai|ser|pfalz** F imperial palace; **Kai|ser|reich** NT empire; **Kai|ser|schma|ren** M, **Kai|ser|schmarrn** M *(Aus)* sugared, cut-up pancake with raisins; **Kai|ser|schnitt** M Caesarean (section); **Kai|ser|sem|mel** F *(S Ger, Aus)* bread roll *(with a raised pattern on top)*, kaiser roll *(US)*; **Kai|ser|stadt** F imperial city

Kai|ser|tum ['kaizɐtu:m] NT -s, **Kaisertümer** [-ty:mɐ] **a** *(= Regierungsform, Reich)* Empire **b** *(= Amt)* emperorship

Kai|ser-: **Kai|ser|wet|ter** NT *(dated)* magnificent sunshine; **Kai|ser|wür|de** F **a** *(= Ehre)* honour *(Brit)* *or* honor *(US)* *or* dignity of an emperor **b** *(= Amt)* emperorship

Ka|jak ['ka:jak] M OR NT -s, -s kayak

Ka|jal [ka'ja:l] M -, *no pl* kohl

Ka|jal|stift M kohl eye pencil

Ka|je ['ka:jə] F -, -n *(N Ger)* quay; *(= Uferdamm auch)* waterfront

Ka|jüt|boot NT cabin boat

Ka|jü|te [ka'jy:tə] F -, -n cabin; *(größer auch)* stateroom

Ka|ka|du ['kakadu] M -s, -s cockatoo

Ka|kao [ka'ka:o, ka'kau] M -s, -s cocoa; **jdn durch den ~ ziehen** *(inf) (= veralbern)* to make fun of sb, to take the mickey out of sb *(Brit inf)*; *(= boshaft reden)* to run *or* do sb down *(Brit)*, to put sb down

Ka|kao-: **Ka|kao|boh|ne** F cocoa bean; **Ka|kao|pul|ver** NT cocoa powder; **Ka|kao|strauch** M cacao palm

ka|keln ['ka:kln] VI *(inf)* to chat, to blether *(Brit inf)*, to blather

Ka|ker|lak ['ka:kɐlak] M -s *or* -en, -en cockroach

ka|ki ['ka:ki] ADJ *pred* khaki

Ka|ki ['ka:ki] F -, -s *(= Frucht)* kaki; *(= Baum auch)* Japanese persimmon

Ka|ki ['ka:ki] M -s, *no pl (= Stoff)* khaki

Ka|ki NT -s, *no pl (= Farbe)* khaki

ka|ki|far|ben [-farbn] ADJ khaki(-coloured *(Brit)*), khaki(-colored *(US)*)

Ka|ko|fo|nie, **Ka|ko|pho|nie** [kakofo'ni:] F -, -n [-'ni:ən] *(geh)* cacophony

Kak|tee [kak'te:] F -, -n [-'te:ən], **Kak|tus** ['kaktʊs] M -, **Kakteen** *or (inf)* **-se** [-'te:ən] cactus

Ka|lab|re|ser [kala'bre:zɐ] M -s, - slouch hat

Ka|lab|ri|en [ka'la:briən] NT -s Calabria

Ka|la|mi|tät [kalami'tɛ:t] F -, -en *(geh)* calamity; *(= heikle Lage)* predicament

Ka|lan|der [ka'landɐ] M -s, - *(Tech)* calender

ka|lan|dern [ka'landɐn] *ptp* **kalandert** VT *(Tech)* to calender

Ka|lasch|ni|kow® [ka'laʃnikɔf] F -, -s *(Mil)* Kalashnikov®

Ka|lau|er ['ka:lauɐ] M -s, - corny joke; *(= Wortspiel)* corny pun; *(= alter Witz)* old chestnut

ka|lau|ern ['ka:lauɐn] VI *(inf)* to joke; *(= Wortspiele machen)* to pun

Kalb [kalp] NT -(e)s, ¨-er ['kɛlbɐ] **a** calf; *(von Rehwild auch)* fawn → **golden ADJ b** *(inf: = Mädchen)* silly young girl *or* thing

Kälb|chen ['kɛlpçən] NT -s, - *dim von* **Kalb**

kal|ben ['kalbn] VI *(Kuh, Gletscher)* to calve

Käl|ber|mast ['kɛlbɐ-] F *(Agr)* calf-fattening

kal|bern ['kalbɐn], **käl|bern** ['kɛlbɐn] VI *(inf)* to fool *or* mess about *or* around *(inf)*

Käl|ber|ne(s) ['kɛlbɐnə] NT *decl as adj (S Ger, Aus)* veal

Kalb-: **Kalb|fell** NT = **Kalbsfell**; **Kalb|fleisch** NT veal; **Kalb|le|der** NT calfskin

Kälb|lein ['kɛlplain] NT -s, - *dim von* **Kalb**

Kalbs-: **Kalbs|bra|ten** M roast veal; **Kalbs|brust** F *(Cook)* breast of veal; **Kalbs|fell** NT **a** *(= Fell)* calfskin **b** *(old: = Trommel)* drum; **Kalbs|hach|se** F, **Kalbs|ha|xe** F *(Cook)* knuckle of veal; **Kalbs|keu|le** F leg of veal; **Kalbs|le|ber** F calves' liver; **Kalbs|le|der** NT calfskin; **Kalbs|schnit|zel** NT veal cutlet

Kal|dau|ne [kal'daunə] F -, -n entrails *pl*

Ka|le|bas|se [kale'basə] F -, -n calabash

Ka|le|do|ni|en [kale'do:niən] NT -s *(liter)* Caledonia

Ka|lei|do|skop [kalaido'sko:p] NT -s, -e kaleidoscope

ka|lei|do|sko|pisch [kalaido'sko:pɪʃ] ADJ kaleidoscopic

ka|len|da|risch [kalɛn'da:rɪʃ] ADJ according to the calendar, calendrical *(spec)*

Ka|len|da|ri|um [kalɛn'da:riʊm] NT -s, **Kalendarien** [-riən] *(geh, Eccl)* calendar

Ka|len|der [ka'lɛndɐ] M -s, - calendar; *(= Taschenkalender)* diary; **etw im ~ rot anstreichen** to make sth a red-letter day

Ka|len|der-: **Ka|len|der|blatt** NT page of a/the calendar; **Ka|len|der|block** M *pl* **-blöcke** *or* **-blocks** day-by-day calendar; **Ka|len|der|jahr** NT calendar year; **Ka|len|der|mo|nat** M calendar month; **Ka|len|der|spruch** M calendar motto; **Ka|len|der|tag** M calendar day; **Ka|len|der|wo|che** F calendar week

Ka|le|sche [ka'lɛʃə] F -, -n *(Hist)* barouche

Kal|fak|ter [kal'faktɐ] M -s, -, **Kal|fak|tor** [kal'fakto:ɐ] M -s, **Kalfaktoren a** *(old: = Heizer)* boilerman, stoker **b** *(= allgemeiner Gehilfe)* odd-jobman

kal|fa|tern [kal'fa:tɐn] *ptp* **kalfatert** VTI *(Naut)* to caulk

Ka|li ['ka:li] NT -s, -s potash

Ka|li|ber [ka'li:bɐ] NT -s, - *(lit, fig)* calibre *(Brit)*, caliber *(US)*; *(zum Messen)* calibrator

Ka|li-: **Ka|li|berg|werk** NT potash mine; **Ka|li|dün|ger** M potash fertilizer

Ka|lif [ka'li:f] M -en, -en caliph

Ka|li|fat [kali'fa:t] NT -(e)s, -e caliphate

Ka|li|for|ni|en [kali'fɔrniən] NT -s California

ka|li|for|nisch [kali'fɔrnɪʃ] ADJ Californian

ka|li|hal|tig ADJ containing potassium

Ka|li|ko ['kaliko] M -s, -s calico; *(für Buchbinderei)* cloth

Ka|li-: **Ka|li|sal|pe|ter** M saltpetre *(Brit)*, saltpeter *(US)*; **Ka|li|salz** NT potassium salt

Ka|li|um ['ka:liʊm] NT -s, *no pl (abbr* **K**) potassium

Ka|li|um|per|man|ga|nat ['ka:liʊmpɛrmaŋga'na:t] NT -s, *no pl (Chem)* potassium permanganate

Kalk [kalk] M -(e)s, -e lime; *(zum Tünchen)* whitewash; *(Anat)* calcium; **gebrannter** ~ quicklime; **gelöschter** ~ slaked lime; **Wände/Decken mit ~ bewerfen** to whitewash walls/ceilings; **bei ihm rieselt schon der** ~ *(inf)* he's going a bit gaga *(Brit inf)*, he's losing his marbles *(inf)*

Kalk-: **kalk|ar|tig** ADJ chalky, calcareous *(form)*; **Kalk|bo|den** M chalky soil; **Kalk|bren|ne|rei** F lime works *sing or pl*

kal|ken ['kalkn] VT **a** *(= tünchen)* to whitewash **b** *(Agr)* to lime

Kalk-: **Kalk|er|de** F chalky soil; **Kalk|gru|be** F lime pit; **kalk|hal|tig** ADJ *Boden* chalky; *Wasser* hard; **Kalk|man|gel** M *(Med)* calcium deficiency; *(von Boden)* lime deficiency; **Kalk|ofen** M limekiln; **Kalk|schie|fer** M calcareous slate; *(Typ)* lithostone; **Kalk|stein** M limestone; **Kalk|stein|bruch** M limestone quarry

Kal|kül [kal'ky:l] M OR NT -s, -e **a** calculation *usu pl* **b** *(Math)* calculus

Kal|ku|la|ti|on [kalkula'tsio:n] F -, -en calculation; *(= Kostenberechnung)* costing

Kal|ku|la|ti|ons|ta|bel|le F *(Comput)* spreadsheet

Kal|ku|la|tor [kalku'la:to:ɐ] M -s, **Kalkulatoren** [-'to:rən], **Kal|ku|la|to|rin** [-'to:rɪn] F -, -nen **a** *(als Beruf)* cost estimator **b** *(= berechnender Mensch)* calculator, calculating person

kal|ku|la|to|risch [kalkula'to:rɪʃ] ADJ arithmetical; *(Fin) Kosten* imputed; **~e Methoden** methods of calculation ADV **das ist ~ einwandfrei, aber ...** the figures are perfect, but ...; **eine ~ notwendige Bedingung** a necessary premise for the calculations

kal|ku|lier|bar ADJ calculable

Kal|ku|lier|bar|keit [kalku'li:ɐba:ɐkait] F -, *no pl* calculability

kal|ku|lie|ren [kalku'li:rən] *ptp* **kalkuliert** VT to calculate

Kal|kut|ta [kal'kʊta] NT -s *(Hist)* Calcutta *(Hist)* → **Kolkata**

Kal|li|gra|fie, **Kal|li|gra|phie** [kaligra'fi:] F -, *no pl* calligraphy

kal|lös [ka'lø:s] ADJ *(Med)* callous

Kal|lus ['kalʊs] M -, **-se** *(Biol, Med)* callus

Kal|mar M *(Zool)* squid

Kal|me ['kalmə] F -, -n *(Naut)* calm

Kal|men|gür|tel M, **Kal|men|zo|ne** F calm belt *or* zones *pl*

Kal|mück [kal'mʏk] M -en, -en, **Kal|mü|cke** [kal'mʏkə] M -n, -n, **Kal|mü|ckin** [-'mʏkɪn] F -, -nen Kalmu(c)k *(member of Mongol tribe)*

Ka|lo|rie [kalo'ri:] F -, -n [-'ri:ən] calorie

Ka|lo|ri|en-: **ka|lo|ri|en|arm** ADJ low-calorie ADV **sich ~ ernähren** to have *or* be on a low-calorie diet; **~ essen** to eat low-calorie food; **~ süßen** to use low-calorie sweeteners; **Ka|lo|ri|en|be|darf** M calorie requirement; **ka|lo|ri|en|be|wusst** ADJ *Ernährungsweise etc* calorie-conscious ADV **sich ~ ernähren** to (only) eat low-calorie foods, to count one's calories *(inf)*; **Ka|lo|ri|en|bom|be** F *(inf)* **das ist eine echte** ~ it's got about sixty million calories *(inf)*; **Ka|lo|ri|en|ge|halt** M calorie content; **ka|lo|ri|en|re|du|ziert** [-redutsi:ɐt] ADJ *Mahlzeit* reduced-calorie; **~e Kost** reduced calorie food; **ka|lo|ri|en|reich** ADJ high-calorie ADV **~ essen** to eat high-calorie food; **sich ~ ernähren** to have *or* be on a high-calorie diet, to eat high-calorie foods

Ka|lo|ri|me|ter [kalori'meːtɐ] M calorimeter

kalt [kalt] ADJ *comp* **⸚er** ['kɛltɐ], *superl* **⸚este(r, s)** ['kɛltəstə] cold; **mir ist/wird ~** I am/I'm getting cold; **im Kalten** in the cold; **~e Platte** *plate of cold meats, cheeses, salad etc*; **jdm die ~e Schulter zeigen** to give sb the cold shoulder, to cold-shoulder sb; **den Sprung ins ~e Wasser wagen** *(fig)* to jump in at the deep end; **~es Grausen** *or* **Entsetzen überkam mich** my blood ran cold; **der Kalte Krieg** the Cold War; **~er Krieger** cold warrior; **ein ~er Staatsstreich** a bloodless coup → **Hundeschnauze, Fuß a, heiß ADV a, Kaffee a**

ADV *comp* **⸚er**, *superl* **am ⸚esten ~ schlafen** to sleep in an unheated room; **~ baden/duschen** to have a cold bath/to take a cold shower; **etw ~ waschen** to wash sth in cold water; **abends essen wir ~** we eat a cold meal in the evening; **etw ~ stellen** to put sth to chill; **etw ~ lagern** to store sth cold; **etw ~ bearbeiten** *(Tech)* to work sth cold; **~ gepresst** *Öl* cold-pressed; **die Wohnung kostet ~ 500 EUR** the flat *(Brit) or* apartment costs 500 euros without heating; **~ rauchen** *(hum)* to have an unlit cigarette in one's mouth; **da kann ich nur ~ lächeln** *(inf)* that makes me laugh; **~ lächelnd** *(iro)* cool as you please; **es überlief** *or* **überrieselte ihn ~** cold shivers ran through him; **jdn ~ erwischen** *(inf)* to shock sb; **es hatte ihn ~ erwischt** *(inf)* he was caught with his trousers down *(inf)*

Kalt-: **kalt+blei|ben** *sep irreg aux sein*, **kalt blei|ben** △ *irreg aux sein* VI *(fig)* to remain unmoved *or* impassive; **Kalt|blut** NT carthorse; **Kalt|blü|ter** [-blyːtɐ] M **-s, -** *(Zool)* cold-blooded animal; **kalt|blü|tig** ADJ **a** *(fig) Mensch, Mord* cold-blooded; *(= gelassen) Handlung* cool; *Mensch* cool, cool-headed, calm **b** *(Zool)* cold-blooded ADV cold-bloodedly; *ermorden* in cold blood, cold-bloodedly; **Kalt|blü|tig|keit** [-blyːtɪçkait] F **-**, *no pl (fig) (von Mensch, Verbrechen)* cold-bloodedness; *(= Gelassenheit) (von Handlung)* cool(ness); *(von Mensch)* cool(ness), cool-headedness

Käl|te ['kɛltə] F **-**, *no pl* **a** *(von Wetter, Material etc)* cold; *(= Kälteperiode)* cold spell; **die ~ des Stahls/Steins** *etc* the coldness *or* cold of the steel/stone *etc*; **fünf Grad ~** five degrees of frost *or* below freezing; **vor ~ zittern** to shiver with cold; **bei dieser ~** in this cold; **hier ist eine solche ~, dass ...** it is so cold here that ... **b** *(fig)* coldness, coolness

Käl|te-: **Käl|te|an|la|ge** F refrigeration plant; **käl|te|be|stän|dig** ADJ cold-resistant, resistant to cold; **Käl|te|brü|cke** F *(Build)* transmitter of cold; **die Fugen wirken als ~n** the gaps introduce cold air; **Käl|te|ein|bruch** M (sudden) cold spell; *(für kurze Zeit)* cold snap; **käl|te|emp|find|lich** ADJ sensitive to cold; *Mensch auch* chilly; **Käl|te|er|zeu|gung** F refrigeration; **käl|te|fest** ADJ cold-resistant, resistant to cold; **Käl|te|ge|fühl** NT feeling of cold(ness); **Käl|te|grad** M degree of frost; **Käl|te|ma|schi|ne** F refrigeration machine; **Käl|te|pe|ri|o|de** F cold spell; **Käl|te|pol** M *(Geog)* cold pole, pole of cold; **käl|te|re|sis|tent** ADJ cold-resistant, resistant to cold; **Käl|te|re|sis|tenz** F cold resistance, resistance to cold; **Käl|te|schutz** M protection against (the) cold; **käl|te|schüt|zend** ADJ **~e Schicht** cold-resistant layer; **käl|te|sen|si|bel** ADJ sensitive to cold; *Mensch auch* chilly; **Käl|te|star|re** F *(Zool)* (cold-induced) torpor; **Käl|te|sturz** M cold spell; **Käl|te|tech|nik** F refrigeration technology; **Käl|te|the|ra|pie** F *(Med)* cryotherapy; **Käl|te|tod** M **den ~ sterben** to freeze to death, to die of exposure; *(Erde)* to freeze over completely; **käl|te|to|le|rant** ADJ tolerant of cold; **käl|te|un|emp|find|lich** ADJ insensitive to cold; **Käl|te|wel|le** F cold spell

Kalt-: **Kalt|front** F *(Met)* cold front; **kalt|ge|presst** [-gəprɛst] ADJ → **kalt ADV**; **kalt|ge|schleu|dert** ADJ → **schleudern VTI b**; **Kalt|haus** NT refrigerated glasshouse; **kalt|her|zig** ADJ cold-hearted; **Kalt|her|zig|keit** [-hɛrtsɪkkait] F **-**, *no pl* cold-heartedness; **kalt|lä|chelnd** ADV → **kalt ADV**; **kalt+las|sen** *sep irreg*, **kalt las|sen** △ *irreg* VT *(fig)* **jdn ~** to leave sb cold; **Kalt|leim** M wood glue; **Kalt|luft** F *(Met)* cold air; **Kalt|luft|front** F *(Met)* cold front; **Kalt|luft|mas|sen** PL *(Met)* cold air mass(es *pl*); **kalt+ma|chen** VT *sep (sl)* to do in *(inf)*; **Kalt|mie|te** F rent exclusive of heating; **Kalt|scha|le** F *(Cook) cold sweet soup*; **kalt|schnäu|zig** [-ʃnɔytsɪç] *(inf)* ADJ *(= gefühllos)* cold, unfeeling, callous; *(= unverschämt)* insolent; *Kritiker* sarky *(Brit inf)*, sarcastic ADV *(= gefühllos)* coldly, unfeelingly, callously; *(= unverschämt)* insolently; **~ sagte sie ...** as cool as you please she said ...; **Kalt|schnäu|zig|keit** F **-**, *no pl (inf) (= Gefühllosigkeit)* coldness, callousness; *(= Unverschämtheit)* insolence; *(von Kritikern)* sarcasm; **Kalt|schwei|ßen** NT **-s**, *no pl* cold weld; **Kalt|start** M *(Aut, Comput)* cold start; *(Comput auch)* cold boot; **Kalt|start|au|to|ma|tik** F automatic choke; **kalt+stel|len** VT *sep* **a** *(inf) jdn* to demote, to put out of harm's way *(inf)* **b** *Sekt etc* → **kalt ADV**; **Kalt|was|ser|kur** F = **Kneippkur**; **Kalt|wel|le** F *(= Frisur)* cold perm *or* wave

Kal|va|ri|en|berg [kal'vaːriən-] M Calvary

kal|vi|nisch [kal'viːnɪʃ] ADJ Calvinistic

Kal|vi|nis|mus [kalvi'nɪsmʊs] M **-**, *no pl* Calvinism

Kal|vi|nist [kalvi'nɪst] M **-en, -en**, **Kal|vi|nis|tin** [-'nɪstɪn] F **-, -nen** Calvinist

kal|vi|nis|tisch [kalvi'nɪstɪʃ] ADJ Calvinist(ic)

Kal|zi|um ['kaltsiʊm] NT **-s**, *no pl (abbr* **Ca**) calcium

Kal|zi|um|kar|bo|nat NT *(Chem)* calcium carbonate

kam *pret von* **kommen**

Ka|ma|ril|la [kama'rɪlja, kama'rɪla] F **-, Kama|ril|len** [-'rɪljən, -'rɪlən] *(geh)* political clique

Kam|bod|scha [kam'bɔdʒa] NT **-s** Cambodia

Kam|bod|scha|ner [kambɔ'dʒaːnɐ] M **-s, -**, **Kam|bod|scha|ne|rin** [-ərɪn] F **-, -nen** Cambodian

kam|bod|scha|nisch [kambɔ'dʒaːnɪʃ] ADJ Cambodian

Ka|mee [ka'meː] F **-, -n** [-'meːən] cameo

Ka|mel [ka'meːl] NT **-(e)s, -e a** camel; **eher geht ein ~ durchs Nadelöhr ...** *(prov)* it is easier for a camel to go through the eye of a needle ... *(prov)* **b** *(inf)* clot *(Brit inf)*, clown *(inf)*; **ich ~!** silly *or* stupid me!

Ka|mel-: **Ka|mel|foh|len** NT, **Ka|mel|fül|len** NT camel foal; **Ka|mel|haar** NT *(Tex)* camel hair

Ka|me|lie [ka'meːliə] F **-, -n** camellia

Ka|mel|le [ka'mɛlə] F **-, -n** *usu pl (inf)* **das sind doch alte** *or* **olle ~n** that's old hat *(inf)*; **er hat nichts als alte** *or* **olle ~n erzählt** he just said the same old things

Ka|mel|trei|ber(in) M(F) camel driver, cameleer

Ka|me|ra ['kamәra, 'kaːmәra] F **-, -s** camera

Ka|me|ra|as|sis|tent(in) M(F) assistant camera operator

Ka|me|rad [kamə'raːt] M **-en, -en** [-dn], **Ka|me|ra|din** [-'raːdɪn] F **-, -nen** *(Mil etc)* comrade; *(= Gefährte, Lebenskamerad)* companion, friend; *(dated: = Arbeitskamerad)* workmate; *(dated: = Freund)* friend, buddy *(inf)*, chum *(inf)*

Ka|me|ra|den|schwein NT *(sl pej)* backstabber

Ka|me|ra|de|rie [kamәradə'riː] F **-**, *no pl (pej)* bonhomie

Ka|me|rad|schaft [kamə'raːtʃaft] F **-, -en** comradeship, camaraderie

ka|me|rad|schaft|lich [kamə'raːtʃaftlɪç] ADJ comradely; **eine ~e Ehe** a companionate marriage ADV **rein ~ zusammenleben** to live together purely as friends; **sich ~ verhalten** to act *or* behave loyally; **~ miteinander umgehen** to be very friendly to each other

Ka|me|rad|schaft|lich|keit F **-**, *no pl* comradeship

Ka|me|rad|schafts-: **Ka|me|rad|schafts|abend** M reunion; **Ka|me|rad|schafts|ehe** F companionate marriage; **Ka|me|rad|schafts|geist** M, *no pl* spirit of comradeship, esprit de corps

Ka|me|ra-: **Ka|me|ra|ein|stel|lung** F shot; **Ka|me|ra|fahrt** F camera movement; **Ka|me|ra|frau** F camerawoman; **Ka|me|ra|füh|rung** F camera work; **ka|me|ra|ge|recht** ADJ suitable for the cameras ADV **sie stellte sich ~ in Pose** she posed for the cameras; **Ka|me|ra|mann** M *pl* **-männer** cameraman; **ka|me|ra|scheu** ADJ camera-shy; **Ka|me|ra|schwenk** M pan; **ka|me|ra|über|wacht** ADJ *Gebäude, Platz* under video surveillance *pred*

Ka|me|ra|lis|tik [kamera'lɪstɪk] F **-**, *no pl* **a** *(old: = Finanzwirtschaft)* finance **b** *(= Buchführung)* governmental accounting

ka|me|ra|lis|tisch [kamera'lɪstɪʃ] ADJ *Rechnungswesen, Buchhaltungsverfahren* governmental

Ka|me|run ['kaməruːn] NT **-s** the Cameroons *pl*

Ka|mi|ka|ze [kami'kaːtsə, kami'kaːzə] M **-, -** kamikaze

Ka|mi|ka|ze- *in cpds* kamikaze; **Ka|mi|ka|ze|an|griff** M kamikaze attack; **Ka|mi|ka|ze|flie|ger(in)** M(F) kamikaze pilot

Ka|mil|le [ka'mɪlə] F **-, -n** camomile

Ka|mil|len|tee M camomile tea

Ka|min [ka'miːn] M OR (DIAL) NT **-s, -e a** *(= Schornstein)* chimney; *(= Abzugsschacht)* flue; **etw in den ~ schreiben** to write sth off **b** *(= offene Feuerstelle)* fireplace; **eine Plauderei am ~** a fireside chat; **wir saßen am** *or* **vor dem ~** we sat by *or* in front of the fire; **ein offener ~** an open fireplace **c** *(Geol: = Felskamin)* chimney

Ka|min-: **Ka|min|be|steck** NT fireside companion set; **Ka|min|feu|er** NT open fire, fire in the grate; **Ka|min|gar|ni|tur** F fireside companion set; **Ka|min|keh|rer** [-keːrɐ] M **-s, -**, **Ka|min|keh|re|rin** [-ərɪn] F **-, -nen** *(dial)* chimney sweep; **Ka|min|sims** M OR NT mantelpiece

Kamm [kam] M **-(e)s, ⸚e** ['kɛmə] **a** *(für Haar, = Webekamm)* comb; **sich** *(dat)* **mit dem ~ durch die Haare fahren** to run a comb through one's hair; **alle/alles über einen ~ scheren** *(fig)* to lump everyone/everything together **b** *(von Vogel, Eidechse etc)* comb → **schwellen VI c** *(von Pferd)* crest **d** *(Cook) (Hammelfleisch)* (middle) neck; *(Schweinefleisch)* shoulder; *(Rindfleisch)* neck **e** *(von Trauben)* stalk **f** *(= Gebirgskamm)* crest, ridge; *(= Wellenkamm)* crest

käm|men ['kɛmən] VT *Haar, Baumwolle* to comb; *Wolle auch* to card, to tease; **sie kämmte ihm die Haare** she combed his hair VR to comb one's hair

Kam|mer ['kamɐ] F **-, -n a** *(allgemein)* chamber; *(Parl)* chamber, house; *(= Ärztekammer, Anwaltskammer)* professional association; *(= Herzkammer)* ventricle; *(Mil)* store *usu pl*; **erste/zweite ~** Upper/Lower House **b** *(= Zimmer)* (small) room, boxroom *(Brit)*; *(dial: = Schlafzimmer)* bedroom

Kam|mer-: **Kam|mer|bul|le** M *(Mil sl)* quartermaster; **Kam|mer|die|ner** M valet

Käm|me|rei [kɛmə'rai] F **-, -en a** *(Hist: = Finanzverwaltung)* treasury *(old)*, finance department **b** *(Tex)* combing works *sing or pl*

Käm|me|rer ['kɛmərɐ] M **-s, - a** *(= Beamter)* finance officer → *auch* **Kämmrerin b** *(Hist, Eccl)* chamberlain

Kam|mer-: **Kam|mer|frau** F *(Hist)* lady-in-waiting; **Kam|mer|ge|richt** NT ≈ Supreme Court; **Kam|mer|herr** M *(Hist)* chamberlain; **Kam|mer|jä|ger(in)** M(F) *(= Schädlingsbekämpfer)* pest controller *(Brit)*, exterminator *(US)*; *(= Leibjäger)* (head) gamekeeper; **Kam|mer|jung|fer** F lady-in-waiting; **Kam|mer|kon|zert** NT chamber concert

Käm|mer|lein ['kɛmɐlain] NT **-s, -** chamber; **im stillen ~** in private

Kam|mer-: **Kam|mer|mäd|chen** NT lady-in-waiting; **Kam|mer|mu|sik** F chamber music; **Kam|mer|or|ches|ter** NT chamber orchestra; **Kam|mer|sän|ger(in)** M(F), **Kam|mer|schau|spie|ler(in)** M(F) *(Titel) title formerly given by Duke etc, now by authorities, to singer/actor for excellence*; **Kam|mer|spiel** NT **a** *(= Schauspiel)* play for a studio theatre *(Brit) or* theater *(US)* **b** *(= Theater)* studio theatre *(Brit) or* theater *(US)*; **Kam|mer|ton** M, *no pl* concert pitch; **Kam|mer|zo|fe** F chambermaid

Kamm-: **Kamm|garn** NT worsted; **Kamm|mu|schel** F scallop; **Kamm|rad** NT cogwheel

Kämm|re|rin ['kɛmrərɪn] F **-, -nen** *(= Beamtin)* finance officer

Kamm|stück NT *(Cook)* shoulder

Kammuschel △ F → **Kammmuschel**

Kamp [kamp] M **-(e)s, ¨-e** ['kɛmpə] *(N Ger)* plot (of land), field

Kam|pag|ne [kam'panjə] F **-, -n** **a** campaign **b** *(bei Ausgrabungen)* stage

Käm|pe ['kɛmpə] M **-n, -n** *(obs, iro)* (old) campaigner *or* soldier

Kampf [kampf] M **-(e)s, ¨-e** ['kɛmpfə] fight, struggle *(um* for); *(Mil auch)* combat; *(Mil: = Gefecht)* battle; *(Mil: = Feindbegegnung)* engagement, encounter; *(= Boxkampf)* fight, bout, contest; **jdm/einer Sache den ~ ansagen** *(fig)* to declare war on sb/sth; **den ~ (gegen jdn/etw) aufnehmen** to commence battle (against sb/sth); *(fig)* to take up the fight *or* struggle (against sb/sth); **den ~/die Kämpfe einstellen** to stop fighting; **den ~ um etw verloren geben** to abandon the struggle for sth; **den ~ aufgeben** to give up the struggle; **den ~ abbrechen** *(Sport)* to stop the fight; **es kam zum ~** clashes occurred, fighting broke out; **auf in den ~!** *(hum)* once more unto the breach! *(hum)*; **er ist im ~ gefallen** he fell in action *or* battle; **im ~ für die Freiheit** in the fight *or* struggle for freedom; **im ~ für Frankreich** in the battle for France; **der ~ ums Dasein** the struggle for existence; **der ~ der Geschlechter** *or* **zwischen den Geschlechtern** the battle of the sexes; **der ~ um die Macht** the battle *or* struggle for power; **ein ~ auf Leben und Tod** a fight to the death; **~ dem Atomtod!** fight the nuclear menace!; **innere Kämpfe** inner conflicts

Kampf-: **Kampf|ab|schnitt** M combat zone *or* sector; **Kampf|ab|stim|mung** F vote; **es kam zur ~** they put it to the vote; **Kampf|ab|zei|chen** NT campaign medal; **Kampf|an|sa|ge** F declaration of war; *(Sport)* announcement; **Kampf|an|zug** M *(Mil etc)* battle dress *no art*, battle uniform; **Kampf|auf|trag** M *(Mil)* mission; **Kampf|aus|bil|dung** F *(Mil)* combat training; **Kampf|bahn** F sports stadium, arena; **Kampf|be|gier|de** F *(liter)* bellicosity *(liter)*; **kampf|be|reit** ADJ ready for battle; **Kampf|be|reit|schaft** F readiness for battle; **kampf|be|tont** ADJ *(Sport) Spiel, Partie* tough, hard, attacking *attr*; **Kampf|bom|ber** M fighter-bomber; **Kampf|ein|heit** F *(Mil)* combat mission; **Kampf|ein|satz** M *(Mil)* combat mission

kämp|fen ['kɛmpfn] VI to fight, to struggle *(um, für* for); *(Sport: = angreifen)* to attack; **gegen etw ~** to fight (against) sth; **die Rangers-Elf kämpft morgen gegen Celtic** Rangers are playing (against) Celtic tomorrow; **mit dem Tode ~** to fight for one's life; **mit den Tränen ~** to fight back one's tears; **gegen die Wellen ~** to battle against the waves; **ich hatte mit schweren Problemen zu ~** I had difficult problems to contend with; **ich habe lange mit mir ~ müssen, ehe ...** I had a long battle with myself before ... VT *(usu fig) Kampf* to fight

Kamp|fer ['kampfɐ] M **-s,** *no pl* camphor

Kämp|fer ['kɛmpfɐ] M **-s, -** *(Archit)* impost

Kämp|fer ['kɛmpfɐ] M **-s, -, Kämp|fe|rin** [-ərɪn] F **-, -nen** fighter; *(= Krieger auch)* warrior

kämp|fe|risch ['kɛmpfərɪʃ] ADJ aggressive; *Spiel auch* attacking ADV aggressively; **sich ~ einsetzen** to fight hard; **sich ~ bewähren** to fight well

Kämp|fer|na|tur F born fighter

kampf|er|probt [-lɛɐpro:pt] ADJ battle-tried

Kampf|es|lust F pugnacity

kampf|es|lus|tig ADJ belligerent, pugnacious

Kampf-: **kampf|fä|hig** ADJ *(Mil)* fit for action; *Boxer* fit to fight; *Gewerkschaft etc* able to fight; **Männer im ~en Alter** men of fighting age; **Kampf|fä|hig|keit** F *(Mil)* fitness for action; *(von Boxer)* fitness to fight; *(von Gewerkschaft etc)* ability to fight; **Kampf|flug|zeug** NT fighter (plane); **Kampf|gas** NT poison gas; **Kampf|geist** M, *no pl* fighting spirit; **Kampf|ge|mein|schaft** F *(Pol)* action group; **Kampf|ge|sche|hen** NT, *no pl* fighting, action; **ins ~ eingreifen** *(lit, fig)* to enter the fray; **Kampf|grup|pe** F task force; *(Mil auch)* combat group; **Kampf|hahn** M *(lit, fig)* fighting cock; **Kampf|hand|lung** F *usu pl* clash *usu pl*; **Kampf|hub|schrau|ber** M helicopter gunship; **Kampf|hund** M fighting dog; **Kampf|kraft** F fighting strength; **kampf|los** ADJ peaceful; *Sieg* uncontested, unopposed ADV peacefully, without a fight; **sich ~ ergeben, ~ aufgeben** to surrender without a fight; **kampf|lus|tig** ADJ belligerent, pugnacious; **Kampf|maß|nah|me** F offensive measure; **~n ergreifen** to go onto the offensive; **Kampf|pan|zer** M combat tank; **Kampf|pau|se** F lull in the fighting *or* battle; **Kampf|platz** M battlefield; *(Sport)* arena, stadium; **Kampf|preis** M **a** *(in Wettkampf)* prize **b** *(Comm)* cut-throat price; **Kampf|rich|ter(in)** M(F) *(Sport)* referee; *(Tennis)* umpire; *(Schwimmen, Skilaufen)* judge; **Kampf|schrift** F broadsheet; **Kampf|sport** M martial art; **kampf|stark** ADJ *Heer, Sportler, Hunderasse* powerful; **Kampf|stär|ke** F *(Mil)* combat strength; **Kampf|stoff** M weapon, warfare agent; **Kampf|tag** M **~ der Arbeiterklasse** *(DDR)* May Day; **Kampf|trin|ker** M *(sl)* pisshead *(inf)*; **kampf|un|fä|hig** ADJ *(Mil)* unfit for action; *Boxer* unfit to fight; **einen Panzer/ein Schiff ~ machen** to put a tank/ship out of action, to cripple a tank/ship; **~ schlagen** *(Boxen)* to put out of the fight; **Kampf|un|fä|hig|keit** F *(Mil)* unfitness for action; *(von Boxer)* unfitness to fight; **Kampf|wa|gen** M chariot

kam|pie|ren [kam'pi:rən] *ptp* **kampiert** VI to camp (out); **im Wohnzimmer ~** *(inf)* to doss down *(Brit) or* camp out *(US)* in the sitting room *(inf)*

Ka|na|an ['ka:naan] NT **-s** *(Bibl)* Canaan

Ka|na|da ['kanada] NT **-s** Canada

Ka|na|di|er [ka'na:diɐ] M **-s, -** **a** Canadian **b** *(Sport)* Canadian canoe

Ka|na|di|e|rin [ka'na:diərɪn] F **-, -nen** Canadian (woman/girl)

ka|na|disch [ka'na:dɪʃ] ADJ Canadian

Ka|nail|le [ka'naljə] F **-, -n** *(dated pej) (= gemeiner Mensch)* scoundrel, rascal; *(= Pöbel, Mob)* rabble, canaille

Ka|na|ke [ka'na:kə] M **-n, -n, Ka|na|kin** [-'na:kɪn] F **-, -nen** *(= Südseeinsulaner)* Kanaka; *(pej sl: = Ausländer, Südländer)* wop *(pej)*, dago *(pej)*

Ka|nal [ka'na:l] M **-s, Ka|nä|le** [ka'nɛ:lə] **a** *(= Schifffahrtsweg)* canal; *(= Wasserlauf)* channel; *(zur Bewässerung)* ditch, canal; *(zur Entwässerung)* drain; *(für Abwässer)* sewer; **der (Ärmel)kanal** the (English) Channel **b** *(Rad, TV, fig: = Weg)* channel; **etw durch die richtigen Kanäle weiterleiten** to pass sth on through the proper channels; **dunkle Kanäle** dubious channels

Ka|nal-: **Ka|nal|ar|bei|ter(in)** M(F) **a** sewerage worker **b** PL *(Pol fig)* pressure group; **Ka|nal|bau** M *pl* **-bauten** canal building *or* construction; **Ka|nal|de|ckel** M drain cover

Ka|nal|in|seln PL **die ~** *(im Ärmelkanal)* the Channel Islands *pl*

Ka|na|li|sa|ti|on [kanaliza'tsio:n] F **-, -en** **a** *(für Abwässer)* sewerage system, sewers *pl*; *(= das Kanalisieren)* sewerage installation **b** *(= Begradigung eines Flusslaufes)* canalization

Ka|na|li|sa|ti|ons|sys|tem NT *(für Abwässer)* sewerage system, sewers *pl*

ka|na|li|sie|ren [kanali'zi:rən] *ptp* **kanalisiert** VT *Fluss* to canalize; *(fig) Energie, Emotionen, Informationen* to channel; *Gebiet* to install *or* lay sewers in

Ka|nal-: **Ka|nal|rohr** NT sewage pipe; **Ka|nal|tun|nel** M Channel Tunnel; **Ka|nal|zo|ne** F canal zone

Ka|na|pee ['kanape] NT **-s, -s** *(old, hum)* sofa, couch, settee

Ka|na|ren [ka'na:rən] PL *(form)* Canaries *pl*, Canary Islands *pl*

Ka|na|ri|en|vo|gel [ka'na:riən-] M canary

Ka|na|ri|sche In|seln [ka'na:rɪʃə] PL Canaries *pl*, Canary Islands *pl*

Kan|da|re [kan'da:rə] F **-, -n** (curb) bit; **jdn an die ~ nehmen** *(fig)* to take sb in hand

Kan|de|la|ber [kande'la:bɐ] M **-s, -** candelabra

Kan|di|dat [kandi'da:t] M **-en, -en, Kan|di|da|tin** [-'da:tɪn] F **-, -nen** candidate; *(bei Bewerbung auch)* applicant; **jdn als ~en aufstellen** to nominate sb, to put sb forward as a candidate

Kan|di|da|ten|lis|te F list of candidates

Kan|di|da|tur [kandida'tu:ɐ] F **-, -en** candidature, candidacy

kan|di|die|ren [kandi'di:rən] *ptp* **kandidiert** VI *(Pol)* to stand, to run *(für* for); **für das Amt des Präsidenten ~** to stand *or* run for president

kan|diert [kan'di:ɐt] ADJ *Frucht* candied

Kan|dis(|zu|cker) ['kandɪs-] M **-,** *no pl* rock candy

Kän|gu|ru ['kɛŋguru] NT **-s, -s, Kän|gu|ruh** △ NT **-s, -s** kangaroo

Ka|nin [ka'ni:n] NT **-s, -e** rabbit (fur)

Ka|nin|chen [ka'ni:nçən] NT **-s, -** rabbit; **sich wie ~ vermehren** *(inf)* to breed like rabbits

Ka|nin|chen-: **Ka|nin|chen|bau** M *pl* **-baue** rabbit warren; **Ka|nin|chen|stall** M rabbit hutch

Ka|nis|ter [ka'nɪstɐ] M **-s, -** can; *(= Blechkanister)* jerry can

kann [kan] *3. pers sing pres von* **können**

Kann|be|stim|mung ['kan-] F *(Jur)* discretionary provision

Känn|chen ['kɛnçən] NT **-s, -** *(für Milch)* jug; *(für Kaffee)* pot; **ein ~ Kaffee** a pot of coffee

Kan|ne ['kanə] F **-, -n** can; *(= Teekanne, Kaffeekanne)* pot; *(= Milchkanne)* churn; *(= Ölkanne)* can, tin; *(= Weinkanne)* ≈ tankard; *(= Gießkanne)* watering can; **sich** *(dat)* **die ~ geben** *(sl: = sich betrinken)* to get pissed *(Brit inf, inf) or* plastered

kan|ne|liert [kanə'li:ɐt] ADJ *(Archit)* fluted

Kan|ni|ba|le [kani'ba:lə] M **-n, -n, Kan|ni|ba|lin** [-'ba:lɪn] F **-, -nen** cannibal

kan|ni|ba|lisch [kani'ba:lɪʃ] ADJ cannibalistic; *(= brutal)* rough; **ich habe ~en Hunger** *(hum inf)* I could eat a horse *(inf)*

Kan|ni|ba|li|sie|rung F *(Ind)* cannibalization

Kan|ni|ba|lis|mus [kaniba'lɪsmʊs] M **-,** *no pl* cannibalism

kann|te *pret von* **kennen**

Ka|non ['ka:nɔn] M **-s, -s** canon

Ka|no|na|de [kano'na:də] F **-, -n** *(Mil)* barrage; *(fig auch)* tirade

Ka|no|ne [ka'no:nə] F **-, -n** **a** gun; *(Hist)* cannon; *(sl: = Pistole)* rod *(US sl)*, gat *(sl)*, shooter *(inf)*; **~n auffahren** *(lit, fig)* to bring up the big guns; **mit ~n auf Spatzen schießen** *(inf)* to take a sledgehammer to crack a nut **b** *(fig inf: = Könner)* ace *(inf)* **c** *(inf)* **das ist unter aller ~** that defies description

Ka|no|nen-: **Ka|no|nen|boot** NT gunboat; **Ka|no|nen|boot|dip|lo|ma|tie** F, **Ka|no|nen|boot|po|li|tik** F gunboat diplomacy; **Ka|no|nen|don|ner** M rumbling of guns; **Ka|no|nen|fut|ter** NT *(inf)* cannon fodder; **Ka|no|nen|ku|gel** F cannon ball; **Ka|no|nen|ofen** M cylindrical iron stove; **Ka|no|nen|rohr** NT gun barrel; **heiliges ~!** *(inf)* good grief! *(inf)*; **Ka|no|nen|schlag** M *(= Feuerwerkskörper)* (fire)cracker

Ka|no|nier [kano'ni:ɐ] **M -s, -e**, **Ka|no|nie|rin** [-'ni:rɪn] **F -, -nen** *(Mil)* gunner

Ka|no|ni|ker [ka'no:nikɐ] **M -s, -**, **Ka|no|ni|kus** [ka'no:nikʊs] **M -, Kanoniker** *(Eccl)* canon

Ka|no|ni|sa|ti|on [kanoniza'tsio:n] **F -, -en** *(Eccl)* canonization

ka|no|nisch [ka'no:nɪʃ] **ADJ** *(Eccl)* canonical; **~es Recht** canon law

ka|no|ni|sie|ren [kanoni'zi:rən] *ptp* **kanonisiert** **VT** *(Eccl)* to canonize

Ka|no|nis|se [kano'nɪsə] **F -, -n**, **Ka|no|nis|sin** [kano'nɪsɪn] **F -, -nen** canoness

Ka|nos|sa *etc* = **Canossa** *etc*

kan|ta|bel [kan'ta:bl] **ADJ** *(Mus)* cantabile; *Musikstück* songlike; *(= sangbar)* singable

Kan|ta|te [kan'ta:tə] **F -, -n** *(Mus)* cantata

Kan|ta|te *no art (Eccl) fourth Sunday after Easter*

Kan|te ['kantə] **F -, -n** *(eines Gegenstandes, einer Fläche)* edge; *(= Rand, Borte)* border; *(= Webkante)* selvage; **wir legten die Steine ~ an ~** we laid the stones end to end; **etw auf ~ kleben** to stick sth with the edges flush; **Geld auf die hohe ~ legen** *(inf)* to put money by *(Brit inf) or* away; **Geld auf der hohen ~ haben** *(inf)* to have (some) money put by *(Brit inf) or* away → **abstoßen VT a, fehlen VI** *impers*

kan|ten ['kantn] **VT a** *(= auf die Kante stellen)* to tilt; **nicht ~!** *(bei Kisten etc)* do not tilt!, this way up! **b** *(= mit Kanten versehen)* to trim, to edge **c** *auch vi (Ski)* to edge

Kan|ten ['kantn] **M -s, -** *(N Ger)* crust, heel *(dial)*

Kan|ter ['kantɐ] **M -s, -** canter

Kan|ter|sieg M *(Sport)* runaway victory, walkover, walkaway *(US)*

Kant-: **Kant|ha|ken** M **jdn beim ~ nehmen** *(inf)* **jdn beim ~ zu fassen kriegen** *(inf)* to haul *(Brit) or* rake sb over the coals *(inf)*; **Kant|holz** NT (piece of) squared timber

kan|tig ['kantɪç] **ADJ** *Holz* edged, squared; *Gesicht* angular; *Charakter* awkward

Kan|ti|le|ne [kanti'le:nə] **F -, -n** *(Mus)* cantilena

Kan|ti|ne [kan'ti:nə] **F -, -n** canteen

Kan|ti|nen|es|sen NT **a** *(einzelnes Gericht)* canteen meal **b** *(= in einer Kantine angebotene Gerichte)* canteen food, canteen meals *pl*

kan|tisch ['kantɪʃ] **ADJ** Kantian

Kan|ton [kan'to:n] **M -s, -e** canton

> **KANTON**
>
> Switzerland is a federal state made up of states called cantons. There are 26 cantons, of which six are demi-cantons (cantons that have been split in two). Cantons are autonomous within the framework of the Federal Constitution. They are responsible for the organization of their own government by means of a cantonal constitution. Thus state authorities differ from canton to canton both in name and structure.

kan|to|nal [kanto'na:l] **ADJ** cantonal **ADV ~ anerkannt** recognized *or* accepted throughout the canton; **~ finanziert** financed by the canton; **~ geregelt** regulated by the cantons *or* at cantonal level; **~ unterschiedliche Praxis** practices that differ from one canton to the other

Kan|to|nal|wahl F *(Sw)* cantonal election

Kan|to|nist [kanto'nɪst] **M -en, -en ein unsicherer ~ sein** to be unreliable

Kan|tons-: **Kan|tons|rat** M *(Sw)* **a** *(= Kantonsparlament)* cantonal council **b** *(= Mitglied des Kantonsrats)* member of a/the cantonal council; **Kan|tons|rä|tin** F *(Sw: = Mitglied des Kantonsrats)* member of a/the cantonal council

Kan|tor ['kanto:ɐ] **M -s, Kantoren** choirmaster; *(in Synagoge)* cantor

Kan|to|rei [kanto'rai] **F -, -en** (church) choir

Kan|to|rin [kan'to:rɪn] **F -, -nen** choirmistress

Ka|nu ['ka:nu] **NT -s, -s** canoe

Ka|nü|le [ka'ny:lə] **F -, -n** *(Med)* cannula

Ka|nu|te [ka'nu:tə] **M -n, -n**, **Ka|nu|tin** [-'nu:tɪn] **F -, -nen** canoeist

Kan|zel ['kantsl] **F -, -n a** pulpit; **auf der ~** in the pulpit; **die ~ besteigen** to get into the pulpit; **von der ~ herab** from the pulpit **b** *(Aviat)* cockpit **c** *(eines Berges)* promontory, spur **d** *(Hunt)* (look-out) platform

Kan|zel-: **Kan|zel|dach** NT canopy; **Kan|zel|red|ner(in)** M(F) orator

kan|ze|ro|gen [kantsero'ge:n] **ADJ** *(Med) Stoff etc* carcinogenic, cancer-causing

Kanz|lei [kants'lai] **F -, -en a** *(= Dienststelle)* office; *(= Büro eines Rechtsanwalts, Notars etc)* chambers *pl* **b** *(Hist, Pol)* chancellery

Kanz|lei-: **Kanz|lei|spra|che** F official language; **Kanz|lei|stil** M *(pej)* officialese

Kanz|ler ['kantslɐ] **M -s, -**, **Kanz|le|rin** [-ərɪn] **F -, -nen a** *(= Regierungschef)* chancellor → **Bundeskanzler(in), Reichskanzler b** *(= diplomatischer Beamter)* chancellor, chief secretary **c** *(Univ)* vice chancellor

Kanz|ler-: **Kanz|ler|amt** NT *(= Gebäude)* chancellery; *(= Posten)* chancellorship; **Kanz|ler|amts|chef(in)** M(F) head of the chancellery; **Kanz|ler|be|ra|ter(in)** M(F) adviser to the chancellor; **Kanz|ler|bo|nus** M advantage of being the chancellor in power

Kanz|le|rin [-ərɪn] F → **Kanzler**

Kanz|ler|kan|di|dat(in) M(F) candidate for the post *(esp Brit) or* position of chancellor

Kanz|ler|kan|di|da|tur F candidacy for the chancellorship

Kanz|list [kants'lɪst] **M -en, -en** *(old)* clerk

Ka|o|lin [kao'li:n] **M OR NT -s, -e** kaolin

Kap [kap] **NT -s, -s** cape, headland; **~ der Guten Hoffnung** Cape of Good Hope; **~ Hoorn** Cape Horn

Ka|paun [ka'paun] **M -s, -e** capon

Ka|pa|zi|tät [kapatsi'tɛ:t] **F -, -en** capacity; *(fig: = Experte)* expert, authority

Ka|pa|zi|täts|gren|ze F limit of capacity, capacity limit, maximum capacity

Ka|pee [ka'pe:] **NT schwer von ~ sein** *(inf)* to be slow on the uptake *(inf)*

Ka|pel|le [ka'pɛlə] **F -, -n a** *(= kleine Kirche etc)* chapel **b** *(Mus)* band, orchestra

Ka|pell|meis|ter(in) M(F) *(Mus)* director of music; *(Mil, von Tanzkapelle etc)* bandmaster, bandleader

Ka|per ['ka:pɐ] **F -, -n** *(Bot, Cook)* caper

Ka|per **M -s, -** *(Naut)* privateer

Ka|per|brief M letter of marque

ka|pern ['ka:pɐn] **VT** *(Naut) Schiff* to seize, to capture; *(fig inf) Ding* to commandeer *(inf)*, to grab; *jdn* to grab; *(= mit Beschlag belegen)* to buttonhole, to collar *(inf)*

Ka|per|schiff NT privateer

ka|pie|ren [ka'pi:rən] *ptp* **kapiert** *(inf)* **VT** to get *(inf)*, to understand **VI** to get it *(inf)*, to understand; **kapiert?** got it? *(inf)*; **kapierst du (denn) jetzt?** do you get it now? *(inf)*; **er hat schnell kapiert** he caught on quick *(inf)*

ka|pil|lar [kapi'la:r] **ADJ** *Blutgefäße, Durchblutung* capillary

Ka|pil|lar|ge|fäß [kapɪ'la:ɐ-] NT *(Anat)* capillary

ka|pi|tal [kapi'ta:l] **ADJ a** *(Hunt) Hirsch* royal; **einen ~en Bock schießen** *(fig)* to make a real bloomer *(Brit inf) or* blooper *(US inf)* **b** *(= grundlegend) Missverständnis etc* major

Ka|pi|tal [kapi'ta:l] **NT -s, -e** *or* **-ien** [-liən] **a** *(Fin)* capital *no pl*; *(= angelegtes Kapital)* capital investments *pl*; **flüssiges** *or* **verfügbares ~** ready *or* available capital; **genehmigtes ~** authorized capital; **er ist mit 35% am ~ dieser Firma beteiligt** he has a 35% stake in this firm **b** *(fig)* asset; **aus etw ~ schlagen** *(pej) (lit, fig)* to make capital out of sth; *(fig auch)* to capitalize on sth

Ka|pi|tal-: **Ka|pi|tal|ab|fluss** M, *no pl* capital outflow; **Ka|pi|tal|ab|wan|de|rung** F exodus of capital; **Ka|pi|tal|an|la|ge** F capital investment, investment of capital; **Ka|pi|tal|an|la|ge|ge|sell|schaft** F investment fund; **Ka|pi|tal|auf|sto|ckung** F capital increase; **Ka|pi|tal|be|darf** M capital requirements *pl*; **Ka|pi|tal|be|tei|li|gungs|ge|sell|schaft** F capital investment company; **Ka|pi|tal|de|cke** F capital resources *pl*; **Ka|pi|tal|ein|la|ge** F capital contribution; **Ka|pi|tal|er|hö|hung** F capital increase; **Ka|pi|tal|er|trags|steu|er** F capital gains tax; **Ka|pi|tal|flucht** F flight of capital; **Ka|pi|tal|ge|sell|schaft** F *(Comm)* joint-stock company; **ka|pi|tal|in|ten|siv** ADJ capital-intensive

ka|pi|ta|li|sie|ren [kapitali'zi:rən] *ptp* **kapitalisiert** **VT** to capitalize

Ka|pi|ta|lis|mus [kapita'lɪsmʊs] **M -,** *no pl* capitalism

Ka|pi|ta|list [kapita'lɪst] **M -en, -en**, **Ka|pi|ta|lis|tin** [-'lɪstɪn] **F -, -nen** capitalist

ka|pi|ta|lis|tisch [kapita'lɪstɪʃ] **ADJ** capitalist

Ka|pi|tal-: **ka|pi|tal|kräf|tig** ADJ financially strong; **~ sein** to have plenty of capital; **Ka|pi|tal|le|bens|ver|si|che|rung** F capital sum life insurance, endowment insurance; **Ka|pi|tal|markt** M money market; **Ka|pi|tal|ren|di|te** F *(Fin)* return on capital; **Ka|pi|tal|sam|mel|stel|le** F institutional investor; **ka|pi|tal|schwach** ADJ financially weak; **kapitalschwäche Länder** countries which are short of capital *or* financially weak; **~ sein** to be short of capital; **ka|pi|tal|stark** ADJ = **kapitalkräftig**; **Ka|pi|tal|stück|kos|ten** PL *(Econ)* unit production costs *pl*; **Ka|pi|tal|über|tra|gung** F *(Fin)* capital transfer; **Ka|pi|tal|über|tra|gungs|steu|er** F *(Fin)* capital transfer tax; **Ka|pi|tal|ver|bre|chen** NT serious crime; *(mit Todesstrafe)* capital crime, capital offence *(Brit) or* offense *(US)*; **Ka|pi|tal|ver|mö|gen** NT *(Fin)* capital assets *pl*; **Ka|pi|tal|ver|si|che|rung** F *(Insur)* capital insurance; **Ka|pi|tal|zu|wachs** M *(Fin)* capital gain

Ka|pi|tän [kapi'tɛ:n] **M -s, -e**, **Ka|pi|tä|nin** [-'tɛ:nɪn] **F -, -nen a** *(Naut, Mil)* captain; *(esp auf kleinerem Schiff)* skipper *(inf)*; **~ zur See** *(Mil)* captain **b** *(Sport)* captain **c** *(Aviat)* captain

Ka|pi|tän|leut|nant M lieutenant commander

Ka|pi|täns|pa|tent NT master's certificate

Ka|pi|tel [ka'pɪtl] **NT -s, - a** chapter; *(fig)* period, chapter; *(= Angelegenheit)* chapter of events, story; **ein dunkles ~ in seinem Leben** a dark chapter in his life; **das ist ein anderes ~** that's another story; **das ist ein ~ für sich** that's a story all to itself; **für mich ist dieses ~ erledigt** as far as I'm concerned the matter is closed **b** *(Eccl: = Domkapitel)* chapter

Ka|pi|tell [kapi'tɛl] **NT -s, -e** capital

Ka|pi|tel-: **Ka|pi|tel|saal** M *(Eccl)* chapter house; **Ka|pi|tel|über|schrift** F chapter heading

Ka|pi|tu|la|ti|on [kapitula'tsio:n] **F -, -en** *(von Armee, Land)* surrender, capitulation *(auch fig)* *(vor +dat* to, in the face of); **bedingungslose ~** unconditional surrender; **das ist eine ~ vor deinen Pflichten** that's refusing to face up to your responsibilities; **das ist eine ~ vor deinen Kindern** that's capitulating to your children

ka|pi|tu|lie|ren [kapitu'li:rən] *ptp* **kapituliert** **VI** *(= sich ergeben)* to surrender, to capitulate; *(fig: = aufgeben)* to give up, to capitulate *(vor +dat* in the face of)

Kap|lan [ka'pla:n] **M -s, Kapläne** [ka'plɛ:nə] *(in Pfarrei)* curate; *(mit besonderen Aufgaben)* chaplain

Ka|po ['kapo] **M -s, -s a** *(= Aufseher)* overseer; *(S Ger inf: = Vorarbeiter)* gaffer *(Brit inf)*, foreman **b** *(Mil sl) (= Unteroffizier)* NCO; *(= Feldwebel)* sarge *(sl)*; *(= Obergefreiter)* corp *(sl)*

Ka|po|das|ter [kapo'dastɐ] **M -s, -** capo

Ka|pok ['kapɔk, 'ka:pɔk] **M -s,** *no pl (Tex)* kapok

Ka|po|si [ka'po:zi] **NT -(s), -s**, **Ka|po|si|sar|kom** NT *(Med)* Kaposi's sarcoma

Kap|pe ['kapə] **F -, -n** cap; *(= Fliegerkappe, Motorradmütze)* helmet; *(= Narrenmütze)* jester's cap; *(von Jude)* skullcap; *(von Füllfederhalter, Saftfla-*

schen) top, cap; *(= Schuhkappe) (vorne)* toe(cap); *(hinten)* heelpiece; *(Archit)* coping; **eine ~ aus Schnee** a snowcap; **das nehme ich auf meine ~** *(fig inf)* I'll take the responsibility for that, on my head be it; **das geht auf meine ~** *(inf) (= ich bezahle)* that's on me; *(= ich übernehme die Verantwortung)* that's my responsibility; **jdm die ~ waschen** *(Sw inf: = tadeln)* to give sb a piece of one's mind

kap|pen ['kapn] VT **a** *(Naut) Tau, Leine* to cut; *Ast* to cut back, to trim; *(Med) Mandeln* to clip (off); *(fig inf) Finanzmittel* to cut (back) **b** *(= kastrieren) Hähne* to caponize

Kap|pen|abend M carnival fancy-dress party *(where fancy-dress hats are worn)*

Kap|pes ['kapəs] M **-, -** *(dial: = Kohl)* cabbage; **~ reden** *(inf)* to talk (a load of) rubbish *or* baloney *(inf)*

Käp|pi ['kɛpi] NT **-s, -s** cap

Kapp|naht F French seam

Kap|pungs|gren|ze ['kapʊŋs-] F *(für Mieten, Kosten etc)* cap

Kap|ri|ce [ka'pri:sə] F **-, -n** caprice

Kap|ri|o|le [kapri'o:lə] F **-, -n** capriole; *(fig)* caper; **~n machen** to cut capers

Kap|ri|ze [ka'pri:tsə] F **-, -n** *(Aus)* caprice

kap|ri|zie|ren [kapri'tsi:rən] *ptp* **kapriziert** VR *(geh)* to insist *(auf +acc* on)

kap|ri|zi|ös [kapri'tsiø:s] ADJ *(geh)* capricious

Kap|sel ['kapsl] F **-, -n** *(= Etui)* container; *(Anat, Bot, Pharm, Space etc)* capsule; *(an einer Flasche)* cap, top; *(= Sprengkapsel)* detonator

Kap|sel|he|ber M **-s, -** bottle-opener

ka|putt [ka'pʊt] ADJ *(inf)* broken; *esp Maschine, Glühbirne etc* kaput *(inf)*; *(= erschöpft) Mensch* shattered *(Brit inf)*, done in *(inf)*, knackered *(Brit inf)*; *Ehe* broken; *Beziehungen, Gesundheit* ruined; *Nerven* shattered; *Firma* bust *pred (inf)*; **das alte Auto/das Dach/ihre Ehe ist ~** *(= irreparabel)* the old car/the roof/her marriage has had it *(inf)*; **irgendetwas muss an deinem Auto ~ sein** something must be wrong with your car; **der Fernseher ist ~** *(zeitweilig)* the TV is on the blink *(inf)*; **mein ~es Bein** my gammy *(Brit inf)* or bad leg; *(gebrochen)* my broken leg; **mein ~es Auge** my bad eye *(inf)*; **meine Jacke ist ~** *(= nicht mehr tragbar)* my jacket has had it *(inf)*; *(= zerrissen)* my jacket is torn *or* ripped; *(am Saum)* my jacket is coming apart; **ein ~es Elternhaus** a broken home; **das ~e Deutschland** the (war-)shattered Germany; **die ~e Welt** this mess of a world; **ein ~er Typ** a wreck *(inf)*

ka|putt-: **ka|putt+ar|bei|ten** VR *sep (inf)* to work oneself to death; **ka|putt+är|gern** VR *sep (inf)* **ich hab mich kaputtgeärgert** *(über jdn/etw)* I was furious; *(über mich selbst)* I could have kicked myself; **ka|putt fah|ren** *irreg*, **ka|putt+fah|ren** *sep irreg* VT *(inf)* to run over; *Auto* to drive or run into the ground, to knacker *(Brit inf)*; *(durch Unfall)* to crash, to smash (up), to write off; **ka|putt+ge|hen** VI *sep irreg aux sein (inf)* to break; *(esp Maschine)* to go kaput *(inf)*; *(esp Glühbirne, Elektronenröhre etc)* to go kaput *(inf)*, to go phut *(inf)*; *(Ehe)* to break up, to go on the rocks *(Brit inf) (an +dat* because of); *(Beziehungen, Gesundheit, Nerven)* to be ruined, to go to pot *(inf)*; *(Firma)* to go bust *(inf)*, to fold (up); *(Waschmaschine, Auto)* to break down, to pack up *(Brit inf)*; *(Kleidung)* to come to pieces; *(= zerrissen werden)* to tear; *(Blumen)* to die off; **der Fernseher ist schon wieder kaputtgegangen** *(zeitweilig)* the TV has gone on the blink again *(inf)*; **in dem Büro/an diesem Job gehe ich noch kaputt** this office/job will be the death of me *(inf)*; **ka|putt+krie|gen** VT *sep (inf, fig) jdn* to wear out; **der Hans ist nicht kaputtzukriegen** Hans just goes on for ever; **ka|putt krie|gen**, **ka|putt+krie|gen** *sep* VT *(inf) Zerbrechliches* to break; *Auto* to ruin; **das Auto ist nicht kaputt zu kriegen** this car just goes on for ever; **ka|putt+la|chen** VR *sep (inf)* to die laughing *(inf)*; **ich lach mich kaputt!** what a laugh!; **ich hätte mich ~ können** I nearly killed myself laughing *(inf)*; **ka|putt+ma|chen** *sep (inf, fig)* VT to ruin; *(= erschöpfen) jdn* to wear out, to knacker *(Brit inf)*; **diese ewigen Sorgen/die Kinder machen mich kaputt** these never-ending worries/the children will be the death of me *(inf)* VR *(= sich überanstrengen)* to wear oneself out, to run oneself into the ground *(inf)*, to knacker oneself *(Brit inf)*; **ka|putt ma|chen**, **ka|putt+ma|chen** *sep (inf)* VT *Auto, Hose* to ruin; *Zerbrechliches* to break, to smash; *Brücke, Sandburg* to knock down; **ka|putt schla|gen** *irreg*, **ka|putt+schla|gen** *sep irreg* VT *(inf)* to break, to smash

Ka|pu|ze [ka'pu:tsə] F **-, -n** hood; *(= Mönchskapuze)* cowl

Ka|pu|zen|ja|cke F hooded jacket

Ka|pu|zen|pul|li M hooded sweater

Ka|pu|zi|ner [kapu'tsi:nɐ] M **-s, -** *(Bot: auch* **Kapuzinerkresse)** nasturtium

Ka|pu|zi|ner [kapu'tsi:nɐ] M **-s, -**, **Ka|pu|zi|ne|rin** [-ərɪn] F **-, -nen** *(Eccl)* Capuchin

Kar [ka:ɐ] NT **-(e)s, -e** corrie, cwm, cirque

Ka|ra|bi|ner [kara'bi:nɐ] M **-s, -** **a** *(= Gewehr)* carbine **b** *(auch* **Karabinerhaken)** karabiner, snap link, crab *(inf)*

Ka|ra|cho [ka'raxo] NT **-s**, *no pl* **mit** *or* **im ~** *(inf)* at full tilt, hell for leather *(esp Brit inf)*; **er rannte/fuhr mit ~ gegen die Wand** he ran/drove smack into the wall *(inf)*

Ka|raf|fe [ka'rafə] F **-, -n** carafe; *(mit Stöpsel)* decanter

Ka|ram|bo|la|ge [karambo'la:ʒə] F **-, -n** *(Aut)* collision, crash; *(Billard)* cannon

Ka|ram|bo|le [karam'bo:lə] F **-, -n** *(Billard)* red (ball)

Ka|ram|bo|le F **-, -n** *(= Frucht)* carambola, star fruit

ka|ram|bo|lie|ren [karambo'li:rən] *ptp* **karamboliert** VI *aux sein (Billard)* to cannon; *(Autos)* to crash *(mit* into), to collide *(mit* with)

Ka|ra|mell [kara'mɛl] M **-s**, *no pl* caramel *no pl*

Ka|ra|mel|le [kara'mɛlə] F **-, -n** caramel (toffee)

Ka|ra|o|ke [kara'o:ke] NT **-**, *no pl* karaoke

Ka|rat [ka'ra:t] NT **-(e)s, -e** *or (bei Zahlenangabe)* **-** *(Measure)* carat; **das Gold dieses Ringes hat 9 ~** this ring is made of 9-carat gold

Ka|ra|te NT **-(s)**, *no pl* karate

Ka|ra|te|hieb M karate chop

-ka|rä|ter [karɛ:tɐ] M *suf in cpds* **-s, - Zehnkaräter** ten-carat stone; *(= Diamant)* ten-carat diamond

-ka|rä|tig [karɛ:tɪç] ADJ *suf* carat; **zehnkarätig** ten-carat

Ka|ra|vel|le [kara'vɛlə] F **-, -n** caravel

Ka|ra|wa|ne [kara'va:nə] F **-, -n** caravan

Ka|ra|wa|nen|stra|ße F caravan route

Kar|bid [kar'bi:t] NT **-(e)s, -e** [-də] carbide

Kar|bid|lam|pe F Davy lamp

Kar|bol [kar'bo:l] NT **-s**, *no pl*, **Kar|bol|säu|re** F carbolic acid

Kar|bo|nat [karbo'na:t] NT **-(e)s, -e** carbonate

kar|bo|ni|sie|ren [karboni'zi:rən] *ptp* **karbonisiert** VT to carbonize; *Getränke* to carbonate

Kar|bun|kel [kar'bʊŋkl] M **-s, -** *(Med)* carbuncle

Kar|da|mom [karda'mo:m] M **-s, -e(n)** cardamom

Kar|dan-: **Kar|dan|ge|lenk** NT universal joint; **Kar|dan|tun|nel** M transmission tunnel; **Kar|dan|wel|le** F prop(eller) shaft

Kar|di|nal [kardi'na:l] M **-s, Kardinäle** [-'nɛ:lə] **a** *(Eccl)* cardinal **b** *(Orn)* cardinal (bird)

Kar|di|nal-: **Kar|di|nal|feh|ler** M cardinal error; **Kar|di|nal|fra|ge** F *(geh)* cardinal *or* crucial question

Kar|di|nals|kol|le|gi|um NT *(Rel)* College of Cardinals, Sacred College

Kar|di|nal-: **Kar|di|nal|tu|gend** F *(Philos, Rel)* cardinal virtue; **Kar|di|nal|zahl** F cardinal (number)

Kar|dio|gramm [kardio'gram] NT *pl* **-gramme** cardiogram

Kar|dio|lo|ge [kardio'lo:gə] M **-n, -n**, **Kar|dio|lo|gin** [-'lo:gɪn] F **-, -nen** cardiologist

Kar|dio|lo|gie [kardiolo'gi:] F **-**, *no pl* cardiology

kar|dio|lo|gisch [kardio'lo:gɪʃ] ADJ cardiological

Ka|renz-: **Ka|renz|tag** M unpaid day of sick leave; **Ka|renz|zeit** F waiting period

Kar|fi|ol [kar'fio:l] M **-s**, *no pl (Aus)* cauliflower; **zwei (Rosen) ~** two cauliflowers

Kar|frei|tag [ka:ɐ'fraita:k] M Good Friday

Kar|fun|kel [kar'fʊŋkl] M **-s, -** **a** *(Med)* carbuncle **b** = **Karfunkelstein**

Kar|fun|kel|stein M *red precious stone such as ruby or garnet*, carbuncle (stone)

karg [kark] ADJ **a** *(= spärlich) Vorrat* meagre *(Brit)*, meager *(US)*, sparse; *(= unfruchtbar) Boden* barren; *(= dürftig) Gehalt, Einkommen* meagre *(Brit)*, meager *(US)* **b** *(= geizig)* mean, sparing ADV **a** *(= spärlich)* **~ ausgestattet sein** *(Mensch)* to have few possessions; **seine Bibliothek ist noch ziemlich ~ ausgestattet** there aren't many books in his library yet; **~ möbliert** sparsely furnished; **~ leben** to lead a meagre *(Brit)* or meager *(US)* existence **b** *(= knapp)* **~ ausfallen/bemessen sein** to be meagre *(Brit)* or meager *(US)*; **etw ~ bemessen** to be mean *(Brit)* or stingy *(inf)* with sth; **die Portionen sind sehr ~ bemessen** they are very mean *(Brit)* or stingy *(inf)* with the helpings

kar|gen ['kargn] VI *(= sparsam sein)* to stint *(mit* on), to scrimp and save *(mit* with); *(= knausern)* to be mean *(Brit)* or stingy *(inf) (mit* with); *(mit Lob)* to be grudging

Karg|heit ['karkhait] F **-**, *no pl (von Vorrat)* meagreness *(Brit)*, meagerness *(US)*; *(von Möblierung)* sparseness; *(von Boden)* barrenness; *(von Gehalt, Einkommen)* meagreness *(Brit)*, meagerness *(US)*

kärg|lich ['kɛrklɪç] ADJ *Vorrat* meagre *(Brit)*, meager *(US)*, sparse; *Mahl* frugal; *(= dürftig) Gehalt, Einkommen* meagre *(Brit)*, meager *(US)*; **unter ~en Bedingungen leben** to live in impoverished conditions ADV **sie leben ~** they lead a meagre *(Brit)* or meager *(US)* existence

Kärg|lich|keit F **-**, *no pl (von Vorrat, Menge)* meagreness *(Brit)*, meagerness *(US)*, sparseness; *(von Mahlzeit)* frugality

Kar|go ['kargo] M **-s, -s** cargo

Ka|ri|be [ka'ri:bə] M **-n, -n**, **Ka|ri|bin** [-'ri:bɪn] F **-, -nen** Carib

Ka|ri|bik [ka'ri:bɪk] F **- die ~** the Caribbean

ka|ri|bisch [ka'ri:bɪʃ] ADJ Caribbean; **das Karibische Meer** the Caribbean Sea; **die Karibischen Inseln** the Caribbean Islands

ka|riert [ka'ri:ɐt] ADJ *Stoff, Muster* checked, checkered *(esp US)*; *Papier* squared ADV *(inf)* **red nicht so ~!** don't talk such rubbish; **~ gucken** to look puzzled

Ka|ri|es ['ka:riɛs] F **-**, *no pl* caries

Ka|ri|ka|tur [karika'tu:ɐ] F **-, -en** caricature; **eine ~ von jdm/etw zeichnen** *(lit)* to draw a caricature of sb/sth; *(lit, fig)* to caricature sb/sth

Ka|ri|ka|tu|rist [karikatu'rɪst] M **-en, -en**, **Ka|ri|ka|tu|ris|tin** [-'rɪstɪn] F **-, -nen** cartoonist; *(= Personenzeichner auch)* caricaturist

ka|ri|ka|tu|ris|tisch [karikatu'rɪstɪʃ] ADJ caricatural *(form)*, caricature; **dieser Artikel ist ~** this article is a caricature ADV **~ wirken** to seem like a caricature; **~ geprägt** caricature-like; **in ~ überspitztem Stil geschrieben** written in a style exaggerated to the point of caricature

ka|ri|kie|ren [kari'ki:rən] *ptp* **karikiert** VT to caricature

ka|ri|ös [ka'riø:s] ADJ *Zahn* carious, decayed

Ka|ri|tas ['ka:ritas] F **-**, *no pl (= Nächstenliebe)* charity

ka|ri|ta|tiv [karita'ti:f] ADJ charitable ADV **sich ~ betätigen, ~ tätig sein** to do charitable work

Kar|kas|se [kar'kasə] F **-, -n** **a** *(Cook)* carcass **b** *(Aut: von Reifen)* casing

Karl [karl] M **-s** Charles; **~ der Große** Charlemagne

Kar|ma ['karma] NT **-s,** *no pl* karma

Kar|me|li|ter [karme'li:tɐ] M **-s, -, Kar|me|li|te|rin** [-ərɪn] F **-, -nen** Carmelite

Kar|me|sin [karme'zi:n] NT **-s,** *no pl* crimson

kar|me|sin(rot) [karme'zi:n-] ADJ crimson

kar|min(rot) [kar'mi:n-] ADJ carmine (red)

Kar|ne|val ['karnəval] M **-s, -e** *or* **-s** carnival

> **KARNEVAL**
>
> **Karneval** is the time between Epiphany and Ash Wednesday, which is also known as the **fünfte Jahreszeit** (fifth season). Among the traditional events are masked balls, and meetings where people make humorous speeches and sing carnival songs. On the so-called **tolle Tage** ("crazy days") normal life in many regions is turned completely upside down. During the **tolle Tage** power is symbolically assumed in many towns by a carnival prince and princess. This is especially so in Rheinland, where **Karneval** has been celebrated in its present form since 1823. **Rosenmontag** is generally a holiday in this region, so that people can watch the processions and join in the celebrations. In Southern Germany and Austria the carnival period is called **Fasching** and the processions take place on Shrove Tuesday. → FASTNACHT, ROSENMONTAG

Kar|ne|vals-: **Kar|ne|vals|or|den** M carnival medal; **Kar|ne|vals|prinz** M carnival prince; **Kar|ne|vals|prin|zes|sin** F carnival princess; **Kar|ne|vals|zug** M carnival procession

Kar|ni|ckel [kar'nɪkl] NT **-s, -** *(inf)* **a** bunny (rabbit) *(inf)*, rabbit; **sich wie die ~ vermehren** *(inf)* to breed like rabbits **b** *(hum: = Schuldiger)* scapegoat

Kar|ni|ckel-: **Kar|ni|ckel|bock** M buck rabbit; **Kar|ni|ckel|stall** M rabbit hutch

kar|ni|vor [karni'vo:ɐ] ADJ *(Biol)* carnivorous

Kar|ni|vo|re [kani'vo:rə] M **-n, -n** *usu pl (Biol)* carnivore

Kärn|ten ['kɛrntn] NT **-s** Carinthia

Ka|ro ['ka:ro] NT **-s, -s** **a** *(= Quadrat)* square; *(auf der Spitze stehend)* diamond, lozenge; *(Muster)* check; *(diagonal)* diamond **b** *no pl (Cards)* diamonds *pl*

Ka|ro|lin|ger ['ka:rolɪŋɐ] M **-s, -, Ka|ro|lin|ge|rin** [-ərɪn] F **-, -nen** Carolingian

ka|ro|lin|gisch ['ka:rolɪŋɪʃ] ADJ Carolingian; **~e Minuskeln** Caroline minuscule

Ka|ro|mus|ter NT checked *or* checkered *(esp US)* pattern

Ka|ros|se [ka'rɔsə] F **-, -n** *(= Prachtkutsche)* (state) coach; *(fig: = großes Auto)* limousine

Ka|ros|se|rie [karɔsə'ri:] F **-, -n** [-'ri:ən] bodywork

Ka|ros|se|rie-: **Ka|ros|se|rie|bau|er(in)** M(F) *pl* **-bauer(innen)** coach-builder; **Ka|ros|se|rie|scha|den** M damage to the bodywork; **Ka|ros|se|rie|schlos|ser(in)** M(F) panel beater; **Ka|ros|se|rie|werk|statt** F body (repair) shop

Ka|ro|tin [karo'ti:n] NT **-s, -e** carotene, carotin

Ka|rot|te [ka'rɔtə] F **-, -n** (small) carrot

Ka|rot|ten|saft M carrot juice

Kar|pa|ten [kar'pa:tn] PL Carpathian Mountains *pl*, Carpathians *pl*

Kar|pell [kar'pɛl] NT **-s, -e** *or* **-a** [-'pɛla] *(Bot)* carpel

Karp|fen ['karpfn] M **-s, -** carp

Karp|fen-: **karp|fen|ar|tig** ADJ *(lit)* carp-like; *(fig) Gesicht, Aussehen* fish-like; **Karp|fen|teich** M carp pond → **Hecht**

Kar|re ['karə] F **-, -n** **a** = **Karren** **b** *(inf: = klappriges Auto)* (old) crate *(inf)* or heap *(inf)*

Kar|ree [ka're:] NT **-s, -s** **a** *(= Viereck)* rectangle; *(= Rhombus)* rhombus; *(= Quadrat)* square; *(= Formation: esp Mil)* square **b** *(= Häuserblock)* block; **einmal ums ~ gehen** to walk round the block **c** *(esp Aus: Cook)* loin

kar|ren ['karən] VT to cart; **jdn ~** *(inf: mit Auto)* to give sb a lift, to drive sb VI *aux sein (inf: mit dem Auto)* to drive (around)

Kar|ren ['karən] M **-s, -** **a** *(= Wagen)* cart; *(esp für Garten, Baustelle)* (wheel)barrow; *(für Gepäck etc)* trolley; **ein ~ voll Obst** a cartload of fruit **b** *(fig inf)* **jdm an den ~ fahren** *or* **pinkeln** to take sb to task; **den ~ einfach laufen lassen** to let things go *or* slide; **den ~ in den Dreck fahren** to ruin things, to get things in a mess; **der ~ ist hoffnungslos verfahren, der ~ steckt im Dreck** we/they *etc* are really in a mess; **den ~ aus dem Dreck ziehen, den ~ wieder flottmachen** to put things back on the rails, to get things sorted out

Kar|ren|gaul M *(pej)* (old) nag

Kar|ret|te [ka'rɛtə] F **-, -n** *(Sw: = Schubkarre)* (hand)cart, trolley

Kar|ri|e|re [ka'rie:rə] F **-, -n** **a** *(= Laufbahn)* career; **~ machen** to make a career for oneself **b** *(= voller Galopp)* (full) gallop; **~ reiten** to gallop, to ride at a gallop

Kar|ri|e|re-: **kar|ri|e|re|be|wusst** ADJ career-conscious; **kar|ri|e|re|dien|lich** ADJ career-enhancing; **Kar|ri|e|re|frau** F career woman; **kar|ri|e|re|geil** ADJ *(pej)* career-mad, career-obsessed; **Kar|ri|e|re|knick** M **es kam zu einem ~** his/her career took a downturn; **Kar|ri|e|re|lei|ter** F ladder of success, career ladder; **die ~ erklimmen** to rise up the ladder; **ganz oben auf der ~ stehen** to be at the top of the ladder *or* tree; **auf der ~ schnell nach oben kommen** to climb the career ladder fast; **Kar|ri|e|re|ma|cher(in)** M(F) careerist; **kar|ri|e|re|süch|tig** ADJ career-driven; **Kar|ri|e|re|typ** M careerist

Kar|ri|e|rist [karie'rɪst] M **-en, -en, Kar|ri|e|ris|tin** [-'rɪstɪn] F **-, -nen** careerist

kar|ri|o|len [ka'rio:lən] *ptp* **karriolt** VI *aux sein (dated inf)* to gallivant (around)

Kärr|ner ['kɛrnɐ] M **-s, -** *(= Fuhrmann)* carter

Kärr|ner|ar|beit F hard labour *(Brit) or* labor *(US)*, hard toil

Kar|sams|tag [ka:ɐ'zamsta:k] M Easter Saturday, Holy Saturday

Karst [karst] M **-(e)s, -e** *(= Hacke)* two-pronged mattock *or* hoe

Karst M **-(e)s, -e** *(Geog, Geol)* karst

kars|tig ['karstɪç] ADJ karstic

Karst|land|schaft F (area of) karst; *(größeres Gebiet)* karst country *no art*

Kar|tät|sche [kar'tɛtʃə] F **-, -n** **a** *(Mil)* case shot **b** *(Build)* plasterer's float, darby

Kar|tau|se [kar'tauzə] F **-, -n** chartreuse, Carthusian monastery

Kar|täu|ser [kar'tɔyzɐ] M **-s, -** *(= Likör)* chartreuse

Kar|täu|ser [kar'tɔyzɐ] M **-s, -, Kar|täu|se|rin** [-ərɪn] F **-, -nen** Carthusian

Kar|te ['kartə] F **-, -n** **a** *(auch Comput)* card **b** *(= Fahrkarte, Eintrittskarte)* ticket; *(= Einladungskarte)* invitation (card); *(= Bezugsschein)* coupon; *(= Essenskarte)* luncheon voucher, meal ticket *(US)*; *(= Mitgliedskarte)* (membership) card; **die ~n, bitte!** tickets, please! **c** *(= Landkarte)* map; *(= Seekarte)* chart; **~n lesen** to mapread **d** *(= Speisekarte)* menu; *(= Weinkarte)* wine list; **nach der ~** à la carte **e** *(= Spielkarte)* (playing) card; **jdm die ~ lesen** to tell sb's fortune from the cards; **mit offenen ~n spielen** *(lit)* to play with one's cards on the table; *(fig)* to put one's cards on the table; **er spielt mit verdeckten ~n** *(fig)* he's playing his cards *or* it very close to his chest; **du solltest deine ~n aufdecken** *(fig)* you ought to show your hand, you ought to put your cards on the table; **alle ~n in der Hand halten** *(fig)* to hold all the cards; **er lässt sich nicht in die ~n sehen** *or* **gucken** *(fig)* he's playing it close to his chest; **jdm in die ~n sehen** *(lit)* to look *or* take a look at sb's cards; **alles auf eine ~ setzen** *(lit)* to stake everything on one card; *(fig)* to stake everything on one chance; *(= andere Möglichkeiten ausschließen)* to put all one's eggs in one basket *(prov)*; **du hast auf die falsche ~ gesetzt** *(fig)* you backed the wrong horse; **schlechte/gute ~n haben** to have a bad/good hand; *(fig)* to be in a difficult/strong position

Kar|tei [kar'tai] F **-, -en** card file, card index

Kar|tei-: **Kar|tei|kar|te** F file *or* index card; **Kar|tei|kas|ten** M file-card box; **Kar|tei|lei|che** F *(inf)* sleeping *or* non-active member; **die meisten Mitglieder sind bloß ~n** most of the members are just names on the files; **Kar|tei|schrank** M filing cabinet

Kar|tell [kar'tɛl] NT **-s, -e** **a** *(Comm)* cartel **b** *(= Interessenvereinigung)* alliance; *(pej)* cartel

Kar|tell-: **Kar|tell|amt** NT, **Kar|tell|be|hör|de** F ≈ Monopolies and Mergers Commission *(Brit)*, anti-trust commission *(esp US)*; **Kar|tell|ge|setz** NT monopolies *or (esp US)* anti-trust law; **Kar|tell|ge|setz|ge|bung** F legislation against monopolies, anti-trust legislation *(esp US)*; **Kar|tell|recht** NT *(= Kartellgesetz)* monopolies *or (esp US)* anti-trust law; *(= Kartellgesetzgebung)* legislation against monopolies, anti-trust legislation *(esp US)*

Kar|ten-: **Kar|ten|be|stel|lung** F ticket reservation(s *pl*); **Kar|ten|blatt** NT map, (map) sheet; **Kar|ten|haus** NT **a** house of cards; **wie ein ~ zusammenstürzen** *or* **in sich zusammenfallen** to collapse like a house of cards **b** *(Naut)* chart room; **Kar|ten|kunst|stück** NT card trick; **Kar|ten|le|gen** NT **-s,** *no pl* **a** = **Kartenlesen b** **b** *(= Patience)* patience; **Kar|ten|le|ger** [-le:gɐ] M **-s, -, Kar|ten|le|ge|rin** [-ərɪn] F **-, -nen** fortune-teller *(who reads cards)*; **Kar|ten|le|se|lam|pe** F *(Aut)* map-reading lamp; **Kar|ten|le|sen** NT **-s,** *no pl* **a** *(von Landkarten etc)* mapreading **b** *(= Wahrsagen)* fortune-telling *(using cards)*, reading the cards, cartomancy *(form)*; **Kar|ten|le|ser(in)** M(F) *(von Landkarten)* mapreader; **Kar|ten|or|ga|ni|sa|ti|on** F credit card company; **Kar|ten|spiel** NT **a** *(= das Spielen)* card-playing; *(= ein Spiel)* card game; **beim ~** when playing cards **b** *(= Karten)* pack *or* deck (of cards); **Kar|ten|te|le|fon** NT cardphone; **Kar|ten|vor|ver|kauf** M advance sale of tickets; *(= Stelle)* advance booking office; **Kar|ten|werk** NT map book, book of maps; **Kar|ten|zei|chen** NT (map) symbol; **Kar|ten|zeich|ner(in)** M(F) cartographer, mapmaker

kar|te|si|a|nisch [karte'zia:nɪʃ], **kar|te|sisch** [kar'te:zɪʃ] ADJ Cartesian

Kar|tha|ger [kar'ta:gɐ] M **-s, -, Kar|tha|ge|rin** [-ərɪn] F **-, -nen** Carthaginian

Kar|tha|go [kar'ta:go] NT **-s** Carthage

kar|tie|ren [kar'ti:rən] *ptp* **kartiert** VT *Gebiet* to map out; *(= in Kartei einordnen)* to file

Kar|tof|fel [kar'tɔfl] F **-, -n** **a** potato; **rin in die ~n, raus aus den ~n** *(inf)* first it's one thing, then (it's) another, you're/he's *etc* always chopping and changing; **etw/jdn fallen lassen wie eine heiße ~** *(inf)* to drop sth/sb like a hot potato → **Bauer a** **b** *(inf) (= Nase)* hooter *(Brit inf)*, conk *(inf)*; *(= Loch)* (gaping) hole

Kar|tof|fel- *in cpds* potato; **Kar|tof|fel|brei** M mashed potatoes *pl*; **Kar|tof|fel|chips** PL potato crisps *pl (Brit)*, potato chips *pl (US)*; **Kar|tof|fel|fe|ri|en** PL *(inf)* autumn holiday(s *pl*) *or* fall holiday *(US, originally in celebration of the potato harvest)*; **Kar|tof|fel|feu|er** NT *fire made from dried potato leaves etc with general celebration after potato harvest*; **Kar|tof|fel|gra|tin** [-gratɛ̃:] NT *(Cook)* gratiné(e) potatoes *pl*; **Kar|tof|fel|kä|fer** M Colorado beetle; **Kar|tof|fel|kloß** NT, **Kar|tof|fel|knö|del** M *(esp S Ger, Aus; Cook)* potato dumpling; **Kar|tof|fel|kraut** NT potato foliage *or* leaves *pl*; **Kar|tof|fel|mehl** NT potato flour; **Kar|tof|fel|mie|te** F *(Agr)* potato clamp; **Kar|tof|fel|puf|fer** M *fried grated potato cakes*; **Kar|tof|fel|pü|ree** NT mashed potatoes *pl*; **Kar|tof|fel|sa|lat** M potato salad; **Kar|tof|-**

fel|scha|len PL potato skin *sing*; *(abgeschält)* potato peel *sing* or peelings *pl*; **Kar|tof|fel|schä|ler** [-ʃɛːlɐ] M **-s, -** potato peeler; **Kar|tof|fel|stamp|fer** M potato masher

Kar|to|graf [karto'graːf] M **-en, -en**, **Kar|to|gra|fin** [-'graːfɪn] F **-, -nen** cartographer

Kar|to|gra|fie [kartogra'fiː] F **-,** *no pl* cartography

kar|to|gra|fisch [karto'graːfɪʃ] ADJ cartographic(al) ADV **diese Gegend ist noch nicht besonders gut ~ erfasst** this area hasn't been mapped very well yet

Kar|to|graph *etc* = **Kartograf** *etc*

Kar|ton [kar'tɔŋ, kar'tõː, kar'toːn] M **-s, -s** **a** (= *steifes Papier, Pappe*) card, cardboard; **ein ~** a piece of card *or* cardboard **b** (= *Schachtel*) cardboard box **c** *(Art)* cartoon **d** (= *Leerblatt*) blank page for one's own notes

Kar|to|na|ge [karto'naːʒə] F **-, -n** (= *Verpackung*) cardboard packaging

kar|to|nie|ren [karto'niːrən] *ptp* **kartoniert** VT *Bücher* to bind in board; **kartoniert** paperback

Kar|to|thek [karto'teːk] F **-, -en** card file, card index

Kar|tu|sche [kar'tʊʃə] F **-, -n** **a** (= *Behälter*) cartridge; *(Hist Mil:* = *Patronentasche)* ammunition pouch **b** *(Archit, Her)* cartouche

Ka|rus|sell [karʊ'sɛl] NT **-s, -s** or **-e** merry-go-round, roundabout *(Brit)*, carousel; **~ fahren** to have a ride on the merry-go-round *etc*

Kar|wo|che ['kaːɐ-] F *(Eccl)* Holy Week

Ka|ry|a|ti|de [karya'tiːdə] F **-, -n** *(Archit)* caryatid

Kar|zer ['kartsɐ] M **-s, -** *(Hist)* **a** (= *Zelle*) detention cell *(in school or university)* **b** (= *Strafe*) detention

kar|zi|no|gen [kartsino'geːn] *(Med)* ADJ carcinogenic ADV **~ wirken** to act as a carcinogen

Kar|zi|no|gen [kartsino'geːn] NT **-s, -e** carcinogen

Kar|zi|no|lo|gie [kartsinolo'giː] F **-,** *no pl (Med)* oncology

Kar|zi|nom [kartsi'noːm] NT **-s, -e** *(Med)* carcinoma, malignant growth

Ka|sack ['kaːzak] M **-s, -s** tunic

Ka|schem|me [ka'ʃɛmə] F **-, -n** low dive

ka|schen ['kaʃn] VT *(inf)* to catch; (= *verhaften)* to nab *(inf)*

ka|schie|ren [ka'ʃiːrən] *ptp* **kaschiert** VT **a** *(fig:* = *überdecken)* to conceal **b** *Bucheinband* to laminate

Kasch|mir ['kaʃmiːɐ] NT **-s** *(Geog)* Kashmir

Kasch|mir M **-s, -e** *(Tex)* cashmere

Ka|schu|be [ka'ʃuːbə] M **-n, -n**, **Ka|schu|bin** [-'ʃuːbɪn] F **-, -nen** Kashub(e)

Kä|se ['kɛːzə] M **-s, -** **a** cheese; **weißer ~** curd cheese; **~ schließt den Magen** cheese rounds off a meal nicely **b** *(inf:* = *Unsinn)* rubbish *(Brit)*, twaddle *(inf)*

Kä|se- *in cpds* cheese; **Kä|se|auf|lauf** M *(Cook)* cheese soufflé; **Kä|se|blatt** NT, **Kä|se|blätt|chen** NT *(inf)* local rag *(inf)*; **Kä|se|brot** NT bread and cheese; **Kä|se|bröt|chen** NT cheese roll; **Kä|se|ecke** F cheese triangle; **Kä|se|fon|due** NT cheese fondue; **Kä|se|fü|ße** PL *(inf)* smelly *or* cheesy feet *pl*; **Kä|se|ge|bäck** NT cheese savouries *pl (Brit) or* savories *pl (US)*; **Kä|se|glo|cke** F cheese cover; *(fig)* dome; **Kä|se|ho|bel** M cheese slice

Ka|se|in [kaze'iːn] NT **-s, -e** casein

Kä|se|ku|chen M cheesecake

Ka|sel ['kaːzl] F **-, -n** *(Eccl)* chasuble

Ka|se|mat|te [kazə'matə] F casemate

kä|sen ['kɛːzn] VI *(rare)* to make cheese

Kä|se|plat|te F cheeseboard

Kä|se|rei [kɛːzə'rai] F **-, -en** **a** (= *Betrieb)* cheese dairy **b** *no pl* (= *Käseherstellung)* cheese-making

Ka|ser|ne [ka'zɛrnə] F **-, -n** barracks *pl*

Ka|ser|nen-: **Ka|ser|nen|ar|rest** M confinement to barracks; **Ka|ser|nen|hof** M barrack square; **Ka|ser|nen|hof|ton** M *pl* **-töne es herrscht ein richtiger ~** it's like being on the parade ground

ka|ser|nie|ren [kazər'niːrən] *ptp* **kaserniert** VT *Truppen* to quarter in barracks; *Flüchtlinge, Obdachlose etc* to quarter, to billet

Kä|se-: **Kä|se|stan|ge** F cheese straw *(Brit)*, cheese stick *(US)*; **Kä|se|tor|te** F cheesecake; **kä|se|weiß** ADJ *(inf)* white *or* pale (as a ghost)

kä|sig ['kɛːzɪç] ADJ **a** *(fig inf) Gesicht, Haut* pasty, pale; *(vor Schreck)* white, pale **b** *(lit)* cheesy

Ka|si|no [ka'ziːno] NT **-s, -s** **a** (= *Spielbank)* casino **b** (= *Offizierskasino)* (officers') mess *or* club; (= *Speiseraum)* dining room, cafeteria

Kas|ka|de [kas'kaːdə] F **-, -n** **a** (= *Wasserfall)* waterfall, cascade *(poet)*; *(in Feuerwerk)* cascade; **die Wasser stürzen in ~n hinab** the waters cascade down **b** (= *Zirkussprung)* acrobatic leap

kas|ko|ver|si|chern ['kasko-] *ptp* **kaskoversichert** VT *insep, only infin and ptp (Aut)* to insure against own damage; ≈ to insure comprehensively; **kaskoversichert sein** ≈ to have comprehensive insurance

Kas|ko|ver|si|che|rung ['kasko-] F *(Aut)* (= *Teilkaskoversicherung)* ≈ third party, fire and theft insurance; (= *Vollkaskoversicherung)* fully comprehensive insurance; *(Naut)* hull insurance

Kas|per ['kaspɐ] M **-s, -**, *(Aus, S Ger)* **Kas|perl** ['kaspɐl] M OR NT **-s, -(n)**, *(S Ger)* **Kas|per|le** ['kaspɐlə] M OR NT **-s, -** **a** *(im Puppenspiel)* Punch *(esp Brit)* **b** *(inf)* clown *(inf)*, fool

Kas|per|le-: **Kas|per|le|fi|gur** F Punch glove *(Brit) or* hand *(US)* puppet; **Kas|per|le|the|a|ter** NT Punch and Judy (show) *(esp Brit)*, puppet show; (= *Gestell)* Punch and Judy theatre *(esp Brit)*, puppet theater *(US)*

kas|pern ['kaspɐn] VI *(inf)* to clown *(inf) or* fool around

Kas|pi|sches Meer ['kaspɪʃəs] NT Caspian Sea

Kas|sa ['kasa] F **-, Kassen** ['kasn] *(esp Aus)* = **Kasse a**

Kas|sa- *(esp Aus)*: **Kas|sa|ge|schäft** NT *(Comm)* cash transaction; *(St Ex)* spot transaction; **Kas|sa|kurs** M spot rate; **Kas|sa|markt** M spot market

Kas|sand|ra|ruf [ka'sandra-] M prophecy of doom, gloomy prediction

Kas|sa|ti|on [kasa'tsioːn] F **-, -en** *(Jur)* quashing, reversal; *(von Urkunde)* annulment

Kas|sa|ti|ons-: **Kas|sa|ti|ons|ge|richt** NT *(Jur)* court of appeal; **Kas|sa|ti|ons|hof** M *(Jur)* Supreme Court of Appeal; *(in der Schweiz) court of appeal in matters of state versus cantonal law*

Kas|se ['kasə] F **-, -n** **a** (= *Zahlstelle)* cash desk *(Brit) or* point, till *(Brit)*, cash register *(US)*, counter *(esp US)*; (= *Zahlraum)* cashier's office; *(Theat etc)* box office; *(in Bank)* bank counter; *(in Supermarkt)* checkout; **an der ~** *(in Geschäft)* at the desk *(esp Brit)*, at the (checkout) counter *(esp US)*

b (= *Geldkasten)* cash box; *(in Läden)* cash register, till *(Brit)*; (= *Geldmittel)* coffers *pl*; *(bei Spielen)* kitty; *(in einer Spielbank)* bank; **in die ~ greifen** *(inf)* to dip into the till *(Brit) or* cashbox; **der Film hat volle ~n gemacht** the film was a big box-office success; **die ~n klingeln** the tills are ringing *(Brit)*, the money is really rolling in

c (= *Bargeld)* cash; **ein Verkauf per ~** *(form)* a cash sale; **netto ~** net payment; **gegen ~** for cash; **bei ~ sein** *(inf)* to be flush *(inf)*, to be in the money *(inf)*; **knapp bei ~ sein** *(inf)* to be short of cash, to be out of pocket *(Brit)*; **gut/schlecht bei ~ sein** *(inf)* to be well-off/badly-off; **~ machen** to check one's finances; *(in Geschäft)* to cash up *(Brit)*, to count up the earnings *(US)*; **die ~ führen** to be in charge of the money; **die ~ stimmt!** *(inf)* the money's OK *(inf)*; **ein Loch in die ~ reißen** *(fig)* to make a dent *or* hole in one's finances; **zur ~ bitten** to ask for money; **jdn zur ~ bitten** to ask sb to pay up

d *(inf:* = *Sparkasse)* (savings) bank

e = **Krankenkasse**

Kas|se|ler ['kasəlɐ] NT **-s, -** *lightly smoked pork loin*

Kas|sen-: **Kas|sen|ab|schluss** M cashing up; **~ machen** to cash up *(Brit)*, to count up the earnings *(US)*; **Kas|sen|arzt** M, **Kas|sen|ärz|tin** F *doctor who treats members of medical insurance schemes*; ≈ National Health general practitioner *(Brit)*, ≈ preferred provider *(US)*; **kas|sen|ärzt|lich** ADJ **~e Behandlung** treatment by a health scheme doctor *(Brit) or* preferred provider *(US)*; **Kas|sen|au|to|mat** M cash dispenser *(Brit)*, automatic teller, money machine *(US)*; *(zum Bezahlen)* pay machine *(at car park etc)*; **Kas|sen|be|leg** M sales receipt *or* check *(US)*; **Kas|sen|be|richt** M financial report; *(in Verein etc auch)* treasurer's report; **Kas|sen|be|stand** M cash balance, cash in hand; **Kas|sen|bon** M sales slip *or* receipt; **Kas|sen|bril|le** F *(pej inf)* NHS specs *pl (Brit inf)*, standard-issue glasses *pl*; **Kas|sen|buch** NT cashbook; **Kas|sen|er|folg** M *(Theat etc)* box-office hit; **Kas|sen|füh|rer(in)** M(F) treasurer; **Kas|sen|fül|ler** M box-office hit; **Kas|sen|la|ge** F *(inf)* state of one's finances, cash flow situation; **die ~ überprüfen** to check how much cash one has; **Kas|sen|ob|li|ga|ti|on** F *(St Ex)* medium-term bond; **Kas|sen|pa|ti|ent(in)** M(F) *patient belonging to medical insurance scheme*, ≈ National Health patient *(Brit)*; **Kas|sen|preis** M cash price, sales price; **Kas|sen|prü|fung** F audit; **Kas|sen|re|kord** M record takings *pl*; **Kas|sen|schal|ter** M = **Kasse a**; **Kas|sen|schla|ger** M *(inf) (Theat etc)* box-office hit; *(Ware)* big seller; **Kas|sen|stand** M *(Comm)* cash in till *(Brit) or* register *(US)*; **Kas|sen|stun|den** PL hours *pl* of business (of cashier's office *etc*); **Kas|sen|sturz** M *(Comm)* cashing up *(Brit)*, counting up the earnings *(US)*; **~ machen** to check one's finances; *(Comm)* to cash up *(Brit)*, to count up the earnings *(US)*; **Kas|sen|wart** [-vart] M **-s, -e**, **Kas|sen|war|tin** [-vartɪn] F **-, -nen** treasurer; **Kas|sen|zet|tel** M sales slip

Kas|se|rol|le [kasə'rɔlə] F **-, -n** saucepan; *(mit Henkeln)* casserole

Kas|set|te [ka'sɛtə] F **-, -n** **a** (= *Kästchen)* case, box **b** *(für Bücher)* slipcase; (= *Bücher in Kassette)* set, pack *(Comm)*; (= *Geschenkkassette)* gift case/set; *(für Schallplatten)* box; set; (= *Tonbandkassette, Filmbehälter)* cassette; (= *Aufbewahrungskassette)* container; *(für Bücher)* library case; *(für Film)* can **c** *(Archit)* coffer

Kas|set|ten-: **Kas|set|ten|deck** NT cassette deck; **Kas|set|ten|de|cke** F coffered ceiling; **Kas|set|ten|film** M *(Phot)* cartridge film; **Kas|set|ten|re|cor|der** M = **Kassettenrekorder**; **Kas|set|ten|re|kor|der** M cassette recorder

Kas|si|ber [ka'siːbɐ] M **-s, -** secret message, stiff *(US inf)*

Kas|sier [ka'siːɐ] M **-s, -e** *(S Ger, Aus, Sw)* = **Kassierer**

kas|sie|ren [ka'siːrən] *ptp* **kassiert** VT **a** *Gelder etc* to collect (up), to take in; *(inf) Abfindung, Finderlohn* to pick up *(inf)*; **nach seinem Tode kassierte sie 50.000 Euro** *(inf)* after his death she collected 50,000 euros; **bei jedem Verkauf kassiert er eine Menge Geld** *(inf)* he makes a packet *(Brit) or* bundle on every sale *(inf)*

b *(inf:* = *wegnehmen)* to take away, to confiscate

c *(inf:* = *verhaften)* to nab *(inf)*

d *(Jur) Urteil* to quash

VI (= *abrechnen)* to take the money; **bei jdm ~** to collect *or* get money from sb; **Sie haben bei mir schon kassiert** I've paid already; **darf ich ~, bitte?** would you like to pay now?

Kas|sie|rer [ka'siːrɐ] M **-s, -**, **Kas|sie|re|rin** [-ərɪn] F **-, -nen** cashier; (= *Bankkassierer)* clerk, teller; (= *Einnehmer)* collector; *(eines Klubs)* treasurer

Kas|sie|rin [ka'siːrɪn] F **-, -nen** *(S Ger, Aus, Sw)* = **Kassiererin**

Kas|tag|net|te [kastan'jɛtə] F -, -n castanet

Kas|ta|nie [kas'ta:niə] F -, -n chestnut; *(= Rosskastanie)* (horse) chestnut; *(= Edelkastanie)* (sweet) chestnut; *(Holz)* chestnut (wood); **glasierte ~n** marrons glacés; **für jdn die ~n aus dem Feuer holen** *(fig)* to pull sb's chestnuts out of the fire

Kas|ta|ni|en-: **Kas|ta|ni|en|baum** M chestnut tree; **kas|ta|ni|en|braun** ADJ maroon; *Pferd, Haar* chestnut; **Kas|ta|ni|en|holz** NT chestnut (wood)

Käst|chen ['kɛstçən] NT -s, - **a** *(= kleiner Kasten)* small box; *(für Schmuck)* case, casket **b** *(auf kariertem Papier)* square

Kas|te ['kastə] F -, -n caste

kas|tei|en [kas'taiən] *ptp* **kasteit** VR *(als Bußübung)* to castigate *or* chastise oneself, to mortify the flesh *(liter)*; *(= sich Entbehrungen auferlegen)* to deny oneself

Kas|tei|ung F -, -en castigation

Kas|tell [kas'tɛl] NT -s, -e (small) fort; *(Naut, Hist)* castle

Kas|tel|lan [kastɛ'la:n] M -s, -e *(= Aufsichtsbeamter, Hausmeister)* steward; (*old dial*: *in Schulen etc*) janitor, caretaker; (*Hist*: *= Schlossvogt*) castellan

Kas|ten ['kastn] M -s, = ['kɛstn] **a** box; *(= Kiste)* crate, case; *(= Truhe)* chest; (*Aus*: *= Schrank*) cupboard; (*N Ger.* *= Schublade*) drawer; *(= Briefkasten)* postbox *(Brit)*, letter box *(Brit)*, mailbox *(US)*; *(= Schaukasten)* showcase, display case; *(= Brotkasten)* breadbin *(Brit)*, breadbox *(US)*; (*Sport*: *= Gerät*) box **b** *(inf)* *(= altes Schiff)* tub *(inf)*; *(= alter Wagen, Flugzeug)* crate *(inf)*; *(= altes großes Haus)* barn (of a place) *(inf)*; *(= Radio, Fernsehapparat etc)* box *(inf)* **c** (*inf*: *= großer, breiter Mann*) heavyweight *(inf)*, big bloke *(Brit inf)* **d** *(inf)* **er hat viel auf dem ~** he's brainy *(inf)* **e** (*inf*: *= Fußballtor*) goal; **sie müssen noch ein Tor in den ~ bringen** they need to put another one in the back of the net *(inf)*; **wer geht in den ~?** who's going in goal?

Kas|ten-: **Kas|ten|form** F *(Cook)* (square) baking tin *(Brit)* *or* pan *(US)*; **kas|ten|för|mig** [-fœrmɪç] ADJ box-shaped; **Kas|ten|geist** M, *no pl* *(Sociol, Rel)* caste spirit; *(von Cliquen)* clannishness, cliquishness; *(= Klassenbewusstsein)* class spirit *or* outlook; **Kas|ten|wa|gen** M *(Aut)* van, truck, panel truck *(US)*; *(auf Bauernhof)* box cart; **Kas|ten|we|sen** NT, *no pl* caste system

Kas|ti|li|en [kas'ti:liən] NT -s Castille

Kast|rat [kas'tra:t] M -en, -en eunuch; *(Mus Hist)* castrato

Kast|ra|ti|on [kastra'tsio:n] F -, -en castration; **chemische ~** chemical castration

Kast|ra|ti|ons-: **Kast|ra|ti|ons|angst** F fear of castration; **Kast|ra|ti|ons|kom|plex** M castration complex

kast|rie|ren [kas'tri:rən] *ptp* **kastriert** VT *(lit, fig)* to castrate; *Tiere auch* to geld

Ka|su|is|tik [kasu'ɪstɪk] F -, *no pl* casuistry

ka|su|is|tisch [kasu'ɪstɪʃ] ADJ casuistic

Ka|sus ['ka:zʊs] M -, - ['ka:zu:s] *(Gram)* case

Ka|sus-: **Ka|sus|bil|dung** F case formation, declension; **Ka|sus|en|dung** F (case) ending

Kat [kat] M -s, -s *(Aut) abbr von* **Katalysator** cat

Ka|ta- [kata] *in cpds* cata-; **Ka|ta|falk** [kata'falk] M -s, -e catafalque

Ka|ta|kom|be [kata'kɔmbə] F -, -n catacomb

Ka|ta|la|ne [kata'la:nə] M -n, -n, **Ka|ta|la|nin** [-'la:nɪn] F -, -nen Catalan

Ka|ta|la|ni|en [kata'la:niən] NT -s Catalonia

ka|ta|la|nisch [kata'la:nɪʃ] ADJ Catalan

Ka|ta|la|nisch(e) [kata'la:nɪʃ] NT Catalan → *auch* **Deutsch(e)**

Ka|ta|log [kata'lo:k] M -(e)s, -e [-gə] catalogue *(Brit)*, catalog *(US)*

ka|ta|lo|gi|sie|ren [katalogi'zi:rən] *ptp* **katalogisiert** VT to catalogue *(Brit)*, to catalog *(US)*

Ka|ta|lo|gi|sie|rung F -, -en cataloguing *(Brit)*, cataloging *(US)*

ka|ta|log|mä|ßig ADJ *Liste* catalogued *(Brit)*, cataloged *(US)* ADV **er erfasste seine Funde ~** he made a catalogue *(Brit)* *or* catalog *(US)* of his finds, he catalogued *(Brit)* *or* cataloged *(US)* his finds

Ka|ta|lo|ni|en [kata'lo:niən] NT -s Catalonia

Ka|ta|ly|sa|tor [kataly'za:toːɐ] M -s, **Katalysatoren** *(lit, fig)* catalyst; *(Aut)* catalytic converter

Ka|ta|ly|sa|tor-: **Ka|ta|ly|sa|tor|au|to** NT car fitted with a catalytic converter; **Ka|ta|ly|sa|tor|mo|dell** NT model with a catalytic converter

Ka|ta|ly|se [kata'ly:zə] F -, -n *(Chem)* catalysis

ka|ta|ly|tisch [kata'ly:tɪʃ] ADJ catalytic

Ka|ta|ma|ran [katama'ra:n] M -s, -e catamaran

Ka|ta|pult [kata'pʊlt] NT OR M -(e)s, -e catapult

ka|ta|pul|tie|ren [katapʊl'ti:rən] *ptp* **katapultiert** VT to catapult VR to catapult oneself; *(Pilot)* to eject

Ka|ta|pult|sitz M ejector *or* ejection seat

Ka|ta|rakt [kata'rakt] M -(e)s, -e cataract

Ka|tarr M -s, -e = **Katarrh**

Ka|tarrh [ka'tar] M -s, -e catarrh

Ka|tas|ter [ka'tastɐ] M OR NT -s, - land register, cadaster *(spec)*

Ka|tas|ter|amt NT land registry

ka|tast|rie|ren [katas'tri:rən] *ptp* **katastriert** VT *Grundstücke* to register, to enter in the land register

ka|ta|stro|phal [katastro'fa:l] ADJ disastrous; *Auswirkungen etc auch* catastrophic; *(= haarsträubend schlecht auch)* atrocious; **der Mangel an Brot ist ~ geworden** the bread shortage has become catastrophic ADV **sich ~ auswirken** to have catastrophic effects; **~ geschwächt** disastrously weakened; **jds Gesundheit ~ beeinträchtigen** to ruin sb's health; **~ unterernährt sein** to be disastrously undernourished; **das Zimmer sieht ja ~ aus** the room looks absolutely disastrous

Ka|ta|stro|phe [katas'tro:fə] F -, -n disaster, catastrophe; *(Theat, Liter)* catastrophe, (tragic) dénouement; **der ist eine ~** *(inf)* he's a real disaster (area) *(inf)* *or* catastrophe *(inf)*

Ka|ta|stro|phen-: **Ka|ta|stro|phen|ab|wehr** F disaster prevention; **Ka|ta|stro|phen|alarm** M emergency alert; **Ka|ta|stro|phen|dienst** M emergency service; **Ka|ta|stro|phen|ein|satz** M duty *or* use in case of disaster; **für den ~** for use in case of disaster; **Ka|ta|stro|phen|ge|biet** NT disaster area; **Ka|ta|stro|phen|op|fer** NT disaster victim; **Ka|ta|stro|phen|schutz** M disaster control; *(im Voraus)*; **Ka|ta|stro|phen|stim|mung** F doomsday atmosphere *or* mood; **Ka|ta|stro|phen|tou|ris|mus** M disaster tourism

Ka|ta|to|nie [katato'ni:] F -, -n [-'ni:ən] *(Psych)* catatonia

Kat|au|to ['kat-] NT *(Mot inf)* cat car

Ka|te ['ka:tə] F -, -n *(N Ger)* cottage, croft *(Scot)*

Ka|te|che|se [katɛ'çe:zə] F -, -n catechesis

Ka|te|chet [katɛ'çe:t] M -en, -en, **Ka|te|che|tin** [-'çe:tɪn] F -, -nen catechist

Ka|te|chis|mus [katɛ'çɪsmʊs] M -, **Katechismen** [-mən] catechism

Ka|te|chist [katɛ'çɪst] M -en, -en, **Ka|te|chis|tin** [-'çɪstɪn] F -, -nen catechist

ka|te|go|ri|al [katego'ria:l] ADJ categorical

Ka|te|go|rie [katego'ri:] F -, -n [-'ri:ən] category; **er gehört auch zur ~ derer, die ...** he's one of those who ..., he's the sort *or* type who ...

ka|te|go|risch [kate'go:rɪʃ] ADJ categorical, absolute; *Ablehnung auch* flat; **der ~e Imperativ** the categorical imperative ADV categorically, absolutely; *ablehnen* categorically, flatly; *behaupten, formulieren* categorically; **ich weigerte mich ~** I refused outright, I absolutely refused; **... erklärte er ~** ... he declared emphatically

ka|te|go|ri|sie|ren [kategori'zi:rən] *ptp* **kategorisiert** VT to categorize

Ka|ter ['ka:tɐ] M -s, - **a** tom(cat); **wie ein verliebter ~** like an amorous tomcat → **gestiefelt** **a b** *(nach Alkoholgenuss)* hangover

Ka|ter-: **Ka|ter|früh|stück** NT *breakfast (of pickled herring etc) to cure a hangover*; **Ka|ter|stim|mung** F depression, the blues *pl* *(inf)*

kat|exo|chen [katlɛksɔ'xe:n] ADV *(liter)* **Demokratie ~** the epitome of democracy

kath. *abbr von* **katholisch**

Ka|thar|sis ['ka:tarzɪs, ka'tarzɪs] F -, *no pl* *(Liter, fig)* catharsis

ka|thar|tisch [ka'tartɪʃ] ADJ *(Liter, fig)* cathartic

Ka|the|der [ka'te:dɐ] M OR NT -s, - *(in Schule)* teacher's desk; *(in Universität)* lectern; **etw vom ~ herab erklären** to declare sth ex cathedra *(hum, form)*

Ka|thed|ra|le [kate'dra:lə] F -, -n cathedral

Ka|the|ter [ka'te:tɐ] M -s, - *(Med)* catheter

Ka|tho|de [ka'to:də] F -, -n *(Phys)* cathode

Ka|tho|den-: **Ka|tho|den|strah|len** PL *(Phys)* cathode rays *pl*; **Ka|tho|den|strahl|röh|re** F *(TV etc)* cathode-ray tube

Ka|tho|le [ka'to:lə] M -n, -n, **Ka|tho|lin** [-'to:lɪn] -, -nen *(inf)* Catholic, Papist *(pej)*

Ka|tho|lik [kato'li:k] M -en, -en, **Ka|tho|li|kin** [-'li:kɪn] F -, -nen (Roman) Catholic

ka|tho|lisch [ka'to:lɪʃ] ADJ (Roman) Catholic; **sie ist streng ~** she's a strict Catholic ADV **~ denken** to have Catholic views; **~ heiraten** to have a Catholic wedding; **~ beerdigt werden** to have a Catholic burial; **~ beeinflusst** influenced by Catholicism; **seine Kinder ~ erziehen** to raise one's children (as) Catholics

Ka|tho|li|zis|mus [katoli'tsɪsmʊs] M -, *no pl* (Roman) Catholicism

Kat-Mo|dell NT *(Aut) abbr von* **Katalysator-Modell**

Katt|an|ker ['katlaŋkɐ] M *(Naut)* kedge

Kat|te|gatt ['katəgat] NT -s Kattegat

Kat|tun [ka'tu:n] M -s, -e *(old)* cotton, calico

katz|bal|gen ['katsbalgn] VR to romp around

Katz|bal|ge|rei [katsbalgə'rai] F romping

katz|bu|ckeln ['katsbʊkln] VI *(pej inf)* to bow and scrape, to grovel

Kätz|chen ['kɛtsçən] NT -s, - **a** *(= junge Katze,* *inf*: *= Mädchen)* kitten; *(= Katze)* pussy *(inf)* **b** *(Bot)* catkin

Kat|ze ['katsə] F -, -n cat; **meine Arbeit war für die Katz** *(fig)* my work was a waste of time; **das hat die ~ gefressen** *(fig)* the fairies took it *(hum inf)*; **Katz und Maus mit jdm spielen** to play cat and mouse with sb; **wie die ~ um den heißen Brei herumschleichen** to beat about the bush; **die ~ aus dem Sack lassen** *(inf)* to let the cat out of the bag; **die ~ im Sack kaufen** to buy a pig in a poke *(prov)*; **die ~ lässt das Mausen nicht** *(Prov)* the leopard cannot change its spots *(Prov)*; **bei Nacht sind alle ~n grau** all cats are grey *(Brit)* *or* gray *(US)* at night; **wenn die ~ aus dem Haus ist, tanzen die Mäuse (auf dem Tisch)** *(Prov)* when the cat's away the mice will play *(Prov)*

Kat|zel|ma|cher(in) M(F) (*S Ger, Aus*: *pej*: *= Italiener)* dago *(pej)*, Eyetie *(Brit pej)*

Kat|zen-: **Kat|zen|au|ge** NT **a** *(= Straßenmarkierung)* Catseye®; *(= Rückstrahler)* reflector **b** *(Min)* cat's-eye; **Kat|zen|bu|ckel** M arched back (of a cat); **einen ~ machen** to arch one's back; **kat|zen|freund|lich** ADJ *(pej)* over-friendly; **Kat|zen|fut|ter** NT cat food; **kat|zen|haft** ADJ cat-like, feline; **Kat|zen|hai** M dogfish; **Kat|zen|jam|mer** M *(inf)* **a** *(= Kater)* hangover **b** *(= jämmerliche Stimmung)* depression, the blues *pl* *(inf)*; **ich habe ~** I feel down (in the dumps) *(inf)*, I've got the blues *(inf)*; **Kat|zen|klo** NT *(inf)* cat litter tray *(Brit)* *or* box *(US)*; **Kat|zen|kopf** M *(fig)* **a** *(= Kopfstein)* cobble(stone) **b** (*Sch*: *= Schlag*) cuff (on the head), box round the ears; **Kat|zen|kraut** NT catnip; **Kat|zen|mu|sik** F *(fig)* caterwauling, din, racket *(inf)*; **Kat|zen|mut|ter** F (doting) cat owner; **Kat|zen|nah|rung** F catfood;

Kat|zen|sprung M *(inf)* stone's throw; **Kat|zen|streu** F cat litter; **Kat|zen|tisch** M *(hum)* children's table; **die Kinder essen am ~** the children are eating at their own table; **Kat|zen|tür** F cat flap; **Kat|zen|wä|sche** F *(hum inf)* a lick and a promise *(inf)*, a cat's lick *(Brit inf)*; **~ machen** to give oneself a lick and a promise; **Kat|zen|zun|ge** F *(= Schokolade)* chocolate langue de chat

Katz-und-Maus-Spiel NT cat-and-mouse game

Kau-: **Kau|ap|pa|rat** M masticatory apparatus; **Kau|be|we|gung** F chewing movement

Kau|der|welsch ['kaudɐvɛlʃ] NT **-(s)**, *no pl (pej)* *(= Fach- oder Geheimsprache)* lingo *(inf)*, jargon; *(= Gemisch aus mehreren Sprachen/Dialekten)* hotchpotch *(Brit)* or hodgepodge or mishmash (of different languages/dialects); *(= unverständliche Sprache)* double Dutch, gibberish

kau|der|wel|schen ['kaudɐvɛlʃn] VI *(unverständlich)* to talk double Dutch, to talk gibberish; *(in Fachsprache)* to talk jargon; *(in Gemisch aus mehreren Sprachen/Dialekten)* to talk a hotchpotch *(Brit)* or hodgepodge or mishmash of languages/dialects

kau|en ['kauən] **VT** to chew; *Nägel* to bite, to chew; *Wein* to taste **VI** to chew; **an etw** *(dat)* **~** to chew (on) sth; **an den Nägeln ~** to bite or chew one's nails; **daran hatte ich lange zu ~** *(fig)* it took me a long time to get over it; **daran wird er zu ~ haben** *(fig)* that will really give him food for thought or something to think about; **gut gekaut ist halb verdaut** *(Prov)* you should chew your food properly; **das Kauen** chewing

kau|ern ['kauɐn] VIR *(vi auch aux sein)* to crouch (down); *(ängstlich)* to cower; *(Schutz suchend)* to be huddled (up)

Kauf [kauf] M **-(e)s, Käu|fe** ['kɔyfə] *(= das Kaufen)* buying *no pl*, purchase *(esp form)*, purchasing *no pl (esp form)*; *(= das Gekaufte)* purchase *(esp form)*, buy; **das war ein günstiger ~** that was a good buy; **diese Käufe haben sich gelohnt** it was worth buying these; **mit diesem Anzug machen Sie bestimmt einen guten ~** this suit is definitely a good buy; **ein ~ auf Kredit** a credit purchase; **etw zum ~ anbieten** to offer sth for sale; **einen ~ abschließen** or **tätigen** *(form)* to complete a purchase; **etw durch ~ erwerben** *(form)* to purchase sth; **etw in ~ nehmen** *(lit)* to accept sth in part exchange; *(fig)* to accept sth

Kauf-: **Kauf|ab|sicht** F intention to buy; **Kauf|an|ge|bot** NT bid; **Kauf|an|reiz** M incentive to buy; **Kauf|auf|trag** M purchasing or buying order; **Kauf|be|reit|schaft** F willingness to buy

Kauf|brief M deed of purchase; *(esp für Grundstücke)* title deed

kau|fen ['kaufn] **VT** **a** *(auch* **sich** *(dat)* **kaufen)** to buy, to purchase *(esp form)*; **ich kauf dir ein Geschenk** I'll buy you a present, I'll buy a present for you; **ich habe (mir) einen neuen Anzug gekauft** I bought (myself) a new suit; **diese Zigaretten werden viel gekauft** we sell a lot of these cigarettes; **diese Zigaretten werden nicht gekauft** nobody buys these cigarettes; **jetzt wird nicht schon wieder eine neue Jacke gekauft!** you're not going to buy another jacket!; **dafür kann ich mir nichts ~** *(iro)*, **was kann man sich** *(dat)* **dafür (schon) ~** *(iro)* what use is that to me!, that's a fat lot of use! *(inf)*
b *(= bestechen)* jdn to bribe, to buy off; *Spiel* to fix; *Stimmen* to buy; **der Sieg war gekauft** it was fixed
c **sich** *(dat)* **jdn ~** *(inf)* to give sb a piece of one's mind *(inf)*; *(tätlich)* to fix sb *(inf)*
d *auch vi (Cards)* to buy
VI to buy; *(= Einkäufe machen)* to shop; **auf dem Markt kauft man billiger** it is cheaper to shop at the market, you can buy things cheaper at the market; **das Kaufen** buying, purchasing *(esp form)*

Kauf|ent|schei|dung F decision to buy *(für etw* sth)

Käu|fer ['kɔyfɐ] M **-s, -**, **Käu|fe|rin** [-ərɪn] F **-, -nen** buyer, purchaser *(esp form)*; *(= Kunde)* customer, shopper

Käu|fer-: **Käu|fer|ge|wohn|hei|ten** PL buying habits *pl*; **Käu|fer|kreis** M group of customers or buyers; **Käu|fer|schicht** F class of customer(s)

Kauf-: **Kauf|fah|rer** M *(old)* merchant ship, merchantman; **Kauf|frau** F businesswoman; **Kauf|hal|le** F department store; *(esp DDR)* small supermarket; **Kauf|haus** NT department store; **Kauf|haus|de|tek|tiv(in)** M(F) store detective; **Kauf|in|te|res|se** NT (buyer) demand; **Kauf|in|te|res|sent(in)** M(F) prospective purchaser or buyer, prospect; **Kauf|kraft** F *(von Geld)* buying or purchasing power; *(vom Käufer)* spending power; **Kunden mit ~** customers with money to spend; **kauf|kräf|tig** ADJ **eine ~e Währung** a currency with good purchasing power; **~e Kunden** customers with money to spend; **ein ~er Markt** a market with strong purchasing power

Kauf|kraft-: **Kauf|kraft|len|kung** F control of (consumer) spending; **Kauf|kraft|schwund** M drop in purchasing power; **Kauf|kraft|über|hang** M excess or surplus (consumer) spending power; **Kauf|kraft|ver|lust** M loss of purchasing power

Kauf-: **Kauf|la|den** M **a** *(rare: = Ladengeschäft)* (small) shop **b** *(= Spielzeug)* toy shop; **Kauf|leu|te** *pl von* **Kaufmann**

käuf|lich ['kɔyflɪç] **ADJ** **a** *(= zu kaufen)* for sale, purchasable *(form)*; **etwas, was nicht ~ ist** something which cannot be bought **b** *(fig)* venal; **~e Liebe** *(geh)* prostitution; **ein ~es Mädchen** *(geh)* a woman of easy virtue; **Freundschaft ist nicht ~** friendship cannot be bought **c** *(fig: = bestechlich)* venal; **~ sein** to be easily bought; **ich bin nicht ~** you cannot buy me! **ADV** **etw ~ erwerben** *(form)* to purchase sth

Käuf|lich|keit F **-**, *no pl* **a** **Kennzeichen des Kapitalismus ist die ~ aller Dinge** it is a characteristic of capitalism that everything can be bought or is for sale **b** *(fig: = Bestechlichkeit)* corruptibility, venality

Kauf-: **Kauf|lust** F desire to buy (things); *(St Ex)* buying; **die ~ hat plötzlich zugenommen** people have suddenly gone on a spending spree; **kauf|lus|tig** ADJ inclined to buy, in a buying mood; **in den Straßen drängten sich die Kauflustigen** the streets were thronged with shoppers

Kauf|mann M *pl* **-leute** **a** *(= Geschäftsmann)* businessman; *(= Händler)* trader; *(= Tabakkaufmann, Gewürzkaufmann, Wollkaufmann etc)* merchant; **gelernter ~** person with qualifications in business or commerce; **jeder ~ lobt seine Ware** *(Prov)* a salesman will always praise his own wares **b** *(= Einzelhandelskaufmann)* small shopkeeper, grocer; **zum ~ gehen** to go to the grocer's

kauf|män|nisch [-mɛnɪʃ] **ADJ** commercial, business *attr*; **~er Angestellter** office worker; **~e Buchführung** commercial book-keeping; **er wollte einen ~en Beruf ergreifen** he wanted to make a career in business or commerce; **er übt einen ~en Beruf aus** he is in business or commerce; **Fachschule für ~e Berufe** commercial college, business school; **alles Kaufmännische** everything commercial, everything to do with business; **alles Kaufmännische macht seine Frau für ihn** his wife looks after the business side of things for him
ADV **sie ist ~ tätig** she is in business, she is a businesswoman; **~ denken** to think in commercial or business terms; **nicht sehr ~ gedacht** not very businesslike; **~ handeln** to act businesslike or like a businessman/-woman

Kauf|mann|schaft ['kaufmanʃaft] F **-**, *no pl (geh)* merchants *pl*

Kauf|manns-: **Kauf|manns|ge|hil|fe** M, **Kauf|manns|ge|hil|fin** F assistant, clerk; *(im Laden)* sales assistant, clerk *(US)*; **Kauf|manns|la|den** M **a** *(dated)* grocer's; *(= Gemischtwarenhandlung)* general store **b** *(= Spielzeug)* toy grocer's shop, miniature grocery store *(US)*; **Kauf|manns|lehr|ling** M management trainee; **Kauf|manns|stand** M merchant class

Kauf-: **Kauf|op|ti|on** F *(St Ex)* call option; *(Comm)* option to buy; **Kauf|preis** M purchase price; **Kauf|rausch** M spending spree; **im ~ sein** to be on a spending spree; **Kauf|sucht** F compulsive shopping; **ihre ~** her shopping addiction; **kauf|süch|tig** ADJ addicted to shopping; **~ sein** to be a compulsive shopper or a shopaholic *(inf)*, to be addicted to shopping; **Kauf|sum|me** F money; **Kauf|un|lust** F consumer resistance; **Kauf|ver|trag** M bill of sale; **Kauf|wert** M market value; **Kauf|zwang** M obligation to buy; **kein/ohne ~** no/without obligation

Kau|gum|mi M OR NT chewing gum

Kau|ka|si|en [kau'ka:ziən] NT **-s** Caucasia

Kau|ka|si|er [kau'ka:ziɐ] M **-s, -**, **Kau|ka|si|e|rin** [-iərɪn] F **-, -nen** Caucasian

kau|ka|sisch [kau'ka:zɪʃ] ADJ Caucasian

Kau|ka|sus ['kaukazʊs] M **- der ~** (the) Caucasus

Kaul|quap|pe ['kaul-] F tadpole

kaum [kaum] **ADV** **a** *(= noch nicht einmal)* hardly, scarcely, barely; **er verdient ~ 1500 Euro** he earns barely 1500 euros; **ich habe ~ noch 10 Liter** I've barely 10 litres *(Brit)* or liters *(US)* left; **das kostet ~ 100 Euro** it doesn't even cost 100 euros; **man braucht ~ 10 Liter** you'll need less than 10 litres *(Brit)* or liters *(US)*; **sie war ~ hereingekommen, als ...** hardly or scarcely or no sooner had she come in when ..., she had hardly *etc* come in when ...; **~ jemand/jemals** hardly or scarcely anyone/ever; **es ist ~ möglich, dass ...** it is hardly or scarcely possible that ...; **es ist ~ zu glauben, wie ...** it's hardly or scarcely believable or to be believed how ...; **wir hatten ~ noch Vorräte** we had hardly or scarcely any supplies left, we hardly had any supplies left; **er kann ~ noch sprechen/laufen** he can hardly *etc* speak/walk any more; **ich hatte ~ noch damit gerechnet, dass ...** I hardly or scarcely thought that ... any more
b *(= wahrscheinlich nicht)* hardly, scarcely; **~!** hardly, scarcely; **wohl ~, ich glaube ~** I hardly or scarcely think so; **ich glaube ~, dass ...** I hardly or scarcely think that ...; **das wird wohl ~ stimmen** *(= richtig sein)* that can hardly be right, surely that can't be right; *(= wahr sein)* that can hardly be true, surely that can't be true; **das wird ~ passieren** that's hardly or scarcely likely to happen
CONJ hardly, scarcely; **~ dass wir das Meer erreicht hatten ...** hardly or scarcely had we reached the sea when ..., no sooner had we reached the sea than ...; **~ gerufen, eilte der Diener herbei** no sooner summoned, the servant hurried in; **er verdient äußerst wenig, ~ dass er davon satt wird** he earns extremely little and can hardly even buy enough to eat

Kau|mus|kel M jaw muscle, masseter *(spec)*

Kau|ri|mu|schel ['kauri-] F cowrie shell

kau|sal [kau'za:l] **ADJ** causal; **~e Therapie** *(Med)* causal therapy; **~ für etw sein** to be the cause of sth **ADV** causally

Kau|sal|be|zie|hung F causal connection

Kau|sal|ge|setz NT law of causality

Kau|sa|li|tät [kauzali'tɛ:t] F **-, -en** causality

Kau|sa|li|täts|prin|zip NT principle of causality

Kau|sal-: **Kau|sal|ket|te** F causal chain, chain of cause and effect; **Kau|sal|ne|xus** [-nɛksʊs] M **-, -** [-nɛksu:s] *(geh)* causal connection; **Kau|sal|satz** M causal clause; **Kau|sal|zu|sam|men|hang** M causal connection

kau|sa|tiv ['kauzati:f] ADJ *(Gram)* causative

Kau|sa|tiv ['kauzati:f] NT **-s, -e** [-və] *(Gram)* causative

kaus|tisch ['kaustɪʃ] ADJ *(Chem, fig)* caustic ADV **~ wirken** *(lit)* to have a caustic effect; **seine Worte wirkten ~** his words were caustic; **sich ~ äußern** to make a caustic remark

Kau|ta|bak M chewing tobacco

Kau|tel [kau'te:l] F **-, -en** *(geh)* proviso

Kau|ti|on [kau'tsio:n] F **-, -en** **a** *(Jur)* bail; **~ stellen** to stand bail; **er stellte 1000 Euro ~** he put up 1000 euros (as) bail; **gegen ~** on bail; **jdn gegen ~ freilassen** to release sb on bail; **gegen ~ freikommen** to get out on bail; **jdn gegen ~ freibekommen** to bail sb out **b** *(Comm)* security **c** *(für Miete)* deposit; **zwei Monatsmieten ~** two months' deposit

Kau|ti|ons|sum|me F **a** *(Jur)* (amount of) bail **b** *(Comm, Jur)* (amount of) security

Kaut|schuk ['kautʃʊk] M **-s, -e** (India) rubber

Kaut|schuk|milch F latex

Kau|werk|zeu|ge PL masticatory organs *pl*

Kauz [kauts] M **-es, Käuze** ['kɔytsə] **a** screech owl **b** *(= Sonderling)* odd *or* strange fellow, oddball *(inf)*; **ein komischer ~** an odd bird; **ein wunderlicher alter ~** a strange old bird

Käuz|chen ['kɔytsçən] NT **-s, -** *dim von* **Kauz a**

kau|zig ['kautsɪç] ADJ odd ADV oddly

Kau|zig|keit F **-,** *no pl* oddness

Ka|va|lier [kava'li:ɐ] M **-s, -e** **a** *(= galanter Mann)* gentleman; **er ist immer ~** he's always a gentleman, he's always chivalrous; **der ~ genießt und schweigt** one does not boast about one's conquests **b** *(dated: = Begleiter einer Dame)* beau *(old)*, young man *(dated)*

Ka|va|liers|de|likt NT trivial offence *(Brit) or* offense *(US)*, (mere) peccadillo

Ka|va|lier(s)-: **Ka|va|lier(s)|start** M *(Aut)* racing start; **Ka|va|lier(s)|tuch** NT *(dated)* handkerchief in one's top pocket

Ka|val|ka|de [kaval'ka:də] F **-, -n** cavalcade

Ka|val|le|rie [kavalə'ri:] F **-, -n** [-'ri:ən] *(Mil)* cavalry

Ka|val|le|rie|pferd NT cavalry horse

Ka|val|le|rist [kavalə'rɪst] M **-en, -en** *(Mil Hist)* cavalryman

Ka|vents|mann [ka'vɛnts-] M *pl* **-männer** *(N Ger inf)* whopper *(inf)*

Ka|ver|ne [ka'vɛrnə] F **-, -n** cavern

Ka|vi|ar ['ka:viar] M **-s, -e** caviar

Ka|vi|ar|brot NT French loaf

KB [ka:'be:] NT **-(s), -(s)**, **KByte** ['ka:bait] NT **-(s), -(s)** *abbr von* **Kilobyte** k, kbyte

kcal *abbr von* **Kilokalorie**

Ke|bab [ke'ba:p, ke'bap] M **-(s), -s** kebab

Keb|se ['ke:psə] F **-, -n**, **Kebs|weib** NT *(old, Bibl)* concubine

keck [kɛk] ADJ **a** *(= frech)* cheeky *(Brit)*, saucy, fresh *(US)* **b** *(= flott)* Mädchen pert; *Kleidungsstück* jaunty, saucy ADV cheekily *(Brit)*, saucily; **sie trug den Hut ~ auf einem Ohr** she wore her hat at a jaunty *or* saucy angle over one ear **a** *(old: = tapfer)* bold

ke|ckern ['kɛkɐn] VI to snarl, to growl

Keck|heit F **-, -en** **a** *(= Frechheit)* cheekiness *(Brit)*, impudence **b** *(old: = Tapferkeit)* boldness

Kee|per ['ki:pɐ] M **-s, -**, **Kee|pe|rin** ['ki:pərɪn] F **-, -nen** *(Aus Sport)* (goal)keeper

Keep|smi|ling [ki:p'smailɪŋ] NT **-(s)**, *no pl* fixed smile

Ke|fir ['ke:fɪr, 'ke:fi:ɐ] M **-s**, *no pl* kefir *(a milk product similar to yoghurt, of Turkish origin)*

Ke|gel ['ke:gl] M **-s, -** **a** *(= Spielfigur)* skittle, ninepin; *(bei Bowling)* pin; **~ schieben** *or (Aus)* **scheiben** to play skittles *or* ninepins; *(bei Bowling)* to play bowls; **~ aufsetzen** to set the skittles/pins up → **Kind** **b** *(Geometrie)* cone; *(= Bergkegel)* peak **c** *(= Lichtkegel, Scheinwerferkegel)* beam (of light) **d** *(Typ)* body, shank

Ke|gel-: **Ke|gel|bahn** F (bowling) lane; *(= Anlage)* skittle alley; *(automatisch)* bowling alley; **Ke|gel|bru|der** M *(inf)* → **kegeln** member of a skittle/bowling club; **ke|gel|för|mig** ADJ conical ADV conically; **Ke|gel|ku|gel** F bowl; **Ke|gel|man|tel** M surface of a cone

ke|geln ['ke:gln] VI to play skittles *or* ninepins; *(bei Bowling)* to play bowls; **~ gehen** to play skittles; to go bowling

Ke|geln ['ke:gln] M (playing) skittles *sing or* ninepins *sing*; *(bei Bowling auf Gras)* (playing) bowls *sing*; *(auf Kegelbahn)* bowling

Ke|gel-: **Ke|gel|rad** NT *(Tech)* bevelled *or* mitre wheel *(Brit)*, beveled *or* miter wheel *(US)*; **ke|gel|schei|ben** [-ʃaibn] *(Aus)*, **ke|gel|schie|ben** VI *sep irreg* → **Kegel a**; **Ke|gel|schnitt** M conic section; **Ke|gel|schwes|ter** F *(inf)* → **kegeln** member of a skittle/bowling club; **Ke|gel|sport** M bowling; **Ke|gel|stumpf** M frustum

Keg|ler ['ke:glɐ] M **-s, -**, **Keg|le|rin** [-ərɪn] F **-, -nen** skittle-player; *(bei Bowling)* bowler

Keh|le ['ke:lə] F **-, -n** **a** *(= Gurgel)* throat; **das ist ihm in die falsche ~ gekommen, er hat das in die falsche ~ bekommen** *(lit)* it went down the wrong way, it got stuck in his throat; *(fig)* he took it the wrong way; **eine raue ~ haben** to be hoarse; **aus voller ~** at the top of one's voice *or* one's lungs; **er hat eine trockene ~** *(inf)* he needs a drink; *(gewohnheitsmäßig)* he likes his *or* a drink *(inf)*; **(sich** *dat***) die ~ schmieren** *(inf) or* **anfeuchten** *(inf)* to wet one's whistle *(inf)*; **jdm die ~ durchschneiden** to cut *or* slit sb's throat; **jetzt geht es ihm an die ~** *(fig)* now things have turned nasty for him → **schreien VR, zuschnüren**
b *(= ausgerundeter Winkel)* moulding *(Brit)*, molding *(US)*; *(= Rille)* groove

keh|lig ['ke:lɪç] ADJ throaty; *Stimme auch* guttural ADV **~ lachen** to give a throaty laugh; **eine ~ klingende Stimme** a throaty voice

Kehl|kopf M larynx

Kehl|kopf-: **Kehl|kopf|ent|zün|dung** F, **Kehl|kopf|ka|tarr(h)** M laryngitis; **Kehl|kopf|krebs** M cancer of the throat; **Kehl|kopf|mik|ro|fon**, **Kehl|kopf|mik|ro|phon** NT throat microphone; **Kehl|kopf|spie|gel** M laryngoscope

Kehl|laut M guttural (sound)

Keh|lung ['ke:lʊŋ] F **-, -en** *(Archit)* groove, flute

Kehl|ver|schluss|laut M *(Phon)* glottal stop

Kehr-: **Kehr|aus** ['ke:ɐlaus] M **-,** *no pl* last dance; *(fig: = Abschiedsfeier)* farewell celebration; **den ~ machen** *(fig)* to have a farewell celebration; **Kehr|be|sen** M broom; **Kehr|blech** NT *(S Ger)* shovel

Keh|re ['ke:rə] F **-, -n** **a** (sharp) turn *or* bend; *(= Haarnadelkurve)* hairpin bend **b** *(= Turnübung)* rear *or* back vault

keh|ren ['ke:rən] VT **a** *(= drehen)* to turn; **die Augen** *or* **den Blick zum Himmel ~** *(liter)* to turn one's eyes heavenwards, to gaze heavenwards; **die Augen** *or* **den Blick zu Boden ~** *(liter)* to cast one's eyes to the ground *(liter)*; **in sich** *(acc)* **gekehrt** *(= versunken)* pensive, wrapped in thought; *(= verschlossen)* introspective, introverted → **Rücken**
b *(= kümmern)* to bother; **was kehrt mich das?** what do I care about that?; **das kehrt mich einen Dreck!** *(inf)* I don't give a damn about that! *(inf)*
VR **a** *(= sich drehen)* to turn; **eines Tages wird sich sein Hochmut gegen ihn ~** one day his arrogance will rebound against him
b **er kehrt sich nicht daran, was die Leute sagen** he doesn't mind *or* care what people say
VI to turn (round); *(Wind)* to turn

keh|ren VTI *(esp S Ger: = fegen)* to sweep; **ich muss noch ~** I've still got to do the sweeping; **jeder kehre vor seiner (eigenen) Tür!** *(prov)* everyone should first put his own house in order → **Besen**

Keh|richt ['ke:rɪçt] M OR NT **-s**, *no pl* **a** *(old, form)* sweepings *pl*; **den ~ zusammenfegen** to sweep up the rubbish → **feucht** **b** *(Sw: = Müll)* rubbish *(Brit)*, trash *(US)*

Keh|richt|sack M *(Sw: = Müllsack)* rubbish *or* refuse bag

Keh|richt|schau|fel F dustpan

Keh|richt|ver|bren|nungs|an|la|ge F *(Sw)* incineration plant

Kehr-: **Kehr|ma|schi|ne** F *(= Straßenkehrmaschine)* road-sweeper, road sweeping machine; *(= Teppichkehrmaschine)* carpet-sweeper; **Kehr|platz** M *(Sw)* turning area; **Kehr|reim** M chorus, refrain; **Kehr|schau|fel** F shovel; **Kehr|sei|te** F **a** *(von Münze)* reverse **b** *(inf: = Rücken)* back; *(hum: = Gesäß)* backside *(inf)*, behind; *(fig: = Nachteil)* drawback; **jdm seine ~ zuwenden** to turn one's back on sb **c** *(fig: = Schattenseite)* other side; **die ~ der Medaille** the other side of the coin

kehrt [ke:ɐt] INTERJ *(Mil)* **ganze Abteilung ~!** company, about turn!

Kehrt-: **kehrt+ma|chen** VI *sep* to turn round, to do an about-turn; *(= zurückgehen)* to turn back; *(Mil)* to about-turn; **Kehrt|wen|de** F, **Kehrt|wen|dung** F about-turn; **diese plötzliche Kehrtwendung wurde scharf kritisiert** this sudden about-turn *or* volte-face was sharply criticized

Kehr|wert M reciprocal value

> **KEHRWOCHE**
>
> The **Kehrwoche** is the week when a tenant living in a building containing several flats is responsible for keeping the staircase and/or pavement clean. The **Kehrwoche** is observed especially strictly in Swabia.

kei|fen ['kaifn] VI to bicker

Kei|fe|rei [kaifə'rai] F **-, -en** *(inf)* bickering

Keil [kail] M **-(e)s, -e** wedge *(auch Mil)*; *(als Hemmvorrichtung auch)* chock; *(= Faustkeil)* hand-axe *(Brit)*, hand-ax *(US)*; *(Sew: = Zwickel)* gusset; *(= Kopfkeil)* headrest; **einen ~ in etw** *(acc)* **treiben** to put a wedge in sth; *(zum Befestigen auch)* to wedge sth; **einen ~ zwischen zwei Freunde treiben** *(fig)* to drive a wedge between two friends → **grob**

Keil-: **Keil|ab|satz** M wedge heel, wedge; **Keil|bein** NT sphenoid (bone)

Kei|le ['kailə] PL *(inf)* thrashing, hiding; **~ bekommen** *or* **kriegen** *or* **beziehen** to get *or* to be given a thrashing *or* hiding; **dahinten gibts gleich ~** there's going to be a fight over there

kei|len ['kailən] VT **a** *(mit Keil)* to wedge **b** *(dated sl: = anwerben)* Mitglieder to rope in *(inf)*
VR *(dial inf: = sich prügeln)* to fight

Kei|ler ['kailɐ] M **-s, -** wild boar

Kei|le|rei [kailə'rai] F **-, -en** *(inf)* punch-up *(inf)*, brawl, fight

Keil-: **keil|för|mig** ADJ wedge-shaped ADV **sich ~ zuspitzen** to form a wedge; *(Turmspitze)* to form a point; **ein Auto mit ~ gestylter Karosserie** a car with a wedge-shaped body; **Keil|haue** F *(Min)* pick(axe) *(Brit)*, pick(ax) *(US)*; **Keil|ho|se** F, **Keil|ho|sen** PL slacks *pl*, ski pants *pl*; **Keil|kis|sen** NT, *(Aus)* **Keil|pols|ter** NT wedge-shaped pillow *(used as a headrest)*; **Keil|rah|men** M stretcher *(for artist's canvas)*; **Keil|rie|men** M drive belt; *(Aut)* fan belt; **Keil|schrift** F cuneiform script

Keim [kaim] M **-(e)s, -e** **a** *(= kleiner Trieb)* shoot, sprout; **die ersten ~e ihrer jungen Liebe** *(liter)* the first blossomings *or* burgeoning of their young love *(liter)* **b** *(= Embryo, fig)* embryo, germ; *(= Krankheitskeim)* germ; **im ~e** *(fig)* in embryo, in embryonic form; **etw im ~ ersticken** to nip sth in the bud **c** *(fig: des Hasses, der Liebe etc)* seed *usu pl*; **den ~ zu etw legen** to sow the seeds of sth; **den ~ zu etw in sich** *(dat)* **tragen** to carry the seeds of sth

Keim-: **Keim|blatt** NT **a** *(Bot)* cotyledon **b** *(Zool)* blastema; **Keim|drü|se** F gonad; **Keim|drü|sen|hor|mon** NT sex hormone

kei|men ['kaimən] VI **a** *(Saat)* to germinate; *(Pflanzen)* to put out shoots, to shoot; *(Knollen)* to sprout **b** *(Verdacht)* to be aroused; *(Hoff-*

nung) to stir (in one's breast *(liter)*); **das ~de Leben** *(geh)* the seeds of a new life

Keim-: **keim|frei** ADJ germ-free, free of germs *pred*; *(Med, auch fig)* sterile; **~ machen** to sterilize; **keim|haft** ADJ *(geh)* embryonic, seminal; **~ vorhanden sein** to be present in embryo *or* in embryonic form *or* in seminal form; **Keim|ling** ['kaimlıŋ] M **-s, -e** a *(= Embryo)* embryo b *(= Keimpflanze)* sprout, shoot; **Keim|öl** NT wheat germ oil, seed oil; **Keim|plas|ma** NT germ plasma; **keim|tö|tend** ADJ germicidal; **~es Mittel** germicide; **Keim|trä|ger(in)** M(F) carrier

Kei|mung ['kaimʊŋ] F **-, -en** germination

Keim|zel|le F germ cell; *(fig)* nucleus

kein [kain], **kei|ne, kein** INDEF PRON a *(adjektivisch)* no; *(mit sing n)* no, not a; *(mit pl n, bei Sammelbegriffen, bei Abstrakten)* no, not any; **~ Mann/~e Häuser/~ Whisky ...** no man/houses/whisky ...; **hast du ~ Herz?** have you no heart? *(esp Brit)*, don't you have a heart?; **hast du ~ Gefühl?** have you no feeling? *(esp Brit)*, haven't you got *(esp Brit) or* don't you have any feeling?; **hast du ~en Bleistift?** haven't you got *(esp Brit) or* don't you have a pencil?, have you no pencil? *(esp Brit)*; **hast du ~e Vorschläge/Geschwister?** haven't you got any *or* have you no suggestions/brothers and sisters? *(esp Brit)*, don't you have any suggestions/brothers and sisters?; **ich sehe da ~en Unterschied** I see no difference, I don't see any *or* a difference; **da sind ~e Häuser** there are no houses there, there aren't any houses there; **er hatte ~e Chance** he had no chance, he didn't have a *or* any chance; **er ist ~ echter Schotte** he is no true Scot, he is not a true Scot; **er ist ~ Lehrer** he is not a teacher; *(= kein guter auch)* he's no teacher; **~e Widerrede/Ahnung!** no arguing/idea!; **~e schlechte Idee** not a bad idea; **~e Lust!** don't want to; **~e Angst!** don't worry; **das ist ~e Antwort auf unsere Frage** that's not an *or* the answer to our question; **er ist noch ~ erfahrener Lehrer** he is not yet an experienced teacher; **~ bisschen** not a bit; **ich habe ~ bisschen Lust/Zeit** I've absolutely no desire to/time; **ich bin doch ~ Kind mehr!** I am not a child any longer, I am no longer a child; **~ anderer als er ...** only he ..., no-one else but he ...; **das habe ich ~em anderen als dir gesagt** I have told nobody else apart from you, I haven't told anybody else apart from you; **~ Einziger** *(= niemand)* not a single one *or* person; **~ einziges Mal** not a single time; **in ~ster Weise** *(strictly incorrect)* not in the least b *(= nicht einmal)* less than; **~e Stunde/drei Monate** less than an hour/three months; **~e 5 Euro** under 5 euros

kei|ne(r, s) ['kainə] INDEF PRON *(substantivisch) (= niemand)* nobody *(auch subj)*, no-one *(auch subj)*, not anybody, not anyone; *(von Gegenstand)* not one, none; *(bei Abstraktum)* none; *(obj)* not any, none; *(von Gegenständen, bei Abstrakta)* none; *(obj)* not any, none; **~r liebt mich** nobody *or* no-one loves me; **es war ~r da** there was nobody *etc* there, there wasn't anybody *etc* there; *(Gegenstand)* there wasn't one there; **es waren ~ da** there wasn't anybody *etc* there; *(Gegenstände)* there weren't any there, there were none there; **ich habe ~s** I haven't got one; **von diesen Platten ist ~ ...** none *or* not one of these records is ...; **haben Sie Avocados? – nein, leider haben wir ~** have you *(esp Brit) or* do you have any avocados? – no, I'm afraid we haven't (any); **hast du schon ein Glas? – nein, ich habe (noch) kein(e)s** have you a glass? – no, I haven't (got one) *or* no, I don't *(US)*; **~r von uns/von uns beiden** none/neither of us; *(betont)* not one of us; **er hat ~n von beiden angetroffen** he didn't meet either of them, he met neither of them; **~s der (beiden) Kinder/Bücher** neither of the children/books; **~s der sechs Kinder/Bücher** none of the six children/books; *(betont)* not one of the six children/books; **er kannte ~s der (fünf) Kinder** he didn't know any of the (five) children, he knew none of the (five) children; **ist Bier da? – nein, ich habe kein(e)s gekauft** is there any beer? – no, I didn't buy any

kei|ner|lei ['kainɐ'lai] ADJ *attr inv* no ... what(-so)ever *or* at all; **dafür gibt es ~ Beweise** there is no proof of it what(so)ever *or* at all

kei|ner|seits ['kainɐ'zaits] ADV **sein Vorschlag fand ~ Zustimmung** his suggestion met with no support from any side; **ich möchte mich ~ festlegen** I wouldn't like to commit myself in any direction

kei|nes|falls ['kainəs'fals] ADV under no circumstances, not ... under any circumstances; **~ darfst du ...** under no circumstances *or* on no account must you ...; **das bedeutet jedoch ~, dass ...** however, in no way does this mean that ...

kei|nes|wegs ['kainəs've:ks] ADV not at all, by no means; *(als Antwort)* not in the least, not at all; **ich fühle mich ~ schuldig** I do not feel in the least guilty *or* in any way guilty

kein|mal ['kainma:l] ADV never once, not once; **ich bin ihr noch ~ begegnet** I've never met her → **einmal**

keins [kains] = **keines**

Keks [ke:ks] M **-es, -e** *or (Aus) nt* **-, -** biscuit *(Brit)*, cookie *(US)*; **jdm auf den ~ gehen** *(inf)* to get on sb's nerves

Kelch [kɛlç] M **-(e)s, -e** a *(= Trinkglas)* goblet; *(Eccl)* chalice, communion cup; **den (bitteren) ~ (des Leidens) bis zur Neige leeren** *(fig)* to drain the (bitter) cup of sorrow (to the last); **möge dieser ~ an mir vorübergehen** *(Bibl)* let this cup pass from me; **dieser ~ ist noch einmal an mir vorübergegangen** I have been spared again, the Good Lord has spared me again b *(Bot)* calyx

Kelch-: **Kelch|blatt** NT sepal; **kelch|för|mig** ADJ cup-shaped, bell-shaped; **Kelch|glas** NT goblet, goblet-shaped glass

Ke|lim ['ke:lım] M **-(s), -(s)** kilim *(Eastern carpet)*

Kel|le ['kɛlə] F **-, -n** a *(= Suppenkelle etc)* ladle; *(= Schaumlöffel)* strainer, straining spoon b *(= Maurerkelle)* trowel c *(= Signalstab)* signalling *(Brit) or* signaling *(US)* disc

Kel|ler ['kɛlɐ] M **-s, -** cellar; *(= Geschoss)* basement; *(= Esslokal)* (cellar) restaurant; *(= Kneipe)* (cellar) bar; **im ~ sein** *(fig)* to be at rock-bottom; **in den ~ rutschen** *or* **fallen** *(fig)* to reach rock-bottom; *(Preise etc auch)* to go *or* fall through the floor; **im ~ sitzen** *(inf: beim Kartenspiel)* to have minus points

Kel|ler-: **Kel|ler|as|sel** F woodlouse; **Kel|ler|bar** F cellar *or* basement bar

Kel|le|rei [kɛlə'rai] F **-, -en** *(= Weinkellerei)* wine producer's; *(= Sektkellerei)* champagne producer's; *(= Lagerraum)* cellar(s *pl*); **Wein direkt von der ~ kaufen** to buy wine direct from the producer's

Kel|ler-: **Kel|ler|ge|schoss** NT basement; **Kel|ler|ge|wöl|be** NT vaulted cellar roof; *(= Keller)* cellars *pl*; *(= Verlies)* dungeon; **Kel|ler|kind** NT unhealthy slum kid; **Kel|ler|knei|pe** F *(inf)*, **Kel|ler|lo|kal** NT cellar bar; **Kel|ler|meis|ter(in)** M(F) vintner; *(in Kloster)* cellarer; **Kel|ler|woh|nung** F basement flat *(Brit) or* apartment

Kell|ner ['kɛlnɐ] M **-s, -** waiter

Kell|ne|rin ['kɛlnərın] F **-, -nen** waitress

kell|nern ['kɛlnɐn] VI *(inf)* to work as a waiter/waitress, to wait on tables *(US)*

Kel|te ['kɛltə] M **-n, -n**, **Kel|tin** ['kɛltın] F **-, -nen** Celt

Kel|ter ['kɛltɐ] F **-, -n** winepress; *(= Obstkelter)* press

kel|tern ['kɛltɐn] VT *Trauben, Wein* to press

kel|tisch ['kɛltıʃ] ADJ Celtic

Kel|vin ['kɛlvın] NT **-s**, *no pl (Phys)* Kelvin

Ke|me|na|te [keme'na:tə] F **-, -n** lady's heated apartment(s *pl*) *(in a castle)*; *(fig)* boudoir

Ke|nia ['ke:nia] NT **-s** Kenya

Ke|ni|a|ner [ke'nia:nɐ] M **-s, -**, **Ke|ni|a|ne|rin** [-ərın] F **-, -nen** Kenyan

ke|ni|a|nisch [ke'nia:nıʃ] ADJ Kenyan

ken|nen ['kɛnən] *pret* **kannte** ['kantə], *ptp* **gekannt** [gə'kant] VT to know; *(= kennengelernt haben auch)* to be acquainted with; *(geh: = erkennen)* to recognize; **er kennt das Leben** he knows the ways of the world, he knows about life; **er kennt den Hunger nicht** he has never known hunger, he doesn't know what hunger is; **er kennt keine Müdigkeit** he never gets tired, he doesn't know what tiredness means; **kein Erbarmen/Mitleid** *etc* **~** to know no mercy/pity *etc*; **ich habe mich nicht mehr gekannt vor Wut** I was beside myself with anger; **so was ~ wir hier nicht!** we don't have that sort of thing here; **jdn als etw ~** to know sb to be sth; **~ Sie sich schon?** do you know each other (already)?; **~ Sie den (schon)?** *(Witz)* have you heard this one?; **das ~ wir (schon)** *(iro)* we know all about that; **kennst du mich noch?** do you remember me?; **wie ich ihn kenne ...** if I know him (at all) ...; **du kennst dich doch!** you know what you're like; **so kenne ich dich ja (noch) gar nicht!** I've never known you like this before; **da kennst du mich aber schlecht** you don't know me, that just shows how little you know me; **da kennt er gar nichts** *(inf) (= hat keine Hemmungen)* he has no scruples whatsoever; *(= ihm ist alles egal)* he doesn't give a damn *(inf)*

ken|nen+ler|nen *sep*, **ken|nen ler|nen** VT to get to know, to become acquainted with *(form)*; *(= zum ersten Mal treffen)* to meet; **sich ~** to get to know each other; to meet each other; **jdn/etw näher ~** to get to know sb/sth better, to become better acquainted with sb/sth; **ich freue mich, Sie kennenzulernen** *(form)* (I am) pleased to meet you *or* to make your acquaintance *(form)*; **ich habe ihn als einen zuverlässigen Mitarbeiter kennengelernt** I came to know him as a reliable colleague; **der soll** *or* **wird mich noch ~** *(inf)* he'll have me to reckon with *(inf)*; **bei näherem Kennenlernen erwies er sich als ...** on closer acquaintance he proved to be ...

Ken|ner ['kɛnɐ] M **-s, -**, **Ken|ne|rin** [-ərın] F **-, -nen** a *(= Sachverständiger)* expert (*von, +gen* on *or* in), authority (*von, +gen* on); **~ der internen Vorgänge** those who know about the internal procedures; **da zeigt sich der ~, da merkt man den ~** there you (can) see the (touch of the) expert b *(= Weinkenner etc)* connoisseur, co(g)noscente *(esp Art)*

Ken|ner|blick M expert's eye

ken|ner|haft ADJ like a connoisseur; **mit ~em Blick/Griff** with the eye/touch of an expert ADV expertly; *lächeln, nicken* knowingly

ken|ne|risch ['kɛnərıʃ] ADJ = **kennerhaft**

Ken|ner-: **Ken|ner|mie|ne** F connoisseur's expression; **mit ~ betrachtete er ...** he looked at ... like a connoisseur; **er versuchte, eine ~ aufzusetzen** he tried to look like a connoisseur; *(bei Erklärung etc)* he tried to look knowledgeable; **Ken|ner|schaft** ['kɛnɐʃaft] F **-**, *no pl* connoisseurship *(rare)*; *(= Fachkenntnis)* expertise

Kenn-: **Kenn|kar|te** F *(dated)* identity card; **Kenn|mar|ke** F identity tag

kennt|lich ['kɛntlıç] ADJ *(= zu erkennen)* recognizable, distinguishable (*an +dat* by); *(= deutlich)* clear; **etw ~ machen** to identify *or* indicate sth (clearly); **etw für jdn ~ machen** to make sth clear to sb, to indicate sth to sb; **bei Dunkelheit gut ~ sein** to be easily visible *or* distinguishable in the dark

Kennt|nis ['kɛntnıs] ✪ 46.2, 46.3 F **-, -se** a *(= Wissen)* knowledge *no pl*; **über ~se von etw verfügen** to be knowledgeable about sth, to know about sth; **gute ~se in Mathematik haben** to have a good knowledge of mathematics; **ohne ~ des Englischen** without any *or* a knowledge of English, without knowing English **b** *no pl (form)* **etw zur ~ nehmen, von etw ~ nehmen** to note sth, to take note of sth; **ich nehme zur ~, dass ...** I note that ...; **zu Ihrer ~** for your information; **jdn von etw in ~ setzen** to inform *or* advise (*Comm, form*) sb about sth; **von etw ~ erhalten** to learn *or* hear about sth; **das entzieht sich meiner ~** I have no knowledge of it; **bei voller ~ der Sachlage** in full knowledge of the situation; **ohne ~ der Umstände** without any knowledge of the circumstances

Kẹnnt|nis-: **Kẹnnt|nis|nah|me** [-naːmə] F -, *no pl (form)* **zur ~ an ...** for the attention of ...; **nach ~** after perusal *(form)*; **kẹnnt|nis|reich** *(geh)* ADJ knowledgeable ADV knowledgeably; **Kẹnnt|nis|reich|tum** M *(geh)* knowledgeableness; **ihr ~** her breadth *or* wealth of knowledge, her knowledgeableness

-kennt|nis|se [kɛntnɪsə] PL *suf in cpds* knowledge of ...; **Sprach-/Englischkenntnisse** knowledge of languages/English

Kẹnnt|nis|stand M, *no pl* **nach dem neuesten ~** according to the latest information

Kẹn|nung [ˈkɛnʊŋ] F -, -en *(Telec)* call sign; *(von Leuchtfeuern)* signal; *(Comput)* password

Kẹnn-: **Kẹnn|wort** NT *pl* **-wörter** *(= Chiffre)* code name; *(= Losungswort)* password, code word; *(Comm)* reference; **bitte geben Sie Ihr ~ ein** please enter your password; **Kẹnn|zahl** F code *or* identification number; *(Telec auch)* code

Kẹnn|zei|chen NT **a** *(Aut)* number plate *(Brit)*, license plate *(US)*; *(Aviat)* markings *pl*; **amtliches** *or* **polizeiliches ~** registration number *(Brit)*, license number *(US)*; **ein Hamburger/Berliner ~** a Hamburg/Berlin registration (number) *(Brit) or* license number *(US)* **b** *(= Markierung)* mark, sign; *(bei Tier)* marking(s *pl*); *(in Personenbeschreibung)* **unveränderliche ~** distinguishing marks *or* features; **besondere ~** particular characteristics **c** *(= Eigenart, Charakteristikum)* (typical) characteristic *(für, +gen* of); *(für Qualität)* hallmark; *(= Erkennungszeichen)* mark, sign; **ein typisches ~ des Intellektuellen** a typical mark *or* sign of the intellectual; **als ~ eine Nelke im Knopfloch vereinbaren** to agree on a carnation in one's buttonhole as a means of identification; **ein ~ des Genies** a mark *or* sign *or* hallmark of genius **d** *(= Anzeichen)* symptom *(für* of)

kẹnn|zeich|nen *insep* VT **a** *(= markieren)* to mark, to indicate; *(durch Etikett)* to label; *Weg etc* to mark, to signpost; *(Logik)* to denote; **etw als zerbrechlich ~** to mark *or* label sth fragile **b** *(= charakterisieren)* to characterize; **jdn als etw ~** to show sb to be sth, to mark sb out as sth VR to be characterized

kẹnn|zeich|nend ADJ *(= charakteristisch)* typical, characteristic *(für* of)

Kẹnn|zeich|nungs|pflicht F obligation to label products accurately

kẹnn|zeich|nungs|pflich|tig ADJ *Waren* subject to the accurate labelling *(Brit) or* labeling *(US)* of products

Kẹnn|zif|fer F (code) number; *(Math)* characteristic; *(Comm)* reference number; *(bei Zeitungsinserat)* box number

Ke|no|taph [kenoˈtaːf] NT -s, -e cenotaph

Ken|taur [kɛnˈtauɐ] M -en, -en centaur

kẹn|tern [ˈkɛntɐn] VI *aux sein* **a** *(Schiff)* to capsize **b** **die Ebbe/Flut kentert** the tide is turning

kẹp|ler|sche Ge|sẹt|ze [ˈkɛplɐʃə] PL Kepler's laws *pl*

kẹp|peln [ˈkɛpln] VI *(Aus inf: = keifen)* to bicker

Ke|ra|mik [keˈraːmɪk] F -, -en **a** *no pl (Art)* ceramics *pl*; *(als Gebrauchsgegenstände)* pottery, ceramics *pl*; *(= Arbeitszweig)* ceramics *sing* **b** *(= Kunstgegenstand)* ceramic; *(= Gebrauchsgegenstand)* piece of pottery, ceramic; **~en** ceramics/pottery

ke|ra|misch [keˈraːmɪʃ] ADJ ceramic; *Gebrauchsgegenstand auch* pottery

Kẹr|be [ˈkɛrbə] F -, -n notch; *(kleiner)* nick; **in die gleiche** *or* **dieselbe ~ hauen** *or* **schlagen** *(fig inf)* to take the same line

Kẹr|bel [ˈkɛrbl] M -s, *no pl* chervil

kẹr|ben [ˈkɛrbn] VT *Holz* to cut *or* carve a notch/notches in, to notch; *Inschrift, Namen* to carve

Kẹrb|holz NT *(fig inf)* **etwas auf dem ~ haben** to have done something wrong *or* bad; **er hat so manches auf dem ~** he has quite a record; **er hat Ladendiebstahl auf dem ~** he has a record for shoplifting; **es gab fast keinen, der nichts auf dem ~ hatte** there was hardly anybody who had a completely clean record

Kẹrb|tier NT insect

Kẹr|bung [ˈkɛrbʊŋ] F -, -en *(= das Kerben)* notching; *(= die Kerben)* notches *pl*; *(kleiner)* nicks *pl*

Kẹr|ker [ˈkɛrkɐ] M -s, - **a** *(Hist, geh)* dungeon *(esp Hist)*, prison; *(= Strafe)* imprisonment **b** *(Aus)* = **Zuchthaus**

Kẹr|ker-: **Kẹr|ker|haft** F **a** *(Hist)* imprisonment in the dungeons; **drei Jahre ~** three years in the dungeons **b** *(Aus: = Zuchthausstrafe)* imprisonment; **Kẹr|ker|meis|ter(in)** M(F) *(Hist, geh)* gaoler, jailer; **Kẹr|ker|stra|fe** F **a** *(Hist)* imprisonment in the dungeons **b** *(Aus: = Zuchthausstrafe)* prison sentence

Kẹrl [kɛrl] M -s, -e *or* -s *(inf)* chap, fellow, guy, bloke *(Brit, all inf)*; *(pej)* character; *(= Mädchen)* girl, lass *(Brit inf)*; **du gemeiner ~!** you mean thing *(inf)*, you swine *(inf)*; **ein ganzer** *or* **richtiger ~** a real man; **er ist nicht ~ genug dazu** he is not man enough to do that; **sie hat schon wieder einen neuen ~** she's already got another guy *(inf) or* bloke *(Brit inf)*; **die langen ~s** *(Hist)* (soldiers of) the bodyguard of the King of Prussia

Kẹrn [kɛrn] M -(e)s, -e *(von Obst)* pip, seed; *(von Steinobst)* stone; *(= Nusskern)* kernel; *(Phys, Biol)* nucleus; *(= Holzkern)* heartwood; *(fig) (von Problem, Sache)* heart, crux, core; *(von Stadt)* centre *(Brit)*, center *(US)*; *(von Gruppe)* core; **jede Legende hat einen wahren ~** at the heart of every legend there is a core of truth; **in ihr steckt ein guter ~** there's some good in her somewhere; **bis zum ~ einer Sache vordringen** to get to the heart *or* the bottom of a matter; **der harte ~** *(fig)* the hard core

Kẹrn-: **Kẹrn|ar|beits|zeit** F core time; **Kẹrn|bei|ßer** [-baisɐ] M -s, - *(Orn)* hawfinch; **Kẹrn|be|reich** M **a** *(= Kernzone)* centre *(Brit)*, center *(US)*, central part **b** *(= Hauptgebiet)* fundamental *or* key area; **die ~e der Informatik** the fundamentals of computer science **c** *(Aus Sch: = Stoffbereich für Reifeprüfung)* core area *or* field; **Kẹrn|brenn|stab** M nuclear fuel rod; **Kẹrn|brenn|stoff** M nuclear fuel; **Kẹrn|che|mie** F nuclear chemistry; **Kẹrn|ener|gie** F nuclear energy; **Kẹrn|ener|gie|geg|ner(in)** M(F) opponent of nuclear energy; **Kẹrn|ex|plo|si|on** F nuclear explosion; **Kẹrn|fach** NT *(Sch)* core subject; **Kẹrn|fa|mi|lie** F *(Sociol)* nuclear family; **Kẹrn|for|scher(in)** M(F) nuclear scientist *or* researcher; **Kẹrn|for|schung** F nuclear research; **Kẹrn|for|schungs|an|la|ge** F nuclear research facility; **Kẹrn|for|schungs|zent|rum** NT nuclear research centre *(Brit) or* center *(US)*; **Kẹrn|fra|ge** F **a** central issue, central question **b** *(Aus Sch: = Prüfungsfrage aus Kerngebiet)* core subject question; **Kẹrn|frucht** F malaceous fruit *(form)*, pome *(form)*; **Kẹrn|fu|si|on** F nuclear fusion; **Kẹrn|ge|biet** NT **a** *(von Land)* heartland **b** *(von Fach, Wissenschaft etc)* central *or* core area **c** *(Aus Sch: = Stoffbereich für Reifeprüfung)* core area *or* field; **Kẹrn|ge|dan|ke** M central idea; **Kẹrn|ge|häu|se** NT core; **Kẹrn|ge|schäft** NT *(Econ)* core (business) activity; **kẹrn|ge|sund** ADJ as fit as a fiddle, completely fit; *(fig) Staatshaushalt, Firma, Land* very healthy; **Kẹrn|grup|pe** F nucleus; **Kẹrn|holz** NT heartwood

kẹr|nig [ˈkɛrnɪç] ADJ **a** *(fig) Ausspruch* pithy; *(= urwüchsig)* earthy; *(= kraftvoll)* robust, powerful; *(sl: = gut)* great *(inf)* **b** *(lit) Frucht* full of pips ADV pithily

Kẹrn|ket|ten|re|ak|ti|on F nuclear chain reaction

Kẹrn|kraft F -, *no pl* nuclear power

Kẹrn|kraft- *in cpds* nuclear power; **Kẹrn|kraft|be|für|wor|ter(in)** M(F) supporter of nuclear power

Kẹrn|kräf|te PL forces *pl* in the nucleus, nuclear forces *pl*

Kẹrn|kraft-: **Kẹrn|kraft|geg|ner(in)** M(F) opponent of nuclear power; **Kẹrn|kraft|werk** NT nuclear power station, nuke *(US inf)*

Kẹrn-: **Kẹrn|la|dungs|zahl** F atomic number; **Kẹrn|land** NT *(= Zentrum, wichtigster Teil)* heartland; *(= wichtigstes Land)* core country; **kẹrn|los** ADJ seedless; *(Biol) Bakterium, Blutkörperchen* containing no nucleus; **Kẹrn|mann|schaft** F *(Sport, fig)* core *or* nucleus of a/the team; *(von Partei)* central caucus; *(von Regierung)* inner cabinet; **Kẹrn|mo|dell** NT model of the nucleus; **Kẹrn|obst** NT pomes *pl (spec)*; **Kẹrn|phy|sik** F nuclear physics *sing*; **Kẹrn|phy|si|ker(in)** M(F) nuclear physicist; **Kẹrn|plas|ma** NT nucleoplasm; **Kẹrn|prob|lem** NT central problem; **Kẹrn|punkt** M central point, crux; **Kẹrn|re|ak|ti|on** F nuclear reaction; **Kẹrn|re|ak|tor** M nuclear reactor; **Kẹrn|satz** M **a** key sentence, key phrase **b** *(Ling)* kernel sentence; *(Satzform)* simple sentence; **Kẹrn|schat|ten** M complete shadow; *(Astron)* umbra; **Kẹrn|schmel|ze** F meltdown; **Kẹrn|sei|fe** F washing soap; **Kẹrn|spal|tung** F nuclear fission; **die erste ~** the first splitting of the atom; **Kẹrn|spei|cher** M core memory; **Kẹrn|spin|to|mo|graf** [ˈkɛrnspɪn-] M MRI scanner; **Kẹrn|spin|to|mo|gra|fie** F magnetic resonance imaging; **Kẹrn|spin|to|mo|graph** *etc* = **Kernspintomograf** *etc*; **Kẹrn|spreng|kopf** M nuclear warhead; **Kẹrn|spruch** M pithy saying; **Kẹrn|stück** NT *(fig)* main item, centrepiece *(Brit)*, centerpiece *(US)*; *(von Theorie etc)* crucial *or* central element, crucial *or* central part, core; *(von Roman etc)* crucial *or* key passage; **Kẹrn|tech|nik** F nuclear technology, nucleonics *sing*; **kẹrn|tech|nisch** ADJ **~e Anlage** nuclear plant; **~e Entwicklung** development of nuclear technology; **Kẹrn|teil|chen** NT nuclear particle; **Kẹrn|tei|lung** F *(Biol)* nuclear division; **Kẹrn|trup|pe** F *(Mil)* core unit *or* division; *(fig)* core team; **Kẹrn|un|ter|richt** M *(Sch)* core curriculum; **Kẹrn|ver|schmel|zung** F **a** *(Phys)* nuclear fusion **b** *(Biol)* cell union

Kẹrn|waf|fe F nuclear weapon

Kẹrn|waf|fen-: **kẹrn|waf|fen|frei** ADJ nuclear-free; **Kẹrn|waf|fen|sperr|ver|trag** M Nuclear Nonproliferation Treaty; **Kẹrn|waf|fen|ver|such** M nuclear (weapons) test

Kẹrn|zeit F core time

Ke|ro|sin [keroˈziːn] NT -s, -e kerosene

Ke|rub [ˈkeːrʊp] M -s, -im *or* -e [-rubiːm, -bə] cherub

Kẹr|ze [ˈkɛrtsə] F -, -n **a** *(= Wachskerze)* candle; *(= Blüte der Kastanie)* candle, thyrus *(form)* **b** *(Aut)* plug **c** *(Turnen)* shoulder-stand **d** *(Ftbl)* skyer

Kẹr|zen-: **Kẹr|zen|be|leuch|tung** F candlelight; **Kẹr|zen|bir|ne** F *(Elec)* candle bulb; **Kẹr|zen|docht** M candle wick; **Kẹr|zen|form** F *(einer Glühbirne)* candle shape; **kẹr|zen|för|mig** ADJ candle-shaped; **kẹr|zen|ge|ra|de** ADJ *(lit)* totally *or* perfectly straight; *(fig) Mensch* (as) straight as a die *(Brit) or* an arrow *(US)*; **Kẹr|zen|ge|sicht** NT *(Tech)* appearance *or* look of a/the (spark) plug; **Kẹr|zen|hal|ter** M candlestick; *(am Weihnachtsbaum, auf Kuchen etc)* candle holder; **Kẹr|zen|leuch|ter** M candlestick; **Kẹr|zen|licht** NT, *no pl* candlelight; **Kẹr|zen|schein** M candlelight; **im ~ des Weihnachtsbaumes** in the light of the Christmas-tree candles, in the candle-lit glow of the Christmas-tree; **Ker|zen|schlüs|sel** M (spark) plug spanner *(Brit)*, (spark) plug wrench *(US)*; **Ker|zen|stän|der** M *(für mehrere Kerzen)* candelabra; *(für eine einzige Kerze)* candlestick; **Ker|zen|stum|mel** M, **Ker|zen|stumpf** M candle stump *or* stub

Ke|scher ['kɛʃɐ] M **-s, -** fishing net; *(= Hamen)* landing net

kess [kɛs] ADJ *(= flott)* saucy; *Kleid, Hut etc* jaunty; *(= vorwitzig)* cheeky *(Brit)*, fresh *(US)*; *(= frech)* fresh *(US)*, impudent; **eine ~e Lippe riskieren** to be cheeky *(Brit)* or fresh *(US)* ADV saucily

Kes|sel ['kɛsl] M **-s, -** **a** *(= Teekessel)* kettle; *(= Waschkessel)* copper; *(= Kochkessel)* pot; *(für offenes Feuer)* cauldron; *(esp in Brauerei)* vat; *(= Dampfkessel)* boiler; *(= Behälter für Flüssigkeiten etc)* tank **b** *(= Mulde)* basin, basin-shaped valley; *(Hunt)* semi-circular ring of hunters; *(Mil)* encircled area

Kes|sel-: **Kes|sel|fleisch** NT *(Cook)* boiled pork belly; **Kes|sel|fli|cker** [-flɪkɐ] M **-s, -**, **Kes|sel|fli|cke|rin** [-ərɪn] F **-, -nen** tinker; **Kes|sel|haus** NT boiler house; **Kes|sel|jagd** F = **Kesseltreiben**; **Kes|sel|pau|ke** F kettle drum; **Kes|sel|raum** M boiler room; **Kes|sel|schlacht** F *(Mil)* battle of encirclement; **Kes|sel|stein** M scale, fur; **Kes|sel|trei|ben** NT *(Hunt)* *hunt using a circle of beaters (fig: in Zeitung etc)* witch-hunt; **Kes|sel|wa|gen** M *(Rail)* tank wagon *or* car

Kess|heit F **-, -en** sauciness; *(= Vorwitzigkeit)* cheekiness *(Brit)*, impudence

Ketch|up ['kɛtʃap] M OR NT **-(s), -s** ketchup

Ketsch [kɛtʃ] F **-, -en** *(Naut)* ketch

Ketsch|up ['kɛtʃap] M OR NT → **Ketchup**

Ket|te ['kɛtə] F **-, -n** **a** chain; *(von Kettenfahrzeug)* chain track; **einen Hund an die ~ legen** to put a dog on the chain, to chain up a dog; **jdn in ~n legen** *or* **schlagen** *(liter)* to put sb in chains; **jdn an die ~ legen** *(fig)* to keep sb on a tight leash *or* rein; **in ~n liegen** *(fig geh)* to be in chains *or* bondage; **seine ~n zerreißen** *or* **sprengen** *(fig geh)* to throw off one's chains *or* shackles *or* fetters
b *(fig)* *(= ununterbrochene Reihe)* chain; *(von Menschen)* line, chain; *(von Fahrzeugen)* line, string; *(von Unfällen, Erfahrungen etc)* series, string; **eine ~ von Ereignissen** a chain of events
c *(= Bergkette, Seenkette)* chain
d *(Hunt)* *(von Rebhühnern)* covey; *(von Wildenten)* skein
e *(Aviat, Mil)* flight
f *(Comm: von Läden etc)* chain
g *(Tex)* warp

Ket|tel ['kɛtl] M **-s, -** *or f* **-, -n** *(dial: = Krampe)* staple

ket|ten ['kɛtn] VT to chain *(an +acc* to); **jdn an sich ~** *(fig)* to bind sb to oneself; **sich an jdn/etw ~** *(fig)* to tie *or* bind oneself to sb/sth

Ket|ten-: **Ket|ten|an|trieb** M chain drive; **mit ~** chain-driven; **Ket|ten|arm|band** NT chain bracelet; **Ket|ten|brief** M chain letter; **Ket|ten|brü|cke** F chain bridge; **Ket|ten|fahr|zeug** NT tracked vehicle, track-laying vehicle; **Ket|ten|ge|bir|ge** NT mountain chain; **Ket|ten|glied** NT (chain-)link; **Ket|ten|hemd** NT *(Hist)* coat of (chain) mail; **Ket|ten|hund** M guard dog, watchdog; **Ket|ten|ka|rus|sell** NT merry-go-round *(with gondolas or seats suspended on chains)*; **Ket|ten|rad** NT sprocket (wheel); **Ket|ten|rau|chen** NT chain-smoking; **Ket|ten|rau|cher(in)** M(F) chain-smoker; **Ket|ten|re|ak|ti|on** F chain reaction; **Ket|ten|reim** M *(Poet)* interlaced rhyme; **Ket|ten|sä|ge** F chain saw; **Ket|ten|schal|tung** F dérailleur gear; **Ket|ten|schluss** M *(Logik)* sorites; **Ket|ten|schutz** M chain guard; **Ket|ten|span|ner** M *(bei Fahrrad etc)* chain adjuster; **Ket|ten|stich** M *(Sew)* chain stitch

Ket|zer ['kɛtsɐ] M **-s, -**, **Ket|ze|rin** [-ərɪn] F **-, -nen** *(Eccl, fig)* heretic

Ket|ze|rei [kɛtsə'rai] F **-,** *no pl* heresy

Ket|zer|ge|richt NT *(Hist)* (court of) inquisition

ket|ze|risch ['kɛtsərɪʃ] ADJ *(Eccl, fig)* heretical ADV heretically; **~ klingen** to sound like heresy

Ket|zer|tau|fe F *(Hist)* heretical baptism

keu|chen ['kɔyçn] VI **a** *(= schwer atmen)* to pant, to puff, to gasp (for breath); *(Asthmatiker etc)* to wheeze; **mit ~dem Atem** panting, puffing; wheezing **b** *aux sein (= sich schwer atmend fortbewegen)* to pant, to puff; *(Zug)* to puff, to chug

Keuch|hus|ten M whooping cough

Keu|le ['kɔylə] F **-, -n** **a** club, cudgel; *(Sport)* (Indian) club **b** *(Cook)* leg; *(von Wild)* leg, haunch **c** **chemische ~** *(bei Polizeieinsatz)* Chemical Mace®; **die chemische ~ einsetzen** *(Agr: zur Insektenvernichtung etc)* to use chemical agents

keu|len ['kɔylən] VT *(Vet)* to cull; **das massenhafte Keulen von Schafen** the mass cull of sheep

Keu|len-: **Keu|len|hieb** M, **Keu|len|schlag** M blow with a club *or* cudgel; **er bekam einen ~ auf den Kopf** he was hit on the head with a club *or* cudgel; **es traf ihn wie ein Keulenschlag** *(fig)* it hit him like a thunderbolt; **Keu|len|schwin|gen** NT **-s,** *no pl (Sport)* (Indian) club swinging

Keu|lung F **-, -en** *(von Rindern)* contiguous cull

Keu|per M **-s,** *no pl (Geol)* Keuper

keusch [kɔyʃ] ADJ *(lit, fig)* chaste; **~ und züchtig** pure and chaste ADV chastely

Keu|sche ['kɔyʃə] F **-, -n** *(Aus inf)* cottage; *(pej: = baufälliges Haus)* hovel

Keusch|heit F **-,** *no pl* chastity

Keusch|heits-: **Keusch|heits|ge|lüb|de** NT vow of chastity; **Keusch|heits|gür|tel** M chastity belt

Key|board ['ki:bɔ:ɐd] NT **-s, -s** *(Comput, Mus)* keyboard; **sie spielt ~** she plays keyboards

Key|board|spie|ler(in) ['ki:bɔ:ɐd-] M(F) *(Mus)* keyboards player

kfm. *abbr von* **kaufmännisch**

Kfz [ka:ɛf'tsɛt] NT **-(s), -(s)** *(form) abbr von* **Kraftfahrzeug** motor vehicle

Kfz- *in cpds* = **Kraftfahrzeug-**

> **KFZ-KENNZEICHEN**
>
> German **Kfz-Kennzeichen** are number plates which indicate where a particular vehicle is registered. The first letters before the hyphen are an abbreviation for the administrative district: a single letter for a city, eg "M" for **München** or "K" for **Köln**, and two or three letters for towns or districts. The number plate also bears the stamp of the licensing authority and a disc indicating when the next **TÜV** test and test of emission levels are due. → TÜV

kg *abbr von* **Kilogramm** kg

KG [ka'ge:] F **-, -s** *abbr von* **Kommanditgesellschaft** ≈ limited partnership

KGB [ka:ge:'be:] M **-(s),** *no pl* KGB

KGB-Chef(in) [ka:ge:'be:-] M(F) head of the KGB

kgl. *abbr von* **königlich** royal

K-Grup|pe ['ka:-] F *(Pol)* Communist splinter group

k.g.V., kgV *abbr von* **kleinstes gemeinsames Vielfaches** lowest common multiple, lcm

kha|ki ['ka:ki] *etc* = **kaki** *etc*

Khar|tum ['kartʊm, kar'tu:m] NT **-s** Khartoum

Khmer [kme:ɐ] M **-s, -** *(= Volksstamm in Kambodscha)* Khmer; **die ~** *pl* the Khmer

Khmer NT **-s,** *no pl (Ling)* Khmer

KHz, kHz *abbr von* **Kilohertz** kHz

kib|beln ['kɪbln] VIR *(dial)* to bicker, to squabble

Kib|buz [kɪ'bu:ts] M **-, Kibbuzim** *or* **-e** [kibu-'tsi:m] kibbutz

Ki|be|rer ['ki:bərɐ] M **-s, -** *(Aus inf: = Polizist)* copper, rozzer *(Brit sl)*, pig *(US sl)*

Ki|che|rei [kɪçə'rai] F **-, -en** giggling

Ki|cher|erb|se F chickpea

ki|chern ['kɪçɐn] VI to giggle

Kick [kɪk] M **-(s), -s** *(inf: = Stoß)* kick; *(sl: = Spiel)* kick-about, kick-around; *(fig inf: = Nervenkitzel)* kick *(inf)*

Kick-: **Kick|board** NT *(= Roler)* kickboard (scooter), skate scooter; **Kick|bo|xen** NT kick boxing; **Kick|bo|xer(in)** M(F) kick boxer; **Kick-down** [kɪk'daun] NT **-s,** *no pl*, **Kick|-down** NT **-s,** *no pl (Aut)* kickdown

ki|cken ['kɪkn] *(Ftbl inf)* VT to kick, to boot *(inf)* VI to play football *(Brit)* or soccer; *(= den Ball kicken)* to kick; **für eine Mannschaft ~** to play for a team

Ki|cker ['kɪkɐ] M **-s, -**, **Ki|cke|rin** [-ərɪn] F **-, -nen** *(Ftbl inf)* player

Kick-off [kɪk'ɔf] M **-s, -s**, **Kick|off** M **-s, -s** *(Ftbl: esp Sw)* kick-off

Kick|star|ter M *(bei Motorrad)* kick-starter

Kid [kɪt] NT **-s, -s** **a** *usu pl (inf: = Jugendlicher)* kid *(inf)* **b** *(Leder)* kid (leather) **c** *usu pl (Handschuh)* kid glove

kid|nap|pen ['kɪtnɛpn] VT *insep* to kidnap

Kid|nap|per ['kɪtnɛpɐ] M **-s, -**, **Kid|nap|pe|rin** [-ərɪn] F **-, -nen** kidnapper

Kid|nap|ping ['kɪtnɛpɪŋ] NT **-s, -s** kidnapping

kie|big ['ki:bɪç] ADJ *(inf) (= vorlaut, frech)* cheeky *(Brit)*, fresh *(US)*; *(= gereizt)* tetchy

Kie|bitz ['ki:bɪts] M **-es, -e** *(Orn)* lapwing, peewit, green plover; *(Cards inf)* kibitzer

kie|bit|zen ['ki:bɪtsn] VI *(inf)* to spy; *(Cards)* to kibitz

Kie|fer ['ki:fɐ] F **-, -n** pine (tree); *(= Holz)* pine (wood)

Kie|fer M **-s, -** jaw; *(= Kieferknochen)* jawbone

Kie|fer-: **Kie|fer|ano|ma|lie** F malformation of the jaw; **Kie|fer|bruch** M broken *or* fractured jaw; **Kie|fer|chi|rurg(in)** M(F) oral surgeon; **Kie|fer|chi|rur|gie** F oral surgery

Kie|fer|höh|le F *(Anat)* maxillary sinus

Kie|fer|höh|len-: **Kie|fer|höh|len|ent|zün|dung** F sinusitis; **Kie|fer|höh|len|ver|ei|te|rung** F sinus infection

Kie|fer|kno|chen M *(Anat)* jawbone

Kie|fern-: **Kie|fern|holz** NT pine(wood); **Kie|fern|na|del** F pine needle; **Kie|fern|scho|nung** F pinery, pine plantation; **Kie|fern|wald** M pine wood; *(größer)* pine forest; **Kie|fern|zap|fen** M pine cone

Kie|fer-: **Kie|fer|or|tho|pä|de** M, **Kie|fer|or|tho|pä|din** F orthodontist; **Kie|fer|or|tho|pä|die** F orthodontics *sing*; **kie|fer|or|tho|pä|disch** ADJ orthodontic

kie|ken ['ki:kn] VI *(dial)* = **gucken**

Kie|ker ['ki:kɐ] M **-s, -** **a** *(N Ger inf)* binoculars *pl* **b** **jdn auf dem ~ haben** *(inf)* to have it in for sb *(inf)*

Kiel [ki:l] M **-(e)s, -e** **a** *(= Schiffskiel)* keel; **ein Schiff auf ~ legen** to lay down a ship **b** *(= Federkiel)* quill

Kiel-: **Kiel|boot** NT keel boat; **Kiel|fe|der** F quill pen; **kiel|ho|len** VT *insep (Naut)* **a** *Schiff* to careen **b** *Matrosen* to keelhaul; **Kiel|li|nie** F line ahead; **kiel|oben** ADV bottom up; **Kiel|raum** M bilge; **Kiel|was|ser** NT wake, wash; **in jds ~** *(dat)* **segeln** *or* **schwimmen** *(fig)* to follow in sb's wake

Kie|me ['ki:mə] F **-, -n** gill

Kie|men- *(Zool)*: **Kie|men|at|mer** [-la:tmɐ] M **-s, -** gill-breather; **Kie|men|at|mung** F gill-breathing

Kien [ki:n] M **-(e)s,** *no pl* pine

Kien-: **Kien|ap|fel** M pine cone; **Kien|holz** NT pine(wood); **Kien|span** M pinewood spill; **Kien|zap|fen** M pine cone

Kie|pe ['ki:pə] F **-, -n** *(dial)* pannier, dosser

Kie|pen|hut M poke bonnet

Kies [ki:s] M **-es, -e** **a** gravel; *(am Strand)* shingle **b** *no pl (inf: = Geld)* dough *(inf)*, lolly *(inf)*

Kie|sel ['ki:zl] M **-s, -** pebble

Kie|sel|er|de F silica

kie|seln ['ki:zln] VT to gravel

Kie|sel-: **kie|sel|sau|er** ADJ *(Chem)* silicic; **kieselsaures Natrium** silicate of sodium; **Kie|sel|säu|re** F *(Chem)* **a** silicic acid **b** *(= Siliziumdioxyd)* silica; **Kie|sel|stein** M pebble; **Kie|sel|strand** M pebble beach, shingle beach

Kies|gru|be F gravel pit

kie|sig ['ki:zıç] ADJ gravelly; *Strand* shingly

Kies-: **Kies|strand** M shingle *or* pebble beach; **Kies|weg** M gravel path

Kiez [ki:ts] M **-es, -e** *(dial)* **a** *(= Stadtgegend)* district, area **b** *(inf: = Bordellgegend)* red-light district

kif|fen ['kıfn] VI *(inf)* to smoke pot *(inf) or* grass *(inf)*, to smoke *(inf)*

Kif|fer ['kıfɐ] M **-s, -**, **Kif|fe|rin** [-ərın] F **-, -nen** *(inf)* pot-smoker *(inf)*

ki|ke|ri|ki [kikəri'ki:] INTERJ cock-a-doodle-doo

Ki|ke|ri|ki [kikəri'ki:] NT **-s, -s** *(= Hahnenschrei)* cock-a-doodle-doo

Kil|bi ['kılbi] F **-, Kilbenen** ['kılbənən] *(Sw)* fair, kermis *(US)*

kil|le|kil|le ['kılə'kılə] INTERJ *(baby-talk)* tickle, tickle, kitchie, kitchie; **(bei jdm) ~ machen** to tickle sb

kil|len ['kılən] *(sl)* **VT** to bump off *(inf)*, to do in *(inf)*, to kill; *(esp mit Auftrag)* to hit *(inf)* **VI** to kill, to murder

kil|len VI *(Naut)* to shake, to shiver

Kil|ler ['kılɐ] M **-s, -**, **Kil|le|rin** [-ərın] F **-, -nen** *(inf)* killer, murderer; *(gedungener)* hit man/woman

Kil|ler- *in cpds* killer; **Kil|ler|ins|tinkt** M *(inf)* killer instinct; **Kil|ler|kom|man|do** NT death squad; **Kil|ler|wal** M killer whale, orca; **Kil|ler|zel|le** F *(Physiol)* killer cell

Ki|lo ['ki:lo] NT **-s, -(s)** kilo

Ki|lo- *in cpds* kilo-; **Ki|lo|byte** NT kilobyte; **Ki|lo|gramm** [kilo'gram] NT kilogram(me); **Ki|lo|hertz** [kilo'hɛrts, 'kilo-] NT kilohertz; **Ki|lo|joule** NT kilojoule; **Ki|lo|ka|lo|rie** F kilocalorie

Ki|lo|me|ter [kilo'me:tɐ] M kilometre *(Brit)*, kilometer *(US)*; *(inf: = Stundenkilometer)* k *(inf)*; **bei ~ 547** *(= Kilometerstein)* at kilometre *(Brit) or* kilometer *(US)* 547; **wir konnten nur 80 ~ fahren** we could only do 80

Ki|lo|me|ter-: **Ki|lo|me|ter|be|gren|zung** F *(bei Mietwagen)* mileage limit; **Ki|lo|me|ter|fres|ser(in)** M(F) *(inf)* long-haul driver; **er ist ein richtiger ~** he really eats up the miles *(inf)*; **Ki|lo|me|ter|geld** NT mileage (allowance); **ki|lo|me|ter|lang** **ADJ** miles long; **~e Strände** miles and miles of beaches; **ein ~er Stau** a traffic jam several miles/kilometres *(Brit) or* kilometers *(US)* long **ADV** for miles (and miles), for miles on end; **Ki|lo|me|ter|pau|scha|le** F mileage allowance (against tax); **Ki|lo|me|ter|stand** M mileage; **der ~ des Autos ist ...** the car has done ..., the car has ... on the clock *(Brit inf)*, the mileage on the car is ...; **Ki|lo|me|ter|stein** M milestone; **ki|lo|me|ter|weit** **ADJ** miles long; **in ~er Entfernung** miles away in the distance; **ein ~er Marsch** a march of several miles/kilometres *(Brit) or* kilometers *(US)* **ADV** for miles (and miles); **man konnte ~ sehen** you could see for miles (and miles); **Ki|lo|me|ter|zahl** F **unbegrenzte ~** *(bei Mietwagen)* unlimited mileage; **Ki|lo|me|ter|zäh|ler** M mileage indicator *or* counter, mileometer *(Brit)*, odometer *(esp US)*

Ki|lo-: **Ki|lo|watt** [kilo'vat, 'kilo-] NT kilowatt; **Ki|lo|watt|stun|de** F kilowatt hour

ki|lo|wei|se [-vaizə] ADV by the kilo

Kim|bern ['kımbɐn] PL *(Hist)* Cimbri *pl*

Kimm [kım] F **-**, *no pl (Naut)* **a** *(= Horizont)* apparent *or* visual horizon **b** *(am Schiffskörper)* bilge

Kim|me ['kımə] F **-, -n** **a** *(von Gewehr)* back sight **b** *(inf: = Gesäßfalte)* cleft between the buttocks, great divide *(hum)* **c** *(rare)* = **Kerbe**

Kim|mung ['kımʊŋ] F **-, -en** *(Naut)* **a** *(= Horizont)* visual horizon **b** *(= Luftspiegelung)* mirage

Ki|mo|no ['ki:mono, ki'mo:no, 'kımono] M **-s, -s** kimono

Kind [kınt] NT **-(e)s, -er** [-dɐ] child, kid *(inf)*; *(= Kleinkind)* baby; *(esp Psych, Med)* infant; **ein ~ erwarten** to be expecting a baby; **ein ~ bekommen** *or* **kriegen** to have a baby *or* child; **sie kriegt ein ~** she's going to have a baby *or* child; **von ~ an** *or* **auf hat er ...** since he was a child *or* from childhood he has ...; **von ~ an** *or* **auf haben wir ...** since we were children *or* from childhood we have ...; **einem Mädchen ein ~ machen** *(inf)* to knock a girl up *(inf)*, to put a girl in the club *(Brit inf)*; **aber ~!** child, child; **schönes ~!** *(old: als Anrede)* my pretty maid *(old)*; **die ~er Gottes** *(geh)* the children of the Lord; **ein echtes Wiener ~** *(dated)* a true son/daughter of Vienna; **ein ~ seiner Zeit sein** to be a child of one's times; **sie ist kein ~ von Traurigkeit** *(hum)* she enjoys life; **er ist ein großes ~** he's a big baby; **sich freuen wie ein ~** to be as pleased as Punch; **er kann sich wie ein ~ freuen** he takes a childlike pleasure in (simple) things; **das weiß doch jedes ~!** any five-year-old would tell you that!; **du bist aber ein kluges ~!** *(iro)* clever kid!; **da kommt das ~ im Manne durch** all men are boys at heart; **wie sag ichs meinem ~e?** *(hum)* I don't know how to put it; *(bei Aufklärung)* what to tell your children; **das ist nichts für kleine ~er** *(fig inf)* that's not for your innocent *or* your young ears/eyes; **aus ~ern werden Leute** *(prov)* children grow up quickly, don't they?; **~er und Narren** *or* **Betrunkene sagen die Wahrheit** *(fig)* children and fools speak the truth; **ein ~ des Todes sein** *(dated)* to be a goner *(inf)*; **mit ~ und Kegel** *(hum inf)* with the whole family; **das ~ muss einen Namen haben** *(fig)* you/we *etc* have to call it something; **das ~ mit dem Bade ausschütten** *(prov)* to throw out the baby with the bathwater *(prov)*; **wir werden das ~ schon schaukeln** *(inf)* we'll soon have that *or* everything sorted out; **los, ~er!** let's go, kids!; **hört mal alle her, ~er!** listen, kids; **~er, ~er!** dear, dear!, goodness me!, good heavens!

Kind-: **Kind|bett** NT *(old)* childbed *(old)*; **im ~** in confinement; **Kind|bett|fieber** NT childbed fever

Kind|chen ['kıntçən] NT **-s, -** *dim von* **Kind** child; *(zu Erwachsenen)* kid(do) *(inf)*

Kin|del ['kındl] NT **-s, -(n)** *(dial) dim von* **Kind** kiddy

Kin|der-: **Kin|der|ar|beit** F child labour *(Brit) or* labor *(US)*; **kin|der|arm** ADJ with few children; *Familie* small; **ein ~es Land** a country with a low birth rate; **Kin|der|ar|mut** F **a** *(= Bedürftigkeit)* child poverty **b** *(= Mangel an Kindern)* small number of children; **Kin|der|art** F the way children are; **Kin|der|arzt** M, **Kin|der|ärz|tin** F paediatrician *(Brit)*, pediatrician *(US)*; **Kin|der|au|gen** PL children's eyes *pl*; **etw mit ~ anschauen** to gaze wide-eyed at sth; **vor Erstaunen ~ machen/bekommen** to be wide-eyed with astonishment; **Kin|der|bei|hil|fe** F *(Aus)* child benefit *(Brit)*, *benefit paid for having children*; **Kin|der|bei|la|ge** F children's supplement, children's page; **Kin|der|be|klei|dung** F children's wear; **Kin|der|be|steck** NT child's cutlery; **Kin|der|bett** NT cot; **Kin|der|bild** NT childhood photograph; **das ist ein ~ (von) meiner Mutter** that's a photograph of my mother as a child *or* when she was a child; **Kin|der|buch** NT children's book; **Kin|der|bü|ro** NT children's advice bureau *(for complaints, suggestions etc)*

Kin|der|chen ['kındɐçən] PL children *pl*

Kin|der-: **Kin|der|chor** M children's choir; **Kin|der|dorf** NT children's village

Kin|de|rei [kındə'rai] F **-, -en** childishness *no pl*; **~en** childishness, childish nonsense

Kin|der-: **Kin|der|er|zie|hung** F bringing up of children; *(durch Schule)* education of children; **sie versteht nichts von ~** she knows nothing about bringing up/educating children; **Kin|der|fahr|kar|te** F child's ticket; **Kin|der|fahr|rad** NT child's *or* children's bicycle; **Kin|der|feind(in)** M(F) child-hater; **kin|der|feind|lich** **ADJ** hostile to children, anti-child; *Architektur, Planung* not catering for children; **~e Steuerpolitik** tax policies which penalize having children; **eine ~e Gesellschaft** a society hostile to children **ADV** without regard to children; **sich ~ verhalten** to be hostile to children; **Kin|der|feind|lich|keit** F hostility to children, anti-child attitude; *(von Architektur)* failure to cater for children; **Kin|der|fern|se|hen** NT children's television; **Kin|der|fest** NT children's party *or (von Stadt etc)* fête; **Kin|der|film** M children's film; **Kin|der|frau** F, **Kin|der|fräu|lein** NT *(dated)* nanny, children's nurse; **Kin|der|frei|be|trag** M child allowance; **Kin|der|freund(in)** M(F) **~ sein** to be fond of children; **kin|der|freund|lich** **ADJ** *Mensch* fond of children; *Gesellschaft* child-orientated; *Möbel, Architektur etc* child-friendly; **eine ~e Steuerpolitik** a tax policy which encourages one to have children **ADV** with children in mind; **sich ~ äußern** to say one is fond of children; **sich ~ verhalten** to be tolerant of children; **sich ~ geben** to show a fondness for children; *(heucheln)* to pretend to be fond of children; **Kin|der|freund|lich|keit** F *(von Mensch)* fondness for children; *(von Möbeln, Architektur etc)* child-friendliness; **der Autor beklagt die mangelnde ~ in Deutschland** the author laments the fact that German society is not child-orientated; **Kin|der|freund|schaft** F friendship between children; **Kin|der|funk** M children's radio *or* programmes *pl (Brit) or* programs *pl (US)*; **Kin|der|gar|ten** M ≈ nursery school, ≈ kindergarten; **Kin|der|gärt|ner(in)** M(F) ≈ nursery-school *or* kindergarten teacher

KINDERGARTEN

A **Kindergarten** takes preschool children between the ages of three and five. The emphasis is on games, singing and group activities rather than the three Rs. This is designed to encourage children to develop their capabilities and powers of concentration at their own pace. Most **Kindergärten** are run by churches or local authorities. Attendance is voluntary and a fee is payable.

Kin|der-: **Kin|der|ge|burts|tag** M *(= Feier)* children's birthday party; **Kin|der|geld** NT child benefit *(Brit)*, *benefit paid for having children*; **Kin|der|ge|schrei** NT screams *pl* of children; **er kann ~ nicht vertragen** he can't stand children screaming; **dieses ~ ...!** these children *or* kids *(inf)* screaming; **Kin|der|ge|sicht** NT baby face; **Kin|der|glau|be** M child-like faith; **Kin|der|got|tes|dienst** M children's service; **Kin|der|heil|kun|de** F paediatrics *sing (Brit)*, pediatrics *sing (US)*; **Facharzt für ~** paediatrician *(Brit)*, pediatrician *(US)*; **Kin|der|heim** NT children's home; **Kin|der|hort** M day-nursery *(Brit)*, crèche *(Brit)*, daycare centre *(Brit) or* center *(US)*; **Kin|der|jah|re** PL childhood years *pl*; **Kin|der|ka|nal** M *(TV)* children's channel; **Kin|der|klei|dung** F children's clothes *pl*; **Kin|der|kli|nik** F children's clinic, paediatric *(Brit) or* pediatric *(US)* clinic; **Kin|der|kram** M *(inf)* kids' stuff *(inf)*; **Kin|der|kran|ken|haus** NT children's hospital; **Kin|der|kran|ken|schwes|ter** F (sick) children's nurse, paediatric *(Brit) or* pediatric *(US)* nurse; **Kin|der|krank|heit** F childhood illness *or* disease; *(fig)* teething troubles *pl*; **Kin|der|kreuz|zug**

M *(Eccl Hist)* Children's Crusade; **Kin|der|krie|gen** NT **-s**, *no pl* **sie hat keine Lust zum ~** she doesn't want to have children; **Kin|der|krip|pe** F day-nursery *(Brit)*, crèche *(Brit)*, daycare centre *(Brit) or* center *(US)*; **Kin|der|la|den** M (left-wing) playgroup; **Kin|der|läh|mung** F poliomyelitis, polio; **Kin|der|läh|mungs|imp|fung** F polio vaccination *or* inoculation; **kin|der|leicht** ADJ childishly simple, dead easy *(inf)*; **es ist ~** it's child's play *or* kid's stuff *(inf)* ADV easily

Kin|der|lein ['kındelain] PL children *pl*

Kin|der-: **kin|der|lieb** ADJ fond of children; **Kin|der|lie|be** F *(= Liebe zwischen Kindern)* children's love, children's affection; *(= Liebe zu Kindern)* love of *or* for children; **Kin|der|lied** NT nursery rhyme; **kin|der|los** ADJ childless; **Kin|der|lo|sig|keit** F -, *no pl* childlessness; **Kin|der|mäd|chen** F nanny; **Kin|der|mär|chen** NT (children's) fairy tale, fairy story; **Kin|der|mo|den** PL children's fashions *pl*; **Kin|der|mord** M child murder; *(Jur)* infanticide; **der bethlehemitische ~** *(Bibl)* **der ~ zu Bethlehem** *(Bibl)* the massacre of the innocents; **Kin|der|mör|der** M child-murderer; **Kin|der|mör|de|rin** F child-murderess; **Kin|der|mund** M *(fig)* children's talk, child's way of talking; **das wirkt spaßig, weil es aus ~ kommt** that sounds funny coming from a child; **~ tut Wahrheit kund** *(Prov)* out of the mouths of babes and sucklings *(prov)*; **Kin|der|narr** M, **Kin|der|När|rin** F great lover of children; **er ist ein ~** he adores children; **Kin|der|pa|ra|dies** NT children's paradise; **Kin|der|pfle|ger** M paediatric *(Brit) or* pediatric *(US)* nurse; **Kin|der|pfle|ge|rin** F paediatric *(Brit) or* pediatric *(US)* nurse; *(= Kindermädchen)* nanny; **Kin|der|po|po** M *(inf)* baby's bottom *(inf)*; **glatt wie ein ~** smooth as a baby's bottom *(inf)*; **Kin|der|por|no** M *(inf)* child-porn *or* kiddy-porn *(inf)* video; **Kin|der|por|no|gra|fie**, **Kin|der|por|no|gra|phie** F child pornography; **Kin|der|pros|ti|tu|ti|on** F child prostitution; **Kin|der|psy|cho|lo|gie** F child psychology; **Kin|der|raub** M baby-snatching; *(= Entführung)* kidnapping (of a child/children); **kin|der|reich** ADJ with many children; *Familie* large; **Kin|der|reich|tum** M an abundance of children; **der ~ Kenias** the abundance of children in Kenya; **Kin|der|reim** M nursery rhyme; **Kin|der|rei|se|bett** NT travel cot; **Kin|der|sa|chen** PL *(= Kleidung)* children's clothes *pl*; *(= Gegenstände)* children's things *pl*; *(= Spielsachen)* toys *pl*; **Kin|der|schän|der** [-ʃɛndɐ] M **-s, -**, **Kin|der|schän|de|rin** [-ərın] F **-, -nen** child abuser; **Kin|der|schar** F swarm of children; **Kin|der|schreck** M bog(e)yman; **Kin|der|schuh** M child's shoe; **~e sind teuer** children's shoes are dear; **etw steckt noch in den ~en** *(fig)* sth is still in its infancy; **Kin|der|schutz** M protection of children; **Kin|der|schutz|bund** M *pl* **-bünde** child protection agency, ≈ NSPCC *(Brit)*; **Kin|der|schwes|ter** F paediatric *(Brit) or* pediatric *(US)* nurse; **Kin|der|se|gen** M *(dated)* children *pl*; **es war ihnen kein ~ beschert** they were not blessed with children; **kin|der|si|cher** ADJ childproof ADV *aufbewahren* out of reach of children; **die Autotür lässt sich ~ verschließen** the car door has a child lock; **die Flasche lässt sich ~ verschließen** the bottle has a childproof cap; **Kin|der|si|che|rung** F *(Aut)* childproof safety catch; *(an Flasche)* childproof cap; **Kin|der|sitz** M child's seat; *(im Auto)* child seat; **Kin|der|spiel** NT children's game; *(fig)* child's play *no art*; **Kin|der|spiel|platz** M children's playground; **Kin|der|spiel|zeug** NT (children's) toys *pl*; **Kin|der|spra|che** F *(von Kindern)* children's language; *(verniedlichend von Erwachsenen)* baby talk *no art*; **Kin|der|sta|ti|on** F children's ward; **Kin|der|sterb|lich|keit** F infant mortality; **Kin|der|stim|me** F child's voice; **Kin|der|streich** M childish prank; **Kin|der|stu|be** F *(fig)* upbringing; **Kin|der|stuhl** M child's chair; *(= Hochstuhl)* high chair; **Kin|der|stun|de** F children's hour; **Kin|der|ta|ges|heim** NT, **Kin|der|ta|ges|stät|te** F day nursery *(Brit)*, crèche *(Brit)*, daycare centre *(Brit) or* center *(US)*

> **KINDERTAGESSTÄTTE/KITA**
>
> **Kindertagesstätten**, or **Kitas** for short, are daycare centres for children whose parents are in full-time employment. They range from crèches for babies, playgroups for children between the ages of one and three, and day centres for children of school age.

Kin|der-: **Kin|der|tau|fe** F infant baptism; **Kin|der|tel|ler** M *(in Restaurant)* children's portion; **Kin|der|the|a|ter** NT children's theatre *(Brit) or* theater *(US)*; *(= Jugendtheater)* youth theatre *(Brit) or* theater *(US)*; **Kin|der|trom|mel** F toy drum; **Kin|der|vers** M nursery rhyme; **Kin|der|vor|stel|lung** F *(Theater, Kino etc)* children's performance *or* show; **Kin|der|wa|gen** M pram *(Brit)*, baby carriage *(US)*, perambulator *(form)*; *(= Sportwagen)* pushchair *(Brit)*, (baby-)stroller *(esp US)*; **Kin|der|welt** F world of children; **Kin|der|wunsch** M *(von Frau, Paar)* desire for *or* to have children/a child; **ihr ~ blieb unerfüllt** she wanted to have children (but couldn't); **Kin|der|zahl** F number of children; **Kin|der|zim|mer** NT child's/children's room; *(esp für Kleinkinder)* nursery; **Kin|der|zu|la|ge** F, **Kin|der|zu|schlag** M child benefit *(Brit)*, *benefit paid for having children*

Kin|des-: **Kin|des|ab|trei|bung** F abortion; **Kin|des|al|ter** NT childhood; **im ~** at an early age; **Kin|des|aus|set|zung** F abandoning of children; **~en** cases of children being abandoned; **Kin|des|bei|ne** PL **von ~n an** from childhood, from an early age; **Kin|des|ent|füh|rung** F kidnapping (of a child/children); **Kin|des|ent|zie|hung** F *(Jur)* child abduction; **Kin|des|kind** NT grandchild; **Kin|des|lie|be** F child's/children's love; **Kin|des|miss|brauch** M child abuse; **Kin|des|miss|hand|lung** F child abuse; **Kin|des|mord** M child-murder, murder of a child; **Kin|des|mör|der** M child-murderer; **Kin|des|mör|de|rin** F child-murderess; **Kin|des|nö|te** PL *(old)* travail *(old)*; **Kin|des|raub** M = **Kinderraub**; **Kin|des|tö|tung** F *(Jur: von eigenem Säugling)* infanticide; **Kin|des|ver|wechs|lung** F confusion of children's identity

Kind-: **Kind|frau** F Lolita; **kind|ge|mäß** ADJ suitable for children/a child ADV appropriately for children/a child; *ausdrücken, formulieren* in children's terms; **kind|ge|recht** ADJ suitable for children/a child ADV *entwickeln, ausrichten* to suit children/a child; **kind|haft** ADJ childlike

Kind|heit F **-, -en** childhood; *(= früheste Kindheit)* infancy

Kind|heits-: **Kind|heits|er|in|ne|rung** F childhood memory; **Kind|heits|traum** M childhood dream

Kin|di ['kındi] M **-s, -** *(inf: = Kindergarten)* nursery

kin|disch ['kındıʃ] *(pej)* ADJ childish ADV childishly; **sich ~ über etw** *(acc)* **freuen** to be as pleased as Punch about sth; **er kann sich ~ freuen** he takes a childlike pleasure in (simple) things

Kindl ['kındl] NT **-s, -(n)** *(dial) dim von* **Kind**

kind|lich ['kıntlıç] ADJ childlike ADV like a child; **~ wirken** to be childlike

Kind|lich|keit F **-**, *no pl* childlikeness

Kinds- *in cpds* = **Kindes-**: **Kinds|be|we|gun|gen** PL *(Med)* foetal *(Brit) or* fetal *(US)* movements *pl*; **Kinds|kopf** M *(inf)* big kid *(inf)*; **sei kein ~** don't be so childish; **Kinds|la|ge** F *(Med)* presentation of the foetus *(Brit) or* fetus *(US)*; **Kinds|tod** M **plötzlicher ~** cot death *(Brit)*, crib death *(US)*

Kind|tau|fe F *(old)* christening

Ki|ne|ma|thek [kinema'te:k] F **-, -en** film library *or* archive

Ki|ne|ma|to|gra|fie, **Ki|ne|ma|to|gra|phie** [kinematogra'fi:] F **-**, *no pl* cinematography

Ki|ne|tik [ki'ne:tık] F **-**, *no pl* kinetics *sing*

ki|ne|tisch [ki'ne:tıʃ] ADJ kinetic

King [kıŋ] M **-(s), -s** *(inf)* king

Ki|ni|gel|ha|se ['kınıgl-] M *(Aus, dial: = Kaninchen)* rabbit

Kin|ker|litz|chen ['kıŋkɐlıtsçən] PL *(inf)* knick-knacks *pl (inf)*; *(= dumme Streiche)* horseplay *sing*

Kinn [kın] NT **-(e)s, -e** chin

Kinn-: **Kinn|ba|cke** F *(S Ger)* jaw; **Kinn|bart** M goatee (beard); **Kinn|ha|ken** M hook to the chin; **Kinn|la|de** F jaw(-bone); **Kinn|rie|men** M *(am Helm)* chinstrap; **Kinn|schutz** M *(Hockey)* chin-guard

Ki|no ['ki:no] NT **-s, -s** cinema; *(= Gebäude)* cinema, movie theater *(US)*; **ins ~ gehen** to go to the cinema *or* pictures *(Brit) or* movies *(esp US)*

Ki|no- *in cpds* cinema, movie *(esp US)*; **Ki|no|be|such** M visit to the cinema; *(= Besucherrate)* cinema attendances *pl*; **Ki|no|be|su|cher(in)** M(F) cinemagoer *(Brit)*, moviegoer *(US)*; **Ki|no|er|folg** M screen hit *or* success; **Ki|no|film** M cinema film; **ki|no|freu|dig** ADJ cinema-loving; **Ki|no|gän|ger** [-gɛŋɐ] M **-s, -**, **Ki|no|gän|ge|rin** [-ərın] F **-, -nen** cinemagoer *(Brit)*, moviegoer *(US)*; **Ki|no|hit** M blockbuster; **Ki|no|kar|te** F cinema ticket; **Ki|no|kas|se** F cinema box office; **Ki|no|pro|gramm** NT film programme *(Brit) or* program *(US)*; *(= Übersicht)* film guide; **Ki|no|pub|li|kum** NT cinema *(Brit) or* movie *(US)* audience(s *pl*), cinemagoers *pl (Brit)*, moviegoers *pl (US)*; **Ki|no|re|kla|me** F *(= Werbespot)* cinema advertisement; *(= Werbung)* cinema advertising; **Ki|no|vor|stel|lung** F performance, programme *(Brit)*, program *(US)*; **Ki|no|wer|bung** F cinema advertising

Kin|topp ['ki:ntɔp] M OR NT **-s, -s** *or* **⸚e** [-tœpə] *(dated)* **a** pictures *pl (Brit)*, movies *pl (US)*; **im ~ sein** to be at the pictures *(Brit) or* movies *(US)* **b** *(als Kulturphänomen)* cinema

Ki|osk ['ki:ɔsk, kiɔsk] M **-(e)s, -e** kiosk

Ki|pa ['kıpa] F **-, -s** kippa

Kipf [kıpf] M **-(e)s, -e** *(S Ger)* (stick) loaf

Kip|fe(r)l ['kıpfl, 'kıpfɐl] NT **-s, -(n)** *(Aus)* croissant

Kipf|ler ['kıpflɐ] PL *(Aus)* salad potatoes *pl*

Kip|pa ['kıpa] F **-, -s** kippa

Kip|pe ['kıpə] F **-, -n** **a** *(Sport)* spring **b** **auf der ~ stehen** *(Gegenstand)* to be balanced precariously; **sie steht auf der ~** *(fig)* it's touch and go with her; **es steht auf der ~, ob …** *(fig)* it's touch and go whether …; **zwei Schüler stehen auf der ~** two pupils might have to repeat the year **c** *(inf) (= Zigarettenstummel)* cigarette stub, fag-end *(Brit inf)*, dog-end *(Brit inf)*; *(= Zigarette)* fag *(Brit inf)*, butt *(US inf)* **d** *(= Müllkippe, Min)* tip

kip|pe|lig ['kıpəlıç] *(inf)* ADJ *(= wackelig)* wobbly; *Möbel auch* rickety; *Angelegenheit* shaky ADV **der Tisch steht ~** the table's wobbly; **in Mathe stehts ~ bei mir aus** I'm a little shaky in maths

kip|peln ['kıpln] VI *(inf)* to wobble, to be wobbly *or* rickety; **(mit dem Stuhl) ~** to tilt (on one's chair)

kip|pen ['kıpn] VT **a** *Behälter, Fenster* to tilt; *Ladefläche, Tisch* to tip *or* tilt (up); *(fig: = umstoßen) Urteil* to overturn; *Regierung, Minister* to topple; **etw aus dem Gleichgewicht ~** to tilt sth; **„bitte nicht ~"** "please do not tilt"; **einen ~** *(inf: = trinken)* to have a drink; **ein paar** *or* **einen hinter die Binde** *or* **hinter den Latz ~** *(inf)* to have a couple *(inf)*
b *(mit Ortsangabe: = schütten)* to tip
VI *aux sein* to tip over; *(esp höhere Gegenstände)* to topple (over); *(Fahrzeug, Schiff)* to overturn; *(Mensch)* to topple, to fall; *(Wechselkurse, Ge-*

winne) to plummet; **aus den Latschen** *or* **Pantinen ~** *(fig inf) (= überrascht sein)* to fall through the floor *(inf)*; *(= ohnmächtig werden)* to pass out

Kip|per ['kɪpɐ] M **-s, -** *(Aut)* tipper, dump(er) truck; *(Rail)* (tipper) wagon

Kipp|fens|ter NT tilt window

kipp|lig ['kɪplɪç] ADJ = **kippelig**

Kipp-: **Kipp|lo|re** F tipper wagon; **Kipp|schal|ter** M toggle switch; **Kipp|wa|gen** M = **Kipper**

Kir [kiːɐ] M **-s, -s** kir

Kir|che ['kɪrçə] F **-, -n** *(= Gebäude, Organisation)* church; *(= bestimmte Glaubensgemeinschaft)* Church; *(= Gottesdienst)* church *no art*; **zur ~ gehen** to go to church; **die ~ im Dorf lassen** *(fig)* not to get carried away

Kir|chen- *in cpds* church; **Kir|chen|äl|tes|te(r)** MF *decl as adj* church elder; **Kir|chen|amt** NT **a** ecclesiastical office **b** *(= Verwaltungsstelle)* church offices *pl*; **Kir|chen|aus|tritt** M leaving the Church *no art*; **~e** (cases of) people leaving the Church; **Kir|chen|bank** F *pl* **-bänke** (church) pew; **Kir|chen|bann** M anathema; *(= Interdikt)* interdict; **den ~ über jdn verhängen** to excommunicate sb; *(= Interdikt verhängen)* to interdict sb; **Kir|chen|be|such** M church-going; **Kir|chen|be|su|cher(in)** M(F) churchgoer; **Kir|chen|blatt** NT parish magazine; **Kir|chen|buch** NT church register; **Kir|chen|chor** M church choir; **Kir|chen|dieb|stahl** M theft from a/the church; **Kir|chen|die|ner(in)** M(F) sexton; **kir|chen|feind|lich** ADJ anticlerical ADV **sich ~ äußern** to make anticlerical remarks; **~ eingestellt sein** to be opposed to the Church; **Kir|chen|fens|ter** NT church window; **Kir|chen|fest** NT religious *or* church festival; **Kir|chen|frau** F churchwoman; **Kir|chen|fürst** M high dignitary of the Church; *(katholisch)* prince of the Church; **Kir|chen|ge|mein|de** F parish; **Kir|chen|ge|schich|te** F church *or* ecclesiastical history; **Kir|chen|glo|cke** F church bell; **Kir|chen|gut** NT church property; **Kir|chen|jahr** NT church *or* ecclesiastical year; **Kir|chen|kampf** M struggle between Church and state; **Kir|chen|la|tein** NT Church Latin; **Kir|chen|leh|rer(in)** M(F) Doctor of the Church; **Kir|chen|lei|tung** F government of the Church; *(= Gremium)* governing body of the Church; **Kir|chen|licht** NT **kein (großes) ~ sein** *(fig inf)* to be not very bright; **Kir|chen|lied** NT hymn; **Kir|chen|mann** M *pl* **-männer** churchman; **Kir|chen|maus** F **arm wie eine ~** poor as a church mouse; **Kir|chen|mu|sik** F church *or* sacred music; **Kir|chen|pat|ron(in)** M(F) (church's) patron saint; **Kir|chen|po|li|tik** F church policy; **kir|chen|po|li|tisch** ADJ relating to church policy ADV in relation to church policy; **Kir|chen|rat** M *(= Gremium)* Church Council; **Kir|chen|rat** M, **Kir|chen|rä|tin** F member of the Church Council; **Kir|chen|raub** M theft from a/the church; *(von geweihtem Gegenstand)* sacrilege; **Kir|chen|räu|ber(in)** M(F) church-robber; **Kir|chen|recht** NT canon law; **kir|chen|recht|lich** ADJ canonical; **Kir|chen|schän|der** [-ʃɛndɐ] M **-s, -**, **Kir|chen|schän|de|rin** [-ərɪn] F **-, -nen** desecrator, profaner; **Kir|chen|schiff** NT *(= Längsschiff)* nave; *(= Querschiff)* transept; **Kir|chen|spal|tung** F schism; **Kir|chen|staat** M *(Hist)* Papal States *pl*; *(= Vatikanstaat)* Vatican City; **Kir|chen|steu|er** F church tax; **Kir|chen|stra|fe** F ecclesiastical punishment; **Kir|chen|tag** M Church congress; **Kir|chen|ton|art** F church *or* ecclesiastical mode; **Kir|chen|va|ter** M Father of the Church, Church Father; **Kir|chen|ver|fol|gung** F persecution of the Church; **Kir|chen|vor|stand** M parish council

Kirch-: **Kirch|gang** M *pl* **-gänge** going to church *no art*; **der sonntägliche ~** going to church on Sunday; **Kirch|gän|ger** [-gɛŋɐ] M **-s, -**, **Kirch|gän|ge|rin** [-ərɪn] F **-, -nen** churchgoer; **Kirch|hof** M churchyard; *(= Friedhof)* graveyard

kirch|lich ['kɪrçlɪç] ADJ church *attr*; *Zustimmung, Missbilligung* by the church; *Amt* church *attr*, ecclesiastical; *Gebot, Gericht* ecclesiastical; *Musik* church *attr*, sacred, religious; *Feiertag* church *attr*, religious; *Land, Mensch* religious, devout; *Recht* canon ADV **sich ~ trauen lassen** to get married in church, to have a church wedding; **~ bestattet werden** to have a Christian funeral

Kirch-: **Kirch|spiel** NT, **Kirch|spren|gel** M parish; **Kirch|tag** M *(Aus, S Ger)* fair, kermis *(US)*; **Kirch|turm** M church steeple; **Kirch|turm|spit|ze** F church spire; **Kirch|weih** [-vai] F **-, -en** fair, kermis *(US)*; **Kirch|wei|he** F consecration of a/the church

> **KIRCHWEIH**
>
> The **Kirchweih** – also called **Kirmes** or **Kerwe** in some regions and **Chilbi** or **Kilbi** in Switzerland – is a celebration that takes place every year in villages, districts or small towns in commemoration of the consecration of the local church. There are all sorts of customs associated with the **Kirchweih**, but common to them all is a fair lasting several days.

Kir|gi|se [kɪr'giːzə] M **-n, -n**, **Kir|gi|sin** [-'giːzɪn] F **-, -nen** Kirghiz

Kir|gi|si|en [kɪr'giːziən] NT **-s** Kirghizia

kir|gi|sisch [kɪr'giːzɪʃ] ADJ Kirghiz, Kirghizian

Kir|gis|tan ['kɪrgɪstaːn] NT **-s**, **Kir|gi|sis|tan** [kɪr'giːzɪstaːn] NT **-s** Kirghizia

Kir|mes ['kɪrmɛs, 'kɪrməs] F **-, -sen** *(dial)* fair, kermis *(US)*

kir|re ['kɪrə] ADJ *pred (inf) Tier* tame; *Mensch* compliant; **jdn ~ machen** to soften sb up *(inf)*

kir|re+ma|chen VT *sep* → **kirre**

Kirsch [kɪrʃ] M **-(e)s, -** kirsch

Kirsch- *in cpds* cherry; **Kirsch|baum** M cherry tree; *(= Holz)* cherry (wood); **Kirsch|blü|te** F cherry blossom; *(= Zeit)* cherry blossom time

Kir|sche ['kɪrʃə] F **-, -n** cherry; *(= Holz)* cherry (-wood); **mit ihm ist nicht gut ~n essen** *(fig)* it's best not to tangle with him

Kir|schen|mund M *(poet)* cherry (red) lips *pl*

Kirsch-: **Kirsch|ent|ker|ner** [-lɛntkɛrnɐ] M **-s, -**, **Kirsch|ent|stei|ner** [-lɛntʃtainɐ] M **-s, -** cherry-stoner; **Kirsch|kern** M cherry stone; **Kirsch|ku|chen** M cherry cake; **Kirsch|li|kör** M cherry brandy; **kirsch|rot** ADJ cherry(-red); **Kirsch|stein** M cherry stone; **Kirsch|to|ma|te** F cherry tomato; **Kirsch|tor|te** F cherry gateau *(Brit) or* cake; **Schwarzwälder ~** Black Forest gateau *(Brit) or* cake *(US)*; **Kirsch|was|ser** NT kirsch

Kis|met ['kɪsmɛt] M **-s,** *no pl* kismet *no pl*, fate, destiny

Kis|sen ['kɪsn] NT **-s, -** cushion; *(= Kopfkissen)* pillow; *(= Stempelkissen, an Heftpflaster)* pad; *(= Duftkissen, Haarshampookissen)* sachet

Kis|sen-: **Kis|sen|be|zug** M cushion cover; *(von Kopfkissen)* pillow case; **Kis|sen|schlacht** F pillow fight; **Kis|sen|über|zug** M cushion cover; *(von Kopfkissen)* pillowcase

Kis|te ['kɪstə] F **-, -n** **a** *(= Behälter)* box; *(für Obst)* box, case; *(für Wein etc)* case; *(= Lattenkiste)* crate; *(= Truhe)* chest; *(sl: = Bett)* sack *(inf)*; **eine ~ Wein** a case of wine; **eine ~ Zigarren** a box of cigars; **(mit jdm) in die ~ springen** *(sl: = ins Bett gehen)* to jump into the sack (with sb) *(inf)* **b** *(inf) (= Auto, Flugzeug)* crate *(inf)*; *(= Schiff)* tub *(inf)*; *(= Fernsehen)* box *(inf)*; *(= Computer)* computer **c** *(inf) (= Angelegenheit)* affair; *(= Beziehungskiste)* relationship; **fertig ist die ~!** that's that (done)!; **das ist eine faule ~!** that's a fishy business! *(inf)*; **immer dieselbe ~** always the same old thing; **eine schwere ~** a big problem; **eine alte ~** an old chestnut; **sie hat die (ganze) ~ allein geschmissen** *(inf)* she did everything herself

kis|ten|wei|se ['kɪstnvaizə] ADV → **Kiste a** by the box/case *etc*

Kit|che|nette [kɪtʃə'nɛt] F **-, -s** kitchenette

Kitsch [kɪtʃ] M **-es,** *no pl* kitsch

kit|schig ['kɪtʃɪç] ADJ kitschy ADV in a kitschy way

Kitt [kɪt] M **-(e)s, -e** *(= Fensterkitt)* putty; *(für Porzellan, Stein etc)* cement; *(fig)* bond; **der ganze ~** *(inf)* the whole (kit and) caboodle *(inf)*

Kitt|chen ['kɪtçən] NT **-s, -** *(inf)* clink *(inf)*

Kit|tel ['kɪtl] M **-s, -** **a** *(= Arbeitskittel)* overall; *(von Arzt, Laborant etc)* (white) coat **b** *(= blusenartiges Kleidungsstück)* smock **c** *(Aus: = Damenrock)* skirt

Kit|tel-: **Kit|tel|kleid** NT frock; **Kit|tel|schür|ze** F overall

kit|ten ['kɪtn] VT to cement, to stick together with cement; *Fenster* to putty; *(= füllen)* to fill; *(fig)* to patch up

Kitz [kɪts] NT **-es, -e** *(= Rehkitz)* fawn; *(= Ziegenkitz, Gämsenkitz)* kid

Kit|zel ['kɪtsl] M **-s, -** tickle; *(= Kitzelgefühl)* tickling feeling; *(fig)* thrill

Kit|zel|ge|fühl NT tickling feeling

kit|ze|lig ['kɪtsəlɪç] ADJ *(lit, fig)* ticklish

Kit|ze|lig|keit F **-, -en** *(lit, fig)* ticklishness

kit|zeln ['kɪtsln] VT *(lit, fig)* to tickle; **jdn unter den Armen/am Bauch ~** to tickle sb under the arms/sb's stomach; **jdm das Zwerchfell ~** *(fig)* to make sb laugh; **ihn kitzelt der Reiz des Neuen** he cannot resist the challenge of something new VI to tickle VT *impers* **es kitzelt mich** I've got a tickle; **es kitzelt mich, das zu tun** I'm itching to do it

Kit|zeln NT **-s,** *no pl* tickling; **er findet das ~ angenehm** he likes being tickled; **ein angenehmes ~** a nice tickle

Kitz|ler ['kɪtslɐ] M **-s, -** *(Anat)* clitoris

kitz|lig ['kɪtslɪç] ADJ *(lit, fig)* ticklish

Ki|wi ['kiːvi] F **-, -s** *(= Frucht)* kiwi

Ki|wi M **-s, -s** *(Orn)* kiwi; *(inf: = Neuseeländer)* Kiwi

KKW [kaːkaː'veː] NT **-s, -s** *abbr von* **Kernkraftwerk**

kla|bas|tern [kla'bastɐn] *ptp* **klabastert** VI *aux sein (N Ger)* to plod, to clump, to stump

Kla|bau|ter|mann [kla'bautɐ-] M *pl* **-männer** *(Naut)* ship's kobold

klack [klak] INTERJ click; *(platschend)* splosh

kla|cken ['klakn] VI *(inf)* to click; *(bei Aufprall)* to crash; *(= klappern)* to rattle

kla|ckern ['klakɐn] VTI *(dial)* = **kleckern**

klacks [klaks] INTERJ splosh

Klacks [klaks] M **-es, -e** *(inf)* **a** *(= Geräusch)* splosh **b** *(von Kartoffelbrei, Sahne etc)* dollop *(inf)*; *(von Senf, Farbe etc)* blob *(inf)*, dollop *(inf)* **c** *(fig)* **das ist ein ~** *(= einfach)* that's a piece of cake *(inf)*; *(= wenig)* that's nothing *(inf)*; **die 500 Euro sind für ihn ein ~** the 500 euros are peanuts *or* chicken feed to him *(inf)*

klack|sen ['klaksn] *(inf)* VT *Sahne, Kartoffelbrei etc* to dollop *(inf)*; *Farbe* to splash; **die Sahne/den Kartoffelbrei** *etc* **auf etw** *(acc)* **~** to put a dollop of cream/mashed potato on sth *(inf)* VI *(Brei, Sahne)* to go smack; *(Farbe)* to splash

Klad|de ['kladə] F **-, -n** *(Sch)* rough book; *(= Notizbuch)* notebook; *(= Block)* scribbling pad; *(= Hilfsmittel)* crib *(inf)*; **in ~** *(inf)* in rough; **~ führen** to take notes

klad|de|ra|datsch [kladəra'datʃ] INTERJ crash-bang-wallop

Klad|de|ra|datsch [kladəra'datʃ] M **-(e)s, -e** *(inf)* **a** *(Geräusch)* crash-bang-wallop *(inf)* **b** *(fig) (= Kram, Durcheinander)* mess; *(= Streit)* bust-up *(inf)*; *(= Skandal)* scandal; **da haben wir den ~!** what a mess!

klaf|fen ['klafn] VI to gape; *(Spalte, Abgrund auch)* to yawn; **da klafft eine Wunde/ein Loch** there is a gaping wound/hole; **zwischen uns beiden klafft ein Abgrund** *(fig)* we are poles apart

kläf|fen ['klɛfn] VI *(pej, fig)* to yap

klaf|fend ADJ gaping; *Spalte, Abgrund auch* yawning; *(fig)* irreconcilable; *Widerspruch* blatant

Kläf|fer ['klɛfɐ] M **-s, -, Kläf|fe|rin** [-ərın] F **-, -nen** *(lit, fig: pej)* yapper

Klaf|ter ['klaftɐ] M OR NT **-s, -** *or (rare)* f **-, -n** fathom

klaf|ter|wei|se ADV *(fig)* by the ton

klag|bar ADJ *(Jur) Sache* actionable; *Anspruch, Forderung* enforceable

Kla|ge ['kla:gə] F **-, -n** **a** *(= Beschwerde)* complaint; **(bei jdm) über jdn/etw ~ führen** to lodge a complaint (with sb) about sb/sth; **~n (über jdn/etw) vorbringen** to make complaints (about sb/sth); **Grund zu ~n** *or* **zur ~** reason for complaint *or* to complain; **dass mir keine ~n kommen!** *(inf)* don't let me hear any complaints **b** *(= Äußerung von Schmerz)* complaint; *(= Äußerung von Trauer)* lament(ation) *(um, über +acc* for); *(= Klagelaut)* plaintive cry **c** *(Jur) (im Zivilrecht)* action, suit; *(im Strafrecht)* charge, action; *(= Scheidungsklage)* petition, action; *(= Klageschrift, Wortlaut) (im Strafrecht)* charge; *(im Zivilrecht)* charge, plaint; **eine ~ gegen jdn einreichen** *or* **erheben** to institute proceedings against sb; **eine ~ abweisen** to reject a charge; **über eine ~ entscheiden** to reach a decision on a charge; **eine ~ auf etw** *(acc)* an action for sth; **öffentliche ~** criminal charge

Kla|ge-: **Kla|ge|ab|wei|sung** F *(Jur)* dismissal of an action; **Kla|ge|er|he|bung** F *(Jur)* institution of proceedings; **Kla|ge|frist** F *(Jur)* period for instituting proceedings; **kla|ge|füh|rend** ADJ *(Jur)* suing; **die ~e Partei** the plaintiff; **Kla|ge|ge|sang** M lament; **Kla|ge|ge|schrei** NT wailing; **Kla|ge|grund** M *(Jur)* cause of action; **Kla|ge|laut** M plaintive cry; *(schmerzerfüllt)* cry of pain; **Kla|ge|lied** NT lament; **ein ~ über jdn/etw anstimmen** *(fig)* to complain about sb/sth; **Kla|ge|mau|er** F **die ~** the Wailing Wall

kla|gen ['kla:gn] VI **a** *(= jammern)* to moan, to wail; *(Tiere)* to cry **b** *(= trauern, Trauer äußern)* to lament *(um jdn/etw* sb/sth), to wail **c** *(= sich beklagen)* to complain; **über etw** *(acc)* **~** to complain about sth; **über Rückenschmerzen/Schlaflosigkeit ~** to complain of backache/insomnia; **ohne zu ~** without complaining; **ich kann nicht ~** *(inf)* mustn't grumble *(inf)* **d** *(Jur)* to sue *(auf +acc* for) VT **a** **jdm sein Leid/seine Not/seinen Kummer ~** to pour out one's sorrow/distress/grief to sb; **Gott** *or* **dem Himmel seis geklagt** alas, alack **b** *(Aus)* = **verklagen**

kla|gend ADJ *(= trauererfüllt) Mensch* lamenting; *Blick, Ton, Schrei* plaintive; *Gesicht* sorrowful; *(= schmerzerfüllt)* pained; *(= jammernd, sich beklagend)* complaining; **der ~e Teil, die ~e Partei** *(Jur)* the plaintiff ADV *singen* mournfully; *klingen* plaintively; **jdn laut ~ beweinen** to loudly lament the loss of sb

Kla|ge-: **Kla|ge|par|tei** F *(Jur)* plaintiff; **Kla|ge|punkt** M *usu pl* → **Klage c** particular of a charge/petition/plaint

Klä|ger ['klɛ:gɐ] M **-s, -, Klä|ge|rin** [-ərın] F **-, -nen** *(Jur) (im Zivilrecht)* plaintiff; *(im Strafrecht auch)* prosecuting party; *(in Scheidungssachen)* petitioner; **wo kein ~ ist, ist auch kein Richter** *(Prov)* well, if no-one complains ...

Kla|ge-: **Kla|ge|ruf** M plaintive cry; *(= Schmerzensschrei)* cry of pain; **Kla|ge|schrift** F *(Jur)* charge; *(bei Scheidung)* petition; **Kla|ge|ton** M plaintive sound; *(pej)* whine; **Kla|ge|weg** M *(Jur)* **auf dem** *or* **im ~(e)** by (taking *or* bringing) legal action; **den ~ beschreiten** to take legal action; **Kla|ge|weib** NT wailer, mourner

kläg|lich ['klɛ:klıç] ADJ pitiful; *Ende auch* wretched; *Leistung auch, Einwand* pathetic; *Rest* miserable; *Niederlage* pathetic, miserable; *Verhalten* despicable ADV *fehlschlagen, scheitern, misslingen* miserably; *miauen, blöken, wimmern, betteln* pitifully; **~ versagen** to fail miserably

Kläg|lich|keit F **-,** *no pl* **die ~ des Angebots** the pathetic choice

klag|los ADJ *(Jur) Schuld, Forderung* non-actionable ADV *(= ohne Klagen)* uncomplainingly; **etw ~ hinnehmen** *(ohne zu klagen)* to accept sth without complaint; *(ohne zu widersprechen)* to accept sth without objection

Kla|mauk [kla'mauk] M **-s,** *no pl (inf) (= Alberei)* horseplay; *(im Theater etc)* slapstick; *(= Lärm)* racket *(inf)*; *(= Reklamewirbel)* hullabaloo; *(= Aufheben)* fuss, to-do; **~ machen** *(= albern)* to fool about; **lass den ~** stop fooling about/making this racket/making such a fuss

klamm [klam] ADJ **a** *(= steif vor Kälte)* numb **b** *(= feucht)* damp **c** *(inf: finanziell)* hard up *(inf)*

Klamm [klam] F **-, -en** gorge

Klam|mer ['klamɐ] F **-, -n** **a** *(= Wäscheklammer)* peg; *(= Hosenklammer)* clip; *(= Büroklammer)* paperclip; *(= Heftklammer)* staple **b** *(= Haarklammer)* (hair)grip **c** *(Med) (= Wundklammer)* clip; *(= Zahnklammer)* brace **d** *(in Text, Math, = Klammerausdruck)* bracket; *(Mus)* brace; **~ auf/zu** open/close brackets *or* parentheses *(esp US)*; **in ~n** in brackets *or* parentheses *(esp US)*; **runde ~n** round brackets, parentheses *(esp US)*; **eckige ~n** square brackets, (square) brackets *(US)*; **geschweifte** *or* **geschwungene ~n** braces; **spitze ~n** pointed *or* angle brackets; **eine ~ auflösen** *(Math)* to eliminate the brackets *or* parentheses *(esp US)* **e** *(= Bauklammer)* clamp, cramp; *(zur Verpackung)* cramp

Klam|mer-: **Klam|mer|af|fe** M **a** *(Zool)* spider monkey; **er ist ein richtiger ~** *(fig inf)* he's always clinging on to you; **sie saß wie ein ~ auf dem Motorrad** *(inf)* she sat on the motorcycle clinging on for dear life **b** *(Typ)* at-sign, "@"; **Klam|mer|beu|tel** M peg bag; **dich haben sie wohl mit dem ~ gepudert** *(inf)* you must be off your rocker *(Brit inf)*, you must be crazy; **Klam|mer|griff** M tight grip, clinch; **Klam|mer|hef|ter** M stapler

klam|mern ['klamɐn] VT *(an +acc* to) *Wäsche* to peg; *Papier etc* to staple; *(Tech)* to clamp; *(Med) Wunde* to clip; *Zähne* to brace VR **sich an jdn/etw ~** *(lit, fig)* to cling to sb/sth VI *(Sport)* to clinch

klamm|heim|lich *(inf)* ADJ clandestine, on the quiet; **eine ~e Freude empfinden** to be secretly delighted ADV on the quiet; **~ aus dem Haus gehen** to sneak out of the house

Kla|mot|te [kla'mɔtə] F **-, -n** **a** **Klamotten** PL *(inf) (= Kleider)* gear *sing (inf)* **b** *(pej: = Theaterstück, Film)* rubbishy old play/film *etc*; **das ist doch eine alte ~** *(inf)* **das sind doch alte ~n** *(inf)* that's old hat *(inf)*

Kla|mot|ten|kis|te F **aus der ~ hervorholen** *(pej inf)* to dig up again

Klamp|fe ['klampfə] F **-, -n** *(inf)* guitar

kla|mü|sern [kla'my:zɐn] *ptp* **klamüsert** VT *(N Ger inf)* to puzzle over

Klan [kla:n] M **-s, -e** *(lit, fig)* clan

klang *pret von* **klingen**

Klang [klaŋ] M **-(e)s, =e** ['klɛŋə] sound; *(= Tonqualität)* tone; *(= Melodie)* tune; **der ~ von Glocken** the chiming of bells; **der ~ von Glöckchen** the tinkling of small bells; **der ~ von Gläsern** the clinking of glasses; **Klänge** *pl (= Musik)* sounds, tones; **unter den Klängen** *(+gen)* to the sound of; **der Name hat einen guten ~** the name has a good ring to it; *(= guten Ruf)* the name has a good reputation → **Sang**

Klang-: **Klang|bild** NT sound; *(Phys)* sound pattern; **Klang|bo|den** M sounding board; **Klang|ef|fekt** M sound effect; **Klang|far|be** F tone colour *(Brit) or* color *(US)*; **Klang|fol|ge** F tonal sequence; **Klang|fül|le** F richness of tone; *(von Stimme, Gedicht)* sonority; **Klang|kör|per** M *(von Musikinstrument)* body; *(= Orchester)* orchestra; *(= Klangbild)* body of sound

klang|lich ['klaŋlıç] ADJ *Qualität* tonal; **~e Unterschiede** differences in sound; *(von Tonqualität)* tonal difference ADV tonally; **~ gut sein** *(Musik, Lied, Gedicht, Stimme)* to sound good; *(Instrument, Gerät)* to have a good tone *or* sound; **~ ähnlich** similar as far as tone is concerned; **die Flöte könnte ~ reiner sein** the tone of the flute could be purer

klang|los ADJ toneless → **sang- und klanglos**

Klang-: **Klang|qua|li|tät** F *(von Ton)* tonal quality; *(von Wiedergabe)* sound quality; **Klang|reg|ler** M *(Rad etc)* tone control; **klang|rein** ADJ pure; **~ sein** to have a pure tone; **Klang|rein|heit** F purity of tone; **klang|schön** ADJ beautiful-sounding; **Klang|schön|heit** F *(von Stimme)* beautiful sound; **Klang|spekt|rum** NT range of sound(s), tonal palette; **klang|treu** ADJ *Wiedergabe* faithful; *Empfänger* high-fidelity; *Ton* true; **~ sein** to have high fidelity; **Klang|treue** F fidelity; **klang|voll** ADJ *Stimme, Sprache* sonorous, euphonic *(liter)*; *Wiedergabe* full; *Melodie* tuneful; *(fig) Titel, Name* fine-sounding; **Klang|wort** NT *pl* **-wörter** onomatopoeia

klapp [klap] INTERJ snap; *(beim Türschließen)* click → **klipp**

Klapp-: **Klapp|bett** NT folding bed; **Klapp|brü|cke** F bascule bridge; **Klapp|de|ckel** M hinged lid

Klap|pe ['klapə] F **-, -n** **a** flap; *(an Lastwagen)* tailgate; *(seitlich)* side-gate; *(an Kombiwagen)* back; *(von Tisch)* leaf; *(von Ofen)* shutter, flap; *(= Klappdeckel)* (hinged) lid; *(an Oboe etc)* key; *(= Falltür)* trapdoor; *(Film)* clapperboard; **die ~ fällt** *(es ist Schluss)* it's over **b** *(= Schulterklappe, an Tasche)* strap; *(= Hosenklappe, an Tasche)* flap; *(= Augenklappe)* patch; *(von Visier)* shutter; **wenn er schon das Wort Überstunden hört, geht bei ihm die ~ runter** *(inf)* as soon as he hears the word overtime, the shutters come down *(inf)* **c** *(= Fliegenklappe)* (fly) swat **d** *(= Herzklappe)* valve **e** *(inf: = Mund)* trap *(inf)*; **die ~ halten** to shut one's trap *(inf)*; **eine große ~ haben** to have a big mouth *(inf)* **f** *(Aus Telec)* extension **g** *(sl: von Homosexuellen)* pick-up spot, cottage *(sl)*

klap|pen ['klapn] VT **etw nach oben/unten ~** *(Sitz, Bett)* to fold sth up/down; *Kragen* to turn sth up/down; *Deckel* to lift sth up/to put sth down, to raise/lower sth; **etw nach vorn/hinten ~** *(Sitz)* to tip sth forward/back; *Deckel* to lift sth forward/back VI **a** *(fig inf) (= gelingen)* to work; *(= gut gehen)* to work (out); *(= reibungslos stattfinden: Aufführung, Abend)* to go (off) smoothly; **wenn das mal klappt** if that works out; **hat es mit den Karten/dem Job geklappt?** did you get the tickets/job all right *or* OK *(inf)*?; **mit dem Flug hat alles geklappt** the flight went all right, there was no problem with the flight **b** *(geräuschvoll, = schlagen)* to bang

Klap|pen-: **Klap|pen|feh|ler** M *(Med)* valvular defect; **Klap|pen|text** M *(Typ)* blurb

Klap|per ['klapɐ] F **-, -n** rattle

Klap|per-: **klap|per|dürr** ADJ *(inf)* thin as a rake *(Brit) or* rail *(US)*; **Klap|per|ge|stell** NT *(hum inf) (= Mensch)* bag of bones; *(= Fahrzeug)* boneshaker *(Brit inf)*, jalopy *(inf)*

klap|pe|rig ['klapərıç] ADJ = **klapprig**

Klap|per|kas|ten M, **Klap|per|kis|te** F *(pej)* boneshaker *(Brit inf)*, jalopy *(inf)*

klap|pern ['klapɐn] VI **a** *(= Geräusch machen)* to clatter; *(Klapperschlange, Fenster, Baby)* to rattle; *(Lider)* to bat; *(Mühle)* to clack; *(auf der Schreibmaschine)* to clatter away; *(mit Stricknadeln)* to click; **er klapperte vor Kälte/Angst mit den Zähnen** his teeth were chattering with cold/fear; **Klappern gehört zum Handwerk** *(prov)* making a big noise is part of the business **b** *aux sein (= sich klappernd fortbewegen)* to clatter along; *(Auto etc auch)* to rattle along

klap|pernd ADJ clattering; *Auto* rattling; *Zähne* chattering

Klạp|per-: **Klạp|per|schlan|ge** F *(Zool)* rattlesnake; *(fig)* rattletrap; **Klạp|per|storch** M *(baby-talk)* stork; **er glaubt noch immer an den ~** he still thinks babies are found under the gooseberry bush *(Brit)*, he still believes in the stork

Klạpp-: **Klạpp|fahr|rad** NT folding bicycle *or* bike *(inf)*; **Klạpp|fens|ter** NT top-hung window; **Klạpp|han|dy** NT clamshell, flip phone, flip-open mobile (phone) *(Brit)*, flip-open cell(phone) *(US)*; **Klạpp|hut** M crush-hat; **Klạpp|la|den** M folding shutter; **Klạpp|mes|ser** NT flick knife *(Brit)*, switchblade *(US)*; **Klạpp|rad** NT folding bicycle *or* bike *(inf)*

klạpp|rig ['klaprɪç] ADJ rickety, shaky; *(fig inf) Mensch* shaky, tottery

Klạpp-: **Klạpp|sitz** M folding seat; **Klạpp|stuhl** M folding chair; **Klạpp|stul|le** F *(N Ger)* sandwich; **Klạpp|tisch** M folding table; **Klạpp|tür** F trapdoor; **Klạpp|ver|deck** NT folding *or* collapsible hood; **Klạpp|zy|lin|der** M opera hat

Klạps [klaps] M **-es, -e** **a** *(inf)* **einen ~ haben** to have a screw loose *(inf)*, to be off one's rocker *(inf)* **b** *(= Schlag)* smack, slap

Klạps|müh|le F *(pej inf)*, **Klạp|se** F *(pej inf)* loony bin *(inf)*, nut house *(inf)*

klar [klaːɐ] ✪ 42.1, 53.6 ADJ clear; *(= fertig)* ready; **~ zum Gefecht** *or* **Einsatz** *(Mil)* ready for action; **~ zum Start** *(Sport)* ready (for the start); **~ Schiff machen** *(lit, fig, Naut)* to clear the decks; **ein ~er Fall** *(inf)* sure thing *(inf)*; **ein ~er Fall von ...** *(inf)* a clear case of ...; **das ist doch ~!** *(inf)* of course; **alles ~?** everything all right *or* OK? *(inf)*; **jetzt ist** *or* **wird mir alles ~!** now I understand; **einen ~en Augenblick haben** to have a lucid moment; **geistig ~ sein, bei ~em Verstand sein** to be in full possession of one's faculties; *(inf)* to be in one's right mind; **~ wie Kloßbrühe** *or* **dicke Tinte** *(inf)* clear as mud *(inf)*; **sich** *(dat)* **über etw** *(acc)* **im Klaren sein** to be aware of sth; **sich** *(dat)* **darüber im Klaren sein, dass ...** to realize that ...; **ins Klare kommen** to get things straight; **mit jdm ins Klare kommen** to straighten things out with sb; **mit seinem Privatlaben ins Klare kommen** to sort out one's private life
ADV clearly; **~ denkend** clear-thinking; **immer ~er hervortreten** to become more and more apparent; **habe ich mich ~ genug ausgedrückt?** have I made myself perfectly clear?; **na ~!** *(inf)* of course!, sure! *(inf)*; **etw ~ und deutlich sagen** to spell sth out; **jdm etw ~ und deutlich sagen** to tell sb sth straight *(inf)*; **etw tritt ~ zutage** sth becomes apparent *or* obvious *or* clear; **~ auf der Hand liegen** to be perfectly obvious *or* clear → **klipp**

Klar [klaːɐ] NT **-(e)s, -(e)** *(Aus: = Eiweiß)* (egg) white, white of an egg

Klär-: **Klär|an|la|ge** F sewage plant; *(von Fabrik)* purification plant; **Klär|be|cken** NT *(von Kläranlage)* clearing tank

Klar-: **Klar|ap|fel** M early dessert apple; **Klar|blick** M *(fig)* clear-sightedness; **klar|den|kend** ADJ → **klar ADV**

klä|ren ['klɛːrən] VT to clear; *Wasser, Luft* to purify; *Abwasser* to treat; *Bier, Wein* to fine; *Fall, Sachlage* to clarify, to clear up; *Frage* to settle VI *(Sport)* to clear (the ball) VR *(Wasser, Himmel)* to clear; *(Wetter)* to clear up; *(Meinungen, Sachlage)* to become clear; *(Streitpunkte)* to be clarified; *(Frage)* to be settled

Kla|re(r) ['klaːrə] M *decl as adj (inf)* schnapps

klar+ge|hen VI *sep irreg aux sein (inf)* to be all right *or* OK *(inf)*; **ist es mit dem Examen klargegangen?** did the exam go all right *or* OK? *(inf)*

Klär|gru|be F cesspit

Klar|heit F **-, -en** **a** *(fig) (= Deutlichkeit)* clarity; *(= geistige Klarheit)* lucidity; **sich** *(dat)* **~ über etw** *(acc)* **verschaffen** to find out about sth, to get clear about sth; *über Sachlage* to clarify sth; **~ über etw** *(acc)* **haben** to be clear about sth; **darüber besteht (völlige) ~** that is (completely) clear; **an ~ nichts zu wünschen übrig lassen** to be completely clear; **jdm etw in aller ~ sagen** to tell sb sth in plain language; **in dieser Frage müssen wir für ~ sorgen** we must clarify the issue; **alle ~en (restlos) beseitigt!** *(hum)* (it's as) clear as mud! *(inf)* **b** *(von Wasser, Fluss)* clarity, clearness

kla|rie|ren [kla'riːrən] *ptp* **klariert** VT **a** *(Naut)* to make ready **b** *(Zoll)* to clear (through customs)

Kla|ri|net|te [klari'nɛtə] F **-, -n** clarinet

Kla|ri|net|tist [klarinɛ'tɪst] M **-en, -en**, **Kla|ri|net|tis|tin** [-'tɪstɪn] F **-, -nen** clarinettist

Kla|ris|se [kla'rɪsə] F **-, -n**, **Kla|ris|sin** [kla'rɪsɪn] F **-, -nen** nun of the order of St Clare

Klar-: **klar+kom|men** VI *sep irreg aux sein (inf)* to manage, to get by *(inf)*; **mit etw ~** to be able to cope with sth; **mit jdm ~** to be able to deal *or* cope with sb; **klar+krie|gen** VT *sep (inf)* to sort out; **ein Problem ~** to sort out *or* crack *(inf)* a problem; **Klar|lack** M clear varnish; **klar|lack|be|han|delt** ADJ varnished; **klar+le|gen** VT *sep* to make clear, to explain; **Klar|luft|tur|bu|lenz** F *(Aviat)* clear air turbulence

klar+ma|chen *sep* VT **a** to make clear, to explain; **jdm etw ~** to make sth clear to sb; **sich** *(dat)* **etw ~** to realize sth; **sich** *(dat)* **die Unterschiede ~** to get the differences clear in one's own mind; **sich** *(dat)* **ein Thema ~** to get a subject sorted out in one's mind **b** *Schiff* to make ready, to get ready; *Flugzeug* to clear; VI *(Naut)* to make ready, to get ready; **zum Gefecht ~** to clear the decks for action

klar ma|chen △ VT → **klarmachen VT a**

Klar|na|me M *(von Agent)* real name

Klär|schlamm M sludge

Klar|schrift|le|ser M **(optischer) ~** optical character reader

klar+se|hen *sep irreg*, **klar se|hen** △ *irreg* VI to see clearly; **in etw** *(dat)* **~** to have understood sth

Klar|sicht- *in cpds* transparent; **Klar|sicht|fo|lie** F clear film; **Klar|sicht|hül|le** F clear plastic folder; **Klar|sicht|pa|ckung** F see-through pack; **Klar|sicht|schei|be** F *(Aut)* anti-mist panel

Klar-: **klar+spü|len** VTI *sep* to rinse; **klar+stel|len** VT *sep (= klären)* to clear up, to clarify; *(= klarmachen)* to make clear; **ich möchte ~, dass ...** I would like to make it clear that ...; **Klar|stel|lung** F clarification; **Klar|text** M uncoded text, text in clear; **im ~** in clear; *(fig inf)* in plain English; **wir sollten endlich ~ reden** *(fig inf)* let's not beat about the bush anymore *(inf)*; **mit jdm ~ reden** *(fig inf)* to give sb a piece of one's mind

Klä|rung ['klɛːrʊŋ] F **-, -en** **a** purification **b** *(fig)* clarification

klar wer|den *irreg aux sein*, **klar+wer|den** *sep irreg aux sein* VR **sich** *(dat)* **(über etw** *acc)* **~** to get (sth) clear in one's mind VI **jdm wird etw klar** sth becomes clear to sb; **es muss ~, dass ...** it must be made clear that ...; **ist dir das noch immer nicht klar geworden?** do you still not understand?

klạss [klas] ADJ *(Aus inf)* = **klasse**

klạs|se ['klasə] *(inf)* ADJ great *(inf)*, brilliant; **das finde ich ~** I think that's great *(inf) or* brilliant; **das ist ~!** *(inf)* that's great *or* tremendous *or* marvellous *(Brit) or* marvelous *(US)*! *(all inf)* ADV brilliantly

Klạs|se ['klasə] F **-, -n** **a** class; *(= Steuerklasse auch)* bracket; *(= Wertklasse auch)* rate; *(= Spielklasse)* league; *(= Güteklasse)* grade; *(= Führerscheinklasse, Gewinnklasse)* category; **ein Maler erster ~** a first-class *or* first-rate painter; **ein Fahrschein zweiter ~** a second-class ticket; **das ist große ~!** *(inf)* that's great *or* tremendous *or* marvellous *(Brit) or* marvelous *(US)*! *(all inf)* **b** *(Sch)* class, form; *(= Raum)* classroom

Klạs|se- *in cpds (inf)* top-class; **eine Klassemannschaft** a top-class team; **Petra ist eine Klassefrau** Petra is a great *or* wonderful woman; *(= gut aussehend)* Petra is a gorgeous woman

Klạs|se|frau F *(inf)* **das ist eine ~** she's a wonderful person; *(= eine Schönheit)* she's a real looker, she's quite stunning

Klas|se|ment [klasə'mãː] NT **-s, -s** *(Sport)* (list of) rankings *pl*

Klạs|sen-: **Klạs|sen|äl|tes|te(r)** MF *decl as adj* oldest pupil (in the class); **Klạs|sen|ar|beit** F (written) class test; **Klạs|sen|auf|satz** M essay written in class; **Klạs|sen|aus|flug** M class outing *(esp Brit)*, field trip; **Klạs|sen|bes|te(r)** MF *decl as adj* best pupil (in the class); **wer ist ~(r)?** who is top of the class?; **klạs|sen|be|wusst** ADJ class-conscious; **Klạs|sen|be|wusst|sein** NT class consciousness; **Klạs|sen|bild** NT class photograph; **Klạs|sen|buch** NT (class-)register; **Klạs|sen|buch|füh|rer(in)** M(F) pupil in charge of the class-register; **Klạs|sen|dün|kel** M snobbishness, snobbery; **Klạs|sen|durch|schnitt** M class average; **Klạs|sen|er|halt** M *(Sport)* staying up; **um den ~ kämpfen** to fight to stay up, to fight against relegation; **Klạs|sen|ers|te(r)** MF *decl as adj* = **Klassenbeste(r)**; **Klạs|sen|fahrt** F *(Sch)* class trip; **Klạs|sen|feind(in)** M(F) *(Pol)* class enemy; **Klạs|sen|fo|to** NT class photograph; **Klạs|sen|fre|quenz** F size of a/the class/the classes; **Klạs|sen|ge|gen|satz** M *usu pl (Sociol)* class difference; **Klạs|sen|geist** M *(Sch dated, Sociol)* class spirit; **Klạs|sen|ge|sell|schaft** F class society; **Klạs|sen|hass** M *(Sociol)* class hatred; **Klạs|sen|herr|schaft** F class rule; **Klạs|sen|in|te|res|se** NT *(Sociol)* class interest; **Klạs|sen|jus|tiz** F *(Pol)* legal system with class bias; **Klạs|sen|ka|me|rad(in)** M(F) classmate; **Klạs|sen|kampf** M class struggle; **Klạs|sen|kei|le** F *(Sch dated)* a thrashing from the rest of the class, a thrashing from one's classmates; **Klạs|sen|krieg** M class warfare; **Klạs|sen|la|ge** F *(Sociol)* class position; **Klạs|sen|leh|rer** M, **Klạs|sen|lei|ter** M class teacher, form teacher *or* master *(Brit)*, homeroom teacher *(US Highschool)*; **Klạs|sen|leh|re|rin** F, **Klạs|sen|lei|te|rin** F class teacher, form teacher *or* mistress *(Brit)*; **Klạs|sen|lek|tü|re** F class reading; **klạs|sen|los** ADJ *Gesellschaft* classless; *Krankenhaus* one-class; **Klạs|sen|los** NT *draw ticket in a Klassenlotterie*; **Klạs|sen|lot|te|rie** F *lottery in which draws are made on a number of different days and in which tickets can be bought for each individual draw*; **Klạs|sen|raum** M classroom; **Klạs|sen|schrank** M classroom cupboard; **Klạs|sen|schran|ke** F class barrier; **Klạs|sen|spie|gel** M *(Sch)* seating plan of the class; **Klạs|sen|spre|cher(in)** M(F) *(Sch)* class representative, ≈ form captain *(Brit)*; **Klạs|sen|staat** M *(Pol)* state governed by one class; **Klạs|sen|stär|ke** F *(Sch)* size of a/the class/the classes; **Klạs|sen|tref|fen** NT *(Sch)* class reunion; **Klạs|sen|un|ter|schied** M class difference; **Klạs|sen|ver|band** M **im ~** as a class; **Klạs|sen|vor|stand** M *(esp Aus)* = **Klassenlehrer(in)**; **Klạs|sen|wahl|recht** NT, **Klạs|sen|wahl|sys|tem** NT electoral system based on class, class system of franchise; **klạs|sen|wei|se** ADJ by class; **~r Aufbau** arrangement by class ADV *sitzen, sich aufstellen* in classes; *erscheinen* as a class; **Klạs|sen|ziel** NT *(Sch)* required standard; **das ~ nicht erreichen** not to reach the required standard; *(fig)* not to make the grade; **Klạs|sen|zim|mer** NT classroom

Klạs|se|spiel NT *(inf: Sport)* great *or* brilliant game

Klas|si|fi|ka|ti|on [klasifika'tsioːn] F **-, -en** classification

klas|si|fi|zier|bar ADJ classifiable

klas|si|fi|zie|ren [klasifi'tsiːrən] *ptp* **klassifiziert** VT to classify; **~d** classificatory

Klas|si|fi|zie|rung F -, -en classification

-klas|sig [klasıç] ADJ *suf* -class; **erst-/zweitklassig** first-/second-class

Klas|sik ['klasık] F -, *no pl* classical period; (*inf:* = *klassische Musik, Literatur*) classical music/literature; **die antike ~** Classical Antiquity

Klas|si|ker ['klasikɐ] M -s, -, **Klas|si|ke|rin** [-ərın] F -, -nen classic; **ein ~ des Jazz** a jazz classic; **ein ~ der modernen Musik** a classic of modern music; **die antiken ~** the classics

klas|sisch ['klasıʃ] ADJ **a** (= *die Klassik betreffend, antik, traditionell*) classical **b** (= *typisch, vorbildlich, zeitlos*) classic **c** (*iro inf:* = *prächtig*) classic ADV classically

Klas|si|zis|mus [klasi'tsısmʊs] M -, *no pl* classicism

klas|si|zis|tisch [klasi'tsıstıʃ] ADJ classical

Klass|leh|rer M (*S Ger, Aus*) = **Klassenlehrer**

Klass|leh|re|rin F (*S Ger, Aus*) = **Klassenlehrerin**

-kläss|ler [klɛslɐ] M -s, -, **-kläss|le|rin** [-ərın] F -, -nen *in cpds (Sch)* -former; **Erst-/Zweitklässler(in)** first-/second-former

klatsch [klatʃ] INTERJ splash, splosh; (*bei Schlag, Aufprall*) smack

Klatsch [klatʃ] M -(e)s, -e **a** splosh, splash; (*bei Schlag, Aufprall*) smack **b** *no pl* (*pej inf:* = *Tratsch*) gossip, scandal

Klatsch|ba|se F (*pej inf*) (*tratschend*) scandalmonger, gossip; (*redselig*) chatterbox (*inf*)

Klat|sche ['klatʃə] F -, -n (*inf*) **a** (*pej:* = *Klatschbase*) gossip **b** (*Sch*) (= *Denunziant*) sneak, telltale (*inf*); (= *Hilfsmittel*) crib (*Brit inf*), cheat sheet (*US inf*) **c** (= *Fliegenklappe*) fly swatter

klat|schen ['klatʃn] VI **a** (= *Geräusch machen*) to clap; **in die Hände ~** to clap one's hands **b** (= *einen Klaps geben*) to slap; **jdm auf die Schenkel/sich** (*dat*) **gegen die Stirn ~** to slap sb's thighs/one's forehead **c** *aux sein* (= *aufschlagen*) (*harte Gegenstände*) to go smack; (*Flüssigkeiten*) to splash; **der Regen klatschte gegen die Fenster** the rain beat against the windows **d** (*pej inf*) (= *tratschen*) to gossip; (*dial:* = *petzen*) to sneak, to tell tales (*bei* to); **über jdn/etw ~** to gossip *or* spread gossip about sb/sth VT **a** (= *geräuschvoll schlagen*) to clap; *Takt* to clap out; **jdm Beifall ~** to applaud *or* clap sb; **den Rhythmus ~** (*Mus*) to clap (out) the rhythm; (*mitklatschen*) to clap along **b** (= *knallen*) to smack, to slap; (= *werfen*) to throw; *Fliegen* to swat; (*sl:* = *zusammenschlagen*) to beat up (*inf*), to bash up (*Brit inf*); **jdm eine ~** (*inf*) to give sb a clip round the ear (*inf*)

Klat|schen NT -s, *no pl* **a** (= *Beifallklatschen*) applause **b** (*inf:* = *Tratschen*) gossiping

klat|sche|nass ADJ (*inf*) **klatschnass**

Klat|scher ['klatʃɐ] M -s, -, **Klat|sche|rin** [-ərın] F -, -nen **a** (*pej:* = *Klatschmaul*) gossip **b** (= *Beifallklatscher*) applauder

Klat|sche|rei [klatʃə'rai] F -, -en (*pej inf*) **a** (= *Beifallklatscherei*) clapping **b** (= *Tratscherei*) gossiping, gossipmongering

Klatsch-: **Klatsch|ge|schich|te** F (*pej*) gossip *no pl*; **eine ~** a piece of gossip; **klatsch|haft** ADJ gossipy; **Klatsch|ko|lum|nist(in)** M(F) (*inf*) gossip columnist; **Klatsch|maul** NT (*pej inf*) **a** big mouth **b** (= *Mensch*) gossip (merchant), scandalmonger; **Klatsch|mohn** M (corn) poppy; **klatsch|nass** ADJ (*inf*) sopping wet (*inf*); **Klatsch|spal|te** F (*Press inf*) gossip column; **klatsch|süch|tig** ADJ extremely gossipy; **Klatsch|tan|te** F, **Klatsch|weib** NT (*pej inf*) gossip(monger), scandalmonger

klau|ben ['klaubn] VT **a** (*S Ger, Aus, Sw*) (= *auflesen*) to pick up; (= *auslesen*) to pick out; **etw in einen Korb ~** to pick sth up and put it in a basket; **etw aus etw ~** to pick sth out from sth **b** (*Aus:* = *sammeln*) to collect; *Holz, Pilze, Kräuter* to gather, to collect; *Beeren* to pick **c** (*Sw:* = *kneifen*) to pinch; **Worte ~** (*dial*) to split hairs

Klaue ['klauə] F -, -n claw; (= *Huf*) hoof; (*pej inf*) (= *Hand*) talons *pl* (*pej inf*); (= *Schrift*) scrawl (*pej*); **in den ~n der Verbrecher** *etc* in the clutches of the criminals *etc*; **den ~n des Todes entkommen** to escape from the jaws of death

klau|en ['klauən] (*inf*) VT to nick (*Brit inf*), to pinch (*inf*) (*jdm etw* sth from sb); *Ideen auch* to crib (*jdm etw* sth from sb) VI to steal, to nick (*Brit inf*) *or* pinch things (*inf*)

Klau|en|seu|che F → **Maul- und Klauenseuche**

Klau|se ['klauzə] F -, -n **a** (*von Mönch, Einsiedler*) hermitage; (= *Klosterzelle*) cell; (*fig hum*) den **b** (mountain) defile

Klau|sel ['klauzl] F -, -n clause; (= *Vorbehalt*) proviso; (= *Bedingung*) condition, stipulation

Klaus|ner ['klausnɐ] M -s, -, **Klaus|ne|rin** [-ərın] F hermit

Klaust|ro|pho|bie [klaustrofo'biː] F -, -n [-'biːən] (*Psych*) claustrophobia

klaust|ro|pho|bisch [klaustro'foːbıʃ] ADJ (*Psych*) claustrophobic

klau|su|lie|ren [klauzu'liːrən] *ptp* **klausuliert** VT = **verklausulieren**

Klau|sur [klau'zuːɐ] F -, -en **a** (*Univ auch* **Klausurarbeit**) exam, paper; **~en korrigieren** to mark exam papers **b** *no pl* (= *Abgeschlossenheit*) seclusion; **eine Arbeit unter** *or* **in ~ schreiben** to write an essay under examination conditions **c** (*Eccl:* = *Räume*) enclosure, cloister

Klau|sur|ta|gung F convention, conference

Kla|vi|a|tur [klavia'tuːɐ] F -, -en keyboard

Kla|vi|chord [klavi'kɔrt] NT -(e)s, -e [-də] clavichord

Kla|vier [kla'viːɐ] NT -s, -e piano; **~ spielen** to play the piano

Kla|vier- *in cpds* piano; **Kla|vier|aus|zug** M piano score; **Kla|vier|abend** M piano recital; **Kla|vier|bau|er** M -s, -, **Kla|vier|bau|e|rin** F -, -nen piano-maker; **Kla|vier|be|ar|bei|tung** F piano arrangement; **Kla|vier|be|glei|tung** F piano accompaniment; **Kla|vier|de|ckel** M piano lid; **Kla|vier|ho|cker** M piano stool; **Kla|vier|kon|zert** NT **a** (= *Musik*) piano concerto **b** (= *Vorstellung*) piano recital; **Kla|vier|schu|le** F (= *Lehrbuch*) piano tutor; **Kla|vier|so|na|te** F piano sonata; **Kla|vier|spiel** NT piano playing; **Kla|vier|spie|ler(in)** M(F) pianist, piano player; **Kla|vier|stim|mer(in)** M(F) piano tuner; **Kla|vier|stück** NT piano piece, piece of piano music; **Kla|vier|stun|de** F piano lesson; **~nehmen** to have *or* to take piano lessons

Kle|be-: **Kle|be|band** [-bant] NT *pl* **-bänder** adhesive tape, sticky tape; **Kle|be|bin|dung** F (*Typ*) adhesive binding; **Kle|be|falz** M (gummed) stamp hinge *or* mount; **Kle|be|fo|lie** F = **Klebfolie**; **Kle|be|mit|tel** NT adhesive

kle|ben ['kleːbn] VI **a** (= *festkleben*) to stick; **an etw** (*dat*) **~** (*lit*) to stick to sth; **am Vordermann ~** (*Aut inf*) to tailgate the person in front; **an den Traditionen ~** to cling *or* stick to tradition; **an seinen Händen klebt Blut** (*fig*) he has blood on his hands; **sein schlechter Ruf klebte an ihm** his bad reputation stuck; **klebt nicht so am Text** don't stick so much *or* so close to the text **b** (*inf: für Sozialversicherung*) to pay stamps VT to stick; (*mit Klebstoff auch*) to glue; (*mit Leim auch*) to paste; *Film, Tonband* to splice; **Marken ~** (*Insur inf*) to pay stamps; **jdm eine ~** (*inf*) to belt sb (one) (*inf*)

kle|ben+blei|ben VI *sep irreg aux sein(fig inf)* = **kleben bleiben b, c**

kle|ben blei|ben VI *irreg aux sein* **a** to stick (*an +dat* to) **b** (*Sch inf*) to stay down a year (*Brit*), to repeat a year **c** (*fig inf:* = *nicht wegkommen*) to get stuck

Kle|be-: **Kle|be|pflas|ter** NT sticking plaster (*Brit*), adhesive tape (*US*); **Kle|be|pres|se** F splicer

Kle|ber ['kleːbɐ] M -s, - **a** (*inf:* = *Klebstoff*) glue **b** (*im Mehl*) gluten

Kle|be-: **Kle|be|stel|le** F join; (*an Film*) splice; **Kle|be|stift** M glue stick; **Kle|be|stoff** M adhesive; **Kle|be|strei|fen** M = **Klebstreifen**; **Kle|be|ver|band** M adhesive dressing; **Kle|be|zet|tel** M gummed label

Kleb-: **Kleb|fes|tig|keit** F adhesiveness; **Kleb|flä|che** F surface to be stuck; **Kleb|fo|lie** F adhesive film; (= *d-c-fix®*) Fablon®; (*für Lebensmittel*) clingfilm; **Kleb|kraft** F adhesive strength; **Kleb|mit|tel** NT adhesive

kleb|rig ['kleːbrıç] ADJ sticky; *Farbe* tacky; (*Geld*)*geschäfte* shady; (= *klebfähig*) adhesive

Kleb|rig|keit F -, *no pl* stickiness; (*von Farbe*) tackiness

Kleb-: **Kleb|stoff** M adhesive; **Kleb|strei|fen** M adhesive tape; (*selbstklebend auch*) sticky tape; (*zum Befeuchten*) gummed tape; (*durchscheinend*) Sellotape® (*esp Brit*)

Kle|bung ['kleːbʊŋ] F -, -en bond

Kle|cke|rei [klɛkə'rai] F -, -en mess; **ohne ~ gehts nicht** you can't do it without making a mess

Kle|cker|kram ['klɛkɐ-] M -s, *no pl* (*inf, pej*) dribs and drabs *pl* (*inf*)

kle|ckern ['klɛkɐn] VT to spill; *Farbe auch* to splash VI **a** (= *Kleckse machen*) to make a mess **b** (= *tropfen*) to spill; (*Farbe*) to spill, to splash **c** (*inf:* = *stückchenweise arbeiten*) to fiddle around; **nicht ~, sondern klotzen** (*inf*) to do things in a big way (*inf*), to think big (*inf*); **gekleckert kommen** to come in dribs and drabs

kle|cker|wei|se ['klɛkɐvaizə] ADV in dribs and drabs

Klecks [klɛks] M -es, -e (= *Tintenklecks*) (ink)blot; (= *Farbklecks*) blob; (= *Fleck*) stain

kleck|sen ['klɛksn] VI (*mit Tinte*) to make blots/a blot; (*Kugelschreiber etc auch*) to blot; (*pej inf:* = *malen*) to daub

Kleck|se|rei [klɛksə'rai] F -, -en (*pej inf*) daubing; (*von Schüler, Kugelschreiber*) making blots

Klee [kleː] M -s, *no pl* clover; **jdn/etw über den grünen ~ loben** to praise sb/sth to the skies

Klee|blatt NT cloverleaf; (*Mot*) cloverleaf (intersection); (*fig:* = *Menschen*) threesome, trio; **vierblättriges ~** four-leaf clover; **das irische ~** the (Irish) shamrock

Klei|ber ['klaibɐ] M -s, - (*Orn*) nuthatch

Kleid [klait] NT -(e)s, -er [-dɐ] **a** (= *Damenkleid*) dress; **ein zweiteiliges ~** a two-piece (suit) **b Kleider** PL (= *Kleidung*) clothes *pl*, clothing *sing* (*esp Comm*), garments *pl* (*Comm*); **warme ~er mitbringen** to bring warm clothes *or* clothing; **jdm die ~er vom Leib reißen** to tear sb's clothes off; **~er machen Leute** (*Prov*) fine feathers make fine birds (*Prov*); **ich bin zwei Tage nicht aus den ~ern gekommen** I haven't been to bed for two days **c** (*old:* = *Gewand*) garment; (*old, Sw, S Ger:* = *Herrenanzug*) suit; (*liter:* = *Uniform*) uniform **d** (*liter*) (= *Federkleid*) plumage; (= *Pelz*) coat, fur; (*fig: von Natur, Bäumen etc*) mantle (*liter*), cloak (*liter*); **der Winter hatte der Erde ein weißes ~ angezogen** winter had clad the earth in white (*liter*)

-kleid NT *suf in cpds* **Sommerkleid** summer dress; **Ordenskleid** monastic robe; **Herbstkleid** autumn cloak *or* mantle (*liter*)

Kleid|chen ['klaitçən] NT -s, - *dim von* **Kleid** little dress; (*leicht*) flimsy dress

klei|den ['klaidn] VR to dress; (*geh:* = *Kleider anziehen auch*) to dress oneself, to clothe oneself (*liter, form*); **sie kleidet sich sportlich** she dresses casually; **gut/schlecht gekleidet sein** to be well/badly dressed; **weiß/schwarz gekleidet** dressed in white/black; **die Natur kleidet sich in Weiß** (*liter*) nature dons a cloak *or* mantle of white (*liter*) VT (*geh*) **a** (= *mit Kleidern versehen*) to clothe, to dress; (*fig*) *Gedanken, Ideen* to clothe, to couch; **die Armen ~** to clothe the poor; **etw in schöne Worte ~** to dress sth up *or* to couch sth in fancy words; **ich kann meine Gefühle nicht in Worte ~** I cannot put my feelings into words **b jdn ~** (= *jdm stehen*) to suit sb

Klei|der-: **Klei|der|ab|la|ge** F (= *Raum*) cloakroom; (= *Garderobenablage*) coat rack; (= *Stän-*

der) hat stand, coat stand; **Klei|der|bü|gel** M coat hanger; **Klei|der|bürs|te** F clothes brush; **Klei|der|ha|ken** M coat hook; **Klei|der|kam|mer** F *(Mil etc)* uniform store; **Klei|der|kas|ten** M *(Aus, Sw)* wardrobe *(esp Brit)*, closet *(US)*; **Klei|der|ma|cher(in)** M(F) *(Aus)* tailor; *(= Damenschneiderin auch)* dressmaker; **Klei|der|ord|nung** F dress regulations *pl*; **Klei|der|sack** M suit bag; **Klei|der|schrank** M **a** wardrobe **b** *(inf: Mensch)* great hulk (of a man) *(inf)*

kleid|sam ['klaitza:m] ADJ flattering

Klei|dung ['klaidʊŋ] F -, *no pl* clothes *pl*, clothing *(esp Comm)*; **warme** ~ warm clothing *or* clothes; **für jds (Nahrung und)** ~ **sorgen** to (feed and) clothe sb

Klei|dungs|stück NT garment; ~**e** *pl* clothes *pl*; **ein warmes** ~ **mitnehmen** to bring something warm (to wear)

Kleie ['klaiə] F -, *no pl* bran

klein [klain] ADJ **a** little, small; *Finger* little; *Format, Gehalt, Rente, Zahl, (Hand)schrift, Buchstabe* small; *(Mus) Terz* minor; **die Kleinen Antillen** *etc* the lesser Antilles *etc*; **Klein Paris** little *or* miniature Paris; **der Kleine Bär** *or* **Wagen** the Little Bear, Ursa Minor; **die Kleine Strafkammer** *(Jur)* the lower criminal court; **x ist ~er als 10** *(Math)* x is less than ten; **haben Sie es nicht ~er?** don't you have anything smaller?; **ein ~ bisschen** *or* **wenig** a little (bit); **ein ~ bisschen** *or* **wenig Salat** a little (bit of) salad; **ein ~es Bier, ein Kleines** *(inf)* a small beer, ≈ half a pint *(Brit)*, ≈ a half *(Brit)*; **~es Geld** small change; **Klein Roland** little Roland; **du ~er Teufel!** you little devil!; **ein süßes ~es Püppchen** a sweet little thing; **hallo, ~er Mann!** hello, little man; **ein schönes ~es Auto** a nice little car; **er fährt ein ~es Auto** he drives a small car; **mit seiner ~en Frau** with his little wife; **ich wusste nicht, dass seine Frau so ~ ist** I didn't know his wife was so small *or* little; **eine ~e, hübsche Wohnung** a small, pretty flat *(Brit)* *or* apartment; **eine hübsche ~e Wohnung** a nice little flat *(Brit)* *or* apartment; **mein ~er Bruder** my little brother; **er ist ~er als sein Bruder** he's smaller than his brother; **als ich (noch) ~ war** when I was little; ~ **für sein Alter** small *or* little for his age; **jdn/sich ~ machen** → **kleinmachen**; **macht euch ein bisschen ~er!** squeeze up closer; **den mach ich SO ~ (mit Hut)!** *(hum)* I'll cut him down to size, I'll make him look THAT big; ~ **aber oho** *(inf)* small but impressive; **ganz ~ (und hässlich) werden** *(inf)* to look humiliated *or* deflated; **im Kleinen** in miniature; **bis ins Kleinste** in every possible detail, in minute detail, right down to the smallest detail; **von ~ an** *or* **auf** *(= von Kindheit an)* from his childhood *or* early days; *(= von Anfang an)* from the very beginning, from scratch; **~e Kinder ~e Sorgen, große Kinder große Sorgen** *(prov)* bigger children just mean bigger problems; **um ein Kleines zu ...** *(geh)* a little *or* a trifle too ... → **Finger, Geschenk**

b *(= kurz) Wuchs, Schritt* little, small, short; *Weile, Pause* little, short; *Vortrag* short; **~en Augenblick, bitte!** just one moment, please; **einen Kopf ~er als jd sein** to be a head shorter than sb

c *(= geringfügig)* little, small, slight; *Betrag, Summe* little, small; **beim ~sten Schreck** at the slightest *or* smallest shock; **das ~ere Übel** the lesser evil; **ein paar ~ere Fehler** a few minor mistakes; **eine ~ere Unpässlichkeit** a minor ailment

d *(= unbedeutend)* petty *(pej)*; *Leute* ordinary; **er ist ein ~er Geist** he is small-minded; **der ~e Mann** the ordinary citizen, the man in the street; **ein ~er Ganove** a small-time *or* petty crook; **die Kleinen fängt man** *or* **werden gehängt, die Großen lässt man laufen** *(prov)* it's always the big fish that get away; **sein Vater war (ein) ~er Beamter** his father was a minor civil servant; **~e Leute übersieht man** *(hum)* I'm *etc* so small and insignificant → **Fisch a**

e *(= armselig) Verhältnisse* humble, lowly, modest

f *Prüfung* intermediate

ADV **a** *(= in kleiner Schrift)* small; **er schreibt sehr ~** he writes very small, his writing is very small; **ein Wort ~ drucken** to print a word without a capital; **~ gedruckt** in small print; **~ Gedruckte(s)** = **Kleingedruckte(s)**; **~ gemustert** small-patterned; **~ kariert** *(Stoff)* finely checked *or* chequered *(Brit)* *or* checkered *(US)* → **kleinkariert, kleinschreiben**

b *(auf kleine Hitze)* **etw ~ stellen** *or* **drehen** to put sth on low *or* on a low heat; **etw ~er stellen** *or* **drehen** to turn sth down

c *(in Wendungen)* **~ anfangen** to start off in a small way; **~ beigeben** *(inf)* to give in; **~ geraten sein** *(Gegenstand)* to have come out a little (too) small; *(Mensch)* to be a bit small; **~ gewachsen** short, small; *(Baum)* small; **etw ~ halten** *(Anzahl, Kosten)* to keep sth down; *(Party, Feier)* to keep sth small

-klein NT *suf in cpds* **-s**, *no pl* → **Gänseklein, Hasenklein** *etc*

Klein-: **Klein|ak|ti|o|när(in)** M(F) small shareholder; **Klein|an|le|ger(in)** M(F) *(Fin)* small investor; **Klein|an|zei|ge** F classified advertisement, small ad *(inf)*; **Klein|ar|beit** F detailed work; **in zäher/mühseliger ~** with rigorous/painstaking attention to detail; **Klein|asi|en** NT Asia Minor; **klein|asi|a|tisch** ADJ of *or* from Asia Minor *pred*; **im ~en Raum** in Asia Minor; **Klein|au|to** NT small car; **Klein|bahn** F narrow-gauge railway *(Brit)* *or* railroad *(US)*; **Klein|bau|er** M *pl* **-bauern**, **Klein|bäu|e|rin** F -, **-nen** small farmer, smallholder; **klein+be|kom|men** VT *sep irreg* = **kleinkriegen**; **Klein|be|trieb** M small business; **bäuerlicher ~** smallholding; **handwerklicher ~** (small) workshop; **industrieller ~** small factory; **Klein|bild|ka|me|ra** F 35mm camera; **Klein|buch|sta|be** M small letter, lowercase letter *(Typ)*; **Klein|bür|ger(in)** M(F) petty bourgeois; **klein|bür|ger|lich** ADJ lower middle-class, petty bourgeois *(pej)*; **er reagierte typisch ~** his reaction was typically lower middle-class *or* typically petty bourgeois; **Klein|bür|ger|tum** NT *(Sociol)* lower middle class, petty bourgeoisie; **Klein|bus** M minibus

Klei|ne|leu|te|mil|lieu NT world of ordinary people

Klei|ne(r) ['klainə] MF *decl as adj* **a** little one *or* child; *(= Junge)* little boy; *(= Mädchen)* little girl; *(= Säugling)* baby; **unser ~r** *(= Jüngster)* our youngest (child); **die lieben ~n** *(iro)* the dear *or* sweet little things; **eine hübsche ~** a pretty little girl *or* thing; **die Katze mit ihren ~n** the cat with its kittens *or* babies *(inf)* **b** *(inf: auch* **Kleines**: *= Schatz, Liebling)* baby *(inf)*; **na ~/~r!** *(zu einem Kind)* hello little girl/boy!; **na ~r!** *(Prostituierte zu einem Passanten)* hello, love *(esp Brit)* *or* dear

Klei|ne(s) ['klainə] NT *decl as adj* **etwas ~s** *(inf)* a little baby *or* stranger *(hum)*

Klein-: **Klein|fa|mi|lie** F *(Sociol)* nuclear family; **Klein|for|mat** NT small format; **ein Buch/Bild im ~** a small-format book/picture; **klein|for|ma|tig** ADJ small-format; **Klein|gar|ten** M allotment *(Brit)*, garden plot; **Klein|gärt|ner(in)** M(F) allotment holder *(Brit)*, garden plot holder; **Klein|ge|bäck** NT biscuits *pl* *(Brit)*, cookies *pl* *(US)*; **klein|ge|druckt** ADJ *attr* → **klein ADV a**; **Klein|ge|druck|te(s)** [-gədrʊktə] NT *decl as adj* small print; **Klein|geist** M *(pej)* small-minded person; **klein|geis|tig** ADJ *(pej)* small-minded, petty; **Klein|geis|tig|keit** F *(pej)* small-mindedness, pettiness; **Klein|geld** NT (small) change; **das nötige ~ haben** *(fig)* to have the necessary wherewithal *(inf)*; **klein|ge|mus|tert** ADJ → **klein ADV a**; **klein|ge|wach|sen** ADJ → **klein ADV a**; **klein|gläu|big** ADJ **a** *(Rel)* doubting, sceptical *(Brit)*, skeptical *(US)*; **der ~e Thomas** doubting Thomas; **ihr Kleingläubigen!** *(Bibl)* o ye of little faith **b** *(= zweiflerisch)* timid; **~ sein** to lack conviction; **sei doch nicht so ~!** don't be so timid; **Klein|grup|pe** F *(Sociol)* small group; **klein ha|cken**, **klein+ha|cken** *sep* VT to chop up small; **Klein|häus|ler** [-hɔyslɐ] M **-s**, **-**, **Klein|häus|le|rin** [-ərɪn] F **-**, **-nen** *(Aus)* small farmer; **Klein|heit** F **-**, **-en** smallness, small size; **klein|her|zig** ADJ faint-hearted ADV faintheartedly; *sich verhalten* timidly; **Klein|hirn** NT *(Anat)* cerebellum; **Klein|holz** NT, *no pl* firewood, kindling; **~ aus jdm machen** *(inf)* to make mincemeat out of sb *(inf)*

Klei|nig|keit ['klainɪçkait] F **-**, **-en** **a** little *or* small thing; *(= Bagatelle)* small *or* trifling *or* trivial matter *or* thing, trifle; *(= Einzelheit)* minor detail *or* point, small point; **ich habe noch ein paar ~en in der Stadt zu erledigen** I still have a few little things to attend to in town; **es war nur eine ~ zu reparieren** there was only something minor to be repaired; **die Reparatur/Prüfung war eine ~** the repair job/exam was no trouble at all; **eine ~ essen** to have a bite to eat, to eat a little something; **jdm eine ~ schenken/bezahlen** to give/pay sb a little something; **die ~ von 1.000 Euro** *(iro)* the small matter of 1,000 euros; **das kostet eine ~** *(iro)* that'll cost a pretty penny *(esp Brit)*; **wegen** *or* **bei jeder ~** for the slightest reason; **sich um jede ~ selbst kümmern müssen** to have to take care of every little detail personally; **das war doch (nur) eine ~!** it was nothing; **das ist doch eine ~!** that isn't (asking) much; **das ist für mich keine ~** that is no small matter for me; **wir haben noch ein paar ~en geändert** we've changed one or two details, we've made one or two small changes; **großen Wert auf ~en legen** to be a stickler for detail(s); **bis auf die letzten ~en ist alles fertig** everything is ready apart from the last-minute odds and ends; **sich nicht mit ~en abgeben** *or* **befassen** not to bother over details

b *(= ein bisschen)* **eine ~** a little (bit), a trifle, a shade; **eine ~ zu groß/nach rechts** a little (bit) *etc* too big/to the right; **das wird eine ~ dauern** it will take a little while

Klei|nig|keits-: **Klei|nig|keits|krä|mer(in)** M(F) *(pej)* stickler for detail, pedant; **Klei|nig|keits|krä|me|rei** [-krɛːməˈrai] F **-**, **-en** *(pej)* pernicketiness, pedantry

Klein-: **Klein|ka|li|ber** NT small bore; **Klein|ka|li|ber|ge|wehr** NT small-bore rifle; **klein|ka|lib|rig** [-kaliːbrɪç] ADJ *Waffe* small-bore *attr*; **klein|ka|riert** ADJ *(fig)* tuppenny-ha'penny *attr* *(Brit inf)*, small-time *(inf)*; **~ sein** *(fig)* to be small-minded *or* petty-minded ADV *reagieren* narrow-mindedly; **~ denken** to think small; **~ handeln, sich ~ verhalten** to be narrow-minded → *auch* **klein ADV a**; **Klein|ka|riert|heit** F **-**, *no pl (fig)* small-mindedness, petty-mindedness; **Klein|kind** NT small child, toddler *(inf)*, infant *(Psych)*; **Klein|kind|schwim|men** NT toddler swimming; **Klein|kli|ma** NT *(Met)* microclimate; **Klein|kram** M *(inf)* odds and ends *pl*; *(= kleinere Arbeiten)* odd jobs *pl*; *(= Trivialitäten)* trivialities *pl*, trivia *pl*; **Klein|krä|mer(in)** M(F) *(pej)* small-minded person; **klein|krä|me|risch** ADJ *Person* small-minded; *Vorbehalte* petty, trivial; **Klein|kre|dit** M personal loan; **Klein|krieg** M *(fig)* battle; **einen ~ mit jdm führen** to be fighting a running battle with sb

klein+krie|gen VT *sep* **a** *(lit) Holz* to chop (up); *Nuss* to break; **er kann das Fleisch mit dem Messer nicht ~** he can't cut up the meat with his knife

b *(inf: = kaputt machen)* to smash, to break

c *(inf) (= gefügig machen)* to bring into line *(inf)*; *(= unterkriegen, müde machen)* to get down; *(körperlich)* to tire out; **er ist einfach nicht kleinzukriegen** he just won't be beaten; **unser altes Auto ist einfach nicht kleinzukriegen** our old car just goes on for ever; **er ließ sich auch trotz erpresserischer Drohungen nicht ~** in spite being blackmailed he was not to be intimidated

d *(inf) Geld* to blow *(inf)*, to get through

Klein|kri|mi|nel|le(r) MF *decl as adj* petty criminal
Klein|kunst F cabaret
Klein|kunst|büh|ne F cabaret
Klein|las|ter M pickup truck
klein|laut ADJ abashed, subdued, meek; **dann wurde er ganz ~** it took the wind out of his sails, that made him shut up ADV *fragen* meekly; **etw ~ zugeben** to admit sth shamefacedly; **~ um Verzeihung bitten** to apologize rather sheepishly
klein|lich ['klainlıç] ADJ petty; *(= knauserig)* mean *(esp Brit)*, stingy *(inf)*; *(= engstirnig)* narrow-minded ADV *(= knauserig)* stingily; *(= engstirnig)* narrow-mindedly
Klein|lich|keit F -, -en pettiness; *(= Knauserigkeit)* meanness *(esp Brit)*, stinginess *(inf)*; *(= Engstirnigkeit)* narrow-mindedness
klein+ma|chen *sep*, **klein ma|chen** △ VT **a** *(inf) Geld (= wechseln)* to change; *(= ausgeben)* to blow *(inf)* **b** *(inf: = erniedrigen)* **jdn ~** to make sb look small; **jdn klein- und hässlichmachen** *(inf)* to make sb feel small → *auch* **klein ADJ a c** = **klein machen** VR *(= sich bücken)* to bend down low; *(= sich zusammenrollen)* to curl up tight; **um durch die enge Tür zu kommen, muss man sich ~** to get through this narrow door you have to squeeze yourself in
klein ma|chen VT *(= zerkleinern)* to chop up, to cut up
Klein-: **Klein|mö|bel** PL smaller items *pl* of furniture; **Klein|mut** M faintheartedness, timidity; **klein|mü|tig** [-myːtıç] ADJ fainthearted, timid ADV timidly
Klein|od ['klainloːt] NT **-(e)s, -ien** *or* **-e** [-'loːdiən, -də] *(lit, fig)* jewel, gem; **sie war sein ~** *(liter)* she was his treasure *or* his pride and joy
Klein-: **klein|räu|mig** ADJ *Gebiet, Wohnung* small; **Klein|rent|ner(in)** M(F) *person living on small pension*; **klein schnei|den** *irreg*, **klein+schnei|den** *sep irreg* VT to cut up small, to cut up into small pieces; **klein+schrei|ben** VT *sep irreg* **a** *(mit kleinem Anfangsbuchstaben)* to write without a capital; **ein Wort ~** to write a word without a capital **b** *(fig)* to set little store by; **kleingeschrieben werden** to count for (very) little; **klein schrei|ben** △ VT *irreg* → **kleinschreiben b**; **Klein|schrei|bung** F use of small initial letters; *(Typ, Comput)* lowercase; **Klein|spa|rer(in)** M(F) small saver; **Klein|staat** M small state; **Klein|stadt** F small town; **Klein|städ|ter(in)** M(F) small-town dweller, provincial *(pej)*; **klein|städ|tisch** ADJ provincial *(pej)*, small-town *attr*
Kleinstbetrag ['klainst-] M small sum; *(bei Wetten)* minimum stake; **Kleinstbeträge unter EUR 1 sind unzulässig** sums below the minimum of 1 euro are not acceptable
kleins|te(r, s) ['klainstə] *superl von* **klein**
Kleinst-: **Kleinst|for|mat** NT **ein Radio im ~** a tiny *or* miniature radio; **kleinst|mög|lich** ADJ smallest possible; **Kleinst|wa|gen** M *(Aut)* minicar; **Kleinst|woh|nung** F one-room flatlet *(Brit) or* apartment
Klein-: **klein|tei|lig** ADJ *Struktur* divided into small sections; **~es Denken** excessive concern with small details ADV **ein ~ angelegter Park** a park laid out in small sections; **~ denken** to be excessively concerned with small details; **Klein|tier** NT small animal; **Klein|tier|hal|tung** F keeping of small livestock; **Klein|tier|pra|xis** F small animal (veterinary) practice; **Klein|trans|por|ter** M *(Aut)* pickup (truck); **Klein|vieh** NT **~ macht auch Mist** *(prov)* many a mickle makes a muckle *(Scot)*, every little helps; **Klein|wa|gen** M small car; **klein|weis** ['klainvais] ADV *(Aus)* gradually; **Klein|wild** NT small game; **Klein|woh|nung** F flatlet *(Brit)*, small apartment; **klein|wüch|sig** [-vyːksıç] ADJ *(geh)* small; *Volk auch* small in stature; **Klein|wüch|sig|keit** F *(Med)* restricted growth; **Klein|zeug** NT, *no pl (inf)* small odds and ends *pl*
Kleis|ter ['klaistɐ] M **-s, -** *(= Klebstoff)* paste; *(pej: dicke Speise)* goo *(inf)*
kleis|te|rig ['klaistərıç] ADJ *(pej inf)* gooey *(inf)*
kleis|tern ['klaistɐn] VT **a** *(= zusammenkleben)* to paste **b** *(dated inf)* **jdm eine ~** to slap sb in the face, to slap sb's face
kleist|rig ['klaistrıç] ADJ *(pej inf)* gooey *(inf)*
Kle|ma|tis [kle'maːtıs, 'kleːmatıs] F -, - *(Bot)* clematis
Kle|men|ti|ne [klemen'tiːnə] F -, -n clementine
Klemmappe △ F → **Klemmmappe**
Klemm|brett NT clipboard
Klem|me ['klɛmə] F -, -n **a** *(= Haarklemme, für Papiere etc)* clip; *(Elec)* crocodile clamp *or* clip; *(Med)* clamp **b** *(fig inf)* **in der ~ sitzen** *or* **sein** to be in a fix *or* tight spot *or* jam *(all inf)*; **jdm aus der ~ helfen** to help sb out of a fix *or* tight spot *or* jam *(all inf)*
klem|men ['klɛmən] VT *Draht etc* to clamp, to clip; *(in Spalt)* to stick, to wedge, to jam; **sich** *(dat)* **den Finger in etw** *(dat)* **~** to catch *or* trap one's finger in sth; **sich** *(dat)* **etw unter den Arm ~** to stick *or* tuck sth under one's arm; **sich** *(dat)* **eine Zigarette zwischen die Lippen ~** *(inf)* to stick a cigarette in one's mouth VR to catch oneself *(in +dat* in); **sich hinter etw** *(acc)* **~** *(inf)* to get stuck into sth *(inf)*; **sich hinter jdn ~** *(inf)* to get on to sb VI *(Tür, Schloss etc)* to stick, to jam
Klem|mer ['klɛmɐ] M **-s, -** pince-nez
Klemm-: **Klemm|lam|pe** F clamp-on lamp; **Klemm|map|pe** F spring folder *or* binder
Klemp|ner ['klɛmpnɐ] M **-s, -**, **Klemp|ne|rin** [-ərın] F -, -nen plumber
Klemp|ne|rei [klɛmpnə'rai] F -, -en **a** *no pl* plumbing **b** *(= Werkstatt)* plumber's workshop
Klemp|ner|la|den M plumber's (shop); **der General trägt** *or* **hat einen ganzen ~ auf der Brust** *(hum)* the general has a whole load of ironmongery on his breast *(Brit hum inf)*, the general is covered in medals
klemp|nern ['klɛmpnɐn] VI to do plumbing
Kle|o|pat|ra [kle'oːpatra] F -s Cleopatra
Klep|per ['klɛpɐ] M **-s, -** nag, hack
Klep|per-®: **Klep|per|boot** NT faltboat, foldboat, folding boat; **Klep|per|man|tel** M mackintosh *(Brit)*, mac *(Brit inf)*, trench coat
Klep|to|ma|ne [klɛpto'maːnə] M -n, -n, **Klep|to|ma|nin** [-'maːnın] F -, -nen kleptomaniac
Klep|to|ma|nie [klɛptoma'niː] F -, *no pl* kleptomania
kle|ri|kal [kleri'kaːl] ADJ *(pej)* clerical ADV *gesinnt, eingestellt* clerically
Kle|ri|ka|lis|mus [klerika'lısmʊs] M -, *no pl (pej)* clericalism
Kle|ri|ker ['kleːrikɐ] M **-s, -**, **Kle|ri|ke|rin** [-ərın] F -, -nen cleric
Kle|rus ['kleːrʊs] M -, *no pl* clergy
Klett|band ['klɛtbant] NT *pl* **-bänder** Velcro® (strip)
Klet|te ['klɛtə] F -, -n *(Bot)* burdock; *(= Blütenkopf)* bur(r); *(pej: = lästiger Mensch)* nuisance, bind *(inf)*; **sich wie eine ~ an jdn hängen** to cling to sb like a bur *or* like a limpet *or* barnacle *(Brit)*; **wie die ~n zusammenhalten** to stick together
Klet|ter-: **Klet|ter|af|fe** M *(inf)* **er ist ein richtiger ~** he can climb like a monkey; **Klet|ter|baum** M climbing tree
Klet|te|rer ['klɛtərɐ] M **-s, -**, **Klet|te|rin** [-ərın] F -, -nen climber
Klet|ter|ge|rüst NT climbing frame
Klet|ter|max ['klɛtɐmaks] M **-es, -e**, **Klet|ter|ma|xe** [-maksə] M **-n, -n** *(inf)* steeplejack
klet|tern ['klɛtɐn] VI *aux sein* to climb; *(mühsam)* to clamber; **auf Bäume ~** to climb trees
Klet|ter-: **Klet|ter|par|tie** F climbing trip *or* outing; **Klet|ter|pflan|ze** F climbing plant, climber; **Klet|ter|ro|se** F climbing rose; **Klet|ter|stan|ge** F climbing pole; **Klet|ter|tour** F climbing trip
Klett|ver|schluss® ['klɛt-] M ≈ Velcro® fastener
Klet|ze ['klɛtsə] F -, -n *(S Ger, Aus)* dried pear
Klet|zen|brot NT *(S Ger, Aus)* fruit bread
Klick [klık] M **-s, -s** *(Comput)* click
kli|cken ['klıkn] VI to click; **mit der Maus auf etw** *(acc)* **~** *(Comput)* to click (on) sth with the mouse
Kli|cker ['klıkɐ] M **-s, -** marble; *(= Spiel)* marbles *sing*
kli|ckern ['klıkɐn] VI to play marbles
Kli|ent [kli'ɛnt] M **-en, -en**, **Kli|en|tin** [-'ɛntın] F -, -nen client
Kli|en|tel [kliɛn'teːl] F -, -en clients *pl*, clientele
klie|ren ['kliːrən] VI *(dial)* to scrawl
Kliff [klıf] NT **-(e)s, -e** cliff
Kliff|küs|te F cliffs *pl*
Kli|ma ['kliːma] NT **-s, -s** *or* **Klimate** [kli'maːtə] *(lit, fig)* climate; *(fig auch)* atmosphere
Kli|ma-: **Kli|ma|än|de|rung** F climatic change; **Kli|ma|an|la|ge** F air conditioning (system); **mit ~** air-conditioned; **Kli|ma|for|scher(in)** M(F) climatologist; **Kli|ma|gip|fel** M *(inf)* climate conference *or* summit; **Kli|ma|kam|mer** F climatic chamber; **Kli|ma|ka|ta|stro|phe** F climatic disaster; **Kli|ma|kol|laps** M climatic breakdown
Kli|mak|te|ri|um [klimak'teːriʊm] NT **-s**, *no pl* climacteric, menopause
Kli|ma-: **Kli|ma|kun|de** F climatology; **Kli|ma|schwan|kung** F climatic variation
kli|ma|tisch [kli'maːtıʃ] ADJ *no pred* climatic ADV **~ günstige Verhältnisse** a favourable *(Brit) or* favorable *(US)* climate; **ein ~ ungünstiger Ort** a location with an unfavourable *(Brit) or* unfavorable *(US)* climate; **eine ~ angenehme Gegend** an area with a pleasant climate; **~ bedingt sein** *(Wachstum)* to be dependent on the climate; *(Krankheit)* to be caused by climatic conditions
kli|ma|ti|sie|ren [klimati'ziːrən] *ptp* **klimatisiert** VT to air-condition
Kli|ma|to|lo|gie [klimatolo'giː] F -, *no pl* climatology
Kli|ma|ver|än|de|rung F, **Kli|ma|wech|sel** M *(lit, fig)* climate change, change in (the) climate
Kli|max ['kliːmaks] F -, *(rare)* **-e** *(geh: = Höhepunkt)* climax
Kli|ma|zo|ne F (climatic) zone
Klim|bim [klım'bım] M **-s**, *no pl (inf)* odds and ends *pl*; *(= Umstände)* fuss (and bother)
klim|men ['klımən] *pret* **klomm** *or* **klimmte** [klɔm, 'klımtə], *ptp* **geklommen** *or* **geklimmt** [gə'klɔmən, gə'klımt] VI *aux sein (geh)* to clamber, to scramble
Klimm|zug M *(Sport)* pull-up; **geistige Klimmzüge machen** *(fig)* to do intellectual *or* mental acrobatics
Klim|pe|rei [klımpə'rai] F -, -en *(inf)* tinkling; *(stümperhaft)* plonking *(inf)*; *(auf Banjo etc)* twanging
Klim|per|kas|ten M *(inf)* piano, joanna *(inf)*
klim|pern ['klımpɐn] VI to tinkle; *(= stümperhaft klimpern)* to plonk away *(inf)*; *(auf Banjo)* to twang; **mit Geld ~** to jingle coins; **mit den Wimpern ~** *(inf)* to flutter one's eyelashes
kling [klıŋ] INTERJ clink, ting, ding; **~ machen** *(Metall, Glas etc)* to clink; **mit Kling und Klang** *(old)* to the sound of music
Klin|ge ['klıŋə] F -, -n blade; *(liter: = Schwert)* sword, blade *(liter)*; **eine gute ~ schlagen** *(Fechten)* to be a good swordsman; **mit blanker ~** *(liter)* with drawn sword; **er führt eine scharfe ~** *(fig)* he is a dangerous opponent; **mit jdm die ~(n) kreuzen** *(lit, fig)* to cross swords with sb; **jdn über die ~ springen lassen** *(inf) (= umbringen)* to bump sb off *(inf)*, to rub sb out *(inf)*; *(= opfern)* to leave sb to be killed
Klin|gel ['klıŋl] F -, -n bell
Klin|gel-: **Klin|gel|an|la|ge** F bell system; **Klin|gel|beu|tel** M collection bag; **Klin|gel|draht** M bell wire
klin|ge|ling [klıŋə'lıŋ] INTERJ ding-a-ling

Klin|gel|knopf M bell button *or* push

klin|geln ['klɪŋln] VI to ring (*nach* for); *(Motor)* to pink, to knock; **es hat schon zum ersten/zweiten/dritten Mal geklingelt** *(in Konzert, Theater)* the three-/two-/one-minute bell has already gone; **es hat schon geklingelt** *(in Schule)* the bell has already gone; **es hat geklingelt** *(Telefon)* the phone just rang; *(an Tür)* somebody just rang the doorbell; **es klingelt an der Tür** *(als Bühnenanweisung)* there is a ring at the door; **hat es jetzt endlich (bei dir) geklingelt?** *(fig inf)* has the penny finally dropped? *(inf)*; **Klingeln** ringing

Klin|gel-: **Klin|gel|schnur** F bell pull; **Klin|gel|zei|chen** NT ring; *(auf Handy auch)* ring tone; *(bei Anruf)* ring-up; **auf ein ~ hin** at the ring of a bell; **auf ein besonderes ~ hin** in response to a special ring; **Klin|gel|zug** M bell pull

klin|gen ['klɪŋən] ✪ 38 *pret* **klang**, [klaŋ] *ptp* **geklungen** VI [gə'klʊŋən] to sound; *(Glocke, Ohr)* to ring; *(Glas)* to clink; *(Metall)* to clang; **nach etw ~** to sound like sth; **mein linkes Ohr klingt** I have a ringing (sound) in my left ear; **das klingt mir wie Musik in den Ohren** that is music to my ears; **die Gläser ~ lassen** to clink glasses; **die Glocke klingt dumpf/hell** the bell has a dull/clear ring → **Münze**

klin|gend ADJ **mit ~em Spiel** *(old Mil)* with fife and drum; **in** *or* **mit ~er Münze** *(old, liter)* in coin of the realm; **~e Register** *(Mus)* (sounding) stops *pl*; **~er Reim** *(Poet)* feminine rhyme

Kli|nik ['kli:nɪk] F -, -en clinic; *(= Universitätsklinik)* (university) hospital

Kli|ni|ka, **Kli|ni|ken** *pl von* **Klinikum**

Kli|ni|ker ['kli:nikɐ] M -s, -, **Kli|ni|ke|rin** [-ərɪn] F -, -nen *(Med)* clinician; *(Univ)* medical student attached to a hospital

Kli|ni|kum ['kli:nikʊm] NT -s, **Klinika** *or* **Kliniken** [-ka, -kn] *(Univ)* **a** medical centre *(Brit) or* center *(US)* **b** *(= Ausbildung)* internship

kli|nisch ['kli:nɪʃ] ADJ clinical; **~er Blick** cold glance ADV clinically; **~ tot** clinically dead

Klin|ke ['klɪŋkə] F -, -n *(= Türklinke)* (door) handle; *(= Sperrklinke)* catch, ratchet, pawl; *(Telec)* jack; **~n putzen** *(inf)* to go *or* canvass from door to door, to go *or* do door-to-door canvassing; *(um Ware zu verkaufen)* to sell from door to door, to go *or* do door-to-door selling; **die Interessenten geben sich** *(dat)* **die ~ in die Hand** there's a constant stream of interested parties

Klin|ken|put|zer [-pʊtsɐ] M -s, -, **Klin|ken|put|ze|rin** [-ərɪn] F -, -nen *(inf) (= Hausierer)* hawker; *(= Vertreter)* door-to-door salesman/saleswoman; *(= Wahlkandidat)* door-to-door canvasser; *(= Bettler)* beggar

Klin|ker ['klɪŋkɐ] M -s, - **a** *(= Ziegelstein)* clinker brick, (Dutch) clinker **b** *(Naut)* clinker

Klin|ker-: **Klin|ker|bau** M *pl* **-bauten** clinker building; **Klin|ker|boot** NT clinker(-built) boat; **Klin|ker|stein** M clinker brick, (Dutch) clinker

Kli|no|mo|bil [klinomo'bi:l] NT -s, -e mobile clinic

klipp [klɪp] INTERJ **~, klapp** click, clack; *(Schuhe, Hufe)* clip, clop ADV **~ und klar** clearly, plainly; *(= offen)* frankly, openly

Klipp [klɪp] M -s, -s clip

Klip|pe ['klɪpə] F -, -n *(= Felsklippe)* cliff; *(im Meer)* rock; *(fig)* hurdle, obstacle; **~n umschiffen** *(lit, fig)* to negotiate obstacles

Klip|pen-: **Klip|pen|küs|te** F rocky coast; **klip|pen|reich** ADJ rocky

Klipp-: **Klipp|fisch** M dried, salted cod; **Klipp|schu|le** F *(pej)* second-rate school

Klips [klɪps] M -es, -e = **Clip**

klir|ren ['klɪrən] VI to clink; *(Glas auch)* to tinkle; *(Fensterscheiben)* to rattle; *(Waffen)* to clash; *(Ketten, Sporen)* to jangle; *(Lautsprecher, Mikrofon)* to crackle; *(Eis)* to crunch; **~de Kälte** crisp cold; **~der Frost** sharp frost; **~de Töne** tinny sounds

Klirr|fak|tor M distortion (factor)

Kli|schee [kli'ʃe:] NT -s, -s *(Typ)* plate, block; *(fig: = Ausdruck, Phrase)* cliché

Kli|schee-: **Kli|schee|an|stalt** F *(Typ)* plate-maker's; **kli|schee|haft** ADJ *(fig)* stereotyped, hackneyed ADV stereotypically; **Kli|schee|vor|stel|lung** F cliché, stereotype

kli|schie|ren [kli'ʃi:rən] *ptp* **klischiert** VT *(Typ)* to make plates for, to stereotype

Klis|tier [klɪs'ti:ɐ] NT -s, -e enema, clyster *(spec)*

Klis|tier|sprit|ze F enema (syringe)

Kli|to|ris ['kli:torɪs] F -, - *or* **Klitorides** [kli'to:ride:s] clitoris

Klitsch [klɪtʃ] M -(e)s, -e *(dial)* **a** *(= Schlag)* slap, smack **b** *(= Brei)* doughy *or* soggy mass

klitsch [klɪtʃ] INTERJ **~, klatsch** slip, slop

Klit|sche ['klɪtʃə] F -, -n *(pej inf)* dilapidated building; *(Theat)* small-time theatre *(Brit) or* theater *(US)*; *(= Kleinbetrieb)* tiny outfit *(inf)*

klit|schig ['klɪtʃɪç] ADJ *(dial)* doughy, soggy

klitsch|nass ADJ *(inf)* drenched, soaking *or* sopping *(inf)* wet

klit|tern ['klɪtɐn] VT *Geschichte* to concoct

Klit|te|rung F -, -en → **Geschichtsklitterung**

klit|ze|klein ['klɪtsə'klain] ADJ *(inf)* tiny, teeny-weeny *(inf)* ADV *schneiden, schreiben, kopieren* very small

Kli|vie ['kli:viə] F -, -n *(Bot)* clivia

Klo [klo:] NT -s, -s *(inf)* loo *(Brit inf)*, john *(US inf)*; **aufs ~ gehen** to go to the loo *(Brit inf) or* john *(US inf)*

Klo|a|ke [klo'a:kə] F -, -n sewer; *(fig auch)* cesspool; *(Zool)* cloaca

Klo|a|ken-: **Klo|a|ken|jour|na|lis|mus** M gutter journalism; **Klo|a|ken|tie|re** PL the monotremes *pl (form)*

Klo|ben ['klo:bn] M -s, - **a** *(= Holzklotz)* log **b** *(= Eisenhaken)* hook

klo|big ['klo:bɪç] ADJ hefty *(inf)*, bulky; *Mensch* hulking great *(inf)*; *Schuhe* clumpy; *Benehmen* boorish; *Hände* massive, hefty *(inf)* ADV *aussehen* bulky; *bauen, sich abheben* massively; **~ wirken** *(Gebäude)* to look big and clumsy; *(Schuhe)* to seem clumpy

Klo-: **Klo|bril|le** F *(inf)* toilet *or* loo *(Brit inf)* seat; **Klo|bürs|te** F *(inf)* toilet *or* loo *(Brit inf)* brush; **Klo|frau** F, **Klo|mann** M *pl* **-männer** *(inf)* toilet *or* loo *(Brit inf)* attendant

klomm *pret von* **klimmen**

Klon [klo:n] M -s, -e clone

klo|nen ['klo:nən] VTI to clone

Klo|nen NT -s, *no pl* cloning; **das ~ von Menschen** human cloning; **therapeutisches ~** therapeutic cloning

klö|nen ['klø:nən] VI *(inf)* to (have a) natter *(Brit inf) or* chat

Klon|schaf NT cloned sheep

Klön|schnack M *(N Ger inf)* natter *(Brit inf)*, chat

Klon|ver|bot NT cloning ban, ban on cloning

Klo|pa|pier NT *(inf)* toilet *or* loo *(Brit inf)* paper

Klöp|fel ['klœpfl] M -s, - **a** *(= Holzhammer)* square mallet; *(= Steinmetzwerkzeug)* stonemason's maul **b** *(old: = Glockenklöpfel)* tongue, clapper

klop|fen ['klɔpfn] VT to knock; *Fleisch, Teppich* to beat; *Steine* to knock down; **den Takt ~** to beat time
VI to knock; *(leicht auch)* to tap; *(Herz)* to beat; *(vor Aufregung, Anstrengung)* to pound; *(Puls, Schläfe)* to throb; *(Specht)* to tap, to hammer; *(Motor)* to knock, to pink; *(beim Kartenspiel)* to pass; **klopf doch noch mal!** give another knock, knock again; **sie klopften wiederholt heftig an die Tür** they kept pounding away at the door; **der Winter klopft an die Tür** winter is approaching; **es klopft** *(Theat)* there is a knock at the door; **es hat geklopft** there's someone knocking at the door; **„bitte laut ~"** "please knock loudly"; **jdm auf die Schulter ~** to tap sb on the shoulder; **jdm auf den Rücken/den Hintern ~** to pat sb on the back/the bottom; **jdm auf die Finger ~** *(lit, fig)* to give sb a rap on the knuckles, to rap sb on the knuckles; **mit ~dem Herzen** with beating *or* pounding heart; **ein ~der Schmerz** a throbbing pain → **Busch**

Klop|fen ['klɔpfn] M -s, *no pl* knock(ing); *(leise)* tap(ping); *(von Motor)* knock(ing)

Klop|fer ['klɔpfɐ] M -s, - *(= Türklopfer)* (door) knocker; *(= Fleischklopfer)* (meat) mallet; *(= Teppichklopfer)* carpet beater

Klopf-: **klopf|fest** ADJ antiknock; **Klopf|fes|tig|keit** F antiknock quality; **Klopf|zei|chen** NT knock

Klop|pe ['klɔpə] PL *(dial inf)* **~ kriegen** to be given a hiding *or* thrashing

Klöp|pel ['klœpl] M -s, - *(= Glockenklöppel)* tongue, clapper; *(= Spitzenklöppel)* bobbin; *(= Trommelklöppel)* stick

Klöp|pel|ar|beit F pillow lace

Klöp|pe|lei [klœpə'lai] F -, -en (pillow) lace making

klöp|peln ['klœpln] VI to make (pillow) lace; **eine Tischdecke ~** to make a lace tablecloth

Klöp|pel|spit|ze F pillow lace

klop|pen ['klɔpn] *(N Ger inf)* VT to hit → **Griff, Skat** VR to fight, to scrap *(inf)*, to brawl

Klop|pe|rei [klɔpə'rai] F -, -en *(N Ger inf)* fight, brawl

Klöpp|ler ['klœplɐ] M -s, -, **Klöpp|le|rin** [-ərɪn] F -, -nen (pillow) lace maker

Klops [klɔps] M -es, -e *(Cook)* meatball; *(dated inf: = schwerer Fehler)* howler *(inf)*, clanger *(Brit inf)*

Klo|schüs|sel F *(inf)* loo *(Brit inf) or* toilet bowl, lavatory pan *(Brit)*

Klo|sett [klo'zɛt] NT -s, -e *or* -s lavatory, toilet

Klo|sett-: **Klo|sett|be|cken** NT lavatory *(esp Brit) or* toilet bowl, lavatory pan *(Brit)*; **Klo|sett|bril|le** F toilet seat; **Klo|sett|bürs|te** F lavatory *(esp Brit) or* toilet brush; **Klo|sett|de|ckel** M lavatory *(esp Brit) or* toilet seat lid; **Klo|sett|frau** F, **Klo|sett|mann** M *pl* **-männer** lavatory *(esp Brit) or* toilet attendant; **Klo|sett|pa|pier** NT lavatory *(esp Brit) or* toilet paper

Kloß [klo:s] M -es, ⸚e ['klø:sə] dumpling; *(= Fleischkloß)* meatball; *(= Bulette)* rissole; **einen ~ im Hals haben** *(fig)* to have a lump in one's throat

Kloß|brü|he F **klar wie ~** *(inf) (= völlig klar)* as clear as day; *(iro: = unklar)* as clear as mud

Klos|ter ['klo:stɐ] NT -s, ⸚ ['klø:stɐ] cloister; *(= Mönchskloster auch)* monastery; *(= Nonnenkloster auch)* convent, nunnery *(old)*; **ins ~ gehen** to enter a monastery/convent, to become a monk/nun

Klos|ter-: **Klos|ter|bru|der** M *(old)* monk; **Klos|ter|frau** F *(old)* nun; **Klos|ter|kir|che** F monastery/convent church; **Klos|ter|le|ben** NT monastic/convent life

klös|ter|lich ['klø:stɐlɪç] ADJ *Leben* monastic/convent; *Stille, Abgeschiedenheit* cloistered

Klos|ter|schu|le F monastic/convent school

Klos|ter|schwes|ter F *(old)* nun

Klö|ten ['klø:tn] PL *(sl)* balls *pl (sl)*

Klotz [klɔts] M -es, ⸚e *or (inf)* ⸚er ['klœtsə] *(= Holzklotz)* block (of wood); *(pej: = Betonklotz)* concrete block *or* monstrosity; *(inf: = Person)* great lump *(inf) or* clod *(inf)*; **sich** *(dat)* **einen ~ ans Bein binden** *(inf)* to tie a millstone around one's neck; **jdm ein ~ am Bein sein** to be a hindrance to sb, to be a millstone around sb's neck; **schlafen wie ein ~** *(inf)* to sleep like a log; **auf die Klötzer treten** *(Aut inf)* to slam on the brakes

Klötz|chen ['klœtsçən] NT -s, - (building) block; **etw aus ~ bauen** to build sth with blocks

klot|zen ['klɔtsn] VT *(inf)* **Hochhäuser in die Stadt ~** to throw up skyscrapers in the town VI *(sl) (= hart arbeiten)* to slog (away) *(inf)* → **kleckern**

klot|zig ['klɔtsɪç] *(inf)* ADJ huge, massive ADV **a** *werben* like crazy *(inf)*; **~ verdienen/absah-**

nen to rake it in *(inf)* **b** *(= klobig)* massively; **~ wirken** to seem bulky

Klub [klʊb] **M -s, -s a** club **b** *(Aus: = Parlamentsfraktion)* (parliamentary) party

Klub-: **Klub|abend** M club night; **Klub|gar|ni|tur** F club-style (three-piece) suite; **Klub|haus** NT clubhouse; **Klub|ja|cke** F blazer; **Klub|le|ben** NT club life; **Klub|lo|kal** NT club bar; **Klub|ob|frau** F **-, -en** *(Aus)* (parliamentary) party leader, floor leader *(US)*; **Klub|ob|mann** M *(Aus)* (parliamentary) party leader, floor leader *(US)*; **Klub|ses|sel** M club chair; **Klub|ur|laub** M club holiday

klu|ckern [ˈklʊken] VI = **gluckern**

Kluft [klʊft] **F -, ⸚e** [ˈklʏftə] **a** *(= Erdspalte)* cleft; *(zwischen Felsenrändern)* ravine; *(in Bergen)* crevasse; *(= Abgrund)* chasm **b** *(fig)* gulf, gap; **in der Partei tat sich eine tiefe ~ auf** a deep rift opened up in the party **c** *no pl (= Uniform, Kleidung)* uniform; *(inf: = Kleidung)* gear *(inf)*, garb *(hum)*; **sich in seine gute** *or* **beste ~ werfen** *(inf)* to put on one's Sunday best *or* to put on one's glad rags *(hum)*

klug [kluːk] ADJ *comp* **⸚er** [ˈklyːgɐ], *superl* **⸚ste(r, s)** [ˈklyːkstə] clever, intelligent; *Augen* intelligent; *Humor* witty, sophisticated; *(= vernünftig) Entscheidung, Rat* wise, sound; *Überlegung* prudent; *(= geschickt) Antwort, Analyse, Geschäftsmann* shrewd, clever; **es wird am klügsten sein, wenn …** it would be most sensible if …, it would be the best idea if …; **es wäre politisch/geschäftlich ~ …** it would make good political/business sense …; **ein ~er Philosoph** an astute philosopher; **ein ~er Kopf** a capable person; **ein ~er Kopf, der Kleine** he's a bright boy; **in ~er Voraussicht** with shrewd foresight; **ich werde daraus nicht ~, da soll einer draus ~ werden** I cannot make head or tail *(Brit)* or heads or tails *(US)* of it, I can't make it out; **aus ihm werde ich nicht ~** I don't know what to make of him, I can't make him out; **im Nachhinein ist man immer klüger** one learns by experience; **~e Reden halten** *or* **führen** *(iro)* to make fine-sounding speeches; **~e Bemerkungen/Ratschläge** *(iro)* clever *or* helpful remarks/advice *(iro)*; **wer war denn so ~ …** *(iro)* who was the bright *or* clever one …; **so ~ bin ich auch** *(iro)* you don't say!; **nun bin ich genauso ~ wie zuvor** *or* **vorher** I am still none the wiser; **der Klügere gibt nach** *(Prov)* discretion is the better part of valour *(Brit) or* valor *(US, Prov)*; **der ~e Mann baut vor** *(Prov)* the wise man takes precautions; **wer ~ ist, fährt mit der Bahn** it makes more sense to go by train; **wenn du ~ bist, haust du sofort ab** if you're smart you'll beat it *(inf)*

ADV *comp* **⸚er**, *superl* **am ⸚sten a** *(= gescheit)* cleverly; **~ geschrieben/durchdacht** cleverly *or* intelligently written/thought out; **~ reden** *or* **tun kann jeder …** anyone can talk …

b *(iro: = dumm)* cleverly

klü|geln [ˈklyːgln] VI to puzzle *(wie/was* as to how/what); **wieder etwas zum Klügeln für unsere Rätselfreunde** another brain-teaser for our puzzle fans

klu|ger|wei|se [ˈkluːgɐˈvaizə] ADV (very) cleverly, (very) wisely

Klug|heit F -, *no pl* cleverness, intelligence; *(= Vernünftigkeit: von Entscheidung, Rat)* wisdom, soundness; *(= Geschicktheit: von Antwort, Geschäftsmann)* shrewdness; **aus ~** (very) wisely; **die ~ eines Sokrates** the astuteness of a Socrates; **deine ~en kannst du dir sparen** *(iro)* you can save your clever remarks

Klüg|ler [ˈklyːglɐ] **M -s, -**, **Klüg|le|rin** [-ərɪn] **F -, -nen** fiddle, fiddly person

Klug-: **klug+re|den** *sep* VI to talk big, to make fine-sounding speeches; **Klug|red|ner(in)** M(F) know-all *(Brit)*, know-it-all *(US)*; **klug+schei|ßen** VI *sep irreg (inf)* to shoot one's mouth off *(inf)*; **Klug|schei|ßer(in)** M(F) *(inf)* big mouth *(inf)*, smart aleck *(inf)*, smart-ass *(esp US sl)*; **klug+schna|cken** *sep* VI *(N Ger inf)* = **klugreden**; **Klug|schna|cker** [-ʃnakɐ] **M -s, -**, **Klug|schna|cke|rin** [-ərɪn] **F -, -nen** *(N Ger inf)* = **Klugredner(in)**

Klump [klʊmp] *no art (inf)* **ein Auto zu ~ fahren** to smash up a car; **jdn zu ~ hauen** to beat sb to a pulp *(inf)*

Klum|patsch [ˈklʊmpatʃ] **M -s**, *no pl (inf)* **der ganze ~** the whole (kit and) caboodle *(inf)*

Klümp|chen [ˈklʏmpçən] **NT -s, -** *dim von* **Klumpen**

klum|pen [ˈklʊmpn] VI *(Sauce)* to go lumpy

Klum|pen [ˈklʊmpn] **M -s, -** lump; *(= Erdklumpen auch)* clod; *(= Goldklumpen)* nugget; *(= Blutklumpen)* clot; **~ bilden** *(Mehl etc)* to go lumpy; *(Blut)* to clot; **steht doch nicht alle auf einem ~!** don't all stand in a huddle

Klum|pert [ˈklʊmpɐt] **NT -s**, *no pl (Aus)* = **Klumpatsch**

Klump-: **Klump|fuß** M club foot; **klump|fü|ßig** ADJ club-footed

klum|pig [ˈklʊmpɪç] ADJ lumpy

Klün|gel [ˈklʏŋl] **M -s, -** *(inf: = Clique)* clique; *(dial: = Kram)* mess

Klün|gel|wirt|schaft F *(inf)* nepotism *no pl*

Klun|ker [ˈklʊŋkɐ] **M -s, -** *(inf: = Edelstein)* rock *(inf)*; *(= großer Modeschmuck)* chunky jewellery *(Brit) or* jewelry *(US)*

Klup|perl [ˈklʊpɐl] **NT -s, -(n)** *(Aus: = Wäscheklammer)* clothes peg, clothes pin *(US)*

Klü|se [ˈklyːzə] **F -, -n a** *(Naut)* hawsehole **b**

Klüsen PL *(N Ger inf)* eyes *pl*

Klü|ver [ˈklyːvɐ] **M -s, -** *(Naut)* jib

Klü|ver|baum M *(Naut)* jib boom

km *abbr von* **Kilometer** km

km/h *abbr von* **Kilometer pro Stunde** kph

kn *(Naut) abbr von* **Knoten** kt

knab|bern [ˈknabɐn] VTI to nibble; **etwas zum Knabbern holen** to get something to nibble on *(inf) or* something to eat; **nichts zu ~ haben** *(inf)* to have nothing to eat; **daran wirst du noch zu ~ haben** *(fig inf)* it will really give you something to think about *or* to get your teeth into; **an dieser Aufgabe habe ich lange zu ~ gehabt** *(fig inf)* I spent ages puzzling over this exercise

Kna|be [ˈknaːbə] **M -n, -n** *(liter)* boy, lad *(esp Brit inf)*; **na alter ~!** *(inf)* well old boy *(inf) or* chap *(inf)*

Kna|ben-: **Kna|ben|al|ter** NT boyhood; **im ~** in his boyhood; **Kna|ben|chor** M boys' choir; **kna|ben|haft** ADJ boyish; **Kna|ben|kraut** NT (wild) orchid; **Kna|ben|lie|be** F *(liter)* paederasty *(Brit)*, pederasty *(US)*; **Kna|ben|schu|le** F *(old)* boys' school; **Kna|ben|stim|me** F boy's voice; *(Mus auch)* treble voice

knack [knak] INTERJ crack; **~ machen** to crack, to go crack

Knack [knak] **M -(e)s, -e** crack

Knä|cke|brot [ˈknɛkə-] NT crispbread

kna|cken [ˈknakn] **VT a** *Nüsse* to crack; *Läuse* to squash, to crush

b *(inf) Auto* to break into, to burgle; *Geldschrank* to crack; *(Mil sl) Panzer* to knock out

c *(fig inf: = bezwingen) Rätsel, Code, Organisation* to crack; *Tabu* to break

VI a *(= brechen)* to crack, to snap; *(Glas etc)* to crack; *(Dielen, Stuhl)* to creak; *(Holz: = knistern)* to crackle; **mit den Fingern ~** to crack one's fingers; **es knackt im Radio** the radio is crackling; **die Leitung knackt** *(Telec)* the line is crackly; **es knackt im Gebälk** the beams are creaking; **an etw** *(dat)* **zu ~ haben** *(inf)* to have sth to think about *or* to chew on *(inf)*; *(= darüber hinwegkommen)* to have a rough time getting over sth; **an dieser Aufgabe hatte ich ganz schön zu ~** *(inf)* I really had to sweat over this exercise

b *(inf: = schlafen)* to kip *(Brit inf)*, to sleep

Kna|cker [ˈknakɐ] **M -s, - a** = **Knackwurst b** *(pej inf)* **alter ~** old fog(e)y *(inf)*

knack|frisch ADJ *(inf)* (nice and) crisp, crunchy

Kna|cki [ˈknaki] **M -s, -s** *(inf: = Knastbruder)* jailbird *(inf)*; *(sl: = alter Mann)* old bloke *(Brit inf) or* guy *(inf)*

kna|ckig [ˈknakɪç] ADJ crisp; *Apfel auch, Salat, Gemüse* crunchy; *(inf) Mädchen* tasty *(inf)*; *Figur, Rock, Hose* sexy; *Musik* hot; *Tonfall, Sprüche* snappy *(inf)* ADV *(inf)* **a** *(= mit Schwung)* **~ rangehen** *(bei Arbeit)* to get a move on *(inf)*; *(beim anderen Geschlecht)* to move in fast *(inf)* **b** *(= ordentlich)* **~ braun sein** to have a fantastic tan

Knack-: **Knack|laut** M glottal stop; **Knack|man|del** F almond in the shell; **Knack|punkt** M *(inf)* crunch *(inf)*

knacks [knaks] INTERJ crack, crash

Knacks [knaks] **M -es, -e a** *(= Sprung, Geräusch)* crack **b** *(inf: = Schaden)* **das Radio/der Fernseher hat einen ~** there is something wrong with the radio/television; **die Ehe der beiden hat schon lange einen ~** their marriage has been breaking up for a long time; **er hat einen ~ (weg)bekommen** he *or (gesundheitlich)* his health *or (psychisch)* his nerves took a knock; **er hat einen ~ weg** he's a bit screwy *(inf)*; *(gesundheitlich)* his health isn't so good

knacksen [ˈknaksn] VI *(inf)* to crack

Knack|wurst F *type of frankfurter, the skin of which makes a cracking sound when bitten*

Knall [knal] **M -(e)s, -e** bang; *(mit Peitsche)* crack; *(bei Tür)* bang, slam; *(von Korken)* pop; *(inf: = Krach)* trouble; **der ~ eines Schusses** a shot; **~ auf Fall** *(inf)* all of a sudden; **jdn ~ auf Fall entlassen** *(inf)* to dismiss sb completely out of the blue *(inf)*; **einen ~ haben** *(inf)* to be crazy *(inf) or* crackers *(Brit inf)*; **der große ~ kommt noch** *(inf)* there's big trouble coming

Knall-: **Knall|bon|bon** NT (Christmas) cracker; **knall|bunt** ADJ *(inf)* brightly coloured *(Brit) or* colored *(US)*; **Knall|ef|fekt** M *(inf)* bombshell *(inf)*; **einen ~ haben** to come as a real bombshell; **ein ~ sein** to be a real bombshell

knal|len [ˈknalən] **VI a** *(= krachen)* to bang; *(= explodieren)* to explode; *(Schuss)* to ring out; *(Feuerwerk)* to (go) bang; *(Korken)* to (go) pop; *(Peitsche)* to crack; *(Tür etc)* to bang, to slam; *(Auspuff)* to misfire; *(aux sein: = auftreffen)* to bang; **mit der Tür ~** to bang *or* slam the door; **mit den Absätzen ~** *(Soldaten etc)* to click one's heels; **die Korken ~ lassen** *(fig)* to pop a cork; **die Sektkorken knallten** *(fig)* the champagne was flowing; **draußen knallte es** there was a shot/were shots outside; **bleib stehen, sonst knallts** *(inf: = es wird geschossen)* freeze or I'll shoot; **sei nicht so frech, sonst knallts** *(inf: = es gibt Prügel)* don't be so cheeky *(Brit) or* fresh *(US)*, or there'll be trouble; **der Fahrer ist gegen die Windschutzscheibe geknallt** the driver hit the windscreen *(Brit) or* windshield *(US)*; **der Ball knallte gegen den Pfosten** *(inf)* the ball banged *or* slammed against the post

b *(inf: Sonne)* to blaze *or* beat down

VT to bang; *Tür, Buch auch* to slam; *Ball auch* to belt *(inf)*, to slam; *Peitsche* to crack; **den Hörer auf die Gabel ~** *(inf)* to slam *or* bang down the receiver; **jdm eine ~** *(inf)* to clout sb (one) *(Brit inf)*, to belt sb (one) *(inf)*; **jdm ein paar vor den Latz ~** *(inf)* to clout sb one *(Brit inf)*, to stick one on sb *(Brit inf)*, to belt sb (one) *(inf)*

knal|lend ADJ *Farbe* bright, loud, gaudy; *Sonne* scorching, blazing

knall|eng ADJ *(inf)* skintight

Knal|ler [ˈknalɐ] **M -s, -** *(inf)* **a** *(= Knallkörper)* banger *(Brit)*, firecracker *(esp US)* **b** *(fig: = Sensation)* sensation **c** *(= Sonderpreis)* fantastic *or* incredible price

Knall|erb|se F toy torpedo

Knal|le|rei [knaləˈrai] **F -, -en** *(inf) (= Schießerei)* shooting; *(Feuerwerk)* banging of fireworks

Knall-: **Knall|frosch** M jumping jack; **Knall|gas** NT oxyhydrogen; **knall|gelb** ADJ *(inf)* bright yellow; **knall|grün** ADJ *(inf)* bright green; **knall|hart** *(inf)* ADJ *Film* brutal; *Porno* hardcore; *Job, Geschäft, Wettbewerb* really tough;

Truppen, Mensch really tough, as hard as nails; *Schuss, Schlag* really hard; *Methode* brutal; *Forderung* uncompromising; **ein ~er Schuss/Schlag** a real humdinger (of a shot/punch) *(inf)* ADV brutally; **der Film zeigt ~, wie ...** the film shows brutally *or* without pulling any punches how ...; **~ verhandeln** to drive a hard bargain; **knall|heiß** ADJ *(inf)* blazing *or* boiling hot; **Knall|hit|ze** F *(inf)* blazing heat, heat wave

knal|lig ['knalıç] *(inf)* ADJ *Farben* loud, gaudy ADV **~ gelb** gaudy yellow; **~ bunt** gaudy

Knall-: **Knall|kopf** M *(inf)*, **Knall|kopp** [-kɔp] *(inf)* M **-s, -köppe** [-kœpə] fathead *(inf)*, blockhead *(inf)*; **Knall|kör|per** M firecracker; **knall|rot** ADJ *(inf)* bright red, scarlet; *Gesicht* as red as a beetroot *(Brit inf) or* beet *(US inf)*; **Knall|schlep|pe** F *(Aviat)* sonic boom; **knall|voll** ADJ *(inf)* **a** *(= total überfüllt)* jam-packed *(inf)*, chock-a-block *(inf)* **b** *(= völlig betrunken)* completely plastered, paralytic *(Brit inf)*, pissed *(Brit inf) or* drunk *(US)* out of one's mind

knapp [knap] ADJ **a** *(= nicht ausreichend vorhanden) Vorräte, Arbeitsstellen* scarce, in short supply; *Geld* tight, scarce; *Taschengeld* meagre *(Brit)*, meager *(US)*; *Gehalt* low, meagre *(Brit)*, meager *(US)*; **mein Geld ist ~** I'm short of money; **mein Geld wird ~** I am running short of *or* out of money; **das Essen wird ~** we/they *etc* are running short of *or* out of food; **~ mit (dem) Geld sein** *(inf)* to be short of money → **Kasse**

b *(= gerade noch ausreichend) Zeit, Geld, Miete* just *or* barely sufficient, just *or* barely enough; *Mehrheit* narrow, small, bare; *Sieg* narrow; *Kleidungsstück etc (= eng)* tight; *(= kurz)* short; *Bikini* scanty

c *(= nicht ganz)* almost; **ein ~es Pfund Mehl** just under a pound of flour; **seit einem ~en** *or* **~ einem Jahr wohne ich hier** I have been living here for almost a year

d *(= kurz und präzis) Stil, Worte* concise; *Geste* terse; *(= lakonisch) Antwort* pithy

e *(= gerade so eben)* just; **mit ~er Not** only just, by the skin of one's teeth

ADV **a** *(= nicht reichlich) rechnen, kalkulieren* conservatively; *bemessen* too closely; **mein Geld/meine Zeit ist ~ bemessen** I am short of money/time; **er hat ihr das Taschengeld ~ bemessen** he was mean *(Brit) or* stingy *(inf)* with her pocket money

b *(= haarscharf)* **wir haben ~ verloren/gewonnen** we only just lost/won; **er ist ~ an mir vorbeigefahren** he just got *or* scraped past me; **der Rock endete ~ über dem Knie** the skirt came to just above the knee; **es war ~ daneben** it was a near miss; **~ vorbei ist auch daneben** *(inf)* a miss is as good as a mile *(prov)*; **ich verprügele dich, aber nicht zu ~** I'll give you a thrashing, and how!

c *(= nicht ganz)* not quite; **~ zwei Wochen** not quite two weeks

Knap|pe ['knapə] M **-n, -n a** *(Hist: eines Ritters)* squire **b** *(Min)* qualified miner

knapp+hal|ten *sep irreg*, **knapp hal|ten** △ *irreg* VT **jdn ~** to keep sb short *(mit* of)

Knapp|heit F **-,** *no pl (= Lebensmittelknappheit)* scarcity, shortage; *(von Zeit, Geld, Produkt)* shortage; *(fig: des Ausdrucks)* conciseness, concision; **wegen der ~ der uns zur Verfügung stehenden Zeit** because of the shortness of the time at our disposal

Knapp|schaft ['knapʃaft] F **-, -en** *(Min)* miners' guild

knap|sen ['knapsn] VI *(inf)* to scrimp *(mit, an +dat* on), to be stingy *(mit, an +dat* with) *(inf)*; **an etw** *(dat)* **zu ~ haben** to have a rough time getting over sth

Knar|re ['knarə] F **-, -n a** *(sl: = Gewehr)* shooter *(inf)* **b** *(= Rassel)* rattle

knar|ren ['knarən] VI to creak; **eine ~de Stimme** a rasping *or* grating voice

Knast M **-(e)s, ¨-e** *or* **-e** *(inf)* clink *(inf)*, can *(US sl)*; **in den ~ wandern** to be put behind bars

Knast|bru|der M *(inf)* jailbird *(inf)*

Knas|ter ['knastɐ] M **-s, -** *(dated inf)* baccy *(Brit inf)*, tobacco; **was rauchst du denn für einen ~!** what's that foul-smelling stuff you're smoking!

Knas|ti ['knasti] M **-s, -s** *(hum inf: = Gefangener)* jailbird *(inf)*

Knas|to|lo|ge [knasto'lo:gə] M **-n, -n**, **Knas|to|lo|gin** [-'lo:gın] F **-, -nen** *(hum)* jailbird *(inf)*

Knast|schwes|ter F *(inf)* jailbird *(inf)*

Knatsch [kna:tʃ] M **-es,** *no pl (inf)* trouble; **das gibt ~** that means trouble

knat|schig ['kna:tʃıç] ADJ *(inf) (= verärgert)* miffed *(inf)*; *(= schlecht gelaunt)* grumpy *(inf)*

knat|tern ['knatɐn] VI *(Motorrad)* to roar; *(Presslufthammer)* to hammer; *(Maschinengewehr)* to rattle, to chatter; *(Schüsse)* to rattle out; *(Fahne im Wind)* to flap

Knäu|el ['knɔyəl] M OR NT **-s, -** ball; *(wirres)* tangle; *(fig: = Durcheinander)* muddle; *(von Menschen)* group, knot; *(in Problemen)* knot, tangle; *(hum: Hund)* bundle of fluff *(inf)*

Knauf [knauf] M **-(e)s, Knäufe** ['knɔyfə] *(= Türknauf)* knob; *(von Schwert etc)* pommel

Knau|ser ['knauzɐ] M **-s, -**, **Knau|se|rin** [-ərın] F **-, -nen** *(inf)* scrooge *(inf)*

Knau|se|rei [knauzə'rai] F **-,** *no pl (inf)* meanness *(esp Brit)*, stinginess *(inf)*

knau|se|rig ['knauzərıç] ADJ *(inf)* mean *(esp Brit)*, stingy *(inf)*

Knau|se|rig|keit F **-,** *no pl (inf)* meanness *(esp Brit)*, stinginess *(inf)*

Knau|se|rin [-ərın] F **-, -nen** *(inf)* scrooge *(inf)*

knau|sern ['knauzɐn] VI *(inf)* to be mean *(esp Brit) or* stingy *(inf) (mit* with)

Knaus-Ogi|no-Me|tho|de ['knauslo'gi:no-] F *(Med)* rhythm method

knaus|rig ADJ *(inf)* mean *(esp Brit)*, stingy *(inf)*

Knaus|rig|keit F **-,** *no pl (inf)* meanness *(esp Brit)*, stinginess *(inf)*

knaut|schen ['knautʃn] VTI *(inf)* to crumple (up); *Kleid etc auch* to crease

knaut|schig ['knautʃıç] ADJ *(inf) Anzug, Kleid* crumpled-up, crumply *(inf)*

Knautsch-: **Knautsch|lack** M, **Knautsch|(lack)|le|der** NT wet-look leather; **Knautsch|zo|ne** F *(Aut)* crumple zone

Kne|bel ['kne:bl] M **-s, -** *(= Mundknebel)* gag; *(= Paketknebel)* (wooden) handle; *(an Mänteln)* toggle; *(= Fensterknebel)* (handle of) window catch

Kne|bel-: **Kne|bel|bart** M Van Dyke (beard); **Kne|bel|knopf** M toggle fastening

kne|beln ['kne:bln] VT *jdn, Presse* to gag

Kne|be|lung ['kne:bəlʊŋ] F **-,** *no pl (lit, fig)* gagging

Kne|bel|ver|trag M oppressive contract; **jdn durch einen ~ binden** to screw sb down with a tight contract *(inf)*

Knecht [knεçt] M **-(e)s, -e a** servant; *(beim Bauern)* (farm) labourer *(Brit) or* laborer *(US)*, farm worker; *(= Stallknecht)* stableboy **b** *(fig: = Sklave)* slave *(+gen* to) **c ~ Ruprecht** *helper to St Nicholas (Santa Claus)*

knech|ten ['knεçtn] VT *(geh)* to subjugate, to oppress; **alle unterdrückten und geknechteten Völker ...** all oppressed and enslaved peoples ...; **sie wollten sich nicht mehr von ihm ~ lassen** they refused to be his slaves any longer

knech|tisch ['knεçtıʃ] ADJ *(geh) Charakter* subservient, submissive; *Unterwürfigkeit, Verhalten auch* servile, slavish ADV **sich ~ verhalten** to be servile; **jdm/einer Sache ~ ergeben sein** to be a complete slave *or* to be totally enslaved to sb/sth

Knecht|schaft ['knεçtʃaft] F **-, -en** slavery, servitude, bondage

Knech|tung ['knεçtʊŋ] F **-,** *no pl (geh)* enslavement, subjugation

knei|fen ['knaifn] *pret* **kniff** [knıf], *ptp* **gekniffen** [gə'knıfn] VT to pinch; **jdn ~** to pinch sb; **jdn** *or* **jdm in den Arm ~** to pinch sb's arm; **der Hund kniff den Schwanz zwischen die Beine** the dog put his tail between his legs VI **a** *(= zwicken)* to pinch; **die Bluse kneift** the blouse is too tight **b** *(inf) (= ausweichen)* to chicken out *(inf)*, to get *or* back out *(vor +dat* of); *(vor Arbeit)* to duck *or* back out *(vor +dat* of); *(vor Auseinandersetzung)* to back out **c** *(Univ sl) to fail to remain motionless during a student duel*

Knei|fer ['knaifɐ] M **-s, -a** *(= Brille)* pince-nez

Kneif|zan|ge F pliers *pl*; *(kleine)* pincers *pl*; **eine ~** (a pair of) pliers/pincers

Knei|pe ['knaipə] F **-, -n** *(inf: = Lokal)* pub *(Brit)*, bar, saloon *(US)*

Knei|pen-: **Knei|pen|bum|mel** M pub crawl *(Brit)*, bar hop *(US)*; **Knei|pen|wirt(in)** M(F) *(inf)* publican *(Brit)*, pub owner *(Brit)*, (pub) landlord/landlady *(Brit)*, barkeeper, saloon-keeper *(US)*

Knei|per ['knaipɐ] M **-s, -**, **Knei|pe|rin** [-ərın] F **-, -nen**, **Knei|pier** [knai'pie:] M **-s, -s** *(inf)* = **Kneipenwirt(in)**

kneip|pen ['knaipn] VI to undergo a Kneipp cure

Kneipp|kur F Kneipp cure *(type of hydropathic treatment combined with diet, rest etc)*

knei|sen ['knaizn] VT *(Aus inf)* to notice

Knes|set(h) ['knεsεt] F **-,** *no pl* Knesset

Knet [kne:t] M **-s,** *no pl* modelling *(Brit) or* modeling *(US)* clay; *(= Plastilin)* Plasticine®

knet|bar ADJ workable; *Teig auch* kneadable

Kne|te ['kne:tə] F **-,** *no pl (dated sl: = Geld)* dough *(inf)*

kne|ten ['kne:tn] VT *Teig* to knead; *Plastilin, Ton* to work; *Figuren* to model; *(= formen)* to form, to shape; *Muskeln, Rücken* to knead, to work VI *(= mit Plastilin spielen)* to play with Plasticine® *or* modelling *(Brit) or* modeling *(US)* clay

Knet-: **Knet|gum|mi** M OR NT Plasticine®; **Knet|ma|schi|ne** F kneading machine; **Knet|mas|se** F modelling *(Brit) or* modeling *(US)* clay

Knick [knık] M **-(e)s, -e** *or* **-s a** *(= leichter Sprung)* crack **b** *(= Kniff, Falte)* crease, crinkle; *(= Eselsohr)* dog-ear; *(= Biegung)* (sharp) bend; *(bei Draht, auf Oberfläche)* kink; **einen ~ machen** to bend sharply → **Optik c** *(fig: in Karriere etc)* downturn **d** *pl* **-s** *(N Ger: = Hecke)* hedgerow

Kni|cke|bein ['knıkə-] M **-s,** *no pl* advocaat

kni|cken ['knıkn] VI *aux sein* to snap VT to snap; *Papier* to fold, to crease; **„nicht ~!"** "do not bend *or* fold" → *auch* **geknickt**

Kni|cker ['knıkɐ] M **-s, -**, **Kni|cke|rin** [-ərın] F **-, -nen** *(inf)* scrooge *(inf)*

Kni|cker|bo|cker ['knıkɐbɔkɐ] PL knickerbockers *pl (old)*, plus fours *pl*

kni|cke|rig ['knıkərıç] ADJ *(inf)* stingy *(inf)*, mean *(esp Brit)*

Kni|cke|rig|keit F **-,** *no pl (inf)* stinginess *(inf)*, meanness *(esp Brit)*

Kni|cke|rin [-ərın] F **-, -nen** *(inf)* scrooge *(inf)*

kni|ckern ['knıkɐn] VI *(inf)* to be stingy *(inf) (mit* with)

Knick|fuß M *(Med)* (type of) club foot

knick|rig ['knıkrıç] ADJ *(inf)* stingy *(inf)*, mean *(esp Brit)*

Knick|rig|keit F **-,** *no pl (inf)* stinginess *(inf)*, meanness *(esp Brit)*

Knicks [knıks] M **-es, -e a** bob; *(tiefer)* curts(e)y; **einen ~ machen** to drop a curts(e)y, to curts(e)y *(vor +dat* to) **b** *(= heller Knacks)* crack, click

knick|sen ['knıksn] VI to curts(e)y, to drop a curts(e)y *(vor +dat* to)

Knie [kni:] NT **-s, - a** knee; **auf ~n** on one's knees, on bended knee; **(vor jdm) auf die ~ fallen** *or* **in die ~ sinken** to fall on *or* drop to one's knees (before sb); **sich vor jdm auf die ~ werfen** to throw oneself on one's knees in front of sb; **jdn auf ~n bitten** to go down on bended knees to sb (and beg); **jdm auf ~n danken** to go down on one's knees and thank sb; **bis zu den ~n im Sumpf stecken** *(lit)* to be up to one's knees in mud; **in die ~ gehen** to kneel, to fall on one's knees; *(fig)* to be brought to one's knees; **jdn in** *or* **auf die ~ zwingen** *(esp fig)* to bring sb to his/her knees; **jdn übers ~ legen** *(inf)* to put sb across one's knee; **etw übers ~ brechen** *(fig)* to rush (at) sth; **die ~ beugen** to bend one's knees; *(vor dem Altar)* to bow, to genuflect *(form)*; *(fig)* to give in, to bend the knee **b** *(= Flussknie)* sharp bend; *(in Rohr)* elbow **c** *(Tech: = Winkelstück)* elbow

Knie-: **Knie|beu|ge** F *(Sport)* knee bend; **in die ~ gehen** to bend one's knees; **Knie|bund|hose** F knee breeches *pl*; **Knie|fall** M genuflection *(form)*; **einen ~ vor jdm tun** *(geh) or* **machen** *(lit, fig)* to kneel before sb; *(fig auch)* to bow before sb; **knie|fäl|lig** ADJ *Verehrung* humble, lowly ADV on one's knees, on bended knee; **knie|frei** ADJ *Rock* above the knee; **Knie|ge|lenk** NT knee joint; **knie|hoch** ADJ *Schnee, Wasser* knee-deep; *Gras* knee-high; **Knie|ho|se** F knee breeches *pl*; **Knie|keh|le** F back *or* hollow of the knee; **Knie|kis|sen** NT *(Eccl)* hassock; **knie|lang** ADJ knee-length

knien [kni:n, ˈkni:ən] VI to kneel; **im Knien** on one's knees, kneeling VR to kneel (down); **sich in die Arbeit ~** *(fig)* to get down to *or* to get stuck into *(inf)* one's work

Knie|rohr NT elbow (pipe)

Knies [kni:s] M -, *no pl (dial inf)* row, argument

Knie-: **Knie|schei|be** F kneecap; **Knie|schei|ben|re|flex** M, **Knie|seh|nen|re|flex** M knee *or* patellar *(spec)* reflex; **Knie|schnack|ler** [-ʃnaklɐ] M **-s, -** *(dial inf)* wobbly knees *pl*; **Knie|scho|ner** M = **Knieschützer**; **Knie|schüt|zer** [-ʃʏtsɐ] M **-s, -** kneepad, kneeguard; **Knie|strumpf** M knee sock, knee-length sock; **Knie|stück** NT elbow joint; **knie|tief** ADJ knee-deep; **Knie|wel|le** F knee circle

kniff *pret von* **kneifen**

Kniff [knɪf] M **-(e)s, -e a** *(inf)* trick; **den ~ bei etw heraushaben** to have the knack of sth *(inf)*; **es ist ein ~ dabei** there is a (special) knack to it *(inf)* **b** *(= Falte)* crease, fold **c** *(= Kneifen)* pinch

Knif|fe|lei [knɪfəˈlai] F **-, -en** *(inf)* fiddly job

knif|fe|lig [ˈknɪfəlɪç], **kniff|lig** [ˈknɪflɪç] ADJ *(inf)* fiddly; *(= heikel)* tricky

Knig|ge [ˈknɪgə] M **-(s), -** etiquette manual

Knilch [knɪlç] M **-s, -e** *(pej inf)* twit *(Brit inf)*, clown *(inf)*

knips [knɪps] INTERJ click

knip|sen [ˈknɪpsn] VT **a** *Fahrschein* to punch, to clip **b** *(Phot inf)* to snap *(inf)* VI **a** *(Phot inf)* to take pictures **b** *(= klicken)* to click; **mit den Fingern ~** to snap one's fingers

Knip|ser [ˈknɪpsɐ] M **-s, -** *(inf)*, **Knips|schal|ter** M shutter

Knirps [knɪrps] M **-es, -e a** *(= Junge)* whippersnapper; *(pej)* squirt **b** ~® folding *or* telescopic umbrella

knir|schen [ˈknɪrʃn] VI *(Sand, Schnee)* to crunch; *(Getriebe)* to grind; **mit den Zähnen ~** to grind one's teeth; *(vor Wut auch)* to gnash one's teeth

knis|tern [ˈknɪstɐn] VI *(Feuer)* to crackle; *(Papier, Seide)* to rustle; **mit Papier** *etc* **~** to rustle paper *etc*; **zwischen den beiden knistert es** *(inf)* there's a real spark between them; **es knistert im Gebälk** *(fig)* there is trouble brewing *or* afoot (+*gen* in)

Knit|tel [ˈknɪtl] M **-s, -** *(dial)* = **Knüppel a**

Knit|tel|vers M rhyming couplets (using a four-stress line)

knit|ter-: **knit|ter|arm** ADJ crease-resistant; **Knit|ter|fal|te** F crease, wrinkle *(esp US)*; **knit|ter|fest** ADJ = **knitterfrei**; **knit|ter|frei** ADJ *Stoff, Kleid* non-crease

knit|te|rig ADJ creased

knit|tern [ˈknɪtɐn] VTI to crease, to crush

knitt|rig ADJ creased

Kno|bel|be|cher M **a** dice cup **b** *(Mil sl)* army boot

kno|beln [ˈkno:bln] VI **a** *(= würfeln)* to play dice; *(um eine Entscheidung)* to toss for it *(inf)*; **sie knobelten darum, wer bezahlen sollte** they tossed (for it) to decide who should pay **b** *(= nachdenken)* to puzzle *(an +dat* over)

Knob|lauch [ˈkno:plaux, ˈkno:blaux, ˈknɔplaux, ˈknɔblaux] M, *no pl* garlic

Knob|lauch-: **Knob|lauch|ba|guette** NT garlic baguette; **Knob|lauch|brot** NT garlic bread; **Knob|lauch|but|ter** F garlic butter; **Knob|lauch|ge|ruch** M smell of garlic; **Knob|lauch|pres|se** F garlic press; **Knob|lauch|pul|ver** NT garlic powder; **Knob|lauch|ze|he** F clove of garlic

Knö|chel [ˈknœçl] M **-s, - a** *(= Fußknöchel)* ankle; **bis über die ~** up to the ankles, ankle-deep **b** *(= Fingerknöchel)* knuckle

Knö|chel-: **Knö|chel|bruch** M broken ankle; **knö|chel|lang** ADJ ankle-length; **knö|chel|tief** ADJ ankle-deep

Kno|chen [ˈknɔxn] M **-s, - a** bone; **Fleisch mit/ohne ~** meat on/off the bone; **die Wunde geht bis auf den ~** the wound has penetrated to the bone; **mir tun alle ~ weh** *(inf)* every bone in my body is aching; **er ist bis auf die ~ abgemagert** he is just (a bag of) skin and bones; **brich dir nicht die ~!** *(inf)* don't break anything *or* your neck!; **dem breche ich alle ~ einzeln** *(inf)* I'll break every bone in his body; **das geht auf die ~** *(inf)* it knackers you *(Brit inf)*, it breaks your back; **ihm steckt** *or* **sitzt die Grippe in den ~** *(inf)* he's got flu; **ihm steckt** *or* **sitzt die Angst in den ~** *(inf)* he's scared stiff *(inf)*; **die Angst ist ihm in die ~ gefahren** it gave him a real fright; **der Schreck fuhr ihm in die ~** he was paralyzed with shock; **nass bis auf die ~** *(inf)* soaked to the skin; **kein Mark** *or* **keinen Mumm in den ~ haben** *(inf)* to have no guts *or* spunk *(inf)*; **sich bis auf die ~ blamieren** *(inf)* to make a proper fool of oneself *(inf)*; **er ist konservativ bis in** *or* **auf die ~** *(inf)* he is conservative through and through, he is a dyed-in-the-wool conservative **b** *(sl: = Kerl)* chap *(inf)*, bloke *(Brit inf)*; **du fauler/müder ~** you lazy/indolent so-and-so *(inf)*

Kno|chen-: **Kno|chen|ar|beit** F hard graft *(inf)*; **Kno|chen|bau** M, *no pl* bone structure; **Kno|chen|bruch** M fracture; **Kno|chen|er|wei|chung** [-lɛɐvaiçʊŋ] F **-, -en** *(Med)* softening of the bones, osteomalacia *(spec)*; **Kno|chen|ge|rüst** NT skeleton; **kno|chen|hart** *(inf)* ADJ rock-hard; *(fig) Job, Kerl* really tough ADV *vorgehen* ruthlessly; *trainieren, fordern, verhandeln* rigorously; **Kno|chen|haut** F periosteum *(spec)*; **Kno|chen|haut|ent|zün|dung** F periostitis *(spec)*; **Kno|chen|leim** M bone glue; **Kno|chen|mann** M, *no pl (liter)* Death; **Kno|chen|mark** NT bone marrow; **Kno|chen|mark|ent|zün|dung** F osteomyelitis; **Kno|chen|mehl** NT bone meal; **Kno|chen|naht** F *(Anat)* bone suture; **Kno|chen|schin|ken** M ham on the bone; **Kno|chen|schwund** M bone atrophy, atrophy of the bone; **kno|chen|tro|cken** *(inf)* ADJ bone-dry *(inf)*; *(fig) Humor etc* very dry ADV very dryly; **Kno|chen|tu|ber|ku|lo|se** F bone tuberculosis, tuberculosis of the bone

knö|che|rig [ˈknœçərɪç] ADJ **a** *(= knochenartig)* bony, bone-like, osseous *(form)* **b** = **knöchern**

knö|chern [ˈknœçɐn] ADJ *Gerät etc* bone *attr*, of bone; *Material auch* bony, osseous *(form)*; *(inf: = großknochig) Mensch, Körperbau* bony; *(pej inf: = nicht anpassungsfähig)* set in one's ways

kno|chig [ˈknɔxɪç] ADJ bony

knöch|rig [ˈknœçrɪç] ADJ = **knöcherig**

Knock-down [nɔkˈdaun] M **-(s), -s**, **Knock|down** M **-(s), -s** knockdown

Knock-out [nɔkˈlaut] M **-(s), -s**, **Knock|out** M **-(s), -s** knockout

Knö|del [ˈknø:dl] M **-s, -** dumpling

knö|deln [ˈknø:dln] VI to sing in a strangled voice

Kno|fel [ˈkno:fl] M **-s**, *no pl (inf)* garlic

Knöll|chen [ˈknœlçən] NT **-s, - a** *dim von* **Knolle b** *(inf: = Strafzettel)* (parking) ticket

Knöll|chen|bak|te|rien PL rhizobin *pl*

Knol|le [ˈknɔlə] F **-, -n** *(Bot)* nodule, tubercule; *(von Kartoffel, Dahlie)* tuber; *(= Kartoffel)* potato; *(inf: = Nase)* conk *(Brit inf)*, honker *(US inf)*

Knol|len [ˈknɔlən] M **-s, - a** = **Knolle b** *(= Klumpen)* lump

Knol|len-: **Knol|len|blät|ter|pilz** M, **Knol|len|blät|ter|schwamm** M amanita; **Grüner ~** deadly amanita, death cap, death angel; **Weißer ~** destroying angel; **Knol|len|na|se** F *(Med)* rhinophyma *(spec)*, (nodular) swelling of the nose; *(inf)* conk *(Brit inf)*, honker *(US inf)*

knol|lig [ˈknɔlɪç] ADJ *Wurzel* tuberous; *Auswuchs* knobbly, knotty; *Nase* bulbous; *(inf: = klumpig)* lumpy

Knopf [knɔpf] M **-(e)s, ¨-e** [ˈknœpfə] **a** *(an Kleidungsstück etc)* button; **etw an den Knöpfen abzählen** to decide sth by counting off one's buttons **b** *(an Gerät, elektrischer Anlage etc)* (push) button; *(an Akkordeon)* button **c** *(an Tür, Stock)* knob; *(= Sattelknopf, Degenknopf)* pommel **d** *(S Ger, Aus: = Knoten)* knob **e** *(inf) (= Junge)* little chap *or* fellow; *(= Mädchen)* little lass *(Brit) or* lassie *(esp Scot)*, little girl; *(= Kerl)* chap, fellow; **ein fieser ~** a nasty so-and-so

Knopf-: **Knopf|au|gen** PL big round eyes *pl*; **Knopf|druck** M, *no pl* **auf ~, mit einem ~** at the touch *or* press of a button, at the flick of a switch *(fig)*

knöp|fen [ˈknœpfn], *(Aus)* **knöp|feln** [ˈknœpfln] *(inf)* VT to button (up); **einen Kragen auf ein Kleid ~** to button a collar to a dress; **ein Kleid zum Knöpfen** a dress that buttons up

Knopf-: **Knopf|leis|te** F button tape *or* facing; **Mantel mit verdeckter ~** coat with a fly *or* button-down *(esp US)* front; **Knopf|loch** NT buttonhole; **aus allen Knopflöchern platzen** *(inf)* to be bursting at the seams; **Knopf|loch|chi|rur|gie** F *(inf)* keyhole surgery *(inf)*; **Knopf|zel|le** F round cell battery

Knopp [knɔp] M **-s, ¨-e** [ˈknœpə] *(dial)* = **Knopf**

knor|ke [ˈknɔrkə] *(dated sl)* ADJ smashing *(Brit inf)*, swell *(esp US inf)* ADV terrifically

Knor|pel [ˈknɔrpl] M **-s, -** *(Anat, Zool)* cartilage; *(Cook)* gristle

knor|pe|lig [ˈknɔrpəlɪç] ADJ *(Anat)* cartilaginous; *Fleisch* gristly

Knor|ren [ˈknɔrən] M **-s, -** *(im Holz)* knot; *(an Weide)* burl, burr; *(= Baumstumpf)* (tree) stump; *(= Aststumpf)* snag

knor|rig [ˈknɔrɪç] ADJ *Baum* gnarled; *Holz, Klotz* knotty; *(fig) alter Mann* rugged; *(= eigenwillig) Mensch, Charakter* surly, gruff

Knos|pe [ˈknɔspə] F **-, -n** bud; **~n ansetzen** *or* **treiben** to bud; **die zarte ~ ihrer Liebe** *(liter)* the tender bud of their love

knos|pen [ˈknɔspən] VI to bud; **~d** *(lit, fig: liter)* budding

Knöt|chen [ˈknø:tçən] NT **-s, -** *dim von* **Knoten**

kno|ten [ˈkno:tn] VT *Seil etc* to (tie into a) knot, to tie a knot in

Kno|ten [ˈkno:tn] M **-s, - a** knot; *(Med) (= Geschwulst)* lump; *(= Gichtknoten)* tophus *(spec)*; *(Phys, Bot, Math, Astron)* node; *(fig: = Verwicklung)* plot; **sich** *(dat)* **einen ~ ins Taschentuch machen** *(inf)* to tie a knot in one's handkerchief **b** *(Naut)* knot **c** *(= Haarknoten)* bun, knot **d** = **Knotenpunkt**

Kno|ten-: **Kno|ten|bahn|hof** M junction; **Kno|ten|punkt** M *(Mot)* (road) junction, (road) intersection; *(Rail)* junction; *(fig)* centre *(Brit)*, center *(US)*; *(von Argumentation, Handlung etc)* nodal point

Knö|te|rich [ˈknø:tərɪç] M **-s, -e** knotgrass

kno|tig [ˈkno:tɪç] ADJ knotty, knotted, full of knots; *Äste, Finger, Hände* gnarled; *Geschwulst* nodular

Know-how [ˈno:hau, no:ˈhau] NT **-s**, *no pl* know-how

Knub|bel [ˈknʊbl] M **-s, -** *(inf)* lump

knud|de|lig [ˈknʊdəlɪç] ADJ *(inf: = niedlich)* cuddly

knud|deln ['knʊdln] VT *(dial)* to kiss and cuddle

Knuff [knʊf] M **-(e)s, ⸚e** ['knʏfə] *(inf)* poke; *(mit Ellbogen)* nudge

knuf|fen ['knʊfn] VTI *(inf)* to poke *(inf)*; *(mit Ellbogen)* to nudge

knül|le ['knʏlə] ADJ *pred (dial inf)* tight *(inf)*

knül|len ['knʏlən] VT to crumple, to crease (up)

Knül|ler ['knʏlɐ] M **-s, -** *(inf)* sensation; *(Press)* scoop

knüp|fen ['knʏpfn] VT *Knoten* to tie; *Band* to knot, to tie (up); *Teppich* to knot; *Netz* to mesh; *Freundschaft* to form, to strike up; **jdn an den nächsten Baum/den Galgen ~** *(inf)* to hang sb from the nearest tree/the gallows, to string sb up *(inf)*; **etw an etw** *(acc)* **~** *(lit)* to tie *or* knot sth to sth; *(fig) Bedingungen* to attach sth to sth; *Hoffnungen* to pin sth on sth; **große Erwartungen an etw** *(acc)* **~** to have great expectations of sth; **Kontakte ~ (zu** *or* **mit)** to establish contact (with); **Freundschaftsbande enger ~** to strengthen *or* tighten the bonds of friendship → **Band**

VR **sich an etw** *(acc)* **~** to be linked to *or* connected with sth; **an diese Bemerkung knüpften sich einige Fragen** this remark raised several questions; **an diese Zeit ~ sich für mich viele Erinnerungen** I have many memories of this time; **an diese Erfindung ~ sich viele technische Möglichkeiten** this discovery has many technical possibilities

Knüp|pel ['knʏpl] M **-s, -** **a** stick; *(= Waffe)* cudgel, club; *(= Polizeiknüppel)* truncheon; *(Metal)* billet; **Politik des großen ~s** big stick policy; **den ~ aus dem Sack holen** *(fig inf)* to wield a big stick *(inf)*; **man sollte mit dem ~ dreinschlagen** *(fig)* someone ought to get tough *or* to wave the big stick; **jdm (einen) ~ zwischen die Beine werfen** *(fig)* to put a spoke in sb's wheel *(Brit)*, to throw a spanner *(Brit) or* (monkey) wrench *(US)* in the works **b** *(Aviat)* control stick, joystick; *(Aut)* gear stick *(Brit)*, gearshift *(US)* **c** *(dial: = Brötchen)* ≈ crusty bridge roll

Knüp|pel-: **Knüp|pel|damm** M log road; **knüp|pel|dick** ADJ *(inf) Steak, Schicht* very thick, good and thick *pred*; **knüp|pel|hart** *(inf)* ADJ rock-hard; *(fig) Job, Kerl* really tough ADV ruthlessly

knüp|peln ['knʏpln] VI to use one's truncheon; *(Sport sl)* to hack, to kick wildly VT to club, to beat with a club *or* stick; *(Polizei)* to use one's truncheon on, to beat with one's truncheon

Knüp|pel-: **Knüp|pel|schal|tung** F *(Aut)* floor-mounted gear change *(Brit)*, floor shift *(US)*; **knüp|pel|voll** ADJ *(inf)* jam-packed, packed solid

knur|ren ['knʊrən] VI *(Hund etc)* to growl; *(wütend)* to snarl; *(Magen)* to rumble; *(fig: = sich beklagen)* to moan, to groan *(über +acc* about) VTI *(= mürrisch sagen)* to growl

Knur|ren NT **-s,** *no pl (von Hund)* growl(ing); *(wütend)* snarl(ing); *(von Magen)* rumble, rumbling; *(= Klagen)* moan(ing)

Knurr|hahn M gurnard

knur|rig ['knʊrɪç] ADJ grumpy; *Angestellte etc* disgruntled

Knus|per|häus|chen [-hɔysçən] NT gingerbread house

knus|pe|rig ['knʊspərɪç] ADJ = **knusprig**

knus|pern ['knʊspɐn] VTI to crunch; **etwas zum Knuspern** something to nibble; **an etw** *(dat)* **~** to crunch away at sth

knusp|rig ['knʊsprɪç] ADJ *Braten* crisp; *Gebäck auch* crunchy; *Brötchen auch* crusty; *(fig) Mädchen* scrumptious *(inf)* ADV *gebacken, gebraten* crisply; **~ braun** *(Hähnchen)* crispy brown; *Mensch* with a super tan; **etw ~ grillen** to grill sth until it is crispy

Knust [knuːst] M **-(e)s, -e** *or* **⸚e** ['knyːstə] *(N Ger)* (end) crust, heel

Knu|te ['knuːtə] F **-, -n** *(old)* knout *(old)*, lash; **jds ~ zu spüren bekommen** to feel sb's lash; **unter jds ~** *(dat)* **stehen/leben** to be completely dominated by sb; **jdn unter seine ~ bringen** to get sb in one's clutches

knut|schen ['knuːtʃn] *(inf)* VT to pet with, to smooch with *(inf)*, to neck with *(inf)* VR to pet, to smooch *(inf)*, to neck *(inf)*

Knut|sche|rei [knuːtʃə'rai] F **-, -en** petting, smooching *(inf)*, necking *(inf)*

Knutsch|fleck M *(inf)* lovebite *(inf)*

k. o. [kaː'loː] ADJ *pred (Sport)* knocked out; *(fig inf)* whacked *(inf)*, all in *(inf)*; **jdn ~ schlagen** to knock sb out

K. o. [kaː'loː] M **-(s), -s** knockout, K.O.; **Sieg durch ~** victory by a knockout

Knüt|tel ['knʏtl] M **-s, -** = **Knüppel a**

Knüt|tel|vers M = **Knittelvers**

ko|a|gu|lie|ren [kolagu'liːrən] *ptp* **koaguliert** VTI *(Med, Chem)* to coagulate, to clot

Ko|a|la [ko'aːla] M **-s, -s**, **Ko|a|la|bär** M koala (bear)

ko|a|lie|ren [kola'liːrən] *ptp* **koaliert** VI *(esp Pol)* to form a coalition *(mit* with)

Ko|a|li|ti|on [kolali'tsioːn] F **-, -en** *(esp Pol)* coalition; **Kleine/Große ~** little/grand coalition

> **KOALITION**
>
> There are various names for the groupings of political parties which form governments. A **Große Koalition** is an alliance between the two large parties **CDU/CSU** and **SPD**, something which seldom happens on account of the incompatibility of their policies. A **Kleine Koalition** is an alliance between a large and a small party. Recently there has also been an **Ampelkoalition** – red for **SPD**, yellow for **FDP** and green for **Bündnis 90/Die Grünen**. → BÜNDNIS 90/DIE GRÜNEN, CDU/CSU, FDP, SPD

Ko|a|li|ti|o|när [kolalitsio'nɛːɐ] M **-s, -e**, **Ko|a|li|ti|o|nä|rin** [-'nɛːrɪn] F **-, -nen** *(Pol) (= Abgeordneter)* coalition member; *(= Partei auch)* coalition party

Ko|a|li|ti|ons- *in cpds* coalition; **Ko|a|li|ti|ons|ab|spra|che** F coalition agreement; **Ko|a|li|ti|ons|aus|sage** F statement of willingness to form a coalition; **ko|a|li|ti|ons|fä|hig** ADJ **~ sein** to be suitable as a coalition partner, to be in a position to form a coalition; **Ko|a|li|ti|ons|fä|hig|keit** F suitability as a coalition partner; **Ko|a|li|ti|ons|frei|heit** F freedom to form a coalition; **Ko|a|li|ti|ons|ge|spräch** NT coalition talks *pl*; **Ko|a|li|ti|ons|krieg** M *(Hist)* coalition war; **Ko|a|li|ti|ons|kri|se** F crisis within a/the coalition; **Ko|a|li|ti|ons|par|tner(in)** M(F) coalition partner; **Ko|a|li|ti|ons|recht** NT right of combination; **Ko|a|li|ti|ons|re|gie|rung** F coalition government; **Ko|a|li|ti|ons|ver|ein|ba|rung** F coalition agreement, agreement on a coalition

Ko|a|li|ti|ons|ver|trag M coalition agreement

Ko|au|tor(in) ['koː-] M(F) co-author

ko|axi|al [kola'ksiaːl] ADJ *(Tech)* coaxial

Ko|axi|al|ka|bel NT *(Tech)* coaxial cable

Ko|balt ['koːbalt] NT **-s,** *no pl (abbr* **Co**) cobalt

ko|balt|blau ADJ cobalt blue

Ko|bel ['koːbl] M **-s, -** *(S Ger, Aus)*, **Ko|ben** ['koːbn] M **-s, -** **a** = **Schuppen a** **b** = **Stall a**

Ko|bold ['koːbɔlt] M **-(e)s, -e** [-də] goblin, imp

Ko|bolz ['koːbɔlts] M **~ schießen** to turn *or* do somersaults

Ko|bra ['koːbra] F **-, -s** cobra

Koch [kɔx] M **-s, ⸚e** ['kœçə], **Kö|chin** ['kœçɪn] F **-, -nen** cook; *(von Restaurant etc)* chef, cook; **viele Köche verderben den Brei** *(Prov)* too many cooks spoil the broth *(Prov)*

Koch NT **-s,** *no pl (Aus) (= Brei) (= Apfelmus etc)* purée; *(= Griesbrei etc)* pudding

Koch-: **Koch|an|lei|tung** F cooking instructions *pl*; **Koch|ap|fel** M cooking apple, cooker; **koch|bar** ADJ suitable for boiling, that may be boiled; **Koch|beu|tel** M **Reis im ~** boil-in-the-bag rice; **Koch|buch** NT cookery book, cookbook; **koch|echt** ADJ *(Tex) Farbe* fast at 100°, fast even in boiling water; *Wäsche etc* suitable for boiling, that may be boiled; **Koch|ecke** F kitchen *or* cooking area

kö|cheln ['kœçln] VI *(lit, fig)* to simmer

Kö|chel|ver|zeich|nis ['kœçl-] NT *(Mus)* Köchel index; **~ 25** Köchel *or* K. (number) 25

ko|chen ['kɔxn] VI **a** *(Flüssigkeit, Speise)* to boil; **etw langsam** *or* **auf kleiner Flamme ~ lassen** to let sth simmer *or* to simmer sth (over a low heat); **etw zum Kochen bringen** to bring sth to the boil; **jdn zum Kochen bringen** *(fig inf)* to make sb's blood boil; **der Kühler/das Auto kocht** *(inf)* the cooling system/car is overheating; **er kochte vor Wut** *(inf)* he was boiling *or* seething with rage

b *(= Speisen zubereiten)* to cook; *(= als Koch fungieren)* to do the cooking; *(= als Koch arbeiten)* to work as a cook; **er kocht gut** he's a good cook, he is good at cooking; **er kocht pikant** his cooking is (always) highly seasoned

VT **a** *Flüssigkeit, Teer, Nahrungsmittel, Wäsche* to boil; **etw langsam** *or* **auf kleiner Flamme ~** to simmer sth over a low heat

b *(= zubereiten) Essen* to cook; *Kakao* to make; *(= aufgießen) Kaffee, Tee* to make, to brew; **etw gar/weich ~** to cook sth through/until (it is) soft; **Eier weich/hart ~** to soft-boil/hard-boil eggs

VI *impers (fig)* to be boiling; **es kocht in ihm** he is boiling *or* seething with rage; **im Stadion kochte es wie in einem Hexenkessel** the atmosphere in the stadium was electric

VR **sich gut/schlecht ~** to cook/not to cook well

ko|chend ADJ *(lit, fig)* boiling; *(liter) See* raging ADV **~ heiß sein** to be boiling hot; *(Suppe etc)* to be piping hot

ko|chend|heiß △ ADJ *attr* → **kochend ADV**

Ko|cher ['kɔxɐ] M **-s, -** *(= Herd)* cooker, stove; *(= Campingkocher)* (Primus®) stove; *(= Kochplatte)* hotplate; *(= Wasserkocher)* ≈ (electric) kettle

Kö|cher ['kœçɐ] M **-s, -** *(für Pfeile)* quiver; *(für Golfschläger)* golf bag; *(für Kameraobjektiv etc)* case

Ko|che|rei [kɔxə'rai] F **-,** *no pl (inf)* cooking

Koch-: **Koch|feld** NT ceramic hob; **koch|fer|tig** ADJ ready-to-cook *attr*, ready to cook *pred*; **koch|fest** ADJ *(Tex)* = **kochecht**; **Koch|fleisch** NT stewing *or* braising meat; **Koch|ge|le|gen|heit** F cooking facilities *pl*; **Koch|ge|schirr** NT *(esp Mil)* billy(can), mess tin *(Mil)*; **Koch|herd** M cooker, stove

Kö|chin ['kœçɪn] F → **Koch**

Koch-: **Koch|kä|se** M (type of) soft cheese; **Koch|kunst** F culinary art, art of cooking; **seine ~** *or* **Kochkünste** his cooking (ability); **Koch|künst|ler(in)** M(F) cookery expert, expert cook; **Koch|kurs** M cookery course; **Koch|löf|fel** M cooking spoon; **Koch|ni|sche** F kitchenette; **Koch|plat|te** F **a** *(= Herdplatte)* hotplate **b** *(= Kocher)* cooker; **Koch|re|zept** NT recipe; **Koch|salz** NT common salt; *(Chem auch)* sodium chloride; *(Cook)* cooking salt; **Koch|salz|in|fu|si|on** F *(Med)* saline infusion; **Koch|schin|ken** M boiled ham; **Koch|stel|le** F **a** *(im Freien)* campfire hearth **b** *(= Kochplatte)* hotplate; **Koch|topf** M (cooking) pot; *(mit Stiel)* saucepan; **Koch|wä|sche** F washing that can be boiled; **Koch|was|ser** NT, *no pl* cooking water, water in which (the) vegetables have been boiled; **Koch|zeit** F cooking time

kod|de|rig ['kɔdərɪç], **kodd|rig** ['kɔdrɪç] ADJ *(N Ger inf)* **a** *(= unwohl)* sick, queasy; **mir ist ganz ~** I feel sick *or* queasy **b** *(= frech)* insolent, impudent

Ko|de [koːt, 'koːdə] M **-s, -s** = **Code**

Ko|de|in [kode'iːn] NT **-s,** *no pl* codeine

Kö|der ['køːdɐ] M **-s, -** bait; *(fig auch)* lure

Kö|der|fisch M bait fish

kö|dern ['køːdɐn] VT *(lit)* to lure; *(fig)* to tempt, to entice; **er will dich mit diesen Versprechun-**

gen nur ~ these promises of his are only a bait (to lure you); **jdn zu ~ versuchen** to woo sb; **jdn für etw** ~ to rope sb into sth *(inf)*; **sich von jdm/etw nicht ~ lassen** not to be tempted by sb/sth; **sie köderte ihn mit ihrem Charme** she seduced him with her charms; **sie köderte ihn mit ihrem Geld** she lured him with her money

Ko|dex ['ko:dɛks] M - *or* **-es, -e** *or* **Kodices** *or* **Kodizes** ['ko:ditse:s] *(= Gesetzbuch)* codex, code; *(= Handschrift)* codex, manuscript; *(fig)* (moral) code

ko|die|ren [ko'di:rən] *ptp* **kodiert** VT = **codieren**

Ko|die|rung F -, -en = **Codierung**

Ko|di|fi|ka|ti|on [kodifika'tsio:n] F -, -en codification

ko|di|fi|zie|ren [kodifi'tsi:rən] *ptp* **kodifiziert** VT to codify; *(fig geh)* to write down; **kodifiziertes Recht** codified *or* statute law

Ko|edu|ka|ti|on ['ko:ledukatsio:n, koleduka'tsio:n] F -, *no pl* coeducation

Ko|ef|fi|zi|ent [koleﬁ'tsiɛnt] M -en, -en coefficient

Ko|exis|tenz ['ko:lɛksɪstɛnts, kolɛksɪs'tɛnts] F, *no pl* coexistence

Ko|fel ['ko:fl] M -s, - *(Aus, S Ger)* rounded *or* dome-shaped mountain top

Kof|fe|in [kɔfe'i:n] NT -s, *no pl* caffeine

kof|fe|in|frei ADJ decaffeinated

kof|fe|in|hal|tig ADJ caffeinated, containing caffeine *pred*

Kof|fer ['kɔfɐ] M -s, - **a** (suit)case, bag; *(= Überseekoffer, Schrankkoffer)* trunk; *(= Arztkoffer)* bag; *(für Schreibmaschine, Kosmetika etc)* (carrying) case; **die ~ packen** *(lit, fig)* to pack one's bags; **aus dem ~ leben** to live out of a suitcase **b** *(Mil sl)* heavy shell

Kof|fer|an|hän|ger M luggage *or* baggage label *or* tag

Köf|fer|chen ['kœfɐçən] NT -s, - *dim von* **Koffer**

Kof|fer-: **Kof|fer|ge|rät** NT portable (set); **Kof|fer|ku|li** M (luggage) trolley *(Brit)*, cart *(US)*; **Kof|fer|ra|dio** NT portable radio; **Kof|fer|raum** M *(Aut)* boot *(Brit)*, trunk *(US)*; *(= Volumen)* luggage *or* baggage space; **Kof|fer|schreib|ma|schi|ne** F portable (typewriter); **Kof|fer|trä|ger(in)** M(F) porter

Ko|gel ['ko:gl] M -s, - *(Aus, S Ger)* = **Kofel**

Kog|ge ['kɔgə] F -, -n *(Naut)* cog

Kog|nak ['kɔnjak] M -s, -s *or* -e brandy

Kog|nak-: **Kog|nak|glas** NT brandy glass; **Kog|nak|schwen|ker** [-ʃvɛŋkɐ] M -s, - brandy glass *or* balloon, balloon glass

kog|ni|tiv [kɔgni'ti:f] ADJ *(Philos, Psych)* cognitive

Ko|ha|bi|ta|ti|on [kohabita'tsio:n] F -, -en *(form)* cohabitation

Ko|hä|si|on [kohɛ'zio:n] F -, *no pl (Phys, geh)* cohesion

Ko|hä|si|ons|kraft F *(Phys, geh)* cohesive force

Kohl [ko:l] M -(e)s, -e **a** cabbage; **das macht den ~ auch nicht fett** *(inf)* that's not much help **b** *(inf: = Unsinn)* rubbish *(Brit inf)*, nonsense; **aufgewärmter** ~ old stuff *or* story

Kohl|dampf M, *no pl (inf)* ~ **haben** *or* **schieben** to be starving *or* famished

Koh|le ['ko:lə] F -, -n **a** *(= Brennstoff)* coal; *(= Stück Kohle)* (lump of) coal; *(dial: = Brikett)* briquette; **wir haben keine ~n mehr** we have no coal left; **weiße** ~ white coal, water power, hydroelectric power; **glühende ~n** *(lit)* (glowing) embers; **glühende** *or* **feurige ~n auf jds Haupt sammeln** *(geh)* to heap coals of fire on sb's head; **(wie) auf (glühenden** *or* **heißen) ~n sitzen** to be like a cat on hot bricks *(Brit) or* on a hot tin roof, to be on tenterhooks *(esp Brit)*; **die ~n aus dem Feuer holen** *(fig)* to pull the chestnuts out of the fire
b *(= Verkohltes, Holzkohle)* charcoal; **(tierische** *or* **medizinische)** ~ animal charcoal
c *(Art: = Kohlestift)* (stick of) charcoal; **mit ~ zeichnen** to draw with *or* in charcoal
d *(Tech)* carbon
e *(inf: = Geld)* dough *(inf)*, cash *(inf)*; **die ~ stimmt** the money's right; **gut** *or* **fett ~ machen** *(sl: = gut verdienen)* to make a packet *(Brit inf)*, to make a lot of money

Koh|le-: **Koh|le|fil|ter** M charcoal filter; **Koh|le|hyd|rat** NT carbohydrate, carb *(inf)*; **Koh|le|hyd|rie|rung** [-hydri:rʊŋ] F -, *no pl (Tech)* hydrogenation of coal; **Koh|le|kraft|werk** NT coal-fired power station

koh|len[1] ['ko:lən] VI **a** *(Naut, Rail)* to take on coal **b** *(= verkohlen)* to char, to carbonize **c** *(= Ruß erzeugen)* to smoke

koh|len[2] VTI *(inf)* to talk a load of rubbish *(Brit inf) or* nonsense; *(= lügen)* to lie, to tell lies; **unglaublich, was der wieder kohlt** it's incredible the nonsense he's been talking again/the lies he's been telling again

Koh|len- *in cpds* coal; **Koh|len|berg|bau** M coal-mining; **Koh|len|berg|werk** NT coal mine, pit, colliery; **Koh|len|bun|ker** M coal bunker; **Koh|len|di|oxid, Koh|len|di|oxyd** NT carbon dioxide; **Koh|len|gas** NT coal gas; **Koh|len|ge|biet** NT coal-mining area; **Koh|len|gru|be** F coal mine, pit; **Koh|len|grus** M (coal) slack; **Koh|len|hal|de** F pile of coal; **Koh|len|hal|den** PL coal stocks *pl*; **Koh|len|hei|zung** F coal heating; *(= Anlage)* coal heating system; **Koh|len|herd** M range; **Koh|len|hyd|rat** NT = **Kohlehydrat**; **Koh|len|in|dust|rie** F coal industry; **Koh|len|kas|ten** M coal box; **Koh|len|kel|ler** M coal cellar; **Koh|len|la|ger** NT **a** *(= Vorrat)* coal depot **b** *(im Stollen, Berg)* coal seam *or* bed; **Koh|len|mon|oxid, Koh|len|mon|oxyd** NT carbon monoxide; **Koh|len|ofen** M (coal-)burning) stove; **Koh|len|pott** M *(inf)* **a** coal-mining area **b** *(inf: = Ruhrgebiet)* Ruhr (basin *or* valley); **Koh|len|re|vier** NT coal-mining area; **Koh|len|sack** M coal sack; **koh|len|sau|er** ADJ **kohlensaurer Kalk** calcium carbonate; **kohlensaures Natrium** sodium carbonate; **Koh|len|säu|re** F **a** *(Chem)* carbonic acid **b** *(inf: in Getränken)* fizz *(inf)*; **koh|len|säu|re|hal|tig** ADJ *Getränke* carbonated; **Koh|len|schau|fel** F coal shovel; **Koh|len|staub** M coal dust; **Koh|len|staub|lun|ge** F anthracosis

Koh|len|stoff M *(abbr* **C***)* carbon

Koh|len|stoff|da|tie|rung [-dati:rʊŋ] F -, -en (radio)carbon dating

Koh|len-: **Koh|len|trim|mer** [-trɪmɐ] M -s, - (coal) trimmer; **Koh|len|wa|gen** M **a** *(Rail)* *(= Tender)* tender; *(= Waggon)* coal truck **b** *(= LKW)* coal lorry *(Brit) or* truck; **Koh|len|was|ser|stoff** M hydrocarbon; **Koh|len|zan|ge** F (pair of) fire *or* coal tongs *pl*; **Koh|len|ze|che** F coal mine, pit, colliery

Koh|le-: **Koh|le|ofen** M coal(-burning) stove; **Koh|le|pa|pier** NT carbon paper; **Koh|le|pfen|nig** M, *no pl (Hist) special tax paid on electricity to subsidize the coal industry*

Köh|ler ['kø:lɐ] M -s, -, **Köh|le|rin** [-ərɪn] F -, -nen charcoal burner

Köh|le|rei [kølə'rai] F -, *no pl* charcoal burning

Koh|le-: **Koh|le|stab** M *(Tech)* carbon rod; **Koh|le|stift** M *(Art)* piece *or* stick of charcoal; **Koh|le|tab|let|te** F *(Med)* charcoal tablet; **Koh|le|vor|kom|men** NT coal deposit(s *pl*); **Koh|le|zeich|nung** F charcoal drawing

Kohl-: **Kohl|kopf** M cabbage; **Kohl|mei|se** F great tit; **kohl|(pech)|ra|ben|schwarz** ADJ **a** *Haar* jet black, raven *attr*, raven-black; *Nacht* pitch-black **b** *(inf: = sehr schmutzig)* as black as coal; **Kohl|ra|bi** [ko:l'ra:bi] M -(s), - kohlrabi; **Kohl|rou|la|de** F *(Cook)* stuffed cabbage leaves *pl*; **Kohl|rü|be** F *(Bot)* swede *(Brit)*, rutabaga *(US)*; **Kohl|sa|lat** M coleslaw; **kohl|schwarz** ADJ *Haare, Augen* jet black; *Gesicht, Hände* black as coal; **Kohl|spros|se** F *(Aus)* (Brussels) sprout; **Kohl|weiß|ling** [-vaislɪŋ] M -s, -e cabbage white (butterfly)

Ko|hor|te [ko'hɔrtə] F -, -n *(Hist)* cohort

ko|i|tie|ren [koi'ti:rən] *ptp* **koitiert** VI *(esp Med)* to engage in coitus *or* sexual intercourse

Ko|i|tus ['ko:itʊs] M -, -se *or* - ['ko:itu:s] *(esp Med)* coitus, coition

Ko|je ['ko:jə] F -, -n **a** *(esp Naut)* bunk, berth; *(inf: = Bett)* bed; **sich in die ~ hauen** *(inf)* to hit the sack *(inf) or* the hay *(inf)* **b** *(= Ausstellungskoje)* stand

Ko|jo|te [ko'jo:tə] M -n, -n coyote

Ko|ka ['ko:ka] F -, - *(Bot)* coca

Ko|ka|in [koka'i:n] NT -s, *no pl* cocaine

ko|ka|in|süch|tig ADJ addicted to cocaine; **ein Kokainsüchtiger** a cocaine addict

Ko|kar|de [ko'kardə] F -, -n cockade

ko|keln ['ko:kln] VI *(inf)* to play with fire; **mit Kerzen/Streichhölzern** ~ to play with (lighted) candles/matches

Ko|ke|rei [ko:kə'rai] F -, -en *(= Tätigkeit)* coking; *(= Anlage)* coking plant

ko|kett [ko'kɛt] ADJ coquettish, flirtatious ADV coquettishly

Ko|ket|te|rie [kokɛtə'ri:] F -, -n [-'ri:ən] **a** *no pl (= Eigenschaft)* coquettishness, coquetry, flirtatiousness **b** *(= Bemerkung)* coquettish *or* flirtatious remark, coquetry

ko|ket|tie|ren [koke'ti:rən] *ptp* **kokettiert** VI to flirt; **mit seinem Alter** ~ to play up *or* upon one's age; **mit einem Gedanken/System** *etc* ~ to toy with an idea/method *etc*

Ko|ko|lo|res [koko'lo:rɛs] M -, *no pl (inf)* **a** *(= Unsinn)* rubbish *(Brit inf)*, nonsense, twaddle *(Brit inf)* **b** *(= Umstände)* palaver *(inf)*, fuss; **mach doch nicht solchen** ~ don't make such a palaver *(inf) or* fuss

Ko|kon [ko'kõ:] M -s, -s *(Zool)* cocoon

Ko|kos[1] ['ko:kɔs] F -, - *(= Palme)* coconut palm *or* tree

Ko|kos[2] NT -, *no pl* coconut

Ko|kos- *in cpds* coconut; **Ko|kos|fa|ser** F coconut fibre *(Brit) or* fiber *(US)*; **Ko|kos|fett** NT coconut oil; **Ko|kos|flo|cken** PL desiccated coconut; **Ko|kos|läu|fer** M coconut matting; **Ko|kos|mat|te** F coconut mat(ting), coir mat(ting); **Ko|kos|milch** F coconut milk; **Ko|kos|nuss** F coconut; **Ko|kos|öl** NT coconut oil; **Ko|kos|pal|me** F coconut palm *or* tree; **Ko|kos|ras|peln** PL desiccated coconut

Ko|kot|te [ko'kɔtə] F -, -n *(old)* cocotte

Koks[1] [ko:ks] M -es, -e coke; *(inf) (= Unsinn)* rubbish *(Brit inf)*, nonsense; *(= Geld)* dough *(inf)*, cash *(inf)*

Koks[2] M OR NT -es, *no pl (inf: = Kokain)* coke *(inf)*

kok|sen ['ko:ksn] VI *(inf: = Kokain nehmen)* to take coke *(inf)*

Kok|ser ['ko:ksɐ] M -s, -, **Kok|se|rin** [-ərɪn] F -, -nen *(inf)* cocaine *or* coke *(inf)* addict

Ko|la[1] ['ko:la] F -, *no pl (Nuss)* cola *or* kola nut

Ko|la[2] *pl von* **Kolon**

Ko|la-: **Ko|la|baum** M cola *or* kola tree; **Ko|la|nuss** F cola *or* kola nut

Kol|ben ['kɔlbn] M -s, - **a** *(= dickes Ende, Gewehrkolben)* butt; *(Tech: = Motorkolben, Pumpenkolben)* piston; *(Chem: = Destillierkolben)* retort; *(von Glühlampe)* bulb; *(von Lötapparat)* bit; *(sl: = Penis)* prick *(sl)*, cock *(sl)*, tool *(sl)* **b** *(Bot)* spadix; *(= Maiskolben)* cob

Kol|ben-: **kol|ben|för|mig** ADJ club-shaped ADV **etw verdickt sich** ~ sth widens into a club shape; **Kol|ben|fres|ser** M *(inf)* piston seizure; **(den)** ~ **haben** to have piston seizure; **Kol|ben|hal|ter** M plunger refill (fountain) pen; **Kol|ben|hub** M *(von Pumpe)* plunger stroke; *(Aut)* piston stroke; **Kol|ben|ring** M piston ring

Kol|chos ['kɔlçɔs] M OR NT -, **Kolchose** [-'ço:zə], **Kol|cho|se** [kɔl'ço:zə] F -, -n collective farm, kolkhoz

Kol|chos|bau|er M *pl* **-bauern**, **Kol|chos|bäu|e|rin** F -, -nen worker on a collective farm

Ko|li|bak|te|ri|en ['ko:li-] PL E.coli *pl*

Ko|lib|ri ['ko:libri] M -s, -s humming bird, colibri *(spec)*

Ko|lik ['ko:lɪk] F -, -en colic

ko|lik|ar|tig ADJ colicky

Kol|ka|ta [kɔl'ka:ta] NT -s Kolkata *(neuer offizieller Name für Kalkutta)*

Kolk|ra|be ['kɔlk-] M raven

kol|la|bie|ren [kɔla'bi:rən] *ptp* **kollabiert** VI *aux sein (Med, fig)* to collapse

Kol|la|bo|ra|teur [kɔlabora'tø:ɐ] M -s, -e, **Kol|la|bo|ra|teu|rin** [-'tø:rɪn] F -, -nen *(Pol)* collaborator

Kol|la|bo|ra|ti|on [kɔlabora'tsio:n] F -, -en collaboration

kol|la|bo|rie|ren *ptp* **kollaboriert** VI to collaborate

Kol|la|ge [kɔ'la:ʒə] F -, -n = **Collage**

Kol|laps ['kɔlaps, kɔ'laps] M -es, -e *(Med, fig)* collapse; **einen ~ erleiden** to collapse

Kol|la|te|ral|scha|den [kɔlate'ra:l-] M *(Mil; euph)* collateral damage

Kol|la|ti|on [kɔla'tsio:n] F -, -en *(Liter)* collation, comparison; *(Typ)* collation

kol|la|ti|o|nie|ren [kɔlatsio'ni:rən] *ptp* **kollationiert** VT *(Liter)* to collate, to compare; *(Typ)* to collate

Kol|leg [kɔ'le:k] NT -s, -s *or* -ien [-giən] **a** *(Univ)* (= *Vorlesung*) lecture; (= *Vorlesungsreihe*) (course of) lectures *pl* **b** *(Sch)* college **c** *(Eccl)* theological college

Kol|le|ge [kɔ'le:gə] M -n, -n, **Kol|le|gin** [-'le:gɪn] F -, -nen colleague; *(Arbeiter auch)* workmate; **seine ~n vom Fach** his professional colleagues; **meine ~n** the people I work with, my colleagues; **seine ~n in der Ärzteschaft** his fellow doctors; **~ kommt gleich!** somebody will be with you right away; **Herr ~!** Mr X; **der (Herr) ~ (Müller)** *(Parl)* the honourable *(Brit) or* honorable *(US)* member

Kol|le|gen-: **Kol|le|gen|kreis** M **im ~** among colleagues; **Kol|le|gen|ra|batt** M trade discount; **Kol|le|gen|schaft** [kɔ'le:gnʃaft] F -, -en colleagues *pl*

Kol|leg-: **Kol|leg|geld** NT lecture fee; **Kol|leg|heft** NT (student's) notebook

kol|le|gi|al [kɔle'gia:l] ADJ **das war nicht sehr ~ von ihm** that wasn't what you would expect from a colleague; **mit ~en Grüßen** ≈ yours sincerely *(Brit)*, sincerely yours *(US)* ADV loyally; **sich ~ verhalten** to be a good colleague; **~ eingestellt sein** to be cooperative

Kol|le|gi|a|li|tät [kɔlegiali'tɛ:t] F -, *no pl* loyalty (to one's colleagues)

Kol|le|gi|at [kɔle'gia:t] M -n, -n, **Kol|le|gi|a|tin** [kɔle'gia:tɪn] F -, -nen **a** *(Univ)* college student *on a course for university entrance qualification* **b** *(Sch:* = *Schüler der Kollegstufe)* ≈ sixth form college *(Brit) or* junior college *(US)* student

Kol|le|gin [-'le:gɪn] F → **Kollege**

Kol|le|gi|um [kɔ'le:gium] NT -s, **Kollegien** [-giən] **a** (= *Lehrerkollegium etc*) staff; (= *Ausschuss*) working party **b** = **Kolleg**

Kol|leg|map|pe F document case

KOLLEGSTUFE

The **Kollegstufe**, or **reformierte gymnasiale Oberstufe**, refers to the final two school years in a **Gymnasium** (two and a half years in some **Länder**). Students can choose which subjects to study, according to their abilities and interests, and can follow courses for one semester only. This system is designed to prepare pupils for university. → GYMNASIUM

Kol|lek|te [kɔ'lɛktə] F -, -n *(Eccl)* offering, collection, offertory

Kol|lek|ti|on [kɔlɛk'tsio:n] F -, -en collection; (= *Sortiment*) range; *(Fashion)* collection; **~ (an Mustern)** (set of) samples

kol|lek|tiv [kɔlɛk'ti:f] ADJ collective ADV collectively

Kol|lek|tiv [kɔlɛk'ti:f] NT -s, -e [-və] collective

Kol|lek|tiv-: **Kol|lek|tiv|ar|beit** F (= *Tätigkeit*) collective work, collaboration; (= *Ergebnis*) collective piece of work; **Kol|lek|tiv|be|griff** M *(Ling)* collective (term); **Kol|lek|tiv|geist** M corporate *or* collective spirit

kol|lek|ti|vie|ren [kɔlɛkti'vi:rən] *ptp* **kollektiviert** VT to collectivize

Kol|lek|ti|vis|mus [kɔlɛkti'vɪsmʊs] M -, *no pl* collectivism

Kol|lek|ti|vist [kɔlɛkti'vɪst] M -en, -en, **Kol|lek|ti|vis|tin** [-'vɪstɪn] F -, -nen collectivist

Kol|lek|tiv-: **Kol|lek|tiv|schuld** F collective guilt; **Kol|lek|tiv|stra|fe** F collective punishment

Kol|lek|ti|vum [kɔlɛk'ti:vʊm] NT -s, **Kollektiva** *or* **Kollektiven** [-va, -vn] *(Ling)* collective (noun)

Kol|lek|tiv-: **Kol|lek|tiv|ver|trag** M collective agreement; **Kol|lek|tiv|wirt|schaft** F *(Econ)* collective economy

Kol|lek|tor [kɔ'lɛkto:ɐ] M -s, **Kollektoren** [-'to:rən] *(Elec)* collector; (= *Sonnenkollektor*) solar collector *or* panel

Kol|ler ['kɔlɐ] M -s, - **a** *(inf)* (= *Anfall*) silly *or* funny mood; (= *Wutanfall*) rage; (= *Tropenkoller*) tropical madness; (= *Gefängniskoller*) prison madness; **seinen ~ bekommen/haben** to get into/to be in one of one's silly *or* funny moods; **einen ~ haben/bekommen** to be in/fly into a rage **b** *(Vet: bei Pferden)* staggers *sing*

kol|lern ['kɔlɐn] VI **a** *(Truthahn etc)* to gobble; *(Magen, Darm)* to rumble **b** *aux sein (dial:* = *kullern)* to roll VI *impers* **es kollert in seinem Bauch** his stomach is rumbling

kol|li|die|ren [kɔli'di:rən] *ptp* **kollidiert** VI *(geh)* **a** *aux sein (Fahrzeuge)* to collide, to be in collision **b** *aux sein or haben (fig)* to conflict, to be in conflict, to clash; *(Termine)* to clash; **miteinander ~** to conflict, to clash, to be in conflict (with each other); **er ist mit dem Gesetz kollidiert** he has collided with the law

Kol|li|er [kɔ'lie:] NT -s, -s necklet, necklace

Kol|li|si|on [kɔli'zio:n] F -, -en *(geh)* (= *Zusammenstoß*) collision; (= *Streit*) conflict, clash; *(von Terminen)* clash; **mit dem Gesetz in ~ geraten** *or* **kommen** to come into conflict with the law, to collide with the law

Kol|li|si|ons|kurs M *(Naut, Aviat)* collision course; **auf ~ gehen, einen ~ ansteuern** *(fig)* to be heading for trouble

Kol|lo|id [kɔlo'i:t] NT -s, -e [-də] *(Chem)* colloid

Kol|lo|ka|ti|on [kɔloka'tsio:n] F -, -en *(Ling)* collocation

Kol|lo|qui|um [kɔ'lo:kvium, kɔ'lɔkvium] NT -s, **Kolloquien** [-kviən] colloquium; *(Aus Univ:* = *Prüfung)* examination

Köln [kœln] NT -s Cologne

Köl|ner ['kœlnɐ] ADJ *attr* Cologne; **der ~ Dom** Cologne Cathedral

Köl|ner ['kœlnɐ] M -s, -, **Köl|ne|rin** [-ərɪn] F -, -nen inhabitant *or* (*gebürtiger*) native of Cologne; **er ist ~** *(wohnhaft)* he lives in Cologne; *(kommt aus Köln)* he comes from Cologne

köl|nisch ['kœlnɪʃ] ADJ Cologne *attr*; **er spricht Kölnisch** he speaks (the) Cologne dialect

Köl|nisch|was|ser NT, *no pl*, **köl|nisch Was|ser** NT, *no pl* eau de Cologne, cologne

Ko|lo|fo|ni|um [kolo'fo:niʊm] △ NT -s, *no pl* → **Kolophonium**

Ko|lom|bi|ne [kolɔm'bi:nə] F -, -n *(Theat)* Columbine

Ko|lon ['ko:lɔn] NT -s, -s *or* **Kola** [-la] *(Typ, Anat)* colon

Ko|lo|nia|kü|bel [ko'lo:nia-] M *(Aus)* dustbin *(Brit)*, trash *or* garbage can *(US)*

ko|lo|ni|al [kolo'nia:l] ADJ *(rare)* colonial

Ko|lo|ni|al- *in cpds* colonial; **Ko|lo|ni|al|be|sitz** M colonial possessions *pl*; **das Land ist in ~** that country is a colony; **Ko|lo|ni|al|herr** M colonial master; (= *Herrscher*) colonial ruler; **Ko|lo|ni|al|herr|schaft** F colonial rule

ko|lo|ni|a|li|sie|ren [koloniali'zi:rən] *ptp* **kolonialisiert** VT to colonize

Ko|lo|ni|a|lis|mus [kolonia'lɪsmʊs] M -, *no pl* colonialism

Ko|lo|ni|al-: **Ko|lo|ni|al|macht** F colonial power; **Ko|lo|ni|al|reich** NT colonial empire; **Ko|lo|ni|al|stil** M Colonial (style); **Ko|lo|ni|al|wa|ren** PL groceries *pl*; (= *Erzeugnisse der Kolonien*) colonial produce; **Ko|lo|ni|al|wa|ren|händ|ler(in)** M(F) *(dated)* grocer; **Ko|lo|ni|al|wa|ren|hand|lung** F, **Ko|lo|ni|al|wa|ren|ge|schäft** NT *(dated)* grocer's (shop); **Ko|lo|ni|al|zeit** F colonial times *pl*; **ein Relikt aus der ~** a relic of the colonial past *or* of colonial times

Ko|lo|ni|a|wa|gen [ko'lo:nia-] M *(Aus)* refuse lorry *(Brit) or* truck

Ko|lo|nie [kolo'ni:] F -, -n [-'ni:ən] *(alle Bedeutungen)* colony; (= *Ansiedlung auch*) settlement; (= *Ferienkolonie*) camp

Ko|lo|ni|sa|ti|on [koloniza'tsio:n] F -, *no pl* **a** (= *Erschließung: von Gebiet*) settlement **b** (= *Kolonisieren: von Land*) colonization

ko|lo|ni|sie|ren [koloni'zi:rən] *ptp* **kolonisiert** VT **a** (= *erschließen*) *Gebiet* to settle in **b** (= *zur Kolonie machen*) *Land* to colonize

Ko|lo|nist [kolo'nɪst] M -en, -en, **Ko|lo|nis|tin** [-'nɪstɪn] F -, -nen colonist; (= *Siedler*) settler

Ko|lon|na|de [kolɔ'na:də] F -, -n colonnade

Ko|lon|ne [ko'lɔnə] F -, -n column; (= *Autoschlange, fig:* = *Menge*) queue *(Brit)*, line; *(zur Begleitung esp Mil)* convoy; (= *Arbeitskolonne*) gang; **„Achtung ~!"** "convoy"; **~ fahren** to drive in (a) convoy; **fünfte ~** fifth column

Ko|lon|nen-: **Ko|lon|nen|fah|ren** NT -s, *no pl* driving in (a) convoy; **Ko|lon|nen|sprin|gen** NT jumping the (traffic) queue *(Brit) or* line *(US)*; **Ko|lon|nen|sprin|ger(in)** M(F) queue-jumper *(Brit)*, line-jumper *(US)*; **Ko|lon|nen|ver|kehr** M a queue/queues of traffic *(Brit)*, a line/lines of traffic, a tailback *(Brit)*

Ko|lo|pho|ni|um [kolo'fo:niʊm] NT -s, *no pl* rosin, resin, colophony *(spec)*

Ko|lo|ra|tur [kolora'tu:ɐ] F -, -en coloratura

ko|lo|rie|ren [kolo'ri:rən] *ptp* **koloriert** VT to colour *(Brit)*, to color *(US)*

Ko|lo|rit [kolo'ri:t] NT -(e)s, -e *(Art)* colouring *(Brit)*, coloring *(US)*; *(Mus)* (tone) colour *(Brit) or* color *(US)*; *(Liter, fig)* atmosphere, colour *(Brit)*, color *(US)*

Ko|lo|sko|pie [kolosko'pi:] F -, -n [-'pi:ən] *(Med)* colonoscopy

Ko|loss [ko'lɔs] M -es, -e colossus; *(fig auch)* giant; **der ~ von Rhodos** the Colossus of Rhodes

ko|los|sal [kolɔ'sa:l] ADJ *Gebäude, Figur* colossal, enormous; *Glück, Gefühl* tremendous; *Dummheit* crass ADV *(inf)* tremendously, enormously; **sich ~ verschätzen** to make a colossal mistake

Ko|los|sal-: **Ko|los|sal|film** M epic film, (film) epic; **Ko|los|sal|ge|mäl|de** NT *(inf)* spectacular painting; **Ko|los|sal|schin|ken** M *(pej geh)* spectacular

Ko|los|ser [ko'lɔsɐ] M -s, -, **Ko|los|se|rin** [-ərɪn] F -, -nen **a** *(Hist)* Colossian **b** *(Bibl)* = **Kolosserbrief**

Ko|los|ser|brief M Epistle to the Colossians, Colossians *sing, no def art*

Ko|los|se|um [kolɔ'se:ʊm] NT -s, *no pl* **das ~** the Colosseum

Kol|por|ta|ge [kɔlpɔr'ta:ʒə] F -, -n **a** *(Press)* cheap sensationalism **b** (= *minderwertige Literatur*) trash, rubbish *(esp Brit inf)* **c** *(old:* = *Wandergewerbe)* peddling

Kol|por|ta|ge-: **Kol|por|ta|ge|li|te|ra|tur** F trashy literature; **Kol|por|ta|ge|ro|man** M trashy novel

kol|por|tie|ren [kɔlpɔr'ti:rən] *ptp* **kolportiert** VT **a** *Nachricht* to spread, to circulate; *Gerüchte* to spread, to peddle; **die Zeitung kolportierte, dass ...** the paper spread the story that ... **b** *(old) Bücher etc* to peddle

kölsch [kœlʃ] ADJ = **kölnisch**

Kölsch [kœlʃ] NT -, - **a** *(= Bier)* ≈ (strong) lager **b** *(= Dialekt)* **er spricht ~** he speaks (the) Cologne dialect

Ko|lum|bi|a|ner [kolʊm'bia:nɐ] M -s, -, **Ko|lum|bi|a|ne|rin** [-ərɪn] F -, -nen Colombian

ko|lum|bi|a|nisch [kolʊm'bia:nɪʃ] ADJ Colombian

Ko|lum|bi|en [ko'lʊmbiən] NT -s Colombia

Ko|lum|bi|er [ko'lʊmbiɐ] M -s, -, **Ko|lum|bi|e|rin** [-iərɪn] F -, -nen Colombian

Ko|lum|bi|ne [kolʊm'bi:nə] F -, -n *(Theat)* Columbine

ko|lum|bisch [ko'lʊmbɪʃ] ADJ Colombian

Ko|lum|bus [ko'lʊmbʊs] M -' **Christoph ~** Christopher Columbus → **Ei**

Ko|lum|ne [ko'lʊmnə] F -, -n *(Typ, Press)* column

Ko|lum|nen|ti|tel M *(Typ)* headline, running head; **toter ~** folio, page number; **lebender ~** running head

Ko|lum|nist [kolʊm'nɪst] M -en, -en, **Ko|lum|nis|tin** [-'nɪstɪn] F -, -nen columnist

Ko|ma ['ko:ma] NT -s, -s *or* -ta [-ta] *(Med)* coma; **im ~ liegen** to be in a coma; **ins ~ fallen** to go *or* fall into a coma

Kom|bat|tant [kɔmba'tant] M -en, -en, **Kom|bat|tan|tin** [-'tantɪn] F -, -nen *(geh)* combatant

Kom|bi ['kɔmbi] M -s, -s *(Aut)* estate (car) *(Brit)*, station wagon *(esp US)*

Kom|bi|kar|te F *(= Fahr- und Eintrittskarte)* combined ticket *(for travel and admission)*

Kom|bi|lohn M *wage subsidized by the state*

Kom|bi|nat [kɔmbi'na:t] NT -s, -e *(Econ)* combine

Kom|bi|na|ti|on [kɔmbina'tsio:n] F -, -en **a** *(= Verbindung, Zusammenstellung, Zahlenkombination)* combination; *(Sport: = Zusammenspiel)* concerted move, (piece of) teamwork; **alpine/nordische ~** *(Ski)* Alpine/Nordic combination **b** *(= Schlussfolgerung)* deduction, reasoning; *(= Vermutung)* conjecture **c** *(= Kleidung)* suit, ensemble; *(= Hemdhose)* combinations *pl*, combs *pl (inf)*; *(= Arbeitsanzug)* overalls *pl*, boiler suit; *(= Fliegerkombination)* flying suit

Kom|bi|na|ti|ons-: **Kom|bi|na|ti|ons|feld** NT *(Comput)* cobo box; **Kom|bi|na|ti|ons|ga|be** F powers *pl* of deduction *or* reasoning; **Kom|bi|na|ti|ons|mög|lich|keit** F possible combination; **Kom|bi|na|ti|ons|prä|pa|rat** NT *(Pharm)* compound preparation; **Kom|bi|na|ti|ons|schloss** NT combination lock; **Kom|bi|na|ti|ons|ver|mö|gen** NT powers *pl* of deduction

Kom|bi|na|to|rik [kɔmbina'to:rɪk] F -, *no pl* *(Math)* combination theory, theory of combinations

kom|bi|na|to|risch [kɔmbina'to:rɪʃ] ADJ **a** *Fähigkeiten* deductive; *Problem, Logik* combinatory **b** *(Ling)* **~er Lautwandel** conditioned sound change

kom|bi|nier|bar [-ba:ɐ] ADJ combinable; *Kleidungsstücke* mix-and-match *attr*

kom|bi|nie|ren [kɔmbi'ni:rən] *ptp* **kombiniert** VT to combine; *Kleidungsstücke auch* to wear together; **Möbel zum Kombinieren** unit furniture; **zum beliebigen Kombinieren** to mix and match VI **a** *(= folgern)* to deduce; *(= vermuten)* to suppose; **gut ~ können** to be good at deducing *or* deduction; **ich kombiniere: ...** I conclude: ...; **du hast richtig kombiniert** your conclusion is right, you have come to the right conclusion **b** *(Sport)* to make a concerted move

Kom|bi|nie|rer M -s, -, **Kom|bi|nie|re|rin** F -, -nen *(Ski)* competitor in the combination (event)

Kom|bi-: **Kom|bi|wa|gen** M estate (car) *(Brit)*, station wagon *(esp US)*; **Kom|bi|zan|ge** F combination pliers *pl*

Kom|bü|se [kɔm'by:zə] F -, -n *(Naut)* galley

Ko|met [ko'me:t] M -en, -en comet; *(fig)* meteor

ko|me|ten-: **ko|me|ten|ar|tig** ADJ **a** *(Astron)* comet-like **b** *(fig)* = **kometenhaft**; **ko|me|ten|haft** ADJ *(fig) Aufstieg, Karriere* meteoric; *Aufschwung* rapid

Kom|fort [kɔm'fo:ɐ] M -s, *no pl (von Hotel etc)* luxury; *(von Möbel etc)* comfort; *(von Auto)* luxury features *pl*; *(von Gerät)* extras *pl*; *(von Wohnung)* amenities *pl*, mod cons *pl (Brit inf)*; **ein Auto mit allem ~** a luxury car, a car with many luxury features

-kom|fort M *suf in cpds* comfort; **Fahrkomfort** (motoring) comfort; **ein Fernsehgerät mit großem Bedienungskomfort** a television set with easy-to-use controls

kom|for|ta|bel [kɔmfɔr'ta:bl] ADJ *(= mit Komfort ausgestattet)* luxurious, luxury *attr*; *Haus, Wohnung* well-appointed; *(= bequem) Sessel, Bett* comfortable; *(= praktisch) Bedienung* convenient ADV *(= bequem)* comfortably; *(= mit viel Komfort)* luxuriously

Kom|fort|woh|nung [kɔm'fo:ɐ-] F luxury flat *(Brit) or* apartment

Ko|mik ['ko:mɪk] F -, *no pl (= das Komische)* comic; *(= komische Wirkung)* comic effect; *(= lustiges Element: von Situation)* comic element; **tragische ~** tragicomedy; **ein Sinn für ~** a sense of the comic

Ko|mi|ker ['ko:mɪkɐ] M -s, -, **Ko|mi|ke|rin** [-ərɪn] F -, -nen comedian, comic; *(fig auch)* joker *(inf)*; **Sie ~** you must be joking

Kom|in|form [komɪn'fɔrm] NT -s, *no pl (Hist)* **das ~** the Cominform

Kom|in|tern [komɪn'tɛrn] F -, *no pl (Hist)* **die ~** the Comintern

ko|misch ['ko:mɪʃ] ADJ **a** *(= spaßhaft, ulkig)* funny, comical; *(Theat) Rolle, Person, Oper* comic; **der ~e Alte** *(Theat)* the comic old man; **das Komische** *(Liter)* the comic; **das Komische daran** the funny thing about it **b** *(= seltsam, verdächtig)* funny, strange, odd; **das Komische daran ist ...** the funny *or* strange *or* odd thing about it is ...; **~, ich hab schon wieder Hunger** funny, I'm hungry again already; **~, dass ich das übersehen habe** it's funny *or* odd that I should have missed that; **mir ist/wird so ~** *(inf)* I feel funny *or* strange *or* odd; **er war so ~ zu mir** he acted so strangely towards *(Brit) or* toward *(US)* me ADV strangely; *riechen, schmecken, sich fühlen* strange; **jdm ~ vorkommen** to seem strange to sb

ko|mi|scher|wei|se ['ko:mɪʃɐ'vaizə] ADV funnily enough

Ko|mi|tee [komi'te:] NT -s, -s committee

Kom|ma ['kɔma] NT -s, -s *or* -ta [-ta] comma; *(Math)* decimal point; **fünf/null ~ drei** five/nought point three

Kom|man|dant [kɔman'dant] M -en, -en, **Kom|man|dan|tin** [-'dantɪn] F -, -nen *(Mil)* commanding officer; *(von Festung auch)* commander; *(Naut)* captain; *(von Stadt)* commandant

Kom|man|dan|tur [kɔmandan'tu:ɐ] F -, -en *(= Funktion)* command; *(= Gebäude auch)* headquarters *sing*

Kom|man|deur [kɔman'dø:ɐ] M -s, -e, **Kom|man|deu|rin** [-'dø:rɪn] F -, -nen commander

kom|man|die|ren [kɔman'di:rən] *ptp* **kommandiert** VT **a** *(= befehligen)* to command, to be in command of **b** *(= befehlen)* **jdn an einen Ort ~** to order sb to a place; **ich kommandierte ihn zu mir** I ordered him to appear before me; **sich von jdm ~ lassen** to let oneself be ordered about by sb VI **a** *(= Befehlsgewalt haben)* to be in command; **~der General/Offizier** commanding general/officer **b** *(= Befehle geben)* to command, to give (the) orders; **er kommandiert gern** he likes to be the one to give (the) orders, he likes ordering people about

Kom|man|dit|ge|sell|schaft [kɔman'di:t-] F *(Comm)* ≈ limited partnership

Kom|man|di|tist [kɔmandi'tɪst] M -en, -en, **Kom|man|di|tis|tin** [-'tɪstɪn] F -, -nen ≈ limited partner

Kom|man|do [kɔ'mando] NT -s, -s **a** *(= Befehl)* command, order; **das ~ zum Schießen geben** to give the command *or* order to fire; **auf ~ schreit ihr alle ...** (up)on the command (you) all shout ...; **ich mache nichts auf ~** I don't do things to order *or* on command; **wie auf ~ stehen bleiben** to stand still as if by command; **der Hund gehorcht auf ~** the dog obeys on command **b** *(= Befehlsgewalt)* command; **wer hat das ~?** who is in command?; **das ~ haben** *or* **führen/übernehmen** to be in *or* have/take command *(über +acc* of); **dem ~ von ... unterstehen** to be under the command of ... **c** *(Mil) (= Behörde)* command; *(= Abteilung)* commando

Kom|man|do-: **Kom|man|do|brü|cke** F *(Naut)* bridge; **Kom|man|do|kap|sel** F *(Space)* command module; **Kom|man|do|raum** M control room; **Kom|man|do|stab** M command (staff); **Kom|man|do|stand** M, **Kom|man|do|turm** M *(Naut)* conning tower; **Kom|man|do|un|ter|neh|men** NT commando operation; **Kom|man|do|wirt|schaft** F controlled economy; **Kom|man|do|zent|ra|le** F control centre *(Brit) or* center *(US)*; *(Mil etc)* command headquarters *sing or pl*

Kom|ma|set|zung F **a** *(= Regeln der Kommasetzung)* comma rules *pl*, rules *pl* for the use of commas **b** *(persönlicher Gebrauch)* use of commas

kom|men ['kɔmən] *aux sein*
pret **kam** [ka:m], *ptp* **gekommen** [gə'kɔmən]

1 INTRANSITIVES VERB	3 TRANSITIVES VERB
2 UNPERSÖNLICHES VERB	

1 – INTRANSITIVES VERB

a allgemein to come; **komm sofort her!** come here at once!; **wenn meine Eltern kommen, gibt es immer Erbsensuppe** when my parents come (over) they always get pea soup; **wenn ich zu meinen Eltern komme, gibt es immer Erbsensuppe** when I go over to my parents I always get pea soup; **ich komme (schon)** I'm (just) coming; **er wird gleich kommen** he'll be here right away; **da kommt er ja!** here he comes!; **ich habe zwei Stunden gewartet, aber sie kam und kam nicht** I waited two hours but she just didn't come; **der Nachtisch kommt gleich** the dessert is coming right now *or* is just coming; **er schießt auf alles, was ihm vor die Flinte kommt** he shoots at everything he gets in his sights; **da kann** *or* **könnte ja jeder kommen und sagen ...** anybody could come along and say ...; **wann soll das Baby kommen?** when's the baby due?; **wann kommt Ihr Baby?** when is your baby due?; **das Baby kam zu früh/an Heiligabend** the baby arrived early/on Christmas Eve; **das Kind ist gestern Nacht gekommen** the baby arrived last night; **bei Schmidts kommt ein Baby** the Schmidts are going to have a baby; **komm ich heut nicht, komm ich morgen** *(prov)* you'll see me when you see me; **kommt Zeit, kommt Rat** *(Prov)* things have a way of working themselves out; **wer zuerst kommt, mahlt zuerst** *(Prov)* first come first served *(prov)*; **Torwart zu sein ist langweilig, wenn nie ein Ball kommt** being goalkeeper is boring if the ball never comes your way; **wann kommt der Bus endlich?** when is the bus going to come?; **wann soll der Zug kommen?** when's the train due?; **der Winter ist dieses Jahr sehr früh gekommen** winter has come very early this year; **der Winter kommt mit großen Schritten** winter is fast approaching; **der Mai ist gekommen** May is here; **ich glaube, es kommt ein Unwetter** I think there's some bad weather on the way; **nach dem Krieg kam noch die Hungersnot** after the war came the famine; **der Motor kommt nicht in Gang** the car is difficult to get started, the car won't start; **das Feuer kommt nicht richtig in Gang** it's difficult to get the fire going properly

♦ **(nach Hause) kommen** *(= ankommen)* to get home; *(= zurückkehren)* to come home; **ich komme oft erst um 6 Uhr nach Hause** I often don't get home until 6 o'clock; **wann kommst du heute nach Hause?** when will you get *or* be home today?; **ich komme heute etwas später nach Hause** I'll get *or* be home a bit later today; **bitte komm nach Hause!** please come home!; **wann kommst du endlich nach Hause?** when are you going to come home?; **mein Mann kommt alle drei Wochen nach Hause** my husband comes home every three weeks; **wann kommt er von der Arbeit?** when does he get home from work?; **ich komme manchmal erst spät von der Arbeit** I sometimes get home from work really late; **zum Essen kommen** to come home for lunch/dinner *etc*

♦ **komm!** come on!; **komm, wir gehen** come on, we're going; **komm, sag schon** come on, tell me; **komm, sei nicht so stur** come on don't be so obstinate; **ach komm!** come on!; **komm, fang bloß nicht wieder damit an** come on, don't start that again

♦ **komm, komm!** come on!; **komm, komm, wir müssen uns beeilen!** come on, we must hurry!; **komm, komm, werd nicht frech!** now now, don't be cheeky *(Brit) or* fresh *(US)!*

b = aufgenommen werden to go; **ins Gefängnis kommen** to go to prison; **auf die Universität kommen** to go to university; **ins Altersheim/Krankenhaus kommen** to go into an old people's home *(esp Brit) or* senior citizens' home *(US)*/into hospital; **in die** *or* **zur Schule kommen** to start school

c = hingehören to go; **das Buch kommt ins oberste Fach** the book goes on the top shelf; **der Kühlschrank kommt hier in die Ecke** the fridge is going in this corner; **das kommt unter „Sonstiges"** that comes under "miscellaneous"; **da kommt ein Deckel drauf** it has to have a lid on it

d = erscheinen, folgen to come; *(Zähne)* to come (through); **das Zitat/Lied kommt gleich** that line/song is coming now; **das Zitat/Lied kommt erst später** that line/song doesn't come till later; **das Lied kommt als Nächstes** that song is next; **ich komme zuerst an die Reihe** I'm first; **bohren, bis Öl/Grundwasser kommt** to bore until one strikes oil/finds water; **pass auf, ob hier eine Tankstelle kommt** watch out for a filling station; **jetzt muss bald die Grenze/Hannover kommen** we should soon be at the border/in Hanover; **die Kreuzung/das Zitat muss noch kommen** we haven't come to the crossing/that line yet; **das Schlimmste kommt noch** the worst is yet to come; **warte, das kommt noch** wait, that comes later; **jetzt kommts!** wait for it! *(inf)*; **wie sie (gerade) kommen** just as they come

e = gelangen, erreichen können to get; *(= mit Hand etc erreichen können)* to reach; **wie komme ich nach London?** how do I get to London?; **ich komme zurzeit nicht an die frische Luft/aus dem Haus** at the moment I never get out into the fresh air/out of the house; **durch den Zoll/die Prüfung kommen** to get through customs/the exam; **ich komme mit meiner Hand bis an die Decke** I can reach *or* touch the ceiling with my hand; **in das Alter kommen, wo ...** to reach the age when ...; **die Entwicklung kam zu ihrem Höhepunkt** developments reached their climax

f = aufgeführt oder gesendet werden *TV, Rad, Theat etc* to be on; **was kommt im Fernsehen?** what's on TV?; **was kommt diese Woche im Kino/Theater?** what's on at the cinema/theatre *(Brit) or* theater *(US)* this week?; **Kobra 13, bitte kommen!** come in Kobra 13!

g = geschehen, sich zutragen to happen; **egal, was kommt, ich fahre morgen nach Paris** whatever happens, I'm going to Paris tomorrow; **komme, was da wolle** come what may; **seine Hochzeit kam für alle überraschend** his wedding came as a surprise to everyone; **das musste ja so kommen, so musste es ja kommen** it had to happen; **das hätte nicht kommen dürfen** that shouldn't have happened → *auch* **2**

♦ **davon** *oder* **daher kommen daher kommt es, dass ...** that's why ...; **das kommt davon, dass ...** that's because ...; **das kommt davon** *or* **daher, dass es so viel geregnet hat** it's because of all the rain we've had; **das kommt davon, wenn man nicht zuhört** that comes of *(Brit) or* from not listening; **das kommt davon!** see what happens?

h = geraten **ins Wackeln kommen** to start shaking *or* to shake; **in Bewegung kommen** to start moving; **jetzt müssen wir mit dem Gerede aufhören und endlich in Bewegung kommen** now we must stop gossiping and get moving; **ins Reden kommen** to start talking; **ins Erzählen kommen** to start telling a story; **zum Blühen kommen** to start flowering *or* to flower; **zum Wachsen kommen** to start growing *or* to grow; **zum Stehen** *or* **Stillstand kommen** to come to a halt *or* standstill

i = sich entwickeln *Samen, Pflanzen* to come on; **der Schnittlauch kommt schön** the chives are coming on well; **schau mal, da kommen die Sonnenblumen!** look how the sunflowers are coming on!; **die Petersilie will dieses Jahr gar nicht kommen** the parsley won't come this year

j inf *= einen Orgasmus haben* to come *(sl)*; **es kommt ihm** he's coming *(inf)*

k mit Dativ

> Wenn *kommen* mit dem Dativ und einem Substantiv oder Adjektiv verwendet wird, siehe auch unter dem Eintrag für das entsprechende Substantiv oder Adjektiv.

ihm kamen Zweifel he started to have doubts; **jdm kommen die Tränen** tears come to sb's eyes; **mir kommen die Tränen!** you're going to make me cry!; **ihm kam das Grausen** he was seized by terror; **mir kommt ein Gedanke** *or* **eine Idee** I've just had a thought; **langsam kam ihm das Verständnis** understanding slowly came to him; **es kommt mir gerade, dass ...** it has just occurred to me that ...; **das Wort/sein Name kommt mir im Moment nicht** the word/his name escapes me for the moment; **du kommst mir gerade recht** *(iro)* you're just what I need; **das kommt mir gerade recht** that's just fine; **jdm frech kommen** to be cheeky *(Brit) or* fresh *(US)* to sb; **jdm dumm kommen** to act stupid; **komm mir nur nicht so!** don't take that attitude with me!; **wie kommst du mir denn?** what kind of attitude is that?; **so darfst du mir nicht kommen!** you'd better not take that attitude with me!

l mit Verb

> Wenn *kommen* mit einem Verb verbunden ist, siehe auch unter dem Eintrag für das jeweilige Verb.

wir standen an der Ecke, und der kleine Johannes kam angelaufen we were standing on the corner and little Johannes came running up to us; **bei einem Unfall kommen immer Schaulustige herbeigelaufen** whenever there's an accident curious spectators come running; **da kommt ein Vogel geflogen** there's a bird; **ich komme dann zu dir gefahren** I'll drive over to your place then; **kommt essen!** come and eat!; **jdn besuchen kommen** to come and see sb; **wann kommt ihr mich mal besuchen?** when are you going to come and see me?; **auf dem Sessel/neben jdm zu sitzen kommen** to get to sit in the armchair/next to sb; **jdn kommen sehen** to see sb coming; **ich habe es ja kommen sehen** I saw it coming

♦ **jdn kommen lassen** to send for sb

♦ **etw kommen lassen** *Mahlzeit, Taxi* to order sth; *Seil* to let sth come; **den Motor kommen lassen** to rev the engine; **und jetzt müssen Sie die Kupplung langsam kommen lassen** and now let the clutch in gently *or* slowly

m mit Präposition

> Wenn *kommen* mit einer Präposition verwendet wird, siehe auch unter dem Eintrag für die entsprechende Präposition.

♦ **an etw** *(acc)* **kommen** *(= sich verschaffen)* to get hold of sth; **ich bin mit der Hand an die Kochplatte gekommen** I touched the hotplate; **er ist an das Glasregal gekommen und hat es umgeworfen** he brushed against the glass shelf and knocked it over

♦ **auf etw** *(acc)* **kommen** *(= kosten, sich belaufen, sprechen über)* to come to; *(= sich erinnern, sich ausdenken)* to think of; **und dann kamen wir auf das leidige Thema Überstunden** then we came onto the vexed question of overtime; **auf eine Idee kommen** to get an idea; **auf einen Gedanken kommen** to get an idea; **wie kommst du darauf?** what makes you think that?; **darauf bin ich nicht gekommen** I didn't think of that; **der Wagen kommt in 16 Sekunden auf 100 km/h** the car reaches 100 km/h in 16 seconds; **auf jeden Haushalt kommen 100 Liter Wasser pro Tag** each household gets 100 litres *(Brit) or* liters *(US)* of water per day; **das kommt auf die Rechnung/auf mein Konto** that goes onto the bill/into my account; **ich komme im Moment nicht auf seinen Namen** his name escapes me for the moment; **auf ihn/darauf lasse ich nichts kommen** *(inf)* I won't hear a word against him/it

♦ **hinter etw** *(acc)* **kommen** *(= herausfinden)* to find sth out, to find out sth

♦ **mit etw/jdm kommen da kommt sie mit ihrem kleinen Bruder** here she comes *or* there she is with her little brother; **mit einer Frage/einem Anliegen kommen** to have a question/a request; **komm mir nicht wieder damit!** don't start that all over again!; **komm (mir) bloß nicht mit DER Entschuldigung** don't come to me with THAT excuse; **damit kann ich ihm nicht kommen** *(mit Entschuldigung)* I can't give him that; *(mit Bitte)* I can't ask him that; **komm mir nicht schon wieder mit deinem Vater!** don't start going on about your father again!; **eine Sache, die mit dem Alter kommt** a thing that develops with age

♦ **um etw kommen** *(= verlieren) um Geld, Besitz, Leben* to lose sth; *um Essen, Schlaf* to go without sth

♦ **zu etw kommen** *(= Zeit finden für)* to get round to sth; *(= erhalten)* to come by sth; *zu Ehre* to receive sth; *(= erben)* to come into sth; **wie komme ich zu der Ehre?** to what do I owe this honour *(Brit) or* honor *(US)?*; **wie bin ich zu der Ehre gekommen, bei Ihnen eingeladen zu werden?** how come I've had the honour *(Brit) or* honor *(US)* of an invitation from you?; **zu einem Entschluss/einer Entscheidung/einer Einigung kommen** to come *or* get to a conclusion/a decision/an agreement

♦ **zu nichts kommen** *(zeitlich)* not to get (a)round to anything; *(= erreichen)* to achieve nothing

♦ **zu sich kommen** *(= Bewusstsein wiedererlangen)* to come round; *(= aufwachen)* to come to one's senses; *(= sich fassen)* to get over it; *(= sich finden)* to find oneself

2 – UNPERSÖNLICHES VERB

a es kommen jetzt die Clowns and now the clowns; **es kommen jetzt die Nachrichten** and now the news

b im übertragenen Sinn **es ist weit gekommen!** it has come to that!; **es kommt noch einmal so weit** *or* **dahin, dass ...** it will get to the point where ...; **so weit kommt es (noch)** that'll be the day *(inf)*; **ich wusste, dass es so kommen würde** I knew that would happen; **wie kommt**

es, dass du ...? how is it that you ...?, how come you ...? *(inf)*; **dazu kam es gar nicht mehr** it didn't come to that; **wir wollten noch eine Reise nach Italien machen, aber es kam nicht mehr dazu** we would have liked to have gone to Italy, but it wasn't to be; **es kam zum Streit** there was a quarrel; **es kam eins zum anderen** one thing led to another; **und so kam es, dass ...** and that is how it came about *or* happened that ...; **es kam, wie es kommen musste** the inevitable happened; **es kommt immer anders, als man denkt** *(prov)*, **erstens kommt es anders und zweitens als man denkt** *(hum inf)* things never turn out the way you expect; **es mag kommen, wie es kommen will** come what may; **vielleicht gehe ich ins Kino oder einen trinken, wie es (gerade) kommt** *(inf)* maybe I'll go to the cinema, or for a drink, whatever *(inf)*

3 – TRANSITIVES VERB

(inf: = kosten) to cost; **das kommt Sie auf 200 Euro** that'll cost you 200 euros; **das kommt mich auf die Dauer teurer** that'll cost me more in the long term

Kom|men NT **-s,** *no pl* coming; **ein einziges ~ und Gehen** a constant coming and going; **etw ist im ~** sth is coming in, sth is on the way in; **jd ist im ~** sb is on his/her way up

kom|mend ADJ *Jahr, Woche, Generation* coming; *Ereignisse, Mode* future; **die nach uns Kommenden** *(geh)* the coming generations, generations to come; **(am) ~en Montag** next Monday; **~e Weihnachten** next Christmas; **in den ~en Jahren** in the coming years, in the years to come; **der ~e Meister** the future champion; **er ist der ~e Mann in der Partei** he is the rising star in the party

kom|men+las|sen VT *sep irreg (fig)* → **kommen I**

kom|men|su|ra|bel [kɔmɛnzu'ra:bl] ADJ *(Math, fig geh)* commensurable

Kom|ment [kɔ'mã:] M **-s, -s** *(Univ)* code of conduct *(of student fraternity)*

Kom|men|tar [kɔmɛn'ta:ɐ] M **-s, -e** *(= Bemerkung, Stellungnahme)* comment; *(Press, Jur, Liter)* commentary; **jeden (weiteren) ~ ablehnen** to decline to comment (further) *or* to make any (further) comment; **kein ~!** no comment; **~ überflüssig!** no comment (necessary)!; **einen ~ (zu etw) abgeben** to (make a) comment (on sth); **musst du zu allem deinen ~ abgeben?** *(inf)* do you have a comment to make about everything?

kom|men|tar|los [-lo:s] ADV without comment

Kom|men|ta|tor [kɔmɛn'ta:to:ɐ] M **-s, Kommentatoren** [-'to:rən], **Kom|men|ta|to|rin** [-'to:rɪn] F **-, -nen** commentator

kom|men|tie|ren [kɔmɛn'ti:rən] *ptp* **kommentiert** VT *(Press etc)* to comment on; *(Jur, Liter)* to write a commentary on; **kommentierte Ausgabe** *(Liter)* annotated edition

Kom|mers [kɔ'mɛrs] M **-es, -e** *evening meeting of student fraternity with drinking ceremony*

Kom|merz [kɔ'mɛrts] M **-es,** *no pl (pej)* commercialism; **reiner ~** pure commercialism; **nur auf ~ aus sein** to have purely commercial interests, to be out for profit

kom|mer|zi|a|li|sie|ren [kɔmɛrtsiali'zi:rən] *ptp* **kommerzialisiert** VT **a** *(= vermarkten)* to commercialize **b** *(= Schulden umwandeln)* **eine öffentliche Schuld ~** to convert a public debt into a private loan

Kom|mer|zi|a|li|sie|rung F **-, -en** **a** *(= Vermarktung)* commercialization **b** *(= Schuldenumwandlung)* **die ~ einer öffentlichen Schuld** the conversion of a public debt into a private loan

Kom|mer|zi|al|rat [kɔmɛr'tsia:l-] M *(Aus)* = **Kommerzienrat**

kom|mer|zi|ell [kɔmɛr'tsiɛl] ADJ commercial ADV commercially; **rein ~ denken** to think purely in commercial terms *or* purely commercially

Kom|mer|zi|en|rat [kɔ'mɛrtsiən-] M *(old) title conferred on distinguished businessman*

Kom|mi|li|to|ne [kɔmili'to:nə] M **-n, -n, Kom|mi|li|to|nin** [-'to:nɪn] F **-, -nen** fellow student; **wir brauchen noch drei ~n, die Flugblätter verteilen** we need three more people *or* students to hand out leaflets

Kom|miss [kɔ'mɪs] M **-es,** *no pl (dated inf)* army; **beim ~ sein** to be in the army; **zum ~ müssen** to have to go into the army

Kom|mis|sar [kɔmɪ'sa:ɐ] M **-s, -e, Kom|mis|sa|rin** [-'sa:rɪn] F **-, -nen,** *(esp Aus)* **Kom|mis|sär** [kɔmɪ'sɛ:ɐ] M **-s, -e, Kom|mis|sä|rin** [-'sɛ:rɪn] F **-, -nen** *(Admin)* commissioner; *(= Polizeikommissar)* inspector; *(ranghöher)* (police) superintendent

Kom|mis|sa|ri|at [kɔmɪsa'ria:t] NT **-(e)s, -e** **a** *(Admin) (= Amt)* commissionership; *(= Dienststelle, Amtsbereich)* commissioner's department **b** *(Polizei) (= Amt)* office of inspector; office of superintendent; *(= Dienststelle, Amtsbereich)* superintendent's department; *(Aus: = Polizeidienststelle)* police station

Kom|mis|sa|rin [-'sa:rɪn] F, **Kom|mis|sä|rin** [-'sɛ:rɪn] F → **Kommissar**

kom|mis|sa|risch [kɔmɪ'sa:rɪʃ] ADJ temporary ADV temporarily

Kom|miss|brot NT rye bread; *(= Armeebrot)* army bread

Kom|mis|si|on [kɔmɪ'sio:n] F **-, -en** **a** *(= Ausschuss)* committee; *(zur Untersuchung)* commission **b** *(Comm)* commission; **etw in ~ geben** to give sth (to a dealer) for sale on commission; **etw in ~ nehmen/haben** to take/have sth on commission

Kom|mis|si|o|när [kɔmɪsio'nɛ:ɐ] M **-s, -e, Kom|mis|si|o|nä|rin** [-'nɛ:rɪn] F **-, -nen** commission agent; *(im Verlagswesen)* wholesale bookseller, wholesaler

kom|mis|si|o|nie|ren [kɔmɪsio'ni:rən] *ptp* **kommissioniert** VT *(Aus)* to commission

Kom|mis|si|ons-: **Kom|mis|si|ons|buch|han|del** M wholesale book trade; **Kom|mis|si|ons|ge|bühr** F commission; **Kom|mis|si|ons|ge|schäft** NT commission *or* agency business

Kom|miss|stie|fel M army boot; *(fig pej)* jackboot

kom|mod [kɔ'mo:t] *(old, dial)* ADJ comfortable ADV comfortably

Kom|mo|de [kɔ'mo:də] F **-, -n** chest of drawers; *(hohe)* tallboy, highboy *(US)*

Kom|mo|di|tät [kɔmodi'tɛ:t] F **-, -en** *(old)* comfort

Kom|mo|do|re [kɔmo'do:rə] M **-s, -n** *or* **-s, Kom|mo|do|rin** [-'do:rɪn] F **-, -nen** *(Naut)* commodore; *(Aviat)* wing commander *(Brit)*, lieutenant colonel *(US)*

kom|mu|nal [kɔmu'na:l] ADJ local; *(= städtisch auch)* municipal; **~es Wahlrecht** right to vote in local elections ADV locally; *(= städtisch auch)* municipally

Kom|mu|nal-: **Kom|mu|nal|ab|ga|ben** PL local rates and taxes *pl*; **Kom|mu|nal|an|lei|he** F municipal loan

kom|mu|na|li|sie|ren [kɔmunali'zi:rən] *ptp* **kommunalisiert** VT to put under the control of the local authorities

Kom|mu|nal-: **Kom|mu|nal|ob|li|ga|ti|on** F municipal bond; **Kom|mu|nal|po|li|tik** F local government politics *sing or pl*; **Kom|mu|nal|ver|wal|tung** F local government; **Kom|mu|nal|wah|len** PL local (government) elections *pl*

Kom|mu|nar|de [kɔmu'nardə] M **-n, -n, Kom|mu|nar|din** [-'nardɪn] F **-, -nen** **a** *(Hist)* Communard **b** *(dated: = Mitglied einer Wohngemeinschaft)* member of a commune, commune-dweller, communard; **er ist ein ~** he lives in a commune

Kom|mu|ne [kɔ'mu:nə] F **-, -n** **a** local authority district **b** *(= Wohngemeinschaft)* commune **c** *(Hist: = Pariser Kommune)* (Paris) Commune

Kom|mu|ni|kant [kɔmuni'kant] M **-en, -en, Kom|mu|ni|kan|tin** [-'kantɪn] F **-, -nen** *(Eccl)* communicant; *(= Erstkommunikant)* first communicant

Kom|mu|ni|ka|ti|on [kɔmunika'tsio:n] F **-, -en** communication; **die ~ ist unmöglich geworden** communication has become impossible

Kom|mu|ni|ka|ti|ons-: **Kom|mu|ni|ka|ti|ons|mit|tel** NT means *sing* of communication; **Kom|mu|ni|ka|ti|ons|sa|tel|lit** M communications satellite; **Kom|mu|ni|ka|ti|ons|schwie|rig|kei|ten** PL communication difficulties *pl*; **Kom|mu|ni|ka|ti|ons|wis|sen|schaf|ten** PL communication studies *pl*

kom|mu|ni|ka|tiv [kɔmunika'ti:f] ADJ communicative; *Brief etc auch* informative

Kom|mu|ni|kee [kɔmuni'ke:] NT **-s, -s** communiqué

Kom|mu|ni|on [kɔmu'nio:n] F **-, -en** *(Eccl)* (Holy) Communion; *(= Erstkommunion)* first Communion

Kom|mu|ni|on-: **Kom|mu|ni|on|bank** F *pl* **-bänke** Communion rail; **Kom|mu|ni|on|kind** NT first communicant; **Kom|mu|ni|on|kleid** NT first communicant's (white) dress

Kom|mu|ni|qué [kɔmyni'ke:, kɔmuni'ke:] NT **-s, -s** communiqué

Kom|mu|nis|mus [kɔmu'nɪsmʊs] M **-,** *no pl* communism

Kom|mu|nist [kɔmu'nɪst] M **-en, -en, Kom|mu|nis|tin** [-'nɪstɪn] F **-, -nen** Communist

Kom|mu|nis|ten|fres|ser(in) M(F) *(pej inf)* Commie basher *(inf)*

kom|mu|nis|tisch [kɔmu'nɪstɪʃ] ADJ communist; **das Kommunistische Manifest** the Communist Manifesto

kom|mu|ni|zie|ren [kɔmuni'tsi:rən] *ptp* **kommuniziert** VI **a** *(= in Kommunikation sein)* to communicate; **~de Röhren** *(Phys)* communicating tubes **b** *(Eccl)* to receive (Holy) Communion

Ko|mö|di|ant [komø'diant] M **-en, -en, Ko|mö|di|an|tin** [-'diantɪn] F **-, -nen** **a** *(old)* actor/actress, player *(old)* **b** *(fig)* play-actor

Ko|mö|di|an|ten-: **ko|mö|di|an|ten|haft** ADJ *Gebaren* theatrical; *(pej)* histrionic ADV *sich benehmen* theatrically; *(pej)* histrionically; **Ko|mö|di|an|ten|tum** [komø'diantntu:m] NT **-s,** *no pl (pej)* histrionics *pl*

Ko|mö|di|an|tin [-'diantɪn] F → **Komödiant**

ko|mö|di|an|tisch [komø'diantɪʃ] ADJ *(= schauspielerisch)* acting; *(pej)* theatrical, histrionic ADV comically

Ko|mö|die [ko'mø:diə] F **-, -n** comedy; *(fig) (= heiteres Ereignis)* farce; *(= Täuschung)* play-acting; **die Stuttgarter ~** the Stuttgart Comedy Theatre *(Brit) or* Theater *(US)*; **~ spielen** *(fig)* to put on an act

Kom|pag|non [kɔmpan'jõ:, 'kɔmpanjõ] M **-s, -s** *(Comm)* partner, associate; *(iro)* pal *(inf)*, chum *(inf)*, buddy *(inf)*

kom|pakt [kɔm'pakt] ADJ compact; *Gestein, Schicht, Brot, Masse auch* solid; *(inf: = gedrungen) Mensch* stocky ADV compactly

Kom|pakt-: **Kom|pakt|an|la|ge** F *(Rad)* audio system; **Kom|pakt|au|to** NT compact *(US)*, medium-sized family saloon; **Kom|pakt|bau|wei|se** F compact functional style; **Kom|pakt|ka|me|ra** F compact camera; **Kom|pakt|ski** M compact ski; **Kom|pakt|wa|gen** M *(Aut)* small family car, subcompact *(US)*

Kom|pa|nie [kɔmpa'ni:] F **-, -n** [-'ni:ən] *(Mil)* company; *(old Comm)* trading company; *(= Firma)* firm; **damit kann man ja eine ganze ~ füttern** that's enough to feed a whole army

Kom|pa|nie|chef(in) M(F), **Kom|pa|nie|füh|rer(in)** M(F) *(Mil)* company commander

Kom|pa|ra|ti|on [kɔmpara'tsio:n] F **-, -en** *(Gram)* comparison

Kom|pa|ra|tis|tik [kɔmpara'tɪstɪk] F -, *no pl* comparative literature

Kom|pa|ra|tiv ['kɔmparatiːf] M -s, -e [-və] *(Gram)* comparative

Kom|par|se [kɔm'parzə] M -n, -n, **Kom|par|sin** [-'parzɪn] F -, -nen *(Film)* extra; *(Theat)* supernumerary; **er war nur ein ~** he only had a walk-on part

Kom|par|se|rie [kɔmparzə'riː] F -, -n [-'riːən] extras *pl*; supernumeraries *pl*; **die ganze ~ ...** all those with walk-on parts ...

Kom|pass ['kɔmpas] M -es, -e compass; **nach dem ~** by the compass

Kom|pass-: **Kom|pass|häus|chen** [-hɔysçən] NT *(Naut)* binnacle; **Kom|pass|na|del** F compass needle

kom|pa|ti|bel [kɔmpa'tiːbl] ADJ *(liter, Tech, Comput)* compatible

Kom|pa|ti|bi|li|tät [kɔmpatibili'tɛːt] F -, -en *(liter, Tech)* compatibility

Kom|pen|di|um [kɔm'pɛndiʊm] NT -s, **Kompendien** [-diən] **a** (= *Abriss*) compendium **b** *(Phot)* lens hood (with bellows extension)

Kom|pen|sa|ti|on [kɔmpɛnza'tsioːn] F -, -en compensation

Kom|pen|sa|ti|ons|ge|schäft NT barter (transaction)

Kom|pen|sa|tor [kɔmpɛn'zaːtoːɐ] M -s, **Kompensatoren** [-'toːrən] *(Tech)* compensator

kom|pen|sie|ren [kɔmpɛn'ziːrən] *ptp* **kompensiert** VT to compensate for, to offset

kom|pe|tent [kɔmpe'tɛnt] ADJ competent; (= *befugt auch*) authorized; **für solche Fälle ist dieses Gericht nicht ~** this court has no jurisdiction in such cases, this court is not competent to decide such cases; **der dafür ~e Kollege** the man responsible for that; **dafür bin ich nicht ~** I'm not responsible for that ADV competently; **der Minister hat sich zu dieser Frage nicht besonders ~ geäußert** the minister did not speak very competently on the issue; **jdm ~ Auskunft geben** to inform sb knowledgeably

Kom|pe|tenz [kɔmpe'tɛnts] F -, -en **a** (area of) authority *or* competence; *(eines Gerichts)* jurisdiction, competence; **da hat er ganz eindeutig seine ~en überschritten** he has quite clearly exceeded his authority *or* powers here; **er hat die alleinige ~, hierüber zu entscheiden** he alone has the authority *or* competence *or* is competent to decide on this issue; **ich will dir nicht deine ~(en) streitig machen** I don't want to infringe on your field; **das fällt in die ~ dieses Amtes** that's the responsibility of this office; **seine mangelnde ~ in dieser Frage** his lack of competence in this issue **b** *(Ling)* competence

Kom|pe|tenz-: **Kom|pe|tenz|be|reich** M area of competence; **Kom|pe|tenz|ge|ran|gel** NT bickering over responsibilities; **Kom|pe|tenz|strei|tig|kei|ten** PL dispute over respective areas of responsibility; **Kom|pe|tenz|ver|tei|lung** F distribution of powers; **Kom|pe|tenz|wirr|warr** M confusion about areas of responsibilities

Kom|pi|la|ti|on [kɔmpila'tsioːn] F -, -en *(geh)* compilation

kom|pi|lie|ren [kɔmpi'liːrən] *ptp* **kompiliert** VT *(geh)* to compile

kompl. *abbr von* **komplett** complete

Kom|ple|ment [kɔmple'mɛnt] NT -(e)s, -e *(Math)* complement

kom|ple|men|tär [kɔmplemɛn'tɛːɐ] ADJ complementary

Kom|ple|men|tär [kɔmplemɛn'tɛːɐ] M -s, -e, **Kom|ple|men|tä|rin** [-'tɛːrɪn] F -, -nen *fully liable partner in a limited partnership*

Kom|ple|men|tär|far|be F complementary colour *(Brit) or* color *(US)*

kom|ple|men|tie|ren [kɔmplemɛn'tiːrən] *ptp* **komplementiert** VT *(geh)* to complement

Kom|plet [kõ'pleː, kɔm'pleː] NT -(s), -s *(Fashion)* matching dress/skirt and coat

Kom|plet [kɔm'pleːt] F -, -e *(Eccl)* complin(e)

kom|plett [kɔm'plɛt] ADJ complete; **ein ~es Frühstück** a full breakfast; **ein ~es Menü** a (full) three course meal ADV completely

kom|plet|tie|ren [kɔmplɛ'tiːrən] *ptp* **komplettiert** VT *(geh)* to complete

Kom|plett-: **Kom|plett|lö|sung** F complete solution; **Kom|plett|preis** M all-inclusive *or* all-in *(Brit)* price

kom|plex [kɔm'plɛks] ADJ complex ADV complexly; **die Situation stellt sich ~ dar** the situation appears to be complex; **~ aufgebaut** complex in structure

Kom|plex [kɔm'plɛks] M -es, -e **a** (= *Gebäudekomplex*) complex; (= *Fragen-/Themenkomplex*) group *or* set of questions/issues **b** *(Psych)* complex; **er steckt voller ~e** he has so many complexes *or* hang-ups *(inf)*

Kom|ple|xi|tät [kɔmplɛksi'tɛːt] F -, *no pl* complexity

Kom|pli|ce [kɔm'pliːtsə] M -n, -n accomplice

Kom|pli|ka|ti|on [komplika'tsioːn] F -, -en complication

Kom|pli|ment [kɔmpli'mɛnt] NT -(e)s, -e compliment; **jdm ~e machen** to pay sb compliments, to compliment sb (*wegen* on); **mein ~!** my compliments!

Kom|pli|ze [kɔm'pliːtsə] M -n, -n accomplice

kom|pli|zie|ren [kɔmpli'tsiːrən] *ptp* **kompliziert** VT to complicate

kom|pli|ziert [kɔmpli'tsiːɐt] ADJ complicated, involved; *(Med) Bruch* compound; **sei doch nicht so ~** don't be so complicated ADV *aufgebaut* in a complicated way; **sich ~ ausdrücken** to express oneself in a complicated *or* an involved way; **das ist sehr ~ dargestellt** the presentation is quite complicated; **die Angelegenheit hat sich ~ entwickelt** the matter has become very complicated

Kom|pli|ziert|heit F -, *no pl* complexity

Kom|pli|zin [-'pliːtsɪn] F -, -nen accomplice

Kom|plott [kɔm'plɔt] NT -(e)s, -e plot, conspiracy; **ein ~ schmieden** to hatch a plot; **ein ~ zur Ermordung ...** a plot *or* conspiracy to murder ...

Kom|po|nen|te [kɔmpo'nɛntə] F -, -n component

kom|po|nie|ren [kɔmpo'niːrən] *ptp* **komponiert** VTI to compose; *(Liter auch)* to construct

Kom|po|nist [kɔmpo'nɪst] M -en, -en, **Kom|po|nis|tin** [-'nɪstɪn] F -, -nen composer

Kom|po|si|ta *pl von* **Kompositum**

Kom|po|si|ti|on [kɔmpozi'tsioːn] F -, -en composition; *(Liter auch)* construction

kom|po|si|to|risch [kɔmpozi'toːrɪʃ] ADJ compositional

Kom|po|si|tum [kɔm'poːzitʊm] NT -s, **Komposita** [-ta] *(Gram, Pharm)* compound

Kom|post [kɔm'pɔst, 'kɔmpɔst] M -(e)s, -e compost

Kom|pos|ter [kɔm'pɔstɐ] M -s, - compost maker

Kom|post-: **Kom|post|er|de** F compost; **Kom|post|hau|fen** M compost heap

Kom|pos|tier|an|la|ge F composting facility *or* station

kom|pos|tier|bar ADJ *Abfälle, Kunststoffe* compostible

kom|pos|tie|ren [kɔmpɔs'tiːrən] *ptp* **kompostiert** VT to compost VI to make compost

Kom|pott [kɔm'pɔt] NT -(e)s, -e stewed fruit, compote

kom|press [kɔm'prɛs] ADV *(Typ)* solid

Kom|pres|se [kɔm'prɛsə] F -, -n compress

Kom|pres|si|on [kɔmprɛ'sioːn] F -, -en *(Tech)* compression

Kom|pres|si|ons-: **Kom|pres|si|ons|pro|gramm** NT *(Comput)* compression program; **Kom|pres|si|ons|pum|pe** F pressure pump; **Kom|pres|si|ons|ver|band** M compression *or* pressure bandage

Kom|pres|sor [kɔm'prɛsoːɐ] M -s, **Kompressoren** [-'soːrən] compressor

kom|pri|mie|ren [kɔmpri'miːrən] *ptp* **komprimiert** VT to compress *(auch Daten)*; *(fig)* to condense

Kom|pri|mie|rer [kɔmpri'miːrɐ] M -s, - *(Comput)* compressor

Kom|pri|mie|rung [kɔmpri'miːrʊŋ] F -, -en *(Comput)* compression

Kom|pri|mie|rungs|pro|gramm [kɔmpri'miːrʊŋs-] NT *(Comput)* compression program, compressor

Kom|pro|miss [kɔmpro'mɪs] M -es, -e compromise; **einen ~ schließen** to (make a) compromise; **sie sind zu keinem ~ bereit** they are not prepared to compromise

Kom|pro|miss-: **kom|pro|miss|be|reit** ADJ prepared *or* willing to compromise *pred*; **Kom|pro|miss|be|reit|schaft** F willingness to compromise; **kom|pro|miss|fä|hig** ADJ able to compromise *pred*, capable of compromise *pred*; **kom|pro|miss|los** ADJ uncompromising; **Kom|pro|miss|lo|sig|keit** F -, *no pl (von Mensch)* uncompromising attitude; *(von Haltung, Politik)* uncompromising nature; **Kom|pro|miss|lö|sung** F compromise solution; **Kom|pro|miss|vor|schlag** M compromise proposal

kom|pro|mit|tie|ren [kɔmpromɪ'tiːrən] *ptp* **kompromittiert** VT to compromise VR to compromise oneself

Kom|so|mol [kɔmzo'mɔl] M -, *no pl* Comsomol

Kom|so|mol|ze [kɔmzo'mɔltsə] M -n, -n, **Kom|so|mol|zin** [-'mɔltsɪn] F -, -nen member of the Comsomol

Kom|tess [kɔm'tɛs, kõ'tɛs] F - *or* -e, -en countess

Kom|tur [kɔm'tuːɐ] M -s, -e commander (of a knightly order)

Kon|den|sat [kɔndɛn'zaːt] NT -(e)s, -e condensate; *(fig)* distillation, condensation

Kon|den|sa|ti|on [kɔndɛnza'tsioːn] F -, -en *(Chem, Phys)* condensation

Kon|den|sa|tor [kɔndɛn'zaːtoːɐ] M -s, **Kondensatoren** [-'toːrən] *(Aut, Chem)* condenser; *(Elec auch)* capacitor

kon|den|sie|ren [kɔndɛn'ziːrən] *ptp* **kondensiert** VTI *(vi: aux haben or sein) (lit, fig)* to condense; *(fig auch)* to distil *(Brit)*, to distill *(US)*

Kon|dens-: **Kon|dens|milch** F evaporated milk; **Kon|dens|strei|fen** M *(Aviat)* vapour *(Brit) or* vapor *(US)* trail; **Kon|dens|was|ser** NT condensation

Kon|di|ti|on [kɔndi'tsioːn] F -, -en **a** condition, shape, form; (= *Durchhaltevermögen*) stamina; **wie ist seine ~?** what sort of condition *etc* is he in?; **er hat überhaupt keine ~** he is completely unfit; *(fig)* he has absolutely no stamina; **er zeigte heute eine ausgezeichnete ~** he was in top form today **b** *usu pl (Comm: = Bedingung)* condition; **zu den üblichen ~en** under the usual terms

kon|di|ti|o|nal [kɔnditsio'naːl] ADJ conditional

Kon|di|ti|o|nal|satz M conditional clause

kon|di|ti|o|nie|ren [kɔnditsio'niːrən] *ptp* **konditioniert** VT *(Biol, Psych)* to condition

Kon|di|ti|ons-: **kon|di|ti|ons|schwach** ADJ (very) unfit; **Kon|di|ti|ons|schwä|che** F lack *no pl* of fitness; **kon|di|ti|ons|stark** ADJ very fit; **Kon|di|ti|ons|trai|ning** NT fitness training

Kon|di|tor [kɔn'diːtoːɐ] M -s, **Konditoren** [-'toːrən], **Kon|di|to|rin** [-'toːrɪn] F -, -nen pastry cook *(Brit)*, confectioner *(US)*

Kon|di|to|rei F -, -en cake shop *(Brit)*, confectioner's shop *(US)*; *(mit Café)* café

Kon|di|tor|wa|ren PL cakes and pastries *pl*

Kon|do|lenz- *in cpds* of condolence; **Kon|do|lenz|be|such** M visit of condolence; **Kon|do|lenz|buch** NT book of condolence; **Kon|do|lenz|schrei|ben** NT (= *Kondolenzbrief*) letter of condolence

kon|do|lie|ren [kɔndo'liːrən] *ptp* **kondoliert** VI **(jdm) ~** to offer one's condolences (to sb), to condole with sb; **schriftlich** ~ to write a letter of condolence

Kon|dom [kɔn'do:m] M OR NT -s, -e condom, contraceptive sheath

Kon|do|me|rie [kɔndomə'ri:] F -, -n [-'ri:ən] *(inf)* condom shop *(esp Brit)* or store *(US)*

Kon|do|mi|ni|um [kɔndo'mi:niʊm] NT -s, **Kondominien** [-niən] condominium

Kon|dor ['kɔndo:ɐ] M -s, -e condor

Kon|duk|teur [kɔndʊk'tø:ɐ] M -s, -e *(Aus, Sw)* conductor

Kon|duk|teu|rin [kɔndʊk'tø:rɪn] F -, -nen *(Aus, Sw)* conductress

Ko|nen *pl von* **Konus**

Kon|fekt [kɔn'fɛkt] NT -(e)s, -e confectionery

Kon|fek|ti|on [kɔnfɛk'tsio:n] F -, -en *(= Herstellung)* manufacture of off-the-peg *(Brit)* or ready-made or ready-to-wear clothing; *(= Industrie)* clothing industry, rag trade *(inf)*; *(= Bekleidung)* off-the-peg *(Brit)* or ready-made or ready-to-wear clothes *pl* or clothing

Kon|fek|ti|o|när [kɔnfɛktsio'nɛ:ɐ] M -s, -e, **Kon|fek|ti|o|nä|rin** [-'nɛ:rɪn] F -, -nen clothing manufacturer

kon|fek|ti|o|nie|ren [kɔnfɛktsio'ni:rən] *ptp* **konfektioniert** VT *Kleidung* to make

Kon|fek|ti|o|nie|rung [kɔnfɛktsio'ni:rʊŋ] F -, -en *(= serienmäßiges Herstellen)* manufacture, (assembly-line) production

Kon|fek|ti|ons- *in cpds* off-the-peg *(Brit)*, ready-made, ready-to-wear; **Kon|fek|ti|ons|an|zug** M off-the-peg *etc* suit; **Kon|fek|ti|ons|ge|schäft** NT (off-the-peg *etc*) clothes shop or store; **Kon|fek|ti|ons|grö|ße** F (clothing) size; **welche ~ haben Sie?** what size are you?; **Kon|fek|ti|ons|wa|re** F off-the-peg *etc* clothing

Kon|fe|renz [kɔnfe'rɛnts] F -, -en conference; *(= Besprechung)* meeting; *(= Ausschuss)* committee

Kon|fe|renz- *in cpds* conference; **Kon|fe|renz|raum** M conference room; **Kon|fe|renz|schal|tung** F *(Telec)* conference circuit; *(Rad, TV)* (television/radio) linkup; **Kon|fe|renz|teil|neh|mer(in)** M(F) → **Konferenz** person attending a conference/meeting; **Kon|fe|renz|zim|mer** NT conference room

kon|fe|rie|ren [kɔnfe'ri:rən] *ptp* **konferiert** VI to confer, to have or hold a conference or discussion *(über +acc* on or about)

Kon|fes|si|on [kɔnfɛ'sio:n] F -, -en (religious) denomination; **welche ~ haben Sie?** what denomination are you?; **die Augsburger ~** the Augsburg Confession

kon|fes|si|o|nell [kɔnfɛsio'nɛl] ADJ denominational ADV **~ gebundene Schulen** schools which are affiliated with a specific denomination; **~ verschiedene Ehen** marriages between different religions

Kon|fes|si|ons-: **kon|fes|si|ons|los** ADJ nondenominational, undenominational; **Kon|fes|si|ons|schu|le** F denominational school

Kon|fet|ti [kɔn'fɛti] NT -s, *no pl* confetti

Kon|fet|ti-: **Kon|fet|ti|re|gen** M shower of confetti; *(in US: bei Empfängen)* shower of ticker tape; **Kon|fet|ti|schlacht** F confetti battle

Kon|fi|dent [kɔnfi'dɛnt] M -en, -en *(old)* confidant; *(Aus)* police informer

Kon|fi|den|tin [kɔnfi'dɛntɪn] F -, -nen *(old)* confidante; *(Aus)* police informer

Kon|fi|gu|ra|ti|on [kɔnfigura'tsio:n] F -, -en configuration

kon|fi|gu|rie|ren [kɔnfigu'ri:rən] *ptp* **konfiguriert** VT *Computer, Software* to configure

Kon|fir|mand [kɔnfɪr'mant] M -en, -en [-dn], **Kon|fir|man|din** [-'mandɪn] F -, -nen *(Eccl)* candidate for confirmation, confirmand

Kon|fir|man|den|bla|se F *(inf)* weak or Chinese *(hum sl)* bladder

Kon|fir|man|den|un|ter|richt M confirmation classes *pl*

Kon|fir|ma|ti|on [kɔnfɪrma'tsio:n] F -, -en *(Eccl)* confirmation

Kon|fir|ma|ti|ons- *in cpds* confirmation; **Kon|fir|ma|ti|ons|spruch** M confirmation text *(chosen by confirmand as motto)*

kon|fir|mie|ren [kɔnfɪr'mi:rən] *ptp* **konfirmiert** VT *(Eccl)* to confirm

Kon|fi|se|rie [kõfizə'ri:] F -, -n [-'ri:ən] *(Sw)* **a** *(= Konditorei)* cake shop *(Brit)*, confectioner's (shop) *(US)*; *(mit Café)* café **b** *(= Konfekt)* confectionery

Kon|fis|ka|ti|on [kɔnfɪska'tsio:n] F -, -en confiscation

kon|fis|zie|ren [kɔnfɪs'tsi:rən] *ptp* **konfisziert** VT to confiscate

Kon|fi|tü|re [kɔnfi'ty:rə] F -, -n jam

Kon|flikt [kɔn'flɪkt] M -s, -e conflict; **bewaffneter ~** armed conflict; **mit etw in ~ geraten** to come into conflict with sth; **kommst du da nicht mit deinem Gewissen in ~?** how can you reconcile that with your conscience?; **er befindet sich in einem ~** he is in a state of inner conflict

Kon|flikt-: **Kon|flikt|be|ra|tung** F *(vor Abtreibung)* abortion counselling *(Brit)* or counseling *(US)*; **kon|flikt|fä|hig** ADJ **~ sein** to be able to deal with conflict; **wir benötigen einen ~en Manager** we need a manager who is able to deal with conflict; **er ist nicht ~** he isn't good at dealing with conflict; **Kon|flikt|fall** M conflict; **im ~** in case of conflict; **Kon|flikt|feld** NT area of conflict; **Kon|flikt|for|scher(in)** M(F) researcher into conflict; **Kon|flikt|for|schung** F conflict studies *pl*, research into the subject of conflict; **kon|flikt|frei** ADJ conflict-free ADV without conflict; **kon|flikt|freu|dig** ADJ combative; **er ist sehr ~** he is very combative, he thrives on conflict; **kon|flikt|ge|la|den** ADJ conflict-ridden; *Situation* explosive; **Kon|flikt|herd** M *(esp Pol)* centre *(Brit)* or center *(US)* of conflict; **kon|flikt|los** ADJ, ADV without conflict; **kon|flikt|reich** ADJ full of conflict; **kon|flikt|scheu** ADJ **~ sein** to be afraid of conflict; **ein ~er Mensch** someone who is afraid of dealing with conflict; **Kon|flikt|si|tu|a|ti|on** F conflict situation; **Kon|flikt|stoff** M cause for conflict; **kon|flikt|träch|tig** ADJ *Situation* likely to lead to conflict

Kon|fö|de|ra|ti|on [kɔnfødera'tsio:n] F -, -en confederacy

kon|fö|de|rie|ren [kɔnføde'ri:rən] *ptp* **konföderiert** VR *(liter)* to confederate

Kon|fö|de|rier|te(r) [kɔnføde'ri:ɐtə] MF *decl as adj* confederate

kon|form [kɔn'fɔrm] ADJ *Ansichten etc* concurring; **in etw** *(dat)* **~ sein** to agree on sth ADV **mit jdm/etw ~ gehen** to agree with sb/sth *(in +dat* about), to be in agreement with sb/sth *(in +dat* about)

-kon|form ADJ SUF in conformity with; **CSU-konforme Kandidaten** candidates adhering to the CSU line

kon|form+ge|hen VI *sep irreg* → **konform**

Kon|for|mis|mus [kɔnfɔr'mɪsmʊs] M -, *no pl* conformism

Kon|for|mist [kɔnfɔr'mɪst] M -en, -en, **Kon|for|mis|tin** [-'mɪstɪn] F -, -nen *(pej)* conformist

kon|for|mis|tisch [kɔnfɔr'mɪstɪʃ] ADJ conformist, conforming ADV **~ eingestellt sein** to tend to conform with everything; **sich ~ verhalten** to be a conformist

Kon|for|mi|tät [kɔnfɔrmi'tɛ:t] F -, -en conformity

Kon|fra|ter [kɔn'fra:tɐ] M *(Eccl)* fellow clergyman; fellow monk

Kon|fron|ta|ti|on [kɔnfrɔnta'tsio:n] F -, -en confrontation

Kon|fron|ta|ti|ons|kurs M **auf ~ gehen, ~ steuern** to be heading for a confrontation

kon|fron|tie|ren [kɔnfrɔn'ti:rən] *ptp* **konfrontiert** VT to confront *(mit* with); **zwei Parteien ~** to bring two parties face to face, to confront two parties with one another

Kon|fron|tie|rung F -, -en confrontation

kon|fus [kɔn'fu:s] ADJ confused, muddled ADV confusedly; **~ klingen** to sound confused; **ein ~ geschriebener Bericht** a report written in a confused style

Kon|fu|si|on F -, -en confusion

kon|fu|zi|a|nisch [kɔnfu'tsia:nɪʃ] ADJ Confucian

Kon|fu|zi|a|nis|mus M -, *no pl* Confucianism

Kon|fu|zi|us [kɔn'fu:tsiʊs] M -' Confucius

kon|ge|ni|al [kɔnge'nia:l] ADJ *(geh)* sympathetic; **~e Geister** kindred or congenial spirits

Kon|glo|me|rat [kɔnglome'ra:t, kɔŋ-] NT -(e)s, -e **a** *(Geol)* conglomerate **b** *(= Ansammlung)* conglomeration

Kon|go ['kɔŋgo] M -(s) **a** *(auch* **Demokratische Republik Kongo***)* (Democratic Republic of the) Congo; *(auch* **Republik Kongo***)* (Republic of the) Congo **b** *(= Fluss)* Congo

Kon|go|le|se [kɔŋgo'le:zə] M -n, -n, **Kon|go|le|sin** [-'le:zɪn] F -, -nen Congolese

kon|go|le|sisch [kɔŋgo'le:zɪʃ] ADJ Congolese

Kon|gress [kɔn'grɛs, kɔŋ-] M -es, -e **a** *(Pol)* congress; *(fachlich)* convention, conference; **der Wiener ~** the Congress of Vienna **b** *(in USA)* Congress

Kon|gress-: **Kon|gress|hal|le** F congress or conference hall, convention hall *(esp US)*; **Kon|gress|mit|glied** NT **a** → **Kongress a** person attending a congress/conference or convention **b** *(in USA)* congressman/-woman; **Kon|gress|teil|neh|mer(in)** M(F) → **Kongress a** person attending a congress/conference or convention; **Kon|gress|zent|rum** NT → **Kongress a** congress/conference centre *(Brit)* or center *(US)*

kon|gru|ent [kɔngru'ɛnt, kɔŋ-] ADJ *(Math)* congruent; *(Gram)* concordant, congruent; *(geh) Ansichten* concurring

Kon|gru|enz [kɔngru'ɛnts, kɔŋ-] F -, -en *(Math)* congruence; *(Gram)* concord, agreement, congruence; *(geh: von Ansichten)* concurrence

kon|gru|ie|ren [kɔngru'i:rən, kɔŋ-] *ptp* **kongruiert** VI to be congruent; *(geh: Ansichten)* to concur, to correspond

K.-o.-Nie|der|la|ge [ka:'lo:-] F KO defeat

Ko|ni|fe|re [koni'fe:rə] F -, -n conifer

Kö|nig ['kø:nɪç] M -s, -e [-gə] king; **des ~s Rock** *(old, liter)* the king's uniform; **die Heiligen Drei ~e** The Three Kings or Magi; **der ~ der Tiere** the king of the beasts; **der ~ der Lüfte** the lord of the skies; **während der Weltmeisterschaft regierte in Deutschland ~ Fußball** during the World Cup Germany went football mad *(Brit)* or soccer crazy *(US)*; **der Kunde ist ~** the customer is always right

Kö|ni|gin ['kø:nigɪn] F -, -nen *(auch Zool)* queen; **~ der Nacht** *(Bot)* queen of the night, night-flowering cereus

Kö|ni|gin-: **Kö|ni|gin|mut|ter** F *pl* **-mütter** queen mother; **Kö|ni|gin|pas|te|te** F vol-au-vent; **Kö|ni|gin|wit|we** F dowager queen

kö|nig|lich ['kø:nɪklɪç] ADJ royal; *Auftreten, Stolz etc auch* regal; *Geschenk, Gehalt* princely; **das ~e Spiel** chess, the royal game, the game of kings; **Seine/Ihre Königliche Hoheit** His/Her Royal Highness; **~-preußisch/bayrisch** Royal Prussian/Bavarian ADV **a** *(inf: = köstlich, ungeheuer)* **sich ~ freuen** to be as pleased as Punch *(inf)*; **sich ~ amüsieren** to have the time of one's life *(inf)* **b** *(= fürstlich) bewirten* like royalty; *belohnen* richly

Kö|nig|reich NT kingdom, realm *(poet)*

Kö|nigs-: **kö|nigs|blau** ADJ royal blue; **Kö|nigs|hof** M royal or king's court; **Kö|nigs|ker|ze** F *(Bot)* mullein; **Kö|nigs|kind** NT *(liter)* royal son/daughter; **Kö|nigs|kro|ne** F royal crown; **Kö|nigs|paar** NT royal couple; **Kö|nigs|mord** M regicide; **Kö|nigs|ma|cher(in)** M(F) *(lit, fig)* kingmaker; **Kö|nigs|sohn** M *(liter)* king's son, prince; **Kö|nigs|ti|ger** M Bengal tiger; **Kö|nigs|toch|ter** F *(liter)* king's daughter, princess; **kö|nigs|treu** ADJ royalist; **Kö|nigs|was|ser** NT, *no pl (Chem)* aqua regia;

Kö|nigs|weg M (*fig: = idealer Weg*) ideal way; **Kö|nigs|wür|de** F royal dignity

Kö|nig|tum ['kø:nıçtu:m] NT **-s, Königtümer** [-ty:mɐ] **a** *no pl* kingship **b** (*= Reich*) kingdom

ko|nisch ['ko:nıʃ] ADJ conical ADV conically

Kon|jek|tur [kɔnjɛk'tu:ɐ] F **-, -en** (*= Vermutung*) conjecture; (*Liter: = Lesart*) conjectured version

Kon|ju|ga|ti|on [kɔnjuga'tsio:n] F **-, -en** conjugation

kon|ju|gie|ren [kɔnju'gi:rən] *ptp* **konjugiert** VT to conjugate

Kon|junk|ti|on [kɔnjʊŋk'tsio:n] F **-, -en** (*Astron, Gram*) conjunction

Kon|junk|ti|o|nal|satz [kɔnjʊŋktsio'na:l-] M (*Gram*) conjunctional clause

Kon|junk|tiv ['kɔnjʊŋktıf] M **-s, -e** [-və] (*Gram*) subjunctive

kon|junk|ti|visch ['kɔnjʊŋkti:vıʃ] ADJ subjunctive

Kon|junk|tur [kɔnjʊŋk'tu:ɐ] F **-, -en** economic situation, economy; (*= Hochkonjunktur*) boom; **steigende/fallende** *or* **rückläufige ~** upward/downward economic trend, increasing/decreasing economic activity

Kon|junk|tur-: **kon|junk|tur|ab|hän|gig** ADJ dependent on economic factors; **Kon|junk|tur|ab|hän|gig|keit** F dependence on economic factors; **Kon|junk|tur|ab|schwung** M economic downturn; **Kon|junk|tur|auf|schwung** M economic upturn; **kon|junk|tur|be|dingt** ADJ influenced by *or* due to economic factors; **Kon|junk|tur|be|le|bung** F business revival; (*= aktives Beleben der Konjunktur*) stimulation of the economy

kon|junk|tu|rell [kɔnjʊŋktu'rɛl] ADJ economic; *Arbeitslosigkeit* resulting from the economic situation, due to economic factors ADV economically; **~ bedingt** caused by economic factors

Kon|junk|tur-: **Kon|junk|tur|flau|te** F economic slowdown; (*= ernsthafte Krise*) slump, recession; **Kon|junk|tur|kli|ma** NT economic *or* business climate; **Kon|junk|tur|po|li|tik** F *measures or policies aimed at preventing economic fluctuation*; **Kon|junk|tur|rück|gang** M slowdown in the economy; **Kon|junk|tur|schwä|che** F weakness in the economy; **Kon|junk|tur|zu|schlag** M *refundable increase in taxation paid into the Bundesbank to help the national economy*

kon|kav [kɔn'ka:f, kɔŋ-] ADJ concave ADV concavely

Kon|kav|spie|gel M concave mirror

Kon|kla|ve [kɔn'kla:və, kɔŋ-] NT **-s, -n** (*Eccl*) conclave

Kon|klu|si|on [kɔnklu'zio:n, kɔŋ-] F **-, -en** (*geh, Philos*) conclusion

Kon|kor|danz [kɔnkɔr'dants, kɔŋ-] F **-, -en** concordance

Kon|kor|dat [kɔnkɔr'da:t, kɔŋ-] NT **-(e)s, -e** concordat

kon|kret [kɔn'kre:t, kɔŋ-] ADJ concrete; **ich kann dir nichts Konkretes sagen** I can't tell you anything definite *or* concrete ADV **drück dich etwas ~er aus** would you put that in rather more concrete terms; **ich kann mir ~ vorstellen, wie ...** I can very clearly imagine how ...; **ich kann es dir noch nicht ~ sagen** I can't tell you definitely

kon|kre|ti|sie|ren [kɔnkreti'zi:rən, kɔŋ-] *ptp* **konkretisiert** VT to put in concrete form *or* terms

Kon|ku|bi|nat [kɔnkubi'na:t, kɔŋ-] **-(e)s, -e** NT concubinage

Kon|ku|bi|ne [kɔnku'bi:nə, kɔŋ-] F **-, -n** concubine

Kon|kur|rent [kɔnku'rɛnt, kɔŋ-] M **-en, -en**, **Kon|kur|ren|tin** [-'rɛntın] F **-, -nen** rival; (*Comm auch*) competitor

Kon|kur|renz [kɔnku'rɛnts, kɔŋ-] F **-, -en** (*= Wettbewerb*) competition, rivalry; (*= Konkurrenzbetrieb*) competitors *pl*; (*= Gesamtheit der Konkurrenten*) competition, competitors *pl*; **die ~ in diesem Sport/auf diesem Gebiet ist größer geworden** the competition in this sport/field has increased; **jdm ~ machen** (*Comm, fig*) to compete with sb; (*Comm auch*) to be in competition with sb; **zur ~ (über)gehen** to go over to the competition; **als ~ zu etw** as competition for sth; **außer ~ sein** to have no competition; **dieser Film läuft außer ~** (*bei Festival etc*) the film is running outside of the main competition

Kon|kur|renz-: **Kon|kur|renz|den|ken** NT competitive mentality; **Kon|kur|renz|druck** M, *no pl* pressure of competition; **kon|kur|renz|fä|hig** ADJ competitive; **Kon|kur|renz|fä|hig|keit** F competitiveness; **Kon|kur|renz|kampf** M competition; (*zwischen zwei Menschen auch*) rivalry; **wir müssen mit einem sehr harten ~ rechnen** we have to reckon with some very tough competition; **ein ~, bei dem wir uns durchgesetzt haben** a competitive situation in which we won out; **Kon|kur|renz|klau|sel** F (*in Vertrag*) noncompetition clause; **kon|kur|renz|los** ADJ without competition ADV **das Angebot ist ~ günstig** you won't find a better offer anywhere else; **~ billig** undoubtedly the cheapest; **Kon|kur|renz|neid** M, *no pl* professional jealousy; **Kon|kur|renz|pro|dukt** NT rival product; **Kon|kur|renz|ver|bot** NT (agreement on) restraint of trade

kon|kur|rie|ren [kɔnku'ri:rən, kɔŋ-] *ptp* **konkurriert** VI to compete; (*Comm auch*) to be in competition

Kon|kurs [kɔn'kʊrs, kɔŋ-] M **-es, -e** bankruptcy; **in ~ gehen** to go bankrupt, to go into receivership (*esp form*); **~ machen** (*inf*) to go bankrupt *or* bust (*inf*) → **anmelden**

Kon|kurs-: **Kon|kurs|er|öff|nung** F opening of bankruptcy proceedings; **Kon|kurs|mas|se** F bankrupt's estate; **Kon|kurs|ver|fah|ren** NT bankruptcy proceedings *pl*; **Kon|kurs|ver|wal|ter(in)** M(F) receiver; (*von Gläubigern bevollmächtigt*) trustee

kön|nen ['kœnən] ✪ 36, 37.4, 42.3, 42.4, 43.3, 43.4, 52.2 *pret* **konnte**, ['kɔntə] *ptp* **gekonnt** *or* (*bei modal aux vb*) **können** VTI, MODAL AUX VB [gə'kɔnt, 'kœnən] **a** (*= vermögen*) to be able to; **ich kann es/das machen** I can do it, I am able to do it; **ich kann es/das nicht machen** I cannot *or* can't do it, I am not able to do it; **man konnte ihn retten** they were able to save him, they managed to save him; **man konnte ihn nicht retten** they couldn't save him, they were unable to save him; **ich konnte es nicht verstehen** I could not *or* couldn't understand it, I was unable to understand it; **ich habe es sehen ~** I could see it, I was able to see it; **es ist furchtbar, nicht schlafen zu ~** it's terrible not to be able to sleep; **er hat es gekonnt** he could do it, he was able to do it; **morgen kann ich nicht** I can't (manage) tomorrow; **das hättest du gleich sagen ~** you could *or* might have said that straight away; **das hätte ich dir gleich sagen ~** I could have told you that straight away; **ich kann das nicht mehr sehen** I can't stand the sight of it any more; **ich kann das nicht mehr hören** I don't want to hear that again; **ich kann nicht mehr** I can't go on; (*ertragen*) I can't take any more; (*essen*) I can't manage *or* eat any more; **kannst du noch?** can you go on?; (*essen*) can you manage some more?; **mir kann keiner!** (*inf*) I'm all right, Jack (*Brit inf*), it's not my problem; **ich habe das alles schriftlich, mir kann keiner!** I've got it all in writing, they can't touch me; **so schnell er konnte** as fast as he could *or* was able to; **~ vor Lachen!** (*inf*) I wish I could, chance would be a fine thing (*inf*); **man kann alles, wenn man (nur) will** where there's a will there's a way (*Prov*)

b (*= beherrschen*) *Sprache* to (be able to) speak; *Schach* to be able to play; *Klavier spielen, lesen, schwimmen, Ski laufen etc* to be able to, to know how to; **er kann seine Schulaufgabe wieder nicht** he can't do his homework again; (*= nicht gemacht*) he hasn't done his homework again; **was ~ Sie?** what can you do?; **was du alles kannst!** the things you can do!; **er kann was** he's very capable *or* able; **unser Chef kann viel** our boss is a very capable *or* able man; **unser Chef kann nichts** our boss is incapable *or* useless; **er kann gut Englisch** he speaks English well; **er kann kein Französisch** he doesn't speak French; **er kann/er kann nicht schwimmen** he can/can't swim → *auch* **gekonnt**

c (*= dürfen*) to be allowed to, to be permitted to; **kann ich jetzt gehen?** can I go now?; **könnte ich ...?** could I ...?; **er kann sich nicht beklagen** he can't complain; **man kann wohl sagen, dass ...** one could well say that ...; **du kannst mich (gernhaben)!** (*inf*) get lost! (*inf*); **er kann mich (mal)** (*inf*) he can get stuffed (*Brit inf*), he can go to hell (*inf*)

d (*= möglich sein*) **Sie könnten recht haben** you could *or* might *or* may be right; **er kann jeden Augenblick kommen** he could *or* might *or* may come any minute; **das kann nur er gewesen sein** it can only have been him; **das kann nicht sein** that can't be true; **das kann fast nicht sein** that can't be true, it's almost unbelievable; **es kann sein, dass er dabei war** he could *or* might *or* may have been there; **es kann nicht sein, dass er dabei war** he couldn't *or* can't possibly have been there; **kann sein** maybe, could be

e (*mit Partikel*) **für etw ~** to be responsible for sth, to be to blame for sth → **dafürkönnen, dazukönnen**

Kön|nen NT **-s**, *no pl* ability, skill

Kön|ner ['kœnɐ] M **-s, -**, **Kön|ne|rin** [-ərın] F **-, -nen** expert

Kon|nex [kɔ'nɛks] M **-es, -e** (*geh*) connection; (*= Verbindung auch*) contact

Kon|nos|se|ment [kɔnɔsə'mɛnt] NT **-s, -s** (*Comm*) bill of lading

konn|te *pret von* **können**

Kon|rek|tor ['kɔn-] M, **Kon|rek|to|rin** F (*an Schule*) deputy head teacher (*Brit*), assistant principal; (*an Universität*) deputy vice chancellor (*Brit*), vice president (*US*)

Kon|sek|ra|ti|on [kɔnzekra'tsio:n] F **-, -en** (*Eccl*) consecration

kon|sek|rie|ren [kɔnze'kri:rən] *ptp* **konsekriert** VT (*Eccl*) to consecrate

kon|se|ku|tiv ['kɔnzekuti:f, kɔnzeku'ti:f] ADJ consecutive

Kon|se|ku|tiv|satz M consecutive clause

Kon|sens [kɔn'zɛns] M **-es, -e** [-zə] agreement, assent, consent

kon|se|quent [kɔnze'kvɛnt] ADJ consistent; (*Sport*) *Deckung* close, tight; **~e Weiterentwicklung eines Stils** logically consistent development of a style ADV *sich weigern, einhalten, befolgen* strictly; *ablehnen* emphatically; *verfechten, eintreten für* rigorously; *behandeln, argumentieren, verbieten* consistently; **~ handeln** to be consistent; **er hat ~ „Nein" gesagt** he stuck to his answer of "no"; **wir werden ~ durchgreifen** we will take rigorous action; **wenn du das ~ durchdenkst** if you follow it through to its logical conclusion; **eine Spur ~ verfolgen** to follow up a clue rigorously; **ein Ziel ~ verfolgen** to pursue an objective single-mindedly; **einen Fall ~ untersuchen** to investigate a case rigorously *or* thoroughly

Kon|se|quenz [kɔnze'kvɛnts] F **-, -en** **a** (*= Schlussfolgerung*) consequence; **die ~en tragen** to take the consequences; **(aus etw) die ~en ziehen** to come to the obvious conclusion, to take the appropriate *or* logical step; **wenn es dir hier nicht gefällt, solltest du die entsprechenden ~en ziehen und gehen** if you don't like it here, you should do something about it and go; **ich werde meine ~en ziehen** there's only one thing for me to do

b (*= Beharrlichkeit*) consistency; (*bei Maßnahmen*) rigorousness, strictness; **die ~, mit der er sein Ziel verfolgte** the single-mindedness with which he pursued his aim

Kon|ser|va|tis|mus [kɔnzɛrva'tısmʊs] M **-**, *no pl* conservatism

kon|ser|va|tiv [kɔnzɛrva'ti:f, 'kɔnzɛrvati:f] ADJ conservative; *(Brit Pol)* Conservative, Tory ADV conservatively; **das ist ~ gerechnet** that's a conservative estimate

Kon|ser|va|ti|ve(r) [kɔnzɛrva'ti:və] MF *decl as adj* conservative; *(Brit Pol)* Conservative, Tory

Kon|ser|va|ti|vis|mus [kɔnzɛrvati'vɪsmʊs] M -, *no pl* conservatism

Kon|ser|va|tor [kɔnzɛr'va:to:ɐ] M **-s, Konserva|toren** [-'to:rən], **Kon|ser|va|to|rin** [-'to:rɪn] F **-, -nen** curator, keeper

Kon|ser|va|to|ri|um [kɔnzɛrva'to:riʊm] NT **-s, Konservatorien** [-riən] conservatory

Kon|ser|ve [kɔn'zɛrvə] F **-, -n** preserved food; *(in Dosen)* tinned *(Brit)* or canned food; *(= Konservendose)* tin *(Brit)*, can; *(Med: = Blutkonserve etc)* stored blood *etc*; blood bottle; *(Rad, TV)* prerecorded *or* canned *(inf)* material; *(= Tonkonserve)* recorded music; *(auf Band)* taped music; **sich aus** *or* **von ~n ernähren** to live out of tins *(Brit) or* cans

Kon|ser|ven|büch|se F, **Kon|ser|ven|do|se** F tin *(Brit)*, can

kon|ser|vie|ren [kɔnzɛr'vi:rən] *ptp* **konserviert** VT to preserve, to conserve; *Leichen* to preserve; *Auto* to wax

Kon|ser|vie|rung F -, *no pl* preservation, conservation; *(der Umwelt)* conservation; *(von Leichen)* preservation

Kon|ser|vie|rungs|mit|tel NT, **Kon|ser|vie|rungs|stoff** M preservative

kon|sis|tent [kɔnzɪs'tɛnt] ADJ **a** *(fest) Masse* solid **b** *(konsequent) Politik, Antwort* consistent **c** *(Comput) Daten, Oberfläche* consistent ADV *durchführen, behaupten* consistently

Kon|sis|tenz [kɔnzɪs'tɛnts] F **-, -en** consistency; *(von Gewebe)* texture

Kon|so|le [kɔn'zo:lə] F **-, -n** *(Archit: = Kragstein)* console, corbel; *(old: an Möbeln)* bracket; *(Comput: = Bedienerkonsole)* console

kon|so|li|die|ren [kɔnzoli'di:rən] *ptp* **konsolidiert** VT *(auch Fin, Econ)* to consolidate VR to consolidate

Kon|so|li|die|rung F **-, -en** consolidation

Kon|so|li|die|rungs|pha|se F consolidation phase

Kon|so|nant [kɔnzo'nant] M **-en, -en** consonant

kon|so|nan|tisch [kɔnzo'nantɪʃ] ADJ consonant(al)

Kon|so|nanz [kɔnzo'nants] F **-, -en** *(Mus)* consonance

Kon|sor|ten [kɔn'zɔrtn] PL *(pej inf)* gang *(inf)*, mob *(inf)*, crowd *(inf)*; **X und** ~ X and his gang *etc (inf)*

Kon|sor|ti|al|bank [kɔnzɔr'tsia:l-] F *pl* **-banken** *(Comm)* consortium bank

Kon|sor|ti|um [kɔn'zɔrtsiʊm] NT **-s, Konsortien** [-tsiən] *(Comm)* consortium, syndicate, group

Kon|spi|ra|ti|on [kɔnspira'tsio:n] F **-, -en** conspiracy, plot

kon|spi|ra|tiv [kɔnspira'ti:f] ADJ conspiratorial; **~er Treff** meeting place *(for terrorists etc)*, meet; **~e Wohnung** safe house

kon|spi|rie|ren [kɔnspi'ri:rən] *ptp* **konspiriert** VI to conspire, to plot

kon|stant [kɔn'stant] ADJ constant ADV *gut, schlecht, niedrig, hoch* consistently

Kon|stan|te [kɔn'stantə] F **-(n), -n** constant

Kon|stan|tin ['kɔnstanti:n] M **-s** Constantine

Kon|stan|ti|no|pel [kɔnstanti'no:pl] NT **-s** *(old)* Constantinople

Kon|stanz [kɔn'stants] F -, *no pl (geh)* constancy

Kon|stanz ['kɔnstants] NT *(Geog)* **-** Constance

kon|sta|tie|ren [kɔnsta'ti:rən] *ptp* **konstatiert** VT to see, to notice; **ich konstatiere, Sie haben schon wieder Ihre Hausaufgaben nicht gemacht** I see *or* notice you haven't done your homework once again; **in ihrer Rede konstatierte sie, dass ...** in her speech she made the point that ...

Kons|tel|la|ti|on [kɔnstɛla'tsio:n] F **-, -en** **a** constellation **b** *(fig)* line-up; *(von Umständen, Faktoren etc)* combination; **diese wirtschaftliche/politische ~** this economic/political situation; **die neue ~ in der Partei** the new line-up in the party; **die ~ in dem Gremium** the make-up of the committee

kons|ter|nie|ren [kɔnstɛr'ni:rən] *ptp* **konsterniert** VT to scandalize

kon|sti|tu|ie|ren [kɔnstitu'i:rən] *ptp* **konstituiert** VT to constitute, to set up; **~de Versammlung** constituent assembly VR to be constituted, to be set up

Kon|sti|tu|ie|rung [kɔnstitu'i:rʊŋ] F **-, -en** *(= Gründung)* constitution

Kon|sti|tu|ti|on [kɔnstitu'tsio:n] F **-, -en** *(Pol, Med)* constitution; *(Phys auch)* structure

kon|sti|tu|ti|o|nell [kɔnstitutsio'nɛl] ADJ constitutional ADV **a** *(Pol: = verfassungsmäßig)* constitutionally **b** *(Med: = körperlich)* **er war ~ im Vorteil** he had a better constitution; **für etw ~ anfällig sein** to be intrinsically susceptible to sth

kon|sti|tu|tiv [kɔnstitu'ti:f] ADJ constitutive

kon|stru|ie|ren [kɔnstru'i:rən] *ptp* **konstruiert** VT to construct *(auch Math)*; *(Gram auch)* to construe; **ein konstruierter Fall** a hypothetical case; **ein konstruiertes Wort** a made-up word; **der Satz klingt sehr konstruiert** the sentence sounds very artificial

Kon|strukt [kɔn'strʊkt] NT **-(e)s, -e** *(Ling)* construct

Kon|struk|teur [kɔnstrʊk'tø:ɐ] M **-s, -e**, **Kon|struk|teu|rin** [-'tø:rɪn] F **-, -nen** designer

Kon|struk|ti|on [kɔnstrʊk'tsio:n] F **-, -en** construction; *(= Entwurf, Bauart auch)* design; *(gedanklich, philosophisch auch)* construct; **erlauben Sie mir die ~ des folgenden Falles** allow me to make up *or* construct the following case; **es bieten sich folgende ~en des Handlungsvorganges an** there are several possible reconstructions of the event

Kon|struk|ti|ons-: **Kon|struk|ti|ons|bü|ro** NT drawing office; **Kon|struk|ti|ons|feh|ler** M *(im Entwurf)* design fault; *(im Aufbau)* structural defect; **Kon|struk|ti|ons|plan** M structural plan

kon|struk|tiv [kɔnstrʊk'ti:f] ADJ constructive; **~e Kritik** constructive criticism ADV constructively

Kon|struk|ti|vis|mus [kɔnstrʊkti'vɪsmʊs] M -, *no pl (Art)* constructivism

Kon|sul ['kɔnzʊl] M **-s, -n**, **Kon|su|lin** [-lɪn] F **-, -nen** consul

kon|su|la|risch [kɔnzu'la:rɪʃ] ADJ consular

Kon|su|lat [kɔnzu'la:t] NT **-(e)s, -e** consulate

Kon|sul|ta|ti|on [kɔnzʊlta'tio:n] F **-, -en** *(form)* consultation; **jdn zur ~ hinzuziehen** to consult sb

kon|sul|tie|ren [kɔnzʊl'ti:rən] *ptp* **konsultiert** VT *(form)* to consult

Kon|sum M **-s, -s** **a** [kɔn'zu:m] *no pl (= Verbrauch)* consumption **b** ['kɔnzu:m, 'kɔnzʊm] *(= Genossenschaft)* cooperative society; *(= Laden)* cooperative store, co-op *(inf)*

Kon|sum|ar|ti|kel [kɔn'zu:m-] M consumer item; ~ *pl* consumer goods *pl*

Kon|su|ma|ti|on [kɔnzuma'tsio:n] F **-, -en** *(Aus, Sw) food and drink consumed in a restaurant*

Kon|su|ment [kɔnzu'mɛnt] M **-en, -en**, **Kon|su|men|tin** [-'mɛntɪn] F **-, -nen** consumer

Kon|su|men|ten|hal|tung F *(pej)* passive *or* nonparticipating attitude

Kon|sum-: **Kon|sum|ge|nos|sen|schaft** [kɔn'zu:m-] F co-operative society; **Kon|sum|ge|sell|schaft** F consumer society; **Kon|sum|gut** NT *usu pl* consumer item; **Konsumgüter** *pl* consumer goods *pl*; **kon|sum|hung|rig** ADJ consumption-oriented; *Gesellschaft auch* consumerist

kon|su|mie|ren [kɔnzu'mi:rən] *ptp* **konsumiert** VT to consume

Kon|su|mis|mus [kɔnzu'mɪsmʊs] M -, *no pl* consumerism

Kon|sum-: **Kon|sum|kli|ma** NT consumer demand *or* confidence; **das ~ ist gut/schlecht** consumer *or* buyer demand is up/down; **Kon|sum|müll** M *(pej)* consumer waste; **Kon|sum|tem|pel** [kɔn'zu:m-] M shrine to consumerism; **Kon|sum|ter|ror** M *(pej)* pressures *pl* of a materialistic society; **Kon|sum|ver|zicht** M non-consumption; ~ **üben** to practise *(Brit) or* practice *(US)* non-consumption; **Kon|sum|zwang** M *(Sociol)* compulsion to buy

Kon|takt [kɔn'takt] M **-(e)s, -e** contact *(auch Elec)*; **~e** *pl (Aut)* contact breakers *pl*; **mit jdm/etw in ~ kommen** to come into contact with sb/sth; **mit jdm ~ bekommen, zu jdm ~ finden** to get to know sb; **ich bekomme mit ihm keinen ~** I don't feel I really know him; **mit jdm ~ aufnehmen** to get in contact *or* touch with sb, to contact sb; **mit jdm in ~ stehen** to be in contact *or* touch with sb; **~ herstellen** to make *or* establish contact; **den ~ unterbrechen** to break contact; **keinen ~ mehr haben, den ~ verloren haben** to have lost contact *or* touch, to be out of touch; **sie hat keinen ~ zu ihrer Familie** she has no contact with her family

Kon|takt-: **Kon|takt|ab|zug** M *(Phot)* contact print; **Kon|takt|ad|res|se** F accommodation address; **er hinterließ eine ~** he left behind an address where he could be contacted; **Kon|takt|an|zei|ge** F lonely hearts ad *(Brit)*, personal ad; **Kon|takt|an|zei|gen** PL personal column; **kon|takt|arm** ADJ **er ist ~** he lacks contact with other people; **Kon|takt|ar|mut** F lack of human contact; **Kon|takt|bild|schirm** M touch-sensitive screen; **Kon|takt|frau** F *(= Agentin)* contact; **Kon|takt|freu|de** F sociability; **kon|takt|freu|dig** ADJ sociable, outgoing; **sie ist ~** she makes friends easily; **Kon|takt|freu|dig|keit** F sociability; **Kon|takt|lin|se** F contact lens; **~n tragen** to wear contact lenses; **Kon|takt|man|gel** M lack of contact; **Kon|takt|mann** M *pl* **-männer** *(= Agent)* contact; **Kon|takt|nah|me** [-na:mə] F **-, -n** *(form)* contacting; **Kon|takt|per|son** F contact; **Kon|takt|pfle|ge** F staying in contact, keeping in touch; **kon|takt|scheu** ADJ shy; **sie ist ~** she doesn't like socializing

Kon|ta|mi|na|ti|on [kɔntamina'tsio:n] F **-, -en** *(auch Kerntechnik)* contamination; *(Gram)* blend(ing); **die ~ der Luft durch gefährliche Stoffe** the contamination of the air by dangerous substances

kon|ta|mi|nie|ren [kɔntami'ni:rən] *ptp* **kontaminiert** VI to contaminate, to pollute; *(Gram)* to blend

Kon|temp|la|ti|on [kɔntɛmpla'tsio:n] F **-, -en** contemplation

kon|temp|la|tiv [kɔntɛmpla'ti:f] ADJ contemplative

Kon|ten *pl von* **Konto**

Kon|te|nan|ce [kɔntə'nã:s] F -, *no pl* = **Contenance**

Kon|ter ['kɔntɐ] M **-s, -** **a** *(Boxen)* counter (-punch); *(Ballspiele)* counterattack, break; **sich** *(dat)* **einen ~ einfangen** to be caught by a counterpunch **b** *(fig: = Handlung)* countermove; *(= Äußerung)* rejoinder, parry

Kon|ter- *in cpds (Sport)* counter-; **Kon|ter|ad|mi|ral(in)** M(F) rear admiral; **Kon|ter|an|griff** M counterattack; **Kon|ter|ban|de** F -, *no pl* contraband

Kon|ter|fei ['kɔntɐfai, kɔntɐ'fai] NT **-s, -s** *or* **-e** *(old, hum)* likeness, portrait

kon|ter|fei|en [kɔntɐ'faiən, 'kɔntɐfaiən] *ptp* **konterfeit** VT to portray

kon|ter|ka|rie|ren [kɔntɐka'ri:rən] *ptp* **konterkariert** VT to counteract; *Aussage* to contradict

kon|tern ['kɔntɐn] VT *Angriff, Vorwurf* to counter VI to counter; *(Sport)* to counterattack

kon|ter-: **kon|ter|pro|duk|tiv** ADJ = **kontraproduktiv**; **Kon|ter|re|vo|lu|ti|on** F counter-revolution; **kon|ter|re|vo|lu|ti|o|när** ADJ counter-revolutionary; **Kon|ter|schlag** M *(Sport, fig)* counterattack; *(Boxen)* counter (-blow), counterpunch

Kon|text ['kɔntɛkst] M context

Kon|text|me|nü NT *(Comput)* context-sensitive menu, context menu

Kon|ti *pl von* **Konto**

Kon|ti|nent ['kɔntinɛnt, kɔnti'nɛnt] M **-(e)s, -e** continent

kon|ti|nen|tal [kɔntinɛn'ta:l] ADJ continental

Kon|ti|nen|tal-: **Kon|ti|nen|tal|drift** F continental drift; **Kon|ti|nen|tal|eu|ro|pa** NT the Continent; **kon|ti|nen|tal|eu|ro|pä|isch** ADJ Continental; **Kon|ti|nen|tal|kli|ma** NT continental climate; **Kon|ti|nen|tal|so|ckel** M continental shelf; **Kon|ti|nen|tal|sper|re** F *(Hist)* Continental System; **Kon|ti|nen|tal|ver|schie|bung** F *(Geol)* continental drift

Kon|tin|gent [kɔntɪŋ'gɛnt] NT **-(e)s, -e** *(Mil: = Truppenkontingent)* contingent; *(Comm)* quota, share; *(= Zuteilung)* allotment, allocation

kon|tin|gen|tie|ren [kɔntɪŋgɛn'ti:rən] *ptp* **kontingentiert** VT *(Comm)* to allocate, to apportion; **den Import** ~ to fix *or* impose import quotas

Kon|tin|genz [kɔntɪŋ'gɛnts] F **-, -en** *(Philos)* contingency

Kon|ti|nua *pl von* **Kontinuum**

kon|ti|nu|ier|lich [kɔntinu'i:ɐlɪç] ADJ continuous ADV continuously

Kon|ti|nu|i|tät [kɔntinui'tɛ:t] F **-,** *no pl* continuity

Kon|ti|nu|um [kɔn'ti:nuʊm] NT **-s, Kontinua** [-ua] continuum

Kon|to ['kɔnto] NT **-s, Konten** *or* **Konti** ['kɔntn, 'kɔnti] account; **auf meinem/mein** ~ in my/into my account; **das geht auf mein** ~ *(inf) (= ich bin schuldig)* I am responsible *or* to blame for this; *(= ich zahle)* this is on me *(inf)*

Kon|to-: **Kon|to|aus|zug** M (bank) statement, statement (of account); **Kon|to|aus|zugs|dru|cker** M *bank statement machine*; **Kon|to|be|we|gung** F transaction; **kon|to|füh|rend** ADJ *Bank* where an account is held; **Kon|to|füh|rung** F running of an account; **Kon|to|füh|rungs|ge|bühr** F bank charge; **Kon|to|in|ha|ber(in)** M(F) account holder; **Kon|to|num|mer** F account number

Kon|tor [kɔn'to:ɐ] NT **-s, -e** **a** *(= Büro)* office → **Schlag** **b** *(= Handelsniederlassung)* branch office

Kon|to|rist [kɔnto'rɪst] M **-en, -en** clerk

Kon|to|ris|tin [kɔnto'rɪstɪn] F **-, -nen** clerkess

Kon|to|stand M balance, state of an account

kont|ra ['kɔntra] PREP *+acc* against; *(Jur)* versus

Kont|ra ['kɔntra] NT **-s, -s** *(Cards)* double; ~ **geben** *(Cards)* to double; **jdm** ~ **geben** *(fig)* to contradict sb

Kont|ra-: **Kont|ra|bass** M double bass; **kont|ra|dik|to|risch** [kɔntradɪk'to:rɪʃ] ADJ contradictory ADV **sich** ~ **äußern/ausdrücken** to contradict oneself

Kon|tra|hent [kɔntra'hɛnt] M **-en, -en**, **Kon|tra|hen|tin** [-'hɛntɪn] F **-, -nen** *(= Vertragsschließender)* contracting party; *(= Gegner)* opponent, adversary

kon|tra|hie|ren [kɔntra'hi:rən] *ptp* **kontrahiert** VT *(Ling, Med)* to contract

Kont|ra|in|di|ka|ti|on [kɔntra-, 'kɔntra-] F *(Med)* contraindication

Kon|trakt [kɔn'trakt] M **-(e)s, -e** contract

Kon|trak|ti|on [kɔntrak'tsio:n] F **-, -en** *(Med)* contraction

Kont|ra-: **Kont|ra|post** [kɔntra'pɔst] M **-(e)s, -e** *(Art)* contrapposto; **kont|ra|pro|duk|tiv** ADJ counterproductive; **Kont|ra|punkt** M *(Mus)* counterpoint; **kont|ra|punk|tisch** [kɔntra'pʊŋktɪʃ] ADJ *(Mus)* contrapuntal

kont|rär [kɔn'trɛ:ɐ] ADJ *(geh) Meinungen* contrary, opposite

Kon|trast [kɔn'trast] M **-(e)s, -e** contrast

Kon|trast-: **kon|trast|arm** ADJ ~ **sein** to be lacking in contrast; *(Programm, Landschaft)* to be monotonous; **Kon|trast|brei** M *(Med)* barium meal; **Kon|trast|far|be** F contrasting colour *(Brit) or* color *(US)*; **Kon|trast|fil|ter** M *(Phot)* yellow filter

kon|tras|tie|ren [kɔntras'ti:rən] *ptp* **kontrastiert** VI to contrast

kon|tras|tiv [kɔntras'ti:f] ADJ *(Ling)* contrastive

Kon|trast-: **Kon|trast|mit|tel** NT *(Med)* contrast medium; **Kon|trast|pro|gramm** NT alternative programme *(Brit) or* program *(US)*; **Kon|trast|re|ge|lung** F contrast control; **Kon|trast|reg|ler** M contrast (control); **kon|trast|reich** ADJ ~ **sein** to be full of contrast

Kont|ra|te|nor [-teno:ɐ] M countertenor

Kont|ra|zep|ti|on [kɔntratsɛp'tsio:n] F **-,** *no pl (form)* contraception

kon|tri|bu|ie|ren [kɔntribu'i:rən] *ptp* **kontribuiert** VT *(old)* to contribute

Kon|tri|bu|ti|on [kɔntribu'tsio:n] F **-, -en** *(old)* contribution

Kon|troll-: **Kon|troll|ab|schnitt** M *(Comm)* counterfoil, stub; **Kontrollampe** △ F → **Kontrolllampe**; **Kon|troll|be|am|te(r)** M *decl as adj*, **Kon|troll|be|am|tin** F **-, -nen** inspector; *(an der Grenze)* frontier guard; *(zur Passkontrolle)* passport officer; *(zur Zollkontrolle)* customs officer; *(zur Überwachung)* security officer; **Kon|troll|be|hör|de** F supervisory body

Kon|trol|le [kɔn'trɔlə] F **-, -n** **a** *(= Beherrschung, Regulierung)* control; **über jdn/etw die** ~ **verlieren** to lose control of sb/sth; **jdn/etw unter** ~ **haben/halten** to have/keep sb/sth under control; **der Brand geriet außer** ~ the fire got out of control **b** *(= Nachprüfung)* check (+*gen* on); *(= Aufsicht)* supervision; *(= Schutz)* safeguard; *(= Passkontrolle)* passport control; *(= Zollkontrolle)* customs examination; **jdn/etw einer** ~ **unterziehen** to check sb/sth; **zur** ~ **haben wir noch einmal alles nachgerechnet** we went over all the figures again to check; **~n durchführen** to carry out *or* make checks; **der Luftverkehr ist unter ständiger** ~ air traffic is kept under constant surveillance, a constant check is kept on air traffic; **die ~n an der Grenze wurden verschärft** the border controls were tightened; **nach einer sorgfältigen** ~ **der Waren** after a careful inspection of the goods, after a careful check on *or* of the goods; **die** ~ **von Lebensmitteln** the inspection of foodstuffs **c** *(= Stelle) (für Überprüfung, Verkehr)* checkpoint; *(= Pass-/Zollkontrolle)* passport control/customs; *(vor Fabrik)* gatehouse; *(an der Grenze)* border post; *(in Bibliothek etc)* checkout desk **d** *(= Person)* inspector; *(= Pass-/Zollkontrolle)* passport/customs officer; *(in Fabrik)* security officer; *(= Polizist) (im Verkehr)* traffic police; *(an der Grenze)* frontier guard; *(in Bibliotheken etc)* person at the checkout desk

Kon|trol|leur [kɔntrɔ'lø:ɐ] M **-s, -e**, **Kon|trol|leu|rin** [-'lø:rɪn] F **-, -nen** inspector

Kon|troll-: **Kon|troll|funk|ti|on** F controlling function; **Kon|troll|gang** M *pl* **-gänge** (inspection) round; **Kon|troll|grup|pe** F **a** *(Med, Psych)* control group **b** *(= Aufsichtsorgan)* surveillance group

kon|trol|lier|bar ADJ controllable; *Behauptung* checkable, verifiable

kon|trol|lie|ren [kɔntrɔ'li:rən] *ptp* **kontrolliert** VT **a** *(= regulieren, beherrschen)* to control **b** *(= nachprüfen, überwachen)* to check; *Pass, Fahrkarte etc* to inspect, to check; *(= Aufsicht haben über)* to supervise; **die Qualität der Waren muss streng kontrolliert werden** a strict check must be kept on the quality of the goods; **jdn/etw nach etw** *or* **auf etw** *(acc)* ~ to check sb/sth for sth; **Gemüse aus kontrolliert biologischem Anbau** organically grown vegetables; **kontrollierte Drogenabgabe** medical prescription of narcotics; **staatlich kontrolliert** state-controlled

Kontrollliste △ F → **Kontrollliste**

Kon|troll-: **Kon|troll|käst|chen** NT *(Comput)* check box; **Kon|troll|kom|mis|si|on** F control commission; **Kon|troll|lam|pe** F, **Kon|troll|leuch|te** F pilot lamp; *(Aut: für Ölstand)* warning light *or* lamp; **Kon|troll|lis|te** F check list; **Kon|troll|or|gan** NT monitoring body; **Kon|troll|pflicht** F control; **seine** ~ **vernachlässigen** to neglect one's supervisory responsibilities; **Kon|troll|punkt** M checkpoint; **Kon|troll|rat** M **Alliierter** ~ Allied Control Council; **Kon|troll|stel|le** F checkpoint; **Kon|troll|stem|pel** M inspection stamp; **Kon|troll|sys|tem** NT control system; **Kon|troll|turm** M control tower; **Kon|troll|uhr** F time clock; **Kon|troll|un|ter|su|chung** F control test; **Kon|troll|waa|ge** F *(in Verpackungs-, Pharmaindustrie)* checkweigher; **Kon|troll|zent|rum** NT control centre *(Brit) or* center *(US)*; *(Space auch)* mission control

kont|ro|vers [kɔntro'vɛrs] ADJ controversial ADV **(etw)** ~ **diskutieren** to have a controversial discussion (on sth)

Kont|ro|ver|se [kɔntro'vɛrzə] F **-, -n** controversy

Kon|tur [kɔn'tu:ɐ] F **-, -en** outline, contour; **~en annehmen** to take shape

Kon|tu|ren|stift M liner

kon|tu|rie|ren [kɔntu'ri:rən] *ptp* **konturiert** VT *(lit, fig)* to outline

kon|tur|los ADJ shapeless, flat; *Person, Politiker* faceless

Kon|tur|sitz M contoured seat

Ko|nus ['ko:nʊs] M **-, -se** *or (Tech)* **Konen** ['ko:nən] *(Math)* cone; *(Tech)* taper; *(Typ)* body

Kon|va|les|zenz [kɔnvalɛs'tsɛnts] **-,** *(rare)* **-en** F *(Med)* convalescence

Kon|vek|tor [kɔn'vɛktɔr] **-s, Konvektoren** [-'to:rən] M convector (heater)

Kon|ve|ni|enz [kɔnve'niɛnts] F **-, -en** *(geh)* propriety; *(= Bequemlichkeit)* convenience

Kon|vent [kɔn'vɛnt] M **-(e)s, -e** **a** *(= Versammlung)* convention **b** *(= Kloster)* convent; *(= Mönchskonvent)* monastery

Kon|ven|ti|on [kɔnvɛn'tsio:n] F **-, -en** **a** *(= Herkommen)* convention; **sich über die ~en hinwegsetzen** to sweep aside *or* ignore (social) conventions **b** *(im Völkerrecht)* convention

Kon|ven|ti|o|nal|stra|fe [kɔnvɛntsio'na:l-] F penalty *or* fine (for breach of contract)

kon|ven|ti|o|nell [kɔnvɛntsio'nɛl] ADJ conventional ADV conventionally

kon|ver|gent [kɔnvɛr'gɛnt] ADJ convergent, converging

Kon|ver|genz [kɔnvɛr'gɛnts] F **-, -en** convergence

Kon|ver|genz-: **Kon|ver|genz|kri|te|rien** PL convergence criteria *pl*; **Kon|ver|genz|the|o|rie** F theory of convergence

kon|ver|gie|ren [kɔnvɛr'gi:rən] *ptp* **konvergiert** VI to converge

Kon|ver|sa|ti|on [kɔnvɛrza'tsio:n] F **-, -en** conversation; ~ **machen** to make conversation *or* small talk *(inf)*

Kon|ver|sa|ti|ons|le|xi|kon NT encyclopaedia *(Brit)*, encyclopedia *(US)*

Kon|ver|si|on [kɔnvɛr'zio:n] F **-, -en** conversion

Kon|ver|ter [kɔn'vɛrtɐ] M **-s, -** converter

kon|ver|ti|bel [kɔnvɛr'ti:bl] ADJ *(Fin)* convertible

Kon|ver|ti|bi|li|tät [kɔnvɛrtibili'tɛ:t] F **-,** *no pl (Fin)* convertibility

kon|ver|tier|bar [kɔnvɛr'ti:ɐba:ɐ] ADJ *(Fin)* convertible

Kon|ver|tier|bar|keit F **-,** *no pl (Fin)* convertibility

kon|ver|tie|ren [kɔnvɛr'ti:rən] *ptp* **konvertiert** VT *Datenformat etc* to convert (in *+acc* to) VI *aux haben or sein* to be converted

Kon|ver|tie|rung [kɔnvɛr'ti:rʊŋ] F **-, -en** *(Comput)* conversion

Kon|ver|tit [kɔnvɛr'ti:t] M **-en, -en**, **Kon|ver|ti|tin** [-'ti:tɪn] F **-, -nen** convert

kon|vex [kɔn'vɛks] ADJ convex ADV convexly

Kon|vex-: **kon|vex|kon|kav** ADJ convexo-concave; **Kon|vex|lin|se** F convex lens; **Kon|vex|spie|gel** M convex mirror

Kon|vikt [kɔnˈvɪkt] NT -(e)s, -e seminary

Kon|voi [ˈkɔnvɔy, kɔnˈvɔy] M -s, -s convoy; **im ~ fahren** to drive in convoy

Kon|vo|lut [kɔnvoˈluːt] NT -(e)s, -e *(geh)* bundle (of papers)

Kon|vul|si|on [kɔnvʊlˈzioːn] F -, -en *usu pl (Med)* convulsion

kon|vul|si|visch [kɔnvʊlˈziːvɪʃ] *(Med)* ADJ convulsive ADV convulsively

kon|ze|die|ren [kɔntseˈdiːrən] *ptp* **konzediert** VT *(geh)* to concede, to grant *(jdm etw* sb sth)

Kon|zent|rat [kɔntsɛnˈtraːt] NT -(e)s, -e concentrate; *(fig: eines Buches etc)* condensed version

Kon|zent|ra|ti|on [kɔntsɛntraˈtsioːn] F -, -en concentration *(auf +acc* on)

Kon|zent|ra|ti|ons-: **Kon|zent|ra|ti|ons|fä|hig|keit** F powers *pl* of concentration; **Kon|zent|ra|ti|ons|la|ger** NT concentration camp; **Kon|zent|ra|ti|ons|man|gel** M lack of concentration; **Kon|zent|ra|ti|ons|schwä|che** F weak *or* poor concentration; **Kon|zent|ra|ti|ons|ver|mö|gen** NT powers *pl* of concentration

kon|zent|rie|ren [kɔntsɛnˈtriːrən] *ptp* **konzentriert** VT to concentrate *(auf +acc* on); *Truppen auch* to mass VR to concentrate *(auf +acc* on); *(Untersuchung, Arbeit etc)* to be concentrated *(auf +acc* on)

kon|zent|riert [kɔntsɛnˈtriːɐt] ADJ **a** *(Chem)* concentrated **b** **mit ~er Aufmerksamkeit** with all one's concentration ADV *arbeiten, zuhören* intently; *nachdenken, spielen* intensely; *rechnen* carefully

kon|zent|risch [kɔnˈtsɛntrɪʃ] *(Math, Mil)* ADJ concentric ADV concentrically

Kon|zept [kɔnˈtsɛpt] NT -(e)s, -e *(= Rohentwurf)* draft, notes *pl*; *(für Aufsatz etc auch)* rough copy; *(= Plan, Programm)* plan, programme *(Brit)*, program *(US)*; *(= Begriff, Vorstellung)* concept; **es ist jetzt wenigstens als** *or* **im ~ fertig** at least the draft *etc* is ready now; **jdn aus dem ~ bringen** to put sb off *(esp Brit)*, to break sb's train of thought; *(inf: aus dem Gleichgewicht)* to upset sb; **aus dem ~ geraten** to lose one's thread; *(inf: aus dem Gleichgewicht)* to get upset; **das passt mir nicht ins ~** that doesn't fit in with my plans *or* doesn't suit my plans; *(= gefällt mir nicht)* I don't like the idea; **jdm das ~ verderben** to spoil sb's plans

Kon|zep|ti|on [kɔntsɛpˈtsioːn] F -, -en **a** *(Med)* conception **b** *(geh) (= Gedankengang)* idea; *(= Entwurf)* conception; **seine ~ der Außenpolitik** his idea *or* conception of foreign policy; **ein schon in der ~ verfehltes Gedicht** a poem which in its (very) conception was a failure

kon|zep|ti|o|nell [kɔntsɛptsioˈnɛl] *(geh)* ADJ conceptional ADV conceptionally

Kon|zep|ti|ons-: **Kon|zep|ti|ons|furcht** F *(Psych)* conception phobia, fear of conceiving; **kon|zep|ti|ons|los** ADJ without a definite line; **das Programm wirkt auf mich recht ~** the programme *(Brit) or* program *(US)* strikes me as lacking any definite line; **Kon|zep|ti|ons|lo|sig|keit** F -, *no pl* lack of any definite line

Kon|zept-: **Kon|zept|kunst** F conceptual art; **Kon|zept|pa|pier** NT rough paper

Kon|zern [kɔnˈtsɛrn] M -s, -e combine, group (of companies); **die ~e haben zu viel Macht** the big companies have too much power

Kon|zern-: **Kon|zern|bil|dung** F formation of combines; **Kon|zern|lei|tung** F, *no pl* **a** *(= Leitung als Aufgabengebiet)* (central) management of a group of companies **b** *(= leitende Personen)* group management; **Kon|zern|spit|ze** F top management *(of a/the group of companies)*, (a/the) group's top management

Kon|zert [kɔnˈtsɛrt] NT -(e)s, -e concert; *(von klassischen Solisten auch)* recital; *(= Komposition)* concerto; **die Kinder heulten im ~** the children cried in unison

Kon|zert-: **Kon|zert|abend** M concert evening; **Kon|zert|agen|tur** F concert artists' agency

kon|zer|tant [kɔntsɛrˈtant] ADJ *(Mus)* in concerto form; *Sinfonie* concertante

Kon|zert-: **Kon|zert|be|su|cher(in)** M(F) concertgoer; **Kon|zert|flü|gel** M concert grand *(Brit)*, grand piano; **Kon|zert|gi|tar|re** F classical guitar; **Kon|zert|hal|le** F concert hall *or* auditorium

kon|zer|tie|ren [kɔntsɛrˈtiːrən] *ptp* **konzertiert** VI to give a concert; *(= als Solist mitwirken)* to play in a concert VT *(geh: = abstimmen)* to concert

kon|zer|tiert [kɔntsɛrˈtiːɐt] ADJ **~e Aktion** *(Fin, Pol)* concerted action

Kon|zer|ti|na [kɔntsɛrˈtiːna] F -, **Konzertinen** [-ˈtiːnən] concertina

Kon|zert-: **Kon|zert|meis|ter(in)** M(F) leader *(Brit)*, concertmaster *(US)*; **Kon|zert|pa|vil|lon** M bandstand; **Kon|zert|pi|a|nist(in)** M(F) concert pianist; **Kon|zert|rei|he** F series of concerts, concert series; **Kon|zert|saal** M concert hall, auditorium; **Kon|zert|sän|ger(in)** M(F) concert singer

Kon|zes|si|on [kɔntsɛˈsioːn] F -, -en **a** *(= Gewerbeerlaubnis)* concession, licence *(Brit)*, license *(US)*, franchise **b** *(= Zugeständnis)* concession *(an +acc* to)

Kon|zes|si|o|när [kɔntsɛsioˈnɛːɐ] M -s, -e, **Kon|zes|si|o|nä|rin** [-ˈnɛːrɪn] F -, -nen concessionaire, licensee

Kon|zes|si|ons-: **kon|zes|si|ons|be|reit** ADJ ready *or* willing to make concessions; **Kon|zes|si|ons|be|reit|schaft** F readiness to make concessions; **kon|zes|si|ons|pflich|tig** ADJ requiring a licence *(Brit) or* license *(US) pred*

kon|zes|siv [kɔntsɛˈsiːf] ADJ *(Gram)* concessive

Kon|zes|siv|satz M *(Gram)* concessive clause

Kon|zil [kɔnˈtsiːl] NT -s, -e *or* -ien [-liən] *(Eccl, Univ)* council

kon|zi|li|ant [kɔntsiˈliant] ADJ *(= versöhnlich)* conciliatory; *(= entgegenkommend)* generous ADV **sich ~ geben** to be conciliatory; **~ gestimmt sein** to be inclined to be conciliatory

Kon|zi|pi|ent [kɔntsiˈpiɛnt] M -en, -en, **Kon|zi|pi|en|tin** [-ˈpiɛntɪn] F -, -nen *(Aus)* articled clerk

kon|zi|pie|ren [kɔntsiˈpiːrən] *ptp* **konzipiert** VT to conceive; *(= entwerfen auch)* to design VI *(Med)* to conceive

kon|zis [kɔnˈtsiːs] *(liter)* ADJ concise ADV concisely

Koof|mich [ˈkoːfmɪç] M -s, -s *or* -e *(pej inf)* businessman type

Koog [koːk] M -es, **Köge** [ˈkøːgə] *(N Ger)* polder

Ko|ope|ra|ti|on [kolopera'tsioːn] F -, -en cooperation

Ko|ope|ra|ti|ons|part|ner(in) M(F) cooperative partner, joint venture partner

ko|ope|ra|tiv [kolopera'tiːf] ADJ cooperative ADV cooperatively

Ko|ope|ra|ti|ve [kolopera'tiːvə] F -, -n *(Econ)* cooperative

Ko|ope|ra|tor [koloperatoːɐ] M -s, **Kooperatoren** [-ˈtoːrən], **Ko|ope|ra|to|rin** [-ˈtoːrɪn] F -, -nen **a** *(Aus)* curate **b** *(rare)* cooperator

ko|ope|rie|ren [koloperiːrən] *ptp* **kooperiert** VI to cooperate

Ko|op|ta|ti|on [kolɔptaˈtsioːn] F -, -en cooption, cooption

Ko|or|di|na|te [kolɔrdiˈnaːtə] F -, -n *(Math)* coordinate

Ko|or|di|na|ten- *(Math)*: **Ko|or|di|na|ten|ach|se** F coordinate axis; **Ko|or|di|na|ten|kreuz** NT, **Ko|or|di|na|ten|sys|tem** NT coordinate system

Ko|or|di|na|ti|on [kolɔrdinaˈtsioːn] F -, -en coordination

Ko|or|di|na|tor [kolɔrdiˈnaːtoːɐ] M -s, **Koordinatoren** [-ˈtoːrən], **Ko|or|di|na|to|rin** [-ˈtoːrɪn] F -, -nen coordinator

ko|or|di|nie|ren [kolɔrdiˈniːrən] *ptp* **koordiniert** VT to coordinate

ko|or|di|nie|rend ADJ *(auch Gram)* coordinating

Ko|pe|ke [koˈpeːkə] F -, -n copeck, kopeck

Ko|pen|ha|gen [koːpnˈhaːgn] NT -s Copenhagen

Ko|pen|ha|ge|ner [koːpnˈhaːgənɐ] ADJ Copenhagen *attr*

Ko|pen|ha|ge|ner [koːpnˈhaːgənɐ] M -s, -, **Ko|pen|ha|ge|ne|rin** [-ərɪn] F -, -nen person from Copenhagen

Kö|pe|ni|cki|a|de [køːpənɪˈkiaːdə] F -, -n hoax involving impersonation

Kö|per [ˈkøːpɐ] M -s, *no pl (Tex)* twill

ko|per|ni|ka|nisch [kopɛrniˈkaːnɪʃ] ADJ Copernican

Kopf [kɔpf] -(e)s, ⸚e [ˈkœpfə]

SUBSTANTIV (M)

a allgemein head; **eine zehn Köpfe starke Gruppe** a group of ten people; **Kopf hoch!** chin up!; **sie sprang Kopf voraus ins Wasser** she jumped into the water headfirst; **sie stürzte sich Kopf voraus in ihr Unglück** she rushed headlong into disaster; **Kopf weg!** *(inf)* mind your head!; **Kopf runter** *or* **ab!** off with his/her head!; **von Kopf bis Fuß** from head to foot; **einen schweren** *or* **dicken** *(inf)* **Kopf haben** to be groggy; *(von Alkohol)* to have a hangover → **Schlinge, Sand**, → *auch* **d, e**

b = Teil *von Plattenspieler, Zug, Nagel, Stecknadel, Münze, Blume* head; *(= Zeitungskopf)* head; *(= Nachrichtenüberschrift)* heading; *(= Briefkopf)* (letter)head; *(= Pfeifenkopf)* bowl; *(= Sprengkopf, Gefechtskopf)* warhead; **Salatkopf** head of lettuce; **Kohlkopf** head of cabbage; **Kopf oder Zahl?** heads or tails?; **am Kopf der Tafel sitzen** to sit at the head of the table

c im übertragenen Sinn = *Verstand* head; *(= Sinn)* head, mind; *(= Denker)* thinker; *(= leitende Persönlichkeit)* leader; *(= Bandenführer)* brains *sing*; **ein kluger/findiger Kopf** an intelligent/ingenious person; **er ist ein fähiger Kopf** he's a very capable person; **in seinem Team sitzen einige hervorragende Köpfe** there are some outstanding people in his team; **die besten Köpfe** the best brains; **ich habe den Kopf voll genug** *(inf)* I've got enough on my mind; **seinen eigenen Kopf haben** *(inf)* to have a mind of one's own; **der Kopf der Gruppe ist Herr Meier** Herr Meier is the leader of the group; **sie war der Kopf der Bande** she was the brains of the gang → *auch* **d, e**

d mit Präposition

♦ **an + Kopf Kopf an Kopf** shoulder to shoulder; *(Sport, Pferderennen)* neck and neck; **jdm etw an den Kopf werfen** *or* **schmeißen** *(inf)* to chuck *(inf) or* sling *(inf)* sth at sb; **jdm Beschimpfungen** *or* **Beleidigungen an den Kopf werfen** *(inf)* to hurl insults at sb; **sich** *(dat)* **an den Kopf fassen** *or* **schlagen** *(verständnislos)* to be left speechless

♦ **auf + Kopf auf dem Kopf stehen** to stand on one's head; **die ganze Gesellschaftsordnung steht auf dem Kopf** the whole social system is stood on its head; **er hat bei seiner Sauftour sein ganzes Gehalt auf den Kopf gehauen** *(inf)* he blew all his wages on his drinking spree; **jdm auf den Kopf spucken können** *(inf)* to tower above sb; **jdm auf dem Kopf herumtrampeln** *(inf)* to walk all over sb *(inf)*; **er ist nicht auf den Kopf gefallen** he's no fool; **etw auf den Kopf stellen** to turn sth upside down; **Tatsachen auf den Kopf stellen** to stand facts on their heads, to turn facts upside down; **du kannst dich auf den Kopf stellen, du wirst ihn**

nicht umstimmen *(inf)* you can talk till you're blue in the face, you won't get him to change his mind *(inf)*; **jdm etw auf den Kopf zusagen** to say sth straight out to sb *(esp Brit)*, to tell sb sth to his/her face; **auf jds Kopf** *(acc)* **20.000 EUR aussetzen** to put 20,000 euros on sb's head

♦ **aus dem Kopf der Gedanke will mir nicht aus dem Kopf** I can't get the thought out of my head *or* mind; **diese Melodie geht mit einfach nicht mehr aus dem Kopf** I just can't get this tune out of my head; **sich** *(dat)* **etw aus dem Kopf schlagen** to put sth out of one's mind

♦ **durch den Kopf sich** *(dat)* **etw durch den Kopf gehen lassen** to think about sth

♦ **im Kopf** in one's head; **etw im Kopf haben** to have sth in one's head; **ich habe die Melodie genau im Kopf** I know the tune exactly; **was man nicht im Kopf hat, muss man in den Beinen haben** *(inf)* a bit of thought would save a lot of legwork; **im Kopf muss mans haben** *(inf)* you need brains; **nichts als Tanzen/Fußball im Kopf haben** to think of nothing but dancing/ football; **andere Dinge im Kopf haben** to have other things on one's mind; **der Gedanke geht mir im Kopf herum** I can't get the thought out of my head *or* mind; **etw im Kopf rechnen** to work sth out in one's head; **er ist nicht ganz richtig** *or* **klar im Kopf** *(inf)* he is not quite right in the head *(inf)*; **das hältst du** *or* **hält man ja im Kopf nicht aus!** *(inf)* it's absolutely incredible! *(inf)*

♦ **in den Kopf mir ist neulich in den Kopf gekommen, dass ...** the other day it *or* the idea crossed my mind that ...; **es will mir nicht in den Kopf** I can't figure it out; **sie hat es sich** *(dat)* **in den Kopf gesetzt, das zu tun** she's dead set on doing it

♦ **mit + Kopf mit bloßem Kopf** bareheaded; **mit besoffenem Kopf** *(inf)* drunk out of one's mind *(inf)*; **mit dem Kopf durch die Wand wollen** *(inf)* to be hell-bent on getting one's own way(, regardless)

♦ **nach + Kopf es muss ja nicht immer alles nach deinem Kopf gehen** you can't have things your own way all the time; **immer muss alles nach deinem Kopf gehen!** you always want things your own way!

♦ **pro Kopf also 20 Euro, das gibt dann 5 Euro pro Kopf** so 20 euros, that means 5 euros each; **das Einkommen pro Kopf** the per capita income

♦ **über + Kopf jdm über den Kopf wachsen** *(lit)* to outgrow sb; *(fig) (Sorgen etc)* to be more than sb can cope with; *(Konkurrent etc)* to outstrip sb; **das könnt ihr nicht einfach über ihren Kopf hinweg entscheiden** you can't just decide without consulting her; **er ist bis über den Kopf in Schulden** he's up to his neck *or* ears in debt

♦ **um + Kopf sich um seinen Kopf reden** to sign one's own death warrant

♦ **vor den Kopf ich war wie vor den Kopf geschlagen** I was dumbfounded; **musst du den Chef immer so vor den Kopf stoßen?** must you always antagonize the boss?; **da hat er mit einem einzigen Satz die Gewerkschaften vor den Kopf gestoßen** with a single phrase he alienated the unions

♦ **zu Kopf(e) (jdm) zu Kopf(e) steigen** to go to sb's head

e mit Verb

> Die in Verbindung mit *Kopf* verwendeten Verben sind alphabetisch angeordnet (siehe auch unter dem Eintrag für das jeweilige Verb).

er wird uns nicht gleich den Kopf abschlagen *or* **abreißen, wenn wir fünf Minuten zu spät kommen** he won't kill us if we're five minutes late; **den Kopf oben behalten** to keep one's chin up; **einen kühlen Kopf behalten** *or* **bewahren** to keep a cool head; **seinen Kopf durchsetzen** to get one's own way; **jds Kopf fordern** *(fig)* to bay for sb's blood; **dafür halte ich meinen Kopf nicht hin** *(inf)* I'm not putting my head on the block for that; **den Kopf hängen lassen** *(lit)* to hang one's head; *(fig)* to be despondent; **die Rosen lassen schon den Kopf hängen** the roses are drooping already; **den Kopf für jdn/etw hinhalten** *(inf)* to take the blame *or* rap *(inf)* for sb/sth; **jdn den Kopf kosten** *(fig)* to cost sb his career *or* job; **das hat ihn den Kopf gekostet** *(fig)* that was the end of the road for him; **sich einen/keinen Kopf um** *or* **über etw** *(acc)* **machen** to think/not think about sth; **mach dir keinen Kopf!** *(inf: = keine Sorgen)* don't worry yourself *(inf)*; **jdn einen Kopf kürzer machen** *(inf)* to cut *or* chop sb's head off; **für etw Kopf und Kragen riskieren** to risk one's neck for sth; **es werden Köpfe rollen** heads will roll; **Kopf stehen** → **kopfstehen**; **ich weiß schon gar nicht mehr** *or* **kaum mehr, wo mir der Kopf steht** I don't know if I'm coming or going; **mir steht der Kopf nach Tanzen** I'm in the mood for dancing; **jdm den Kopf verdrehen** to turn sb's head; **den Kopf verlieren** to lose one's head; **den Kopf nicht verlieren** to keep one's head, not to lose one's head; **nur nicht den Kopf verlieren!** don't lose your head!; **Kopf und Kragen wagen** *(inf) (körperlich)* to risk life and limb; *(beruflich etc)* to risk one's neck; **jdm den Kopf waschen** *(lit)* to wash sb's hair; *(fig inf)* to give sb a telling-off; **sich** *(dat)* **den Kopf waschen** to wash one's hair; **den Kopf in den Nacken werfen** to throw one's head back; **sich** *(dat)* **über etw** *(acc)* **den Kopf zerbrechen** to rack one's brains over sth; **jdm den Kopf zurechtsetzen** *or* **zurechtrücken** to bring sb to his/her senses, to give sb a talking-to; **die Köpfe zusammenstecken** to go into a huddle *(inf)*; **sich** *(dat)* **den Kopf zuschütten** to get tanked up *(inf)* → *auch* **d**

Kopf-: **Kopf-an-Kopf-Ren|nen** NT neck-and-neck race; **Kopf|ar|beit** F brainwork; **Kopf|ar|bei|ter(in)** M(F) brainworker; **Kopf|bahn|hof** M terminus (station) *(Brit)*, terminal (station)

Kopf|ball M *(Ftbl)* header

Kopf|ball-: **Kopf|ball|du|ell** NT *(Ftbl)* aerial duel; **sich ein ~ liefern** to have an aerial duel; **kopf|ball|stark** ADJ *(Ftbl)* strong in the air *pred*; **ein ~er Spieler** a good header of the ball; **Kopf|ball|tor** NT *(Ftbl)* headed goal

Kopf-: **Kopf|be|de|ckung** F headgear; **als ~ trug er ...** on his head he wore ...; **ohne ~** without a hat; **Kopf|be|trag** M per capita sum, sum per head; **Kopf|be|we|gung** F movement of the head, head movement; **Kopf|bild** NT (portrait of sb's) head

Köpf|chen ['kœpfçən] NT **-s, -** *dim von* **Kopf** little head; *(fig hum)* brains *pl*; **~, ~!** clever stuff!; **~ haben** to have brains, to be brainy *(inf)*; **du bist aber ein kluges ~** *(iro)* clever *or* smart cookie, eh! *(inf)*

köp|feln ['kœpfln] *(Aus)* VI *(= einen Kopfsprung machen)* to dive (headfirst), to take a header VTI *(Ftbl)* to head; **ins Tor ~** to head a goal, to head the ball in

köp|fen ['kœpfn] VT **a** *jdn* to behead, to decapitate; *(hum) Flasche Wein* to crack (open); **ein Ei ~** to cut the top off an egg **b** *(Ftbl)* to head VI **a** *(als Todesstrafe)* **in Saudi-Arabien wird immer noch geköpft** they still behead *or* decapitate people in Saudi Arabia; **das Köpfen** beheading, decapitation **b** *(Ftbl)* **ins Tor ~** to head a goal, to head the ball in

Kopf-: **Kopf|en|de** NT head; **Kopf|form** F shape of (the) head; **Kopf|fü|ßer** [-fy:sɐ] M **-s, -** *(Zool)* cephalopod *(spec)*; **Kopf|ge|burt** F *(fig)* intellectual creation; **Kopf|geld** NT bounty *(on sb's head)*; **Kopf|geld|jä|ger** M bounty hunter; **kopf|ge|steu|ert** ADJ *Person, Handeln etc* rational; **Kopf|griff** M *(Rettungsschwimmen)* chinhold; *(Ringen)* headlock; **Kopf|grip|pe** F flu (and headache), (epidemic) encephalitis *(spec)*; **Kopf|haar** NT hair on one's head; *(einzelnes)* hair from the head; **Kopf|hal|tung** F **eine gerade ~ haben** to hold one's head straight; **Kopf|haut** F scalp; **Kopf|hö|rer** M headphone

-köp|fig [kœpfıç] ADJ *suf* -headed; **eine fünfköpfige Familie** a family of five

Kopf-: **Kopf|jä|ger(in)** M(F) head-hunter; **Kopf|ju|cken** NT **-s,** *no pl* itching of the scalp; **Kopf|keil** M (wedge-shaped) bolster; **Kopf|kis|sen** NT pillow; **Kopf|kis|sen|be|zug** M pillow case *or* slip; **Kopf|la|ge** F *(Med)* head presentation; **Kopf|län|ge** F **um eine ~** by a head; **kopf|las|tig** [-lastıç] ADJ *(lit, fig)* top-heavy; *Flugzeug* nose-heavy; **Kopf|las|tig|keit** F **-,** *no pl* top-heaviness; *(von Flugzeug)* nose-heaviness; **Kopf|laus** F head louse; **Kopf|leis|te** F *(Typ)* head rule; **kopf|los** ADJ *(fig)* in a panic, panicky, in a flap *(Brit inf)*; *(lit)* headless; **~ werden** to lose one's head, to get into a flap *(Brit inf)* ADV **~ handeln** to lose one's head; **~ reagieren** to lose one's head; **~ durch die Gegend laufen** to run about like a headless chicken *(Brit)*, to run around like a chicken with its head cut off *(US)*; **Kopf|lo|sig|keit** F **-,** *no pl (= Panik)* panic; **Kopf|ni|cken** NT **-s,** *no pl* nod (of the head); **Kopf|nuss** F *(inf)* clip (round the earhole) *(inf)*; **Kopf|prä|mie** F reward; **Kopf|putz** [-pʊts] M **-es, -e** headdress; **kopf|rech|nen** VI *infin only* to do mental arithmetic; **Kopf|rech|nen** NT mental arithmetic; **Kopf|sa|lat** M lettuce; **kopf|scheu** ADJ timid, nervous, shy; **jdn ~ machen** to intimidate sb; **Kopf|schmer|zen** PL headache; **~ haben** to have a headache; **sich** *(dat)* **über** *or* **um etw** *(acc) or* **wegen etw ~ machen** *(fig)* to worry about sth; **Kopf|schmerz|tab|let|te** F aspirin, headache tablet; **Kopf|schup|pe** F flake of dandruff; **er hat ~n** he's got dandruff *sing*; **Kopf|schmuck** M headgear; *(bei Tracht)* headdress; **Kopf|schuss** M shot in the head; **Kopf|schüt|teln** NT **-s,** *no pl* shaking the head; **mit einem ~** with a shake of the *or* one's head; **sein ~ zeigte mir, dass er ...** the way he shook his head told me that he ...; **kopf|schüt|telnd** ADJ shaking one's head ADV with a shake of one's head, shaking one's head; **Kopf|schutz** M protection for the head; *(= Kopfschützer)* headguard; **Kopf|schüt|zer** [-ʃʏtsɐ] M **-s, -** headguard; **Kopf|sei|te** F *(von Münze)* heads, face side; *(von Zeitung)* front page; **Kopf|spiel** NT *(Ftbl)* heading; **Kopf|sprung** M header, dive; **einen ~ machen** to take a header, to dive (headfirst); **Kopf|stand** M headstand; **einen ~ machen** to stand on one's head; **kopf|stark** ADJ *(inf)* brainy *(inf)*; **kopf+ste|hen** VI *sep irreg (S Ger, Aus, Sw: aux sein) (lit)* to stand on one's head; *(fig) (vor Ausgelassenheit)* to go wild (with excitement); *(vor Aufregung)* to be in a state of excitement; *(vor Empörung)* to be in a (state of) turmoil; *(durcheinander sein: Haus etc)* to be upside down; **Kopf|stein** M cobblestone; **Kopf|stein|pflas|ter** NT cobblestones *pl*; **eine Gasse mit ~** a cobbled street; **Kopf|stein|pflas|te|rung** F cobblestone pavement; **Kopf|steu|er** F poll tax; **Kopf|stim|me** F *(Mus)* falsetto; *(Phon)* head voice; **Kopf|stoß** M *(Billard)* massé; **Kopf|stück** NT *(Cook)* head end; **Kopf|stüt|ze** F headrest; *(Aut)* head restraint; **Kopf|tuch** NT *pl* **-tücher** (head)scarf; **kopf|über** ADV *(lit, fig)* headfirst, headlong; **Kopf|ver|band** M *(Med)* head bandage; **Kopf|ver|let|zung** F head injury; **Kopf|wä|sche** F hair wash; **Kopf|weh** NT headache; **~ haben** to have a headache; **Kopf|wei|de** F *(Bot)* pollarded willow; **Kopf|wun|de** F head wound; **Kopf|zahl** F number of persons; **Kopf|zei|le** F *(Comput)* header; **Kopf|zer|bre|chen** NT **-s,** *no pl* **jdm ~ machen** to be a worry to sb, to be a headache for sb *(inf)*; **sich** *(dat)* **über etw** *(acc)* **~ machen** to worry about sth

Ko|pie [ko'pi: -'pi:ən, *(Aus)* -piən] F -, -n copy; *(= Durchschlag auch)* carbon (copy); *(= Ablichtung)* photocopy; *(Phot)* print; *(Film)* print, copy; *(von Statue)* copy, replica; *(fig)* carbon copy; **das ist nicht das Original sondern eine ~** it's not the original but a copy *or* imitation

Ko|pier-: **Ko|pier|an|stalt** F *(Film)* printing laboratory, print lab *(inf)*; **Ko|pier|ap|pa|rat** M photocopier; **Ko|pier|be|fehl** M *(Comput)* copy command

ko|pie|ren [ko'pi:rən] *ptp* **kopiert** VT to copy; *(= nachahmen)* to imitate; *(= ablichten)* to photocopy; *(= durchpausen)* to trace; *(Phot) Film* to print; **eine Datei auf die Festplatte ~** to copy a file onto the hard disk; **oft kopiert, nie erreicht** often imitated but never equalled *(Brit) or* equaled *(US)* VI to copy; *(= fotokopieren)* to photocopy

Ko|pie|rer [ko'pi:rɐ] M -s, - copier

Ko|pier-: **Ko|pier|funk|ti|on** F *(Comput)* copy function; **Ko|pier|ge|rät** NT photocopier; **ko|pier|ge|schützt** ADJ *(Comput, HiFi)* copy-protected; **Ko|pier|pa|pier** NT photocopy paper; **Ko|pier|rad** NT *(Sew)* tracing wheel; **Ko|pier|rah|men** M printing frame; **Ko|pier|schutz** M *(Comput, HiFi)* copy protection; **mit ~** copy-protected; **Ko|pier|sper|re** F anti-copy device; **Ko|pier|stift** M indelible pencil; **Ko|pier|ver|fah|ren** NT photocopying process

Ko|pi|lot(in) ['ko:-] M(F) copilot

Ko|pist [ko'pɪst] M -en, -en, **Ko|pis|tin** [-'pɪstɪn] F -, -nen *(= Nachahmer)* imitator; *(Art)* copyist

Kop|pe ['kɔpə] F -, -n (rounded) hilltop

Kop|pel [kɔpl] NT -s, - *or (Aus) f* -, -n *(Mil)* belt

Kop|pel F -, -n **a** *(= Weide)* paddock, enclosure; **auf** *or* **in der ~** in the paddock *etc* **b** *(= Hundekoppel)* pack; *(= Pferdekoppel)* string **c** *(Mus: = Registerzug)* coupler

Kop|pel|ge|schäft NT tie-in deal

kop|peln ['kɔpln] VT **a** *(= zusammenbinden) Tiere* to tie together **b** *(= verbinden)* to couple, to join *(etw an etw acc* sth to sth); *zwei Dinge* to couple together, to join together; *Raumschiffe* to link up; *(fig)* to link, to couple; *(als Bedingung)* to tie; *Ziele, Zwecke* to conjoin, to combine; **eine Dienstreise mit einem Urlaub ~** to combine a business trip with a holiday *(esp Brit) or* vacation *(US)*; **einen Vertrag mit einer Klausel ~** to attach a clause to a contract **c** *(Elec)* to couple **d** *(Typ) Wort* to hyphenate

Kop|pel-: **Kop|pel|rick** [-rɪk] NT -s, -e *(Pferderennen)* fence; **Kop|pel|schloss** NT *(Mil)* belt buckle

Kop|pe|lung ['kɔpəlʊŋ] F -, -en **a** *(Elec)* coupling **b** *(= Verbindung) (lit)* coupling, joining; *(fig, von Raumschiffen)* linkup **c** *(Mus)* coupler

Kop|pe|lungs|ma|nö|ver NT *(Space)* docking manoeuvre *(Brit) or* maneuver *(US)*; **ein ~ durchführen** to link up

Köp|per ['kœpɐ] M -s, - *(N Ger inf)* header; **einen ~ machen** to take a header, to dive headfirst

kopp|heis|ter [kɔp'haistɐ] ADV *(N Ger)* headfirst, headlong; **~ schießen** to do a somersault

Kopp|lung ['kɔplʊŋ] F = **Koppelung**

Kopp|lungs|ge|schäft F *(Econ)* package *or* tie-in *(US)* deal

Kop|ra ['ko:pra] F -, *no pl* copra

Ko|pro|duk|ti|on ['ko:-] F coproduction

Ko|pro|du|zent(in) ['ko:-] M(F) coproducer

Kop|ro|pha|gie [koprofa'gi:] F -, *no pl (Psych)* coprophagy

Ko|pro|zes|sor ['ko:-] M *(Comput)* coprocessor

Kop|te ['kɔptə] M -n, -n, **Kop|tin** [-tɪn] F -, -nen Copt

kop|tisch ['kɔptɪʃ] ADJ Coptic

Ko|pu|la ['ko:pula] F -, -s *or* -e [-lɛ:] *(Gram)* copula

Ko|pu|la|ti|on [kopula'tsio:n] F -, -en *(Biol)* copulation, coupling; *(Hort)* splice grafting; *(old Jur* = *Trauung)* union

ko|pu|la|tiv [kopula'ti:f] ADJ *(Gram)* copulative

ko|pu|lie|ren [kopu'li:rən] *ptp* **kopuliert** VT *(Hort)* to splice-graft; *(old Jur.* = *trauen)* to unite VI *(= koitieren)* to copulate

kor *pret von* **küren**

Ko|ral|le [ko'ralə] F -, -n coral

Ko|ral|len-: **Ko|ral|len|bank** F *pl* -bänke coral reef; **Ko|ral|len|fi|scher(in)** M(F) coral fisherman; **Ko|ral|len|pilz** M goatsbeard; **Ko|ral|len|riff** NT coral reef; **ko|ral|len|rot** ADJ coral(-red); **Ko|ral|len|tie|re** PL coral

Ko|ran [ko'ra:n, 'ko:ra(:)n] M -s, *no pl* Koran

Ko|ran|schu|le F Koranic school

Korb [kɔrp] M -(e)s, ⸗e ['kœrbə] **a** basket *(auch Econ, Fin)*; *(= Tragkorb für Lasttiere auch)* pannier; *(= Fischkorb auch)* creel; *(= Bienenkorb)* hive; *(= Förderkorb)* cage; *(= Degenkorb, Säbelkorb)* basket hilt; **ein ~ Äpfel** a basket of apples; **ein ~ ausländischer Währungen** a basket of foreign currencies **b** *(= Korbgeflecht)* wicker; **ein Sessel aus ~** a wicker(work) chair, a basket(work) chair **c** *(inf: = Abweisung)* refusal, rebuff; **einen ~ bekommen/kriegen, sich** *(dat)* **einen ~ holen** to get a refusal, to be turned down; **jdm einen ~ geben** to turn sb down

Korb-: **Korb|ar|beit** F wickerwork *no pl*; **Korb|ball** M basketball; **Korb|blüt|ler** [-bly:tlɐ] M -s, - *(Bot)* composite (flower)

Körb|chen ['kœrpçən] NT -s, - **a** *dim von* **Korb** *(von Hund)* basket; **ins ~!** *(baby-talk)* off to *or* time for beddy-bye(s) *(baby-talk)* **b** *(von Biene)* (pollen) basket; *(von Büstenhalter)* cup

Korb-: **Korb|fla|sche** F demijohn; **Korb|flech|ter** [-flɛçtɐ] M -s, -, **Korb|flech|te|rin** [-ərɪn] F -, -nen basket maker; **Korb|flech|te|rei** [-flɛçtə'rai] F -, *no pl* basket-making; **Korb|ge|flecht** NT basketwork, wickerwork; **Korb|macher(in)** M(F) basket maker; **Korb|mö|bel** PL wicker(work) furniture; **Korb|ses|sel** M, **Korb|stuhl** M wicker(work) chair; **Korb|wa|gen** M bassinet; **Korb|wa|ren** PL wickerwork (articles *pl*); **Korb|wei|de** F osier; **korb|wei|se** ADV by the basketful

Kord *etc* = **Cord** *etc*

Kor|del ['kɔrdl] F -, -n cord

Kor|del|zug M drawstring; **eine Kapuze mit ~** a drawstring hood

Kor|dil|le|ren [kɔrdɪl'je:rən] PL *(Geog)* Cordilleras *pl*

Kor|don M [kɔr'dõ:, *(Aus)* kɔr'do:n] -s, -s *or (Aus)* -e *(Mil, Bot)* cordon; *(= Ordensband auch)* ribbon

Ko|re ['ko:rə] F -, -n *(Archit)* caryatid

Ko|rea [ko're:a] NT -s Korea

Ko|re|a|ner [kore'a:nɐ] M -s, -, **Ko|re|a|ne|rin** [-ərɪn] F -, -nen Korean

ko|re|a|nisch [kore'a:nɪʃ] ADJ Korean

Ko|re|a|nisch(e) [kore'a:nɪʃ] NT Korean → *auch* **Deutsch(e)**

Ko|rea|stra|ße F **die ~** the Korea Strait

Ko|re|fe|rat ['ko:-] NT = **Korreferat**

Ko|re|fe|rent(in) ['ko:-] M(F) = **Korreferent(in)**

kö|ren ['kø:rən] VT to select for breeding purposes

Kor|fi|ot [kɔr'fio:t] M -en, -en, **Kor|fi|o|tin** [-'fio:tɪn] F -, -nen Corfuan, Corfiote

Kor|fu ['kɔrfu, kɔr'fu:] NT -s Corfu

Kör|hengst M stud

Ko|ri|an|der [ko'riandɐ] M -s, *no pl* coriander

Ko|rinth [ko'rɪnt] NT -s Corinth

Ko|rin|the [ko'rɪntə] F -, -n currant

Ko|rin|then|ka|cker [-kakɐ] M -s, -, **Ko|rin|then|ka|cke|rin** [-ərɪn] F -, -nen *(inf)* fusspot *(Brit inf)*, fussbudget *(US inf)*

Ko|rin|ther [ko'rɪntɐ] M -s, - Corinthian

Ko|rin|ther|brief M Epistle to the Corinthians, Corinthians *sing, no def art*

ko|rin|thisch [ko'rɪntɪʃ] ADJ Corinthian

Kork [kɔrk] M -(e)s, -e **a** *(Bot)* cork **b** *(= Korken)* cork; *(aus Plastik)* stopper

Kork|ei|che F cork oak *or* tree

Kor|ken ['kɔrkn] M -s, - cork; *(aus Plastik)* stopper

Kor|ken-: **Kor|ken|zie|her** [-tsi:ɐ] M -s, - corkscrew; **Kor|ken|zie|her|lo|cken** PL corkscrew curls *pl*

kor|kig ['kɔrkɪç] ADJ corky ADV **~ schmecken** *(Wein)* to be corked

Kork|mund|stück NT cork filter

Kor|mo|ran [kɔrmo'ra:n] M -s, -e cormorant

Korn [kɔrn] NT -(e)s, ⸗er ['kœrnɐ] **a** *(= Samenkorn)* seed, grain; *(= Pfefferkorn)* corn; *(= Salzkorn, Sandkorn, Tech, Phot, Typ)* grain; *(= Hagelkorn)* stone; *(= Staubkorn)* speck **b** *no pl (= Getreide)* grain, corn *(Brit)*; **das ~ steht gut** the grain *or* corn *(Brit)* looks promising

Korn M -(e)s, - *or* -s *(= Kornbranntwein)* corn schnapps

Korn NT -(e)s, -e *(am Gewehr)* front sight, bead; **jdn/etw aufs ~ nehmen** *(lit)* to draw a bead on sb/sth; *(fig)* to hit out at sth; **jdn aufs ~ nehmen** *(fig)* to start keeping tabs on sb

Korn-: **Korn|äh|re** F ear of corn *(Brit) or* grain; **Korn|blu|me** F cornflower; **korn|blu|men|blau** ADJ cornflower blue; *(hum: = volltrunken)* as drunk as a lord *(Brit) or* sailor *(US)*; **Korn|brannt|wein** M *(form)* corn schnapps

Körn|chen ['kœrnçən] NT -s, - *dim von* **Korn** small grain, granule; **ein ~ Wahrheit** a grain of truth

Körndl|bau|er ['kœrndl-] M *pl* -bauern, **Körndl|bäu|e|rin** F *(Aus)* corn-growing *(Brit) or* grain-growing farmer

kör|nen ['kœrnən] VT to granulate, to grain; *(= aufrauen)* to roughen

Kör|ner ['kœrnɐ] M -s, - centre *(Brit) or* center *(US)* punch

Kör|ner-: **Kör|ner|fres|ser** M *(Zool)* grain-eating bird, granivore *(form)*; **Kör|ner|fres|ser(in)** M(F) *(inf)* health food freak *(inf)*; **Kör|ner|fut|ter** NT grain *or* corn *(Brit)* (for animal feeding)

Kor|nett [kɔr'nɛt] NT -s, -e *or* -s *(Mus)* cornet

Kor|nett M -(e)s, -e *or* -s *(old Mil)* cornet *(old)*

Korn|feld NT cornfield *(Brit)*, grain field

kör|nig ['kœrnɪç] ADJ granular, grainy

-kör|nig ADJ *suf* -grained; **grob-/feinkörnig** coarse-/fine-grained

kor|nisch ['kɔrnɪʃ] ADJ Cornish

Korn-: **Korn|kä|fer** M corn weevil; **Korn|kam|mer** F *(lit, fig)* granary; **Korn|ra|de** F *(Bot)* corncockle; **Korn|spei|cher** M granary

Kör|nung ['kœrnʊŋ] F -, -en *(Tech)* grain size; *(Phot)* granularity; *(Hunt)* decoy place; **Schmirgelpapier mit feiner ~** fine-grain sandpaper

Ko|ro|na [ko'ro:na] F -, **Koronen** [-nən] corona; *(inf)* crowd *(inf)*, gang *(inf)*

Ko|ro|nar- *(Anat, Med) in cpds* coronary; **Ko|ro|nar|ar|te|rie** F coronary artery; **Ko|ro|nar|ge|fäß** NT coronary vessel

Kör|per ['kœrpɐ] M -s, - *(alle Bedeutungen)* body; *(= Schiffskörper)* hull; **~ und Geist** mind and body; **das braucht der ~** it's good for you; **am ganzen ~ beben** *or* **zittern/frieren** to tremble/to be cold all over

Kör|per-: **Kör|per|bau** M, *no pl* physique, build; **Kör|per|bau|typ** M physical type; **Kör|per|be|herr|schung** F physical control; **kör|per|be|hin|dert** [-bəhɪndɐt] ADJ physically handicapped *or* disabled; **Kör|per|be|hin|der|te(r)** MF *decl as adj* physically handicapped *or* disabled person; **die ~n** the disabled, the physically handicapped; **kör|per|be|tont** ADJ *(Sport)* (very) physical; *(Fashion) Kleid etc* figure-hugging ADV **~ geschnitten** *(Kleid etc)* cut to emphasize the figure; **kör|per|ei|gen** ADJ produced *or* occurring naturally in the body; **Kör|per|er|tüch|ti|gung** F physical training, keep-fit exercises *pl*; **das dient der ~** it helps keep you fit; **Kör|per|fül|le** F *(euph)* corpulence; **Kör|per|ge|ruch** M body odour *(Brit) or* odor *(US)*, BO *(inf)*; **Kör|per|ge|wicht** NT weight; **Kör|per|grö|ße** F height; **Kör|per|hal|tung** F posture, bearing; **Kör|per|kon|takt** M physical *or* bodily contact; **Kör|per|kraft** F physical *or* bodily strength; **Kör|per|-**

län|ge F height; *(von Schlange etc)* (body) length
kör|per|lich ['kœrpelɪç] ADJ physical; *(= stofflich)* material, corporeal; **~e Arbeit** manual work; **~e Gewalt** physical violence; **~e Züchtigung** corporal punishment ADV physically; **sich ~ ertüchtigen** to keep oneself physically fit
Kör|per-: **kör|per|los** ADJ bodiless, incorporeal; **Kör|per|lo|ti|on** F body lotion; **Kör|per|ma|ße** PL measurements *pl*; **Kör|per|öff|nung** F *(Anat)* orifice of the body; **Kör|per|pfle|ge** F personal hygiene; **Kör|per|pu|der** M OR NT body powder; **kör|per|reich** ADJ *Wein* full-bodied; **Kör|per|säf|te** PL *(liter)* blood *sing*; *(= Körperflüssigkeit)* body *or* bodily fluids *pl*
Kör|per|schaft ['kœrpeʃaft] F -, -en corporation, (corporate) body; **gesetzgebende ~** legislative body
Kör|per|schaft(s)|steu|er F corporation tax
Kör|per-: **Kör|per|schwä|che** F physical weakness; **Kör|per|spra|che** F body language; **Kör|per|spray** M OR NT body spray; **Kör|per|teil** M part of the body; **Kör|per|tem|pe|ra|tur** F body temperature; **Kör|per|ver|let|zung** F *(Jur)* bodily *or* physical injury; **fahrlässige ~** physical injury resulting from negligence; **einfache ~** actual bodily harm; **schwere ~** grievous bodily harm; **~ im Amt** *injury caused by a policeman/public official*; **~ mit tödlichem Ausgang** manslaughter; **Kör|per|wär|me** F body heat; **Kör|per|zel|le** F body cell
Kor|po|ral [kɔrpo'ra:l] M -s, -e *or* **Korporäle** [-'rɛ:lə], **Kor|po|ra|lin** [-'ra:lɪn] F -, -nen corporal
Kor|po|ra|ti|on [kɔrpora'tsio:n] F -, -en **a** *(= Studentenverbindung)* student society, fraternity *(US)* **b** *(= Körperschaft)* corporation
kor|po|ra|tiv [kɔrpora'ti:f] ADJ *Staat* corporate
kor|po|riert [kɔrpo'ri:ɐt] ADJ *pred* **~ sein** to be a member of a students' society *(which fights duels)*
Korps [ko:ɐ] NT -, - [ko:ɐs, ko:ɐs] *(Mil)* corps; *(Univ)* (duelling *(Brit)* or dueling *(US)*) corps
Korps-: **Korps|bru|der** M fellow member of a student (duelling *(Brit)* or dueling *(US)*) society; **Korps|geist** M esprit de corps; **Korps|stu|dent** M student belonging to a (duelling *(Brit)* or dueling *(US)*) society
kor|pu|lent [kɔrpu'lɛnt] ADJ corpulent
Kor|pu|lenz [kɔrpu'lɛnts] F -, *no pl* corpulence
Kor|pus ['kɔrpʊs] M -, -se *(Art)* body of Christ; *(hum inf: = Körper)* body
Kor|pus NT -, **Korpora** ['kɔrpora] **a** *(Ling)* corpus **b** *(Mus)* resonance box
kor|pus|ba|siert ADJ *(Ling) Lexikografie* corpus-based
Kor|pus|kel [kɔr'pʊskl] NT -s, -n *or f* -, -n *(Phys)* particle, corpuscle
Kor|pus|lin|gu|is|tik F *(Ling)* corpus linguistics *sing*
Kor|re|fe|rat ['kɔ-] NT **a** *(= Vortrag)* supplementary paper *or* report **b** *(= Prüfung)* second marking *or* assessment
Kor|re|fe|rent(in) ['kɔ-] M(F) **a** *(= Redner)* reader of a supplementary paper **b** *(= Prüfer)* second examiner
kor|rekt [kɔ'rɛkt] ADJ **a** *(= richtig, anständig)* correct; *Frage* civil; **politisch ~** politically correct **b** *(sl: = toll)* shit-hot *(Brit sl)*, wicked *(sl)* ADV correctly; *gekleidet* appropriately; *darstellen* accurately
kor|rek|ter|wei|se [kɔ'rɛktɐ'vaizə] ADV to be correct, by rights
Kor|rekt|heit F -, *no pl* correctness; **politische ~** political correctness
Kor|rek|tiv [kɔrɛk'ti:f] NT -s, -e [-və] corrective
Kor|rek|tor [kɔ'rɛkto:ɐ] M -s, **Korrektoren** [-'to:rən], **Kor|rek|to|rin** [-'to:rɪn] F -, -nen *(Typ)* proofreader
Kor|rek|tur [kɔrɛk'tu:ɐ] F -, -en correction; *(Typ) (= Vorgang)* proofreading; *(= Verbesserung)* proof correction; *(= Korrekturfahne)* proof; **~ lesen** to read *or* correct (the) proofs, to do (the) proofreading (*bei etw* for sth), to proofread (*bei etw* sth); **kann er ~ lesen?** can he proofread?
Kor|rek|tur-: **Kor|rek|tur|ab|zug** M galley (proof); **Kor|rek|tur|band** [-bant] NT *pl* **-bänder** correction tape; **Kor|rek|tur|bo|gen** M page proof; **Kor|rek|tur|fah|ne** F galley (proof); **Kor|rek|tur|flüs|sig|keit** F correction fluid, White-Out® *(US)*; **Kor|rek|tur|le|sen** NT proofreading; **Kor|rek|tur|spei|cher** M correction memory; **Kor|rek|tur|tas|te** F correction key; **Kor|rek|tur|zei|chen** NT proofreader's mark
Kor|re|lat [kɔre'la:t] NT -(e)s, -e correlate
kor|re|lie|ren [kɔre'li:rən] *ptp* **korreliert** VI to correlate
kor|re|pe|tie|ren [kɔrepe'ti:rən] *ptp* **korrepetiert** VI to act as a repetiteur, to coach opera singers
Kor|re|pe|ti|tor [kɔrepe'ti:to:ɐ] M -s, **Korrepetitoren** [-'to:rən] *(Mus)* répétiteur, coach
Kor|re|pe|ti|to|rin [kɔrepeti'to:rɪn] F -, -nen *(Mus)* répétiteuse, coach
Kor|res|pon|dent [kɔrɛspɔn'dɛnt] M -en, -en, **Kor|res|pon|den|tin** [-'dɛntɪn] F -, -nen correspondent
Kor|res|pon|denz [kɔrɛspɔn'dɛnts] F -, -en correspondence; **mit jdm in ~ stehen** to be in correspondence with sb
Kor|res|pon|denz-: **Kor|res|pon|denz|bü|ro** NT news *or* press agency; **Kor|res|pon|denz|schrift** F *(Comput)* letter quality
kor|res|pon|die|ren [kɔrɛspɔn'di:rən] *ptp* **korrespondiert** VI **a** *(in Briefwechsel stehen)* to correspond; **~des Mitglied** corresponding member **b** *(= entsprechen)* to correspond (*mit* to, with); **~der Winkel** corresponding angle
Kor|ri|dor ['kɔrido:ɐ] M -s, -e *(= auch Luftkorridor etc)* corridor; *(= Flur)* hall; **der (Polnische) ~** *(Hist)* the Polish Corridor
kor|ri|gier|bar ADJ able to be corrected, corrigible *(form)*; **ein nicht so leicht ~er Sprachfehler** a speech defect which is not so easy to put right *or* to correct
kor|ri|gie|ren [kɔri'gi:rən] *ptp* **korrigiert** VT *(= berichtigen)* to correct; *Aufsätze etc auch* to mark; *Meinung, Einstellung* to alter, to change; **nach oben ~** to adjust upwards; *Gehaltsangebot etc auch* to top up; **nach unten ~** to adjust downwards; *Gehaltsforderung etc auch* to trim down
kor|ro|die|ren [kɔro'di:rən] *ptp* **korrodiert** VTI *(vi: aux sein)* to corrode
Kor|ro|si|on [kɔro'zio:n] F -, -en corrosion
Kor|ro|si|ons-: **kor|ro|si|ons|an|fäl|lig** ADJ corrosion-prone; **kor|ro|si|ons|be|stän|dig**, **kor|ro|si|ons|fest** ADJ corrosion-resistant; **kor|ro|si|ons|frei** ADJ noncorrosive, noncorroding; **Kor|ro|si|ons|schutz** M corrosion prevention
kor|ro|siv [kɔro'zi:f] ADJ corrosive
kor|rum|pie|ren [kɔrʊm'pi:rən] *ptp* **korrumpiert** VT to corrupt
kor|rum|piert [kɔrʊm'pi:ɐt] ADJ corrupt
kor|rupt [kɔ'rʊpt] ADJ corrupt ADV *handeln* corruptly; **als ~ gelten** to be considered corrupt
Kor|rupt|heit F -, *no pl* corruptness
Kor|rup|ti|on [kɔrʊp'tsio:n] F -, *no pl* corruption
Kor|rup|ti|ons|af|fä|re F corruption scandal
Kor|sa|ge [kɔr'za:ʒə] F -, -n corsage
Kor|sar [kɔr'za:ɐ] M -en, -en *(Hist)* corsair
Kor|se ['kɔrzə] M -n, -n, **Kor|sin** ['kɔrzɪn] F -, -nen Corsican
Kor|se|lett [kɔrzə'lɛt] NT -(e)s, -e *or* -s corselet
Kor|sett [kɔr'zɛt] NT -s, -s *or* -e corset, corsets *pl*
Kor|sett|stan|ge F stay
Kor|si|ka ['kɔrzika] NT -s Corsica
Kor|sin ['kɔrzɪn] F -, -nen Corsican
kor|sisch ['kɔrzɪʃ] ADJ Corsican
Kor|sisch(e) NT Corsican → *auch* **Deutsch(e)**
Kor|so ['kɔrso] M -s, -s *(= Umzug)* parade, procession; *(= breite Straße)* avenue; *(old: = Pferderennen)* horse race
Kor|tex ['kɔrtɛks] M -(es), **Kortizes** ['kɔrtitse:s] *(Anat)* cortex
kor|ti|kal [kɔrti'ka:l] ADJ *(Anat)* cortical
Kor|ti|son [kɔrti'zo:n] NT -s, -e *(Med)* cortisone
Ko|rund [ko'rʊnt] M -(e)s, -e [-də] *(Geol)* corundum
Kö|rung ['kø:rʊŋ] F -, -en selection for breeding purposes
Kor|vet|te [kɔr'vɛtə] F -, -n *(Naut)* corvette; *(Sport)* jump to handstand
Kor|vet|ten|ka|pi|tän(in) M(F) lieutenant commander
Ko|ry|phäe [kory'fɛ:ə] F -, -n genius; *(auf einem Gebiet)* eminent authority
Ko|sak [ko'zak] M -en, -en Cossack
Ko|sa|ken|müt|ze F cossack hat
Ko|sche|nil|le [kɔʃə'nɪljə] F -, *no pl* cochineal
ko|scher ['ko:ʃɐ] ADJ *(Rel, fig inf)* kosher ADV **a** **~ kochen/schlachten** to cook/slaughter according to kosher requirements **b** *(fig inf)* **dabei ist es nicht ganz ~ zugegangen** that wasn't quite kosher *(inf)*
K.-o.-Schlag [ka:'lo:-] M knockout blow; **durch ~ siegen** to win by a knockout
Ko|se|form F affectionate *or* familiar form *(of proper name)*
ko|sen ['ko:zn] VTI *(dated, geh)* **jdn ~, mit jdm ~** to fondle *or* caress sb; **~d** caressingly; **miteinander ~** to bill and coo
Ko|se-: **Ko|se|na|me** M pet name; **Ko|se|wort** NT *pl* **-wörter** *or* **-worte** term of endearment *or* affection
K.-o.-Sieg [ka:'lo:-] M knockout victory
Ko|si|nus ['ko:zinʊs] M *(Math)* cosine
Kos|me|tik [kɔs'me:tɪk] F -, *no pl* beauty culture; *(= Kosmetika, fig)* cosmetics *pl*; **eine Reform, die sich nicht nur auf ~ beschränkt** a reform which is not merely cosmetic
Kos|me|ti|ker [kɔs'me:tɪkɐ] M -s, -, **Kos|me|ti|ke|rin** [-ərɪn] F -, -nen beautician, cosmetician
Kos|me|tik-: **Kos|me|tik|in|sti|tut** NT beauty parlour *(Brit)* or parlor *(US)*; **Kos|me|tik|kof|fer** M vanity case; **Kos|me|tik|sa|lon** beauty parlour *(Brit)*, beauty parlor *(US)*; **Kos|me|tik|tuch** NT *pl* **-tücher** paper tissue
Kos|me|ti|kum [kɔs'me:tɪkʊm] NT -s, **Kosmetika** [-ka] cosmetic
kos|me|tisch [kɔs'me:tɪʃ] ADJ cosmetic; **ein ~es Mittel** a cosmetic ADV *behandeln* cosmetically
kos|misch ['kɔsmɪʃ] ADJ cosmic; **~ beeinflusst werden** to be influenced by the stars *or* the cosmos
Kos|mo-: **Kos|mo|bio|lo|gie** F space *or* cosmic biology; **Kos|mo|lo|ge** [kɔsmo'lo:gə] M -n, -n, **Kos|mo|lo|gin** [-'lo:gɪn] F -, -nen cosmologist; **Kos|mo|lo|gie** [kɔsmolo'gi:] F -, -n [-'gi:ən] cosmology; **Kos|mo|naut** [kɔsmo'naut] M -en, -en, **Kos|mo|nau|tin** [-'nautɪn] F -, -nen cosmonaut; **Kos|mo|po|lit** [kɔsmopo'li:t] M -en, -en, **Kos|mo|po|li|tin** [-'li:tɪn] F -, -nen cosmopolitan; **kos|mo|po|li|tisch** [kɔsmopo'li:tɪʃ] ADJ cosmopolitan
Kos|mo- [kɔsmo-]: **Kos|mo|go|nie** [kɔsmogo'ni:] F -, -n [-'ni:ən] cosmogony
Kos|mos ['kɔsmɔs] M -, *no pl* cosmos
Ko|so|va|re [kɔso'va:rə] M -n, -n Kosovar, **Ko|so|va|rin** [kɔso'va:rɪn] F -, -nen Kosovar woman *or* girl
Ko|so|vo ['kɔsovo] M -s *(Geog)* **(der) ~** Kosovo
Ko|so|vo-Al|ba|ner(in) M(F) Kosovo Albanian
Kost [kɔst] F -, *no pl* **a** *(= Nahrung, Essen)* food, fare; **vegetarische/fleischlose ~** vegetarian/meatless diet; **geistige ~** *(fig)* intellectual fare; **leichte/schwere ~** *(fig)* easy/heavy going, heavy stuff *(inf)* **b** *(dated: = Beköstigung)* board; **jdn in ~ nehmen** to take sb as a boarder; **(freie) ~ und Logis** *or* **Wohnung** (free) board and lodging

kost|bar ADJ *(= wertvoll)* valuable, precious; *(= luxuriös)* luxurious, sumptuous ADV *verziert, geschmückt, geschnitzt, gearbeitet* sumptuously; *sich kleiden* luxuriously

Kost|bar|keit ['kɔstbaːɐkait] F -, -en *(= Gegenstand)* treasure, precious object; *(= Leckerbissen)* delicacy

kos|ten ['kɔstn] VT **a** *(lit, fig)* to cost; **was kostet das?** how much *or* what does it cost?, how much is it?; **was soll das ~?** what's it going to cost?; **das kostet nicht die Welt** it doesn't cost the earth; **koste es, was es wolle** whatever the cost; **das/die lasse ich mich etwas ~** I don't mind spending a bit of money on it/them; **jdn sein Leben/den Sieg ~** to cost sb his life/the victory; **was kostet die Welt?** *(inf)* the world's your/their *etc* oyster
b *(= in Anspruch nehmen) Zeit, Geduld etc* to take
VI to cost; **das kostet** *(inf)* it costs something *or* a bit; **das hat gekostet** *(inf)* it cost something *or* a bit

kos|ten VT *(= probieren)* to taste, to try, to sample; *(fig)* to taste; *Freuden etc* to taste, to taste of *(liter)* VI to taste; **willst du mal ~?** would you like a taste?; **von etw ~** to taste *or* try *or* sample sth

Kos|ten ['kɔstn] PL cost(s); *(Jur)* costs *pl*; *(= Unkosten)* expenses *pl*; **die ~ tragen** to bear the cost(s); **auf ~ von** *or +gen (fig)* at the expense of; **auf ~ des Steuerzahlers** at the expense of the taxpayer, at the taxpayer's expense; **auf meine ~** *(lit, fig)* at my expense; **auf seine ~ kommen** to cover one's expenses; *(fig)* to get one's money's worth, to have a very good time; **~ spielen keine Rolle** money's no object; **~ deckend** = **kostendeckend**; **~ sparend** = **kostensparend**; **~ zuweisen** to allocate costs

Kos|ten-: **Kos|ten|auf|stel|lung** F statement of costs; **Kos|ten|auf|wand** M expense; **mit einem ~ von 50.000 EUR** at a cost of 50,000 euros; **kos|ten|be|wusst** ADJ cost-conscious; **Kos|ten|be|wusst|sein** NT cost-consciousness, cost-awareness; **Kos|ten|bin|dung** F cost controls *pl*; **Kos|ten|brem|se** F *(inf)* **auf die ~ treten, die ~ anziehen** to curb costs; **Kos|ten|dämp|fung** F curbing cost expansion; **kos|ten|de|ckend** ADJ **~e Preise** prices that cover one's costs ADV without a loss, cost-effectively; **~ arbeiten** to cover one's costs, to break even; **~ wirtschaften** to avoid a deficit; **Kos|ten|de|ckung** F cost-effectiveness; **Kos|ten|de|ckungs|grad** M level of cost-effectiveness; **Kos|ten|er|spar|nis** F cost saving; **Kos|ten|er|stat|tung** F reimbursement of costs *or* expenses; **Kos|ten|ex|plo|si|on** F *(inf)* costs explosion; **Kos|ten|fak|tor** M cost factor; **Kos|ten|fra|ge** F question of cost(s); **kos|ten|frei** ADJ cost-free, free of cost ADV free of cost; **kos|ten|güns|tig** ADJ economical ADV *arbeiten, produzieren* economically; **kos|ten|in|ten|siv** ADJ *(Econ)* cost-intensive; **Kos|ten|la|wi|ne** F spiralling *(Brit)* or spiraling *(US)* costs *pl*; **eine ~ auslösen** *or* **lostreten** to cause costs to spiral; **kos|ten|los** ADJ ADV free (of charge); **Kos|ten|mie|te** F rent which covers costs; **kos|ten|neut|ral** ADJ self-financing; **Kos|ten-Nut|zen-Ana|ly|se** F, **Kos|ten-Nut|zen-Rechnung** F cost-benefit analysis, CBA; **kos|ten|pflich|tig** [-pflɪçtɪç] ADJ liable to pay costs, with costs ADV **eine Klage ~ abweisen** to dismiss a case with costs; **~ verwarnt werden** to be fined; **~ verurteilt werden** to have costs awarded against one, to have to pay costs; **ein Kfz ~ abschleppen** to tow away a car at the owner's expense, to impound a car; **Kos|ten|pla|nung** F costing; **Kos|ten|punkt** M cost question; **~?** *(inf)* what'll it cost?, how much?; **~: 100 EUR** *(inf)* cost, 100 euros; **Kos|ten|rech|nung** F calculation of costs; **Kos|ten|satz** M rate; **Kos|ten|schrau|be** F cost spiral; **an der ~ drehen** to (try to) cut down on costs; **kos|ten|spa|rend** ADJ cost-saving ADV **etw ~ herstellen** to produce sth at low cost; **~er arbeiten** to reduce costs; **Kos|ten|stei|ge|rung** F increase in costs; **Kos|ten|stel|le** F cost centre *(Brit)* or center *(US)*; **Kos|ten|trä|ger(in)** M(F) **(der) ~ sein** to bear the cost; **Kos|ten|vor|an|schlag** M (costs) estimate; **Kos|ten|vor|schuss** M advance

Kost-: **Kost|gän|ger** [-gɛŋɐ] M -s, -, **Kost|gän|ge|rin** [-ərɪn] F -, -nen *(dated)* boarder; **Kost|geld** NT board

köst|lich ['kœstlɪç] ADJ **a** *Wein, Speise* exquisite; *Luft* magnificent **b** *(= amüsant)* priceless; **~, wie er darauf reagiert hat** it was priceless the way he reacted; **du bist ja ~** you're priceless ADV **a** *(= gut) schmecken* delicious **b sich ~ amüsieren/unterhalten** to have a great time

Köst|lich|keit F -, -en **a** *(= köstliche Sache)* treat, delight; **eine kulinarische ~** a culinary delicacy; **eine literarische ~** a literary gem **b** *no pl (von Speise, Getränk)* **ein Wein von einmaliger ~** a uniquely exquisite wine

Kost-: **Kost|pro|be** F *(von Wein, Käse etc)* taste; *(fig)* sample; **bei der ~** while tasting; **warst du auch bei der ~?** were you at the tasting too?; **kost|spie|lig** [-ʃpiːlɪç] ADJ costly, expensive

Kos|tüm [kɔs'tyːm] NT -s, -e **a** *(Theat: = Tracht)* costume **b** *(= Maskenkostüm)* fancy dress **c** *(= Damenkostüm)* suit

Kos|tüm-: **Kos|tüm|ball** M fancy-dress ball; **Kos|tüm|bild|ner(in)** M(F) costume designer; **Kos|tüm|fest** NT fancy-dress ball; **Kos|tüm|film** M period film *or* picture

kos|tü|mie|ren [kɔsty'miːrən] *ptp* **kostümiert** VR to dress up

Kos|tüm-: **Kos|tüm|pro|be** F *(Theat)* dress rehearsal; **Kos|tüm|ver|leih** M (theatrical) costume agency

Kost|ver|äch|ter(in) M(F) **kein ~/keine ~in sein** *(hum) (= Feinschmecker sein)* to be fond of one's food, to enjoy one's food; **bei Frauen ist er kein ~** he's one for the ladies *(Brit)*, he's a bit of a lad *(Brit inf)* or a womanizer

Kot [koːt] M -(e)s, *no pl (form)* excrement, faeces *pl (Brit form)*, feces *pl (US form)*; *(liter: = Schmutz, Dreck)* mire, filth

Ko|tan|gens ['koː-] M *(Math)* cotangent

Ko|tau ['koːtau] M -s, -s **(einen) ~ machen** *(pej)* to kowtow *(vor jdm* to sb)

Ko|te ['koːtə] F -, -n *(Surv)* spot height

Ko|te F -, -n *(= Lappenzelt)* tent

Ko|te|lett ['kɔtlɛt, kɔt'lɛt] NT -(e)s, -s *or (rare)* -e chop, cutlet

Ko|te|let|te [kotə'lɛtə] F -, -n *usu pl* (side) whisker, sideboard *(Brit)*, sideburn

ko|ten ['koːtn] VI *(form)* to defecate *(form)*

Kö|ter ['køːtɐ] M -s, - *(pej)* damn dog *(inf)*

Kot|flü|gel M *(Aut)* wing

ko|tig ['koːtɪç] ADJ filthy

K.-o.-Trop|fen [kaː'loː-] PL *(inf)* knockout drops *pl (inf)*

Kotz|bro|cken M *(inf)* mean bastard *(Brit sl)*, son of a bitch *(esp US sl)*

Kot|ze ['kɔtsə] F -, *no pl (vulg: = Erbrochenes)* vomit, puke *(sl)*; **dabei krieg ich die ~** it makes me want to puke *(sl)*; **da kommt einem die ~ hoch** it makes you want to puke *(sl)*

Kot|ze F -, -n *(S Ger, Aus: = Umhang aus Wolle)* woollen *(Brit)* or woolen *(US)* cape

kot|zen ['kɔtsn] VI *(sl)* to throw up *(inf)*, to puke *(sl)*; **das ist zum Kotzen** it makes you sick; **du bist zum Kotzen** you make me sick, you make me want to throw up *(inf)* or puke *(sl)*; **da kann man das große Kotzen kriegen** it makes you want to throw up *(inf)* or puke *(sl)*

kotz|übel ADJ *(inf)* **mir ist ~** I feel like throwing up *(inf)*

KP [kaː'peː] F -, -s *abbr von* **Kommunistische Partei**

KPD [kaːpeː'deː] F - *abbr von* **Kommunistische Partei Deutschlands**

KPdSU [kaːpeːdeːlɛs'luː] F - *(Hist) abbr von* **Kommunistische Partei der Sowjetunion** Communist Party of the Soviet Union

Kraal [kraːl] M -s, -e kraal

Krab|be ['krabə] F -, -n **a** *(Zool) (klein)* shrimp; *(größer)* prawn **b** *(dated inf: = Kind)* tot *(inf)*, mite *(Brit inf)*; **eine süße kleine ~** a sweet little thing **c** *(Archit)* crocket

Krab|bel-: **Krab|bel|al|ter** NT crawling stage *(of a baby)*; **Krab|bel|grup|pe** F playgroup

krab|beln ['krabln] VI *aux sein* to crawl VT *(= kitzeln)* to tickle VTI *impers (= kitzeln)* to tickle; *(= jucken)* to itch → **kribbeln**

Krab|ben|cock|tail M prawn cocktail

krach [krax] INTERJ crash, bang

Krach [krax] M -(e)s, ¨-e ['krɛçə] **a** *no pl (= Lärm)* noise, din, racket *(inf)*; *(= Schlag)* crash, bang; **~ machen** to make a noise *etc* **b** *(inf: = Zank, Streit)* row, quarrel, fight *(um* about); **mit jdm ~ haben** to have a row *etc* with sb, to row *or* quarrel *or* fight with sb; **mit jdm ~ kriegen** to get into trouble with sb, to have a row with sb; **~ schlagen** to make a fuss **c** *(= Börsenkrach)* crash

kra|chen ['kraxn] VI **a** *(= Lärm machen)* to crash, to bang; *(Holz)* to creak; *(Schuss)* to ring out; *(Donner)* to crash; **~d fallen** *etc* to fall *etc* with a crash *or* bang; **..., dass es nur so krachte** *(lit)* ... with a bang *or* crash; *(fig)* ... with a vengeance; **sonst kracht's!** *(inf)* or there'll be trouble; **gleich krachts** *(inf)* there's going to be trouble; **es hat gekracht** *(inf: Zusammenstoß)* there's been a crash **b** *aux sein (inf) (= aufplatzen)* to rip (open), to split; *(= brechen)* to break; *(Eis)* to crack; *(Betrieb)* to crash **c** *aux sein (inf: = aufprallen)* to crash VR *(inf)* to have a row *or* fight *or* quarrel

Kra|cher ['kraxɐ] M -s, - banger *(Brit)*, firecracker *(US)*

Kra|cherl ['kraxɐl] NT -s, -(n) *(Aus inf)* fizzy pop *(Brit inf)* or drink

Krach-: **krach|le|dern** ['kraxleːdɐn] ADJ *(fig hum)* rustic; **Krach|le|der|ne** ['kraxleːdɐnə] F *decl as adj* leather shorts *pl*, lederhosen *pl*; **Krach|ma|cher(in)** M(F) *(inf) (lit)* noisy person *or* character; *(fig)* troublemaker; **hör auf, du ~!** must you make so much noise!

krä̈ch|zen ['krɛçtsn] VI to croak; *(Vogel)* to caw; **eine ~de Stimme** a croaky voice

Krä̈ch|zen NT -s, *no pl* croak(ing); *(von Vogel)* caw(ing)

kra|cken ['krakn, 'krɛkn] VT *(Chem)* to crack

Krä|cker ['krɛkɐ] M -s, - *(Cook)* cracker

Krad [kraːt] NT -(e)s, ¨-er ['krɛːdɐ] *(Mil, dated)* motorcycle

Krad-: **Krad|fah|rer(in)** M(F) *(dated)* motor cyclist; **Krad|mel|der(in)** M(F) *(Mil)* motorcycle despatch rider

kraft [kraft] PREP +gen *(form)* by virtue of; *(= mittels)* by use of; **~ meines Amtes** by virtue of my office; **~ meiner Befugnisse** on the strength of *or* by virtue of my authority

Kraft [kraft] F -, ¨-e ['krɛftə] **a** *(körperlich, sittlich)* strength *no pl*; *(geistig, schöpferisch)* powers *pl*; *(militärisch, wirtschaftlich)* strength, power; *(von Prosa, Stimme)* strength, power, force; *(= Energie)* energy, energies *pl*; **er weiß nicht wohin mit seiner ~** *(inf)* he's just bubbling over with energy; **er kann vor ~ nicht mehr laufen** *(hum)* he's so muscle-bound he can hardly move; **die Kräfte (mit jdm) messen** to try *or* pit one's strength (against sb); *(fig)* to pit oneself against sb; **wenn man alle Kräfte anspannt** *or* **zusammennimmt** if you summon up all your strength; **seine Kräfte sammeln** to build up *or* recover one's strength; **mit frischer ~** with renewed strength; **mit letzter ~** with one's last ounce of strength; **die ~ aufbringen, etw zu tun** to find the strength to do sth; **mit vereinten Kräften werden wir ...** if we combine our efforts *or* if we join forces we will ...; **die ~ der Verzweiflung** the strength born of desperation; **das geht über meine Kräfte, das übersteigt meine Kräfte** it's more than I can take, it's too much for me; **ich bin am Ende meiner ~** I can't take any more; **mit aller** *or* **voller ~** with all one's might or strength; **er will mit aller ~ durchsetzen, dass ...** he will do his utmost to ensure that ...; **aus eigener ~** by oneself; *(fig auch)* by one's own efforts, single-handedly; **nach (besten) Kräften** to the best of one's ability; **er tat, was in seinen Kräften stand** he did everything (with)in his power; **nicht bei Kräften sein** not to be in very good shape; **wieder bei Kräften sein** to have (got) one's strength back; **wieder zu Kräften kommen** to regain one's strength → **messen VT**

b *(Phys: einer Reaktion etc)* force; *(der Sonne etc)* strength, power *(no pl: = Wirksamkeit, liter, Bibl: = Macht)* power;; **die treibende ~** *(fig)* the driving force; **das Gleichgewicht der Kräfte** *(Pol)* the balance of power; **das Parallelogramm der Kräfte** *(Phys)* the parallelogram of forces; **die heilende ~ der Sonne** the healing power of the sun; **die tröstende ~ der Musik** the comforting power of music

c *(usu pl: in Wirtschaft, Politik etc)* force

d *no pl (Jur: = Geltung)* force; **in ~ sein/treten/setzen** to be in/come into/bring into force; **außer ~ sein** to have ceased to be in force, to be no longer in force; **außer ~ treten** to cease to be in force; **außer ~ setzen** to cancel, to annul

e *no pl (Naut: = Geschwindigkeit)* **halbe/volle ~ voraus!** half/full speed ahead

f *(= Arbeitskraft)* employee, worker; *(= Haushaltskraft)* domestic help; *(= Lehrkraft)* teacher

Kraft-: **Kraft|akt** M strongman act; *(fig)* show of strength; **Kraft|an|stren|gung** F exertion; **Kraft|an|trieb** M power drive; **mit ~** power-driven; **Kraft|arm** M *(Phys)* lever arm to which force is applied; **Kraft|auf|wand** M effort; **unnützer ~** wasted effort, waste of energy; **Kraft|aus|druck** M *pl* **-ausdrücke** swearword; **Kraftausdrücke** strong language; **Kraft|brü|he** F beef tea; **Kraft|drosch|ke** F *(form)* hackney carriage *(form)*, taxicab; **Kraft|ein|heit** F *(Phys)* unit of force

Kräf|te|pa|ral|le|lo|gramm NT parallelogram of forces

Kraft|er|spar|nis F saving of energy *or* effort

Kräf|te-: **Kräf|te|spiel** NT power play; **Kräf|te|ver|fall** M loss of strength; **Kräf|te|ver|hält|nis** NT *(Pol)* balance of power; *(von Mannschaften etc)* relative strength; **Kräf|te|ver|la|ge|rung** F *(Pol)* power shift; **Kräf|te|ver|schleiß** M waste of energy

Kraft|fah|rer(in) M(F) *(form)* motorist, driver; *(als Beruf)* driver

Kraft|fahr-: **Kraft|fahr|park** M fleet of motor vehicles; **kraft|fahr|tech|nisch** ADJ *attr* mechanical; **~e Ausbildung** training in motor mechanics ADV mechanically; **Kraft|fahr|trup|pe** F *(Mil)* motorized unit

Kraft|fahr|zeug NT motor vehicle

Kraft|fahr|zeug-: **Kraft|fahr|zeug|brief** M (vehicle) registration document, logbook *(Brit)*; **Kraft|fahr|zeug|kenn|zei|chen** NT (vehicle) registration; **Kraft|fahr|zeug|me|cha|ni|ker(in)** M(F) motor mechanic; **Kraft|fahr|zeug|schein** M (vehicle) registration document; **Kraft|fahr|zeug|steu|er** F motor vehicle tax, road tax *(Brit)*; **Kraft|fahr|zeug|ver|si|che|rung** F car insurance

Kraft-: **Kraft|feld** NT *(Phys)* force field; **Kraft|fut|ter** NT concentrated feed(stuff)

kräf|tig [ˈkrɛftɪç] ADJ strong; *Mann, Geschmack, Muskel, Stimme auch* powerful; *Ausdrucksweise auch* powerful, forceful; *Haarwuchs* healthy, strong; *Pflanze* healthy; *Farbe* rich, strong; *Schlag* hard, powerful, hefty *(inf)*; *Händedruck* firm, powerful; *Fluch* violent; *Suppe, Essen* nourishing; *(= groß) Portion, Preiserhöhung* big, massive; *Beifall* loud; **~e Ausdrücke** strong language; **einen ~en Schluck nehmen** to take a good *or* big swig; **eine ~e Tracht Prügel** a good *or* sound *or* thorough beating

ADV **a** *gebaut* strongly, powerfully; *zuschlagen, treten, pressen, drücken, blasen* hard; *klatschen* loudly; *lachen, mitsingen* heartily; *fluchen, niesen* violently; **etw ~ schütteln/polieren/umrühren** to shake/polish/stir sth vigorously, to give sth a good shake/polish/stir; **jdn ~ verprügeln** to give sb a sound *or* good *or* thorough beating; **~ essen** to eat well; **~ trinken** to drink a lot; **husten Sie mal ~** have a good cough; **er hat sich ~ dagegen gewehrt** he objected most strongly; *(körperlich)* he put up a strong resistance; **sich für etw ~ einsetzen** to support sth strongly *or* energetically

b *(zur Verstärkung)* really; **es hat ~ geregnet/geschneit** it really rained/snowed, it rained/snowed heavily; **die Preise sind ~ gestiegen** prices have gone up a lot, prices have really gone up; **jdn ~ ausschimpfen** to give sb a good bawling out *(inf)*, **sich ~ täuschen** *(inf)* to be really *or* very much *or* greatly mistaken; **jdn ~ belügen** *(inf)* to tell sb a pack of lies; to really give sb a bawling out *(inf)*; **sich ~ ausweinen** to have a good cry; **sich ~ ärgern** to get really *or* mighty *(inf)* annoyed

kräf|ti|gen [ˈkrɛftɪgn] VT *(geh) Körper, Muskeln* to strengthen; **jdn ~** to build up sb's strength; *(Luft, Bad etc)* to invigorate sb; *(Essen, Mittel etc)* to fortify sb

Kräf|ti|gung [ˈkrɛftɪgʊŋ] F -, *no pl (geh)* strengthening; *(durch Luft, Bad)* invigoration; *(durch Essen, Mittel)* fortification

Kräf|ti|gungs|mit|tel NT tonic

Kraft|li|ni|en PL *(Phys)* lines *pl* of force

kraft|los ADJ *(= schwach)* feeble, weak; *(= schlaff)* limp; *(= machtlos)* powerless; *(Jur)* invalid ADV weakly; **~ zur Seite fallen** to fall limply to one side; **~ sank er zurück** he fell feebly back

Kraft|los|er|klä|rung F *(Jur)* invalidation, annulment

Kraft|lo|sig|keit F -, *no pl* feebleness, weakness

Kraft-: **Kraft|mei|er** [-maiɐ] M **-s, -** *(inf)* muscle man *(inf)*; *(fig)* strongman; **Kraft|mei|e|rei** [-maiəˈrai] F -, *no pl* strong-arm tactics *pl*; **verbale ~** tough talking; **Kraft|mensch** M strongman, muscle man *(inf)*; **Kraft|mes|ser** M **-s, -** dynamometer *(form)*; *(auf Jahrmarkt)* test-your-strength machine; **Kraft|pa|ket** NT *(= Mensch)* powerhouse; *(= Auto, Maschine)* powerful machine; **Kraft|post** F post(al) bus service; **Kraft|pro|be** F test of strength; *(zwischen zwei Gruppen, Menschen)* trial of strength; **Kraft|protz** M *(inf)* muscle man *(inf)*; **Kraft|rad** NT motorcycle, motorbike; **Kraft|raum** M power training gym; **Kraft|re|ser|ven** PL energy reserves *pl*, reserves *pl* of strength; **Kraft|sport** M sport(s *pl*) involving strength; **Kraft|sport|ler(in)** M(F) power athlete; **Kraft|spruch** M strong words *pl*

Kraft|stoff M fuel

Kraft|stoff-: **Kraft|stoff|an|zei|ge** F, **Kraft|stoff|an|zei|ger** M fuel gauge; **Kraft|stoff|ver|brauch** M fuel consumption

Kraft-: **kraft|strot|zend** ADJ exuding vitality, vigorous; *Pflanze* healthy-looking, vigorous; *(= muskulös)* with bulging muscles; **ein ~es Baby** a big strong bouncing baby; **Kraft|trai|ning** NT power training; **Kraft|über|tra|gung** F power transmission; **Kraft|ver|geu|dung** F waste of energy *or* effort; **Kraft|ver|kehr** M motor traffic; **Kraft|ver|schwen|dung** F waste of energy *or* effort; **kraft|voll** ADJ *(geh) Stimme* powerful ADV powerfully; **bei etw ~ zubeißen können** to be able to sink one's teeth into sth; **Kraft|wa|gen** M motor vehicle; **Kraft|werk** NT power station; **Kraft|wort** NT *pl* **-wörter** swearword; **Kraftwörter** strong language

Krag|dach [ˈkraːg-] NT overhanging roof

Kra|gen [ˈkraːgn] M **-s, -** *or (S Ger, Sw auch)* = [ˈkrɛːgn] collar; **jdn am** *or* **beim ~ packen** to grab sb by the collar; *(fig inf)* to collar sb; **mir platzte der ~** *(inf)* I blew my top *(inf)*; **jetzt platzt mir aber der ~!** this is the last straw!; **jetzt gehts ihm an den ~** *(inf)* he's in for it now *(inf)* → **Kopf e**

Kra|gen-: **Kra|gen|knopf** M collar stud; **Kra|gen|num|mer** F collar size; **Kra|gen|spie|gel** M *(Mil)* collar patch; **Kra|gen|wei|te** F *(lit)* collar size; **eine ~ zu groß für jdn sein** *(fig inf)* to be too much for sb (to handle); **das ist nicht meine ~** *(fig inf)* that's not my cup of tea *(inf)*

Krag|stein [ˈkraːg-] M *(Archit)* console

Krä|he [ˈkrɛːə] F **-, -n** crow; **eine ~ hackt der anderen kein Auge aus** *(Prov)* birds of a feather stick *or* flock together *(Prov)*

krä|hen [ˈkrɛːən] VI to crow → **Hahn a**

Krä|hen-: **Krä|hen|fuß** M *(= Eisenkralle)* crowbar; **Krä|hen|fü|ße** PL *(an den Augen)* crow's-feet *pl*; *(= Schriftkrakel)* scrawl *sing*; **Krä|hen|nest** NT *(Naut)* crow's-nest

Kräh|win|kel M *(pej)* cultural backwater

Kra|kau [ˈkraːkau] NT **-s** Cracow

Kra|kau|er [ˈkrakauɐ] F **-, -** *(Cook)* spicy smoked sausage with garlic

Kra|kau|er [ˈkrakauɐ] M **-s, -**, **Kra|kau|e|rin** [-ərɪn] F **-, -nen** Cracovian

Kra|ke [ˈkraːkə] M **-n, -n** octopus; *(Myth)* Kraken

Kra|keel [kraˈkeːl] M **-s**, *no pl (inf)* row; **~ machen** *(inf)* to kick up a row *or* racket *(inf)*

kra|kee|len [kraˈkeːlən] *ptp* **krakeelt** VI *(inf)* to make *or* kick up a row *or* racket *(inf)*

Kra|kee|ler [kraˈkeːlɐ] M **-s, -**, **Kra|kee|le|rin** [-ərɪn] F **-, -nen** *(inf)* rowdy *(inf)*, rowdy type *(inf)*

Kra|kel [ˈkraːkl] M **-s, -** *(inf)* scrawl, scribble

Kra|ke|lei [krakəˈlai] F **-, -en** *(inf)* scrawl, scribble

kra|ke|lig [ˈkrakəlɪç] ADJ scrawly ADV **~ schreiben** to scrawl, to scribble; **~ unterschreiben** to scrawl one's signature; **meine Kinder malen ~** my children do scribbly drawings

kra|keln [ˈkraːkln] VTI to scrawl, to scribble

Kra|kel|schrift [ˈkraːkl-] F *(inf pej)* spidery handwriting *or* scrawl

Kral [kraːl] M **-s, -e** kraal

Kral|le [ˈkralə] F **-, -n** claw; *(von Raubvogel auch)* talon; *(pej: = Fingernagel)* claw, talon; *(= Parkkralle)* wheel clamp *(Brit)*, Denver boot *(US)*; **jdn/etw in seinen ~n haben** *(fig inf)* to have sb/sth in one's clutches; **(jdm) die ~n zeigen** *(fig)* to show (sb) one's claws; **die ~n einziehen** *(fig)* to put one's claws away; **jdn aus den ~n des Todes retten** to rescue sb from the jaws of death; **(bar) auf die ~** *(inf)* (cash) on the nail *(Brit inf)* *or* on the barrelhead *(US inf)*

kral|len [ˈkralən] VR **sich an jdn/etw ~** *(lit, fig)* to cling to sb/sth; *(Tier)* to dig its claws into sb/sth; **sich in etw** *(acc)* **~** to sink its claws into sth; *(mit Fingern)* to dig one's fingers into sth

VT **a die Finger in etw** *(acc)* **~** to dig one's fingers into sth; **die Finger um etw ~** to clutch sth **b** *(sl)* to pinch *(Brit inf)*, to swipe *(inf)*; **er krallte vor Schmerz die Finger in die Stuhllehne** he clawed (at) the back of the chair in pain; **sich** *(dat)* **etw ~** to pinch *(Brit)* *or* swipe sth *(inf)*; **den haben sich die Bullen gekrallt** the cops nicked *(Brit)* *or* nabbed him *(inf)*

c *(Aut)* to clamp *(Brit)*, to (Denver) boot *(US)*

VI to claw *(an +dat* at)

Kram [kraːm] M **-(e)s**, *no pl (inf) (= Gerümpel)* junk; *(= Zeug)* things *pl*, stuff *(inf)*; *(= Angelegenheit)* business; **den ~ satthaben/hinschmeißen** to be fed up with/to chuck the whole thing *or* business *(inf)*; **das passt mir nicht in den ~** it's a confounded nuisance; **mach doch deinen ~ allein!** do it yourself!; **lass mich meinen ~ alleine machen** don't tell me what to do

kra|men [ˈkraːmən] VI **a** *(= wühlen)* to rummage about *(in +dat* in, *nach* for) **b** *(Sw inf)* to do a bit of shopping VT **etw aus etw ~** to fish sth out of sth

Krä|mer [ˈkrɛːmɐ] M **-s, -**, **Krä|me|rin** [-ərɪn] F **-, -nen** small shopkeeper, grocer; *(= Laden)* small general store, grocer's; **ein Volk von ~n** a nation of shopkeepers

Krä|mer|geist M, **Krä|mer|see|le** F small-minded *or* petty-minded person; **ein ~** *or* **eine**

Krämerseele sein to be small-minded *or* petty-minded; **einen ~** *or* **eine Krämerseele haben** to have a small *or* petty mind

Kram|la|den M *(pej inf)* tatty little shop *(inf)*; *(= Trödelladen)* junk shop

Kram|pe ['krampə] F -, -n staple

Kram|pen ['krampn] M -s, - staple; *(Aus: = Spitzhacke)* pick(axe) *(Brit)*, pick(ax) *(US)*

Krampf [krampf] M -(e)s, ⸚e ['krɛmpfə] **a** *(= Zustand)* cramp; *(= Verkrampfung, Zuckung)* spasm; *(wiederholt)* convulsion(s *pl*); *(= Anfall, Lachkrampf)* fit; **einen ~ haben/bekommen** to have/get (a) cramp **b** *no pl (inf) (= Getue)* palaver *(inf)*; *(= Unsinn)* nonsense, rubbish **c** *(esp Sw inf: = krampfhaftes Tun, Bemühen)* strain; **einen ~ drehen** to do a job *(inf)*

Krampf-: **Krampf|ader** F varicose vein; **krampf|ar|tig** ADJ convulsive ADV convulsively

kramp|fen ['krampfn] VT *Finger, Hand* to clench *(um etw* around sth); **die Finger in etw** *(acc)* **~** to dig one's fingers into sth VR **sich um etw ~** to clench sth VI **a** *(= Krämpfe haben)* to have a convulsion/convulsions **b** *(Sw inf: = hart arbeiten)* to slave away *(inf)*

Kramp|fer ['krampfɐ] M -s, -, **Kramp|fe|rin** [-ərɪn] F -, -nen *(sl)* grafter *(Brit inf)*, hard worker

Krampf-: **krampf|haft** ADJ *Zuckung* convulsive; *(inf: = angestrengt, verzweifelt)* frantic, desperate; *Lachen* forced *no adv* ADV **sich ~ bemühen** to try desperately hard; **~ nachdenken** to rack one's brains; **sich ~ an etw** *(dat)* **festhalten** *(lit, fig inf)* to cling desperately to sth; **Krampf|hus|ten** M *(Aus inf)* whooping cough; **krampf|lin|dernd** ADJ antispasmodic *(spec)*; **krampf|lö|send** ADJ antispasmodic *(spec)*

Kram|pus ['krampʊs] M -, -se *(Aus)* companion of St Nicholas

Kran [kra:n] M -(e)s, ⸚e *or* -e ['krɛ:nə] **a** crane **b** *(dial: = Hahn)* tap *(esp Brit)*, faucet *(US)*

Kran|füh|rer(in) M(F) crane driver *or* operator

krän|gen ['krɛŋən] VI *(Naut)* to heel (over)

Kra|nich ['kra:nɪç] M -s, -e *(Orn)* crane

krank [kraŋk] ADJ *comp* ⸚**er** ['krɛŋkɐ], *superl* ⸚**ste(r, s)** ['krɛŋkstə] **a** *(= nicht gesund)* ill *usu pred*, sick *(auch fig)*, not well; *(= leidend)* invalid; *Pflanze, Organ* diseased; *Zahn, Bein* bad; *Wirtschaft, Firma* ailing; *(Hunt) Wild* wounded; **~ werden** to fall ill *or* sick, to be taken ill *or* sick; **schwer ~** seriously ill; **~ am Herzen** *or* **an der Seele** *(liter)* sick at heart *(liter)*; **vor Aufregung/Angst ~** sick with excitement/fear; **vor Heimweh ~** homesick; **vor Liebe ~** lovesick; **du bist wohl ~!** *(inf iro)* there must be something wrong with you!; **der ~e Mann am Bosporus** the Sick Man of Europe **b** *(sl: = verrückt)* off one's head *(inf)* ADV *comp* ⸚**er**, *superl* **am** ⸚**sten sich ~ stellen** to pretend to be ill *or* sick, to malinger; **das macht/du machst mich ~!** *(inf)* it gets/you get on my nerves! *(inf)*, it drives/you drive me crazy *or* (a)round the bend! *(inf)*

krän|keln ['krɛŋkln] VI to be ailing *(auch Wirtschaft, Firma)*, to be sickly, to be in bad *or* poor health; **sie ~ leicht** they're often poorly *(Brit) or* sick

kran|ken ['kraŋkn] VI to suffer *(an +dat* from); **das krankt daran, dass ...** *(fig)* it suffers from the fact that ...

krän|ken ['krɛŋkn] VT **jdn ~** to hurt sb('s feelings), to wound sb; **sie war sehr gekränkt** she was very hurt; **es kränkt mich, dass ...** it hurts *or* grieves me that ...; **jdn in seiner Ehre ~** to offend sb's pride; **~d** hurtful VR **sich über etw** *(acc)* **~** *(dated, dial)* to feel upset about sth

Kran|ken-: **Kran|ken|ak|te** F medical file; **Kran|ken|an|stalt** F *usu pl* hospital; **Kran|ken|au|to** NT ambulance; **Kran|ken|be|richt** M medical report; **Kran|ken|be|such** M visit (to a sick person); *(von Arzt)* (sick) call; **Kran|ken|bett** NT sickbed; **Kran|ken|blatt** NT medical report, doctor's notes *pl*; **Kran|ken|geld** NT sickness benefit; *(von Firma)* sick pay; **Kran|ken|ge|schich|te** F medical history; **Kran|ken|gym|nast** [-gymnast] M -en, -en, **Kran|ken|gym|nas|tin** [-gymnastɪn] F -, -nen physiotherapist; **Kran|ken|gym|nas|tik** F physiotherapy

Kran|ken|haus NT hospital; **ins ~ gehen** *(als Patient)* to go into (the *US*) hospital; **im ~ liegen** to be in (the *US*) hospital; **jdn in einem ~ unterbringen** to put sb in a hospital, to hospitalize sb; **an einem ~ sein** *(Arzt, Schwester etc)* to work in a hospital

Kran|ken|haus- *in cpds* hospital; **Kran|ken|haus|arzt** M, **Kran|ken|haus|ärz|tin** F hospital doctor; **Kran|ken|haus|auf|ent|halt** M stay in hospital; **Kran|ken|haus|kos|ten** PL hospital charges *pl or* costs *pl*; **Kran|ken|haus|rech|nung** F bill for hospital treatment; **kran|ken|haus|reif** ADJ in need of hospital treatment; **jdn ~ schlagen** to make a stretcher-case out of sb *(Brit inf)*, to beat the hell out of sb *(inf)*; **Kran|ken|haus|seel|sor|ger(in)** M(F) hospital chaplain; **Kran|ken|haus|ta|ge|geld** NT (hospital) daily benefit

Kran|ken-: **Kran|ken|kas|se** F *(= Versicherung)* medical *or* health insurance; *(= Gesellschaft)* medical *or* health insurance company; **ich bin in einer privaten ~** I am in a private medical insurance scheme, I'm privately insured; **er ist in keiner ~** he has no medical insurance; **Kran|ken|kas|sen|bei|trag** M health insurance contribution, contribution to a/the medical insurance scheme; **Kran|ken|la|ger** NT *(= Krankenbett)* sickbed; *(= Kranksein)* illness; **das Fieber warf ihn aufs ~** *(geh)* the fever confined him to his sickbed; **Kran|ken|pfle|ge** F nursing; **Kran|ken|pfle|ge|hel|fer(in)** M(F) nursing auxiliary *(Brit)*, auxiliary nurse; **Kran|ken|pfle|ger** M orderly; *(mit Schwesternausbildung)* male nurse; **Kran|ken|pfle|ge|rin** F nurse; **Kran|ken|pfle|ge|schü|ler(in)** M(F) student nurse; **Kran|ken|saal** M ward; **Kran|ken|sal|bung** F *(Eccl)* anointing of the sick; **Kran|ken|schein** M medical insurance record card; **Kran|ken|schwes|ter** F nurse; **Kran|ken|stand** M **a** *(von Firma)* level of sickness, number of employees sick **b im ~ sein** to be sick *or* ill; **Kran|ken|stuhl** M invalid chair, Bath chair; *(= Nachtstuhl)* commode; **Kran|ken|trans|port** M transportation of sick people; *(mittels Krankenwagen)* ambulance service; *(die Kranken selbst)* shipload/busload *etc* of sick people; **kran|ken|ver|si|chern** *ptp* **krankenversichert** VT to take out medical *or* health insurance *(jdn* for); **sich ~** to take out medical *or* health insurance; **krankenversichert** medically insured; **sind Sie krankenversichert?** do you have medical *or* health insurance *or* cover?; **Kran|ken|ver|si|che|rung** F medical *or* health insurance; **soziale/private ~** state *or* national/private health insurance; **Kran|ken|ver|si|che|rungs|aus|weis** M health insurance card, medical card *(Brit)*; **Kran|ken|wa|gen** M ambulance; **Kran|ken|wär|ter** M orderly; **Kran|ken|wär|te|rin** F nurse; **Kran|ken|zim|mer** NT sickroom; *(im Krankenhaus)* hospital room

Kran|ke(r) ['kraŋkə] MF *decl as adj* sick person, invalid; *(= Patient)* patient; **die ~n** the sick

krank+fei|ern VI *sep (inf)* to be off sick, to skive off work *(Brit inf)*; **das Krankfeiern ist ein großes Problem** absenteeism is a great problem; **geh doch heute nicht ins Büro, feier doch krank** don't go in to the office today, say you're not feeling well; **ich glaube, ich muss morgen ~** I think I'll have to be off sick tomorrow

krank|haft ADJ **a** *Stelle, Zelle* diseased; *Vergrößerung, Zustand* morbid; *Aussehen* sickly; *Augen* ill-looking; **die Untersuchungen haben keinen ~en Befund ergeben** the examinations revealed no sign(s) of disease; **~er Befund der Leber** affected *or* diseased liver; **~e Veränderung** affection; **der ~e Zustand der britischen Wirtschaft** the ailing condition of the British economy; **das Krankhafte an unserer Gesellschaft** the sickness affecting our society **b** *(seelisch)* pathological; *Misstrauen, Eifersucht etc* chronic, pathological; **sein Geiz/diese Vorstellung ist schon ~** his meanness/this idea is almost pathological *or* has reached almost pathological proportions ADV **a** *(Med)* abnormally; **sich ~ verändern** to show pathological changes **b** *(auf seelische Zustände bezogen)* pathologically

Krank|heit F -, -en *(lit, fig)* illness, sickness; *(eine bestimmte Krankheit wie Krebs, Masern etc auch)* disease; *(von Pflanzen)* disease; **wegen ~** due to illness; **eine ~ durchmachen, an einer ~ leiden** to suffer from *or* have a disease *or* an illness; **einer ~ vorbeugen** to take preventive measures against an illness *or* a disease; **(eine) ~ vorschützen, eine ~ vortäuschen** to pretend to be ill, to fake an illness; **sich** *(dat)* **eine ~ zuziehen** to catch *or* contract *(form)* an illness *or* a disease; **von einer ~ befallen werden** to catch *or* contract *(form)* an illness *or* a disease; *(Pflanze, Organ)* to become diseased; **von einer ~ genesen** to recuperate from an illness; **nach langer/schwerer ~** after a long/serious illness; **während/seit meiner ~** during/since my illness; **das soll ein Auto sein? das ist eine ~!** *(fig inf)* call that a car? that's just an apology *or* excuse for one!

-krank|heit F *suf in cpds* disease; **Lungenkrankheit** lung disease; **Blutkrankheit** disease of the blood

Krank|heits-: **krank|heits|be|dingt** ADJ due to illness *or* sickness *pred* ADV due to illness *or* sickness; **Krank|heits|bild** NT symptoms *pl*, syndrome *(spec)*; **Krank|heits|er|re|ger** M pathogen, disease-causing agent; **krank|heits|hal|ber** ADV due to illness; **Krank|heits|herd** M focus of a/the disease; **Krank|heits|keim** M germ (of a/the disease); **Krank|heits|tag** M day of illness *or* sickness

krank+la|chen VR *(inf)* to kill oneself (laughing) *(inf)*; **er hat sich bei dem Film krankgelacht** he just about killed himself (laughing) *(inf) or* died laughing when he saw the film

kränk|lich ['krɛŋklɪç] ADJ sickly, in poor *or* bad health

Krank-: **krank+ma|chen** VI *sep (inf)* = **krankfeiern**; **krank+mel|den** VR *sep* to let sb/one's boss *etc* know that one is sick *or* ill; *(telefonisch)* to phone in sick; *(esp Mil)* to report sick; **sie hat sich krankgemeldet** she is off sick; **Krank|mel|dung** F notification of illness *or* sickness; **krank+schrei|ben** VT *sep irreg* to give sb a medical certificate; *(esp Mil)* to put sb on the sick list; **er ist schon seit einem halben Jahr krankgeschrieben** he's been off sick for six months; **Krank|schrei|bung** F medical certificate, doctor's certificate *(US)*, sick note *(inf)*

Krän|kung ['krɛŋkʊŋ] F -, -en **a** insult; **etw als ~ empfinden** to take offence *(Brit) or* offense *(US)* at sth, to be hurt by sth; **jdm eine (tiefe) ~ zufügen** to hurt sb (deeply) **b** *(= Kränken)* offending, insulting; **das war eine ~ seiner Gefühle** that hurt his feelings

Kranz [krants] M -es, ⸚e ['krɛntsə] **a** wreath; *(= Siegerkranz, Dichterkranz, Brautkranz auch)* garland; *(fig: von Geschichten, Anekdoten etc)* cycle; **da kannst du dir gleich einen ~ schicken lassen** *(inf)* you'll be signing your own death warrant **b** *(= kreisförmig Angeordnetes)* ring, circle; *(= Haarkranz)* plaits *pl* round one's head *(Brit)*, braids *pl* around one's head *(US)*; *(obs: von Mädchen)* bevy **c** *(Tech: = Radkranz)* rim; *(von Glocke auch)* lip **d** *(dial Cook)* ring

Kranz|ar|te|rie F coronary artery

Kränz|chen ['krɛntsçən] NT -s, - **a** → **Kranz a** small wreath/garland **b** *(fig: = Kaffeekränzchen)* coffee circle

krän|zen ['krɛntsn] VT *(liter)* to garland, to adorn (with garlands)

Kranz-: **Kranz|ge|fäß** NT *(Anat)* coronary artery; **Kranz|geld** NT *(Jur)* *money paid by a man to a woman as a fine for having sexual intercourse with her after pretending to make her an offer of marriage*; **Kranz|ge|sims** NT *(Archit)* cornice; **Kranz|jung|fer** F *(dial)* bridesmaid; **Kranz|nie|der|le|gung** F wreath laying

Krap|fen ['krapfn] M **-s, -** *(dial Cook)* ≈ doughnut *(Brit)*, ≈ donut *(US)*

Krapp M **-(e)s,** *no pl* madder

Kräp|pel ['krɛpl] M **-s, -** *(dial Cook)* ≈ doughnut *(Brit)*, ≈ donut *(US)*

Krapp-: **Krapp|lack** M madder paint; **Krapp|rot** NT madder red

krass [kras] **ADJ** **a** *(= auffallend) Beispiel* glaring; *Widerspruch, Gegensatz* glaring, stark; *Farben* garish, glaring; *Dissonanz* harsh, jarring; *Unterschied* extreme; *(= unerhört) Ungerechtigkeit, Lüge* blatant, gross; *(= extrem) Fall, Haltung, Lage* extreme; *Materialist, Unkenntnis* crass; *Egoist* out-and-out, blatant; *Außenseiter* rank, complete; *(= unverblümt) Schilderung, Worte, Stil* stark; **etw ~ finden** *(inf)* to find sth gross
b *(sl: = unmöglich)* gross *(inf)*; **das ist echt ~** that's a real bummer *(inf)* or pisser *(Brit sl)*
c *(sl: = toll)* wicked *(sl)*
ADV *sich ausdrücken* crudely; *schildern* garishly; *widersprechen* completely; *kontrastieren* sharply; **sich ~ von etw abheben** to contrast sharply with sth; **das war ~ gelogen** that was a blatant lie; **um es ~ zu sagen, ~ gesagt** to put it bluntly

Kra|ter ['kra:tɐ] M **-s, -** crater

Kra|ter-: **Kra|ter|land|schaft** F crater(ed) landscape; **Kra|ter|see** M *(Geol)* crater lake

Krät|ten ['krɛtn] M **-s, -** *(S Ger, Sw)* (small) basket

Kratz-: **Kratz|bee|re** F *(dial: = Brombeere)* blackberry, bramble; **Kratz|bürs|te** F wire brush; *(inf)* prickly character; **kratz|bürs|tig** [-bʏrstɪç] ADJ *(inf)* prickly

Krätz|chen ['krɛtsçən] NT **-s, -** *(Mil sl)* forage cap

Krat|ze ['kratsə] F **-, -n** scraper; *(Tex)* carding machine

Krät|ze ['krɛtsə] F **-,** *no pl* **a** *(Med)* scabies; **da kriegt man doch die ~** *(fig inf)* it drives you up the wall *(inf)* **b** *(Tech)* scrapings *pl*, (metal) waste

Krät|ze F **-, -n** *(S Ger)* basket

krat|zen ['kratsn] **VT** **a** *(mit Nägeln, Werkzeug)* to scratch; *(= abkratzen)* to scrape *(von* off); **seinen Namen in die Wand ~** to scratch one's name on the wall; **der Rauch kratzt (mich) im Hals** the smoke irritates my throat; **es kratzt (mich) im Hals** my throat feels rough
b *(inf: = stören)* to bother; **das kratzt mich nicht** *(inf)* **das soll** *or* **kann mich nicht ~** *(inf)* I couldn't care less (about that), I don't give a damn (about that) *(inf)*; **was kratzt mich das?** what do I care about that?; **das braucht dich (doch) nicht (zu) ~** it's nothing to do with you
c *(Tex)* to card, to tease
VI to scratch; **der Pulli kratzt fürchterlich** the pullover scratches terribly *or* is terribly scratchy *(inf)*; **es kratzt (mir) im Hals** my throat feels rough; **an etw** *(dat)* **~** *(fig)* to scratch away at sth; **diese Sache hat an seinem guten Ruf gekratzt** this business has tarnished his reputation
VR to scratch oneself

Krat|zer ['kratsɐ] M **-s, -** *(= Schramme)* scratch

Krät|zer ['krɛtsɐ] M **-s, -** *(inf)* rough *or* vinegary wine, plonk *no pl (Brit inf)*; *(Aus) sweet young Tyrolean wine*

kratz|fest ADJ non-scratch *attr*, scratchproof

Kratz|fuß M *(dated inf)* (low) bow *(with one foot drawn backwards)*; **einen ~ machen** to bow low

krat|zig ['kratsɪç] ADJ *(inf)* scratchy *(inf)*

krät|zig ['krɛtsɪç] ADJ scabious

Krätz|mil|be F *(Zool)* itch mite

Kratz-: **Kratz|putz** M sgraffito; **Kratz|spur** F scratch (mark); **Kratz|wun|de** F scratch

krau|chen ['krauxn] VI *aux sein (dial)* to crawl

krau|eln ['krauəln], **krau|en** ['krauən] VT = **kraulen**

Kraul [kraul] NT **-(s),** *no pl (Schwimmen)* crawl; **(im) ~ schwimmen** to do the crawl

krau|len ['kraulən] *aux haben or sein (Schwimmen)* **VI** to do *or* swim the crawl **VT** **er hat** *or* **ist die Strecke gekrault** he swam the stretch front crawl; **er hat** *or* **ist 100 m gekrault** he did a 100m crawl

krau|len VT to fondle; **jdn am Kinn ~** to chuck *(Brit)* *or* tickle sb under the chin; **jdn in den Haaren ~** to run one's fingers through sb's hair

kraus [kraus] ADJ crinkly; *Haar, Kopf* frizzy; *Stirn* wrinkled, furrowed; *(= zerknittert)* crumpled, wrinkled; *(fig: = verworren)* muddled, confused → **krausziehen**

Krau|se ['krauzə] F **-, -n** **a** *(= Halskrause)* ruff; *(an Ärmeln etc)* ruffle, frill **b** *(inf) (= Krausheit)* crinkliness; *(von Haar, Kopf)* frizziness; *(= Frisur)* frizzy hair; **im Regen bekomme ich eine ~** my hair goes frizzy in the rain

Kräu|sel-: **Kräu|sel|band** [-bant] NT *pl* **-bänder** decorative ribbon; **Kräu|sel|krepp** M *(Tex)* crepe; *(= Streifenkrepp)* seersucker

kräu|seln ['krɔyzln] **VT** **a** *Haar* to make frizzy; *(Sew)* to gather; *(Tex)* to crimp; *Stirn* to knit, to wrinkle; *Nase* to screw up **b** *Lippen, Mund* to pucker; *Wasseroberfläche* to ruffle **VR** **a** *(Haare)* to go frizzy; *(Stoff)* to go crinkly; *(Stirn, Nase)* to wrinkle up; **gekräuselte Haare** frizzy hair **b** *(Lippen)* to pucker; *(Wasser)* to ripple; *(Rauch)* to curl (up)

krau|sen ['krauzn] VTR = **kräuseln VT a VR a**

Kraus-: **kraus|haa|rig** ADJ frizzy-haired; **Kraus|kopf** M frizzy head; *(= Frisur)* frizzy hair/hairstyle; *(= Mensch)* curly-head; **kraus+zie|hen** VT *sep irreg* **die Stirn ~** to wrinkle up *or* knit one's brow; *(missbilligend)* to frown; **die Nase ~** to screw up one's nose

Kraut [kraut] NT **-(e)s, Kräuter** ['krɔytɐ] **a** *(Pflanze: = esp Heilkraut, Würzkraut)* herb; **dagegen ist kein ~ gewachsen** *(fig)* there is no remedy for that, there's nothing anyone can do about that
b *no pl (= grüne Teile von Pflanzen)* foliage, stems and leaves *pl*, herbage; *(von Gemüse)* tops *pl*; *(= Kartoffelkraut)* potato foliage; *(= Spargelkraut)* asparagus leaves *pl*; **wie ~ und Rüben durcheinanderliegen** *(inf)* to lie (about *(Brit) or* around) all over the place *(inf)*; **ins ~ schießen** *(lit)* to go to seed; *(fig)* to get out of control, to run wild
c *no pl (= Rotkraut, Weißkraut)* cabbage; *(= Sauerkraut)* sauerkraut
d *(pej: = Tabak)* tobacco

Krau|ter M **-s, -** *(pej)* small-timer *(inf)*

Kräu|ter-: **Kräu|ter|but|ter** F herb butter; **Kräu|ter|frau** F herb woman; **Kräu|ter|gar|ten** M herb garden; *(am Fensterbrett)* potted herbs *pl*; **Kräu|ter|he|xe** F *(pej)* herb woman; *(fig)* old hag *(pej)*; **Kräu|ter|kä|se** M herb cheese; **Kräu|ter|li|kör** M herbal liqueur; **Kräu|ter|müh|le** F herb mill; **Kräu|ter|samm|ler(in)** M(F) herbalist; **Kräu|ter|tee** M herb(al) tea; **Kräu|ter|weib|lein** NT herb woman

Kraut-: **Kraut|jun|ker** M *(pej)* country squire; **Kraut|kopf** M *(S Ger, Aus)* (head of) cabbage; **Kraut|sa|lat** M ≈ coleslaw; **Kraut|wi|ckel** M *(S Ger, Aus: Cook)* stuffed cabbage leaves *pl*

Kra|wall [kra'val] M **-s, -e** *(= Aufruhr)* riot; *(inf) (= Rauferei)* brawl; *(= Lärm)* racket *(inf)*, din *(inf)*; **~ machen** *(inf)* to kick up a row; *(= randalieren)* to go on the rampage; *(auch* **Krawall schlagen**: *= sich beschweren)* to kick up a fuss

Kra|wall|bru|der M, **Kra|wall|ma|cher(in)** M(F) *(inf)* hooligan; *(= Krakeeler)* rowdy *(inf)*

Kra|wal|lo [kra'valo] M **-s, -s** *(inf)* hooligan

Kra|wall|tou|rist(in) M(F) *(inf)* professional rioter

Kra|wat|te [kra'vatə] F **-, -n** tie, necktie *(esp US)*; *(= kleiner Pelzkragen)* tippet; *(Ringkampf)* headlock

Kra|wat|ten-: **Kra|wat|ten|hal|ter** M, **Kra|wat|ten|klem|me** F tie clip; **Kra|wat|ten|kno|ten** M tie knot; **Kra|wat|ten|na|del** F tiepin; **Kra|wat|ten|zwang** M **da ist ~** you have to wear a tie there; **der ~ ...** the fact that you have to wear a tie ...

kra|xeln ['kraksln] VI *aux sein (S Ger)* to clamber (up)

Kre|a|ti|on [krea'tsio:n] F **-, -en** *(Fashion etc)* creation

kre|a|tiv [krea'ti:f] **ADJ** creative **ADV** creatively; **~ veranlagt** creatively inclined; **~ begabt** creative

Kre|a|ti|ve(r) [krea'ti:və] MF *decl as adj (inf)* creative person; **er ist einer der ~n** he's one of the creators

Kre|a|ti|vi|tät [kreativi'tɛ:t] F **-,** *no pl* creativity

Kre|a|tur [krea'tu:ɐ] F **-, -en** **a** *(lit, fig, pej)* creature; *(= abhängiger Mensch)* minion, creature *(liter)* **b** *no pl (= alle Lebewesen)* creation; **die ~** all creation

kre|a|tür|lich [krea'ty:ɐlɪç] ADJ *(= naturhaft)* natural; *Angst etc* animal *attr*

Krebs [kre:ps] M **-es, -e** **a** *(= Taschenkrebs, Einsiedlerkrebs)* crab; *(= Flusskrebs)* crayfish, crawfish *(US)*; **rot wie ein ~** red as a lobster **b** *(Gattung)* crustacean; *(= Hummer, Krabbe etc)* crayfish, crawfish *(US)* **c** *(Astrol)* Cancer; **der ~** *(Astron)* Cancer, the Crab **d** *(Med)* cancer; *(Bot)* canker; **~ erzeugend** *or* **auslösend** carcinogenic; **~ erregend** = **krebserregend** **e** *(Typ inf)* return

krebs-: **krebs|ar|tig** **ADJ** *(Zool)* crablike; crayfish-like; crustaceous; *(Med)* cancerous **ADV** *(Med)* **~ wuchern** to spread like cancer; **sich ~ verändern** to become cancerous; **krebs|aus|lö|send** ADJ, ADV → **Krebs d**

kreb|sen ['kre:psn] VI **a** *(inf: = sich abmühen)* to struggle; *(Umsatz, Industrie)* to languish; **in den Umfragen krebst die Partei bei 6 Prozent** the party is languishing at 6 per cent in the polls; **er hat schwer zu ~** he really has to struggle, he finds it really hard going **b** *(= Krebse fangen)* to go crabbing, to catch crabs

Krebs-: **krebs|er|re|gend** **ADJ** carcinogenic **ADV** **~ wirken** to cause cancer, to be carcinogenic; **krebs|er|zeu|gend** ADJ, ADV → **Krebs d**; **krebs|för|dernd** **ADJ** cancer-inducing; **eine ~e Wirkung haben** to increase the risk of cancer **ADV** **~ wirken** to increase the risk of (getting) cancer; **Krebs|for|schung** F cancer research; **Krebs|früh|er|ken|nung** F early detection of cancer; **Krebs|gang** [-gaŋ] M, *no pl (fig)* retrogression; **im ~ gehen** to regress, to go backwards; **Krebs|ge|schwulst** F *(Med)* cancer, cancerous tumour *(Brit) or* tumor *(US)*, cancerous growth; **Krebs|ge|schwür** NT *(Med)* cancerous ulcer; *(fig)* cancer, cancerous growth; **krebs|hem|mend** **ADJ** cancer-inhibiting; **eine ~e Wirkung haben** to reduce the risk of cancer **ADV** **~ wirken** to reduce the risk of (getting) cancer; **Krebs|kli|nik** F cancer clinic; **krebs|krank** ADJ suffering from cancer; **~ sein** to have cancer; **Krebs|kran|ke(r)** MF *decl as adj* cancer victim; *(= Patient)* cancer patient; **Krebs|krank|heit** F cancer; **krebs|rot** ADJ red as a lobster; **Krebs|sche|re** F → **Krebs a** claws *pl or* pincers *pl* of the crab/crayfish; **Krebs|tie|re** PL crustaceans *pl*, crustacea *pl*; **Krebs|vor|sor|ge** F, **Krebs|vor|sor|ge|un|ter|su|chung** F cancer checkup; **Krebs|zel|le** F *(Med)* cancer cell

Kre|denz [kre'dɛnts] F **-, -en** *(dated, Aus)* sideboard

kre|den|zen [kre'dɛntsn] *ptp* **kredenzt** VT *(liter)* **jdm etw ~** to proffer sb sth *(liter)*

Kre|dit [kre'di:t] M **-(e)s, -e** credit; *(= Darlehen auch)* loan; *(fig auch)* standing, (good) repute; **auf ~** on credit; **jdm einen ~ gewähren** to grant sb credit/a loan; **einen ~ kündigen** to withdraw credit facilities *or* a credit; to call in a loan; **er hat bei uns/der Bank ~** his credit is good with us/the bank; **in seiner Stammkneipe hat er ~**

he gets credit at his local; **~ haben** *(fig)* to have standing *or* a good reputation

Kre|dit ['kre:dɪt] NT **-s, -s** *(= Habenseite)* credit (side)

Kre|dit-: Kre|dit|an|stalt F credit institution, credit *or* loan bank; **Kre|dit|auf|nah|me** F borrowing; **sich zu einer ~ entschließen** to decide to obtain a loan; **Kre|dit|bank** M *pl* **-banken** credit bank; **Kre|dit|be|darf** M borrowing requirement(s *pl*), credit demand; **Kre|dit|be|din|gung|en** PL credit terms *pl*; **Kre|dit|brief** M letter of credit; **kre|dit|fä|hig** ADJ credit-worthy; **Kre|dit|fä|hig|keit** F credit-worthiness; **Kre|dit|ge|ber(in)** M(F) creditor; **Kre|dit|hai** M *(inf)* loan shark *(inf)*

kre|di|tie|ren [kredi'ti:rən] *ptp* **kreditiert** VT **jdm einen Betrag ~, jdn für einen Betrag ~** to advance sb an amount, to credit sb with an amount

Kre|dit-: Kre|dit|in|sti|tut [kre'di:t-] NT bank; **Kre|dit|kar|te** F credit card; **Kre|dit|kar|ten|or|ga|ni|sa|ti|on** F credit card company; **Kre|dit|kauf** M credit sale; **Kre|dit|lauf|zeit** F credit period; **Kre|dit|li|mit** NT credit limit; *(für Bankkonto)* overdraft limit; **Kre|dit|li|nie** F line of credit; **Kre|dit|neh|mer(in)** M(F) borrower; **Kre|dit|po|li|tik** F lending policy; **kre|dit|po|li|tisch** ADJ *Maßnahme, Beschluss* on lending ADV in terms of lending policy; **~ sinnvoll sein** to be good lending policy; **Kre|dit|rah|men** M credit range; **den ~ ausschöpfen/sprengen** to use up/exceed the credit range; **Kre|dit|ri|si|ko** NT credit risk; **Kre|dit|sper|re** F credit freeze; **Kre|dit|sprit|ze** F *(fig inf)* credit injection; **Kre|dit|ver|ein|ba|rung** F *usu pl* credit agreement; **Kre|dit|vo|lu|men** NT lending volume, total lending; **Kre|dit|wirt|schaft** F, *no pl* banking industry; **kre|dit|wür|dig** ADJ creditworthy; **Kre|dit|wür|dig|keit** F creditworthiness; **Kre|dit|zins** M lending rate

Kre|do ['kre:do] NT **-s, -s** *(lit, fig)* creed, credo

kre|gel ['kre:gl] *(dial)* ADJ lively ADV in a lively manner

Krei|de ['kraidə] F **-, -n** chalk; *(Geol: = Kreidezeit)* Cretaceous (period); **eine ~** a piece of chalk; **bei jdm (tief) in der ~ sein** *or* **stehen** to be (deep) in debt to sb, to owe sb (a lot of) money

Krei|de-: krei|de|bleich ADJ (as) white as chalk *or* a sheet; **Krei|de|fel|sen** M chalk cliff; **Krei|de|for|ma|ti|on** F *(Geol)* Cretaceous (formation); **krei|de|hal|tig** ADJ chalky, cretaceous *(spec)*; **Krei|de|stift** M chalk; **krei|de|weiß** ADJ = **kreidebleich**; **Krei|de|zeich|nung** F chalk drawing; **Krei|de|zeit** F, *no pl (Geol)* Cretaceous period

krei|dig ['kraidɪç] ADJ chalky

kre|ie|ren [kre'i:rən] *ptp* **kreiert** VT *(Fashion, Theat etc, Eccl)* to create; **jdn zum Kardinal ~** *(form)* to create *or* appoint sb (a) cardinal

Kreis [krais] M **-es, -e** [-zə] **a** circle; **einen ~ beschreiben** *or* **schlagen** *or* **ziehen** to describe a circle; **einen ~ um jdn bilden** *or* **schließen** to form *or* make a circle around sb, to encircle sb; **im ~ (gehen/sitzen)** (to go (a)round/sit) in a circle; **~e ziehen** *(lit)* to circle; **(weite) ~e ziehen** *(fig)* to have (wide) repercussions; **sich im ~ bewegen** *or* **drehen** *(lit)* to go *or* turn (a)round in a circle; *(fig)* to go (a)round in circles; **mir dreht sich alles im ~e** everything's going (a)round and (a)round, my head is reeling *or* spinning; **der ~ schließt sich** *(fig)* we *etc* come full circle, the wheel turns full circle; **störe meine ~e nicht!** *(fig)* leave me in peace!

b *(Elec: = Stromkreis)* circuit

c *(= Stadtkreis, Landkreis)* district; *(= Gemeindewahlkreis)* ward; *(= Landeswahlkreis)* constituency; **~ Leipzig** Leipzig District, the District of Leipzig

d *(fig: von Menschen)* circle; **der ~ seiner Leser** his readership, his readers *pl*; **weite ~e der Bevölkerung** wide sections of the population; **im ~e von Freunden/seiner Familie** among *or* with friends/his family, in the family circle; **eine Feier im engen** *or* **kleinen ~e** a celebration for a few close friends and relatives; **in seinen/ihren** *etc* **~en** in the circles in which he/she *etc* moves; **das kommt (auch) in den besten ~en vor** that happens even in the best society *or* the best of circles

e *(= Bereich: von Interessen, Tätigkeit etc)* sphere; *(= Ideenkreis)* body of ideas; *(= Sagenkreis)* cycle; **im ~ des Scheinwerferlichtes** in the arc *or* pool of light thrown by the headlamps

Kreis-: Kreis|ab|schnitt M segment; **Kreis|aus|schnitt** M sector; **Kreis|bahn** F *(Astron, Space)* orbit; **Kreis|be|we|gung** F rotation, circular motion; **Kreis|bo|gen** M arc (of a circle)

krei|schen ['kraiʃn] VI *pret* **kreischte** *or (old, hum)* **krisch** [krɪʃ], *ptp* **gekreischt** *or (old, hum)* **gekrischen** [gə'krɪʃn] to screech; *(Vogel auch)* to squawk; *(Reifen, Bremsen auch)* to squeal; *(Mensch auch)* to shriek, to squeal

Kreis-: Kreis|dia|gramm NT pie *or* circular chart; **Kreis|durch|mes|ser** M diameter (of a/the circle)

Krei|sel ['kraizl] M **-s, -** *(Tech)* gyroscope; *(= Spielzeug)* (spinning) top; *(inf: im Verkehr)* roundabout *(Brit)*, traffic circle *(US)*, rotary *(US)*; **den ~ schlagen** to spin the top

Krei|sel-: Krei|sel|be|we|gung F gyration; **Krei|sel|kom|pass** M gyroscopic compass, gyrocompass

krei|seln ['kraizln] VI **a** *aux sein or haben (= sich drehen)* to spin around, to gyrate **b** *(= mit Kreisel spielen)* to play with a top, to spin a top

krei|sen ['kraizn] VI *aux sein or haben* to circle *(um* (a)round, *über +dat* over); *(um eine Achse)* to revolve *(um* around); *(Satellit, Planet)* to orbit *(um etw* sth), to circle *(um etw* (a)round sth); *(Blut, Öl etc)* to circulate *(in +dat* through); *(fig: Gedanken, Wünsche, Gespräch)* to revolve *(um* around); **die Arme ~ lassen** to swing one's arms around (in a circle); **den Becher ~ lassen** to hand the cup (a)round

Kreis-: Kreis|flä|che F circle; *(= Kreisinhalt)* area of a/the circle; **kreis|för|mig** ADJ circular ADV **sich ~ bewegen** to move in a circle; **~ angelegt** arranged in a circle; **sich ~ aufstellen** to form a circle; **kreis|frei** ADJ **~e Stadt** *town which is an administrative district in its own right*; **Kreis|in|halt** M area of a/the circle; **Kreis|kol|ben|mo|tor** M rotary piston engine; **Kreis|kran|ken|haus** NT district hospital

Kreis|lauf M *(= Blutkreislauf, Ölkreislauf, von Geld)* circulation; *(der Natur, des Wassers)* cycle

Kreis|lauf-: Kreis|lauf|kol|laps M circulatory collapse; **Kreis|lauf|mit|tel** NT cardiac stimulant; **kreis|lauf|sta|bi|li|sie|rend** ADJ stabilizing blood circulation; **Kreis|lauf|stö|run|gen** PL circulation *or* circulatory trouble *sing or* disorders *pl*

Kreis-: Kreis|li|nie F circle; **vom Mittelpunkt durch die ~** from the centre *(Brit) or* center *(US)* through the circumference (of a/the circle); **kreis|rund** ADJ (perfectly) circular; **Kreis|sä|ge** F circular saw; *(inf: = Hut)* boater; **Kreis|seg|ment** NT segment (of a/the circle)

krei|ßen ['kraisn] VI *(old)* to be in labour *(Brit) or* labor *(US)*; **der Berg kreißt und gebiert eine Maus** *(prov)* the mountain laboured *(Brit) or* labored *(US)* and brought forth a mouse

Kreiß|saal M delivery room

Kreis-: Kreis|stadt F chief town of a district, district town, ≈ county town *(Brit)*; **Kreis|tag** M district assembly, ≈ county council *(Brit)*; **Kreis|um|fang** M circumference (of a/the circle); **Kreis|ver|kehr** M roundabout *(Brit) or* rotary *(US)* traffic; *(= Kreisel)* roundabout *(Brit)*, traffic circle *(US)*, rotary *(US)*; **im ~ muss man ...** on a roundabout *etc* one must ...; **dort gibt es viel ~** there are a lot of roundabouts *etc* there; **Kreis|ver|wal|tung** F district administration; *(= Behörde)* district *or* local *(esp Brit)* authority; **Kreis|wehr|er|satz|amt** NT district recruiting office; **Kreis|zahl** F, *no pl (Math)* pi

Kre|ma|to|ri|um [krema'to:riʊm] NT **-s, Krematorien** [-riən] crematorium

Kre|me *etc* = **Creme** *etc*

kre|mig ['kre:mɪç] ADJ = **cremig**

Kreml ['kre:ml, 'krɛml] M **-s der ~** the Kremlin

Kreml-: Kreml-Ast|ro|lo|ge M, **Kreml-Ast|ro|lo|gin** F *(Pol sl)* Kremlin watcher; **Kreml|chef(in)** M(F) Kremlin chief

Krem|pe ['krɛmpə] F **-, -n** *(= Hutkrempe)* brim; **ein Hut mit breiter ~** a broad-brimmed hat

Krem|pel ['krɛmpl] M **-s,** *no pl (inf) (= Sachen)* stuff *(inf)*, things *pl*; *(= wertloses Zeug)* junk, rubbish; **ich werfe den ganzen ~ hin** I'm chucking the whole lot *or* business in *(inf)*; **dann kannst du deinen ~ allein machen** then you can (damn well *(inf)*) do it yourself

Krem|pel F **-, -n** carding machine

Krem|pel|arm M *(Fashion)* rolled sleeve

krem|peln ['krɛmpln] VT **a** *(Tex)* to card **b** → **hochkrempeln, umkrempeln** *etc*

Kren [kre:n] M **-s,** *no pl (Aus)* horseradish

Kre|o|le [kre'o:lə] M **-n, -n**, **Kre|o|lin** [-'o:lɪn] F **-, -nen** Creole

kre|o|lisch [kre'o:lɪʃ] ADJ Creole

Kre|o|lisch(e) NT Creole → *auch* **Deutsch(e)**

kre|pie|ren [kre'pi:rən] *ptp* **krepiert** VI *aux sein* **a** *(= platzen)* to explode, to go off **b** *(inf) (= sterben)* to croak (it) *(inf)*, to snuff it *(Brit inf)*, to kick the bucket *(inf)*; *(= elend sterben)* to die a wretched death; **das Tier ist ihm krepiert** the animal died on him *(inf)*

Krepp [krɛp] M **-s, -e** *or* **-s** crepe

Krepp [krɛp] F **-, -s** *(Cook)* crêpe

Krepp|pa|pier NT crepe paper

Krepp|soh|le F crepe sole

Kres|se ['krɛsə] F **-,** *no pl* cress

Kre|ta ['kre:ta] NT **-s** Crete

Kre|ter ['kre:tɐ] M **-s, -**, **Kre|te|rin** [-ərɪn] F **-, -nen** Cretan

Kre|thi und Ple|thi ['kre:ti ʊnt 'ple:ti] PL *no art (inf)* every Tom, Dick and Harry

Kre|tin [kre'tɛ̃:] M **-s, -s** *(Med, pej)* cretin

Kre|ti|nis|mus [kreti'nɪsmʊs] M **-,** *no pl (Med)* cretinism

kre|tisch ['kre:tɪʃ] ADJ Cretan

Kre|ton [kre'to:n] M **-s, -e** *(Aus)*, **Kre|ton|ne** [kre'tɔn] M OR F **-, -s** *(Tex)* cretonne

kreucht [krɔyçt] *(obs, poet) 3. pers sing pres von* **kriechen**; **alles was da ~ und fleucht** all living creatures, all things that do creep and fly *(poet)*

kreuz [krɔyts] ADV **~ und quer** all over; **~ und quer durch die Gegend fahren** to travel *or (im Auto)* drive all over the place

Kreuz [krɔyts] NT **-es, -e** **a** cross; *(als Anhänger etc)* crucifix; **das ~ des Südens** *(Astron)* the Southern Cross; **jdn ans ~ schlagen** *or* **nageln** to nail sb to the cross; **ein ~ schlagen** *or* **machen** to make the sign of the cross; *(= sich bekreuzigen auch)* to cross oneself; **zwei Gegenstände über ~ legen** to put two objects crosswise one on top of the other; **mit jdm über ~ sein** *or* **stehen** *(fig)* to be on bad terms with sb; **sein ~ auf sich nehmen** *(fig)* to take up one's cross; **es ist ein** *or* **ich habe mein ~ mit ihm/damit** he's/it's an awful problem; **ich mache drei ~e, wenn er geht** *(inf)* it'll be such a relief when he has gone; **er machte ein ~ (als Unterschrift/am Rand)** he put a cross (for his signature/in the margin); **zu ~e kriechen** *(fig)* to eat humble pie, to eat crow *(US)*

b *(Anat)* small of the back; *(von Tier)* back; **ich habe Schmerzen im ~** I've got (a) backache; **ich habs im ~** *(inf)* I have back trouble; **aufs ~ fallen** to fall on one's back; *(fig inf)* to be staggered *(inf)*, to fall through the floor *(inf)*; **jdn aufs ~ legen** to throw sb on his back; *(fig inf)* to take sb for a ride *(inf)* → **leiern**

c *(Archit: = Fensterkreuz)* mullion and transom

d *(Mus)* sharp

e *(= Autobahnkreuz)* intersection **f** *(Cards) (= Farbe)* clubs *pl*; *(= Karte)* club; **die ~dame** the Queen of Clubs **g** *(Typ)* dagger, obelisk

Kreuz F **in die ~ und in die Quer** this way and that

Kreuz-: **Kreuz|ab|nah|me** F Descent from the Cross; **Kreuz|band** [-bant] NT *pl* **-bänder a** *(Anat)* cruciate ligament **b** *(Post: = Streifband)* wrapper; **kreuz|bar** ADJ *(Biol)* crossable; **Kreuz|bein** NT *(Anat)* sacrum; *(von Tieren)* rump-bone; **Kreuz|blu|me** F *(Bot)* milkwort; *(Archit)* finial; **Kreuz|blüt|ler** [-blyːtlɐ] M **-s, -** cruciferous plant; **kreuz|brav** ADJ *Kind* terribly good *or* well-behaved, as good as gold; *Benehmen, Karriere* faultless; *Film, Theaterstück etc* conventional ADV *inszenieren, aufführen* conventionally; **sich ~ benehmen** to be terribly well-behaved

kreu|zen [ˈkrɔytsn] VT to cross *(auch Biol)*; **die Degen** *or* **Klingen** *or* **Schwerter mit jdm ~** *(lit, fig)* to cross swords with sb; **die Arme ~** to fold *or* cross one's arms; **die Beine ~** to cross one's legs; **jds Weg ~** to cross sb's path VR to cross; *(Meinungen, Interessen)* to clash; *(Biol)* to interbreed; **unsere Wege haben sich nie wieder gekreuzt** our paths have never crossed again; **die Briefe haben sich gekreuzt** the letters crossed in the post *(Brit)* or mail VI *aux haben or sein (Naut)* to cruise; *(= Zickzack fahren)* to tack

Kreu|zer [ˈkrɔytsɐ] M **-s, - a** *(Naut)* cruiser **b** *(Hist: = Münze)* kreutzer

Kreu|zes-: **Kreu|zes|tod** [ˈkrɔytsəs-] M (death by) crucifixion; **den ~ erleiden** to die on the cross; **Kreu|zes|zei|chen** NT sign of the cross

Kreuz-: **Kreuz|fah|rer** M *(Hist)* crusader; **Kreuz|fahrt** F **a** *(Naut)* cruise; **eine ~ machen** to go on a cruise **b** *(Hist)* crusade; **Kreuz|feu|er** NT *(Mil, fig)* crossfire; **im ~ (der Kritik) stehen** *(fig)* to be under fire (from all sides); **ins ~ (der Kritik) geraten** *(fig)* to come under fire (from all sides); **kreuz|fi|del** ADJ *(inf)* happy as a sandboy *(Brit inf)* or lark; **kreuz|för|mig** ADJ cross-shaped, cruciform *(form)* ADV in the shape of a cross; **etw ~ anordnen** to arrange sth crossways *or* crosswise; **Kreuz|gang** M *pl* **-gänge** cloister; **Kreuz|ge|lenk** NT *(Tech)* universal joint; **Kreuz|ge|wöl|be** NT *(Archit)* cross *or* groin vault

kreu|zi|gen [ˈkrɔytsɪgn] VT to crucify

Kreu|zi|gung [ˈkrɔytsɪgʊŋ] F **-, -en** crucifixion

Kreuz-: **Kreuz|kno|ten** M reef knot; **Kreuz|küm|mel** M cumin; **kreuz|lahm** ADJ *Pferd* broken-backed; *(inf) Mensch* exhausted; **Kreuz|läh|me** [-lɛːmə] **-, -n** F *(Vet)* paralysis of the hindquarters; **Kreuz|mast** M *(Naut)* mizzen mast; **Kreuz|ot|ter** F *(Zool)* adder, viper; **Kreuz|reim** M *(Liter)* alternate rhyme; **Kreuz|rip|pen|ge|wöl|be** NT *(Archit)* ribbed vault; **Kreuz|rit|ter** M *(Hist)* crusader; *(vom deutschen Ritterorden)* knight of the Teutonic Order; **Kreuz|schiff** NT **a** *(Naut)* cruise ship; *(größer)* cruise liner **b** *(Archit: in Kirche)* transept; **Kreuz|schlitz|schrau|be** F Phillips® screw; **Kreuz|schlitz|schrau|ben|zie|her** M Phillips® screwdriver; **Kreuz|schlüs|sel** M wheel brace; **Kreuz|schmer|zen** PL backache *sing*, pains *pl* in the small of the back; **Kreuz|schna|bel** M *(Orn)* crossbill; **Kreuz|spin|ne** F *(Zool)* garden *or* cross spider; **kreuz|stän|dig** ADJ *(Bot)* decussate; **Kreuz|stich** M *(Sew)* cross-stitch

Kreu|zung [ˈkrɔytsʊŋ] F **-, -en a** *(= Straßenkreuzung)* crossroads *sing*, intersection *(esp US)* **b** *(= das Kreuzen)* crossing; *(von Tieren)* crossing, cross-breeding, interbreeding **c** *(= Rasse)* hybrid; *(= Tiere)* cross, cross-breed

kreuz|un|glück|lich ADJ absolutely miserable

kreu|zungs|frei ADJ *Strecke, Ausbau* without crossroads

Kreuz-: **Kreuz|ver|band** M *(Med)* crossed bandage; *(Build)* cross bond; **Kreuz|ver|hör** NT cross-examination; **jdn ins ~ nehmen** to cross-examine sb; **Kreuz|weg** M **a** *(= Wegkreuzung, fig)* crossroads *sing* **b** *(Rel: = Christi Leidensweg)* way of the cross; **den ~ beten** to do the stations of the cross; **Kreuz|weh** NT *(inf)* backache; **kreuz|wei|se** ADV crosswise, crossways; **du kannst mich ~!** *(inf)* (you can) get stuffed! *(Brit inf)*, you can kiss my ass! *(US sl)*; **Kreuz|wort|rät|sel** NT crossword puzzle; **Kreuz|zei|chen** NT sign of the cross; **Kreuz|zug** M *(lit, fig)* crusade

Kre|vet|te [kreˈvɛtə] F **-, -n** shrimp

krib|be|lig [ˈkrɪbəlɪç] ADJ *(inf)* fidgety, edgy *(inf)*; *(= kribbelnd)* tingly *(inf)*

krib|beln [ˈkrɪbln] VT *(= kitzeln)* to tickle; *(= jucken)* to make itch; *(= prickeln)* to make tingle VI **a** *(= jucken)* to itch, to tickle; *(= prickeln)* to prickle, to tingle; **auf der Haut ~** to cause a prickling sensation; *(angenehm)* to make the skin tingle; **es kribbelt mir im Fuß** *(lit)* I have pins and needles in my foot; **es kribbelt mir in den Fingern, etw zu tun** *(inf)* I'm itching to do sth; **ein Kribbeln im Bauch haben** to have a feeling of anticipation in one's stomach **b** *aux sein (Insekten)* **~ (und krabbeln)** to scurry *or* swarm (around); **es kribbelt von Ameisen** the place is crawling *or* swarming *or* teeming with ants; **es kribbelt und krabbelt wie in einem Ameisenhaufen** it's like an ant hill

kribb|lig [ˈkrɪblɪç] ADJ = **kribbelig**

kri|cke|lig [ˈkrɪkəlɪç] ADJ, ADV *(inf)* = **krakelig**

Kri|ckel|kra|kel [ˈkrɪklˈkraːkl] NT **-s, -** *(inf)* scrawl, scribble; *(= Krakeln)* scrawling, scribbling

kri|ckeln [ˈkrɪkln] VI *(inf)* to scrawl, to scribble

Kri|cket [ˈkrɪkət] NT **-s, -s** *(Sport)* cricket

Kri|da [ˈkriːda] F **-**, *no pl* faked bankruptcy

krie|chen [ˈkriːçn] *pret* **kroch** [krɔx], *ptp* **gekrochen** [gəˈkrɔxn] VI *aux sein* to creep *(auch Pflanze, Tech)*, to crawl *(auch Schlange)*; *(= langsam fahren)* to creep *or* crawl (along); *(fig: Zeit)* to creep by; *(fig: = unterwürfig sein)* to grovel *(vor +dat* before), to crawl *(vor +dat* to); **aus dem Ei ~** to hatch (out); **ins Bett ~** *(inf)* to go to bed; *(sehr müde, erschöpft)* to crawl into bed; **auf allen vieren ~** to crawl on all fours; **unter die Bettdecke ~** to slip under the covers *or* blankets; **die Kälte kroch mir in die Knochen** the cold seeped into my bones → **Arsch, Kreuz, Leim**

Krie|cher [ˈkriːçɐ] M **-s, -**, **Krie|che|rin** [-ərɪn] F **-, -nen** *(inf)* groveller *(Brit)*, groveler *(US)*, bootlicker *(inf)*, crawler *(Brit inf)*

krie|che|risch [ˈkriːçərɪʃ] *(inf)* ADJ grovelling *(Brit)*, groveling *(US)*, servile, bootlicking *attr (inf)* ADV **sich ~ benehmen/verhalten** to grovel

Kriech-: **Kriech|gang** [-gaŋ] M, *no pl* crawling gear; **Kriech|spur** F crawler lane; **Kriech|strom** M *(Elec)* leakage current; **Kriech|tier** NT *(Zool)* reptile

Krieg [kriːk] M **-(e)s, -e** [-gə] war; *(= Art der Kriegsführung)* warfare; **~ der Sterne** *(Pol)* Star Wars; **~ anfangen mit** to start a war with; **einer Partei** *etc* **den ~ erklären** *(fig)* to declare war on a party *etc*; **~ führen (mit** *or* **gegen)** to wage war (on); **~ führend** belligerent, warring; **in ~ und Frieden** in war and in peace; **im ~(e)** in war; *(als Soldat)* away in the war, away fighting; **im ~ sein** *or* **stehen (mit), ~ haben (mit), sich im ~ befinden (mit)** to be at war (with); **im ~e fallen, im ~ bleiben** to be killed in the war *or* in action; **in den ~ ziehen** to go to war; **in einem ständigen ~ leben** *(fig)* to be constantly feuding

krie|gen [ˈkriːgn] VT *(inf)* to get; *Zug, Bus, Schnupfen, Weglaufenden auch* to catch; *Schlaganfall, eine Spritze, Besuch auch* to have; *Junge, ein Kind* to have; **sie kriegt ein Kind** she's going to have a baby; **graue Haare ~** to get grey *(Brit) or* gray *(US)* hairs, to go grey *(Brit) or* gray *(US)*; **eine Glatze ~** to go bald; **es mit jdm zu tun ~** to be in trouble with sb; **wenn ich dich kriege!** just you wait till I catch you!; **sie ~ sich** *(in Kitschroman)* boy gets girl; **dann kriege ich zu viel** then it gets too much for me; **was kriegt der Herr?** yes sir, what will you have?; **ich kriege ein Steak** I'll have a steak; **~ Sie schon?** are you being *or* have you been served?; **wenn du nicht sofort aufhörst, kriegst du ein paar!** *(inf)* if you don't stop that right now, I'll belt you! *(inf)*; **ich kriegs im Kopf** *(inf)* I'm about to go nuts *(inf)*; **jdn dazu ~, etw zu tun** to get sb to do sth; **etw gemacht ~** to get sth done; **das kriege ich einfach nicht übersetzt** I just can't get it translated; **kann ich das bestätigt ~?** can I have *or* get that confirmed? → **Kurve**

Krie|gen NT **-s**, *no pl* (game of) tag

Krie|ger [ˈkriːgɐ] M **-s, -**, **Krie|ge|rin** [-ərɪn] F **-, -nen** warrior; *(= Indianerkrieger)* brave; **alter ~** veteran (soldier), old campaigner *or* warhorse; **ein müder ~ sein** *(fig inf)* to have no go left in one

Krie|ger|denk|mal NT war memorial

krie|ge|risch [ˈkriːgərɪʃ] ADJ warlike *no adv*; *Haltung auch* belligerent; *Einsatz* military; **eine ~e Auseinandersetzung** fighting *no pl*, military conflict ADV *auftreten, eingestellt sein* belligerently; **sich ~ auseinandersetzen** to engage in military conflict; **einen Konflikt ~ austragen** to resolve a conflict by military means

Krie|ger|wit|we F war widow

Krieg-: **krieg|füh|rend** ADJ → **Krieg**; **Krieg|füh|ren|de(r)** MF *decl as adj* **die ~n** the belligerents; **Krieg|füh|rung** F warfare *no art*; *(eines Feldherrn)* conduct of the war

Kriegs-: **Kriegs|an|lei|he** F war loan; **Kriegs|aus|bruch** M outbreak of war; **es kam zum ~** war broke out; **kriegs|be|dingt** ADJ resulting from *or* caused by (the) war; **Kriegs|be|ginn** M start of the war; **Kriegs|beil** NT tomahawk; **das ~ begraben** *(fig)* to bury the hatchet; **das ~ ausgraben** *(fig)* to start a fight; **Kriegs|be|ma|lung** F *(lit, hum)* war paint; **Kriegs|be|richt|er|stat|ter(in)** M(F) war correspondent; **kriegs|be|schä|digt** [-bəʃɛːdɪçt] ADJ war-disabled; **Kriegs|be|schä|dig|te(r)** MF *decl as adj* war-disabled person; **die ~n** the war disabled; **Kriegs|blin|de(r)** MF *decl as adj* **die ~n** the war-blind

Kriegs|dienst M *(old, form)* military service; **den ~ verweigern** to be a conscientious objector

Kriegs|dienst-: **Kriegs|dienst|ver|wei|ge|rer** [-fɛɐvaigərɐ] M **-s, -**, **Kriegs|dienst|ver|wei|ge|rin** [-ərɪn] F **-, -nen** conscientious objector; **Kriegs|dienst|ver|wei|ge|rung** F refusal to fight in a war

Kriegs-: **Kriegs|ein|wir|kung** F effects *pl or* aftermath *no pl* of war; **Kriegs|en|de** NT end of the war; **Kriegs|ent|schä|di|gun|gen** PL reparations *pl*; **Kriegs|er|klä|rung** F declaration of war; **Kriegs|er|leb|nis** NT wartime experience; **Kriegs|fall** M (eventuality of a) war; **dann träte der ~ ein** then war would break out; **Kriegs|film** M war film; **Kriegs|flag|ge** F naval ensign; **Kriegs|flot|te** F navy, fleet; **Kriegs|fol|ge** F consequence of (a/the) war; **Kriegs|frei|wil|li|ge(r)** MF *decl as adj* (wartime) volunteer; **Kriegs|fuß** M *(inf)* **mit jdm auf ~ stehen** to be at loggerheads with sb *(esp Brit)*, to be at odds with sb; **Kriegs|ge|biet** NT war zone; **Kriegs|ge|fahr** F danger of war; **~ zieht herauf** *(geh)* the war clouds are gathering; **Kriegs|ge|fan|ge|ne(r)** MF *decl as adj* prisoner of war, P.O.W.; **Kriegs|ge|fan|gen|schaft** F captivity; **in ~ sein** to be a prisoner of war; **aus der ~ kommen** to return *or* be released from captivity; **Kriegs|geg|ner(in)** M(F) **a** opponent of a/the war; *(= Pazifist)* pacifist, opponent of war **b** *(= Gegner im Krieg)* wartime enemy; **Kriegs|ge|rät** NT military equipment; **Kriegs|ge|richt** NT (wartime) court martial; **jdn vor ein ~ stellen** to court-martial sb; **kriegs|ge|schä|digt** [-gəʃɛːdɪçt] ADJ war-damaged; **Kriegs|ge|schrei** NT war cry; **Kriegs|ge|winn|ler** [-gəvɪnlɐ] M **-s, -**, **Kriegs|ge|winn|le|rin** [-ərɪn] F **-, -nen** *(pej)* war-profiteer; **Kriegs|glück** NT *(liter)* fortunes *pl* of war; **dann verließ Hannibal sein ~** then the fortunes of war turned against *or* deserted Hannibal; **Kriegs|gott** M god of war; **Kriegs|göt|tin** F goddess of war; **Kriegs|grä|ber|für|sor|ge** F War Graves Commission; **Kriegs|gräu|el** PL war atrocities *pl*; **Kriegs|grund** M reason for war; **Kriegs|ha|fen** M naval port, naval harbour *(Brit) or* harbor *(US)*; **Kriegs|hand|werk** NT *(old)* soldiering; **Kriegs|held** M great warrior; *(in moderner Zeit)* military hero; **Kriegs|hel|din** F great warrior; *(in moderner Zeit)* military heroine; **Kriegs|herr(in)** M(F) warlord; **oberster ~** *(Hist)* commander-in-chief; **Kriegs|het|ze** F war-mongering; **Kriegs|in|va|li|de** M, **Kriegs|in|va|li|din** F *decl as adj* war-disabled person; **Kriegs|jahr** NT year of war; **die ~e** the war years; **im ~ 1945** (during the war) in 1945; **im dritten ~** in the third year of the war; **Kriegs|ka|me|rad(in)** M(F) fellow soldier, war(time) comrade; **Kriegs|kas|se** F war chest; **Kriegs|kind** NT war baby; **Kriegs|kos|ten** PL cost of the war *sing*; **Kriegs|kunst** F art of war(fare); **Kriegs|list** F *(old, liter)* ruse of war, stratagem; **Kriegs|ma|ri|ne** F navy; **Kriegs|ma|schi|ne|rie** F machinery of war; **kriegs|mä|ßig** ADJ for war; *Kleidung, Bemalung* war- ADV **~ gekleidet/ausgerüstet** dressed/equipped for war; **die Indianer waren ~ bemalt** the Indians wore war paint; **ein ~ vorbereitetes Land** a country prepared for war; **~ klingende Musik** martial music; **Kriegs|mi|nis|ter(in)** M(F) *(Hist, Pol pej)* minister of war; **Kriegs|mi|nis|te|ri|um** NT *(Hist)* War Office *(Brit)*, War Department *(US)*; **kriegs|mü|de** ADJ war-weary; **Kriegs|op|fer** NT war victim; **Kriegs|pfad** M *(liter)* **auf dem ~** on the warpath; **Kriegs|rat** M council of war; **~ halten** *(fig)* to have a pow-wow *(inf)*; **Kriegs|recht** NT conventions of war *pl*; *(Mil)* martial law; **Kriegs|schä|den** PL war damage; **Kriegs|schau|platz** M theatre *(Brit) or* theater *(US)* of war; **Kriegs|schiff** NT warship, man-of--war; **Kriegs|schuld** F war guilt; **Kriegs|schul|den** PL war debts *pl*; **Kriegs|spiel** NT war game; **Kriegs|spiel|zeug** NT war toy; **Kriegs|stär|ke** F war establishment; **die Armee auf ~ bringen** to make the army ready for war; **Kriegs|teil|neh|mer** M combatant; *(= Staat)* combatant nation, belligerent; *(= ehemaliger Soldat)* ex-serviceman; **Kriegs|teil|neh|me|rin** F combatant; *(= ehemalige Soldatin)* ex--servicewoman; **Kriegs|to|te(r)** MF *decl as adj* war dead; **30.000 ~** 30,000 killed in action; **Kriegs|trau|ung** F war wedding; **Kriegs|trei|ber** M **-s, -**, **Kriegs|trei|be|rin** F **-, -nen** *(pej)* warmonger; **kriegs|tüch|tig** ADJ *(old)* fit for active service; **kriegs|un|taug|lich** ADJ unfit for active service; **Kriegs|ver|bre|chen** NT war crime; **Kriegs|ver|bre|cher(in)** M(F) war criminal; **Kriegs|ver|let|zung** F war wound; **kriegs|ver|sehrt** ADJ war-disabled; **Kriegs|ver|sehr|te(r)** MF *decl as adj* war-disabled person; **die Kriegsversehrten** the war-disabled; **kriegs|ver|wen|dungs|fä|hig** ADJ *(form)* fit for active service; **Kriegs|waf|fe** F weapon of war; **Kriegs|wir|ren** PL *(geh)* chaos of war *sing*; **Kriegs|wirt|schaft** F war economy; **Kriegs|zeit** F wartime; **in ~en** in times of war; **sie erzählten von ihrer ~** they told about their wartime experiences; **kriegs|zer|stört** ADJ destroyed in (the) war *pred*; **Kriegs|zug** M *(old)* campaign, military expedition; **Kriegs|zu|stand** M state of war; **im ~** at war

Kriek|en|te ['kri:k-] F (green-winged) teal

Krill [krɪl] M **-(s)**, *no pl (Biol)* krill

Krim [krɪm] F **- die ~** the Crimea

Kri|mi ['kri:mi] M **-s, -s** *(inf)* (crime) thriller; *(rätselhaft)* murder mystery, whodunnit *(inf)*; *(= Buch: mit Detektiv als Held)* detective novel

Kri|mi|nal|be|am|te(r) [krimi'na:l-] M *decl as adj*, **Kri|mi|nal|be|am|tin** F detective, CID officer *(Brit)*

Kri|mi|na|le(r) [krimi'na:lə] M *decl as adj (sl)* plain-clothes man, detective, CID officer *(Brit)*

Kri|mi|nal-: **Kri|mi|nal|film** M crime thriller *or* film *or* movie *(esp US)*; *(rätselhaft)* murder mystery, whodunnit *(inf)*; **Kri|mi|nal|ge|richt** NT criminal court; **Kri|mi|nal|gro|tes|ke** F black comedy; **Kri|mi|nal|hör|spiel** NT radio thriller; *(rätselhaft)* murder mystery, whodunnit *(inf)*

kri|mi|na|li|sie|ren *ptp* **kriminalisiert** VT to criminalize

Kri|mi|na|list M **-en, -en**, **Kri|mi|na|lis|tin** F **-, -nen** criminologist

Kri|mi|na|lis|tik F **-**, *no pl* criminology

kri|mi|na|lis|tisch ADJ criminological; **~er Spürsinn besitzen** to have a nose for solving crimes ADV **~ begabt sein** to have a talent for solving crimes

Kri|mi|na|li|tät F **-**, *no pl* crime; *(= Ziffer)* crime rate; **organisierte ~** organized crime

Kri|mi|nal-: **Kri|mi|nal|kom|mis|sar(in)** M(F) detective superintendent; **Kri|mi|nal|ko|mö|die** F comedy thriller; **Kri|mi|nal|li|te|ra|tur** F crime literature; **Kri|mi|nal|mu|se|um** NT crime museum; **Kri|mi|nal|po|li|zei** F criminal investigation department; **Kri|mi|nal|po|li|zist(in)** M(F) detective, CID officer *(Brit)*; **Kri|mi|nal|ro|man** M → **Krimi** (crime) thriller; detective novel; murder mystery, whodunnit *(inf)*; **Kri|mi|nal|stück** NT → **Krimi** thriller; detective play; murder mystery, whodunnit *(inf)*; **kri|mi|nal|tech|nisch** ADJ forensic ADV forensically

kri|mi|nell [krimi'nɛl] ADJ *(lit, fig inf)* criminal; **~ werden** to turn to crime, to become a criminal; *(junger Mensch auch)* to become delinquent; **~e Energie** criminal resolve ADV **a** *fährlässig* criminally **b** *(inf: = gefährlich) glatt, schlüpfrig, schnell* dangerously

Kri|mi|nel|le(r) [krimi'nɛlə] MF *decl as adj* criminal

Kri|mi|no|lo|ge [krimino'lo:gə] M **-n, -n**, **Kri|mi|no|lo|gin** [-'lo:gɪn] F **-, -nen** criminologist

Kri|mi|no|lo|gie [kriminolo'gi:] F **-**, *no pl* criminology

kri|mi|no|lo|gisch [krimino'lo:gɪʃ] ADJ criminological

Krim|krieg M Crimean War

Krims|krams ['krɪmskrams] M **-es**, *no pl (inf)* odds and ends *pl*, bits and pieces *pl*, rubbish

Krin|gel ['krɪŋl] M **-s, -** *(der Schrift)* squiggle; *(Cook: = Zuckerkringel etc)* ring

krin|ge|lig ['krɪŋəlɪç] ADJ crinkly; **sich ~ lachen** *(inf)* to laugh oneself silly *(inf)*, to kill oneself (laughing) *(inf)*

krin|geln ['krɪŋln] VR to go frizzy, to curl; **sich ~ vor Lachen** *(inf)* to kill oneself (laughing) *(inf)*

Kri|no|li|ne [krino'li:nə] F **-, -n** *(Hist)* crinoline

Kri|po ['kri:po, 'krɪpo] F **-, -s** *(inf) abbr von* **Kriminalpolizei**; **die ~** the cops *pl (inf)*, the CID *(Brit)*

Kri|po- *in cpds (inf)* police; **Kri|po|be|am|te(r)** M *decl as adj*, **Kri|po|be|am|tin** F police detective

Krip|pe ['krɪpə] F **-, -n** **a** *(= Futterkrippe)* (hay)-rack, (hay)box; **sich an die ~ drängen** *(fig)* to start jockeying for position; **an der ~ sitzen** *(fig)* to live a life of ease, to live in comfort **b** *(= Kinderkrippe, Weihnachtskrippe)* crib; *(Bibl)* crib, manger **c** *(= Kinderhort)* crèche *(Brit)*, daycare centre *(Brit) or* center *(US)* **d** *(Astron)* Manger

Krip|pen-: **Krip|pen|spiel** NT nativity play; **Krip|pen|tod** M cot death *(Brit)*, crib death *(US)*

krisch *(old, hum) pret von* **kreischen**

Kri|se ['kri:zə] F **-, -n** crisis; **in eine ~ geraten** to enter a state of crisis; **er hatte eine schwere ~** he was going through a difficult crisis; **die ~ kriegen** *(inf)* to do one's nut *(Brit inf)*, to go crazy *(inf)*

kri|seln ['kri:zln] VI *impers (inf)* **es kriselt** there is a crisis looming, trouble is brewing; **in seiner Ehe kriselt es** trouble's brewing in his marriage

Kri|sen-: **kri|sen|an|fäl|lig** ADJ crisis-prone; **Kri|sen|an|fäl|lig|keit** F **wegen der ~ dieser Gegend** as this area is so crisis-prone; **kri|sen|fest** ADJ stable, crisis-proof ADV **Geld ~ in Grundbesitz anlegen** to invest money in property to secure it against *or* to hedge against economic crises; **Kri|sen|fes|tig|keit** F stability (in the face of a crisis); **Kri|sen|ge|biet** NT crisis area; **kri|sen|ge|schüt|telt** [-gəʃʏtlt] ADJ crisis-ridden; **kri|sen|haft** ADJ *Situation, Entwicklung* critical ADV critically; **Kri|sen|herd** M flash point, trouble spot; **Kri|sen|ma|nage|ment** NT crisis management; **Kri|sen|ma|na|ger(in)** M(F) crisis manager; **Kri|sen|plan** M contingency plan; **Kri|sen|re|gi|on** F trouble spot; **kri|sen|si|cher** ADJ stable, crisis-proof ADV **Geld ~ in Grundbesitz anlegen** to invest money in property to secure it against *or* to hedge against economic crises; **Kri|sen|si|tu|a|ti|on** F crisis (situation); **Kri|sen|sit|zung** F emergency session; **Kri|sen|stab** M (special) action *or* crisis committee; **Kri|sen|stim|mung** F crisis mood, mood of crisis

Kri|sis ['kri:zɪs] F **-, Krisen** ['kri:zn] *(liter)* crisis

Kris|tall [krɪs'tal] M **-s, -e** crystal; **~e bilden** to crystallize, to form crystals

Kris|tall NT **-s**, *no pl (= Kristallglas)* crystal (glass); *(= Kristallwaren)* crystalware, crystal goods *pl*

Kris|tall|bil|dung F crystallization

kris|tal|len [krɪs'talən] ADJ (made of) crystal; *Stimme* crystal-clear

Kristalleuchter △ M → **Kristallleuchter**

Kris|tall-: **Kris|tall|git|ter** NT crystal lattice; **Kris|tall|glas** NT crystal glass

kris|tal|lin [krɪsta'li:n], **kris|tal|li|nisch** [krɪsta'li:nɪʃ] ADJ crystalline

Kris|tal|li|sa|ti|on [krɪstaliza'tsio:n] F **-, -en** crystallization

Kris|tal|li|sa|ti|ons|punkt M *(fig)* focal point

kris|tal|li|sie|ren [krɪstali'zi:rən] *ptp* **kristallisiert** VIR *(lit, fig)* to crystallize

Kris|tall-: **kris|tall|klar** ADJ crystal-clear; **Kris|tall|leuch|ter** M, **Kris|tall|lüs|ter** M *(geh)* crystal chandelier; **Kris|tall|nacht** F *(Hist)* Crystal night, *night of 9th/10th November 1938, during which the Nazis organized a pogrom throughout Germany, burning synagogues and breaking windows of Jewish shops*

Kristallüster △ M → **Kristalllüster**

Kris|tall-: **Kris|tall|wa|ren** PL crystalware *sing*, crystal goods *pl*; **Kris|tall|zu|cker** M refined sugar (in) crystals

Kri|te|ri|um [kri'te:riʊm] NT **-s, Kriterien** [-riən] **a** criterion **b** *(Radfahren)* circuit race

Kri|tik [kri'ti:k] F **-, -en** **a** *no pl* criticism *(an +dat* of); **an jdm/etw ~ üben** to criticize sb/sth; **auf (heftige) ~ stoßen** to come in for *or* to come under (severe) criticism; **Gesellschafts-/ /Literaturkritik** social/literary criticism; **unter aller *or* jeder ~ sein** *(inf)* to be beneath contempt **b** *(= Rezensieren)* criticism; *(= Rezension)* review, notice, crit *(inf)*; **eine gute ~ haben** to get good reviews *etc*; **der Film bekam schlechte ~en** the film got bad reviews *etc* **c** *no pl (= die Kritiker)* critics *pl* **d** *no pl (= Urteilsfähigkeit)* discrimination; **ohne jede ~** uncritically **e** *(Philos: = kritische Analyse)* critique

Kri|ti|kas|ter [kriti'kastɐ] M **-s, -**, **Kri|ti|kas|te|rin** [-ərɪn] F **-, -nen** *(dated pej)* caviller *(Brit)*, caviler *(US)*, fault-finder, criticaster *(rare)*

Kri|ti|ker ['kri:tikɐ] M **-s, -**, **Kri|ti|ke|rin** [-ərɪn] F **-, -nen** critic

Kri|tik-: **kri|tik|fä|hig** ADJ able to criticize; **Kri|tik|fä|hig|keit** F critical faculty; **kri|tik|-**

los ADJ uncritical ADV uncritically; **etw ~ hinnehmen** to accept sth without criticism *or* protest; **Kri|tik|punkt** M point of criticism; **es gibt noch einen weiteren ~** and there's another point which is open to criticism; **kri|tik|wür|dig** ADJ reprehensible

kri|tisch ['kri:tɪʃ] ADJ *(alle Bedeutungen)* critical; **wenn dieser Mitarbeiter auch noch ausfällt, dann wird es ~** if we lose this worker too things will become critical ADV *kommentieren, bewerten, sich äußern* critically; **~ eingestellt sein** to be critical; **sich jdm gegenüber ~ verhalten** to be critical of sb; **die Lage ~ beurteilen** to make a critical appraisal of the situation; **jdm/einer Sache ~ gegenüberstehen** to be critical of sb/sth, to regard *or* consider sb/sth critically

kri|ti|sie|ren [kriti'zi:rən] *ptp* **kritisiert** VTI to criticize; **er hat** *or* **findet an allem etwas zu ~** he always has *or* finds something to criticize

Kri|ti|zis|mus [kriti'tsɪsmʊs] M **-**, *no pl (Philos)* critical philosophy

Krit|te|lei [krɪtə'lai] F **-, -en** fault-finding *no pl*, cavilling *no pl (Brit)*, caviling *no pl (US)*

krit|teln ['krɪtln] VI to find fault *(an +dat, über +acc* with), to cavil *(an +dat, über +acc* at)

Krit|ze|lei [krɪtsə'lai] F **-, -en** scribble; *(= das Kritzeln)* scribbling; *(= Männchenmalen etc)* doodle; doodling; *(an Wänden)* graffiti

krit|zeln ['krɪtsln] VTI to scribble, to scrawl; *(= Männchen malen etc)* to doodle

Kro|a|te [kro'a:tə] M **-n, -n**, **Kro|a|tin** [-'a:tɪn] F **-, -nen** Croat, Croatian

Kro|a|ti|en [kro'a:tsiən] NT **-s** Croatia

kro|a|tisch [kro'a:tɪʃ] ADJ Croat, Croatian

Kro|a|tisch(e) [kro'a:tɪʃ] NT Croatian → *auch* **Deutsch(e)**

Kro|atz|bee|re [kro'ats-] F *(esp S Ger: = Brombeere)* blackberry, bramble

kroch *pret von* **kriechen**

Kro|cket(spiel) ['krɔkət-, krɔ'kɛt-] NT **-s**, *no pl* croquet

Kro|kant [kro'kant] M **-s**, *no pl (Cook)* cracknel

Kro|ket|te [kro'kɛtə] F **-, -n** *(Cook)* croquette

Kro|ko ['kro:ko] NT **-s**, *no pl* crocodile leather

Kro|ko|dil [kroko'di:l] NT **-s, -e** crocodile

Kro|ko|dil|le|der NT crocodile leather *or* skin

Kro|ko|dils|trä|nen PL crocodile tears *pl*

Kro|kus ['kro:kʊs] M **-, -** *or* **-se** crocus

Krön|chen ['krø:nçən] NT **-s, -** *dim von* **Krone**

Kro|ne ['kro:nə] F **-, -n** **a** crown; *(eines Grafen etc)* coronet; **die ~** *(fig)* the Crown **b** *(= Mauerkrone)* coping; *(= Schaumkrone)* cap, crest; *(= Zahnkrone)* crown, cap; *(an Uhr)* winder; *(= Geweihkrone)* surroyal (antler); *(= Baumkrone)* top; *(= Erntekrone)* harvest wreath *or* crown; **die ~ der Schöpfung** the pride of creation, creation's crowning glory; **die ~ des Lebens** *(Bibl)* (a) crown of life; **die ~ des Ganzen war, dass ...** *(fig)* (but) what crowned *or* capped it all was that ...; **das setzt doch allem die ~ auf** *(inf)* that beats everything; **das setzt der Dummheit die ~ auf** *(inf)* that beats everything for stupidity; **einen in der ~ haben** *(inf)* to be tipsy, to have had a drop too much; **dabei fällt dir keine Perle** *or* **kein Stein** *or* **Zacken aus der ~** *(inf)* it won't hurt you **c** *(= Währungseinheit) (in Tschechien, Slowakei)* crown; *(in Dänemark, Norwegen)* krone; *(in Schweden, Island)* krona

krö|nen ['krø:nən] VT *(lit, fig)* to crown; *Bauwerk* to crown, to top, to cap; **jdn zum König ~** to crown sb king; **von Erfolg gekrönt sein/werden** to be crowned with success; **gekrönte Häupter** crowned heads; **damit wurde ihre glänzende Laufbahn gekrönt** this was the crowning achievement in *or* the culmination of her career; **der ~de Abschluss** the culmination

Kro|nen-: **Kro|nen|kor|ken** M crown cap; **Kro|nen|mut|ter** F *pl* **-muttern** *(Tech)* castle nut

Kron- ['kro:n-]: **Kron|er|be** M heir to the crown *or* throne; **Kron|er|bin** F heiress to the crown *or* throne; **Kron|gut** NT crown estate; **Kron|ju|we|len** PL crown jewels *pl*; **Kron|ko|lo|nie** F crown colony; **Kron|kor|ken** M crown cap; **Kron|land** NT crown land; **Kron|leuch|ter** M chandelier; **Kron|prä|ten|dent(in)** M(F) pretender (to the crown); **Kron|prinz** M crown prince; *(in Großbritannien auch)* Prince of Wales; *(fig)* heir apparent; **Kron|prin|zes|sin** F crown princess; *(fig)* heir apparent

Krön|lein ['krø:nlain] NT **-s, -** *dim von* **Krone**

Kron|rat M crown council

Krons|bee|re ['kro:ns-] F *(N Ger: = Preiselbeere)* cranberry

Krö|nung ['krø:nʊŋ] F **-, -en** coronation; *(fig)* culmination; *(von Veranstaltung)* high point, culmination; *(Archit)* coping stone

Kron|zeu|ge ['kro:n-] M, **Kron|zeu|gin** F *(Jur)* person who gives *or* turns King's/Queen's evidence *(Brit) or* State's evidence *(US)*; *(= Hauptzeuge)* principal witness; *(fig)* main authority; **~ sein, als ~ auftreten** to turn King's/Queen's evidence *(Brit) or* State's evidence *(US)*; to appear as principal witness

Kron|zeu|gen|re|ge|lung ['kro:n-] F *(Jur) regulation guaranteeing a state witness from a terrorist background immunity from prosecution or a lenient sentence*

Kropf [krɔpf] M **-(e)s, =e** ['krœpfə] **a** *(von Vogel)* crop **b** *(Med)* goitre *(Brit)*, goiter *(US)*; **überflüssig wie ein ~** totally superfluous

Kröpf|chen ['krœpfçən] NT **-s, -** *dim von* **Kropf a**

kröp|fen ['krœpfn] VT *(= füttern, nudeln)* to cram VI *(= fressen: Raubvögel)* to gorge

Kropf|tau|be F pouter (pigeon)

Kropp|zeug ['krɔp-] NT, *no pl (pej inf: = Gesindel)* scum; **dieses ganze ~** all this junk *(inf)*

kross [krɔs] *(N Ger)* ADJ crisp; *Brötchen auch* crusty ADV *backen, braten* until crisp

Krö|sus ['krø:zʊs] M **-, -se** Croesus; **ich bin doch kein ~** *(inf)* I'm not made of money *(inf)*

Krö|te ['krø:tə] F **-, -n** **a** *(Zool)* toad; **eine freche (kleine) ~** *(inf)* a cheeky (little) minx *(Brit inf)*, a little devil *(esp US inf)*; **eine giftige ~** *(inf)* a spiteful creature; **eine ~ schlucken** *(fig inf)* to bite the bullet **b** **Kröten** PL *(inf)* pennies *(inf)*; **die paar ~n** the few pounds

Krö|ten|test M *(Med)* Hogben (pregnancy) test

Krü|cke ['krʏkə] F **-, -n** **a** crutch; *(fig)* prop, stay; **auf** *or* **an ~n** *(dat)* **gehen** to walk on crutches **b** *(= Schirmkrücke)* crook **c** *(zum Harken etc)* rake **d** *(inf) (= Nichtskönner)* dead loss *(inf)*, washout *(inf)*; *(= altes Fahrrad)* unfashionable bike

Krück|stock M walking stick → **Blinde(r)**

krud [kru:t], **kru|de** ['kru:də] *(geh)* ADJ crude ADV *sich ausdrücken* crudely

Krug [kru:k] M **-(e)s, =e** ['kry:gə] **a** *(= Milchkrug etc)* jug, pitcher *(old)*; *(= Weinkrug)* jug; *(= Bierkrug)* (beer) mug, stein, tankard; *(= Maßkrug)* litre *(Brit) or* liter *(US)* mug; *(= Kruke)* jar; **der ~ geht so lange zum Brunnen, bis er bricht** *(Prov)* one day you/they *etc* will come unstuck *or* come to grief **b** *(N Ger: = Wirtshaus)* inn, pub *(Brit)*

Krü|gel ['kry:gl] NT **-s, -** *(Aus)* half-litre *(Brit) or* half-liter *(US)* mug

Kru|ke ['kru:kə] F **-, -n** stone jar; *(= Wärmkruke)* bed-warmer, earthenware *or* stone hot-water bottle

Kru|me ['kru:mə] F **-, -n** *(geh)* **a** *(= Brotkrume)* crumb **b** *(liter: = Ackerkrume)* (top)soil

Krü|mel ['kry:ml] M **-s, -** **a** *(= Brotkrümel etc)* crumb **b** *(inf: = Kind)* little one, tiny tot *(inf)*

krü|me|lig ['kry:məlɪç] ADJ crumbly

krü|meln ['kry:mln] VTI to crumble; *(beim Essen)* to make crumbs

krumm [krʊm] ADJ **a** crooked; *(= verbogen)* bent, crooked; *(= hakenförmig)* hooked; *Beine* bandy; *Rücken* hunched; **~e Nase** hook(ed) nose; **etw ~ biegen** to bend sth; **~ und schief** askew, skewwhiff *(Brit inf)*; **jdn ~ und lahm schlagen** to beat sb black and blue; **eine ~e Hand machen** *(inf)* to hold one's hand out; **einen ~en Rücken machen** to stoop; *(fig)* to bow and scrape; **mach nicht solchen ~en Rücken!** straighten your shoulders, hold yourself straight **b** *(inf: = unehrlich)* crooked *(inf)*; **~er Hund** *(pej)* crooked swine; **ein ~es Ding drehen** *(sl)* to do something crooked; **er hat während seiner Zeit als Buchhalter viele ~e Dinger gedreht** *(sl)* while he was a book-keeper he got up to all sorts of crooked tricks *(inf)*; **etw auf die ~e Tour versuchen** to try to fiddle *(inf) or* wangle *(inf)* sth; **er hat sie auf die ~e Tour herumgekriegt** he conned her *(inf)*; **~e Wege gehen** to err from the straight and narrow ADV *(= nicht gerade)* **~ stehen/sitzen** to slouch; **steh/sitz nicht so ~ da!** stand/sit up straight, don't slouch; **~ gehen** to walk with a stoop; **~ wachsen** to grow crooked; **~ gewachsen** crooked; **keinen Finger ~ machen** *(inf)* not to lift a finger

Krumm-: **krumm|bei|nig** ADJ bow-legged, bandy(-legged); **krumm+bie|gen** VT *sep irreg* → **krumm a**; **Krumm|dolch** M curved dagger, jhambaia *(spec)*

krüm|men ['krʏmən] VT to bend; **die Katze krümmte den Buckel** the cat arched its back; **gekrümmte Oberfläche** curved surface → **Haar c** VR to bend; *(Fluss)* to wind; *(Straße)* to bend, to curve; *(Wurm)* to writhe; *(Mensch)* to double up; **sich vor Lachen ~** to double up with laughter, to crease up *(inf)*; **sich vor Schmerzen** *(dat)* **~** to double up *or* writhe with pain

Krumm-: **Krumm|horn** NT crumhorn, krummhorn; **krumm+la|chen** VR *sep (inf)* **sich ~** *or* **krumm- und schieflachen** to double up laughing *or* with laughter, to fall about laughing *or* with laughter; **krumm+le|gen** *sep*, **krumm le|gen** △ VR *(inf)* to pinch and scrape *(inf)*; **krumm+ma|chen** VT *sep* → **krumm b**; **krumm|na|sig** ADJ *(pej)* hook-nosed; **krumm+neh|men** *sep irreg*, **krumm neh|men** △ *irreg* VT *(inf)* **(jdm) etw ~** to take offence *(Brit) or* offense *(US)* at sth, to take sth amiss *(esp Brit)*; **Krumm|sä|bel** M scimitar; **Krumm|schwert** NT scimitar; **Krumm|stab** M crook, crozier

Krüm|mung ['krʏmʊŋ] F **-, -en** **a** *(= das Krümmen)* bending **b** *(= Biegung) (von Weg, Fluss)* bend, turn; *(Math, Med, von Fläche)* curvature; *(Opt: von Linse)* curve, curvature, figure

krum|pe|lig ['krʊmpəlɪç], **krump|lig** ['krʊmplɪç] ADJ *(dial)* creased, crumpled

Krup|pe ['krʊpə] F **-, -n** *(Zool)* croup, crupper

Krüp|pel ['krʏpl] M **-s, -** cripple; **ein seelischer/geistiger ~ sein** to be an emotional/intellectual cripple, to be emotionally/intellectually stunted; **zum ~ werden** to be crippled; **jdn zum ~ machen** to cripple sb; **jdn zum ~ schlagen** to (beat and) cripple sb

krüp|pe|lig ['krʏpəlɪç], **krüpp|lig** ['krʏplɪç] ADJ *Mensch* crippled, deformed; *Baum, Wuchs* stunted ADV **~ gewachsen** misshapen

Krupp|hus|ten ['krʊp-] M *(Med)* croupy cough

Krus|ta|ze|en [krʊsta'tse:ən] PL *(spec)* crustacea *pl*

Krus|te ['krʊstə] F **-, -n** crust; *(von Schweinebraten)* crackling; *(von Braten)* crisped outside

Krus|ten|tie|re PL crustaceans *pl*, crustacea *pl (spec)*

krus|tig ['krʊstɪç] ADJ crusty; *Topf etc* encrusted

Krux [krʊks] F **-**, *no pl* = **Crux**

Kru|zi|fix ['kru:tsifɪks, krutsi'fɪks] NT **-es, -e** crucifix; **~!** *(inf)* Christ almighty! *(sl)*

Kru|zi|tür|ken [krutsi'tʏrkn] INTERJ *(S Ger inf)* confound it, curse it

kryo|kon|ser|vie|ren [kryokɔnzɛr'vi:rən] *ptp* **kryokonserviert** VT to preserve cryogenically

Kryp|ta ['krʏpta] F **-, Krypten** ['krʏptn] crypt

kryp|tisch ['krʏptɪʃ] ADJ *Bemerkung* cryptic; **sich ~ ausdrücken** to express oneself cryptically

Kryp|to-, kryp|to- *in cpds* crypto-; **Kryp|to|fa|schist(in)** M(F) crypto-fascist; **Kryp|to|-**

gramm NT cryptogram; **Kryp|to|gra|fie** △, **Kryp|to|gra|phie** [kryptogra'fi:] F **a** (= *Geheimschrift*) cryptography **b** (*Psych*: = *Kritzelzeichnung*) doodle (*used in psychoanalysis*); **Kryp|to|lo|ge** [krypto'lo:gə] M **-n, -n**, **Kryp|to|lo|gin** [-'lo:gɪn] F **-, -nen** cryptologist

Kryp|ton ['kryptɔn, kryp'to:n] NT **-s**, *no pl* (*abbr* **Kr**) krypton

KSZE [ka:lɛstsɛt'le:] F **-** (*Hist*) *abbr von* **Konferenz über Sicherheit und Zusammenarbeit in Europa** CSCE

Ku|ba ['ku:ba] NT **-s** Cuba

Ku|ba|ner [ku'ba:nɐ] M **-s, -**, **Ku|ba|ne|rin** [-ərɪn] F **-s, -** Cuban

ku|ba|nisch [ku'ba:nɪʃ] ADJ Cuban

Kü|bel ['ky:bl] M **-s, -** bucket, pail; (*für Jauche etc*) container; (*inf: im Gefängnis*) latrine *or* toilet bucket, crapper (*inf*); (*für Bäume*) tub; **es regnet (wie) aus** *or* **mit ~n** it's bucketing down (*Brit*), it's coming down in buckets (*US*); **~ von Schmutz** *or* **Unrat** (*fig geh*) torrents of abuse

kü|beln ['ky:bln] VI (*sl*: = *sich übergeben*) to puke (*inf*)

Kü|bel|pflan|ze F tub plant

Ku|ben *pl von* **Kubus**

Ku|bik [ku'bi:k] NT **-, -** (*Aut inf*: = *Hubraum*) cc

Ku|bik-: **Ku|bik|me|ter** M OR NT cubic metre (*Brit*) *or* meter (*US*); **Ku|bik|wur|zel** F cube root; **Ku|bik|zahl** F cube number; **Ku|bik|zen|ti|me|ter** M OR NT cubic centimetre (*Brit*) *or* centimeter (*US*)

ku|bisch ['ku:bɪʃ] ADJ cubic(al); *Gleichung* cubic; *Lampen* cube-shaped

Ku|bis|mus [ku'bɪsmʊs] M **-**, *no pl* (*Art*) cubism

Ku|bist [ku'bɪst] M **-en, -en**, **Ku|bis|tin** [-'bɪstɪn] F **-, -nen** (*Art*) cubist

ku|bis|tisch [ku'bɪstɪʃ] ADJ (*Art*) cubist(ic)

Ku|bus ['ku:bʊs] M **-, Kuben** *or* **-** ['ku:bn] cube

Kü|che ['kʏçə] F **-, -n** **a** kitchen; (*klein*) kitchenette; **es wurde alles aufgetischt, was ~ und Keller zu bieten hatten** he/they *etc* served up a meal fit for a king **b** (= *Kochkunst*) **gutbürgerliche** ~ good home cooking; **chinesische** ~ Chinese cooking **c** (= *Speisen*) meals *pl*, dishes *pl*, food; **warme/kalte** ~ hot/cold food

Ku|chen ['ku:xn] M **-s, -** cake; (= *Torte*) cake, gateau (*Brit*); (*mit Obst gedeckt*) (fruit) flan, gateau (*Brit*)

Kü|chen-: **Kü|chen|ab|fäl|le** PL kitchen scraps *pl*; **Kü|chen|ab|zugs|hau|be** F extractor hood (*Brit*), fan hood (*US*); **Kü|chen|be|nut|zung** F use of kitchen

Ku|chen|blech NT baking sheet *or* tin (*Brit*) *or* pan (*US*)

Kü|chen-: **Kü|chen|bul|le** M (*Mil sl*) cookhouse wallah (*Mil sl*); **Kü|chen|chef(in)** M(F) chef; **Kü|chen|ein|rich|tung** F (fitted) kitchen; **Kü|chen|fee** F (*hum inf*) (lady) cook

Ku|chen-: **Ku|chen|form** F cake tin (*Brit*) *or* pan (*US*); **Ku|chen|ga|bel** F pastry fork

Kü|chen-: **Kü|chen|ge|rät** NT kitchen utensil; (*kollektiv*) kitchen utensils *pl*; (*elektrisch*) kitchen appliance; **Kü|chen|ge|schirr** NT kitchenware *no pl*; **Kü|chen|hand|tuch** NT kitchen towel; **Kü|chen|herd** M cooker (*Brit*), range (*US*); **Kü|chen|hil|fe** F kitchen help; **Kü|chen|ho|bel** M slicer, cutter; **Kü|chen|jun|ge** M (*dated*) apprentice cook *or* chef; **Kü|chen|ka|bi|nett** NT (*Pol*) inner circle, kitchen cabinet (*inf*); **Kü|chen|la|tein** NT dog Latin; **Kü|chen|ma|schi|ne** F food processor; **Kü|chen|meis|ter(in)** M(F) chef; **Kü|chen|mes|ser** NT kitchen knife; **Kü|chen|per|so|nal** NT kitchen staff; **Kü|chen|rol|le** F kitchen roll; **Kü|chen|scha|be** F (*Zool*) cockroach; **Kü|chen|schel|le** F (*Bot*) pasqueflower; **Kü|chen|schrank** M (kitchen) cupboard

Ku|chen|teig M cake mixture; (= *Hefeteig*) dough

Kü|chen-: **Kü|chen|tisch** M kitchen table; **Kü|chen|tuch** NT *pl* **-tücher** kitchen towel; **Kü|chen|uhr** F kitchen clock; **Kü|chen|waa|ge** F kitchen scales *pl*; **Kü|chen|wa|gen** M (*Mil*) mobile field-kitchen; **Kü|chen|zei|le** F kitchen units *pl*; **Kü|chen|zet|tel** M menu

Küch|lein ['ky:çlain] NT **-s, -** **a** small cake **b** (= *Küken*) chick

ku|cken ['kʊkn] VI (*N Ger inf*) = **gucken**

Kü|cken ['kʏkn] NT **-s, -** (*Aus*) = **Küken**

ku|ckuck ['kʊkʊk] INTERJ cuckoo

Ku|ckuck ['kʊkʊk] M **-s, -e** **a** cuckoo **b** (*inf*: = *Siegel des Gerichtsvollziehers*) bailiff's seal (for distraint of goods) **c** (*euph inf*: = *Teufel*) devil; **zum ~ (noch mal)!** hell's bells! (*inf*), darn it! (*esp US inf*); **hols der ~!** botheration! (*inf*); **geh zum ~, scher dich zum ~** go to blazes (*inf*); **(das) weiß der ~** heaven (only) knows (*inf*)

Ku|ckucks-: **Ku|ckucks|ei** NT cuckoo's egg; (*inf*: = *bei einem Seitensprung einer Ehefrau gezeugtes Kind, das ihr Ehemann für sein eigenes hält*) *etwa* illegitimate child; **man hat uns ein ~ untergeschoben** (*inf*) we've been left holding the baby (*inf*); *bei unangenehmer Zusatzarbeit* we've been/we were left to do the dirty work; **jdm ein ~ ins Nest legen** (*inf*) to foist something on sb; **Ku|ckucks|uhr** F cuckoo clock

Kud|del|mud|del ['kʊdlmʊdl] M OR NT **-s**, *no pl* (*inf*) muddle, mess, confusion; (= *Aufsatz etc auch*) hotchpotch (*Brit inf*), hodgepodge (*US inf*)

Ku|fe ['ku:fə] F **-, -n** **a** (*von Schlitten, Schlittschuh etc*) runner; (*von Flugzeug*) skid **b** (= *Holzbottich*) tub

Kü|fer ['ky:fɐ] M **-s, -** cellarman; (*S Ger*: = *Böttcher*) cooper

Kü|fe|rin ['ky:fərɪn] F **-, -nen** cellarwoman; (*S Ger*: = *Böttcherin*) cooper

Ku|gel ['ku:gl] F **-, -n** **a** ball; (*geometrische Figur*) sphere; (= *Erdkugel*) sphere, globe; (*Sport sl*: = *Ball*) ball; (= *Kegelkugel*) bowl; (= *Gewehrkugel*) bullet; (*für Luftgewehr*) pellet; (= *Kanonenkugel*) (cannon)ball; (*Sport*: = *Stoßkugel*) shot; (= *Murmel*) marble; (= *Papierkugel*) ball; (*kleine*) pellet; (= *Christbaumkugel*) glitter ball; **sich** (*dat*) **eine ~ durch den Kopf jagen** *or* **schießen** to blow one's brains out; **ich geb mir die ~** (*sl*: = *erschieße mich*) I'll shoot myself (*inf*); **eine ruhige ~ schieben** (*inf*) to have a cushy number *or* job (*inf*); (*aus Faulheit*) to swing the lead (*Brit inf*), to play hookey (*US inf*); **rund wie eine ~** (*inf*) like a barrel; **die ~ rollt** (*fig*) the roulette wheels are spinning **b** (= *Gelenkkugel*) head (of a bone)

Ku|gel-: **Ku|gel|ab|schnitt** M (*Math*) spherical segment; **Ku|gel|aus|schnitt** M (*Math*) spherical sector; **Ku|gel|bauch** M pot belly, paunch; **Ku|gel|blitz** M (*Met*) ball lightning

Kü|gel|chen ['ky:glçən] NT **-s, -** *dim von* **Kugel** small ball; (*aus Schrot, Papier etc*) pellet

Ku|gel-: **Ku|gel|fang** M butt; **die Leibwächter sollen als ~ dienen** the bodyguards are meant to act as a bullet-screen; **ku|gel|fest** ADJ = **kugelsicher**; **Ku|gel|fisch** M globefish, puffer; **Ku|gel|flä|che** F (*Math*) spherical surface; **ku|gel|för|mig** ADJ spherical ADV spherically; **Ku|gel|ge|lenk** NT (*Anat, Tech*) ball-and-socket joint; **Ku|gel|ha|gel** M hail of bullets

ku|ge|lig ['ku:gəlɪç] ADJ (= *kugelförmig*) spherical; (*inf*) *Person* tubby, dumpy; *Bauch* plump ADV **a** spherically **b** (*inf*) **sich ~ lachen** to double up (laughing)

Ku|gel-: **Ku|gel|kopf** M golf ball; **Ku|gel|kopf|schreib|ma|schi|ne** F golf-ball typewriter; **Ku|gel|la|ger** NT ball bearing

ku|geln ['ku:gln] VI *aux sein* (= *rollen, fallen*) to roll VR to roll (about); **sich (vor Lachen) ~** (*inf*) to double up (laughing); **ich könnte mich ~** (*inf*) it's killingly funny (*inf*)

Ku|gel-: **Ku|gel|re|gen** M hail of bullets; **ku|gel|rund** ADJ as round as a ball; (*inf*) *Mensch* tubby, barrel-shaped (*inf*); **Ku|gel|schrei|ber** M ballpoint (pen), Biro® (*Brit*); **Ku|gel|schrei|ber|mi|ne** F refill (for a ballpoint pen); **ku|gel|si|cher** ADJ bullet-proof; **Ku|gel|sto|ßen** NT **-s**, *no pl* shot-putting, putting the shot; **Sieger im ~** winner in the shot(-put); **Ku|gel|sto|ßer** [-ʃto:sɐ] M **-s, -**, **Ku|gel|sto|ße|rin** [-ərɪn] F **-, -nen** shot-putter; **Ku|gel|ven|til** NT (*Tech*) ball valve; **Ku|gel|wech|sel** M exchange of shots

Kuh [ku:] F **-, ¨-e** ['ky:ə] cow; (*pej inf*: = *Mädchen, Frau*) cow (*inf*); **wie die ~ vorm neuen Tor dastehen** (*inf*) to be completely bewildered; **die ~ vom Eis bringen** (*fig inf*) to save the situation; **heilige ~** (*lit, fig*) sacred cow

Kuh-: **Kuh|au|gen** PL (*pej inf*) goggle eyes *pl* (*inf*); **Kuh|dorf** NT (*pej inf*) one-horse town (*inf*); **Kuh|fla|den** M cowpat; **Kuh|fuß** M (*Tech*) crowbar; **Kuh|glo|cke** F cowbell; **Kuh|han|del** M (*pej inf*) horse-trading (*inf*) *no pl*; **ein ~** a bit of horse-trading; **kuh|han|deln** VI *insep* (*inf*) to do horse-trading; **Kuh|haut** F cowhide; **das geht auf keine ~** (*inf*) that is absolutely staggering *or* incredible; **Kuh|her|de** F herd of cows; **Kuh|hirt** M, **Kuh|hir|te** M, **Kuh|hir|tin** F cowhand, cowherd

kühl [ky:l] ADJ (*lit, fig*) cool; (= *abweisend*) cold; **mir wird etwas ~** I'm getting rather chilly; **abends wurde es ~** in the evenings it got cool; **ein ~er Kopf** (*fig*) a cool-headed person; **einen ~en Kopf bewahren** to keep a cool head, to keep cool; **ein ~er Rechner** a cool, calculating person ADV coolly; (= *nüchtern*) coolly, calmly; **etw ~ lagern** to store sth in a cool place; **„kühl servieren"** "serve chilled"

Kühl-: **Kühl|ag|gre|gat** NT refrigeration unit; **Kühl|an|la|ge** F refrigeration plant, cold storage plant; **Kühl|be|cken** NT (*für Brennelemente*) cooling pond; **Kühl|box** F cold box (*Brit*), cooler

Ku|hle ['ku:lə] F **-, -n** (*N Ger*) hollow; (= *Grube*) pit

Küh|le ['ky:lə] F **-**, *no pl* (*lit*) cool(ness); (*fig*) coolness; (= *Abweisung*) coldness

küh|len ['ky:lən] VT to cool; (*auf Eis*) to chill → **Mütchen**, → *auch* **gekühlt** VI to be cooling, to have a cooling effect; **bei großer Hitze kühlt Tee am besten** in very hot weather tea cools you down best

Küh|ler ['ky:lɐ] M **-s, -** (*Tech*) cooler; (*Aut*) radiator; (*inf*: = *Kühlerhaube*) bonnet (*Brit*), hood (*US*); (= *Sektkühler*) ice bucket; **ich hätte die alte Frau beinahe auf den ~ genommen** (*inf*) the old lady almost ended up on my bonnet (*Brit*) *or* car hood (*US*); **jdm vor den ~ rennen** (*inf*) to run (out) right in front of sb *or* right under sb's front wheels

Küh|ler-: **Küh|ler|fi|gur** F (*Aut*) radiator mascot (*Brit*), hood ornament (*US*); **Küh|ler|grill** M radiator grill; **Küh|ler|hau|be** F (*Aut*) bonnet (*Brit*), hood (*US*)

Kühl-: **Kühl|fach** NT freezer *or* ice compartment (*Brit*), deep freeze; **Kühl|flüs|sig|keit** F coolant; **Kühl-Ge|frier-Kom|bi|na|ti|on** F fridge-freezer (*esp Brit*); **Kühl|haus** NT cold storage depot; **Kühl|ket|te** F chain of cold storage units; **Kühl|la|ge|rung** F cold storage; **Kühl|mit|tel** NT (*Tech*) coolant, cooling agent; **Kühl|ofen** M (*Tech*) annealing oven; **Kühl|raum** M cold store *or* storage room; **Kühl|rip|pe** F (*Aut*) cooling fin; **Kühl|schiff** NT refrigerator ship; **Kühl|schrank** M refrigerator, fridge, icebox (*US*); **Kühl|ta|sche** F cold bag, cool bag; **Kühl|the|ke** F (*in Lebensmittelgeschäft*) refrigerated counter *or* cabinet; **Kühl|tru|he** F (chest) freezer, deep freeze; (*in Lebensmittelgeschäft*) freezer (cabinet); **Kühl|turm** M (*Tech*) cooling tower

Küh|lung ['ky:lʊŋ] F **-**, *no pl* (= *das Kühlen*) cooling; (= *Kühle*) coolness; **zur ~ des Motors** to cool the engine; **der Wind brachte etwas ~** the wind cooled things down a little; **sich** (*dat*) **~ verschaffen** to cool oneself (down); **er ging in den Schatten, um sich ~ zu verschaffen** he went into the shade to cool down *or* off; **auch bei ~ nur begrenzt haltbar** perishable even when kept in cold storage

Kühl-: **Kühl|vit|ri|ne** F refrigerated counter *or* cabinet; **Kühl|wa|gen** M **a** (*Rail*) refrigerator or refrigerated wagon, cold storage wagon **b** *(= Lastwagen)* refrigerator *or* refrigerated truck, cold storage truck; **Kühl|was|ser** NT coolant; *(Aut)* radiator water; **Kühl|was|ser|turm** M cooling tower; **Kühl|wir|kung** F cooling effect

Kuh-: **Kuh|magd** F *(dated)* milkmaid, dairymaid; **Kuh|milch** F cow's milk; **Kuh|mist** M cow dung

kühn [ky:n] ADJ *(lit, fig)* bold; **das übertrifft meine ~sten Erwartungen** it's beyond *or* it surpasses my wildest hopes or dreams ADV *(lit, fig)* boldly; **~ formuliert** radically stated; **eine ~ geschwungene Nase** an aquiline nose

Kühn|heit F -, -en **a** *no pl* boldness **b** *(Handlung)* bold act

Kuh-: **Kuh|po|cken** PL cowpox *sing*; **Kuh|schei|ße** F *(inf)* cowshit *(sl)*; **Kuh|schel|le** F *(Bot)* pasqueflower; **Kuh|stall** M cowshed, byre; **kuh|warm** ADJ *Milch* warm *or* fresh from the cow; **Kuh|wei|de** F pasture

k. u. k. ['ka:lʊnt'ka:] *abbr von* **kaiserlich und königlich** imperial and royal

Kuh-: **Kuh|stall|wär|me** F *(fig)* cosy camaraderie

ku|jo|nie|ren [kujo'ni:rən] *ptp* **kujoniert** VT *(old)* to bully, to harass

Kü|ken ['ky:kn] NT **-s, -** **a** *(= Huhn)* chick; *(inf) (= junges Mädchen)* young goose *(inf)*; *(= Nesthäkchen)* youngest child, baby of the family *(inf)*; *(= jüngste Person)* baby **b** *(Tech)* plug

Ku-Klux-Klan [kuklʊks'kla:n] M **-s** Ku Klux Klan

Ku|ku|ruz ['kʊkurʊts, 'ku:kurʊts] M **-(es)**, *no pl (Aus)* maize, corn

ku|lant [ku'lant] ADJ obliging, accommodating; *Bedingungen* fair ADV accommodatingly

Ku|lanz [ku'lants] F -, *no pl* **auf** *or* **aus ~** as a courtesy; **kann ich auf Ihre ~ zählen?** I wonder if you could oblige me in this

Ku|lanz|leis|tung F gesture of goodwill

Ku|li ['ku:li] M **-s, -s** **a** *(= Lastträger)* coolie; *(fig)* slave; **wie ein ~ arbeiten** *(inf)* to work like a slave *(inf)* **b** *(inf: = Kugelschreiber)* ballpoint (pen), Biro® *(Brit)*

ku|li|na|risch [kuli'na:rɪʃ] ADJ culinary; *(fig)* entertainment-orientated

Ku|lis|se [ku'lɪsə] F **-, -n** scenery *no pl*; *(= Teilstück)* flat, piece of scenery; *(hinten auf Bühne)* backdrop; *(an den Seiten)* wing; *(fig: = Hintergrund)* background, backdrop, backcloth; *(St Ex)* unofficial market; **die ~n für das Stück** the scenery for the play; **vor der ~ der Schweizer Alpen** against the backdrop of the Swiss Alps; **das ist alles nur ~** *(fig)* that is only a façade; **hinter den ~n** *(fig)* behind the scenes; **jdm/einer Sache als ~ dienen** *(fig)* to serve as a backdrop for sb/to sth; **die ~ für etw bilden** *(lit, fig)* to provide the backdrop for *or* to sth

Ku|lis|sen-: **Ku|lis|sen|ma|ler(in)** M(F) scene-painter; **Ku|lis|sen|schie|ber** [-ʃi:bɐ] M **-s, -**, **Ku|lis|sen|schie|be|rin** [-ərɪn] F **-, -nen** scene-shifter

Kul|ler-: **Kul|ler|au|gen** PL *(inf)* big wide eyes *pl*; **Kul|ler|ball** M *(baby-talk)* little ball

kul|lern ['kʊlɐn] VTI *(vi: aux sein) (inf)* to roll

Kul|mi|na|ti|on [kʊlmina'tsio:n] F **-, -en** culmination; *(fig auch)* apex; **obere/untere ~** highest/lowest point

Kul|mi|na|ti|ons|punkt M *(Astron)* point of culmination; *(fig)* culmination, apex

kul|mi|nie|ren [kʊlmi'ni:rən] *ptp* **kulminiert** VI to culminate; *(fig auch)* to reach its peak

Kult [kʊlt] M **-(e)s, -e** cult; *(= Verehrung)* worship; **einen ~ mit jdm/etw treiben** to make a cult out of sb/sth, to idolize sb; **mit denen wird jetzt so ein ~ getrieben** they have become such cult figures

Kult- *in cpds* cult-; **Kult|bild** NT religious symbol; **Kult|buch** NT cult book; **Kult|fi|gur** F cult figure; **Kult|film** M cult film; **Kult|ge|mein|schaft** F cult; **Kult|hand|lung** F ritual(istic) act

kul|tig ['kʊltɪç] ADJ *(sl)* cult; **voll ~: die neue CD von XY** a real cult object: XY's new CD

kul|tisch ['kʊltɪʃ] ADJ ritual(istic), cultic *(rare)* ADV ritualistically; **er wird geradezu ~ verehrt** they almost make a god out of him

kul|ti|vier|bar ADJ *Land, Mikroorganismen* cultiv(at)able; **dieser Boden ist nur schwer ~** the soil is very hard to cultivate

kul|ti|vie|ren [kʊlti'vi:rən] *ptp* **kultiviert** VT *(lit, fig)* to cultivate

kul|ti|viert [kʊlti'vi:ɐt] ADJ cultivated, cultured, refined; **Kerzen beim Essen, das ist sehr ~** meals by candlelight, very civilized ADV *speisen, sich einrichten* stylishly; *sich ausdrücken* in a refined manner; **könnt ihr euch nicht etwas ~er unterhalten?** couldn't you make your language just a little more refined?; **in dieser Familie musst du dich ein bisschen ~er benehmen als sonst** in this family you'll have to behave with a little more refinement *or* class *(inf)* than usual; **wenn Sie ~ reisen wollen** if you want to travel in style; **wenn man mal ~ essen will** if you want a civilized meal

Kul|ti|viert|heit F -, *no pl* refinement

Kul|ti|vie|rung F **-, -en** *(lit, fig)* cultivation

Kult-: **Kult|spra|che** F language of worship; **Kult|stät|te** F place of worship; **Kult|sta|tus** M cult status; **~ haben/genießen** to have/enjoy cult status; **Kult|sym|bol** NT ritual symbol

Kul|tur [kʊl'tu:ɐ] F **-, -en** **a** *(no pl: = Kunst und Wissenschaft)* culture; **ein Volk von hoher ~** a highly cultured *or* civilized people; **er hat keine ~** he is uncultured; **politische ~** political culture **b** *(= Lebensform)* civilization; **dort leben verschiedene ~en harmonisch zusammen** different cultures live harmoniously together there **c** *(= Bakterienkultur, Pilzkultur etc)* culture **d** *no pl (von Mikroben etc)* culture; *(des Bodens)* culture, cultivation **e** *(= Bestand angebauter Pflanzen)* plantation

Kul|tur-: **Kul|tur|ab|kom|men** NT cultural agreement; **Kul|tur|an|ge|bot** NT programme *(Brit) or* program *(US)* of cultural events, cultural scene; **Münchens vielfältiges ~** Munich's rich and varied cultural life; **Kul|tur|an|thro|po|lo|gie** F cultural anthropology; **Kul|tur|ar|beit** F cultural activities *pl*; **Kul|tur|at|ta|ché(e)** M cultural attaché; **Kul|tur|aus|tausch** M cultural exchange; **Kul|tur|au|to|no|mie** F independence in cultural (and educational) matters; **Kul|tur|ba|nau|se** M, **Kul|tur|ba|nau|sin** F *(inf)* philistine; **kul|tur|be|flis|sen** ADJ *(geh)* (very) culturally-minded; **sie ist sehr ~** she's a real culture vulture *(inf)*; **Kul|tur|bei|la|ge** F cultural *or* arts supplement *or* review; **Kul|tur|be|trieb** M *(inf)* culture industry; **Kul|tur|beu|tel** M sponge *or* toilet bag *(Brit)*, washbag, cosmetic case *(US)*; **Kul|tur|bo|den** M cultivated *or* arable land; **Kul|tur|denk|mal** NT cultural monument

kul|tu|rell [kʊltu'rɛl] ADJ cultural ADV culturally

Kul|tur-: **Kul|tur|er|be** NT cultural heritage; **Kul|tur|film** M documentary film; **Kul|tur|fö|de|ra|lis|mus** M *(Pol)* cultural and educational devolution; **Kul|tur|för|de|rung** F (state) promotion of the arts; **Kul|tur|geo|gra|fie**, **Kul|tur|geo|gra|phie** F human geography; **Kul|tur|ge|schich|te** F history of civilization; **Sozial- und ~ der Etrusker** social and cultural history of the Etruscans; **kul|tur|ge|schicht|lich** ADJ historico-cultural, concerning the history of civilization ADV **eine ~ interessante Ära** an era interesting from a cultural and historical point of view;; **Kul|tur|gut** NT cultural possessions *pl or* assets *pl*; **Kul|tur|haupt|stadt** F cultural capital; **~ Europas, Europäische ~** European City of Culture; **kul|tur|his|to|risch** ADJ, ADV = **kulturgeschichtlich**; **Kul|tur|ho|heit** F independence in matters of education and culture; **Kul|tur|in|dust|rie** F culture industry; **Kul|tur|kampf** M, *no pl* cultural war; *(Hist)* Kulturkampf *(struggle between Church and State 1872-1887)*; **Kul|tur|kon|sum** [-kɔnzu:m] M *(inf)* consumption of culture, cultural consumption; **Kul|tur|kreis** M culture group *or* area; **Kul|tur|kri|tik** F critique of (our) civilization *or* culture; **Kul|tur|land** NT cultivated *or* arable land; **Kul|tur|land|schaft** F land developed and cultivated by man; *(fig)* cultural landscape; **Kul|tur|le|ben** NT cultural life; **kul|tur|los** ADJ lacking culture; *Mensch auch* uncultured; **Kul|tur|lo|sig|keit** F -, *no pl* lack of culture; **Kul|tur|mi|nis|ter(in)** M(F) minister of education and the arts; **Kul|tur|mi|nis|te|ri|um** NT ministry of education and the arts; **Kul|tur|na|ti|on** F cultural nation, nation with a great cultural hisory; **Kul|tur|pa|last** M *(esp DDR)* palace of culture *or* the arts; *(pej)* cultured extravagance; **Kul|tur|pes|si|mis|mus** M despair of civilization; **Kul|tur|pflan|ze** F cultivated plant; **Kul|tur|po|li|tik** F cultural and educational policy; **Kul|tur|po|li|ti|ker(in)** M(F) politician who concerns himself mainly with cultural and educational policies; **kul|tur|po|li|tisch** ADJ politico-cultural; **~e Fragen** matters with both a cultural and a political aspect ADV from a politico-cultural point of view; **~ bedeutsame Vorschläge** propositions that are significant from both a cultural and a political point of view; **Kul|tur|psy|cho|lo|gie** F psychology of culture; **Kul|tur|raum** M cultural area; **im südostasiatischen ~** in the Southeast Asian cultural area; **Kul|tur|re|fe|rat** NT *(einer Gemeinde, Stadt etc)* cultural affairs department; **Kul|tur|re|vo|lu|ti|on** F cultural revolution; **Kul|tur|schaf|fen|de(r)** [-ʃafndə] MF *decl as adj* creative artist; **Kul|tur|scha|le** F Petri dish; **Kul|tur|schan|de** F crime against civilization, cultural outrage; *(fig inf)* insult to good taste, offence *(Brit) or* offense *(US)* against good taste; **Kul|tur|schock** M culture shock; **Kul|tur|so|zio|lo|gie** F cultural sociology, sociology of culture; **kul|tur|so|zio|lo|gisch** ADJ socio-cultural ADV *betrachten* from a sociological and cultural *or* socio-cultural viewpoint; **Kul|tur|spra|che** F language of the civilized world; **Kul|tur|stät|te** F place of cultural interest; **Kul|tur|step|pe** F *(Geog)* cultivated steppe; **Kul|tur|stu|fe** F stage *or* level of civilization; **Kul|tur|teil** M *(von Zeitung)* arts section; **Kul|tur|trä|ger(in)** M(F) vehicle of culture *or* civilization; **Kul|tur|volk** NT civilized people *sing or* nation; **Kul|tur|wan|del** M cultural change; **Kul|tur|wis|sen|schaft** F study of civilization; **~en** cultural studies; **Kul|tur|zent|rum** NT **a** *(= Stadt)* centre *(Brit) or* center *(US)* of cultural life, cultural centre *(Brit) or* center *(US)* **b** *(= Anlage)* arts centre *(Brit) or* center *(US)*

Kul|tus- ['kʊltʊs-]: **Kul|tus|frei|heit** F religious freedom, freedom of worship; **Kul|tus|ge|mein|de** F religious community; **Kul|tus|mi|nis|ter(in)** M(F) minister of education and the arts; **Kul|tus|mi|nis|te|ri|um** NT ministry of education and the arts

Kum|me ['kʊmə] F **-, -n** *(N Ger)* bowl

Küm|mel ['kyml] M **-s, -** **a** *no pl (= Gewürz)* caraway (seed) **b** *(inf: = Schnaps)* kümmel

Küm|mel-: **Küm|mel|brannt|wein** M *(form)* kümmel; **Küm|mel|öl** NT caraway oil; **Küm|mel|tür|ke** M, **Küm|mel|tür|kin** F *(pej inf: = Türke)* Turk, wog *(pej sl)*

Kum|mer ['kʊmɐ] M **-s**, *no pl (= Gram, Betrübtheit)* grief, sorrow; *(= Unannehmlichkeit, Ärger)* trouble, problems *pl*; **hast du ~?** is something wrong?, have you got problems? *(esp Brit)*; **aus** *or* **vor ~ sterben** to die of sorrow *or* grief; **vor ~ vergehen** to be pining away with sorrow *or* grief; **aus** *or* **vor ~ nahm er sich** *(dat)* **das Leben** grief-stricken *or* in his grief he took his life; **er fand vor ~ keinen Schlaf mehr** such was his grief *or* sorrow that he was unable to sleep;

jdm ~ machen *or* **bereiten** to cause sb worry; **zu jds ~** to sb's dismay; **wenn das dein einziger ~ ist** if that's your only problem *or* worry; **wir sind (an) ~ gewöhnt** *(inf)* it happens all the time, nothing's ever perfect

Kum|mer|bund M -(e)s, -e cummerbund

Kum|mer|fal|ten PL wrinkles *pl*; **das sind ~** that's the worry

Kum|mer|kas|ten M *(inf: in Zeitung, Zeitschrift)* agony column *(Brit)*, advice column

Kum|mer|kas|ten|on|kel M *(inf)* agony uncle *(Brit inf)*, advice columnist

Kum|mer|kas|ten|tan|te F *(inf)* agony aunt *(Brit inf)*, advice columnist

küm|mer|lich ['kʏmɐlɪç] ADJ **a** *(= karg, armselig)* wretched, miserable; *Reste, Ausbeute, Rente* miserable, meagre *(Brit)*, meager *(US)*, paltry; *Lohn, Mahlzeit* paltry, measly *(inf)*; *Aufsatz* scanty **b** *(= schwächlich)* puny; *Vegetation, Baum* stunted ADV *leben, wachsen, sich entwickeln* poorly; **sich ~ ernähren** to live on a meagre *(Brit)* *or* meager *(US)* diet

Küm|mer|ling ['kʏmɐlɪŋ] M -s, -e **a** *(Zool)* stunted person/plant/animal; **die Pflanze war von Anfang an ein ~** the plant always was a sickly thing **b** *(inf: = Schwächling)* weakling, weed *(pej inf)*

küm|mern ['kʏmɐn] VI *(Hunt, Zool)* to become *or* grow stunted; *(fig)* to shrivel

küm|mern VT to concern; **was kümmert mich die Firma?** why should I worry about the firm?, what do I care about the firm?; **was kümmert Sie das?** what business *or* concern is that of yours?; **was kümmert mich das?** what's that to me?

VR **sich um jdn/etw ~** to look after sb/sth; **sich um einen Kranken/jds Kinder ~** to look after *or* take care of a sick person/sb's children; **sich um die Karten/das Essen ~** to look after *or* take care of *or* see to the tickets/the food; **sich darum ~, dass ...** to see to it that ...; **aber darum kümmert sich im Stadtrat ja keiner** but nobody on the council does anything about it; **kümmere dich nicht um Sachen, die dich nichts angehen** don't worry about things that don't concern you; **kümmere dich gefälligst um deine eigenen Angelegenheiten!** mind your own business!; **er kümmert sich nicht darum, was die Leute denken** he doesn't mind *or* isn't worried about *or* doesn't care (about) what people think → **Dreck b**

Küm|mer|nis ['kʏmɐnɪs] F -, -se *(liter)* troubles *pl*, worries *pl*

Kum|mer-: **Kum|mer|speck** M *(inf)* flab *caused by overeating because of emotional problems*; **sie hat ganz schön ~ angesetzt** she's been putting on weight through comfort eating; **kum|mer|voll** ADJ sorrowful, sad, woebegone *no adv*

Küm|mer|wuchs M stunted growth

Kum|met ['kʊmət] NT -s, -e horse collar

Kü|mo ['ky:mo] NT -s, -s *abbr von* **Küstenmotorschiff** coaster

Kum|pan [kʊm'pa:n] M -s, -e, **Kum|pa|nin** [-'pa:nɪn] F -, -nen *(dated inf)* pal *(inf)*, chum *(inf)*, mate *(Brit inf)*, buddy *(esp US inf)*

Kum|pa|nei [kʊmpa'nai] F -, *no pl (pej)* chumminess

Kum|pel ['kʊmpl] M -s, - *or (inf)* -s *or (Aus)* -n **a** *(Min: = Bergmann)* pitman, miner **b** *(inf: = Arbeitskollege, Kamerad)* pal *(inf)*, chum *(inf)*, mate *(Brit inf)*, buddy *(esp US inf)*

kum|pel|haft [-haft] ADJ *(inf)* pally *(inf)*, chummy *(inf)*

Kumt [kʊmt] NT -(e)s, -e horse collar

Ku|mu|la|ti|on [kumula'tsio:n] F -, -en **a** *(von Ämtern)* plurality **b** *(von Wahlstimmen)* accumulation

ku|mu|la|tiv [kumula'ti:f] ADJ cumulative ADV cumulatively

ku|mu|lie|ren [kumu'li:rən] *ptp* **kumuliert** VT to accumulate; **~de Bibliografie** cumulative bibliography

Ku|mu|lie|rung F -, -en cumulative voting; *(von Wahlstimmen)* accumulation

Ku|mu|lus ['ku:mulʊs] M -, **Kumuli** ['ku:muli], **Ku|mu|lus|wol|ke** F cumulus (cloud)

kund [kʊnt] ADJ *inv (obs)* **jdm etw ~ und zu wissen tun** to make sth known to sb

künd|bar ADJ *Vertrag* terminable; *Anleihe* redeemable; **Beamte sind nicht ohne Weiteres ~** civil servants cannot be given (their) notice *or* cannot be dismissed just like that; **die Mitgliedschaft ist sehr schwer ~** it is very difficult to terminate *or* cancel one's membership

Künd|bar|keit ['kʏntba:ɐkait] F -, *no pl* **die ~ von Verträgen ist gesetzlich geregelt** the termination of contracts is controlled by law

Kun|de ['kʊndə] F -, *no pl (geh)* news *sing*, tidings *pl (old)*; **der Welt von etw ~ geben** to proclaim sth to the world; **von etw ~ geben** *or* **ablegen** to bear witness to sth

Kun|de ['kʊndə] M -n, -n, **Kun|din** [-dɪn] F -, -nen customer; *(pej inf)* customer *(inf)*, character

-kun|de ['kʊndə] F *suf in cpds* study of; **Denkmalskunde** study of historical monuments; **Erdkunde** geography; **Pflanzenkunde** botany

kün|den ['kʏndn] VT *(geh)* to announce, to herald VI *(geh)* **von etw ~** to tell of sth, to bear witness to sth

Kun|den-: **Kun|den|be|ra|tung** F customer advisory service; **Kun|den|dienst** M customer *or* after-sales service; *(= Abteilung)* service department; **Kun|den|fang** M *(pej)* touting *or* looking for customers; **auf ~ sein** to be touting *or* looking for customers; **kun|den|freund|lich** ADJ customer-friendly; **~e Öffnungszeiten** opening times to suit the customer; **Kun|den|kar|te** F *(von Firma, Organisation)* charge card; *(von Kaufhaus etc)* (department *(US)*) store card; *(von Bank)* bank card; **Kun|den|kar|tei** F customer file; **Kun|den|kom|mu|ni|ka|ti|on** F communication *or* dialogue with the customer; **Kun|den|kreis** M customers *pl*, clientele; **Kun|den|num|mer** F customer number; **kun|den|ori|en|tiert** ADJ customer-oriented, customer-friendly; **Kun|den|park|platz** M customer car park, customer parking lot *(US)*; **Kun|den|ser|vice** M customer service, after-sales service; **Kun|den|spra|che** F thieves' cant *(Brit)*, argot, slang; **Kun|den|stamm** M, **Kun|den|stock** M *(Aus)* (regular) customers *pl*, clientèle; **Kun|den|wer|bung** F publicity aimed at attracting custom *(Brit)* *or* customers

Kün|der ['kʏndɐ] M -s, -, **Kün|de|rin** [-ərɪn] F -, -nen *(rare)* messenger, harbinger *(obs, liter)*

kund+ge|ben ['kʊntge:bn] *sep irreg* VT *(dated)* to make known, to announce; *Meinung, Gefühle* to express, to declare; **etw ~** to announce sth *(jdm* to sb), to make sth known *(jdm* to sb) VR to be revealed

Kund|ge|bung ['kʊntge:bʊŋ] F -, -en **a** *(Pol)* rally **b** *(= Bekanntgabe)* declaration, demonstration

kun|dig ['kʊndɪç] ADJ *(geh)* well-informed, knowledgeable; *(= sachkundig)* expert; **einer Sache** *(gen)* **~ sein** to have a knowledge of sth; **sich ~ machen** to inform oneself

-kun|dig ADJ *suf* with a good knowledge of; **fachkundig** with a good knowledge of the subject; **gesetzkundig** well-versed in the law

kün|di|gen ['kʏndɪgn] VT *Stellung* to hand in one's notice for; *Abonnement, Mitgliedschaft, Kredite* to cancel, to discontinue, to terminate; *Vertrag* to terminate; *Tarife* to discontinue; *Hypothek (Bank)* to foreclose (on); *(Hausbesitzer)* to terminate; *(Aus) Person* to sack *(inf)*, to fire *(inf)*, to dismiss; **jdm die Wohnung ~, jdn aus einer Wohnung ~** *(Aus)* to give sb notice to quit his/her flat *(Brit)* *or* to vacate his/her apartment *(US)*; **ich habe meine Wohnung gekündigt** I've given in (my) notice that I'm leaving my flat *(Brit)* *or* apartment, I've given in my notice for my flat *(Brit)* *or* apartment; **die Stellung ~** to hand *or* give in one's notice; **jdm die Stellung ~** to give sb his/her notice; **ihm wurde sein Kredit gekündigt** his credit was cancelled *(Brit)* *or* canceled *(US)* *or* withdrawn; **Beträge über ... muss man ~** for sums in excess of ... notification must be given in advance; **jdm die Freundschaft ~** to break off a friendship with sb

VI *(Arbeitnehmer)* to hand *or* give in one's notice; *(Mieter)* to give in one's notice, to give notice; **jdm ~** *(Arbeitgeber)* to give sb his/her notice, to dismiss sb; *(Arbeitnehmer)* to hand *or* give in one's notice to sb; *(Vermieter)* to give sb notice to quit *(Brit)* *or* to vacate his apartment *(US)*; *(Mieter)* to give in one's notice to sb; **zum 1. April ~** to give *or* hand in one's notice for April 1st; *(Mieter)* to give notice for *or* give in one's notice for April 1st; *(bei Mitgliedschaft)* to cancel one's membership as of April 1st; **ihm ist zum 1. Februar gekündigt worden** he's been given his notice for February 1st *or* as from February 1st; *(bei Wohnung)* he's been given notice to quit *(Brit)* *or* to vacate his apartment *(US)* for February 1st; **ich kann nur mit Monatsfrist ~** I have to give a clear *(Brit)* *or* one month's notice; **bei jdm/einer Firma ~** to give *or* hand in one's notice to sb/a firm

Kün|di|gung ['kʏndɪgʊŋ] F -, -en **a** *(= Mitteilung) (von Vermieter)* notice to quit *(Brit)* *or* to vacate one's apartment *(US)*; *(von Mieter)* notice; *(von Stellung)* notice; *(von Vertrag)* termination; *(von Hypothek)* notice of foreclosure; *(von Anleihe)* notice of withdrawal; *(von Mitgliedschaft, Abonnement)* (letter of) cancellation

b *(= das Kündigen) (von Mieter, Vermieter)* giving notice; *(von Arbeitgeber)* dismissal; *(von Arbeitnehmer)* handing *or* giving in one's notice; *(von Vertrag)* termination; *(von Hypothek)* foreclosure; *(von Anleihe)* withdrawal; *(von Tarifen)* discontinuation; *(von Mitgliedschaft, Abonnement)* cancellation; **wegen schlechten Betragens des Mieters entschloss sich der Vermieter zur ~** the landlord decided to give the tenant his notice (to quit *(Brit)* *or* to vacate his apartment *(US)*) because of his unruly conduct; **ich drohte (dem Chef) mit der ~** I threatened to give *or* hand in my notice (to my boss), I threatened to quit; **ihm wurde gestern die ~ ausgesprochen** he was given his notice yesterday; **ich erwäge eine ~ meiner Stelle** I'm considering handing *or* giving in my notice; **Vertrag mit vierteljährlicher ~** contract with three months' notice on either side; **vierteljährliche ~ haben** to have (to give) three months' notice

Kün|di|gungs-: **Kün|di|gungs|frist** F period of notice; **Kün|di|gungs|geld** NT *(Fin)* deposits *pl* at notice; **Kün|di|gungs|grund** M reason *or* grounds *pl* for giving notice; *(von Arbeitgeber auch)* grounds *pl* for dismissal; **Kün|di|gungs|schrei|ben** NT written notice; *(des Arbeitgebers)* letter of dismissal; **Kün|di|gungs|schutz** M protection against wrongful dismissal

Kun|din [-dɪn] F -, -nen customer; *(pej inf)* customer *(inf)*, character

kund+ma|chen ['kʊntmaxn] VT *sep (old, liter)* = **kundgeben VT**

Kund|ma|chung ['kʊntmaxʊŋ] F -, -en *(Aus, Sw, S Ger)* = **Bekanntmachung**

Kund|schaft ['kʊntʃaft] F -, -en **a** customers *pl*; **~!** shop!, service!; **es ist ~ im Geschäft** there are customers in the shop; **die ~ bleibt neuerdings aus** customers have been staying away recently **b** *(= Erkundung)* reconnaissance; **jdn auf ~ ausschicken** *or* **senden** *(Mil)* to send sb out to reconnoitre *(Brit)* *or* reconnoiter *(US)* *or* on reconnaissance; **auf ~ (aus)gehen** *(Mil)* to go out on reconnaissance **c** *(old: = Nachricht)* news *sing*, tidings *pl (old)*

kund|schaf|ten ['kʊntʃaftn] VI *insep (Mil)* to reconnoitre *(Brit)*, to reconnoiter *(US)*

Kund|schaf|ter ['kʊntʃaftɐ] M -s, -, **Kund|schaf|te|rin** [-ərɪn] F -, -nen spy; *(Mil)* scout

kund+tun ['kʊnttu:n] VT *sep irreg (geh)* to make known, to proclaim

kund+wer|den ['kʊntveːrdn] VI *sep irreg aux sein* *(liter)* to become known

künf|tig ['kynftɪç] ADJ future; **das ~e Leben** the next life, the life to come; **meine ~e Frau** my future wife, my wife-to-be; **mein ~er Schwager** my future brother-in-law, my brother-in-law to be ADV in future

Kun|ge|lei [kʊŋə'lai] F -, -en *(inf)* scheming, wheeling and dealing

kun|geln ['kʊŋln] VI *(inf)* to scheme; **mit denen hat er viel gekungelt** he did a lot of wheeling and dealing with them

Kung-Fu [kʊŋ'fuː] NT -, *no pl* kung fu

Kunst [kʊnst] F -, ⸚e ['kʏnstə] **a** art; **die schönen Künste** fine art *sing*, the fine arts → **bildend, darstellen VT a, schwarz ADJ a** **b** *(= Können, Fertigkeit)* art, skill; **seine ~ an jdm versuchen** to try *or* practise *(Brit)* *or* practice *(US)* one's skills on sb; **seine ~ zeigen** to show what one can do; **mit seiner ~ am** *or* **zu Ende sein** to be at one's wits' end; **die ~ besteht darin, …** the art *or* knack is in …; **ärztliche ~** medical skill → **Regel a** **c** *(= Kunststück)* trick; **er wandte alle Künste der Rhetorik an** he used all the arts *or* tricks of rhetoric; **sie versuchte all ihre Künste an ihm** she used all her charms and wiles on him; **das ist keine ~!** it's like taking candy from a baby *(inf)*; *(= ein Kinderspiel)* it's a piece of cake *(inf)*; **so einfach ist das, das ist die ganze ~** it's that easy, that's all there is to it **d** *(inf)* **das ist eine brotlose ~** there's no money in that; **was macht die ~?** how are things?, how's tricks? *(Brit inf)*

Kunst- *in cpds (Art)* art; *(= künstlich)* artificial; **Kunst|aka|de|mie** F college of art, art college; **Kunst|aus|stel|lung** F art exhibition; **Kunst|ba|nau|se** M, **Kunst|ba|nau|sin** F *(pej)* philistine; **kunst|be|flis|sen** ADJ *(hum)* ~ **sein** to be keen on art; **~e Menschen/Museumsbesucher** people who are keen on art/visiting museums; **Kunst|darm** M artificial sausage skin; **Kunst|denk|mal** NT work of art *(from an older culture)*; **Kunst|druck** M *pl* **-drucke** art print; **Kunst|druck|pa|pier** NT art paper; **Kunst|dün|ger** M chemical *or* artificial fertilizer

Küns|te|lei [kʏnstə'lai] F -, -en affectation

Kunst-: **kunst|emp|fäng|lich** ADJ artistic, appreciative of art; **Kunst|er|zie|her(in)** M(F) art teacher; **Kunst|er|zie|hung** F *(Sch)* art; **Kunst|fa|ser** F man-made *or* synthetic fibre *(Brit)* *or* fiber *(US)*; **Kunst|feh|ler** M professional error; *(weniger ernst)* slip; **wegen eines ärztlichen ~s** because of medical malpractice; **kunst|fer|tig** *(geh)* ADJ skilful *(Brit)*, skillful *(US)* ADV skilfully *(Brit)*, skillfully *(US)*; **Kunst|fer|tig|keit** F skill, skilfulness *(Brit)*, skillfulness *(US)*; **Kunst|fi|gur** F fictional character; **Kunst|flie|ger(in)** M(F) stunt *or* aerobatic pilot, stunt flyer; **Kunst|flug** M aerobatics *sing*, aerobatic *or* stunt flying; **ein ~** a piece of aerobatic *or* stunt flying; **Kunst|freund(in)** M(F) art lover, patron *or* lover of the arts; **Kunst|ge|gen|stand** M objet d'art, art object; *(Gemälde)* work of art; **kunst|ge|mäß, kunst|ge|recht** ADJ *(= fachmännisch)* proficient, skilful *(Brit)*, skillful *(US)* ADV proficiently, skilfully *(Brit)*, skillfully *(US)*; **Kunst|ge|nuss** M *(= Freude an der Kunst)* enjoyment of art; *(= Konzert, Theateraufführung etc)* aesthetic treat; **Kunst|ge|schich|te** F history of art, art history; **kunst|ge|schicht|lich** ADJ, ADV = **kunsthistorisch**; **Kunst|ge|wer|be** NT arts and crafts *pl*; **ein Fachgeschäft für ~** an arts and crafts shop, a craft shop; **Kunst|ge|werb|ler** [-gəvɛrplɐ] M -s, -, **Kunst|ge|werb|le|rin** [-ərɪn] F -, -nen artisan, craftsman/-woman; **kunst|ge|werb|lich** ADJ **~e Gegenstände** craft objects; **~er Zweig** arts and crafts department; **Kunst|griff** M trick, dodge *(inf)*; **Kunst|han|del** M art trade; **Kunst|händ|ler(in)** M(F) art dealer; **Kunst|hand|werk** NT craft industry; **Kunst|harz** NT synthetic resin; **Kunst|herz** NT artificial heart; **kunst|his|to|risch** ADJ art-historical, relating to art history; **~es Museum** art history museum; **~es Interesse** interest in art history ADV from the point of view of art history; **Kunst|hoch|schu|le** F college of art, art college; **Kunst|ho|nig** M artificial *or* synthetic honey; **Kunst|ken|ner(in)** M(F) art connoisseur; **Kunst|kri|tik** F, *no pl* art criticism; *(= die Kritiker)* art critics *pl*; *(= Rezension)* art review; **Kunst|kri|ti|ker(in)** M(F) art critic; **Kunst|le|der** NT artificial *or* imitation leather

Künst|ler ['kʏnstlɐ] M -s, -, **Künst|le|rin** [-ərɪn] F -, -nen **a** artist; *(= Unterhaltungskünstler)* artiste; **bildender ~** visual artist **b** *(= Könner)* genius *(in +dat* at)

Künst|ler|ein|gang M stage door

künst|le|risch ['kʏnstlərɪʃ] ADJ artistic ADV artistically; **~ wertvoll** of *or* having artistic value

Künst|ler-: **Künst|ler|knei|pe** F bar popular with *or* frequented by artists; **Künst|ler|ko|lo|nie** F artists' colony, colony of artists; **Künst|ler|le|ben** NT life of an artist; **ein ~** an artist's life; **Künst|ler|mäh|ne** F *(inf)* mane of hair; **Künst|ler|na|me** M pseudonym; *(von Schriftsteller auch)* pen name, nom de plume; *(von Schauspieler auch)* stage name; **Künst|ler|pech** NT *(inf)* hard luck; **Künst|ler|tum** ['kʏnstlɐtuːm] NT -s, *no pl* artistry, artistic genius; **Künst|ler|ver|band** M artists' association

künst|lich ['kʏnstlɪç] ADJ artificial; *Auge auch* glass; *Zähne, Wimpern, Fingernägel* false; *Faserstoffe* synthetic, man-made; *Diamanten* imitation, fake *(inf)*; **~e Intelligenz** artificial intelligence → **Befruchtung** ADV **a** *fertigen, herstellen* artificially, synthetically **b** *(mit Apparaten)* **jdm ~ Insulin zuführen** to administer insulin to sb; **jdn ~ ernähren** *(Med)* to feed sb artificially → **beatmen** **c** *(inf: = übertrieben)* **sich ~ aufregen** to get all worked up *(inf)* *or* excited about nothing

Künst|lich|keit F -, *no pl* artificiality

Kunst-: **Kunst|licht** NT *(Phot)* artificial light; **Kunst|lied** NT composed *or* art song, Kunstlied; **kunst|los** ADJ unsophisticated, simple ADV simply; **Kunst|lo|sig|keit** F -, *no pl* simplicity; **Kunst|maler(in)** M(F) artist, painter; **Kunst|mär|chen** NT literary fairy tale; **Kunst|ob|jekt** NT art object, objet d'art; **Kunst|pau|se** F *(als Spannungsmoment)* dramatic pause, pause for effect; *(iro: beim Stocken)* awkward pause, hesitation; **eine ~ machen** to pause for effect; to pause awkwardly; **Kunst|ra|sen** M artificial turf; **Kunst|raub** M art theft; **kunst|reich** ADJ, ADV *(geh)* = **kunstvoll**; **Kunst|rei|se** F art tour; **Kunst|rei|ter(in)** M(F) trick *or* circus rider; **Kunst|samm|lung** F art collection; **Kunst|schät|ze** PL art treasures *pl*; **Kunst|schnee** M artificial snow; **Kunst|schnee|pis|te** F artificial snow piste; **Kunst|schwim|men** NT exhibition swimming; **Kunst|sei|de** F artificial silk; **Kunst|sinn** M artistic sense *or* taste, appreciation of art, feeling for art; **kunst|sin|nig** ADJ artistic, appreciative of art; **Kunst|spra|che** F artificial *or* invented language; **Kunst|sprin|gen** NT diving

Kunst|stoff M man-made *or* synthetic material *or* substance

Kunst|stoff-: **kunst|stoff|be|schich|tet** ADJ synthetic-coated; **Kunst|stoff|flasche** F plastic bottle; **Kunst|stoff|ka|ros|se|rie** F fibreglass *(Brit)* *or* fiberglass *(US)* body

Kunst-: **kunst+stop|fen** *sep infin and ptp only* VT to repair by invisible mending, to mend invisibly VI to do invisible mending; **Kunst|stück** NT trick; **~!** *(iro)* hardly surprising!, no wonder!; **das ist kein ~** *(fig)* there's nothing to it; *(= keine große Leistung)* that's nothing to write home about; **Kunst|sze|ne** F art scene; **Kunst|tisch|ler(in)** M(F) cabinet-maker; **Kunst|tur|nen** NT gymnastics *sing*; **Kunst|ver|stand** M feeling for art, appreciation of art, artistic taste *or* sense; **kunst|ver|stän|dig** ADJ appreciative of art, having artistic sense *or* taste ADV **er äußerte sich ~** he showed his appreciation of art; **Kunst|ver|ständ|nis** NT feeling for art, appreciation of art, artistic taste *or* sense; **kunst|voll** ADJ artistic; *(= kompliziert)* elaborate ADV elaborately; **Kunst|werk** NT work of art; **Kunst|wis|sen|schaft** F aesthetics *sing*, art; **Kunst|wort** NT *pl* **-wörter** artificial *or* made-up word

kun|ter|bunt ['kʊntɐbʊnt] ADJ *Sammlung, Gruppe etc* motley *attr*; *(= vielfarbig auch)* multi-coloured *(Brit)*, multi-colored *(US)*, many-coloured *(Brit)*, many-colored *(US)*; *Programm* varied; *Leben* chequered *(Brit)*, checkered *(US)* ADV chaotically; **eine ~ zusammengewürfelte Gruppe** a motley assortment; **~ durcheinander** all jumbled up, higgledy-piggledy *(inf)*; **hier geht es ~ zu** it's pretty chaotic here

Kunz [kʊnts] M → **Hinz**

Ku|pee [ku'peː] NT -s, -s coupé

Kup|fer ['kʊpfɐ] NT -s, *no pl (abbr* **Cu***)* **a** *no pl (Chem)* copper; **etw in ~ stechen** to do a copper engraving of sth, to engrave *or* etch sth on copper **b** *no pl (= Gegenstände aus Kupfer)* copper; *(= Kupfergeld)* coppers *pl* **c** *(= Kupferstich)* copperplate

Kup|fer- *in cpds* copper; **Kup|fer|blech** NT sheet copper; **Kup|fer|draht** M copper wire; **Kup|fer|druck** M *pl* **-drucke** copperplate engraving *or* etching; **Kup|fer|geld** NT coppers *pl*, copper coins *pl*; **kup|fer|hal|tig** ADJ containing copper, cupriferous *(form)*

kup|fe|rig ['kʊpfərɪç] ADJ coppery

kup|fern ['kʊpfɐn] ADJ copper; **~e Hochzeit** 7th wedding anniversary

Kup|fer-: **kup|fer|rot** ADJ copper-red, copper-coloured *(Brit)*, copper-colored *(US)*; **Kup|fer|schmied(in)** M(F) coppersmith; **Kup|fer|ste|cher** [-ʃtɛçɐ] M -s, -, **Kup|fer|ste|che|rin** [-ərɪn] F -, -nen copper(plate) engraver; **mein lieber Freund und ~** *(inf)* now then my dear old chap; **Kup|fer|stich** M **a** copperplate (engraving *or* etching) **b** *(Kunst)* copper(plate) engraving *or* etching; **Kup|fer|vit|ri|ol** NT blue vitriol; *(dated Chem)* copper sulphate

kupf|rig ['kʊpfrɪç] ADJ = **kupferig**

ku|pie|ren [ku'piːrən] *ptp* **kupiert** VT *Schwanz, Ohren* to crop, to dock; *Karten* to cut; *(form) Wein* to blend; *(Med) Krankheit* to check, to arrest

Ku|pon [ku'põː] M -s, -s = **Coupon**

Ku|pon- [ku'põː-]: **Ku|pon|steu|er** F *(Fin)* coupon tax; **Ku|pon|ter|min** M *(Fin)* coupon date

Kup|pe ['kʊpə] F -, -n *(= Bergkuppe)* (rounded) hilltop; *(von Straße)* hump; *(= Fingerkuppe)* tip

Kup|pel ['kʊpl] F -, -n dome, cupola

Kup|pel|dach NT domed *or* dome-shaped roof

Kup|pe|lei [kʊpə'lai] F -, *no pl (Jur)* procuring, procuration

Kup|pel|mut|ter F *pl* **-mütter** procuress, bawd

kup|peln ['kʊpln] VT **a** = **koppeln a, b** **b** *(Tech)* to couple VI **a** *(Aut)* to operate *or* use the clutch **b** *(inf: = Paare zusammenführen)* to match-make

Kup|pel|pelz M **sich** *(dat)* **einen ~ verdienen** *(fig)* to arrange *or* make a match

Kup|pe|lung ['kʊpəlʊŋ] F -, -en coupling

Kup|pel|zelt NT dome tent

Kupp|ler ['kʊplɐ] M -s, -, **Kupp|le|rin** [-ərɪn] F -, -nen matchmaker *(+gen* for); *(Jur)* procurer/procuress

Kupp|lung ['kʊplʊŋ] F -, -en **a** *(Tech)* coupling; *(Aut etc)* clutch; **die ~ (durch)treten** to disengage the clutch; **die ~ kommen lassen** *(Aut)* to let the clutch up *or* in **b** *(= das Koppeln)* coupling

Kupp|lungs- *in cpds (Aut)* clutch; **Kupp|lungs|be|lag** M clutch lining; **Kupp|lungs|pe|dal** NT clutch pedal; **Kupp|lungs|schei|be** F clutch plate; **Kupp|lungs|seil** NT, **Kupp|lungs|zug** M clutch cable

Kur [kuːɐ] F -, -en *(in Badeort)* (health) cure; *(= Haarkur etc)* treatment *no pl*; *(= Schlankheitskur, Diätkur)* diet; **er ist zur ~ in Baden-Baden** he's on a health cure *or* he is taking a cure *or* he is taking the waters in Baden-Baden; **in** *or* **zur ~ fahren** to go to a health resort *or* spa; **jdm eine ~ verordnen** to prescribe a stay in a health resort *or* a spa for sb; **jdn zur ~ schicken** to send sb to a health resort *or* to a spa; **eine ~ machen** to take *or* undergo a cure; *(= Schlankheitskur)* to diet; **ich mache zurzeit eine ~ gegen meinen Ausschlag** *(mit Cremes etc)* I'm taking a course of treatment for my rash

Kür [kyːɐ] F -, -en **a** *(Sport)* free section; **eine ~ laufen** to do the free skating; **eine ~ tanzen/turnen** to do the free section **b** *(old: = Wahl)* election

Ku|rant [kuˈrant] M -en, -en, **Ku|ran|tin** [-ˈrantɪn] F -, -nen *(Sw)* = **Kurgast**

Kü|rass [ˈkyːras] M -es, -e cuirass

Kü|ras|sier [kyraˈsiːɐ] M -s, -e *(Mil Hist)* cuirassier

Ku|rat [kuˈraːt] M -en, -en curate

Ku|ra|tel [kuraˈteːl] F -, -en *(old)* *(= Pflegschaft)* trusteeship; *(= Vormundschaft)* guardianship; **unter (jds)** *(dat)* **~ stehen** *(fig dated)* to be under sb's thumb; **jdn unter ~ stellen** *(old)* to keep a watch on sb

ku|ra|tiv [kuraˈtiːf] ADJ *(Med)* curative

Ku|ra|tor [kuˈraːtoːɐ] M -s, **Kuratoren** [-ˈtoːrən], **Ku|ra|to|rin** [-ˈtoːrɪn] F -, -nen **a** *(= Vormund)* guardian **b** *(= Verwalter einer Geldstiftung)* trustee **c** *(von Museum)* curator **d** *(Univ)* ≈ registrar

Ku|ra|to|ri|um [kuraˈtoːriʊm] NT -s, **Kuratorien** [-riən] **a** *(Vereinigung)* committee **b** *(Amt)* curatorship

Kur-: **Kur|au|fent|halt** M stay at a health resort *or* spa; **Kur|bad** NT spa, watering place *(old)*

Kur|bel [ˈkʊrbl] F -, -n crank; *(an Fenstern, Rollläden etc)* winder

kur|beln VTI to turn, to wind; *(inf: = filmen)* to film, to shoot; **wenn du daran kurbelst ...** if you turn *or* wind it ...; **die Markise vors Fenster ~** to wind up the awning in front of the window

Kur|bel-: **Kur|bel|stan|ge** F connecting rod; **Kur|bel|wel|le** F crankshaft

Kür|bis [ˈkyrbɪs] M -ses, -se pumpkin; *(inf: = Kopf)* nut *(inf)*

Kür|bis|fla|sche F gourd

Kur|de [ˈkʊrdə] M -n, -n, **Kur|din** [-dɪn] F -, -nen Kurd

Kur|dis|tan [ˈkʊrdɪstaːn, ˈkʊrdɪstan] NT -s Kurdistan

ku|ren [ˈkuːrən] VI *(Sw inf)* to take a cure; *(in Mineralbad)* to take the waters

kü|ren [ˈkyːrən] *pret* **kürte** *or (rare)* **kor** [ˈkyːɐtə, koːɐ], *ptp* **gekürt** *or* **gekoren** [gəˈkyːɐt, gəˈkoːrən] VT *(old, geh)* to choose, to elect *(zu* as)

Kur|fürst M Elector, electoral prince

Kur|fürs|ten|tum NT electorate

kur|fürst|lich ADJ electoral

Kur-: **Kur|gast** M *(Patient)* patient at a spa *or* health resort; *(Tourist)* visitor to a spa *or* health resort; **Kur|haus** NT assembly rooms *pl* (at a spa *or* health resort), spa rooms *pl*

Ku|rie [ˈkuːriə] F -, *no pl* **a** *(Eccl)* Curia **b** *(Hist)* curia

Ku|rier [kuˈriːɐ] M -s, -e, **Ku|rie|rin** [-ˈriːrɪn] F -, -nen courier; *(Hist)* messenger

Ku|rier|dienst M courier service

ku|rie|ren [kuˈriːrən] *ptp* **kuriert** VT *(lit, fig)* to cure *(von* of); **von dieser Stadt/Idee/ihm bin ich kuriert** I've gone right off *(Brit)* *or* I've had enough of this town/this idea/him

Ku|rier|post F mail sent by courier

ku|ri|os [kuˈrioːs] ADJ *(= merkwürdig)* strange, odd, curious ADV strangely, oddly, curiously

Ku|ri|o|sa *pl von* **Kuriosum**

Ku|ri|o|si|tät [kuriozi'tɛːt] F -, -en **a** *(Gegenstand)* curio(sity) **b** *(= Eigenart)* peculiarity, oddity

Ku|ri|o|si|tä|ten|ka|bi|nett NT collection of curios; *(fig)* collection of odd people

Ku|ri|o|sum [kuˈrioːzʊm] NT -s, **Kuriosa** [-za] *(geh)* curious *or* strange *or* odd thing

Kur|kon|zert NT concert (at a spa *or* health resort), spa concert

Kur|ku|ma [ˈkʊrkuma] F -, **Kurkumen** [-ˈkuːmən] turmeric

Kur|laub [ˈkuːɐlaup] M -(e)s, -e health spa holiday *(Brit)* *or* vacation *(US)*

Kür|lauf M free skating

Kur-: **Kur|ort** M spa, health resort; **Kur|pa|ckung** F *(für Haare)* hair repair kit; **Kur|park** M spa gardens *pl*; **Kur|pfalz** F Palatinate, Palatine electorate; **kur|pfäl|zisch** ADJ Palatine; **kur|pfu|schen** [ˈkuːɐpfʊʃn] VI *insep* to play the quack; **Kur|pfu|scher(in)** M(F) *(pej inf)* quack (doctor); **Kur|pfu|sche|rei** [kuːɐpfʊʃəˈrai] F *(pej inf)* quackery; **Kur|prinz** M heir of an Elector; **Kur|pro|me|na|de** F promenade (at a spa *or* health resort)

> **KURORT**
>
> A **Kurort** is an area specializing in natural health remedies such as springs, mud and salt water. When patients are sent by their doctors to a **Kurort**, insurance companies pay most of the cost. **Kurorte** also levy a **Kurtaxe** on every patient. This charge helps cover the cost of the many recreational and leisure facilities available in the resort.

Kur|re [ˈkʊrə] F -, -n *(Naut)* trawl (net)

kur|rent [kʊˈrɛnt] ADJ, ADV *(Aus)* in gothic handwriting

Kur|rent|schrift [kʊˈrɛnt-] F **a** cursive writing *or* script **b** *(Aus)* gothic handwriting

Kur|ri|ku|lum [kʊˈriːkulʊm] NT -s, **Kurrikula** [-la] = **Curriculum**

Kurs [kʊrs] M -es, -e [-zə] **a** *(Naut, Aviat, fig)* course; *(Pol: = Richtung)* line, course; **den ~ halten** to hold (the) course; **vom ~ abkommen** to deviate from one's/its course; **~ nehmen auf** *(+acc)* to set course for, to head for; **auf (südwestlichen) ~ gehen** to set a (southwesterly) course; **auf (südwestlichem) ~ sein** to be on (a southwesterly) course; **~ haben auf** *(+acc)* to be heading for; **harter/weicher ~** *(Pol)* hard/soft line; **den ~ ändern** *(lit, fig)* to change *or* alter (one's) course; **einen neuen ~ einschlagen** *(lit, fig)* to go in a new direction, to follow a new course; **den ~ beibehalten** *(lit, fig)* to stick to *or* hold (one's) course; **jdn/etw wieder auf ~ bringen** *(fig)* to bring sb/sth back on course **b** *(Fin)* *(= Wechselkurs)* rate of exchange, exchange rate; *(= Börsenkurs, Aktienkurs)* price, (going) rate; *(= Marktpreis)* market value *or* price, going rate; **zum ~ von** at the rate of; **der amtliche ~ des Dollars** the official dollar exchange rate; **die ~e fallen/steigen** prices *or* rates are falling/rising; **hoch im ~ stehen** *(Aktien)* to be high; *(fig)* to be popular *(bei* with); **etw außer ~ setzen** to withdraw sth from circulation **c** *(= Lehrgang)* course *(in +dat, für* in); **einen ~ belegen** to do a course; **einen ~ besuchen** *or* **mitmachen** to attend a course

Kurs-: **Kurs|ab|schlag** M *(Fin)* markdown, backwardation *(Brit)*; **Kurs|än|de|rung** F *(lit, fig)* change of course; **Kurs|an|stieg** M *(St Ex)* rise in (market) prices; **Kurs|auf|schlag** M *(Fin)* markup, contango *(Brit)*; **Kurs|be|richt** M *(Fin)* stock market report; **Kurs|be|we|gung** F *(Fin)* price movement; **Kurs|bil|dung** F formation of rates; **Kurs|blatt** NT *(Fin)* stock-exchange (price) list, list of quotations; **Kurs|buch** NT *(Rail)* (railway) timetable, Bradshaw *(dated Brit)*

Kur|schat|ten M -s, - *(hum inf)* lady/gentleman friend *(met during a stay at a spa)*; **sie war zuerst nur sein ~** he first met her at a spa

Kürsch|ner [ˈkʏrʃnɐ] M -s, -, **Kürsch|ne|rin** [-ərɪn] F -, -nen furrier

Kürsch|ne|rei [kʏrʃnəˈrai] F -, -en **a** *(= Handwerk)* furrier's trade **b** *(= Werkstatt)* furrier's workshop

Kur|se *pl von* **Kursus**

Kurs-: **Kurs|ein|bruch** M *(Fin)* sudden fall in prices; **Kurs|ein|bu|ße** F decrease *or* fall in value; **das Pfund hat weitere ~n hinnehmen müssen** the pound suffered further losses (on the exchange market); **Kurs|ent|wick|lung** F *(Fin)* price trend; **Kurs|er|ho|lung** F *(Fin)* rally in prices, price rally; **Kurs|fest|set|zung** F *(Fin)* exchange rate fixing; **Kurs|ge|winn** M profit (on the stock exchange *or (bei Wechsel)* foreign exchange market); **der jüngste ~ des Pfundes** the recent increase in the value of the pound; **einen ~ haben** to make a profit

kur|sie|ren [kʊrˈziːrən] *ptp* **kursiert** VI *aux haben or sein* to be in circulation, to circulate; *(fig)* to circulate, to go (a)round

kur|siv [kʊrˈziːf] ADJ italic; **Anmerkungen sind ~** notes are in italics ADV in italics; **etw ~ drucken** to print sth in italics, to italicize sth

Kur|si|ve [kʊrˈziːvə] F -, -n, **Kur|siv|schrift** F italics *pl*; **in ~ gesetzt** printed in italics, italicized

Kur|siv|druck M *(Typ)* italics *pl*; **in ~ erscheinen** to appear in italics

Kurs-: **Kurs|kor|rek|tur** F *(lit, fig)* course correction *or* adjustment; *(St Ex)* corrective price adjustment, corrective rate adjustment; **Kurs|lei|ter(in)** M(F) course tutor *(esp Brit)*; **Kurs|mak|ler(in)** M(F) *(St Ex)* market maker; **Kurs|no|tie|rung** F (market) quotation, quotation (of stock exchange prices)

kur|so|risch [kʊrˈzoːrɪʃ] ADJ *Behandlung, Lektüre* cursory ADV **etw ~ lesen/überfliegen** to skim through sth

Kurs-: **Kurs|pfle|ge** F price support; **Kurs|ri|si|ko** NT market risk; **Kurs|rück|gang** M fall in prices; **Kurs|schwan|kung** F fluctuation in rates of exchange *or* exchange rates; *(St Ex)* fluctuation in market rates *or* prices; **Kurs|si|che|rung** F price support; **Kurs|si|che|rungs|ge|schäft** NT price support operation; **Kurs|stei|ge|rung** F *(Fin)* price increase; **Kurs|sturz** M sharp fall in prices; **Kurs|sys|tem** NT *(Sch, Univ)* course system

Kur|sus [ˈkʊrzʊs] M -, **Kurse** [ˈkʊrzə] *(geh: = Lehrgang)* course

Kurs-: **Kurs|ver|lust** M *(Fin)* loss (on the stock exchange *or* foreign exchange market); **das Pfund musste ~e hinnehmen** the pound suffered losses on the foreign exchange market; **Kurs|wa|gen** M *(Rail)* through coach; **Kurs|wech|sel** M change of direction; **Kurs|wert** M *(Fin)* market value *or* price; **Kurs|zet|tel** M *(Fin)* stock exchange (price) list, list of quotations; **Kurs|zu|satz** M excess supply and demand indicator

Kur|ta|xe F visitors' tax (at spa *or* health resort)

Kur|ti|sa|ne [kʊrtiˈzaːnə] F -, -n courtesan

Kurt|scha|to|vi|um [kʊrtʃaˈtoːviʊm] NT -s, *no pl (abbr* **Ku**) rutherfordium, kurchatovium

Kür|übung F *(Sport)* free section

Kur|ve [ˈkʊrvə, ˈkʊrfə] F -, -n *(Math, inf: = Körperrundung)* curve; *(= Biegung, Straßenkurve)* bend; *(an Kreuzung)* corner; *(von Geschoss)* trajectory; *(statistisch, = Fieberkurve etc)* graph; **die Straße macht eine ~** the road bends; **eine ~ fliegen** *(Aviat)* to bank, to do a banking turn; **die ~ kratzen** *(inf)* to scrape through *(inf)*; *(= schnell weggehen)* to make tracks *(inf)*; **die ~ kriegen** *(inf) (mit Auto etc)* to make the corner; *(fig)* to make it, to manage it; **die ~ nicht kriegen** *(inf) (mit Auto etc)* not to make the corner; *(fig)* not to get round to it

kur|ven [ˈkʊrvn, ˈkʊrfn] VI *aux sein (inf) (Aviat)* to circle; **durch Italien ~** to drive around Italy

Kur|ven-: **Kur|ven|dia|gramm** NT graph; **Kur|ven|la|ge** F *(Mot)* roadholding (in bends *or* curves *(US)*), cornering (ability); **eine gute ~**

haben to hold the road well (in bends *or* curves *(US)*), to corner well; **Kur|ven|li|ne|al** NT curve template *or* templet, French curve; **kur|ven|reich** ADJ *Straße, Strecke* bendy, winding; *(inf) Frau* curvaceous, shapely; **„kurvenreiche Strecke"** "(series of) bends"; **Kur|ven|tech|nik** F *(Sport)* cornering technique

Kur|ver|wal|tung F spa authorities *pl*

kur|vig [ˈkʊrvɪç] ADJ winding, twisting ADV **die Straße verläuft sehr ~** the street bends sharply; **eine ~ geschwungene Treppe** a winding staircase; **ihr ~ geformter Körper** her curvy build

kurz [kʊrts] ADJ *comp* **⸗er** [ˈkʏrtsɐ], *superl* **⸗es|te(r, s)** [ˈkʏrtsəstə] short; *Zeit, Aufenthalt, Besuch, Bericht, Antwort etc auch* brief; *Gedächtnis auch* short-lived; *Blick, Folge* quick; *(= klein und stämmig)* stocky, squat; **etw kürzer machen** to make sth shorter, to shorten sth; **ich will es ~ machen** I'll make it brief, I'll be brief; **machs ~!** make it brief *or* quick, be brief, keep it short; **~e Hosen** short trousers; *(= Shorts)* shorts; **~e See** *(Naut)* choppy sea; **den Kürzeren ziehen** *(fig inf)* to come off worst, to get the worst of it; **~ verliert, lang gewinnt** whoever draws the shortest (straw) loses; **in** *or* **mit ein paar ~en Worten** in a few brief words, briefly; **in kürzester Frist** before very long; **Pippin der Kurze** Pippin the Short → **Prozess a**

ADV *comp* **⸗er**, *superl* **am ⸗esten** **a** **~ atmen** to take short breaths; **X hat ~ abgespielt** *(Sport)* X's pass was short [ˈkʏrtsɐ]; **(zu) ~ schießen/werfen** *etc* to shoot/throw *etc* (too) short; **die Hundeleine ~ halten** to keep the dog on a short lead *(Brit) or* line *(US)*; **eine Sache ~ abtun** to dismiss sth out of hand; **zu ~ kommen** to come off badly, to get a raw deal *(inf)*; **zu ~ greifen** not to go far enough; **zu ~ denken** to see things too simply; **~ entschlossen** without a moment's hesitation, without the slightest hesitation; **~ gesagt** in a nutshell, in a word; **sich ~ fassen** → **kurzfassen**; **~ gefasst** concise; **~ geschnitten** cropped; **~ und bündig** concisely, tersely *(pej)*; **~ und gut** in short, in a word; **~ und schmerzlos** *(inf)* short and sweet; **jdn ~ und klein hauen** *or* **schlagen** to beat sb up; **etw ~ und klein hauen** *or* **schlagen** to smash sth to pieces

b *(= für eine kurze Zeit)* briefly; **ich bleibe nur ~** I'll only stay for a short while; **darf ich mal ~ stören?** could I just interrupt for a moment *or* second?; **ich muss mal ~ weg** I'll just have to go for a moment *or* second; **darf ich mal ~ fragen ...?** could I just quickly ask ...?; **ich werde ~ mal gucken** I'll have a quick look

c *(zeitlich, räumlich: = nicht lang, nicht weit)* shortly, just; **~ bevor/nachdem** shortly *or* just before/after; **~ vor Köln/Ostern** shortly *or* just before Cologne/Easter; **binnen Kurzem** *(form)* shortly, before long; **er hat den Wagen erst seit Kurzem** he's only had the car for a short *or* little while; **seit Kurzem gibt es Bier in der Kantine** recently there's been beer in the canteen; **über ~ oder lang** sooner or later; **(bis) vor Kurzem** (until) recently; **~ nacheinander** shortly after each other

Kurz-: **Kurz|ar|beit** F short time; **kurz+ar|bei|ten** VI *sep* to be on short time, to work short time; **Kurz|ar|bei|ter(in)** M(F) short-time worker; **Kurz|ar|bei|ter|geld** NT short-time allowance

> **KURZARBEIT**
>
> **Kurzarbeit** is a temporary reduction in working hours due to a lack of orders. The firm reports the situation to the employment office, which then makes up part of the shortfall in employees' wages, or – in cases where working hours have been drastically reduced – pays out **Kurzarbeitergeld** amounting to about two-thirds of an employee's recent net salary. This measure is intended to help firms through short-term economic difficulties: employees do not have to be dismissed and are ready to resume full-time work as soon as the situation improves.

Kurz-: **kurz|är|me|lig, kurz|ärm|lig** ADJ short-sleeved; **kurz|at|mig** [-laːtmɪç] ADJ *(Med)* short of breath; *(fig)* short-winded; **Kurz|at|mig|keit** F -, *no pl (Med)* shortness of breath; *(fig)* short-windedness; **Kurz|aus|bil|dung** F short training course; **Kurz|au|to** NT short-wheelbase car; **Kurz|be|richt** M brief report; *(= Zusammenfassung)* summary; **Kurz|be|schrei|bung** F brief description; **Kurz|be|such** M brief *or* flying visit; **Kurz|brief** M memo

Kür|ze [ˈkʏrtsə] F **-, -n** **a** *no pl* shortness; *(von Besuch, Bericht etc)* brevity, briefness, shortness; *(fig) (= Bündigkeit)* brevity, conciseness; *(= Barschheit)* abruptness, curtness, bluntness; **in ~** *(= bald)* shortly, soon; *(= kurz umrissen)* briefly *or* in brief; **in aller ~** very briefly; **der ~ halber** for the sake of brevity; **in der ~ liegt die Würze** *(Prov)* brevity is the soul of wit **b** *(Poet: = Silbe)* short (syllable)

Kür|zel [ˈkʏrtsl] NT **-s, -** *(= stenografisches Zeichen)* shorthand symbol; *(Ling: = Kurzwort)* contraction; *(= Abkürzung)* abbreviation

kür|zen [ˈkʏrtsn] VT *Kleid, Rede etc* to shorten; *Buch auch* to abridge; *(Math) Bruch* to cancel (down); *Gehalt, Etat, Ausgaben, Produktion* to cut (back)

Kurz|ent|schlos|se|ne(r) [-ɛntʃlɔsənə] MF *decl as adj* last-minute decision-maker; **ein Schnäppchen für ~** *(bei Urlaubsbuchung)* last-minute deals *pl*

Kur|ze(r) [ˈkʊrtsə] M *decl as adj (inf)* **a** *(= Schnaps)* short **b** *(= Kurzschluss)* short (circuit)

Kur|ze(r) MF *decl as adj (inf: = Kind)* kid *(inf)*

kur|zer|hand [ˈkʊrtsɐˈhant] ADV without further ado; *entlassen* on the spot; **etw ~ ablehnen** to reject sth out of hand

Kurz-: **kurz+fas|sen** VR *sep* to be brief; **Kurz|fas|sung** F abridged version; **Kurz|film** M short (film); **Kurz|form** F shortened form (*von, zu* of, for); **kurz|fris|tig** [-frɪstɪç] ADJ short-term; *Wettervorhersage* short-range ADV *(= auf kurze Sicht)* for the short term; *(= für kurze Zeit)* for a short time; **etw ~ erledigen** to do sth without delay; **~ seine Pläne ändern** to change one's plans at short notice; **~ gesehen** looked at in the short term; **kurz|ge|fasst**, **kurz|ge|faßt** △ ADJ → **kurz ADV a**; **Kurz|ge|schich|te** F short story; **kurz|ge|schnit|ten** ADJ *attr* → **kurz ADV a**; **Kurz|haar|da|ckel** M short-haired dachshund; **kurz|haa|rig** ADJ short-haired; **Kurz|haar|schnitt** M short haircut, crop; **einen ~ haben** to wear one's hair short; **kurz|hal|sig** ADJ short-necked; **kurz+hal|ten** *sep irreg*, **kurz hal|ten** △ *irreg* VT **jdn ~** to keep sb short; **Kurz|han|tel** F dumbbell; **Kurz|in|for|ma|ti|on** F information summary; *(= Blatt)* information sheet; **Kurz|läu|fer** M *(Fin)* short-dated bond; **kurz|le|big** [-leːbɪç] ADJ short-lived; *(Konsumgut)* with a short lifespan; **Kurz|le|big|keit** F -, *no pl (von Mensch, Tier)* short lifespan; **ich bin von der ~ dieser Mode überzeugt** I'm convinced this fashion won't last; **aufgrund der ~ dieser Maschine ...** since this machine is not built to last ...

kürz|lich [ˈkʏrtslɪç] ADV recently, lately; **erst** *or* **gerade ~** only *or* just recently, only a short time ago ADJ recent

Kurz-: **Kurz|mel|dung** F newsflash; **Kurz|mit|tei|lungs|dienst** M *(Telec)* short message(s) service; **Kurz|nach|richt** F **a** *(= Information)* **~en** *pl* the news headlines *pl*; *(in Zeitung auch)* the news *sing* in brief, news brief **b** *(= SMS)* text message; **Kurz|par|ker** [-parkɐ] M **-s, -** **„nur für ~"** "short-stay *(Brit) or* short-term parking only"; **Kurz|park|zo|ne** F short-stay *(Brit) or* short-term parking zone; **Kurz|pass|spiel** NT *(Ftbl)* short passing (game); **Kurz|rei|se** F short trip; **Kurz|rei|se|kof|fer** M overnight bag; **kurz+schal|ten** VR *sep* to get in contact (*mit* with); **kurz+schlie|ßen** *sep irreg* VT to short-circuit VR *(= in Verbindung treten)* to get in contact (*mit* with); **Kurz|schluss** M **a** *(Elec)* short circuit; **einen ~ haben** to be short-circuited; **einen ~ bekommen** to short-circuit **b** *(fig: auch* **Kurzschlusshandlung***)* rash action; **das war ein ~** *or* **eine ~handlung** something just went snap; **Kurz|schluss|re|ak|ti|on** F knee-jerk *or* rash reaction; **Kurz|schrift** F shorthand; **kurz|schrift|lich** ADJ shorthand ADV in shorthand; **kurz|sich|tig** [-zɪçtɪç] *(lit, fig)* ADJ short-sighted ADV short-sightedly; **Kurz|sich|tig|keit** F -, *no pl (lit, fig)* short-sightedness

Kurz|stre|cken-: **Kurz|stre|cken|flug|zeug** NT short-haul *or* short-range aircraft; **Kurz|stre|cken|jet** M short-range jet; **Kurz|stre|cken|läu|fer(in)** M(F) *(Sport)* sprinter, short distance runner; **Kurz|stre|cken|ra|ke|te** F short-range missile; **Kurz|stre|cken|waf|fe** F short-range weapon

kurz-: **kurz+tre|ten** *sep irreg*, **kurz tre|ten** △ *irreg* VI *(fig inf)* to go easy; **kurz tre|ten** VI *irreg (Mil)* to march with short steps; **Kurz|trip** M *(inf)* short holiday; **kurz|um** [kʊrtsˈlʊm, ˈkʊrtsˈlʊm] ADV in short, in a word

Kür|zung [ˈkʏrtsʊŋ] F **-, -en** shortening; *(eines Berichts, Buchs etc)* abridgement; *(von Gehältern, von Etat, der Produktion)* cut (*+gen* in)

Kurz-: **Kurz|ur|laub** M short holiday *(esp Brit) or* vacation *(US)*; *(Mil)* short leave; **Kurz|wahl** F one-touch dialling *(Brit) or* dialing *(US)*, quick *or* speed *(US)* dial; **Kurz|wahl|spei|cher** M quick-dial number memory; **Kurz|wa|ren** PL haberdashery *(Brit)*, notions *pl (US)*; **Kurz|weil** [-vail] F **-**, *no pl (old)* pastime, diversion; **allerlei ~ treiben** to amuse oneself; **zur ~** as a pastime; **kurz|wei|lig** [-vailɪç] ADJ entertaining; **Kurz|wel|le** F *(Rad)* short wave; **Kurz|wel|len|sen|der** M short-wave transmitter; **Kurz|wort** NT *pl* **-wörter** abbreviation, abbreviated word

Kurz|zeit- *in cpds* short-term; **Kurz|zeit|ef|fekt** M short-term effect; **Kurz|zeit|ge|dächt|nis** NT short-term memory

kurz|zei|tig ADJ *(= für kurze Zeit)* short, brief; *(= kurzlebig)* short-lived *attr* ADV for a short time, briefly

Kurz|zeit-: **Kurz|zeit|mes|ser** M **-s, -** timer; **Kurz|zeit|spei|cher** M short-term memory

kusch [kʊʃ] INTERJ *(an Hund)* down

ku|sche|lig [ˈkʊʃəlɪç] *(inf)* ADJ cosy *(Brit)*, cozy *(US)*, snug ADV **~ weich** soft and cosy *(Brit) or* cozy *(US)*; **~ warm** snug and warm

ku|scheln [ˈkʊʃln] VI to cuddle (*mit* with) VR **sich an jdn ~** to snuggle up to sb, to cuddle up to sb; **sich in etw** *(acc)* **~** to snuggle up in sth, to cuddle up in sth

Ku|schel-: **Ku|schel|rock** M *(Mus inf)* soft rock; **Ku|schel|sex** M loving sex; **wir machen nur ~** we don't have full sex, we just cuddle up together in bed; **Ku|schel|tier** NT cuddly toy

ku|schen [ˈkʊʃn] VI *(Hund etc)* to get down; *(fig)* to knuckle under

Ku|si|ne [kuˈziːnə] F **-, -n** (female) cousin

Kuss [kʊs] M **-es, ⸗e** [ˈkʏsə] kiss; **Gruß und ~ dein X** *(hum inf)* love and kisses, yours X

Küss|chen [ˈkʏsçən] NT **-s, -** little kiss, peck *(inf)*; **gib ~** give us a kiss

kuss|echt ADJ *Lippenstift* kiss-proof

küs|sen [ˈkʏsn] VTI to kiss; **jdm die Hand ~** to kiss sb's hand VR to kiss (each other); **küss die Hand** *(Aus)* your servant *(old)*; *(= guten Tag)* your servant *(old)*, how do you do? *(Brit)*; *(= auf Wiedersehen auch)* good day *(form)*

Kuss-: **kuss|fest** ADJ = **kussecht**; **Kuss|hand** F **jdm eine ~ zuwerfen** to blow sb a kiss; **mit ~!** with (the greatest) pleasure!, gladly!; **jdn/etw mit ~ nehmen** *(inf)* to be only too glad to take sb/sth; **Kuss|mund** M puckered lips *pl*

Küs|te ['kʏstə] F -, -n coast; *(= Ufer)* shore; **die zerklüftete ~ Schottlands** the jagged coastline *or* coast of Scotland

Küs|ten- *in cpds* coastal; **Küs|ten|be|woh|ner(in)** M(F) coast-dweller; **die ~ Englands** people who live on the English coast; **Küs|ten|fi|sche|rei** F inshore fishing *or* fishery *(form)*; **Küs|ten|ge|biet** NT coastal area; **Küs|ten|ge|wäs|ser** PL, **Küs|ten|meer** NT coastal waters *pl*; **Küs|ten|mo|tor|schiff** NT coaster; **Küs|ten|nä|he** F **in ~** near the coast; **Küs|ten|re|gi|on** F coastal area; **Küs|ten|schiff|fahrt** F coastal shipping; **Küs|ten|strich** M stretch of coast; **Küs|ten|wa|che** F, **Küs|ten|wacht** F coastguard(s *pl*)

Küs|ter ['kʏstɐ] M -s, -, **Küs|te|rin** [-ərɪn] F -, -nen verger, sexton

Küs|te|rei [kʏstə'rai] F -, -en verger's *or* sexton's house

Kus|to|de [kʊs'toːdə] M -n, -n, **Kus|to|din** [-'toːdɪn] F -, -nen, **Kus|tos** ['kʊstɔs] M -, **Kustoden** [-'toːdn] *(in Museum)* curator

Ku|ti|ku|la [ku'tiːkula] F -, -s *(spec)* cuticle, cuticula *(spec)*

Kutsch|bock M coach box

Kut|sche ['kʊtʃə] F -, -n coach, carriage; *(inf: = Auto)* jalopy *(inf)*

kut|schen ['kʊtʃn] VTI *(old)* = **kutschieren**

Kut|scher ['kʊtʃɐ] M -s, - coachman, driver

Kut|sche|rin ['kʊtʃərɪn] F -, -nen driver

Kut|scher-: **Kut|scher|ma|nie|ren** PL *(pej)* manners *pl* like a navvy; **Kut|scher|sitz** M coach box

kut|schie|ren [kʊ'tʃiːrən] *ptp* **kutschiert** VI *aux sein* to drive, to ride; **durch die Gegend ~** *(inf)* to drive *or* ride around VT to drive; **jdn im Auto durch die Gegend ~** to drive sb around

Kutsch|kas|ten M luggage compartment on a coach

Kut|te ['kʊtə] F -, -n habit

Kut|tel ['kʊtl] F -, -n *usu pl (S Ger, Aus, Sw)* entrails *pl*

Kut|ter ['kʊtɐ] M -s, - *(Naut)* cutter

Ku|vert [ku'veːɐ, ku'vɛːɐ, ku'vɛrt] NT -s, -s *or (bei dt. Aussprache)* -(e)s, -e **a** *(= Briefkuvert)* envelope **b** *(= Gedeck)* cover

ku|ver|tie|ren [kuvɛr'tiːrən] *ptp* **kuvertiert** VT *(form)* to put into an envelope

Ku|ver|tü|re [kuvɛr'tyːrə] F -, -n *(Cook)* (chocolate) coating

Ku|wait [ku'vait, 'kuːvait] NT -s Kuwait

Ku|wai|ter [ku'vaitɐ, 'kuːvaitɐ] M -s, -, **Ku|wai|te|rin** [-ərɪn] F -, -nen Kuwaiti

Ku|wai|ti [ku'vaiti] M -s, -s Kuwaiti

ku|wai|tisch [ku'vaitɪʃ, 'kuːvaitɪʃ] ADJ Kuwaiti

KV *abbr von* **Köchelverzeichnis**

kW *abbr von* **Kilowatt**

KW *abbr von* **Kalenderwoche**

kWh *abbr* = **Kilowattstunde**

Ky|ber|ne|tik [kybɛr'neːtɪk] F -, *no pl* cybernetics *sing*

Ky|ber|ne|ti|ker [kybɛr'neːtikɐ] M -s, -, **Ky|ber|ne|ti|ke|rin** [-ərɪn] F -, -nen cybernetician

ky|ber|ne|tisch [kybɛr'neːtɪʃ] ADJ cybernetic

Kyk|la|den [ky'klaːdn] PL Cyclades *pl*

kym|risch ['kymrɪʃ] ADJ Cymric, Welsh

Ky|rie ['kyːrie] NT -, -s, **Ky|rie|elei|son** ['kyːriele'laizɔn, -le'leːizɔn] NT -s, -s Kyrie (eleison)

ky|ril|lisch [ky'rɪlɪʃ] ADJ Cyrillic

KZ [kaː'tsɛt] NT -s, -s *abbr von* **Konzentrationslager**

KZler [kaː'tsɛtlɐ] M -s, -, **KZle|rin** [-ərɪn] F -, -nen *(inf)* concentration camp prisoner

L

L, l [ɛl] NT -, - L, l
l [ɛl] *abbr von* **Liter**
Lab [la:p] NT **-(e)s, -e** [-bə] rennin
lab|be|rig ['labərıç], **labb|rig** ['labrıç] ADJ *(dial) Bier, Suppe* watery; *Kaffee, Tee auch* weak; *Essen* mushy; *Stoff etc* floppy, limp; *Hose* flappy
La|bel ['le:bl] NT **-s, -** label
la|ben ['la:bn] *(liter)* VR to feast (oneself) *(an +dat* on); *(an einer Quelle etc)* to refresh oneself *(mit, an +dat* with); **wir labten uns an dem Anblick** we drank in the view, we feasted our eyes on the view VT *(Mensch)* to feast; *(Quelle)* to refresh
la|bern ['la:bɐn] *(inf)* VI to prattle (on *or* away) *(inf)*, to jabber (on *or* away) *(inf)* VT to talk; **was laberst du denn da?** what are you prattling *etc* on about? *(inf)*
la|bi|al [la'bia:l] ADJ *(Ling)* labial
La|bi|al(laut) [la'bia:l-] M **-s, -e** labial
la|bil [la'bi:l] ADJ *Gesundheitszustand, Gleichgewicht, Lage, Markt* unstable; *Gesundheit* delicate; *Kreislauf* poor; *Patient* frail; *(psychisch) Mensch* with no strength of character; *Charakter* weak ADV **die Situation wird als ~ eingeschätzt** the situation is considered to be unstable; **jdn als psychisch ~ einstufen** to consider sb emotionally unstable
La|bi|li|tät [labili'tɛ:t] F -, *no pl* instability; *(von Patient)* frailness; **wegen der ~ seiner Gesundheit** because of his unstable state of health; **die ~ seines Kreislaufs/Charakters** his poor circulation/weak character; **er ist von einer großen ~** he has no strength of character at all
la|bio|den|tal [labiodɛn'ta:l] ADJ *(Ling)* labiodental
Lab-: **Lab|kraut** NT *(Bot)* bedstraw; **Lab|ma|gen** M *(Zool)* abomasum *(spec)*, fourth stomach
La|bor [la'bo:ɐ] NT **-s, -s** *or* **-e** laboratory, lab *(inf)*
La|bo|rant [labo'rant] M **-en, -en**, **La|bo|ran|tin** [-'rantın] F **-, -nen** lab(oratory) technician
La|bo|ra|to|ri|um [labora'to:rium] NT **-s, Laboratorien** [-riən] laboratory
La|bor|be|fund M laboratory findings *pl*
la|bo|rie|ren [labo'ri:rən] *ptp* **laboriert** VI to labour *(Brit)*, to labor *(US) (an +dat* at); *(= leiden)* to be plagued *(an +dat* by)
La|bor-: **La|bor|schiff** NT laboratory ship; **La|bor|un|ter|su|chung** F laboratory test, lab test; **La|bor|ver|such** M laboratory experiment; **La|bor|wer|te** PL laboratory results *pl*
La|bra|dor [labra'do:ɐ] M **-s, -e**, **La|bra|dor|hund** M *(Zool)* labrador
Lab|sal ['la:pza:l] NT **-(e)s, -e** *(or Aus auch)* F **-, -e** *(old, liter)* refreshment
Labs|kaus ['lapskaus] NT -, *no pl (N Ger) stew made of meat, fish and mashed potato*
La|bung ['la:buŋ] F **-, -en** *(liter)* refreshment
La|by|rinth [laby'rınt] NT **-(e)s, -e** *(lit, Med)* labyrinth; *(fig auch)* maze
la|by|rin|thisch ADJ labyrinthine, maze-like ADV **der Weg verläuft ~** the road follows a maze-like path
Lach|an|fall M laughing fit
La|che ['laxə, 'la:xə] F **-, -n** puddle; *(von Benzin, Blut etc auch)* pool

La|che ['laxə] F **-, -n** *(inf)* laugh
lä|cheln ['lɛçln] VI to smile; **verlegen/freundlich ~** to give an embarrassed/a friendly smile
Lä|cheln NT **-s**, *no pl* smile
la|chen ['laxn] VI to laugh *(über +acc* at); **jdn zum Lachen bringen, jdn ~ machen** to make sb laugh; **zum Lachen sein** *(= lustig)* to be hilarious; *(= lächerlich)* to be laughable; **mir ist nicht zum Lachen (zumute)** I'm in no laughing mood; **dass ich nicht lache!** *(inf)* don't make me laugh! *(inf)*; **da kann ich doch nur ~** I can't help laughing (at that); **du hast gut ~!** it's all right for you to laugh! *(inf)*; **lach du nur!** you can laugh!; **gezwungen/verlegen/herzlich ~** to give a forced/an embarrassed/a hearty laugh; **wer zuletzt lacht, lacht am besten** *(Prov)* he who laughs last, laughs longest *(Prov)*; **die ~den Erben** *(hum)* the joyful heirs; **die Sonne** *or* **der Himmel lacht** the sun is shining brightly; **ihm lachte das Glück/der Erfolg** fortune/success smiled on him *or* favoured *(Brit) or* favored *(US)* him → **Dritte(r)**
VT **da gibt es gar nichts zu ~** that's nothing to laugh about; *(= es ist etwas Ernstes auch)* that's no laughing matter, that's not funny; **was gibt es denn da zu ~?** what's so funny about that?; **er hat bei seiner Frau nichts zu ~** *(inf)* he has a hard time of it with his wife; **wenn dieses Versehen herauskommt, hast du nichts zu ~** *(inf)* you won't have anything to laugh about *or* it won't be funny if that mistake comes to light; **das wäre doch gelacht** it would be ridiculous; **sich** *(dat)* **einen Ast** *or* **Bruch ~** *(inf)* to split one's sides (laughing) *(inf)*, to kill oneself *(inf)*, to laugh oneself silly *(inf)*; **sich** *(dat)* **eins (ins Fäustchen) ~** *(inf)* to have a little snigger → **scheckiglachen, Träne**
La|chen NT **-s**, *no pl* laughter, laughing; *(= Art des Lachens)* laugh; **vor ~ schreien** to shriek with laughter; **dir wird das ~ schon noch vergehen!** you'll soon be laughing on the other side of your face *(Brit) or* out of the other side of your mouth *(US)*
La|cher ['laxɐ] M **-s, -** **a** laugher; **die ~ auf seiner Seite haben** to have the last laugh; *(= einen Lacherfolg verbuchen)* to get a laugh **b** *(inf: = Lache)* laugh
Lach|er|folg M **ein ~ sein, einen ~ haben** *or* **erzielen** to make everybody laugh
lä|cher|lich ['lɛçɐlıç] ADJ **a** ridiculous, absurd, ludicrous; *(= komisch)* comical, funny; **jdn/etw ~ machen** to make sb/sth look silly *or* stupid *(vor jdm* in front of sb); **jdn/sich ~ machen** to make a fool of sb/oneself *(vor jdm* in front of sb); **etw ins Lächerliche ziehen** to make fun of sth **b** *(= geringfügig) Kleinigkeit, Anlass* trivial, petty; *Preis* ridiculously *or* absurdly low ADV ridiculously, absurdly
lä|cher|li|cher|wei|se ['lɛçɐlıçɐ'vaizə] ADV ridiculously enough
Lä|cher|lich|keit F **-, -en** **a** *no pl (von Argument etc)* absurdity; **die ~ seiner Bemerkung/ihrer Verkleidung** his ridiculous comment/her ridiculous get-up *(inf)*; **jdn der ~ preisgeben** to make a laughing stock of sb **b** *(= Geringfügigkeit)* triviality

Lach-: **Lach|fal|ten** PL laughter lines *pl*, laugh lines *pl (US)*; **Lach|gas** NT laughing gas; **lach|haft** ADJ ridiculous, ludicrous; *Ansichten, Argument auch* laughable; **Lach|krampf** M paroxysm (of laughter); **einen ~ bekommen** to go (off) into fits of laughter; **Lach|mö|we** F black-headed gull; **Lach|mus|kel** M *(Anat)* risorius; **das ist was für Ihre ~n** this will really make you laugh; **Lach|num|mer** F *(inf: = Witz, Mensch)* joke *(inf)*
Lachs [laks] M **-es, -e** salmon
Lach|sal|ve F burst *or* roar of laughter
Lachs-: **lachs|far|ben** [-farbn], **lachs|far|big** ADJ salmon pink, salmon(-coloured) *(Brit)*, salmon(-colored) *(US)*; **Lachs|fo|rel|le** F salmon *or* sea trout; **Lachs|schin|ken** M *smoked, rolled fillet of ham*
Lach|tau|be F ringdove, Barbary dove
Lack [lak] M **-(e)s, -e** *(= Holzlack, Nagellack)* varnish; *(= Autolack)* paint; *(für Lackarbeiten)* lacquer → **fertig ADJ a**
Lack-: **Lack|af|fe** M *(pej inf)* flash Harry *(Brit inf)*, real flashy dude *(US inf)*; **Lack|ar|beit** F lacquerwork
La|cke ['lakə] F **-, -n** *(Aus)* puddle
La|ckel ['lakl] M **-s, -** *(S Ger, Aus)* oaf
la|cken ['lakn] VTI *(Tech)* to lacquer
Lack|far|be F gloss paint
La|ckier|ar|bei|ten PL *(von Möbeln etc)* varnishing; *(von Autos)* spraying
la|ckie|ren [la'ki:rən] *ptp* **lackiert** VTI *Holz* to varnish; *Fingernägel auch* to paint; *Auto* to spray; **am Ende war ich der Lackierte** *(inf)* I ended up looking a fool
La|ckie|rer [la'ki:rɐ] M **-s, -**, **La|ckie|re|rin** [-ərın] F **-, -nen** varnisher; *(von Autos)* sprayer
La|ckie|re|rei [laki:rə'rai] F **-, -en** **a** *(= Autolackiererei)* paint shop; *(= Möbellackiererei)* varnisher's **b** *(Handwerk)* lacquerwork
La|ckie|rung F **-, -en** **a** *(= das Lackieren) (von Autos)* spraying; *(von Möbeln)* varnishing **b** *(= der Lack) (von Auto)* paintwork; *(= Holzlackierung)* varnish; *(für Lackarbeiten)* lacquer
La|ckier|werk|statt F, **La|ckier|werk|stät|te** F *(für Autos)* paint shop; *(für Möbel)* varnisher's
Lack|le|der NT patent leather
lack|mei|ern ['lakmaiɐn] VT → **gelackmeiert**
Lack|mus ['lakmus] NT OR M -, *no pl* litmus
Lack|mus|pa|pier NT litmus paper
Lack-: **Lack|scha|den** M damage to the paintwork; **Lack|schuh** M patent-leather shoe
lad|bar ADJ *(Comput)* loadable, download(able); **~e Schriften** *pl (Comput)* soft fonts
La|de ['la:də] F **-, -n** chest; *(inf: = Schublade)* drawer
La|de-: **La|de|baum** M derrick; **La|de|brü|cke** F loading bridge; **La|de|bucht** F *(Space)* loading bay; **La|de|büh|ne** F loading ramp; **La|de|flä|che** F load area; **La|de|ge|rät** NT battery charger; **La|de|ge|wicht** NT load capacity; **La|de|gut** NT *(= Ladung)* load; *(= Fracht)* freight *no pl*; **La|de|hem|mung** F **das Gewehr hat ~** the gun is jammed; **er hatte plötzlich ~** *(inf)* he had a sudden mental block; **La|de|hö|he** F **Lkw mit einer ~ bis zu ... Meter** loads not exceeding ... metres *(Brit) or* meters

(US) (in height); **La|de|klap|pe** F tailboard, tailgate; **La|de|kon|trol|le** F *(Aut)* (generator) charge indicator; **La|de|lu|ke** F cargo *or* loading hatch

la|den ['la:dn] *pret* **lud** [lu:t], *ptp* **geladen** [gə'la:dn] VT **a** *(= beladen)* to load; **einen Sack Mehl auf den Rücken ~** to load *or* hump a sack of flour on one's back; **das Schiff hat Autos geladen** the ship has a cargo of cars; **der Lkw hat zu viel geladen** the lorry is overloaded; **Verantwortung/Schulden auf sich** *(acc)* **~** to saddle *or* load oneself with responsibility/debts; **eine schwere Schuld auf sich** *(acc)* **~** to place oneself under a heavy burden of guilt; **da habe ich ja etwas auf mich geladen** I've taken on more than I'd bargained for → *auch* **geladen**

b *Schusswaffe* to load; *(= wiederaufladen) Batterie, Akku* to recharge; *(Phys)* to charge

c *(Comput)* to load; *Schrift, Datei* to (down)-load; *Laufwerk, Datenträger* to mount

VI **a** *(auch Comput)* to load (up)

b *(Phys)* to charge

la|den *pret* **lud** [lu:t], *ptp* **geladen** [gə'la:dn] VT **a** *(liter: = einladen)* to invite; **nur für geladene Gäste** by invitation only **b** *(form: vor Gericht)* to summon

La|den ['la:dn] M **-s,** ¨ ['lɛ:dn] *(= Geschäft)* shop *(esp Brit)*, store *(US)*; *(inf: = Betrieb, Unternehmung)* outfit *(inf)*; **der ~ läuft** *(inf)* business is good; **es wird eine Zeit dauern, bis der ~ läuft** *(inf)* it will be some time before the business gets going *or* gets off the ground; **dann kann er den ~ zumachen** *or* **dichtmachen** *(inf)* he might as well shut up shop (and go home) *(inf)*; **den ~ schmeißen** *(inf)* to run the show; *(= zurechtkommen)* to manage; **den (ganzen) ~ hinschmeißen** *(inf)* to chuck the whole thing in *(inf)*

La|den M **-s,** ¨ *or* **-** *(= Fensterladen)* shutter

La|den-: **La|den|be|sit|zer(in)** M(F) shopowner *(esp Brit)*, shopkeeper *(esp Brit)*, storekeeper *(US)*; **La|den|de|tek|tiv(in)** M(F) store detective; **La|den|dieb(in)** M(F) shoplifter; **La|den|dieb|stahl** M shoplifting; **La|den|ein|rich|tung** F shop fittings *pl*, store fixtures *pl*; **La|den|ge|schäft** NT retail business; **La|den|hü|ter** M non-seller; **La|den|kas|se** F cash desk, till; **La|den|ket|te** F chain of shops *(esp Brit) or* stores; **La|den|lo|kal** NT shop *or* store *(US)* premises *pl*; **La|den|öff|nungs|zeit** F *usu pl* shop *(esp Brit) or* store *(US)* opening hours *pl*; **La|den|preis** M shop *(esp Brit) or* store *(US)* price; **La|den|schild** NT shop *(esp Brit) or* store *(US)* sign

La|den|schluss M **nach/vor ~** after/before the shops *(esp Brit) or* stores *(US)* shut; **kurz vor ~** *(lit, fig)* just before we/they shut up shop; **um fünf Uhr ist ~** the shops *(esp Brit) or* stores *(US)* shut at five o'clock

La|den|schluss-: **La|den|schluss|ge|setz** NT *law governing the hours of trading*; **La|den|schluss|zeit** F (shop *(esp Brit) or* store *(US)*) closing time

La|den-: **La|den|stra|ße** F shopping street; **La|den|tisch** M shop counter; **über den/unter dem ~** over/under the counter; **La|den|toch|ter** F *(Sw)* shop *(esp Brit) or* sales assistant, salesgirl

La|de-: **La|de|platz** M loading bay *or* area; **La|de|ram|pe** F loading ramp; **La|de|raum** M load room; *(Aviat, Naut)* hold; **La|de|sta|ti|on** F *(Elec, für Gerät, Akku)* base unit; **La|de|stock** M ramrod; **La|de|zo|ne** F loading bay *or* area

lä|die|ren [lɛ'di:rən] *ptp* **lädiert** VT *Kunstwerk, Briefmarke* to damage; *Körperteil* to injure; **lädiert sein/aussehen** *(hum)* to be/look the worse for wear; **sein lädiertes Image** his tarnished image

Lad|ne|rin ['la:dnərɪn] F **-, -nen** *(old: S Ger, Aus)* shop assistant

lädt [lɛ:t] *3. pers sing pres von* **laden**

La|dung ['la:dʊŋ] F **-, -en** **a** load; *(von Schnee, Steinen, Unflätigkeiten etc)* whole load *(inf)*; *(von Sprengstoff)* charge; **eine geballte ~ Schnee/Dreck** *(inf)* a handful of snow/mud; **eine geballte ~ von Schimpfwörtern** a whole torrent of abuse **b** *(= Vorladung)* summons *sing*

La|dy ['le:di] F **-, -s** lady; *(Adlige)* Lady

La|fet|te [la'fɛtə] F **-, -n** *(Mil)* (gun) carriage

Laf|fe ['lafə] M **-n, -n** *(pej)* flash Harry *(Brit inf)*, real flashy dude *(US inf)*

lag *pret von* **liegen**

La|ge ['la:gə] ✪ 39.2, 42.4, 43.4 F **-, -n** **a** *(= geografische Lage)* situation, location; **in günstiger ~** well-situated; **eine gute/ruhige ~ haben** to be in a good/quiet location; **in höheren ~n Schneefall** snow on higher ground

b *(= Art des Liegens)* position; **eine bequeme ~ haben, sich in einer bequemen ~ befinden** to be lying comfortably, to be (lying) in a comfortable position

c *(= Situation)* situation; **in der ~ sein, etw zu tun** *(befähigt sein)* to be able to do sth, to be capable of doing sth; **dazu bin ich nicht in der ~** I'm not in a position to do that; **er wird wohl nie in die ~ kommen, das zu tun** he'll never be in a position to do it; **in der glücklichen/beneidenswerten ~ sein, etw zu tun** to be in the happy/enviable position of doing sth; **Herr der ~ sein/bleiben** to be/remain master of *or* in control of the situation; **nach ~ der Dinge** as things stand; **die ~ der Dinge erfordert es, dass ...** the situation requires that ... → **peilen**

d *(= Schicht)* layer

e *(Mus) (= Stimmlage)* register; *(= Tonlage)* pitch; *(auf Instrument)* position; **enge/weite ~** close/open harmony

f *(= Runde)* round

La|ge-: **La|ge|be|richt** M report; *(Mil)* situation report; **La|ge|be|spre|chung** F discussion of the situation; **eine ~ abhalten** to discuss the situation

La|gen-: **La|gen|schwim|men** NT, *no pl (Sport)* individual medley; **La|gen|staf|fel** F *(Sport) (Schwimmen)* medley relay; *(= Mannschaft)* medley relay team

la|gen|wei|se ['la:gnvaizə] ADV in layers

La|ge|plan M ground plan

La|ger ['la:gɐ] NT **-s, -** **a** *(= Unterkunft)* camp; **sein ~ aufschlagen** to set up camp

b *(liter: = Schlafstätte)* bed; **die Krankheit fesselte ihn wochenlang ans ~** the illness kept him abed *(old) or* in bed for weeks; **sie wachten am ~ des Königs** they kept watch at the King's bedside

c *(fig) (= Partei)* camp; *(von Staaten)* bloc; **ins andere ~ überwechseln** to change camps *or* sides

d *pl auch* **Läger** *(= Vorratsraum)* store(room); *(von Laden)* stockroom; *(= Lagerhalle)* warehouse ['lɛ:gɐ]; *(= Vorrat)* stock; **am ~ sein** to be in stock; **etw auf ~ legen** *(Comm)* to store sth; **etw auf ~ haben** to have sth in stock; *(fig) Witz etc* to have sth on tap *(inf)*, to have sth (at the) ready

e *(Tech)* bearing

f *(Geol)* bed; *(= Lagerstätte)* deposit

La|ger-: **La|ger|be|stand** M stock, inventory *(US)*; **den ~ aufnehmen** to do the stocktaking *(Brit) or* inventory; **La|ger|den|ken** NT *(Pol)* stereotype thinking, thinking in stereotypes; **la|ger|fä|hig** ADJ storable; **La|ger|feu|er** NT campfire; **La|ger|flä|che** F storage area; *(gemessen)* storage *or* floor space; **La|ger|ge|bühr** F, **La|ger|geld** NT storage charge; **La|ger|haft** F detention in a (prison) camp; **nach sieben Jahren ~** after seven years in a prison camp; **La|ger|hal|le** F warehouse; **La|ger|hal|tung** F storekeeping; **~ rentiert sich bei uns nicht** it doesn't pay us to keep a large stock; **La|ger|haus** NT warehouse

La|ge|rist [lagə'rɪst] M **-en, -en** storeman

La|ge|ris|tin [lagə'rɪstɪn] F **-, -nen** storewoman

La|ger-: **La|ger|kol|ler** M *(inf)* **er hat einen ~ gekriegt** life in the camp turned his mind; **La|ger|kos|ten** PL storage charges *pl*, storage *sing*; **La|ger|le|ben** NT camp life; **La|ger|lei|ter(in)** M(F) camp commander; *(in Ferienlager etc)* camp leader

la|gern ['la:gɐn] VT **a** *(= aufbewahren)* to store; **kühl ~!** keep *or* store in a cool place **b** *(= hinlegen)* **jdn** to lay down; *Bein etc* to rest; **den Kopf/einen Kranken weich ~** to rest one's head/lay an invalid on something soft; **das Bein hoch ~** to put one's leg up; **die Patienten müssen bequem gelagert werden** the patients must be bedded down *or* must lie comfortably → *auch* **gelagert** VI **a** *(Vorräte, Waren, Abfall etc)* to be stored *or* kept **b** *(= liegen)* to lie; **vor der Küste lagert Erdöl** there are deposits of oil lying off the coast **c** *(Truppen etc)* to camp, to be encamped VR *(geh)* to settle oneself (down)

La|ger-: **La|ger|platz** M **a** *(über Nacht)* place to spend the night **b** *(Econ: = Warenlager)* storage place; **La|ger|raum** M storeroom; *(in Geschäft)* stockroom; **La|ger|statt** F *pl* **-stätten** [-ʃtɛtn] *(old liter)* bed, couch *(liter)*; **La|ger|stät|te** F **a** *(old liter: = Bett)* bed, couch *(liter)* **b** *(Geol)* deposit; **La|ger|the|o|rie** F *(Pol)* theory of political stereotypes

La|ge|rung ['la:gərʊŋ] F **-, -en** storage; *(= das Lagern auch)* storing

La|ger-: **La|ger|ver|kauf** M warehouse sale; **La|ger|ver|wal|ter(in)** M(F) stores supervisor; **La|ger|vor|rat** M stock, supply

La|ge|skiz|ze F sketch-map

La|gu|ne [la'gu:nə] F **-, -n** lagoon

La|gu|nen|stadt F town built on a lagoon; **die ~** *(= Venedig)* Venice

lahm [la:m] ADJ **a** *(= gelähmt) Bein, Mensch, Tier* lame; *(inf: = steif)* stiff; **er ist auf dem linken Bein ~** he is lame in his *or* the left leg; **er hat ein ~es Bein** he is lame in one leg, he has a gammy *(Brit) or* gimpy *(US)* leg *(inf)* **b** *(inf: = langsam, langweilig)* dreary, dull; *Ausrede, Entschuldigung* lame; *Geschäftsgang* slow, sluggish; **eine ~e Ente sein** *(inf)* to have no zip *(inf)* ADV *(inf) (= langsam)* slowly; *(= wenig überzeugend)* lamely; **eine ~ verfilmte Story** a dully filmed story

Lahm-: **Lahm|arsch** M *(inf)* slowcoach *(Brit inf)*, slowpoke *(US inf)*; **lahm|ar|schig** [-larʃɪç] *(inf)* ADJ bloody *(Brit inf) or* damn *(inf)* slow ADV bloody *(Brit inf) or* damn *(inf)* slowly

lah|men ['la:mən] VI to be lame *(auf +dat* in)

läh|men ['lɛ:mən] VT to paralyze; *(fig) Industrie, Regierung auch* to cripple; *Verhandlungen, Verkehr* to hold up; **er ist durch einen Unfall gelähmt** he was paralyzed in an accident; **~des Entsetzen befiel die Zuschauer** the onlookers were paralyzed with horror → *auch* **gelähmt**

Lah|me(r) ['la:mə] MF *decl as adj (old)* cripple

Lahm|heit F **-,** *no pl* **a** *(von Mensch, Tier, Bein)* lameness **b** *(inf: = Langsamkeit, Langeweile)* dreariness, dullness; *(von Geschäft, Konjunktur)* slowness, sluggishness

lahm+le|gen *sep*, **lahm le|gen** △ VT *Verkehr, Produktion* to bring to a standstill *or* halt; *Industrie auch, Stromversorgung* to paralyze; **einen Flughafen ~** to bring an airport to a standstill

Läh|mung ['lɛ:mʊŋ] F **-, -en** *(lit)* paralysis; *(fig)* immobilization

Läh|mungs|er|schei|nun|gen PL signs *pl* of paralysis

Lahn [la:n] F **-, -en** *(Aus)* avalanche

Laib [laip] M **-(e)s, -e** [-bə] *(esp S Ger)* loaf

Laich [laiç] M **-(e)s, -e** spawn

lai|chen ['laiçn] VI to spawn

Laich-: **Laich|platz** M spawning ground; **Laich|zeit** F spawning season

Laie ['laiə] M **-n, -n** *(lit, fig)* layman, layperson; **er ist ein ökonomischer ~** he is no expert in economics; **~n** the lay public; **die ~n** *pl (Eccl)* the laity; **da staunt der ~, der Fachmann wundert sich** *(hum inf)* that's a real turn-up for the book(s) *(Brit inf)*, that's a real unexpected surprise

Lai|en-: **Lai|en|apos|to|lat** [-lapɔstola:t] NT **-(e)s, -e** lay apostolate; **Lai|en|bru|der** M lay brother; **Lai|en|büh|ne** F amateur dramatic society; *(Gebäude)* amateur theatre *(Brit) or* theater *(US)*; **Lai|en|dar|stel|ler(in)** M(F) amateur actor/actress; **lai|en|haft** ADJ *Arbeit* amateurish, unprofessional; *Urteil, Meinung* lay *attr* ADV *spielen* amateurishly, unprofessionally; **etw ~ ausdrücken** to put sth in simple terms; **etw ~ übersetzen** to do an amateurish translation of sth; **ich benutze den Computer ~** I am an amateur when it comes to computers; **Lai|en|pre|di|ger(in)** M(F), **Lai|en|pries|ter(in)** M(F) lay preacher; **Lai|en|rich|ter(in)** M(F) lay judge; **Lai|en|schwes|ter** F lay sister; **Lai|en|spiel** NT amateur play; **Lai|en|spiel|grup|pe** F amateur theatre *(Brit) or* theater *(US)* group; **Lai|en|stand** M laity; **Lai|en|the|a|ter** NT amateur theatre *(Brit) or* theater *(US)*; *(Ensemble)* amateur theatre *(Brit) or* theater *(US)* group; **Lai|en|tum** [ˈlaiəntu:m] NT **-s,** *no pl* laity; **er musste sich zwischen Priestertum und ~ entscheiden** he had to decide whether to become a priest or remain a layman; **Lai|en|ver|stand** M lay mind, layman's *or* layperson's knowledge

la|i|sie|ren [laiˈzi:rən] *ptp* **laisiert** VT to unfrock

Lais|ser-faire [lɛseˈfɛ:r] NT **-,** *no pl (Econ, fig)* laisser-faire, laissez-faire

La|i|zis|mus [laiˈtsɪsmʊs] M **-,** *no pl* laicism

la|i|zis|tisch [laiˈtsɪstɪʃ] ADJ laicist

La|kai [laˈkai] M **-en, -en** *(lit, fig)* lackey

la|kai|en|haft ADJ servile ADV *sich benehmen* in a servile way

La|ke [ˈla:kə] F **-, -n** brine

La|ken [ˈla:kn] NT **-s, -** sheet

la|ko|nisch [laˈko:nɪʃ] ADJ laconic ADV laconically

Lak|ritz [laˈkrɪts] M **-es, -e** *(dial)*, **Lak|rit|ze** [laˈkrɪtsə] F **-, -n** liquorice *(Brit)*, licorice

Lak|to|se [lakˈto:zə] F **-,** *no pl* lactose

la|la [ˈlaˈla] ADV *(inf)* **so ~** so-so *(inf)*, not too bad *(inf)*

lal|len [ˈlalən] VTI to babble; *(Betrunkener)* to mumble

La|ma [ˈla:ma] NT **-s, -s** *(Zool)* llama

La|ma M **-(s), -s** *(Rel)* lama

La|ma|is|mus [lamaˈɪsmʊs] M **-,** *no pl* Lamaism

La|ma|klos|ter NT lamasery

La|mäng [laˈmɛŋ] F **aus der (kalten) ~** *(sl)* just like that

Lamb|da-Son|de [ˈlampda-] F *(Aut)* Lambda probe

La|mé, La|mee [laˈme:] M **-s, -s** *(Tex)* lamé

La|mel|le [laˈmɛlə] F **-, -n** **a** *(Biol)* lamella **b** *(Tech)* commutator bar *or* segment; *(von Jalousien)* slat

la|mel|len|för|mig ADJ lamellate, lamellar

La|mel|len|pilz M agaric

la|men|tie|ren [lamɛnˈti:rən] *ptp* **lamentiert** VI to moan, to complain

La|men|to [laˈmɛnto] NT **-s, -s** *(Mus)* lament; **wegen etw ein ~ anstimmen** *(fig)* to bewail sth

La|met|ta [laˈmɛta] NT **-s,** *no pl* lametta; *(hum: = Orden)* gongs *pl (inf)*

La|mi|nat [lamiˈna:t] NT **-s, -e** laminate

la|mi|nie|ren [lamiˈni:rən] *ptp* **laminiert** VT *(Tex)* to draw; *(Typ)* to laminate

Lamm [lam] NT **-(e)s, ¨-er** [ˈlɛmɐ] lamb; **das ~ Gottes** the Lamb of God

Lamm-: **Lamm|bra|ten** M roast lamb; **Lamm|fell** NT lambskin; **Lamm|fleisch** NT lamb; **lamm|fromm** ADJ *Gesicht, Miene* innocent; **~ sein** to be like a (little) lamb ADV like a little lamb/little lambs; **sie saßen ~ auf ihren Plätzen** they were sitting in their seats like little lambs *or* as good as gold; **Lamm|ko|te|lett** NT lamb chop; **Lamm|rü|cken** M *(Cook)* saddle of lamb; **Lamm|wol|le** F lambswool

Läm|mer|wölk|chen PL fleecy *or* cotton-wool clouds *pl (inf)*

Lam|mes|ge|duld F patience of a saint

Lamms|ge|duld F patience of a saint

Lam|pe [ˈlampə] F **-, -n** light; *(= Öllampe, Stehlampe, Tischlampe)* lamp; *(= Glühlampe)* bulb; **die ~n auf der Straße** the street lights; **einen auf die ~ gießen** *(inf)* to wet one's whistle *(inf)*

Lam|pen-: **Lam|pen|fie|ber** NT stage fright; **Lam|pen|licht** NT artificial light; **Lam|pen|schirm** M lampshade

Lam|pi|on [lamˈpiõ:, lamˈpiɔŋ] M **-s, -s** Chinese lantern

LAN [lɛn] NT **-(s), -s** *abbr von* **local area network** *(Comput)* LAN

lan|cie|ren [lãˈsi:rən] *ptp* **lanciert** VT *Produkt, Künstler, Initiative* to launch; *Meldung, Nachricht* to put out; **jdn/etw in etw** *(acc)* **~** to get sb/sth into sth; **sein Onkel hat ihn in diese hohe Stellung lanciert** his uncle got him (into) that high position; **etw an die Presse ~** to leak sth to the press

Land [lant] NT **-(e)s, ¨-er** [ˈlɛndɐ] **a** *(= Gelände, Festland)* land; *(= Landschaft)* country, landscape; **ein Stück ~** a plot of land *or* ground; **~ bestellen** to till the soil *or* land; **~ bebauen** to cultivate the land; **~ gewinnen** *(lit) (am Meer)* to reclaim land; *(Agr)* to cultivate land; *(fig)* to gain ground; **an ~ gehen** to go ashore; **jdn an ~ setzen** to put sb ashore; **an ~ schwimmen** to swim to the shore; **~ sehen** *(lit)* to see *or* sight land; **endlich können wir ~ sehen/sehe ich ~** *(fig)* at last we/I can see the light at the end of the tunnel; **kein ~ mehr sehen (können)** *(fig)* to be completely muddled, to be in a complete muddle; **etw an ~ ziehen** to pull sth ashore; **ein Boot an ~ ziehen** to beach a boat; **einen Fisch an ~ ziehen** to land a fish; **einen Millionär/einen Auftrag an ~ ziehen** *(inf)* to land a millionaire/an order; **~ in Sicht!** land ahoy!; **~ unter!** land submerged!; **bei uns/euch zu ~e** back home, where we/you come from *or* live, in our/your country **b** *(= ländliches Gebiet)* country; **aufs ~** (in)to the country; **auf dem ~(e)** in the country; **vom ~(e)** from the country; **über ~ fahren** *(mit Auto etc)* to drive/travel across country; *(Fahrschüler)* to drive on country roads; *(old: = reisen)* to travel **c** *(= Staat)* country, land *(esp liter)*; *(= Bundesland) (in BRD)* Land, state; *(in Österreich)* province; **das ~ Hessen** the state of Hesse; **das ~ Tirol** the province of Tyrol, Tyrol province; **außer ~es sein/gehen** to be out of/leave the country; **~ und Leute kennenlernen** to get to know the country and its inhabitants; **das ~ der unbegrenzten Möglichkeiten** the new world, the land of limitless opportunity; **das ~ der aufgehenden Sonne** the land of the rising sun; **aus aller Herren Länder(n)** from all over the world, from the four corners of the earth; **der Frühling war ins ~ gezogen** *(liter)* spring had arrived; **seitdem waren viele Jahre ins ~ gegangen** *or* **gezogen** *(liter)* many years had passed since then; **bleibe im ~e und nähre dich redlich** *(prov)* stay put and prosper → **Milch** **d** **Lande** PL *(poet)* lands *pl*; **in fernen ~en** *(liter)* in distant lands, in faraway lands; **durch die ~e ziehen** *(liter)* to roam abroad

> **LAND**
>
> Germany is a federal republic made up of 16 **Länder**: Baden-Württemberg, Bavaria, Berlin, Bremen, Hamburg, Hesse, Lower Saxony, North Rhine-Westphalia, Rhineland-Palatinate, Saarland, Schleswig-Holstein and the so-called **neue Länder** which acceded to the constitution after re-unification on 3rd October 1990: Brandenburg, Saxony, Saxony-Anhalt, Mecklenburg-West Pomerania and Thuringia. The **Länder** have their own state authorities and their own legislation. However, the rule that "Federal law takes precedence over **Land** law" means that in many cases **Land** legislation is no longer observed. The **Länder** are responsible for education and policing, and for implementing Federal laws.
>
> Austria is also a federal state consisting of nine **Länder**: Burgenland, Carinthia, Lower Austria, Upper Austria, Salzburg, Styria, Tyrol, Vorarlberg and Vienna.

Land-: **land|ab** [lantˈlap] ADV → **landauf**; **Land|adel** M landed gentry; **Land|am|mann** M *(Sw) highest official in a Swiss canton*; **Land|ar|beit** F agricultural work; **Land|ar|bei|ter(in)** M(F) agricultural worker; **Land|aris|to|kra|tie** F landed aristocracy; **Land|arzt** M, **Land|ärz|tin** F country doctor

Lan|dau|er [ˈlandauɐ] M **-s, -** landau

Land-: **land|auf** [lantˈlauf] ADV **~, landab** all over the country, the length and breadth of the country; **land|aus** [lantˈlaus] ADV **~, landein** all over the world; **Land|bau** M, *no pl* = **Ackerbau**; **Land|be|sitz** M landholding; **~ haben** to be a landowner, to own land; **Land|be|sit|zer(in)** M(F) landowner; **Land|be|völ|ke|rung** F rural population; **Land|be|woh|ner(in)** M(F) country dweller; **~ sind ...** people who live in the country are ...; **Land|brot** NT *brown bread usually made from rye flour*; **Land|brü|cke** F land bridge; **Land|but|ter** F farm butter

Län|de [ˈlɛndə] F **-, -n** *(dial)* landing stage

Lan|de-: **Lan|de|an|flug** M approach; **Lan|de|bahn** F runway; **Lan|de|brü|cke** F jetty, landing stage; **Lan|de|er|laub|nis** F landing permission, permission to land; **Lan|de|fäh|re** F *(Space)* landing module

Land-: **Land|ei** NT farm egg; *(pej sl)* country bumpkin *(inf)*; **land|ein** [lantˈlain] ADV → **landaus**; **land|ein|wärts** [lantˈlainvɛrts] ADV inland

Lan|de-: **Lan|de|klap|pe** F landing flap; **Lan|de|kopf** M *(Mil)* beachhead; **Lan|de|kor|ri|dor** M *(Space)* re-entry corridor *or* window; **Lan|de|ma|nö|ver** NT landing manoeuvre *(Brit) or* maneuver *(US)*

lan|den [ˈlandn] VI *aux sein* to land; *(inf) (= enden)* to land up; *(= Eindruck machen)* to get somewhere; **weich ~** to make a soft landing; **alle anonymen Briefe ~ sofort im Papierkorb** all anonymous letters go straight into the wastepaper basket; **mit deinen Komplimenten kannst du bei mir nicht ~** your compliments won't get you anywhere *or* very far with me VT *(lit, fig)* to land → **Coup**

län|den [ˈlɛndn] VT *(dial) Leiche* to recover *(aus* from)

Land|en|ge F isthmus

Lan|de-: **Lan|de|pis|te** F landing strip; **Lan|de|platz** M *(für Flugzeuge)* place to land; *(ausgebaut)* landing strip; *(für Schiffe)* landing place; **Lan|de|recht** NT *(Aviat)* landing rights *pl*

Län|de|rei|en [lɛndəˈraiən] PL estates *pl*

Län|der-: **Län|der|ein|stel|lun|gen** PL *(Comput)* regional settings; **Län|der|fi|nanz|aus|gleich** M, *no pl* balancing of federal budgets; **Län|der|kampf** M *(Sport)* international contest; *(= Länderspiel)* international (match); **Län|der|kun|de** F regional studies *pl*; **Län|der|na|me** M name of a/the country; **Län|der|spiel** NT international (match); **län|der|über|grei|fend** ADJ **a** *(Ger)* at federal level **b** *(international)* at international level

Lan|des-: **Lan|des|bank** F *pl* **-banken** regional bank; **Lan|des|be|am|te(r)** M *decl as adj*, **Lan|des|be|am|tin** F *civil servant employed by a Land rather than the nation*; **Lan|des|be|hör|de** F regional authorities *pl*; **Lan|des|bo|den|brief** M land mortgage certificate; **Lan|des|brauch** M national custom, custom of the country; **nach ~ ist es hier üblich ...** in this country it is customary ...; **Lan|des|ebe|ne** F **auf ~** at state level; **lan|des|ei|gen** ADJ → **Land c** owned by the country/state *or* Land/province; **Lan|des|far|ben** PL *(von Staat)* national colours *pl (Brit) or* colors *pl (US)*; *(von Bundesland)* state colours *pl (Brit) or* colors *pl (US)*; *(in Österreich)* colours *pl (Brit) or* colors *pl (US)* of the province; **Lan|des|fürst(in)** M(F) prince/princess; *(inf: = Ministerpräsident)* state boss; **Lan|des|ge|richt** NT district court; **Lan|des|gren|ze** F *(von Staat)* national boundary;

(von Bundesland) state *or (Aus)* provincial boundary; **Lan|des|haupt|mann** M *(Aus) head of the government of a province*; **Lan|des|haupt|stadt** F capital of a Land; *(Aus)* capital of a province, provincial capital; **Lan|des|herr(in)** M(F) *(Hist)* sovereign, ruler; **Lan|des|ho|heit** F sovereignty; **Lan|des|in|ne|re(s)** NT *decl as adj* interior; **Lan|des|kenn|zahl** F *(Telec)* country code; **Lan|des|kind** NT *(von Staat)* native of a/the country; *(von Bundesland)* native of a/the Land *or (Aus)* province; **Lan|des|kir|che** F national church; *(in Deutschland) established Protestant church in some Länder*; **Lan|des|kun|de** F knowledge of the/a country; *(Univ)* regional and cultural studies *pl*; **lan|des|kun|dig** ADJ **~er Reiseleiter** courier who knows the country; **lan|des|kund|lich** [-kʊntlɪç] ADJ *Kenntnisse, Aspekte* of a/the country's geography and culture ADV in geography and culture; **Lan|des|lis|te** F *(Parl) regional list of parliamentary candidates for election to Federal parliament*; **Lan|des|me|di|en|ge|setz** NT *law relating to the running and content of regional media*; **Lan|des|meis|ter(in)** M(F) *(Sport)* regional champion; **Lan|des|mut|ter** F *pl* **-mütter** *(liter)* mother of the people *(liter)*; **die britische ~** the mother of the British nation *(liter)*; **Lan|des|par|tei|tag** M regional party conference; **Lan|des|po|li|ti|ker(in)** M(F) regional *or* provincial politician; **lan|des|po|li|tisch** ADJ relation to regional *or* provincial politics; **Lan|des|rat** M, **Lan|des|rä|tin** F *(Aus) highest official of an administrative district*; **Lan|des|recht** NT law of a Land *or (Aus)* province; **Lan|des|re|gie|rung** F government of a Land; *(Aus)* provincial government; **Lan|des|spra|che** F national language; **der ~ unkundig sein** not to know the language

Lan|de|steg M landing stage

Lan|des-: **Lan|des|teil** M region, area; **Lan|des|tracht** F national dress *or* costume; **lan|des|üb|lich** ADJ customary; **das ist dort ~** that's the custom there; **Lan|des|va|ter** M *(liter)* father of the people *(liter)*; **Lan|des|ver|rat** M treason; **Lan|des|ver|rä|ter(in)** M(F) traitor; **Lan|des|ver|si|che|rungs|an|stalt** F regional pensions office *(for waged employees)*; **Lan|des|ver|tei|di|gung** F national defence *(Brit) or* defense *(US)*; **lan|des|ver|wie|sen** ADJ *(rare)* expelled, banished *(old)*; *(= exiliert)* exiled; **Lan|des|wäh|rung** F national *or* local currency; **Lan|des|zent|ral|bank** F *pl* **-banken** State Central Bank

Lan|de-: **Lan|de|übung** F landing exercise; **Lan|de|ver|bot** NT refusal of landing permission; **~ erhalten** to be refused landing permission *or* permission to land

Land-: **Land|fah|rer(in)** M(F) *(form)* vagrant; **land|fein** ADJ *(dated)* spruced up; **Land|flucht** F migration from the land, emigration to the cities; **Land|frau** F countrywoman; **Land|frie|de(n)** M *(Hist)* King's/Queen's Peace; **Land|frie|dens|bruch** M *(Jur)* breach of the peace; **Land|funk** M farming (radio) programme *(Brit) or* program *(US)*; **Land|gang** M *pl* **-gänge** shore leave; **Land|ge|mein|de** F country community; **Land|ge|richt** NT district court; **land|ge|stützt** [-gəʃtʏtst] ADJ *Raketen* land-based; **Land|ge|win|nung** F land reclamation; **Land|graf** M landgrave; **Land|gut** NT estate; **Land|haus** NT country house; **Land|heer** NT army; **Land|heim** NT = **Schullandheim**; **Land|jä|ger** M **a** *(Hist)* country policeman **b** *(= Wurst) pressed smoked sausage*; **Land|kar|te** F map; **Land|kli|ma** NT continental climate; **Land|kreis** M administrative district; **Land|krieg** M land warfare; **Luft- und ~** war in the air and on the ground; **See- und ~** war at sea and on land; **Land|kriegs|ord|nung** F **Haager ~** Hague Land Warfare Convention; **land|läu|fig** ADJ popular, common; **entgegen ~er** *or* **der ~en Meinung** contrary to popular opinion ADV commonly

Länd|le ['lɛntlə] NT **-s,** *no pl* **das ~** *(inf)* Baden-Württemberg

Land|le|ben NT country life

Länd|ler ['lɛntlɐ] M **-s, -** *(S Ger) country dance*

Land|leu|te PL country people *pl or* folk *pl*

länd|lich ['lɛntlɪç] ADJ rural; *Tracht* country *attr*; *Tanz* country *attr*, folk *attr*; *Idylle* pastoral; *Stille, Frieden* of the countryside, rural ADV **eine ~ geprägte Region** a rural area; **eine ~ wirkende Stadt** a town which gives a rural impression

Land-: **land|lie|bend** ADJ country-loving *attr*; **Land|luft** F country air; **Land|macht** F land power; **Land|mann** M *pl* **-männer** *(old, liter)* husbandman *(old, liter)*; **Land|ma|schi|nen** PL agricultural machinery *sing or* machines *pl*; **Land|mes|ser** [-mɛsɐ] M **-s, -**, **Land|mes|se|rin** [-ərɪn] F **-, -nen** land surveyor; **Land|mi|ne** F landmine; **Land|nah|me** [-na:mə] F **-, -n** *(Hist)* acquisition of land; **Land|par|tie** F *(old)* country outing; **Land|pfar|rer(in)** M(F) country parson; **Land|pfle|ger** M *(Bibl)* governor; **Land|pla|ge** F plague; *(fig inf)* pest; **Land|po|me|ran|ze** F *(dated pej)* country cousin; **Land|pra|xis** F *(Med)* country practice; **Land|rat** M *(Sw) cantonal parliament*; **Land|rat** M, **Land|rä|tin** F *(Ger) head of the administration of a Landkreis*; **Land|rat|te** F *(hum)* landlubber; **Land|re|form** F land reform; **Land|re|gen** M steady rain; **Land|rü|cken** M ridge of land; **Land|sas|se** ['lantzasə] M **-n, -n** *(Hist)* freeholder

Land|schaft ['lantʃaft] F **-, -en** scenery *no pl*; *(Gemälde)* landscape; *(= ländliche Gegend)* countryside; *(fig)* landscape, scene; **eine öde ~** a barren landscape *or* region; **die ~ um London** the countryside around London; **die ~en Italiens** the types of countryside in Italy; **wir sahen eine reizvolle ~** we saw some delightful scenery; **vor uns tat sich eine liebliche ~ auf** *(geh)* a lovely view appeared before us; **in der ~ herumstehen** *(inf)* to stand around; **da stand einsam ein Hochhaus in der ~ (herum)** *(inf)* there was one solitary skyscraper to be seen; **die politische ~** the political scene *or* landscape; **die kulinarische/kulturelle ~** the culinary/cultural scene

land|schaft|lich ['lantʃaftlɪç] ADJ *Schönheiten etc* scenic; *Besonderheiten* regional ADV *abwechslungsreich, eintönig* scenically; **das Dorf liegt ~ einmalig** *(inf)* the village is surrounded by the most fantastic scenery; **diese Gegend ist ~ ausgesprochen reizvoll** the scenery in this area is particularly delightful; **das ist ~ unterschiedlich** it differs from one part of the country to another, it differs in various parts of the country; **„Klempner" heißt ~ auch „Spengler"** in some areas the word "Spengler" is used for "Klempner"

Land|schafts-: **Land|schafts|bild** NT view; *(Gemälde)* landscape (painting); *(Fotografie)* landscape (photograph); **Land|schafts|form** F land form; **Land|schafts|gärt|ner(in)** M(F) landscape gardener; **Land|schafts|ma|ler(in)** M(F) landscape painter; **Land|schafts|pfle|ge** F, **Land|schafts|schutz** M protection of the countryside; **Land|schafts|schutz|ge|biet** NT nature reserve; **Land|schafts|ver|brauch** M encroachment on the countryside

Land|schul|heim NT = **Schullandheim**

Land|ser ['lantsɐ] M **-s, -** *(dated inf)* private

Lands|frau F *(= Landsmännin)* compatriot, fellow countrywoman

Land|sitz M country seat

Lands-: **Lands|knecht** M *(Hist)* lansquenet; **fluchen wie ein ~** to swear like a trooper; **Lands|mann** M *pl* **-leute** compatriot, fellow countryman; **Lands|män|nin** [-mɛnɪn] F **-, -nen** compatriot, fellow countrywoman; **Lands|mann|schaft** F *welfare and cultural association for Germans born in the eastern areas of the former Reich*

Land-: **Land|spit|ze** F point, promontory, headland; **Land|stän|de** PL *(Hist) body of representatives of various classes in medieval provincial politics*; **Land|stra|ße** F country road; *(= Straße zweiter Ordnung)* secondary *or* B *(Brit)* road; *(im Gegensatz zur Autobahn)* ordinary road; **Land|strei|cher** [-ʃtraiçɐ] M **-s, -**, **Land|strei|che|rin** [-ərɪn] F **-, -nen** *(pej)* tramp, hobo *(US)*; **Land|strei|che|rei** [lantʃtraiçə'rai] F **-,** *no pl* vagrancy; **Land|streit|kräf|te** PL land forces *pl*; **Land|strich** M area; **ein flacher ~** a flat belt of land; **Land|sturm** M *conscripted militia in times of war*, ≈ Home Guard *(Brit)*; **Land|tag** M Landtag *(state parliament)*; **Land|tags|wahl** PL *(Ger)* elections *pl* for the Land *or* state parliament; *(Aus)* elections *pl* for the provincial parliament; **Land|tags|wah|len** PL (West) German regional elections *pl*; **Land|trup|pen** PL land forces *pl*

Lan|dung ['landʊŋ] F **-, -en** *(von Flugzeug, Truppen etc)* landing; **zur ~ gezwungen werden** to be forced to land, to be forced down

Lan|dungs-: **Lan|dungs|boot** NT landing craft; **Lan|dungs|brü|cke** F jetty, landing stage; **Lan|dungs|platz** M landing place; **Lan|dungs|steg** M landing stage; **Lan|dungs|trup|pen** PL land assault forces *pl*

Land-: **Land|ur|laub** M shore leave; **Land|ver|mes|ser** [-fɛɐmɛsɐ] M **-s, -**, **Land|ver|mes|se|rin** [-ərɪn] F **-, -nen** land surveyor; **Land|ver|mes|sung** F land surveying; **Land|vogt** M *(Hist)* landvogt *(governor of a royal province)*; **Land|volk** NT country people *pl or* folk *pl*

landw. *abbr von* **landwirtschaftlich**

Land-: **land|wärts** ['lantvɛrts] ADV landwards; **Land|weg** M **auf dem ~** by land; **Land|wein** M vin ordinaire *(Brit)*, homegrown wine; **Land|wind** M offshore wind; **Land|wirt(in)** M(F) farmer

Land|wirt|schaft F agriculture, farming; *(Betrieb)* farm; *(= Landwirte)* farmers *pl*; **~ betreiben** to farm; **~ haben** *(inf)* to have a farm

land|wirt|schaft|lich ADJ agricultural; **~e Geräte** agricultural *or* farm implements ADV *tätig sein* agriculturally; *geprägt sein* by agriculture; **~ genutzt** used for agricultural purposes

Land|wirt|schafts- *in cpds* agricultural; **Land|wirt|schafts|be|ra|ter(in)** M(F) agricultural adviser; **Land|wirt|schafts|brief** M *(Fin)* agricultural bond; **Land|wirt|schafts|mi|nis|te|ri|um** NT ministry of agriculture, ≈ Department of Agriculture *(US)*; **Land|wirt|schafts|schu|le** F agricultural college *(Brit) or* school *(US)*

Land|zun|ge F spit (of land), promontory

lang [laŋ] ADJ *comp* **=er** ['lɛŋɐ], *superl* ['lɛŋɐ] **=ste(r, s)** ['lɛŋstə] **a** long ['lɛŋstn]; *Film, Roman, Aufenthalt, Rede* long, lengthy; **das ist seit Langem geplant** that has been planned (for) a long time; **das war seit Langem geplant** it was planned a long time ago; **vor ~er Zeit** a long time ago; **in nicht allzu ~er Zeit** before too *or* very long, in the not too distant future; **das hat die längste Zeit gedauert!** that's gone on long enough!; **hier wird mir der Tag** *or* **die Zeit nicht ~** I won't get bored here; **etw länger machen** to make sth longer, to lengthen sth; **es ist eine ~e Strecke bis Bristol, jedenfalls länger, als ich gedacht hatte** it's a long way to Bristol, at least, further than I thought; **die Tage werden wieder länger** the days are drawing out, the days are getting longer; **er machte ein ~es Gesicht** his face fell; **man sah überall nur ~e Gesichter** you saw nothing but long faces; **etw von ~er Hand vorbereiten** to prepare sth carefully; **des Langen und Breiten** at great length; **einen ~en Hals machen** *(inf)* to crane one's neck → **Leine, Sicht a, Bank a, Leitung d, Rede a**

b (*inf:* = *groß gewachsen*) *Mensch* tall; **eine ~e Latte sein, ein ~er Lulatsch sein, ein ~es Elend** *or* **Ende sein** to be a (real) beanpole *(inf)*; **er ist so ~ wie er dumm ist** he's as thick as two short planks *(inf)*

ADV *comp* **≃er**, *superl* **am ≃sten der ~ erwartete Regen** the long-awaited rain; [ˈlɛŋɐ] **der ~ ersehnte Tag/Urlaub** the longed-for day/holiday *(esp Brit)* or vacation *(US)*; **~ anhaltender Beifall** prolonged *or* long applause; **~ gehegt** *(Wunsch)* long-cherished; **~ gestreckt** long; *Dorf auch* strung-out; **~ gezogen** *(Ton, Schrei)* long-drawn-out; *Kurve* long; **nur einen Augenblick ~** only for a moment *or* second; **zwei Stunden ~** for two hours; **mein ganzes Leben ~** all my life, my whole life; **~ und breit** at great length → *auch* **lange, entlang**

lạng-: **lạng|an|hal|tend** ADJ → **lang ADV**; **lạng|är|me|lig** ADJ long-sleeved; **lạng|ar|mig** ADJ long-armed; **lạng|ärm|lig** ADJ long-sleeved; **lạng|at|mig** [-la:tmɪç] ADJ long-winded ADV in a long-winded way; **er schreibt ~** his style of writing is long-winded; **Lạng|at|mig|keit** F -, *no pl* long-windedness; **lạng|bei|nig** ADJ long-legged

lạn|ge [ˈlaŋə], *(S Ger)* **lạng** [laŋ], *(Aus)* ADV [ˈlɛŋɐ] *comp* **≃er** [ˈlɛŋɐ], [ˈlɛŋstə] *superl* **am längsten** [ˈlɛŋstn] **a** *(zeitlich)* a long time; *(in Fragen, Negativsätzen)* long; **die Sitzung hat heute ~/nicht ~ gedauert** the meeting went on (for) a long time/didn't go on (for) long today; **wie ~ lernst du schon Deutsch/bist du schon hier?** how long have you been learning German (for)/been here (for)?; **es ist noch gar nicht ~ her, dass wir diese Frage diskutiert haben** we discussed this question not long ago, it's not long since we discussed this question; **er wird es nicht mehr ~ machen** *(inf)* he won't last long, he's not got long to go; **bis Weihnachten ist es ja noch ~ hin** it's still a long time till Christmas, we're a long way from Christmas; **~ nicht gesehen** *(inf)* long time no see *(inf)*; **je länger, je lieber** the more the better; *(zeitlich)* the longer the better

b (*inf:* = *längst*) **noch ~ nicht** not by any means, not by a long chalk *(Brit inf)* or shot; **~ nicht so ...** nowhere near as ..., not nearly as ...; **er verdient ~ nicht so viel** he doesn't earn nearly as much, he doesn't earn anywhere near as much; **wenn er das schafft, kannst du das schon ~** if he can do it, you can do it easily

Lạ̈n|ge [ˈlɛŋə] F -, -n **a** *(zeitlich, räumlich)* length; (*inf:* *von Mensch*) height; **eine ~ von 10 Metern haben** to be 10 metres *(Brit)* or meters *(US)* long *or* in length; **ein Seil von 10 Meter ~** a rope 10 metres *(Brit)* or meters *(US)* long; **ein Vortrag von einer Stunde ~** an hour-long lecture; **eine Fahrt von einer Stunde ~** an hour's journey; **Bauarbeiten auf 5 km ~** roadworks *(Brit)* or road construction *(US)* for 5 kms; **etw der ~ nach falten** to fold sth lengthways *or* lengthwise; **der ~ nach hinfallen** to fall flat, to go sprawling; **in die ~ gehen** *(Kleidungsstücke)* to stretch; **in die ~ schießen** *or* **wachsen** to shoot up; **etw in die ~ ziehen** to protract sth, to drag sth out *(inf)*; **sich in die ~ ziehen** to go on and on; **einen Artikel in seiner vollen ~ abdrucken** to print an article in its entirety

b *(Sport)* length; **mit einer ~ gewinnen** to win by a length; **die anderen Wagen kamen mit einigen ~n Abstand** the other cars came in several lengths behind; **(jdm/etw) um ~n voraus sein** *(fig)* to be streets ahead (of sb/sth); **um ~n geschlagen werden** *(fig)* to be well beaten

c *(Geog)* longitude; **der Ort liegt auf** *or* **unter 20 Grad östlicher ~** the town has a longitude of 20 degrees east

d *(in Buch)* long-drawn-out passage; *(in Film)* long-drawn-out scene

lạn|gen [ˈlaŋən] *(dial inf)* VI **a** (= *sich erstrecken, greifen*) to reach (*nach* for, *in +acc* in, into); **bis an etw** *(acc)* **~** to reach sth **b** (= *fassen*) to touch (*an etw (acc)* sth) **c** (= *ausreichen*) to be enough; (= *auskommen*) to get by, to manage; **mir** *or* **für mich langt es** I've had enough; **das Geld langt nicht** there isn't *or* we *etc* haven't enough money; **jetzt langts mir aber!** I've had just about enough! → **hinten e** VT (= *reichen*) **jdm etw ~** to give *or* pass *or* hand sb sth; **jdm eine ~** to give sb a clip on the ear *(inf)*; **sich** *(dat)* **etw ~** to take sth

Lạ̈n|gen-: **Lạ̈n|gen|grad** M **a** degree of longitude **b** (*auch* **Längenkreis**) meridian; **Lạ̈n|gen|maß** NT measure of length, linear measure *(form)*

lạ̈n|ger *comp von* **lang, lange**

lạ̈n|ger|fris|tig [-frɪstɪç] ADJ longer-term ADV in the longer term; *planen* for the longer term

lạ̈n|ger|hans|sche In|seln [ˈlaŋɐhansʃə] PL *(Med)* islets *pl* of Langerhans

lạng|er|sehnt ADJ *attr* → **lang ADV**

lạng|er|war|tet ADJ *attr* → **lang ADV**

Lạn|ge|wei|le [ˈlaŋəvailə, laŋəˈvailə] F *gen* - *or* **langen Weile** [ˈlaŋənvailə], *dat* - *or* **langer Weile** [ˈlaŋɐvailə] *no pl* boredom; **~ haben** to be bored

Lạng-: **lạng|fä|dig** [-fɛːdɪç] *(Sw)* ADJ long-winded ADV in a long-winded way; **er schreibt sehr ~** his style of writing is very long-winded; **Lạng|fin|ger** M *(hum)* pickpocket; **lạng|fin|ge|rig** [-fɪŋərɪç], **lạng|fing|rig** [-fɪŋrɪç] ADJ long-fingered; *(hum)* light-fingered; **Lạng|for|mat** NT **Briefumschläge im ~** long envelopes; **Zigaretten im ~** long(-length) cigarettes; **lạng|fris|tig** [-frɪstɪç] ADJ long-term ADV in the long term; *planen* for the long term; **lạng|ge|hegt** ADJ *attr* → **lang ADV**; **lạng+ge|hen** *sep irreg* VI **a** *(Weg etc)* **wo gehts hier lang?** where does this (road *etc*) go? **b** **sie weiß, wo es langgeht** she knows what's what; **hier bestimme ich, wo es langgeht** I decide what's what here VT to go along; **lạng|ge|streckt** ADJ → **lang ADV**; **lạng|ge|zo|gen** ADJ **lang ADV**; **lạng|glie|de|rig** [-gliːdərɪç], **lạng|glied|rig** [-gliːdrɪç] ADJ long-limbed; **lạng|haa|rig** ADJ long-haired; **Lạng|haa|ri|ge(r)** [-haːrɪgə] MF *decl as adj* long-haired man/woman *etc*; **so ein ~r** some long-haired type; **diese dreckigen ~n** *(pej)* these long-haired layabouts *(Brit)* or good-for-nothings; **Lạng|haar|pe|rü|cke** F long wig; **Lạng|haar|schnei|der** M (= *Gerät*) trimmer (attachment); **Lạng|han|tel** F barbell; **Lạng|haus** NT nave; **Lạng|holz** NT uncut timber; **Lạng|holz|wa|gen** M timber lorry *(Brit)* or truck; **lạng|jäh|rig** ADJ *Freundschaft, Bekannter, Gewohnheit* long-standing; *Erfahrung, Verhandlungen, Recherchen* many years of; *Mitarbeiter* of many years' standing ADV for many years; **Lạng|lauf** M *(Ski)* cross-country (skiing); **Sieger im ~** winner of the cross-country (event); **Lạng|läu|fer** M *(Fin)* long(-dated security); **Lạng|läu|fer(in)** M(F) *(Ski)* cross-country skier; **Lạng|lauf|ski** M cross-country ski; **lạng|le|big** [-leːbɪç] ADJ long-lasting; *Stoff, Waren etc auch* durable; *Gerücht* persistent; *Melodie* enduring; *Mensch, Tier* long-lived; **~ sein** to last a long time; to have a long life, to be durable; to be persistent; to live to an old age; **Lạng|le|big|keit** F -, *no pl (von Stoff, Waren)* durability; *(von Gerücht)* persistence; *(von Mensch, Tier)* longevity; **die ~ dieser giftigen Substanzen** the fact that these toxic substances last so long; **lạng+le|gen** VR *sep* to have a lie-down

lạ̈ng|lich [ˈlɛŋlɪç] ADJ long, elongated

Lạng-: **lạng+lie|gen** VI *sep irreg (inf)* to be in bed; **lạng+ma|chen** VR *sep* (*inf:* = *sich ausruhen*) to have a lie-down *or* a rest *(US)*, to stretch out (on the bed/sofa *etc*); **lạng|mäh|nig** [-mɛːnɪç] ADJ with a long mane, long-maned; *(inf) Mensch* long-haired; **Lạng|mut** [ˈlaŋmuːt] F -, *no pl* patience, forbearance; **lạng|mü|tig** [ˈlaŋmyːtɪç] ADJ patient, forbearing; **Lạng|mü|tig|keit** F -, *no pl* forbearance; **Lạng|ohr** NT *(hum)* rabbit, bunny *(inf)*; (= *Hase*) hare; **Meister ~** Master Longears; **Lạng|pferd** NT *(Sport)* (long) horse

lạ̈ngs [lɛŋs] ADV lengthways, lengthwise; **~ gestreift** *(Stoff)* with lengthways stripes; *Kleid, Vorhang etc auch* with vertical stripes PREP *+gen* along; **~ der Straße stehen Kastanien** chestnut trees line the road, there are chestnut trees along the road; **die Bäume ~ des Flusses** the trees along (the banks of) the river

Lạ̈ngs|ach|se F longitudinal axis

lạng|sam [ˈlaŋzaːm] ADJ slow

ADV **a** slowly; **geh/fahr/sprich ~er!** slow down!, walk/drive/speak (a bit) more slowly or (a bit) slower! *(inf)*; **~, ~!, immer schön ~!** *(inf)* (take it) easy!, easy does it!; **~, aber sicher** slowly but surely

b (= *allmählich, endlich*) **es wird ~ Zeit, dass ...** it's about time that ..., it's high time that ...; **~ müsstest du das aber wissen** it's about time you knew that, it's high time you knew that; **ich muss jetzt ~ gehen** I must be getting on my way, I'd better be thinking about going; **kannst du dich ~ mal entscheiden?** could you start making up your mind?; **~ (aber sicher) reicht es mir** I've just about had enough; **ist das ~ fertig?** is it ready yet?

Lạng|sam|keit F -, *no pl* slowness

lạng|sam+tre|ten *sep irreg*, **lạng|sam tre|ten** △ *irreg* VI *(inf)* to go easy *(inf)*; *(gesundheitlich auch)* to take things easy

Lạng-: **Lạng|schäf|ter** [ˈlaŋʃɛftɐ] M -s, - high boot; *(aus Gummi)* wader; **lạng|schäf|tig** [ˈlaŋʃɛftɪç] ADJ *Stiefel* high; **Lạng|schiff** NT nave; **Lạng|schlä|fer(in)** M(F) late-riser; **Lạng|schrift** F longhand; **Lạng|sei|te** F long side

Lạ̈ngs-: **Lạ̈ngs|fa|den** M warp; **Lạ̈ngs|fal|te** F lengthways fold; **lạ̈ngs|ge|streift** ADJ → **längs ADV**; **Lạ̈ngs|li|nie** F vertical line, line down

Lạng|spiel-: **Lạng|spiel|band** [-bant] NT *pl* -**bänder** long-playing tape; **Lạng|spiel|plat|te** F long-playing record

Lạ̈ngs-: **Lạ̈ngs|rich|tung** F longitudinal direction; **in ~ zu etw verlaufen** to run longitudinally along sth; **lạ̈ngs|schiffs** [ˈlɛŋsʃɪfs] ADV broadside on; **Lạ̈ngs|schnitt** M longitudinal section; **Lạ̈ngs|sei|te** F long side; *(Naut)* broadside; **lạ̈ngs|seit(s)** [ˈlɛŋszait(s)] ADV PREP *+gen* alongside; **die beiden Boote lagen längsseits** the boats were lying alongside one another; **Lạ̈ngs|strei|fen** PL lengthways stripes *pl*; *(von Kleid, Vorhängen auch)* vertical stripes *pl*

lạ̈ngst [lɛŋst] ADV **a** (= *seit Langem, schon lange*) for a long time; (= *vor langer Zeit*) a long time ago, long ago; **er ist inzwischen ~ gestorben** he has been dead (for) a long time now; **als wir ankamen, war der Zug ~ weg** when we arrived the train had long since gone **b** → **lange b**

Lạ̈ngs|tal NT longitudinal valley

lạ̈ngs|tens [ˈlɛŋstns] ADV **a** (= *höchstens*) at the most **b** (= *spätestens*) at the latest

lạ̈ngs|te(r, s) [ˈlɛŋstə] *superl von* **lang**

lạng|stie|lig [-ʃtiːlɪç] ADJ long-stemmed

Lạng|stre|cken-: **Lạng|stre|cken|flug** M long-distance flight; **Lạng|stre|cken|flug|zeug** NT long-range *or* long-haul aircraft; **Lạng|stre|cken|lauf** M *(Disziplin)* long-distance running; *(Wettkampf)* long-distance race; **Lạng|stre|cken|läu|fer(in)** M(F) long-distance runner; **Lạng|stre|cken|ra|ke|te** F long-range missile; **Lạng|stre|cken|waf|fe** F long-range weapon

Lạng|streck|ler [-ʃtrɛklɐ] M -s, -, **Lạng|streck|le|rin** [-ərɪn] F -, -nen *(inf)* long-distance runner

Lạ̈ngs|wand F long wall

Lạng|text M *(esp Sch)* longer text

Lan|gus|te [laŋˈgʊstə] F -, -n crayfish, crawfish *(US)*

lạng|wei|len [ˈlaŋvailən] *insep* VT to bore VI to be boring VR to be bored; **sich tödlich** *or* **zu Tode ~** to be bored to death *or* to tears → *auch* **gelangweilt**

Lang|wei|ler ['laŋvailɐ] M -s, -, **Lang|wei|le|rin** [-ərın] F -, -nen bore; *(= langsamer Mensch)* slowcoach *(Brit inf)*, slowpoke *(US inf)*

lang|wei|lig ['laŋvailıç] ADJ **a** boring **b** *(inf: = langsam)* slow; **er ist so ~ mit allem** he's so slow or such a slowcoach *(Brit inf)* or such a slowpoke *(US inf)* at everything ADV boringly

Lang|wei|lig|keit F -, *no pl* **aufgrund der ~ ihres Unterrichts/des Buches** because her teaching/the book is so boring; **seine Geschichten sind von einer extremen ~** his stories are so incredibly boring

Lang-: **Lang|wel|le** F long wave; **lang|wel|lig** ADJ long-wave; **lang|wie|rig** ['laŋvi:rıç] ADJ long, lengthy; *Verhandlungen, Behandlung, Krankheit auch* prolonged ADV over a long period; **~ planen** to plan long-term; **eine ~ verlaufende Krankheit** a long-term illness; **~ über etw** *(acc)* **beraten** to have lengthy or prolonged discussions about sth; **Lang|wie|rig|keit** F -, *no pl* lengthiness

Lang|zeit- *in cpds* long-term; **Lang|zeit|ar|beits|lo|se(r)** MF *decl as adj* **ein ~r** someone who is long-term unemployed; **die ~n** the long-term unemployed; **Lang|zeit|ge|dächt|nis** NT long-term memory; **Lang|zeit|pro|gramm** NT long-term programme *(Brit)* or program *(US)*; **Lang|zeit|ri|si|ko** NT long--term risk; **Lang|zeit|stu|die** F long-range study; **Lang|zeit|ver|such** M long-term trial; **Lang|zeit|wert** M, *no pl* long-term result; **Lang|zeit|wir|kung** F long-term effect

lang zie|hen *irreg*, **lang+zie|hen** *sep irreg* VT to stretch → **Ohr, Hammelbeine**

La|no|lin [lano'li:n] NT -s, *no pl* lanolin

LAN-Par|ty *(Comput)* LAN party

Lan|than [lan'ta:n] NT -s, *no pl (abbr* **La***)* lanthanum

Lan|ze ['lantsə] F -, -n **a** *(= Waffe)* lance; *(zum Werfen)* spear; **für jdn eine ~ brechen** *(fig)* to take up the cudgels for sb *(Brit)*, to go to bat for sb *(esp US)* **b** *(sl: = Penis)* tool *(sl)*

Lan|zen-: **Lan|zen|spit|ze** F tip of a lance; *(von Wurfwaffe)* tip of a spear; **Lan|zen|stich** M lance thrust; *(von Wurfwaffe)* spear thrust; *(Wunde)* lance/spear wound; **er wurde von einem ~ getroffen** he was hit by a lance/spear; **Lan|zen|stoß** M lance thrust; *(von Wurfwaffe)* spear thrust

Lan|zet|te [lan'tsɛtə] F -, -n *(Med)* lancet

Lan|zett-: **Lan|zett|fisch** M, **Lan|zett|fisch|chen** [lan'tsɛtfıʃçən] NT -s, - lancelet; **lan|zett|för|mig** ADJ *(Bot)* lanceolate *(spec)*

La|os ['la:ɔs] NT -' Laos

La|o|te [la'o:tə] M -n, -n, **La|o|tin** [la'o:tın] F -, -nen Laotian

la|o|tisch [la'o:tıʃ] ADJ Laotian

La|ot|se [la'o:tsə, 'lautsə] M -s Lao-Tse

La|pa|ro|sko|pie [laparosko'pi:] F -, -n [-'pi:ən] *(Med)* laparoscopy

la|pa|ro|sko|pisch [laparo'sko:pıʃ] ADJ *(Med)* laparoscopic

la|pi|dar [lapi'da:ɐ] ADJ succinct ADV succinctly

La|pis|la|zu|li [lapıs'la:tsuli] M -, - lapis lazuli

Lap|pa|lie [la'pa:liə] F -, -n trifle, petty little matter

Läpp|chen ['lɛpçən] NT -s, - (small) cloth

Lap|pe ['lapə] M -n, -n, **Lap|pin** ['lapın] F -, -nen Lapp, Lapplander

Lap|pen ['lapn] M -s, - **a** *(= Stück Stoff)* cloth; *(= Waschlappen)* face cloth, flannel *(Brit)*, washcloth *(US)* **b** *(inf: = Geldschein)* note, bill *(US)*; **die paar ~** ≈ a couple of quid *(Brit inf)* or dollars *(US)* **c** *(sl: = Führerschein)* licence *(Brit)*, license *(US)* **d** *(= Hautstück)* fold of skin **e** *(inf)* **jdm durch die ~ gehen** to slip through sb's fingers; **die Sendung ist mir durch die ~ gegangen** I missed the programme *(Brit)* or program *(US)*

läp|pern ['lɛpɐn] VR *impers (inf)* **es läppert sich** it (all) mounts up

lap|pig ['lapıç] ADJ *(inf)* limp

Lap|pin ['lapın] F -, -nen Lapp, Lapplander

läp|pisch ['lɛpıʃ] ADJ silly; **wegen ~en zwei Euro macht er so ein Theater** *(inf)* he makes such a fuss about a mere two euros ADV *sich verhalten* foolishly

Lapp|land ['laplant] NT -s Lapland

Lapp|län|der ['laplɛndɐ] M -s, -, **Lapp|län|de|rin** [-ərın] F -, -nen Lapp, Lapplander

lapp|län|disch ['laplɛndıʃ] ADJ Lapp

Lap|sus ['lapsʊs] M -, - ['lapsu:s] mistake, slip; *(gesellschaftlich, diplomatisch)* faux pas; **~ Linguae** slip of the tongue; **mir ist ein ~ unterlaufen** or **passiert, ich habe einen ~ begangen** I've made a mistake/faux pas

Lap|top ['lɛptɔp] M -s, -s *(Comput)* laptop (computer), portable

Lär|che ['lɛrçə] F -, -n larch

large [larʒ] ADJ *(Sw)* generous

Lär|ge ['lɛrgə] F -, -n *(dial, pej)* Silesian

Lar|go ['largo] NT -s, -s or **Lar|ghi** ['largi] *(Mus)* largo

la|ri|fa|ri [lari'fa:ri] INTERJ nonsense, fiddlesticks, fiddle-de-dee ADJ *inv* airy-fairy

La|ri|fa|ri [lari'fa:ri] NT -s, *no pl (inf)* nonsense

Lärm [lɛrm] M -(e)s, *no pl* noise; *(= Geräuschbelästigung auch)* din, row, racket; *(= Aufsehen)* fuss; **~ schlagen** *(lit)* to raise the alarm; *(fig)* to kick up a fuss, to raise a commotion; **„Viel ~ um nichts"** "Much Ado about Nothing"; **viel ~ um nichts machen** to make a lot of fuss or a lot of ado or a big to-do *(inf)* about nothing; **viel ~ um jdn/etw machen** to make a big fuss about sb/sth

Lärm-: **Lärm|be|kämp|fung** F noise abatement; **Lärm|be|läs|ti|gung** F noise pollution or nuisance; **sie beschwerten sich wegen der unzumutbaren ~** they complained about the unacceptable noise level; **lärm|emp|find|lich** ADJ sensitive to noise; **Lärm|emp|find|lich|keit** F sensitivity to noise

lär|men ['lɛrmən] VI to make a noise; **~d** noisy

Lärm-: **lärm|ge|plagt** [-gəpla:kt] ADJ plagued with noise; **lärm|ge|schä|digt** [-gəʃɛ:dıçt] ADJ suffering physical damage as a result of exposure to noise

lär|mig ADJ *(esp Sw)* noisy

Lärm-: **Lärm|mess|ge|rät** NT noise meter; **lärm|min|dernd** ADJ *Straßenbelag, Maßnahmen* noise-reducing

lar|mo|yant [larmoa'jant] *(geh)* ADJ lachrymose *(liter)* ADV lachrymosely *(liter)*

Lar|mo|yanz [larmoa'jants] F -, *no pl (geh)* sentimentality

Lärm-: **Lärm|pe|gel** M noise level; **Lärm|quel|le** F source of noise/the noise; **Lärm|schä|den** PL, **Lärm|schä|di|gun|gen** PL injuries *pl* caused by excessive noise

Lärm|schutz M noise prevention

Lärm|schutz-: **Lärm|schutz|maß|nah|men** PL noise prevention measures *pl*; **Lärm|schutz|wall** M, **Lärm|schutz|wand** F sound or noise barrier

Lärv|chen ['lɛrfçən] NT -s, - **a** *dim von* **Larve** **b** *(dated inf: = Gesicht)* baby-doll face

Lar|ve ['larfə] F -, -n **a** *(= Tierlarve)* larva **b** *(= Maske)* mask

las *pret von* **lesen**

La|sag|ne [la'zanjə] PL lasagne *sing*

lasch [laʃ] *(inf)* ADJ **a** *Erziehung, Gesetz, Kontrolle, Polizei, Eltern* lax; *Vorgehen* feeble **b** *(= schlaff) Bewegungen* feeble; *Händedruck* limp **c** *Speisen* insipid, wishy-washy *(inf)* ADV **a** *(= nicht streng)* in a lax way; *vorgehen* feebly **b** *(= schlaff) bewegen* feebly; *die Hände drücken* limply

La|sche ['laʃə] F -, -n *(= Schlaufe)* loop; *(= Schuhlasche)* tongue; *(als Schmuck, Verschluss)* tab, flap; *(Tech)* splicing plate; *(von Kette)* sideplate; *(Rail)* fishplate

Lasch|heit F -, *no pl* **a** *(von Erziehung, Gesetz, Kontrolle etc)* laxity; *(von Vorgehen)* feebleness **b** *(= Schlaffheit) (von Bewegungen)* feebleness; *(von Händedruck)* limpness

La|ser ['le:zɐ] M -s, - laser

La|ser- *in cpds* laser; **La|ser|chi|rur|gie** F laser surgery; **La|ser|dru|cker** M *(Typ)* laser (printer); **La|ser|ka|no|ne** F laser gun

la|sern ['le:zɐn] VTI *(Med)* to treat with laser

La|ser-: **La|ser|pis|to|le** F laser gun; *(bei Geschwindigkeitskontrollen)* radar gun; **La|ser|strahl** M laser beam; **La|ser|tech|nik** F, *no pl* laser technology; **La|ser|waf|fe** F laser weapon

la|sie|ren [la'zi:rən] *ptp* **lasiert** VT *Bild, Holz* to varnish; *Glas* to glaze

Las|sa|fie|ber ['lasa-] NT, *no pl* Lassa fever

las|sen ['lasn]

pret **ließ** [li:s], *ptp* **gelassen** [gə'lasn]

1 MODALVERB	3 INTRANSITIVES VERB
2 TRANSITIVES VERB	4 REFLEXIVES VERB

1 – MODALVERB *ptp* lassen

Die Übersetzung hängt oft vom Vollverb ab, siehe auch dort.

a = veranlassen **etw tun lassen** to have or get sth done; **ich muss mich mal untersuchen lassen** I'll have to have a checkup; **sich** *(dat)* **einen Zahn ziehen lassen** to have a tooth out; **jdm mitteilen lassen, dass ...** to let sb know that ...; **jdn etw wissen lassen** to let sb know sth; **jdm ausrichten lassen, dass ...** to leave a message for sb that ...; **er lässt Ihnen mitteilen, dass ...** he wants or wishes *(form)* you to know that ...; **jdn rufen** or **kommen lassen** to send for sb; **sich** *(dat)* **etw kommen lassen** to have sth delivered; **eine Versammlung einberufen lassen** to have a meeting called; **mein Vater wollte mich studieren lassen** my father wanted me to study; **Goethe lässt Faust sagen ...** Goethe has Faust say ...

b = zulassen

Bei absichtlichen Handlungen wird *lassen* mit *to let* übersetzt, bei versehentlichen Handlungen mit *to leave*.

die Bohnen fünf Minuten kochen lassen let the beans boil for five minutes; **Wasser in die Badewanne laufen lassen** to run water into the bath; **sich** *(dat)* **einen Bart/die Haare wachsen lassen** to grow a beard/one's hair, to let one's beard/hair grow; **warum hast du das Licht brennen lassen?** why did you leave the light on?; **hast du den Motor absichtlich laufen lassen?** have you left the engine running on purpose?; **jdn warten lassen** to keep sb waiting; **den Tee ziehen lassen** to let the tea draw *(Brit)* or steep *(US)*; **etw kochen lassen** to boil sth

c = erlauben to let, to allow; **er hat mich nicht ausreden lassen** he didn't allow me to finish speaking, he didn't let me finish speaking; **jdn etw sehen/hören lassen** to let sb see/hear sth; **er hat sich überreden lassen** he let himself be persuaded, he allowed himself to be persuaded; **er hat sich nicht überreden lassen** he couldn't be persuaded; **ich lasse mich nicht belügen/zwingen** I won't be lied to/coerced; **ich lasse gern mit mir handeln** I'm quite willing to negotiate; **lass mich machen!** let me do it!; **lass das sein!** don't (do it)!; *(= hör auf)* stop it!; **lass doch die Arbeit Arbeit sein** forget about work *(inf)*

d = Möglichkeit bieten **das Fenster lässt sich leicht öffnen** the window opens easily; **das Fenster lässt sich nicht öffnen** *(grundsätzlich nicht)* the window doesn't open; *(momentan nicht)* the window won't open; **das Wort lässt sich schwer/nicht übersetzen** the word is hard to translate/can't be translated or is untranslatable; **das lässt sich machen** that's possible, that can be done; **es lässt sich essen/trinken** it's edible/drinkable; **hier lässt es sich bequem sitzen** it's nice sitting here; **das lässt sich zehn Jahre später nicht mehr feststellen** ten years on this can no longer be established, ten years on it is too late to establish this; **das lässt sich nicht mehr ändern** it's too late to do anything about it now; **daraus lässt sich schließen** *or* **folgern, dass …** one can conclude from this that …

e [im Imperativ] **lass uns gehen!** let's go!; **lass uns all das vergessen!** let's forget all this!; **lass es dir gut gehen!** take care of yourself!; **lass dir das gesagt sein!** let me tell you this!; **lass ihn nur kommen!** just let him show his face!, just let him come!; **lasset uns beten** let us pray; **lasset die Kindlein zu mir kommen** *(Bibl)* suffer the little children to come unto me *(Bibl)*

2 – TRANSITIVES VERB

a [= unterlassen] to stop; *(= momentan aufhören)* to leave; **das lassen wir fürs Erste** let's leave this for the moment; **lass das!** don't do it!; *(= hör auf)* stop that!; **lass das Jammern** stop your moaning; **lass diese Bemerkungen!** that's enough of that kind of remark!; **lassen wir das!** let's leave it!; **er kann das Rauchen/Trinken nicht lassen** he can't stop smoking/drinking; **tu was du nicht lassen kannst!** if you must, you must!

♦ **es lassen er kann es nicht lassen!** he will keep on doing it!; **er hat es versucht, aber er kann es nicht lassen** he's tried, but he can't help it *or* himself; **dann lassen wir es eben** let's drop the whole idea; **ich will aber nicht! – dann lassen wir es eben** but I don't want to! – let's not bother then; **wenn du nicht willst, dann lass es doch** if you don't want to, then don't; **ich habe es dann doch gelassen** in the end I didn't

b [= zurücklassen, loslassen] to leave; **jdn allein lassen** to leave sb alone; **er hat dort viel Geld gelassen** he left with his pockets a lot lighter; **lass mich (los)!** let me go!; **lass mich (in Ruhe)!** leave me alone!

c [= überlassen] **jdm etw lassen** to let sb have sth; *(= behalten lassen)* to let sb keep sth; **Peter will mir meinen Ball nicht lassen** *(= nicht geben)* Peter won't let go of my ball; **lass ihr schon den Ball, sonst weint sie wieder** let her keep the ball otherwise she'll start crying again; **das muss man ihr lassen** *(= zugestehen)* you've got to give *or* grant her that

d [= hineinlassen, hinauslassen] to let *(in +acc* into, *aus* out of); **er ließ mich nicht aus dem Haus** he wouldn't let me out of the house; **Wasser in die Badewanne lassen** to run water into the bath; **lass bloß den Hund nicht auf das Sofa!** don't let the dog get on the sofa!; **einen (Furz) lassen** *(inf)* to let off *(inf)*

e [= belassen] to leave; **etw lassen, wie es ist** to leave sth (just) as it is; **etw ungesagt/ungetan lassen** *(geh)* to leave sth unsaid/undone

3 – INTRANSITIVES VERB

♦ **von jdm/etw lassen** *(= ablassen)* to give sb/sth up; **sie konnte vom Gin nicht lassen** she couldn't give up the gin *(inf)*; **wir wollen von unserem Anspruch nicht lassen** we're determined not to give up our claim

♦ **lass mal lass mal, ich mach das schon** leave it, I'll do it; **lass mal, ich zahle das schon** no, that's all right, I'll pay

4 – REFLEXIVES VERB

♦ **sich lassen sich vor Freude nicht zu lassen wissen** *or* **nicht lassen können** to be beside oneself with joy

läs|sig ['lɛsɪç] ADJ *(= ungezwungen)* casual; *(= nachlässig)* careless; *(inf: = gekonnt)* cool *(inf)* ADV *(= ungezwungen)* casually; *(= nachlässig)* carelessly; *(inf: = leicht)* easily; **die heutigen Kinder bedienen den Computer ganz ~** using a computer seems to come naturally to today's children; **das hat er ganz ~ hingekriegt** pretty cool, the way he did that *(inf)*

Läs|sig|keit F -, *no pl (= Ungezwungenheit)* casualness; *(= Nachlässigkeit)* carelessness; *(inf: = Gekonntheit)* coolness *(inf)*

läss|lich ['lɛslɪç] ADJ *(Eccl) Sünde* venial, pardonable

Läss|lich|keit F -, -en *(= Fehlverhalten)* misdemeanour *(Brit)*, misdemeanor *(US)*

Las|so ['laso] M OR NT -s, -s lasso

lässt [lɛst] *3. pers sing pres von* **lassen**

Last [last] F -, -en **a** load; *(= Traglast)* load, burden; *(lit, fig: = Gewicht)* weight; **Aufzug nur für ~en** goods lift *or* hoist; **des Lebens ~ und Mühe** *(liter)* the trials and tribulations of life **b** *(fig: = Bürde)* burden; **eine ~ für jdn sein** to be a burden on sb; **jdm zur ~ fallen/werden** to be/become a burden on sb; **die ~ der Verantwortung** the burden of responsibility; **die ~ des Amtes** the weight of office; **sich** *(dat)* **selbst eine ~ sein** to be a burden to oneself; **damit war uns eine schwere ~ vom Herzen** *or* **von der Seele genommen** that took a load off our minds; **jdm eine ~ abnehmen** to take a load off sb's shoulders; **jdm etw zur ~ legen** to accuse sb of sth; **zu ~en = zulasten** **c Lasten** PL *(= Kosten)* costs; *(des Steuerzahlers)* charges; **soziale ~en** welfare costs *or* charges; **die steuerlichen ~en für die kleinen Unternehmen** the tax burden for small concerns; **zu jds ~en gehen** to be chargeable to sb

Last-: **Last|arm** M *(Phys)* load arm; **Last|au|to** NT van, truck

las|ten ['lastn] VI to weigh heavily *(auf +dat* on); **eine schwere Sorge hat auf ihr gelastet** a terrible worry weighed her down; **eine lähmende Schwüle lastete über der Stadt** *(geh)* an oppressive heat hung heavily over the town; **auf dem Haus lastet noch eine Hypothek** the house is still encumbered (with a mortgage) *(form)*; **auf ihm lastet die ganze Verantwortung** all the responsibility rests on him; **auf ihm lastet die ganze Arbeit** all the work falls on him

Las|ten-: **Las|ten|auf|zug** M hoist, goods lift *(Brit) or* elevator *(US)*; **Las|ten|aus|gleich** M *system of financial compensation for losses suffered in the Second World War*

las|tend ADJ *(geh) Stille, Schwüle* oppressive

Las|ten-: **las|ten|frei** ADJ *Grundstück* unencumbered; **Las|ten|ta|xi** NT *van plus driver to rent*

Las|ter ['lastɐ] M -s, - *(inf: = Lastwagen)* lorry *(Brit)*, truck

Las|ter NT -s, - *(= Untugend)* vice → **Müßiggang**

Läs|te|rei [lɛstə'rai] F -, -en *(inf)* **a** *no pl (= das Lästern)* running down *(über +acc* of), nasty comments *pl* **b** *(= Lästerwort)* nasty remark

Läs|te|rer ['lɛstərɐ] M -s, -, **Läs|te|rin** [-ərɪn] F -, -nen **a ein ~ sein** to have a vicious tongue (in one's head) **b** *(= Gotteslästerer)* blasphemer

las|ter|haft ADJ depraved ADV **~ leben** to lead a depraved life *or* a life of depravity

Las|ter|haf|tig|keit ['lastɐhaftɪçkait] F - depravity

Las|ter|höh|le F den of vice *or* iniquity

Läs|te|rin [-ərɪn] F -, -nen → **Lästerer**

Las|ter|le|ben NT *(old, iro)* life of sin and depravity

läs|ter|lich ['lɛstɐlɪç] ADJ malicious; *(= gotteslästerlich)* blasphemous; **~e Bemerkung** gibe *(über +acc* at)

Läs|ter|maul NT *(inf)* = **Lästerer a**

läs|tern ['lɛstɐn] VI to bitch *(inf)*; **über jdn/etw ~** to bitch about sb/sth *(inf)*, to run sb/sth down; **wir haben gerade über dich gelästert** *(hum)* we were just talking about you, we were just taking your name in vain *(hum)* VT **Gott** to blaspheme against, to curse

Läs|ter-: **Läs|ter|wort** NT *pl* **-worte a** gibe **b** *(gegen Gott)* blasphemy; **~e** blasphemous words; **Läs|ter|zun|ge** F vicious tongue

Last|esel M pack mule

Las|tex® ['lastɛks] NT -, *no pl* stretch fabric

Las|tex-® *in cpds* stretch; **Las|tex|ho|se** F stretch fabric trousers *pl (Brit)*, stretch pants *pl*

Last-: **Last|fahr|zeug** NT goods vehicle; **Last|fuh|re** F **mit dem Mietwagen dürfen keine ~n unternommen werden** the hired car is not to be used for the carriage of goods

läs|tig ['lɛstɪç] ADJ tiresome; *(= ärgerlich auch)* annoying, irksome, aggravating; *Husten, Kopfschuppen etc* troublesome; **wie ~!** what a nuisance!; **jdm ~ sein** to bother sb; **der Regenschirm ist mir ~** the umbrella is a nuisance to me; **dieser Verband ist mir ~** this bandage is bothering me; **jdm ~ fallen** to be a nuisance to sb; **jdm ~ werden** to become a nuisance (to sb); *(= zum Ärgernis werden)* to get annoying (to sb); **etw als ~ empfinden** to think sth is annoying *or* a pain *(inf)*

läs|tig+fal|len VI *sep irreg aux sein* → **lästig**

Last-: **Last|kahn** M barge; **Last|kraft|wa|gen** M *(form)* heavy goods vehicle

Last-Mi|nute-: **Last-Mi|nute-Flug** M late availability flight *(Brit)*, standby flight; **Last-Mi|nute-Rei|se** F late availability holiday *(esp Brit) or* vacation *(US)*; **Last-Mi|nute-Ti|cket** NT standby ticket

Last-: **Last|schiff** NT freighter, cargo ship; **Last|schrift** F debit; *(Eintrag)* debit entry; **Last|tier** NT beast of burden, pack animal; **Last|trä|ger(in)** M(F) carrier, porter; **Last|wa|gen** M lorry *(Brit)*, truck; **Last|wa|gen|fah|rer(in)** M(F) lorry *(Brit) or* truck driver; **Last|zug** M truck-trailer *(US)*, juggernaut *(Brit inf)*

La|sur [la'zuːɐ] F -, -en *(auf Holz, Bild)* varnish; *(auf Glas, Email)* glaze

La|sur|stein M lapis lazuli

las|ziv [las'tsiːf] *(geh)* ADJ lascivious ADV lasciviously

Las|zi|vi|tät [lastsivi'tɛːt] F -, *no pl (geh)* lasciviousness

Lä|ta|re [lɛ'taːrə] *no art (Eccl)* Laetare Sunday, 3rd Sunday before Easter

La|tein [la'tain] NT -s Latin; **mit seinem ~ am Ende sein** to be stumped *(inf)*

La|tein-: **La|tein|ame|ri|ka** NT Latin America; **La|tein|ame|ri|ka|ner(in)** M(F) Latin American; **la|tein|ame|ri|ka|nisch** ADJ Latin-American

La|tei|ner [la'tainɐ] M -s, -, **La|tei|ne|rin** [-ərɪn] F -, -nen Latin scholar; *(Sch)* Latin pupil

la|tei|nisch [la'tainɪʃ] ADJ Latin

La|tein|schu|le F *(Hist)* grammar school

la|tent [la'tɛnt] ADJ latent; *Selbstmörder* potential ADV latently; **~ vorhanden sein** to be latent

La|tenz [la'tɛnts] F -, *no pl* latency

La|tenz-: **La|tenz|pe|ri|o|de** F latency period; **La|tenz|zeit** F latent period

la|te|ral [late'raːl] ADJ *(Sci)* lateral

La|ter|na ma|gi|ca [la'tɛrna 'maːgika] F - -, **Laternae magicae** [la'tɛrnɛ 'maːgitsɛ] magic lantern

La|ter|ne [la'tɛrnə] F -, -n *(= Leuchte, Archit)* lantern; *(= Straßenlaterne)* streetlight, streetlamp

La|ter|nen-: **La|ter|nen|licht** NT light of the street lamp(s); **La|ter|nen|par|ker(in)** M(F) *(inf)* kerbside *(Brit) or* curbside *(US)* parker; **La|ter|nen|pfahl** M lamppost

La|tex ['laːtɛks] M -, **Latizes** ['laːtitseːs] latex

La|ti|fun|di|um [lati'fʊndiʊm] NT -s, **Latifundien** [-diən] *usu pl* latifundium

la|ti|ni|sie|ren [latini'ziːrən] *ptp* **latinisiert** VT to latinize

La|ti|nist [lati'nɪst] M -en, -en, **La|ti|nis|tin** [-'nɪstɪn] F -, -nen Latinist, Latin scholar

La|ti|no [la'tiːno] M -s, -s Latino *(esp US)*

La|ti|num [la'tiːnʊm] NT -s, *no pl* **kleines/großes ~** Latin O-level/A-level (exam) *(Brit)*, basic/advanced Latin exam

La|ti|um ['laːtsiʊm] NT -s Latium

Lat|ri|ne [la'triːnə] F -, -n latrine

Lat|sche ['laːtʃə] F -, -n *(Bot)* mountain pine

lat|schen ['la:tʃn] VI *aux sein (inf)* to wander; *(durch die Stadt etc)* to traipse; *(schlurfend)* to slouch along

Lat|schen ['la:tʃn] M **-s, -** *(inf) (= Hausschuh)* slipper; *(pej: = Schuh)* worn-out shoe

Lat|schen|kie|fer F mountain pine

lat|schig ['la:tʃıç] *(inf)* ADJ slovenly, sloppy *(inf)* ADV slovenly, sloppily *(inf)*

Lat|te ['latə] F **-, -n** **a** *(= schmales Brett)* slat **b** *(Sport)* bar; *(Ftbl)* (cross)bar **c** *(inf: = Liste)* **eine (ganze) ~ von Wünschen/Vorstrafen** a whole string of things that he *etc* wants/of previous convictions → **lang ADJ b** **d** *(sl)* **eine ~ haben** to have a hard-on *(sl)*

Lat|ten-: **Lat|ten|holz** NT lath wood; **Lat|ten|kis|te** F crate; **Lat|ten|kreuz** NT corner of the goalpost; **Lat|ten|rost** M duckboards *pl*, lath floor; *(in Bett)* slatted frame; **Lat|ten|schuss** M *(Ftbl)* shot against the bar; **nach dem ~ von Matthäus** after Matthäus hit the crossbar; **Lat|ten|ver|schlag** M crate; *(abgeteilte Fläche)* enclosure; *(für Hühner etc)* run; **Lat|ten|zaun** M wooden fence, paling

Lat|tich ['latıç] M **-s, -e** *(Bot)* lettuce

La|tüch|te [la'tʏçtə] F **-, -n** *(hum)* = **Laterne**

Latz [lats] M **-es, ⸗e** or *(Aus)* **-e** ['lɛtsə] *(bei Kleidung = Lätzchen)* bib; *(= Hosenlatz)* (front) flap; **jdm eins vor den ~ knallen** *(inf)* or **ballern** *(inf)* to sock sb one *(inf)*

Lätz|chen ['lɛtsçən] NT **-s, -** bib

Latz|ho|se F (pair of) dungarees *pl (Brit)* or overalls *pl (US)*

lau [lau] ADJ **a** *(= mild) Wind, Abend* mild **b** *(= lauwarm) Flüssigkeit* tepid, lukewarm; *(fig) Freundschaft, Begeisterung, Haltung* lukewarm, half-hearted ADV **a** *(= mild) wehen* gently **b** *(fig) empfangen, behandeln* half-heartedly

Laub [laup] NT **-(e)s** [-bəs], *no pl* leaves *pl*; *(an Bäumen etc auch)* foliage; **~ tragend** deciduous

Laub-: **Laub|baum** M deciduous tree; **Laub|blatt** NT (fallen) leaf; **Laub|dach** NT leafy canopy *(liter)*

Lau|be ['laubə] F **-, -n** **a** *(= Gartenhäuschen)* summerhouse **b** *(= Gang)* arbour *(Brit)*, arbor *(US)*, pergola; *(= Arkade)* arcade → **fertig ADJ a**

Lau|ben-: **Lau|ben|gang** M *pl* **-gänge** arbour *(Brit)*, arbor *(US)*, pergola; **Lau|ben|ko|lo|nie** F area of allotments *(Brit)* or garden plots; **Lau|ben|pie|per** [-pi:pɐ] M **-s, -**, **Lau|ben|pie|pe|rin** [-ərın] F **-, -nen** *(dial)* allotment gardener *(Brit)*, plot gardener

Laub-: **Laub|fall** M **vor dem ~** before the leaves fall; **Laub|fär|bung** F colouring *(Brit)* or coloring *(US)* of the leaves; **Laub|frosch** M (European) tree frog; **Laub|höl|zer** PL deciduous trees *pl*; **Laub|hüt|ten|fest** NT Feast of Tabernacles, Sukkoth; **Laub|kro|ne** F treetop; **Laub|sä|ge** F fret saw; **Laub|sä|ge|ar|beit** F fretwork; **laub|tra|gend** ADJ → **Laub**; **Laub|wald** M deciduous wood or *(größer)* forest; **Laub|werk** NT foliage *(auch Art)*

Lauch [laux] M **-(e)s, -e** allium *(form)*; *(esp S Ger: = Porree)* leek

Lauch|zwie|bel F spring onion *(Brit)*, scallion *(US)*

Lau|da|tio [lau'da:tsio] F **-, Laudationes** [lauda'tsio:ne:s] encomium, eulogy

Laue ['lauə] F **-, -nen**, **Laue|ne** ['lauənə] F **-, -n** *(esp Sw)* avalanche

Lau|er ['lauɐ] F **-,** *no pl* **auf der ~ sein** or **liegen** to lie in wait; **sich auf die ~ legen** to settle down to lie in wait

lau|ern ['lauɐn] VI *(lit, fig)* to lurk, to lie in wait *(auf +acc* for); *(inf)* to wait *(auf +acc* for); **ein ~der Blick** a furtive glance

Lauf [lauf] M **-(e)s, Läufe** ['lɔyfə] **a** *(= schneller Schritt)* run; *(Sport: = Wettlauf, -fahrt)* race; *(= Durchgang)* run, race, heat; **sein ~ wurde immer schneller** he ran faster and faster; **im ~ innehalten** to stop running for a moment

b *(= Verlauf)* course; **im ~e der Jahre** in the course of the years, over or through the years; **im ~e der Zeit** in the course of time; **im ~e des Gesprächs** in the course of the conversation, during the conversation; **einer Entwicklung** *(dat)* **freien ~ lassen** to allow a development to take its (own) course; **seiner Fantasie freien ~ lassen** to give free rein to one's imagination; **sie ließ ihren Gefühlen freien ~** she gave way to her feelings; **seinen ~ nehmen** to take its course; **den Dingen ihren ~ lassen** to let matters or things take their course; **das ist der ~ der Dinge** or **der Welt** that's the way of the world, that's the way things go

c *(= Gang, Arbeit)* running, operation; *(Comput)* run

d *(= Flusslauf, auch Astron)* course; **der obere/untere ~ der Donau** the upper/lower reaches of the Danube

e *(= Gewehrlauf)* barrel; **ein Tier vor den ~ bekommen** to get an animal in one's sights

f *(Hunt: = Bein)* leg

g *(Mus)* run

Lauf-: **Lauf|bahn** F career; **die ~ des Beamten einschlagen** to embark or enter on a career as a civil servant; **Lauf|band** [-bant] NT *pl* **-bänder** *(= Förderband)* conveyor belt; *(in Flughafen etc)* travelator *(Brit)*, moving sidewalk *(US)*; *(= Sportgerät)* treadmill; **Lauf|bur|sche** M errand boy, messenger boy

lau|fen ['laufn] *pret* **lief** [li:f], *ptp* **gelaufen** [gə'laufn] VI *aux sein* **a** *(= rennen)* to run; **lauf doch!** get a move on! *(inf)*

b *(inf) (= gehen)* to go; *(= seine Notdurft verrichten)* to run (to the toilet) *(inf)*; **er läuft dauernd ins Kino/auf die Polizei** he's always off to the cinema/always running to the police

c *(= zu Fuß gehen)* to walk; **das Kind läuft schon** the child can already walk or is already walking; **das Laufen lernen** to learn to walk; **er läuft sehr unsicher** he's very unsteady on his feet; **es sind noch/nur 10 Minuten zu ~** it's another/only 10 minutes' walk

d *(= fließen)* to run; *(= schmelzen: Käse, Butter)* to melt; **in Strömen ~** to stream or pour (in/out/down *etc*); **Wasser in einen Eimer/die Badewanne ~ lassen** to run water into a bucket/the bath; **das Bier muss ~** the beer must be kept flowing

e *(= undicht sein) (Gefäß, Wasserhahn)* to leak; *(Wunde)* to weep; **seine Nase läuft, ihm läuft die Nase** his nose is running, he's got a runny nose

f *(= in Betrieb sein)* to run, to go; *(Uhr)* to go; *(Gerät, Maschine) (= eingeschaltet sein)* to be on; *(= funktionieren)* to work; **wir haben jetzt drei neue Maschinen ~** *(inf)* we've got three new machines going *(inf)*; **er hat vier Mädchen ~** *(sl)* he's got four girls out on the game *(inf)*, he's got four girls hustling for him *(inf)*

g *(Comput)* to run; **ein Programm ~ lassen** to run a program

h *(fig: = im Gange sein) (Prozess, Verhandlung)* to go on, to be in progress; *(Bewerbung, Antrag)* to be under consideration; *(= gezeigt werden) (Film)* to be on, to be showing; *(Stück)* to be on, to be playing; **der Film lief schon, als wir ankamen** the film had already started when we arrived; **der Film läuft über drei Stunden** the film goes on for three hours; **etw läuft gut/schlecht** sth is going well/badly; **die Sache/das Geschäft läuft jetzt** it/the shop is going well now; **sehen wie die Sache läuft** to see how things go; **alles/die Dinge ~ lassen** to let everything/things slide; **die Sache ist gelaufen** *(inf)* it's in the bag *(inf)*, it's all wrapped up *(inf)*; **jdm zeigen, wie es läuft** *(inf)* to show sb the ropes *(inf)*

i *(= gültig sein: Vertrag, Abkommen)* to run; **der Kredit läuft über zwei Jahre** the loan is repayable over two years

j *(= bezeichnet werden)* **das Auto läuft unter meinem Namen** or **auf meinen Namen** the car is in my name; **das Konto läuft unter der Nummer ...** the number of the account is ...; **der Agent läuft unter dem Decknamen „Spinne"** the agent goes by the cover name of "Spider"; **das läuft unter „Sonderausgaben"** that comes under "special expenses"

k *(= sich bewegen)* to run; **auf eine Mine ~** to hit a mine; **auf Grund ~** to run aground; **in den Hafen ~** to enter port; **es lief mir eiskalt über den Rücken** a chill ran or went up my spine → **Geld a, Stapel c**

l *(= verlaufen) (Fluss etc)* to run; *(Weg)* to go, to run

VT **a** *aux haben or sein (Sport) Rekordzeit* to run; *Rekord* to set; **Rennen ~** to run (in races); **Ski ~** to ski; **Schlittschuh ~** to skate; **Rollschuh ~** to roller-skate → **Gefahr b**

b *aux sein (= fahren: Auto etc) Strecke* to do

c *aux sein (= zu Fuß gehen)* to walk; *(schnell)* to run

d sich *(dat)* **eine Blase ~** to give oneself a blister; **sich** *(dat)* **ein Loch in die Sohlen ~** to wear a hole in one's soles

VR **sich warm ~** to warm up; **sich müde ~** to tire oneself out; **in den Schuhen läuft es sich gut/schlecht** these shoes are good/bad for walking/running in; **zu zweit läuft es sich besser** it's better walking/running in twos

lau|fend ADJ *attr (= ständig) Arbeiten, Ausgaben* regular; *Kredit* outstanding; *(= regelmäßig) Wartung* routine; *Monat, Jahr, Konto (form)* current; **15 EUR der ~e Meter** EUR 15 per metre *(Brit)* or meter *(US)*; **~e Nummer** serial number; *(von Konto)* number; **auf dem Laufenden bleiben/sein** to keep (oneself)/be in the picture or up-to-date or up to speed; **jdn auf dem Laufenden halten** to keep sb posted or up-to-date or informed; **mit etw auf dem Laufenden sein** to be up-to-date on sth → **Band** ADV continually, constantly

lau|fen las|sen *ptp* **laufen lassen** or *(rare)* **laufen gelassen** *irreg*, **lau|fen+las|sen** *ptp* **laufenlassen** or *(rare)* **laufengelassen** *sep irreg* VT *(inf)* **jdn ~** to let sb go

Läu|fer ['lɔyfɐ] M **-s, -** **a** *(Chess)* bishop **b** *(Teppich)* rug; *(= Treppenläufer, Tischläufer)* runner **c** *(Tech) (= Laufkatze)* crab; *(= Laufgewicht)* sliding weight **d** *(Build)* stretcher **e** *(= junges Schwein)* young pig

Läu|fer ['lɔyfɐ] M **-s, -**, **Läu|fe|rin** [-ərın] F **-, -nen** *(Sport)* runner; *(= Hürdenläufer)* hurdler; *(Ftbl)* halfback; **rechter/linker ~** *(Ftbl)* right/left half

Lau|fe|rei [laufə'rai] F **-, -en** *(inf)* running about *no pl*

Läu|fer|stan|ge F stair rod

Lauf-: **lauf|fä|hig** ADJ *(Comput)* **das Programm ist unter Windows ~** the program can be run under Windows; **lauf|faul** ADJ lazy; **das Kind ist ~** the child isn't keen on running; **er war während des Spiels ~** he didn't run around very much during the game; **Lauf|feu|er** NT **sich wie ein ~ verbreiten** to spread like wildfire; **Lauf|flä|che** F *(von Reifen)* tread; **lauf|freu|dig** ADJ *Fußballer etc* keen on walking; *(= wanderfreudig)* keen on walking; **Lauf|ge|wicht** NT sliding weight; **Lauf|git|ter** NT playpen; **Lauf|gra|ben** M approach trench

läu|fig ['lɔyfıç] ADJ on *(Brit)* or in heat

Lauf-: **Lauf|jun|ge** M errand boy; **Lauf|kat|ze** F *(Tech)* crab; **Lauf|kran** M (overhead) travelling *(Brit)* or traveling *(US)* crane; **Lauf|kun|de** M, **Lauf|kun|din** F occasional customer; **Lauf|kund|schaft** F occasional customers *pl*; **Lauf|leis|tung** F *(Mot, von Reifen, Fahrzeug)* mileage; **~en von mehr als 500.000 km haben** *(Motor)* to cover more than 300,000 miles (without overhaul); **Lauf|ma|sche** F ladder *(Brit)*, run; **~n aufnehmen** to mend ladders *(Brit)* or runs; **Lauf|pass** M **jdm den ~ geben** *(inf)* to give sb his marching orders *(inf)*; *Freundin etc auch* to chuck sb *(inf)*; **Lauf|plan|ke** F *(Naut)* gangplank; **Lauf|rad** NT traversing wheel; *(ohne Antrieb)* trailing wheel; *(in Turbine)* rotor; **Lauf|rich|tung** F *(Mech)* direction of travel; **Lauf|rol|le** F roller; *(unter Möbeln)* castor; **Lauf|rost** M duckboards *pl (Brit)*, lath floor; **lauf|ru|hig** ADJ *Motor* quiet; **Lauf|schritt** M trot; *(Mil)* double-quick, double time; **im ~** *(Mil)* at the double; **er näherte sich im ~** he came trotting up; **Lauf|schuh** M *(inf)* walking shoe; **Lauf|sport** M running; **Lauf|stall** M **a** playpen **b** *(für Tiere)* pen; **lauf|stark** ADJ *Sportler* good at running *pred*; **er ist sehr ~** he's a strong runner; **Lauf|steg** M catwalk

läuft [lɔyft] *3. pers sing pres von* **laufen**

Lauf-: **Lauf|werk** NT running gear; *(Comput)* drive; **Lauf|werk(s)|buch|sta|be** M *(Comput)* drive letter; **Lauf|zeit** F **a** *(von Wechsel, Vertrag)* term, period of validity; *(von Kredit)* period **b** *(von Maschine) (= Lebensdauer)* (operational) life; *(= Betriebszeit)* running time **c** *(von Brief, Postsendung)* delivery time **d** *(Comput: von Programm)* run-time **e** *(Sport)* time **f** *(Zool: = Brunstzeit)* **während der ~** while on *(Brit)* or in heat; **Lauf|zet|tel** M *(an Akten, Maschinen)* docket

Lau|ge [ˈlaugə] F **-, -n** *(Chem)* lye, leach; *(= Seifenlauge)* soapy water; *(= Salzlauge)* salt solution

Lau|gen|bre|zel F pretzel stick

Lau|heit [ˈlauhait] F **-,** *no pl (von Wind, Abend)* mildness; *(von Haltung)* half-heartedness

Lau|ne [ˈlaunə] F **-, -n** **a** *(= Stimmung)* mood; **(je) nach (Lust und) ~** just as the mood *or* fancy takes one; **gute/schlechte ~ haben, (bei** *or* **in) guter/schlechter ~ sein** to be in a good/bad mood *or* temper; **jdn bei guter ~** *or* **bei ~** *(inf)* **halten** to keep sb happy *or* in a good mood; **was hat er für ~?** what sort of (a) mood is he in?; **seine ~ an jdm auslassen** to take one's temper out on sb; **~ machen** to be fun **b** *(= Grille, Einfall)* whim, caprice; **die ~n des Glücks** the vagaries of fortune; **eine ~ der Natur** a whim *or* caprice of nature; **etw aus einer ~ heraus tun** to do sth on a whim

lau|nen|haft ADJ moody; *(= unberechenbar)* capricious; *Wetter* changeable ADV moodily; *(= unberechenbar)* capriciously

Lau|nen|haf|tig|keit [ˈlaunənhaftɪçkait] F **-,** *no pl* moodiness; *(= Unberechenbarkeit)* capriciousness; *(von Wetter)* changeability

lau|nig [ˈlaunɪç] *(dated)* ADJ witty ADV **~ gestimmt sein** to be witty *or* in a witty mood; **eine ~ formulierte Rede** a witty speech

Lau|nig|keit F **-,** *no pl* wittiness

lau|nisch [ˈlaunɪʃ] ADJ, ADV = **launenhaft**

Lau|re|at [laureˈaːt] M **-en, -en, Lau|re|a|tin** [-ˈaːtɪn] F **-, -nen** *(geh)* laureate

Laus [laus] F **-, Läu|se** [ˈlɔyzə] louse; *(= Blattlaus)* greenfly, blackfly; **jdm/sich eine ~ in den Pelz setzen** *(inf)* to land sb/oneself in it *(Brit inf)*, to let sb/oneself in for it *(inf)*; **ihm ist (wohl) eine ~ über die Leber gelaufen** *or* **gekrochen** *(inf)* something's eating at him *(inf)*

Laus|bub M *(dated)* rascal, scamp, scallywag; *(= jungenhaftes Mädchen)* tomboy

Laus|bu|ben|ge|sicht NT *(dated)* scampish *or* roguish face

Laus|bü|be|rei [lausbyːbəˈrai] F **-, -en** *(dated)* devilry, prank(s *pl*)

laus|bü|bisch [ˈlausbyːbɪʃ] *(dated)* ADJ roguish, scampish, rascally; *Mädchen* tomboyish ADV **sich ~ benehmen** *(Junge)* to behave like a rascal; *(Mädchen)* to behave like a tomboy

Lausch|an|griff M bugging operation *(gegen* on)

Läus|chen [ˈlɔysçən] NT **-s, -** *dim von* **Laus**

lau|schen [ˈlauʃn] VI **a** *(geh)* to listen (+*dat*, *auf +acc* to) **b** *(= heimlich zuhören)* to eavesdrop

Lau|scher [ˈlauʃɐ] M **-s, -** *(Hunt: = Ohr)* ear

Lau|scher [ˈlauʃɐ] M **-s, -, Lau|sche|rin** [-ərɪn] F **-, -nen** eavesdropper; **der ~ an der Wand hört seine eigene Schand** *(Prov)* people who listen at doors never hear any good of themselves

lau|schig [ˈlauʃɪç] ADJ *Plätzchen* cosy *(Brit)*, cozy *(US)*, snug; *(im Freien)* secluded

Lau|se-: **Lau|se|ben|gel** M *(inf)*, **Lau|se|jun|ge** M *(inf)* blighter *(Brit inf)*, little devil *(inf)*; *(wohlwollend)* scamp, rascal; **lau|se|kalt** ADJ *(inf)* perishing *(inf)*, freezing (cold); **Lau|se|käl|te** F *(inf)* freezing *or* perishing *(inf)* cold

lau|sen [ˈlauzn] VT to delouse; **jdn ~** *(inf: = übervorteilen)* to fleece sb *(inf)*; **ich glaub, mich laust der Affe!** *(inf)* well blow me down! *(inf)*, well I'll be blowed! *(Brit inf)*

Lau|ser [ˈlauzɐ] M **-s, -** *(S Ger: = Lausbub)* rascal, scamp, scallywag

lau|sig [ˈlauzɪç] *(inf)* ADJ lousy *(inf)*, awful; *Kälte* freezing, perishing ADV awfully; *(vor Adjektiv auch)* damn(ed) *(inf)*, bloody *(Brit inf)*

Lau|sitz [ˈlauzɪts] F **- die ~** Lusatia

laut [laut] ADJ **a** *(= nicht leise)* loud **b** *(= lärmend, voll Lärm)* noisy; *(= auffällig, aufdringlich) Mensch* loudmouthed; *Farbe etc* loud; **er wird immer gleich/wird niemals ~** he always/never gets obstreperous **c** *(= hörbar)* out loud *pred, adv*, aloud *pred, adv*; **~ werden** *(= bekannt)* to become known; **etw ~ werden lassen** to make sth known, to let sth be known **d** *(Hunt: = windstill)* still ADV loudly; **~er sprechen** to speak louder *or* more loudly, to speak up; **etw ~(er) stellen** to turn sth up (loud); **~ auflachen** to burst out laughing, to laugh out loud; **~ nachdenken** to think aloud; **etw ~ sagen** *(lit)* to say sth out loud; *(fig)* to shout sth from the rooftops, to tell sth to the whole world; **das kannst du aber ~ sagen** *(fig inf)* you can say that again

laut PREP *+gen or dat (geh)* according to

Laut [laut] M **-(e)s, -e** sound; **heimatliche ~e** sounds of home; **wir hörten bayerische ~e** we heard Bavarian accents; **keinen ~ von sich** *(dat)* **geben** not to make a sound; **~ geben** *(Hund)* to give tongue; *(fig inf)* to give a shout

laut|bar ADJ **~ werden** to become known

Laut|bil|dung F articulation

Lau|te [ˈlautə] F **-, -n** lute

lau|ten [ˈlautn] VI to be; *(Rede, Argumentation)* to go; *(Schriftstück)* to read, to go; *(= sich belaufen)* to amount *(auf +acc* to); **dieser Erlass lautet wörtlich …** the exact text of this decree is …; **auf den Namen … ~** *(Pass)* to be in the name of …; *(Scheck)* to be payable to …, to be made out to …; **die Anklage lautet auf Mord** the charge is (one of) murder

läu|ten [ˈlɔytn] VTI **a** *(Glocke, Mensch)* to ring; *(Wecker)* to go (off); **es hat geläutet** the bell rang *or* went; **es läutet zur Stunde** *(Sch)* the bell is ringing *or* going for the next lesson; **jdn zu Grabe ~** *(liter)* to sound sb's funeral knell, to toll the bells for sb's funeral; **(nach) jdm ~** to ring for sb → **Sturm a b er hat davon (etwas) ~ hören** *(inf)* he has heard something about it

Lau|te|nist [lautəˈnɪst] M **-en, -en, Lau|te|nis|tin** [-ˈnɪstɪn] F **-, -nen, Lau|ten|spie|ler(in)** M(F) lute player, lutenist

lau|ter [ˈlautɐ] ADJ *inv (= nur)* nothing but; **~ Unsinn/Freude** *etc* pure *or* sheer nonsense/joy *etc*; **das sind ~ Lügen** that's nothing but lies, that's all a pack of lies; **vor ~ Rauch/Autos kann man nichts sehen** you can't see anything for all the smoke/cars; **das sind ~ Idioten** they are nothing but idiots

lau|ter ADJ **a** *(liter: = rein) Gold, Wein* pure **b** *(geh: = aufrichtig) Mensch, Absichten* honourable *(Brit)*, honorable *(US)*; *Wahrheit* honest; **~er Wettbewerb** fair competition

Lau|ter|keit F **-,** *no pl (geh: = Aufrichtigkeit)* integrity

läu|tern [ˈlɔytɐn] VT *(liter)* to purify; *(fig)* to reform

Läu|te|rung [ˈlɔytərʊŋ] F **-, -en** *(liter)* purification; *(fig)* reformation

Läu|te|werk NT *(Rail)* signal bell

Laut-: **laut|ge|treu** ADJ phonetic; **laut|hals** [ˈlauthals] ADV at the top of one's voice; **Laut|leh|re** F phonetics *sing*, phonology; **laut|lich** [ˈlautlɪç] ADJ phonetic ADV phonetically; **laut|los** ADJ silent; *Schritt, Bewegung auch* soundless, noiseless; *Stille* utter, complete ADV silently; *fallen, sich bewegen auch* soundlessly, noiselessly; **laut|ma|lend** ADJ onomatopoeic; **Laut|ma|le|rei** F onomatopoeia; *(Ausdruck auch)* onomatopoeic word; **laut|ma|le|risch** ADJ onomatopoeic; **Laut|schrift** F phonetics *pl*; *(System auch)* phonetic alphabet *or* script

Laut|spre|cher M (loud)speaker; **über ~** over the loudspeaker(s)

Laut|spre|cher-: **Laut|spre|cher|an|la|ge** F **öffentliche ~** public address *or* PA system, Tannoy® *(Brit)*; **Laut|spre|cher|box** F speaker; **Laut|spre|cher|durch|sa|ge** F announcement over the public address, PA announcement; **Laut|spre|cher|wa|gen** M loudspeaker car *or (größer)* van

Laut-: **Laut|stand** M *(Ling)* stage of development of the sound system; **laut|stark** ADJ loud; *(Rad, TV etc)* high-volume; *Partei, Protest* vociferous ADV loudly; *protestieren auch* vociferously; **Laut|stär|ke** F **a** loudness; *(von Protest etc)* vociferousness **b** *(Rad, TV etc)* volume; **das Radio auf volle ~ einstellen** to turn the radio right up, to turn the radio up to full volume; **Laut|stär|ke|re|ge|lung** F *(Rad, TV etc)* volume control; **Laut|stär|ke|reg|ler** M *(Rad, TV etc)* volume control; **laut|treu** ADJ phonetic

Lau|tung [ˈlautʊŋ] F **-, -en** *(geh)* articulation

Laut-: **Laut|ver|schie|bung** F sound shift; **Laut|wan|del** M sound change; **laut+wer|den** VI *sep irreg aux sein (fig)* → **laut c**

Läut|werk NT *(Rail)* signal bell

Laut|zei|chen NT phonetic symbol

lau|warm ADJ slightly warm; *Flüssigkeit* lukewarm; *(fig)* lukewarm, half-hearted ADV *(fig)* half-heartedly

La|va [ˈlaːva] F **-, Laven** [ˈlaːvn] lava

La|va|bo NT **-(s), -s** **a** [laˈvaːbo] *(Rel)* lavabo **b** [ˈlaːvabo] *(Sw)* washbasin, sink

La|va-: **La|va|mas|se** F mass of (molten) lava; **La|va|strom** M stream *or* flow of (molten) lava

La|ven|del [laˈvɛndl] M **-s, -** lavender

la|vie|ren [laˈviːrən] *ptp* **laviert** VI **a** *(Naut)* to tack **b** *(fig)* to manoeuvre *(Brit)*, to maneuver *(US)*

la|vie|ren *ptp* **laviert** VT *(Art)* to wash; **lavierte Zeichnung** wash drawing

La|voir [laˈvoaːɐ] NT **-s, -s** *(old, Aus)* washbasin, washbowl, sink

Law and or|der [lɔːləndˈlɔːdɐ] *no art* law and order

Law-and-or|der- *in cpds* law-and-order; **Law-and-or|der-Kurs** M law-and-order campaign; **Law-and-or|der-Pro|gramm** NT law-and-order policy

La|wi|ne [laˈviːnə] F **-, -n** *(lit, fig)* avalanche

La|wi|nen-: **la|wi|nen|ar|tig** ADJ like an avalanche ADV like an avalanche; **~ anwachsen** to snowball; **La|wi|nen|ge|fahr** F danger of avalanches; **La|wi|nen|op|fer** NT avalanche victim; **La|wi|nen|schutz|wald** M barrier forest; **la|wi|nen|si|cher** ADJ *Ort* secure from avalanches ADV *gebaut* to withstand avalanches; **La|wi|nen|ver|bau|ung** [-fɛɐbauʊŋ] F **-, -en** avalanche barrier; **La|wi|nen|war|nung** F avalanche warning

Law|ren|ci|um [loˈrɛntsiʊm] NT **-s,** *no pl (abbr* **Lr)** lawrencium

lax [laks] ADJ lax ADV laxly

Lax|heit F **-,** *no pl* laxity, laxness

Lay|out [ˈleːlaut] NT **-s, -s, Lay-out** NT **-s, -s** layout

Lay|ou|ter [ˈleːlautɐ] M **-s, -, Lay|ou|te|rin** [-ərɪn] F **-, -nen** designer

La|za|rett [latsaˈrɛt] NT **-(e)s, -e** *(Mil) (in Kaserne etc)* sickbay; *(selbstständiges Krankenhaus)* hospital

La|za|rett-: **La|za|rett|schiff** NT hospital ship; **La|za|rett|zug** M hospital train

La|za|rus [ˈlaːtsarʊs] M **-, -se** *(Bibl)* Lazarus; **armer ~!** poor beggar *(Brit) or* devil!

LCD- *in cpds* LCD; **LCD-An|zei|ge** F LCD display; **LCD-Mo|ni|tor** M LCD monitor; **LCD-TV** NT LCD-TV

Lead|sän|ger(in) ['li:d-] M(F) lead singer

lea|sen ['li:zn] VT *(Comm)* to lease

Lea|sing ['li:zıŋ] NT **-s, -s** *(Comm)* leasing; **etw im ~ bekommen** to lease sth

Lea|sing-: **Lea|sing|ge|ber(in)** M(F) lessor; **Lea|sing|neh|mer(in)** M(F) lessee; **Lea|sing|ra|te** F leasing payment; **Lea|sing|ver|trag** M lease

Le|be|da|me ['le:bə-] F courtesan

Le|be|hoch [le:bə'ho:x] NT **-(s), -(s)** ≈ three cheers; **~ rufen** ≈ to give three cheers; **ein (dreifaches) ~ auf jdn ausbringen** ≈ to give sb three cheers

Le|be|mann ['le:bə-] M *pl* **-männer** roué, rake, playboy

le|ben ['le:bn] VI to live; *(= am Leben sein)* to be alive; *(= weiterleben)* to live on; **er lebt noch** he is still alive; **er lebt nicht mehr** he is no longer alive; **er hat nicht lange gelebt** he didn't live (for) long; **ich möchte nicht mehr ~** I don't want to go on living; **er wird nicht mehr lange zu ~ haben** he won't live much longer; **von etw ~** to live on sth; **es lebe** *or* **lang lebe der König!** long live the King!; **so wahr ich lebe!** *(obs)* 'pon my life! *(obs)*; **wie geht es dir? – man lebt (so)** *(inf)* how are you? – surviving; **lebst du noch?** *(hum inf)* are you still in the land of the living? *(hum)*; **genug zu ~ haben** to have enough to live on; **~ und ~ lassen** to live and let live; **so was lebt, und Schiller musste sterben!** *(hum inf)* some mothers do have 'em *(inf)*, it's a sad case *(inf)*; **zum Leben zu wenig, zum Sterben zu viel, davon kann man nicht ~ und nicht sterben** it's barely enough to keep body and soul together; **man lebt nur einmal!** you only live once; **einsam/christlich/gesund ~** to live *or* lead a lonely/Christian/healthy life; **allein/glücklich ~** to live alone/happily; **ganz für sich ~** to live a secluded life; **für etw ~, einer Sache** *(dat)* **~** *(geh)* to live for sth; **leb(e) wohl!** *(liter)* farewell! *(liter)*; **hier lebt es sich gut, hier lässt es sich (gut) ~** it's a good life here; **mit etw (gut) ~ können** to be able to live with sth → **hoch 2 e**

VT to live; **jeder muss sein eigenes Leben ~** we've all got our own lives to live *or* lead

Le|ben ['le:bn] NT **-s, - a** life; **das ~** life; **das ~ des Menschen/der Tiere** *etc* the life of man/animals *etc*; **am ~ sein/bleiben** to be/stay alive; **das ~ als Milchmann** life as a milkman, a milkman's life; **das ~ Hemingways** Hemingway's life, the life of Hemingway; **das ~ vor/hinter sich** *(dat)* **haben** to have one's life ahead of *or* in front of *or* before/behind one; **solange ich am ~ bin** as long as I live; **sich des ~s freuen, das** *or* **sein ~ genießen** to enjoy life; **das** *or* **sein ~ verlieren** to lose one's life; **jdm das ~ retten** to save sb's life; **es geht um ~ und Tod, es ist eine Sache auf ~ und Tod** it's a matter of life and death; **wenn dir dein ~ lieb ist** if you value your life; **ein glückliches** *etc* **~ führen** to lead a happy *etc* life; **mit dem ~ davonkommen** to escape with one's life; **mit dem ~ spielen, sein ~ aufs Spiel setzen** to take one's life in one's hands, to dice with death; **mit dem ~ abschließen** to prepare for death; **seinem ~ ein Ende machen** *or* **bereiten** to put an end to one's life; **einer Sache** *(dat)* **zu neuem ~ verhelfen** to breathe new life into sth, to revitalize sth; **etw ins ~ rufen** to bring sth into being; **jdn vom ~ zum Tode bringen** *(form)* or **befördern** *(inf)* to kill sb, to take sb's life, to take care of sb *(inf)*; *(bei Hinrichtung auch)* to put sb to death; **seines ~s nicht mehr sicher sein** to fear for one's life; **ums ~ kommen** to die, to lose one's life; **sein ~ lassen (müssen)** to lose one's life; **jdn am ~ lassen** to spare sb's life; **um sein ~ laufen** *or* **rennen** to run for one's life *or* for dear life; **sich** *(dat)* **das ~ nehmen** to take one's (own) life; **jdn wieder ins ~ zurückrufen** to bring sb back to life; *Bewusstlosen* to revive sb, to bring sb round *(Brit)* or around *(US)*; **was ist das für ein ~?** what kind of (a) life is that?; **der Mann/die Frau meines ~s** my ideal man/woman; **etw für sein ~ gern tun** to love doing sth, to be mad about doing sth *(inf)*; **etw für sein ~ gern essen/trinken** to be mad about sth *(inf)*, to love sth; **jdn künstlich am ~ erhalten** to keep sb alive artificially; **ein ~ in Frieden/in Armut** *etc* a life of peace/poverty *etc*; **er hat es nie leicht gehabt im ~** he has never had an easy life; **ein ~ lang** one's whole life (long); **zum ersten Mal** *or* **das erste Mal im ~** for the first time in one's life; **ich habe noch nie im** *or* **in meinem ~ geraucht** I have never smoked (in) all my life *or* in my whole life; **nie im ~!** never!; **sich durchs ~ schlagen** to struggle through (life); **ins ~ treten** to go out into the world; **im ~ stehen** to have some standing in the world; *(= nicht weltfremd sein)* to know what life is all about; **(draußen) im ~ ist das ganz anders** in real life it's very different; **ein Roman, den das ~ schrieb** a novel of real life; **ein Film nach dem ~** a film from real life; **das ~ geht weiter** life goes on; **unser ~ währet siebenzig Jahr ...** *(Bibl)* the days of our years are three score years and ten *(Bibl)*; **so ist das ~ (eben)** that's life, such is life, that's the way the cookie crumbles *(inf)*

b *(= Betriebsamkeit)* life; **auf dem Markt herrscht reges ~** the market is a hive of activity; **in dieser Stadt ist wenigstens ~** at least there is some life in this town; **~ in etw** *(acc)* **bringen** *(inf)* to liven *or* brighten sth up; **voller ~ stecken** to be full of life; **es war überhaupt kein ~ in seinem Vortrag** there wasn't a spark of life in his lecture → **Bude c**

le|bend ADJ live *attr*, alive *pred*; *Wesen, Seele, Beispiel, Sprache* living; **„Vorsicht, ~e Tiere"** "attention *or* with care, live animals"; **ein noch ~er Zeuge** a witness who is still alive *or* living today; **~es Inventar** livestock; **die Lebenden** the living; **~es Bild** tableau ADV alive; **ein Tier ~ fangen** to catch an animal alive; **~ gebärend** viviparous, live-bearing

Le|bend-: **le|bend|ge|bä|rend** ADJ → **lebend** ADV; **Le|bend|ge|burt** F live birth; **Le|bend|ge|wicht** NT live weight; *(von Rindern auch)* weight on the hoof

le|ben|dig [le'bɛndıç] ADJ **a** *(= nicht tot)* live *attr*, alive *pred*; *Wesen* living; **~e Junge** live young; **~e Junge gebären** to bear one's young live; **die Lebendigen und die Toten** *(Bibl)* the Quick and the Dead *(Bibl)*; **jdn bei ~em Leibe verbrennen, jdn ~en Leibes verbrennen** *(liter)* to burn sb alive; **wieder ~ werden** to come back to life; **er nimmts von den Lebendigen** *(hum inf)* he'll have the shirt off your back *(inf)*, it's daylight robbery *(Brit)* or highway robbery what he charges *(inf)*

b *(fig: = lebhaft)* lively *no adv*; *Darstellung, Bild, Erinnerung* lively, vivid; *Glaube* fervent

ADV **a** *(= lebend)* alive; **er ist dort ~ begraben** *(fig inf)* it's a living death for him there

b *(fig: = lebhaft)* vividly

Le|ben|dig|keit F **-,** *no pl (fig: = Lebhaftigkeit)* liveliness; *(von Darstellung, Bild, Erinnerung auch)* vividness

Le|bend|spen|der(in) M(F) *(Med)* living donor

Le|bens-: **Le|bens|abend** M old age, autumn *(Brit)* or twilight of one's life *(liter)*; **Le|bens|ab|schnitt** M phase in *or* of one's life; **Le|bens|ab|schnitts|part|ner(in)** M(F) *(inf, usu hum)* companion for a while; **ihr aktueller ~** her present companion *or* cohabitee; **Le|bens|ader** F *(fig)* lifeline; **Le|bens|al|ter** NT age; **ein hohes ~ erreichen** to have a long life; *(Mensch auch)* to reach a ripe old age *(inf)*; **Le|bens|angst** F angst; **Le|bens|an|schau|ung** F philosophy of life; **Le|bens|ar|beits|zeit** F working life; **Le|bens|ar|beits|zeit|ver|kür|zung** F shortening of one's working life; **Le|bens|art** F, *no pl* **a** *(= Lebensweise)* way of life **b** *(= Manieren)* manners *pl*; *(= Stil)* style, savoir-vivre; **eine feine ~ haben** to have exquisite manners/style; **eine kultivierte ~ haben** to be cultivated; **Le|bens|auf|fas|sung** F attitude to life; **Le|bens|auf|ga|be** F life's work; **Le|bens|äu|ße|rung** F sign of life; **Le|bens|baum** M *(Bot)* arbor vitae; *(fig, Art)* tree of life; **Le|bens|be|din|gun|gen** PL living conditions *pl*; **le|bens|be|dro|hend, le|bens|be|droh|lich** ADJ life-threatening ADV *krank, verletzt* critically; **le|bens|be|ja|hend** ADJ positive; **eine ~e Einstellung** a positive approach to life; **Le|bens|be|ja|hung** F positive attitude to life; **Le|bens|be|rech|ti|gung** F right to exist; *(von Menschen, Tieren auch)* right to live; **Le|bens|be|reich** M area of life; **Le|bens|be|schrei|bung** F biography; **Le|bens|bild** NT *(fig)* picture of sb's life; **Le|bens|dau|er** F life(span); *(von Maschine)* life; **le|bens|echt** ADJ true-to-life ADV realistically, authentically; **Le|bens|ein|stel|lung** F attitude *or* approach to life, take on life; **Le|bens|eli|xier** NT elixir of life; **Le|bens|en|de** NT end (of sb's/one's life); **sie lebte bis an ihr ~ in Armut** she lived in poverty till the day she died; **Le|bens|ener|gie** F, *no pl* vitality; **Le|bens|ent|wurf** M life plan; **Le|bens|er|fah|rung** F experience of life; **le|bens|er|hal|tend** ADJ life-preserving; *Geräte* life-support *attr*; **Le|bens|er|hal|tungs|sys|tem** NT life-support system; **Le|bens|er|in|ne|run|gen** PL memoirs *pl*; **Le|bens|er|war|tung** F life expectancy; **le|bens|fä|hig** ADJ *(Med)* capable of life *or* of living, viable; *(fig)* capable of surviving, viable; **Le|bens|fä|hig|keit** F *(Med, fig)* viability; **Le|bens|form** F *(Biol)* life form; *(Psych, Philos)* form of life, type of man; *(= Form menschlichen Zusammenlebens)* way of life; **Le|bens|fra|ge** F vital matter; **le|bens|fremd** ADJ remote from life, out of touch with life; **Le|bens|freu|de** F joie de vivre, zest for life; **le|bens|freu|dig** ADJ **~ sein** to enjoy life; **le|bens|froh** ADJ merry, full of the joys of life; **Le|bens|füh|rung** F lifestyle; **Le|bens|ge|fahr** F (mortal) danger; **„Lebensgefahr!"** "danger!"; **es besteht (akute) ~** there is danger (to life); **er ist** *or* **schwebt in (akuter) ~** his life is in danger, he is in danger of his life; *(Patient)* he is in a critical condition; **außer ~ sein** to be out of danger; **etw unter ~** *(dat)* **tun** to risk one's life doing sth; **der Film wurde unter ~ gedreht** the film was made at great personal risk to the crew; **le|bens|ge|fähr|lich** ADJ highly dangerous; *Krankheit, Verletzung* critical ADV *verletzt* critically; *(inf) glatt, schnell* dangerously; **Le|bens|ge|fähr|te** M, **Le|bens|ge|fähr|tin** F partner; **Le|bens|ge|fühl** NT, *no pl* awareness of life, feeling of being alive; **ein ganz neues ~ haben** to feel (like) a different person; *(= neuen Auftrieb haben)* to have a new lease of life *(Brit)* or on life; **Le|bens|geis|ter** PL *(hum inf)* **jds/seine ~ auffrischen** *or* **wecken** to pep sb/oneself up *(inf)*, to put some life into sb/oneself; **Le|bens|ge|mein|schaft** F long-term relationship; *(Biol, Zool)* symbiosis; **Le|bens|ge|nuss** M enjoyment of life; **Le|bens|ge|schich|te** F life story, life history; **Le|bens|ge|wohn|heit** F habit; **Le|bens|glück** NT happiness; **le|bens|groß** ADJ, ADV life-size; **Le|bens|grö|ße** F life-size; **eine Figur in ~** a life-size figure; **etw in ~ malen** to paint sth life-size; **da stand er in voller ~** *(hum)* there he was (as) large as life (and twice as ugly) *(inf)*; **er erhob sich zu seiner vollen ~** *(hum)* he drew himself up to his full height; **Le|bens|grund|la|ge** F (basis for one's) livelihood

Le|bens|hal|tung F **a** *(= Unterhaltskosten)* cost of living **b** *(= Lebensführung)* lifestyle

Le|bens|hal|tungs-: **Le|bens|hal|tungs|in|dex** M cost-of-living index; **Le|bens|hal|tungs|kos|ten** PL cost of living *sing*

Le|bens-: **Le|bens|hauch** M *(liter)* breath of life; **Le|bens|hil|fe** F counselling *(Brit)*, counseling *(US)*; **er missversteht Literatur als ~** he makes the mistake of thinking that literature can help him with the problems of life; **Le|bens|hun|ger** M thirst for life; **le|bens|hun|grig** ADJ eager *or* thirsty for life; **Le|bens|in|halt** M purpose in life, raison d'être; **etw zu seinem ~ machen** to devote oneself to sth, to make sth one's mission in life; **das ist sein ganzer ~** his whole life revolves (a)round it, it's the be-all and end-all of his existence; **Le|bens|jahr** NT year of (one's) life; **in seinem fünften ~** in the fifth year of his life; **nach Vollendung des 18. ~es** on attaining the age of 18; **Le|bens|ka|me|rad(in)** M(F) longtime companion; **Le|bens|kampf** M struggle for life *or* existence; **le|bens|klug** ADJ experienced; **Le|bens|klug|heit** F experience of life; **Le|bens|kraft** F vitality; **Le|bens|kreis** M *(= Lebensbereich)* sphere of life; **Le|bens|künst|ler(in)** M(F) **er ist ein echter ~** he really knows how to live *or* how to enjoy life; **Le|bens|la|ge** F situation; **in jeder ~** in any situation; **le|bens|lang** ADJ *Freundschaft, Siechtum* lifelong; *Haft, Gefangenschaft* life *attr*, for life; **~es Lernen** lifelong learning *or* education ADV for the rest of one's life; *mit jdm verbunden sein* for one's entire life; **Le|bens|lang** NT -, *no pl* life (sentence); **le|bens|läng|lich** ADJ *Rente, Strafe* for life; *Gefangenschaft auch* life *attr*; **ein Lebenslänglicher** *(inf)* a lifer *(inf)*; **sie hat „lebenslänglich"** *or* **Lebenslänglich bekommen** *(inf)* she got life *(inf)* ADV for life; **~ im Zuchthaus** *or* **hinter Gittern sitzen** *(inf)* to be inside for life *(inf)*, to be behind bars for life *(inf)*; **Le|bens|lauf** ✪ 46.2 M life; *(bei Bewerbungen)* curriculum vitae *(Brit)*, résumé *(US)*; **Le|bens|licht** NT **a** *(fig)* flame of life *(liter)*; **jdm das ~ ausblasen** *or* **auslöschen** *(liter)* to snuff out sb's life **b** *(als Geburtstagskerze)* candle; **Le|bens|li|nie** F lifeline; **Le|bens|lü|ge** F sham existence; **mit einer ~ leben** to live a lie; **Le|bens|lust** F zest for life, joie de vivre; **le|bens|lus|tig** ADJ in love with life; **Le|bens|mit|te** F middle years *pl*; **die Krise in der ~** the midlife crisis

Le|bens|mit|tel PL food *sing*, food(stuff)s *pl (form)*; *(als Kaufware auch)* groceries *pl*

Le|bens|mit|tel-: **Le|bens|mit|tel|che|mie** F food chemistry; **le|bens|mit|tel|ge|recht** ADJ suitable for putting food in ADV *verpacken* suitably for food; **Le|bens|mit|tel|ge|schäft** NT grocer's (shop); **Le|bens|mit|tel|ge|setz** NT food law; **Le|bens|mit|tel|kar|te** F food ration card; **Le|bens|mit|tel|ver|gif|tung** F food poisoning; **Le|bens|mit|tel|vor|rat** M food supplies *pl*, provisions *pl*

Le|bens-: **Le|bens|mo|nat** M **in den ersten ~en** in *or* during the first few months of life; **le|bens|mü|de** ADJ weary *or* tired of life; **ein Lebensmüder** a potential suicide; **ich bin doch nicht ~!** *(inf: = verrückt)* I'm not completely mad! *(inf)*; **Le|bens|mü|dig|keit** F weariness of life; **Le|bens|mut** M courage to face life; **le|bens|nah** ADJ true-to-life ADV realistically; **Le|bens|nerv** M *(fig)* **eine Industrie/eine Stadt an ihrem ~ treffen** to cripple an industry/a town; **der Tourismus ist der ~ Mallorcas** tourism is Majorca's lifeblood; **le|bens|not|wen|dig** ADJ essential, vitally necessary; *Organ, Sauerstoff etc* vital (for life), essential for life; **Le|bens|not|wen|dig|keit** F necessity of life, essential; **Le|bens|ord|nung** F way of life; *(Eccl)* canons and ordinances *pl (of the German Protestant Church)*; **Le|bens|part|ner|schaft** F long-term relationship; **eingetragene ~** registered *or* civil *(Brit)* partnership; **Le|bens|pfad** M, *no pl (liter)* journey through life; **Le|bens|phi|lo|so|phie** F philosophy of life; **Le|bens|pla|nung** F career planning; **Le|bens|qua|li|tät** F quality of life; **Le|bens|raum** M *(Pol)* lebensraum; *(Biol)* habitat; **Le|bens|re|gel** F rule (of life); **Le|bens|rei|se** F, *no pl (liter)* journey through life; **le|bens|ret|tend** ADJ lifesaving; **Le|bens|ret|ter(in)** M(F) rescuer; **du bist mein ~** you've saved my life; **Le|bens|ret|tungs|me|dail|le** F lifesaving medal; **Le|bens|rhyth|mus** M rhythm of life; **Le|bens|span|ne** F lifespan; **Le|bens|stan|dard** M standard of living; **Le|bens|stel|lung** F job for life; **Le|bens|stil** M lifestyle, style of life; **le|bens|tüch|tig** ADJ able to cope with life; **Le|bens|über|druss** M weariness with life, world-weariness; **Le|bens|um|stän|de** PL circumstances *pl*; **damals waren die ~ schwierig** conditions made life difficult in those days; **le|bens|un|fä|hig** ADJ *Lebewesen, System* nonviable; **Le|bens|un|ter|halt** M **a seinen ~ verdienen** to earn one's living; **seinen ~ bestreiten** to make one's living, to support oneself; **sie verdient den ~ für die Familie** she is the breadwinner of the family, she supports the family; **für jds ~ sorgen** to support sb; **etw zu seinem ~ tun** to do sth for a living *or* livelihood; **nur das Nötigste zum ~ haben** to have just enough to live on **b** *(= Unterhaltskosten)* cost of living, living expenses *pl*; **le|bens|un|tüch|tig** ADJ unable to cope with life; **le|bens|ver|län|gernd** ADJ *Maßnahme* life-prolonging; **le|bens|ver|nei|nend** ADJ negative; **eine ~e Einstellung** a negative approach to life; **Le|bens|ver|si|che|rung** F life assurance *(Brit) or* insurance; **eine ~ abschließen** to take out a life assurance *(Brit) or* insurance policy; **Le|bens|wan|del** M way of life; **einen einwandfreien/zweifelhaften** *etc* **~ führen** to lead an irreproachable/a dubious *etc* life; **Le|bens|weg** M journey through life; **den gemeinsamen ~ antreten** to begin one's life together; **alles Gute für den weiteren** *or* **ferneren ~** all the best for the future; **Le|bens|wei|se** F way of life; **Le|bens|weis|heit** F maxim; *(= Lebenserfahrung)* wisdom; **Le|bens|wen|de** F *(geh)* turning point in (one's/sb's) life; **Le|bens|werk** NT life's work, lifework; **le|bens|wert** ADJ worth living; **le|bens|wich|tig** ADJ essential, vital; *Organ, Bedürfnisse, Entscheidung* vital; *Nährstoffe* essential; **~e Verbindungslinie** vital link, lifeline; **Le|bens|wil|le** M will to live; **Le|bens|zei|chen** NT sign of life; **kein ~ mehr von sich geben** to show no sign(s) of life; **Le|bens|zeit** F life(time); **auf ~** for life; **Beamter auf ~** permanent *(Brit) or* tenured *(US)* civil servant; **Mitglied auf ~** life member; **Le|bens|ziel** NT goal *or* aim in life; **Le|bens|zweck** M purpose in life

Le|ber [ˈleːbɐ] F -, -n liver; **ich habe es mit der ~ zu tun** *(inf)* **ich habe es an der ~** *(inf)* I've got liver trouble; **frei** *or* **frisch von der ~ weg reden** *(inf)* to speak out, to speak frankly; **sich** *(dat)* **etw von der ~ reden** *(inf)* to get sth off one's chest → **Laus**

Le|ber-: **Le|ber|blüm|chen** NT liverleaf; **Le|ber|ent|zün|dung** F hepatitis, inflammation of the liver; **Le|ber|fleck** M mole; *(Hautfärbung)* liver spot; **Le|ber|ha|ken** M *(Sport)* hook to the liver; **Le|ber|kä|se** M, *no pl* ≈ meat loaf; **Le|ber|knö|del** M liver dumpling; **le|ber|krank** ADJ suffering from a liver disorder; **Le|ber|krebs** M cancer of the liver; **Le|ber|lei|den** NT liver disorder; **Le|ber|pas|te|te** F liver pâté; **Le|ber|scha|den** M damaged liver, liver damage; **Le|ber|tran** M cod-liver oil; **Le|ber|wert** M liver function reading; **Le|ber|wurst** F liver sausage → **beleidigt**; **Le|ber|zir|rho|se** [-tsiroːzə] F -, -n *(Med)* cirrhosis of the liver, hepatocirrhosis *(spec)*

Le|be|we|sen NT living thing; **kleinste ~** micro-organisms

Le|be|wohl [leːbəˈvoːl] NT -s, *no pl (liter)* farewell *(liter)*; **die Stunde des ~s** the hour of farewell; **jdm ~ sagen** to bid sb farewell *or* adieu

leb|haft ADJ **a** *(= voll Leben, rege)* lively *no adv*; *alter Mensch* sprightly, lively; *Temperament* vivacious, lively; *Gespräch, Streit* animated; *(Comm) Geschäfte, Verkehr, Nachfrage* brisk **b** *(= deutlich) Erinnerung, Eindruck, Vorstellungsvermögen* vivid; *(= einfallsreich) Fantasie* lively; **in ~er Erinnerung bleiben** to remain a vivid memory; **etw in ~er Erinnerung haben** to remember sth vividly **c** *(= kräftig) Muster, Interesse, Beifall* lively; *Farbe* bright, lively

ADV **a** *(= rege) reagieren, strampeln* strongly; **~ diskutieren** to have a lively discussion; **es geht ~ zu** it is lively, things are lively; **das Geschäft geht ~** business is brisk *or* lively; **die Börse schloss ~** business was brisk *or* lively on the Stock Exchange at the close of the day **b** *(= deutlich)* vividly, clearly; **ich kann mir ~ vorstellen, dass ...** I can (very) well imagine that ... **c** *(= intensiv)* intensely; **eine ~ geführte Debatte** a lively debate; **~ bedauern** to regret deeply, to be really sorry about

Leb|haf|tig|keit [ˈleːphaftɪçkait] F -, *no pl* liveliness; *(Comm: von Geschäften)* briskness; *(= Deutlichkeit: von Erinnerung, Eindruck)* vividness; *(von Farbe)* brightness

Leb|ku|chen M gingerbread

> **LEBKUCHEN**
>
> **Lebkuchen** are a sort of Christmas gingerbread. They are generally round and made with syrup or honey and lots of spices, including cinnamon, cardamom and allspice. They are then often coated with chocolate or sugar icing.

Leb-: **leb|los** ADJ *Körper, Augen, Stadt, Text* lifeless; *Pracht* empty; **~er Gegenstand** inanimate object; **Leb|lo|sig|keit** F -, *no pl* lifelessness; **Leb|tag** M *(inf)* **mein/dein** *etc* **~** all my/your *etc* life, all my/your *etc* born days; **das habe ich mein ~ noch nicht gesehen** I've never seen the like (of it) in all my life *or* in all my born days; **das werde ich mein ~ nicht vergessen** I'll never forget that as long as I live; **Leb|zei|ten** PL **zu jds ~** *(= Leben)* while sb is/was alive, in sb's lifetime; *(= Zeit)* in sb's day; **sie war schon zu ~ eine Legende** she was a legend in her own lifetime

lech|zen [ˈlɛçtsn] VI to pant; *(Hund auch)* to have its tongue hanging out; **nach etw ~** to thirst for sth, to crave sth, to long for sth; **mit ~der Zunge** with one's tongue hanging out → **Blut**

Le|ci|thin [lɛtsiˈtiːn] NT -s, *no pl* lecithin

leck [lɛk] ADJ leaky; **~ sein** to leak

Leck [lɛk] NT -(e)s, -s leak

Le|cka|ge [lɛˈkaːʒə] F -, -n **a** *(= Gewichtsverlust)* leakage **b** *(= Leck)* leak

Le|cke [ˈlɛkə] F -, -n *(Hunt)* salt lick

le|cken¹ [ˈlɛkn] VI *(= undicht sein)* to leak

le|cken² VTI to lick; **an jdm/etw ~** to lick sb/sth; **sich** *(dat)* **die Wunden ~** to lick one's wounds → **Arsch a, Finger**

le|cker [ˈlɛkɐ] ADJ *Speisen* delicious, lovely, yummy *(inf)*; *(inf) Mädchen* lovely, delectable ADV *zubereitet* deliciously; **~ schmecken/aussehen** to taste/look delicious

Le|cker|bis|sen M **a** *(Speise)* delicacy, titbit *(Brit)*, tidbit *(US)* **b** *(fig)* gem

Le|cke|rei F -, -en **a** *(= Leckerbissen)* delicacy, titbit *(Brit)*, tidbit *(US)* **b** *(= Süßigkeit)* dainty

Le|cker|maul NT, **Le|cker|mäul|chen** [-mɔylçən] NT -s, - *(inf)* sweet-toothed child/person *etc*; **ein ~ sein** to have a sweet tooth

leck+schla|gen VTI *sep irreg* to hole

Leck|stein M licking stone

LED [ɛleːˈdeː] F -, -s LED

led. *abbr von* **ledig**

Le|der [ˈleːdɐ] NT -s, - **a** leather; *(= Fensterleder)* chamois, chammy; *(= Wildleder)* suede; **in ~ gebunden** leather-bound; **zäh wie ~** as tough as old boots *(Brit inf)*, as tough as shoe leather *(US)*; **vom ~ ziehen** *(inf)* to let rip *(inf) or* fly *(inf)*; **was das ~ hält** *(inf, kämpfen, lügen)* like mad, like crazy **b** *(dated inf: = Haut)* hide *(inf)*; **jdm das ~ gerben** *or* **versohlen** to tan sb's hide; **jdm ans ~ wollen** to want to get one's hands on sb **c** *(inf: = Fußball)* ball; **am ~ bleiben** to stick with the ball

Le|der- *in cpds* leather; **le|der|ar|tig** ADJ *Stoff* leatherlike; **Le|der|band** [-bant] M *pl* **-bände** *(Buch)* leather-bound volume; **Le|der|fett** NT dubbin; **Le|der|gar|ni|tur** F leather-upholstered suite; **Le|der|haut** F *(Anat)* dermis *(spec)*, derma *(spec)*; *(um den Augapfel)* sclera *(spec)*; **Le|der|ho|se** F leather trousers *pl (esp Brit)* or pants *pl (esp US)*; *(aus Wildleder)* suede trousers *pl (esp Brit)* or pants *pl (esp US)*; *(kurz)* lederhosen *pl*; *(von Tracht)* leather shorts *pl*; *(Bundhose)* leather breeches *pl*; **Le|der|ja|cke** F leather jacket; *(aus Wildleder)* suede jacket; **Le|der|man|tel** M leather coat; *(aus Wildleder)* suede coat

LEDERHOSE

Contrary to popular belief abroad, **Lederhosen** are not the traditional costume for the whole of Germany. Only in Bavaria and Austria are leather knee-breeches and the **Gamsbart** hat the traditional male costume. The women in these areas wear a **Dirndl**: a dress with a bodice and apron. Other parts of Germany have different costumes – for example, in the Black Forest the traditional costume for women includes a wide black hat with three large red bobbles on top.

le|dern ['le:dɐn] ADJ **a** *(= aus Leder)* leather **b** *(= zäh) Fleisch, Haut* leathery; *(fig) Vortrag etc* dry (as dust) VT **a** *(= gerben)* to tan **b** *(= putzen)* to leather

Le|der-: **Le|der|na|cken** PL leathernecks *pl*; **Le|der|rü|cken** M *(von Buch)* leather spine; **Le|der|schurz** M leather apron; **Le|der|wa|ren** PL leather goods *pl*; **Le|der|zeug** NT, *no pl* leather gear; *(Mil)* leathers *pl*

le|dig ['le:dɪç] ADJ **a** *(= unverheiratet)* single; *(inf) Mutter* unmarried; *(S Ger) Kind* illegitimate **b** *(geh: = unabhängig)* free; **(los und) ~ sein** to be footloose and fancy free; **aller Pflichten** *(gen)* **(los und) ~ sein** to be free of all commitments

Le|di|ge(r) ['le:dɪgə] MF *decl as adj* single person

le|dig|lich ['le:dɪklɪç] ADV merely, simply

Lee [le:] F -, *no pl (Naut)* lee; **in ~ liegen** to be on the lee side; **nach ~ drehen** to turn to leeward

leer [le:ɐ] ADJ empty; *Blätter, Seite auch* blank; *Gesichtsausdruck, Blick* blank, vacant;; *(Comput) Ordner, Datei* empty; *DVD, CD* blank **der ~e Raum** *(geh)* the cosmos; **eine ~e Stelle** an empty space; **vor einem ~en Haus** *or* **vor ~en Bänken spielen** *(Theat)* to play to an empty house; **ins Leere starren/treten** to stare/step into space; **ins Leere greifen** to clutch at thin air; **ins Leere laufen** *(fig)* to come to nothing, to get nowhere; **mit ~en Händen** *(fig)* empty-handed
ADV **eine Zeile ~ lassen** to leave a line (blank *or* free); **etw ~ machen** to empty sth; **den Teller ~ essen** to eat everything on the plate; **(wie) ~ gefegt** *(Straßen, Stadt etc)* deserted; **etw ~ trinken** to empty sth; **etw ~ pumpen** to pump sth dry; **~ stehen** to stand empty; **~ stehend** empty; **einen Laden ~ kaufen** to buy a shop *(esp Brit)* or store *(US)* out → **leerlaufen**

Lee|re ['le:rə] F -, *no pl (lit, fig)* emptiness; **(eine) geistige ~** a mental vacuum; **(eine) gähnende ~** a gaping *or* yawning void

lee|ren ['le:rən] VT to empty *(auch Papierkorb von Computer)*; *Briefkasten auch* to clear; **jdm die Taschen ~** *(inf)* to clean sb out *(inf)* VR to empty

Leer-: **leer+es|sen** VT *sep irreg* → **leer** ADV; **Leer|fahrt** F *(von Bus, Lkw)* empty trip; **Leer|for|mel** F empty phrase; **leer+fres|sen** VT *sep irreg* → **fressen** VT **a**; **leer|ge|fegt** [-gəfe:kt] ADJ *(fig)* → **leer** ADV; **Leer|ge|wicht** NT unladen weight, tare; *(von Behälter)* empty weight; **Leer|gut** NT empties *pl*; **leer+kau|fen** VT *sep* → **leer** ADV; **Leer|lauf** M **a** *(Aut)* neutral; *(von Fahrrad)* freewheel; **im ~ fahren** to coast; **das Auto ist im ~** the engine is in neutral; *(= stehend mit laufendem Motor)* the engine is idling **b** *(fig)* slack; **leer+lau|fen** *sep irreg aux sein*, **leer lau|fen** △ *irreg aux sein* VI **a** *(Fass etc)* to run dry; **~ lassen** to empty, to drain **b** *(Motor)* to idle; *(Maschine)* to run idle; *(Betrieb etc)* to be idle; **leer+ma|chen** VT *sep* → **leer** ADV; **Leer|pa|ckung** F (empty) display package, dummy; **Leer|po|si|ti|on** F *(St Ex)* short position; **leer+pum|pen** VT *sep* → **leer** ADV; **Leer|schlag** M *(auf Tastatur)* space; **leer|ste|hend** ADJ → **leer** ADV; **Leer|stel|le** F blank (space); **Leer|tas|te** F *((auf Tastatur)* space bar; **leer+trin|ken** VT *sep irreg* → **leer** ADV

Lee|rung ['le:rʊŋ] F -, **-en** emptying; **die ~ der Mülltonnen erfolgt wöchentlich** the dustbins *(Brit)* or garbage cans *(US)* are emptied once a week; **nächste ~ 18 Uhr** *(an Briefkasten)* next collection *(Brit)* or pickup *(US)* 6 p.m.

Leer-: **Leer|ver|kauf** M *(St Ex)* short sale; **Leer|zei|chen** NT *(Comput)* blank (character), space (character); **Leer|zei|le** F *(Typ)* blank line; **zwei ~n lassen** to leave two lines free *or* blank, to leave two empty lines

Lef|ze ['lɛftsə] F -, **-n** *usu pl* chaps *pl*; *(von Pferd)* lip

le|gal [le'ga:l] ADJ legal, lawful ADV legally

le|ga|li|sie|ren [legali'zi:rən] *ptp* **legalisiert** VT to legalize

le|ga|lis|tisch [lega'lɪstɪʃ] ADJ legalistic ADV legalistically

Le|ga|li|tät [legali'tɛ:t] F -, *no pl* legality; **(etwas) außerhalb der ~** *(euph)* (slightly) outside the law

Le|gas|the|nie [legaste'ni:] F -, **-n** [-'ni:ən] dyslexia

Le|gas|the|ni|ker [legas'te:nikɐ] M **-s, -**, **Le|gas|the|ni|ke|rin** [-ərɪn] F -, **-nen** dyslexic

le|gas|the|nisch [legas'te:nɪʃ] ADJ dyslexic

Le|gat [le'ga:t] NT **-(e)s, -e** *(Jur)* legacy

Le|gat M **-en, -en** *(Eccl, Hist)* legate

Le|ga|ti|on [lega'tsio:n] F -, **-en** legation

Le|ga|ti|ons|rat M, **Le|ga|ti|ons|rä|tin** F counsellor to a legation *(Brit)*, legation counselor *(US)*

Le|ga|to [le'ga:to] NT **-(s), -s** *or* **Legati** [-ti] *(Mus)* legato

Le|ge|bat|te|rie F hen battery

Le|ge|hen|ne F, **Le|ge|huhn** NT layer, laying hen

Le|gel ['le:gl] M **-s, -** *(Naut)* cringle, grummet

le|gen ['le:gn] VT **a** *(= lagern)* to lay down; *(mit adv)* to lay; *Flasche etc* to lay on its side; *(= zusammenlegen) Wäsche* to fold; *(dial) Kartoffeln etc* to plant, to put in; *(Sport)* to bring down
b *(mit Raumangabe)* to put, to place; **wir müssen uns ein paar Flaschen Wein in den Keller ~** we must lay down a few bottles of wine; **beiseite ~** → **beiseitelegen**; **etw in Essig** *etc* **~** to preserve sth in vinegar *etc*; **ein Tier an die Kette ~** to chain an animal (up); **jdn in Ketten** *or* **Fesseln ~** to put sb in chains, to chain sb; *(fig hum)* to (en)snare sb
c *(mit Angabe des Zustandes)* **etw in Falten ~** to fold sth; **er legte die Stirn in Falten** he frowned, he creased his brow; **eine Stadt in Schutt und Asche ~** to reduce a town to rubble
d *(= verlegen) Fliesen, Leitungen, Schienen, Minen etc* to lay, to put down; *Bomben* to plant; **Feuer** *or* **einen Brand ~** to start a fire; **sich** *(dat)* **die Haare ~ lassen** to have one's hair set; **sich** *(dat)* **Dauerwellen** *etc* **~ lassen** to have a perm *etc*, to have one's hair permed *etc*
e *(Huhn) Eier* to lay
VI *(Huhn)* to lay
VR **a** *(= hinlegen)* to lie down *(auf +acc* on); **sich ins** *or (geh)* **zu Bett ~** to go to bed, to retire *(form)*; **sich in die Sonne ~** to lie in the sun; **leg dich!** *(zum Hund)* lie down! → **schlafen VI**
b *(mit Ortsangabe)* (= *niederlegen: Nebel, Rauch)* to settle *(auf +acc* on); **sich auf die Seite ~** to lie on one's side; *(Boot)* to heel over, to go over onto its side; **sich in die Kurve ~** to lean into the corner; **sich auf ein Spezialgebiet ~** to concentrate on *or* specialize in a particular field
c *(= abnehmen) (Lärm)* to die down, to abate; *(Sturm, Wind auch, Kälte)* to let up; *(Rauch, Nebel)* to clear; *(Zorn, Begeisterung auch, Arroganz, Nervosität)* to wear off; *(Anfangsschwierigkeiten)* to sort themselves out; **das Fieber legt sich bald** his/her *etc* temperature will come down soon

le|gen|där [legen'dɛ:ɐ] ADJ legendary; *(= obskur)* apocryphal; **er/das ist schon fast ~** he/it has already become almost legendary

Le|gen|de [le'gɛndə] F -, **-n** *(alle Bedeutungen)* legend; **sich** *(dat)* **eine ~ zulegen** to assume a false identity

le|gen|den|um|woben [-lʊmvo:bn] ADJ fabled, surrounded by legends

le|ger [le'ʒe:ɐ, le'ʒɛ:ɐ] ADJ **a** *(= bequem) Kleidung* casual; *Sitz* comfortable **b** *(= ungezwungen) Benehmen, Ausdrucksweise* casual; *Typ* casual, informal; *Atmosphäre* relaxed, informal ADV **a** *(= bequem) sich kleiden* casually; **etw sitzt ~** sth is comfortable; **etw fällt ~** sth is comfortably fitting **b** *(= ungezwungen)* casually; *sich ausdrücken* informally

Le|ge|zeit F laying season *or* time

Leg|föh|re ['le:k-] F mountain pine

Leg|gings ['lɛgɪŋs] PL, **Leg|gins** ['lɛgɪns] PL leggings *pl*

Leg|hen|ne ['le:k-] F layer, laying hen

le|gie|ren [le'gi:rən] *ptp* **legiert** VT **a** *Metall* to alloy **b** *(Cook) Suppe etc* to thicken

Le|gie|rung [le'gi:rʊŋ] F -, **-en** alloy; *(Verfahren)* alloying

Le|gi|on [le'gio:n] F -, **-en** legion; **die Zahl der Toten war ~** *(geh)* the number of the dead was legion *(liter)*

Le|gi|o|när [legio'nɛ:ɐ] M **-s, -e** legionary, legionnaire

Le|gi|o|närs|krank|heit F legionnaire's disease

le|gis|la|tiv [legɪsla'ti:f] ADJ legislative ADV **~ handeln** to take legislative action; **eine Reform ~ absichern** to validate a reform through legislation

Le|gis|la|ti|ve [legɪsla'ti:və] F -, **-n** legislature, legislative assembly *or* body

Le|gis|la|tur [legɪsla'tu:ɐ] F -, **-en** **a** *(rare: = Gesetzgebung)* legislation; *(obs: = gesetzgebende Gewalt)* legislature **b** *(inf: = Legislaturperiode)* parliamentary term *(Brit)*, legislative period *(US)*

Le|gis|la|tur|pe|ri|o|de F parliamentary term *(Brit)*, legislative period *(US)*

le|gi|tim [legi'ti:m] ADJ legitimate; **als ~ anerkannt** recognized as legitimate; **etw als ~ betrachten** to consider sth legitimate; **ich finde seine Kritik ~** I find his criticism legitimate; **deine Vorwürfe erscheinen mir ~** I think your accusations are justified ADV legitimately; **der Zusammenschluss ist nicht ganz ~ zustande gekommen** the merger wasn't set up in a strictly legal way

Le|gi|ti|ma|ti|on [legitima'tsio:n] F -, **-en** identification; *(= Berechtigung)* authorization; *(eines Kindes)* legitimation

le|gi|ti|mie|ren [legiti'mi:rən] *ptp* **legitimiert** VT *Beziehung, Kind* to legitimize; *(= berechtigen)* to entitle; *(= berechtigt erscheinen lassen)* to justify, to warrant; *(= Erlaubnis geben)* to authorize; **die demokratisch legitimierte Regierung** the democratically elected government VR to show (proof of) authorization; *(= sich ausweisen)* to identify oneself, to show proof of one's identity

Le|gi|ti|mie|rung [legiti'mi:rʊŋ] F legitimizing, legitimization; *(= Berechtigung)* justification

Le|gi|ti|mi|tät [legitimi'tɛ:t] F -, *no pl* legitimacy

Le|go|stein® ['le:go-] M Lego® brick

Le|gu|an [le:gu'a:n, 'le:gua:n] M **-s, -e** iguana

Le|hen ['le:ən] NT **-s, -** *(Hist)* fief, feoff, feu *(Scot)*; **jdm ein Gut zu ~ geben** to enfeoff sb

Le|hens- *in cpds* = **Lehns-**

Lehm [leːm] M -(e)s, -e loam; (= Ton) clay

Lehm-: **Lehm|bau** M pl -bauten, **Lehm|bau|wei|se** F clay building; **Lehm|bo|den** M clay soil; **lehm|far|ben** [-farbn], **lehm|far|big** ADJ clay-coloured (Brit), clay-colored (US); **Lehm|hüt|te** F mud hut

leh|mig ['leːmɪç] ADJ loamy; (= tonartig) claylike, clayey

Lehm-: **Lehm|pa|ckung** F mudpack; **Lehm|zie|gel** M clay brick

Lehn [leːn] NT -s, - = Lehen

Lehn|bil|dung F (Ling) loan formation

Leh|ne ['leːnə] F -, -n a (= Armlehne) arm(rest); (= Rückenlehne) back (rest) b (old, S Ger. = Berghang) slope

leh|nen ['leːnən] VT to lean (an +acc against) VI to be leaning (an +dat against) VR to lean (an +acc against, auf +acc on); „nicht aus dem Fenster ~!" (Rail) "do not lean out of the window"

Lehns|dienst ['leːns-] M (Hist) vassalage

Lehn-: **Lehn|ses|sel** M, **Lehn|stuhl** M easy chair

Lehns-: **Lehns|herr** M (Hist) feudal lord; **Lehns|mann** M pl -männer or -leute (Hist) vassal; **Lehns|pflicht** F (Hist) feudal duty

Lehn|stuhl M easy chair

Lehns|wesen ['leːns-] NT (Hist) feudal system, feudalism

Lehn|über|set|zung F (Ling) loan translation

Lehn|wort NT pl -wörter (Ling) loan word, borrowing

Lehr|amt NT das ~ the teaching profession; (= Lehrerposten) teaching post (esp Brit) or position; ein ~ ausüben to hold a teaching post (esp Brit) or position; Prüfung für das höhere ~ examination for secondary school teachers; das ~ an Gymnasien ≈ grammar school teaching (Brit), ≈ high school teaching (US); sie studiert ~ für Französisch und Englisch she's studying to be a teacher of French and English; sein ~ ernst nehmen (Univ) to take one's teaching responsibilities seriously

Lehr|amts-: **Lehr|amts|an|wär|ter(in)** M(F), **Lehr|amts|kan|di|dat(in)** M(F) prospective teacher; **Lehr|amts|stu|di|um** NT teacher training

Lehr-: **Lehr|an|stalt** F (form) educational establishment; höhere ~ establishment of secondary education; **Lehr|auf|trag** M (als Sonderlehrer) special teaching post (esp Brit) or position; (Univ) einen ~ für etw haben to give lectures on sth; **lehr|bar** ADJ teachable; **Lehr|be|auf|trag|te(r)** MF decl as adj (Univ) ~(r) für etw sein to give lectures on sth; **Lehr|be|fä|hi|gung** F teaching qualification; **Lehr|be|halt** [-bəhalt] M -s, -e (Aus) teaching aid; (pl auch) teaching materials pl; **Lehr|be|rech|ti|gung** F jdm die ~ erteilen to register sb as a teacher; ihm wurde die ~ entzogen he was struck off the register of teachers; für Latein hat er keine ~ he isn't qualified to teach Latin; **Lehr|be|ruf** M a (als Lehrer) teaching profession; den ~ ergreifen to go into teaching b (= Beruf mit Lehrzeit) trade requiring an apprenticeship, skilled trade; **Lehr|be|trieb** M (Univ) teaching; **Lehr|brief** M a (= Zeugnis) apprenticeship certificate b (= Lektion) correspondence lesson; **Lehr|bub** M apprentice; **Lehr|buch** NT textbook; **lehr|buch|ge|recht** ADJ a die ~e Bearbeitung eines Textes the editing of a text for a school edition b (= gut ausgeführt) textbook attr, perfect; **Lehr|buch|wis|sen** NT (pej) textbook knowledge; **Lehr|bur|sche** M (dial) apprentice; **Lehr|dich|tung** F didactic poetry

Leh|re ['leːrə] F -, -n a (= das Lehren) teaching b (von Christus, Buddha, Marx etc) teachings pl; (= Lehrmeinung) doctrine; (von Galilei, Kant, Freud etc) theory; (von Erdaufbau, Leben etc) science; die christliche ~ Christian doctrine/teaching c (= negative Erfahrung) lesson; (= Ratschlag) (piece of) advice; (einer Fabel) moral; jdm eine ~ erteilen to teach sb a lesson; seine ~(n) aus etw ziehen to learn a lesson from sth; (aus einer Fabel etc) to draw a moral from sth; lass dir das eine ~ sein let that be a lesson to you! d (= Berufslehre) apprenticeship; (in nicht handwerklichem Beruf) training; eine ~ machen to train; (in Handwerk) to do an apprenticeship; bei jdm die ~ (durch)machen, bei jdm in die ~ gehen to serve one's apprenticeship with or under sb; sie machte eine ~ als or zur Bürokauffrau she trained as an office administrator; du kannst bei ihm noch in die ~ gehen (fig) he could teach you a thing or two e (Tech) gauge; (= Muster) template

> **LEHRE**
>
> **Lehre** is the name for vocational training in trade and industry. It is strictly regulated and usually lasts three years, although those who have their **Abitur** are often allowed to reduce this by one year. The trainees, so-called **Auszubildende** or **Azubis** for short, work in a company and become familiar with all the different areas of their future profession. They also have classes at a vocational college for two days a week, or in blocks of seminars. At the end of the training period they take their **Gesellenprüfung**. → ABITUR

leh|ren ['leːrən] VTI to teach; (Univ auch) to lecture (ein Fach in a subject); die Wissenschaft lehrt, dass ... science tells us that ...; jdn or jdm (inf) lesen etc ~ to teach sb to read etc; die Zukunft wird es ~ time (alone) will tell; ich werde dich ~, so frech zu antworten! I'll teach you to answer back! (inf) → auch gelehrt

Leh|rer ['leːrɐ] M -s, -, **Leh|re|rin** [-ərɪn] F -, -nen teacher; (= Privatlehrer, Nachhilfelehrer auch) tutor; (= Fluglehrer, Fahrlehrer etc) instructor/instructress; er ist ~ he's a (school)teacher; ~(in) für Philosophie/Naturwissenschaften teacher of philosophy/science; (in der Schule) philosophy/science teacher

Leh|rer-: **Leh|rer|aus|bil|dung** F teacher training; **Leh|rer|be|ruf** M teaching profession, career as a teacher; **Leh|rer|hand|rei|chung|en** PL teacher's notes pl; **Leh|rer|kol|le|gi|um** NT (teaching) staff; in diesem ~ amongst the teaching staff of this school; **Leh|rer|kon|fe|renz** F (Sch) staff meeting

Lehr|er|laub|nis F → Lehrberechtigung

Leh|rer-: **Leh|rer|man|gel** M teacher shortage; **Leh|rer|schaft** ['leːrɐʃaft] F -, -en (form) (teaching) staff; **Leh|rer|schwem|me** F surplus of teachers; **Leh|rer|se|mi|nar** NT (für Referendare, inf: = Pädagogische Hochschule) teacher training college; (Kurs) in-service course for teachers; **Leh|rer|zim|mer** NT staff (esp Brit) or teachers' room

Lehr-: **Lehr|fach** NT subject; **Lehr|film** M educational film; **Lehr|frei|heit** F freedom to teach as one sees fit; **Lehr|gang** M pl -gänge course (für in); **Lehr|ge|bäu|de** NT (fig) system of theories; (Eccl) doctrinal system; **Lehr|ge|gen|stand** M subject; **Lehr|geld** NT (Hist) (apprenticeship) premium; (teures) ~ für etw zahlen müssen (fig) to pay dearly for sth; lass dir dein ~ zurückgeben! (hum inf) go to the bottom of the class! (hum inf); **Lehr|ge|rüst** NT centring (Brit), centering (US); **lehr|haft** ADJ didactic; **Lehr|herr(in)** M(F) master (of an apprentice); **Lehr|jahr** NT year as an apprentice; ~e sind keine Herrenjahre (Prov) life's not easy at the bottom; **Lehr|jun|ge** M (dated) apprentice; **Lehr|kan|zel** F (Aus) = Lehrstuhl; **Lehr|kör|per** M (form) teaching staff; (Univ auch) academic staff; **Lehr|kraft** F (form) teacher

Lehr|ling ['leːɐlɪŋ] M -s, -e apprentice; (in nicht handwerklichem Beruf) trainee

Lehr-: **Lehr|mäd|chen** NT (dated) apprentice; **Lehr|mei|nung** F opinion; (von einer bestimmten Gruppe vertreten) school of thought; (Eccl) doctrine; **Lehr|meis|ter(in)** M(F) master; seinen ~ finden to meet one's master; du bist mir ein schöner ~ you're a fine example; **Lehr|me|tho|de** F teaching method; **Lehr|mit|tel** NT teaching aid; (pl auch) teaching materials pl; **Lehr|plan** M (teaching) curriculum; (für ein Schuljahr) syllabus; **Lehr|pro|be** F demonstration lesson, crit (Brit inf); **Lehr|pro|gramm** NT teaching programme (Brit) or program (US); **lehr|reich** ADJ (= informativ) instructive; Erfahrung educational; **Lehr|satz** M (Math, Philos) theorem; (Eccl) dogma; **Lehr|schwimm|be|cken** NT beginners' or teaching pool; **Lehr|stel|le** F position for an apprentice; (in nicht handwerklichem Beruf) position for a trainee; (aus Sicht des Auszubildenden) position as an apprentice/a trainee; wir haben zwei ~n zu vergeben we have vacancies for two apprentices/trainees; **Lehr|stoff** M subject; (eines Jahres) syllabus; das ist ~ der dritten Klasse that's on the syllabus for the third year; **Lehr|stuhl** M (Univ) chair (für of); jdn auf einen ~ berufen to offer sb a chair; **Lehr|tä|tig|keit** F (Univ) (= Unterrichten) teaching; (= Stelle) teaching post or job; eine ~ ausüben to teach; **Lehr|toch|ter** F (Sw) apprentice; (in nicht handwerklichem Beruf) trainee; **Lehr|ver|an|stal|tung** F (Univ) (= Vorlesung) lecture; (= Seminar) seminar; **Lehr|ver|hält|nis** NT contractual relationship (between apprentice and master/trainee and employer); in einem ~ stehen (form) to be apprenticed (bei to); **Lehr|ver|trag** M indentures pl; (in nicht handwerklichem Beruf) contract as a trainee; **Lehr|werk** NT (form) textbook; (Buchreihe) series of textbooks; **Lehr|werk|statt** F training workshop; **Lehr|zeit** F apprenticeship

Leib [laip] M -(e)s, -er [-bɐ] a (= Körper) body; der ~ des Herrn (Eccl) the Body of Christ; Gefahr für ~ und Leben (geh) danger to life and limb; ~ und Leben wagen (geh) to risk life and limb; mit ~ und Seele heart and soul; wünschen with all one's heart; mit ~ und Seele singen to sing one's heart out; mit ~ und Seele dabei sein to put one's heart and soul or one's whole heart into it; etw am eigenen ~(e) erfahren or (ver)spüren to experience sth for oneself; kein Hemd mehr am ~ haben to be completely destitute; keinen trockenen Faden am ~ haben (inf) to be soaked to the skin (inf); der hat vielleicht einen Ton am ~! (inf) talk about rude!; am ganzen ~(e) zittern/frieren/schwitzen to be shaking/freezing/sweating all over; sich (dat) alles an den ~ hängen (inf) to spend everything on clothes; die Rolle ist ihr wie auf den ~ geschrieben the part is tailor-made for her; der Beruf ist ihr wie auf den ~ geschnitten that job is tailor-made for her, that job suits her to a T (esp Brit inf); kein Herz im ~e haben to have no heart at all, to be completely heartless; sich (dat) jdn/etw vom ~e halten to keep or hold sb/sth at bay; halt ihn mir vom ~ keep him away from me; jdm vom ~ bleiben to keep away from sb; geh mir vom ~! get away (from me)!; (= lass mich in Ruhe) get off my back! (inf); bleib mir damit vom ~e! (inf) stop pestering me with it (inf) → rücken VI b (old, dial: = Bauch) stomach; (= Mutterleib) womb; ich habe noch nichts im ~(e) I haven't eaten yet; gut bei ~e sein (iro) to be well-upholstered (iro)

Leib-: **Leib|arzt** M, **Leib|ärz|tin** F personal physician; **Leib|bin|de** F truss; (nach Geburt) abdominal binder (Brit) or belt (US)

Leib|chen ['laipçən] NT -s, - a (old) bodice b (= Unterhemd) vest (Brit), undershirt (US); (= Hemdchen) top

Leib-: **leib|ei|gen** ADJ unfree, in bondage; (im Mittelalter) serf attr; ~ sein not to be a free man/woman; (im Mittelalter) to be a serf; **Leib|ei|ge|ne(r)** ['laiplaigənə] MF decl as adj bond(s)man/-woman; (im Mittelalter) serf; er behandelt seine Frau wie eine ~ he treats his wife as though she were one of his possessions; **Leib|ei|gen|schaft** F bondage; *(im Mittelalter)* serfdom

lei|ben ['laibn] VI **wie er leibt und lebt** to the life, to a T *(esp Brit inf)*

Lei|bes-: **Lei|bes|er|zie|hung** F physical education; **Lei|bes|frucht** F *(geh)* unborn child, fruit of one's/sb's womb *(poet)*; **Lei|bes|fül|le** F, *no pl (geh)* corpulence *(form)*; *(von Mann)* portliness *(geh)*; **Lei|bes|kraft** F **aus Leibeskräften schreien** *etc* to shout *etc* with all one's might (and main); **Lei|bes|übung** F (physical) exercise; **~en** *(Schulfach)* physical education *no pl*; **Lei|bes|vi|si|ta|ti|on** F body search; *(Mil)* physical inspection, medical

Leib-: **Leib|gar|de** F *(Mil)* bodyguard; **die ~ der englischen Königin** the Queen's Guards *pl*; **Leib|gar|dist** M soldier in a bodyguard; **Leib|ge|richt** NT favourite *(Brit)* or favorite *(US)* meal

leib|haft ADJ *(rare)* = **leibhaftig**

leib|haf|tig [laip'haftɪç, 'laiphaftɪç] ADJ personified, incarnate; **die ~e Güte** *etc* goodness *etc* personified *or* incarnate; **(wie) der ~e Teufel, (wie) der Leibhaftige** (as) the devil himself ADV in person, in the flesh

Leib|koch M, **Leib|kö|chin** F personal chef

leib|lich ['laiplɪç] ADJ **a** *(= körperlich)* physical, bodily; **die ~en Genüsse** the pleasures of the flesh; **die ~e Hülle** *(geh)* the mortal remains *pl*; **für das ~e Wohl sorgen** to take care of our/their *etc* bodily needs **b** *Mutter, Vater* natural; *Kind* by birth; *Bruder, Schwester* full; *Verwandte* blood; *(emph: = eigen)* (very) own

Leib-: **Leib|pacht** F *(old)* life tenancy, lease for life; **Leib|ren|te** F life annuity; **Leib|rie|men** M *(old)* belt; **Leib|schmer|zen** PL *(old, dial)* stomach pains *pl*; **Leib|spei|se** F favourite *(Brit)* or favorite *(US)* food; **Leib|wa|che** F bodyguard; **Leib|wäch|ter(in)** M(F) bodyguard; **Leib|wä|sche** F underwear, underclothes *pl*; **Leib|weh** NT *(old)* stomachache

Leich [laiç] M **-(e)s, -e** *(Liter)* lay

Lei|che ['laiçə] F **-, -n** **a** body, corpse; *(inf: = Bierleiche, Schnapsleiche)* drunken body *(inf)*; **die Insassen konnten nur noch als ~n geborgen werden** the passengers were dead when the rescuers arrived; **eine lebende** *or* **wandelnde ~** *(inf)* a corpse; **wie eine lebende** *or* **wandelnde ~ aussehen** to look like death (warmed up *(Brit inf)* or over *(US inf)*); **er geht über ~n** *(inf)* he'd stop at nothing, he'd sell his own grandmother *(inf)*; **nur über meine ~!** *(inf)* over my dead body!; **eine ~ im Keller haben** *(fig)* to have a skeleton in the cupboard *(Brit)* or closet **b** *(S Ger) (= Beerdigung)* funeral; *(= Leichenschmaus)* funeral meal; **die ~ begießen** *(inf)* to drink the dead man's health **c** *(Typ)* omission

Lei|chen-: **Lei|chen|be|gäng|nis** [-bəgɛŋnɪs] NT **-ses, -se** *(form)*, **Lei|chen|be|gräb|nis** NT funeral; **Lei|chen|be|schau|er** [-bəʃauɐ] M **-s, -**, **Lei|chen|be|schau|e|rin** [-ərɪn] F **-, -nen** doctor conducting a postmortem; **Lei|chen|bit|ter|mie|ne** F *(inf)* mournful *or* doleful expression; **lei|chen|blass** ADJ deathly pale, as pale as death; **Lei|chen|fled|de|rei** [-flɛdərai] F **-, -en** robbing of dead people; **das ist die reinste ~** *(fig)* what vultures!; **Lei|chen|fled|de|rer** M **-s, -**, **Lei|chen|fled|de|rin** F **-, -nen** person who robs dead people; *(fig)* vulture; **Lei|chen|frau** F layer-out; **Lei|chen|hal|le** F, **Lei|chen|haus** NT mortuary; **Lei|chen|hemd** NT shroud; **Lei|chen|kon|ser|vie|rung** F preservation of corpses; **Lei|chen|öff|nung** F autopsy; **Lei|chen|re|de** F funeral oration *(liter) or* address; **Lei|chen|schän|dung** F desecration of corpses; *(sexuell)* necrophilia; **Lei|chen|schau** F postmortem (examination); **Lei|chen|schau|haus** NT morgue; **Lei|chen|schmaus** M funeral meal; **Lei|chen|star|re** F rigor mortis *no art*; **Lei|chen|tuch** NT *pl* **-tücher** shroud; **Lei|chen|ver|bren|nung** F cremation; **Lei|chen|wa|gen** M hearse; **Lei|chen|zug** M funeral procession

Leich|nam ['laiçna:m] M **-s, -e** *(form)* body

leicht [laiçt] ADJ **a** *(= von geringem Gewicht, nicht schwerfällig, Mil)* light; *(= aus leichtem Material) Koffer, Kleidung* lightweight; **einen ~en Gang haben** to have an easy walk; **mit ~er Hand** lightly; *(fig)* effortlessly; **eine ~e Hand mit jdm/für etw haben** to have a way with sb/sth; **~en Fußes** *(liter)* with a spring in one's step; **gewogen und zu ~ befunden** *(fig)* tried and found wanting; **jdn um einiges ~er machen** to relieve sb of some of his money → **Feder**

b *(= schwach, geringfügig, nicht wichtig)* slight; *Regen, Wind, Frost, Schläge, Schlaf, Berührung, Atmen* light; *(Jur) Diebstahl, Vergehen etc* minor, petty

c *(von geringem Gehalt) Essen, Musik, Lektüre etc* light

d *(= ohne Schwierigkeiten, einfach)* easy; **~er Absatz** *(Comm)* quick turnover (*von* in); **mit dem werden wir (ein) ~es Spiel haben** he'll be a pushover *(inf)* or walkover *(inf)*, he'll be no problem; **keinen ~en Stand haben** not to have an easy time (of it) (*bei, mit* with); **das ist ihr ein Leichtes** *(geh)* that will present no problem to *or* for her; **nichts ~er als das!** nothing (could be) easier *or* simpler

e *(= moralisch locker) Lebenswandel* loose; **~es Mädchen** tart *(Brit inf)*, floozy *(inf)*

f *(= unbeschwert) Herz, Gefühl* light; **etw ~en Herzens** *or* **Sinnes tun** to do sth with a light heart → **Schulter**

ADV **a** *(= einfach)* easily; **jdm etw ~ machen** to make it easy for sb; **es sich** *(dat)* **(bei etw) ~ machen** not to make much of an effort (with sth); **sie hat es immer ~ gehabt (im Leben)** she's always had it easy, she's always had an easy time of it; **man hats nicht ~** *(inf)* it's a hard life; **das ist** *or* **geht ganz ~** it's quite easy *or* simple; **die Aufgabe ist ~ zu lösen** *or* **lässt sich ~ lösen** the exercise is easy to do; **mach es dir nicht zu ~** *(= bequem)* don't make things too easy for yourself; *(= sei gewissenhaft auch)* don't take the easy way out; *(= vereinfache es nicht)* don't oversimplify things; **das ist ~er gesagt als getan** that's easier said than done; **du hast ~ reden/lachen** it's all very well for you *or* it's all right for you to talk/laugh

b *(= problemlos)* easily; **~ zu beantworten/verstehen** easily answered/understood, easy to answer/understand; **~ verständlich** readily *or* easily understood; **er ist ~ herumzukriegen/zu überzeugen** he's easy to win round/convince, he's easily won round/convinced; **~ begreifen** to understand quickly *or* readily; **das kann ich mir ~ vorstellen** *or* **denken** I can easily *or* well imagine (it); **~ verdaulich** *(Speisen, Informationen)* easily digestible; *Kunst, Musik etc* not too demanding

c *(= unbekümmert)*; **~ beschwingt** *(Musik)* light; **~beschwingte Melodien** melodies for easy listening; **sich ~ und beschwingt fühlen** to be walking on air, to be up in the clouds; **mir ist so ~ ums Herz** my heart is so light; **mir ist jetzt viel ~er** I feel a lot easier now; **nimm das nicht zu ~** don't take it too lightly; **etw leicht nehmen** → **leichtnehmen**

d *(= schnell, unversehens)* easily; **er wird ~ böse/ist ~ beleidigt** *etc* he is quick to get angry/take offence *(Brit)* or offense *(US) etc*, he gets angry/takes offence *(Brit)* or offense *(US) etc* easily; **~ zerbrechlich** very fragile; **~ verderblich** highly perishable; **man kann einen Fehler ~ übersehen** it's easy to miss a mistake, mistakes are easily missed; **das ist ~ möglich** that's quite possible; **~ entzündlich** *(Brennstoff etc)* highly (in)flammable; **~ entzündliche Haut** skin which easily becomes inflamed; **~ entzündlich sein** *(Gas, Brennstoff)* to be highly inflammable; *(Haut)* to become easily inflamed; **man hat ~ etwas gesagt, was man nachher bereut** it's easy to say something (without thinking) that you regret later; **das passiert mir so ~ nicht wieder** I won't let that happen again in a hurry *(inf)*; **das passiert mir so ~ nicht wieder, dass ich dir Geld borge** I won't lend you money again in a hurry *(inf)*

e *(= geringfügig, nicht schwer) gewebt* finely; *bewaffnet* not heavily, lightly; **das Haus ist ~ gebaut** the house is built of light materials; **ein zu ~ gebautes Haus/Auto** a flimsily built house/car; **~ bekleidet sein** to be scantily clad *or* dressed; **~ gekleidet sein** to be (dressed) in light clothes; **~ geschürzt** *(hum)* scantily clad *or* dressed

f *(= schwach) regnen* not hard; **es hat ~ gefroren** there was a light frost; **~ gewürzt/gesalzen** lightly seasoned/salted; **zu ~ gewürzt/gesalzen** not seasoned/salted enough; **~ waschen** to wash gently

g *(= nicht ernsthaft) beschädigt* slightly; *gekränkt auch* a little; **~ verletzt** slightly injured; *(in Gefecht, Schlägerei etc auch)* slightly wounded; **~er verletzt** not as seriously injured; **~ Verletzte(r)** = **Leichtverletzte(r)**; **~ verwundet** slightly wounded; **~ Verwundete(r)** = **Leichtverwundete(r)**

Leicht-: **Leicht|ath|let(in)** M(F) (track and field) athlete; **Leicht|ath|le|tik** F (track and field) athletics *sing*; **leicht|ath|le|tisch** ADJ athletic *attr* ADV as regards (track and field) athletics; **Leicht|bau** M *pl* **-bauten** lightweight construction; **in ~** using lightweight materials; **Leicht|bau|stoff** M lightweight building material; **Leicht|bau|wei|se** F = **Leichtbau**; **Leicht|ben|zin** NT benzine; **leicht|be|schwingt** ADJ *attr* → **leicht ADV c**; **Leicht|be|ton** M lightweight concrete; **leicht|be|waff|net** ADJ *attr* → **leicht ADV e**; **leicht|ent|zünd|lich** ADJ *attr* → **leicht ADV d**

Leich|ter ['laiçtɐ] M **-s, -** *(Naut)* lighter

leich|tern ['laiçtɐn] VT *(Naut)* to lighten *(form)*

Leicht-: **leicht+fal|len** *sep irreg aux sein*, △ **leicht fal|len** △ *irreg aux sein* VI to be easy (*jdm* for sb); **Sprachen sind mir schon immer leichtgefallen** I've always found languages easy; **leicht|fer|tig** ADJ thoughtless; *(moralisch)* of easy virtue ADV thoughtlessly; **~ handeln** to act without thinking; **etw ~ aufs Spiel setzen** to risk sth without giving it a thought; **Leicht|fer|tig|keit** F thoughtlessness; *(moralisch)* loose morals *pl*; **leicht|flüs|sig** ADJ *attr* (easily) fusible; **Leicht|fuß** M *(old)* **(Bruder) ~** adventurer; **leicht|fü|ßig** *(liter)* ADJ light-footed ADV light-footedly; **leicht|gän|gig** ADJ *Getriebe* smooth; *Motor auch* smooth-running; **leicht|ge|schürzt** [-gəʃʏrtst] ADJ *attr* → **leicht ADV e**; **Leicht|ge|wicht** NT *(Sport, fig)* lightweight; **Weltmeister im ~** world lightweight champion; **leicht|ge|wich|tig** ADJ *(lit, fig)* lightweight; **Leicht|ge|wicht|ler** [-gəvɪçtlɐ] M **-s, -**, **Leicht|ge|wicht|le|rin** [-ərɪn] F **-, -nen** *(Sport)* lightweight; **Leicht|ge|wichts|klas|se** F lightweight class; **leicht|gläu|big** ADJ credulous; *(= leicht zu täuschen)* gullible; **Leicht|gläu|big|keit** F credulity; *(= Arglosigkeit)* gullibility

Leicht|heit F **-**, *no pl* lightness; *(= Geringfügigkeit)* slightness; *(= Einfachheit: von Aufgabe etc)* easiness

leicht|her|zig ADJ light-hearted ADV naively, light-heartedly

leicht|hin ['laiçthɪn] ADV lightly

Leich|tig|keit ['laiçtɪçkait] F **-**, *no pl* **a** *(= Mühelosigkeit)* ease; **mit ~** easily, with no trouble (at all) **b** *(= Unbekümmertheit)* light-heartedness

Leicht-: **Leicht|in|dust|rie** F light industry; **Leicht|kraft|rad** NT moped; **leicht|le|big** [-le:bɪç] ADJ happy-go-lucky, easygoing; **Leicht|le|big|keit** F **-**, *no pl* happy-go-lucky *or* easygoing nature; **Leicht|lohn|grup|pe** F *group of (usually female) workers paid less than workers in comparable jobs*; **leicht ma|chen** , **leicht+ma|chen** *sep* VT **(jdm)**

etw ~ to make sth easy (for sb); **sich** *(dat)* **etw ~, sich** *(dat)* **es mit etw ~** *(= es sich bequem machen)* to make things easy for oneself with sth; *(= nicht gewissenhaft sein)* to take it easy with sth; *(= vereinfachen)* to oversimplify sth; **er machte es sich** *(dat)* **leicht und vermied eine Entscheidung** he took the easy way out and avoided making a decision; **Leicht|mat|ro|se** M, **Leicht|ma|tro|sin** F ordinary seaman; **Leicht|me|tall** NT light metal; **leicht+neh|men** *sep irreg,* **leicht neh|men** △ *irreg* VT **etw ~** *(= nicht ernsthaft behandeln)* to take sth lightly; *(= sich keine Sorgen machen)* not to worry about sth; **das Leben ~** not to take things too seriously; **das Leben nicht ~** to take everything too seriously → *auch* **leicht ADV c**; **Leicht|öl** NT light oil

Leicht|sinn M *(= unvorsichtige Haltung)* foolishness; *(= Unbesorgtheit, Sorglosigkeit)* thoughtlessness; **sträflicher ~** criminal negligence; **unverzeihlicher ~** unforgivable stupidity; **das ist (ein) ~** that's foolish *or* silly; **so ein ~!** how silly (can you get)!

leicht|sin|nig ADJ foolish; *(= unüberlegt)* thoughtless ADV *handeln, mit etw umgehen* thoughtlessly, carelessly; **~ schnell fahren** to drive recklessly; **~ mit etw umgehen** to be careless with sth

Leicht|sin|nig|keit F **-, -en** foolishness; *(= Unüberlegtheit)* thoughtlessness

Leicht|sinns|feh|ler M careless mistake, slip

Leicht-: **leicht+tun** *sep irreg,* **leicht tun** △ *irreg* VR **sich** *(acc or dat)* **mit** *or* **bei etw ~** to have no problems with sth; **leicht|ver|dau|lich** ADJ *attr* → **leicht ADV b**; **leicht|ver|derb|lich** ADJ *attr* → **leicht ADV d**; **leicht|ver|letzt** [-fɛɐlɛtst] ADJ *attr* → **leicht ADV g**; **Leicht|ver|letz|te(r)** MF *decl as adj* **die ~n** the slightly injured; *(in Gefecht, Schlägerei auch)* the slightly wounded; **leicht|ver|ständ|lich** ADJ *attr* → **leicht ADV b**; **leicht|ver|wun|det** ADJ *attr* → **leicht ADV g**; **Leicht|ver|wun|de|te(r)** MF *decl as adj* slightly wounded soldier/man *etc*; **die ~n** the walking wounded; **Leicht|was|ser|re|ak|tor** M light water reactor

leid [lait] ADJ *pred (= überdrüssig)* **jdn/etw ~ sein** to be tired of sb/sth; **das lange Warten bin ich ~ geworden** I'm tired of all this waiting → **leidtun**

Leid [lait] ✪ 39.3, 45.1, 45.3, 48.1 NT **-(e)s,** [-dəs] *no pl* **a** *(= Kummer, Sorge)* sorrow, grief *no indef art*; *(= Unglück)* misfortune; *(= Böses, Schaden)* harm; **jdm in seinem tiefen ~ beistehen** to stand by sb in his/her (hour of) affliction *or* sorrow; **um jdn ~ tragen** *(geh)* to mourn sb; **ihm ist großes ~ widerfahren** he has suffered great misfortune; **viel ~ erfahren/ertragen (müssen)** to suffer/have to suffer a great deal; **es soll dir kein ~ zugefügt werden** *or* **geschehen** you will come to no harm, no harm will come to you; **jdm ein ~ antun** *(liter)* to harm sb; *(moralisch)* to wrong sb, to do sb wrong; **sich** *(dat)* **ein ~ antun** *(liter)* to injure oneself; **jdm sein ~ klagen** to tell sb one's troubles, to cry on sb's shoulder; **zu ~e = zuleide**; → *auch* **leidtun, leid**

b *(Sw: = Begräbnis)* funeral

c *(Sw: = Trauerkleidung)* mourning; **(um jdn) ~ tragen, im ~ sein** to wear mourning (for sb), to be in mourning (for sb)

Lei|de|form ['laidə-] F *(Gram)* passive (voice)

lei|den ['laidn] *pret* **litt** [lɪt], *ptp* **ge|lit|ten** [gə'lɪtn] VT **a** *(= ertragen müssen) Schaden, Hunger, Schmerz, Unrecht etc* to suffer; **viel zu ~ haben** to have a great deal to bear *or* endure

b ich kann *or* **mag ihn/es (gut) ~** I like him/it (very much); **ich kann** *or* **mag ihn/es nicht (gut) ~** I don't like him/it very much, I'm not very fond of him/it

c *(geh: = zulassen, dulden)* to allow, to permit, to suffer *(old)*; **er ist bei allen wohl gelitten** everybody holds him in high regard *or* great esteem

VI to suffer *(an +dat, unter +dat* from); **die Farbe hat durch die grelle Sonne sehr gelitten** the harsh sun hasn't done the paint any good → **leidend**

Lei|den ['laidn] NT **-s, - a** suffering; **das sind (nun mal) die Freuden und ~ des Lebens!** ah, the ups and downs *or* the trials and tribulations of life!; **du siehst aus wie das ~ Christi** *(inf)* you look like death warmed up *(Brit inf)* or over *(US inf)* **b** *(= Krankheit)* illness; *(= Beschwerden)* complaint; **das ist ja eben das ~!** *(inf)* that's just the trouble **c** *(hum inf: Mensch)* **ein langes ~** a beanpole *(inf)*

-lei|den NT *suf in cpds* complaint, condition; **Augen-/Leberleiden** eye/liver complaint *or* condition

lei|dend ADJ *(= kränklich)* ailing; *(inf) Miene* long-suffering; **~ aussehen** to look ill; **sich ~ fühlen** *(form)* to feel ill

Lei|den|de(r) ['laidndə] MF *decl as adj* sufferer; **die ~n** the afflicted *pl*

Lei|den|schaft ['laidnʃaft] F **-, -en** passion; **seine ~ für etw entdecken** to develop a passion for sth; **etw mit ~ tun** to do sth with passionate enthusiasm; **ich koche mit großer ~** cooking is a great passion of mine; **er ist Lehrer aus ~** he teaches for the love of it

lei|den|schaft|lich ['laidnʃaftlɪç] ADJ passionate; *Liebhaber auch* ardent; *Rede auch* impassioned ADV passionately; **etw ~ gern tun** to be mad about doing sth *(inf)*, to be passionately fond of doing sth

Lei|den|schaft|lich|keit F **-,** *no pl* passion; *(von Mensch)* passionate nature; *(im Beruf)* dedication; *(bei Hobby)* burning enthusiasm

lei|den|schafts|los ADJ dispassionate ADV dispassionately

Lei|dens-: **Lei|dens|druck** M, *no pl* mental trauma, level of suffering *or* pain; **lei|dens|fä|hig** ADJ **wir sind nicht unbegrenzt ~** we do not have an unlimited capacity for suffering; **Lei|dens|fä|hig|keit** F capacity for suffering; **Lei|dens|ge|fähr|te** M, **Lei|dens|ge|fähr|tin** F, **Lei|dens|ge|nos|se** M, **Lei|dens|ge|nos|sin** F fellow-sufferer; **Lei|dens|ge|schich|te** F tale of woe; **die ~ (Christi)** *(Bibl)* Christ's Passion; **Lei|dens|mie|ne** F *(hum inf)* (long-)suffering expression; **Lei|dens|weg** M life of suffering; **Christi ~** Christ's suffering; **seinen ~ gehen** to bear one's cross

lei|der ['laidɐ] ✪ 36.3, 39, 45.3, 47.2, 47.4, 48.3, 52.4, 52.5 ADV unfortunately; **~ (Gottes) ja!, ja ~!** (yes,) more's the pity *(inf)*, I'm afraid so, yes, unfortunately; **~ (Gottes) nein/nicht!** unfortunately not, I'm afraid not, no, worse luck *(inf)*; **ich kann ~ nicht kommen** unfortunately I can't come, I'm afraid I can't come

leid-: **leid|ge|beugt** [-gəbɔykt] ADJ bowed down with sorrow; **leid|ge|prüft** [-gəpry:ft] ADJ sorely afflicted

lei|dig ['laidɪç] ADJ *attr* tiresome; **wenn bloß das ~e Geld nicht wäre** if only we didn't have to worry about money

leid|lich ['laitlɪç] ADJ reasonable, fair ADV reasonably; **wie gehts? – danke, ~!** how are you? – not too bad *or* all right, thanks; **sie ist noch so ~ davongekommen** she didn't come out of it too badly

Leid|tra|gen|de(r) ['laittragndə] MF *decl as adj* **a** *(= Hinterbliebener eines Verstorbenen)* **ein ~r** a bereaved man; **eine ~** a bereaved woman; **die ~n** the bereaved **b** *(= Benachteiligter)* **der/die ~** the sufferer, the one to suffer

leid+tun *sep irreg,* **Leid tun** △ *irreg,* **leid tun** △ *irreg* VI **etw tut jdm leid** sb is sorry about *or* for sth; **es tut jdm leid, dass ...** sb is sorry that ...; **tut mir leid!** (I'm) sorry!; **es tut mir leid, dass ich so spät gekommen bin** I'm sorry for coming so late *or* (that) I came so late; **es tut mir nur leid, dass ...** I'm only sorry that ..., my only regret is that ..., I only regret that ...; **es tut uns leid, Ihnen mitteilen zu müssen ...** we regret to have to inform you ...; **es tut einem leid, zu sehen, wie ...** it makes you feel sorry when you see how ...; **er/sie tut mir leid** I'm sorry for him/her, I pity him/her; **er/sie kann einem ~** you can't help feeling sorry for him/her, you can't (help) but feel sorry for him/her; **du kannst einem ~** you really are to be pitied; **es kann einem ~, wenn ...** you can't help feeling sorry when ...; **es tut mir um ihn/darum leid** I'm sorry about him/that; **das wird dir noch ~** you'll regret it, you'll be sorry

leid|voll ADJ *(geh) Miene* sorrowful; *Erfahrung* painful

Leid|we|sen ['laitve:zn] NT **zu jds ~** (much) to sb's disappointment *or* chagrin

Lei|er ['laiɐ] F **-, -n a** *(Mus)* lyre; *(= Drehleier)* hurdy-gurdy; **es ist immer dieselbe** *or* **die alte** *or* **die gleiche ~** *(inf)* it's always the same old story **b** *(Astron)* Lyra

Lei|er|kas|ten M barrel organ, hurdy-gurdy

Lei|er|kas|ten|frau F, **Lei|er|kas|ten|mann** M *pl* **-männer** organ-grinder

lei|ern ['laiɐn] VT *Drehorgel* to grind, to play; *(inf: = kurbeln)* to wind; *(inf) Gedicht, Gebete etc* to drone (out); **jdm etw aus dem Kreuz** *or* **den Rippen ~** to squeeze sth out of sb *(inf)* VI *(= Drehorgel spielen)* to grind *or* play a barrel organ; *(inf: = drehen)* to crank *(an etw (dat)* sth); *(inf: beim Beten, Gedichteaufsagen etc)* to drone

Lei|er|schwanz M lyrebird

Leih-: **Leih|ar|beit** F, *no pl* subcontracted work; **Leih|ar|bei|ter(in)** M(F) subcontracted worker; **Leih|au|to** NT hire(d) car *(Brit)*, rental (car) *(US)*; **Leih|bib|lio|thek** F, **Leih|bü|che|rei** F lending library

Lei|he ['laiə] F **-, -n** *(= das Verleihen)* lending; *(= das Vermieten)* hiring; *(= das Verpfänden)* pawning; *(inf: = Leihhaus)* pawnshop; **etw in ~** *or* **in die ~** *(inf)* **geben** to pawn *or* pop *(inf)* sth; **etw in ~ nehmen** to take sth in pawn

lei|hen ['laiən] *pret* **lieh** [li:], *ptp* **ge|lie|hen** [gə'li:ən] VT *(= verleihen) Geld* to lend; *Sachen auch* to loan; *(= entleihen)* to borrow; *(= mieten, ausleihen)* to hire; **ich habe es (mir) geliehen** I've borrowed *or (gemietet)* hired it, I've got it on loan *or (gemietet)* hire; **jdm seinen Beistand/sein Ohr/seine Aufmerksamkeit ~** *(geh)* to lend sb one's support/one's ear/one's attention; **jdm seine Stimme ~** *(Synchronsprecher)* to lend one's voice to sb

Leih-: **Leih|fla|sche** F returnable bottle; **Leih|ga|be** F loan; **dieses Bild ist eine ~ der Tate Gallery** this picture is on loan from the Tate Gallery; **Leih|ge|bühr** F hire *or* rental charge; *(für Buch)* lending charge; **Leih|haus** NT pawnshop; **Leih|mut|ter** F *pl* **-mütter** surrogate mother; **Leih|mut|ter|schaft** F surrogate motherhood, surrogacy; **Leih|schein** M *(in der Bibliothek)* borrowing slip; *(im Leihhaus)* pawn ticket; **Leih|schwan|ger|schaft** F surrogate pregnancy; **Leih|stim|me** F *(Pol)* tactical vote; **Leih|ver|kehr** M **ein Buch über den auswärtigen ~ bestellen** to order a book on interlibrary loan; **im ~ erhältlich** available on loan; **Leih|wa|gen** M hire(d) car *(Brit)*, rental (car) *(US)*; **leih|wei|se** ADV on loan

Leim [laim] M **-(e)s, -e** glue; *(zum Vogelfangen)* (bird)lime; **jdn auf den ~ führen** *or* **locken** *(inf)* to take sb in; **jdm auf den ~ gehen** *or* **kriechen** *(inf)* to be taken in by sb; **aus dem ~ gehen** *(inf) (Sache)* to fall apart *or* to pieces; *(Mensch)* to lose one's figure

lei|men ['laimən] VT *(= zusammenkleben)* to glue (together); *(= mit Leim bestreichen)* to spread with glue; *(zum Vogelfangen)* to lime; *(inf) Ehe* to patch up *(inf)*; **jdn ~** *(inf)* to take sb for a ride *(inf)*; **der Geleimte** the mug *(inf)*

Leim|far|be F distemper

lei|mig ['laimɪç] ADJ sticky, gluey

Leim|ru|te F lime twig

Lei|mung ['laimʊŋ] F **-,** *no pl* sizing

Lein [lain] M **-(e)s, -e** flax

Lei|ne ['lainə] F **-, -n** cord; *(= Tau, Zeltleine)* rope; *(= Schnur)* string; *(= Angelleine, Wäscheleine, Naut)* line; *(= Hundeleine)* lead *(Brit)*, leash; **Hunde bitte an der ~ führen!** dogs should *or* must be kept on a leash; **den Hund an die ~ nehmen** to put the dog on the lead *(Brit) or* leash; **jdn an der ~ halten** *or* **haben** *(inf)* to keep sb on a tight rein; **jdn an die ~ legen** *(inf)* to hook sb *(inf)*, to drag sb to the altar *(inf)*; **jdn an die kurze ~ nehmen** *or* **legen** *(inf)* to keep sb on a short leash; **jdn an die lange ~ legen** to give sb his/her head; **~ ziehen** *(inf)* to clear out *(inf)*, to push off *(inf)*; **~n los!** cast off!

lei|nen ['lainən] ADJ linen; *(grob)* canvas; *Bucheinband* cloth

Lei|nen ['lainən] NT **-s, -** linen; *(grob, segeltuchartig)* canvas; *(als Bucheinband)* cloth

Lei|nen-: **Lei|nen|band** [-bant] M *pl* **-bände** cloth(bound) volume; **ein Buch als ~ haben** to have the clothbound edition of a book; **Lei|nen|ho|se** F linen trousers *(esp Brit) or* pants *(esp US)*; **Lei|nen|schlaf|sack** M sheet sleeping bag; **Lei|nen|ta|sche** F canvas bag; **Lei|nen|tuch** NT *pl* **-tücher** linen (cloth); *(grob, segeltuchartig)* canvas; **Lei|nen|zeug** NT linen

Lei|ne|we|ber(in) M(F) linen weaver

Lei|ne|we|be|rei F *(Fabrik)* linen mill; *(Herstellung)* linen weaving

Lein-: **Lein|kraut** NT toadflax; **Lein|öl** NT linseed oil; **Lein|pfad** M towpath; **Lein|sa|men** M linseed; **Lein|tuch** NT *pl* **-tücher** *(S Ger, Aus, Sw)* sheet

Lein|wand F **-,** *no pl* canvas; *(für Dias)* screen; **wenn der Film über die ~ läuft** when the film is being shown *or* screened; **Dias auf die ~ werfen** to show *or* project slides

lei|se ['laizə] ADJ **a** quiet; *Stimme, Schritt, Klopfen* soft, quiet; *Radio* low; *(aus der Ferne)* faint; **auf ~n Sohlen** treading softly; **... sagte er mit ~r Stimme** ... he said in a low voice, ... he said quietly
b *(= gering, schwach)* slight, faint; *Schlaf, Regen, Berührung* light; *Wind, Wellenschlag* light, gentle; **nicht die ~ste Ahnung haben** not to have the slightest *or* faintest *or* foggiest *(inf)* (idea); **ich habe nicht die ~ste Veranlassung, ...** there isn't the slightest *or* faintest reason why I ...
c *(= sanft, zart)* soft, gentle; *Musik* soft
ADV *(= nicht laut)* quietly, softly; **~r singen** to sing more quietly; **ein ~ geführtes Gespräch** a quiet talk; **das Radio (etwas) ~r stellen** to turn the radio down (slightly); **sprich doch ~r!** keep your voice down a bit

Lei|se|tre|ter [-tre:tɐ] M **-s, -**, **Lei|se|tre|te|rin** [-ərın] F **-, -nen** *(pej inf)* pussyfoot(er) *(pej inf)*; *(= Duckmäuser)* creep *(pej inf)*

Leis|te ['laistə] F **-, -n** **a** *(= Holzleiste etc)* strip (of wood *etc*); *(= Zierleiste)* trim; *(= Umrandung)* border; *(zur Bilderaufhängung, zur Führung von Arbeitsstücken etc)* rail; *(= Scheuerleiste)* skirting (board) *(Brit)*, baseboard *(US)*; *(Comput)* bar
b *(Anat)* groin

leis|ten ['laistn] VT **a** *(= erringen, erreichen)* to achieve; *Arbeit, Überstunden* to do; *(Maschine)* to manage; *(= ableisten) Wehrdienst etc* to complete; **etwas/viel/nichts ~** *(Mensch) (= arbeiten)* to do something/a lot/nothing; *(= schaffen auch)* to get something/a lot/nothing done; *(= vollbringen)* to achieve something/a great deal/nothing; *(Maschine)* to be quite good/very good/no good at all; *(Auto, Motor etc)* to be quite powerful/very powerful/to have no power; **der Motor des Autos leistet 150 PS** the car has a 150-hp engine; **Großartiges/Erstaunliches/Überragendes** *etc* **~** to do *or* achieve something really great/amazing/excellent *etc*; **gute/ganze Arbeit ~** to do a good/thorough job; **in meiner Position muss ich schon etwas ~** in my position I have to do my work and do it well; **er leistet genauso viel wie ich** he's just as efficient as I am; **was eine Mutter alles ~ muss** the things that a mother has to cope with; **er hat immer das Gefühl, nichts zu ~** he always has the feeling that he isn't doing a good job; **seine Arbeit ~** to do one's work well; **ich muss genauso meine Arbeit ~ wie jeder andere auch** I've got my job to do like everybody else
b *(in festen Verbindungen mit n siehe auch dort)* **(jdm) Beistand ~** to lend (sb) one's support; **jdm Hilfe ~** to give sb some help; **jdm gute Dienste ~** *(Gegenstand)* to serve sb well; *(Mensch)* to be useful to sb; **Folge ~** to comply (*+dat* with); **Zahlungen ~** to make payments; **jdm eine Garantie ~** to give sb a guarantee *(auf etw (acc)* on sth); **jdm Gewähr ~** to give sb a guarantee *(für etw* for sth, *dafür, dass* ... that ...)
c **sich** *(dat)* **etw ~** to allow oneself sth; *(= sich gönnen)* to treat oneself to sth; *(= kaufen)* to buy sth; **sich** *(dat)* **etw ~ können** *(finanziell)* to be able to afford sth; **sich** *(dat)* **eine Frechheit/Frechheiten ~** to be cheeky *(Brit) or* impudent; **er leistete sich die Frechheit, ungebeten zu erscheinen** he had the cheek *(Brit) or* gall to turn up uninvited; **da hast du dir ja was (Schönes** *or* **Nettes) geleistet** *(iro)* you've really done it now; **er hat sich tolle Sachen/Streiche geleistet** he got up to the craziest things/pranks

Leis|ten ['laistn] M **-s, -** *(= Schuhleisten)* last; **alle/alles über einen ~ schlagen** *(fig)* to measure everyone/everything by the same yardstick → **Schuster**

Leis|ten-: **Leis|ten|bruch** M *(Med)* hernia, rupture; **Leis|ten|ge|gend** F inguinal region *(form)*, groin

Leis|tung ['laistʊŋ] F **-, -en** **a** *(= Geleistetes)* performance; *(großartige, gute, Sociol)* achievement; *(= Ergebnis)* result(s); *(= geleistete Arbeit)* work *no pl*; **eine große ~ vollbringen** to achieve a great success; **das ist eine ~!** that's quite *or* really something *(inf)*, that's quite an achievement *or* quite a feat; **das ist keine besondere ~** that's nothing special; **nach ~ bezahlt werden** to be paid on results; **nicht das Geschlecht, nur die ~ zählt** your sex isn't important, it's how you do the job that counts; **das liegt weit unter der üblichen ~** that is well below the usual standard; **die ~en sind besser geworden** the levels of performance have improved; *(in Fabrik, Schule auch)* the standard of work has improved; **seine schulischen/sportlichen ~en haben nachgelassen** his school work/athletic ability has deteriorated; **er ist auf seine sportlichen ~en stolz** he's proud of his athletic achievement(s); **eine ~ der Technik** a feat of engineering; **schwache ~!** poor show! *(dated inf)*, that's not very good
b *(= Leistungsfähigkeit)* capacity *(auch Comput)*; *(von Motor, Energiequelle)* power; *(von Fabrik, Firma)* potential output
c *(Jur) (= Übernahme einer Verpflichtung)* obligation; *(= Zahlung)* payment; **die ~en des Reiseveranstalters** what the travel company offers; **~ eines Ersatzes** obligation to provide a replacement
d *(= Aufwendungen: einer Versicherung, Krankenkasse, sozial)* benefit; *(= Dienstleistung)* service; *(= Zahlungsleistung)* payment
e *(= Ableistung)* completion; **die ~ des Wehrdienstes ist Pflicht** completion of national service is obligatory

Leis|tungs-: **Leis|tungs|ab|fall** M *(in Bezug auf Qualität)* drop in performance; *(in Bezug auf Quantität)* drop in productivity; **Leis|tungs|aus|fall** M loss of productivity; **leis|tungs|be|zo|gen** ADJ performance-related; **Leis|tungs|bi|lanz** F *(einer Firma)* current balance including investments; *(eines Landes)* balance of payments including invisible trade; **Leis|tungs|druck** M, *no pl* pressure (to do well); **Leis|tungs|emp|fän|ger(in)** M(F) beneficiary; **Leis|tungs|fach** NT *(Sch)* special subject; **leis|tungs|fä|hig** ADJ *(= konkurrenzfähig)* competitive; *(= produktiv)* efficient, productive; *Motor* powerful; *Maschine* productive; *(Fin)* able to pay, solvent; *Mensch* able, capable; *Arbeiter* efficient; *Organ, Verdauungssystem etc* functioning properly; **Leis|tungs|fä|hig|keit** F *(= Konkurrenzfähigkeit)* competitiveness; *(= Produktivität)* efficiency, productivity; *(von Motor)* power(fulness); *(von Maschine, Körperorgan etc)* capacity; *(Fin)* ability to pay, solvency; *(von Mensch)* ability, capability; *(von Arbeiter)* efficiency; **das übersteigt meine ~** that's beyond my capabilities; **leis|tungs|feind|lich** ADJ **hohe Steuern sind ~** high taxes inhibit productivity; **leis|tungs|för|dernd** ADJ conducive to efficiency; *(in Schule, Universität etc)* conducive to learning; *Substanz* performance-enhancing ADV to improve performance; **leis|tungs|ge|recht** ADJ *Bezahlung* preformance-related; **Leis|tungs|ge|sell|schaft** F meritocracy, achievement-orientated society *(pej)*; **Leis|tungs|gren|ze** F upper limit; **Leis|tungs|kla|ge** F *(Jur)* suit for fulfilment *(Brit) or* fulfillment *(US)* of obligations; **Leis|tungs|klas|se** F *(Sport)* class; **Leis|tungs|kon|trol|le** F *(Sch, Univ)* assessment; *(in der Fabrik)* productivity check; **zur ~** (in order) to assess progress/check productivity; **Leis|tungs|kraft** F power; **eine hohe ~ haben** to be very powerful; **Leis|tungs|kurs** M advanced course in specialist subjects

> **LEISTUNGSKURS**
>
> **Leistungskurse** are the two specialist subjects chosen by students in the upper classes of a **Gymnasium**, during the **Kollegstufe**. Six hours a week are devoted to each subject, allowing more time for special projects and the students' own work. Those taking the **Abitur** have to write a **Facharbeit** – similar to a short university seminar paper – on one of the subjects. Together with examinations in the two subjects, this makes up a third of the overall mark for the **Abitur**.
> In a **Gesamtschule**, **Leistungskurse** are more advanced courses. → ABITUR, GESAMTSCHULE, GYMNASIUM, KOLLEGSTUFE

Leis|tungs-: **Leis|tungs|kur|ve** F productivity curve; **Leis|tungs|kür|zung** F reduction of benefit *or* payment; **Leis|tungs|lohn** M piece rates *pl*; **Leis|tungs|merk|mal** NT performance feature; **Leis|tungs|mes|ser** M **-s, -** *(Phys)* power output meter; *(Elec)* wattmeter; **Leis|tungs|mes|sung** F assessment of achievement; *(in Fabrik)* measuring *or* assessment of productivity; *(Phys, Elec)* measurement of power; **Leis|tungs|mo|ti|va|ti|on** F achievement motivation; **Leis|tungs|nach|weis** M certificate *(of academic achievement)*; **leis|tungs|ori|en|tiert** ADJ *Gesellschaft* competitive; *Lohn* performance-related; **Leis|tungs|prä|mie** F productivity bonus; **Leis|tungs|prin|zip** NT achievement principle; **Leis|tungs|prü|fung** F *(Sch)* achievement test; *(Tech)* performance test; **Leis|tungs|schau** F exhibition, show; **Leis|tungs|sport** M competitive sport; **leis|tungs|stark** ADJ *(= konkurrenzfähig)* highly competitive; *(= produktiv)* highly efficient *or* productive; *Motor* very powerful; *Maschine* highly productive; **Leis|tungs|stei|ge|rung** F → **Leistung a, b** increase in performance/achievement *etc*; **Leis|tungs|stu|fe** F *(Sch)* special subject class; **Leis|tungs|test** M *(Sch)* achievement test; *(Tech)* performance test; **Leis|tungs|trä|ger(in)** M(F) **a** *(esp Sport)* key player **b** *(von Sozialleistungen)* (health care *etc*) service provider; **Leis|tungs|ver|mö|gen** NT capabilities *pl*; **Leis|tungs|wett|kampf** M competition; **Leis|tungs|wil|le** M motivation; **Leis|tungs|zu|la|ge** F, **Leis|tungs|zu|schlag** M productivity bonus; **Leis|tungs|zwang** M pressure to do well

Leit- ['lait-]: **Leit|ar|ti|kel** M leader *(Brit)*, editorial; **leit|ar|ti|keln** [-larti:kln, -lartıkln] *ptp* **leitartikelt** VTI *insep (inf)* to lead; **Leit|ar|tik|ler** [-larti:klɐ, -lartıklɐ] M **-s, -**, **Leit|ar|tik|le|rin** [-ərın] F **-, -nen** leader writer *(Brit)*, editorial writer; **Leit|bild** NT model; **Leit|bün|del** NT *(Bot)* vascular bundle

lei|ten ['laitn] VT **a** *(= in bestimmte Richtung lenken)* to lead; *(= begleiten, führen)* to conduct, to lead; *(fig) Leser, Schüler etc* to guide; *Verkehr* to route; *Gas, Wasser* to conduct; *(= umleiten)* to divert; **etw an die zuständige Stelle ~** to pass sth on to the proper authority; **sich von jdm/etw ~ lassen** *(lit, fig)* to (let oneself) be guided by sb/sth; *von Vorstellung, Idee, Emotion* to be governed by sth; **das Öl wird (durch Rohre) zum Hafen geleitet** the oil is piped to the port
b *(= verantwortlich sein für)* to be in charge of; *(administrativ)* to run, to be in charge of; *Expedition, Partei, Regierung, Bewegung etc* to lead, to head; *Betrieb* to manage, to be in charge of; *Theater* to run; *Orchester, Theatergruppe etc* to direct, to run; *Sitzung, Diskussion, Gespräch, Verhandlungen* to lead; *(als Vorsitzender)* to chair; *Geschick(e)* to determine, to guide
c *(Phys) Wärme, Strom, Licht* to conduct; **(etw) gut/schlecht ~** to be a good/bad conductor (of sth)

lei|tend ADJ leading; *Gedanke, Idee* central, dominant; *Stellung, Position* managerial; *Ingenieur, Beamter* in charge; *(Phys)* conductive; **nicht ~** *(Phys)* nonconductive; **~e(r) Angestellte(r)** executive; **~er Beamter, ~e Beamtin** senior official; **die ~e Hand** *(fig)* the guiding hand

Lei|ter ['laitɐ] F -, -n *(lit, fig)* ladder; *(= Stehleiter)* steps *pl*, stepladder; *(Sport)* wall bars *pl*; **an der ~ turnen** to work on the wall bars

Lei|ter M -s, - **a** leader; *(von Hotel, Restaurant, Geschäft)* manager; *(= Abteilungsleiter, in Firma)* head; *(von Schule)* head *(esp Brit)*, principal *(esp US)*; *(von Orchester, Chor, Theatergruppe etc)* director; *(von Kirchenchor)* choirmaster; **kaufmännischer/künstlerischer ~** sales/artistic director → *auch* **Leiterin** **b** *(Phys)* conductor

Lei|ter|bahn F *(Comput)* strip conductor

Lei|te|rin ['laitərɪn] F -, -nen leader; *(von Hotel, Restaurant)* manager; *(von Geschäft)* manageress; *(= Abteilungsleiterin, in Firma)* head; *(von Schule)* head *(esp Brit)*, principal *(esp US)*; *(von Orchester, Chor, Theatergruppe etc)* director; *(von Kirchenchor)* choirmistress; **kaufmännische/künstlerische ~** sales/artistic director

Lei|ter-: **Lei|ter|plat|te** F *(Comput)* circuit board; **Lei|ter|spros|se** F rung; **eine ~ des Erfolgs höher kommen** t; **Lei|ter|wa|gen** M handcart

Leit-: **Leit|fa|den** M *(fig)* main connecting thread *or* theme; *(Fachbuch)* introduction; *(= Gebrauchsanleitung)* manual; **leit|fä|hig** ADJ *(Phys)* conductive; **Leit|fä|hig|keit** F *(Phys)* conductivity; **Leit|feu|er** NT beacon; **Leit|fos|sil** NT index fossil; **Leit|fra|ge** F *(auch Sch: in schriftlichen Prüfungen)* guiding question; **Leit|ge|dan|ke** M central idea; **er machte diesen Spruch zum ~n seines Lebens** he made this saying his motto in life; **Leit|ge|ra|de** F *(Math)* directrix; **Leit|ge|we|be** NT *(Biol)* vascular tissue; **Leit|ham|mel** M bellwether; *(fig inf)* leader, bellwether *(liter)*; **Leit|hund** M *(Hunt)* leader of the pack; **Leit|idee** F central idea; **Leit|kul|tur** F defining *or* guiding culture; **Leit|li|nie** F *(im Verkehr)* broken (white) line; *(fig)* broad outline; *(= Bestimmung)* guideline; *(Math)* directrix; **Leit|mo|tiv** NT *(Mus, Liter, fig)* leitmotif; **Leit|pfos|ten** M reflector post; **Leit|plan|ke** F crash barrier; **Leit|preis** M guide price; **Leit|satz** M basic principle; **Leit|schie|ne** F guide rail; **Leit|spin|del** F *(Tech)* lead screw; **Leit|spruch** M motto; **Leit|stel|le** F regional headquarters *pl*; *(= Funkleitstelle)* control centre *(Brit) or* center *(US)*; **Leit|stern** M *(lit)* lodestar; *(fig auch)* guiding star; **Leit|strahl** M *(Aviat, Mil, Space)* control beam; *(Math)* radius vector; **Leit|tier** NT leader *(of a herd etc)*; **Leit|ton** M *pl* **-töne** *(Mus)* leading note; **Leit|trieb** M *(Bot)* leader

Lei|tung ['laitʊŋ] F -, -en **a** *no pl (= das Leiten)* leading; *(= Begleitung, Führung)* conducting; *(von Verkehr)* routing; *(von Gas, Wasser)* conducting
b *no pl (von Menschen, Organisationen)* running; *(von Partei, Regierung)* leadership; *(von Betrieb)* management; *(von Schule)* headship *(esp Brit)*, principalship *(esp US)*; **die ~ einer Sache** *(gen)* **haben** to be in charge of sth; **unter der ~ von jdm** *(Mus)* conducted by sb; **die ~ des Gesprächs hat Horst Bauer** Horst Bauer is leading the discussion
c *(= die Leitenden)* leaders *pl*; *(eines Betriebes etc)* management *sing or pl*; *(einer Schule)* head teachers *pl*
d *(für Gas, Wasser, Elektrizität etc bis zum Haus)* main; *(für Gas, Wasser im Haus)* pipe; *(für Elektrizität im Haus)* wire; *(dicker)* cable; *(= Überlandleitung für Elektrizität)* line; *(= Telefonleitung) (= Draht)* wire; *(dicker)* cable; *(= Verbindung)* line; **die ~ ist ganz fürchterlich gestört** *(Telec)* it's a terrible line, there's a lot of interference on the line; **die ~ is tot** *(Telec inf)* the line is dead; **gehen Sie aus der ~!** *(Telec inf)* get off the line; **da ist jemand in der ~** *(Telec inf)* there's somebody else on the line; **eine lange ~ haben** *(hum inf)* to be slow on the uptake, to be slow to catch on; **bei dir steht wohl jemand** *or* **du stehst wohl auf der ~** *(hum inf)* you're slow on the uptake, you're slow to catch on

Lei|tungs-: **Lei|tungs|an|äs|the|sie** F *(Med)* nerve-block *or* conduction anaesthesia *(Brit) or* anesthesia *(US)*; **Lei|tungs|draht** M wire; **Lei|tungs|mast** M *(Elec)* (electricity) pylon; **Lei|tungs|netz** NT *(Elec)* (electricity) grid; *(für Wasser, Gas)* mains system; *(Telec)* (telephone) network; **Lei|tungs|rohr** NT main; *(im Haus)* (supply) pipe; **Lei|tungs|was|ser** NT tap water, mains water; **Lei|tungs|wi|der|stand** M *(Elec)* resistance

Leit-: **Leit|ver|mö|gen** NT *(Phys)* conductivity; **Leit|wäh|rung** F reserve currency; **Leit|werk** NT *(Aviat)* tail unit, empennage *(spec)*; **Leit|wert** M conductance; **Leit|wolf** M *(Zool, fig)* leader of the pack, alpha male; **Leit|wort** NT *pl* **-wörter** motto

Leit|zins M base rate, (central bank) discount rate, prime rate *(US)*

Leit|zins-: **Leit|zins|er|hö|hung** F increase in the base rate; **Leit|zins|satz** M bank rate

Leitz-Ord|ner® ['laits-] M lever-arch file

lei|wand ['laivant] ADJ *(Aus inf)* brilliant, fantastic

Lek|ti|on [lɛk'tsio:n] F -, -en lesson; **jdm eine ~ erteilen** *(fig)* to teach sb a lesson

Lek|tor ['lɛkto:ɐ] M -s, **Lektoren** [-'to:rən], **Lek|to|rin** [-'to:rɪn] F -, -nen *(Univ)* foreign language assistant, lector; *(= Verlagslektor)* editor

Lek|to|rat [lɛkto'ra:t] NT -(e)s, -e *(im Verlag)* editorial office; *(Gutachten)* editorial report

lek|to|rie|ren [lɛkto'ri:rən] *ptp* **lektoriert** VT **etw ~** to edit sth, to prepare sth for press VI to work as an editor

Lek|tü|re [lɛk'ty:rə] F -, -n *(no pl: = das Lesen)* reading; *(= Lesestoff)* reading matter; **das wird zur ~ empfohlen** that is recommended reading; **das ist eine gute/interessante** *etc* **~** it makes good/interesting *etc* reading, it's a good/an interesting *etc* read; **das ist eine schlechte ~** it doesn't make good reading, it's not a good read; **das ist keine (passende) ~ für dich/Kinder** that's not suitable reading for you/children, that's not suitable for you/children to read; **ich muss noch (etwas) leichte ~ besorgen** I've still got to get something light to read

Lem|ma ['lɛma] NT -s, -ta [-ta] lemma

Lem|ming ['lɛmɪŋ] M -s, -e lemming

Len|de ['lɛndə] F -, -n *(Anat, Cook)* loin

Len|den-: **Len|den|bra|ten** M loin roast *(Brit)*, porterhouse (steak); **Len|den|ge|gend** F lumbar region; **len|den|lahm** ADJ **a** *(dated) Pferd* broken-backed; **er ist ~** his back is crippling him **b** *(inf: = impotent)* **er ist ~** he can't get it up *(inf)*; **Len|den|schurz** M loincloth; **Len|den|stück** NT piece of loin; **Len|den|wir|bel** M lumbar vertebra

Le|ni|nis|mus [leni'nɪsmʊs] M -, *no pl* Leninism

Le|ni|nist [leni'nɪst] M -en, -en, **Le|ni|nis|tin** [-'nɪstɪn] F -, -nen Leninist

le|ni|nis|tisch [leni'nɪstɪʃ] ADJ Leninist ADV **~ klingend** Leninist-sounding; **~ gesinnt** Leninist; **~ beeinflusst** influenced by (the teachings of) Lenin

Lenk-: **Lenk|ach|se** F pivoted axle; **lenk|bar** ADJ *(Tech)* steerable; *Kind* tractable; *Rakete* guided; **leicht/schwer ~ sein** to be easy/difficult to steer, to have light/heavy steering; **das Kind ist leicht/schwer ~** the child can be easily guided/won't be guided; **Lenk|bar|keit** F -, *no pl* *(Tech)* steerability; **die schwere ~ des Fahrzeugs** the vehicle's heavy steering; **Lenk|com|pu|ter** M guide computer

len|ken ['lɛŋkn] VT **a** *(= führen, leiten)* to direct, to guide; *(fig: = beeinflussen) Sprache, Presse etc* to influence; *Kind* to guide; **gelenkte Wirtschaft** planned economy; **staatlich gelenkte Medien** state-controlled media
b *(= steuern) Auto, Flugzeug, Schiff etc* to steer; *Pferde* to drive; **sich leicht ~ lassen** to be easy to steer/drive
c *(fig) Schritte, Gedanken, seine Aufmerksamkeit, Blick* to direct *(auf +acc* to); *jds Aufmerksamkeit, Blicke* to draw *(auf +acc* to); *Verdacht* to throw, to draw *(auf +acc* onto); *Gespräch* to lead, to steer; *Schicksal* to guide; **das Gespräch in eine andere Richtung ~** to steer the conversation in another direction; **die Geschicke des Landes/der Partei ~** to control the future of the country/party
VI *(= steuern)* to steer **seine Schritte heimwärts ~** *(liter, hum inf)* to wend one's way homewards *(liter, hum)*, to turn one's steps to home *(liter, hum)*

Len|ker ['lɛŋkɐ] M -s, - **a** *(= Fahrradlenker etc)* handlebars *pl* **b** *(Tech)* guide; *(= Lenkung)* steering gear

Len|ker ['lɛŋkɐ] M -s, -, **Len|ke|rin** [-ərɪn] F -, -nen driver; *(fig)* guide

Lenk|ge|trie|be NT steering gear

Lenk|rad NT (steering) wheel; **jdm ins ~ greifen** to grab the (steering) wheel from sb

Lenk|rad- *(Aut)*: **Lenk|rad|schal|tung** F column(-mounted) (gear) change *(Brit) or* shift *(US)*; **Lenk|rad|schloss** NT steering (wheel) lock; **Lenk|rad|sper|re** F steering wheel lock

Lenk|säu|le F steering column

Lenk|stan|ge F *(von Fahrrad etc)* handlebars *pl*

Len|kung ['lɛŋkʊŋ] F -, -en **a** *(= das Lenken)* direction, guidance; *(fig: = Beeinflussung)* influencing; *(= das Steuern)* steering **b** *(Tech: = Lenkeinrichtung)* steering

Len|kungs|aus|schuss M *(Pol)* steering committee

Lenk-: **Lenk|ver|hal|ten** NT *(von Auto)* steering *no indef art*; **Lenk|waf|fe** F guided missile

Len|ti|vi|rus [lɛnti'vi:rʊs] NT OR M lentivirus

len|to ['lɛnto] ADV *(Mus)* lento

Lenz [lɛnts] M -es, -e *(liter: = Frühling)* spring(-time), springtide *(liter)*; **der ~ des Lebens** the springtime of one's life *(liter)*; **sie zählt 20 ~e** *(hum)* she has seen 20 summers *(liter, hum)*; **einen ~ schieben** *or* **haben** *(inf)* **sich** *(dat)* **einen (faulen** *or* **schönen) ~ machen** *(inf)* to laze about *(Brit) or* around, to swing the lead *(Brit inf)*

len|zen ['lɛntsn] *(Naut)* VT *(= leer pumpen)* to pump out VI *(= vor dem Wind segeln)* to scud

Lenz-: **Lenz|pum|pe** F *(Naut)* bilge pump; **Lenz|tag** M *(liter)* spring day

Le|o|pard [leo'part] M -en, -en [-dn] leopard

Le|o|par|din [leo'pardɪn] F -, -nen leopardess

Le|po|rel|lo [lepo'rɛlo] NT OR M -s, -s concertina folder

Lep|ra ['le:pra] F -, *no pl* leprosy

Lep|rom [le'pro:m] NT -s, -e leprous lesion

lep|ros [le'pro:s], **lep|rös** [le'prø:s] ADJ leprous

Lep|rö|se(r) [le'prø:zə] MF *decl as adj* leper

Lep|ro|so|ri|um [lepro'zo:riʊm] NT -s, **Leprosorien** [-riən] leprosarium

lep|to|som [lɛpto'zo:m] ADJ *(form)* asthenic *(form)*, leptosome *(form)*

Lẹr|che ['lɛrçə] **F -, -n** lark

Lẹrn-: **lẹrn|bar ADJ** learnable; **Lẹrn|be|gier|(-de) F** eagerness to learn; **lẹrn|be|gie|rig ADJ** eager to learn; **lẹrn|be|hin|dert** [-bəhɪndɐt] **ADJ** with learning difficulties; **Lẹrn|be|hin|der|te(r) MF** *decl as adj* child/person *etc* with learning difficulties; **Lẹrn|dis|ket|te F** tutorial disk *or* diskette; **Lẹrn|ef|fekt M** pedagogical benefit; **Lẹrn|ei|fer M** eagerness to learn; **lẹrn|eif|rig ADJ** eager to learn

lẹr|nen ['lɛrnən] **VT a** *(= Fertigkeit erwerben in)* to learn; **lesen/schwimmen** *etc* ~ to learn to read/swim *etc*; **Stenografie/Schreibmaschine** ~ to learn shorthand/typing *or* to type; **~, etw zu tun** to learn to do sth; *(= sich Fähigkeit, Können aneignen auch)* to learn how to do sth; **etw von/bei jdm** ~ to learn sth from sb; **jdn lieben/schätzen** ~ to come *or* learn to love/appreciate sb; **er lernts nie** he never learns; **er wirds nie** ~ he'll never learn → **Hänschen**

b *Beruf* to learn; *Bäcker, Schlosser etc* to train as, to learn the trade of; **er hat zwei Jahre gelernt** he trained for two years, he did two years' training; *(in Handwerk)* he did a two-year apprenticeship; **das will gelernt sein** it's a question of practice; **gelernt ist gelernt** *(Prov)* once you've learned something ...; **lerne was, so kannst/bist du was** *(prov)* it never hurt anyone to learn anything → *auch* **gelernt**

VI a *(= Kenntnisse erwerben)* to learn; *(= arbeiten)* to study; *(= Schulaufgaben machen)* to do (one's) homework; **die Mutter lernte drei Stunden mit ihm** his mother spent three hours helping him with his homework; **lerne fleißig in der Schule** work hard at school; **von ihm kannst du noch (was) ~!** he could teach you a thing or two; **nicht für die Schule, sondern für das Leben ~ wir** *(prov)* learning is not just for school but for life

b *(= sich in der Ausbildung befinden)* to go to school; *(in Universität)* to study; *(in Beruf)* to train; **er lernt bei der Firma Braun** he's training at Braun's, Braun's are training him

VR der Text/die Rolle lernt sich leicht/schwer/schnell the text/part is easy/hard to learn/doesn't take long to learn

Lẹr|ner ['lɛrnɐ] **M -s, -, Lẹr|ne|rin** [-ərɪn] **F -, -nen** learner

Lẹrn|er|folg M learning success; **den ~ messen** to measure the success of the learning process

Lẹrn-: **lẹrn|fä|hig ADJ** capable of learning *pred*; **Lẹrn|hil|fe F** educational aid; **Lẹrn|kur|ve F** *(Psych)* learning curve; **Lẹrn|ma|schi|ne F** teaching machine; **Lẹrn|mit|tel PL** schoolbooks and equipment *pl*; **Lẹrn|mit|tel|frei|heit F** free provision of schoolbooks and equipment; **Lẹrn|pro|gramm NT** *(Comput) (für Software)* tutorial (program); *(= didaktisches Programm)* learning software *or* tool; *(= Selbstlernprogramm)* self-study course; *(auf Sprache bezogen)* CALL application; **multimediale ~e** multimedia(-based) learning tools; **Lẹrn|pro|zess M** learning process; **Lẹrn|psy|cho|lo|gie F** psychology of learning; **Lẹrn|schwes|ter F** student nurse; **Lẹrn|soft|ware F** learning software; **lẹrn|wil|lig ADJ** willing to learn *pred*; **Lẹrn|ziel NT** learning goal

Lẹs-: **Lẹs|art F** *(lit, fig)* version; **lẹs|bar ADJ a** *(= leserlich)* legible; *(Comput)* readable; **nicht ~** *Daten, Datei* corrupt **b** *(= verständlich) Buch* readable **ADV a** *(= leserlich)* legibly; **gut ~ angebracht** very visible **b** *(= verständlich)* readably

Lẹs|be ['lɛsbə] **F -, -n** *(inf)* lesbian

Lẹs|bie|rin ['lɛsbiərɪn] **F -, -nen** lesbian

lẹs|bisch ['lɛsbɪʃ] **ADJ** lesbian

Le̱|se ['le:zə] **F -, -n** *(= Ernte)* harvest; *(= Weinart)* vintage; *(= Beerenlese)* picking

Le̱|se-: **Le̱|se|abend M** evening of readings; **Le̱|se|bril|le F** reading glasses *pl*; **Le̱|se|buch NT** reader; **Le̱|se|ecke F** reading *or* readers' corner; **Le̱|se|ge|rät NT** *(Comput)* reading device, reader; **le̱|se|ge|schützt ADJ** *(Comput)* write-only *attr*; **Le̱|se|ge|schwin|dig|keit F** *(auch Comput)* reading speed; **Le̱|se|ge|wohn|hei|ten PL** reading habits *pl*; **Le̱|se|kar|te F** reader's ticket; **Le̱|se|kopf M** *(Comput)* read head; **Le̱|se|kreis M** reading circle; **Le̱|se|lam|pe F** reading lamp; **Le̱|se|lis|te F** reading list; **Le̱|se|map|pe F** *(= Zeitschrift)* magazine in a folder

le̱|sen ['le:zn] *pret* **las** [la:s], *ptp* **gelesen** [gə'le:zn] **VTI a** *Geschriebenes* to read *(auch Comput)*; *(Eccl) Messe* to say; **hier/in der Zeitung steht** *or* **ist zu ~, dass ...** it says here/in the paper that ...; **die Schrift ist kaum zu ~** the writing is scarcely legible → **Leviten**

b *(= deuten) Gedanken* to read; **jdm (sein Schicksal) aus der Hand ~** to read sb's palm; **in den Sternen ~** to read *or* see in the stars; **aus ihren Zeilen habe ich einen Vorwurf/eine gewisse Unsicherheit gelesen** I could tell from what she had written that she was reproaching me/felt a certain amount of uncertainty; **etw in jds Augen/Miene** *(dat)* ~ to see sth in sb's eyes/from sb's manner; **es war in ihrem Gesicht zu ~** it was written all over her face, you could see it in her face

c *(Univ)* to lecture; **er liest Englisch an der Universität** he lectures in English at the university

VR *(Buch, Bericht etc)* to read; **bei diesem Licht liest es sich nicht gut** this light isn't good for reading (in); **sich in den Schlaf ~** to read oneself to sleep

le̱|sen *pret* **las** [la:s], *ptp* **gelesen** [gə'le:zn] **VT a** *(= sammeln) Trauben, Beeren* to pick; *(nach der Ernte) Ähren* to glean **b** *(= verlesen) Erbsen, Linsen etc* to sort; *Salat* to clean

le̱|sens|wert ADJ worth reading

Le̱|se-: **Le̱|se|pro|be F a** *(Theat)* reading **b** *(= Ausschnitt aus Buch)* extract, excerpt; **Le̱|se|pult NT** lectern

Le̱|ser ['le:zɐ] **M -s, -, Le̱|se|rin** [-ərɪn] **F -, -nen** reader; **seine Romane haben viele ~ gefunden** his novels have gained a large readership

Le̱|se|rat|te F *(inf)* bookworm *(inf)*

Le̱|ser|brief M (reader's) letter; **einen ~ an eine Zeitung schreiben** to write a letter to a newspaper; **„Leserbriefe"** "letters to the editor", "readers' letters"

Le|se|rei [le:zə'rai] **F -,** *no pl (inf)* reading; **kannst du jetzt nicht endlich mit der ~ aufhören?** can't you take your nose out of your books? *(inf)*

le̱|ser|freund|lich ADJ easy-to-read *attr*, easy to read *pred*; **wenig ~** difficult to read, hard on the eyes; **~e Gestaltung** reader-friendly layout **ADV ~ gestaltet** designed to be easy to read; *Nachschlagewerk* designed for easy reference

Le̱|se|rin [-ərɪn] **F** → **Leser**

Le̱|se|ring® M book club

Le̱|ser-: **Le̱|ser|kreis M** readership; **le̱|ser|lich** ['le:zɐlɪç] **ADJ** legible **ADV** legibly; **Le̱|ser|lich|keit F -,** *no pl* legibility; **Le̱|ser|schaft** ['le:zɐʃaft] **F -, -en** readership; **Le̱|ser|stamm M** regular readers *pl*; **Le̱|ser|wunsch M** wish(es) of the readers; **auf vielfachen ~** at the request of many readers; **Le̱|ser|zu|schrift F = Leserbrief**

Le̱|se-: **Le̱|se|saal M** reading room; **Le̱|se|spei|cher M** *(Comput)* read-only memory, ROM; **Le̱|se|stift M** *(für Barcodes)* barcode scanner; *(Comput)* wand; **Le̱|se|stoff M** reading material; **ich brauche noch ~** I need something to read; **Le̱|se|stück NT** reading passage; **Le̱|se|wut F** craze for reading; **von (der) ~ gepackt sein** to have caught the reading bug *(inf)*; **Le̱|se|zei|chen NT** bookmark(er); *(Comput)* bookmark; **Le̱|se|zim|mer NT** reading room; **Le̱|se|zir|kel M** magazine subscription club

Le̱|sung ['le:zʊŋ] **F -, -en** *(= Dichterlesung, Parl)* reading; *(Eccl auch)* lesson

le|tal [le'ta:l] **ADJ** *(Med)* lethal

Le|thar|gie [letar'gi:] **F -, -n** [-'gi:ən] *(Med, fig)* lethargy

le|thar|gisch [le'targɪʃ] *(Med, fig)* **ADJ** lethargic **ADV** lethargically

Le̱|the ['le:tə] **F -** *(Myth)* Lethe; *(poet: = Vergessenheit)* waters *pl* of oblivion

Lẹt|te ['lɛtə] **M -n, -n, Lẹt|tin** ['lɛtɪn] **F -, -nen** Lett, Latvian

Lẹt|ten ['lɛtn] **M -s, -** (potter's) clay

Lẹt|ter ['lɛtɐ] **F -, -n** character

lẹt|tisch ['lɛtɪʃ] **ADJ** Lettish, Latvian

Lẹt|tisch(e) ['lɛtɪʃ] **NT** Latvian → *auch* **Deutsch(e)**

Lẹtt|land ['lɛtlant] **NT -s** Latvia

Lẹtt|ner ['lɛtnɐ] **M -s, -** *(Archit)* choir screen

Lẹt|ze|bur|gisch(e) **NT** *(Ling)* Letzeburgesch → *auch* **Deutsch(e)**

Lẹtzt [lɛtst] **F zu guter ~** finally, in the end

lẹtz|temal △ **ADV** → **letzte(r, s) a**

lẹtzt|ẹnd|lich ['lɛtst'lɛntlɪç] **ADV** at (long) last; *(= letzten Endes)* at the end of the day

lẹtz|tens ['lɛtstns] **ADV** recently; **erst ~, ~ erst** just *or* only recently

Lẹtz|te(r) ['lɛtstə] **MF** *decl as adj* **der ~ seines Stammes** the last of his line; **der ~ des Monats** the last (day) of the month; **der/die ~ in der Klasse sein** to be bottom *(Brit) or* at the bottom of the class; **die ~n werden die Ersten sein** *(Bibl)* the last shall be first *(Bibl)*; **~(r) werden** to be last; **als ~(r) (an)kommen/(weg)gehen/fertig sein** to arrive/leave/finish last, to be the last to arrive/leave/finish; **als ~(r) gehen** to be the last to go; *(in Reihenfolge auch)* to go last; *(in Prozession etc)* to bring up the rear; **er wäre der ~, dem ich ...** he would be the last person I'd ...; **den ~n beißen die Hunde** *(Prov)* (the) devil take the hindmost *(prov)*

lẹtz|te(r, s) ['lɛtstə] **ADJ a** *(örtlich, zeitlich)* last; *(= endgültig, allerletzte)* final, last; *(= restlich)* last (remaining); **auf dem ~n Platz** *or* **an ~r Stelle liegen** to be (lying) last; *(in Tabelle, Liga auch)* to be (lying) bottom *(Brit)*, to be (lying) at the bottom; **mein ~s Geld** the last of my money; **das ~ Mal** (the) last time; **zum ~n Mal** (for) the last time; **die ~n zwei Tage/Jahre** the last two days/years; *(vor heute/diesem Jahr auch)* the past two days/years; **in ~r Zeit** recently; **jdm die ~ Ehre erweisen, jdm das ~ Geleit geben** to pay one's last respects to sb; **die Letzten Dinge** death and the life to come; **die Lehre der Letzten Dinge** eschatology; **das ~ und höchste Ziel meines Lebens/des Werkes** the ultimate aim of my life/of the work; **der Letzte Wille** the last will and testament

b *(= neueste) Mode, Nachricht, Neuigkeit etc* latest

c *(= schlechtester)* most terrible; **das ist der ~ Schund** *or* **Dreck** that's absolute trash; **er ist der ~ Mensch** *(inf)* he's a terrible person; **jdn wie den ~n Dreck/Sklaven** *etc* **behandeln** to treat sb like dirt/a slave *etc*

lẹtz|te|re(r, s) ['lɛtstərə] **ADJ** the latter

Lẹtz|te(s) ['lɛtstə] **NT** *decl as adj* **a** *(= Äußerste)* last thing; **es geht ums ~** everything is at stake; **sein ~s (her)geben** to give one's all, to do one's utmost; **bis zum ~n gehen** to do all that one possibly can; **das ist das ~, was ich tun würde** that's the last thing I'd do; **das ist ja das ~!** *(inf)* that really is the limit → **bis 1 b**

b zum Dritten und zum ~n *(bei Auktion)* for the (third and) last time of asking; **bis aufs ~** completely, totally; **bis ins ~** (right) down to the last detail; **etw bis ins ~ kennen** to know sth like the back of one's hand; **bis zum ~n** to the utmost; **am** *or* **zum ~n** last; **fürs ~** lastly

Lẹtzt-: **lẹtzt|ge|nannt ADJ** last-named; **lẹtzt|hin** ['lɛtst'hɪn] **ADV = letztens**; **lẹtzt|in|stanz|lich** ['lɛtstlinstantslɪç] **ADJ** *Urteil* in the court of last instance; *(fig)* in the last instance **ADV** by the court of last instance; **etw ~ entscheiden** *(fig)* to have the final decision on sth; **lẹtzt|jäh|rig** ['lɛtstjɛ:rɪç] **ADJ** *attr* last year's *no art*; **lẹtzt|lich** ['lɛtstlɪç] **ADV** in the end; **das ist ~ egal** it comes down to the same thing in the end; **lẹtzt|ma|lig** ['lɛtstma:lɪç] **ADJ** *attr* last **ADV** for the last time; **lẹtzt|mals** ['lɛtstma:ls] **ADV** for the last time; **lẹtzt|mög|lich ADJ** *attr* last possible; **Letzt|num|mern|spei|cher** M last number redial; **letzt|wil|lig** *(form)* ADJ **~e Verfügung** last will and testament ADV **~ verfügen, dass ...** to state in one's last will and testament that ...

Leu [lɔy] M **-en, -en** *(obs, poet)* lion

Leucht-: **Leucht|an|zei|ge** F illuminated display; **Leucht|bo|je** F light buoy; **Leucht|di|o|de** F light-emitting diode; **Leucht|di|o|den|an|zei|ge** F LED display

Leuch|te ['lɔyçtə] F **-, -n** *(= Leuchtkörper)* light; *(old: = Laterne)* lamp, lantern; *(inf: Mensch)* genius; **auf einem Gebiet/in einem Fach eine ~ sein** to shine in a particular field/subject

leuch|ten ['lɔyçtn] VI **a** *(Licht)* to shine; *(Flammen, Feuer, Lava, Zifferblatt)* to glow; *(= aufleuchten)* to flash **b** *(Mensch)* **mit einer Lampe in/auf etw** *(acc)* **~** to shine a lamp into/onto sth; **musst du mir direkt in die Augen ~?** do you have to shine that thing straight into my eyes?; **kannst du (mir) nicht mal ~?** can you point *or* shine the lamp *or (mit Taschenlampe)* the torch *(Brit) or* flashlight (for me)?; **leuchte mal hierher!** shine some light over here

leuch|tend ADJ *(lit, fig)* shining; *Farbe* bright, radiant; **etw in den ~sten Farben schildern/preisen** to paint sth/speak of sth in glowing colours *(Brit) or* colors *(US)*; **ein ~es Vorbild** a shining example ADV *rot, gelb* radiant, bright; **etw ~ gelb malen** to paint sth a radiant *or* bright yellow; **der Nachthimmel war ~ hell** the night sky was brightly lit

Leuch|ter ['lɔyçtɐ] M **-s, -** *(= Kerzenleuchter)* candlestick; *(= Armleuchter)* candelabra; *(= Kronleuchter)* chandelier; *(= Wandleuchter)* sconce

Leucht-: **Leucht|far|be** F fluorescent colour *(Brit) or* color *(US)*; *(= Anstrichfarbe)* fluorescent paint; *(für Farbbad)* fluorescent dye; *(= Druckfarbe)* fluorescent ink; **Leucht|feu|er** NT navigational light; **Leucht|gas** NT town gas; **Leucht|ge|schoss** NT flare; **Leucht|kä|fer** M glow-worm; **Leucht|kraft** F brightness; *(von Birne etc auch)* luminous power *(form)*; *(von Stern auch)* luminosity *(form)*; **Leucht|ku|gel** F flare; **Leucht|pat|ro|ne** F flare; **Leucht|pis|to|le** F flare pistol; **Leucht|pult** NT light box; **Leucht|ra|ke|te** F signal rocket; **Leucht|rek|la|me** F neon sign; **Leucht|röh|re** F fluorescent tube; **Leucht|schirm** M fluorescent screen; **Leucht|schrift** F neon writing; **eine ~** a neon sign

Leucht|spur F trail of light

Leucht|spur-: **Leucht|spur|ge|schoss** NT *(Mil)* tracer bullet; **Leucht|spur|mu|ni|ti|on** F *(Mil)* tracer bullets *pl*

Leucht-: **Leucht|stift** M highlighter; **Leucht|ton|ne** F light buoy; **Leucht|turm** M lighthouse; **Leucht|zei|ger** M luminous hand; **Leucht|zif|fer|blatt** NT luminous face *or* dial

leug|nen ['lɔygnən] ✪ 42.1 VT to deny; **~, etw getan zu haben** to deny having done sth; **es ist nicht zu ~, dass ...** it cannot be denied that ...; **der Angeklagte leugnete die Tat** the defendant denied the offence *(Brit) or* offense *(US)*; *(vor Gericht)* the defendant pleaded not guilty VI to deny everything

Leug|nung ['lɔygnʊŋ] F **-, -en** denial

Leu|kä|mie [lɔykɛ'mi:] F **-, -n** [-'mi:ən] leukaemia *(Brit)*, leukemia *(US)*

Leu|kä|mie|kran|ke(r) MF *decl as adj* leukaemia *(Brit) or* leukemia *(US)* sufferer

leu|kä|misch [lɔy'kɛ:mɪʃ] ADJ leukaemic *(Brit)*, leukemic *(US)*

Leu|ko|plast® [lɔyko'plast] NT **-(e)s, -e** sticking plaster *(Brit)*, ≈ Elastoplast® *(Brit)*, ≈ Band-Aid® *(US)*

Leu|ko|zy|t [lɔyko'tsy:t] M **-en, -en** leucocyte *(spec)*, white corpuscle

Leu|ko|zy|ten|zäh|lung F blood count *(of the white corpuscles)*

Leu|mund ['lɔymʊnt] M **-(e)s** [-dəs], *no pl* reputation, name

Leu|munds|zeug|nis NT character reference

Leut|chen ['lɔytçən] PL *(inf)* people *pl*, folk *pl (inf)*; **kommt, ~!** come on everyone *or* folks *(inf)*

Leu|te ['lɔytə] PL **a** people *pl*; *(inf: = Eltern)* folks *pl (inf)*, people *pl*; *(inf: = Verwandte)* people *pl*; **arme/reiche/alte/junge ~** poor/rich/old/young folk(s) *(inf) or* people; **alle ~** everybody; **vor allen ~n** in front of everybody; **kleine ~** *(fig)* ordinary folk *(inf) or* people; **die kleinen ~** *(hum, inf: Kinder)* the little ones; **die ~ waren von dem Stück begeistert** people were enthusiastic about the play; **was sollen denn die ~ davon denken?** what will people think?; **aber liebe ~!** *(inf)* come on now! *(inf)*; **~, ~!** *(inf)* dear me, (dear) oh dear; **kommt, ~!** come on folks; **aber die Sache ist doch in aller ~ Mund!** but everybody's talking about it!; **es ist nicht wie bei armen ~n** *(hum inf)* we're not on the breadline yet *(hum inf)*; **ich kenne meine ~!** *(inf)* I know them/him *etc*; **etw unter die ~ bringen** *(inf, Gerücht, Geschichte)* to spread sth around, to put sth about; *Geld* to spend sth; **unter die ~ kommen** *(inf) (Mensch)* to meet people; *(Gerüchte etc)* to go around, to go *or* do the rounds *(inf)*; **das sind wohl nicht die richtigen ~** they're not the right kind of people **b** *(= Mannschaft, Arbeiter etc)* **der Offizier ließ seine ~ antreten** the officer ordered his men to fall in; **dafür brauchen wir mehr ~** we need more people *or (Personal)* staff for that

Leu|te|schin|der [-ʃɪndɐ] M **-s, -**, **Leu|te|schin|de|rin** [-ərɪn] F **-, -nen** slave driver

Leut|nant ['lɔytnant] M **-s, -s** *or* **-e** (second) lieutenant; *(bei der Luftwaffe)* pilot officer *(Brit)*, second lieutenant *(US)*; **~ zur See** sublieutenant *(Brit)*, lieutenant junior grade *(US)*; **jawohl, Herr ~!** yes, sir; *(Naut)* aye aye, sir

leut|se|lig ['lɔytze:lɪç] ADJ affable, genial ADV affably, genially

Leut|se|lig|keit F **-**, *no pl (= Umgänglichkeit)* affability

Le|van|te [le'vantə] F **-**, *no pl* Levant

le|van|ti|nisch [levan'ti:nɪʃ] ADJ Levantine

Le|vi|a|than M **-s**, **Le|vi|a|tan** [le'via:tan, levia'ta:n] M **-s** *(Myth)* leviathan

Le|vit [le'vi:t] M **-en, -en** *(Bibl)* Levite; *(Eccl)* deacon

Le|vi|ten [le'vi:tn] PL **jdm die ~ lesen** *(inf)* to haul sb over the coals *(inf)*, to read sb the riot act *(inf)*

Lev|ko|je [lɛf'ko:jə] F **-, -n** *(Bot)* stock

Lex [lɛks] F **-, Leges** ['le:gəs] (parliamentary) bill; **~ Smythe/Braun** *etc* Smythe's/Braun's *etc* bill

Le|xem [le'kse:m] NT **-s, -e** *(Ling)* lexeme

Le|xik ['lɛksɪk] F **-**, *no pl (Ling)* lexis

le|xi|ka|lisch [lɛksi'ka:lɪʃ] ADJ lexical ADV lexically

Le|xi|ko|graf [lɛksiko'gra:f] M **-en, -en**, **Le|xi|ko|gra|fin** [-'gra:fɪn] F **-, -nen** lexicographer

Le|xi|ko|gra|fie [lɛksikogra'fi:] F **-, -n** [-'fi:ən] lexicography

le|xi|ko|gra|fisch [lɛksiko'gra:fɪʃ] ADJ lexicographic(al) ADV lexicographically

Le|xi|ko|graph *etc* = **Lexikograf** *etc*

Le|xi|ko|lo|ge [lɛksiko'lo:gə] M **-n, -n**, **Le|xi|ko|lo|gin** [-'lo:gɪn] F **-, -nen** lexicologist

Le|xi|ko|lo|gie [lɛksikolo'gi:] F **-**, *no pl* lexicology

le|xi|ko|lo|gisch [lɛksiko'lo:gɪʃ] ADJ lexicological ADV lexicologically

Le|xi|kon ['lɛksikɔn] NT **-s, Lexika** [-ka] encyclopedia; *(= Wörterbuch)* dictionary, lexicon

lfd. *abbr von* **laufend**

Li|ai|son [liɛ'zõ:] F **-, -s** liaison

Li|a|ne ['lia:nə] F **-, -n** liana

Li|ba|ne|se [liba'ne:zə] M **-n, -n**, **Li|ba|ne|sin** [-'ne:zɪn] F **-, -nen** Lebanese

li|ba|ne|sisch [liba'ne:zɪʃ] ADJ Lebanese

Li|ba|non ['li:banɔn] M **-(s) der ~** *(Land)* the Lebanon; *(Gebirge)* the Lebanon Mountains *pl*

Li|ba|non|ze|der F cedar of Lebanon

Li|bel|le [li'bɛlə] F **-, -n** *(Zool)* dragonfly; *(in Wasserwaage)* spirit level

li|be|ral [libe'ra:l] ADJ liberal ADV liberally; **~ eingestellt sein** to be liberal

Li|be|ra|le(r) [libe'ra:lə] MF *decl as adj (Pol)* Liberal

li|be|ra|li|sie|ren [liberali'zi:rən] *ptp* **liberalisiert** VT to liberalize

Li|be|ra|li|sie|rung F **-, -en** liberalization

Li|be|ra|lis|mus [libera'lɪsmʊs] M **-**, *no pl* liberalism

li|be|ra|lis|tisch [libera'lɪstɪʃ] ADJ liberalist

Li|be|ra|li|tät [liberali'tɛ:t] F **-**, *no pl* liberality

Li|be|ro ['li:bero] M **-s, -s** *(Ftbl)* sweeper

Li|ber|tin [libɛr'tɛ̃:] M **-s, -s** *(old, geh)* libertine *(old)*

li|bi|di|nös [libidi'nø:s] ADJ *(Psych)* libidinous, libidinal

Li|bi|do [li'bi:do, 'li:bido] F **-**, *no pl (Psych)* libido

Lib|ret|tist [libre'tɪst] M **-en, -en**, **Lib|ret|tis|tin** [-'tɪstɪn] F **-, -nen** librettist

Lib|ret|to [li'brɛto] NT **-s, -s** *or* **Libretti** [-ti] libretto

Li|by|en ['li:byən] NT **-s** Libya

Li|by|er ['li:byɐ] M **-s, -**, **Li|by|e|rin** [-ərɪn] F **-, -nen** Libyan

li|bysch ['li:byʃ] ADJ Libyan

licht [lɪçt] ADJ **a** *(= hell)* light; *(liter) Morgen* bright; **am ~en Tag** in broad daylight; **es wird schon ~** *(geh)* it is getting light, (the) day is dawning *(liter)*; **einen ~en Augenblick** *or* **Moment haben** to have a lucid moment; *(fig inf)* to have a brainwave *(inf)*; **auch ich habe ~e Augenblicke** even I have my lucid moments **b** *Wald* sparse; *Haar* thin, sparse; **eine ~e Stelle im Wald** a sparsely-wooded spot in the forest **c** *(Tech)* **~e Höhe** headroom; **~e Weite** (internal) width; **~er Durchmesser** internal diameter

Licht [lɪçt] NT **-(e)s, -er** *or (rare)* **-e a** *no pl* light; **~ machen** *(= anschalten)* to turn *or* switch *or* put on a light; *(= anzünden)* to light a candle/lantern *etc*; **das ~ brennt** *or* **ist an** the light is on *or* is burning; *(Kerze)* the candle is burning; **das ~ des Tages/der Sonne** the light of day/the sun; **ich möchte es noch bei ~ fertig bekommen** I'd like to get it finished in daylight *or* while it's still light; **~ ins Zimmer lassen** to let light into the room; **in der ganzen Stadt fiel das ~ aus** all the lights in the town went out; **hier gehen bald die ~er aus** *(fig)* we're about to hit troubled waters; **etw gegen das ~ halten** to hold sth up to the light; **gegen das ~ fotografieren** to take a photograph into the light; **bei ~e besehen** *or* **betrachtet** *(lit)* in the daylight; *(fig)* in the cold light of day; **das ist nicht das richtige ~** that's not the right sort of light; **das Bild hängt hier nicht im richtigen ~** the light is wrong for the picture here; **du nimmst mir das ganze ~ weg** you're in the *or* my light; **jdm im ~ stehen** *(lit)* to stand in sb's light; **(jdm) aus dem ~ gehen** to move *or* get out of the *or* sb's light; **~ und Schatten** light and shade *(auch Art)*; **wo ~ ist, ist auch Schatten** *(Prov)* there's no joy without sorrow *(prov)*; **das ~ der Welt erblicken** *(geh)* to (first) see the light of day; **das ~ scheuen** *(lit)* to shun the light (of day); **Geschäfte, die das ~ scheuen** shady deals; **grünes ~ (für etw) geben** to give the green light (to *or* for sth); **~ am Ende des Tunnels sehen** *(fig)* to see a light at the end of the tunnel; **sein ~ leuchten lassen** *(fig)* to shine → **Scheffel b** *(fig)* light; *(= Könner)* genius; **das ~ der Wahrheit/Erkenntnis** *etc* the light of truth/knowledge *etc*; **~ in eine (dunkle) Sache bringen** to cast *or* shed some light on a matter; **im ~(e) unserer Erfahrungen** in the light of our experiences; **etw ans ~ bringen/zerren** to bring/drag sth out into the open; **ans ~ kommen** to come *or* get out, to come to light; **jdn hinters ~ führen** to pull the wool over sb's eyes, to lead sb up *(Brit) or* down *(US)* the garden path; **mir geht ein ~ auf(, warum ...)** now it's dawned on me (why ...), now I see (why ...); **etw in milderem**

~ sehen to see sth in a more favourable *(Brit)* or favorable *(US)* light; **ein schiefes/schlechtes** or **kein gutes ~ auf jdn/etw werfen** to show sb/sth in the wrong/a bad light; **das wirft ein bezeichnendes ~ auf seinen Charakter** that shows him for what he really is; **in ein schiefes** or **falsches ~ geraten** to be seen in the wrong light; **etw ins rechte ~ rücken** or **setzen** to show sth in a favourable *(Brit)* or favorable *(US)* light; *(= richtigstellen)* to show sth in its true light; **etw ins falsche ~ rücken** or **setzen** to show sth in an unfavourable *(Brit)* or unfavorable *(US)* light; *(= falsch darstellen)* to put a wrong complexion on sth, to misrepresent sth

c *(= Lichtquelle)* light; *(= Kerze)* candle; **die ~er der Großstadt** the bright lights of the big city; **~er führen** *(Naut)* to display or show lights; **jdm ein ~ aufstecken** or **aufsetzen** *(fig inf)* to put sb wise *(inf)*

d *(Hunt)* eye *(of deer etc)*

Licht-: **Licht|an|la|ge** F lights *pl*; **er hat sich** *(dat)* **eine ganze ~ gebastelt** he put together a whole lighting system; **Licht|be|hand|lung** F *(Med)* phototherapy; **licht|be|stän|dig** ADJ lightproof; *Farben, Stoff* non-fade; **Licht|bild** NT *(= Dia)* transparency, slide; *(form: = Foto)* photograph; **Licht|bil|der|vor|trag** M illustrated talk or lecture; **Licht|blick** M *(fig)* ray of hope; **Licht|bo|gen** M arc; **licht|bre|chend** ADJ *(Opt)* refractive; **Licht|bre|chung** F refraction; **Licht|brü|cke** F lighting rig; **Licht|bün|del** NT pencil (of rays); **Licht|druck** M *pl* **-drucke** *(Typ)* collotype; *(Phys) no pl* light pressure; **licht|durch|flu|tet** ADJ flooded with light, bathed in light; **licht|durch|läs|sig** ADJ pervious to light, light-transmissive *(form)*; *Stoff* that lets the light through; **dieser Stoff ist ~er/zu ~** this material lets more/too much light through; **Licht|durch|läs|sig|keit** F perviousness to light

Lich|te ['lɪçtə] F **-**, *no pl* (internal) width

Licht-: **licht|echt** ADJ non-fade; **Licht|echt|heit** F non-fade properties *pl*; **Licht|ef|fekt** M lighting effect; **Licht|ein|fall** M incidence of light; **Licht|ein|wir|kung** F action of light; **licht|elek|trisch** ADJ photoelectric; **licht|emp|find|lich** ADJ sensitive to light, photosensitive *(Tech)*; **Licht|emp|find|lich|keit** F sensitivity to light, photosensitivity *(Tech)*; *(Phot)* film speed

lich|ten ['lɪçtn] VT *Wald* to thin (out); **den Steuerdschungel ~** *(fig)* to cut through the jungle of tax regulations VR *(Reihen, Wald, Dickicht, Haare)* to thin (out); *(Nebel)* to clear, to lift; *(Wolken, Dunkel)* to lift; *(Bestände)* to go down, to dwindle; *(fig: Angelegenheit)* to be cleared up

lich|ten VT *Anker* to weigh

Lich|ter-: **Lich|ter|baum** M Christmas tree; **Lich|ter|fest** NT **a** *(liter: = Weihnachten)* Yule *(old)*, Christmas **b** *(jüdisches Fest)* Festival of Lights, Hanuk(k)ah; **Lich|ter|glanz** M blaze of lights; **in festlichem ~ erstrahlen** to be a blaze of festive lights; **Lich|ter|ket|te** F *(an Weihnachtsbaum)* fairy lights *pl*; *(von Menschen)* long line of demonstrators carrying lights; **lich|ter|loh** ['lɪçtɐ'lo:] ADV **~ brennen** *(lit)* to be ablaze; *(fig: Herz)* to be aflame; **Lich|ter|meer** NT *(liter)* sea of light; **das ~ von New York** the sea of light that is New York

Licht-: **Licht|fil|ter** NT OR M (light) filter; **Licht|ge|schwin|dig|keit** F the speed of light; **Licht|ge|stalt** F *(fig)* shining light; **Licht|grif|fel** M *(Comput)* light pen; **Licht|hof** M **a** *(Archit)* air well **b** *(Phot)* halation *(spec)* **c** *(des Mondes)* halo; **Licht|hu|pe** F *(Aut)* flash (of the headlights); **jdn durch ~ warnen** to warn sb by flashing one's lights; **Licht|jahr** NT light year; **~e entfernt sein** *(fig)* to be light years away *(von* from); **jdm um ~e voraus sein** to be light years ahead of sb; **etw um ~e zurückwerfen** to set sth back a long way; **Licht|ke|gel** M *(Phys)* cone of light; *(von Scheinwerfer)* beam (of light); **er stand im ~** he stood in the spotlight; *(von Autoscheinwerfer)* he stood in the beam of the headlights; **Licht|kreis** M circle or pool of light; **Licht|lei|tung** F lighting wire; **licht|los** ADJ dark; **ein ~es Zimmer** a room which doesn't get any light; **Licht|man|gel** M lack of light; **Licht|ma|schi|ne** F *(für Gleichstrom)* dynamo; *(für Drehstrom)* alternator; **Licht|mast** M lamppost; **Licht|mess** ['lɪçtmɛs] *no art* **Mariä ~** Candlemas; **Licht|mes|ser** M light meter; **Licht|mess|ver|fah|ren** NT *(Mil)* flash ranging; **Licht|nel|ke** F catchfly, lychnis *(form)*; **Licht|or|gel** F clavilux, colour *(Brit)* or color *(US)* organ; **Licht|pau|se** F photocopy; *(bei Blaupausverfahren)* blueprint; **Licht|punkt** M point of light; **Licht|quant** NT photon; **Licht|quel|le** F source of light; **Licht|rek|la|me** F neon sign; **Licht|satz** M *(Typ)* filmsetting, photocomposition; **in ~ hergestellt** filmset; **Licht|schacht** M air shaft; **Licht|schal|ter** M light switch; **Licht|schein** M gleam of light; **licht|scheu** ADJ averse to light; *(fig) Gesindel* shady; **Licht|schim|mer** M gleam of light; **Licht|schran|ke** F photoelectric barrier

Licht|schutz-: **Licht|schutz|fak|tor** M protection factor; **Licht|schutz|fil|ter** M light filter

Licht-: **Licht|setz|ma|schi|ne** F *(Typ)* photo-setting machine; **Licht|sig|nal** NT light signal; **Licht|spiel|haus** NT, **Licht|spiel|the|a|ter** NT *(dated)* cinema, picture palace *(Brit old)*; **licht|stark** ADJ *(Opt)* intense; *(Phot)* fast; **Licht|stär|ke** F *(Opt)* luminous intensity; *(Phot)* speed; **Licht|stift** M *(Comput)* light pen; **Licht|stock** M *(= Kerze)* wax taper; **Licht|strahl** M beam or ray of light; *(fig)* ray of sunshine; **Licht|strom** M *(Opt)* luminous or light flux; **Licht|the|ra|pie** F *(Med)* light therapy; **licht|un|durch|läs|sig** ADJ opaque

Lich|tung ['lɪçtʊŋ] F **-**, **-en** clearing, glade

Licht-: **Licht|ver|hält|nis|se** PL lighting conditions *pl*; **Licht|ver|schmut|zung** F light pollution; **Licht|wech|sel** M change of light; *(Astron)* light variation; **Licht|weg** M light path; **licht|wen|dig** ADJ *(Bot)* phototropic

Lid [li:t] NT **-(e)s, -er** [-dɐ] eyelid

Lid-: **Lid|schat|ten** M eye shadow; **Lid|schlag** M blink; **Lid|strich** M eyeliner

lieb [li:p] ADJ **a** *(= liebenswürdig, hilfsbereit)* kind; *(= nett, reizend)* nice; *(= niedlich) Kerl(chen), Ding* sweet, lovely, cute *(inf)*; *(= artig) Kind, Schulklasse* good; **(es sendet dir) (viele) ~e Grüße deine Silvia** love Silvia; **~e Grüße an deine Eltern** give my best wishes to your parents; **würdest du (bitte) so ~ sein und das Fenster aufmachen** or **das Fenster aufzumachen?, sei bitte so ~ und mache das Fenster auf** would you do me a favour *(Brit)* or favor *(US)* or (would you) be an angel *(inf)* and open the window?; **willst du wohl (endlich) ~ sein?!** are you going to be good or to behave now?; **bei jdm ~ Kind sein** *(pej)* to be sb's (little) darling or pet; **beim Lehrer ~ Kind sein** *(pej)* to be teacher's pet; **sich bei jdm ~ Kind machen** *(pej)* to suck up to sb, to worm one's way into sb's good books

b *Gast, Besuch (= angenehm)* pleasant; *(= willkommen)* welcome; **bei uns bist du jederzeit ein ~er Gast** you're always welcome, we're always pleased to see you

c *(= angenehm)* **etw ist jdm ~** sb likes sth; **es wäre mir ~, wenn ...** I'd be glad if ..., I'd like it if ...; **es ist mir ~, dass ...** I'm glad that ...; **es wäre ihm ~er** he would prefer it → *auch* **lieber ADV, liebste(r, s) ADV**

d *(= geliebt, geschätzt)* dear, beloved *(iro, form)*; *(in Briefanrede)* dear; **~e Monika, das geht doch nicht** (my) dear Monika, that's just not on; **~e Brüder und Schwestern** *(Rel)* dearly beloved; **der ~e Gott** the Good Lord; **~er Gott** *(Anrede)* dear God or Lord; **unsere Liebe Frau** *(Eccl)* Our Lady; **Liebe Anna, ~er Klaus! ...** Dear Anna and Klaus, ...; **(mein) Liebes** (my) love or pet, honey *(esp US)*; **er ist mir ~ und wert** or **teuer** he's very dear to me; **~ geworden** well-loved; *Klischee* much-loved; **eine mir ~ gewordene Gewohnheit** a habit of which I've grown very fond; **den ~en langen Tag** *(inf)* the whole livelong day; **das ~e Geld!** the money, the money!; **(ach) du ~er Himmel/~er Gott/~e Güte/~e Zeit/~es Lieschen** or **Lottchen/~es bisschen** *(inf)* good heavens or Lord!, goodness me! → **Not**

e ~ste(r, s) favourite *(Brit)*, favorite *(US)*; **sie ist mir die Liebste von allen** she is my favourite *(Brit)* or favorite *(US)*

ADV **a** *(= liebenswürdig) danken, grüßen* sweetly, nicely; **jdm ~ schreiben** to write a sweet letter to sb; **jdn ~ beschenken** to give sb a sweet present; **sich ~ um jdn kümmern** to be very kind to sb; **er hat mir wirklich ~ geholfen** it was really sweet the way he helped me

b *(= artig)* nicely; **geh jetzt ~ nach Hause** be a sweetie, go home

lieb|äu|geln ['li:plɔygln] VI *insep* **mit etw ~** to have one's eye on sth; **mit einem neuen Auto ~** to be toying with the idea of getting a new car; **mit dem Gedanken ~, etw zu tun** to be toying or flirting with the idea of doing sth

lieb be|hal|ten *irreg*, **lieb+be|hal|ten** *sep irreg* to stay fond of sb

Lieb|chen ['li:pçən] NT **-s, -** *(old)* sweetheart

Lie|be ['li:bə] F **-**, **-n** **a** love *(zu jdm, für jdn* for or of sb, *zu etw* of sth); **die große ~** the love of one's life, the real thing *(inf)*; **Heirat aus ~** love match; **aus ~ zu jdm/einer Sache** for the love of sb/sth; **ein Kind der ~** *(liter)* a love child; **etw mit viel ~ tun** to do sth with loving care; **bei aller ~** with the best will in the world; **in ~** with love; **in ~ dein Theobald** with all my love, Theobald; **~ macht blind** *(Prov)* love is blind *(Prov)*; **wo die ~ hinfällt!** love is a funny thing

b *(= Sex)* sex; **eine Nacht der ~** a night of love; **von der ~ leben** *(Prostituierte etc)* to live off sex, to live off one's favours *(Brit)* or favors *(US, euph)*; **ein Meister der ~** an expert at lovemaking, an expert in love; **sie/er ist gut in der ~** *(inf)* she/he is good at making love

c *(inf: = Gefälligkeit)* favour *(Brit)*, favor *(US)*; **tu mir doch bitte die ~ und ...** would you do me a favour *(Brit)* or favor *(US)* and ...

d *(= Geliebte(r))* love, darling; **sie ist eine alte ~ von mir** she is an old flame of mine

Lie|be-: **lie|be|be|dürf|tig** ADJ **~ sein, ein ~es Wesen haben** or **sein** to need a lot of love or affection; **Lie|be|die|ne|rei** [-di:nə'rai] F **-**, *no pl (pej)* subservience, fawning *(gegenüber* to); **lie|be|die|nern** [-di:nɐn] VI *insep (pej)* to fawn *(jdm* to sb); **lie|be|leer** ADJ *Leben, Dasein* loveless

Lie|be|lei [li:bə'lai] F **-**, **-en** *(inf)* flirtation, affair

lie|ben ['li:bn] VT to love; *(als Liebesakt)* to make love *(jdn* to sb); **etw nicht ~** not to like sth; **ich liebe es nicht, wenn man mich unterbricht** I do not like being interrupted; **das liebe ich (gerade)!** *(iro)* marvellous *(Brit)* or marvelous *(US)*, isn't it? *(iro)*; **sich** or **einander ~** to love one another or each other; *(euph)* to make love → *auch* **geliebt** VI to love; **etw ~d gern tun** to love to do sth

Lie|ben|de(r) ['li:bndə] MF *decl as adj* lover

lie|ben ler|nen VT to come to love

lie|bens|wert ADJ lovable, endearing

lie|bens|wür|dig ADJ kind; *(= liebenswert)* charming; **würden Sie so ~ sein und die Tür schließen?** would you be so kind as to shut the door? ADV kindly

lie|bens|wür|di|ger|wei|se ['li:bnsvʏrdɪgə'vaizə] ADV kindly

Lie|bens|wür|dig|keit F **-**, **-en** **a** *(= Höflichkeit)* politeness; *(= Freundlichkeit)* kindness; **würden Sie die ~ haben, das zu tun** or **und das tun?** *(form)* would you be kind or good enough to do that?, would you have the goodness to do that? **b** *(iro: = giftige Bemerkung)* charming remark *(iro)*

lie|ber ['li:bɐ] ✪ 31, 33.3, 34, 35.5, 36.3 ADJ *comp von* **lieb**

ADV comp von **gern** **a** (= *vorzugsweise*) rather, sooner; **das tue ich ~** (*im Augenblick*) I would *or* I'd rather *or* I'd sooner do that; (*grundsätzlich auch*) I prefer doing that; **das würde ich ~ tun** I would *or* I'd rather *or* I'd sooner do that, I would prefer to do that; **ich trinke ~ Wein als Bier** I prefer wine to beer; **(das möchte ich) ~ nicht!** I would *or* I'd sooner *or* rather not, I would *or* I'd prefer not to; **er sieht es ~, wenn du das nicht tust** he would *or* he'd prefer you not to do that, he would *or* he'd prefer it if you didn't do that, he would *or* he'd sooner *or* he'd rather you didn't do that; (*grundsätzlich*) he prefers you not to do that, he prefers it if you don't do that

b (= *besser, vernünftigerweise*) better; **bleibe ~ im Bett** you had *or* you'd better stay in bed, I would *or* I'd stay in bed if I were you; **ich hätte ~ nachgeben sollen** I would have done better *or* I'd have done better to have given in; **sollen wir gehen? – ~ nicht!** should we go? – better not; **nichts ~ als das** there's nothing I'd rather do/have *etc*

Lie|be(r) [ˈliːbə] MF *decl as adj* dear; **meine ~n** my dears

Lie|bes- *in cpds* love; **Lie|bes|aben|teu|er** NT amorous adventure; **Lie|bes|af|fä|re** F (love) affair; **Lie|bes|akt** M love *or* sex act; **Lie|bes|ap|fel** M (*obs*) tomato; **Lie|bes|ban|de** PL (*liter*) bonds *pl* of love; **Lie|bes|be|zie|hung** F romantic attachment, (sexual) relationship; **Lie|bes|bo|te** M, **Lie|bes|bo|tin** F messenger of love; **Lie|bes|brief** M love letter; **Lie|bes|die|ne|rin** F (*inf*) lady of the night (*euph*); **Lie|bes|dienst** M labour (*Brit*) *or* labor (*US*) of love; (*fig:* = *Gefallen*) favour (*Brit*), favor (*US*); **jdm einen ~ erweisen** to do sb a service of love/a favour (*Brit*) *or* favor (*US*); **Lie|bes|ent|zug** M, *no pl* withdrawal of affection; **Lie|bes|er|klä|rung** F declaration of love; **jdm eine ~ machen** to declare one's love to sb; **Lie|bes|film** M love film; **Lie|bes|ge|dicht** NT love poem; **Lie|bes|ge|schich|te** F **a** (*Liter*) love story **b** (*inf:* = *Liebschaft*) love affair; **Lie|bes|glück** NT joy(s *pl*) of love; (= *glückliche Liebe*) happy love affair; **Lie|bes|gott** M god of love; **Lie|bes|göt|tin** F goddess of love; **Lie|bes|han|del** M, **Lie|bes|hän|del** [-hɛndl] M **-s, -** (*obs*) love affair; **Lie|bes|hei|rat** F love match; **Lie|bes|kum|mer** M lovesickness; **~ haben** to be lovesick; **vor ~ konnte sie nicht mehr essen** she was so lovesick that she couldn't eat; **Lie|bes|kunst** F art of love; **Lie|bes|lau|be** F (*hum*) love nest; **Lie|bes|le|ben** NT love life; **Lie|bes|lied** NT love song; **Lie|bes|müh** F **das ist vergebliche** *or* **verlorene ~** that is futile; **Lie|bes|nacht** F night of love; **Lie|bes|nest** NT (*inf*) love nest; **Lie|bes|paar** NT lovers *pl*; **Lie|bes|part|ner(in)** M(F) lover; **Lie|bes|per|len** PL hundreds and thousands *pl* (*Brit*); **Lie|bes|ro|man** M romantic novel; **Lie|bes|scha|tul|le** F (*hum sl:* = *Vagina*) love hole (*sl*); **Lie|bes|spiel** NT love play; **Lie|bes|schwur** M lover's oath; **Lie|bes|sze|ne** F love scene; **lie|bes|toll** ADJ love-stricken, lovelorn; **Lie|bes|tö|ter** [-tøːtɐ] PL (*hum*) long johns *pl*, passion killers *pl* (*Brit hum*); **Lie|bes|trank** M (*liter*) love potion; **lie|bes|trun|ken** ADJ (*geh*) in an ecstasy of love; **Lie|bes|ver|hält|nis** NT (sexual) relationship, liaison

lie|be|voll ADJ loving; *Umarmung* affectionate ADV lovingly; *umarmen* affectionately; **sie sah ihn ~ an** she looked at him lovingly *or* with affection; **alle nannten ihn ~ Blacky** he was affectionately known to all as Blacky

lieb-: **lieb ge|win|nen** *irreg*, **lieb+ge|win|nen** *sep irreg* VT to get *or* grow fond of; **liebge|wor|den** ADJ *attr* → **lieb ADJ d**; **lieb ha|ben** *irreg*, **lieb+ha|ben** *sep irreg* VT to love; (*weniger stark*) to be (very) fond of

Lieb|ha|ber [-haːbɐ] M **-s, -**, **Lieb|ha|be|rin** [-ərɪn] F **-, -nen** **a** lover **b** (= *Interessent, Freund*) enthusiast; (= *Sammler*) collector; **ein ~ von etw** a lover of sth; **das ist nur etwas für ~** it's an acquired taste; **das ist ein Wein/Auto für ~** that is a wine/car for connoisseurs

Lieb|ha|be|rei [-haːbəˈrai] F **-, -en** (*fig:* = *Steckenpferd, Hobby*) hobby; **etw aus ~ tun** to do sth as a hobby

Lieb|ha|ber-: **Lieb|ha|ber|preis** M collector's price; **Lieb|ha|ber|stück** NT collector's item; **Lieb|ha|ber|wert** M collector's value

lieb|ko|sen [liːpˈkoːzn] *ptp* **liebkost** VT *insep* (*liter*) to caress, to fondle

Lieb|ko|sung F **-, -en** (*liter*) caress

lieb|lich [ˈliːplɪç] ADJ charming, lovely, delightful; *Landschaft* lovely, delightful; *Duft, Geschmack, Wein* sweet ADV *singen* delightfully; **~ klingen** to sound delightful; **~ aussehen** to look sweet *or* lovely; **~ duften/schmecken** to smell/taste sweet

Lieb|lich|keit F **-, -en** loveliness, delightfulness; (*von Duft, Geschmack, Wein*) sweetness; **Ihre ~, Prinzessin Sylvia** (*im Fasching*) Her Sweetness Princess Sylvia (*title of carnival princess*)

Lieb|ling [ˈliːplɪŋ] M **-s, -e** darling; (= *bevorzugter Mensch*) favourite (*Brit*), favorite (*US*)

Lieb|lings- ✪ 34.1, 34.3 *in cpds* favourite (*Brit*), favorite (*US*); **mein Lieblingsgericht** my favo(u)rite meal

Lieb-: **lieb|los** ADJ *Ehemann, Eltern* unloving; *Bemerkung, Behandlung* unkind; *Benehmen* inconsiderate ADV unkindly; (= *ohne Sorgfalt*) carelessly, thoughtlessly; **~ gekocht/zubereitet** *etc* cooked/prepared *etc* any old how (*Brit inf*) *or* any old way (*inf*); **Lieb|lo|sig|keit** F **-, -en** **a** *no pl* (= *liebloser Charakter*) (*von Ehemann, Eltern*) unloving nature; (*von Bemerkung, Behandlung*) unkindness; (*von Benehmen*) inconsiderateness **b** (*Äußerung*) unkind remark; (*Tat*) unkind act; **~en** (*Benehmen*) unkind behaviour *sing* (*Brit*) *or* behavior *sing* (*US*); **Lieb|reiz** M (*liter*) charm; **lieb|rei|zend** (*liter*) ADJ charming ADV charmingly; **Lieb|schaft** [ˈliːpʃaft] F **-, -en** affair

liebs|ten [ˈliːpstn] ADV **am ~** → **liebste(r, s) ADV**

Liebs|te(r) [ˈliːpstə] MF *decl as adj* sweetheart

liebs|te(r, s) [ˈliːpstə] ADJ *superl von* **lieb** ADV *superl von* **gern**; **am ~n** best; **am ~n hätte ich ...** what I'd like most would be (to have) ..., most of all *or* best of all I'd like (to have) ...; **am ~n würde ich ...** what I'd like most would be to ..., most of all *or* best of all I'd like to ...; **am ~n lese ich Kriminalromane/esse ich scharfe Speisen/gehe ich ins Kino** most *or* best of all I like detective novels/spicy food/going to the cinema; **am ~n hätte ich ihm eine geklebt!** (*inf*) I could have belted him (one) (*inf*); **das würde ich am ~n tun** that's what I'd like to do best, that's what I'd prefer to do

Lieb|stö|ckel [ˈliːpʃtœkl] M OR NT **-s, -** (*Bot*) lovage

Liech|ten|stein [ˈlɪçtnʃtain] NT **-s** Liechtenstein

Liech|ten|stei|ner [ˈlɪçtnʃtainɐ] M **-s, -**, **Liech|ten|stei|ne|rin** [-ərɪn] F **-, -nen** Liechtensteiner

liech|ten|stei|nisch [ˈlɪçtnʃtainɪʃ] ADJ Liechtenstein, of Liechtenstein

Lied [liːt] NT **-(e)s, -er** [-dəs, -dɐ] song; (= *Kirchenlied*) hymn; (= *Weihnachtslied*) carol; (*Mus*) lied (*spec*); **das Ende vom ~** (*fig inf*) the upshot *or* outcome (of all this); **das ist dann immer das Ende vom ~** it always ends like that; **es ist immer dasselbe** *or* **das alte** *or* **gleiche ~** (*inf*) it's always the same old story (*inf*); **davon kann ich ein ~ singen, davon weiß ich ein ~ zu singen** I could tell you a thing or two about that (*inf*)

Lie|der-: **Lie|der|abend** M evening of songs; (*von Sänger*) song recital; **Lie|der|buch** NT → **Lied** songbook; hymn book; book of carols; **Lie|der|dich|ter(in)** M(F) lyrical poet; (*des Mittelalters*) minstrel; **Lie|der|hand|schrift** F collection of ballads

Lie|der|jan [ˈliːdɐjaːn] M **-(e)s, -e** (*dated inf*) wastrel

lie|der|lich [ˈliːdɐlɪç] ADJ (= *schlampig*) slovenly *attr, pred*; (= *nachlässig auch*) sloppy; (= *unmoralisch*) *Leben, Mann* dissolute, dissipated; *Frau, Mädchen* loose; **ein ~es Frauenzimmer** (*pej*) a slut (*pej*); **Bruder Liederlich** (*old*) wastrel ADV (= *schlampig*) sloppily; (= *unmoralisch*) dissolutely

Lie|der|lich|keit F **-,** *no pl* (= *Schlampigkeit*) slovenliness; (= *Nachlässigkeit auch*) sloppiness

Lie|der-: **Lie|der|ma|cher(in)** M(F) singer-songwriter; **Lie|der|zyk|lus** M song cycle

Lied-: **Lied|gut** NT, *no pl* song literature, body of song; **deutsches ~** German song; **Lied|text** M lyrics *pl*, words *pl*

lief *pret von* **laufen**

Lie|fe|rant [lifəˈrant] M **-en, -en**, **Lie|fe|ran|tin** [-ˈrantɪn] F **-, -nen** supplier; (= *Auslieferer*) deliveryman/-woman

Lie|fe|ran|ten|ein|gang M tradesmen's entrance; (*von Warenhaus etc*) goods entrance

Lie|fer-: **Lie|fer|auf|trag** M order; **Lie|fer|au|to** NT van, delivery van *or* truck (*US*); **lie|fer|bar** ADJ (= *vorrätig*) available; (= *zustellbar*) deliverable (*rare*); **die Ware ist sofort ~** the article can be supplied/delivered at once; **diese Sachen sind auch kurzfristig ~** these goods can be supplied/delivered at short notice; **Lie|fer|be|din|gun|gen** PL conditions *pl* or terms *pl* of supply *or* (*für Zustellung*) delivery; **Lie|fer|fir|ma** F supplier; (= *Zusteller*) delivery firm; **Lie|fer|frist** F delivery period; **die ~ einhalten** to meet the delivery date; **Lie|fer|kos|ten** PL delivery charges *pl*, shipping costs *pl*; **Lie|fer|land** NT supplier country; **Lie|fer|men|ge** F quantity delivered *or* ordered; **Lie|fer|mo|nat** M (*Comm*) contract month, delivery month

lie|fern [ˈliːfɐn] VT **a** *Waren* to supply; (= *zustellen*) to deliver (*an +acc* to); **jdm etw ~** to supply sb with sth/deliver sth to sb

b (= *zur Verfügung stellen*) to supply; *Beweise, Gesprächsstoff, Informationen, Sensationen* to provide, to furnish, to supply; *Ertrag* to yield; (= *hervorbringen*) *Ergebnis* to produce; (*inf:* = *stellen*) to provide; **jdm eine Schlacht/ein Wortgefecht ~** to do battle/verbal battle with sb; **sie lieferten sich eine regelrechte Schlacht** they had a real battle; (*Sport*) they put up a real fight; **ein spannendes Spiel ~** (*Sport*) to put on an exciting game; **jdm eine gute/schlechte Partie ~** to give/not to give sb a good game; **jdm einen Vorwand ~** to give sb an excuse → *auch* **geliefert**

VI to supply; (= *zustellen*) to deliver; **wir ~ nicht ins Ausland/nach Frankreich** we don't supply the foreign market/(to) France; **eine Firma, die wegen eines Streiks nicht mehr ~ kann** a firm which is no longer able to deliver because of a strike

Lie|fer-: **Lie|fer|schein** M delivery note; **Lie|fer|schwie|rig|kei|ten** PL delivery problems *pl*; **Lie|fer|ter|min** M delivery date

Lie|fe|rung [ˈliːfərʊŋ] F **-, -en** **a** (= *Versand, Versandgut*) delivery; (= *Versorgung*) supply; **bei ~ zu bezahlen** payable on delivery; **Zahlung bis 14 Tage nach ~** account payable within 14 days of delivery; **~ frei Haus** free home delivery **b** (*von Buch*) instalment (*Brit*), installment (*US*)

Lie|fe|rungs|be|din|gun|gen PL = **Lieferbedingungen**

Lie|fer-: **Lie|fer|ver|kehr** M delivery traffic; **„Lieferverkehr frei"** "delivery vehicles only"; **Lie|fer|ver|trag** M contract of sale, sale contract; **ein ~ über 5.000 Autos** a contract to supply *or* (*für Zustellung*) deliver 5,000 cars; **Lie|fer|wa|gen** M van, delivery van *or* truck (*US*); (*offen*) pick-up; **Lie|fer|zeit** F delivery period, lead time (*Comm*); **Lie|fer|zet|tel** M delivery order

Lie|ge [ˈliːgə] F **-, -n** couch; (= *Campingliege*) camp bed (*Brit*), cot (*US*); (*für Garten*) lounger (*Brit*), lounge chair (*US*)

Lie|ge-: **Lie|ge|deck** NT *(Naut)* sun deck; **Lie|ge|geld** NT *(Naut)* demurrage; **Lie|ge|kar|te** F *(Rail)* couchette ticket; **Lie|ge|kur** F rest-cure

lie|gen ['li:gn]
pret **lag** [la:g], *ptp* **gelegen** [gə'le:gn] *aux haben or (S Ger) sein*

INTRANSITIVES VERB

Siehe auch *liegen bleiben, liegen lassen, gelegen.*

a = flach liegen: Mensch to lie; (*inf*: = *krank sein*) to be laid up *(inf)*; **er lag auf dem Boden** he was lying on the floor; **vom stundenlangen Liegen auf dem harten Boden war ich ganz steif** I was stiff after lying for hours on the hard ground; **ich liege nicht gerne weich** I don't like sleeping on a soft mattress; **ich liege lieber hart** I prefer (to sleep on) a hard mattress; **unbequem liegen** to lie uncomfortably *or* in an uncomfortable position; **in diesem Bett liegt es sich** *or* **liegt man hart/weich** this bed is hard/soft; **im Bett/Krankenhaus liegen** to be in bed/hospital; **zu Bett liegen** *(form)* to have retired *(form)*; (= *krank sein*) to have taken to one's bed *(form)*; **der Kranke muss unbedingt liegen** the patient really must stay *or* keep lying down; **das lange Liegen** *(von Patient etc)* being in bed a long time; **in diesem Grab liegen meine Eltern** my parents are in this grave; **auf welchem Friedhof liegt dein Vater?** which cemetery is your father buried in?; **auf den Knien liegen** to be on one's knees

b = flach liegen: Gegenstand to lie; *(Flasche etc)* to lie on its side; *(Schnee)* to be; *(Hitze, Nebel)* to hang; **auf dem Boden haben sie teure Teppiche liegen** they have expensive carpets on the floor; **ich habe noch einen guten Wein im Keller liegen** I've got a good wine in the cellar; **die Stadt lag in dichtem Nebel** the town was enveloped in thick fog, thick fog hung over the town; **über dem Tal lag Nebel** fog hung over the valley; **der Schnee lag 4 m hoch** the snow was 4m deep; **der Schnee bleibt nicht liegen** the snow isn't lying *(esp Brit) or* sticking *(US)*; **auf den Bergen lag schon Schnee** there was already snow on the mountains; **der Kopf muss hoch/tief liegen** the head must be higher/lower than the rest of the body; **etw liegen lassen** to leave sth (there); **meine Haare liegen heute nicht richtig** my hair doesn't look right today; **wenn ich Ihre Haare so schneide, liegen sie viel besser** if I cut your hair in this style it'll look much better; **der Stoff liegt 90 cm breit** the material is 90 cm wide; **der Vogel/das Flugzeug lag ganz ruhig in der Luft** the bird/plane was gliding through the air; **in der Kurve liegen** *(Auto)* to hold the corner; *(Rennfahrer)* to corner; **der Wagen liegt gut auf der Straße** the car holds the road well

c = sich befinden to be; **das Schiff liegt am Kai** the ship is (tied up) alongside the quay; **das Schiff liegt vor Anker** the ship is lying at anchor; **die Betonung liegt auf der zweiten Silbe** the stress is on the second syllable; **ein Lächeln lag auf ihrem Gesicht** there was a smile on her face; **die Preise liegen zwischen 60 und 80 Euro** the prices are between 60 and 80 euros; **seine Fähigkeiten liegen auf einem anderen Gebiet** his abilities lie in a different direction; **in jds Absicht** *(dat)* **liegen** to be sb's intention; **so, wie die Dinge jetzt liegen** as things are *or* stand at the moment; **damit liegst du goldrichtig** *(inf)* you're (dead *(inf) or* absolutely) right there → **richtigliegen**

d = eine bestimmte Lage haben to be; *(Haus, Stadt etc)* to be (situated *or* located); **verstreut liegen** to be scattered; **nach Süden/der Straße liegen** to face south/the road; **das Haus liegt ganz ruhig** the house is in a very quiet position *or* location; **das liegt doch ganz in der Nähe** it's quite close; **das liegt doch auf dem Weg** it's on the way; **einen Ort links/rechts liegen lassen** to pass by a place

e = einen bestimmten Rang haben to be; **auf den hintersten Plätzen/in Führung/an der Spitze liegen** to be at the bottom/in the lead/right out in front; **der zweite Läufer liegt weit hinter dem ersten** the second runner is a long way behind the first

f = lasten **auf dieser Familie scheint ein Fluch zu liegen** there seems to be a curse on this family; **die Verantwortung/Schuld dafür liegt bei ihm** the responsibility/blame for that lies *or* rests with him; **die Schuld liegt schwer auf mir** my guilt weighs heavily on me; **damit liegt die ganze Arbeit auf mir** that means all the work falls on me; **die Entscheidung liegt beim Volk/bei Ihnen** the decision rests with the people/with you; **das liegt ganz bei dir** that is completely up to you; **es liegt in seiner Gewalt, das zu tun** it is *or* lies within his power to do that

g = geeignet sein, passen **das liegt mir/ihm nicht** it doesn't suit me/him; *(Beruf)* it doesn't appeal to me/him; *(jds Art)* I don't/he doesn't like it; *(Mathematik etc)* I have/he has no aptitude for it; **Krankenschwester liegt mir nicht** *(inf)* nursing doesn't appeal to me; **diese Rolle liegt ihr** this part is perfect for her

h Redewendungen

♦ **liegen an es liegt mir viel daran** (= *ist mir wichtig*) that matters a lot to me, that is important to me; **es liegt mir wenig/nichts daran** that doesn't matter much/at all to me, that isn't very important/isn't at all important to me; **es liegt mir viel an ihm/an meinem Beruf** he/my job is very important to me *or* matters a lot to me; **mir liegt an einer schnellen Fertigstellung des Hauses** I am concerned that the house should be finished quickly; **was liegt (dir) schon daran?** what does it matter (to you)?; **an jdm/etw liegen** (= *als Grund haben*) to be because of sb/sth; **woran liegt es?** why is that?; **das liegt daran, dass ...** that is because...; **an mir soll es nicht liegen!** I'll go along with that; **an mir soll es nicht liegen, dass** *or* **wenn die Sache schiefgeht** it won't be my fault if things go wrong

lie|gen+blei|ben VI *sep irreg aux sein* = **liegen bleiben b-f**

lie|gen blei|ben VI *irreg aux sein* **a** (= *nicht aufstehen*) to remain lying (down); **(im Bett) ~** to stay in bed; **er blieb bewusstlos auf dem Boden liegen** he lay unconscious on the floor; **bleib liegen!** don't get up!, stay down! **b** (= *vergessen werden*) to be *or* get left behind; **mein Schirm muss irgendwo liegen geblieben sein** I must have left my umbrella somewhere **c** (= *nicht verkauft werden*) not to sell, to be left unsold; **wenn uns diese Sachen ~** if we are left with these things (on our hands) **d** (= *nicht ausgeführt werden*) to get *or* be left (undone), not to get done **e** (= *auf einer Stelle bleiben*) to lie about; *(Schnee)* to lie **f** *(Auto)* to conk out *(inf)*

lie|gend ADJ *(Art)* reclining; **~e Güter** immovable property *sing (form)*, real estate ADV **a** (= *flach*) **~ aufbewahren** to store flat; *Flasche etc* to store on its side **b** (= *im Liegen*) while lying down

Lie|gen|de(r) ['li:gndə] MF *decl as adj (Art)* reclining figure

lie|gen las|sen *ptp* **liegen lassen** *or (rare)* **liegen gelassen** *irreg*, **lie|gen+las|sen** *ptp* **liegenlassen** *or (rare)* **liegengelassen** *sep irreg* VT (= *nicht erledigen*) to leave; (= *vergessen*) to leave (behind); (= *herumliegen lassen*) to leave lying about *or* around; **sie hat alles liegen gelassen, um dem Kind zu helfen** she dropped everything to (go and) help the child → **links ADV a, stehen lassen**

Lie|gen|schaft ['li:gnʃaft] F **-, -en**, **Lie|gen|schaf|ten** PL real estate *sing*, property *sing*

Lie|ge-: **Lie|ge|platz** M place to lie; *(auf Schiff, in Zug etc)* berth; (= *Ankerplatz*) moorings *pl*; *(von großem Schiff)* berth; **Lie|ge|rad** NT (= *Fahrrad*) recumbent (bike); **Lie|ge|sitz** M reclining seat; *(auf Boot)* couchette; **Lie|ge|statt** F *pl* **-stätten** [-ʃtɛtn] *(old, dial)* bed; **Lie|ge|stuhl** M *(mit Holzgestell)* deck chair; *(mit Metallgestell)* lounger *(Brit)*, lounge chair *(US)*; **Lie|ge|stütz** [-ʃtʏts] M **-es, -e** *(Sport)* press-up *(Brit)*, push-up *(US)*; **~e machen** to do press-ups *(Brit) or* push-ups *(US)*; **in den ~!** press-ups! *(Brit)*, push-ups! *(US)*; **Lie|ge|wa|gen** M *(Rail)* couchette coach *or* car *(esp US)*; **~ buchen** to book a couchette; **Lie|ge|wie|se** F lawn *(for sunbathing)*; **Lie|ge|zeit** F **a** *(Naut)* lay days *pl (form)* **b** rest period

lieh *pret von* **leihen**

Liek [li:k] NT **-(e)s, -en** *(Naut)* boltrope

lies [li:s] IMPER *sing von* **lesen**

Lies|chen ['li:sçən] NT **-s, -** Liz(zie); **~ Müller** *(inf)* the average woman in the street → **fleißig ADJ a, lieb ADJ d**

ließ *pret von* **lassen**

liest [li:st] *3. pers sing pres von* **lesen**

Life|style ['laifstail] M **-s, -s** lifestyle

Life|style|dro|ge F lifestyle drug

Lift [lɪft] M **-(e)s, -e** *or* **-s** (= *Personenlift*) lift *(Brit)*, elevator *(esp US)*; (= *Güterlift*) lift *(Brit)*, hoist; (= *Skilift*) ski lift

Lift|boy ['lɪftbɔy] M liftboy *(Brit)*, elevator boy *(US)*

lif|ten ['lɪftn] VT to lift; **sich** *(dat)* **das Gesicht ~ lassen** to have a face-lift

Lift-off [lɪft'ɔf] M **-(s), -s** liftoff

Li|ga ['li:ga] F **-, Li|gen** [-gn] league

Li|ga|tur [liga'tu:ɐ] F **-, -en** ligature; *(Mus*: = *Verbindung zweier Noten)* tie

light [lait] ADJ *pred inv* **a** light; **Limo ~** diet lemonade, low calorie lemonade **b** (*iro*: = *seicht*) lightweight

Light- [lait] *in cpds* light, lite; (= *kalorienarm auch*) low-calorie, diet *attr*

Lightpen ['laitpɛn] M **-s, -s** light pen

Lig|nin [lɪ'gni:n] NT **-s, -e** lignin(e)

Li|gus|ter [li'gʊstɐ] M **-s, -** privet

li|ie|ren [li'i:rən] *ptp* **liiert** VT to bring *or* get together; *Firmen etc* to get to work together; **liiert sein** to have joined forces; *(Firmen etc)* to be working together; *(Pol)* to be allied; (= *ein Verhältnis haben*) to have a relationship VR to join forces; *(Firmen etc)* to work together; *(Pol)* to enter into an alliance; (= *ein Verhältnis eingehen*) to get together, to form a liaison

Li|kör [li'kø:ɐ] M **-s, -e** liqueur

li|la ['li:la] ADJ *inv* purple

Li|la ['li:la] NT **-s** *(inf)* **-s** purple

Li|lie ['li:liə] F **-, -n** lily; **keusch wie eine ~** as pure as the driven snow

Li|li|put- ['li:lipʊt] *in cpds* miniature; **eine Liliputeisenbahn** a miniature railway; **im Liliputformat** in miniature

Li|li|pu|ta|ner [lilipu'ta:nɐ] M **-s, -**, **Li|li|pu|ta|ne|rin** [-ərɪn] F **-, -nen** dwarf, midget; (= *Bewohner von Liliput*) Lilliputian

Lim|bo ['lɪmbo] M **-s, -s** limbo

Lim|bur|ger (Kä|se) ['lɪmbʊrgɐ] M **-s, -** Limburger, Limburg cheese

Li|me|rick ['lɪmərɪk] M **-(s), -s** limerick

Li|mes ['li:mɛs] M **-, -** **a** *no pl (Hist)* limes **b** *(Math)* limit

Li|met|te [li'mɛtə] F **-, -n** sweet lime

Li|mit ['lɪmɪt] NT **-s, -s** *or* **-e** limit; *(Fin)* ceiling; **jdm ein ~ setzen** to set sb a limit

li|mi|tie|ren [limi'ti:rən] *ptp* **limitiert** VT *(form)* to limit; *(Fin)* to put a ceiling on; **nicht limitiert** unlimited, open-ended; **eine streng limitierte Auflage** a strictly limited edition

Li|mo ['lɪmo, 'li:mo] F **-, -s** *(inf)* = **Limonade**

Li|mo|na|de [limo'na:də] F **-, -n** lemonade; *(in weiterem Sinn)* soft drink

Li|mo|ne [li'mo:nə] F **-, -n** lime

Li|mou|si|ne [limu'zi:nə] F -, -n saloon *(Brit)*, sedan *(US)*

lind [lɪnt] ADJ *(liter)* balmy; *Regen* gentle ADV **a** *(liter: = mild)* gently **b** *(Sw)* ~ **(gewürzt)** lightly spiced; ~ **gewürzter Käse** mild cheese

Lin|dan [lɪn'da:n] NT - lindane

Lin|de ['lɪndə] F -, -n *(= Baum)* linden *or* lime (tree); *(= Holz)* limewood

Lin|den|blü|ten|tee M lime blossom tea

lin|dern ['lɪndɐn] VT to ease, to relieve, to alleviate; *Hustenreiz, Sonnenbrand etc auch* to soothe

Lin|de|rung ['lɪndərʊŋ] F -, -en easing, relief, alleviation; *(von Hustenreiz, Sonnenbrand etc auch)* soothing

Lin|de|rungs|mit|tel NT pain reliever, analgesic

Lind-: **lind|grün** ADJ lime green; **Lind|wurm** M *(Myth)* lindworm *(type of wingless dragon)*

Li|ne|al [line'a:l] NT -s, -e ruler; **einen Strich mit dem ~ ziehen** to rule a line *(esp Brit)*, to draw a line with a ruler; **er geht, als ob er ein ~ verschluckt hätte** *(inf)* he walks with his back as stiff as a ramrod

li|ne|ar [line'a:ɐ] ADJ linear; **~e Abschreibung** *(Fin)* straight-line depreciation ADV linearly

Li|ne|ar|be|schleu|ni|ger M *(Phys)* linear accelerator

Li|ne|ar|schrift F linear script; ~ **B** Linear B

Li|ne|a|tur [linea'tu:ɐ] F -, -en ruling, lines *pl*

Li|ner ['lainɐ] M -s, - *(Naut)* liner

Lin|ge|rie [lɛ̃ʒə'ri:] F -, -n *(Sw)* lingerie

lin|gu|al [lɪŋ'gua:l] ADJ *(form)* lingual

Lin|gu|ist [lɪŋ'guɪst] M -en, -en, **Lin|gu|is|tin** [-'guɪstɪn] F -, -nen linguist

Lin|gu|is|tik [lɪŋ'guɪstɪk] F -, *no pl* linguistics *sing*

lin|gu|is|tisch [lɪŋ'guɪstɪʃ] ADJ linguistic ADV linguistically; ~ **interessiert** interested in linguistics

Li|ni|a|tur [linia'tu:ɐ] F -, -en ruling, lines *pl*

Li|nie ['li:niə] ✪ 53.5 F -, -n **a** line *(auch Sport, Pol, Naut)*; *(= Umriss)* (out)line; **ein Schreibblock mit ~n** a ruled *(esp Brit) or* lined notepad; **die ~n (in) seiner Hand** the lines of *or* on his hand; **in einer ~ stehen** to be in a line; **sich in einer ~ aufstellen** to line up; **die Buchstaben halten nicht ~** *(Typ)* the letters are not in line; **auf der gleichen ~** along the same lines; **einer Sache** *(dat)* **fehlt die klare ~** there's no clear line to sth; **eine klare ~ für sein Leben finden, seinem Leben eine klare ~ geben** to give one's life a clear sense of direction; **eine ~ ziehen zwischen ...** *(+dat) (fig)* to draw a distinction between ...; **auf der ganzen ~** *(fig)* all along the line; **auf ~ bleiben** *(fig)* to toe the line; **sie hat ein Gesicht mit klaren/verschwommenen ~n** she has clear-cut/ill-defined features; **auf die (schlanke) ~ achten** to watch one's figure; **in direkter ~ von jdm abstammen** to be a direct descendant of sb; **die männliche/weibliche ~ eines Geschlechts** the male/female line of a family; **in erster/zweiter ~ kommen** *(fig)* to come first/second, to take first/second place; **in erster ~ muss die Arbeitslosigkeit bekämpft werden** the fight against unemployment must come first *or* must take priority → **erste(r, s) a**

b *(Mil) (= Stellung)* line; *(= Formation)* rank; **in ~ antreten!** fall in!; **in ~ zu drei Gliedern** in ranks three deep; **die feindliche/vorderste ~** the enemy lines *pl*/front line

c *(= Verkehrsverbindung, -strecke)* route; *(= Buslinie, Eisenbahnlinie)* line, route; **fahren Sie mit der ~ 2** take a *or* the (number) 2; **auf einer ~ verkehren** to work a route; **die ~ Köln-Bonn** the Cologne-Bonn line

Li|ni|en-: **Li|ni|en|ball** M *(Tennis)* ball (right) on the line; **Li|ni|en|blatt** NT ruled *(esp Brit) or* lined sheet *(placed under writing paper)*, line guide; **Li|ni|en|bus** M public service bus, regular bus; **Li|ni|en|dampf|er** M regular service steamer; **Li|ni|en|dienst** M regular service; *(Aviat)* scheduled service; **Li|ni|en|flug** M scheduled flight; **Li|ni|en|flug|zeug** NT scheduled (service) plane; **Li|ni|en|füh|rung** F **a** *(Art etc)* lines *pl* **b** *(von Bus etc)* route; **Li|ni|en|ma|schi|ne** F scheduled flight; **mit einer ~** on a scheduled flight; **Li|ni|en|netz** NT network of routes; **das ~ der U-Bahn** the underground *(Brit) or* subway *(US)* (system); **das ~ der Straßenbahnen** the tram *(esp Brit) or* streetcar *(US)* system; **Li|ni|en|pa|pier** NT ruled *(esp Brit) or* lined paper; **Li|ni|en|rich|ter** M *(Sport)* linesman; *(Tennis)* line judge; **Li|ni|en|rich|te|rin** F *(Sport)* lineswoman; *(Tennis)* line judge; **Li|ni|en|schiff** NT regular service ship; **li|ni|en|treu** ADJ loyal to the party line; **~ sein** to follow *or* toe the party line; **Li|ni|en|treue** F loyalty to the party line; **Li|ni|en|ver|kehr** M regular traffic; *(Aviat)* scheduled traffic; **im ~ fliegen** to fly on scheduled services; **im ~ fahren** to operate on regular services

li|nie|ren [li'ni:rən] *ptp* **liniert**, **li|ni|ie|ren** [lini'i:rən] *ptp* **liniiert** VT to rule, to rule *(esp Brit) or* draw lines on; **lini(i)ert** lined, feint *(spec)*

Li|nie|rung F -, -en, **Li|ni|ie|rung** F -, -en ruling

link [lɪŋk] *(inf)* ADJ *Typ* underhanded, double-crossing; *Masche, Tour* dirty, low-down *(US inf)*; **ein ganz ~er Hund** *(pej)* a nasty piece of work *(pej inf)*; **ein ganz ~es Ding drehen** to get up to a bit of no good *(inf)* ADV **jdn ~ behandeln, sich jdm gegenüber ~ verhalten** to mess *(Brit) or* jerk *(esp US)* sb around *(inf)*; **komm mir nicht so ~** stop messing *(Brit) or* jerking *(esp US)* me around *(inf)*

Link M -s, -s *(Comput)* link

Lin|ke ['lɪŋkə] F *decl as adj* **a** *(Hand)* left hand; *(Seite)* left(-hand) side; *(Boxen)* left; **zur ~n (des Königs) saß ...** to the left (of the king) *or* on the (king's) left sat ... **b** *(Pol)* **die ~** the Left

lin|ken ['lɪŋkn] VT *(inf: = hereinlegen)* to con *(inf)*

Lin|ke(r) ['lɪŋkə] MF *decl as adj (Pol)* left-winger, leftist *(pej)*, lefty *(pej inf)*

lin|ke(r, s) ['lɪŋkə] ADJ *attr* **a** left; *Rand, Spur etc* left(-hand); **die ~ Seite** the left(-hand) side; *(von Stoff)* the wrong side, the reverse (side); **auf der ~n Seite** on the left-hand side, on the left; **~r Hand, zur ~n Hand** to the left, on the left, on one's left; **~ Masche** *(Stricken)* purl (stitch); **eine ~ Masche stricken** to purl one; **zwei ~ Hände haben** *(inf)* to have two left hands *(inf)*; **das mache ich mit der ~n Hand** *(inf)* I can do that with my eyes shut *(inf)*; **er ist heute mit dem ~n Bein** *or* **Fuß zuerst aufgestanden** *(inf)* he got out of bed on the wrong side this morning *(inf)*

b *(Pol)* left-wing, leftist *(pej)*, lefty *(pej inf)*; *Flügel* left

lin|ker|seits ['lɪŋkɐzaits] ADV to the left, on the left-hand side

lin|kisch ['lɪŋkɪʃ] ADJ clumsy, awkward ADV clumsily, awkwardly; *tanzen, begrüßen* awkwardly

links [lɪŋks] ADV **a** on the left; *schauen, abbiegen* (to the) left; **nach ~** (to the) left; **von ~** from the left; **~ von etw** (to the *or* on the) left of sth; **~ von jdm** to *or* on sb's left; **sich ~ halten** to keep to the left; **weiter ~** further to the left; **sich ~ einordnen** to move into *or* take the left-hand lane; **jdn ~ liegen lassen** *(fig inf)* to ignore sb; **weder ~ noch rechts schauen** *(lit)* to look neither left nor right; *(fig)* not to let oneself be distracted; **~ von der Mitte** *(Pol)* (to the) left of centre *(Brit) or* center *(US)*; **~ stehen** *or* **sein** *(Pol)* to be left-wing *or* on the left *or* a left-winger; **mit ~** *(inf)* just like that, without any trouble; **das mache ich mit ~** *(inf)* I can do that with my eyes shut *(inf)*; **Augen ~!** *(Mil)* eyes left!; **~ um!** *(Mil)* left about turn; **~ schwenkt, marsch!** *(Mil)* left wheel!

b *(= verkehrt) bügeln* on the reverse *or* wrong side; *tragen* reverse *or* wrong side out; *liegen* reverse *or* wrong side up; **~ stricken** to purl; **eine (Masche) ~, drei (Maschen) rechts** purl one, knit three; **der Pullover ist nur ~ gestrickt** the pullover is knitted all in purl

PREP *+gen* on *or* to the left of

Links-: **Links|ab|bie|ger** [-lapbi:gɐ] M -s, - *(= Spur)* left-hand turn-off lane; **Links|ab|bie|ger** [-lapbi:gɐ] M -s, -, **Links|ab|bie|ge|rin** [-ərɪn] F -, -nen motorist/cyclist/car *etc* turning left; **Links|ab|bie|ger|spur** F left-hand turn-off lane; **Links|ab|weich|ler(in)** M(F) *(Pol inf)* left-wing dissenter; **Links|au|ßen** [-'lausn] M -, - *(Ftbl)* outside left; *(Pol)* extreme left-winger; **links|bün|dig** ADJ *(Typ)* ranged *or* flush left, left-aligned; *(Comput: als Option)* align left ADV flush left; **Links|drall** M *(lit) (im Gewehrlauf)* anticlockwise rifling *(Brit)*, counterclockwise rifling *(US)*; *(von Geschoss, Billardball)* swerve to the left; *(von Auto, Pferd)* pull to the left; *(fig)* leaning to the left; **einen ~ haben** to swerve/pull/lean to the left; **links|dre|hend** ADJ *(Chem)* laevorotatory *(Brit spec)*, levorotatory *(US spec)*; **Links|dre|hung** F anticlockwise rotation, counter-rotation *(US)*; **Links|ext|re|mist(in)** M(F) left-wing extremist; **Links|gang** M *pl* **-gänge** *(Tech)* left-handed thread; **links|gän|gig** ADJ *(Tech)* left-handed; **links|ge|richtet** [-gərɪçtət] ADJ *(Pol)* left-wing; **Links|ge|win|de** NT left-handed thread; **Links|ha|ken** M left hook; **Links|hän|der** [-hendɐ] M -s, -, **Links|hän|de|rin** [-ərɪn] F -, -nen left-hander, left-handed person; **~ sein** to be left-handed; **links|hän|dig** ADJ ADV left-handed; **Links|hän|dig|keit** F -, *no pl* left-handedness; **links|her** ['lɪŋkshe:ɐ] ADV *(old)* from the left; **links|he|ran** ['lɪŋksheran] ADV over to the left; **links|he|rum** ['lɪŋksherʊm] ADV (round) to the left; *sich drehen etc* anticlockwise *(Brit)*, counterclockwise *(US)*; **links|hin** ['lɪŋkshɪn] ADV *(old)* (to the) left; **Links|in|tel|lek|tu|el|le(r)** MF *decl as adj* left-wing intellectual; **Links|kur|ve** F *(von Straße)* left-hand bend; *(von Bahn auch)* left-hand curve; **links|las|tig** [-lastɪç] ADJ *(lit) Boot* listing to the left; *Auto* down at the left; *(fig)* leftist *(pej)*, leaning to the left; **links|läu|fig** ADJ *Gewinde* left-handed; *Schrift* right-to-left; **Links|par|tei** F left-wing party; **links|ra|di|kal** ADJ *(Pol)* radically left-wing; **die Linksradikalen** the left-wing radicals ADV **~ eingestellt sein** to be a left-wing radical; **~ klingen** to sound radically left-wing; **Links|ra|di|ka|lis|mus** M *(Pol)* left-wing radicalism; **links|rhei|nisch** ADJ, ADV to *or* on the left of the Rhine; **Links|ruck** M, **Links|rutsch** M *(Pol)* shift to the left; **links|rum** ['lɪŋksrʊm] ADV *(inf)* = **linksherum**; **Links|schwenk** M = **Linksruck**; **links|sei|tig** [-zaitɪç] ADJ, ADV on the left(-hand) side; **~ gelähmt** paralyzed on the left side; **~ blind** blind in the left eye; **er war ~ amputiert** his left arm/leg was amputated; **Links|steu|e|rung** F *(Mot)* left-hand drive; **links|um** [lɪŋks'lʊm, 'lɪŋkslʊm] ADV *(Mil)* to the left; **~ machen** *(inf)* to do a left turn; **~ kehrt!** to the left about turn!; **Links|ver|kehr** M, *no pl* driving on the left *no def art*; **in Großbritannien ist ~** they drive on the left in Britain; **im ~ muss man ...** when driving on the left one must ...

lin|nen ['lɪnən] ADJ *(liter)* = **leinen**

Lin|nen ['lɪnən] NT -s, - *(liter)* linen

Li|no|le|um [li'no:leʊm] NT -s, *no pl* linoleum, lino

Li|nol-: **Li|nol|säu|re** F linoleic acid; **Li|nol|schnitt** M *(Art)* linocut

Li|non [li:'nõ:] M -(s), -s *(Tex)* lawn

Lin|se ['lɪnzə] F -, -n **a** *(Bot, Cook)* lentil **b** *(Opt)* lens

lin|sen ['lɪnzn] VI *(inf)* to peep, to peek *(inf)*; *(Sch)* to copy *(bei* off, from)

Lin|sen-: **Lin|sen|ge|richt** NT lentil dish; *(Bibl, fig)* mess of potage; **Lin|sen|sup|pe** F lentil soup; **Lin|sen|trü|bung** F *(Med)* cataract

Lip|gloss ['lɪpglɔs] NT -, - lip gloss

Lip|pe ['lɪpə] F -, -n lip; *(Bot auch)* labium; **eine (große** *or* **dicke) ~ riskieren** *(inf)* to be brazen;

das bringe ich nicht über die ~n I can't bring myself to say it; **es wird** *or* **soll kein Wort über meine ~n kommen** not a word shall cross *or* pass my lips; **er brachte kein Wort über die ~n** he couldn't say *or* utter a word; **das Wort erstarb ihm auf den ~n** *(liter)* the word froze on his lips; **von den ~n lesen** to read lips → **hängen 1 d, beißen VR**

Lip|pen-: **Lip|pen|bal|sam** M lip balm; **Lip|pen|be|kennt|nis** NT lip service; **ein ~ ablegen** to pay lip service (to one's ideals *etc*); **Lip|pen|blüt|ler** [-bly:tlɐ] M **-s, -** *(Bot)* labiate; **Lip|pen|laut** M *(Ling)* labial; **Lip|pen|pfle|ge|stift** M lip salve (stick) *(Brit)*, chapstick®; **Lip|pen|stift** M lipstick

li|quid [li'kvi:t] ADJ = **liquide**

Li|qui|da ['li:kvida] F **-, Liquidä** *or* **Liquiden** [-dɛ:, li'kvi:dn] *(Ling)* liquid

Li|qui|da|ti|on [likvida'tsio:n] F **-, -en** *(form)* **a** *(= Auflösung)* liquidation; **in ~ treten** to go into liquidation; **sie haben die ~ beschlossen** they decided to go into liquidation **b** *(= Rechnung)* account

Li|qui|da|ti|ons|wert M *(Fin)* net asset value, break-up value

Li|qui|da|tor [likvi'da:to:ɐ] M **-s, Liquidatoren** [-'to:rən], **Li|qui|da|to|rin** [-'to:rɪn] F **-, -nen** *(Fin)* liquidator

li|qui|de [li'kvi:də] ADJ *(Econ) Geld, Mittel* liquid; *Firma, Geschäftsmann* solvent; **ich bin nicht ~** *(inf)* I'm out of funds *(inf)*, I'm short of the readies *(Brit inf)*

li|qui|die|ren [likvi'di:rən] *ptp* **liquidiert** VT **a** *Geschäft* to put into liquidation, to wind up; *Betrag* to charge; **einen Kontrakt in bar ~** to settle a contract in cash **b** *Firma* to liquidate; *jdn* to eliminate

Li|qui|die|rung F **-, -en** *(von Firma)* liquidation; *(von Person)* elimination

Li|qui|di|tät [likvidi'tɛ:t] F **-,** *no pl (Econ)* liquidity

lis|men ['lɪsmən] VTI *(Sw)* to knit

lis|peln ['lɪspln] VTI to lisp; *(= flüstern)* to whisper

Lis|sa|bon ['lɪsabɔn, lɪsa'bɔn] NT **-s** Lisbon

Lis|sa|bon|ner ['lɪsabɔnɐ, lɪsa'bɔnɐ] ADJ *attr* Lisbon

Lis|sa|bon|ner ['lɪsabɔnɐ, lɪsa'bɔnɐ] M **-s, -, Lis|sa|bon|ne|rin** [-ərɪn] F **-, -nen** native of Lisbon; *(Einwohner)* inhabitant of Lisbon

List [lɪst] F **-, -en** *(= Täuschung)* cunning, artfulness; *(= trickreicher Plan)* trick, ruse; **mit ~ und Tücke** *(inf)* with a lot of coaxing; **zu einer ~ greifen, (eine) ~ anwenden** to use a bit of cunning, to resort to a ruse

Lis|te ['lɪstə] F **-, -n** *(= Aufstellung)* list; *(= Wählerliste)* register; *(von Parteien)* (party) list *(of candidates under the proportional representation system)*; **sich in eine ~ eintragen** *or* **(ein)schreiben** to put oneself *or* one's name (down) on a list

Lis|ten-: **Lis|ten|feld** NT *(Comput)* list box; **Lis|ten|füh|rer(in)** M(F) list keeper; **Lis|ten|platz** M *(Pol)* place on the party list *(of candidates under the proportional representation system)*; **Lis|ten|preis** M list price; **Lis|ten|wahl** F *electoral system in which a vote is cast for a party rather than a specific candidate*

lis|tig ['lɪstɪç] ADJ cunning, crafty, wily *no adv* ADV cunningly

lis|ti|ger|wei|se ['lɪstɪgɐ'vaizə] ADV cunningly, craftily

Li|ta|nei [lita'nai] F **-, -en** *(Eccl, fig)* litany; **eine ~ von Klagen/Beschwerden** *etc* a long list *or* catalogue *(Brit) or* catalog *(US)* of complaints; **immer dieselbe ~ beten** to go on about the same old things all the time *(inf)*

Li|tau|en ['li:tauən, 'lɪtauən] NT **-s** Lithuania

Li|tau|er ['li:tauɐ, 'lɪtauɐ] M **-s, -, Li|tau|e|rin** [-ərɪn] F **-, -nen** Lithuanian

li|tau|isch ['li:tauɪʃ, 'lɪtauɪʃ] ADJ Lithuanian

Li|tau|isch(e) NT *(Ling)* Lithuanian → *auch* **Deutsch(e)**

Li|ter ['li:tɐ, 'lɪtɐ] M OR NT **-s, -** litre *(Brit)*, liter *(US)*

li|te|rar|his|to|risch [lɪtəˈra:ɐ-] ADJ literary historical *attr*; *Buch, Artikel auch* relating to literary history ADV from a literary historical point of view; **~ interessant** of interest to literary history

li|te|ra|risch [lɪtə'ra:rɪʃ] ADJ literary ADV **~ gebildet/informiert sein** to be knowledgeable in literature; **~ interessiert** interested in literature

Li|te|rat [lɪtə'ra:t] M **-en, -en** man of letters; *(= Schriftsteller)* literary figure; **die ~en** the literati *(form)*

Li|te|ra|tin [lɪtə'ra:tɪn] F **-, -nen** woman of letters; *(= Schriftstellerin)* literary figure

Li|te|ra|tur [lɪtəra'tu:ɐ] F **-, -en** literature

Li|te|ra|tur-: **Li|te|ra|tur|an|ga|be** F bibliographical reference; *(Zusammenfassung)* bibliography; **Li|te|ra|tur|be|trieb** M, *no pl* literary scene; **Li|te|ra|tur|denk|mal** NT literary monument; **Li|te|ra|tur|gat|tung** F literary genre; **Li|te|ra|tur|ge|schich|te** F history of literature; **li|te|ra|tur|ge|schicht|lich** ADJ, ADV = **literarhistorisch**; **Li|te|ra|tur|hin|weis** M literary reference *(auf +acc* to); **Li|te|ra|tur|kri|tik** F literary criticism; *(= Kritikerschaft)* literary critics *pl*; **Li|te|ra|tur|kri|ti|ker(in)** M(F) literary critic; **Li|te|ra|tur|nach|weis** M bibliographical reference; *(Zusammenfassung)* bibliography; **Li|te|ra|tur|papst** M, **Li|te|ra|tur|päps|tin** F literary pundit; **Li|te|ra|tur|preis** M prize *or* award for literature, literary prize *or* award; **Li|te|ra|tur|ver|zeich|nis** NT bibliography; **Li|te|ra|tur|wis|sen|schaft** F literary studies *pl*; **vergleichende ~** comparative literature; **Li|te|ra|tur|wis|sen|schaft|ler(in)** M(F) literary *or* literature specialist

Li|ter-: **Li|ter|fla|sche** F litre *(Brit) or* liter *(US)* bottle; **Li|ter|leis|tung** F power output per litre *(Brit) or* liter *(US)*; **Li|ter|maß** NT litre *(Brit) or* liter *(US)* measure; **li|ter|wei|se** ADV *(lit)* by the litre *(Brit) or* liter *(US)*; *(fig)* by the gallon

Lit|faß|säu|le ['lɪtfas-] F advertisement pillar

Li|thi|um ['li:tiʊm] NT **-s,** *no pl (abbr* **Li)** lithium

Li|tho ['li:to] NT **-s, -s** *(inf) abbr von* **Lithografie**

Li|tho-: **Li|tho|graf** [lito'gra:f] M **-en, -en**, **Li|tho|gra|fin** [-'gra:fɪn] F **-, -nen** lithographer; **Li|tho|gra|fie** [litogra'fi:] F **-, -n** [-'fi:ən] **a** *(Verfahren)* lithography **b** *(Druck)* lithograph; **li|tho|gra|fie|ren** [litogra'fi:rən] *ptp* **lithografiert** VT to lithograph; **li|tho|gra|fisch** [lito'grafɪʃ] ADJ lithographic(al); **Li|tho|graph** [lito'gra:f] *etc* = **Lithograf** *etc*

Li|to|tes [li'to:tɛs] F **-, -** *(Liter)* litotes

Lit|schi ['lɪtʃi] F **-, -s** lychee, litchi

litt *ptp von* **leiden**

Li|tur|gie [litʊr'gi:] F **-, -n** [-'gi:ən] liturgy

li|tur|gisch [li'tʊrgɪʃ] ADJ liturgical

Lit|ze ['lɪtsə] F **-, -n** braid; *(Elec)* flex

live [laif] ADJ *pred* ADV *(Rad, TV)* live; **wir konnten ~ dabei sein** we were able to see everything live; **„live im ZDF"** "live on ZDF"

Live-: **Live|be|richt** [laif-] M *(Sport)* live commentary; *(= Reportage)* on-the-spot report; **das war ein Livebericht von X in Basra** that was X reporting live from Basra; **Live|mit|schnitt** ['laifmɪtʃnɪt] M live recording; **Live|mu|sik** [laif-] F live music; **Live|sen|dung** [laif-] F live programme *(Brit) or* program *(US)*, live broadcast; **Live|über|tra|gung** [laif-] F live transmission

Liv|ree [li'vre:] F **-, -n** [-'re:ən] livery

liv|riert [li'vri:ɐt] ADJ liveried

Li|zenz [li'tsɛnts] F **-, -en** licence *(Brit)*, license *(US)*; **eine ~ dafür haben, etw zu tun** to have a licence *(Brit) or* license *(US)* to do sth, to be licensed to do sth; **etw in ~ herstellen** to manufacture sth under licence *(Brit) or* license *(US)*

Li|zenz-: **Li|zenz|ab|ga|be** F licence *(Brit) or* license *(US)* fee; *(im Verlagswesen)* royalty; **Li|zenz|ab|kom|men** NT licensing agreement; **Li|zenz|aus|ga|be** F licensed edition; **Li|zenz|ge|ber(in)** M(F) licenser; *(Behörde)* licensing authority; **Li|zenz|ge|bühr** F licence *(Brit) or* license *(US)* fee; *(im Verlagswesen)* royalty

li|zen|zie|ren [litsɛn'tsi:rən] *ptp* **lizenziert** VT *(form)* to license

Li|zenz-: **Li|zenz|in|ha|ber(in)** M(F) licensee, licence *(Brit) or* license *(US)* holder; **er ist ~** he has a licence *(Brit) or* license *(US)*, he is licensed; **Li|zenz|neh|mer(in)** M(F) licensee; **Li|zenz|pres|se** F *(Pol)* licensed press; **Li|zenz|spie|ler(in)** M(F) *(Ftbl)* professional player; **Li|zenz|trä|ger(in)** M(F) licensee

Lkw M, **LKW** ['ɛlka:ve:, ɛlka:'ve:] M **-(s), -(s)** *abbr von* **Lastkraftwagen**

Lkw-Maut F, **LKW-Maut** F lorry toll *(Brit)*, truck toll *(US)*

Lob [lo:p] NT **-(e)s** [-bəs], *no pl* praise; *(= Belobigung)* commendation; **~ verdienen** to deserve praise, to deserve to be praised; **(viel) ~ für etw bekommen** to come in for (a lot of) praise for sth, to be (highly) praised for sth; **(über jdn/etw) des ~es voll sein** *(geh)* to be full of praise (for sb/sth); **ein ~ der Köchin** (my/our) compliments to the chef!; **den Schülern wurde für ihre hervorragenden Leistungen ein ~ erteilt** the pupils were commended for their outstanding achievements; **Gott sei ~ und Dank** praise be to God, God be praised; **zum ~e Gottes** in praise of the Lord; **über jedes ~ erhaben sein** to be beyond praise; **sein eigenes ~ singen** *(inf)* to sing one's own praises, to blow one's own trumpet *(inf)*; **jdm ~ spenden** *or* **zollen** to praise sb

Lob [lo:p] [lɔp] M [-bəs] **-(s), -s** *(Tennis, Volleyball)* lob

lob|ben ['lɔbn] VTI *(Tennis, Volleyball)* to lob

Lob|by ['lɔbɪ] F **-, -s** lobby

Lob|by|is|mus [lɔbi'ɪsmʊs] M **-,** *no pl* lobbyism

Lob|by|ist [lɔbi'ɪst] M **-en, -en**, **Lob|by|is|tin** [-'ɪstɪn] F **-, -nen** lobbyist

Lo|be|lie [lo'be:liə] F **-, -n** *(Bot)* lobelia

lo|ben ['lo:bn] ✪ 40.4 VT to praise; **sein neues Werk wurde allgemein sehr gelobt** his new work was universally acclaimed; **jdn/etw ~d erwähnen** to commend sb/sth; **das lob ich mir** that's what I like (to see/hear *etc*); **seinen Fleiß lob ich mir** his diligence is most laudable; **da lob ich mir doch ein gutes Glas Wein** I always say you can't beat a good glass of wine → **Abend a, Klee**

lo|bens|wert ADJ praiseworthy, laudable ADV praiseworthily, laudably

lo|be|sam ['lo:bəza:m] *(obs)* ADJ virtuous ADV virtuously

Lo|bes|hym|ne F *(fig)* hymn of praise, panegyric

Lob-: **Lob|ge|sang** M song *or* hymn of praise; **einen ~ auf jdn/etw anstimmen** *(fig)* to sing sb's praises/the praises of sth; **Lob|hu|de|lei** [lo:phu:də'lai] F **-, -en** *(pej)* gushing; **lob|hu|deln** ['lo:phu:dln] VI *insep* **jdm ~** *(pej)* to gush over sb *(inf)*

löb|lich ['lø:plɪç] ADJ *(auch iro)* commendable, laudable; **die ~e Ausnahme sein** to be the notable exception

Lob-: **Lob|lied** NT song *or* hymn of praise; **ein ~ auf jdn/etw anstimmen** *or* **singen** *(fig)* to sing sb's praises/the praises of sth; **Lob|preis** M *(liter)* praise *no art*; **lob|prei|sen** *ptp* **lob(ge)priesen** VT *insep (liter)* to praise; *Gott auch* to glorify; **Lob|re|de** F eulogy, panegyric; **eine ~ auf jdn halten** *(lit)* to make a speech in sb's honour *(Brit) or* honor *(US)*; *(fig)* to eulogize *or* extol sb; **sich in ~n über jdn/etw ergehen** to eulogize *or* extol sb/sth; **Lob|red|ner(in)** M(F) *(lit)* speaker; *(fig)* eulogist; **lob|sin|gen** *ptp* **lobgesungen** VI *sep irreg +dat Gott* to praise; *(fig)* to sing the praises of; **Lob|spruch** M eulogy (*über +acc* of), encomium *(form)*; *(Gedicht)* panegyric

Lo|cal-Bus ['lo:kəlbas] **M** *(Comput)* local bus

Loch [lɔx] **NT -(e)s, ⸗er** ['lœçɐ] *(= Öffnung, Lücke, Defizit)* hole; *(in Zahn auch)* cavity; *(in Reifen)* puncture; *(= Luftloch)* gap; *(Billard)* pocket; *(fig inf: = elende Wohnung, Raum)* dump *(inf)*, hole *(inf)*; *(inf: = Kneipe)* dive *(inf)*; *(inf: = Gefängnis)* jug *(inf)*, clink *(inf)*, can *(esp US inf)*; *(vulg: = Vagina)* cunt *(vulg)*, hole *(sl)*; **sich** *(dat)* **ein ~ in den Kopf/ins Knie** *etc* **schlagen** to gash one's head/knee *etc*, to cut one's head/knee *etc* open; **jdm ein ~** *or* **Löcher in den Bauch fragen** *(inf)* to pester the living daylights out of sb (with all one's questions) *(inf)*; **sie redet einem ein ~** *or* **Löcher in den Bauch** *(inf)* she could talk the hind legs off a donkey *(inf)*; **ein ~** *or* **Löcher in die Luft gucken** *or* **starren** *or* **in die Wand stieren** *(inf)* to gaze into space *or* thin air; **in ein ~ fallen** *(fig)* to come off the rails; **ein großes ~ in jds (Geld)beutel** *(acc) or* **Tasche** *(acc)* **reißen** *(inf)* to make a big hole in sb's pocket; **jdn ins ~ stecken** *(inf: = ins Gefängnis)* to put sb in the clink *(inf)* → **pfeifen**

Loch|ei|sen **NT** punch

lo|chen ['lɔxn] **VT** to punch holes/a hole in; *(= perforieren)* to perforate; *Fahrkarte* to punch, to clip; **gelochter Schreibblock** tear-off file pad

Lo|cher ['lɔxɐ] **M -s, -** *(= Gerät)* punch

Lo|cher ['lɔxɐ] **M -s, -, Lo|che|rin** [-ərın] **F -, -nen** punch card operator

lö|che|rig ['lœçərıç] **ADJ** *(lit, fig)* full of holes; **ganz ~ sein** to be full of holes

lö|chern ['lœçɐn] **VT** *(inf)* to pester (to death) with questions *(inf)*; **er löchert mich seit Wochen, wann ...** he's been pestering me for weeks wanting to know when ...

Loch-: **Loch|ka|me|ra** **F** pinhole camera; **Loch|kar|te** **F** punch card; **Loch|kar|ten|ma|schi|ne** **F** punch card machine

löch|rig ['lœçrıç] **ADJ** = **löcherig**

Loch-: **Loch|sä|ge** **F** keyhole saw; **Loch|sti|cke|rei** **F** broderie anglaise; **Loch|strei|fen** **M** (punched) paper tape

Lo|chung ['lɔxʊŋ] **F -, -en** punching; *(= Perforation)* perforation

Loch-: **Loch|ver|stär|ker** **M** paper reinforcement ring; **Loch|zan|ge** **F** punch; **Loch|zie|gel** **M** airbrick *(esp Brit)*

Lo|cke ['lɔkə] **F -, -n** *(Haar)* curl; **~n haben** to have curly hair

Lo|cke **F -, -n** *(Pfeife)* (bird) call

lo|cken ['lɔkn] **VTR** *Haar* to curl; **gelockt** *(Haar)* curly; *Mensch* curly-haired, curly-headed

lo|cken **VT** **a** *Tier* to lure; **die Henne lockte ihre Küken** the hen called to its chicks **b** *jdn* to tempt; *(mit Ortsangabe)* to lure; **es lockt mich in den Süden** I can feel the call of the south; **jdn in einen Hinterhalt ~** to lead *or* lure sb into a trap; **das Angebot lockt mich sehr** I'm very tempted by the offer → **Falle a, Tasche b**

lö|cken ['lœkn] **VI** **wider den Stachel ~** *(geh)* to kick against the pricks *(Brit liter)*, to oppose authority

lo|ckend **ADJ** tempting, enticing, alluring

Lo|cken-: **Lo|cken|kopf** **M** curly hairstyle; *(Mensch)* curly-head; **Lo|cken|pracht** **F** (magnificent) head of curls; **Lo|cken|sche|re** **F** curling tongs *pl (Brit)*, curling iron *(US)*; **Lo|cken|stab** **M** (electric) curling tongs *pl (Brit)*, (electric) curling iron *(US)*; **Lo|cken|wi|ckel** **M**, **Lo|cken|wick|ler** [-vıklɐ] **M -s, -** (hair) curler; **das Haar auf ~ drehen** to put one's hair in curlers

lo|cker ['lɔkɐ] **ADJ** *(lit, fig)* loose; *Schnee, Erdreich auch* loose-packed; *Kuchen, Schaum* light; *(= nicht gespannt)* slack; *Haltung, Sitzweise, Muskulatur* relaxed; *(inf: = liberal, unkompliziert)* laid-back *(inf)*; **~ werden** *(lit, fig)* to get loose; *(Muskeln, Mensch)* to loosen up; *(Seil)* to get *or* go slack; *(Verhältnis)* to get more relaxed; *(Kuchen)* to be light; **eine ~e Hand haben** *(fig: = schnell zuschlagen)* to be quick to hit out; *(beim Schreiben)* to have a flowing hand; **ein ~er Vogel** *(inf) or* **Zeisig** *(dated inf)* a bit of a lad *(inf) or* rake *(dated)*, a gay dog *(dated)* → **Mundwerk, Schraube a**

ADV **a** *(= nicht stramm)* loosely; **etw ~ machen** to loosen sth; *Seil etc* to slacken sth; **etw ~ lassen** to slacken sth off; *Bremse* to let sth off; **~ sitzen** *(Ziegel, Schraube etc)* to be loose; **bei ihm sitzt das Geld ~** he is free with money; **bei ihr sitzt die Hand ziemlich ~** she's quick to lash out *(inf)*; **bei ihm sitzt der Revolver ~** he's trigger-happy; **bei ihm sitzt das Messer ~** he'd pull a knife at the slightest excuse

b *(= nicht verkrampft) laufen* loosely; *schreiben* naturally; **etw ~ sehen** to be relaxed about sth; **jdn ~ machen** to relax sb; **~ sitzen** *(Mensch)* to relax, to sit in a relaxed position; **~ drauf sein** *(inf)* to be laid-back *(inf)*

c *(= oberflächlich) kennen, bekannt sein* casually

d *(inf: = leicht)* easily; **~ vom Hocker** *(sl)* just like that *(inf)*; **das mache ich ganz ~** I can do it just like that *(inf)*

lo|cker-flo|ckig **ADJ** *(inf)* easy-going, laid-back

Lo|cker|heit **F -,** *no pl* looseness; *(von Kuchen etc)* lightness; *(von Seil etc)* slackness; *(= Entspanntheit)* relaxed state; **etw in aller ~ tun** to do sth in a relaxed way

lo|cker-: **lo|cker+las|sen** **VI** *sep irreg (inf)* **nicht ~** not to give up, not to let up; **lo|cker+ma|chen** **VT** *sep (inf) Geld* to shell out *(inf)*, to part with; **bei jdm 100 Euro ~** to get sb to shell out *(inf) or* part with 100 euros

lo|ckern ['lɔkɐn] **VT** **a** *(= locker machen)* to loosen; *Boden* to break up; *Griff* to relax, to loosen; *Seil* to slacken; *(lit, fig) Zügel* to slacken **b** *(= entspannen) Arme, Beine, Muskeln* to loosen up; *(fig) Vorschriften, Atmosphäre* to relax **VR** to work itself loose; *(Moral)* to become loose *or* lax; *(Sport)* to loosen up; *(zum Warmwerden)* to limber up, to warm up; *(Verkrampfung, Spannung)* to ease off; *(Atmosphäre, Beziehungen, Mensch)* to get more relaxed

Lo|cke|rung ['lɔkərʊŋ] **F -, -en** **a** loosening; *(von Griff)* relaxation, loosening; *(von Seil)* slackening **b** *(von Armen, Beinen, Muskeln)* loosening up; *(von Beziehungen)* easing, relaxation

Lo|cke|rungs-: **Lo|cke|rungs|mit|tel** **NT** raising agent; **Lo|cke|rungs|übung** **F** loosening-up exercise; *(zum Warmwerden)* limbering-up exercise, warm-up exercise

lo|ckig ['lɔkıç] **ADJ** *Haar* curly; *Mensch* curly-headed

Lock-: **Lock|mit|tel** **NT** lure; **Lock|pfei|fe** **F** (bird) call; *(für Hund)* whistle; **Lock|ruf** **M** call; **Lock|spit|zel** **M** agent provocateur; **Lock|stoff|fal|le** **F** pheromone-baited insect trap

Lo|ckung ['lɔkʊŋ] **F -, -en** lure; *(= Versuchung)* temptation

Lock|vo|gel **M** decoy (bird); *(fig)* lure, decoy

Lock|vo|gel|an|ge|bot **NT** inducement

Lod|del ['lɔdl] **M -s, -** *(inf)* ponce *(esp Brit inf)*, pimp

Lo|den ['lo:dn] **M -s, -** loden (cloth)

Lo|den|man|tel **M** loden (coat)

lo|dern ['lo:dɐn] **VI** *(lit, fig)* to blaze; *(= emporlodern)* to blaze up; **in seinen Augen loderte Hass/Gier** his eyes blazed with hatred/greed

Löf|fel ['lœfl] **M -s, -** **a** *(als Besteck)* spoon; *(als Maßangabe)* spoonful; *(von Bagger)* bucket; **den ~ abgeben** *(inf)* to kick the bucket *(inf)*; **mit einem silbernen** *or* **goldenen ~ im Mund geboren sein** to be born with a silver spoon in one's mouth → **balbieren**

b *(Hunt)* ear; *(inf: von Mensch)* ear, lug *(Brit inf)*; **jdm ein paar hinter die ~ hauen** *(inf)* **jdm eins hinter die ~ geben** *(inf)* to give sb a clip (a)round the ear; **ein paar hinter die ~ kriegen** *(inf)* to get a clip (a)round the ear; **sich** *(dat)* **etw hinter die ~ schreiben** *(inf)* to get sth into one's head *(inf)*; **sperr doch deine ~ auf** *(inf)* pin back your lugholes *(Brit inf)*, listen properly; **die ~ spitzen** *(inf)* to prick up one's ears

Löf|fel|bag|ger **M** excavator, mechanical shovel

Löf|fel|bis|kuit **M OR NT** sponge finger, ladyfinger *(US)*

löf|feln ['lœfln] **VT** to spoon; *(mit der Kelle)* to ladle

Löf|fel-: **Löf|fel|stiel** **M** spoon handle; **löf|fel|wei|se** **ADV** by the spoonful

Löff|ler ['lœflɐ] **M -s, -** *(Zool)* spoonbill

Loft [lɔft] **NT -s, -s** *(Build)* luxury attic flat *(Brit) or* apartment

log *pret von* **lügen**

log *abbr von* **Logarithmus**

Log [lɔk] **NT -s, -e** [-gə] *(Naut)* log

Lo|ga|rith|men|ta|fel **F** log table

lo|ga|rith|mie|ren [logarıt'mi:rən] *ptp* **logarithmiert** **VT** to find the log(arithm) of **VI** to find the log(arithm)

lo|ga|rith|misch [loga'rıtmıʃ] **ADJ** logarithmic

Lo|ga|rith|mus [loga'rıtmʊs] **-, Logarithmen** [-mən] **M** logarithm, log

Log|buch **NT** log(book)

Lo|ge ['lo:ʒə] **F -, -n** **a** *(Theat)* box **b** *(= Freimaurerloge)* lodge **c** *(= Pförtnerloge)* lodge

Lo|gen-: **Lo|gen|bru|der** **M** lodge brother; **Lo|gen|meis|ter** **M** master of a/the lodge; **Lo|gen|platz** **M** *(Theat)* seat in a box

Log|ger ['lɔgɐ] **M -s, -** *(Naut)* lugger

Log|gia ['lɔdʒa] **F -, Loggien** [-dʒiən] *(= Bogenhalle)* loggia; *(= Balkon auch)* balcony

Log|glas **NT** log glass

Lo|gier|be|such **M** *(dated)* house guest(s *pl*)

lo|gie|ren [lo'ʒi:rən] *ptp* **logiert** *(dated)* **VI** to stay; *(als Zimmerherr)* to lodge **VT** **jdn ~** to put sb up

Lo|gier|gast **M** *(dated) (= Besuch)* house guest; *(= Untermieter)* lodger

Lo|gik ['lo:gık] **F -,** *no pl* logic; **in der ~** in logic; **du hast vielleicht eine ~!** your logic is a bit quaint; **dieser Aussage fehlt die ~** this statement is illogical *or* is lacking in logic

Lo|gi|ker ['lo:gikɐ] **M -s, -, Lo|gi|ke|rin** [-ərın] **F -, -nen** logician

Lo|gis [lo'ʒi:] **NT -, -** *(dated)* lodgings *pl*, rooms *pl*; *(Naut)* forecastle, crew's quarters *pl*; **Kost und ~** board and lodging; **bei jdm in** *or* **zu ~ wohnen** to lodge with sb

lo|gisch ['lo:gıʃ] **ADJ** logical; *(inf: = selbstverständlich)* natural; **gehst du auch hin? – ~** are you going too? – of course **ADV** logically; **~ denken** to think logically; **~ folgern** to come to a logical conclusion

lo|gi|scher|wei|se ['lo:gıʃɐ'vaizə] **ADV** logically

Lo|gis|tik [lo'gıstık] **F -,** *no pl* **a** *(Math)* logic **b** *(Mil, Econ)* logistics *sing*

lo|gis|tisch [lo'gıstıʃ] **ADJ** logistic **ADV** logistically

Log|lei|ne **F** *(Naut)* log line

lo|go ['lo:go] **INTERJ** *(inf)* you bet *(inf)*

Lo|go ['lo:go] **NT -(s), -s** *(= Firmenlogo)* logo

Lo|go|pä|de [logo'pɛ:də] **M -n, -n**, **Lo|go|pä|din** [-'pɛ:dın] **F -, -nen** speech therapist

Lo|go|pä|die [logopɛ'di:] **F -,** *no pl* speech therapy

Lo|gos ['lɔgɔs] **M -, Logoi** ['lɔgɔy] *(Philos)* logos; *(Rel)* Logos

Lo|go|ty|pe [logo'ty:pə] **F -, -n** logotype

Lo|he ['lo:ə] **F -, -n** *(liter)* raging flames *pl*

Lo|he **F -, -n** *(= Gerbrinde)* tan

lo|hen ['lo:ən] **VI** *(liter)* to blaze

lo|hen **VT** *Felle* to tan

Loh-: **Loh|ger|ber(in)** **M(F)** tanner; **Loh|ger|bung** **F** tanning

Lohn [lo:n] **M -(e)s, ⸗e** ['lø:nə] **a** *(= Arbeitsentgelt)* wage(s), pay *no pl, no indef art*; **wie viel ~ bekommst du?** how much do you get (paid)?, what are your wages?; **2% mehr ~ verlangen** to demand a 2% pay rise *(Brit) or* pay raise *(US)*; **gleicher ~ für gleiche Arbeit** equal pay for equal work; **bei jdm in ~ und Brot stehen** *(old)* to be in sb's employ *(old)*; **jdn um ~ und Brot bringen** *(old)* to deprive sb of a living *or* livelihood; **jdn in ~ und Brot nehmen** *(old)* to

take sb into one's employ *(old)*
b *(fig) (= Belohnung/Vergeltung)* reward; *(= Strafe)* punishment; **als** *or* **zum ~ für …** as a reward/punishment for …; **sein verdienter ~** one's just reward; **das ist nun der ~ für meine Mühe!** *(iro)* **das ist ein schlechter ~ für all die Mühe** that's what I get for my trouble, that's all the thanks I get for my trouble

Lohn-: **Lohn|ab|bau** M reduction of earnings; **lohn|ab|hän|gig** ADJ *Arbeiter* wage-earning; *Leistungen, Rente* wage-linked; **Lohn|ab|hän|gi|ge(r)** MF *decl as adj* wage earner; **Lohn|ab|kom|men** NT wages *or* pay agreement; **Lohn|ab|rech|nung** F wages slip *(Brit)*, pay slip; **Lohn|ab|schluss** M wage *or* pay agreement; **Lohn|ab|zug** M deduction from one's wages; **Lohn|ar|beit** F labour *(Brit)*, labor *(US)*; **Lohn|auf|trag** M **etw im ~ herstellen** *or* **fertigen** to manufacture sth under a contracting-out agreement; **Lohn|aus|fall** M loss of earnings; **Lohn|aus|gleich** M wage adjustment; **bei vollem ~** with full pay; **Lohn|aus|zah|lung** F payment of wages; **Lohn|buch|hal|ter(in)** M(F) wages clerk *(Brit)*, pay clerk; **Lohn|buch|hal|tung** F wages accounting; *(= Büro)* wages office *(Brit)*, pay(roll) office; **Lohn|bü|ro** NT wages office *(Brit)*, pay(roll) office; **Lohn|dum|ping** NT reduction in wage levels *(due to an influx of cheap labour)*; **Lohn|emp|fän|ger(in)** M(F) wage earner

loh|nen ['lo:nən] VIR to be worthwhile, to be worth it; **es lohnt (sich), etw zu tun** it is worth *or* worthwhile doing sth; **die Mühe lohnt sich** it is worth the effort, the effort is worthwhile; **der Film lohnt sich wirklich** the film is really worth seeing; **Fleiß lohnt sich immer** hard work always pays (off) *or* is always worthwhile; **das lohnt sich nicht für mich** it's not worth my while
VT **a** *(= es wert sein)* to be worth; **das Ergebnis lohnt die Mühe** the result makes all the effort worthwhile, the result amply repays all the effort
b *(= danken)* **jdm etw ~** to reward sb for sth; **er hat mir meine Hilfe mit Undank gelohnt** he repaid my help with ingratitude

löh|nen ['lø:nən] VI *(inf: = viel bezahlen)* to pay up, to cough up *(inf)*, to shell out *(inf)* VT **a** *(inf: = bezahlen)* to shell out *(inf)* **b** *(old: = mit Lohn versehen)* to pay

loh|nend ADJ rewarding; *(= nutzbringend)* worthwhile; *(= einträglich)* profitable; *(= sehens-/hörenswert)* worth seeing/hearing

loh|nens|wert ADJ worthwhile; **es ist ~, etw zu tun** it is worth(while) doing sth

Lohn-: **Lohn|er|hö|hung** F (wage *or* pay) rise *(Brit)*, (wage *or* pay) raise *(US)*; **Lohn|for|de|rung** F wage demand *or* claim; **Lohn|fort|zah|lung** F continued payment of wages; **Anspruch auf ~ haben** *(im Krankheitsfall)* to be entitled to (receive) statutory sick pay; **Lohn|ge|fäl|le** NT pay differential; **Lohn|grup|pe** F wage group; **Lohn|herr(in)** M(F) *(old)* employer; **lohn|in|ten|siv** ADJ *Arbeit, Betrieb* wage-intensive; **Lohn|kos|ten** PL wage costs *pl (Brit)*, labor costs *pl (US)*; **Lohn|kos|ten|zu|schuss** M *allowance towards wage costs paid to the employer of a long-term unemployed person*; **Lohn|kür|zung** F wage *or* pay cut; **~ im Krankheitsfall** sick-leave cuts *pl*; **Lohn|lis|te** F payroll; **Lohn|ne|ben|kos|ten** PL additional wage costs *pl (Brit) or* labor costs *pl (US)*; **Lohn|ni|veau** NT wage level; **Lohn|po|ker** NT *(fig)* wages haggling; **Lohn|po|li|tik** F pay policy; **Lohn-Preis-Spi|ra|le** F *(Econ)* wage-price spiral; **Lohn|run|de** F pay round; **Lohn|sen|kung** F cut in wages *or* pay; **Lohn|ska|la** F pay *or* wages scale

Lohn|steu|er F income tax *(paid on earned income)*

Lohn|steu|er-: **Lohn|steu|er|jah|res|aus|gleich** M annual adjustment of income tax; **beim letzten ~ habe ich 500 Euro zurückbekommen** at the end of the last tax year I got back 500 euros; **Lohn|steu|er|kar|te** F (income) tax card

> **LOHNSTEUERKARTE**
>
> The **Lohnsteuerkarte** is a card showing income tax and social security contributions paid in a particular year. If the employee changes jobs, this card and their **Sozialversicherungsausweis** must be given to the new employer. At the end of the year the **Lohnsteuerkarte** is returned to the employee. They can then present it to the tax office together with their income tax return and claim any tax rebates they may be entitled to. → SOZIALVERSICHERUNGSAUSWEIS

Lohn-: **Lohn|stopp** M wages *or* pay freeze; **Lohn|strei|fen** M pay slip; **Lohn|stück|kos|ten** PL *(Comm)* unit wage costs *pl (Brit) or* labor costs *pl (US)*; **Lohn|ta|rif** M wage rate; **Lohn|tü|te** F pay packet

Löh|nung ['lø:nʊŋ] F -, -en **a** *(= Auszahlung)* payment; *(auch* **Löhnungstag***)* pay day **b** *(= Lohn)* pay

Lohn-: **Lohn|ver|hand|lung** F pay *or* wage negotiations *pl*; **Lohn|ver|zicht** M **~ üben** to take a cut in wages *or* pay; **wir mussten einen ~ hinnehmen** we had to accept a cut in wages *or* pay; **Lohn|zah|lung** F payment of wages; **Lohn|zet|tel** M pay slip

Loi|pe ['lɔypə] F -, -n cross-country ski run

Lok [lɔk] F -, -s *abbr von* **Lokomotive** engine

lo|kal [lo'ka:l] ADJ **a** *(= örtlich)* local; **~es Rechnernetz** *(Comput)* local area network **b** *(Gram)* of place ADV locally; **jdn ~ betäuben** to give sb a local anaesthetic *(Brit) or* anesthetic *(US)*; **ein ~ wirkendes Schmerzmittel** a local painkiller

Lo|kal [lo'ka:l] NT -s, -e **a** *(= Gaststätte)* pub *(esp Brit)*, bar; *(esp auf dem Land)* inn *(esp Brit)*, restaurant *(esp US)*; *(= Restaurant)* restaurant **b** *(= Versammlungsraum)* meeting place

Lo|kal- *in cpds* local; **Lo|kal|an|äs|the|sie** F *(Med)* local anaesthetic *(Brit) or* anesthetic *(US)*; **Lo|kal|au|gen|schein** M *(Aus Jur)* visit to the scene of the crime; **Lo|kal|aus|ga|be** F *(von Zeitung)* local edition; **Lo|kal|blatt** NT local paper; **Lo|kal|der|by** NT local derby

Lo|ka|le(s) [lo'ka:lə] NT *decl as adj* local news *sing*

Lo|kal|fern|se|hen NT local television

Lo|ka|li|sa|ti|on [lokaliza'tsio:n] F -, -en **a** *(= Ortsfeststellung)* location **b** *(Med)* localization; *(= Beschränkung auf einen Ort)* limiting **c** *(Comput)* localization

lo|ka|li|sie|ren [lokali'zi:rən] *ptp* **lokalisiert** VT **a** *(= Ort feststellen)* to locate **b** *(Med)* to localize; *(auf einen Ort)* to limit *(auf +acc* to)

Lo|ka|li|sie|rung F = **Lokalisation**

Lo|ka|li|tät [lokali'tɛ:t] F -, -en **a** *(= örtliche Beschaffenheit)* locality; *(= Raum)* facilities *pl*; **sich mit den ~en auskennen** to know the district; **die ~en verlassen** to leave the premises **b** *(hum inf: = Lokal)* pub *(esp Brit)*, bar **c** *(hum inf: = WC)* cloakroom *(euph)*, washroom, bathroom *(esp US)*

Lo|kal-: **Lo|kal|ko|lo|rit** NT local colour *(Brit) or* color *(US)*; **Lo|kal|ma|ta|dor(in)** M(F) local hero/heroine; **Lo|kal|nach|rich|ten** PL local news *sing*; **Lo|kal|pat|ri|o|tis|mus** M local patriotism; **Lo|kal|re|dak|ti|on** F local newsroom; **Lo|kal|re|por|ter(in)** M(F) local reporter; **Lo|kal|run|de** F **eine ~ ausgeben** *or* **schmeißen** to buy drinks *or* a round for everyone (in the house); **Lo|kal|satz** M *(Gram)* (adverbial) clause of place; **Lo|kal|teil** M local section; **Lo|kal|ter|min** M *(Jur)* visit to the scene of the crime; **Lo|kal|ver|bot** NT ban; **~ haben** to be barred *or* banned from a pub *(esp Brit) or* bar; **Lo|kal|zei|tung** F local newspaper

Lo|ka|tiv ['lo:kati:f] M -s, -e [-və] *(Gram)* locative (case)

Lok|füh|rer(in) M(F) engine driver, engineer *(US)*

Lo|ko|ge|schäft ['lo:ko-] NT *(St Ex)* spot deal

Lo|ko|mo|ti|ve [lokomo'ti:və, lokomi'ti:fə] F -, -n locomotive, (railway) engine

Lo|ko|mo|tiv-: **Lo|ko|mo|tiv|füh|rer(in)** M(F) engine driver, engineer *(US)*; **Lo|ko|mo|tiv|schup|pen** M engine shed

Lo|ko|preis ['lo:ko-] M *(St Ex)* spot price

Lo|ko|wa|re ['lo:ko-] F *(Comm, St Ex)* spot goods *pl*

Lo|kus ['lo:kʊs] M - *or* -ses, - *or* -se *(inf)* toilet, bathroom *(esp US)*

Lol|li ['lɔli] M -(s), -s *(inf)* lollipop, lolly *(esp Brit)*

Lol|lo ros|so M - -s *(= Salat)* lollo rosso

Lom|bard ['lɔmbart] M OR NT -(e)s, -e [-də] *(Fin)* loan on security

Lom|bard|ge|schäft NT loan on security

lom|bar|die|ren [lɔmbar'di:rən] *ptp* **lombardiert** VT *(Fin)* to accept as collateral

Lom|bard-: **Lom|bard|kas|se** F guaranty authority; **Lom|bard|kre|dit** [-kre'di:t] M collateral loan; **Lom|bard|satz** M rate for loans on security

Lon|don ['lɔndɔn] NT -s London

Lon|do|ner ['lɔndɔnɐ] ADJ *attr* London

Lon|do|ner ['lɔndɔnɐ] M -s, -, **Lon|do|ne|rin** [-ərɪn] F -, -nen Londoner

Long|drink ['lɔŋdrɪŋk] M long drink

Lon|ge ['lõ:ʒə] F -, -n *(für Pferde)* lunge; *(für Akrobaten)* harness

lon|gie|ren [lõ'ʒi:rən] *ptp* **longiert** VT *Pferd* to lunge

Look [lʊk] M -s, -s *(Fashion)* look

Loo|ping ['lu:pɪŋ] M OR NT -s, -s *(Aviat)* looping the loop; **einen ~ machen** to loop the loop

Lor|bass ['lɔrbas] M -es, -e *(dial inf)* sly devil *(inf)*, sharp one *(inf)*

Lor|beer ['lɔrbe:ɐ] M -s, -en **a** *(lit: Gewächs)* laurel; *(als Gewürz)* bay leaf; *(= Lorbeerkranz)* laurel wreath **b** **Lorbeeren** PL *(fig: = Erfolg)* laurels *pl*; **sich auf seinen ~en ausruhen** *(inf)* to rest on one's laurels; **seine ersten ~en ernten** to win one's first laurels; **damit kannst du keine ~en ernten** that's no great achievement

Lor|beer-: **Lor|beer|baum** M laurel (tree); **Lor|beer|blatt** NT bay leaf; **Lor|beer|kranz** M laurel wreath

Lor|do|se [lɔr'do:zə] F -, -n *(Med)* lordosis *(spec)*

Lo|re ['lo:rə] F -, -n **a** *(Rail)* truck, wagon; *(= Kipplore)* tipper, dumper **b** *(Kohlenmaß: = 200 Zentner)* 10,000 kilos (of coal)

Lorg|net|te [lɔrn'jɛtə] F -, -n lorgnette

Lorg|non [lɔrn'jõ:] NT -s, -s lorgnon

los [lo:s] ADJ *pred* **a** *(= nicht befestigt)* loose; **der Hund ist von der Leine ~** the dog is off the lead *(Brit) or* leash
b *(= frei)* **jdn/etw ~ sein** *(inf)* to be rid *or* shot *(Brit inf)* of sb/sth, to have got *or* gotten *(US)* rid of sb/sth; **ich bin mein ganzes Geld ~** *(inf)* I'm cleaned out *(inf)*
c *(inf)* **etwas ist ~/es ist nichts ~** *(= geschieht)* there's something/nothing going on *or* happening; *(= nicht in/in Ordnung)* there's something/nothing wrong *or* the matter, something's/nothing's up; **mit jdm/etw ist etwas/nichts ~** there's something/nothing wrong *or* the matter with sb/sth; **mit jdm/etw ist nichts (mehr) ~** *(inf)* sb/sth isn't up to much (any more), sb/sth is a dead loss (now) *(inf)*; **was ist denn hier/da ~?** what's going on here/there (then)?, what's up here/there (then)?; **was ist ~?** what's up?, what's wrong?, what's the matter?; **was ist da abends ~?** what is there going on there in the evenings?; **wo ist denn hier was ~?** where's the action here *(inf)*?; **als mein Vater das hörte, da war was ~!** when my father heard about it all hell broke loose *(inf)*
ADV **a** *(Aufforderung)* **~!** come on!; *(= geh/lauf*

schon) go on!, get going!; **nun aber ~!** let's get going; *(zu andern)* get going *or* moving *(inf)*; **nichts wie ~!** let's get going; **(na) ~, mach schon!** (come on,) get on with it; **~, schreib/fahr** *etc* **doch endlich** come on, start writing/driving *etc*; **auf die Plätze** *or* **Achtung, fertig, ~** on your marks, get set, go!, ready, steady, go!

b *(= weg)* **sie wollen ~ vom Reich/Kapitalismus** they want to break away from the Reich/from capitalism; **wir wollen früh ~** we want to leave early, we want to be off early

Los [lo:s] NT **-es, -e** [-zə] **a** *(für Entscheidung)* lot; *(in der Lotterie, auf Jahrmarkt etc)* ticket; **das große ~ gewinnen** *or* **ziehen** *(lit, fig)* to hit the jackpot; **etw durch das ~ entscheiden** *or* **bestimmen** *or* **ermitteln** to decide sth by drawing *or* casting lots; **jdn durch das ~ bestimmen** to pick sb by drawing lots; **etw durch das ~ gewinnen** to win sth in a lottery *or (bei Tombola)* raffle *or (auf Jahrmarkt)* tombola; **auf dieses ~ entfiel der Hauptgewinn** this ticket won first prize; **das ~ hat mich getroffen** it fell to my lot

b *no pl (= Schicksal)* lot; **er hat ein hartes** *or* **schweres ~** his is a hard *or* not an easy lot; **das gleiche ~ erfahren** to share the same lot; **jds ~ teilen** to share sb's lot

c *(Comm)* lot

-los ADJ *suf* -less; **vater-/mutterlos** father-/motherless; **richtungslos** without direction

los+bal|lern VI *sep (inf)* to start banging away *(inf)*; *(stärker)* to start blazing away

lös|bar ADJ soluble

los-: **los+bel|len** VI *sep (Hund)* to start barking; *(Mensch)* to start yelling; **los+bin|den** VT *sep irreg* to untie *(von* from); **los+bre|chen** *sep irreg* VT to break off VI *aux sein (Gelächter etc)* to break out; *(Sturm, Gewitter)* to break

Lösch-: **Lösch|ar|beit** F *usu pl* firefighting operations *pl*; **lösch|bar** ADJ **a** *Feuer, Flammen* extinguishable; *Kalk* slakable; *Durst* quenchable; *Schrift, Daten, Tonband* erasable; **die Hypothek/Schuld ist ~** the mortgage/debt can be paid off; **die Eintragung ist ~** the entry can be deleted; **das Konto ist ~** the account can be closed **b** *(Naut)* unloadable; **Lösch|blatt** NT sheet *or* piece of blotting paper; **Lösch|ei|mer** M fire bucket

lö|schen ['lœʃn] VT **a** *Feuer, Brand, Flammen, Kerze* to put out, to extinguish; *Licht* to switch out *or* off, to turn out *or* off; *Kalk, Durst* to slake; *Durst* to quench; *Schrift (an Tafel), Tonband etc* to wipe *or* rub off, to erase; *Tafel* to wipe; *Schuld* to cancel; *Eintragung, Zeile* to delete; *Konto* to close; *Firma, Name* to strike *(Brit) or* cross off; *(= aufsaugen) Tinte* to blot; *(Comput) Datei, Programm* to remove; *Speicher, Bildschirm* to clear; *Festplatte* to wipe; *Daten, Information* to erase, to delete

b *(Naut) Ladung* to unload

VI **a** *(Feuerwehr etc)* to put out a/the fire

b *(= aufsaugen)* to blot

c *(Naut)* to unload

Lö|scher ['lœʃɐ] M **-s, -** (fire-)extinguisher; *(= Tintenlöscher)* blotter

Lösch-: **Lösch|fahr|zeug** NT fire engine; **Lösch|flug|zeug** NT firefighting plane; **Lösch|kalk** M slaked lime; **Lösch|mann|schaft** F team of firemen *or* firefighters; **Lösch|mit|tel** NT (fire-)extinguishing agent; **Lösch|pa|pier** NT (piece of) blotting paper; **Lösch|schaum** M extinguishant foam; **Lösch|tas|te** F *(Comput)* delete key; **Lösch|trupp** M fire-fighting team *or* squad

Lö|schung ['lœʃʊŋ] F **-, -en a** *(von Schuld, Hypothek)* paying off; *(von Eintragung)* deletion; *(von Konto)* closing; *(von Firma, Namen)* striking *(Brit) or crossing off*; *(Comput: von Daten)* erasing, deletion **b** *(Naut: von Ladung)* unloading

Lösch-: **Lösch|was|ser** NT, *no pl* water for firefighting; **Lösch|zug** M convoy of fire engines, set of appliances *(form)*

los+don|nern VI *sep (lit, fig)* to start to thunder

lo|se ['lo:zə] ADJ *(lit, fig)* loose; *(= nicht gespannt) Seil* slack; *(= schelmisch) Streich* mischievous; **etw ~ verkaufen** to sell sth loose → **Zunge** ADV loosely; **~ sitzen** to be loose

Lo|se|blatt|aus|ga|be F loose-leaf edition

Lö|se|geld NT ransom (money)

los+ei|sen *sep (inf)* VT to get *or* prise away *(bei* from); **jdn von einer Verpflichtung ~** to get sb out of an obligation VR to get away *(bei* from); *(von Verpflichtung etc)* to get out *(von* of)

lo|sen ['lo:zn] VI to draw lots *(um* for); **wir ~, wer ...** we'll draw lots to decide who ...

lö|sen ['lø:zn] VT **a** *(= losmachen, abtrennen, entfernen)* to remove *(von* from); *Boot* to cast off *(von* from); *(= ablösen) Fleisch, Briefmarken, Tapete etc* to get off *(von etw* sth), to remove *(von* from); *(= herauslösen)* to get out *(aus* of), to remove *(aus* from); *(= aufbinden) Knoten, Fesseln, Gürtel, Haare* to undo; *Arme* to unfold; *Hände* to unclasp; *Handbremse* to take *or* let off; *Husten, Krampf* to ease; *Muskeln* to loosen up; *(lit, fig: = lockern)* to loosen; **sie löste ihre Hand aus der seinen** she slipped her hand out of his → *auch* **gelöst**

b *(= klären, Lösung finden für) Aufgabe, Problem* to solve; *Konflikt, Schwierigkeiten* to resolve

c *(= annullieren) Vertrag* to cancel; *Verlobung* to break off; *Verbindung, Verhältnis* to sever; *Ehe* to dissolve

d *(= zergehen lassen)* to dissolve *(auch Chem)*

e *(= kaufen) Karte* to buy, to get

VR **a** *(= sich losmachen)* to detach oneself *(von* from); *(= sich ablösen)* to come off *(von etw* sth); *(Knoten, Haare)* to come undone; *(Schuss)* to go off; *(Husten, Krampf, Spannung)* to ease; *(Schleim, Schmutz)* to loosen; *(Atmosphäre)* to relax; *(Muskeln)* to loosen up; *(lit, fig: = sich lockern)* to (be)come loose; *(Lawine)* to break away; **sich von jdm ~** to break away from sb *(auch Sport)*; **sich von etw ~** *(von Verpflichtungen)* to free oneself of sth; *von Vorstellung, Vorurteilen, Gedanken* to rid oneself of sth; *von Partnern, Vaterland, Vergangenheit* to break with sth, to break away from sth; **das Boot hat sich aus der Verankerung gelöst** the boat has broken (away from) its moorings; **eine Gestalt löste sich aus der Dunkelheit** *(liter)* a figure detached itself *or* emerged from the darkness

b *(= sich aufklären)* to be solved; **sich von selbst ~** *(Verbrechen)* to solve itself; *(Problem auch)* to clear itself up, to resolve itself

c *(= zergehen)* to dissolve *(in +dat* in) *(auch Chem)*; **die Tablette löst sich gut/schlecht** the tablet dissolves easily/doesn't dissolve easily; **ihre Anspannung/ihr Schmerz löste sich in Tränen** her tension/pain found relief in tears

Los|ent|scheid M drawing (of) lots; **die Gewinner werden durch Losentscheid ermittelt** the winners are established by drawing lots

Lo|ser ['lu:zɐ] M **-s, -** *(inf: = Verlierer)* loser

los-: **los+fah|ren** VI *sep irreg aux sein* **a** *(= abfahren)* to set off; *(Fahrzeug)* to move off; *(Auto)* to drive off **b** *(inf: = schimpfen, anfallen)* **auf jdn ~** to lay into sb *(inf)*, to attack sb; **los+ge|hen** VI *sep irreg aux sein* **a** *(= weggehen)* to set off; *(Schuss, Bombe etc)* to go off; **(mit dem Messer) auf jdn ~** to go for sb (with a knife) **b** *(inf: = anfangen)* to start; *(Geschrei der Menge)* to go up; **gleich gehts los** it's just about to start; *(bei Streit)* any minute now; **jetzt gehts los!** here we go!; *(Vorstellung)* it's starting!; *(Rennen)* they're off!; *(Reise, Bewegung)* we're/you're *etc* off!; **jetzt gehts wieder los (mit ihren Klagen)** here we go again (with all her moans); **gehts bald los?** will it start soon?; *(Reise etc)* are we off soon?; **bei drei gehts los** you/they *etc* start on the count of three; **jetzt gehts aber los!** *(inf)* you're kidding! *(inf)*; *(bei Frechheit)* do you mind! **c** *(inf: = abgehen)* to come off; **los+ha|ben** VT *sep irreg (inf)* **etwas/nichts ~** to be pretty clever *(inf)*/pretty stupid *(inf)*; **los+heu|len** VI *sep* to burst out crying

-lo|sig|keit *suf* **-, -en** -lessness; **Hoffnungslosigkeit** hopelessness

los-: **los+kau|fen** *sep* VT to buy out; *Entführten* to ransom VR to buy oneself out *(aus* of); **los+knüp|fen** VT *sep* to untie, to undo; **los+kom|men** VI *sep irreg aux sein (Mensch)* to get away *(von* from); *(= sich befreien)* to free oneself, to get free *(von* of); **das Boot kam von der Sandbank los/nicht los** the boat came off/wouldn't come off the sandbank; **von Schulden ~** to get out of debt; **von einer Sucht ~** to get free of an addiction; **los+kön|nen** VI *sep irreg (inf)* to be able to get away; **los+krie|gen** VT *sep (inf) (= ablösen)* to get off; *(= loswerden)* to get rid *or* shot *(Brit inf)* of; **los+la|chen** VI *sep* to burst out laughing; **laut ~** to laugh out loud; **los+las|sen** VT *sep irreg* **a** *(= nicht mehr festhalten)* to let go of; *(fig: = nicht fesseln) Mensch* to let go; **das Seil ~** to let go of the rope; **der Gedanke/die Frage** *etc* **lässt mich nicht mehr los** the thought/problem haunts me *or* won't go out of my mind; **das Buch lässt mich nicht mehr los** I can't put the book down **b** *(inf) (= abfeuern) Feuerwerk, Bombe* to let off; *(fig) Rede, Witze, Geschichte* to come out with; *Beschwerden, Schimpfkanonade* to launch into; *Schrift* to launch; *Brief* to send off **c** **jdn (auf jdn) ~** *(fig inf)* to let sb loose (on sb); **die Hunde auf jdn ~** to put *or* set the dogs on(to) sb; **und so was lässt man nun auf die Menschheit los!** *(hum inf)* what a thing to unleash on an unsuspecting world; **wehe, wenn sie losgelassen ...** *(hum inf)* once let them off the leash ...; **los+lau|fen** VI *sep irreg aux sein (= zu laufen anfangen)* to start to run; *(= weggehen)* to run out; **los+le|gen** VI *sep (inf)* to get going *or* started; *(mit Schimpfen)* to let fly *(inf) or* rip *(inf)*; **er legte gleich mit seinen Ideen los** he started on about his ideas; **nun leg mal los und erzähle ...** now come on and tell me/us ...

lös|lich ['lø:slɪç] ADJ soluble; **leicht/schwer ~** readily/not readily soluble; **~er Kaffee** instant coffee

Lös|lich|keit F **-,** *no pl (Chem)* solubility

los-: **los+lö|sen** *sep* VT to remove *(von* from); *(= ablösen auch)* to take off *(von etw* sth); *(= herauslösen auch)* to take out *(aus* of); *(= lockern)* to loosen VR to detach oneself *(von* from); *(= sich ablösen auch)* to come off *(von etw* sth); *(= lockern)* to become loose; **sich von jdm ~** to break away from sb; **los+ma|chen** *sep* VT *(= befreien)* to free; *(= losbinden)* to untie; *Handbremse* to let *or* take off; **jdn von einer Kette ~** to unchain sb VI **a** *(Naut)* to cast off **b** *(inf: = sich beeilen)* to step on it *(inf)*, to get a move on *(inf)* VR to get away *(von* from); **der Hund hat sich losgemacht** the dog has got loose; **los+müs|sen** VI *sep irreg (inf)* to have to go

Los|num|mer F ticket number

los-: **los+plat|zen** VI *sep aux sein (inf) (= lachen)* to burst out laughing; *(spontan, vorzeitig äußern)* to start yapping *(inf)*; **mit etw ~** to burst out with sth; **platz nicht immer gleich los** think before you speak; **los+prus|ten** VI *sep (inf)* to explode (with laughter); **los+quat|schen** [-kvatʃn] VI *sep (inf)* to prattle away *(inf)*; **los+ra|sen** VI *sep aux sein (inf)* to race *or* tear off; **los+rei|ßen** *sep irreg* VT *(= abreißen)* to tear *or* rip off *(von etw* sth); *(= herunterreißen)* to tear *or* rip down *(von etw* from sth); *(= herausreißen)* to tear *or* rip out *(aus* of); **jdn ~** to tear sb away VR **sich (von etw) ~** *(Hund etc)* to break free *or* loose (from sth); *(fig)* to tear oneself away (from sth); **los+ren|nen** VI *sep irreg aux sein (inf)* to run off; *(= anfangen zu laufen)* to start to run

Löss [lœs] M **-es, -e**, **Löß** [lø:s] M **-es, -e** *(Geol)* loess

los+sa|gen VR *sep* **sich von etw ~** to renounce sth; **sich von jdm/seiner Vergangenheit ~** to dissociate oneself from *or* break with sb/the *or* one's past

Los|sa|gung ['lo:sza:gʊŋ] F -, *no pl* renunciation (*von* of); dissociation (*von* from)

Löss|bo|den M, **Löß|bo|den** M loess soil

los-: **los+schi|cken** VT *sep* to send off; **los+schie|ßen** VI *sep irreg* **a** (*= zu schießen anfangen*) to open fire; **schieß los!** (*fig inf*) fire away! (*inf*) **b** *aux sein* (*= schnell starten*) to shoot *or* race off; **auf jdn ~** to race toward(s) sb; **los+schla|gen** *sep irreg* VI to hit out; (*Mil*) to (launch one's) attack; **auf jdn/aufeinander ~** to go for sb/one another *or* each other VT **a** (*= abschlagen*) to knock off **b** (*inf: = verkaufen*) to get rid of; **los+schnal|len** VT *sep* to unbuckle; **los+schrau|ben** VT *sep* to unscrew; (*= lockern auch*) to loosen; **los+sprin|gen** VI *sep irreg aux sein* to jump; **auf jdn/etw ~** to leap for sb/sth; **los+steu|ern** VI *sep aux sein* **auf jdn/etw ~** to head *or* make for sb/sth; **los+stür|zen** VI *sep aux sein* to rush off; **auf jdn/etw ~** to pounce on sb/sth

Lost [lɔst] M -(e)s, *no pl* (*Chem*) mustard gas

los-: **los+ti|gern** VI *sep aux sein* (*inf*) to toddle off (*inf*); **los+tren|nen** VT *sep* = **abtrennen a**; **los+tre|ten** VT *sep irreg* to kick off

Los|trom|mel F drum (*containing lottery tickets*)

Lo|sung ['lo:zʊŋ] F -, -en **a** (*= Devise, Parole*) motto **b** (*= Kennwort*) password

Lo|sung F -, -en (*Hunt*) droppings *pl*

Lö|sung ['lø:zʊŋ] F -, -en **a** solution (+*gen* to); (*= das Lösen*) solution (+*gen* of); (*eines Konfliktes, von Schwierigkeiten*) resolving; **zur ~ dieser Schwierigkeiten** to resolve these problems **b** (*= Annullierung*) (*eines Vertrages*) cancellation; (*von Beziehungen, einer Verlobung*) breaking off; (*einer Verbindung, eines Verhältnisses*) severing, severance; (*einer Ehe*) dissolving **c** (*Chem*) solution

Lö|sungs-: **Lö|sungs|mit|tel** NT solvent; **Lö|sungs|vor|schlag** M suggested solution; (*bei Frage, Rätsel etc*) suggested answer; **Lö|sungs|weg** M path towards a solution

Lo|sungs|wort NT *pl* **-worte** password

Lö|sungs|wort NT *pl* **-wörter** answer

Los-: **Los|ver|fah|ren** NT decision by lot; **etw im ~ entscheiden** to decide sth by drawing lots; **Los|ver|käu|fer(in)** M(F) ticket seller (*for lottery, raffle etc*); **los+wer|den** VT *sep irreg aux sein* to get rid of; *Angst etc auch* to rid oneself of; *Hemmungen auch* to lose; *Gedanken* to get away from, to get out of one's mind; *Geld* (*beim Spiel etc*), *Hab und Gut* to lose; *Geld* (*= ausgeben*) to spend; **er wird seine Erkältung einfach nicht los** he can't shake off *or* get rid of his cold; **los+zie|hen** VI *sep irreg aux sein* **a** (*= aufbrechen*) to set out *or* off (*in +acc, nach* for) **b gegen jdn/etw ~** (*inf*) to lay into sb/sth (*inf*)

Lot [lo:t] NT -(e)s, -e **a** (*= Senkblei*) plumb line; (*Naut*) sounding line, plumb line; **im ~ sein** to be in plumb **b** (*Math*) perpendicular; **das ~ fällen** to drop a perpendicular; **seine Finanzen wieder ins ~ bringen** to put one's finances back on an even keel; **die Sache ist wieder im ~** things have been straightened out; **die Sache wieder ins (rechte) ~ bringen** to put things right, to put the record straight (*inf*); **aus dem ~ geraten** to be thrown out of kilter **c** (*old*) *old unit of weight varying between 14 and 18 grams* **d** (*= Lötmetall*) solder

Lot M -s (*Bibl*) Lot

Löt|ap|pa|rat M soldering appliance

löt|bar ADJ solderable

lo|ten ['lo:tn] VT to plumb

lö|ten ['lø:tn] VTI to solder

Loth|rin|gen ['lo:trɪŋən] NT -s Lorraine

Loth|rin|ger ['lo:trɪŋɐ] M -s, -, **Loth|rin|ge|rin** [-ərɪn] F -, -nen Lorrainer

loth|rin|gisch ['lo:trɪŋɪʃ] ADJ of Lorraine, Lorrainese

Lo|ti|on [lo'tsio:n] F -, -en lotion

Löt-: **Löt|kol|ben** M soldering iron; **Löt|lam|pe** F blowlamp

Lot|lei|ne F plumb line

Löt|me|tall NT solder

Lo|to|pha|ge [loto'fa:gə] M -n, -n, **Lo|to|pha|gin** [-'fa:gɪn] F -, -nen (*Myth*) lotus-eater

Lo|tos ['lo:tɔs] M -, - lotus

Lo|tos-: **Lo|tos|blu|me** F lotus (flower); **Lo|tos|sitz** M lotus position

lot|recht ADJ perpendicular ADV perpendicularly

Lot|rech|te F *decl as adj* (*Math*) perpendicular

Löt|rohr NT blowpipe

Lot|se ['lo:tsə] M -n, -n, **Lot|sin** [-tsɪn] F -, -nen (*Naut*) pilot; (*= Fluglotse*) air-traffic *or* flight controller; (*Aut*) navigator; (*fig*) guide

lot|sen ['lo:tsn] VT to guide; *Schiff auch* to pilot; **jdn irgendwohin ~** (*inf*) to drag sb somewhere (*inf*) → **Geld a**

Lot|sen-: **Lot|sen|boot** NT pilot boat; **Lot|sen|dienst** M pilot service; (*Aut*) driver-guide service; **Lot|sen|fisch** M pilot fish; **Lot|sen|geld** NT pilotage; **Lot|sen|zwang** M compulsory pilotage

Lot|sin [-tsɪn] F → **Lotse**

Löt-: **Löt|stein** M sal ammoniac block; **Löt|stel|le** F soldered point

Lot|te ['lɔtə] F - *contr von* **Charlotte**

Lot|ter|bett ['lɔtɐ-] NT (*old, hum*) old bed

Lot|te|rie [lɔtə'ri:] F -, -n [-'ri:ən] lottery; (*= Tombola*) raffle

Lot|te|rie-: **Lot|te|rie|ge|winn** M → **Lotterie** lottery/raffle prize *or* (*Geld*) winnings *pl*; **Lot|te|rie|los** NT → **Lotterie** lottery/raffle ticket; **Lot|te|rie|spiel** NT (*lit*) lottery; (*fig*) gamble

lot|te|rig ['lɔtərɪç] (*inf*) ADJ slovenly *no adv*; *Mensch, Arbeit auch* sloppy (*inf*) ADV **~ herumlaufen** to go around looking a mess (*inf*)

Lot|ter|le|ben NT (*inf*) dissolute life

lot|tern ['lɔtɐn] VI (*S Ger, Sw: = lose sein*) to wobble

Lot|ter|wirt|schaft F (*inf*) muddle, slovenly mess

Lot|to ['lɔto] NT -s, -s **a** lottery, ≈ National Lottery (*Brit*); **(im) ~ spielen** to do (*Brit*) *or* play the lottery; **du hast wohl im ~ gewonnen** you must have won the pools (*Brit*) *or* the lottery **b** (*= Gesellschaftsspiel*) lotto

Lot|to-: **Lot|to|ge|schäft** NT, **Lot|to|la|den** M (*inf*) lottery agency; **Lot|to|ge|winn** M lottery win; (*Geld*) lottery winnings *pl*; **Lot|to|kö|nig(in)** M(F) (*inf*) jackpot winner; **Lot|to|schein** M lottery coupon; **Lot|to|spie|ler(in)** M(F) lottery player *or* participant; **Lot|to- und To|to|an|nah|me|stel|le** F lottery and football pools agency; **Lot|to|zah|len** PL winning lottery numbers *pl*

lott|rig ['lɔtrɪç] ADJ, ADV (*inf*) = **lotterig**

Lö|tung ['lø:tʊŋ] F -, -en (*= das Löten*) soldering; (*= Lötstelle*) soldered joint

Lo|tus ['lo:tʊs] M -, - (*Bot*) **a** (*= Hornklee*) bird's-foot trefoil **b** = **Lotos**

Lo|tus|ef|fekt M lotus effect

Löt|zinn M solder

Louis|dor [lui'do:ɐ] M -s, -e *or* (*bei Zahlenangaben*) - (*Hist*) louis (d'or)

Lo|ver ['lavɐ] M -s, - (*inf: = Liebhaber*) lover

Low-Bud|get- *in cpds* low-budget; **Low-Bud|get-Pro|duk|ti|on** F low-budget production; **Low-Bud|get-Sen|dung** F low-budget programme (*Brit*) *or* program (*US*)

Lö|we ['lø:və] M -n, -n lion; **der ~** (*Astron*) Leo, the Lion; (*Astrol*) Leo; **im Zeichen des ~n geboren sein** to be born under (the sign of) Leo; **~ sein** to be (a) Leo; **sich in die Höhle des ~n begeben** (*inf*) to beard the lion in his den (*Brit prov*), to go into the lion's den

Lö|wen-: **Lö|wen|an|teil** M (*inf*) lion's share; **Lö|wen|bän|di|ger(in)** M(F) lion tamer; **Lö|wen|gru|be** F (*Bibl*) lions' den; **Lö|wen|herz** NT **Richard ~** *m* Richard (the) Lionheart; **Lö|wen|jagd** F lion hunt; **Lö|wen|mäh|ne** F (*lit*) lion's mane; (*fig*) flowing mane; **Lö|wen|maul** NT, **Lö|wen|mäul|chen** [-mɔylçən] NT -s, - snapdragon, antirrhinum; **Lö|wen|mut** M (*liter*) leonine courage (*liter*); **mit ~** as brave as a lion; **Lö|wen|zahn** M dandelion

Lö|win ['lø:vɪn] F -, -nen lioness

lo|yal [loa'ja:l] ADJ loyal ADV loyally; **sich jdm gegenüber ~ verhalten** to be loyal to(wards) sb

Lo|ya|li|tät [loajali'tɛ:t] F -, -en loyalty (*jdm gegenüber* to sb)

LP [ɛl'pe:] F -, -s LP

LPG [ɛlpe:'ge:] F -, -s (*DDR*) *abbr von* **Landwirtschaftliche Produktionsgenossenschaft**

LSD [ɛlɛs'de:] NT -(s) LSD

lt. *abbr von* **laut**

Luch [lu:x] F -, ⸗e ['ly:çə] *or nt* -(e)s, -e (*dial*) marsh

Luchs [lʊks] M -es, -e lynx; **Augen wie ein ~ haben** (*inf*) to have eyes like a hawk, to be eagle-eyed

Luchs|au|gen PL (*inf*) eagle eyes *pl*

luch|sen ['lʊksn] VI (*inf*) to peep

Lü|cke ['lʏkə] F -, -n (*lit, fig*) gap; (*zwischen Wörtern auch, auf Formularen etc*) space; (*= Ungereimtheit, Unvollständigkeit etc*) hole; (*= Gesetzeslücke*) loophole; (*in Versorgung*) break; **~n (im Wissen) haben** to have gaps in one's knowledge; **sein Tod hinterließ eine schmerzliche ~** (*geh*) his death has left a void in our lives

Lü|cken-: **Lü|cken|bü|ßer(in)** M(F) (*inf*) stopgap; **~ spielen** to be used as a stopgap; **lü|cken|haft** ADJ full of gaps; *Bericht, Sammlung, Beweis etc auch* incomplete; *Kenntnisse auch* sketchy; *Versorgung* deficient; *Gesetz, Alibi* full of holes; **sein Wissen ist sehr ~** there are great gaps in his knowledge ADV *sich erinnern* vaguely; *informieren, zusammenstellen* sketchily; *ausbilden, versorgen* deficiently; **Lü|cken|haf|tig|keit** ['lʏknhaftɪçkait] F -, -en incompleteness; (*von Kenntnissen auch*) sketchiness; (*von Versorgung*) deficiency; **wegen der ~ des Berichts/des Gesetzes** because of all the gaps in the report/all the loopholes in the law; **lü|cken|los** ADJ complete; *Kontrolle auch, Überwachung* thorough; *Kenntnisse* perfect; (*Mil*) *Abwehr* perfect; *Aufklärung* full ADV completely; **Lü|cken|test** M (*Sch*) completion test (*Brit*), fill-in-the-gaps test; **Lü|cken|text** M (*Sch*) completion exercise

lud *pret von* **laden**, *von* **laden**

Lu|de ['lu:də] M -n, -n (*sl*) ponce (*Brit inf*), pimp

Lu|der ['lu:dɐ] NT -s, - **a** (*Hunt: = Aas*) bait **b** (*inf*) minx; **armes/dummes ~** poor/stupid creature; **so ein ordinäres ~!** what a common little hussy!

Lu|der|jan ['lu:dɐja:n] M -(e)s, -e (*inf*) wastrel

Lud|wig ['lu:dvɪç] M -s Ludwig; (*= französischer Königsname*) Louis

Lu|es ['lu:ɛs] F -, *no pl* (*Med*) syphilis, lues (*spec*)

lu|e|tisch [lu'e:tɪʃ] ADJ (*Med*) syphilitic, luetic (*spec*)

Luft [lʊft] F -, (*liter*) ⸗e ['lʏftə] **a** air *no pl*; **die Lüfte** *pl* (*liter*) the skies, the air *sing*; **frische ~ hereinlassen** to let some fresh air in; **im Zimmer ist schlechte ~** the room is stuffy, the air *or* it is stuffy in the room; **bei schlechter ~ kann ich nicht schlafen** I can't sleep when it's stuffy; **dicke ~** (*inf*) a bad atmosphere; **~ an etw** (*acc*) **kommen lassen** to let the air get to sth; **an** *or* **in die/der (frischen) ~** in the fresh air; **an die (frische) ~ gehen/kommen** to get out in the fresh air; **(frische) ~ schnappen** (*inf*) *or* **schöpfen** (*geh*) to get some fresh air; **die ~ ist rein** (*inf*) the coast is clear; **die ~ reinigen** (*lit, fig*) to clear the air; **jetzt ist das Flugzeug in der ~** the plane is now airborne *or* in the air; **aus der ~** from the air; **die ~ aus etw lassen** to let the air out of sth; **die ~ ist raus** (*fig inf*) the fizz has gone; **jdn an die (frische) ~ setzen** (*inf*) to show sb the door; (*Sch*) to send sb out; (*= entlassen*) to give sb the push (*inf*); **in die ~ fliegen** (*inf*) to explode, to go up; **etw in die ~ jagen** (*inf*) *or* **sprengen** to blow sth up; **leicht** *or* **schnell in die ~ gehen** (*fig*) to be quick to blow one's top (*inf*), to be very quick-tempered; **er geht gleich in die ~** (*fig*) he's about to blow his top; **es**

liegt ein Gewitter in der ~ there's a storm brewing; **es liegt etwas in der ~** there's something in the air; **in die ~ starren** *or* **gucken** to stare into space *or* thin air; **in die ~ gucken** *(fig inf: = leer ausgehen)* to come away empty-handed *(inf)*; **jdn/etw in der ~ zerreißen** *(inf)* to tear sb/sth to pieces; **das kann sich doch nicht in ~ aufgelöst haben** it can't have vanished into thin air; **in der ~ hängen** *(Sache)* to be (very much) up in the air; *(Mensch)* to be in (a state of) limbo, to be dangling; **die Behauptung ist aus der ~ gegriffen** this statement is (a) pure invention; **vor Freude in die ~ springen** to jump for *or* with joy; **von ~ und Liebe/von ~ leben** to live on love/air; **jdn wie ~ behandeln** to treat sb as though he/she just didn't exist; **er ist ~ für mich** I'm not speaking to him

b *(= Atem)* breath; **der Kragen schnürt mir die ~ ab** this collar is choking me, I can't breathe in this collar; **nach ~ schnappen** to gasp for breath *or* air; **die ~ anhalten** *(lit)* to hold one's breath; **nun halt mal die ~ an!** *(inf) (= rede nicht)* hold your tongue!, put a sock in it! *(inf)*; *(= übertreibe nicht)* come off it! *(inf)*, come on! *(inf)*; **keine ~ mehr kriegen** not to be able to breathe; **nach ~ ringen** to struggle for breath; **tief ~ holen** *(lit, fig)* to take a deep breath; **... da musste ich erst mal tief ~ holen** *(fig: = war perplex)* it really made me gasp; **mir blieb vor Schreck/Schmerz die ~ weg** I was breathless with shock/pain; **wieder ~ bekommen** *or* **kriegen/haben** *(nach Sport etc)* to get/have got one's breath back; *(nach Schnupfen etc)* to be able to breathe again; *(fig)* to get/have a chance to catch one's breath

c *(= Wind)* breeze; **linde/laue Lüfte** *(liter)* gentle/warm breezes; **sich** *(dat)* **~ machen** *(= fächeln)* to fan oneself; **sich** *(dat)* **~ machen** *(fig)*, **seinem Herzen ~ machen** *(fig)* to get everything off one's chest; **seinem Ärger/Zorn** *etc* **~ machen** to give vent to one's annoyance/anger *etc*

d *(fig: = Spielraum, Platz)* space, room; **zwischen Wand und Regal etwas ~ lassen** to leave a space between the wall and the bookcase

Luft-: **Luft|ab|wehr** F *(Mil)* anti-aircraft defence *(Brit) or* defense *(US)*; **Luft|ab|wehr|ra|ke|te** F anti-aircraft missile; **Luft|ab|zug** M air vent; **Luft|alarm** M air-raid alarm; **Luft|an|griff** M air raid *(auf +acc* on); **einen ~ auf eine Stadt fliegen** to bomb a town, to carry out an air raid on a town; **Luft|auf|klä|rung** F aerial *or* air reconnaissance; **Luft|auf|nah|me** F aerial photo(graph); **Luft|auf|sicht** F *(Aviat)* air traffic control; **Luft|bal|lon** M balloon; **Luft|be|feuch|ter** [-bəfɔyçtɐ] M **-s, -** humidifier; **Luft|be|las|tung** F, *no pl* atmospheric pollution; **Luft|be|tan|kung** [-bətaŋkʊŋ] F **-, -en** *(Aviat)* in-flight refuelling *(Brit) or* refueling *(US)*; **Luft|be|we|gung** F movement of the air; **Luft|bild** NT aerial picture; **Luft|bläs|chen** [-blɛːsçən] NT *(Anat)* air sac; **Luft|bla|se** F air bubble, bubble of air; **Luft-Bo|den-Flug|kör|per** M air-to-surface ballistic missile; **Luft|brem|se** F air brake; **Luft|brü|cke** F airlift; **über eine ~** by airlift

Lüft|chen ['lʏftçən] NT **-s, -** breeze

Luft-: **luft|dicht** ADJ airtight *no adv* ADV **die Ware ist ~ verpackt** the article is in airtight packaging; **ein ~ verschlossener Behälter** an airtight container, a container with an airtight seal; **Luft|druck** M, *no pl* air pressure; **Luft|druck|wel|le** F *(Met)* pressure wave; *(= Knallwelle)* blast; **luft|durch|läs|sig** ADJ pervious to air; *Pflaster, Binde* breathable; **Luft|durch|läs|sig|keit** F perviousness to air; **ein Pflaster von größerer ~** a more breathable plaster

lüf|ten ['lʏftn] VT **a** *Raum, Kleidung, Bett* to air; *(ständig, systematisch)* to ventilate **b** *(= hochheben) Hut, Schleier* to raise, to lift; **das Geheimnis war gelüftet** the secret was out VI *(= Luft hereinlassen)* to let some air in; *(Betten, Kleider etc)* to air

Lüf|ter ['lʏftɐ] M **-s, -** fan

Luft|fahrt F aeronautics *sing*; *(mit Flugzeugen)* aviation *no art*

Luft|fahrt-: **Luft|fahrt|ge|sell|schaft** F airline (company); **Luft|fahrt|in|ge|nieur(in)** M(F) aviation engineer; **Luft|fahrt|kar|te** F aviation chart; **Luft|fahrt|me|di|zin** F aeromedicine; **Luft|fahrt|schau** F air show

Luft-: **Luft|fahr|zeug** NT aircraft; **Luft|feuch|tig|keit** F (atmospheric) humidity; **Luft|fil|ter** NT OR M air filter; **Luft|flot|te** F air fleet; **Luft|fracht** F air freight; **Luft|geist** M *(Myth)* spirit of the air; **luft|ge|kühlt** ADJ air-cooled; **luft|ge|schützt** ADJ sheltered ADV **etw ~ aufbewahren** to keep sth in an airtight container; **luft|ge|stützt** [-gəʃtʏtst] ADJ *Flugkörper* air-launched; **luft|ge|trock|net** [-gətrɔknət] ADJ air-dried; **Luft|ge|wehr** NT air rifle, air gun; **Luft|hauch** M *(geh)* gentle breeze; **Luft|herr|schaft** F air supremacy; **Luft|ho|heit** F air sovereignty; **Luft|ho|len** NT **-s,** *no pl* breathing; **zum ~ an die Oberfläche kommen** to come up for air; **Luft|hül|le** F mantle of air; **luft|hung|rig** ADJ longing for fresh air; **ein ~er Mensch** a fresh-air fiend

luf|tig ['lʊftɪç] ADJ *Zimmer* airy; *Plätzchen* breezy; *Kleidung* light; **in ~er Höhe** *(liter)* at a dizzy height ADV **~ gekleidet** lightly dressed; **das Restaurant war hell und ~ eingerichtet** the restaurant's furnishings lent it a light, airy feeling

Luf|ti|kus ['lʊftikʊs] M **-(ses), -se** *(inf)* happy-go-lucky sort of fellow

Luft-: **Luft|kampf** M air *or* aerial battle; **Luft|kis|sen** NT air cushion; *(von Luftkissenboot)* cushion of air; **Luft|kis|sen|boot** NT, **Luft|kis|sen|fahr|zeug** NT hovercraft; **Luft|klap|pe** F ventilation flap; **Luft|kor|ri|dor** M air corridor; **luft|krank** ADJ airsick; **Luft|krank|heit** F airsickness; **Luft|kreuz** NT, **Luft|kreu|zung** F centre *(Brit) or* center *(US)* of air routes; **Luft|krieg** M aerial warfare; **Luft- und Seekrieg** warfare at sea and in the air; **Luft|küh|lung** F air-cooling; **Luft|kur|ort** M (climatic) health resort; **Luft|lan|de|trup|pe** F airborne troops *pl*; **luft|leer** ADJ **(völlig) ~ sein** to be a vacuum; **~er Raum** vacuum; **etw im ~en Raum diskutieren** *(fig)* to discuss sth in a vacuum *or* in the abstract; **Luft|li|nie** F **200 km** *etc* **~** 200 km *etc* as the crow flies

Lüftl|ma|le|rei ['lʏftl-] F *(Art) (Gemälde)* (outdoor) wall *or* mural painting(s *pl*), façade painting(s *pl*), outdoor mural(s *pl*); *(Kunstart)* (oudoor) wall *or* mural painting, façade painting

Luft-: **Luft|loch** NT air hole; *(Aviat)* air pocket; **Luft|man|gel** M lack of air; **Luft|ma|sche** F *(Sew)* chain stitch; **Luft|mas|sen** PL air masses *pl*; **Luft|mat|rat|ze** F air bed *(Brit)*, Lilo® *(Brit)*, air mattress *(esp US)*; **Luft|pi|rat(in)** M(F) (aircraft) hijacker, skyjacker *(esp US)*; **Luft|pols|ter** NT air cushion

Luft|post F airmail; **mit ~** by airmail

Luft|post-: **Luft|post|auf|kle|ber** M airmail sticker; **Luft|post|leicht|brief** M aerogramme, air letter *(Brit)*; **Luft|post|pa|pier** NT airmail paper

Luft-: **Luft|pum|pe** F air *or* pneumatic pump; *(für Fahrrad)* (bicycle) pump; **Luft|qua|li|tät** F air quality; **Luft|raum** M airspace; **Luft|raum|über|wa|chung** F air traffic control; **Luft|recht** NT air traffic law; **Luft|rei|fen** M pneumatic tyre *(Brit) or* tire *(US)*; **Luft|rein|hal|tung** F prevention of air pollution; **Luft|rei|ni|ger** M air purifier; **Luft|ret|tungs|dienst** M air rescue service; **Luft|röh|re** F *(Anat)* windpipe, trachea; **Luft|röh|ren|schnitt** M tracheotomy; **Luft|sack** M *(Aut)* air bag; *(Orn)* air sac; **Luft|schacht** M ventilation shaft; **Luft|schau|kel** F swingboat; **Luft|schicht** F *(Met)* layer of air; **Luft|schiff** NT airship; **Luft|schiff|fahrt** F aeronautics *sing*; **Luft|schlacht** F air battle; **die ~ um England** the Battle of Britain; **Luft|schlan|ge** F (paper) streamer; **Luft|schlitz** M *(Aut)* ventilation slit; **Luft|schloss** NT *(fig)* castle in the air, pipe dream; **Luftschlösser bauen** to build castles in the air; **Luft|schnei|se** F air lane; **Luft|schrau|be** F propeller, airscrew

Luft|schutz M anti-aircraft defence *(Brit) or* defense *(US)*

Luft|schutz-: **Luft|schutz|bun|ker** M, **Luft|schutz|kel|ler** M, **Luft|schutz|raum** M air-raid shelter; **Luft|schutz|übung** F air-raid drill

Luft-: **Luft|sieg** M air victory; **Luft|sper|re** F *(Mil)* aerial barrage; **Luft|spie|ge|lung** F mirage; **Luft|sprung** M jump in the air; **vor Freude einen ~** *or* **Luftsprünge machen** to jump for *or* with joy; **Luft|stoß** M gust (of wind); **Luft|stra|ße** F air route; **Luft|stre|cke** F air route; **Luft|streit|kräf|te** PL air force *sing*; **Luft|strom** M stream of air; **Luft|strö|mung** F current of air; **Luft|stütz|punkt** M air base; **Luft|tan|ken** NT **-s,** *no pl* in-flight refuelling *(Brit) or* refueling *(US)*; **Luft|ta|xi** NT air taxi; **Luft|tem|pe|ra|tur** F air temperature; **Luft|tor|pe|do** M aerial torpedo; **luft|tro|cken** ADJ air-dry; **luft|tüch|tig** ADJ *Flugzeug* airworthy; **Luft|über|wa|chung** F air surveillance; **Luft|über|wa|chungs|flug|kör|per** M airborne warning and control system; **Luft- und Raum|fahrt|in|dust|rie** F aerospace industry; **Luft- und Raum|fahrt|tech|nik** F aerospace technology

Lüf|tung ['lʏftʊŋ] F **-, -en** airing; *(ständig, systematisch)* ventilation

Lüf|tungs-: **Lüf|tungs|an|la|ge** F ventilation (system); **Lüf|tungs|klap|pe** F ventilation flap; **Lüf|tungs|rohr** NT ventilation pipe; **Lüf|tungs|schacht** M ventilation shaft

Luft-: **Luft|un|ter|stüt|zung** F *(Mil)* air support; **Luft|ver|än|de|rung** F change of air; **Luft|ver|flüs|si|gung** F liquefaction of air; **Luft|ver|kehr** M air traffic; **Luft|ver|kehrs|ge|sell|schaft** F airline; **Luft|ver|kehrs|li|nie** F air route; **Luft|ver|pes|tung** F *(pej)*, **Luft|ver|schmut|zung** F air pollution; **Luft|ver|sor|gung** F air supplies *pl*; **Luft|ver|tei|di|gung** F air defence *(Brit) or* defense *(US)*; **Luft|waf|fe** F *(Mil)* air force; **die (deutsche) ~** the Luftwaffe; **Luft|waf|fen|stütz|punkt** M air-force base; **Luft|weg** M *(= Flugweg)* air route; *(= Atemweg)* respiratory tract; **etw auf dem ~ befördern** to transport by air; **Luft|wi|der|stand** M air resistance; **Luft|wi|der|stands|bei|wert** M drag coefficient; **Luft|zu|fuhr** F air supply; **Luft|zug** M wind, (mild) breeze; *(in Gebäude)* draught *(Brit)*, draft *(US)*

Lug [luːk] M **~ und Trug** lies *pl* (and deception)

Lü|ge ['lyːgə] F **-, -n** lie, falsehood; **jdn einer ~ beschuldigen** *or* **bezichtigen** to accuse sb of lying; **jdn der ~ überführen** to catch sb (out) lying; **das ist alles ~** that's all lies; **jdn/etw ~n strafen** to give the lie to sb/sth, to belie sth; **~n haben kurze Beine** *(prov)* truth will out *(esp Brit prov)*, truth will prevail

lu|gen ['luːgn] VI *(dial)* to peep, to peek

lü|gen ['lyːgn] *pret* **log** [loːk], *ptp* **gelogen** [gə'loːgn] VI to lie; **ich müsste ~, wenn ...** I would be lying if ...; **sie lügt, wenn sie nur den Mund aufmacht** she's a born liar; **wie gedruckt ~** *(inf)* to lie like mad *(inf)*; **wer einmal lügt, dem glaubt man nicht, und wenn er auch die Wahrheit spricht** *(Prov)* remember the boy who cried "wolf" *(prov)* VT **das ist gelogen!, das lügst du doch!** *(inf)* that's a lie!, you're lying! → **Blaue(s) a**

Lü|gen-: **Lü|gen|be|richt** M fabrication; **Lü|gen|bold** [-bɔlt] M **-(e)s, -e** [-də] *(dated inf)* (inveterate) liar; **Lü|gen|de|tek|tor** M lie detector; **Lü|gen|dich|tung** F *(lit, fig)* wildly improbable story, tall tale *(lit, Liter)*; **Lü|gen|ge|bäu|de** NT, **Lü|gen|ge|spinst** NT *(geh)*, **Lü|gen|ge|we|be** NT *(liter)* tissue *or* web of lies; **Lü|gen|ge|schich|te** F pack of lies; **lü|gen|haft** ADJ *Erzählung* made-up, mendacious *(form)*; *Bericht auch* false; **seine ~en Geschich-**

ten his tall stories; **Lü|gen|kam|pag|ne** F campaign of lies; **Lü|gen|mär|chen** NT tall story, cock-and-bull story; **Lü|gen|maul** NT *(pej inf)* liar; **Lü|gen|pro|pa|gan|da** F propagandist lies *pl*, mendacious propaganda

Lü|ge|rei [ly:gə'rai] F -, -en lying *no pl*, fibbing *no pl*

Lüg|ner ['ly:gnɐ] M -s, -, **Lüg|ne|rin** [-ərɪn] F -, -nen liar

lüg|ne|risch ['ly:gnərɪʃ] ADJ *Mensch, Worte* lying *attr*, untruthful, mendacious *(form)*

Lu|kas ['lu:kas] M -' Luke

Lu|kas|evan|ge|li|um NT Gospel according to St. Luke, St. Luke's Gospel

Lu|ke ['lu:kə] F -, -n hatch; *(= Dachluke)* skylight

luk|ra|tiv [lukra'ti:f] ADJ lucrative ADV lucratively

lu|kul|lisch [lu'kʊlɪʃ] ADJ epicurean ADV exquisitely

Lu|kul|lus [lu'kʊlʊs] M -, -se *(fig)* epicure, gourmet, gastronome

Lu|latsch ['lu:la(:)tʃ] M -(es), -e *(hum inf)* **langer ~** beanpole *(inf)*

lul|len ['lʊlən] VT *(dated)* **ein Kind in den Schlaf ~** to lull a child to sleep

Lum|ba|go [lʊm'ba:go] F -, *no pl* lumbago

lum|be|cken ['lʊmbɛkn] VT *(Typ)* to adhesive-bind

Lum|ber|jack ['lambɐdʒɛk] M -s, -s *(dated)* lumber jacket

Lum|me ['lʊmə] F -, -n guillemot

Lüm|mel ['lʏml] M -s, - **a** *(pej)* lout, oaf; **du ~, du** you rascal *or* rogue you **b** *(hum inf: = Penis)* willie *(Brit inf)*, weenie *(US inf)*

Lüm|me|lei [lʏmə'lai] F -, -en *(inf)* sprawling about; *(= Flegelei)* rudeness *no pl*

lüm|mel|haft *(pej)* ADJ ill-mannered ADV ill-manneredly

lüm|meln ['lʏmln] VR *(inf)* to sprawl; *(= sich hinlümmeln)* to flop down

Lüm|mel|tü|te F *(hum inf: = Kondom)* French letter *(Brit inf)*, rubber *(US inf)*

Lum|mer ['lʊmɐ] M -s, - *(S Ger: Cook)* roast loin; *(vom Rind)* sirloin

Lump [lʊmp] M -en, -en *(pej)* rogue, blackguard *(dated)*

lum|pen ['lʊmpn] VT *(inf)* **sich nicht ~ lassen** to splash out *(inf)* VI *(old, dial)* to go out on the tiles *(inf)*

Lum|pen ['lʊmpn] M -s, - **a** rag **b** *(S Ger: = Lappen)* cloth

Lum|pen-: **Lum|pen|ge|sin|del** NT *(pej)* rabble *pl (pej)*, riffraff *pl (pej)*; **Lum|pen|händ|ler** M rag-and-bone man; **Lum|pen|pack** NT *(pej inf)* rabble *pl (pej)*, riffraff *pl (pej)*; **Lum|pen|pro|le|ta|ri|at** NT *(Sociol)* lumpenproletariat; **Lum|pen|samm|ler** M **a** *(= Lumpenhändler)* rag-and-bone man **b** *(hum: = Bus/Bahn/Zug)* last bus/tram/train, drunks' special *(hum)*

Lum|pe|rei [lʊmpə'rai] F -, -en *(inf)* mean *or* dirty trick

lum|pig ['lʊmpɪç] ADJ **a** *Kleidung* ragged, tattered **b** *Gesinnung, Tat* shabby, mean **c** *attr (inf: = geringfügig)* paltry, measly *(inf)*; **~e 10 Euro** 10 paltry *or* measly *(inf)* euros ADV **a** *(= zerlumpt)* raggedly; **~ aussehen** to look tattered; **~ herumlaufen** to go around in rags; **sich ~ anziehen** to be dressed in rags **b** *(= gemein)* shabbily

Lu|na|tis|mus [luna'tɪsmʊs] M -, *no pl (Psych)* sleepwalking, somnambulism *(form)*

Lunch [lanʃ, lantʃ] M -(es) *or* -s, -e(s) *or* -s lunch, luncheon *(form)*

lun|chen ['lanʃn, 'lantʃn] VI *(geh)* to lunch *(form)*

Lunch|pa|ket ['lanʃ-, 'lantʃ-] NT packed lunch, lunchbox, box lunch *(US)*

Lü|ne|bur|ger Hei|de ['ly:nəbʊrgɐ] F Lüneburg Heath

Lun|ge ['lʊŋə] F -, -n lungs *pl*; *(= Lungenflügel)* lung; **(auf) ~ rauchen** to inhale; **sich** *(dat)* **die ~ aus dem Hals** *or* **Leib schreien** *(inf)* to yell till one is blue in the face *(inf)*; **sich** *(dat)* **die ~ aus dem Leib husten** *(inf)* to cough one's lungs up *(Brit inf) or* out *(esp US inf)*; **die (grünen) ~n einer Großstadt** the lungs of a city → **eisern ADJ a**

Lun|gen-: **Lun|gen|bläs|chen** [-blɛ:sçən] NT pulmonary alveolus *(spec)*; **Lun|gen|bra|ten** M *(Aus)* loin roast *(Brit)*, porterhouse (steak); **Lun|gen|em|bo|lie** F pulmonary embolism *(spec)*; **Lun|gen|em|phy|sem** [-lɛmfyze:m] NT -s, -e pulmonary emphysema; **Lun|gen|ent|zün|dung** F pneumonia; **Lun|gen|fisch** M lungfish; **Lun|gen|flü|gel** M lung; **Lun|gen|ha|schee** NT *(Cook) hash made with calf's lights*; **Lun|gen|heil|stät|te** F TB *or* tuberculosis sanitarium *(US) or* sanatorium; **lun|gen|krank** ADJ **~ sein** to have a lung *or* pulmonary *(form)* disease; **Lun|gen|kran|ke(r)** MF *decl as adj* person suffering from a lung *or* pulmonary *(form)* disease; **Lun|gen|krank|heit** F lung *or* pulmonary *(form)* disease; **Lun|gen|kraut** NT *(Bot)* lungwort; **Lun|gen|krebs** M lung cancer; **Lun|gen|sa|na|to|ri|um** NT tuberculosis sanitarium *(US) or* sanatorium; **Lun|gen|tu|ber|ku|lo|se** F tuberculosis (of the lung), TB; **Lun|gen|tu|mor** M lung tumour *(Brit) or* tumor *(US)*; **Lun|gen|zug** M deep drag *(inf)*; **einen ~ machen** to inhale deeply, to take a deep drag *(inf)*

lun|gern ['lʊŋɐn] VI *(inf)* to loaf or hang about *(Brit inf) or* around

Lun|te ['lʊntə] F -, -n **a** *(Hist)* fuse; **~ riechen** *(= Verdacht schöpfen)* to smell a rat *(inf)*; *(= Gefahr wittern)* to smell *(inf) or* sense danger **b** *(Hunt: = Fuchsschwanz)* brush

Lu|pe ['lu:pə] F -, -n magnifying glass; **so etwas/solche Leute kannst du mit der ~ suchen** things/people like that are few and far between; **jdn/etw unter die ~ nehmen** *(inf) (= beobachten)* to keep a close eye on sb/sth; *(= prüfen)* to examine sb/sth closely

lu|pen|rein ADJ *(lit) Edelstein* flawless; *Diamant auch* of the first water; *(fig) Vergangenheit etc auch* unimpeachable, unblemished; *Englisch, Bayrisch auch* perfect; *Gentleman, Intellektueller, Demokrat* through and through *pred*; **das Geschäft war nicht ganz ~** the deal wouldn't stand close scrutiny *or* wasn't quite all above board ADV *trennen* absolutely; *darstellen* flawlessly

lup|fen ['lʊpfn], **lüp|fen** ['lʏpfn] VT *(S Ger, Aus, Sw)* to lift, to raise

Lu|pi|ne [lu'pi:nə] F -, -n lupin

Lurch [lʊrç] M -(e)s, -e amphibian

Lu|re ['lu:rə] F -, -n lur

Lu|rex® ['lu:rɛks] NT -, *no pl* Lurex®

Lu|sche ['lʊʃə] F -, -n *(Cards)* low card; *(fig)* cipher

Lust [lʊst] F -, ⸚e ['lʏstə] **a** *no pl (= Freude)* pleasure, joy; **er hat die ~ daran verloren, die ~ daran ist ihm vergangen** he has lost all interest in it; **da kann einem die (ganze)** *or* **alle ~ vergehen, da vergeht einem die ganze ~** it puts you off; **jdm die ~ an etw** *(dat)* **nehmen** to take all the fun out of sth for sb; **ich habe immer mit ~ und Liebe gekocht** I've always enjoyed cooking; **sie ging mit/ohne ~ an die Arbeit** she set to work enthusiastically/without enthusiasm **b** *no pl (= Neigung)* inclination; **zu etw ~ (und Liebe) haben** to feel like sth; **ich habe keine ~, das zu tun** I don't really want to do that; *(= bin nicht dazu aufgelegt)* I don't feel like doing that; **ich habe keine ~ zu arbeiten** I'm not in the mood to work *or* for working, I don't feel like work *or* working; **ich habe ~, das zu tun** I'd like to do that; *(= bin dazu aufgelegt)* I feel like doing that; **ich habe jetzt keine ~** I'm not in the mood just now; **ich hätte ~ dazu** I'd like to; **das mache ich erst, wenn ich ~ dazu habe** I'll do that when I feel like it *or* when I'm in the mood; **hast du ~?** how about it?; **auf etw** *(acc)* **~ haben** to feel like sth, to fancy sth; **jdm ~ zu etw** *or* **auf etw** *(acc)* **machen** to put sb in the mood for sth; **mach, wie du ~ hast** *(inf)* do as you like; **er kann bleiben, solange er ~ hat** he can stay as long as he likes; **~ kriegen, etw zu tun** to feel like doing sth; **ich habe nicht übel ~, ... zu ...** I've a good *or* half a mind to ...; **ganz** *or* **je nach ~ und Laune** *(inf)* just depending on how I/you *etc* feel, just depending on my/your *etc* mood **c** *(= sinnliche Begierde)* desire; *(sexuell)* desire, lust *(usu pej)*; **~ haben** to feel desire; **er/sie hat ~** *(inf)* he's/she's in the mood *(inf)*; **seinen Lüsten leben** *or* **frönen** to indulge one's desires/lusts *(pej)*

Lust|aus|ter F *(hum sl: = Vagina)* love hole *(sl)*

Lust|bar|keit ['lʊstba:ɐkait] F -, -en *(dated)* jollity

lust|be|tont ADJ pleasure-orientated, governed by the pleasure principle; *Beziehung, Mensch* sensual ADV sensually; **~ unterrichten** to teach in such a way that learning is fun; **sein Leben so ~ wie möglich gestalten** to live one's life as enjoyably as possible

Lus|ter ['lʊstɐ] M -s, - *(Aus: = Leuchter)* chandelier

Lüs|ter ['lʏstɐ] M -s, - **a** *(= Leuchter)* chandelier **b** *(= Stoff, Glanzüberzug)* lustre *(Brit)*, luster *(US)*

Lüs|ter|klem|me F *(Elec)* connector

lüs|tern ['lʏstɐn] ADJ lascivious; *Mann auch* lecherous; **nach etw ~ sein** to lust after *or* for sth ADV lecherously; lasciviously

Lüs|tern|heit F -, *no pl* lasciviousness; *(von Mann auch)* lecherousness

Lust-: **lust|feind|lich** ADJ *(geh)* opposed to carnal pleasures; **Lust|film** M *(dated)* comedy film; **Lust|gar|ten** M *(old)* pleasance; **Lust|ge|fühl** NT feeling of pleasure; *(sexuell auch)* desire; **Lust|ge|winn** M pleasure; **Lust|greis** M *(hum)* dirty old man *(inf)*, old lecher; **Lust|haus** NT *(dated)* summer house, garden pavilion; **Lust|höh|le** F *(hum sl: = Vagina)* love hole *(sl)*

lus|tig ['lʊstɪç] ADJ *(= munter)* merry, jolly; *Mensch auch* jovial; *(= humorvoll)* funny, amusing; *(= emsig)* happy, merry, cheerful; **es wurde ~** things got quite merry; **seid ~!** liven up and have a bit of fun; **Lustige Person** *(Theat)* clown, fool, buffoon; **Die Lustige Witwe** the Merry Widow; **Bruder Lustig** *(old)* jolly *or* merry fellow *(dated)*; **das ist ja ~!** *(iro)* **das finde ich aber ~!** *(iro)* (that's) very *or* most amusing *(iro)*; **das kann ja ~ werden!** *(iro)* that's going to be fun *(iro)*; **das kannst du tun, solange du ~ bist** *(inf)* you can do that as long as you like *or* please; **sich über jdn/etw ~ machen** to make fun of sb/sth ADV **a** *(= fröhlich)* **sich ~ unterhalten** to have a lot of fun; **auf ihren Partys geht es ~ zu** her parties are always a lot of fun; **schau doch ein bisschen ~er** come on, cheer up **b** *(= humorvoll)* amusingly **c** *(inf: = unbekümmert)* happily

Lus|tig|keit F -, *no pl (= Munterkeit)* merriness *(dated)*; *(von Mensch auch)* joviality; *(von Geschichte)* funniness

Lust|kna|be M *(old, hum)* catamite

Lüst|ling ['lʏstlɪŋ] M -s, -e debauchee, lecher; **ein alter ~** an old lecher, a debauched old man

Lust-: **lust|los** ADJ unenthusiastic; *(Fin) Börse* slack, dull ADV unenthusiastically; **Lust|lo|sig|keit** F -, *no pl* lack of enthusiasm; *(Fin: von Börse)* slackness; **Lust|molch** M *(hum inf)* sex maniac *(inf)*; *(bewundernd)* sexy beast *(inf)*, sexpot *(inf)*; **Lust|mord** M sex murder; **Lust|mör|der(in)** M(F) sex killer *or* murderer; **Lust|ob|jekt** NT sex object; **Lust|prin|zip** NT *(Psych)* pleasure principle; **Lust|schloss** NT summer residence; **Lust|spiel** NT comedy; **Lust|spiel|dich|ter(in)** M(F) comedy writer, writer of comedies; **Lust|ver|lust** M, *no pl* **unter ~ leiden** to have lost one's zest for life; **lust|voll** ADJ full of relish ADV with relish; **lust|wan|deln** VI *insep aux sein or haben (liter)* to (take a) stroll, to promenade *(old)*

Lu|te|ti|um [lu'te:tsiʊm] **NT -s,** *no pl* (*abbr* **Lu**) lutecium

luth. *abbr von* **lutherisch**

Lu|the|ra|ner [lutə'ra:nɐ] **M -s, -, Lu|the|ra|ne|rin** [-ərɪn] **F -, -nen** Lutheran

Lu|ther|bi|bel F Lutheran translation *(of the Bible)*

lu|the|risch ['lʊtərɪʃ], **lu|thersch** ['lʊtɐʃ] **ADJ** Lutheran

lut|schen ['lʊtʃn] **VTI** to suck (*an etw (dat)* sth)

Lut|scher ['lʊtʃɐ] **M -s, -** lollipop

Lutsch|tab|let|te F *(Med)* lozenge

lütt [lʏt] **ADJ** *(N Ger inf)* little, wee *(esp Scot)*; **die Lütten** *(= Kinder)* the kids

Lüt|tich ['lʏtɪç] **NT -s** Liège

Luv [lu:f] **F -,** *no pl (Naut)* windward *or* weather side; **nach ~** to windward

lu|ven ['lu:vn, 'lu:fn] **VI** *(Naut)* to luff (up)

Luv|sei|te F windward side

Lux [lʊks] **NT -, -** *(Phys)* lux

Lu|xa|ti|on [lʊksa'tsio:n] **F -, -en** *(Med)* dislocation

Lu|xem|burg ['lʊksmbʊrk] **NT -s** Luxembourg

Lu|xem|bur|ger ['lʊksmbʊrgɐ] **M -s, -, Lu|xem|bur|ge|rin** [-ərɪn] **F -, -nen** Luxembourger

lu|xem|bur|gisch ['lʊksmbʊrgɪʃ] **ADJ** Luxembourgian

lu|xu|ri|ös [lʊksu'riø:s] **ADJ** luxurious; **ein ~es Leben** a life of luxury **ADV** luxuriously; **~ Urlaub machen** to take a luxurious holiday *(esp Brit) or* vacation *(US)*

Lu|xus ['lʊksʊs] **M -,** *no pl* luxury; (*pej:* = *Verschwendung, Überfluss*) extravagance; **im ~ leben/schwelgen** to live in (the lap of) luxury; **den ~ lieben** to love luxury; **mit etw ~ treiben** to be extravagant with sth, to lash out on sth *(inf)*; **ich leiste mir den ~ und …** I'll treat myself to the luxury of …

Lu|xus- *in cpds* luxury; **Lu|xus|ar|ti|kel M** luxury article; **~** *pl* luxury goods *pl*; **Lu|xus|aus|füh|rung F** de luxe model; **Lu|xus|aus|ga|be F** de luxe edition; **Lu|xus|damp|fer M** luxury cruise ship; **Lu|xus|frau F** *(inf)* piece of class *(inf)*, classy woman; **Lu|xus|gü|ter PL** luxury goods *pl*; **Lu|xus|ho|tel NT** luxury hotel; **Lu|xus|klas|se F,** *no pl* **der ~** *(nachgestellt)* de luxe *attr*, luxury-class *attr*, deluxe *attr (US)*, luxury *attr*; **Lu|xus|kör|per M** *(hum)* beautiful body; **Lu|xus|li|mou|si|ne F** limousine; **Lu|xus|res|tau|rant NT** first-class restaurant; **Lu|xus|schlit|ten M** *(inf)* classy car *(inf) or* job *(inf)*; **Lu|xus|weib|chen NT** *(pej)* classy piece *(inf)*; **Lu|xus|zug M** Pullman (train)

Lu|zern [lu'tsɛrn] **NT -s** Lucerne

Lu|zer|ne [lu'tsɛrnə] **F -, -n** *(Bot)* lucerne

lu|zid [lu'tsi:t] **ADJ** *(liter)* lucid; *(= durchsichtig)* translucent

Lu|zi|fer ['lu:tsifɛr] **M -s** Lucifer

lu|zi|fe|risch [lutsi'fe:rɪʃ] **ADJ** diabolical, satanic

LVA [ɛlfau'la:] **F -, -s** *abbr von* **Landesversicherungsanstalt**

LW [ɛl've:] *abbr von* **Langwelle** LW

Ly|chee ['lɪtʃi] **F -, -s** lychee, litchi

Lymph-: **Lymph|bahn F** lymph vessel; **Lymph|drä|na|ge F** lymphatic drainage; **Lymph|drü|se F** lymph(atic) gland

Lym|phe ['lʏmfə] **F -, -n** lymph

Lymph|kno|ten ['lʏmf-] **M** lymph node, lymph(atic) gland

Lymph|kno|ten-: **Lymph|kno|ten|ent|zün|dung F** inflammation of the lymph node; **Lymph|kno|ten|schwel|lung F** swelling of the lymph node

Lym|pho|zyt [lʏmfo'tsy:t] **M -en, -en** lymphocyte

lyn|chen ['lʏnçn, 'lɪnçn] **VT** *(lit)* to lynch; *(fig)* to kill

Lynch-: **Lynch|jus|tiz F** lynch law; **Lynch|mord M** lynching

Ly|o|ner ['lio:nɐ] **F -, -** *(= Wurst) type of pork or veal sausage*

Ly|ra ['ly:ra] **F -, Lyren** [-rən] *(Mus)* lyre; **die ~** *(Astron)* Lyra, the Lyre

Ly|rik ['ly:rɪk] **F -,** *no pl* lyric poetry *or* verse

Ly|ri|ker ['ly:rikɐ] **M -s, -, Ly|ri|ke|rin** [-ərɪn] **F -, -nen** lyric poet, lyricist

ly|risch ['ly:rɪʃ] **ADJ** *(lit, fig)* lyrical; *Dichtung, Dichter* lyric **ADV** lyrically

Ly|ze|um [ly'tse:ʊm] **NT -s, Lyzeen** [ly'tse:ən] **a** *(= Gymnasium)* girls' grammar school *(Brit)*, girls' high school **b** *(Sw:* = *Oberstufe)* upper school

M, m [ɛm] NT **-, -** M, m
m [ɛm] *abbr von* **Meter**
MA. *abbr von* **Mittelalter**
M.A. [ɛm'la:] *(Univ) abbr von* **Magister Artium** MA, M.A. *(US)*
Mä|an|der [mɛ'andɐ] M **-s, -** *(Geog, Art)* meander
mä|an|dern [mɛ'andɐn] *ptp* **mäandert** VI *(Geog)* to meander VT *(Art)* to decorate with meanders
mä|and|risch [mɛ'andrɪʃ] ADJ meandering ADV **sich ~ schlängeln** to meander; **~ verziert** *(Art)* decorated with meanders
Maar [ma:ɐ] NT **-(e)s, -e** *(Geol)* maar *(spec)*, volcanic lake
Maas [ma:s] F **-** Meuse, Maas
Maas|tricht-Ver|trag [ma:s'trɪçt] M Maastricht Treaty
Maat [ma:t] M **-(e)s, -e** *or* **-en** *(Naut)* (ship's) mate
Mac|chi|a ['makia] F **-, Macchien, Mac|chi|e** ['makiə] F **-, Macchien** *(Bot)* maquis, macchia
Mach [max] NT **-(s), -** *(Phys)* Mach
Ma|chan|del [ma'xandl] M **-s, -, Ma|chan|del|baum** M *(N Ger)* juniper (tree)
Mach|art F make; *(= Muster)* design; *(lit, fig: = Stil)* style
mach|bar ADJ feasible, possible
Mach|bar|keit ['maxba:ɐkait] F **-,** *no pl* feasibility
Mach|bar|keits|stu|die F feasibility study
Ma|che ['maxə] F **-, -n** *(inf)* **a** *(= Technik)* structure **b** *(= Vortäuschung)* sham; **reine** *or* **pure ~ sein** to be (a) sham **c etw in der ~ haben** *(inf)* to be working on sth, to have sth on the stocks; **in der ~ sein** *(inf)* to be in the making; **der Film war noch in der ~** *(inf)* the film was still being made

ma|chen ['maxn]

1 TRANSITIVES VERB
2 INTRANSITIVES VERB
3 REFLEXIVES VERB

1 – TRANSITIVES VERB

Wenn *machen* sich auf eine nicht näher gekennzeichnete Aktivität bezieht oder stellvertretend für ein anderes Verb steht, wird es in den meisten Fällen mit *to do* übersetzt.

a = tun to do; **was machst du heute Abend?** what are you doing this evening?; **was machen wir mit dem restlichen Brot?** what shall we do with the rest of the bread?; **die Hausarbeit/den Garten machen** to do the housework/the garden; **er machte sich** *(dat)* **Zucker in den Kaffee** *(inf)* he put sugar in his coffee; **ich muss noch so viel machen** I still have so much to do; **ich mache dir das schon** I'll do that for you; **ich mache das schon** *(= bringe das in Ordnung)* I'll see to that; *(= erledige das)* I'll do that; **gut, wird gemacht** right, will do *(inf)*; **gut, mache ich** right, will do *(inf)* or I'll do that; **wie mans macht, ists verkehrt** whatever you do is wrong; **was habe ich nur falsch gemacht?** what have I done wrong?; **er macht, was er will** he does what he likes; **soll ich ihn nach seinem Gehalt fragen? – so etwas macht man nicht!** shall I ask how much he earns? – you don't ask that (question)!; **wie machen Sie das nur?** how do you do it?; **das lässt sich machen/nicht machen** that can/can't be done; **das ist zu/nicht zu machen** that can/can't be done; **(da ist) nichts zu machen** *(= geht nicht)* (there's) nothing to be done; *(= kommt nicht infrage)* nothing doing; **ich kann da auch nichts machen** I can't do anything about it either; **ich mache es wohl am besten so, dass ich etwas früher komme** I would do best to come a bit earlier; **es ist schon gut gemacht, wie sie die Rolle der Ophelia mit echtem Leben erfüllt** it's wonderful how she brings the role of Ophelia to life; **damit/mit ihr kann man etwas machen** you could do something with it/her; **das lässt er nicht mit sich machen** he won't stand for that → *auch* **gemacht**

♦ **was macht jd/etw? was machst du da?** what are you doing (there)?; **was hast du denn nun wieder gemacht?** what have you done now?; **was machst du denn hier?** what (on earth) are you doing here?; **was macht denn das Fahrrad hier im Hausflur?** what's this bicycle doing in the hall?; **was macht die Arbeit?** how's the work going?; **was macht dein Bruder (beruflich)?** what does your brother do (for a living)?; **was macht dein Bruder?** *(= wie geht es ihm?)* how's your brother doing?

♦ **es machen machs kurz!** make it short!; **machs gut!** all the best!; **er wirds nicht mehr lange machen** *(inf)* he won't last long; **es mit jdm machen** *(inf: = Sex haben)* to make *or* do it with sb *(inf)*; **es jdm machen** *(sl: = befriedigen)* to bring sb off *(sl)*; **es sich** *(dat)* **selber machen** *(sl)* to bring oneself off *(inf)*; **mit mir kann mans ja machen!** *(inf)* the things I put up with! *(inf)*

b = anfertigen, zubereiten to make; **Bier wird aus Gerste gemacht** beer is made from barley; **aus Holz gemacht** made of wood; **sich/jdm etw machen lassen** to have sth made for oneself/sb; **er ist für den Beruf wie gemacht** he's made for the job; **das Essen machen** to make the meal; **jdm einen Drink machen** *(Cocktail)* to make *or* mix sb a drink

c = verursachen, bewirken *Schwierigkeiten, Arbeit* to make (*jdm* for sb); *Mühe, Schmerzen* to cause (*jdm* for sb); **jdm Angst/Sorgen/Freude machen** to make sb afraid/worried/happy; **jdm Hoffnung/Mut/Kopfschmerzen machen** to give sb hope/courage/a headache; **das macht Appetit** that gives you an appetite; **das macht Hunger** that makes you hungry; **das macht die Kälte** it's the cold that does that; **jdn lachen/weinen/etw vergessen machen** to make sb laugh/cry/forget sth; **machen, dass etw geschieht** to make sth happen; **mach, dass er gesund wird!** make him better!; **das machen die vielen Zigaretten, dass du hustest** it's all those cigarettes that make you cough; **(viel) von sich reden machen** to be much talked about → **schaffen**

d = hervorbringen *Laut, Geräusch* to make; **mäh/miau machen** to baa/miaow; **brumm machen** to go "brumm"; **wie macht das Kindchen?** say please!; **wie macht das feine Hündchen?** be a clever dog!

e = bilden *Kreuzzeichen, Kreis* to make; **die Straße macht einen Knick** the road bends

f machen + Substantiv

Siehe auch unter dem Eintrag für das jeweilige Substantiv.

einen Ausflug machen to go on an outing; **Bilder machen** to take photos; **ein Defizit machen** to make a loss; **ein Diplom machen** to do a diploma; **einen Doktor machen** to do a doctorate; **ein Fest machen** to have a party; **Fotos machen** to take photos; **das Geschirr machen** to do the dishes; **einen Gewinn machen** to make a profit; **Grimassen machen** to make a face; **Halt machen** = **haltmachen**; **einen Handstand machen** to do a handstand; **auf jdn/etw Jagd machen** to hunt sb/sth; **einen Kopfsprung machen** to take a header *(Brit)*, to dive (headfirst); **einen Kurs machen** *(= teilnehmen)* to do a course; **Nachtdienst machen** to do night duty; **eine Party machen** to have a party; **Pause machen** to have a break; **mach mir mal einen (guten) Preis!** make me an offer!; **eine Prüfung machen** to do *(esp Brit)* or take an exam; **Punkte machen** to get points; **jdm die Rechnung machen** to make up sb's bill; **Schicht machen** to work shifts; **einen Spaziergang machen** to go for a walk; **ein Spiel machen** to play a game

g machen + Adjektiv

Siehe auch unter dem Eintrag für das jeweilige Adjektiv.

to make; **jdn nervös/unglücklich machen** to make sb nervous/unhappy; **etw größer/kleiner machen** to make sth bigger/smaller; **etw sauber/schmutzig machen** to get sth clean/dirty; **etw leer machen** to empty sth; **etw kürzer machen** to shorten sth; **einen Stuhl frei machen** to vacate a chair; **jdn alt/jung machen** *(= aussehen lassen)* to make sb look old/young; **jdn wieder sehend machen** to make sb see again; **machs dir doch bequem/gemütlich** make yourself comfortable/at home; **mach es ihm nicht noch schwerer** don't make it harder for him; **er macht es sich** *(dat)* **nicht leicht** he doesn't make it easy for himself

h = ergeben *inf* to make; *Summe, Preis* to be; **das macht (zusammen) 23** that makes 23 altogether; **drei und fünf macht** *or* **machen acht** three and five makes *or* is eight; **fünf mal vier macht** *or* **machen zwanzig** five fours are twenty, five times four is twenty; **was macht die Rechnung?** how much is the bill?, what does the bill come to?; **was** *or* **wie viel macht sechs geteilt durch zwei?** what is six divided by two?; **100 cm machen einen Meter** 100 cm make a metre *(Brit)* or meter *(US)*; **was** *or* **wie viel macht das (alles zusammen)?** how much is that altogether?

i = spielen *inf, Theat* to play; *Dolmetscher, Schiedsrichter etc* to be; **den Weihnachtsmann machen** to play Santa Claus; **den Ghostwriter für jdn machen** to be sb's ghostwriter

j [= Notdurft verrichten] *inf* **einen Haufen** *or* **sein Geschäft machen** (*euph:*) *(Hund)* to do its business *(euph)* → **Aa, Pipi** *etc*

k [= ordnen, reparieren, säubern] to do; **die Küche muss mal wieder gemacht werden** *(= gereinigt, gestrichen)* the kitchen needs doing again; **das Auto machen lassen** to have the car seen to *or* done; **er macht mir die Haare** *(inf)* he does my hair; **das Bett machen** to make the bed; **ich muss noch die Betten machen** I've still got the beds to make; **mach den Fleck aus der Bluse, ehe du sie wäschst** get the stain out of the blouse before you wash it

l [andere Wendungen]

♦ **machen + aus etw aus jdm/etw machen** *(= verwandeln in)* to turn sb/sth into sth; *(= darstellen, interpretieren als)* to make sth of sb/sth; **aus dem Haus könnte man schon etwas machen** you could really make something of that house; **eine große Sache aus etw machen** to make a big thing of sth; **etwas aus sich** *(dat)* **machen** to make something of oneself; **was soll ich aus dieser Sache machen?** *(= verstehen, interpretieren)* what am I to make of this?

♦ **machen + zu jdn/etw zu etw machen** *(= verwandeln in)* to turn sb/sth into sth; **jdn zum Star/Helden machen** to turn sb into a star/hero; **jdn zum Wortführer/Sklaven/zu seiner Frau machen** to make sb spokesman/a slave/one's wife; **jdm etw zur Hölle/Qual machen** to make sth hell/a misery for sb

♦ **nichts/etwas machen** *(= ausmachen, schaden)* **macht nichts!** it doesn't matter!; **macht das was?** does that matter?; **das macht durchaus etwas** it does indeed matter; **das macht mir doch nichts!** that doesn't matter to me!; **der Regen/die Kälte macht mir nichts** I don't mind the rain/cold; **die Kälte macht dem Motor nichts** the cold doesn't hurt the engine; **es macht mir nichts, durch den Regen zu gehen** I don't mind walking in the rain

♦ **sich etw machen sich** *(dat)* **viel aus jdm/etw machen** to like sb/sth; **sich** *(dat)* **wenig aus jdm/etw machen** not to be very keen on *(esp Brit) or* thrilled with *(esp US)* sb/sth; **sich** *(dat)* **nichts aus etw machen** *(= keinen Wert legen auf)* not to be very keen on *(esp Brit) or* thrilled with *(esp US)* sth; *(= sich nicht ärgern)* not to let sth bother one; **mach dir nichts draus!** don't let it bother you!; **sich** *(dat)* **einen schönen Abend/ein paar gemütliche Stunden machen** to have a nice evening/a few pleasant hours; **ein Vergnügen aus etw machen** to take delight in sth; **sich** *(dat)* **Umstände/Mühe machen** to go to a lot of bother/trouble; **machen Sie sich keine Umstände** don't go to any trouble; **sich** *(dat)* **Sorgen machen** to worry; **sich** *(dat)* **(auf etw** *acc***) Hoffnungen machen** to have hopes (of sth); **sich** *(dat)* **jdn zum Freund/Feind machen** to make sb one's friend/enemy; **sich** *(dat)* **etw zur Aufgabe/zum Grundsatz/Motto machen** to make sth one's job/a principle/one's watchword

2 – INTRANSITIVES VERB

a [= tun] **lass ihn nur machen** *(= hindre ihn nicht)* just let him do it; *(= verlass dich auf ihn)* just leave it to him; **lass mich mal machen** let me do it; *(= ich bringe das in Ordnung)* let me see to that

b [machen + Adjektiv] **das macht müde/gesund/schlank** that makes you tired/healthy/slim; **das Kleid macht alt/schlank** that dress makes you look old/slim

c [= sich beeilen] *inf* to get a move on *(inf)*, to hurry up; **mach schon!, mach schnell** *or* **schneller!** get a move on! *(inf)*, hurry up!; **ich mach ja schon!** I'm being as quick as I can!; **sie machten, dass sie nach Hause kamen** they hurried home; **mach, dass du hier wegkommst** *or* **verschwindest!** (you just) get out of here!

d [= Notdurft verrichten] *inf* to go to the toilet *(esp Brit) or* bathroom *(esp US) or* restroom *(US)*; *(Hund etc)* to do its business *(euph)*; **(sich** *dat***) in die Hosen machen** *(lit, fig)* to wet oneself; **ins Bett machen** to wet the bed; **groß/klein machen** *(baby-talk)* to do a poo/wee *(baby-talk)*

e [= reisen] *dial* to go; **nach Amerika machen** to go to America; **über die (grüne) Grenze machen** to go over the border

f [Redewendungen]

♦ **machen auf etw** *(acc) (inf)* **jetzt macht sie auf große Dame** she's playing the grand lady now; **er macht auf Staatsmann** he's playing the statesman; **sie macht auf verständnisvoll/gebildet** she's doing her understanding/cultured bit *(inf)*; **jetzt macht sie auf beleidigt** now she's acting the injured innocent *(Brit)*, now she's acting insulted *(esp US)*; **er macht auf Schau** he's out for effect *(inf)*

♦ **machen in etw** *(dat) (inf, beruflich)* to be in sth; **er macht in Politik** he's in politics; **er macht in Nächstenliebe/Großzügigkeit** he puts on a show of compassion/generosity

3 – REFLEXIVES VERB

♦ **sich machen**

a [= sich entwickeln] to come on; **wie macht sich der Garten?** how is the garden coming on?

b [= aussehen] to look; **der Schal macht sich sehr hübsch zu dem Kleid** the scarf looks very pretty with that dress

c [andere Wendungen] **sich an etw** *(acc)* **machen** to get down to sth; **sich auf den Weg machen** to get going; **sich über das Essen machen** *(inf)* to get stuck in *(inf)*; **sich zum Fürsprecher/Anwalt machen** to make oneself spokesman/advocate; **sich verständlich machen** to make oneself understood; **sich bei jdm beliebt/verhasst machen** *(inf)* to make oneself popular with/hated by sb → **wichtigmachen**

Ma|chen|schaf|ten ['maxn∫aftn] PL wheelings and dealings *pl*, machinations *pl*

Ma|cher ['maxɐ] M **-s, -**, **Ma|che|rin** [-ərın] F **-, -nen** *(inf)* doer, man/woman of action

-ma|cher(in) M(F) *suf in cpds* -maker; **Kleider-/Möbelmacher(in)** clothes/furniture-maker

Ma|cher|lohn M labour *(Brit) or* labor *(US)* charge; *(bei Kleidung)* making-up charge

Ma|che|te [ma'xe:tə, ma't∫e:tə] F **-, -n** machete

Ma|chi|a|vel|lis|mus M Machiavellianism

ma|chi|a|vel|lis|tisch [makiave'lıstı∫] ADJ Machiavellian ADV like a true Machiavellian

Ma|chis|mo [ma't∫ısmo] M **-s**, *no pl* machismo

Ma|cho ['mat∫o] M **-s, -s** macho *(inf)*

Macht [maxt] F **-, ⸚e** ['mεçtə] **a** *no pl (= Einfluss, Kraft)* power; *(= Stärke)* might, power; **die ~ der Gewohnheit/Verhältnisse/des Schicksals** the force of habit/circumstance(s)/destiny; **alles, was in unserer ~ steht, alles in unserer ~ Stehende** everything (with)in our power; **es stand nicht in seiner ~, zu ...** it was not *or* did not lie within his power to ...; **mit ~** with a vengeance; **mit aller ~** with might and main, with all one's might; **~ geht vor Recht** *(Prov)* might is right *(Prov)*

b *no pl (= Herrschaft, Befehlsgewalt)* power; **die ~ ergreifen/erringen** to seize/gain power; **an die ~ gelangen** *(form) or* **kommen** to come to power; **jdn an die ~ bringen** to bring sb to power; **an der ~ sein/bleiben** to be/remain in power; **seine ~ behaupten** to maintain control, to continue to hold sway; **die ~ übernehmen** to assume power, to take over

c *(= außerirdische Kraft, Großmacht)* power; **die Mächte der Finsternis** *(old, liter)* the Powers of Darkness *(old, liter)*

d *(dated: = Heeresmacht)* forces *pl*

Macht-: **Macht|an|spruch** M claim to power; **Macht|ap|pa|rat** M *(Pol)* machinery of power; **Macht|aus|übung** F exercise of power; **jdn an der ~ hindern** to prevent sb from exercising his power; **Macht|be|fug|nis** F power, authority *no pl*; **Macht|be|reich** M sphere of influence *or* control; **macht|be|ses|sen** ADJ power-crazed; **Macht|block** M *pl* **-blöcke** power bloc

Mäch|te|grup|pie|rung F grouping of the powers

Macht-: **Macht|er|grei|fung** F seizure of power; **Macht|erhalt** M retention of power; **der Regierungspartei geht es nur um den ~** the ruling party is only interested in staying in power; **Macht|fül|le** F power *no indef art*; **Macht|ge|fü|ge** NT power structure; **Macht|gier** F lust for power; **Macht|ha|ber** [-ha:bɐ] M **-s, -**, **Macht|ha|be|rin** [-ərın] F **-, -nen** ruler; *(pej)* dictator; **die ~ in Ruritanien** the rulers of *or* powers-that-be in Ruritania; **Macht|hun|ger** M *(liter)* craving *or* hunger for power; **macht|hung|rig** ADJ *(liter)* power-hungry; **~ sein** to crave power

mäch|tig ADJ **a** *(= einflussreich)* powerful; **die Mächtigen (dieser Erde)** the powerful (of this world)

b *(= sehr groß)* mighty; *Baum, Felsen* massive, mighty; *Körper* massive; *Stimme, Wirkung, Schlag, Schultern* powerful, mighty; *Essen* heavy; *(inf: = enorm) Hunger, Durst, Glück* terrific *(inf)*, tremendous; **~e Angst** *or* **einen ~en Bammel haben** *(inf)* to be scared stiff

c *(liter)* **seiner selbst** *(gen) or* **seiner Sinne** *(gen)* **nicht ~ sein** not to be in control of oneself; **einer Sprache** *(gen)* **~ sein** to have a good command of a language

ADV *(inf: = sehr)* terrifically *(inf)*, tremendously; *schneien, brüllen, sich beeilen* like mad *(inf)*; **sich ~ anstrengen** to make a terrific *(inf) or* tremendous effort; **da hast du dich ~ getäuscht** you've made a big mistake there; **darüber hat sie sich ~ geärgert** she got really angry about it

Mäch|tig|keit F **-**, *no pl* powerfulness, power; *(von Felsen, Körper)* massiveness

Macht-: **Macht|kampf** M power struggle, struggle for power; **macht|los** ADJ powerless; *(= hilflos)* helpless; **gegen diese Argumente war ich ~** I was powerless against these arguments ADV powerlessly; *(= hilflos)* helplessly; **Macht|lo|sig|keit** F **-**, *no pl* powerlessness; *(= Hilflosigkeit)* helplessness; **Macht|mensch** M power-seeker; **Macht|miss|brauch** M abuse *or* misuse of power; **Macht|mit|tel** NT instrument of power; **Macht|mo|no|pol** NT monopoly of power; **Macht|po|li|tik** F power politics *pl*; **Macht|po|si|ti|on** F position of power; **Macht|pro|be** F trial of strength; **Macht|stel|lung** F position of power; *(= einflussreiche Stellung auch)* powerful position; **Macht|stre|ben** NT striving for power; **Macht|struk|tur** F power structure; **Macht|tech|ni|ker(in)** M(F) powermonger; **Macht|über|nah|me** F takeover *(durch* by); **Macht|va|ku|um** NT power vacuum; **Macht|ver|hält|nis|se** PL balance *sing* of power; **Macht|ver|lust** M loss of power; **Macht|ver|schie|bung** F shift of power; **macht|voll** ADJ powerful ADV powerfully; *eingreifen* decisively; **~ auftrumpfen** to flex one's muscles; **Macht|voll|kom|men|heit** F absolute power; **Macht|wech|sel** M changeover of power; **Macht|wort** NT *pl* **-worte** word (+*gen* from); **ein ~ sprechen** to exercise one's authority

Mach|werk NT *(pej)* sorry effort; **das ist ein ~ des Teufels** that is the work of the devil

Mach|zahl F *(Phys)* Mach number

Ma|cke ['makə] F **-, -n** *(inf)* **a** *(= Tick, Knall)* quirk; **eine ~ haben** *(inf)* to be cracked *(inf)*, to have a screw loose *(inf)* **b** *(= Fehler, Schadstelle)* fault; *(bei Maschinen)* defect, fault; *(bei Kartoffeln etc)* bad patch

Ma|cker ['makɐ] M **-s, -** *(inf)* fellow *(inf)*, bloke *(Brit inf)*, guy *(inf)*; **spiel hier nicht den ~** don't come *(Brit) or* play the tough guy here *(inf)*

MAD [εmla:'de:] M - *abbr von* **Militärischer Abschirmdienst** ≈ MI5 *(Brit)*, ≈ CIA *(US)*

Ma|da|gas|kar [mada'gaskaːr] NT **-s** Madagascar; (*Pol: heutzutage*) Malagasy Republic
Ma|da|gas|se [mada'gasə] M **-n, -n**, **Ma|da|gas|sin** [-'gasɪn] F **-, -nen** Madagascan; Malagasy
ma|da|gas|sisch [mada'gasɪʃ] ADJ Madagascan; Malagasy
Ma|dam [ma'dam] F **-, -s** *or* **-en** **a** (*hum dated*) lady; **meine ~** my old woman *or* lady (*inf*) **b** (*in Bordell*) madam
Mäd|chen ['mɛːtçən] NT **-s, -** girl; (*= Tochter auch*) daughter; (*dated: = Freundin*) girl(friend); (*= Dienstmädchen*) maid; **ein unberührtes ~** a virgin; **ein ~ für alles** (*inf*) a dogsbody (*Brit*), a gofer; (*im Haushalt auch*) a maid-of-all-work → **spät ADJ, leicht ADJ e**
Mäd|chen-: **Mäd|chen|buch** NT book for girls; **mäd|chen|haft** ADJ girlish ADV *sich bewegen, aussehen* like a (young) girl; *kichern auch* girlishly (*pej*); **sich ~ kleiden** to dress like a girl; **Mäd|chen|han|del** M white slave trade; **Mäd|chen|händ|ler(in)** M(F) white-slaver; **Mäd|chen|klas|se** F girls' class, girls' form (*Brit*); **Mäd|chen|klei|dung** F girls' clothing *or* clothes *pl*; **Mäd|chen|na|me** M **a** (*Vorname*) girl's name; **~n** girls' names **b** (*von verheirateter Frau*) maiden name; **Mäd|chen|pen|si|o|nat** NT girls' boarding school; **diese Kaserne ist kein ~!** (*hum*) these barracks aren't a finishing school; **Mäd|chen|schu|le** F girls' school; **Mäd|chen|zim|mer** NT (*dated*) maid's room; (*für Tochter*) girl's room
Ma|de ['maːdə] F **-, -n** maggot; **wie die ~ im Speck leben** (*inf*) to live *or* be in clover, to live in (the lap of) luxury
Ma|dei|ra [ma'deːra] M **-s, -s** (*= Wein*) Madeira
Mä|del ['mɛːdl] NT **-s, -(s)** (*dial*), **Ma|del** ['maːdl] NT **-s, -n** (*Aus*) lass (*dial*), girl → *auch* **Mädchen**
Ma|den|wurm M threadworm
Mä|derl ['mɛːdɐl] NT **-s, -n** (*Aus*) little lass (*dial*) *or* girl
ma|dig ['maːdɪç] ADJ maggoty; *Obst auch* worm-eaten → **madigmachen**
ma|dig+ma|chen VT *sep* **jdn/etw ~** (*inf*) to run sb/sth down; **jdm etw ~** (*inf*) to put sb off sth
Mad|jar [ma'djaːɐ] M **-en, -en** Magyar
Madl ['maːdl] NT **-s, -n** (*Aus*), **Mäd|le** ['mɛːdlə] NT **-s, -** (*S Ger*) lass (*dial*), girl → *auch* **Mädchen**
Ma|don|na [ma'dɔna] F **-, Madonnen** [-'dɔnən] Madonna
Ma|don|nen-: **Ma|don|nen|bild** NT (picture of the) Madonna; **ma|don|nen|haft** ADJ madonna-like ADV *schön, unschuldig* as a madonna
Mad|rid [ma'drɪt] NT **-s** Madrid
Mad|ri|der[1] [ma'drɪdɐ] ADJ *attr* Madrid
Mad|ri|der[2] [ma'drɪdɐ] M **-s, -**, **Mad|ri|de|rin** [-ərɪn] F **-, -nen** native of Madrid; (*Einwohner*) inhabitant of Madrid
Mad|ri|gal [madri'gaːl] NT **-s, -e** madrigal
Ma|est|ro [ma'ɛstro] M **-s, -s** *or* **Maestri** [-tri] maestro
Ma|fia ['mafia] F, **Maf|fia** ['mafia] F **-**, *no pl* Mafia
Ma|fia-Boss M, **Maf|fia-Boss** M Mafia boss
Ma|fia|me|tho|den PL Mafia(-type) methods *pl*
ma|fi|os [ma'fioːs] ADJ Mafia *attr*; *Zustände* Mafia-like
Ma|fi|o|so [ma'fioːzo] M **-, Mafiosi** [-zi] mafioso
mag [maːk] *3. pers sing pres von* **mögen**
Ma|ga|zin [maga'tsiːn] NT **-s, -e** **a** (*= Lager*) storeroom; (*esp für Sprengstoff, Waffen, old: = Speicher*) magazine; (*= Bibliotheksmagazin*) stockroom **b** (*am Gewehr*) magazine **c** (*= Zeitschrift*) magazine, journal; (*TV, Rad*) magazine programme (*Brit*) *or* program (*US*)
Ma|ga|zi|ner [maga'tsiːnɐ] M **-s, -** (*Sw*), **Ma|ga|zi|neur** [magatsi'nøːɐ] M **-s, -e** (*Aus*) storeman
Ma|ga|zi|ne|rin [maga'tsiːnərɪn] F **-, -nen** (*Sw*), **Ma|ga|zi|neu|rin** [magatsi'nøːrɪn] F **-, -nen** (*Aus*) storewoman
Ma|ga|zin|sen|dung F (*Rad, TV*) magazine programme (*Brit*) *or* program (*US*)
Magd [maːkt] F **-, ⸚e** ['mɛːkdə] **a** (*old*) (*= Dienstmagd*) maid; (*= Landarbeiterin*) farm lass (*dial*) *or* girl; (*= Kuhmagd*) milkmaid **b** (*liter: = Mädchen, Jungfrau*) maid(en) (*old, liter*); **Maria, die reine ~** Mary, the holy virgin; **Maria, die ~ des Herrn** Mary, the handmaid of the Lord
Mäg|de|lein ['mɛːkdəlain] NT **-s, -**, **Mägd|lein** ['mɛːktlain] NT **-s, -** (*obs, poet*) maid(en) (*old, liter*)
Ma|gen ['maːgn] M **-s, ⸚** *or* **-** ['mɛːgn] stomach, tummy (*inf*); **mit leerem ~, auf nüchternen ~** on an empty stomach; **mein ~ rebelliert** (*= mir ist schlecht*) I feel sick; **(die) Liebe geht durch den ~** (*Prov*) the way to a man's heart is through his stomach (*prov*); **etw liegt jdm (schwer** *or* **wie Blei** *or* **bleiern) im ~** (*inf*) sth lies heavily on *or* in sb's stomach; (*fig*) sth preys on sb's mind; **jdm auf den ~ schlagen** (*inf*) to upset sb's stomach, to give sb an upset stomach; (*fig*) to upset sb; **sich** (*dat*) **den ~ verderben** *or* **verkorksen** (*inf*) to get an upset stomach, to upset one's stomach → **umdrehen VR, verrenken VT**
Ma|gen-: **Ma|gen|aus|gang** M (*Anat*) pyloric orifice (*spec*); **Ma|gen|band** NT **-s, ⸚er** gastric band; **Ma|gen|be|schwer|den** PL stomach *or* tummy (*inf*) trouble *sing*; **Ma|gen|bit|ter** M bitters *pl*; **Ma|gen|blu|tung** F stomach bleeding, stomach haemorrhaging (*Brit*) *or* hemorrhaging (*US*); **Ma|gen-Darm-Ka|tarr(h)** M gastroenteritis; **Ma|gen-Darm-Trakt** M gastrointestinal tract; **Ma|gen|drü|cken** NT **-s, -** stomachache; **Ma|gen|ge|gend** F stomach region; **Ma|gen|ge|schwür** NT stomach ulcer; **Ma|gen|gru|be** F pit of the stomach; **ein Schlag in die ~** a blow in the solar plexus; **Ma|gen|knur|ren** NT **-s**, *no pl* tummy (*inf*) *or* stomach rumbles *pl*; **Ma|gen|krampf** M stomach cramp; **ma|gen|krank** ADJ with stomach trouble; **~ sein** to have stomach trouble; **jdn ~ machen** to give sb stomach trouble; **Ma|gen|krebs** M stomach cancer, cancer of the stomach; **Ma|gen|lei|den** NT stomach disorder *or* complaint; **ma|gen|lei|dend** ADJ = **magenkrank**; **Ma|gen|mit|tel** NT stomachic (*spec*); **jdm ein ~ verschreiben** to give sb something for his stomach; **Ma|gen|saft** M gastric juice; **Ma|gen|säu|re** F gastric acid; **Ma|gen|schleim|haut** F stomach lining; **Ma|gen|schleim|haut|ent|zün|dung** F gastritis; **Ma|gen|schmer|zen** PL stomachache *sing*, tummy-ache *sing* (*inf*); (*= Krämpfe auch*) stomach pains *pl*; **Ma|gen|son|de** F stomach probe; **Ma|gen|spie|ge|lung** F gastroscopy (*spec*); **Ma|gen|spü|lung** F irrigation of the stomach
Ma|gen|ta [ma'dʒɛnta] NT **-**, *no pl* magenta
Ma|gen-: **Ma|gen|ver|stim|mung** F upset stomach, stomach upset; **Ma|gen|weh** NT = **Magenschmerzen**
ma|ger ['maːgɐ] ADJ **a** (*= fettarm*) *Fleisch* lean; *Kost* low-fat, low in fat **b** (*= dünn*) thin, skinny (*inf*); (*= abgemagert*) emaciated; (*Typ*) *Druck* roman **c** (*= unfruchtbar*) *Boden, Felder* poor, infertile **d** (*= dürftig*) meagre (*Brit*), meager (*US*); *Ernte, Ertrag* lean, meagre (*Brit*), meager (*US*); (*Tech*) *Mischung* weak; *Ergebnis* poor; **die sieben ~en Jahre** the seven lean years
ADV **a** (*= fettarm*) **~ essen** to be on a low-fat diet; **~ kochen** to cook low-fat meals; **etw ist ~ zubereitet** sth is low-fat **b** (*= dürftig*) meagrely (*Brit*), meagerly (*US*); **~ ausfallen** to be meagre (*Brit*) *or* meager (*US*) **c** (*Typ*) **~ drucken/setzen** to print/typeset in roman
Ma|ger|keit F **-**, *no pl* **a** (*= Fettarmut*) (*von Fleisch*) leanness; (*von Kost*) low fat content **b** (*von Mensch*) thinness; (*= Abgemagertheit*) emaciation
Ma|ger-: **Ma|ger|milch** F skimmed milk; **Ma|ger|quark** [-kvark] M low-fat cottage cheese (*US*) *or* curd cheese; **Ma|ger|sucht** F (*Med*) anorexia; **ma|ger|süch|tig** ADJ (*Med*) anorexic; **~ sein** to be anorexic
Ma|gie [ma'giː] F **-**, *no pl* magic
Ma|gier ['maːgiɐ] M **-s, -**, **Ma|gie|rin** [-iərɪn] F **-, -nen** magician; **die drei ~** the three Magi
Ma|gi|not-Li|nie F, **Ma|gi|not|linie** [maʒi'no-] F Maginot Line
ma|gisch ['maːgɪʃ] ADJ magic(al); *Quadrat, (Tech) Auge, (Econ) Dreieck, (Phys) Zahlen* magic; **nach ~en Vorstellungen** according to various concepts of magic; **mit ~er Gewalt** with magical force; (*fig*) as if by magic ADV magically; **von jdm/etw ~ angezogen werden** to be attracted to sb/sth as if by magic
Ma|gis|ter [ma'gɪstɐ] M **-s, - ~ (Artium)** (*Univ*) M.A., Master of Arts; **~ (Pharmaciae)** (*Aus*) MSc *or* Master of Science in pharmacology

> **MAGISTER**
>
> In Germany **Magister** is an academic degree awarded in the arts. Students must study for at least eight semesters, write a **Magisterarbeit** and take an examination in one principal subject and two subsidiary subjects.

Ma|gis|tra|le [magɪs'traːlə] F **-, -n** (*Mot*) main thoroughfare
Ma|gist|rat [magɪs'traːt] M **-(e)s, -e** municipal authorities *pl*
Mag|ma ['magma] NT **-s, Magmen** [-mən] (*Geol*) magma
mag|na cum lau|de ['magna 'kʊm 'laudə] ADV (*Univ*) magna cum laude
Mag|nat [ma'gnaːt] M **-en, -en**, **Mag|na|tin** [ma'gnaːtɪn] F **-, -nen** magnate (*auch Hist*)
Mag|ne|sia [ma'gneːzia] F **-**, *no pl* (*Chem*) magnesia; (*Sport*) chalk
Mag|ne|si|um [ma'gneːziʊm] NT **-s**, *no pl* (*abbr* **Mg**) magnesium
Mag|net [ma'gneːt] M **-s** *or* **-en, -e(n)** (*lit, fig*) magnet
Mag|net- *in cpds* magnetic; **Mag|net|auf|zeich|nung** F magnetic recording; **Mag|net|bahn** F magnetic railway; **Mag|net|band** [-bant] NT *pl* **-bänder** magnetic tape; **Mag|net|berg** M (*liter*) *mountain believed to draw ships to their doom by its magnetic properties*; **Mag|net|bild|ver|fah|ren** NT video recording; **Mag|net|ei|sen|stein** M lodestone, magnetite; **Mag|net|feld** NT magnetic field
mag|ne|tisch [ma'gneːtɪʃ] ADJ (*lit, fig*) magnetic; **eine ~e Anziehungskraft auf jdn ausüben** (*fig*) to have a magnetic attraction for sb ADV magnetically; **von etw ~ angezogen werden** (*fig*) to be drawn to sth like a magnet
mag|ne|ti|sie|ren [magneti'ziːrən] *ptp* **magnetisiert** VT *Metall* to magnetize; *jdn* to use animal magnetism on
Mag|ne|tis|mus [magne'tɪsmʊs] M **-**, *no pl* magnetism; (*= Mesmerismus*) animal magnetism; (*heutzutage*) *form of healing where the illness is supposedly drawn out by the magnetic power of the healer*
Mag|net-: **Mag|net|kar|te** F magnetic card; (*von Bank etc auch*) cashpoint card (*Brit*), ATM card (*US*); **Mag|net|kar|ten|le|ser** M magnetic card reader; **Mag|net|kern** M (magnet) core; **Mag|net|kom|pass** M magnetic compass; **Mag|net|na|del** F magnetic needle
Mag|ne|to- [magneto-]: **Mag|ne|to|fon** [magneto'foːn] NT **-(e)s, -e** steel tape recorder, Magnetophone®; **Mag|ne|to|fon|band** [-bant] NT *pl* **-bänder** steel recording tape; **Mag|ne|to|phon®** [magneto'foːn] *etc* → **Magnetofon** *etc*; **Mag|ne|to|sphä|re** F magnetosphere
Mag|net-: **Mag|net|plat|te** F (*Comput*) magnetic disk; **Mag|net|pol** M magnetic pole; **Mag|net|schal|ter** M (*Aut*) solenoid switch; **Mag|net|schwe|be|bahn** F magnetic levitation railway; **Mag|net|spu|le** F coil; **Mag|net|strei|fen** M magnetic strip; **Mag|net|-**

streifenkarte F magnetic strip card; **Magnettonband** NT magnetic tape; **Magnettongerät** NT magnetic (sound) recorder; **Magnettonverfahren** NT magnetic (sound) recording; **Magnetzündung** F *(Aut)* magneto ignition

Magnifikat [ma'gni:fikat] NT **-(s)**, *no pl* Magnificat

Magnifizenz [magnifi'tsɛnts] F **-, -en** *(Univ)* **(Euer** *or* **Eure)/Seine** ~ Your/His Magnificence *(title given to German university rectors)*

Magnolie [mag'no:liə] F **-, -n** magnolia

Magnumflasche ['magnʊm-] F magnum (bottle)

Magyar [ma'dja:ɐ] M **-en, -en**, **Magyarin** [ma'dja:rɪn] F **-, -nen** *(Aus liter)* Magyar

magyarisch [ma'dja:rɪʃ] ADJ *(Aus liter)* Magyar

mäh [mɛ:] INTERJ baa

Mahagoni [maha'go:ni] NT **-s**, *no pl* mahogany

Maharadscha [maha'ra:dʒa] M **-s, -s** maharaja(h)

Maharani [maha'ra:ni] F **-, -s** maharani

Mähbinder M reaper-binder, reaping-and-binding machine

Mahd [ma:t] F **-, -en** [-dn] *(dial)* reaping; *(= das Abgemähte)* cut grass

Mahd NT **-(e)s, ¨-er** ['mɛ:dɐ] *(Sw, Aus)* mountain pasture

Mähder ['mɛ:dɐ] M **-s, -**, **Mähderin** [-ərɪn] F **-, -nen** *(dial: = Mäher)* mower; *(von Getreide)* reaper

Mähdrescher M combine (harvester)

mähen¹ ['mɛ:ən] **VT** *Gras* to cut; *Getreide auch* to reap; *Rasen* to mow **VI** to reap; *(= Rasen mähen)* to mow

mähen² VI *(Schaf)* to bleat

Mäher ['mɛ:ɐ] M **-s, -**, **Mäherin** [-ərɪn] F **-, -nen** mower; *(von Getreide)* reaper

Mahl [ma:l] NT **-(e)s, -e** *or* **¨-er** ['mɛ:lɐ] *(liter)* meal, repast *(form)*; *(= Gastmahl)* banquet; **beim ~e sitzen** *(liter)* to be at table

mahlen ['ma:lən] *pret* **mahlte** ['ma:ltə], *ptp* **gemahlen** [gə'ma:lən] **VT** to grind **VI** to grind; *(Räder)* to spin

Mahl-: **Mahlgang** M *pl* **-gänge** *(Tech)* pair of millstones; **Mahlgut** NT material to be ground; *(= Getreide)* grain (to be ground), grist

mählich ['mɛ:lɪç] ADJ, ADV *(poet)* = **allmählich**

Mahl-: **Mahlstatt** F *pl* **-stätte** [-ʃtɛtə], **Mahlstätte** F *(Hist) meeting place of the Teutons*; **Mahlstein** M millstone; *(prähistorisch)* quern; **Mahlstrom** M = **Malstrom**; **Mahlwerk** NT mill, milling device; **Mahlzahn** M grinder

Mahlzeit F meal; **~!** *(inf) greeting used around mealtimes (= guten Appetit)* enjoy your meal; **(prost) ~!** *(iro inf)* that's just great *(inf) or* swell *(esp US inf)*

Mähmaschine F mower; *(= Rasenmähmaschine auch)* mowing machine; *(= Getreidemähmaschine)* reaper

Mahnbescheid M, **Mahnbrief** M reminder

Mähne ['mɛ:nə] F **-, -n** *(lit, fig)* mane; **du hast wieder eine ~!** *(inf)* you're looking rather wild and woolly again *(inf)*

mahnen ['ma:nən] **VT** **a** *(= erinnern)* to remind *(wegen, an +acc* of); *(warnend, missbilligend)* to admonish *(wegen, an +acc* on account of); *Schuldner* to send a reminder to; **jdn schriftlich/brieflich ~** to remind sb in writing/by letter; **gemahnt werden** *(Schuldner)* to receive a reminder; **eine ~de Stimme** *(liter)* an admonishing *or* admonitory voice

b *(= auffordern)* **jdn zur Eile/Geduld/Ruhe** *etc* **~** to urge *or (warnend, missbilligend)* admonish sb to hurry/be patient/be quiet *etc*; **jdn zur Mäßigkeit ~** to urge sb to be moderate, to urge moderation on sb

VI **a** *(wegen Schulden etc)* to send a reminder

b **zur Eile/Geduld/Vorsicht ~** to urge haste/patience/caution; **der Lehrer mahnte zur Ruhe** the teacher called for quiet; **die Uhr mahnte zur Eile** the clock indicated that haste was called for

Mahner ['ma:nɐ] M **-s, -**, **Mahnerin** ['ma:nərɪn] F **-, -nen** *(geh)* admonisher *(geh)*

Mahn-: **Mahngebühr** F reminder fee; **Mahnmal** NT memorial; **Mahnruf** M *(liter)* exhortation; **Mahnschreiben** NT reminder

Mahnung ['ma:nʊŋ] F **-, -en** **a** *(= Ermahnung)* exhortation; *(warnend, missbilligend)* admonition **b** *(geh: = warnende Erinnerung)* reminder; **zur ~ an** *(+acc)* in memory of **c** *(= Mahnbrief)* reminder

Mahn-: **Mahnverfahren** NT collection proceedings *pl*; **Mahnwache** F *(Pol)* picket; **eine demonstrative ~** a protest picket; **jdn als institutionelle ~ einstellen** to appoint sb as an official watchdog

Mähre ['mɛ:rə] F **-, -n** *(old, pej)* nag, jade

Mähren ['mɛ:rən] NT **-s** Moravia

mährisch ['mɛ:rɪʃ] ADJ Moravian

Mai [mai] M **-(e)s** *or* **-** *or (poet)* **-en, -e** May; **der Erste ~** May Day; **des Lebens ~** *(poet)* the springtime of one's life *(poet)*; **wie einst im ~** (as if) in the first flush of youth, as if young again → *auch* **März**

Mai- *in cpds* May; *(Pol)* May Day; **Maiandacht** F May devotions *pl*; **Maibaum** M maypole; **Maibowle** F white wine punch *(flavoured with woodruff)*

Maid [mait] F **-, -en** [-dn] *(old, liter)* maid(en) *(old, liter)*; *(hum)* wench *(old, hum)*

Mai-: **Maifeier** F May Day celebrations *pl*; **Maifeiertag** M *(form)* May Day *no art*; **Maiglöckchen** NT lily of the valley; **Maikäfer** M cockchafer; **Maikönigin** F Queen of (the) May; **Maikundgebung** F May Day rally

Mail [me:l] F **-, -s** *(Comput)* e-mail, mail

Mailand ['mailant] NT **-s** Milan

Mailänder ['mailɛndɐ] ADJ *attr* Milan; **die ~ Scala** La Scala (in Milan)

Mailänder ['mailɛndɐ] M **-s, -**, **Mailänderin** [-ərɪn] F **-, -nen** Milanese

mailändisch ['mailɛndɪʃ] ADJ Milanese

Mailbox ['me:lbɔks] F *(Comput)* mailbox

mailen ['me:ln] VTI *(Comput)* to e-mail, to mail

Mailing ['me:lɪŋ, 'meɪlɪŋ] NT **-s, -s** mailing, mailshot *(Brit)*; **etw per ~ erhalten** to receive sth in a mailing; **ein ~ an alle Kunden durchführen** to send a mailing *or* mailshot *(Brit)* to all customers

Mailingliste F *(Comput)* mailing list

Mailprogramm ['me:l-] NT *(Comput)* (e)mail program

Mailserver ['me:l-] M *(Comput)* (e)mail server

Main [main] M **-s** Main

Mainlinie F *line formed by the River Main roughly dividing North and South Germany*

Mainstream M mainstream

Mais [mais] M **-es**, *no pl* maize, (Indian) corn *(esp US)*

Mais-: **Maisbrei** M thick maize porridge; **Maisbrot** NT corn bread

Maischbottich M mash tub; *(für Wein)* fermenting vat

Maische ['maiʃə] F **-, -n** *(= Biermaische)* mash; *(= Weinmaische)* must; *(= Schnapsmaische)* wort

maischen ['maiʃn] VT to mash; *Trauben* to ferment

Mais-: **Maisflocken** PL cornflakes *pl*; **maisgelb** ADJ corn-coloured *(Brit)*, corn-colored *(US)*; **Maiskolben** M corn cob; *(Gericht)* corn on the cob; **Maiskorn** NT *pl* **-körner** grain of maize *or* corn *(esp US)*; *(als Sammelbegriff)* maize *or* corn *(esp US)* grain; **Maismehl** NT maize *or* corn *(esp US)* meal

Maisonette [mɛzo'nɛt] F **-, -n**, **Maisonettewohnung** F maisonette

Maisstärke F cornflour *(Brit)*, cornstarch *(US)*

Maître de Plaisir [mɛtrə(də)plɛ'zi:r] M **- - -, -s - -** *(old, hum)* Master of Ceremonies

Maître d'Hôtel [mɛtrado'tɛl] M **- -, -s -** maître d'hôtel

Majestät [majɛs'tɛ:t] F **-, -en** **a** *(Titel)* Majesty; **Seine/Ihre/Eure** *or* **Euer ~** His/Her/Your Majesty; **die (kaiserlichen** *etc***) ~en ...** their (Imperial *etc*) Majesties ... **b** *(liter)* majesty, grandeur

majestätisch [majɛs'tɛ:tɪʃ] **ADJ** majestic **ADV** majestically

Majestäts-: **Majestätsbeleidigung** F lèse-majesté; **Majestätsverbrechen** NT *(Jur)* crime against the crown

Majo ['ma:jo] F **-, -s** *(inf: = Majonäse)* mayo *(inf)*

Majolika [ma'jo:lika] F **-, -s** *or* **Majoliken** [-kn] majolica

Majonäse [majo'nɛ:zə] F **-, -n** mayonnaise

Major [ma'jo:ɐ] M **-s, -e**, **Majorin** [ma'jo:rɪn] F **-, -nen** *(Mil)* major; *(in Luftwaffe)* squadron leader *(Brit)*, major *(US)*

Majoran ['majora:n, 'ma:joran] M **-s, -e** marjoram

Majorat [majo'ra:t] NT **-(e)s, -e** *(old)* **a** *(Jur)* primogeniture **b** *(= Erbgut) estate to which the eldest son is entitled*

Majorette [majo'rɛtə] F **-, -n** *or* **-s** majorette

Majorin [ma'jo:rɪn] F → **Major**

majorisieren [majori'zi:rən] *ptp* **majorisiert** VT to outvote

Majorität [majori'tɛ:t] F **-, -en** majority; **die ~ haben** to have a majority

Majoritäts-: **Majoritätsbeschluss** M majority decision; **Majoritätsprinzip** NT principle of majority rule; **Majoritätswahl** F election by a simple majority, first-past-the-post election *(Brit)*

Majorsrang M *(Mil)* rank of major; **im ~ sein** to hold the rank of major

Majorz [ma'jɔrts] M **-es**, *no pl (Sw)* first-past-the-post system; *(= Mehrheit)* majority

Majuskel [ma'jʊskl] F **-, -n** *(geh)* majuscule *(spec)*, capital (letter)

MAK [ɛmla:'ka:] *abbr von* **Maximale Arbeitsplatzkonzentration** *maximum permitted exposure level of pollution at the place of work* **~-Liste** *list of products or materials which are harmful to health*

makaber [ma'ka:bɐ] ADJ macabre; *Witz, Geschichte* sick

Makak [ma'ka:k, 'ma:kak] M **-s or -en, -e**, *(Zool)* macaque

Makedonien [make'do:niən] NT **-s** Macedonia

Makedonier [make'do:niɐ] M **-s, -**, **Makedonierin** [-iərɪn] F **-, -nen** Macedonian

makedonisch [make'do:nɪʃ] ADJ Macedonian

Makel ['ma:kl] M **-s, -** **a** *(= Schandfleck)* stigma; **ohne ~** without a stain on one's reputation; *(Rel)* unblemished; **ein ~ auf seiner blütenreinen Weste** a blot on his escutcheon *(Brit)*, a stain on his reputation; **mit einem ~ behaftet sein** *(liter)* to be stigmatized **b** *(= Fehler)* blemish; *(von Charakter)* flaw; *(bei Waren)* flaw, defect; **ohne ~** without blemish, flawless

Mäkelei [mɛkə'lai] F **-, -en** carping *no pl*, fault-finding *no pl* *(an +dat, über +acc* about, over)

mäkelig ['mɛ:kəlɪç] ADJ *(inf)* finicky *(inf)*

makellos **ADJ** *Reinheit, Frische* spotless; *Charakter, Lebenswandel, Gesinnung* unimpeachable; *Figur, Haut, Frisur* perfect, flawless; *Kleidung, Haare* immaculate; *Alibi* watertight; *Vortrag, Spiel* flawless; *Klang (von Instrument)* perfect; *Englisch, Deutsch* flawless, perfect **ADV** *rein* spotlessly; **~ gekleidet sein** to be impeccably dressed; **~ weiß** spotless white

Makellosigkeit F **-**, *no pl (= Reinheit)* spotlessness; *(moralisch)* unimpeachability; *(von Haut, Vortrag, Spiel)* flawlessness

makeln ['ma:kln] **VI** **a** *(St Ex, Fin)* to act as a broker **b** *(Telec)* to make a conference call **VT** *(St Ex, Fin)* to be a broker for

mä|keln ['mɛ:kln] VI *(inf) (= nörgeln)* to carp, to cavil *(an +dat* at); *(= zu wählerisch sein)* to be finicky *(inf) (an +dat* about, over)

Make-up [me:k'lap] NT **-s, -s** make-up; *(flüssig)* foundation, liquid make-up; **sie braucht zwei Stunden fürs ~** she needs two hours for her make-up *or* to put on her make-up

Mak|ka|bä|er [maka'bɛ:ɐ] PL Maccabees *pl*

Mak|ka|ro|ni [maka'ro:ni] PL macaroni *sing*

Mak|ler ['ma:klɐ] M **-s, -, Mak|le|rin** [-ərın] F **-, -nen** broker; *(= Grundstücksmakler)* estate agent *(Brit)*, real-estate agent *(US)*; *(fig)* middleman; **der ehrliche ~** *(fig)* the honest broker

Mäk|ler M **-s, -, Mäk|le|rin** F **-, -nen** **a** *(inf) (nörglerisch)* fault-finder, carper; *(wählerisch)* fusspot *(inf)* **b** *(= Makler)* broker; *(= Grundstücksmakler)* estate agent *(Brit)*, real-estate agent *(US)*

Mak|ler-: **Mak|ler|bü|ro** NT *(St Ex)* broker's office; *(für Immobilien)* estate agent's office *(Brit)*, realtor's office *(US)*; **Mak|ler|ge|bühr** F *(St Ex)* broker's commission, brokerage; *(für Immobilie)* estate agent's fee *(Brit)*, realtor's fee *(US)*

mäk|lig ['mɛ:klıç] ADJ *(inf)* finicky *(inf)*

Ma|ko ['mako] M OR F OR NT **-(s), -s** *(Tex)* Egyptian cotton

Mak|re|le [ma'kre:lə] F **-, -n** mackerel

Mak|ro ['makro] NT **-s, -s** *(Comput)* macro

Mak|ro-, mak|ro- [makro] *in cpds* macro-; **Mak|ro|be|fehl** M *(Comput)* macro command; **mak|ro|bi|o|tisch** [-'bio:tıʃ] ADJ macrobiotic ADV **sich ~ ernähren** to be on a macrobiotic diet; **Mak|ro|kli|ma** NT macroclimate; **Mak|ro|kos|mos** M macrocosm

Mak|ro|ne [ma'kro:nə] F **-, -n** macaroon

Mak|ro-: **Mak|ro|öko|no|mie** F macroeconomics *sing*; **Mak|ro|pha|ge** [makro'fa:gə] F **-, -n** *(Med: = Fresszelle)* macrophage; **mak|ro|ze|phal** [-tse'fa:l] ADJ megacephalic

Ma|ku|la|tur [makula'tu:ɐ] F **-, -en** *(Typ)* wastepaper; *(fig pej)* rubbish; **~ reden** *(inf)* to talk rubbish *(Brit inf) or* trash *(inf)*

Ma|ku|la|tur|bo|gen M *pl* **-bogen** *(Typ)* waste *or* spoiled sheet

ma|ku|lie|ren [maku'li:rən] *ptp* **makuliert** VT to pulp

mal [ma:l] ADV *(Math)* times; *(bei Maßangaben)* by; **ein ~ eins ist eins** one times one is one; **zwei ~ zwei** *(Math)* two times two, two twos, twice two *(Brit)*; **zwei ~ drei ist (gleich) sechs** two times *or* twice *(Brit)* three is *or* equals *or* are six

mal ADV *(inf)* = **einmal**

-mal ADV *suf* times; **drei-/fünfmal** three/five times

Mal [ma:l] NT **-(e)s, -e** *or (poet)* **=er** ['mɛ:lɐ] **a** *(= Fleck)* mark; *(fig liter: = Kennzeichen)* brand, mark, sign **b** *(liter: = Ehrenmal)* memorial, monument **c** *(Sport) (Schlagball)* base; *(Rugby)* posts *pl*; *(= Malfeld)* touch

Mal NT **-(e)s, -e** time; **das eine ~** once; **erinnerst du dich an das eine ~ in Düsseldorf?** do you remember that time in Düsseldorf?; **nur das eine ~** just (the) once; **(nur) dieses eine ~** (just) this once; **das eine oder andere ~** now and then *or* again, from time to time; **ein/kein einziges ~** once/not once; **wenn du bloß ein einziges ~ auf mich hören würdest** if you would only listen to me for once; **manch liebes ~** *(dated)*, **manches liebe ~** *(dated)* many a time; **ein für alle ~(e)** once and for all; **ein über das andere ~, ein ums andere ~, ein ~ über das** *or* **ums andere ~** time after time; **voriges** *or* **das vorige ~** the time before; **das soundsovielte** *or* **x-te ~** *(inf)* the umpteenth *(inf) or* nth time; **ein erstes ~** *(liter)* for the first time ever; **ein letztes ~** *(liter)* one last time; **als ich letztes** *or* **das letzte ~ in London war** (the) last time I was in London; **beim ersten ~(e)** the first time; **beim zweiten/letzten** *etc* **~** the second/last *etc* time; **zum ersten/letzten** *etc* **~** for the first/last *etc* time; **zu verschiedenen ~en** at various times; **zu wiederholten ~en** repeatedly, time and again; **von ~ zu ~** each *or* every time; **er wird von ~ zu ~ besser/dümmer** he gets better and better/more and more stupid, he gets better/more stupid each *or* every time; **für dieses ~** for the time being, for now; **mit einem ~(e)** all at once, all of a sudden, suddenly

Ma|la|chit [mala'xi:t] M **-s, -e** malachite

ma|lad [ma'la:t]

ma|la|de [ma'la:də] ADJ *(dial)* ill, sick *(esp US)*

Ma|la|ga(wein) ['ma(:)laga-] M **-s, -s** Malaga

Ma|laie [ma'laiə] M **-n, -n, Ma|lai|in** [ma'laiın] F **-, -nen** Malay

ma|lai|isch [ma'laiıʃ] ADJ Malayan, Malay *attr*; **der Malaiische Archipel** the Malay Archipelago; **Malaiischer Bund** *(Hist)* Federation of Malaya

Ma|lai|isch(e) [ma'laiıʃ] NT Malay → *auch* **Deutsch(e)**

Ma|lai|se [ma'lɛ:zə] F **-, -n** *or (Sw) nt* **-s, -** *(geh)* malaise

Ma|la|ria [ma'la:ria] F **-,** *no pl* malaria

Ma|la|ria|pro|phy|la|xe F *(= Vorsorge)* malaria prophylaxis; *(= Medikament)* malaria tablets *pl*; *(= Therapie)* course of malaria tablets

Ma|lä|se [ma'lɛ:zə] F **-, -n** *or (Sw) nt* **-s, -** *(geh)* malaise

Ma|la|wi [ma'la:vi] NT **-s** Malawi

Ma|la|wi|er [ma'la:viɐ] M **-s, -, Ma|la|wi|e|rin** [-iərın] F **-, -nen** Malawian

ma|la|wisch [ma'la:vıʃ] ADJ Malawian, Malawi *attr*

Ma|lay|sia [ma'laizia] NT **-s** Malaysia

Ma|lay|si|er [ma'laiziɐ] M **-s, -, Ma|lay|si|e|rin** [-iərın] F **-, -nen** Malaysian

ma|lay|sisch [ma'laizıʃ] ADJ Malaysian

Mal|buch NT colouring *(Brit) or* coloring *(US)* book

Ma|le|di|ven [male'di:vn] PL Maldives *pl*, Maldive Islands *pl*

ma|len ['ma:lən] VTI **a** *(mit Pinsel und Farbe)* to paint; *(= zeichnen)* to draw; *(= langsam schreiben)* to write with painstaking care; **sich/jdn ~ lassen** to have one's/sb's portrait painted; **er hat während des Vortrags (Männchen) gemalt** he was doodling during the talk; **er malt** *(als Beruf)* he's a painter *or* an artist → **Teufel b, rosigmalen, schwarzmalen b** *(inf: = streichen)* to paint VR **a** *(= Selbstbildnis machen)* to paint *or* do a self-portrait, to paint a picture of oneself **b** *(fig liter)* to show itself, to be reflected

Ma|ler ['ma:lɐ] M **-s, -, Ma|le|rin** [-ərın] F **-, -nen** painter; *(= Kunstmaler auch)* artist

Ma|le|rei [malə'rai] F **-, -en** **a** *(no pl: = Malkunst)* art **b** *(= Bild)* painting; *(= Zeichnung)* drawing

Ma|ler|far|be F paint

Ma|le|rin [-ərın] F **-, -nen** (woman) painter; *(= Kunstmalerin auch)* artist

ma|le|risch ['ma:lərıʃ] ADJ **a** *(= bildnerisch)* in painting; *Talent, Können* as a painter; **das ~e Schaffen Leonardos** Leonardo's painting; **seine ~en Mittel** his technique as a painter **b** *(= pittoresk)* picturesque; *Landschaft* picturesque, scenic ADV *(= pittoresk)* picturesquely

Ma|ler-: **Ma|ler|lein|wand** F artist's canvas; **Ma|ler|meis|ter(in)** M(F) (master) painter; **Ma|ler|schu|le** F school of painting

Mal|heur [ma'lø:ɐ] NT **-s, -s** *or* **-e** mishap; **ihm ist ein kleines ~ passiert** *(inf)* he's had a little accident *(auch euph) or* a mishap; **das ist doch kein ~!** it's not serious

Ma|li ['ma:li] NT **-s** Mali

Ma|li|er ['ma:liɐ] M **-s, -, Ma|li|e|rin** [-iərın] F **-, -nen** Malian

ma|lig|ne [ma'lıgnə] ADJ *(Med)* malignant

ma|li|zi|ös [mali'tsiø:s] ADJ malicious ADV maliciously

Mal-: **Mal|kas|ten** M paintbox; **Mal|krei|de** F artist's chalk

mall [mal] ADJ *(Naut)* variable; *(N Ger inf)* barmy *(Brit inf)*, batty *(inf)*

Mal|lor|ca [ma'jɔrka, ma'lɔrka] NT **-s** Majorca, Mallorca

mal|lor|qui|nisch [malɔr'ki:nıʃ] ADJ Majorcan

mal+neh|men VTI *sep irreg* to multiply *(mit* by)

Ma|lo|che [ma'lɔxə, ma'lo:xə] F **-,** *no pl (inf)* graft *(Brit inf)*, hard work; **auf ~ sein** to be grafting *(Brit inf) or* working hard; **du musst zur ~** you've got to go to work

ma|lo|chen [ma'lɔxn, ma'lo:xn] *ptp* **malocht** VI *(inf)* to graft *(Brit inf)*, to sweat away *(inf)*

Ma|lo|cher [ma'lɔxɐ, ma'lo:xɐ] M **-s, -, Ma|lo|che|rin** [-ərın] F **-, -nen** *(inf)* grafter *(Brit inf)*, hard worker

Mal|stift M crayon

Mal|strom M Maelstrom; *(fig liter)* maelstrom

Mal|ta ['malta] NT **-s** Malta

Mal|tech|nik F painting technique

Mal|te|ser [mal'te:zɐ] M **-s, -, Mal|te|se|rin** [-'te:zərın] F **-, -nen** Maltese

Mal|te|ser-: **Mal|te|ser|kreuz** NT Maltese cross *(auch Tech)*; **Mal|te|ser|or|den** M (Order of the) Knights *pl* of Malta *or* of St John; **Mal|te|ser|rit|ter** M Knight of Malta, (Knight) Hospitaller

mal|te|sisch [mal'te:zıʃ] ADJ Maltese

Mal|to|se [mal'to:zə] F **-,** *no pl* maltose

mal|trä|tie|ren [maltrɛ'ti:rən] *ptp* **malträtiert** VT to ill-treat, to maltreat

Ma|lus ['ma:lʊs] M **-ses, -** *or* **-se** [-lu:s] *(Insur)* supplementary (high-risk) premium; *(Univ)* minus point; **sein ~ ist ihr Bonus** his loss is her gain

Mal|ve ['malvə] F **-, -n** *(Bot)* mallow; *(= Stockrose)* hollyhock

mal|ven|far|ben [-farbn], **mal|ven|far|big** ADJ mauve

Mal|vi|nen [mal'vi:nən] PL = **Malwinen**

Mal|wi|nen [mal'vi:nən] PL Falklands *pl*, Malvinas *pl*

Malz [malts] NT **-es,** *no pl* malt → **Hopfen**

Malz-: **Malz|bier** NT malt beer, ≈ stout *(Brit)*; **Malz|bon|bon** NT OR M malt lozenge

Mal|zei|chen NT multiplication sign

mäl|zen ['mɛltsn] VTI to malt

Mäl|zer ['mɛltsɐ] M **-s, -, Mäl|ze|rin** [-ərın] F **-, -nen** maltster

Mäl|ze|rei [mɛltsə'rai] F **-, -en** malt house, malting

Malz-: **Malz|ex|trakt** M malt extract; **Malz|kaf|fee** M *coffee substitute made from barley malt*; **Malz|zu|cker** M maltose, malt sugar

Ma|ma ['mama] F **-, -s** *(inf)* mummy *(Brit)*, mommy *(US)*

Ma|ma [ma'ma:] F **-, -s** *(dated)* mama *(dated)*

Ma|ma-: **Ma|ma|kind** NT *(pej)* mummy's boy/girl *(Brit)*, mommy's boy/girl *(US)*; **Ma|ma|söhn|chen** NT *(pej)* mummy's darling *(Brit)*, mommy's darling *(US)*

Mam|ba ['mamba] F **-, -s** *(Zool)* mamba; **Schwarze ~** black mamba; **Grüne ~** West African mamba

Ma|me|luck [mamə'lʊk] M **-en, -en** *(Hist)* Mameluke

Ma|mi ['mami] F **-, -s** *(inf)* mummy, mommy *(US)*

Mam|mo|gra|fie, **Mam|mo|gra|phie** [mamogra'fi:] F **-, -n** [-'fi:ən] mammography

Mam|mon ['mamɔn] M **-s,** *no pl* Mammon; **der schnöde ~** Mammon, filthy lucre; **dem ~ dienen** to serve Mammon

Mam|mons|die|ner(in) M(F) *(pej)* servant of Mammon

Mam|mut ['mamʊt, 'mamu:t] NT **-s, -s** *or* **-e** mammoth

Mam|mut- *in cpds (lit, fig)* mammoth; *(= lange dauernd)* marathon; **Mam|mut|baum** M sequoia, giant redwood; **Mam|mut|pro|gramm** NT huge programme *(Brit) or* program *(US)*; *(lange dauernd)* marathon programme *(Brit) or* program *(US)*; **Mam|mut|pro|zess** M marathon trial; **Mam|mut|sit|zung** F marathon meeting

mampf|en ['mampfn] VTI *(inf)* to munch, to chomp *(inf)*; **ich brauche was zu ~** I want something to eat

Mam|sell [mam'zɛl] F -, -en *or* -s *(dated hum)* lady; *(old: = Wirtschafterin)* housekeeper

man [man] INDEF PRON *dat* **einem**, *acc* **einen** **a** you, one; *(= ich)* one; *(= wir)* we; **~ kann nie wissen** you *or* one can never tell, there's no knowing; **das tut ~ nicht** that's not done; **~ wird doch wohl noch fragen dürfen** there's no law against asking
b *(= jemand)* somebody, someone; **~ hat mir gesagt …** I was told …, somebody told me …; **~ hat mir erklärt, dass …** it was explained *or* somebody explained to me that …; **~ hat festgestellt, dass …** it has been established that …
c *(= die Leute)* they *pl*, people *pl*; **früher glaubte ~, dass …** they *or* people used to believe that …; **~ will die alten Häuser niederreißen** they want to pull down the old houses; **diese Hemden trägt ~ nicht mehr** people don't wear these shirts any more; **~ hat öfters versucht, …** many attempts have been made …
d **~ wende sich an …** apply to … → **nehmen c**

man ADV *(N Ger inf)* just; **denn ~ los!** let's go then!; **~ sachte!** (just) take it easy!; **jetzt ~ schnell!** we'd/you'd *etc* better hurry

Ma|na|ge|ment ['mɛnɛdʒmənt] NT -s, -s management

Ma|nage|ment-Buy-out ['mɛnɛdʒmənt-baiaut] NT -s, -s *(Ind)* management buyout

ma|na|gen ['mɛnɛdʒn] VT *(inf)* to manage; *(= hinkriegen auch)* to fix; **ich manage das schon!** I'll manage *or* fix it somehow!

Ma|na|ger ['mɛnɛdʒɐ] M -s, -, **Ma|na|ge|rin** [-ərɪn] F -, -nen manager

Ma|na|ger-: **Ma|na|ger|krank|heit** F *(inf)* executivitis *(hum)*; **Ma|na|ger|typ** M management *or* executive type

manch [manç] INDEF PRON **a** *inv (in Zusammensetzung mit ein, eine(r, s), substantiviertem Adjektiv und (geh) Substantiv)* many a; **~ eine(r), ~ ein Mensch** many a person, (a good) many people, quite a few people; **~ einem kann man nie Vernunft beibringen** you can never teach sense to some people; **~ anderer** many another; **~ Schönes** *(geh)* many a beautiful thing; **~ Erlebnis/schöne Geschichte/Kind** *(all liter)* many an experience/a lovely story/a child
b *(adjektivisch)* **~e(r, s)** a good many *+pl*, a fair number *+pl*, quite a few *+pl*, many a *+sing*; *(pl: = einige)* some *+pl*; **~er, der …** many a person who …, many *pl* who …, a good many people *pl* who …, some (people) *pl* who …; **~e hundert Euro** some *or* several hundreds of euros; **~es Schöne** a number of beautiful things, quite a few beautiful things
c *(substantivisch)* **~e(r)** a good many people *pl*, many a person/man/woman *etc*; *(pl: = einige)* some (people); **~er lernts nie** some people never learn; **~es** *(= vieles)* a good many things *pl*, a number of things *pl*, quite a few things *pl*; *(= einiges)* some things *pl*; **in ~em hat er recht** he's right about a lot of/some things; **so** *or* **gar** *(old)* **~es** a good many things *pl*, quite a few things *pl*

man|chen|orts ['mançn'ɔrts] ADV = **mancherorts**

man|cher|lei ['mançɐ'lai] ADJ *inv (adjektivisch mit pl n)* various, a number of; *(substantivisch)* various things *pl*, a number of things

man|cher|orts ['mançɐ'ɔrts], **man|cher|or|ten** ['mançɐ'ɔrtn] ADV in a number of places, in many a place

Man|ches|ter [man'ʃɛstɐ] M -s, *no pl (Tex)* broad-ribbed cord(uroy)

manch|mal ['mançma:l] ADV sometimes

Man|dant [man'dant] M -en, -en, **Man|dan|tin** [-'dantɪn] F -, -nen *(Jur)* client

Man|da|rin [manda'ri:n] M -s, -e *(Hist)* mandarin

Man|da|ri|ne [manda'ri:nə] F -, -n mandarin (orange), tangerine

Man|dat [man'da:t] NT -(e)s, -e **a** *(= Auftrag, Vollmacht)* mandate *(auch Pol)*, authorization (*+gen* from); *(von Anwalt)* brief; *(Parl: = Abgeordnetensitz)* seat; **sein ~ niederlegen** *(Parl)* to resign one's seat; **imperatives ~** *(Pol)* fixed mandate **b** *(= Gebiet)* mandated territory, mandate

Man|da|tar [manda'ta:ɐ] M -s, -e **a** *(rare: = Beauftragter)* mandatary *(form)*, agent **b** *(Aus)* member of parliament, representative

Man|da|tar|staat M mandatary

Man|dats-: **Man|dats|ge|biet** NT mandated territory, mandate; **Man|dats|macht** F mandatory power; **Man|dats|trä|ger(in)** M(F) mandate holder; **Man|dats|ver|lust** M loss of a seat

Man|del ['mandl] F -, -n **a** almond **b** *(Anat)* tonsil **c** *(obs: Measure)* fifteen

Man|del-: **Man|del|au|gen** PL *(poet)* almond eyes *pl*; **man|del|äu|gig** ADJ *(poet)* almond-eyed; **Man|del|baum** M almond tree; **Man|del|ent|zün|dung** F tonsillitis; **man|del|för|mig** ADJ almond-shaped; **Man|del|kern** M almond (kernel); **Man|del|kleie** F almond meal; **Man|del|öl** NT almond oil

Man|derl ['mandɐl] NT -s, -n *(Aus)*, **Mandl** ['mandl] NT -s, -n *(S Ger, inf)* **a** *(= Männchen)* little man **b** *(= Vogelscheuche)* scarecrow

Man|do|li|ne [mando'li:nə] F -, -n mandolin

Mand|ra|go|ra [man'dra:gora] F -, **Mandragoren** [-'go:rən] *(Bot)* mandrake

Mand|rill [man'drɪl] M -s, -e *(Zool)* mandrill

Mand|schu ['mandʒu, 'mantʃu] NT -(s), *no pl (Ling)* Manchu

Mand|schu|rei [mandʒu'rai, mantʃu'rai] F - **die ~** Manchuria

mand|schu|risch [man'dʒu:rɪʃ, man'tʃu:rɪʃ] ADJ Manchurian

Ma|ne|ge [ma'ne:ʒə] F -, -n ring, arena

mang [maŋ] PREP *+dat or acc (N Ger inf)* among(st)

Man|gan [maŋ'ga:n] NT -s, *no pl (abbr* **Mn***)* manganese

Man|ga|nat [maŋga'na:t] NT -s, -e *(Chem)* manganate

Man|gan-: **Man|gan|ei|sen** NT ferro-manganese; **Man|gan|erz** NT manganese ore; **Man|gan|stahl** M manganese steel

-man|gel M *suf in cpds* shortage of …; *(Med)* … deficiency; **Ärztemangel** shortage of doctors; **Vitaminmangel** vitamin deficiency

Man|gel ['maŋəl] F -, -n mangle; *(= Heißmangel)* rotary iron; **durch die ~ drehen** to put through the mangle; *(fig inf)* to put through it *(inf)*; *Prüfling etc* to put through the mill; **jdn in die ~ nehmen/in der ~ haben** *(fig inf)* to give sb a going-over *(inf)*; *(= ausfragen auch)* to give sb a grilling *(inf)*

Man|gel M -s, = ['mɛŋl] **a** *(= Fehler)* fault; *(bei Maschine)* defect, fault; *(= Unzulänglichkeit)* fault, shortcoming; *(= Charaktermangel)* flaw
b *no pl (= das Fehlen)* lack *(an +dat* of); *(= Knappheit)* shortage *(an +dat* of); *(Med)* deficiency *(an +dat* of); **aus ~** *or* **wegen ~s an** *(+dat)* for lack of, due to a lack of; **wegen ~s an Beweisen** for lack of evidence; **~ an Vitamin C** lack of vitamin C, vitamin C deficiency; **es besteht** *or* **herrscht ~ an etw** *(dat)* there is a lack/shortage of sth; **~ an etw** *(dat)* **haben** *or* **leiden** *(liter)* to be short of sth, to lack sth, to have a lack of sth
c *no pl (= Entbehrung)* privation, need, want; **~ leiden** *(liter)* to go short, to suffer hardship *or* privation; **keinen ~ leiden** to want for nothing

Män|gel-: **Män|gel|an|zei|ge** F notification of defects; **Män|gel|be|richt** M list of faults

Man|gel-: **Man|gel|be|ruf** M undersubscribed *or* understaffed profession; **Man|gel|er|näh|rung** F malnutrition; **Man|gel|er|schei|nung** F *(Med)* deficiency symptom; **eine ~ sein** *(fig)* to be in short supply *(bei* with)

man|gel|frei, män|gel|frei ADJ free of faults *or* defects

man|gel|haft ADJ *(= unzulänglich, schlecht)* poor; *Beleuchtung, Ausrüstung auch* inadequate; *Informationen, Interesse* insufficient; *(= fehlerhaft) Sprachkenntnisse, Ware* faulty; *(Schulnote)* unsatisfactory, poor ADV poorly, inadequately; **sich in der Stadt nur ~ auskennen** not to know one's way around town very well; **er spricht nur ~ Englisch** he doesn't speak English very well

Män|gel|haf|tung F *(Jur)* liability for faults *or* defects

Man|gel|krank|heit F deficiency disease

Män|gel|lis|te F list of faults *or* defects

man|geln ['maŋln] VT *Wäsche* to (put through the) mangle; *(= heiß mangeln)* to iron, to press VI to use the mangle; *(mit Heißmangel)* to use the rotary iron

man|geln VI *impers* **es mangelt an etw** *(dat)* there is a lack of sth; *(= unzureichend vorhanden auch)* there is a shortage of sth; **er ließ es an nichts ~** he made sure that he/they *etc* lacked nothing, he made sure that nothing was lacking; **es mangelt jdm an etw** *(dat)* sb lacks sth; **es mangelt ihm an Selbstvertrauen/Erfahrung** he is lacking in *or* he lacks self-confidence/experience; **~des Selbstvertrauen/Verständnis** *etc* a lack of self-confidence/understanding *etc*; **wegen ~der Aufmerksamkeit** through not paying attention; **das Kino wurde wegen ~der Sicherheit geschlossen** the cinema was closed because of inadequate safety precautions
VI **etw mangelt jdm/einer Sache** sb/sth lacks sth; *(Verständnis, Selbstvertrauen, Erfahrung auch)* sb is lacking in sth

Män|gel|rü|ge F *(Admin)* (letter of) complaint

man|gels ['maŋls] PREP *+gen (form)* for lack of

Man|gel-: **Man|gel|wa|re** F scarce commodity, commodity in short supply; **~ sein** *(fig)* to be a rare thing; *(Ärzte, gute Lehrer etc)* not to grow on trees; **Man|gel|wä|sche** F ironing *(to be done in a rotary iron)*; **Man|gel|wirt|schaft** F, *no pl* economy of scarcity

Man|go ['maŋgo] F -, -s *or* -nen *(auch* **Mangopflaume***)* mango

Man|go|baum M mango tree

Man|gold ['maŋgɔlt] M -(e)s, -e [-də] mangel (-wurzel)

Mang|ro|ve [maŋ'gro:və] F -, -n mangrove

Mang|ro|ven|sumpf M mangrove swamp

Ma|nie [ma'ni:] F -, -n [-'ni:ən] *(Med, fig)* mania; *(fig auch)* obsession

Ma|nier [ma'ni:ɐ] F -, -en **a** *no pl (= Art und Weise)* manner; *(eines Künstlers etc)* style; **in überzeugender ~** in a most convincing manner **b** **Manieren** PL *(= Umgangsformen)* manners; **jdm ~en beibringen** to teach sb (some) manners; **~en lernen** to learn (some) manners, to learn (how) to behave; **was sind das für ~en?** *(inf)* that's no way to behave **c** *(= Angewohnheit)* affectation

ma|nie|riert [mani'ri:ɐt] ADJ affected; *Benehmen auch* mannered

Ma|nie|riert|heit F -, -en affectation

Ma|nie|ris|mus [mani'rɪsmʊs] M -, *no pl (Liter, Art)* mannerism

ma|nie|ris|tisch [mani'rɪstɪʃ] ADJ *(Liter, Art, fig)* mannerist, manneristic

ma|nier|lich [ma'ni:ɐlɪç] ADJ **a** *Kind* well-mannered, well-behaved; *Benehmen* good **b** *(inf: = einigermaßen gut)* decent, reasonable; *Aussehen, Frisur, Kleidung* respectable ADV *essen* politely; *sich benehmen* properly; *sich kleiden* respectably

ma|ni|fest [mani'fɛst] ADJ *(liter)* manifest

Ma|ni|fest [mani'fɛst] NT -(e)s, -e **a** manifesto **b** *(Naut)* manifest

Ma|ni|fes|tant [manifɛs'tant] M -en, -en, **Ma|ni|fes|tan|tin** [-'tantɪn] F -, -nen *(Sw)* demonstrator

Ma|ni|fes|ta|ti|on [manifɛsta'tsio:n] F -, -en manifestation; *(Sw: = Kundgebung)* demonstration; *(Sw: = Kundgebung)* demonstration

ma|ni|fes|tie|ren [manifɛs'ti:rən] *ptp* **manifestiert** *(geh)* VT to demonstrate, to manifest VI *(Sw)* to demonstrate VR to manifest oneself

Ma|ni|kü|re [mani'ky:rə] F -, -n **a** *(= Handpflege)* manicure **b** *(= Handpflegerin)* manicurist

ma|ni|kü|ren [mani'ky:rən] *ptp* **manikürt** VT to manicure

Ma|ni|la [ma'ni:la] NT -s Manil(l)a
Ma|ni|la-: **Ma|ni|la|hanf** M Manil(l)a (hemp); **Ma|ni|la|zi|gar|re** F Manil(l)a (cigar)
Ma|ni|ok [ma'niɔk] M -s, -s *(Bot)* cassava
Ma|ni|ok|wur|zel F cassava root
Ma|ni|pu|lant [manipu'lant] M -en, -en, **Ma|ni|pu|lan|tin** [-'lantın] F -, -nen manipulator; *(Aus: = Amtshelfer)* assistant
Ma|ni|pu|la|ti|on [manipula'tsio:n] F -, -en manipulation; *(= Trick)* manoeuvre *(Brit)*, maneuver *(US)*
Ma|ni|pu|la|tor [manipu'la:to:ɐ] M -s, **Manipulatoren** [-'to:rən] *(Tech)* manipulator
Ma|ni|pu|la|tor [manipu'la:to:ɐ] M -s, **Manipulatoren** [-'to:rəm], **Ma|ni|pu|la|to|rin** [-'to:rın] F -, -nen *(fig)* conjurer, magician
ma|ni|pu|lier|bar ADJ manipulable; **leicht ~** easily manipulated; **schwer ~** difficult to manipulate; **beliebig ~** manipulable at will
Ma|ni|pu|lier|bar|keit [manipu'li:ɐba:ɐkait] F -, *no pl* manipulability
ma|ni|pu|lie|ren [manipu'li:rən] *ptp* **manipuliert** VT to manipulate
Ma|ni|pu|lie|rung F -, -en manipulation
ma|nisch ['ma:nıʃ] ADJ manic; **~-depressiv, ~-melancholisch** manic-depressive; **~-melancholische Krankheit** manic depression
Ma|ni|tu ['ma:nitu] M -s Manitou
Man|ko ['maŋko] NT -s, -s **a** *(Comm: = Fehlbetrag)* deficit; **~ haben** *(inf) or* **machen** *(inf)* to be short *(inf)*; **~ machen** *(inf: bei Verkauf)* to make a loss **b** *(fig: = Nachteil)* shortcoming
Mann [man] M -(e)s, =er ['mɛnɐ] **a** man; **ein Überschuss an Männern** a surplus of males *or* men; **der böse** *or* **schwarze ~** the bogeyman; **ein feiner ~** a (perfect) gentleman; **ein ~ aus dem Volk(e)** a man of the people; **der erste ~ sein** *(fig)* to be in charge; **der ~ im Mond(e)** the man in the moon; **ein ~ der Feder/Wissenschaft** a man of letters/science; **ein ~ des Todes** a dead man, a man marked for death; **ein ~ von Wort** a man of his word; **wo Männer noch Männer sind** where men are men; **er ist unser ~** he's the man for us, he's our man; **er ist nicht der ~ dafür** *or* **danach** he's not the man for that; *(= nicht seine Art)* he's not the sort; **drei ~ hoch** *(inf)* three of them together; **wie ein ~** as a *or* one man; **auf den ~ dressiert sein** to be trained to go for people; **etw an den ~ bringen** *(inf)* to get rid of sth; **seinen ~ stehen** to hold one's own; *(= auf eigenen Füßen stehen)* to stand on one's own two feet; **einen kleinen ~ im Ohr haben** *(hum)* to be crazy *(inf)*; **und ein ~, ein Wort, er hats auch gemacht** and, as good as his word, he did it; **~ an ~** close together, next to one another; **~ für ~** *(= einzeln hintereinander)* one after the other; *(= allesamt)* every single one; **~ gegen ~** man against man; **pro ~** per head; **ein Gespräch unter Männern** *or* **von ~ zu ~** a man-to-man talk → **Mannen, Not a, tot a**
b *(= Ehemann)* husband; **jdn an den ~ bringen** *(inf)* to marry sb off *(inf)*, to find sb a husband; **~ und Frau werden** to become man and wife
c *pl* **Leute** *(= Besatzungsmitglied)* hand, man; **20 ~** 20 hands *or* men; **mit ~ und Maus untergehen** to go down with all hands; *(Passagierschiff)* to go down with no survivors → **Bord**
d *pl* **Leute** *(= Teilnehmer, Sport, Cards)* player, man; **auf den ~ spielen** to play the ball at one's opponent; *(beim Zuspielen)* to pass accurately; **den dritten ~ spielen** *(Cards)* to play *or* take the third hand
e *(inf: als Interjektion)* (my) God *(inf)*; *(auffordernd, bewundernd, erstaunt)* (my) God *(inf)*, hey, (hey) man *(inf)*; **~, das kannst du doch nicht machen!** hey, you can't do that!; **mach schnell, ~!** hurry up, man!; **~, oh ~!** oh boy! *(inf)*; **(mein) lieber ~!** my God! *(inf)*; *(erstaunt, bewundernd auch)* wow! *(inf)*
Man|na ['mana] NT -(s), *no pl* F -, *no pl (Bibl, fig)* manna (from heaven)
mann|bar ADJ **a** *Junge* sexually mature; *(= mutig)* brave **b** *Mädchen* marriageable
Männ|chen ['mɛnçən] NT -s, - *dim von* **Mann a** little man; *(= Zwerg)* man(n)ikin; **~ malen** to draw (little) matchstick men *(Brit) or* stickmen *(US)*, ≈ to doodle **b** *(Biol)* male; *(= Vogelmännchen)* male, cock **c ~ machen** *(Tier)* to sit up on its hind legs; *(Hund)* to (sit up and) beg; *(pej inf) (Mensch)* to grovel; *(hum: Soldat)* to jump smartly to attention
Mann|de|ckung F *(Sport)* man-to-man marking, one-on-one defense *(US)*; **einen Spieler in ~ nehmen** to mark *or* guard *(US)* a player man-to-man *or* closely
Män|ne ['mɛnə] M -, *no pl* **a** *(dial) dim von* **Hermann b** *(inf: = Ehemann)* hubby *(inf)*
Man|nen ['manən] PL *(Hist: = Gefolgsleute)* men *pl*
Man|ne|quin [manə'kɛ̃:, 'manəkɛ̃] NT -s, -s (fashion) model
Män|ner *pl von* **Mann**
Män|ner- *in cpds* men's; *(= eines bestimmten Mannes)* man's; **Män|ner|be|kannt|schaft** F *usu pl* man friend, boyfriend; **von ~en leben** to earn one's living from prostitution; **Män|ner|be|ruf** M male profession; **Män|ner|bund** M *pl* **-bünde** male organization; **Män|ner|chor** M male-voice choir; **Män|ner|do|mä|ne** F male domain; **technische Berufe waren früher ~** the technical professions used to be a male preserve *or* domain; **Män|ner|fang** M **auf ~ ausgehen/sein** to go/be looking for a man/men; *(zwecks Heirat)* to go/be husband-hunting; **Män|ner|freund|schaft** F friendship between men; **er hat immer ~en vorgezogen** he has always preferred friendship(s) with other men; **Män|ner|ge|fäng|nis** NT men's prison; **Män|ner|ge|sang|ver|ein** M male choral society, men's glee club *(US)*; **Män|ner|ge|schich|te** F affair with a man; *(= Erlebnisse)* sexploits *(hum inf)*, experiences with men; **Män|ner|ge|sell|schaft** F *(Sociol)* male-dominated society; *(= Gesellschaft von Männern)* all-male company; **Män|ner|grup|pe** F men's group; **Män|ner|hass** M hatred of men; **Män|ner|haus** NT men's house; **Män|ner|herr|schaft** F male domination; **Män|ner|klos|ter** NT monastery; **Män|ner|ma|ga|zin** NT magazine for men; **män|ner|mor|dend** ADJ man-eating; **Män|ner|sa|che** F *(Angelegenheit)* man's business; *(Arbeit)* job for a man, man's job; **~n** men's affairs; **Fußball war früher ~** football used to be a male preserve *or* domain; **Män|ner|sport** M men's sport; **Män|ner|stim|me** F man's voice; *(Mus)* male voice; **Män|ner|treu** [-trɔy] F -, - *(Bot)* speedwell; **Män|ner|über|schuss** M surplus of men; **Män|ner|welt** F *(dated hum)* **die ~** men *pl*
Man|nes-: **Man|nes|al|ter** NT manhood *no art*; **im besten ~ sein** to be in one's prime, to be in the prime of (one's) life; **Man|nes|jah|re** PL years *pl* of manhood; **in die ~ kommen** to reach manhood; **Man|nes|kraft** F *(dated, hum)* virility
Man|nes|mann|rohr® NT seamless metal tube, Mannesmann tube
Man|nes-: **Man|nes|stolz** M masculine pride; **Man|nes|wür|de** F *(old)* accoutrements *pl (Brit) or* accouterments *pl (US)* of manhood; *(hum)* dignity as a man
mann|haft ADJ manly *no adv*; *(= tapfer)* manful, valiant; *(= entschlossen)* resolute; *Widerstand* stout ADV *(= tapfer)* valiantly; *(= entschlossen)* resolutely
man|nig|fach ['manıçfax] ADJ *attr* manifold, multifarious
man|nig|fal|tig ['manıçfaltıç] ADJ diverse, varied
Mann|jahr NT *(Ind)* man-year
Männ|lein ['mɛnlain] NT -s, - *dim von* **Mann** little man; *(= Zwerg)* man(n)ikin; **~ und Weiblein** *(hum inf)* boys and girls
männ|lich ['mɛnlıç] ADJ **a** male; *Reim, Wort* masculine **b** *(fig: = mannhaft) Stärke, Mut, Entschluss, Wesen* manly; *Stimme* masculine, manly; *Auftreten* masculine; *Frau* masculine, mannish ADV **~ dominiert** male-dominated; **~ geprägt** masculine
Männ|lich|keit F -, *no pl (fig)* manliness; *(von Stimme auch)* masculinity; *(von Auftreten)* masculinity; *(von Frau)* masculinity, mannishness
Männ|lich|keits|wahn M machismo
Mann|loch NT *(Tech)* manhole
man|no ['mano], **man|no|mann** ['manoman] INTERJ *(inf)* boy, boy oh boy
Manns|bild NT *(dated pej)* fellow, male
Mann|schaft ['manʃaft] F -, -en *(Sport, fig)* team; *(Naut, Aviat)* crew; **~(en)** *(Mil)* men *pl*
mann|schaft|lich ADJ *(Sport)* as a team *pred*; **Schalkes Stärke ist die ~e Geschlossenheit** Schalke's strength is that they play together as a team
Mann|schafts- *in cpds (Sport)* team; **Mann|schafts|auf|stel|lung** F team line-up; *(das Aufstellen)* selection of the team; **Mann|schafts|dienst|grad** M *(Mil)* other rank *usu pl*; **Mann|schafts|füh|rer(in)** M(F) *(Sport)* (team) captain; **Mann|schafts|geist** M team spirit; **Mann|schafts|kampf** M *(Sport)* team event; **Mann|schafts|ka|pi|tän** M *(Sport)* (team) captain, skipper *(inf)*; **Mann|schafts|kost** F *(Sport)* team fare; *(Mil)* troops' rations *pl*; *(Naut, Aviat)* crew's rations *pl*; **Mann|schafts|raum** M *(Sport)* team quarters *pl*; *(Mil)* men's quarters *pl*; *(Naut)* crew's quarters *pl*; *(= Umkleideraum)* changing rooms *pl*, locker rooms *pl*; **Mann|schafts|sie|ger** M *(Sport)* winning team; **Mann|schafts|spiel** NT, **Mann|schafts|sport** M team sport; **Mann|schafts|ver|pfle|gung** F = **Mannschaftskost**; **Mann|schafts|wa|gen** M police van; *(Mil)* troop carrier; **Mann|schafts|wer|tung** F *(Sport)* team score
Manns-: **manns|hoch** ADJ as high as a man; **der Schnee liegt ~** the snow is six feet deep; **Manns|leu|te** PL *(dated inf)* men *pl*; **Manns|per|son** F *(dated pej)* fellow, male; **manns|toll** ADJ man-mad *(esp Brit inf)*, mad about men; **Manns|toll|heit** F nymphomania; **Manns|volk** NT *(dated inf)* men *pl*
Mann|weib NT *(pej)* masculine *or* mannish woman
Ma|no|me|ter [mano'me:tɐ] NT -s, - *(Tech)* pressure gauge; **~!** *(inf)* wow! *(inf)*, boy oh boy! *(inf)*
Ma|nö|ver [ma'nø:vɐ] NT -s, - *(lit, fig)* manoeuvre *(Brit)*, maneuver *(US)*; **ins ~ gehen** *or* **ziehen** to go on manoeuvres *(Brit) or* maneuvers *(US)*; **nach größeren ~n ...** *(Mot, fig etc)* after a lot of manoeuvring *(Brit) or* maneuvering *(US)* ...
Ma|nö|ver-: **Ma|nö|ver|ge|län|de** NT exercise area; *(ständig)* ranges *pl*; **Ma|nö|ver|kri|tik** F *(fig)* inquest, postmortem; **Ma|nö|ver|scha|den** M damage resulting from military manoeuvres *(Brit) or* maneuvers *(US)*
ma|növ|rie|ren [manø'vri:rən] *ptp* **manövriert** VTI *(lit, fig)* to manoeuvre *(Brit)*, to maneuver *(US)*
Ma|növ|rier-: **ma|növ|rier|fä|hig** ADJ manoeuvrable *(Brit)*, maneuverable *(US)*; *(fig)* flexible; **Ma|növ|rier|fä|hig|keit** F manoeuvrability *(Brit)*, maneuverability *(US)*; *(fig)* flexibility; **Ma|növ|rier|mas|se** F *(= Geldsumme)* transferable sum; *(fig: = Menschen)* pawns *pl* who can be pushed around; **ma|növ|rier|un|fä|hig** ADJ disabled
Man|sar|de [man'za:rdə] F -, -n garret; *(Boden)* attic
Man|sar|den- *in cpds* attic; **Man|sar|den|woh|nung** F attic flat *(Brit) or* apartment; **Man|sar|den|zim|mer** NT attic room
Mansch [manʃ] M -es, *no pl (inf) (= Brei)* mush; *(= Schlamm)* mud
man|schen ['manʃn] VI *(inf)* to mess around *(inf)*
Man|schet|te [man'ʃɛtə] F -, -n **a** *(= Ärmelaufschlag)* cuff; *(zur Blutdruckmessung)* blood pres-

sure cuff **b** *(= Umhüllung)* frill **c** *(Tech: = Dichtung)* seal **d** *(Sport: = Würgegriff)* stranglehold; **~n haben** *(inf)* to be scared stupid *(inf)*; **vor seinem Vater/der Prüfung hat er mächtige ~n** *(inf)* his father/the thought of the exam scares him stupid *(inf)*; **~n kriegen** *(inf)* to get cold feet

Man|schet|ten|knopf M cufflink

Man|tel ['mantl] M **-s,** ⸚ ['mɛntl] **a** coat; *(= Umhang)* cloak → **Wind a b** *(Tech) (= Glockenmantel)* cope; *(= Rohrmantel)* jacket; *(= Geschossmantel)* jacket, casing; *(= Kabelmantel)* casing; *(= Reifenmantel)* outer tyre *(Brit)* or tire *(US)*, casing **c** *(fig)* cloak, mantle; **etw mit dem ~ der christlichen Nächstenliebe zudecken** to forgive and forget sth **d** *(Fin)* share certificate **e** *(Comm: = Firmenmantel)* form **f** *(Zool)* mantle, pallium **g** *(Math)* curved surface

Män|tel|chen ['mɛntlçən] NT **-s,** - *dim von* **Mantel**; **einer Sache** *(dat)* **ein ~ umhängen** to cover sth up → **Wind a**

Man|tel- *in cpds (Tex)* coat; **Man|tel|fut|ter** NT coat lining; **Man|tel|ge|schoss** NT jacketed bullet; **Man|tel|ge|setz** NT *general outline of a law providing guidelines for specific elaboration*; **Man|tel|pa|vi|an** M sacred or hamadryas baboon; **Man|tel|stoff** M coating, coat fabric; **Man|tel|ta|rif|ver|trag** M *(Ind)* general agreement on conditions of employment; **Man|tel|tie|re** PL tunicates *pl (spec)*

Man|tel-und-De|gen- *in cpds* swashbuckling

Man|tel-und-De|gen-Film M swashbuckling film

Man|tra ['mantra] NT **-(s), -s** mantra

Mantsch [mantʃ] M **-es,** *no pl (inf) (= Brei)* mush; *(= Schlamm)* mud

mant|schen ['mantʃn] VI *(inf)* to mess around *(inf)*

Ma|nu|al [ma'nua:l] NT **-s, -e a** *(Mus)* manual **b** *(old Comm)* daily ledger

ma|nu|ell [ma'nuɛl] ADJ *Arbeit, Bedienung* manual ADV manually, by hand

Ma|nu|fak|tur [manufak'tu:ɐ] F **-, -en** *(old, Sociol)* **a** *no pl* manufacture **b** *(= Fabrik)* factory, manufactory *(old)*

Ma|nu|fak|tur|wa|ren PL manufactured goods *pl*; *(= Textilien)* textiles *pl*

Ma|nu|skript [manu'skrɪpt] NT **-(e)s, -e** manuscript; *(Rad, Film, TV)* script

Ma|o|is|mus [mao'ɪsmʊs] M **-,** *no pl* Maoism

Ma|o|ist [mao'ɪst] M **-en, -en, Ma|o|is|tin** [-'ɪstɪn] F **-, -nen** Maoist

ma|o|is|tisch [mao'ɪstɪʃ] ADJ Maoist ADV **~ gesinnt** Maoist; **~ beeinflusst** influenced by (the teachings) of Mao; **~ klingend** Maoist-sounding

Ma|o|ri ['mauri, ma'o:ri] M **-(s), -(s)** *or f* **-, -(s)** Maori

Map|pe ['mapə] F **-, -n** *(= Aktenhefter)* folder, file; *(= Aktentasche)* briefcase; *(= Schulmappe)* (school) bag; *(= Federmappe, Bleistiftmappe)* pencil case

Map|ping ['mɛpɪŋ] NT **-s, -s** *(Comput)* mapping

Mär [mɛ:ɐ] F **-, -en** *(old) (= Nachricht)* tidings *pl*, news *sing*; *(= Märchen)* (fairy) tale; *(hum inf)* fairy story

Ma|ra|bu ['ma:rabu] M **-s, -s** *(Orn)* marabou

Ma|ra|but [mara'bu:t] M **-(s), -(s)** *(Rel)* marabout

Ma|ra|cu|ja [mara'ku:ja] F **-, -s** passion fruit

Ma|ra|thon ['ma:ratɔn, 'maratɔn] M **-s, -s** marathon

Ma|ra|thon NT **-s, -s** *(fig)* marathon

Ma|ra|thon- *in cpds* marathon; **Ma|ra|thon|lauf** M marathon; **Ma|ra|thon|läu|fer(in)** M(F) marathon runner; **Ma|ra|thon|sit|zung** F marathon meeting *or* session

Mär|chen ['mɛ:ɐçən] NT **-s,** - fairy tale, fairy story; *(inf)* tall story

Mär|chen- *in cpds* fairy-tale; **Mär|chen|buch** NT book of fairy tales; **Mär|chen|er|zäh|ler(in)** M(F) teller of fairy tales; *(fig)* storyteller; **Mär|chen|film** M film of a fairy tale; **mär|chen|haft** ADJ fairy-tale *attr*, fabulous; *(fig)* fabulous, fantastic ADV *reich* fabulously; *singen, malen* beautifully; **~ schön** incredibly beautiful; **Mär|chen|land** NT fairyland; **Mär|chen|prinz** M Prince Charming; *(fig auch)* fairy-tale prince; **Mär|chen|prin|zes|sin** F *(fig)* fairy-tale princess; **Mär|chen|stun|de** F story time

Mar|der ['mardɐ] M **-s,** - marten

Mar|der|fell NT, **Mar|der|pelz** M marten (fur)

Mä|re ['mɛ:rə] F **-, -n** *(old) (= Nachricht)* tidings *pl*, news *sing*; *(= Märchen)* (fairy) tale; *(hum inf)* fairy story

Mar|ga|re|te [marga're:tə] F - Margaret

Mar|ga|ri|ne [marga'ri:nə, *(Aus)* -'ri:n] F **-, -n** margarine

Mar|ge ['marʒə] F **-, -n** *(Comm)* margin

Mar|ge|ri|te [margə'ri:tə] F **-, -n** daisy, marguerite

mar|gi|nal [margi'na:l] ADJ marginal ADV marginally; *betreffen, interessieren* slightly

Mar|gi|na|lie [margi'na:liə] F **-, -n** *usu pl* marginalia *pl*

Ma|ria [ma'ri:a] F **-s** Mary; **die Mutter ~** the Virgin Mary, Our (Blessed) Lady

Ma|riä- [ma'ri:ɛ]: **Ma|riä Emp|fäng|nis** F the Immaculate Conception; **Ma|riä Ge|burt** F (the) Nativity of Mary; **Ma|riä Him|mel|fahrt** F Assumption

Ma|ria|the|re|si|en|ta|ler [-te're:ziən-] M Maria Theresa thaler, Levant dollar

Ma|ri|en-: **Ma|ri|en|al|tar** M Lady altar; **Ma|ri|en|bild** NT picture of the Virgin Mary; **Ma|ri|en|dich|tung** F hymns *pl* and poems *pl* in praise of the Virgin Mary; **Ma|ri|en|fest** NT Lady Day; **Ma|ri|en|kä|fer** M ladybird *(Brit)*, ladybug *(US)*; **Ma|ri|en|kult** M Mariolatry *(form)*, cult of the Virgin Mary; **Ma|ri|en|le|ben** NT *(Art, Liter)* Life of the Virgin Mary; **Ma|ri|en|ver|eh|rung** F adoration *or* veneration of the Virgin Mary

Ma|ri|hu|a|na [mari'hua:na] NT **-s,** *no pl* marijuana

Ma|ril|le [ma'rɪlə] F **-, -n** *(Aus)* apricot

Ma|ri|na [ma'ri:na] F **-, -s** marina

Ma|ri|na|de [mari'na:də] F **-, -n a** *(Cook)* marinade; *(= Soße)* mayonnaise-based sauce **b Marinaden** PL *(= Fischkonserven)* canned *or* tinned *(Brit)* fish

Ma|ri|ne [ma'ri:nə] F **-, -n** navy

Ma|ri|ne- *in cpds* naval; **ma|ri|ne|blau** ADJ navy-blue; **Ma|ri|ne|flie|ger(in)** M(F) naval pilot; **Ma|ri|ne|flug|zeug** NT naval aircraft *or* plane; **Ma|ri|ne|in|fan|te|rie** F marines *pl*; **Ma|ri|ne|in|fan|te|rist(in)** M(F) marine; **Ma|ri|ne|ma|ler(in)** M(F) marine *or* seascape painter; **Ma|ri|ne|mi|nis|ter(in)** M(F) minister of naval affairs, ≈ Secretary of the Navy *(US)*; **Ma|ri|ne|mi|nis|te|ri|um** NT ministry of naval affairs, ≈ Navy Department *(US)*; **Ma|ri|ne|of|fi|zier** M naval officer

Ma|ri|ner [ma'ri:nɐ] M **-s,** - *(inf)* sailor

Ma|ri|ne-: **Ma|ri|ne|sol|dat(in)** M(F) marine; **Ma|ri|ne|stütz|punkt** M naval base; **Ma|ri|ne|trup|pen** PL marines *pl*; **Ma|ri|ne|we|sen** NT navy; **ein Begriff aus dem ~** a nautical term

ma|ri|nie|ren [mari'ni:rən] *ptp* **mariniert** VT *Fisch, Fleisch* to marinate, to marinade; **marinierter Hering** pickled herring

Ma|ri|o|net|te [mario'nɛtə] F **-, -n** marionette, puppet; *(fig)* puppet

Ma|ri|o|net|ten- *in cpds* puppet; **Ma|ri|o|net|ten|re|gie|rung** F puppet government; **Ma|ri|o|net|ten|spie|ler(in)** M(F) puppeteer; **Ma|ri|o|net|ten|the|a|ter** NT puppet theatre *(Brit)* or theater *(US)*

ma|ri|tim [mari'ti:m] ADJ maritime

Mark [mark] NT **-(e)s,** *no pl (= Knochenmark)* marrow; *(Bot: = Gewebemark)* medulla, pith; *(= Fruchtfleisch)* purée; **Brühe mit ~** *(Cook)* consommé *or* broth with beef marrow; **bis ins ~** *(fig)* to the core; **jdn bis ins ~ treffen** *(fig)* to cut sb to the quick; **es geht mir durch ~ und Bein** *(inf)* it goes right through me; **kein ~ in den Knochen haben** *(fig)* to have no guts *or* backbone; **jdm das ~ aus den Knochen saugen** *(liter)* to bleed sb dry

Mark F **-, -en a** *(= Grenzland)* borderland, march *(rare)*; **die ~ Brandenburg, die ~** *(inf)* the Mark Brandenburg, the Brandenburg Marches; **die ~en** *(Hist)* the Marches **b** *(Rugby)* touch

Mark F **-, -** *or (hum)* ⸚**er** *(Hist)* mark; **Deutsche ~** German mark, Deutschmark; **vier ~ zwanzig** four marks twenty (pfennigs); **mit jeder ~ rechnen, die** *or* **jede ~ umdrehen** to think twice before spending anything; **mit jeder ~ rechnen müssen** to have to count every penny

mar|kant [mar'kant] ADJ *(= ausgeprägt)* clear-cut; *Schriftzüge* clearly defined; *(= hervorstechend) Kinn etc* prominent; *(= auffallend) Erscheinung, Persönlichkeit* striking ADV *(= auffallend)* strikingly; **sich ~ unterscheiden** to be strikingly different

Mark Au|rel ['mark au're:l] M **- -s** Marcus Aurelius

mark|durch|drin|gend ADJ, ADV = **markerschütternd**

Mar|ke ['markə] F **-, -n a** *(bei Lebens- und Genussmitteln)* brand; *(bei Industriegütern)* make; **du bist (vielleicht) eine ~!** *(inf)* you're a right one *or* fine one *(inf)*; **eine komische ~** *(fig inf)* a queer *or* rum *(dated)* customer *or* character *(Brit)*, an odd *or* a strange customer *or* character

b *(= Briefmarke)* stamp; **zehn ~n à** *or* **zu fünfzig** ten fifty-cent stamps

c *(= Essenmarke)* voucher; *(= Rabattmarke)* (trading) stamp; *(= Lebensmittelmarke)* coupon; *(old: = Rentenmarke)* stamp; **~n kleben** *(inf)* to buy one's stamps

d *(= Erkennungsmarke)* disc, tag; *(= Hundemarke)* dog licence disc *(Brit)*, dog tag *(US)*; *(= Garderobenmarke)* cloakroom counter; *(Zettel)* cloakroom ticket *or* check *(US)*; *(= Polizeimarke)* badge; *(= Spielmarke)* chip; *(= Pfandmarke etc)* token

e *(= Rekordmarke)* record; *(= Wasserstandsmarke)* watermark; *(= Stand, Niveau)* level

mär|ken ['mɛrkn] VT *(Aus) Wäsche* to mark

Mar|ken-: **Mar|ken|al|bum** NT *(inf)* stamp album; **Mar|ken|ar|ti|kel** M proprietary article; **Mar|ken|ar|tik|ler** M *(Comm)* branded company; **Mar|ken|be|wusst|sein** NT brand awareness; **Mar|ken|but|ter** F nonblended butter, best quality butter; **Mar|ken|er|zeug|nis** NT, **Mar|ken|fab|ri|kat** NT proprietary article; **mar|ken|frei** ADJ **a** *(= ohne Lebensmittelmarken etc)* unrationed, not on coupons **b** *(= ohne Warenzeichen)* nonbranded *(Brit)*, generic *(US)*; **Mar|ken|her|stel|ler(in)** M(F) manufacturer of proprietary goods; **Mar|ken|na|me** M brand *or* proprietary name; **Mar|ken|pi|ra|te|rie** F brand name piracy; **Mar|ken|qua|li|tät** F brand quality; **Mar|ken|schutz** M protection of trademarks; **Mar|ken|treu|e** F brand loyalty; **Mar|ken|wa|re** F proprietary goods *pl*; **Mar|ken|zei|chen** NT *(lit, fig)* trademark

Mar|ker ['markɐ] M **-s, -(s) a** *(Med)* marker **b** *(= Markierstift)* highlighter

mark|er|schüt|ternd *(geh)* ADJ bloodcurdling ADV **er schrie ~** his screams were bloodcurdling

Mar|ke|ten|der [markə'tɛndɐ] M **-s, -, Mar|ke|ten|de|rin** [-ərɪn] F **-, -nen** *(Hist)* sutler

Mar|ke|ten|der|wa|re F *(Mil)* goods *pl or (einzelner Artikel)* article sold at army stores

Mar|ke|ting ['markətɪŋ] NT **-s,** *no pl* marketing

Mar|ke|ting-: **Mar|ke|ting|di|rek|tor(in)** M(F) marketing director *or* manager; **Mar|ke|ting|ma|na|ger(in)** M(F) marketing manager

Mark- *(Hist)*: **Mark|graf** M margrave; **Mark|grä|fin** F margravine; **mark|gräf|lich** ADJ margravial; **Mark|graf|schaft** F margravate

mar|kie|ren [mar'ki:rən] *ptp* **markiert** VT *(lit, fig, Sport)* to mark; *(Comput auch) text* to highlight; *(inf: = vortäuschen)* to play, to fake; **den starken**

Mann ~ to come *(Brit) or* play the strong man; **den Dummen** *or* **Dusseligen ~** *(inf)* to act daft *(Brit inf)* or dumb *(inf)*; **eine Zelle ~** *(Comput)* to mark a cell; **den Text ~** *(Comput)* to highlight the text; **alles ~** *(Comput: Option)* select all VI *(inf: = so tun, als ob)* to put it on *(inf)*; **markier doch nicht!** stop putting it on *(inf)*

Mar|kier|stift M highlighter

Mar|kie|rung F -, -en marking; *(= Hervorhebung)* highlighting; *(= Zeichen)* mark; *(Comput: = Textauswahl)* selection; **eine ~ aufheben** to deselect

Mar|kie|rungs-: **Mar|kie|rungs|li|nie** F (marking) line; **Mar|kie|rungs|punkt** M marker; **Mar|kie|rungs|zei|chen** NT *(Comput)* marker

mar|kig ['markɪç] ADJ *(= kraftvoll, kernig) Spruch, Worte* pithy; *Drohung* strong; *(iro: = großsprecherisch)* grandiloquent, bombastic ADV *(iro: = großsprecherisch)* bombastically; **sich ~ ausdrücken** to be fond of strong expressions; **~ schallen** to ring out sharply

mär|kisch ['mɛrkɪʃ] ADJ of the Mark Brandenburg

Mar|ki|se [mar'kiːzə] F -, -n awning, (sun) blind

Mark-: **Mark|klöß|chen** NT *(Cook)* bone marrow dumpling; **Mark|kno|chen** M *(Cook)* marrowbone; **Mark|schei|de** F *(Min)* boundary line; **Mark|schei|de|kun|de** F, **Mark|schei|de|kunst** F mine surveying; **Mark|schei|der** [-ʃaidɐ] M -s, -, **Mark|schei|de|rin** [-ərɪn] F -, -nen mine surveyor; **Mark|stein** M *(lit, fig)* milestone; *(an Feldern etc)* boundary stone; **Mark|stück** NT *(Hist)* (one-)mark piece; **mark|stück|groß** ADJ *(fig)* the size of a one-mark piece

Markt [markt] M -(e)s, ⸚e ['mɛrktə] **a** market; *(= Jahrmarkt)* fair; **zum** *or* **auf den ~ gehen** to go to (the) market/to the fair; **~ abhalten** to hold *or* have a market; **dienstags/jede Woche einmal ist ~** *or* **wird ~ abgehalten** there is a market every Tuesday/week

b *(Comm)* market; *(= Warenverkehr)* trade; **auf dem** *or* **am ~** on the market; **auf den ~ bringen** to put on the market; **neue Märkte erschließen** to develop new markets; **etw in großen Mengen auf den ~ werfen** to flood the market with sth; **auf den ~ kommen** *or* **gebracht werden** to come on the market; **etw vom ~ nehmen** to withdraw sth from the market

c *(= Marktplatz)* marketplace, market square; **am ~** in the marketplace; **am ~ wohnen** to live on the marketplace

d *(geh: = Marktflecken)* small market town

Markt- *in cpds* market; **Markt|ab|spra|che** F marketing agreement; **Markt|ana|ly|se** F market analysis; **Markt|an|teil** M market share, share of the market; **markt|be|herr|schend** ADJ **~ sein, eine ~e Stellung einnehmen** to control *or* dominate the market; **Markt|be|rei|ni|gung** F market adjustment *or* cleansing, shakeout *(inf)*; **Markt|be|richt** M *(Fin)* stock market report; **Markt|bu|de** F market stall; **Markt|chan|ce** F *usu pl* sales opportunity; **Markt|er|folg** M sales success, success on the market; **markt|fä|hig** ADJ *Produkt, Unternehmen* marketable; **Markt|fä|hig|keit** F marketability; **Markt|fah|rer(in)** M(F) *(Aus)* (travelling *(Brit) or* traveling *(US))* market trader; **Markt|fle|cken** M small market town; **Markt|for|scher(in)** M(F) market researcher; **Markt|for|schung** F market research; **Markt|frau** F market woman, (woman) stallholder; **Markt|füh|rer(in)** M(F) market leader; **markt|gän|gig** ADJ *(= marktfähig)* marketable; *(= marktüblich)* current; **markt|ge|recht** ADJ in line with market requirements, geared to market requirements ADV **etw ~ einführen/präsentieren** to introduce/present sth in line with market requirements; **das Produkt war nicht ~ verpackt** the packaging of the product was not in line with market requirements; **Markt|hal|le** F covered market; **Markt|hel|fer(in)** M(F) market hand; **Markt|la|ge** F state of the market; **Markt|lü|cke** F gap in the market; **eine ~ erkennen/finden** to spot *or* find a gap in the market; **in eine ~ stoßen** to fill a gap in the market; **Markt|macht** F, *no pl* market power; **Markt|ni|sche** F (market) niche; **eine ~ besetzen** to fill a gap in the market; **eine ~ besetzt halten** to retain a market niche; **Markt|ord|nung** F market regulations *pl*; **Markt|ort** M (small) market town; **Markt|platz** M marketplace, market square; **am/auf dem ~** on/in the marketplace; **Markt|preis** M market price; **Markt|psy|cho|lo|gie** F marketing psychology; **Markt|recht** NT *(Hist)* market rights *pl*; **markt|reif** ADJ *Produkt* ready for the market; **Markt|rei|fe** F **ein Produkt zur ~ entwickeln** to develop a product into a marketable commodity; **Markt|schrei|er(in)** M(F) barker, market crier; **markt|schrei|e|risch** [-ʃraiərɪʃ] ADJ loud and vociferous; *(fig)* blatant ADV loudly and vociferously; *(fig)* blatantly; **Markt|seg|ment** NT market segment *or* sector; **Markt|stand** M market stall *or* stand; **Markt|stu|die** F market survey; **markt|üb|lich** ADJ *Preis, Konditionen* current; **zu ~en Konditionen** at usual market terms; **Markt|weib** NT *(pej)* market woman; *(fig)* fishwife; **Markt|wert** M market value; **Markt|wirt|schaft** F market economy → **frei b**; **markt|wirt|schaft|lich** ADJ *attr* market-economy *attr* ADV **~ orientiert** market-economy-based; **~ organisiert** with a market-based economy; **eine ~ sinnvolle Änderung** an economically worthwhile change; **~ arbeiten** to work economically

Mar|kus ['markʊs] M -' Mark

Mar|kus|evan|ge|li|um NT St Mark's Gospel, Gospel according to St Mark

Mar|ma|ra|meer ['marmara-] NT Sea of Marmara

Mar|mel ['marml] F -, -n marble

Mar|me|la|de [marmə'laːdə] F -, -n jam *(Brit)*, jelly *(US)*; *(= Orangenmarmelade)* marmalade

Mar|me|la|den-: **Mar|me|la|den|brot** NT jam *(Brit) or* jelly *(US)* sandwich; *(Scheibe)* slice of bread and jam *(Brit) or* bread and jelly *(US)*; **Mar|me|la|den|glas** NT jam jar *(Brit)*, jelly jar *(US)*

mar|meln ['marmln] VI to play marbles

Mar|mor ['marmoːɐ] M -s, -e marble

Mar|mor- *in cpds* marble; **Mar|mor|bild** NT *(liter)* marble statue; **Mar|mor|bruch** M marble quarry

mar|mo|rie|ren [marmo'riːrən] *ptp* **marmoriert** VT to marble; **mit marmoriertem Schnitt** with marbled edges, marbled

Mar|mor|ku|chen M marble cake

mar|morn ['marmɔrn, 'marmoːɐn] ADJ marble

ma|ro|de [ma'roːdə] ADJ *(inf)* washed-out *(inf)*; *Gebäude, Anlagen* ramshackle; *Wirtschaft etc* ailing

Ma|ro|deur [maro'døːɐ] M -s, -e marauder

ma|ro|die|ren [maro'diːrən] *ptp* **marodiert** VI to maraud

Ma|rok|ka|ner [marɔ'kaːnɐ] M -s, -, **Ma|rok|ka|ne|rin** [-ərɪn] F -, -nen Moroccan

ma|rok|ka|nisch [marɔ'kaːnɪʃ] ADJ Moroccan

Ma|rok|ko [ma'rɔko] NT -s Morocco

Ma|ro|ne [ma'roːnə] F -, -n, **Ma|ro|ni** [ma'roːni] F -, - (sweet *or* Spanish) chestnut

Ma|ro|ne F -, -n, **Ma|ro|nen|pilz** M, **Ma|ro|nen|röhr|ling** M chestnut boletus, boletus badius *(spec)*

Ma|ro|ni|bra|ter [-braːtɐ] M -s, -, **Ma|ro|ni|bra|te|rin** [-ərɪn] F -, -nen *(Aus)* chestnut vendor

Ma|ro|nit [maro'niːt] M -en, -en, **Ma|ro|ni|tin** [-'niːtɪn] F -, -nen Maronite

Ma|rot|te [ma'rɔtə] F -, -n quirk; **das ist ihre ~** that's one of her little quirks

Mar|quis [mar'kiː] M -, - marquis, marquess

Mar|qui|se [mar'kiːzə] F -, -n marquise, marchioness

Mars [mars] M -, *no pl (Myth, Astron)* Mars

Mars M -, -e *(Naut)* top

Mars|be|woh|ner(in) M(F) Martian

marsch [marʃ] INTERJ **a** *(Mil)* march; **vorwärts ~!** forward march!; **(im Laufschritt,) ~! ~!** (at the double,) quick march! **b** *(inf)* off with you; **~ ins Bett!** off to bed with you at the double! *(inf)*; **raus hier, ~! ~!** get out of here at the double! *(inf)*

Marsch [marʃ] M -(e)s, ⸚e ['mɛrʃə] **a** *(= das Marschieren)* march; *(= Wanderung)* hike; **einen ~ machen** to go on a march/hike; **sich in ~ setzen** to move off **b** *(= Marschmusik)* march; **jdm den ~ blasen** *(inf)* to give sb a rocket *(inf)*

Marsch F -, -en marsh, fen

Mar|schall ['marʃal] M -s, **Marschälle** [-ʃɛlə] (field) marshal

Mar|schall|stab M (field) marshal's baton; **den ~ im Tornister haben** *(fig)* to be a potential leader of men

Marsch-: **Marsch|be|fehl** M *(Mil) (für Truppen)* marching orders *pl*; *(für Einzelnen)* travel orders *pl*; **marsch|be|reit** ADJ ready to move; **Marsch|bo|den** M marshy soil

Mar|schen|dorf NT fenland village

Marsch-: **marsch|fer|tig** ADJ = **marschbereit**; **Marsch|flug|kör|per** M cruise missile; **Marsch|ge|päck** NT pack

mar|schie|ren [mar'ʃiːrən] *ptp* **marschiert** VI *aux sein* to march; *(fig)* to march off, to take oneself off; **getrennt ~, vereint schlagen** to unite for the attack

Marsch-: **Marsch|ko|lon|ne** F column; **Marsch|kom|pass** M compass; **Marsch|land** NT marsh(land), fen; **marsch|mä|ßig** ADJ *Ausrüstung etc* marching *attr*; *(für Wanderung)* hiking *attr* ADV **~ angezogen** dressed for marching/hiking; **Marsch|mu|sik** F military marches *pl*; **Marsch|or|der** F *(Mil)* marching orders *pl*; *(fig)* go-ahead; **Marsch|ord|nung** F marching order; **Marsch|pau|se** F halt; **Marsch|rich|tung** F, **Marsch|rou|te** F *(lit)* route of march; *(fig)* line of approach; **Marsch|tem|po** NT marching time; *(Mus)* march time *or* tempo; **Marsch|ver|pfle|gung** F rations *pl*; *(Mil)* field rations *pl*; **Marsch|ziel** NT destination

Mar|seil|lai|se [marzɛjɛːzə, marsɛ'jɛːz] F -, *no pl* **die ~** the Marseillaise

Mar|seille [mar'zɛːj, mar'sɛːj] NT -s Marseilles

Mars|feld NT *(in Rom)* Campus Martius; *(in Paris)* Champs de Mars

Mar|shall|plan ['marʃal-] M *(Pol)* Marshall Plan

Mars|mensch M Martian

Mars|se|gel NT *(Naut)* topsail

Mar|stall ['marʃtal] M -(e)s, **Marställe** [-ʃtɛlə] *(Hist)* royal stables *pl*

Mar|ter ['martɐ] F -, -n *(liter)* torment; **das kann zur ~ werden** it can be a painful ordeal

Mar|ter|ge|rät NT, **Mar|ter|in|stru|ment** NT instrument of torture

Mar|terl ['martɐl] NT -s, -n *(S Ger, Aus)* wayside shrine with a crucifix

mar|tern ['martɐn] *(liter)* VT to torture, to torment; **jdn zu Tode ~** to torture sb to death VR to torment *or* torture oneself

Mar|ter-: **Mar|ter|pfahl** M stake; **Mar|ter|tod** M *(liter)* = **Märtyrertod**

Mar|te|rung ['martərʊŋ] F -, -en *(liter)* torment

mar|ti|a|lisch [mar'tsiaːlɪʃ] *(geh)* ADJ martial, warlike ADV *brüllen, aussehen* in a warlike manner

Mar|tin-Horn® ['martiːn-] NT = **Martinshorn**

Mar|ti|ni [mar'tiːni] NT -, *no pl (Eccl)* Martinmas

Mar|tins-: **Mar|tins|fest** NT Martinmas; **Mar|tins|gans** F Martinmas goose; **Mar|tins|horn** NT *(von Polizei und Feuerwehr)* siren; **mit ~** with its siren blaring *or* going; **Mar|tins|tag** M Martinmas

MARTINSTAG

November 11th is **Martinstag** (Martinmas), which is celebrated throughout Germany in a variety of ways. Processions are common: as soon as darkness falls, groups of young children with lanterns go singing through the streets. Sometimes the story of St Martin of Tours is acted out, describing how he tore his cloak in two and shared it with a beggar. A special meal of roast goose – the **Martinsgans** – is often eaten.

Mär|ty|rer ['mɛrtyrɐ] M **-s, -, Mär|ty|re|rin** [-ərın] F **-, -nen** *(Eccl, fig)* martyr; **jdn zum ~ machen** to make a martyr of sb; **sich als ~ aufspielen** *(pej)* to make a martyr of oneself

Mär|ty|rer-: **Mär|ty|rer|kro|ne** F martyr's crown; **Mär|ty|rer|tod** M martyr's death; **den ~ sterben** to die a martyr's death; **Mär|ty|rer|tum** ['mɛrtyrɐtu:m] NT **-s,** *no pl* martyrdom

Mar|ty|ri|um [mar'ty:riʊm] NT **-s, Martyrien** [-riən] **a** *(= Opfertod)* martyrdom; *(fig)* ordeal **b** *(= Grabkirche)* martyry

Mar|xis|mus [mar'ksɪsmʊs] M **-,** *no pl* Marxism

Mar|xis|mus-Le|ni|nis|mus M Marxism-Leninism

Mar|xist [mar'ksɪst] M **-en, -en, Mar|xis|tin** [-'ksɪstɪn] F **-, -nen** Marxist

mar|xis|tisch [mar'ksɪstɪʃ] ADJ Marxist ADV *klingen etc* Marxist; **~ gesinnte Kreise** Marxist groups; **seine Lehre ist ~ beeinflusst** he is influenced by (the teachings of) Marx

marxsch [marksʃ] ADJ *attr* Marxian; **die ~e Dialektik** Marx's *or* Marxian dialectic

März [mɛrts] M **-(es)** *or (poet)* **-en, -e** March; **im ~** in March; **Berlin, im ~ 2001** *(in Brief)* Berlin, March 2001; **im Monat ~** in the month of March; **heute ist der zweite ~** today is the second of March, today is March the second *or* March second *(US)*; *(geschrieben)* today is 2nd March *or* March 2nd; *(in Brief)* **Berlin, den 4. ~ 2001** Berlin, March 4th, 2001, Berlin, 4th March 2001; **am Mittwoch, dem** *or* **den 4. ~** on Wednesday the 4th of March; **am ersten ~ fahren wir nach ...** on the first of March we are going to ...; **in diesem ~** this March; **im Laufe des ~** during March; **der ~ war sehr warm** March was very warm; **Anfang/Ende/Mitte ~** at the beginning/at the end/in the middle of March

März|be|cher M *(Bot)* snowflake; *(inf: = Narzisse)* narcissus

März|bier NT, **Mär|zen** ['mɛrtsn] NT **-(s), -** *strong light beer*

Mär|zen|be|cher M *(Bot)* snowflake; *(inf: = Narzisse)* narcissus

Mär|zen|bier NT *strong light beer*

Mar|zi|pan [martsi'pa:n, 'martsipa:n] NT **-s, -e** marzipan

März-: **März|re|vo|lu|ti|on** F *(Hist) Revolution of March 1848*; **März|veil|chen** NT sweet violet

Ma|sche ['maʃə] F **-, -n a** *(= Strickmasche, Häkelmasche)* stitch; *(von Netz)* hole; *(von Kettenhemd)* link; *(= Laufmasche)* ladder *(Brit)*, run; **die ~n eines Netzes** the mesh *sing* of a net; **eine ~ aufnehmen/fallen lassen** to pick up/drop a stitch; **rechte/linke ~n** *(beim Stricken)* plain/purl stitches; **jdm durch die ~n schlüpfen** to slip through sb's net; *(fig auch)* to slip through sb's fingers; **durch die ~n des Gesetzes schlüpfen** to slip through a loophole in the law
b *(S Ger, Aus: = Schleife)* bow
c *(inf) (= Trick)* trick, dodge *(inf)*; *(= Eigenart)* fad, craze; **die ~ raushaben** to know how to do it; **er versucht es immer noch auf die alte ~** he's still trying the same old trick; **das ist seine neueste ~, das ist die neueste ~ von ihm** that's his latest (fad *or* craze); **eine ~ abziehen** to pull a stunt/trick

Ma|schen-: **Ma|schen|draht** M wire netting; **Ma|schen|draht|zaun** M wire-netting fence; **ma|schen|fest** ADJ *Strümpfe* non-run; **Ma|schen|netz** NT mesh, net; **Ma|schen|werk** NT *(fig)* **sich im ~ von etw verfangen** to become enmeshed in sth

Ma|scherl ['maʃɐl] NT **-s, -n** *(Aus inf: = Fliege, Zierschleife)* bow tie

Ma|schin- [ma'ʃi:n] *(Aus) in cpds* = **Maschine(n)-**

Ma|schi|ne [ma'ʃi:nə] F **-, -n** machine *(auch Comput)*; *(= Motor)* engine; *(= Flugzeug)* plane; *(= Schreibmaschine)* typewriter; *(inf: = Motorrad)* bike; **eine bloße ~ sein** *(fig)* to be no more than a machine; **zur ~ werden** *(fig)* to become a machine; **Kaffee mit der ~ machen** to make coffee in the coffee-maker; **etw in der ~ waschen** to machine-wash sth; **etw auf** *or* **mit der ~ schreiben, etw in die ~ tippen** *or* **schreiben** to type sth; **~ schreiben** to type; **sie schreibt ~** she types

ma|schi|ne|ge|schrie|ben ADJ typewritten, typed

ma|schi|nell [maʃi'nɛl] ADJ *Herstellung, Bearbeitung* mechanical, machine *attr*; *Anlage, Übersetzung* machine *attr*; **~e Ausstattung** machines *pl* ADV mechanically, by machine; **die Produktion erfolgt weitgehend ~** production is predominantly mechanized

Ma|schi|nen-: **Ma|schi|nen|an|trieb** M machine drive; **mit ~** machine-driven, mechanically driven; **Ma|schi|nen|ar|beit** F machine work; **Ma|schi|nen|bau** M mechanical engineering; **Ma|schi|nen|bau|er(in)** M(F) *pl* **-bauer(innen)** mechanical engineer; **Ma|schi|nen|bau|in|ge|ni|eur(in)** M(F) mechanical engineer; **Ma|schi|nen|de|fekt** M mechanical fault; **Ma|schi|nen|dik|tat** NT *typing directly from dictation*; **Ma|schi|nen|ele|ment** NT machine component; **Ma|schi|nen|fab|rik** F engineering works *sing or pl*; **Ma|schi|nen|garn** NT machine thread; **ma|schi|nen|ge|schrie|ben** ADJ typewritten, typed; **Ma|schi|nen|ge|schütz** NT machine gun; **ma|schi|nen|ge|strickt** [-gəʃtrɪkt] ADJ machine-knitted; **Ma|schi|nen|ge|wehr** NT machine gun; **mit ~(en) beschießen** to machine-gun; **Ma|schi|nen|ge|wehr-Schüt|ze** M, **Ma|schi|nen|ge|wehr-Schüt|zin** F machine-gunner; **Ma|schi|nen|haus** NT machine room; **Ma|schi|nen|in|dust|rie** F engineering industry; **Ma|schi|nen|kraft** F mechanical power; **Ma|schi|nen|lauf|zeit** F machine running time; **ma|schi|nen|les|bar** ADJ machine-readable; **Ma|schi|nen|les|bar|keit** [-le:sba:ɐkait] F **-,** *no pl* machine-readability; **ma|schi|nen|mä|ßig** ADJ in terms of machinery; **~e Ausstattung** machinery; **Ma|schi|nen|meis|ter(in)** M(F) *(= Aufseher)* machine minder; *(Theat)* stage technician; *(Typ)* pressman; **Ma|schi|nen|öl** NT lubricating oil; **Ma|schi|nen|park** M plant; **Ma|schi|nen|pis|to|le** F submachine gun; **Ma|schi|nen|raum** M plant room; *(Naut)* engine room; **Ma|schi|nen|re|vi|si|on** F *(Typ)* press proof; **Ma|schi|nen|saal** M machine room; *(Typ)* pressroom; *(in Setzerei)* caseroom; **Ma|schi|nen|satz** M **a** machine unit **b** *(Typ)* machine setting *or* composition; **Ma|schi|nen|scha|den** M mechanical fault; *(Aviat etc)* engine fault; **Ma|schi|nen|schlos|ser(in)** M(F) machine fitter; **ma|schi|nen+schrei|ben** △ VI *sep irreg* → **Maschine**; **Ma|schi|nen|schrei|ben** NT typing, typewriting; **Ma|schi|nen|schrei|ber(in)** M(F) typist; **Ma|schi|nen|schrift** F typescript, typing; *(Schriftart)* typeface; **in ~** typed, typewritten; **ma|schi|nen|schrift|lich** ADJ typewritten *no adv* ADV **sich ~ bewerben** to submit a typewritten application; **ein ~ präsentierter Text** a typewritten text; **Ma|schi|nen|set|zer(in)** M(F) machine compositor *or* typesetter; **Ma|schi|nen|spra|che** F machine language; **Ma|schi|nen|stür|mer** M *(Hist, fig)* Luddite; **Ma|schi|nen|stür|me|rei** [-ʃtʏrmə'rai] F **-,** *no pl* Luddism; **Ma|schi|nen|teil** NT machine part; **Ma|schi|nen|wär|ter(in)** M(F) machine minder; **Ma|schi|nen|wä|sche** F *(= Wäsche)* machine-washed clothes *pl or* laundry; *(= das Waschen)* machine washing; *(Etikett)* machine-wash; **Ma|schi|nen|zeit|al|ter** NT machine age

Ma|schi|ne|rie [maʃinə'ri:] F **-, -n** [-'ri:ən] **a** *(dated: = Mechanismus)* piece of machinery **b** *(= Bühnenmaschinerie)* stage machinery **c** *(fig: = Getriebe)* machinery

Ma|schi|ne-: **ma|schi|ne+schrei|ben** △ VI *sep irreg* → **Maschine**; **Ma|schi|ne|schrei|ben** NT typing, typewriting; **Ma|schi|ne|schrei|ber(in)** M(F) typist

Ma|schi|nist [maʃi'nɪst] M **-en, -en, Ma|schi|nis|tin** [-'nɪstɪn] F **-, -nen** *(= Schiffsmaschinist)* engineer; *(= Eisenbahnmaschinist)* engine driver, engineer *(US)*

Ma|ser ['ma:zɐ] F **-, -n** vein; **Holz mit feinen ~n** wood with a fine grain

Ma|ser ['me:zɐ, 'ma:zɐ] M **-s, -** *(Phys)* maser

Ma|ser|holz NT grained wood

ma|se|rig ['ma:zərɪç] ADJ grained

ma|sern ['ma:zɐn] VT to grain → *auch* **gemasert** VI to become grained

Ma|sern ['ma:zɐn] PL measles *sing*; **die ~ haben** to have (the) measles

Ma|se|rung ['ma:zərʊŋ] F **-, -en** grain

Mas|ke ['maskə] F **-, -n a** *(lit, fig, Sport, Med)* mask; **sein Gesicht wurde** *or* **erstarrte zur ~** his face froze (into a mask); **eine ~ aufsetzen** *(lit, fig)* to put on a mask; **die ~ abnehmen** *or* **ablegen** to take off one's mask, to unmask; *(fig)* to drop all pretence *(Brit) or* pretense *(US)*, to let fall one's mask; **die ~ fallen lassen** *or* **abwerfen** *(fig)* to throw off one's mask; **jdm die ~ herunterreißen** *or* **vom Gesicht reißen** *(fig)* to unmask sb; **ohne ~** *(fig)* undisguised; **unter der ~ von etw** *(fig)* under the guise of sth; **das ist alles nur ~** that's all just pretence *(Brit) or* pretense *(US)*
b *(Theat: = Aufmachung)* make-up; **~ machen** to make up
c *(Typ, Comput)* mask
d *(= maskierte Person)* mask, domino *(old)*; *(fig)* phony *(inf)*
e *(Tech)* frame

Mas|ken-: **Mas|ken|ball** M masked ball; **Mas|ken|bild|ner(in)** M(F) make-up artist; **mas|ken|haft** ADJ ADV mask-like, like a mask; **Mas|ken|kleid** NT, **Mas|ken|kos|tüm** NT fancy-dress costume; **Mas|ken|spie|le** PL *(Liter)* masques *pl*; **Mas|ken|ver|leih** M fancy-dress hire, costume shop *(US)*; **Mas|ken|zug** M carnival procession; **Mas|ken|zwang** M, *no pl* requirement to wear masks; *(auf Einladungsschreiben)* masks will be worn

Mas|ke|ra|de [maskə'ra:də] F **-, -n** *(= Verkleidung)* costume; *(old: = Kostümfest)* masquerade

mas|kie|ren [mas'ki:rən] *ptp* **maskiert** VT **a** *(= verkleiden)* to dress up; *(= unkenntlich machen)* to disguise **b** *(= verbergen)* to mask, to disguise VR to dress up; *(= sich unkenntlich machen)* to disguise oneself; **sich als jd/etw ~** *(fig)* to masquerade as sb/sth

mas|kiert [mas'ki:ɐt] ADJ masked

Mas|kie|rung F **-, -en a** *(= das Verkleiden)* dressing up; *(= Sich-Unkenntlichmachen)* disguising oneself **b** *(= Verkleidung)* fancy-dress costume; *(von Spion etc)* disguise **c** *(= Verhüllung)* masking

Mas|kott|chen [mas'kɔtçən] NT **-s, -** (lucky) mascot

mas|ku|lin [masku'li:n] ADJ **a** *(Gram, Poet)* masculine **b** *(= betont männlich)* masculine

Mas|ku|li|num ['maskuli:nʊm] NT **-s, Maskulina** [-na] masculine noun

Ma|so ['ma:zo] M **-s,** *no pl (inf) abbr von* **Masochismus**

Ma|so|chis|mus [mazɔ'xɪsmʊs] M **-,** *no pl* masochism

Ma|so|chist [mazɔ'xɪst] M **-en, -en, Ma|so|chis|tin** [-'xɪstɪn] F **-, -nen** masochist

ma|so|chis|tisch [mazɔ'xɪstɪʃ] ADJ masochistic ADV **~ veranlagt sein** to be a masochist, to have masochistic inclinations

maß *pret von* **messen**

Maß [ma:s] NT **-es, -e a** *(= Maßeinheit)* measure *(für* of); *(= Zollstock)* rule; *(= Bandmaß)* tape measure; **~e und Gewichte** weights and meas-

ures; **das ~ aller Dinge** *(fig)* the measure of all things; **das richtige** *or* **rechte ~ halten** *(fig)* to strike the right balance; **mit zweierlei** *or* **verschiedenem ~ messen** *(fig)* to operate a double standard; **das ~ ist voll** *(fig)* that's enough (of that), enough's enough; **das macht das ~ voll** *(fig)* that's the last straw, enough's enough; **und, um das ~ vollzumachen …** *(fig)* and to cap it all … *(esp Brit)*, and to top it all off … *(esp US)*; **in reichem ~(e)** abundantly; **in reichem ~(e) vorhanden sein** to be abundant; *(Energie, Zeit etc)* to be plentiful; **das (übliche) ~ überschreiten** to overstep the mark; **ihr Engagement im Beruf geht weit über das übliche ~ hinaus** her commitment to the job far exceeds the norm; **die edlen ~e dieser Plastik** *(geh)* the noble proportions of this statue
b *(= Abmessung)* measurement; *(von Zimmer, Möbelstück)* dimension, measurement; **ihre ~e sind: …** her measurements are …, her vital statistics are … *(inf)*; **sich** *(dat)* **etw nach ~ anfertigen lassen** to have sth made to measure *or* order; **~ nehmen** to measure up; **bei jdm ~ nehmen** to measure sb, to take sb's measurements; **Schuhe/Hemden nach ~** shoes/shirts made to measure *or* order, custom-made shoes/shirts
c *(= Ausmaß)* extent, degree; **ein solches/gewisses ~ an** *or* **von …** such a degree/a certain degree of …; **in hohem ~(e)** to a high degree; **in solchem ~(e) dass …, in einem ~(e), dass …** to such an extent that …; **in nicht geringem ~(e)** in no small measure; **in geringem ~(e)** to a small extent; **in großem ~e** to a great extent; **in vollem ~e** fully; **in demselben** *or* **gleichem ~e wie die Produktion steigt auch der Verbrauch** when production increases, consumption increases accordingly; **die Drucker verlangen eine Lohnerhöhung in demselben** *or* **in gleichem ~e wie die Metaller** the print workers are demanding a pay rise comparable to *or* with that of the metal workers; **in besonderem ~e** especially; **in gewissem/höherem** *or* **stärkerem/beschränktem/erheblichem ~** to a certain/greater/limited/considerable degree *or* extent; **in höchstem ~e** extremely; **über alle ~en** *(liter)* beyond (all) measure
d *(= Mäßigung)* moderation; **~ halten** = **maßhalten**; **in** *or* **mit ~en** in moderation; **weder ~ noch Ziel kennen** to know no bounds; **ohne ~ und Ziel** immoderately

Maß F -, - *(S Ger, Aus)* litre *(Brit) or* liter *(US)* (tankard) of beer; **zwei ~ Bier** two litres *(Brit) or* liters *(US)* of beer

Mas|sa|ge [ma'saːʒə] F -, -n massage; **~n nehmen** to have massage treatment

Mas|sa|ge-: **Mas|sa|ge|in|sti|tut** NT *(euph)* massage parlour *(Brit) or* parlor *(US)*; **Mas|sa|ge|öl** NT massage oil; **Mas|sa|ge|pra|xis** F physiotherapy centre *(Brit) or* center *(US)*; **Mas|sa|ge|sa|lon** M *(euph)* massage parlour *(Brit) or* parlor *(US)*; **Mas|sa|ge|stab** M vibrator

Mas|sa|ker [ma'saːkɐ] NT -s, - massacre

mas|sak|rie|ren [masa'kriːrən] *ptp* **massakriert** VT *(dated inf)* to massacre

Maß-: **Maß|ana|lyse** F *(Chem)* volumetric analysis; **Maß|an|fer|ti|gung** F **a** *no pl (von Kleidung)* (custom *or* bespoke) tailoring; *(von Möbeln)* custom building; **das Hemd ist ~** the shirt is made to measure *or* custom-made **b** *(= Kleidungsstück)* made-to-measure item, tailor-made item, bespoke item *(geh)*; *(= Möbelstück)* specially made item, custom-made *or* custom-built item; **Maß|an|ga|be** F measurement; *(bei Hohlmaßen)* volume *no pl*; **Gläser in Restaurants müssen eine ~ haben** glasses in restaurants must show how much they hold; **Maß|an|zug** M made-to-measure *or* bespoke *or* made-to-order *(US)* suit, custom-made suit; **Maß|ar|beit** F *(inf)* **das war ~** that was a neat bit of work

Mas|se ['masə] F -, -n **a** *(= Stoff)* mass; *(Cook)* mixture
b *(= große Menge)* heaps *pl (inf)*, stacks *pl (inf)*; *(von Besuchern etc)* host; **die (breite) ~ der Bevölkerung** the bulk of the population; **eine ganze ~** *(inf)* a lot, a great deal; **sie kamen in wahren ~n** they came in droves, they came in their thousands; **die ~ muss es bringen** *(Comm)* the profit only comes with quantity; **die wenigen guten Bücher gehen in der ~ der Neuerscheinungen unter** the few good books are lost in the mass of new titles
c *(= Menschenmenge)* crowd; **in der ~ untertauchen** to disappear into the crowd
d *(= Bevölkerungsmasse)* masses *pl (auch pej)*; **die namenlose** *or* **graue** *or* **breite ~** the masses *pl*; **der Geschmack der ~** the taste of the masses; **mit der ~ gehen** to go with the flow *(inf)*
e *(= Konkursmasse)* assets *pl*; *(= Erbmasse)* estate
f *(Phys)* mass

Mas|se|gläu|bi|ger(in) M(F) *(Jur)* preferential creditor

Maß-: **Maß|ein|heit** F unit of measurement; **Maß|ein|tei|lung** F (measuring) scale

Mas|se|ka|bel NT ground cable

Mas|sen- *in cpds* mass; **Mas|sen|ab|fer|ti|gung** F *(usu pej)* mass *or* wholesale processing; **Mas|sen|ab|füt|te|rung** F *(inf pej)* feeding of the masses; **Mas|sen|ab|satz** M bulk selling; **das ist kein Artikel für den ~** that isn't intended for the mass market; **Mas|sen|an|drang** M crush; **Mas|sen|an|ge|bot** NT glut; **sie waren im ~ auf dem Markt** there was a glut of them on the market; **Mas|sen|an|zie|hung** F *(Phys)* gravitation; **Mas|sen|ar|beits|lo|sig|keit** F mass unemployment; **Mas|sen|ar|ti|kel** M mass-produced article; **Mas|sen|auf|ge|bot** NT large body; **in einem ~ erscheinen** to turn up in force; **Mas|sen|auf|lauf** M, *no pl* crowds *pl* of people; **es gab einen ~ am Unfallort** huge crowds of people gathered at the scene of the accident; **Mas|sen|be|darf** M requirements *pl* of the masses; *(Comm)* requirements *pl* of the mass market; **Mas|sen|be|darfs|gü|ter** PL basic consumer goods *pl*; **Mas|sen|be|ein|flus|sung** F mass propaganda; **Mas|sen|be|för|de|rungs|mit|tel** NT means *sing* of mass transportation; **Mas|sen|druck|sa|che** F bulk printed matter; **„Massendrucksache"** "(bulk) printed matter"; **Mas|sen|ent|las|sung** F mass redundancy; **Mas|sen|fab|ri|ka|ti|on** F, **Mas|sen|fer|ti|gung** F mass production; **Mas|sen|flucht** F mass exodus; *(panikartig)* mass stampede; **Mas|sen|ge|sell|schaft** F faceless society; **Mas|sen|grab** NT mass grave; **Mas|sen|gü|ter** PL bulk goods *pl*; **mas|sen|haft** ADJ on a huge *or* massive scale; **~ Fanbriefe/Sekt** *etc (inf)* masses of fan letters/champagne *etc (inf)* ADV on a huge *or* massive scale; *kommen, erscheinen, eingehen, austreten* in droves; **Mas|sen|her|stel|lung** F mass production; **Mas|sen|hys|te|rie** F mass hysteria; **Mas|sen|ka|ram|bo|la|ge** F multiple (car) crash, pile-up *(inf)*; **Mas|sen|kom|mu|ni|ka|ti|ons|mit|tel** NT mass medium *usu pl*; **Mas|sen|me|di|en** PL mass media *pl*; **Mas|sen|mord** M mass murder; **Mas|sen|mör|der(in)** M(F) mass murderer; **Mas|sen|par|tei** F party of the masses; **Mas|sen|pres|se** F popular press; **Mas|sen|pro|duk|ti|on** F mass production; **Mas|sen|psy|cho|lo|gie** F crowd psychology; **Mas|sen|psy|cho|se** F mass hysteria; **Mas|sen|quar|tier** NT camp; **Mas|sen|spei|cher** M *(Comput)* mass storage (device); **Mas|sen|ster|ben** NT mass of deaths; **Mas|sen|sze|ne** F crowd scene; **Mas|sen|ter|ror** M mass terror; **Mas|sen|tier|hal|tung** F intensive livestock farming; **Mas|sen|ver|an|stal|tung** F huge event; **Mas|sen|ver|kehrs|mit|tel** NT means *sing* of mass transportation

Mas|sen|ver|nich|tung F mass extermination

Mas|sen|ver|nich|tungs-: **Mas|sen|ver|nich|tungs|la|ger** NT extermination camp; **Mas|sen|ver|nich|tungs|mit|tel** PL means *sing* of mass extermination; **Mas|sen|ver|nich|tungs|waf|fe** F weapon of mass destruction

Mas|sen-: **Mas|sen|ver|samm|lung** F mass meeting; **Mas|sen|wahn** M mass hysteria; **Mas|sen|wa|re** F mass-produced article; **mas|sen|wei|se** ADJ ADV = **massenhaft**; **Mas|sen|wir|kung** F mass effect

Mas|sen|zu|strom M *(von Asylanten etc)* mass influx

Mas|seur [ma'søːɐ] M -s, -e masseur

Mas|seu|rin [ma'søːrɪn] F -, -nen *(Berufsbezeichnung)* masseuse

Mas|seu|se [ma'søːzə] F -, -n *(in Eros-Center etc)* masseuse

Maß|ga|be F *(form)* stipulation; **mit der ~, dass …** with the proviso that …, on (the) condition that …; **nach ~** *(+gen)* according to

maß|ge|bend ADJ *(= ausschlaggebend) Einfluss* decisive; *Meinung, Ansicht* definitive; *Text* definitive, authoritative; *Fachmann* authoritative; *(= wichtig) Persönlichkeit* leading; *(= zuständig)* competent; **das Verhalten des Chefs ist ~ für die Mitarbeiter** the boss's behaviour *(Brit) or* behavior *(US)* sets the standard for his employees; **das ist hier nicht ~** that doesn't weigh *or* signify here; **das war für mich nicht ~** that didn't weigh with me ADV **er hat ~ dazu beigetragen** he made a significant contribution to it

maß|geb|lich ADJ *(= entscheidend) Einfluss* decisive; *Faktor* deciding, decisive; *(= führend) Person, Firma, Rolle* leading; *Beteiligung* substantial; **~en Anteil an etw** *(dat)* **haben** to make a major contribution to sth ADV decisively; **~ an etw** *(dat)* **beteiligt sein** to play a substantial role in sth

maß|ge|schnei|dert [-gəʃnaidɐt] ADJ *Anzug* made-to-measure, made-to-order *(US)*, custom-made; *(fig) Lösung, Produkte* tailor-made

Maß|hal|te|ap|pell M, **Maß|hal|te|pa|ro|le** F appeal for moderation

maß+hal|ten VI *sep irreg* to be moderate, to practise *(Brit) or* practice *(US)* moderation → *auch* **Maß a**

mas|sie|ren [ma'siːrən] *ptp* **massiert** VT *Körper, Haut* to massage VI to give (a) massage

mas|sie|ren *ptp* **massiert** VT *Truppen* to mass VR to amass; *(Truppen)* to mass

mas|sig ['masɪç] ADJ massive, huge ADV *(inf: = sehr viel)* **~ Arbeit/Geld** *etc* masses *or* stacks of work/money *etc (inf)*

mä|ßig ['mɛːsɪç] ADJ **a** *(= bescheiden)* moderate; *Preise* moderate, reasonable; **in etw** *(dat)* **~ sein** to be moderate in sth **b** *(= unterdurchschnittlich) Leistung, Schulnote etc* mediocre, indifferent; *Begabung, Beifall, Erfolg* moderate; *Gesundheit* middling, indifferent ADV **a** *(= nicht viel)* moderately; **etw ~ tun** to do sth in moderation; **~ essen** to eat with moderation; **~ rauchen** to be a moderate smoker, to smoke in moderation; **~, aber regelmäßig** in moderation but regularly **b** *(= nicht besonders)* moderately; *groß* reasonably; **sich nur ~ anstrengen** not to make much of an effort

-mä|ßig ADJ ADV *suf* **a** *(in einer bestimmten Art)* -like; **geschäftsmäßiges Verhalten** businesslike behaviour *(Brit) or* behavior *(US)* **b** *(bezüglich einer Sache)* -wise; **geldmäßig haben wir Probleme** we are having problems moneywise

mä|ßi|gen ['mɛːsɪgn] VT *(= mildern) Anforderungen* to moderate; *Sprache auch* to tone down; *Zorn, Ungeduld* to curb, to check; **sein Tempo ~** to slacken one's pace, to slow down → *auch* **gemäßigt** VR *(im Essen, Trinken, Temperament)* to restrain *or* control oneself; *(Sturm)* to abate, to die down; **~ Sie sich!** control yourself!; **sich in seinem Temperament ~** to control *or* restrain oneself; **sich im Ton ~** to moderate one's tone; **~ Sie sich in Ihren Worten!** tone down your language!

Mas|sig|keit F -, *no pl* massiveness, hugeness

Mä|ßig|keit F -, *no pl* **a** *(beim Essen, Trinken)* moderation, restraint; *(von Forderungen, Preisen etc)* moderateness; **~ üben** to exercise *or* show moderation *or* restraint **b** *(= Mittelmäßigkeit)* mediocrity; *(von Begabung, Beifall)* moderateness

Mä|ßi|gung F -, *no pl* restraint; *(beim Essen etc auch)* moderation

mas|siv [ma'si:f] ADJ **a** *(= pur, nicht hohl, stabil)* solid **b** *(= heftig) Beleidigung* gross; *Drohung, Kritik* serious; *Anschuldigung* severe; *Protest, Forderung, Unterstützung* strong; **~ werden** *(inf)* to turn nasty ADV **a** *(= wuchtig) gebaut* massively **b** *(= heftig)* severely; *protestieren, fördern, unterstützen* strongly; **jdm ~ drohen** to issue a serious threat to sb; **jdn ~ kritisieren** to severely criticize sb **c** *(= stark) zunehmen, verstärken* greatly; *erhöhen* massively; *steigen* strongly; *einschränken, behindern* severely; **sich ~ verschlechtern** to deteriorate *or* worsen sharply

Mas|siv [ma'si:f] NT **-s, -e** [-və] *(Geol)* massif

Mas|siv|bau|wei|se F masonry construction

Mas|si|vi|tät [masivi'tɛ:t] F -, *no pl* **a** *(= Stabilität)* solidness **b** *(= Heftigkeit)* **die ~ seiner Kritik** his serious criticism

mas|siv+wer|den VI *sep irreg aux sein* → **massiv ADJ b**

Maß-: **Maß|klei|dung** F made-to-measure *or* made-to-order *(US) or* custom-made clothing; **Maß|krug** M litre *(Brit) or* liter *(US)* beer mug; *(= Steinkrug)* stein; **Maß|lieb** ['ma:sli:p] NT **-(e)s, -e** [-bə], **Maß|lieb|chen** ['ma:sli:pçən] NT **-s, -** daisy, marguerite

maß|los ADJ extreme; *(= übermäßig) Forderungen auch* excessive; *(= grenzenlos) Trauer, Freude, Ehrgeiz auch* boundless; *Mensch (in Forderungen etc auch, im Essen etc)* immoderate; **er war ~ in seiner Wut/Freude** *etc* his rage/joy *etc* knew no bounds ADV *(= äußerst)* extremely; *übertreiben* grossly, hugely; **es ist alles ~ traurig** *(inf)* it's all very *or* terribly *(inf)* sad; **er raucht/trinkt ~** he smokes/drinks to excess

Maß|lo|sig|keit F **-, -en** extremeness; *(= Übermäßigkeit)* excessiveness; *(= Grenzenlosigkeit)* boundlessness; *(im Essen etc)* lack of moderation; **die ~ seiner Forderungen** his excessive demands

Maß|nah|me [-na:mə] F **-, -n** measure; **~n treffen** *or* **ergreifen, um etw zu tun** to take steps *or* measures to do sth; **~n gegen jdn/etw treffen** *or* **ergreifen** to take measures against sb/sth; **vor ~n zurückschrecken** to shrink from taking action; **sich zu ~n gezwungen sehen** to be forced to take action

Maß|nah|men|ka|ta|log M catalogue *(Brit) or* catalog *(US)* of measures

Maß|nah|men|pa|ket NT package of measures

Maß|re|gel F rule

maß|re|geln VT *insep (= zurechtweisen)* to reprimand, to rebuke, to reprove; *(= bestrafen)* to discipline; *(Sport)* to penalize

Maß|re|ge|lung F **a** *no pl (= Zurechtweisung)* reprimanding, rebuking, reproval; *(= Bestrafung)* disciplining; *(Sport)* penalizing **b** *(= Rüge)* reprimand, rebuke; *(von Beamten)* disciplinary action; *(Sport)* penalty

Maß|schnei|der(in) M(F) bespoke *or* custom *(US)* tailor

Maß|stab M **a** *(= Lineal)* ruler; *(= Zollstock)* rule **b** *(= Kartenmaßstab, Modell)* scale; *(= Ausmaß)* scale; **die Karte hat einen kleinen/großen ~** it's a small-scale/large-scale map, the map is on a small/large scale; **im ~ 1:1000** on a scale of 1:1000; **im ~ 1:25000 gezeichnet** drawn to a scale of 1:25000; **etw in verkleinertem ~ darstellen** to scale sth down; **Klimaverschiebungen im großen ~** large-scale climate changes **c** *(fig: = Richtlinie, Kriterium)* standard; **einen hohen/strengen ~ anlegen** to apply a high/strict standard *(an +acc* to); **für jdn als** *or* **zum ~ dienen, für jdn einen ~ abgeben** to serve as a model for sb; **sich** *(dat)* **jdn/etw zum** *or* **als ~ nehmen** to take sb/sth as a yardstick, to take sth as a benchmark; **das ist für mich kein ~** I don't take that as my yardstick *or* benchmark

maß|stäb|lich [-ʃtɛ:plɪç] ADJ scale *attr,* to scale

maß|stab(s)|ge|recht, maß|stab(s)|ge|treu ADJ ADV (true) to scale; **eine ~e Karte** an accurate scale map

Maß-: **Maß|sys|tem** NT system of measures; **maß|voll** ADJ moderate ADV moderately; **Maß|vor|la|ge** F *(Ftbl)* spot-on *(inf) or* accurate pass; **Maß|werk** NT *(Archit)* tracery

Mast [mast] M **-(e)s, -en** *or* **-e** *(Naut, Rad, TV)* mast; *(= Stange)* pole; *(Elec)* pylon

Mast F **-, -en** *(= das Mästen)* fattening; *(= Futter)* feed; *(= Schweinemast)* mast

Mast-: **Mast|baum** M mast; **Mast|darm** M rectum

mäs|ten ['mɛstn] VT to fatten VR *(inf)* to gorge *or* stuff *(inf)* oneself

Mäs|te|rei [mɛstə'rai] F **-, -en** *(= Schweinemästerei)* pig fattening unit

Mast|fut|ter NT (fattening) feed; *(für Schweine)* mast

Mas|ti|no [mas'ti:no] M **-s, Mastini** [-ni] mastiff

Mast-: **Mast|korb** M *(Naut)* top; **Mast|kur** F *(hum inf)* fattening diet; **Mast|schwein** NT *(zu mästen)* porker; *(gemästet)* fattened pig; **er sieht wie ein ~ aus** he looks like a little (fat) piggy

Mas|tung ['mastʊŋ] F **-, -en** = **Mästung**

Mäs|tung ['mɛstʊŋ] F **-, -en** fattening

Mas|tur|ba|ti|on [mastʊrba'tsio:n] F **-, -en** masturbation

mas|tur|bie|ren [mastʊr'bi:rən] *ptp* **masturbiert** VTI to masturbate

Mast|vieh NT fat stock; *(zu mästendes Vieh)* fattening stock

Ma|sur|ka [ma'zʊrka] F **-, -s** mazurka

Ma|ta|dor [mata'do:ɐ] M **-s, -e**, **Ma|ta|do|rin** [-'do:rɪn] F **-, -nen** *(= Stierkämpfer)* matador; *(fig)* kingpin

Match [mɛtʃ] NT OR M **-(e)s, -e(s)** match

Match-: **Match|ball** M *(Tennis)* match point; **Match|beutel** M, **Match|sack** M duffel bag

Ma|te ['ma:tə] M -, *no pl* maté, Paraguay tea

Ma|ter ['ma:tɐ] F **-, -n** *(Typ)* matrix, mould *(Brit)*, mold *(US)*

Ma|te|ri|al [mate'ria:l] NT **-s, -ien** [-liən] material; *(= Baumaterial, Utensilien, Gerät)* materials *pl;* *(= Beweismaterial, Belastungsmaterial)* evidence; **rollendes ~** *(Rail)* rolling stock

Ma|te|ri|al-: **Ma|te|ri|al|aus|ga|be** F **a** *(Raum)* stores *pl* **b** *(Vorgang)* issue of stores and equipment; **Ma|te|ri|al|be|darf** M material requirements *pl;* **Ma|te|ri|al|er|mü|dung** F *(von Metall)* metal fatigue; **Ma|te|ri|al|feh|ler** M material defect, defect in the material

Ma|te|ri|a|li|sa|ti|on [materializa'tsio:n] F **-, -en** materialization

ma|te|ri|a|li|sie|ren [materiali'zi:rən] *ptp* **materialisiert** VTR to materialize

Ma|te|ri|a|lis|mus [materia'lɪsmʊs] M **-** materialism

Ma|te|ri|a|list [materia'lɪst] M **-en, -en**, **Ma|te|ri|a|lis|tin** [-'lɪstɪn] F **-, -nen** materialist

ma|te|ri|a|lis|tisch [materia'lɪstɪʃ] ADJ materialist(ic); *(pej)* materialistic ADV materialistically

Ma|te|ri|al-: **Ma|te|ri|al|kos|ten** PL cost of materials *sing;* **Ma|te|ri|al|la|ger** NT stores *pl,* inventory *(US);* **Ma|te|ri|al|prü|fung** F testing of materials; **Ma|te|ri|al|samm|lung** F collection of material; **ich habe jetzt die ~ abgeschlossen** I have now finished collecting *or* gathering the material; **Ma|te|ri|al|scha|den** M material defect, defect in the material; **Ma|te|ri|al|schlacht** F *(Mil)* matériel battle; **Ma|te|ri|al|wert** M material value; *(von Münzen)* intrinsic value

Ma|te|rie [ma'te:riə] F **-, -n a** *no pl (Phys, Philos)* matter *no art* **b** *(= Stoff, Thema)* subject matter *no indef art;* **die ~ beherrschen** to know one's stuff

ma|te|ri|ell [mate'riɛl] ADJ **a** *(Philos)* material, physical; *Recht* substantive **b** *(= wirtschaftlich) Not, Versorgung, Vorteile* material, financial; *(= gewinnsüchtig)* materialistic; **nur ~e Interessen haben** to be only interested in material things ADV **a** *(= finanziell)* financially; *(pej: = materialistisch)* materialistically; **~ eingestellt sein** *(pej)* to be materialistic **b** *(= das Material betreffend)* materially; **die Behörde war ~ und personell umfangreich ausgestattet** the authority was fully provided for with resources and staff

ma|tern ['ma:tɐn] VT *(Typ)* to make a plate for

Ma|te|tee ['ma:tə-] M maté, Paraguay tea

Math. *abbr von* **Mathematik**

Ma|the ['matə] F -, *no pl (Sch inf)* maths *sing (Brit inf)*, math *(US inf)*

Ma|the|ma|tik [matema'ti:k] F -, *no pl* mathematics *sing, no art*

Ma|the|ma|ti|ker [mate'ma:tikɐ] M **-s, -**, **Ma|the|ma|ti|ke|rin** [-ərɪn] F **-, -nen** mathematician

ma|the|ma|tisch [mate'ma:tɪʃ] ADJ mathematical ADV mathematically

Ma|ti|nee [mati'ne:] F **-, -n** [-'ne:ən] matinée

Mat|jes ['matjəs] M **-, -**, **Mat|jes|he|ring** M young herring

Mat|rat|ze [ma'tratsə] F **-, -n** mattress

Mat|rat|zen|la|ger NT **für die Kinder ein ~ herrichten** to put down a mattress for the children

Mät|res|se [mɛ'trɛsə] F **-, -n** mistress

mat|ri|ar|cha|lisch [matriar'ça:lɪʃ] ADJ matriarchal ADV **eine ~ orientierte Bewegung** a matriarchal movement; **sie regiert die Familie ~** she rules the family like a matriarch

Mat|ri|ar|chat [matriar'ça:t] NT **-(e)s, -e** matriarchy, matriarchate

Mat|ri|kel [ma'tri:kl] F **-, -n** *(old, Aus)* register; *(Univ: = Aufnahmeverzeichnis)* matriculation register *(Brit)*, registration list *(US);* **Student mit kleiner/großer ~** occasional/full-time student

Mat|ri|kel|num|mer F *(Univ)* registration *or* matriculation number

Mat|rix ['ma:trɪks] F **-, Matrizen** *or* **Matrizes** [ma'tri:tsn, ma'tri:tse:s] *(Math, Med, Biol)* matrix

Mat|rix|dru|cker M dot-matrix (printer)

Mat|ri|ze [ma'tri:tsə, ma'trɪtsə] F **-, -n** *(Typ)* matrix, mould *(Brit)*, mold *(US);* *(für Schreibmaschine)* stencil; **etw auf ~ schreiben** to stencil sth

Mat|ro|ne [ma'tro:nə] F **-, -n** matron

mat|ro|nen|haft ADJ matronly ADV in a matronly way

Mat|ro|se [ma'tro:zə] M **-n, -n**, **Mat|ro|sin** [-'tro:zɪn] F sailor; *(als Rang)* rating *(Brit)*, ordinary seaman

Mat|ro|sen- *in cpds* sailor; **Mat|ro|sen|an|zug** M sailor suit; **Mat|ro|sen|müt|ze** F sailor's cap; **Mat|ro|sen|uni|form** F sailor's uniform

Mat|ro|sin [-'tro:zɪn] F → **Matrose**

matsch [matʃ] ADJ *pred (dial)* **a** *Obst* rotten, bad **b** *(Cards)* beaten; **~ werden** to be beaten **c sich ~ fühlen** to feel whacked *(Brit inf) or* beat *(esp US inf)*

Matsch [matʃ] M **-(e)s**, *no pl (inf) (= breiige Masse)* mush; *(= Schlamm)* mud, sludge; *(= Schneematsch)* slush; **~ aus jdm machen** *(sl)* to beat sb to a pulp *(inf)*

Matsch|bir|ne F *(inf)* bad head *(inf)*

mat|schen ['matʃn] VI *(inf)* to splash (about *or* around)

mat|schig ['matʃɪç] ADJ *(inf) (= breiig) Obst* mushy; *(= schlammig) Straße, Weg* muddy, sludgy; *Schnee* slushy

Matsch|wet|ter NT *(inf)* muddy *or (mit Schneematsch)* slushy weather

matt [mat] ADJ **a** *(= schwach) Kranker* weak; *Stimme, Lächeln* weak, faint; *Glieder* weary; **sich ~ fühlen** to have no energy **b** *(= glanzlos) Augen, Metall, Farbe* dull; *(= nicht glänzend) Farbe, Papier, Foto* mat(t); *(= trübe) Licht* dim, subdued; *Glühbirne* opal, pearl; *Spiegel* cloudy, dull **c** *(= undurchsichtig) Glas* frosted, opaque **d** *(fig) Entschuldigung, Widerspruch, Entgegnung* feeble; *Echo* faint; *(St Ex: = flau)* slack **e** *(Chess)* (check)-mate; **jdn ~ setzen** to (check)mate sb → *auch* **mattsetzen** ADV **a** *(= schwach)* weakly; *lächeln*

faintly, weakly **b** *(= nicht hell)* dimly; **~ glänzend** dull **c** *(= ohne Nachdruck)* lamely
Matt [mat] NT **-s, -s** *(Chess)* (check)mate
matt|blau ADJ pale blue
Mat|te ['matə] F **-, -n** mat; **auf der ~ stehen** *(inf: = bereit sein)* to be there and ready for action; **du musst um sechs bei mir auf der ~ stehen** you must be at my place at six; **jdn auf die ~ legen** *(= niederschlagen)* to floor sb; *(fig inf)* to make mincemeat of sb *(inf)*; *(= übervorteilen)* to put one over on sb *(inf)*
Mat|te F **-, -n** *(liter, Sw, Aus)* alpine meadow
Mat|ter|horn ['matɐhɔrn] NT **-s das ~** the Matterhorn
Matt-: **Matt|glanz** M mat(t) finish; **Matt|glas** NT frosted *or* ground glass; **Matt|gold** NT dull gold; *(Farbe)* pale gold
Mat|thäi [ma'tɛːi] *gen von* **Matthäus bei ihm ist ~ am letzten** he's had it *(inf)*
Mat|thä|us [ma'tɛːʊs] M **Matthäi** [ma'tɛːi] Matthew
Mat|thä|us|evan|ge|li|um NT St Matthew's Gospel, Gospel according to St Matthew
Matt|heit F **-,** *no pl* **a** *(= Schwäche)* weakness; *(von Stimme)* weakness, faintness; *(von Gliedern)* weariness; *(= Energielosigkeit)* lack of energy **b** *(= Glanzlosigkeit: von Augen, Farbe)* dullness; *(= Trübheit: von Licht)* dimness
mat|tie|ren [ma'tiːrən] *ptp* **mattiert** VT to give a mat(t) finish to; **mattiert sein** to have a mat(t) finish; **mattierte Gläser** frosted glasses
Mat|tig|keit ['matɪçkait] F **-,** *no pl* weariness; *(von Kranken)* weakness
Matt-: **Matt|lack** M dull *or* mat(t) lacquer *or* varnish; **Matt|pa|pier** NT mat(t) *or* unglazed paper
Matt|schei|be F **a** *(Phot)* focus(s)ing screen; *(inf: = Fernseher)* telly *(Brit inf)*, (goggle)box *(Brit inf)*, tube *(US inf)* **b** *(inf)* **eine ~ haben/kriegen** *(= dumm sein)* to be soft/go soft in the head *(inf)*; *(= nicht klar denken können)* to have/get a mental block; **als ich das gesagt habe, muss ich wohl eine ~ gehabt haben** I can't have been really with it when I said that *(inf)*
matt+set|zen VT *sep (fig)* to (check)mate → *auch* **matt ADJ e**
Ma|tur [ma'tuːɐ] NT **-s,** *no pl,* **Ma|tu|rum** [ma'tuːrʊm] NT **-s,** *no pl (old),* **Ma|tu|ra** [ma'tuːra] F **-,** *no pl (Aus, Sw)* → **Abitur**
Ma|tu|rand [matu'rant] M **-en, -en** [-dn], **Ma|tu|ran|din** [-'randɪn] F **-, -nen** *(old, Sw),* **Ma|tu|rant** [matu'rant] M **-en, -en** [-tn], **Ma|tu|ran|tin** [-'rantɪn] F **-, -nen** *(Aus)* → **Abiturient(in)**
ma|tu|rie|ren [matu'riːrən] *ptp* **maturiert** VI *(Aus: = Abitur machen)* to take one's school-leaving exam *(Brit)*, to graduate (from high school) *(US)*
Ma|tu|ri|tät [maturi'tɛːt] F **-,** *no pl (Sw: = Hochschulreife)* matriculation exam(ination) *(Brit)*, high school diploma *(US)*
Ma|tu|ri|täts- *in cpds* = **Reife-**
Matz [mats] M **-es, ⸚e** ['mɛtsə] *(dated inf)* laddie *(Scot inf)*, guy *(inf)*
Mätz|chen ['mɛtsçən] NT **-s, -** *(inf)* **a** antic; **~ machen** to play *or* fool around *(inf)*; **mach keine ~, schmeiß die Pistole weg!** don't try anything funny, just drop the gun! **b** *dim von* **Matz**
Mat|ze ['matsə] F **-, -n, Mat|zen** ['matsn] M **-s, -** *(Cook)* matzo
mau [mau] ADJ *pred (inf)* poor, bad; **mir ist ~** I feel poorly *(Brit inf) or* sick ADV **die Geschäfte gehen ~** business is slack
Mau|er ['mauɐ] F **-, -n** **a** wall; **etw mit einer ~ umgeben** to wall sth in; **in den ~n der Stadt** *(fig)* in the city; **die (Berliner) ~** *(Hist)* the (Berlin) Wall **b** *(fig)* wall; **gegen eine ~ des Schweigens anrennen** *(fig)* to run up against a wall of silence; **die ~n einreißen** to tear down the barriers
Mau|er-: **Mau|er|ab|satz** M ledge; **Mau|er|ar|beit** F bricklaying (work) *no pl*; **Mau|er|as|sel** F woodlouse; **Mau|er|bau** M, *no pl (Hist)* building of the Berlin Wall; **Mau|er|blüm|chen** NT *(fig inf) (beim Tanzen)* wallflower; *(= schüchternes Mädchen)* shy young thing; **Mau|er|bre|cher** M *(Mil)* battering ram; **Mau|er|durch|bruch** M *(= das Durchbrechen)* breaching of a/the wall; *(= Stelle)* breach in a/the wall; **Mau|er|fall** M, *no pl (Hist)* fall of the Berlin Wall; **beim ~** when the Berlin Wall came down *or* fell; **Mau|er|ha|ken** M *(Bergsteigen)* piton, peg; **Mau|er|kel|le** F (bricklayer's) trowel; **Mau|er|kro|ne** F wall coping
mau|ern ['mauɐn] VI **a** *(= Maurerarbeit machen)* to build, to lay bricks **b** *(Cards)* to hold back; *(Ftbl sl)* to stonewall, to play defensively; *(fig)* to stall, to stonewall *(esp Parl)* VT to build; *(= mit Zement verfugen)* to build with mortar; **der Beckenrand muss gemauert werden** the edge of the pool must be bedded in mortar
Mau|er-: **Mau|er|schau** F, *no pl (Liter) reporting of offstage events (by a character on stage)*; **Mau|er|schüt|ze** M *East German border guard who shot people fleeing west*; **Mau|er|schwal|be** F, **Mau|er|seg|ler** M swift; **Mau|er|speis** [-ʃpais] M **-es,** *no pl,* **Mau|er|spei|se** F *(esp S Ger: = Mörtel)* mortar; **Mau|er|stein** M building stone; **Mau|er|ver|band** M bond; **Mau|er|vor|sprung** M projection on a/the wall; **Mau|er|werk** NT **a** *(= Steinmauer)* stonework, masonry; *(= Ziegelmauer)* brickwork; **ein mittelalterliches ~** a medieval stone structure **b** *(= die Mauern)* walls *pl*; **Mau|er|zie|gel** M (building) brick
Mau|ke ['maukə] F **-,** *no pl (Vet)* malanders *pl*
Mau|ken ['maukn] PL *(dial inf)* hooves *pl (hum)*
Maul [maul] NT **-(e)s, Mäuler** ['mɔylɐ] mouth; *(von Löwe etc, von Zange)* jaws *pl*; *(inf: von Menschen)* gob *(Brit inf)*, trap *(esp US sl)*; *(von Schraubenschlüssel)* head; **ein böses** *or* **ungewaschenes** *or* **gottloses ~** *(inf)* an evil *or* a wicked *or* a malicious tongue; **jdm übers ~ fahren** *(inf)* to choke sb off *(inf)*; **das ~ zu weit aufreißen** *(sl)* **das ~ zu voll nehmen** *(sl)* to be too cocksure *(inf)*; **ein großes ~ haben** *(inf)* to have a big mouth, to be a bigmouth *(inf)*; **(hungrige) Mäuler stopfen** *(inf)* to feed *or* fill (hungry) mouths; **darüber werden sich die Leute das ~ zerreißen** *(inf)* that will start people's tongues wagging; **dem Volk** *or* **den Leuten aufs ~ schauen** *(inf)* to listen to what people really say; *(= Meinung ermitteln)* to sound out public opinion, to listen to the man in the street; **halt's ~!** *(vulg)* **~ halten!** *(vulg)* shut your face *(sl) or* trap *(sl) or* gob *(Brit inf)*; **halt dein ungewaschenes ~** *(sl)* keep your dirty mouth shut *(inf)*; **sich** *(dat)* **das ~ verbrennen** *(inf)* to talk one's way *or* oneself into trouble
Maul-: **Maul|af|fen** PL *(dated inf)* **~ feilhalten** to stand gawping *or* gaping; **Maul|beer|baum** M mulberry (tree); **Maul|bee|re** F mulberry
maul|len ['maulən] VI *(inf)* to moan
Maul-: **Maul|esel** M mule, hinny; **maul|faul** ADJ *(inf)* uncommunicative; **Maul|held(in)** M(F) *(pej)* loudmouth *(inf)*, show-off; **Maul|hu|re|rei** F *(geh)* foul-mouthedness
Maul|korb M *(lit, fig)* muzzle; **einem Hund/jdm einen ~ umhängen** to put a muzzle on a dog/sb, to muzzle a dog/sb
Maul|korb- *(fig inf)*: **Maul|korb|er|lass** M decree muzzling freedom of speech; **Maul|korb|ge|setz** NT law muzzling freedom of speech
Maul-: **Maul|schel|le** F *(dated inf)* slap in the face; **Maul|sper|re** F **er kriegte die ~** *(inf)* his mouth dropped open; **Maul|ta|schen** PL *(Cook)* pasta squares *pl*; **Maul|tier** NT mule; **Maul|trom|mel** F Jew's harp; *(politisch korrekt)* jaw('s) *or* juice harp; **Maul- und Klau|en|seu|che** F *(Vet)* foot-and-mouth disease *(Brit)*, hoof-and-mouth disease *(US)*
Maul|wurf ['maulvʊrf] M **-(e)s, Maulwürfe** [-vʏrfə] *(auch fig)* mole
Maul|wurfs|hau|fen M, **Maul|wurfs|hü|gel** M molehill
maun|zen ['mauntsn] VI *(S Ger) (= winseln)* to whine; *(Katze)* to mew
Mau|re ['maurə] M **-n, -n, Mau|rin** ['maurɪn] F **-, -nen** *(Hist)* Moor
Mau|rer ['maurɐ] M **-s, -, Mau|re|rin** [-ərɪn] F **-, -nen** bricklayer, brickie *(Brit inf)*; **~ lernen** to learn bricklaying, to learn to be a bricklayer; **pünktlich wie die ~** *(hum)* super-punctual; **pünktlich wie die ~ ließ er seinen Kugelschreiber fallen** bang on the dot he put down his pen
Mau|rer-: **Mau|rer|ar|beit** F bricklaying (work) *no pl*; **Mau|rer|ge|sel|le** M, **Mau|rer|ge|sel|lin** F journeyman bricklayer; **Mau|rer|ham|mer** M bricklayer's hammer; **Mau|rer|hand|werk** NT bricklaying
Mau|re|rin [-ərɪn] F → **Maurer**
Mau|rer-: **Mau|rer|kel|le** F (bricklayer's) trowel; **Mau|rer|ko|lon|ne** F bricklaying gang; **Mau|rer|meis|ter(in)** M(F) master builder; **Mau|rer|po|lier(in)** M(F) foreman/-woman (bricklayer)
Mau|re|ta|ni|en [maure'taːniən] NT **-s** Mauritania, Mauretania
Mau|re|ta|ni|er [maure'taːniɐ] M **-s, -, Mau|re|ta|ni|e|rin** [-iərɪn] F **-, -nen** Mauritanian
mau|re|ta|nisch [maure'taːnɪʃ] ADJ Mauritanian
Mau|rin ['maurɪn] F **-, -nen** *(Hist)* Moor
mau|risch ['maurɪʃ] ADJ Moorish
Mau|ri|ti|er [mau'riːtsiɐ] M **-s, -, Mau|ri|ti|e|rin** [-iərɪn] F **-, -nen** Mauritian
Mau|ri|ti|us [mau'riːtsiʊs] NT **-'** Mauritius
Maus [maus] F **-, Mäuse** ['mɔyzə] **a** mouse; **weiße ~** *(fig inf)* traffic cop *(inf)*; **weiße Mäuse sehen** *(fig inf)* to see pink elephants *(inf)*; **da beißt die ~ keinen Faden ab** *(inf: = nicht zu ändern)* there's no changing that **b** *(inf) (= Frau)* woman; *(= Mädchen, Freundin)* bird *(esp Brit inf)*, chick *(esp US inf)*; **eine süße ~** *(= Kind)* a sweet little thing *(inf)*; **eine graue ~** *(inf)* a mouse *(inf)* **c** *(Comput)* mouse **d Mäuse** PL *(dated sl: = Geld)* bread *(inf)*, dough *(inf)*
Maus|arm M *(Med inf) tennis elbow as a result of intensive computer use,* mouse elbow *(inf)*
Mau|sche|lei [mauʃə'lai] F **-, -en** *(inf: = Korruption)* fiddle *(Brit inf)*, swindle; **das war bestimmt ~** it was definitely a fiddle *(Brit inf) or* a swindle
mau|scheln ['mauʃln] VI *(= jiddisch sprechen)* to talk Yiddish VTI *(= manipulieren)* to fiddle *(inf)*
Mau|scheln NT **-s** *(Cards)* cheat
Mäus|chen ['mɔysçən] NT **-s, -** **a** little mouse; **da möchte ich mal ~ sein** *or* **spielen** *(inf)* I'd like to be a fly on the wall **b** *(fig)* sweetheart *(inf)*, love *(Brit inf)*, honey *(esp US inf)* **c** *(= Musikantenknochen)* funny bone *(Brit inf)*, crazy bone *(US inf)*
mäus|chen|still ['mɔysçən'ʃtɪl] ADJ dead quiet; *Mensch auch* (as) quiet as a mouse; *(= reglos)* stock-still ADV quiet as a mouse
Mäu|se|bus|sard M (common) buzzard
Mau|se|fal|le F, **Mäu|se|fal|le** F *(rare)* mousetrap; *(fig)* police roadblock; **in eine ~ kommen** *or* **geraten** to get caught in a police roadblock
Mäu|se|gift NT mouse poison
Mau|se|loch NT, **Mäu|se|loch** NT *(rare)* mousehole; **sich in ein ~ verkriechen** *(fig)* to crawl into a hole in the ground
Mäu|se|mel|ken NT **-s,** *no pl* **das/es ist zum ~** *(dated inf)* it's enough to drive you up the wall *(inf)*
mau|sen ['mauzn] VI to catch mice; **diese Katze maust gut** the cat is a good mouser VT *(dated inf)* to pinch *(inf)*, to nick *(Brit inf)*
Mau|ser ['mauzɐ] F **-,** *no pl (Orn)* moult *(Brit)*, molt *(US)*; **in der ~ sein** to be moulting *(Brit) or* molting *(US)*
Mau|ser® F **-, -** *(= Pistole)* Mauser
Mau|ser|ge|wehr NT Mauser (rifle)
Mäu|se|rich ['mɔyzərɪç] M **-s, -e** *(hum)* Mr Mouse *(hum)*

mau|sern ['mauzɐn] VR **a** *(Orn)* to moult *(Brit)*, to molt *(US)* **b** *(inf)* to blossom out *(inf)*

Mau|ser|pis|to|le F -, -n Mauser

mau|se|tot ['mauzə'to:t] ADJ *(inf)* stone-dead, as dead as a doornail

maus|ge|steu|ert [-gəʃtɔyɐt] ADJ *(Comput)* mouse-driven, mouse-controlled

maus|grau ADJ **a** *(= mausfarben)* mouse-grey *(Brit)*, mouse-gray *(US)* **b** *(= unauffällig)* mousy

mau|sig+ma|chen ['mauzɪç-] VR *sep (inf)* to get uppity *(inf)*

Maus-: **Maus|klick** [-klɪk] M -s, -s *(Comput)* mouse click; **etw per ~ steuern/aktivieren** to control/activate sth by clicking the mouse; **Maus|ku|gel** F *(Comput)* mouse ball; **Maus|loch** NT = **Mauseloch**; **Maus|mat|te** F *(Comput)* mouse pad

Mau|so|le|um [mauzo'le:ʊm] NT -s, **Mausoleen** [-'le:ən] mausoleum

Maus-: **Maus|pad** [-pɛt] NT *(Comput)* mouse mat *or* pad; **Maus|rad** NT *(Comput)* mouse wheel; **Maus|steu|e|rung** F *(Comput)* mouse control; **Maus|tas|te** F *(Comput)* mouse button; **Maus|zei|ger** M *(Comput)* mouse pointer

Maut [maut] F -, -en toll

Maut-: **Maut|ge|bühr** F toll (charge); **maut|pflich|tig** ADJ toll *attr*, subject to a toll *pred*; **Maut|schran|ke** F toll barrier *(Brit)*, turnpike *(US)*; **Maut|stel|le** F tollgate; **Maut|stra|ße** F toll road, turnpike *(US)*

max. *abbr von* **maximal**

ma|xi ['maksi] ADJ *pred (Fashion)* maxi; **Maxi tragen** to wear maxi *or* ankle-length skirts/dresses

Ma|xi- ['maksi] *in cpds* maxi- **a** *(= Riesen-)* giant-sized; **eine Maxiflasche** a giant-sized bottle **b** *(Fashion)* (really) long; **ein Maxikleid** a long dress

ma|xi|mal [maksi'ma:l] ADJ maximum ADV *(= höchstens)* at most; **bis zu ~ £ 100** up to a maximum of £100

Ma|xi|mal- *in cpds* maximum; **Ma|xi|mal|ge|schwin|dig|keit** F maximum *or* top speed; **zulässige ~** maximum permitted speed; **Ma|xi|mal|ge|wicht** NT maximum weight

Ma|xi|me [ma'ksi:mə] F -, -n *(Liter, Philos)* maxim

ma|xi|mie|ren [maksi'mi:rən] *ptp* **maximiert** VT to maximize

Ma|xi|mie|rung F -, -en maximization

Ma|xi|mum ['maksimʊm] NT -s, **Maxima** [-ma] maximum *(an +dat* of)

Ma|xi|sin|gle [-sɪŋgl] F twelve-inch single

Ma|ya ['ma:ja] M -(s), -(s) *or f* -, -(s) Maya

Ma|yo ['ma:jo] F -, -s *(inf)* mayonnaise, mayo *(inf)*

Ma|yon|nai|se [majɔ'nɛ:zə] F -, -n mayonnaise

Ma|ze|do|ni|en [matse'do:niən] NT -s Macedonia

Mä|zen [mɛ'tse:n] M -s, -e, **Mä|ze|nin** [-'tse:nɪn] F -, -nen patron

Mä|ze|na|ten|tum [mɛtse'na:tntu:m] NT -s, *no pl* **a** *(= Kunstförderung)* patronage (of the arts) **b** *(= Wesen eines Mäzens)* spirit of patronage

Ma|zur|ka [ma'zʊrka] F -, -s mazurka

MB [ɛm'be:] *abbr von* **Megabyte** Mb

MByte, **Mbyte** ['ɛmbait] *abbr von* **Megabyte** mbyte

Mc-Job ['mɛkdʒɔp] M *(sl)* McJob

MdB M, **M. d. B.** [ɛmde:'be:] M -s, -s *abbr von* **Mitglied des Bundestages** Member of the Bundestag

MdE [ɛmde:'e:] M -s, -s, **MdEP** M -s, -s *abbr von* **Mitglied des Europäischen Parlaments** MEP

MdL M, **M. d. L.** [ɛmde:'ɛl] M -s, -s *abbr von* **Mitglied des Landtages** Member of the Landtag

MDR [ɛmde:'ɛr] M - *abbr von* **Mitteldeutscher Rundfunk**

m. E. *abbr von* **meines Erachtens** in my opinion

mech. *abbr von* **mechanisch**

Me|cha|nik [me'ça:nɪk] F -, -en **a** *no pl (Phys)* mechanics *sing* **b** *(rare: = Mechanismus)* mechanism

Me|cha|ni|ker [me'ça:nikɐ] M -s, -, **Me|cha|ni|ke|rin** [-ərɪn] F -, -nen mechanic

me|cha|nisch [me'ça:nɪʃ] ADJ *(alle Bedeutungen)* mechanical; **~er Webstuhl** power loom ADV mechanically

me|cha|ni|sie|ren [meçani'zi:rən] *ptp* **mechanisiert** VT to mechanize

Me|cha|ni|sie|rung F -, -en mechanization

Me|cha|ni|sie|rungs|pro|zess M process of mechanization

Me|cha|nis|mus [meça'nɪsmʊs] M -, **Mechanismen** [-mən] mechanism; *(= Methode, Arbeitsablauf)* machinery

me|cha|nis|tisch [meça'nɪstɪʃ] ADJ *(Philos, Psych)* mechanistic

meck [mɛk] INTERJ *(Ziege)* ~, ~! meh, meh!

Me|cker|ecke F *(inf, in Zeitung, Zeitschrift)* complaints column

Me|cke|rei [mɛkə'rai] F -, -en *(inf)* moaning, grumbling, griping *(inf)*

Me|cke|rer ['mɛkərɐ] M -s, -, **Me|cke|rin** [-ərɪn] F *(inf)* moaner, grumbler, griper *(inf)*

Me|cker-: **Me|cker|frit|ze** M *(inf)* bellyacher *(inf)*, wailing Willie *(Brit inf)*; **Me|cker|lie|se** [-li:zə] F -, -n *(inf)* moaning minnie *(Brit inf)*, moaner *(inf)*

me|ckern ['mɛkɐn] VI *(Ziege)* to bleat; *(inf: Mensch)* to moan, to bleat *(inf)*, to gripe *(inf)*; **über jdn/etw** *(acc)* ~ *(inf)* to moan *or* bleat *(inf)* about sb/sth

Me|cker|zie|ge F *(inf)* sourpuss *(inf)*, ratbag *(Brit inf)*

Meck|len|burg-Vor|pom|mern ['me:klən-bʊrkfo:ɐpɔmɐn, 'mɛklənbʊrk-] NT Mecklenburg-West Pomerania

med. *abbr von* **medizinisch**

Me|dail|le [me'daljə] F -, -n *(= Gedenkmünze)* medallion; *(bei Wettbewerben)* medal

Me|dail|len-: **Me|dail|len|ge|win|ner(in)** M(F) medallist, medal winner; **Me|dail|len|spie|gel** M medals table

Me|dail|lon [medal'jõ:] NT -s, -s **a** *(= Bildchen)* medallion; *(= Schmuckkapsel)* locket **b** *(Cook)* médaillon

me|di|al [me'dia:l] ADJ **a** *(= die Medien betreffend)* media *attr* **b** *(Gram)* middle **c** *(Med)* medial, median; *(Psych)* mediumistic ADV **wir leben in einer ~ vernetzten Welt** we live in a world interconnected through the media; **ein Ereignis ~ ausschlachten** to exploit an event in the media

Me|dia|thek [media'te:k] F -, -en multimedia centre *(Brit) or* center *(US)*

Me|di|a|ti|on [media'tsio:n] F -, -en mediation

Me|di|ä|vist [mediɛ'vɪst] M -en, -en, **Me|di|ä|vis|tin** F [-'vɪstɪn] -, -nen medievalist

Me|di|ä|vis|tik [mediɛ'vɪstɪk] F -, *no pl* medieval studies *sing or pl*

Me|di|en ['me:diən] PL media *pl*

Me|di|en-: **Me|di|en|be|ra|ter(in)** M(F) press adviser; **Me|di|en|be|richt** M *usu pl* media report, report in the media; **~en zufolge** according to media reports; **Me|di|en|er|eig|nis** NT media event; **Me|di|en|for|schung** F media research; **me|di|en|ge|recht** ADJ suited to the media ADV in a manner *or* way suited to the media; **Me|di|en|ge|setz** NT media law; **Me|di|en|gi|gant** M media giant; **Me|di|en|kom|pe|tenz** F media competence; **Me|di|en|kon|zern** M media group *or* concern; **Me|di|en|land|schaft** F, *no pl* media landscape; **Me|di|en|mo|gul** M media mogul; **Me|di|en|po|li|tik** F (mass) media policy; **me|di|en|po|li|tisch** ADJ media-political; **der ~e Sprecher der SPD-Fraktion** the SPD party spokesman on media policy; **Me|di|en|prä|senz** F, *no pl* media presence; **Me|di|en|re|fe|rent(in)** M(F) press officer; **Me|di|en|re|so|nanz** F media response *or* resonance; **Me|di|en|rum|mel** M media excitement; **Me|di|en|schel|te** F media-bashing *(inf)*; **~ betreiben** to knock the media; **Me|di|en|spek|ta|kel** NT media circus; **Me|di|en|ver|bund** M **etw im ~ lernen** to learn sth using the multimedia system; **Me|di|en|wie|der|ga|be** F *(Comput: Programm)* media player; **me|di|en|wirk|sam** ADJ *Ereignis, Politiker* mediagenic; **eine ~e Kampagne** a campaign geared toward(s) the media ADV **etw ~ präsentieren** to gear sth toward(s) the media

Me|di|en|zar M media mogul

Me|di|ka|ment [medika'mɛnt] NT -(e)s, -e medicine

Me|di|ka|men|ten-: **me|di|ka|men|ten|ab|hän|gig** ADJ **~ sein** to be addicted to medical drugs; **Me|di|ka|men|ten|ab|hän|gig|keit** F addiction to medical drugs; **Me|di|ka|men|ten|miss|brauch** M drug abuse; **Me|di|ka|men|ten|sucht** F, *no pl* drug dependency

me|di|ka|men|tös [medikamɛn'tø:s] ADJ *Behandlung, Therapie* medicinal ADV *behandeln* medicinally

Me|di|kus ['me:dikʊs] M -, **Medizi** *or* **-se** [-tsi] *(hum)* quack *(hum inf)*, doc *(inf)*; *(esp Student)* medic *(inf)*

Me|dio ['me:dio] M -(s), -s *(Fin)* middle of the month, mid-month

me|di|o|ker [me'dio:kɐ] *(geh)* ADJ mediocre ADV **der Schüler hat ~ abgeschnitten** the pupil got mediocre marks *(Brit) or* grades *(US)*

Me|di|ok|ri|tät F -, -en *(geh)* mediocrity

Me|dio|thek [medio'te:k] F -, -en multimedia centre *(Brit) or* center *(US)*

Me|dio|wech|sel M *(Fin)* bill for payment mid-month

Me|di|sance [medi'zã:sə] F -, -n *(geh)* malicious remark

Me|di|ta|ti|on [medita'tsio:n] F -, -en meditation

me|di|ta|tiv [medita'ti:f] ADJ meditative; **in ~er Versunkenheit** lost in meditation ADV meditatively

me|di|ter|ran [meditɛ'ra:n] ADJ Mediterranean

me|di|tie|ren [medi'ti:rən] *ptp* **meditiert** VI to meditate

Me|di|um ['me:diʊm] NT -s, **Medien** [-diən] medium; *(Gram)* middle (voice)

Me|di|zin [medi'tsi:n] F -, -en **a** *no pl (= Heilkunde)* medicine **b** *(inf: = Heilmittel)* medicine; **das ist ~ für ihn** that's his medicine; *(fig: Lektion, Denkzettel)* that'll teach him a lesson

Me|di|zi|nal- [meditsina:l-]: **Me|di|zi|nal|as|sis|tent(in)** M(F) houseman *(Brit)*, intern *(US)*; **Me|di|zi|nal|rat** M, **Me|di|zi|nal|rä|tin** F medical officer of health; **Me|di|zi|nal|sta|tis|tik** F medical statistics *pl*

Me|di|zin|ball M *(Sport)* medicine ball

Me|di|zi|ner [medi'tsi:nɐ] M -s, -, **Me|di|zi|ne|rin** [-ərɪn] F -, -nen **a** doctor **b** *(Univ)* medic *(inf)*

me|di|zi|nisch [medi'tsi:nɪʃ] ADJ **a** *(= ärztlich)* medical; **~e Fakultät** school *or* faculty of medicine; **~e Klinik** clinic for internal medicine; **~-technische Assistentin, ~-technischer Assistent** medical technician **b** *(= heilend) Kräuter, Bäder* medicinal; *Shampoo* medicated ADV **a** *(von einem Arzt)* medically; **sich ~ beraten lassen** to get medical advice; **jdn ~ behandeln** to treat sb (medically); **~ betreut werden** to be in medical care, to be treated; **~ beobachtet werden** to be under (medical) observation **b** *(= heilkundlich) ausbilden* medically; **~ wirksame Kräuter** medicinal herbs

Me|di|zin-: **Me|di|zin|mann** M *pl* **-männer** medicine man, witch doctor; *(hum: = Arzt)* quack *(inf)*, medico *(US inf)*; **Me|di|zin|schränk|chen** NT medicine cabinet *or* cupboard; **Me|di|zin|stu|dent(in)** M(F) medical student; **Me|di|zin|stu|di|um** NT study of medicine

Med|ley ['mɛdli] NT -s, -s *(Mus)* medley

Me|du|se [me'du:zə] F -, -n **a** *(Myth)* Medusa **b** *(Zool)* medusa *(spec)*, jellyfish

Me|du|sen|haupt NT **a** *(Liter)* head of Medusa **b** *(Med)* caput medusae *(spec)*

Meer [meːɐ] NT **-(e)s, -e** **a** sea; *(= Weltmeer)* ocean; **am ~(e)** by the sea; **diesseits des ~es** at home; **jenseits des ~es** across the sea; **übers ~ fahren** to travel (across) the seas; **ans ~ fahren** to go to the sea(side); **über dem ~** above sea level **b** *(fig: = riesige Menge)* sea

Meer-: **Meer|aal** M *(Zool)* conger (eel); **Meer|äsche** F *(Zool)* grey *(Brit) or* gray *(US)* mullet; **Meer|bu|sen** M gulf, bay; **Bottnischer ~** Gulf of Bothnia; **Meer|en|ge** F straits *pl*, strait

Mee|res-: **Mee|res|al|gen** PL seaweed, marine algae *pl (spec)*; **Mee|res|arm** M arm of the sea, inlet; **Mee|res|bio|lo|ge** M, **Mee|res|bio|lo|gin** F marine biologist; **Mee|res|bio|lo|gie** F marine biology; **Mee|res|bo|den** M seabed, sea bottom, bottom of the sea; **Mee|res|fau|na** F marine fauna; **Mee|res|fisch** M saltwater fish; **Mee|res|flo|ra** F marine flora; **Mee|res|for|schung** F oceanography; **Mee|res|frei|heit** F *(Jur)* freedom of the seas; **Mee|res|früch|te** PL seafood *sing*; **Mee|res|grund** M seabed, sea bottom, bottom of the sea; **Mee|res|hö|he** F sea level; **Mee|res|kli|ma** NT maritime climate; **Mee|res|kun|de** F oceanography; **mee|res|kund|lich** [-kʊntlɪç] ADJ oceanographic(al); **Mee|res|leuch|ten** NT **-s**, *no pl* marine phosphorescence; **Mee|res|ober|flä|che** F surface of the sea; **Mee|res|schild|krö|te** F turtle; **Mee|res|schne|cke** F conch; **Mee|res|spie|gel** M sea level; **über/unter dem ~** above/below sea level; **Mee|res|stil|le** F calm (at sea); **Mee|res|strand** M *(liter)* seashore, strand *(poet)*; **Mee|res|stra|ße** F waterway; **Mee|res|strö|mung** F ocean current; **Mee|res|tie|fe** F depth (of the sea *or* ocean); **Mee|res|tier** NT marine creature; **Mee|res|ufer** NT seashore, coast

Meer-: **Meer|gott** M *(Myth)* sea god; **Meer|göt|tin** F sea goddess; **meer|grün** ADJ sea-green; **Meer|jung|fer** F, **Meer|jung|frau** F mermaid; **Meer|kat|ze** F long-tailed monkey, guenon; **Meer|ret|tich** M horseradish; **Meer|salz** NT sea salt; **Meer|schaum** M *(Miner)* meerschaum; **Meer|schaum|pfei|fe** F meerschaum (pipe); **Meer|schwein|chen** NT guinea pig, cavy *(spec)*; **meer|um|schlun|gen** ADJ *(poet)* seagirt *(poet)*, seabound; **Meer|un|ge|heu|er** NT sea monster; **meer|wärts** [ˈmeːɐvɛrts] ADV seawards

Meer|was|ser NT sea water

Meer|was|ser-: **Meer|was|ser|auf|be|rei|tung** F treatment of sea water; **Meer|was|ser|ent|sal|zung** F desalination of sea water; **Meer|was|ser|ent|sal|zungs|an|la|ge** F desalination plant

Mee|ting [ˈmiːtɪŋ] NT **-s, -s** meeting

Me|ga-, **me|ga-** [ˈmeːga] *in cpds (eine Million)* mega-; *(inf: = Super-)* mega- *(inf)*; **Me|ga|bit** NT megabit; **Me|ga|bit|chip** M megabit chip; **Me|ga|byte** [-ˈbait] NT megabyte; **Me|ga|fon** [megaˈfoːn] NT **-s, -e** megaphone; **me|ga|geil** ADJ *(sl)* mega *(inf)*; **Me|ga|hertz** NT megahertz; **me|ga-in** ADJ *pred (inf)* mega cool *(inf)*

Me|ga|lith [megaˈliːt] M **-en, -en** *(Archeol)* megalith

Me|ga|lith-: **Me|ga|lith|grab** NT *(Archeol)* dolmen, megalithic tomb; **Me|ga|lith|kul|tur** F *(Hist)* megalithic culture

Me|ga|lo-: **me|ga|lo|man** [megaloˈmaːn] ADJ *(geh)* megalomanic; **Me|ga|lo|ma|nie** [megalomaˈniː] F *(geh)* megalomania; **Me|ga|lo|po|lis** [megaˈloːpolɪs] F **-, Megalopolen** [megaloˈpoːlən] megalopolis

Me|ga-: **me|ga-out** [ˈmegaˈlaut] ADJ *pred (inf)* mega uncool *(inf)*; **Me|ga|phon** [megaˈfoːn] NT **-s, -e** = **Megafon**

Me|gä|re [meˈgɛːrə] F **-, -n** **a** *(Myth)* Megaera **b** *(fig liter)* shrew, termagant *(liter)*

Me|ga-: **Me|ga|star** M *(inf)* megastar; **Me|ga|ton|ne** F megaton; **Me|ga|ton|nen|bom|be** F megaton bomb; **me|ga|tren|dy** ADJ *(inf)* super trendy *(inf)*; **Me|ga|watt** NT **-s, -** megawatt

Mehl [meːl] NT **-(e)s, -e** flour; *(gröber)* meal; *(= Knochenmehl)* bone meal; *(= Pulver, Zementmehl)* powder

Mehl-: **mehl|ar|tig** ADJ floury, mealy; **Mehl|bee|re** F berry of the whitebeam; **Mehl|brei** M pap, flummery

meh|lig [ˈmeːlɪç] ADJ *Äpfel, Kartoffeln* mealy ADV **~ schmecken** to taste mealy; **~ kochend** mealy

Mehl-: **Mehl|kleis|ter** M flour paste; **Mehl|kloß** M dumpling; **Mehl|papp** M *(inf)* mush *(inf)*; **Mehl|sack** M flour bag; **wie ein ~** *(inf)* like a sack of potatoes; **Mehl|schwal|be** F *(Orn)* house martin; **Mehl|schwit|ze** F *(Cook)* roux; **Mehl|spei|se** F **a** *(= Gericht)* flummery **b** *(Aus) (= Nachspeise)* sweet, dessert; *(= Kuchen)* pastry; **Mehl|sup|pe** F gruel; **Mehl|tau** M *(Bot)* mildew; **Mehl|wurm** M *(Zool)* mealworm

mehr [meːɐ] INDEF PRON INV *comp von* **viel, sehr** more; **was wollen Sie ~?** what more do you want?; **zu ~ hat es nicht gelangt** *or* **gereicht** that was all I/you *etc* could manage; **~ will er nicht bezahlen** he doesn't want to pay (any) more; **ist das alles, ~ kostet das nicht?** is that all it costs?; **je ~ er hat, je ~ er will** *(Prov)* the more he has, the more he wants; **sich für ~ halten** *(inf)* to think one is something more; **mit ~ oder weniger Erfolg** with a greater or lesser degree of success

ADV **a** *(= in höherem Maße)* more; **immer ~** more and more; **~ oder weniger** *or* **minder** *(geh)* more or less; **~ lang als breit** more long than wide, longer than it is/they are wide; **~ ein juristisches Problem** more (of) a legal problem; **war er brav/sind Sie beleidigt/hat es Ihnen geschmeckt? – ~ als das** was he good/are you insulted/did you like it? – "good/insulted/like" is not the word for it; **würden Sie das gerne tun? – ja, nichts ~ als das** would you like to? – there's nothing I'd rather do

b *(+neg: = sonst, länger)* **ich habe kein Geld ~** I have no more money, I haven't *or* I don't have any more money; **du bist doch kein Kind ~!** you're not a child any longer *or* any more!, you're no longer a child!; **es hat sich keiner ~ beworben** nobody else has applied; **es besteht keine Hoffnung ~** there's no hope left; **kein Wort ~!** not another word!; **es war niemand ~ da** there was no-one left, everyone had gone; **daran erinnert sich niemand ~** nobody can remember that any more; **wenn niemand ~ einsteigt, …** if nobody else gets in …; **nicht ~** not any longer, not any more, no more, no longer; **nicht ~ lange** not much longer; **das benutzt man nicht ~** that's not used any more *or* any longer, it's no longer used; **er lebt nicht ~** he is dead; **das darf nicht ~ vorkommen** that must not *or* never happen again; **wenn unser Opa nicht ~ ist** *(euph)* when Grandpa is no longer with us; **nichts ~** nothing more; **ich kann nichts ~ sagen** I can say nothing more, I can't say anything more; **nie ~** never again, nevermore *(liter)*; **ich will dich nie ~ wiedersehen** I never want to see you again, I don't ever want to see you again

Mehr [meːɐ] NT **-**, *no pl* **a** *(esp Sw: = Mehrheit)* majority **b** *(= Zuwachs)* increase; **mit einem ~ an Mühe** with more effort; **auf das ~ oder Weniger an Erfahrung kommt es nicht an** it's not a question of having more or less experience

Mehr-: **Mehr|ar|beit** F overtime, extra time *or* work; **Mehr|auf|wand** M *(= Kosten)* additional expenditure; *(= Mühe)* additional effort; **Mehr|aus|ga|be** F extra *or* additional expense(s *pl*); **mehr|bän|dig** ADJ in several volumes, multi-volume; **Mehr|be|darf** M greater need *(an +dat* of, for); *(Comm)* increased demand, increase in demand *(an +dat* for); **Mehr|be|las|tung** F excess load; *(fig)* extra *or* additional burden; **Mehr|be|nut|zer-** *in cpds (Comput)* = **Mehrplatz-**; **Mehr|be|reichs|öl** NT *(Aut)* multigrade oil; **Mehr|be|trag** M **a** *(= zusätzliche Zahlung)* extra *or* additional amount **b** *(= Überschuss)* surplus; **mehr|deu|tig** [-dɔytɪç] ADJ ambiguous, equivocal ADV ambiguously; **Mehr|deu|tig|keit** F **-, -en** ambiguity, equivocalness; **mehr|di|men|si|o|nal** ADJ multi-dimensional ADV *darstellen* multi-dimensionally; **eine ~ arbeitendes Programm** a multi-dimensional program; **Mehr|ein|nah|me** F additional revenue

meh|ren [ˈmeːrən] VT *(liter) (= vergrößern)* to augment, to increase; *(= fördern)* to further VR *(geh: = sich vermehren)* to multiply; **seid fruchtbar und mehret Euch!** *(Bibl)* be fruitful and multiply!

Meh|rer [ˈmeːrɐ] M **-s, -**, **Meh|re|rin** [-ərɪn] F **-, -nen** *(liter)* augmenter *(form)*

meh|re|re [ˈmeːrərə] INDEF PRON several; *(= verschiedene auch)* various

meh|re|res [ˈmeːrərəs] INDEF PRON several *or* various things *pl*

meh|rer|lei [ˈmeːrɐˈlai] INDEF PRON *inv* **a** *(substantivisch)* several things *pl* **b** *(adjektivisch)* several kinds of

Mehr-: **Mehr|er|lös** M additional revenue; **Mehr|er|trag** M additional yield, increase in yield

mehrf. *abbr von* **mehrfach**

mehr|fach [ˈmeːɐfax] ADJ multiple; *(= zahlreich)* numerous; *(= wiederholt)* repeated; **ein ~er Millionär** a multimillionaire; **der ~e Meister im Weitsprung** the man who has been the long jump champion several times; **die Unterlagen in ~er Ausfertigung einsenden** to send in several copies of the documents ADV *(= öfter)* many *or* several times; *(= wiederholt)* repeatedly

Mehr|fach-: **Mehr|fach|be|hin|der|te(r)** MF *decl as adj* person with multiple disabilities; **Mehr|fach|be|steu|e|rung** F multiple taxation

Mehr|fa|che(s) [ˈmeːɐfaxə] NT *decl as adj* **das ~** *or* **ein ~s des Kostenvoranschlags** several times the estimated cost; **verdient er wirklich mehr? – ja, das ~** *or* **ein ~s** does he earn more? – yes, several times as much

Mehr|fach-: **Mehr|fach|fahr|schein** M multi-journey ticket; **Mehr|fach|steck|do|se** F *(Elec)* multiple socket; **Mehr|fach|ste|cker** M *(Elec)* multiple adaptor; **Mehr|fach|tä|ter(in)** M(F) multiple offender

Mehr-: **Mehr|fahr|ten|kar|te** F multi-journey ticket; **Mehr|fa|mi|li|en|haus** NT multiple dwelling *(form)*, house for several families; **Mehr|far|ben|druck** M *pl* **-drucke** **a** *no pl (= Verfahren)* colour *(Brit) or* color *(US) or* polychromatic *(form)* printing **b** *(= Druck)* colour *(Brit) or* color *(US) or* polychromatic *(form)* print; **mehr|far|big** ADJ multicoloured *(Brit)*, multicolored *(US)*, polychromatic *(form)*; **Mehr|ge|päck** NT excess baggage; **Mehr|ge|wicht** NT additional *or* excess weight; *(= Übergewicht)* excess weight; **Mehr|ge|winn** M additional *or* surplus profits *pl*

Mehr|heit F **-, -en** **a** *no pl (= größerer Teil)* majority *(with sing or pl vb)*; **weitaus in der ~** decidedly in the majority **b** *(= Stimmenmehrheit)* majority; **die absolute/einfache** *or* **relative ~** an absolute/a simple *or* relative majority; **die ~ haben** *or* **besitzen/gewinnen** *or* **erringen** to have/win *or* gain a majority; **die ~ der Stimmen auf sich vereinigen** to secure a majority of votes; **die ~ verlieren** to lose one's majority; **mit zwei Stimmen ~** with a majority of two (votes)

mehr|heit|lich [-haitlɪç] ADV **wir sind ~ der Ansicht, dass …** the majority of us think(s) that …; **der Stadtrat hat ~ beschlossen …** the town council has reached a majority decision …; **an einer Gesellschaft ~ beteiligt sein** to be the majority shareholder *or* to have the majority holding in a company; **eine Gesellschaft ~ übernehmen** to become the majority shareholder in a company

Mehr|heits-: **Mehr|heits|be|schaf|fer** M **-s, -**, **Mehr|heits|be|schaf|fe|rin** F **-, -nen** *(Pol)* junior coalition partner *(securing majority)*; **Mehr|heits|be|schluss** M majority decision; **Mehr|heits|be|tei|li|gung** F *(Econ)* majority holding; **Mehr|heits|ent|schei|dung** F majority decision; **mehr|heits|fä|hig** ADJ capable of winning a majority; **Mehr|heits|füh|rer(in)** M(F) leader of the majority faction; **Mehr|heits|grund|satz** M principle of majority rule; **Mehr|heits|par|tei|en** PL majority parties *pl*; **Mehr|heits|prin|zip** NT principle of majority rule; **Mehr|heits|ver|hält|nis** NT majority; **~se** *pl* distribution of power; **Mehr|heits|wahl** F first-past-the-post election; **Mehr|heits|wahl|recht** NT first-past-the-post system, majority vote system

Mehr-: **mehr|jäh|rig** ADJ *attr* of several years; **~e Klinikerfahrung** several years of clinical experience; **Mehr|kampf** M *(Sport)* multidiscipline event; **Mehr|kämp|fer(in)** M(F) *(Sport)* all-round *(Brit) or* all-around *(US)* athlete, all--rounder *(Brit)*;; **mehr|köpf|ig** ADJ *attr* **eine ~e Familie** a multi-member family; **Mehr|kos|ten** PL additional costs *pl*; *(in Hotel etc)* additional expenses *pl*; **Mehr|la|de|ge|wehr** NT, **Mehr|la|der** [-la:dɐ] M **-s, -** repeater, repeater rifle; **mehr|ma|lig** ['me:ɐma:lɪç] ADJ *attr* repeated; **mehr|mals** ['me:ɐma:ls] ADV several times, repeatedly; **Mehr|par|tei|en|sys|tem** NT multiparty system; **Mehr|pha|sen|strom** M *(Elec)* multiphase *or* polyphase current

Mehr|platz- *in cpds (Comput)* multi-user; **mehr|platz|fä|hig** ADJ *(Comput)* capable of supporting multi-user operation; **Mehr|platz|rech|ner** M *(Comput)* multi-user system

Mehr-: **Mehr|rumpf|boot** NT multihull (boat); **mehr|schich|tig** [-ʃɪçtɪç] ADJ *(lit, fig)* multilayered; **mehr|sei|tig** ADJ *Dokument, Brief etc* multipage *attr*; of several pages *pred*; **mehr|sil|big** ADJ polysyllabic, multisyllabic; **mehr|spal|tig** ADJ *Dokument, Tabelle etc* multiple-column *attr*; with several columns *pred*; **mehr|spra|chig** ADJ *Person, Wörterbuch* multilingual, polyglot *(form)*; *Brief, Fragebogen etc* in several languages ADV in more than one language, in several languages; **~ aufwachsen** to grow up multilingual, to grow up speaking several languages; **Mehr|spra|chig|keit** F **-,** *no pl* multilingualism; **mehr|stel|lig** ADJ *attr Zahl, Betrag* multidigit; **mehr|stim|mig** ADJ *(Mus)* for several voices; **~es Lied** part-song ADV *spielen* in more than one voice; **~ singen** to sing in harmony; **Mehr|stim|mig|keit** F *(Mus)* polyphony; **mehr|stö|ckig** ADJ multistorey *(Brit)*, multistory *(US)* ADV **~ bauen** to build *or* erect multistorey *(Brit) or* multistory *(US)* buildings; **~ planen** to plan a multistorey *(Brit) or* multistory *(US)* building; **Mehr|stu|fen|ra|ke|te** F multistage rocket; **mehr|stu|fig** ADJ multistage; **mehr|stün|dig** ADJ *attr Verhandlungen* lasting several hours; **mit ~er Verspätung eintreffen** to arrive several hours late; **mehr|tä|gig** ADJ *attr Konferenz* lasting several days; **nach ~er Abwesenheit** after an absence of several days, after several days' absence; **Mehr|tei|ler** M **a** *(= Kleidungsstück)* combination; *(= Anzug)* suit **b** *(TV) (= Serie)* series; *(= Film)* serial; **mehr|tei|lig** ADJ in several parts

Meh|rung ['me:rʊŋ] F **-,** *no pl (liter)* increase

Mehr|ver|brauch M additional consumption

Mehr|weg- *in cpds* reusable; **Mehr|weg|fla|sche** F returnable bottle; **Mehr|weg|sys|tem** NT (bottle *or* packaging) return system; **Mehr|weg|ver|pa|ckung** F reusable packaging

Mehr-: **Mehr|wert** M *(Econ)* added value; **mehr|wer|tig** ADJ *(Chem)* polyvalent, multivalent; **Mehr|wert|steu|er** F value added tax, VAT; **mehr|wö|chig** [-vœçɪç] ADJ *attr* lasting several weeks; *Abwesenheit* of several weeks; **Mehr|zahl** F, *no pl* **a** *(Gram)* plural **b** *(= Mehrheit)* majority; **mehr|zei|lig** ADJ of several lines; **mehr|zel|lig** [-tsɛlɪç] ADJ multicellular

Mehr|zweck- *in cpds* multipurpose; **Mehr|zweck|ge|rät** NT multipurpose gadget; **Mehr|zweck|hal|le** F multipurpose room

mei|den ['maidn] *pret* **mied** [mi:t], *ptp* **gemieden** [gə'mi:dn] VT to avoid

Mei|e|rei [maiə'rai] F **-, -en** **a** *(dial: = Molkerei)* dairy (farm) **b** *(old: = Pachtgut)* leasehold farm

Mei|le ['mailə] F **-, -n** mile; *(old: = 4,8 km)* league; **das riecht man drei ~n gegen den Wind** *(inf)* you can smell *or* tell that a mile off *(Brit) or* away *(inf)*

Mei|len-: **mei|len|lang** ADJ mile-long ADV for miles; **Mei|len|stein** M *(lit, fig)* milestone; **Mei|len|stie|fel** PL seven-league boots *pl*; **mei|len|weit** ADJ of many miles; **~e Sandstrände** miles and miles of sandy beaches ADV for miles; **~ auseinander/entfernt** *(lit, fig)* miles apart/away; **Mei|len|zahl** F mileage; **Mei|len|zäh|ler** M mileometer *(Brit)*, clock *(Brit inf)*, odometer

Mei|ler ['mailɐ] M **-s, -** *(= Kohlenmeiler)* charcoal kiln *or* pile; *(= Atommeiler)* (atomic) pile

mein [main] POSS PRON **a** *(adjektivisch)* my; **~ verdammtes Auto** *(inf)* this damn car of mine *(inf)*; **ich trinke so ~e fünf Flaschen Bier pro Tag** I drink my five bottles of beer a day **b** *(old: substantivisch)* mine; **Mein und Dein verwechseln** *(euph)* to take what doesn't belong to one PERS PRON *gen von* **ich** *(old, poet)* of me

Mein|eid ['mainlait] M perjury *no indef art*; **einen ~ leisten** *or* **ablegen** to perjure oneself, to commit perjury

mein|ei|dig ['mainlaidɪç] ADJ perjured; **~ werden** to commit perjury, to perjure oneself

Mein|ei|di|ge(r) ['mainlaidɪgə] MF *decl as adj* perjurer

mei|nen ['mainən] ✪ 29.1, 53.2 VI *(= denken, glauben)* to think; **ich würde/man möchte ~** I/one would think; **ich meine, ...** I think ..., I reckon ... *(inf)*; **~ Sie?** (do) you think so?, do you reckon? *(inf)*; **wie ~ Sie?** I beg your pardon?; **ich meine nur so** *(inf)* it was just a thought; **wie Sie ~!** as you wish; *(drohend auch)* have it your own way; **wenn du meinst!** if you like, I don't mind; **man sollte ~** one would have thought

VT **a** *(= der Ansicht sein)* to think; **was ~ Sie dazu?** what do you think *or* say?; **~ Sie das im Ernst?** are you serious about that?; **das will ich ~!** I quite agree!; **das sollte man ~!** one would think so

b *(= sagen wollen)* to mean; *(inf: = sagen)* to say; **was ~ Sie damit?, wie ~ Sie das?** what *or* how do you mean?; *(drohend)* (just) what do you mean by that?

c *(geh: = bedeuten)* to mean

d *(= bezeichnen wollen)* to mean; **damit bin ich gemeint** that's meant for me, they mean/he means *etc* me

e *(= beabsichtigen)* to mean, to intend; **so war es nicht gemeint** it wasn't meant like that; **sie meint es gut** she means well; **sie meint es nicht böse** she means no harm, she doesn't mean any harm; **die Sonne hat es aber heute wieder gut (mit uns) gemeint!** the sun's done its best for us again today

mei|ner ['mainɐ] PERS PRON *gen von* **ich** of me

mei|ne(r, s) ['mainə] POSS PRON *(substantivisch)* mine; **der/die/das Meine** *(geh)* mine; **ich tu das Meine** *(geh)* I'll do my bit; **das Meine** *(geh: = Besitz)* what is mine; **die Meinen** *(geh: = Familie)* my people, my family

mei|ner|seits ['mainɐzaits] ADV as far as I'm concerned, for my part; **ich ~** I personally, I myself, I for my part; **Vorschläge/Einwände ~** suggestions/objections from me; **ganz ~!** the pleasure's (all) mine

mei|nes-: **mei|nes|glei|chen** ['mainəs'glaiçn] PRON *inv (= meiner Art)* people such as I *or* me, people like me *or* myself; *(= gleichrangig)* my own kind, my equals; **Leute** *or* **Menschen ~** *(= meiner Art)* people like me *or* myself; *(= gleichrangig)* people of my own kind, my equals; **mei|nes|teils** ['mainəs'tails] ADV for my part

mei|net-: **mei|net|hal|ben** ['mainət'halbn] *(dated)* = **meinetwegen**; **mei|net|we|gen** ['mainət've:gn] ADV **a** *(= wegen mir)* because of me, on account of me, on my account; *(= mir zuliebe)* for my sake; *(= um mich)* about me; *(= für mich)* on my behalf **b** *(= von mir aus)* as far as I'm concerned; **~!** if you like; **wenn Ihr das tun wollt, ~, aber ...** if you want to do that, fair enough *(inf)*, but ...; **mei|net|wil|len** ['mainət'vɪlən] ADV **um ~** *(= mir zuliebe)* for my sake; *(= wegen mir)* on my account

mei|ni|ge ['mainɪgə] POSS PRON **der/die/das Meinige** *or* **~** *(form, old)* mine; **die Meinigen** *(geh)* my family, my people

meins [mains] POSS PRON mine

Mei|nung ['mainʊŋ] ✪ 29.2, 33, 34.5, 38.1, 39.1, 40.1, 40.4, 41, 53.3, 53.5 F **-, -en** opinion; *(= Anschauung auch)* view; *(= Urteil)* judgement, estimation; **eine vorgefasste ~** a preconceived idea; **nach meiner ~, meiner ~ nach** in my opinion *or* view; **ich bin der ~, dass ...** I'm of the opinion that ..., I take the view that ...; **eine/keine hohe ~ von jdm/etw haben** to think/not to think highly of sb/sth, to have a high/low opinion of sb/sth; **seine ~ ändern** to change one's opinion *or* mind; **einer ~ sein** to share the same opinion, to think the same; **geteilter ~ sein** to have different opinions; **was ist Ihre ~ dazu?** what's your opinion *or* view (about *or* on that)?; **von seiner ~ eingenommen sein** to be opinionated; **ganz meine ~!** I completely agree!, hear, hear!; **das ist auch meine ~!** that's just what I think; **jdm (kräftig** *or* **vernünftig) die ~ sagen** *(inf)* to give sb a piece of one's mind *(inf)*

Mei|nungs-: **Mei|nungs|än|de|rung** F change of opinion; **Mei|nungs|äu|ße|rung** F (expression of) opinion; **Mei|nungs|aus|tausch** M exchange of views *(über +acc* on, about*)*; **mei|nungs|bil|dend** ADJ opinion-forming ADV **~ wirken** to shape public opinion; **Mei|nungs|bil|dung** F formation of opinion; **der Prozess der ~ ist noch nicht abgeschlossen** we have not yet formed an opinion; **Mei|nungs|bil|dungs|pro|zess** M opinion-forming process; **Mei|nungs|for|scher(in)** M(F) (opinion) pollster; **Mei|nungs|for|schung** F (public) opinion polling *or* research; **Mei|nungs|for|schungs|in|sti|tut** NT opinion research institute; **Mei|nungs|frei|heit** F freedom of speech; **Mei|nungs|füh|rer(in)** M(F) opinion leader; **die Rolle als ~ verlieren** *(Pol)* to no longer set the (political) agenda; **Mei|nungs|kli|ma** NT climate of public opinion; **mei|nungs|los** ADJ without opinions, viewless; **~ sein** to have no opinions; **Mei|nungs|ma|che** F *(pej inf)* propaganda; **Mei|nungs|ma|cher(in)** M(F) *(inf)* opinion-maker, opinion--leader; **Mei|nungs|ma|ni|pu|la|ti|on** F manipulation of (public) opinion; **Mei|nungs|mo|no|pol** NT monopoly of opinion; **Mei|nungs|streit** M conflict of views *or* opinions, controversy, dispute; **Mei|nungs|um|fra|ge** F (public) opinion poll; **Mei|nungs|um|schwung** M swing of opinion; **Mei|nungs|un|ter|schied** M *usu pl* difference of opinion; **da gibt es ~e** opinions are divided on that; **zwischen Herrn Meier und mir gibt es erhebliche ~e, was ... angeht** where ... is *or* are concerned, Mr Meier and I have considerable differences of opinion *or* think quite differently; **Mei|nungs|ver|schie|den|heit** F difference of opinion

Mei|se ['maizə] F **-, -n** titmouse; **eine ~ haben** *(inf)* to be crackers *(Brit) or* crazy *(inf)*

Mei|sen-: **Mei|sen|knö|del** M *(= Vogelfutter)* fat ball; **Mei|sen|ring** M bird-feeding ring

Mei|ßel ['maisl] M **-s, -** chisel

mei|ßeln ['maisln] VTI to chisel

Mei|ße|ner ['maisənɐ], **Meiß|ner** ['maisnɐ] ADJ **Meiß(e)ner Porzellan** Dresden *or* Meissen china

meist [maist] ADV = **meistens**

Meist-: **meist|be|güns|tigt** [-bəgynstıçt] ADJ *(Econ)* most-favoured *(Brit)*, most-favored *(US)*; **Meist|be|güns|ti|gung** F *(Econ, Pol)* most-favoured-nation *(Brit)* or most-favored-nation *(US)* treatment; **Meist|be|güns|ti|gungs|klau|sel** F *(Econ, Pol)* most-favoured-nation *(Brit)* or most-favored-nation *(US)* clause; **meist|bie|tend** ADJ highest bidding; **Meistbietender** highest bidder; ~ *or* **an den Meistbietenden versteigern** to sell *or* auction (off) to the highest bidder

meis|ten ['maistn] **am** ~ ADV **a** *superl von* **viel** the most **b** *superl von* **sehr** most of all; **am ~ bekannt** best known

meis|tens ['maistns] ADV mostly, more often than not; *(= zum größten Teil)* for the most part

meis|ten|teils ['maistn'tails] ADV = **meistens**

Meis|ter ['maistɐ] M **-s, - a** *(= Handwerksmeister)* master (craftsman); *(in Laden)* boss *(inf)*; *(in Fabrik)* foreman, boss *(inf)*; *(sl: als Anrede)* guv *(Brit inf)*, chief *(Brit inf)*, mac *(US inf)*; *(Sport)* champion; *(Mannschaft)* champions *pl*; **seinen ~ machen** to take one's master craftsman's diploma
b *(= Lehrmeister, Künstler)* master *(auch fig)*; **alter ~** *(Art)* old master; **~ vom Stuhl** *(fig)* Master of the Lodge; **er hat seinen ~ gefunden** *(fig)* he's met his match; **~ einer Sache** *(gen) or* **in etw** *(dat)* past master at sth; **ein ~ seines Faches sein** to be a master of one's craft; **es ist noch kein ~ vom Himmel gefallen** *(Prov)* no-one is born a master
c *(old liter)* master; **~ Zwirn** Snip, the tailor; **~ Knieriem** *or* **Pfriem/Lampe** Master Cobbler/Hare; **~ Urian** Old Nick

meis|te(r, s) ['maistə] INDEF PRON *superl von* **viel a** *(adjektivisch)* **die ~n Leute** most people; **die ~n Leute, die ...** most people who ..., most of the people who ...; **du hast die ~ Zeit** you have (the) most time **b** *(substantivisch)* **die ~n** most people; **die ~n (von ihnen)** most (of them), the majority (of them); **das ~** most of it; **du hast das ~** you have (the) most

Meis|ter- *in cpds* master; **Meis|ter|brief** M master craftsman's diploma *or* certificate; **Meis|ter|ge|sang** M *(Liter)* poetry of the Meistersingers; **meis|ter|haft** ADJ masterly ADV brilliantly; **er versteht es ~ zu lügen** he is brilliant at lying; **Meis|ter|hand** F **von ~** by a master hand

Meis|te|rin ['maistərın] F **-, -nen** *(= Handwerksmeisterin)* master craftswoman; *(= Frau von Handwerksmeister)* master craftsman's wife; *(in Fabrik)* forewoman; *(Sport)* champion; **Frau ~!** madam!

Meis|ter-: **Meis|ter|klas|se** F master class; **Meis|ter|leis|tung** F masterly performance; *(iro)* brilliant achievement

meis|ter|lich ['maistɐlıç] ADJ ADV = **meisterhaft**

meis|tern ['maistɐn] VT to master; *Schwierigkeiten* to overcome; **sein Leben ~** to come to grips with one's life

Meis|ter|prü|fung F examination for master craftsman's diploma *or* certificate

Meis|ter|schaft ['maistɐʃaft] F **-, -en a** *(Sport)* championship; *(Veranstaltung)* championships *pl* **b** *no pl (= Können)* mastery; **es zu wahrer ~ bringen** *(als Künstler etc)* to become really proficient *or* expert, to achieve real mastery *or* proficiency; *(als Dieb etc)* to get it down to a fine art

Meis|ter|schafts-: **Meis|ter|schafts|fei|er** F *(Sport)* title-winners' celebration; **Meis|ter|schafts|spiel** NT *(Sport)* league match

Meis|ter-: **Meis|ter|schu|le** F school for master craftspeople; **Meis|ter|schü|ler(in)** M(F) *(Art, Mus)* pupil *(in a master class)*; **Meis|ter|schuss** M brilliant shot; **Meis|ter|schüt|ze** M marksman, crack shot; **Meis|ter|schüt|zin** F markswoman, crack shot; **Meis|ter|sin|ger** [-zıŋɐ] M **-s, -** *(Hist)* meistersinger, mastersinger; **Meis|ter|stück** NT *(von Handwerker) work done to qualify as master craftsman (fig)* masterpiece; *(= geniale Tat)* master stroke; **Meis|ter|ti|tel** M *(im Handwerk)* title of master craftsman; *(Sport)* championship title

Meis|te|rung ['maistəruŋ] F **-**, *no pl* mastery

Meis|ter|werk NT masterpiece

Meist-: **Meist|ge|bot** NT highest bid, best offer; **meist|ge|bräuch|lich** ADJ *attr* commonest; **meist|ge|fragt** ADJ *attr* most popular, most in demand; *Wohngegend auch* most sought-after; **meist|ge|kauft** [-gəkauft] ADJ *attr* best-selling; **meist|ge|le|sen** ADJ *attr* most widely read; **meist|ge|nannt** ADJ *attr* most frequently mentioned; **meist|ver|kauft** [-fɛɐkauft] ADJ *attr* best-selling

Meit|ne|ri|um [mait'ne:rium] NT **-s**, *no pl (abbr* **Mt)** meitnerium

Mek|ka ['mɛka] NT **-s** *(Geog, fig)* Mecca

Me|lan|cho|lie [melaŋko'li:] F **-, -n** [-'li:ən] melancholy

Me|lan|cho|li|ker [melaŋ'ko:likɐ] M **-s, -**, **Me|lan|cho|li|ke|rin** [-ərın] F **-, -nen** melancholic

me|lan|cho|lisch [melaŋ'ko:lıʃ] ADJ melancholy ADV *sagen* in a melancholy voice; **er schreibt ~** his writing is melancholy; **sie sann ~ vor sich hin** she was thinking melancholy thoughts

Me|la|ne|si|en [mela'ne:ziən] NT **-s** Melanesia

Me|la|ne|si|er [mela'ne:ziɐ] M **-s, -**, **Me|la|ne|si|e|rin** [-iərın] F **-, -nen** Melanesian

me|la|ne|sisch [mela'ne:zıʃ] ADJ Melanesian

Me|lan|ge [me'lã:ʒə] F **-, -n a** *(rare: = Mischung)* blend **b** *(Aus: = Milchkaffee)* white coffee *(Brit)*, coffee with milk

Me|la|nin [mela'ni:n] NT **-s, -e** *(Chem)* melanin

Me|la|nom [mela'no:m] NT **-s, -e** *(Med)* melanoma

Me|lan|za|ni [melan'tsa:ni] F **-, -** *(Aus)* aubergine, eggplant *(esp US)*

Me|las|se [me'lasə] F **-, -n** molasses

Mel|de-: **Mel|de|amt** NT, **Mel|de|bü|ro** *(inf)* NT registration office; **Mel|de|be|hör|de** F registration authorities *pl*; **Mel|de|fah|rer(in)** M(F) *(Mil)* dispatch rider; **Mel|de|frist** F registration period

mel|den ['mɛldn] ✪ 27.5, 27.7 VT **a** *(= anzeigen) Unfall, Verlust, ansteckende Erkrankungen* to report; *(= berichten)* to report; *(= registrieren lassen)* to register; *(= denunzieren)* to report; **eine Geburt/Änderungen (der Behörde** *dat)* **~** to notify the authorities of a birth/changes; **wie soeben gemeldet wird** *(Rad, TV)* according to reports just coming in; **das wird gemeldet!** *(Sch)* I'll tell on you *(Sch inf)*; **(bei jdm) nichts zu ~ haben** *(inf)* to have no say; **er hat hier nichts zu ~** *(inf)* he has no say in this; **melde gehorsamst** *(old Mil)* beg to report; **(als) arbeitslos gemeldet sein** to be registered unemployed
b *(= ankündigen)* to announce; **ich ging zur Sekretärin und ließ mich beim Direktor ~** I went to the secretary and asked her to tell the director that I was there; **wen darf ich ~?** who(m) shall I say (is here)?, who(m) shall I announce?
VR **a** *(= antreten)* to report *(zu* for); **sich zum Dienst ~** to report for work; **sich freiwillig ~** to volunteer; **sich zu** *or* **für etw ~** *(esp Mil)* to sign up for sth, to volunteer for sth; *(für Arbeitsplatz)* to apply for sth; *(für Lehrgang)* to enrol *(Brit) or* enroll *(US)* for sth, to sign on for sth; **sich auf eine Anzeige ~** to answer an advertisement; **sich polizeilich** *or* **bei der Polizei ~** to register with the police; **sich arbeitslos ~** to register as unemployed, to sign on → **krankmelden**
b *(fig: = sich ankündigen)* to announce one's presence; *(Alter, Hunger)* to make itself *or* its presence felt; *(Winter, Dunkelheit)* to draw *or* set in; *(Sport, zur Prüfung)* to enter (one's name) *(zu* for); *(durch Handaufheben)* to put one's hand up, to hold up one's hand; *(Rad, TV)* to come on the air → **Wort c**
c *(esp Telec: = antworten)* to answer; **bitte ~!** *(Telec)* come in, please; **es meldet sich niemand** there's no answer
d *(= von sich hören lassen)* to get in touch *(bei* with); **melde dich wieder** keep in touch; **seitdem hat er sich nicht mehr gemeldet** he hasn't been heard of since; **wenn du was brauchst, melde dich** if you need anything give (me) a shout *(inf)*

Mel|de-: **Mel|de|pflicht** F **a** *(beim Ordnungsamt)* compulsory registration, obligation to register *(when moving house)*; **polizeiliche ~** obligation to register with the police **b ~ des Arztes** the doctor's obligation to notify the authorities *(of people with certain contagious diseases)*; **mel|de|pflich|tig** [-pflıçtıç] ADJ **a** *Mensch* obliged to register **b** *Krankheit* notifiable; *Unfall, Schadensfall* that must be reported

MELDEPFLICHT

A **Meldepflicht** is a regulation requiring people to notify the authorities of things such as a change of address or a birth. Everyone who takes up residence in Germany is obliged to register with the **Einwohnermeldeamt** within a week (three days in Austria). If you move to a different address, you must first inform the authorities in your previous place of residence. In Switzerland regulations vary from canton to canton.

Mel|der ['mɛldɐ] M **-s, -**, **Mel|de|rin** [-ərın] F **-, -nen** dispatch rider

Mel|de-: **Mel|de|re|gis|ter** NT register (of residents); **Mel|de|schein** M registration form; **Mel|de|schluss** M closing date; **Mel|de|stel|le** F place of registration; **Mel|de|we|sen** NT, *no pl* registration system; **Mel|de|zet|tel** M *(Aus)* certificate of registration

Mel|dung ['mɛlduŋ] F **-, -en a** *(= Mitteilung)* announcement **b** *(Press, Rad, TV)* report *(über +acc* on, about); **~en in Kürze** news headlines *pl*; **~en vom Sport** sports news *sing* **c** *(dienstlich)* report; **(eine) ~ machen** to make a report **d** *(bei der Polizei)* report **e** *(Sport: = Examensmeldung)* entry; **seine ~ zurückziehen** to withdraw **f** *(Comput)* (on-screen) message

me|liert [me'li:ɐt] ADJ *Haar* greying *(Brit)*, graying *(US)*, streaked with grey *(Brit) or* gray *(US)*; *Wolle* flecked; **sein Haar war grau ~** his hair was streaked with grey *(Brit) or* gray *(US)*

Me|li|o|ra|ti|on [meliora'tsio:n] F **-, -en** *(Agr)* soil improvement

Me|lis|se [me'lısə] F **-, -n** balm

Me|lis|sen|geist® M medicinal spirit

Melk- *in cpds* milking; **Melk|an|la|ge** F milking plant

mel|ken ['mɛlkn] *pres* **melkt** *or (old)* **milkt** [mɛlkt, mılkt], *pret* **melkte** *or (old)* **molk** ['mɛlktə, mɔlk], *ptp* **gemolken** *or (rare)* **gemelkt** [gə'mɔlkn, gə'mɛlkt] VT **a** *Kuh, Ziege etc* to milk; **frisch gemolkene Milch** milk fresh from the cow **b** *(fig inf)* to milk *(inf)*, to fleece *(inf)* VI to milk

Mel|ker ['mɛlkɐ] M **-s, -** milker

Mel|ke|rei [mɛlkə'rai] F **-, -en** *(= Milchwirtschaft)* dairy (farm)

Mel|ke|rin ['mɛlkərın] F **-, -en** milkmaid

Me|lo|die [melo'di:] F **-, -n** [-'di:ən] melody; *(= Weise auch)* tune; **nach der ~ von ...** to the tune of ...

Me|lo|die|ins|tru|ment NT melodic instrument

Me|lo|di|en|fol|ge [-'di:ən-] F, **Me|lo|di|en|rei|gen** [-'di:ən-] M *(Rad)* medley of tunes

Me|lo|dik [me'lo:dık] F **-**, *no pl* **a** *(Theorie)* melodics *sing* **b** *(= musikalische Eigenart)* musical idiom

me|lo|di|ös [melo'diø:s] *(geh)* ADJ melodious ADV melodiously; **~ klingen** to sound melodious

me|lo|disch [me'lo:dıʃ] ADJ *Musik* melodic, tuneful; *Sprache, Wort* melodic ADV **~ klingen** to sound melodic

Me|lo|dram [melo'dra:m] NT **-s, Melodramen** *(liter)*, **Me|lo|dra|ma** NT melodrama *(auch fig)*

me|lo|dra|ma|tisch [melodra'ma:tɪʃ] ADJ melodramatic (*auch fig*) ADV melodramatically; ~ **klingen** to sound melodramatic

Me|lo|ne [me'lo:nə] F -, -n **a** melon **b** (*Hut*) bowler (*Brit*), derby (*US*)

Mem|bran [mɛm'bra:n] F -, -en, **Mem|bra|ne** [mɛm'bra:nə] F -, -n **a** (*Anat*) membrane **b** (*Phys, Tech*) diaphragm

Me|men|to [me'mɛnto] NT -s, -s (*liter*) admonition, warning

Mem|me ['mɛmə] F -, -n (*inf*) sissy (*inf*), yellow-belly (*inf*)

mem|men|haft (*inf*) ADJ lily-livered (*inf*), yellow-bellied (*inf*) ADV like a yellow-belly (*inf*)

Me|mo ['me:mo] NT -s, -s memo

Me|moire [me'moa:r(ə)] NT -s, -s (*Pol*) memorandum

Me|moi|ren [me'moa:rən] PL memoirs *pl*

Me|mo|ran|dum [memo'randʊm] NT -s, **Memoranden** *or* **Memoranda** [-dn, -da] (*Pol*) memorandum

me|mo|rie|ren [memo'ri:rən] *ptp* **memoriert** VT (*old*) **a** (= *sich einprägen*) to memorize, to commit to memory **b** (= *aufsagen*) to recite (from memory)

Me|na|ge [me'na:ʒə] F -, -n **a** (= *Gewürzständer*) cruet (set) **b** (*Aus*: = *Verpflegung*) rations *pl*

Me|na|ge|rie [menaʒə'ri:] F -, -n [-'ri:ən] menagerie

Me|nar|che [me'narçə] F -, *no pl* (*Med*) menarche (*spec*), first menstruation

Men|de|le|vi|um [mɛnde'le:viʊm] NT -s, *no pl* (*abbr* **Md**) mendelevium

men|deln ['mɛndln] VI (*Biol*) to mendelize (*spec*), to conform to Mendel's laws

men|del|sche Re|geln ['mɛndlʃə] PL (*Biol*) Mendel's laws *pl*

Me|ne|te|kel [mene'te:kl] NT -s, - (*liter*) warning sign, portent; **das ~ an der Wand** the writing on the wall

Men|ge ['mɛŋə] F -, -n **a** (= *Quantum*) amount, quantity; **in ~n zu** in quantities of
b (*inf*) (= *große Anzahl*) lot, load (*inf*); (= *Haufen*) pile (*inf*), heap (*inf*); **eine ~** a lot, lots (*inf*); **eine ~ Zeit/Häuser** a lot *or* lots (*inf*) of time/houses; **jede ~** masses *pl* (*inf*), loads *pl* (*inf*); **jede ~ Zeit/Geld** masses (*inf*) *or* loads (*inf*) of time/money; **wir haben jede ~ getrunken** we drank an enormous amount, we drank a hell of a lot (*inf*); **es gab Wein jede ~** *or* **jede ~ Wein** there was masses *or* loads of wine (*inf*); **eine ganze ~** quite a lot; **sie bildet sich eine ~ auf ihre Schönheit ein** she's incredibly conceited about her looks; **Bücher in ~n** any amount of books → **rau e**
c (= *Menschenmenge*) crowd; (*geh*) (= *Masse*) mass; (= *das Volk*) people; (*pej*: = *Pöbel*) mob; **in der ~ untertauchen** to disappear into the crowd
d (*Math*) set

men|gen ['mɛŋən] VT (*geh*) to mix (*unter +acc* with) VR to mingle (*unter +acc* with); (*fig*: = *sich einmischen*) to meddle, to interfere (*in +acc* with, in)

Men|gen-: **Men|gen|an|ga|be** F quantity, indication of quantity; **Men|gen|be|griff** M uncountable noun; (*Math*) concept of the set; **Men|gen|be|zeich|nung** F unit of quantity; **Men|gen|leh|re** F (*Math*) set theory; **men|gen|mä|ßig** ADJ as far as quantity is concerned, quantitative ADV as far as quantity is concerned; **Men|gen|preis** M bulk price; **Men|gen|ra|batt** M bulk *or* quantity discount; **Men|gen|ver|hält|nis** NT relative proportions *pl* (*zwischen +dat* of), quantitative ratio (*form*) (*zwischen +dat* between)

Meng|sel ['mɛŋzl] NT -s, - (*dial*) mixture

Men|hir ['mɛnhi:ɐ] M -s, -e (*Archeol*) standing stone, menhir

Me|nin|gi|tis [menɪŋ'gi:tɪs] F -, **Meningitiden** [menɪŋgi'ti:dn] (*Med*) meningitis

Me|nis|kus [me'nɪskʊs] M -, **Menisken** [-kn] (*Anat, Phys*) meniscus; (*Phot auch*) meniscal lens

Me|nis|kus|riss M torn meniscus

Men|jou|bärt|chen ['mɛnʒu-] NT pencil moustache (*Brit*) *or* mustache (*US*)

Men|ken|ke [mɛŋ'kɛŋkə] F -, -s *or* -n (*dial*) fuss

Men|ni|ge ['mɛnɪgə] F -, *no pl* minium, red lead

Men|no|nit [mɛno'ni:t] M -en, -en, **Men|no|ni|tin** [-'ni:tɪn] F -, -nen Mennonite

Me|no|pau|se [meno'pauzə] F (*Med*) menopause

Me|no|sta|se [meno'sta:zə] F -, -n (*Med*) menostasis

Men|sa ['mɛnza] F -, **Mensen** [-zn] (*Univ*) canteen, refectory (*Brit*), dining hall

Men|sa|es|sen NT (*Univ*) (= *Mahlzeit*) college meal; (= *Kost*) college food

Mensch [mɛnʃ] M -en, -en **a** (= *Person*) person, man/woman; **ein anderer ~ werden** to become a different person *or* man/woman; **ein neuer ~ werden** to become a new person *or* man/woman; **von ~ zu ~** man-to-man/woman-to-woman; **es war kein ~ da** there was nobody there, there was not a soul there; **als ~** as a person; **des ~en Wille ist sein Himmelreich** (*Prov*) do what you want if it makes you happy (*inf*); **das konnte kein ~ ahnen!** no-one (on earth) could have foreseen that!; **viel unter (die) ~en kommen** to meet a lot of people, to get around (a lot); **man muss die ~en nehmen, wie sie sind** you have to take people as they are *or* come; **Aktion ~** *charity for people with disabilities*
b (*als Gattung*) **der ~** man; **die ~en** man *sing*, human beings *pl*, people *pl*; **die Ruritanier sind gutmütige ~en** the Ruritanians are a good-natured race *or* are good-natured people; **ein Tier, das keine ~en mag** an animal that doesn't like people *or* humans; **~ bleiben** (*inf*) to stay human; **ich bin auch nur ein ~!** I'm only human; **wer so etwas macht, ist kein ~ mehr** somebody who does something like that is not human; **wie die ersten** *or* **letzten ~en** (*inf*) like animals; **~ und Tier** man and beast; **alle ~en müssen sterben** we are all mortal; **alle ~en haben tierische Gelüste** all human beings have animal cravings; **~en verachtend** = **menschenverachtend**
c (= *die Menschheit*) **die ~en** mankind, man, humankind (*esp US*); **des ~en Sohn** (*Bibl*) the Son of Man; **Jesus ist gekommen, um die ~en zu retten** Jesus came to save mankind *or* humankind (*esp US*); **alle ~en** everyone; **so sind die ~en** that's human nature
d (*inf*: *als Interjektion*) hey; (*erstaunt*) hey, wow, blimey (*Brit sl*); **~, hat die Beine!** hey *or* wow! has she got a pair of legs! (*inf*); **~, das habe ich ganz vergessen** damn, I completely forgot (*inf*); **~, da habe ich mich aber getäuscht** boy, was I wrong! (*inf*); **~, habe ich mich beeilt/geärgert!** boy, did I rush/was I angry! (*inf*); **~ Meier!** golly! (*dated inf*), gosh! (*dated inf*)

Mensch NT -(e)s, -er (*sl*) cow (*inf*); (*gemein*) bitch (*sl*)

Mensch är|ge|re dich nicht® [mɛnʃ 'ɛrgərə dɪç nɪçt] NT - - - -, *no pl* (= *Spiel*) ≈ ludo (*Brit*), ≈ aggravation (*US*)

men|scheln ['mɛnʃln] VI *impers* **a es menschelt** there's no escaping (from) one's humanity **b** (*in Märchen*) **es menschelt** I smell or sense a human

Men|schen- *in cpds* human; **Men|schen|af|fe** M ape, anthropoid (ape); **men|schen|ähn|lich** ADJ manlike, humanlike (*esp US*), like a human being/human beings; **Men|schen|al|ter** NT **a** (= *30 Jahre*) generation **b** (= *Lebensdauer*) lifetime; **Men|schen|an|samm|lung** F gathering (of people); **Men|schen|art** F **a nach ~** like human beings/a human being **b** (= *menschliche Schwäche*) human nature; **Men|schen|auf|lauf** M crowd (of people); **Men|schen|feind(in)** M(F) misanthropist; **men|schen|feind|lich** ADJ *Mensch* misanthropic; *Landschaft etc* hostile to man, inhospitable; *Politik, Gesellschaft* inhumane; **Men|schen|fleisch** NT human flesh; **Men|schen|fres|ser(in)** M(F) **a** (*inf*) (= *Kannibale*) cannibal; (= *Raubtier*) man-eater; **ich bin doch kein ~!** I won't eat you! **b** (*Myth*) ogre; **Men|schen|fres|se|rei** F (*inf*) cannibalism; **Men|schen|freund(in)** M(F) philanthropist; **men|schen|freund|lich** ADJ *Mensch* philanthropic, benevolent; *Gegend* hospitable; *Politik, Gesellschaft* humane; **diese Affenart ist nicht sehr ~** this species of ape does not like humans ADV **sich ~ geben** to like to give the impression of being a philanthropist; **Men|schen|freund|lich|keit** F philanthropy, benevolence; **aus reiner ~** out of the sheer goodness of one's heart; **Men|schen|füh|rung** F leadership; **Men|schen|ge|den|ken** NT **der kälteste Winter seit ~** the coldest winter in living memory; **hier hat sich seit ~ nichts geändert** nothing has changed here from time immemorial; **Men|schen|ge|stalt** F human form; **ein Teufel** *or* **Satan in ~** a devil in disguise; **Men|schen|ge|wühl** NT milling crowd; **Men|schen|hai** M man-eating shark, man-eater; **Men|schen|hand** F human hand; **von ~ geschaffen** fashioned by the hand of man; **das liegt nicht in ~** that is beyond man's control; **Men|schen|han|del** M slave trade; (*Jur*) trafficking (in human beings); **Men|schen|händ|ler(in)** M(F) slave-trader; (*Jur*) trafficker (in human beings); **Men|schen|hass** M misanthropy, hatred of people; **Men|schen|has|ser** [-hasɐ] M -s, -, **Men|schen|has|se|rin** [-ərɪn] F -, -nen misanthropist; **Men|schen|jagd** F manhunts *pl*, manhunting; **eine ~** a manhunt; **Men|schen|jä|ger(in)** M(F) manhunter; **Men|schen|ken|ner(in)** M(F) judge of character, connoisseur of human nature; **Men|schen|kennt|nis** F, *no pl* knowledge of human nature; **~ haben** to know human nature; **Men|schen|ket|te** F human chain; **Men|schen|kind** NT creature, soul; **Men|schen|kun|de** F anthropology; **Men|schen|le|ben** NT human life; **ein ~ lang** a whole lifetime; **~ beklagen** to report fatalities; **~ waren nicht zu beklagen** there was no loss of life, no fatalities were reported; **Verluste an ~** loss of human life; **das Unglück hat zwei ~ gefordert** the accident claimed two lives; **men|schen|leer** ADJ deserted; **Men|schen|lie|be** F **a** (*Bibl*) human love **b** (= *Nächstenliebe*) love of mankind *or* humanity, philanthropy; **aus reiner ~** from the sheer goodness of one's heart; **tätige ~** concrete humanitarianism, active philanthropy; **Men|schen|mas|se** F crowd *or* mass (of people); **Men|schen|ma|te|ri|al** NT manpower; **Men|schen|men|ge** F crowd (of people); **men|schen|mög|lich** ADJ humanly possible; **das Menschenmögliche tun** to do all that is humanly possible; **Men|schen|op|fer** NT **a** human sacrifice **b** (= *Menschenleben*) **es waren ~ zu beklagen** there were (some) fatalities; **Men|schen|raub** M (*Jur*) kidnapping; **Men|schen|räu|ber(in)** M(F) (*Jur*) kidnapper

Men|schen|recht NT human right; **die Allgemeine Erklärung** *or* **Deklaration der ~e** the Universal Declaration of Human Rights

Men|schen|rechts-: **Men|schen|rechts|kom|mis|si|on** F Commission on Human Rights; **Men|schen|rechts|kon|ven|ti|on** F Human Rights Convention; **Men|schen|rechts|or|ga|ni|sa|ti|on** F human rights organization; **Men|schen|rechts|ver|let|zung** F violation of human rights

Men|schen-: **men|schen|scheu** ADJ afraid of people; **Men|schen|scheu** F fear of people; **krankhafte ~** anthropophobia (*spec*); **Men|schen|schin|der(in)** M(F) slave-driver; **Men|schen|schlag** M (*inf*) kind of people, breed (*inf*); **Men|schen|schlan|ge** F queue (of people) (*Brit*), line (of people) (*US*); **Men|schen|see|le** F human soul; **keine ~** (*fig*) not a (living) soul

Men|schens|kind INTERJ good heavens, heavens above

Men|schen-: **Men|schen|sohn** M *(Bibl)* Son of Man; **Men|schen|strom** M stream *or* flood of people; **Men|schen|trau|be** F cluster of people; **men|schen|un|mög|lich** ADJ absolutely impossible; **das Menschenunmögliche versuchen/vollbringen** to attempt/achieve the impossible; **men|schen|un|wür|dig** ADJ beneath human dignity; *Behandlung* inhumane; *Behausung* unfit for human habitation ADV *behandeln* inhumanely; *hausen, unterbringen* under inhuman conditions; **men|schen|ver|ach|tend** ADJ inhuman ADV inhumanely; **Men|schen|ver|äch|ter(in)** M(F) despiser of mankind *or* humanity; **Men|schen|ver|ach|tung** F contempt for mankind *or* humanity; **Men|schen|ver|stand** M human understanding *no art*; **gesunder ~** common sense; **Men|schen|ver|such** M human experiment; **Men|schen|werk** NT *(old, liter)* work of man *or* humans *(esp US)*; **alles ~ ist vergänglich** all works of men *or* humans *(esp US)* are transient; **Men|schen|wür|de** F human dignity *no art*; **men|schen|wür|dig** ADJ *Behandlung* humane; *Leben, Tod* dignified; *Lebensbedingungen* fit for human beings; *Unterkunft* fit for human habitation; **~e Entlohnung** decent living wage ADV *behandeln* humanely; *unterbringen, wohnen* in decent conditions; **~ leben** to live in conditions fit for human beings

Men|sche|wik [mɛnʃe'vɪk] M **-en, -en** *or* **-i** [-ki], **Men|sche|wi|kin** [-'vɪkɪn] F **-, -nen** *(Hist)* Menshevik

Men|sche|wis|mus [mɛnʃe'vɪsmʊs] M **-,** *no pl* *(Hist)* Menshevism

Mensch|heit F **-,** *no pl* **die ~** mankind, humanity; **zum Wohle der ~** for the benefit of mankind *or* humanity; **eine Geißel der ~** the scourge of humanity; **Verdienste um die ~** services to humanity; **Verdienste im Namen der ~** services in the name of humanity; **Verbrechen gegen die** *or* **an der ~** crimes against humanity

Mensch|heits-: **Mensch|heits|ent|wick|lung** F development of mankind *or* humanity; **Mensch|heits|ge|schich|te** F history of the human race *or* of mankind

mensch|lich ['mɛnʃlɪç] ADJ **a** human; **das ~e Leben** human life; **der ~e Körper/Geist** the human body/mind; **die ~e Gesellschaft** the society of man; **die ~e Gemeinschaft** the human community; **jede ~e Hilfe kam zu spät für sie** she was beyond human help **b** *(inf: = zivilisiert)* human **c** *(= human) Behandlung etc* humane; **eine ~e Seite haben** to have a human side to one ADV **a** *(= human)* humanely **b** *(inf: = zivilisiert)* decently; **(einigermaßen) ~ aussehen** *(inf)* to look more or less human; **sich wieder ~ fühlen** to feel more human (again) **c** *(= als Mensch)* personally, as a person; **sie ist mir ~ sympathisch** I like her as a person

Mensch|lich|keit F **-,** *no pl* humanity *no art*; **aus reiner ~** on purely humanitarian grounds; **Verbrechen gegen die ~** crimes against humanity

Mensch|wer|dung [-veːdʊŋ] F **-,** *no pl* **a** *(Bibl)* incarnation **b** *(Biol)* anthropogenesis

Men|ses ['mɛnzeːs] PL *(geh euph: = Menstruation)* menstruation

Menst|ru|a|ti|on [mɛnstrua'tsioːn] F **-, -en** menstruation

Menst|ru|a|ti|ons|be|schwer|den PL *(= Schmerzen)* period pains *pl*; *(= Spannung etc)* premenstrual tension *or* syndrome

menst|ru|ie|ren [mɛnstru'iːrən] *ptp* **menstruiert** VI to menstruate

Men|sur [mɛn'zuːɐ] F **-, -en** *(Univ)* (students') fencing bout; **eine ~ schlagen** *or* **fechten** to fight a duel

men|tal [mɛn'taːl] ADJ *Einstellung, Reaktion* mental; **~es Training** mental training, mind training ADV mentally; **körperlich und ~** physically and mentally

Men|ta|li|tät [mɛntali'tɛːt] F **-, -en** mentality

Men|thol [mɛn'toːl] NT **-s, -e** menthol

Men|tor ['mɛntoːɐ] M **-s, Mentoren** [-'toːrən], **Men|to|rin** [-'toːrɪn] F **-, -nen** **a** *(dated, geh)* mentor **b** *(Sch)* ≈ tutor

Me|nü [me'nyː] NT **-s, -s** **a** *(= Tagesmenü)* set meal *or* menu, table d'hôte *(form)*; **~ essen** to have one of the set meals, to have the set menu; **~ des Tages** (set) meal of the day *(Brit)*, (daily) special **b** *(Comput)* menu

Me|nü- *in cpds (Comput)* menu; **Me|nü|be|fehl** M menu command *or* item *or* point; **Me|nü|ein|trag** M menu item

Me|nu|ett [me'nuɛt] NT **-s, -e** *(Tanz, Kunstmusik)* minuet

Me|nü- *(Comput)*: **Me|nü|füh|rung** F menu-driven operation; **me|nü|ge|steu|ert** [-gəʃtɔyɐt] ADJ menu-driven; **Me|nü|leis|te** F menu bar; **Me|nü|op|ti|on** F menu option; **Me|nü|steu|e|rung** F menu-driven operation; **Me|nü|zei|le** F menu line

me|phis|to|phe|lisch [mefɪsto'feːlɪʃ] *(liter)* ADJ Mephistophelian ADV *lachen, grinsen* devilishly

Mer|chan|di|sing ['mœrtʃəndaizɪŋ] NT **-s,** *no pl* merchandising

Mer|gel ['mɛrgl] M **-s, -** *(Geol)* marl

Mer|gel|bo|den M *(Geol)* marly *or* marlacious *(spec)* soil

mer|ge|lig ['mɛrgəlɪç], **merg|lig** ['mɛrglɪç] ADJ marly, marlacious *(spec)*

Me|ri|di|an [meri'diaːn] M **-s, -e** *(Astron, Geog)* meridian

Me|ri|di|an|kreis M *(Astron)* meridian circle

Me|rin|ge [me'rɪŋə] F **-, -n, Me|rin|gel** [me'rɪŋl] NT **-s, -, Me|ringue** [me'rɛ̃ːk] F **-, -s** *(Sw)* meringue

Me|ri|no [me'riːno] M **-s, -s, Me|ri|no|schaf** NT merino (sheep)

Me|ri|no|wol|le F merino wool

Me|ri|ten [me'riːtn] PL *(geh)* merits *pl*; **sich** *(dat)* **~ um etw erwerben** to receive plaudits for sth; **auf seinen alten ~ ruhen** to rest on one's laurels, to rest on one's past merits

mer|kan|til [mɛrkan'tiːl] ADJ *(Hist, geh)* mercantile

Mer|kan|ti|lis|mus [mɛrkanti'lɪsmʊs] M **-,** *no pl* *(Hist)* mercantilism

mer|kan|ti|lis|tisch [mɛrkanti'lɪstɪʃ] ADJ *(Hist)* mercantilist(ic)

Merk-: **merk|bar** ADJ **a** *(= wahrnehmbar)* noticeable **b** *(= im Gedächtnis zu behalten)* retainable; **leicht/schwer ~** easy/difficult to remember *or* retain ADV noticeably; **Merk|blatt** NT leaflet; *(mit Anweisungen auch)* instructions *pl*; **Merk|buch** NT notebook

mer|ken ['mɛrkn] VT **a** *(= wahrnehmen, entdecken)* to notice; *(= spüren)* to feel; *(= erkennen)* to realize; **ich merke nichts!** I can't feel anything!; **davon habe ich nichts gemerkt** I didn't notice anything; **das kann man leicht ~** that's easy to see; **jdn etw ~ lassen** to make sb feel sth; **seine Gefühle ~ lassen** to let one's feelings show; **hat er dich etwas ~ lassen?** did you notice anything in the way he behaved?; **woran hast du das gemerkt?** how could you tell that?; **wie soll ich das ~?** how am I supposed to tell (that)?; **du merkst auch alles!** *(iro)* nothing escapes you, does it?, you ARE observant(, aren't you?); **das merkt jeder/keiner!** everyone/no-one will notice!; **das ist kaum zu ~, davon merkt man kaum etwas** it's hardly noticeable; **das ist zu ~** you can tell; **ich merke keinen Unterschied** I can't tell the difference; *(weil es keinen gibt)* I can't see a difference **b** *(= im Gedächtnis behalten)* to remember, to retain; **merke: …** NB *or* note: …; **sich** *(dat)* **jdn/etw ~** to remember sb/sth; **sich** *(dat)* **eine Autonummer ~** to make a (mental) note of a licence *(Brit)* *or* license *(US)* *or* registration number; **das werde ich mir ~!, ich werds mir ~!** *(inf)* I'll remember that, I won't forget that; **das hat er sich gemerkt** he's taken it to heart; **merk dir das!** mark my words! **c** *(= im Auge behalten)* **sich** *(dat)* **etw ~** to remember sth, to make a note of sth; **~ Sie sich** *(dat)* **den Mann!** keep an eye on that man; **diesen Schriftsteller wird man sich** *(dat)* **~ müssen** this author is someone to take note of

Merk-: **Merk|fä|hig|keit** F memory capacity; **Merk|heft** NT notebook; **Merk|hil|fe** F mnemonic (aid)

merk|lich ['mɛrklɪç] ADJ noticeable, marked, distinct; **kein ~er Unterschied** no noticeable difference ADV noticeably; **kaum ~** almost imperceptibly

Merk|mal ['mɛrkmaːl] NT **-s, -e** characteristic, feature; *(Biol, Zool)* distinctive mark *or* marking; **„besondere ~e …"** "distinguishing marks …"

Merk- *(Sch)*: **Merk|satz** M mnemonic (sentence); **Merk|spruch** M mnemonic *(form)*, memory aid

Mer|kur [mɛr'kuːɐ] M **-s,** *no pl* *(Myth, Astron)* Mercury; *(obs: = Quecksilber)* quicksilver, mercury

Merk-: **Merk|vers** M *(Sch)* jingle, mnemonic (rhyme) *(form)*; **Merk|wort** NT *(Theat)* cue; **merk|wür|dig** ['mɛrkvʏrdɪç] ADJ strange, odd, curious ADV strangely, oddly; **~ riechen** to have a strange smell; **er hat sich ganz ~ verändert** he has undergone a curious change; **merk|wür|di|ger|wei|se** ['mɛrkvʏrdɪgɐ'vaizə] ADV strangely *or* oddly *or* curiously enough; **Merk|wür|dig|keit** F **-, -en** **a** *no pl (= Seltsamkeit)* strangeness, oddness **b** *(= Eigentümlichkeit)* peculiarity; **Merk|zet|tel** M (reminder) note

Mer|le ['mɛrlə] F **-, -n** *(dial: Orn)* blackbird

Me|sal|li|ance [meza'liãːs] F **-, -n** *(liter)* misalliance, mésalliance *(liter)*

me|schug|ge [me'ʃʊgə] ADJ *(inf)* nuts *(inf)*, barmy *(Brit inf)*

Mes|ka|lin [mɛska'liːn] NT **-s,** *no pl* mescalin(e)

Mes|me|ris|mus [mɛsmə'rɪsmʊs] M **-,** *no pl* mesmerism

Mes|ner ['mɛsnɐ] M **-s, -, Mes|ne|rin** [-ərɪn] F **-, -nen** *(dial)* verger, sexton

Me|so|karp [mezo'karp] NT **-s, -e** *(Bot)* mesocarp

Me|so|li|thi|kum [mezo'liːtikʊm] NT **-s,** *no pl* *(Geol)* Mesolithic period

me|so|li|thisch [mezo'liːtɪʃ] ADJ *(Geol)* Mesolithic

Me|son ['meːzɔn] NT **-s, -en** [-'zoːnən] *(Phys)* meson, mesotron

Me|so|po|ta|mi|en [mezopo'taːmiən] NT **-s** Mesopotamia

Me|so|po|ta|mi|er [mezopo'taːmiɐ] M **-s, -, Me|so|po|ta|mi|e|rin** [-iərɪn] F **-, -nen** Mesopotamian

me|so|po|ta|misch [mezopo'taːmɪʃ] ADJ Mesopotamian

Me|so|ze|pha|le(r) [mezotse'faːlə] MF *decl as adj* mesocephalic

Me|so|zo|i|kum [mezo'tsoːikʊm] NT **-s,** *no pl* *(Geol)* Mesozoic

Mess-: **Mess|band** [-bant] NT *pl* **-bänder** tape measure; **mess|bar** ADJ measurable ADV measurably; **er hat ~ an Zustimmung verloren** he has lost a measurable amount of support; **Mess|be|cher** M *(Cook)* measuring jug; **Mess|be|reich** M measuring range; **Mess|buch** NT *(Eccl)* missal, Mass book; **Mess|da|ten** PL readings *pl*; **Mess|die|ner(in)** M(F) *(Eccl)* server, acolyte *(form)*

Mes|se ['mɛsə] F **-, -n** *(Eccl, Mus)* mass; **in die** *or* **zur ~ gehen** to go to mass; **die ~ lesen** *or* **halten** to say mass; **für jdn eine ~ lesen lassen** to have a mass said for sb; **die Hohe ~** High Mass

Mes|se F **-, -n** (trade) fair; **auf der ~** at the fair

Mes|se F **-, -n** *(Naut, Mil)* mess

Mes|se- *in cpds* fair; **Mes|se|an|ge|bot** NT exhibits *pl* (at a/the fair), fair exhibits *pl*; **Mes|se|gast** M visitor to a/the fair, fair visitor; **Mes|se|ge|län|de** NT exhibition centre *(Brit)* *or* center *(US)*; **Mes|se|hal|le** F fair pavilion

mes|sen ['mɛsn] *pret* **maß** [maːs], *ptp* **gemessen** [gə'mɛsn] VT to measure; *(Tech: = anzeigen* *auch)* to gauge; *Verlauf* to time; *(= abschätzen) Entfernung etc* to judge, to gauge; **jds Blutdruck/Temperatur ~** *(Arzt)* to take sb's blood pressure/temperature; *(Instrument)* to measure sb's blood pressure/temperature; **während ich lief, maß er die Zeit** I ran and he timed me *or* he took the time; **er misst 1,90 m** he is 1.90 m tall; **seine Kräfte/Fähigkeiten mit jdm ~** to match one's strength/skills against sb's, to try *or* measure one's strength/skills with sb; **seine Kräfte/Fähigkeiten an etw** *(dat)* **~** to test one's strength/skills on sth; **etw an etw** *(dat)* **~** *(= ausprobieren)* to try sth out on sth; *(= vergleichen)* to compare sth with sth; **jdn mit den Blicken ~** *(geh)* to look sb up and down → *auch* **gemessen**

VI to measure

VR **a sich mit jdm ~** *(geh: im Wettkampf)* to compete with sb; *(in geistigem Wettstreit)* to pit oneself against sb

b sich mit jdm/etw nicht ~ können to be no match for sb/sth

Mes|se|neu|heit F new product *(shown at a trade fair)*

Mes|ser ['mɛsɐ] NT **-s, -** knife; *(Tech auch)* cutter, blade; *(= Rasiermesser)* (cut-throat) razor; **jdm ein ~ in den Leib stoßen, jdm ein ~ in den Bauch jagen** *(inf)* to stick a knife into sb; **unters ~ kommen** *(Med inf)* to go under the knife; **jdn unters ~ nehmen** *(Med inf)* to put sb under the knife; **jdm das ~ an die Kehle setzen** *(lit, fig)* to hold a knife to sb's throat; **die ~ wetzen** *(fig)* to get ready *or* to prepare for the kill; **damit würden wir ihn ans ~ liefern** *(fig)* that would be putting his head on the block; **jdn der Mafia ans ~ liefern** to shop sb to the Mafia *(Brit inf)*, to rat on sb to the Mafia *(sl)*; **ins (offene) ~ laufen** to walk straight into the trap; **ein Kampf/sich bekämpfen bis aufs ~** *(fig)* a fight/to fight to the finish; **ihm ging das ~ in der Tasche auf** *(inf)* he lost the place; **auf des ~s Schneide stehen** *(fig)* to be *or* hang (very much) in the balance, to be on a razor-edge *or* razor's edge; **es steht auf des ~s Schneide, ob ...** it's touch and go whether ..., it's very much in the balance whether ...; **es wird eine Nacht der langen ~ geben** *(fig)* heads will roll → **locker**

Mes|ser- *in cpds* knife; **Mes|ser|block** M *pl* **-blöcke** knife block *or* holder; **Mes|ser|griff** M, **Mes|ser|heft** NT knife handle; **Mes|ser|held(in)** M(F) *(inf)* knifer *(inf)*; **Mes|ser|rü|cken** M back of a/the knife; **mes|ser|scharf** ADJ *(lit, fig)* razor-sharp; *Folgerung* clear-cut ADV *argumentieren* shrewdly; **~ schließen** *(iro)* to conclude shrewdly *(iro)*; **Mes|ser|schmied(in)** M(F) cutler; **Mes|ser|schnei|de** F knife edge; **Mes|ser|spit|ze** F knife point; **eine ~ (voll)** *(Cook)* a pinch; **Mes|ser|ste|cher** [-ʃtɛçɐ] M **-s, -**, **Mes|ser|ste|che|rin** [-ərɪn] F **-, -nen** knifer *(inf)*; **Mes|ser|ste|che|rei** [-ʃtɛçə'rai] F **-, -en** knife fight; **in eine** *or* **zur ~ ausarten** to end up in a knife fight; **Mes|ser|stich** M knife thrust; *(Wunde)* stab wound; **Mes|ser|wer|fer(in)** M(F) knife-thrower

Mes|se-: **Mes|se|stadt** F (town with an) exhibition centre *(Brit)* or center *(US)*; **Mes|se|stand** M stand (at the/a fair)

Mess-: **Mess|füh|ler** M probe, detector; *(Met)* gauge; **Mess|ge|rät** NT **a** *(für Öl, Druck etc)* measuring instrument, gauge **b** *(Eccl)* Mass requisites *pl*; **Mess|ge|wand** NT chasuble; **Mess|glas** NT graduated measure

mes|si|a|nisch [mɛ'siaːnɪʃ] ADJ *(Rel, Philos)* Messianic

Mes|si|as [mɛ'siːas] M **-, -se** *(Rel, fig)* Messiah

Mes|sie ['mɛsi] M **-s, -s** *(inf: = krankhaft unordentlicher Mensch)* messy person

Mes|sing ['mɛsɪŋ] NT **-s**, *no pl* brass; **mit ~ beschlagen** brass-bound

Mes|sing- *in cpds* brass; **Mes|sing|blech** NT sheet brass; **Mes|sing|schild** NT brass plate

Mess-: **Mess|in|stru|ment** NT gauge; **Mess|lat|te** F measuring stick; *(fig: = Maßstab)* threshold; **die ~ hochlegen** *(fig)* to set a high standard

Mess|ner ['mɛsnɐ] M **-s, -**, **Mess|ne|rin** [-ərɪn] F **-, -nen** *(dial)* verger, sexton

Mess-: **Mess|op|fer** NT *(Eccl)* Sacrifice of the Mass; **Mess|ord|nung** F *(Eccl)* ordinary (of the Mass); **Mess|plat|te** F *(Surv)* surveyor's staff *or* rod; **Mess|stab** M **a** *(Surv)* surveyor's staff **b** *(Aut: = Ölmessstab etc)* dipstick; **Mess|sta|ti|on** F survey (control) station; **Mess|tech|nik** F measurement technology, metrology; **Mess|tisch** M *(Surv)* surveyor's table; **Mess|tisch|blatt** NT ordnance survey map; **Mess|uhr** F *(Tech)* meter, gauge

Mes|sung ['mɛsʊŋ] F **-, -en a** *(= das Messen)* measuring; *(= das Ablesen)* reading; *(von Blutdruck)* taking; *(Tech: = das Anzeigen)* gauging **b** *(= Messergebnis)* measurement; *(= Ableseergebnis)* reading

Mess-: **Mess|wein** M *(Eccl)* Communion wine; **Mess|wert** M measurement; *(= Ableseergebnis)* reading; **Mess|zahl** F measurement; **Mess|zy|lin|der** M measuring cylinder, graduated measure

Mes|ti|ze [mɛs'tiːtsə] M **-n, -n** mestizo

Mes|ti|zin [mɛs'tiːtsɪn] F **-, -nen** mestiza

MESZ *abbr von* **mitteleuropäische Sommerzeit**

Met [meːt] M **-(e)s**, *no pl* mead

Me|ta|bo|lis|mus [metabo'lɪsmʊs] M **-, Metabolismen** *(Physiol)* metabolism

Me|tall [me'tal] NT **-s, -e a** metal; **~ verarbeitend** *(Industrie, Unternehmen)* metal-processing *attr*, metal-working *attr* **b** *(geh: der Stimme)* metallic ring, metallic timbre *(Brit)* or timber *(US)*

Me|tall- *in cpds* metal-; **Me|tall|ar|bei|ter(in)** M(F) metalworker; **me|tall|ar|tig** ADJ metallic ADV metallically; **~ aussehen** to look metallic; **sich ~ anfühlen** to feel like metal; **Me|tall|be|ar|bei|tung** F metal processing, metalworking

me|tal|len [me'talən] ADJ metal; *(geh) Klang, Stimme* metallic ADV *glänzen* metallically; **~ klingen** to sound tinny

Me|tal|ler [me'talɐ] M **-s, -**, **Me|tal|le|rin** [-ərɪn] F **-, -nen** *(inf)* metalworker

Me|tall-: **Me|tall|er|mü|dung** F metal fatigue; **Me|tall|geld** NT specie, metallic currency; **me|tall|hal|tig** ADJ metalliferous, metalline

me|tal|lic [me'talɪk] ADJ metallic

Me|tal|lic- *in cpds* metallic; **me|tal|lic|blau** ADJ metallic blue; **Me|tal|lic|lack** M metallic paint

Me|tall|in|dus|trie F, *no pl* metal industry

me|tal|lisch [me'talɪʃ] ADJ *(= aus Metall)* metal; *(fig: = metallartig) Stimme, Klang* metallic ADV metallically; **~ glänzen** to gleam like metal; **~ schmecken** to have a metallic taste; **zu ~ klingen** to sound too tinny

Me|tall-: **Me|tall|kun|de** F metallurgy; **Me|tall|sä|ge** F hacksaw; **Me|tall|stift** M metal pin

Me|tal|lurg [meta'lʊrk] M **-en, -en** [-gn], **Me|tal|lur|ge** [meta'lʊrgə] M **-n, -n**, **Me|tal|lur|gin** [-'lʊrgɪn] F **-, -nen** metallurgist

Me|tal|lur|gie [metalʊr'giː] F **-**, *no pl* metallurgy

me|tal|lur|gisch [meta'lʊrgɪʃ] ADJ metallurgical ADV metallurgically

Me|tall-: **me|tall|ver|ar|bei|tend** ADJ → **Metall a**; **Me|tall|ver|ar|bei|tung** F metal processing; **Me|tall|wa|ren** PL hardware *sing*

Me|ta|mor|pho|se [metamɔr'foːzə] F **-, -n** metamorphosis

Me|ta|pher [me'tafɐ] F **-, -n** *(Liter, Poet)* metaphor

Me|ta|pho|rik [meta'foːrɪk] F **-**, *no pl (Liter, Poet)* imagery

me|ta|pho|risch [meta'foːrɪʃ] *(Liter, Poet)* ADJ metaphoric(al) ADV metaphorically; **ein ~ reicher Text** a text full of metaphors; **ein ~ überladener Roman** a novel with too many metaphors

Me|ta|phy|sik [meta-] F metaphysics *sing*

me|ta|phy|sisch ADJ metaphysical

Me|ta|psy|cho|lo|gie F metapsychology

Me|ta|spra|che F metalanguage

Me|ta|sta|se [meta'staːzə] F **-, -n** *(Med)* metastasis

Me|ta|the|se [meta'teːzə] F, **Me|ta|the|sis** [me'taːtezɪs] F **-, Metathesen** [-'teːzn] *(Ling)* metathesis

Me|te|or [mete'oːɐ, 'meːteoːɐ] M OR NT **-s, -e** [-'oːrə] meteor

Me|te|or|ei|sen NT meteoric iron

Me|te|o|rit [meteo'riːt] M **-en, -en** meteorite

Me|te|o|ro|lo|ge [meteoro'loːgə] M **-n, -n**, **Me|te|o|ro|lo|gin** [-'loːgɪn] F **-, -nen** meteorologist; *(im Wetterdienst)* weather forecaster, weatherman/-woman *(inf)*

Me|te|o|ro|lo|gie [meteorolo'giː] F **-**, *no pl* meteorology

me|te|o|ro|lo|gisch [meteoro'loːgɪʃ] ADJ meteorological ADV meteorologically; **sich ~ auswirken** to have a meteorological effect

Me|te|or|stein M meteorite

Me|ter ['meːtɐ] M OR NT **-s, - a** metre *(Brit)*, meter *(US)*; **in einer Entfernung von 40 ~(n)** at a distance of 40 metres *(Brit)* or meters *(US)*; **in/auf 500 ~(n) Höhe** at a height of 500 metres *(Brit)* or meters *(US)*; **nach ~n** by the metre *(Brit)* or meter *(US)* **b** *(= Meterstab)* metric measure **c** *(inf)* = **Metermaß**

Me|ter-: **me|ter|dick** ADJ metres *(Brit)* or meters *(US)* thick ADV **Schlammmassen bedeckten die Straßen ~** layers of mud several metres *(Brit)* or meters *(US)* thick covered the streets; **der Betonbelag war ~ aufgetragen** the cement covering was several metres *(Brit)* or meters *(US)* thick; **er hat seine Botschaft ~ aufgetragen** *(pej)* he laid it on too thick *(inf)*; **me|ter|hoch** ADJ *Wellen, Mauer, Pflanze* metres *(Brit)* or meters *(US)* high; *Schnee* metres *(Brit)* or meters *(US)* deep ADV **das Grundstück war ~ eingezäunt** the estate was bordered by a very high fence; **der Schnee lag ~** the snow was very deep; **die Akten türmten sich ~ auf seinem Schreibtisch** the files were piled three feet high on his desk; **me|ter|lang** ADJ metres *(Brit)* or meters *(US)* long; **~e Lochstreifen** yards and yards of punch tape; **Me|ter|maß** NT **a** *(= Bandmaß)* tape measure, measuring tape **b** *(= Stab)* (metre *(Brit)* or meter *(US)*) rule; **Me|ter|wa|re** F *(Tex)* piece goods; **me|ter|wei|se** ADV by the metre *(Brit)* or meter *(US)*; **me|ter|weit** ADJ *(breit)* metres *(Brit)* or meters *(US)* wide; *(lang)* metres *(Brit)* or meters *(US)* long ADV for yards; **er schoss ~ vorbei** his shot was yards *or* miles *(inf)* off target

Me|tha|don [meta'doːn] NT **-s**, *no pl* methadone

Me|than [me'taːn] NT **-s**, *no pl*, **Me|than|gas** NT methane

Me|tha|nol [meta'noːl] NT **-s**, *no pl* methyl *or* wood alcohol

Me|tho|de [me'toːdə] ✪ 39.2 F **-, -n a** method; **etw mit ~ machen** to do sth methodically *or* systematically; **das hat ~** *(inf)* there's (a) method behind it; **er hat ~ in den Laden gebracht** *(inf)* he knocked things into shape; **er hat (so) seine ~n** *(inf)* he's got his methods **b Methoden** PL *(= Sitten)* behaviour *(Brit)*, behavior *(US)*; **was sind denn das für ~n?** what sort of way is that to behave?

Me|tho|den|leh|re F methodology

Me|tho|dik [me'toːdɪk] F **-, -en** methodology

Me|tho|di|ker [me'toːdikɐ] M **-s, -**, **Me|tho|di|ke|rin** [-ərɪn] F **-, -nen** methodologist

me|tho|disch [me'toːdɪʃ] ADJ methodical ADV methodically

Me|tho|dist [meto'dɪst] M **-en, -en**, **Me|tho|dis|tin** [-'dɪstɪn] F **-, -nen** Methodist

me|tho|dis|tisch [meto'dɪstɪʃ] ADJ Methodist

Me|tho|do|lo|gie [metodolo'giː] F **-, -n** [-'giːən] methodology

me|tho|do|lo|gisch [metodo'loːgɪʃ] ADJ methodological

Me|thu|sa|lem [me'tu:zalɛm] M **-s** Methuselah; **alt wie ~** as old as Methuselah

Me|thyl|al|ko|hol [me'ty:l-] M methyl *or* wood alcohol

Me|ti|er [me'tie:] NT **-s, -s** job, profession; **sich auf sein ~ verstehen** to be good at one's job

Me|to|ny|mie [metony'mi:] F **-, -n** [-'mi:ən] *(Liter)* metonymy

me|to|ny|misch [meto'ny:mɪʃ] ADJ *(Liter)* metonymical

Met|rik ['me:trɪk] F **-, -en** *(Poet, Mus)* metrics *sing*

met|risch ['me:trɪʃ] ADJ *(Sci) Maß* metric; *(Poet, Mus auch)* metrical ADV metrically, in metres *(Brit) or* meters *(US)*

Met|ro ['me:tro, 'mɛtro] F **-, -s** metro

Met|ro|nom [metro'no:m] NT **-s, -e** *(Mus)* metronome

Met|ro|po|le [metro'po:lə] F **-, -n** **a** *(= größte Stadt)* metropolis **b** *(= Zentrum)* capital, centre *(Brit)*, center *(US)* **c** *(Pol: = Mutterland)* home country

Met|ro|po|lit [metropo'li:t] M **-en, -en** metropolitan

Met|rum ['me:trum] NT **-s, Metren** ['me:trən] metre *(Brit)*, meter *(US)*

Mett [mɛt] NT **-(e)s,** *no pl (Cook)* (lean) minced *(Brit) or* ground *(US)* pork/beef

Met|ta|ge [mɛ'ta:ʒə] F **-, -n** *(Typ)* make-up; *(Arbeitsort)* make-up room

Met|te ['mɛtə] F **-, -n** *(Eccl)* matins *sing*; *(= Abendmette)* vespers *sing*

Met|teur [mɛ'tø:ɐ] M **-s, -e, Met|teu|rin** [-'tø:rɪn] F **-, -nen** *(Typ)* make-up man/woman

Mett|wurst F (smoked) pork/beef sausage

Met|ze ['mɛtsə] F **-, -n** *(obs: = Hure)* strumpet *(old)*

Met|ze|lei [mɛtsə'lai] F **-, -en** butchery, slaughter

met|zeln ['mɛtsln] VT to slaughter, to butcher; *(S Ger: = schlachten)* to slaughter

Met|zel|sup|pe ['mɛtsl-] F *(S Ger)* meat broth

Metz|ger ['mɛtsgɐ] M **-s, -, Metz|ge|rin** [-ərɪn] F **-, -nen** butcher

Metz|ger- *in cpds* → **Fleischer-**

Metz|ge|rei [mɛtsgə'rai] F **-, -en** butcher's (shop)

Meu|chel-: **Meu|chel|mord** M (treacherous) murder; **Meu|chel|mör|der(in)** M(F) (treacherous) assassin

meu|cheln ['mɔyçln] VT *(old)* to assassinate

meuch|le|risch ['mɔyçlərɪʃ] ADJ *(old)* murderous; *Mörder* treacherous

meuch|lings ['mɔyçlɪŋs] ADV treacherously

Meu|te ['mɔytə] F **-, -n** pack (of hounds); *(fig pej)* mob; **die ~ loslassen** *or* **loskoppeln** to release the hounds

Meu|te|rei [mɔytə'rai] F **-, -en** mutiny; *(fig auch)* rebellion

meu|tern ['mɔyten] VI to mutiny; *(inf auch)* to rebel; *(dial inf: = meckern)* to moan, to grouch *(inf)*; **die ~den Soldaten** the mutinous soldiers

Me|xi|ka|ner [mɛksi'ka:nɐ] M **-s, -, Me|xi|ka|ne|rin** [-ərɪn] F **-, -nen** Mexican

me|xi|ka|nisch [mɛksi'ka:nɪʃ] ADJ Mexican

Me|xi|ko ['mɛksiko] NT **-s** Mexico; **~ City, ~-Stadt** Mexico City

MEZ *abbr von* **mitteleuropäische Zeit**

Mez|za|nin [mɛtsa'ni:n] M OR NT **-s, -e** *(Archit)* mezzanine; *(unter dem Dach)* attic

Mez|za|nin|woh|nung F *(Aus)* mezzanine flat *(Brit) or* apartment

mez|zo|for|te ['mɛtso-] ADJ *(Mus)* mezzo forte

mez|zo|pi|a|no ['mɛtso-] ADJ *(Mus)* mezzo piano

Mez|zo|sop|ran ['mɛtso-] M mezzo-soprano

mg *abbr von* **Milligramm** mg

MG [ɛm'ge:] NT **-(s), -(s)** *abbr von* **Maschinengewehr**

mhd *abbr von* **mittelhochdeutsch**

MHz *abbr von* **Megahertz**

mi|au [mi'au] INTERJ miaow *(Brit)*, meow

mi|au|en [mi'auən] *ptp* **miaut** VI to miaow *(Brit)*, to meow

mich [mɪç] PERS PRON *acc von* **ich** me REFL PRON myself; **ich fühle ~ wohl** I feel fine

Mi|cha|el ['mɪçae:l, 'mɪçaɛl] M **-s** Michael

Mi|cha|e|li(s) [mɪça'e:li, mɪça'e:lɪs] NT **-,** *no pl* Michaelmas

Mi|chel ['mɪçl] M **-s** Mike, Mick; **der deutsche ~** *(fig)* the plain honest German

Mi|chi|gan|see ['mɪʃɪgən-] M Lake Michigan

mi|cke|rig ['mɪkərɪç], **mick|rig** ['mɪkrɪç] *(inf)* ADJ pathetic; *Betrag auch* paltry; *altes Männchen* puny ADV pathetically

Mi|cky|maus ['mɪki-] F Mickey Mouse

Mic|ro|blog ['mi:kroblɔg, 'maikroblɔg] NT OR M *(Internet)* microblog

mi|di ['mɪdi] ADJ *pred (Fashion)* midi; **Midi tragen** to wear midi *or* mid-length skirts/dresses

Mi|di- ['mɪdi] *in cpds* midi; **Mi|di-An|la|ge** F, **Mi|di-Sys|tem** NT midi (system)

mied *pret von* **meiden**

Mie|der ['mi:dɐ] NT **-s, -** **a** *(= Leibchen)* bodice **b** *(= Korsage)* girdle

Mie|der-: **Mie|der|hös|chen** [-hø:sçən] NT panty girdle; **Mie|der|wa|ren** PL corsetry *sing*

Mief [mi:f] M **-s,** *no pl (inf)* fug; *(muffig)* stale air; *(= Gestank)* stink, pong *(Brit inf)*; **der ~ der Provinz/des Kleinbürgertums** *(fig)* the oppressive claustrophobic atmosphere of the provinces/petty bourgeoisie

mie|fen ['mi:fn] VI *(inf)* to stink, to pong *(Brit inf)*; *(= furzen)* to make a smell; **hier mieft es** there's a pong *(Brit inf) or* smell in here; *(muffig)* the air in here is so stale; **was mieft denn hier so?** what's this awful pong *(Brit inf) or* smell?

Mief|quirl M *(inf, hum)* fan

Mie|ne ['mi:nə] F **-, -n** *(= Gesichtsausdruck)* expression, face, mien *(liter)*; **eine finstere ~ machen** to look grim; **gute ~ zum bösen Spiel machen** to grin and bear it; **~ machen, etw zu tun** to make a move to do sth; **seine ~ verfinsterte** *or* **verdüsterte sich** his face darkened; **sich** *(dat)* **etw mit eisiger ~ anhören** to listen to sth in stony silence → **verziehen VT a**

Mie|nen|spiel NT facial expressions *pl*; **ein lebhaftes ~ haben** to express a lot with one's face

mies [mi:s] *(inf)* ADJ rotten *(inf)*, lousy *(inf)*; *Lokal auch* crummy *(inf)*; *Laune auch* foul; *Qualität* poor; **mir ist ~** I feel lousy *(inf) or* rotten *(inf)* ADV badly; **er hat sich ihr gegenüber ~ verhalten** he was rotten to her *(inf)*; **er hat das ~ übersetzt** his translation was lousy *(inf) or* crummy *(inf)*

Mie|se ['mi:zə] PL *(inf)* **in den ~n sein** *(bei der Bank)* to be in the red; *(beim Kartenspiel)* to be down on points; **in die ~n kommen** *(bei der Bank)* to get into the red; *(beim Kartenspiel)* to get minus points

Mie|se|pe|ter ['mi:zəpe:tɐ] M **-s, -** *(inf)* misery-guts *(Brit inf)*, grouch *(inf)*

mie|se|pe|te|rig ['mi:zəpe:tərɪç], **mie|se|pet|rig** ['mi:zəpe:trɪç] ADJ *(inf)* miserable, grouchy *(inf)*

Mie|se|pet|rig|keit F **-,** *no pl (inf)* grouchiness *(inf)*

mies+machen *sep*, **mies machen** △ VT *(inf)* to run down

Mies|ma|cher(in) M(F) *(inf)* killjoy

Mies|ma|che|rei [mi:smaxə'rai] F **-, -en** *(inf)* belly-aching *(inf)*

Mies|mu|schel F mussel

Miet-: **Miet|aus|fall** M loss of rent; **Miet|au|to** NT hire(d) car; **Miet|bei|hil|fe** F rent allowance *or* subsidy

Mie|te[1] ['mi:tə] F **-, -n** *(für Wohnung)* rent; *(für Gegenstände)* rental; *(für Dienstleistungen)* charge; **rückständige ~** (rent) arrears; **zur ~ wohnen** to live in rented accommodation; **das ist die halbe ~** *(fig inf)* that's half the battle

Mie|te[2] F **-, -n** *(= Kartoffelmiete)* clamp *(Brit)*, pit; *(= Schober)* stack

Miet|ein|nah|me F *usu pl* rental income *sing*

mie|ten ['mi:tn] VT to rent; *Boot, Auto* to rent, to hire *(esp Brit)*

Mie|ter ['mi:tɐ] M **-s, -, Mie|te|rin** [-ərɪn] F **-, -nen** tenant; *(= Untermieter)* lodger

Miet|er|hö|hung F rent increase

Mie|ter-: **Mie|ter|schaft** ['mi:tɐʃaft] F **-, -en** tenants *pl*; **Mie|ter|schutz** M rent control; **Mie|ter|schutz|bund** M tenants' (rights) association; **Mie|ter|schutz|ge|setz** NT Rent Act

Miet-: **Miet|er|trag** M rent(al) (income); **miet|frei** ADJ ADV rent-free; **Miet|ga|ran|tie** F proof of ability to pay rent; **Miet|kauf** M *(Comm)* lease-purchase agreement *(with option to buy at the end of the lease period)*, hire purchase *(Brit)*; **Miet|kau|ti|on** F deposit; **Miet|par|tei** F tenant (and family); **Miet|preis** M rent; *(für Sachen)* rental (fee *or* rate *(US)*), hire charge *(Brit)*; **Miet|recht** NT rent law; **Miet|rück|stän|de** PL rent arrears *pl*; **Miet|schuld** F back rent; **~en** rent arrears *pl*

Miets-: **Miets|haus** NT block of (rented) flats *(Brit)*, apartment house *(US)*; **Miets|ka|ser|ne** F *(pej)* tenement house

Miet-: **Miet|spie|gel** M rent level; **Miet|stei|ge|rung** F rent increase; **Miet|ver|hält|nis** NT tenancy; **Miet|ver|trag** M lease; *(von Auto)* rental agreement; **Miet|wa|gen** M hire(d) car *(Brit)*, rental (car) *(US)*; **Miet|wa|gen|bu|chung** F car hire *(Brit) or* rental *(US)* booking; **Miet|wa|gen|fir|ma** F car hire *(Brit) or* rental *(US)* firm *or* company; **Miet|wert** M letting *or* rental value; **Miet|woh|nung** F rented flat *(Brit) or* apartment; **Miet|wu|cher** M exorbitant rent; **~ ist strafbar** charging exorbitant rent(s) is a punishable offence *(Brit) or* offense *(US)*; **Miet|zah|lung** F payment of the rent; **Miet|zins** M *(S Ger, Aus)* rent

Mie|ze ['mi:tsə] F **-, -n** *(inf)* **a** *(= Katze)* pussy (-cat) *(inf)* **b** *(Mädchen)* chick *(inf)*, bird *(Brit inf)*; *(als Anrede)* baby *(inf)*, honey *(inf)*

Mie|ze-: **Mie|ze|kätz|chen** NT *(baby-talk)* (little) pussy(-cat); **Mie|ze|kat|ze** F *(baby-talk)* pussy(-cat)

MiG [mɪg] F **-s, -s** *(Mil)* MiG

Mig|rä|ne [mi'grɛ:nə] F **-,** *no pl* migraine

Mig|rä|ne|an|fall M attack of migraine

Mi|grant [mi'grant] M **-en, -en, Mi|gran|tin** [mi'grantɪn] F **-, -nen** migrant

Mig|ra|ti|on [migra'tsio:n] F **-, -en** *(Sociol, Comput, Biol)* migration

Mi|ka|do[1] [mi'ka:do] NT **-s, -s** *(= Spiel)* pick-a-stick

Mi|ka|do[2] M **-s, -s** *(old: = Kaiser von Japan)* mikado

Mik|ro ['mi:kro] NT **-s, -s** *(inf) abbr von* **Mikrofon** mike *(inf)*

Mik|ro|be [mi'kro:bə] F **-, -n** microbe

Mik|ro- *in cpds* micro-; **Mik|ro|bio|lo|gie** F microbiology; **Mik|ro|chip** M microchip; **Mik|ro|com|pu|ter** M microcomputer, micro; **Mik|ro|elekt|ro|nik** F microelectronics *sing*; **Mik|ro|fa|ser** F microfibre *(Brit)*, microfiber *(US)*; **Mik|ro|fiche** ['mi:krofi:ʃ] M OR NT **-s, -s** microfiche

Mik|ro|fon [mikro'fo:n, 'mi:krofo:n] NT **-s, -e** microphone

Mik|ro|gramm NT microgram(me)

Mik|ro|kos|mos M microcosm

Mik|ro|me|ter NT micron; *(Gerät)* micrometer

Mik|ron ['mi:krɔn] NT **-s, -** micron

Mik|ro|or|ga|nis|mus M microorganism

Mik|ro|phon [mikro'fo:n, 'mi:krofo:n] NT **-s, -e** microphone

Mik|ro-: **Mik|ro|pil|le** F *(Med)* ≈ mini-pill; **Mik|ro|pro|zes|sor** M microprocessor; **Mik|ro|se|kun|de** F microsecond; **Mik|ro|sen|der** M microtransmitter

Mik|ro|skop [mikro'sko:p] NT **-s, -e** microscope

Mik|ro|sko|pie [mikrosko'pi:] F **-,** *no pl* microscopy

mik|ro|sko|pie|ren [mikrosko'pi:rən] *ptp* **mikroskopiert** VT *(rare)* to examine under *or* with the microscope VI to work with a/the microscope

mik|ro|sko|pisch [mikro'sko:pɪʃ] ADJ microscopic ADV microscopically; **etw ~ untersuchen** to examine sth under the microscope; **~ klein** *(fig)* microscopically small

Mik|ro|struk|tur F microstructure

Mik|ro|wel|le F microwave

Mik|ro|wel|len|herd M microwave (oven)

Mik|ro|zen|sus M sample census

Mik|ro|ze|pha|le(r) [mikrotse'fa:lə] MF *decl as adj* microcephalic

Mi|lan ['mi:lan, mi'la:n] M **-s, -e** *(Orn)* kite

Mil|be ['mɪlbə] F **-, -n** mite

Milch [mɪlç] F **-,** *no pl (alle Bedeutungen)* milk; *(= Fischsamen)* milt, soft roe; **dicke ~** curd(s); **~ geben** *(Kuh)* to yield milk; **das Land, wo ~ und Honig fließt** the land of *or* flowing with milk and honey; **aussehen wie ~ und Blut** to have a peaches-and-cream complexion

Milch- *in cpds* milk; **milch|ar|tig** ADJ milky; **Milch|bar** F milk bar; *(sl: = Busen)* tits *pl (sl)*; **Milch|bart** M *(inf)* downy *or* fluffy beard, bum-fluff *(Brit inf)*, peach fuzz *(US inf)*; *(fig pej: = Jüngling)* milksop; **Milch|brei** M ≈ milk pudding; **Milch|bröt|chen** NT *roll made with milk and sugar*; **Milch|drü|se** F mammary gland; **Milch|eis** NT milk-based ice cream; **Milch|ei|weiß** NT lactoprotein; **Milch|fett** NT milk fat; **Milch|fla|sche** F milk bottle; **Milch|fluss** M *(Med)* galactorrhoea *(Brit)*, galactorrhea *(US)*; **Milch|frau** F *(inf)* dairywoman; **Milch|ge|biss** NT milk teeth *pl*; **Milch|ge|schäft** NT dairy; **Milch|ge|sicht** NT *(inf)* baby-face; **Milch|glas** NT frosted glass; **Milch|han|del** M dairy business; **Milch|händ|ler** M dairyman; **Milch|händ|le|rin** F dairywoman

mil|chig ['mɪlçɪç] ADJ milky ADV **~ trüb** opaque; **~ blau** pale blue; **~ bleich** milk-white

Milch-: **Milch|kaf|fee** M milky coffee; **Milch|kalb** NT sucking calf; **Milch|kan|ne** F milk can; *(größer)* (milk) churn; **Milch|kuh** F milk *or* milch *(spec)* cow; *(fig inf)* milch cow *(Brit inf)*, source of easy income; **Milch|la|den** M dairy; **Milch|mäd|chen** NT *(= Milchverkäuferin)* dairy girl; *(= Milchkassiererin)* milk girl; **Milch|mäd|chen|rech|nung** F *(inf)* naïve fallacy; **Milch|mann** M *pl* **-männer** milkman; **Milch|mix|ge|tränk** NT milk shake

Milch|ner ['mɪlçnɐ] M **-s, -** milter

Milch-: **Milch|pro|dukt** NT milk product; **Milch|pul|ver** NT dried *or* powdered milk; **Milch|pum|pe** F breast pump; **Milch|quo|te** F *(in der EU)* milk quota; **Milch|reis** M round-grain rice; *(als Gericht)* rice pudding; **Milch|saft** M *(Bot)* latex; **Milch|säu|re** F lactic acid; **Milch|scho|ko|la|de** F milk chocolate; **Milch|schorf** M cradle cap; **Milch|see** M *(in der EU)* milk lake; **Milch|spei|se** F milky *or* milk-based food; **Milch|stra|ße** F Milky Way; **Milch|stra|ßen|sys|tem** NT Milky Way system *or* galaxy; **Milch|sup|pe** F **a** ≈ warm blancmange *(Brit)*, milk soup *(US)* **b** *(dated inf: = Nebel)* peasouper *(Brit inf)*, thick fog; **Milch|tü|te** F milk carton; **Milch|vieh** NT dairy cattle *pl*; **Milch|wirt|schaft** F dairy farming; **Milch|zahn** M milk tooth; **Milch|zu|cker** M lactose

mild [mɪlt], **mil|de** ['mɪldə] ADJ **a** *(= sanft, lind) Wetter, Abend* mild; *Luft* gentle, mild **b** *(= nachsichtig, barmherzig) Behandlung, Beurteilung, Strafe, Richter* lenient; *Worte* mild; **eine ~e Gabe** alms *pl* **c** *Käse, Zigaretten* mild; *Seife* gentle, mild; *Speisen* light ADV **a** *(= sanft)* mildly, gently **b** *(= nachsichtig)* leniently; **das Urteil fiel ~/~er aus** the sentence was lenient/more lenient; **jdn ~ stimmen** to put sb in a generous mood; **~e gesagt** *or* **ausgedrückt** to put it mildly **c** *(= nicht stark) gewürzt* mildly; **~ schmecken** to taste mild; **die Seife riecht ~** the soap is mildly scented

Mil|de ['mɪldə] F **-,** *no pl* **a** *(= Sanftheit, Lindheit)* mildness, gentleness **b** *(= Nachsichtigkeit, Barmherzigkeit)* leniency; **~ walten lassen** to be lenient

mil|dern ['mɪldɐn] VT *(geh) Schmerz* to ease, to soothe, to alleviate; *Kälte* to alleviate; *Angst* to calm; *Strafe, Urteil* to moderate, to mitigate; *Gegensätze* to reduce, to make less crass *or* severe; *Schärfe, Konflikt, Problem, Härte, Druck* to reduce; *Ausdrucksweise, Zorn* to moderate; *Sanktionen* to relax; *Folgen* to make less severe; **~de Umstände** *(Jur)* mitigating *or* extenuating circumstances VR *(Wetter)* to become milder; *(Gegensätze)* to become less crass; *(Zorn)* to abate; *(Schmerz)* to ease

Mil|de|rung ['mɪldərʊŋ] F **-,** *no pl (von Schmerz)* easing, soothing, alleviation; *(von Ausdruck, des Klimas)* moderation; *(von Strafe)* moderation, mitigation; **spüren Sie schon eine ~?** can you feel any easing (of the pain)?

Mil|de|rungs|grund M mitigating cause *or* circumstance

Mild-: **mild|her|zig** ADJ *(old)* = **barmherzig**; **mild|tä|tig** ADJ *(geh)* charitable; **er war sein ganzes Leben lang ~** he performed charitable deeds throughout his life; **für ~e Zwecke** for charity; **Mild|tä|tig|keit** F *(geh)* charity

Mi|li|eu [mi'liø:] NT **-s, -s** *(= Umwelt)* environment, milieu; *(= Lokalkolorit)* atmosphere; *(= Verbrechermilieu)* underworld; *(von Prostitution)* world of prostitutes

Mi|li|eu-: **mi|li|eu|ge|schä|digt** [-gəʃɛ:dɪçt], **mi|li|eu|ge|stört** ADJ maladjusted *(due to adverse social factors)*; **Mi|li|eu|scha|den** M effects *pl* of adverse social factors; **Mi|li|eu|schil|de|rung** F background description; **Mi|li|eu|stu|di|en** PL **~ treiben** *(usu hum)* to study the locals *(hum)*; **Mi|li|eu|the|o|rie** F *(Sociol)* environmentalism *no art*; **Mi|li|eu|wech|sel** M change of environment; *(= Abwechslung)* change of scene

mi|li|tant [mili'tant] ADJ militant ADV **~ kommunistisch/antikommunistisch sein** to be a militant communist/anticommunist; **der ~ auftretende Präsident** the militant president

Mi|li|tanz [mili'tants] F **-,** *no pl* militancy

Mi|li|tär [mili'tɛ:ɐ] NT **-s,** *no pl* military, armed forces *pl*; **beim ~ sein** *(inf)* to be in the forces; **zum ~ einberufen werden** to be called up *(Brit)* *or* drafted *(US)*; **zum ~ müssen** *(inf)* to have to join up *(Brit)* *or* join the army; **zum ~ gehen** to join up *(Brit)*, to join the army; **vom ~ entlassen werden** to be discharged from the armed forces; **(gegen jdn) ~ einsetzen** to use the military (against sb); **wir sind doch hier nicht beim ~!** we're not in the army, you know!; **da geht es zu wie beim ~** the place is run like an army *(Brit)* *or* military camp

Mi|li|tär M **-s, -s** (army) officer

Mi|li|tär- *in cpds* military; **Mi|li|tär|aka|de|mie** F military academy; **Mi|li|tär|ak|ti|on** F military action; **Mi|li|tär|arzt** M, **Mi|li|tär|ärz|tin** F army doctor; *(= Offizier)* medical officer; **Mi|li|tär|dienst** M military service; **(seinen) ~ ableisten** to do national service; **Mi|li|tär|dik|ta|tur** F military dictatorship; **Mi|li|tär|ein|satz** M *(= Einsatz von Militär)* deployment of troops; *(= Kampfhandlung)* military action; **Mi|li|tär|geist|li|che(r)** MF *decl as adj* (army) chaplain; **Mi|li|tär|ge|län|de** NT military property; **Mi|li|tär|ge|richt** NT military court, court martial; **Internationales ~** International Military Tribunal; **vor ein ~ gestellt werden** to be tried by a court martial; **wenn Sie das machen, werden Sie vor ein ~ gestellt** if you do that you'll be court-martialled *(Brit)* *or* court-martialed *(US)*; **Mi|li|tär|hil|fe** F military aid

Mi|li|ta|ria [mili'ta:ria] PL things *pl* military

mi|li|tä|risch [mili'tɛ:rɪʃ] ADJ military; **jdm ~e** *or* **die ~en Ehren erweisen** to give sb military honours *(Brit)* *or* honors *(US)*; **mit allen ~en Ehren** with full military honours *(Brit)* *or* honors *(US)*; **einen Konflikt mit ~en Mitteln lösen** to resolve a conflict with the use of troops ADV militarily; **~ grüßen** to salute; **es geht dort streng ~ zu** it's very regimented there; **sich ~ geben** to behave in a military fashion

mi|li|ta|ri|sie|ren [militari'zi:rən] *ptp* **militarisiert** VT to militarize

Mi|li|ta|ris|mus [milita'rɪsmʊs] M **-,** *no pl* militarism

Mi|li|ta|rist [milita'rɪst] M **-en, -en**, **Mi|li|ta|ris|tin** [-'rɪstɪn] F **-, -nen** militarist

mi|li|ta|ris|tisch [milita'rɪstɪʃ] ADJ militaristic

Mi|li|tär-: **Mi|li|tär|macht** F military power; **Mi|li|tär|mu|sik** F military marches *pl*, military music; **Mi|li|tär|pa|ra|de** F military parade; **Mi|li|tär|putsch** M military putsch; **Mi|li|tär|re|gime** NT military regime; **Mi|li|tär|schlag** M military strike *or* action; **Mi|li|tär|seel|sor|ge** F spiritual welfare of the armed forces; **Mi|li|tär|we|sen** NT military affairs *pl*; **Mi|li|tär|wis|sen|schaft** F military science

Mi|li|ta|ry ['mɪlɪtəri] F **-, -s** *(Sport)* three-day event

Mi|li|tär|zeit F army days *pl*, days *pl* as a soldier

Mi|liz [mi'li:ts] F **-, -en** militia; *(in Osteuropa: = Polizei)* police

Mi|li|zi|o|när [militsio'nɛ:ɐ] M **-s, -e**, **Mi|li|zi|o|nä|rin** [-'nɛ:rɪn] F **-, -nen** militiaman/-woman; *(in Osteuropa: = Polizist)* policeman/-woman

Mi|liz|sol|dat M *(old)* militiaman

milkt [mɪlkt] *(old) 3. pers sing pres von* **melken**

Mill. *abbr von* **Million(en)**

mil|le ['mɪlə] **pro ~** = **Promille**

Mil|le ['mɪlə] F **-, -** *(inf)* grand *(inf)*; **5 ~** 5 grand *(inf)*

Mil|len|ni|um [mɪ'lɛniʊm] NT **-s, Millennien** [-niən] *(geh)* millennium

Mil|li|ar|där [mɪliar'dɛ:ɐ] M **-s, -e**, **Mil|li|ar|dä|rin** [-'dɛ:rɪn] F **-, -nen** multi-millionaire, billionaire

Mil|li|ar|de [mɪ'liardə] F **-, -n** thousand millions *(Brit)*, billion *(US)*; **zwei ~n Euro** two thousand million euros *(Brit)*, two billion euros *(US)*; **~n (von) Menschen** thousands of millions of people, billions of people

Mil|li|ar|den-: **Mil|li|ar|den|be|trag** M (amount of) thousands of millions *pl (Brit)*, billions *pl (US)*; **Mil|li|ar|den|de|fi|zit** NT (mulit)billion dollar/euro *etc* deficit; **Mil|li|ar|den|grab** NT *(inf)* expensive white elephant; **dieses neue Projekt ist ein ~** this new project is gobbling up vast amounts of money; **Mil|li|ar|den|hö|he** F **in ~** amounting to a billion/billions; **ein Kredit in ~** a (multi)billion dollar/euro *etc* loan

mil|li|ards|tel [mɪ'liartstl] ADJ thousand millionth *(Brit)*, billionth *(US)*; **ein ~ Meter** a *or* one thousand millionth of a metre *(Brit)*, a *or* one billionth of a meter *(US)*, a *or* one bicron *(US)*

Mil|li|ards|tel [mɪ'liartstl] NT **-s, -** thousand millionth part *(Brit)*, billionth part *(US)*

mil|li|ards|te(r, s) [mɪ'liartstə] ADJ thousand millionth *(Brit)*, billionth *(US)*

Mil|li- *in cpds* milli-; **Mil|li|bar** NT millibar; **Mil|li|gramm** NT milligram(me); **Mil|li|me|ter** M OR NT millimetre *(Brit)*, millimeter *(US)*; **mil|li|me|ter|ge|nau** ADJ *Berechnung, Planung* extremely precise ADV to the millimetre *(Brit)* *or* millimeter *(US)*; **Mil|li|me|ter|pa|pier** NT graph paper

Mil|li|on [mɪ'lio:n] F **-, -en** million; **eine ~ Londoner ist** *or* **sind unterwegs** a million Londoners are on their way; **zwei ~en** two millions; **zwei ~en Einwohner** two million inhabitants; **~en begeisterter Zuschauer** *or* **von begeisterten Zuschauern** millions of enthusiastic viewers; **~en Mal** a million times

Mil|li|o|när [mɪlio'nɛːɐ] M **-s, -e** millionaire; **vom Tellerwäscher zum ~** from rags to riches; **es zum ~ bringen** to make a million

Mil|li|o|nä|rin [mɪlio'nɛːrɪn] F **-, -nen** millionairess

Mil|li|o|nen-: **Mil|li|o|nen|auf|la|ge** F million copies *pl*; millions of copies *pl*; **Mil|li|o|nen|auf|trag** M contract worth millions; **Mil|li|o|nen|er|be** M, **Mil|li|o|nen|er|bin** F inheritor of millions; **mil|li|o|nen|fach** ADJ millionfold; **der ~e Mord an den Juden** the murder of millions of Jews ADV a million times; **Mil|li|o|nen|ge|schäft** NT multi-million-pound/dollar *etc* industry; **ein ~ abschließen** to conclude a (business) deal worth millions; **Mil|li|o|nen|ge|winn** M **a** *(= Ertrag)* profit of millions; **manche Firmen haben ~e gemacht** some firms have made profits running into millions **b** *(= Lotteriegewinn)* prize of a million; **Mil|li|o|nen|heer** NT army of millions; **Mil|li|o|nen|hö|he** F **in ~** amounting to a million/millions; **die Explosion verursachte einen Schaden in ~** the explosion caused damage running into millions of dollars *etc*; **mil|li|o|nen|mal** △ ADV → **Million**; **Mil|li|o|nen|scha|den** M damage *no pl* amounting to millions, damage *no pl* running into millions; **mil|li|o|nen|schwer** ADJ *(inf) Person* worth a few million; *Verlust, Schuld* of a few million; *Maßnahme* costing a few million; **Mil|li|o|nen|stadt** F town with over a million inhabitants

mil|li|ons|tel [mɪ'lioːnstl] ADJ millionth

Mil|li|ons|tel [mɪ'lioːnstl] NT **-s, -** millionth part

mil|li|ons|te(r, s) [mɪ'lioːnstə] ADJ millionth

Mil|li|rem NT millirem

Milz [mɪlts] F **-, -en** spleen

Milz|brand M *(Med, Vet)* anthrax

Mi|me ['miːmə] M **-n, -n**, **Mi|min** ['miːmɪn] F **-, -nen** *(old, liter)* mime *(old)*, Thespian

mi|men ['miːmən] VT to mime; **er mimt den Unschuldigen** *(inf)* he's acting innocent *or* the innocent *(Brit)*; **er mimt den Kranken** *(inf)* he's pretending to be sick VI to play-act

Mi|me|sis ['miːmezɪs] F **-, Mimesen** [mi'meːzn] *(Liter, Philos)* mimesis

mi|me|tisch [mi'meːtɪʃ] ADJ *(Liter, Philos)* mimetic

Mi|mik ['miːmɪk] F **-**, *no pl* facial expression; **etw durch ~ ausdrücken** to express sth facially

Mi|mi|ker ['miːmikɐ] M **-s, -**, **Mi|mi|ke|rin** [-ərɪn] F **-, -nen** mime(r)

Mi|mik|ry ['mɪmikri] F **-**, *no pl (Zool, fig)* mimicry

Mi|min ['miːmɪn] F → **Mime**

mi|misch ['miːmɪʃ] ADJ mimic ADV *darstellen* using mime; *sich verständigen, zum Ausdruck bringen* by using mime, by miming

Mi|mo|se [mi'moːzə] F **-, -n** mimosa; **empfindlich wie eine ~ sein** to be oversensitive

mi|mo|sen|haft ADJ *(fig)* oversensitive ADV *(fig) reagieren* oversensitively

mim|sen ['mɪmzn] VTI *(Telec: inf)* to send an MMS (message)

min. *abbr von* **minimal**

Min., min. *abbr von* **Minute(n)**

Mi|na|rett [mina'rɛt] NT **-s, -e** *or* **-s** minaret

min|der ['mɪndɐ] ADV less; **mehr oder ~** more or less; **nicht mehr und nicht ~** neither more nor less, no more and no less; **nicht ~ wichtig als** no less important than; **und das nicht ~** and no less so

Min|der-: **Min|der|aus|ga|ben** PL reduced expenditure *sing*; **min|der|be|gabt** ADJ less gifted; **Min|der|be|gab|te** PL *decl as adj* less gifted people *pl*; **min|der|be|gü|tert** ADJ less well-off; **Min|der|be|gü|ter|te** [-bəgyːtɐtə] PL *decl as adj* people *pl* in the lower income brackets; **Min|der|be|las|te|te(r)** [-bəlastətə] MF *decl as adj (Jur)* less incriminated person; **min|der|be|mit|telt** ADJ less well-off; **geistig ~** *(iro)* mentally less gifted; **Min|der|be|mit|tel|te** [-bəmɪtltə] PL *decl as adj (dated)* people *pl* with a limited income; *(iro)* not very bright people *pl*; **Min|der|ein|nah|men** PL decrease *sing* in receipts

min|de|re(r, s) ADJ *attr* lesser; *Güte, Qualität* inferior

Min|der|ge|wicht NT short weight

Min|der|heit F **-, -en** minority

Min|der|hei|ten- *(Pol)*: **Min|der|hei|ten|fra|ge** F minorities problem; **Min|der|hei|ten|schutz** M protection of minorities

Min|der|heits- *(Pol)*: **Min|der|heits|rech|te** PL rights *pl* of minorities; **Min|der|heits|re|gie|rung** F minority government

Min|der-: **min|der|jäh|rig** [-jɛːrɪç] ADJ who is (still) a minor; **Min|der|jäh|ri|ge(r)** [-jɛːrɪgə] MF *decl as adj* minor; **Min|der|jäh|rig|keit** [-jɛːrɪçkait] F **-**, *no pl* minority

min|dern ['mɪndɐn] VT *(= herabsetzen) Ansehen* to diminish; *(= verringern) Wert, Qualität* to reduce, to diminish, to erode; *Rechte* to erode; *Freude, Vergnügen* to detract from, to lessen; *Risiko, Chancen* to reduce VR *(Ansehen, Wert, Qualität)* to diminish; *(Freude, Vergnügen)* to lessen

Min|de|rung ['mɪndərʊŋ] F **-, -en** *(= Herabsetzung)* diminishing *no indef art*; *(von Wert, Qualität)* reduction (+*gen* in); *(von Rechten)* erosion; *(von Freude, Vergnügen)* lessening

Min|der|wert M *(Jur)* decrease in value

min|der|wer|tig ADJ inferior; *Waren, Material auch* poor-quality, low-quality; *Arbeit auch* poor(-quality); *Qualität auch* low; *Charakter* low, base

Min|der|wer|tig|keit F inferiority; **die ~ der Qualität** the low quality

Min|der|wer|tig|keits-: **Min|der|wer|tig|keits|ge|fühl** NT feeling of inferiority; **~e haben** to feel inferior; **Min|der|wer|tig|keits|kom|plex** M inferiority complex

Min|der|zahl F minority; **in der ~ sein** to be in the minority

Min|dest- *in cpds* minimum; **Min|dest|ab|stand** M minimum distance; **Min|dest|al|ter** NT minimum age; **Min|dest|be|steu|e|rung** F lowest *or* minimum tax rate; **Min|dest|be|trag** M minimum amount; **Waren für einen ~ von EUR 100** goods to a minimum value of 100 euros; **Min|dest|ein|kom|men** NT minimum income

min|des|tens ['mɪndəstns] ADV at least

min|des|te(r, s) ['mɪndəstə] *superl von* **wenig** ADJ *attr* least, slightest; *Ahnung auch* faintest, foggiest *(inf)*; **nicht die ~ Angst** not the slightest *or* least trace of fear; **er hat nicht das ~ bisschen Arbeit geleistet** he didn't do a single stroke (of work); **das Mindeste** the (very) least; **ich verstehe nicht das Mindeste von (der) Kunst** I don't know the slightest thing about art; **das wäre das Mindeste gewesen** that's the least he/she *etc* could have done

ADV **zum Mindesten** at least, at the very least; **(nicht) im Mindesten** (not) in the least; **das bezweifle ich nicht im Mindesten** I don't doubt that at all, I don't doubt that in the slightest

Min|dest-: **Min|dest|for|de|rung** F minimum demand; **Min|dest|ge|bot** NT *(bei Auktionen)* reserve *or* knockdown price; **Min|dest|ge|schwin|dig|keit** F minimum speed; **Min|dest|grö|ße** F minimum size; *(von Menschen)* minimum height; **Min|dest|halt|bar|keits|da|tum** NT best-before date; **Min|dest|lohn** M minimum wage; **Min|dest|maß** NT minimum, minimum amount (*an +dat* of); **sich auf das ~ beschränken** to limit oneself to the (absolute) minimum; **Min|dest|preis** M minimum price; **Min|dest|ren|te** F minimum pension; **Min|dest|re|ser|ve** F *(Fin)* minimum reserves *pl*; **Min|dest|re|ser|ve|satz** M *(Fin)* minimum reserve ratio; **Min|dest|stra|fe** F minimum penalty; **Min|dest|um|tausch** M minimum obligatory exchange; **Min|dest|ur|laub** M minimum holiday *(esp Brit) or* vacation *(US)* entitlement; **Min|dest|wert** M minimum value; **im ~ von** to a minimum value of; **Min|dest|zins|satz** M minimum lending rate, MLR

Mi|ne ['miːnə] F **-, -n** **a** *(Min)* mine; **in den ~n arbeiten** to work down *or* in the mines **b** *(Mil)* mine; **auf eine ~ fahren/treten/laufen** to drive over/to step on/to strike *or* hit a mine; **~n legen** to lay mines **c** *(= Bleistiftmine)* lead; *(= Kugelschreibermine, Filzstiftmine)* reservoir; *(= Farbmine)* cartridge; *(austauschbar)* refill; **die ~ ist leer/läuft aus** *(von Kugelschreiber)* the Biro® *(Brit) or* pen has run out/is leaking; *(von Filzstift)* the felt-tip has run out/is leaking; **eine neue ~** a refill; *(für Bleistift)* a new lead

Mi|nen-: **Mi|nen|feld** NT *(Mil)* minefield; **Mi|nen|le|ger** [-leːgɐ] M **-s, -** *(Mil, Naut)* minelayer; **Mi|nen|räum|boot** NT minesweeper; **Mi|nen|sper|re** F *(Mil)* mine barrage; **Mi|nen|such|boot** NT, **Mi|nen|su|cher** M *(inf)* minesweeper; **Mi|nen|such|ge|rät** NT mine detector; **Mi|nen|wer|fer** M *(old Mil)* mortar

Mi|ne|ral [mine'raːl] NT **-s, -e** *or* **-ien** [-liən] mineral

Mi|ne|ral-: **Mi|ne|ral|bad** NT mineral bath; *(= Ort)* spa; *(= Schwimmbad) swimming pool fed from a mineral spring*; **Mi|ne|ral|brun|nen** M mineral spring; **Mi|ne|ral|dün|ger** M inorganic fertilizer

Mi|ne|ra|li|en|samm|lung [-liən-] F collection of minerals

mi|ne|ra|lisch [mine'raːlɪʃ] ADJ mineral

Mi|ne|ra|lo|ge [minera'loːgə] M **-n, -n**, **Mi|ne|ra|lo|gin** [-'loːgɪn] F **-, -nen** mineralogist

Mi|ne|ra|lo|gie [mineralo'giː] F **-**, *no pl* mineralogy

mi|ne|ra|lo|gisch [minera'loːgɪʃ] ADJ mineralogical

Mi|ne|ral-: **Mi|ne|ral|öl** NT (mineral) oil; **Mi|ne|ral|öl|ge|sell|schaft** F oil company; **Mi|ne|ral|öl|steu|er** F tax on oil; **Mi|ne|ral|quel|le** F mineral spring; **Mi|ne|ral|salz** NT mineral salt; **Mi|ne|ral|was|ser** NT mineral water

mi|ni ['mɪni] ADJ *inv (Fashion)* mini; **Mini tragen** to wear a mini

Mi|ni ['mɪni] M **-s, -s** *(inf: = Minirock)* mini

Mi|ni- *in cpds* mini-; **Mi|ni-An|la|ge** F mini hi-fi

Mi|ni|a|tur [minia'tuːɐ] F **-, -en** *(Art)* miniature; *(fig, Liter)* thumbnail sketch

Mi|ni|a|tur- *in cpds* miniature; **Mi|ni|a|tur|an|sicht** F *(Comput)* thumbnail; **Mi|ni|a|tur|aus|ga|be** F miniature version; *(Buch)* miniature edition; **Mi|ni|a|tur|bild** NT miniature; **Mi|ni|a|tur|bild|nis** NT miniature portrait; **Mi|ni|a|tur|for|mat** NT miniature format; **eine Bibel in ~** a miniature Bible; **Mi|ni|a|tur|ge|mäl|de** NT miniature; **Mi|ni|a|tur|ma|le|rei** F miniature painting; **Mi|ni|a|tur|ma|ler(in)** M(F) miniaturist; **Mi|ni|a|tur|staat** M tiny state *or* country

Mi|ni-: **Mi|ni|bar** F *(im Hotel etc)* minibar; **Mi|ni|bi|ki|ni** M scanty bikini; **Mi|ni|bus** M minibus; **Mi|ni|car** M minicab; **Mi|ni|com|pu|ter** M minicomputer; **Mi|ni|disk**, **Mi|ni|disc** [-dɪsk] F **-, -s** *(= Tonträger)* Minidisc®; *(Comput)* minidisk; **Mi|ni|golf** NT crazy golf *(Brit)*, putt-putt golf *(US)*; **Mi|ni|job** M minijob; **Mi|ni|kas|set|te** F mini-cassette

mi|ni|mal [mini'maːl] ADJ *Unterschied, Aufwand* minimal; *Verlust, Verbesserung, Steigerung* marginal; *Gewinn, Chance* very small; *Preise, Benzinverbrauch, Gehalt* very low; **mit ~er Anstrengung** with a minimum of effort ADV *(= wenigstens)* at least; *(= geringfügig)* minimally, marginally

Mi|ni|mal- *in cpds* minimum; **Mi|ni|mal|be|trag** M minimum amount; **Mi|ni|mal|for|de|rung** F minimum demand; **mi|ni|mal|in|va|siv** [-ɪnva'ziːf] ADJ minimally invasive; **~e Chirurgie** minimally invasive surgery; **Mi|ni|mal|kon|sen|sus** M basic area of agreement; **Mi|ni|mal|lö|sung** F minimal solution; **Mi|ni|mal|pro|gramm** NT basic programme *(Brit) or* program *(US)*

mi|ni|mie|ren [mini'mi:rən] *ptp* **minimiert** VT to minimize

Mi|ni|mie|rung F -, **-en** minimization

Mi|ni|mum ['mi:nimʊm] NT **-s, Minima** [-ma] minimum *(an +dat* of); **barometrisches ~** *(Met)* barometric low

Mi|ni-: **Mi|ni|note|book** M *(Comput)* mini notebook; **Mi|ni|pil|le** F minipill; **Mi|ni|rock** M miniskirt; **Mi|ni|spi|on** M miniaturized bugging device

Mi|nis|ter [mi'nɪstɐ] M **-s, -**, **Mi|nis|te|rin** [-tərɪn] F **-, -nen** *(Pol)* minister *(Brit)* *(für* of), secretary *(für* for)

Mi|nis|ter-: **Mi|nis|ter|amt** NT ministerial office; **Mi|nis|ter|bank** F *pl* **-bänke** government front bench

Mi|nis|te|ri|al-: **Mi|nis|te|ri|al|be|am|te(r)** M *decl as adj*, **Mi|nis|te|ri|al|be|am|tin** F ministry official; **Mi|nis|te|ri|al|di|rek|tor(in)** M(F) head of a government department, permanent secretary *(Brit)*; **Mi|nis|te|ri|al|di|ri|gent(in)** M(F), **Mi|nis|te|ri|al|rat** M, **Mi|nis|te|ri|al|rä|tin** F assistant head of a government department, assistant secretary *(Brit)*

mi|nis|te|ri|ell [minɪste'riɛl] ADJ *attr* ministerial

Mi|nis|te|rin [-tərɪn] F → **Minister**

Mi|nis|te|ri|um [minɪs'te:riʊm] NT **-s, Ministerien** [-riən] ministry *(Brit)*, department

Mi|nis|ter-: **Mi|nis|ter|kon|fe|renz** F conference of ministers, ministerial conference; **Mi|nis|ter|prä|si|dent(in)** M(F) prime minister; *(eines Bundeslandes)* leader of a Federal German state; **Mi|nis|ter|rat** M council of ministers; *(von EG)* Council of Ministers; **Mi|nis|ter|ses|sel** M ministerial post *(esp Brit)* or position

mi|nist|ra|bel [minɪs'tra:bl] ADJ *(Pol inf)* suitable for ministerial office

Mi|nist|rant [minɪs'trant] M **-en, -en**, **Mi|nist|ran|tin** [-'trantɪn] F **-, -nen** *(Eccl)* server

mi|nist|rie|ren [minɪs'tri:rən] *ptp* **ministriert** VI *(Eccl)* to serve, to act as server

Min|na ['mɪna] F -, *no pl* *(dated: = Hausangestellte)* maid; *(fig inf)* skivvy *(Brit inf)*, maid; **jdn zur ~ machen** *(inf)* to give sb a piece of one's mind, to tear a strip off sb *(Brit inf)* → **grün**

Min|ne ['mɪnə] F -, *no pl* *(Liter, Hist)* courtly love

Min|ne-: **Min|ne|dienst** M homage rendered by a knight to his lady; **Min|ne|ge|sang** M minnesong; **Min|ne|lied** NT minnelied

Minneola [mɪne'o:la] F **-, -s** *(= Mandarinenart)* minneola

Min|ne-: **Min|ne|sang** M minnesong; **Min|ne|sän|ger** M, **Min|ne|sin|ger** M **-s, -** minnesinger

mi|no|isch [mi'no:ɪʃ] ADJ Minoan

Mi|no|ri|tät [minori'tɛ:t] F **-, -en** minority

Mi|nu|end [mi'nuɛnt] M **-en, -en** [-dn] *(Math)* minuend

mi|nus ['mi:nʊs] PREP *+gen* minus, less; *(Math)* minus ADV minus; *(Elec)* negative; **~ 10 Grad, 10 Grad ~** minus 10 degrees, 10 degrees below (zero); **~ machen** *(inf)* to make a loss

Mi|nus ['mi:nʊs] NT **-, -** a *(= Fehlbetrag)* deficit; *(auf Konto)* overdraft; *(fig: = Nachteil)* bad point; *(in Beruf etc)* disadvantage b *(= Minuszeichen)* minus (sign)

Mi|nus|kel [mi'nʊskl] F **-, -n** *(geh)* minuscule *(spec)*, small *or* lower-case letter

Mi|nus-: **Mi|nus|pol** M negative pole; **Mi|nus|punkt** M minus *or* penalty point; *(fig)* minus point; **ein ~ für jdn sein** to count against sb, to be a point against sb; **Mi|nus|tem|pe|ra|tur** F temperature below freezing *or* zero; **Mi|nus|zei|chen** NT minus sign

Mi|nu|te [mi'nu:tə] F **-, -n** minute; *(fig: = Augenblick auch)* moment; **es ist 10 Uhr und 21 ~n** *(form)* it is 21 minutes past 10 o'clock; **auf die ~ (genau** *or* **pünktlich)** (right) on the dot; **in letzter ~** at the last moment *or* minute; **~ auf** *or* **um ~ verging** *or* **verstrich** *or* **verrann** *(liter)* the minutes ticked by *or* went by; **auf die ~ kommt es nicht an** a few minutes one way or another don't matter; **es vergeht keine ~, ohne dass ...** not a moment goes by without ...

Mi|nu|ten-: **mi|nu|ten|lang** ADJ *attr* several minutes of; **~es Schweigen** several minutes' silence, silence for several minutes ADV for several minutes; **Mi|nu|ten|schnel|le** F **in ~** in minutes, in a matter of minutes; **Mi|nu|ten|takt** M **im ~** *(Telefongebühren)* (charged) per minute *or* by the minute; *(fig: = schnell, häufig)* one a minute; **die Tore fielen jetzt im ~** the goals came thick and fast; **Mi|nu|ten|zei|ger** M minute hand

mi|nu|ti|ös [minu'tsiø:s], **mi|nu|zi|ös** [minu'tsiø:s] *(geh)* ADJ *Nachbildung, Mensch* meticulous; *Schilderung auch, Fragen* detailed ADV meticulously; *erklären* in great detail

Min|ze ['mɪntsə] F **-, -n** *(Bot)* mint

Mio. *abbr von* **Million(en)** m

mir [mi:ɐ] PERS PRON *dat von* **ich** to me; *(nach Präpositionen)* me; **ein Freund von ~** a friend of mine; **von ~ aus!** *(inf)* I don't mind, fair enough; **~ nichts, dir nichts** *(inf: unhöflich)* without so much as a by-your-leave; **es war ~ nichts, dir nichts weg** the next thing I knew it had gone; **wie du ~, so ich dir** *(prov)* tit for tat *(inf)*; *(als Drohung)* I'll get my own back (on you); **und das ~!** why me (of all people)?; **dass ihr ~ nicht an die Bücher geht!** *(inf)* don't you touch those books!; **du bist ~ vielleicht einer!** *(inf)* you're a right one, you are! *(inf)* → *auch* **ihm**

Mi|ra|bel|le [mira'bɛlə] F **-, -n** mirabelle, small yellow plum

Mi|ra|kel [mi'ra:kl] NT **-s, -** *(old, liter)* miracle

Mi|santh|rop [mizan'tro:p] M **-en, -en**, **Mi|santh|ro|pin** [-'tro:pɪn] F **-, -nen** *(geh)* misanthropist

Mi|santh|ro|pie [mizantro'pi:] F -, *no pl* *(geh)* misanthropy

Misch-: **Misch|ar|beits|platz** M *(Comput)* mixed work station; **misch|bar** ADJ mixable, miscible *(form)*; **~ sein** to mix; **Misch|bat|te|rie** F mixer tap; **Misch|brot** NT *bread made from more than one kind of flour*; **Misch|ehe** F mixed marriage

mi|schen ['mɪʃn] VT to mix; *Tabak-, Tee-, Kaffeesorten auch* to blend; *Karten* to shuffle; *(Comput) Dateien* to merge; **sie mischt Realität und Einbildung** she mixes up reality and fantasy; **die Karten neu ~** *(lit, fig)* to reshuffle the pack → *auch* **gemischt** VR *(= sich vermengen)* to mix; **sich unter jdn ~** to mix *or* mingle with sb; **sich unter etw** *(acc)* **~** to mix with sth; **sich in etw** *(acc)* **~** to meddle *or* interfere in sth; **sich in das Gespräch ~** to butt *or* cut into the conversation VI *(Cards)* to shuffle; **wer mischt?** whose turn is it to shuffle?

Mi|scher ['mɪʃɐ] M **-s, -** *(inf)* a *(= Mischpult)* mixing desk *or* panel; *(von Band)* sound mixer b *(= Zementmischer)* cement-mixer

Misch-: **misch|er|big** ADJ *(Biol)* heterozygous *(spec)*; **Misch|far|be** F mixed *or* blended colour *(Brit)* *or* color *(US)*; *(Phys)* secondary colour *(Brit)* *or* color *(US)*; **Misch|fi|nan|zie|rung** F mixed financing; **Misch|form** F mixture; *(von zwei Elementen auch)* hybrid (form); **Misch|fut|ter** NT *(Agr)* compound feed; **Misch|gas** NT *mixture of coal gas and water gas*; **Misch|ge|mü|se** NT mixed vegetables *pl*; **Misch|ge|we|be** NT mixed fibres *(Brit)* *or* fibers *(US)* *pl*; **Misch|hahn** M *(an Waschbecken etc)* mixer tap *(Brit)*, mixing faucet *(US)*; **Misch|haut** F combination skin; **Misch|kal|ku|la|ti|on** F mixed calculation; **Misch|kon|zern** M conglomerate; **Misch|kost** F mixed diet; **Misch|kul|tur** F a *(Agr)* mixed cultivation; **~en anbauen** to grow different crops side by side *or* in the same field b *(Sociol)* mixed culture

Misch|ling ['mɪʃlɪŋ] M **-s, -e** a *(Mensch)* half-caste, half-breed b *(Zool)* half-breed

Misch|lings|kind NT half-caste child

Misch-: **Misch|masch** ['mɪʃmaʃ] M **-(e)s, -e** *(inf)* *(aus* of) hotchpotch *(Brit)*, hodgepodge *(US)*, mishmash; *(Essen auch)* concoction; **sie redet einen fürchterlichen ~** she speaks a horrible jumble *or* hotchpotch *(Brit)* *or* hodgepodge *(US)* of different languages; **Misch|ma|schi|ne** F cement-mixer; **Misch|po|ke** [mɪʃ'po:kə] F -, *no pl*, **Misch|po|che** [mɪʃ'po:xə] F -, *no pl* *(sl)* clan *(inf)*, mob *(inf)*; **Misch|pult** NT *(Rad, TV)* mixing desk *or* panel; *(von Band)* sound mixer; **Misch|ras|se** F a *(Tiere)* crossbreed b *(Menschen)* mixed race; **Misch|trom|mel** F (drum in) cement-mixer

Mi|schung ['mɪʃʊŋ] F **-, -en** a *(= das Mischen)* mixing; *(von Tee-, Kaffee-, Tabaksorten)* blending, mixing b *(lit, fig: = Gemischtes)* mixture; *(von Tee etc)* blend, mixture; *(von Süßigkeiten etc)* assortment, mixture; *(fig)* mixture, combination *(aus* of) c *(Chem)* mixture

Mi|schungs|ver|hält|nis NT ratio (of a mixture)

Misch-: **Misch|volk** NT mixed race; **Misch|wald** M mixed (deciduous and coniferous) woodland; **Misch|wort** NT *pl* **-wörter** hybrid word

mi|se|ra|bel [mizə'ra:bl] *(inf)* ADJ lousy *(inf)*; *Leistungen auch* pathetic; *Gesundheit* miserable, wretched; *Gefühl* ghastly; *Benehmen* dreadful; *Qualität* poor; *Ruf* terrible; *(= gemein) Kerl etc* nasty ADV dreadfully; **~ schmecken** to taste lousy *(inf)*; **man isst dort ~** the food there is just lousy *(inf)*; **~ riechen** to smell horrible; **er hat ~ abgeschnitten** he got lousy marks *(Brit inf)* *or* grades *(US inf)*

Mi|se|re [mi'ze:rə] F **-, -n** *(von Leuten, Wirtschaft etc)* plight; *(von Hunger, Krieg etc)* misery, miseries *pl*; **in einer ~ stecken** to be in a terrible *or* dreadful state; *(Mensch)* to be in a mess, to have run into trouble; **jdn aus einer ~ herausholen** to get sb out of trouble *or* a mess; **das war eine einzige ~** that was a real disaster; **es ist eine ~, wie/dass ...** it is dreadful how/that ...; **es ist die ~ des Alltags, dass ...** it is one of life's hardships that ...

Mi|se|re|re [mize're:rə] NT **-(s)**, *no pl* a *(Eccl)* miserere b *(Med)* faecal *(Brit)* *or* fecal *(US)* vomiting

Mi|so|gyn [mizo'gy:n] M **-s** *or* **-en, -en** *(liter)* misogynist

Mis|pel ['mɪspl] F **-, -n** medlar (tree)

miss *imper sing von* **messen**

Miss [mɪs] F **-, -es** ['mɪsɪz] Miss

miss|ach|ten [mɪs'laxtn, 'mɪs-] *ptp* **missachtet** VT *insep* a *(= ignorieren) Warnung, Ratschlag* to ignore, to disregard; *Gesetz, Verbot* to flout b *(= gering schätzen) jdn* to despise; *Hilfe, Angebot* to disdain

Miss|ach|tung F a *(= Ignorieren)* disregard *(gen* for); *(von Gesetz, Verbot)* flouting *(gen* of) b *(= Geringschätzung)* disrespect *(+gen* for); disdain *(+gen* of, for)

miss|be|ha|gen ['mɪsbəha:gn] *ptp* **missbehagt** VI *insep +dat* **das missbehagte ihm** that was not to his liking; **es missbehagt mir, schon wieder umziehen zu müssen** it ill suits me to have to move again

Miss|be|ha|gen NT *(geh)* *(= Unbehagen)* uneasiness; *(= Missfallen)* discontent(ment); **jdm ~ bereiten** to cause sb uneasiness/discontent (-ment)

miss|bil|den ['mɪsbɪldn] VT to deform

Miss|bil|dung F deformity, malformation

miss|bil|li|gen [mɪs'bɪlɪgn] *ptp* **missbilligt** VT *insep* to disapprove of, to object to

miss|bil|li|gend ADJ disapproving ADV disapprovingly

Miss|bil|li|gung F disapproval

Miss|brauch ['mɪsbraux] M abuse; *(= falsche Anwendung)* misuse; *(von Notbremse, Feuerlöscher, Kreditkarte)* improper use; *(geh: einer Person)* sexual assault *(+gen, von* on); **~ mit etw betreiben** to abuse *or* misuse sth; **~ zur Unzucht** *(Jur)* *sexual offence committed by person in position* *of authority over victim;* **vor ~ wird gewarnt** use only as directed; *(an Notbremse etc)* do not misuse; **unter ~ seines Amtes** in abuse of his office; **„Missbrauch strafbar!"** "penalty for misuse"

miss|brau|chen [mɪsˈbrauxn] *ptp* **missbraucht** VT *insep Vertrauen* to abuse; *(geh: = vergewaltigen)* to assault; **den Namen Gottes ~** *(liter)* to take the Lord's name in vain; **jdn für** *or* **zu etw ~** to use sb for sth, to use sb to do sth; **etw für politische Zwecke ~** to abuse sth for political purposes; **jdn zu allem Möglichen ~** to impose on sb; **sexuell missbraucht** sexually abused

miss|bräuch|lich [ˈmɪsbrɔyçlɪç] ADJ incorrect; *(= unerlaubt)* improper ADV incorrectly; *(= unerlaubterweise)* improperly

miss|deu|ten [mɪsˈdɔytn] *ptp* **missdeutet** VT *insep* to misinterpret

Miss|deu|tung F misinterpretation

mis|sen [ˈmɪsn] VT *(geh)* to go *or* do without; *Erfahrung* to miss; **das möchte ich nicht ~** I wouldn't do without it/miss it (for the world); **ich möchte meine Kinder nicht ~** I could not do without my children

Miss|er|folg M failure; *(Theat, Buch etc auch)* flop

Miss|ern|te F crop failure

Mis|se|tat [ˈmɪsəta:t] F *(old, liter)* misdeed, misdemeanour *(Brit)*, misdemeanor *(US)*

Mis|se|tä|ter(in) M(F) *(old, liter)* culprit; *(= Verbrecher auch)* wrongdoer

miss|fal|len [mɪsˈfalən] *ptp* **missfallen** VI *insep irreg +dat* to displease; **es missfällt mir, wie er ...** I dislike the way he ...

Miss|fal|len NT **-s,** *no pl* displeasure *(über +acc* at), disapproval *(über +acc* of); **jds ~ erregen** to incur sb's displeasure

Miss|fal|lens-: **Miss|fal|lens|äu|ße|rung** F expression of disapproval *or* displeasure; **Miss|fal|lens|be|kun|dung** F, **Miss|fal|lens|kund|ge|bung** F expression *or* demonstration of disapproval *or* displeasure

miss|fäl|lig [ˈmɪsfɛlɪç] ADJ *Bemerkung* disparaging, deprecatory ADV disparagingly

miss|ge|bil|det [ˈmɪsgəbɪldət] ADJ deformed

Miss|ge|burt F deformed person/animal; *(fig inf)* failure; **das Kind ist eine ~** the child was born deformed; **du ~!** *(sl)* you spastic! *(Brit pej sl)*, you psycho! *(pej sl)*

miss|ge|launt [ˈmɪsgəlaunt] ADJ *(geh)* bad-tempered, ill-humoured *(Brit)*, ill-humored *(US)*

Miss|ge|schick NT mishap; *(= Pech, Unglück)* misfortune; **ein kleines ~** a slight mishap; **vom ~ verfolgt werden** *(geh)* to be dogged by misfortune

miss|ge|stalt [ˈmɪsgəʃtalt] *(liter)*, **miss|ge|stal|tet** [ˈmɪsgəʃtaltət] *(geh)* ADJ misshapen

Miss|ge|stalt F *(liter)* misshapen figure

miss|ge|stimmt [ˈmɪsgəʃtɪmt] ADJ *(geh)* ill-humoured *(Brit)*, ill-humored *(US)*; **~ sein** to be in an ill humour *(Brit) or* humor *(US)*

miss|glü|cken [mɪsˈglʏkn] *ptp* **missglückt** VI *insep aux sein* to fail, to be unsuccessful; **der Versuch ist missglückt** the attempt failed; **der Versuch ist ihm missglückt** his attempt failed; **das ist ihr missglückt** she failed; **der Kuchen ist (mir) missglückt** the cake didn't turn out; **ihm missglückt alles** everything he does goes wrong; **ein missglückter Versuch** an unsuccessful attempt

miss|gön|nen [mɪsˈgœnən] *ptp* **missgönnt** VT *insep* **jdm etw ~** to (be)grudge sb sth; **sie missgönnt es ihm, dass er erfolgreich ist** she (be)grudges him his success, she resents his success

Miss|griff M mistake

Miss|gunst F enviousness *(gegenüber* of)

miss|güns|tig ADJ envious *(auf +acc* of) ADV enviously

miss|han|deln [mɪsˈhandln] *ptp* **misshandelt** VT *insep* to ill-treat, to maltreat

Miss|hand|lung F ill-treatment, maltreatment; *(= Kindesmisshandlung)* cruelty (to children)

Miss|hel|lig|keit [ˈmɪshɛlɪçkait] F **-, -en** *(geh)* difference, disagreement

Mis|singsch [ˈmɪsɪŋʃ] NT **-,** *no pl mixture of High and Low German*

Mis|si|on [mɪˈsio:n] F **-, -en** *(Eccl, Pol, fig)* mission; *(= diplomatische Vertretung)* legation, mission *(US)*; *(= Gruppe)* delegation; **~ treiben** to do missionary work; **in der ~ tätig sein** to be a missionary

Mis|si|o|nar [mɪsioˈna:ɐ] M **-s, -e**, **Mis|si|o|na|rin** [-ˈna:rɪn] F **-, -nen**, *(Aus)* **Mis|si|o|när** [mɪsioˈnɛ:ɐ] M **-s, -e**, **Mis|si|o|nä|rin** [-ˈnɛ:rɪn] F **-, -nen** missionary

mis|si|o|na|risch [mɪsioˈna:rɪʃ] ADJ missionary; **mit ~em Eifer** with missionary zeal ADV with missionary zeal

Mis|si|o|nars|stel|lung F *(fig)* missionary position

mis|si|o|nie|ren [mɪsioˈni:rən] *ptp* **missioniert** VI to do missionary work, to proselytize; *(fig)* to preach, to proselytize VT *Land, Mensch* to (work to) convert, to proselytize; *(fig)* to convert, to proselytize

Mis|si|o|nie|rung F **-,** *no pl* conversion, proselytization

Mis|si|ons-: **Mis|si|ons|chef(in)** M(F) *(Pol)* head of a legation; *(einer Gruppe)* leader of a delegation; **Mis|si|ons|ge|sell|schaft** F missionary society; **Mis|si|ons|schu|le** F mission school; **Mis|si|ons|schwes|ter** F nun working at a mission

Miss|klang M discord *(auch Mus)*, dissonance; *(= Misston)* discordant note; **ein ~** *(fig)* a note of discord, a discordant note

Miss|kre|dit [-kreˈdi:t] M, *no pl* discredit; **jdn/etw in ~ bringen** to bring sb/sth into discredit, to discredit sb/sth; **in ~ geraten** *or* **kommen** to be discredited

miss|lang *pret von* **misslingen**

miss|lau|nig [ˈmɪslaunɪç] ADJ bad-tempered, ill-humoured *(Brit)*, ill-humored *(US)*

miss|lich [ˈmɪslɪç] ADJ *(geh) Lage* awkward, difficult; *Umstand auch, Verzögerung* unfortunate, regrettable; **das ist ja eine ~e Sache** that is a bit awkward/unfortunate; **es steht ~ um dieses Vorhaben** the outlook for this plan is not good

Miss|lich|keit F **-, -en** *(Umstand)* unfortunate *or* regrettable situation; **tägliche ~en** everyday difficulties

miss|lie|big [ˈmɪsli:bɪç] ADJ unpopular; **sich (bei jdm) ~ machen** to make oneself unpopular (with sb); **politisch ~e Personen** people who have fallen out of favour *(Brit) or* favor *(US)* with the government

miss|lin|gen [mɪsˈlɪŋən] *pret* **misslang** [mɪsˈlaŋ], *ptp* **misslungen** [mɪsˈlʊŋən] VI *insep aux sein* = **missglücken**

Miss|lin|gen NT **-s,** *no pl* failure

miss|lun|gen *ptp von* **misslingen**

Miss|ma|na|ge|ment NT mismanagement

Miss|mut M sullenness, moroseness; *(= Unzufriedenheit)* displeasure, discontent; **seinen ~ über etw** *(acc)* **zeigen/äußern** to show/express one's displeasure *or* discontent at sth

miss|mu|tig [ˈmɪsmu:tɪç] ADJ sullen, morose; *(= unzufrieden)* discontented; *Äußerung, Aussehen* disgruntled; **mach nicht so ein ~es Gesicht** don't look so morose ADV sullenly, morosely; *(= unzufrieden)* discontentedly; *sagen, sich äußern* disgruntledly

miss|ra|ten¹ [mɪsˈra:tn] *ptp* **missraten** VI *insep irreg aux sein* to go wrong; *(Kind)* to become wayward; **der Kuchen ist (mir) ~** the cake didn't turn out

miss|ra|ten² [mɪsˈra:tn] ADJ *Kind* wayward; **der ~e Kuchen** the cake which went wrong

Miss|stand M disgrace *no pl*, outrage; *(allgemeiner Zustand)* bad *or* deplorable state of affairs *no pl*; *(= Ungerechtigkeit)* abuse; *(= Mangel)* defect; **einen ~/Missstände beseitigen** to remedy something which is wrong/things which are wrong; **Missstände in der Regierung/im Management anprangern** to denounce misgovernment/mismanagement

Miss|stim|mung F **a** *(= Uneinigkeit)* friction, discord; **eine ~** a note of discord, a discordant note **b** *(= Missmut)* ill feeling *no indef art*

misst [mɪst] *3. pers sing pres von* **messen**

Miss|ton M *pl* **-töne** *(Mus, fig)* discordant note; *(fig auch)* note of discord; **Misstöne** *(Klang)* discordant sound; *(fig)* discord

miss|tö|nend [ˈmɪstø:nənd], **miss|tö|nig** *(rare)* [ˈmɪstø:nɪç] ADJ discordant; *Stimme, Instrument* unpleasant(-sounding)

miss|trau|en [mɪsˈtrauən] *ptp* **misstraut** VI *insep +dat* to mistrust, to be suspicious *or* wary of

Miss|trau|en [ˈmɪstrauən] NT **-s,** *no pl* mistrust, distrust *(gegenüber* of); *(esp einer Sache, Handlung gegenüber)* suspiciousness *(gegenüber* of); **~ gegen jdn/etw haben** *or* **hegen** *(liter)*, **jdm/einer Sache ~ entgegenbringen** to mistrust sb/sth, to be suspicious of sth

Miss|trau|ens- *(Parl)*: **Miss|trau|ens|an|trag** M motion of no confidence; **Miss|trau|ens|vo|tum** NT vote of no confidence

miss|trau|isch [ˈmɪstrauɪʃ] ADJ mistrustful, distrustful; *(= argwöhnisch)* suspicious ADV sceptically *(Brit)*, skeptically *(US)*

Miss|ver|gnü|gen NT *(geh)* displeasure, disgruntlement

miss|ver|gnügt [ˈmɪsfɛɐgny:kt] ADJ *(geh)* disgruntled, displeased

Miss|ver|hält|nis NT discrepancy, disparity; *(in Proportionen)* imbalance; **seine Leistung steht im ~ zu seiner Bezahlung** there is a discrepancy *or* disparity between the work he does and his salary

miss|ver|ständ|lich [ˈmɪsfɛɐʃtɛntlɪç] ADJ unclear; **~e Ausdrücke** expressions which could be misunderstood *or* misleading ADV unclearly; **ich habe mich ~ ausgedrückt** I didn't express myself clearly

Miss|ver|ständ|nis NT **a** misunderstanding; *(= falsche Vorstellung)* misconception **b** *usu pl (= Meinungsverschiedenheit)* misunderstanding, disagreement

miss|ver|ste|hen [ˈmɪsfɛɐʃte:ən] *ptp* **missverstanden** VT *insep irreg* to misunderstand; **Sie dürfen mich nicht ~** please do not misunderstand me; **in nicht misszuverstehender Weise** unequivocally

Miss|wahl F beauty contest

Miss|wei|sung F *(form) (von Kompass)* magnetic declination *or* variation; *(von Radar)* indication error

Miss|wirt|schaft F maladministration, mismanagement

Miss|wuchs M malformed growth, malformation

Mist [mɪst] M **-es,** *no pl* **a** *(= Tierkot)* droppings *pl*; *(= Pferdemist, Kuhmist etc)* dung; *(= Dünger)* manure; *(= Misthaufen)* manure *or* muck heap; **~ streuen** *or* **fahren** to spread manure *or* muck; **das ist nicht auf seinem ~ gewachsen** *(inf)* he didn't think that up himself

b *(inf) (= Unsinn)* rubbish *(esp Brit)*, nonsense; *(= Schund)* rubbish, trash; **~!** blow!, blast! *(inf)*; **so ein ~!** what a darned *or* blasted nuisance *(inf)*; **was soll der ~?** what's all this rubbish *(esp Brit) or* nonsense?; **er hat einen ~ geredet** he talked a load of rubbish *(esp Brit) or* nonsense; **da hat er ~ gemacht** *or* **gebaut** he really messed that up *(inf)*; **~ verzapfen** *(= dummes Zeug reden)* to talk rubbish *(Brit inf) or* nonsense; **allerlei ~ machen** to do all sorts of stupid things; **mach keinen ~!** don't be a fool!

Mist|beet NT *(Hort)* hotbed

Mis|tel [ˈmɪstl] F **-, -n** mistletoe *no pl*

Mis|tel|zweig M sprig of mistletoe; **ein Kuss unterm ~** a kiss under the mistletoe

mis|ten [ˈmɪstn] VT **a** *Stall* to muck out; *Acker* to manure **b** *(inf) Schrank etc* to tidy out; *Zim-*

mer to clean out **VI** *(im Stall)* to do the mucking out; *(= düngen)* to do the manuring

mis|ten VI *impers (Naut)* **es mistet** it is misting over

Mist-: **Mist|ga|bel** F pitchfork *(used for shifting manure)*; **Mist|gru|be** F manure pit; **Mist|hau|fen** M manure heap; **Mist|kä|fer** M dung beetle; **Mist|kerl** M *(inf)* dirty swine *(Brit inf)*, dirty *or* rotten pig *(inf)*; **Mist|kü|bel** M *(Aus)* = **Abfalleimer**; **Mist|stück** NT *(inf)*, **Mist|vieh** NT *(inf) (= Mann)* bastard *(sl)*; *(= Frau auch)* bitch *(sl)*; **Mist|wa|gen** M dung cart; **Mist|wet|ter** NT *(inf)* lousy weather

Mis|zel|len [mɪsˈtsɛlən] PL *(liter)* short articles *or* items *pl*; **das fällt unter ~** that comes under miscellaneous

mit [mɪt] **PREP** *+dat* **a** with; **Tee ~ Zitrone** lemon tea, tea with lemon; **~ dem Hut in der Hand** (with) his hat in his hand; **ein Topf ~ Suppe** a pot of soup; **ein Kleid ~ Jacke** a dress and jacket; **wie wärs ~ einem Bier?** *(inf)* how about a beer?

b *(= mit Hilfe von)* with; **~ einer Zange** with *or* using a pair of pliers; **~ der Bahn/dem Bus/dem Auto** by train/bus/car; **ich fahre ~ meinem eigenen Auto zur Arbeit** I drive to work in my own car; **~ der Post®** by post *(Brit) or* mail; **~ Gewalt** by force; **~ Bleistift/Tinte/dem Kugelschreiber schreiben** to write in pencil/ink/ballpoint; **~ dem nächsten Flugzeug/Bus kommen** to come on the next plane/bus; **~ etwas Liebe/Verständnis** with a little love/understanding; **~ einem Wort** in a word

c *(zeitlich)* **~ achtzehn Jahren** at (the age of) eighteen; **~ einem Mal** all at once, suddenly, all of a sudden; **~ heutigem Tage** *(form)* as from today; **~ beginnendem Sommer** at the start of summer; **~ der Zeit** in time

d *(bei Maß-, Mengenangaben)* **~ 1 Sekunde Vorsprung gewinnen** to win by 1 second; **etw ~ 50.000 EUR versichern** to insure sth for EUR 50,000; **~ 80 km/h** at 80 km/h; **~ 4:2 gewinnen** to win 4-2

e *(= einschließlich)* with, including; **~ mir waren es 5** there were 5 with *or* including *or* counting me

f *(Begleitumstand, Art und Weise, Eigenschaft)* with; **er ~ seinem Herzfehler kann das nicht** he can't do that with his heart condition; **du ~ deinen dummen Ideen** *(inf)* you and your stupid ideas; **~ Muße** at (one's) leisure; **ein junger Dichter, Rosenholz ~ Namen** *(old)* a young poet, Rosenholz by name *or* called Rosenholz; **~ einem Schlage** in a flash; **~ lauter Stimme** in a loud voice; **~ Verlust** at a loss

g *(= betreffend)* **was ist ~ ihr los?** what's the matter with her?, what's up with her?; **wie geht** *or* **steht es ~ deiner Arbeit?** how is your work going?, how are you getting on with your work?; **~ meiner Reise wird es nichts** my trip is off

ADV **er war ~ dabei** he went *or* came too; **er ist ~ der Beste der Gruppe/Mannschaft** he is one of *or* among the best in the group/the team; **das gehört ~ dazu** that's part and parcel of it; **etw ~ in Betracht ziehen** to consider sth as well

Mit|an|ge|klag|te(r) MF *decl as adj* co-defendant

Mit|ar|beit F cooperation, collaboration; *(= Hilfe auch)* assistance; *(= Teilnahme)* participation *(auch Sch)*; **~ bei** *or* **an etw** *(dat)* work on sth; **er ist an einer ~ bei diesem Projekt interessiert** he is interested in working on this project; **unter ~ von** in collaboration with

mit+ar|bei|ten VI *sep (= mithelfen)* to cooperate *(bei* on); *(bei Projekt etc)* to collaborate; **an** *or* **bei etw ~** to work on sth; **er hat beim Bau des Hauses mitgearbeitet** he helped build the house; **im Unterricht ~** to take an active part in lessons; **seine Frau arbeitet mit** *(inf)* his wife works too

Mit|ar|bei|ter(in) M(F) *(= Betriebsangehöriger)* employee; *(= Kollege)* colleague; *(an Projekt etc)* collaborator; **die ~ an diesem Projekt/bei dieser Firma** those who work on this project/for this firm; **freier ~** freelance; **inoffizieller ~** *(DDR: von Stasi)* unofficial collaborator

Mit|ar|bei|ter-: **Mit|ar|bei|ter|mo|ti|va|ti|on** F staff *or* employee motivation; **Mit|ar|bei|ter|stab** M staff

Mit|ar|beits|fest|stel|lung F *(Aus Sch: = kürzer schriftlicher Test)* participation assessment

Mit|ar|beits|no|te F *(Sch: bei Schülerbeurteilung)* participation mark *(Brit) or* grade *(US)*

Mit|be|grün|der(in) M(F) co-founder

mit+be|kom|men *ptp* **mitbekommen** VT *sep irreg* **a** **etw ~** to get *or* be given sth to take with one; *Rat, Ausbildung* to get *or* be given sth; *(als Mitgift)* to be given sth as a dowry **b** *(inf) (= verstehen)* to get *(inf)*; *(= bemerken)* to realize; **hast du das noch nicht ~?** *(= erfahren)* you mean you didn't know that?

mit+be|nut|zen *ptp* **mitbenutzt**, *(esp S Ger, Aus, Sw)* **mit+be|nüt|zen** *ptp* **mitbenützt** VT *sep* to share (the use of)

Mit|be|nut|zung F, *(esp S Ger, Aus, Sw)* **Mit|be|nüt|zung** F **-, -en** joint use

Mit|be|sitz M co-ownership, joint ownership; **~ an etw** *(dat)* **haben** to have a share in the ownership of sth

Mit|be|sit|zer(in) M(F) joint owner, co-owner

mit+be|stim|men *ptp* **mitbestimmt** *sep* **VI** to have a say *(bei* in); **~d sein** *or* **wirken** to have an influence *(bei, für* on) **VT** to have an influence on

Mit|be|stim|mung F co-determination, participation *(bei* in); **~ der Arbeiter** *or* **am Arbeitsplatz** worker participation

Mit|be|stim|mungs-: **Mit|be|stim|mungs|ge|setz** NT worker participation law; **Mit|be|stim|mungs|recht** NT right of participation *(in decision-making etc)*

Mit|be|wer|ber(in) M(F) (fellow) competitor; *(für Stelle)* (fellow) applicant

Mit|be|woh|ner(in) M(F) (fellow) occupant; **die ~ in unserem Haus** the other occupants of the house

mit+brin|gen VT *sep irreg* **a** *Geschenk etc* to bring; *Freund, Begleiter* to bring along; *(beim Zurückkommen)* to bring back; **jdm etw ~** to bring sth for sb, to bring sb sth; **jdm etw von** *or* **aus der Stadt ~** to bring (sb) sth back from town; **jdm etw vom Bäcker ~** to get (sb) sth from the baker's; **was sollen wir der Gastgeberin ~?** what should we take to our hostess?; **die richtige Einstellung ~** to have the right attitude; **bring gute Laune mit** come ready to enjoy yourself; **Sie haben schönes Wetter mitgebracht!** lovely weather you've brought with you!

b *Mitgift, Kinder, Kapital* to bring with one; **etw in die Ehe ~** to have sth when one gets married; **sie hat ein ansehnliches Vermögen in die Ehe mitgebracht** she brought a considerable fortune with her when she got married; **meine Frau hat den Hund in die Ehe mitgebracht** my wife had the dog before our marriage; **sie hat zwei Kinder aus der ersten Ehe mitgebracht** she has two children from her first marriage

c *(fig) Befähigung, Voraussetzung etc* to have, to possess

Mit|bring|sel [ˈmɪtbrɪŋzl] NT **-s, -** *(Geschenk)* small present; *(Andenken)* souvenir

Mit|bür|ger(in) M(F) fellow citizen; **meine Stuttgarter ~** my fellow citizens from Stuttgart; *(in Anrede)* fellow citizens of Stuttgart; **die älteren ~** senior citizens

mit+den|ken VI *sep irreg (= Gedankengänge/Beweisführung mitvollziehen)* to follow sb's train of thought/line of argument; *(= Ideen einbringen)* to make a contribution; **zum Glück hat er mitgedacht** luckily he did not let me/us *etc* forget; **du denkst ja mit!** good thinking; **denk mal mit** help me/us *etc* think

mit+dür|fen VI *sep irreg* **wir durften nicht mit** we weren't allowed to go along

Mit|ei|gen|tum NT = **Mitbesitz**

Mit|ei|gen|tü|mer(in) M(F) joint owner, co-owner

mit|ei|nan|der [mɪtlaiˈnandɐ] ADV with each other, with one another; *(= gemeinsam)* together; **alle ~!** all together; **wir haben lange ~ geredet** we had a long talk; **sie reden nicht mehr ~** they are not talking (to each other *or* to one another) any more; **guten Tag ~** *(esp S Ger)* hello everybody *or* all

Mit|ei|nan|der [mɪtlaiˈnandɐ] NT **-s**, *no pl* cooperation; **ein ~ ist besser als ein Gegeneinander** it is better to work with each other than against each other

mit+emp|fin|den *ptp* **mitempfunden** *sep irreg* **VT** to feel too, to share **VI** **mit jdm ~** to feel for sb, to sympathize with sb

Mit|emp|fin|den NT sympathy

mit|ent|schei|dend ADJ **~ sein** to be a decisive factor *or* one of the decisive factors

Mit|er|be M, **Mit|er|bin** F joint heir; **außer ihm sind es noch 4 ~n** there are 4 other heirs apart from him

mit+er|le|ben VT *sep* to experience; *Krieg auch* to live through; *(im Fernsehen)* to watch

mit+es|sen *sep irreg* **VT** *Schale etc* to eat as well; *Mahlzeit* to share **VI** **(bei jdm) ~** to eat with sb, to have a meal with sb; **willst du nicht ~?** why don't you have something to eat too?

Mit|es|ser M blackhead

mit+fah|ren VI *sep irreg aux sein* to go (with sb); **sie fährt mit** she is going too; *(mit mir/uns zusammen)* she is going with me/us; **(mit jdm) ~** to go with sb; *(auf Reise auch)* to travel with sb; *(= mitgenommen werden)* to get a lift *or* ride *(esp US)* with sb, to be given a lift *or* ride *(esp US)* by sb; **jdn ~ lassen** to allow sb to go; *(= jdn mitnehmen)* to give sb a lift *or* ride *(esp US)*; **kann ich (mit Ihnen) ~?** can you give me a lift *or* a ride *(esp US)*?; **er fährt jeden Morgen mit mir im Auto mit** I give him a lift *or* ride *(esp US)* in my car every morning; **wie viel Leute können bei dir ~?** how many people can you take (with you)?; **ich fahre nicht gern mit ihr im Auto mit** I don't like going in her car; **auf der Lokomotive ~** to ride with the driver

Mit|fah|rer(in) M(F) fellow passenger; *(vom Fahrer aus gesehen)* passenger

Mit|fahr-: **Mit|fahr|ge|le|gen|heit** F lift; **~en nach Rom** lifts *or* rides *(esp US)* offered to Rome; **Mit|fahr|zent|ra|le** F agency for arranging lifts *or* rides *(esp US)*

mit+fie|bern VI *sep (inf)* to join the fever

mit+fi|nan|zie|ren VT *sep* to help to finance

mit+füh|len VI *sep* **mit jdm ~** to feel for sb

mit|füh|lend **ADJ** sympathetic, compassionate **ADV** sympathetically, compassionately

mit+füh|ren VT *sep Papiere, Ware, Waffen etc* to carry (with one); *(Fluss)* to carry along

mit+ge|ben VT *sep irreg* **jdn jdm ~** to send sb along with sb; **jdm etw ~** to give sb sth to take with them; *Rat, Erziehung* to give sb sth; **das gebe ich dir noch mit** take that (with you) too

Mit|ge|fan|ge|ne(r) MF *decl as adj* fellow prisoner

Mit|ge|fühl NT sympathy

mit+ge|hen VI *sep irreg aux sein* **a** *(= mit anderen gehen)* to go too *or* along; **mit jdm ~** to go with sb; *(= begleiten auch)* to accompany sb; **gehen Sie mit?** are you going (too)?; **ich gehe bis zur Ecke mit** I'll go to the corner with you/him *etc*; **er ging bis 25.000 Euro mit** *(bei Auktion)* he went with the bidding until it reached 25,000 euros; **mit der Zeit ~** to move with the times; **mit der Mode ~** to keep up with fashion; **mitgegangen, (mitgefangen,) mitgehangen** *(Prov)* fly with the crows, get shot with the crows *(prov)*

b *(fig: Publikum etc)* to respond (favourably *(Brit) or* favorably *(US)*) *(mit* to); **man merkt, wie die Zuhörer richtig (mit ihm) ~** you can see

that the audience is really with him
c *(inf)* **etw ~ lassen** to lift *or* pinch sth *(Brit inf)*, to steal sth

Mit|gift ['mɪtgɪft] F **-, -en** dowry

Mit|gift|jä|ger M *(inf)* dowry-hunter *(Brit)*, fortune-hunter

Mit|glied ['mɪtgliːt] NT member (*+gen, bei, in +dat* of); **~ eines Komitees sein** to sit on a committee, to be a member of a committee

Mit|glie|der-: **Mit|glie|der|lis|te** F list of members; **Mit|glie|der|schwund** M dwindling membership (numbers *pl*); **Mit|glie|der|ver|samm|lung** F general meeting; **Mit|glie|der|zahl** F membership, number of members; **Mit|glie|der|zu|wachs** M increase *or* growth in membership

Mit|glieds-: **Mit|glieds|aus|weis** M membership card; **Mit|glieds|bei|trag** M membership subscription *or* fee, membership dues *pl*

Mit|glied|schaft ['mɪtgliːtʃaft] F **-, -en** membership

Mit|glieds|staat M member state *or* country

mit+ha|ben VT *sep irreg* **etw ~** to have sth (with one); **jdn ~** to have brought sb with one; **hast du alles mit?** have you got everything?

Mit|häft|ling M fellow prisoner; **die ~e** *pl* the other prisoners

Mit|haf|tung F *(Jur)* joint liability

mit+hal|ten ✪ 32.3 VI *sep irreg (= sich beteiligen)* to join in (*mit* with); *(= bei Leistung, Tempo etc nachkommen)* (*mit* with) to keep up, to keep pace; *(bei Versteigerung)* to stay in the bidding; **beim Trinken hat er immer feste mitgehalten** he would always drink as much as the rest; **bei einer Diskussion ~ können** to be able to hold one's own in a discussion; **er kann so erstklassig Englisch, da kann keiner ~** he speaks such excellent English, no-one can touch him *(inf)*; **ich halte mit** *(= mitmachen)* count me in (on that)

mit+hel|fen VI *sep irreg* to help; **beim Bau des Hauses ~** to help build the house; **hilf doch ein bisschen mit** give us *or* lend us a hand

Mit|he|raus|ge|ber(in) M(F) co-editor, joint editor; *(Verlag)* co-publisher

mit|hil|fe, **mit Hil|fe** [mɪt'hɪlfə] PREP *+gen* with the help *or* aid (*+gen* of)

Mit|hil|fe F assistance, aid; **unter ~ der Kollegen** with the aid *or* assistance of colleagues

mit|hin [mɪt'hɪn] ADV *(dated)* therefore, consequently

mit+hö|ren *sep* VT to listen to (too); *Gespräch* to overhear; *(heimlich)* to listen in on; *Vorlesung* to attend, to go to; **ich habe alles mitgehört** I heard everything VI *(zusammen mit jdm)* to listen (too); *(= Radio hören, Gespräch belauschen)* to listen in (*bei* on); *(zufällig)* to overhear; **Feind hört mit** *(Mil prov)* careless talk costs lives; *(fig hum)* someone may be listening VI *impers* **es hört jd mit** sb is listening

Mit|in|ha|ber(in) M(F) *(von Haus etc)* joint owner, co-owner; *(von Firma auch)* joint proprietor

mit+kämp|fen VI *sep* to fight; **mit jdm ~** to fight alongside sb

Mit|kämp|fer(in) M(F) *(im Krieg)* comrade-in--arms; *(Sport) (= Teamkollege)* team-mate; *(= Partner)* partner

mit+klin|gen VI *sep irreg (Ton, Saite)* to sound, to resonate; **bei dem ersten Lied klangen eigenartige Töne mit** there were some odd notes in the first song; **in ihrer Äußerung klang Traurigkeit/ein leichter Vorwurf mit** there was sadness/a slight note of reproach in her remark; **Assoziationen, die bei diesem Wort ~** associations contained in this word

mit+kom|men VI *sep irreg aux sein* **a** *(= mit anderen kommen)* to come along (*mit* with); *(Sendung, Brief etc)* to come, to arrive; **kommst du auch mit?** are you coming too?; **ich kann nicht ~** I can't come; **komm doch mit!** (do) come with us/me *etc!*, why don't you come too?; **kommst du mit ins Kino?** are you coming to the cinema (with me/us)?; **bis zum Bahnhof ~** to come as far as the station; **ich bin gerade noch mit dem Zug mitgekommen** I just caught the train
b *(inf) (= mithalten)* to keep up; *(= verstehen)* to follow; **da komme ich nicht mit** that's beyond me; **sie kommt in der Schule/in Französisch gut mit** she is getting on well at school/with French

mit+kön|nen VI *sep irreg (inf)* **a** *(= mitkommen können)* to be able to come (*mit* with); *(= mitgehen können)* to be able to go (*mit* with) **b** *(usu neg) (= verstehen)* to be able to follow; **da kann ich nicht mehr mit** I can't follow that

mit+krie|gen VT *sep (inf)* = **mitbekommen**

mit+lau|fen VI *sep irreg aux sein* to run (*mit* with); *(Rad, Zeiger etc)* to turn; *(Kamera, Tonband)* to run; **er läuft beim 100-Meter-Lauf mit** he's running in the 100 metres *(Brit) or* meters *(US)*

Mit|läu|fer(in) M(F) *(Pol, pej)* fellow traveller *(Brit) or* traveler *(US)*

Mit|laut M consonant

Mit|leid NT, *no pl* pity, compassion (*mit* for); *(= Mitgefühl)* sympathy (*mit* with, for); **~ erregend** = **mitleiderregend**

Mit|lei|den|schaft F **jdn/etw in ~ ziehen** to affect sb/sth (detrimentally)

mit|leid|er|re|gend ADJ pitiable, pitiful

mit|lei|dig ['mɪtlaidɪç] ADJ pitying; *(= mitfühlend)* sympathetic; *Mensch* compassionate, sympathetic ADV pityingly; *(= mitfühlend)* compassionately

Mit|leid(s)-: **mit|leid(s)|los** ADJ pitiless, heartless ADV pitilessly, heartlessly; **mit|leid(s)|voll** ADJ sympathetic, compassionate ADV sympathetically, compassionately

mit+ler|nen VTI *sep* to learn too; *(= durch jdn lernen)* to learn (*mit* from)

mit+le|sen VTI *sep irreg* to read too; *Text* to follow; **etw (mit jdm) ~** to read sth at the same time (as sb)

mit+ma|chen VTI *sep* **a** *(= teilnehmen) Spiel, Singen etc* to join in; *Reise, Expedition, Ausflug* to go on; *Kurs* to do; *Mode* to follow; *Wettbewerb* to take part in; **(bei) etw ~** to join in sth; **er hat schon viele Partys mitgemacht** he has been to lots of parties; **er macht alles mit** he always joins in (all the fun); **jede Mode ~** to follow every fashion; **da mache ich nicht mit** *(= ist nicht mein Fall)* that's not my scene; *(= ohne mich)* count me out!; **meine Augen/meine Beine machen nicht mehr mit** my eyes/legs are giving up; **wenn das Wetter mitmacht** if the weather cooperates
b *(inf: = einverstanden sein)* **da kann ich nicht ~** I can't go along with that; **da macht mein Chef nicht mit** my boss won't go along with that; **das mache ich nicht mehr mit** I've had quite enough (of that); **ich mache das nicht mehr lange mit** I won't take that much longer
c *(= erleben)* to live through; *(= erleiden)* to go through; **sie hat viel mitgemacht** she has been through a lot in her time

Mit|mensch M fellow man *or* creature, neighbour *(Brit)*, neighbor *(US)*; **wir müssen in jedem den ~en sehen** we must see people as neighbours *(Brit) or* neighbors *(US)*

mit|mensch|lich ADJ *Kontakte, Probleme etc* human; *Verhalten* considerate

Mit|mensch|lich|keit F humanity

mit+mi|schen VI *sep (inf) (= sich beteiligen)* to be involved (*in +dat, bei* in)

mit+müs|sen VI *sep irreg (= mitkommen müssen)* to have to come too; *(= mitgehen müssen)* to have to go too

Mit|nah|me [-naːmə] F **-,** *no pl* **(jdm) die ~ von etw empfehlen** to recommend sb to take sth with them

Mit|nah|me-: **Mit|nah|me|ar|ti|kel** M impulse buy; **Mit|nah|me|markt** M cash-and-carry

mit+neh|men VT *sep irreg* **a** *(= mit sich nehmen)* to take (with one); *(= ausleihen)* to borrow; *(= kaufen)* to take; **jdn (im Auto) ~** to give sb a lift *or* ride *(esp US)*; **der Bus konnte nicht alle ~** the bus couldn't take everyone; **sie nimmt alles mit, was sich bietet** she makes the most of everything life has to offer; **(das ist) zum Mitnehmen** please take one; **einmal Pommes frites zum Mitnehmen** a bag of chips to take away *(Brit)*, French fries to go *(US)*; **Gewinne ~** *(St Ex)* to take profits
b *(= erschöpfen) jdn* to exhaust, to weaken; *(= beschädigen)* to be bad for; **mitgenommen aussehen** to look the worse for wear
c *(= stehlen)* to walk off with
d *(inf) Sehenswürdigkeit, Veranstaltung* to take in

mit|nich|ten [mɪt'nɪçtn] ADV *(old)* not at all, by no means, in no way

Mit|ra ['miːtra] F **-, Mit|ren** [-trən] *(Eccl)* mitre *(Brit)*, miter *(US)*

Mit|rau|chen NT **-s**, *no pl* passive smoking

Mit|rau|cher(in) M(F) passive smoker

mit+rech|nen VT *sep* to count; *Betrag* to count in; **Feiertage nicht mitgerechnet** excluding public holidays

mit+re|den *sep* VI *(= Meinung äußern)* to join in (*bei etw* sth); *(= mitbestimmen)* to have a say (*bei* in); **da kann er nicht ~** he wouldn't know anything about that; **da kann ich ~** I should know; **da kann ich aus Erfahrung ~** I know from my own experience; **sie will überall ~** *(inf)* she always has to have her say VT **da möchte ich auch ein Wörtchen ~** I'd like to have some say (in this) too; **Sie haben hier nichts mitzureden** this is none of your concern

mit+rei|sen VI *sep aux sein* to travel (too) (*mit* with)

Mit|rei|sen|de(r) MF *decl as adj* fellow passenger

mit+rei|ßen VT *sep irreg (Fluss, Lawine)* to sweep *or* carry away; *(Fahrzeug)* to carry along; **sich ~ lassen** *(fig)* to allow oneself to be carried away; **der Schauspieler/seine Rede hat alle mitgerissen** everyone was carried away by the actor's performance/his speech

mit|rei|ßend ADJ *Rhythmus, Enthusiasmus* infectious; *Reden, Musik* rousing; *Film, Fußballspiel* thrilling, exciting ADV *vortragen* infectiously; **er redete ~** he gave a rousing speech

mit|samt [mɪt'zamt] PREP *+dat* together with

mit+schi|cken VT *sep (in Brief etc)* to enclose

mit+schlei|fen VT *sep* to drag along

mit+schlep|pen VT *sep* **jdn/etw ~** to drag *or* cart *(inf)* sb/sth along

mit+schnei|den VT *sep irreg* to record

Mit|schnitt M recording

mit+schrei|ben *sep irreg* VT **etw ~** to write *or* take sth down; *(Sekretärin)* to take sth down; **er hat ein Stück Zeitgeschichte mitgeschrieben** he helped shape recent history VI to take notes; **nicht so schnell, ich kann nicht mehr ~** not so fast, I can't keep up

Mit|schrift F record; *(von Vorlesung etc)* notes *pl*; **zur ~** for the record; **nicht zur ~ bestimmt** *or* **gedacht** off the record

Mit|schuld F share of the blame *or* responsibility (*an +dat* for); *(an einem Verbrechen)* complicity (*an +dat* in); **ihn trifft eine ~** a share of the blame falls on him *or* must be taken by him; *(an Verbrechen)* he is implicated (*an +dat* in)

mit|schul|dig ADJ *(an Verbrechen)* implicated (*an +dat* in); *(an Unfall)* partly responsible *or* to blame (*an +dat* for); **sich ~ machen** to incur (some) blame (*an +dat* for); *(an Verbrechen)* to become implicated (*an +dat* in)

Mit|schul|di|ge(r) MF *decl as adj* accomplice; *(= Helfershelfer)* accessory

Mit|schü|ler(in) M(F) school-friend; *(in derselben Klasse)* classmate

mit+schwin|gen VI *sep irreg (lit)* to resonate too; **was bei** *or* **in diesem Wort mitschwingt** the overtones *or* associations contained in *or* conjured up by this word; **in seiner Stimme schwang ein Ton von Enttäuschung mit** there was a note of disappointment in his voice

mit+sin|gen *sep irreg* VT to join in (singing) VI to join in the singing, to sing along; **in einer Oper/einem Chor** *etc* ~ to sing in an opera/ choir *etc*

mit+spie|len VI *sep* **a** *(= auch spielen)* to play too; *(in Mannschaft etc)* to play *(bei* in); **in einem Film/bei einem Theaterstück** ~ to be in a film/ play; **bei einem Orchester** ~ to play in an orchestra; **wer spielt mit?** who wants to play?; *(in Mannschaft)* who's playing?; *(Theat etc)* who's in it?
b *(fig inf) (= mitmachen)* to play along *(inf)*; *(= sich beteiligen)* to be involved in; **wenn das Wetter mitspielt** if the weather's OK *(inf)*
c *(Gründe, Motive)* to play a part *or* role *(bei* in), to be involved *(bei* in)
d *(= Schaden zufügen)* **er hat ihr übel** *or* **schlimm** *or* **arg** *or* **hart mitgespielt** he has treated her badly; **das Leben hat ihr übel** *etc* **mitgespielt** she has had a hard life, life has been hard to her

Mit|spie|ler(in) M(F) *(Sport)* player; *(Theat)* member of the cast; **seine** ~ *(Sport)* his team-mates; *(Theat)* the other members of the cast

Mit|spra|che F a say

Mit|spra|che|recht NT right to a say in a matter; **jdm ein ~ einräumen** *or* **gewähren** to allow *or* grant sb a say *(bei* in); **bei dieser Entscheidung möchte ich ein** ~ I want to have a say in this matter

mit+spre|chen *sep irreg* VT *Gebet etc* to join in (saying); **etw (mit jdm)** ~ to say sth with sb, to say sth at the same time as sb VI to join in; **bei etw** ~ to join in sth; *(= mitbestimmen)* to have a say in sth; **sie will überall** ~ she always wants to have her say

Mit|strei|ter(in) M(F) *(geh)* comrade-in-arms

mit|tag △ ['mɪta:k] ADV → **Mittag a**

Mit|tag ['mɪta:k] M **-(e)s, -e** **a** midday; **gegen** ~ around *or* about midday *or* noon; **über** ~ at midday, at lunchtime(s); **am** ~ at midday, at lunchtime; **jeden** ~ every day at midday, every lunchtime; **jeden ~ gegen halb eins** every day at half past twelve; **gestern/heute/morgen** ~ at midday yesterday/today/tomorrow, yesterday/ today/tomorrow lunchtime; **kurz vor/nach** ~ shortly before/after midday; **des ~s** *(geh)* around noon *or* midday; **eines ~s** *(geh)* one day around noon *or* midday; **zu ~ essen** to have lunch *or* dinner, to have one's midday meal; **etwas Warmes zu ~ essen** to have a cooked lunch *(Brit) or* warm lunch *(US)*
b *(inf: Pause)* lunch hour, lunch-break; ~ **machen/haben** to take/have one's lunch hour *or* lunch-break; **sie macht gerade** ~ she's (off) at lunch → **Dienstagmittag** *etc*
c *(old, liter: = Süden)* south

Mit|tag NT **-s**, *no pl (inf: = Mittagessen)* lunch

Mit|tag|es|sen NT lunch, midday meal; **er kam zum** ~ he came to lunch; **sie saßen beim** ~ they were having lunch, they were having their midday meal

mit|tä|gig ADJ *attr* midday

mit|täg|lich ADJ *attr* midday, lunchtime; *Schläfchen* afternoon ADV at lunchtimes

mit|tags ADV at lunchtime; **die Deutschen essen ~ warm** the Germans have a hot meal at midday; ~ **(um) 12 Uhr, (um) 12 Uhr** ~ at 12 noon, at 12 o'clock midday; **sonnabends** ~ Saturday lunchtime → **dienstagmittags** *etc*

Mit|tags-: **Mit|tags|aus|ga|be** F midday *or* lunchtime edition; **Mit|tags|brot** NT *(dial)* lunch; **Mit|tags|glut** F *(liter)*, **Mit|tags|hit|ze** F midday *or* noonday heat, heat of midday; **Mit|tags|mahl** NT *(liter)*, **Mit|tags|mahl|zeit** F midday meal; **Mit|tags|pau|se** F lunch hour, lunch-break; ~ **machen/haben** to take/ have one's lunch hour *or* lunch-break; *(Geschäft etc)* to close at lunchtime; **Mit|tags|ru|he** F period of quiet (after lunch); *(in Geschäft)* midday-closing; ~ **halten** to have a period of quiet after lunch; *(Geschäft)* to close for lunch; **Mit|tags|schlaf** M afternoon nap; **Mit|tags|son|ne** F midday sun; **Mit|tags|stun|de** F midday, noon; **um die** *or* **zur** *(geh)* ~ around midday *or* noon; **Mit|tags|tisch** M **a** dinner table; **den ~ decken** to lay *(esp Brit) or* set the table for lunch; **am ~ sitzen** to be sitting (at the table) having lunch **b** *(im Restaurant)* businessman's lunch; **Mit|tags|zeit** F lunchtime; **während** *or* **in der** ~ at lunchtime; **um die** ~ around midday *or* lunchtime; **zur** ~ *(geh)* at midday

Mit|tä|ter(in) M(F) accomplice

Mit|tä|ter|schaft F complicity; **die ~ leugnen** *or* **abstreiten** to deny complicity

Mitt|drei|ßi|ger ['mɪtdraisɪgɐ] M **-s, -**, **Mitt|drei|ßi|ge|rin** [-ərɪn] F **-, -nen** man/woman in his/her mid-thirties

Mit|te ['mɪtə] F **-, -n** **a** *(= Mittelpunkt, mittlerer Teil)* middle; *(von Kreis, Kugel, Stadt)* centre *(Brit)*, center *(US)*; *(Sport)* centre *(Brit)*, center *(US)*; **ein Buch bis zur ~ lesen** to read half of a book; ~ **August** in the middle of August; ~ **des Jahres/des Monats** halfway through the year/ month; ~ **der siebziger Jahre** in the mid-seventies; **er ist ~ vierzig** *or* **der Vierziger** he's in his mid-forties; **die goldene** ~ the golden mean; **die rechte** ~ a happy medium; **in der** ~ in the middle; *(zwischen zwei Menschen)* in between (them/us *etc*); *(zwischen Ortschaften)* halfway, midway; **sie nahmen sie in die** ~ they took her between them → **ab ADV, Reich a**
b *(Pol)* centre *(Brit)*, center *(US)*; **die linke/ rechte** ~ centre-left/-right *(Brit)*, center-left/-right *(US)*; **in der ~ stehen** to be moderate; **in der ~ zwischen** midway between; **rechts/links von der** ~ right/left of centre *(Brit) or* center *(US)*
c *(von Gruppe, Gesellschaft)* **einer aus unserer** ~ one of us, one of our number; **ich bin gern in eurer** ~ I like being with you; **in unserer** ~ with us, in our midst, among(st) us; **wir haben ihn in unserer ~ willkommen geheißen** we welcomed him into our midst; **er wurde aus unserer ~ gerissen** he was taken from our midst *or* from amongst us

mit|teil|bar ADJ communicable

mit+tei|len *sep* ✪ 31, 45.3, 46.5, 48.3, 51.4 VT **jdm etw** ~ to tell sb sth; *(= benachrichtigen)* to inform sb of *or* about sth, to communicate sth to sb *(form)*; *(= bekannt geben)* to announce sth to sb; *(Comm, Admin)* to inform *or* notify sb of sth; **hiermit teilen wir Ihnen mit, dass …** we hereby inform you that …; **teile ihm die Nachricht schonend mit** break the news to him gently; **es wurde mitgeteilt, dass …** it was announced that …; **wie die Polizei mitteilt, …** as announced by the police …
VR **a** *(= kommunizieren)* to communicate *(jdm* with sb); **er kann sich gut/schlecht** ~ he finds it easy/difficult to communicate
b *(geh: Stimmung)* to communicate itself *(jdm* to sb)

mit|teil|sam ['mɪttailza:m] ADJ communicative; *(pej)* talkative, garrulous

Mit|tei|lung F *(= Bekanntgabe)* announcement; *(= Erklärung)* statement; *(= Benachrichtigung)* notification; *(Comm, Admin)* communication; *(an Mitarbeiter etc)* memo; *(von Korrespondenten, Reporter etc)* report; **jdm (eine) ~ (von etw) machen** *(form)* to inform sb (of sth), to report (sth) to sb; *(= bekannt geben)* to announce sth to sb; *(= Erklärung abgeben)* to make a statement (about sth) to sb; *(= benachrichtigen)* to inform *or* notify sb (of sth); **eine ~ bekommen, dass …** to hear that …

Mit|tei|lungs|be|dürf|nis NT need to talk to other people

mit|tel ['mɪtl] ADJ = **mittlere(r, s) b**

Mit|tel ['mɪtl] NT **-s, -** **a** *(Math: = Durchschnitt)* average; **im** ~ on average; **arithmetisches/geometrisches** ~ arithmetical/geometrical mean
b *(= Mittel zum Zweck, Transportmittel etc)* means *sing*; *(= Maßnahme, Methode)* way, method; *(= Werbemittel, Propagandamittel, zur Verkehrsbeeinflussung)* device; *(= Lehrmittel)* aid; ~ **und Wege finden** to find ways and means; ~ **zum Zweck** a means to an end; **kein ~ unversucht lassen** to try everything; ~ **gegen die Inflation** ways of beating inflation; **als letztes** *or* **äußerstes** ~ as a last resort; **zu anderen ~n greifen, andere ~ anwenden** to use *or* employ other means *or* methods; **ihm ist jedes ~ recht** he will do anything (to achieve his ends); **ihm war jedes ~ recht, dazu war ihm jedes ~ recht** he did not care how he did it *or* what means he used to achieve his ends; **er ist in der Wahl seiner ~ nicht zimperlich** he is not fussy about what methods he chooses; **etw mit allen ~n verhindern/bekämpfen** to do one's utmost *or* to do everything one can to prevent/oppose sth; **etw mit allen ~n versuchen** to try one's utmost to do sth; **sie hat mit allen ~n gekämpft, um …** she fought tooth and nail to …
c PL *(= Geldmittel)* funds *pl*, resources *pl*; *(= Privatmittel)* means *pl*, resources *pl* **d** *(= Medikament, kosmetisch)* preparation; *(Med)* drug, preparation; *(= Medizin)* medicine; *(= Putzmittel)* cleaning agent; *(= Fleckenmittel)* spot *or* stain remover; *(= Waschmittel)* detergent; *(= Haarwaschmittel)* shampoo; **welches ~ nimmst du?** what do you use?; *(Med: = einnehmen)* what do you take?; **ein ~ zum Einreiben** *(flüssig)* something *or* a lotion to be rubbed in; *(Salbe)* an ointment to be rubbed in; *(Creme)* a cream to be rubbed in; **das ist ein ~ gegen meine Erkältung/Schuppen** that is for my cold/dandruff; ~ **zum Putzen** cleaning things *pl or* stuff; **sich** *(dat)* **ein ~ (gegen Kopfschmerzen/Husten** *etc*) **verschreiben lassen** to get the doctor to prescribe something (for headaches/a cough *etc*); **welches ~ hat der Arzt dir verschrieben?** what did the doctor give you?; **es gibt kein ~ gegen Schnupfen** there is no cure for the common cold; **das beste ~ für** *or* **gegen etw** the best cure *or* remedy for sth
e *(Phys, Chem: = Medium)* medium

Mit|tel-: **Mit|tel|ach|se** F *(von Fläche, Körper)* central axis; *(von Auto)* central axle; **mit|tel|ak|tiv** ADJ *Atommüll etc* intermediate-level; **Mit|tel|al|ter** NT Middle Ages *pl*; **da herrschen Zustände wie im ~!** *(inf)* it is positively medieval there; **mit|tel|al|ter|lich** [-laltɛlɪç] ADJ medieval ADV **eine ~ anmutende Stadt** a medieval-looking town; ~ **geprägt sein** to show a medieval influence; **Mit|tel|ame|ri|ka** NT Central America (and the Caribbean); **mit|tel|ameri|ka|nisch** ADJ Central American; **mit|tel|bar** ADJ indirect *(auch Jur)*; *Schaden* consequential ADV indirectly; **Mit|tel|bau** M *pl* **-bauten** **a** *(Gebäude)* central block **b** *no pl (Univ)* non-professorial teaching staff; **mit|tel|deutsch** ADJ *(Geog, Ling)* Central German; *(dated Pol)* East German; **Mit|tel|deutsch(e)** NT Central German dialects *pl*; **Mit|tel|deutsch|land** NT *Germany east of the Harz Mountains excluding Pomerania etc* *(dated Pol: = DDR)* East Germany; **Mit|tel|ding** NT *(= Mischung)* cross *(zwischen +dat, aus* between); **Mit|tel|eu|ro|pa** NT Central Europe; **Mit|tel|eu|ro|pä|er(in)** M(F) Central European; **ich als normaler** ~ *(inf)* any average person like myself; **mit|tel|eu|ro|pä|isch** ADJ Central European; **~e Zeit** Central European Time; **mit|tel|fein** ADJ *Erbsen etc* medium-sized; *Kaffee, Mehl etc* medium-ground ADV **den Kaffee/das Mehl ~ mahlen** to grind the coffee/flour medium-fine; **Mit|tel|feld** NT *(Sport)* midfield; *(die Spieler auch)* midfield players *pl*; **Mit|tel|feld|spie|ler(in)** M(F) *(Sport)* midfielder; **Mit|tel|fin|ger** M middle finger; **Mit|tel|fran|ken** [-fraŋkn] NT **-s** Central Franconia; **mit|tel|fris|tig** [-frɪstɪç] ADJ *Finanzplanung, Kredite* medium-term; *Voraussage* medium-range ADV in the medium term; **Mit|tel|gang** M centre aisle *(Brit)*, center aisle *(US)*; **Mit|tel|ge|bir|ge** NT low mountain range; **Mit|tel|ge|wicht** NT middleweight; **Meister im** ~ middleweight champion; **mit|tel|groß** ADJ medium-sized; **mit|tel|hoch|deutsch** ADJ Middle High German; **Mit|tel|hoch|deutsch(e)** NT Middle High German; **Mit|tel|klas|se** F **a** *(Comm)* middle of the market; **ein Wagen der ~** a mid-range car **b** *(Sociol)* middle classes *pl*; **Mit|tel|klas|se|wa|gen** M mid-range car, middle of the range car; **Mit|tel|kon|so|le** F *(Aut)* centre *(Brit)* or center *(US)* console; **mit|tel|län|disch** [-lɛndɪʃ] ADJ Mediterranean; **das Mittelländische Meer** *(form)* the Mediterranean Sea; **Mit|tel|lauf** M *(eines Flusses)* middle reaches *pl*; **Mit|tel|läu|fer(in)** M(F) *(Sport)* centre-half *(Brit)*, center-half *(US)*; **Mit|tel|li|nie** F centre *(Brit)* or center *(US)* line; **mit|tel|los** ADJ without means; *(= arm)* impoverished; **Mit|tel|lo|sig|keit** F **-, -en** lack of means; **Mit|tel|maß** NT mediocrity *no art*; **das (gesunde) ~** the happy medium; **~ sein** to be average; **seine Leistungen bewegen sich im ~, seine Leistungen gehen nicht über das ~ hinaus** his performance is mediocre; **mit|tel|mä|ßig** ADJ mediocre; *Schriftsteller, Spieler etc auch* indifferent; **als Redner gibt er eine recht ~e Figur ab** he's a pretty mediocre *or* indifferent speaker ADV indifferently; *begabt, gebildet* moderately; *ausgestattet* modestly; **~ ausgebildet** moderately well-trained; **wie gefällt es dir hier? – so ~** how do you like it here? – so-so *(inf)*; **Mit|tel|mä|ßig|keit** F mediocrity

Mit|tel|meer NT Mediterranean (Sea), Med *(inf)*

Mit|tel|meer- *in cpds* Mediterranean; **Mit|tel|meer|raum** M Mediterranean (region), Med *(inf)*

Mit|tel|ohr|ent|zün|dung F, **Mit|tel|ohr|ver|ei|te|rung** F inflammation of the middle ear, otitis (media) *(spec)*

Mit|tel-: **mit|tel|präch|tig** *(hum inf)* ADJ reasonable, not bad *pred*, so-so *pred (inf)*; *(= ziemlich schlecht)* pretty awful *(inf)* ADV not bad; **sich ~ fühlen** to feel not too bad; **Mit|tel|punkt** M *(Math, räumlich)* centre *(Brit)*, center *(US)*; *(fig: visuell)* focal point; **er muss immer ~ sein** *or* **im ~ stehen** he always has to be the centre *(Brit)* or center *(US)* of attention; **er steht im ~ des Interesses** he is the centre *(Brit)* or center *(US)* of attention; **Mit|tel|punkt|schu|le** F *school at the centre of a rural catchment area or rural service area*

mit|tels ['mɪtls] PREP *+gen or dat (geh)* by means of

Mit|tel-: **Mit|tel|schei|tel** M centre parting *(Brit)*, center part *(US)*; **Mit|tel|schicht** F *(Sociol)* middle class; **Mit|tel|schiff** NT *(Archit)* nave; **Mit|tel|schu|le** F **a** *(inf: = Realschule)* ≈ secondary modern school *(dated Brit)*, ≈ junior high *(US)* **b** *(Sw, Aus: = Oberschule)* secondary school, high school *(US)*; **mit|tel|schwer** ADJ *Text etc* of medium difficulty *pred*; *Verletzungen* moderately severe; *Unfall, Katastrophe* fairly serious; **etw als ~ einstufen** to classify sth as intermediate ADV *verletzt* seriously

Mit|tels|mann M *pl* **-männer** *or* **-leute**, **Mit|tels|per|son** F intermediary

mit|telst PREP *(old)* by means of

Mit|tel-: **Mit|tel|stand** M middle classes *pl*; **mit|tel|stän|dig** ADJ *(Bot)* perigynous *(spec)*;; **mit|tel|stän|disch** ADJ **a** middle-class **b** *Betrieb* medium-sized **c** *(Pol)* centrist; **Mit|tel|ständ|ler** [-ʃtɛndlɐ] M **-s, -**, **Mit|tel|ständ|le|rin** [-ərɪn] F **-, -nen a** middle-class person **b** *(Pol)* centrist; **Mit|tel|stein|zeit** F Mesolithic period; **Mit|tel|stel|lung** F medium setting; *(fig)* intermediate position; **Mit|tel|stim|me** F *(Mus)* middle part

Mit|tel|stre|cke F *(Sport)* middle-distance event; *(Aviat)* medium haul; *(von Rakete etc)* medium range

Mit|tel|stre|cken-: **Mit|tel|stre|cken|flug|zeug** NT medium-haul aircraft; **Mit|tel|stre|cken|lauf** M middle-distance race; *(Disziplin)* middle-distance running; **Mit|tel|stre|cken|läu|fer(in)** M(F) middle-distance runner; **Mit|tel|stre|cken|ra|ke|te** F intermediate-range *or* medium-range missile; **Mit|tel|stre|cken|waf|fe** F intermediate-range weapon

Mit|tel-: **Mit|tel|strei|fen** M central reservation *(Brit)*, median (strip) *(US)*; **Mit|tel|stück** NT middle part, centre *(Brit)* or center *(US)* part; *(von Braten etc)* middle; **Mit|tel|stu|fe** F *(Sch)* middle school *(Brit)*, junior high *(US)*; **Mit|tel|stür|mer(in)** M(F) *(Sport)* centre-forward *(Brit)*, center-forward *(US)*; **Mit|tel|teil** M OR NT middle section; **Mit|tel|weg** M middle course; **der goldene ~** the happy medium, the golden mean; **einen ~ gehen** *or* **einschlagen** to steer a middle course; **einen ~ suchen** to try to find a happy medium; **Mit|tel|wel|le** F *(Rad)* medium wave(band); **auf ~ senden** to broadcast on the medium waveband *or* on (the) medium wave; **Mit|tel|wert** M mean; **Mit|tel|wort** NT *pl* **-wörter** *(Gram)* participle; **~ der Gegenwart/Vergangenheit** present/past participle

mit|ten ['mɪtn] ADV **~ an etw** *(dat)*/**auf etw** *(dat)*/**in etw** *(dat)*/**bei etw** (right) in the middle of sth; **~ aus etw** (right) from the middle of sth; *(aus Gedränge etc auch)* from the midst of sth; **~ durch etw** (right) through the middle of sth; **~ darin/darein** (right) in the middle of it; **~ darunter** *(räumlich)* right under it/them; *(= dabei)* right amongst it/them, right in the middle of it/them; **~ (hin)durch** right through the middle; **~ im Urwald** in the middle *or* depths of the jungle; **~ in der Luft/im Atlantik** in mid-air/mid-Atlantic; **~ ins Gesicht** right in the face; **es ist noch ~ in der Nacht** it's still the middle of the night; **~ im Leben** in the middle of life; **~ in** *or* **bei der Arbeit** in the middle of working; **~ beim Frühstück/Essen sein** to be in the middle of (one's) breakfast/of eating; **~ unter uns** (right) in our midst; **der Stock brach ~ entzwei** the stick broke clean in two

mit|ten-: **mit|ten|drin** [mɪtn'drɪn] ADV (right) in the middle of it; **~ in der Stadt/der Arbeit** (right) in the middle of the town/one's work; **~, etw zu tun** (right) in the middle of doing sth; **mit|ten|durch** [mɪtn'dʊrç] ADV (right) through the middle; **mit|ten|mang** [mɪtn'maŋ] *(dial inf)* PREP *+dat or (sl) acc* among ADV (right) in the middle of it/them

Mit|ter|nacht F midnight *no art*

mit|ter|näch|tig [-nɛçtɪç], **mit|ter|nächt|lich** ADJ *attr* midnight; **zu ~er Stunde** *(geh)* at the midnight hour

Mit|ter|nachts-: **Mit|ter|nachts|son|ne** F midnight sun; **Mit|ter|nachts|stun|de** F witching hour; **Mit|ter|nachts|va|se** F *(hum)* chamber pot

Mitt|fünf|zi|ger ['mɪtfʏnftsɪgɐ] M **-s, -**, **Mitt|fünf|zi|ge|rin** [-ərɪn] F **-, -nen** man/woman in his/her mid-fifties

Mitt|ler ['mɪtlɐ] M **-s, -**, **Mitt|le|rin** [-ərɪn] F **-, -nen** mediator; *(liter: Ideen, Sprache etc)* medium

Mitt|ler|amt NT mediatory position

mitt|le|re(r, s) ['mɪtlərə] ADJ *attr* **a** *(= dazwischenliegend)* middle; **der/die/das ~** the middle one; **der Mittlere Osten** the Middle East; **der ~ Weg** *(fig)* the middle course **b** *(= den Mittelwert bildend)* medium; *(= mittelschwer) Kursus, Aufgabe* intermediate; *(= durchschnittlich)* average; *(Math)* mean; *(= von mittlerer Größe) Betrieb* medium-sized; **von ~m Wert** of medium value; **~r Beamter** *person in the section of the civil service for which the entry requirement is the Abitur*, ≈ civil servant of the administrative class *(Brit)*; **~n Alters** middle-aged; **~ Reife** *(Sch) first public examination in secondary school*, ≈ O-levels *(Brit)*

MITTLERE REIFE

mittlere Reife is the term still generally used for the intermediate school certificate. This is normally gained after successful completion of the six years (four in many **Länder**) in a **Realschule**. All pupils who complete their tenth year at a **Gymnasium** also automatically receive their **mittlere Reife**. If pupils from a **Realschule** achieve good examination results, they can move up to the eleventh year of a **Gymnasium** and try for the **Abitur**. The **mittlere Reife** entitles a pupil to attend a **Fachoberschule** and take the **Fachabitur** there after two years. → ABITUR, GYMNASIUM, REALSCHULE

Mitt|ler-: **Mitt|ler|funk|ti|on** F mediating role, role as (a) mediator; **Mitt|ler|rol|le** F role of mediator, mediatory role

mitt|ler|wei|le ['mɪtlɐ'vailə] ADV in the meantime; **ich habe mich ~ daran gewöhnt** I've got used to it in the meantime

mit-: **mit+tra|gen** VT *sep irreg Last* to help (to) carry; *Kosten, Verantwortung, Schuld* to share; *Entscheidung, Planung* to share responsibility for; *Politik, Programm, Vorschlag* to lend one's support to; **mit+trin|ken** *sep irreg* VT to drink with us/them *etc*; **er wollte nichts ~** he didn't want to join us/them *etc* in a drink VI to have a drink with us/them *etc*

Mitt-: **mitt|schiffs** ['mɪtʃɪfs] ADV *(Naut)* (a)midships; **Mitt|sech|zi|ger** ['mɪtzɛçtsɪgɐ] M **-s, -**, **Mitt|sech|zi|ge|rin** [-ərɪn] F **-, -nen** man/woman in his/her mid-sixties; **Mitt|sieb|zi|ger** ['mɪtzi:ptsɪgɐ] M **-s, -**, **Mitt|sieb|zi|ge|rin** [-ərɪn] F **-, -nen** man/woman in his/her mid-seventies; **Mitt|som|mer** ['mɪtzɔmɐ] M midsummer; **Mitt|som|mer|nacht** F Midsummer's Night

mit+tun VI *sep irreg (inf)* to join in

Mitt-: **Mitt|vier|zi|ger** ['mɪtfɪrtsɪgɐ] M **-s, -**, **Mitt|vier|zi|ge|rin** [-ərɪn] F **-, -nen** man/woman in his/her mid-forties; **mitt|wegs** ['mɪtve:ks] ADV *(old)* midway; **Mitt|woch** ['mɪtvɔx] M **-s, -e** Wednesday → *auch* **Dienstag**; **mitt|wochs** ['mɪtvɔxs] ADV on Wednesdays → *auch* **dienstags**; **Mitt|wochs|zie|hung** F *(im Lotto)* Wednesday draw; **Mitt|zwan|zi|ger** ['mɪttsvantsɪgɐ] M **-s, -**, **Mitt|zwan|zi|ge|rin** [-ərɪn] F **-, -nen** man/woman in his/her mid-twenties

mit|un|ter [mɪt'ʊntɐ] ADV from time to time, now and then *or* again, (every) once in a while

mit+un|ter|schrei|ben *ptp* **mitunterschrieben** VTI *sep irreg* to sign too

Mit|ver|an|stal|ter(in) M(F) co-organizer; *(von Konzert etc)* co-promoter

mit|ver|ant|wort|lich ADJ jointly responsible *pred*

Mit|ver|ant|wort|lich|keit F joint responsibility

Mit|ver|ant|wor|tung F share of the responsibility; **~ haben** to have *or* bear a share of the responsibility; **die** *or* **jede ~ ablehnen** to abnegate (all) responsibility

mit+ver|die|nen *ptp* **mitverdient** VI *sep* to (go out to) work as well

Mit|ver|fas|ser(in) M(F) co-author

Mit|ver|schul|den NT **ihm wurde ein ~ nachgewiesen** he was shown to have been partially *or* partly to blame; **ihn trifft ein ~ an diesem Vorfall** he was partially *or* partly to blame for this incident

Mit|ver|schwo|re|ne(r) [-fɛɐʃvo:rənə] MF *decl as adj* crony *(hum inf)*; *(pej, bei Verbrechen)* conspirator

Mit|ver|schwö|rer(in) M(F) conspirator

mit+ver|si|chern *ptp* **mitversichert** VT *sep* to include in the insurance; **bei seinen Eltern mitversichert sein** to be included on one's parents' insurance (policy)

Mit|ver|si|cher|te(r) MF *decl as adj* jointly insured (party)

Mit|welt F **die ~** the people *or* those about one; **es dauerte lange, bis die ~ seine Leistungen würdigte** it was a long time before his contemporaries learned to appreciate his achievements *(Brit)*

mit+wir|ken VI *sep* to play a part (*an +dat, bei* in); *(Fakten, Faktoren etc auch)* to contribute (*an +dat, bei* to); *(= beteiligt sein)* to be involved (*an +dat, bei* in); *(Schriftsteller, Regisseur etc)* to collaborate (*an +dat, bei* on); *(= mitspielen) (Schauspieler, Diskussionsteilnehmer)* to take part (*an +dat, bei* in); *(in Film)* to appear (*an +dat* in); *(in Chor, Orchester etc)* to perform (*in +dat* in); *(Tänzer, Orchester, Chor)* to perform (*an +dat, bei* in); **ohne sein Mitwirken wäre das unmöglich gewesen** it would have been impossible without his involvement

Mit|wir|ken|de(r) [-vɪrkndə] MF *decl as adj* participant (*an +dat, bei* in); *(= Mitspieler)* performer (*an +dat, bei* in); *(= Schauspieler)* actor (*an +dat, bei* in); **die ~n** *(Theat)* the cast *pl*

Mit|wir|kung F *(= Beteiligung, Mitarbeit)* involvement (*an +dat, bei* in); *(= Zusammenarbeit)* co-operation (*an +dat, bei* in); *(an Buch, Film)* collaboration (*an +dat, bei* on); *(= Teilnahme) (an Diskussion, Projekt)* participation (*an +dat, bei* in); *(von Schauspieler)* appearance (*an +dat, bei* in); *(von Tänzer, Orchester, Chor)* performance (*an +dat, bei* in); **unter ~ von** with the assistance *or* aid *or* help of

Mit|wir|kungs-: **Mit|wir|kungs|pflicht** F, *no pl (Jur)* duty to cooperate; **Mit|wir|kungs|recht** NT, *no pl (Jur)* right of participation

Mit|wis|ser [-vɪsɐ] M **-s, -**, **Mit|wis|se|rin** [-ərɪn] F **-, -nen** *(Jur)* accessory (*+gen* to); **~ sein** to know about it; **~ einer Sache** *(gen)* **sein** to know about sth; **jdn zum ~ machen** to tell sb (all) about it; *(Jur)* to make sb an accessory; **er wollte nicht so viele ~ haben** he didn't want so many people to know about it

Mit|wis|ser|schaft [-vɪsɐʃaft] F **-**, *no pl* **er wurde wegen ~ angeklagt** he was charged with being an accessory (to the crime); **an seiner ~ kann kein Zweifel bestehen** there can be no doubt that he was an accessory (to it) *(Jur)*, there can be no doubt that he knew about it

Mit|wohn|zent|ra|le F *agency for arranging shared accommodation*

mit+wol|len VI *sep (= mitgehen wollen)* to want to go along; *(= mitkommen wollen)* to want to come along

mit+zäh|len VTI *sep* to count; *Betrag* to count in

mit+zie|hen VI *sep irreg aux sein (fig inf)* to go along with it

Mix [mɪks] M **-, -e** mixture

Mix|be|cher M (cocktail) shaker

Mixed [mɪkst] NT **-(s), -(s)** *(Sport) (= Spiel)* mixed doubles *sing*; *(= Mannschaft)* mixed doubles pair

mi|xen [ˈmɪksn] VT *Getränke* to mix; *(Rad, TV)* to mix

Mi|xer [ˈmɪksɐ] M **-s, -** *(= Küchenmixer)* blender; *(= Rührmaschine)* mixer

Mi|xer [ˈmɪksɐ] M **-s, -**, **Mi|xe|rin** [-ərɪn] F **-, -nen** **a** *(= Barmixer)* cocktail waiter/waitress **b** *(Film, Rad, TV)* mixer

Mix|ge|tränk NT mixed drink; *(alkoholisch)* cocktail; *(= Milchmixgetränk)* milk shake

Mix|tur [mɪksˈtuːɐ] F **-, -en** *(Pharm, Mus, fig)* mixture

MKS *abbr von* **Maul- und Klauenseuche** FMD, foot and mouth disease

ml *abbr von* **Milliliter** millilitre *(Brit)*, milliliter *(US)*

mm *abbr von* **Millimeter** millimetre *(Brit)*, millimeter *(US)*

MM *(in Annoncen) abbr von* **Monatsmiete(n)**

MMC-Kar|te F *(Comput)* MMC *or* multimedia card

MMS [ɛmlɛmˈlɛs] F **-, -** *abbr von* **Multimedia Messaging Service** MMS; **jdm eine ~ schicken** to send sb an MMS (message)

Mne|mo-: **Mne|mo|tech|nik** F mnemonics *sing*; **mne|mo|tech|nisch** ADJ mnemonic ADV mnemonically

Mob [mɔp] M **-s**, *no pl (pej)* mob

mob|ben [ˈmɔbn] VT to harass *or* bully (at work)

Mob|bing [ˈmɔbɪŋ] NT **-s**, *no pl* workplace bullying

Mö|bel [ˈmøːbl] NT **-s, -** *(= Möbelstück)* piece of furniture; **~** *pl* furniture *sing*; **~ rücken** to shift the furniture

Mö|bel- *in cpds* furniture; **Mö|bel|haus** NT furniture shop *(Brit) or* store *(US)*; **Mö|bel|la|ger** NT furniture showroom; **Mö|bel|pa|cker(in)** M(F) furniture packer; **Mö|bel|schrei|ner(in)** M(F) cabinet-maker; **Mö|bel|spe|di|ti|on** F removal firm *(Brit)*, moving company *(US)*; **Mö|bel|stoff** M furnishing fabric; **Mö|bel|stück** NT piece of furniture; **Mö|bel|tisch|ler(in)** M(F) cabinet-maker; **Mö|bel|wa|gen** M removal van *(Brit)*, moving van *or* truck *(US)*, pantechnicon *(Brit)*

mo|bil [moˈbiːl] ADJ **a** mobile; *(Comm, Jur) Vermögen, Kapital* movable; *(= mitnehmbar) Drucker* portable; **~es Vermögen** movables *pl*; **~ machen** *(Mil)* to mobilize **b** *(inf: = flink, munter)* lively; **jdn ~ machen** to liven sb up ADV **mit jdm ~ telefonieren** to call sb on one's mobile (phone)

Mo|bi|le [ˈmoːbilə] NT **-s, -s** mobile

Mo|bil|funk M cellular radio

Mo|bil|funk|an|bie|ter M mobile phone *(Brit) or* cell phone *(US)* company

Mo|bil|funk|netz NT cellular network

Mo|bi|li|ar [mobiˈliaːɐ] NT **-s**, *no pl* furnishings *pl*

Mo|bi|li|en [moˈbiːliən] PL *(old)* furnishings *pl*; *(Jur)* chattels *pl*, movables *pl*

mo|bi|li|sie|ren [mobiliˈziːrən] *ptp* **mobilisiert** VT *(Mil, fig)* to mobilize; *(Comm) Kapital* to make liquid; **die Straße** *or* **den Mob ~** to rouse the mob

Mo|bi|li|sie|rung F mobilization; *(Econ)* realization

Mo|bi|li|tät [mobiliˈtɛːt] F **-**, *no pl* mobility *(auch Sociol)*; *(geistig)* agility

Mo|bil-: **Mo|bil|ma|chung** [moˈbiːlmaxʊŋ] F **-, -en** *(Mil)* mobilization; **die ~ ausrufen/beschließen** to mobilize/decide to mobilize; **Mo|bil|te|le|fon** NT mobile phone

möbl. *abbr von* **möbliert** furnished

möb|lie|ren [møˈbliːrən] *ptp* **möbliert** VT to furnish; **neu ~** to refurnish; **ein möbliertes Zimmer** a furnished room; **ein möblierter Herr** *(hum inf)* a lodger; **möbliert wohnen** to live in furnished accommodation

Moc|ca [ˈmɔka] M **-s, -s** mocha

moch|te *pret von* **mögen**

Möch|te|gern- [ˈmœçtəgɛrn] *in cpds (iro)* would-be; **ein ~Schauspieler** a would-be actor

mod. *abbr von* **modern**

mo|dal [moˈdaːl] ADJ *(Gram)* modal

Mo|da|li|tät [modaliˈtɛːt] F **-, -en** **a** *usu pl (von Plan, Vertrag etc)* arrangement; *(von Verfahren, Arbeit)* procedure **b** *(Philos)* modality

Mo|dal- *(Gram)*: **Mo|dal|satz** M (adverbial) clause of manner; **Mo|dal|verb** NT modal verb

Mod|der [ˈmɔdɐ] M **-s**, *no pl (N Ger)* mud

mod|de|rig [ˈmɔdərɪç], **modd|rig** [ˈmɔdrɪç] ADJ *(N Ger)* muddy

Mo|de [ˈmoːdə] F **-, -n** fashion; *(= Sitte)* custom; **~n** *(= Kleider)* fashions, fashionwear *sing*, apparel *sing (esp US)*; **~ sein** to be fashionable, to be the fashion, to be in vogue; *(Sitte)* to be the custom; **das ist jetzt ~** that's the latest fashion; **Radfahren/Alaska wird jetzt große ~** cycling/Alaska is becoming very fashionable nowadays; **in ~/aus der ~ kommen** to come into/go out of fashion; **die ~** *or* **alle ~n mitmachen, mit** *or* **nach der ~ gehen, sich nach der ~ richten** to keep up with the latest fashions; **sich nach der (neuesten) ~ kleiden** to wear the latest fashions; **wir wollen keine neuen ~n einführen** *(inf)* we don't want any new-fangled ideas

Mo|de-: **Mo|de|ar|ti|kel** M **a** fashion accessory **b** *(in Zeitung)* fashion article; **Mo|de|arzt** M, **Mo|de|ärz|tin** F fashionable doctor; **Mo|de|aus|druck** M *pl* **-ausdrücke** in-phrase, trendy expression *(inf)*; *(Wort)* in-word, vogue *or* trendy *(inf)* word, buzz word; **mo|de|be|wusst** ADJ fashion-conscious; **Mo|de|be|wusst|sein** F fashion-consciousness; **Mo|de|de|sig|ner(in)** M(F) fashion designer; **Mo|de|dro|ge** F recreational drug; **Mo|de|er|schei|nung** F vogue, (passing) fashion; **Mo|de|far|be** F fashionable colour *(Brit) or* color *(US)*, in-colour *(Brit inf)*, in-color *(US inf)*; **mo|de|ge|recht** ADJ fashionable; **Mo|de|ge|schäft** NT fashion shop; **Mo|de|haus** NT fashion house; **Mo|de|heft** NT, **Mo|de|jour|nal** NT fashion magazine; **Mo|de|krank|heit** F fashionable complaint

Mo|del [ˈmɔdl] NT **-s, -s** *(Fashion)* model

Mo|del [ˈmoːdl] NT **-s, -** *(Cook)* wooden mould *(Brit) or* mold *(US)*

Mo|dell [moˈdɛl] NT **-s, -e** **a** model; *(= naturgetreue Nachbildung)* mock-up, model **b** *(Art: = Fotomodell)* model; **zu etw ~ stehen** to be the model for sth; **jdm ~ stehen/sitzen** to sit for sb

Mo|dell-: **Mo|dell|cha|rak|ter** M, *no pl* **~ haben** to serve as a model; **Mo|dell|ei|sen|bahn** F model railway *(esp Brit) or* railroad *(US)*; *(als Spielzeug)* train set; **Mo|dell|flug|zeug** NT model aeroplane *(Brit) or* airplane *(US)*

mo|del|lie|ren [modɛˈliːrən] *ptp* **modelliert** VTI to model

Mo|del|lier|mas|se F modelling *(Brit) or* modeling *(US)* clay

Mo|dell-: **Mo|dell|kleid** NT model (dress); **Mo|dell|ver|such** M *(esp Sch)* experiment; **Mo|dell|zeich|nung** F drawing of a model; *(Art)* drawing from a model

mo|deln [ˈmɔdln] VI *(Fashion)* to model

mo|deln [ˈmoːdln] VT to model

Mo|dem [ˈmoːdɛm] NT **-s, -e** modem

Mo|de|ma|cher(in) M(F) *(inf)* fashion designer

Mo|den-: **Mo|den|schau** F fashion show; **Mo|den|zei|tung** F fashion magazine

Mo|de|pup|pe F, **Mo|de|püpp|chen** NT model type *(inf)*

Mo|der [ˈmoːdɐ] M **-s**, *no pl* mustiness; *(geh: = Verwesung)* decay; *(= Schimmel)* mildew; **es riecht nach ~** it smells musty; **in ~ übergehen** to decay; *(Grabsteine etc)* to become mildewed

mo|de|rat [modeˈraːt] ADJ moderate, reasonable; **nach außen hin gibt sich der Parteichef ~** outwardly the party leader gives the impression of being a moderate ADV moderately; **die Krankenkassenbeiträge sollen ~ erhöht werden** there are to be moderate increases in health insurance contributions

Mo|de|ra|ti|on [moderaˈtsioːn] F **-, -en** *(Rad, TV)* presentation; **die ~ heute Abend hat: ...** tonight's presenter is ...

Mo|de|ra|to [modeˈraːto] NT **-s, -s** or **Moderati** *(Mus)* moderato

Mo|de|ra|tor [modeˈraːtoːɐ] M **-s, Moderatoren** [-ˈtoːrən], **Mo|de|ra|to|rin** [-ˈtoːrɪn] F **-, -nen** presenter

Mo|der|ge|ruch M musty odour *(Brit) or* odor *(US)*

mo|de|rie|ren [modeˈriːrən] *ptp* **moderiert** VTI *(Rad, TV)* to present; **das Moderieren** the presentation

mo|de|rig [ˈmoːdərɪç] ADJ *Geruch* musty ADV **~ riechen** to smell musty; *(Raum etc)* to be filled with a damp smell; **~ schmecken** to taste mouldy *(Brit) or* moldy *(US)*

mo|dern [ˈmoːdɐn] VI *aux sein or haben* to rot

mo|dern [moˈdɛrn] ADJ modern *no adv*; *(= zeitgemäß) Maschine, Vorrichtung auch* up-to-date *no adv*; *(= modisch)* fashionable; *Politik, Ansichten, Eltern, Lehrer* progressive; **~ sein** *(Kleidung, Möbel)* to be fashionable; **~ werden** to come into fashion, to become fashionable; **der ~e Mensch** modern man ADV *bauen, ausstatten* in a modern style; *sich kleiden* fashionably; *denken* open-mindedly; ~ **wohnen** to live in modern housing; **eine ~ eingerichtete Wohnung** an apartment furnished in a modern style; ~ **eingestellt sein** to be modern

Mo|der|ne [mo'dɛrnə] F -, *no pl (geh)* modern age; **das Zeitalter der ~** the modern age

mo|der|ni|sie|ren [modɛrni'zi:rən] *ptp* **modernisiert** VT *Gebäude* to modernize; *Gesetz, Arbeitsmethoden, Wirtschaft, Unternehmen auch* to bring up to date; *Kleidung* to revamp, to make more fashionable VI to get up to date

Mo|der|nis|mus [modɛr'nɪsmʊs] M -, *no pl* modernism

mo|der|nis|tisch [modɛr'nɪstɪʃ] ADJ modernistic ADV modernistically

Mo|der|ni|tät [modɛrni'tɛ:t] F -, *no pl (geh)* modernity

Mo|de-: **Mo|de|sa|che** F **das ist reine ~** it's just the fashion; **Mo|de|sa|lon** M fashion house; **Mo|de|schau** F fashion show; **Mo|de|schmuck** M costume jewellery *(Brit) or* jewelry *(US)*; **Mo|de|schöp|fer** M fashion designer, couturier; **Mo|de|schöp|fe|rin** F fashion designer, couturière; **Mo|de|schrei** M **der letzte ~** the latest fashion; **Mo|de|schrift|stel|ler(in)** M(F) popular writer; **Mo|de|tanz** M popular dance; **Mo|de|tor|heit** F fashion fad; **Mo|de|trend** M fashion(able) trend; **Mo|de|wort** NT *pl* **-wörter** in-word, vogue *or* trendy *(inf)* word, buzz word; **Mo|de|zeich|ner(in)** M(F) fashion illustrator; **Mo|de|zeit|schrift** F fashion magazine; **Mo|de|zen|trum** NT *(= Gebäude)* fashion centre *(Brit) or* center *(US)*; *(= Stadt, Region)* centre *(Brit) or* center *(US)* of fashion

Mo|di *pl von* **Modus**

Mo|di|fi|ka|ti|on [modifika'tsio:n] F -, **-en** modification

mo|di|fi|zie|ren [modifi'tsi:rən] *ptp* **modifiziert** VT to modify

Mo|di|fi|zie|rung F -, **-en** modification

mo|disch ['mo:dɪʃ] ADJ stylish, fashionable, modish ADV fashionably, stylishly, modishly

Mo|dis|tin [mo'dɪstɪn] F -, **-nen** milliner

mod|rig ['mo:drɪç] ADJ, ADV = **moderig**

Mo|dul ['mo:dʊl] M **-s, -n** *(Archit)* module; *(Math)* modulus

Mo|dul [mo'du:l] NT **-s, -e** *(Comput)* module

mo|du|lar [modu'la:ɐ] ADJ modular ADV of modules

Mo|du|la|ti|on [modula'tsio:n] F -, **-en** modulation

mo|du|lie|ren [modu'li:rən] *ptp* **moduliert** VT to modulate

Mo|dus ['mo:dʊs, 'mɔdʊs] M -, **Modi** ['mo:di, 'mɔdi] **a** way; ~ **Vivendi** *(geh)* modus vivendi **b** *(Gram)* mood **c** *(Comput)* mode

MOF *(inf) abbrvon* **Mensch ohne Freunde** Billy no-mates *(Brit)*

Mo|fa ['mo:fa] NT **-s, -s** small moped, motor-assisted bicycle *(form)*

Mo|ge|lei [mogə'lai] F -, **-en** cheating *no pl*

mo|geln ['mo:gln] VI to cheat; **beim Kartenspiel/bei der Prüfung ~** to cheat at cards/in an exam; **nicht ~!** no cheating!

Mo|gel-: **Mo|gel|pa|ckung** F misleading packaging; *(fig)* sham, fraud; **den Wählern eine ~ verkaufen** *(fig)* to sell the electorate false promises; **Mo|gel|zet|tel** M *(Sch)* crib *(Brit)*, cheat sheet *(US inf)*

mö|gen ['mø:gn] ✪ 34, 35, 36.3 *pret* **mochte**, ['mɔxtə] *ptp* **gemocht** VT [gə'mɔxt] to like; **~ Sie ihn/Operettenmusik?** do you like him/operetta?; **ich mag ihn/Operettenmusik nicht** I don't like him/operetta, I don't care for him/operetta; **sie mag das (gern)** she (really) likes that; **sie mag kein Sauerkraut** she doesn't like sauerkraut; **was möchten Sie, bitte?** what would you like?; *(Verkäufer)* what can I do for you?; **~ Sie eine Praline/etwas Wein?** *(form)* would you like a chocolate/some wine?, would you care for a chocolate/some wine?; **nein danke, ich möchte lieber Tee** no thank you, I would prefer tea *or* would rather have tea

VI **a** *(eine Praline/etwas Wein etc mögen)* to like one/some; *(= etw tun mögen)* to like to; **ich mag nicht mehr** I've had enough; *(= bin am Ende)* I can't take any more; **kommen Sie mit? – ich möchte gern, aber ...** are you coming too? – I'd like to, but ...

b *(= gehen/fahren wollen)* to want to go; **ich möchte (gern) nach Hause** I want to go home; **ich möchte lieber in die Stadt** I would prefer to go *or* I would rather go into town *ptp* **mögen**

MODAL AUX VB **a** *(im Konjunktiv: Wunsch)* to like to *+infin*; **möchten Sie etwas essen?** would you like something to eat?, would you care for something to eat?; **wir möchten (gern) etwas trinken** we would like something to drink; **ich möchte gern Herrn Schmidt sprechen** I would like to speak to Mr Schmidt; **hier möchte ich nicht wohnen** *(= würde nicht gern)* I wouldn't like to live here; *(= will nicht)* I don't want to live here; **ich möchte dazu nichts sagen** I don't want to say anything about that, no comment; **ich hätte gern dabei sein ~** I would like *or* have liked to have been there; **ich hätte lieber dabei sein ~** I would prefer *or* have preferred to have been there; **das möchte ich auch wissen** I'd like to know that too; **möge er/mögest du Erfolg haben** *(old)* may he/you be successful

b *(im Konjunktiv: einschränkend)* **man möchte meinen, dass ...** you would think that ...; **ich möchte fast sagen ...** I would almost say ...

c *(geh: Einräumung)* **es mag wohl sein, dass er recht hat, aber ...** he may well be right, but ...; **wie dem auch sein mag** however that may be; **was sie auch sagen mag** whatever she says; **oder wie er auch heißen mag** or whatever he is *or* might be *or* may be called; **es mag dieses Mal gehen** it's all right this time; **mag kommen was da will** come what may; **mag es schneien, so viel es will** it can snow as much as it likes, let it snow as much as it likes; **von mir aus mag er warten** as far as I'm concerned he can wait; **man mag es tun, wie man will, aber ...** you can do it how you like, but ...

d *(Vermutung)* **es mochten etwa fünf Stunden vergangen sein** about five hours must *or* would have passed; **sie mag/mochte etwa zwanzig sein** she must *or* would be/have been about twenty; **wie alt mag sie sein?** how old might *or* would she be?, how old is she, I wonder?; **wo mag sie das gehört haben?** where could *or* might she have heard that?; **was mag das wohl heißen?** what might that mean?

e *(= wollen)* to want; **sie mag nicht bleiben** she doesn't want to stay

f *(Aufforderung, indirekte Rede)* **(sagen Sie ihm,) er möchte zu mir kommen** would you tell him to come and see me; **Sie möchten zu Hause anrufen** you should call home; **du möchtest dich brieflich melden** you should write

Mög|ler ['mo:glɐ] M **-s, -**, **Mog|le|rin** [-ərɪn] F **-, -nen** cheat

mög|lich ['mø:klɪç] ✪ 36.1, 39.2, 42.3, 43.3, 46.6 ADJ **a** possible; **alles Mögliche** everything you *or* one can think of; **alles Mögliche tun** to do everything possible, to do everything one can; **er tat sein Möglichstes** he did his utmost, he did all he could; **aus allen ~en Richtungen** from all directions; **er hat allen ~en Blödsinn gemacht** he did all sorts of stupid things; **so viel/bald wie ~** as much/soon as possible; **das ist schon** *or* **wohl** *or* **durchaus ~** that's quite possible; **wenn es irgend ~ ist** if (it's) at all possible; **können Sie es ~ machen, dass Sie schon morgen kommen** *or* **schon morgen zu kommen?** could you manage to come tomorrow?;; **es war mir nicht ~ mitzukommen** I couldn't manage to come, it wasn't possible for me to come; **das ist doch nicht ~!** that's impossible; **nicht ~!** never!, impossible!; **das wäre woanders nicht ~** that couldn't happen anywhere else; **ist denn so was ~?** would you credit it? *(inf)*; **im Bereich** *or* **Rahmen des Möglichen** within the realms of possibility

b *(attr: = eventuell) Kunden, Interessenten, Nachfolger* potential, possible; **alle ~en Fälle** every eventuality; **alles Mögliche bedenken** to consider everything

ADV = **möglichst**

mög|li|cher|wei|se ['mø:klɪçɐ'vaizə] ADV possibly; **~ kommt er morgen** he may *or* might (possibly) come tomorrow; **da liegt ~ ein Missverständnis vor** it's possible that there is a misunderstanding, there is possibly a misunderstanding

Mög|lich|keit ✪ 39.2, 42.3, 43.3, 46.1 F **-, -en a** possibility; **es besteht die ~, dass ...** there is a possibility that ..., it is possible that ...; **es besteht die ~ zu kündigen** it would (always) be possible to hand in your notice; **alle ~en in Betracht ziehen** to take all the possibilities into account; **nach ~** if possible; **ist denn das die ~?** *(inf)* **ist es die ~!** *(inf)* it's impossible!, I don't believe it!

b *(= Aussicht)* chance; *(= Gelegenheit)* opportunity, chance; **die ~ haben, etw zu tun** to have the chance/opportunity to do sth *or* of doing sth; **er hatte keine andere ~** he had no other choice *or* alternative; **das Land der unbegrenzten ~en** the land of unlimited opportunity; **ungeahnte ~en eröffnen** to open up undreamed-of opportunities *(Brit)*

c *usu pl (= Fähigkeiten)* capabilities; **der Mietpreis übersteigt meine finanziellen ~en** the rent is beyond my means

mög|lichst ['mø:klɪçst] ADV **~ genau/schnell/oft** as accurately/quickly/often as possible; **in ~ kurzer Zeit** as quickly as possible

Mo|gul ['mo:gʊl, mo'gu:l] M **-s, -n** *or* **-e** *(Hist, fig)* mogul

Mo|hair [mo'hɛ:ɐ] M **-s, -e**, **Mo|här** [mo'hɛ:ɐ] M **-s, -e** *(Tex)* mohair

Mo|ham|me|da|ner [mohame'da:nɐ] M **-s, -** *(Hist) (neg!)*, **Mo|ham|me|da|ne|rin** [-ərɪn] F **-, -nen** *(Hist) (neg!)* Mohammedan *(dated)*

mo|ham|me|da|nisch [mohame'da:nɪʃ] *(Hist) (neg!)* ADJ Mohammedan *(dated)* ADV *erziehen* as a Mohammedan *(dated)*; *aufwachsen* Mohammedan *(dated)*

Mo|hi|ka|ner [mohi'ka:nɐ] M **-s, -**, **Mo|hi|ka|ne|rin** [-ərɪn] F **-, -nen** Mohican; **der letzte ~** *(fig)* the very last one

Mohn [mo:n] M **-(e)s, -e a** poppy **b** *(= Mohnsamen)* poppy seed

Mohn- *in cpds* poppy; *(Cook)* (poppy-)seed; **Mohn|blu|me** F poppy; **Mohn|bröt|chen** NT poppy, *roll sprinkled with poppy seeds*; **Mohn|ku|chen** M poppy-seed cake

Mohr [mo:ɐ] M **-en, -en**, **Moh|rin** [-rɪn] F **-, -nen** *(old)* (blacka)moor *(old)*; **Othello, der ~ von Venedig** Othello, the Moor of Venice; **schwarz** *or* **braun gebrannt wie ein ~** *(dated inf)* as brown as a berry; **der ~ hat seine Schuldigkeit getan, der ~ kann gehen** *(prov)* as soon as you've served your purpose they've no further interest in you

Möh|re ['mø:rə] F **-, -n** carrot

Moh|ren|kopf M *small chocolate-covered cream cake (= Schokokuss) chocolate marshmallow with biscuit base*

Mohr|rü|be F carrot

moin [mɔyn] INTERJ *(N Ger inf)* **~(, ~)!** morning *(inf)*; *(= hallo)* hi *(inf)*

Moi|ré [moa're:] M OR NT **-s, -s** *(Tex)* moiré

mo|kant [mo'kant] *(geh)* ADJ sardonic, mocking ADV sardonically

Mo|kas|sin [moka'si:n, 'mɔkasi:n] M **-s, -s** moccasin

Mo|kick ['mo:kɪk] NT **-s, -s** moped with a kick-starter

mo|kie|ren [mo'ki:rən] *ptp* **mokiert** VR to sneer *(über +acc* at)

Mok|ka ['mɔka] M **-s, -s** mocha

Mok|ka-: **Mok|ka|löf|fel** M coffee spoon; **Mok|ka|tas|se** F, **Mok|ka|täss|chen** NT coffee cup

Mol [mo:l] NT **-s, -e** *(Chem)* mole

Mo|lar [mo'la:ɐ] M **-s, -en**, **Mo|lar|zahn** M molar (tooth)

Molch [mɔlç] M **-(e)s, -e** salamander

Mol|dau ['mɔldau] F - **a** *(Fluss)* Vltava **b** *(Republik)* = **Moldawien**

Mol|da|wi|en [mɔl'da:viən] NT **-s** Moldavia

Mo|le ['mo:lə] F **-, -n** *(Naut)* mole

Mo|le|kel [mo'le:kl] *(old)* NT **-s, -** *or f* **-, -n** = **Molekül**

Mo|le|kül [mole'ky:l] NT **-s, -e** molecule

mo|le|ku|lar [moleku'la:ɐ] ADJ molecular

Mo|le|ku|lar-: **Mo|le|ku|lar|bio|lo|ge** M, **Mo|le|ku|lar|bio|lo|gin** F molecular biologist; **Mo|le|ku|lar|bio|lo|gie** F molecular biology

molk *pret von* **melken**

Mol|ke ['mɔlkə] F **-**, *no pl*, **Mol|ken** ['mɔlkn] M **-s**, *no pl (dial)* whey

Mol|ke|rei [mɔlkə'rai] F **-, -en** dairy

Mol|ke|rei-: **Mol|ke|rei|but|ter** F blended butter; **Mol|ke|rei|ge|nos|sen|schaft** F dairy cooperative; **Mol|ke|rei|pro|dukt** NT dairy product

Moll [mɔl] NT **-, -** *(Mus)* minor (key); **in ~ übergehen** to go into the minor; **a-~** A minor; **a-~-Tonleiter** scale of A minor; **Violinkonzert Nummer 4 a-~** violin concerto Number 4 in A minor; **alles in ~ sehen** to see only the gloomy side of things

Mol|le ['mɔlə] F **-, -n** *(dial)* beer; **eine ~ mit Korn** a beer and a (glass of) schnapps

mol|lert ['mɔlɐt] ADJ *(Aus inf)* plump

mol|lig ['mɔlıç] *(inf)* ADJ **a** cosy *(Brit)*, cozy *(US)*; *(= warm, behaglich)* snug, cosy *(Brit)*, cozy *(US)* **b** *(= rundlich)* plump ADV **~ warm** warm and cosy *(Brit) or* cozy *(US)*

Moll-: **Moll|ton|art** F minor key; **Moll|ton|lei|ter** F minor scale

Mol|lus|ke [mɔ'lʊskə] F **-, -n** *(spec)* mollusc

Mo|loch ['mo:lɔx] M **-s, -e** Moloch

Mo|lo|tow|cock|tail ['mo:lotɔf-] M Molotov cocktail

Mo|luk|ken [mo'lʊkn] PL *(Geog)* Moluccas *pl*, Spice Islands *pl*

Mo|lyb|dän [molʏp'dɛ:n] NT **-s**, *no pl (abbr* **Mo**) molybdenum

Mo|ment [mo'mɛnt] M **-(e)s, -e** moment; **einen ~ lang** for a moment; **jeden ~** any time *or* minute *or* moment; **einen ~, bitte** one minute *or* moment please; **kleinen ~!** just a tick *(Brit inf) or* a second!; **~ mal!** just a minute!; **im ~** at the moment; **im letzten/richtigen** *etc* **~** at the last/right *etc* moment; **im ersten ~** for a moment

Mo|ment NT **-(e)s, -e** **a** *(= Bestandteil)* element **b** *(= Umstand)* fact; *(= Faktor)* factor **c** *(Phys)* moment; *(= Kraftwirkung)* momentum

mo|men|tan [momɛn'ta:n] ADJ **a** *(= vorübergehend)* momentary **b** *(= augenblicklich)* present *attr* ADV **a** *(= vorübergehend)* for a moment, momentarily **b** *(= augenblicklich)* at the moment, at present

Mo|ment|auf|nah|me F *(Phot)* photo(graph)

Mo|na|co ['mo:nako, mo'nako] NT **-s** Monaco

Mo|na|de [mo'na:də] F **-, -n** *(Philos)* monad

Mo|na|den|leh|re F, **Mo|na|do|lo|gie** [monadolo'gi:] F **-**, *no pl (Philos)* monadology

Mo|narch [mo'narç] M **-en, -en**, **Mo|nar|chin** [-'narçın] F **-, -nen** monarch

Mo|nar|chie [monar'çi:] F **-, -n** [-'çi:ən] monarchy

mo|nar|chisch [mo'narçıʃ] ADJ monarchic(al)

Mo|nar|chist [monar'çıst] M **-en, -en**, **Mo|nar|chis|tin** [-'çıstın] F **-, -nen** monarchist

mo|nar|chis|tisch [monar'çıstıʃ] ADJ pro-monarchist ADV **eine ~ orientierte Partei** a pro-monarchist party

Mo|nat ['mo:nat] M **-(e)s, -e** month; **der ~ Mai** the month of May; **im ~ Mai** in the month of May; **sie ist im sechsten ~ (schwanger)** she's over five months pregnant *or* gone *(inf)*, she's in the sixth month; **was verdient er im ~?** how much does he earn a month?; **am 12. dieses ~s** *or* **des laufenden ~s** on the 12th (of this month); **auf ~e hinaus** months ahead; **jdn zu drei ~en (Haft) verurteilen** to sentence sb to three months' imprisonment, to send sb down for three months *(inf)*; **von ~ zu ~** month by month

mo|na|te|lang ADJ *attr Verhandlungen, Kämpfe* which go on for months; **seine ~e Abwesenheit** his months of absence; **nach ~em Warten** after waiting for months, after months of waiting; **mit ~er Verspätung** months late ADV for months

-mo|na|tig [mo:natıç] ADJ *suf* -month; **ein dreimonatiger Urlaub** a three-month holiday *(esp Brit) or* vacation *(US)*

mo|nat|lich ['mo:natlıç] ADJ monthly ADV every month, monthly; **er zahlt ~ 500 Euro** he pays 500 euros a month

-mo|nat|lich ADJ *suf* **zwei-/dreimonatlich** every two/three months; **allmonatlich** every month

Mo|nats-: **Mo|nats|an|fang** M beginning of the month; **Mo|nats|bei|trag** M monthly contribution; *(bei Abonnement)* monthly subscription; **Mo|nats|bin|de** F sanitary towel *(Brit)*, sanitary napkin *(US)*; **Mo|nats|blu|tung** F menstrual period; **Mo|nats|ein|kom|men** NT monthly income; **Mo|nats|en|de** NT end of the month; **Mo|nats|ers|te(r)** M *decl as adj* first (day) of the month; **Mo|nats|frist** F **innerhalb** *or* **binnen ~** within a month; **Mo|nats|ge|halt** NT monthly salary; **ein ~** one month's salary; **Mo|nats|hälf|te** F half of the month; **Mo|nats|heft** NT monthly (journal *or* periodical); **Mo|nats|kar|te** F monthly season ticket; **Mo|nats|lohn** M monthly wage; **~ bekommen** to be paid monthly; **Mo|nats|mie|te** F monthly rent; **zwei ~n als Kaution** two months' rent in advance (as a deposit); **Mo|nats|mit|te** F middle of the month; **Mo|nats|mit|tel** NT monthly average; **im ~** on average for a month; **Mo|nats|na|me** M name of the/a month; **Mo|nats|ra|te** F monthly instalment *(Brit) or* installment *(US)*; **Mo|nats|schrift** F monthly (journal *or* periodical); **Mo|nats|wech|sel** M monthly allowance

mo|nat(s)|wei|se ADV every month, monthly ADJ monthly

Mönch [mœnç] M **-(e)s, -e** monk; *(= Bettelmönch auch)* friar; **wie ein ~ leben** to live like a monk

mön|chisch ['mœnçıʃ] ADJ *Geduld, Fleiß* monastic; **ein ~es Leben führen** *(fig)* to live like a monk ADV **~ enthaltsam/zurückgezogen leben** to live like a monk/hermit

Mönchs-: **Mönchs|ka|pu|ze** F cowl; **Mönchs|klos|ter** NT monastery; *(von Bettelmönchen)* friary; **Mönchs|kut|te** F → **Mönch** monk's/friar's habit; **Mönchs|le|ben** NT monastic life; **Mönchs|or|den** M monastic order

Mönchs|tum ['mœnçstu:m] NT **-s**, *no pl* monasticism

Mönchs-: **Mönchs|we|sen** NT monasticism; **Mönchs|zel|le** F monastic cell

Mönch|tum ['mœnçtu:m] NT **-s**, *no pl* monasticism

Mond [mo:nt] M **-(e)s, -e** [-də] **a** moon; **den ~ anbellen** *(fig)* to bay at the moon; **auf** *or* **hinter dem ~ leben** *(inf)* to be *or* live behind the times; **du lebst wohl auf dem ~!** *(inf)* where have you been?; **drei Meilen hinter dem ~** *(inf)* in the Stone Age *(hum)*; **in den ~ gucken** *(inf)* to go empty-handed; **deine Armbanduhr geht nach dem ~** *(inf)* your watch is way out *(inf)*; **ich hätte ihn auf den ~ schießen können** *(inf)* I could have killed him *(inf)*; **das Geld können wir in den ~ schreiben** *(inf)* we can write the money off **b** *(old: = Monat)* moon *(old)*, month

mon|dän [mɔn'dɛ:n] ADJ chic; **dort geht es mir zu ~ zu** it's too chic for me there

Mond-: **Mond|auf|gang** M moonrise; **Mond|au|to** NT moon buggy *or* rover; **Mond|bahn** F moon's orbit, orbit of the moon; *(Space)* lunar orbit; **mond|be|schie|nen** [-bəʃi:nən] ADJ *(geh)* bathed in moonlight, moonlit

Mon|den|schein M *(geh)* moonlight

Mon|des|glanz M *(poet)* moonlight

Mond-: **Mond|fäh|re** F *(Space)* lunar module; **Mond|fins|ter|nis** F eclipse of the moon, lunar eclipse; **Mond|ge|bir|ge** NT mountains *pl* of the moon; **Mond|ge|sicht** NT moonface; *(gemalt) simple representation of a face*; **Mond|ge|stein** NT moon rocks *pl*; **Mond|göt|tin** F moon goddess; **mond|hell** ADJ moonlit ADV **~ erleuchtet** lit by the moon, moonlit; **Mond|jahr** NT lunar year; **Mond|kalb** NT *(dated inf: = Dummkopf)* mooncalf; **Mond|kra|ter** M lunar crater; **Mond|lan|de|fäh|re** F *(Space)* lunar module; **Mond|land|schaft** F lunar landscape; **Mond|lan|dung** F lunar *or* moon landing; **Mond|licht** NT moonlight; **mond|los** ADJ *(geh)* moonless; **Mond|nacht** F *(geh)* moonlit night; **Mond|ober|flä|che** F surface of the moon; **Mond|pha|sen** PL phases *pl* of the moon; **Mond|preis** M *(inf)* astronomical price *(inf)*; **Mond|schein** M moonlight; **Mond|si|chel** F crescent moon; **Mond|son|de** F *(Space)* lunar probe; **Mond|stein** M moonstone; **mond|süch|tig** ADJ **~ sein** to sleepwalk; **Mond|süch|tig|keit** F sleepwalking, somnambulism *(form)*; **Mond|um|lauf|bahn** F *(Space)* lunar orbit; **Mond|un|ter|gang** F moonset

Mo|ne|gas|se [mone'gasə] M **-n, -n**, **Mo|ne|gas|sin** [-'gasın] F **-, -nen** Monegasque

mo|ne|gas|sisch [mone'gasıʃ] ADJ Monegasque

mo|ne|tär [mone'tɛ:ɐ] ADJ monetary ADV **ihre Politik ist ~ geprägt** her policy is monetary; **eine ~ orientierte Denkweise** monetary thinking

Mo|ne|ta|ris|mus [moneta'rısmʊs] M **-**, *no pl (Econ)* monetarism

Mo|ne|ta|rist [moneta'rıst] M **-en, -en**, **Mo|ne|ta|ris|tin** [-'rıstın] F **-, -nen** *(Econ)* monetarist

Mo|ne|ten [mo'ne:tn] PL *(inf)* bread *sing (inf)*, dough *sing (inf)*; **~ machen** to make some bread *(inf) or* dough *(inf)*

Mon|go|le [mɔŋ'go:lə] M **-n, -n**, **Mon|go|lin** [-'go:lın] F **-, -nen** Mongolian, Mongol

Mon|go|lei [mɔŋgo'lai] F **- die ~** Mongolia; **die Innere/Äußere ~** Inner/Outer Mongolia

Mon|go|len-: **Mon|go|len|fal|te** F epicanthus; **Mon|go|len|fleck** M Mongolian spot

mon|go|lid [mɔŋgo'li:t] ADJ Mongoloid

Mon|go|li|de(r) [mɔŋgo'li:də] MF *decl as adj* Mongoloid

Mon|go|lin F **-, -nen** Mongolian, Mongol

mon|go|lisch [mɔŋ'go:lıʃ] ADJ Mongolian

Mon|go|lisch(e) NT Mongolian → *auch* **Deutsch(e)**

Mon|go|lis|mus [mɔŋgo'lısmʊs] M **-**, *no pl (Med) (neg!)* Down's syndrome

mon|go|lo|id [mɔŋgolo'i:t] ADJ Mongol; *(Med) (neg!)* affected with Down's syndrome

Mon|go|lo|i|de(r) [mɔŋgolo'i:də] MF *decl as adj* Mongol; *(Med) (neg!)* person with Down's syndrome

mo|nie|ren [mo'ni:rən] *ptp* **moniert** VT to complain about; **sie hat moniert, dass ...** she complained that ... VI to complain

Mo|nis|mus [mo'nısmʊs] M **-**, *no pl (Philos)* monism

Mo|ni|tor ['mo:nito:ɐ] M **-s, -e** *or* **Monitoren** [-'to:rən] *(TV, Phys)* monitor

Mo|no-, mo|no- ['mo:no, 'mɔno] *in cpds* mono-; **mo|no|chrom** [mono'kro:m] ADJ monochrome; **mo|no|co|lor** [monoko'lo:ɐ] ADJ *(Aus)* **eine ~e Regierung** a single-party government; **mo|no|gam** [mono'ga:m] ADJ monogamous ADV *leben* monogamously; **Mo|no|ga|mie** [monoga'mi:] F **-**, *no pl* monogamy; **Mo|-**

no|gra|fie [monogra'fi:] F -, -n [-'fi:ən] monograph; **Mo|no|gramm** [mono'gram] NT pl -gramme monogram; **Mo|no|gra|phie** [monogra'fi:] F -, -n [-'fi:ən] monograph; **mo|no|kau|sal** [monokau'za:l] ADJ *Erklärung* monocausal ADV **ein Problem ~ sehen** to see only one aspect of a problem; **ein Problem ~ erklären** to attribute a problem to a single cause

Mo|no|kel [mo'nɔkl] NT -s, - monocle

mo|no|klo|nal [monoklo'na:l] ADJ **~e Antikörper** monoclonal antibodies

Mo|no|kul|tur F *(Agr)* monoculture

Mo|no|lith [mono'li:t] M -en, -e(n) monolith

mo|no|li|thisch [mono'li:tɪʃ] *(lit, fig)* ADJ monolithic ADV monolithically

Mo|no|log [mono'lo:k] M -(e)s, -e [-gə] *(Liter, fig)* monologue; *(= Selbstgespräch)* soliloquy; **einen ~ sprechen** to hold a monologue/give a soliloquy; **einen ~ halten** *(fig)* to hold a monologue, to talk on and on

mo|no|lo|gisch [mono'lo:gɪʃ] ADJ monologic(al) ADV **etw ~ erzählen** to give a monologue about sth

mo|no|lo|gi|sie|ren [monologi'zi:rən] ptp **monologisiert** VI to hold a monologue; *(= ein Selbstgespräch führen)* to soliloquize

mo|no|man [mono'ma:n] ADJ *(geh)* monomaniacal

Mo|no|ma|ne [mono'ma:nə] M -n, -n, **Mo|no|ma|nin** [-'ma:nɪn] F -, -nen *(geh)* monomaniac

Mo|no|ma|nie [monoma'ni:] F -, -n [-'niən] *(geh)* monomania; *(fig)* obsession

mo|no|ma|nisch ADJ *(geh)* monomaniacal

Mo|noph|thong [mono'ftɔŋ] M -s, -e *(Ling)* monophthong

Mo|no|pol [mono'po:l] NT -s, -e monopoly *(auf +acc, für* on)

Mo|no|pol- *in cpds* monopoly; **Mo|no|pol|bil|dung** F monopolization *no pl*

mo|no|po|li|sie|ren [monopoli'zi:rən] ptp **monopolisiert** VT *(lit, fig)* to monopolize

Mo|no|po|li|sie|rung F -, -en monopolization

Mo|no|po|list [monopo'lɪst] M -en, -en, **Mo|no|po|lis|tin** [-'lɪstɪn] F -, -nen monopolist

Mo|no|pol-: **Mo|no|pol|ka|pi|tal** NT *(Kapital)* monopoly capital; *(Kapitalisten)* monopoly capitalism; **Mo|no|pol|ka|pi|ta|lis|mus** M monopoly capitalism; **Mo|no|pol|ka|pi|ta|list(in)** M(F) monopolist; **mo|no|pol|ka|pi|ta|lis|tisch** ADJ monopolistic; **Mo|no|pol|kom|mis|si|on** F monopolies commission; **Mo|no|pol|stel|lung** F monopoly

Mo|no|po|ly® [mo'no:poli] NT -, *no pl* Monopoly®

Mo|no|se|mie [monoze'mi:] F -, *no pl (Ling)* monosemy

Mo|no|the|is|mus [monote'ɪsmʊs] M monotheism

mo|no|ton [mono'to:n] ADJ monotonous ADV monotonously

Mo|no|to|nie [monoto'ni:] F -, -n [-'ni:ən] monotony

Mon|oxid, Mon|oxyd ['mo:nɔksi:t, 'mɔnɔksi:t, mɔnɔ'ksi:t] NT monoxide

Mons|ter ['mɔnstɐ] NT -s, - *(inf)* = **Monstrum**

Mons|ter- *in cpds (usu pej)* mammoth, monster; **Mons|ter|film** M mammoth (film) production

Monst|ranz [mɔn'strants] F -, -en *(Eccl)* monstrance

Monst|ren *pl von* **Monstrum**

monst|rös [mɔn'strø:s] ADJ monstrous; *(= riesig groß)* monster ADV *sich benehmen* monstrously; **~ aussehen** to look monstrous; **~ aussehende Kreaturen** monstrous-looking creatures

Monst|ro|si|tät [mɔnstrozi'tɛ:t] F -, -en monstrosity; *(= riesige Größe)* monstrous size; *(= Ungeheuer)* monster

Monst|rum ['mɔnstrʊm] NT -s, **Monstren** *or (geh)* **Monstra** [-trən, -tra] *(= Ungeheuer)* monster; *(fig: = Missbildung)* monstrosity; *(inf: = schweres Möbel)* hulking great piece of furniture *(inf)*

Mon|sun [mɔn'zu:n] M -s, -e monsoon

Mon|sun|re|gen M monsoon rain

Mon|tag ['mo:nta:k] M Monday → **blau c, Dienstag**

Mon|ta|ge [mɔn'ta:ʒə] F -, -n **a** *(Tech) (= Aufstellung)* installation; *(von Gerüst)* erection; *(= Zusammenbau)* assembly; *(Typ)* stripping; **auf ~ (dat) sein** to be away on a job **b** *(Art, Liter)* montage; *(Film)* editing

Mon|ta|ge-: **Mon|ta|ge|an|lei|tung** F assembly instructions *pl*; **Mon|ta|ge|band** [-bant] NT *pl* **-bänder** assembly line; **Mon|ta|ge|hal|le** F assembly shop; **Mon|ta|ge|werk** NT assembly plant

mon|tags ['mo:nta:ks] ADV on Mondays → *auch* **dienstags**

Mon|tags|au|to NT *(hum)* problem car, Friday-afternoon car *(Brit hum)*

Mon|tan-: **Mon|tan|in|dust|rie** F coal and steel industry; **Mon|tan|uni|on** F European Coal and Steel Community

Mon|te Car|lo ['mɔntə 'karlo] NT - -s Monte Carlo

Mon|te|neg|ro [,mɔnte'ne:gro] NT -s Montenegro

Mon|teur [mɔn'tø:ɐ] M -s, -e, **Mon|teu|rin** [-'tø:rɪn] F -, -nen *(Tech)* fitter; *(Aut)* mechanic; *(= Heizungsmonteur, Fernmeldemonteur, Elektromonteur)* engineer; *(Elec)* electrician

Mon|teur|an|zug [-'tø:ɐ-] M boiler suit *(Brit)*, overalls *pl*

mon|tie|ren [mɔn'ti:rən] ptp **montiert** VT **a** *(Tech)* to install; *(= zusammenbauen)* to assemble; *(= befestigen) Bauteil* to fit *(auf +acc, an +acc* to); *Dachantenne* to put up; *(= aufstellen) Gerüst* to erect; **etw an die Wand ~** to fix sth to the wall **b** *(Art, Film, Liter) Einzelteile* to create a montage from; **aus etw montiert sein** to be a montage of sth

Mon|tur [mɔn'tu:ɐ] F -, -en *(inf) (hum: = Arbeitskleidung)* gear *(inf)*, rig-out *(Brit inf)*; *(Aus: = Uniform)* uniform

Mo|nu|ment [monu'mɛnt] NT -(e)s, -e monument

mo|nu|men|tal [monumɛn'ta:l] ADJ *Gebäude, Gemälde, Roman* monumental ADV monumentally; **~ anmutende Architektur** monumental architecture

Mo|nu|men|tal- *in cpds* monumental; **Mo|nu|men|tal|bau** M monumental building; **Mo|nu|men|tal|film** M (screen) epic, (Hollywood) spectacular; **Mo|nu|men|tal|werk** NT monumental work; *(Literatur auch)* epic work

Moon|boots ['mu:nbu:ts] PL moon boots *pl*

Moor [mo:ɐ] NT -(e)s, -e bog; *(= Hochmoor)* moor

Moor-: **Moor|bad** NT mud bath; **Moor|bo|den** M marshy soil; **Moor|huhn** NT grouse; **Moor|huhn|jagd** F **a** *(= Jagd)* grouse shoot, grouse hunt *(US)*; *(= das Jagen)* grouse shooting **b** *(= Computerspiel)* moorhen-chicken chase

moo|rig ['mo:rɪç] ADJ boggy

Moor-: **Moor|ko|lo|nie** F fen community; **Moor|kul|tur** F cultivation of peat bogs; **Moor|land** NT marshland; *(= Hochmoorland)* moorland; **Moor|pa|ckung** F mudpack; **Moor|sied|lung** F fen community

Moos [mo:s] NT -es, -e moss; **von ~ überzogen** overgrown with moss, moss-grown; **~ ansetzen** to become covered with moss, to become moss-grown; *(fig)* to become hoary with age

moos-: **moos|be|deckt** ADJ moss-covered; **moos|grün** ADJ moss-green

moo|sig ['mo:zɪç] ADJ mossy

Moos|ro|se F, **Moos|rös|chen** [-rø:sçən] NT moss rose

Mop △ [mɔp] M -s, -s → **Mopp**

Möp △ [mœp] M -s, -s *or f* -, -s → **Möpp**

Mo|ped ['mo:pɛt, 'mo:pe:t] NT -s, -s moped

Mo|ped|fah|rer(in) M(F) moped rider

Mopp [mɔp] M -s, -s mop

Möpp [mœp] M -s, -s *or f* -, -s **ein fieser** *or* **eine fiese ~** *(dial inf)* a nasty piece of work *(inf)*

Mop|pel ['mɔpl] M -s, - *(inf)* tubby *(inf)*

mop|pen ['mɔpn] VT to mop

Mops [mɔps] M -es, ⸚e ['mœpsə] **a** *(Hund)* pug (dog) **b** *(= Dickwanst)* roly-poly *(inf)*, dumpling *(inf)* **c** **Möpse** PL *(sl: = Busen)* tits *pl (sl)*

möp|seln ['mœpsln] VI *(dial)* to be smelly

mop|sen ['mɔpsn] VT *(dated inf)* to nick *(Brit inf)*, to pinch *(inf)*

Mops-: **mops|fi|del** ADJ *(dated inf)* chirpy *(inf)*; **Mops|ge|sicht** NT *(inf)* pug-face, puggy face *(inf)*

mop|sig ['mɔpsɪç] ADJ *(inf)* **a** *Kerl, Gesicht* podgy *(inf)* **b** *(= frech)* **sich ~ machen, ~ werden** to get cheeky *(Brit)* or fresh *(US)* **c** *(= langweilig)* boring

Mo|ral [mo'ra:l] F -, *no pl* **a** *(= Sittlichkeit)* morals *pl*; *(= gesellschaftliche Norm)* morality, morals *pl*; **eine hohe/keine ~ haben** to have high moral standards/no morals; **private ~** personal morals; **die ~ sinkt/steigt** moral standards are declining/rising; **die bürgerliche/sozialistische ~** bourgeois/socialist morality; **gegen die (geltende) ~ verstoßen** to violate the (accepted) moral code; **eine doppelte ~** double standards *pl*, a double standard; **~ predigen** to moralize *(jdm* to sb)

b *(= Lehre, Nutzanwendung)* moral; **und die ~ von der Geschicht': …** and the moral of this story is …

c *(= Ethik)* ethics *pl*, moral code; **nach christlicher ~** according to Christian ethics, according to the Christian (moral) code

d *(= Disziplin: von Volk, Soldaten)* morale; **die ~ sinkt** morale is falling, morale is getting lower

Mo|ral- *in cpds* moral; **Mo|ral|apos|tel** M *(pej)* upholder of moral standards

Mo|ra|lin [mora'li:n] NT -s, *no pl (hum)* priggishness

mo|ra|lin|sau|er *(hum)* ADJ priggish ADV priggishly; **~ reden** to talk like a prig; **~ klingen** to sound priggish

mo|ra|lisch [mo'ra:lɪʃ] ADJ moral; **das war eine ~e Ohrfeige für die Regierung** that was one in the eye *(Brit)* or that was a black eye *(US)* for the government *(inf)*; **einen** *or* **seinen Moralischen haben** *(inf)* to have (a fit of) the blues *(inf)*, to be down in the dumps *(inf)* ADV *bedenklich, verpflichtet* morally; **ein ~ hochstehender Mensch** a person of high moral standing

mo|ra|li|sie|ren [morali'zi:rən] ptp **moralisiert** VI to moralize

Mo|ra|lis|mus [mora'lɪsmʊs] M -, *no pl (geh)* morality; **einem unbestechlichen ~ leben** to live a life of incorruptible morality

Mo|ra|list [mora'lɪst] M -en, -en, **Mo|ra|lis|tin** [-'lɪstɪn] F -, -nen moralist

mo|ra|lis|tisch [mora'lɪstɪʃ] ADJ moralistic

Mo|ra|li|tät [morali'tɛ:t] F -, -en morality; *(Theat)* morality play

Mo|ral-: **Mo|ral|ko|dex** M moral code; **Mo|ral|phi|lo|so|phie** F moral philosophy; **Mo|ral|pre|di|ger(in)** M(F) moralizer; **Mo|ral|pre|digt** F homily, sermon; **~en halten** to moralize; **jdm eine ~ halten** to give sb a homily *or* sermon; **Mo|ral|theo|lo|gie** F moral theology; **Mo|ral|vor|stel|lung** F moral *or* ethical standards *pl*

Mo|rä|ne [mo'rɛ:nə] F -, -n *(Geol)* moraine

Mo|rast [mo'rast] M -(e)s, -e *or* **Moräste** [mo'rɛstə] *(lit, fig)* mire, quagmire; *(= Sumpf auch)* morass

mo|ras|tig [mo'rastɪç] ADJ marshy; *(= schlammig)* muddy

Mo|ra|to|ri|um [mora'to:riʊm] NT -s, **Moratorien** [-riən] moratorium

mor|bid [mɔr'bi:t] ADJ *(Med)* morbid; *(fig geh)* degenerate

Mor|bi|di|tät [mɔrbidi'tɛ:t] F -, *no pl (Med)* morbidity; *(fig geh)* degeneracy

Mor|bus-Down-Syn|drom ['mɔrbʊs'daun-] NT Down's syndrome

Mor|chel ['mɔrçl] F -, -n *(Bot)* morel

Mord [mɔrt] M -(e)s, -e [-də] murder, homicide *(US) (an +dat* of); *(an Politiker etc)* assassination (*an +dat* of); **wegen ~es** for murder *or* homicide *(US)*; **„Mord an altem Mann"** "old man slain *or* murdered"; **politischer ~** political killing; **auf ~ sinnen** *(old, liter)* to devise murderous schemes; **das ist ja ~!** *(inf)* it's (sheer) murder! *(inf)*; **dann gibt es ~ und Totschlag** *(inf)* all hell will be let loose *(Brit inf) or* will break out *(inf)*, there'll be hell to pay *(inf)*; **von ~ und Totschlag handeln** to be full of violence

Mord-: **Mord|an|kla|ge** F murder charge, charge of homicide *(US)*; **~ erheben** to file a murder charge, to file a charge of homicide *(US)*; **unter ~ stehen** to be on a murder charge, to be on a charge of homicide *(US)*; **Mord|an|schlag** M assassination (*auf +acc* of); *(erfolglos)* assassination attempt (*auf +acc* on), attempted assassination (*auf +acc* of); **einen ~ verüben** to carry out an assassination attempt; **einen ~ auf jdn verüben** to try to assassinate sb; *(erfolgreich)* to assassinate sb; **Mord|bren|ner(in)** M(F) *(old, liter)* arsonist, incendiary; **Mord|bu|be** M *(obs)* murderer; **Mord|dro|hung** F threat on one's life, murder *or* death threat

mor|den ['mɔrdn] VTI *(liter)* to murder, to kill, to slay *(liter)*; **das sinnlose Morden** senseless killing

Mör|der ['mœrdɐ] M **-s, -**, **Mör|de|rin** [-ərɪn] F **-, -nen** murderer *(auch Jur)*, killer; *(Frau auch)* murderess; *(= Attentäter)* assassin

Mör|der-: **Mör|der|ban|de** F gang *or* bunch of murderers *or* killers; **Mör|der|gru|be** F **aus seinem Herzen keine ~ machen** to speak frankly; **Mör|der|hand** F *(old, liter)* **durch ~ fallen** *or* **sterben** to die *or* perish *(old)* at the hands of a murderer

Mör|de|rin [-ərɪn] F → **Mörder**

mör|de|risch ['mœrdərɪʃ] ADJ *(lit) Anschlag* murderous; *(fig) (= schrecklich)* dreadful, terrible; *Tempo* breakneck *attr*; *Preise* iniquitous; *Konkurrenzkampf* cutthroat ADV *(inf) (= entsetzlich)* dreadfully, terribly; *stinken* like hell *(inf)*; *wehtun* like crazy *(inf)*; **~ fluchen** to curse like blazes *(inf)*; **~ schreien** to scream blue murder *(Brit) or* bloody murder *(inf)*

Mord-: **Mord|fall** M murder *or* homicide *(US)* (case); **der ~ Dr. Praun** the Dr Praun murder *or* homicide *(US)* (case); **Mord|gier** F *(geh)* desire to kill; **mord|gie|rig** ADJ *(geh)* bloodthirsty; **Mord|in|stru|ment** NT murder weapon

mor|dio ['mɔrdio] INTERJ *(old)* → **zetermordio, Zeter**

Mord-: **Mord|kom|mis|si|on** F murder squad, homicide squad *or* division *(US)*; **Mord|lust** F desire to kill; **Mord|pro|zess** M murder trial

Mords- *in cpds (inf)* incredible, terrible, awful; *(= toll, prima)* hell of a *(inf)*; **Mords|ding** NT *(inf)* whopper *(inf)*; **Mords|du|sel** M *(inf)* tremendous stroke of luck; **einen ~ haben** to be dead *(Brit inf) or* completely lucky; **Mords|gau|di** F *(S Ger inf)* whale of a time *(inf)*; **Mords|geld** NT *(inf)* fantastic amount of money; **Mords|glück** NT *(inf)* = **Mordsdusel**; **Mords|hit|ze** F *(inf)* scorching heat; **es ist eine ~ heute!** it's a real scorcher today *(inf)*; **Mords|hun|ger** M *(inf)* **einen ~ haben** to be famished *or* ravenous, to be dying of hunger; **Mords|kerl** M *(inf)* **a** *(= verwegener Mensch)* hell of a guy *(inf)* **b** *(= starker Mann)* enormous fellow *or* guy *(inf)*; **Mords|krach** M *(inf)* hell of a din *(inf)*, fearful *or* terrible din; *(= Streit)* hell of a row *(inf)*; **Mords|lärm** M *(inf)* hell of a noise *(inf)*, fearful *or* terrible noise; **mords|mä|ßig** *(inf)* ADJ incredible; **ich habe einen ~en Hunger** I could eat a horse *(inf)* ADV *(= sehr)* incredibly; *(= furchtbar)* dreadfully, terribly; **Mords|spaß** M *(inf)* **einen ~ haben** to have a great time; **etw macht ~** sth is great fun; **Mords|wut** F *(inf)* terrible temper *or* rage; **eine ~ im Bauch haben** to be in a hell of a *(inf) or* in a terrible temper *or* rage

Mord-: **Mord|tat** F *(liter)* murderous deed; **Mord|ver|dacht** M suspicion of murder; **unter ~ (dat) stehen** to be suspected of murder; **Mord|waf|fe** F murder weapon

Mo|rel|le [mo'rɛlə] F **-, -n** *(Bot)* morello cherry

Mo|res ['mo:re:s] PL **jdn ~ lehren** *(dated inf)* to teach sb some manners

mor|gen ['mɔrgn] ADV tomorrow; **~ früh/Mittag/Abend** tomorrow morning/lunchtime/evening; **~ in acht Tagen** tomorrow week, a week (from) tomorrow; **~ um diese** *or* **dieselbe Zeit** this time tomorrow; **bis ~/~ früh!** see you tomorrow/in the morning; **Kartoffeln gibt es erst wieder ~** we/they *etc* won't have any potatoes till tomorrow; **hast du ~ Zeit?** are you free tomorrow?; **~, ~, nur nicht heute, sagen alle faulen Leute** *(Prov)* tomorrow never comes *(Prov)*; **~ ist auch (noch) ein Tag!** *(Prov)* tomorrow is another day *(prov)*; **die Technik von ~** the technology of tomorrow → **heute a, Morgen a**

Mor|gen ['mɔrgn] M **-s, -** **a** *(= Tagesanfang)* morning; **am ~, des ~s** *(geh)* in the morning; **gegen ~** toward(s) (the) morning; **gestern ~** yesterday morning; **heute ~** this morning; **bis in den ~ (hinein)** into the wee small hours *(Brit)*, into the early hours; **am nächsten** *or* **den nächsten ~** the next morning; **früh/spät am ~** early/late in the morning; **eines ~s** one morning; **den ganzen ~ (über)** the whole morning; **es wird ~** day is breaking; **der ~ dämmert** *or* **bricht an** *(liter)* **der ~ graut** *or* **zieht herauf** *(liter)* dawn is breaking; **guten ~!** good morning; **~!** *(inf)* morning, hello, hi *(inf)*; **(jdm) guten ~ sagen** to say good morning (to sb); *(= morgens kurz besuchen)* to say hello (to sb); **schön** *or* **frisch wie der junge ~** *(liter)* fresh as a daisy **b** *no pl (old, liter: = Osten)* East **c** *(liter: = Zukunft)* dawn; **der ~ einer neuen Zeit bricht an** a new age is dawning

Mor|gen M **-s, -** *(Measure)* ≈ acre; **drei ~ Land** ≈ three acres of land

Mor|gen- *in cpds* morning; **Mor|gen|aus|ga|be** F morning edition; **Mor|gen|däm|me|rung** F dawn, daybreak; **in der ~** at first light, at the first light of dawn

mor|gend|lich ['mɔrgntlɪç] ADJ morning *attr*; *(= frühmorgendlich)* early morning *attr*; **die ~e Stille** the quiet of the early morning ADV **es war ~ kühl** *or* **frisch** it was cool as it often is in the morning; **~ frisch aussehen** to look as fresh as a daisy

Mor|gen-: **Mor|gen|dunst** M early morning mist; **Mor|gen|es|sen** NT *(Sw: = Frühstück)* breakfast; **Mor|gen|frü|he** F early morning; **sie brachen in aller ~ auf** they left at (the) break of dawn; **Mor|gen|ga|be** F *(Hist)* gift given to a bride by her husband after the wedding night; **Mor|gen|grau|en** [-grauən] NT **-s, -** dawn, daybreak; **im** *or* **beim ~** in the first light of dawn; **Mor|gen|gym|nas|tik** F morning exercises *pl*; **~ machen** to do one's morning exercises; **Mor|gen|land** NT *(old, liter)* Orient, East; **die Weisen aus dem ~** the Wise Men from the East; **Mor|gen|län|der** [-lɛndɐ] M **-s, -**, **Mor|gen|län|de|rin** [-ərɪn] F **-, -nen** *(old, iro)* Oriental; **mor|gen|län|disch** [-lɛndɪʃ] ADJ *(old, iro)* Oriental, Eastern; **Mor|gen|lat|te** F *(sl)* early-morning hard-on *(sl)*; **Mor|gen|licht** NT early morning light; **Mor|gen|luft** F early morning air; **~ wittern** *(fig inf)* to see one's chance; **Mor|gen|man|tel** M dressing gown; *(für Damen auch)* housecoat; **Mor|gen|muf|fel** M *(inf)* **sie ist ein schrecklicher ~** she's terribly grumpy in the mornings *(inf)*; **Mor|gen|ne|bel** M early morning mist; **Mor|gen|post** F morning post *(Brit) or* mail; **Mor|gen|rock** M housecoat; **Mor|gen|rot** NT **-s**, *no pl*, **Mor|gen|rö|te** F **-, -n** sunrise; *(fig)* dawn(ing); **~ deutet auf schlechtes Wetter hin** red sky in the morning, shepherd's warning *(prov)*

mor|gens ['mɔrgns] ADV in the morning; **(um) drei Uhr ~, ~ (um) drei Uhr** at three o'clock in the morning, at three a.m.; **~ und abends** morning and evening; *(fig: = dauernd)* morning, noon and night; **von ~ bis mittags** in the morning; **von ~ bis abends** from morning to night; **nur ~** mornings only → **dienstagmorgens** *etc*

Mor|gen-: **Mor|gen|son|ne** F morning sun; **~ haben** to get *or* catch the morning sun; **Mor|gen|stern** M morning star; *(Schlagwaffe auch)* flail; **Mor|gen|stun|de** F morning hour; **zu früher ~** early in the morning; **bis in die frühen ~n** into the early hours, into the wee small hours *(Brit)*; **Morgenstund(e) hat Gold im Mund(e)** *(Prov)* the early bird catches the worm *(Prov)*; **Mor|gen|to|i|let|te** F, *no pl (geh)* morning ablutions *pl*; **Mor|gen|zug** M early (morning) train

mor|gig ['mɔrgɪç] ADJ *attr* tomorrow's; **die ~e Veranstaltung/Zeitung** tomorrow's event/paper; **der ~e Tag** tomorrow; **sein ~er Besuch** his visit tomorrow

mo|ri|bund [mori'bʊnt] ADJ *(Med, fig)* moribund

Mo|ri|tat ['mo:rita:t] F **-, -en** **a** *(= Vortrag)* street ballad **b** *(= Geschehen)* murderous deed

Mor|mo|ne [mɔr'mo:nə] M **-n, -n**, **Mor|mo|nin** [-'mo:nɪn] F **-, -nen** Mormon

mor|mo|nisch [mɔr'mo:nɪʃ] ADJ Mormon ADV *erziehen* as a Mormon; *aufwachsen* Mormon

Mor|phem [mɔr'fe:m] NT **-s, -e** morpheme

Mor|pheus ['mɔrfɔys] M **-'** Morpheus; **in ~' Armen ruhen** *(liter)* to be in the arms of Morpheus *(liter)*

Mor|phin [mɔr'fi:n] NT **-s**, *no pl (Chem)* morphine, morphia

Mor|phi|nis|mus [mɔrfi'nɪsmʊs] M **-**, *no pl* morphine addiction

Mor|phi|nist [mɔrfi'nɪst] M **-en, -en**, **Mor|phi|nis|tin** [-'nɪstɪn] F **-, -nen** morphine addict

Mor|phi|um ['mɔrfiʊm] NT **-s**, *no pl* morphine, morphia

mor|phi|um|süch|tig ADJ addicted to morphine

Mor|pho|lo|gie [mɔrfolo'gi:] F **-**, *no pl* morphology

mor|pho|lo|gisch [mɔrfo'lo:gɪʃ] ADJ morphological

morsch [mɔrʃ] ADJ *(lit, fig)* rotten; *Knochen* brittle; *Gebäude* ramshackle

Morse-: **Mor|se|al|pha|bet** NT Morse (code); **im ~** in Morse (code); **Mor|se|ap|pa|rat** M Morse telegraph

mor|sen ['mɔrzn] VI to send a message in Morse (code) VT to send in Morse (code)

Mör|ser ['mœrzɐ] M **-s, -** mortar *(auch Mil)*; **etw im ~ zerstoßen** to crush sth with a pestle and mortar

Mor|se|zei|chen ['mɔrzə-] NT Morse signal

Mor|ta|del|la [mɔrta'dɛla] F **-**, *no pl* mortadella, baloney *(US)*

Mor|ta|li|tät [mɔrtali'tɛ:t] F **-**, *no pl* mortality rate

Mör|tel ['mœrtl] M **-s, -** *(zum Mauern)* mortar; *(= Putz)* stucco

Mo|sa|ik [moza'i:k] NT **-s, -e(n)** *(lit, fig)* mosaic

Mo|sa|ik- *in cpds* mosaic; **mo|sa|ik|ar|tig** ADJ like a mosaic, tessellated *no adv* ADV like a mosaic; **Mo|sa|ik|fuß|bo|den** M mosaic *or* tessellated floor; **Mo|sa|ik|stein** M tessera

mo|sa|isch [mo'za:ɪʃ] ADJ Mosaic

Mo|sam|bik [mozam'bɪk, -'bi:k] NT **-s** Mozambique

Mo|schee [mɔ'ʃe:] F **-, -n** [-'ʃe:ən] mosque

Mo|schus ['mɔʃʊs] M **-**, *no pl* musk

Mo|schus|och|se M musk ox

Mo|se ['mo:zə, 'mo:zɛ] M = **Moses**, → **Buch a**

Mö|se ['mø:zə] F **-, -n** *(vulg)* cunt *(vulg)*

Mo|sel ['mo:zl] F **-** *(Geog)* Moselle

Mo|sel M **-s, -**, **Mo|sel|wein** M Moselle (wine)

mo|sern ['mo:zɐn] VI *(dial inf)* to gripe *(inf)*, to bellyache *(inf)*; **er hat immer was zu ~** he always has something to gripe *or* bellyache about *(inf)*

Mo|ses ['mo:zəs, 'mo:zɛs] M -' *or (liter)* **Mosis** ['mo:zɪs] Moses; **bin ich ~?** *(hum inf)* don't ask me
Mo|ses M -, - *(Naut inf)* ship's boy
Mos|kau ['mɔskau] NT -s Moscow
Mos|kau|er ['mɔskauɐ] ADJ *attr* Moscow *attr*
Mos|kau|er ['mɔskauɐ] M -s, -, **Mos|kau|e|rin** [-ərɪn] F -, -nen Muscovite
Mos|ki|to [mɔs'ki:to] M -s, -s mosquito
Mos|ki|to|netz NT mosquito net
Mos|ko|wi|ter [mɔsko'vi:tɐ] ADJ *attr* Muscovite
Mos|ko|wi|ter [mɔsko'vi:tɐ] M -s, -, **Mos|ko|wi|te|rin** [-ərɪn] F -, -nen Muscovite
Mos|lem ['mɔslɛm] M -s, -s, **Mos|le|min** [mɔs'le:mɪn] F -, -nen Moslem, Muslim
mos|le|misch [mɔs'le:mɪʃ] ADJ *attr* Moslem, Muslim ADV *erziehen* as a Moslem; *aufwachsen* Moslem
Mos|li|me [mɔs'li:mə] F -, -n Moslem, Muslim
Most [mɔst] M -(e)s, *no pl* **a** (unfermented) fruit juice; *(für Wein)* must **b** *(S Ger, Sw) (= Obstwein)* fruit wine; *(= Birnenmost)* perry; *(= Apfelmost)* cider
Most|ap|fel M cider apple
Most|ge|wicht NT specific gravity of the must
Most|rich ['mɔstrɪç] M -s, *no pl (dial)* mustard
Mo|tel [mo'tɛl] NT -s, -s motel
Mo|tet|te [mo'tɛtə] F -, -n *(Mus)* motet
Mo|ti|on [mo'tsio:n] F -, -en **a** *(Sw: = Antrag)* motion **b** *(Gram: = Abwandlung)* inflection (for gender)
Mo|tiv [mo'ti:f] NT -s, -e [-və] **a** *(Psych, Jur, fig)* motive; **das ~ einer Tat** the motive for a deed; **aus welchem ~ heraus?** for what motive?, what are your/his *etc* motives?; **er wurde aus politischen ~en umgebracht** his murder was politically motivated; **ohne erkennbares ~** without any apparent motive **b** *(Art, Liter)* subject; *(= Leitmotiv, Topos, Mus)* motif
Mo|ti|va|ti|on [motiva'tsio:n] F -, -en motivation
mo|ti|va|ti|ons|för|dernd ADJ motivational; **~e Maßnahmen** incentives
Mo|tiv-: **Mo|tiv|for|schung** F motivation research; **mo|tiv|gleich** ADJ with the same theme *or* motif; **~ sein** to have the same motif
mo|ti|vie|ren [moti'vi:rən] *ptp* **motiviert** VT **a** *Mitarbeiter (= anregen)* to motivate; **politisch motiviert** politically motivated **b** *(= begründen)* **etw (jdm gegenüber) ~** to give (sb) reasons for sth; *(rechtfertigend)* to justify sth (to sb); *Verhalten, Abwesenheit* to account for sth (to sb)
Mo|ti|vie|rung F -, -en motivation; *(= erklärende Rechtfertigung)* explanation
Mo|ti|vik [mo'ti:vɪk] F -, *no pl* motifs *pl*
Mo|to-Cross ['motokrɔs] NT -, -e, **Mo|to|cross** NT -, -e motocross
Mo|tor ['mo:tɔr, mo'to:ɐ] M -s, -en [-'to:rən] motor; *(von Fahrzeug)* engine; *(fig)* driving force (+*gen* in)
Mo|tor-: **Mo|tor|an|trieb** M motor drive; **mit ~** motor-driven; **Mo|tor|block** M *pl* -blöcke engine block; **Mo|tor|boot** NT motorboat
Mo|to|ren-: **Mo|to|ren|ge|räusch** NT sound of the/an engine/engines; **Mo|to|ren|lärm** M noise *or* roar of (the) engines; **Mo|to|ren|öl** NT engine oil
Mo|tor|hau|be F bonnet *(Brit)*, hood *(US)*; *(Aviat)* engine cowling
-mo|to|rig [moto:rɪç] ADJ *suf* -engined; **einmotorig** one-engined, single-engined; **zweimotorig** twin-engined
Mo|to|rik [mo'to:rɪk] F -, *no pl (Physiol)* motor activity; *(= Lehre)* study of motor activity
Mo|to|ri|ker [mo'to:rikɐ] M -s, -, **Mo|to|ri|ke|rin** [-ərɪn] F -, -nen *(Psych)* motor type
mo|to|risch [mo'to:rɪʃ] ADJ *(Physiol) Nerv, Störung* motor *attr*; **~e Fähigkeiten** motor skills ADV **sie ist ~ gestört** she suffers from an impairment of the motor nerves; **~ geschickt** well coordinated

mo|to|ri|sie|ren [motori'zi:rən] *ptp* **motorisiert** VT to motorize; *Landwirtschaft* to mechanize; *(= mit Motor ausstatten)* to fit with an engine; **sich ~** to get motorized; **motorisiertes Zweirad** motorized bike
Mo|to|ri|sie|rung F -, *no pl* motorization; *(der Landwirtschaft)* mechanization; *(= Ausstattung mit Motor)* fitting with an engine
Mo|tor-: **Mo|tor|jacht** F motor yacht; **Mo|tor|küh|lung** F engine cooling system; **Mo|tor|lärm** M noise *or* roar of the engine; **Mo|tor|leis|tung** F engine performance; **Mo|tor|öl** NT engine oil
Mo|tor|rad ['mo:tɔrra:t, mo'to:ɐra:t] NT motorbike, motorcycle; **fahren Sie (ein) ~?** do you ride a motorbike?
Mo|tor|rad-: **Mo|tor|rad|fah|rer(in)** M(F) motorcyclist; **Mo|tor|rad|helm** M (motorcylce *or* motorcyclist's) crash helmet; **Mo|tor|rad|ren|nen** NT motorcycle race; *(= Sportart)* motorcycle racing; **Mo|tor|rad|renn|fah|rer(in)** M(F) motorcycle racer; **Mo|tor|rad|sport** M motorcycle racing
Mo|tor-: **Mo|tor|raum** M engine compartment; **Mo|tor|rol|ler** M (motor) scooter; **Mo|tor|sä|ge** F power saw; **Mo|tor|scha|den** M engine trouble *no pl*; **Mo|tor|schiff** NT motor vessel *or* ship; **Mo|tor|schlit|ten** M motorized sleigh; **Mo|tor|sport** M motor sport
Mot|te ['mɔtə] F -, -n moth; **von ~n zerfressen** moth-eaten; **angezogen wie die ~n vom Licht** attracted like moths to a flame; **du kriegst die ~n!** *(inf)* blow me! *(inf)*
Mot|ten-: **mot|ten|fest** ADJ mothproof; **Mot|ten|kis|te** F *(fig)* **etw aus der ~ hervorholen** to dig sth out; **aus der ~ des 19. Jahrhunderts stammen** *(inf)* to be a relic of the 19th century; **Mot|ten|ku|gel** F mothball; **Mot|ten|pul|ver** NT moth powder; **mot|ten|zer|fres|sen** ADJ moth-eaten
Mot|to ['mɔto] NT -s, -s **a** *(= Wahlspruch)* motto; **unter dem ~ ... stehen** to have ... as a *or* one's motto **b** *(in Buch)* epigraph **c** *(= Kennwort)* password
mot|zen ['mɔtsn] VI *(inf)* to beef *(inf)*, to gripe *(inf)*; **was hast du jetzt zu ~?** what are you beefing *or* griping about now? *(inf)*
mouil|lie|ren [mu'ji:rən] *ptp* **mouilliert** VT *(Ling)* to palatalize
Moun|tain|bike ['mauntɪnbaik] NT -s, -s mountain bike
mous|sie|ren [mʊ'si:rən] *ptp* **moussiert** VI to effervesce; **~d** *(Wein)* sparkling
Mö|we ['mø:və] F -, -n seagull, gull
Mo|zart-: **Mo|zart|ku|gel** F *chocolate truffle with marzipan soaked in liqueur*; **Mo|zart|schlei|fe** F Mozart cravat
MP F -, -s **a** [ɛm'pe:] *abbr von* **Militärpolizei** Military Police **b** [ɛm'pi:] *abbr von* **Maschinenpistole**
MP3 *(Comput: = Komprimierungsformat)* MP3
MP3-Play|er M -s, - MP3 player
Mrd. *abbr von* **Milliarde**
MS [ɛm'lɛs] *abbr von* **Multiple Sklerose** MS
Ms., Mskr. *abbr von* **Manuskript** ms
MS-: **MS-krank** ADJ suffering from MS; **MS-Kran|ke(r)** MF *decl as adj* MS sufferer, person with MS
MTA [ɛmte:'la:] M -s, -s *abbr von* **medizinisch-technischer Assistent**
MTA [ɛmte:'la:] F -, -s *abbr von* **medizinisch-technische Assistentin**
mtl. *abbr von* **monatlich**
Mü|cke ['mʏkə] F -, -n *(= Insekt)* mosquito, midge *(Brit)*, gnat; **aus einer ~ einen Elefanten machen** *(inf)* to make a mountain out of a molehill
Mu|cke|fuck ['mʊkəfʊk] M -s, *no pl (inf)* coffee substitute, ersatz coffee
mu|cken ['mʊkn] VI *(inf)* to mutter; **ohne zu ~** without a murmur VR to make a sound
Mu|cken ['mʊkn] PL *(inf)* moods *pl*; **(seine) ~ haben** to be moody; *(Sache)* to be temperamental; *(zu diesem Zeitpunkt) (Mensch)* to be in one of one's moods; *(Sache)* to play up; **jdm die ~ austreiben** to sort sb out *(inf)*
Mü|cken|pla|ge F plague of mosquitoes *or* midges *(Brit)*
Mü|cken|stich M mosquito *or* gnat bite, midge bite *(Brit)*
Mu|cki|bu|de F *(inf: = Fitnesscenter)* muscle factory *(inf)*
Mu|ckis PL *(inf hum: = Muskeln)* (bulging) muscles *pl*; *(= Bauch- und Brustmuskeln)* abs *pl* and pecs *pl (hum)*
mu|ckisch ['mʊkɪʃ], **mucksch** [mʊkʃ] ADJ *(dial)* peeved
Mucks [mʊks] M -es, -e *(inf)* sound; **einen/keinen ~ sagen** to make/not to make a sound; *(widersprechend)* to say/not to say a word; **ohne einen ~** *(= widerspruchslos)* without a murmur
muck|sen ['mʊksn] VR *(inf)* **sich nicht ~** not to budge *(inf)*, not to move (a muscle); *(= sich nicht äußern)* not to make a sound; *(Mensch)* not to say a dickybird *(Brit inf)*, not to make a peep
mucks|mäus|chen|still [-mɔysçən-] ADJ ADV *(inf)* (as) quiet as a mouse
Mud [mʊt] M -s, *no pl*, **Mudd** [mʊt] M -s, *no pl (Naut)* mud
mü|de ['my:də] ADJ **a** tired; *(= erschöpft)* weary, tired; *Haupt* weary
b *(= überdrüssig)* tired, weary; **einer Sache** *(gen)* **~ werden** to tire *or* weary of sth, to grow tired *or* weary of sth; **einer Sache** *(gen)* **~ sein** to be tired *or* weary of sth; **des Wartens ~ sein** to be tired of waiting; **ich bin es ~, das zu tun** I'm tired *or* weary of doing that; **sie wird nicht ~, das zu tun** she never tires *or* wearies of doing that; **keine ~ Mark** *(inf)* not a single penny
ADV **a** *(= erschöpft)* **sich ~ reden/kämpfen** to tire oneself out talking/fighting; **sich ~ laufen** to tire oneself out running about
b *(= gelangweilt)* **~ lächeln** to give a weary smile; **~ lächelnd** with a weary smile; **~ abwinken** to make a weary gesture (with one's hand)
-mü|de ADJ *suf* tired *or* weary of ...; **amtsmüde** tired of office; **kampfmüde** tired *or* weary of fighting
Mü|dig|keit ['my:dɪçkait] F -, *no pl (= Schlafbedürfnis)* tiredness; *(= Schläfrigkeit)* sleepiness; *(= Erschöpfung)* weariness, fatigue, tiredness; **die ~ überwinden** to overcome one's tiredness; **sich** *(dat)* **die ~ vertreiben, gegen die ~ ankämpfen** to fight one's tiredness; **vor ~** *(dat)* **umfallen** to drop from exhaustion; **alle ~ fiel von ihm ab** all of his tiredness melted away; **nur keine ~ vorschützen!** *(inf)* don't (you) tell me you're tired
Mud|scha|hed|din [mʊdʒahe'di:n] M -(s), -, **Mud|scha|hi|din** [mʊdʒahɪ'di:n] M -(s), - Mujaheddin
Mües|li ['my:ɛsli] NT -s, -s *(Sw)* muesli
Mu|ez|zin [mu'ɛtsi:n] M -s, -s muezzin
Muff [mʊf] M -s, *no pl (N Ger)* **a** *(= Modergeruch)* musty smell, mustiness; *(fig: = Rückständigkeit)* fustiness **b** *(= Schimmel, Moder)* mildew
Muff M -(e)s, -e muff
Muf|fe ['mʊfə] F -, -n **a** *(Tech)* sleeve **b** *(inf)* **~ kriegen/haben** to be scared stiff *(inf)*, to get/have the shits *(sl)*; **ihm geht die ~ (eins zu hunderttausend)** he's scared stiff *(inf)*
Muf|fel ['mʊfl] M -s, - **a** *(Hunt: = Maul)* muzzle **b** *(inf: = Murrkopf)* grouch *(inf)*, griper *(inf)*
-muf|fel M *suf in cpds (inf)* **ein Mode-/Computermuffel sein** to have no time for fashion/computers; **er ist ein fürchterlicher Krawattenmuffel** he hates wearing ties
muf|fe|lig ['mʊfəlɪç] *(inf)* ADJ grumpy ADV grumpily; **~ aussehen** to look grumpy; **~ an die Arbeit herangehen** to start work with a grumpy attitude
muf|feln ['mʊfln] *(inf)* VI **a** *(= mürrisch sein)* to be grumpy **b** *(dial inf)* = **müffeln** VTI *(= mürrisch reden)* to mutter
müf|feln ['mʏfln] VI *(dial inf)* to smell musty; **es müffelt** there's a musty smell

Muf|fen|sau|sen ['mʊfnzauzn] NT *(inf)* ~ **kriegen/haben** to get/be scared stiff *(inf)*

muf|fig ['mʊfɪç] ADJ **a** *Geruch, Zimmer* musty; *(fig) Tradition, Institution* stuffy **b** *(inf) Gesicht* grumpy ADV **a** *riechen* musty **b** *(inf: = lustlos)* grumpily; ~ **dreinsehen** to look grumpy

müf|fig ['mʏfɪç] *(dial)* ADJ musty ADV *riechen* musty

muff|lig ['mʊflɪç] ADJ ADV *(inf)* = **muffelig**

Muff|lon ['mʊflɔn] M **-s, -s** *(Zool)* mouflon, moufflon

Muf|ti ['mʊfti] M **-s, -s** mufti

Mu|gel ['mu:gl] M **-s, -n**, **Mugl** ['mugl] M **-s, -(n)** *(Aus inf)* hillock, hummock

Mug|ge ['mʊgə] F **-, -n** *abbr von* **musikalisches Gelegenheitsgeschäft** *(inf)* gig *(inf)*

muh [mu:] INTERJ moo

Mü|he ['my:ə] F **-, -n** trouble; *(= Anstrengung auch)* effort; *(= Arbeitsaufwand auch)* bother; **ohne ~** without any trouble *or* bother; **nur mit ~** only just; **mit Müh und Not** *(inf)* with great difficulty; **unter (großen) ~n** with a great deal of effort; **er kann mit Müh und Not seinen Namen schreiben** *(inf)* he can just about write his name; **alle/viel ~ haben** to have a tremendous amount of/a great deal of trouble *or* bother *(etw zu tun* doing sth); **wenig/keine ~ haben** not to have much trouble *or* bother *(etw zu tun* doing sth); **das ist mit einigen ~n** *or* **einiger ~ verbunden** that involves considerable effort; **mit jdm/etw seine ~ haben** to have a great deal of trouble *or* bother with sb/sth; **es ist der** *(gen) or* **die ~ wert, es lohnt die ~** it's worth the trouble *or* bother *(etw zu tun* of doing sth); **die kleine ~ hat sich gelohnt** it was worth the little bit of trouble; **sich** *(dat)* **etwas/mehr/keine ~ geben** to take some/more/no trouble; **er hat sich** *(dat)* **große ~ gegeben** he has taken great pains, he has taken a lot of trouble; **gib dir keine ~!** *(= sei still)* save your breath; *(= hör auf)* don't bother, save yourself the trouble; **sich** *(dat)* **die ~ machen, etw zu tun** to take the trouble to do sth, to go to the trouble *or* bother of doing sth; **sich** *(dat)* **nicht die ~ machen, etw zu tun** not to take the trouble to do sth, not to bother to do sth; **machen Sie sich** *(dat)* **keine ~!** (please) don't go to any trouble *or* bother; **sie hatte sich die ~ umsonst gemacht** her efforts were wasted; **jdm ~ machen** to give sb some trouble *or* bother; **wenn es Ihnen keine ~ macht** if it isn't too much *or* any trouble *or* bother; **viel ~ auf etw** *(acc)* **verwenden** to take a lot of trouble *or* bother with sth; **es hat viel ~ gekostet** it took a great deal of trouble; **verlorene ~** a waste of effort

mü|he|los ADJ effortless; *Sieg, Aufstieg auch* easy ADV effortlessly

Mü|he|lo|sig|keit F **-**, *no pl* effortlessness; *(von Sieg, Aufstieg auch)* ease

mu|hen ['mu:ən] VI to moo, to low

mü|hen ['my:ən] VR to strive *(um* for); **sosehr er sich auch mühte ...** strive as he might ...

mü|he|voll ADJ laborious, arduous; *Leben* arduous ADV with difficulty; ~ **verdientes Geld** hard-earned money

Muh|kuh F *(baby-talk)* moo-cow *(baby-talk)*

Mühl|bach M mill stream

Müh|le ['my:lə] F **-, -n** **a** mill; *(= Kaffeemühle)* grinder **b** *(fig) (= Routine)* treadmill; *(= Bürokratie)* wheels *pl* of bureaucracy; **die ~n der Justiz mahlen langsam** the wheels of justice grind slowly **c** *(= Mühlespiel)* nine men's morris *(esp Brit)* **d** *(inf) (Auto)* banger *(Brit inf)*, jalopy *(inf)*; *(Fahrrad)* boneshaker *(Brit inf)*; *(Flugzeug)* crate *(inf)*

Müh|len- *in cpds* = **Mühl-**

Müh|le|spiel NT **das** ~ nine men's morris *(esp Brit)*

Mühl- *in cpds* mill; **Mühl|gra|ben** M mill race; **Mühl|rad** NT millwheel; **Mühl|stein** M millstone

Muh|me ['mu:mə] F **-, -n** *(obs)* aunt

Müh|sal ['my:za:l] F **-, -e** *(geh)* tribulation; *(= Strapaze)* toil; **die ~e des Lebens** the trials and tribulations of life

müh|sam ['my:za:m] ADJ *Aufstieg, Weg, Leben* arduous; *Aufgabe, Amt auch* laborious; **ein ~es Geschäft sein** to be a painstaking business ADV with difficulty; **nur ~ vorwärtskommen** to make painfully slow progress; ~ **verdientes Geld** hard-earned money

müh|se|lig ['my:ze:lɪç] ADJ arduous, toilsome *(liter)*; **Ihr Mühseligen und Beladenen** *(Bibl)* ye that labour *(Brit) or* labor *(US)* and are heavy laden ADV **sich ~ ernähren** *or* **durchschlagen** to toil for one's living

mu|kös [mu'kø:s] ADJ *(Med)* mucous

Mu|ko|vis|zi|do|se [mukovɪstsi'do:zə] F **-**, *no pl (Med)* mucoviscidosis *(spec)*, cystic fibrosis

Mu|lat|te [mu'latə] M **-n, -n**, **Mu|lat|tin** [-'latɪn] F **-, -nen** mulatto

Mulch [mʊlç] M **-(e)s, -e** *(Agr)* mulch

Mul|de ['mʊldə] F **-, -n** **a** *(= Geländesenkung)* hollow **b** *(= Trog)* trough **c** *(für Bauschutt)* skip

Mu|li ['mu:li] NT OR M **-s, -(s)** **a** *(= Maultier)* mule **b** *(Ind inf: = Gabelstapler)* fork-lift *(inf)*

Mull [mʊl] M **-(e)s, -e** **a** *(= Torfmull)* garden peat **b** *(= Gewebe)* muslin; *(Med)* gauze

Müll [mʏl] M **-(e)s**, *no pl (= Haushaltsmüll)* rubbish, garbage *(esp US)*, trash *(US)*, refuse *(form)*; *(= Gerümpel)* rubbish, junk, garbage *(esp US)*; *(= Industriemüll)* waste; *(inf: = Unsinn)* rubbish *(Brit inf)*, trash *(inf)*; **etw in den ~ werfen** to throw sth out; **„Müll abladen verboten"** "dumping prohibited", "no tipping" *(Brit)*

Müll-: **Müll|ab|fuhr** F *(= Müllabholung)* refuse *or* garbage *(US) or* trash *(US)* collection; *(= Stadtreinigung)* refuse *etc* collection department; **Müll|ab|ho|lung** F refuse *or* garbage *(US) or* trash *(US)* collection; **Müll|ab|la|de|platz** M rubbish dump *or* tip *(Brit)*, garbage dump *(US)*, dump

Mul|lah ['mʊla] M **-s, -s** Mullah

Müll-: **Müll|au|to** NT = **Müllwagen**; **Müll|berg** M rubbish heap *(Brit)*, garbage dump *(US)*; **Müll|beu|tel** M bin liner *(Brit)*, garbage can liner *(US)*

Mull|bin|de F gauze bandage

Müll-: **Müll|con|tai|ner** M rubbish *or* garbage *(US)* skip, dumpster *(US)*; **Müll|de|po|nie** F waste disposal site *(form)*, sanitary (land)fill *(US form)*; **Müll|ei|mer** M rubbish bin *(Brit)*, garbage can *(US)*

Mül|ler ['mʏlɐ] M **-s, -** miller

Mül|le|rin ['mʏlərɪn] F **-, -nen** miller; *(obs: = Frau des Müllers)* miller's wife; ~ **Art** *(Cook)* meunière; **Forelle (nach) ~ Art** trout meunière

Mül|ler-Thur|gau [-'tu:ɐgau] M **-, -** *(= Rebe, = Weinsorte)* Müller-Thurgau

Müll-: **Müll|fah|rer(in)** M(F) dustman *(Brit)*, garbage man *(US)*, trash collector *(US)*, refuse collector *(esp US)*; **Müll|gru|be** F rubbish *(Brit) or* refuse pit; **Müll|hal|de** F rubbish heap *(Brit)*, garbage dump *(US)*; **Müll|hau|fen** M rubbish *or* garbage *(US) or* trash *(US)* heap; **Müll|heiz|kraft|werk** NT *power station using refuse-derived fuel*; **Müll|kas|ten** M *(dial)* dustbin *(Brit)*, ashcan *(US)*, trash can *(US)*; **Müll|kip|pe** F rubbish *or* garbage *(US)* dump; **Müll|kut|scher** M *(N Ger)*, **Müll|mann** M *pl* **-männer** *or* **-leute** *(inf)* dustman *(Brit)*, garbage man *(US)*, trash collector *(US)*, refuse collector *(esp US)*; **Müll|sack** M refuse *or* garbage *(US)* bag; **Müll|schau|fel** F, **Müll|schip|pe** F dustpan; **Müll|schlu|cker** M refuse chute; **Müll|sor|tier|an|la|ge** F refuse sorting plant; **Müll|sor|tie|rung** F **-**, *no pl* sifting of waste; **Müll|ton|ne** F dustbin *(Brit)*, ashcan *(US)*, trash can *(US)*; **Müll|tou|ris|mus** M, *no pl shipment of waste to other countries*; **Müll|tren|nung** F waste separation; **Müll|tü|te** F bin liner *(Brit)*, trash-can liner *(US)*

Müll|ver|bren|nungs-: **Müll|ver|bren|nungs|an|la|ge** F incinerating plant; **Müll|ver|bren|nungs|ofen** M incinerator

Müll-: **Müll|ver|fül|lung** [-vɛɐfʏlʊŋ] F **-**, *no pl* waste relocation; **Müll|ver|mei|dung** F waste prevention *or* avoidance; **Müll|ver|wer|tung** F refuse utilization; **Müll|ver|wer|tungs|werk** NT waste reprocessing plant; **Müll|wa|gen** M dust-cart *(Brit)*, garbage truck *(US)*

Mull|win|del F gauze nappy *(Brit) or* diaper *(US)*

mul|mig ['mʊlmɪç] ADJ **a** *(= morsch) Holz etc* rotten **b** *(inf: = bedenklich)* uncomfortable; **es wird ~** things are getting (a bit) uncomfortable; **ich hatte ein ~es Gefühl im Magen, mir war ~ zumute** *or* **zu Mute** *(lit)* I felt queasy; *(fig)* I had butterflies (in my tummy) *(inf)*

Mul|ti ['mʊlti] M **-s, -s** *(inf)* multinational (organization)

Mul|ti-, mul|ti- [mʊlti] *in cpds* multi-; **mul|ti|dis|zi|pli|när** ADJ multidisciplinary; **mul|ti|funk|ti|o|nal** ADJ multi-function(al); **Mul|ti|funk|ti|ons|tas|ta|tur** F *(Comput)* multi-functional keyboard; **Mul|ti|funk|ti|ons|trai|ner** M *(Sport)* multigym; **mul|ti|kau|sal** ADJ ~ **sein** to have multiple causes; **Mul|ti|kul|ti** ['mʊltikʊlti] NT **-s**, *no pl (inf)* multiculturalism; **die ~-Gesellschaft** the multicultural society; **mul|ti|kul|tu|rell** ADJ multicultural; **~e Gesellschaft** multicultural society; **mul|ti|la|te|ral** ADJ multilateral ADV multilaterally

Mul|ti|me|dia [mʊlti'me:dia] PL multimedia *pl*

Mul|ti|me|dia- *in cpds* multimedia; **mul|ti|me|dia|fä|hig** ADJ *PC* capable of multimedia, multimedia-compliant

Mul|ti-: **mul|ti|me|di|al** [mʊltime'dia:l] ADJ multimedia *attr*; **das ~e Zeitalter** the age of multimedia ADV **eine ~ geprägte Welt** a world dominated by multimedia; **der Computer kann ~ genutzt werden** the computer is equipped for multimedia use; **Mul|ti|mil|li|o|när(in)** M(F) multimillionaire; **mul|ti|na|ti|o|nal** ADJ multinational ADV multinationally

mul|ti|pel [mʊl'ti:pl] ADJ multiple; **multiple Sklerose** multiple sclerosis

Mul|ti|ple-Choice-Ver|fah|ren ['maltɪpl'tʃɔys-] NT, **Mul|ti|ple|choice|ver|fah|ren** △ NT multiple choice (method)

Mul|ti|plex-Ki|no NT, **Mul|ti|plex|ki|no** ['mʊltiplɛks-] NT multiplex (cinema)

Mul|ti|pli|kand [mʊltipli'kant] M **-en, -en** [-dn] *(Math)* multiplicand

Mul|ti|pli|ka|ti|on [mʊltiplika'tsio:n] F **-, -en** multiplication

Mul|ti|pli|ka|ti|ons-: **Mul|ti|pli|ka|ti|ons|punkt** M multiplication point; **Mul|ti|pli|ka|ti|ons|zei|chen** NT multiplication sign

Mul|ti|pli|ka|tor [mʊltipli'ka:to:ɐ] M **-s, Multiplikatoren** [-'to:rən] *(Math)* multiplier

Mul|ti|pli|ka|tor [mʊltipli'ka:to:ɐ] M **-s, Multiplikatoren** [-'to:rən], **Mul|ti|pli|ka|to|rin** [-'to:rɪn] F **-, -nen** *(fig)* disseminator

mul|ti|pli|zier|bar ADJ multipliable

mul|ti|pli|zie|ren [mʊltipli'tsi:rən] *ptp* **multipliziert** VT *(lit, fig)* to multiply *(mit* by) VR *(fig)* to multiply

Mul|ti|ta|lent NT all-rounder *(Brit)*, multi-talent *(US)*

Mul|ti|tas|king ['maltita:skɪŋ] NT **-(s)**, *no pl (Comput)* multitasking

Mul|ti|vi|ta|min|prä|pa|rat NT multivitamin preparation

Mul|ti|vi|ta|min|tab|let|te F multivitamin tablet

Mum|bai ['mʊmbai] NT **-s** Mumbai *(neuer offizieller Name für Bombay)*

Mu|mie ['mu:miə] F **-, -n** mummy; **wie eine wandelnde ~** *(inf)* like death warmed up *(inf)*

mu|mi|en|haft [-iən-] ADJ like a mummy

Mu|mi|en|schlaf|sack M mummy(-style) sleeping bag

mu|mi|fi|zie|ren [mumifi'tsi:rən] *ptp* **mumifiziert** VT to mummify

Mumm [mʊm] M **-s,** *no pl (inf)* **a** *(= Kraft)* strength **b** *(= Mut)* spunk *(dated inf)*, guts *pl (inf)*

Mum|mel|greis(in) ['mʊml-] M(F) *(inf)* old fogey *(inf)*

Müm|mel|mann ['mʏml-] M *pl* **-männer** *(hum)* hare

mum|meln ['mʊmln] VTI **a** *(= undeutlich reden)* to mumble **b** *(= behaglich kauen)* to chew slowly, to munch VTR *(= einhüllen)* **jdn/sich in etw** *(acc)* **~** to wrap *or* muffle sb/oneself up in sth; **sich ins Bett ~** to huddle up in bed

müm|meln ['mʏmln] VI to nibble

Mum|men|schanz ['mʊmənʃants] M **-es,** *no pl* masquerade

Mum|pitz ['mʊmpɪts] M **-es,** *no pl (inf)* balderdash *(dated inf)*

Mumps [mʊmps] M OR (INF) F **-,** *no pl* (the) mumps *sing*

Mün|chen ['mʏnçən] NT **-s** Munich

Mün|che|ner ['mʏnçənɐ] ADJ *attr* Munich; **das ~ Abkommen** *(Hist)* the Munich Agreement

Mün|che|ner ['mʏnçənɐ] M **-s, -, Mün|che|ne|rin** [-ərɪn] F **-, -nen** native of Munich; *(Einwohner)* inhabitant of Munich

Münch|hau|sen ['mʏnçhauzn] M **-s, -(s)** *(fig)* yarn-spinner

Münch|hau|se|ni|a|de [mʏnçhauzə'nia:də] F **-, -n, Münch|hau|si|a|de** [mʏnçhau'zia:də] F **-, -n** cock-and-bull story, tall story

Münch|ner ['mʏnçnɐ] = **Münchener**

Mund [mʊnt] M **-(e)s, ¨er** *or (rare)* **-e** *or* **¨e** ['mʏndɐ, -də, 'mʏndə] mouth; *(inf: = Mundwerk)* tongue; **ein Glas an den ~ setzen** to raise a glass to one's mouth *or* lips; **~ und Nase aufsperren** to gape (with astonishment *or* amazement); **etw in den ~ nehmen** to put sth in one's mouth; **dieses Wort nehme ich nicht in den ~** I never use that word; **den ~ aufmachen** *or* **auftun** *(lit, fig)* to open one's mouth; *(fig: = seine Meinung sagen)* to speak up; **einen großen ~ haben** *(fig) (= aufschneiden)* to talk big *(inf)*; *(= frech sein)* to be cheeky *(Brit) or* fresh *(US)*; **jdm den ~ verbieten** to order sb to be quiet; **halt den ~!** shut up! *(inf)*, hold your tongue!; **er kann den ~ einfach nicht halten** *(inf)* he can't keep his big mouth shut *(inf)*; **jdm über den ~ fahren** to cut sb short; **jdm den ~ stopfen** *(inf)* to shut sb up *(inf)*; **Sie haben mir das in den ~ gelegt** you're putting words into my mouth; **in aller ~e sein** to be on everyone's lips; **wie aus einem ~e** with one voice; **von ~ zu ~ gehen** to be passed on from person to person; **und das** *or* **so etwas aus deinem/seinem** *etc* **~(e)!** and (that) coming from you/him *etc* too!; **an jds ~(e)** *(dat)* **hängen** *(fig)* to hang on sb's every word; **Sie nehmen mir das Wort aus dem ~(e)** you've taken the (very) words out of my mouth; **jdm nach dem ~(e) reden** *(inf)* to say what sb wants to hear; **sie ist nicht auf den ~ gefallen** *(inf)* she's never at a loss for words; **den ~ zu/reichlich voll nehmen** *(inf)* to talk too/pretty big *(inf)*; **den ~ aufreißen/vollnehmen** *(inf)* to talk big *(inf)*; **~ voll** = **Mundvoll**

Mund|art F dialect; **~ sprechen** to speak dialect

Mund|art-: **Mund|art|dich|ter(in)** M(F) dialect poet; **Mund|art|dich|tung** F dialect poetry

Mund|ar|ten|for|schung F, **Mund|art|for|schung** F dialect research

mund|art|lich ['mʊntla:ɐtlɪç] ADJ dialect(al) ADV in dialect; **das Wort wird ~ gebraucht** it's a dialect word, the word is used in dialect

Mund|art-: **Mund|art|spre|cher(in)** M(F) dialect speaker; **Mund|art|wör|ter|buch** NT dialect dictionary

Mund-: **Mund|at|mung** F oral breathing; **Mund|du|sche** F water jet

Mün|del ['mʏndl] NT OR (JUR) M **-s, -** ward

mün|del|si|cher *(St Ex)* ADJ ≈ gilt-edged *no adv* ADV **anlegen** in secure gilt-edged investments

mun|den ['mʊndn] VI *(liter)* **jdm trefflich/köstlich ~** to taste excellent/delicious to sb; **südländisch ~** to have a Mediterranean flavour *(Brit) or* flavor *(US)*; **sich** *(dat)* **etw ~ lassen** to savour *(Brit) or* savor *(US)* sth; **es mundete ihm nicht, es wollte ihm nicht ~** he found it unpalatable

mün|den ['mʏndn] VI *aux sein or haben (Bach, Fluss)* to flow *(in +acc* into); *(Straße, Gang)* to lead *(in +acc, auf +acc* into); *(fig: Fragen, Probleme)* to lead *(in +acc or dat* to); **die B 3 mündet bei Celle in die B 1** the B3 joins the B1 at Celle

Mund-: **mund|faul** ADJ *(inf)* too lazy to say much; **sei doch nicht so ~!** make an effort and say something!; **Mund|fäu|le** F *(Med)* stomatitis; **Mund|flo|ra** F *(Med)* (bacterial) flora of the oral cavity *or* of the mouth; **mund|ge|bla|sen** ADJ *Glas* (mouth-)blown; **mund|ge|recht** ADJ bite-sized; **jdm etw ~ machen** *(fig)* to make sth attractive *or* palatable to sb ADV *zubereiten, schneiden* in bite-sized pieces; **Mund|ge|ruch** M bad breath, halitosis; **etwas gegen ~ tun** to do something about one's (bad) breath; **Mund|har|mo|ni|ka** F mouth organ, harmonica; **Mund|höh|le** F oral cavity; **Mund|hy|gi|e|ne** F oral hygiene

mun|dig ['mʊndɪç] ADJ *(geh)* appetizing, savoury *(Brit)*, savory *(US)*; *Wein* full-bodied

mün|dig ['mʏndɪç] ADJ of age; *(fig)* mature, responsible; **~ werden** to come of age, to reach *or* attain one's majority; **jdn (für) ~ erklären** to declare sb of age; **der ~e Bürger** the politically mature citizen

Mün|dig|keit F **-,** *no pl* majority; *(fig)* maturity, responsibility

Mün|dig-: **mün|dig spre|chen** *irreg*, **mün|dig+spre|chen** *sep irreg* VT to declare of age; **Mün|dig|spre|chung** [-ʃprɛçʊŋ] F **-,** *no pl* declaration of majority

münd|lich ['mʏntlɪç] ADJ verbal; *Prüfung, Leistung* oral; **~e Verhandlung** *(Jur)* hearing; **etw durch ~e Überlieferung weitergeben** to pass sth on by word of mouth; **das Mündliche** *(inf: Sch, Univ) (in Fremdsprache)* the oral; *(bei Doktorprüfung etc)* the oral, the viva (voce) *(Brit)* ADV *testen* orally; *informieren, besprechen* personally; **jdn ~ prüfen** to submit sb to an oral examination; **etw ~ abmachen** to have a verbal agreement; **etw ~ überliefern** to pass sth on by word of mouth; **einen Fall ~ verhandeln** *(Jur)* to hear a case; **alles andere** *or* **Weitere ~!** I'll tell you the rest when I see you

Mund-: **Mund|or|gel** F cheng; **Mund|pfle|ge** F oral hygiene *no art*; **Mund|pro|pa|gan|da** F verbal propaganda; **Mund|raub** M *(Jur)* theft of comestibles for personal consumption; **Mund|schenk** ['mʊntʃɛŋk] M **-en, -en** *(Hist)* cupbearer; *(fig)* wine-waiter; **Mund|schleim|haut** F mucous membrane of the oral cavity *or* of the mouth; **Mund|schutz** M mask (over one's mouth); **Mund|spal|te** F oral fissure

M-und-S-Rei|fen ['ɛmʊnt'ɛs-] M winter tyre *(Brit) or* tire *(US)*

Mund-: **Mund|stel|lung** F position of the mouth, embouchure; **Mund|stück** NT *(von Pfeife, Blasinstrument)* mouthpiece; *(von Zigarette)* tip; **ohne ~** untipped; **mit ~** tipped; **mund|tot** ADJ *(inf)* **jdn ~ machen** to silence sb; **Mund|tuch** NT *pl* **-tücher** serviette *(Brit)*, napkin

Mün|dung ['mʏndʊŋ] F **-, -en** *(von Fluss)* mouth; *(= Trichtermündung)* estuary; *(von Rohr)* mouth; *(von Straße)* end; *(= Gewehrmündung, Kanonenmündung)* muzzle; **die ~ des Missouri in den Mississippi** the confluence of the Missouri and the Mississippi, the point where the Missouri flows into the Mississippi; **die ~ der Straße auf die B 11** the point where the road joins the B11

Mün|dungs-: **Mün|dungs|feu|er** NT flash from the muzzle; **Mün|dungs|ge|biet** NT *(eines Flusses)* estuary (area)

Mund-: **Mund|ver|kehr** M oral intercourse; **Mund|voll** M **ein ~** a mouthful; **ein paar ~** a few mouthfuls; **Mund|vor|rat** M provisions *pl*; **Mund|was|ser** NT mouthwash; **Mund|werk** NT *(inf)* **ein gutes** *or* **flinkes ~ haben** to be a fast talker *(inf)*; **ein böses ~ haben** to have a vicious tongue (in one's head); **ein freches ~ haben** to be cheeky *(Brit) or* fresh *(US)*; **ein loses** *or* **lockeres ~ haben** to have a big mouth *(inf)*; **ein großes ~ haben** to talk big *(inf)*; **der mit seinem großen ~!** him with all his big talk *(inf)*; **ihr ~ steht nie still** her tongue never stops wagging *(inf)*; **Mund|werk|zeu|ge** PL *(Zool)* mouth parts *pl*; **Mund|win|kel** M corner of one's mouth; **Mund-zu-Mund-Be|at|mung** F mouth-to-mouth resuscitation

Mun|go ['mʊŋgo] M **-(s), -s** *(Zool)* mongoose

Mun|go M **-(s), -s** *(Tex)* mungo

Mu|ni|ti|on [muni'tsio:n] F **-, -en** ammunition; *(Mil: als Sammelbegriff)* munitions *pl*; **~ fassen** *(Mil)* to be supplied with ammunition/munitions; **keine ~ mehr haben** *(lit, fig)* to have run out of ammunition; **seine ~ verschießen** *(lit)* to use up one's ammunition; *(fig)* to shoot one's bolt; **jdm ~ liefern** *(fig)* to provide sb with ammunition

mu|ni|ti|o|nie|ren [munitsio'ni:rən] *ptp* **munitioniert** VT to provide with ammunition

Mu|ni|ti|ons-: **Mu|ni|ti|ons|de|pot** NT munitions *or* ammunition dump *or* store; **Mu|ni|ti|ons|fab|rik** F munitions *or* ordnance factory; **Mu|ni|ti|ons|la|ger** NT munitions *or* ammunition dump *or* store; **Mu|ni|ti|ons|zug** M *(Rail)* ammunition train

mun|keln ['mʊŋkln] VTI **man munkelt** *or* **es wird gemunkelt, dass ...** it's rumoured *(Brit) or* rumored *(US)* that ..., there's a rumour *(Brit) or* rumor *(US)* that ...; **ich habe ~ hören, dass ...** I've heard it rumoured *(Brit) or* rumored *(US)* that ...; **man munkelt allerlei, allerlei wird gemunkelt** you hear all kinds of rumours *(Brit) or* rumors *(US)*; **im Dunkeln ist gut ~** darkness is the friend of thieves/lovers

Mun-Sek|te ['mu:n-] F Moonies *pl*

Müns|ter ['mʏnstɐ] NT **-s, -** minster, cathedral

Müns|ter ['mʏnstɐ] NT **-s, -, Müns|ter|kä|se** M Münster cheese

mun|ter ['mʊntɐ] ADJ **a** *(= lebhaft)* lively *no adv*; *Farben* bright, gay; *(= fröhlich)* cheerful, merry; **~ werden** to liven up; **~ und vergnügt** bright and cheery → **Fisch a b** *(= wach)* awake; *(= aufgestanden)* up and about; **jdn ~ machen** to wake sb up; **jdn wieder ~ machen** to wake sb up (again) ADV *(= unbekümmert)* blithely; **~ drauflosreden** to prattle away merrily; **~ drauflosgehen** to go at it with a will; **sie redete ~ weiter** she just kept on talking regardless

Mun|ter|keit F **-,** *no pl (= Lebhaftigkeit)* liveliness; *(von Farben)* brightness; *(= Fröhlichkeit)* cheerfulness

mun|ter+ma|chen VT *sep* → **munter ADJ b**

Mun|ter|ma|cher M *(Med inf)* stimulant, pick-me-up *(inf)*

Münz-: **Münz|an|stalt** F mint; **Münz|au|to|mat** M slot machine

Mün|ze ['mʏntsə] F **-, -n a** *(= Geldstück)* coin; *(= Münzsystem)* coinage; **jdm etw mit** *or* **in gleicher ~ heimzahlen** *(fig)* to pay sb back in his own coin for sth → **bar a b** *(= Münzanstalt)* mint

Münz|ein|wurf M (coin) slot

mün|zen ['mʏntsn] VT to mint, to coin; **das war auf ihn gemünzt** *(fig)* that was aimed at him, that was meant for him

Mün|zen|samm|lung F coin *or* numismatic *(form)* collection

Münz-: **Münz|fäl|scher(in)** M(F) *(Jur)* counterfeiter *(of coins)*; **Münz|fäl|schung** F *(Jur)* counterfeiting of coins; **Münz|fern|spre|cher** M *(form)* pay phone; *(= Telefonzelle)* pay phone, call box *(Brit)*; **Münz|fund** M find of coins; **Münz|gas|zäh|ler** M slot gas meter; **Münz|geld** NT coin; **Münz|ge|wicht** NT coin weight; **Münz|ho|heit** F prerogative of coinage; **Münz|kun|de** F numismatics *sing*; **Münz|samm|lung** F coin *or* numismatic *(form)* collection; **Münz|schacht** M coin slot; **Münz|spiel|au|to|mat** M, **Münz|spiel|ge|rät** NT *(form)* coin-operated gaming machine *(form)*, slot machine; **Münz|sys|tem** NT coinage; **Münz|tank** M coin-operated petrol *(Brit)* or gas(oline) *(US)* pump; **Münz|te|le|fon** NT pay phone; *(= Telefonzelle)* pay phone, call box *(Brit)*; **Münz|wechs|ler** M change machine; **Münz|we|sen** NT coinage

Mur [muːɐ] F -, -en *(Aus)* mud

Mu|rä|ne [muˈrɛːnə] F -, -n moray

mür|be [ˈmʏrbə], *(esp Aus, S Ger)* **mürb** [mʏrp] ADJ **a** crumbly; *(= zerbröckelnd)* crumbling; *Stoff, Gewebe* worn through; *Holz* rotten **b** *Fleisch* tender; *(= abgehangen)* well-hung; ~ **klopfen** to tenderize, to hammer **c** *Obst* soft; **etw ~ werden lassen** to let sth ripen **d** *(fig: = zermürbt)* ~ **werden/sein** to be worn down → **mürbekriegen, mürbemachen**

Mür|be-: **mür|be+klop|fen** VT *sep* → **mürbe b**; **mür|be+krie|gen** VT *sep (fig)* to break sb; **mür|be+ma|chen** VT *sep (fig)* to wear sb down; **Mür|be|teig** M short(-crust) pastry; **mür|be+wer|den** VI *sep irreg aux sein (fig)* → **mürbe d**

Mu|re [ˈmuːrə] F -, -n *(Geol)* mudflow

Mur|kel [ˈmʊrkl] M -s, - *(dial inf)* squirt *(inf)*, shrimp *(inf)*

mur|ke|lig [ˈmʊrkəlɪç], **murk|lig** [ˈmʊrklɪç] ADJ *(dial inf)* tiny, wee *(esp Scot)*

Murks [mʊrks] M -es, *no pl (inf)* ~ **machen** *or* **bauen** to bungle things *(inf)*, to botch things up *(inf)*; **das ist ~!** that's a botch-up *(inf)*; **so ein ~!** what a botch-up! *(inf)*

murk|sen [ˈmʊrksn] VI *(inf)* to fiddle around; *(= vermurksen)* to bungle things *(inf)*, to botch things up *(inf)*

Murk|se|rei [mʊrksəˈrai] F -, -en *(inf)* botching things up *(inf)*; **eine ~** a botch-up *(inf)*

Mur|mel [ˈmʊrml] F -, -n marble

mur|meln [ˈmʊrmln] VTI to murmur; *(undeutlich)* to mumble; *(= brummeln)* to mutter; **etw vor sich** *(acc)* **hin ~** to mutter sth to oneself VI *(= mit Murmeln spielen)* to play marbles

Mur|mel|tier NT marmot → **schlafen VI**

mur|ren [ˈmʊrən] VI to grumble *(über +acc* about); **etw ohne Murren** *or* **ohne zu ~ ertragen** to put up with sth without grumbling

mür|risch [ˈmʏrɪʃ] ADJ *(= abweisend)* sullen, morose, surly; *(= schlecht gelaunt)* grumpy ADV *(= abweisend)* sullenly, morosely, surlily; *(= schlecht gelaunt)* grumpily

Mus [muːs] NT OR M -es, -e mush; *(= Apfelmus, Kartoffelmus)* puree; *(= Pflaumenmus)* jam *(Brit)*, jelly *(US)*; ~ **aus Kartoffeln machen** to cream *or* mash potatoes; **sie wurden fast zu ~ zerdrückt** *or* **zerquetscht** *(inf)* they were (nearly) squeezed to death; **jdn zu ~ schlagen** *(inf)* to make mincemeat of sb *(inf)*

Mu|schel [ˈmʊʃl] F -, -n **a** mussel *(auch Cook)*, bivalve; *(Schale)* shell **b** *(= Ohrmuschel)* external ear, pinna **c** *(Telec) (= Sprechmuschel)* mouthpiece; *(= Hörmuschel)* ear piece

Mu|schel-: **Mu|schel|bank** F *pl* **-bänke** mussel bed; **Mu|schel|kalk** M Muschelkalk *(spec)*

Mu|schi [ˈmʊʃi] F -, -s *(inf)* pussy *(sl)*

Musch|ko|te [mʊʃˈkoːtə] M -n, -n *(Mil sl)* private

Mu|se [ˈmuːzə] F -, -n *(Myth)* Muse; **die heitere** *or* **leichte ~** *(fig)* light entertainment; **von der ~ geküsst werden** *(fig)* to be inspired

mu|se|al [muzeˈaːl] ADJ **a** *(geh)* museum *attr*; **das Haus sieht zu ~ aus** the house looks too much like a museum **b** *(fig)* out-of-date; *Gerät, Auto etc* antiquated, ancient

Mu|sel|man [ˈmuːzlmaːn] M -en, -en, **Mu|sel|ma|nin** [-ˈmaːnɪn] F -, -nen, **Mu|sel|mann** [ˈmuːzlman] M *pl* **-männer** *(dated)*, **Mu|sel|män|nin** [-mɛnɪn] F -, -nen *(dated)* Moslem

Mu|sen-: **Mu|sen|al|ma|nach** M *(old) poetry periodical published in the 17th and 18th centuries*; **Mu|sen|tem|pel** M *(old, liter)* theatre *(Brit)*, theater *(US)*

Mu|se|um [muˈzeːʊm] NT -s, **Museen** [-ˈzeːən] museum

Mu|se|ums-: **Mu|se|ums|die|ner(in)** M(F) *(dated)* museum attendant; **Mu|se|ums|füh|rer(in)** M(F) museum guide; **mu|se|ums|reif** ADJ *(hum)* antique; ~ **sein** to be almost a museum piece; **Mu|se|ums|stück** NT museum piece

Mu|si|cal [ˈmjuːzikl] NT -s, -s musical

Mu|sic|box [ˈmjuːzik-] F jukebox

Mu|sik [muˈziːk] F -, -en **a** music; **die ~ lieben** to love music; **etw in ~ setzen** *(geh)* to set *or* put sth to music; ~ **machen** to play some music; **das ist ~ in meinen Ohren** *(fig)* that's music to my ears **b** *(= Musikkapelle)* band; **hier ist** *or* **spielt die ~!** *(fig inf)* this is where it's at *(inf)*

Mu|sik|aka|de|mie F musical academy, academy of music

Mu|si|ka|li|en [muziˈkaːliən] PL music *sing*

Mu|si|ka|li|en|hand|lung F music shop *(Brit)* or store

mu|si|ka|lisch [muziˈkaːlɪʃ] ADJ musical ADV *begabt* musically; **jdn ~ ausbilden** to give sb a musical training, to give sb a training in music

Mu|si|ka|li|tät [muzikaliˈtɛːt] F -, *no pl* musicality

Mu|si|kant [muziˈkant] M -en, -en, **Mu|si|kan|tin** [-ˈkantɪn] F -, -nen musician, minstrel *(old)*

Mu|si|kan|ten|kno|chen M funny bone, crazy bone *(US)*

Mu|sik-: **Mu|sik|au|to|mat** M musical box *(Brit)*, music box; *(= Musikbox)* jukebox; **mu|sik|be|geis|tert** ADJ fond of music, music-loving *attr*; **Mu|sik|be|glei|tung** F musical accompaniment; **unter ~** accompanied by music, to the accompaniment of music; **Mu|sik|be|rie|se|lung** F *(inf)* constant background music; **Mu|sik|be|trieb** M music industry; **Mu|sik|box** F jukebox; **Mu|sik|dra|ma** NT music drama

Mu|si|ker [ˈmuːzikɐ] M -s, -, **Mu|si|ke|rin** [-ərɪn] F -, -nen musician

Mu|sik-: **Mu|sik|er|zie|hung** F *(form)* musical education; **Mu|sik|freund(in)** M(F) music-lover; **Mu|sik|ge|schich|te** F history of music; **Mu|sik|hoch|schu|le** F college of music; **Mu|sik|in|stru|ment** NT musical instrument; **Mu|sik|ka|pel|le** F band; **Mu|sik|kas|set|te** F music cassette; **Mu|sik|kon|ser|ve** F *(inf)* canned music *no pl*; **Mu|sik|korps** NT music corps *sing*; **Mu|sik|kri|tik** F music criticism; *(= Rezension)* music criticism, music crit *(Brit)*; *(= Kritikerschaft)* music critics *pl*; **Mu|sik|kri|ti|ker(in)** M(F) music critic; **Mu|sik|leh|rer(in)** M(F) music teacher; **Mu|sik|le|xi|kon** NT encyclopaedia of music; *(Wörterbuch)* dictionary of music; **Mu|sik|lieb|ha|ber(in)** M(F) music-lover; **Mu|sik|pro|gramm** NT music station; *(Sendung)* music programme *(Brit)* or program *(US)*; **Mu|sik|rich|tung** F kind of music, musical trend *or* genre; **Mu|sik|saal** M music room; **Mu|sik|schu|le** F music school; **Mu|sik|sen|dung** F music programme *(Brit)* or program *(US)*; **Mu|sik|stück** NT piece of music; **Mu|sik|stun|de** F music lesson; **Mu|sik|the|a|ter** NT music theatre *(Brit)* or theater *(US)*; **Mu|sik|tru|he** F radiogram, radio-phonograph *(US)*; **Mu|sik|un|ter|richt** M music lessons *pl*; *(Sch)* music; **Mu|sik|wunsch** M *(Rad)* listener's request *(for a piece of music)*

Mu|si|kus [ˈmuːzikʊs] M -, **Musizi** [-tsi] *(hum)* musician

Mu|sik-: **Mu|sik|werk** NT *(geh)* musical composition *or* work; **Mu|sik|wis|sen|schaft** F musicology; **Mu|sik|wis|sen|schaft|ler(in)** M(F) musicologist; **Mu|sik|zim|mer** NT music room

mu|sisch [ˈmuːzɪʃ] ADJ *Fächer, Gymnasium* (fine) arts *attr*; *Begabung* for the arts; *Erziehung* in the (fine) arts; *Veranlagung, Mensch* artistic ADV ~ **begabt/interessiert** gifted/interested in the (fine) arts; ~ **talentiert sein** to have artistic talent; ~ **veranlagt** artistically inclined

Mu|si|zi *pl von* **Musikus**

mu|si|zie|ren [muziˈtsiːrən] *ptp* **musiziert** VI to play a musical instrument; **sie saßen auf dem Marktplatz und musizierten** they sat in the market place playing their instruments; **sonntags abends wird bei uns immer musiziert** we always have a musical evening on Sundays

Mus|kat [mʊsˈkaːt, ˈmʊskat] M -(e)s, -e nutmeg

Mus|kat|blü|te F mace

Mus|ka|tel|ler [mʊskaˈtɛlɐ] M -s, -, **Mus|ka|tel|ler|wein** M muscatel

Mus|kat|nuss F nutmeg

Mus|kat|rei|be F nutmeg grater

Mus|kel [ˈmʊskl] M -s, -n muscle; **(viele) ~n haben** to be muscular; **seine ~n spielen lassen** *(lit, fig)* to flex one's muscles

Mus|kel-: **Mus|kel|auf|bau** M muscle building; **mus|kel|be|packt** ADJ *(inf)* muscly, with bulging muscles *(nachgestellt)*, musclebound *(pej)*; **Mus|kel|dys|tro|phie** [-dʏstrofiː] F -, -n [-ˈfiːən] muscular dystrophy; **Mus|kel|fa|ser** F muscle fibre *(Brit)* or fiber *(US)*; **Mus|kel|fa|ser|riss** M torn muscle fibre *(Brit)* or fiber *(US)*; **Mus|kel|fleisch** NT flesh; **Mus|kel|ka|ter** M aching muscles *pl*; ~ **haben** to be stiff; **er hatte (einen) ~ in den Beinen** his legs were stiff; **Mus|kel|kraft** F physical strength; **Mus|kel|krampf** M muscle cramp *no indef art*; **Mus|kel|mann** M *pl* **-männer**, **Mus|kel|pa|ket** NT, **Mus|kel|protz** M *(inf)* muscleman *(inf)*; **Mus|kel|riss** M torn muscle; **sich** *(dat)* **einen ~ zuziehen** to tear a muscle; **Mus|kel|schmer|zen** PL muscle pains *pl*; **Mus|kel|schwä|che** F *(Med)* myasthenia *(spec)*, muscle weakness; **Mus|kel|schwund** M muscular atrophy *or* wasting; **Mus|kel|spiel** NT muscle play; **Mus|kel|star|re** F muscular rigidity; **Mus|kel|zer|rung** F pulled muscle

Mus|ke|te [mʊsˈkeːtə] F -, -n musket

Mus|ke|tier [mʊskeˈtiːɐ] M -s, -e musketeer

Mus|ku|la|tur [mʊskulaˈtuːɐ] F -, -en muscular system, musculature *(spec)*

mus|ku|lös [mʊskuˈløːs] ADJ muscular ADV ~ **gebaut sein** to have a muscular build

Müs|li [ˈmyːsli] NT -(s), -s muesli

Müs|li|rie|gel M cereal bar

Mus|lim [ˈmʊslɪm] M -s, -s Muslim, Moslem

Mus|li|me [mʊsˈliːmə] F -, -n Muslim, Moslem

Mus|li|min [mʊsˈliːmɪn] F -, -nen Muslim, Moslem

mus|li|misch [mʊsˈliːmɪʃ] ADJ *attr* Muslim, Moslem ADV *erziehen* as a Muslim; *aufwachsen* Muslim

muss [mʊs] *3. pers sing pres von* **müssen**

Muss [mʊs] NT -, *no pl* **es ist ein/kein ~** it's/it's not a must

Muss|be|stim|mung F fixed regulation

Mu|ße [ˈmuːsə] F -, *no pl* leisure; **(die) ~ für** *or* **zu etw finden** to find the time and leisure for sth; **dafür fehlt mir die ~** I don't have the time or leisure; **sich** *(dat)* **~ gönnen** to allow oneself some (time for) leisure; **etw mit ~ tun** to do sth in a leisurely way

Muss|ehe F *(inf)* shotgun wedding *(inf)*

müs|sen [ˈmʏsn] ✪ 27.7, 37, 39.3, 42, 45.1, 48.1, 48.3 MODAL AUX VB *pret* **musste**, [ˈmʊstə] *ptp* **müssen** **a** *(Zwang)* to have to; *(Notwendigkeit)* to need to, to have to; **ich muss** *(Zwang)* I have to, I must *only pres*, I've got to *(esp Brit)*; *(Notwendigkeit auch)* I need to; **ich muss nicht** *(Zwang)* I don't have to, I haven't got to *(esp Brit)*; *(Notwendigkeit auch)* I don't need to, I needn't; **muss er?** must he?, does he have to?, has he got to? *(esp Brit)*; **musstest du?** did you have to?; **das hat er tun/nicht tun ~** he had to/didn't have to do it; **er hatte es tun ~** he had had to do it; **es musste ins Haus gebracht werden** it had to be brought inside; **das muss irgendwann mal gemacht werden** it will have to be done some time; **er sagte, er müsse**

bald gehen he said he would have to go soon; **ich hätte es sonst allein tun ~** otherwise I would have had to do it alone; **dafür ~/müssten Sie einen Polizisten fragen** you'll/you'd have *or* need to ask a policeman about that; **ich muss jeden Tag um sechs Uhr aufstehen** I have to get up at six every day; **ich muss jetzt gehen** *or* **weg** *(inf)* I must be going now *or* be off now, I must go now, I'll have to go now; **man musste lachen/weinen** *etc* you couldn't help laughing/crying *etc*, you had to laugh/cry *etc*; **wir ~ Ihnen leider mitteilen, dass ...** we regret to (have to) inform you (that) ...; **muss das (denn) sein?** is that (really) necessary?; must you/he?, do you/does he have to?; **das muss sein** it's necessary; I do/he does have to; **das musste (ja so) kommen** that had to happen, that was bound to happen; **das muss man sich** *(dat)* **mal vorstellen!** (just) imagine that!, think of it!; **jetzt muss ich dir mal was sagen** now let me tell you something; **was habe ich da hören ~?** what's this I hear?

b *(= sollen)* **das müsste ich/müsstest du eigentlich wissen** I/you ought to know that, I/you should know that; **ich hätte es gestern tun ~** I ought to *or* should have done it yesterday; **das musst du nicht tun!** you oughtn't to do that, you shouldn't do that

c *(Vermutung, Wahrscheinlichkeit)* **es muss geregnet haben** it must have rained; **es muss wahr sein** it must be true, it has to be true, it's got to be true; **es muss nicht wahr sein** it needn't be true; **er muss es gewesen sein** it must have been him, it has to have been him, it's got to have been him; **es müssten zehntausend Zuschauer im Stadion gewesen sein** there must have been ten thousand spectators in the stadium; **er müsste schon da sein** he should be there by now; **so muss es gewesen sein** that's how it must have been; **was ~ bloß die Leute (von uns) denken!** what must people think (of us); **was muss bloß in ihm vorgehen?** what goes on in his mind?

d *(Wunsch)* **(viel) Geld müsste man haben!** if only I were rich!; **man müsste noch mal von vorn anfangen können!** if only one could begin again!; **man müsste noch mal zwanzig sein!** oh, to be twenty again!

VI *pret* **musste**, *ptp* **gemusst** **a** ['mʊstə] *(= weggehen, -fahren müssen)* to have to go; [gə'mʊst] **ich muss jetzt zur Schule** I must go to school now, I've got to *(esp Brit)* or I have to go to school now; **wann müsst ihr zur Schule?** when do you have to go to school?; **der Brief muss heute noch zur Post®** the letter must be *or* has to be posted *(Brit)* or mailed *(esp US)* today

b *(inf: = austreten müssen)* **ich muss mal** I need to go to the loo *(Brit inf)* or bathroom *(esp US)*

c *(= gezwungen sein)* to have to; **hast du gewollt? – nein, gemusst** did you want to? – no, I had to; **kein Mensch muss ~** *(hum)* there's no such thing as 'must'

Mu|ße|stun|de F hour of leisure; **seine ~n** one's leisure hours

Muss|hei|rat F *(inf)* shotgun wedding *(inf)*

mü|ßig ['my:sɪç] ADJ *(= untätig)* idle; *Leben, Tage, Stunden* of leisure; *(= überflüssig, unnütz)* futile, pointless ADV *(= untätig)* idly

Mü|ßig-: **Mü|ßig|gang** [-gaŋ] M, *no pl (liter: = Untätigkeit)* idleness; **sich dem ~ hingeben** to lead a life of idleness, to lead an idle life; **~ ist aller Laster Anfang** *(Prov)* the devil finds work for idle hands *(Prov)*; **Mü|ßig|gän|ger** [-gɛŋɐ] M **-s, -**, **Mü|ßig|gän|ge|rin** [-ərɪn] F **-, -nen** *(liter)* idler

Mü|ßig|keit F **-**, *no pl (= Überflüssigkeit)* futility, pointlessness

muss|te *pret von* **müssen**

Muss|vor|schrift F fixed regulation

Mus|tang ['mʊstaŋ] M **-s, -s** mustang

Mus|ter ['mʊstɐ] NT **-s, -** **a** *(= Vorlage, Dessin)* pattern; *(für Brief, Bewerbung etc)* specimen; **nach einem ~ stricken** *etc* to knit *etc* from a pattern; **die Parade läuft immer nach demselben ~ ab** the parade always takes the same form

b *(= Probestück) sample; (Buch, Korrekturfahne etc)* specimen; **~ ohne Wert** sample of no commercial value

c *(fig: = Vorbild)* model *(an +dat* of); *(= Verhaltensmuster)* pattern; **als ~ dienen** to serve as a model; **sich** *(dat)* **ein ~ an jdm nehmen** to take sb as an example; **er ist ein ~ von einem Schüler/Ehemann/Staatsbürger** he is a model student/husband/citizen; **ein ~ an Tugend** a paragon of virtue

Mus|ter- *in cpds* model; **Mus|ter|bei|spiel** NT classic *or* prime example; **Mus|ter|be|trieb** M model business; **Mus|ter|brief** M specimen letter; **Mus|ter|buch** NT pattern book; **Mus|ter|dorf** NT model village; **Mus|ter|ehe** F perfect marriage; **Mus|ter|ex|emp|lar** NT fine specimen; **ein ~ von einer Frau** a model wife; **ein ~ von einem Idioten** a perfect idiot; **Mus|ter|fall** M model case; *(positiv)* perfect *or* classic example; **Mus|ter|gat|te** M model husband; **Mus|ter|gat|tin** F model wife; **mus|ter|gül|tig** ADJ exemplary ADV **sich ~ benehmen** to be a model of good behaviour *(Brit)* or behavior *(US)*; **Mus|ter|gül|tig|keit** F **die ~ seines Benehmens** his exemplary behaviour *(Brit)* or behavior *(US)*; **Mus|ter|gut** NT model farm; **mus|ter|haft** ADJ exemplary ADV exemplarily; **er hat sich ~ verhalten** his conduct was exemplary; **Mus|ter|haus** NT show house *(Brit)*, model house *(US)*; **Mus|ter|kna|be** M *(iro)* paragon; **Mus|ter|kof|fer** M sample case; **Mus|ter|kol|lek|ti|on** F collection of samples; *(Fashion)* collection of models; **Mus|ter|länd|le** NT *(inf)* **das ~** Baden-Württemberg; **Mus|ter|mes|se** F trade fair

mus|tern ['mʊstɐn] VT **a** *(= betrachten)* to scrutinize, to look over, to survey; **jdn kühl/skeptisch ~** to survey *or* eye sb coolly/sceptically *(Brit)* or skeptically *(US)*; **jdn von oben bis unten ~** *or* **von Kopf bis Fuß ~** to look sb up and down, to scrutinize sb from head to toe **b** *(Mil: = inspizieren)* to inspect, to review **c** *(Mil: für Wehrdienst)* **jdn ~** to give sb his/her medical **d** *(Tex)* → **gemustert**

Mus|ter-: **Mus|ter|pa|ckung** F sample pack; *(= Attrappe)* display pack; **Mus|ter|pro|zess** M test case; **Mus|ter|schü|ler(in)** M(F) model pupil; *(fig)* star pupil; **Mus|ter|schutz** M protection of patterns and designs; **Mus|ter|sen|dung** F selection of samples; **Mus|ter|stadt** F model town; **Mus|ter|stück** NT *(usu iro)* = **Musterexemplar**

Mus|te|rung F **-, -en** **a** *(= Muster)* pattern **b** *(Mil) (von Truppen)* inspection, review; *(von Rekruten)* medical examination for military service **c** *(durch Blicke)* scrutiny

Mus|te|rungs-: **Mus|te|rungs|aus|schuss** M recruiting *or* draft *(US)* board; **Mus|te|rungs|be|scheid** M notification of the recruiting *or* draft *(US)* board's decision; **Mus|te|rungs|kom|mis|si|on** F recruiting *or* draft *(US)* board

Mus|ter|ver|gleich M *(Comput)* pattern matching

Mut [mu:t] M **-(e)s**, *no pl* **a** courage, pluck *(inf)* *(zu +dat* for); *(= Zuversicht)* heart; **(wieder) ~ fassen** to pluck up courage (again); **~ haben** to have (a lot of) courage; **keinen ~ haben** not to have any courage; **mit frischem ~** with new heart; **nur ~!** don't lose heart!, cheer up!, keep your pecker up! *(Brit inf)*; **jdm den ~ nehmen** to discourage sb, to make sb lose heart; **den ~ verlieren** to lose heart; **~ bekommen** to gain confidence; **wieder ~ bekommen** to take heart; **den ~ aufbringen, etw zu tun** to find the courage to do sth; **jdm ~ zusprechen** *or* **machen** to encourage sb; **sich gegenseitig ~ machen** to keep each other's spirits up; **das gab ihr wieder neuen ~** that gave her new heart; **ihm sank der ~** his heart sank; **mit dem ~ der Verzweiflung** with the courage born of desperation *or* despair; **der ~ zum Leben** the will to live; **der ~ zur Lücke** *(hum)* the courage to admit when one doesn't know something; **zu ~e** = **zumute**

b *(old: = Laune, Stimmung)* spirits *pl*; **frohen** *or* **guten ~es sein** to be of good cheer *(old)*, to be in good spirits; **mit frohem ~** with good cheer *(old)*

Mu|tant [mu'tant] M **-en, -en**, **Mu|tan|te** [mu'tantə] F **-, -n** *(Biol)* mutant, mutation; **du ~!** *(sl)* you spastic! *(Brit pej sl)*, you psycho! *(pej sl)*

Mu|ta|ti|on [muta'tsio:n] F **-, -en** **a** mutation **b** *(Med)* breaking of the voice; **er hat die ~ gerade hinter sich** his voice has just broken

Mut|be|weis M proof of his *etc* courage

Müt|chen ['my:tçən] NT **-s**, *no pl* **sein ~ an jdm kühlen** *(inf)* to take it out on sb *(inf)*

mu|ten ['mu:tn] VI *(Min)* to divine

Mu|ter ['mu:tɐ] M **-s, -**, **Mu|te|rin** [-ərɪn] F **-, -nen** *(Min)* diviner

mu|tie|ren [mu'ti:rən] *ptp* **mutiert** VI to mutate **a** *(= sich erblich ändern)* to mutate **b** *(Med, Aus)* **er hat schon mutiert** his voice has already broken

mu|tig ['mu:tɪç] ADJ courageous, brave; **dem Mutigen gehört die Welt** *(Prov)* fortune favours *(Brit)* or favors *(US)* the brave *(Prov)* ADV courageously, bravely

Mut-: **mut|los** ADJ *(= niedergeschlagen)* discouraged *no adv*, disheartened *no adv*; *(= bedrückt)* despondent, dejected; **jdn ~ machen** to discourage sb, to make sb lose heart ADV dejectedly; **~ wirken** to seem discouraged; **~ dastehen** *(vor Aufgabe)* to stand there discouraged; **Mut|lo|sig|keit** F **-**, *no pl (= Niedergeschlagenheit)* discouragement; *(= Bedrücktheit)* despondency, dejection

mut|ma|ßen ['mu:tma:sn] VTI *insep* to conjecture; **es wurde viel über seine Abwesenheit gemutmaßt** there was a lot of conjecture as to the reason for his absence

mut|maß|lich ['mu:tma:slɪç] ADJ *attr Vater* presumed; *Täter, Terrorist* suspected ADV **alle Fahrgäste sind ~ ums Leben gekommen** it is presumed that all the passengers were killed; **~ soll er der Vater sein** he is presumed to be the father

Mut|ma|ßung ['mu:tma:sʊŋ] F **-, -en** conjecture; **wir müssen uns auf ~en stützen** we can only conjecture

Mut|pro|be F test of courage

Mutt|chen ['mʊtçən] NT **-s, -** *(inf)* **a** *(= Mutter)* mummy *(Brit inf)*, mommy *(US inf)* **b** *(= biedere Hausfrau)* little housewife **c** *(= alte Frau)* grandma

Mut|ter ['mʊtɐ] F **-, =** ['mʏtɐ] mother; **sie ist jetzt ~** she's a mother now; **~ werden** to have a baby; **sie ist ~ von drei Kindern** she's a mother of three; **als Frau und ~** as a wife and a mother; **~ Natur/Erde** *(liter)* Mother Nature/Earth; **die ~ der Kompanie** *(Mil hum)* the sergeant major; **wie bei ~n** *(dial)* just like (at) home; *(Essen)* just like mother makes; **die ~ aller ...** *(fig)* the mother of all ...

Mut|ter F **-, -n** *(Tech)* nut

Müt|ter|be|ra|tungs|stel|le F child welfare clinic

Mut|ter-: **Mut|ter|bin|dung** F *(Psych)* mother fixation; **Mut|ter|bo|den** M topsoil; **Mut|ter|brust** F mother's breast; *(Ernährung)* mother's milk; **an der ~** at one's mother's breast; **da war ich ja noch an der ~!** I was just a babe-in-arms then

Müt|ter|chen ['mʏtɐçən] NT **-s, -** **a** *(= Mutter)* mummy *(Brit inf)*, mommy *(US inf)* **b** *(= alte Frau)* grandma **c** **~ Russland** Mother Russia

Mut|ter-: **Mut|ter|er|de** F topsoil; *(liter: = Heimaterde)* native soil; **Mut|ter|fahr|zeug** NT *(Space)* mother *or* parent ship; **Mut|ter|fi|gur** F mother figure; **Mut|ter|freu|den** PL the joys *pl* of motherhood

Müt|ter|ge|ne|sungs-: **Müt|ter|ge|ne|sungs|heim** NT *rest centre for mothers, es-*

pecially of large families; **Müt|ter|ge|ne|sungs|werk** NT *organization providing rest for mothers*

Mut|ter-: **Mut|ter|ge|sell|schaft** F *(Comm)* parent company; **Mut|ter|ge|win|de** NT *(Tech)* female thread; **Mut|ter|glück** NT **das ~** the joy of motherhood; **Mut|ter|got|tes** [mʊtɐˈgɔtəs] F **-**, *no pl* Mother of God; *(Abbild)* Madonna; **Mut|ter|got|tes|bild** NT (image of the) Madonna; **Mut|ter|haus** NT *(Rel)* training centre *(Brit) or* center *(US)*; *(von Kloster)* mother house; **Mut|ter|herz** NT maternal heart; **Mut|ter|ins|tinkt** M maternal instinct; **Mut|ter|kir|che** F mother church; **Mut|ter|kom|plex** M mother complex; **Mut|ter|korn** NT *pl* **-korne** *(Bot)* ergot; **Mut|ter|ku|chen** M *(Anat)* placenta; **Mut|ter|kult** M mother cult; **Mut|ter|land** NT mother country; **Mut|ter|leib** M womb

Müt|ter|lein [ˈmʏtɐlain] NT **-s, -** = **Mütterchen a, b**

müt|ter|lich [ˈmʏtɐlɪç] ADJ **a** maternal; *Seite, Linie* maternal, distaff; **die ~en Pflichten** one's duties as a mother; **auf ~er Seite** on his/her *etc* mother's side, on the distaff side **b** *(= liebevoll besorgt)* motherly *no adv* ADV like a mother; **jdn ~ umsorgen** to mother sb

müt|ter|li|cher|seits ADV on his/her *etc* mother's side, on the distaff side; **sein Großvater ~** his maternal grandfather

Müt|ter|lich|keit F **-**, *no pl* motherliness

Mut|ter-: **Mut|ter|lie|be** F motherly love; **mut|ter|los** ADJ motherless; **Mut|ter|mal** NT *pl* **-male** birthmark, mole; **Mut|ter|milch** F mother's milk; **etw mit der ~ einsaugen** *(fig)* to learn sth from the cradle; **Mut|ter|mord** M matricide; **Mut|ter|mund** M *(Anat)* cervix, neck of the uterus *or* womb

Mut|tern|schlüs|sel M *(Tech)* spanner *(Brit)*, wrench *(US)*

Mut|ter-: **Mut|ter|pass** M *document held by expectant mothers in which the details of the pregnancy are entered,* ≈ antenatal card *(Brit)*; **Mut|ter|pferd** NT dam; **Mut|ter|pflan|ze** F parent (plant); **Mut|ter|pla|ti|ne** F *(Comput)* motherboard; **Mut|ter|recht** NT *(Sociol)* matriarchy; **mut|ter|recht|lich** ADJ *(Sociol)* matriarch(al); **Mut|ter|schaf** NT ewe

Mut|ter|schaft [ˈmʊtɐʃaft] F **-**, *no pl* motherhood; *(nach Entbindung)* maternity

Mut|ter|schafts-: **Mut|ter|schafts|geld** NT maternity pay *(esp Brit)*; **Mut|ter|schafts|hil|fe** F maternity benefit *(esp Brit)*; **Mut|ter|schafts|ur|laub** M maternity leave; **Mut|ter|schafts|ver|tre|tung** F maternity cover

Mut|ter-: **Mut|ter|schiff** NT *(Space)* mother *or* parent ship; **Mut|ter|schutz** M legal protection of expectant and nursing mothers; **Mut|ter|schutz|ge|setz** NT law for the protection of expectant and nursing mothers; **Mut|ter|schwein** NT sow; **mut|ter|see|len|al|lein** ADJ ADV all alone, all on one's own; **Mut|ter|söhn|chen** NT *(pej)* mummy's boy *(Brit)*, mommy's boy *(US)*; **Mut|ter|spra|che** F native language, mother tongue; **Gälisch ist seine ~** Gaelic is his native language, he's a native speaker of Gaelic; **Mut|ter|sprach|ler** [-ʃpraːxlɐ] M **-s, -**, **Mut|ter|sprach|le|rin** [-ərɪn] F **-, -nen** native speaker; **mut|ter|sprach|lich** ADJ native-language *attr*; **~er Unterricht für Ausländer** language lessons for foreigners in their mother tongue; **Mut|ter|stel|le** F **bei jdm ~ vertreten** to be like a mother to sb; *(Jur)* to stand in loco parentis to sb

Müt|ter|sterb|lich|keit F mortality in childbirth

Mut|ter-: **Mut|ter|stu|te** F dam; **Mut|ter|tag** M Mother's Day; **Mut|ter|tier** NT mother (animal); *(= Zuchttier)* brood animal; **Mut|ter|witz** M *(= Schläue)* mother wit; *(= Humor)* natural wit

Mut|ti [ˈmʊti] F **-, -s** *(inf)* mummy *(Brit inf)*, mum *(Brit inf)*, mommy *(US inf)*

Mut|wil|le [ˈmuːtvɪlə] M **-ns**, *no pl* **a** *(geh: = Übermut)* mischief; **aus bloßem** *or* **reinem ~n** out of pure mischief **b** *(= böse Absicht)* malice; **etw mit** *or* **aus ~n tun** to do sth out of malice

mut|wil|lig [ˈmuːtvɪlɪç] ADJ **a** *(geh: = übermütig) Streiche, Dummheiten* mischievous **b** *(= böswillig)* malicious; *Beschädigung, Zerstörung* wilful, malicious ADV *(= absichtlich) zerstören etc* wilfully

Mut|wil|lig|keit F = **Mutwille**

Müt|ze [ˈmʏtsə] F **-, -n** cap; *(= Pudelmütze, Pelzmütze)* hat; **die ~ ziehen** to doff one's cap *(dated)*; *(fig)* to take one's hat off (*vor jdm* to sb); **was** *or* **eins auf die ~ kriegen** *(inf)* to get a ticking-off *(Brit inf) or* telling-off *(inf)*; *(= verprügelt werden)* to get thumped *(Brit inf) or* bashed *(inf)*; **eine ~ voll Schlaf** *(inf)* a good kip *(Brit inf)*, a long nap

Müt|zen|schirm M peak

MW *abbr von* **Megawatt**

MwSt., **MWSt.** *abbr von* **Mehrwertsteuer** VAT

My|an|mar [myːˈanmaːɐ] NT **-s** Myanmar

My|ke|nä [myˈkeːnɛ] NT **-s**, **My|ke|ne** [myˈkeːnə] NT **-s** Mycenae

my|ke|nisch [myˈkeːnɪʃ] ADJ Mycenaean

My|om [myˈoːm] NT **-s, -e** *(Med)* myoma

My|ri|a|de [myˈriaːdə] F **-, -n** *(lit, fig)* myriad

Myr|re [ˈmʏrə] F **-, -n** = **Myrrhe**

Myr|ren|öl NT → **Myrrhenöl**

Myr|rhe [ˈmʏrə] F **-, -n** myrrh

Myr|rhen|öl NT oil of myrrh

Myr|te [ˈmʏrtə] F **-, -n** myrtle

Myr|ten|kranz M myrtle wreath

Mys|te|ri|en- *(Hist)*: **Mys|te|ri|en|kult** M mystery cult; **Mys|te|ri|en|spiel** NT *(Theat)* mystery play

mys|te|ri|ös [mʏsteˈriøːs] ADJ mysterious ADV *(= unter mysteriösen Umständen) sterben* mysteriously; **~ verschwundene Gelder** money that disappeared mysteriously

Mys|te|ri|um [mʏsˈteːriʊm] NT **-s, Mysterien** [-riən] *(alle Bedeutungen)* mystery

Mys|ti|fi|ka|ti|on [mʏstifikaˈtsioːn] F **-, -en** mystification

mys|ti|fi|zie|ren [mʏstifiˈtsiːrən] *ptp* **mystifiziert** VT to mysticize

Mys|ti|fi|zie|rung F **-, -en** mystification

Mys|tik [ˈmʏstɪk] F **-**, *no pl* mysticism *no art*

Mys|ti|ker [ˈmʏstikɐ] M **-s, -**, **Mys|ti|ke|rin** [-ərɪn] F **-, -nen** mystic

mys|tisch [ˈmʏstɪʃ] ADJ mystic(al); *(fig: = geheimnisvoll)* mysterious

Mys|ti|zis|mus [mʏstiˈtsɪsmʊs] M **-**, *no pl* mysticism

My|then-: **My|then|bil|dung** F **zur ~ beitragen** to help to create a myth; **my|then|haft** ADJ mythical

my|thisch [ˈmyːtɪʃ] ADJ mythical

My|tho|lo|gie [mytoloˈgiː] F **-, -n** [-ˈgiːən] mythology

my|tho|lo|gisch [mytoˈloːgɪʃ] ADJ mythological

My|thos [ˈmyːtɔs] M **-, Mythen** [ˈmyːtn], **My|thus** [ˈmyːtʊs] M **-, Mythen** [ˈmyːtn] *(lit, fig)* myth; **er war zeitlebens von einem ~ umgeben** he was a legend in his time

N

N, n [ɛn] NT -, - N, n; **n-te** nth

N *abbr von* **Norden**

'n [n] *(inf) abbr von* **ein, einen**

na [na] INTERJ *(inf)* **a** *(Frage, Anrede)* well; *(Aufforderung)* then; **na, kommst du mit?** well, are you coming?, are you coming then?; **na du?** hey, you!
b *(zögernde Zustimmung, Resignation)* well; **na ja** well; **na ja, aber nur noch zehn Minuten** well yes *or* I suppose so, but only another ten minutes; **na gut, na schön** all right, OK *(inf)*
c *(Bestätigung, Erleichterung)* well; **na also!, na eben!** (well,) there you are (then)!; **na, endlich!** about time!, at last!; **na und ob!** *(= auf jeden Fall)* you bet! *(inf)*, not half! *(Brit inf)*; *(= und wie)* and how! *(inf)*
d *(Beschwichtigung)* come (on) (now)
e *(Ermahnung)* now; *(Zurückweisung)* well; **na (na)!** now, now!, now then!; **na warte!** just you wait!; **na so was** *or* **so etwas!** well, I never!; **na und?** so what?; **na ich danke!** no thank you!; **na, wirds bald?** come on, aren't you ready yet?
f *(Zweifel)* well; **na, wenn das mal klappt!** well, if it comes off

na [na:] ADV *(S Ger, Aus inf)* = **nein**

Na|be ['na:bə] F -, -n hub

Na|bel ['na:bl] M -s, - *(Anat)* navel, umbilicus *(spec)*; *(Bot)* hilum; **der ~ der Welt** *(fig)* the hub of the universe, the centre *(Brit) or* center *(US)* of the world

Na|bel-: **Na|bel|bin|de** F umbilical bandage; **Na|bel|bruch** M umbilical hernia; **na|bel|frei** ADJ **~es T-Shirt** crop top ADV **~ gehen** to wear a crop top, to bare one's navel; **Na|bel|schau** F **~ betreiben** to be bound up in oneself; **Na|bel|schnur** F, **Na|bel|strang** M *(Anat)* umbilical cord

Na|ben|schal|tung F *(beim Fahrrad)* hub gear

Na|bob ['na:bɔp] M -s, -s nabob

nach [na:x] PREP +*dat* **a** *(örtlich)* to; **ich nahm den Zug ~ Mailand** *(= bis)* I took the train to Milan; *(= in Richtung)* I took the Milan train, I took the train for Milan; **das Schiff/der Zug fährt ~ Kiel** the boat/train is bound for Kiel, the boat/train is going to Kiel; **er ist schon ~ London abgefahren** he has already left for London; **~ Osten** eastward(s), to the east; **~ Westen** westward(s), to the west; **von Osten ~ Westen** from (the) east to (the) west; **~ links/rechts** (to the) left/right; **von links ~ rechts** from (the) left to (the) right; **~ jeder Richtung, ~ allen Richtungen** *(lit)* in all directions; *(fig)* on all sides; **~ hinten/vorn** to the back/front; *(in Wagen/Zug etc auch)* to the rear/front; **~ … zu** towards … *(Brit)*, toward … *(US)*; **~ Norden zu** *or* **hin** to(wards) the north
b *(in Verbindung mit vb siehe auch dort)* **~ jdm/etw suchen** to look for sb/sth; **sich ~ etw sehnen** to long for sth; **~ etw schmecken/riechen** to taste/smell of sth
c *(zeitlich)* after; **fünf (Minuten) ~ drei** five (minutes) past *or* after *(US)* three; **~ Christi Geburt, ~ unserer Zeitrechnung** AD, anno Domini *(form)*; **sie kam ~ zehn Minuten** she came ten minutes later, she came after ten minutes; **~ zehn Minuten war sie wieder da** she was back in ten minutes, she was back ten minutes later; **~ zehn Minuten wurde ich schon unruhig** after ten minutes I was getting worried; **was wird man ~ zehn Jahren über ihn sagen?** what will people be saying about him in ten years *or* in ten years' time?; **~ Empfang** *or* **Erhalt** *or* **Eingang** on receipt; **drei Tage ~ Empfang** three days after receipt; **~ allem, was geschehen ist** after all that has happened
d *(Reihenfolge)* after; **eine(r, s) ~ dem/der anderen** one after another *or* the other; **die dritte Straße ~ dem Rathaus** the third road after *or* past the town hall; **ich komme ~ Ihnen!** I'm *or* I come after you; **(bitte) ~ Ihnen!** after you!; **der Leutnant kommt ~ dem Major** *(inf)* a lieutenant comes after a major; **~ „mit" steht der Dativ** "mit" is followed by *or* takes the dative
e *(= laut, entsprechend)* according to; *(= im Einklang mit)* in accordance with; **~ dem Gesetz, dem Gesetz ~** according to the law; **~ römischem Gesetz** according to *or* under Roman law; **~ Artikel 142c** under article 142c; **manche Arbeiter werden ~ Zeit, andere ~ Leistung bezahlt** some workers are paid by the hour, others according to productivity; **etw ~ Gewicht kaufen** to buy sth by weight; **~ Verfassern/Gedichtanfängen** in order of *or* according to authors/first lines; **die Uhr ~ dem Radio stellen** to put a clock right by the radio; **seinem Wesen** *or* **seiner Natur ~ ist er sehr sanft** he's very gentle by nature; **seiner Veranlagung ~ hätte er Musiker werden sollen** with his temperament he should have been a musician; **ihrer Sprache ~ (zu urteilen)** from her language, judging by her language; **~ dem, was er gesagt hat** from what he's said, according to what he's said; **~ allem, was ich gehört habe** from what I've heard; **~ allem, was ich weiß** as far as I know; **Knödel ~ schwäbischer Art** Swabian dumplings
f *(= angelehnt an)* after; **~ dem Russischen** after the Russian; **~ einem Gedicht von Schiller** after a poem by Schiller
g er wurde ~ seinem Großvater genannt he was named after *(Brit) or* for *(US)* his grandfather
ADV **a** *(räumlich)* **mir ~!** *(old, liter)* follow me!
b *(zeitlich)* **~ und ~** little by little, gradually; **~ wie vor** still; **wir treffen uns ~ wie vor im „Goldenen Handschuh"** we still meet in the "Golden Glove" as always

nach+äf|fen VT *sep (pej) Moden, Ideen, Stil* to ape; *jdn* to take off *(Brit)*, to mimic; *(= imitieren)* to copy

Nach|äf|fe|rei [na:xlɛfə'rai] F -, *no pl (pej) (von Mode, Ideen)* aping; *(von Menschen)* mimicry; *(= das Imitieren)* copying

nach+ah|men ['na:xla:mən] VT *sep* to imitate; *(= nacheifern auch)* to emulate; *(= karikieren)* to take off *(Brit)*, to mimic; *(= kopieren)* to copy

nach|ah|mens|wert ADJ exemplary ADV exemplarily; **~ leben** to lead an exemplary life

Nach|ah|mer ['na:xla:mɐ] M -s, -, **Nach|ah|me|rin** [-ərɪn] F -, -nen imitator; *(eines großen Vorbilds)* emulator; *(pej: Art, Liter)* copyist

Nach|ah|mer|me|di|ka|ment NT, **Nach|ah|mer|prä|pa|rat** NT generic drug

Nach|ah|mung ['na:xla:mʊŋ] F -, -en **a** *(= das Imitieren)* imitation; *(= das Nacheifern)* emulation; *(= das Karikieren)* taking off *(Brit)*, mimicking; *(= das Kopieren)* copying; **etw zur ~ anraten** *or* **empfehlen** to recommend sth as an example **b** *(= die Imitation)* imitation; *(= Karikatur)* take-off *(Brit)*, impression; *(= Kopie)* copy

Nach|ah|mungs-: **Nach|ah|mungs|tä|ter(in)** M(F) imitator, copy-cat criminal; **man muss damit rechnen, dass es ~ geben wird** copy-cat crimes have to be expected; **Nach|ah|mungs|trieb** M imitative instinct

nach+ar|bei|ten *sep* VT **a** *(= aufholen)* to make up **b** *(= überarbeiten)* to work over; *(Art etc)* to touch up **c** *(= nachbilden)* to copy, to reproduce VI **wir müssen morgen ~** we'll have to make up the work tomorrow

Nach|bar ['naxba:ɐ] M -n *or* -s, -n, **Nach|ba|rin** [-rɪn] F -, -nen neighbour *(Brit)*, neighbor *(US)*; *(in Nachbarwohnung, Nachbarhaus auch)* next-door neighbo(u)r; *(= Nachbarland auch)* neighbo(u)ring country; **Herr X war beim Konzert mein ~** Mr X sat next to me at the concert; **ich war eben bei ~s** *(inf)* I've just been round to the neighbo(u)rs'; **~s Garten** the next-door garden; **die lieben ~n** *(iro)* the neighbo(u)rs

Nach|bar-: **Nach|bar|dorf** NT neighbouring *(Brit) or* neighboring *(US)* village; **Nach|bar|grund|stück** NT property next door, neighbouring *(Brit) or* neighboring *(US)* property; **Nach|bar|haus** NT house next door, neighbouring *(Brit) or* neighboring *(US)* house; **in unserem ~, bei uns im ~** in the house next door (to us)

Nach|ba|rin [-rɪn] F -, -nen → **Nachbar**

Nach|bar|land NT neighbouring *(Brit) or* neighboring *(US)* country

nach|bar|lich ['naxba:ɐlɪç] ADJ *(= freundlich)* neighbourly *no adv (Brit)*, neighborly *no adv (US)*; *(= benachbart)* neighbo(u)ring *no adv*; **~e Freundlichkeit** neighbo(u)rliness

Nach|bar|schaft ['naxba:ɐʃaft] F -, *no pl (= Gegend)* neighbourhood *(Brit)*, neighborhood *(US)*; *(= Nachbarn)* neighbo(u)rs *pl*; *(= Nähe)* vicinity; **gute ~ halten** *or* **pflegen** to keep on good terms with the neighbo(u)rs

Nach|bar|schafts|hil|fe F neighbourly *(Brit) or* neighborly *(US)* help; **man ist ja wohl zu ein bisschen ~ verpflichtet** you have to help your neighbo(u)rs a bit

Nach|bars-: **Nach|bars|fa|mi|lie** F next-door family, family next door; **Nach|bars|frau** F lady next door; **Nach|bars|kind** NT child next door; **Nach|bars|leu|te** PL neighbours *pl (Brit)*, neighbors *pl (US)*; *(von nebenan auch)* people *pl* next door

Nach|bar-: **Nach|bar|stadt** F neighbouring *(Brit) or* neighboring *(US)* town; **Nach|bar|tisch** M next table; **am ~** at the next table

nach+be|ar|bei|ten *ptp* **nachbearbeitet** VT *sep Text, Musikstück etc* to rework; *(Comput)* to post-edit

Nach|be|ben NT aftershock

nach+be|han|deln *ptp* **nachbehandelt** VT *sep (Med)* **jdn/etw ~** to give sb aftercare, to give sb/sth follow-up treatment

Nach|be|hand|lung F (Med) follow-up treatment *no indef art*

nach+be|rei|ten *ptp* **nachbereitet** VT *sep (Sch)* to assess *or* evaluate afterwards

nach+bes|sern *sep* VT *Lackierung* to retouch; *Gesetz, Vertrag* to amend; *Angebot* to improve VI to make improvements

Nach|bes|se|rung F -, -en *(von Gesetz, Beschluss)* amendment; **~en vornehmen/fordern** to make/demand improvements

Nach|bes|se|rungs|klau|sel F clause improving the terms of a/the contract

nach+be|stel|len *ptp* **nachbestellt** VT *sep* to order some more; *(Comm)* to reorder, to put in a repeat order for; *(nachträglich)* to put in *or* make a late order for; **ich habe gerade noch Sekt/noch zwei Flaschen Sekt nachbestellt** I've just ordered some more champagne/another two bottles of champagne

Nach|be|stel|lung F repeat order (*gen* for); *(= nachträgliche Bestellung)* late order (*gen* for)

nach+be|ten VT *sep (inf)* to repeat parrot-fashion, to parrot

Nach|be|ter ['na:xbe:tɐ] M -s, -, **Nach|be|te|rin** [-ərɪn] F -, -nen *(inf)* echoer, parrot *(inf)*

nach+be|zah|len *ptp* **nachbezahlt** *sep* VT to pay; *(später)* to pay later; **Steuern ~** to pay back-tax VI to pay the rest

Nach|bild NT *(Opt)* afterimage

nach+bil|den VT *sep* to copy; *(exakt)* to reproduce; **einer Sache** *(dat)* **nachgebildet sein** to be modelled *(Brit) or* modeled *(US)* on sth, to be a copy/reproduction of sth

Nach|bil|dung F copy; *(exakt)* reproduction

nach+blät|tern VI *sep* to have a quick look; **in etw** *(dat)* ~ to flick through sth again

nach+blei|ben VI *sep irreg aux sein (dial)* to stay behind

nach+bli|cken VI *sep* = **nachsehen VI a**

Nach|blu|tung F *(Med)* secondary haemorrhage *(Brit) or* hemorrhage *(US)*; *(nach Operation)* postoperative h(a)emorrhage; *(nach Geburt)* postpartum h(a)emorrhage

nach+boh|ren *sep* VT *Öffnung* to drill out VI *(lit)* to drill out some more; **(bei jdm)** ~ *(fig inf)* to probe

Nach|bör|se F *(St Ex)* after-hours market, kerb market

nach|börs|lich ADJ *(St Ex)* **~e Kurse** after-hours prices; **~e Notierung** after-hours quotation

Nach|bren|ner M *(Aviat)* afterburner

nach+brin|gen VT *sep irreg (= hinterherbringen)* to bring afterwards; *(= zusätzlich servieren)* to bring some more; **er brachte mir den Schirm nach** he came after me with my umbrella

nach|christ|lich ADJ **in den ersten ~en Jahrhunderten** in the first centuries AD

nach+da|tie|ren *ptp* **nachdatiert** VT *sep* to postdate

nach|dem [na:x'de:m] CONJ **a** *(zeitlich)* after **b** *(modal)* → **je** CONJ **b** **c** *(S Ger. = da, weil)* since

nach+den|ken VI *sep irreg* to think (*über +acc* about); **darüber darf man gar nicht ~** it doesn't bear thinking about; **laut ~** to think aloud, to think out loud; **denk doch mal nach!** think about it!; **denk mal gut** *or* **scharf nach!** think carefully!

Nach|den|ken NT thought, reflection; **nach langem ~** after (giving the matter) considerable thought; **gib mir ein bisschen Zeit zum ~** give me a bit of time to think (about it)

nach|denk|lich ['na:xdɛŋklɪç] ADJ *Mensch, Miene* thoughtful, pensive; *Geschichte, Worte* thought-provoking; **jdn ~ stimmen** *or* **machen** to set sb thinking; **~ gestimmt sein** to be in a thoughtful mood

Nach|denk|lich|keit F -, *no pl* thoughtfulness

nach+dich|ten VT *sep (Liter)* to give a free rendering of

Nach|dich|tung F *(Liter)* free rendering

nach+drän|gen VI *sep aux sein* to push from behind; **jdm ~** to throng after sb *(liter)*

Nach|druck M *pl* **-drucke** **a** *no pl (= Betonung)* stress, emphasis; *(= Tatkraft)* vigour *(Brit)*, vigor *(US)*, energy; **einer Sache** *(dat)* **~ verleihen** to lend weight to sth; **besonderen ~ darauf legen, dass ...** to put special emphasis on the fact that ..., to stress *or* emphasize particularly that ...; **mit ~** vigorously, emphatically; **etw mit ~ betreiben** to pursue sth with vigo(u)r; **etw mit ~ sagen** to say sth emphatically **b** *(= das Nachdrucken)* reprinting; *(= das Nachgedruckte)* reprint; **„Nachdruck verboten"** "no part of this publication may be reproduced without the prior permission of the publishers"

nach+dru|cken VT *sep* to reprint

nach|drück|lich ['na:xdrʏklɪç] ADJ emphatic; *Warnung auch* firm; **jdm den ~en Rat geben, etw zu tun** to advise sb strongly *or* urge sb to do sth ADV firmly; **sich ~ für/gegen etw aussprechen** to come out firmly in favour *(Brit) or* favor *(US)* of sth/against sth; **jdm ~ raten, etw zu tun** to advise sb strongly *or* to urge sb to do sth; **jdn ~ warnen** to give sb a firm warning

Nach|drück|lich|keit F -, *no pl* insistence

nach|drucks|voll ADJ emphatic ADV emphatically

nach+dun|keln VI *sep aux sein* to get *or* grow darker; *(Bild)* to darken

Nach|durst M *(nach Alkoholgenuss)* dehydration; **~ haben** to be dehydrated

nach+ei|fern VI *sep* **jdm/einer Sache ~** to emulate sb/sth

nach|ei|ferns|wert ADJ worth emulating, worthy of emulation

nach+ei|len VI *sep aux sein (geh)* **jdm/einer Sache ~** to run *or* hurry after sb/sth

nach|ei|nan|der [na:xlai'nandɐ] ADV *(räumlich)* one after another, one after the other; *(zeitlich auch)* in succession; **zweimal ~** twice running, twice in a row; **kurz/unmittelbar ~** shortly/immediately after each other

nach+emp|fin|den *ptp* **nachempfunden** VT *sep irreg* **a** *Stimmung* to feel; *Text, Musik* to relate to; *(= nachvollziehen)* to understand; **niemand kann solchen Schmerz ~** no-one can really feel such grief; **ich kann (Ihnen) Ihre Entrüstung ~** I can understand how horrified you must be; **das kann ich ihr ~** I can understand her feelings *or* how she feels **b** *(= nachgestalten)* to adapt (*+dat* from); **etw jdm ~** *(= nachahmen)* to base sth on sb; **etw einer Sache ~** to model sth on sth

Na|chen ['naxn] M -s, - *(liter)* barque *(poet)*

Nach|ern|te F second harvest; *(= Ährennachernte)* gleaning; *(= Ertrag)* gleanings *pl*; **~ halten** to glean the remains of the harvest

nach+er|zäh|len *ptp* **nacherzählt** VT *sep* to retell; **dem Türkischen nacherzählt** *(geh)* adapted from the Turkish

Nach|er|zäh|lung F retelling; *(Sch)* (story) reproduction

nach+ex|er|zie|ren *ptp* **nachexerziert** VI *sep (Mil)* to do extra drill

Nachf. *abbr von* **Nachfolger**

Nach|fahr ['na:xfa:ɐ] M -s, -en, **Nach|fah|rin** [-rɪn] F -, -nen *(liter)* descendant

nach+fah|ren VI *sep irreg aux sein* to follow (on); **jdm ~** to follow sb

Nach|fass|ak|ti|on F *(in der Werbung)* follow-up campaign

nach+fas|sen *sep* VI **a** *(= nachgreifen)* to get a firmer grip; *(= noch einmal zufassen)* to regain one's grip **b** *(inf. = nachforschen)* to probe a bit deeper **c** *(inf. = Essen nachfassen)* to have a second helping VT *(inf. = nachholen)* to have a second helping of; **Essen ~** to have a second helping

Nach|fei|er F continuation of the party; *(später) celebration (held some time after the event)*

nach+fei|ern VI *sep* **a** *auch vt (= später feiern)* to celebrate later **b** *(= weiterfeiern)* to carry on celebrating

nach+fei|len VT *sep* to file off

nach+fi|nan|zie|ren *ptp* **nachfinanziert** VT *sep* to find additional finance for

Nach|fi|nan|zie|rung F additional financing

Nach|fol|ge F, *no pl* **a** succession; **jds ~ antreten** to succeed sb, to be sb's successor **b** *(= Nacheiferung)* emulation; **in jds ~ stehen** to emulate sb; **in der ~ seines Lehrmeisters** in emulation of his master; **die ~ Christi** the imitation of Christ

Nach|fol|ge- *in cpds* follow-up; **Nach|fol|ge|mo|dell** NT *(von Produkt, Auto)* successor, follow-up model (*+gen* to)

nach+fol|gen VI *sep aux sein* **a** *(= hinterherkommen)* to follow (on); **jdm ~** to follow sb; **jdm im Amt ~** to succeed sb in office; **sie ist ihrem Gatten nachgefolgt** *(euph)* she has gone to join her husband *(euph)* **b** *+dat (= Anhänger sein)* to follow

nach|fol|gend ADJ following; **wie im Nachfolgenden ausgeführt** as detailed below; **Nachfolgendes, das Nachfolgende** the following

Nach|fol|ge|or|ga|ni|sa|ti|on F successor organization

Nach|fol|ger ['na:xfɔlgɐ] M -s, -, **Nach|fol|ge|rin** [-ərɪn] F -, -nen *(im Amt etc)* successor; **Friedrich Reißnagel ~** successors to Friedrich Reißnagel

Nach|fol|ge|re|ge|lung F regulations *pl* governing the succession; *(in einer Firma, Partei etc)* succession planning

Nach|fol|ge|staat M succession state

nach+for|dern VT *sep* to put in another demand for

Nach|for|de|rung F subsequent demand

nach+for|schen VI *sep* to try to find out; *(polizeilich etc)* to carry out an investigation (*+dat* into); *(amtlich etc)* to make inquiries (*+dat* into)

Nach|for|schung F enquiry; *(polizeilich etc)* investigation; **~en anstellen** to make inquiries

Nach|fra|ge F **a** *(Comm)* demand (*nach, +dat* for); **danach besteht eine rege/keine ~** there is a great/no demand for it **b** *(= Erkundigung)* inquiry; **danke der ~** *(form)* thank you for your concern; *(inf)* nice of you to ask

nach+fra|gen ✪ 46.1, 48.1 VI *sep* to ask, to inquire

Nach|fra|ge-: **Nach|fra|ge|rück|gang** M drop *or* fall in demand; **Nach|fra|ge|schub** M surge in demand; **Nach|fra|ge|schwä|che** F weak demand; **Nach|fra|ge|über|hang** M surplus demand

Nach|frist F extension; **jdm eine ~ setzen** to extend sb's deadline, to give *or* grant sb an extension

nach+füh|len VT *sep* = **nachempfinden a**

nach+fül|len VT *sep leeres Glas etc* to refill; *halbleeres Glas, Batterie etc* to top up *(Brit) or* off *(US)*; **Öl ~** to top up *(Brit) or* off *(US)* with oil; **darf ich (Ihr Glas) ~?** can I fill/top you up *(Brit) or* off *(US)* ?, would you like a refill?

Nach|füll|pack M, **Nach|füll|pa|ckung** F refill pack; **etw im ~ kaufen** to buy the refill pack of sth

nach+gä|ren VI *sep irreg aux haben or sein* to be lagered

Nach|gä|rung F lagering

nach+ge|ben *sep irreg* VI **a** *(Boden, Untergrund)* to give way (*+dat* to); *(= federn)* to give; *(fig) (Mensch)* to give in *or* way (*+dat* to); *(= aufgeben)* to give up *or* in **b** *(Comm: Preise, Kurse)* to drop, to fall VT *(= noch mehr geben)* **darf ich Ihnen noch etwas Gemüse ~?** may I give you a few more vegetables?; **er ließ sich** *(dat)* **Fleisch ~** he had another helping of meat

nach|ge|bo|ren ADJ **a** *(mit großem Altersunterschied)* late(r)-born; **die Nachgeborenen** *(geh)* future generations **b** *(= nach Tod des Vaters geboren)* posthumous

Nach|ge|bühr F excess (postage)

Nach|ge|burt F *(= Gewebe)* afterbirth; *(= Vorgang)* expulsion of the afterbirth

Nach|ge|fühl NT feeling

nach+ge|hen VI *sep irreg aux sein* **a** *+dat (= hinterhergehen)* to follow; *jdm* to go after, to follow **b** *(Uhr)* to be slow; **deine Uhr geht fünf Minuten nach** your clock is five minutes slow **c** *+dat (= ausüben) Beruf* to practise *(Brit)*, to practice *(US)*; *Studium, Vergnügungen, Interesse etc* to pursue; *Geschäften* to go about; **welcher Tätigkeit gehen Sie nach?** what is your occupation?; **seiner Arbeit ~** to do one's job **d** *+dat (= erforschen)* to investigate, to look into **e** *+dat (= zu denken geben)* to haunt

nach|ge|las|sen ADJ *Werke, Briefe, Papiere* posthumously published; **seine ~en, bis heute nicht veröffentlichten Fragmente** the fragments he left which remain unpublished to this day → *auch* **nachlassen**

nach|ge|macht ADJ *Gold, Leder etc* imitation; *Geld* counterfeit → *auch* **nachmachen**

nach|ge|ord|net ADJ *(form) Behörde, Dienststelle* subordinate

nach|ge|ra|de ['na:xgə'ra:də] ADV *(= geradezu)* practically, virtually; *(= nach wie vor)* still

nach+ge|ra|ten *ptp* **nachgeraten** VI *sep irreg aux sein* **jdm ~** to take after sb; **sie ist ganz ihrer Mutter ~** she's just like her mother

Nach|ge|schmack M *(lit, fig)* aftertaste; **einen üblen ~ hinterlassen** *(fig)* to leave a bad *or* nasty taste in one's *or* the mouth

nach|ge|wie|se|ner|ma|ßen ['na:xgəvi:znɐ'ma:sn] ADV = **erwiesenermaßen**

nach|gie|big ['na:xgi:bɪç] ADJ **a** *Material* pliable; *Boden* soft; **~ sein** to be pliable/soft **b** *(fig) Mensch, Haltung* soft; *(= entgegenkommend)* accommodating, compliant; **jdn ~ machen** to soften sb up ADV **sie behandelt die Kinder zu ~** she's too soft with the children

Nach|gie|big|keit F -, *no pl* **a** *(von Material)* pliability; *(von Boden)* softness **b** *(fig) (von Mensch, Haltung)* softness; *(= Entgegenkommen)* compliance; **~ zeigen** to be accommodating; **er tendiert zur ~** he tends to be soft; **es darf keine ~ gegenüber Schulschwänzern geben** we must stand firm against truancy

nach+gie|ßen *sep irreg* VT *Wasser, Milch, Benzin* to add; **darf ich Ihnen noch etwas Wein ~?** would you like some more wine? VI **er trinkt so schnell, dass man ständig ~ muss** he drinks so fast that you keep having to top up *(Brit) or* off *(US)* his glass; **darf ich (Ihnen) ~?** would you like some more?

nach+glü|hen VI *sep* to go on glowing

nach+grei|fen VI *sep irreg* = **nachfassen VI a**

nach+grü|beln VI *sep* to think *(über +acc* about); *(= sich Gedanken machen)* to ponder *(über +acc* on), to muse *(über +acc* about)

nach+gu|cken VTI *sep* = **nachsehen**

nach+ha|ken VI *sep (inf)* to dig deeper; **bei jdm ~** to pump sb *(inf)*

Nach|hall M reverberation; *(= Nachklang)* echo; *(fig: = Anklang)* response *(auf +acc* to); **künstlicher ~** echo effect, artificial echo; **das Echo hatte einen langen ~** the echo went on reverberating a long while

nach+hal|len VI *sep* to reverberate

nach|hal|tig ['na:xhaltɪç] ADJ lasting; *Wachstum auch, Widerstand* sustained; **~e Entwicklung** sustainable development; **~e Nutzung** *(von Energie, Rohstoffen etc)* sustainable use; **~es Wirtschaften** sustainable management ADV **a** *(= mit langer Wirkung)* with lasting effect; **ihre Gesundheit hat sich ~ gebessert** there has been a lasting improvement in her health; **sich ~ verschlechtern** to continue to deteriorate; **etw ~ verändern** to change sth permanently; **~ beeindruckt** deeply impressed; **etw ~ beeinflussen** to have a profound effect on sth **b** *(= ökologisch bewusst)* with a view to sustainability

Nach|hal|tig|keit F -, *no pl* sustainability

nach+hän|gen VI *sep irreg +dat* to give oneself up to, to abandon oneself to; **seinen Erinnerungen ~** to lose oneself in one's memories

nach|hau|se [na:x'hauzə] ADV home

Nach|hau|se|weg [na:x'hauzəve:k] M way home

nach+hel|fen VI *sep irreg* to help; **jdm ~** to help sb, to give sb a hand; **sie hat ihrer Schönheit etwas nachgeholfen** she has improved a little on Mother Nature, she has given nature a helping hand; **er hat dem Glück ein bisschen nachgeholfen** he engineered himself a little luck; **jds Gedächtnis ~** to jog sb's memory; **meine Güte, bist du braun! – na, ich hab auch ein bisschen nachgeholfen** good heavens, you're brown! – well, I did help it *or* things along a bit

nach|her [na:x'he:ɐ, 'na:x-] ADV **a** *(= danach)* afterwards; *(= später)* later; **bis ~** see you later! **b** *(inf: = möglicherweise)* **~ stimmt das gar nicht** that might not be true at all, (it) could be that's not true at all

Nach|hil|fe F help, assistance; *(Sch)* private coaching *or* tuition *or* tutoring *(US)*

Nach|hil|fe-: **Nach|hil|fe|leh|rer(in)** M(F) private tutor, crammer *(Brit inf)*; **Nach|hil|fe|schü|ler(in)** M(F) private pupil; **Nach|hil|fe|stun|de** F private lesson; **Nach|hil|fe|un|ter|richt** M private coaching *or* tuition *or* tutoring *(US)*

Nach|hi|nein ['na:xhɪnain] ADV **im ~** afterwards; *(rückblickend)* in retrospect → **klug**

nach+hin|ken VI *sep aux sein (fig inf)* to lag behind; **hinter jdm/etw ~** to lag behind sb/sth

Nach|hol|be|darf M **einen ~ an etw** *(dat)* **haben** to have a lot of sth to catch up on

nach+ho|len VT *sep* **a** *(= aufholen) Versäumtes* to make up; **den Schulabschluss ~** to sit one's school exams as an adult **b** **jdn ~** *(= nachkommen lassen)* to get sb to join one; *(von Übersee)* to bring sb over

Nach|hut [na:xhu:t] F -, **-en** *(Mil)* rearguard; **bei der ~** in the rearguard

Nach|imp|fung F *(= Zweitimpfung)* reinoculation; *(= Wiederholungsimpfung)* booster

nach|in|dust|ri|ell ADJ *(Sociol)* post-industrial

nach+ja|gen VI *sep aux sein +dat* to chase (after); *Vergnügungen, dem Glück auch* to pursue

nach+kar|ten VI *sep (inf)* to reopen the subject

nach+kau|en VT *sep (inf)* to regurgitate

Nach|kauf M further purchase; **10 Jahre ~ garantiert** availability guaranteed for 10 years

nach+kau|fen VT *sep* to buy later; **kann man diese Knöpfe auch ~?** is it possible to buy replacements for these buttons?

Nach|kauf|ga|ran|tie F availability guarantee

Nach|klang M **der ~ der Mandolinen** the sound of the mandolins dying away; **ein ferner ~ von Mallarmé** a distant echo of Mallarmé

nach|klas|sisch ADJ post-classical

nach+klin|gen VI *sep irreg aux sein (Ton, Echo)* to go on sounding; *(Worte, Erinnerung)* to linger on, to linger; **die Melodie klang noch lange in mir nach** the tune stayed in my head for some time

nach+ko|chen VT *sep (Cook)* to cook (according to a recipe)

Nach|kom|me ['na:xkɔmə] M **-n, -n** descendant; **ohne ~n** without issue *(form)*

nach+kom|men ✪ 39.3 VI *sep irreg aux sein* **a** *(= später kommen)* to follow later, to come (on) later; **jdm ~** to follow sb; **wir kommen gleich nach** we'll follow *or* come in just a couple of minutes; **Sie können Ihre Familie/Ihr Gepäck ~ lassen** you can let your family join you later/ have your luggage *or* baggage sent on (after) **b** *(= mitkommen, Schritt halten)* to keep up; **ich komme nicht nach!** I can't keep up (with you/ them *etc*) **c** *+dat (= erfüllen) seiner Pflicht* to fulfil *(Brit)*, to fulfill *(US)*, to carry out; *einer Anordnung, Forderung, einem Wunsch* to comply with

Nach|kom|men|schaft ['na:xkɔmənʃaft] F -, **-en** descendants *pl*, issue *(form)*; **seine zahlreiche ~** his numerous progeny *pl or* descendants

Nach|kömm|ling ['na:xkœmlɪŋ] M **-s, -e** **a** *(= Nachzügler)* late arrival, latecomer; *(Kind)* afterthought *(hum)* **b** *(old: = Nachkomme)* descendant

nach+kon|trol|lie|ren *ptp* **nachkontrolliert** VT *sep* to check (over)

Nach|kriegs- *in cpds* post-war; **nach|kriegs|deutsch** ADJ post-war German; **Nach|kriegs|deutsch|land** NT post-war Germany; **Nach|kriegs|zeit** F postwar era, postwar years *pl*

Nach|kühl|strang ['na:xky:l-] M *(bei Kraftwerk)* cooling phase

Nach|kur F follow-up cure

nach+la|den VTI *sep irreg* to reload

Nach|lass ['na:xlas] M **-es, -e** *or* **-lässe** [-lɛsə] **a** *(= Preisnachlass)* discount, reduction *(auf +acc* on) **b** *(= Erbschaft)* estate; **den ~ eröffnen** to read the will; **den ~ verwalten** to administer the estate; **literarischer ~** literary estate; **Gedichte aus dem ~** unpublished poems; **aus dem ~ des Dichters** from the poet's estate

nach+las|sen *sep irreg* VT **a** *Preis, Summe* to reduce; **10% vom Preis ~** to give a 10% discount *or* reduction **b** *(= locker lassen) Zügel, Seil* to slacken; *Schraube* to loosen **c** *(old: = hinterlassen)* to bequeath → *auch* **nachgelassen** VI to decrease, to diminish; *(Interesse auch)* to flag, to wane; *(Sehvermögen, Gedächtnis, Gehör auch)* to deteriorate; *(Regen, Sturm, Nasenbluten)* to ease off *or* up; *(Hitze)* to ease off; *(Leistung, Geschäfte)* to fall *or* drop off; *(Preise)* to fall, to drop; **nicht ~!** keep it up!; **bei der Suche nach etw nicht ~** not to let up in the search for sth; **er hat in letzter Zeit sehr nachgelassen** he hasn't been nearly as good recently; **er hat in** *or* **mit seinem Eifer sehr nachgelassen** he's lost a lot of his enthusiasm; **das hat nachgelassen** it's got better; **sobald die Kälte nachlässt** as soon as it gets a bit warmer

Nach|las|sen|schaft ['na:xlasnʃaft] F -, **-en** = **Hinterlassenschaft**

Nach|lass-: **Nach|lass|ge|richt** NT probate court; **Nach|lass|gläu|bi|ger(in)** M(F) *(Jur)* creditor of the estate

nach|läs|sig ['na:xlɛsɪç] ADJ careless, negligent; *Arbeit auch* slipshod; *(= unachtsam)* thoughtless ADV carelessly; *(= unachtsam)* thoughtlessly; **~ gekleidet** carelessly dressed

nach|läs|si|ger|wei|se ['na:xlɛsɪgɐ'vaizə] ADV thoughtlessly

Nach|läs|sig|keit F **a** carelessness; *(= Unachtsamkeit)* thoughtlessness **b** **~en** sloppy practices

Nach|lass-: **Nach|lass|pfle|ger(in)** M(F), **Nach|lass|ver|wal|ter(in)** M(F) executor; **Nach|lass|steu|er** F inheritance tax, estate tax *(US)*; **Nach|lass|ver|wal|tung** F administration of the estate

nach+lau|fen VI *sep irreg aux sein +dat* **jdm/einer Sache ~** to run after sb/sth; *(fig auch)* to chase sb/sth; **den Mädchen ~** to chase girls

nach+le|ben VI *sep* **jdm ~** to model one's life on sb's; **einem Ideal ~** to live according to an ideal

nach+le|gen *sep* VT **noch Kohlen/Holz ~** to put some more coal/wood on (the fire); **Geld/ein verbessertes Angebot ~** to come up with extra money/a better offer VI to make up the fire; *(fig)* to come up with something better; **wir müssen ~** *(fig)* we have to do better

Nach|le|se F second harvest; *(= Ährennachlese)* gleaning; *(Ertrag)* gleanings *pl*; *(Liter)* further selection

nach+le|sen *sep irreg* VT **a** *(in einem Buch)* to read; *(= nachschlagen)* to look up; *(= nachprüfen)* to check up; **man kann das in der Bibel ~** it says so in the Bible; **das kannst du bei Goethe ~** you can find it in Goethe **b** *Ähren* to glean; **Beeren/Kartoffeln ~** to gather late berries/potatoes VI **a** *(= nachschlagen)* to look it up; *(= nachprüfen)* to check up **b** *(Agr)* to have a second harvest; *(= Ähren nachlesen)* to glean

nach+lie|fern *sep* VT *(= später liefern)* to deliver at a later date; *(= zuzüglich liefern)* to make a further delivery of; *(inf: = später abgeben) Unterlagen* to hand in later; *(fig) Begründung etc* to give later; **könnten Sie noch 25 Stück ~?** could you deliver another 25? VI to make further deliveries

Nach|lie|fe|rung F delivery; **wir warten auf die ~** we're waiting for the rest to be delivered

nach+lö|sen *sep* VI to pay on the train; *(zur Weiterfahrt)* to pay the extra VT *Fahrkarte* to buy on the train; *(zur Weiterfahrt)* to buy another

nachm. *abbr von* **nachmittags** p.m.

nach+ma|chen VT *sep* **a** *(= nachahmen)* to copy; *(= nachäffen)* to take off *(Brit)*, to mimic; **sie macht mir alles nach** she copies everything I do; **das mach mir mal einer nach!, das macht mir so schnell keiner nach!, das soll erst mal einer ~!** I'd like to see anyone else do that! **b** *(= fälschen) Unterschrift* to forge; *Geld* to forge, to counterfeit; *(= imitieren)* to copy → *auch* **nachgemacht** **c** *(inf: = nachholen)* to make up; **er hat das Abitur in der Abendschule nachgemacht** ≈ he did A levels at night school *(Brit)*, ≈ he completed his high school diploma at night school *(US)*

nach+ma|len VT *sep* to copy; *(= übermalen)* to touch up

nach|ma|lig ['na:xma:lıç] ADJ *(old)* **der ~e Präsident** the future president; **der ~e Präsident X** President X, as he was to become

nach|mals ['na:xma:ls] ADV *(old)* later, subsequently

nach+mes|sen *sep irreg* VT to measure again; *Temperatur* to take again; *(= prüfend messen)* to check VI to check

Nach|mie|ter(in) M(F) next tenant; **unser ~** the tenant after us; **wir müssen einen ~ finden** we have to find someone to take over the apartment *etc*

nach|mit|tag △ ['na:xmıta:k] ADV → **Nachmittag**

Nach|mit|tag ['na:xmıta:k] M afternoon; **am ~** in the afternoon; **gestern/morgen/heute ~** yesterday/tomorrow/Tuesday/this afternoon; **am heutigen ~** this afternoon; **am ~ des 14. Oktober** on the afternoon of October 14th; **den ganzen ~** (for) the whole afternoon; **im Laufe** *or* **während des ~s** during *or* in the course of the afternoon; *(heute)* some time this afternoon; **vom ~ an** from about two o'clock; **bis zum ~** till the afternoon; **des ~s** *(geh)* in the afternoon → **Dienstagnachmittag** *etc*

nach|mit|tä|gig ['na:xmıtɛ:gıç] ADJ *attr* afternoon

nach|mit|täg|lich ['na:xmıtɛ:glıç] ADJ *no pred* afternoon *attr* ADV in the afternoon; **die ~ stattfindenden Kurse** the afternoon courses

nach|mit|tags ['na:xmıta:ks] ADV in the afternoon; *(= jeden Nachmittag)* in the afternoon(s); **von ~ an** from about two o'clock; **dienstags ~** every Tuesday afternoon, on Tuesday afternoons; **er isst immer erst ~** he never eats till (the) afternoon → **dienstagnachmittags** *etc*

Nach|mit|tags-: **Nach|mit|tags|schlaf** M **~ halten** to have a sleep after lunch; **Nach|mit|tags|schläf|chen** NT *(inf)* **sein ~ halten** to have one's afternoon nap, to have one's postprandial snooze *(Brit hum)*; **Nach|mit|tags|sen|dung** F *(TV)* afternoon programme *(Brit)* or program *(US)*, afternoon show *(esp US)*; **Nach|mit|tags|stun|de** F hour of the afternoon; **Nach|mit|tags|vor|stel|lung** F matinée (performance)

Nach|mus|te|rung F *(Mil)* medical re-examination

Nach|nah|me ['na:xna:mə] F **-, -n** cash *or* collect *(US)* on delivery, COD; *(inf: = Nachnahmesendung)* COD parcel *(esp Brit) or* package; **etw als** *or* **per ~ schicken** to send sth COD

Nach|nah|me-: **Nach|nah|me|ge|bühr** F COD charge; **Nach|nah|me|sen|dung** F COD parcel *(esp Brit) or* package

Nach|na|me M surname, family *or* last name; **wie heißt du mit ~n?** what is your surname?

nach+neh|men VTI *sep irreg* to take (some) more

nach+plap|pern VT *sep* to repeat parrot-fashion; **jdm alles ~** to repeat everything sb says parrot-fashion

Nach|por|to NT excess (postage)

nach+prä|gen VT *sep (= nachträglich prägen)* to mint *or* strike some more; *(= fälschen)* to forge; **es wurden 200 Stück nachgeprägt** a further 200 copies were struck

nach|prüf|bar ADJ verifiable; **die Ergebnisse sind jederzeit ~** the results can be verified *or* checked at any time ADV *(= nachweislich) wahr, falsch* demonstrably; **was er sagte, war ~ wahr** what he said could be proved *(Brit) or* proven to be true

Nach|prüf|bar|keit ['na:xpry:fba:ɐkait] F **-**, *no pl* verifiability

nach+prü|fen *sep* VT **a** *Aussagen, Tatsachen* to verify, to check **b** *Kandidaten (= nochmals prüfen)* to re-examine; *(= später prüfen)* to examine at a later date VI to check

Nach|prü|fung F **a** *(von Aussagen, Tatsachen)* check (*+gen* on); **bei der ~ der Meldungen** when the reports were checked **b** *(= nochmalige Prüfung)* re-examination; *(Termin)* resit; *(= spätere Prüfung)* later examination

nach+ra|sen VI *sep aux sein +dat* to race *or* chase after

nach+rech|nen VTI *sep* to check; **rechne noch einmal nach!** you'd better do your sums again, you'd better check your arithmetic

Nach|re|de F **a** *(= Verunglimpfung)* **üble ~** *(Jur)* defamation of character; **jdn in üble ~ bringen** to damage sb's reputation, to bring sb into ill repute; **üble ~ über jdn verbreiten** *or* **führen** to cast aspersions on sb's character; **in üble ~ geraten** *or* **kommen** to get a bad reputation **b** *(= Epilog)* epilogue *(Brit)*, epilog *(US)*

nach+re|den VT *sep* **a** *(= wiederholen)* to repeat; **er redet dir alles nach** he repeats everything you say **b** **jdm (etwas) Übles/Schlechtes ~** to speak ill/badly of sb

Nach|red|ner(in) M(F) later *or* subsequent speaker; **mein ~** the speaker after me

nach+rei|chen VT *sep* to hand in later

Nach|rei|fe F after-ripening

nach+rei|fen VI *sep aux sein* to after-ripen

nach+rei|sen VI *sep aux sein* **jdm ~** to follow sb

nach+rei|ten VI *sep irreg aux sein +dat* to ride after

nach+ren|nen VI *sep irreg aux sein (inf)* = **nachlaufen**

Nach|richt ['na:xrıçt] ✪ 27.6, 51.3, 51.4 F **-, -en** **a** *(= Mitteilung, Botschaft)* message *(auch Comput)*; *(= Meldung)* (piece of) news *sing*; **eine ~** a message; some news *sing*, a piece of news *sing*; **die ~en** the news *sing (auch Rad, TV)*; **~en aus Politik und Kultur** news from the world of politics and culture; **~en hören** to listen to the news; **„Sie hören ~en"** "this *or* here is the news"; **das sind aber schlechte ~en** that's bad news; **wer teilt ihm diese unangenehme ~ mit?** who's going to break this unpleasant (piece of) news to him?; **die letzte ~ von ihm kam aus Indien** the last news of him was from India; **~ erhalten, dass ...** to receive (the) news that ...; **wir geben Ihnen ~** we'll let you know **b** *(= Bestätigung)* confirmation; **wir sind bezüglich unserer Bestellung immer noch ohne ~** we are still awaiting confirmation of our order

Nach|rich|ten-: **Nach|rich|ten|agen|tur** F news agency; **nach|rich|ten|arm** ADJ **in ~en Monaten** in the silly season *(Brit) or* off season *(US)*; **Nach|rich|ten|bü|ro** NT news agency; **Nach|rich|ten|dienst** M **a** *(Rad, TV)* news service **b** *(Pol, Mil)* intelligence (service); **nach|rich|ten|dienst|lich** ADJ *Erkenntnisse, Tätigkeit, Mittel etc* intelligence *attr*; *Vorschriften etc* intelligence service *attr* ADV **~ erfasst sein** to be on the files of the intelligence service; **~ beobachtet werden** to be under surveillance; **Nach|rich|ten|ma|ga|zin** NT news magazine; **Nach|rich|ten|re|dak|ti|on** F news department *or* room; **wie wir von der ~ erfahren, ...** as we hear from the news desk, ...; **Nach|rich|ten|sa|tel|lit** M (tele)communications satellite; news satellite; **Nach|rich|ten|sen|der** M *(Rad, TV)* news station; *(TV auch)* news channel; **Nach|rich|ten|sper|re** F news blackout *or* embargo; **Nach|rich|ten|spre|cher(in)** M(F) newsreader, newscaster; **Nach|rich|ten|tech|nik** F telecommunications *sing*; **Nach|rich|ten|über|mitt|lung** F communication; **Nach|rich|ten|ver|bin|dung** F line of communication (*zu* with, to); **Nach|rich|ten|we|sen** NT communications *pl*

nach|richt|lich ['na:xrıçtlıç] ADJ *Sendung etc* news *attr* ADV *(form)* **~ an** *+acc* copy to

nach+rü|cken VI *sep aux sein* to move up; *(auf Stelle, Posten)* to succeed *(auf +acc* to); *(Mil)* to advance; **dem Feind/nach Hanoi ~** to advance on the enemy/on Hanoi

Nach|rü|cker ['na:xrʏkɐ] M **-s, -**, **Nach|rü|cke|rin** [-ərın] F **-, -nen** successor, replacement

Nach|rü|cker|pha|se F period of succession, transition period

Nach|ruf M obituary

nach+ru|fen VTI *sep irreg +dat* to shout after

Nach|ruhm M fame after death

nach+rüh|men VT *sep* **jdm etw ~** to praise sb for sth

nach+rüs|ten *sep* VI *(Mil)* to deploy new arms; *(= modernisieren)* to modernize VT *Kraftwerk etc* to modernize; **ein Auto mit einem Airbag/einen Computer mit einer Soundkarte ~** to fit a car with an air bag/a computer with a sound card

Nach|rüst|satz M *(Aut)* additional components *pl*; *(von Spiel)* supplement

Nach|rüs|tung F **a** *(Mil)* deployment of new arms; *(= Modernisierung)* arms modernization **b** *(Tech) (von Kraftwerk etc)* modernization; *(von Auto etc)* refit

Nach|rüs|tungs-: **Nach|rüs|tungs|ab|kom|men** NT *(Mil)* agreement to deploy new arms; **Nach|rüs|tungs|be|schluss** M *(Mil)* decision to deploy new arms

nach+sa|gen VT *sep* **a** *(= wiederholen)* to repeat; **jdm alles ~** to repeat everything sb says; **das ist kein Grund für dich, es nachzusagen** that's no reason for you to say it too **b** **jdm etw ~** to attribute sth to sb; **jdm Schlechtes ~** to speak ill of sb; **man kann ihr nichts ~** you can't say anything against her; **ihm wird nachgesagt, dass ...** it's said that he ...; **das kannst du mir nicht ~** you can't accuse me of that; **das lasse ich mir nicht ~!** I'm not having that said of me!

Nach|sai|son F off season

nach+sal|zen *sep irreg* VT to add more salt to VI to add more salt

Nach|satz M **a** *(= Nachschrift)* postscript; *(= Nachtrag)* afterthought; **in einem ~ sagte er, dass ...** he added, as an afterthought, that ... **b** *(Gram)* clause in sentence final position

nach+schaf|fen VT *sep irreg* to reproduce

nach+schau|en VTI *sep (esp dial)* = **nachsehen VI VT a**

nach+schen|ken VTI *sep* **jdm etw ~** to top sb up *(Brit) or* off *(US)* with sth; **darf ich Ihnen noch (etwas) ~?** may I top you up *(Brit) or* off *(US)*?, may I top up *(Brit) or* off *(US)* your glass/cup/mug?, may I give you a refill?; **darf ich (dir) noch etwas Wein ~?** can I give you a little *or* a drop more wine?

nach+schi|cken VT *sep* to send on, to forward; **bitte ~!** please forward

nach+schie|ben VT *sep irreg (inf) Erklärung, Begründung etc* to provide afterwards; **einer Sache** *(dat)* **etw ~** to follow sth up with sth; **nachgeschobene Gründe** rationalizations

nach+schie|ßen *sep irreg* VI **a** *(Ftbl)* to shoot again **b** *(inf: = Geld nachschießen)* to add something to it VT *(inf) Geld* to add (to it)

Nach|schlag M **a** *(inf)* second helping **b** *(Mus)* nachschlag *(spec, turn ending a trill)*; **freier ~** *any grace note following the main note*

nach+schla|gen *sep irreg* VT *Stelle, Zitat, Wort* to look up VI **a** *aux sein (= ähneln)* **jdm ~** to take after sb **b** *(in Lexikon)* to look **c** *(Ftbl) (= sich revanchieren)* to retaliate; *(von hinten foulen)* to foul (one's opponent) from behind

Nach|schla|ge|werk NT reference book *or* work

nach+schlei|chen VI *sep irreg aux sein +dat* to creep after

nach+schlei|fen VT *sep (= hinterherschleifen)* to drag along

nach+schlei|fen VT *sep irreg* **eine Linse ~** to grind a lens a little more; **ein Messer ~** to sharpen up a knife

nach+schlep|pen VT *sep* **jdm etw ~** to lug sth after *(Brit) or* behind sb

nach+schleu|dern VT *sep (fig)* **jdm etw ~** to fling *or* hurl sth after sb *(Brit) or* at sb's back *(US)*

Nach|schlüs|sel M duplicate key; *(= Dietrich)* skeleton key

nach+schmei|ßen VT *sep irreg (inf)* **jdm etw ~** to fling sth after sb *(Brit) or* at sb's back *(US)*; **das ist ja nachgeschmissen!** it's a real bargain

nach+schmin|ken VT *sep* **sich ~** to touch up one's make-up

nach+schnei|den VT *sep irreg Haare* to recut

nach+schnüf|feln VI *sep (inf)* to poke *or* sniff around *(inf)*; **jdm ~** to spy on sb

nach+schrei|ben VT *sep irreg (= nachträglich schreiben)* to write later; *(= abschreiben)* to write out

Nach|schrift F *(= Protokoll)* transcript; *(= Zugefügtes) (abbr* **NS***)* postscript, PS; **er hat eine ~ der Vorlesung angefertigt** he wrote up the lecture afterwards

Nach|schub M *(Mil)* supplies *pl (an +dat* of*)*; *(Material)* reinforcements *pl*

Nach|schub- *(Mil)*: **Nach|schub|ba|sis** F supply base; **Nach|schub|li|nie** F supply line; **Nach|schub|weg** M supply route

Nach|schu|lung F further training; *(= Kurs, Lehrgang)* further training course

Nach|schuss M **a** *(Comm)* additional payment; *(St Ex)* marginal call **b** *(Ftbl)* second shot

nach+schüt|ten VT *sep Kies, Sand* to pour in (some) more; *Kohlen* to put on (some) more; *(inf: = nachgießen)* to pour (some) more

nach+schwat|zen, *(S Ger, Aus)* **nach+schwät|zen** VT *sep (inf)* = **nachplappern**

nach+schwin|gen VI *sep irreg* = **nachklingen**

nach+se|hen *sep irreg* VI **a** **jdm/einer Sache ~** to follow sb/sth with one's eyes, to watch sb/sth; *(= hinterherschauen)* to gaze after sb/sth **b** *(= gucken)* to have a look (and see), to look and see; *(= nachschlagen)* to (have a) look; **in der Schublade ~** to (have a) look in the drawer VT **a** to (have a) look at; *(= prüfen)* to check; *Schulaufgaben etc (= durchsehen)* to read through, to check; *(= korrigieren)* to mark; *(= nachschlagen)* to look up **b** *(= verzeihen)* **jdm etw ~** to forgive sb (for) sth

Nach|se|hen NT **das ~ haben** to be left standing; *(= keine Chance haben)* not to get a look-in *(inf)*, not to get anywhere; *(= nichts bekommen)* to be left empty-handed

Nach|sen|de-: **Nach|sen|de|an|schrift** F forwarding address; **Nach|sen|de|an|trag** M *application to have one's mail forwarded*; **Nach|sen|de|auf|trag** M *application to have one's mail forwarded or redirected*

nach+sen|den VT *sep irreg* to forward; **bitte ~!** please forward

nach+set|zen *sep* VI **jdm ~** to pursue sb VT **a** *Fuß* to drag **b** = **nachstellen VT a**

Nach|sicht ['na:xzɪçt] F -, *no pl (= Milde)* leniency, clemency; *(= Geduld)* forbearance; **er wurde ohne ~ bestraft** he was punished without mercy; **er kennt keine ~** he knows no mercy; **~ üben** to be lenient/forbearing; **mit jdm/etw (keine) ~ haben** to make (no) allowances for sb/sth; **jdn mit ~ behandeln** to show leniency or clemency to sb; *(= geduldig)* to be forbearing with sb; **jdn um ~ bitten** to ask sb to be lenient/forbearing

nach|sich|tig ['na:xzɪçtɪç], **nach|sichts|voll** ADJ *(= milde)* lenient; *(= geduldig)* forbearing *(gegen, mit* with*)* ADV leniently; **~ mit jdm umgehen** to be understanding with sb; **jdn ~ behandeln** to be lenient with sb

Nach|sich|tig|keit F -, *no pl* = **Nachsicht**

Nach|sil|be F suffix

nach+sin|gen VT *sep irreg* to sing

nach+sin|nen VI *sep irreg* to ponder *(über +acc* over, about*)*

nach+sit|zen VI *sep irreg (Sch)* **~ (müssen)** to be kept in, to have detention; **jdn ~ lassen** to keep sb in, to give sb detention

Nach|som|mer M Indian summer

Nach|sor|ge F *(Med)* aftercare

Nach|sor|ge|kli|nik F aftercare clinic

nach+spä|hen VI *sep* **jdm ~** to watch sb closely

Nach|spann ['na:xʃpan] M **-s, -e** credits *pl*

Nach|spei|se F dessert, sweet *(Brit)*; **als ~** for dessert

Nach|spiel NT *(Theat)* epilogue *(Brit)*, epilog *(US)*; *(Mus)* closing section, postlude *(form)*; *(fig)* sequel; **das geht nicht ohne ~ ab** that's bound to have repercussions; **das wird noch ein (unangenehmes) ~ haben** that will have (unpleasant) consequences; **ein gerichtliches ~ haben** to have legal repercussions

nach+spie|len *sep* VT to play VI *(Sport)* to play stoppage time *(Brit) or* overtime *(US)*; *(wegen Verletzungen)* to play injury time *(Brit) or* injury overtime *(US)*; **der Schiedsrichter ließ ~** the referee allowed stoppage time/injury time *(Brit)*, the referee allowed (injury) overtime *(US)*

Nach|spiel|zeit F *(Sport) (wegen Unterbrechung)* stoppage time; *(wegen Verletzungen)* injury time

nach+spi|o|nie|ren *ptp* **nachspioniert** VI *sep (inf)* **jdm ~** to spy on sb

nach+spre|chen *sep irreg* VT to repeat; **jdm etw ~** to repeat sth after sb VI **wir mussten ihm ~** we had to repeat what he said

nach+spü|len VTI *sep* to rinse; **ein Bier zum Nachspülen** *(inf)* a beer to wash it down

nach+spü|ren VI *sep +dat* to track *or* hunt down; *einem Tier* to track; *einer Fährte* to follow; *einem Verbrechen, Fehler* to go *or* look into

nächst [nɛ:çst] PREP *+dat (geh) (örtlich)* next to, beside; *(= außer)* apart *or* aside from

nach+star|ren VI *sep irreg* **jdm ~** to stare after sb; **er starrte ihr einfach nach** he couldn't take his eyes off her

nächst|bes|te ['nɛ:çst'bɛstə] ADJ *attr* **der ~ Zug/Job** the first train/job that comes along; **der/die/das Nächstbeste ...** the first ... I/you *etc* see; **das Nächstbeste (zu tun) wäre ...** the first thing to do would be ...

nach+ste|hen VI *sep irreg* **jdm/etw ~** to take second place to sb/sth; **keinem ~** to be second to none *(in +dat* in*)*; **jdm in nichts** *(dat)* **~** to be sb's equal in every way; **jdm an Intelligenz** *(dat)* **nicht ~** to be every bit as intelligent as sb

nach|ste|hend ADJ *attr Bemerkung, Ausführungen* following; *(Gram)* postpositive *(form)*; **im Nachstehenden** below, in the following; **im Nachstehenden der Kläger genannt** here(in)after referred to as the plaintiff; **Nachstehendes müssen Sie beachten** you must take note of the following; **das ~e Adjektiv** the adjective which follows the noun ADV *(= weiter unten)* below

nach+stei|gen VI *sep irreg aux sein* **jdm ~** *(lit)* to climb up after sb; *(fig inf)* to run after *or* chase sb

nach+stel|len *sep* VT **a** *(Gram)* **nachgestellt** postpositive; **im Französischen wird das Adjektiv (dem Substantiv) nachgestellt** in French the adjective is put after the noun **b** *(Tech) (= neu einstellen)* to adjust; *(= zurückstellen)* to put back **c** **einen Vorfall/den Unfallhergang ~** to reconstruct an incident/the accident; **eine Szene ~** to recreate a scene; **etw in einem Roman ~** to reproduce sth in a novel VI **jdm ~** to follow sb; *(= aufdringlich umwerben)* to pester sb; **einem Tier ~** to hunt an animal

Nach|stel|lung F **a** *(Gram)* postposition *(form)* **b** *(Tech)* adjustment; *(= Zurückstellung)* putting back **c** *usu pl (old) (= Verfolgung)* pursuit *no pl*; *(= Aufdringlichkeit)* pestering *no pl*; *(= Versuchung)* temptation, snare

Nächs|ten|lie|be F brotherly love; *(= Barmherzigkeit)* compassion; **~ üben** to love one's neighbour *(Brit) or* neighbor *(US)* as oneself → **Mantel c**

nächs|tens ['nɛ:çstns] ADV **a** *(= das nächste Mal)* (the) next time; *(= bald einmal)* some time soon, before long **b** *(= am Ende)* next

Nächs|te(r) ['nɛ:çstə] MF *decl as adj* **a** next one; **der ~, bitte** next please, first please *(US, Scot)* **b** *(fig: = Mitmensch)* neighbour *(Brit)*, neighbor *(US)*; **jeder ist sich selbst der ~** *(Prov)* charity begins at home *(Prov)*; **du sollst deinen ~n lieben wie dich selbst** *(Bibl)* (thou shalt) love thy neighbo(u)r as thyself

nächs|te(r, s) ['nɛ:çstə] ADJ *superl von* **nah(e)** **a** *(= nächstgelegen)* nearest; **der ~ Nachbar/das ~ Telefon** the nearest neighbour *(Brit) or* neighbor *(US)*/telephone; **ist dies der ~ Weg zum Bahnhof?** is this the shortest *or* quickest way to the station?; **in ~r Nähe** in the immediate vicinity; **in ~r Entfernung** not far away; **aus ~r Entfernung** *or* **Nähe** from close by; *sehen, betrachten* at close quarters; *schießen* at close range

b *(= unmittelbar folgend)* next; **im ~n Haus** next door

c *(zeitlich)* next; **~s Mal** next time; **bis zum ~n Mal!** till the next time!, see you (some time)!; **Dienstag ~r Woche** Tuesday next week; **Ende ~n Monats** at the end of next month; **am ~n Morgen/Tag(e)** (the) next morning/day; **~r Tage, in den ~n Tagen** in the next few days; **bei ~r** *or* **bei der ~n Gelegenheit** at the earliest opportunity; **in ~r Zukunft** in the near future; **in den ~n Jahren** in the next few years; **in ~r Zeit** some time soon

d *Angehörige, Freunde etc* closest; **die ~n Verwandten** the immediate family; **der ~ Angehörige** the next of kin

e *(in Adverbialkonstruktionen)* **am ~n** closest; *(räumlich auch)* nearest

Nächs|te(s) ['nɛ:çstə] NT *decl as adj* **das ~** the next thing; *(= das erste)* the first thing; **als ~s** next/first; **das ~ wäre, ...** the next/first thing *or* step would be ...; **fürs ~** for the time being

nächst-: **nächst|fol|gend** ADJ *attr* next; **nächst|ge|le|gen** ADJ *attr* nearest; **nächst|hö|her** ['nɛ:çst'hø:ɐ] ADJ *attr* one higher; **die ~e Klasse** one class higher; **nächst|jäh|rig** ['nɛ:çstjɛ:rɪç] ADJ *attr* next year's; **nächst|lie|gend** ['nɛ:çstli:gnt] ADJ *attr (lit)* nearest; *(fig)* most obvious; **das Nächstliegende** the most obvious thing (to do); **nächst|mög|lich** ['nɛ:çst'mø:klɪç] ADJ *attr* next possible; **zum ~en Zeitpunkt/Termin** at the earliest possible date

nach+stre|ben VI *sep (geh)* **jdm ~** to emulate sb; **einer Sache ~** to strive after sth

nach+stür|zen VI *sep aux sein (Geröll)* to cave in; **jdm ~** *(fig)* to dash *or* rush after sb

nach+su|chen VI *sep* **a** *(= suchen)* to look; **such mal nach, ob ...** (have a) look and see if ... **b** *(form: = beantragen)* **um etw ~** to request sth *(bei jdm* of sb*)*, to apply for sth *(bei jdm* to sb*)*

Nach|su|chung ['na:xzu:xʊŋ] F -, -en *(form)* application (*um* for), request (*um* for)

nacht △ [naxt] ADV → **Nacht**

Nacht [naxt] F -, ⸗e ['nɛçtə] *(lit, fig)* night; **es wird/ist/war ~** it's getting/it is/it was dark; **heute ~** tonight; *(= letzte Nacht)* last night; **12 Uhr ~** *(Aus)* midnight; **als die ~ hereinbrach** at nightfall, as night fell; **in der** *or* **bei ~** at night; **in der ~ vom 12. zum 13. April** during the night of April 12th to 13th; **in der ~ auf** *or* **zum Dienstag** during Monday night; **diese ~** tonight; **des ~s** *(geh)* at night; **spät in der ~** late in the *or* at night; **in tiefster ~** at dead of night; **bis tief in die ~ arbeiten, bis in die späte ~ arbeiten** to work late *or* far into the night; **vor der ~** *(S Ger)* before evening; **über ~** *(lit, fig)* overnight; **über ~ bleiben** to stay the night; **zu(r) ~ essen** *(S Ger, Aus)* to have supper; **sich** *(dat)* **die ~ um die Ohren schlagen** *(inf)* to make a night of it; **die ~ zum Tage machen** to stay up all night (working *etc*); **eines ~s** one night; **letzte** *or* **vergangene ~** last night; **ganze Nächte** for nights (on end); **die ganze ~ (lang)** all night long; **vier Nächte lang** for four nights; **gute ~!** good night!; **na, dann gute ~!** *(inf)* what a prospect!, what an outlook!; **bei ~ und Nebel** *(inf)* at dead of night; **die ~ des Wahnsinns/der Barbarei/des Krieges** *(liter)* the darkness of insanity/barbarism/war *(liter)*; **es wurde ~ über Deutschland** *(liter)* the sun went down on Germany *(liter)*; **die ~ hat (viele) Augen** *(prov)* the night has a thousand eyes → **Dienstagnacht** *etc*

nach+tan|ken *sep* **VI** to get some more petrol *(Brit) or* gas *(US)* **VT** **fünf Liter ~** to put in another five litres *(Brit) or* liters *(US)*

Nacht- *in cpds* night; **nacht|ak|tiv** ADJ *(Zool)* nocutrnal; **Nacht|ar|beit** F night-work; **Nacht|asyl** NT night shelter; **Nacht|aus|ga|be** F late final (edition); **nacht|blind** ADJ nightblind; **Nacht|blind|heit** F night blindness; **Nacht|bus** M night bus; **Nacht|club** M night club; **Nacht|dienst** M *(von Person)* night duty; *(von Apotheke)* all-night service; **~ haben** *(Person)* to be on night duty; *(Apotheke)* to be open all night

Nach|teil ['na:xtail] ✪ 53.3, 53.4 M -(e)s, -e disadvantage; *(= Schaden auch)* detriment; **~e von** *or* **durch etw haben** to lose by sth; **jdm ~e bringen** to bring sb disadvantages, to be disadvantageous to sb; **im ~ sein, sich im ~ befinden** to be at a disadvantage (*jdm gegenüber* with sb); **daraus entstanden** *or* **erwuchsen ihm ~e** this brought its disadvantages for him; **der ~, allein zu leben** the disadvantage of living alone; **er hat sich zu seinem ~ verändert** he has changed for the worse; **das soll nicht Ihr ~ sein** you won't lose by it; **zu jds ~** to sb's disadvantage/detriment

nach|tei|lig ['na:xtailɪç] **ADJ** *(= ungünstig)* disadvantageous; *(= schädlich)* detrimental; **es ist nichts Nachteiliges über ihn bekannt** nothing unfavourable *(Brit) or* unfavorable *(US)* is known about him **ADV** *behandeln* unfavourably *(Brit)*, unfavorably *(US)*; **er hat sich sehr ~ über mich geäußert** he spoke very unfavo(u)rably about me; **sich ~ auf etw** *(acc)* **auswirken** to have a detrimental effect on sth

näch|te|lang ['nɛçtəlaŋ] ADV night after night, for nights (on end)

nach|ten ['naxtn] VI *impers (Sw, poet)* **es nachtet** it's growing dark, darkness *or* night is falling

Nacht-: **Nacht|es|sen** NT *(S Ger, Aus)* supper; **Nacht|eu|le** F *(fig inf)* night owl; **Nacht|fal|ter** M moth; **Nacht|flug** M night flight; **Nacht|flug|ver|bot** NT ban on night flights; **Nacht|frost** M night frost; **Nacht|ge|bet** NT evening prayer; **sein** *or* **das ~ sprechen** to say one's bedtime prayers; **Nacht|ge|schirr** NT *(old, hum)* chamber pot; **Nacht|ge|spenst** NT ghost *(that walks at night)*; **Nacht|ge|wand** NT *(geh)* nightrobe; **Nacht|hemd** NT *(für Damen)* nightie, nightdress; *(für Herren)* nightshirt; **Nacht|him|mel** M night sky, sky at night

Nach|ti|gall ['naxtɪgal] F -, -en nightingale; **~, ick hör dir trapsen** *(dial hum)* I see it all now, now I see what you're/he's *etc* after

näch|ti|gen ['nɛçtɪgn] VI *(geh)* to spend the night

Nach|tisch M dessert, sweet *(Brit)*; *(zu Hause)* dessert, sweet *(Brit)*, pudding *(Brit)*

Nacht-: **Nacht|käst|chen** NT *(S Ger, Aus)* bedside table; **Nacht|klub** M night club; **Nacht|la|ger** NT *(= Unterkunft)* place for the night; *(Mil auch)* bivouac; **sein ~ aufschlagen** to settle down *or* to bed down for the night; *(Mil)* to bivouac; **Nacht|le|ben** NT night life

nächt|lich ['nɛçtlɪç] ADJ *attr (= jede Nacht)* nightly; *(= in der Nacht)* night; **die ~e Stadt** the town at night; **zu ~er Stunde** at a late hour; **~e Ausgangssperre** night-time curfew; **~e Ruhestörung** *(Jur) breach of the peace during the night*

Nacht-: **Nacht|lo|kal** NT night club; **Nacht|luft** F night air; **Nacht|mahl** NT *(Aus)* supper; **nacht|mah|len** ['naxtma:lən] VI *insep (Aus)* to have supper; **Nacht|mahr** ['naxtma:ɐ] M -(e)s, -e *(old, liter)* nightmare; **Nacht|mensch** M night person; **Nacht|müt|ze** F nightcap *(lit)*

nach+tö|nen *sep* **VI** *(Glocke)* to resound **VT** *Haare* to recolour, to retint

Nacht-: **Nacht|por|ti|er** M night porter; **Nacht|pro|gramm** NT late-night programme *(Brit) or* program *(US)*; **Nacht|quar|tier** NT **ein ~** somewhere for the night, a place to sleep; **sein ~ aufschlagen** to bed down (for the night)

Nach|trag ['na:xtra:k] M -(e)s, **Nachträge** [-trɛ:gə] postscript; *(zu einem Buch)* supplement

nach+tra|gen VT *sep irreg* **a** *(= hinterhertragen)* **jdm etw ~** *(lit)* to go after sb with sth, to take sth after sb; *(fig)* to hold sth against sb, to bear sb a grudge for sth **b** *(= hinzufügen)* to add; *Summe* to enter up

nach|tra|gend ADJ unforgiving; **er war nicht ~** he didn't bear a grudge

nach|träg|lich ['na:xtrɛ:klɪç] **ADJ** *(= zusätzlich)* additional; *(= später)* later; *(= verspätet)* belated; *(= nach dem Tod)* posthumous **ADV** *(= zusätzlich)* additionally; *(= später)* later; *(= verspätet)* belatedly; *(= nach dem Tod)* posthumously

Nach|trags- *in cpds* supplementary; **Nach|trags|etat** M, **Nach|trags|haus|halt** M *(Pol)* supplementary budget; **Nach|trags|haus|halt** M *(Pol)* supplementary budget

nach+trau|ern VI *sep +dat* to mourn

Nacht|ru|he F night's rest *or* sleep; *(in Anstalten)* lights-out

nachts [naxts] ADV at night; **dienstags ~** (on) Tuesday nights → **dienstagnachts** *etc*

Nacht-: **Nacht|schal|ter** M night desk; **Nacht|schat|ten** M, *no pl (Bot)* nightshade; **Nacht|schat|ten|ge|wächs** NT *(Bot)* solanum *(spec)*; *(fig inf)* night bird; **Nacht|schicht** F night shift; **~ haben** to be on night shift *or* on nights; **nacht|schla|fend** ADJ **bei** *or* **zu ~er Zeit** *or* **Stunde** in the middle of the night; **Nacht|schwär|mer** M *(Zool)* moth; **Nacht|schwär|mer(in)** M(F) *(hum)* night owl; **Nacht|schwes|ter** F night nurse; **Nacht|sicht|ge|rät** NT night vision aid; **Nacht|spei|cher|ofen** M storage heater; **Nacht|strom** M off-peak electricity; **Nacht|stuhl** M *(old)* commode

nachts|über ['naxtsly:bɐ] ADV by night

Nacht-: **Nacht|ta|rif** M *(bei Verkehrsmitteln)* night fares *pl*; *(bei Strom etc)* off-peak rate; **Nacht|tier** NT nocturnal animal; **Nacht|tisch** M bedside table; **Nacht|tisch|lam|pe** F, **Nacht|tisch|leuch|te** F bedside lamp; **Nacht|topf** M chamber pot

nach+tun ['na:xtu:n] VT *sep irreg* **es jdm ~** to copy *or* emulate sb

Nacht-: **Nacht-und-Ne|bel-Ak|ti|on** F cloak-and-dagger operation; **Nacht|vo|gel** M nocturnal *or* night bird; **Nacht|vor|stel|lung** F late-night performance; **Nacht|wa|che** F night watch; *(im Krankenhaus)* night duty; **bei einem Kranken ~ halten** to sit with a patient through the night; **~ haben** to be on night duty *or* on nights; **Nacht|wäch|ter(in)** M(F) *(Hist)* (night) watch; *(in Betrieben etc)* night watchman; *(inf)* dope *(inf)*; **nacht|wan|deln** VI *insep aux sein or haben* to sleepwalk, to walk in one's sleep; **Nacht|wan|de|rung** F night ramble *or* walk; **Nacht|wand|ler** ['naxtvandlɐ] M -s, -, **Nacht|wand|le|rin** [-ərɪn] F -, -nen sleepwalker; **nacht|wand|le|risch** ['naxtvandlərɪʃ] ADJ **mit ~er Sicherheit** with instinctive assurance; **Nacht|zeit** F night-time; **Nacht|zeug** NT night things *pl*; **Nacht|zug** M night train; **Nacht|zu|schlag** M night supplement

Nach|un|ter|su|chung F *(= weitere Untersuchung)* further examination; *(= spätere Untersuchung)* check-up

nach+ver|an|la|gen *ptp* **nachveranlagt** VT *sep (Fin)* **jdn ~** to assess sb further

Nach|ver|an|la|gung F *(Fin, von Steuern)* supplementary assessment

Nach|ver|bren|nung F *(Tech)* after-burning *no pl*

nach+ver|fol|gen *ptp* **nachverfolgt** VT *sep (Comput)* to track

nach+ver|lan|gen *ptp* **nachverlangt** VT *sep* **20 Euro ~** to demand an additional 20 euros

nach+ver|si|chern *ptp* **nachversichert** VT *sep* **Sie müssen neu erworbene Wertgegenstände ~** you must revise your insurance to cover newly-acquired valuables

nach+ver|steu|ern *ptp* **nachversteuert** VT *sep (Fin)* **etw ~** to pay supplementary tax on sth; *Steuerrückstände* to pay back tax on sth

nach|voll|zieh|bar ADJ comprehensible

nach+voll|zie|hen *ptp* **nachvollzogen** VT *sep irreg* to understand, to comprehend

nach+wach|sen VI *sep irreg aux sein* to grow again; **die neue Generation, die jetzt nachwächst** the young generation who are now taking their place in society

nach|wach|send ADJ *Rohstoff* renewable; *Generation* up-and-coming, younger

Nach|wahl F *(Pol)* ≈ by-election

Nach|we|hen PL after-pains *pl*; *(fig)* painful aftermath *sing*

nach+wei|nen VI *sep +dat* to mourn; **dieser Sache weine ich nicht nach** *or* **keine Träne nach** I won't shed any tears over that

Nach|weis ['na:xvais] M -es, -e *(= Beweis)* proof (*+gen, für, über +acc* of); *(= Zeugnis)* certificate; *(= Zahlungsnachweis)* proof of payment (*über +acc* of); **als** *or* **zum ~** as proof; **den ~ für etw erbringen** *or* **führen** *or* **liefern** to furnish proof of sth; **der ~ seiner Bedürftigkeit ist ihm geglückt** he succeeded in proving his need

-nach|weis M *suf in cpds* **a** *(= Vermittlungsstelle)* agency; **Zimmernachweis** accommodation office; **Hotelnachweis** *(von Fremdenverkehrsbüro)* accommodation service **b** *(= Aufstellung)* directory, list; **Zimmernachweis** accommodation list; **Hotelnachweis** hotel directory, list of hotels

nach|weis|bar **ADJ** *(= beweisbar)* provable; *Fehler, Irrtum* demonstrable; *(Tech, Chem)* detectable; **dem Angeklagten ist keinerlei Schuld ~** it cannot be proved that the accused is in any way guilty **ADV** **ich war ~ 500 Kilometer entfernt** it can be proved that I was 500 kilometres *(Brit) or* kilometers *(US)* away; **Sie irren sich ~** it can be proved that you are wrong; **Radioaktivität ist ~ vorhanden** radioactivity is present in detectable amounts

Nach|weis|bar|keit ['na:xvaisba:ɐkait] F -, *no pl (Tech, Chem)* detectability

nach+wei|sen ['na:xvaizn] ✪ 53.4 VT *sep irreg (= beweisen, aufzeigen)* to prove; *Staatsangehörigkeit, Identität auch* to establish proof of; *(Tech, Med)* to detect; **die Polizei konnte ihm nichts ~** the police could not prove anything against him; **dem Angeklagten konnte seine Schuld**

nicht nachgewiesen werden the accused's guilt could not be proved *(Brit)* or proven

nach|weis|lich ['na:xvaislıç] ADJ provable; *Fehler, Irrtum* demonstrable ADV *falsch* demonstrably; **er war ~ in London** it can be proved *(Brit)* or proven that he was in London; **ich habe das ~ nicht gewusst** it can be proved *(Brit)* or proven that I knew nothing about it

Nach|welt F **die ~** posterity

nach+wer|fen VT *sep irreg* **jdm etw ~** *(lit)* to throw sth after *(Brit)* or at sb; **das ist nachgeworfen** *(inf)* that's dirt cheap *(inf)*, that's a gift

nach+wie|gen *sep irreg* VT to weigh again VI to check the weight

nach+win|ken VI *sep* **jdm ~** to wave (goodbye) to sb

Nach|win|ter M late winter

nach+wir|ken VI *sep* to continue to have an effect

Nach|wir|kung F aftereffect; *(fig)* consequence

Nach|wort NT *pl* **-worte** epilogue *(Brit)*, epilog *(US)*

Nach|wuchs M **a** *(fig: = junge Kräfte)* young people *pl*; **es mangelt an ~** there's a lack of young blood; **der wissenschaftliche ~** the new generation of academics, the up-and-coming academics **b** *(hum: = Nachkommen)* offspring *pl*

Nach|wuchs-: **Nach|wuchs|ar|beit** F *(esp Ftbl)* youth development; **Nach|wuchs|au|tor(in)** M(F) up-and-coming young author; **Nach|wuchs|kraft** F junior member of (the) staff; **Nach|wuchs|par|la|men|ta|ri|er(in)** M(F) junior parliamentarian; **Nach|wuchs|schau|spie|ler(in)** M(F) talented young actor/actress; **Nach|wuchs|sor|gen** PL recruitment problems *pl*; **Nach|wuchs|spie|ler(in)** M(F) *(Sport)* junior

nach+wür|zen VTI *sep* to season to taste

nach+zah|len VTI *sep* to pay extra; *(= später zahlen)* to pay later; **20 Euro ~** to pay 20 euros extra

nach+zäh|len VTI *sep* to check

Nach|zah|lung F *(nachträglich)* back-payment; *(zusätzlich)* additional payment

nach+zeich|nen VT *sep Linie, Umriss* to go over; *(fig: = wiedergeben)* to reproduce

Nach|zei|tig|keit ['na:xtsaitıçkait] F **-**, *no pl (Gram)* posteriority

nach+zie|hen *sep irreg* VT **a** *(= hinterherziehen)* **etw ~** to pull or drag sth behind one; **das rechte Bein ~** to drag one's right leg **b** *Linie, Umriss* to go over; *Lippen* to paint over or in; *Augenbrauen* to pencil over or in **c** *Schraube, Seil* to tighten (up) VI **a** *aux sein +dat (= folgen)* to follow **b** *(Schach etc)* to make the next move; *(inf: = gleichtun)* to follow suit

nach+zot|teln VI *sep aux sein (inf)* to lag behind

Nach|zug ['na:xtsu:k] M **a** *(Rail)* relief train **b** *(von Familie, Ehepartner)* joining one's family *(in country of immigration)*; **der ~ wurde nur Kindern unter 10 gestattet** only children under 10 were allowed to join their families

Nach|züg|ler ['na:xtsy:klɐ] M **-s, -**, **Nach|züg|le|rin** [-ərın] F **-, -nen** latecomer, late arrival *(auch fig)*

Na|cke|dei ['nakədai] M **-(e)s, -e** or **-s** *(hum inf)* naked body or person; *(Kind)* little bare monkey *(hum inf)*

Na|cken ['nakn] M **-s, -** (nape of the) neck; **den ~ beugen** *(fig)* to submit; **jdm den ~ steifen** to encourage sb, to back sb up; **jdn im ~ haben** *(inf)* to have sb after one, to have sb on one's tail; **jdm im ~ sitzen** *(inf)* to breathe down sb's neck; **ihm sitzt die Furcht im ~** he's frightened out of his wits *(inf)*; **ihm sitzt der Geiz im ~** he's a stingy so-and-so *(inf)*; **den ~ steifhalten** *(inf)* to stand one's ground, to stand fast; **er hat einen starren/störrischen/unbeugsamen ~** he's an obstinate/hard-headed/unbending character

na|ckend ['naknt] *(inf)* ADJ *Mensch* naked ADV in the nude

Na|cken-: **Na|cken|haar** NT hair at the nape of the neck; **Na|cken|he|bel** M *(Sport)* nelson; **Na|cken|rol|le** F bolster; **Na|cken|schlag** M rabbit punch; *(fig)* hard knock; **Na|cken|schutz** M neck guard; **Na|cken|star|re** F stiffness of the neck; **~ kriegen** to get a stiff neck; **Na|cken|stüt|ze** F *(Aut)* headrest, head restraint

na|ckig ['nakıç], *(Aus)* **na|ckert** (*(inf)* ADJ bare; *Mensch* bare, starkers *pred (Brit inf)* ADV in the nude

nackt [nakt] ADJ **a** *Mensch* naked, nude *(esp Art)*; *Arm, Kinn, Haut etc* bare; *neugeborenes Tier* naked; **einem ~en Mann in die Tasche greifen** *(fig inf)* to look for money where there is none **b** *(= unbewachsen, unbedeckt) Erde, Wand* bare **c** *(fig) (= unverblümt)* naked; *Wahrheit* plain, naked; *Wirklichkeit* stark; *Tatsachen, Zahlen* bare; **mit ~en Worten** without mincing one's words; **die ~e Armut** naked or sheer poverty; **das ~e Leben retten** to escape with one's life ADV *baden, schlafen* in the nude; *tanzen, herumlaufen auch* naked; **er stand ganz ~ da** he was standing there absolutely starkers *(Brit inf)* or stark naked

Nackt-: **Nackt|ba|den** NT **-s**, *no pl* nude bathing, swimming in the nude; **Nackt|ba|de|strand** M nudist beach

Nack|te(r) ['naktə] MF *decl as adj* nude

Nackt-: **Nackt|heit** F **-**, *no pl* nakedness; *(von Mensch auch)* nudity; *(= Kahlheit)* bareness; *(von Landschaft)* starkness, bareness; **Nackt|kul|tur** F nudism, naturism; **Nackt|mo|dell** NT nude model; **Nackt|sa|mer** M **-s, -** *(Bot)* gymnosperm *(spec)*; **Nackt|schne|cke** F slug; **Nackt|tän|zer(in)** M(F) nude dancer

Na|del ['na:dl] F **-, -n** **a** needle; *(von Plattenspieler)* stylus, needle; *(= Stecknadel, Comput: von Drucker)* pin; *(= Häkelnadel)* hook; *(inf: = Spritze)* needle; **mit ~ und Faden umgehen können** to be able to wield a needle and thread; **etw mit heißer ~ nähen** *(fig inf)* to cobble sth together quickly *(inf)*; **nach einer ~ im Heuhaufen suchen** *(fig)* to look for a needle in a haystack; **er sitzt wie auf ~n** *(inf)* he's like a cat on hot bricks *(Brit inf)* or on a hot tin roof; **an der ~ hängen** *(inf)* to be hooked on heroin **b** *(= Haarnadel, Hutnadel, Krawattennadel)* pin; *(= Brosche)* brooch **c** *(= Blattnadel, Eisnadel, Kristallnadel)* needle

Na|del-: **Na|del|ab|wei|chung** F magnetic deviation or declination; **Na|del|ar|beit** F needlework *no pl*; **eine ~** a piece of needlework; **Na|del|baum** M conifer; **Na|del|brief** M packet of needles; **Na|del|büch|se** F pin tin; **Na|del|dru|cker** M dot-matrix printer; **Na|del|ein|fäd|ler** [-lainfɛ:dlɐ] M **-s, -** needle-threader; **Na|del|filz** M needle felting; **na|del|för|mig** ADJ needlelike, needle-shaped; **Na|del|höl|zer** PL conifers *pl*; **Na|del|kis|sen** NT pincushion; **Na|del|kopf** M pinhead

na|deln ['na:dln] VI *(Baum)* to shed (its needles)

Na|del-: **Na|del|öhr** NT eye of a needle; *(fig)* narrow passage → **Kamel**; **Na|del|spit|ze** F point or tip (of a needle); *(Handarbeit)* needlepoint (lace); **Na|del|stär|ke** F size of needle; **Na|del|stich** M prick; *(beim Nähen, Med)* stitch; **jdm ~e versetzen** *(fig)* to needle sb; **eine Politik der ~e** a policy of pinpricks; **Na|del|strei|fen** PL pinstripes *pl*; **Na|del|strei|fen|an|zug** M pinstripe(d) suit; **Na|del|wald** M coniferous forest

Na|dir [na'di:ɐ, 'na:dır] M **-s**, *no pl* nadir

-Nad|ler [na:dlɐ] M *suf* **-s, -** *(Comput inf)* **24-Nadler** 24-pin printer

Na|gel ['na:gl] M **-s, =** ['nɛ:gl] nail *(auch Anat)*; *(= Zwecke)* tack; *(aus Holz)* peg; *(an Schuhen)* hobnail, stud; *(Med)* pin; **sich** *(dat)* **etw unter den ~ reißen** or **ritzen** *(inf)* to pinch *(Brit)* or swipe sth *(inf)*; **etw an den ~ hängen** *(fig)* to chuck sth in *(inf)*; **den ~ auf den Kopf treffen** *(fig)* to hit the nail on the head; **Nägel mit Köpfen machen** *(inf)* to do the job or thing *(inf)* properly → **Sarg, brennen VI**

Na|gel-: **Na|gel|bett** NT *(Anat)* bed of the nail; **Na|gel|boh|rer** M gimlet; **Na|gel|brett** NT *(von Fakir)* bed of nails; **Na|gel|bürs|te** F nailbrush; **Na|gel|fei|le** F nailfile; **na|gel|fest** ADJ → **niet- und nagelfest**; **Na|gel|haut** F cuticle; **Na|gel|haut|ent|fer|ner** [-lɛntfɛrnɐ] M **-s, -** cuticle remover

Nä|gel|kau|en NT **-s**, *no pl* nail-biting

Na|gel-: **Na|gel|knip|ser** [-knıpsɐ] M **-s, -** nail clippers *pl*; **Na|gel|kopf** M head (of a/the nail); **Na|gel|lack** M nail varnish or polish; **Na|gel|lack|ent|fer|ner** [-lɛntfɛrnɐ] M **-s, -** nail varnish remover

na|geln ['na:gln] VT to nail *(an +acc, auf +acc* (on)to); *(Med)* to pin; *(= mit Nägeln versehen)* to hobnail, to stud; *(vulg: = koitieren)* to screw *(sl)*

Na|gel-: **na|gel|neu** ADJ *(inf)* brand new; **Na|gel|pfle|ge** F nail care; **~ machen** to give oneself a manicure; **Na|gel|pro|be** F *(fig)* acid test; **Na|gel|rei|ni|ger** M nail-cleaner; **Na|gel|sche|re** F (pair of) nail scissors *pl*; **Na|gel|schuh** M hobnailed boot; *(= Bergstiefel)* climbing boot; **Na|gel|zan|ge** F nail clippers *pl*; *(Tech)* (pair of) pincers *pl*

na|gen ['na:gn] VI *(lit, fig)* to gnaw *(an +dat* at); *(= knabbern)* to nibble *(an +dat* at); *(Rost, Wasser)* to eat *(an +dat* into); **an einem Knochen ~** to gnaw (on or at) a bone VT to gnaw; **wir haben nichts zu ~ noch zu beißen** *(old)* we've eaten our last crust

na|gend ADJ *Hunger* gnawing; *Zweifel, Gewissen* nagging

Na|ger ['na:gɐ] M **-s, -**, **Na|ge|tier** NT rodent

nah [na:] ADJ ADV = **nahe**

Näh|ar|beit F sewing *no pl*; **eine ~** a piece of sewing

Nah|auf|nah|me F *(Phot)* close-up

Nah|be|reich M **a** *(= unmittelbare Nachbarschaft)* neighbourhood *(Brit)*, neighborhood *(US)*, vicinity; *(= Umgebung)* surroundings *pl*, environs *pl*; *(= Vorstädte)* suburbs *pl*, suburban areas *pl*; **der ~ von München** the Munich area; **Geschäfte/Züge im ~** nearby shops/local trains **b** *(Phot)* close-up range; **im ~** at close range

na|he ['na:ə] ADJ *comp* **näher** ['nɛ:ɐ], *superl* **nächs|te(r, s)** ['nɛ:çstə] **a** *(örtlich)* near *pred*, close *pred*, nearby; **der Nahe Osten** the Middle East; **von Nahem** from close to, at close quarters; **jdm nah sein** to be near (to) sb; **Gott ist uns nah** *(liter)* God is nigh *(liter)*; **Rettung** or **Hilfe ist nah** help is at hand **b** *(zeitlich)* near *pred*, approaching, nigh *(liter) pred*; **die ~ Zukunft** the near future **c** *(= eng) Freund, Beziehung etc* close; **~ Verwandte** close relatives

ADV *comp* **näher**, *superl* **am nächsten** **a** *(örtlich)* ['nɛ:ɐ] near, close; **~ an** near or close to; **nah(e) bei** close to or by, near; **nah beieinander** close together; **nah(e) liegend** *Ort* nearby → *auch* **naheliegend**; **~ vor** right in front of; **von nah und fern** from near and far; **jdm zu nah(e) treten** *(fig)* to offend sb; **jdm/einer Sache zu nah(e) kommen** to get too close to sb/sth; **wir stehen uns (geistig) sehr ~** our views are very close → **daran** **b** *(zeitlich)* **mein Prüfungstermin rückt allmählich nah(e)** my examination is getting close; **Weihnachten steht nah(e) bevor** Christmas is just (a)round the corner, Christmas is almost upon us; **nah(e) bevorstehend** approaching; **sie ist nah an die Achtzig** she's almost or nearing eighty **c** *(= eng)* closely; **nah verwandt** closely-related; **mit jdm nah(e) verwandt sein** to be a near relative of sb's, to be closely related to sb

PREP *+dat* near (to), close to; **der Ohnmacht/dem Wahnsinn** *etc* **nah(e) sein** to be on the verge of fainting/madness *etc*

Nä|he [ˈnɛːə] F -, no pl **a** (örtlich) (= Nahesein) nearness, closeness, proximity; (= Umgebung, Nachbarschaft) vicinity, neighbourhood (Brit), neighborhood (US); **in meiner ~** near me; **in der ~ des Gebäudes** near the building, in the vicinity of the building; **in unmittelbarer ~** (+gen) right next to; **aus der ~** from close to, at close quarters **b** (zeitlich) closeness **c** (emotional etc) closeness

na|he|bei [naːəˈbai] ADV nearby, close to or by

na|he+brin|gen sep irreg +dat, **na|he brin|gen** △ irreg +dat VT (fig) **jdm etw ~** to bring sth home to sb, to impress sth on sb; **jdn jdm ~** to bring sb close to sb

na|he+ge|hen sep irreg aux sein +dat, **na|he ge|hen** △ irreg aux sein +dat VI (fig) to upset

Nah|ein|stel|lung F (Film) close-up (shot)

na|he+kom|men sep irreg aux sein +dat, **na|he kom|men** △ irreg aux sein +dat VI (fig) **jdm ~** (= vertraut werden) to get on close terms with sb, to get close to sb; **jdm/einer Sache ~** (= fast gleichen) to come close or near to sb/sth; **sich** or **einander ~** to become close; **das kommt der Wahrheit schon eher nahe** that is getting nearer the truth → auch **nahe ADV b**

na|he+le|gen sep +dat, **na|he le|gen** △ +dat VT (fig) **jdm etw ~** to suggest sth to sb; **jdm ~, etw zu tun** to advise sb to do sth; **er legte es mir nahe, von mir aus zu kündigen** he put it to me that I should resign

na|he+lie|gen sep irreg (S Ger, Aus, Sw: aux sein), **na|he lie|gen** △ irreg (S Ger, Aus, Sw: aux sein) VI (fig: Idee, Frage, Lösung) to suggest itself; **die Vermutung/die Annahme/der Verdacht liegt nahe, dass ...** it seems reasonable to suppose/assume/suspect that ...; **der Gedanke lag nahe, ihn zum Teilhaber zu machen** the idea of making him a partner seemed to suggest itself

na|he|lie|gend ADJ **a** (fig) (Gedanke, Lösung) which suggests itself; (Verdacht, Vermutung) natural; **aus ~en Gründen** for obvious reasons **b** (räumlich) → **nahe ADV a**

Na|he|lie|gen|de(s) NT decl as adj **das ~ wäre ...** the obvious thing to do would be ...

na|hen [ˈnaːən] VIR aux sein (liter) to approach (jdm/einer Sache sb/sth), to draw near or nigh (liter) (jdm/einer Sache to sb/sth)

nä|hen [ˈnɛːən] VT to sew; (= mit Stichen befestigen auch) to stitch; Kleid to make; Wunde, Verletzten to stitch (up), to suture (spec); **mit der Maschine/mit der** or **von Hand genäht** machine-/ /hand-sewn, sewn by machine/hand; **er musste genäht werden** he had to have stitches → **doppelt ADV, wund** VI to sew

nä|her [ˈnɛːɐ] comp von **nah(e)** ADJ **a** (örtlich) closer, nearer; **jdm/einer Sache ~** closer to sb/ sth, nearer (to) sb/sth; **dieser Weg ist ~** this road is shorter or quicker; **die ~e Umgebung** the immediate vicinity → **Hemd**
b (zeitlich) closer, sooner pred
c (= genauer) Auskünfte, Einzelheiten further attr, more detailed or precise
d (= enger) Verwandter, Bekannter, Beziehungen closer; **die ~e Verwandtschaft** the immediate family
ADV **a** (örtlich, zeitlich) closer, nearer; **~ kommen** or **rücken** to come or draw nearer, to approach; **bitte treten Sie ~** just step up!; (Beamter, Arzt) please come over here
b (= genauer) more closely; besprechen, erklären, ausführen in more detail; **ich habe mir das Bild ~ angesehen** I had a closer look at the picture; **sich mit etw ~ befassen** or **beschäftigen** to go into sth; **jdn/etw ~ kennenlernen** to get to know sb/sth better; **ich kenne ihn nicht ~** I don't know him well; **der Sache** (dat) **~ kommen** to be nearer the mark

Nä|her [ˈnɛːɐ] M -s, -, **Nä|he|rin** [-ərɪn] F -, -nen sewing worker; (Frau auch) seamstress

nä|her+brin|gen sep irreg +dat, **nä|her brin|gen** △ irreg +dat VT (fig) **jdm etw ~** to give sb an understanding of sth

Nä|he|rei [nɛːəˈrai] F -, -en **a** (no pl: = das Nähen) sewing; (= Näharbeit) piece of sewing **b** (Betrieb) sewing works sing or pl; (für Kleider) garment factory

Nä|he|re(s) [ˈnɛːərə] NT decl as adj details pl; (über Stellenangebot etc) further details pl; **alles ~** all details; **~s erfahren Sie von ...** further details from ...; **ich kann mich des ~n nicht entsinnen** (geh) I can't remember the (precise) details

Nah|er|ho|lungs|ge|biet NT recreational area (close to a town)

Nä|he|rin [-ərɪn] F → **Näher**

nä|her+kom|men sep irreg aux sein +dat, **nä|her kom|men** △ irreg aux sein +dat VI (fig) **jdm ~** to get closer to sb; **sie sind sich** or **einander nähergekommen** they've become closer

nä|her+lie|gen sep irreg (S Ger, Aus, Sw: aux sein), **nä|her lie|gen** △ irreg (S Ger, Aus, Sw: aux sein) VI (fig) to be more obvious; (Verdacht auch) to be more natural; **was liegt näher, als ...** what could be more obvious than ...

Nä|her|lie|gen|de(s) NT decl as adj **das ~** the more obvious course

nä|hern [ˈnɛːɐn] VR **sich (jdm/einer Sache) ~** to approach (sb/sth), to get closer (to sb/sth), to draw nearer (to sb/sth); **der Abend näherte sich seinem Ende** the evening was drawing to a close VT to bring or draw closer

nä|her+ste|hen sep irreg (S Ger, Aus, Sw: aux sein) +dat, **nä|her ste|hen** △ irreg (S Ger, Aus, Sw: aux sein) +dat VI (fig) to be closer to

nä|her+tre|ten sep irreg aux sein +dat, **nä|her tre|ten** △ irreg aux sein +dat VI (fig) to get closer to; **ich werde Ihrem Vorschlag ~** (form) I shall give full consideration to your proposal

Nä|he|rung [ˈnɛːərʊŋ] F -, -en (Math) approximation

Nä|he|rungs|wert M (Math) approximate value

na|he+ste|hen sep irreg (S Ger, Aus, Sw: aux sein) +dat, **na|he ste|hen** △ irreg (S Ger, Aus, Sw: aux sein) +dat VI (fig) to be close to; (Pol) to sympathize with; **sich ~** (Menschen, Ideen) to be close; **wir stehen uns (geistig) sehr nahe** our views are very close; **dem Präsidenten ~de Kreise** circles close to the president; **eine der Regierung ~de Zeitung** a pro-government newspaper → auch **nahe ADV b**

na|he|zu [ˈnaːəˈtsuː] ADV nearly, almost, virtually; **das ist ja ~ Wucher** that's little short of profiteering

Näh|fa|den M, **Näh|garn** NT (sewing) cotton (Brit) or thread

Nah|kampf M (Mil) close combat, hand-to-hand fighting

Nah|kampf|mit|tel PL, **Nah|kampf|waf|fen** PL close-range or short-range weapons pl

Näh-: **Näh|käst|chen** NT, **Näh|kas|ten** M workbox, sewing box; **aus dem ~ plaudern** (inf) to give away private details; **Näh|korb** M work basket, sewing basket

nahm pret von **nehmen**

Näh-: **Näh|ma|schi|ne** F sewing machine; **Näh|na|del** F needle

Nah|ost [naːˈlɔst] M **in/aus ~** in/from the Middle East

Nah|ost|kon|flikt M, no pl (Pol) Middle East conflict

nah|öst|lich [naːˈlœstlɪç] ADJ attr Middle East (-ern)

Nähr-: **Nähr|bo|den** M (lit) fertile soil; (für Bakterien) culture medium; (fig) breeding-ground; **ein guter ~** (lit) fertile or good soil or land; **diese Ideen fanden keinen guten ~** these ideas didn't take root; **Nähr|brü|he** F nutrient solution; **Nähr|cre|me** F skin food (Brit), skin-care product

näh|ren [ˈnɛːrən] (geh) VT to feed; (fig) (= steigern) to increase, to feed; Hoffnung to build up; (= haben) Hoffnungen, Zweifel, Verdacht to nurture, to nurse; **er sieht gut genährt aus** he looks well-fed; **das Handwerk nährt seinen Mann** there's a good living to be made as a craftsman; **er nährt den Wunsch, berühmt zu werden** he has fond hopes of becoming famous VR to feed oneself; (Tiere) to feed; **sich von** or **mit etw ~** to live on sth → **Eichhörnchen** VI to be nourishing

nahr|haft ADJ Kost nourishing, nutritious; Boden fertile, rich; **ein ~es Essen** a square meal

Nähr-: **Nähr|kraft** F nutritional value; **Nähr|lö|sung** F nutrient solution; **Nähr|mit|tel** PL cereal products pl; **Nähr|salz** NT nutrient salt; **Nähr|stoff** M usu pl nutrient, nutriment; **nähr|stoff|arm** ADJ low-nutrient attr, low in nutrients pred; **Nähr|stoff|ge|halt** M nutrient content

Nah|rung [ˈnaːrʊŋ] F -, no pl food; **flüssige ~** liquids pl; **feste ~** solids pl; **geistige ~** intellectual stimulation; **keine ~ zu sich** (dat) **nehmen** to take no nourishment; **sie verweigerten jegliche ~** they refused all nourishment; **einer Sache** (dat) **(neue) ~ geben** to help to nourish or feed sth; **dadurch fand** or **erhielt** or **bekam die ganze Sache neue ~** that just added fuel to the fire; **dem Feuer ~ geben** (liter) to build up the fire

Nah|rungs-: **Nah|rungs|auf|nah|me** F eating, ingestion (of food) (form); **die ~ verweigern** to refuse food or sustenance; **Nah|rungs|ket|te** F (Biol) food chain; **Nah|rungs|man|gel** M food shortage

Nah|rungs|mit|tel NT food(stuff)

Nah|rungs|mit|tel-: **Nah|rungs|mit|tel|al|ler|gie** F food allergy; **Nah|rungs|mit|tel|che|mie** F food chemistry; **Nah|rungs|mit|tel|che|mi|ker(in)** M(F) food chemist; **Nah|rungs|mit|tel|in|dust|rie** F, no pl food industry; **Nah|rungs|mit|tel|pro|duk|ti|on** F food production; **Nah|rungs|mit|tel|ver|gif|tung** F food poisoning

Nah|rungs-: **Nah|rungs|quel|le** F source of food; **Nah|rungs|su|che** F search for food; **Nah|rungs- und Ge|nuss|mit|tel|in|dust|rie** F food and allied industries pl; **Nah|rungs|ver|wei|ge|rung** F refusal of food, refusal to eat; **durch ~** by refusing food or to eat

Nähr|wert M nutritional value; **hat das einen praktischen ~?** (inf) does that have any practical value?; **das hat doch keinen (praktischen) ~** (inf) it's pretty pointless

Näh|sei|de F sewing-silk, silk thread

Naht [naːt] F -, **=e** [ˈnɛːtə] seam; (Tech auch) join; (Med) stitches pl, suture (spec); (Anat) suture; **aus allen Nähten platzen** to be bursting at the seams

Näh|tisch M, **Näh|tisch|chen** NT sewing table

naht|los ADJ (lit) Teil, Anzug seamless; (fig) Übergang smooth, imperceptible; Bräune perfect ADV **Vorlesung und Diskussion gingen ~ ineinander über** there was a smooth transition from the lecture to the discussion; **die Diskussion schloss (sich) ~ an den Vortrag an** the discussion followed on smoothly from the lecture; **sich ~ in etw** (acc) **einfügen** to fit right in with sth; **etw ~ fortsetzen** to carry sth on without interruption; **die Aussagen deckten sich ~** the statements concurred exactly; **~ braun** tanned all over

Nah|tod|er|fah|rung F, **Nah|tod|er|leb|nis** NT near-death experience

Naht|stel|le F **a** (Tech) seam, joint **b** (fig) link

Nah|ver|kehr M local traffic; **der öffentliche ~** local public transport; **im ~** on local runs or journeys

Nah|ver|kehrs-: **Nah|ver|kehrs|mit|tel** PL means pl of local transport; **Nah|ver|kehrs|zug** M local train

nah|ver|wandt ADJ → **nahe ADV c**

Näh|zeug NT pl **-zeuge** sewing kit, sewing things pl

Nah|ziel NT immediate aim or objective

na|iv [na'i:f] ADJ naive; **die Naive** *(Theat)* the Ingénue ADV naively; **sich ~ geben** to give the impression of being naive

Na|i|vi|tät [naivi'tɛ:t] F -, *no pl* naivety

Na|iv|ling [na'i:flɪŋ] M -s, - *(inf)* simpleton; **wie kann man bloß so ein ~ sein!** how can anyone be so naive!

Na|ja|de [na'ja:də] F -, -n naiad

Na|me ['na:mə] M -ns, -n, **Na|men** ['na:mən] M -s, - (= *Benennung*) name; *(fig: = Ruf)* name, reputation; **ein angenommener ~** an assumed name; *(von Autoren etc)* a pen name, a nom de plume, a pseudonym; **unter falschem ~n** under a false name; **der volle ~** his/her/their full name; **mit ~n, des ~ns** *(geh)* by the name of, called; **dem ~n nach** by name; **ich kenne das Stück nur dem ~n nach** I've heard of the play but that's all; **dem ~n nach müsste sie Schottin sein** judging by her name she must be Scottish; **auf jds ~n** *(acc)* in sb's name; **unter dem ~n** under the name of; **er war unter dem ~n Schmidt bekannt** he was known under *or* by the name of Schmidt, he was known as Schmidt; **er nannte seinen ~n** he gave his name; **ich möchte keine ~n nennen, aber ...** I don't want to mention any names but ...; **Ihr ~, bitte?** your *or* the name, please?; **wie war doch gleich Ihr ~?** what was the name?; **dazu gebe ich meinen ~n nicht her** I won't lend my name to that; **der ~ tut nichts zur Sache** his/my *etc* name's irrelevant; **einen ~n haben** *(fig)* to have a name; **sich** *(dat)* **(mit etw) einen ~n machen** to make a name for oneself (with sth); **etw beim ~n nennen** *(fig)* to call a spade a spade, to face facts; **im ~n** *(+gen)* on *or* in *(US)* behalf of; **im ~n des Volkes** in the name of the people; **im ~n des Gesetzes** in the name of the law; **in Gottes ~n!** *(inf)* for heaven's sake *(inf)*

Na|men-: **Na|men|ge|bung** [-ge:bʊŋ] F -, -en = **Namensgebung**; **Na|men|ge|dächt|nis** NT memory for names; **Na|men|kun|de** F science of names, onomastics *(spec) sing*; **Na|men|lis|te** F list of names, name list

na|men|los ADJ **a** nameless *(auch fig)*, unnamed; *Helfer* anonymous; **er will ~ bleiben** he wishes to remain anonymous; **die Millionen der Namenlosen** the nameless millions **b** *(geh: = unsäglich)* nameless, unspeakable, unutterable ADV *(geh: = äußerst)* unspeakably, unutterably

na|mens ['na:məns] ADV (= *mit Namen*) by the name of, called, named PREP *+gen (form: = im Auftrag)* in the name of

Na|mens- *in cpds* name; **Na|mens|ak|tie** F *(St Ex)* registered *or* personal share; **Na|mens|än|de|rung** F change of name; **Na|mens|ge|bung** [-ge:bʊŋ] F -, -en naming; **eine unglückliche ~ für eine Ware** an unfortunate choice of name for a product; **Na|mens|lis|te** F list of names, name list; **Na|mens|nen|nung** F naming names; **auf ~ wollen wir doch verzichten** we don't need to name names; **Na|mens|pa|pier** NT *(Fin)* registered security; **Na|mens|pat|ron(in)** M(F) name saint; **Na|mens|recht** NT, *no pl (Jur) law relating to the use of names*; **Na|mens|re|gis|ter** NT list of names, name list; **Na|mens|schild** NT nameplate; **Na|mens|schuld|ver|schrei|bung** F *(Fin)* registered bond; **Na|mens|schwes|ter** F namesake; **Na|mens|tag** M name day, Saint's day

> **NAMENSTAG**
>
> In many regions of Germany, particularly in Catholic regions, a person's **Namenstag** is more important than their birthday. This is the day in the Church calendar dedicated to the saint after whom the person is named. On their name day people receive gifts and celebrate the occasion with family and friends.

Na|mens-: **Na|mens|vet|ter** M namesake; **Na|mens|ver|zeich|nis** NT list of names, name list; **Na|mens|zei|chen** NT initials *pl*; **Na|mens|zug** M signature; (= *Monogramm*) monogram

na|ment|lich ['na:məntlɪç] ADJ by name; **wir bitten, von einer ~en Aufführung der Spender abzusehen** we would request you to refrain from naming the donors; **~e Abstimmung** roll call vote; **~er Aufruf** roll call ADV **a** (= *insbesondere*) (e)specially, in particular, particularly **b** (= *mit Namen*) by name; **~ nicht genannt** not mentioned by name, not mentioned as such; **es wurde ~ abgestimmt** there was a roll call vote

Na|men-: **Na|men|ver|zeich|nis** NT list of names, name list; **Na|men|wech|sel** M change of name

nam|haft ADJ **a** (= *bekannt*) famous, well-known; **~ machen** *(form)* to identify **b** (= *beträchtlich*) considerable, substantial ADV (= *beträchtlich*) considerably, substantially

Na|mi|bia [na'mi:bia] NT -s Namibia

Na|mi|bi|er [na'mi:biɐ] M -s, -, **Na|mi|bi|e|rin** [-ərɪn] F -, -nen Namibian

na|mi|bisch [na'mi:bɪʃ] ADJ Namibian

näm|lich ['nɛ:mlɪç] ADV **a** (= *und zwar*) namely, to wit *(Jur, hum)*; *(geschrieben)* viz; (= *genauer gesagt*) to be exact **b** (= *denn*) since; **..., es ist ~ sehr regnerisch** ... since it's very rainy; **es ging nicht schneller, wir haben ~ einen Umweg machen müssen** we couldn't be any quicker, we had to take a detour you see ADJ **der/die/das Nämliche** *(old)* the same

nann|te *pret von* **nennen**

Na|no-: **Na|no|bot** M *(Tech)* nanobot; **Na|no|gramm** NT nanogram; **Na|no|me|ter** M OR NT nanometer; **Na|no|se|kun|de** F nanosecond; **Na|no|tech|nik** F, **Na|no|tech|no|lo|gie** F nanotechnology

na|nu [na'nu:] INTERJ well I never; **~, wer ist das denn?** hello (hello), who's this?

Na|palm® ['na:palm] NT -s, *no pl* napalm

Na|palm|bom|be F napalm bomb

Napf [napf] M -(e)s, =e ['nɛpfə] bowl

Napf|ku|chen M ≈ ring-shaped pound cake

Naph|tha ['nafta] NT -s *or f* -, *no pl* naphtha

Naph|tha|lin [nafta'li:n] NT -s, *no pl* naphthalene

na|po|le|o|nisch [napole'o:nɪʃ] ADJ Napoleonic

Nap|pa(le|der) ['napa-] NT -(s), -s nappa leather

Nar|be ['narbə] F -, -n **a** *(lit, fig)* scar; (= *Pockennarbe*) pock(mark); **eine ~ hinterlassen** to leave a scar; **die ~ bleibt, auch wenn die Wunde heilt** *(Prov)* deep down, I/you *etc* still bear the scars **b** *(Bot)* stigma **c** (= *Grasnarbe*) turf **d** (= *Ledernarbe*) grain

Nar|ben ['narbn] M -s, - grain

Nar|ben-: **Nar|ben|bil|dung** F scarring; **Nar|ben|ge|sicht** NT scarred face; *(als Name)* scarface

nar|big ['narbɪç] ADJ scarred

Nar|ko|se [nar'ko:zə] F -, -n anaesthesia *(Brit)*, anesthesia *(US)*; **jdm eine ~ geben** to put sb under anaesthetic *(Brit)* or anesthetic *(US)*; **in der ~ liegen** to be under an(a)esthetic; **ohne ~** without an(a)esthetic; **unter ~** under an(a)esthetic; **aus der ~ aufwachen** to come out of the an(a)esthetic

Nar|ko|se-: **Nar|ko|se|ap|pa|rat** M anaesthetic *(Brit)* or anesthetic *(US)* apparatus *no indef art*; **Nar|ko|se|arzt** M, **Nar|ko|se|ärz|tin** F anaesthetist *(Brit)*, anesthesiologist *(US)*; **Nar|ko|se|mas|ke** F anaesthetic *(Brit)* or anesthetic *(US)* mask; **Nar|ko|se|mit|tel** NT anaesthetic *(Brit)*, anesthetic *(US)*; **Nar|ko|se|zwi|schen|fall** M complication during anaesthesia *(Brit)* or anesthesia *(US)*

Nar|ko|ti|kum [nar'ko:tikʊm] NT -s, **Narkotika** [-ka] *(Med)* narcotic

nar|ko|tisch [nar'ko:tɪʃ] ADJ narcotic; *Düfte* overpowering ADV *duften* overpowering; **der süße Geruch wirkte ~ auf uns** the sweet smell had a druglike effect on us

nar|ko|ti|sie|ren [narkoti'zi:rən] *ptp* **narkotisiert** VT *(lit, fig)* to drug

Narr [nar] M -en, -en, **När|rin** ['nɛrɪn] F -, -nen fool; (= *Hofnarr auch*) jester; (= *Teilnehmer am Karneval*) carnival reveller *(Brit)* or reveler *(US)*; **den ~en spielen** to act *or* play the fool; **die ~en werden nicht alle** *(Prov)* there's one born every minute *(inf)*; **jdn zum ~en haben** *or* **halten** to make a fool of sb; **er ist ein verliebter ~** he is love's dupe *or* fool; **dieser verliebte ~** this love-lorn fool → **fressen VT b**

nar|ra|tiv [nara'ti:f] ADJ narrative

nar|ren ['narən] VT *(geh)* **jdn ~** (= *zum Besten haben*) to make a fool of sb, to fool sb; (= *täuschen*) to dupe sb, to fool sb

Nar|ren-: **Nar|ren|frei|heit** F freedom to do whatever one wants; **sie hat bei ihm ~** he gives her (a) free rein; **nar|ren|haft** ADJ foolish ADV foolishly; **Nar|ren|hän|de** PL **~ beschmieren Tisch und Wände** *(Prov)* only fools go around defacing things; **Nar|ren|haus** NT madhouse; **du gehörst ins ~** you need locking up *or* putting away; **Nar|ren|kap|pe** F fool's *or* jester's cap; **nar|ren|si|cher** ADJ ADV foolproof; **Nar|ren|streich** M *(old)* prank; (= *dumme Tat*) act of stupidity; **Nar|ren|zep|ter** NT fool's sceptre *(Brit)* or scepter *(US)*, jester's bauble; **das ~ führen** to carry the fool's sceptre *(Brit)* or scepter *(US)*

Nar|re|tei [narə'tai] F -, -en *(geh)* folly

Narr|heit F -, -en **a** *no pl* folly, stupidity **b** (= *Streich*) prank; (= *dumme Tat*) act of stupidity, stupid thing to do

När|rin ['nɛrɪn] F -, -nen fool

när|risch ['nɛrɪʃ] ADJ foolish, silly; (= *verrückt*) mad; *(inf: = sehr)* madly; **die ~en Tage** *Fasching and the period leading up to it*; **das ~e Treiben** *Fasching celebrations*; **sich wie ~ gebärden** to act like a madman, to act crazy; **ganz ~ auf jdn/etw sein** *(inf)* to be crazy about sb/sth *(inf)*, to be mad (keen) on sb/sth *(Brit inf)* ADV foolishly, silly; **es ~ treiben** to go wild; **sie hüpfte ganz ~ durchs Haus** she was bouncing around the house like crazy *(inf)*

Nar|ziss [nar'tsɪs] M -es, -e *(liter)* Narcissus

Nar|zis|se [nar'tsɪsə] F -, -n narcissus

Nar|ziss|mus [nar'tsɪsmʊs] M -, *no pl* narcissism

Nar|zisst [nar'tsɪst] M -en, -en, **Nar|ziss|tin** [-'tsɪstɪn] F -, -nen *(Psych)* narcissist

nar|ziss|tisch [nar'tsɪstɪʃ] ADJ narcissistic; **~e Persönlichkeitsstörung** *(Med)* narcissistic personality disorder

NASA F -, **Na|sa** ['na:za] F - NASA

na|sal [na'za:l] ADJ nasal; **~er Ton** nasal twang ADV nasally; **~ klingen** to sound nasal

Na|sal [na'za:l] M -s, -e nasal

na|sa|lie|ren [naza'li:rən] *ptp* **nasaliert** VT *(Ling)* to nasalize

Na|sal|laut M nasal (sound)

na|schen ['naʃn] VI to eat sweet things; (= *heimlich kosten*) to pinch *(Brit)* or snitch *(esp US)* a bit *(inf)*; **darf ich mal ~?** can I try a bit?; **an etw** *(dat)* **~** to pinch *(Brit)* or snitch *(esp US)* a bit of sth *(inf)*; (= *anknabbern*) to (have a) nibble at sth; **er hat von allem nur genascht** he had only a taste of everything; **die Kinder haben den ganzen Tag nur genascht** the children have been nibbling all day VT to nibble; **sie nascht gern Süßigkeiten** she has a sweet tooth; **hast du was zum Naschen?** have you got something for my sweet tooth?

Näs|chen ['nɛ:sçən] NT -s, - *dim von* **Nase**

Na|scher ['naʃɐ] M -s, -, **Na|sche|rin** [-ərɪn] F -, -nen nibbler; *(der Süßes mag)* sweet-eater

Na|sche|rei [naʃə'rai] F -, -en **a** *no pl* nibbling; *(von Süßigkeiten)* sweet-eating **b** **Naschereien** PL (= *Süßigkeiten*) sweets and biscuits *pl (Brit)*, candy and cookies *pl (US)*

Nasch-: **nasch|haft** ADJ fond of sweet things; **die Kinder sind so ~** the children are always nibbling at things; **sei nicht so ~** you and your sweet tooth; **Nasch|haf|tig|keit** ['naʃhaftɪkkait] F -, no pl constant snacking; **Nasch|kat|ze** F (inf) guzzler (inf); ich bin halt so eine alte ~ I've got such a sweet tooth; **Nasch|sucht** F craving for sweet things; **Nasch|werk** NT, no pl (old) dainties pl, sweetmeats pl (old)

Na|se ['na:zə] F -, -n **a** (Organ, Sinn, fig) nose; durch die ~ reden to talk through one's nose; mir blutet die ~, meine ~ blutet I've got a nosebleed, my nose is bleeding; jdm die ~ putzen to wipe sb's nose; sich (dat) die ~ putzen (= sich schnäuzen) to blow one's nose; pro ~ (hum) per head; es liegt vor deiner ~ (inf) it's right in front of your nose or right under your nose (inf); wir haben die Weinberge genau vor der ~ (inf) the vine slopes are right on our doorstep; (immer) der ~ nachgehen (inf) to follow one's nose; eine gute ~ für etw haben (inf) to have a good nose for sth; die richtige ~ für etw haben (inf) to have a nose for sth; fass dich an deine eigene ~! (inf) you can (iro) or can't talk!; jdm etw/die Würmer aus der ~ ziehen (inf) to drag sth/it all out of sb; jdm etw unter die ~ reiben (inf) to rub sb's nose or face in sth (inf); die ~ rümpfen to turn up one's nose (über +acc at); jdm auf der ~ herumtanzen (inf) to play sb up (Brit inf), to act up with sb (inf); seine ~ gefällt mir nicht (inf) I don't like his face; es muss nicht immer nach deiner ~ gehen (inf) you can't always have things your way; ihm wurde ein Neuer vor die ~ gesetzt (inf) they put a new man over him; ich sah es ihm an der ~ an (inf) I could see it on his face or written all over his face (inf); auf der ~ liegen (inf) (= krank sein) to be laid up; (= hingefallen sein) to be flat on one's face (inf); steck deine ~ ins Buch! (inf) get on with your book; auf die ~ fallen (lit, fig) or fliegen (fig, inf) to fall flat on one's face; jdm etw vor der ~ wegschnappen (inf) just to beat sb to sth; die Katze hat dem Hund das Futter vor der ~ weggeschnappt the cat took the dog's food away from right under its nose; der Zug fuhr ihm vor der ~ weg (inf) he missed the train by inches or seconds; jdm eine (lange) ~ drehen or machen (inf) to cock a snook at sb (Brit), to thumb one's nose at sb; jdm etw unter die ~ halten to shove sth right under sb's nose (inf); jdn mit der ~ auf etw stoßen (inf: = überdeutlich werden) to make it more than obvious to sb, to (really) spell it out to sb; jdm eins auf die ~ geben (lit) to punch sb on (Brit) or in (US) the nose; (fig) to tell sb what's what, to put sb in his place; sich (dat) eine blutige ~ holen (lit, fig) to get a bloody nose; die ~ voll haben (inf) to be fed up (inf), to have had enough; die ~ von jdm/etw voll haben (inf) to be sick (to death) of sb/sth (inf), to be fed up to the back teeth with sb/sth (Brit inf); jdn an der ~ herumführen to give sb the runaround (inf); (als Scherz) to pull sb's leg; an der ~ herumgeführt werden to get the runaround (inf); jdm etw auf die ~ binden (inf) to tell sb all about sth; jdm auf die ~ binden, dass ... (inf) to tell sb that ...; das werde ich ihm gerade auf die ~ binden (iro) you think I'd tell him that!; er steckt seine ~ in alles (hinein) (inf) he sticks his nose into everything; er sieht nicht weiter als seine ~ (inf) he can't see further than the end of his nose; die ~ vorn haben (inf) to be ahead by a nose; (in Forschung etc auch) to be one step ahead → Mund, Tür, Wind a, hoch 2 b
b (Mech) handle, horn
c (= Farbtropfen) run
d (= Halbinsel) promontory, headland, naze; (= Felsnase) overhang

na|se|lang ADV alle ~ all the time, again and again

nä|seln ['nɛ:zln] VI to talk or speak through one's nose

nä|selnd ADJ Stimme, Ton nasal ADV nasally; ~ sprechen to talk through one's nose

Na|sen-: **Na|sen|af|fe** M proboscis monkey; **Na|sen|at|mung** F breathing through the nose; **Na|sen|bär** M coati; **Na|sen|bein** NT nose bone, nasal bone; **Na|sen|blu|ten** NT -s, no pl ~ haben to have a nosebleed; häufiges ~ frequent nosebleeds; ich habe ~ my nose is bleeding, I have a nosebleed; **Na|sen|flü|gel** M side of the nose; seine ~ fingen an zu zittern his nose or nostrils began to twitch; **Na|sen|höh|le** F nasal cavity; **na|sen|lang** ADV = naselang; **Na|sen|län|ge** F (fig) mit einer or um eine ~ gewinnen to win by a nose; jdm eine ~ voraus sein to be a hair's breadth ahead of sb; **Na|sen|loch** NT nostril; verliebte Nasenlöcher machen (hum) to make eyes; **Na|sen|ring** M (nose) ring; **Na|sen|rü|cken** M bridge of the nose; **Na|sen|schei|de|wand** F nasal septum (spec); **Na|sen|schleim** M nasal mucus; **Na|sen|schleim|haut** F mucous membrane (of the nose); **Na|sen|schmuck** M nose ornament(s pl); **Na|sen|spit|ze** F tip of the/sb's nose; ich seh es dir an der ~ an I can tell by your face, I can see it written all over your face; **Na|sen|spray** M OR NT nasal or nose spray; **Na|sen|stü|ber** [-ʃty:bɐ] M -s, - bump on the nose; jdm einen ~ versetzen (lit) to bash sb on the nose (inf); (fig) to tick (Brit) or tell sb off; **Na|sen|trop|fen** PL nose drops pl; **Na|sen|was|ser** NT ein ~ (inf: = so gut wie nichts) next to nothing; **Na|sen|wur|zel** F bridge (of the nose)

Na|se-: **Na|se|rümp|fen** NT -s, no pl wrinkling (up) or screwing up (Brit) one's nose; auf etw (acc) mit ~ reagieren to turn one's nose up at sth; **na|se|rümp|fend** ADV er sagte ~ ... screwing up (Brit) or wrinkling (up) his nose, he said ...; die ~en Eltern the disapproving parents; **na|se|weis** ['na:zəvais] ADJ cheeky (Brit), fresh (US), saucy; (= vorlaut) forward, precocious; (= neugierig) nosy (inf), inquisitive ADV (= frech) cheekily (Brit), impudently; (= vorlaut) precociously; (= neugierig) nosily; **Na|se|weis** ['na:zəvais] M -es, -e (= Vorlauter) cheeky (Brit) or precocious brat or monkey (inf); (= Neugieriger) nosy parker (Brit inf), curious George (US inf); (= Überschlauer) know-all (Brit inf), know-it-all (US inf), clever dick (Brit inf), wise guy (inf)

nas|füh|ren ['na:sfy:rən] VT insep jdn ~ (als Täuschung) to lead sb by the nose; (als Scherz) to pull sb's leg (inf); ich war der/die Genasführte I was the dupe

Nas|horn ['na:shɔrn] NT rhinoceros, rhino

-na|sig [nasıç] ADJ suf -nosed; plattnasig flat-nosed

nas|lang ['na:slaŋ] ADV = naselang

nass [nas] ADJ comp nasser or nässer ['nɛsɐ], superl nasseste(r, s) or nässeste(r, s) wet; etw ~ machen to make sth wet; (für bestimmten Zweck) to wet sth; Bügelwäsche to dampen sth; sich ~ machen (inf) to wet oneself; das Bett ~ machen to wet the bed; nun mach dich bloß nicht ~! (inf) keep your shirt (inf) or hair (Brit inf) or pantyhose (US inf) on!, don't get your knickers in a twist! (Brit inf); durch und durch ~ wet through; mit ~en Augen with moist eyes, moist-eyed; wie ein ~er Sack (inf) like a wet rag (inf); ein ~es Grab (fig) a watery grave; der ~e Tod (fig) a watery death
ADV comp nasser or nässer, superl am nassesten or nässesten Staub wischen with a damp cloth; den Boden ~ wischen to mop the floor

Nass [nas] NT -es, no pl (liter, hum) water; (Getränk) liquid; hinein ins kühle ~ (hum) into the foaming brine; gierig trank er das erfrischende ~ (liter) eagerly he drank of the refreshing waters (liter)

Nas|sauer ['nasauɐ] M -s, -, **Nas|saue|rin** [-ərın] F -, -nen (inf) sponger (inf), scrounger

nas|sau|ern ['nasauɐn] VI (inf) to sponge (inf), to scrounge (bei jdm on or off sb)

Näs|se ['nɛsə] F -, no pl wetness, damp(ness), moisture; in der ~ stehen to stand in the wet; „vor ~ schützen" "keep dry"; vor ~ triefen to be dripping or wringing wet

näs|sen ['nɛsn] VI (Wunde) to weep, to discharge VT (liter: = feucht machen) to dampen, to wet, to moisten; Bett to wet

Nass-: **nass|forsch** (inf) ADJ brash ADV brashly; **nass|kalt** ADJ cold or chilly and damp, raw; **nass+ma|chen** VTR sep → nass ADJ; **Nass|ra|sur** F die ~ wet shaving; eine ~ a wet shave; **Nass-Tro|cken-Ra|sie|rer** M wet/dry shaver; **Nass|wä|sche** F wet washing; **Nass|zel|le** F wet cell

Nas|tuch ['na:stu:x] NT pl -tücher (S Ger, Aus, Sw) handkerchief

Na|tal ['na:tal] NT -s Natal

Na|ti ['na:ti] F (Sw: inf) -, -s (= Nationalmannschaft) national team

Na|ti|on [na'tsio:n] F -, -en nation; Held der ~ national hero; der Liebling der ~ the nation's favourite (Brit) or favorite (US); die Vereinten ~en the United Nations

na|ti|o|nal [natsio'na:l] ADJ national; (= patriotisch) nationalist, nationalistic (usu pej) ADV (= auf nationaler Ebene) nationwide; regeln nationally; (= patriotisch) nationalistically; ~ eingestellt sein, ~ denken to be nationalist or nationalistic (usu pej); die Inflation muss ~ eingedämmt werden inflation must be checked nationally or at the national level

Na|ti|o|nal- in cpds national; **Na|ti|o|nal|bank** F pl -banken national bank; **na|ti|o|nal|be|wusst** ADJ nationally conscious; **Na|ti|o|nal|be|wusst|sein** NT national consciousness; **Na|ti|o|nal|bib|lio|thek** F national library; **Na|ti|o|nal|cha|rak|ter** M national character; **Na|ti|o|nal|chi|na** NT Nationalist China; **na|ti|o|nal|chi|ne|sisch** ADJ Chinese Nationalist; **Na|ti|o|nal|ein|kom|men** NT national income; **Na|ti|o|nal|elf** F national (football) team; die italienische ~ the Italian (national) team, the Italian eleven; er hat dreimal in der ~ gespielt he's played for his country three times, he's been capped three times; **Na|ti|o|nal|epos** NT national epic; **Na|ti|o|nal|far|ben** PL national colours pl (Brit) or colors pl (US); **Na|ti|o|nal|fei|er|tag** M national holiday; **Na|ti|o|nal|flag|ge** F national flag; **Na|ti|o|nal|gar|de** F National Guard; **Na|ti|o|nal|ge|fühl** NT national feeling or sentiment; **Na|ti|o|nal|ge|richt** NT national dish; **Na|ti|o|nal|ge|tränk** NT national drink; **Na|ti|o|nal|held** M national hero; **Na|ti|o|nal|hel|din** F national heroine; **Na|ti|o|nal|hym|ne** F national anthem

na|ti|o|na|li|sie|ren [natsionali'zi:rən] ptp nationalisiert VT **a** (= einbürgern) to naturalize **b** (= verstaatlichen) to nationalize

Na|ti|o|na|li|sie|rung F -, -en **a** (= Einbürgerung) naturalization **b** (= Verstaatlichung) nationalization

Na|ti|o|na|lis|mus [natsiona'lısmʊs] M -, no pl nationalism

Na|ti|o|na|list [natsiona'lıst] M -en, -en, **Na|ti|o|na|lis|tin** [-'lıstın] F -, -nen nationalist

na|ti|o|na|lis|tisch [natsiona'lıstıʃ] ADJ nationalist, nationalistic (usu pej) ADV nationalistically

Na|ti|o|na|li|tät [natsionali'tɛ:t] F -, -en nationality

Na|ti|o|na|li|tä|ten-: **Na|ti|o|na|li|tä|ten|fra|ge** F problem of different nationalities (within one state); **Na|ti|o|na|li|tä|ten|staat** M multinational state

Na|ti|o|na|li|täts|kenn|zei|chen NT nationality sticker or (aus Metall) plate

Na|ti|o|nal-: **na|ti|o|nal|kon|ser|va|tiv** ADJ conservative and nationalist or nationalistic (usu pej) ADV ~ eingestellt sein, ~ denken to be conservative and nationalist or nationalistic (usu pej); **na|ti|o|nal|li|be|ral** ADJ liberal and nationalist or nationalistic (usu pej) ADV ~ eingestellt sein, ~ denken to be liberal and nationalist or nationalistic (usu pej); **Na|ti|o|nal|mann|schaft** F national team; er spielt in der schottischen ~ he plays for Scotland, he plays in *(Brit)* or on *(US)* the Scotland team; **die Fußball-~** the national football team; **er wurde mit der ~ Europameister** he played in *(Brit)* or on *(US)* the national team that won the European Championship; **Na|ti|o|nal|mu|se|um** NT national museum; **Na|ti|o|nal|öko|no|mie** F economics *sing*; **Na|ti|o|nal|park** M national park; **Na|ti|o|nal|rat** M *(Gremium) (Sw)* National Council; *(Aus)* National Assembly; **Na|ti|o|nal|rat** M, **Na|ti|o|nal|rä|tin** F *(Sw)* member of the National Council, ≈ MP; *(Aus)* deputy of or to the National Assembly, ≈ MP

NATIONALRAT

The Austrian **Nationalrat** is the representative body elected for a period of four years. It is made up of 183 members whose main duties are to pass laws and to exercise political and financial control over the Federal government.

The Swiss **Nationalrat** is one of the two chambers of the **Bundesversammlung**. It consists of 200 members who are elected for four years by voters in the cantons and demi-cantons. Each canton has the right to at least one seat; the remaining seats are allocated in proportion to each canton's population. → BUNDESVERSAMMLUNG

Na|ti|o|nal-: **Na|ti|o|nal|so|zi|a|lis|mus** M National Socialism; **Na|ti|o|nal|so|zi|a|list(in)** M(F) National Socialist; **na|ti|o|nal|so|zi|a|lis|tisch** ADJ National Socialist ADV **~ denken** to be a follower of National Socialism; **Na|ti|o|nal|spie|ler(in)** M(F) international (footballer *etc*); **Na|ti|o|nal|staat** M nation-state; **na|ti|o|nal|staat|lich** ADJ of a nation-state/nation-states; *Ordnung* as a nation-state; **Na|ti|o|nal|stolz** M national pride; **Na|ti|o|nal|stra|ße** F *(Aus, Sw)* national highway; **Na|ti|o|nal|the|a|ter** NT national theatre *(Brit)* or theater *(US)*; **Na|ti|o|nal|tracht** F national dress or costume; **Na|ti|o|nal|trai|ner(in)** M(F) manager of the national team; **Deutschlands ~ Meier** German manager Meier; **Na|ti|o|nal|tri|kot** NT *(Sport)* national strip *(Brit)* or jersey *(US)*; **Na|ti|o|nal|ver|samm|lung** F National Assembly

NATO F -, **Na|to** [ˈnaːto] F - **die ~** NATO

Na|to-: **Na|to-Dop|pel|be|schluss** M NATO twin-track policy; **Na|to|land** NT *usu pl* NATO country, NATO member, member of NATO; **Na|to|mit|glied** NT, **Na|to|mit|glied(s)|staat** M NATO member, member of NATO; **Na|to-Ost|er|wei|te|rung** F NATO eastern or eastward expansion, NATO's expansion to the east; **Na|to-Stütz|punkt** M NATO base

Nat|ri|um [ˈnaːtriʊm] NT -s, *no pl (abbr* **Na**) sodium

Nat|ri|um|chlo|rid [ˈnaːtriʊmkloriːt] NT *(abbr* **NaCl**) sodium chloride

Nat|ron [ˈnaːtrɔn] NT -s, *no pl (Chem)* bicarbonate of soda; *(= Backzutat)* bicarbonate of soda, baking soda, bicarb *(inf)*; **kohlensaures ~** sodium carbonate; **doppeltkohlensaures ~** sodium bicarbonate, bicarbonate of soda

Nat|ron|lau|ge F caustic soda, sodium hydroxide

Nat|ter [ˈnatɐ] F -, -n adder, viper; *(fig)* snake, serpent; **eine ~ am Busen nähren** *(liter)* to nurture a viper at one's breast or bosom

Nat|tern|brut F, **Nat|tern|ge|zücht** NT *(fig liter)* viper's brood

Na|tur [naˈtuːɐ] F -, -en **a** *no pl (= Kosmos, Schöpfungsordnung)* nature; **die Giraffe ist ein Meisterwerk der ~** the giraffe is one of Nature's masterpieces; **die drei Reiche der ~** the three kingdoms of nature, the three natural kingdoms; **~ und Kultur** nature and civilization; **wider** or **gegen die ~ sein** to be unnatural, to be against nature; **wie sich dieses Tier in der freien ~ verhält** how this animal behaves in the wild

b *no pl (= freies Land)* countryside; **die freie ~, Gottes freie ~** *(liter)* the open country(side); **in der freien ~** in the open countryside

c *no pl (= Naturzustand)* nature; **ist ihr Haar gefärbt? – nein, das ist alles ~** is her hair dyed? – no, it's natural; **sie sind von ~ so gewachsen** they grew that way naturally; **ich bin von ~ (aus) schüchtern** I am shy by nature; **sein Haar ist von ~ aus blond** his hair is naturally blond; **zurück zur ~!** back to nature; **nach der ~ zeichnen/malen** to draw/paint from nature

d *(Cook)* **Schnitzel/Fisch ~** *cutlet/fish not cooked in breadcrumbs*; **Zitrone ~** freshly-squeezed lemon juice

e *(= Beschaffenheit, Wesensart)* nature; *(Mensch)* type; **die menschliche ~** human nature; **es liegt in der ~ der Sache** or **der Dinge** it is in the nature of things; **das geht gegen meine ~** it goes against the grain; **das entspricht nicht meiner ~, das ist meiner ~ zuwider** it's not in my nature; **eine Frage allgemeiner ~** a question of a general nature; **zurückhaltender ~ sein** to be of a retiring nature; **das ist ihm zur zweiten ~ geworden** it's become second nature to him; **eine eiserne ~ haben** to have a cast-iron constitution; **sie ist eine gutmütige ~** she's a good-natured type or soul; **das ist nichts für zarte ~en** that's not for sensitive types

Na|tu|ra|li|en [natuˈraːliən] PL **a** natural produce; **in ~ bezahlen** to pay in kind; **Handel mit ~** barter(ing) with goods **b** *(Naturgeschichte)* natural history specimens *pl*

na|tu|ra|li|sie|ren [naturaliˈziːrən] *ptp* **naturalisiert** VT **a** *(Jur)* to naturalize **b** *(Biol, Zool)* **naturalisiert werden, sich ~** to be naturalized, to naturalize

Na|tu|ra|li|sie|rung F -, *no pl* naturalization

Na|tu|ra|lis|mus [naturaˈlɪsmʊs] M -, *no pl* naturalism

Na|tu|ra|list [naturaˈlɪst] M -en, -en, **Na|tu|ra|lis|tin** [-ˈlɪstɪn] F -, -nen naturalist

na|tu|ra|lis|tisch [naturaˈlɪstɪʃ] ADJ naturalistic ADV naturalistically

Na|tu|ral|lohn M payment in kind

Na|tur-: **Na|tur|apos|tel** M *(hum)* health fiend *(inf)*; **na|tur|be|las|sen** ADJ *Lebensmittel, Material* natural; **Na|tur|be|ob|ach|tung** F observation of nature; **Na|tur|be|schrei|bung** F description of nature; **Na|tur|bur|sche** M *(dated)* nature-boy *(inf)*; **Na|tur|denk|mal** NT natural monument

na|ture [naˈtyːɐ] *(Sw)*, **na|tu|rell** [natuˈrɛl] *(geh)* ADJ *inv (Cook)* = **Natur d**

Na|tu|rell [natuˈrɛl] NT -s, -e temperament, disposition

Na|tur-: **Na|tur|er|eig|nis** NT (impressive) natural phenomenon, phenomenon of nature; **Na|tur|er|schei|nung** F natural phenomenon; **Na|tur|er|zeug|nis** NT natural product; **Na|tur|far|be** F **a** natural colour *(Brit)* or color *(US)* **b** *(auch* **Naturfarbstoff**) natural dye; **na|tur|far|ben** [-farbn] ADJ natural-coloured *(Brit)*, natural-colored *(US)*; **Na|tur|fa|ser** F natural fibre *(Brit)* or fiber *(US)*; **Na|tur|for|scher(in)** M(F) natural scientist; **Na|tur|for|schung** F natural science; **Na|tur|freund(in)** M(F) nature-lover; **Na|tur|gas** NT *(S Ger, Sw)* natural gas; **Na|tur|ge|fühl** NT feeling for nature; **na|tur|ge|ge|ben** ADJ *(lit)* natural; *(fig auch)* normal; **na|tur|ge|mäß** ADJ **~e Waldwirtschaft** natural forestry methods ADV naturally; **Na|tur|ge|schich|te** F natural history; **na|tur|ge|schicht|lich** ADJ natural history *attr*; **Na|tur|ge|setz** NT law of nature; **na|tur|ge|treu** ADJ *Darstellung* lifelike, true to life; *(= in Lebensgröße)* life-size, full-scale ADV realistically; **etw ~ wiedergeben** to reproduce sth true to life; **Na|tur|ge|walt** F *usu pl* element; **na|tur|haft** *(geh)* ADJ natural ADV **~ gegebene Eigenschaften** natural characteristics; **Na|tur|haus|halt** M balance of nature, nature's balance, ecological balance; **Na|tur|heil|kun|de** F nature healing; **Na|tur|heil|ver|fah|ren** NT natural cure or remedy; **Na|tur|ka|ta|stro|phe** F natural disaster; **Na|tur|kind** NT child of nature; **Na|tur|kos|me|tik** F natural make-up; **Na|tur|kost** F health food(s *pl*); **Na|tur|kost|la|den** M health-food shop; **Na|tur|kraft** F natural energy or force; **Na|tur|kun|de** F natural history; **na|tur|kund|lich** [-kʊntlɪç] ADJ *Forschung, Zeitschrift, Museum* natural history *attr*; **Na|tur|land|schaft** F natural or virgin landscape; **Na|tur|leh|re** F *(Sch)* (physical) science; **Na|tur|lehr|pfad** M nature trail

na|tür|lich [naˈtyːɐlɪç] ADJ *(alle Bedeutungen)* natural; **in seiner ~en Größe** life-size; **eines ~en Todes sterben** to die from or of natural causes, to die a natural death; **es ist doch (nur zu) ~, dass ...** it's (only) natural that ...; **~e Person** *(Jur)* natural person; **~e Zahl** natural number; **die ~ste Sache (von) der Welt** the most natural thing in the world; **es geht nicht mit ~en Dingen zu** there's something odd or fishy *(inf)* going on, I smell a rat *(inf)*; **~e Grenze** natural frontier or boundary; **~e Auslese** *(Biol)* natural selection

ADV **a** naturally; **die Krankheit verlief ganz ~** the illness took its natural course

b *(= selbstverständlich)* naturally, of course; **~!** naturally!, of course!, certainly!

na|tür|li|cher|wei|se [naˈtyːɐlɪçɐˈvaizə] ADV naturally, of course

Na|tür|lich|keit F -, *no pl* naturalness

Na|tur-: **Na|tur|lo|cken** PL natural curls *pl*; **Na|tur|mensch** M child of nature; **na|tur|nah** ADJ *Stoffe* natural; **~e Tierhaltung** keeping livestock in natural conditions; **~e Landwirtschaft** ≈ organic farming; **das ~e Wohnen ist ...** living close to nature is ... ADV **Tiere ~ halten** to keep animals in conditions close to their natural habitat or *(in der Landwirtschaft)* in natural conditions; **die Ferien ~ verbringen** to get close to nature on one's holidays *(esp Brit)* or vacation *(US)*; **der Park sollte möglichst ~ gestaltet sein** the park should be laid out as naturally as possible; **Na|tur|park** M ≈ national park; **Na|tur|phi|lo|so|phie** F philosophy of nature; **Na|tur|pro|dukt** NT natural product; **~e** *pl* natural produce *sing*; **Na|tur|recht** NT natural right; **na|tur|recht|lich** ADJ *Wertvorstellungen, Begründungen* based on natural rights; **na|tur|rein** ADJ natural, pure, unadulterated; **Na|tur|reis** M brown rice; **Na|tur|schät|ze** PL natural resources *pl*; **Na|tur|schau|spiel** NT natural spectacle, spectacle of nature; **Na|tur|schutz** M conservation, nature conservancy; **unter (strengem) ~ stehen** *(Pflanze, Tier)* to be a protected species; **dieses Gebiet steht unter ~** this is a conservation or protected area; **etw unter ~ stellen** to classify sth as a protected species; **Na|tur|schüt|zer** [-ʃʏtsɐ] M -s, -, **Na|tur|schüt|ze|rin** [-ʃytsərɪn] F -, -nen conservationist; **Na|tur|schutz|ge|biet** NT conservation or protected area; **Na|tur|schutz|park** M ≈ national park; **Na|tur|sei|de** F natural silk; **Na|tur|stein** M natural stone; **Na|tur|ta|lent** NT *(Person)* naturally talented or gifted person; *(Begabung)* natural talent or gift; **sie ist ein ~** she is a natural; **Na|tur|the|a|ter** NT open-air theatre *(Brit)* or theater *(US)*; **Na|tur|treue** F trueness to life, faithfulness, fidelity; **Na|tur|trieb** M (natural) instinct; **na|tur|trüb** ADJ *Saft, Bier* (naturally) cloudy; **na|tur|ver|bun|den** ADJ nature-loving, attached to nature; **Na|tur|ver|bun|den|heit** F love of nature; **Na|tur|ver|eh|rung** F nature worship; **na|tur|ver|träg|lich** ADJ compatible with the environment ADV **etw ~ bauen** to build sth so that it is compatible with the environment; **etw ~ düngen** to use organic fertilizer on sth; **Na|tur|volk** NT primitive people

naturw. *abbr von* **naturwissenschaftlich**

Na|tur-: **na|tur|wid|rig** ADJ unnatural, against nature; *(= nicht normal)* abnormal; **Na|tur|wis|sen|schaft** F natural sciences *pl*; *(Zweig)* natural science; **Na|tur|wis|sen|schaft|ler(in)** M(F) (natural) scientist; **na|tur|wis|sen|schaft|lich** ADJ scientific ADV scientifically; **~ forschen/arbeiten** to do scientific research/work; **~ interessiert sein** to be interested in science; **na|tur|wüch|sig** ADJ *Entwicklung* natural; *Kunst* native; **Na|tur|wun|der** NT miracle of nature, natural wonder; **Na|tur|zu|stand** M natural state

'nauf [nauf] ADV *(dial)* = **hinauf**

'naus [naus] ADV *(dial)* = **hinaus**

Nau|tik ['nautɪk] F -, *no pl* nautical science, navigation

nau|tisch ['nautɪʃ] ADJ navigational; *Instrumente auch, Ausbildung, Ausdruck* nautical; **~e Meile** nautical *or* sea mile

Na|vel|oran|ge F navel orange

Na|vi|ga|ti|on [naviga'tsio:n] F -, *no pl* navigation

Na|vi|ga|ti|ons-: **Na|vi|ga|ti|ons|feh|ler** M navigational error; **Na|vi|ga|ti|ons|ge|rät** NT navigation system; **Na|vi|ga|ti|ons|kar|te** F navigation chart; **Na|vi|ga|ti|ons|leis|te** F *(Comput)* navigation bar; **Na|vi|ga|ti|ons|of|fi|zier(in)** M(F) navigation officer; **Na|vi|ga|ti|ons|raum** M charthouse, chartroom; **Na|vi|ga|ti|ons|soft|ware** F navigation(al) software; **Na|vi|ga|ti|ons|sys|tem** NT navigation system; **ein ~ fürs Auto** a car navigation system

Na|vi|ga|tor [navi'ga:to:ɐ] F -s, **Navigatoren** [-'to:rən], **Na|vi|ga|to|rin** [-'to:rɪn] F -, **-nen** *(Aviat)* navigator, navigation officer

na|vi|gie|ren [navi'gi:rən] *ptp* **navigiert** VTI to navigate

Na|za|re|ner [natsa're:nɐ] M -s, - Nazarene

Na|zi ['na:tsi] M -s, -s Nazi

Na|zi|re|gime NT Nazi regime

Na|zis|mus [na'tsɪsmʊs] M -, **Nazismen** [-mən] **a** *(pej: = Nationalsozialismus)* Nazism **b** *(= Ausdruck)* Nazi term *or* expression

na|zis|tisch [na'tsɪstɪʃ] *(pej)* ADJ Nazi ADV **~ orientierte Kreise** Nazi groups; **~ angehaucht sein** to be a Nazi sympathizer; **~ anmutende Parolen** Nazi-sounding slogans

Na|zi- *in cpds* Nazi; **Na|zi|ver|bre|chen** NT Nazi crime, Nazi atrocity; **Na|zi|zeit** F Nazi period

NB [ɛn'be:] *abbr von* **nota bene** NB

n. Br. *abbr von* **nördlicher Breite**

NC [ɛn'tse:] M -(s), -(s) *(Univ) abbr von* **Numerus clausus**

NC-Fach NT *(Univ)* subject with restricted entry

n. Chr. *abbr von* **nach Christus** AD

nd *abbr von* **niederdeutsch**

NDR [ɛnde:'lɛr] M -s *abbr von* **Norddeutscher Rundfunk**

ne [ne:] ADV *(inf)* = **nee**

'ne [nə] *(inf) abbr von* **eine**

Ne|an|der|ta|ler [ne'andɐta:lɐ] M -s, - Neanderthal man

Ne|a|pel [ne'a:pl] NT -s Naples

Ne|a|po|li|ta|ner [neapoli'ta:nɐ] M -s, - *(Aus: = Waffel)* waffle

Ne|a|po|li|ta|ner [neapoli'ta:nɐ] M -s, -, **Ne|a|po|li|ta|ne|rin** [-ərɪn] F -, **-nen** Neapolitan

Ne|bel ['ne:bl] M -s, - mist; *(dichter)* fog; *(mit Abgasen)* smog; *(Mil: künstlich)* smoke; *(Astron)* nebula; *(fig)* mist, haze; **bei (dichtem) ~** in thick mist/fog; **im ~ liegen** *(lit)* to be shrouded in mist/fog; *(fig)* to be shrouded in mystery; **im ~ verschwinden** *(lit)* to vanish into the mist/fog; *(fig)* to vanish into the mist; **im ~ stochern** *(fig)* to stumble *or* grope about in the dark → **Nacht**

Ne|bel-: **Ne|bel|auf|lö|sung** F **nach ~** after the fog has lifted; **Ne|bel|bank** F *pl* **-bänke** fog bank; **Ne|bel|bil|dung** F fog; **stellenweise ~** foggy patches; **Ne|bel|fleck** M **a** *(Astron)* nebula **b** *(Zool)* leucoma *(spec)*, clouding (of the eye); **Ne|bel|gra|na|te** F smoke grenade *or* canister

ne|bel|haft ADJ *(fig) Erklärung, Ausdrucksweise* nebulous, vague; **es liegt in ~er Ferne** it's in the dim distance; *(Vergangenes)* it's in the dim and distant past; *(Zukünftiges)* it's in the dim and distant future

Ne|bel|horn NT *(Naut)* foghorn

ne|be|lig ['ne:bəlɪç] ADJ misty; *(bei dichterem Nebel)* foggy

Ne|bel-: **Ne|bel|kam|mer** F *(Phys)* cloud chamber; **Ne|bel|krä|he** F hooded crow; **Ne|bel|leuch|te** F *(Aut)* rear fog light; **Ne|bel|meer** NT sea of mist; **Ne|bel|mo|nat** M *(liter)* November

ne|beln ['ne:bln] VI *impers* **es nebelt** it's misty/foggy

Ne|bel-: **Ne|bel|schein|wer|fer** M *(Aut)* fog lamp; **Ne|bel|schlei|er** M *(geh)* veil of mist; **Ne|bel|schluss|leuch|te** F *(Aut)* rear fog light; **Ne|bel|schwa|den** M *usu pl* waft of mist

Ne|be|lung ['ne:bəlʊŋ] M -s, -e *(obs)* November

Ne|bel-: **Ne|bel|wand** F wall *or* bank of fog; *(Mil)* smokescreen; **Ne|bel|wer|fer** M *(Mil)* multiple rocket launcher; **Ne|bel|wet|ter** NT misty weather; *(mit dichtem Nebel)* foggy weather

ne|ben ['ne:bn] PREP **a** *(örtlich: +dat or (mit Bewegungsverben) +acc)* beside, next to; **er fuhr ~ dem Zug her** he kept level with the train; **er ging ~ ihr** he walked beside her; **ich stelle ihn ~ die größten Denker des 17. Jahrhunderts** I rank him among *or* with the greatest thinkers of the 17th century **b** *(= außer: +dat)* apart from, besides, aside from *(esp US)*; **du sollst keine anderen Götter haben ~ mir** *(Bibl)* thou shalt have no other gods before me *(Bibl)*; **~ anderen Dingen** along with *or* as well as *or* amongst other things **c** *(= verglichen mit: +dat)* compared with *or* to

Ne|ben-: **Ne|ben|ab|re|de** F *(Jur)* supplementary agreement, sub-agreement; **Ne|ben|ab|sicht** F secondary aim *or* objective; **eine ~ haben** *or* **verfolgen** to have a secondary aim *or* objective; **Ne|ben|ak|zent** M *(Ling)* secondary stress; **Ne|ben|al|tar** M side altar; **Ne|ben|amt** NT **a** *(= Nebenberuf)* secondary *or* additional office **b** *(Telec)* branch *or* local exchange; **ne|ben|amt|lich** ADJ *Tätigkeit* secondary, additional ADV as a second job; **er unterrichtet ~** he also works as a teacher; **Ne|ben|aus|ga|ben** PL extras *pl*; *(Econ)* incidental expenses *pl*

ne|ben|an [ne:bn'lan] ADV next door; **die Tür ~** the next door

Ne|ben-: **Ne|ben|an|schluss** M *(Telec)* extension; **Ne|ben|ar|beit** F **a** *(= Zusatzarbeit)* extra work *no indef art, no pl*, extra job **b** *(= Zweitberuf)* second *or* extra job, sideline; **Ne|ben|arm** M *(von Fluss)* branch; **Ne|ben|aus|ga|be** F incidental expense; **~n** incidentals, incidental expenses; **Ne|ben|aus|gang** M side exit; **Ne|ben|be|deu|tung** F secondary meaning *or* connotation

ne|ben|bei [ne:bn'bai] ADV **a** *(= gleichzeitig)* at the same time; **etw ~ machen** to do sth on the side **b** *(= außerdem)* additionally, in addition; **die ~ entstandenen Kosten** the additional expenses **c** *(= beiläufig)* incidentally; **~ bemerkt** *or* **gesagt** by the way, incidentally, by the by(e); **das mache ich so ~** *(inf)* that's just a sideline; *(= kein Problem)* I'll do that with no bother *(Brit inf) or* without any problem

Ne|ben-: **Ne|ben|be|mer|kung** F aside; **Ne|ben|be|ruf** M second *or* extra job, sideline; **er ist im ~ Nachtwächter** he has a second job as a night watchman; **ne|ben|be|ruf|lich** ADJ extra, supplementary; **~e Arbeit/Tätigkeit** extra work/job, sideline, side job ADV as a second job, as a sideline *(inf)*, as a side job *(inf)*; **er verdient ~ mehr als hauptberuflich** he earns more from his second job than he does from his main job; **Ne|ben|blatt** NT *(Bot)* stipule *(spec)*; **Ne|ben|be|schäf|ti|gung** F, **Ne|ben|be|tä|ti|gung** F **a** *(= Zweitberuf)* second *or* extra job, sideline **b** *(= Ablenkung)* **beim Fernsehen brauche ich immer eine kleine ~** I always need something else to do while I'm watching television; **Ne|ben|be|trieb** M **a** branch industry **b** *(= Filiale) (Büro)* branch (office); *(Werk)* subsidiary factory; **Ne|ben|buh|ler(in)** M(F) rival; **Ne|ben|buh|ler|schaft** ['ne:bnbu:lɐʃaft] F -, *no pl* rivalry; **Ne|ben|dar|stel|ler** M supporting actor; **die ~** the supporting cast *sing*; **Ne|ben|dar|stel|le|rin** F supporting actress; **Ne|ben|din|ge** PL secondary matters *pl*; **Ne|ben|ef|fekt** M side effect

ne|ben|ei|nan|der [ne:bnlai'nandɐ] ADV **a** *(räumlich)* side by side; *sitzen, liegen* next to each other, side by side; *(bei Rennen)* neck and neck; **sie gingen ~ durchs Ziel** they were neck and neck at the finish; **drei ~, zu dritt ~** three abreast; **~ anordnen** *(Comput) Fenster* to tile **b** *(zeitlich)* simultaneously, at the same time

Ne|ben|ei|nan|der [ne:bnlai'nandɐ, 'ne:bn-] NT -s, *no pl* juxtaposition

ne|ben|ei|nan|der|her ADV side by side; **sie leben nur noch ~** *(Ehepaar etc)* they're just two people living in the same house

ne|ben|ei|nan|der-: **ne|ben|ei|nan|der+le|gen** *sep*, **ne|ben|ei|nan|der le|gen** △ VT to lay side by side *or* next to each other; **ne|ben|ei|nan|der+rei|hen** *sep*, **ne|ben|ei|nan|der rei|hen** △ VT to place *or* put side by side, to place *or* put next to each other; **ne|ben|ei|nan|der+schal|ten** *sep*, **ne|ben|ei|nan|der schal|ten** △ VT *(Elec)* to put in parallel; **ne|ben|ei|nan|der+set|zen** *sep*, **ne|ben|ei|nan|der set|zen** △ VT to place *or* put side by side, to place *or* put next to each other; **ne|ben|ei|nan|der+sit|zen** *sep irreg (S Ger, Aus, Sw: aux sein)*, **ne|ben|ei|nan|der sit|zen** △ *irreg (S Ger, Aus, Sw: aux sein)* VI to sit side by side *or* next to each other; **ne|ben|ei|nan|der+stel|len** *sep*, **ne|ben|ei|nan|der stel|len** △ VT to place *or* put side by side, to place *or* put next to each other; *(fig: = vergleichen)* to compare

Ne|ben-: **Ne|ben|ein|gang** M side entrance; **Ne|ben|ein|künf|te** PL, **Ne|ben|ein|nah|men** PL additional *or* supplementary income *sing*, extra income *sing*; **Ne|ben|er|schei|nung** F concomitant; *(von Krankheit)* secondary symptom; *(von Medikament)* side effect; *(von Tourismus etc)* knock-on effect; **Ne|ben|er|werb** M second occupation; **Ne|ben|er|werbs|land|wirt(in)** M(F) part-time farmer; **Ne|ben|fach** NT *(Sch, Univ)* subsidiary (subject), minor *(US)*; **Ne|ben|fi|gur** F minor character; **Ne|ben|flü|gel** M side wing; **Ne|ben|fluss** M tributary; **Ne|ben|form** F *(Biol)* variety; *(Ling)* variant; **Ne|ben|fra|ge** F side issue; **Ne|ben|frau** F concubine; **Ne|ben|ge|bäu|de** NT **a** *(= Zusatzgebäude)* annexe *(Brit)*, annex, outbuilding **b** *(= Nachbargebäude)* neighbouring *(Brit) or* neighboring *(US)* building, adjacent building; **Ne|ben|ge|büh|ren** PL extra charges *pl*; **Ne|ben|ge|dan|ke** M ulterior motive; **Ne|ben|ge|räusch** NT *(Rad, Telec)* interference, noise; **Ne|ben|ge|schäft** NT sideline; **Ne|ben|ge|stein** NT *(Min)* country rock; **Ne|ben|ge|wer|be** NT second trade; **Ne|ben|gleis** NT *(Rail)* siding, sidetrack *(US)*; **Ne|ben|hand|lung** F *(Liter)* subplot; **Ne|ben|haus** NT house next door, neighbouring *(Brit) or* neighboring *(US)* house

ne|ben|her [ne:bn'he:ɐ] ADV **a** *(= zusätzlich)* in addition, on the side **b** *(= gleichzeitig)* at the same time, simultaneously

ne|ben|her- [ne:bn'he:ɐ] PREF alongside, beside it/him *etc*; **neben etw nebenherfahren** *(mit Auto)* to drive alongside sth; *(mit Fahrrad)* to ride alongside sth; **nebenherlaufen** to run alongside

ne|ben|hin [neːbnˈhɪn] ADV (= *beiläufig*) in passing, by the way, casually

Ne|ben-: **Ne|ben|höh|le** F (*Physiol*) sinus (of the nose); **Ne|ben|höh|len|ent|zün|dung** F (*Med*) sinusitis; **Ne|ben|job** M (*inf*) second *or* extra job, sideline; **Ne|ben|kla|ge** F (*Jur*) incidental action; **Ne|ben|klä|ger(in)** M(F) (*Jur*) joint plaintiff; **Ne|ben|kos|ten** PL additional costs *pl*; **es kostet £ 300 die Woche inklusive ~** it's £300 a week including bills; **Ne|ben|kriegs|schau|platz** M secondary theatre (*Brit*) *or* theater (*US*) of war; (*fig*) secondary area of confrontation; **Ne|ben|li|nie** F **a** (*von Familie*) collateral line **b** (*Rail*) branch line; **Ne|ben|mann** M *pl* **-männer** neighbour (*Brit*), neighbor (*US*); (*Mann neben Ehemann*) lover; **Ihr ~** the person next to you, your neighbour (*Brit*) *or* neighbor (*US*); **Ne|ben|nie|re** F suprarenal gland, adrenal body

ne|ben+ord|nen VT *sep infin and ptp only* (*Gram*) to coordinate

Ne|ben-: **Ne|ben|ord|nung** F (*Gram*) coordination; **Ne|ben|per|son** F minor character; **Ne|ben|platz** M (= *Sitzplatz*) next seat; (*Ftbl*) training ground; (*Tennis*) outside court; **auf meinem ~** in the seat next to me; **Ne|ben|pro|dukt** NT by-product; **Ne|ben|raum** M (*benachbart*) adjoining *or* next room; (*weniger wichtig*) side room; **Ne|ben|rech|te** PL (*Jur*) subsidiary rights *pl*; **Ne|ben|rol|le** F supporting role; (*fig*) minor role; **eine ~ spielen** (*lit, fig*) to play a supporting role; **das spielt für mich nur eine ~** that's only of minor concern to me; **Ne|ben|sa|che** F minor matter, trifle, triviality; **das ist (für mich) ~** that's irrelevant *or* that's not the point (as far as I'm concerned); **die schönste ~ der Welt** the greatest trivial pursuit in the world; **ne|ben|säch|lich** ADJ minor, trivial, of minor importance; **etw als ~ abtun** to dismiss sth as irrelevant *or* beside the point; **Nebensächliches** minor matters *pl*, trifles *pl*, trivia(lities) *pl*; **es ist doch völlig ~, wann er kommt** it doesn't matter a bit when he comes, it's quite irrelevant when he comes; **Ne|ben|säch|lich|keit** [ˈneːbnzɛçlɪçkait] F -, -en side issue; **Ne|ben|sai|son** F low season; **Ne|ben|satz** M (*Gram*) subordinate clause

ne|ben+schal|ten VT *sep* (*Elec*) to wire *or* connect in parallel

Ne|ben-: **Ne|ben|schluss** M (*Tech*) parallel connection, side (of a parallel circuit); **Ne|ben|son|ne** F mock sun, sundog, parhelion (*spec*); **ne|ben|ste|hend** ADJ **~e Erklärungen/Verbesserung** explanations/correction in the margin; **~e Abbildung** illustration opposite; **im Nebenstehenden wird erklärt ...** the marginal note explains ...; **Ne|ben|stel|le** F (*Telec*) extension; (*Comm*) branch; (*Post*) sub-post office; **Ne|ben|stel|len|an|la|ge** F (*Telec*) private branch exchange; **Ne|ben|stra|fe** F additional penalty; **Ne|ben|stra|ße** F (*in der Stadt*) side street; (= *Landstraße*) minor road, by-road; **Ne|ben|stre|cke** F (*Rail*) branch *or* local line; (*Aut*) minor road; **Ne|ben|the|ma** NT (*Mus*) minor theme; **Ne|ben|tisch** M adjacent table; **am ~** at the next table; **sie saßen an einem ~** they were sitting at a table near us; **Ne|ben|ton** M *pl* **-töne** (*Ling*) secondary stress; **Ne|ben|ur|sa|che** F secondary cause; **Ne|ben|ver|dienst** M secondary income; **Ne|ben|weg** M byway; **auf ~en** (*lit, fig*) by a roundabout route; **Ne|ben|win|kel** M (*Math*) adjacent angle; **Ne|ben|wir|kung** F side effect; **Ne|ben|woh|nung** F **a** next(-door) flat (*Brit*) *or* apartment, flat (*Brit*) *or* apartment next door; **in einer ~** in one of the flats (*Brit*) *or* apartments next door **b** (= *Zweitwohnung*) second flat (*Brit*) *or* apartment; **Ne|ben|wohn|sitz** M second residence *or* domicile (*form*); **Ne|ben|zim|mer** NT (= *benachbarter Raum*) next *or* adjoining room; (= *Nebengelass*) side room; **in einem ~** in an adjoining room/a side room; **Ne|ben|zweck** M secondary aim

neb|lig [ˈneːblɪç] ADJ = **nebelig**

nebst [neːpst] PREP +*dat* together with; **viele Grüße, Onkel Otto ~ Familie** greetings from Uncle Otto and family

ne|bu|los [nebuˈloːs], **ne|bu|lös** [nebuˈløːs] ADJ nebulous, vague; **er redete so ~es Zeug** he was so vague ADV vaguely, nebulously

Ne|ces|saire [neseˈsɛːɐ] NT -s, -s (= *Kulturbeutel*) vanity bag *or* case; (*zur Nagelpflege*) manicure case; (= *Nähzeug*) sewing bag

ne|cken [ˈnɛkn] VT to tease; **jdn mit jdm/etw ~** to tease sb about sb/sth VR **sich** *or* **einander ~**, **sich mit jdm ~** to tease each other, to have a tease (*inf*); **was sich liebt, das neckt sich** (*Prov*) teasing is a sign of affection

Ne|cke|rei [nɛkəˈrai] F -, -en teasing *no pl*

Neck|hol|der-BH [ˈnɛkhoːldɐ-] M neckholder bra, halterneck bra

ne|ckisch [ˈnɛkɪʃ] ADJ (= *scherzhaft*) merry, teasing; *Einfall, Melodie* amusing; *Unterhaltung* bantering; (*inf*: = *kokett, kess*) *Kleid, Frisur* coquettish, saucy; *Spielchen* mischievous, naughty ADV (= *scherzhaft*) teasingly; (= *kokett*) coquettishly

nee [neː] ADV (*inf*) no, nope (*inf*); **~, so was!** no, really!

Neer [neːɐ] F -, -en (*N Ger*) eddy

Nef|fe [ˈnɛfə] M -n, -n nephew

neg. ADJ *abbr von* **negativ** neg.

Ne|ga|ti|on [negaˈtsioːn] F -, -en negation

ne|ga|tiv [ˈneːgatiːf, negaˈtiːf] ADJ negative ADV **a** (= *ablehnend*) *antworten* negatively, in the negative; **jdm auf eine Frage ~ antworten** to answer sb's question in the negative; **sich ~ zu etw stellen** to adopt a negative attitude toward(s) sth; **sich ~ zu etw äußern** to speak negatively about sth; (*ablehnen*) to be against sth; **ich beurteile seine Arbeit sehr ~** I have a very negative view of his work; **die Untersuchung verlief ~** the examination proved negative; **die Antwort/Beurteilung fiel ~er aus als erwartet** the answer/assessment was less favourable (*Brit*) *or* favorable (*US*) than expected; **zu etw ~ eingestellt sein** to have reservations about sth; **alles ~ sehen** to be pessimistic **b** (= *ungünstig*) **sich ~ auf etw** (*acc*) **auswirken** to be detrimental to *or* for sth; **die Umsatzentwicklung wird ~ eingeschätzt** the prognosis for turnover is negative **c** (*Elec*) **etw ~ (auf)laden** to put a negative charge on sth

Ne|ga|tiv [ˈneːgatiːf, negaˈtiːf] NT -s, -e [-və] (*Phot*) negative

Ne|ga|tiv-: **Ne|ga|tiv|bei|spiel** NT negative example; **Ne|ga|tiv|bi|lanz** F debit balance; **Ne|ga|tiv|bild** NT negative; **Ne|ga|tiv|druck** M *pl* **-drucke etw im ~ herstellen** to reverse sth out; **Ne|ga|tiv|film** M negative (film); **Ne|ga|tiv|i|mage** [-ɪmɪtʃ] NT negative image

Ne|ga|ti|vi|tät [negativiˈtɛːt] F -, *no pl* negativity

Ne|ga|tiv-: **Ne|ga|tiv|ko|pie** F (*Typ*) negative copy; **Ne|ga|tiv|lis|te** F **a** (*Med, Pharm*) drug exclusion list **b** (*allgemein*: *pej*) black list

ne|ger [ˈneːgɐ] ADJ *pred* (*Aus inf*: = *pleite*) broke (*inf*)

Ne|ger [ˈneːgɐ] M -s, - **a** (*neg!*) black (man *or* person), Negro (*neg!*) **b** (*TV sl*) (= *Gedächtnishilfe*) idiot board (*Brit inf*), Teleprompter® (*US*); (= *Verdunklungstafel*) gobo

Ne|ge|rin [ˈneːgərɪn] F -, -nen (*neg!*) black (woman *or* lady), Negress (*neg!*), Negro woman (*neg!*)

Ne|ger-: **Ne|ger|kuss** M (*neg!*) *chocolate marshmallow with biscuit base*; **Ne|ger|lein** [ˈneːgɐlain] NT -s, - (*neg!*) *dim von* **Neger** little black, little Negro (*neg!*); **Ne|ger|mu|sik** F (*usu pej*) black music, Negro music (*neg!*); **Ne|ger|skla|ve** M (*neg!*), **Ne|ger|skla|vin** F (*neg!*) black slave, Negro slave (*neg!*)

ne|gie|ren [neˈgiːrən] *ptp* **negiert** VT (= *verneinen*) *Satz* to negate; (= *bestreiten*) *Tatsache, Behauptung* to deny

Neg|li|gé [negliˈʒeː] NT -s, -s, **Neg|li|gee** NT -s, -s negligee, négligé

neg|rid [neˈgriːt] ADJ *Rasse* negro

neg|ro|id [negroˈiːt] ADJ negroid

neh|men [ˈneːmən] *pret* **nahm** [naːm], *ptp* **ge|nom|men** [gəˈnɔmən] VTI **a** (= *ergreifen*) to take; **etw in die Hand ~** (*lit*) to pick sth up; (*fig*) to take sth in hand; **etw an sich** (*acc*) **~** (= *aufbewahren*) to take care *or* charge of sth, to look after sth; (= *sich aneignen*) to take sth (for oneself) **b** (= *wegnehmen*) to take; *Schmerz* to take away, to relieve; (= *versperren*) *Blick, Sicht* to block; **jdm etw ~** to take sth (away) from sb; **jdm die Hoffnung/den Glauben/die Freude ~** to take away sb's hope/faith/joy, to rob *or* deprive sb of his hope/faith/joy; **um ihm die Angst zu ~** to stop him being afraid; **ihm sind seine Illusionen genommen worden** his illusions were shattered; **er ließ es sich** (*dat*) **nicht ~, mich persönlich hinauszubegleiten** he insisted on showing me out himself; **diesen Erfolg lasse ich mir nicht ~** I won't be robbed of this success; **woher ~ und nicht stehlen?** (*inf*) where on earth am I going to find any/one *etc*?; **sie ~ sich** (*dat*) **nichts** (*inf*) there's nothing to choose between them, one's as good as the other; **sich** (*dat*) **vom Brot/Fleisch ~** to help oneself to bread/meat; **~ Sie sich doch bitte!** please help yourself **c** (= *benutzen*) *Auto, Zug etc* to take; *Bürste, Zutaten, Farbe* to use; **man nehme ...** (*Cook*) take ...; **sich** (*dat*) **etw ~** (*Zimmer, Wohnung*) to take sth; (= *sich bedienen auch*) to help oneself to sth; **sich** (*dat*) **einen Anwalt/eine Hilfe ~** to get a lawyer/some help **d** (= *annehmen*) *Geschenk, Stelle, Bewerber, Anwalt* to take; (= *berechnen*) to charge; **was ~ Sie dafür?** how much will you take for it?; **jdn zu sich ~** to take sb in; **Gott hat ihn zu sich genommen** (*euph*) he has been called home to his maker; **etw ~, wie es kommt** to take sth as it comes; **jdn ~, wie er ist** to take sb as he is; **etw auf sich** (*acc*) **~** to take sth upon oneself; **er ist immer der Nehmende** he does all the taking, with him it's just take take take (*inf*); **die Nehmenden und die Gebenden** the takers and the givers **e** (= *einnehmen*) to take; *Essen* to have, to take; **sie nimmt Rauschgift/die Pille** she's on drugs/the pill, she takes drugs/the pill; **etw zu sich ~** to take sth, to partake of sth (*liter*); **der Patient hat nichts zu sich ~ können** the patient has been unable to take nourishment **f** (= *auffassen*) to take; (= *behandeln*) to handle, to treat; **wenn Sie das so ~ wollen** if you care *or* choose to take it that way; **etw für ein** *or* **als Zeichen ~** to take sth as a sign *or* an omen; **wie mans nimmt** (*inf*) depending on your point of view; **wissen, wie man jdn ~ muss** *or* **soll** to know how to take sb **g** (= *auswählen*) to take; *Essen, Menü* to have, to take; **sich** (*dat*) **einen Mann/eine Frau ~** to take a husband/wife **h** *Hürde, Festung, Stadt, Frau* to take; *Schwierigkeiten* to overcome; **das Auto nahm den Berg im dritten Gang** the car took the hill in third gear **i** (*in festen Verbindungen mit n und adv siehe dort*)

Neh|mer [ˈneːmɐ] M -s, -, **Neh|me|rin** [-ərɪn] F -, -nen **a** recipient **b** (= *Käufer*) taker

Neh|rung [ˈneːrʊŋ] F -, -en spit (of land)

Neid [nait] M -(e)s [-dəs], *no pl* envy, jealousy (*auf* +*acc* of); **aus ~** out of envy *or* jealousy; **der ~ der Besitzlosen** (*inf*) sour grapes (*inf*); **nur kein ~!** don't be envious *or* jealous!; **grün (und gelb) vor ~** (*inf*) green with envy; **das muss ihm der ~ lassen** (*inf*) you have to say that much for him, give the devil his due; **mit ~ auf etw** (*acc*) **blicken** to view sth with envy; **jds** (*acc*) *or* **bei jdm ~ erregen** *or* **(er)wecken** to make sb jealous *or* envious, to arouse sb's jealousy; **~ erregend** = **neiderregend**; **vor ~ platzen** (*inf*) *or* **vergehen** to die of envy → **erblassen**

nei|den ['naidn] VT **jdm etw ~** to envy sb (for) sth

Nei|der ['naidɐ] M **-s, -, Nei|de|rin** [-ərın] F **-, -nen** envious *or* jealous person; **reiche Leute haben viele ~** rich people are much envied; **ih|re/seine** *etc* **~** those who envy her/him *etc*

Neid-: **neid|er|füllt** [-lɛɐfʏlt] ADJ *Blick* filled with *or* full of envy, envious, jealous ADV enviously; **~ auf jdn blicken** to look at sb enviously *or* jealously; **neid|er|re|gend** ADJ envy-rousing, causing envy *pred*; **Neid|ham|mel** M *(inf)* jealous *or* envious person; **der alte/du alter ~!** he's/you're just jealous

nei|disch ['naidıʃ], *(S Ger, Aus)* **nei|dig** ['naidıç] ADJ jealous, envious; **auf jdn/etw ~ sein** to be jealous of sb/sth; **etw mit ~en Blicken betrachten** to look enviously at sth, to cast covetous glances at sth ADV jealously, enviously; **etw ~ kommentieren** to make envious comments about sth

neid|los ADJ ungrudging, without envy ADV graciously, gracefully; **das gebe ich ~ zu** I'm willing to admit it graciously; **etw ~ anerkennen** to acknowledge sth graciously

Nei|ge ['naigə] F **-, -n** a *(= Überrest)* remains *pl*; **das Glas bis zur ~ leeren** *(liter)* to drain the cup to the dregs; **den Kelch bis zur ~ leeren** *or* **trinken** *(fig liter)* to drain the bitter cup *(liter)*; **etw bis zur ~ auskosten** *(= genießen)* to savour *(Brit) or* savor *(US)* sth to the full; **etw bis zur bitteren ~ auskosten** *or* **kennenlernen** to suffer sth to the full b *no pl (geh: = Ende)* **zur ~ gehen** to draw to an end *or* a close; **die Vorräte gehen zur ~** the provisions are fast becoming exhausted

nei|gen ['naign] ✪ 53.1 VT *(= beugen) Kopf, Körper* to bend; *(zum Gruß)* to bow; *(= kippen) Behälter, Glas* to tip, to tilt, to incline; **die Bäume ~ ihre Zweige bis zur Erde** *(geh)* the trees bow their branches to the ground; **geneigte Ebene** *(Math)* sloping surface

VR *(Ebene)* to slope, to incline; *(Mensch)* to bend; *(liter: = sich verneigen)* to bow; *(unter Last: Bäume etc)* to bow, to bend; *(Gebäude etc)* to lean; *(= kippen)* to tip (up), to tilt (up); *(Schiff)* to list; *(liter. Tag, Leben)* to draw to a close *or* an end; **sich nach vorne/nach hinten/zur Seite ~** *(Mensch)* to lean *or* bend forward/backwards/to one side; **ein leicht zur Seite geneigtes Gebäude** a building which is leaning *or* tilting over slightly; **mit seitwärtsgeneigtem Kopf** with his/her head held on *or* to one side; **die Waagschale neigt sich zu seinen Gunsten** *(geh)* the scales are tipping *or* the tide is turning in his favour *(Brit) or* favor *(US)*

VI **zu etw ~** to tend toward(s) sth, to have a tendency toward(s) sth; *(= für etw anfällig sein)* to be susceptible *or* prone to sth; **er neigt zum Alkohol** he has a tendency to drink; **er neigt zum Sozialismus** he tends *or* leans toward(s) socialism, he has socialist leanings; **zu der Ansicht** *or* **Annahme ~, dass ...** to tend *or* lean toward(s) the view that ..., to be inclined to take the view that ...; **ich neige eher zur klassischen Musik** I tend rather toward(s) classical music → *auch* **geneigt**

Nei|ge-: **Nei|ge|tech|nik** F, *no pl (Rail)* tilting technology; **Nei|ge|tech|nik|zug** M, **Nei|ge|zug** M *(Rail)* tilting train

Nei|gung ['naigʊŋ] F **-, -en** a *(= das Neigen)* inclination; *(= Gefälle)* incline, slope; *(esp Rail)* gradient *(Brit)*, grade *(US)*; *(= Schräglage)* tilt; *(von Schiff)* list; *(von Magnetnadel)* dip; *(Astron)* inclination

b *(= Tendenz)* tendency; *(Med: = Anfälligkeit)* proneness, tendency; *(= Hingezogensein, Veranlagung)* leaning *usu pl*; *(= Hang, Lust)* inclination; **er hat eine ~ zum Geiz/zum Trinken/zur Kritik** he has a tendency to be mean/to drink/to criticize, he inclines *or* tends to be mean/to drink/to criticize; **künstlerische/politische ~en** artistic/political leanings; **etw aus ~ tun** to do sth by inclination; **keine/geringe ~ verspüren, etw zu tun** to have *or* feel no/little inclination to do sth

c *(= Zuneigung)* affection, fondness; **zu jdm eine ~ fassen** to take a liking to sb; **jds ~ erwidern** to return sb's affection

Nei|gungs-: **Nei|gungs|ehe** F *(geh)* love match; **Nei|gungs|grup|pe** F *(Sch)* club; **~ Fußball** (school) football club; **Nei|gungs|mes|ser** M **-s, -** inclinometer; **Nei|gungs|win|kel** M angle of inclination

nein [nain] ADV no; *(Überraschung)* no; **kommt er? – ~!** is he coming? – no(, he isn't); **ich sage nicht Nein** I wouldn't say no; **da sage ich nicht Nein** I wouldn't say no to that; **~, ~ und nochmals ~** for the last time, no!; **Hunderte, ~ Tausende, hunderte, ~ tausende** hundreds, no *or* nay *(liter)* thousands; **~, so was!** well I never!, you don't say!; **~ doch!** no!; **o ~!, aber ~!** certainly not!, of course not!; **~, dass du dich auch mal wieder sehen lässt!** fancy seeing you again; **~ wie nett, dass du mich mal besuchst!** well, how nice of you to visit me

Nein [nain] NT **-s**, *no pl* no; **bei seinem ~ bleiben** to stick to one's refusal, to remain adamant; **mit Ja oder ~ stimmen** to vote yes or no; *(Parl auch)* to vote yea *or* aye *(Brit)* or nay

Nein-: **Nein|sa|ger** [-za:gɐ] M **-s, -, Nein|sa|ge|rin** [-ərın] F **-, -nen er ist ein ewiger ~** he always says no; **Nein|stim|me** F *(Pol)* no (-vote), nay

Nek|ro-: **Nek|ro|log** [nekro'lo:k] M **-(e)s, -e** [-gə] *(liter)* obituary (notice), necrology *(form)*; **Nek|ro|po|le** [nekro'po:lə] F **-, -n** necropolis; **Nek|ro|phi|lie** [nekrofi'li:] F **-,** *no pl* necrophilia

Nek|tar ['nɛktar] M **-s,** *no pl (Myth, Bot: = Fruchtnektar)* nectar

Nek|ta|ri|ne [nɛkta'ri:nə] F **-, -n** nectarine

Nel|ke ['nɛlkə] F **-, -n** a pink; *(gefüllt)* carnation b *(Gewürz)* clove

Nel|son ['nɛlzɔn] M **-(s), -(s)** *(Sport)* nelson

'nem [nəm] *abbr von* **einem**

Ne|me|sis ['ne:mezıs] F **-,** *no pl* nemesis

'nen [nən] *abbr von* **einen**

nenn|bar ADJ specifiable; *Gefühl, Phänomen, Gedanke etc* nam(e)able; **nicht ~** unspecifiable; unnam(e)able

Nenn|be|trag M *(Comm)* = **Nennwert**

nen|nen ['nɛnən] *pret* **nannte** ['nantə], *ptp* **genannt** [gə'nant] VT a *(= bezeichnen)* to call; *(= einen bestimmten Namen geben)* to name, to call; **jdn nach jdm ~** to name sb after *(Brit) or* for *(US)* sb; **Friedrich II., genannt „der Große"** Frederick II, known as Frederick the Great; **das nenne ich Mut!** that's what I call courage!; **das nennst du schön?** you call that beautiful? → **eigen, Name, so ADV b**

b *(= angeben, aufzählen)* to name; *Beispiel, Grund, Details* to give; **die genannten Namen** the names mentioned; **können Sie mir einen guten Anwalt ~?** could you give me the name of a good lawyer?

c *(= erwähnen)* to mention; **das (weiter oben) Genannte** the above; **das genannte Schloss** the above-mentioned castle, the castle referred to

VR to call oneself; *(= heißen)* to be called, to call oneself; **er nennt sich nur so** that's just what he calls himself; **und so was nennt sich Liebe/modern** *(inf)* and they call that love/modern; **und so was (wie er) nennt sich modern/Dichter** *(inf)* and he calls himself modern/a poet

nen|nens|wert ADJ considerable, not inconsiderable; **nicht ~** negligible, not worth mentioning; **keine ~en Schwierigkeiten** no great difficulties, no difficulties worth mentioning; **nichts Nennenswertes** nothing worth mentioning, nothing of any consequence; **die Demonstration verlief ohne ~e Zwischenfälle** the demonstration went off without major incident ADV significantly; **sich nicht ~ unterscheiden** not to be significantly different

Nen|ner ['nɛnɐ] M **-s, -** *(Math)* denominator; **kleinster gemeinsamer ~** *(lit, fig)* lowest common denominator; **etw auf einen (gemeinsamen) ~ bringen** *(lit, fig)* to reduce sth to a common denominator

Nenn-: **Nenn|fall** M nominative; **Nenn|form** F infinitive; **Nenn|on|kel** M **er ist nur ein ~** I just call him uncle; **ich bin nur ihr ~** she just calls me uncle; **Nenn|tan|te** F **sie ist nur eine ~** I just call her aunt; **ich bin nur seine ~** he just calls me aunt

Nen|nung ['nɛnʊŋ] F **-, -en** *(= das Nennen)* naming; *(Sport)* entry

Nenn-: **Nenn|wert** M *(Fin)* nominal *or* face *or* par value; **zum ~** at par; **über/unter dem ~** above/below par; **eine Aktie im** *or* **zum ~ von 50 EUR** a share with a nominal *or* face *or* par value of 50 euros; **nenn|wert|los** ADJ *Aktie* nonpar; **Nenn|wort** NT *pl* **-wörter** noun

neo-, Neo- [neo] *in cpds* neo-

Neo|dym [neo'dy:m] NT **-s,** *no pl (abbr* **Nd**) neodymium

Neo-: **Neo|fa|schis|mus** M neo-fascism; **Neo|klas|si|zis|mus** M neoclassicism; **neo|kon|ser|va|tiv** ADJ neo-conservative, neo-con *(inf)*; **neo|li|be|ral** ADJ neo-liberal, neo-lib *(inf)*; **Neo|li|be|ra|lis|mus** M neoliberalism

Neo|li|thi|kum [neo'li:tikʊm] NT **-s,** *no pl* Neolithic period

neo|li|thisch [neo'li:tıʃ] ADJ *attr* Neolithic

Neo|lo|gis|mus [neolo'gısmʊs] M **-, Neologismen** [-mən] neologism

Ne|on ['ne:ɔn] NT **-s,** *no pl (abbr* **Ne**) neon

Neo-: **Neo|na|zi** ['ne:ona:tsi] M neo-Nazi; **Neo|na|zis|mus** [neona'tsısmʊs, 'ne:o-] M neo-Nazism; **neo|na|zis|tisch** [neona'tsıstıʃ, 'ne:o-] ADJ neo-Nazi ADV **~ klingende Parolen** neo-Nazi sounding slogans; **~ ausgerichtete Kreise** neo-Nazi groups; **~ angehauchtes Denken** a mentality tainted by neo-Nazism

Ne|on-: **Ne|on|licht** NT neon light; **Ne|on|re|kla|me** F neon sign; **Ne|on|röh|re** F neon tube *or* strip

Neo|pren|an|zug [neo'pre:n-] M wet suit

Ne|pal ['ne:pal, ne'pa:l] NT **-s** Nepal

Ne|pa|le|se [nepa'le:zə] M **-, -n, Ne|pa|le|sin** [-'le:zın] F **-, -nen** Nepalese

ne|pa|le|sisch [nepa'le:zıʃ] ADJ Nepalese

Neph|ri|tis [ne'fri:tıs] F **-, Nephritiden** [nefri'ti:dn] *(Med)* nephritis

Neph|rom [ne'fro:m] NT **-s, -e** *(Med)* nephroma

Ne|po|tis|mus [nepo'tısmʊs] M **-,** *no pl (geh)* nepotism

Nepp [nɛp] M **-s,** *no pl (inf)* **so ein ~!, das ist ja ~!** that's daylight *(Brit) or* highway robbery! *(inf)*, it's a rip-off! *(inf)*

nep|pen ['nɛpn] VT *(inf)* to fleece *(inf)*, to rip off *(inf)*; **da bist du aber geneppt worden!** they must have seen you coming *(inf)*

Nepp|lo|kal NT *(inf)* clip joint *(inf)*

Nep|tun [nɛp'tu:n] M **-s** Neptune

Nep|tu|ni|um [nɛp'tu:niʊm] NT **-s,** *no pl (abbr* **Np**) neptunium

Nerv [nɛrf] M **-s** *or* **-en, -en** nerve; *(Bot auch)* vein; *(obs: = Sehne)* sinew; **(leicht) die ~en verlieren** to scare (easily), to get nervous (easily); **er hat trotz allem die ~en behalten** *or* **nicht verloren** in spite of everything he kept calm *or* kept his cool *(inf)*; *(die Selbstbeherrschung nicht verloren)* in spite of everything he didn't lose control; **die ~en sind (mit) ihm durchgegangen** he lost control *or* his cool *(inf)*, he snapped *(inf)*; **gute/schlechte** *or* **schwache ~en haben** to have strong *or* good/bad *or* weak nerves; **sie kennt** *or* **hat keine ~en** she doesn't get nervous; **der hat (vielleicht) ~en!** *(inf)* he's got a nerve! *(inf)*; **er hat ~en wie Drahtseile** *or* **Bindfäden** *or* **Stricke** he has nerves of steel; **es geht** *or* **fällt mir auf die ~en** *(inf)* it gets on my nerves; **jdm den (letzten) ~ töten** *or* **rauben** *(inf)* to get on sb's nerves *or* wick *(inf)*; **bei ihm liegen die ~en blank** *or* **bloß** he's a bag of nerves *(inf)*; **den ~ haben, etw zu tun** to have the nerve to do sth; **dafür fehlt mir der ~** I don't have the nerve for that; **jdn am ~ treffen** to touch a raw nerve; **den ~ von etw treffen** to touch *or* mention the essential part of sth; **jds ~ treffen** *(inf, positiv)* to be sb's kind of thing *(inf)*; **das kostet ~en** it's a strain on the nerves; **das kostete ihn ~en** it was a strain on his nerves; **~en zeigen** to show nerves → **herunter sein**

nẹr|ven ['nɛrfn] *(inf)* VT **jdn (mit etw) ~** to get on sb's nerves (with sth); **genervt sein** *(= nervös sein)* to be worked up; *(= gereizt sein)* to be irritated VI **das nervt** it gets on your nerves; **du nervst!** *(inf)* you're bugging me! *(inf)*

Nẹr|ven-: **Nẹr|ven|an|span|nung** F nervous tension; **Nẹr|ven|arzt** M, **Nẹr|ven|ärz|tin** F neurologist; **nẹr|ven|auf|rei|bend** ADJ nerve-racking ADV **die Klasse ist ~ laut** the noise of the class plays on the nerves; **Nẹr|ven|bahn** F nerve; **Nẹr|ven|be|las|tung** F strain on the nerves; **nẹr|ven|be|ru|hi|gend** ADJ sedative; **Nẹr|ven|be|ru|hi|gungs|mit|tel** NT sedative, tranquillizer; **Nẹr|ven|bün|del** NT fascicle; *(fig inf)* bag *or* bundle of nerves *(inf)*; **Nẹr|ven|chi|rur|gie** F neurosurgery; **Nẹr|ven|ent|zün|dung** F neuritis; **Nẹr|ven|fa|ser** F nerve fibre *(Brit)* *or* fiber *(US)*; **Nẹr|ven|gas** NT *(Mil)* nerve gas; **Nẹr|ven|gift** NT neurotoxin; **Nẹr|ven|heil|an|stalt** F psychiatric *or* mental hospital; **Nẹr|ven|heil|kun|de** F neurology; **Nẹr|ven|kit|zel** M *(fig)* thrill; **etw als einen äußersten ~ empfinden** to get a big thrill *or* kick *(inf)* out of sth, to find sth really thrilling; **er liebt/sucht den ~** he gets a kick out of it *(inf)*; **Nẹr|ven|kli|nik** F psychiatric clinic; **Nẹr|ven|kos|tüm** NT *(hum)* **ein starkes/schwaches ~ haben** to have strong/weak nerves; **Nẹr|ven|kraft** F strong nerves *pl*; **es erforderte einige ~** it took strong nerves; **meine ~ ist erschöpft** my nerves can't take any more; **nẹr|ven|krank** ADJ *(geistig)* mentally ill *or* disturbed; *(körperlich)* suffering from a nervous disease; **Nẹr|ven|krank|heit** F *(geistig)* mental illness *or* disorder; *(körperlich)* nervous disease *or* disorder; **Nẹr|ven|krieg** M *(fig)* war of nerves; **Nẹr|ven|läh|mung** F neuroparalysis; **Nẹr|ven|lei|den** NT nervous complaint *or* condition; **Nẹr|ven|mit|tel** NT sedative, tranquillizer *(Brit)*, tranquilizer *(US)*; **Nẹr|ven|nah|rung** F *(fig)* **das ist ~** it's good for my *etc* nerves; **Nẹr|ven|pro|be** F trial; **Nẹr|ven|sa|che** F *(inf)* question of nerves; **reine ~!** it's all a question of nerves; **Nẹr|ven|sä|ge** F *(inf)* pain (in the neck) *(inf)*; **nẹr|ven|schä|di|gend** ADJ damaging to the nerves; **Nẹr|ven|schmerz** M neuralgia *no pl*; **Nẹr|ven|schock** M nervous shock; **nẹr|ven|schwach** ADJ with weak nerves, neurasthenic *(spec)*; **er ist ~** he has weak nerves; **Nẹr|ven|schwä|che** F weak nerves *pl*, neurasthenia *(spec)*; **nẹr|ven|stark** ADJ *Mensch* with strong nerves; *Leistung* determined; **er ist ~** he has strong nerves; **Nẹr|ven|stär|ke** F strong nerves *pl*; **es erforderte meine ganze ~** I needed nerves of steel to do it; **nẹr|ven|stär|kend** ADJ nerve-strengthening, tonic; **Nẹr|ven|strang** M nerve fibre *(Brit)* *or* fiber *(US)*; **Nẹr|ven|sys|tem** NT nervous system; **Nẹr|ven|zel|le** F nerve cell; **Nẹr|ven|zent|rum** NT *(Physiol, fig)* nerve centre *(Brit)* *or* center *(US)*; **Nẹr|ven|zu|sam|men|bruch** M nervous breakdown, crackup *(inf)*

nẹr|vig ['nɛrfɪç, 'nɛrvɪç] ADJ a *(inf: = irritierend) Musik, Lärm, Mensch* irritating; **Mensch, wie ~!** God, how irritating!; **der ist vielleicht ~** he gets on your nerves b *Faust, Hand* sinewy; *Gestalt* wiry

nẹrv|lich ['nɛrflɪç] ADJ *Belastung, Anspannung* nervous; **der ~e Zustand des Patienten** the state of the patient's nerves; **ein ~es Wrack** a nervous wreck ADV **er ist ~ erschöpft** he suffers from nervous exhaustion; **~ bedingt** nervous; **~ angespannt sein** to be suffering from nervous exhaustion; **~ überlastet** *or* **überanstrengt sein** to be under a great deal of stress

ner|vös [nɛr'vøːs] ADJ nervous; *(= aufgeregt auch)* jumpy *(inf)*, jittery *(inf)*, on edge; *(Med) Magen* nervous; **jdn ~ machen** to make sb nervous; *(= ärgern)* to get on sb's nerves ADV nervously; **er schreckt beim kleinsten Geräusch ~ zusammen** he jumps nervously at the slightest noise; **die Krankheit ist rein ~ bedingt** the illness is purely nervous in origin

Ner|vo|si|tät [nɛrvozi'tɛːt] F -, *no pl* nervousness; *(Stimmung)* tension

nẹrv|tö|tend ['nɛrf-] *(inf)* ADJ *Geräusch, Gerede* nerve-racking; *Arbeit* soul-destroying ADV *langsam, langweilig, laut* irritatingly

Nẹrz [nɛrts] M **-es, -e** mink

Nẹrz|man|tel M mink coat

Nẹs|sel ['nɛsl] F **-, -n** a *(Bot)* nettle; **sich in die ~n setzen** *(inf)* to put oneself in a spot *(inf)* b **Nesseln** PL *(= Quaddeln)* nettle rash

Nẹs|sel M **-s, -** *(auch* **Nesseltuch, Nesselstoff***)* (untreated) cotton

Nẹs|sel-: **Nẹs|sel|aus|schlag** M, **Nẹs|sel|fie|ber** NT nettle rash; **Nẹs|sel|ge|wächs** NT urticaceae *(spec)*; **Nẹs|sel|schlaf|sack** M sheet sleeping bag; **Nẹs|sel|tier** NT cnidarian *(spec)*

Nẹs|ses|sär NT **-s, -s** → **Necessaire**

Nẹst [nɛst] NT **-(e)s, -er** a *(= Brutstätte)* nest b *(fig: = Schlupfwinkel)* hideout, lair; **ein ~ von Dieben** a den of thieves; **das ~ leer finden** to find the bird has/the birds have flown c *(fig: = Heim)* nest, home; **sein eigenes ~ beschmutzen** to foul one's own nest; **sich ins gemachte** *or* **warme ~ setzen** *(inf) (durch Heirat)* to marry (into) money; *(beruflich)* to move straight into a good job; **da hat er sich ins gemachte** *or* **warme ~ gesetzt** *(inf)* he's got it made *(inf)* d *(fig inf: = Bett)* bed; **raus aus dem ~!** rise and shine! *(inf)*, show a leg! *(Brit inf)* e *(pej inf: Ort) (schäbig)* dump *(inf)*, hole *(inf)*, one-horse town *(inf)*; *(klein)* little place

Nẹst-: **Nẹst|bau** M, *no pl* nest-building; **Nẹst|be|schmut|zer** [-bəʃmʊtsɐ] M **-s, -**, **Nẹst|be|schmut|ze|rin** [-ərɪn] F **-, -nen** *(pej)* runner-down *(inf)* *or* denigrator of one's family/country; **Nẹst|be|schmut|zung** F *(pej)* running-down *(inf)* *or* denigration of one's family/country

nẹs|teln ['nɛstln] VI **an etw** *(dat)* **~** to fumble *or* fiddle (around) with sth VT *(rare)* to fasten

Nẹst-: **Nẹst|flüch|ter** [-flʏçtɐ] M **-s, -**, **Nẹst|flüch|te|rin** [-ərɪn] F **-, -nen** *bird that leaves the nest early (fig) person who leaves the family home at an early age*; **Nẹst|häk|chen** NT baby of the family; **Nẹst|ho|cker** [-hɔkɐ] M **-s, -**, **Nẹst|ho|cke|rin** [-ərɪn] F **-, -nen** *bird that stays a long time in the nest (fig) person who stays in the family home for a long time*

Nẹs|tor ['nɛstoːɐ] M **-s, Nestoren** [-'toːrən] Nestor; *(fig)* doyen

Nes|to|rin [nɛs'toːrɪn] F **-, -nen** *(fig)* doyenne

Nẹst-: **nẹst|warm** ADJ warm from the nest; **Nẹst|wär|me** F *(fig)* happy home life

Ne|ti|kẹt|te [nɛti'kɛt(ə)] F **-**, *no pl*, **Ne|ti|quẹt|te** [nɛti'kɛt(ə)] F **-**, *no pl* *(Comput: im Internet)* netiquette

Net-Sur|fer(in) ['nɛt-] M(F) *(inf)* Net-surfer *(inf)*

nẹtt [nɛt] ADJ nice; *(= hübsch auch)* pretty, cute; **ein ganz ~es Sümmchen** a nice little sum; **eine ~e Stange Geld kosten** *(inf)* to cost a pretty penny *(inf)* *or* a tidy sum *(inf)*; **das kann ja ~ werden!** *(iro)* that'll be nice *or* great *(inf)* (I don't think!); **sei so ~ und räum auf!** would you mind clearing up?, would you like to clear up?; **Oma war so ~ und hat schon abgewaschen** Grandma very nicely *or* kindly washed the dishes; **~, dass Sie gekommen sind!** nice *or* good of you to come; **das war ~/nicht ~ von ihm** that was nice/wasn't very nice of him; **was Netteres ist dir wohl nicht eingefallen?** *(iro)* you do say/do some nice things ADV nicely, nice; **wir haben uns ~ unterhalten** we had a nice chat; **hier werden die Gäste ~ bedient** the waiters are very friendly here; **~ aussehen** to be nice-looking; **die Geschenk war ~ gemeint** the gift was well-meant; **sie plaudert ~** she's nice to talk to

nẹt|ter|wei|se ['nɛtɐvaizə] ADV kindly

Nẹt|tig|keit ['nɛtɪçkait] F **-, -en** a *no pl (= nette Art)* kindness, goodness b **Nettigkeiten** PL *(= nette Worte)* kind words, nice things

Net|ti|kẹt|te [nɛti'kɛt(ə)] F **-**, *no pl*, **Net|ti|quẹt|te** [nɛti'kɛt(ə)] F **-**, *no pl* *(Comput: im Internet)* netiquette

nẹt|to ['nɛto] ADV *(Comm)* net; **ich verdiene ~ £ 1500** *or* **£ 1500 ~ im Monat** I earn £1500 net a month, I net £1500 a month

Nẹt|to- *in cpds* net; **Nẹt|to|ein|kom|men** NT, **Nẹt|to|ein|künf|te** PL net income *no pl*; **Nẹt|to|er|trag** M net profit; **Nẹt|to|ge|halt** NT net salary; **mein ~ ist …** *(auch)* I net …, I take home …; **Nẹt|to|ge|wicht** NT net weight; **Nẹt|to|ge|winn** M clear profit; **Nẹt|to|kre|dit|auf|nah|me** [-kre'diːt-] F net borrowing; **Nẹt|to|kurs** M net rate; **Nẹt|to|lohn** M take-home pay; **Nẹt|to|um|satz** M net turnover, net sales *pl*; **Nẹt|to|ver|dienst** M net income *sing*

Nẹtz [nɛts] NT **-es, -e** a net; *(= Spinnennetz)* web; *(= Haarnetz)* (hair)net; *(= Einkaufsnetz)* string bag, net bag; *(= Gepäcknetz)* (luggage) rack; *(fig: von Lügen, Heuchelei)* tissue, web; *(= Maschenwerk)* netting; **Fische mit dem ~ fangen** to catch fish with nets, to net fish; **ans ~ gehen** *(Sport)* to go up to the net; **ins ~ gehen** *(Ftbl)* to go into the (back of the) net; *(Tennis)* to hit the net; **ins ~ schlagen** to play into the net; **~!** *(Sport)* let!; **ohne ~ und doppelten Boden** without a safety net; **in jds ~ geraten** *(fig)* to fall into sb's clutches; **sich im eigenen ~ verstricken** to be caught in one's own trap, to be hoist with *(Brit)* *or* on *(US)* one's own petard *(prov)*; **jdm ins ~ gehen** *(fig)* to fall into sb's trap; **jdm durchs ~ gehen** *(fig)* to give sb the slip
b *(= System)* network; *(= Stromnetz)* mains *sing or pl*; *(= Überlandnetz)* (national) grid; *(Comput)* network; **das soziale ~** the social security net; **ans ~ gehen** *(Kraftwerk)* to be connected to the grid; **Strom geht ins ~** the grid is supplied with electricity; **das Kraftwerk musste vom ~ genommen werden** the power station had to be shut down
c *(= Internet)* **das ~** the Net; **im ~ surfen** *(inf)* to surf the Net *(inf)*; **ins ~ gehen** to get connected to the Net; **etw übers ~ bestellen** to order sth online *or* through the Net
d *(Math)* net; *(= Kartengitter)* grid
e *(Anat)* omentum *(spec)*, caul (of the stomach)

Nẹtz-: **Nẹtz|ad|mi|nist|ra|tor** M, **Nẹtz|ad|mi|nist|ra|to|rin** F *(Comput)* network administrator; **Nẹtz|an|bie|ter** [-lanbiːtɐ] M **-s, -** *(Telec)* network provider; *(Comput)* Internet (service) provider; **Nẹtz|an|schluss** M *(Elec)* mains connection; **nẹtz|ar|tig** ADJ netlike, reticulate *(form)*; **Nẹtz|auf|schlag** M *(Tennis)* net let; **Nẹtz|au|ge** NT compound eye; **Nẹtz|ball** M *(Tennis etc)* net ball; **Nẹtz|be|trei|ber** M *(Telec)* network operator; *(Comput)* Internet *or* Net operator; **Nẹtz|com|pu|ter** M network computer

nẹt|zen ['nɛtsn] VTI to moisten, to wet

Nẹtz-: **Nẹtz|flüg|ler** [-flyːglɐ] M **-s, -** neuropter *(spec)*, lacewing; **die ~** the Neuroptera *(spec)*; **Nẹtz|fre|quenz** F mains frequency; **Nẹtz|gar|di|ne** F net curtain; **Nẹtz|garn** NT netting yarn; **Nẹtz|ge|rät** NT mains receiver; **Nẹtz|ge|we|be** NT gauze; **Nẹtz|ge|wöl|be** NT *(Archit)* fan vault

Nẹtz|haut F retina

Nẹtz|haut-: **Nẹtz|haut|ab|lö|sung** F detachment of the retina; **Nẹtz|haut|ent|zün|dung** F retinitis

Netz-: **Netz|hemd** NT string vest *(Brit)*, mesh undershirt *(US)*; **Netz|kar|te** F *(Rail)* unlimited travel ticket, runabout ticket *(Brit)*; **Netz|lauf|werk** NT *(Comput)* network drive; **Netz|ma|gen** M *(Zool)* second stomach; **Netz|nut|zer(in)** M(F) Internet *or* Net user; **Netz|plan** M critical path (diagram); **Netz|plan|tech|nik** F critical path method; **Netz|pro|vi|der** M *(Internet)* Internet service provider, ISP; **Netz|rol|ler** F *(Tennis, Volleyball etc)* net cord; **Netz|si|cher|heit** F -, *no pl (Comput)* cybersecurity; **Netz|span|nung** F mains voltage; **Netz|spiel** NT net game; **Netz|spie|ler(in)** M(F) *(Volleyball)* forward; *(Tennis)* net player; **Netz|ste|cker** M mains plug, power *or* electrical *(esp US)* outlet; **Netz|strümp|fe** PL fishnet stockings *pl*; **Netz|sur|fer(in)** M(F) *(inf)* Net-surfer *(inf)*; **Netz|teil** NT mains adaptor

Netz|werk NT *(Elec, Comput, fig)* network; *(aus Draht)* netting

Netz|werk- *(Comput)*: **Netz|werk|kar|te** F network card; **Netz|werk|ser|ver** M network server; **Netz|werk|spiel** NT Net *or* on-line game; **Netz|werk|tech|ni|ker(in)** M(F) network technician; **Netz|werk|trei|ber** M network driver; **Netz|werk|um|ge|bung** F network neighbo(u)rhood

Netz|zu|gang M *(Comput, Telec)* network access; *(Internet)* Internet access, access to the Internet

neu [nɔy] ✪ 50.2 ADJ new; *Seite, Kräfte, Hoffnung, Truppen auch* fresh; *(= kürzlich entstanden auch)* recent; *(= frisch gewaschen) Hemd, Socken* clean; *Wein* young; **das Neue Testament** the New Testament; **die Neue Welt** the New World; **jdm zum ~en Jahr Glück wünschen** to wish sb (a) Happy New Year; **ein ~er Anfang** a fresh *or* new start; **~eren Datums** of (more) recent date; **~e Hoffnung schöpfen** to take new *or* fresh hope; **eine ~e Mode** a new fashion; **ein ~er Tanz** a new dance; **die ~(e)ste Mode** the latest fashion; **der ~(e)ste Tanz** the latest dance; **die ~esten Nachrichten** the latest news; **die ~eren Sprachen** modern languages; **ein ganz ~er Wagen** a brand-new car; **das ist mir ~!** that's new(s) to me; **mir ist die Sache ~** this is all new to me; **schlechte Laune ist mir ~ an ihm** it's something new for me to see him in a bad mood; **sich wie ein ~er Mensch fühlen** to feel like a new person; **eine ~e Bearbeitung** a revised edition; *(von Oper etc)* a new version; **Geschichte der ~eren Zeit** recent *or* modern history; **in ~erer Zeit** in modern times; **erst in ~erer Zeit** only recently; **viele alte Leute finden sich in der ~en Zeit nicht mehr zurecht** a lot of old people can't get on in the modern world; **seit Neu(e)stem** recently; **seit Neu(e)stem gibt es …** since recently there has been …; **aufs Neue** *(geh)* afresh, anew; **auf ein Neues!** *(als Toast)* (here's) to the New Year!; *(Aufmunterung)* let's try again; **der/die Neue** the newcomer, the new man/boy/woman/girl *etc*; **Neue Welle** new wave; **die Neuen** the newcomers, the new people; **was ist das Neue an dem Buch?** what's new about the book?; **das Neu(e)ste in der Mode/auf dem Gebiet der Weltraumforschung** the latest in fashion/in the field of space research; **weißt du schon das Neu(e)ste?** have you heard the latest (news)?; **was gibts Neues?** *(inf)* what's the latest?, what's new?; **das Neu(e)ste vom Tage** the latest news, up-to-the-minute news; **das Neu(e)ste vom Neuen** the very latest (things); **von Neuem** *(= von vorn)* from the beginning, afresh, from scratch; *(= wieder)* again → **Besen a, Weg a, alt a**

ADV **a** *(= von vorn)* **~ anfangen** to start all over (again); **~ beginnen** to make a fresh start, to start again from scratch; **~ starten** *Computer* to restart, to reboot; **Vorhänge/ein Kleid ~ anfertigen lassen** to have new curtains/a new dress made; **~ entwickelt** newly developed; **sich/jdn ~ einkleiden** to buy oneself/sb a new set of clothes; **etw ~ anschaffen** to buy sth new; **~ bauen** to build a new house; **~ geschaffen** newly created

b *(= zusätzlich)* **~ hinzukommen zu etw** to join sth; **Mitarbeiter ~ einstellen** to hire new employees; **Tierarten ~ entdecken** to discover new species of animals; **~ entdeckt** newly *or* recently discovered

c *(= erneut)* **etw ~ auflegen** to publish a new edition of sth; **~ drucken** to reprint; **~ bearbeiten** to revise; **~ bearbeitet** revised; **ein Zimmer ~ einrichten** to refurnish a room; **frei werdende Stellen werden nicht ~ besetzt** vacant positions will not be filled; **ich hatte das Buch verloren und musste es ~ kaufen** I lost the book and had to buy another copy; **~ eröffnet** *(= wiedereröffnet)* reopened; **~ ordnen** to reorganize; **sich ~ verschulden** to borrow money again, to take out another loan; **die Rollen ~ besetzen** to recast the roles; **die Akten ~ ordnen** to reorganize the files

d *(= seit kurzer Zeit)* **ich habe mir das ganz ~ gekauft** I just bought it; **~ gebacken** fresh-baked, newly-baked → *auch* **neugebacken**; **das Buch ist ~ erschienen** the book is a recent publication *or* has just come out; **er ist ~ hinzugekommen** he's joined (him/them) recently; **~ gewählt** newly elected; **hier ist ein Supermarkt ~ entstanden/gebaut worden** a supermarket has just been opened/built here; **~ eröffnet** newly-opened; **wir sind ~ hierhergezogen** we have just moved here; **der Schüler ist ganz ~ in unserer Klasse** the pupil is new in our class, the pupil has just joined our class; **dieser Artikel ist ~ eingetroffen/~ im Sortiment** this article has just come in/has just been added to the range; **~ vermählt** newly married *or* wed

Neu-: **Neu|an|fang** M new beginning; **einen ~ machen** to start again from the scratch *or* from the beginning; **Neu|an|fer|ti|gung** F *(= das Neuanfertigen)* making (up), production (from scratch); *(Produkt)* newly-made article; **die ~ eines Anzugs dauert vier Wochen** it takes four weeks to make up a suit; **Neu|an|kömm|ling** M newcomer; **Neu|an|schaf|fung** F new purchase *or* acquisition; **eine ~ würde sich rentieren** it would be worth buying a new machine/part *etc*; **neu|apos|to|lisch** ADJ New Apostolic ADV **jdn ~ erziehen** to raise sb as a member of the New Apostolic Church

neu|ar|tig ADJ new; **ein ~es Wörterbuch** a new type of dictionary; **es ist ganz ~** it is of a completely new type, it is a completely new departure

Neu|ar|tig|keit [ˈnɔylaːrtɪçkait] F -, -en novelty

Neu-: **Neu|auf|la|ge** F reprint; *(mit Verbesserungen)* new edition; **Neu|aus|ga|be** F new edition

Neu|bau M *pl* **-bauten** new house/building

Neu|bau-: **Neu|bau|ge|biet** NT development area; **Neu|bau|sied|lung** F new housing estate; **Neu|bau|vier|tel** NT new district; **Neu|bau|woh|nung** F newly-built flat *(Brit) or* apartment

Neu-: **neu|be|ar|bei|tet** [-bəlarbaitət] ADJ → **neu ADV c**; **Neu|be|ar|bei|tung** F revised edition; *(von Oper etc)* new version; *(= das Neubearbeiten)* revision; **Neu|be|ginn** M new beginning(s *pl*); **Neu|be|le|bung** F revival; **Neu|be|set|zung** F replacement; *(Theat)* recasting; **in der ~** in the recast version; **eine ~ dieses Postens wurde nötig** it was necessary to find a replacement for this position; **Neu|bil|dung** F *(= das Neubilden)* forming, formation; *(= neues Gebilde)* new entity; *(Ling)* neologism; *(Med)* renewal, repair; **eine staatliche ~** a newly-formed state; **bei der ~ von Begriffen** in the formation of new concepts; **Neu|bür|ger(in)** M(F) new citizen; **Neu-Del|hi** [nɔyˈdeːli] NT **-s** New Delhi; **neu|deutsch** *(iro, pej)* ADJ new German, neo-German ADV in the new German manner; *sprechen* in new German; **Neu|druck** M *pl* **-drucke** reprint; **Neu|ein|rich|tung** F refurnishing; *(= Möbel)* new furnishings *pl or* furniture; **Neu|ein|stei|ger(in)** M(F) newcomer; **Neu|ein|stel|lung** F new appointment; **Neu|ein|stu|die|rung** F new production

Neu|en|burg [ˈnɔyənbʊrk] NT **-s** *(Kanton)* Neuchâtel

Neu-: **Neu|eng|land** NT New England; **neu|eng|lisch** ADJ **a** modern English **b** *(= zu Neuengland gehörend)* New England *attr*; **neu|ent|deckt** ADJ → **neu ADV b**; **Neu|ent|de|ckung** F rediscovery; *(Mensch)* new discovery; *(Ort)* newly discovered place; **neu|ent|wi|ckelt** [-lɛntvɪklt] ADJ → **neu ADV a**; **Neu|ent|wick|lung** F new development

neu|er|dings [ˈnɔyɐˈdɪŋs] ADV recently; *(rare: = von Neuem)* again

Neu|e|rer [ˈnɔyərɐ] M **-s, -**, **Neu|e|rin** [-ərɪn] F **-, -nen** innovator

neu|er|lich [ˈnɔyɐlɪç] ADV lately, recently, of late; *(= nochmals, wieder)* again ADJ recent; *(= wiederholt)* further

Neu-: **neu|er|öff|net** [-lɛrlœfnət] ADJ → **neu ADV c, d**; **Neu|er|öff|nung** F (new) opening; *(= Wiedereröffnung)* reopening; **die ~ der Filiale** the opening of the new branch; **es gab zwanzig Geschäftsschließungen und nur zwei ~en** twenty shops *(Brit) or* stores were closed and only two new ones opened; **Neu|er|schei|nung** F *(Buch)* new *or* recent publication; *(CD)* new release; *(= Neuheit)* new *or* recent phenomenon

Neu|e|rung [ˈnɔyərʊŋ] F **-, -en** innovation; *(= Reform)* reform

neu|e|rungs|süch|tig ADJ over-anxious to carry out reforms, reform-mad *(Brit inf)*, reform-crazy *(inf)*

Neu|er|wer|bung F new acquisition; *(= Sportler)* new signing; **die ~ von Büchern** the acquisition of new books

neu|es|tens [ˈnɔyəstns] ADV lately, recently

Neu-: **Neu|fas|sung** F new *or* revised version; **Neu|fest|set|zung** F reassessment; **Neu|fund|land** [nɔyˈfʊntlant] NT **-s** Newfoundland; **Neu|fund|län|der**[1] [nɔyˈfʊntlɛndɐ] M **-s, -** *(Hund)* Newfoundland (dog); **Neu|fund|län|der**[2] [nɔyˈfʊntlɛndɐ] M **-s, -**, **Neu|fund|län|de|rin** [-ərɪn] F **-, -nen** Newfoundlander; **neu|fund|län|disch** [nɔyˈfʊntlɛndɪʃ] ADJ Newfoundland; **neu|ge|ba|cken** ADJ **a** *(fig)* newly-fledged, brand-new **b** *(Brot)* → **neu ADV d**; **neu|ge|bo|ren** ADJ newborn; **sich wie ~ fühlen** to feel (like) a new man/woman; **Neu|ge|bo|re|ne(s)** [-gəboːrənə] NT *decl as adj* newborn child; **Neu|ge|bo|re|nen|scree|ning** NT *(Med)* new-born screening; **Neu|ge|burt** F *(= Neugeborenes)* newborn child/animal; *(= Neuerscheinung)* new phenomenon; *(= Wiedergeburt)* rebirth; **die ~en** the newborn; **neu|ge|schaf|fen** ADJ → **neu ADV a**; **neu ge|stal|ten** VT to rearrange, to reorder; *Beziehungen, Ordnung* to reorganize; *Platz, Stadion* to redesign, to give a new layout; **Neu|ge|stal|tung** F rearrangement, reordering; *(von Platz, Stadion)* redesigning; *(von Beziehungen, Ordnung)* reorganization; **die ~ eines alten Themas** the reworking of an old theme; **neu|ge|wählt** [-gəvɛːlt] ADJ → **neu ADV d**

Neu|gier [ˈnɔygiːɐ] F **-**, *no pl*, **Neu|gier|de** [ˈnɔygiːɐdə] F **-**, *no pl* curiosity, inquisitiveness (*auf +acc* about); *(pej auch)* nosiness *(inf)*; **aus (reiner) ~** out of (sheer) curiosity; **seine ~ befriedigen** to satisfy one's curiosity; **vor ~ platzen** to be bursting with curiosity

neu|gie|rig [ˈnɔygiːrɪç] ADJ inquisitive, curious (*auf +acc* about); *(pej)* prying, nosy *(inf)*; *(= gespannt)* longing *or* curious to know; *Blick, Fragen* inquisitive; **ein Neugieriger** an inquisitive person; *(pej auch)* a nos(e)y parker *(Brit inf)*, a curious George *(US inf)*; **jdn ~ machen** to excite *or* arouse sb's curiosity; **ich bin ~, ob** I wonder if; **da bin ich aber ~!** this should be interesting, I can hardly wait *(inf)*; **sei nicht so ~!** don't be so inquisitive *or* nosy *(inf) or* such a nos(e)y parker *(Brit inf) or* curious George *(US inf)*!

ADV full of curiosity; **etw ~ untersuchen** to

study sth curiously; *(Tier)* to examine sth inquisitively; **er fragt zu ~** he's too curious

Neu-: **Neu|glie|de|rung** F reorganization, restructuring; **Neu|go|tik** F Gothic revival, neo-Gothic style; **neu|go|tisch** ADJ neo-Gothic; **neu|grie|chisch** ADJ Modern Greek; **Neu|grie|chisch(e)** NT Modern Greek → *auch* **Deutsch(e)**; **Neu|grün|dung** F *(= Wiederbegründung)* re-establishment, refoundation; **die ~ von Universitäten** the founding of new universities; **der Verein ist eine ~** the club was only recently founded; **Neu|grup|pie|rung** F regroupment, rearrangement; **Neu|gui|nea** [nɔygi'ne:a] NT New Guinea

Neu|heit ['nɔyhait] F **-, -en** **a** *no pl (= das Neusein)* novelty; **es wird bald den Reiz der ~ verlieren** the novelty will soon wear off **b** *(= neue Sache)* innovation, new thing/idea; **dieses Gerät ist eine ~ auf dem Markt** this item is new on the market

neu|hoch|deutsch ADJ New High German; **das Neuhochdeutsche** New High German

Neu|ig|keit ['nɔyıçkait] F **-, -en** **a** (piece of) news; **die ~en** the news *sing*; **die ~ des Tages** the (big) news of the day **b** *(= das Neusein)* novelty

Neu|ins|tal|la|ti|on F *(Comput)* new installation

Neu|in|sze|nie|rung F new production

Neu|jahr ['nɔyja:ɐ, nɔy'ja:ɐ] NT New Year; **an ~** on New Year's Day; **jdm zu(m) ~ gratulieren** to wish sb a Happy New Year; **~ begehen** *or* **feiern** to celebrate the New Year; **Pros(i)t ~!** (here's) to the New Year!

Neu|jahrs-: **Neu|jahrs|abend** M New Year's Eve, Hogmanay *(Scot)*; **Neu|jahrs|an|spra|che** F New Year speech; **Neu|jahrs|emp|fang** M New Year reception; **Neu|jahrs|fest** NT New Year's Day; *(= Feier)* New Year celebrations *pl*; **Neu|jahrs|glück|wunsch** M New Year greeting; **Neu|jahrs|kar|te** F New Year card; **Neu|jahrs|kon|zert** NT New Year concert; **Neu|jahrs|tag** M New Year's Day

Neu-: **Neu|ka|le|do|ni|en** [nɔykale'do:niən] NT **-s** New Caledonia; **Neu|ka|le|do|ni|er** [nɔykale'do:niɐ] M **-s, -**, **Neu|ka|le|do|ni|e|rin** [-iərın] F **-, -nen** New Caledonian; **Neu|kun|de** M, **Neu|kun|din** F *(Comm)* new customer; **neu|ka|le|do|nisch** [nɔykale'do:nıʃ] ADJ New Caledonian; **Neu|land** NT, *no pl* virgin land *or* territory, uncultivated land; *(fig)* new territory *or* ground; **~ gewinnen** *(lit)* to reclaim land; **~ betreten** *or* **beschreiten** to break new ground; **er betrat wissenschaftliches/geistiges ~** he broke new ground in science/intellectually; **neu|la|tei|nisch** ADJ neo-Latin, new Latin

neu|lich ['nɔylıç] ADV recently, the other day; **~ Abend** *or* **abends** the other evening ADJ *(strictly incorrect)* recent

Neu|ling ['nɔylıŋ] M **-s, -e** newcomer, new man/woman/boy/girl; *(pej auch)* beginner, greenhorn *(inf)*

neu|mo|disch *(pej)* ADJ new-fangled *(pej)*, fashionable ADV **sich ~ anziehen** to dress in the latest fashions; **~ einrichten** to be furnished according to the latest style; **sich ~ ausdrücken** to use new-fangled words; **~ unterrichten** *(mit neuen Methoden)* to teach in a new-fangled way; *(modernes Wissen)* to teach new-fangled stuff

Neu|mond M new moon; **bei ~** at new moon; **heute ist ~** there's a new moon today

neun [nɔyn] NUM nine; **alle ~(e)!** *(beim Kegeln)* strike!; **er warf alle ~(e)** he got a strike → *auch* **vier**

Neun [nɔyn] F **-, -en** nine; **er hat die ~ ausgespielt** he played the nine; **ach du grüne ~e!** *(inf)* well I'm blowed *(Brit inf)* *or* I'll be damned! → *auch* **Vier**

Neun-: **Neun|au|ge** NT lamprey; **Neun|eck** NT nonagon; **neun|eckig** ADJ nonagonal

Neu|ner|pro|be ['nɔynɐ-] F *(Math)* casting out nines

Neun-: **neun|hun|dert** ['nɔyn'hʊndɐt] NUM nine hundred; **neun|mal** ['nɔynma:l] ADV nine times → *auch* **viermal**; **neun|mal|klug** *(iro)* ADJ smart-aleck *attr (inf)*; **du bist ein ganz Neunmalkluger!** you're a real smart-aleck *(inf)* ADV like a smart-aleck *(inf)*; **sie redet so ~ daher** she talks as if she knows it all; **neun|schwän|zig** [-ʃvɛntsıç] ADJ **die ~e Katze** the cat-o'-nine-tails; **neun|tau|send** ['nɔyn'tauznt] NUM nine thousand

Neun|tel ['nɔyntl] NT **-s, -** ninth → *auch* **Viertel**

neun|tens ['nɔyntns] ADV ninth(ly), in the ninth place

neun|te(r, s) ['nɔyntə] ADJ ninth → *auch* **vierte(r, s)**

neun|zehn ['nɔyntse:n] NUM nineteen → *auch* **vierzehn**

neun|zehn|te(r, s) ['nɔyntse:ntə] ADJ nineteenth → *auch* **vierte(r, s)**

19-Zöl|ler M **-s, -** *(Comput)* 19-inch *or* 19" monitor

neun|zig ['nɔyntsıç] NUM ninety; **auf ~ sein** *(inf)* to be in a blind fury *or* a filthy temper *(inf)* → *auch* **vierzig**

Neun|zi|ger ['nɔyntsıgɐ] M **-s, -**, **Neun|zi|ge|rin** [-ərın] F **-, -nen** *(Mensch)* ninety-year-old, nonagenarian → *auch* **Vierziger**

neun|zigs|te(r, s) ['nɔyntsıçstə] ADJ ninetieth → **vierte(r, s)**

Neu-: **Neu|ord|nung** F reorganization, reordering; *(= Reform)* reform; **Neu|or|ga|ni|sa|ti|on** F reorganization; **Neu|ori|en|tie|rung** F reorientation; **Neu|phi|lo|lo|ge** M, **Neu|phi|lo|lo|gin** F modern linguist; **Neu|phi|lo|lo|gie** F modern languages *sing or pl*; **Neu|prä|gung** F *(Münze)* new minting; *(Begriff)* new coinage

neu|ral [nɔy'ra:l] ADJ neural; **~es Netzwerk** *(Comput)* neural network

Neu|ral|gie [nɔyral'gi:] F **-, -n** [-'gi:ən] neuralgia

neu|ral|gisch [nɔy'ralgıʃ] ADJ neuralgic; **ein ~er Punkt** a trouble area; **diese Kreuzung/Zypern ist ein ~er Punkt** this crossroads/Cyprus is a trouble area *or* trouble spot

Neu|ral|the|ra|pie [nɔy'ral-] F neural therapy

Neu|ras|the|nie [nɔyraste'ni:] F **-, -n** [-'ni:ən] neurasthenia

Neu|ras|the|ni|ker [nɔyras'te:nikɐ] M **-s, -**, **Neu|ras|the|ni|ke|rin** [-ərın] F **-, -nen** neurasthenic

neu|ras|the|nisch [nɔyras'te:nıʃ] ADJ neurasthenic

Neu-: **Neu|re|ge|lung** F adjustment, revision; **eine ~ des Verkehrs** a new traffic management scheme; **neu|reich** ADJ nouveau riche; **Neu|rei|che(r)** MF *decl as adj* nouveau riche; **die ~n** the nouveaux riches

Neu|ri|tis [nɔy'ri:tıs] F **-, Neuritiden** [-ri'ti:dn] neuritis

Neu|ro- *in cpds* neuro; **Neu|ro|chi|rur|gie** F neurosurgery; **Neu|ro|der|mi|tis** [nɔyrodɛr'mi:tıs] F **-, Neurodermitiden** [-mi'ti:dn] *(Med)* neurodermatitis; **Neu|ro|lep|ti|kum** [nɔyro'lɛptikʊm] NT **-s, Neuroleptika** [-ka] *(Pharm)* neuroleptic (drug); **Neu|ro|lo|ge** [nɔyro'lo:gə] M **-n, -n**, **Neu|ro|lo|gin** [-'lo:gın] F **-, -nen** neurologist; **Neu|ro|lo|gie** [nɔyrolo'gi:] F **-, -n** [-'gi:ən] neurology; **neu|ro|lo|gisch** [nɔyro'lo:gıʃ] ADJ neurological ADV neurologically; **~ erkrankt sein** to have a neurological disease

Neu|ron ['nɔyrɔn] NT **-s, -e(n)** [-'ro:nə͜n] neuron

Neu|ro-: **Neu|ro|na|vi|ga|ti|on** F *(Med)* neuronavigation; **Neu|ro|pa|thie** [nɔyropa'ti:] F **-, -n** [-'ti:ən] neuropathy; **Neu|ro|pa|tho|lo|gie** F neuropathology

Neu|ro|se [nɔy'ro:zə] F **-, -n** neurosis

Neu|ro|ti|ker [nɔy'ro:tikɐ] M **-s, -**, **Neu|ro|ti|ke|rin** [-ərın] F **-, -nen** neurotic

neu|ro|tisch [nɔy'ro:tıʃ] ADJ neurotic ADV neurotically; **~ klingen** to sound neurotic; **dein Misstrauen wirkt ~** you are neurotically suspicious

Neu|ro|trans|mit|ter [-transmıtɐ] M **-s, -** *(Med)* neurotransmitter

Neu-: **Neu|satz** M *(Typ)* new setting; **Neu|schnee** M fresh snow; **über Nacht gab es bis zu 37 Zentimeter ~** up to 37 cm of fresh snow fell overnight; **Neu|schöp|fung** F new creation; *(Ausdruck)* invention; **Neu|see|land** [nɔy'ze:lant] NT **-s** New Zealand; **Neu|see|län|der** [nɔy'ze:lɛndɐ] M **-s, -**, **Neu|see|län|de|rin** [-ərın] F **-, -nen** New Zealander; **neu|see|län|disch** [nɔy'ze:lɛndıʃ] ADJ New Zealand; **Neu|sil|ber** NT nickel silver; **Neu|sprach|ler** [-ʃpraxlɐ] M **-s, -**, **Neu|sprach|le|rin** [-ərın] F **-, -nen** modern linguist; **neu|sprach|lich** ADJ modern language *attr*; **~er Zweig** *(Sch)* modern language side; **~es Gymnasium** ≈ grammar school *(Brit)*, ≈ high school *(esp US, Scot, stressing modern languages)*; **Neu|stadt** F new town

Neu|start M **a** *(= Neuanfang)* new start **b** *(Comput)* restart, reboot

neus|tens ['nɔystns] ADV = **neuestens**

Neu|struk|tu|rie|rung F restructuring

Neu|tö|ner [-tø:nɐ] M **-s, -**, **Neu|tö|ne|rin** [-ərın] F **-, -nen** *(Mus)* exponent of the New Music

neut|ral [nɔy'tra:l] ADJ neutral; *(rare: Gram)* neuter; **die Neutralen** *(Pol)* the neutrals ADV neutrally; **etw ~ bewerten** to give a neutral assessment of sth

Neut|ra|li|sa|ti|on [nɔytraliza'tsio:n] F **-, -en** neutralization; *(Sport: von Rennen)* suspension

neut|ra|li|sie|ren [nɔytrali'zi:rən] *ptp* **neutralisiert** VT to neutralize; *(Sport) Rennen* to suspend

Neut|ra|li|sie|rung F **-, -en** neutralization

Neut|ra|lis|mus [nɔytra'lısmʊs] M **-,** *no pl (Pol)* neutralism

Neut|ra|li|tät [nɔytrali'tɛ:t] F **-,** *no pl* neutrality

Neut|ra|li|täts-: **Neut|ra|li|täts|ab|kom|men** NT treaty of neutrality; **Neut|ra|li|täts|er|klä|rung** F declaration of neutrality; **Neut|ra|li|täts|po|li|tik** F policy of neutrality; **Neut|ra|li|täts|ver|let|zung** F violation of neutrality; **Neut|ra|li|täts|zei|chen** NT sign of neutrality

Neut|ri|no [nɔy'tri:no] NT **-s, -s** neutrino

Neut|ron ['nɔytrɔn] NT **-s, -en** [-'tro:nən] neutron

Neut|ro|nen- *in cpds* neutron; **Neut|ro|nen|bom|be** F neutron bomb; **Neut|ro|nen|strah|len** PL neutron rays *pl*; **Neut|ro|nen|strah|lung** F neutron radiation

Neut|rum ['nɔytrʊm] NT **-s, Neutra** *or* **Neutren** [-tra, -trən] *(Gram, fig)* neuter; **ein ~** *(Gram)* a neuter noun; **sie wirkt auf mich wie ein ~** I don't think of her as a woman

Neu-: **Neu|ver|an|la|gung** F *(Fin)* reassessment; **Neu|ver|fil|mung** F remake; **Neu|ver|hand|lung** F *usu pl* renegotiation; **neu|ver|mählt** [-fɛɐmɛ:lt] ADJ → **neu ADV d**; **Neu|ver|mähl|te(r)** [-fɛɐmɛ:ltə] MF *decl as adj* **die ~n** the newly-weds; **Neu|ver|schul|dung** F new borrowings *pl*; **Neu|wa|gen** M new car; **Neu|wahl** F *(Pol)* new election, re-election; **die ~ des Präsidenten** the election of a new president; **es gab vorgezogene ~en** the elections were brought forward; **neu|welt|lich** ADJ *(geh)* new world; **Neu|wert** M value when new; **neu|wer|tig** ADJ as new; **Neu|wert|ver|si|che|rung** F new-for-old insurance *(Brit)*, replacement value insurance; **Neu|zeit** F modern age *or* era, modern times *pl*; **Literatur/Gesellschaft der ~** modern literature/society; **die Olympischen Spiele der ~** the modern Olympics; **neu|zeit|lich** ADJ modern; **Neu|züch|tung** F *(Tier)* new breed; *(= Pflanze)* new variety; **die ~ von Tieren** the breeding of new types of animal; **die ~ von Pflanzen** the cultivation of new types of plant; **Neu|zu|gang** M new entry; **Neu|zu|las|sung** F *(Aut)* ≈ registration of a new vehicle; *(von Arzneimittel)* licensing; **die meisten gestohlenen Autos waren ~en** most of the stolen cars were *or* had new registrations; **die Zahl der ~en steigt** the number of new vehicles being registered is increasing

New Age ['nju: 'e:dʒ] **NT -,** *no pl* new age

New|co|mer ['nju:kamɐ] **M -(s), -** newcomer

News|group ['nju:zgru:p] **F -, -s** *(Comput, Internet)* newsgroup

News|let|ter ['nju:zlɛtɐ] **M -s, -s** *(Comput: im Internet)* newsletter

New Wave [nju:'we:v] **F -,** *no pl* new wave

New York ['nju:'jɔ:k] **NT -s** New York

New Yor|ker [nju:'jɔ:kɐ] **ADJ** *attr* New York

New Yor|ker [nju:'jɔ:kɐ] **M - -s, - -, New Yor|ke|rin** [-ərɪn] **F - -, - -nen** New Yorker

nhd. *abbr (Ling) von* **neuhochdeutsch**

Ni|be|lun|gen|treue [ni:bə'lʊŋən-] **F** unshakeable loyalty

nicht [nɪçt] **ADV a** *(Verneinung)* not; **~ amtlich** unofficial; **~ berufstätig** non-employed; **~ christlich** non-Christian; **~ druckbar** *Zeichen* nonprintable; **~ ehelich** = **nichtehelich**; **~ flüchtig** *(Chem, Comput)* non-volatile; **~ geschäftsfähig** = **geschäftsunfähig**; **~ leitend** *(Phys)* non-conducting; **~ metallisch** nonmetallic; **~ öffentlich** not open to the public, private; **~ öffentliche Sitzung/Konferenz** meeting/conference in camera *(Jur) or* behind closed doors; **~ organisiert** *(Arbeiter)* non-organized, non-union(ized); **~ rostend** rustproof, non-rust; *(Stahl)* stainless; **~ Sesshafte(r)** = **Nichtsesshafte(r)**; **~ staatlich** non-governmental; *(= privat)* private; **~ Zutreffende(s)** = **Nichtzutreffende(s)**; **er raucht ~** *(augenblicklich)* he is not *or* isn't smoking; *(gewöhnlich)* he does not *or* doesn't smoke; **alle lachten, nur er ~** everybody laughed except him, everybody laughed, only he didn't; **kommst du? – nein, ich komme ~** are you coming? – no, I'm not (coming); **ich weiß auch ~, warum** I really don't know why; **ich kann das ~ – ich auch ~** I can't do it – neither *or* nor can I; **~ mehr** *or* **länger** not any longer; **~ mehr als** no *or* not more than; **~ mehr und ~ weniger als** no more and no less than; **~ heute und ~ morgen** neither today nor tomorrow; **~ ihn meinte ich, sondern sie** I didn't mean him, I meant her, it's not him I meant but her; **er ~!** not him, not he *(form)*; **~ (ein)mal** not even

b *(Bitte, Gebot, Verbot)* **~ berühren!** do not touch; *(gesprochen)* don't touch; **ärgere dich ~!** don't be angry, do not be angry *(often liter)*; **~ rauchen!** no smoking; **~!** don't!, no!; **tus ~!** don't do it!; **~ doch!** stop it!, don't!; **bitte ~!** please don't; **nur das ~!** anything but that!; **nun wein mal ~ gleich!** now don't start crying

c *(rhetorisch)* **er kommt, ~ (wahr)?** he's coming, isn't he *or* is he not *(esp Brit)*?; **sie kommen, ~ (wahr)?** they're coming, aren't they *or* are they not *(esp Brit)*?; **er kommt ~, ~ wahr?** he isn't coming, is he?; **ich darf kommen, ~ (wahr)?** I can come, can't I *or* can I?; **das ist schön, ~ (wahr)?** it's nice, isn't it?; **jetzt wollen wir Schluss machen, ~?** let's leave it now, right *or* OK?

d *(doppelte Verneinung)* **~ uninteressant/unschön** *etc* not uninteresting/unattractive *etc*

e *(Verwunderung, Resignation etc)* **was die Kinder ~ alles wissen!** the things children know about!; **was ich ~ alles durchmachen muss!** the things I have to go through!

Nicht-, nicht- [nɪçt] **PREF** non-; **Nicht|ach|tung F** (*+gen* for) disregard, lack of regard; **jdn mit ~ strafen** to send sb to Coventry *(Brit)*, to give sb the silent treatment; **~ des Gerichts** contempt of court; **nicht|amt|lich ADJ** unofficial; **Nicht|an|er|ken|nung F** non-recognition; **Nicht|an|griffs|pakt M** non-aggression pact; **Nicht|ari|er(in) M(F)** non-Aryan; **Nicht|be|ach|tung F, Nicht|be|fol|gung F** non-observance; **Nicht|be|nut|zung F** *(form)* non-utilization *(form)*; **bei ~ der Maschine** when the machine is not in use *or* being used; **nicht|be|rufs|tä|tig ADJ → nicht a**; **Nicht|be|zah|lung F** non-payment; **nicht|christ|lich ADJ** non-Christian

nicht|druck|bar ADJ *(Typ, Comput)* **→ nicht a**

Nich|te ['nɪçtə] **F -, -n** niece

Nicht-: **nicht|ehe|lich ADJ** *(Jur) Kinder, Abstammung* illegitimate; *Mutter, Vater* unmarried; **in ~er Lebensgemeinschaft leben** to cohabit; **~e Beziehungen zu jdm unterhalten** to cohabit with sb; **Kinder aus ~en Beziehungen** children born outside wedlock *(form)*; **Nicht|ein|hal|tung F** non-compliance (*+gen* with), non-observance (*+gen* of); **Nicht|ein|mi|schung F** *(Pol)* non-intervention, non-interference; **Nicht|er|fül|lung F** *(Jur)* non-fulfilment (*+gen* of), default; **Nicht|er|schei|nen NT** non-appearance, failure to appear; **Nicht|fach|frau F, Nicht|fach|mann M** non-specialist, non-expert; **nicht|flüch|tig ADJ** *(Chem, Comput)* non-volatile; **Nicht|ge|brauch M** = **Nichtbenutzung**; **Nicht|ge|fal|len NT bei ~ (zurück)** if not satisfied (return); **nicht|ge|schäfts|fä|hig ADJ** *attr* = **geschäftsunfähig**

nich|tig ['nɪçtɪç] **ADJ a** *(Jur: = ungültig)* invalid, void; **etw für ~ erklären** to declare sth invalid; *Ehe auch* to annul sth; **dadurch** *or* **hierdurch ist der Vertrag ~ geworden** the treaty has thereby become invalid **→ null b** *(= unbedeutend)* trifling, trivial; *Versuch* vain; *Drohung* empty, vain; **die ~en Dinge dieser Welt** *(liter)* the vain things *or* the vanities *(liter)* of this life

Nich|tig|keit F -, -en a *(Jur: = Ungültigkeit)* invalidity, nullity **b** *usu pl (= Kleinigkeit)* trifle, triviality, trivia *pl*

Nich|tig|keits-: **Nich|tig|keits|er|klä|rung F** *(Jur)* annulment; **Nich|tig|keits|kla|ge F** *(Jur)* nullity suit *(Brit)*, filing for an annulment

Nicht-: **Nicht|kom|bat|tant(in) M(F)** *(form)* non-combatant; **nicht|lei|tend ADJ** *(Elec)* **→ nicht a**; **Nicht|lei|ter M** *(Elec)* non-conductor; **Nicht|me|tall NT** nonmetal; **nicht|me|tal|lisch ADJ** nonmetallic; **Nicht|mit|glied NT** non-member; **nicht|öf|fent|lich ADJ → nicht a**; **nicht|or|ga|ni|siert ADJ** *attr* **→ nicht a**; **Nicht|rau|cher(in) M(F)** non-smoker; **ich bin ~** I don't smoke, I'm a non-smoker; **„Nichtraucher"** *(Rail)* "no smoking" *(Brit)*, "non-smoking car" *(US)*; *(Aviat)* "non-smoking seats"; **Nicht|rau|cher|ab|teil NT** no-smoking compartment; **Nicht|rau|cher|zo|ne F** no-smoking area; **nicht|ros|tend ADJ → nicht a**

nichts [nɪçts] **INDEF PRON** *inv* nothing; *(fragend, bedingend auch)* not … anything; **ich weiß ~** I know nothing, I don't know anything; **~ als** nothing but; **~ anderes als** not … anything but *or* except; **~ von Bedeutung** nothing of (any) importance; **~ Besseres/Neues** *etc* nothing better/new *etc*; **~ gegen Volksmusik, aber …** (I've got) nothing against folk music, but …; **~ da!** *(inf) (= weg da)* no you don't!; *(= ausgeschlossen)* nothing doing *(inf)*, no chance *(inf)*; **~ ahnend** *(adjektivisch)* unsuspecting; *(adverbial)* unsuspectingly; **~ sagend** = **nichtssagend**; **~ zu danken!** don't mention it, not at all; **für** *or* **um ~** for nothing; **das ist ~ für mich** that's not (for) me, that's not my thing *(inf)*, that's not my cup of tea *(Brit inf)*; **für ~ und wieder ~** *(inf)* for nothing at all, for damn all *(inf)*; **~ und niemand** nothing and nobody; **~ zu machen** nothing doing *(inf)*, nix *(inf)*; **(es war) ~ mehr zu machen** there was nothing more that could be done; **~ mehr** nothing more, not … anything more; **ich weiß ~ Näheres** *or* **Genaues** I don't know any details; **das war wohl ~** *(inf)* you can't win them all *(inf)*; **~ wie raus/rein/hin** *etc (inf)* let's get out/in/over there *etc* (on the double); **aus ~ wird ~** *(Prov)* **von ~ kommt ~** *(Prov)* you can't make something out of nothing; **ich mag** *or* **will ~ mehr davon hören** I don't want to hear any more about it; **er ist zu ~ nutze** *or* **zu gebrauchen** he's useless *or* hopeless

Nichts [nɪçts] **NT -,** *no pl (Philos)* nothingness; *(= Leere)* emptiness, void; *(= Kleinigkeit)* trifle, triviality, trivia *pl*; **etw aus dem ~ erschaffen** to create sth out of nothing(ness) *or* the void; **etw aus dem ~ aufbauen** to build sth up from nothing; **dieser Schriftsteller ist aus dem ~ aufgetaucht** this author sprang up from nowhere; **vor dem ~ stehen** to be left with nothing; **alle seine Hoffnungen endeten im ~** *(liter)* all his hopes came to nothing *or* nought

Nichts NT -es, -e *(= Mensch)* nobody, nonentity, (mere) cipher

nichts|ah|nend ADJ → nichts

Nicht|schwim|mer(in) M(F) non-swimmer; **er ist ~** he's a non-swimmer

Nicht|schwim|mer|be|cken NT pool for non-swimmers

nichts-: **nichts|des|to|trotz** [nɪçtsdɛsto'trɔts] **ADV** notwithstanding *(form)*, nonetheless; **nichts|des|to|we|ni|ger** [nɪçtsdɛsto've:nɪgɐ] **ADV** nevertheless, nonetheless

Nicht|sein ['nɪçtzain] **NT** non-existence, non-being

Nicht|sess|haf|te(r) ['nɪçtzɛshaftə] **MF** *decl as adj (form)* person of no fixed abode *(form)*

Nichts-: **Nichts|kön|ner(in) M(F)** washout *(inf)*, incompetent person; **er ist ein ~** he's (worse than) useless; **Nichts|nutz** ['nɪçtsnʊts] **M -es, -e** good-for-nothing, useless bungler; **nichts|nut|zig** ['nɪçtsnʊtsɪç] **ADJ** useless, hopeless; *(= unartig)* good-for-nothing; **nichts|sa|gend ADJ** *(Buch, Rede, Worte)* empty, meaningless; *(Vergnügen)* trivial, trite, frivolous; *(Mensch)* insignificant; *(Gesichtsausdruck)* blank, vacant, expressionless; *(Erklärung, Redensart)* meaningless **ADV** *antworten* non-committally, vaguely

nicht|staat|lich ADJ → nicht a

Nichts-: **Nichts|tu|er** ['nɪçtstu:ɐ] **M -s, -, Nichts|tu|e|rin** [-ərɪn] **F -, -nen** idler, loafer; **Nichts|tun** ['nɪçtstu:n] **NT** idleness, inactivity; *(= Muße)* leisure; **das süße ~** dolce far niente *(Brit)*, idle bliss; **viel Zeit mit ~ verbringen** to spend a lot of time doing nothing; **nichts|wür|dig** ['nɪçtsvʏrdɪç] **ADJ** base, despicable; *Mensch auch* worthless; **(du) Nichtswürdiger!** *(old, liter)* vile *or* base wretch! *(old, liter)*

Nicht-: **Nicht|tän|zer(in) M(F)** non-dancer; **ich bin ~** I don't dance; **Nicht|trin|ker(in) M(F)** non-drinker; **er ist ~** he doesn't drink; **Nicht|über|ein|stim|mung F** discrepancy (*+gen* in, of, between); *(= Meinungsunterschied)* differences *pl*, disagreement; **Nicht|ver|an|la|gungs|be|scheid M** *(Fin)* non-assessment declaration; **Nicht|ver|an|la|gungs|be|schei|ni|gung F** *(Fin)* non-assessment note; **Nicht|ver|brei|tung F** *(von Kernwaffen etc)* non-proliferation; **Nicht|ver|fol|ger|land NT, Nicht|ver|fol|ger|staat M** *(Pol)* non-repressive country; **Nicht|vor|han|den|sein NT** absence; **Nicht|wähl|bar|keit** ['nɪçtvɛ:lba:ɐkait] **F -,** *no pl* ineligibility (for office); **Nicht|wäh|ler(in) M(F)** non-voter; **Nicht|wei|ter|ver|brei|tung F** *(von Gefahrenstoffen, Atomwaffen)* non-proliferation; **Nicht|wis|sen NT** ignorance (*um* about); **sich mit ~ entschuldigen** to plead ignorance; **Nicht|zah|lung F** *(form)* non-payment; **im Falle der ~, bei ~** in default of payment; **nicht|zie|lend ADJ** = **intransitiv**; **Nicht-zu|stan|de-Kom|men NT** *(form)* non-completion; **Nicht|zu|tref|fen|de(s)** [-tsu:trɛfndə] **NT** *decl as adj* **(etwas) ~s** something incorrect; **~s (bitte) streichen!** (please) delete as applicable

Ni|ckel ['nɪkl] **NT -s,** *no pl (abbr* **Ni**) nickel

Ni|ckel|bril|le F metal-rimmed glasses *pl*

ni|cken ['nɪkn] **VI a** *(lit, fig)* to nod; **mit dem Kopf ~** to nod one's head; **ein leichtes Nicken** a slight nod **b** *(inf: = schlummern)* to snooze *(inf)*, to doze, to nod

Ni|cker|chen ['nɪkɐçən] **NT -s, -** *(inf)* nap, snooze *(inf)*, forty winks *(inf)*; **ein ~ machen** *or* **halten** to take *or* have forty winks *(inf)* or a nap *or* a snooze *(inf)*

Ni|cki ['nɪki] **M -s, -s** velour(s) pullover

nid [ni:t] PREP +*dat (old)* beneath, under, 'neath *(poet)*

nie [ni:] ADV never; **~ im Leben** never ever; **machst du das? – ~ im Leben!** will you do it? – not on your life; **~ und nimmer** never ever; **~ wieder** *or* **mehr** never again; **ein ~ wiedergutzumachender Fehler** a mistake that can never be put right; **fast ~** hardly ever

nie|der ['ni:dɐ] ADJ *attr* **a** *Triebe, Instinkt, Motiv* low, base; *Arbeit* menial **b** *(= primitiv) Kulturstufe* low, primitive; *Entwicklungsstufe* low, early **c** *(= weniger bedeutend)* lower; *Beamter* minor, lower; *(= geringer) Geburt, Herkunft* lowly; *Volk* common; *Klasse, Stand* lower; *(Comput) Programmiersprache* lower(-level); *(Biol) Lebensformen, Organismen* lower; **der ~e Adel** the gentry, the lower *or* lesser aristocracy; **Hohe und Niedere** *(liter)*, **Hoch und Nieder** *(liter)* (both) the high and the low **d** *(esp S Ger: = niedrig)* low; **die ~e Jagd** small game hunting
ADV down; **die Waffen ~!** lay down your arms; **auf und ~** up and down; **das Auf und Nieder** *(lit)* the bobbing up and down; *(fig)* the ups and (the) downs *pl*; **~ mit dem Kaiser!** down with the Kaiser!

Nie|der-, nie|der- ['ni:dɐ] PREF *(Geog)* Lower, lower; **Niederbayern** Lower Bavaria; **nieder|bay(e)risch** lower Bavarian

nie|der+beu|gen *sep* VT *(lit, fig)* to bow down VR to bend down

nie|der+bren|nen VTI *sep irreg (vi: aux sein)* to burn down

nie|der+brin|gen VT *sep irreg Bohrung* to sink

nie|der+brül|len VT *sep Redner* to shout down

nie|der+bü|geln VT *sep (inf) Person, Einwand, Argument* to demolish; **jdn rhetorisch ~** to demolish sb with rhetoric

nie|der|deutsch ADJ **a** *(Geog)* North German **b** *(Ling)* Low German

Nie|der|deutsch(e) NT Low German → *auch* **Deutsch(e)**

nie|der+don|nern VI *sep aux sein (Lawine)* to thunder down

Nie|der|druck M, *no pl (Tech)* low pressure

nie|der+drü|cken VT *sep* **a** *(lit)* to press down; *Taste, Hebel* to press (down), to push, to depress *(form)* **b** *(= bedrücken)* **jdn ~** to depress sb, to get sb down *(inf)*; **~d** depressing → **niedergedrückt**

nie|der+fah|ren VI *sep irreg aux sein (liter)* to descend

nie|der+fal|len VI *sep irreg aux sein (liter)* to fall *or* drop down

nie|der|fre|quent ADJ low-frequency *attr*

Nie|der|fre|quenz F low frequency; *(Akustik)* audio frequency

Nie|der|gang M *pl* **-gänge a** *(liter: der Sonne)* setting, going down *(poet)*; *(fig: = Verfall)* decline, fall **b** *(Naut)* companionway

nie|der|ge|drückt ADJ depressed, dejected

nie|der+ge|hen VI *sep irreg aux sein* to descend; *(Aviat)* to descend, to come down; *(Bomben, Regen, Giftstoff, Komet)* to fall; *(Fallschirmspringer)* to drop; *(Vorhang)* to fall, to drop; *(Gewitter)* to break *(auch fig)*; *(Boxer)* to go down

nie|der|ge|schla|gen ADJ dejected, despondent ADV dejectedly, despondently → *auch* **niederschlagen**

Nie|der|ge|schla|gen|heit [-gəʃla:gnhait] F -, *no pl* dejection, despondency

nie|der+hal|ten VT *sep irreg* to hold *or* keep down; *Volk* to oppress; *(Mil)* to pin *or* hold down

nie|der+hau|en VT *sep irreg Baum* to cut *or* chop down, to fell; *Gegner* to floor, to knock down, to fell

nie|der+ho|len VT *sep Segel, Flagge* to haul down, to lower; *Ballon* to bring down

Nie|der|holz NT, *no pl* underwood, underbrush

nie|der+kämp|fen VT *sep Feuer* to fight down *or* back; *Gegner* to overcome; *Tränen* to fight back; *Aufstand* to suppress

nie|der+kau|ern VIR *(vi: aux sein)* to crouch *or* cower down

nie|der+knal|len VT *sep* to shoot down

nie|der+kni|en VI *sep aux sein* to kneel down

nie|der+knüp|peln VT *sep* to club down

nie|der+kom|men VI *sep irreg aux sein (old)* to be delivered *(old)* (*mit* of)

Nie|der|kunft [-kʊnft] F -, **⸚e** [-kʏnftə] *(old)* delivery

Nie|der|la|ge F **a** *(Mil, Sport, fig)* defeat *(gegen* by); *(= Misserfolg)* failure, defeat; **eine ~ einstecken müssen** *or* **hinnehmen müssen** *or* **erleiden** to suffer a defeat; **jdm eine ~ zufügen** *or* **beibringen** to defeat sb, to inflict a defeat on sb **b** *(= Lager)* warehouse, store, depot **c** *(= Filiale)* branch (office)

Nie|der|lan|de ['ni:dɐlandə] PL **die ~** the Netherlands *sing or pl*, the Low Countries *pl*

Nie|der|län|der ['ni:dɐlɛndɐ] M **-s, -** Dutchman; **die ~** the Dutch

Nie|der|län|de|rin ['ni:dɐlɛndərɪn] F **-, -nen** Dutchwoman

nie|der|län|disch ['ni:dɐlɛndɪʃ] ADJ Dutch, Netherlands

Nie|der|län|disch(e) ['ni:dɐlɛndɪʃ] NT Dutch → *auch* **Deutsch(e)**

nie|der+las|sen VR *sep irreg* **a** *(= sich setzen)* to sit down; *(= sich niederlegen)* to lie down; *(Vögel)* to land, to alight *(form)* **b** *(= Wohnsitz nehmen)* to settle (down); *(in Amtsitz)* to take up official residence **c** *(= Praxis, Geschäft eröffnen)* to set up in business, to establish oneself, to set up shop *(inf)*; **sich als Arzt/Rechtsanwalt ~** to set up (a practice) as a doctor/lawyer; **die niedergelassenen Ärzte** *registered doctors/specialists with their own practices*; **die niedergelassenen Rechtsanwälte** lawyers in private practice

Nie|der|las|sung [-lasʊŋ] F **-, -en a** *no pl (= das Niederlassen)* settling, settlement; *(eines Arztes etc)* establishment, setting-up **b** *(= Siedlung)* settlement **c** *(Comm)* registered office; *(= Zweigstelle)* branch

Nie|der|las|sungs-: Nie|der|las|sungs|be|wil|li|gung F *(Sw)* residence permit; **Nie|der|las|sungs|frei|heit** F, *no pl (Jur)* freedom of establishment; **Nie|der|las|sungs|recht** NT, *no pl (Jur)* right of establishment

nie|der+le|gen *sep* VT **a** *(= hinlegen)* to lay *or* put *or* set down; *Kranz, Blumen* to lay; *Waffen* to lay down **b** *(= aufgeben) Dienst, Amt, Mandat* to resign (from), to give up; *Krone, Führung* to renounce, to give up; **die Arbeit ~** *(= aufhören)* to stop work(ing); *(= streiken)* to down tools **c** *(= schriftlich festlegen)* to write *or* set down VR to lie down; **da legst di nieder!** *(S Ger inf)* well I'm blowed *(Brit inf)* *or* I'll be damned!, by 'eck! *(N Engl inf)*

Nie|der|le|gung [-le:gʊŋ] F **-, -en a** *(von Kranz)* laying; *(von Waffen)* laying down **b** *(von Amt, Dienst, Mandat)* resignation (from); *(von Kommando)* resignation (of); *(der Krone)* abdication; **~ der Arbeit** walkout **c** *(schriftlich)* setting-out; **eine schriftliche ~ meiner Gedanken** setting out *or* putting down my thoughts in writing

nie|der+ma|chen VT *sep* **a** *(= töten)* to massacre, to butcher **b** *(fig: = heftig kritisieren)* to run down, to disparage *(form)*

nie|der+mä|hen VT *sep (lit, fig)* to mow down

nie|der+met|zeln VT *sep* to massacre, to butcher

Nie|der|ös|ter|reich NT Lower Austria

nie|der+pras|seln VI *sep aux sein (Regen, Hagel etc)* to beat down, to hammer down; *(fig: Beschimpfungen, Vorwürfe etc)* to rain *or* hail down

nie|der+rei|ßen VT *sep irreg jdn* to pull *or* drag down; *Gebäude* to pull *or* knock down; *(fig) Schranken* to tear down

Nie|der|rhein M Lower Rhine

nie|der|rhei|nisch ADJ lower Rhine

nie|der+rin|gen VT *sep irreg* to fight down; *(im Ringkampf auch)* to floor

Nie|der|sach|sen NT Lower Saxony

nie|der|säch|sisch ADJ of Lower Saxony

nie|der+sau|sen VI *sep aux sein* to rain *or* hail down

nie|der+schie|ßen *sep irreg* VT to shoot down VI *aux sein (Vogel etc)* to shoot *or* plummet down

Nie|der|schlag M **a** *(Met)* precipitation *(form)*; *(Chem)* precipitate; *(= Bodensatz)* sediment, dregs *pl*; *(fig: = Ausdruck)* expression; **radioaktiver ~** (radioactive) fallout; **für morgen sind heftige Niederschläge gemeldet** tomorrow there will be heavy rain/hail/snow; **in diesem Gedicht haben seine eigenen Erfahrungen ihren ~ gefunden** his own experiences are reflected *or* find expression in this poem **b** *(Mus)* downbeat **c** *(Boxen)* knockdown blow; *(über 10 Sekunden)* knockout, KO; **~ bis 10** knockout, KO; **Sieg durch ~** win by a knockout

nie|der+schla|gen *sep irreg* VT **a** *jdn* to knock down, to fell; *(Regen, Hagel) Getreide* to beat down, to flatten; *Kragen, Hutkrempe* to turn down; *Aufstand, Revolte* to quell, to put down, to suppress; *Augen, Blick* to lower, to cast down *(liter)* → *auch* **niedergeschlagen b** *(= erlassen) Steuerschuld* to waive; **ein Verfahren ~** *(Jur)* to dismiss a case **c** *(Chem)* to precipitate VR *(Flüssigkeit)* to condense; *(Bodensatz)* to settle; *(Chem)* to precipitate; *(Met)* to fall; **die Untersuchung schlug sich in einer Reform nieder** the investigation resulted in a reform; **sich in etw** *(dat)* **~** *(Erfahrungen, Vorfälle etc)* to find expression in sth; *in Statistik* to be reflected in sth

Nie|der|schlags-: nie|der|schlags|arm ADJ *Wetter* not very rainy/snowy; **eine ~e Gegend** an area which gets little rain/snow; **die Südinsel ist niederschlagsärmer** the south island has a lower rainfall/gets less snow, the south island has a lower level of precipitation *(form)*; **nie|der|schlags|frei** ADJ dry, without precipitation *(form)*; **Nie|der|schlags|men|ge** F rainfall/snowfall, precipitation *(form)*; **nie|der|schlags|reich** ADJ *Wetter* very rainy/snowy; **eine ~e Gegend** an area which gets a lot of rain/snow

Nie|der|schla|gung [-ʃla:gʊŋ] F **-, -en** *(von Strafverfahren)* dismissal; *(von Steuerschuld)* waiving, writing-off; *(eines Aufstands)* suppression

nie|der+schmet|tern VT *sep* to smash *or* batter down; *(fig)* to shatter

nie|der|schmet|ternd ADJ *Nachricht, Ergebnis, Erlebnis* shattering

nie|der+schrei|ben VT *sep irreg* to write down

nie|der+schrei|en VT *sep irreg* to shout down

Nie|der|schrift F *(= das Niederschreiben)* writing down; *(= Niedergeschriebenes)* notes *pl*; *(= Schulaufsatz)* composition, essay; *(= Protokoll) (einer Sitzung)* minutes *pl*; *(Jur)* record; *(von Bandaufzeichnung)* transcript; **er brauchte viel Zeit für die ~ seiner Gedanken** he needed a lot of time to write down his thoughts; **die erste ~ eines Gedichts/Romans** the first draft of a poem/novel

nie|der+set|zen *sep* VT *Kind, Glas, Last* to put *or* set down VR to sit down; *(Vogel)* to perch, to settle, to alight

nie|der+sin|ken VI *sep irreg aux sein (geh)* to sink down

nie|der+sit|zen VI *sep irreg (S Ger, Aus, Sw)* to sit down

Nie|der|span|nung F *(Elec)* low voltage *or* tension

nie|der+ste|chen VT *sep irreg* to stab, to knife

nie|der+stei|gen VI *sep irreg aux sein (liter)* to descend

nie|der+stel|len VT *sep* to put down, to set down

nie|der+stim|men VT *sep* to vote down

nie|der+sto|ßen *sep irreg* VT to knock down VI *aux sein (Raubvogel)* to shoot *or* plummet down

nie|der+stre|cken *sep (geh)* VT to lay low VR to lie down, to stretch out

nie|der+stür|zen VI *sep aux sein* to crash down

nie|der|tou|rig [-tu:rɪç] ADJ *Motor, Maschine* low-revving ADV ~ **fahren** to drive with low revs

Nie|der|tracht ['ni:dɐtraxt] F -, *no pl* despicableness, vileness; *(als Rache)* malice, spite; *(= niederträchtige Tat)* vile *or* despicable act; **so viel ~ hätte ich ihm nicht zugetraut** I would not have suspected him of such a despicable *or* vile act; **die ~, mit der er bei seinen Betrügereien vorgegangen ist** the despicable way he went about his deceptions

nie|der|träch|tig ['ni:dɐtrɛçtɪç] ADJ despicable, vile; *(= rachsüchtig)* malicious, spiteful ADV despicably; *verleumden* maliciously; **jdn ~ verraten** to maliciously betray sb

Nie|der|träch|tig|keit F -, **-en** **a** *no pl* = **Niedertracht** **b** *(Tat)* despicable behaviour *no pl (Brit) or* behavior *no pl (US)*; *(rachsüchtig)* malicious behaviour *no pl (Brit) or* behavior *no pl (US)*; **das ist eine ~** that's despicable; **eine ~ begehen** to commit a vile *or* despicable act

nie|der+tram|peln VT *sep* to trample underfoot

nie|der+tre|ten VT *sep irreg* to trample down; *Erde auch* to stamp down; *Teppich* to wear (down)

Nie|de|rung ['ni:dərʊŋ] F -, **-en** *(= Senke)* depression; *(= Mündungsgebiet)* flats *pl*; *(sumpfig)* marsh; **die ~en des Alltags** the down side of everyday life; **in solche ~en begebe ich mich nicht** *(fig)* I will not sink to such depths

Nie|der|wald M *(Forest)* copse

nie|der+wal|zen VT *sep* to flatten

nie|der|wärts ['ni:dɐvɛrts] ADV *(obs)* down, downward(s)

nie|der+wer|fen *sep irreg* VT to throw *or* hurl *or* cast *(liter)* down; *Aufstand* to suppress, to put down; *Gegner (lit)* to throw down, to floor; *(fig)* to defeat, to overcome; **er wurde von einer Krankheit niedergeworfen** he was laid low with an illness VR to throw oneself down, to prostrate oneself

Nie|der|wer|fung [-vɛrfʊŋ] F -, *no pl (von Aufstand)* suppression; *(von Gegner)* defeat, overthrow

Nie|der|wild NT small game

nie|der+zwin|gen VT *sep irreg (lit)* to force down; *(fig)* to defeat, to vanquish; **er zwang seinen Gegner auf die Knie nieder** *(lit, fig)* he brought his enemy to his knees

nied|lich ['ni:tlɪç] ADJ sweet, cute, pretty little *attr* ADV cutely, sweetly; ~ **aussehen** to look sweet; **sie hat das Lied ~ gesungen** she sang that song sweetly; **das Kätzchen lag so ~ auf meinem Bett** the kitten looked so sweet lying on my bed

Nied|na|gel ['ni:t-] M agnail, hangnail

nied|rig ['ni:drɪç] ADJ **a** *(= tief)* low **b** *(= gering)* low; *Stand, Herkunft, Geburt* low(ly), humble; **~ste Preise** lowest *or* rock-bottom prices **c** *(= gemein)* low *no adv*, base ADV **a** *(= tief) fliegen, schießen* low **b** *(= gering)* **etw ~er berechnen** to charge less for sth; **etw zu ~ veranschlagen** to underestimate sth; **etw ~ einstufen** to give sth a low classification; **jdn gehaltsmäßig ~er einstufen** to pay sb a lower salary; **ich schätze seine Chancen sehr ~ ein** I don't think much of his chances, I think his chances are very slim *or* small; ~ **denken** to think base thoughts; **von jdm ~ denken, jdn ~ einschätzen** to have a low *or* poor opinion of sb; ~ **stehend** *(Volk, Kultur)* undeveloped, primitive

Nied|rig|ener|gie|haus NT low-energy house

nied|ri|ger+schrau|ben VT *sep (fig)* to lower

Nied|rig|keit F -, *no pl* **a** lowness; **die ~ der Häuser** the low-built style of the houses **b** *(von Gedanken, Beweggründen)* baseness

Nied|rig-: **Nied|rig|lohn** M low wages *pl*; **Nied|rig|lohn|grup|pe** F low-wage bracket; **Nied|rig|lohn|land** NT low-wage country; **Nied|rig|lohn|sek|tor** M low-wage sector

nied|rig|ste|hend ADJ → **niedrig ADV b**

Nied|rig|strah|lung F low-level radiation

Nied|rig|was|ser NT *pl* **-wasser** *(Naut)* low tide, low water

nie|mals ['ni:ma:ls] ADV never

nie|mand ['ni:mant] INDEF PRON nobody, no-one; **es war ~ zu Hause** there was nobody *or* no-one at home, there wasn't anybody *or* anyone at home; ~ **anders** *or* **anderer** *(S Ger)* **kam** nobody else came; ~ **anders** *or* **anderer** *(S Ger)* **war da** there wasn't anybody else there, nobody else was there; **ich habe ~ anders** *or* **anderen** *(S Ger)* **gesehen** I didn't see anybody else; **herein kam ~ anders** *or* **anderer** *(S Ger)* **als der Kanzler selbst** in came the Chancellor himself, no less, in came none other than the Chancellor himself; ~ **Fremdes** no strangers, not ... any strangers; **er hat es ~(em) gesagt** he hasn't told anyone, he has told no-one; **sag das ~(em)!** don't tell anyone

Nie|mand ['ni:mant] M -s, *no pl* **er ist ein ~** he's a nobody

Nie|mands|land NT no-man's-land

Nie|re ['ni:rə] F -, **-n** kidney; **künstliche ~** kidney machine, artificial kidney; **es geht mir an die ~n** *(inf)* it gets me down *(inf)*; **er hat es an der ~** *or* **den ~n** he has kidney problems

Nie|ren- *in cpds (Anat)* renal; **Nie|ren|be|cken** NT pelvis of the kidney; **Nie|ren|be|cken|ent|zün|dung** F pyelitis *(spec)*; **Nie|ren|ent|zün|dung** F nephritis *(spec)*; **nie|ren|för|mig** ADJ kidney-shaped; **Nie|ren|gurt** M *(Aut)* kidney belt; **Nie|ren|ko|lik** F renal colic; **nie|ren|krank** ADJ suffering from a kidney disease; **Nie|ren|krank|heit** F, **Nie|ren|lei|den** NT kidney disease; **Nie|ren|scha|le** F kidney dish; **Nie|ren|schüt|zer** [-ʃʏtsɐ] M -s, - kidney belt; **Nie|ren|spen|der(in)** M(F) kidney donor; **Nie|ren|stein** M kidney stone, renal calculus *(spec)*; **Nie|ren|stein|zer|trüm|me|rer** [-tsɛɐtrʏmərɐ] M -s, - lithotripter *(spec)*; **Nie|ren|ta|sche** F bum bag *(Brit)*, fanny pack *(US)*; **Nie|ren|tisch** M kidney-shaped table; **Nie|ren|trans|plan|ta|ti|on** F kidney transplant; **Nie|ren|ver|sa|gen** NT kidney failure; **Nie|ren|wär|mer** [-vɛrmɐ] M -s, - kidney warmer

nie|seln ['ni:zln] VI *impers* to drizzle

Nie|sel|priem ['ni:zlpri:m] M -s, -e *(inf)* misery-guts *(Brit inf)*, moaner

Nie|sel|re|gen M drizzle

nie|sen ['ni:zn] VI to sneeze

Nies|pul|ver NT sneezing powder

Nieß-: **Nieß|brauch** M *(Jur)* usufruct; **Nieß|brau|cher** [-brauxɐ] M -s, -, **Nieß|brau|che|rin** [-ərɪn] F -, **-nen**, **Nieß|nut|zer** [-nʊtsɐ] M -s, -, **Nieß|nut|ze|rin** [-ərɪn] F -, **-nen** *(Jur)* usufructuary

Nies|wurz ['ni:svʊrts] F -, *no pl (Bot)* hellebore

Niet [ni:t] [ni:t] M **-(e)s, -e** *(spec)*, **Nie|te** ['ni:tə] F -, **-n** rivet; *(auf Kleidung)* stud

Nie|te F -, **-n** *(= Los)* blank; *(inf: = Mensch)* dead loss *(inf)*, washout *(inf)*; **eine ~ ziehen** *(lit)* to draw a blank; **mit ihm haben wir eine ~ gezogen** he is a dead loss *(inf)*; **~n in Nadelstreifen** *(inf)* incompetent managers

nie|ten ['ni:tn] VT to rivet

Nie|ten|ho|se F (pair of) studded jeans *pl*

niet- und na|gel|fest ['ni:tlunt 'na:glfɛst] ADJ *(inf)* nailed *or* screwed down

ni|gel|na|gel|neu ['ni:gl'na:gl'nɔy] ADJ *(inf)* brand spanking new *(inf)*

Ni|ger ['ni:gɐ] M -s *(= Fluss)* Niger

Ni|ger NT -s *(= Staat)* Niger

Ni|ge|ria [ni'ge:ria] NT -s Nigeria

Ni|ge|ri|a|ner [nigeri'a:nɐ] M -s, -, **Ni|ge|ri|a|ne|rin** [-ərɪn] F -, **-nen** Nigerian

ni|ge|ri|a|nisch [nigeri'a:nɪʃ] ADJ Nigerian

Nig|ger ['nɪgɐ] M -s, - *(pej)* nigger *(pej)*, coon *(pej)*

Nig|rer ['ni:grɐ] M -s, -, **Nig|re|rin** [-ərɪn] F -, **-nen** Nigerian

nig|risch ['ni:grɪʃ] ADJ Nigerian

Ni|hi|lis|mus [nihi'lɪsmʊs] M -, *no pl* nihilism

Ni|hi|list [nihi'lɪst] M **-en, -en**, **Ni|hi|lis|tin** [-'lɪstɪn] F -, **-nen** nihilist

ni|hi|lis|tisch [nihi'lɪstɪʃ] ADJ nihilistic

Nik|kei-In|dex ['nɪkei-] M -, *no pl (St Ex)* Nikkei Index

Ni|ko|laus ['nɪkolaus, 'ni:kolaus] M **a** -' *(= Name)* Nicholas **b** -, **-e** *or (hum inf)* **Nikoläuse** [-lɔyzə] St Nicholas; *(= Nikolaustag)* St Nicholas' Day

> **NIKOLAUS**
>
> **Nikolaus** (known as **Samichlaus** in Switzerland) is a saint, usually represented as wearing a tall hat, long gown and white bushy beard, who traditionally brings gifts for children on December 6th. He either puts them in boots left outside the front door the night before, or arrives in person. In many regions he is accompanied by **Knecht Ruprecht** or, particularly in Austria, by **Krampus**, who beats naughty children with a birch or carries them off in a sack. Increasingly, **Nikolaus** is presented as a benevolent character similar to Santa Claus.

Ni|ko|tin [niko'ti:n] NT -s, *no pl* nicotine

Ni|ko|tin-: **ni|ko|tin|arm** ADJ low-nicotine; **ni|ko|tin|frei** ADJ nicotine-free; **Ni|ko|tin|ge|halt** M nicotine content; **ni|ko|tin|hal|tig** ADJ containing nicotine; **Zigarren sind ~er als Zigaretten** cigars contain more nicotine than cigarettes; **Ni|ko|tin|pflas|ter** NT nicotine patch; **ni|ko|tin|süch|tig** ADJ nicotine-addicted *attr*, addicted to nicotine *pred*; **Ni|ko|tin|ver|gif|tung** F nicotine poisoning

Nil [ni:l] M -s Nile

Nil-: **Nil|del|ta** NT Nile Delta; **Nil|pferd** NT hippopotamus, hippo

Nim|bus ['nɪmbʊs] M -, **-se** *(= Heiligenschein)* halo, aureole; *(fig)* aura; **sich mit dem ~ der Anständigkeit umgeben** to surround oneself with an aura of respectability; **im ~ der Heiligkeit stehen** to be thought of as a saint; **einen ~ zerstören** to shatter *or* destroy a myth

nimm [nɪm] *imper sing von* **nehmen**

nim|mer ['nɪmɐ] ADV **a** *(liter: = niemals)* never **b** *(S Ger, Aus)* = **nicht mehr**

Nim|mer|leins|tag ['nɪmɐlainsta:k] M = **Sankt-Nimmerleins-Tag**

nim|mer|mehr ['nɪmɐme:ɐ] ADV *(liter)* nevermore *(liter)*, never again; **nie und ~** never ever

nim|mer|mü|de ['nɪmɐ'my:də] ADJ *attr* tireless, untiring

nim|mer|satt ['nɪmɐzat] ADJ gluttonous, insatiable

Nim|mer|satt ['nɪmɐzat] M **-(e)s, -e** glutton; **ein ~ sein** to be insatiable

Nim|mer|wie|der|se|hen NT *(inf)* **auf ~!** I don't *or* I never want to see you again; **ich habe meinen Koffer da stehen lassen – na dann, auf ~** I left my case there – well, you've seen the last of that; **auf ~ verschwinden** to disappear never to be seen again; **ich habe es ihm geborgt, hoffentlich nicht auf ~** I lent it to him, not permanently I hope *or* I hope not for ever

nimmt [nɪmt] *3. pers sing pres von* **nehmen**

Nim|rod ['nɪmrɔt] M -s, -e [-də] Nimrod

Ni|ob ['nio:p] NT -s, *no pl*, **Ni|o|bi|um** ['nio:biʊm] NT -s, *no pl (abbr* **Nb**) niobium

Nip|pel ['nɪpl] M -s, - **a** *(Tech)* nipple **b** *(inf: = Brustwarze)* nipple

nip|pen ['nɪpn] VTI to nip *(an +dat* at); *(an Glas etc)* to sip from; **am** *or* **vom Wein ~** to sip (at) the wine

Nip|pes ['nɪpəs] PL, **Nipp|sa|chen** ['nɪp-] PL ornaments *pl*, knick-knacks *pl*, bric-à-brac *sing*

Nipp|flut F, **Nipp|zeit** ['nɪp-] F neap tide

Nip|pon ['nɪpɔn] NT **-s** Japan

nir|gend|her ['nɪrgnt'heːɐ] ADV = **nirgendsher**

nir|gend|hin ['nɪrgnt'hɪn] ADV = **nirgendwohin**

nir|gends ['nɪrgnts] ADV nowhere, not ... anywhere; **ihm gefällt es ~** he doesn't like it anywhere; **überall und ~** here, there and everywhere; **er ist überall und ~ zu Hause** he has no real home; **er fühlt sich ~ so wohl wie ...** there's nowhere *or* there isn't anywhere he feels so happy as ...; **~ sonst** nowhere else; **das sieht man fast ~ mehr** you hardly see that any more

nir|gends|her ['nɪrgnts'heːɐ] ADV from nowhere, not ... from anywhere

nir|gends|hin ['nɪrgnts'hɪn] ADV = **nirgendwohin**

nir|gend|wo ['nɪrgnt'voː] ADV = **nirgends**

nir|gend|wo|hin ['nɪrgntvo'hɪn] ADV nowhere, not ... anywhere; **wohin gehst du? – ~** where are you going? – nowhere; **wenn man ~ gehen kann, um zu übernachten** if you've got nowhere to spend the night, if you haven't got anywhere to spend the night

Ni|ros|ta® [ni'rɔsta] M **-**, *no pl* stainless steel

Nir|wa|na [nɪr'vaːna] NT **-(s)**, **Nir|va|na** [nɪr'vaːna] NT **-(s)** nirvana

Ni|sche ['niːʃə] F **-, -n** niche, alcove; *(= Kochnische etc)* recess; *(fig)* niche

Nis|se ['nɪsə] F **-, -n** nit

Nis|sen|hüt|te F Nissen hut *(Brit)*, Quonset hut *(US)*

nis|ten ['nɪstn] VI to nest; *(fig)* to take possession *(in +dat* of); **dieses Vorurteil nistete in seinem Hirn** this prejudice lodged in his mind; **in ihm nistete tiefes Misstrauen** he was filled with a deep mistrust VR **Hass nistete sich in ihr Herz** *(liter)* hatred gripped *or* filled her heart

Nist-: **Nist|kas|ten** M nest(ing) box; **Nist|platz** M nesting place; **Nist|zeit** F nesting time, (the) nesting season

Nit|rat [ni'traːt] NT **-(e)s, -e** nitrate

Nit|rat|ge|halt M nitrate level; *(im Boden auch)* nitrate levels *pl*

nit|rie|ren [ni'triːrən] *ptp* **nitriert** VT to nitrate

Nit|rit [ni'triːt] NT **-s, -e** nitrite

Nit|ro- *in cpds* nitro; **Nit|ro|ben|zol** NT nitrobenzene; **Nit|ro|gly|ze|rin** NT nitroglycerine; **Nit|ro|lack** M nitrocellulose paint; **Nit|ro|ver|dün|nung** F cellulose thinner; **Nit|ro|ver|gif|tung** F nitrate poisoning

Ni|veau [ni'voː] NT **-s, -s** *(lit, fig)* level; **auf gleichem ~ liegen** to be on the same level; **auf hohem/niedrigem ~ liegen** *(fig)* to be at a high/low level; **intelligenzmäßig steht er auf dem ~ eines Dreijährigen** he has the mental age of a three-year-old; **diese Schule hat ein hohes ~** this school has high standards; **seine Arbeit hat ein sehr schlechtes ~** the level *or* standard of his work is very poor; **unter ~** below par; **unter meinem ~** beneath me; **~/kein/wenig ~ haben** to be of a high/low/fairly low standard; *(Mensch)* to be cultured/not at all/not very cultured; **ein Hotel mit ~** a hotel with class

Ni|veau-: **Ni|veau|li|nie** F contour line; **ni|veau|los** ADJ *Film etc* mediocre; *Unterhaltung* mindless ADV **sich ~ unterhalten** to have a mindless conversation; **sich ~ amüsieren** to amuse oneself with mindless things; **Ni|veau|un|ter|schied** M *(lit, fig)* difference of level; **ni|veau|voll** ADJ *Unterhaltung, Film etc* high-class ADV **sich ~ unterhalten** to have a quality conversation; **eine ~ inszenierte Komödie** a high-class comedy

ni|vel|lie|ren [nivɛ'liːrən] *ptp* **nivelliert** VT *(lit, fig)* to level off *or* out VI *(Surv)* to level

Ni|vel|lie|rung F **-, -en** *(Surv)* levelling *(Brit)*, leveling *(US)*; *(= Ausgleichung)* level(l)ing out

nix [nɪks] INDEF PRON *(inf)* = **nichts**

Nix [nɪks] M **-es, -e** water sprite *(esp Brit)*, water pixie *(US)*; *(mit Fischschwanz)* merman

Ni|xe ['nɪksə] F **-, -n** water sprite *(esp Brit)*, water nymph, nix(ie); *(mit Fischschwanz)* mermaid; *(hum: = Badenixe)* bathing belle

Niz|za ['nɪtsa] NT **-s** Nice

NN *abbr von* **Normalnull**

N.N. *abbr von* **nomen nescio** N.N., name not known *or* unkown

NNO *abbr von* **Nordnordost** NNE

NNW *abbr von* **Nordnordwest** NNW

NO *abbr von* **Nordosten**

no|bel ['noːbl] ADJ *(= edelmütig)* noble; *(inf) (= großzügig)* generous, lavish; *(= kostspielig)* extravagant; *(= elegant)* posh *(inf)*; **ein nobler Kunde** *(iro inf)* a pleasant customer, a nice type of person ADV *(= edelmütig)* nobly; *(= großzügig)* generously; **~ wohnen** to live in posh surroundings; **das war ~ gedacht** that was a noble thought; **~ geht die Welt zugrunde** *(iro)* there's nothing like going out in style; **sich ~ zeigen** *(inf)* to be generous; **er zeigte sich sehr ~ und verzieh ihm** he nobly forgave him

No|bel|her|ber|ge F *(inf)* posh *or* classy hotel *(inf)*

No|be|li|um [no'beːliʊm] NT **-s**, *no pl (abbr* **No**) nobelium

No|bel|preis [no'bɛl-] M Nobel prize

No|bel|preis|trä|ger(in) M(F) Nobel prizewinner

No|bel|schup|pen M *(inf, usu iro)* posh place, classy joint *(inf)*

No|bel|vier|tel NT *(inf, usu iro)* posh *or* upmarket *(US)* area

Nob|les|se [no'blɛsə] F **-**, *no pl (geh)* noblesse; **dafür hat er zu viel ~** he's much too high-minded for that; **noblesse oblige** noblesse oblige *(form)*

No|bo|dy ['noːbɔdi] M **-(s), -s** *(usu pej)* nobody

noch [nɔx] ADV **a** *(= weiterhin, bis jetzt, wie zuvor)* still; **~ nicht** still not, not yet; **bist du fertig? – ~ nicht** are you ready? – not yet; **er ist ~ nicht da** he still isn't here, he isn't here yet; **immer ~, ~ immer** still; **sie ist immer ~ nicht fertig** she still isn't ready (yet), she isn't ready yet; **er dachte ~ lange an sie** it was a long time before he stopped thinking of her; **du bist ~ zu klein** you're still too young; **sie ist ~ jung** she's only *or* still young; **er schläft ~** he's still asleep; **~ nie** never; **das habe ich ~ nie gehört** I've never known that (before); **ich gehe kaum ~ aus** I hardly go out any more; **ich möchte gerne ~ bleiben** I'd like to stay on longer

b *(= irgendwann)* some time, one day; **er wird sich (schon) ~ daran gewöhnen** he'll get used to it (some time *or* one day); **das kann ~ passieren** that just might happen, that might still happen; **er wird ~ kommen** he'll come (yet)

c *(= eben, nicht später als)* **das muss ~ vor Dienstag fertig sein** it has to be ready by Tuesday; **ich habe ihn ~ vor zwei Tagen gesehen** I saw him only two days ago; **er ist ~ am selben Tag gestorben** he died the very same day; **ich tue das ~ heute** *or* **heute ~** I'll do it today *or* this very day; **~ im 18. Jahrhundert** as late as the 18th century; **gerade ~** (only) just; **~ gestern war er frisch und munter** (only) yesterday he was still bright and cheerful; **~ keine drei Tage** not three days

d *(einschränkend)* (only) just; **(gerade) ~ gut genug** (only) just good enough

e *(= außerdem, zusätzlich)* **wer war ~ da?** who else was there?; **(gibt es) ~ etwas?** (is there) anything else?; **ich will ~ etwas sagen** there's something else *or* another thing I want to say; **~ etwas Fleisch** some more meat, a bit more meat; **~ einer** another (one); **~ ein Bier** another beer; **~ zwei Bier** two more beers, another two beers; **~ einmal** *or* **mal** (once) again, once more; **und es regnete auch ~** *or* **~ dazu** and on top of that it was raining; **dumm und ~ dazu frech** stupid and impudent with it *(inf)*; **ich gebe Ihnen ~ zwei dazu** I'll give you two extra; **~ ein Wort!** (not) another word!

f *(bei Vergleichen)* even, still, yet; **~ größer** even *or* still *or* yet bigger; **er will ~ mehr haben** he wants even *or* still more; **das ist ~ besser** that's even better, that's better still *or* still better; **das ist ~ viel wichtiger als ...** that is far more important yet *or* still than ...; **(und) seien sie auch ~ so klein** however small they may *or* might be; **und wenn du auch ~ so bittest ...** however much you ask ...

g *(inf)* **wir fanden Fehler ~ und nöcher** *(hum inf)* we found tons *(inf) or* loads *(inf)* of mistakes; **Geld ~ und nöcher** *(hum inf)* heaps and heaps of money *(inf)*; **er kann ~ und nöcher erzählen** he can go on telling stories for ever; **ich kann Ihnen Beispiele ~ und nöcher geben** I can give you any number of examples; **sie hat ~ und nöcher versucht, ...** she tried again and again to ...

CONJ *(weder ... noch ...)* nor; **nicht X, ~ Y, ~ Z** not X nor Y nor Z

Noch|ge|schäft NT *(Fin)* option to double

noch|mal ADV *(inf)* → **noch e**

noch|ma|lig ['nɔxmaːlɪç] ADJ *attr* renewed; **eine ~e Überprüfung** another check

noch|mals ['nɔxmaːls] ADV again

No|cken|wel|le ['nɔkn-] F camshaft

No|ckerl ['nɔkɐl] NT **-s, -n** *usu pl (Aus Cook)* dumpling; **Salzburger ~n** *type of sweet whipped pudding eaten hot*

Noc|turne [nɔk'tʏrn] NT **-s, -s** *or f* **-, -s** *(Mus)* nocturne

No-Fu|ture-, **No|fu|ture-** △ *in cpds* no-future; **No-Fu|ture-Ge|ne|ra|ti|on** F no-future generation

Noi|set|te [noa'zɛt] F **-, -s** noisette

NOK [ɛnloː'kaː] NT **-s** *abbr von* **Nationales Olympisches Komitee**

nö|len ['nøːlən] VI *(inf)* to moan

no|lens vo|lens ['noːlɛns 'voːlɛns] ADV *(geh)* like it or not *or* no, willy-nilly

No|li|me|tan|ge|re ['noːlime'taŋgerə] NT **-, -** *(Bot)* touch-me-not

No|ma|de [no'maːdə] M **-n, -n**, **No|ma|din** [no'maːdɪn] F **-, -nen** *(lit, fig)* nomad

No|ma|den- *in cpds* nomadic; **no|ma|den|haft** ADJ *(lit, fig)* nomadic; **No|ma|den|le|ben** NT nomadic life; **No|ma|den|tum** [no'maːdntuːm] NT **-s**, *no pl* nomadism; **No|ma|den|volk** NT nomadic tribe *or* people; **No|ma|den|zelt** NT nomad('s) tent

No|ma|din [no'maːdɪn] F **-, -nen** *(lit, fig)* nomad

no|ma|disch [no'maːdɪʃ] ADJ nomadic ADV **~ leben** to live a nomadic lifestyle

no|ma|di|sie|ren [nomadi'ziːrən] *ptp* **nomadisiert** VI to lead a nomadic existence; **~de Stämme** nomadic tribes

No|men ['noːmən] NT **-s, Nomina** ['noːmina] *(Gram)* noun; **nomen est omen** *(geh)* true to your/his *etc* name

No|men|kla|tur [nomɛnkla'tuːɐ] F **-, -en** nomenclature

No|men|kla|tu|ra [nomɛnkla'tuːra] F **-**, *no pl (= Führungsschicht)* top-ranking officials *pl*

No|mi|na *pl von* **Nomen**

no|mi|nal [nomi'naːl] *(Econ)* ADJ nominal ADV nominally

No|mi|nal- *in cpds (Gram, Fin)* nominal; **No|mi|nal|lohn** M nominal *or* money wages *pl*; **No|mi|nal|stil** M nominal style; **No|mi|nal|wert** M *(Fin)* nominal *or* face *or* par value; **No|mi|nal|zins** M *(Fin)* nominal interest rate

No|mi|na|ti|on [nomina'tsioːn] F **-, -en** *(Eccl)* nomination

No|mi|na|tiv ['nominatiːf] M **-s, -e** [-və] nominative

no|mi|nell [nomi'nɛl] ADJ *Regierungschef, Unabhängigkeit* nominal, in name only ADV in name only

no|mi|nie|ren [nomi'niːrən] *ptp* **nominiert** VT to nominate

No|mi|nie|rung [nomi'niːrʊŋ] F nomination

No-Name-Pro|dukt ['no:ne:m-] NT *(Econ)* no--name product, own-label *or* house-brand *(US)* product

Non|cha|lance [nõʃa'lã:s] F -, *no pl (geh)* nonchalance

non|cha|lant [nõʃa'lã:] *(geh)* ADJ nonchalant ADV nonchalantly; **sich ~ geben** to appear nonchalant

No|ne ['no:nə] F -, -n **a** *(Mus)* ninth **b** *(Eccl, Gebetsstunde)* nones *with sing vb*

Non-Food-Ab|tei|lung [nɔn'fu:d-] F non--food section

No|ni|us ['no:niʊs] M -, -se *or* **Nonien** [-niən] vernier (scale)

Non|kon|for|mist(in) M(F) nonconformist

non|kon|for|mis|tisch ADJ nonconformist ADV **sich ~ verhalten** to act unconventionally

Non|ne ['nɔnə] F -, -n **a** nun **b** *(Schmetterling)* nun moth **c** *(Dachziegel)* concave tile

Non|nen-: **non|nen|haft** ADJ nunlike ADV **sie lebte ~** she lived like a nun; **sie tut so ~** she pretends to be so chaste; **Non|nen|klos|ter** NT convent, nunnery *(old, hum)*

Non|plus|ult|ra [nɔnplʊs'ʊltra, no:nplʊs'ʊltra] NT -s, *no pl (geh)* ultimate, non plus ultra *(Brit)*

Non-Pro|fit-Un|ter|neh|men NT non-profit company

Non|sens ['nɔnzɛns] M -(es), *no pl* nonsense

non|stop [nɔn'ʃtɔp, -'stɔp] ADV non-stop

Non|stop-, Non-Stop- △ *in cpds* non-stop; **Non|stop-Be|trieb** M **im ~** non-stop; **Non|stop-Flug** M non-stop flight; **Non|stop-Ki|no** NT cinema with a continuous programme *(Brit) or* program *(US)*

non|ver|bal [nɔnvɛr'ba:l] ADJ non-verbal ADV non-verbally

Nop|pe ['nɔpə] F -, -n *(= Gumminoppe)* nipple, knob; *(von Tischtennisschläger, Gummisohle auch)* pimple; *(= Knoten)* burl; *(= Schlinge)* loop; *(= Stricknoppe)* bobble; *(bei Blindenschrift)* braille dot; **Garn mit ~n** bouclé; **ein Teppich mit ~n** a loop pile carpet

nop|pen ['nɔpn] VT **a** *(= Noppen auszupfen) Rohgewebe* to burl **b** *(= mit Noppen versehen)* → *auch* **genoppt**

Nord [nɔrt] M -(e)s, *(rare)* -e [-də] **a** *(Naut, Met, liter)* north; **aus** *or* **von/nach ~** from the/to the north **b** *(liter. Wind)* north wind

Nord-, nord- *in cpds (in Ländernamen) (politisch)* North; *(geografisch auch)* the North of ..., Northern; **Nord|af|ri|ka** NT North Africa; **Nord|ame|ri|ka** NT North America; **Nord|at|lan|tik** M North Atlantic; **Nord|at|lan|tik|pakt** M North Atlantic Treaty; **nord|at|lan|tisch** ADJ North Atlantic; **~es Verteidigungsbündnis, ~e Allianz** NATO Alliance; **nord|deutsch** ADJ North German; *Dialekt, Spezialität, Mentalität auch* Northern German; **die ~e Tiefebene** the North German lowlands *pl*; **die Norddeutschen** the North Germans; **Nord|deutsch|land** NT North(ern) Germany, the North of Germany

nor|den ['nɔrdn] VT *Karte* to orient(ate)

Nor|den ['nɔrdn] M -s, *no pl* north; *(von Land)* North; **aus dem ~, von ~ (her)** from the north; **gegen** *or* **gen** *(liter) or* **nach ~** north(wards), to the north; **der Balkon liegt nach ~** the balcony faces north(wards); **nach ~ hin** to the north; **im ~ der Stadt/des Landes** in the north of the town/country; **im/aus dem hohen ~** in/from the far north; **weiter** *or* **höher im ~** further north; **im Münchner ~** on the north side of Munich; **im ~ Frankreichs** in the north of France, in northern France

Nord-: **Nord|eng|land** NT the North of England; **Nord|eu|ro|pa** NT Northern Europe; **nord|frie|sisch** ADJ North Frisian; **Nord|halb|ku|gel** F northern hemisphere; **Nord|hang** M northern *or* north-facing slope; **nord|irisch** ADJ Northern Irish; **Nord|ir|land** NT Northern Ireland, Ulster; **Nord|ir|land|kon|flikt** M **der ~** the conflict in Northern Ireland, the Troubles *pl (euph)*

nor|disch ['nɔrdɪʃ] ADJ *Wälder* northern; *Völker, Sprache, Mythologie* Nordic; *(Ski)* nordic; **Ski ~** nordic skiing; **~e Kombination** *(Ski)* nordic combined

Nor|dist [nɔr'dɪst] M -en, -en, **Nor|dis|tin** [-'dɪstɪn] F -, -nen expert on Nordic languages; *(Student)* student of Nordic languages

Nor|dis|tik [nɔr'dɪstɪk] F -, *no pl* Nordic studies *sing*

Nord-: **Nord|kap** NT North Cape; **Nord|ko|rea** NT North Korea; **Nord|küs|te** F north (-ern) coast; **Nord|län|der** ['nɔrtlɛndɐ] M -s, -, **Nord|län|de|rin** [-ərɪn] F -, -nen northerner; *(= Skandinavier)* Scandinavian

nörd|lich ['nœrtlɪç] ADJ northern; *Kurs, Wind, Richtung* northerly; **der ~e Polarkreis** the Arctic Circle; **der ~e Wendekreis** the Tropic of Cancer; **52 Grad ~er Breite** 52 degrees north ADV (to the) north; **~ von Köln (gelegen)** north of Cologne; **es liegt ~er** *or* **weiter ~** it is further (to the) north PREP *+gen* (to the) north of

Nord|licht NT northern lights *pl*, aurora borealis; *(fig hum: Mensch)* Northerner

Nord|nord-: **Nord|nord|ost** M **a** *(Naut, Met, liter)* north-north-east, nor'-nor'-east *(Naut)* **b** *(liter. Wind)* nor'-nor'-easterly;; **Nord|nord|os|ten** M north-north-east, nor'-nor'-east *(Naut)*; **nord|nord|öst|lich** ADJ north-north--east(erly), nor'-nor'-east(erly) *(Naut)*; **Nord|nord|west** M **a** *(Naut, Met, liter)* north-north--west, nor'-nor'-west *(Naut)* **b** *(liter. Wind)* nor'-nor'-westerly; **Nord|nord|wes|ten** M north-north-west, nor'-nor'-west *(Naut)*; **nord|nord|west|lich** ADJ north-north-west (-erly), nor'-nor'-west(erly) *(Naut)*

Nord|ost M **a** *(Met, Naut, liter)* north-east, nor'-east *(Naut)*; **aus ~** from the north-east **b** *(liter. Wind)* north-east(erly) wind, north-easter, nor'-easter *(Naut)*

Nord|ost- *in cpds* north-east; *(bei Namen)* North-East; **Nordostengland** North-East England

Nord|os|ten M north-east; *(von Land)* North East; **aus** *or* **von ~** from the north-east; **nach ~** to the north-east, north-east(wards); **im ~ Brasiliens** in the North East of Brazil, in north--east Brazil

nord|öst|lich ADJ *Gegend* north-eastern; *Wind* north-east(erly) ADV (to the) north-east; **~ von ...** north-east of ... PREP *+gen* (to the) north-east of

Nord-Ost|see-Ka|nal M Kiel Canal

Nord|pol M North Pole

Nord|po|lar-: **Nord|po|lar|ge|biet** NT Arctic (Zone); **Nord|po|lar|meer** NT Arctic Ocean

Nord|rhein-West|fa|len ['nɔrtrainvɛst'fa:lən] NT North Rhine-Westphalia

nord|rhein-west|fä|lisch ['nɔrtrainvɛst'fɛ:lɪʃ] ADJ North Rhine-Westphalian

Nord-: **Nord|see** ['nɔrtze:] F North Sea; **Nord|see|insel** F island in the North Sea; **Nord|see|küs|te** F North Sea coast; **Nord|sei|te** F north(ern) side; *(von Berg)* north(ern) face; **Nord|staa|ten** PL *(Hist)* northern states *pl*, Union; **Nord|stern** M North Star, Polar Star; **Nord-Süd-Di|a|log** ['nɔrt'zy:t-] M north-south dialogue *(Brit) or* dialog *(US)*; **Nord-Süd-Ge|fäl|le** ['nɔrt'zy:t-] NT north--south divide; **Nord|wand** F *(von Berg)* north face

nord|wärts ['nɔrtvɛrts] ADV north(wards); **der Wind dreht ~** the wind is moving round to the north

Nord|west M **a** *(Met, Naut, liter)* north-west; **aus ~** from the north-west **b** *(liter. Wind)* north-west(erly) wind, north-wester, nor'-wester *(Naut)*

Nord|west- *in cpds* north-west; *(bei Namen)* North-West; **Nordwestengland** North-West England

Nord|wes|ten M north-west; *(von Land)* North West; **aus** *or* **von ~** from the north-west; **nach ~** to the north-west, north-west(wards); **im ~ Englands** in the North West of England, in north-west England

nord|west|lich ADJ *Gegend* north-western; *Wind* north-west(erly) ADV (to the) north-west; **~ von** (to the) north-west of PREP *+gen* (to the) north-west of

Nord|wind M north wind

Nör|ge|lei [nœrgə'lai] F -, -en moaning, grumbling; *(= Krittelei)* carping, nit-picking *(inf)*

nör|ge|lig ['nœrgəlɪç] ADJ grumbly *(inf)*, moaning; *(= krittelig)* carping, nit-picking *(inf)*

nör|geln ['nœrgln] VI to moan, to grumble; *(= kritteln)* to carp, to niggle *(an +dat, über +acc* about); **er hat immer an allem zu ~** he always finds something to moan about

Nörg|ler ['nœrglɐ] M -s, -, **Nörg|le|rin** [-ərɪn] F -, -nen grumbler, moaner; *(= Krittler)* carper, niggler, nit-picker *(inf)*

nörg|lig ['nœrglɪç] ADJ = **nörgelig**

Norm [nɔrm] F -, -en **a** norm; *(= Größenvorschrift)* standard (specification); **als ~ gelten, die ~ sein** to be (considered) normal, to be the usual thing; **gegen die ~ verstoßen** to be an exception to the norm; **der ~ entsprechen** to conform to the norm **b** *(= Leistungssoll)* quota, norm; **die ~ erfüllen/erreichen** to achieve one's quota, to meet one's target **c** *(Typ)* signature *(at foot of page)*

nor|mal [nɔr'ma:l] ADJ normal; *Format, Maß, Gewicht* standard; **bist du noch ~?** *(inf)* have you gone mad? ADV normally; **er ist ~ groß** his height is normal; **seine Nase ist nicht ~ lang** his nose is not normal length; **~ aussehen/riechen** to look/smell normal; **benimm dich ganz ~** act naturally; **benimm dich doch mal ~!** act like a normal human being, can't you?; **so hohe Trinkgelder sind ~ nicht üblich** such good tips aren't usual

Nor|mal- *in cpds (= üblich)* normal; *(= genormt)* standard; **Nor|mal|an|sicht** F *(Comput)* normal view; **Nor|mal|ben|zin** NT regular (petrol *(Brit) or* gas *(US))*; **Nor|mal|bür|ger(in)** M(F) average citizen, man/woman in the street

Nor|ma|le [nɔr'ma:lə] F -(n), -n *(Math)* normal

nor|ma|ler|wei|se [nɔr'ma:lɐ'vaizə] ADV normally, usually

Nor|mal-: **Nor|mal|fall** M normal case; **im ~** normally, usually; **das ist der ~** that is the norm; **Nor|mal|film** M standard film; **Nor|mal|ge|wicht** NT normal weight; *(genormt)* standard weight

nor|ma|li|sie|ren [nɔrmali'zi:rən] *ptp* **normalisiert** VT to normalize VR to return to normal, to get back to normal

Nor|ma|li|sie|rung F -, -en normalization

Nor|ma|li|tät [nɔrmali'tɛ:t] F -, -en normality, normalcy

Nor|mal-: **Nor|mal|maß** NT standard (measure); **Nor|mal|null** NT -s, *no pl (abbr* **NN**) ≈ sea level; **Nor|mal|spur** F *(Rail)* standard gauge; **Nor|mal|sterb|li|che(r)** MF *decl as adj* lesser mortal; **Nor|mal|uhr** F *(old)* (synchronized) clock; **Nor|mal|ver|brau|cher(in)** M(F) average consumer; **(geistiger) ~** *(inf)* middlebrow; **Otto ~** *(inf)* Joe Bloggs *(Brit inf)*, John Doe *(US inf)*, the man in the street; **Nor|mal|zeit** F standard time; **Nor|mal|zu|stand** M normal state; *(= normale Verhältnisse)* normal conditions *pl*; *(Chem, Phys)* natural state

Nor|man|die [nɔrman'di:, nɔrmãdi:] F - Normandy

Nor|man|ne [nɔr'manə] M -n, -n, **Nor|man|nin** [-'manɪn] F -, -nen Norman

nor|man|nisch [nɔr'manɪʃ] ADJ Norman

nor|ma|tiv [nɔrma'ti:f] ADJ normative ADV **Arbeitszeiten ~ verbindlich regeln** to establish certain working hours as the norm

Nor|ma|tiv|be|stim|mun|gen PL *(Jur)* basic stipulations *pl*

Norm|blatt NT standard specifications sheet

nor|men ['nɔrmən] VT to standardize

Nor|men|kon|troll|kla|ge F *(Jur) legal proceedings brought to ask for judicial review*

nor|mie|ren [nɔr'miːrən] *ptp* **normiert** VT *(Tech, Jur)* to standardize

Nor|mie|rung F -, -en standardization

Norm|teil NT *(Tech)* standard part

Nor|mung ['nɔrmʊŋ] F -, -en *(Tech)* standardization

norm|wid|rig ADJ deviant; *(Tech)* non-standard

Nor|we|gen ['nɔrveːgn] NT -s Norway

Nor|we|ger ['nɔrveːgɐ] M -s, -, **Nor|we|ge|rin** [-ərɪn] F -, -nen Norwegian

Nor|we|ger|pul|lo|ver M Norwegian pullover

nor|we|gisch ['nɔrveːgɪʃ] ADJ Norwegian

Nor|we|gisch(e) ['nɔrveːgɪʃ] NT Norwegian → *auch* **Deutsch(e)**

Nos|tal|gie [nɔstal'giː] F -, *no pl* nostalgia

Nos|tal|gi|ker [nɔs'talgikɐ] M -s, -, **Nos|tal|gi|ke|rin** [-ərɪn] F -, -nen nostalgic person

nos|tal|gisch [nɔs'talgɪʃ] ADJ nostalgic ADV nostalgically; **~ anmutende Bilder** nostalgic pictures; **ein ~ gestimmtes Publikum** a nostalgic audience; **~ klingende Lieder** nostalgic(sounding) songs

not △ [noːt] ADJ *(geh)* → **Not d**

Not [noːt] F -, ¨-e ['nøːtə] a *no pl (= Mangel, Elend)* need(iness), want, poverty; **hier herrscht große ~** there is great poverty here; **eine Zeit der ~** a time of need, a lean time; **aus ~** out of poverty; **~ leiden** to suffer deprivation; **~ leidend** *(Bevölkerung, Land)* impoverished; *Unternehmen, Wirtschaft* ailing; *(Comm) Wechsel, Wertpapier* dishonoured *(Brit)*, dishonored *(US)*; *Kredit* unsecured; **jds ~** *(acc)* **lindern** to improve sb's lot; **in ~ leben** to live in poverty; **~ macht erfinderisch** *(Prov)* necessity is the mother of invention *(Prov)*; **in der ~ frisst der Teufel Fliegen** *(Prov)* **in der ~ schmeckt jedes Brot** *(Prov)* beggars can't be choosers *(prov)*; **~ kennt kein Gebot** *(Prov)* necessity knows no law *(Prov)* → **Geldnot, Zeitnot**

b *(= Bedrängnis)* distress *no pl*, affliction; *(= Problem)* problem; **die Nöte des Alltags** the problems of everyday living; **in seiner ~** in his hour of need; **in unserer ~ blieb uns nichts anderes übrig** in this emergency we had no choice; **jdm seine ~ klagen** to tell sb one's troubles, to cry on sb's shoulder *(inf)*; **in ~ sein** to be in distress; **in ~ geraten** to get into serious difficulties; **wenn ~ am Mann ist** if the need arises; *(= im Notfall)* in an emergency; **Freunde in der ~ (gehen tausend auf ein Lot)** *(Prov)* a friend in need (is a friend indeed) *(Prov)*; **der Retter in der ~** the knight in shining armour *(Brit)* or armor *(US)*; **Hilfe in höchster ~** help in the nick of time; **in höchster ~ sein, sich in höchster ~ befinden** to be in dire straits; **in Ängsten und Nöten schweben** to be in fear and trembling; **jdm in der ~ beistehen** to help sb in *or* through times of trouble, to help sb in his need; **jetzt ist Holland in ~!** now we're in dire straits!

c *no pl (= Sorge, Mühe)* difficulty, trouble; **er hat seine liebe ~ mit ihr/damit** he really has problems with her/it, he really has his work cut out with her/it *(inf)*; **die Eltern hatten ~, ihre fünf Kinder zu ernähren** the parents had difficulty in feeding their five children; **es hat** *or* **damit hat's keine ~** *(old)* there's no rush → **knapp, Mühe**

d *(= Zwang, Notwendigkeit)* necessity; **der ~ gehorchend** bowing to necessity; **etw nicht ohne ~ tun** not to do sth without having to; **ohne ~** without good cause; **zur ~** if necessary, if need(s) be; *(= gerade noch)* at a pinch, just about; **aus der ~ geboren sein** to be born of necessity; **aus der ~ eine Tugend machen** to make a virtue (out) of necessity; **~ sein** to be necessary; **Not tun** → **nottun**

No|ta|beln [no'taːbln] PL *(geh)* notabilities *pl*

no|ta|be|ne [nota'beːnə] ADV *(geh)* please note, let it be noted

Not|an|ker M sheet anchor

No|tar [no'taːɐ] M -s, -e, **No|ta|rin** [-'taːrɪn] F -, -nen notary public

No|ta|ri|at [nota'riaːt] NT -(e)s, -e notary's office

no|ta|ri|ell [nota'riɛl] *(Jur)* ADJ notarial ADV ~ **beglaubigt** legally certified; **~ beurkunden** to notarize

Not-: **Not|arzt** M, **Not|ärz|tin** F emergency doctor; **Not|arzt|wa|gen** M emergency doctor's car; **den ~ rufen** to call the emergency doctor

No|ta|ti|on [nota'tsioːn] F -, -en *(Comput, Mus)* notation

Not-: **Not|auf|nah|me|la|ger** NT reception centre *(Brit)* or center *(US)*, transit camp; **Not|aus|gang** M emergency exit; **Not|be|helf** M stopgap (measure), makeshift; **Not|be|leuch|tung** F emergency lighting; **Not|brem|se** F emergency brake, communication cord *(Brit)*; **die ~ ziehen** *(lit)* to pull the communication cord *(Brit)* or emergency brake; *(fig)* to put the brakes on; *(Ftbl sl: = foulen)* to commit a blatant foul; **Not|brem|sung** F emergency stop; **Not|brü|cke** F temporary bridge; **Not|dienst** M **~ haben** *(Apotheke)* to be open 24 hours; *(Arzt, Elektriker etc)* to be on call; **Not|durft** ['noːtdʊrft] F -, *no pl* a *(euph geh)* call of nature *(euph)*; **seine ~ verrichten** to relieve oneself, to answer the *or* a call of nature *(euph)* b *(old)* need; **des Lebens ~** the bare necessities of life; **des Leibes ~** enough to keep body and soul together

not|dürf|tig ['noːtdʏrftɪç] ADJ *(= kaum ausreichend)* meagre *(Brit)*, meager *(US)*, poor; *(= behelfsmäßig)* makeshift *no adv*, rough and ready *no adv*; *Kleidung* scanty ADV *bekleidet* scantily; *reparieren* in a makeshift way; *versorgen* meagrely *(Brit)*, meagerly *(US)*, poorly; **wir konnten uns mit den Einheimischen ~ verständigen** we could just about communicate with the natives; **damit Sie sich wenigstens ~ verständigen können** so that you can at least communicate to some extent; **nachdem wir das Netz ~ geflickt hatten** when we had patched up the net in a makeshift *or* rough-and-ready way

No|te ['noːtə] F -, -n a *(Mus)* note b **Noten** PL music; **~n lesen** to read music; **nach ~n spielen/singen** to play/sing from music; **nach ~n** *(fig inf)* thoroughly c *(Sch)* mark; **jdm/einer Sache gute/schlechte ~n geben** to give sb/sth good/bad marks d *(Pol)* note e *(= Banknote)* (bank)note, bill *(US)* f *no pl (= Eigenart) (in Bezug auf Gespräch, Brief etc)* note; *(in Bezug auf Beziehungen, Atmosphäre)* tone, character; *(in Bezug auf Einrichtung, Kleidung)* touch; **das ist meine persönliche ~** that's my trademark; **einer Sache** *(dat)* **eine persönliche ~ verleihen** to give sth a personal touch; **ein Parfüm mit einer herben ~** a perfume with something tangy about it *or* with a tangy quality g *(Sport)* mark

Note|book ['noːtbʊk] M OR NT -s, -s *(Comput)* notebook (computer)

Note|book|com|pu|ter ['noːtbʊk-] M notebook computer

No|ten-: **No|ten|aus|tausch** M *(Pol)* exchange of notes; **No|ten|bank** F *pl* **-banken** issuing bank, bank of issue; **No|ten|blatt** NT sheet of music; **No|ten|de|ckung** F *(Fin)* (bank)-note cover; **No|ten|durch|schnitt** M *(Sch)* average mark *or* grade *(esp US)*; **No|ten|ge|bung** F *(Sch: = das Benoten)* marking; **No|ten|heft** NT *(mit Noten)* book of music; *(ohne Noten)* manuscript book; **No|ten|li|nie** F lines *pl* (of a stave); **Papier mit ~n** manuscript paper; **No|ten|pa|pier** NT manuscript paper; **No|ten|pres|se** F money press; **No|ten|pult** NT music stand; **No|ten|schlüs|sel** M clef; **No|ten|schrift** F musical notation; **No|ten|stän|der** M music stand; **No|ten|um|lauf** M *(Fin)* circulation (of banknotes *(Brit)* or bills *(US)*); **No|ten|wech|sel** M *(Pol)* exchange of notes

Note|pad ['noːtpɛθ] NT -s, -s *(Comput)* notepad

Not|fall M emergency; **für den ~ nehme ich einen Schirm mit** I'll take an umbrella (just) in case; **im ~** if necessary, if need(s) be; **bei einem ~** in case of emergency; **im äußersten ~** in an extreme emergency; **er ist ein ~** *(Kranker)* he is an emergency case

Not|fall|me|di|zin F, *no pl (= Heilkunde)* emergency medicine

not|falls ['noːtfals] ADV if necessary, if need(s) be

Not|flag|ge F distress flag

not|ge|drun|gen ['noːtgədrʊŋən] ADJ enforced ADV of necessity, perforce *(form)*; **ich muss mich ~ dazu bereit erklären** I'm forced to agree, I've no choice but to agree, I must perforce agree *(form)*

Not-: **Not|geld** NT emergency money; **Not|ge|mein|schaft** F emergency organization; *(= Zwangsbündnis)* union of convenience; **im Kampf gegen die Schlammmassen waren wir alle eine ~** in the fight against the mud we all had to pull together; **Not|gro|schen** M nest egg; **sich** *(dat)* **einen ~** *or* **eine Summe als ~ zurücklegen** to put some money away for a rainy day; **Not|ha|fen** M harbour *(Brit)* or harbor *(US)* of refuge; **wegen der Epidemie musste das Schiff einen ~ anlaufen** because of the epidemic the ship had to make an emergency stop; **Not|hel|fer(in)** M(F) *(Rel)* auxiliary saint; **Not|hil|fe** F assistance in an emergency

no|tie|ren [no'tiːrən] *ptp* **notiert** VTI a *(= Notizen machen)* to note down, to make a note of; *(schnell)* to jot down; *(= bemerken)* to note; **ich notiere (mir) den Namen** I'll make a note of the name; **Frau Becker, bitte ~ Sie!** please take a note/a letter *etc*, Ms Becker; **was möchten Sie bestellen? ich notiere** what would you like to order? I'll make a note of it *or* I'll take it down b *(= vormerken) Auftrag* to note, to book; **zu welchem Termin waren Sie notiert?** what time was your appointment?; **jdn (für etw) ~** to put sb's name *or* sb down (for sth) c *(St Ex: = festlegen)* to quote *(mit* at) VI *(St Ex: = wert sein)* to be quoted *(auf +acc* at); **an der Börse notiert sein** to be quoted *or* listed on the stock market

No|tie|rung F -, -en a *(Comm)* note b *(St Ex)* quotation c *(Mus)* notation

nö|tig ['nøːtɪç] ✪ 37.2 ADJ necessary; **das für die Reise ~e Geld** the necessary money for the journey, the money needed *or* necessary for the journey; **ist das unbedingt ~?** is that really *or* absolutely necessary?; **es ist nicht ~, zu sagen, wie ...** it's not necessary *or* there's no need to say how ...; **es ist nicht ~, dass er kommt** it's not necessary *or* there's no need for him to come, he doesn't need to come; **das war wirklich nicht ~** that really wasn't necessary, there was no need for that; *(nach spitzer Bemerkung auch)* that was uncalled for; **die ~en Unkosten** the unavoidable costs; **wenn ~** if necessary, if need(s) be; **etw ~ haben** to need sth; **etw bitter ~ haben** to need sth badly; **er hat das natürlich nicht ~** *(iro)* but, of course, he's different; **ich habe es nicht ~, mich von dir anschreien zu lassen** I don't need *or* I don't have to let you shout at me; **die habens gerade ~** *(inf)* that's the last thing they need; **du hast es gerade ~, so zu reden** *(inf)* you can *or* can't talk *(inf)*, you're a fine one to talk *(inf)*; **das habe ich nicht ~!** I can do without that, I don't need that; **etw ~ machen** to necessitate sth, to make sth necessary; **das Nötige** the necessary; **das Nötigste** the (bare) necessities *or* essentials; **alles zum Bergsteigen unbedingt Nötige** everything necessary *or* needed for mountaineering ADV *(= dringend)* **etwas ~ brauchen** to need something urgently; **ich muss mal ~** *(inf)* I'm dying to go *(inf)*

nö|ti|gen ['nøːtɪgn] VT *(geh: = zwingen)* to force, to compel; *(Jur)* to coerce; *(= auffordern)* to urge, to press; **jdn ins Zimmer ~** to urge *or* press sb to go into a room; **sich ~ lassen** to need prompting *or* urging; **lassen Sie sich nicht (erst) ~!** don't wait to be asked → *auch* **genötigt**

nö|ti|gen|falls ['nøːtɪgnfals] ADV *(form)* if necessary, if need(s) be

Nö|ti|gung ['nøːtɪgʊŋ] F -, -en *(= Zwang)* compulsion; *(Jur)* coercion; **~ zum Diebstahl** coercion to commit theft; **sexuelle ~** sexual assault

No|tiz [no'tiːts] F -, -en **a** *(= Vermerk)* note; *(= Zeitungsnotiz)* item; **sich** *(dat)* **~en machen** to make *or* take notes; **sich** *(dat)* **eine ~ von etw machen** to make a note of sth **b ~ nehmen von** to pay attention to, to take notice of; **keine ~ nehmen von** to ignore; **kaum ~ nehmen von** to hardly take any notice of; **nimm keine ~!** take no notice, don't take any notice **c** *(St Ex: = Notierung)* quotation

No|tiz-: **No|tiz|block** M *pl* **-blöcke** notepad, jotter; **No|tiz|buch** NT notebook; **No|tiz|zet|tel** M piece of paper; **er hinterließ mir einen ~ mit seiner Adresse** he left me a note of his address on a piece of paper

Not-: **Not|jahr** NT year of need, difficult year; **Not|kühl|sys|tem** NT emergency cooling system; **Not|la|ge** F crisis; *(= Elend)* plight; **in ~n** in an emergency; **die wirtschaftliche ~ Mittelamerikas** Central America's economic plight; **jds ~** *(acc)* **ausnutzen** to exploit sb's situation; **in eine ~ geraten** to get into serious difficulties; **sich in einer (finanziellen** *etc*) **~ befinden** to find oneself in serious (financial *etc*) difficulties

not|lan|den ['noːtlandn] *pret* **notlandete**, *ptp* **notgelandet** ['noːtgəlandət] VI *aux sein* to make a forced landing, to make an emergency landing

Not|lan|dung F forced *or* emergency landing

not|lei|dend ADJ → **Not a**

Not|lei|den|de(r) MF *decl as adj* **die ~n** the needy

Not-: **Not|lei|ne** F emergency cord; **Not|lö|sung** F compromise *or* less-than-ideal solution; *(provisorisch)* temporary solution; **Not|lü|ge** F white lie; **Not|maß|nah|me** F emergency measure; **Not|na|gel** M *(fig inf)* last resort; **Not|ope|ra|ti|on** F emergency operation; **Not|op|fer** NT emergency levy

no|to|risch [no'toːrɪʃ] ADJ **a** *(= gewohnheitsmäßig)* habitual **b** *(= allbekannt)* notorious ADV habitually

Not-: **Not|pro|gramm** NT *(Pol, Econ)* emergency measures *pl*; **Not|rad** NT *(Aut)* spare wheel; **Not|ra|ti|on** F emergency ration; **Not|ruf** M *(Telec) (Gespräch)* emergency call; *(Nummer)* emergency number; **Not|ruf|säu|le** F emergency telephone; **Not|rut|sche** F *(Aviat)* escape chute

not|schlach|ten ['noːtʃlaxtn] *pret* **notschlachtete**, *ptp* **notgeschlachtet** ['noːtgəʃlaxtət] VT to destroy, to put down

Not-: **Not|schlach|tung** F putting down; **Not|schrei** M *(liter)* cry of distress, cry for help; **Not|sig|nal** NT distress signal; **Not|si|tu|a|ti|on** F emergency; **Not|sitz** M foldaway seat, tip-up seat

Not|stand M crisis; *(Pol)* state of emergency; *(Jur)* emergency; **innerer ~** domestic *or* internal state of emergency; **äußerer ~** threat of invasion *or* attack; **nationaler ~** national (state of) emergency; **ziviler ~** disaster; **übergesetzlicher ~** *emergency situation in which a law no longer holds*; **den ~ ausrufen** to declare a state of emergency; **einen ~ beheben** to end *or* put an end to a crisis; **einen ~ abwenden** to avert a crisis/an emergency

Not|stands-: **Not|stands|ge|biet** NT *(wirtschaftlich)* depressed *or* deprived area; *(bei Katastrophen)* disaster area; **Not|stands|ge|set|ze** PL, **Not|stands|ver|fas|sung** F *(Pol)* emergency laws *pl*

Not-: **Not|strom|ag|gre|gat** NT emergency power generator; **Not|tau|fe** F emergency baptism; **not|tau|fen** ['noːttaufn] *pret* **nottaufte**, *ptp* **notgetauft** ['noːtgətauft] VT **jdn ~** to administer an emergency baptism to sb; **not+tun** VI *sep irreg* to be necessary; **ihm tat Hilfe not** he needed help; **uns allen täte ein bisschen mehr Bescheidenheit not** we could all benefit from a little more modesty

Not|tur|no [nɔ'tʊrno] NT -s, -s *or* **Notturni** [-ni] nocturne

Not-: **Not|un|ter|kunft** F emergency accommodation; **Not|ver|band** M emergency *or* first-aid dressing; **Not|ver|ord|nung** F emergency decree; **not|was|sern** ['noːtvasɐn] *pret* **notwasserte**, *ptp* **notgewassert** ['noːtgəvasɐt] VI to ditch (*Aviat sl*), to make a crash-landing in the sea; **Not|wehr** ['noːtveːɐ] F, *no pl* self-defence *(Brit)*, self-defense *(US)*; **in** *or* **aus ~** in self-defence *(Brit) or* self-defense *(US)*

not|wen|dig ['noːtvɛndɪç, noːt'vɛndɪç] ADJ necessary; *(= unvermeidlich auch)* inevitable; **es ist ~, dass sie selbst kommt** it is necessary that she come(s) herself; **das Notwendige** the necessary, what is necessary; **ich habe alles Notwendige erledigt** I've done everything (that's) necessary; **das Notwendigste** the (bare) necessities *or* essentials; **sich auf das Notwendigste beschränken** to stick to essentials → **Übel b** ADV necessarily; **eine rationale Denkweise ist ~ geboten** rational thinking is strongly recommended; **~ brauchen** to need urgently; **es folgt ~** it necessarily follows; **es musste ~ zum Zusammenstoß kommen** the collision was inevitable

not|wen|di|ger|wei|se ['noːtvɛndɪgɐ'vaizə] ADV of necessity, necessarily, inevitably

Not|wen|dig|keit F -, -en **a** *no pl* necessity; **mit ~** of necessity; **die ~, etw zu tun** the necessity of doing sth; **die/keine ~ für etw sehen** to see the/no necessity for sth; **keine ~ sehen, etw zu tun** to see no necessity to do sth **b** *(= notwendige Sache)* necessity, essential

Not|zei|chen NT distress signal

Not|zucht F *(Jur)* rape; **~ begehen** *or* **verüben** to commit rape *(an +dat* on)

not|züch|ti|gen ['noːttsʏçtɪgn] *pret* **notzüchtigte**, *ptp* **genotzüchtigt** [gə'noːttsʏçtɪçt] VT *(Jur)* to rape, to ravish *(form)*, to violate

Not|zucht|ver|bre|chen NT crime of rape

Nou|gat ['nuːgat] M OR NT -s, -s nougat

No|va *pl von* **Novum**

No|vel|le [no'vɛlə] F -, -n **a** novella **b** *(Pol)* amendment

no|vel|lie|ren [novɛ'liːrən] *ptp* **novelliert** VT *(Pol)* to amend

No|vel|lie|rung F -, *no pl (Pol)* amendment

No|vel|list [novɛ'lɪst] M -en, -en, **No|vel|lis|tin** [-'lɪstɪn] F -, -nen novella writer

no|vel|lis|tisch [novɛ'lɪstɪʃ] ADJ novella-like ADV **den Stoff ~ behandeln** to use the material for *or* in a novella; **eine ~ erzählte Geschichte** a novella-like story

No|vem|ber [no'vɛmbɐ] M -(s), - November → *auch* **März**

no|vem|ber|lich [no'vɛmbɐlɪç] ADJ November-like

No|ve|ne [no'veːnə] F -, -n novena

No|vi|tät [novi'tɛːt] F -, -en *(geh)* new product; *(Buch)* new publication; *(Theat)* new play; **das ist keine ~** that's nothing new

No|vi|ze [no'viːtsə] M -n, -n F -, -n, **No|vi|zin** [-'viːtsɪn] F -, -nen novice

No|vi|zi|at [novi'tsiaːt] NT -(e)s, -e novitiate

No|vum ['noːvʊm] NT -s, **Nova** [-va] novelty

NPD [ɛnpeː'deː] F - *abbr von* **Nationaldemokratische Partei Deutschlands**

NR *(in Annoncen) abbr von* **Nichtraucher**

Nr. *abbr von* **Numero, Nummer** No.

NRW [ɛnlɛr'veː] *abbr von* **Nordrhein-Westfalen** North Rhine-Westphalia

NS [ɛn'lɛs] **a** *abbr von* **Nachschrift** PS **b** *abbr von* **nationalsozialistisch**

NS- *in cpds* Nazi; **NS-Dik|ta|tur** F Nazi dictatorship; **NS-Ver|bre|chen** NT Nazi crime *or* atrocity; **NS-Zeit** F Nazi era, (period of) Nazi rule

N. T. *abbr von* **Neues Testament** NT

nu [nuː] ADV *(dial inf)* = **nun**

Nu [nuː] M **im Nu** in no time, in a flash *or* trice

Nu|an|ce ['nyãːsə] F -, -n *(= kleiner Unterschied)* nuance; *(= Kleinigkeit)* shade; **um eine ~ zu laut** a shade too loud; **sie unterscheiden sich nur in ~n voneinander** they differ only very slightly

nu|an|cen|reich ADJ ADV full of nuances

nu|an|cie|ren [nyã'siːrən] *ptp* **nuanciert** VT to nuance

'nü|ber ['nyːbɐ] ADV *(dial)* = **hinüber**

Nu|buk ['nʊbʊk, 'nuːbʊk] NT -(s), *no pl*, **Nu|buk|le|der** NT nubuk

nüch|tern ['nʏçtɐn] ADJ **a** *(ohne Essen)* **der Patient muss ~ sein** the patient must have an empty stomach; **eine Medizin ~ einnehmen** to take a medicine on an empty stomach; **mit ~em/auf ~en Magen** with/on an empty stomach; **das war ein Schreck auf ~en Magen** *(hum)* my heart skipped a beat **b** *(= nicht betrunken)* sober; **wieder ~ werden** to sober up **c** *(= sachlich, vernünftig)* down-to-earth *no adv*, rational; *Zahlen, Tatsachen* bare, plain **d** *(= schmucklos)* sober ADV **a** *(= sachlich)* unemotionally, objectively **b** *(= schlicht)* **~ gestaltete Räume** soberly decorated rooms; **~ graue Wände** bare grey *(Brit) or* gray *(US)* walls; **~ schmucklose Häuser** plain unadorned buildings

Nüch|tern|heit F -, *no pl* **a überzeugen Sie sich von der ~ des Patienten** make sure that the patient's stomach is empty **b** *(= unbetrunkener Zustand)* soberness **c** *(= Sachlichkeit, Vernünftigkeit)* rationality **d** *(= Schmucklosigkeit)* soberness

Nu|ckel ['nʊkl] M -s, - *(inf) (auf Fläschchen)* teat *(Brit)*, nipple *(US)*; *(= Schnuller)* dummy *(Brit)*, pacifier *(US)*

nu|ckeln ['nʊkln] VI *(inf) (Mensch)* to suck *(an +dat* at); *(Tier)* to suckle *(an +dat* from); **am Daumen ~** to suck one's thumb

Nu|ckel|pin|ne F *(inf)* old banger *(Brit inf) or* crate *(inf)*

Nu|cki ['nʊki] M -s, - *(Sw)* dummy *(Brit)*, pacifier *(US)*

Nu|del ['nuːdl] F -, -n *usu pl* **a** *(als Beilage)* pasta *no pl*; *(als Suppeneinlage, chinesische)* noodle; *(= Fadennudel)* vermicelli *pl* **b** *(inf: Mensch) (dick)* dumpling *(inf)*; *(komisch)* character

Nu|del-: **Nu|del|brett** NT pastryboard; **nu|del|dick** ADJ *(inf)* podgy *(Brit inf)*, pudgy *(US inf)*; **Nu|del|holz** NT rolling pin

nu|deln ['nuːdln] VT *Gans* to force-feed; *(inf) Kind etc* to stuff *(inf)*, to overfeed; **ich bin genudelt** *(inf)* I'm full to bursting *(inf)*

Nu|del-: **Nu|del|sa|lat** M pasta salad; **Nu|del|sup|pe** F noodle soup; **Nu|del|teig** M pasta dough; *(für Suppennudeln, chinesische Nudeln)* noodle dough

Nu|dis|mus [nu'dɪsmʊs] M -, *no pl* nudism

Nu|dist [nu'dɪst] M -en, -en, **Nu|dis|tin** [-'dɪstɪn] F -, -nen nudist

Nu|di|tät [nudi'tɛːt] F -, -en *usu pl (geh: = Nacktbild)* nude (picture); *(= Nacktheit)* nudity

Nu|gat ['nuːgat] M OR NT -s, -s nougat

nuk|le|ar [nukle'aːɐ] ADJ *attr* nuclear ADV with nuclear weapons; **jdn ~ bestrahlen** to expose sb to nuclear radiation

Nuk|le|ar- *in cpds* nuclear; **Nuk|le|ar|macht** F nuclear power; **Nuk|le|ar|me|di|zin** F nuclear medicine; **Nuk|le|ar|schlag** M nuclear strike; **Nuk|le|ar|test** M nuclear test; **Nuk|le|ar|waf|fe** F nuclear weapon

Nuk|le|in|säu|re F nucleic acid

Nuk|le|on ['nuːkleɔn] NT -s, **Nukleonen** [nukle'oːnən] nucleon

Nuk|leo|tid [nukleo'ti:t] NT **-s, -e** [-'ti:də] nucleotide

Nuk|le|us ['nu:kleʊs] M **-, Nuklei** [-klei] nucleus

Nuk|lid [nu'kli:t] NT **-s, -e** [-də] nuclide

null [nʊl] NUM zero; (inf: = kein) zero (inf); (Telec) O (Brit), zero; (Sport) nil, nothing; (Tennis) love; ~ **Komma eins** (nought) point one; **es ist ~ Uhr zehn** it's ten past twelve or midnight; **zwei Minuten ~ Sekunden** (bei Zeitansagen) two minutes precisely; (bei Rennen) two minutes dead or flat; ~ **Grad** zero degrees; ~ **Fehler** no or zero (inf) mistakes; **es steht ~ zu ~** there's no score; **das Spiel wurde ~ zu ~ beendet** the game was a goalless (Brit) or no-score draw; **eins zu ~** one-nil, one-nothing; ~ **und nichtig** (Jur) null and void; **für ~ und nichtig erklären** (Jur) to declare null and void, to annul; ~ **Ahnung haben** to have absolutely no idea; **das Thermometer steht auf ~** the thermometer is at or on zero; **Temperaturen unter ~** sub-zero temperatures; **gleich ~ sein** to be absolutely nil or zero; **in ~ Komma nichts** (inf) in less than no time; ~ **Komma ~** (inf) damn-all (inf), sweet Fanny Adams (Brit inf); **jdn auf ~ bringen** (inf) to fix sb for good (inf); **von ~ auf hundert in 20 Sekunden** (Aut) ≈ from nought (esp Brit) or zero to sixty in 20 seconds; **bei ~ anfangen** to start from scratch; **gegen ~ gehen** or **tendieren** to be virtually non-existent; (Math) to tend to zero; **seine Stimmung sank auf** or **unter ~** (inf) he sank into the depths of gloom; **im Jahre ~** in the year zero; **die Stunde ~** the new starting point → **Bock f**

Null [nʊl] F **-, -en** **a** (Zahl) nought, naught (US), zero; (= Gefrierpunkt) zero; **die ~** the figure nought, zero; **eine schwarze ~ schreiben** (Fin) to break even **b** (inf: Mensch) dead loss (inf)

Null M OR NT **-(s), -s** (Cards) nullo

null|acht|fünf|zehn [nʊlaxt'fʏnftse:n], **null|acht|fuff|zehn** [nʊlaxt'fʊftse:n] (inf) ADJ inv run-of-the-mill (inf) ADV in a run-of-the-mill way

Null|acht|fünf|zehn- [nʊlaxt'fʏnftse:n], **Null|acht|fuff|zehn-** [nʊlaxt'fʊftse:n] in cpds (inf) run-of-the-mill; **ein ~Restaurant** a run-of-the-mill restaurant; **er fährt ein ~Auto** he drives a pretty ordinary car

Null-Bock- ['nʊl'bɔk] (inf) in cpds apathetic; **~Generation** *generation characterized by general apathy*, "couldn't care less" generation, disaffected youth; **~Haltung** "couldn't care less" attitude

Null|di|ät F starvation diet

Nulleiter △ M → **Nullleiter**

Nul|li ['nʊli] M **-s, -s** (sl) loser (inf)

Nullinie △ F → **Nulllinie**

Null-: **Null|lei|ter** M (Elec) earth (wire) (Brit), ground (wire) (US); **Null|li|nie** F zero, nought, naught (US); **Null|lö|sung** F (Pol) zero option; **Null|men|ge** F (Math) empty set; **Null|me|ri|di|an** M Greenwich or prime Meridian; **Null-Null** ['nʊl'nʊl] NT OR M **-,** no pl (inf) loo (Brit inf), restroom (US); **Null|num|mer** F **a** (von Zeitung etc) pilot **b** (= Misserfolg) flop (inf), washout (inf); (= Nichtskönner) no-hoper (inf)

Nullösung △ F → **Nulllösung**

Null-: **Null ou|vert** ['nʊl u've:ɐ] M OR (RARE) NT **- -, - -s** (Cards) null ouvert; **Null|punkt** M zero; **absoluter ~** absolute zero; **die Stimmung sank unter den ~** the atmosphere froze; **auf den ~ sinken, den ~ erreichen** to reach or hit rock-bottom; **auf dem ~ angekommen sein** or **am ~ angelangt sein** (fig) to have hit or reached rock-bottom; **Null|run|de** F **in diesem Jahr gab es eine ~ für Beamte** there has been no pay increase this year for civil servants; **ich bin gegen eine ~ bei den Renten** I am in favour (Brit) or favor (US) of an increase in pensions; **Null|spiel** NT (Cards) nullo; **Null|stel|lung** F zero position; **in der ~ sein** to be on zero; **Null|sum|men|spiel** NT zero-sum game; **Null|ta|rif** M (für Verkehrsmittel) free travel; (= freier Eintritt) free admission; **zum ~** (hum) free of charge; **Null|wachs|tum** NT (Pol) zero growth

Nul|pe ['nʊlpə] F **-, -n** (inf) clot (Brit inf), dope (inf), jerk (inf)

Nu|me|ra|le [nume'ra:lə] NT **-s, Numeralia** or **Numeralien** [-lia, -liən] (Gram) numeral

Nu|me|ri pl von **Numerus**

nu|me|rie|ren △ [nume'ri:rən] ptp **numeriert** VT → **nummerieren**

Nu|me|rie|rung △ F **-, -en** → **Nummerierung**

nu|me|risch [nu:'me:rɪʃ] ADJ numeric(al); **~er Tastenblock** (Comput) numeric keypad ADV numerically; **~ überlegen/unterlegen sein** to be superior/inferior in number

Nu|me|ro ['nu:mero, 'nʊmero] NT **-s, -s** (old, hum) **~ eins/zwei** number one/two

Nu|me|rus ['nu:merʊs, 'nʊmerʊs] M **-, Numeri** [-ri] (Gram) number; **~ clausus** (Univ) restricted entry; **sozialer ~ clausus** *restricted access to higher education on basis of financial means*

NUMERUS CLAUSUS

The **Numerus clausus**, or **NC**, controls admissions to certain over-subscribed university courses such as medicine, information technology and architecture. The main admission criterion is the mark obtained in the **Abitur**. Places are allocated by the **Zentralstelle für die Vergabe von Studienplätzen**, or **ZVS**. → ABITUR

NUM-Fest|stell|tas|te ['nʊm-] F (Comput) num lock key

Nu|mis|ma|tik [numɪs'ma:tɪk] F **-,** no pl numismatics sing

Num|mer ['nʊmɐ] ✪ 27 F **-, -n** (Math, von Zeitschrift, in Varieté) number; (= Größe) size; (inf: Mensch) character; (inf: = Koitus) screw (sl); (mit Prostituierter) trick (inf); **unser Haus hat die ~ 25** our house is number 25; **Bahnhofstraße ~ 15** number 15 Bahnhofstraße; **nur eine ~ unter vielen sein** (fig) to be a cog (in the machine); **er hat** or **schiebt eine ruhige ~** (inf) he's onto a cushy number (inf); **auf ~ sicher gehen** (inf) to play (it) safe; **Gesprächsthema ~ eins** the number one talking point; **sie ist die ~ eins in Hollywood** she's number one or the number one star in Hollywood; **bei jdm eine gute ~ haben** (inf) to be well in with sb (inf); **eine ~ abziehen** (inf) to put on an act; **eine ~ machen** or **schieben** (inf) to have it off or away (inf); **dieses Geschäft ist eine ~/ein paar ~n zu groß für ihn** this business is out of/well out of his league; **der Pullover ist eine ~ zu klein** the jumper is one size too small

num|me|rie|ren [nʊme'ri:rən] ptp **nummeriert** VT to number

Num|me|rie|rung F **-, -en** numbering

Num|mern-: **Num|mern|block** M (Comput: auf Tastatur) numeric keypad; **Num|mern|girl** [-gø:ɐl] NT **-s, -s** ring card girl; **Num|mern|kon|to** NT (Fin) numbered account; **Num|mern|schei|be** F (Telec) dial; **Num|mern|schild** NT (Aut) number plate (Brit), registration plate (Brit), license plate (US); **Num|mern|spei|cher** M (Telec) memory; **Num|mern|zei|chen** NT (Typ) number sign

nun [nu:n] ADV **a** (= jetzt) now; **von ~ an** from now on, as of now, from here on in (esp US); **~ und nimmer(mehr)** (liter) nevermore (liter); **~, da er da ist, können wir anfangen** now that he's here we can get started; **~ erst, erst ~** only now; **~ ist aber genug!** now that's enough; **~ endlich** (now) at last; **was ~?** what now?; **was ~ (schon wieder)?** what (is it) now?

b (= danach) then; **~ erst ging er** only then did he go

c **ich bin ~ eben dumm** I'm just stupid, that's all; **er will ~ mal nicht** he simply doesn't want to; **wir hatten uns ~ eben entschlossen zu gehen ...** after all, we had decided to go ...; **dann muss ich das ~ wohl tun!** then I'll just have to do it; **~, wenns unbedingt sein muss** well, if I/you etc really must; **~, du hast ja recht, wenn du das sagst, aber ...** well or OK (inf) or fair enough (inf) what you say is true but ...; **das ist ~ (ein)mal so** that's just the way things are; **~ ja** or **gut, aber ...** all right or OK (inf) but ...; **~ ja** well yes; **~ gut** (well) all right, (well) OK (inf); **~, meinetwegen** well, as far as I'm concerned; **er mag ~ wollen oder nicht** (liter) whether he wants to or not or no; **~ gerade erst!, ~ erst recht!** just for that (I'll do it)!; **~ taten wirs erst recht nicht** just because they/he/she etc said/did that, we didn't do it

d (Folge) now; **das hast du ~ davon!** (it) serves you right

e (Aufforderung) come on, go on; **~ denn** (geh) well then; **~, wirds bald?** (inf) come on then, hurry up then

f (bei Fragen) well; **~?** well?

g (beschwichtigend) come on; **~, ~!** (warnend) come on now, come, come, now, now; (tröstend) there, there

CONJ (obs) since (that (obs)), now that

nun|mehr ['nu:n'me:ɐ] ADV (geh) (= jetzt) now, at this point; (= von jetzt an) henceforth (form), from now on, as of now; **die ~ herrschende Partei** the currently ruling party

nun|meh|rig ['nu:n'me:rɪç] ADJ attr (form) present, current

'nun|ter ['nʊntɐ] ADV (dial) abbr von **hinunter**

Nun|ti|us ['nʊntsiʊs] M **-, Nuntien** [-tsiən] nuncio

nur [nu:ɐ] ADV **a** (einschränkend) only, just; **er ist ein sehr schneller Arbeiter, ~ müsste er etwas gründlicher sein** he is a very fast worker but or only he should be rather more thorough; **ich habe ~ ein Stück Brot gegessen** I've only eaten a piece of bread, I've eaten only or just a piece of bread; **alle, ~ ich nicht** everyone except or but me; **~ ich weiß** I'm the only one who knows, only I know; **~ schade, dass ...** it's just a pity that ...; **~ dass ...** it's just that ..., only ...; **~ noch zwei Minuten** only or just two minutes left or to go; **der Kranke isst fast ~ noch Obst** the sick man eats virtually nothing but fruit these days; **nicht ~ ..., sondern auch** not only or just ... but also; **alles, ~ das nicht!** anything but that!; **warum möchtest du das denn wissen? – ach, ~ so!** why do you want to know? – oh I just do or oh just because or oh no special reason; **ich hab das ~ so gesagt** I was just talking; **warum hast du das gemacht? – ~ so** why did you do that? – I just did; **~ kann man nie wissen, ob ...** only or but you never can or can never tell if ...

b (verstärkend) just; **wie schnell er ~ redet** doesn't he speak fast!; **dass es ~ so krachte** making a terrible din or racket; **er fuhr, so schnell er ~ (fahren) konnte** he drove just as fast as he possibly could, he drove for all he was worth

c (mit Fragepronomen) -ever, on earth (inf); **was/wer/wie** etc **~?** but what/who/how etc?; **was hat er ~?** whatever is or what on earth (inf) is the matter with him?; **wie kannst du ~ (so etwas sagen)?** how could you (say such a thing)?; **sie bekommt alles, was sie ~ will** she gets whatever she wants

d (Wunsch, Bedingung) **wenn er ~ (erst) käme** if only he would come, if he would only come; **wüsste ich ~, wie** if only I knew how, if I only knew how; **es wird klappen, wenn er ~ nicht die Nerven verliert** it will be all right as long as or so long as (inf) or provided (that) he doesn't lose his nerve

e (mit Negationen) just, ... whatever you do; **lass das ~ niemand(en) wissen!** just don't let anyone find out, (but) don't let anyone find out whatever you do; **sagen Sie das ~ nicht Ihrer Frau!** just don't tell your wife (whatever you do)

f (Aufforderung) just; **geh ~!** just go, go on; ~

zu! go on; **sieh ~** just look; **~ her damit!** *(inf)* let's have it; **sagen Sie es ~, Sie brauchen es ~ zu sagen** just say (the word), you only have to say (the word); **er soll ~ lachen!** let him laugh **g ~ mehr** *(dial, esp Aus)* only ... left; **ich habe ~ mehr einen Euro** I've only one euro left

Nur|haus|frau F full-time housewife

Nürn|berg ['nʏrnbɛrk] NT **-s** Nuremberg; **jdm etw mit dem ~er Trichter beibringen** *(inf)* to drum sth into sb; **die ~er Prozesse** the Nuremberg (war) trials

nu|scheln ['nʊʃln] VTI *(inf)* to mutter, to mumble

Nuss [nʊs] F **-, ⸗e** ['nʏsə] **a** nut; **eine harte ~ zu knacken haben** *(fig)* to have a tough nut to crack **b** *(inf: Mensch)* drip *(inf)*, jerk *(inf)*; **eine taube ~** a dead loss *(inf)*, a washout *(inf)*; **eine doofe ~** a stupid twit *(Brit inf)* or clown *(inf)* **c** *(inf: = Kopfnuss)* punch (in the head) **d Nüsse** *(sl: = Hoden)* nuts *pl (sl)*

Nuss-: **Nuss|baum** M *(Baum)* walnut tree; *(Holz)* walnut; **nuss|braun** ADJ nut-brown, hazel; **Nuss|ecke** F *(Cook)* nut pastry; **Nuss|kna|cker** M nutcracker, (pair of) nutcrackers *pl*; **Nuss|koh|le** F nut coal; **Nuss|scha|le** F nutshell; *(fig: Boot)* cockleshell, frail little boat

Nüs|ter ['nʏstɐ] F **-, -n** nostril

Nut [nu:t] F **-, -en** *(spec)*, **Nu|te** ['nu:tə] F **-, -n** groove, flute, chase; *(zur Einfügung)* rabbet, slot; *(= Keilnut)* keyway, key seat; **~ und Feder** tongue and groove; **~ und Zapfen** mortise and tenon

nu|ten ['nu:tn] VT → **Nut** to groove, to flute; to rabbet, to slot; to cut a keyway in, to key seat

Nut|ria ['nu:tria] F **-, -s** *(Tier, Pelz)* coypu, nutria *(rare)*

Nut|te ['nʊtə] F **-, -n** *(inf)* tart *(inf)*, pro *(inf)*, hooker *(esp US inf)*

nut|tig ['nʊtɪç] ADJ *(inf)* tarty *(inf)*

Nut- und Fe|der|brett NT tongue and groove board

nutz [nʊts] ADJ *(S Ger, Aus)* = **nütze**

Nutz [nʊts] M **zu ~ und Frommen** *+gen (old liter)* for the greater good of *(form)*; **sich** *(dat)* **etw zu ~e machen** → **zunutze**

Nutz|an|wen|dung F practical application; *(einer Geschichte)* moral

nutz|bar ADJ *Rohstoffe, Gebäude, Wasserstraßen* us(e)able; *Boden* productive; *Bodenschätze* exploitable; **~e Fläche** *(in Gebäude)* us(e)able floor space; **landwirtschaftlich ~e Fläche** agriculturally productive land; **~ machen** to make us(e)able or utilizable; *Sonnenenergie* to utilize, to harness, to turn to good use; *Sümpfe* to reclaim; *Bodenschätze* to exploit

Nutz|bar|keit ['nʊtsba:ɐkait] F **-,** *no pl (von Rohstoffen, Gebäude)* us(e)ability; **die ~ des Bodens lässt nach** the soil is becoming less and less productive

Nutz|bar|ma|chung ['nʊtsba:ɐmaxʊŋ] F **-,** *no pl* utilization; *(von Sümpfen)* reclamation; *(von Bodenschätzen)* exploitation

Nutz|bau M *pl* **-bauten** functional building

nutz|brin|gend ADJ profitable ADV profitably; **etw ~ anwenden** to use sth profitably *or* to good effect, to put sth to good use, to turn sth to good account

nüt|ze ['nʏtsə] ADJ *pred* **zu etw ~ sein** to be useful for sth; **zu nichts ~ sein** to be no use for anything

Nutz|ef|fekt M effectiveness, efficiency

nut|zen ['nʊtsn] VI to be of use, to be useful *(jdm zu etw* to sb for sth); **die Ermahnungen haben genutzt/nichts genutzt** the warnings had the desired effect/didn't do any good; **es nutzt nichts** it's no use *or* good, it's useless; **alle Anstrengungen haben nichts genutzt** all our efforts were useless *or* in vain; **da nutzt alles nichts** there's nothing to be done; **das nutzt (mir/dir) nichts** that won't help (me/you); **das nutzt niemandem** that's of no use to anybody; **es nutzt wenig** it isn't much use *or* good; **wozu soll das alles ~?** what's the use *or* point of that?

VT to make use of, to use; *Gelegenheit* to take advantage of; *Bodenschätze, Energien* to use, to exploit; **nutze den Tag!** gather ye rosebuds while ye may *(liter)*

Nut|zen ['nʊtsn] M **-s, - a** use; *(= Nützlichkeit)* usefulness; **es hat keinen ~, das zu tun** there's no use *or* point (in) doing that; **zum ~ der Öffentlichkeit** for the benefit of the public; **jdm von ~ sein** to be useful *or* of use to sb; *(einer anderen Person auch)* to be of service to sb; **von großem/geringem ~ sein** to be of great/little use

b *(= Vorteil)* advantage, benefit; *(= Gewinn)* profit; **jdm ~ bringen** *(Vorteil)* to be of advantage to sb; *(Gewinn)* to bring sb profit, to prove profitable to sb; **sich** *(dat)* **großen ~ von etw versprechen** to expect to benefit *or* profit greatly from sth; **von etw ~ haben** to gain *or* profit by sth; **aus etw ~ ziehen** to reap the benefits of sth

nüt|zen ['nʏtsn] VTI = **nutzen**

Nut|zer ['nʊtsɐ] M **-s, -**, **Nut|ze|rin** [-ərɪn] F **-, -nen** user

Nut|zer|end|ge|rät NT *(Comput)* user terminal

nut|zer|freund|lich, **nut|zer|ge|recht** ADJ user-friendly ADV **~ geschrieben** written in a user-friendly way/style; **~ gestaltet/eingerichtet sein** to be user-friendly

Nutz-: **Nutz|fahr|zeug** NT farm vehicle; military vehicle *etc*; *(Comm)* commercial vehicle, goods vehicle; *(= Straßenbahn etc)* public vehicle; **Nutz|flä|che** F utilizable *or* us(e)able floor space; **(landwirtschaftliche) ~** *(Agr)* (agriculturally) productive land; **Nutz|gar|ten** M vegetable *or* kitchen garden; **Nutz|ge|gen|stand** M article of purely practical value; **Nutz|holz** NT (utilizable) timber; **Nutz|last** F payload; **Nutz|leis|tung** F efficiency, effective capacity *or* output; *(Aut)* performance

nütz|lich ['nʏtslɪç] ADJ useful; *Hinweis, Wissen, Kenntnisse, Buch auch* helpful; **~ für die Gesundheit** beneficial for the health; **er könnte dir eines Tages sehr ~ werden** he might be very useful to you one day; **sich ~ machen** to make oneself useful; **kann ich Ihnen ~ sein?** may I be of service to you?

Nütz|lich|keit F **-,** *no pl* usefulness

Nütz|lich|keits-: **Nütz|lich|keits|den|ken** NT utilitarian thinking; **Nütz|lich|keits|prin|zip** NT utility principle

Nütz|ling ['nʏtslɪŋ] M **-s, -en** beneficial insect

nutz|los ADJ **a** useless; *(= unergiebig, vergeblich)* futile, vain *attr*, in vain *pred*; **es ist völlig ~, das zu tun** it's absolutely useless *or* pointless *or* futile doing that **b** *(= unnötig)* needless ADV **a** *(= ohne Nutzen)* uselessly; **ich fühle mich ~** I feel useless **b** *(= unnötig)* futilely, in vain; **er hat seine Zeit ~ mit Spielen zugebracht** he frittered away *or* wasted his time playing; **sein Leben ~ aufs Spiel setzen** to risk one's life needlessly *or* unnecessarily

Nutz|lo|sig|keit F **-,** *no pl* uselessness; *(= Uneinträglichkeit, Vergeblichkeit)* futility

Nutz|nie|ßer ['nʊtsni:sɐ] M **-s, -**, **Nutz|nie|ße|rin** [-ərɪn] F **-, -nen** beneficiary; *(Jur)* usufructuary

Nutz|nie|ßung ['nʊtsni:sʊŋ] F **-, -en** *(Jur)* usufruct

Nutz-: **Nutz|pflan|ze** F useful plant, crop; **Nutz|tier** NT working animal

Nut|zung ['nʊtsʊŋ] F **-, -en** *(= Gebrauch)* use; *(= das Ausnutzen)* exploitation; *(von Ressourcen, Technologie)* use; *(Jur: = Ertrag)* benefit; *(= Einkommen)* revenue (*+gen* from), return(s *pl*) (*+gen* on); **jdm etw zur ~ überlassen** to give sb *or* let sb have the use of sth; **die ~en aus etw ziehen** *(Jur)* to enjoy the benefit of sth

Nut|zungs-: **Nut|zungs|dau|er** F (useful) life; **Nut|zungs|ge|bühr** F user fee; **Nut|zungs|recht** NT *(Jur)* usufruct; **Nut|zungs|ver|trag** M *contract granting use (im Verlagswesen)* rights contract

n. u. Z. *abbr von* **nach unserer Zeitrechnung** by our calendar

NVA [ɛnfau'a:] **-,** *no pl (Hist) abbr von* **Nationale Volksarmee** National People's Army

NW *abbr von* **Nordwesten** NW

Ny|lon® ['nailɔn] NT **-(s),** *no pl* nylon

Ny|lons ['nailɔns] PL nylons *pl*, nylon stockings *pl*

Ny|lon|strumpf ['nailɔn-] M nylon (stocking)

Nymph|chen ['nʏmfçən] NT **-s, -** nymphet

Nym|phe ['nʏmfə] F **-, -n** *(Myth)* nymph; *(fig)* sylph; *(Zool)* nymph(a); **die ~n** *(Anat)* the nymphae *pl*

Nym|pho|ma|nie [nʏmfoma'ni:] F **-,** *no pl* nymphomania

Nym|pho|ma|nin [nʏmfo'ma:nɪn] F **-, -nen** nymphomaniac

nym|pho|ma|nisch [nʏmfo'ma:nɪʃ] ADJ nymphomaniac

O

O, o [oː] NT -, - O, o

o [oː] INTERJ oh; **o Sünder!** *(liter)* O sinner; **O Gott!** O God!

O *abbr von* **Osten**

Oa|se [oˈaːzə] F -, -n oasis; *(fig)* haven, oasis

ob [ɔp] CONJ **a** *(indirekte Frage)* if, whether; **wir gehen spazieren, ob es regnet oder nicht** we're going for a walk whether it rains or not; **Sie müssen kommen, ob Sie (nun) wollen oder nicht** like it or not, you have to come; **ob reich, ob arm** whether rich or poor; **ob er (wohl) morgen kommt?** I wonder if he'll come tomorrow?; **ob wir jetzt Pause machen?** shall we take a break now?; **ob ich nicht lieber gehe?** maybe I'd better go, hadn't I better go?; **ich muss mal nachsehen, ob sie nicht schon kommen** I must look and see if they're coming yet; **ob ich keine Angst gehabt hätte, fragte er** hadn't I been afraid, he asked; **er hat gefragt, ob dus geklaut hast – ob ich was?** *(inf)* he asked if you pinched *(Brit)* or swiped it – if I what? *(inf)*; **kommst du mit? – was? – ob du mitkommen willst?** are you coming? – what? – are you coming?; **ob Sie mir wohl mal helfen können?** could you possibly help me?, I wonder if you could help me?
b *(verstärkend)* **und ob** *(inf)* you bet *(inf)*, of course; **und ob ich das gesehen habe!** you bet *(inf)* or of course I saw it!
c *(vergleichend)* **als ob** as if; **(so) tun als ob** *(inf)* to pretend; **tu nicht so als ob!** stop pretending!
d *(liter)* **ob … auch, ob … gleich** even though
PREP +*gen* **a** *(old, liter)* on account of
b *(in Ortsnamen)* (up)on

OB [oːˈbeː] M -s, -s *abbr von* **Oberbürgermeister**

o. B. *abbr von* **ohne Befund**

Ob|acht [ˈoːbaxt] F -, *no pl (esp S Ger)* **(aber) ~!** watch out!, look out!, careful!; **~ geben auf** (+*acc*) *(= aufmerken)* to pay attention to; *(= bewachen)* to keep an eye on; **du musst ~ geben, dass du keine Fehler machst** you must be careful not to make any mistakes; **gib** *or* **hab doch ~!** *(inf)* be careful!, watch it! *(inf)*

ÖBB *abbr von* **Österreichische Bundesbahnen**

Ob|dach [ˈɔpdax] NT, *no pl (geh)* shelter; **jdm (ein) ~ gewähren** *or* **geben** to give *or* offer sb shelter; **kein ~ haben** to be homeless; *(vorübergehend)* to have no shelter; **Menschen ohne ~** homeless people

ob|dach|los ADJ homeless; **~ werden** to be made homeless ADV **die Flüchtlinge zogen ~ umher** the refugees wandered around with no home to go to

Ob|dach|lo|sen-: **Ob|dach|lo|sen|asyl** NT, **Ob|dach|lo|sen|heim** NT hostel for the homeless; **Ob|dach|lo|sen|sied|lung** F settlement for the homeless

Ob|dach|lo|se(r) [ˈɔpdaxloːzə] MF *decl as adj* homeless person; **die ~n** the homeless

Ob|dach|lo|sig|keit F -, *no pl* homelessness

Ob|duk|ti|on [ɔpdʊkˈtsioːn] F -, -en postmortem (examination), autopsy

Ob|duk|ti|ons|be|fund M postmortem findings *pl*, autopsy result

ob|du|zie|ren [ɔpduˈtsiːrən] *ptp* **obduziert** VT to carry out *or* do a postmortem *or* autopsy on

O-Bei|ne [ˈoː-] PL *(inf)* bow *or* bandy *(Brit)* legs *pl*

o-bei|nig [ˈoː-], **O-bei|nig** ADJ bow-legged, bandy-legged *(Brit)*

Obe|lisk [obəˈlɪsk] M -en, -en obelisk

oben [ˈoːbn] ADV **a** *(= am oberen Ende)* at the top; *(= an der Oberfläche)* on the surface; *(im Hause)* upstairs; *(= in der Höhe)* up; **(hier) ~!** *(auf Kisten etc)* this way up!, this side up!; **so ist das Leben, mal bist du ~, mal bist du unten** that's life, sometimes you're up, sometimes you're down; **~ und unten (von etw) verwechseln** to get sth upside down; **wo ist ~ (bei dem Bild)?** which is the top (of the picture)?, which is the right way up (for the picture)?; **die Leute, die ~ wohnen** the people on the floor above us/you *etc*, the people (who live) upstairs; **wir möchten lieber ~ wohnen** we'd rather live high(er) up; **möchten Sie lieber ~ schlafen?** *(im oberen Bett)* would you like the top bunk?, would you like to sleep on top?; **wir wohnen rechts ~** *or* **~ rechts** we live on the top floor to the right; **~ rechts** *or* **rechts ~ (in der Ecke)** in the top right-hand corner; **die Abbildung ~ links** *or* **links ~ auf der Schautafel** the illustration on the top left corner *or* in the top left-hand corner of the diagram; **der ist ~ nicht ganz richtig** *(inf)* he's not quite right up top *(inf)*; **~ ohne gehen** *or* **tragen** *(inf)* to be topless; **ganz ~** right at the top; **ganz ~ auf dem Stapel/in der Rangordnung** right at the top of the pile/of the hierarchy; **hier/dort ~** up here/there; **die ganze Sache steht mir bis hier ~** *(inf)* I'm sick to death of the whole thing *(inf)*, I'm fed up to the back teeth with the whole thing *(Brit inf)*; **bis ~ (hin)** to the top; **hoch ~** high (up) above; **beim Festessen saß er weiter ~ an der Tafel** at the banquet he sat nearer the top of the table; **~ auf dem Berg/der Leiter/dem Dach** on top of the mountain/ladder/roof; **~ am Himmel** up in the sky; **~ im Himmel** up in heaven, in heaven above *(liter)*; **~ in Schottland** up in Scotland; **~ im Norden** up (in the) north; **~ herum** (a)round the top; *(von Frau)* up top; *(von Jacke)* (a)round the chest; **nach ~** up, upwards; *(im Hause)* upstairs; **der Fahrstuhl fährt nach ~** the lift *(Brit)* or elevator *(US)* is going up; **wir sind mit dem Fahrstuhl nach ~ gefahren** we went up in the lift *(Brit)* or elevator *(US)*; **die Bergsteiger sind auf dem Weg nach ~** the climbers are on their way up; **der Weg nach ~** *(fig)* the road to the top; **endlich hat sie den Weg nach ~ geschafft** *(fig)* she finally got to the top *or* made it (to the top); **nach ~ zu** *or* **hin** towards *(Brit)* or toward *(US)* the top; **von ~ (her)** down; *(im Hause)* down(stairs); **ich komme gerade von ~** *(am Berg)* I've just come from the top; *(im Hause)* I've just been upstairs; **von ~ (aus) hat man eine schöne Aussicht** there's a nice view from the top; **von ~ bis unten** from top to bottom; *(von Mensch)* from top to toe; **jdn von ~ bis unten mustern** to look sb up and down; **jdn von ~ herab behandeln** to be condescending to sb, to treat sb condescendingly; **jdn von ~ herab ansehen** to look down on sb; **weiter ~** further up; **das Gehöft liegt weiter ~ (am Berg/im Tal)** the farm is further *or* higher up (the mountain/valley)
b *(inf: = die Vorgesetzten)* **die da ~** the powers that be *(inf)*, the top brass *(inf)*; **das wird ~ entschieden** that's decided higher up; **er will sich nur ~ beliebt machen** he's just sucking up to the management *(inf)*; **etw nach ~ (weiter)melden/weitergeben** to report sth/to pass sth on to a superior; **der Befehl kommt von ~** it's orders from above
c *(= vorher)* above; **siehe ~** see above; **~ erwähnt** *attr*, **~ genannt** *attr* above-mentioned; **wie ~ erwähnt** *or* **genannt** as mentioned above; **der ~ schon erwähnte Herr** the above-mentioned *or* aforementioned gentleman; **der weiter ~ erwähnte Fall** the case referred to before *or* above

oben-: **oben|an** [ˈoːbnˈlan] ADV at the top, on (the) top; **sein Name steht ~ (auf der Liste)** his name is (at the) top (of the list); **an der Tafel saß er ~** he sat at the top of the table; **er will immer ~ sein** *(fig)* he always wants to be on top; **oben|auf** [ˈoːbnˈlauf] ADV on (the) top; *(= an der Oberfläche)* on the top *or* surface; **gestern war er krank, aber heute ist er wieder ~** *(inf)* he wasn't well yesterday, but he's back on *(Brit)* or in *(US)* form today; **sie ist immer ~** *(inf)* she is always bright and cheery *(inf)*; **oben|drauf** [ˈoːbnˈdrauf] ADV *(inf)* on top; **oben|drein** [ˈoːbnˈdrain] ADV *(inf)* on top of everything *(inf)*; **oben|drü|ber** [ˈoːbnˈdryːbɐ] ADV *(inf: = über)* above; *(= obendrauf)* on top; **oben|er|wähnt** [ˈoːbnlɛɐvɛːnt] **oben|ge|nannt** [ˈoːbnlgənant] ADJ *attr* → **oben c**; **oben|he|rum** [ˈoːbnhɛrʊm] ADV around the top; *(euph: am Körper)* around the chest; **oben|hin** [ˈoːbnˈhɪn] ADV superficially; **etw nur so ~ sagen** to say sth lightly *or* casually *or* in an offhand way

Oben-oh|ne- *in cpds* topless; **Oben-oh|ne-Be|die|nung** F topless waitress service

Ober [ˈoːbɐ] M -s, - **a** *(= Kellner)* waiter; **Herr ~!** waiter! **b** *(Cards)* ≈ Queen

ober- [ˈoːbɐ], **Ober-** *in cpds (Geog)* Upper; *(im Rang)* senior, chief; *(inf: = besonders)* really

Ober|arm M upper arm

Ober|arzt M, **Ober|ärz|tin** F senior physician

Ober|auf|se|her(in) M(F) (head) supervisor, superintendent; *(im Gefängnis)* head warder *(Brit)* or warden *(US)* or guard

Ober|auf|sicht F supervision, superintendence; **die ~ haben** *or* **führen** to be in *or* have overall control *(über +acc* of); **unter (der) ~** *(+gen)* under the supervision *or* overall control (of)

Ober|bau M *pl* **-bauten a** *(von Brücke)* superstructure **b** *(Rail)* permanent way **c akademischer ~** *academic teaching staff at professorial level*

Ober|be|fehl M *(Mil)* supreme command; **den ~ haben** to be commander-in-chief *or* supreme commander, to be in supreme command *(über +acc* of)

Ober|be|fehls|ha|ber(in) M(F) *(Mil)* commander-in-chief, supreme commander

Ober|be|griff M generic term

O|ber|be|klei|dung F outer clothing, top clothes *pl*
Ober|bett NT quilt
Ober|bun|des|an|walt M, **Ober|bun|des|an|wäl|tin** F chief public prosecutor
Ober|bür|ger|meis|ter M Lord Mayor, Lord Provost *(Scot)*
Ober|bür|ger|meis|te|rin F mayoress, Lord Provost *(Scot)*
Ober|deck NT upper *or* top deck
ober|deutsch ADJ *(Ling)* Upper German
obe|re(r, s) [ˈoːbərə] ADJ *attr Ende, Stockwerke, (Schul)klassen* upper, top; *Flusslauf* upper; **die Oberen** *(inf)* the top brass *(inf)*, the bosses; *(Eccl)* the superiors; **die ~n Zehntausend** *(inf)* high society → **oberste(r, s)**
Ober-: **ober|faul** ADJ *(inf)* very peculiar *or* odd *or* funny *(inf)*; **Ober|feld** M **-s, -s** *(Mil sl)* sarge *(inf)*; **Ober|feld|we|bel(in)** M(F) **a** *(Heer)* staff sergeant *(Brit)*, first sergeant *(US)* **b** *(Luftwaffe)* flight sergeant *(Brit)*, master sergeant *(US)*
Ober|flä|che F surface *(auch fig)*; *(Tech, Math)* surface area; *(Comput)* (user) interface; **an die ~ kommen** *(lit)* to come to the surface, to surface; *(fig)* to emerge; **an der ~ schwimmen** to float; **an der ~ bleiben** *(lit)* to remain on the surface; **das Buch bleibt an der ~** *(fig)* the book doesn't go very deep; **grafische ~** *(Comput)* graphical (user) interface
ober|fläch|lich [-flɛçlɪç] ADJ **a** *(= an der Oberfläche)* superficial; **~e Verletzung** surface wound
b *(= flüchtig)* superficial; *Kenntnisse* superficial, shallow; **bei ~er Betrachtung** at a quick glance; **seine Englischkenntnisse sind nur ~** his knowledge of English is only superficial; **er ist sehr ~ in seiner Arbeit** his work is very superficial; **nach ~er Schätzung** at a rough estimate *or* guess
c *(= seicht) Mensch, Unterhaltung* superficial, shallow
ADV **a** *(= an der Oberfläche)* superficially, on the surface; **er ist nur ~ verletzt** he's only got superficial injuries
b *(= flüchtig)* superficially, not thoroughly; **sie arbeitet ~** she doesn't do her work thoroughly; **er hat die Arbeit sehr ~ gemacht** he didn't do the work very thoroughly; **etw ~ lesen** to skim through sth; **jdn (nur) ~ kennen** to know sb (only) slightly, to have a nodding acquaintance with sb; **etw (nur) ~ kennen** to have (only) a shallow *or* superficial knowledge of sth
c *(= seicht)* superficially; **sich ~ unterhalten** to have a superficial conversation; **~ leben** to lead a superficial life
Ober|fläch|lich|keit F **-, -en** **a** *no pl* superficiality **b** *(Bemerkung)* superficial remark
Ober-: **Ober|förs|ter(in)** M(F) head forester; **Ober|fran|ken** [ˈoːbɐfraŋkn] NT **-s** Upper Franconia; **ober|gä|rig** [-gɛːrɪç] ADJ *Bier* top-fermented; **Ober|ge|frei|te(r)** MF *decl as adj* **a** *(Heer)* lance corporal *(Brit)*, private first class *(US)* **b** *(Luftwaffe)* senior aircraftsman *(Brit)*, airman first class *(US)* **c** *(Marine)* seaman first class *(Brit)*, seaman *(US)*; **Ober|ge|schoss** NT upper floor; *(bei zwei Stockwerken)* top floor; **im zweiten ~** on the second *(Brit) or* third *(US)* floor; **Ober|gren|ze** F upper limit; **ober|halb** [ˈoːbɐhalp] PREP +*gen* above ADV above; **~ von Basel** above Basel; **weiter ~** further *or* higher up; **Ober|hand** F *(fig)* upper hand; **die ~ über jdn/etw gewinnen** to get *or* gain the upper hand over sb/sth, to get the better of sb/sth; **die ~ (über jdn/etw) haben/behalten** to have/keep the upper hand (over sb/sth); **Ober|haupt** NT *(= Repräsentant)* head; *(= Anführer)* leader; **Ober|haus** NT *(Pol)* upper house; *(in GB)* House of Lords; **Ober|hemd** NT shirt; **Ober|herr(in)** M(F) *(old)* sovereign; **Ober|herr|schaft** F sovereignty, supremacy *(über +acc* over); **unter der ~ Englands** under English rule; **Ober|hir|te** M, **Ober|hir|tin** F spiritual head *or* leader; **Ober|hit|ze** F *(Cook)* top heat; **(nur) mit ~ backen** to bake in the top oven; **Ober|ho|heit** F supremacy, sovereignty; **unter UN-~ stehen** to be under UN authority *or* control; **unter polnischer ~** under Polish sovereignty; **die ~ über jdn gewinnen** to gain *or* win supremacy over sb
Obe|rin [ˈoːbərɪn] F **-, -nen** **a** *(im Krankenhaus)* matron **b** *(Eccl)* Mother Superior
Ober-: **Ober|in|ge|ni|eur(in)** M(F) chief engineer; **Ober|in|spek|tor(in)** M(F) senior inspector; **ober|ir|disch** ADJ above ground *pred* ADV above ground; **Ober|kell|ner** M head waiter; **Ober|kell|ne|rin** F head waitress; **Ober|kie|fer** M upper jaw; **Ober|kir|chen|rat** M *(Gremium)* church assembly; **Ober|kir|chen|rat** M, **Ober|kir|chen|rä|tin** F member of the church assembly; **Ober|klas|se** F **a** *(Sch)* **~n** top classes *or* forms **b** *(Sociol)* upper class **c** **ein Auto/eine Stereoanlage der ~** a top-of-the-range car/stereo; **Ober|kleid** NT *(liter)* outer garment(s *pl*); **Ober|klei|dung** F outer clothing; **Ober|kom|man|die|ren|de(r)** [-kɔmandiːrəndə] MF *decl as adj* Commander-in-Chief, Supreme Commander; **Ober|kom|man|do** NT *(= Oberbefehl)* Supreme Command; *(= Befehlsstab)* headquarters *pl*; **Ober|kör|per** M upper part of the body; **mit bloßem** *or* **freiem** *or* **nacktem ~** stripped to the waist; **den ~ freimachen** to strip to the waist; **Ober|land** NT, *no pl (Geog)* uplands *pl*; **das Berner ~** the Bernese Oberland; **Ober|lan|des|ge|richt** NT *provincial high court and court of appeal*; **Ober|län|ge** F upstroke; *(Typ)* ascender; **ober|las|tig** [-lastɪç] ADJ *(Naut)* top-heavy; **Ober|lauf** M upper reaches *pl*; **am ~ des Rheins** in the upper reaches of the Rhine; **Ober|le|der** NT (leather) uppers *pl*; **Ober|leh|rer(in)** M(F) *(old)* senior primary school teacher; **Ober|lei|tung** F **a** *(= Führung)* direction; **die ~ eines Projekts haben** to be in overall charge of a project **b** *(Elec)* overhead cable; **Ober|leut|nant** M **a** *(Heer)* lieutenant *(Brit)*, first lieutenant *(US)* **b** *(Luftwaffe)* flying officer *(Brit)*, first lieutenant *(US)* **c** *(Marine)* **~ zur See** lieutenant; **Ober|licht** NT *(= hoch gelegenes Fenster)* small, high window; *(= Lüftungsklappe, über einer Tür)* fanlight, transom (window); **Ober|lid** NT upper lid; **Ober|li|ga** F *(Sport)* top *or* first league; **Ober|lip|pe** F upper lip; **Ober|maat** M *(Naut)* ≈ leading seaman; **Ober|ma|te|ri|al** NT *(von Schuh)* upper; **Ober|meis|ter(in)** M(F) **a** *head of craft guild* **b** *(bei Polizei)* ≈ sergeant; **Ober|ös|ter|reich** NT Upper Austria; **Ober|post|di|rek|ti|on** F *(Behörde)* regional post office (administration); *(Bezirk)* postal area *or* district; **~ Köln** Cologne postal district; **Ober|pries|ter** M high priest; **Ober|pries|te|rin** F high priestess; **Ober|pri|ma** F *(dated) top class of German grammar school*, ≈ upper sixth *(Brit)*, ≈ senior grade *(US)*; **Ober|pri|ma|ner(in)** M(F) *(dated)* ≈ sixth former *(Brit)*, ≈ senior *(US)*; **ober|rhei|nisch** ADJ upper Rhine; **die Oberrheinische Tiefebene** the Upper Rhine Valley; **im Oberrheinischen** along *or* around the upper Rhine; **Ober|rich|ter(in)** M(F) *(Sw)* ≈ high court judge
Obers [ˈoːbɐs] NT **-**, *no pl (Aus)* cream
Ober-: **Ober|schen|kel** M thigh; **Ober|schen|kel|bruch** M broken thighbone *or* femur, fracture of the thighbone *or* femur; **Ober|schen|kel|hals** M head of the thighbone *or* femur; **Ober|schen|kel|hals|bruch** M femoral neck fracture; **Ober|schen|kel|kno|chen** M thighbone, femur; **Ober|schicht** F top layer; *(Sociol)* upper strata (of society) *pl*; **ober|schläch|tig** [-ʃlɛçtɪç] ADJ *Mühle* overshot; **ober|schlau** *(inf)* ADJ really clever ADV really cleverly; **sie redet schon wieder so ~ daher** she's talking again as if she knows it all; **Ober|schu|le** F *(old: = Gymnasium)* ≈ grammar school *(Brit)*, ≈ high school *(US)*; *(weiterführende Schule)* secondary school; **Ober|schü|ler(in)** M(F) *(old: = Gymnasiast)* ≈ grammar school pupil *(Brit)*, ≈ high school student *(US)*; *(an weiterführenden Schulen)* secondary school pupil; **Ober|schul|rat** M, **Ober|schul|rä|tin** F school inspector, HMI *(Brit inf)*; **Ober|schur|ke** M, **Ober|schur|kin** F *(inf)* chief villain, baddie *(inf)*; **Ober|schwes|ter** F senior nursing officer; **Ober|sei|te** F top (side); **Ober|se|kun|da** F *(dated) seventh year of German secondary school*; **Ober|se|kun|da|ner(in)** M(F) *(dated) pupil in seventh year of German secondary school*
Oberst [ˈoːbɛst] M **-en, -e(n)** **a** *(Heer)* colonel **b** *(Luftwaffe)* group captain *(Brit)*, colonel *(US)*
Ober-: **Ober|staats|an|walt** M, **Ober|staats|an|wäl|tin** F public prosecutor, procurator fiscal *(Scot)*, district attorney *(US)*; **Ober|stadt** F upper town, upper part of a town; **Ober|stadt|di|rek|tor(in)** M(F) town clerk; **Ober|stei|ger** M head foreman (in a mine)
obers|te(r, s) [ˈoːbɛstə] ADJ **a** *(= ganz oben) Stockwerk, Schicht* topmost, uppermost, very top; **das Oberste zuunterst kehren** to turn everything *or* things upside down **b** *Gebot, Gesetz, Prinzip* supreme; *Dienstgrad* highest, most senior, top; **die ~n Kreise der Gesellschaft** the upper circles *or* echelons of society; **Oberstes Gericht, Oberster Gerichtshof** supreme court; *(in GB)* High Court (of Justice); *(in USA)* Supreme Court
Ober|stim|me F soprano; *(= Knabenoberstimme)* treble; *(= Diskant)* descant
Oberst|leut|nant M **a** *(Heer)* lieutenant colonel **b** *(Luftwaffe)* wing commander *(Brit)*, lieutenant colonel *(US)*
Ober-: **Ober|stüb|chen** NT *(inf)* **er ist nicht ganz richtig im ~** he's not quite right up top *(inf)*; **Ober|stu|di|en|di|rek|tor** M headmaster *(esp Brit)*, principal *(US)*; **Ober|stu|di|en|di|rek|to|rin** F headmistress *(esp Brit)*, principal *(US)*; **Ober|stu|di|en|rat** M, **Ober|stu|di|en|rä|tin** F senior teacher; **Ober|stu|fe** F upper school; *(Univ)* advanced level; **Ober|teil** NT OR M upper part, top; **Ober|ter|tia** F *(dated) fifth year of German secondary school*; **Ober|ter|ti|a|ner(in)** M(F) *(dated) pupil in fifth year of German secondary school*; **Ober|tö|ne** PL *(Mus, fig)* overtone(s *pl*); **Ober|trot|tel** M *(inf)* prize *or* first-class idiot; **Ober|vol|ta** [oːbɐˈvɔlta] NT **-s** Upper Volta; **Ober|was|ser** NT *pl* **-wasser** **a** *(von Wehr)* backwater **b** *(fig inf)* **~ haben** to feel better; **sobald sein älterer Bruder dabei ist, hat er (wieder) ~** he feels much braver when his elder brother is around; **wieder ~ gewinnen** *or* **bekommen** to be in a better position; **Ober|wei|te** F bust measurement; **sie hat ~ 94** ≈ she has a 38-inch bust; **die hat eine ganz schöne ~!** she's very well-endowed
Ob|frau F representative
ob|gleich [ɔpˈglaiç] CONJ although, (even) though
Ob|hut [ˈɔphuːt] F **-**, *no pl (geh) (= Aufsicht)* care; *(= Verwahrung)* keeping, care; **jdn/etw jds ~ (dat) anvertrauen** to place *or* put sb/sth in sb's care; **jdn in ~ nehmen** to take care of sb, to look after sb; **jdn bei jdm in ~ geben, jdn in jds ~ (acc) geben** to put *or* place sb in sb's care; **sich in jds ~ (dat) befinden, unter jds ~ (dat) sein** to be in sb's care
obi|ge(r, s) [ˈoːbɪgə] ADJ *attr* above; **vergleiche ~ Abbildung** compare the illustration above *or* the above illustration; **der Obige** *(form)* the above *(form)*
Ob|jekt [ɔpˈjɛkt] NT **-(e)s, -e** *(auch Gram)* object; *(Comm: = Grundstück etc)* property; *(Phot)* subject; **das ~ der Untersuchung** the object under

examination; **zum ~ der Forschung werden** to become the object of research
Ob|jękt|feld NT *(Comput)* object frame
ob|jek|tiv [ɔpjɛk'ti:f] ADJ objective ADV objectively; **~ Stellung nehmen** to take an objective stance; **~ über etw** *(acc)* **urteilen** to make an objective judgement about sth, to judge sth objectively; **etw ~ betrachten** to view sth objectively; **~ gesehen** *or* **betrachtet ist das falsch** seen *or* viewed objectively this is wrong
Ob|jek|tiv [ɔpjɛk'ti:f] NT **-s, -e** [-və] (object) lens, objective
ob|jek|ti|vie|ren [ɔpjɛkti'vi:rən] *ptp* **objektiviert** VI to objectify; **~des Denken** objective thinking VT *Problem, Aussage* to treat objectively, to objectivize
Ob|jek|ti|vi|tät [ɔpjɛktivi'tɛ:t] F -, *no pl* objectivity; **sich um größte ~ bemühen** to try to be as objective as possible
Ob|jękt-: **ob|jękt|ori|en|tiert** ADJ *(Comput)* object-orient(at)ed; **Ob|jękt|satz** M *(Gram)* object clause; **Ob|jękt|schutz** M protection of property; **Ob|jękt|spra|che** F *(Ling)* object language; **Ob|jękt|trä|ger** M slide
Ob|la|te [o'bla:tə] F **-, -n** wafer; *(Eccl)* host
ọb|lie|gen ['ɔpli:gn, ɔp'li:gn] *ptp* **ọblegen** *or (rare)* **ọbgelegen** [ɔp'le:gn, 'ɔpgəle:gn] *irreg aux haben or sein (+dat)* VI *impers insep or (rare) sep (form)* **es obliegt ihm, es liegt ihm ob** it is incumbent upon him *(form)*; **ihm oblag die Betreuung der Flüchtlinge** he was responsible for looking after the refugees; **diese Entscheidung obliegt dem Präsidenten** this decision lies with the President VI *sep or insep (old: = sich widmen)* to apply oneself to *(form)*
Ọb|lie|gen|heit [ɔp'li:gnhait] F **-, -en** *(form)* obligation, incumbency *(form)*
ob|li|gat [obli'ga:t] ADJ obligatory; **der ~e Dudelsackpfeifer** the obligatory (bag)piper; **mit ~em Cembalo** *(Mus)* with (a) cembalo obbligato
Ob|li|ga|ti|on [obliga'tsio:n] F **-, -en** *(auch Fin)* obligation; **die Firma übernimmt keine ~** the firm is under no obligation
ob|li|ga|to|risch [obliga'to:rɪʃ] ADJ obligatory; *Fächer, Vorlesung* compulsory; *Qualifikationen* necessary, requisite
Ọb|li|go ['o:bligo, 'ɔbligo] NT **-s, -s** **a** *(Fin)* guarantee; **ohne ~** without recourse **b** *(= Verpflichtung)* obligation; **bei der Sicherung der Renten ist die Regierung im ~** the government has an obligation to safeguard pensions
Ọb|mann ['ɔpman] M *pl* **-männer** *or* **-leute**, **Ọb|män|nin** ['ɔpmɛnɪn] F **-, -nen** representative
Oboe [o'bo:ə] F **-, -n** oboe
Obo|ist [obo'ɪst] M **-en, -en**, **Obo|is|tin** [-'ɪstɪn] F **-, -nen** oboist, oboe player
Obo|lus ['o:bolʊs] M **-, -se** contribution
Ob|rig|keit ['o:brɪçkait] F **-, -en** **a** *(als Begriff, Konzept)* authority **b** *(= Behörden)* **die ~** the authorities *pl*; **die geistliche/weltliche ~** the spiritual/secular authorities
ob|rig|keit|lich ['o:brɪçkaitlɪç] ADJ authoritarian ADV in an authoritarian manner
Ob|rig|keits|staat M authoritarian state
Ob|rist [o'brɪst] M **-en, -en** colonel
ob|schon [ɔp'ʃo:n] CONJ *(liter)* although, albeit *(nur in verbloser Konstruktion)*
Ob|ser|vanz [ɔpzɛr'vants] F **-, -en** observance; **ein Orden (von) der strengen ~** a strict *or* closed order
Ob|ser|va|to|ri|um [ɔpzɛrva'to:riʊm] NT **-s, Observatorien** [-riən] observatory
ob|ser|vie|ren [ɔpzɛr'vi:rən] *ptp* **observiert** VT *(form)* to observe; **er ist schon einige Monate observiert worden** he has been under surveillance for several months
Ob|ses|si|on [ɔpzɛ'sio:n] F **-, -en** obsession
ob|ses|siv [ɔpzɛ'si:f] ADJ obsessive ADV obsessively
ọb|sie|gen [ɔp'zi:gn, 'ɔpzi:gn] *ptp* **ọbsiegt** *or (rare)* **ọbgesiegt** [ɔp'zi:kt, 'ɔpgəzi:kt] VI *insep or (rare) sep (obs, Jur)* to prevail *(+dat* over)

obs|kur [ɔps'ku:ɐ] ADJ *(= fragwürdig, zweifelhaft) Quellen* obscure; *(= verdächtig) Gestalten, Kneipe, Geschäfte* suspect, dubious; **diese ~en Gestalten der Unterwelt** these twilight figures of the underworld ADV obscurely; **~ aussehen/erscheinen** to look/seem obscure
Obs|ku|ran|tis|mus [ɔpskuran'tɪsmʊs] M -, *no pl* obscurantism
ob|so|let [ɔpzo'le:t] ADJ obsolete
Obst [o:pst] NT **-(e)s**, *no pl* fruit
Obst-: **Obst|bau** M, *no pl* fruit-growing; **Obst|baum** M fruit tree; **Obst|gar|ten** M orchard; **Obst|jahr** NT **ein gutes ~** a good year for fruit; **Obst|ku|chen** M fruit flan; *(gedeckt)* fruit tart
obs|ti|nat [ɔpsti'na:t] ADJ *(geh)* obstinate
Obst|ler ['o:pstlɐ] M **-s, -** *(dial)* fruit schnapps
Obst-: **Obst|mes|ser** NT fruit knife; **Obst|sa|lat** M fruit salad
Ob|struk|ti|on [ɔpstrʊk'tsio:n] F **-, -en** **a** *(Med)* obstruction, blockage **b** *(Pol)* obstruction, filibuster; **die Gesetzesvorlage scheiterte an der ~ der Opposition** the bill failed because of the Opposition's obstructive *or* filibustering tactics *or* obstructionism; **~ betreiben** to obstruct, to block, to filibuster
Obst-: **Obst|saft** M fruit juice; **Obst|tag** M **legen Sie jede Woche einen ~ ein** eat only fruit one day a week; **meine Frau hat heute ihren ~** my wife's on her fruit diet today; **Obst|tor|te** F fruit flan; *(gedeckt)* fruit tart; **Obst|was|ser** NT *pl* **-wässer** fruit schnapps; **Obst|wein** M fruit wine
obs|zön [ɔps'tsø:n] ADJ obscene ADV obscenely; **~ klingen** to sound obscene; **~ gestikulieren** to make obscene gestures
Obs|zö|ni|tät [ɔpstsøni'tɛ:t] F **-, -en** obscenity
Obus ['o:bʊs] M **-ses, -se** *(inf)* trolley *(Brit inf)*, trolley bus
ọb|wal|ten [ɔp'valtn, ɔp'valtn] *ptp* **ọbwaltet** *or (rare)* **ọbgewaltet** [ɔp'valtət, 'ɔpgəvaltət] VI *insep or (rare) sep (form: = herrschen)* to prevail
ob|wohl [ɔp'vo:l] CONJ although, (even) though
ob|zwar [ɔp'tsva:ɐ] CONJ *(rare)* although, (even) though
Oc|ca|si|on [ɔka'zio:n] F **-, -en** *(Aus, Sw)* → **Okkasion**
Ochs [ɔks] M **-en, -en**, **Och|se** ['ɔksə] M **-n, -n** **a** ox; *(junger Ochse)* bullock; **~ am Spieß** roast ox; **er stand da wie der ~ vorm** *or* **am Berg** *or* **vorm (neuen) Scheunentor** *(inf)* he stood there like a cow at a five-barred gate *(inf)* **b** *(inf: = Dummkopf)* twit *(Brit inf)*, ass *(inf)*, dope *(inf)*
och|sen ['ɔksn] *(Sch inf)* VT to swot up *(Brit inf)*, to mug up *(Brit inf)*, to study up on *(US inf)* VI to swot (up) *(Brit inf)*, to mug (up) *(Brit inf)*, to cram *(inf)*
Och|sen-: **Ọch|sen|frosch** M bullfrog; **Ọch|sen|ge|spann** NT yoke of oxen; **Ọch|sen|schwanz|sup|pe** F oxtail soup; **Ọch|sen|tour** F *(inf)* **a** *(= Schinderei)* slog *(inf)*, sweat *(inf)* **b** **er brauchte sich nicht über die ~ heraufzudienen** he did not have to work his way up the hard way; **Ọch|sen|zie|mer** M bull's pizzle, bullwhip
Öchs|le ['œkslə] NT **-s, -** *measure of alcohol content of drink according to its specific gravity*
Ọcker ['ɔkɐ] M OR NT **-s, -** ochre *(Brit)*, ocher *(US)*
ọcker|braun, **ọcker|gelb** ADJ ochre *(Brit)*, ocher *(US)*
OCR [o:tse:'lɛr] *(Comput) abbr von* **optical character recognition**
OCR-Schrift [o:tse:'lɛr-] F OCR font
öd [ø:t] ADJ = **öde**
od. *abbr von* **oder**
Ode ['o:də] F **-, -n** ode
öde ['ø:də] ADJ **a** *(= verlassen) Stadt, Strand* deserted, empty, abandoned; *(= unbewohnt)* desolate, empty; *(= unbebaut)* waste, barren; **öd und leer** dreary and desolate **b** *(fig: = fade)* dull, dreary, tedious; *Dasein* dreary; *(inf: = langweilig)* grim *(inf)*
Öde ['ø:də] F **-, -n** *(liter)* **a** *(= einsame Gegend)* desert, wasteland **b** *no pl (= Langeweile)* dreariness
Odem ['o:dəm] M **-s**, *no pl (poet, Bibl)* breath
Ödem [ø'de:m] NT **-s, -e** oedema, edema
oder ['o:dɐ] CONJ **a** or; **~ aber** or else; **~ auch** or even, or maybe, or perhaps; **eins ~ das andere** one or the other, it's either or; **entweder ...** **~** either ... or; **~ so** *(am Satzende)* or something; **~ so ähnlich** or something like that **b** *(in Fragen)* **so wars doch, ~ (etwa) nicht?** that was what happened, wasn't it?, wasn't that how it happened?, it happened like that, didn't it?; **du kommst doch, ~?** you're coming, aren't you?; **der Mörder hat sein Opfer nie vorher gesehen, ~ doch?** the murderer had never seen his victim before, or had he?; **damit war der Fall erledigt, ~ doch nicht?** with that the case was closed, or perhaps not?; **~ soll ich lieber mitkommen?** maybe I should come along?; **lassen wir es so, ~?** let's leave it at that, right *or* OK?
Oder ['o:dɐ] F - Oder
Oder-Nei|ße-Gren|ze F, **Oder-Nei|ße-Li|nie** ['o:dɐ'naisə-] F Oder-Neisse Line
ödi|pal [ødi'pa:l] ADJ oedipal
Ödi|pus|kom|plex ['ø:dipʊs-] M Oedipus complex
Odi|um ['o:diʊm] NT **-s**, *no pl (liter)* odium
Öd|land ['ø:tlant] NT wasteland
Öd|nis ['ø:tnɪs] F **-, -se** *(geh)* = **Öde**
Odys|see [ody'se:] F **-, -n** [-'se:ən] *(Liter)* Odyssey; *(fig)* odyssey
OECD-Land [o:le:tse:'de:-] NT OECD member country
Oeuv|re ['ø:vɐ, 'ø:vrə] NT **-, -s** *(Liter)* work, works *pl*
OEZ *abbr von* **Osteuropäische Zeit**
OF *abbr von* **Originalfassung**
Öf|chen ['ø:fçən] NT **-s, -** *dim von* **Ofen**
Ofen [o:fn] M **-s, =** ['ø:fn] **a** *(= Heizofen)* heater; *(= Elektroofen, Gasofen)* fire, heater; *(= Ölofen, Petroleumofen)* stove, heater; *(= Kohleofen)* stove; *(= Heizungsofen)* boiler; *(= Kachelofen)* tiled stove; **hinter dem ~ hocken** to be a stay-at-home; **jdn hinter dem ~ hervorlocken** to tempt sb; **jetzt ist der ~ aus** *(inf)* that's it *(inf)*, that does it *(inf)*
b *(= Herd)* oven, stove; *(= Kohleofen)* stove, range; *(= Backofen)* oven
c *(Tech)* furnace, oven; *(= Brennofen)* kiln; *(= Trockenofen)* drying oven *or* kiln; *(= Hochofen)* blast furnace; *(= Schmelzofen)* smelting furnace; *(= Müllverbrennungsofen)* incinerator
d *(inf: = Motorrad)* **ein heißer ~** a fast bike *(inf)*
Ofen-: **Ofen|bank** F *pl* **-bänke** fireside (bench), hearth; **auf der ~** by the hearth *or* fire *or* fireside; **Ofen|blech** NT *tray for catching falling coals*; **Ofen|ecke** F inglenook; **ofen|fer|tig** ADJ *Gericht* oven-ready ADV oven-ready; **ofen|frisch** ADJ *Brot* oven-fresh; **Ofen|hei|zung** F stove heating; **Zimmer mit ~** room with stove (heater); **Ofen|kar|tof|fel** F jacket potato; **Ofen|klap|pe** F **a** *(= Ofentür)* stove door **b** *(= Lüftungsklappe)* damper; **Ofen|loch** NT stove door; **Ofen|rohr** NT stovepipe; *(old inf: = Zylinder)* stovepipe (hat); **Ofen|röh|re** F (slow) oven; **Ofen|schirm** M firescreen; **Ofen|set|zer(in)** M(F) stove fitter; **Ofen|tür** F stove door
Off [ɔf] NT **-**, *no pl (TV, Theat)* offstage; **aus dem ~** offstage; **eine Stimme aus dem ~** a voice off; **aus dem ~ kommen** to come onstage, to come from offstage
of|fen ['ɔfn] ADJ **a** open; *Bein* ulcerated; *Flamme, Licht* naked; *Feuer* open; *Haare* loose; **ein ~er Brief** an open letter; **er geht mit ~em Hemd** he is wearing an open-neck shirt; **der Laden hat bis 10 Uhr ~** the shop *(esp Brit)* or store is *or* stays open until 10 o'clock; **das Turnier ist**

für alle ~ the tournament is open to everybody; **die Teilnahme ist für alle ~** anyone can take part; **~er Wein** wine by the carafe/glass; **auf ~er Strecke** *(Straße)* on the open road; *(Rail)* between stations; **wir hielten auf ~er Strecke** we stopped in the middle of nowhere; **auf ~er Straße** in the middle of the street; *(Landstraße)* on the open road; **auf ~er See** on the open sea; **Beifall auf ~er Szene** spontaneous applause, an outburst of applause; **bei ~er Szene** *or* **Bühne verwandelt sich das Bild** the scene changed without a curtain; **~e Flanke** *(Mil)* open *or* exposed flank; **~e Stadt** *(Mil)* open *or* undefended town **mit ~em Mund dastehen** *(fig)* to stand gaping; **mit ~em Mund atmen** to breathe with one's mouth open; **Tag der ~en Tür** open day; **ein ~es Haus haben** *or* **führen** to keep open house; **überall ~e Türen finden** *(fig)* to find a warm welcome everywhere; **Haus der ~en Tür** open house; **Politik der ~en Tür** open-door policy; **mit ~en Augen** *or* **Sinnen durchs Leben gehen** to go through life with one's eyes open; **eine ~e Hand haben** *(fig)* to be open-handed; **allem Neuen gegenüber ~ sein** to be open *or* receptive to (all) new ideas; **~e Handelsgesellschaft** general partnership → **Arm, Buch, Karte, Tür**

b *(= frei) Stelle* vacant; **~e Stellen** vacancies; **„offene Stellen"** "vacancies", "situations vacant" *(Brit)*

c *(= unerledigt, unentschieden) Frage, Ausgang, Partie* open; *Rechnung* outstanding

d *(= aufrichtig, freimütig) Mensch, Bekenntnis, Aussprache* open; **er hat einen ~en Blick** he's got an open *or* honest face; **er hat keinen ~en Blick** he's got a shifty look in his eyes; **ein ~es Wort mit jdm reden** to have a frank talk with sb

ADV **a** *(= freimütig)* candidly; *kritisieren, zugeben, als Lügner bezeichnen, sich zu etw bekennen* openly; **ein ~ schwul lebender Mensch** a person living openly as a homosexual; **die Karten ~ auf den Tisch legen** to lay one's cards on the table; **etw ~ aussprechen** to say sth out loud; **etw ~ einräumen** to be perfectly willing to admit sth; **sich ~ für/gegen etw aussprechen** to openly speak out for/against sth; **~ gestanden** *or* **gesagt** to tell you the truth, quite honestly, to be frank; **etw ~ eingestehen** *or* **zugeben** to confess *or* admit (to) sth openly *or* frankly; **seine Meinung ~ sagen** to speak one's mind, to say what one thinks; **sag mir ganz ~ deine Meinung** tell me your honest opinion; **~ mit jdm reden** to speak openly to sb, to be frank with sb

b *(= deutlich)* clearly; **die Probleme treten ~ zutage** the problems can be clearly identified; **damit war der Krieg ~ ausgebrochen** with that the war had clearly begun; **wir sollten den Konflikt ~ austragen** we should bring the matter out in the open

c *(= lose)* **die Haare ~ tragen** to wear one's hair loose *or* down; **Wein ~ verkaufen** to sell wine on draught *(Brit) or* draft *(US)*; *(glasweise)* to sell wine by the glass; **Schrauben ~ kaufen** to buy screws loose

d *(= unverstellt)* **endlich lag das Ziel ~ vor ihnen (da)** at last their goal lay before them; **das Land erstreckte sich ~ vor ihnen** the countryside stretched out before them

of|fen|bar ADJ obvious; **sein Zögern machte ~, dass ...** it showed *or* was obvious from the way he hesitated that ...; **~ werden** to become obvious *or* clear, to emerge ADV *(= vermutlich)* apparently; **er hat ~ den Zug verpasst** he must have missed the train; **da haben Sie sich ~ geirrt** you seem to have made a mistake

of|fen|ba|ren [ɔfn'baːrən] *insep ptp* **offenbart** *or (old)* **geoffenbart** [ɔfn'baːɐt, gəlɔfn'baːɐt] VT to reveal VR **a** *(= erweisen)* to show *or* reveal itself/oneself; **sich als etw ~** to show oneself to be sth **b** *(= kundtun)* **sich jdm ~** to reveal oneself to sb; *(= Liebe erklären)* to reveal one's feelings to sb

Of|fen|ba|rung [ɔfn'baːrʊŋ] F **-, -en** revelation

Of|fen|ba|rungs|eid M *(Jur)* oath of disclosure *or* manifestation; **den ~ leisten** *(lit)* to swear an oath of disclosure *or* manifestation; *(fig)* to admit defeat; **mit diesem Programm hat die Partei ihren ~ geleistet** with this programme *(Brit) or* program *(US)* the party has revealed its political bankruptcy; **vor dem ~ stehen** *(fig)* to be on the verge of defeat

of|fen-: **of|fen+blei|ben** *sep irreg aux sein,* **of|fen blei|ben** △ *irreg aux sein* VI *(fig)* to remain open; **alle offengebliebenen Probleme** all unsolved *or* remaining problems; **of|fen blei|ben** VI *irreg aux sein (Fenster etc)* to remain open; **of|fen+hal|ten** *sep irreg,* **of|fen hal|ten** △ *irreg* VT *(fig)* to keep open; **die Ohren ~** to keep one's ear open *or* to the ground; **jdm eine Stelle** *or* **eine Stelle für jdn ~** to keep a job open for sb; **(sich** *dat*) **eine Option ~** to keep an option open; **of|fen hal|ten** VT *irreg (Fenster etc)* to keep open

Of|fen|heit F **-,** *no pl (gegenüber* about) openness, frankness, candour *(Brit)*, candor *(US)*; **schonungslose ~** brutal frankness; **in aller** *or* **schöner ~** quite openly

of|fen-: **of|fen|her|zig** ADJ **a** open, frank, candid **b** *(hum inf) Kleid* revealing; **sie ist ja heute wieder sehr ~** she's being very revealing again today *(hum inf)* ADV *(= ehrlich)* openly, frankly; **Of|fen|her|zig|keit** [-hɛrtsɪçkait] F **-,** *no pl* openness, frankness, candour *(Brit)*, candor *(US)*; **of|fen|kun|dig** ADJ obvious, clear; *Beweise* clear; *Lüge, Interesse* obvious, manifest; **es ist ~, dass ...** it is obvious *or* clear *or* evident that ... ADV blatantly, clearly; **of|fen+las|sen** *sep irreg,* **of|fen las|sen** △ *irreg* VT *(fig)* to leave open; **of|fen las|sen** VT *irreg (Tür etc)* to leave open; **of|fen+le|gen** *sep,* **of|fen le|gen** △ VT *(fig)* to disclose; **Of|fen|le|gung** [-leːgʊŋ] F **-, -en** disclosure; **Of|fen|markt|po|li|tik** F *(Fin)* free market policy; **of|fen|sicht|lich** ['ɔfnzɪçtlɪç, ɔfn'zɪçtlɪç] ADJ obvious; *Irrtum, Lüge auch* blatant; *Unterschied auch* clear; **es war ~, dass er uns mied** it was plain *or* evident *or* obvious he was avoiding us, he was obviously avoiding us ADV obviously, clearly, evidently

of|fen|siv ADJ offensive ADV offensively; *verkaufen* aggressively; **sich ungewohnt ~ zeigen** to be unusually aggressive; **es wurde ~ geworben** the advertising campaign was aggressive

Of|fen|si|ve F **-, -n** offensive; **in die ~ gehen** to take the offensive; **die ~** *(Sport: = die Offensivspieler)* the forward line

Of|fen|siv-: **Of|fen|siv|krieg** M offensive war; **Of|fen|siv|ra|ke|te** F offensive missile; **Of|fen|siv|waf|fe** F offensive weapon

of|fen+ste|hen *sep irreg (S Ger, Aus, Sw: aux sein),* **of|fen ste|hen** △ VI *irreg (S Ger, Aus, Sw: aux sein)* **a** *(Comm: Rechnung, Betrag)* to be *or* remain unpaid *or* unsettled, to be outstanding **b jdm ~** *(fig: = zugänglich sein)* to be open to sb; **uns stehen zwei Möglichkeiten offen** there are two possibilities *or* options open to us; **dir stehen noch alle Möglichkeiten offen** you still have plenty of options; **die (ganze) Welt steht ihm offen** he has the (whole) world at his feet, the world's his oyster; **es steht ihr offen, sich uns anzuschließen** she's free to join us; **die Teilnahme an der Veranstaltung steht auch Nichtmitgliedern offen** the function is also open to non-members **c** *(= unbesetzt sein: Stelle)* to be available; **of|fen ste|hen** VI *irreg (S Ger, Aus, Sw: aux sein) (Tür etc)* to be open; *(Knopf)* to be undone; **der Mund stand ihr offen** her mouth was hanging open

öf|fent|lich ADJ **a** *(= allgemein zugänglich, sichtbar) (attr)* public; *(pred)* open to the public, public; **eine Persönlichkeit des ~en Lebens** a person in public life *or* in the public eye; **im ~en Leben stehen** to be in public life; **ein ~es Haus** *(euph)* a house of ill repute *(euph)* **b** *attr (= die Allgemeinheit betreffend) Wohl, Interesse* public; **die ~e Meinung/Moral** public opinion/morality; **die ~e Ordnung** law and order; **~es Recht** *(Jur)* public law; **Anstalt/Körperschaft des ~en Rechts** public institution/corporation *or* body

c *(= staatlich)* public; **~e Schule** state school, public school *(US)*; **der ~e Dienst** the civil service; **die ~e Hand** *(= der Staat)* (central) government; *(= die Gemeinde)* local government; **Ausgaben der ~en Hand** public spending; **etw in die ~e Hand überführen** to take sth into public ownership, to take sth under public control

ADV publicly; **sich ~ äußern** to voice one's opinion in public; **etw ~ bekannt machen** to make sth public, to publicize sth; **~ versteigern** to sell by public auction, to auction publicly; **jdn ~ anschuldigen/hinrichten** to accuse/execute sb publicly

Öf|fent|lich|keit F **-,** *no pl* **a** *(= Zugänglichkeit)* **der Verteidiger bestand auf der ~ der Verhandlung** the defence *(Brit) or* defense *(US)* counsel insisted that the trial take place in public; **~ der Rechtsprechung** administration of justice in open court; **~ der Prüfungen war eine Hauptforderung der Studenten** one of the students' main demands was that exams should be open to the public; **die ~ einer Versammlung herstellen** to make a meeting public

b *(= Allgemeinheit)* the (general) public; **die ~ scheuen** to shun publicity; **in** *or* **vor aller ~** in public; **die/eine breite ~** the/a broad public; **unter Ausschluss der ~** in secret *or* private; *(Jur)* in camera; **als er das erste Mal vor die ~ trat** when he made his first public appearance; **mit etw an** *or* **vor die ~ treten** *or* **gehen, etw vor die ~ bringen** to bring sth to public attention *or* into the public eye; **etw in** *or* **an die ~ tragen** to go public with sth; **etw der ~ übergeben** *(form)* *(= eröffnen)* to declare sth officially open; *(= veröffentlichen)* to publish sth; **etw der ~ zugänglich machen** to open sth to the public; **im Licht der ~ stehen** to be in the public eye; **ans** *or* **ins Licht der ~ geraten** to end up in the public eye; **das Licht der ~ scheuen** to keep out of the public eye

Öf|fent|lich|keits-: **Öf|fent|lich|keits|ar|beit** F public relations work; **öf|fent|lich|keits|scheu** ADJ publicity-shy; **öf|fent|lich|keits|wirk|sam** ADJ **~ sein** to be effective (as) publicity, to be good publicity ADV **wir müssen besonders ~ werben** we need particularly effective publicity

öf|fent|lich-recht|lich ['œfntlɪç'rɛçtlɪç] ADJ *attr* (under) public law; **~er Rundfunk/~es Fernsehen** ≈ public-service broadcasting

of|fe|rie|ren [ɔfə'riːrən] *ptp* **offeriert** VT *(Comm, form)* to offer

Of|fer|te [ɔ'fɛrtə] F **-, -n** *(Comm)* offer

Of|fi|zi|al|de|likt [ɔfi'tsiaːl-] NT *(Jur)* offence *for which proceedings are brought directly by the public prosecutor's department*

of|fi|zi|ell [ɔfi'tsiɛl] ADJ *Meinung, Erklärung, Besuch* official; *Einladung, Besuch auch* formal; **wie von ~er Seite verlautet** according to official sources; **auf dem Empfang ging es schrecklich ~ zu** the reception was extremely formal ADV officially; **etw ~ bekannt geben** to announce sth officially

Of|fi|zier [ɔfi'tsiːɐ] M **-s, -e** *(Chess)* piece *(except pawn)*

Of|fi|zier [ɔfi'tsiːɐ] M **-s, -e, Of|fi|zie|rin** [-'tsiːrɪn] F **-, -nen** officer; **~ werden** to become an officer, to get *or* be given *or* gain a commission; *(als Beruf)* to become *or* be an army officer; **erster/zweiter ~** first/second officer

Of|fi|ziers-: **Of|fi|ziers|an|wär|ter(in)** M(F) officer cadet; **Of|fi|ziers|ka|si|no** NT officers' mess; **Of|fi|ziers|korps** NT officer corps, the officers *pl*; **Of|fi|ziers|lauf|bahn** F officer's career, career as an officer; **Of|fi|ziers|mes|se** F officers' mess; **Of|fi|ziers|pa|tent** NT *(old)* commission

of|fi|zi|ös [ɔfi'tsiøːs] ADJ semiofficial

Off-Ki|no ['ɔf-] NT art-house *or* repertory *(US)* cinema

off|line ['ɔflain] ADV *(Comput)* offline

Off|line|be|trieb ['ɔflain-] M *(Comput)* offline mode

öff|nen ['œfnən] VT to open; **jdm den Blick für etw ~** to open sb's eyes to sth, to make sb aware *or* conscious of sth; **eine Leiche ~** to open (up) a corpse; **das Museum wird um 10 geöffnet** the museum is open *or* opens at 10; **die Messe öffnet heute ihre Tore** *or* **Pforten** the (trade) fair opens its doors *or* gates today; **„hier ~"** "open here"; **eine Datei ~** *(Comput)* to open a file

VI to open; **es hat geklingelt, könnten Sie mal ~?** that was the doorbell, would you answer it *or* would you get it?; **der Nachtportier öffnete mir** the night porter opened the door for me

VR *(Tür, Blume, Augen)* to open; *(= weiter werden)* to open out; **sich jdm ~** to confide in sb, to open up to sb; **die Erde öffnete sich** the ground opened (up); **nach Norden hin öffnete sich die Schlucht** the gully widens *or* opens out *or* is open to the north; **die Landschaft öffnet sich** the landscape opens out; **vom Bürofenster aus öffnete sich der Blick auf die Berge** the office window offered a view of the mountains

Öff|ner ['œfnɐ] M **-s, -** opener

Öff|nung ['œfnʊŋ] F **-, -en** **a** no pl *(= das Öffnen)* opening; *(von Partei, Bewegung)* opening up; **~ der Leiche** postmortem, autopsy; **eine Politik der ~ gegenüber dem Westen** a policy of opening up to the West **b** *(= offene Stelle)* opening

Öff|nungs-: **Öff|nungs|klau|sel** F *(Jur)* escape clause; *(fig: = Schlupfloch)* loophole; **Öff|nungs|kurs** M *(Pol)* process of opening up; **Öff|nungs|po|li|tik** F policy of openness; **Öff|nungs|zei|ten** PL hours *pl* of business

Off|set|druck ['ɔfsɛt-] M *pl* **-drucke** offset (printing)

oft [ɔft] ADV *comp* **=er** ['œftɐ], *(rare) superl* **am =esten** ['œftəstn] *(= häufig)* often, frequently; *(= in kurzen Abständen)* frequently; **der Bus fährt nicht ~, die Bahn verkehrt öfter** the bus doesn't go very often, the train goes more often; **schon so ~, ~ genug** often enough; **wie ~ fährt der Bus?** how often *or* frequently does the bus go?; **wie ~ warst du schon in Deutschland?** how often *or* how many times have you been to Germany?; **wie ~ wir das schon gehört haben!** how often we've heard that!, how many times have we heard that before!; **des Öfteren** quite often *or* frequently; **je öfter ...** the more often ...

öf|ter(s) ['œftɐ(s)] ADV on occasion, (every) once in a while; *(= wiederholt)* from time to time, (every) now and then; **öfter mal was Neues** *(inf)* variety is the spice of life *(prov)*

oft|mals ['ɔftma:ls] ADV *(geh)* often, oft *(poet)*, ofttimes *(poet)*

o.g. *abbr von* **oben genannt**

oh [o:] INTERJ = **o**

Oheim ['o:haim] M **-s, -e** *(old)* uncle

OHG [o:ha:'ge:] F **-, -s** *abbr von* **offene Handelsgesellschaft**

Ohm [o:m] NT **-(s), -** ohm; **ohmsches Gesetz** Ohm's Law

Ohm M **-s, -e** *(old)* uncle

oh|ne ['o:nə] PREP +*acc* **a** without; **~ (die) Vororte hat die Stadt 100.000 Einwohner** excluding *or* not including *or* not counting the suburbs, the city has 100,000 inhabitants; **~ mich!** count me out!; **er ist nicht ~** *(inf)* he's not bad *(inf)*, he's got what it takes *(inf)*; **die Sache ist (gar) nicht (so) ~** *(inf) (= interessant)* it's not bad; *(= schwierig)* it's not that easy *(inf)*; **~ ihn wären wir immer noch dort** without him *or* but for him *or* if it weren't for him we'd still be there; **~ etw sein** to be without *or* minus *(inf)* sth; **~ Auto** without a *or* one's car; **~ Mehrwertsteuer** excluding VAT; **er ist ~ jede Begabung (für Musik)** he lacks *or* is without any (musical) talent; **~ einen** *or* **jeden Pfennig Geld** penniless, without a penny *or* dime *(US)*, without two ha'pennies to rub together; **ich rauche immer ~** *(inf)* I always smoke untipped cigarettes

b **ich hätte das ~ Weiteres getan** I'd have done it without a second thought, I'd have done it without thinking twice about it; **so etwas kann man ~ Weiteres sagen** it's quite all right to say that; **so etwas kann man in feiner Gesellschaft nicht ~ Weiteres sagen** you can't say that sort of thing in polite society; **ich würde ~ Weiteres sagen, dass ...** I would not hesitate to say that ...; **er hat den Brief ~ Weiteres unterschrieben** he signed the letter straight away *or* just like that; **das Darlehen ist ~ Weiteres bewilligt worden** the loan was granted straight away *or* without any bother *or* problem; **ihm können Sie ~ Weiteres vertrauen** you can trust him implicitly; **das lässt sich ~ Weiteres arrangieren** that can easily be arranged; **das ist nicht (so) ~ Weiteres möglich** it can't be done just like that; **hast du das Geld gekriegt? – ja, ~ Weiteres** did you get the money? – yes, no problem *(inf)*; **dem Kerl kann man nicht ~ Weiteres glauben** you can't just believe anything *or* whatever that guy says; **das kann man nicht ~ Weiteres voraussetzen** you can't just assume that automatically; **diesem Vorschlag kann ich nicht ~ Weiteres zustimmen** I can't just accept the suggestion without question; **du kannst doch nicht so ~ Weiteres aus der Schule weglaufen** you can't just run away from school like that

CONJ **~ zu zögern** without hesitating; **~ dass ich ihn darum gebeten hätte, kam er mich besuchen** he came to see me without my *(Brit) or* me inviting him; **wer redet, ~ gefragt zu sein ...** anybody who talks without being asked ...

oh|ne-: **oh|ne|dem** [o:nə'de:m] *(old)*, **oh|ne|dies** [o:nə'di:s] ADV = **ohnehin**; **oh|ne|ei|nan|der** [o:nəlai'nandɐ] ADV without one another, without each other; **oh|ne|glei|chen** [o:nə'glaiçn] ADJ *inv* unparalleled; **ein Erfolg ~** an unparalleled success; **diese Frechheit ist ~!** I've never known such a nerve!; **seine Frechheit ist ~** I've never known anybody have such a nerve; **er singt ~** as a singer he is without compare *or* he's in a class by himself; **oh|ne|hin** [o:nə'hɪn] ADV anyway; **wir sind ~ zu viel Leute** there are too many of us already *or* as it is; **es ist ~ schon spät** it's already late, it's late enough already, it's late enough as it is; **das hat ~ keinen Zweck** there is no point in (doing) that anyway

Ohn|macht ['o:nmaxt] F **-, -en** **a** *(Med)* faint, swoon *(old)*; **in ~ fallen** to faint, to swoon *(old)*; **aus der ~ erwachen** to come round *or* to, to recover consciousness **b** *(geh: = Machtlosigkeit)* powerlessness, helplessness, impotence

ohn|mäch|tig ['o:nmɛçtɪç] ADJ **a** *(= bewusstlos)* unconscious; **~ werden** to faint, to pass out; **Hilfe, sie ist ~!** help, she's fainted!; **~ sank sie in seine Arme** she fainted into his arms, she collapsed unconscious into his arms **b** *(geh: = machtlos)* powerless, impotent, helpless; **~e Wut, ~er Zorn** impotent *or* helpless rage ADV *(= hilflos)* helplessly, powerlessly, impotently; **einer Sache** *(dat)* **~ gegenüberstehen** to be helpless *or* powerless in the face of sth; **~ zusehen** to look on helplessly

Ohn|machts|an|fall M *(lit, fig)* fainting fit; **als ich das hörte, habe ich fast einen ~ bekommen** *(inf)* when I heard that I nearly fainted *or* nearly passed out

oho [o'ho:] INTERJ oho, hello → **klein**

Ohr [o:ɐ] NT **-(e)s, -en** ear; **seine ~en sind nicht mehr so gut** his hearing isn't too good any more; **auf einem ~ taub sein** to be deaf in one ear; **auf dem ~ bin ich taub** *(fig)* nothing doing *(inf)*, I won't hear of it; **auf taube/offene ~en stoßen** to fall on deaf/sympathetic ears; **bei jdm ein aufmerksames/geneigtes/offenes ~ finden** to find sb a ready/willing/sympathetic listener; **ein offenes ~ für jdn/etw haben** to be ready to listen to sb/sth; **jdm ein geneigtes ~ leihen** *or* **schenken** *(geh)* to lend sb an ear *or* a sympathetic ear; **lange ~en machen** *(inf)* to prick up one's ears; **ein musikalisches ~ haben** to have a musical ear *or* an ear for music; **ein scharfes** *or* **feines ~ haben** to have a good ear; **die ~en hängen lassen** *(inf)* to look down in the mouth *(inf) or* down in the dumps *(inf)*; **die ~en steifhalten** *(inf)* to keep one's chin up; **die ~en anlegen** to put its ears back; **mach** *or* **sperr die ~en auf!** *(inf)* wash *or* clean out your ears *(inf)*; **mir klingen die ~en** my ears are burning; **seine Kritik klingt ihnen noch immer in den ~en** his criticism is still ringing in their ears; **jdm die ~en volljammern** *(inf)* to keep (going) on *or* moaning at sb; **die Wände haben ~en** walls have ears; **ganz ~ sein** *(hum)* to be all ears; **sich aufs ~ legen** *or* **hauen** *(inf)* to turn in *(inf)*, to hit the hay *or* the sack *(inf)*, to kip down *(Brit inf)*; **sitzt er auf seinen ~en?** *(inf)* is he deaf or something?; **jdn bei den ~en nehmen, jdm die ~en lang ziehen** *(inf)* to tweak sb's ear(s); **für deutsche/englische ~en klingt das komisch** that sounds odd to German/English ears; **diese Nachricht war nicht für fremde ~en bestimmt** this piece of news was not meant for other ears; **jdm eins** *or* **ein paar hinter die ~en geben** *(inf)* to give sb a clip round *(Brit) or* a smack on the ear; **ein paar** *or* **eins hinter die ~en kriegen** *(inf)* to get a clip round *(Brit) or* a smack on the ear; **jdm etw um die ~en hauen** *(inf) or* **schlagen** *(inf)* to hit sb over the head with sth; **schreib es dir hinter die ~en** *(inf)* will you (finally) get that into your (thick) head *(inf)*, has that sunk in? *(inf)*; **noch nass** *or* **feucht** *or* **nicht trocken hinter den ~en sein** to be still wet behind the ears; **jdm etw ins ~ sagen** to whisper sth in sb's ear; **die Melodie geht (leicht) ins ~** the tune is very catchy; **du hast wohl Dreck** *or* **Watte in den ~en!** *(inf)* are you deaf or something?, is there something wrong with your ears?; **ich habe seine Worte noch deutlich im ~** I can still hear his words clearly, his words are still ringing in my ears; **jdm (mit etw) in den ~en liegen** to badger sb (about sth), to keep on at sb (about sth) *(inf)*; **mit halbem ~(e) hinhören** *or* **zuhören** to half listen, to listen with half an ear; **jdn übers ~ hauen** to take sb for a ride *(inf)*, to pull a fast one on sb *(inf)*; **bis über die** *or* **beide ~en verliebt sein** to be head over heels in love; **bis über die** *or* **beide ~en verschuldet sein** to be up to one's ears *or* eyes *(Brit)* in debt; **viel um die ~en haben** *(inf)* to have a lot on (one's plate) *(inf)*, to be rushed off one's feet *(inf)*; **es ist mir zu ~en gekommen** it has come to my ears *(form)*; **zum einen ~ hinein und zum anderen wieder hinaus gehen** *(inf)* to go in one ear and out the other *(inf)*; **dein Wort in Gottes ~** God willing

Öhr [ø:ɐ] NT **-(e)s, -e** eye

Oh|ren-: **Oh|ren|arzt** M, **Oh|ren|ärz|tin** F ear specialist; **Oh|ren|beich|te** F (auricular) confession; **oh|ren|be|täu|bend** ADJ *(fig)* deafening; *Lärm auch* earsplitting ADV **~ laut** deafeningly loud; **Oh|ren|ent|zün|dung** F ear infection; **Oh|ren|klap|pe** F earflap; **Oh|ren|krie|cher** M *(= Ohrwurm)* earwig; **Oh|ren|sau|sen** NT **-s,** *no pl (Med)* buzzing in one's ears; **Oh|ren|schmalz** NT earwax; **Oh|ren|schmaus** M **das Konzert war ein richtiger ~** the concert was a real delight to hear *or* a treat for the ears; **moderne Musik ist oft kein ~** modern music is often far from easy on the ear; **Oh|ren|schmer|zen** PL earache; **Oh|ren|schüt|zer** PL earmuffs *pl*; **Oh|ren|ses|sel** M wing chair; **Oh|ren|stöp|sel** M earplug; **Oh|ren|zeu|ge** M, **Oh|ren|zeu|gin** F earwitness

Ohr|fei|ge ['o:ɐfaigə] F **-, -n** slap (on *or* round *(Brit)* the face); *(als Strafe)* box on the ears *(dated)*, clip round the ear *(Brit)*, smack on the ear; **jdm eine ~ geben** *or* **verabreichen** *or*

verpassen *(inf)* to slap sb's face; **eine ~ bekommen** to get a slap round *(Brit) or* in *(US)* the face; **wenn du nicht gleich ruhig bist, bekommst du eine ~** if you don't shut up I'll box your ears *(dated) or* I'll give you a clip round the ear *(Brit) or* a smack on the ear

ohr|fei|gen ['o:ɐfaign] VT *insep* **jdn ~** to slap *or* hit sb; *(als Strafe)* to box sb's ears *(dated)*, to give sb a clip round the ear *(Brit) or* a smack on the ear; **ich könnte mich selbst ~, dass ich das gemacht habe** I could kick myself for doing it

Ohr|fei|gen|ge|sicht NT *(inf)* fish face *(inf)*; **er hat so ein richtiges ~** he's got the sort of face you'd like to put your fist into

Ohr-: **Ohr|ge|hän|ge** NT *(form)* drop earrings *pl*; *(hum)* dangly earrings *pl*; **Ohr|hän|ger** M earring; **Ohr|läpp|chen** NT (ear)lobe; **Ohr|mu|schel** F (outer) ear, auricle *(form)*

Oh|ro|pax® ['o:ropaks, o:ro'paks] NT **-, -** earplugs *pl*

Ohr-: **Ohr|ring** M earring; **Ohr|ste|cker** M stud earring; **Ohr|stöp|sel** PL earplugs *pl*; **Ohr|ther|mo|me|ter** NT *(Med)* ear thermometer; **Ohr|wurm** M *(Zool)* earwig; **der Schlager ist ein richtiger ~** *(inf)* that's a really catchy record *(inf)*

o.J. *abbr von* **ohne Jahr** n.d. *(no date)*

oje [o'je:], **oje|mi|ne** [o'je:mine] INTERJ oh dear

OK[1] [o:'ka:] NT **-, -s** *abbr von* **Organisationskomitee**

OK[2] [o:'ka:] *abbr von* **organisierte Kriminalität**

o.k., O.K. [o'ke:] *abbr von* **okay** OK

Oka|pi [o'ka:pi] NT **-s, -s** okapi

okay [o'ke:] INTERJ okay, OK

Okay [o'ke:] NT **-s, -s** okay, OK

Ok|ka|si|on [ɔka'zio:n] F **-, -en** *(Comm)* **a** *(= Ware aus zweiter Hand)* second-hand article **b** *(= Gelegenheitskauf)* (second-hand) bargain

ok|kult [ɔ'kʊlt] ADJ occult; **das Okkulte** the occult

Ok|kul|tis|mus [ɔkʊl'tɪsmʊs] M **-,** *no pl* occultism

Ok|ku|pant [ɔku'pant] M **-en, -en**, **Ok|ku|pan|tin** [-'pantɪn] F **-, -nen** occupier; **die ~en** the occupying forces *or* powers

Ok|ku|pa|ti|on [ɔkupa'tsio:n] F **-, -en** occupation

ok|ku|pie|ren [ɔku'pi:rən] *ptp* **okkupiert** VT to occupy

Öko ['ø:ko] M **-s, -s** *(inf: = Umweltschützer)* Green

Öko- *in cpds* eco-, ecological; *(= die Umwelt betreffend auch)* environmental; **Öko-Au|dit** [-'audɪt] M OR NT **-s, -s** green *or* environmental audit; **Öko|bau|er** M **-n, -n**, **Öko|bäu|e|rin** F **-, -nen** *(inf)* ecologically-minded farmer; **Öko|bi|lanz** F ecological balance; **Öko|fonds** M eco fund, green fund; **Öko|kri|mi|nel|le(r)** MF *decl as adj* environmental criminal; **Öko|kri|se** F ecological crisis; **Öko|la|den** M wholefood shop

Öko|lo|ge [øko'lo:gə] M **-n, -n**, **Öko|lo|gin** [-'lo:gɪn] F **-, -nen** ecologist

Öko|lo|gie [økolo'gi:] F **-,** *no pl* ecology

Öko|lo|gie|be|we|gung F ecology movement

öko|lo|gisch [øko'lo:gɪʃ] ADJ ecological, environmental ADV ecologically; *anbauen, aufziehen* organically; **~ wirtschaftende Betriebe** companies saving on natural resources

Öko|nom [øko'no:m] M **-en, -en**, **Öko|no|min** [-'no:mɪn] F **-, -nen** **a** economist **b** *(obs)* bailiff

Öko|no|mie [økono'mi:] F **-, -n** **a** *no pl (= Wirtschaftlichkeit)* economy; **durch kluge ~ hat er das Unternehmen wieder auf die Beine gestellt** by clever economies he put the concern back on its feet again **b** *(= Wirtschaft)* economy **c** *no pl (= Wirtschaftswissenschaft)* economics *sing*; **politische ~ studieren** to study political economy **d** *(Aus: = Landwirtschaftsbetrieb)* farm

öko|no|misch [øko'no:mɪʃ] ADJ **a** economic **b** *(= sparsam)* economic(al) ADV economically; **~ mit etw umgehen** to be sparing with sth; **etw ~ einsetzen** to use sth sparingly; **~ wirtschaften** to be economical

Öko-: **Öko|pa|pier** NT recycled paper; **Öko|par|tei** F ecology party; **Öko|pax** ['ø:kopaks] M **-, -e** *(inf)* campaigner for peace and the environment; **Öko|pa|zi|fis|mus** M environmental pacifism; **Öko|po|li|ti|ker(in)** M(F) ecologist politician; **Öko|sie|gel** NT eco-label; **Öko|sphä|re** F ecosphere; **Öko|steu|er** F *(Econ)* ecotax, ecological tax, green tax; **Öko|sys|tem** NT ecosystem

Öko|tro|pho|lo|gie [økotrofolo'gi:] F **-,** *no pl* home economics *sing*

Ok|ta|e|der [ɔkta'le:dɐ] NT **-s, -** octahedron

Ok|tan|zahl [ɔk'ta:n-] F octane number *or* rating; **Benzin mit einer hohen ~** high octane petrol

Ok|tav [ɔk'ta:f] NT **-s, -e** [-və] octavo

Ok|tav|band [-bant] M *pl* **-bände** octavo volume

Ok|ta|ve [ɔk'ta:və] F **-, -n** octave

Ok|tett [ɔk'tɛt] NT **-s, -e** octet

Ok|to|ber [ɔk'to:bɐ] M **-(s), -** October → *auch* **März**

Ok|to|ber|fest NT *Munich beer festival*

OKTOBERFEST

The beer festival known as the **Oktoberfest** takes place annually in Munich from the middle of September until the first weekend in October. Beer tents representing Munich's breweries are set up on the **Wies'n**, a large festival site in the city. In the tents local people and tourists sit at long wooden tables and drink a particularly strong festival beer served only in one-litre mugs. Pretzels and various kinds of sausage are available, and people sing along with the brass bands that are often in attendance.

Ok|to|ber|re|vo|lu|ti|on F October Revolution

ok|tro|yie|ren [ɔktroa'ji:rən] *ptp* **oktroyiert** VT *(geh)* to force, to impose *(jdm etw* sth on sb)

Oku|lar [oku'la:ɐ] NT **-s, -e** eyepiece, ocular

oku|lie|ren [oku'li:rən] *ptp* **okuliert** VT *Obstbäume, Rosen* to graft, to bud

Öku|me|ne [øku'me:nə] F **-,** *no pl* ecumenical movement

öku|me|nisch [øku'me:nɪʃ] ADJ ecumenical; **~es Konzil** Ecumenical Council ADV **~ denken** to be ecumenically minded; **~ getraut werden** *to be married by a priest and a minister together*

Ok|zi|dent ['ɔktsidɛnt, ɔktsi'dɛnt] M **-s,** *no pl (liter)* occident

Öl [ø:l] NT **-(e)s, -e** oil; **auf Öl stoßen** to strike oil; **Öl fördern** to extract oil; **nach Öl bohren** to drill for oil; **ätherische Öle** *(Chem)* essential oils; **in Öl malen** to paint in oils; **T(h)unfisch in Öl** tuna (fish) in oil; **Öl auf die Wogen gießen** *(prov)* to pour oil on troubled waters; **Öl ins Feuer gießen** *(prov)* to add fuel to the fire *(prov)*; **solche Schmeicheleien gehen ihm runter wie Öl** *(inf)* he laps up compliments like that

Öl-: **Öl|ab|schei|der** [-lapʃaidɐ] M **-s, -** oil separator; **Öl|baum** M olive tree; **Öl|berg** M **a** Mount of Olives **b** *(Art) sculpture or painting showing Christ with 12 sleeping Apostles on the Mount of Olives*; **Öl|bild** NT oil painting, oil; **Öl|boh|rung** F oil drilling, drilling for oil

Old|die ['o:ldi] M **-s, -s** *(inf: = Schlager)* (golden) oldie *(inf)*

Öl-: **Öl|druck** M **a** *pl* **-drucke** *(Bild)* oleograph **b** *no pl (Tech)* oil pressure; **Öl|druck|brem|se** F hydraulic brake

OLE [olel'le:] *(Comput) abbr von* **object linking and embedding**

Old|ti|mer ['o:ldtaimɐ] M **-s, -** **a** *(= Auto)* veteran car; *(Rail)* historic train; *(Aviat)* veteran plane, old bus *or* crate *(pej inf)* **b** *(Sport)* veteran, old timer **c** *(= Pferd)* old *or* retired racehorse

Ole|an|der [ole'andɐ] M **-s, -** oleander

Öl|em|bar|go NT oil embargo

ölen ['ø:lən] VT to oil; **wie geölt** *(inf)* like clockwork *(inf)*

Öl-: **Öl|ex|port|land** NT oil-exporting country; **Öl|far|be** F oil-based paint; *(Art)* oil (paint *or* colour *(Brit) or* color *(US))*; **mit ~n malen** to paint in oil colours *(Brit) or* colors *(US)*, to paint in oils; **Öl|feld** NT oil field; **Öl|film** M film of oil; **Öl|för|der|land** NT oil-producing country; **Öl|ge|mäl|de** NT oil painting; **Öl|ge|sell|schaft** F oil company; **Öl|göt|ze** M *(inf)* **wie ein ~** like a stuffed *or* tailor's dummy *(inf)*; **Öl|hei|zung** F oil-fired central heating

ölig ['ø:lɪç] ADJ oily; *(fig auch)* greasy ADV **~ verschmierte Gesichter** faces smeared with oil *or (fettig)* grease; **~ glänzende Gesichter** shiny faces; **~ triefender Fisch** fish dripping with oil

Oli|gar|chie [oligar'çi:] F **-, -n** [-'çi:ən] oligarchy

Oli|go|pol [oligo'po:l] NT **-s, -e** oligopoly

Öl|in|dust|rie F oil industry

oliv [o'li:f] ADJ *pred* olive(-green); **ein Kleid in Oliv** an olive-green dress

Oli|ve [o'li:və] F **-, -n** olive

Oli|ven-: **Oli|ven|baum** M olive tree; **oli|ven|far|ben** [-farbn], **oli|ven|far|big** ADJ *attr* olive-green; **Oli|ven|hain** M olive grove; **Oli|ven|öl** NT olive oil

oliv|grün ADJ olive-green

Öl-: **Öl|ka|nal** M oil duct; **Öl|kan|ne** F, **Öl|känn|chen** NT oil can; **Öl|ka|tas|tro|phe** F *(= Tankerunglück)* oil spill disaster; **Öl|kon|zern** M oil company; **Öl|kri|se** F oil crisis; **Öl|ku|chen** M oil cake; **Öl|kühl|ung** F oil cooling; **mit ~** oil-cooled

oll [ɔl] ADJ *(N Ger inf)* old; **je ~er, je** *or* **desto doller** *(prov inf)* there's no fox like an old fox *(prov inf)* → **Kamelle**

Öl|la|che [-'laxə, -'la:xə] F patch of oil

Ol|le(r) ['ɔlə] MF *decl as adj (N Ger)* old man/woman; *(= Chef, Chefin)* boss; **mein ~r** *(inf) (= Vater)* the old man *(inf)*; *(= Ehemann)* my old man *(inf)*; **meine ~** *(inf) (= Mutter, Ehefrau, Freundin)* the old lady *(inf)*

Öl-: **Öl|lie|fe|rant(in)** M(F) oil producer; **Öl|ma|le|rei** F oil painting; **Öl|mess|stab** M *(Aut)* dipstick; **Öl|müh|le** F oil mill; **Öl|mul|ti** M *(inf)* oil conglomerate; **Öl|ofen** M oil stove *or* heater; **Öl|pa|pier** NT oil paper; **Öl|pest** F oil pollution; **Öl|platt|form** F oil rig; **Öl|preis** M oil price; **Öl|quel|le** F oil well; **öl|reich** ADJ *Pflanze, Gegend* oil-rich; **Öl|reich|tum** F *(von Land)* rich oil reserves *pl*; **Öl|sar|di|ne** F sardine; **6 Leute im Auto, da sitzt ihr ja wie die ~n** *(inf)* with 6 people in the car, you must be crammed in like sardines *(inf)*; **Öl|schal|ter** M *(Elec)* oil switch; **Öl|scheich** M *(pej)* oil sheik; **Öl|schicht** F layer of oil; **Öl|schie|fer** M oil shale; **Öl|sper|re** F oil barrier *(for containing oil spills)*; **Öl|stand** M oil level; **Öl|stands|an|zei|ger** M oil pressure gauge; **Öl|tep|pich** M oil slick

Ölung ['ø:lʊŋ] F **-, -en** oiling; **die Letzte ~** *(Eccl)* extreme unction, the last rites

Öl-: **Öl|ver|brauch** M oil consumption; **Öl|ver|knap|pung** [-fɛɐknapʊŋ] F **-, -en** oil shortage; **Öl|vor|kom|men** NT oil deposit; **Öl|wan|ne** F *(Aut)* sump *(Brit)*, oil pan *(US)*; **Öl|wech|sel** M oil change; **ich muss mit dem Auto zum ~** I must take my car in for an oil change; **den ~ machen** to change the oil, to do an oil change

Olymp [o'lʏmp] M **-s** **a** *(Berg)* Mount Olympus; **die Götter des ~** the gods of *or* on Mount Olympus; **in den ~ der Baukunst/der Politik aufsteigen** to climb to the top of the architectural/political world **b** *(Theat)* **der ~** the gods

Olym|pia [o'lʏmpia] NT **-(s),** *no pl (liter)* the Olympic Games *pl*, the Olympics *pl*

Olym|pi|a|de [olym'pia:də] **F -, -n** **a** *(= Olympische Spiele)* Olympic Games *pl*, Olympics *pl* **b** *(liter. Zeitraum)* Olympiad

Olym|pia-: **Olym|pi|a|mann|schaft** **F** Olympic team; **Olym|pi|a|me|dail|le** **F** Olympic medal; **Olym|pi|a|sie|ger(in)** **M(F)** Olympic champion, Olympic gold medallist *(Brit) or* medalist *(US)*; **Olym|pi|a|sta|di|on** **NT** Olympic stadium; **Olym|pi|a|teil|neh|mer(in)** **M(F)** participant in the Olympic Games

Olym|pi|er [o'lympiɐ] **M -s, -**, **Olym|pi|e|rin** [-iərɪn] **F -, -nen** *(liter)* Olympian *(liter)*

Olym|pi|o|ni|ke [olympio'ni:kə] **M -n, -n**, **Olym|pi|o|ni|kin** [-'ni:kɪn] **F -, -nen** *(liter)* Olympic athlete

olym|pisch [o'lympɪʃ] **ADJ** **a** *(= den Olymp betreffend)* Olympian *(auch fig)*; **die ~en Götter, die Olympischen** *(liter)* the gods of *or* on Mount Olympus, the Olympian deities *(liter)* **b** *(= die Olympiade betreffend)* Olympic; **die Olympischen Spiele** the Olympic Games

Öl-: **Öl|zeug** **NT** oilskins *pl*; **Öl|zweig** **M** *(lit, fig)* olive branch

Oma ['o:ma] **F -, -s** *(inf)* granny *(inf)*, grandma *(inf)*; **die alte ~ da drüben** the old dear *(inf) or* old granny *(inf)* over there

Oman [o'ma:n] **NT -s** Oman

Oma|ner [o'ma:nɐ] **M -s, -**, **Oma|ne|rin** [-ərɪn] **F -, -nen** Omani

oma|nisch [o'ma:nɪʃ] **ADJ** Omani

Om|buds|frau ['ɔmbʊts-] **F** ombudswoman

Om|buds|mann ['ɔmbʊts-] **M** *pl* **-männer** ombudsman

Ome|lett [ɔm(ə)'lɛt] **NT -(e)s, -e** *or* **-s**, **Ome|lette** [ɔm,ə,'lɛt] **F -, -n** omelette

Omen ['o:mən] **NT -s, -** *or* **Omina** ['o:mina] omen

omi|nös [omi'nø:s] *(geh)* **ADJ** ominous, sinister **ADV** ominously

Om|ni|bus ['ɔmnibʊs] **M** bus; *(im Überlandverkehr)* bus, coach *(Brit)*

Om|ni|bus-: **Om|ni|bus|li|nie** **F** bus route; **Om|ni|bus|ver|kehr** **M** *(Stadtverkehr)* bus service; *(Überlandverkehr)* bus *or* coach *(Brit)* service

Om|ni|plex-Ki|no **NT** Omniplex cinema

om|ni|po|tent [ɔmnipo'tɛnt, 'ɔmni-] **ADJ** *(liter)* omnipotent

Om|ni|po|tenz [ɔmnipo'tɛnts, 'ɔmni-] **F -, no pl** *(liter)* omnipotence

om|ni|prä|sent [ɔmniprɛ'zɛnt] **ADJ** *(geh)* omnipresent

Om|ni|prä|senz [ɔmniprɛ'zɛnts] **F -, no pl** *(geh)* omnipresence

Om|ni|vo|re [ɔmni'vo:rə] **M -n, -n** *usu pl (Zool)* omnivore

OmU *abbr von* **Original(fassung) mit Untertiteln**

Ona|nie [ona'ni:] **F -, no pl** masturbation, onanism

ona|nie|ren [ona'ni:rən] *ptp* **onaniert** **VI** to masturbate

Ona|nist [ona'nɪst] **M -en, -en** masturbator

On|dit [õ'di:] **NT -, -s** *(geh)* **einem ~ zufolge** as rumour *(Brit) or* rumor *(US)* has it, as is being noised abroad *(liter)*

on|du|lie|ren [ɔndu'li:rən] *ptp* **onduliert** **VT** to crimp

On|kel ['ɔŋkl] **M -s, -** **a** uncle; **~ Sam** *(= USA)* Uncle Sam **b** *(Kindersprache: = erwachsener Mann)* uncle; **sag dem ~ guten Tag!** say hello to the nice man!; **sieh mal den komischen ~ da!** look at the funny (old) man *or* guy *(inf)* over there!; **der ~ Doktor** the nice doctor **c** *(inf)* **der große** *or* **dicke ~** your/his *etc* big toe; **über den ~ gehen** to walk pigeon-toed

On|kel-: **On|kel|ehe** **F** *cohabitation of widow with a man so that she keeps pension rights etc*; **on|kel|haft** **ADJ** avuncular *(form)* **ADV** avuncularly *(form)*; *(pej)* patronizingly

On|ko|gen [ɔŋko'ge:n] **NT -s, -e** *(Med)* oncogene

On|ko|lo|ge [ɔŋko'lo:gə] **M -n, -n**, **On|ko|lo|gin** [-'lo:gɪn] **F -, -nen** oncologist

On|ko|lo|gie [ɔŋkolo'gi:] **F -, no pl** *(Med)* oncology

on|line ['ɔnlain] **ADJ** *pred (Comput)* online; **~ arbeiten** to work online

On|line- ['ɔnlain] *in cpds (Comput)* online; **On|line|an|bie|ter** **M** online (service) provider; **On|line|auk|ti|on** **F** online auction; **On|line|bank** **F** online bank; **On|line|ban|king** **NT** online banking; **On|line|be|trieb** **M** online mode; **On|line|da|ten|bank** **F** *pl* **-banken** online database; **On|line|dienst** **M** online service; **On|line|ein|kauf** **M** online shopping; **On|line|händ|ler(in)** **M(F)** online trader *or* dealer; **On|line|hil|fe** online help; **On|line|pub|li|shing** **NT** online publishing; **On|line|ser|vice** [-zø:ɐvɪs, -zœrvɪs] **M** online service; **On|line|shop** **NT** online store; **On|line|shop|per(in)** **M(F)** oline shopper; **On|line|shop|ping** **NT** online shopping; **On|line|um|satz** **M** online profits *pl or* turnover; **On|line|ver|bin|dung** **F** online connection; **On|line|zu|gang** **M** online access

ONO *abbr von* **Ostnordost** ENE

Ono|ma|si|o|lo|gie [onomaziolo'gi:] **F -, no pl** onomastics *sing*

ono|ma|to|po|e|tisch [onomatopo'e:tɪʃ] *(form)* **ADJ** onomatopoeic **ADV** onomatopoeically

Önorm ['ø:nɔrm] **F -, no pl** *abbr von* **Österreichische Norm** Austrian standard

on|tisch ['ɔntɪʃ] **ADJ** ontic

On|to|ge|ne|se [ɔntoge'ne:zə] **F -, no pl** ontogenesis, ontogeny

on|to|ge|ne|tisch [ɔntoge'ne:tɪʃ] **ADJ** ontogenetic, ontogenic

On|to|lo|gie [ɔntolo'gi:] **F -, no pl** ontology

on|to|lo|gisch [ɔnto'lo:gɪʃ] **ADJ** ontological; **der ~e Gottesbeweis** the ontological proof *or* argument

Onyx ['o:nyks] **M -(es), -e** onyx

OP [o:'pe:] **M -s, -s** *abbr von* **Operationssaal**

o. P. *abbr von* **ordentlicher Professor**

Opa ['o:pa] **M -s, -s** *(inf)* grandpa *(inf)*, grandad *(inf)*; *(fig)* old grandpa *or* grandad *(inf)*; **na ~, nun mach mal schneller!** come on grandpa, hurry up! *(inf)*

opak [o'pa:k] **ADJ** opaque

Opal [o'pa:l] **M -s, -e** opal

Op-Art ['ɔpla:ɐt] **F -, no pl** op art

Opa|zi|tät [opatsi'tɛ:t] **F -, no pl** opacity

OPEC ['o:pɛk] **F - die ~** OPEC; **~-Länder** OPEC countries *pl*

Open Air ['o:pn 'ɛɐ] **NT -s, -s** *(= Festival)* open-air festival

Oper ['o:pɐ] **F -, -n** opera; *(Ensemble)* Opera; *(= Opernhaus)* opera, opera house; **in die ~ gehen** to go to the opera; **an die** *or* **zur ~ gehen** to take up opera-singing, to become an opera singer; **die Wiener/Zürcher ~** the Vienna/Zurich Opera; **quatsch keine ~!** *(inf)* stop going on! *(inf)*

Ope|rand [opə'rant] **M -en, -en** *(Comput)* operand

Ope|ra|teur [opəra'tø:ɐ] **M -s, -e**, **Ope|ra|teu|rin** [-'tø:rɪn] **F -, -nen** **a** *(Med)* surgeon **b** *(old: im Kino)* projectionist

Ope|ra|ti|on [opəra'tsio:n] **F -, -en** operation

Ope|ra|ti|ons-: **Ope|ra|ti|ons|nar|be** **F** operation scar; **Ope|ra|ti|ons|saal** **M** operating theatre *(Brit) or* room *(US)*; **Ope|ra|ti|ons|schwes|ter** **F** theatre sister *(Brit)*, operating room nurse *(US)*; **Ope|ra|ti|ons|tisch** **M** operating table

ope|ra|tiv [opəra'ti:f] **ADJ** **a** *(Med)* operative, surgical; **das ist nur durch einen ~en Eingriff zu beseitigen** that can only be removed by (means of) surgery **b** *(Mil) Pläne, Planung, Stab* operational, strategic **c** *(Econ) Ergebnis, Verluste* operational **ADV** **a** *(Med)* surgically; **eine Geschwulst ~ entfernen** to remove a growth surgically *or* by surgery **b** *(Mil)* strategically; **~ denken** to think strategically; **wir sollten ~ vorgehen** we should attempt to develop a strategy **c** *(Econ)* **das Unternehmen steckt ~ in den roten Zahlen** the company is operating in the red; **die Firma wirtschaftet seit geraumer Zeit ~ mit Verlust** the firm has been operating at a loss for quite some time; **unser Betrieb ist auch in den USA ~ tätig** our company also has operations in the USA; **die Behörde sollte in dieser Sache ~ tätig werden** the authorities should take action on this matter

Ope|ra|tor [opə'ra:to:ɐ] **M -s, -en** [-'to:rən] *(Comput)* operator

Ope|ra|tor ['ɔpəre:tɐ, opə'ra:to:ɐ] **M -s, -s,** *or (bei dt. Aussprache)* **Operatoren** [-'to:rən], **Ope|ra|to|rin** [-'to:rɪn] **F -, -nen** *(= Beruf)* (computer) operator

Ope|ret|te [opə'rɛtə] **F -, -n** operetta

Ope|ret|ten|kai|ser **M** *(hum)* stage emperor

ope|rie|ren [opə'ri:rən] *ptp* **operiert** **VT** *Patienten, Krebs, Magen* to operate on; **jdn am Magen ~** to operate on sb's stomach, to perform an operation on sb's stomach; **der Blinddarm muss sofort operiert werden** that appendix must be operated on at once, that appendix needs immediate surgery **VI** **a** *(Med)* to operate; **die Ärzte haben drei Stunden an ihm operiert** the doctors operated on him for three hours; **sich ~ lassen** to have an operation; **ambulant ~** to operate on an out-patient basis **b** *(Mil)* to operate **c** *(fig: = agieren, arbeiten)* to operate; **Arbeiter, die mit großen Maschinen ~** workers who operate large machines; **wir müssen in den Verhandlungen sehr vorsichtig ~** we must go *or* tread very carefully in the negotiations; **ein weltweit ~des Unternehmen** a worldwide business

Opern-: **Opern|arie** **F** (operatic) aria; **Opern|ball** **M** opera ball; **Opern|führer** **M** *(Buch)* opera guide; **Opern|glas** **NT** opera glasses *pl*; **Opern|haus** **NT** opera house; **Opern|sän|ger(in)** **M(F)** opera singer; **Opern|text** **M** libretto

Op|fer ['ɔpfɐ] **NT -s, -** **a** *(= Opfergabe)* sacrifice *(auch fig)*; **zum** *or* **als ~** as a sacrifice; **die Gottheit verlangte zehn Jungfrauen zum** *or* **als ~** the god demanded the sacrifice of ten virgins; **sie brachten ein ~ aus Wein und Wasser dar** they made an offering of water and wine; **jdm etw zum ~ bringen, jdm etw als ~ darbringen** to offer sth as a sacrifice to sb, to make a sacrificial offering of sth to sb; **für ihre Kinder scheut sie keine ~** she sacrifices everything for her children, for her children she considers no sacrifice too great; **ein ~ bringen** to make a sacrifice **b** *(= Geschädigte)* victim; **jdm/einer Sache zum ~ fallen** to be (the) victim of sb/sth; **sie fiel seinem Charme zum ~** she fell victim to his charm; **ein ~ einer Sache** *(gen)* **werden** to be a victim of sth, to fall victim to sth; **täglich werden 28 Kinder ~ des Straßenverkehrs** every day 28 children are the victims of road accidents; **das Erdbeben forderte viele ~** the earthquake took a heavy toll *or* claimed many victims

Op|fer-: **op|fer|be|reit** **ADJ** ready *or* willing to make sacrifices; **Op|fer|be|reit|schaft** **F** readiness *or* willingness to make sacrifices; **op|fer|freu|dig** **ADJ** willing to make sacrifices; **Op|fer|ga|be** **F** *(liter)* (sacrificial) offering; *(Eccl)* offering; **Op|fer|gang** **M** *pl* **-gänge einen ~ antreten** *(fig liter)* to make a huge sacrifice; **Op|fer|lamm** **NT** sacrificial lamb; **der Bräutigam schritt wie ein ~ zum Altar** the groom walked to the altar like a lamb to the slaughter; **Op|fer|mut** **M** self-sacrifice

op|fern ['ɔpfɐn] **VT** **a** *(= als Opfer darbringen)* to sacrifice, to immolate *(form)*; *Feldfrüchte etc* to offer (up); **sein Leben ~** to give up *or* sacrifice one's life; **die soziale Idee wurde auf dem Altar des freien Marktes geopfert** the idea of social responsibility was sacrificed on the altar of the

free market
b (*fig: = aufgeben*) to give up, to sacrifice
VI to make a sacrifice, to sacrifice; **einem Gotte ~** (*liter*) to pay homage to a god (*liter*), to worship a god
VR a sich für etw ~ (*= hingeben*) to devote *or* dedicate one's life to sth; **sich** *or* **sein Leben für jdn/etw ~** to sacrifice oneself *or* one's life for sb/sth
b (*inf: = sich bereit erklären*) to be a martyr (*inf*); **wer opfert sich und isst die Reste auf?** who's going to be a martyr and eat up the leftovers? (*inf*), who's going to volunteer to eat up the leftovers?

Op|fer-: **Op|fer|pfen|nig** M small contribution; **Op|fer|rol|le** F role of (a/the) victim; **Op|fer|stät|te** F sacrificial altar; **Op|fer|stock** M offertory box; **Op|fer|tier** NT sacrificial animal; **Op|fer|tod** M self-sacrifice, sacrificial death; **er rettete durch seinen ~ den anderen das Leben** by sacrificing his own life, he saved the lives of the others; **Christus starb den ~ (für unsere Sünden)** Christ gave up his life (for our sins)

Op|fe|rung ['ɔpfərʊŋ] F -, -en (*= das Opfern*) sacrifice; (*Eccl*) offertory

Op|fer-: **Op|fer|wil|le** M spirit of sacrifice; **op|fer|wil|lig** ADJ self-sacrificing, willing to make sacrifices

Opi|at [o'pia:t] NT -(e)s, -e opiate

Opi|um ['o:piʊm] NT -s, *no pl* opium

Opi|um-: **Opi|um|han|del** M opium trade *or* traffic(king); **Opi|um|höh|le** F opium den; **Opi|um|rau|cher(in)** M(F) opium smoker

ÖPNV *abbr von* **öffentlicher Personennahverkehr**

Opos|sum [o'pɔsʊm] NT -s, -s (*Zool*) opossum, possum (*inf*)

Op|po|nent [ɔpo'nɛnt] M -en, -en, **Op|po|nen|tin** [-'nɛntɪn] F -, -nen opponent

op|po|nie|ren [ɔpo'ni:rən] *ptp* **opponiert** VI to oppose (*gegen jdn/etw* sb/sth), to offer opposition (*gegen* to); **ihr müsst auch immer ~** do you always have to oppose everything *or* be against everything?

op|por|tun [ɔpɔr'tu:n] ADJ (*geh*) opportune

Op|por|tu|nis|mus [ɔpɔrtu'nɪsmʊs] M -, *no pl* opportunism

Op|por|tu|nist [ɔpɔrtu'nɪst] M -en, -en, **Op|por|tu|nis|tin** [-'nɪstɪn] F -, -nen opportunist

op|por|tu|nis|tisch [ɔpɔrtu'nɪstɪʃ] ADJ opportunistic, opportunist; **~e Infektion** (*Med*) secondary infection ADV opportunistically; **~ handeln** to act in an opportunist fashion; **da hat er sehr ~ gehandelt** that was very opportunist(ic) of him

Op|por|tu|ni|tät [ɔpɔrtuni'tɛ:t] F -, -en (*geh*) appropriateness

Op|por|tu|ni|täts|prin|zip NT, *no pl* (*Jur*) discretionary prosecution principle (*principle allowing the public prosecutor to judge whether legal proceedings are appropriate in certain cases*)

Op|po|si|ti|on [ɔpozi'tsio:n] F -, -en opposition (*auch Pol, Astron*); **etw aus (lauter) ~ tun** to do sth out of *or* from (sheer) contrariness; **diese Gruppe macht ständig ~ (gegen den Klassenlehrer)** (*inf*) this group is always making trouble (for the teacher); **in ~ zu etw stehen** to stand in opposition to sth; **in die ~ gehen** (*Pol*) to go into opposition

op|po|si|ti|o|nell [ɔpozitsio'nɛl] ADJ *Gruppen, Kräfte* opposition

Op|po|si|ti|ons- *in cpds* opposition; **Op|po|si|ti|ons|bank** F *pl* -bänke (*Pol*) opposition bench; **auf der ~ sitzen** to be in the opposition, to sit on the opposition benches; **Op|po|si|ti|ons|füh|rer(in)** M(F) (*Pol*) opposition leader; **Op|po|si|ti|ons|par|tei** F (*Pol*) opposition, opposition party

OP-Schwes|ter [o:'pe:-] F *abbr von* **Operationsschwester**

Op|ta|tiv ['ɔptati:f] M -s, -e [-və] optative

op|tie|ren [ɔp'ti:rən] *ptp* **optiert** VI (*form: auch Pol*) ~ **für** to opt for

Op|tik ['ɔptɪk] F -, -en **a** *no pl* (*Phys*) optics
b (*= Linsensystem*) lens system; **du hast wohl einen Knick in der ~!** (*inf*) can't you see straight? (*inf*), are you blind?
c (*= Sicht, Sehweise*) point of view, perspective; **das ist eine Frage der ~** (*fig*) it depends on your point of view; **in** *or* **aus seiner ~** in his eyes
d (*= Mode, Aussehen*) look; (*= Schein*) appearances *pl*; **das ist nur hier wegen der ~** it's just here because it looks good, it's just here for visual *or* optical effect; **die Partei muss sehen, dass sie die ~ ihrer Politik ein bisschen verbessert** the party must try to present their policies in a better light; **etw in die rechte ~ bringen** to put sth into the right perspective

Op|ti|ker ['ɔptikɐ] M -s, -, **Op|ti|ke|rin** [-ərɪn] F -, -nen optician

op|ti|mal [ɔpti'ma:l] ADJ optimal, optimum *attr* ADV perfectly; **etw ~ nutzen** to put sth to the best possible use

op|ti|mie|ren [ɔpti'mi:rən] *ptp* **optimiert** VT to optimize

Op|ti|mis|mus [ɔpti'mɪsmʊs] M -, *no pl* optimism

Op|ti|mist [ɔpti'mɪst] M -en, -en, **Op|ti|mis|tin** [-'mɪstɪn] F -, -nen optimist

op|ti|mis|tisch [ɔpti'mɪstɪʃ] ADJ optimistic ADV optimistically; **etw ~ sehen** *or* **einschätzen** to be optimistic about sth

Op|ti|mum ['ɔptimʊm] NT -s, **Optima** [-ma] optimum

Op|ti|on [ɔp'tsio:n] F -, -en **a** (*= Wahl*) option (*für* in favour of) **b** (*= Anrecht*) option (*auf +acc* on)

Op|ti|ons-: **Op|ti|ons|an|lei|he** F optional bond; **Op|ti|ons|aus|übung** F exercise (of option); **Op|ti|ons|emp|fän|ger(in)** M(F) grantee (of an option); **Op|ti|ons|fi|xie|rer** [-fɪksi:rɐ] M -s, -, **Op|ti|ons|fi|xie|re|rin** [-ərɪn] F -, -nen option issuer; **Op|ti|ons|frist** F option period; **Op|ti|ons|ge|schäft** NT dealing in options; (*einzelne Transaktion*) option transaction; **Op|ti|ons|preis** M option price; **Op|ti|ons|recht** NT option right; **Op|ti|ons|schein** M warrant

op|tisch ['ɔptɪʃ] ADJ visual; *Gesetze, Instrumente* optical; **~er Eindruck** visual *or* optical effect; **~e Täuschung** optical illusion ADV **a** (*= vom Eindruck her*) optically, visually; **die Bepflanzung lockert die Betonbauten ~ auf** the landscaping softens the appearance of the concrete structures; **dieser Bezirk unterscheidet sich schon rein ~ von ...** the very appearance of this area distinguishes it from ... **b** (*= mit optischen Mitteln*) optically; **die Daten werden ~ eingelesen** the data is read in optically

opu|lent [opu'lɛnt] (*geh*) ADJ *Kostüme, Geldsumme, Feier* lavish; *Mahl, Inszenierung auch* sumptuous ADV lavishly, sumptuously

Opu|lenz F -, *no pl* (*geh*) lavishness

Opus ['o:pʊs, 'ɔpʊs] NT -, **Opera** ['o:pəra] (*pl rare*) work; (*Mus, hum*) opus; (*= Gesamtwerk*) (complete) works *pl*, opus

Ora|kel [o'ra:kl] NT -s, - oracle; **das ~ befragen** to consult the oracle; **er spricht in ~n** (*fig*) he talks in riddles → **Delphi**

ora|kel|haft (*liter*) ADJ oracular, delphic (*liter*) ADV ambiguously, mysteriously; **sich ~ ausdrücken** to talk in riddles

ora|keln [o'ra:kln] *ptp* **orakelt** VI **a** (*= rätseln*) **wir haben lange orakelt, was der Satz bedeuten sollte** we spent a long time trying to figure out what the sentence meant *or* trying to decipher the sentence **b** (*über die Zukunft*) to prophesy, to prognosticate (*hum*)

oral [o'ra:l] ADJ oral ADV orally; **~ mit jdm verkehren** to have oral sex with sb

Oral|ero|tik F, *no pl* oral eroticism

Oral|sex M oral sex

oran|ge [o'rã:ʒə] ADJ *inv* orange; **ein ~** *or* **~ner** (*inf*) **Rock** an orange skirt

Oran|ge [o'rã:ʒə] F -, -n (*Frucht*) orange

Oran|ge NT -, - *or* (*inf*) -s orange

O|ran|gea|de [orã'ʒa:də] F -, -n orangeade (*esp Brit*), orange juice

Oran|geat [orã'ʒa:t] NT -s, -e candied (orange) peel

oran|ge(n)|far|ben [o'rã:ʒə(n)farbn], **oran|ge(n)|far|big** ADJ orange(-coloured) (*Brit*), orange(-colored) (*US*)

Oran|gen-: **Oran|gen|haut** F, *no pl* (*Med*) orange-peel skin; **Oran|gen|mar|me|la|de** F orange marmalade; **Oran|gen|saft** M orange juice

Oran|ge|rie [orãʒə'ri:] F -, -n [-'ri:ən] orangery

Orang-Utan ['o:raŋ-'lu:tan] M -s, -s orang-utan, orang-outang

Ora|ni|en [o'ra:niən] NT -s Orange; **Wilhelm von ~** William of Orange; **der ~-Orden** the Orange Order

Oran|je|frei|staat [o'ranjə-] M Orange Free State

Ora|to|ri|um [ora'to:riʊm] NT -s, **Oratorien** [-riən] **a** (*Mus*) oratorio **b** (*= Betraum*) oratory

ORB [o:lɛr'be:] M - *abbr von* **Ostdeutscher Rundfunk Brandenburg**

Or|bit ['ɔrbɪt] M -s, -s orbit

Or|bi|ter ['ɔrbitɐ] M -s, -s orbiter

Or|ches|ter [ɔr'kɛstɐ, (*old*) ɔr'çɛstɐ] NT -s, - **a** orchestra **b** (*= Orchesterraum*) orchestra (pit)

Or|ches|ter-: **Or|ches|ter|be|glei|tung** F orchestral accompaniment; **Or|ches|ter|fas|sung** F orchestral version; **Or|ches|ter|gra|ben** M orchestra pit

or|chest|ral [ɔrkɛs'tra:l, (*old*) ɔrçɛs'tra:l] ADJ orchestral

or|chest|rie|ren [ɔrkɛs'tri:rən, (*old*) ɔrçɛs'tri:rən] *ptp* **orchestriert** VT to orchestrate

Or|chest|rie|rung F -, -en orchestration

Or|chi|dee [ɔrçi'de:(ə)] F -, -n [-'de:ən] orchid

Or|den ['ɔrdn] M -s, - **a** (*Gemeinschaft*) (holy) order **b** (*= Ehrenzeichen*) decoration; (*Mil*) medal, decoration; **~ tragen** to wear one's decorations; **jdm einen ~ (für etw) verleihen** to decorate sb (for sth); **einen ~ bekommen** to be decorated, to receive a decoration

or|den|ge|schmückt [-gəʃmʏkt] ADJ decorated, covered in decorations *or* (*Mil auch*) medals

Or|dens-: **Or|dens|band** [-bant] NT *pl* -bänder ribbon; (*Mil*) medal ribbon; **Or|dens|bru|der** M **a** (*Eccl*) monk; **meine Ordensbrüder** my brother monks **b** (*von Ritterorden etc*) brother member (of an order); **Or|dens|burg** F *medieval castle built by a religious order*; **Or|dens|frau** F (*old*) nun; **Or|dens|geist|li|che(r)** M *decl as adj* priest (*in a religious order*); **Or|dens|ge|mein|schaft** F (*= Orden*) (religious) order; (*= Mitglieder*) (total) membership of an order; **Or|dens|kleid** NT (*liter*) habit; **Or|dens|meis|ter** M master of an order; **Or|dens|re|gel** F rule (of the order); **Or|dens|schwes|ter** F nun; (*= Krankenschwester*) (nursing) sister; **Or|dens|tracht** F habit

or|dent|lich ['ɔrdntlɪç] ADJ **a** *Mensch, Zimmer* tidy, neat, orderly
b (*= ordnungsgemäß*) **~es Gericht** court of law, law court; **~es Mitglied** full member; **~er Professor** (full) professor
c (*= anständig*) respectable
d (*inf: = tüchtig*) **ein ~es Frühstück** a proper *or* good breakfast; **eine ~e Tracht Prügel** a real beating, a proper hiding (*inf*)
e (*inf: = richtig*) real, proper
f (*= annehmbar, ganz gut*) *Preis, Leistung* reasonable
ADV **a** (*= geordnet*) *zusammenlegen, stapeln, untereinanderschreiben* neatly; **hier geht es ~ zu** we do things by the book here; **in ihrem Haushalt geht es sehr ~ zu** she runs a very orderly household; **bei ihr sieht es immer ~ aus** her house always looks neat and tidy
b (*= ordnungsgemäß*) *anmelden, abmelden, regeln* correctly; *studieren, lernen* seriously; **~ arbeiten**

to be a thorough and precise worker **c** *(= anständig) sich kleiden* appropriately; *hinlegen, aufhängen* properly, right; **sich ~ benehmen** to behave properly **d** *(inf: = tüchtig)* **~ essen** to eat heartily, to eat (really) well; **nicht ~ essen** not to eat properly; **~ trinken** to drink a lot; **ihr habt sicher Hunger, greift ~ zu** you're sure to be hungry, tuck in *(Brit inf)* or dig in *(inf)*; **alle haben ~ zugelangt** everyone got stuck in *(inf)*; **jdn ~ verprügeln** to give sb a real beating; **~ was wegschaffen** *(S Ger)* to get a lot done; **wir haben ~ gearbeitet** we really got down to it; **~ fluchen** to swear like a trooper *(Brit)* or sailor *(US)*; **sich ~ vertun** to be way off *(inf)*; **es hat ~ geregnet** it really rained; **~ Geld verdienen** to make a pile of money *(inf)* **e** *(= annehmbar)* **ganz** or **recht ~** quite well

Or|der ['ɔrdɐ] **F -, -s** or **-n** **a** *(Comm: = Auftrag)* order; **an ~ lautend** made out to order **b** *(dated: = Anweisung)* order; **jdm ~ erteilen** to order or direct or instruct sb; **jdm die ~ geben, etw zu tun** to give sb the order to do sth; **~ erhalten** or **bekommen, etw zu tun** to receive orders to do sth; **sich an eine ~ halten** to keep to one's orders; **ich habe meine ~ und daran halte ich mich** orders are orders, I have my orders and I'm sticking to them

or|dern ['ɔrdɐn] **VT** *(Comm)* to order

Or|di|na|lia [ɔrdi'na:lia] **PL** ordinals *pl*

Or|di|nal|zahl [ɔrdi'na:l-] **F** ordinal number

or|di|när [ɔrdi'nɛ:ɐ] **ADJ** **a** *(= gemein, unfein)* vulgar, common **b** *(= alltäglich)* ordinary; **was, Sie wollen so viel für eine ganz ~e Kiste?** what, you're wanting that much for a perfectly ordinary box or for that old box? **c** *(old Comm: = regulär) Preis* regular, normal **ADV** vulgarly; **~ aussehen** to look like a tart *(Brit inf)* or tramp *(US inf)*; **wenn du dich so ~ schminkst, dann …** if you wear such tarty *(Brit)* or trampy *(US)* make-up, then …

Or|di|na|ri|at [ɔrdina'ria:t] **NT -(e)s, -e** **a** *(Univ)* chair **b** **(erz)bischöfliches ~** archbishop's palace; *(Amt)* bishopric

Or|di|na|ri|us [ɔrdi'na:riʊs] **M -, Ordinarien** [-riən] **a** *(Univ)* professor *(für* of) **b** *(Eccl)* bishop, ordinary **c** *(old Sch)* form or class teacher

Or|di|na|te [ɔrdi'na:tə] **F -, -n** ordinate

Or|di|na|ten|ach|se **F** axis of ordinates

Or|di|na|ti|on [ɔrdina'tsio:n] **F -, -en** **a** *(Eccl)* ordination, ordaining **b** *(Med: = Verordnung)* prescription; *(old: = Sprechstunde)* surgery **c** *(Aus)* (doctor's) surgery *(Brit)* or office *(US)*

or|di|nie|ren [ɔrdi'ni:rən] *ptp* **ordiniert** **VT** **a** *(Eccl)* to ordain; **sich ~ lassen** to be ordained **b** *(Med)* to prescribe **VI** *(Med: old, Aus)* to hold or have surgery (hours) *(Brit)* or office (hours) *(US)*

ord|nen ['ɔrdnən] **VT** **a** *Gedanken, Ideen, Material* to order, to organize; *Sammlung* to sort out; *Sektor, Markt* to organize; *Akten, Finanzen, Hinterlassenschaft, Privatleben* to put in order, to straighten out; **neu ~** *(Struktur, Verhältnisse)* to reorganize; *Kleidung, Haar* to straighten up; **das Steuerrecht wird neu geordnet** tax law is being reformed → *auch* **geordnet** **b** *(= sortieren)* to order, to arrange; *(Comput)* to sort
VR to get into order; **allmählich ordnete sich das Bild** *(fig)* the picture gradually became clear, things gradually fell into place; **die Menge ordnete sich zu einem Festzug** the crowd formed itself into a procession

Ord|ner ['ɔrdnɐ] **M -s, -** *(= Aktenordner)* file; *(Comput)* folder

Ord|ner ['ɔrdnɐ] **M -s, -, Ord|ne|rin** [-ərɪn] **F -, -nen** steward; *(bei Demonstration auch)* marshal

Ord|nung ['ɔrdnʊŋ] ✪ 36.1 **F -, -en** **a** *(= das Ordnen)* ordering; **bei der ~ der Papiere** when putting the papers in order **b** *(= geordneter Zustand)* order; **~ halten** to keep things tidy; **du musst mal ein bisschen ~ in deinen Sachen halten** you must keep your affairs a bit more in order, you must order your affairs a bit more; **in dem Aufsatz sehe ich keine ~** I can see no order or coherence in the essay; **~ schaffen, für ~ sorgen** to sort things out, to put things in order, to tidy things up; **seid ruhig, sonst schaff ich gleich mal ~** *(inf)* be quiet or I'll come and sort you out *(inf)*; **Sie müssen mehr für ~ in Ihrer Klasse sorgen** you'll have to keep more discipline in your class, you'll have to keep your class in better order; **auf ~ halten** or **sehen** to be tidy; **etw in ~ halten** to keep sth in order; *Garten, Haus etc auch* to keep sth tidy; **etw in ~ bringen** *(= reparieren)* to fix sth; *(= herrichten)* to put sth in order; *(= bereinigen)* to clear sth up, to sort sth out; **ich finde es (ganz) in ~, dass …** I think or find it quite right that …; **ich finde es nicht in ~, dass …** I don't think it's right that …; **(das ist) in ~!** *(inf)* (that's) OK *(inf)* or all right!; **geht in ~** *(inf)* sure *(inf)*, that's all right or fine or OK *(inf)*; **Ihre Bestellung geht in ~** we'll see to your order, we'll put your order through; **der ist in ~** *(inf)* he's OK *(inf)* or all right *(inf)*; **da ist etwas nicht in ~** there's something wrong there; **mit ihm/der Maschine ist etwas nicht in ~** there's something wrong or there's something the matter with him/the machine; **die Maschine ist (wieder) in ~** the machine's fixed or in order or all right (again); **das kommt schon wieder in ~** *(inf)* that will soon sort itself out; **es ist alles in bester** or **schönster ~** everything's fine, things couldn't be better; **jetzt ist die/seine Welt wieder in ~** all is right with the/his world again; **jdn zur ~ rufen** to call sb to order; **jdn zur ~ anhalten** to tell sb to be tidy; **jdn zur ~ erziehen** to teach sb tidy habits; **~ muss sein!** we must have order!; **~ ist das halbe Leben** *(Prov)* a tidy mind or tidiness is half the battle; **hier** or **bei uns herrscht ~** we like to have a little order around here; **hier herrscht ja eine schöne ~** *(iro)* this is a nice mess → **Ruhe** **c** *(= Gesetzmäßigkeit)* routine; **alles muss (bei ihm) seine ~ haben** *(räumlich)* he has to have everything in its right or proper place; *(zeitlich)* he does everything according to a fixed schedule; **das Kind braucht seine ~** the child needs a routine **d** *(= Vorschrift)* rules *pl*; **sich an eine ~ halten** to stick or keep to the rules; **ich frage nur der ~ halber** it's only a routine or formal question, I'm only asking as a matter of form; **der ~ gemäß** according to the rules or the rule book **e** *(= Rang, auch Biol)* order; **Straße erster ~** first-class road; **das war ein Skandal erster ~** *(inf)* that was a scandal of the first water *(Brit inf)* or first order; **ein Stern fünfter ~** a star of the fifth magnitude; **die ~ der Nagetiere** the order of rodents

Ord|nungs-: **Ord|nungs|amt** **NT** ≈ town clerk's office; **Ord|nungs|fa|na|ti|ker(in)** **M(F)** fanatic for order; **nicht alle Deutschen sind ~** not all Germans have a mania or passion for order; **Ord|nungs|geld** **NT** = **Ordnungsstrafe**; **ord|nungs|ge|mäß** **ADJ** according to or in accordance with the regulations, proper; **ich werde mich selbst um die ~e Abwicklung Ihrer Bestellung kümmern** I will see to it myself that your order is properly or correctly dealt with **ADV** correctly, properly; **der Prozess ist ~ abgelaufen** the trial took its proper course; **ord|nungs|hal|ber** **ADV** as a matter of form, for the sake of form; **Ord|nungs|hü|ter(in)** **M(F)** *(hum)* custodian of the law *(hum)*; **Ord|nungs|lie|be** **F** love of order; **ord|nungs|lie|bend** **ADJ** tidy, tidy-minded; **Ord|nungs|macht** **F** law enforcement agency; *(im Ausland)* peacekeeper, peacekeeping power; **Ord|nungs|ruf** **M** call to order; **in der Debatte musste der Präsident mehrere ~e erteilen** during the debate the chairman had to call the meeting to order several times; **einen ~ erhalten** to be called to order; **Ord|nungs|sinn** **M**, *no pl* idea or conception of tidiness or order; **Ord|nungs|stra|fe** **F** fine; **jdn mit einer ~ belegen** to fine sb; **ord|nungs|wid|rig** **ADJ** irregular; *Parken, Verhalten (im Straßenverkehr)* illegal **ADV** *parken* illegally; **~ handeln** to go against or to infringe rules or regulations; *(ungesetzlich)* to act illegally; **Ord|nungs|wid|rig|keit** **F** infringement; **Ord|nungs|zahl** **F** **a** *(Math)* ordinal number **b** *(Phys)* atomic number

Or|don|nanz [ɔrdo'nants] **F -, -en** orderly

Or|don|nanz|of|fi|zier **M** aide-de-camp, ADC

Ore|ga|no [o're:gano] **M -, *no pl* *(Bot)* oregano

> **ORF**
>
> **ORF** – short for **Österreichischer Rundfunk** – is a public service broadcasting station, which transmits three radio and two television channels from nine studios in the Austrian **Länder**. Since 1984 it has been operating the culture channel **3sat** in collaboration with **ZDF** and **SRG**. → SRG, ZDF

Or|gan [ɔr'ga:n] **NT -s, -e** **a** *(Med, Biol)* organ; **kein ~ für etw haben** *(inf)* not to have any feel for sth **b** *(inf: = Stimme)* voice **c** *(fig: = Zeitschrift)* organ, mouthpiece **d** *(= Behörde, Einrichtung)* organ, instrument; *(= Beauftragter)* agent; *(von Polizei)* branch, division; **die ausführenden ~e** the executors; **wir sind nur ausführendes ~** we are only responsible for implementing orders; **beratendes ~** advisory body; **die staatlichen ~e** state organs

Or|gan-: **Or|gan|bank** **F** *pl* **-banken** *(Med)* organ bank; **Or|gan|emp|fän|ger(in)** **M(F)** *(Med)* organ recipient; **Or|gan|ent|nah|me** **F** *(Med)* organ removal; **Or|gan|han|del** **M** trade in transplant organs; **Or|gan|händ|ler(in)** **M(F)** organ dealer

Or|ga|ni|gramm [ɔrgani'gram] **NT -s, -e** organization chart

Or|ga|ni|sa|ti|on [ɔrganiza'tsio:n] **F -, -en** organization

Or|ga|ni|sa|ti|ons-: **Or|ga|ni|sa|ti|ons|plan** **M** organization chart; **Or|ga|ni|sa|ti|ons|pro|gram|mie|rer(in)** **M(F)** *(Comput)* application programmer *(Brit)* or programer *(US)*; **Or|ga|ni|sa|ti|ons|ta|lent** **NT** talent or flair for organization; **er ist ein ~** he has a talent or flair for organization

Or|ga|ni|sa|tor [ɔrgani'za:to:ɐ] **M -s, Organisatoren** [-'to:rən], **Or|ga|ni|sa|to|rin** [-'to:rɪn] **F -, -nen** organizer

or|ga|ni|sa|to|risch [ɔrganiza'to:rɪʃ] **ADJ** *Schwierigkeiten, Maßnahmen* organizational; **eine ~e Höchstleistung** a masterpiece of organization; **er ist ein ~es Talent** he has a talent or flair for organization **ADV** organizationally; **er betätigt sich lieber ~, die Durchführung überlässt er anderen** he prefers organizing, leaving others to carry things out; **~ hatte einiges nicht geklappt** the organization left something to be desired; **so viele Leute zu koordinieren, dürfte ~ nicht so einfach sein** coordinating everything for so many people can't be very easy to organize; **dazu brauchen wir einen ~ versierten Menschen** we need someone with good organizational skills

or|ga|nisch [ɔr'ga:nɪʃ] **ADJ** *Chemie, Verbindung, Salze* organic; *Erkrankung, Leiden* physical; **ein ~es Ganzes** an organic whole **ADV** **a** *(Med)* organically, physically; *gesund* physically **b** *(= sinnvoll)* **sich ~ einfügen** to merge, to blend *(in +acc* with, into)

or|ga|ni|sie|ren [ɔrgani'zi:rən] *ptp* **organisiert** **VTI** *(= veranstalten, aufbauen)* to organize; **er kann ausgezeichnet ~** he's excellent at organizing; **etw neu ~** to reorganize sth **VR** to organize

or|ga|ni|siert [ɔrgani'zi:ɐt] **ADJ** organized; **die ~e Kriminalität** organized crime

Or|ga|nis|mus [ɔrga'nɪsmʊs] **M -, Organismen** [-mən] organism

Or|ga|nist [ɔrga'nɪst] M **-en, -en, Or|ga|nis|tin** [-'nɪstɪn] F **-, -nen** *(Mus)* organist

Or|ga|ni|zer ['ɔrganaizɐ] M **-s, -** *(Comput)* organizer

Or|gan-: **Or|gan|kla|ge** F *action brought against the Bundestag or Bundesrat by a Land or political party*; **Or|gan|spen|de** F organ donation; **Or|gan|spen|der|aus|weis** M donor card; **Or|gan|spen|der(in)** M(F) donor *(of an organ)*; **Or|gan|ver|mitt|lung** F transplant coordination; **Or|gan|ver|pflan|zung** F transplant(ation) *(of organs)*

Or|gan|za [ɔr'gantsa] M **-s**, *no pl* organza

Or|gas|mus [ɔr'gasmʊs] M **-, Orgasmen** [-mən] orgasm

or|gas|tisch [ɔr'gastɪʃ] ADJ orgasmic ADV **~ gestört sein** to have problems experiencing an orgasm

Or|gel ['ɔrgl] F **-, -n** *(Mus)* organ

Or|gel|mu|sik F organ music

or|geln ['ɔrgln] VI **a** *(inf: = Orgel spielen)* to play the organ **b** *(Hunt: Hirsch)* to bell **c** *(= tiefes Geräusch machen) (Motor)* to growl; *(Wind)* to howl **d** *(sl: = koitieren)* to screw *(sl)*

Or|gel|pfei|fe F organ pipe; **die Kinder standen da wie die ~n** *(hum)* the children were standing in order of height, the children were standing like a row of Russian dolls

or|gi|as|tisch [ɔr'giastɪʃ] *(geh)* ADJ orgiastic ADV **~ feiern** to celebrate wildly

Or|gie ['ɔrgiə] F **-, -n** orgy; **~n feiern** *(lit)* to have orgies; *(fig)* to go wild; *(Phantasie etc)* to run riot

Ori|ent ['o:riɛnt, o'riɛnt] M **-s**, *no pl* **a** *(liter: = der Osten)* Orient; **das Denken des ~s** Eastern thought; **vom ~ zum Okzident** from east to west **b** *(= arabische Welt)* ≈ Middle East; **der Vordere ~** the Near East; **der Alte ~** the ancient Orient

Ori|en|ta|le [oriɛn'ta:lə] M **-n, -n, Ori|en|ta|lin** [-'ta:lɪn] F **-, -nen** person from the Middle East

ori|en|ta|lisch [oriɛn'ta:lɪʃ] ADJ Middle Eastern

Ori|en|ta|list [oriɛnta'lɪst] M **-en, -en, Ori|en|ta|lis|tin** [-'lɪstɪn] F **-, -nen** ≈ specialist in Middle Eastern and oriental studies; *(= Student)* ≈ student of Middle Eastern and oriental studies

Ori|en|ta|lis|tik [oriɛnta'lɪstɪk] F **-**, *no pl* ≈ Middle Eastern and oriental studies *pl*; **~ studieren** ≈ to do Middle Eastern and oriental studies

ori|en|tie|ren [oriɛn'ti:rən] *ptp* **orientiert** VT **a** *(= unterrichten)* **jdn ~** to put sb in the picture *(über +acc* about); **unsere Broschüre orientiert Sie über unsere Sonderangebote** our brochure gives you information on *or* about our special offers; **darüber ist er gut/falsch/nicht orientiert** he is well/wrongly/not informed on *or* about that

b *(= ausrichten: lit, fig)* to orient, to orientate *(nach, auf +acc* to, towards); **ein positivistisch orientierter Denker** a positivistically orientated thinker; **am Text orientierte Illustrationen** text-related illustrations; **links orientiert sein** to tend to the left; **links orientierte Gruppen** left-wing groups

c *(= hinweisen)* to orient, to orientate *(nach, auf +acc* to, towards)

VI *(= informieren)* **unsere Broschüre orientiert über unsere Sonderangebote** our brochure gives information on *or* about our special offers

VR **a** *(= sich unterrichten)* to inform oneself *(über +acc* about, on)

b *(= sich zurechtfinden)* to orientate oneself *(an +dat, nach* by), to find *or* get one's bearings; **in einer fremden Stadt kann ich mich gar nicht ~** I just can't find my way around in a strange city; **von da an kann ich mich alleine ~** I can find my own way from there

c *(= sich einstellen)* to adapt *or* orientate (oneself) *(an +dat, auf +acc* to)

d *(= sich ausrichten)* to be orientated *(nach, an +dat* towards); **sich nach Norden/links ~** to bear north/left

Ori|en|tie|rung F **-, -en a** *(= Unterrichtung)* information; **zu Ihrer ~** for your information **b** *(= das Zurechtfinden)* orientation; **hier fällt einem die ~ schwer** it's difficult to find *or* get one's bearings here; **die ~ verlieren** to lose one's bearings **c** *(= das Ausrichten)* orientation *(an +dat* according to, *auf +acc* towards) **d** *(= Ausrichtung)* orientation *(an +dat* towards, *auf +acc* to); **sexuelle/politische ~** sexual/political orientation

Ori|en|tie|rungs-: **Ori|en|tie|rungs|punkt** M point of reference; **Ori|en|tie|rungs|sinn** M, *no pl* sense of direction

Ori|ent|tep|pich M Oriental carpet; *(= Brücke)* Oriental rug

Orig. *abbr von* **Original**

Ori|ga|mi [ori'ga:mi] NT **-(s)**, *no pl* origami

Ori|ga|no [o'ri:gano] M **-**, *no pl (Bot)* oregano

ori|gi|nal [origi'na:l] ADJ original ADV **~ Meißener Porzellan** real *or* genuine Meissen porcelain; **Jeans ~ aus (den) USA** original American jeans; **~ verpackt sein** to be in the original packaging; **diese Tapete ist noch ~ erhalten** this is still the original wallpaper; **einige Häuser in der Altstadt sind noch ~ erhalten** some of the houses in the old town are original

Ori|gi|nal [origi'na:l] NT **-s, -e a** original **b** *(Mensch)* character

Ori|gi|nal-: **Ori|gi|nal|aus|ga|be** F first edition; **Ori|gi|nal|ein|zug** M *(bei Kopierer)* automatic sheet feed; **Ori|gi|nal|fas|sung** F original (version); **in ~** in the original; **in der englischen ~** in the original English; **ori|gi|nal|ge|treu** ADJ true to the original ADV **etw ~ nachmalen** to paint a very faithful copy of sth; **die Kopie sieht sehr ~ aus** the copy looks very much like the original; **Farben werden ~ wiedergegeben** colours *(Brit) or* colors *(US)* are faithfully reproduced; **etw ~ übersetzen** to give a true translation of sth

Ori|gi|na|li|tät [originali'tɛ:t] F **-**, *no pl* **a** *(= Echtheit)* authenticity, genuineness **b** *(= Urtümlichkeit)* originality

Ori|gi|nal-: **Ori|gi|nal|ton** M *pl* **-töne** original soundtrack; **(im) ~ Thatcher** *(fig)* in Thatcher's own words; **Ori|gi|nal|über|tra|gung** F live broadcast; **Ori|gi|nal|ver|pa|ckung** F original packaging; **in ~** *(= ungeöffnet)* unopened; *(= in ursprünglicher Verpackung)* in the original packaging

ori|gi|när [origi'nɛ:ɐ] ADJ *Idee, Rechte, Aufgaben* original ADV **eine ~ bayerische Trachtengruppe** an original Bavarian folk dance group; **~ katholische Bräuche** originally Catholic customs

ori|gi|nell [origi'nɛl] ADJ *(= selbstständig) Idee, Argumentation, Interpretation* original; *(= neu)* novel; *(= geistreich)* witty; **sie ist ein ~er Kopf** she's got an original mind; **das finde ich ~ (von ihm)** that's pretty original/witty (of him) ADV originally; *(= witzig)* wittily; **sie denkt/argumentiert ~** her way of thinking/her arguments are very original; **das hat er sich** *(dat)* **sehr ~ ausgedacht** that's a very original idea of his

Or|kan [ɔr'ka:n] M **-(e)s, -e a** hurricane; **der Sturm schwoll zum ~ an** the storm increased to hurricane force **b** *(fig)* storm; **ein ~ der Entrüstung brach los** a storm of indignation broke out

Or|kan-: **or|kan|ar|tig** ADJ *Wind* gale-force; *Beifall* thunderous; *Geschwindigkeit* tremendous; **Or|kan|stär|ke** F hurricane force; **Or|kan|tief** NT hurricane-force depression *or* cyclone *or* low

Or|kus ['ɔrkʊs] M **-**, *no pl (Myth)* Orcus, Hades; **etw im ~ verschwinden lassen** *(hum)* to consign sth to oblivion

Or|na|ment [ɔrna'mɛnt] NT **-(e)s, -e** decoration, ornament; **der Fries ist reines ~** the frieze is purely ornamental *or* decorative; **eine Vase mit figürlichen ~en** a vase decorated with figures; **etw mit ~en versehen** to put ornaments on/in sth

or|na|men|tal [ɔrnamɛn'ta:l] ADJ ornamental ADV ornamentally

or|na|men|tie|ren [ɔrnamɛn'ti:rən] *ptp* **ornamentiert** VT to embellish, to ornament

Or|na|men|tik [ɔrna'mɛntɪk] F **-**, *no pl (Art)* **a** *(= Verzierung)* ornamentation **b** *(Stil eine Epoche)* decorative art

Or|nat [ɔr'na:t] M **-(e)s, -e** regalia *pl*; *(Eccl)* vestments *pl*; *(Jur)* official robes *pl*; **in vollem ~** *(inf)* dressed up to the nines *(Brit inf) or* hilt *(US inf)*

Or|ni|tho|lo|ge [ɔrnito'lo:gə] M **-n, -n, Or|ni|tho|lo|gin** [-'lo:gɪn] F **-, -nen** ornithologist

Or|pheus ['ɔrfɔys] M **-'** Orpheus

or|phisch ['ɔrfɪʃ] ADJ Orphic

Ort [ɔrt] M **-(e)s, -e a** *(= Platz, Stelle)* place; **~ des Treffens** meeting place, venue; **hier bin ich wohl nicht am rechten ~** I've obviously not come to the right place; **das Bügeleisen ist nicht an seinem ~** the iron is not in its usual place; **ein ~ der Stille/des Friedens** a place of quiet/of peace; **ein ~ der Einkehr** a place for thinking quietly; **~ der Handlung** *(Theat)* scene of the action; **an den ~ der Tat** *or* **des Verbrechens zurückkehren** to return to the scene of the crime; **hier ist nicht der ~, darüber zu sprechen** this is not the (time or) place to talk about that; **am angegebenen ~** in the place quoted, loc cit *abbr*; **ohne ~ und Jahr** without indication of place and date of publication; **an ~ und Stelle** on the spot, there and then; **an ~ und Stelle ankommen** to arrive (at one's destination); **das ist höheren ~(e)s entschieden worden** *(hum, form)* the decision came from higher places *or* from above; **höheren ~(e)s ist das bemerkt worden** *(hum, form)* it's been noticed in high places; **an ~ treten** *(Sw fig)* to make no progress *or* headway

b *(= Ortschaft)* place; *(= Dorf)* village; *(= Stadt)* town; **in einem kleinen ~ in Cornwall** in a little spot in Cornwall; **jeder größere ~ hat ein Postamt** a place of any size has a post office; **~e über 100.000 Einwohner** places with more than *or* with over 100,000 inhabitants; **er ist im ganzen ~ bekannt** everyone knows him, the whole village/town *etc* knows him; **wir sind mit dem halben ~ verwandt** we're related to half the people in the place; **am ~** in the place; **das beste Hotel am ~** the best hotel in town; **wir haben keinen Arzt am ~** we have no resident doctor; **am ~ wohnen** to live in the same village/town; **mitten im ~** in the centre *(Brit) or* center *(US)* (of the place/town); **der nächste ~** the next village/town *etc*; **von ~ zu ~** from place to place

Ort M **-(e)s, ¨-er** ['œrtɐ] **a** position *(auch Astron)*; *(Math)* locus **b** *(Min)* coal face, (working) face; **vor ~** at the (coal) face; *(fig)* on the spot; **Wartungsarbeiten vor ~ durchführen** to carry out on-the-spot *or* on-site servicing

Ört|chen ['œrtçən] NT **-s, -** *(= kleiner Ort)* small place; **das (stille** *or* **gewisse) ~** *(inf)* the smallest room *(inf)*

or|ten ['ɔrtn] VT *U-Boot, Flugzeug* to locate, to fix the position of, to get a fix on; *Fischschwarm, Gegenstand* to locate; *(fig: = ausfindig machen)* to locate

or|tho|dox [ɔrto'dɔks] ADJ *(lit, fig)* orthodox ADV **a** *(Rel)* **~ leben** to lead an orthodox life; **~ heiraten** to be married in the Eastern Orthodox Church; *(jüdisch)* to be married in an orthodox Jewish ceremony **b** *(= starr) denken* conventionally; **~ an etw** *(dat)* **festhalten** to stick rigidly to sth

Or|tho|do|xie [ɔrtodɔ'ksi:] F **-**, *no pl* orthodoxy

Or|tho|gra|fie [ɔrtogra'fi:] F **-, -n** [-'fi:ən] orthography

or|tho|gra|fisch [ɔrto'gra:fɪʃ] ADJ orthographic(al) ADV orthographically; **ein ~ schwieriges Wort** a hard *or* difficult word to spell; **er schreibt nicht immer ~ richtig** his spelling is not always correct

Or|tho|gra|phie [ɔrtogra'fi:] *etc* = **Orthografie** *etc*

Or|tho|pä|de [ɔrtoˈpɛːdə] M **-n, -n, Or|tho|pä|din** [-ˈpɛːdɪn] F **-, -nen** orthopaedist *(Brit)*, orthopedist *(US)*, orthopaedic *(Brit) or* orthopedic *(US)* specialist

Or|tho|pä|die [ɔrtopeˈdiː] F **-,** *no pl* **a** *(= Wissenschaft)* orthopaedics *pl (Brit)*, orthopedics *pl (US)* **b** *(inf: = Abteilung)* orthopaedic *(Brit) or* orthopedic *(US)* department; **auf der ~ liegen** to be in an orthopaedic *(Brit) or* orthopedic *(US)* ward, to be in an orthopaedic *(Brit) or* orthopedic *(US)* ward

or|tho|pä|disch [ɔrtoˈpɛːdɪʃ] ADJ orthopaedic *(Brit)*, orthopedic *(US)*

ört|lich [ˈœrtlɪç] ADJ local ADV locally; **das ist ~ verschieden** it varies from place to place; **der Konflikt war ~ begrenzt** the conflict was limited to one area; **jdn/etw ~ betäuben** to give sb/sth a local anaesthetic *(Brit) or* anesthetic *(US)*; **er war nur ~ betäubt** he was only under local anaesthetic *(Brit) or* anesthetic *(US)*, he had only had a local anaesthetic *(Brit) or* anesthetic *(US)*; **~ desorientiert sein** to be disoriented

Ört|lich|keit F **-, -en** locality; **sich mit der ~/den ~en vertraut machen** to get to know the place; **er ist mit den ~en gut vertraut** he knows his way about; **die ~en** *(euph)* the cloakroom *(euph)*

Orts-: **Orts|an|ga|be** F place of publication; *(bei Anschriften)* (name of the) town; *(= Standortangabe)* (name of) location; *(Theat: = Szenenbeschreibung)* location; **ohne ~** no place of publication indicated; **orts|an|säs|sig** ADJ local; **eine schon lange ~e Firma** a long established local firm; **sind Sie schon lange ~?** have you been living here *or* locally for a long time?; **die Ortsansässigen** the local residents; **Orts|aus|gang** M way out of the village/town; **am ~** as you leave the village/town; **Orts|be|reich** M local area; **im ~ München** in the Munich area; **Orts|be|stim|mung** F **Fehler bei der ~** navigational error; **die ~ mit dem Kompass** getting one's bearings with a compass; **die ~ einer Partei vornehmen** to locate a party's political position; **Orts|bild** NT town's/village's apperance; *(architektonisch)* townscape; *(von Großstadt)* cityscape

Ort|schaft [ˈɔrtʃaft] F **-, -en** village; *(größer)* town; **geschlossene ~** built-up *or* restricted area

Orts-: **Orts|ein|gang** M way into the village/town; **orts|fest** ADJ fixed; **orts|fremd** ADJ non-local; **ich bin hier ~** I'm a stranger here; **ein Ortsfremder** a stranger; **orts|ge|bun|den** ADJ local; *(= stationär)* stationary; *Person* tied to the locality *pred*; *Industrie* resources-bound; **Orts|ge|spräch** NT *(Telec)* local call; **Orts|grup|pe** F local branch *or* group; **Orts|kennt|nis** F local knowledge; **(gute) ~se haben** to know one's way around (well); **Orts|kenn|zahl** F *(Telec)* dialling code *(Brit)*, area code *(US)*; **Orts|kern** M centre *(Brit) or* center *(US)*(of the village/town); **Orts|klas|se** F *classification of area according to cost of living for estimating salary weighting allowances*; **Orts|kran|ken|kas|se** F **Allgemeine ~** *compulsory medical insurance scheme*; **orts|kun|dig** ADJ **nehmen Sie sich einen ~en Führer** get a guide who knows his way around; **ich bin nicht sehr ~** I don't know my way around very well; **ein Ortskundiger** somebody who knows his way around *or* who knows the area; **Orts|mit|te** F centre *(Brit)*, center *(US)*; **Orts|na|me** M place name; **Orts|netz** NT *(Telec)* local (telephone) exchange area; *(Elec)* local grid; **Orts|netz|kenn|zahl** F *(Telec)* dialling *(Brit) or* dialing *(US)* code; **Orts|re|gis|ter** NT index of places; **Orts|schild** NT place name sign; **Orts|sinn** M sense of direction; **Orts|ta|rif** M *(bei Briefen)* local postal charge; *(Telec)* charge for local phone call; **orts|üb|lich** ADJ local; **~e Mieten** standard local rents; **das ist hier ~** it is usual *or* customary here, it is (a) local custom here; **Orts|um|ge|hung** F *(Straße)* bypass; **Orts|ver|band** M local committee; **Orts|ver|kehr** M local traffic; **selbst im ~ hat der Brief noch drei Tage gebraucht** even a local letter took three days; **Gebühren im ~** *(Telec)* charges for local (phone) calls; *(von Briefen)* local postage rates; **Orts|zeit** F local time; **Orts|zu|la|ge** F, **Orts|zu|schlag** M (local) weighting allowance

Or|tung [ˈɔrtʊŋ] F **-, -en** locating; **bei (der) ~ eines feindlichen U-Boots ...** when locating an *or* fixing the position of *or* getting a fix on an enemy submarine ...

O-Saft [ˈoː-] M *(inf)* orange juice, O-J *(US inf)*

Os|car [ˈɔskar] M **-(s), -s** Oscar

Os|car|preis|trä|ger(in) M(F) Oscar winner

Os|car|ver|leih|ung F Oscar award ceremony; **die ~** the Oscars *pl (inf)*

Öse [ˈøːzə] F **-, -n** loop; *(an Kleidung)* eye → **Haken**

Ösen|zan|ge F eyelet punch

Ösi [ˈøːzi] M **-s, -s** *(inf)* Austrian

Os|lo [ˈɔslo] NT **-s** Oslo

Os|lo|er [ˈɔsloːɐ] M **-s, -, Os|lo|e|rin** [-ərɪn] F **-, -nen** person from Oslo

Os|ma|ne [ɔsˈmaːnə] M **-n, -n, Os|ma|nin** [-ˈmaːnɪn] F **-, -nen** Ottoman

os|ma|nisch [ɔsˈmaːnɪʃ] ADJ Ottoman; **das Osmanische Reich** the Ottoman Empire

Os|mi|um [ˈɔsmiʊm] NT **-s,** *no pl (abbr* **Os**) osmium

Os|mo|se [ɔsˈmoːzə] F **-,** *no pl* osmosis

OSO *abbr von* **Ostsüdost**

Os|si [ˈɔsi] M **-s, -s** *(inf)* Easterner, East German

> **OSSI**
>
> **Ossi** is the jocular (or sometimes derogatory) term for a citizen of the former East Germany. The 40-year separation of the two Germanies and the differences between their two political systems caused West and East Germans to grow apart from each other. There are still prejudices on both sides about what exactly is typical of an **Ossi** or a **Wessi**.
> → Wessi

Ost [ɔst] M **-(e)s,** *no pl (liter)* **a** East; **aus ~ und West** from East and West; **von ~ nach West** from East to West; **in ~ und West** in East and West, in the East and the West; **der Wind kommt aus ~** the wind is coming from the East; **wo ~ und West zusammentreffen** where East and West meet, where East meets West; **10 Mark ~** *(DDR Hist)* 10 East German marks **b** *(liter: = Ostwind)* east or easterly wind

Ost-, ost- *in cpds (bei Ländern, Erdteilen) (als politische Einheit)* East; *(geografisch auch)* Eastern, the East of ...; *(bei Städten, Inseln)* East; **Ost|af|ri|ka** NT East Africa

Os|tal|gie [ɔstalˈgiː] F **-,** *no pl (inf)* ostalgia, *nostalgia for the good old days of the GDR*

Ost-: **Ost|asi|en** NT Eastern Asia; **Ost|ber|lin** NT *(Hist)* East Berlin; **Ost|ber|li|ner** ADJ *attr* East Berlin; **Ost|ber|li|ner(in)** M(F) East Berliner; **Ost|block** M, *no pl (Hist) (neg!)* Eastern bloc; **Ost|block|land** NT *(Hist) (neg!)*, **Ost|block|staat** M *(Hist) (neg!)* country belonging to the Eastern bloc, Eastern bloc country, Iron Curtain country; **ost|deutsch** ADJ East German; **Ost|deutsch|land** NT *(Geog)* East(ern) Germany

Os|ten [ˈɔstn] M **-s,** *no pl* **a** east; *(von Land)* East; **der Ferne ~** the Far East; **der Nahe ~** the Middle East, the Near East; **der Mittlere ~** *area stretching from Iran and Iraq to India*, the Middle East; **im Nahen und Mittleren ~** in the Middle East; **aus dem ~, von ~ her** from the east; **Flüchtlinge aus dem ~** *(Hist: aus ehemaligen deutschen Ostgebieten) German refugees displaced from former German territories in the East after World War II*; **gegen** *or* **gen** *(liter) or* **nach ~** east(wards), to the east; **nach ~ (hin)** to the east; **im ~ der Stadt/des Landes** in the east of the town/country; **weiter im ~** further east; **im ~ Frankreichs** in the east of France, in eastern France **b** *(Pol)* **der ~** *(= Ostdeutschland)* East Germany; *(dated: = Ostblock)* the East

os|ten|ta|tiv [ɔstɛntaˈtiːf] ADJ pointed ADV pointedly

Os|teo|path [ɔsteoˈpaːt] M **-n, -n, Os|teo|pa|thin** [-ˈpaːtɪn] F **-, -nen** *(Med)* osteopath

Os|teo|po|ro|se [ɔsteopoˈroːzə] F **-,** *no pl (Med)* osteoporosis

Os|ter- [ˈoːstɐ-]: **Os|ter|ei** NT Easter egg; **Os|ter|fei|er|tag** M Easter holiday; **am 2. ~** on Easter Monday; **an den ~en** at the Easter weekend; **über die ~e fahren wir weg** we're going away over the Easter weekend; **Os|ter|fest** NT Easter; **das jüdische ~** the Jewish Feast of the Passover; **Os|ter|feu|er** NT *bonfire lit on Easter Saturday*; **Os|ter|glo|cke** F daffodil; **Os|ter|ha|se** M Easter bunny; **Os|ter|in|sel** F Easter Island; **Os|ter|ker|ze** F paschal candle; **Os|ter|lamm** NT paschal lamb

ös|ter|lich [ˈøːstɐlɪç] ADJ Easter

Os|ter- [ˈoːstɐ-]: **Os|ter|marsch** M Easter peace march; **Os|ter|mon|tag** [ˈoːstɐˈmoːntaːk] M Easter Monday; **Os|ter|mor|gen** M Easter morning

Os|tern [ˈoːstɐn] NT **-, -** Easter; **frohe** *or* **fröhliche ~!** Happy Easter!; **ein verregnetes ~, verregnete ~** a rainy Easter; **an ~** on Easter Day; **zu** *or* **an ~** at Easter; **(zu** *or* **über) ~ fahren wir weg** we're going away at *or* over Easter; **wenn ~ und Pfingsten auf einen Tag fällt** *(hum)* if pigs could fly *(hum)*; **das ist ein Gefühl wie Weihnachten und ~ (zusammen)** it's like having Christmas and Easter rolled into one, it's like having all your Christmases come at once

Os|ter|nacht [ˈoːstɐ-] F Easter eve; *(kirchliche Feier)* Easter eve service

Ös|ter|reich [ˈøːstəraiç] NT **-s** Austria; **~-Ungarn** *(Hist)* Austria-Hungary

Ös|ter|rei|cher [ˈøːstəraiçɐ] M **-s, -, Ös|ter|rei|che|rin** [-ərɪn] F **-, -nen** Austrian; **er ist ~** he's (an) Austrian

ös|ter|rei|chisch [ˈøːstəraiçɪʃ] ADJ Austrian; **~-ungarisch** *(Hist)* Austro-Hungarian; **das Österreichische** *(Ling)* Austrian

Os|ter- [ˈoːstɐ-]: **Os|ter|sonn|tag** [ˈoːstɐˈzɔntaːk] M Easter Sunday; **Os|ter|spiel** NT Easter (passion) play

Ost|er|wei|te|rung [ˈɔst-] F *(von Nato, EU)* eastward expansion

Os|ter|wo|che [ˈoːstɐ-] [ˈoːstɐ-] F Easter week

Ost-: **Ost|eu|ro|pa** NT East(ern) Europe; **ost|eu|ro|pä|isch** ADJ East(ern) European; **Ost|frie|se** [-friːzə] M, **Ost|frie|sin** [-friːzɪn] F East Frisian; **ost|frie|sisch** ADJ East Frisian; **Ost|frie|si|sche In|seln** PL East Frisian Islands *pl*; **Ost|fries|land** [-ˈfriːslant] NT **-s** East Frisia; **Ost|geld** NT *(DDR)* East German money; **ost|ger|ma|nisch** ADJ *(Ling)* East Germanic; **Ost|go|ten** PL *(Hist)* Ostrogoths *pl*

os|ti|nat [ɔstiˈnaːt] ADJ *(Mus)* ostinato; **~er Bass** ground bass, bass ostinato

Os|ti|na|to [ɔstiˈnaːto] NT OR M **-s, -s** *or* **Ostinati** [-ti] ostinato

Ost-: **ost|in|disch** [ˈɔstˈɪndɪʃ] ADJ East Indian; **Ostindische Kompanie** East India Company; **Ost|ju|de** M, **Ost|jü|din** F East European Jew; **Ost|kir|che** F Orthodox *or* Eastern Church; **Ost|ko|lo|ni|sa|ti|on** F *(Hist) German medieval colonization of Eastern Europe*; **Ost|küs|te** F East coast

Ost|ler [ˈɔstlɐ] M **-s, -, Ost|le|rin** [-ərɪn] F **-, -nen** *(inf)* East German

öst|lich [ˈœstlɪç] ADJ *Richtung, Winde* easterly; *Gebiete* eastern; **30° ~er Länge** 30° (longitude) east ADV **~ von Hamburg/des Rheins** (to the) east of Hamburg/of the Rhine PREP *+gen* (to the) east of

Ost-: **Ost|mark** F **a** *no pl (Hist)* Austria **b** *pl* **-mark** *(DDR Hist inf)* East German Mark; **Ost|**

nord|ost M east-north-east; **Ost|nord|os|ten** M east-north-east; **Ost|po|li|tik** F *(Hist)* Ostpolitik, *West German foreign policy regarding the Eastern bloc especially East Germany and East Berlin*; **Ost|preu|ße** M, **Ost|preu|ßin** F East Prussian; **Ost|preu|ßen** NT East Prussia; **ost|preu|ßisch** ADJ East Prussian

Öst|ro|gen [œstro'ge:n] NT **-s, -e** oestrogen *(Brit)*, estrogen *(US)*

Ost-: **Ost|rom** NT *(Hist)* Eastern (Roman) Empire, Byzantine Empire; **ost|rö|misch** ADJ Byzantine

Ost|see ['ɔstze:] F **die ~** the Baltic (Sea)

Ost|see- *in cpds* Baltic; **Ost|see|ha|fen** M Baltic port; **Ost|see|in|sel** F island in the Baltic; **Ost|see|küs|te** F Baltic coast; **Ost|see|rat** M Baltic Council

Ost-: **Ost|staa|ten** PL *(in USA)* the Eastern states *pl*, the East coast states *pl*; **Ost|süd|ost** M east-south-east; **Ost|süd|os|ten** M east-south-east; **Ost|ver|trä|ge** PL *(Pol) political, social and economic agreements made between West Germany and some Eastern bloc countries in the early 1970s*; **ost|wärts** [-vɛrts] ADV eastwards

Ost-West-: **Ost-West-Ach|se** [-'vɛst-] F East-West link; **Ost-West-Be|zie|hung|en** F *pl* East-West relations *pl*; **Ost-West-Ver|hand|lun|gen** PL East-West negotiations *pl*

Ost|wind M east *or* easterly wind

OSZE [o:lɛstsɛt'le:] F *abbr von* **Organisation für Sicherheit und Zusammenarbeit in Europa** OSCE

os|zil|lie|ren [ɔstsɪ'li:rən] *ptp* **oszilliert** VI to oscillate

Os|zil|lo|graf, **Os|zil|lo|graph** [ɔstsɪlo'gra:f] M **-en, -en** oscillograph

O-Ton ['o:-] M *pl* **-Töne** *abbr von* **Originalton**

Ot|ter ['ɔtɐ] M **-s, -** otter

Ot|ter F **-, -n** viper, adder

Ot|tern|ge|zücht NT *(Bibl)* brood of vipers

Ot|to|ma|ne [ɔto'ma:nə] F **-, -n** ottoman

Ot|to|mo|tor ['ɔto-] M internal combustion engine, otto engine

ÖTV [ø:te:'fau] F - *abbr von* **Gewerkschaft Öffentliche Dienste, Transport und Verkehr** ≈ TGWU *(Brit)*, ≈ TWU *(US)*

Öt|zi ['œtsi] M **-s** Otzi, the Iceman, *frozen mummified corpse found in the Alps in 1991 (fig inf)* dinosaur

out [aut] ADJ *pred Mode etc* out

Out|door-: **Out|door|ja|cke** F outdoor jacket; **Out|door|sport** M outdoor sports *pl*

ou|ten ['autn] *(inf)* VT *(als Homosexuellen)* to out *(inf)*; *(als Trinker, Spitzel etc)* to reveal, to expose VR *(als Homosexueller)* to come out *(inf)*; **du solltest dich endlich ~** you really should come out *(inf)*; **er outete sich als Schwuler** he came out *(inf)*

Out|fit ['autfɪt] NT **-(s), -s** outfit

Ou|ting ['autɪŋ] NT **-s** *(inf: als Homosexueller)* outing *(inf)*; **er hat Angst vor dem ~** *(geoutet zu werden)* he's afraid of being outed *(inf)*; *(sich zu outen)* he's afraid of coming out *(inf)*

Out|sour|cing ['autsɔ:rsɪŋ] NT **-s**, *no pl* outsourcing

Ou|ver|tü|re [uvɛr'ty:rə] F **-, -n** overture

oval [o'va:l] ADJ oval ADV **ein ~ geformter Spiegel** an oval mirror; **ein ~ gerahmtes Bild** a picture with an oval frame

Oval [o'va:l] NT **-s, -e** oval

Ova|ti|on [ova'tsio:n] F **-, -en** ovation *(für jdn/etw* for sb/sth); **jdm eine ~** *or* **~en darbringen** to give sb an ovation *or* a standing ovation; **stehende ~en** standing ovations

Over|all ['o:vərɔ:l] M **-s, -s** overalls *pl*

Over|head-: **Over|head|fo|lie** F transparency; **Over|head|pro|jek|tor** M overhead projector

Over|kill ['o:vɐkɪl] M **-(s)** overkill

Ovo|lac|to|ve|ge|ta|bi|le(r) [ovo'laktovegeta-'bi:lə] MF *decl as adj* ovo-lacto-vegetarian

ÖVP [ø:fau'pe:] F - *abbr von* **Österreichische Volkspartei**

Ovu|la|ti|on [ovula'tsio:n] F **-, -en** ovulation

Ovu|la|ti|ons|hem|mer [-hɛmɐ] M **-s, -** ovulation inhibitor

Oxer ['ɔksɐ] M **-s, -** *(Sport)* oxer

Oxid [ɔ'ksi:t] NT **-(e)s, -e**, **Oxyd** [ɔ'ksy:t] NT **-(e)s, -e** [-də] oxide

Oxi|da|ti|on [ɔksida'tsio:n] F **-, -en**, **Oxy|da|ti|on** [ɔksyda'tsio:n] F **-, -en** oxidation

oxi|die|ren [ɔksi'di:rən] *ptp* **oxidiert**, **oxy|die|ren** [ɔksy'di:rən] *ptp* **oxydiert** VTI *(vi: aux sein or haben)* to oxidize

OZ *abbr von* **Oktanzahl**

Oze|an ['o:tsea:n, otse'a:n] M **-s, -e** ocean; **ein ~ von Tränen** an ocean of tears

Oze|an|damp|fer M ocean steamer

Oze|a|ni|en [otse'a:niən] NT **-s** Oceania

oze|a|nisch [otse'a:nɪʃ] ADJ *Flora, Klima* oceanic; *Sprachen, Kunst* Oceanic

Oze|a|no|gra|fie, **Oze|a|no|gra|phie** [otseanogra'fi:] F **-**, *no pl* oceanography

Oze|an|rie|se M *(inf)* ocean liner

Oze|lot ['o:tselɔt, 'ɔtselɔt] M **-s, -e** ocelot

Ozon [o'tso:n] NT OR (INF) M **-s**, *no pl* ozone

Ozon-, **ozon-** *in cpds* ozone; **Ozon|alarm** M ozone warning; **Ozon|ge|halt** M ozone content; **Ozon|hül|le** F ozone layer; **Ozon|loch** NT hole in the ozone layer; **Ozon|schicht** F ozone layer; **Ozon|schild** M, *no pl* ozone shield; **Ozon|the|ra|pie** F ozone therapy; **Ozon|war|nung** F ozone warning; **Ozon|wert** M ozone level

P

P, p [peː] NT -, - P, p

paar [paːɐ] ADJ *inv* **ein ~** a few; *(= zwei oder drei auch)* a couple of; **ein ~ Mal(e)** a few times; *(= zwei- oder dreimal auch)* a couple of times, once or twice; **schreiben Sie mir ein ~ Zeilen** drop me a line; **die ~ Cent, die es kostet ...** the few cents that it costs ...; **der Bus fährt alle ~ Minuten** there's a bus every few minutes; **wenn er alle ~ Minuten mit einer Frage kommt ...** if he comes along with a question every other minute ...; **du kriegst ein ~!** *(inf)* I'll land you one! *(Brit inf)*, I'll kick your butt *(US inf)*

Paar [paːɐ] NT -s, -e pair; *(= Mann und Frau auch)* couple; **ein ~ Schuhe** a pair of shoes; **zwei ~ Socken** two pairs of socks; **ein ~ Ochsen** a yoke of oxen; **ein ~ Würstchen** two sausages; **ein ~ bilden** to make *or* form a pair; **ein ~ mit jdm bilden** to pair off with sb **ein ~ werden** *(liter: = heiraten)* to become man and wife *(form)*, to be made one *(liter)*; **ein ungleiches ~** an odd pair; *(Menschen auch)* an odd *or* unlikely couple; **ein ~ sein** to be a couple *or* an item *(inf)*; **das sind zwei ~ Stiefel** *or* **Schuhe** *(fig)* they are two completely different things

Paar|be|zie|hung F relationship, partnership

paa|ren [ˈpaːrən] VT *Tiere* to mate, to pair; *(Sport)* to match; *(Chem)* to pair; *(fig)* to combine; **in seinen Bemerkungen sind Witz und Geist gepaart** his remarks show a combination of wit and intellect, in his remarks wit is coupled with intellect VR *(Tiere)* to mate, to copulate; *(Chem)* to be paired; *(fig)* to be coupled *or* combined

Paar|hu|fer [-huːfɐ] M *(Zool)* cloven-hoofed animal, even-toed ungulate *(spec)*

paa|rig [ˈpaːrɪç] ADJ in pairs; **~e Blätter** paired leaves

Paar-: **Paar|lauf** M, **Paar|lau|fen** NT pair-skating, pairs *pl*; **paar+lau|fen** VI *sep irreg aux sein infin, ptp only* to pair-skate

paar|mal △ [ˈpaːɐmaːl] ADV → **paar**

Paar|reim M *(Poet)* rhyming couplet

Paa|rung [ˈpaːrʊŋ] F -, -en **a** *(Sport, fig liter)* combination; *(Sport: = Gegnerschaft)* draw, match **b** *(= Kopulation)* mating, copulation; *(= Kreuzung)* crossing, mating

Paa|rungs|zeit F mating season

Paar-: **paar|wei|se** ADV in pairs, in twos; **Paar|ze|her** [-tseːɐ] M -s, - cloven-hoofed animal, even-toed ungulate *(spec)*

Pacht [paxt] F -, -en lease; *(Entgelt)* rent; **etw in ~ geben** to lease sth (out), to let out sth on lease; **etw in ~ nehmen** to take sth on lease, to lease sth; **etw in** *or* **zur ~ haben** to have sth on lease *or* (on) leasehold

Pacht|brief M lease

pach|ten [ˈpaxtn] VT to take a lease on, to lease; **du hast das Sofa doch nicht für dich gepachtet** *(inf)* don't hog the sofa *(inf)*, you haven't got a monopoly on the sofa *(inf)*; **er tat so, als hätte er die Weisheit für sich (allein) gepachtet** *(inf)* he behaved as though he was the only clever person around

Päch|ter [ˈpɛçtɐ] M -s, -, **Päch|te|rin** [-ərɪn] F -, -nen tenant, leaseholder, lessee *(form)*; **er ist ~ eines Bauernhofs** *or* **auf einem Bauernhof** he's a tenant farmer

Pacht-: **Pacht|er|trag** M net rent; **Pacht|geld** NT rent; **Pacht|grund|stück** NT leasehold property; **Pacht|gut** NT, **Pacht|hof** M smallholding; **Pacht|ver|trag** M lease; **ein ~ über 20 Jahre** a 20-year lease; **Pacht|zins** M rent

Pach|tung [ˈpaxtʊŋ] F -, -en leasing

pacht|wei|se ADV leasehold, on lease

Pack [pak] M -(e)s, -e *or* ⸚e [ˈpɛkə] *(von Zeitungen, Büchern, Wäsche)* stack, pile; *(zusammengeschnürt)* bundle, pack; **zwei ~(e) Spielkarten** two packs of (playing) cards

Pack NT -s, *no pl (pej)* rabble *pl (pej)*, riffraff *pl (pej)*; **~ schlägt sich, ~ verträgt sich** *(Prov)* riffraff like that are at each other's throats one minute and friends again the next *(pej)*

Pack NT -s, -s *(= Paket)* pack, package

Päck|chen [ˈpɛkçən] NT -s, - package, (small) parcel; *(Post)* small packet; *(= Packung)* packet, pack; **ein ~ Zigaretten** a packet *or* pack *(esp US)* of cigarettes; **ein ~ Spielkarten** a pack of (playing) cards; **ein ~ aufgeben** to post *(Brit)* *or* mail *(esp US)* a small parcel; **jeder hat sein ~ zu tragen** *(fig inf)* we all have our cross to bear

Pack|eis NT pack ice

pa|ckeln [ˈpakln] VI *(Aus inf: = paktieren)* to make a deal *(inf)*

pa|cken [ˈpakn] VT **a** *Koffer* to pack; *Paket* to make up; *(= verstauen)* to stow *or* pack (away); *(Comput: = komprimieren) Daten* to pack; **Sachen in ein Paket ~** to make things up into a parcel; **etw ins Paket ~** to put *or* pack sth into the parcel; **etw in Holzwolle ~** to pack sth (up) in wood shavings; **etw in Watte ~** to pack *or* wrap sth (up) in cotton wool; **jdn ins Bett ~** *(inf)* to tuck sb up (in bed) → **Watte**

b *(= fassen)* to grab (hold of), to seize, to grasp; *(Gefühle)* to grip, to seize; **jdn am** *or* **beim Kragen ~** *(inf)* to grab *or* seize sb by the collar; **von der Leidenschaft gepackt** in the grip of passion; **jdn bei der Ehre ~** to appeal to sb's sense of honour *(Brit)* *or* honor *(US)*; **den hat es aber ganz schön gepackt** *(inf)* he's got it bad *(inf)*

c *(fig: = mitreißen)* to grip, to thrill, to enthral; **das Theaterstück hat mich gepackt** I was really gripped by the play

d *(inf: = schaffen)* to manage; **hast du die Prüfung gepackt?** did you (manage to) get through the exam?; **du packst das schon** you'll manage it OK

e *(inf: = gehen)* **~ wirs!** let's go

VI **a** *(= den Koffer packen)* to pack

b *(fig: = mitreißen)* to thrill

VR **a** *(inf: = abhauen)* to clear off *(Brit inf)* *or* out *(inf)*; **packt euch (fort)!** clear off! *(inf)*, beat it! *(inf)*; **pack dich nach Hause!** clear off home! *(Brit inf)*, clear out and go home! *(inf)*

b *(inf: = sich hinlegen)* to crash out *(inf)*; **sich aufs Sofa ~** to crash out on the couch *(inf)*

Pa|cken [ˈpakn] M -s, - heap, pile, stack; *(zusammengeschnürt)* package, bundle; **ein ~ Arbeit** *(inf)* a pile of work

Pa|cker [ˈpakɐ] M -s, - *(Hunt)* boarhound

Pa|cker [ˈpakɐ] M -s, -, **Pa|cke|rin** [-ərɪn] F -, -nen packer

Pa|cke|rei [pakəˈrai] F -, -en **a** packing department **b** *no pl (inf)* packing

Pa|ckerl NT -s, - *(Aus)* packet

Pack-: **Pack|esel** M packass, packmule; *(fig)* packhorse; **Pack|lei|nen** NT, **Pack|lein|wand** F burlap, gunny, bagging; **Pack|ma|te|ri|al** NT packing material; **Pack|pa|pier** NT wrapping *or* brown paper; **Pack|pferd** NT packhorse; **Pack|raum** M packing room; **Pack|sat|tel** M pack-saddle; **Pack|ta|sche** F saddlebag; **Pack|tier** NT pack animal, beast of burden

Pa|ckung [ˈpakʊŋ] F -, -en **a** *(= Schachtel)* packet, pack; *(von Pralinen)* box; **eine ~ Zigaretten** a packet *or* pack *(esp US)* of cigarettes **b** *(Med)* compress, pack; *(Kosmetik)* face pack *or* mask; **sich** *(dat)* **eine ~ machen** to have a face pack *or* mask; **jdm eine ~ machen** to put a face pack *or* mask on sb **c** *(Tech)* gasket; *(Straßenbau)* pitching *no pl*, ballast *no pl* **d** *(inf: = Niederlage)* thrashing, hammering *(inf)*

Pa|ckungs|bei|la|ge F *(bei Medikamenten)* enclosed instructions *pl* for use, patient information leaflet

Pack-: **Pack|wa|gen** M luggage van *(Brit)*, baggage car *(US)*; **Pack|zet|tel** M packing slip, docket

Pä|da|go|ge [pɛdaˈgoːgə] M -n, -n, **Pä|da|go|gin** [-ˈgoːgɪn] F -, -nen educationalist, pedagogue *(form)*

Pä|da|go|gik [pɛdaˈgoːgɪk] F -, *no pl* education, educational theory, pedagogy *(rare)*

pä|da|go|gisch [pɛdaˈgoːgɪʃ] ADJ educational, pedagogical *(form)*; **~e Hochschule** college of education, teacher-training college *(for primary teachers)*; **eine ~e Ausbildung** a training in education, a pedagogical training; **seine ~en Fähigkeiten** his ability to teach, his teaching ability; **das ist nicht sehr ~** that's not a very educationally sound thing to do ADV educationally, pedagogically; **~ falsch** wrong from an educational point of view; **das Spielzeug ist ~ wertvoll** it is an educational toy

pä|da|go|gi|sie|ren [pɛdagogiˈziːrən] *ptp* **pädagogisiert** VT *(= pädagogisch ausrichten)* to bring into line with educational *or* pedagogical theory VI *(inf: = über Pädagogik reden)* to talk education

Pad|del [ˈpadl] NT -s, - paddle

Pad|del-: **Pad|del|boot** NT canoe; **Pad|del|boot|fah|rer(in)** M(F) canoeist

pad|deln [ˈpadln] VI *aux sein or haben* to paddle; *(als Sport)* to canoe; *(= schwimmen)* to dog-paddle

Padd|ler [ˈpadlɐ] M -s, -, **Padd|le|rin** [-ərɪn] F -, -nen canoeist

Pä|de|rast [pɛdeˈrast] M -en, -en pederast

Pä|de|ras|tie [pɛderasˈtiː] F -, *no pl* pederasty

Pä|di|at|rie [pɛdiaˈtriː] F -, *no pl* paediatrics *sing (Brit)*, pediatrics *sing (US)*

pä|di|at|risch [pɛˈdiaːtrɪʃ] ADJ paediatric *(Brit)*, pediatric *(US)*

Pä|do|phi|le(r) [pɛdoˈfiːlə] MF *decl as adj* paedophile *(Brit)*, pedophile *(US)*

Pä|do|phi|lie [pɛdofiˈliː] F -, *no pl* paedophilia *(Brit)*, pedophilia *(US)*

paff [paf] INTERJ bang

paf|fen ['pafn] (inf) VI a (= heftig rauchen) to puff away b (= nicht inhalieren) to puff; **du paffst ja bloß!** you're just puffing at it! VT to puff (away) at

Pa|ge ['pa:ʒə] M -n, -n (Hist) page; (= Hotelpage) page (boy), bellboy, bellhop (US)

Pa|gen|fri|sur F, **Pa|gen|kopf** M page-boy (hairstyle or haircut)

Pa|ger ['pe:dʒɐ] M -s, - (Telec) pager

Pa|ging-Dienst ['pe:dʒɪŋ-] M paging service

pa|gi|nie|ren [pagi'ni:rən] ptp **paginiert** VT to paginate

Pa|gi|nie|rung [pagi'ni:rʊŋ] F pagination, page numbering

Pa|go|de [pa'go:də] F -, -n pagoda

pah [pa:] INTERJ bah, pooh, poof

Pail|let|te [pai'jɛtə] F -, -n sequin

pail|let|ten|be|setzt [pai'jɛtnbəzɛtst] ADJ attr Kleidungsstück sequin(n)ed

Pak [pak] F -, -s abbr von **Panzerabwehrkanone** anti-tank gun

Pa|ket [pa'ke:t] NT -s, -e (= Bündel) pile, stack; (zusammengeschnürt) bundle, package; (= Packung) packet; (Post) parcel; (fig: von Angeboten, Gesetzesvorschlägen) package; (= Aktienpaket) dossier; (Comput) package; **ein ~ von Maßnahmen** a package of measures

Pa|ket-: **Pa|ket|ad|res|se** F stick-on address label; **Pa|ket|an|nah|me** F parcels office; **Pa|ket|aus|ga|be** F parcels office; **Pa|ket|bom|be** F parcel bomb; **Pa|ket|boot** NT packet (boat), mailboat; **Pa|ket|dienst** M parcel service, parcel post; **Pa|ket|kar|te** F dispatch form; **Pa|ket|post** F parcel post; **Pa|ket|schal|ter** M parcels counter; **Pa|ket|schnur** F parcel string, twine; **Pa|ket|ver|mitt|lung** F (Comput) packet switching

Pa|kis|tan ['pa:kɪsta:n] NT -s Pakistan

Pa|kis|ta|ner [pakɪs'ta:nɐ] M -s, -, **Pa|kis|ta|ne|rin** [-ərɪn] F -, -nen, **Pa|kis|ta|ni** [pakɪs'ta:ni] M -(s), -(s) or f -, -s Pakistani

pa|kis|ta|nisch [pakɪs'ta:nɪʃ] ADJ Pakistani

Pakt [pakt] M -(e)s, -e pact, agreement; **einen ~ (ab)schließen (mit)** to make a pact or agreement or deal (inf) (with); **einem ~ beitreten** to enter into an agreement

pak|tie|ren [pak'ti:rən] ptp **paktiert** VI a (old: = Bündnis schließen) to make a pact or an agreement b (pej) to make a deal (inf)

Pa|la|din [pala'di:n, 'pa:ladi:n, 'paladi:n] M -s, -e (Hist) paladin; (pej) (= Gefolgsmann) henchman, hireling; (= Land) satellite

Pa|lais [pa'lɛ:] NT -, - palace

Pa|läo-, **pa|läo-** [palɛo] PREF palaeo- (Brit), paleo- (US)

Pa|läo|li|thi|kum [palɛo'li:tɪkʊm] NT -s Palaeolithic (Brit), Paleolithic (US)

Pa|lä|on|to|lo|gie [palɛɔntolo'gi:] F -, no pl palaeontology (Brit), paleontology (US)

Pa|last [pa'last] M -(e)s, **Paläste** [pa'lɛstə] (lit, fig) palace

pa|last|ar|tig ADJ palatial

Pa|läs|ti|na [palɛ'sti:na] NT -s Palestine

Pa|läs|ti|nen|ser [palɛsti'nɛnzɐ] M -s, -, **Pa|läs|ti|nen|se|rin** [-ərɪn] F -, -nen Palestinian

Pa|läs|ti|nen|ser|füh|rer M Palestinian leader

Pa|läs|ti|nen|ser|tuch NT pl **-tücher** keffiyeh (esp Brit), kaffiyeh

pa|läs|ti|nen|sisch [palɛsti'nɛnzɪʃ], **pa|läs|ti|nisch** [palɛ'sti:nɪʃ] ADJ Palestinian

Pa|last-: **Pa|last|re|vo|lu|ti|on** F (lit, fig) palace revolution; **Pa|last|wa|che** F palace guard

pa|la|tal [pala'ta:l] ADJ palatal

Pa|la|tal|laut [pala'ta:l-] M palatal (sound)

Pa|lat|schin|ke [pala'tʃɪŋkə] F -, -n (Aus) stuffed pancake

Pa|la|ver [pa'la:vɐ] NT -s, - (lit, fig inf) palaver (inf)

pa|la|vern [pa'la:vɐn] ptp **palavert** VI (lit, fig inf) to palaver (inf)

Pa|le|tot ['paləto] M -s, -s (obs) greatcoat, overcoat

Pa|let|te [pa'lɛtə] F -, -n a (Malerei) palette; (fig) range b (= Stapelplatte) pallet

pa|let|ti [pa'lɛti] ADV (inf) OK (inf); **alles ~!** everything's OK! (inf)

Pa|li|sa|de [pali'za:də] F -, -n palisade

Pa|li|sa|den|wand F, **Pa|li|sa|den|zaun** M palisade, stockade

Pa|li|san|der M -s, -, **Pa|li|san|der|holz** NT jacaranda

Pal|la|di|um [pa'la:diʊm] NT -s, no pl (abbr **Pd**) palladium

Pal|li|a|tiv [palia'ti:f] NT -s, -e [-və], **Pal|li|a|ti|vum** [palia'ti:vʊm] NT -s, **Palliativa** [-va] (Med) palliative

Pal|li|a|tiv|me|di|zin F palliative medicine

Pal|me ['palmə] F -, -n palm; **jdn auf die ~ bringen** (inf) to make sb see red (inf), to make sb's blood boil (inf); **unter ~n** under (the) palm trees; **einen von der ~ locken** (sl: = onanieren) to visit palm and her five sisters (Brit sl), to have a date with Mrs Handy (US sl)

Palm|fett NT (= Palmbutter) palm butter; (= Palmöl) palm oil

Pal|min® [pal'mi:n] NT -s, no pl cooking fat (made from coconut oil)

Palm-: **Palm|kätz|chen** NT pussy willow, catkin (Brit); **Palm|li|lie** F yucca; **Palm|öl** NT palm oil; **Palm|sonn|tag** M Palm Sunday

Palm|top ['pa:mtɔp] M -s, -s palmtop

Palm|top-Or|ga|ni|zer M (Comput) palmtop organizer

Palm-: **Palm|we|del** M palm leaf; **Palm|wein** M palm wine; **Palm|zweig** M palm leaf

Pam|pa ['pampa] F -, -s pampas pl

Pam|pas|gras ['pampas-] NT pampas grass

Pam|pe ['pampə] F -, no pl paste; (pej) slop (inf), mush (inf)

Pam|pel|mu|se [pampl'mu:zə] F -, -n grapefruit

Pam|pers® ['pɛmpɐs] PL Pampers® pl, (disposable) nappies pl (Brit) or diapers pl (US)

Pamph|let [pam'fle:t] NT -(e)s, -e lampoon

pam|pig ['pampɪç] (inf) ADJ a (= breiig) gooey (inf); Kartoffeln soggy b (= frech) stroppy (Brit inf), bad-tempered ADV (= frech) **jdm ~ antworten** to talk back to sb; **jdm ~ kommen** to be stroppy (Brit inf) or bad-tempered with sb

Pan [pa:n] M -s (Myth) Pan

pan- [pa:n] PREF pan-; **panafrikanisch** pan-African; **panamerikanisch** pan-American; **panarabisch** pan-Arab; **Panslawismus** pan-Slavism

Pa|na|de [pa'na:də] F -, -en (Cook) coating (of eggs, flour and breadcrumbs)

Pa|na|ma ['panama, 'pa:nama] NT -s, -s a Panama b (auch **Panamahut**) Panama (hat)

Pa|na|ma|ka|nal M, no pl Panama Canal

pa|na|schie|ren [pana'ʃi:rən] ptp **panaschiert** VI (Pol) to split one's ticket VT **panaschierte Blätter** variegated leaves

pan|chro|ma|tisch [pankro'ma:tɪʃ] ADJ panchromatic

Pan|da ['panda] M -s, -s panda

Pan|dä|mo|ni|um [pandɛ'mo:niʊm] NT -s, **Pandämonien** [-niən] (Myth, fig) pandemonium

Pan|dek|ten [pan'dɛktn] PL (Jur) Pandects pl, Digest

Pan|de|mie [pande'mi:] F -, -n [-'mi:ən] (Med) pandemic

Pa|neel [pa'ne:l] NT -s, -e (form) (einzeln) panel; (= Täfelung) panelling (Brit), paneling (US), wainscoting

pa|nee|lie|ren [pane'li:rən] ptp **paneeliert** VT (form) to panel

Pan|flö|te ['pa:n-] F panpipes pl, Pan's pipes pl

päng [pɛŋ] INTERJ bang

Pa|nier [pa'ni:ɐ] NT -s, -e (obs) banner, standard; **Freiheit sei euer ~!** (liter) let freedom be your slogan or motto! (liter); **unter dem ~ der Freiheit kämpfen** (liter) to fight under the banner of freedom; **sich (dat) etw aufs ~ schreiben** (fig) to take or adopt sth as one's motto

pa|nie|ren [pa'ni:rən] ptp **paniert** VT to bread, to coat with breadcrumbs

Pa|nier|mehl NT breadcrumbs pl

Pa|nik ['pa:nɪk] F -, -en panic; **(eine) ~ brach aus** or **breitete sich aus** panic broke out or spread, there was panic; **in ~ ausbrechen** or **geraten** to panic, to get into a panic; **jdn in ~ versetzen** to throw sb into a state of panic; **von ~ ergriffen** panic-stricken; **nur keine ~!** don't panic!; **kein Grund zur ~!** no reason to panic!; **die ~, die ihn zu überwältigen drohte** the feeling of panic that threatened to overwhelm him

Pa|nik-: **Pa|nik|kauf** M (Comm) panic buying; **Pa|nik|ma|che** F (inf) panicmongering (Brit), inciting panic; **Pa|nik|stim|mung** F state of panic; **Pa|nik|ver|kauf** M (Comm) panic selling; **Panikverkäufe** panic selling sing

pa|nisch ['pa:nɪʃ] ADJ no pred panic-stricken; **~e Angst** panic-stricken fear, terror; **sie hat ~e Angst vor Schlangen** she's terrified of snakes, snakes scare her out of her wits; **er hatte eine ~e Angst zu ertrinken** he was terrified of drowning; **~er Schrecken** panic ADV in panic, frantically; **~ reagieren** to panic; **sich ~ fürchten (vor)** to be terrified or petrified (by); **sie rannten ~ durcheinander** they ran about frantically or in panic

Pank|re|as ['pankreas] NT -, **Pankreaten** [pankre'a:tn] (Anat) pancreas

Pan|ne ['panə] F -, -n a (= technische Störung) hitch (inf), breakdown, trouble no indef art; (= Reifenpanne) puncture, flat (tyre (Brit) or tire (US)), blow-out (inf); **ich hatte eine ~ mit dem Fahrrad, mein Fahrrad hatte eine ~** I had some trouble with my bike; (Reifenpanne) I had a puncture (Brit) or flat; **ich hatte eine ~ mit dem Auto, mein Auto hatte eine ~** my car broke down; **mit der neuen Maschine passieren dauernd ~n** things keep going wrong with the new machine, the new machine keeps breaking down

b (fig inf) slip, boob (esp Brit inf), goof (US inf) (bei etw with sth); **mit jdm/etw eine ~ erleben** to have (a bit of) trouble with sb/sth; **uns ist eine ~ passiert** we've made a slip, we've slipped up, we've boobed (esp Brit inf) or goofed (US inf); **da ist eine ~ passiert mit dem Brief** something has gone wrong with the letter

Pan|nen-: **Pan|nen|dienst** M, **Pan|nen|hil|fe** F breakdown service; **Pan|nen|kof|fer** M emergency toolkit; **Pan|nen|kurs** M car maintenance course

Pa|nop|ti|kum [pa'nɔptikʊm] NT -s, **Panoptiken** [-kn] (von Kuriositäten) collection of curios; (von Wachsfiguren) waxworks pl

Pa|no|ra|ma [pano'ra:ma] NT -s, **Panoramen** [-mən] panorama

Pa|no|ra|ma-: **Pa|no|ra|ma|auf|nah|me** F panorama, panoramic view; **Pa|no|ra|ma|bus** M coach with panoramic windows, panorama coach; **Pa|no|ra|ma|ge|mäl|de** NT panoramic painting; **Pa|no|ra|ma|spie|gel** M (Aut) panoramic mirror

pan|schen ['panʃn] VT to adulterate; (= verdünnen) to water down, to dilute VI (inf) to splash (about)

Pan|scher ['panʃɐ] M -s, -, **Pan|sche|rin** [-ərɪn] F -, -nen (inf) a (pej) adulterator b **du bist vielleicht ein ~!** you're a messy thing!

Pan|sche|rei [panʃə'rai] F -, -en a (= Vermischen) adulteration; (mit Wasser) watering down, dilution b (inf: = Herumspritzen) splashing (about); **was für eine ~ du gemacht hast!** what a mess you've made!

Pan|sen ['panzn] M -s, - (Zool) rumen; (N Ger inf) belly (inf)

Pan|ta|lons [pãta'lõ:s] PL (Hist) pantaloons pl

Pan|ter ['pantɐ] M -s, - = **Panther**

Pan|the|is|mus [pante'ɪsmʊs] M -, no pl pantheism

Pan|the|ist [pante'ɪst] M -en, -en, **Pan|the|is|tin** [-'ɪstɪn] F -, -nen pantheist

pan|the|is|tisch [pante'ɪstɪʃ] ADJ pantheistic

Pan|ther ['pantɐ] M -s, - panther

Pan|ti|ne [pan'ti:nə] F -, -n (N Ger) clog → **kippen**

Pan|tof|fel [pan'tɔfl] M **-s, -n** slipper; **unterm ~ stehen** *(inf)* to be henpecked *(inf)*; **unter den ~ kommen** *or* **geraten** *(inf)* to become henpecked *(inf)*; **den ~ schwingen** to wear the trousers *(esp Brit inf)* or pants *(esp US inf)*

Pan|tof|fel|blu|me F slipper flower, calceolaria

Pan|töf|fel|chen [pan'tœflçən] NT **-s, -** slipper

Pan|tof|fel-: **Pan|tof|fel|held** M *(inf)* henpecked husband *(inf)*; **Pan|tof|fel|ki|no** NT *(inf)* telly *(Brit inf)*, (goggle)box *(Brit inf)*, tube *(US inf)*; **Pan|tof|fel|tier|chen** NT *(Biol)* slipper animalcule, paramecium *(spec)*

Pan|to|let|te [panto'lɛtə] F **-, -n** slip-on (shoe)

Pan|to|mi|me [panto'mi:mə] F **-, -n** mime

Pan|to|mi|me [panto'mi:mə] M **-n, -n**, **Pan|to|mi|min** [-'mi:mɪn] F **-, -nen** mime

pan|to|mi|misch [panto'mi:mɪʃ] ADJ *Darstellung* in mime ADV in mime; **sich ~ verständlich machen** to communicate with gestures *or* in mime

pant|schen ['pantʃn] VTI = **panschen**

Pan|zer ['pantsɐ] M **-s, -** **a** *(Mil)* tank; **die deutschen ~** the German tanks *pl or* armour *sing (Brit) or* armor *sing (US)* **b** *(Hist: = Rüstung)* armour *no indef art (Brit)*, armor *no indef art (US)*, suit of armo(u)r **c** *(= Panzerung)* armour *(Brit) or* armor *(US)* plating, armour *(Brit) or* armor *(US)* plate **d** *(von Schildkröte, Insekt)* shell; *(= dicke Haut)* armour *(Brit)*, armor *(US)* **e** *(fig)* shield; **sich mit einem ~ (gegen etw) umgeben** to harden oneself (against sth); **sich mit einem ~ aus etw umgeben** to put up *or* erect a defensive barrier of sth; **ein ~ der Gleichgültigkeit** a wall of indifference

Pan|zer-: **Pan|zer|ab|wehr** F anti-tank defence *(Brit) or* defense *(US)*; *(Truppe)* anti-tank unit; **Pan|zer|ab|wehr|hub|schrau|ber** M anti-tank helicopter; **Pan|zer|ab|wehr|ka|no|ne** F anti-tank gun; **Pan|zer|be|sat|zung** F tank crew; **pan|zer|bre|chend** ADJ armour-piercing *(Brit)*, armor-piercing *(US)*; **Pan|zer|di|vi|si|on** F armoured *(Brit) or* armored *(US)* division; **Pan|zer|fal|le** F tank trap; **Pan|zer|faust** F bazooka; **Pan|zer|glas** NT bulletproof glass; **Pan|zer|gra|ben** M anti-tank ditch; **Pan|zer|gra|na|te** F armour-piercing *(Brit) or* armor-piercing *(US)* shell; **Pan|zer|gre|na|dier** M armoured *(Brit) or* armored *(US)* infantryman; **Pan|zer|hemd** NT coat of mail; **Pan|zer|kampf|wa|gen** M armoured *(Brit) or* armored *(US)* vehicle; **Pan|zer|ket|te** F tank-track; **Pan|zer|kreu|zer** M *(Naut)* (armoured *(Brit) or* armored *(US)*) cruiser

pan|zern ['pantsɐn] VT to armour-plate *(Brit)*, to armor-plate *(US)*; **gepanzerte Fahrzeuge** armoured *(Brit) or* armored *(US)* vehicles; **gepanzerte Tiere** shell-bearing animals VR *(lit)* to put on one's armour *(Brit) or* armor *(US)*; *(fig)* to arm oneself

Pan|zer-: **Pan|zer|plat|te** F armour *(Brit) or* armor *(US)* plating *no pl*, armour *(Brit) or* armor *(US)* plate; **Pan|zer|schrank** M safe; **Pan|zer|späh|wa|gen** M armoured *(Brit) or* armored *(US)* scout car; **Pan|zer|sper|re** F anti-tank obstacle, tank trap; **Pan|zer|trup|pe** F tanks *pl*, tank division; **Pan|zer|turm** M tank turret

Pan|ze|rung ['pantsərʊŋ] F **-, -en** armour *(Brit) or* armor *(US)* plating; *(fig)* shield

Pan|zer-: **Pan|zer|wa|gen** M armoured *(Brit) or* armored *(US)* car; **Pan|zer|wes|te** F bulletproof vest

Pa|pa ['papa] M **-s, -s** *(inf)* daddy *(inf)*, pa *(US inf)*, pop(s) *(US inf)*

Pa|pa [pa'pa:] M **-s, -s** papa

Pa|pa|gal|lo [papa'galo] M **-s, Papagalli** [-li] *(pej)* (Latin) wolf *or* romeo

Pa|pa|gei [papa'gai, 'papagai] M **-s, -en** parrot; **er plappert alles wie ein ~ nach** he repeats everything parrot fashion

Pa|pa|gei|en|krank|heit F *(Med)* parrot fever, psittacosis

Pa|pa|gei|en|tau|cher M puffin

Pa|pa|mo|bil NT *(inf)* popemobile

Pa|pa|raz|zo [papa'ratso] M **-s, Paparazzi** [-tsi] *(inf)* paparazzo

Pa|pa|ya [pa'pa:ja] F **-, -s** papaya

Pa|per ['pe:pɐ] NT **-s, -** paper

Pa|per|back ['pe:pɐbɛk] NT **-s, -s** paperback

Pa|pe|te|rie [papɛtə'ri:] F **-, -n** [-ri:ən] *(Sw)* stationer's

Pa|pi ['papi] M **-s, -s** *(inf)* daddy *(inf)*, pappy *(US inf)*

Pa|pier [pa'pi:ɐ] NT **-s, -e** **a** *no pl (Material)* paper; **ein Blatt ~** a sheet *or* piece of paper; **~ verarbeitend** *(Industrie)* paper-processing; **das existiert nur auf dem ~** it only exists on paper; **das steht nur auf dem ~** that's only on paper, that's only in theory; **etw zu ~ bringen** to set *or* put sth down on paper *or* in writing, to commit sth to paper; **~ ist geduldig** *(Prov)* you can say what you like on paper, you can write what you like; **das Abkommen ist das ~ nicht wert, auf dem es gedruckt ist** the agreement isn't worth the paper it's written on **b** *(= politisches Dokument, Schriftstück)* paper **c** **Papiere** PL (identity) papers *pl*; *(= Urkunden)* documents *pl*; **er hatte keine ~e bei sich** he had no *or* he was carrying no means of identification on him; **seine ~e bekommen** *(= entlassen werden)* to get one's cards **d** *(Fin: = Wertpapier)* security

Pa|pier-: **Pa|pier|deutsch** NT officialese, gobbledygook *(inf)*; **Pa|pier|ein|zug** M paper feed

pa|pie|ren [pa'pi:rən] ADJ **a** *(lit form)* paper **b** *(fig) Stil, Sprache* prosy, bookish ADV *(fig)* **die Sprache wirkt ~** the language seems stilted

Pa|pier-: **Pa|pier|fab|rik** F paper mill; **Pa|pier|fet|zen** M scrap *or* (little) bit of paper; **Pa|pier|for|mat** NT paper format *or* size; **Pa|pier|geld** NT paper money; **Pa|pier|grö|ße** F paper size; **Pa|pier|korb** M (waste)paper basket *or* bin; *(Comput)* recycle bin, trash(can); **Pa|pier|kram** M *(inf)* bumf *(Brit inf)*, stuff (to read) *(inf)*; **Pa|pier|krieg** M *(inf)* **vor lauter ~ kommen wir nicht zur Forschung** there's so much paperwork we can't get on with our research; **erst nach einem langen ~** after going through a lot of red tape; **einen ~ (mit jdm) führen** to go through a lot of red tape (with sb); **pa|pier|los** ADJ *Datenverkehr, Kommunikation* paperless; **das ~e Büro** the paperless *or* paper-free office ADV **Daten ~ versenden** to send data electronically; **Pa|pier|ma|ché** [papie:ma'ʃe:] NT **-s, -s** → **Papiermaschee**; **Pa|pier|man|schet|te** F paper frill; *(am Ärmel)* false cuff; **Pa|pier|ma|schee** [papie:ma'ʃe:] NT **-s, -s** papier-mâché; **Pa|pier|müh|le** F paper mill

pa|piern [pa'pi:ɐn] ADJ ADV = **papieren**

Pa|pier-: **Pa|pier|schacht** M *(von Drucker, Kopierer)* paper tray; **Pa|pier|sche|re** F paper scissors *pl*; **Pa|pier|schlan|ge** F streamer; **Pa|pier|schnit|zel** M OR NT scrap of paper; *(pl: = Konfetti)* confetti; **Pa|pier|ser|vi|et|te** F paper serviette *(esp Brit) or* napkin; **Pa|pier|stau** M *(in Drucker, Kopierer)* paper jam; **Pa|pier|ta|schen|tuch** NT paper hankie *or* handkerchief, tissue; **Pa|pier|ti|ger** M *(fig)* paper tiger; **Pa|pier|tü|te** F paper bag; **pa|pier|ver|ar|bei|tend** ADJ *attr* → **Papier a**; **Pa|pier|ver|schwen|dung** F waste of paper; **Pa|pier|vor|schub** M paper feed; **Pa|pier|wäh|rung** F paper currency; **Pa|pier|wa|ren** PL stationery *no pl*; **Pa|pier|wa|ren|ge|schäft** NT, **Pa|pier|wa|ren|hand|lung** F stationer's (shop); **Pa|pier|zu|fuhr** F, **Pa|pier|zu|füh|rung** F *(Comput, von Drucker)* paper source *or* feed, sheetfeed

Pa|pist [pa'pɪst] M **-en, -en**, **Pa|pis|tin** [-'pɪstɪn] F **-, -nen** *(pej)* papist *(pej)*

pa|pis|tisch [pa'pɪstɪʃ] ADJ *(Hist)* papal; *(pej)* popish

papp [pap] ADJ *(inf)* **ich kann nicht mehr ~ sagen** I'm full to bursting *(Brit inf)*, I'm about to go pop *(inf)*

Papp [pap] M **-s**, *no pl (S Ger)* = **Pappe b**

Papp-: **Papp|band** [-bant] M *pl* **-bände** *(Einband)* pasteboard; *(Buch)* hardback; **Papp|be|cher** M paper cup; **Papp|de|ckel** M (thin) cardboard; **einen ~ unterlegen** to put a piece of cardboard underneath

Pap|pe ['papə] F **-, -n** **a** *(= Pappdeckel)* cardboard; *(= Dachpappe)* roofing felt; **dieser linke Haken war nicht von ~** *(inf)* that left hook really had some weight *or* force behind it, that was a mean left hook; **X ist ein guter Sprinter, aber Y ist auch nicht von ~** *(inf)* X is good but Y is no mean sprinter either *(Brit)*, X is a fast sprinter but Y is no slacker *(esp US inf)* **b** *(S Ger inf) (= Leim)* glue; *(= Brei)* paste; *(pej)* slop *(pej inf)*, mush *(pej inf)*; **ich kann diese ~ von Porridge nicht essen** I can't eat this porridge slop *(pej inf)*

Papp|ein|band M pasteboard

Pap|pel ['papl] F **-, -n** poplar

Pap|pel|al|lee F avenue of poplars

päp|peln ['pɛpln] VT *(inf)* to nourish

pap|pen ['papn] *(inf)* VT to stick, to glue *(an +acc, auf +acc* on) VI *(inf) (= klebrig sein)* to be sticky; *(Schnee)* to pack; **der Leim pappt gut** the glue sticks *or* holds well; **das Hemd pappt an mir** my shirt is sticking to me

Pap|pen-: **Pap|pen|de|ckel** M *(S Ger)* = **Pappdeckel**; **Pap|pen|hei|mer** [-haime] PL **ich kenne meine ~** *(inf)* I know you lot/that lot (inside out) *(inf)*; **Pap|pen|stiel** M, *no pl (fig inf)* **das ist doch ein/kein ~** *(= billig)* that's chicken feed/not exactly chicken feed *(inf)*; *(= leicht)* that's child's play/not exactly child's play *(inf)*; *(Geldbetrag)* that's peanuts/not exactly peanuts *(inf)*; **das ist keinen ~ wert** that's not worth a thing *or* a penny *or* a straw; **das hab ich für einen ~ gekauft** I bought it for a song *(inf) or* for next to nothing

pap|per|la|papp [papɐla'pap] INTERJ *(inf)* rubbish *(Brit inf)*, (stuff and) nonsense

pap|pig ['papɪç] *(inf)* ADJ sticky; *Brot* doughy ADV **der Kartoffelbrei klebte ~ am Löffel/an meinem Gaumen** mashed potato was stuck to the spoon/to the roof of my mouth

Papp-: **Papp|ka|me|rad** M *(Mil sl)* silhouette target; **Papp|kar|ton** M *(= Schachtel)* cardboard box; *(Material)* cardboard; **Papp|ma|ché** ['papmaʃe:] NT **-s, -s** = **Pappmaschee**; **Papp|ma|schee** ['papmaʃe:] NT **-s, -s** papier-mâché; **Papp|na|se** F false nose; **papp|satt** ADJ *(inf)* really full; **ich bin ~** I've really had enough; **Papp|schach|tel** F cardboard box; **Papp|schnee** M wet *or* sticky snow; **Papp|tel|ler** M paper plate

Pap|ri|ka ['paprika, 'pa:prika] M **-s, -(s)** *(no pl: = Gewürz)* paprika; *(= Paprikaschote)* pepper; *(Sw: = Peperoni)* chilli *(Brit)*, chili

Pap|ri|ka|scho|te F pepper; *(= rote Paprikaschote)* pepper, pimento *(US)*; **gefüllte ~n** stuffed peppers

Paps [paps] M **-**, *no pl (inf)* dad *(inf)*, daddy *(inf)*, pops *(US inf)*

Papst [pa:pst] M **-(e)s, ¨-e** ['pɛ:pstə] pope; *(fig)* high priest

Papst-: **Papst|au|di|enz** F audience with the Pope; **Papst|be|such** M papal visit

Päps|tin ['pɛ:pstɪn] F **-, -nen** popess; *(fig)* high priestess

päpst|lich ['pɛ:pstlɪç] ADJ papal; *(fig pej)* pontifical; **~er als der Papst sein** to be more Catholic than the Pope, to be more royal than the king

Papst-: **Papst|tum** ['pa:psttu:m] NT **-(e)s**, *no pl* papacy; **Papst|wahl** F papal elections *pl*; **Papst|wür|de** F papal office

Pa|pua ['pa:pua, pa'pu:a] M **-(s), -(s)** *or f* **-, -s** Papuan

Pa|pua-Neu|gui|nea ['pa:puanɔygi'ne:a] NT **-s** Papua New Guinea

pa|pu|a|nisch [papu:'a:nɪʃ] ADJ Papuan

Pa|py|rus [pa'py:rʊs] M -, **Papyri** [-ri] papyrus
Pa|py|rus|rol|le F papyrus (scroll)
Pa|ra|bel [pa'ra:bl] F -, -n **a** *(Liter)* parable **b** *(Math)* parabola, parabolic curve
Pa|ra|bol|an|ten|ne F satellite dish, parabolic receiving dish
pa|ra|bo|lisch [para'bo:lɪʃ] ADJ **a** *(Liter)* parabolic; **eine ~e Erzählung** a parable **b** *(Math)* parabolic
Pa|ra|bol|spie|gel M parabolic reflector *or* mirror
Pa|ra|de [pa'ra:də] F -, -n **a** parade *(auch Mil)*; **die ~ abnehmen** to take the salute **b** *(Sport) (Fechten, Boxen)* parry; *(Ballspiele)* save; *(Reiten)* check; **jdm in die ~ fahren** *(fig)* to cut sb off short
Pa|ra|de-: **Pa|ra|de|an|zug** M *(Mil)* dress uniform; (*inf*: *= gute Kleidung*) best bib and tucker *(dated inf)*, Sunday best *(inf)*; **Pa|ra|de|bei|spiel** NT prime example; **Pa|ra|de|bett** NT fourposter (bed); **Pa|ra|de|fall** M prime example
Pa|ra|dei|ser [para'daizɐ] M -s, - *(Aus)* tomato
Pa|ra|de-: **Pa|ra|de|kis|sen** NT scatter cushion; **Pa|ra|de|marsch** M **a** *(= Paradeschritt)* parade step; *(= Stechschritt)* goose step; **im ~ marschieren** to march in parade step/to goose-step **b** *(= Aufmarsch)* march in parade step **c** *(Marschmusik)* (military) march; **Pa|ra|de|pferd** NT show horse; *(fig)* showpiece; **Pa|ra|de|platz** M parade ground; **Pa|ra|de|rol|le** F *(von Schauspieler)* most famous role; **der Hamlet war seine ~** he was best known for his role as Hamlet; **Pa|ra|de|schritt** M = **Parademarsch a**; **Pa|ra|de|stück** NT *(fig)* showpiece; *(Gegenstand auch)* pièce de résistance; **Pa|ra|de|uni|form** F dress uniform
pa|ra|die|ren [para'di:rən] *ptp* **paradiert** VI to parade; **mit etw ~** *(fig)* to show off *or* flaunt sth
Pa|ra|dies [para'di:s] NT -es, -e [-zə] **a** *(lit, fig)* paradise; **die Vertreibung aus dem ~** the expulsion from Paradise; **das verlorene ~** the lost paradise; **hier ist es so schön wie im ~** it's like paradise here, this is paradise; **da haben sie wie im ~ gelebt** they were living in paradise; **ein ~ für Kinder** a children's paradise, a paradise for children; **das ~ auf Erden** heaven on earth **b** *(Archit)* galilee
pa|ra|die|sisch [para'di:zɪʃ] ADJ *(fig)* heavenly, paradisiac(al) *(liter)*; **dort herrschen ~e Zustände für Autofahrer** it's heaven for car drivers there ADV *leer* blissfully; *schön* incredibly; **hier ist es ~ ruhig** it's incredibly peaceful here; **sich ~ wohl fühlen** to be blissfully happy, to be in paradise
Pa|ra|dies|vo|gel M bird of paradise; *(fig inf)* exotic creature
Pa|ra|dig|ma [para'dɪgma] NT -s, **Paradigmen** [-mən] paradigm
pa|ra|dig|ma|tisch [paradɪ'gma:tɪʃ] ADJ paradigmatic
Pa|ra|dig|men|wech|sel M *(Pol)* paradigm shift
pa|ra|dox [para'dɔks] ADJ paradoxical ADV paradoxically
Pa|ra|dox [para'dɔks] NT -es, -e paradox
pa|ra|do|xer|wei|se [para'dɔksɐ'vaizə] ADV paradoxically
Pa|ra|do|xie [paradɔ'ksi:] F -, -n [-'ksi:ən] paradox
Pa|ra|do|xon [pa'ra:dɔksɔn] NT -s, **Paradoxa** [-ksa] *(geh)* paradox
Pa|raf|fin [para'fi:n] NT -s, -e *(Chem)* *(= Paraffinöl)* (liquid) paraffin; *(= Paraffinwachs)* paraffin wax
Pa|ra|gli|der M -s, - *(= Schirm)* paraglider
Pa|ra|gli|der M -s, -, **Pa|ra|gli|de|rin** F -, -nen paraglider
Pa|ra|gli|ding ['pa:raglaidɪŋ] NT -s, *no pl* paragliding
Pa|ra|graf [para'gra:f] M -en, -en *(Jur)* section; *(= Abschnitt)* paragraph

> **PARAGRAF 218**
>
> **Paragraf 218** of the criminal code concerns abortion, which is a very controversial issue. **Paragraf 218** is used as shorthand for the entire abortion debate. In Germany abortion is legal up to the third month of pregnancy, provided the pregnant woman has undergone thorough counselling.

Pa|ra|gra|fen- : **Pa|ra|gra|fen|rei|ter(in)** M(F) *(inf)* pedant, stickler for the rules; **pa|ra|gra|fen|wei|se** ADV in paragraphs; **Pa|ra|gra|fen|werk** NT rules and regulations *pl*; **Pa|ra|gra|fen|zei|chen** NT *(Typ)* paragraph (marker *or* sign), section mark
Pa|ra|graph [para'gra:f] *etc* = **Paragraf** *etc*
Pa|ral|la|xe [para'laksə] F -, -n *(Math)* parallax
pa|ral|lel [para'le:l] ADJ parallel *(auch Comput)* ADV parallel; **~ laufen** to run parallel; **der Weg (ver)läuft ~ zum Fluss** the path runs *or* is parallel to the river; **die Entwicklung dort verläuft ~ zu der in Deutschland** the development there is parallel to *or* parallels that of Germany; **~ schalten** *(Elec)* to connect in parallel
Pa|ral|lel|com|pu|ter [para'le:l-] M parallel computer
Pa|ral|lel|dru|cker M *(Comput)* parallel printer
Pa|ral|le|le [para'le:lə] F -, -n *(lit)* parallel (line); *(fig)* parallel; **eine ~/~n zu etw ziehen** *(lit)* to draw a line/lines parallel to sth; *(fig)* to draw a parallel/parallels to sth; **dafür gibt es keine ~** there are no parallels; **~n sehen zwischen ...** to see parallels between ...
Pa|ral|lel- [para'le:l-]: **Pa|ral|lel|er|schei|nung** F parallel; **Pa|ral|lel|fall** M parallel (case)
Pa|ral|le|lis|mus [parale'lɪsmʊs] M -, **Parallelismen** [-mən] parallelism
Pa|ral|le|li|tät [paraleli'tɛ:t] F -, -en parallelism
Pa|ral|lel-: **Pa|ral|lel|klas|se** F parallel class; **Pa|ral|lel|kreis** M parallel (of latitude)
Pa|ral|le|lo|gramm [paralelo'gram] NT -s, -e parallelogram
Pa|ral|lel-: **Pa|ral|lel|rech|ner** M *(Comput)* parallel computer; **Pa|ral|lel|schal|tung** F parallel connection; **Pa|ral|lel|schnitt|stel|le** F *(Comput)* parallel interface; **Pa|ral|lel|schwung** M *(Ski)* parallel turn; **Pa|ral|lel|ver|ar|bei|tung** F *(Comput)* parallel processing
Pa|ra|lym|pics [para'lʏmpɪks] PL Paralympics *pl*
Pa|ra|ly|se [para'ly:zə] F -, -n *(Med, fig)* paralysis
pa|ra|ly|sie|ren [paraly'zi:rən] *ptp* **paralysiert** VT *(Med, fig)* to paralyze
Pa|ra|ly|ti|ker [para'ly:tikɐ] M -s, -, **Pa|ra|ly|ti|ke|rin** [-ərɪn] F -, -nen *(Med)* paralytic
pa|ra|ly|tisch [para'ly:tɪʃ] ADJ paralytic
Pa|ra|me|di|zin ['pa:ra-] F alternative medicine
Pa|ra|me|ter [pa'ra:metɐ] M -s, - parameter
pa|ra|mi|li|tä|risch ['pa:ra-] ADJ paramilitary
Pa|ra|noia [para'nɔya] F -, *no pl* paranoia
pa|ra|no|id [parano'i:t] ADJ paranoid
Pa|ra|no|i|ker [para'no:ikɐ] M -s, -, **Pa|ra|no|i|ke|rin** [-ərɪn] F -, -nen paranoiac
pa|ra|no|isch [para'no:ɪʃ] ADJ paranoiac
Pa|ra|nuss ['para-] F *(Bot)* Brazil nut
Pa|ra|phe [pa'ra:fə] F -, -n *(form)* *(= Namenszug)* signature; *(= Namenszeichen)* initials *pl*; *(= Stempel)* signature stamp
pa|ra|phie|ren [para'fi:rən] *ptp* **paraphiert** VT *(Pol)* to initial
Pa|ra|phra|se [para-] F paraphrase; *(Mus)* variation
pa|ra|phra|sie|ren [parafra'zi:rən] *ptp* **paraphrasiert** VT to paraphrase; *(Mus)* to write variations on
Pa|ra|psy|cho|lo|gie ['pa:ra-] F parapsychology
Pa|ra|sit [para'zi:t] M -en, -en *(Biol, fig)* parasite
pa|ra|si|tär [parazi'tɛ:ɐ], **pa|ra|si|tisch** [para'zi:tɪʃ] ADJ *(Biol, fig)* parasitic(al) ADV **~ leben** to live parasitically
Pa|ra|sol [para'zo:l] M OR NT -s, -s *or* -e *(old)* parasol, sunshade
pa|rat [pa'ra:t] ADJ *Antwort, Beispiel etc* ready, prepared; *Werkzeug etc* handy, ready; **halte dich ~** be ready; **er hatte immer eine Ausrede ~** he always had an excuse ready *or* on tap *(inf)*, he was always ready with an excuse; **seine stets ~e Ausrede** his ever-ready excuse
pa|ra|tak|tisch [para'taktɪʃ] ADJ *(Ling)* coordinated; *(ohne Konjunktion)* paratactic(al)
Pa|ra|ta|xe [para'taksə] F *(Ling)* coordination; *(ohne Konjunktion)* parataxis
Pär|chen ['pɛ:ɐçən] NT -s, - (courting) couple; **ihr seid mir so ein ~!** *(iro)* you're a fine pair!
pär|chen|wei|se ADV in pairs
Par|cours [par'ku:ɐ] M -, - [-'ku:ɐs, -'ku:ɐs] *(Reiten)* showjumping course; *(Sportart)* showjumping; *(= Rennstrecke, Hindernisstrecke)* course; **einen ~ reiten** to jump a course; **sie reitet nicht gern ~** she doesn't like showjumping
par|dauz [par'dauts] INTERJ *(old)* whoops
par|don [par'dõ:] INTERJ *(= Verzeihung)* sorry; *(= nicht verstanden)* sorry, beg (your) pardon, pardon me *(US)*; **o ~!** sorry!, I'm so sorry!; *(empört)* excuse me!
Par|don [par'dõ:] M OR NT -s, *no pl* **a** pardon; **jdn um ~ bitten** to ask sb's pardon; **jdm kein (-en) ~ geben** *(old)* to show sb no mercy, to give sb no quarter **b** *(inf)* **kein ~ kennen** to be ruthless; **wenn er sich** *(dat)* **was in den Kopf gesetzt hat, gibts kein ~** *or* **kennt er kein ~** once he's set on something he's merciless *or* ruthless; **das Zeug räumst du auf, da gibts kein ~** you'll clear that stuff up and that's that! *(inf)*
Pa|ren|the|se [parɛn'te:zə] F parenthesis; **in ~** in parenthesis *or* parentheses; **etw in ~ setzen** to put sth in parentheses
pa|ren|the|tisch [parɛn'te:tɪʃ] ADJ parenthetic(al)
par ex|cel|lence [par ɛksɛ'lã:s] ADV par excellence
Par|fait [par'fɛ] NT -s, -s *(Art Sorbet)* parfait
Par|force- [par'fɔrs-]: **Par|force|jagd** F hunt, course; *(Jagdart)* coursing; **wir machen eine ~** we're going hunting, we're going on a hunt; **Par|force|ritt** M forced ride
Par|fum [par'fœ̃:] NT -s, -s, **Par|füm** [par'fy:m] NT -s, -e *or* -s perfume, scent
Par|fü|me|rie [parfymə'ri:] F -, -n [-'ri:ən] perfumery
Par|füm|fläsch|chen NT scent *or* perfume bottle
par|fü|mie|ren [parfy'mi:rən] *ptp* **parfümiert** VT to scent, to perfume VR to put perfume *or* scent on; **du parfümierst dich zu stark** you put too much scent *or* perfume on
Par|füm|wol|ke F cloud of perfume
Par|füm|zer|stäu|ber M scent spray, perfume *or* scent atomizer
pa|ri ['pa:ri] ADV *(Fin)* par; **al ~, zu ~** at par (value), at nominal value; **über ~** above par, at a premium; **unter ~** below par, at a discount; **die Chancen stehen ~ (~)** the odds are even *or* fifty-fifty
Pa|ria ['pa:ria] M -s, -s *(lit, fig)* pariah
pa|rie|ren [pa'ri:rən] *ptp* **pariert** VT **a** *(Fechten, fig)* to parry; *(Ftbl)* to save; **super pariert!** what a brilliant save! **b** *(Reiten)* to rein in VI to obey, to do what one is told; **aufs Wort ~** to jump to it
Pa|ri|kurs ['pa:ri-] M *(Fin)* par of exchange
Pa|ris [pa'ri:s] NT -' Paris
Pa|ri|ser [pa'ri:zɐ] ADJ *attr* Parisian, Paris
Pa|ri|ser M -s, - **a** Parisian **b** (*inf*: *= Kondom*) French letter *(inf)*
Pa|ri|se|rin [pa'ri:zərɪn] F -, -nen Parisienne
Pa|ri|tät [pari'tɛ:t] F -, -en *(= Gleichstellung)* parity, equality; *(in Gremium)* parity; *(von Währung)* parity, par of exchange; *(Comput)* parity
pa|ri|tä|tisch [pari'tɛ:tɪʃ] ADJ equal; **~e Mitbestimmung** equal representation ADV equally; **eine Kommission ~ besetzen** to provide equal representation on a committee

Park [park] M **-s, -s** **a** park; *(von Schloss)* grounds *pl* **b** *(rare: = Fuhrpark)* fleet (of vehicles)

Par|ka ['parka] M **-(s), -s** *or f* **-, -s** parka

Park-and-ride-Sys|tem ['pa:kənd'raid-] NT park and ride system

Park-: Park|an|la|ge F park; **park|ar|tig** ADJ park-like ADV like a park; **Park|aus|weis** M parking permit; **Park|bahn** F *(Space)* parking orbit; **Park|bank** F *pl* **-bänke** park bench; **Park|bucht** F parking bay; **Park|dau|er** F parking period; **Park|deck** NT parking level

par|ken ['parkn] VTI *(auch Comput)* to park; **ein ~des Auto** a parked car; **„Parken verboten!"** "No Parking"; **falsch ~** to park illegally; **sein Auto parkte ...** his car was parked ...

Par|kett [par'kɛt] NT **-s, -e** **a** *(= Fußboden)* parquet (flooring); **ein Zimmer mit ~ auslegen** to lay parquet (flooring) in a room; **sich auf jedem ~ bewegen können** *(fig)* to be able to move in any society; **auf dem internationalen ~** in international circles; **sich auf glattem ~ bewegen** *(fig)* to be skating on thin ice **b** *(= Tanzfläche)* (dance) floor; **eine tolle Nummer aufs ~ legen** *(inf)* to put on a great show → **Sohle** **c** *(Theat)* stalls *pl*, parquet *(US)*; **das ~ klatschte Beifall** there was applause from the stalls; **im ~ sitzen** to sit in the stalls **d** *(St Ex)* trading floor; **auf dem ~** on the trading floor

Par|kett(fuß)|bo|den M parquet floor

Par|kett|han|del M *(St Ex)* floor trading

par|ket|tie|ren [parkɛ'ti:rən] *ptp* **parkettiert** VT to lay with parquet, to lay *or* put down parquet in, to parquet

Par|kett|platz M, **Par|kett|sitz** M *(Theat)* seat in the stalls *or* parquet *(US)*

Park-: Park|ge|bühr F parking fee; **Park|haus** NT multi-storey *(Brit)* or multi-story *(US)* car park

par|kie|ren [par'ki:rən] *ptp* **parkiert** VTI *(Sw)* = **parken**

Par|king|me|ter ['parkɪŋ-] M *(Sw)* parking meter

Par|kin|son|kran|ke(r) ['pa:ɐkɪnzən-] MF *decl as adj* person suffering from Parkinson's disease

par|kin|son|sche Krank|heit ['pa:ɐkɪnzənʃə-] F Parkinson's disease

Park-: Park|kral|le F wheel clamp *(Brit)*, Denver boot *(US)*; **Park|land|schaft** F parkland; **Park|leit|sys|tem** NT parking guidance system; **Park|licht** NT parking light; **Park|lü|cke** F parking space; **Park|mög|lich|keit** F parking facility; **Park|platz** M car park, parking lot *(esp US)*; *(für Einzelwagen)* (parking) space *(Brit)* or spot *(US)*, place to park; **bewachter/unbewachter ~** car park with/without an attendant; **Park|platz|not** F shortage of parking spaces; **Park|raum** M parking space; **Park|raum|not** F shortage of parking space; **Park|schei|be** F parking disc; **Park|schein** M car-parking ticket, parking slip *(US)* or check *(US)*; **Park|schein|au|to|mat** M *(Mot)* ticket machine *(for parking)*; **Park|stu|di|um** NT *(Univ)* interim course of study *(while waiting for a place)*; **Park|sün|der(in)** M(F) parking offender *(Brit)*, illegal parker; **Park|uhr** F parking meter; **Park|ver|bot** NT parking ban; **hier ist ~** there's no parking here, you're not allowed to park here; **im ~ stehen** to be parked illegally; **Park|ver|bots|schild** NT no-parking sign; **Park|wäch|ter(in)** M(F) *(auf Parkplatz)* car-park attendant; *(= Politesse)* traffic warden; *(von Anlagen)* park keeper *or* attendant; **Park|zeit** F parking time

Par|la|ment [parla'mɛnt] NT **-(e)s, -e** parliament; **das ~ auflösen** to dissolve parliament; **jdn ins ~ wählen** to elect sb to parliament; **im ~ vertreten sein** to be represented in parliament

Par|la|men|tär [parlamɛn'tɛ:ɐ] M **-s, -e**, **Par|la|men|tä|rin** [-'tɛ:rɪn] F **-, -nen** peace envoy, negotiator

Par|la|men|tär|flag|ge F flag of truce

Par|la|men|ta|ri|er [parlamɛn'ta:riɐ] M **-s, -**, **Par|la|men|ta|rie|rin** [-iərɪn] F **-, -nen** parliamentarian

par|la|men|ta|risch [parlamɛn'ta:rɪʃ] ADJ parliamentary; **~er Staatssekretär im Verteidigungsministerium** *non-Cabinet minister with special responsibility for defence*; **~er Geschäftsführer** ≈ party whip; **der Parlamentarische Rat** the Parliamentary Council; **~e Demokratie** parliamentary democracy ADV **~ regieren** to govern by a parliament; **~ vertreten sein** to be represented in parliament

Par|la|men|ta|ris|mus [parlamɛnta'rɪsmʊs] M **-**, *no pl* parliamentarianism

Par|la|ments-: Par|la|ments|aus|schuss M parliamentary committee; **Par|la|ments|be|schluss** M vote *or* decision of parliament; **Par|la|ments|fe|ri|en** PL recess; **in die ~ gehen** to go into recess; **Par|la|ments|ge|bäu|de** NT parliamentary building(s *pl*); *(in London)* Houses of Parliament *pl*; *(in Washington)* Capitol; **Par|la|ments|mehr|heit** F parliamentary majority, majority in parliament; **Par|la|ments|mit|glied** NT member of parliament; *(in GB)* Member of Parliament, MP; *(in USA)* Congressman; **Par|la|ments|prä|si|dent(in)** M(F) (parliamentary) president; *(in GB)* Speaker; **Par|la|ments|sit|zung** F sitting (of parliament); **Par|la|ments|wahl** F *usu pl* parliamentary election(s *pl*)

Par|lan|do [par'lando] NT **-s, -s** *or* **Parlandi** [-di] *(Mus)* parlando

par|lie|ren [par'li:rən] *ptp* **parliert** VI to talk away; **Italienisch ~** to chat away in Italian; **er ist so schüchtern, ich hätte nie geglaubt, dass er so ~ könnte** he's so shy I'd never have believed that he could talk so fluently

Par|ma|schin|ken ['parma-] M Parma ham

Par|me|san(|kä|se) [parme'za:n-] M **-s**, *no pl* Parmesan (cheese)

Par|nass [par'nas] M **-es** *(liter)* (Mount) Parnassus

Pa|ro|die [paro'di:] F **-, -n** [-'di:ən] parody, takeoff *(Brit)* *(auf +acc* on, *zu* of); **er ist nur noch eine ~ seiner selbst** he is now only a parody of his former self; **eine ~ von jdm geben** to do a parody *or* takeoff *(Brit)* of sb, to take sb off *(Brit)*

pa|ro|die|ren [paro'di:rən] *ptp* **parodiert** VT **a** *(= Parodie schreiben auf)* to parody **b** *(= karikieren)* to take off *(Brit)*, to parody

Pa|ro|dist [paro'dɪst] M **-en, -en**, **Pa|ro|dis|tin** [-'dɪstɪn] F **-, -nen** parodist; *(von Persönlichkeiten)* impersonator

pa|ro|dis|tisch [paro'dɪstɪʃ] ADJ parodistic *(liter)*; **~e Sendung** parody, takeoff *(Brit)*; **er hat ~e Fähigkeiten** he's good at taking people off, he's a good impersonator; **~e Literatur** literary parodies

Pa|ro|don|to|se [parodɔn'to:zə] F **-, -n** periodontosis *(spec)*, receding gums *pl*

Pa|ro|le [pa'ro:lə] F **-, -n** **a** *(Mil)* password **b** *(fig: = Wahlspruch)* motto, watchword; *(Pol)* slogan

Pa|ro|li [pa'ro:li] NT **jdm ~ bieten** *(geh)* to defy sb

par|sen ['pa:ɐsn] VT *(Comput, Ling)* to parse

Par|ser ['pa:ɐsɐ] M **-s, -** *(Comput)* parser

Par|sing ['pa:ɐsɪŋ] NT **-s** *(Comput)* parsing

Part [part] M **-s, -e** **a** *(= Anteil)* share **b** *(Theat, Mus)* part

Par|tei [par'tai] F **-, -en** **a** *(Pol)* party; **bei** *or* **in der ~** in the party; **die ~ wechseln** to change parties; **als Bundespräsident steht er über den ~en** as Federal President he takes no part in party politics **b** *(Jur)* party; **die streitenden ~en** the disputing parties; **die vertragsschließenden ~en** the contracting parties; **meine ~** my client **c** *(fig)* **~ sein** to be biased *(Brit)* or biassed; **jds ~ (acc) ergreifen, für jdn ~ ergreifen** *or* **nehmen** to take sb's side *or* part, to side with sb; **gegen jdn ~ ergreifen** *or* **nehmen** to side *or* to take sides against sb; **es mit keiner ~ halten, es mit keiner von beiden ~en halten** to be on neither side, to be neutral; **es mit beiden ~en halten** to run with the hare and hunt with the hounds *(prov)*; **ein Richter sollte über den ~en stehen** a judge should be impartial **d** *(im Mietshaus)* tenant, party *(form)*

Par|tei-: Par|tei|ab|zei|chen NT party badge; **Par|tei|an|hän|ger(in)** M(F) party supporter; **Par|tei|ap|pa|rat** M party machinery *or* apparatus; **Par|tei|aus|schluss|ver|fah|ren** NT expulsion proceedings *pl*; **Par|tei|ba|sis** F rank and file, grassroots (members) *pl*; **Par|tei|bon|ze** M *(pej)* party bigwig *or* boss; **Par|tei|buch** NT party membership book; **das richtige/falsche ~ haben** to belong to the right/wrong party; **das ~ ab-** *or* **zurückgeben** to leave the party; **Par|tei|chef(in)** M(F) party leader *or* boss; **Partei|chi|ne|sisch** NT *(pej)* party jargon

Par|teien-: Par|tei|en|fi|nan|zie|rung F party financing; **Par|tei|en|ge|setz** NT *(Jur)* political parties act; **Par|tei|en|land|schaft** F party (political) scene, political constellation

Par|tei|en|streit M (inter-)party disputes *pl*; *(innerparteilich)* intra-party disputes *pl*

Par|tei-: Par|tei|frau F *(Pol)* female politician; **Par|tei|freund(in)** M(F) fellow party member; **Par|tei|füh|rer(in)** M(F) party leader; **Par|tei|füh|rung** F leadership of a party; *(Vorstand)* party leaders *pl or* executive; **Par|tei|gän|ger** [-gɛŋɐ] M **-s, -**, **Par|tei|gän|ge|rin** [-ərɪn] F **-, -nen** party supporter *or* follower; **Par|tei|ge|nos|se** M, **Par|tei|ge|nos|sin** F party member; **par|tei|in|tern** ADJ internal party *attr*; **~e Kritik** criticism from within the party ADV within the party

par|tei|isch [par'taiɪʃ] ADJ biased *(Brit)*, biassed; partial ADV **~ urteilen** to be biased (in one's judgement)

Par|tei|kon|gress M convention, party congress

par|tei|lich [par'tailɪç] ADJ **a** *(rare: = parteiisch)* bias(s)ed **b** *(= eine Partei betreffend)* party *attr* ADV **~ organisiert sein** to belong to a (political) party; **Maßnahmen, die nicht ~ gebunden sind** measures which are independent of party politics; **ein ~ ungebundener Kandidat** an independent candidate

Par|tei|lich|keit F **-**, *no pl* bias, partiality

Par|tei|li|nie F party line; **auf die ~ einschwenken** to toe the party line

par|tei|los ADJ *Abgeordneter, Kandidat* independent, non-party; **der Journalist war ~** the journalist wasn't attached to *or* aligned with any party

Par|tei|lo|se(r) [par'tailo:zə] MF *decl as adj* independent

Par|tei|lo|sig|keit F **-**, *no pl* independence; **seine ~** the fact that he is not a member of any political party; **~ ist oft ein Vorteil** it's often an advantage not to belong to any party

Par|tei-: Par|tei|mit|glied NT party member; **Par|tei|nah|me** [-na:mə] F **-, -n** partisanship; **Par|tei|or|gan** NT party organ; **Par|tei|po|li|tik** F party politics *pl*; **par|tei|po|li|tisch** ADJ party political ADV as far as party politics go; **dieser Schritt ist ~ geboten** party politics demand this step; **etw ~ ausschlachten** to make party political capital out of sth; **Par|tei|prä|si|di|um** NT party executive committee; **Par|tei|pro|gramm** NT (party) manifesto, (party) programme *(Brit)* or program *(US)*; **Par|tei|sol|dat(in)** M(F) *(inf)* party activist; **Par|tei|spen|de** F party donation; **Par|tei|spen|den|af|fä|re** F party donations scandal; **Par|tei|spit|ze** F party leadership, party leaders *pl*; **Par|tei|tag** M party conference *or* convention

Par|tei|un|gen [par'taiʊŋən] PL *(old)* factions *pl*

Par|tei-: Par|tei|ver|samm|lung F party meeting; **Par|tei|volk** NT grass roots *pl* of the party; **Par|tei|vor|sit|zen|de(r)** MF *decl as adj* party leader; **Par|tei|vor|stand** M party executive; **Par|tei|we|sen** NT, *no pl* party system; **Par|tei|zu|ge|hö|rig|keit** F party membership; **was hat er für eine ~?** what party does he belong to?

par|terre [parˈtɛr] ADV on the ground *(esp Brit) or first (US)* floor

Par|ter|re [parˈtɛr(ə)] NT **-s, -s** **a** *(von Gebäude)* ground floor *(esp Brit)*, first floor *(US)*; **im ~ wohnen** to live on the ground floor *(esp Brit)* or first floor *(US)* **b** *(old Theat)* rear stalls *pl*, pit *(Brit)*, parterre *(US)*

Par|ter|re|woh|nung F ground-floor flat *(Brit)*, first-floor apartment *(US)*

Par|tie [parˈtiː] F **-, -n** [-ˈtiːən] **a** *(= Teil, Ausschnitt)* part; *(eines Buchs)* part, section **b** *(Theat)* part, role; *(Mus)* part **c** *(Sport)* game; *(Fechten)* round; **eine ~ Schach spielen** to play *or* have a game of chess; **die ~ verloren geben** *(lit, fig)* to give the game up as lost; **eine gute/schlechte ~ liefern** to give a good/bad performance **d** *(old: = Landpartie)* outing, trip; **eine ~ machen** to go on an outing, to go for *or* on a trip **e** *(Comm)* lot, batch **f** *(inf)* catch *(inf)*; **eine gute ~ (für jdn) sein** to be a good catch (for sb) *(inf)*; **eine gute ~ machen** to marry (into) money **g** **mit von der ~ sein** to join in, to be in on it; **da bin ich mit von der ~** count me in, I'm with you **h** *(Aus: = Arbeitergruppe)* gang

par|ti|ell [parˈtsiɛl] ADJ partial ADV partially, partly; **diese Lösung ist ~ richtig** this solution is partly *or* partially right; **~ differenzieren** *(Math)* to form a partial derivative

par|ti|en|wei|se [parˈtiːənvaizə] ADV *(Comm)* in lots

Par|ti|kel [parˈtiːkl, parˈtɪkl] F **-, -n** *(Gram, Phys)* particle

Par|ti|kel|schleu|der F *(Phys)* particle accelerator

Par|ti|ku|la|ris|mus [partikulaˈrɪsmʊs] M **-,** *no pl* particularism

Par|ti|ku|la|rist [partikulaˈrɪst] M **-en, -en, Par|ti|ku|la|ris|tin** [-ˈrɪstɪn] F **-, -nen** particularist

par|ti|ku|la|ris|tisch [partikulaˈrɪstɪʃ] ADJ particularistic

Par|ti|san [partiˈzaːn] M **-s** *or* **-en, -en, Par|ti|sa|nin** [-ˈzaːnɪn] F **-, -nen** partisan

Par|ti|sa|nen-: **Par|ti|sa|nen|kampf** M guerrilla warfare; *(Kampfhandlung)* guerrilla battle; **Par|ti|sa|nen|krieg** M partisan war; *(Art des Krieges)* guerrilla warfare

Par|ti|ta [parˈtiːta] F **-, Par|ti|ten** [-tn] *(Mus)* partita

Par|ti|ti|on [partiˈtsioːn] F **-, -en** *(Comput)* partition

par|ti|tiv [partiˈtiːf] ADJ *(Gram)* partitive

Par|ti|tur [partiˈtuːɐ] F **-, -en** [-ˈtuːrən] *(Mus)* score

Par|ti|zip [partiˈtsiːp] NT **-s, -ien** [-piən] *(Gram)* participle; **~ I** *or* **Präsens** present participle; **~ II** *or* **Perfekt** past participle

Par|ti|zi|pa|ti|on [partitsipaˈtsioːn] F **-, -en** participation *(an +dat* in)

Par|ti|zi|pa|ti|ons|ge|schäft NT *(Comm)* transaction conducted by several parties

Par|ti|zi|pi|al-: **Par|ti|zi|pi|al|kon|struk|ti|on** F participial construction; **Par|ti|zi|pi|al|satz** M participial clause

par|ti|zi|pie|ren [partitsiˈpiːrən] *ptp* **partizipiert** VI to participate *(an +dat* in)

Part|ner [ˈpartnɐ] M **-s, -, Part|ne|rin** [-ərɪn] F **-, -nen** partner; *(Film)* co-star; **als jds ~ spielen** *(in Film)* to play opposite sb; *(Sport)* to be partnered by sb, to be sb's partner → **Gesprächspartner(in)**

Part|ner|look [-lʊk] M matching clothes *pl*

Part|ner|schaft [ˈpartnɐʃaft] F **-, -en** partnership; *(= Städtepartnerschaft)* twinning

part|ner|schaft|lich [ˈpartnɐʃaftlɪç] ADJ **~es Verhältnis** (relationship based on) partnership; **in unserer Ehe haben wir ein ~es Verhältnis** our marriage is a partnership; **~e Zusammenarbeit** working together as partners; **in gutem ~em Einvernehmen** in a spirit of partnership ADV **~ zusammenarbeiten** to work in partnership; **~ zusammenleben** to live together as equal partners; **das haben wir ~ gelöst** we solved it together *or* jointly

Part|ner-: **Part|ner|staat** M partner (country); **Part|ner|stadt** F twin town *(Brit)*, sister city *(US)*; **Part|ner|su|che** F finding a/the right partner, finding a mate *(inf)*; **auf ~ sein** to be looking for a partner *or* a mate *(inf)*; **Part|ner|tausch** M **a** *(Tanz, Tennis)* change of partners **b** *(sexuell)* partner-swopping; **Part|ner|ver|mitt|lung** F dating agency; *(= Institut)* marriage bureau; **~ per Computer** computer dating; **Part|ner|wahl** F choice of partner; **jetzt ist ~** *(beim Tanz)* take *or* choose your partners, please!; **Part|ner|wech|sel** M = **Partnertausch**

par|tout [parˈtuː] ADV *(dated)* **er will ~ nach Hause gehen** he insists on going home; **sie will ~ nicht nach Hause gehen** she just doesn't want to go home

Par|ty [ˈpaːɐti] F **-, -s** party; **eine ~ geben** *or* **veranstalten** to give *or* have a party; **bei** *or* **auf einer ~** at a party; **auf eine** *or* **zu einer ~ gehen** to go to a party

Par|ty-: **Par|ty|dro|ge** F party *or* recreational drug; **Par|ty|lö|we** M, **Par|ty|lö|win** F *(iro)* socialite; **Par|ty|lu|der** NT *(inf)* socialite, It girl *(inf)*; **Par|ty|raum** M party room; **Par|ty|ser|vice** [-zøːɐvɪs, -zœrvɪs] M party catering service

Par|ve|nü [parveˈnyː, -vəˈnyː] M **-s, -s** *(dated)* parvenu, upstart

Par|ze [ˈpartsə] F **-, -n** *(Myth)* Parca; **die ~n** the Fates

Par|zel|le [parˈtsɛlə] F **-, -n** plot, lot, parcel of land

par|zel|lie|ren [partsɛˈliːrən] *ptp* **parzelliert** VT to parcel out

Pasch [paʃ] M **-(e)s, -e** *or* **⸚e** [ˈpɛʃə] *(beim Würfelspiel)* doublets *pl* → **Viererpasch**

Pa|scha [ˈpaʃa] M **-s, -s** pasha; **wie ein ~** like Lord Muck *(Brit)* or His Highness *(inf)*

Pas|pel [ˈpaspl] F **-, -n** piping *no pl*

pas|pe|lie|ren [paspəˈliːrən] *ptp* **paspeliert**, **pas|peln** [ˈpaspln] VT to pipe

Pass [pas] M **-es, ⸚e** [ˈpɛsə] **a** passport **b** *(im Gebirge etc)* pass **c** *(Ballspiele)* pass; **öffnender ~** *(Ftbl)* through pass *or* ball; **~ auf die andere Seite** *(Ftbl)* switch of play; **~ in den freien Raum** *(Ftbl)* pass into space **d** *(Reitsport)* amble; **im ~ gehen** to amble

pas|sa|bel [paˈsaːbl] ADJ passable, reasonable; *Aussehen auch* presentable ADV reasonably well; *schmecken* passable; *aussehen* presentable; **mir gehts ganz ~** I'm OK *(inf)*, I'm all right

Pas|sa|ge [paˈsaːʒə] F **-, -n** *(alle Bedeutungen)* passage; *(= Ladenstraße)* arcade

Pas|sa|gier [pasaˈʒiːɐ] M **-s, -e, Pas|sa|gie|rin** [-ʒiːrɪn] F **-, -nen** passenger; **ein blinder ~** a stowaway

Pas|sa|gier-: **Pas|sa|gier|damp|fer** M passenger steamer; **Pas|sa|gier|flug|zeug** NT passenger aircraft, airliner; **Pas|sa|gier|lis|te** F passenger list

Pas|sah [ˈpasa] **-s,** *no pl*, **Pas|sah|fest** NT (Feast of the) Passover

Pas|sah|mahl NT Passover meal; *(jüdisch)* Seder

Pass|amt NT passport office

Pas|sant [paˈsant] M **-en, -en, Pas|san|tin** [-ˈsantɪn] F **-, -nen** passer-by

Pas|sat [paˈsaːt] M **-s, -e, Pas|sat|wind** M trade wind

Pass|bild NT passport photo(graph)

Pass|bild|au|to|mat M photo booth

Pas|se [ˈpasə] F **-, -n** yoke

pas|sé [paˈseː], **pas|see** ADJ *pred* passé; **diese Mode ist längst ~** this fashion went out long ago; **die Sache ist längst ~** that's all ancient history *(inf)*, that's all in the past

pas|sen [pasn] VI **a** *(= die richtige Größe, Form haben)* to fit; **die Schuhe ~ (mir) gut** the shoes fit (me) well, the shoes are a good fit (for me); **dieser Schlüssel passt nicht (ins Schloss)** this key doesn't *or* won't fit (the lock); **der Deckel passt nicht** the lid doesn't *or* won't fit (on) **b** *(= harmonieren)* **zu etw ~** to go with sth; *(im Ton)* to match sth; **zu jdm ~** *(Mensch)* to be suited to sb, to suit sb; **zueinander ~ = zueinanderpassen; sie passt gut zu ihm** she's well suited to him, she's just right for him; **das passt zu ihm, so etwas zu sagen** that's just like him to say that; **es passt nicht zu dir, Bier zu trinken** it doesn't look right for you to drink beer, you don't look right drinking beer; **es passt nicht zu ihr, dass sie so freundlich ist** it's not like her to be so friendly; **diese Einstellung passt gut zu ihm** that attitude is typical of him, that attitude is just like him; **diese Einstellung passt nicht mehr in die heutige Zeit** this attitude is not acceptable nowadays; **so ein formeller Ausdruck passt nicht in diesen Satz** such a formal expression is out of place *or* is all wrong in this sentence; **Streiks ~ nicht in die konjunkturelle Landschaft** strike action is inappropriate in the current economic situation; **das Rot passt da nicht** the red is all wrong there; **das Bild passt besser in das andere Zimmer** the picture would look *or* go better in the other room; **er passt nicht in diese Welt/in dieses Team** he doesn't fit *or* he is out of place in this world/in this team; **ins Bild ~** to fit the picture **c** *(= genehm sein)* to suit, to be suitable *or* convenient; **er passt mir (einfach) nicht** I (just) don't like him; **Sonntag passt uns nicht/gut** Sunday is no good for us/suits us fine; **das passt mir gar nicht** *(= kommt ungelegen)* that isn't at all convenient, that doesn't suit me at all; *(= gefällt mir nicht)* I don't like that at all, I don't think much of that; **das passt mir gar nicht, dass du schon gehst** I don't want you to go now; **wenns dem Chef passt ...** if it suits the boss ..., if the boss gets the idea into his head ...; **du kannst doch nicht einfach kommen, wann es dir passt** you can't just come when it suits you *or* when you like; **das könnte dir so ~!** *(inf)* you'd like *or* love that, wouldn't you?; **ihre Raucherei passt mir schon lange nicht** this smoking of hers has been annoying me for a long time

VR *(inf)* to be proper; **ein solches Benehmen passt sich nicht hier** you can't behave like that here

VT to fix

pas|sen VI *(Cards, fig)* to pass; **(ich) passe!** (I) pass!; **~ müssen** to have to pass; **bei dieser Frage muss ich ~** I'll have to pass on this question

pas|sen VTI *(Ftbl)* to pass

pas|send ADJ **a** *(in Größe, Form)* **gut/schlecht ~** well-/ill-fitting; **er trägt kaum mal einen ~en Anzug** he hardly ever wears a suit that fits; **ein ~er Schlüssel (zu diesem Schloss)** a key that fits *or* to fit (this lock) **b** *(in Farbe, Stil)* matching; **etwas dazu Passendes** something that goes with it *or* to go with it, something to match; **ich muss jetzt dazu ~e Schuhe kaufen** now I must buy some matching shoes *or* some shoes that go with it; **eine im Ton genau dazu ~e Tasche** a bag which matches it exactly **c** *(= genehm) Zeit, Termin* convenient, suitable; **er kam zu jeder ~en und unpassenden Zeit** he came at any time, no matter how inconvenient **d** *(= angemessen) Bemerkung, Benehmen, Kleidung* suitable, appropriate, fitting; *Wort* right, proper; **sie trägt zu jeder Gelegenheit einen ~en Hut** she always wears a hat to suit *or* match the occasion; **er findet immer das ~e Wort** he always knows the right thing to say; **bei jeder ~en**

und unpassenden Gelegenheit at every opportunity, whether appropriate or not
e *Geld* exact
ADV **a** **etw ~ machen** *(Kleidung)* to alter sth; *Brett etc* to fit sth; **etw ~ kürzen** to shorten sth to fit
b *(= abgezählt)* **den Fahrpreis ~ bereithalten** to have the exact fare ready; **haben Sie es ~?** have you got it exactly?, have you got the right money?

Pas|se|par|tout [paspar'tu:] M OR NT **-s, -s** *(alle Bedeutungen)* passe-partout

Pass-: **Pass|form** F fit; **eine gute ~ haben** to be a good fit; **Pass|fo|to** NT passport photo(graph); **Pass|gang** [-gaŋ] M, *no pl* amble; **im ~ gehen** to amble; **Pass|gän|ger** [-gɛŋɐ] M **-s, -** ambler; **Pass|hö|he** F top of the pass

pas|sier|bar ADJ *Brücke, Grenze* passable; *Fluss, Kanal, Pass* negotiable

pas|sie|ren [pa'si:rən] *ptp* **passiert** VI *aux sein* **a** *(= sich ereignen)* to happen *(mit* to); **ihm ist etwas Schreckliches passiert** something terrible has happened to him; **ihm ist beim Bergsteigen etwas passiert** he had an accident while mountaineering; **ist ihm etwas passiert?** has anything happened to him?; **beim Sturz ist ihm erstaunlicherweise nichts passiert** miraculously he wasn't hurt *or* injured in the fall; **was ist denn passiert?** what's the matter?; **es wird dir schon nichts ~** nobody's going to hurt you, nothing is going to happen to you; **es ist ein Unfall passiert** there has been an accident; **das kann auch nur mir ~!** that could only happen to me!, just my luck!; **dass mir das ja nicht mehr** *or* **nicht noch mal passiert!** see that it doesn't happen again!; **jetzt ist es passiert! ich hatte dich gewarnt** now it's happened! I warned you; **jetzt ist es passiert! jetzt kriegen wir Ärger** that's done it *or* torn it *(Brit inf) or* that does it, now we'll be in trouble; **so was ist mir noch nie passiert!** that's never happened to me before!; *(empört)* I've never known anything like it!
b *(= durchgehen)* to pass; *(Gesetz)* to be passed, to go through; **jdn ungehindert ~ lassen** to let sb pass
VT **a** *(= vorbeigehen an)* to pass; **der Zug passierte die Brücke** the train crossed *or* went over *or* passed over the bridge; **der Zug passierte zwei Stationen** the train went through *or* passed (through) two stations; **die Grenze ~** to cross (over) *or* pass (over *or* through) the border; **die Zensur ~** to get through the censor, to be passed by the censor; **das Parlament ~** *(Gesetz)* to be passed by parliament, to get through parliament
b *(Cook)* to strain

Pas|sier-: **Pas|sier|schein** M pass, permit; **Pas|sier|schlag** M *(Tennis)* passing shot; **Pas|sier|sieb** NT strainer; **Pas|sier|stel|le** F crossing point

Pas|si|on [pa'sio:n] F **-, -en** passion; *(religiös)* Passion; **er ist Jäger aus ~** he has a passion for hunting

pas|si|o|niert [pasio'ni:ɐt] ADJ enthusiastic, passionate

Pas|si|ons-: **Pas|si|ons|blu|me** F passion flower; **Pas|si|ons|frucht** F passion fruit; **Pas|si|ons|spiel** NT Passion play; **Pas|si|ons|wo|che** F Holy Week, Passion Week; **Pas|si|ons|zeit** F *(= Karwoche)* Holy *or* Passion Week; *(= Fastenzeit)* Lent

pas|siv ['pasi:f, pa'si:f] ADJ passive; **~e Bestechung** corruption *no pl*, corrupt practices *pl*; **~es Mitglied** non-active member; **~es Rauchen** passive smoking; **~e Sicherheit** *(Aut)* passive safety; **~er Widerstand** passive resistance; **~er Wortschatz** passive vocabulary; **~e Handelsbilanz** *(Comm)* adverse trade balance → **Wahlrecht**
ADV passively; **sich ~ verhalten** to be passive

Pas|siv ['pasi:f] NT **-s, -e** [-və] *(Gram)* passive (voice); **das Verb steht im ~** the verb is in the passive (voice)

Pas|si|va [pa'si:va] PL, **Pas|si|ven** [-vn] PL *(Comm)* liabilities *pl*

Pas|siv-: **Pas|siv|bil|dung** F *(Gram)* formation of the passive; **Pas|siv|fä|hig|keit** F *(Gram)* ability to form the passive; **Pas|siv|ge|schäft** NT *(Fin)* deposit business

Pas|si|vi|tät [pasivi'tɛ:t] F **-,** *no pl* passiveness, passivity; *(Chem)* passivity

Pas|siv-: **Pas|siv|pos|ten** M *(Comm)* debit entry; **Pas|siv|rau|chen** NT passive smoking; **Pas|siv|sal|do** M *(Comm)* debit account; **Pas|siv|sei|te** F *(Comm)* debit side

Pas|si|vum [pa'si:vʊm] NT **-s, Passiva** [-va] *(Gram)* = **Passiv**

Pass-: **Pass|kon|trol|le** F passport control; **~!** (your) passports please!; **durch die ~ gehen** to go through passport control; **Pass|stel|le** F passport office; **Pass|stra|ße** F (mountain) pass

Pas|sung ['pasʊŋ] F **-, -en** *(Tech)* fit

Pas|sus ['pasʊs] M **-, -** ['pasu:s] passage

Pass|ver|län|ge|rung F passport renewal

Pass|wort NT *pl* **-wörter** *(Comput)* password

Pass|wort|schutz M password protection

Pass|zwang M, *no pl* requirement to carry a passport; **es besteht kein ~** you don't have to carry a passport

Pas|te ['pastə] F **-, -n**, **Pas|ta** ['pasta] F **-, Pasten** ['pastn] paste

Pas|tell [pas'tɛl] NT **-s, -e** pastel; *(= Pastellfarbe auch)* pastel shade *or* colour *(Brit) or* color *(US)*; **in ~ arbeiten** to work in pastels; **ein schönes ~** a beautiful pastel (drawing)

Pas|tell-: **Pas|tell|far|be** F pastel (crayon); *(Farbton)* pastel (shade *or* colour *(Brit) or* color *(US))*; **pas|tell|far|ben** [-farbn] ADJ pastel (-coloured) *(Brit)*, pastel(-colored) *(US)* ADV in pastel colours *(Brit) or* colors *(US)*, in pastels; **etw ~ streichen** to paint sth in pastel colo(u)rs *or* in pastels; **Pas|tell|ma|ler(in)** M(F) pastellist *(Brit)*, pastelist *(US)*; **Pas|tell|ma|le|rei** F drawing in pastels, pastel drawing; **Pas|tell|stift** M pastel (crayon); **Pas|tell|ton** M *pl* **-töne** pastel shade *or* tone

Pas|tet|chen [pas'te:tçən] NT **-s, -** vol-au-vent

Pas|te|te [pas'te:tə] F **-, -n** **a** *(= Schüsselpastete)* pie; *(= Pastetchen)* vol-au-vent; *(ungefüllt)* vol-au-vent case **b** *(= Leberpastete etc)* pâté

Pas|teu|ri|sa|ti|on [pastøriza'tsio:n] F **-, -en** pasteurization

pas|teu|ri|sie|ren [pastøri'zi:rən] *ptp* **pasteurisiert** VT to pasteurize

Pas|teu|ri|sie|rung F **-, -en** pasteurization

Pas|til|le [pas'tɪlə] F **-, -n** pastille

Pas|ti|nak ['pastinak] M **-s, -e**, **Pas|ti|na|ke** [pasti'na:kə] F **-, -n** *(Bot)* parsnip

Pas|tor ['pasto:ɐ, pas'to:ɐ] M **-s, Pastoren** [-'to:rən], **Pas|to|rin** [-'to:rɪn] F **-, -nen** → **Pfarrer**

pas|to|ral [pasto'ra:l] ADJ pastoral

Pas|to|ra|le [pasto'ra:lə] NT **-s, -s** *or f* **-, -n** *(Mus)* pastorale; *(Art, Liter)* pastoral; **Beethovens ~** Beethoven's Pastoral Symphony

Patch [pɛtʃ] NT **-s, -es** [-ɪz] *(Comput)* patch

Patch|work ['pɛtʃwø:ɐk, -wœrk] NT **-s,** *no pl* *(Tex, fig)* patchwork

Pa|te ['pa:tə] M **-n, -n** **a** *(= Taufzeuge)* godfather, godparent; *(= Mafiaboss)* godfather; *(= Firmzeuge)* sponsor; **bei einem Kind ~ stehen** to be a child's godparent/sponsor; **bei etw ~ gestanden haben** *(fig)* to be the force behind sth **b** *(obs: = Täufling)* godchild

Pa|te|ne [pa'te:nə] F **-, -n** *(Eccl)* paten

Pa|ten-: **Pa|ten|kind** NT godchild; godson; goddaughter; **Pa|ten|on|kel** M godfather; **Pa|ten|schaft** ['pa:tnʃaft] F **-, -en** godparenthood; sponsorship; **er übernimmt die ~ für das Kind** he's going to be the child's godfather; **die ~ für** *or* **über jdn/etw übernehmen** *(fig)* to take on the responsibility for sb/sth; **er nahm seine ~ nicht ernst** he didn't take his responsibilities as godfather *or* godparent very seriously; **Pa|ten|sohn** M godson; **Pa|ten|stadt** F twin(ned) town *(Brit)*, sister city *(US)*

pa|tent [pa'tɛnt] ADJ ingenious, clever; *Lösung auch* neat; *Werkzeug auch* nifty *(inf)*; **ein ~er Kerl** a great guy/girl *(inf)*; **sie ist eine ~e Frau** she's a tremendous woman

Pa|tent [pa'tɛnt] NT **-(e)s, -e** **a** *(= Erfindung, Urkunde)* patent *(für etw* for sth, *auf etw* on sth); **etw als** *or* **zum ~ anmelden, ein ~ auf** *or* **für etw anmelden** to apply for a patent on *or* for sth; **ein ~ auf eine Erfindung haben** to have a patent on an invention; **für etw** *or* **auf etw das ~ erteilen** to grant a patent on sth; **„(zum) ~ angemeldet"** "patent pending" **b** *(= Ernennungsurkunde)* commission **c** *(Sw)* permit, licence *(Brit)*, license *(US)* **d** *(inf: = Mechanismus)* apparatus; **der Haken, so ein blödes ~** this hook, the stupid thing

Pa|tent-: **Pa|tent|amt** NT Patent Office; **Pa|tent|an|mel|dung** F application for a patent

Pa|ten|tan|te F godmother

Pa|tent-: **Pa|tent|an|walt** M, **Pa|tent|an|wäl|tin** F patent agent *or* attorney; **Pa|tent|dau|er** F life of a patent; **pa|tent|fä|hig** ADJ patentable; **Pa|tent|fä|hig|keit** F patentability; **Pa|tent|ge|ber(in)** M(F) patentor; **Pa|tent|ge|bühr** F *(bei Anmeldung)* (patent) filing fee; *(jährlich)* patent annuity; **Pa|tent|ge|setz** NT Patents Act

pa|ten|tier|bar ADJ patentable

pa|ten|tie|ren [patɛn'ti:rən] *ptp* **patentiert** VT to patent; **sich** *(dat)* **etw ~ lassen** to take out a patent on sth, to have sth patented

Pa|tent-: **Pa|tent|in|ha|ber(in)** M(F) patentee, patent-holder; **Pa|tent|lö|sung** F *(fig)* easy answer, patent remedy; **bei der Kindererziehung gibt es keine ~** there's no instant recipe for success in bringing up children

Pa|ten|toch|ter F goddaughter

Pa|tent-: **Pa|tent|recht** NT patent law; **pa|tent|recht|lich** ADJ, ADV under patent law; **~ geschützt** patented, protected (by patent); **Pa|tent|re|gis|ter** NT Patent Rolls *pl*; **Pa|tent|re|zept** NT *(fig)* = **Patentlösung**; **Pa|tent|schrift** F patent specification; **Pa|tent|schutz** M patent right, protection by (letters) patent; **Pa|tent|ur|kun|de** F letters patent *pl*; **Pa|tent|ver|let|zung** F patent infringement

Pa|ter ['pa:tɐ] M **-s, -** *or* **Patres** ['patre:s] *(Eccl)* Father

Pa|ter|nos|ter [pate'nɔstɐ] NT **-s, -** *(= Gebet)* Lord's Prayer, paternoster

Pa|ter|nos|ter M **-s, -** *(= Aufzug)* paternoster

pa|the|tisch [pa'te:tɪʃ] ADJ emotional; *Beschreibung auch* dramatic; *Rede, Stil auch* emotive; *Gehabe auch* histrionic ADV dramatically; **das war zu ~ gespielt** it was overacted

pa|tho|gen [pato'ge:n] ADJ *(Med)* pathogenic

Pa|tho|lo|ge [pato'lo:gə] M **-n, -n**, **Pa|tho|lo|gin** [-'lo:gɪn] F **-, -nen** pathologist

Pa|tho|lo|gie [patolo'gi:] F **-, -n** [-'gi:ən] pathology

pa|tho|lo|gisch [pato'lo:gɪʃ] *(Med, fig)* ADJ pathological ADV pathologically

Pa|thos ['pa:tɔs] NT **-,** *no pl* emotiveness, emotionalism; **ein Gedicht mit/ohne ~ vortragen** to recite a poem with great drama/without drama; **die Rede enthielt zu viel falsches ~** the speech contained too much false emotionalism; **mit viel ~ in der Stimme** in a voice charged with emotion; **mit viel ~ versuchte sie, ihn zu überzeugen** she made a highly emotional attempt to persuade him

Pa|ti|ence [pa'siã:s] F **-, -n** patience *no pl*; **~n legen** to play patience; **eine ~ legen** to play (a game of) patience

Pa|ti|ent [pa'tsiɛnt] M **-en, -en**, **Pa|ti|en|tin** [-'tsiɛntɪn] F **-, -nen** patient; **ich bin ~ von** *or* **bei Dr X** I'm Dr X's patient, I'm being treated by Dr X; **~en mit Lungenentzündung** pneumonia patients

Pa|ti|en|ten|tes|ta|ment NT *(Jur)* living will

Pa|ti|en|ten|ver|fü|gung F patient's provision

Pa|tin ['pa:tɪn] **F -, -nen** godmother, godparent; *(= Firmpatin)* sponsor

Pa|ti|na ['pa:tina] **F -,** *no pl (lit, fig)* patina; **~ ansetzen** *(lit)* to patinate, to become coated with a patina; *(fig)* to take on a hallowed air of tradition

pa|ti|nie|ren [pati'ni:rən] *ptp* **patiniert** **VT** to patinate, to coat with a patina

Pa|tio ['pa:tio] **M -s, -s** *(Archit)* patio

Pa|tis|se|rie [patɪsə'ri:] **F -, Patisserien** [-'ri:ən] *(Sw)* **a** *(= Konditorei)* patisserie **b** *(= Gebäck)* pastries *pl*

Pat|res *pl von* **Pater**

Pat|ri|arch [patri'arç] **M -en, -en** *(lit, fig)* patriarch

pat|ri|ar|cha|lisch [patriar'ça:lɪʃ] *(lit, fig)* **ADJ** patriarchal **ADV** patriarchally; **er regiert ~** his rule is patriarchal; **eine noch stark ~ organisierte Gesellschaft** a still very patriarchal society

Pat|ri|ar|chat [patriar'ça:t] **NT -(e)s, -e** patriarchy

Pat|ri|ot [patri'o:t] **M -en, -en**, **Pat|ri|o|tin** [-'o:tɪn] **F -, -nen** patriot

pat|ri|o|tisch [patri'o:tɪʃ] **ADJ** patriotic **ADV** *reden, sich verhalten, denken* patriotically; **~ gesinnt** *or* **eingestellt** patriotically-minded, patriotic; **~ klingen** to sound patriotic

Pat|ri|o|tis|mus [patrio'tɪsmʊs] **M -,** *no pl* patriotism

Pat|ri|ze [pa'tri:tsə] **F -, -n** punch

Pat|ri|zi|at [patri'tsia:t] **NT -(e)s, -e** patriciate

Pat|ri|zi|er [pa'tri:tsiɐ] **M -s, -**, **Pat|ri|zie|rin** [-iərɪn] **F -, -nen** patrician

Pat|ri|zi|er|ge|schlecht **NT** patrician family

pat|ri|zisch [pa'tri:tsɪʃ] **ADJ** patrician

Pat|ron [pa'tro:n] **M -s, -e** **a** *(Eccl)* patron saint **b** *(old: = Schirmherr)* patron **c** *(inf)* **frecher ~** cheeky beggar *(Brit inf)*, real (impudent) so-and-so *(inf)* **d** *(Sw, S Ger: = Inhaber)* owner

Pat|ro|na|ge [patro'na:ʒə] **F -, -n** patronage

Pat|ro|nat [patro'na:t] **NT -(e)s, -e** patronage *(über +acc* of); **unter jds ~** *(dat)* **stehen** to be under sb's patronage

Pat|ro|ne [pa'tro:nə] **F -, -n** *(Film, Mil, von Füller, von Drucker)* cartridge; *(Tex)* point paper design

Pat|ro|nen-: **Pat|ro|nen|gurt** **M** ammunition belt; **Pat|ro|nen|gür|tel** **M** cartridge belt, bandolier; **Pat|ro|nen|hül|se** **F** cartridge case; **Pat|ro|nen|rah|men** **M** (cartridge) clip; **Pat|ro|nen|ta|sche** **F** ammunition pouch

Pat|ro|nin **F -, -nen** **a** *(Eccl)* patron saint **b** *(old: = Schirmherrin)* patron, patroness

Pat|ro|nym [patro'ny:m] **NT -s, -e**, **Pat|ro|ny|mi|kon** [patro'ny:mikɔn] **NT -s, Patronymika** [-ka] patronymic

Pat|rouil|le [pa'trʊljə] **F -, -n** patrol; **(auf) ~ gehen** to patrol

Pat|rouil|len-: **Pat|rouil|len|boot** **NT** patrol boat; **Pat|rouil|len|gang** **M** *pl* **-gänge** patrol

pat|rouil|lie|ren [patrʊl'ji:rən] *ptp* **patrouilliert** **VI** to patrol

patsch [patʃ] **INTERJ** splash, splat; *(bei Ohrfeige)* smack; **wenn du so frech bist, machts gleich ~!** if you go on being so naughty you'll get a good smack

Patsch [patʃ] **M -es, -e** *(inf)* smack, slap

Pat|sche ['patʃə] **F -, -n** *(inf)* **a** *(= Hand)* paw *(inf)*, mitt *(inf)* **b** *(= Matsch)* mud; *(= Schneematsch)* slush; *(fig)* jam *(inf)*, fix *(inf)*, (tight) spot *(inf)*; **in der ~ sitzen** *or* **stecken** to be in a jam *(inf)*; **jdm aus der ~ helfen, jdn aus der ~ ziehen** to get sb out of a jam *(inf)*; **jdn in der ~ (sitzen) lassen** to leave sb in the lurch; **jdn in die ~ reiten** to get sb into a jam *(inf)* **c** *(= Feuerpatsche)* beater; *(= Fliegenpatsche)* swat

pat|schen ['patʃn] **VI** **a** *(mit Flüssigkeit)* to splash; **das Baby patschte mit der Hand in die Suppe** the baby went splat *or* splash with his hand in the soup; **er ist durch die Pfützen gepatscht** he splashed *or* went splashing through the puddles **b** *(inf: mit Hand, Fuß)* **das Baby patschte auf den Tisch/an die Möbel** the baby smacked the table/the furniture; **die Kinder ~ mit den Händen** the children clap their hands (together); **der Hund patschte über den Flur** the dog padded across the hall; **er patschte der Sekretärin auf den Hintern** he gave his secretary a pat on the bottom, he patted his secretary on the bottom

Patsch|hand **F** *(inf)*, **Patsch|händ|chen** **NT** *(inf)* paw *(inf)*, mitt *(inf)*; *(von Kindern)* (little) hand

patsch|nass ['patʃ'nas] **ADJ** *(inf)* soaking *or* dripping wet; **draußen ist es ~!** it's soaking wet outside

Pat|schu|li|öl [pa'tʃu:liø:l] **NT -s, -e** pa(t)chouli oil, patchouly oil

patt [pat] **ADJ** *pred* **ADV** *(Chess, fig)* in stalemate; **das Spiel endete ~** the game ended in (a) stalemate; **jetzt sind wir beide ~** now we've both reached a stalemate

Patt [pat] **NT -s, -s** *(lit, fig)* stalemate; **ein ~ erreichen** to reach (a) stalemate, to come to (a) stalemate

Patt|si|tu|a|ti|on **F** *(lit, fig)* stalemate; **aus einer ~ herauskommen** to get out of a stalemate, to break the deadlock

pat|zen ['patsn] **VI** *(inf)* to slip up, to boob *(esp Brit inf)*, to goof *(US inf)*; **der Pianist hat gepatzt** the pianist fluffed a passage *or* boobed *etc*; **der Schauspieler hat gepatzt** the actor fluffed his lines *or* boobed *etc*

Pat|zen ['patsn] **M -s, -** *(Aus)* blotch, splodge; *(Tinte auch)* blot

Pat|zer ['patsɐ] **M -s, -** *(inf: = Fehler)* slip, boob *(esp Brit inf)*, goof *(US inf)*; **mir ist ein ~ unterlaufen** I made a boob *(esp Brit inf)* *or* slip

pat|zig ['patsɪç] *(inf)* **ADJ** snotty *(inf)* **ADV** **jdm ~ kommen** to be snotty to sb *(inf)*

Pau|kant [pau'kant] **M -en, -en** *(Univ sl)* duellist *(Brit)*, duelist *(US)*

Pauk|bo|den **M** *(Univ sl)* duelling *(Brit)* *or* dueling *(US)* floor

Pau|ke ['paukə] **F -, -n** **a** *(Mus)* kettledrum; **jdn mit ~n und Trompeten empfangen** to roll out the red carpet for sb, to give sb the red-carpet treatment; **mit ~n und Trompeten durchfallen** *(inf)* to fail miserably *or* dismally; **auf die ~ hauen** *(inf)* *(= angeben)* to blow one's own trumpet, to brag; *(= feiern)* to paint the town red **b** *(Sch inf: = Schule)* swot-shop *(Brit dated sl)*, school

pau|ken ['paukn] **VI** **a** *(inf: = Pauke spielen)* to drum **b** *(von Korpsstudenten)* to fence **c** *(inf: = lernen)* to swot *(Brit inf)*, to cram *(inf)*; **meine Mutter hat immer mit mir gepaukt** my mother always helped me with my swotting *(Brit inf)* *or* cramming *(inf)* **VT** to swot up *(Brit inf)*, to study up on *(US)*; **mit jdm Geschichtszahlen ~** to help sb swot up *(Brit inf)* *or* study up on *(US)* their dates; **Englisch ~** to swot up on *(Brit inf)* *or* study up on *(US)* English

Pau|ken-: **Pau|ken|schlag** **M** drum beat; **wie ein ~** *(fig)* like a thunderbolt; **die Sinfonie mit dem ~** the Surprise Symphony; **Pau|ken|schlä|gel** **M** drumstick; **Pau|ken|schlä|ger(in)** **M(F)** drummer; **Pau|ken|spie|ler(in)** **M(F)** drummer

Pau|ker ['paukɐ] **M -s, -**, **Pau|ke|rin** [-ərɪn] **F -, -nen** **a** *(inf: = Paukenspieler)* timpanist **b** *(Sch inf: = Lehrer)* teacher; **da geht unser ~** there's sir *(Brit inf)*, there's the teach *(US inf)*

Pau|ke|rei [paukə'rai] **F -, -en** **a** *(inf: = das Paukespielen)* drumming **b** *(Sch inf)* swotting *(Brit inf)*, cramming *(inf)*; **ich hab diese ~ satt** I'm fed up with school

Pau|kist [pau'kɪst] **M -en, -en**, **Pau|kis|tin** [-'kɪstɪn] **F -en, -en** timpanist

Pau|lus|brief ['paulʊs-] **M** Paul's Epistle

Paus|ba|cken ['paus-] **PL** chubby cheeks *pl*

paus|bä|ckig ['pausbɛkɪç] **ADJ** chubby-cheeked

pau|schal [pau'ʃa:l] **ADJ** **a** *(= vorläufig geschätzt)* estimated; *(= einheitlich)* flat-rate *attr only* **b** *(fig) Behauptung, Kritik, Urteil* sweeping **ADV** **a** *(= nicht spezifiziert)* at a flat *or* set rate; **ich schätze die Baukosten ~ auf etwa eine Million Euro** I'd estimate the overall building costs to be 1 million euros; **die Werkstatt berechnet ~ pro Inspektion 100 Euro** the garage has a flat rate of 100 euros per service; **die Einkommensteuer kann ~ festgesetzt werden** income tax can be set at a flat rate; **die Gebühren werden ~ bezahlt** the charges are paid in a lump sum; **Strom berechnen wir Ihnen ~** we'll charge you a flat rate for electricity; **die Kosten verstehen sich ~** the costs are fixed; **alle bekommen ~ £ 20 pro Woche mehr** there will be an across-the-board increase of £20 a week, they'll get £20 a week more across the board **b** *(= nicht differenziert) abwerten* categorically; **so ~ kann man das nicht sagen** that's much too sweeping a statement; **ein Volk ~ verurteilen** to condemn a people wholesale, to condemn a people lock, stock and barrel; **diese Probleme hat er ganz ~ behandelt** he dealt with these problems all lumped together

Pau|schal|be|trag [pau'ʃa:l-] **M** lump sum; *(= Preis)* inclusive price

Pau|scha|le [pau'ʃa:lə] **F -, -n** *(= Einheitspreis)* flat rate; *(= vorläufig geschätzter Betrag)* estimated amount

Pau|schal-: **Pau|schal|ge|bühr** **F** *(= Einheitsgebühr)* flat rate (charge); *(= vorläufig geschätzter Betrag)* estimated charge; **Pau|schal|ho|no|rar** **NT** flat-rate fee

pau|scha|lie|ren [pauʃa'li:rən] *ptp* **pauschaliert** **VT** to estimate at a flat rate *or* in a lump sum

Pau|scha|lie|rung [pauʃa'li:rʊŋ] **F** **a** *(von Beträgen)* consolidation into a lump sum **b** *(Fin: = Besteuerung)* lump-sum taxation, taxation based on average figures

pau|scha|li|sie|ren [pauʃali'zi:rən] *ptp* **pauschalisiert** **VTI** *(geh)* *(= verallgemeinern)* to generalize; *(= nicht differenzieren)* to lump everything together, to tar everything with the same brush *(inf)*; **das kann man nicht ~** you can't generalize *or* make generalizations like that

Pau|schal-: **Pau|schal|preis** **M** *(= Einheitspreis)* flat rate; *(= vorläufig geschätzter Betrag)* estimated price; *(= Inklusivpreis)* inclusive *or* all-in price; **Pau|schal|rei|se** **F** package holiday *(esp Brit)* *or* tour; **Pau|schal|steu|er** **F** *(= vorläufige Steuer)* estimated tax; *(= einheitliche Steuer)* tax at a flat rate; **Pau|schal|sum|me** **F** lump sum; **Pau|schal|ta|rif** **M** flat rate; **Pau|schal|ur|laub** **M** package holiday; **Pau|schal|ur|teil** **NT** sweeping statement; **er neigt sehr zu ~en** he tends to make sweeping statements; **Pau|schal|ver|si|che|rung** **F** comprehensive insurance *no pl*

Pausch|be|trag ['pauʃ-] **M** flat rate

Pau|se **F -, -n** **a** *(= Unterbrechung)* break; *(= Rast)* rest; *(= das Innehalten)* pause; *(Theat)* interval, intermission; *(Sch)* break, recess *(US)*; *(Pol)* recess; *(Liter)* caesura; **(eine) ~ machen, eine ~ einlegen** *(= sich entspannen)* to take *or* have *or* make a break; *(= rasten)* to rest, to have *or* take a rest; *(= innehalten)* to pause, to make a pause; **du hast jetzt mal ~!** *(inf)* now, you keep quiet!; **nach einer langen ~ sagte er ...** after a long silence he said ...; **immer wieder entstanden ~n in der Unterhaltung** the conversation was full of gaps *or* silences; **ohne ~ arbeiten** to work nonstop *or* without stopping *or* continuously; **die große ~** *(Sch)* (the) break *(Brit)*, recess *(US)*; *(in Grundschule)* playtime; **zur ~ stand es 3:1** *(Ftbl)* it was 3-1 at half-time **b** *(Mus)* rest; **die ~n einhalten** to make the rests; **eine halbe/ganze ~** a minim *(Brit)* *or* half-note *(US)*/semibreve *(Brit)* *or* whole-note *(US)* rest

Pau|se **F -, -n** *(= Durchzeichnung)* tracing

pau|sen ['pauzn] **VT** to trace

Pau|sen-: **Pau|sen|brot** **NT** something to eat at break; **Pau|sen|clown** **M** **ich bin doch hier nicht der ~!** *(inf)* I'm not going to play the clown; **Pau|sen|fül|ler** **M** stopgap; **Pau|sen|hal|le** **F** break *or* recess *(US)* hall; **Pau|sen|-**

hof M playground, schoolyard; **pau|sen|los** ADJ *no pred* nonstop, continuous, incessant ADV continuously; **er arbeitet ~** he works nonstop; **Pau|sen|pfiff** M *(Sport)* time-out whistle; *(zur Halbzeit)* half-time whistle; **Pau|sen|stand** M half-time score; score at the interval; **Pau|sen|zei|chen** NT *(Mus)* rest; *(Rad)* call sign

pau|sie|ren [pau'zi:rən] *ptp* **pausiert** VI to (take *or* have a) break; **der Torwart musste wegen einer Verletzung ~** the goalkeeper had to rest up because of injury

Paus|pa|pier ['paus-] NT tracing paper; *(= Kohlepapier)* carbon paper

Pa|vi|an ['pa:via:n] M **-s, -e** baboon

Pa|vil|lon ['pavıljõ:] M **-s, -s** pavilion

Pay-TV ['pe:ti:vi:] NT **-s,** *no pl* pay TV

Pay|wall ['pe:vɔ:l] F **-, -s** *(Internet)* paywall

Pa|zi|fik [pa'tsi:fık, 'pa:tsifık] M **-s** Pacific

pa|zi|fisch [pa'tsi:fıʃ] ADJ Pacific; **der Pazifische Ozean** the Pacific (Ocean); **der (asiatisch-)pazifische Raum** the Pacific Rim

Pa|zi|fis|mus [patsi'fısmʊs] M **-,** *no pl* pacifism

Pa|zi|fist [patsi'fıst] M **-en, -en, Pa|zi|fis|tin** [-'fıstın] F **-, -nen** pacifist

pa|zi|fis|tisch [patsi'fıstıʃ] ADJ pacifist ADV **~ eingestellt sein** to be a pacifist; **~ klingen** to sound pacifist; **sich ~ geben** to give the impression of being a pacifist

PC [pe:'tse:] M **-s, -s** *abbr von* **Personal Computer** PC

PC-Be|nut|zer(in) M(F) PC user

PDA[1] M **-s, -s** *abbr von* **Personal Digital Assistant** PDA

PDA[2] F **-, -s** *abbr von* **Periduralanästhesie** peridural anaesthesia *(Brit) or* anesthesia *(US)*, epidural analgesia

PDF NT **-s, -s** *abbr von* **portable document format** PDF

PDF-Da|tei F PDF file

PDS [pe:de:'ǀɛs] F **-** *abbr von* **Partei des Demokratischen Sozialismus**

> **PDS**
>
> The **PDS (Partei des Demokratischen Sozialismus)** emerged in 1989/90 from the **Sozialistische Einheitspartei Deutschlands (SED)**, which was the official ruling party of the former East Germany. The **PDS** championed people's rights in the new **Länder** and aimed to establish itself as a left-wing socialist party throughout Germany. In 2005 it changed its name to **die Linkspartei.**

Pearl-In|dex ['pø:ɐl-] M *(= Versagerquote einer Verhütungsmethode)* Pearl index

Pech [pɛç] NT **-(e)s, -e** **a** *(Stoff)* pitch; **schwarz wie ~** (as) black as pitch; **ihr Haar ist schwarz wie ~** her hair is jet black; **die beiden halten zusammen wie ~ und Schwefel** *(inf)* the two are as thick as thieves *(Brit) or* are inseparable **b** *no pl (inf: = Missgeschick)* bad *or* hard *or* tough *(inf)* luck; **bei etw ~ haben** to be unlucky in *or* with sth, to have bad *or* tough *(inf) or* lousy *(inf)* luck in *or* with sth; **~ gehabt!** tough! *(inf)*; **sie ist vom ~ verfolgt** bad luck follows her around; **das ist sein ~!** that's his hard *or* bad *or* tough *(inf)* luck!; **so ein ~!** just my/our *etc* luck!; **~ im Spiel, Glück in der Liebe** *(prov)* unlucky at cards, lucky in love *(prov)*

Pech-: **Pech|blen|de** F *(Min)* pitchblende; **Pech|draht** M waxed thread; **Pech|fa|ckel** F (pitch) torch, link; **Pech|koh|le** F bituminous coal; **pech|(ra|ben)|schwarz** ADJ *(inf)* pitch-black; *Haar* jet-black; **Pech|sträh|ne** F *(inf)* run *or* streak of bad luck, unlucky patch; **eine ~ haben** to have a run *or* streak of bad luck; **Pech|vo|gel** M *(inf)* unlucky person, walking disaster area *(hum inf)*; *(Frau auch)* Calamity Jane

Pe|dal [pe'da:l] NT **-s, -e** pedal; **(fest) in die ~e treten** to pedal (hard)

Pe|dant [pe'dant] M **-en, -en, Pe|dan|tin** [-'dantın] F **-, -nen** pedant

Pe|dan|te|rie [pedantə'ri:] F **-, -n** [-'ri:ən] pedantry

pe|dan|tisch [pe'dantıʃ] ADJ pedantic ADV pedantically

Ped|dig|rohr ['pɛdıç-] NT cane

Pe|dell [pe'dɛl] M **-s, -e** *(old) (Sch)* caretaker, janitor; *(Univ)* porter

Pe|di|kü|re [pedi'ky:rə] F **-, -n** **a** *no pl (= Fußpflege)* pedicure **b** *(= Fußpflegerin)* chiropodist

pe|di|kü|ren [pedi'ky:rən] *ptp* **pedikürt** VT to give a pedicure to

Pee|ling ['pi:lıŋ] NT **-s, -s** *(Hautpflege)* peeling, exfoliation

Pee|ling-Creme, Peel|ing|creme ['pi:lıŋ-kre:m] F *(Hautpflege)* body scrub, *(für Gesicht)* face scrub

Peep|show ['pi:pʃo:] F peep show

Pe|ga|sus ['pe:gazʊs] M **-'** Pegasus

Pe|gel ['pe:gl] M **-s, -** *(in Flüssen, Kanälen, Meer)* water depth gauge; *(Elec)* level recorder

Pe|gel|stand M water level

Peil-: **Peil|an|la|ge** F direction-finding equipment, direction finder; *(Naut)* sounding equipment; **Peil|an|ten|ne** F directional antenna

pei|len ['pailən] VT *Wassertiefe* to sound, to plumb; *U-Boot, Sender, Standort* to get a fix on, to get *or* take the bearings of; *Richtung* to plot; *(= entdecken)* to detect; **die Lage ~** *(inf)* to see how the land lies, to see which way the wind's blowing; **über den Daumen ~** *(inf)* to guess roughly; **über den Daumen gepeilt** *(inf)* roughly speaking, at a rough estimate; **es ~** *(sl: = durchblicken)* to get it *(inf)*

Pei|ler ['pailɐ] M **-s, -** detector

Peil-: **Peil|funk** M radio direction finder; **Peil|ge|rät** NT direction finder; **Peil|lot** NT plumb line; **Peil|sen|der** M tracking device; **Peil|sta|ti|on** F direction finding station

Pei|lung ['pailʊŋ] F **-, -en** *(von Wassertiefe)* sounding, plumbing; *(von U-Boot, Sender, Standort)* locating; *(von Richtung)* plotting; **eine ~ vornehmen** to take a bearing; **was für eine ~ haben wir für das U-Boot?** what's our bearing on the submarine?

Pein [pain] F **-,** *no pl (geh)* agony, suffering; **sein Leben war eine einzige ~** his life was one long torment; **jdm das Leben zur ~ machen** to make sb's life a misery

pei|ni|gen ['painıgn] VT to torture; *(fig)* to torment; **jdn bis aufs Blut ~** to torture sb till he bleeds; *(fig)* to torment sb mercilessly; **von Schmerzen/Zweifeln gepeinigt** tormented by pain/doubt, racked with pain/doubt

Pei|ni|ger ['painıgɐ] M **-s, -, Pei|ni|ge|rin** [-ərın] F **-, -nen** *(liter)* torturer; *(fig)* tormentor

Pei|ni|gung F **-, -en** *(liter)* torture; *(fig)* torment

pein|lich ['painlıç] ADJ **a** *(= unangenehm)* (painfully) embarrassing; *Lage, Fragen auch* awkward; *Überraschung* nasty; **ich habe das ~e Gefühl, dass ...** I have a terrible feeling that ...; **es war ihm ~(, dass ...)** he was *or* felt embarrassed (because ...); **es ist mir sehr ~, aber ich muss es Ihnen einmal sagen** I don't know how to put it, but you really ought to know; **es ist mir sehr ~, aber die Arbeit ist immer noch nicht fertig** I'm really sorry but the work still isn't finished; **das ist mir ja so ~** I feel awful about it; **es war so schlecht, dass es schon ~ war** *(inf)* it was so bad it was (really) painful *(inf)* **b** *(= gewissenhaft)* painstaking, meticulous; *Sparsamkeit* careful; **in seinem Zimmer/auf seinem Schreibtisch herrschte ~e** *or* **~ste Ordnung** his room/his desk was meticulously *or* scrupulously tidy; **jdn einem ~en Verhör unterziehen** to question sb very closely ADV **a** *(= unangenehm)* **~ berührt sein** *(hum)* to be profoundly shocked *(iro)*; **~ wirken** to be embarrassing, to cause embarrassment **b** *(= gründlich)* painstakingly; *sauber* meticulously, scrupulously; **der Koffer wurde ~ genau untersucht** the case was gone through very thoroughly, the case was given a very thorough going-over *(inf)*; **er vermied es ~st, davon zu sprechen** he was at pains not to talk about it; **etw ~st geheim halten** to keep sth strictly secret *or* top secret

Pein|lich|keit F **-, -en** *(= Unangenehmheit)* awkwardness; **die ~ der Situation** the awkwardness of the situation, the embarrassing *or* awkward situation; **die ~ seines Benehmens** his embarrassing behaviour *(Brit) or* behavior *(US)*; **diese ~en auf der Bühne** these embarrassing *or* painful scenes on stage

pein|sam ['painza:m] ADJ *(hum)* painful, embarrassing

pein|voll ['painfɔl] ADJ *(old)* painful

Peit|sche ['paitʃə] F **-, -n** whip; **er gab seinem Pferd die ~** he whipped his horse on; **mit der ~ knallen** *(lit, fig)* to crack the whip → **Zuckerbrot**

peit|schen ['paitʃn] VTI to whip; *(fig)* to lash

Peit|schen-: **Peit|schen|hieb** M stroke, lash; **Peit|schen|knall** M crack of a whip; **Peit|schen|leuch|te** F streetlamp; **Peit|schen|schlag** M stroke *or* lash of a whip; **Peit|schen|schnur** F (whip)lash, thong; **Peit|schen|stiel** M whip handle, whipstock

pe|jo|ra|tiv [pejora'ti:f] ADJ pejorative ADV pejoratively

Pe|ki|ne|se [peki'ne:zə] M **-n, -n** pekinese, peke *(inf)*

Pe|king ['pe:kıŋ] NT **-s** Peking, Beijing

Pe|king-: **Pe|king|en|te** F Peking duck; **Pe|king|oper** F Peking Opera

Pek|tin [pɛk'ti:n] NT **-s, -e** pectin

pe|ku|ni|är [pekuni'ɛ:ɐ] *(dated)* ADJ pecuniary, financial ADV financially

Pe|lar|go|nie [pelar'go:niə] F **-, -n** *(Bot)* pelargonium

Pe|le|ri|ne [pelə'ri:nə] F **-, -n** *(old)* pelerine *(old)*, cape

Pe|li|kan ['pe:lika:n, peli'ka:n] M **-s, -e** pelican

Pel|le ['pɛlə] F **-, -n** *(inf)* skin; *(abgeschält)* peel; **der Chef sitzt mir auf der ~** *(inf)* I've got the boss on my back *(inf)*; **er geht mir nicht von der ~** *(inf)* he won't stop pestering me → **rücken**

pel|len ['pɛlən] *(inf)* VT *Kartoffeln, Wurst* to skin, to peel; *Ei* to take the shell off → **Ei** VR *(Mensch, Körperhaut)* to peel; **meine Haut pellt sich** my skin's peeling, I'm peeling; **sie pellt sich aus dem nassen Kleid** she peeled off her wet dress

Pell|kar|tof|feln PL potatoes *pl* boiled in their jackets *or* skins

Pe|lo|pon|nes [pelopɔ'ne:s] M **-(es)** *or f* **-** Peloponnese

Pelz [pɛlts] M **-es, -e** fur; *(nicht gegerbt auch)* pelt, hide, skin; *(Kleidung)* fur; *(fig: = Haarwuchs)* fur *no pl*; **jdm eins auf den ~ brennen** *(inf)* to singe sb's hide; **sich** *(dat)* **die Sonne auf den ~ brennen lassen** *(inf)* to toast oneself *(inf)*; **wasch mir den ~, aber mach mich nicht nass** *(prov)* give me all of the benefits and none of the hassle *(inf)* → **rücken**

Pelz-: **Pelz|be|satz** M fur trimming; **pelz|be|setzt** ADJ trimmed with fur, fur-trimmed; **Pelz|fut|ter** NT fur lining; **pelz|ge|füt|tert** [-gəfʏtɐt] ADJ fur-lined, lined with fur; **Pelz|händ|ler(in)** M(F) furrier; *(= Fellhändler)* fur trader; **Pelz|hand|schuh** M fur glove

pel|zig ['pɛltsıç] ADJ furry; *Zunge* furred(-over), furry

Pelz-: **Pelz|imi|ta|ti|on** F imitation fur; **Pelz|jä|ger(in)** M(F) skin-hunter; *(= Fallensteller)* (fur) trapper; **Pelz|kra|gen** M fur collar; **Pelz|man|tel** M fur coat; **Pelz|müt|ze** F fur hat; **Pelz|stie|fel** M fur *or* furry *(inf)* boot; *(pelzgefüttert)* fur-lined boot; **Pelz|stoff** M fur fabric; **Pelz|tier** NT animal with a valuable fur, animal prized for its fur; **~e jagen** to hunt animals for their fur; *(mit Fallen)* to go trapping; **Pelz|tier|farm** F fur farm; **Pelz|tier|jä|ger(in)** M(F) skin-hunter; *(= Fallensteller)* (fur) trapper; **Pelz|tier|zucht** F fur farming; **pelz|ver|brämt** [-fɛɐbrɛ:mt] ADJ *(liter)* = **pelzbesetzt**; **Pelz|wa|ren** PL furs *pl*; **Pelz|werk** NT fur

Pe|nal|ty ['pɛnlti] M **-(s), -s** *(Sport)* **a** *(Eishockey)* penalty **b** *(Aus, Sw Ftbl)* penalty

P.E.N-Club, **PEN-Club** ['pɛn-] M PEN Club

Pen|dant [pã'dã:] NT -s, -s counterpart, opposite number

Pen|del ['pɛndl] NT -s, - pendulum; **keiner kann das ~ der Zeit aufhalten** time and tide wait for no man *(prov)*; **das ~ schlug nach der entgegengesetzten Seite aus** *(fig)* the pendulum swung in the other direction

Pen|del-: **Pen|del|aus|schlag** M swing of a/the pendulum; **Pen|del|bus** M shuttle bus; **Pen|del|flug|dienst** M shuttle service

pen|deln ['pɛndln] VI **a** *(= schwingen)* to swing (to and fro), to oscillate *(form)*; *(Boxer)* to weave; **er ließ die Beine ~** he let his legs dangle, he dangled his legs; **der DAX pendelte um die 3000-Marke** the DAX index fluctuated around the 3000 level **b** *aux sein (= hin und her fahren) (Zug, Fähre etc)* to shuttle; *(Mensch)* to commute; *(fig)* to vacillate, to fluctuate

Pen|del-: **Pen|del|schlag** M swing of the pendulum; **er spielte zum ~ des Metronoms** he played in time to the metronome; **der ~ der Zeit** the march of time; **Pen|del|schwin|gung** F swing of the pendulum; *(Phys auch)* oscillation (of a pendulum); **Pen|del|tür** F swing door; **Pen|del|uhr** F pendulum clock; **Pen|del|ver|kehr** M shuttle service; *(= Berufsverkehr)* commuter traffic; **Pen|del|zug** M shuttle train

Pend|ler ['pɛndlɐ] M -s, -, **Pend|le|rin** [-ərɪn] F -, -nen commuter

Pend|ler-

Pend|ler|bus M commuter bus

Pend|ler|pau|scha|le F commuter allowance

Pend|ler|zug M commuter train

Pen|do|li|no [pɛndo'li:no] M -s, -s *(Rail)* tilting train

pe|net|rant [pene'trant] ADJ **a** *Gestank, Geschmack* penetrating, pungent; *Gestank, Parfüm auch* overpowering **b** *(fig: = aufdringlich)* pushing, insistent; **der Typ war mir zu ~** he was too pushing *or* pushy *(inf)* for my liking; **seine Selbstsicherheit ist schon ~** his self-confidence is overpowering; **ein ~er Kerl** a pest *(inf)*, a nuisance ADV **a** *(= stark)* **das Parfüm riecht ~** the perfume is overpowering; **das schmeckt ~ nach Knoblauch** you can't taste anything for garlic, it has a very strong taste of garlic **b** *(= aufdringlich)* **jdn ~ nach etw ausfragen** to ask sb insistent questions about sth; **er ist mir ~ auf die Pelle gerückt** he just wouldn't take no for an answer

Pe|net|ranz [pene'trants] F -, *no pl (von Geruch, Geschmack)* pungency; *(fig: = Aufdringlichkeit)* pushiness; **er ist von einer unausstehlichen ~** he's unbearably pushy *(inf)*

Pe|net|ra|ti|on [penetra'tsio:n] F -, -en penetration

pe|net|rie|ren [pene'tri:rən] *ptp* **penetriert** VT to penetrate

peng [pɛŋ] INTERJ bang

pe|ni|bel [pe'ni:bl] ADJ **a** *(= gründlich, genau)* pernickety *(inf)*, precise, exact **b** *(dial: = peinlich) Lage, Angelegenheit* painful, embarrassing ADV *sauber* meticulously; **ein ~ ordentliches Zimmer** an immaculately clean and tidy room; **sie räumt ihr Zimmer immer ~ auf** she always keeps her room immaculate; **mein Mann rechnet mir jeden Cent ~ vor** my husband knows exactly where every penny I spend goes; **er macht seine Buchführung äußerst ~** he is very meticulous about his bookkeeping; **sie zählte ~ jeden Cent einzeln nach** she checked every single penny

Pe|ni|cil|lin [penitsɪ'li:n] NT -s, -e penicillin

Pe|nis ['pe:nɪs] M -, -se *or* **Penes** ['pe:ne:s] penis

Pe|nis|neid M *(Psych)* penis envy

Pe|ni|zil|lin [penitsɪ'li:n] NT -s, -e penicillin

Pen|näl|ler [pɛ'nɛ:lɐ] M -s, -, **Pen|nä|le|rin** [-ərɪn] F -, -nen *(dated)* high-school boy/girl, grammar-school boy/girl *(Brit)*

Penn|bru|der ['pɛn-] M *(inf)* tramp, bum *(inf)*, hobo *(US)*

Pen|ne ['pɛnə] F -, -n *(Sch inf)* school

Pen|ne ['pɛnə] PL *(= Nudeln)* penne *sing*

pen|nen ['pɛnən] VI *(inf: = schlafen)* to kip *(Brit inf)*, to sleep; *(= dösen)* to be half-asleep; **ich habe gerade ein bisschen gepennt** I've just been having a kip *(Brit inf)* or a sleep; **der Meier pennt schon wieder im Unterricht** Meier's having a little nap again during the lesson; **du bist dran, penn nicht!** it's your turn, wake up!; **was das Arbeitslosenproblem betrifft, haben die Politiker wieder einmal gepennt** as far as the unemployment problem is concerned the politicians were once again caught napping

Pen|ner ['pɛnɐ] M -s, -, **Pen|ne|rin** [-ərɪn] F -, -nen *(inf)* **a** tramp, bum *(inf)*, hobo *(US)* **b** *(= verschlafener Mensch)* sleepyhead *(inf)* **c** *(= Blödmann)* plonker *(inf)*

Pen|sa *pl*, **Pen|sen** *pl von* **Pensum**

Pen|si|on [pã'zio:n, pã'sio:n, pɛn'zio:n] F -, -en **a** *(= Fremdenheim)* guesthouse, pension **b** *no pl (= Verpflegung, Kostgeld)* board; **halbe/volle ~** half/full board; **die ~ pro Tag macht 70 Euro** half/full board is 70 euros a day **c** *(= Ruhegehalt)* pension, superannuation **d** *no pl (= Ruhestand)* retirement; **in ~ gehen** to retire, to go into retirement; **in ~ sein** to be retired, to be in retirement; **jdn in ~ schicken** to retire sb

Pen|si|o|när [pãzio'nɛ:ɐ, pãsio'nɛ:ɐ, pɛnzio'nɛ:ɐ] M -s, -e, **Pen|si|o|nä|rin** [-'nɛ:rɪn] F -, -nen **a** *(Pension beziehend)* pensioner; *(im Ruhestand befindlich)* retired person **b** *(= Pensionsgast)* paying guest; *(= ständiger Pensionsgast)* boarder

Pen|si|o|nat [pãzio'na:t, pãsio'na:t, pɛnzio'na:t] NT -(e)s, -e *(dated)* boarding school

pen|si|o|nie|ren [pãzio'ni:rən, pãsio'ni:rən, pɛnsio'ni:rən] *ptp* **pensioniert** VT to pension off, to retire; **sich ~ lassen** to retire; **sich vorzeitig ~ lassen** to take early retirement

pen|si|o|niert [pãzio'ni:ɐt, pãsio'ni:ɐt, pɛnzio'ni:ɐt] ADJ retired, in retirement

Pen|si|o|nie|rung F -, -en *(Zustand)* retirement; *(Vorgang)* pensioning-off; **das Finanzamt entschloss sich zur ~ der älteren Mitarbeiter** the tax office decided to pension off the older workers

Pen|si|o|nist [pãzio'nɪst, pãsio'nɪst, pɛnzio'nɪst] M -en, -en, **Pen|si|o|nis|tin** [-'nɪstɪn] F -, -nen *(S Ger, Aus) (Pension beziehend)* pensioner; *(im Ruhestand befindlich)* retired person

Pen|si|ons-: **Pen|si|ons|al|ter** NT retiring *or* retirement age; **Pen|si|ons|an|spruch** M right to a pension; **pen|si|ons|be|rech|tigt** ADJ entitled to a pension; **Pen|si|ons|fonds** M pension fund; **Pen|si|ons|gast** M paying guest; **Pen|si|ons|kas|se** F pension fund; **Pen|si|ons|preis** M price for full board; **~ 70 Euro** full board 70 euros; **pen|si|ons|reif** ADJ *(inf)* ready for retirement; **Pen|si|ons|rück|stel|lun|gen** PL pension reserve(s *pl*)

Pen|sum ['pɛnzʊm] NT -s, **Pensa** *or* **Pensen** [-za, -sn] workload; *(Sch)* curriculum; *(= Trainingspensum)* quota, programme *(Brit)*, program *(US)*; **tägliches ~** daily quota; **er hat sein ~ nicht geschafft** *or* **bewältigt** he didn't achieve his target; **ein hohes** *or* **großes ~ an Arbeit** a heavy workload

Pen|ta|gon [pɛnta'go:n] NT -s, -e Pentagon

Pen|ta|gramm [pɛnta'gram] NT *pl* **-gramme** pentagram

Pen|ta|me|ter [pɛn'ta:metɐ] M *(Poet)* pentameter

Pen|ta|teuch [pɛnta'tɔyç] M -s Pentateuch

Pent|house ['pɛnthaus] NT -, -s, **Pent|house-Woh|nung** F penthouse (flat *(Brit)* or apartment)

Pen|ti|um® ['pɛntsiʊm] M -(s), -s *(Comput)* Pentium® PC; *(Chip)* Pentium® chip

Pen|ti|um-Pro|zes|sor® M Pentium® processor

Pen|top ['pɛntɔp] M -s, -s *(Comput)* pentop

Pep [pɛp] M -(s), *no pl (inf)* pep *(inf)*, life; **etw mit ~ machen** to put a bit of pep *(inf)* or life *or* zip *(inf)* into doing sth; **das Kleid hat ~** that dress has style *or* flair; **auch torlose Spiele haben manchmal ~** even goalless *(esp Brit)* or scoreless games can be full of action

Pe|pe|ro|ni [pepe'ro:ni] PL chillies *pl (Brit)*, chilies *pl*; *(Sw: = Paprika)* pepper

Pe|pi|ta [pe'pi:ta] M OR NT -s, -s shepherd('s) check *or* plaid

pep|pig ['pɛpɪç] *(inf)* ADJ *Musik, Show* lively, upbeat; *Kleidung* jolly ADV **die Band spielte ~** the band played lively music; **sie war ~ zurechtgemacht** she was really dolled up *(inf)*

Pep|sin [pɛ'psi:n] NT -s, -e pepsin

Pep|tid [pɛp'ti:t] NT -(e)s, -e [-də] peptide

per [pɛr] PREP **a** *(= mittels, durch)* by; **~ Adresse** *(Comm)* care of, c/o; **mit jdm ~ du sein** *(inf)* to be on Christian-name terms *or* first-name terms with sb; **~ Kreditkarte zahlen** to pay by credit card; **~ procura** *(Comm)* per procura, pp *abbr*, for; **~ Saldo** *(Fin)* net; **~ pedes** *(hum)* on shanks's pony *(Brit hum)* or mare *(US hum)*, on foot; **~ se** per se; **~ definitionem** by definition **b** *(Comm: = gegen)* against; **~ cassa** *(old)*, **~ Kasse** *(old)* against cash **c** *(Comm, Econ: = bis, am)* by **d** *(Comm: = pro)* per; **~ annum** per annum

Per NT -s, *no pl*, **PER** [pɛr] NT -s, *no pl abbr von* **Perchloräthylen** perchloroethylene

Per|cus|sion [pə:ɐ'kaʃn] F -, -s *(Mus: = Instrumente)* percussion

per|du [pɛr'dy:] ADJ *pred (inf)* lost

pe|ren|nie|rend [pere'ni:rənt] ADJ perennial

per|fekt [pɛr'fɛkt] ADJ **a** *(= vollkommen)* perfect **b** *pred (= abgemacht)* settled; **etw ~ machen** to settle *or* conclude sth; **die Sache ~ machen** to clinch the deal, to settle the matter; **der Vertrag ist ~** the contract is signed, sealed and delivered *(inf)*, the contract is all settled; **damit war die Niederlage ~** total defeat was then inevitable ADV *(= sehr gut)* perfectly; **~ kochen** to be a perfect cook; **~ Englisch sprechen** to speak perfect English, to speak English perfectly

Per|fekt ['pɛrfɛkt] NT -s, -e perfect (tense)

Per|fek|ti|on [pɛrfɛk'tsio:n] F -, *no pl* perfection; **das war Artistik in höchster ~** that was the epitome of artistry, that was perfect artistry; **etw (bis) zur ~ entwickeln** *(Produkt)* to hone sth; *Betrugsmanöver, Ausreden etc* to get sth down to a fine art

per|fek|ti|o|nie|ren [pɛrfɛktsio'ni:rən] *ptp* **perfektioniert** VT to perfect

Per|fek|ti|o|nis|mus [pɛrfɛktsio'nɪsmʊs] M -, *no pl* perfectionism

Per|fek|ti|o|nist [pɛrfɛktsio'nɪst] M -en, -en, **Per|fek|ti|o|nis|tin** [-'nɪstɪn] F -, -nen perfectionist

per|fek|ti|o|nis|tisch [pɛrfɛktsio'nɪstɪʃ] ADJ perfectionist ADV **du musst nicht alles so ~ machen** you don't have to be such a perfectionist; **~ eingestellt sein** to be a perfectionist

per|fek|tiv [pɛrfɛk'ti:f] ADJ perfective

Per|fek|tum [pɛr'fɛktʊm] NT -s, **Perfekta** [-ta] perfect (tense)

per|fid [pɛr'fi:t], **per|fi|de** [pɛr'fi:də] *(liter)* ADJ perfidious *(liter)* ADV perfidiously *(liter)*

Per|fi|die [pɛrfi'di:] F -, -n [-'di:ən] *(liter)* perfidy

Per|fo|ra|ti|on [pɛrfora'tsio:n] F -, -en perforation

per|fo|rie|ren [pɛrfo'ri:rən] *ptp* **perforiert** VT to perforate

Per|for|mance [pœr'fɔ:məns] F -, -s [-mənsɪz] *(Art, Fin)* performance

Per|for|mance-In|dex M *(Econ, Fin)* performance indicator

Per|for|manz [pɛrfɔr'mants] F -, *no pl (Ling)* performance

Per|ga|ment [pɛrga'mɛnt] NT -(e)s, -e **a** *(= präparierte Tierhaut)* parchment; *(= Kalbspergament auch)* vellum; **dieses Buch ist in ~ gebunden** this book is vellum-bound *or* bound in vellum **b** *(= Handschrift)* parchment **c** *(= Pergamentpapier)* greaseproof paper

Per|ga|ment|band [-bant] M *pl* **-bände** vellum(-bound) book

per|ga|men|ten [pɛrga'mɛntn] ADJ *(liter)* parchment; *(aus Kalbshaut)* vellum

Per|ga|ment-: **Per|ga|ment|pa|pier** NT greaseproof paper; **Per|ga|ment|rol|le** F (parchment) scroll; **Per|ga|ment|rü|cken** M vellum spine

Per|go|la ['pɛrgola] F -, **Pergolen** [-lən] arbour *(Brit)*, arbor *(US)*, bower

Pe|ri|du|ral|an|äs|the|sie F *(Med)* peridural anaesthesia *(Brit)* or anesthesia *(US)*

Pe|ri|o|de [pe'rio:də] F -, -n period *(auch Physiol)*; *(von Wetter auch)* spell; *(Math)* repetend; *(Elec)* cycle; **0,33 ~** 0.33 recurring; **ihre ~ ist ausgeblieben** she didn't get *or* have her period; **~n pro Sekunde** cycles per second

Pe|ri|o|den|sys|tem NT periodic system; *(Tafel)* periodic table

Pe|ri|o|di|kum [pe'rio:dikʊm] NT -s, **Periodika** [-ka] *usu pl* periodical

pe|ri|o|disch [pe'rio:dɪʃ] ADJ periodic(al); *(= regelmäßig)* regular; *(Phys)* periodic; **~er Dezimalbruch** recurring fraction ADV periodically

pe|ri|o|di|sie|ren [periodi'zi:rən] *ptp* **periodisiert** VT to divide up into periods

Pe|ri|o|di|zi|tät [periodizi'tɛ:t] F -, *no pl* periodicity; *(Math: von Bruch)* recurrence

Pe|ri|pe|tie [peripe'ti:] F -, -n [-'ti:ən] peripeteia

pe|ri|pher [peri'fe:ɐ] *(geh, Med)* ADJ peripheral ADV peripherally

Pe|ri|phe|rie [perife'ri:] F -, -n [-'ri:ən] periphery; *(von Kreis)* circumference; *(von Stadt)* outskirts *pl*; *(von Computer)* periphery; **an der ~ Bonns** in *or* on the outskirts of Bonn

Pe|ri|phe|rie|ge|rät NT *(Comput)* peripheral

Pe|ri|skop [peri'sko:p] NT -s, -e periscope

pe|ri|sko|pisch [peri'sko:pɪʃ] ADJ periscopic

Pe|ris|tal|tik [peri'staltɪk] F -, *no pl* peristalsis

Per|le ['pɛrlə] F -, -n **a** *(= Muschelperle)* pearl; **~n vor die Säue werfen** *(prov)* to cast pearls before swine *(prov)* → **Krone** **b** *(aus Glas, Holz etc)* bead; *(= Luftbläschen)* bubble; *(von Wasser, Schweiß)* bead, drop, droplet **c** *(fig)* pearl, gem; *(dated inf: = Hausmädchen)* maid

per|len ['pɛrlən] VI *(= sprudeln)* to sparkle, to bubble, to effervesce; *(Champagner)* to fizz; *(= fallen, rollen)* to trickle, to roll; **~des Lachen** *(liter)* rippling *or* bubbling laughter; **der Tau perlt auf den Blättern** drops *or* beads of dew glisten on the leaves; **der Schweiß perlte ihm von/auf der Stirn** beads of sweat were running down/stood out on his forehead; **Wasser perlt auf einer Fettschicht** water forms into droplets on a greasy surface

Per|len-: **Per|len|aus|ter** F pearl oyster; **per|len|be|setzt** ADJ set with pearls; **per|len|be|stickt** [-bəʃtɪkt] ADJ embroidered *or* decorated with pearls; **Per|len|fi|scher(in)** M(F) pearl fisher, pearler; **Per|len|fi|sche|rei** F pearl fishing; **Per|len|ket|te** F, **Per|len|kol|lier** NT string of pearls, pearl necklace, pearls *pl*; **Per|len|schnur** F string of beads, beads *pl*; **Per|len|sti|cke|rei** F beadwork; **Per|len|tau|cher(in)** M(F) pearl diver

Perl-: **Perl|fang** M, *no pl (Sew)* knit one, purl one; **Perl|garn** NT mercerized yarn; **perl|grau** ADJ pearl-grey *(Brit)*, pearl-gray *(US)*; **Perl|huhn** NT guinea fowl; **Perl|mu|schel** F pearl oyster; **Perl|mutt** ['pɛrlmʊt, pɛrl'mʊt] NT -s, *no pl*, **Perl|mut|ter** ['pɛrlmʊtɐ, pɛrl'mʊtɐ] F - *no pl or nt* -s, *no pl* mother-of-pearl; **Perl|mut|ter|knopf**, **Perl|mutt|knopf** M (mother-of) -pearl button; **perl|mut|tern** ['pɛrlmʊtɐn, pɛrl'mʊtɐn] ADJ mother-of-pearl; *(fig)* pearly

Per|lon® ['pɛrlɔn] NT -s, *no pl a special type of nylon*

Per|lon|strümp|fe PL nylons *pl*, nylon stockings *pl*

Perl-: **Perl|schrift** F *(Typ)* pearl; **Perl|wein** M sparkling wine; **perl|weiß** ADJ pearly white; **Perl|zwie|bel** F cocktail *or* pearl onion

Per|ma|frost ['pɛrmafrɔst] M permafrost

Per|ma|frost|bo|den M permafrost

per|ma|nent [pɛrma'nɛnt] ADJ permanent ADV constantly, continually

Per|ma|nenz [pɛrma'nɛnts] F -, *no pl* permanence; **in ~** continually, constantly

Per|man|ga|nat [pɛrmaŋga'na:t] NT -s, -e *(Chem)* permanganate

per|me|a|bel [pɛrme'a:bl] ADJ *(Bot, Phys, Tech)* permeable

per|mis|siv [pɛrmɪ'si:f] ADJ permissive

Per|mis|si|vi|tät [pɛrmɪsivi'tɛ:t] F -, *no pl* permissiveness

per|ni|zi|ös [pɛrni'tsiø:s] ADJ *(Med)* malignant

Per|pen|di|kel [pɛrpɛn'di:kl] M OR NT -s, - *(von Uhr)* pendulum

per|pe|tu|ie|ren [pɛrpetu'i:rən] *ptp* **perpetuiert** VT to perpetuate

Per|pe|tu|um mo|bi|le [pɛr'pe:tuʊm 'mo:bilə] NT - -, - -(s) perpetual motion machine

per|plex [pɛr'plɛks] ADJ dumbfounded, thunderstruck

Per|ron [pɛ'rõ:] M -s, -s *(old, Sw, Aus)* platform

Per|sen|ning [pɛr'zɛnɪŋ] F -, -e(n) tarpaulin, tarp *(US inf)*

Per|ser ['pɛrzɐ] M -s, - *(inf) (= Teppich)* Persian carpet; *(= Brücke)* Persian rug

Per|ser ['pɛrzɐ] M -s, -, **Per|se|rin** [-ərɪn] F -, -nen Persian

Per|ser|tep|pich M Persian carpet; *(= Brücke)* Persian rug

Per|shing ['pø:ɐʃɪŋ, 'pœrʃɪŋ] F -, -s *(inf)*, **Per|shing|ra|ke|te** F Pershing missile

Per|si|a|ner [pɛr'zia:nɐ] M -s, - **a** *(Pelz)* Persian lamb **b** *(auch* **Persianermantel***)* Persian lamb (coat)

Per|si|en ['pɛrziən] NT -s Persia

Per|sif|la|ge [pɛrzi'fla:ʒə] F -, -n pastiche, satire (+*gen*, *auf* +*acc* on, of)

per|sif|lie|ren [pɛrzi'fli:rən] *ptp* **persifliert** VT to satirize, to write a pastiche of

Per|sil|schein [pɛr'zi:l-] M *(Hist)* denazification certificate; *(hum inf)* clean bill of health *(inf)*; **jdm einen ~ ausstellen** *(hum inf)* to absolve sb of all responsibility

per|sisch ['pɛrzɪʃ] ADJ Persian; **Persischer Golf** Persian Gulf

Per|sisch(e) NT Persian → *auch* **Deutsch(e)**

Per|son [pɛr'zo:n] F -, -en **a** *(= Einzelperson)* person, individual; *(= Charakter)* character; **~en** people, persons *(form)*; **jede ~ bezahlt ...** each person *or* everybody pays ...; **eine aus 6 ~en bestehende Familie** a family of 6; **ein Vier-~en-Haushalt** a four-person household; **pro ~** per person; **die eigene ~** oneself; **was seine (eigene) ~ betrifft** as for himself; **ich für meine ~ ...** I myself ..., as for myself I ..., I for my part ...; **in (eigener) ~ erscheinen** to appear in person *or* personally; **er ist Vorsitzender und Schatzmeister in einer ~** he's the chairman and treasurer rolled into one; **jdn zur ~ vernehmen** *(Jur)* to question sb concerning his identity; **Angaben zur ~ machen** to give one's personal details; **von ~ bekannt** *(Jur)* of known identity; **natürliche/juristische ~** *(Jur)* natural/juristic *or* artificial person; **die drei göttlichen ~en** the Holy Trinity, God in three persons; **eine hochgestellte ~** a high-ranking personage *or* person **b** *(= Mensch)* person; *(pej: = Frau)* female; **sie ist die Geduld in ~** she's patience personified; **Tiere treten in Fabeln als ~en auf** animals figure in fables as human beings *or* as people; **die ~ des Königs ist unantastbar** (the person of) the king is inviolable; **es geht um die ~ des Kanzlers, nicht um das Amt** it concerns the chancellor as a person, not the office; **lassen wir seine ~ aus dem Spiel** let's leave personalities out of it; **wir müssen die ~ von der Sache trennen** we must keep the personal and the factual aspects separate **c** *(Liter, Theat)* character; **die ~en der Handlung** the characters (in the action); *(Theat auch)* the dramatis personae; **eine stumme ~** a nonspeaking part **d** *(Gram)* person; **das Verb steht in der ersten ~ Plural** the verb is in the first person plural

Per|so|nal [pɛrzo'na:l] NT -s, *no pl* personnel, staff; *(= Dienerschaft auch)* servants *pl*; *(Liter: = Romanfiguren)* characters *pl*; **fliegendes ~** aircrew; **ungenügend/ausreichend mit ~ versehen sein** to be understaffed/adequately staffed; **beim ~ sparen** to save money on personnel costs

Per|so|nal-: **Per|so|nal|ab|bau** M, *no pl* reductions *pl* in staff *or* in personnel, personnel *or* staff cuts *pl*; **Per|so|nal|ab|tei|lung** F personnel (department); **Per|so|nal|ak|te** F personal file; **Per|so|nal|an|ga|ben** PL particulars *pl*; **Per|so|nal|auf|wand** M personnel expenditure, staff costs *pl*; **hohen ~ erfordern** to be very labour-intensive *(Brit)* or labor-intensive *(US)*; **Per|so|nal|aus|weis** M identity card; **Per|so|nal|be|ra|ter(in)** M(F) personnel adviser *or* consultant; **Per|so|nal|be|stand** M number of staff *or* employees *or* personnel; **Per|so|nal|bü|ro** NT personnel (department); **Per|so|nal|chef(in)** M(F) personnel manager, head of the personnel department; **Per|so|nal Com|pu|ter** M personal computer; **Per|so|nal|de|cke** F personnel cover; **eine dünne ~** a very tight personnel situation; **Per|so|nal|di|rek|tor(in)** M(F) personnel director; **Per|so|nal|ein|spa|rung** F reduction *or* cut in personnel; **Per|so|nal|ge|sell|schaft** F unlimited company

Per|so|na|lie [pɛrzo'na:liə] F -, -n **a** *(= Angabe zur Person)* personal detail; **~n** *pl* particulars *pl* **b** *(= Personalangelegenheit)* personnel matter

Per|so|na|li|en|über|prü|fung F checking of one's/my/his *etc* particulars

per|so|na|li|sie|ren [pɛrzonali'zi:rən] *ptp* **personalisiert** VTI to personalize; **er personalisiert immer alles** he always personalizes everything, he always reduces everything to a personal level

Per|so|na|li|sie|rung F -, -en personalization

Per|so|na|li|tät [pɛrzonali'tɛ:t] F -, -en *(geh)* personality

Per|so|nal-: **Per|so|nal|kar|tei** F personnel index; **Per|so|nal|kos|ten** PL personnel costs *pl*; **Per|so|nal|lei|ter(in)** M(F) personnel manager, head of the personnel department; **Per|so|nal|man|gel** M staff shortage(s *pl*), shortage of staff; **an ~ leiden** to be understaffed; **Per|so|nal|pla|nung** F staff planning; **Per|so|nal|po|li|tik** F staff *or* personnel policy; **Per|so|nal|pro|no|men** NT personal pronoun; **Per|so|nal|ra|batt** M staff discount; **Per|so|nal|rat** M *(Ausschuss) staff council for civil servants*; **Per|so|nal|rat** M, **Per|so|nal|rä|tin** F *representative on a staff council for civil servants*; **Per|so|nal-Ser|vice-A|gen|tur** F temporary employment service *(offered by the state employment service as an intermediate solution to jobseekers)*; **Per|so|nal|stand** M staff number, number of persons employed; **Per|so|nal|stands|re|du|zie|rung** F staff cuts *pl*, manpower reductions *pl*, redundancies *pl*; **Per|so|nal|uni|on** F personal union; **er ist Kanzler und Parteivorsitzender in ~** he is at the same time Prime Minister and party chairman; **Per|so|nal|ver|tre|tungs|ge|setz** NT employees' representation law; **Per|so|nal|we|sen** NT, *no pl* personnel (matters *pl*)

Per|so|na non gra|ta [pɛr'zo:na nɔn 'gra:ta] F - - -, *no pl* persona non grata

Per|sön|chen [pɛr'zø:nçən] NT -s, - *(inf)* little lady *(inf)*

per|so|nell [pɛrzo'nɛl] ADJ staff *attr*, personnel *attr*; *Konsequenzen* for staff, for personnel; **unsere Schwierigkeiten sind rein ~** our difficulties are simply to do with staffing *or* personnel

ADV **die Abteilung wird ~ aufgestockt** more staff will be taken on in the department; **~ unzureichend/zu großzügig ausgestattet sein** to be understaffed/overstaffed; **die Verzögerungen der Produktion sind ~ bedingt** the delays in production are caused by staff *or* personnel problems

Per|so|nen-: **Per|so|nen|auf|zug** M (passenger) lift *(Brit)*, elevator *(US)*; **Per|so|nen|au|to** NT car, automobile *(US)*; **Per|so|nen|be|för|de|rung** F carriage *or* conveyance of passengers; **die Bahn hat ein Defizit bei der ~** the railways' passenger(-carrying) services show a deficit; **Per|so|nen|be|schrei|bung** F (personal) description; **per|so|nen|be|zo|gen** ADJ *Daten, Informationen* personal; **Per|so|nen|fern|ver|kehr** M *(esp Rail)* long-distance passenger services *pl*; **Per|so|nen|ge|dächt|nis** NT memory for faces; **Per|so|nen|ge|sell|schaft** F partnership; **Per|so|nen|kon|trol|le** F identity check; **Per|so|nen|kraft|wa|gen** M *(form)* (private) car, motorcar *(form)*, automobile *(US)*; **Per|so|nen|kreis** M group of people; **Per|so|nen|kult** M personality cult; **mit Che Guevara wird viel ~ getrieben** a great personality cult has been built up around Che Guevara; **Per|so|nen|nah|ver|kehr** M local passenger services *pl*; **öffentlicher ~** local public transport; **Per|so|nen|re|gis|ter** NT index of names; **Per|so|nen|ruf|an|la|ge** F pager, bleeper *(Brit)*, beeper *(esp US)*; **Per|so|nen|scha|den** M injury to persons; **ein Unfall mit/ohne ~** an accident in which people were injured/in which nobody was injured; **es gab keine ~** no-one was injured; **Per|so|nen|schutz** M personal security; **Per|so|nen|stand** M marital status; **Per|so|nen|stands|re|gis|ter** NT register of births, marriages and deaths; **Per|so|nen|ver|kehr** M passenger services *pl*; **Per|so|nen|ver|si|che|rung** F personal injury insurance; **Per|so|nen|ver|zeich|nis** NT register (of persons); *(Liter)* list of characters; **Per|so|nen|waa|ge** F scales *pl*, pair of scales; **Per|so|nen|wa|gen** M *(Aut)* car, automobile *(US)*; **Per|so|nen|zahl** F number of persons *(form)* or people; **Per|so|nen|zug** M *(Gegensatz: Schnellzug)* slow *or* stopping train; *(Gegensatz: Güterzug)* passenger train

Per|so|ni|fi|ka|ti|on [pɛrzonifika'tsio:n] F -, -en personification

per|so|ni|fi|zie|ren [pɛrzonifi'tsi:rən] *ptp* **personifiziert** VT to personify; **er läuft herum wie das personifizierte schlechte Gewissen** he's going around with guilt written all over his face

Per|so|ni|fi|zie|rung F -, -en personification

per|sön|lich [pɛr'zø:nlɪç] ✪ 33.1, 33.2, 53.5 ADJ personal; *Atmosphäre, Umgangsformen* friendly; **~e Auslagen** out-of-pocket *or* personal expenses; **~e Meinung** personal opinion, one's own opinion; **~es Fürwort** personal pronoun; **~ werden** to get personal; **nun werden Sie doch nicht gleich ~!** there's no need to get personal ADV personally; *(auf Briefen)* private (and confidential); **der Chef ~** the boss himself *or* in person *or* personally; **etw ~ meinen/nehmen** *or* **auffassen** to mean/take sth personally; **er interessiert sich ~ für seine Leute** he takes a personal interest in his people; **Sie müssen ~ erscheinen** you are required to appear in person *or* personally; **~ haften** *(Comm)* to be personally liable

Per|sön|lich|keit F -, -en **a** *no pl (= Charakter)* personality; *(von Hotel, Einrichtung)* character; **er besitzt wenig ~** he hasn't got much personality **b** *(= bedeutender Mensch)* personality; **er ist eine ~** he's quite a personality; **~en des öffentlichen Lebens** public figures

Per|sön|lich|keits-: **Per|sön|lich|keits|ent|fal|tung** F personality development, development of the personality; **Per|sön|lich|keits|merk|mal** NT personality trait; **Per|sön|lich|keits|pro|fil** NT psychological profile; **Per|sön|lich|keits|test** M personality test; **Per|sön|lich|keits|ver|än|de|rung** F personality change; **Per|sön|lich|keits|wahl** F *electoral system in which a vote is cast for a candidate rather than a party*; **diese Wahl war eine reine ~** *(inf)* this election boiled down to a question of the candidates' personalities

Per|spek|tiv [pɛrspɛk'ti:f] NT -(e)s, -e [-və] small telescope, perspective *(obs)*

Per|spek|ti|ve [pɛrspɛk'ti:və] F -, -n *(Art, Opt)* perspective; *(= Blickpunkt)* angle; *(= Gesichtspunkt)* point of view, angle; *(fig: = Zukunftsausblick)* prospects *pl*; **aus dieser ~ wirkt das Haus viel größer** the house looks much bigger from this angle; **das eröffnet ganz neue ~n für uns** that opens new horizons for us; **für etw keine ~ sehen** to see no future for sth

per|spek|ti|visch [pɛrspɛk'ti:vɪʃ] ADJ **a** perspective *attr*; **die Zeichnung ist nicht ~** the drawing is not in perspective; **~e Verkürzung** foreshortening **b** *(= auf die Zukunft gerichtet)* prospective ADV in perspective; **~ verkürzt** foreshortened; **dieses Bild ist ~ korrekt/verzerrt** the perspective in this picture is correct/distorted

per|spek|tiv|los ADJ without prospects

Per|spek|tiv|lo|sig|keit F -, *no pl* lack of prospects

Pe|ru [pe'ru:] NT -s Peru

Pe|ru|a|ner [pe'rua:nɐ] M -s, -, **Pe|ru|a|ne|rin** [-ərɪn] F -, -nen Peruvian

pe|ru|a|nisch [pe'rua:nɪʃ] ADJ Peruvian

Pe|rü|cke [pe'rʏkə] F -, -n wig

per|vers [pɛr'vɛrs] ADJ perverted, warped *(inf)*; **ein ~er Mensch** a pervert ADV perversely; **~ veranlagt sein** to be a pervert

Per|ver|si|on [pɛrvɛr'zio:n] F -, -en perversion

Per|ver|si|tät [pɛrvɛrzi'tɛ:t] F -, -en perversion

per|ver|tie|ren [pɛrvɛr'ti:rən] *ptp* **pervertiert** VT to pervert, to warp VI *aux sein* to become *or* get perverted

Per|ver|tiert|heit F -, -en pervertedness, perversion

pe|sen ['pe:zn] VI *aux sein (inf)* to belt *(inf)*, to charge *(inf)*

Pes|sar [pɛ'sa:ɐ] NT -s, -e pessary; *(zur Empfängnisverhütung)* cap, diaphragm

Pes|si|mis|mus [pɛsi'mɪsmʊs] M -, *no pl* pessimism; **immer dieser ~!** you're/he's *etc* always so pessimistic!, this eternal pessimism!; **in ~ machen** *(inf)* to be pessimistic

Pes|si|mist [pɛsi'mɪst] M -en, -en, **Pes|si|mis|tin** [-'mɪstɪn] F -, -nen pessimist

pes|si|mis|tisch [pɛsi'mɪstɪʃ] ADJ pessimistic ADV pessimistically; **etw ~ beurteilen** to take a pessimistic view of sth, to view sth pessimistically; **~ eingestellt sein** to be pessimistic

Pest [pɛst] F -, *no pl (Hist, Med)* plague, pestilence, pest; *(fig)* plague; **die Schwarze ~** the black plague; **sich wie die ~ ausbreiten** to spread like the plague *or* like wildfire; **jdn/etw wie die ~ hassen** *(inf)* to loathe (and detest) sb/sth, to hate sb's guts *(inf)*; **jdn wie die ~ meiden** *(inf)* to avoid sb like the plague; **wie die ~ stinken** *(inf)* to stink to high heaven *(inf)*; **jdm die ~ an den Hals wünschen** *(inf)* to wish sb would drop dead *(inf)*

Pest-: **pest|ar|tig** ADJ *(Med)* pestilential; *(fig) Gestank* fetid, miasmic *(liter)* ADV **~ stinken** to stink to high heaven *(inf)*; **sich ~ verbreiten** to spread like the plague; **Pest|beu|le** F plague spot; **Pest|ge|ruch** M, **Pest|ge|stank** M (foul) stench, stink; **Pest|hauch** M *(poet)* miasma *(liter)*, fetor *(liter)*

Pes|ti|lenz [pɛsti'lɛnts] F -, -en *(old)* pestilence

Pes|ti|zid [pɛsti'tsi:t] NT -(e)s, -e [-də] pesticide

Pest-: **pest|krank** ADJ sick of the plague *(old)*, plague-stricken; **Pest|kran|ke(r)** MF *decl as adj* person with the plague

PET [pet] NT **a** *abbr von* **Polyethylenterephthalat** PET, polyethylene terephthalate **b** *(Med) abbr von* **Positronen-Emissions-Tomografie** PET, positron emission tomography

Pe|ter|si|lie [petɐ'zi:liə] F -, -n parsley; **du siehst aus, als hätte es dir die ~ verhagelt** *(inf)* you look as though you've lost a pound and found a sixpence *(Brit inf)*, you look as though you lost a buck and found a penny *(US inf)*

Pe|ters|kir|che ['pe:tɐs-] F, *no pl* St Peter's

Pe|ter|wa|gen ['pe:tɐ-] M *(inf)* police *or* patrol car, panda car *(Brit)*

PET-Fla|sche ['pet-] F PET bottle

Pe|ti|tes|se [pəti'tɛsə] F -, -n *(geh)* small *or* trifling matter; *(Summe)* small *or* trifling sum

Pe|ti|ti|on [peti'tsio:n] F -, -en petition

Pe|ti|ti|ons-: **Pe|ti|ti|ons|aus|schuss** M committee on petitions; **Pe|ti|ti|ons|recht** NT right to petition

Pe|tri Heil ['pe:tri-] INTERJ *(Anglergruß)* tight lines!

Pet|ri|scha|le ['pe:tri-] F Petri dish

Pet|ro-: **Pet|ro|che|mie** [petroçe'mi:, 'pe:tro-] F petrochemistry; **pet|ro|che|misch** ADJ petrochemical; **Pet|ro|dol|lar** M petrodollar

Pet|ro|le|um [pe'tro:leʊm] NT -s, *no pl* paraffin (oil) *(Brit)*, kerosene *(esp US)*

Pet|ro|le|um-: **Pet|ro|le|um|ko|cher** M paraffin *(Brit) or* kerosene *(esp US)* stove, primus (stove)® *(Brit)*; **Pet|ro|le|um|lam|pe** F, **Pet|ro|le|um|licht** NT paraffin *(Brit) or* oil *or* kerosene *(esp US)* lamp

Pet|rus ['pe:trʊs] M -' *(Bibl)* Peter

Pet|schaft ['pɛtʃaft] NT -s, -e *(old)* seal

Pet|ti|coat ['pɛtiko:t] M -s, -s stiff(ened) petticoat

Pet|ting ['pɛtɪŋ] NT -s, -s petting

pet|to ['pɛto] ADV **etw in ~ haben** *(inf)* to have sth up one's sleeve *(inf)*

Pe|tu|nie [pe'tu:niə] F -, -n petunia

Petz [pɛts] M -es, -e *(liter)* **Meister ~** (Master) Bruin

Pet|ze ['pɛtsə] F -, -n *(Sch inf)* sneak *(dated Brit Sch inf)*, telltale (tit) *(Brit Sch inf)*, snitch *(Sch inf)*

pet|zen ['pɛtsn] *(inf)* VT **der petzt alles** he always tells; **er hat gepetzt, dass ...** he (went and) told that ...; **er hats dem Lehrer gepetzt** he told sir *(Brit Sch inf)*, he told the teacher VI to tell (tales) *(bei* to)

Pet|zer ['pɛtsɐ] M -s, -, **Pet|ze|rin** [-ərɪn] F -, -nen *(Sch inf)* sneak *(dated Brit Sch inf)*, telltale (tit) *(Brit Sch inf)*, snitch *(Sch inf)*

peu à peu [pø a 'pø] ADV *(inf)* gradually, little by little

Pf *(Hist) abbr von* **Pfennig**

Pfad [pfa:t] M -(e)s, -e [-də] path, track; *(Comput)* path; **auf dem ~ der Tugend wandeln** *(liter)* to follow the path of virtue; **neue ~e in der Medizin** new directions in medicine

Pfad|fin|der M, **Pfa|der** ['pfa:dɐ] M -s, - *(Sw)* (Boy) Scout; **er ist bei den Pfadern** he's in the (Boy) Scouts

Pfad|fin|der|be|we|gung F (Boy) Scout movement, (Boy) Scouts *pl*

Pfad|fin|de|rin F, **Pfa|de|rin** [-ərɪn] F -, -nen *(Sw)* Girl Guide *(Brit)*, Girl Scout *(US)*

Pfad|na|me M *(Comput)* path name

Pfaf|fe ['pfafə] M -n, -n *(pej)* cleric *(pej)*, parson

pfäf|fisch ['pfɛfɪʃ] ADJ *(pej)* sanctimonious *(pej)*

Pfahl [pfa:l] M -s, ⸗e ['pfɛ:lə] post; *(= Zaunpfahl auch)* stake; *(= Stütze auch)* support; *(= Palisade)* palisade, pale, stake; *(= Brückenpfahl)* pile, pier; *(= Marterpfahl)* stake; **jdm ein ~ im Fleisch sein** *(liter)* to be a thorn in sb's flesh

Pfahl-: **Pfahl|bau** M *pl* -bauten **a** *no pl (Bauweise)* building on stilts; **im ~** on stilts **b** *(Haus)* pile dwelling, house built on stilts; **Pfahl|brü|cke** F pile bridge; **Pfahl|dorf** NT pile village

pfäh|len ['pfɛ:lən] VT **a** *(Hort)* to stake **b** *(hinrichten)* to impale

Pfahl-: **Pfahl|werk** NT *(= Stützwand)* pilework; *(= Palisade)* palisade, paling

Pfahl|wur|zel F taproot

Pfalz [pfalts] F -, -en **a** *no pl (= Rheinpfalz)* Rhineland *or* Lower Palatinate, Rheinpfalz **b** *no pl (= Oberpfalz)* Upper Palatinate **c** *(Hist) (= Burg)* palace; *(= Gebiet eines Pfalzgrafen)* palatinate

Pfäl|zer ['pfɛltsɐ] M -s, - *(Wein) wine from the Rhineland Palatinate*

Pfäl|zer ['pfɛltsɐ] M -s, -, **Pfäl|ze|rin** [-ərɪn] F -, -nen *(aus Rheinpfalz)* person from the Rhineland; *(aus der Oberpfalz)* person from the Upper Palatinate; **er ist (ein) ~** he comes from the (Rhineland/Upper) Palatinate

Pfäl|zer ['pfɛltsɐ] ADJ *attr* Palatine, of the (Rhineland) Palatinate

Pfalz-: **Pfalz|graf** M *(Hist)* count palatine; **pfalz|gräf|lich** ADJ of a/the count palatine

pfäl|zisch ['pfɛltsɪʃ] ADJ Palatine, of the (Rhineland) Palatinate

Pfand [pfant] NT -(e)s, ¨-er ['pfɛndɐ] security, pledge; *(beim Pfänderspiel)* forfeit; *(= Verpackungspfand, Nutzungspfand)* deposit; *(fig)* pledge; **etw als ~ geben, etw zum ~ setzen** *(liter)* to pledge sth, to give sth as (a) security; *(fig)* to pledge sth; *(beim Pfänderspiel)* to pay sth as a forfeit; **ich gebe mein Wort als ~** I pledge my word; **etw gegen ~ leihen** to lend sth against a security *or* pledge; *Fahrrad, Schlittschuh etc* to hire *(Brit) or* rent *(US)* sth out in return for a deposit; **auf dem Glas ist ~** there's something (back) on the glass *(inf)*, there's a deposit on the glass; **auf der Flasche sind 50 Pf ~** there's 50Pf (back) on the bottle *(inf)*; **ein ~ einlösen** to redeem a pledge; **etw als ~ behalten** to keep sth as (a) security, to hold sth in pledge

pfänd|bar ADJ *(Jur)* distrainable *(form)*, attachable *(form)*; **der Fernseher ist nicht ~** the bailiffs can't take the television

Pfand|brief M *(von Bank, Regierung)* bond, debenture

pfän|den ['pfɛndn] VT *(Jur)* to impound, to seize, to distrain upon *(form)*; *Konto, Lohn, Gehalt* to seize; **man hat ihm die Möbel gepfändet** the bailiffs *or* they took away his furniture; **jdn ~** to impound *or* seize some of sb's possessions; **jdn ~ lassen** to get the bailiffs onto sb

Pfän|der|spiel NT (game of) forfeits

Pfand-: **Pfand|fla|sche** F returnable bottle; **Pfand|haus** NT pawnshop, pawnbroker's; **Pfand|lei|he** F **a** *(das Leihen)* pawnbroking **b** *(= Pfandhaus)* pawnshop, pawnbroker's; **Pfand|lei|her** [-laiɐ] M -s, -, **Pfand|lei|he|rin** [-ərɪn] F -, -nen pawnbroker; **Pfand|pflicht** F (a) compulsory deposit *(on bottles, tins, cans, etc)*; **Pfand|recht** NT right of distraint *(an +dat* upon) *(form)*, lien *(an +dat* on) *(form)*; **wenn du deine Miete nicht bezahlst, hat der Vermieter ein ~ an deinen Möbeln** if you don't pay your rent the landlord is entitled to seize *or* impound your furniture; **Pfand|schein** M pawn ticket

Pfän|dung ['pfɛndʊŋ] F -, -en seizure, distraint *(form)*, attachment *(form)*; **der Gerichtsvollzieher kam zur ~** the bailiff came to seize *or* impound their possessions

Pfän|dungs|be|fehl M, **Pfän|dungs|ver|fü|gung** F distress warrant

Pfan|ne ['pfanə] F -, -n *(Cook)* pan; *(Anat)* socket; *(= Dachpfanne)* pantile; *(= Zündpfanne)* pan; *(= Gießpfanne)* ladle; **ein paar Eier in die ~ schlagen** *or* **hauen** *(inf)* to bung a couple of eggs in the pan *(Brit inf)*, to fry up a couple of eggs; **jdn in die ~ hauen** *(inf)* to do the dirty on sb *(inf)*; **etw auf der ~ haben** *(inf: = in petto)* to have sth up one's sleeve *(inf)*; **etwas auf der ~ haben** *(inf: geistig)* to have it up there *(inf)*

Pfan|nen|ge|richt NT *(Cook)* fry-up

Pfan|nen|ku|chen M, **Pfann|ku|chen** M *(= Eierpfannkuchen)* pancake; *(= Berliner)* (jam) doughnut *(Brit) or* donut *(US)*; **aufgehen wie ein ~** *(inf)* to turn into *or* to get to be a real dumpling *(Brit inf) or* roly-poly *(inf)*

Pfarr|amt NT priest's office

Pfarr|be|zirk M, **Pfar|re** ['pfarə] F -, -n *(old)* parish

Pfar|rei [pfa'rai] F -, -en *(= Gemeinde)* parish; *(= Amtsräume)* priest's office

Pfar|rer ['pfarɐ] M -s, -, **Pfar|re|rin** [-ərɪn] F -, -nen *(katholisch, evangelisch)* parish priest; *(anglikanisch auch)* vicar; *(von Freikirchen)* minister; *(= Gefängnispfarrer, Militärpfarrer etc)* chaplain, padre; **guten Morgen, Herr ~!** good morning, *(katholisch)* Father *or (evangelisch, anglikanisch)* Vicar *or (von Freikirchen)* Mr ... *or (Gefängnis etc)* Padre; **als nächster wird Herr ~ Schmidt sprechen** the Reverend Michael Schmidt is going to speak next

Pfarr-: **Pfarr|ge|mein|de** F parish; **Pfarr|ge|mein|de|rat** M *(= Gremium)* parish council; **Pfarr|haus** NT *(anglikanisch)* vicarage; *(methodistisch, Scot)* manse; *(katholisch)* presbytery; **Pfarr|hel|fer(in)** M(F) curate; **Pfarr|kind** NT parishioner; **Pfarr|kir|che** F parish church; **Pfarr|stel|le** F parish, (church) living, benefice

Pfau [pfau] M -(e)s *or* -en, -en peacock; **er stolziert daher wie ein ~** he struts around like a peacock; **aufgedonnert wie ein ~** *(inf)* dressed *or* done up to the nines *(Brit inf) or* hilt *(US inf)*

Pfau|en-: **Pfau|en|au|ge** NT *(= Tagpfauenauge)* peacock butterfly; *(= Nachtpfauenauge)* peacock moth; **Pfau|en|fe|der** F peacock feather; **Pfau|en|hen|ne** F peahen

Pfef|fer ['pfɛfɐ] M -s, - pepper; **~ und Salz** *(lit)* salt and pepper; *(Stoffmuster)* pepper-and-salt; **das brennt wie ~** that's red-hot; *(Schmerz)* that really stings; **er kann hingehen** *or* **bleiben, wo der ~ wächst!** *(inf)* he can go to hell *(inf)*, he can take a running jump *(Brit inf) or* flying leap *(US inf)*; **sie hat ~ im Hintern** *(inf) or* **Arsch** *(sl)* she's a lot of get-up-and-go *(inf)*

pfef|fe|rig ['pfɛfərɪç] ADJ peppery

Pfef|fer-: **Pfef|fer|korn** NT *pl* -körner peppercorn; **Pfef|fer|ku|chen** M gingerbread; **Pfef|fer|ku|chen|häus|chen** [-hɔysçən] NT gingerbread house

Pfef|fer|minz ['pfɛfɐmɪnts, -'mɪnts] NT -es, -(e), **Pfef|fer|minz|bon|bon** NT OR M peppermint

Pfef|fer|min|ze ['pfɛfɐmɪntsə, -'mɪntsə] F -, *no pl* peppermint

Pfef|fer|minz-: **Pfef|fer|minz|ge|schmack** M peppermint flavour *(Brit) or* flavor *(US)*; **Pfef|fer|minz|li|kör** M crème de menthe; **Pfef|fer|minz|plätz|chen** NT peppermint; **Pfef|fer|minz|tee** M peppermint tea

Pfef|fer|müh|le F pepper mill

pfef|fern ['pfɛfɐn] VT **a** *(Cook)* to season with pepper, to pepper; *(fig)* to pepper → *auch* **gepfeffert** **b** *(inf) (= heftig werfen)* to fling, to hurl; *(= hinauswerfen)* to chuck out *(inf)*, to sling out *(inf)*; **jdm eine ~** to give sb a clout *(Brit inf) or* a slap, to clout sb one *(Brit inf)*

Pfef|fer-: **Pfef|fer|nuss** F gingerbread biscuit; **Pfef|fer|spray** NT pepper spray; **Pfef|fer|steak** NT pepper steak; **Pfef|fer|strauch** M pepper (plant); **Pfef|fer|streu|er** M pepper pot *or* shaker; **Pfef|fer-und-Salz-Mus|ter** ['pfɛfɐlʊnt'zalts-] NT pepper-and-salt (pattern)

pfeff|rig ['pfɛfrɪç] ADJ = **pfefferig**

Pfeif|chen ['pfaifçən] NT -s, - *dim von* **Pfeife** pipe; **ein ~ rauchen** to smoke *or* have a pipe

Pfei|fe ['pfaifə] F -, -n **a** whistle; *(= Querpfeife)* fife *(esp Mil)*, piccolo; *(= Bootsmannspfeife, Orgelpfeife)* pipe; **nach jds ~ tanzen** to dance to sb's tune **b** *(zum Rauchen)* pipe; **eine ~ rauchen** to smoke *or* have a pipe; **~ rauchen** *(= Pfeifenraucher sein)* to smoke a pipe, to be a pipe-smoker **c** *(inf: = Versager)* wash-out *(inf)*

pfei|fen ['pfaifn] *pret* **pfiff** [pfɪf], *ptp* **gepfiffen** [gə'pfɪfn] VI to whistle (*+dat* for); *(auf einer Trillerpfeife)* to blow one's whistle; *(Mus: = auf einer Pfeife spielen)* to pipe; *(Wind)* to whistle; *(Radio)* to whine; **mit Pfeifen und Trommeln zogen sie durch die Stadt** they made their way through the town amid piping and drumming *or* with pipes piping and drums beating; **aus** *or* **auf dem letzten Loch ~** *(inf) (= erschöpft sein)* to be on one's last legs *(inf)*; *(finanziell)* to be on one's beam-ends *(Brit inf)*, to be broke *(inf)*; **ich pfeife darauf!** *(inf)* I couldn't care less, I don't give a damn *(inf)*; **ich pfeife auf seine Meinung** *(inf)* I couldn't care less about what he thinks; **~der Atem** wheezing; **sein Atem ging ~d** he was wheezing

VT to whistle; *(Mus)* to pipe; *(Sport inf) Spiel* to ref *(inf)*; *Abseits, Foul* to give; **das ~ ja schon die Spatzen von den Dächern** that's common knowledge, it's all over town

Pfei|fen-: **Pfei|fen|de|ckel** M pipe lid; **Pfei|fen|kopf** M bowl (of a pipe); **Pfei|fen|rei|ni|ger** M pipe cleaner; **Pfei|fen|stän|der** M pipe stand *or* rack; **Pfei|fen|stiel** M pipe stem; **Pfei|fen|stop|fer** M tamper; **Pfei|fen|ta|bak** M pipe tobacco; **Pfei|fen|werk** NT pipes *pl*, pipework

Pfei|fer ['pfaifɐ] M -s, -, **Pfei|fe|rin** [-ərɪn] F -, -nen piper, fifer *(esp Mil)*

Pfei|fe|rei [pfaifə'rai] F -, -en *(inf)* whistling

Pfeif|fer|sches Drü|sen|fie|ber ['pfaifɐʃəs-] NT *(Med)* Pfeiffer's glandular fever, infectious mononucleosis *(US)*

Pfeif-: **Pfeif|kes|sel** M whistling kettle; **Pfeif|kon|zert** NT barrage *or* hail of catcalls *or* whistles; **Pfeif|ton** M *pl* -töne whistle, whistling sound *or* tone

Pfeil [pfail] M -s, -e arrow; *(bei Armbrust auch)* bolt; *(= Wurfpfeil)* dart; **~ und Bogen** bow and arrow; **die ~e seines Spotts** *(liter)* the barbs of his mockery; **vergiftete ~e abschießen** *(fig)* to fire poisoned darts at sb; **alle seine ~e verschossen haben** *(fig)* to have run out of arguments, to have shot one's bolt; **Amors ~** Cupid's arrow *or* dart; **er schoss (schnell) wie ein ~ davon** he was off like a shot *(inf)*; **der grüne ~** *(Mot)* the filter (arrow)

Pfei|ler ['pfailɐ] M -s, - *(lit, fig)* pillar; *(= Brückenpfeiler auch)* pier; *(von Hängebrücke)* pylon; *(= Stützpfeiler)* buttress

Pfeil-: **pfeil|för|mig** ADJ arrow-shaped, V-shaped ADV **~ angeordnet** arranged in the shape of an arrow, arranged in a V; **pfeil|ge|ra|de** ADJ as straight as a die; **eine ~ Linie** a dead straight line ADV **sie kam ~ auf uns zu** she made a beeline for us, she headed straight for us; **der Vogel flog ~ von einem Baum zum nächsten** the bird flew straight as an arrow from one tree to the next; **Pfeil|gift** NT arrow poison; **Pfeil|kö|cher** M quiver; **Pfeil|rich|tung** F **in ~** in the direction of the arrow; **in ~ gehen** to follow the arrows; **pfeil|schnell** ADJ as quick as lightning ADV like an arrow, like a shot *(inf)*; **er startete ~** he was off like a shot *(inf)*; **Pfeil|schuss** M arrow shot; **durch einen ~ getötet** killed by an arrow; **Pfeil|schüt|ze** M bowman, archer; **Pfeil|schüt|zin** F archer; **Pfeil|spit|ze** F arrowhead, tip of an arrow; **Pfeil|tas|te** F *(Comput)* arrow key; **Pfeil|wurf|spiel** NT darts *pl*; **Pfeil|wurz** [-vʊrts] F -, -en arrowroot *no pl*

Pfen|nig ['pfɛnɪç] M -s, -e *or (nach Zahlenangabe)* - [-gə] *(Hist)* pfennig *(one hundredth of a mark)*; **30 ~** 30 pfennigs; **er hat keinen ~ (Geld)** he hasn't got a penny to his name, he hasn't got two pennies to rub together, he hasn't got a dime *(US)*; **ohne einen ~ dasitzen** *(inf)* to be left without a penny *(Brit) or* cent *(US)*; **es ist keinen ~ wert** *(fig)* it's not worth a thing *or* a red cent *(US)*; **dem/dafür gebe ich keinen ~** *(lit)* I won't give him/it a penny; **für seine Chancen gebe ich keinen ~** I don't give much for his chances *(inf)*, I wouldn't put much money on his chances *(inf)*; **nicht für fünf ~** *(inf)* not the slightest (bit of); **er hat nicht für fünf ~ Anstand/Verstand** *(inf)* he hasn't an ounce of respectability/intelligence; **das interessiert mich nicht für fünf ~** *(inf)* that doesn't interest me in the slightest; **auf den ~ sehen** *(fig)* to watch *or* count every penny; **mit dem** *or*

jedem ~ rechnen müssen *(fig)* to have to watch *or* count every penny; **jeden ~ (dreimal) umdrehen** *(fig inf)* to think twice about every penny one spends; **wer den ~ nicht ehrt, ist des Talers nicht wert** *(Prov)* ≈ take care of the pennies, and the pounds will take care of themselves *(Brit Prov)*, ≈ a penny saved is a penny earned *(US)* → **Groschen, Heller**

Pfen|nig-: **Pfen|nig|ab|satz** M stiletto heel; **Pfen|nig|be|trag** M *(Hist, fig)* **es war nur ein ~** it was only a matter of pence *or* pennies; **Pfen|nig|fuch|ser** [-fʊksɐ] M **-s, -**, **Pfen|nig|fuch|se|rin** [-ərɪn] F **-, -nen** *(fig inf)* skinflint *(inf)*, miser *(inf)*; **pfen|nig|groß** ADJ **ein ~es Geschwür** a boil the size of a penny (coin) *or* a cent *(US)*; **Pfen|nig|stück** NT *(Hist)* pfennig (piece); **pfen|nig|wei|se** ADV *(Hist)* penny by penny, one penny at a time

Pferch [pfɛrç] M **-es, -e** fold, pen

pfer|chen [ˈpfɛrçn] VT to cram, to pack

Pferd [pfeːɐt] NT **-(e)s, -e** [-də] *(Tier, Turngerät)* horse; *(= Reitpferd auch)* mount; *(Chess)* knight, horse *(US inf)*; **zu ~(e)** on horseback; **aufs falsche/richtige ~ setzen** *(lit, fig)* to back the wrong/right horse; **mitten im Strom die ~e wechseln** *(fig)* to change horses in midstream; **die ~e gehen ihm leicht durch** *(fig)* he flies off the handle easily *(inf)*; **immer langsam** *or* **sachte mit den jungen ~en** *(inf)* hold your horses *(inf)*; **wie ein ~ arbeiten** *or* **schuften** *(inf)* to work like a Trojan; **das hält ja kein ~ aus** *(inf)* it's more than flesh and blood can stand; **keine zehn ~e brächten mich dahin** *(inf)* wild horses couldn't drag me there; **mit ihm kann man ~e stehlen** *(inf)* he's a great sport *(inf)*; **er ist unser bestes ~ im Stall** he's our best man; **ich glaub, mich tritt ein ~** *(inf)* blow me down *(dated inf)*, struth *(Brit inf)*

Pfer|de-: **Pfer|de|ap|fel** M piece of horse dung; **Pferdeäpfel** horse droppings *pl or* dung *no pl*; **Pfer|de|bahn** F horse-drawn tram *(esp Brit)*, horsecar *(US)*; **pfer|de|be|spannt** [-bəʃpant] ADJ horse-drawn; **Pfer|de|brem|se** F horsefly; **Pfer|de|de|cke** F horse blanket; **Pfer|de|dieb(in)** M(F) horse thief; **Pfer|de|drosch|ke** F hackney cab; **Pfer|de|fleisch** NT horse meat, horseflesh; **Pfer|de|flie|ge** F horsefly; **Pfer|de|fuhr|werk** NT horse and cart; **Pfer|de|fuß** M *(von Teufel)* cloven hoof; *(fig)* snag; **die Sache hat aber einen ~** there's just one snag; **Pfer|de|ge|biss** NT horsey mouth *or* teeth; **Pfer|de|ge|sicht** NT horsey face, face like a horse; **Pfer|de|haar** NT horsehair; **Pfer|de|händ|ler(in)** M(F) horse dealer; **Pfer|de|huf** M horse's hoof; **Pfer|de|knecht** M groom; **Pfer|de|kop|pel** F paddock; **Pfer|de|län|ge** F length; **Pfer|de|renn|bahn** F race course *or* track; **Pfer|de|ren|nen** NT *(Sportart)* (horse) racing; *(einzelnes Rennen)* (horse) race; **Pfer|de|schlach|ter(in)** M(F) knacker *(Brit inf)*, butcher; **Pfer|de|schlach|te|rei** F knacker's *(Brit inf)*, slaughterhouse; **Pfer|de|schlit|ten** M horse-drawn sleigh; **Pfer|de|schwanz** M horse's tail; *(Frisur)* ponytail; **Pfer|de|sport** M equestrian sport; **Pfer|de|stall** M stable; **Pfer|de|stär|ke** F horse power *no pl*, hp *abbr*; **Pfer|de|wa|gen** M *(für Personen)* horse and carriage, trap *(Brit)*, horse buggy *(US)*; *(für Lasten)* horse and cart; **Pfer|de|zucht** F horse breeding; *(= Gestüt)* stud farm; **Pfer|de|züch|ter(in)** M(F) horse breeder

pfet|zen [ˈpfɛtsn] VT *(S Ger: = kneifen)* to pinch

pfiff *pret von* **pfeifen**

Pfiff [pfɪf] M **-s, -e** **a** whistle; *(Theat auch)* catcall; **auf ~ reagieren** *(fig)* to obey on command **b** *(= Reiz)* flair, style; **der Soße fehlt noch der letzte ~** the sauce still needs that extra something; **einem Kleid den richtigen ~ geben** to give a dress real style; **eine Inneneinrichtung mit ~** a stylish interior **c** *(inf: = Trick)* knack; **jetzt hast du den ~ heraus** you've got the knack *or* hang *(inf)* of it now; **das ist ein Ding mit 'nem ~** there's a special knack to it

Pfif|fer|ling [ˈpfɪfɐlɪŋ] M **-s, -e** chanterelle; **er kümmert sich keinen ~ um seine Kinder** *(inf)* he doesn't give a fig *(inf)* or couldn't care less about his children; **keinen ~ wert** *(inf)* not worth a thing

pfif|fig [ˈpfɪfɪç] ADJ smart, sharp, cute; *Idee* smart, clever ADV cleverly

Pfif|fig|keit F **-,** *no pl* sharpness, cuteness; *(von Idee)* cleverness

Pfif|fi|kus [ˈpfɪfikʊs] M **-** *or* **-ses, -se** *(dated)* crafty thing *(inf)*

Pfingst|ten [ˈpfɪŋstn] NT **-, -** Whitsun *(Brit)*, Pentecost; **zu** *or* **an ~** at Whitsun *(Brit) or* Pentecost

Pfingst-: **Pfingst|fe|ri|en** PL Whit(sun) holiday(s *pl*) *(Brit)*, Pentecost holiday(s *pl*) *(US)*; **Pfingst|fest** NT Whitsun *(Brit)*, Pentecost

pfingst|lich [ˈpfɪŋstlɪç] ADJ *no pred* Whit(sun) *attr (Brit)*, Pentecost *attr* ADV **der Altar war ~ geschmückt** the altar was decorated for Whitsun *(Brit) or* Pentecost

Pfingst-: **Pfingst|mon|tag** M Whit Monday *(Brit)*, Pentecost Monday *(US)*; **Pfingst|och|se** M **herausgeputzt wie ein ~** *(inf)* dressed *or* done up to the nines *(Brit inf) or* hilt *(US inf)*; **Pfingst|ro|se** F peony; **Pfingst|sonn|tag** M Whit Sunday *(Brit)*, Pentecost; **Pfingst|wo|che** F Whit week *(Brit)*, the week of the Pentecost holiday *(US)*; **Pfingst|zeit** F Whitsun (-tide) *(Brit)*, the time before Pentecost

Pfir|sich [ˈpfɪrzɪç] M **-s, -e** peach

Pfir|sich-: **Pfir|sich|baum** M peach tree; **Pfir|sich|blü|te** F peach blossom; **pfir|sich|far|ben** [-farbn] ADJ peach(-coloured) *(Brit)*, peach(-colored) *(US)*; **Pfir|sich|haut** F, *no pl* *(lit)* peach skin; *(fig)* peaches-and-cream complexion

Pflanz [pflants] M **-,** *no pl (Aus inf)* fraud, swindle

Pflan|ze [ˈpflantsə] F **-, -n** **a** *(= Gewächs)* plant; **~n fressend** = **pflanzenfressend** **b** *(inf: Mensch)* **er/sie ist eine komische** *or* **seltsame ~** he/she is a strange fish *(inf)*; **eine Berliner ~** *(dated)* a typical Berlin lass *(Brit) or* girl

pflan|zen [ˈpflantsn] VT to plant; **einem Kind etw ins Herz ~** *(liter)* to implant sth in the heart of a child *(liter)* VR *(inf)* to plant *(inf) or* plonk *(Brit inf)* oneself

Pflan|zen-: **Pflan|zen|but|ter** F vegetable butter; **Pflan|zen|farb|stoff** M vegetable dye; **Pflan|zen|fa|ser** F plant fibre *(Brit) or* fiber *(US)*; **Pflan|zen|fett** NT vegetable fat; **pflan|zen|fres|send** ADJ herbivorous; **Pflan|zen|fres|ser** M herbivore; **Pflan|zen|kost** F vegetable foodstuffs *pl*; **Pflan|zen|kun|de** F, **Pflan|zen|leh|re** F, *no pl* botany; **Pflan|zen|mar|ga|ri|ne** F vegetable margarine; **Pflan|zen|öl** NT vegetable oil; **Pflan|zen|reich** NT vegetable kingdom; **Pflan|zen|schäd|ling** M pest; garden pest; **Pflan|zen|schutz** M protection of plants; *(gegen Ungeziefer)* pest control; **Pflan|zen|schutz|mit|tel** NT pesticide; **Pflan|zen|welt** F plant world; **die ~ des Mittelmeers** the plant life *or* the flora of the Mediterranean

Pflan|zer [ˈpflantsɐ] M **-s, -**, **Pflan|ze|rin** [-ərɪn] F **-, -nen** planter

Pflanz|kar|tof|fel F seed potato

pflanz|lich [ˈpflantslɪç] ADJ *Fette, Nahrung* vegetable *attr*; *Zellen, Organismen* plant *attr* ADV **sich rein ~ ernähren** to eat no animal products; *(Tier)* to be a herbivore

Pflänz|ling [ˈpflɛntslɪŋ] M **-s, -e** seedling

Pflanz-: **Pflanz|scha|le** F planting dish; **Pflanz|trog** M plant trough

Pflan|zung [ˈpflantsʊŋ] F **-, -en** *(= das Pflanzen)* planting; *(= Plantage)* plantation

Pflas|ter [ˈpflastɐ] NT **-s, -** **a** *(= Heftpflaster)* (sticking) plaster *(Brit)*, adhesive tape *(US)*; *(fig: = Entschädigung)* sop (*auf +acc* to); **das ~ erneuern** to put on a fresh *or* new (piece of) (sticking) plaster *(Brit) or* adhesive tape *(US)* **b** *(= Straßenpflaster)* (road) surface; *(= Kopfsteinpflaster)* cobbles *pl*; **~ treten** *(inf)* to trudge the streets, to trudge *or* traipse around; **ein gefährliches** *or* **heißes ~** *(inf)* a dangerous place; **ein teures ~** *(inf)* a pricey place *(inf)*; **das Berliner ~** *(inf)* the streets of Berlin

Pflas|te|rer [ˈpflastərɐ] M **-s, -**, **Pflas|te|rin** [-ərɪn] F **-, -nen** road worker

Pflas|ter-: **Pflas|ter|ma|ler(in)** M(F) pavement artist; **pflas|ter|mü|de** ADJ *(inf)* dead on one's feet *(inf)*

pflas|tern [ˈpflastɐn] VT **a** *Straße, Hof* to surface; *(mit Kopfsteinpflaster)* to cobble; *(mit Steinplatten)* to pave; **eine Straße neu ~** to resurface a road; **ihre Filmkarriere war mit unzähligen Misserfolgen gepflastert** her film career was made up of a series of failures → **Weg a** **b** *(inf: = ohrfeigen)* **jdm eine ~** to sock sb (one) *(inf)*; **du kriegst gleich eine gepflastert** I'll sock you one in a minute *(inf)*

Pflas|ter|stein M *(= Kopfstein)* cobble(stone); *(= Steinplatte)* paving stone, flag(stone); *(inf: = Pfefferkuchen)* ≈ gingerbread

Pflas|te|rung F **-, -en** surfacing; *(mit Kopfsteinpflaster)* cobbling; *(mit Steinplatten)* paving; *(= Pflaster)* surface; *(= Kopfsteinpflaster)* cobbles *pl*; *(= Steinplatten)* paving *no pl*

Pflau|me [ˈpflaumə] F **-, -n** **a** plum; **getrocknete ~** prune **b** *(inf: Mensch)* dope *(inf)*, twit *(inf)* **c** *(sl: = Vagina)* cunt *(vulg)*

Pflau|men-: **Pflau|men|baum** M plum (tree); **Pflau|men|kern** M plum stone; **Pflau|men|kom|pott** NT stewed plums *pl*; **Pflau|men|ku|chen** M plum tart; **Pflau|men|mus** NT plum jam; **pflau|men|weich** ADJ *(inf)* soft; *(pej) Haltung* spineless

Pfle|ge [ˈpfleːgə] F **-,** *no pl* care; *(von Kranken auch)* nursing; *(von Garten auch)* attention; *(von Beziehungen, Künsten)* fostering, cultivation; *(von Maschinen, Gebäuden)* maintenance, upkeep; **jdn/etw in ~ nehmen** to look after sb/sth; **jdn/etw in ~ geben** to have sb/sth looked after; **sie gaben den Hund bei ihrem Sohn in ~** they gave their dog to their son to look after; **ein Kind in ~ nehmen** *(dauernd)* to foster a child; **ein Kind in ~ geben** to have a child fostered; *(stundenweise)* to have a child looked after; *(Behörde)* to foster a child out (*zu jdm* with sb); **die ~ von jdm/etw übernehmen** to look after sb/sth; **der Garten/Kranke braucht viel ~** the garden/sick man needs a lot of care and attention; **das Kind/der Hund hat bei uns gute ~** the child/dog is well looked after *or* cared for by us; **jdm gute ~ angedeihen lassen** to take good care of sb, to look after sb well; **häusliche ~** care in the home

Pfle|ge-: **pfle|ge|be|dürf|tig** ADJ in need of care (and attention); **wenn alte Leute ~ werden** when old people start to need looking after; **Pfle|ge|be|dürf|tig|keit** F need for care; **Pfle|ge|be|ruf** M caring profession; **Pfle|ge|dienst** M home nursing service; **Pfle|ge|el|tern** PL foster parents *pl*; **Pfle|ge|fall** M case for nursing *or* care; **sie ist ein ~** she needs constant care; **Pfle|ge|geld** NT *(für Pflegekinder)* boarding-out allowance; *(für Kranke)* attendance allowance; **Pfle|ge|heim** NT nursing home; **Pfle|ge|kind** NT foster child; **Pfle|ge|kos|ten** PL nursing fees *pl*; **Pfle|ge|kos|ten|ver|si|che|rung** F private nursing insurance; **pfle|ge|leicht** ADJ easy-care; *(fig auch)* easy to handle; **Pfle|ge|mit|tel** NT *(= Kosmetikum)* cosmetic care product; *(Aut)* cleaning product; **Pfle|ge|mut|ter** F *pl* **-mütter** foster mother

pfle|gen [ˈpfleːgn] VT to look after, to care for; *Kranke auch* to nurse; *Garten, Blumen, Rasen* to tend, to look after; *Haar, Bart* to groom, to look after; *Beziehungen, Kunst, Freundschaft* to foster, to cultivate; *Maschinen, Gebäude, Denkmäler* to maintain, to keep up; **etw regelmäßig ~** to attend to sth regularly, to pay regular attention to sth; **eine Creme, die die Haut pflegt** a cream

which is good for the skin → *auch* **gepflegt, Umgang**
VI *(= gewöhnlich tun)* to be in the habit *(zu* of), to be accustomed *(zu* to); **sie pflegte zu sagen** she used to say, she was in the habit of saying; **zum Mittagessen pflegt er Bier zu trinken** he's in the habit of drinking beer with his lunch, he usually drinks beer with his lunch; **wie es so zu gehen pflegt** as usually happens; **wie man zu sagen pflegt** as they say
VR **a** *(= sein Äußeres pflegen)* to care about one's appearance
b *(= sich schonen)* to take it *or* things easy *(inf)*

Pfle|ge-: **Pfle|ge|not|stand** M shortage of nursing staff; **Pfle|ge|per|so|nal** NT nursing staff; **Pfle|ge|pro|dukt** NT care product; **~e für die Haut/das Auto** skin/car care products

Pfle|ger ['pfle:gɐ] M **-s, -** *(im Krankenhaus)* orderly; *(voll qualifiziert)* (male) nurse; *(= Vormund)* guardian; *(= Nachlasspfleger)* trustee

Pfle|ge|rin ['pfle:gərɪn] F **-, -nen** nurse → *auch* **Pfleger**

pfle|ge|risch ['pfle:gərɪʃ] ADJ nursing ADV **~ ausgebildet sein** to be a trained nurse; **~ tätig sein** to do nursing

Pfle|ge-: **Pfle|ge|satz** M hospital and nursing charges *pl*; **Pfle|ge|se|rie** F *(= Kosmetika)* line of cosmetic products; **Pfle|ge|sohn** M foster son; **Pfle|ge|sta|ti|on** F nursing ward; **Pfle|ge|toch|ter** F foster daughter; **Pfle|ge|va|ter** M foster father; **Pfle|ge|ver|si|che|rung** F nursing care insurance

> **PFLEGEVERSICHERUNG**
>
> **Pflegeversicherung** was introduced in Germany in 1995 and is compulsory for members of state and private health insurance schemes. It covers the costs of long-term nursing care for the old or disabled. The **Pflegeversicherung** also pays a certain amount to those who care for relatives at home and covers their social security contributions. **Pflegeversicherung** costs are borne jointly by employee and employer.

pfleg|lich ['pfle:klɪç] ADJ careful ADV *behandeln, umgehen* carefully, with care

Pfleg|ling ['pfle:klɪŋ] M **-s, -e** foster child; *(= Mündel)* ward

Pflegs|chaft ['pfle:kʃaft] F **-, -en** *(= Vormundschaft)* guardianship, tutelage *(form)*; *(= Vermögenspflegschaft)* trusteeship

Pflicht [pflɪçt] F **-, -en** **a** *(= Verpflichtung)* duty *(zu* to); **ich habe die traurige ~ ...** it is my sad duty ...; **als Abteilungsleiter hat er die ~, ...** it's his duty *or* responsibility as head of (the) department ...; **Rechte und ~en** rights and responsibilities; **seine ~ erfüllen** *or* **tun** to do one's duty; **der ~ gehorchen** *(geh)* to obey the call of duty; **jdn in die ~ nehmen** to remind sb of his duty; **eheliche ~en** conjugal *or* marital duties; **die bürgerlichen ~en** one's civic duties *or* responsibilities; **die ~ ruft** duty calls; **ich habe es mir zur ~ gemacht** I've taken it upon myself, I've made it my duty; **ich tue nur meine ~** I'm only doing my duty; **etw nur aus ~ tun** to do sth merely because one has to; **das ist ~** you have to do that, it's compulsory; **Schulbesuch ist ~** you have to go to school, going to school is compulsory; **es ist seine (verdammte** *inf*) **~ und Schuldigkeit(, das zu tun)** he damn well *or* jolly well *(Brit)* ought to (do it) *(inf)*
b *(Sport)* compulsory section *or* exercises *pl*; **bei der ~** in the compulsory section *or* exercises

Pflicht-: **Pflicht|be|such** M duty visit; **pflicht|be|wusst** ADJ conscientious, conscious of one's duties; **er ist sehr ~** he takes his duties very seriously, he has a great sense of duty; **Pflicht|be|wusst|sein** NT sense of duty; **Pflicht|ei|fer** M zeal; **pflicht|eif|rig** ADJ zealous ADV zealously

Pflich|ten|heft NT *(= Anforderungsprofil) (für Geräte)* specification; *(für Arbeitsstelle)* job description

Pflich|ten|kreis M duties *pl*

Pflicht-: **Pflicht|er|fül|lung** F fulfilment *(Brit) or* fulfillment *(US)* of one's duty; **Pflicht|ex|emp|lar** NT deposit copy; **Pflicht|fach** NT compulsory subject; **Deutsch ist ~** German is compulsory, German is a compulsory subject; **Pflicht|ge|fühl** NT sense of duty; **pflicht|ge|mäß** ADJ dutiful; **~es Ermessen** proper discretion ADV dutifully; **ich teile Ihnen ~ mit** it is my duty to inform you; **etw ~ tun müssen** to be required to do sth; **pflicht|ge|treu** ADJ dutiful ADV dutifully; **Pflicht|jahr** NT *(NS) a year's compulsory community service for girls during Nazi period*; **Pflicht|kür** F compulsory exercise; **Pflicht|lauf** M *(Eiskunstlauf)* compulsory figures *pl*; **Pflicht|lek|tü|re** F compulsory reading; *(Sch auch)* set book(s *pl*); **pflicht|schul|dig** ADJ dutiful ADV dutifully; **Pflicht|teil** M OR NT statutory portion *(of a deceased person's estate that must be left eg to a child)*; **pflicht|treu** ADJ dutiful; **Pflicht|treue** F devotion to duty; **Pflicht|übung** F compulsory exercise; **pflicht|ver|ges|sen** ADJ neglectful of one's duty; **Pflicht|ver|ges|sen|heit** F neglect of duty; **Pflicht|ver|let|zung** F breach of duty; **Pflicht|ver|säum|nis** F neglect *or* dereliction of duty *no pl*; **er machte sich häufiger ~se schuldig** he was frequently guilty of neglecting his duties; **pflicht|ver|si|chert** [-fɛɐzɪçɐt] ADJ compulsorily insured; **Pflicht|ver|si|cher|te(r)** MF *decl as adj* compulsorily insured person; **Pflicht|ver|si|che|rung** F compulsory insurance; **Pflicht|ver|tei|di|ger(in)** M(F) *counsel for the defence appointed by the court and paid from the legal aid fund*; **Pflicht|vor|le|sung** F compulsory lecture; **pflicht|wid|rig** ADJ **~es Verhalten** failure to carry out one's duty ADV **er hat sich ~ verhalten** he failed to carry out his duty

Pflock [pflɔk] M **-(e)s, ¨-e** ['pflœkə] peg; *(für Tiere)* stake; **einen ~** *or* **ein paar Pflöcke zurückstecken** *(dated fig)* to back-pedal a bit; **Pflöcke** *or* **einen ~ einschlagen** *(fig)* to set standards

pflü|cken ['pflʏkn] VT to pick, to pluck; *(= sammeln)* to pick

Pflü|cker ['pflʏkɐ] M **-s, -**, **Pflü|cke|rin** [-ərɪn] F **-, -nen** picker

Pflück|sa|lat M picking salad, *lettuce that is picked a few leaves at a time*

Pflug [pflu:k] M **-es, ¨-e** ['pfly:gə] plough *(Brit)*, plow *(US)*; *(= Schneepflug)* snowplough *(Brit)*, snowplow *(US)*; **unter dem ~ sein** to be under the plough *(Brit) or* plow *(US)*

Pflug|bo|gen M *(Ski)* snowplough *(Brit) or* snowplow *(US)* turn

pflü|gen ['pfly:gn] VTI *(lit, fig)* to plough *(Brit)*, to plow *(US)*; *(lit auch)* to till *(liter)*; **das Boot pflügt durch die Brandung** the boat ploughs *(Brit) or* plows *(US)* (through) the waves

Pflü|ger ['pfly:gɐ] M **-s, -** ploughman *(Brit)*, plowman *(US)*

Pflü|ge|rin ['pfly:gərɪn] F **-, -nen** ploughwoman *(Brit)*, plowwoman *(US)*

Pflug-: **Pflug|schar** F ploughshare *(Brit)*, plowshare *(US)*; **Pflug|sterz** M plough handle *(Brit)*, plow handle *(US)*

Pfort|ader F portal vein

Pfor|te ['pfɔrtə] F **-, -n** *(= Tor)* gate; *(Geog)* gap; **das Theater hat seine ~n für immer geschlossen** the theatre *(Brit) or* theater *(US)* has closed its doors for good; **die Messe öffnet am Sonntag ihre ~n** the (trade) fair opens its doors *or* gates on Sunday; **Nepal, die ~ zum Himalaya** Nepal, the gateway to the Himalayas; **die ~n des Himmels** *(liter)* the gates *or* portals *(liter)* of Heaven; **die Hohe ~** *(Hist)* the Sublime Porte

Pfört|ner ['pfœrtnɐ] M **-s, -** *(Anat)* pylorus

Pfört|ner ['pfœrtnɐ] M **-s, -**, **Pfört|ne|rin** [-ərɪn] F **-, -nen** porter; *(von Fabrik)* gateman/-woman; *(von Wohnhaus, Behörde)* doorman/-woman; *(von Schloss)* gatekeeper

Pfört|ner|lo|ge F porter's office; *(in Fabrik)* gatehouse; *(in Wohnhaus, Büro)* doorman's office

Pfos|ten ['pfɔstn] M **-s, -** post; *(= senkrechter Balken)* upright; *(= Fensterpfosten)* (window) jamb; *(= Türpfosten)* (door) jamb, doorpost; *(= Stütze)* support, prop; *(Ftbl)* (goal)post, upright; **kurzer ~** *(Ftbl)* near post; **langer ~** *(Ftbl)* far post

Pfos|ten|schuss M *(Ftbl)* **das war nur ein ~** it hit the (goal)post *or* upright

Pföt|chen ['pfø:tçən] NT **-s, -** *dim von* **Pfote** little paw; **~ geben** *(fig inf)* to shake hands; **(gib) ~!** *(zu Hund)* give me a paw!

Pfo|te ['pfo:tə] F **-, -n** **a** paw **b** *(inf: = Hand)* mitt *(inf)*, paw *(inf)*; **sich** *(dat)* **die ~n verbrennen** *(inf)* to burn one's fingers; **seine ~n überall drinhaben** *(fig inf)* to have a finger in every pie *(inf)* **c** *(inf: = schlechte Handschrift)* scribble, scrawl

Pfriem [pfri:m] M **-(e)s, -e** awl

Pfropf [pfrɔpf] M **-(e)s, -e** *or* **¨-e** ['pfrœpfə] *(= Stöpsel)* stopper; *(= Kork, Sektpfropf)* cork; *(= Wattepfropf etc)* plug; *(von Fass, Korbflasche)* bung; *(Med: = Blutpfropf)* (blood) clot; *(verstopfend)* blockage; **er hat einen ~ im Ohr** his ears are bunged up *(Brit inf) or* blocked up

pfrop|fen ['pfrɔpfn] VT **a** *Pflanzen* to graft **b** *(= verschließen) Flasche* to bung, to stop up **c** *(inf: = hineinzwängen)* to cram; **er pfropfte den Korken in die Flasche** he shoved the cork in the bottle; **gepfropft voll** jam-packed *(inf)*, crammed full

Pfrop|fen ['pfrɔpfn] M **-s, -** = **Pfropf**

Pfröpf|ling ['pfrœpflɪŋ] M **-s, -e** graft, scion

Pfropf-: **Pfropf|mes|ser** NT grafting knife; **Pfropf|reis** NT, *no pl* graft, scion

Pfrün|de ['pfrʏndə] F **-, -n** *(= Kirchenamt)* (church) living, benefice; *(Einkünfte auch)* prebend; *(fig)* sinecure

Pfuhl [pfu:l] M **-s, -e** *(liter)* mudhole; *(fig)* (quag)mire, slough *(liter)*

Pfühl [pfy:l] M OR NT **-(e)s, -e** *(poet, dial)* *(= Kissen)* pillow; *(= weiches Bett)* downy *or* feather bed

pfui [pfui] INTERJ *(Ekel)* ugh, yuck; *(Missbilligung)* tut tut; *(zu Hunden)* oy, hey; *(Buhruf)* boo; **fass das nicht an, das ist ~** *(inf)* don't touch it, it's dirty *or* nasty; **~ Teufel** *or* **Deibel** *or* **Spinne** *(all inf)* ugh, yuck; **~ schäme dich** shame on you!; **da kann ich nur ~** *or* **Pfui sagen** it's simply disgraceful

Pfui|ruf M boo

Pfund [pfʊnt] NT **-(e)s, -e** *or (nach Zahlenangabe)* **-** [-də] **a** *(= Gewicht) (in Deutschland)* 500 grams, half a kilo(gram); *(in Großbritannien)* pound; **drei ~ Äpfel** three pounds of apples; **er bewegte seine ~e mit Mühe** he moved his great bulk with effort; **überflüssige ~e abspecken** to shed surplus pounds **b** *(= Währungseinheit)* pound; *(= türkisches Pfund)* lira; *(Hist: = irisches Pfund)* punt; **in ~** in pounds; **zwanzig ~ Sterling** twenty pounds sterling; **das ~ sinkt** the pound is falling; **mit seinem ~e** *or* **seinen ~en wuchern** *(liter)* to make the most of one's talents

Pfund- *in cpds* pound; **Pfund|be|trag** M amount in pounds, sterling sum

-pfün|der [pfʏndɐ] M **-s, -** *in cpds* -pounder; **ein Fünfpfünder** *(Fisch)* a five-pounder

pfun|dig ['pfʊndɪç] *(dated inf)* ADJ great *no adv*, fantastic, swell *no adv (US dated inf)* ADV fantastically; **sich ~ amüsieren** to have a great time; **das hast du ~ gemacht** you've made a great job of that

-pfün|dig [pfʏndɪç] ADJ *suf* weighing ... pounds; **ein vierpfündiger Fisch** a fish weighing four pounds

Pfunds- *in cpds (inf)* great *(inf)*, swell *(US dated inf)*, super *(inf)*; **Pfunds|kerl** M *(inf)* great guy *(inf)*

pfund|wei|se ADV by the pound

Pfusch [pfʊʃ] M **-(e)s**, *no pl (inf)* = **Pfuscherei**

Pfusch|ar|beit F, *no pl (inf)* slapdash work; **sie haben richtige ~ geleistet** they did a really sloppy job *(inf)*

pfu|schen ['pfʊʃn] VI **a** *(= schlecht arbeiten)* to bungle; *(= einen Fehler machen)* to slip up, to come unstuck *(inf)*; **jdm ins Handwerk ~** to stick one's nose into sb's affairs *(inf)*, to meddle in sb's affairs **b** *(Sch)* to cheat **c** *(Aus: = schwarzarbeiten)* to (do) work on the side *(esp Brit inf)*, to moonlight *(inf)*

Pfu|scher ['pfʊʃɐ] M **-s, -** *(inf)*, **Pfu|sche|rin** [-ərɪn] F **-, -nen** *(inf)* bungler, botcher *(inf)*

Pfu|sche|rei [pfʊʃə'rai] F **-, -en** *(= das Pfuschen)* bungling *no pl*; *(= gepfuschte Arbeit)* botch-up *(inf)*, botched-up job *(inf)*

Pfüt|ze ['pfʏtsə] F **-, -n** puddle

PH [pe:'ha:] F **-, -s** *abbr von* **pädagogische Hochschule**

Pha|lanx ['fa:laŋks] F **-, Phalangen** [fa'laŋən] *(Hist)* phalanx; *(fig)* battery

Phal|len *pl*, **Phal|li** *pl von* **Phallus**

phal|lisch ['falɪʃ] ADJ phallic

Phal|lus ['falʊs] M **-, -se** *or* **Phalli** *or* **Phallen** ['fali, 'falən] phallus

Phal|lus-: **Phal|lus|kult** M, *no pl* phallus worship; **Phal|lus|sym|bol** NT phallic symbol

Phä|no|men [fɛno'me:n] NT **-s, -e** phenomenon; **dieser Mensch ist ein ~** this person is phenomenal, this person is an absolute phenomenon

phä|no|me|nal [fɛnome'na:l] ADJ phenomenal ADV phenomenally (well); **~ aussehen** to look phenomenal

Phä|no|me|no|lo|gie [fɛnomenolo'gi:] F **-,** *no pl* phenomenology

Phä|no|typ [fɛno'ty:p] M **-s, -en**, **Phä|no|ty|pus** [fɛno'ty:pʊs] M phenotype

Phan|ta|sie [fanta'zi:] F **-, -n** [-'zi:ən] = **Fantasie**

Phan|ta|sie- *in cpds* = **Fantasie-**

phan|ta|sie|ren VTI = **fantasieren**

Phan|tast [fan'tast] M **-en, -en**, **Phan|tas|tin** [-'tastɪn] F **-, -nen** = **Fantast**

Phan|tas|te|rei [fantastə'rai] F **-, -en** = **Fantasterei**

phan|tas|tisch [fan'tastɪʃ] ADJ, ADV = **fantastisch**

Phan|tom [fan'to:m] NT **-s, -e** **a** *(= Trugbild)* phantom; **einem ~ nachjagen** *(fig)* to tilt at windmills **b** *(= Modell) (für Unterricht)* anatomical model, manikin; *(beim Fechten)* dummy

Phan|tom-: **Phan|tom|bild** NT Identikit® (picture), Photofit® (picture); **Phan|tom|schmerz** M phantom limb pain

Pha|rao ['fa:rao] M **-s, Pharaonen** [fara'o:nən] Pharaoh

Pha|ra|o|nen- *in cpds* of the Pharaohs; **Pharaonengräber** tombs of the Pharaohs

Pha|ri|sä|er [fari'zɛ:ɐ] M **-s, -** *(Hist)* pharisee; *(fig auch)* hypocrite

pha|ri|sä|er|haft ADJ pharisaic(al); *(fig auch)* holier-than-thou, self-righteous

Pha|ri|sä|er|tum [fari'zɛ:ɐtu:m] NT **-s,** *no pl (fig)* self-righteousness

pha|ri|sä|isch [fari'zɛ:ɪʃ] ADJ = **pharisäerhaft**

pharm. *abbr von* **pharmazeutisch**

Phar|ma-: **Phar|ma|her|stel|ler(in)** M(F) drug manufacturer; **Phar|ma|in|dust|rie** F pharmaceuticals industry

Phar|ma|ko|lo|ge [farmako'lo:gə] M **-n, -n**, **Phar|ma|ko|lo|gin** [-'lo:gɪn] F **-, -nen** pharmacologist

Phar|ma|ko|lo|gie [farmakolo'gi:] F **-,** *no pl* pharmacology

phar|ma|ko|lo|gisch [farmako'lo:gɪʃ] ADJ pharmacological ADV pharmacologically

Phar|ma-: **Phar|ma|markt** M pharmaceuticals market; **Phar|ma|pro|dukt** NT pharmaceutical product; **Phar|ma|pro|du|zent(in)** M(F) pharmaceuticals producer; **Phar|ma|re|fe|rent(in)** M(F) medical representative; **Phar|ma|rück|stän|de** PL pharmaceutical effluents *pl*; **Phar|ma|un|ter|neh|men** NT pharmaceuticals company

Phar|ma|zeut [farma'tsɔyt] M **-en, -en**, **Phar|ma|zeu|tin** [-'tsɔytɪn] F **-, -nen** pharmacist, druggist *(US)*

Phar|ma|zeu|tik [farma'tsɔytɪk] F **-,** *no pl* pharmacy, pharmaceutics *sing*

phar|ma|zeu|tisch [farma'tsɔytɪʃ] ADJ pharmaceutical; **~-technische Assistentin, ~-technischer Assistent** pharmaceutical assistant ADV pharmaceutically

Phar|ma|zie [farma'tsi:] F **-,** *no pl* pharmacy, pharmaceutics *sing*

Pha|se ['fa:zə] F **-, -n** phase

Pha|sen-: **pha|sen|gleich** ADJ in phase; **Pha|sen|gleich|heit** F phase coincidence; **Pha|sen|span|nung** F voltage to neutral, phase voltage; **Pha|sen|ver|schie|bung** F phase difference *or* displacement

pha|sen|wei|se ADJ **a** *attr (in Abschnitten)* step-by-step, stage-by-sage **b** *(= zeitweilig)* temporary ADV **a** *(= in Phasen)* in phases *or* stages, step by step, stage by stage **b** *(= zeitweise)* temporarily; *(= manchmal)* at times; *(= vereinzelt)* from time to time, now and then

-pha|sig [fa:zɪç] ADJ *suf* -phase; **dreiphasig** three-phase

Phe|nol [fe'no:l] NT **-s,** *no pl* phenol

Phe|nol|gas NT phenol gas

Phe|ro|mon [fero'mo:n] NT **-s, -e** pheromone

Phi|lanth|rop [filan'tro:p] M **-en, -en**, **Phi|lanth|ro|pin** [-'tro:pɪn] F **-, -nen** philanthropist

Phi|lanth|ro|pie [filantro'pi:] F **-,** *no pl* philanthropy

phi|lanth|ro|pisch [filan'tro:pɪʃ] ADJ philanthropic(al)

Phi|la|te|lie [filate'li:] F **-,** *no pl* philately

Phi|la|te|list [filate'lɪst] M **-en, -en**, **Phi|la|te|lis|tin** [-'lɪstɪn] F **-, -nen** philatelist

phi|la|te|lis|tisch [filate'lɪstɪʃ] ADJ philatelic

Phil|har|mo|nie [fɪlharmo'ni:, fi:lharmo'ni:] F **-, -n** [-'ni:ən] *(= Orchester)* philharmonia, philharmonic (orchestra); *(= Konzertsaal)* philharmonic hall

Phil|har|mo|ni|ker [fɪlhar'mo:nikɐ, fi:lhar'mo:nikɐ] M **-s, -**, **Phil|har|mo|ni|ke|rin** [-ərɪn] F **-, -nen** *(= Musiker)* member of a philharmonic orchestra; **die (Münchner) ~** the (Munich) philharmonic (orchestra)

phil|har|mo|nisch [fɪlhar'mo:nɪʃ, fi:lhar'mo:nɪʃ] ADJ philharmonic

Phi|lip|pi|ka [fi'lɪpika] F **-, Philippiken** [-kn] *(Hist)* Philippic; *(fig)* philippic

Phi|lip|pi|nen [filɪ'pi:nən] PL Philippines *pl*, Philippine Islands *pl*

Phi|lip|pi|ner [filɪ'pi:nɐ] M **-s, -**, **Phi|lip|pi|ne|rin** [-ərɪn] F **-, -nen** Filipino

phi|lip|pi|nisch [filɪ'pi:nɪʃ] ADJ Filipino

Phi|lis|ter [fi'lɪstɐ] M **-s, -**, **Phi|lis|te|rin** [-ərɪn] F **-, -nen** *(lit)* Philistine; *(fig)* philistine

phi|lis|ter|haft [fi'lɪstɐhaft] *(fig)* ADJ philistine ADV *sich verhalten* like a philistine

Phi|lo|lo|ge [filo'lo:gə] M **-n, -n**, **Phi|lo|lo|gin** [-'lo:gɪn] F **-, -nen** philologist

Phi|lo|lo|gie [filolo'gi:] F **-,** *no pl* philology

phi|lo|lo|gisch [filo'lo:gɪʃ] ADJ philological ADV philologically; **~ gesehen** from a philological point of view

Phi|lo|soph [filo'zo:f] M **-en, -en**, **Phi|lo|so|phin** [-'zo:fɪn] F **-, -nen** philosopher

Phi|lo|so|phie [filozo'fi:] F **-, -n** [-'fi:ən] philosophy

phi|lo|so|phie|ren [filozo'fi:rən] *ptp* **philosophiert** VI to philosophize *(über +acc* about)

phi|lo|so|phisch [filo'zo:fɪʃ] ADJ philosophical ADV philosophically; **~ gesehen** from a philosophical point of view

Phi|mo|se [fi'mo:zə] F **-, -n** phimosis

Phi|o|le ['fio:lə] F **-, -n** phial, vial

Phi|shing ['fɪʃɪŋ] NT *(Internet)* phishing

Phleg|ma ['flɛgma] NT **-s,** *no pl* apathy, torpor

Phleg|ma|ti|ker [flɛ'gma:tikɐ] M **-s, -**, **Phleg|ma|ti|ke|rin** [-ərɪn] F **-, -nen** apathetic person

phleg|ma|tisch [flɛ'gma:tɪʃ] ADJ apathetic ADV apathetically; **~ veranlagt sein** to be apathetic (by nature)

Phlox [flɔks] M **-es, -e** *or f* **-, -e** phlox

Pho|bie [fo'bi:] F **-, -n** [-'bi:ən] phobia *(vor +dat* about)

Phon [fo:n] NT **-s, -s** phon

Pho|nem [fo'ne:m] NT **-s, -e** phoneme

Pho|ne|tik [fo'ne:tɪk] F **-,** *no pl* phonetics *sing*

Pho|ne|ti|ker [fo'ne:tikɐ] M **-s, -**, **Pho|ne|ti|ke|rin** [-ərɪn] F **-, -nen** phonetician

pho|ne|tisch [fo'ne:tɪʃ] ADJ phonetic; **~e Schrift** phonetic transcription *or* script ADV **etw ~ (um)schreiben** to write *or* transcribe sth phonetically *or* in phonetics

Phö|nix ['fø:nɪks] M **-(es), -e** phoenix; **wie ein ~ aus der Asche steigen** to rise like a phoenix from the ashes

Phö|ni|zi|er [fø'ni:tsiɐ] M **-s, -**, **Phö|ni|zi|e|rin** [-iərɪn] F **-, -nen** Phoenician

phö|ni|zisch [fø'ni:tsɪʃ] ADJ Phoenician

Pho|no- ['fono-]: **Pho|no|bran|che** F hi-fi industry; **Pho|no|lo|gie** [fonolo'gi:] F **-,** *no pl* phonology; **pho|no|lo|gisch** [fono'lo:gɪʃ] ADJ phonological; **Pho|no|ty|pist** [fonoty'pɪst] M **-en, -en**, **Pho|no|ty|pis|tin** [-'pɪstɪn] F **-, -nen** audiotypist

Phon-: **phon|stark** ADJ *Lautsprecher* powerful; *Lärm* loud; **Phon|stär|ke** F decibel; **Phon|zahl** F decibel level

Phos|gen [fɔs'ge:n] NT **-s,** *no pl* phosgene

Phos|phat [fɔs'fa:t] NT **-(e)s, -e** phosphate

phos|phat-: **phos|phat|frei** ADJ phosphate-free; **phos|phat|hal|tig** ADJ containing phosphates

Phos|phor ['fɔsfɔɐ] M **-s,** *no pl (abbr* **P***)* phosphorus

Phos|pho|res|zenz [fɔsforɛs'tsɛnts] F **-,** *no pl* phosphorescence

phos|pho|res|zie|ren [fɔsforɛs'tsi:rən] *ptp* **phosphoresziert** VI to phosphoresce

phos|pho|res|zie|rend [fɔsforɛs'tsi:rənt] *prp von* **phosphoreszieren** ADJ phosphorescent

phos|phor|hal|tig ADJ phosphorous

phos|pho|rig ['fɔsforɪç] ADJ **~e Säure** phosphorous acid

Phos|phor-: **Phos|phor|säu|re** F phosphoric acid; **Phos|phor|ver|gif|tung** F phosphorus poisoning

phot. *abbr von* **photographisch**

Pho|to △ ['fo:to] NT **-s, -s** → **Foto**

Pho|to △ M **-s, -s** *(inf)* → **Foto**

Pho|to- = **Foto-**

Pho|to|graph [foto'gra:f] *etc* = **Fotograf** *etc*

Pho|ton ['fo:tɔn, fo'to:n] NT **-s, -en** [-'to:nən] photon

Phra|se ['fra:zə] F **-, -n** phrase; *(pej)* empty *or* hollow phrase; **abgedroschene ~** cliché, hackneyed phrase *(Brit)*; **das sind alles nur ~n** that's just (so many) words, that's just talk; **leere** *or* **hohle ~n** empty *or* hollow words *or* phrases; **~n dreschen** *(inf)* to churn out one cliché after another

Phra|sen-: **Phra|sen|dre|scher(in)** M(F) *(pej)* windbag *(inf)*; **Phra|sen|dre|sche|rei** [-drɛʃə'rai] F **-, -en** *(pej)* phrasemongering; *(= Geschwafel)* hot air; **phra|sen|haft** ADJ empty, hollow ADV **er drückt sich ~ aus** he speaks in clichés; **phra|sen|reich** ADJ cliché-ridden

Phra|seo|lo|gie [frazeolo'gi:] F **-, -n** [-'gi:ən] phraseology; *(Buch)* dictionary of idioms

phra|seo|lo|gisch [frazeo'lo:gɪʃ] ADJ phraseological; **~es Wörterbuch** dictionary of idioms

phra|sie|ren [fra'zi:rən] *ptp* **phrasiert** VT to phrase

Phra|sie|rung F **-, -en** phrasing

pH-Wert [pe:'ha:-] M pH value

Phy|lo|ge|ne|se [fyloge'ne:zə] F **-, -n** *(Biol)* phylogenesis

Phy|sik [fy'zi:k] F **-,** *no pl* physics *sing*

phy|si|ka|lisch [fyzi'ka:lɪʃ] ADJ physical; **~e Experimente durchführen** to carry out physics experiments *or* experiments in physics; **~e Thera-**

pie physiotherapy, physical therapy ADV physically; **das ist ~ nicht erklärbar** that can't be explained by physics; **jdn ~ behandeln** *(Med)* to give sb physiotherapy *or* physical therapy; **etw ~ therapieren** *(Med)* to have physiotherapy *or* physical therapy

Phy|si|ker ['fy:zikɐ] M -s, -, **Phy|si|ke|rin** [-ərɪn] F -, -nen physicist; *(Student auch)* physics student

Phy|sik|saal M physics lab *or* laboratory

Phy|si|kum ['fy:zikʊm] NT -s, *no pl (Univ) preliminary examination in medicine*

Phy|sio|gno|mie [fyziogno'mi:] F -, -n [-'mi:ən] *(liter)* physiognomy

phy|sio|gno|misch [fyzio'gno:mɪʃ] ADJ physiognomical ADV physiognomically

Phy|sio|lo|ge [fyzio'lo:gə] M -n, -n, **Phy|sio|lo|gin** [-'lo:gɪn] F -, -nen physiologist

Phy|sio|lo|gie [fyziolo'gi:] F -, *no pl* physiology

phy|sio|lo|gisch [fyzio'lo:gɪʃ] ADJ physiological ADV physiologically

Phy|sio|the|ra|peut(in) [fyziotera'pɔyt] M(F) physiotherapist

Phy|sio|the|ra|pie [fyziotera'pi:] F physiotherapy, physical therapy

Phy|sis ['fy:zɪs] F -, *no pl (geh)* physical constitution

phy|sisch ['fy:zɪʃ] ADJ physical ADV physically

Phy|to|plank|ton NT *(Biol)* phytoplankton

Phy|to|the|ra|pie [fytotera'pi:] F *(Med)* phytotherapy

Pi [pi:] NT -(s), -s pi; **etw Pi mal Daumen machen** *(inf)* to do sth off the top of one's head

Pi|a|ni|no [pia'ni:no] NT -s, -s pianino, cottage *or* piccolo piano

Pi|a|nist [pia'nɪst] M -en, -en, **Pi|a|nis|tin** [-'nɪstɪn] F -, -nen pianist

pi|a|no ADV *(Mus)* piano

Pi|a|no ['pia:no] NT -s, -s *(geh: = Klavier)* piano

Pi|a|no NT -s, -s *or* **Piani** piano section

Pi|a|no|for|te [piano'fɔrtə] NT -s, -s pianoforte

pi|cheln ['pɪçln] VI *(inf)* to booze *(inf)*, to knock it back *(Brit inf)*, to put it away *(inf)*

Pi|chel|stei|ner ['pɪçlʃtainɐ] M -s, *no pl*, **Pi|chel|stei|ner Topf** M - -(e)s, *no pl (Cook) meat and vegetable stew*

Pi|cke ['pɪkə] F -, -n pick(axe) *(Brit)*, pick(ax) *(US)*

Pi|ckel ['pɪkl] M -s, - **a** spot, pimple **b** *(= Spitzhacke)* pick(axe) *(Brit)*, pick(ax) *(US)*; *(= Eispickel)* ice axe *(Brit)*, ice ax *(US)*

Pi|ckel-: **Pi|ckel|ge|sicht** NT *(inf)* **a** *(Gesicht)* spotty face **b** *(pej: Person)* spotty person, zit face *(US pej)*, pizza face *(pej)*; *(Junge)* pimply youth; **~er** *pl (auch)* the acne brigade; **Pi|ckel|hau|be** F spiked (leather) helmet

pi|cke|lig ['pɪkəlɪç] ADJ spotty, pimply

pi|cken ['pɪkn] VTI to peck *(nach* at)

Pi|ckerl ['pɪkɐl] NT -s, -n *(Aus)* **a** *(= Aufkleber)* sticker **b** *(= Autobahnvignette)* motorway *(Brit) or* tollway *(US)* permit *(in the form of a windscreen sticker)*, motorway tax disc

pick|lig ['pɪklɪç] ADJ spotty, pimply

Pick|nick ['pɪknɪk] NT -s, -s *or* -e picnic; **zum ~ fahren** to go for a picnic; **~ machen** to have a picnic

pick|ni|cken ['pɪknɪkn] VI to (have a) picnic

Pick|nick|korb M picnic basket; *(größer)* picnic hamper

pi|co|bel|lo [pi:ko'bɛlo] *(inf)* ADJ perfect, spot *(Brit) or* right *(US)* on *(inf)* ADV **~ gekleidet** immaculately dressed; **~ sauber** absolutely spotless; **er hat die Wohnung ~ aufgeräumt** he did a beautiful job of tidying the flat *(Brit) or* apartment *(esp US)*; **das Zimmer war ~ aufgeräumt** *(auch)* there wasn't a thing out of place (in the room)

Pi|co|gramm [piko'gram] NT *pl* **-gramme** *or (nach Zahlenangabe)* - picogramme *(Brit)*, picogram *(US)*

Pief|ke ['pi:fkə] M -s, -s **a** *(Aus inf: = Deutscher)* Kraut *(inf)*, Jerry *(inf)* **b ein kleiner ~** a (little) pipsqueak **c** *(= Wichtigtuer)* pompous idiot

pie|ken ['pi:kn] VTI *(inf)* to prick; **es hat nur ein bisschen gepiekt** it was just a bit of a prick, I/he *etc* just felt a bit of a prick

piek|fein ['pi:k'fain] *(inf)* ADJ posh *(inf)*, swish *(Brit inf)* ADV **~ eingerichtet sein** to have classy furnishings *or* posh furniture *(inf)*; **~ angezogen sein** to look snazzy *(inf)*; **~ speisen** to have a really posh meal *(inf)*

piek|sau|ber ['pi:k'zaubɐ] ADJ *(inf)* spotless, clean as a whistle *or* a new penny

piek|sen ['pi:ksn] VTI = **pieken**

piep [pi:p] INTERJ tweet(-tweet), chirp(-chirp), cheep(-cheep); *(von Armbanduhr, Telefon)* beep (-beep)

Piep [pi:p] M -s, -e *(= Piepgeräusch)* peep, beep; *(inf)* **er sagt keinen ~** *or* **gibt keinen ~ von sich** he doesn't say a (single) word; **keinen ~ mehr machen** to have had it *(inf)*; **du hast ja einen ~!** you're off your head *(Brit) or* rocker! *(inf)*; **er traute sich nicht mal, ~ zu sagen** *or* **machen** *(inf)* he wouldn't have dared to say boo to a goose *(inf)*

pie|pe ['pi:pə], **piep|egal** ['pi:ple'ga:l] ADJ *pred (inf)* all one *(inf)*; **das ist mir ~!** *(inf)* I couldn't care less *(inf)*, it's all one to me *(inf)*

pie|pen ['pi:pn] VI *(Vogel)* to cheep, to chirrup; *(Kinderstimme)* to pipe, to squeak; *(Maus)* to squeak; *(Funkgerät etc)* to bleep, to beep; **bei dir piepts wohl!** *(inf)* are you off your head *(Brit) or* rocker? *(inf)*; **es war zum Piepen!** *(inf)* it was a scream! *(inf)*; **mit ~der Stimme** in a piping voice

Pie|pen ['pi:pn] PL *(dated sl)* lolly *(dated inf)*, dough *(inf)*

Piep|matz ['pi:pmats] M -s, **Piepmätze** [-mɛtsə] *(baby-talk: = Vogel)* dickybird *(Brit baby-talk)*, birdy *(baby-talk)*

piep|sen ['pi:psn] VI = **piepen**

Piep|ser ['pi:psɐ] M -s, - *(inf)* **a** = **Piep b** *(Telec)* bleeper

piep|sig ['pi:psɪç] *(inf)* ADJ *Stimme* squeaky ADV **~ reden** to have a squeaky voice; **~ klingen** to sound squeaky

Pieps|stim|me F *(inf)* squeaky voice

Piep|ton M bleep; **sprechen Sie bitte nach dem ~** please speak after the tone

Piep|vo|gel M *(baby-talk)* dickybird *(Brit baby-talk)*, birdy *(baby-talk)*;

Pier [pi:ɐ] M -s, -s *or* -e, *or f* -, -s jetty, pier

pier|cen ['pi:ɐsn] VT to pierce; **sich** *(dat)* **die Zunge ~ lassen** to get one's tongue pierced

Pier|cing ['pi:ɐsɪŋ] NT -s, s **a** *no pl* body piercing **b** *(Körperschmuck)* piece of body jewellery *(Brit) or* jewelry *(US)*; **~s aus Gold** gold body jewellery *(Brit) or* jewelry *(US)*

pie|sa|cken ['pi:zakn] VT *(inf: = quälen)* to torment; *(= belästigen)* to pester; **er piesackt mich schon den ganzen Tag, dass ich ihn mitnehmen soll** he's been pestering me all day to take him with me

pie|seln ['pi:zln] VI *(inf)* **a** *(= nieseln)* to drizzle **b** *(= pinkeln)* to pee, to have a pee; **~ gehen** to go for a pee

Pie|se|pam|pel ['pi:zəpampl] M -s, - *(inf)* square *(inf)*

Pi|e|ta, **Pi|e|tà** [pie'ta] F -, -s, **Pi|e|tà** F -, -s pietà

Pi|e|tät [pie'tɛ:t] F -, *no pl (= Ehrfurcht vor den Toten)* reverence *no pl*; *(= Achtung)* respect *(gegenüber jdm/etw, vor etw (dat)* for sb/sth); *(= Frömmelei)* piety; **das verstößt gegen jede ~** this offends against a proper sense of reverence

pi|e|tät|los ADJ irreverent; *(= ohne Achtung)* lacking in respect, impious ADV irreverently; **~ über Tote sprechen** to speak disrespectfully of the dead

Pi|e|tät|lo|sig|keit F -, -en irreverence; *(Tat)* impiety; **das ist eine ~ sondergleichen!** that shows a complete lack of reverence!

pi|e|tät|voll ADJ pious, reverent ADV respectfully

Pi|e|tis|mus [pie'tɪsmʊs] M -, *no pl* Pietism; *(pej)* pietism, piety, piousness

Pi|e|tist [pie'tɪst] M -en, -en, **Pi|e|tis|tin** [-'tɪstɪn] F -, -nen Pietist; *(pej auch)* holy Joe *(inf)*

pi|e|tis|tisch [pie'tɪstɪʃ] ADJ pietistic; *(pej auch)* pious

piff, paff ['pɪf'paf] INTERJ bang bang, pow pow *(inf)*

Pig|ment [pɪ'gmɛnt] NT -(e)s, -e pigment

Pig|men|ta|ti|on [pɪgmɛnta'tsio:n] F -, -en pigmentation

Pig|ment|fleck M pigmentation mark

pig|men|tie|ren [pɪgmɛn'ti:rən] *ptp* **pigmentiert** *(form)* VI to become pigmented, to pigment VT to pigment

Pik [pi:k] M *(inf)* **einen ~ auf jdn haben** to have something *or* a grudge against sb

Pik NT -s, - *(Cards) (no pl: Farbe)* spades *pl*; *(= Pikkarte)* spade; **~ass** ace of spades; **dastehen wie ~sieben** *(inf)* to look completely bewildered *or* at a loss

pi|kant [pi'kant] ADJ piquant, spicy; *Witz, Geschichte auch* racy ADV piquantly; **~ gewürzt** well-seasoned; **~ schmecken** to taste piquant

Pi|kan|te|rie [pikantə'ri:] F -, -n [-'ri:ən] **a** piquancy; *(von Witz, Geschichte auch)* raciness **b** *(Bemerkung)* piquant *or* racy remark

pi|ka|resk [pika'rɛsk] ADJ *Roman* picaresque

Pi|ke ['pi:kə] F -, -n pike; **von der ~ auf dienen** *(fig)* to rise from the ranks, to work one's way up; **etw von der ~ auf lernen** *(fig)* to learn sth starting from the bottom

Pi|kee [pi'ke:] M OR NT -s, -s piqué

pik|fein ['pi:k'fain] ADJ ADV = **piekfein**

pi|kie|ren [pi'ki:rən] *ptp* **pikiert** VT **a** *Sämlinge* to prick out, to transplant; *Bäume* to transplant **b** *(Sew)* pad *or* prick stitch

pi|kiert [pi'ki:ɐt] *(inf)* ADJ put out, peeved *(inf)*, piqued; **sie machte ein ~es Gesicht** she looked put out *or* peeved *(inf)* ADV **~ reagieren** to be put out *or* peeved *(inf)*; **~ das Gesicht verziehen** to look peeved *(inf)*

Pik|ko|lo ['pɪkolo] M -s, -s **a** *(= Kellnerlehrling)* apprentice *or* trainee waiter **b** *(fig: = kleine Ausgabe)* mini-version, baby; *(auch* **Pikkoloflasche)** quarter bottle of champagne **c** *(Mus: auch* **Pikkoloflöte)** piccolo

pi|ko|bel|lo [piko'bɛlo] *(inf)* ADJ immaculate, impeccable ADV immaculately, impeccably; **ein Zimmer ~ aufräumen** to make a room look immaculate

Pik|to|gramm [pɪkto'gram] NT *pl* **-gramme** pictogram

Pi|la|tes [pi'la:tɛs] NT -, *no pl (= Fitnessprogramm)* Pilates

Pi|lau [pi'lau] M -s, *no pl*, **Pi|law** [pi'laf] M -s, *no pl (Cook)* pilau, pilaf(f)

Pil|ger ['pɪlgɐ] M -s, -, **Pil|ge|rin** [-ərɪn] F -, -nen pilgrim

Pil|ger|fahrt F pilgrimage; **auf ~ gehen** to go on a pilgrimage

pil|gern ['pɪlgɐn] VI *aux sein* to make a pilgrimage; *(inf: = gehen)* to make *or* wend one's way

Pil|ger-: **Pil|ger|schaft** ['pɪlgɐʃaft] F -, -en pilgrimage; **Pil|ger|stab** M pilgrim's staff; **Pil|ger|zug** M procession of pilgrims

Pil|le ['pɪlə] F -, -n pill, tablet; *(= Antibabypille)* pill; **die ~ danach** the morning-after pill; **die ~ für den Mann** the male pill; **eine ~ (ein)nehmen** *or* **schlucken** to take a pill; **sie nimmt die ~** she's on the pill, she takes the pill; **das war eine bittere ~ für ihn** *(fig)* that was a bitter pill for him (to swallow); **jdm eine bittere ~ versüßen** *or* **verzuckern** *(fig)* to sugar *or* sweeten the pill for sb

Pil|len-: **Pil|len|dre|her** M *(Zool)* scarab; **Pil|len|dre|her(in)** M(F) *(inf: = Apotheker)* chemist, druggist *(US)*; **Pil|len|knick** M *slump in the birth rate caused by the pill*; **Pil|len|schach|tel** F pillbox

Pi|lot [pi'lo:t] M -en, -en, **Pi|lo|tin** [-'lo:tɪn] F -, -nen pilot

Pi|lot-: **Pi|lot|an|la|ge** F pilot plant; **Pi|lot|bal|lon** M pilot balloon; **Pi|lot|film** M pilot film

Pi|lo|tin [-'lo:tɪn] F -, -nen pilot

Pi|lot-: **Pi|lot|pro|jekt** NT pilot scheme; **Pi|lot|sen|dung** F *(TV)* pilot broadcast; **Pi|lot|stu|die** F pilot study; **Pi|lot|ver|such** M pilot experiment

Pils [pɪls] NT -, -, **Pil|se|ner** ['pɪlzənɐ] NT -s, -, **Pils|ner** ['pɪlznɐ] NT -s, - Pils, Pilsner

Pilz [pɪlts] M -es, -e **a** fungus; *(giftig)* toadstool; *(essbar)* mushroom; *(= Mikropilz)* mould *(Brit)*, mold *(US)*; *(= Atompilz)* mushroom cloud; **~e sammeln, in die ~e gehen** *(inf)* to go mushrooming *or* mushroom-picking; **wie ~e aus der Erde** *or* **aus dem Boden schießen** *or* **sprießen** to spring up like mushrooms, to mushroom **b** *(= Hautpilz)* fungal skin infection

pilz|för|mig ADJ mushroom-shaped ADV **der Rauch stieg ~ auf** the smoke rose to form a mushroom-shaped cloud

Pilz-: **Pilz|kopf** M *(inf)* Beatle; *(Frisur)* Beatle haircut; **Pilz|krank|heit** F fungal disease; **Pilz|kun|de** F, *no pl* mycology; **pilz|tö|tend** ADJ fungicidal; **Pilz|ver|gif|tung** F fungus poisoning

Pi|ment [pi'mɛnt] M OR NT -(e)s, -e *(= Nelkenpfeffer)* allspice, pimento

Pim|mel ['pɪml] M -s, - *(inf: = Penis)* willie *(inf)*

pim|pe|lig ['pɪmpəlɪç] ADJ *(inf) (= wehleidig)* soppy *(inf)*; *(= verweichlicht auch)* namby-pamby *(Brit inf)*, sissyish

Pim|per|lin|ge ['pɪmpɐlɪŋə] PL *(dated inf)* **die paar ~** the odd penny

pim|pern ['pɪmpɐn] *(inf)* VT to have it off with *(Brit inf)*, to have it with *(US sl)* VI to have it off *(Brit inf)*, to do it *(inf)*

Pimpf [pɪmpf] M -(e)s, -e **a** *(inf)* squirt *(pej)* **b** *(Hist) member of Hitlerian organization for 10-14-year-olds*

pimp|lig ['pɪmplɪç] ADJ = **pimpelig**

PIN [pɪn] F *abbr von* **persönliche Identifikationsnummer** PIN; **~-Code** PIN code; **~-Nummer** PIN number

Pin [pɪn] M -s, -s **a** *(Comput: von Stecker)* pin **b** *(= Anstecknadel)* badge

Pi|na|ko|thek [pinako'te:k] F -, -en art gallery

pin|ge|lig ['pɪŋəlɪç] ADJ *(inf)* finicky *(inf)*, fussy, nit-picking *(inf)*

Ping|pong ['pɪŋpɔŋ] NT -s, -s *(inf)* ping-pong

Pin|gu|in ['pɪŋgui:n] M -s, -e penguin

Pi|nie ['pi:niə] F -, -n *(= Baum)* pine (tree); *(= Holz)* pine (wood)

Pi|ni|en|kern M pine nut

pink [pɪŋk] ADJ shocking pink

Pin|kel ['pɪŋkl] M -s, - *(inf)* **ein feiner** *or* **vornehmer ~** a swell, Lord Muck *(Brit inf)*, His Highness *(inf)*

pin|keln ['pɪŋkln] VI *(inf)* to pee *(inf)*, to piddle *(inf)*; **ich muss mal ~** I need a pee *(inf)*

Pin|kel|pau|se F *(inf)* toilet break; **der Bus hielt zu einer ~** the bus made a toilet stop *or* a convenience stop

Pin|ke(pin|ke) ['pɪŋkə('pɪŋkə)] F -, *no pl (dated inf)* dough *(inf)*, lolly *(dated inf)*; **heute gibts ~** payday today!

pink|far|ben [-farbn] ADJ shocking pink

Pin|ne ['pɪnə] F -, -n **a** *(inf: = Stift)* pin **b** *(für Kompassnadel)* pivot **c** *(= Ruderpinne)* tiller

Pinn|wand [pɪn-] F (notice) board

Pin|scher ['pɪnʃɐ] M -s, - pinscher

Pin|scher ['pɪnʃɐ] M -s, -, **Pin|sche|rin** [-ərɪn] F -, -nen *(inf)* self-important little pipsqueak *(inf)*

Pin|sel ['pɪnzl] M -s, - **a** brush; *(Hunt)* tuft of hair **b** *(inf)* **ein eingebildeter ~** a self-opinionated twit *(Brit inf)*, a jumped-up *(Brit) or* hopped-up *(US)* so-and-so *(inf)* **c** *(sl: = Penis)* willie *(inf)*

Pin|se|lei [pɪnzə'lai] F -, -en *(pej)* daubing *(pej)*; *(= Gemälde auch)* daub *(pej)*

Pin|sel|füh|rung F brushwork

pin|seln ['pɪnzln] VTI *(inf: = streichen)* to paint *(auch Med)*; *(pej: = malen)* to daub; *(inf: = schreiben)* to pen

Pin|sel|strich M stroke (of a brush), brush-stroke

Pin|te ['pɪntə] F -, -n **a** *(inf: = Lokal)* boozer *(Brit inf)*, bar **b** *(Measure)* pint

Pin-up-Girl [pɪn'lap-] NT pin-up (girl)

Pin|zet|te [pɪn'tsɛtə] F -, -n (pair of) tweezers *pl*

Pi|o|nier [pio'ni:ɐ] M -s, -e, **Pi|o|nie|rin** [-'ni:ərɪn] F -, -nen **a** *(Mil)* sapper, engineer **b** *(fig)* pioneer **c** *(DDR) member of a political organization in the former GDR similar to the Boy Scouts*

Pi|o|nier-: **Pi|o|nier|ar|beit** F, *no pl* pioneering work; **Pi|o|nier|geist** M, *no pl* pioneering spirit

Pi|pa|po [pipa'po:] NT -s, *no pl (inf)* **das ganze ~** the whole (kit and) caboodle *(inf)*; **eine Party mit allem ~** a party with all the works

Pipe|line ['paiplain] F -, -s pipeline

Pi|pet|te [pi'pɛtə] F -, -n pipette

Pi|pi [pi'pi:] NT OR M -s, -s *(baby-talk)* wee(-wee) *(baby-talk)*; **~ machen** to do *or* have a wee (-wee)

Pi|pi-: **Pi|pi|fax** ['pɪpifaks] NT OR M -, *no pl (inf)* nonsense; **Pi|pi|mäd|chen** ['pɪpi-] NT *(pej)* bimbo *(inf)*

Pi|ran|ha [pi'ranja] M -(s), -s piranha

Pi|rat [pi'ra:t] M -en, -en, **Pi|ra|tin** [-'ra:tɪn] F -, -nen *(lit, fig)* pirate; *(= Luftpirat)* hijacker

Pi|ra|ten-: **Pi|ra|ten|akt** M act of piracy; **Pi|ra|ten|flag|ge** F Jolly Roger, skull and crossbones; **unter der ~ segeln** to sail under the skull and crossbones; **Pi|ra|ten|schiff** NT pirate ship; **Pi|ra|ten|sen|der** M pirate radio station; **Pi|ra|ten|stück** NT *(fig)* deed *or* act of piracy

Pi|ra|te|rie [piratə'ri:] F -, -n [-'ri:ən] *(lit, fig)* piracy

Pi|ra|tin [-'ra:tɪn] F → **Pirat**

Pi|rog|ge [pi'rɔgə] F -, -n *(Cook)* pirogi, piroshki *pl*

Pi|rol [pi'ro:l] M -s, -e oriole

Pi|rou|et|te [pi'ruɛtə] F -, -n pirouette

Pirsch [pɪrʃ] F -, *no pl* stalk; **auf (die) ~ gehen** to go stalking; **auf der ~ nach etw sein** *(fig)* to be on the lookout for sth

pir|schen ['pɪrʃn] VI to stalk, to go stalking

Pirsch|gang M *pl* **-gänge** stalk; **auf ~ gehen** to go stalking

PI|SA-Schock ['pi:za-] M *(Sch)* PISA shock

PI|SA-Stu|die ['pi:za-] F *(Sch)* PISA study *or* survey

pis|pern ['pɪspɐn] VI *(dial)* to whisper

Piss|ba|cke F *(sl)* nerd *(inf)*

Pis|se ['pɪsə] F -, *no pl (vulg)* piss *(sl)*

pis|sen ['pɪsn] VI *(vulg)* to (have a *(Brit) or* take a) piss *(sl)*; *(sl: = regnen)* to piss down *(Brit vulg)*, to pour down *(inf)*

Piss|nel|ke F *(sl)* nerd *(inf)*

Pis|soir [pɪ'soa:ɐ] NT -s, -s *or* -e *(dated)* urinal

Piss|pott ['pɪspɔt] M *(sl)* potty *(inf)*

Pis|ta|zie [pɪs'ta:tsiə] F -, -n pistachio

Pis|ta|zi|en|kern M (shelled) pistachio

Pis|te ['pɪstə] F -, -n *(Ski)* piste, (ski) run; *(= Rennbahn)* track, circuit; *(Aviat)* runway, tarmac; *(behelfsmäßig)* landing strip, airstrip; *(im Zirkus)* barrier

Pis|ten-: **Pis|ten|rau|pe** F piste caterpillar *or* basher *(inf)*; **Pis|ten|sau** F *(Ski sl)*, **Pis|ten|schreck** M *(Ski inf)* hooligan on the piste

Pis|to|le [pɪs'to:lə] F -, -n **a** pistol; **jdn mit vorgehaltener ~ (zu etw) zwingen** to force sb (to do sth) at gunpoint; **jdn auf ~n fordern** *(old)* to challenge sb to a duel (with pistols); **jdm die ~ auf die Brust setzen** *(fig)* to hold a pistol to sb's head; **wie aus der ~ geschossen** *(fig)* like a shot *(inf)* **b** *(Hist: Goldmünze)* pistole

Pis|to|len-: **Pis|to|len|griff** M pistol butt; **Pis|to|len|ku|gel** F (pistol) bullet; **Pis|to|len|schuss** M pistol shot; **Pis|to|len|ta|sche** F holster

Pit|bull|ter|ri|er ['pɪtbʊl-] M pit bull terrier

pit|sche|nass ['pɪtʃə'nas], **pitsch|nass** ['pɪtʃ'nas] *(inf)* ADJ soaking (wet); *Kleidung, Mensch auch* dripping (wet)

pitsch, patsch ['pɪtʃ 'patʃ] INTERJ pitter-patter

pit|to|resk [pɪto'rɛsk] ADJ picturesque ADV picturesquely; **~ aussehen** to look picturesque

Pi|xel ['pɪksl] NT -s, -s *(Comput)* pixel

Piz|za ['pɪtsa] F -, -s *or* **Pizzen** ['pɪtsn] pizza

Piz|za-: **Piz|za|bä|cker(in)** M(F) pizza chef; **Piz|za|ge|würz** NT pizza spice; **Piz|za|ta|sche** F calzone

Piz|ze|ria [pɪtsə'ri:a] F -, -s *or* **Pizzerien** [-'ri:ən] pizzeria

Pkw ['pe:ka:ve:, pe:ka:'ve:] M -s, -s *abbr von* **Personenkraftwagen** car

pl., **Pl.** *abbr von* **Plural** pl

Pla|ce|bo [pla'tse:bo] NT -s, -s placebo

Pla|ce|bo|ef|fekt M *(lit, fig)* placebo effect

pla|cie|ren △ [pla'tsi:rən] *ptp* **placiert** VT → **platzieren**

Pla|cie|rung △ F -, -en → **Platzierung**

pla|cken ['plakn] VR *(inf)* to slave (away) *(inf)*

Pla|cken ['plakn] M -s, - *(dial)* patch

Pla|cke|rei [plakə'rai] F -, -en *(inf)* grind *(inf)*

plad|dern ['pladɐn] *(N Ger)* VI *aux sein (Regen)* to pelt (down) VI *impers* to pelt down

plä|die|ren [plɛ'di:rən] *ptp* **plädiert** VI *(Jur, fig)* to plead *(für, auf +acc* for)

Plä|do|yer [plɛdoa'je:] NT -s, -s *(Jur)* address to the jury, summation *(US)*, summing up; *(fig)* plea

Pla|fond [pla'fõ:] M -s, -s *(lit, fig)* ceiling

Pla|ge ['pla:gə] F -, -n **a** plague **b** *(fig: = Mühe)* nuisance; *(= Plackerei)* (hard) grind *(inf)*; **sie hat ihre ~ mit ihm** he's a trial for her; **man hat schon seine ~ mit dir** you do make life difficult, you are a nuisance; **zu einer ~ werden** to become a nuisance

Pla|ge|geist M nuisance, pest

pla|gen ['pla:gn] VT to plague, to torment; *(mit Bitten und Fragen auch)* to pester, to harass; **dich plagt doch was, heraus mit der Sprache** something's worrying *or* bothering you, out with it; **ein geplagter Mann** a harassed man; **vom schlechten Gewissen geplagt werden** to be plagued *or* tormented by a guilty conscience VR **a** *(= leiden)* to be troubled *or* bothered *(mit* by); **schon die ganze Woche plage ich mich mit meinem Heuschnupfen** I've been bothered *or* troubled all week by my hay fever, my hay fever's been bothering *or* troubling me all week **b** *(= sich abrackern)* to slave *or* slog *(esp Brit)* away *(inf)*; *(= sich Mühe geben)* to go to *or* take a lot of trouble *or* great pains *(mit* over, with)

Pla|gi|at [pla'gia:t] NT -(e)s, -e **a** *(= geistiger Diebstahl)* plagiarism; **da hat er ein ~ begangen** that's a plagiarism, he plagiarized that **b** *(Buch, Film etc)* book/film *etc* resulting from plagiarism; *(= nachgebildeter Markenartikel)* counterfeit product; **dieses Buch ist ein ~** this book is plagiarism

Pla|gi|a|tor [pla'gia:to:ɐ] M -s, **Plagiatoren** [-'to:rən], **Pla|gi|a|to|rin** [-'to:rɪn] F -, -nen plagiarist

pla|gi|ie|ren [plagi'i:rən] *ptp* **plagiiert** VTI to plagiarize

Plaid [ple:t] NT OR M -s, -s tartan travelling rug *(Brit) or* traveling rug *(US)*

Pla|ka|far|be® ['plaka-] F poster paint

Pla|kat [pla'ka:t] NT -(e)s, -e *(an Litfaßsäulen etc)* poster, bill; *(aus Pappe)* placard

Pla|kat-: **Pla|kat|ak|ti|on** F poster campaign; **Pla|kat|an|kle|ber** [-ankle:bɐ] M -s, -, **Pla|kat|an|kle|be|rin** [-ərɪn] F -, -nen billposter, billsticker; **Pla|kat|far|be** F poster paint

pla|ka|tie|ren [plaka'ti:rən] *ptp* **plakatiert** VT to placard; *(fig)* to broadcast

pla|ka|tiv [plaka'ti:f] ADJ *Wirkung, Farben* striking, bold; *Sprüche* pithy; *Gehabe* showy ADV **~ formuliert** catchy; **etw ~ formulieren** to express sth in a catchy phrase; **~ wirkende Lieder** catchy songs

Pla|kat-: **Pla|kat|ma|ler(in)** M(F) poster painter *or* artist; **Pla|kat|säu|le** F advertisement pillar; **Pla|kat|schrift** F block lettering; **Pla|kat|trä|ger(in)** M(F) sandwich man, man/woman carrying a sandwich board; **Pla|kat|wer|bung** F poster advertising

Pla|ket|te [pla'kɛtə] F -, -n *(= Abzeichen)* badge; *(Münze)* commemorative coin; *(an Wänden)* plaque

plan [pla:n] ADJ flat, level; *Ebene, Fläche* plane *attr*

Plan [pla:n] M -(e)s, ⸗e ['plɛ:nə] **a** plan; **die Pläne zur Renovierung der Häuser** the plans for the renovation of the houses; **den ~ fassen, etw zu tun** to form the intention of doing sth, to plan to do sth; **wir haben den ~, ...** we're planning to ...; **Pläne machen** *or* **schmieden** to make plans, to plan; **nach ~ verlaufen** to run *or* go according to plan; **das passt mir nicht in den ~** *(inf)* it doesn't suit me, it's inconvenient **b** *(= Stadtplan)* (street) map, town plan; *(= Grundriss, Bauplan)* plan, blueprint; *(= Zeittafel)* schedule, timetable; *(= Wirtschaftsplan)* economic plan

Plan M -(e)s, ⸗e ['plɛ:nə] *(obs: = ebene Fläche)* plain; **auf dem ~ erscheinen, auf den ~ treten** *(fig)* to arrive *or* come on the scene; **jdn auf den ~ rufen** *(fig)* to bring sb into the arena

plan|bar ADJ plannable

Pla|ne ['pla:nə] F -, -n tarpaulin, tarp *(US inf)*; *(von LKW)* hood; *(= Schutzdach)* canopy, awning

Plä|ne|ma|cher(in) M(F) planner; **er ist ein großer ~** he's a great one for making plans

pla|nen ['pla:nən] ✪ 35.2, 52.5 VTI to plan; *Attentat, Verbrechen auch* to plot

Pla|ner ['pla:nɐ] M -s, -, **Pla|ne|rin** [-ərɪn] F -, -nen planner

Pla|ner M -s, - *(= Terminkalender)* diary

Plan|er|fül|lung F realization of a/the plan; **uns trennen nur noch 5% von der ~** we're only 5% short of our planned target

pla|ne|risch ['pla:nərɪʃ] ADJ planning; **~e Ausarbeitung** working out of the plans ADV **etw ~ durchdenken** to plan sth from start to finish; **~ ausgearbeitet** planned down to the last detail; **~ vorgehen** to proceed methodically; **ein Projekt ~ betreuen** to be in charge of the planning of a project; **~ hat das Team versagt** the team's planning was a failure

Pla|net [pla'ne:t] M -en, -en planet

pla|ne|ta|risch [plane'ta:rɪʃ] ADJ planetary; **~er Nebel** *(Astron)* planetary nebula

Pla|ne|ta|ri|um [plane'ta:riʊm] NT -s, **Planetarien** [-riən] planetarium

Pla|ne|ten-: **Pla|ne|ten|bahn** F planetary orbit; **Pla|ne|ten|sys|tem** NT planetary system

Pla|ne|to|id [planeto'i:t] M -en, -en [-dn] planetoid, asteroid

Plan-: **Plan|fest|stel|lungs|ver|fah|ren** NT *(Build)* planning permission hearings *pl*; **plan|ge|mäß** ADJ ADV = **planmäßig**

pla|nie|ren [pla'ni:rən] *ptp* **planiert** VT *Boden* to level (off); *Werkstück* to planish

Pla|nier|rau|pe F bulldozer

Plan|ke ['plaŋkə] F -, -n plank, board; *(= Leitplanke)* crash barrier; **~n** *(= Umzäunung)* fencing, boarding (+*gen* round)

Plän|ke|lei [plɛŋkə'lai] F -, -en *(old Mil)* skirmish; *(fig auch)* squabble

plän|keln ['plɛŋkln] VI *(old Mil)* to skirmish, to engage in skirmishes; *(fig)* to squabble, to have a squabble

Plank|ton ['plaŋktɔn] NT -s, *no pl* plankton

plan|los ADJ unmethodical, unsystematic; *(= ziellos)* random ADV *umherirren, durchstreifen* aimlessly; *vorgehen* without any clear direction; *durchsuchen* haphazardly; **etw ~ durchblättern** to flick aimlessly through sth

Plan|lo|sig|keit F -, *no pl* lack of planning

plan|mä|ßig ADJ *(= wie geplant)* as planned, according to plan; *(= pünktlich)* on schedule, as scheduled; *(= methodisch)* methodical; **~e Ankunft/Abfahrt** scheduled time of arrival/departure ADV **a** *(= systematisch)* methodically, systematically **b** *(= fahrplanmäßig)* on schedule, on time; **wir sind ~ um 7 angekommen** we arrived on schedule *or* as scheduled *or* on time at 7; **~ kommt der Zug um 7 Uhr an** the train is scheduled to arrive *or* is due in at 7 o'clock

Plan|mä|ßig|keit F *(= Methodik)* method; *(= Pünktlichkeit)* punctuality; *(= Regelmäßigkeit)* regularity

Plan|quad|rat NT grid square

Plansch|be|cken NT paddling pool *(Brit)*, wading pool *(US)*

plan|schen ['planʃn] VI to splash around

Plan|sche|rei [planʃə'rai] F -, -en splashing around

Plan-: **Plan|soll** NT output target; **Plan|spiel** NT experimental game; *(Mil)* map exercise; *(Econ)* planning *or* experimental game; **Plan|stel|le** F post

Plan|ta|ge [plan'ta:ʒə] F -, -n plantation

Plantsch|be|cken NT paddling pool *(Brit)*, wading pool *(US)*

plant|schen VI to splash around

Plant|sche|rei F -, -en splashing around

Pla|nung ['pla:nʊŋ] F -, -en planning; **diese Straße ist noch in ~** this road is still being planned; **schon in der ~** in *or* at the planning stage

Pla|nungs-: **Pla|nungs|ab|tei|lung** F planning department; **Pla|nungs|aus|schuss** M planning committee; **Pl|anung|schef(in)** M(F) chief planner, head of the planning department; **Pla|nungs|kom|mis|si|on** F planning commission; **Pla|nungs|zeit|raum** M planning period

Plan-: **Plan|wa|gen** M covered wagon; **Plan|wirt|schaft** F planned economy

Plap|pe|rei [plapə'rai] F -, -en *(inf)* chatter(ing), prattling *(esp Brit)*

Plap|per|maul NT *(inf)* *(= Mund)* big mouth *(inf)*; *(= Kind)* chatterbox *(inf)*; *(= Schwätzer)* tittle-tattler *(esp Brit inf)*, windbag *(inf)*

plap|pern ['plapɐn] VI to prattle, to chatter; *(= Geheimnis verraten)* to talk, to blab *(inf)* VT **was plapperst du denn da für Blödsinn?** don't talk rubbish *(Brit) or* nonsense

Plap|per|ta|sche F *(inf)* tittle-tattler *(esp Brit inf)*, windbag *(inf)*

Plaque [plak] F -, -s *(Med)* plaque

plär|ren ['plɛrən] VTI *(inf: = weinen)* to howl, to bawl; *(Radio)* to blare (out); *(= schreien)* to yell, to shriek; *(= unschön singen)* to screech

Plä|sier [plɛ'zi:ɐ] NT -s, -e *(dated)* pleasure, delight; **nun lass ihm doch sein ~** let him have his bit of fun

Plä|sier|chen [plɛ'zi:ɐçən] NT -s, - **jedem Tierchen sein ~** *(hum)* each to his own

Plas|ma ['plasma] NT -s, **Plasmen** [-mən] plasma

Plas|ma-: **Plas|ma|bild|schirm** M *(inf)* plasma screen; **Plas|ma|fern|se|her** M *(inf)* plasma screen TV

Plast [plast] M -(e)s, -e, **Plas|te** ['plastə] F -, -n *(dial)* plastic

Plas|tik ['plastɪk] NT -s, *no pl* *(= Kunststoff)* plastic

Plas|tik F -, -en **a** *(= Bildhauerkunst)* sculpture, plastic art *(form)* **b** *(= Skulptur)* sculpture **c** *(Med)* plastic surgery **d** *(fig: = Anschaulichkeit)* vividness

Plas|tik-: **Plas|tik|beu|tel** M plastic bag, carrier bag; **Plas|tik|bom|be** F plastic bomb; **Plas|tik|fla|sche** F plastic bottle; **Plas|tik|fo|lie** F plastic film; **Plas|tik|geld** NT *(inf)* plastic money; **mit ~ bezahlen** to pay with plastic *(inf)*; **Plas|tik|hül|le** F plastic cover; **Plas|tik|ma|te|ri|al** NT plastic; **Plas|tik|spreng|stoff** M plastic explosive; **Plas|tik|tü|te** F plastic bag

Plas|ti|lin® [plasti'li:n] NT -s, -e ≈ Plasticine®

Plas|ti|na|ti|on [plastina'tsio:n] F -, *no pl* plastination

plas|tisch ['plastɪʃ] ADJ **a** *(= knetbar)* malleable, workable **b** *(= dreidimensional)* three-dimensional, 3-D; *(fig: anschaulich)* vivid; **~es Vorstellungsvermögen** ability to imagine things in three dimensions; **~e Sprache** vivid *or* graphic language **c** *(Art)* plastic; **die ~e Kunst** plastic art; **~e Arbeiten** sculptures, plastic works **d** *(Med) Chirurgie* plastic ADV **a** *(räumlich)* three-dimensionally; **~ wirken** *or* **erscheinen** to appear three-dimensional; **etw ~ ausformen** to mould *(Brit) or* mold *(US)* sth into shape; **~ hervortreten** to stand out **b** *(fig: anschaulich)* **etw ~ schildern** to give a graphic description of sth; **sich** *(dat)* **etw ~ vorstellen** to picture sth clearly; **das kann ich mir ~ vorstellen** I can just imagine *or* picture it

Plas|ti|zi|tät [plastitsi'tɛ:t] F -, *no pl* **a** *(= Formbarkeit)* malleability, workability **b** *(fig: = Anschaulichkeit)* vividness, graphicness

Pla|ta|ne [pla'ta:nə] F -, -n plane tree

Pla|teau [pla'to:] NT -s, -s **a** plateau **b** *(von Schuh)* platform

Pla|teau|schuh [pla'to:-] M platform shoe

Pla|teau|soh|le [pla'to:-] F platform sole

Pla|tin ['pla:ti:n, pla'ti:n] NT -s, *no pl* *(abbr* **Pt***)* platinum

pla|tin|blond ADJ platinum blond(e) ADV **~ gefärbtes Haar** dyed platinum blond(e) hair

Pla|ti|ne [pla'ti:nə] F -, -n *(Comput)* circuit board

Pla|ti|tü|de △ [plati'ty:də] F -, -n → **Plattitüde**

Pla|to(n) ['pla:to, 'pla:tɔn] M -s Plato

Pla|to|ni|ker [pla'to:nikɐ] M -s, -, **Pla|to|ni|ke|rin** [-ərɪn] F -, -nen Platonist

pla|to|nisch [pla'to:nɪʃ] ADJ Platonic, Platonist; *(= nicht sexuell)* platonic; *(geh: = unverbindlich)* noncommittal; **~e Liebe** platonic love ADV platonically

platsch [platʃ] INTERJ splash, splosh

plat|schen ['platʃn] VI *(inf)* to splash; *(= regnen)* to pelt, to pour

plät|schern ['plɛtʃɐn] VI *(Bach)* to babble, to splash; *(Brunnen)* to splash; *(Regen)* to patter; *(= planschen)* to splash (about *(Brit) or* around); **aus dem Radio plätscherte ein altes Lied** an old song was playing softly on the radio; **eine ~de Unterhaltung** light conversation

platsch|nass ADJ *(inf)* soaking (wet); *Kleidung, Mensch auch* dripping (wet), drenched

platt [plat] ADJ **a** *(= flach)* flat; **einen Platten** *(inf) or* **einen ~en Reifen haben** to have a flat *(inf)*, to have a flat tyre *(Brit) or* tire *(US)*; **das ~e Land** the flat country; *(nicht Stadt)* the country **b** *(fig: = geistlos) Bemerkung, Witz* flat, dull; *Mensch* dull, uninspired **c** *(inf: = verblüfft)* **~ sein** to be flabbergasted *(inf)*; **da bist du ~, nicht?** that surprised you, didn't it? **d** *(inf)* *(= erschöpft)* done in *(inf)*, dead beat *(Brit inf)*; *(= bankrott) Betrieb* bust *(inf)* **e** *(sl: = high)* wasted *(sl)* ADV *pressen, walzen* flat; **etw ~ drücken** to press sth flat, to flatten sth → **plattmachen**

Platt [plat] NT -(s), *no pl* *(inf)* Low German, Plattdeutsch

Plätt|brett NT *(dial)* ironing board; *(inf)* skinny Lizzy *(Brit inf)*, skinny Minnie *(US inf)*

Plätt|chen ['plɛtçən] NT -s, - little tile

platt|deutsch ADJ Low German

Platt|deutsch(e) NT Low German, Plattdeutsch → *auch* **Deutsch(e)**

platt+drü|cken VT *sep* → **platt ADV**

Plat|te ['platə] F -, -n **a** *(= Holzplatte)* piece of wood, wood *no pl*, board; *(zur Wandverkleidung)* panel; *(= Tischtennisplatte)* ping-pong table; *(= Glasplatte/Metallplatte/Plastikplatte)* piece *or* sheet of glass/metal/plastic; *(= Betonplatte, Steinplatte)* slab; *(zum Pflastern)* paving stone, flag(stone); *(= Kachel, Fliese)* tile; *(= Grabplatte)* gravestone, slab; *(= Herdplatte)* hotplate; *(= Tischplatte)* (table) top; *(ausziehbare)* leaf; *(= Felsenplatte)* shelf, ledge; *(Geog: = ebenes Land)* flat *or* low land; *(Geol: = tektonische Platte)* (tectonic) plate; *(= Druckstock)* plate; *(= Münzrohling)* coin disc; *(Phot)* plate; *(von Gebiss)* (dental) plate; *(= Gedenktafel)* plaque; *(Comput)* disk; **ein Ereignis auf die ~ bannen** to capture an event on film

b *(= Servierteller)* serving dish, plate; *(= Tortenplatte)* cake plate; *(mit Fuß)* cake stand; **eine ~ Aufschnitt** a plate of selected cold meats
c *(= Schallplatte)* record, disc; **etw auf ~ sprechen/aufnehmen** to make a record of sth, to record sth; **eine ~ mit Marschmusik** a record of march music; **die ~ kenne ich schon** *(fig inf)* I've heard all that before, I know that line; **er legte die alte ~ auf** *(fig inf)* he started on his old theme; **leg doch mal eine neue ~ auf!** *(fig inf)* change the record, can't you!; **die ~ hat einen Sprung** the record's stuck
d *(inf) (= Glatze)* bald head; *(= kahle Stelle)* bald spot *or* patch
e *(Aus: = Verbrecherbande)* gang (of criminals)
f *(sl)* **auf ~ sein** *(= obdachlos)* to be on the streets; **~ machen** *(= als Obdachloser schlafen)* to sleep rough *(Brit) or* on the streets

Plät|te ['plɛtə] F -, -n *(N Ger inf)* iron

Plätt|ei|sen NT *(dial)* iron; *(Hist)* smoothing iron

plät|ten ['plɛtn] VT *(dial)* to iron, to press → *auch* **geplättet**

Plat|ten-: **Plat|ten|bau** M *pl* **-bauten** *(inf: = Haus) prefabricated building*; **Plat|ten|con|trol|ler** M *(Comput)* (hard) disk controller; **Plat|ten|kon|den|sa|tor** M plate condenser; **Plat|ten|la|bel** NT record label; **Plat|ten|lauf|werk** NT *(Comput)* disk drive; **Plat|ten|le|ger** [-le:gɐ] M **-s, -**, **Plat|ten|le|ge|rin** [-ərɪn] F **-, -nen** paver; **Plat|ten|samm|lung** F record collection; **Plat|ten|see** M **der ~** Lake Balaton; **Plat|ten|spie|ler** M record player; **Plat|ten|tel|ler** M turntable; **Plat|ten|wechs|ler** [-vɛkslɐ] M **-s, -** autochanger, record changer; **Plat|ten|weg** M paved path

Plät|ter ['plɛtɐ] M **-s, -**, **Plät|te|rin** [-ərɪn] F **-, -nen** *(dial)* ironer, presser

Plät|te|rei [plɛtə'rai] F **-, -en** *(dial)* **a** *(Betrieb) business which does ironing* **b** *(inf: = das Plätten)* ironing

Platt-: **Platt|fisch** M flatfish; **Platt|form** F platform; *(fig: = Grundlage)* basis; **platt|form|über|grei|fend** ADJ *(Comput)* cross-platform *attr*; **Platt|fuß** M flat foot; *(inf: = Reifenpanne)* flat *(inf)*; **platt|fü|ßig** ADJ ADV flat-footed

Platt|heit F **-, -en** **a** *no pl (= Flachheit)* flatness; *(= Geistlosigkeit)* dullness, flatness **b** *usu pl (= Redensart etc)* commonplace, platitude, cliché

plat|tie|ren [pla'ti:rən] *ptp* **plattiert** VT *Metall* to plate

Plat|ti|tü|de [plati'ty:də] F **-n, -n** platitude

Plätt|li ['plɛtli] NT **-, -** *(Sw: = Fliese, Kachel)* tile

Platt-: **platt+ma|chen** VT *sep (sl) (= dem Erdboden gleichmachen)* to level; *(= pleitegehen lassen) Firma* to bankrupt; *(= heruntermachen)* to knock *(inf)*; *(= töten)* to do in *(inf)*, to take out *(inf)*; *(= fertigmachen)* to lay into *(inf)*; **platt|na|sig** ADJ flat-nosed; **Platt|stich** M satin stitch; **Platt|sti|cke|rei** F satin stitch embroidery

Plätt|wä|sche F *(dial)* ironing

Platz [plats] M **-es, =e** ['plɛtsə] **a** *(= freier Raum)* room, space; **~ für jdn/etw schaffen** to make room for sb/sth; **~ für etw finden** to find room *or* space for sth; **in dem Zelt finden** *or* **haben zwei Personen ~** there is room for two people in the tent; **es wird ~ finden** there'll be room *or* space for it; **~ greifen** to spread, to gain ground; **~ einnehmen** *or* **brauchen** to take up or occupy room *or* space; **~ für etw (frei) lassen** to leave room *or* space for sth; **~ raubend** = **platzraubend**; **~ sparend** = **platzsparend**; **das Buch hat keinen ~ mehr im Regal** there's no more room *or* space on the bookshelf for that book; **mehr als 10 Leute haben hier nicht ~** there's not room *or* space for more than 10 people here; **jdm den (ganzen) ~ wegnehmen** to take up all the room; **jdm ~ machen** to make room for sb; *(= vorbeigehen lassen)* to make way for sb *(auch fig)*; **für etw ~ machen** *or* **schaffen** to make room for sth; **~ machen** to get out of the way *(inf)*; **mach mal ein bisschen ~** make a bit of room; **~ für jdn/etw bieten** to hold sb/sth, to have room for sb/sth; **~ da!** *(inf)* (get) out of the way there! *(inf)*, gangway! *(inf)*
b *(= Sitzplatz)* seat; **~ nehmen** to take a seat; **bitte ~ nehmen zum Mittagessen** please take your seats for lunch; **behalten Sie doch bitte ~!** *(form)* please remain seated *(form)*; **ist hier noch ein ~ frei?** is there a free seat here?; **dieser ~ ist belegt** *or* **besetzt** this seat's taken, this is somebody's seat; **sich von seinem ~ erheben** *(geh)* to rise *(form)*; **der Saal hat 2.000 Plätze** the hall seats 2,000, the hall has seating for 2,000 *or* has 2,000 seats; **mit jdm den ~ tauschen** *or* **wechseln** to change places with sb; **erster/zweiter ~** front/rear stalls; **~!** *(zum Hund)* (lie) down!
c *(= Stelle, Standort, Rang)* place; **das Buch steht nicht an seinem ~** the book isn't in (its) place; **etw (wieder) an seinen ~ stellen** to put sth (back) in (its) place; **fehl** *or* **nicht am ~(e) sein** to be out of place; **am ~(e) sein** to be appropriate; **auf die Plätze, fertig, los!** *(beim Sport)* on your marks, get set, go!, ready, steady, go! *(Brit)*, ready, set, go! *(esp US)*; **er wich nicht vom ~(e)** he wouldn't yield (an inch); **seinen ~ behaupten** to stand one's ground, to hold one's own; **Extremismus hat keinen ~ in der Politik** there is no place for extremism in politics; **alles hat seinen festen ~** everything has its proper place; **die Literatur hat einen festen ~ in ihrem Leben** literature is very much a part of her life; **ihr ~ ist an der Seite ihres Mannes** her (proper) place is at her husband's side; **den ersten ~ einnehmen** *(fig)* to take first place, to come first; **auf ~ zwei** in second place; **jdn auf ~ drei/den zweiten ~ verweisen** to beat sb into third/second place; **jdn auf die Plätze verweisen** *(fig)* to beat sb; **auf ~ wetten** to make a place bet; **ein ~ an der Sonne** *(lit, fig)* a place in the sun → **fehl**
d *(= Arbeitsplatz, Studienplatz, Heimplatz etc)* place; *(= unbesetzter Arbeitsplatz)* vacancy; **im Kindergarten sind noch ein paar Plätze frei** there are still a few vacancies *or* places left in the kindergarten
e *(= umbaute Fläche)* square; **auf dem ~** in *or* on the square; **ein freier ~ vor der Kirche** an open space in front of the church
f *(= Sportplatz)* playing field; *(Ftbl, Hockey)* pitch, field; *(= Handballplatz, Tennisplatz)* court; *(= Golfplatz)* (golf) course, (golf) links *pl*; **einen Spieler vom ~ stellen** *or* **verweisen** to send a player off *(Brit)*, to eject a player *(US)*; **auf gegnerischem ~** away; **auf eigenem ~** at home; **jdn vom ~ fegen** *(inf: = vernichtend schlagen)* to wipe the floor with sb *(inf)*
g *(= Ort)* town, place; *(= Handelsplatz)* centre *(Brit)*, center *(US)*; **das erste Hotel** *or* **Haus am ~(e)** the best hotel in town *or* in the place
h *(= Lagerplatz)* (store *or* storage) yard
i *(= Bauplatz)* site

Platz-: **Platz|angst** F *(inf: = Beklemmung)* claustrophobia; *(auf offenen Plätzen)* agoraphobia; **~ bekommen** to get claustrophobic *or* claustrophobia/agoraphobic *or* agoraphobia; **Platz|an|wei|ser** [-anvaizɐ] M **-s, -** usher; **Platz|an|wei|se|rin** [-anvaizərɪn] F **-, -nen** usherette

Plätz|chen ['plɛtsçən] NT **-s, -** **a** *dim von* **Platz** spot, little place **b** *(Gebäck)* biscuit *(Brit)*, cookie *(US)*

Plätz|chen|form F *(Cook)* biscuit *(Brit) or* cookie *(US)* cutter

plat|zen ['platsn] VI *aux sein* **a** *(= aufreißen)* to burst; *(Naht, Hose, Augenbraue, Haut)* to split; *(= explodieren: Granate, Stinkbombe)* to explode; *(= einen Riss bekommen)* to crack; **mir ist unterwegs ein Reifen geplatzt** I had a blowout on the way *(inf)*, a tyre burst *(Brit) or* a tire blew *(US)* on the way; **ihm ist eine Ader geplatzt** he burst a blood vessel; **wenn du so weiterisst, platzt du!** if you go on eating like that you'll burst; **wir sind vor Lachen fast geplatzt** we split our sides laughing, we laughed till our sides ached *or* split; **ins Zimmer ~** *(inf)* to burst into the room; **jdm ins Haus ~** *(inf)* to descend on sb; **(vor Wut/Neid/Ungeduld) ~** *(inf)* to be bursting (with rage/envy/impatience); **bei ihm ist endlich der Knoten geplatzt** *(inf)* it all eventually clicked (for him) *(inf)* → **Bombe, Kragen, Naht**
b *(inf: = scheitern) (Plan, Geschäft, Termin, Vertrag)* to fall through; *(Freundschaft, Koalition)* to break up; *(Theorie)* to fall down, to collapse; *(Wechsel)* to bounce *(inf)*; **die Verlobung ist geplatzt** the engagement is (all) off; **etw ~ lassen** *(Plan, Geschäft, Termin, Vertrag)* to make sth fall through; *Freundschaft, Verlobung* to break sth off; *Koalition* to break sth up; *Vorstellung* to call sth off; *Theorie* to explode sth; *Wechsel* to make sth bounce *(inf)*

plat|zen+las|sen *ptp* **platzenlassen** *or (rare)* **platzengelassen** VT *sep irreg (inf, fig)* → **platzen b**

Platz-: **Platz|er|spar|nis** F space saving; **aus Gründen der ~** for reasons of space, to save space; **Platz|hal|ter** M place marker; *(Comput, Ling)* placeholder, wildcard (character); **Platz|hal|ter(in)** M(F) custodian; **Platz|her|ren** PL *(Sport inf)* home team; **Platz|hirsch** M *(lit, fig)* dominant male

plat|zie|ren [pla'tsi:rən] *ptp* **platziert** VT **a** *(= Platz anweisen)* to put; *Soldaten, Wächter* to put, to place, to position; *(Tennis)* to seed; **der Kellner platzierte uns in die** *or* **der Nähe der Band** the waiter directed *or* showed us to a place *or* put us near the band; **„Sie werden platziert"** "please wait to be seated"
b *(= zielen) Ball* to place, to position; *Schlag, Faust* to land; **gut platzierte Aufschläge** well-placed *or* well-positioned services; **ein (gut) platzierter Schlag** a well-placed *or* well-aimed blow; **platziert schießen** to position one's shots well; **er hat platziert in die rechte Torecke geschossen** he tucked the ball away neatly in the right corner of the goal
c *(= anlegen) Geld* to put, to place; *Aktien* to place
VR **a** *(inf: = sich setzen, stellen etc)* to plant oneself *(inf)*
b *(Sport)* to be placed, to get a place; *(Tennis)* to be seeded; **der Läufer konnte sich gut/nicht ~** the runner was well-placed/wasn't even placed

Plat|zie|rung F *(bei Rennen)* order; *(Tennis)* seeding; *(= Platz)* place; *(von Aktien, Geld)* placing; **welche ~ hatte er?** where did he come in?, what position did he come in?

Platz-: **Platz|kar|te** F *(Rail)* seat reservation (ticket); **ich bestelle mir eine ~** I'll reserve (myself) a seat, I'll get a seat reservation; **Platz|kon|zert** NT open-air concert; **Platz|man|gel** M, *no pl* shortage *or* lack of space *or* room; **wir leiden sehr unter ~** we're terribly short of space *or* room, we've a space problem; **Platz|mie|te** F *(Theat)* season ticket; *(Sport)* ground rent; **Platz|pat|ro|ne** F blank (cartridge); **platz|rau|bend** ADJ space-consuming; **Platz|re|gen** M cloudburst; **das ist nur ein ~** it's only a (passing) shower; **Platz|re|ser|vie|rung** F seat reservation; **platz|spa|rend** ADJ space-saving *attr*; **das ist ~er** that saves more space ADV *bauen, einbauen, unterbringen* (in order) to save space; **etw ~ stapeln** to stack sth (away) with a minimum use of space; **so kann ~ geparkt werden** it's a way of saving parking space; **Platz|sper|re** F *(Sport)* (home) ground ban, ban on playing on one's home ground; **Platz|ver|hält|nis|se** PL *(Sport)* state *sing* of the pitch *or* field; **Platz|ver|weis** M sending-off *(Brit)*, ejection *(US)*; **es gab drei ~e** three players were sent off *(Brit) or* ejected *(US)*; **Platz|vor|teil** M home advantage; **Platz|wahl** F toss-up; **die ~ haben/verlieren** to win/lose the toss; **die ~ vornehmen** to toss up; **Platz|wart** [-vart] M **-s, -e**, **Platz|war|tin** [-vartɪn] F **-, -nen** *(Sport)* groundsman; **Platz|wech|sel** M change of position; **Plạtz|wet|te** F place bet; **Plạtz|wun|de** F cut, laceration

Plau|de|rei [plaudə'rai] F -, -en chat, conversation; *(Press)* feature; *(TV, Rad)* chat show *(Brit)*, talk show

Plau|de|rer ['plaudərɐ] M -s, -, **Plau|de|rin** [-ərɪn] F -, -nen conversationalist

plau|der|haft ADJ *Ton* conversational, chatty

plau|dern ['plaudɐn] VI to chat, to talk *(über +acc, von* about); *(= verraten)* to talk; **mit ihm lässt sich gut ~** he's easy to talk to → **Schule, Nähkästchen**

Plau|der-: **Plau|der|stünd|chen** NT, **Plau|der|stun|de** F chat; **ein angenehmes ~ zubringen** to have a pleasant chat, to have a cosy *(Brit)* or cozy *(US)* little chat; **Plau|der|ta|sche** F *(inf)* chatterbox *(inf)*; **Plau|der|ton** M, *no pl* conversational *or* chatty tone

Plausch [plauʃ] M -(e)s, -e *(inf)* chat; **einen ~ halten** to have a chat; **das war ein ~** *(Sw: = Freude, Amüsement)* that was a good laugh

plau|schen ['plauʃn] VI *(inf)* to chat, to have a chat *or* a natter *(Brit inf)*

plau|si|bel [plau'zi:bl] ADJ *Erklärung, Grund* plausible ADV plausibly; **jdm etw ~ machen** to make sth clear to sb, to explain sth to sb

Plau|si|bi|li|tät [plauzibili'tɛ:t] F -, *no pl* plausibility

Plau|si|bi|li|täts|kon|trol|le F *(von Daten, Statistik)* plausibility check

plauz [plauts] INTERJ *(inf)* crash, bang

Plauz [plauts] M -es, -e *(inf) (Geräusch)* bang, crash; *(= Fall)* fall

Plau|ze ['plautsə] F -, -n *(dial inf)* chest; **es auf der ~ haben** *(inf)* to have a chesty *(Brit)* or deep *(US inf)* cough, to be chesty *(Brit inf)*; **auf der ~ liegen** *(inf)* to be laid up *(inf)*

Play-: **Play-back** ['ple:bɛk] NT -s, -s, **Play|back** NT -s, -s *(= Band) (bei Musikaufnahme)* backing track; *(TV)* recording; *(= Playbackverfahren) (bei Musikaufnahme)* double-tracking *no pl*; *(TV)* miming *no pl*; **ein ~ von einem Lied machen** to double-track a song; *(TV)* to prerecord a song, to make a recording of a song; **etw im ~ machen** to double-track sth; *(TV)* to mime to (a recording of) sth; **~ singen** to mime, to lip-sync(h); **Play|boy** ['ple:-] M playboy; **Play|girl** ['ple:-] NT playgirl; **Play-off** [ple:'ɔf] NT -(s), -s *(Sport)* play-off; **Play-off-Run|de** [ple:'ɔf-] F *(Sport)* play-off round, play-offs *pl*

Pla|zen|ta [pla'tsɛnta] F -, -s *or* **Plazenten** [-'tsɛntn] placenta

Pla|zet ['pla:tsɛt] NT -s, -s *(geh)* approval; **sein ~ zu etw geben** to approve sth, to give sth one's approval

Pla|zeur [pla'tsø:ɐ] M -s, -e, **Pla|zeu|rin** [-'tsø:rɪn] F -, -nen *(Fin)* securities investor

pla|zie|ren △ [pla'tsi:rən] VT → **platzieren**

Pla|zie|rung △ F -, -en → **Platzierung**

Ple|be|jer [ple'be:jɐ] M -s, -, **Ple|be|je|rin** [-ərɪn] F -, -nen *(lit, fig)* plebeian, pleb *(inf)*

ple|be|jisch [ple'be:jɪʃ] ADJ *(lit)* plebeian *no adv*; *(fig auch)* plebby *(inf)*, common ADV **sich ~ benehmen** to behave like a pleb *(inf)*

Ple|bis|zit [plebɪs'tsi:t] NT -(e)s, -e plebiscite

Plebs [plɛps] F -, *no pl (Hist)* plebs *pl*

Plebs M -es, *no pl (pej)* plebs *pl (inf)*

plei|te ['plaitə] ADJ *pred* ADV *(inf) Mensch* broke *(inf)*; *Firma auch* bust *(inf)*

Plei|te ['plaitə] F -, -n *(inf)* bankruptcy, collapse; *(fig)* flop *(inf)*, washout *(inf)*; **~ machen** to go bankrupt *or* bust *(inf)*; **damit/mit ihm haben wir eine ~ erlebt** it/he was a disaster; **~ gehen** → **pleitegehen**

plei|te+ge|hen VI *sep irreg aux sein* to go bust

Plei|te|gei|er M *(inf)* **a** *(= drohende Pleite)* vulture; **über der Firma schwebt** *or* **kreist der ~** the vultures are hovering over the firm, the threat of bankruptcy is hanging over the firm **b** *(= Bankrotteur)* bankrupt

Plei|ti|er [plai'tie:] M -s, -s *(inf: = Bankrotteur)* bankrupt

Plek|tron ['plɛktrɔn] NT -s, **Plektren** *or* **Plektra** [-trən, -tra], **Plek|trum** ['plɛktrʊm] NT -s, **Plektren** *or* **Plektra** plectrum

Plem|pe ['plɛmpə] F -, -n *(dial)* dishwater

plem|pern ['plɛmpɐn] VI *(inf)* **a** *(= trödeln)* to dawdle **b** *(= verschütten)* to splash

plem|plem [plɛm'plɛm] ADJ *pred (inf)* nuts *(inf)*, round *(Brit)* or around *(US)* the bend *(inf)*; **jdn ~ machen** to drive sb round *(Brit)* or around *(US)* the bend *(inf)*, to drive sb up the wall *(inf)*

Ple|na *pl von* **Plenum**

Ple|nar-: **Ple|nar|saal** M chamber; **Ple|nar|sit|zung** F, **Ple|nar|ver|samm|lung** F plenary session

Ple|num ['ple:nʊm] NT -s, **Plena** [-na] plenum

Ple|o|nas|mus [pleo'nasmʊs] M -, **Pleonasmen** [-mən] pleonasm

ple|o|nas|tisch [pleo'nastɪʃ] ADJ pleonastic

Pleu|el|stan|ge ['plɔyəl-] F connecting rod

Ple|xi|glas® ['plɛksigla:s] NT, *no pl special type of acrylic glass*

plie|ren ['pli:rən], **plin|kern** ['plɪŋkɐn] VI *(N Ger)* to screw up one's eyes *(Brit)*, to squint

Plis|see [plɪ'se:] NT -s, -s pleats *pl*, pleating *no pl*

Plis|see-: **Plis|see|fal|te** F pleat; **Plis|see|rock** M pleated skirt

plis|sie|ren [plɪ'si:rən] *ptp* **plissiert** VT to pleat

PLO [pe:lɛl'o:] F - PLO

PLO-Füh|rung F PLO leadership

Plom|be ['plɔmbə] F -, -n **a** *(= Siegel)* lead seal **b** *(= Zahnplombe)* filling

plom|bie|ren [plɔm'bi:rən] *ptp* **plombiert** VT **a** *(= versiegeln)* to seal, to put a seal on **b** *Zahn* to fill; **er hat mir zwei Zähne plombiert** he did two fillings

Plom|bie|rung F -, -en **a** *(= das Versiegeln)* sealing; *(Vorrichtung)* seal **b** *(beim Zahn)* filling

Plör|re ['plœrə] F -, -n *(dial)* dishwater

Plo|siv [plo'zi:f] M -s, -e, **Plo|siv|laut** M *(Phon)* plosive

Plot [plɔt] M OR NT -s, -s *(Liter)* plot

Plot|ter ['plɔtɐ] M -s, - *(Comput)* plotter

plötz|lich ['plœtslɪç] ADJ sudden ADV suddenly, all of a sudden; **aber etwas ~!** *(inf)*, **aber ein bisschen ~!** *(inf)* (and) make it snappy! *(inf)*, and look sharp (about it)! *(inf)*; **das kommt alles so ~** *(inf)* it all happens so suddenly

Plötz|lich|keit F -, *no pl* suddenness

Plu|der|ho|se ['plu:dɐ-] F harem pants *pl*, Turkish trousers *pl (esp Brit)*

Plug and Play ['plagənd'ple:] NT -, *no pl (Comput)* plug-and-play

Plu|meau [ply'mo:] NT -s, -s eiderdown, quilt

plump [plʊmp] ADJ *Figur, Hände, Form* ungainly *no adv*; *Bewegung, Gang auch* awkward; *Ausdruck* clumsy; *Bemerkung, Benehmen* crass; *Mittel, Schmeichelei, Lüge, Betrug, Trick* obvious, crude; *Film, Roman* crude; **~e Annäherungsversuche** obvious and crude advances ADV *sich bewegen, tanzen* awkwardly; *sagen, sich ausdrücken* clumsily; **~ lügen** to tell a blatant lie; **jdn ~ hereinlegen** to play a blatantly obvious trick on sb; **der Film ist sehr ~ gemacht** the film is very crudely made; **sich ~ verhalten** to behave crassly

Plump|heit F -, -en *(von Figur, Form)* ungainliness; *(von Bewegung auch)* awkwardness; *(von Ausdruck)* clumsiness; *(von Bemerkung, Benehmen)* crassness; *(von Lüge, Trick)* obviousness

plumps [plʊmps] INTERJ bang; *(lauter)* crash; **~, da lag er** crash, he'd fallen over

Plumps [plʊmps] M -es, -e *(inf) (= Fall)* fall, tumble; *(Geräusch)* bump, thud; **einen ~ machen** *(baby-talk)* to fall; **mit einem ~ ins Wasser fallen** to fall into the water with a splash

plump|sen ['plʊmpsn] VI *aux sein (inf) (= fallen)* to tumble, to fall; **ich habe es ~ hören** I heard a bang *or* a thud; **ich ließ mich einfach aufs Bett ~** I just flopped (down) onto the bed; **er plumpste ins Wasser** he went splash into the water, he fell into the water with a splash

Plumps|klo(sett) NT *(inf)* earth closet

plump|ver|trau|lich ADJ overly chummy *(inf)* ADV in an overly chummy way *(inf)*

Plun|der ['plʊndɐ] M -s, *no pl* junk, rubbish *(Brit)*

Plün|de|rer ['plʏndərɐ] M -s, -, **Plün|de|rin** [-ərɪn] F -nen looter, plunderer

Plun|der|ge|bäck NT flaky pastry

plün|dern ['plʏndɐn] VTI to loot, to plunder, to pillage; *(= ausrauben)* to raid; *Obstbaum* to strip; **jemand hat unsere** *or* **auf unserer Obstplantage geplündert** somebody's raided our orchard

Plün|de|rung F -, -en looting, pillage, plunder

Plünd|rer ['plʏndrɐ] M -s, -, **Plünd|re|rin** [-rərɪn] F -, -nen looter, plunderer

Plu|ral ['plu:ra:l] M -s, -e plural; **im ~ stehen** to be (in the) plural; **den ~ zu etw bilden** to form the plural of sth

Plu|ra|le|tan|tum [plura:lə'tantʊm] NT -s, -s *or* **Pluraliatantum** [plura:lia'tantʊm] plural noun

Plu|ral|en|dung F plural ending

plu|ra|lisch [plu'ra:lɪʃ] *(Gram)* ADJ plural ADV **ein Wort ~ gebrauchen** to use a word in the plural

Plu|ra|lis|mus [plura'lɪsmʊs] M -, *no pl* pluralism

plu|ra|lis|tisch [plura'lɪstɪʃ] ADJ pluralistic *(form)* ADV pluralistically *(form)*; **sich ~ organisieren** to create a pluralistic system

Plu|ra|li|tät [plurali'tɛ:t] F -, -en plurality; *(= Mehrheit)* majority, plurality *(US)*

plus [plʊs] PREP *+gen* plus ADV plus; **bei ~ 5 Grad** *or* **5 Grad ~** at 5 degrees (above freezing *or* zero); **~/minus 10** *(= mit Abweichung bis plus oder minus zehn)* plus or minus 10; **das Ergebnis war ~ minus null** nothing was gained, nothing was lost; **mit ~ minus null abschließen** to break even CONJ **Karl ~ Ehefrau** *(inf)* Karl plus wife

Plus [plʊs] NT -, - **a** *(= Pluszeichen)* plus (sign); **ein ~ machen** to put a plus (sign) **b** *(Phys inf: = Pluspol)* positive (pole) **c** *(esp Comm) (= Zuwachs)* increase; *(= Gewinn)* profit; *(= Überschuss)* surplus **d** *(fig: = Vorteil)* advantage; **das ist ein ~ für dich** that's a point in your favour *(Brit)* or favor *(US)*; **das können Sie als ~ für sich buchen** that's one up to *or* for you *(inf)*, you've scored a point there *(inf)*

Plüsch [plʏʃ, ply:ʃ] M -(e)s, -e plush; *(pej)* ostentation; **Stofftiere aus ~** soft toys made of fur fabric

Plüsch- *in cpds* plush; *(von Plüschtier)* furry; **Plüsch|bär** M furry teddy bear

plü|schig ['plʏʃɪç, 'ply:ʃɪç] ADJ plush; *(pej)* ostentatious ADV plushly

Plüsch|tier NT ≈ soft toy

Plüsch|vor|hang M plush curtain

Plus-: **Plus|pol** M *(Elec)* positive pole; **Plus|punkt** M *(Sport)* point; *(Sch)* extra mark; *(fig)* advantage; **einen ~ machen** to win a point; **deine Erfahrung ist ein ~ für dich** your experience counts in your favour *(Brit)* or favor *(US)*, your experience is a point in your favour *(Brit)* or favor *(US)*; **~e sammeln** *(inf)* to score Brownie points; **Plus|quam|per|fekt** ['plʊskvampɛrfɛkt] NT pluperfect, past perfect

plus|tern ['plu:stɐn] VT *Federn* to fluff up VR to fluff oneself up

Plus|zei|chen NT plus sign

Plu|to|krat [pluto'kra:t] M -en, -en, **Plu|to|kra|tin** [-'kra:tɪn] F -, -nen plutocrat

Plu|to|kra|tie [plutokra'ti:] F -, -n [-'ti:ən] plutocracy

Plu|to|ni|um [plu'to:niʊm] NT -s, *no pl (abbr* **Pn**) plutonium

Plu|to|ni|um-: **Plu|to|ni|um|ge|win|nung** F plutonium extraction; **Plu|to|ni|um|wirt|schaft** F, *no pl* plutonium industry

PLZ [pe:lɛl'tsɛt] F - *abbr von* **Postleitzahl**

Pneu [pnø:] M -s, -s *(esp Sw)* tyre *(Brit)*, tire *(US)*

pneu|ma|tisch [pnɔy'ma:tɪʃ] ADJ pneumatic; **~e Kammer** pressure chamber ADV pneumatically

Po [poː] M **-s, -s** *(inf)* bottom, behind *(inf)*

Po|ba|cke F *(inf)* buttock, cheek *(inf)*, bun *(US inf)*

Pö|bel ['pøːbl] M **-s**, *no pl* rabble, mob, riffraff *(pej)*

Pö|be|lei [pøːbe'lai] F **-, -en** vulgarity, bad language *no pl*

Pö|bel-: **pö|bel|haft** ADJ uncouth, vulgar ADV uncouthly, vulgarly; **Pö|bel|herr|schaft** F mob rule

pö|beln ['pøːbln] VI to swear, to use bad language

po|chen ['pɔxn] VI to knock; *(leise auch)* to tap; *(heftig)* to thump, to bang; *(Herz)* to pound, to thump; *(Blut)* to throb, to pound; **auf etw** *(acc)* ~ *(fig)* to insist on sth; **auf sein (gutes) Recht** ~ to insist on one's rights, to stand up for one's rights

po|chie|ren [pɔ'ʃiːrən] *ptp* **pochiert** VT *Ei, Fisch* to poach

Po|cke ['pɔkə] F **-, -n** a pock b **Pocken** PL smallpox

Po|cken-: **Po|cken|nar|be** F pockmark; **po|cken|nar|big** ADJ pockmarked; **Po|cken|(schutz)|imp|fung** F smallpox vaccination

Po|cket- *in cpds* pocket; **Po|cket|for|mat** NT pocket size; **im** ~ pocket-sized; **Po|cket|ka|me|ra** F pocket camera

Po|dest [po'dɛst] NT OR M **-(e)s, -e** *(= Sockel)* pedestal *(auch fig)*; *(= Podium)* platform; *(= Treppenabsatz)* landing

Po|dex ['poːdɛks] M **-es, -e** *(hum inf)* posterior *(hum inf)*, behind *(inf)*

Po|di|um ['poːdiʊm] NT **-s, Podien** [-diən] *(lit, fig)* platform; *(des Dirigenten)* podium; *(bei Diskussion)* panel

Po|di|ums|dis|kus|si|on F, **Po|di|ums|ge|spräch** NT panel discussion, brains trust

Po|em [po'eːm] NT **-s, -e** *(usu pej)* poem, doggerel *(pej) no indef art*

Po|e|sie [poe'ziː] F **-, -n** [-'ziːən] *(lit, fig)* poetry

Po|e|sie|al|bum NT autograph book

Po|et [po'eːt] M **-en, -en**, **Po|e|tin** [-'eːtɪn] F **-, -nen** (*old*: = *Dichter*) poet, bard *(liter)*; *(pej)* poetaster, versifier

Po|e|tas|ter [poe'tastɐ] M **-s, -**, **Po|e|tas|te|rin** [-ərɪn] F **-, -nen** *(old pej)* poetaster

Po|e|tik [po'eːtɪk] F **-, -en** poetics *sing*

po|e|tisch [po'eːtɪʃ] ADJ poetic ADV poetically

po|fen ['poːfn] VI *(dated sl)* to kip *(Brit inf)*, to sleep

po|gen ['poːgn] VI (*Mus inf*: = *Pogo tanzen*) to pogo, to pogo-dance

Pog|rom [po'groːm] NT OR M **-s, -e** pogrom

Pog|rom|stim|mung F bloodthirsty mood

Poin|te ['poɛ̃ːtə] F **-, -n** *(eines Witzes)* punch line; *(einer Geschichte)* point; **die ~ einer Geschichte begreifen** to get the (main) point of a story

poin|tie|ren [poɛ̃'tiːrən] *ptp* **pointiert** [poɛ̃'tiːɐt] VT to emphasize, to stress

poin|tiert [poɛ̃'tiːɐt] ADJ trenchant *(form)*, pithy ADV trenchantly *(form)*, pithily; **~ antworten** to give a pithy *or* trenchant *(form)* answer

Poin|til|lis|mus [pɔɛ̃nti'lɪsmʊs, poɛ̃ti'jɪsmʊs] M **-**, *no pl (Art)* pointillism

Po|kal [po'kaːl] M **-s, -e** *(zum Trinken)* goblet; *(Sport)* cup; **das Endspiel um den** ~ the cup final

Po|kal-: **Po|kal|fi|na|le** NT *(Ftbl)* cup final; **Po|kal|run|de** F round (of the cup); **Po|kal|sie|ger(in)** M(F) cup winners *pl*; **Po|kal|spiel** NT cup tie; **Po|kal|tur|nier** NT cup tournament

Pö|kel ['pøːkl] M **-s, -** brine, pickle

Pö|kel-: **Pö|kel|fleisch** NT salt meat; **Pö|kel|he|ring** M salt *or* pickled herring

pö|keln ['pøːkln] VT *Fleisch, Fisch* to salt, to pickle

Po|ker ['poːkɐ] NT **-s**, *no pl* poker

Po|ker|face ['poːkɐfeːs] NT **-, -s**, **Po|ker|ge|sicht** NT, **Po|ker|mie|ne** F poker face; **ein ~ machen** *or* **aufsetzen** to put on a poker-faced *or* deadpan expression

Po|ker|spiel NT poker; *(einzelnes Spiel)* game of poker

po|kern ['poːkɐn] VI to play poker; *(fig)* to gamble, to take a risk; **um etw ~** *(fig)* to haggle for sth; **hoch ~** *(fig)* to take a big risk

Pol [poːl] M **-s, -e** pole; **der ruhende ~** *(fig)* the calming influence

pol. *abbr von* **politisch, polizeilich**

Po|la|cke [po'lakə] M **-s, -n**, **Po|la|ckin** [po'lakɪn] F **-, -nen** *(pej sl)* Polack *(pej)*

po|lar [po'laːɐ] ADJ a polar; **~e Kälte** arctic coldness b **~e Gegensätze** complete *or* exact opposites ADV ~ **entgegengesetzt** diametrically opposed, poles apart *pred*

Po|lar- *in cpds* polar; **Po|lar|eis** NT polar ice; **Po|lar|fuchs** M arctic fox

po|la|ri|sie|ren [polari'ziːrən] *ptp* **polarisiert** VT to polarize VR to polarize, to become polarized

Po|la|ri|sie|rung F **-, -en** polarization

Po|la|ri|tät [polari'tɛːt] F **-, -en** *(Phys, fig)* polarity

Po|lar-: **Po|lar|kreis** M polar circle; **nördlicher/südlicher ~** Arctic/Antarctic circle; **Po|lar|licht** NT polar lights *pl*, Northern/Southern lights *pl*; **Po|lar|meer** NT **Nördliches/Südliches ~** Arctic/Antarctic Ocean; **Po|lar|stern** M Pole Star, North Star, Polaris

Po|la|roid|ka|me|ra® [polaro'iːt-, pola'rɔyt-] F Polaroid® camera

Po|lar|zo|ne F Frigid Zone *(esp Brit)*, polar region

Pol|der ['pɔldɐ] M **-s, -** polder

Pol|der|deich M polder dyke

Po|le ['poːlə] M **-n, -n** Pole; **er ist ~** he's Polish, he's a Pole

Po|le|mik [po'leːmɪk] F **-, -en** polemics *sing (gegen* against); *(= Streitschrift)* polemic; **die ~ dieses Artikels** the polemic nature of this article; **seine ~ ist kaum mehr erträglich** his polemics are becoming unbearable

Po|le|mi|ker [po'leːmikɐ] M **-s, -**, **Po|le|mi|ke|rin** [-ərɪn] F **-, -nen** controversialist, polemicist

po|le|misch [po'leːmɪʃ] ADJ polemic(al) ADV polemically; **~ argumentieren** to be polemical

po|le|mi|sie|ren [polemi'ziːrən] *ptp* **polemisiert** VI to polemicize; **~ gegen** to inveigh against

po|len ['poːlən] VT to polarize

Po|len ['poːlən] NT **-s** Poland; **noch ist ~ nicht verloren** *(prov)* the day is not yet lost, all is not yet lost

Po|len|ta [po'lɛnta] F **-, -s** *or* **Polenten** *(Cook)* polenta

Po|len|te [po'lɛntə] F **-**, *no pl (dated inf)* cops *pl (inf)*, fuzz *pl (esp Brit dated inf)*

Po|li|ce [po'liːsə] F **-, -n** (insurance) policy

Po|lier [po'liːɐ] M **-s, -e** site foreman

po|lie|ren [po'liːrən] *ptp* **poliert** VT to polish; *Schuhe auch* to shine; *(fig)* to polish *or* brush up; **jdm die Fresse** *or* **Visage ~** *(vulg)* to smash sb's face in *(inf)*

Po|lie|rin [po'liːərɪn] F **-, -nen** site forewoman

Po|lier-: **Po|lier|mit|tel** NT polish; **Po|lier|schei|be** F polishing wheel *or* disc; **Po|lier|tuch** NT *pl* **-tücher** polishing cloth; **Po|lier|wachs** NT wax polish

Po|li|kli|nik ['poːli-] F *(= Krankenhaus)* clinic *(for outpatients only)*; *(Abteilung)* outpatients' department, outpatients *sing*

Po|lin ['poːlɪn] F **-, -nen** Pole, Polish woman

Po|lio ['poːlio] F **-**, *no pl* polio, poliomyelitis

Po|lit- *in cpds (inf)* political; **Po|lit|ba|ro|me|ter** NT *(fig)* political barometer; **Po|lit|büh|ne** F political stage; **Po|lit|bü|ro** NT Politburo

Po|li|tes|se [poli'tɛsə] F **-, -n** (woman) traffic warden

Po|li|tik [poli'tiːk] F **-, -en** a *no pl* politics *sing*; *(= politischer Standpunkt)* politics *pl*; **welche ~ vertritt er?** what are his politics?; **in die ~ gehen** to go into politics; **über ~ sprechen** to talk (about) politics b *(= bestimmte Politik)* policy; **eine ~ der starken Hand treiben** to take a tough line; **eine ~ verfolgen** *or* **betreiben** to pursue a policy; **ihre gesamte ~** all their policies

Po|li|ti|ka *pl von* **Politikum**

Po|li|ti|ker [po'liːtikɐ] M **-s, -**, **Po|li|ti|ke|rin** [-ərɪn] F **-, -nen** politician; **führender ~** leading politician

Po|li|tik-: **po|li|tik|fä|hig** ADJ *Partei* capable of governing responsibly; **der Naturschutz muss ~ werden** conservation must become part of the political debate; **Po|li|tik|fä|hig|keit** F *(von Partei)* ability to govern responsibly

Po|li|ti|kum [po'liːtikʊm] NT **-s, Politika** [-ka] political issue

Po|li|tik-: **po|li|tik|un|fä|hig** ADJ *Partei* incapable of governing responsibly; **Po|li|tik|un|fä|hig|keit** F *(von Partei)* inability to govern responsibly; **po|li|tik|ver|dros|sen** ADJ tired of politics, disenchanted with politics; **Po|li|tik|ver|dros|sen|heit** F disenchantment with politics; **die wachsende ~ der Bevölkerung** the people's growing disenchantment with politics; **Po|li|tik|wis|sen|schaft** F political science, politics *sing*

po|li|tisch [po'liːtɪʃ] ADJ political; *(= klug)* politic, judicious; **er ist ein Politischer** he's a political prisoner ADV politically; **sich ~ betätigen** to be involved in politics; **~ interessiert sein** to be interested in politics; **jdn ~ schulen** to educate sb politically

po|li|ti|sie|ren [politi'ziːrən] *ptp* **politisiert** VI to talk politics, to politicize VT to politicize; *jdn* to make politically aware

Po|li|ti|sie|rung F **-**, *no pl* politicization

Po|lit|öko|no|mie [po'liːt-] F political economy

Po|li|to|lo|ge [polito'loːgə] M **-n, -n**, **Po|li|to|lo|gin** [-'loːgɪn] F **-, -nen** political scientist

Po|li|to|lo|gie [politolo'giː] F **-**, *no pl* political science, politics *sing*

Po|lit|pro|mi|nenz F *(inf)* political top brass *(inf)*, top politicians *pl*

Po|li|tur [poli'tuːɐ] F **-, -en** *(= Poliermittel)* polish; *(= Glanz)* shine, polish; *(= das Polieren)* polishing

Po|li|zei [poli'tsai] F **-, -en** police *pl*; *(Gebäude)* police station; **auf die** *or* **zur ~ gehen** to go to the police; **er ist bei der ~** he's in the police (force); **die ~, dein Freund und Helfer** *(usu iro)* your friendly neighbourhood *(Brit) or* neighborhood *(US)* police force *(iro)* → **dumm**

Po|li|zei- *in cpds* police; **Po|li|zei|ak|ti|on** F police operation; **Po|li|zei|ap|pa|rat** M police force; **Po|li|zei|auf|ge|bot** NT police presence; **Po|li|zei|auf|sicht** F police supervision; **unter ~ stehen** to have to report regularly to the police; **Po|li|zei|be|am|te(r)** M *decl as adj*, **Po|li|zei|be|am|tin** F police official; *(= Polizist)* police officer; **Po|li|zei|be|hör|de** F police authority; **sich bei der ~ anmelden** to register with the police; **Po|li|zei|be|richt** M police report; **Po|li|zei|chef(in)** M(F) chief constable *(Brit)*, chief of police *(US)*; **Po|li|zei|dienst|stel|le** F *(form)* police station; **Po|li|zei|di|rek|ti|on** F police headquarters *pl*; **Po|li|zei|ein|satz** M police action *or* intervention; **Po|li|zei|funk** M police radio; **Po|li|zei|ge|wahr|sam** M police custody; **jdn in ~ nehmen** to take sb into police custody; **Po|li|zei|ge|walt** F **die ~ haben** to have police powers *pl*; **die Menge wurde mit ~ auseinandergetrieben** the police dispersed the crowd by force; **Po|li|zei|griff** M wrist-hold, police hold; **jdn in den ~ nehmen** to put sb in an arm lock; **er wurde im ~ abgeführt** he was frogmarched away *(Brit)*, they put a wrist-hold on him and took him away; **Po|li|zei|haft** F detention; **Po|li|zei|hund** M police dog; **Po|li|zei|in|spek|tor(in)** M(F) police inspector; **Po|li|zei|ket|te** F police cordon; **Po|li|zei|knüp|pel** M truncheon, billy club *(esp US)*;

Po|li|zei|kom|mis|sar(in) M(F) (police) inspector

po|li|zei|lich [poli'tsailıç] ADJ police attr; **~es Führungszeugnis** *certificate issued by the police, stating that the holder has no criminal record* ADV *ermittelt werden* by the police; **~ überwacht werden** to be under police surveillance; **sie wird ~ gesucht** the police are looking for her; **sich ~ melden** to register with the police; **~ verboten** against the law; **„Parken ~ verboten"** "police notice - no parking"; **diese Regelung ist ~ angeordnet** this is a police regulation, this regulation is by order of the police

Po|li|zei-: **Po|li|zei|prä|si|dent(in)** M(F) chief constable *(Brit)*, chief of police *(US)*; **Po|li|zei|prä|si|di|um** NT police headquarters *pl*; **Po|li|zei|re|vier** NT **a** *(= Polizeiwache)* police station; **ins** *or* **aufs** *or* **zum ~ gehen** to go (down) to the (police) station **b** *(Bezirk)* (police) district, precinct *(US)*, patch *(inf)*; **Po|li|zei|schutz** M police protection; **Po|li|zei|si|re|ne** F (police) siren, heehaw *(Brit inf)*; **Po|li|zei|spit|zel** M (police) informer, nark *(inf)*; **Po|li|zei|staat** M police state; **Po|li|zei|strei|fe** F police patrol; **Po|li|zei|stun|de** F closing time; **Po|li|zei|ver|ord|nung** F police regulation; **Po|li|zei|wa|che** F police station; **Po|li|zei|we|sen** NT, *no pl* police force; **po|li|zei|wid|rig** ADJ illegal ADV **sich ~ verhalten** to break the law

Po|li|zist [poli'tsıst] **-en, -en** M policeman

Po|li|zis|tin [poli'tsıstın] F **-, -nen** policewoman

Po|liz|ze [po'lıtsə] F **-, -n** *(Aus: Insur)* (insurance) policy

Pol|ka ['pɔlka] F **-, -s** polka

Pol|kap|pe F polar icecap

pol|len VTI *(Internet)* to poll

Pol|len ['pɔlən] M **-s, -** pollen

Pol|len-: **Pol|len|be|richt** M pollen forecast; **Pol|len|fal|le** F pollen trap; **Pol|len|flug** M pollen count; **Pol|len|sack** M pollen sac; **Pol|len|war|nung** F pollen warning

Pol|ler ['pɔlɐ] M **-s, -** capstan, bollard

Pol|ling NT **-s, -s** *(Internet)* polling

Pol|lu|ti|on [polu'tsio:n] F **-, -en** *(Med)* (seminal) emission

pol|nisch ['pɔlnıʃ] ADJ Polish; **~e Wirtschaft** *(inf)* shambles *sing*

Pol|nisch(e) ['pɔlnıʃ] NT Polish → *auch* **Deutsch(e)**

Po|lo ['po:lo] NT **-s, -s** polo

Po|lo|hemd NT sports shirt; *(für Frau)* casual blouse

Po|lo|nai|se [polo'nɛ:zə] F **-, -n**, **Po|lo|nä|se** [polo'nɛ:zə] F **-, -n** polonaise

Po|lo|ni|um [po'lo:niʊm] NT **-s**, *no pl (abbr* **Po**) polonium

Pols|ter ['pɔlstɐ] NT OR (AUS) M **-s, - a** cushion; *(= Polsterung)* upholstery *no pl*; *(bei Kleidung)* pad, padding *no pl*; **das ~ vom Sessel muss erneuert werden** the chair needs re-upholstering; **sich in die ~ (zurück)fallen lassen** to let oneself fall (back) into the cushions; **seine Jacke als ~ für den Kopf benutzen** to use one's jacket as a pillow
b *(fig) (= Fettpolster)* flab *no pl (inf)*, layer of fat; *(= Bauch)* spare tyre *(Brit)* or tire *(US)*; *(= Reserve)* reserve, cushion; *(= Geldreserve)* reserves *pl*; **er hat ein ganz schönes ~ am Hintern** he's pretty well-upholstered *or* well-padded behind *(Brit)*, he has a pretty well-upholstered *or* well-padded butt *(US inf)*
c *(esp Aus: = Kissen)* cushion

Pöls|ter|chen ['pœlstɐçən] NT **-s, -** *(inf)* **a** *(= Rücklage)* nest egg **b** *(= Fettpolster)* (layer of) fat; *(an Hüften)* spare tyre *(Brit)* or tire *(US)*; **sie hat einige ~** she's well-upholstered *or* well-padded

Pol|ster|ele|ment NT *(von Sitzgruppe)* (upholstered) element

Pols|te|rer ['pɔlstərɐ] M **-s, -**, **Pols|te|rin** [-ərın] F **-, -nen** upholsterer

Pols|ter|gar|ni|tur F three-piece suite

Pols|ter|mö|bel PL upholstered furniture *sing*

pols|tern ['pɔlstɐn] VT to upholster; *Kleidung, Tür* to pad; **etw neu ~** to re-upholster sth; **sie ist gut gepolstert** she's well-upholstered *or* well-padded; **sie ist finanziell gut** *or* **komfortabel gepolstert** she's not short of the odd penny

Pols|ter-: **Pols|ter|ses|sel** M armchair, easy chair; **Pols|ter|sitz** M upholstered *or* padded seat; **Pols|ter|stoff** M upholstery *or* upholstering fabric; **Pols|ter|stuhl** M upholstered *or* padded chair; **Pols|ter|tür** F padded door

Pols|te|rung ['pɔlstərʊŋ] F **-, -en** *(= Polster)* upholstery; *(= das Polstern)* upholstering

Pol|ter|abend M *party on the eve of a wedding, at which old crockery is smashed to bring good luck*

> **POLTERABEND**
>
> **Polterabend** is the evening before a wedding, when crockery is smashed outside the door of the bride's parents or of the bride and groom: the broken pieces are supposed to bring luck to the happy couple. Often the **Polterabend** is extended into an informal party for friends and acquaintances. It is sometimes held a week before the wedding to allow guests time to recover.

Pol|te|rer ['pɔltərɐ] M **-s, -** noisy person; *(beim Sprechen)* ranter, blusterer

Pol|ter|geist M poltergeist

Pol|te|rin F → **Polterer**

pol|tern ['pɔltɐn] VI **a** *(= Krach machen)* to crash about; *(= polternd umfallen)* to go crash; **die Kinder ~ oben** the children are crashing about *or* banging about upstairs, the children are making a din *or* racket *(inf)* upstairs; **was hat da eben so gepoltert?** what was that crash *or* bang?; **es fiel ~d zu Boden** it crashed to the floor, it fell with a crash to the floor; **es polterte fürchterlich, als er ...** there was a terrific crash *or* bang when he ...; **es poltert (an der Tür/vor dem Haus)** there's a real racket *(inf) or* din going on (at the door/ in front of the house); **an die Tür ~** to thump *or* bang on the door
b *aux sein (= sich laut bewegen)* to crash, to bang; **über das Pflaster ~** to clatter over the cobbles
c *(inf: = schimpfen)* to rant (and rave), to carry on *(inf)*
d *(inf: = Polterabend feiern) to celebrate on the eve of a wedding*

Po|ly-: **Po|ly|acryl** NT **a** *(Chem)* polyacrylics *sing* **b** *(Tex)* acrylics *sing*; **Po|ly|amid®** [poly|a'mi:t] NT **-(e)s, -e** polyamide; **po|ly|chlo|riert** [polyklo'ri:ɐt] ADJ polychlorinated; **Po|ly|es|ter** [poly'ɛstɐ] M **-s, -** polyester; **po|ly|fon** ADJ *(Mus, fig)* polyphonic, polyphonous; **Po|ly|fo|nie** F **-**, *no pl (Mus)* polyphony; **po|ly|gam** [poly'ga:m] ADJ polygamous ADV **~ leben** to be polygamous; **Po|ly|ga|mie** [polyga'mi:] F **-**, *no pl* polygamy; **po|ly|glott** [poly'glɔt] ADJ polyglot *no adv*; **po|ly|morph** ADJ polymorphous

Po|ly|ne|si|en [poly'ne:ziən] NT **-s** Polynesia

Po|ly|ne|si|er [poly'ne:ziɐ] M **-s, -**, **Po|ly|ne|si|e|rin** [-iərın] F **-, -nen** Polynesian

po|ly|ne|sisch [poly'ne:zıʃ] ADJ Polynesian

Po|lyp [po'ly:p] M **-en, -en a** *(Zool)* polyp; *(old: = Krake)* octopus **b** *(Med)* **~en** adenoids **c** *(dated inf: = Polizist)* cop *(inf)*

po|ly|phon *etc* → **polyfon** *etc*

po|ly|sem [poly'ze:m] ADJ *(Ling)* polysemous

Po|ly|se|mie [polyze'mi:] F **-**, *no pl (Ling)* polysemy

Po|ly|tech|ni|kum [poly'tɛçnikʊm] NT polytechnic, poly *(inf)*

po|ly|tech|nisch [poly'tɛçnıʃ] ADJ polytechnic

Po|ly|the|is|mus [polyte'ısmʊs] M **-**, *no pl* polytheism

Po|ma|de [po'ma:də] F **-, -n** hair cream; *(Hist, für krause Haare)* pomade

po|ma|dig [po'ma:dıç] ADJ *(inf)* **a** *Haare* greased-back *(inf)*, Brylcreemed® **b** *(= schleimig)* smarmy *(inf)* **c** *(= langsam)* sluggish ADV **~ glänzendes Haar** oiled hair; **~ zurückgekämmte Haare** slicked-back hair

Po|me|ran|ze [pomə'rantsə] F **-, -n** Seville *or* bitter orange

Pom|mer ['pɔmɐ] M **-n, -n**, **Pom|me|rin** [-ərın] F **-, -nen** Pomeranian

pom|me|risch ['pɔmərıʃ] ADJ, **pom|mersch** ['pɔmɐʃ] ADJ Pomeranian

Pom|mern ['pɔmɐn] NT **-s** Pomerania

Pom|mes ['pɔməs] PL *(inf)* chips *pl (Brit)*, (French) fries *pl*

Pom|mes|bu|de F *(inf)* fast food stand, ≈ chip shop *(Brit)*

Pommes frites [pɔm 'frıts] PL chips *pl (Brit)*, French fries *pl*, French fried potatoes *pl (form)*

Pomp [pɔmp] M **-(e)s**, *no pl* pomp

pom|pös [pɔm'pø:s] ADJ grandiose ADV grandiosely

Pon|cho ['pɔntʃo] M **-s, -s** poncho

Pond [pɔnt] NT **-s, -** *(Phys) weight of 1 gram mass under standard gravity*

Pon|ti|fex ['pɔntifɛks] M **-, Pontifizes** [pɔn'ti:fitse:s] Pontifex

Pon|ti|fi|kal|amt [pɔntifi'ka:l-] NT Pontifical Mass

Pon|ti|fi|kat [pɔntifi'ka:t] NT OR M **-(e)s, -e** pontificate

Pon|ti|us ['pɔntsiʊs] M **von ~ zu Pilatus laufen** to rush from pillar to post *(Brit) or* one place to another; **jdn von ~ zu Pilatus schicken** to pass sb from pillar to post *(Brit) or* one place to another

Pon|ton [pō'tō:, pɔn'tō:, 'pɔntō] M **-s, -s** pontoon

Pon|ton|brü|cke F pontoon bridge

Po|ny ['pɔni] NT **-s, -s** pony

Po|ny M **-s, -s** *(Frisur)* fringe *(Brit)*, bangs *pl (US)*

Po|ny|fri|sur F hairstyle with a fringe *(Brit) or* with bangs *(US)*; **sie hat eine ~** she has bangs *(US) or* a fringe *(Brit)*

Pool [pu:l] M **-s, -s** *(alle Bedeutungen)* pool; **Mitarbeiter-~** pool of workers

Pool(bil|lard) ['pu:l-] NT **-s**, *no pl* pool, pocket billiards *no pl*

Pop [pɔp] M **-s**, *no pl (Mus)* pop; *(Art)* pop art; *(Mode)* pop fashion

POP, PoP [pɔp] M **-, -s** *(Telec, Internet) abbr von* **point of presence**

Po|panz ['po:pants] M **-es, -e a** *(= Schreckgespenst)* bogey; **etw/jdn als ~ hinstellen, etw/jdn zum ~ machen** to make a bogey of sth/sb **b** *(= willenloser Mensch)* puppet

Pop|corn ['pɔpkɔ:n] NT **-s**, *no pl* popcorn

Po|pe ['po:pə] M **-n, -n** priest; *(pej)* cleric

Po|pel ['po:pl] M **-s, -** *(inf) (= Nasenpopel)* bogey *(Brit inf)*, booger *(US inf)*, (piece of) snot *(inf)*

po|pe|lig ['po:pəlıç] *(inf)* ADJ **a** *(= knauserig)* stingy *(inf)*; **~e zwei Euro** a lousy two euros *(inf)* **b** *(= dürftig)* crummy *(inf)* **c** *(= spießig)* small-minded, narrow-minded ADV **a** *(= knauserig)* stingily **b** *(= dürftig)* **~ leben** to live on the cheap *(inf)*; **ihr Haus war recht ~ eingerichtet** her house had really crummy furniture *(inf)*

Po|pe|lin [popə'li:n] M **-s, -e**, **Po|pe|li|ne** [popə'li:nə] F **-, -** poplin

po|peln ['po:pln] VI *(inf)* **(in der Nase) ~** to pick one's nose

Pop|grup|pe F pop group

Pop|iko|ne F pop icon

pop|lig ['po:plıç] ADJ, ADV *(inf)* = **popelig**

Pop-: **Pop|kon|zert** NT pop concert; **Pop|mu|sik** F pop music

Po|po [po'po:] M **-s, -s** *(inf)* bottom, behind *(inf)*, botty *(baby-talk)*

Po|po|schei|tel M *(inf)* middle *or* centre parting *(Brit)*, center part *(US)*

pop|pen ['pɔpn] VI *(sl: = koitieren)* to pump *(sl)*

Pop|per ['pɔpɐ] M **-s, -**, **Pop|pe|rin** [-ərɪn] F **-, -nen** preppie

pop|pig ['pɔpɪç] *(inf)* ADJ *(Art, Mus)* pop *no adv*; *Kleidung* loud and trendy; *Farben* bright and cheerful ADV **sich ~ kleiden** to wear loud, trendy clothes; **das Buch war total ~ aufgemacht** the book was brightly presented

Pop-: **Pop|sän|ger(in)** M(F) pop singer; **Pop|star** M pop star; **Pop|sze|ne** F pop scene

po|pu|lär [popu'lɛːɐ] ADJ popular *(bei* with) ADV *schreiben, darstellen, sich ausdrücken* in an accessible way

po|pu|la|ri|sie|ren [populari'ziːrən] *ptp* **popularisiert** VT to popularize

Po|pu|la|ri|tät [populari'tɛːt] F **-,** *no pl* popularity

po|pu|lär|wis|sen|schaft|lich ADJ *Buch* popular science; *Literatur* popular scientific; **seine Bücher sind mehr ~** his books are rather more popular science ADV **etw ~ darstellen** to present sth in a popular scientific way

Po|pu|la|ti|on [popula'tsioːn] F **-, -en** *(Biol, Sociol)* population

Po|pu|lis|mus [popu'lɪsmʊs] M **-,** *no pl (Pol)* populism

Po|pu|list [popu'lɪst] M **-en, -en**, **Po|pu|lis|tin** [-'lɪstɪn] F **-, -nen** populist

po|pu|lis|tisch [popu'lɪstɪʃ] ADJ populist ADV in a populist way; **~ argumentieren** to use populist arguments

Pop-up-Me|nü NT *(Comput)* pop-up (menu)

Po|re ['poːrə] F **-, -n** pore

po|rig ['poːrɪç] ADJ *Gestein, Struktur* porous

-po|rig ADJ *suf* with … pores; **feinporige Haut** skin with fine pores

Por|no ['pɔrno] M **-s, -s** *(inf)* porn *(inf)*

Por|no- *in cpds (inf)* porn *(inf)*; **Por|no|film** M porn *or* blue movie, skin flick *(US inf)*

Por|no|gra|fie [pɔrnogra'fiː] F **-, -n** [-'fiːən] pornography

por|no|gra|fisch [pɔrno'graːfɪʃ] ADJ pornographic

Por|no|gra|phie [pɔrnogra'fiː] *etc* = **Pornografie** *etc*

Por|no|heft NT *(inf)* porn magazine

Por|no|ma|ga|zin NT porn magazine

po|rös [po'røːs] ADJ *(= durchlässig)* porous; *(= brüchig) Gummi, Leder* perished; **~ werden** to perish

Po|ro|si|tät [porozi'tɛːt] F **-,** *no pl* porosity

Por|ree ['pɔre] M **-s, -s** leek

Port [pɔrt] M **-(e)s, -e** **a** *(poet)* haven *(poet)* **b** *(= Portwein)* port

Port M **-s, -s** *(Comput)* port

por|ta|bel [pɔr'taːbl] ADJ *(auch Comput)* portable

Por|ta|bi|li|tät [pɔrtabili'tɛːt] F **-,** *no pl (auch Comput)* portability

Por|ta|ble ['pɔrtəbl] NT **-s, -s** portable TV *or* television (set)

Por|tal [pɔr'taːl] NT **-s, -e** portal

Porte|feuille [pɔrt(ə)'føːj] NT **-s, -s** *(Pol, obs)* portfolio; *(obs: = Brieftasche)* wallet

Porte|mon|naie [pɔrtmɔ'neː, pɔrtmɔ'nɛː] NT **-s, -s** purse

Port|fo|lio [pɔrt'foːlio] NT **-s, -s** **a** *(Fin, St Ex)* portfolio **b** *(= Bildbandmappe)* portfolio

Por|ti|er [pɔr'tieː] M **-s, -s** = **Pförtner**

por|tier|bar [pɔr'tiːɐbaːɐ] ADJ *(Comput) software* portable

por|tie|ren [pɔr'tiːrən] *ptp* **portiert** VT *(Sw Pol)* to put up

Por|ti|er|lo|ge [pɔr'tieːloːʒə] F = **Pförtnerloge**

Por|ti|ers|frau [pɔr'tieːz-] F = **Pförtnerin**

Por|ti|on [pɔr'tsioːn] F **-, -en** **a** *(beim Essen)* portion, helping; **eine halbe ~** a half portion; *(fig inf)* a half pint *(inf)*; **eine zweite ~** a second helping; **eine ~ Kaffee** a pot of coffee; **eine ~ Butter** a portion of butter **b** *(fig inf: = Anteil)* amount; **er besitzt eine gehörige ~ Mut** he's got a fair amount of courage; **sie brachte eine gute ~ Geduld auf** she showed a fair amount of patience *(inf)*

por|ti|o|nen|wei|se [pɔr'tsioːnənvaizə], **por|ti|ons|wei|se** [pɔr'tsioːnsvaizə] ADV in helpings *or* portions

por|ti|o|nie|ren [pɔrtsio'niːrən] *ptp* **portioniert** VT to divide into portions

Por|ti|o|nie|rer [pɔr'tsioːn] M **-s, -** *(für Eis)* scoop

Port|mo|nee [pɔrtmɔ'neː, pɔrtmɔ'nɛː] NT **-s, -s** = **Portemonnaie**

Por|to ['pɔrto] NT **-s, -s** *or* **Por|ti** [-ti] postage *no pl (für* on, for); *(für Kisten etc)* carriage; **~ zahlt Empfänger** postage paid; **das ~ für den Brief macht** *or* **beträgt zwei Euro** the postage on *or* for the letter is two euros

Por|to-: **Por|to|aus|la|gen** PL postal *or* postage expenses *pl*; **por|to|frei** ADJ ADV post-free *(Brit)*, postage paid; **Por|to|kas|se** F ≈ petty cash *(for postal expenses)*; **por|to|pflich|tig** [-pflɪçtɪç] ADJ liable *or* subject to postage

Port|rät [pɔr'trɛː, pɔr'trɛːt] NT **-s, -s** *(lit, fig)* portrait

Port|rät|auf|nah|me F portrait photo(graph)

Port|rät|fo|to|gra|fie, **Port|rät|pho|to|gra|phie** F portrait photography

port|rä|tie|ren [pɔrtrɛ'tiːrən] *ptp* **porträtiert** VT *(fig)* to portray; **jdn ~** to paint a portrait of sb, to paint sb's portrait; *(mit Fotoapparat)* to do a portrait of sb

Port|rä|tist [pɔrtrɛ'tɪst] M **-en, -en**, **Port|rä|tis|tin** [-'tɪstɪn] F **-, -nen** portrait painter, portraitist; *(= Fotograf)* portrait photographer

Port|rät-: **Port|rät|ma|ler(in)** M(F) portrait painter, portraitist; **Port|rät|ma|le|rei** F portraiture; **Port|rät|stu|die** F sketch for a portrait

Por|tu|gal ['pɔrtugal] NT **-s** Portugal

Por|tu|gie|se [pɔrtu'giːzə] M **-n, -n**, **Por|tu|gie|sin** [-'giːzɪn] F **-, -nen** Portuguese

por|tu|gie|sisch [pɔrtu'giːzɪʃ] ADJ Portuguese

Por|tu|gie|sisch(e) [pɔrtu'giːzɪʃ] NT Portuguese → *auch* **Deutsch(e)**

Port|wein ['pɔrt-] M port

Por|zel|lan [pɔrtsɛ'laːn] NT **-s, -e** *(Material)* china, porcelain; *(= Geschirr)* china; **(unnötig) ~ zerbrechen** *or* **zerschlagen** *(fig)* to cause a lot of (unnecessary) bother *or* trouble

Por|zel|lan- *in cpds* china, porcelain; **Por|zel|lan|er|de** F china clay, kaolin; **Por|zel|lan|ge|schirr** NT china, crockery; **Por|zel|lan|la|den** M china shop → **Elefant**; **Por|zel|lan|ma|nu|fak|tur** F porcelain *or* china factory; *(Herstellung)* porcelain *or* china production

Po|sau|ne [po'zaunə] F **-, -n** trombone; *(fig)* trumpet; **die ~n des Jüngsten Gerichts** the last trump

po|sau|nen [po'zaunən] *ptp* **posaunt** *(inf)* VI *(= Posaune spielen)* to play the trombone VTI *(fig: = laut sprechen)* to bellow, to bawl, to yell; **etw in alle Welt** *or* **in die Gegend ~** to shout sth from the rooftops *or* hilltops, to tell *or* proclaim sth to the whole world

Po|sau|nen-: **Po|sau|nen|blä|ser(in)** M(F) trombonist, trombone player; **Po|sau|nen|chor** M trombone band *(usually connected with a church)*; **Po|sau|nen|en|gel** M *(lit)* cherub with a trumpet; *(fig)* (little) chubby-cheeks *(inf)*

Po|sau|nist [pozau'nɪst] M **-en, -en**, **Po|sau|nis|tin** [-'nɪstɪn] F **-, -nen** trombonist, trombone player

Po|se ['poːzə] F **-, -n** pose

Pos-1-Tas|te [pɔs'lains-] F **-, -n** *(Comput)* home key

po|sie|ren [po'ziːrən] *ptp* **posiert** VI to pose; **er posiert in der Rolle des Wohltäters** he's playing the benefactor

Po|si|ti|on [pozi'tsioːn] F **-, -en** position; *(Comm: = Posten einer Liste)* item; **in gesicherter ~ sein** to have a secure position

po|si|ti|o|nie|ren [pozitsio'niːrən] *ptp* **positioniert** VT *(Comput)* to position

Po|si|ti|o|nie|rung F **-, -en** positioning

Po|si|ti|ons-: **Po|si|ti|ons|lam|pe** F, **Po|si|ti|ons|licht** NT navigation light; **Po|si|ti|ons|pa|pier** NT *(Pol)* policy document

po|si|tiv ['poːzitiːf, pozi'tiːf] ADJ positive; **eine ~e Antwort** an answer in the affirmative, an affirmative (answer); **ich weiß nichts Positives** I don't know anything definite ADV positively; **etw ~ wissen** to know sth for certain *or* for a fact; **~ denken** to think positively; **etw ~ (auf)laden** *(Phys)* to put a positive charge on sth; **~ zu etw stehen** to be in favour *(Brit) or* favor *(US)* of sth; **sich ~ zu einer Sache äußern** to respond *or* react positively to sth

Po|si|tiv ['poːzitiːf, pozi'tiːf] M **-s, -e** [-və] *(Gram)* positive

Po|si|tiv NT **-s, -e** [-və] **a** *(Phot)* positive **b** *(= Orgel)* harmonium

Po|si|ti|vis|mus [poziti'vɪsmʊs] M **-,** *no pl* positivism

po|si|ti|vis|tisch [poziti'vɪstɪʃ] ADJ positivist

Po|si|tiv|lis|te F **a** *(Med, Pharm)* approved drug list **b** *(allgemein)* list of recommended products/shops/procedures *etc*

Po|si|tur [pozi'tuːɐ] F **-, -en** posture; *(stehend auch)* stance; **sich in ~ setzen/stellen** to take up a posture; **sie setzte sich vor den Fernsehkameras in ~** she posed for the TV cameras; **sich in ~ werfen** to strike a pose

Pos|se ['pɔsə] F **-, -n** farce

Pos|sen ['pɔsn] M **-s, -** *(dated)* prank, tomfoolery *no pl*; **~ reißen** to lark *or* fool *or* clown around; **jdm einen ~ spielen** to play a prank on sb; **mit jdm ~ treiben** *(old)* to play pranks on sb; **er tat es mir zum ~** he did it just to annoy me

Pos|sen-: **pos|sen|haft** ADJ farcical ADV farcically; **Pos|sen|rei|ßer** [-raisɐ] M **-s, -**, **Pos|sen|rei|ße|rin** [-ərɪn] F **-, -nen** clown, buffoon; **Pos|sen|spiel** NT *(liter)* pranks *pl*

pos|ses|siv ['pɔsɛsiːf, pɔsɛ'siːf] ADJ possessive

Pos|ses|siv ['pɔsɛsiːf, pɔsɛ'siːf] NT **-s, -e**, **Pos|ses|siv|pro|no|men** ['pɔsɛsiːf-, pɔsɛ'siːf-] NT possessive pronoun

Pos|ses|si|vum [pɔsɛ'siːvʊm] NT **-s, Possessiva** = **Possessiv**

pos|sier|lich [pɔ'siːɐlɪç] ADJ comical, funny ADV comically

Post® F **-, -en** **a** post *(Brit)*, mail; *(= Postamt, Postwesen)* post office; **war die ~® schon da?** has the post *(Brit) or* mail come yet?; **ist ~ für mich da?** is there any post *(Brit) or* mail for me?, are there any letters for me?; **etw mit der ~® schicken** to send sth by post *(Brit) or* mail; **etw auf** *or* **in die ~® geben** to post *(Brit) or* mail sth; **auf die** *or* **zur ~® gehen** to go to the post office; **mit gleicher ~** by the same post *(Brit)*, in the same mail *(US)*; **mit getrennter ~** under separate cover; **mit der ersten ~ kommen** to come (with *or* in the) first post *(Brit)*, to come in the first mail *(US)*; **etw durch die ~® beziehen** to order sth by post *(Brit) or* by mail **b** *(= Postkutsche)* stagecoach; *(= Postbus)* post but *(Brit)*, mail bus; **die ~ geht ab** *(fig inf)* things really happen

Post|ab|hol|ler [-laphoːlɐ] M **-s, -**, **Post|ab|ho|le|rin** [-ərɪn] F **-, -nen** *someone who collects his mail from a PO box*

Post|agen|tur F sub-post office *(Brit)*, post office substation *(US)*

pos|ta|lisch [pɔs'taːlɪʃ] ADJ postal ADV by post *(Brit) or* mail

Pos|ta|ment [pɔsta'mɛnt] NT **-(e)s, -e** pedestal, base

Post-: **Post|amt** NT post office; **Post|an|schrift** F postal address; **Post|an|wei|sung** F *remittance paid in at a Post Office and delivered by post*, ≈ postal *(Brit) or* money order; **Post|aus|gang** M, *no pl* outgoing mail, *(in E-Mail-Programmen)* outbox, out mail; **Post|au|to** NT post office van; *(Lieferwagen)* mail van

(Brit) or truck *(US)*; *(Bus)* post bus *(Brit)*, mail bus; **Post|bank** F Post Office Savings Bank; **Post|be|amt|e(r)** M *decl as adj*, **Post|be|am|tin** F post office official; **Post|be|diens|te|te(r)** MF *decl as adj (form)* post office worker; **Post|be|zirk** M postal district *or* area *or* zone *(US)*; **Post|boot** NT mail boat, packet (boat); **Post|bo|te** M postman, mailman *(US)*; **Post|bo|tin** F postwoman, mailwoman *(US)*; **Post|bus** M mail bus

Pöst|chen ['pœstçən] NT **-s, -** *dim von* **Posten** little position *or* job

Post-: **Post|dienst** M postal service, the mail *(US)*; **Post|ein|gang** M, *no pl* incoming mail, *(in E-Mail-Programmen)* inbox, in mail

pos|ten ['pɔstn] *(Sw: = einkaufen)* VT to buy VI to shop

pos|ten ['po:stn] VTI *(Internet)* to post

Pos|ten ['pɔstn] M **-s, -** **a** *(= Anstellung)* post *(esp Brit)*, position, job **b** *(Mil: = Wachmann)* guard; *(am Eingang)* sentry, guard; *(= Stelle)* post; **~ stehen** to stand guard; *(am Eingang auch)* to stand sentry; **~ beziehen** to take up one's post; **~ aufstellen** to post guards, to mount a guard **c** *(fig)* **auf dem ~ sein** *(= aufpassen)* to be awake; *(= gesund sein)* to be fit; **nicht ganz auf dem ~ sein** to be (a bit) under the weather, to be off colour *(Brit) or* off color *(US)* → **verloren, ausharren** **d** *(= Streikposten)* picket; **~ aufstellen** to set up pickets *or* a picket line **e** *(Comm: = Warenmenge)* quantity, lot **f** *(Comm: im Etat)* item, entry

pos|ten ['pɔstn] *(Sw: = einkaufen)* VT to buy VI to shop

Pos|ten-: **Pos|ten|dienst** M guard duty; **~ haben** to be on guard duty; **Pos|ten|ket|te** F cordon

Pos|ter ['pɔstɐ] NT **-s, -(s)** poster

Postf. *abbr von* **Postfach**

Post-: **Post|fach** NT post office *or* PO box; **Post|fach|num|mer** F (PO *or* post office) box number; **post|fer|tig** ADJ ready for posting *(Brit) or* mailing, ready for the post *(Brit) or* mail; **Post|flug|zeug** NT mail plane; **post|frisch** ADJ *Briefmarke* mint; **Post|ge|bühr** F postal charge *or* rate; **Post|ge|heim|nis** NT secrecy of the post *(Brit) or* mail

Post|gi|ro- [-ʒi:ro] *(dated)*: **Post|gi|ro|amt** NT National Giro office *(Brit)*, state-owned bank office *(US)*; **Post|gi|ro|kon|to** NT National *or* Post Office Giro account *(Brit)*, state-owned bank account *(US)*

Post-: **Post|hal|te|rei** [pɔsthaltə'rai] F **-, -en** coaching house *(Brit)*, motor inn *(US)*; **Post|horn** NT post horn

post|hum [pɔst'hu:m, pɔs'tu:m] ADJ ADV = **postum**

pos|tie|ren [pɔs'ti:rən] *ptp* **postiert** VT to post, to station, to position VR to station *or* position oneself

Pos|til|li|on [pɔstɪl'jo:n, 'pɔstɪljo:n] M **-s, -e** stagecoach driver

Pos|til|lon d'Amour [pɔstijõ da'mu:r] M **- -, - -s -** go-between

Pos|ting NT **-s, -s** *(Internet)* posting

Post|kar|te F postcard, postal card *(US)*

Post|kar|ten|for|mat NT, **Post|kar|ten|grö|ße** F postcard size; **in Postkartengröße, im ~** postcard-sized

Post-: **Post|kas|ten** M pillar box *(Brit)*, postbox, mailbox *(US)*; **Post|kut|sche** F stagecoach; **post|la|gernd** ADJ, ADV poste restante *(Brit)*, general delivery *(US)*; **Post|leit|zahl** F post(al) code, Zip code *(US)*

Post|ler ['pɔstlɐ] M **-s, -**, **Post|le|rin** [-ərɪn] F **-, -nen**, *(Sw)* **Pöst|ler** ['pœstlɐ] M **-s, -**, **Pöst|le|rin** [-ərɪn] F **-, -nen** *(inf)* post office worker

Post-: **Post|meis|ter** M *(dated)* postmaster; **Post|meis|te|rin** F *(dated)* postmistress; **Post|mi|nis|ter(in)** M(F) ≈ postmaster general

post|mo|dern [pɔstmo'dɛrn] ADJ postmodern

Post|mo|der|ne [pɔstmo'dɛrnə] F postmodern era

post|na|tal ['pɔstna'ta:l] ADJ *attr* postnatal

post|nuk|le|ar [pɔstnukle'a:ɐ] ADJ post-nuclear

Post-: **Post|pa|ket** NT parcel *(sent by post)*; **Post|sa|che** F matter *no pl* sent postage paid; **Post|sack** M postbag *(Brit)*, mailbag; **Post|schal|ter** M post office counter; **Post|scheck** M *(dated)* (Post Office *or* National) Giro cheque *(Brit)*, state-owned bank check *(US)*

Post|skript [pɔst'skrɪpt] NT **-(e)s, -e**, **Post|skrip|tum** [pɔst'skrɪptʊm] NT **-s, -e** *or* **Postskripta** [-ta] postscript, PS

Post-: **Post|spar|buch** NT Post Office savings book; **Post|spar|kas|se** F *(dated)* Post Office Savings Bank; **Post|stel|le** F sub-post office; **Post|stem|pel** M postmark; **Datum des ~s** date as postmark; **Einsendungen bis zum 17. Juni (Datum des ~s)** entries to be postmarked no later than 17th June; **Post|über|wei|sung** F Girobank transfer *(Brit)*, money transfer from a Post Office Savings Bank

Pos|tu|lat [pɔstu'la:t] NT **-(e)s, -e** *(= Annahme)* postulate; *(Eccl: = Probezeit)* postulancy

pos|tu|lie|ren [pɔstu'li:rən] *ptp* **postuliert** VT to postulate

pos|tum [pɔs'tu:m] ADJ posthumous ADV posthumously

Post-: **Post|ver|merk** M postmark; **Post|wa|gen** M *(Rail)* mail car, mail coach *(Brit)*; **Post|weg** M **auf dem ~** by mail *or* post *(Brit)*, by snail mail *(inf)*; **post|wen|dend** ADV by return (of post) *(Brit)*, by return mail; *(fig)* straight away, immediately; **Post|wert|zei|chen** NT *(form)* postage stamp *(form)*; **Post|we|sen** NT, *no pl* Post Office; **Post|wurf|sen|dung** F direct-mail advertising; **Post|zug** M mail train; **Post|zu|stel|lung** F postal *or* mail delivery; **Post|zu|stel|lungs|ur|kun|de** F registered post *(Brit) or* certified mail *(US)* certificate

Pot [pɔt] NT **-s**, *no pl (sl: = Haschisch)* pot *(inf)*

po|tem|kinsch [po'tɛmkɪnʃ] ADJ sham; **Potemkinsche Dörfer** façade

po|tent [po'tɛnt] ADJ **a** *(sexuell)* potent **b** *(= leistungsfähig, stark) Gegner, Waffe, Fantasie* powerful **c** *(= einflussreich)* high-powered; *(= zahlungskräftig)* financially powerful

Po|ten|tat [potɛn'ta:t] M **-en, -en**, **Po|ten|ta|tin** [-'ta:tɪn] F **-, -nen** potentate

Po|ten|ti|al [potɛn'tsia:l] NT **-s, -e** = **Potenzial**

po|ten|ti|ell [potɛn'tsiɛl] ADJ ADV = **potenziell**

Po|tenz [po'tɛnts] F **-, -en** **a** *(Med)* potency; *(fig)* ability; *(wirtschaftlich etc)* power; **schöpferische ~** creative power **b** *(Math)* power; **zweite ~** square; **dritte ~** cube; **eine Zahl in die sechste ~ erheben** to raise a number to the power of six *(esp Brit) or* to the sixth power; **die zweite/dritte ~ zu zwei ist vier/acht** the square/cube of two is four/eight, two to the power of two/three is four/eight; **die sechste ~ zu zwei** two to the power of six *(esp Brit) or* to the sixth power; **in höchster ~** *(fig)* to the highest degree

Po|ten|zi|al [potɛn'tsia:l] NT **-s, -e** potential

po|ten|zi|ell ADJ potential ADV potentially; **er ist ~ mein Gegner** he's a potential opponent, he's potentially my opponent

po|ten|zie|ren [potɛn'tsi:rən] *ptp* **potenziert** VT *(Math)* to raise to the power; *(fig: = steigern)* to multiply, to increase; **2 mit 5 ~** to raise 2 to the power (of) 5; **3 mit 2 ~** *(auch)* to square 3; **4 mit 3 ~** *(auch)* to cube 4; **2 potenziert mit 4** 2 to the power of 4 *(esp Brit)*, 2 to the fourth

po|tenz|stei|gernd ADJ potency-enhancing; **~es Mittel** potency pill *or* supplement

Pot|pour|ri ['pɔtpʊri] NT **-s, -s** *(Mus)* potpourri, medley *(aus +dat* of); *(fig)* potpourri, assortment

Pott [pɔt] M **-(e)s, ⸚e** ['pœtə] *(inf)* pot; *(= Schiff)* ship, tub *(hum inf)*; **mit etw zu ~e kommen** to see sth through; *(= anfangen)* to get down to sth

Pott-: **Pott|asche** F potash; **Pott|fisch** M sperm whale; **pott|häss|lich** *(inf)* ADJ ugly as sin, plug-ugly *(inf)* ADV **sie war ~ angezogen** the way she was dressed made her look plug-ugly *(inf)*; **wie kann man sein Haus nur so ~ anstreichen?** who would ever paint a house like that, it's ugly as sin *(inf)*; **Pott|wal** M sperm whale

potz Blitz ['pɔts 'blɪts], **potz|tau|send** ['pɔts'tauznt] INTERJ *(old)* upon my soul *(old)*

Pou|lar|de [pu'lardə] F **-, -n** poulard(e)

Pou|let [pu'le:] NT **-s, -s** *(Sw)* chicken

pous|sie|ren [pu'si:rən] *ptp* **poussiert** VI *(dated inf: = flirten)* to flirt VT *(old: = schmeicheln)* **jdn ~** to curry favour *(Brit) or* favor *(US)* with sb

po|wer ['po:vɐ] ADJ *(dial)* poor; *Essen, Geschenke* meagre *(Brit)*, meager *(US)*

Pow|er ['pauɐ] F **-**, *no pl (inf)* power; **die hat ~** she's a powerful person; **ihm fehlt die richtige ~** he's got no oomph *(inf)*

Pow|er|frau ['pauɐ-] F *(inf)* high-powered career woman

pow|ern ['pauɐn] VI *(inf)* to get things moving

Po|widl ['pɔvidl] M **-**, *no pl (Aus: = Pflaumenmus)* plum jam

PR [pe:'|ɛr] *abbr von* **Public Relations** PR

Prä-, prä- [prɛ] PREF pre-

Prä|am|bel [prɛ'ambl] F **-, -n** preamble (*+gen* to)

Pracht [praxt] F **-**, *no pl* splendour *(Brit)*, splendor *(US)*, magnificence; *(fig: = Herrlichkeit)* splendo(u)r; **in seiner vollen** *or* **ganzen ~** in all its splendo(u)r *or* magnificence; **große ~ entfalten** to put on a show *or* display of great splendo(u)r; **es ist eine wahre ~** it's (really) marvellous *(esp Brit) or* marvelous *(US) or* fantastic; **er kann singen, dass es eine ~ ist** he can sing marvellously *(esp Brit) or* marvelously *(US) or* fantastically; **die weiße ~** *(= Schnee)* snowy splendo(u)r

Pracht-: **Pracht|aus|ga|be** F de luxe edition; **Pracht|bau** M *pl* **-bauten** splendid *or* magnificent building; **Pracht|ent|fal|tung** F display of splendour *(Brit) or* splendor *(US)*, magnificent display; **zur vollen ~ kommen** to display its/their full splendour *(Brit) or* splendor *(US)*; **Pracht|ex|emp|lar** NT splendid *or* prime specimen, beauty *(inf)*; *(von Buch: = Prachtausgabe)* de luxe copy; *(fig: Mensch)* fine specimen; **mein ~ von Sohn** *(iro)* my brilliant son *(iro)*

präch|tig ['prɛçtɪç] ADJ *(= prunkvoll)* splendid, magnificent; *(= großartig)* splendid, marvellous *(esp Brit)*, marvelous *(US)* ADV **a** *(= prunkvoll)* magnificently **b** *(= großartig)* splendidly, marvellously *(esp Brit)*, marvelously *(US)*; **sich ~ amüsieren** to have a splendid *or* marvellous *(esp Brit) or* marvelous *(US)* time

Pracht-: **Pracht|kerl** M *(inf)* great guy *(inf)*, good bloke *(Brit inf)*; *(= Prachtexemplar)* beauty *(inf)*; **Pracht|stra|ße** F boulevard, magnificent avenue; **Pracht|stück** NT = **Prachtexemplar**; **pracht|voll** ADJ ADV = **prächtig**; **Pracht|weib** NT *(inf)* fine specimen of a woman *or* of womanhood

Prä|des|ti|na|ti|on [prɛdɛstina'tsio:n] F **-**, *no pl* predestination

prä|des|ti|nie|ren [prɛdɛsti'ni:rən] *ptp* **prädestiniert** VT to predestine, to predetermine *(für* for); **sein diplomatisches Geschick prädestinierte ihn zum Politiker** with his diplomatic skill he was predestined to be a politician; **er ist für diese Aufgabe wie** *or* **geradezu prädestiniert** he seems to have been made for the job

Prä|di|kat [prɛdi'ka:t] NT **-(e)s, -e** *(Gram)* predicate; *(= Bewertung)* rating; *(Sch: = Zensur)* grade; *(= Rangbezeichnung)* title; **Wein mit ~** special quality wine

prä|di|ka|tiv ['prɛ:dikati:f, prɛdika'ti:f] ADJ predicative ADV predicatively

Prä|di|ka|tiv ['prɛ:dikati:f, prɛdika'ti:f] NT **-s, -e** [-və] predicative noun/adjective/pronoun

Prä|di|ka|ti|vum [prɛdika'ti:vʊm] NT **-s, Prädikativa** [-va] = **Prädikativ**

Prä|di|kats-: Prä|di|kats|exa|men NT honours *(Brit)* or honors *(US)* degree; **Prä|di|kats|no|men** NT predicative noun/pronoun; **Prä|di|kats|wein** M top quality wine

prä|dis|po|nie|ren [prɛdɪspo'ni:rən] *ptp* **prädisponiert** VT to predispose (*für* to)

Prä|emp|tiv|schlag [prɛlɛmp'ti:f-] M *(Mil)* pre-emptive strike

Prä|fekt [prɛ'fɛkt] M **-en, -en, Prä|fek|tin** [-'fɛktɪn] F **-, -nen** prefect

Prä|fe|renz [prɛfe'rɛnts] F **-, -en** *(geh)* preference

Prä|fix [prɛ'fɪks, 'prɛ:fɪks] NT **-es, -e** prefix

Prag [pra:k] NT **-s** Prague; **der ~er Frühling** *(Pol)* the Prague Spring

Prä|ge ['prɛ:gə] F **-, -n, Prä|ge|an|stalt** F mint

prä|gen ['prɛ:gn] VT **a** *Münzen* to mint, to strike; *Leder, Papier, Metall* to emboss; *(= erfinden) Begriffe, Wörter* to coin
b *(fig: = formen) Charakter* to shape, to mould *(Brit)*, to mold *(US)*; *(Erlebnis, Kummer, Erfahrungen) jdn* to leave its/their mark on; **ein vom Leid geprägtes Gesicht** a face marked by suffering; **ein katholisch geprägtes Land** a predominantly Catholic country; **das moderne Drama ist durch Brecht geprägt worden** Brecht had a forming *or* formative influence on modern drama
c *(= kennzeichnen) Stadtbild, Landschaft etc* to characterize
VR **seine Worte prägten sich ihr ins Herz** *(liter)* his words engraved themselves on her heart *(liter)*

prä|gend ADJ *Erlebnis* formative

PR-Agen|tur [pe:'lɛr-] F PR agency

Prä|ge-: Prä|ge|ort M *pl* **-orte** mint; **Prä|ge|stem|pel** M die, stamp; **Prä|ge|stock** M punch

Prag|ma|ti|ker [pra'gma:tikɐ] M **-s, -, Prag|ma|ti|ke|rin** [-ərɪn] F **-, -nen** pragmatist

prag|ma|tisch [pra'gma:tɪʃ] ADJ pragmatic ADV pragmatically; **~ eingestellt sein** to be pragmatic

Prag|ma|tis|mus [pragma'tɪsmʊs] M **-**, *no pl* pragmatism

präg|nant [prɛ'gnant] ADJ *Worte* succinct, concise; *Beispiel, Unterschied* striking ADV succinctly, concisely; **die Antwort ist ~ ausgefallen** the answer was concise *or* succinct

Präg|nanz [prɛ'gnants] F **-**, *no pl* succinctness, conciseness

Prä|gung ['prɛ:gʊŋ] F **-, -en a** *(= das Prägen)* stamping; *(von Münzen)* minting, striking; *(von Leder, Papier, Metall)* embossing; *(von Begriffen, Wörtern)* coining; *(fig: von Charakter)* shaping, moulding *(Brit)*, molding *(US)* **b** *(auf Münzen)* strike; *(auf Leder, Metall, Papier)* embossing **c** *(= Eigenart)* character; **Kommunismus sowjetischer ~** soviet-style communism

prä|his|to|risch ADJ prehistoric

prah|len ['pra:lən] VI to boast, to brag, to swank *(Brit inf)* (*mit* about)

Prah|ler ['pra:lɐ] M **-s, -, Prah|le|rin** [-ərɪn] F **-, -nen** boaster, bragger, braggart

Prah|le|rei [pra:lə'rai] F **-, -en** *(= Großsprecherei)* boasting *no pl*, bragging *no pl*; *(= das Zurschaustellen)* showing-off, swank *(Brit inf)*; **~en** boasts; showing-off, swanking *(Brit inf)*

prah|le|risch ['pra:lərɪʃ] ADJ *(= großsprecherisch)* boastful, bragging *attr*; *(= großtuerisch)* swanky *(Brit inf)*, flashy *(inf)* ADV boastfully; **~ reden** to brag; **sich ~ verhalten** to swank about *(Brit inf)*, to strut around *(inf)*

Prahl|hans [-hans] M **-es, -hänse** [-hɛnzə] *(inf)* show-off

Prahm [pra:m] M **-(e)s, -e** *or* **⸚e** ['prɛ:mə] barge, lighter

prä|ju|di|zie|ren [prɛjudi'tsi:rən] *ptp* **präjudiziert** VT *insep (Jur)* to prejudge

Prak|tik ['praktɪk] F **-, -en** *(= Methode)* procedure, method; *(usu pl: = Kniff)* practice, trick; **undurchsichtige ~en** shady *or* dark practices

Prak|ti|ka *pl von* **Praktikum**

prak|ti|ka|bel [prakti'ka:bl] ADJ practicable

Prak|ti|ka|bi|li|tät F **-**, *no pl* practicability

Prak|ti|kant [prakti'kant] M **-en, -en, Prak|ti|kan|tin** [-'kantɪn] F **-, -nen** *student doing a period of practical training*, trainee

Prak|ti|ker ['praktikɐ] M **-s, -, Prak|ti|ke|rin** [-ərɪn] F **-, -nen** practical person *or* man/woman; *(auf wissenschaftlichem Gebiet auch)* practitioner; *(inf: = praktischer Arzt)* GP; **was halten Sie als ~ von der Montessori-Pädagogik?** what do you, as a practising *(Brit) or* practicing *(US)* teacher, think of the Montessori method?; **er ist ein ~ unter den Politikern** he is a practical sort of politician

Prak|ti|kum ['praktikʊm] NT **-s, Praktika** [-ka] practical, (period of) practical training

> **PRAKTIKUM**
>
> A **Praktikum** is a period of practical work experience. It usually entails four to eight weeks of unpaid work in a firm and is generally a compulsory part of an employment training course. Recently, however, increasing numbers of young people and students have been using the **Praktikum** as an opportunity to sample a profession and make useful contacts.

PR-Ak|ti|on [pe:'lɛr-] F PR campaign

prak|tisch ['praktɪʃ] ADJ practical; *(= nützlich auch)* handy; **sie hat einen ~en Verstand** she's practically minded; **~er Arzt** general practitioner; **~es Jahr** practical year; **~e Ausbildung** practical *or* in-job training; **~es Beispiel** concrete example ADV *(= in der Praxis)* in practice; *(= geschickt)* practically; *(= so gut wie)* practically, virtually

prak|ti|zie|ren [prakti'tsi:rən] *ptp* **praktiziert** VI to practise *(Brit)*, to practice *(US)*; **ein ~der Katholik** a practising *(Brit) or* practicing *(US)* Catholic; **sie praktiziert als Ärztin/Rechtsanwältin** she is a practising *(Brit) or* practicing *(US)* doctor/lawyer VT **a** *(pej: = ausführen)* to put into practice, to practise *(Brit)*, to practice *(US)* **b** *(inf: = geschickt an eine Stelle bringen)* to conjure

Prä|lat [prɛ'la:t] M **-en, -en, Prä|la|tin** [-'la:tɪn] F **-, -nen** prelate

Prä|li|mi|na|ri|en [prɛlimi'na:riən] PL preliminary talks *or* discussions *pl*

Pra|li|ne [pra'li:nə] F **-, -n**, *(Aus)* **Pra|li|né** [prali'ne:] NT **-s, -s, Pra|li|nee** [prali'ne:] NT **-s, -s** chocolate, chocolate candy *(US)*

prall [pral] ADJ *Sack, Beutel, Brieftasche* bulging; *Segel* billowing, full; *Tomaten* firm; *Euter* swollen, full; *Luftballon* hard; *Wange* full, chubby; *Brüste* full, well-rounded; *Hintern* well-rounded; *Arme, Schenkel* big strong *attr*; *Sonne* blazing; **das ~e Leben** life in all its colour *(Brit) or* color *(US) or* intensity; **sich ins ~e Leben stürzen** to live life to the full
ADV **etw ~ aufblasen** to blow sth up until it is ready to burst; **~ gefüllt** *(Tasche, Kasse etc)* full to bursting; *Arbeitstag* chock-full *(inf)*; **das Segel war ~ vom Wind gefüllt** the sail billowed out in the wind; **ihre Brüste wölbten sich ~ unter dem Pullover** her breasts swelled firmly under her sweater; **die Shorts spannten sich ~ über seinem Hintern** his shorts stretched tightly over his bottom; **die Sonne brannte ~ auf den Strand** the sun blazed *or* beat down onto the beach

Prall [pral] M **-(e)s, -e** collision (*gegen* with)

pral|len ['pralən] VI *aux sein* **gegen etw ~** to collide with sth, to crash into sth; *(Ball)* to bounce against *or* off sth; **er prallte mit dem Kopf gegen die Windschutzscheibe** he hit *or* crashed his head on *or* against the windscreen; **die Sonne prallte auf** *or* **gegen die Fenster** the sun beat *or* blazed down on the windows

prall|ge|füllt ADJ → **prall**

prall|voll ADJ full to bursting; *Brieftasche* bulging

Prä|lu|di|um [prɛ'lu:diʊm] NT **-s, Präludien** [-diən] prelude; *(sexuell)* foreplay

prä|mens|tru|ell [prɛmɛnstru'ɛl] ADJ premenstrual; **~e Beschwerden** *pl*, **~es Syndrom** premenstrual tension, PMT, premenstrual syndrome *(esp US)*, PMS *(esp US)*

Prä|mie ['prɛ:miə] F **-, -n** premium; *(= Belohnung)* bonus; *(= Preis)* prize

Prä|mi|en-: prä|mi|en|be|güns|tigt [-bəgʏnstɪçt] ADJ carrying a premium, with benefit of premiums; **Prä|mi|en|ge|schäft** NT *(Handel)* option dealing; *(Abschluss)* option; **Prä|mi|en|los** NT winning premium bond; **prä|mi|en|spa|ren** VI *sep infin, ptp only to save on a system benefiting from government premiums in addition to interest*

prä|mie|ren [prɛ'mi:rən] *ptp* **prämiert** VT *(= auszeichnen)* to give an award; *(= belohnen)* to give a bonus; **etw mit dem ersten Preis/mit 1000 Euro ~** to award sth first prize/a prize of 1000 euros *or* a 1000-euro prize; **der prämierte Film** the award-winning film

Prä|mie|rung F **-, -en a** *(= das Prämieren)* **für diesen Film kommt eine ~ nicht in Frage** there's no question of giving this film an award **b** *(Veranstaltung)* presentation; **die ~ der Preisträger** the presentation to the prizewinners

prä|mi|ie|ren [prɛmi'i:rən] *ptp* **prämiiert** VT = **prämieren**

Prä|mi|ie|rung F **-, -en** = **Prämierung**

Prä|mis|se [prɛ'mɪsə] F **-, -n** premise

prä|na|tal [prɛna'ta:l] ADJ *attr Diagnostik* prenatal; *Vorsorge, Untersuchung* antenatal, prenatal *(esp US)*

pran|gen ['praŋən] VI *(liter)* to be resplendent; **an der Tür prangte ein Schild** a notice hung resplendent on the door; **an der Tür prangte sein Name in großen Lettern** his name was emblazoned in big letters on the door

Pran|ger ['praŋɐ] M **-s, -** stocks *pl*, pillory; **jdn/etw an den ~ stellen** *(fig)* to pillory sb/sth; **am ~ stehen** *(lit)* to be in the stocks *or* pillory; *(fig)* to be being pilloried

Pran|ke ['praŋkə] F **-, -n** *(= Tierpranke)* paw; *(inf: = Hand)* paw *(inf)*, mitt *(inf)*

Pran|ken|hieb M swipe *or* blow from a paw; **ein ~ des Löwen streckte die Antilope nieder** one blow *or* swipe from the lion's paw brought the antelope down

PR-An|zei|ge [pe:'lɛr-] F promotional advert

Prä|pa|rat [prɛpa'ra:t] NT **-(e)s, -e** preparation; *(für Mikroskop)* slide preparation

Prä|pa|ra|tor [prɛpa'ra:to:ɐ] M **-s, Präparatoren** [-'to:rən], **Prä|pa|ra|to|rin** [-'to:rɪn] F **-, -nen** lab technician; *(= Tierpräparator)* taxidermist

prä|pa|rie|ren [prɛpa'ri:rən] *ptp* **präpariert** VT **a** *(= konservieren)* to preserve; *Tier* to prepare **b** *(Med: = zerlegen)* to dissect **c** *(geh: = vorbereiten)* to prepare VR *(dated)* to prepare (oneself), to do one's preparation (*für, auf +acc* for)

Prä|po|si|ti|on [prɛpozi'tsio:n] F **-, -en** preposition

prä|po|si|ti|o|nal [prɛpozitsio'na:l] ADJ prepositional

Prä|rie [prɛ'ri:] F **-, -n** [-'ri:ən] prairie

Prä|rie|wolf M prairie wolf, coyote

Prä|sens ['prɛ:zɛns] NT **-, Präsenzien** [prɛ'zɛntsiən] present (tense)

prä|sent [prɛ'zɛnt] ADJ *(= anwesend)* present; *(= geistig rege)* alert; **etw ~ haben** to have sth at hand; **sein Name ist mir nicht ~** his name escapes me

Prä|sent [prɛ'zɛnt] NT **-s, -e** present, gift

prä|sen|ta|bel [prezɛn'ta:bl] ADJ presentable ADV presentably; **~ aussehen** to look presentable; **etw ~ herrichten** to make sth look presentable

Prä|sen|ta|ti|on [prɛzɛnta'tsio:n] F **-, -en** presentation

prä|sen|tie|ren [prɛzɛn'ti:rən] *ptp* **präsentiert** VT to present; **jdm etw ~** to present sb with sth; **jdm die Rechnung (für etw) ~** *(fig)* to make sb pay the price (for sth); **präsentiert das Gewehr!** present arms! VR *(= sich zeigen)* to present oneself; *(= sich vorstellen auch)* to introduce oneself VI *(Mil)* to present arms

Prä|sen|tier|tel|ler M *(old)* salver; **auf dem ~ sitzen** *(fig)* to be on show; **jdm etw auf dem ~ servieren** *(fig)* to hand sb sth on a plate

Prä|sent|korb M gift basket; *(mit Lebensmitteln)* (food) hamper

Prä|senz [prɛ'zɛnts] F **-,** *no pl (geh)* presence; **die ständig abnehmende ~ im Abgeordnetenhaus** the constantly decreasing numbers in parliament

Prä|senz|bib|lio|thek F reference library

Prä|sen|zi|en *pl von* **Präsens**

Prä|senz|lis|te F (attendance) register

Pra|seo|dym [prazeo'dy:m] NT **-s,** *no pl (abbr* **Pr***)* praseodymium

Prä|ser ['prɛ:zɐ] M **-s, -** *(inf) abbr von* **Präservativ**

Prä|ser|va|tiv [prɛzɛrva'ti:f] NT **-s, -e** [-və] contraceptive, condom, sheath

Prä|si|dent [prɛzi'dɛnt] M **-en, -en, Prä|si|den|tin** [-'dɛntɪn] F **-, -nen** president; **Herr ~** Mister President; **Frau ~in** Madam President

Prä|si|den|ten|wahl F presidential election

Prä|si|dent|schaft [prɛzi'dɛntʃaft] F **-, -en** presidency

Prä|si|dent|schafts|kan|di|dat(in) M(F) presidential candidate

Prä|si|di|al|de|mo|kra|tie F presidential democracy

prä|si|die|ren [prɛzi'di:rən] *ptp* **präsidiert** VI to preside; **einem Ausschuss ~** to preside over a committee, to be president of a committee

Prä|si|di|um [prɛ'zi:dium] NT **-s, Präsidien** [-diən] *(= Vorsitz)* presidency; *(= Führungsgruppe)* committee; *(= Gebäude)* headquarters (building); *(= Polizeipräsidium)* (police) headquarters *pl*; **ins ~ gewählt werden** to be elected to the committee; **das ~ übernehmen** to take the chair

pras|seln ['prasln] VI **a** *aux sein* to clatter; *(Regen, Hagel)* to drum; *(fig: Vorwürfe, Fragen)* to rain *or* hail down **b** *(Feuer)* to crackle; **~der Beifall** thunderous applause

pras|sen ['prasn] VI *(= schlemmen)* to feast; *(= in Luxus leben)* to live the high life

Pras|ser ['prasɐ] M **-s, -, Pras|se|rin** [-ərɪn] F **-, -nen** glutton; *(= Verschwender)* spendthrift

Pras|se|rei [prasə'rai] F **-, -en** *(= Schlemmerei)* feasting; *(= Luxusleben)* high life

Prä|ten|dent [prɛtɛn'dɛnt] M **-en, -en, Prä|ten|den|tin** [-'dɛntɪn] F **-, -nen** pretender

prä|ten|ti|ös [prɛtɛn'tsiø:s] ADJ *(geh)* pretentious

Prä|te|ri|tum [prɛ'te:ritʊm] NT **-s, Präterita** [-ta] preterite

Prat|ze ['pratsə] F **-, -n** *(S Ger inf)* paw; *(fig: = Hand)* paw *(inf)*, mitt *(inf)*

Prä|ven|ti|on [prɛvɛn'tsio:n] F **-, -en** prevention *(gegen* of)

prä|ven|tiv [prɛvɛn'ti:f] ADJ prevent(at)ive ADV prevent(at)ively; *wirken, operieren* as a prevent(at)ive measure; **etw ~ bekämpfen** to use prevent(at)ive measures against sth; **die Polizei hat ~ eingegriffen** the police took prevent(at)ive measures

Prä|ven|tiv-: **Prä|ven|tiv|be|hand|lung** F *(Med)* prevent(at)ive treatment; **Prä|ven|tiv|krieg** M prevent(at)ive *or* pre-emptive war; **Prä|ven|tiv|maß|nah|me** F prevent(at)ive measure; **Prä|ven|tiv|me|di|zin** F prevent(at)ive medicine; **Prä|ven|tiv|schlag** M *(Mil)* pre-emptive strike

Pra|xis ['praksɪs] F **-, Praxen** ['praxn] **a** *no pl* practice; *(= Erfahrung)* experience; *(= Brauch)* practice, custom; **in der ~** in practice; **die ~ sieht anders aus** the facts are different; **etw in die ~ umsetzen** to put sth into practice; **ein Mann der ~** a man with practical experience; **ein Beispiel aus der ~** an example from real life; **das lernt man erst durch die** *or* **in der ~** you only learn that by doing it, that's only learned through practical experience; **seine langjährige künstlerische ~** his long years of artistic experience **b** *(eines Arztes, Rechtsanwalts)* practice; *(= Behandlungsräume)* surgery *(Brit)*, doctor's office *(US)*; *(= Anwaltsbüro)* office **c** *(= Sprechstunde)* consultation (hour), surgery *(Brit)*

Pra|xis-: **Pra|xis|be|zug** M foundation in reality; **ohne ~** with no foundation in reality; **pra|xis|fern, pra|xis|fremd** ADJ *Ausbildung* lacking in practical relevance ADV **jdn ~ ausbilden** to provide sb with training lacking in practical relevance; **Pra|xis|fer|ne** F *(von Studium)* lack of practical relevance; *(von Nachwuchs)* lack of practical experience; **Pra|xis|ge|bühr** F *(Med)* practice *(Brit) or* office *(US)* fee; **pra|xis|nah** ADJ *Ausbildung* practically relevant ADV **jdn ~ ausbilden** to provide sb with practically relevant training; **Pra|xis|nä|he** F practical relevance; **pra|xis|ori|en|tiert** [-orienti:ɐt] ADJ *Ausbildung, Lösung, Software* practically orientated ADV **jdn ~ ausbilden** to provide sb with a practically orientated training; **dort wird ~er gearbeitet** their work is practically orientated; **Pra|xis|schock** M reality shock; **Pra|xis|test** M practical *or* practice test, trial; *(von Auto)* test run

Prä|ze|denz|fall M precedent; **einen ~ schaffen** to set *or* create *or* establish a precedent

prä|zis [prɛ'tsi:s], **prä|zi|se** [prɛ'tsi:zə] ADJ precise ADV precisely; *formulieren, schneiden* exactly; **sie arbeitet sehr ~** her work is very precise

prä|zi|sie|ren [prɛtsi'zi:rən] *ptp* **präzisiert** VT to state more precisely; *(= zusammenfassen)* to summarize

Prä|zi|si|on [prɛtsi'zio:n] F **-,** *no pl* precision

Prä|zi|si|ons- *in cpds* precision; **Prä|zi|si|ons|ar|beit** F precision work; **~ leisten** to work with precision; **Prä|zi|si|ons|ins|tru|ment** NT precision instrument

pre|di|gen ['pre:dɪgn] VT **a** *(Rel)* to preach; **solche Leute ~ immer Moral** people like that are always preaching (about) *or* sermonizing about morality **b** *(fig)* **jdm etw ~** to lecture sb on sth; **sie predigt ihm andauernd, dass er sich die Zähne putzen soll** she keeps lecturing him on the importance of cleaning his teeth VI to give a sermon, to preach; *(fig: = mahnen)* to preach, to sermonize; **tauben Ohren ~** to preach to deaf ears

Pre|di|ger ['pre:dɪgɐ] M **-s, -, Pre|di|ge|rin** [-ərɪn] F **-, -nen** preacher

Pre|digt ['pre:dɪçt] F **-, -en** *(lit, fig)* sermon; **jdm eine lange ~ über etw** *(acc)* **halten** *(fig)* to give sb a long sermon on *or* about sth

Pre|digt|text M text for a sermon

Preis [prais] M **-es, -e** **a** price *(für* of); *(= Fahrgeld)* fare *(für* for); *(= Gebühr, Honorar)* fee *(für* of); **der ~ für die Jacke beträgt 90 Euro** the price of the jacket is 90 euros; **(weit) unter(m) ~** cut-price; **etw unter ~ verkaufen/verschleudern** to sell/flog *(Brit inf)* sth off cheap; **zum halben ~** half-price; **um jeden ~** *(fig)* at all costs; **Qualität hat ihren ~** you have to pay for quality; **ich gehe um keinen ~ hier weg** *(fig)* I'm not leaving here at any price; **auch um den ~ seines eignen Glücks** even at the expense of his own happiness **b** *(bei Wettbewerben)* prize; *(= Auszeichnung)* award; **in diesem Rennen ist kein ~ ausgesetzt** there's no prize in *or* for this race; **den ersten ~ gewinnen** to win (the) first prize; **jdm einen ~ zusprechen** *or* **zuerkennen** *or* **verleihen** to award *or* give sb a prize/to give sb an award; **der Große ~ von Deutschland** the German Grand Prix **c** *(= Belohnung)* reward; **einen ~ auf jds Kopf aussetzen** to put a price on sb's head **d** *no pl (liter: = Lob)* praise *(auf +acc* of); **ein Gedicht zum ~ von …** a poem in praise of …; **~ sei Gott** praise be to God

Preis-: **Preis|ab|bau** M, *no pl* price reduction; **Preis|ab|spra|che** F price-fixing *no pl*; **Preis|än|de|rung** F price change; **Preis|an|ga|be** F price quotation; **alle Kleider sind mit ~** all dresses are priced, the prices of all dresses are given; **Preis|an|stieg** M rise in prices; **Preis|auf|ga|be** F prize competition; **Preis|auf|schlag** M supplementary charge, supplement; **Preis|auf|trieb** M price increase; **Preis|aus|schrei|ben** NT competition; **Preis|be|we|gung** F movement of prices; **preis|be|wusst** ADJ price-conscious ADV **~ einkaufen** to shop around; **Preis|bil|dung** F price fixing; **Preis|bin|dung** F price fixing; **~ der zweiten Hand** retail price maintenance; **Preis|bre|cher** M *(Produkt)* (all-time) bargain, snip *(Brit inf)*, steal *(inf)*; *(Firma)* undercutter; **diese Firma wirkt als ~ auf dem Markt** this firm undercuts the market; **Preis|dis|zip|lin** F price restraint; **Preis|ein|bruch** M price collapse

Prei|sel|bee|re ['praizl-] F cranberry

Preis-: **Preis|emp|feh|lung** F recommended price; **unverbindliche ~** recommended retail price, rrp, RRP; **preis|emp|find|lich** ADJ price-sensitive

prei|sen ['praizn] *pret* **pries** [pri:s], *ptp* **gepriesen** [gə'pri:zn] VT *(geh)* to extol, to praise, to laud *(liter)*; **Gott sei gepriesen** praise be to God; **sich glücklich ~** to consider *or* count *or* think oneself lucky

Preis-: **Preis|ent|wick|lung** F price trend; **Preis|er|hö|hung** F price increase; **Preis|er|mä|ßi|gung** F price reduction; **Preis|ex|plo|si|on** F price explosion; **Preis|fra|ge** F **a** question of price **b** *(beim Preisausschreiben)* prize question *(in a competition)*; *(inf: = schwierige Frage)* sixty-four thousand dollar question *(inf)*, big question

Preis|ga|be F *(geh)* *(= Aufgabe)* surrender, relinquishment, abandoning; *(von Gebiet)* abandoning; *(von Geheimnis)* betrayal, divulgence; **sie wurden zur ~ ihrer Position gezwungen** they were forced to surrender *or* abandon *or* relinquish their position

preis+ge|ben VT *sep irreg (geh)* **a** *(= ausliefern)* to expose, to leave to the mercy of; **jdm/einer Sache preisgegeben sein** to be exposed to sb/sth, to be at the mercy of sb/sth **b** *(= aufgeben)* to abandon, to relinquish; *Gebiete* to surrender, to abandon **c** *(= verraten)* to betray; *Geheimnis* to divulge, to betray

Preis-: **Preis|ge|fäl|le** NT price gap; **Preis|ge|fü|ge** NT price structure; **preis|ge|krönt** [-gəkrø:nt] ADJ award-winning; **~ werden** to be given an award; **Preis|geld** NT *(Sport)* prize money; **Preis|ge|richt** NT jury, team of judges; **Preis|ge|stal|tung** F pricing *(bei* of); **eine ganz andere ~** a totally different price structure; **Preis|gren|ze** F price limit; **preis|güns|tig** ADJ inexpensive ADV *kaufen* inexpensively; **etw ~ bekommen** to get sth at a low *or* good price; **am ~sten kauft man im Supermarkt ein** you get the most for your money at the supermarket; **Preis|in|dex** M price index; **Preis|kampf** M price war; **Preis|klas|se** F price range; **die gehobene/mittlere/untere ~** the upper/medium/lower price range; **Preis|kon|trol|le** F price control; **Preis|krieg** M price war; **Preis|la|ge** F price range; **in jeder ~** at all prices, at prices to suit every pocket; **in der mittleren ~** in the medium-priced range; **Preis|la|wi|ne** F *(inf)* snowballing prices *pl*; **Preis-Leis|tungs-Ver|hält|nis** NT cost-effectiveness

preis|lich ['praislɪç] ADJ price *attr*, in price; **~e Wettbewerbsfähigkeit** price competitiveness ADV **~ niedriger/vorteilhaft** lower/favourably *(Brit) or* favorably *(US)* priced; **~ günstig/höher**

reasonably/higher priced; **~ vergleichbar** similarly priced; **sie sind ~ unterschiedlich** they differ in price; **dieses Angebot ist ~ sehr günstig** this offer is a bargain; **die Waren sind nur ~ verschieden** the goods only differ in price

Preis-: **Preis|lis|te** F price list; **Preis|nach|lass** M price reduction; **10% ~ bei Barzahlung** 10% off cash sales; **Preis|ni|veau** NT price level; **Preis|po|li|tik** F pricing policy; **Preis|rät|sel** NT prize competition; **Preis|rich|ter(in)** M(F) judge *(in a competition)*, jury member; **Preis|schie|ßen** NT -s, *no pl* shooting competition *or* contest, shoot; **Preis|schild** NT price tag; **Preis|schla|ger** M (all-time) bargain; **Preis|schwan|kung** F price fluctuation; **Preis|sen|kung** F price cut; **Preis|span|ne** F price margin; **preis|sta|bil** ADJ stable in price; **Preis|sta|bi|li|tät** F price stability; **Preis|stei|ge|rung** F price increase; **Preis|stei|ge|rungs|ra|te** F rate of price increases; **Preis|stopp** M price freeze; **Preis|sturz** M sudden fall *or* drop in prices; **Preis|sys|tem** NT price *or* pricing system, system of prices; **Preis|trä|ger(in)** M(F) prizewinner; *(= Kulturpreisträger)* award-winner; **Preis|trei|ber(in)** M(F) *person who forces prices up*; **Preis|trei|be|rei** [-traibəˈrai] F -, -en forcing up of prices; *(= Wucher)* profiteering; **das ist nur ein Vorwand für die ~ der Industrie** that's only an excuse for industry to force up prices; **Preis|über|wa|chung** F price control; **Preis|un|ter|schied** M difference in price(s), price differential; **Preis|ver|fall** M drop-off in prices; **Preis|ver|gleich** M price comparison; **einen ~ machen** to shop around; **Preis|ver|lei|hung** F presentation (of prizes); *(von Auszeichnung)* presentation (of awards); **preis|wert** ADJ good value *pred*; **ein (sehr) ~es Angebot** a (real) bargain; **ein ~es Kleid** a dress which is good value (for money) ADV inexpensively; **hier kann man ~ einkaufen** you get good value (for money) here; **am ~esten kauft man im Supermarkt ein** you get the most for your money at the supermarket

pre|kär [preˈkɛːɐ] ADJ *(= peinlich)* awkward, embarrassing; *(= schwierig)* precarious

Prell-: **Prell|ball** M *game similar to volleyball in which the ball is bounced over the net*; **Prell|bock** M *(Rail)* buffers *pl*, buffer stop; **der ~ sein** *(fig)* to be the scapegoat *or* fall guy *(esp US inf)*

prel|len [ˈprɛlən] VT **a** *Körperteil* to bruise; *(= anschlagen)* to hit **b** *(fig inf: = betrügen)* to swindle, to cheat; **jdm um etw ~** to swindle *or* cheat sb out of sth → **Zeche c** *(Sport)* to bounce VR to bruise oneself; **ich habe mich am** *or* **mir den Arm geprellt** I've bruised my arm

Prel|le|rei [prɛləˈrai] F -, -en swindle, fraud

Prell|schuss M ricochet, ricocheting bullet

Prel|lung [ˈprɛlʊŋ] F -, -en bruise, contusion

Pre|mi|er [prəˈmieː, pre-] M -s, -s premier

Pre|mi|e|re [prəˈmieːrə, pre-, -ˈmiɛːrə] F -, -n premiere

Pre|mi|e|ren-: **Pre|mi|e|ren|be|su|cher** PL, **Pre|mi|e|ren|pub|li|kum** NT premiere audience *no pl*; **Pre|mi|e|ren|ki|no** NT first-run cinema

Pre|mi|er|mi|nis|ter(in) [prəˈmieː-, pre-] M(F) prime minister

Pre|paid-: **Pre|paid|han|dy** NT prepaid mobile phone *(Brit)*, prepaid cellphone *(US)*; **Pre|paid|kar|te** F *(im Handy)* prepaid card

Pres|by|te|ri|a|ner [prɛsbyteˈriaːnɐ] M -s, -, **Pres|by|te|ri|a|ne|rin** [-ərɪn] F -, -nen Presbyterian

pres|by|te|ri|a|nisch [prɛsbyteˈriaːnɪʃ] ADJ Presbyterian

pre|schen [ˈprɛʃn] VI *aux sein (inf)* to tear, to dash

pres|sant [prɛˈsant] ADJ *(inf)* urgent; **es ~ haben** to be in a hurry

Pres|se [ˈprɛsə] F -, -n **a** *(= mechanische Presse, Druckmaschine)* press; **in die ~ gehen** to go to press; **frisch** *or* **eben aus der ~** hot from the press **b** *(= Zeitungen)* press; **eine gute/schlechte ~ haben** to have *or* get a good/bad press; **von der ~ sein** to be (a member of the) press

Pres|se-: **Pres|se|agen|tur** F press *or* news agency; **Pres|se|amt** NT press office; **Pres|se|at|ta|ché** M press attaché; **Pres|se|aus|weis** M press card; **Pres|se|be|richt** M press report; **Pres|se|bü|ro** NT press *or* news agency; **Pres|se|dienst** M news service; **Pres|se|emp|fang** M press reception; **Pres|se|er|klä|rung** F statement to the press; *(schriftlich)* press release; **Pres|se|fo|to|graf(in)** M(F) press photographer; **Pres|se|frei|heit** F freedom of the press; **Pres|se|ge|setz** NT press law; **Pres|se|jar|gon** M journalese; **Pres|se|kam|pag|ne** F press campaign; **Pres|se|kar|te** F press *or* review ticket; **Pres|se|kom|men|tar** M press commentary; **Pres|se|kon|fe|renz** F press conference; **Pres|se|map|pe** F press kit; **Pres|se|mel|dung** F press report; **Pres|se|mit|tei|lung** F press release *or* announcement

pres|sen [ˈprɛsn] VT **a** *(= quetschen)* to press; *Obst, Saft* to squeeze; *hohe Töne* to squeeze out; *(fig: = zwingen)* to force *(in +acc, zu* into); *(fig dated: = unterdrücken)* to oppress; **frisch gepresster Orangensaft** freshly squeezed orange juice; **eine CD ~** to press a CD; **etw auf CD-ROM ~** to put sth onto CD-ROM; **mit gepresster Stimme** in a strained voice **b** *(Naut)* **Segel ~** to make too much sail

Pres|se-: **Pres|se|no|tiz** F paragraph in the press; **Pres|se|or|gan** NT organ; **Pres|se|pho|to|graph(in)** M(F) press photographer; **Pres|se|recht** NT press laws *pl*; **Pres|se|re|fe|rent(in)** M(F) press officer; **Pres|se|rum|mel** M *(inf)* press furore *(Brit)* *or* furor *(US)*, media frenzy; **Pres|se|spre|cher(in)** M(F) press officer; **Pres|se|stel|le** F press office; **Pres|se|stim|me** F press commentary; *(kulturell)* press review; **Pres|se|tri|bü|ne** F press box; *(Parl)* press gallery; **Pres|se|ver|tre|ter(in)** M(F) representative of the press; **Pres|se|we|sen** NT press; **Pres|se|zar(in)** M(F) *(inf)* press baron

Press|glas NT pressed glass

pres|sie|ren [prɛˈsiːrən] *ptp* **pressiert** *(S Ger, Aus, Sw)* VI to be in a hurry VI *impers* **es pressiert** it's urgent; **(bei) ihm pressiert es immer** he's always in a hurry

Pres|si|on [prɛˈsioːn] F -, -en pressure

Press|kopf M, *no pl* → **Presssack**

Press|koh|le F briquette

Press|luft F compressed air

Press|luft-: **Press|luft|boh|rer** M pneumatic drill; **Press|luft|ham|mer** M pneumatic *or* air hammer

Press|sack M, *no pl (Cook)* brawn *(Brit)*, headcheese *(US)*

Press|we|hen PL *(bei Geburt)* bearing-down pains *pl*, expulsive pains *pl (spec)*

Pres|ti|ge [prɛsˈtiːʒə] NT -s, *no pl* prestige; **~ verlieren** to lose (one's) prestige

Pres|ti|ge-: **Pres|ti|ge|den|ken** NT status mentality; **Pres|ti|ge|fra|ge** F question *or* matter of prestige; **Pres|ti|ge|ge|winn** M gain in prestige; **Pres|ti|ge|sa|che** F question *or* matter of prestige; **Pres|ti|ge|sucht** F status mentality; **pres|ti|ge|süch|tig** ADJ status-minded, preoccupied with one's prestige; **Pres|ti|ge|ver|lust** M loss of prestige

Prêt-à-por|ter- *in cpds* ready-to-wear; **Prêt-à-por|ter-Kol|lek|ti|on** F ready-to-wear collection

pre|ti|ös [preˈtsiøːs] ADJ *(geh)* = **preziös**

Pre|ti|o|sen [preˈtsioːzn] PL *(geh)* valuables *pl*

Preu|ße [ˈprɔysə] M -n, -n, **Preu|ßin** [-sɪn] F -, -nen Prussian; *(fig)* strict disciplinarian; **so schnell schießen die ~n nicht** *(inf)* things don't happen that fast

Preu|ßen [ˈprɔysn] NT -s Prussia

preu|ßisch [ˈprɔysɪʃ] ADJ Prussian

preu|ßisch|blau ADJ Prussian blue

pre|zi|ös [preˈtsiøːs] ADJ *(geh)* precious

Pre|zi|o|sen [preˈtsioːzn] PL *(geh)* valuables *pl*

PR-Fach|frau [peːˈlɛr-] F, **PR-Fach|mann** M PR specialist

Pri|cke [ˈprɪkə] F -, -n *(Naut)* shallows marker

pri|ckeln [ˈprɪkln] VI *(= kribbeln)* to tingle; *(= kitzeln)* to tickle; *(= Bläschen bilden)* to sparkle, to bubble; **die Limonade prickelt in der Nase** the lemonade's tickling my nose; **ein angenehmes Prickeln auf der Haut** a pleasant tingling of the skin; **ich spürte ein Prickeln in meinem Bein** I had pins and needles in my leg; **die Atmosphäre prickelte vor Spannung** the atmosphere was electric

pri|ckelnd ADJ *(= kribbelnd)* tingling; *(= kitzelnd)* tickling; *(= Bläschen bildend)* sparkling, bubbling; *(fig) (= würzig)* piquant; *(= erregend) Gefühl* tingling; **der ~e Reiz der Neuheit** the thrill of novelty; **etwas Prickelndes für den Gaumen** something to titillate the taste buds *(hum)*

Priel [priːl] M -(e)s, -e narrow channel *(in North Sea mud flats)*, tideway

Priem [priːm] M -(e)s, -e quid of tobacco

prie|men [ˈpriːmən] VI to chew tobacco

pries *pret von* **preisen**

Pries|ter [ˈpriːstɐ] M -s, - priest

Pries|ter|amt NT priesthood

Pries|te|rin [ˈpriːstərɪn] F -, -nen (woman) priest; *(Hist)* priestess

pries|ter|lich [ˈpriːstɐlɪç] ADJ priestly *no adv*; *Kleidung auch* clerical ADV **er war ~ gekleidet** he was dressed like a priest

Pries|ter-: **Pries|ter|rock** M cassock; **Pries|ter|schaft** [ˈpriːstɐʃaft] F -, -en priesthood; **Pries|ter|se|mi|nar** NT seminary; **Pries|ter|tum** [ˈpriːstɐtuːm] NT -s, *no pl* priesthood; **Pries|ter|wei|he** F ordination (to the priesthood); **die ~ empfangen** to be ordained (to the priesthood *or* as a priest); **jdm die ~ spenden** to confer holy orders on sb

pri|ma [ˈpriːma] ADJ *inv* **a** *(inf)* fantastic *(inf)*, great *no adv (inf)* **b** *(Comm)* first-class, top-quality ADV *(inf: = sehr gut)* fantastically; **das hast du ~ gemacht** you did that fantastically (well) *or* beautifully *or* just great

Pri|ma [ˈpriːma] F -, **Primen** [-mən] *(dated Sch) eighth and ninth year of German secondary school (Aus) first year of secondary school*

Pri|ma-: **Pri|ma|bal|le|ri|na** [primabaləˈriːna] F prima ballerina; **Pri|ma|don|na** [primaˈdɔna] F -, **Primadonnen** [-ˈdɔnən] prima donna

Pri|ma|ner [priˈmaːnɐ] M -s, -, **Pri|ma|ne|rin** [-ərɪn] F -, -nen *(dated Sch)* ≈ sixth-former *(Brit)*, ≈ twelfth grader *(US)*; *(Aus)* first-former

pri|mär [priˈmɛːɐ] ADJ primary ADV primarily

Pri|mär-: **Pri|mär|ener|gie** F primary energy; **Pri|mär|kreis|lauf** F primary circuit

Pri|mar|leh|rer(in) [priˈmaːɐ-] M(F) *(Sw)* primary school teacher

Pri|mär|li|te|ra|tur F primary literature *or* sources *pl*

Pri|mar|schu|le [priˈmaːɐ-] F *(Sw)* primary *or* junior school

Pri|mas [ˈpriːmas] M -, -se *or* **Primaten** [priˈmaːtn] *(Eccl)* primate; *(in Zigeunerkapelle)* first violin

Pri|mat [priˈmaːt] M OR NT -(e)s, -e priority, primacy *(vor +dat* over); *(des Papstes)* primacy; *(= Erstgeburtsrecht)* primogeniture

Pri|mat M -en, -en *(Zool)* primate

Pri|ma|ten *pl von* **Primas, Primat**

Pri|mel [ˈpriːml] F -, -n *(= Waldprimel)* (wild) primrose; *(= Schlüsselblume)* cowslip; *(= farbige Gartenprimel)* primula; *(mit verzweigtem Stiel)* polyanthus; **wie eine ~ eingehen** *(fig)* to fade *or* wither away

Pri|men *pl von* **Prima**

Pri|mi *pl von* **Primus**

pri|mi|tiv [primiˈtiːf] ADJ primitive; *Maschine auch* crude ADV primitively

Pri|mi|ti|ve(r) [primiˈtiːvə] MF *decl as adj* primitive

Pri|mi|ti|vi|tät [primitiviˈtɛːt] F -, -en primitiveness; *(von Maschine auch)* crudeness

Pri|mi|tiv|ling [primiˈtiːflɪŋ] M -s, -e *(pej inf)* peasant *(pej inf)*, primitive *(pej inf)*

Pri|mus [ˈpriːmʊs] M -, -se *or* **Primi** [-mi] top of the class, top *or* star pupil

Prim|zahl [ˈpriːm-] F prime (number)

Prin|te [ˈprɪntə] F -, -n *(Gebäck)* oblong spiced biscuit

Prin|ter M -s, - *(= Drucker)* printer

Print|me|di|um [ˈprɪntmeːdiʊm] NT *usu pl* printed medium; **die Werbung in Fernsehen und Printmedien** advertising on television and in printed media

Prinz [prɪnts] M -en, -en prince; **wie ein ~ leben** *(inf)* to live like a lord *(Brit) or* a king; **unser kleiner ~** *(inf: = Sohn)* our son and heir *(inf)*; **Johann Georg ~ von Hohenzollern** Johann Georg, Prince of Hohenzollern

Prin|zen-: **Prin|zen|gar|de** F *(im Karneval)* King's Guard; **Prin|zen|paar** NT **a** *(Adelige)* princely couple **b** *(im Karneval)* Carnival King and Queen *or* Prince and Princess

Prin|zes|sin [prɪnˈtsɛsɪn] F -, -nen princess; **Agnes ~ von Polen** Agnes, Princess of Poland; **die ~ auf der Erbse** *(Liter)* the Princess and the Pea; **eine ~ auf der Erbse** *(fig)* a hothouse plant

Prinz|ge|mahl M prince consort

Prin|zip [prɪnˈtsiːp] NT -s, -ien *or (rare)* -e [-piən] principle; **aus ~** on principle; **das hat er aus ~ getan** he did it on principle, he did it as a matter of principle; **im ~** in principle; **das funktioniert nach einem einfachen ~** it works on a simple principle; **nach einem ~ handeln** to act according to a principle; **etw zum ~ erheben** *or* **machen** to make sth into a principle; **er ist ein Mann von** *or* **mit ~ien** he is a man of principle; **das ~ Hoffnung** the principle of hope

Prin|zi|pal [prɪntsiˈpaːl] M -s, -e, **Prin|zi|pa|lin** [-ˈpaːlɪn] F -, -nen **a** *(= Theaterleiter)* theatre *(Brit) or* theater *(US)* director **b** *(old) (= Geschäftsinhaber)* proprietor; *(= Lehrherr)* master

prin|zi|pi|ell [prɪntsiˈpiɛl] ADJ *(= im Prinzip)* in principle; *(= aus Prinzip)* on principle ADV **a** *(= im Prinzip) möglich* theoretically; *dafür/dagegen sein* basically; **~ bin ich einverstanden** I agree in principle **b** *(= aus Prinzip) ablehnen, gegen etw sein, sich weigern* on principle; **das tue ich ~ nicht** I won't do that on principle

Prin|zi|pi|en-: **prin|zi|pi|en|fest** ADJ *Mensch* firm-principled, of firm principles; *Politik* principled; **Prin|zi|pi|en|fra|ge** F matter *or* question of principle; **prin|zi|pi|en|los** ADJ unprincipled ADV **sich ~ verhalten** to be unprincipled; **Prin|zi|pi|en|lo|sig|keit** F -, *no pl* lack of principle(s); **Prin|zi|pi|en|rei|ter(in)** M(F) *(pej)* stickler for one's principles; **Prin|zi|pi|en|rei|te|rei** F *(pej)* going-on about principles *(pej)*; **Prin|zi|pi|en|streit** M dispute about principles

Prinz|re|gent M prince regent

Pri|on [ˈpriːɔn] NT -s, -e [priˈoːnə] *(Biol)* prion

Pri|or [ˈpriːoːɐ] M -s, **Prioren** [priˈoːrən] prior

Pri|o|rin [priˈoːrɪn] F -, -nen prioress

Pri|o|ri|tät [prioriˈtɛːt] F -, -en **a** priority; **~ vor etw** *(dat)* **haben** to have *or* take priority *or* precedence over sth; **erste** *or* **höchste ~ haben** to have top priority; **~en setzen** to establish one's priorities; **die richtigen/falschen ~en setzen** to get one's priorities right/wrong; **jdm/etw (höchste) ~ einräumen** to give sb/sth (top) priority **b Prioritäten** PL *(Comm)* preference shares *pl*, preferred stock *(US)*

Pri|o|ri|tä|ten|lis|te F list of priorities

Pri|se [ˈpriːzə] F -, -n **a** *(= kleine Menge)* pinch; **eine ~ Salz** a pinch of salt; **eine ~ Humor** a touch of humour *(Brit) or* humor *(US)* **b** *(Naut)* prize

Pris|ma [ˈprɪsma] NT -s, **Prismen** [-mən] prism

pris|ma|tisch [prɪsˈmaːtɪʃ] ADJ prismatic

Pris|men *pl von* **Prisma**

Pris|men|glas NT prismatic telescope

Prit|sche [ˈprɪtʃə] F -, -n **a** *(= Narrenpritsche)* fool's wand **b** *(von LKW)* platform **c** *(= Liegestatt)* plank bed

prit|schen [ˈprɪtʃn] VT *(Volleyball)* to pass (the ball) with both hands

Prit|schen|wa|gen M platform truck

pri|vat [priˈvaːt] ADJ private; *Telefonnummer auch* home *attr*; **etw an Privat verkaufen/von Privat kaufen** *(Comm)* to sell sth to/to buy sth from private individuals; **aus ~er Hand** from private individuals

ADV **a** *(= als Privatperson)* privately; **~ wohnt sie in einer Villa** she lives in a villa; **~ ist der Chef sehr freundlich** the boss is very friendly out(side) of work; **~ ist er ganz anders** he's quite different socially; **jdn ~ sprechen** to speak to sb privately *or* in private

b *(von Privatpersonen) finanzieren, unterstützen* privately

c *(= individuell)* **jdn ~ unterbringen** to put sb up privately; **ich sagte es ihm ganz ~** I told him in private

d *(= nicht gesetzlich)* **~ versichert sein** to be privately insured; **~ behandelt werden** to have private treatment; **~ liegen** to be in a private ward

Pri|vat- *in cpds* private; **Pri|vat|ad|res|se** F private *or* home address; **Pri|vat|an|ge|le|gen|heit** F private matter; **das ist eine reine ~** that's a purely *or* strictly private matter; **das ist meine ~** that's my own business, that's a private matter; **Pri|vat|an|le|ger(in)** M(F) *(St Ex)* private investor; **Pri|vat|aus|ga|ben** PL personal expenses *pl*; **Pri|vat|be|sitz** M private property; **viele Gemälde sind** *or* **befinden sich in ~** many paintings are privately owned *or* are in private ownership; **in ~ befindliche Grundstücke** privately owned land; **Pri|vat|de|tek|tiv(in)** M(F) private detective *or* investigator *or* eye *(inf)*; **Pri|vat|do|zent(in)** M(F) outside lecturer; **Pri|vat|ei|gen|tum** NT private property; **Pri|vat|fern|se|hen** NT commercial television; **Pri|vat|funk** M commercial broadcasting; **Pri|vat|ge|brauch** M private use, personal use; **die sind für den ~** they're for your own (personal) use; **Pri|vat|ge|lehr|te(r)** MF *decl as adj* scholar *(working for himself/herself)*; **Pri|vat|ge|spräch** NT private conversation *or* talk; *(am Telefon)* private call; **Pri|vat|grund|stück** NT private property

Pri|va|ti|er [privaˈtieː] M -s, -s *(dated)* man of independent *or* private means

Pri|vat-: **Pri|vat|ini|ti|a|ti|ve** F private initiative; **Pri|vat|in|te|res|se** NT private interest

pri|va|ti|sie|ren [privatiˈziːrən] *ptp* **privatisiert** VT to privatize VI to live on a private income *or* on independent means

Pri|va|ti|sie|rung F -, -en privatization

Pri|vat-: **Pri|vat|kla|ge** F private action *or* suit; **Pri|vat|klä|ger(in)** M(F) private litigant; **Pri|vat|kli|nik** F private clinic *or* hospital, nursing home; **Pri|vat|kun|de** M, **Pri|vat|kun|din** F private customer; **Pri|vat|le|ben** NT private life; **Pri|vat|leh|rer(in)** M(F) private tutor; **Pri|vat|mann** M *pl* **-leute** private person *or* individual; **Pri|vat|ma|schi|ne** F *(Privatflugzeug)* private plane *or* aircraft; **Pri|vat|mit|tel** PL private means *pl*; **Pri|vat|num|mer** F *(= Telefonnummer)* private number, home number; **Pri|vat|pa|ti|ent(in)** M(F) private patient; **Pri|vat|per|son** F private individual *or* person; **Pri|vat|quar|tier** NT private quarters *pl*; **Pri|vat|recht** NT private *or* civil law; **pri|vat|recht|lich** ADJ *Klage, Verfahren* private *or* civil law *attr*; *Gesellschaft* private ADV **~ ist die Frage ganz eindeutig** the matter is quite clear in private *or* civil law; **Pri|vat|ren|te** F private pension scheme; **Pri|vat|sa|che** F private matter; **das ist meine ~** that's my own business, that's a private matter; **das ist reine ~** that's a purely *or* strictly private matter; **Religion ist ~** religion is a private matter; **Pri|vat|schu|le** F private school; *(= Eliteschule auch)* ≈ public school *(Brit)*; **Pri|vat|se|kre|tär(in)** M(F) private secretary; **Pri|vat|sek|tor** M private sector; **Pri|vat|un|ter|neh|men** NT private enterprise; **Pri|vat|un|ter|richt** M private tuition; **Pri|vat|ver|gnü|gen** NT *(inf)* private pleasure; **Pri|vat|ver|mö|gen** NT private fortune; **pri|vat|ver|si|chert** ADJ → **privat ADV d**; **Pri|vat|ver|si|che|rung** F private insurance; **Pri|vat|vor|sor|ge** F *(fürs Alter)* private pension scheme; *(für die Gesundheit)* private health insurance scheme; **Pri|vat|weg** M private way; **Pri|vat|wirt|schaft** F private industry; **Pri|vat|woh|nung** F private flat *(Brit) or* apartment; *(Haus)* private house

Pri|vi|leg [priviˈleːk] NT -(e)s, -gien *or* -e [-giən, -gə] privilege

pri|vi|le|gie|ren [privileˈgiːrən] *ptp* **privilegiert** VT to favour *(Brit)*, to favor *(US)*, to privilege; **die privilegierten Schichten** the privileged classes; **eine privilegierte Stellung innehaben** to hold a privileged position; **steuerlich privilegiert sein** to enjoy tax privileges

pro [proː] PREP per; **~ Tag/Stunde** a *or* per day/hour; **~ Jahr** per annum *(form)*, a *or* per year; **~ Quadratmeter** a *or* per square metre *(Brit) or* meter *(US)*; **~ Person** per person; **~ Kopf** per person, per capita *(form)*; **~ Nase** *(inf)* a *or* per head; **~ Stück** each, apiece; **~ Kopf und Tag** per person per day

Pro [proː] NT **(das) ~ und (das) Kontra** the pros and cons *pl*

pro|ak|tiv [proakˈtiːf] ADJ proactive ADV **~ handeln** to be proactive

Pro|band [proˈbant] M -en, -en [-dn], **Pro|ban|din** [-ˈbandɪn] F -, -nen guinea pig

pro|bat [proˈbaːt] ADJ *no adv (dated)* tried and tested

Pro|be [ˈproːbə] F -, -n **a** *(= Prüfung)* test; **eine ~ auf etw** *(acc)* **machen** to test sth, to do a test on sth; **die ~ (auf eine Rechnung) machen** to check a calculation; **wenn du die ~ gemacht hättest** if you'd checked it, if you'd given it a check; **ein Beamter auf ~** a probationary civil servant; **er ist auf ~ angestellt** he's employed for a probationary period; **jdn/etw auf ~ nehmen** to take sb/sth on trial; **~ fahren** to go for a test drive *or* run; **ein Auto ~ fahren** to test-drive a car; **jdn/etw auf die ~ stellen** to put sb/sth to the test, to try sb/sth; **meine Geduld wurde auf eine harte ~ gestellt** my patience was sorely tried; **jdn/etw einer ~ unterziehen** to subject sb/sth to a test; **zur ~** for a trial, to try out → **Exempel**

b *(Theat, Mus)* rehearsal; **~n abhalten** to rehearse, to hold rehearsals

c *(= Teststück, Beispiel)* sample; **er gab eine ~ seines Könnens** he showed what he could do

Pro|be-: **Pro|be|ab|zug** M proof; **Pro|be|alarm** M practice alarm; **heute ist ~** the alarms will be tested today; **Pro|be|an|ge|bot** NT trial offer; **Pro|be|ar|beit** F test *or* specimen piece, trial work *no pl*; **Pro|be|be|las|tung** F stress test; **Pro|be|boh|rung** F test drill, probe; **Pro|be|druck** M *pl* **-drucke** trial print; **Pro|be|ex|emp|lar** NT specimen (copy); **pro|be|fah|ren** △ VT VI → **Probe a**; **Pro|be|fahrt** F test drive *or* run; *(mit Boot)* trial sail; *(mit Fahrrad)* test ride; **eine ~ machen** to go for a test drive *etc*; **Pro|be|flug** M test flight; **pro|be|hal|ber** ADV for a test; **Pro|be|jahr** NT probationary year; **Pro|be|lauf** M test *or* trial run; *(Sport)* practice run; **Pro|be|leh|rer(in)** M(F) *(Aus)* probationary teacher

pro|ben [ˈproːbn] VTI to rehearse

Pro|ben-: **Pro|ben|ar|beit** F rehearsals *pl*; **Pro|ben|ent|nah|me** F sampling

Pro|be-: **Pro|be|num|mer** F trial copy; **Pro|be|pa|ckung** F sample pack; **Pro|be|sei|te** F specimen *or* sample page; **Pro|be|sen|dung** F *(von Ware)* sample pack; **Pro|be|stück** NT sample, specimen; **pro|be|wei|se** ADV on a trial basis; **ich habe mir ~ einen anderen Kaffee gekauft** I've bought another kind of coffee to try (out); **Pro|be|zeit** F probationary *or* trial period

pro|bie|ren [pro'bi:rən] *ptp* **probiert** VT **a** (= *versuchen*) to try, to have a go *(Brit)* *or* try at; (= *prüfen*) to try (out), to test; **~ Sie es noch mal!** try (it) again!, have another go *(Brit)* *or* try!; **lass (es) mich mal ~!** let me try!, let me have a go *(Brit)* *or* a try!
b (= *kosten*) *Speisen, Getränke* to try, to taste, to sample
c (= *proben*) to rehearse
VI **a** (= *versuchen*) to try, to have a go *(Brit)* *or* a try; **Kinder lernen durch Probieren** children learn by trial and error; **Probieren geht über Studieren** *(Prov)* the proof of the pudding is in the eating *(Prov)*
b (= *kosten*) to have a taste, to try; **probier mal** try some, have a taste
c (= *proben*) to rehearse

Pro|bie|rer [pro'bi:rɐ] M **-s, -**, **Pro|bie|re|rin** [-ərɪn] F **-, -nen** taster

Pro|bier|glas [pro'bi:ɐ-] NT **a** *(zum Kosten)* taster, tasting glass **b** (= *Reagenzglas*) test tube

Prob|lem [pro'ble:m] ✪ 38.3, 44.1, 53.1, 53.2, 53.3 NT **-s, -e** problem; **vor einem ~ stehen** to be faced *or* confronted with a problem; **das wird zum ~** it's becoming (something of) a problem; **~e wälzen** to turn problems over in one's mind

Prob|le|ma|tik [proble'ma:tɪk] F **-, -en** **a** (= *Schwierigkeit, Problem*) problem, difficulty (+*gen* with); **die ~ der modernen Soziologie** the problems of modern sociology **b** (= *Fragwürdigkeit*) questionability, problematic nature

prob|le|ma|tisch [proble'ma:tɪʃ] ADJ problematic; (= *fragwürdig*) questionable

Prob|lem-: **Prob|lem|be|hand|lung** F *(Comput)* troubleshooting; **Prob|lem|be|wusst|sein** NT appreciation of the difficulties *or* problem; **Prob|lem|fall** M problem (case), problematic case; **Prob|lem|kind** NT problem child; **Prob|lem|kreis** M problem area; **prob|lem|los** ADJ trouble-free, problem-free ADV without any problems; **~ ablaufen** to go smoothly, to go without any problems; **prob|lem|ori|en|tiert** ADJ *(auch Comput)* problem-orientated; **Prob|lem|stel|lung** F problem; **Prob|lem|stück** NT problem play; **Prob|lem|zo|ne** F problem area

Pro|ce|de|re [pro:'tse:dərə] NT **-, -** *(geh)* proceedings *pl*

Pro|duct-Place|ment ['prɔdakt'ple:smənt] NT **-s, -s**, **Pro|duct|place|ment** NT **-s, -s** product placement

Pro|dukt [pro'dʊkt] NT **-(e)s, -e** *(lit, fig)* product; **landwirtschaftliche ~e** agricultural produce *no pl* *or* products; **das ~ aus 2 mal 2** the product of 2 times 2; **ein ~ seiner Phantasie** a figment of his imagination

Pro|dukt|be|schrei|bung F product description

Pro|duk|ten-: **Pro|duk|ten|han|del** M produce business *or* trade; **Pro|duk|ten|markt** M produce market

Pro|dukt|haf|tung F product liability

Pro|duk|ti|on [prodʊk'tsio:n] F **-, -en** production

Pro|duk|ti|ons- *in cpds* production; **Pro|duk|ti|ons|ab|lauf** M production process *or* sequence; **Pro|duk|ti|ons|an|la|gen** PL production plant; **Pro|duk|ti|ons|aus|fall** M loss of production; **Pro|duk|ti|ons|be|schrän|kung** F limitation of production; **Pro|duk|ti|ons|ge|nos|sen|schaft** F *(esp DDR)* collective, cooperative; **landwirtschaftliche ~** collective farm; **~ des Handwerks** craftsmen's cooperative; **Pro|duk|ti|ons|kos|ten** PL production costs *pl*; **Pro|duk|ti|ons|kraft** F production capacity; **Pro|duk|ti|ons|leis|tung** F (potential) output, production capacity; **Pro|duk|ti|ons|lei|ter(in)** M(F), **Pro|duk|ti|ons|ma|na|ger(in)** M(F) production manager; **pro|duk|ti|ons|mä|ßig** ADJ production *attr* ADV in terms of production; **Pro|duk|ti|ons|men|ge** F output; **Pro|duk|ti|ons|mit|tel** PL means of production *pl*; **pro|duk|ti|ons|reif** ADJ ready to go into production; **Pro|duk|ti|ons|rei|fe** F **vom Entwurf bis zur ~** from conception to production; **dieser Artikel hat die ~ noch nicht erreicht** this article is not yet ready to go into production; **Pro|duk|ti|ons|rück|gang** M drop in production; **Pro|duk|ti|ons|stand** M production level; **Pro|duk|ti|ons|stät|te** F production centre *(Brit)* *or* center *(US)*; **Pro|duk|ti|ons|zweig** M line of production

pro|duk|tiv [prodʊk'ti:f] ADJ *Autor, Arbeit etc* productive

Pro|duk|ti|vi|tät [prodʊktivi'tɛ:t] F **-, -en** productivity

Pro|duk|ti|vi|täts|stei|ge|rung F increase *or* rise in productivity, increased productivity

Pro|duk|tiv|kräf|te PL *(Sociol)* productive forces *pl*, forces of production *pl*

Pro|duk|tiv|ver|mö|gen NT *(Econ)* productive assets *pl*

Pro|dukt-: **Pro|dukt|ma|na|ger(in)** M(F) product manager; **Pro|dukt|pa|let|te** F product spectrum *or* range, range of products; **Pro|dukt|pi|rat** M product pirate; **Pro|dukt|pi|ra|te|rie** F product piracy

Pro|du|zent [produ'tsɛnt] M **-en, -en**, **Pro|du|zen|tin** [-'tsɛntɪn] F **-, -nen** producer

pro|du|zie|ren [produ'tsi:rən] *ptp* **produziert** VT **a** *auch vi* to produce; **~des Gewerbe** production industry **b** *(inf: = hervorbringen) Lärm* to make; *Entschuldigung* to come up with *(inf)*; *Romane* to churn out *(inf)*; **wer hat denn das produziert?** who's responsible for that? VR *(pej)* to show off

Prof [prɔf] M **-s, -s** *(Univ inf)* prof *(inf)*

Prof. *abbr von* **Professor**

Pro Fa|mi|lia ['pro fa'mi:lia] F **- -**, *no pl* *family planning organization*

pro|fan [pro'fa:n] ADJ (= *weltlich*) secular, profane; (= *gewöhnlich*) mundane

Pro|fan|bau M *pl* **-bauten** secular building

pro|fa|nie|ren [profa'ni:rən] *ptp* **profaniert** VT *(form)* to profane

Pro|fes|si|on [profɛ'sio:n] F **-, -en** *(old, form)* profession; **eine ~ ausüben** to ply a trade *(old)*, to follow a profession *(form)*

Pro|fes|si|o|nal [pro'fɛʃənəl] M **-s, -s** professional

Pro|fes|si|o|na|li|tät [profɛsionali'tɛ:t] F **-**, *no pl* professionalism

pro|fes|si|o|nell [profɛsio'nɛl] ADJ professional; **eine Professionelle** *(inf)* a pro *(inf)*, a tart *(inf)* ADV professionally

Pro|fes|sor [pro'fɛso:ɐ] M **-s, Professoren** [-'so:rən] **a** (= *Hochschulprofessor*) professor; **ordentlicher ~ für Philosophie** (full) professor of philosophy; **außerordentlicher ~** professor not holding a chair, ≈ associate professor *(US)*; **Herr/Frau ~!** Professor!; **Herr ~ Vogel** Professor Vogel **b** *(Aus, S Ger: = Gymnasiallehrer)* teacher; **Herr ~!** Sir!; **Frau ~!** Miss!

pro|fes|so|ral [profɛso'ra:l] *(geh)* ADJ professorial ADV like a professor, professorially *(pej)*

Pro|fes|so|ren|schaft [profɛ'so:rənʃaft] F **-, -en** professors *pl*

Pro|fes|so|rin [profɛ'so:rɪn] F **-, -nen** **a** (= *Hochschulprofessorin*) professor **b** *(Aus, S Ger: = Gymnasiallehrerin)* teacher

Pro|fes|sur [profɛ'su:ɐ] F **-, -en** chair *(für* in, of*)*

Pro|fi ['pro:fi] M **-s, -s** *(inf)* pro *(inf)*

Pro|fi|kil|ler(in) M(F) professional *or* contract killer

Pro|fil [pro'fi:l] NT **-s, -e** **a** *(von Gesicht)* profile; *(Archit)* elevation; *(fig: = Ansehen)* image; **im ~** in profile; **~ haben** *or* **besitzen** *(fig)* to have a (distinctive or personal) image; **die Partei hat in den letzten Jahren mehr ~ bekommen** over the last few years the party has sharpened its image; **dadurch hat er an ~ gewonnen/verloren** that improved/damaged his image; **psychisches ~** state of mind **b** *(von Reifen, Schuhsohle)* tread **c** (= *Querschnitt*) cross section; (= *Längsschnitt*) vertical section; *(Geog)* (vertical) section; *(Aviat)* wing section; *(fig: = Skizze)* profile; **im ~** in section

Pro|fi|la|ger NT *(Sport inf)* **ins ~ (über)wechseln** to turn *or* go professional; **aus dem ~ zurückkehren** to give up being a professional, to give up professional sport

pro|fi|lie|ren [profi'li:rən] *ptp* **profiliert** VT (= *mit Profil versehen*) *Schuhsohlen, Reifen* to put a tread on; *Blech* to profile; *(fig: = scharf umreißen)* to give a distinctive image to VR (= *sich ein Image geben*) to create a distinctive image for oneself; (= *Besonderes leisten*) to distinguish oneself; **er will sich akademisch/politisch** *etc* **~** he wants to make a name for himself academically/in politics *etc*, he wants to make his mark academically/in politics *etc*; **sie hat sich als Expertin für Lexikografie profiliert** she made a name for herself as an expert in lexicography

pro|fi|liert [profi'li:ɐt] ADJ *Schuhe, Reifen* with a tread, treaded; *(fig: = scharf umrissen)* clear-cut *no adv*; *(fig: = hervorstechend)* distinctive; *Persönlichkeit* prominent; **ein ~er Politiker/Wissenschaftler** a politician/scientist who has made his mark

Pro|fi|lie|rung F **-**, *no pl* (= *das Sich-Profilieren*) making one's mark *no art*

Pro|fi|li|ga F *(Sport)* professional league; **die Profiligen** the professional leagues, the pros *(inf)*, the big *or* major leagues *(US)*

Pro|fil-: **pro|fil|los** ADJ *Politiker, Firma* lacking any distinct image; *Sohle, Reifen* treadless; **Pro|fil|neu|ro|se** F *(hum)* neurosis about one's image, image neurosis; **Pro|fil|soh|le** F sole with a tread, treaded sole; **Pro|fil|stahl** M sectional steel

Pro|fi-: **Pro|fi|sport** M professional sport *or* sports *pl* *(US)*; **Pro|fi|sport|ler(in)** M(F) professional sportsperson *or* sportsman/-woman; *(in Leichtathletik)* professional athlete

Pro|fit [pro'fi:t, pro'fɪt] M **-(e)s, -e** profit; **~ aus etw schlagen** *or* **ziehen** *(lit)* to make a profit from *or* out of sth; *(fig)* to reap the benefits from sth, to profit from sth; **~ machen** to make a profit; **~ bringend** *(adjektivisch)* profitable; *(adverbial)* profitably; **den/keinen ~ von etw haben** to profit/not to profit from sth; **ohne/mit ~ arbeiten** to work unprofitably/profitably

pro|fi|ta|bel [profi'ta:bl] ADJ profitable

Pro|fi|ta|bi|li|tät F **-**, *no pl* profitability

Pro|fit-: **pro|fit|brin|gend** △ ADJ → **Profit**; **Pro|fit|cen|ter** ['prɔfɪtsɛntɐ] NT *(Comm)* profit centre *(Brit)* *or* center *(US)*; **Pro|fit|den|ken** NT profit orientation; **Pro|fit|gier** F greed for profit, profit lust; **pro|fit|gie|rig** ADJ greedy for profit, profit-greedy

pro|fi|tie|ren [profi'ti:rən] *ptp* **profitiert** VTI *(von* from, by*)* to profit; *(fig auch)* to gain; **viel/etwas ~** *(lit)* to make a large profit/to make something of a profit; *(fig)* to profit greatly/somewhat; **davon hat er wenig profitiert** *(lit)* he didn't make much of a profit from it; *(fig)* he didn't profit much *or* didn't gain a great deal from it; **dabei kann ich nur ~** I only stand to gain from it, I can't lose; **und was profitierst du dabei** *or* **davon?** what do you stand to gain from *or* by it?

Pro|fit-: **Pro|fit|jä|ger(in)** M(F), **Pro|fit|ma|cher(in)** M(F) *(inf)* profiteer; **Pro|fit|ma|che|rei** [-maxə'rai] F **-, -en** *(inf)* profiteering; **Pro|fit|ma|xi|mie|rung** F maximization of profit(s); **Pro|fit|stre|ben** NT profit seeking

pro for|ma [pro 'fɔrma] ADV as a matter of form, for appearance's sake

Pro-for|ma-Rech|nung [pro'fɔrma-] F pro forma invoice

pro|fund [pro'fʊnt] *(geh)* ADJ profound, deep; **er ist ein ~er Kenner** +*gen* he has a profound *or* deep knowledge of ... ADV profoundly; ~ **recherchiert** thoroughly researched

Prog|no|se [pro'gno:zə] F -, -n prediction, prognosis; *(= Wetterprognose)* forecast; **eine ~ stellen/wagen** to give *or* make/venture a prediction *or* prognosis; **genetische ~** genetic prognosis

prog|nos|tisch [pro'gnɔstɪʃ] ADJ prognostic

prog|nos|ti|zie|ren [prognɔsti'tsi:rən] *ptp* **prognostiziert** VT to predict, to prognosticate *(form)*

Pro|gramm [pro'gram] NT -s, -e **a** programme *(Brit)*, program *(US)*; *(= Tagesordnung)* agenda; *(TV: = Sender)* channel; *(= Sendefolge)* program(me)s *pl*; *(= gedrucktes Radio-Programm)* program(me) guide; *(= gedrucktes TV-Programm)* programme guide *(Brit)*, TV guide; *(= Programmheft)* program(me); *(= Verlagsprogramm)* list; *(beim Pferderennen)* card; *(= Kollektion, Sortiment)* range; **nach ~** as planned; **auf dem ~ stehen** to be on the program(me)/agenda; **ein ~ für das nächste Quartal machen** to work out a programme for the next quarter; **für heute habe ich schon ein ~** I've already got something planned for today; **ein volles ~ haben** to have a full schedule; **unser ~ für den heutigen Abend** *(TV, Rad)* our program(me)s for this evening; **durch das ~ führt XY** the program(me) is presented by XY **b** *(Comput)* program

Pro|gramm|an|bie|ter M *(TV)* programme *(Brit) or* program *(US)* maker

Pro|gram|ma|tik F -, *no pl* aims and objectives *pl*

pro|gram|ma|tisch [progra'ma:tɪʃ] ADJ programmatic ADV **der Titel ist ~ zu verstehen** the title is the central theme of the programme *(Brit) or* program *(US)*; **der Sprecher der Partei hat ~ verkündet, dass dieser Punkt revidiert würde** the party spokesman announced that this point was to be revised in their new programme *(Brit) or* program *(US)*

Pro|gramm-: **Pro|gramm|da|tei** F *(Comput)* executable file, program file; **Pro|gramm|di|rek|tor(in)** M(F) *(TV, Rad)* director of programmes *(Brit) or* programs *(US)*; **Pro|gramm|feh|ler** M *(Comput)* program error, bug; **Pro|gramm|fol|ge** F order of programmes *(Brit) or* program *(US)*; *(Theat)* order of acts; **Pro|gramm|fül|ler** M *(inf)* (programme *(Brit) or* program *(US)*) filler; **pro|gramm|ge|mäß** ADJ ADV according to plan *or* programme *(Brit) or* program *(US)*; **Pro|gramm|ge|stal|tung** F programme *(Brit) or* program *(US)* planning; **pro|gramm|ge|steu|ert** ADJ computer-controlled; **Pro|gramm|grup|pe** F *(Comput)* program group; **Pro|gramm|heft** NT programme *(Brit)*, program *(US)*; **Pro|gramm|hin|weis** M *(Rad, TV)* programme *(Brit) or* program *(US)* announcement; **wir bringen noch einige ~e für morgen** and now a look at some of tomorrow's programmes *(Brit) or* programs *(US)*

pro|gram|mier|bar ADJ programmable

pro|gram|mie|ren [progra'mi:rən] *ptp* **programmiert** VT **a** *auch vi* to programme *(Brit)*, to program *(US)*; *(Comput)* to program; *(fig: = konditionieren)* to programme *(Brit)*, to program *(US)*, to condition; **auf etw** *(acc)* **programmiert sein** *(fig)* to be geared *or* conditioned to sth; **programmiertes Lernen** program(m)ed learning **b** *(= entwerfen)* to draw up a programme *(Brit) or program (US)* for; *(= planen)* to schedule, to plan

Pro|gram|mie|rer [progra'mi:rɐ] M -s, -, **Pro|gram|mie|re|rin** [-ərɪn] F -, -nen programmer *(Brit)*, programer *(US)*

Pro|gram|mier|feh|ler M programming *(Brit) or* programing *(US)* error, bug

Pro|gram|mier|spra|che F programming *(Brit) or* programing *(US)* language

Pro|gram|mie|rung [progra'mi:rʊŋ] F -, -en programming *(Brit)*, programing *(US)*; *(fig auch)* conditioning

Pro|gramm-: **Pro|gramm|ki|no** NT arts *or* repertory *(US)* cinema; **Pro|gramm|mu|sik** F programme *(Brit) or* program *(US)* music; **Pro|gramm|platz** M *(TV, Rad)* programme *(Brit) or* program *(US)* slot; **Pro|gramm|punkt** M item on the agenda; *(TV)* programme *(Brit)*, program *(US)*; *(bei Show)* act; **Pro|gramm|spei|cher** M *(von CD-Spieler etc)* programmable memory; **Pro|gramm|über|sicht** F rundown of the programmes *(Brit) or* programs *(US)*

Programmusik △ F → **Programmmusik**

Pro|gramm-: **Pro|gramm|vor|schau** F preview *(für* of); *(Film)* trailer; **Pro|gramm|zeit|schrift** F *(TV)* programme *(Brit) or* TV guide; **Pro|gramm|zet|tel** M programme *(Brit)*, program *(US)*

Pro|gress [pro'grɛs] M -es, -e progress

Pro|gres|si|on [progrɛ'sio:n] F -, -en progression

pro|gres|siv [progrɛ'si:f] ADJ progressive ADV **a** *(= fortschrittlich)* progressively; **~ eingestellt sein** to be progressive **b** *(in Bezug auf Steuern)* **der Steuertarif ist ~ gestaltet** the tax rates are progressive

Pro|gym|na|si|um ['pro:-] NT secondary school *(for pupils up to 16)*

Pro|hi|bi|ti|on [prohibi'tsio:n] F -, -en Prohibition

Pro|jekt [pro'jɛkt] NT -(e)s, -e project

Pro|jekt|grup|pe F project team

pro|jek|tie|ren [projɛk'ti:rən] *ptp* **projektiert** VT *(= entwerfen)* to plan, to project, to lay plans for; *(= planen)* to project

Pro|jek|til [projɛk'ti:l] NT -s, -e *(form)* projectile

Pro|jek|ti|on [projɛk'tsio:n] F -, -en projection

Pro|jek|ti|ons-: **Pro|jek|ti|ons|ap|pa|rat** M projector; **Pro|jek|ti|ons|ebe|ne** F plane of projection; **Pro|jek|ti|ons|flä|che** F projection surface; **Pro|jek|ti|ons|lam|pe** F projection lamp; **Pro|jek|ti|ons|schirm** M projection screen

Pro|jekt|lei|ter(in) M(F) project leader

Pro|jek|tor [pro'jɛkto:ɐ] M -s, **Projektoren** [-'to:rən] projector

Pro|jekt|un|ter|richt M *(Sch)* project-based teaching

pro|ji|zie|ren [proji'tsi:rən] *ptp* **projiziert** VT to project

Pro|kla|ma|ti|on [proklama'tsio:n] F -, -en proclamation

pro|kla|mie|ren [prokla'mi:rən] *ptp* **proklamiert** VT to proclaim

Pro-Kopf- *in cpds* per capita; **Pro-Kopf-Ein|kom|men** NT per capita income; **Pro-Kopf-Ver|brauch** M per capita consumption

Pro|krus|tes|bett [pro'krʊstəs-] NT Procrustean bed

Pro|ku|ra [pro'ku:ra] F -, **Prokuren** [-rən] *(form)* procuration *(form)*, general commercial power of attorney; **jdm ~ erteilen** to grant sb general commercial power of attorney

Pro|ku|rist [proku'rɪst] M -en, -en, **Pro|ku|ris|tin** [-'rɪstɪn] F -, -nen holder of a general power of attorney, ≈ company secretary *(Brit)*

Pro|let [pro'le:t] M -en, -en, **Pro|le|tin** [-'le:tɪn] F -, -nen *(pej)* prole *(esp Brit pej inf)*, pleb *(pej inf)*

Pro|le|ta|ri|at [proleta'ria:t] NT -(e)s, *no pl* proletariat

Pro|le|ta|ri|er [prole'ta:riɐ] M -s, -, **Pro|le|ta|ri|e|rin** [-iərɪn] F -, -nen proletarian; **~ aller Länder, vereinigt euch!** workers of the world, unite!

pro|le|ta|risch [prole'ta:rɪʃ] ADJ proletarian

pro|le|ta|ri|sie|ren [proletari'zi:rən] *ptp* **proletarisiert** VT to proletarianize

pro|le|ten|haft *(pej)* ADJ plebeian *(pej)*, plebby *(Brit pej inf)* ADV like a pleb *(inf)*

Pro|le|tin [-'le:tɪn] F → **Prolet**

Proll [prɔl] M -s, -s → **Prolo**

prol|lig ['prɔlɪç] ADJ *(pej inf)* → **proletenhaft**

Pro|lo ['pro:lo] M -s, -s *(pej inf: = Prolet)* prole *(esp Brit inf)*, pleb *(pej inf)*

Pro|log [pro'lo:k] M -(e)s, -e [-gə] prologue *(Brit)*, prolog *(US)*

Pro|lon|ga|ti|on [prolɔŋga'tsio:n] F -, -en *(St Ex)* carryover

Pro|lon|ga|ti|ons- *(St Ex)*: **Pro|lon|ga|ti|ons|ge|schäft** NT carryover; **Pro|lon|ga|ti|ons|satz** M carryover rate

pro|lon|gie|ren [prolɔŋ'gi:rən] *ptp* **prolongiert** VT to prolong, to extend

PROM [prɔm] NT -(s), -s *(Comput) abbr von* **program(m)able read only memory** PROM

Pro|me|na|de [promə'na:də] F -, -n *(old: = Spaziergang)* promenade, constitutional *(old, hum)*; *(= Spazierweg)* promenade

Pro|me|na|den-: **Pro|me|na|den|deck** NT promenade deck; **Pro|me|na|den|kon|zert** NT promenade concert; **Pro|me|na|den|mi|schung** F *(hum)* mongrel, crossbreed

pro|me|nie|ren [promə'ni:rən] *ptp* **promeniert** VI *aux sein (geh)* to promenade

pro|me|the|isch [prome'te:ɪʃ] ADJ *(liter)* Promethean *(liter)*

Pro|me|theus [pro'me:tɔys] M -' Prometheus

Pro|me|thi|um [pro'me:tiʊm] NT -s, *no pl (abbr* **Pm***)* promethium

Pro|mi ['pro:mi] M -s, -s *or f* -, -s *(inf)* VIP; *(= Politiker)* star politician

Pro|mil|le [pro'mɪlə] NT -(s), - thousandth; *(inf: = Alkoholspiegel)* alcohol level; **er hat zu viel ~ (im Blut)** he has too much alcohol in his blood, his alcohol level is too high; **0,5 ~ (Alkohol im Blut)** a blood-alcohol level of 50 millilitres *(Brit)*, a blood-alcohol content of 0.5 *(US)*

Pro|mil|le-: **Pro|mil|le|gren|ze** F legal (alcohol) limit; **Pro|mil|le|mes|ser** M -s, - Breathalyzer®

pro|mi|nent [promi'nɛnt] ADJ prominent

Pro|mi|nen|ten- *in cpds* VIP; *(inf: = vornehm)* posh; **Pro|mi|nen|ten|her|ber|ge** F *(inf)* posh hotel *(inf)*; **Pro|mi|nen|ten|suite** F VIP suite

Pro|mi|nen|te(r) [promi'nɛntə] MF *decl as adj* prominent figure, VIP

Pro|mi|nenz [promi'nɛnts] F - VIPs *pl*, prominent figures *pl*

pro|misk [pro'mɪsk] ADJ promiscuous

Pro|mis|ku|i|tät [promɪskui'tɛ:t] F -, *no pl* promiscuity

Pro|mo|ter [pro'mo:tɐ] M -s, -, **Pro|mo|te|rin** [-ərɪn] F -, -nen promoter

Pro|mo|ti|on [promo'tsio:n] F -, -en **a** *(Univ)* doctorate, PhD; *(Aus: = Feier)* doctoral degree ceremony; **während seiner ~** while he was doing his doctorate *or* PhD; **nach seiner ~** after he got his PhD; **jds ~ befürworten** to recommend sb for a doctorate; **das Studium mit einer ~ abschließen** to gain a doctorate *or* PhD **b** *(Sw Sch: = Versetzung)* moving up

Pro|mo|tion [prə'mo:ʃən] F -, -s *(Comm)* promotion

Pro|mo|ti|ons|ord|nung F *(Univ)* doctoral degree regulations *pl*

Pro|mo|tor [pro'mo:to:ɐ] M -s, **Promotoren** [-'to:rən], **Pro|mo|to|rin** [-'to:rɪn] F -, -nen promoter

pro|mo|vie|ren [promo'vi:rən] *ptp* **promoviert** VI to do a doctorate *or* a doctor's degree *or* a PhD *(über +acc* in); *(= Doktorwürde erhalten)* to receive a doctorate *etc* VT to confer a doctorate *or* the degree of doctor on

prompt [prɔmpt] ADJ prompt ADV promptly; *(= natürlich)* naturally, of course

Prompt M -(s), -s *(Comput: = Eingabeaufforderung)* prompt

Prompt|heit F -, *no pl* promptness

Pro|no|men [pro'no:mən] NT -s, - *or* **Pronomina** [-mina] pronoun

pro|no|mi|nal [pronomi'na:l] ADJ pronominal

Pro|no|mi|nal-: **Pro|no|mi|nal|ad|jek|tiv** NT pronominal adjective; **Pro|no|mi|nal|ad|verb** NT pronominal adverb

pro|non|ciert [pronõ'si:ɐt] *(geh)* ADJ *(= deutlich)* distinct, clear; *(= nachdrücklich)* definite ADV *(= deutlich)* clearly; *(= nachdrücklich)* definitely

Pro|pä|deu|tik [propɛ'dɔytɪk] F -, -en preparatory course

pro|pä|deu|tisch [propɛ'dɔytɪʃ] ADJ preparatory

Pro|pa|gan|da [propa'ganda] F -, *no pl* propaganda; *(dated: = Werbung)* publicity; **~ für/gegen etw machen** *or* **betreiben** to make propaganda for/against sth; **~ mit etw machen** to make propaganda out of sth; **das ist (doch) alles nur ~** that's just (so much) propaganda

Pro|pa|gan|da-: **Pro|pa|gan|da|ap|pa|rat** M propaganda machine; **Pro|pa|gan|da|feld|zug** M propaganda campaign; *(= Werbefeldzug)* publicity campaign; **Pro|pa|gan|da|rum|mel** M *(inf)* deluge *or* torrent *or* flood of propaganda; **pro|pa|gan|da|wirk|sam** ADJ which is effective *or* good propaganda ADV **etw ~ nutzen** to use sth as propaganda; **er hat ihre Außenpolitik ~ angegriffen** the way he attacked her foreign policy was strictly for propaganda; **etw ~ ausnutzen** to make effective propaganda out of sth

Pro|pa|gan|dist [propagan'dɪst] M -en, -en, **Pro|pa|gan|dis|tin** [-'dɪstɪn] F -, -nen **a** propagandist **b** *(Comm)* demonstrator

pro|pa|gan|dis|tisch [propagan'dɪstɪʃ] ADJ propagandist(ic) ADV as propaganda; **etw ~ ausnutzen** to use sth as propaganda

pro|pa|gie|ren [propa'gi:rən] *ptp* **propagiert** VT to propagate

Pro|pan [pro'pa:n] NT -s, *no pl* propane

Pro|pan|gas NT, *no pl* propane gas

Pro|pel|ler [pro'pɛlɐ] M -s, - *(= Luftschraube)* propeller, prop *(inf)*, airscrew; *(= Schiffsschraube)* propeller, screw

Pro|pel|ler-: **Pro|pel|ler|an|trieb** M propeller drive; **ein Flugzeug mit ~** a propeller-driven plane; **Pro|pel|ler|flug|zeug** NT, **Pro|pel|ler|ma|schi|ne** F propeller-driven plane; **Pro|pel|ler|tur|bi|ne** F turboprop

pro|per ['prɔpɐ] ADJ *(inf)* trim, neat, (clean and) tidy

Pro|phet [pro'fe:t] M -en, -en prophet; **der ~ gilt nichts in seinem Vaterland** *or* **im eigenen Lande** *(Prov)* a prophet is without honour *(Brit)* *or honor (US)* in his own country *(Prov)*; **beim Barte des ~en!** *(usu hum)* honest to God! *(inf)* → **Berg**

Pro|phe|tie [profe'ti:] F -, -n [-'ti:ən] prophecy

Pro|phe|tin [pro'fe:tɪn] F -, -nen prophetess

pro|phe|tisch [pro'fe:tɪʃ] ADJ *Worte, Gabe* prophetic ADV prophetically

pro|phe|zei|en [profe'tsaiən] *ptp* **prophezeit** VT to prophesy; *(= vorhersagen auch)* to predict, to foretell; **jdm eine glänzende Zukunft ~** to predict a brilliant future for sb; **Kassandra hat den Trojanern ihren Untergang prophezeit** Cassandra prophesied that the Trojans would meet their downfall; **das kann ich dir ~!** I can promise you that!

Pro|phe|zei|ung F -, -en prophecy

Pro|phy|lak|ti|kum [profy'laktikʊm] NT -s, **Prophylaktika** [-ka] *(Med)* prophylactic; *(= Präservativ)* contraceptive

pro|phy|lak|tisch [profy'laktɪʃ] ADJ prophylactic *(form)*, preventative ADV as a preventative measure, as a precaution

Pro|phy|la|xe [profy'laksə] F -, -n prophylaxis

Pro|por|ti|on [propɔr'tsio:n] F -, -en proportion

pro|por|ti|o|nal [propɔrtsio'na:l] ADJ proportional, proportionate; **umgekehrt ~** *(Math)* in inverse proportion ADV proportionally; **die Steuern steigen ~ mit dem Einkommen** *or* **zum Einkommen** taxes increase in proportion to *or* proportionally to income

Pro|por|ti|o|nal-: **Pro|por|ti|o|nal|druck** M, *no pl* proportional printing; **Pro|por|ti|o|nal|schrift** F proportionally spaced font; **Pro|por|ti|o|nal|zo|ne** F *(Fin)* flat rate tax bracket

pro|por|ti|o|niert [propɔrtsio'ni:ɐt] ADJ proportioned

Pro|porz [pro'pɔrts] M -es, -e proportional representation *no art*

Prop|pen ['prɔpn] M -s, - *(N Ger)* **a** *(= Pfropfen)* stopper; *(= Kork, Sektpropfen)* cork; *(von Fass, Korbflasche)* bung **b** *(inf: Mensch)* dumpling *(inf)*

prop|pe(n)|voll ADJ *(inf)* jam-packed *(inf)*

Propst [pro:pst] M -(e)s, ⸚e ['prø:pstə], **Pröps|tin** ['prø:pstɪn] F -, -nen provost

Pro|rek|tor ['pro:rɛkto:ɐ, 'pro:'rɛkto:ɐ] M, **Pro|rek|to|rin** [-'to:rɪn] F *(old Sch)* deputy rector; *(Univ)* deputy vice chancellor

Pro|sa ['pro:za] F -, *no pl* prose; *(fig)* prosaicness

Pro|sa|dich|tung F prose writing

Pro|sa|i|ker [pro'za:ikɐ] M -s, -, **Pro|sa|i|ke|rin** [-ərɪn] F -, -nen **a** *(old: = Prosaist)* prose writer **b** *(fig: = nüchterner Mensch)* prosaic person

pro|sa|isch [pro'za:ɪʃ] ADJ **a** *(= nüchtern)* prosaic **b** *(Liter)* prose *attr*, prosaic *(form)* ADV **a** *(= nüchtern)* prosaically **b** *(Liter)* **ein Thema ~ bearbeiten** to treat a subject in prose

Pro|sa|ist [proza'ɪst] M -en, -en, **Pro|sa|is|tin** [-'ɪstɪn] F -, -nen, **Pro|sa|schrift|stel|ler(in)** M(F) prosewriter

Pro|se|lyt [proze'ly:t] M -en, -en, **Pro|se|ly|tin** [-'ly:tɪn] F -, -nen *(liter)* proselyte; **~en machen** to proselytize

Pro|se|mi|nar ['pro:-] NT *introductory seminar course for students in their first and second year*

pro|sit ['pro:zɪt] INTERJ your health; **~ Neujahr!** Happy New Year!, (here's to) the New Year!

Pro|sit ['pro:zɪt] NT -s, -s toast; **ein ~ der Köchin!** here's to the cook!; **ein ~ auf die Treue** there's to *or* let's drink to loyalty; **auf jdn ein ~ ausbringen** to toast sb, to drink to sb, to drink sb's health; **sie rief mir ein ~ zu** she called out "cheers" to me

Pro|so|die [prozo'di:] F -, -n [-'di:ən] prosody

pro|so|disch [pro'zo:dɪʃ] ADJ prosodic

Pros|pekt [pro'spɛkt] M -(e)s, -e **a** *(= Reklameschrift)* brochure, pamphlet (+*gen* about); *(= Werbezettel)* leaflet; *(= Verzeichnis)* catalogue *(Brit)*, catalog *(US)* **b** *(= Ansicht)* view, prospect *(old)* **c** *(Theat)* backdrop, backcloth *(Brit)*

pros|pek|tie|ren [prospɛk'ti:rən] *ptp* **prospektiert** VT to prospect (in)

pros|pek|tiv [prospɛk'ti:f] ADJ prospective

Pros|pekt|ma|te|ri|al NT brochures *pl*, pamphlets *pl*, literature

pros|pe|rie|ren [prospe'ri:rən] *ptp* **prosperiert** VI *(geh)* to prosper

Pros|pe|ri|tät [prosperi'tɛ:t] F -, *no pl* *(geh)* prosperity

prost [pro:st] INTERJ cheers, cheerio *(Brit)*; *(hum: beim Niesen)* bless you; **na denn ~!** *(= Prosit)* cheers then!, bottoms up! *(hum inf)*; *(iro inf)* that's just great *(inf) or* swell *(esp US dated inf)*; **~ Neujahr!** *(inf)* Happy New Year!, (here's to) the New Year! → **Mahlzeit**

Pros|ta|ta ['prɔstata] F -, *no pl* prostate gland; *(inf: = Prostataleiden)* prostate

Pros|ta|ta|krebs M prostate cancer

pros|ten ['pro:stn] VI to say cheers

prös|ter|chen ['prø:stɐçən] INTERJ *(hum)* cheers, bottoms up *(hum inf)*

pros|ti|tu|ie|ren [prostitu'i:rən] *ptp* **prostituiert** VR *(lit, fig)* to prostitute oneself VT *(old)* to prostitute

Pros|ti|tu|ier|te(r) [prostitu'i:ɐtə] MF *decl as adj* prostitute

Pros|ti|tu|ti|on [prostitu'tsio:n] F -, -en prostitution

Pro|sze|ni|um [pro'stse:niʊm] NT -s, **Proszenien** [-niən] proscenium

Pro|tac|ti|ni|um [protak'ti:niʊm] NT -s, *no pl* *(abbr* **Pa***)* protactinium

Pro|ta|go|nist [protago'nɪst] M -en, -en, **Pro|ta|go|nis|tin** [-'nɪstɪn] F -, -nen *(lit, fig)* protagonist

Pro|te|gé [prote'ʒe:] M -s, -s protégé

pro|te|gie|ren [prote'ʒi:rən] *ptp* **protegiert** VT *Künstler, Persönlichkeit, Projekt* to sponsor; *Land, Regime* to support; **er wird vom Chef protegiert** he's the boss's protégé

Pro|te|in [prote'i:n] NT -s, -e protein

Pro|tek|ti|on [protɛk'tsio:n] F -, -en *(= Schutz)* protection; *(= Begünstigung)* patronage; **unter jds ~** *(dat)* **stehen** *(Schutz)* to be under sb's protection; *(Begünstigung)* to be under sb's patronage

Pro|tek|ti|o|nis|mus [protɛktsio'nɪsmʊs] M -, *no pl* **a** *(Econ)* protectionism **b** *(= Günstlingswirtschaft)* nepotism

pro|tek|ti|o|nis|tisch [protɛktsio'nɪstɪʃ] ADJ protectionist

Pro|tek|tor [pro'tɛkto:ɐ] M -s, **Protektoren** [-'to:rən], **Pro|tek|to|rin** [-'to:rɪn] F -, -nen *(old: = Beschützer)* protector; *(= Schirmherr)* patron

Pro|tek|to|rat [protɛkto'ra:t] NT -(e)s, -e *(= Schirmherrschaft)* patronage; *(= Schutzgebiet)* protectorate

Pro|test [pro'tɛst] M -(e)s, -e **a** protest; **(scharfen) ~ gegen jdn/etw erheben** to make a (strong) protest against sb/sth; **(gegen etw) ~ einlegen** to register a protest (about sth); **etw aus ~ tun** to do sth in protest *or* as a protest; **unter ~** protesting; *(gezwungen)* under protest; **ich machs, aber nur unter ~** I'm only doing it under protest **b** *(Fin)* protest; **~ mangels Annahme/Zahlung** protest for non-acceptance/ /non-payment; **einen Wechsel zu ~ gehen lassen** to protest a bill

Pro|test|ak|ti|on F protest

Pro|tes|tant [protɛs'tant] M -en, -en, **Pro|tes|tan|tin** [-'tantɪn] F -, -nen Protestant

pro|tes|tan|tisch [protɛs'tantɪʃ] ADJ Protestant ADV **~ denken** to have Protestant beliefs; **Kinder ~ erziehen** to raise one's children as Protestants; **~ heiraten** to be married in the Protestant church; **~ beerdigt werden** to be buried as a Protestant; **~ beeinflusst** influenced by Protestantism

Pro|tes|tan|tis|mus [protɛstan'tɪsmʊs] M -, *no pl* Protestantism

Pro|test-: **Pro|test|be|we|gung** F protest movement; **Pro|test|de|monst|ra|ti|on** F (protest) demonstration, demo *(inf)*; **Pro|test|ge|schrei** NT howls *(pl)* of protest; **Pro|test|hal|tung** F attitude of protest, rebellious attitude *or* stance

pro|tes|tie|ren [protɛs'ti:rən] *ptp* **protestiert** VI to protest *(gegen* against, about) VT *(Fin)* to protest

Pro|test|kund|ge|bung F (protest) rally

Pro|test|ler [pro'tɛstlɐ] M -s, -, **Pro|test|le|rin** [-ərɪn] F -, -nen *(inf)* protester

Pro|test-: **Pro|test|marsch** M protest march; **Pro|test|no|te** F *(Pol)* letter of protest; **Pro|test|sän|ger(in)** M(F) protest singer; **Pro|test|schrei|ben** NT letter of protest; **Pro|test|song** M protest song; **Pro|test|stim|me** F protest vote; **Pro|test|streik** M protest strike; **Pro|test|sturm** M storm of protest; **Pro|test|ver|samm|lung** F protest meeting; **Pro|test|wäh|ler(in)** M(F) protest voter; **Pro|test|wel|le** F wave of protest

Pro|the|se [pro'te:zə] F -, -n **a** artificial limb *or (Gelenk)* joint, prosthesis *(Med, form)*; *(= Gebiss)* set of dentures **b** *(Ling)* prothesis

Pro|the|sen|trä|ger(in) M(F) **a** *(von Arm, Bein)* person with an artificial limb; *(von Auge, Nase etc)* person with an artificial eye/nose *etc*; **er ist ~** he has an artificial limb/artificial eye/ artificial nose *etc* **b** *(= Gebissträger)* denture-wearer

Pro|the|tik [pro'te:tɪk] F -, *no pl (Med)* prosthetics *sing*
pro|the|tisch [pro'te:tɪʃ] ADJ prosthetic
Pro|to|koll [proto'kɔl] NT -s, -e **a** *(= Niederschrift)* record; *(= Bericht)* report; *(von Sitzung)* minutes *pl*; *(bei Polizei)* statement; *(bei Gericht)* transcript; *(= Vertragsanhang)* protocol; **das ~ aufnehmen** *(bei Sitzung)* to take (down) the minutes; *(bei Polizei)* to take (down) a statement; *(bei Gericht)* to keep a record of the proceedings, to make a transcript of the proceedings; **(das) ~ führen** *(bei Sitzung)* to take *or* keep the minutes; *(bei Gericht)* to keep a record of *or* make a transcript of the proceedings; *(beim Unterricht)* to write a report; **etw zu ~ geben** to have sth put on record; *(bei Polizei)* to say sth in one's statement; **etw zu ~ nehmen** to take sth down, to record sth; **wenn man auf Dienstreise ist, muss man über alle Ausgaben ~ führen** on a business trip one must keep a record *or* (check)list of all expenses
b *no pl (diplomatisch)* protocol
c *(= Strafzettel)* ticket
d *(Comput) (von Vorgang)* log, history; *(= Netzwerkprotokoll)* protocol
Pro|to|kol|lant [protokɔ'lant] M -en, -en, **Pro|to|kol|lan|tin** [-'lantɪn] F -, -nen secretary; *(Jur)* clerk (of the court)
pro|to|kol|la|risch [protokɔ'la:rɪʃ] ADJ **a** *(= protokolliert)* on record; *(in Sitzung)* minuted **b** *(= zeremoniell)* **~e Vorschriften** rules of protocol; **diese Vorschriften sind rein ~** these are merely rules of protocol ADV **a** *(= per Protokoll)* **folgende Maßnahmen wurden ~ festgelegt** the following measures were agreed on **b** *(= zeremoniell)* according to protocol; **~ ist das so geregelt, dass ...** protocol requires that ...
Pro|to|koll-: **Pro|to|koll|chef(in)** M(F) head of protocol; **Pro|to|koll|füh|rer(in)** M(F) secretary; *(Jur)* clerk (of the court)
pro|to|kol|lie|ren [protokɔ'li:rən] *ptp* **protokolliert** VI *(bei Sitzung)* to take the minutes (down); *(bei Polizei)* to take a/the statement (down); *(in der Schule)* to write notes VT to take down; *Sitzung* to minute; *Unfall, Verbrechen* to take (down) statements about; *Vorgang, Vernehmung, Gerichtsverhandlung* to keep a record of; *Bemerkung* to put *or* enter in the minutes; *Stunde* to write up; *(Comput)* to log, to keep a log of; **protokollierte Zeugenaussagen** recorded witness statements
Pro|ton ['pro:tɔn] NT -s, **Protonen** [pro'to:nən] proton
Pro|to|plas|ma [proto'plasma] NT protoplasm
Pro|to|typ ['pro:toty:p] M *(= Erstanfertigung)* prototype; *(= Inbegriff auch)* archetype
pro|to|ty|pisch ['pro:toty:pɪʃ] ADJ prototypical, archetypal
Pro|to|zo|on [proto'tso:ɔn] NT -s, **Protozoen** [-'tso:ən] *usu pl (Zool)* protozoon
Pro|tu|be|ranz [protube'rants] F -, -en *(Astron)* prominence; *(am Sonnenrand)* solar flare
Protz [prɔts] M -es *or* -en, -e(n) *(inf)* swank *(inf)*
prot|zen ['prɔtsn] VI *(inf)* to show off; **mit etw ~** to show sth off
Prot|ze|rei [prɔtsə'rai] F -, -en *(inf)* showing off, swanking *(inf)*
prot|zig ['prɔtsɪç] *(inf)* ADJ swanky *(inf)*, showy *(inf)* ADV extravagantly; *wohnen* ostentatiously; **~ auftreten** to show off
Pro|ve|ni|enz [prove'niɛnts] F -, -en *(geh)* provenance
Pro|ven|za|le [provɛn'tsa:lə, provɛn'sa:lə, provã-'sa:lə] M -n, -n, **Pro|ven|za|lin** [-'tsa:lɪn, -'sa:-lɪn] F -, -nen Provençal
pro|ven|za|lisch [provɛn'tsa:lɪʃ, provɛn'sa:lɪʃ] ADJ Provençal
Pro|vi|ant [pro'viant] M -s, *(rare)* -e provisions *pl*, supplies *pl (esp Mil)*; *(= Reiseproviant)* food for the journey; **sich mit ~ versehen** to lay in provisions; *(für Reise)* to buy food for the journey
Pro|vi|ant|la|ger NT supply camp
Pro|vi|der [pro'vaidɐ] M -s, - provider
Pro|vinz [pro'vɪnts] F -, -en province; *(im Gegensatz zur Stadt)* provinces *pl (auch pej)*, country; **das ist finsterste** *or* **hinterste ~** *(pej)* it's so provincial, it's a cultural backwater
Pro|vinz- *in cpds* provincial; **Pro|vinz|be|woh|ner(in)** M(F) provincial; **Pro|vinz|blatt** NT *(pej inf)* local rag *(pej inf)*, provincial newspaper; **Pro|vinz|haupt|stadt** F provincial capital
Pro|vin|zi|a|li|tät F -, *no pl (usu pej)* provinciality
pro|vin|zi|ell [provɪn'tsiɛl] ADJ provincial *(auch pej)*
Pro|vinz|ler [pro'vɪntslɐ] M -s, -, **Pro|vinz|le|rin** [-ərɪn] F -, -nen *(pej)* provincial
pro|vinz|le|risch [pro'vɪntslərɪʃ] ADJ *(pej)* provincial
Pro|vinz|nest NT *(pej inf)* provincial backwater *(pej)*, hick town *(US pej)*
Pro|vinz|pos|se F *(pej)* provincial farce
Pro|vi|si|on [provi'zio:n] F -, -en commission; *(bei Bank)* bank charges *pl*; **auf ~** on commission
Pro|vi|si|ons|ba|sis F, *no pl* commission basis; **auf ~ arbeiten** to work on a commission basis
Pro|vi|sor [pro'vi:zo:ɐ] M -s, **Provisoren** [-'zo:rən], **Pro|vi|so|rin** [-'zo:rɪn] F -, -nen *(old) manager of a chemist's shop*
pro|vi|so|risch [provi'zo:rɪʃ] ADJ provisional, temporary; **~e Regierung** caretaker *or* provisional government; **das ist alles noch sehr ~ in unserem Haus** things are still very makeshift in our house; **Straßen mit ~em Belag** roads with a temporary surface ADV temporarily; **wir wollen es ~ so lassen** let's leave it like that for the time being; **ich habe den Stuhl ~ repariert** I've fixed the chair up for the time being
Pro|vi|so|ri|um [provi'zo:riʊm] NT -s, **Provisorien** [-riən] stopgap, temporary *or* provisional arrangement
pro|vo|kant [provo'kant] ADJ provocative, provoking ADV provocatively, provokingly
Pro|vo|ka|teur [provoka'tø:ɐ] M -s, -e, **Pro|vo|ka|teu|rin** [-'tø:rɪn] F -, -nen troublemaker; *(Pol auch)* agitator, agent provocateur
Pro|vo|ka|ti|on [provoka'tsio:n] F -, -en provocation
pro|vo|ka|tiv [provoka'ti:f], **pro|vo|ka|to|risch** [provoka'to:rɪʃ] ADJ provocative, provoking ADV provocatively, provokingly
pro|vo|zie|ren [provo'tsi:rən] *ptp* **provoziert** VTI to provoke
Pro|ze|de|re [pro'tse:dərə] NT -, - *(geh)* proceedings *pl*
Pro|ze|dur [protse'du:ɐ] F -, -en **a** *(= Vorgang)* procedure; **die Ratifizierung des Vertrages ist eine langwierige ~** ratifying the treaty is a lengthy procedure **b** *(pej)* carry-on *(inf)*, palaver *(inf)*; **die ganze ~, bis man endlich zur Universität zugelassen wird** all the rigmarole before you are finally admitted to university; **die ~ beim Zahnarzt** the ordeal at the dentist's **c** *(Comput)* procedure
Pro|zent [pro'tsɛnt] NT -(e)s, -e *or (nach Zahlenangaben)* - per cent *no pl (Brit)*, percent *no pl (US)*; **~e** percentage; **fünf ~** five per cent *(Brit) or* percent *(US)*; **wie viel ~?** what percentage?; **zu zehn ~** at ten per cent *(Brit) or* percent *(US)*; **zu hohen ~en** at a high percentage; **etw in ~en ausdrücken** to express sth as a percentage *or* in per cent *(Brit) or* percent *(US)*; **dieser Whisky hat 35 ~ (Alkoholgehalt)** this whisky contains 35 per cent *(Brit) or* percent *(US)* alcohol; **~e bekommen** *(= Rabatt)* to get a discount
Pro|zent|ba|sis F percentage basis; *(von Vertreter auch)* commission basis; **auf ~ arbeiten** to work on a commission basis
-pro|zen|tig [protsɛntɪç] ADJ *suf* per cent; **hochprozentig** high percentage; **eine zehnprozentige Lohnerhöhung** a ten per cent *(Brit) or* percent *(US)* pay rise
Pro|zent-: **Pro|zent|punkt** M point; **Pro|zent|rech|nung** F percentage calculation; **Pro|zent|satz** M percentage; *(= Zins)* rate of interest, interest rate
pro|zen|tu|al [protsɛn'tua:l] ADJ percentage *attr*; **~er Anteil** percentage ADV **etw ~ ausdrücken/rechnen** to express/calculate sth as a percentage *or* in percentages; **sich an einem Geschäft ~ beteiligen** to have a percentage (share) in a business; **~ gut abschneiden** to get a good percentage
pro|zen|tu|ell [protsɛn'tuɛl] ADJ, ADV *(esp Aus)* = **prozentual**
Pro|zent|zei|chen NT per cent *or* percent *(esp US)* sign
Pro|zess [pro'tsɛs] M -es, -e **a** *(= Strafprozess)* trial (*wegen* for; *um* in the matter of); *(= Rechtsfall)* (court) case; **der ~ gegen XY** the trial of XY, the case against XY; **einen ~ gewinnen/verlieren** to win/lose a case; **gegen jdn einen ~ anstrengen** to take *or* institute legal proceedings against sb, to bring an action against sb; **er führt zurzeit gegen fünf Firmen einen ~** at the moment he's taking five companies to court *or* he is involved in legal action against five companies; **es ist sehr teuer, einen ~ zu führen** going to court is very expensive, taking legal action is very expensive; **es zum ~ kommen lassen** to go to court; **es kann zum ~ kommen** it might come to a court case; **mit jdm im ~ liegen** to be involved in a court case *or* in a lawsuit *or* in litigation *(form)* with sb; **jdm den ~ machen** *(inf)* to take sb to court; **mit jdm/etw kurzen ~ machen** *(fig inf)* to make short work of sb/sth *(inf)*
b *(= Vorgang)* process
Pro|zess-: **Pro|zess|ak|ten** PL case files *pl*; **pro|zess|fä|hig** ADJ entitled to take legal action; **Pro|zess|fä|hig|keit** F entitlement to take legal action; **pro|zess|füh|rend** ADJ **~e Partei** litigant; **die ~e Strafkammer** the criminal court conducting the case; **Pro|zess|füh|rung** F conducting of a case; **Pro|zess|geg|ner(in)** M(F) opposing party; **Pro|zess|han|sel** [-hanzl] M -s, - *(inf)* someone who is always going to law
pro|zes|sie|ren [protsɛ'si:rən] *ptp* **prozessiert** VI to go to court; **er prozessiert mit fünf Firmen** he's got cases going on against five firms; **gegen jdn ~** to bring an action against sb; **sie haben jahrelang gegen mich prozessiert** they've been bringing an action against me for years, they've had a case going on against me for years; **durch alle Instanzen ~** to go through all the courts
Pro|zes|si|on [protsɛ'sio:n] F -, -en procession
Pro|zess-: **Pro|zess|kos|ten** PL legal costs *pl*; **er musste die ~ tragen** he had to pay costs; **Pro|zess|la|wi|ne** F spate of trials
Pro|zes|sor [pro'tsɛso:ɐ] M -s, **Prozessoren** [-'so:rən] *(Comput)* processor
Pro|zess-: **Pro|zess|ord|nung** F code *or* rules *pl* of procedure, legal procedure; **Pro|zess|recht** NT procedural law; **Pro|zess|spra|che** F *(Comput)* processing language; **pro|zess|süch|tig** ADJ litigious; **pro|zess|un|fä|hig** ADJ not entitled to take legal action; **Pro|zess|un|fä|hig|keit** F lack of entitlement to take legal action; **Pro|zess|ver|schlep|pung** F protraction of a case; **Pro|zess|voll|macht** F, *no pl* power of attorney *(for a lawsuit)*; *(Formular)* letter of attorney; **Pro|zess|wär|me** F heat of reaction
prü|de ['pry:də] ADJ prudish
Prü|de|rie [pry:də'ri:] F -, *no pl* prudishness, prudery
prü|fen ['pry:fn] VT **a** *auch vi (Sch, Univ) jdn* to examine; *Kenntnisse* to examine, to test; **jdn in etw** *(dat)* **~** to examine sb in sth; **wer hat bei dir geprüft?** who examined you?; **morgen wird in Englisch geprüft** the English exams are tomorrow; **schriftlich geprüft werden** to have a written examination; **ein staatlich geprüfter**

Dolmetscher a state-certified interpreter
b *(= überprüfen)* to check *(auf +acc* for); *(= untersuchen)* to examine, to check; *(durch Ausprobieren)* to test; *(= auf die Probe stellen)* to test; *Geschäftsbücher* to audit, to check, to examine; *Lebensmittel, Wein* to inspect, to test; **es wird geprüft, ob alle anwesend sind** they check *or* there's a check to see if everyone is present; **den Wein auf sein Aroma ~** to sniff *or* test the bouquet of the wine; **Metall auf den Anteil an Fremdstoffen ~** to check the level of impurities in metal; **jdn auf seine Ehrlichkeit ~** to test *or* try sb's honesty; **wir werden die Beschwerde/Sache ~** we'll look into *or* investigate the complaint/matter; **sie wollte ihn nur ~** she only wanted to test him; **drum prüfe, wer sich ewig bindet** *(prov)* marry in haste, repent at leisure *(Prov)*
c *(= erwägen)* to examine, to consider; **etw nochmals ~** to reconsider *or* review sth
d *(= mustern)* to scrutinize; **ein ~der Blick** a searching look
e *(= heimsuchen)* to try, to afflict; **ein schwer geprüfter Vater** a sorely tried father, a much afflicted father
VI *(Sch, Univ)* to give exams; **er prüft sehr streng** he's a strict examiner
VR *(geh)* to search one's heart; **du musst dich selber ~, ob ...** you must decide for yourself *or* you must inquire of yourself *(liter)* whether ...

Prü|fer ['pry:fɐ] **M -s, -, Prü|fe|rin** [-ərɪn] **F -, -nen** examiner; *(= Wirtschaftsprüfer)* inspector

Prüf-: Prüf|ge|rät NT testing apparatus *or* equipment; **Prüf|lam|pe F** control light tester

Prüf|ling ['pry:flɪŋ] **M -s, -e** examinee, (examination) candidate

Prüf-: Prüf|röhr|chen NT test tube; **Prüf|stand M** test bed; *(Space)* test stand; **auf dem ~ stehen** to be being tested; **Prüf|stand|lauf M** test run; **Prüf|stein M** *(fig)* touchstone *(für* of, for), measure *(für* of); **Prüf|stück NT** specimen; **kostenloses ~** *(= Buch)* inspection *or* specimen copy

Prü|fung ['pry:fʊŋ] **F -, -en a** *(Sch, Univ)* exam, examination; **eine ~ machen** *or* **ablegen** to take *or* do *or* sit *(Brit)* an exam
b *(= Überprüfung)* check, checking *no indef art*; *(= Untersuchung)* examination, checking *no indef art*; *(durch Ausprobieren)* test, testing *no indef art*; *(von Geschäftsbüchern)* audit, examination, checking *no indef art*; *(von Lebensmitteln, Wein)* inspection, testing *no indef art*; **eine gründliche ~ einer Maschine vornehmen** to check *or* examine *or* test a machine thoroughly, to give a machine a thorough check *or* examination *or* test; **jdn/etw einer ~ unterziehen** to subject sb/sth to an examination; **nach der ~ wird das Auto ...** after being checked *or* tested the car is ...; **bei nochmaliger ~ der Rechnung** on rechecking the account; **er führt ~en bei Firmen durch** *(von Geschäftsbüchern)* he audits firms' books; **nach/bei ~ Ihrer Beschwerde/dieser Sache ...** after/on looking into *or* investigating your complaint/the matter
c *(= Erwägung)* examination, consideration; **die ~ seiner Entscheidung** the reconsideration of one's decision
d *(= Heimsuchung)* test, trial
e *(Sport)* test

Prü|fungs-: Prü|fungs|an|for|de|rung F examination requirement; **Prü|fungs|angst F** exam nerves *pl*; **Prü|fungs|ar|beit F** dissertation; **Prü|fungs|auf|ga|be F** exam(ination) question; **Prü|fungs|aus|schuss M** board of examiners, examining board; *(bei Geräten)* board of inspectors; **Prü|fungs|er|geb|nis NT** *(Sch, Univ)* exam(ination) results *pl*; *(Tech)* test result; **Prü|fungs|fra|ge F** examination question; **Prü|fungs|ge|bühr F** examination fee; **Prü|fungs|kan|di|dat(in) M(F)** examinee, (examination) candidate; **Prü|fungs|kom|mis|si|on F** = **Prüfungsausschuss**; **Prü|fungs|ord|nung F** exam(ination) regulations *pl*; **Prü|fungs|ter|min M** *(Sch, Univ)* date of examination *or* test; *(Jur)* meeting of creditors; **Prü|fungs|un|ter|la|gen PL** exam(ination) papers *pl*; **Prü|fungs|zeug|nis NT** exam(ination) certificate

Prüf|ver|fah|ren NT test procedure

Prü|gel ['pry:gl] **M -s, - a** *pl auch* **-n** *(= Stock)* club, cudgel *(Brit)* **b** *pl (inf: = Schläge)* beating, thrashing; **~ bekommen** *or* **beziehen** *(lit, fig)* to get a beating *or* thrashing; **~ einstecken** to take a beating; **jetzt gibt** *or* **setzt es ~** you're/he's *etc* in for a (good) thrashing → **Tracht c** *(sl: = Penis)* tool *(sl)*

Prü|ge|lei [pry:gə'lai] **F -, -en** *(inf)* fight, punch-up *(Brit inf)*

Prü|gel|kna|be M *(fig)* whipping boy

prü|geln ['pry:gln] **VTI** to beat; **unser Lehrer prügelt grundsätzlich nicht** our teacher doesn't use corporal punishment on principle; **jdn zu Tode ~** to beat sb to death **VR** to fight; **sich mit jdm ~** to fight sb; **Eheleute, die sich ~** married people who come to blows; **sich um etw** *(acc)* **~** to fight over sth

Prü|gel-: Prü|gel|stra|fe F corporal punishment; **Prü|gel|sze|ne F** fight; *(Theat)* fight scene

Prunk [prʊŋk] **M -s,** *no pl (= Pracht)* splendour *(Brit)*, splendor *(US)*, magnificence, resplendence; *(von Saal, Rokoko auch)* sumptuousness; *(von Stadt, Gebäude auch)* grandeur; *(von höfischer Zeremonie, Fest auch)* pomp and pageantry; **Protz und ~** pomp and splendo(u)r; **Ludwig XIV liebte ~** Louis XIV had a passion for grandeur; **der ~ im Saal** the splendo(u)r *or* magnificence *or* resplendence of the hall; **die Schlösser sind voller ~** the castles are sumptuously appointed; **großen ~ entfalten** to put on a show of great splendo(u)r

Prunk- *in cpds* magnificent, resplendent; **Prunk|bau M** *pl* **-bauten** magnificent building; **Prunk|bett NT** magnificent bed; *(= Himmelbett)* four-poster bed

prun|ken ['prʊŋkn] **VI** to be resplendent; **an der Decke prunkt ein Gipsbaldachin** on the ceiling is a resplendent plaster baldachin; **mit etw ~** to flaunt sth, to make a great show of sth

Prunk-: Prunk|ge|mach NT state apartment; **prunk|los ADJ** unostentatious, modest **ADV** modestly, unostentatiously; **Prunk|saal M** sumptuous *or* palatial room; **Prunk|stück NT** showpiece; **Prunk|sucht F** great love of splendour *(Brit) or* splendor *(US)*, passion for the grand scale; **prunk|süch|tig ADJ ~ sein** to have a craving for splendour *(Brit) or* splendor *(US)*; **prunk|voll ADJ** splendid, magnificent **ADV** splendidly, magnificently

prus|ten ['pru:stn] **VI** *(inf)* to snort; **vor Lachen ~** to snort with laughter; **sie prustete laut vor Lachen** she gave a loud snort (of laughter)

PS [pe:'ɛs] [pe:'ɛs] **NT -, -** *abbr von* **Pferdestärke** hp

P.S., PS [pe:'ɛs] [pe:'ɛs] **NT -, -** *abbr von* **Postskript(um)** PS

Psalm [psalm] **M -s, -en** psalm

Psal|mist [psal'mɪst] **M -en, -en, Psal|mis|tin** [-'mɪstɪn] **F -, -nen** psalmist

Psal|ter ['psaltɐ] **M -s, - a** *(Eccl)* psalter **b** *(Mus)* psaltery

pseu|do- ['psɔydo] *in cpds* pseudo

Pseu|do|krupp [-krʊp] **M -,** *no pl (Med)* pseudocroup

Pseu|do|nym [psɔydo'ny:m] **NT -s, -e** pseudonym; *(eines Schriftstellers auch)* nom de plume, pen name

psst [pst] **INTERJ** psst; *(ruhig)* sh, hush

Psy|cha|go|ge [psyça'go:gə] **M -n, -n, Psy|cha|go|gin** [-'go:gɪn] **F -, -nen** educational psychotherapist

Psy|che ['psy:çə] **F -, -n** psyche; *(Myth)* Psyche

psy|che|de|lisch [psyçə'de:lɪʃ] **ADJ** psychedelic

Psy|chi|a|ter [psy'çia:tɐ] **M -s, -, Psy|chi|a|te|rin** [-ərɪn] **F -, -nen** psychiatrist

Psy|chi|at|rie [psyçia'tri:] **F -, -n** [-'tri:ən] psychiatry

psy|chi|at|risch [psy'çia:trɪʃ] **ADJ** psychiatric **ADV** psychiatrically; *behandeln, untersuchen* by a psychiatrist; **~ betrachtet** from a psychiatric point of view, (considered) psychiatrically; **~ behandelt werden** to be under psychiatric treatment

psy|chisch ['psy:çɪʃ] **ADJ** *Belastung, Auswirkungen, Defekt* emotional, psychological; *Phänomen, Erscheinung* psychic; *Vorgänge* psychological; **~e Erkrankung** mental illness; **~ unter großem Druck stehen, unter großem ~en Druck stehen** to be under a great deal of emotional *or* psychological pressure
ADV *abnorm, auffällig* psychologically; *krank, gestört, labil* mentally; **~ gesund/unauffällig** psychologically normal; **sich ~ auswirken** to have psychological effects; **~ belastet sein** to be under psychological pressure; **~ erschöpft** emotionally exhausted; **sich ~ schlecht fühlen** to feel bad; **eine ~ bedingte Krankheit** a psychosomatic illness; **~ gestört** emotionally *or* psychologically disturbed; **jdn ~ beanspruchen** to make emotional *or* psychological demands on sb; **er ist ~ völlig am Ende** his nerves can't take any more

Psy|cho-, psy|cho- ['psy:ço] *in cpds* psycho-; **Psy|cho|ana|ly|se** [psyço-] **F** psychoanalysis; **Psy|cho|ana|ly|ti|ker(in)** [psyço-] **M(F)** psychoanalyst; **psy|cho|ana|ly|tisch** [psyço-] **ADJ** psychoanalytic(al) **ADV jdn ~ behandeln** to psychoanalyze sb; **Psy|cho|di|ag|nos|tik** [psyço-] **F** psychodiagnostics *sing*; **Psy|cho|dra|ma** ['psy:ço-] **NT** psychodrama; **psy|cho|gen** [psyço'ge:n] **ADJ** psychogenic; **Psy|cho|gramm** [psyço-] **NT** *pl* **-gramme** profile *(auch fig)*, psychograph; **Psy|cho|ki|ne|se** [psyçoki'ne:zə] **F -,** *no pl* psychokinesis; **Psy|cho|lo|ge** [psyço'lo:gə] **M -n, -n, Psy|cho|lo|gin** [-'lo:gɪn] **F -, -nen** psychologist; **Psy|cho|lo|gie** [psyçolo'gi:] **F -,** *no pl* psychology; **psy|cho|lo|gisch** [psyço'lo:gɪʃ] **ADJ** psychological; **~e Kriegsführung** psychological warfare **ADV** psychologically; **~ erfahrene Kräfte** personnel with experience in psychology; **psy|cho|lo|gi|sie|ren** [psyçologi'zi:rən] *ptp* **psychologisiert VT** to psychologize; **Psy|cho|neu|ro|se** [psyço-] **F** psychoneurosis; **Psy|cho|path** [psyço'pa:t] **M -en, -en, Psy|cho|pa|thin** [-'pa:tɪn] **F -, -nen** psychopath; **Psy|cho|pa|thie** [psyçopa'ti:] **F -, -n** [-'ti:ən] psychopathy; **psy|cho|pa|thisch** [psyço'pa:tɪʃ] **ADJ** psychopathic **ADV** like a psychopath; **~ reagieren** to react psychopathically; **Psy|cho|phar|ma|kon** [psyço'farmakɔn] **NT -s, -pharmaka** [-ka] *usu pl* psychiatric drug

Psy|cho|se [psy'ço:zə] **F -, -n** psychosis

Psy|cho-: Psy|cho|so|ma|tik [psyçozo'ma:tɪk] **F -,** *no pl* psychosomatics *sing*; **psy|cho|so|ma|tisch** [psyçozo'ma:tɪʃ] **ADJ** psychosomatic **ADV** psychosomatically; **psy|cho|so|zi|al ADJ** *(Psych, Sociol)* psychosocial; **Psy|cho|ter|ror** ['psy:ço-] **M** psychological terror; **Psy|cho|test** ['psy:ço-] **M** psychological test; **Psy|cho|the|ra|peut(in)** [psyço-] **M(F)** psychotherapist; **psy|cho|the|ra|peu|tisch** [psyço-] **ADJ** psychotherapeutic **ADV** psychotherapeutically; **Psy|cho|the|ra|pie** [psyço-] **F** psychotherapy; **Psy|cho|thril|ler** [psyço-] **M** psychological thriller

Psy|cho|ti|ker [psy'ço:tikɐ] **M -s, -, Psy|cho|ti|ke|rin** [-ərɪn] **F -, -nen** psychotic

psy|cho|tisch [psy'ço:tɪʃ] **ADJ** psychotic

PTA [pe:te:'la:] **M -s, -s** *abbr von* **pharmazeutisch-technischer Assistent**

PTA [pe:te:'la:] **F -, -s** *abbr von* **pharmazeutisch-technische Assistentin**

pto|le|mä|isch [ptole'mɛ:ɪʃ] **ADJ** Ptolemaic

Pto|le|mä|us [ptole'mɛ:ʊs] **M -'** Ptolemy

pu|ber|tär [pubɛr'tɛ:ɐ] **ADJ** of puberty, adolescent; **ein Junge im ~en Alter** a boy in puberty **ADV ~ bedingte Störungen** disorders caused by puberty, adolescent disorders

Pu|ber|tät [pubɐ'tɛ:t] F -, *no pl* puberty; **er steckt mitten in der ~** he's going through his adolescence
Pu|ber|täts-: **Pu|ber|täts|al|ter** NT age of puberty; **im ~** at the age of puberty; **Pu|ber|täts|er|schei|nung** F symptom of puberty *or* adolescence; **Pu|ber|täts|stö|run|gen** PL adolescent disturbances *pl*, growing-up problems *pl (inf)*; **Pu|ber|täts|zeit** F puberty (period)
pu|ber|tie|ren [pubɐ'ti:rən] *ptp* **pubertiert** VI to reach puberty; **~d** pubescent
Pu|blic-Do|main-Pro|gramm [pablıkdɔ'me:n-] NT *(Comput)* public domain program
Pub|li|ci|ty [pa'blısıtı] F -, *no pl* publicity
pub|li|ci|ty-: **pub|li|ci|ty|scheu** ADJ **er ist ~** he shuns publicity; **pub|li|ci|ty|träch|tig** ADJ which generates (a lot of) publicity
Pub|lic Re|la|tions [pablık rı'le:ʃəns] PL public relations *pl*
pub|lik [pu'bli:k] ADJ *pred* public; **~ werden** to become public knowledge; **etw ~ machen** to make sth public; **die Sache ist längst ~** that's long been common knowledge
Pub|li|ka|ti|on [publika'tsio:n] F -, **-en** publication
pub|lik+ma|chen VT *sep* → **publik**
Pub|li|kum ['pu:blikʊm] NT **-s**, *no pl* public; *(= Zuschauer, Zuhörer)* audience; *(= Leser)* readers *pl*; *(Sport)* crowd; **er muss ja immer ein ~ haben** *(fig)* he always has to have an audience; **das ~ in dem Restaurant ist sehr gemischt** you get a very mixed group of people using this restaurant, this restaurant's customers are very mixed; **in diesem Restaurant verkehrt ein sehr schlechtes ~** this restaurant attracts a very bad type of customer *or* a very bad clientele; **sein ~ finden** to find a public; **vor eigenem ~** *(Sport)* in front of a home crowd
Pub|li|kums-: **Pub|li|kums|er|folg** M success with the public, popular success; **Pub|li|kums|ge|schmack** M public *or* popular taste; **Pub|li|kums|in|te|res|se** NT interest of the public; **Pub|li|kums|lieb|ling** M darling of the public; **Pub|li|kums|mag|net** M crowd puller; **Pub|li|kums|ren|ner** M *(inf)* hit with the public *(inf)*; **Pub|li|kums|ver|kehr** M **~ im Rathaus ist von 8 bis 12 Uhr** the town hall is open to the public from 8 till 12 o'clock; **„heute kein ~"** "closed today for public business"; **für den ~ geschlossen/geöffnet sein** to be closed/open to the public; **wir haben heute viel ~** we've a lot of people coming in today; **pub|li|kums|wirk|sam** ADJ **~ sein** to have public appeal; **sehr ~e Tricks** tricks with great public appeal, tricks which appeal to the public ADV **ein Stück ~ inszenieren** to produce a play in a popular way *or* with a view to public appeal
pub|li|zie|ren [publi'tsi:rən] *ptp* **publiziert** VTI **a** *(= veröffentlichen)* to publish; **er hat in verschiedenen Fachzeitschriften publiziert** he's had things *or* work published *or* he has been published in various journals **b** *(= publik machen)* to publicize
Pub|li|zist [publi'tsıst] M **-en, -en**, **Pub|li|zis|tin** [-'tsıstın] F -, **-nen** publicist; *(= Journalist)* journalist
Pub|li|zis|tik [publi'tsıstık] F -, *no pl* journalism
pub|li|zis|tisch [publi'tsıstıʃ] ADJ journalistic ADV *ausschlachten* in the media; **sich ~ betätigen** to write for newspapers
Pub|li|zi|tät [publitsi'tɛ:t] F -, *no pl* publicity
Pub|li|zi|täts|pflicht F *(St Ex)* duty of public disclosure
pub|li|zi|täts|pflich|tig [-pflıçtıç] ADJ declarable
Puck [pʊk] M **-s, -s** puck
pu|ckern ['pʊkɐn] VI *(inf)* to throb; **es puckert im Zahn** my tooth's throbbing
Pud|ding ['pʊdıŋ] M **-s, -s** *thick custard-based dessert often tasting of vanilla, chocolate etc*, ≈ blancmange; **kaltgerührter ~** instant whip; **Beine/Arme wie ~ haben** to have legs/arms like jelly
Pud|ding|pul|ver NT custard powder
Pu|del ['pu:dl] M **-s, -** **a** *(= Hund)* poodle; **das ist des ~s Kern** *(fig)* that's what it's really all about → **begossen** **b** *(inf: = Fehlwurf beim Kegeln)* miss
Pu|del-: **Pu|del|müt|ze** F bobble cap *or* hat, pompom hat *(inf)*; **pu|del|nackt** ADJ *(inf)* stark-naked, starkers *pred (Brit inf)*; **pu|del|nass** ADJ dripping *or* soaking wet, drenched; **pu|del|wohl** ADJ *(inf)* **sich ~ fühlen** to feel completely contented; **nach der Sauna fühle ich mich ~** after the sauna I feel like a million dollars *(inf) or* I feel on top of the world *(inf)*
Pu|der ['pu:dɐ] M OR (INF) NT **-s, -** powder
Pu|der|do|se F powder tin; *(für Gesichtspuder)* (powder) compact
pu|de|rig ['pu:dərıç] ADJ powdery
pu|dern ['pu:dɐn] VT to powder; **sich** *(dat)* **das Gesicht ~** to powder one's face; **ich muss mir noch die Nase ~** *(euph)* I just have to powder my nose VR *(= Puder auftragen)* to powder oneself; *(= Puder benutzen)* to use powder; **ich muss mich noch ~** I still have to powder my nose *or* face; **sich stark ~** to use a lot of powder
Pu|der-: **Pu|der|quas|te** F powder puff; **Pu|der|zu|cker** M icing sugar
pu|e|ril [pue'ri:l] ADJ *(geh)* puerile; *(= knabenhaft)* boyish
Pu|er|to Ri|ca|ner [puɛrtori'ka:nɐ] M **-s, -**, **Pu|er|to Ri|ca|ne|rin** [-ərın] F -, **-nen** Puerto Rican
pu|er|to-ri|ca|nisch [puɛrtori'ka:nıʃ] ADJ Puerto Rican
Pu|er|to Ri|co [pu'ɛrto 'ri:ko] NT **- -s** Puerto Rico
puff [pʊf] INTERJ bang
Puff [pʊf] M **-(e)s, ¨-e** ['pʏfə] **a** *(= Stoß)* thump, blow; *(in die Seite)* prod, dig; *(vertraulich)* nudge; **einen ~ *or* einige Püffe aushalten können** *(fig)* to be thick-skinned **b** *(Geräusch)* phut *(inf)*
Puff M **-(e)s, -e** **a** *(= Wäschepuff)* linen basket **b** *(= Bausch)* puff **c** *(= Sitzpuff)* pouffe *(Brit)*, pouf *(US)*
Puff M OR NT **-s, -s** *(inf)* brothel, whorehouse *(inf)*, cathouse *(esp US inf)*
Puff|är|mel M puff(ed) sleeve
puf|fen ['pʊfn] VT **a** *(= schlagen)* to thump, to hit; *(in die Seite)* to prod, to dig; *(= vertraulich stoßen)* to nudge **b** *Rauch* to puff **c** *Ärmel* to puff **d** *Mais* to pop VI *(inf) (Dampflokomotive, Rauch, Abgase)* to puff; *(= puff machen)* to go phut *(inf)*
Puf|fer ['pʊfɐ] M **-s, -** **a** *(Rail, Comput)* buffer **b** *(Cook: = Kartoffelpuffer)* potato fritter
Puf|fer|funk|ti|on F *(Comput)* buffer function
puf|fern ['pʊfɐn] VT to buffer
Puf|fer-: **Puf|fer|spei|cher** M *(Comput)* buffer memory; **Puf|fer|staat** M buffer state
Puf|fe|rung F -, **-en** *(Comput)* buffering
Puf|fer|zo|ne F buffer zone
Puff-: **Puff|ge|gend** F *(inf)* red-light district; **Puff|mais** M popcorn; **Puff|mut|ter** F *pl* **-mütter** *(inf)* madam(e), bawd; **Puff|reis** M puffed rice; **Puff|stra|ße** F *(inf)* brothel street
puh [pu:] INTERJ *(Abscheu)* ugh; *(Erleichterung)* phew
pu|len ['pu:lən] VI *(inf)* to pick; **in der Nase ~** to pick one's nose; **an einem Loch/einem Etikett/ einer Narbe ~** to pick at a hole/a label/a scar VT *(N Ger) Krabben* to shell; *Erbsen, Bohnen auch* to pod; **etw aus etw ~** to pick sth out of sth
Pulk [pʊlk] M **-s, -s** *or (rare)* **-e** **a** *(Mil)* group **b** *(= Menge) (von Menschen)* throng; *(von Dingen)* pile; **im ~** in a throng
Pull-down-Me|nü [pʊl'daun-] NT *(Comput)* pull-down menu
Pul|le ['pʊlə] F -, **-n** *(inf)* bottle; **eine ~ Schnaps** a bottle of schnapps; **ein Schluck aus der ~** *(fig)* a fair whack *(Brit inf) or* share; **volle ~ fahren/ arbeiten** *(inf)* to drive/work flat out *(esp Brit)* *or* at full speed; **das Radio volle ~ aufdrehen** *(inf)* to turn the radio on at full blast
pul|len ['pʊlən] VI *(Naut)* to row
pul|len VI, **pul|lern** ['pʊlɐn] VI *(inf)* to pee *(inf)*
Pul|li ['pʊli] M **-s, -s** *(inf)*, **Pul|lo|ver** [pʊ'lo:vɐ] M **-s, -** jumper *(Brit)*, pullover, sweater, jersey
Pul|lun|der [pʊ'lʊndɐ, pʊl'lʊndɐ] M **-s, -** tank top, slipover
Puls [pʊls] M **-es, -e** [-zə] *(lit, fig)* pulse; **sein ~ geht *or* schlägt regelmäßig** his pulse is regular; **jdm den ~ fühlen** *(lit)* to feel *or* take sb's pulse; *(fig)* to take sb's pulse; **am ~ der Zeit sein** to have one's finger on the pulse of the time(s)
Puls|ader F artery; **sich** *(dat)* **die ~(n) aufschneiden** to slash one's wrists
Pul|sar [pʊl'za:ɐ] M **-s, -e** *(Astron)* pulsar
pul|sen ['pʊlzn] VI *(liter)* to pulse, to pulsate, to throb
pul|sie|ren [pʊl'zi:rən] *ptp* **pulsiert** VI *(lit, fig)* to pulsate; **~der Gleichstrom** intermittent direct current
Puls-: **Puls|schlag** M pulse beat; *(fig)* pulse; *(= das Pulsieren)* throbbing, pulsing, pulsation; **an der Börse fühlt man den ~ der Wirtschaft** at the stock exchange you have your finger on the pulse of the economy; **in Schwabing spürte sie den ~ der Großstadt** in Schwabing she felt the throbbing *or* puls(at)ing of the city; **den ~ der Zeit spüren** to feel life pulsing around one; **Puls|wär|mer** [-vɛrmɐ] M **-s, -** wristlet; **Puls|zahl** F pulse count
Pult [pʊlt] NT **-(e)s, -e** desk
Pul|ver ['pʊlfɐ, -vɐ] NT **-s, -** powder; *(= Schießpulver)* gunpowder, powder; **er hat das ~ nicht erfunden** *(fig)* he'll never set the Thames on fire *(prov)*; **sein ~ verschossen haben** *(fig)* to have shot one's bolt → **Schuss**
Pul|ver-: **Pul|ver|dampf** M gunsmoke, gunpowder smoke; **Pul|ver|fab|rik** F gunpowder factory; **Pul|ver|fass** NT barrel of gunpowder, powder barrel *or* keg; *(fig)* powder keg, volcano; **(wie) auf einem ~ sitzen** *(fig)* to be sitting on (top of) a volcano; **Russland gleicht einem ~** Russia is like a powder keg; **die Lunte ans ~ legen** *(fig)* to ignite an explosive situation; **pul|ver|fein** ADJ finely ground ADV *mahlen* finely
pul|ve|rig ['pʊlfərıç, -vərıç] ADJ powdery *no adv* ADV **den Kaffee ~ mahlen** to grind the coffee to a powder
Pul|ve|ri|sa|tor [pʊlveri'za:to:ɐ] M **-s, Pulverisatoren** [-'to:rən] pulverizer
pul|ve|ri|sie|ren [pʊlveri'zi:rən] *ptp* **pulverisiert** VT to pulverize, to powder
Pul|ver-: **Pul|ver|kaf|fee** M *(inf)* instant coffee; **Pul|ver|kam|mer** F *(Hist)*, **Pul|ver|ma|ga|zin** NT magazine; **Pul|ver|müh|le** F gunpowder factory
pul|vern ['pʊlfɐn, -vɐn] VT to pulverize, to powder; **zu Silvester werden Millionenbeträge in die Luft gepulvert** on New Year's Eve vast sums of money go up in smoke VI *(inf)* to shoot
Pul|ver-: **Pul|ver|schnee** M powder snow; **Pul|ver|turm** M *(Hist)* magazine
pulv|rig ['pʊlfrıç, -vrıç] ADJ, ADV = **pulverig**
Pu|ma ['pu:ma] M **-s, -s** puma *(Brit)*, cougar *(US)*
Pum|mel ['pʊml] M **-s, -** *(inf)*, **Pum|mel|chen** ['pʊmlçən] NT **-s, -** *(inf)* dumpling *(Brit inf)*, pudding *(Brit inf)*, roly-poly *(inf)*
pum|me|lig ['pʊməlıç], **pumm|lig** ['pʊmlıç] ADJ *(inf)* chubby, plump
Pump [pʊmp] M **-(e)s**, *no pl (inf)* credit, tick *(Brit inf)*; **etw auf ~ kaufen** to buy sth on tick *(Brit inf) or* on credit; **auf ~ leben** to live on tick *(Brit inf) or* on credit
Pum|pe ['pʊmpə] F -, **-n** **a** pump **b** *(inf: = Herz)* ticker *(inf)*
pum|pen ['pʊmpn] VT **a** *(mit Pumpe)* to pump **b** *(inf: = entleihen)* to borrow; *(= verleihen)* to lend, to loan; **(sich** *dat*) **Geld bei jdm ~** to borrow money from *or* off *(inf)* sb VI to pump
Pum|pen|schwen|gel M pump handle

pum|pern ['pʊmpɐn] VI (*inf: S Ger, Aus*) to thump, to hammer; **sein Herz pumperte vor Aufregung** his heart was thumping (away) *or* hammering away with excitement

Pum|per|ni|ckel ['pʊmpɐnɪkl] M **-s, -** pumpernickel

Pump|ho|se F baggy breeches *pl*, knickerbockers *pl*; (*= Unterhose*) bloomers *pl*

Pumps [pœmps] M **-, -** pump

Pump-: **Pump|spei|cher|kraft|werk** NT, **Pump|spei|cher|werk** NT pumped storage works *sing or pl*; **Pump|spray** NT pump (action) spray; **Pump|sta|ti|on** F pumping station

Punch [pantʃ] M **-s, -s** (*Boxen*) punch; **einen harten ~ haben** to pack a hard punch, to be a hard puncher

punc|to ['pʊŋkto] PREP +*gen* = **punkto**

Pu|ni|er ['pu:niɐ] M **-s, -**, **Pu|ni|e|rin** [-iərɪn] F **-, -nen** Phoenician

pu|nisch ['pu:nɪʃ] ADJ Punic; **die Punischen Kriege** the Punic Wars

Punk [paŋk] M **-s**, *no pl* punk

Pun|ker ['paŋkɐ] M **-s, -**, **Pun|ke|rin** ['paŋkərɪn] F **-, -nen** punk

Punkt [pʊŋkt] M **-(e)s, -e** **a** (*= Tupfen*) spot, dot; **grüne ~e in den Augen** green flecks in one's eyes; **das Schiff war nur noch ein kleiner ~ in der Ferne** the ship was only a small speck *or* dot *or* spot in the distance; **~e pro Zoll** (*Comput etc*) dots per inch
b (*= Satzzeichen*) full stop (*Brit*), period (*esp US*); (*Typ*) point; (*auf dem i, Mus: = Auslassungszeichen, von Punktlinie, Comput, E-Mail-Adresse*) dot; **einen ~ setzen** *or* **machen** to put a full stop (*Brit*) *or* a period (*esp US*); **der Satz endet mit drei ~en** the sentence ends with a row of dots *or* with suspension points (*Brit*) *or* with the ellipsis mark; **der ~ auf dem i sein** (*fig*) to be the final touch; **nun mach aber mal einen ~!** (*inf*) come off it! (*inf*); **einen ~ hinter eine Angelegenheit setzen** to make an end to a matter; **ohne ~ und Komma reden** (*inf*) to talk nineteen to the dozen (*Brit inf*), to rattle on and on (*inf*), to talk up a storm (*US inf*); **und sagte, ~, ~, ~** and said dot, dot, dot
c (*= Stelle, Zeitpunkt, auch Math*) point; **zwischen den ~en A und B** between (the) points A and B; **~ 12 Uhr** at 12 o'clock on the dot; **wir sind auf** *or* **an dem ~ angelangt, wo ...** we have reached the stage *or* point where ...; **ein dunkler ~** (*fig*) a dark chapter; **bis zu einem gewissen ~** up to a certain point → **tot**
d (*= Bewertungseinheit*) point, mark; (*bei Prüfung*) mark; (*bei Verkehrsvergehen*) point; **nach ~en siegen/führen** to win/lead on points
e (*bei Diskussion, von Vertrag etc*) point; **in diesem ~** on this point; **etw ~ für ~ widerlegen** to disprove sth point by point; **etw in allen ~en widerlegen** to refute sth in every respect; **der strittige ~** the disputed point, the area of dispute; **sein Aufsatz ist in vielen ~en anfechtbar** many points in his essay are disputable; **etw auf den ~ bringen** to get to the heart of sth; **damit brachte er das Problem auf den ~** he put his finger on it *or* on the problem

Punkt-: **Punkt|ab|zug** M (*Sport*) points deduction; **Punkt|ball** M punchball (*Brit*), punchbag (*US*), punching ball *or* bag (*US*); **Punkt|be|fehl** M (*Comput*) dot command

Pünkt|chen ['pʏŋktçən] NT **-s, -** little dot *or* spot; **drei ~** three dots; **da fehlt aber auch nicht das ~ auf dem i!** (*fig*) it's got every i dotted and every t crossed

punk|ten ['pʊŋktn] VI (*Sport*) to score (points); (*fig: = Erfolg haben*) to score a hit → *auch* **gepunktet**

Punkt-: **Punkt|feu|er** NT (*Mil*) precision fire; **Punkt|ge|winn** M (*Sport*) point/points won; **punkt|gleich** ADJ (*Sport*) level (*mit* with) ADV **die Mannschaften haben ~ gespielt/abgeschnitten** the score was even, it was a draw (*esp Brit*); **die beiden Mannschaften liegen ~** the two teams are lying level (on points) *or* are level pegging (*Brit*), the two teams are even; **der Boxkampf ging ~ aus** the fight ended in a draw *or* was a draw; **Punkt|gleich|heit** F (*Sport*) level score; **bei ~** if the scores are level; **wegen ~** because the score was level

punk|tie|ren [pʊŋk'ti:rən] *ptp* **punktiert** VT **a** (*Med*) to aspirate **b** (*= mit Punkten versehen*) to dot; (*Mus*) *Note* to dot; **einen Umriss ~** to dot in an outline; **punktierte Linie** dotted line; **punktierte Rhythmen** dotted rhythms

Punk|ti|on [pʊŋk'tsio:n] F **-, -en** (*Med*) aspiration

Punkt|lan|dung F precision landing

pünkt|lich ['pʏŋktlɪç] ADJ **a** punctual; **er ist selten ~** he's a bad timekeeper **b** (*= genau*) exact, precise, meticulous ADV on time; **er kam ~ um 3 Uhr** he came punctually at 3 o'clock *or* at 3 o'clock sharp; **der Zug kommt immer sehr ~** the train is always dead on time *or* very punctual; **~ da sein** to be there on time; **es wird ~ erledigt** it will be promptly dealt with; (*= rechtzeitig*) it will be dealt with on time

Pünkt|lich|keit F **-**, *no pl* punctuality; **~ ist die Höflichkeit der Könige** (*Prov*) punctuality is the politeness of princes

Punkt-: **Punkt|li|nie** F dotted line; **Punkt|mat|rix** F (*Comput*) dot matrix; **Punkt|nie|der|la|ge** F defeat on points, points defeat

punk|to ['pʊŋkto] PREP +*gen* **in ~** with regard to, as regards; **~ X** where X *or* as far as X is concerned; **~ meiner Anfrage** concerning *or* reference (*Comm*) *or* re (*Comm*) my inquiry

Punkt-: **Punkt|rich|ter(in)** M(F) judge; **Punkt|schrift** F Braille; **punkt+schwei|ßen** VTI *sep infin, ptp only* (*Tech*) to spot-weld; **Punkt|sieg** M win on points, points win; **Punkt|sie|ger(in)** M(F) winner on points; **Punkt|spiel** NT league game, game decided on points

punk|tu|ell [pʊŋk'tuɛl] ADJ *Maßnahmen, Streik* selective; *Zusammenarbeit* on certain points; **einige ~e Ergänzungen anbringen** to expand a few points; **~e Verkehrskontrollen** spot checks on traffic ADV *kritisieren* in a few points; **wir haben uns nur ~ mit diesem Thema befasst** we only dealt with certain *or* selected points of this topic; **die Kontrollen erfolgten nur ~** they only did spot checks

Punk|tum ['pʊŋktʊm] INTERJ and that's flat, and that's that; **Schluss, aus, ~!** and that's the end of that!

Punkt-: **Punkt|ver|lust** M loss of points; **Punkt|wer|tung** F points system; **in der ~ liegt er vorne** he's leading on points; **Punkt|zahl** F score

Punsch [pʊnʃ] M **-es, -e** (hot) punch

Punsch|glas NT punch cup

Pun|ze ['pʊntsə] F **-, -n** **a** (*Tech*) punch **b** (*= Güte-, Herstellerzeichen*) hallmark

pun|zen ['pʊntsn] VT **a** (*Tech*) to punch **b** *Gold* to hallmark

Pup [pu:p] M **-(e)s, -e** (*inf*) (*= Furz, Geräusch*) rude noise; (*= Geruch*) nasty smell

pu|pen ['pu:pn] VI (*inf*) to let off (*Brit inf*), to pass gas (*US inf*)

Pu|pil|le [pu'pɪlə] F **-, -n** pupil

Pu|pil|len-: **Pu|pil|len|er|wei|te|rung** F dilation of the pupil; **Pu|pil|len|ver|en|gung** F contraction of the pupil, miosis (*spec*)

Püpp|chen ['pʏpçən] NT **-s, -** **a** (*= kleine Puppe*) little doll *or* dolly (*inf*) **b** (*= hübsches Mädchen*) little sweetie; (*= Teenagerin*) dolly bird (*dated inf*); **ein süßes kleines ~** a sweet little thing

Pup|pe ['pʊpə] F **-, -n** **a** (*= Kinderspielzeug*) doll, dolly (*inf*); (*= Marionette*) puppet, marionette; (*= Schaufensterpuppe, Mil: = Übungspuppe*) dummy; (*inf: = Mädchen*) doll (*inf*), bird (*esp Brit inf*); (*als Anrede*) baby (*inf*), doll (*esp US inf*); **die ~n tanzen lassen** (*inf*) to paint the town red (*inf*), to live it up (*inf*); **bis in die ~n schlafen** (*inf*) to sleep to all hours **b** (*Zool*) pupa

Pup|pen- *in cpds* doll's; **Pup|pen|dok|tor** M, **Pup|pen|dok|to|rin** F dolls' doctor; **Pup|pen|ge|sicht** NT baby-doll face; **pup|pen|haft** ADJ doll-like; **Pup|pen|haus** NT doll's house (*Brit*), dollhouse (*US*); **Pup|pen|kü|che** F doll's kitchen (*Brit*), dollkitchen (*US*); **Pup|pen|spiel** NT puppet show; **Pup|pen|spie|ler(in)** M(F) puppeteer; **Pup|pen|stu|be** F doll's house (*Brit*), dollhouse (*US*); **Pup|pen|the|a|ter** NT puppet theatre (*Brit*) *or* theater (*US*); **Pup|pen|wa|gen** M doll's pram (*Brit*), toy baby carriage (*US*)

pup|pern ['pʊpɐn] VI (*inf*) (*= zittern*) to tremble, to shake, to quake; (*= klopfen*) to thump, to thud

pup|pig ['pʊpɪç] ADJ (*inf*) **a** (*= niedlich*) cute **b** (*= einfach*) easy

Pups [pu:ps] M **-es, -e** (*inf*) = **Pup**

pup|sen ['pu:psn] VI (*inf*) to let off (*Brit inf*), to pass gas (*US inf*)

Pup|ser M **-s, -** (*inf*) = **Pup**

pur [pu:ɐ] ADJ (*= rein*) pure; (*= unverdünnt*) neat, straight; (*= bloß, völlig*) sheer, pure; **~er Unsinn** absolute nonsense; **~er Wahnsinn** sheer *or* pure *or* absolute madness; **~er Zufall** sheer *or* mere coincidence; **Whisky ~** straight *or* neat whisky ADV *anwenden* pure, undiluted; *trinken* straight

Pü|ree [py're:] NT **-s, -s** puree; (*= Kartoffelpüree*) mashed *or* creamed potatoes *pl*

Pur|ga|to|ri|um [pʊrga'to:riʊm] NT **-s**, *no pl* purgatory

pü|rie|ren [py'ri:rən] *ptp* **püriert** VT to puree

Pü|rier|stab M masher

pu|ri|fi|zie|ren [purifi'tsi:rən] *ptp* **purifiziert** VT (*liter*) to purify

Pu|ris|mus [pu'rɪsmʊs] M **-**, *no pl* purism

Pu|rist [pu'rɪst] M **-en, -en**, **Pu|ris|tin** [-'rɪstɪn] F **-, -nen** purist

pu|ris|tisch [pu'rɪstɪʃ] ADJ puristic

Pu|ri|ta|ner [puri'ta:nɐ] M **-s, -**, **Pu|ri|ta|ne|rin** [-ərɪn] F **-, -nen** Puritan

pu|ri|ta|nisch [puri'ta:nɪʃ] ADJ (*Hist*) Puritan; (*pej*) puritanical ADV (*pej*) puritanically; **bei uns geht es ~ zu** ours is a puritanical household; **sie verhält sich sehr ~** she is really puritanical

Pu|ri|ta|nis|mus [purita'nɪsmʊs] M **-**, *no pl* Puritanism

Pur|pur ['pʊrpʊr] M **-s**, *no pl* crimson; (*= purpurner Umhang*) purple; **den ~ tragen** (*fig*) to wear the purple

Pur|pur-: **pur|pur|far|ben** [-farbn], **pur|pur|far|big** ADJ crimson; **der Morgenhimmel strahlte ~** the morning sky shone a deep crimson; **Pur|pur|man|tel** M purple robe

pur|purn ['pʊrpʊrn] ADJ (*liter*) crimson

pur|pur|rot ADJ crimson (red)

Pur|zel|baum ['pʊrtslbaum] M somersault; **einen ~ machen** *or* **schlagen** *or* **schießen** to turn *or* do a somersault

pur|zeln ['pʊrtsln] VI *aux sein* to tumble; **über etw** (*acc*) **~** to trip *or* fall over sth

pu|schen, **pu|shen** ['pʊʃn] VT (*inf*) to push

Pu|schen ['pʊʃn] M **-s, -** (*N Ger*) slipper

Push-up-BH M push-up bra

Pus|sel|ar|beit ['ʊsl-] F (*inf*) fiddly *or* finicky work *no art*

pus|se|lig ['pʊsəlɪç] ADJ (*inf*) *Mensch* pernickety (*inf*), finicky (*inf*), fussy; *Arbeit, Aufgabe* fiddly (*Brit inf*), awkward

pus|seln ['pʊsln] VI (*inf*) **a** (*= geschäftig sein*) to fuss; **sie pusselt den ganzen Tag im Haus** she fusses about the house all day **b** (*= herumbasteln*) to fiddle around (*an etw* (*dat*) with sth)

Puß|ta △ ['pʊsta] F **-, Pußten** [-tn] → **Puszta**

Pus|te ['pu:stə] F **-**, *no pl* (*inf*) puff (*inf*), breath; **aus der** *or* **außer ~ kommen** *or* **geraten** to get out of breath; **außer ~ sein** to be puffed out (*inf*), to be out of puff (*inf*); **(ja) ~!** (*inf*) no chance! (*inf*) → **ausgehen**

Pus|te|blu|me F (*inf*) dandelion clock

Pus|te|ku|chen INTERJ (*inf*) fiddlesticks (*dated inf*); **(ja) ~!** (*inf*) no chance! (*inf*)

Pus|tel ['pʊstl] F -, -n (= *Pickel*) spot, pimple; (*Med*) pustule

pus|ten ['puːstn] (*inf*) VI (= *blasen*) to puff, to blow; (= *keuchen*) to puff (and pant) VT a (= *blasen*) to puff, to blow; **die Fabrik pustet seit Jahren Dreck in die Luft** the factory has been puffing (out) *or* blowing (out) filth into the air for years b (*inf*) **dem werd' ich was ~!** I'll tell him where he can get off! (*inf*)

Pus|te|rohr NT (*inf*) peashooter

Pusz|ta ['pʊsta] F -, **Puszten** [-tn] puszta, Hungarian plain

pu|ta|tiv [puta'tiːf] ADJ (*geh*) putative

Pu|te ['puːtə] F -, -n turkey (hen); **dumme ~** (*inf*) silly goose (*inf*); **eingebildete ~** (*inf*) conceited *or* stuck-up little madam (*Brit inf*) *or* missy (*US inf*)

Pu|ten-: **Pu|ten|brust** F turkey breast; **Pu|ten|fleisch** NT (*Cook*) turkey (meat) *no pl*; **Pu|ten|schin|ken** M turkey ham; **Pu|ten|schnit|zel** NT (*Cook*) turkey breast in breadcrumbs

Pu|ter ['puːtɐ] M -s, - turkey (cock)

pu|ter|rot ADJ scarlet, bright red; **~ werden** to go as red as a beetroot (*inf*), to go scarlet, to go bright red

put put ['pʊt 'pʊt] INTERJ chick, chick, chick

Putsch [pʊtʃ] M -(e)s, -e coup (d'état), revolt, putsch

put|schen ['pʊtʃn] VI to rebel, to revolt; **in Südamerika wird permanent geputscht** they're always having coups *or* revolts in South America; **sich an die Macht ~** to take power by a military coup

Put|schist [pʊ'tʃɪst] M -en, -en, **Put|schis|tin** [-'tʃɪstɪn] F -, -nen rebel

Putsch|ver|such M attempted coup (d'état)

Pütt [pʏt] M -s, -s (*dial*) pit, mine

Put|te ['pʊtə] F -, -n (*Art*) cherub

put|ten ['pʊtn] VT to putt

putt, putt ['pʊt 'pʊt] INTERJ chick, chick, chick

Putz [pʊts] M -es, *no pl* a (*dated*) (= *Kleidung*) finery; (= *Besatz*) frills and furbelows *pl*; **in vollem ~ erscheinen** to arrive all dressed up in one's Sunday best b (*Build*) plaster; (= *Rauputz*) roughcast; **eine Mauer mit ~ verkleiden** *or* **bewerfen** to plaster *or* roughcast a wall; **unter ~** under the plaster c **auf den ~ hauen** (*inf*) (= *angeben*) to show off; (= *ausgelassen feiern*) to have a rave-up (*inf*); (= *meckern*) to kick up a fuss (*inf*)

Putz|dienst M cleaning duty; (= *Dienstleistung*) cleaning service; **~ haben** to be on cleaning duty

put|zen ['pʊtsn] VT a (= *säubern*) to clean; (= *polieren*) to polish; (= *wischen*) to wipe; *Pferd* to brush down, to groom; *Docht* to trim; **die Schuhe ~** to clean *or* polish one's shoes; **Fenster ~** to clean the windows; **sich** (*dat*) **die Nase ~** to wipe one's nose; (= *sich schnäuzen*) to blow one's nose; **sich** (*dat*) **die Zähne ~** to clean (*Brit*) *or* brush one's teeth; **einem Baby den Hintern/die Nase ~** to wipe a baby's bottom/nose; **~ gehen** to work as a cleaner
b (*dated*: = *schmücken*) to decorate
c *Mauer* to roughcast, to plaster
d (*Aus*: = *chemisch reinigen*) to dry-clean
VR a (= *sich säubern*) to wash *or* clean oneself
b (*dated*: = *sich schmücken*) to dress *or* do oneself up

Put|ze|rei [pʊtsə'rai] F -, -en a *no pl* (*inf*) cleaning; **hör doch endlich mal auf mit der ~!** will you stop all this damn cleaning! (*inf*) b (*Aus*: = *Reinigung*) dry cleaner's

Putz-: **Putz|fim|mel** M, *no pl* (*inf*) cleaning mania *or* bug; **einen ~ haben** to be a cleaning maniac; **Putz|frau** F cleaner, cleaning lady, char(woman) (*Brit*)

put|zig ['pʊtsɪç] (*inf*) ADJ (= *komisch*) funny, comical, amusing; (= *niedlich*) cute; (= *merkwürdig*) funny, strange, odd ADV (= *niedlich*) cutely; **das klingt ganz ~** that sounds so cute

Putz-: **Putz|ko|lon|ne** F team of cleaners; **Putz|lap|pen** M cloth; (= *Staubtuch*) duster; **Putz|le|der** NT chamois *or* chammy (leather), wash-leather; **Putz|ma|che|rin** F (*dated*) milliner; **Putz|mann** M *pl* **-männer** cleaning man; **Putz|mit|tel** NT (*zum Scheuern*) cleanser, cleansing agent; (*zum Polieren*) polish; (*pl*) cleaning things *pl*; **putz|mun|ter** ['pʊts'mʊntɐ] ADJ (*inf*) full of beans (*Brit inf*), lively; **Putz|sche|re** F wick trimmer; **Putz|stel|le** F cleaning job; **Putz|tag** M cleaning day; **Putz|teu|fel** M (*inf*) **sie ist ein richtiger ~** she's excessively house-proud (*Brit*), she's a neat-freak (*US sl*); **vom ~ besessen sein, den ~ haben** to have a mania for keeping things clean, to have the cleaning bug (*inf*); **Putz|tuch** NT *pl* **-tücher** (= *Staubtuch*) duster; (= *Wischlappen*) cloth; **Putz|wol|le** F wire *or* steel wool; **Putz|wut** F obsession with cleaning; **Putz|zeug** NT cleaning things *pl*

puz|zeln [pasəln] VI to do a jigsaw (puzzle)

Puz|zle ['pazl, 'pasl] NT -s, -s jigsaw (puzzle)

Puz|zle-: **Puz|zle|spiel** NT jigsaw (puzzle); **Puz|zle|teil** NT (*lit, fig*) piece of a/the puzzle; **die ~e wollen nicht passen** the pieces of the puzzle won't fit together

PVC [peːfau'tseː] NT -(s) PVC

PX-La|den [peː'ɪks-] M (*US Mil*) PX store

Pyg|mäe [pʏ'gmɛːə] M -n, -n, **Pyg|mä|in** [pʏ'gmɛːɪn] F -, -nen Pygmy

pyg|mä|en|haft [pʏ'gmɛːən-] ADJ pygmy-like, pygmy *attr*

Py|ja|ma [py'dʒaːma, py'ʒaːma, pi'dʒaːma, pi'ʒaːma] M -s, -s pair of pyjamas (*Brit*) *or* pajamas (*US*) *sing*, pyjamas *pl* (*Brit*), pajamas *pl* (*US*); **er öffnete die Tür im ~** he opened the door in his pyjamas (*Brit*) *or* pajamas (*US*)

Py|ja|ma|ho|se F pyjama trousers *or* bottoms *pl* (*Brit*), pajama bottoms *pl* (*US*)

Pyk|ni|ker ['pʏknikɐ] M -s, -, **Pyk|ni|ke|rin** [-ərɪn] F -, -nen stocky person

pyk|nisch ['pʏknɪʃ] ADJ stockily built, pyknic (*spec*)

Py|lon [py'loːn] M -en, -en, **Py|lo|ne** [py'loːnə] F -, -n (*Archit, von Brücke, Eingangstor*) pylon; (= *Absperrmarkierung*) traffic cone

Py|ra|mi|de [pyra'miːdə] F -, -n pyramid

py|ra|mi|den|för|mig ADJ pyramid-shaped *no adv*, pyramidal (*form*) ADV in the shape of a pyramid; **die Artisten hatten sich ~ aufgebaut** the acrobats had formed a pyramid

Py|re|nä|en [pyre'nɛːən] PL **die ~** the Pyrenees *pl*

Py|re|nä|en|halb|in|sel F Iberian Peninsula

Py|ro-: **Py|ro|ly|se** [pyro'lyːzə] F -, -n pyrolysis; **Py|ro|ma|ne** [pyro'maːnə] M -n, -n, **Py|ro|ma|nin** [-'maːnɪn] F -, -nen pyromaniac; **Py|ro|ma|nie** [pyroma'niː] F, *no pl* pyromania; **Py|ro|tech|nik** [pyro'tɛçnɪk] F pyrotechnics *sing*; **Py|ro|tech|ni|ker(in)** [pyro'tɛçnikɐ, -ərɪn] M(F) pyrotechnist; **py|ro|tech|nisch** [pyro'tɛçnɪʃ] ADJ pyrotechnic

Pyr|rhus|sieg ['pʏrʊs-] M Pyrrhic victory

py|tha|go|re|isch [pytago'reːɪʃ] ADJ Pythagorean; **~er Lehrsatz** Pythagoras's theorem, law of Pythagoras

Py|thon ['pyːtɔn] M -s, -s python

Py|thon|schlan|ge ['pyːtɔn-] F python

Q

Q, q [kuː] **NT -, -** Q, q
qkm *abbr von* **Quadratkilometer**
qm *abbr von* **Quadratmeter**
qua [kvaː] **ADV** *(geh)* qua
quab|be|lig [ˈkvabəlɪç] **ADJ** *Frosch, Qualle* slimy; *Pudding* wobbly
quab|beln [ˈkvabln] **VI** to wobble
Qua|cke|lei [kvakəˈlai] **F -, -en** *(inf)* nattering *(Brit inf)*, chattering, blethering *(inf)*
Quack|sal|ber [ˈkvakzalbɐ] **M -s, -**, **Quack|sal|be|rin** [-ərɪn] **F -, -nen** *(pej)* quack (doctor)
Quack|sal|be|rei [kvakzalbəˈrai] **F -, -en** quackery, quack medicine
quack|sal|bern [ˈkvakzalbɐn] **VI** *insep* to quack *(rare)*; **sowas nenne ich ~** I'd call that quack medicine *or* quackery
Quad **NT** *(= vierrädriges Motorrad)* Quad (bike), four-wheeler *(inf)*
Quad|del [ˈkvadl] **F -, -n** hives *pl*, rash; *(durch Insekten)* bite; *(von Sonne)* heat spot
Qua|der [ˈkvaːdɐ] **M -s, -** *or* **f -, -n** *(Math)* cuboid, rectangular solid; *(Archit: auch* **Quaderstein***)* ashlar, square stone block
Qua|der|stein **M** ashlar, square stone block
Quad|rant [kvaˈdrant] **-en, -en M** quadrant
Quad|rat [kvaˈdraːt] **NT -(e)s, -e** **a** *no pl (Fläche)* square; **drei Meter im ~** three metres *(Brit) or* meters *(US)* square **b** *no pl (Potenz)* square; **eine Zahl ins ~ erheben** to square a number; **vier zum ~** four squared; **die Geschwindigkeit steigt im ~ zur Entfernung** the speed increases in proportion to the square of the distance; **Pech im ~** *(fig)* incredibly bad luck **c** *(= quadratische Fläche)* square; **magisches ~** magic square
Quad|rat **NT -(e)s, -e(n)** *(Typ)* quad, quadrat
Quad|rat- *in cpds* square; **Quad|rat|fuß** **M** square foot
quad|ra|tisch [kvaˈdraːtɪʃ] **ADJ** *Form* square; *(Math) Gleichung* quadratic
Quad|rat-: **Quad|rat|ki|lo|me|ter** **M** square kilometre *(Brit) or* kilometer *(US)*; **Quad|rat|lat|schen** **PL** *(inf) (= Schuhe)* clodhoppers *pl (inf)*, beetle-crushers *pl (Brit inf)*; *(= Füße)* plates of meat *pl (Brit inf)*; **Quad|rat|me|ter** **M OR NT** square metre *(Brit) or* meter *(US)*; **Quad|rat|me|ter|preis** **M** price per square metre *(Brit) or* meter *(US)*; **Quad|rat|schä|del** **M** *(inf: = Kopf)* big head, great bonce *(Brit inf)*
Quad|ra|tur [kvadraˈtuːɐ] **F -, -en** quadrature; **die ~ des Kreises** *or* **Zirkels** the squaring of the circle; **das käme der ~ des Kreises** *or* **Zirkels gleich** that's like trying to square the circle
Quad|rat-: **Quad|rat|wur|zel** **F** square root; **Quad|rat|zahl** **F** square number
quad|rie|ren [kvaˈdriːrən] *ptp* **quadriert** **VT** **a** *Zahl, Kreis* to square **b** *Wand* to divide into squares
Quad|ri|ga [kvaˈdriːga] **F -, Quadrigen** [-gn] four-horsed chariot
Quad|ril|le [kvaˈdrɪljə, ka-] **F -, -n** quadrille
Quad|ro|fo|nie [kvadrofoˈniː] **F -,** *no pl* quadrophonic sound, quadrophony; **in ~** in quadrophonic, in quad *(inf)*
quad|ro|fo|nisch [kvadroˈfoːnɪʃ] **ADJ** quadrophonic
Quad|ro|pho|nie [kvadrofoˈniː] *etc* → **Quadrofonie** *etc*
Quai [keː, keː] **M OR NT -s, -s** quay; *(= Uferdamm auch)* waterfront
quak [kvaːk] **INTERJ** *(von Frosch)* croak; *(von Ente)* quack
qua|ken [ˈkvaːkn] **VI** *(Frosch)* to croak; *(Ente)* to quack; *(inf: Mensch)* to squawk *(inf)*, to screech *(inf)*
quä|ken [ˈkvɛːkn] **VTI** *(inf)* to screech, to squawk
Quä|ker [ˈkvɛːkɐ] **M -s, -**, **Quä|ke|rin** [-ərɪn] **F -, -nen** Quaker
Qual [kvaːl] **F -, -en** *(= Schmerz) (körperlich)* pain, agony; *(seelisch)* agony, anguish; **tapfer ertrug er alle ~en** he bore all his suffering *or* pain bravely; **jds ~(en) lindern** *or* **mildern** *(liter)* to lessen sb's suffering; **~en erleiden** *or* **leiden** to suffer agonies; **unter großen ~en sterben** to die in agony *or* great pain; **sein Leben war eine einzige ~** his life was a living death; **die letzten Monate waren für mich eine (einzige) ~** the last few months have been sheer agony for me; **es ist eine ~, das mit ansehen zu müssen** it is agonizing to watch; **er machte ihr den Aufenthalt/das Leben/die Tage zur ~** he made her stay/her life/her days a misery; **(jdm) zur ~ werden** to be agony (for sb); **es bereitete ihm ~en, sie so leiden zu sehen** it tormented him to see her suffering so; **die ~en des Gewissens** *(geh)*/**des Zweifels** agonies of conscience/of doubt *or* indecision; **die ~en, die sie seinetwegen** *or* **um ihn ausgestanden hat** the suffering she has gone through because of him → **Wahl**
quä|len [ˈkvɛːlən] **VT** to torment; *Tiere auch* to tease; *(inf) Motor* to punish; *(mit Bitten etc)* to pester, to plague; **jdn zu Tode ~** to torture sb to death → *auch* **gequält**
VR **a** *(seelisch)* to torture *or* torment oneself; *(= leiden)* to suffer, to be in agony
b *(= sich abmühen)* to struggle; **sie quälte sich in das enge Kleid** she struggled into *or* squeezed herself into her tight dress; **er musste sich ~, damit er das schaffte** it took him a lot of effort to do it, it was a struggle for him to do it; **sich durch ein Buch/die Unterlagen ~** to struggle *or* plough *(Brit) or* plow *(US)* through a book/the documents; **ich quäle mich jeden Morgen aus dem Bett** it's a struggle for me to get out of bed every morning; **er quälte sich aus dem Sessel** he heaved himself out of the chair; **das Auto quälte sich über den Berg** the car laboured *(Brit) or* labored *(US) or* struggled over the hill
quä|lend **ADJ** agonizing; *Erinnerungen auch* tormenting; *Krankheit auch* excruciating; **~e Ungewissheit/Zweifel** agonizing uncertainty/doubts, agonies of uncertainty/doubt; **~er Schmerz** agonizing *or* excruciating pain **ADV** agonizingly; **~ langsam** agonizingly slow
Quä|le|rei [kvɛːləˈrai] **F -, -en** **a** *(= Grausamkeit)* atrocity, torture *no pl*; *(= seelische, nervliche Belastung)* agony, torment; **diese Tierversuche sind in meinen Augen ~** in my view these experiments on animals are cruel; **das ist doch eine ~ für das Tier** that is cruel to the animal; **die letzten Monate waren eine einzige ~** the last few months were sheer agony **b** *(= mühsame Arbeit)* struggle; **das war vielleicht eine ~!** that was really a struggle *or* hard going
quä|le|risch [ˈkvɛːlərɪʃ] **ADJ** *attr* tormenting, agonizing
Quäl|geist **M** *(inf)* pest *(inf)*
Qua|li [ˈkvaːli] **M** *(Sch inf) special secondary school leaving certificate*
Qua|li [ˈkvaːli] **F** *abbr von* **Qualifikation** *(Sport inf)* qualification; *(= Runde)* qualifying round
Qua|li|fi|kant [kvalifiˈkant] **M -en, -en**, **Qua|li|fi|kan|tin** [-ɪn] **F -, -nen** *(Sport)* qualifier
Qua|li|fi|ka|ti|on [kvalifikaˈtsioːn] **F -, -en** qualification; *(= Ausscheidungswettkampf)* qualifying round, qualifier; **für diese Arbeit fehlt ihm die nötige ~** he lacks the necessary qualifications for this work; **er hat die ~ zu diesem Amt** he has the qualifications *or* he is qualified for this office; **die ~ für** *or* **zu etw schaffen** to qualify for sth; **zur ~ fehlten ihr nur wenige Sekunden** she only failed to qualify by a few seconds
Qua|li|fi|ka|ti|ons-: **Qua|li|fi|ka|ti|ons|run|de** **F** qualifying round; **Qua|li|fi|ka|ti|ons|spiel** **NT** qualifying match *or* game; **Qua|li|fi|ka|ti|ons|tur|nier** **NT** *(Sport)* qualifying tournament *or* round
qua|li|fi|zie|ren [kvalifiˈtsiːrən] *ptp* **qualifiziert** **VT** **a** *(= befähigen)* to qualify *(für, zu* for) **b** *(geh: = differenzieren)* to qualify **c** *(geh: = einstufen)* to characterize, to label **VR** **a** *(allgemein, Sport)* to qualify; **er hat sich zum Facharbeiter qualifiziert** he qualified as a specialist; **sich wissenschaftlich ~** to gain academic qualifications **b** *(= sich erweisen)* to show *or* reveal oneself *(als* to be)
qua|li|fi|ziert [kvalifiˈtsiːɐt] **ADJ** **a** *Arbeiter, Nachwuchs* qualified; *Arbeit* expert, professional **b** *(Pol) Mehrheit* requisite
Qua|li|tät [kvaliˈtɛːt] **F -, -en** quality; **dieses Leder ist in der ~ besser** this leather is better quality; **von der ~ her** as far as quality is concerned, (as) for quality; **die Ware ist von ausgezeichneter ~** the product is top quality, this is a top-quality product; **er kauft nur ~** he only buys quality (goods)
qua|li|ta|tiv [kvalitaˈtiːf] **ADJ** qualitative **ADV** qualitatively; **~ hochwertige Produkte** high-quality products; **~ ausgezeichnet/minderwertig sein** to be of (an) excellent/(a) substandard quality; **etw ist ~ verbesserungsfähig** the quality of sth could be improved
Qua|li|täts- *in cpds* quality; **Qua|li|täts|ar|beit** **F** quality work; **unsere Firma hat sich durch (ihre) ~ einen Namen gemacht** our firm made its name by the quality of its work, our firm has got itself a reputation for quality; **Qua|li|täts|er|zeug|nis** **NT** quality product; **Qua|li|täts|kon|trol|le** **F** quality check *or* control; **Qua|li|täts|ma|nage|ment** **NT** quality management; **Qua|li|täts|merk|mal** **NT** mark of quality; **Qua|li|täts|si|che|rung** **F**, *no pl* quality assurance *no pl*; **Qua|li|täts|stan|dard** **M** quality standard; **Qua|li|täts|un|ter|schied** **M** difference in quality; **Qua|li|täts|wa|re** **F** quality goods *pl*; **Qua|-**

li|täts|wein M *wine of certified origin and quality*

Qual|le ['kvalə] F -, -n jellyfish

Qualm [kvalm] M -(e)s, *no pl* (thick *or* dense) smoke; *(= Tabaksqualm)* fug

qual|men ['kvalmən] VI **a** *(Feuer)* to give off smoke; *(Ofen, Schornstein)* to (give off) smoke; **es qualmt aus dem Schornstein/hinten aus dem Auto** clouds of smoke are coming *or* billowing from the chimney/from the back of the car; **ihm ~ die Socken** *(inf)* he's rushing around all over the place **b** *(inf: Mensch)* to smoke; **sie qualmt einem die ganze Bude voll** she fills the whole place with smoke → **Schlot** VT *(inf) Zigarette, Pfeife* to puff away at *(inf)*

Qual|me|rei [kvalmə'rai] F -, -en *(inf)* smoking; *(von Ofen, Auto)* smoke

qual|mig ['kvalmıç] ADJ *Zimmer* smoke-filled, smoky; *Flamme* smoky

qual|voll ADJ painful; *Schmerzen* agonizing, excruciating; *Vorstellung, Gedanke* agonizing; *Anblick* harrowing ADV **~ sterben** to die an agonizing death

Quant [kvant] NT -s, -en quantum

Quänt|chen ['kvɛntçən] NT -s, - *(old)* tiny bit, spot; **ein ~ Salz** a speck *or* dash of salt; **ein ~ Mut** a scrap of courage; **kein ~** not a jot, not an iota; **das letzte ~ Glück/Hoffnung** the last little bit of luck/hope

quan|teln ['kvantln] VT to quantize

Quan|ten ['kvantn] *pl von* **Quantum**

Quan|ten-: **Quan|ten|me|cha|nik** F quantum mechanics *sing*; **Quan|ten|phy|sik** F quantum physics *sing*; **Quan|ten|sprung** M quantum leap; **Quan|ten|the|o|rie** F quantum theory

quan|ti|fi|zie|ren [kvantifi'tsi:rən] *ptp* **quantifiziert** VT to quantify

Quan|ti|tät [kvanti'tɛ:t] F -, -en quantity

quan|ti|ta|tiv [kvantita'ti:f] ADJ quantitative ADV quantitatively

Quan|tum ['kvantʊm] NT -s, **Quanten** [-tn] *(= Menge, Anzahl)* quantum, quantity; *(= Anteil)* quota, quantum *(an +dat* of)

Quap|pe ['kvapə] F -, -n **a** *(= Kaulquappe)* tadpole **b** *(= Aalquappe)* burbot

Qua|ran|tä|ne [karan'tɛ:nə] F -, -n quarantine; **in ~ liegen** *or* **sein** to be in quarantine; **unter ~ stellen** *(Personen)* to put in quarantine; *Gebiet, Stadt auch* to put under quarantine, to quarantine off; **unter ~ stehen** *(Person)* to be in quarantine; *(Gebiet, Stadt auch)* to be under quarantine, to be quarantined off; **über das Gebiet wurde sofort ~ verhängt** the area was immediately placed under quarantine *or* was immediately quarantined off

Qua|ran|tä|ne|sta|ti|on F quarantine *or* isolation ward

Quark [kvark] M -s, *no pl* **a** *(= Käse)* quark **b** *(inf) (= Unsinn)* rubbish *(Brit)*, nonsense; *(= unbedeutende Sache)* (little) trifle; **so ein ~!** stuff and nonsense!; **~ reden** to talk rubbish *(Brit)* *or* nonsense; **das geht ihn einen ~ an!** it's none of his business!; **getretener ~ wird breit, nicht stark** *(Prov)* it's quality not quantity that counts

Quark [kva:k] NT -s, -s *(Phys)* quark

Quark-: **Quark|ku|chen** M ≈ cheesecake; **Quark|spei|se** F *uncooked pudding made with quark, sugar, milk, fruit etc*; **Quark|ta|sche** F, **Quark|teil|chen** NT *curd cheese turnover*

Quart [kvart] [kvart] F -, -en **a** *(Mus: auch* **Quarte**) fourth; **ein Sprung über eine ~ nach oben/unten** a jump up/down a fourth; **verminderte/reine ~e** diminished/perfect fourth **b** *(Fechten)* quarte

Quart NT -s, -e **a** *(old: Maß)* ≈ quart **b** *no pl (Typ: = Format)* quarto (format)

Quar|ta ['kvarta] F -, **Quarten** [-tn] *(dated Sch) third year of German secondary school*

Quar|tal [kvar'ta:l] NT -s, -e quarter; **Kündigung zum ~** quarterly notice date; **es muss jedes ~ bezahlt werden** it has to be paid quarterly *or* every quarter

Quar|tal(s)-: **Quar|tal(s)|ab|schluss** M end of the quarter; **Quar|tal(s)|säu|fer(in)** M(F) *(inf)* periodic heavy drinker; **sein Vater ist ein ~** every so often his father goes on a binge *(inf)*; **quar|tal(s)|wei|se** ADJ quarterly ADV quarterly

Quar|ta|ner [kvar'ta:nɐ] M -s, -, **Quar|ta|ne|rin** [-ərın] F -, -nen *(dated Sch) pupil in third year of German secondary school*

Quar|tär [kvar'tɛ:ɐ] NT -s, *no pl* quaternary

Quart|band [-bant] M *pl* -bände quarto volume

Quar|te ['kvartə] F -, -n = **Quart**

Quar|ten *pl von* **Quart** *von* **Quarta** *von* **Quarte**

Quar|tett [kvar'tɛt] NT -(e)s, -e **a** *(Mus)* quartet **b** *(Cards) (= Spiel)* ≈ happy families; *(= Karten)* set of four cards

Quart|for|mat ['kvart-] NT quarto (format)

Quar|tier [kvar'ti:ɐ] NT -s, -e **a** *(= Unterkunft)* accommodation *(Brit)*, accommodations *pl (US)*; **wir sollten uns ein ~ suchen** we should look for accommodation(s) *or* a place to stay; **die Jugendlichen sind in verschiedenen ~en untergebracht/auf mehrere ~e verteilt worden** the youngsters have been accommodated *or* have been given accommodation(s) *or* have been put up in various places; **wir hatten unser ~ in einem alten Bauernhof** we stayed in an old farmhouse **b** *(Mil)* quarters *pl*, billet; **bei jdm in ~ liegen** to be quartered *or* billeted with *or* on sb; **~ machen** to arrange quarters *or* billets; **~ nehmen** to put up, to stop; **(sein) ~ beziehen** to take up (one's) quarters **c** *(= Stadtviertel)* district, quarter

Quar|tier-: **Quar|tier|ma|cher(in)** M(F) *(Mil)* billeting officer; **Quar|tier|meis|ter** M *(old Mil)* quartermaster; **Quar|tier|su|che** F **auf ~ sein** to be looking for accommodation *or* a place to stay

Quarz [kvarts] M -es, -e quartz

Quarz-: **Quarz|glas** NT quartz glass; **quarz|hal|tig** ADJ quartziferous *(form)*, which contains quartz; **Quarz|lam|pe** F quartz lamp; **Quarz|sand** M quartz sand; **Quarz|uhr** F quartz clock; *(= Armbanduhr)* quartz watch

Qua|sar [kva'za:ɐ] M -s, -e quasar

qua|si ['kva:zi] ADV virtually PREF quasi; **~-wissenschaftlich** quasi-scientific

Quas|sel-: **Quas|sel|bu|de** F *(pej inf: = Parlament etc)* talking shop *(inf)*; **Quas|sel|strip|pe** F *(inf)* chatterbox *(inf)*; *(beleidigend)* windbag *(inf)*, blabbermouth *(inf)*

Quas|se|lei [kvasə'lai] F -, -en *(inf)* gabbling *(Brit inf)*, gabbing *(inf)*, blathering *(inf)*

quas|seln ['kvasln] VTI to gabble *(Brit inf)*, to blather *(inf)*; **was quasselst du denn da für ein dummes Zeug?** what are you blathering about now? *(inf)*

Quast [kvast] M -(e)s, -e *(dial)* wide paint brush

Quas|te ['kvastə] F -, -n *(= Troddel)* tassel; *(von Pinsel)* brush, bristles *pl*; *(= Schwanzquaste)* tuft; *(= Puderquaste)* powder puff

Quas|ten|flos|ser [-flɔsɐ] M -s, - *(Zool)* coelacanth

Quäs|tur [kvɛs'tu:ɐ] F -, -en *(Univ)* bursary

Qua|tem|ber [kva'tɛmbɐ] M -s, - *(Eccl)* Ember day

quatsch [kvatʃ] INTERJ squelch

Quatsch [kvatʃ] M -es, *no pl (inf)* **a** *(= Unsinn)* rubbish *(Brit)*, nonsense; **das ist der größte ~, den ich je gehört habe** that is the biggest load of rubbish *(Brit) or* nonsense I have ever heard; **ach ~!** rubbish! *(Brit)*, nonsense!; **ohne ~!** *(= ehrlich)* no kidding! *(inf)*; **alles ~!, so ein ~!** what (a load of) rubbish *(Brit) or* nonsense; **~ mit Soße!** stuff and nonsense! **b** *(= Dummheiten)* nonsense; **hört doch endlich mit dem ~ auf!** stop being so stupid *or* silly!; **was soll denn der ~!** what's all this nonsense in aid of then!; **lass den ~** cut it out! *(inf)*; **~ machen** to mess about *(Brit) or* around *(inf)*; **etw aus ~ machen** to do sth for a laugh *or* for fun; **mach damit keinen ~** don't mess about *(Brit) or* around with it *(inf)*, don't do anything stupid with it; **mach keinen ~, sonst knallts** don't try anything funny or I'll shoot; **mach keinen ~, du kannst doch jetzt nicht schwanger werden** don't be silly, you can't get pregnant now!

quat|schen ['kvatʃn] *(inf)* VTI *(= dummes Zeug reden)* to gab (away) *(inf)*, to blather *(inf)*, to gabble *(Brit inf)*; **sie quatscht mal wieder einen Blödsinn** she's talking a load of rubbish *(Brit) or* nonsense again VI **a** *(= plaudern)* to blather *(inf)*, to chatter, to natter *(Brit inf)*; **er hat stundenlang gequatscht** he blathered *or* gabbled *(Brit)* on for hours *(inf)*; **ich hab mit ihm am Telefon gequatscht** I had a good natter *(Brit inf) or* chat with him on the phone **b** *(= etw ausplaudern)* to squeal *(inf)*, to talk

quat|schen ['kva:tʃn] VI *(Schlamm)* to squelch

Quat|sche|rei [kvatʃə'rai] F -, -en *(inf)* blathering *(inf)*, yacking *(inf)*; *(in der Schule)* chattering

Quatsch-: **Quatsch|kopf** M *(pej inf) (= Schwätzer)* windbag *(inf)*; *(= Dummkopf)* fool, twit *(inf)*; **quatsch|nass** ADJ *(inf)* soaking *or* dripping wet

Que|cke ['kvɛkə] F -, -n couch grass

Queck|sil|ber ['kvɛkzılbɐ] NT **a** *(abbr* **Hg**) mercury, quicksilver *(dated)*; *(inf: = Thermometer)* mercury *(inf)*; **~ im Leib haben** *(fig)* to have ants in one's pants *(inf)* **b** *(dated: Mensch)* fidget

Queck|sil|ber- *in cpds* mercury; **Queck|sil|ber|dampf|lam|pe** F mercury-vapour *(Brit) or* mercury-vapor *(US)* lamp; **queck|sil|ber|hal|tig** ADJ mercurial

queck|sil|be|rig, **queck|silb|rig** ADJ *(fig)* fidgety, restless

Queck|sil|ber-: **Queck|sil|ber|säu|le** F mercury (column); **die ~ ist auf 30 Grad geklettert** the mercury has risen to 30 degrees; **Queck|sil|ber|ver|gif|tung** F mercury poisoning

Quell [kvɛl] M -(e)s, -e *(poet)* spring, source

Quell-: **Quell|an|wen|dung** F *(Comput)* source application; **Quell|be|wöl|kung** F *(Met)* cumulus clouds *pl*; **Quell|code** M *(Comput)* source code; **Quell|da|tei** F *(Comput)* source file

Quel|le ['kvɛlə] F -, -n **a** spring; *(von Fluss)* spring, source; *(= Erdölquelle, Gasquelle)* well; **heiße ~n** hot springs; **eine ~ erschließen** to develop *or* exploit a source **b** *(fig) (= Ursprung, Informant)* source; *(für Waren)* source (of supply), supplier; **die ~ allen Übels** the root of all evil; **eine ~ der Freude** a source of pleasure; **~n der Weisheit** fountain of knowledge; **aus zuverlässiger/sicherer ~** from a reliable/trustworthy source; **an der ~ sitzen** *(fig)* to be well-placed; *(in Organisation)* to be able to get inside information; **kannst du mir einige Bücher besorgen, du sitzt doch an der ~?** can you get me some books, after all you can get them at source **c** *(Comput)* source

quel|len ['kvɛlən] VI *pret* **quoll** [kvɔl], *ptp* **gequollen** [gə'kvɔlən] *aux sein* **a** *(= herausfließen)* to pour, to stream *(aus* out of); **der Bauch quillt ihm über die Hose** his stomach hangs out *or* bulges out over his trousers *(esp Brit) or* pants *(esp US)*; **die Augen quollen ihm aus dem Kopf** his eyes were popping out of his head **b** *(Holz, Reis, Erbsen)* to swell; **lassen Sie die Bohnen über Nacht ~** leave the beans to soak overnight VT *pret* **quellte** ['kvɛltə], *ptp* **gequellt** [gə'kvɛlt] *(rare) Erbsen* to soak

Quel|len-: **Quel|len|an|ga|be** F reference; **achten Sie bei der ~ darauf, dass ...** make sure when doing *or* giving the references that ...; **das Material wurde ohne ~ verwendet** the material was used without reference to its source; **Quel|len|for|schung** F source research; **Quel|len|kri|tik** F verification of sources;

Quel|len|nach|weis M *(= Quellenangabe)* reference; *(Auflistung der Quellen)* bibliography, list of sources; **Quel|len|samm|lung** F (collection of) source material; *(= Quellenwerk)* source book; **Quel|len|steu|er** F *(Econ)* tax at source; **Quel|len|stu|di|um** NT study of sources; **ich bin immer noch mit dem ~ beschäftigt** I am still studying the sources

Quell-: **Quell|fluss** M source (river); **quell|frisch** ADJ *Wasser* spring-fresh *attr*, fresh from the spring *pred*; **Quell|ge|biet** NT headwaters *pl*; **Quell|lauf|werk** NT *(Comput)* source drive; **Quell|pro|gramm** NT *(Comput)* source program; **Quell|spra|che** F source language; **Quell|was|ser** NT spring water

Quen|ge|lei [kvɛŋəˈlai] F -, -en *(inf)* whining

quen|ge|lig [ˈkvɛŋəlɪç], **queng|lig** [ˈkvɛŋlɪç] ADJ whining; **die Kinder wurden ~** the children started to whine; **er ist sonst nicht so ~** he doesn't usually whine so much

quen|geln [ˈkvɛŋln] VI *(inf)* to whine

Queng|ler [ˈkvɛŋlɐ] M -s, -, **Queng|le|rin** [-ərɪn] F -, -nen *(inf)* whiner

Quent|chen △ [ˈkvɛntçən] NT -s, - → **Quäntchen**

quer [kveːɐ] ADV *(= schräg)* crossways, crosswise, diagonally; *(= rechtwinklig)* at right angles; **~ gestreift** horizontally striped, cross-striped; **sollen wir den Teppich lieber ~ legen?** why don't we lay the carpet crosswise *or* crossways *or* diagonally?; **er legte sich ~ aufs Bett** he lay down across the bed; **die Spur verläuft ~ zum Hang** the path runs across the slope; **die Straße/Linie verläuft ~** the road/the line runs at right angles; **der Wagen stand ~ zur Fahrbahn** the car was at right angles to the road; **der Lastzug lag ~ über der Straße** the truck was lying (diagonally/at right angles) across the road; **wenn Sie sich ~ stellen, habe ich mit meinem Wagen auch noch Platz** if you park diagonally/at right angles I'll have room to park my car too; **~ durch etw gehen/laufen** *etc* to cross sth, to go through sth; **~ über etw** *(acc)* **gehen/laufen** to cross sth, to go across sth; **der Hund ist ~ über den Rasen gelaufen** the dog ran straight *or* right across the lawn; **die Kamera ~ nehmen** to hold the camera lengthways *or* crossways; **den Stoff ~ nehmen** to use the cross-grain of the material → **kreuz**

Quer-: **quer|ab** [kveːɐˈlap] ADV *(Naut)* abeam; **Quer|ach|se** F transverse axis; **Quer|bal|ken** M crossbeam; *(von Türrahmen)* transom, lintel; *(Sport)* crossbar; *(Her)* bar; *(Mus) line joining quavers etc*; **quer|beet** [kveːɐˈbeːt, ˈkveːɐbeːt] ADV *(inf) (= wahllos)* at random; *(= durcheinander)* all over the place *(inf)*; *(= querfeldein)* across country; **Quer|den|ker(in)** M(F) open-minded thinker; **quer|durch** [kveːɐˈdʊrç] ADV straight through

Que|re [ˈkveːrə] F -, *no pl* **der ~ nach** widthways, breadthways; **jdm in die ~ kommen** *(= begegnen)* to cross sb's path; *(auch fig: = in den Weg geraten)* to get in sb's way; **es muss ihm etwas in die ~ gekommen sein, sonst hätte er sich nicht verspätet** something must have come up otherwise he would not be late

Quer|ein|stei|ger(in) M(F) lateral entry employee; **sie ist (eine) ~in** she comes from a totally different profession; **bei uns gibt es viele ~** many of our employees *or* colleagues come from a different professional *or* educational background

Que|re|le [kveˈreːlə] F -, -n *usu pl (geh)* dispute, quarrel

que|ren [ˈkveːrən] VTI to cross

quer|feld|ein [kveːɐfɛltˈlain] ADV across country

Quer|feld|ein-: **Quer|feld|ein|lauf** M cross-country (run); *(Wettbewerb)* cross-country (race); **Quer|feld|ein|ren|nen** NT cross-country; *(Autorennen)* autocross; *(Motorradrennen)* motocross; *(Fahrradrennen)* cyclecross; *(Pferderennen)* point-to-point

Quer-: **Quer|flö|te** F (transverse) flute; **Quer|for|mat** NT landscape (format); **im ~** in landscape format; **quer+ge|hen** *sep irreg aux sein*, **quer ge|hen** △ *irreg aux sein* VI *(inf)* to go wrong; **heute geht mir alles quer** I can't do a thing right today; **quer|ge|streift** ADJ *attr* → **quer**; **Quer|holz** NT crossbeam; *(von Türrahmen)* transom, lintel; **Quer|kopf** M *(inf)* awkward so-and-so *(inf) or* customer *(inf)*; **quer|köp|fig** ADJ awkward, perverse; **Quer|la|ge** F *(Med)* transverse presentation, crossbirth; **Quer|lat|te** F crossbar; **quer+le|gen** *sep*, **quer le|gen** △ VR *(fig inf)* to be awkward; **Quer|li|nie** F diagonal line; **Quer|pass** M cross; **Quer|pfei|fe** F fife; **Quer|ru|der** NT aileron; **quer+schie|ßen** *sep irreg*, **quer schie|ßen** △ *irreg* VI *(inf)* to be awkward, to spoil things; **Quer|schiff** NT transept; **Quer|schlä|ger** M ricochet (shot)

Quer|schnitt M *(lit, fig)* cross section

Quer|schnitt(s)-: **quer|schnitt(s)|ge|lähmt** ADJ paraplegic; **seit dem Autounfall ist er ~** since the car accident he has been paralyzed from the waist down; **Quer|schnitt(s)|ge|lähm|te(r)** [-gəlɛːmtə] MF *decl as adj* paraplegic; **Quer|schnitt(s)|läh|mung** F paraplegia; **Quer|schnitt(s)|zeich|nung** F sectional drawing

Quer-: **quer+schrei|ben** *sep irreg*, **quer schrei|ben** △ *irreg* VT *(Fin) Wechsel* to accept, to underwrite; **Quer|schuss** M *(fig)* objection; **quer+stel|len** *sep*, **quer stel|len** △ VR *(fig inf)* to be awkward; **Quer|stra|ße** F *(= Nebenstraße)* side street; *(= Abzweigung)* turning; **das ist eine ~ zur Hauptstraße** it runs at right angles to the main street; **in dieser ~ muss das Geschäft sein** the shop must be down this turning; **bei** *or* **an der zweiten ~ fahren Sie links ab** take the second road *or* turning on your left; **die ~n zur Königstraße sehen alle gleich aus** the streets (going) off Königstraße all look the same; **Quer|strei|fen** M horizontal stripe; **Quer|strich** M (horizontal) stroke *or* line; *(Typ inf: = Gedankenstrich)* dash; *(= Bruchstrich)* line; **einen ~ durch etw machen** to put a line through sth; *(= streichen auch)* to cross sth out; **er macht beim T nie die ~e** he always forgets to cross his T's; **Quer|sum|me** F *(Math)* sum of digits (of a number); **die ~ bilden** to add the digits in a number; **Quer|trei|ber(in)** M(F) *(inf)* troublemaker, awkward customer *(inf)*; **Quer|trei|be|rei** [kveːɐtraibəˈrai] F -, -en *(inf)* awkwardness, troublemaking

Que|ru|lant [kveruˈlant] M -en, -en, **Que|ru|lan|tin** [-ˈlantɪn] F -, -nen grouser *(Brit inf)*, grumbler

que|ru|lie|ren [kveruˈliːrən] *ptp* **queruliert** VI to grouse *(Brit inf)*, to grumble

Quer-: **Quer|ver|bin|dung** F connection, link; *(von Eisenbahn)* connecting line; *(von Straße)* link road; **hier lässt sich doch eine ~ zur deutschen Geschichte herstellen** you can surely make a connection here with German history, you can surely link this up with German history; **Quer|ver|weis** M cross-reference

quet|schen [ˈkvɛtʃn] **VT** **a** *(= drücken)* to squash, to crush; *(aus einer Tube)* to squeeze; *Kartoffeln* to mash; *(Med:) usu pass* to crush; *Stimme* to strain; **etw in etw** *(acc)* **~** to squeeze *or* squash sth into sth; **jdn halbtot ~** to crush sb (nearly) to death; **jdm/sich den Finger ~** to squash sb's/one's finger; **du hast mir den Finger in der Tür gequetscht** you caught my finger in the door **VR** *(= sich klemmen)* to be caught *or* squashed *or* crushed; *(= sich zwängen)* to squeeze (oneself); **du kannst dich noch ins Auto ~** you can still squeeze into the car

Quetsch-: **Quetsch|fal|te** F *(Fashion)* box pleat; **Quetsch|kom|mo|de** F *(hum inf)* squeeze-box *(inf)*

Quet|schung [ˈkvɛtʃʊŋ] F -, -en, **Quetsch|wun|de** F *(Med)* bruise, contusion *(form)*; **~en erleiden** to suffer bruising; **der Fahrer kam mit ~en davon** the driver escaped with bruises *or* bruising; **~ innerer Organe** internal bruising

Queue [kø:] NT OR M -s, -s *(Billard)* cue

Quiche [kɪʃ] F -, -s quiche

quick [kvɪk] ADJ *(esp N Ger)* lively

Qui|ckie [ˈkvɪki] M -s, -s *(inf: = Sex)* quickie *(inf)*

quick|le|ben|dig ADJ *(inf) Kind* lively, active; *ältere Person auch* spry

quiek [kviːk] INTERJ squeak

quie|ken [ˈkviːkən], **quiek|sen** [ˈkviːksn] VI to squeal, to squeak

quiet|schen [ˈkviːtʃn] VI *(Tür, Schloss, Schuhe)* to squeak; *(Reifen, Straßenbahn, Mensch)* to squeal; *Bremsen* to screech; **das Kind quietschte vergnügt** *or* **vor Vergnügen** *(inf)* the child squealed with delight; **das** *or* **es war zum Quietschen!** *(inf)* it was a (real) scream! *(inf)*

quietsch-: **quietsch|fi|del** → **quietschvergnügt**; **quietsch|le|ben|dig** ADJ *(inf) Kind* full of beans *pred (inf)*; *(= sehr wach)* wide awake *pred*; **quietsch|ver|gnügt** ADJ *(inf)* happy as a sandboy

quillt [kvɪlt] *3. pers sing pres von* **quellen**

Quilt [kvɪlt] M -s, -s quilt

Quint [kvɪnt] F -, -en **a** *(Mus)* fifth **b** *(Fechten)* quinte

Quin|ta [ˈkvɪnta] F -, **Quinten** [-tn] *(dated Sch) second year of German secondary school*

Quin|ta|ner [kvɪnˈtaːnɐ] M -s, -, **Quin|ta|ne|rin** [-ərɪn] F -, -nen *(dated Sch) pupil in second year of German secondary school*

Quin|te [ˈkvɪntə] F -, -n *(Mus)* fifth

Quin|ten *pl von* **Quinta** *von* **Quinte**

Quint|es|senz [ˈkvɪntɛsɛnts] F quintessence

Quin|tett [kvɪnˈtɛt] NT -(e)s, -e quintet

Quin|to|le [kvɪnˈtoːlə] F -, -n quintuplet

Quirl [kvɪrl] M -s, -e **a** *(Cook)* whisk, beater **b** *(Bot)* whorl, verticil **c** *(dated inf: Mensch)* live wire *(inf)*

quir|len [ˈkvɪrlən] VT to whisk, to beat

quir|lig [ˈkvɪrlɪç] ADJ *Mensch, Stadt* lively, exuberant

Quis|ling [ˈkvɪslɪŋ] M -s, -e *(Pol pej)* quisling

quitt [kvɪt] ADJ **~ sein (mit jdm)** to be quits *or* even (with sb); **jdn/etw ~ sein** *(dial)* to be rid of sb/sth

Quit|te [ˈkvɪtə] F -, -n quince

quit|te(n)|gelb ADJ (sickly) yellow

Quit|ten|ge|lee NT quince jelly

quit|tie|ren [kvɪˈtiːrən] *ptp* **quittiert** **VT** **a** *(= bestätigen) Betrag, Rechnung, Empfang* to give a receipt for; **lassen Sie sich** *(dat)* **die Rechnung ~** get a receipt for the bill **b** *(= beantworten)* to meet, to answer, to counter *(mit* with) **c** *(= verlassen) Dienst* to quit, to resign **VI** **a** *(= bestätigen)* to sign **b** *(old: = zurücktreten)* to quit, to resign

Quit|tung [ˈkvɪtʊŋ] F -, -en **a** receipt; **gegen ~** on production of a receipt; **eine ~ über 500 Euro** a receipt for 500 euros; **eine ~ ausstellen (über** *or* **für etw)** to make out *or* give a receipt (for sth); **jdm eine ~ für etw ausstellen** to give sb a receipt for sth; **können Sie mir bitte eine ~ geben?** could I have a receipt please? **b** *(fig)* **das ist die ~ für Ihre Unverschämtheit** that is what you get for being so insolent, that's what comes of being so insolent; **das ist die ~ dafür, dass ...** that's the price you have to pay for ...; **jetzt haben Sie die ~!** now you have paid the penalty!; **die ~ für etw bekommen** *or* **erhalten** to pay the penalty for sth; **du wirst schon noch die ~ für deine Faulheit/Frechheit bekommen** you'll pay the penalty for your laziness/impudence *or* for being so lazy/impudent

Quit|tungs|block M *pl* -blöcke, **Quit|tungs|buch** NT *pl* -bücher receipt book

Qui|vive [kiˈviːf] NT, *no pl* **auf dem ~** on the qui vive, on the alert

Quiz [kvɪs] NT -, - quiz

Quiz-: **Quiz|fra|ge** F quiz question; **Quiz|mas|ter** [ˈkvɪsmaːstɐ] M -s, -, **Quiz|mas|te|rin**

[-ərɪn] F -, -nen quizmaster; **Quiz|sen|dung** F quiz show; *(mit Spielen)* gameshow

quoll *pret von* **quellen**

Quo|rum ['kvo:rʊm] NT -s, *no pl* quorum

Quo|te ['kvo:tə] F -, -n **a** *(Statistik) (= Anteilsziffer)* proportion; *(= Rate)* rate; *(TV etc)* ratings *pl* **b** *(Econ: = Quantum)* quota

QUOTE

In German-speaking countries the word **Quote** generally refers to two things. Firstly, it denotes the ratings for a particular television programme. If the **Quote** is not high enough, then the programme in question is likely to be doomed, whether it is on a state or a commercial channel. Secondly, **Quoten** refer to the quota system for the allocation of jobs. This is a commitment on the part of the government, employers and political parties to reserve a certain proportion of available jobs for women, the disabled and members of ethnic minorities. Quota systems, especially those relating to women, are controversial and have given rise to derogatory terms such as **Quotenfrauen**.

Quo|te|lung ['kvo:təlʊŋ] F -, -en apportionment

Quo|ten|frau F *(pej inf)* token woman, *woman who has been given a post just to fulfil the quota system requirements*

Quo|ten|re|ge|lung F quota system

Quo|ti|ent [kvo'tsiɛnt] M -en, -en quotient

quo|tie|ren [kvo'ti:rən] *ptp* **quotiert** VT *(Comm) Preis, Kurs* to quote; *(= Verhältnis regeln)* to set quotas/a quota on; **die Ministerposten sind quotiert** the allocation of ministerial posts *(esp Brit) or* positions is subject to quotas

Quo|tie|rung F -, -en *(Comm)* quotation; *(= Regelung des Verhältnisses)* setting of quotas/a quota

QWER|TY-Tas|ta|tur ['kvɛrti-] F QWERTY keyboard

QWERTZ-Tas|ta|tur ['kvɛrts-] F QWERTZ keyboard

R

R, r [ɛr] NT **-, -** R, r; **das R rollen** to roll one's r's; **R wie Richard** R for Richard

Ra|batt [ra'bat] M **-(e)s, -e** discount (*auf* on); **mit 10%** ~ at *or* with (a) 10% discount

Ra|bat|te [ra'batə] F **-, -n** (= *Beet*) border

Ra|batt|mar|ke F (*Comm*) (trading) stamp, coupon (*US*)

Ra|batz [ra'bats] M **-es,** *no pl* (*inf*) = **Radau**

Ra|bau|ke [ra'baukə] M **-n, -n** (*inf*) hooligan, lout (*inf*), rowdy (*Brit inf*), punk (*US inf*)

Ra|bau|ken|tum [ra'baukntu:m] NT **-s,** *no pl* hooliganism, rowdyism (*Brit*)

Rab|bi ['rabi] M **-(s), -s** *or* **Rabbinen** [ra'bi:nən] rabbi

Rab|bi|ner [ra'bi:nɐ] M **-s, -, Rab|bi|ne|rin** [-ərın] F **-, -en** rabbi

rab|bi|nisch [ra'bi:nıʃ] ADJ rabbinical

Ra|be ['ra:bə] M **-n, -n** raven; **wie ein ~ stehlen** (*inf*) to thieve like a magpie; **ein weißer ~** (*fig*) a rare bird, a rara avis

Ra|ben-: **Ra|ben|aas** NT (*dated inf*) bad lot (*Brit inf*), bad character (*esp US inf*); **Ra|ben|el|tern** PL (*inf*) bad parents *pl*; **Ra|ben|mut|ter** F *pl* **-mütter** (*inf*) bad mother; **ra|ben|schwarz** ADJ *Nacht* pitch-black, black as pitch; *Augen, Seele auch* coal-black, black as coal; *Haare* jet-black, raven(-black); (*fig*) *Tag, Humor* black; **Ra|ben|va|ter** M (*inf*) bad father

ra|bi|at [ra'bia:t] ADJ *Kerl* violent, rough; *Autofahrer* breakneck, wild; *Geschäftsleute* ruthless; *Umgangston* aggressive; *Methoden, Konkurrenz* ruthless, cut-throat; **~ werden** (*wütend*) to go wild; (*aggressiv*) to get violent *or* physical (*inf*) ADV (= *rücksichtslos*) roughly; *vorgehen* ruthlessly; (= *aggressiv*) violently

Ra|bu|list [rabu'lıst] M **-en, -en, Ra|bu|lis|tin** [-'lıstın] F **-, -nen** sophist, quibbler

Ra|bu|lis|te|rei [rabulıstə'rai] F **-, -en, Ra|bu|lis|tik** [rabu'lıstık] F **-,** *no pl* sophistry, quibbling

ra|bu|lis|tisch [rabu'lıstıʃ] ADJ sophistic, quibbling

Ra|che ['raxə] F **-,** *no pl* revenge, vengeance; **die ~ des kleinen Mannes** (*inf*) sweet revenge; **Tag der ~** (*liter*) day of reckoning; **das ist die ~ für deine Untat** this is the retribution for your misdeed; **auf ~ sinnen** to contemplate *or* plot revenge; **~ schwören** to swear vengeance; **(an jdm) ~ nehmen** *or* **üben** to take revenge *or* to have one's revenge (on *or* upon sb); **etw aus ~ tun** to do sth in revenge; **~ ist Blutwurst** (*inf*) you'll/he'll *etc* be sorry (*inf*); **~ ist süß** (*prov*) revenge is sweet (*prov*); **Montezumas ~** (*hum inf*: = *Durchfall*) Montezuma's revenge (*hum*)

Ra|che-: **Ra|che|akt** M act of revenge *or* vengeance; **Ra|che|durst** M thirst *or* longing for revenge *or* vengeance; **ra|che|durs|tig** ADJ thirsting *or* longing for revenge *or* vengeance; **Ra|che|en|gel** M avenging angel; **Ra|che|feld|zug** M retaliation campaign; **Ra|che|ge|fühl** NT feeling of bitter resentment; **~e gegen etw/jdn haben** to feel bitter resentment at sth/against *or* toward(s) sb; **Ra|che|göt|tin** F **wie eine ~** like a Fury

Ra|chen ['raxn] M **-s, -** throat, pharynx (*spec*); (*von großen Tieren*) jaws *pl*; (*fig*) jaws *pl*, abyss, maw; **jdm etw in den ~ werfen** *or* **schmeißen** (*inf*) to shove sth down sb's throat (*inf*); **jdm den ~ stopfen** (*inf*) to give sb what he/she wants

rä|chen ['rɛçn] VT *jdn, Untat* to avenge (*etw an jdm* sth on sb); **er schwor, dieses Unrecht zu ~** he swore to seek vengeance for this injustice, he swore to avenge this injustice; **dieses Unrecht werde ich noch an ihm ~** I intend to avenge myself on him for this injustice VR (*Mensch*) to get one's revenge, to take revenge *or* vengeance (*an jdm für etw* on sb for sth); (*Schuld, Sünde, Untat*) to have dire consequences; **deine Faulheit/Unehrlichkeit wird sich ~** you'll pay for being so lazy/dishonest

Ra|chen-: **Ra|chen|blüt|ler** [-bly:tlɐ] M **-s, -** (*Bot*) figwort; **Ra|chen|höh|le** F pharynx, pharyngeal cavity; **Ra|chen|ka|tarr(h)** M pharyngitis; **Ra|chen|man|del** F pharyngeal tonsil; **Ra|chen|put|zer** [-pʊtsɐ] M **-s, -** (*hum inf*) gut rot (*inf*)

Ra|che|plan M plan of revenge; **Rachepläne schmieden** to plot revenge

Rä|cher ['rɛçɐ] M **-s, -, Rä|che|rin** [-ərın] F **-, -nen** avenger

Ra|che|schwur M oath of revenge *or* vengeance

Rach-: **Rach|gier** F vindictiveness; **rach|gie|rig** ADJ vindictive ADV vindictively

Ra|chi|tis [ra'xi:tıs] F **-, Rachitiden** [raxi'ti:dn] rickets, rachitis (*spec*)

ra|chi|tisch [ra'xi:tıʃ] ADJ *Kind* with rickets, rickety, rachitic (*spec*); *Symptom* of rickets

Rach-: **Rach|sucht** F vindictiveness; **rach|süch|tig** ADJ vindictive

Ra|cker ['rakɐ] M **-s, -** (*inf*: *Kind*) rascal, scamp, monkey (*all inf*)

Ra|cke|rei [rakə'rai] F **-, -en** (*inf*) grind (*inf*)

ra|ckern ['rakɐn] VIR (*inf*) to slave (away) (*inf*)

Ra|cket ['rɛkət, ra'kɛt] NT **-s, -s** (*Aus*) racket, racquet (*Brit*)

Rac|lette ['raklɛt] NT OR F **-s, -s** raclette

Rad [ra:t] NT **-(e)s, ¨-er** ['rɛ:dɐ] **a** wheel; (= *Rolle*) caster; (= *Zahnrad*) gearwheel; (*Sport*) cartwheel; **~ schlagen** to do *or* turn cartwheels; **ein ~ schlagen** (*Sport*) to do *or* turn a cartwheel; **der Pfau schlägt ein ~** the peacock is fanning out its tail *or* spreading its tail *or* opening its fan; **jdn aufs ~ flechten** (*Hist*) to break sb on the wheel; **alle Räder greifen ineinander** (*fig*) **ein ~ greift ins andere** (*fig*) it all knits together, all the parts knit together; **nur ein ~** *or* **Rädchen im Getriebe sein** (*fig*) to be only a cog in the works; **das ~ der Geschichte** the wheels of history; **das ~ der Geschichte** *or* **Zeit lässt sich nicht zurückdrehen** you can't turn *or* put the clock back; **unter die Räder kommen** *or* **geraten** (*inf*) to get *or* fall into bad ways; **ein großes ~ drehen** (*fig*) to be a big businessman/businesswoman; **das ~ neu** *or* **noch einmal erfinden** to reinvent the wheel; **das fünfte ~ am Wagen sein** (*inf*) to be in the way; **ein ~ abhaben** (*inf*) to have a screw loose (*inf*)

b (= *Fahrrad*) bicycle, bike (*inf*), cycle; **~ fahren** to cycle; (*pej inf*: = *kriechen*) to crawl (*Brit inf*), to suck up (*inf*); **ich fahre ~** I ride a bicycle; **kannst du ~ fahren?** can you ride a bike?; **mit dem ~ fahren/kommen** to go/come by bicycle

Rad NT **-(s), -** (*Maßeinheit*) rad

Rad|ach|se F axle(tree)

Ra|dar [ra'da:ɐ, 'ra:da:ɐ] M OR NT **-s, -e** radar

Ra|dar- *in cpds* radar; **Ra|dar|ab|wehr|netz** NT (*Mil*) radar defence (*Brit*) *or* defense (*US*) network; **Ra|dar|an|la|ge** F radar (equipment) *no indef art*; **Ra|dar|fal|le** F speed trap; **Ra|dar|ge|rät** NT radar unit; **ra|dar|ge|steu|ert** [-gəʃtɔyɐt] ADJ radar-controlled; **Ra|dar|kon|trol|le** F radar speed check; **Ra|dar|schirm** M radar screen, radarscope; **Ra|dar|sta|ti|on** F radar station; **Ra|dar|über|wach|ung** F radar monitoring

Ra|dau [ra'dau] M **-s,** *no pl* (*inf*) row, din, racket (*inf*); **~ machen** *or* **schlagen** to kick up a row; (= *Unruhe stiften*) to cause *or* make trouble; (= *Lärm machen*) to make a racket

Ra|dau|bru|der M (*inf*) hooligan, yobbo (*Brit inf*)

Rad|auf|hän|gung F (*Aut*) (wheel) suspension

Ra|dau|ma|cher(in) M(F) (*inf*) hooligan, yobbo (*Brit inf*)

Rad|ball M, *no pl* bicycle polo

Räd|chen ['rɛ:tçən] NT **-s, -** *dim von* **Rad** small wheel; (*für Schnittmuster*) tracing wheel; (*Cook*) pastry wheel → **Rad a**

Rad|dampf|er M paddle steamer

Ra|de ['ra:də] F **-, -n** (*Bot*) corncockle

ra|de|bre|chen ['ra:dəbrɛçn] *insep* VI to speak broken English/German *etc* VT **Englisch/Deutsch ~** to speak broken English/German; **er radebrechte auf Italienisch, er wolle ...** he said in broken Italian that he wanted ...

ra|deln ['ra:dln] VI *aux sein* (*inf*) to cycle

ra|deln, **rä|deln** ['rɛ:dln] VT *Schnittmuster* to trace; (*Cook*) to cut out with a/the pastry wheel

Rä|dels|füh|rer(in) ['rɛ:dls-] M(F) ringleader

-rä|de|rig [rɛdərıç] ADJ *suf* -wheeled; **zwei-/vierräderig** two-/four-wheeled

rä|dern ['rɛdɐn] VT (*Hist*) to break on the wheel → *auch* **gerädert**

Rä|der|werk NT (*Mech*) mechanism, works *pl*; (*fig*) machinery, cogs *pl*

rad+fah|ren △ ['ra:tfa:rən] VI *sep irreg aux sein* → **Rad b**

Rad|fah|ren NT **-s,** *no pl* **~ verboten** no cycling

Rad|fah|rer(in) M(F) **a** cyclist **b** (*pej inf*) crawler (*Brit inf*), brown-noser (*esp US sl*)

Rad|fahr-: **Rad|fahr|sport** M cycling; **Rad|fahr|weg** M cycleway; (*in der Stadt*) cycle lane

Rad|ga|bel F fork

Rad|helm M cycle helmet

Ra|di ['ra:di] M **-s, -** (*S Ger, Aus*) white radish; **einen ~ kriegen** (*inf*) to get a rocket (*Brit inf*), to catch it (*inf*)

ra|di|al [ra'dia:l] ADJ radial ADV radially

Ra|di|al|ge|schwin|dig|keit F (*Phys, Astron*) radial velocity

Ra|di|al|rei|fen M radial (tyre (*Brit*) *or* tire (*US*))

Ra|di|a|tor [ra'dia:to:ɐ] M **-s, Radiatoren** [-'to:rən] radiator

Ra|dic|chio [ra'dıkjo] M **-s, Radicchi** [-'diki] radicchio

ra|die|ren [ra'di:rən] *ptp* **radiert** VT **a** *(mit Radiergummi)* to rub out *(esp Brit)*, to erase; *(mit Messer)* to erase **b** *(Art)* to etch VI **a** *(mit Radiergummi)* to erase, to rub out *(esp Brit)*; **auf dieser Seite hat er dreimal radiert** he's rubbed three things out *(esp Brit)* or he's erased three things on this page **b** *(Art)* to etch

Ra|die|rer [ra'di:rɐ] M **-s, -** *(inf)* rubber *(Brit)*, eraser *(esp US, form)*

Ra|die|rer [ra'di:rɐ] M **-s, -**, **Ra|die|re|rin** [-ərın] F **-, -nen** *(Art)* etcher

Ra|dier-: **Ra|dier|gum|mi** M rubber *(Brit)*, eraser *(esp US, form)*; **Ra|dier|kunst** F *(Art)* etching; **Ra|dier|mes|ser** NT (steel) eraser, erasing knife; **Ra|dier|na|del** F *(Art)* etching needle

Ra|die|rung [ra'di:rʊŋ] F **-, -en** *(Art)* etching

Ra|dies|chen [ra'di:sçən] NT **-s, -** radish; **sich** *(dat)* **die ~ von unten ansehen** *or* **besehen** *(hum)* to be pushing up the daisies *(hum)*

ra|di|kal [radi'ka:l] ADJ radical; *Vereinfachung, Methode auch* drastic; *Vertilgung, Entfernen* total; *Verneinung* categorical; *Ablehnung* flat, categorical

ADV **a** *(Pol) sich verhalten* radically; **~ denken, ~ eingestellt** *or* **gesinnt sein** to be politically radical

b *(= völlig) ausrotten, beseitigen, mit jdm brechen* radically; *ablehnen* flatly; *verneinen* categorically

c *(= tief greifend) ändern, verfahren* radically; **mit diesem Missbrauch muss ~ Schluss gemacht werden** a definitive stop must be put to this abuse; **etw ~ verneinen** to deny sth categorically; **etw ~ ablehnen** to refuse sth flatly; **~ vorgehen** to be drastic; **~ gegen etw vorgehen** to take radical steps against sth

Ra|di|kal [radi'ka:l] NT **-s, -e** *(Math)* root; *(Chem)* radical

Ra|di|ka|len|er|lass M *ban on the employment of teachers and civil servants who are considered to be radical*

Ra|di|ka|le(r) [radi'ka:lə] MF *decl as adj* radical

ra|di|kal-fun|da|men|ta|lis|tisch ADJ *Gruppe, Organisation etc* radical fundamentalist

ra|di|ka|li|sie|ren [radikali'zi:rən] *ptp* **radikalisiert** VT to radicalize

Ra|di|ka|li|sie|rung F **-, -en** radicalization

Ra|di|ka|lis|mus [radika'lısmʊs] M **-**, *no pl (Pol)* radicalism

Ra|di|ka|li|tät [radikali'tɛ:t] F **-**, *no pl (Wesenszug)* radical nature; *(Maßnahmen)* drastic nature; *(in Meinung)* radical approach *or* views *pl*

Ra|di|kal|kur F *(inf)* drastic remedy, kill-or-cure remedy

Ra|dio ['ra:dio] NT OR (SW, S GER AUCH) M **-s, -s** radio, wireless *(esp Brit old)*; *(= Station)* radio; **~ hören** to listen to the radio; **im ~, am ~** *(Sw)* on the radio; **etw aus dem ~ erfahren** to hear sth on the radio; **aus dem ~ ertönte ein Beatles-Hit** a Beatles hit was playing on the radio

Ra|dio- *in cpds* radio; **ra|dio|ak|tiv** [radiolak'ti:f] ADJ radioactive; **~er Niederschlag** (radioactive) fallout ADV radioactively; **~ verseucht** contaminated with radioactivity; **Ra|dio|ak|ti|vi|tät** [radiolaktivi'tɛ:t] F radioactivity; **Ra|dio|ama|teur(in)** M(F) radio ham *(inf)* or amateur; **Ra|dio|ap|pa|rat** M radio (set); **Ra|dio|ast|ro|no|mie** F radio astronomy; **Ra|dio|bio|lo|gie** F radiobiology; **Ra|dio|che|mie** F radiochemistry; **Ra|dio|durch|sa|ge** F radio announcement; **Ra|dio|emp|fän|ger** M radio (set); *(von Funkamateur)* radio receiver; **Ra|dio|ge|häu|se** NT radio cabinet; *(von Kofferradio)* radio casing; **Ra|dio|ge|rät** NT radio (set); **Ra|dio|gra|fie** [radiogra'fi:] F **-, -n** [-'fi:ən] radiography; **Ra|dio|gramm** [radio'gram] NT *pl* **-gramme** *(Med)* X-ray (photograph), radiograph *(esp US)*; **Ra|dio|gra|phie** [radiogra'fi:] F **-, -n** [-'fi:ən] radiography; **Ra|dio|iso|top** NT radioisotope; **Ra|dio|kar|bon|me|tho|de** [radiokar'bo:n-] F radiocarbon (dating) technique *or* method; **Ra|dio|kar|te** F *(Comput)* radio card; **Ra|dio|kom|pass** M *(Aviat, Naut)* radio compass, automatic direction finder

Ra|dio|lo|ge [radio'lo:gə] M **-n, -n**, **Ra|dio|lo|gin** [-'lo:gın] F **-, -nen** *(Med)* radiologist

Ra|dio|lo|gie [radiolo'gi:] F **-**, *no pl (Med)* radiology

ra|dio|lo|gisch [radio'lo:gıʃ] ADJ radiological ADV radiologically; **~ behandelt werden** to undergo radiotherapy; **~ untersucht werden** to undergo a radiological examination

Ra|dio|ly|se [radio'ly:zə] F **-, -n** radiolysis

Ra|dio-: **Ra|dio|me|cha|ni|ker(in)** M(F) radio technician *or* engineer; **Ra|dio|met|rie** [radiome'tri:] F **-**, *no pl* radiometry; **Ra|dio|nuk|lid** M *(Phys)* radionuclide; **Ra|dio|quel|le** F *(Astron)* radio source; **Ra|dio|re|cor|der** M = **Radiorekorder**; **Ra|dio|re|kor|der** M radio recorder; **Ra|dio|röh|re** F radio valve *(esp Brit)* or tube *(esp US)*; **Ra|dio|sen|der** M *(= Rundfunkanstalt)* radio station; *(= Sendeeinrichtung)* radio transmitter; **Ra|dio|sen|dung** F radio programme *(Brit)* or program *(US)*; **Ra|dio|sko|pie** [radiosko'pi:] F **-, -n** [-'pi:ən] radioscopy; **Ra|dio|son|de** F (radio-equipped) weather balloon, radiosonde; **Ra|dio|sta|ti|on** F radio *or* broadcasting station; **Ra|dio|strah|lung** F radio signal; **Ra|dio|tech|nik** F radio technology; **Ra|dio|tech|ni|ker(in)** M(F) radio technician *or* engineer; **Ra|dio|te|le|gra|fie**, **Ra|dio|te|le|gra|phie** F radiotelegraphy; **Ra|dio|te|le|skop** NT radio telescope; **Ra|dio|the|ra|peut(in)** M(F) radiotherapist; **Ra|dio|the|ra|pie** F radiotherapy; **Ra|dio|über|tra|gung** F (radio) broadcast *or* transmission; **Ra|dio|we|cker** M radio alarm (clock); **Ra|dio|wel|len** PL radio waves *pl*

Ra|di|um ['ra:diʊm] NT **-**, *no pl (abbr* **Ra***)* radium

Ra|di|um-: **Ra|di|um|be|hand|lung** F, **Ra|di|um|be|strah|lung** F *(Med)* radium therapy *or* treatment; **ra|di|um|hal|tig** ADJ containing radium; **~ sein** to contain radium; **Ra|di|um|strah|len** PL *(Phys, Med)* radium rays *pl*; **Ra|di|um|the|ra|pie** F radium therapy *or* treatment

Ra|di|us ['ra:diʊs] M **-, Radien** [-diən] radius

Rad-: **Rad|kap|pe** F hubcap; **Rad|kas|ten** M wheel casing; *(Naut)* paddle box; **Rad|kral|le** F wheel clamp, (Denver) boot *(US)*; **Rad|kranz** M rim (of a/the wheel); **Rad|la|ger** NT wheel bearing

Rad|ler ['ra:dlɐ] M **-s, -**, **Rad|le|rin** [-ərın] F **-, -nen** *(inf)* cyclist

Rad|ler|ho|se F cycling shorts *pl*

Rad|ler|maß F *(S Ger inf)* shandy *(esp Brit)*, radler *(US)*

Rad-: **Rad|ma|cher(in)** M(F) wheelwright; **Rad|man|tel** M *(= Bereifung)* bicycle tyre *(Brit)* or tire *(US)*; **Rad|na|be** F (wheel) hub

Ra|don ['ra:dɔn, ra'do:n] NT **-s**, *no pl (abbr* **Rn***)* radon

Rad-: **Rad|pro|fi** M professional (racing) cyclist; **Rad|renn|bahn** F cycle (racing) track; **Rad|ren|nen** NT *(Sportart)* cycle racing; *(einzelnes Rennen)* cycle race; **Rad|renn|fah|rer(in)** M(F) racing cyclist; **Rad|renn|sport** M cycle racing

-räd|rig [rɛ:drıç] ADJ *suf* = **-räderig**

Rad-: **Rad|schau|fel** F blade (of a wheel); **rad+schla|gen** △ ['ra:tʃla:gn] VI *sep irreg* → **Rad a**; **Rad|sport** M cycling; **Rad|sport|ler(in)** M(F) cyclist; **Rad|stand** M *(Aut, Rail)* wheelbase; **Rad|sturz** M *(Aut)* camber; **Rad|tas|te** F *(Comput) (von Maus)* wheel button; **Rad|tour** F bike ride; *(länger)* cycling *or* cycle tour; **Rad|wech|sel** M wheel change; **(einen) ~ machen** *(= Bauteil wechseln)* to change a wheel, to do a wheel change; *(= Fahrrad wechseln)* to change bicycles; **Rad|weg** M cycleway

RAF [ɛrla:'lɛf] F **-**, *no pl abbr von* **Rote-Armee-Fraktion**

Raf|fel ['rafl] F **-, -n** *(dial)* **a** *(= Reibeisen)* grater **b** *(Tex)* hackle, flax comb

raf|feln ['rafln] VTI *(dial)* **a** *(= raspeln)* to grate **b** *(Tex)* to comb, to hackle

raf|fen ['rafn] VT **a** *(= anhäufen)* to pile, to heap; *(hastig)* to grab, to snatch; **er will immer nur (Geld) ~** he's always after money; **sein ganzes Leben hat er nur (Geld) gerafft** he spent his whole life making money; **etw an sich** *(acc)* **~** to grab *or* snatch sth **b** *Stoff, Gardine* to gather; *langes Kleid, Rock* to gather up **c** *(zeitlich)* to shorten, to cut down **d** *(sl: = verstehen)* to get *(inf)*, to work out

Raff-: **Raff|gier** ['rafgi:ɐ] F greed, avarice; **raff|gie|rig** ['rafgi:rıç] ADJ greedy, grasping

Raf|fi|na|de [rafi'na:də] F **-, -n** *(Zucker)* refined sugar

Raf|fi|na|ti|on [rafina'tsio:n] F **-, -en** *(von Öl, Zucker, Metall)* refining

Raf|fi|ne|ment [rafinə'mã:] NT **-s, -s** *(geh)* cunning *no pl*, craftiness *no pl*, wiliness *no pl*; **mit allen ~s** with all one's cunning

Raf|fi|ne|rie [rafinə'ri:] F **-, -n** [-'ri:ən] refinery

Raf|fi|nes|se [rafi'nɛsə] F **-, -n** **a** *(= Feinheit)* refinement, finesse *no pl*; **ein Auto mit allen ~n** a car with all the refinements **b** *(= Schlauheit, Durchtriebenheit)* cunning *no pl*, craftiness *no pl*, wiliness *no pl*; **mit aller ~** with all one's cunning

raf|fi|nie|ren [rafi'ni:rən] *ptp* **raffiniert** VT *Zucker, Öl, Metall* to refine

raf|fi|niert [rafi'ni:ɐt] ADJ **a** *Zucker, Öl* refined **b** *Methoden, Techniken, Mechanismen, Apparat* sophisticated; *(inf) Kleid, Frisur, Kleidung* stylish **c** *(= schlau)* clever, cunning; *(= durchtrieben)* crafty; **sie ist eine ~e Frau** she knows all the tricks in the book; **ein ~es Luder** *or* **Weib** *(pej)* a sly cow *(Brit pej inf)* or bitch *(US sl)* ADV **a** *(= durchtrieben)* cleverly; **~ vorgehen** to be cunning; **da musst du dich ~er anstellen** you have to be a little more clever; **~ einfach** cunningly simple **b** *(= ausgesucht) gewürzt* exquisitely; **sie kleidet sich sehr ~** she certainly knows how to dress

Raf|fi|niert|heit F **-**, *no pl* **a** *(von Kleidung, Frisur)* stylishness **b** *(= Schlauheit)* cleverness; *(= Durchtriebenheit)* cunning, craftiness

Raff|ke ['rafkə] M **-s, -s** *(inf)* money-grubber *(inf)*

RAF-: **RAF-Ka|der** M unit of the Red Army Faction; **RAF-Mit|glied** NT member of the Red Army Faction

Ra|ge ['ra:ʒə] F **-**, *no pl* **a** *(= Wut)* rage, fury; **jdn in ~ bringen** to infuriate sb; **in ~ kommen** *or* **geraten** to get *or* become furious, to fly into a rage *or* fury; **sich in ~ reden** to talk oneself into a rage **b** *(inf: = Aufregung, Eile)* hurry, rush

ra|gen ['ra:gn] VI to rise, to tower, to loom; *(= herausragen)* to jut

Ra|gi|o|nen|buch [ra'dʒo:nən-] NT *(Sw)* business register

Rag|lan- *in cpds* raglan; **Rag|lan|är|mel** M raglan sleeve; **Rag|lan|schnitt** M raglan style

Ra|gout [ra'gu:] NT **-s, -s** ragout

Rag|time ['rɛgtaim] M **-(s)**, *no pl* ragtime

Rah [ra:] F **-, -en**, **Ra|he** ['ra:ə] F **-, -en** *(Naut)* yard

Rahm [ra:m] M **-(e)s**, *no pl (dial)* cream → **abschöpfen**

Rähm|chen ['rɛ:mçən] NT **-s, -** *dim von* **Rahmen** *(= Diarähmchen)* mount

rah|men ['ra:mən] VT to frame; *Dias* to mount

Rah|men ['ra:mən] M **-s, -** **a** frame; *(vom Schuh)* welt; *(Comput)* border

b *(fig)* *(= Bereich, Liter: = Rahmenhandlung)* framework; *(= Atmosphäre)* setting; *(= Größe)* scale; **den ~ zu** *or* **für etw bilden** to provide a backdrop for sth; **im ~** within the framework *(+gen* of*)*; **seine Verdienste wurden im ~ einer kleinen Feier gewürdigt** his services were honoured *(Brit)* or honored *(US)* in a small ceremony; **im ~ des Möglichen** within the bounds of possibility; **im ~ bleiben, sich im ~ halten** to keep within the limits; **aus dem ~ fallen** to be strikingly different; **musst du denn immer aus**

dem ~ fallen! do you always have to show yourself up?; **ein Geschenk/Getränk, das aus dem ~ des Üblichen fällt** a present/drink with a difference; **dieses Buch fällt aus dem ~ unserer normalen Produktion** this book is outside our usual line (of business); **in den ~ von etw passen, sich in den ~ von etw einfügen** to fit (in) *or* blend in with sth, to go with sth; **den ~ von etw sprengen, über den ~ von etw hinausgehen** to go beyond the scope of sth; **das würde den ~ sprengen** it would be beyond my/our *etc* scope; **einer Feier einen würdigen** *or* **den richtigen ~ geben** to provide the appropriate setting for a celebration; **in größerem/kleinerem ~** on a large/small scale; **die Feier fand nur in engem** *or* **in engstem ~ statt** the celebration was just a small-scale affair

Rah|men-: **Rah|men|ab|kom|men** NT *(Pol)* outline agreement; **Rah|men|an|ten|ne** F frame aerial *(esp Brit)* or antenna;; **Rah|men|be|din|gung** F basic condition; **Rah|men|er|zäh|lung** F *(Liter)* framework story; **Rah|men|ge|setz** NT *general outline of a law providing guidelines for specific elaboration*; **Rah|men|hand|lung** F *(Liter)* background story, story which forms the framework; **Rah|men|plan** M framework, outline plan; **Rah|men|pro|gramm** NT **a** *(von Veranstaltung etc)* supporting programme *(Brit)* or program *(US)* **b** *(= Rahmenplan)* framework, outline plan; **Rah|men|richt|li|ni|en** PL guidelines *pl*; **Rah|men|ta|rif|ver|trag** M ≈ general agreement on conditions of employment; **Rah|men|ver|an|stal|tung** F umbrella event; **Rah|men|ver|trag** M *(Ind)* general agreement

rah|mig ['ra:mɪç] ADJ *(dial)* creamy

Rahm-: **Rahm|kä|se** M cream cheese; **Rahm|spi|nat** M creamed spinach *(with sour cream)*

Rah|se|gel ['ra:-] NT *(Naut)* square sail

Rain [rain] M **-(e)s, -e** *(liter)* margin, marge *(poet)*

rä|keln ['rɛ:kln] VR = **rekeln**

Ra|kel|tief|druck ['ra:kl-] M, *no pl* photogravure, rotogravure

Ra|ke|te [ra'ke:tə] F **-, -n** rocket *(auch Space)*; *(Mil auch)* missile; **ferngelenkte** *or* **ferngesteuerte ~** guided missile; **wie eine ~ einschlagen** (*inf*: *Idee etc*) to be a big hit *(inf)*

Ra|ke|ten-, **ra|ke|ten-** *in cpds* rocket; *(Mil auch)* missile; **Ra|ke|ten|ab|schuss** M (rocket) launching *(Brit)* or launch; **Ra|ke|ten|ab|schuss|ba|sis** F *(Mil)* missile *or* rocket base; *(Space)* launching *(Brit) or* launch site

Ra|ke|ten|ab|wehr F antimissile defence *(Brit) or* defense *(US)*

Ra|ke|ten|ab|wehr-: **Ra|ke|ten|ab|wehr|ra|ke|te** F antimissile missile; **Ra|ke|ten|ab|wehr|schirm** M nuclear defence *(Brit) or* defense *(US)* umbrella; **Ra|ke|ten|ab|wehr|stel|lung** F antimissile position; **Ra|ke|ten|ab|wehr|sys|tem** NT missile defence *(Brit) or* defense *(US)* system; **Ra|ke|ten|ab|wehr|waf|fe** F antimissile weapon

Ra|ke|ten-: **Ra|ke|ten|an|trieb** M rocket propulsion; **mit ~** rocket-propelled; **Ra|ke|ten|ap|pa|rat** M rocket(-line) apparatus; **Ra|ke|ten|ba|sis** F = **Raketenabschussbasis**; **ra|ke|ten|be|stückt** [-bəʃtʏkt] ADJ missile-carrying, missile-equipped; **Ra|ke|ten|flug|zeug** NT rocket-propelled aircraft; **Ra|ke|ten|ge|schoss** NT missile; **Ra|ke|ten|satz** M set of rockets; *(Mil auch)* set of missiles; **Ra|ke|ten|si|lo** M rocket silo; **Ra|ke|ten|spreng|kopf** M *(Mil)* missile warhead; **Ra|ke|ten|start** M (rocket) launching *(Brit) or* launch; *(= Start mittels Raketen)* rocket-assisted takeoff; **Ra|ke|ten|stu|fe** F stage (of a rocket *or (Mil auch)* missile); **Ra|ke|ten|stütz|punkt** M missile base; **Ra|ke|ten|ver|suchs|ge|län|de** NT rocket range; *(Space)* launching *(Brit) or* launch site; **Ra|ke|ten|wer|fer** M rocket launcher; **Ra|ke|ten|zeit|al|ter** NT space age

Ra|kett [ra'kɛt] NT **-s, -s** *or* **-e** *(old Sport)* racket, racquet *(Brit)*

Ral|lye ['rali, 'rɛli] F **-, -s** rally; **eine ~ fahren** to drive in a rally; **~ fahren** to go rallying

Ral|lye|fah|rer(in) M(F) rally driver

RAM [rɛm] NT **-s, -s** *(Comput)* RAM

Ra|ma|dan [rama'da:n] M **-(s), -e** Ramadan

Ram|ba|zam|ba ['ramba'tsamba] NT **-s**, *no pl (inf)* **~ machen** to kick up a fuss

Ram|bo ['rambo] M **-s, -s** Rambo, tough guy *(inf)*

Ramm-: **Ramm|bock** M ram(mer); *(für Pfähle)* pile-driver; **ramm|dö|sig** ['ramdø:zɪç] ADJ *(inf)* giddy, dizzy

Ram|me ['ramə] F **-, -n** ram(mer); *(für Pfähle)* pile-driver

Ram|me|lei [ramə'lai] F **-, -en** **a** (*inf*: *= Gedränge*) crush, scrum *(Brit inf)* **b** *(sl)* banging away *(inf)*

ram|meln ['ramln] VT → **gerammelt** VIR (*dial*: *= herumtoben*) to charge about *(Brit) or* around VI *(Hunt)* to mate; *(sl)* to have it off *or* away *(Brit inf)*, to do it *(inf)*

ram|men ['ramən] VT to ram

Ramm|ler ['ramlɐ] M **-s, -** **a** *(= Kaninchen)* buck **b** (*sl*: *= Mann*) stud *(inf)*

Ram|pe ['rampə] F **-, -n** **a** ramp **b** *(Theat)* apron, forestage

Ram|pen|licht NT *(Theat)* footlights *pl*; *(fig)* limelight; **sie möchte im ~ stehen** *(Theat)* she'd like to go on the stage; *(fig)* she wants to be in the limelight; **im ~ der Öffentlichkeit stehen** *(fig)* to be in the limelight; **ins ~ treten** *or* **rücken** *(Theat)* to come down to the footlights; *(fig)* to step into the limelight

ram|po|nie|ren [rampo'ni:rən] *ptp* **ramponiert** VT *(inf)* to ruin; *Möbel* to bash about *(inf)*; **er sah ziemlich ramponiert aus** he looked the worse for wear *(inf)*

Ramsch [ramʃ] M **-(e)s**, *no pl* **a** *(inf)* junk, rubbish *(Brit)*, trash **b** *(Skat)* **(einen) ~ spielen** to play (a) ramsch

ram|schen ['ramʃn] VI **a** *(inf)* to buy cheap junk **b** *(beim Skat)* to play (a) ramsch VT *(Comm)* to buy up

Ramsch-: **Ramsch|händ|ler(in)** M(F) *(pej)* junk dealer; **Ramsch|la|den** M *(pej)* junk shop; **Ramsch|ver|kauf** M oddments sale; **Ramsch|wa|re** F *(pej)* trashy goods *pl*, rubbish *(Brit)*

RAM-Spei|cher ['ram-] M *(Comput)* RAM memory

ran [ran] INTERJ *(inf)* come on, go it *(inf)*; **~ an den Feind!** let's go get 'em! *(inf)*; **~ an die Arbeit!** down to work, shoulders to the wheel → *auch* **heran**

Ranch [rɛntʃ, ra:ntʃ] F **-, -(e)s** ranch

Ran|cher ['rɛntʃɐ, 'ra:ntʃɐ] M **-s, -(s)**, **Ran|che|rin** [-ərɪn] F **-, -nen** rancher

Rand [rant] M **-es, ¨er** ['rɛndɐ] **a** edge; *(von Weg, Straße, Schwimmbecken etc)* side, edge; *(von Brunnen, Gefäß, Tasse)* top, rim, brim; *(von Abgrund)* brink; **voll bis zum ~** full to the brim, brimful; **am ~e** *(erwähnen, zur Sprache kommen)* by the way, in passing; *interessieren* marginally; *beteiligt sein* marginally, on the fringe; *miterleben* from the sidelines; **etw am ~e bemerken** *or* **vermerken** to mention sth in passing *or* in parentheses; **am ~e des Waldes** at the edge of the forest; **am ~e der Stadt** on the outskirts of the town; **am ~e der Veranstaltung** on the fringe(s) of the event; **am ~e der Verzweiflung/des Wahnsinns** on the verge of despair/madness; **am ~e des Grabes** *or* **Todes stehen** to be at death's door; **am ~e des Untergangs** *or* **Ruins** on the brink or verge of ruin; **am ~e eines Krieges** on the brink of war; **die Schweizer haben den Krieg nur am ~e miterlebt** the Swiss were only marginally involved in the war, the Swiss only experienced the war from the sidelines; **er hat die Russische Revolution noch am ~e miterlebt** he was around at the beginning/end of the Russian Revolution; **eine kleine Szene am ~e des Krieges** a small incident on the fringe of the war; **am ~e der Gesellschaft/der politischen Landschaft** on the fringes of society/the political scene; **an den ~ der Gesellschaft gedrängt werden** to be marginalized by society; **am äußersten rechten ~ des politischen Spektrums** on the extreme right of the political spectrum **b** *(= Umrandung)* border; *(= Tellerrand)* edge, side; *(= Brillenrand)* rim; *(von Hut)* brim; *(= Seitenrand, Buchrand, Heftrand)* margin; **wenn er so über die Ränder seiner Brille schielt** when he peers over the top of his glasses like that; **mit schwarzem ~** black-edged, with a black border; **etw an den ~ schreiben** to write sth in the margin **c** *(= Schmutzrand)* ring; *(um Augen)* circle, ring; **rote Ränder um die Augen haben** to have red rims around one's eyes **d** *(fig)* **das versteht sich am ~e** that goes without saying; **sie waren außer ~ und Band** there was no holding them, they were going wild; *(sl)* **halt den ~!** *(sl)* shut your face! *(sl)*; **zu ~e** = **zurande**

Rand M **-s, -(s)** *(= Währung)* rand

Ran|da|le [ran'da:lə] F **-**, *no pl* rioting; **~ machen** to riot

ran|da|lie|ren [randa'li:rən] *ptp* **randaliert** VI to rampage (about); **~de Jugendliche** (young) hooligans; **~de Studenten** rioting students; **die Jugendlichen zogen ~d durch die Straßen** the youths rampaged *or* went on the rampage *or* ran wild through the streets; **die Gefangenen fingen an zu ~** the prisoners started to go on the rampage

Ran|da|lie|rer [randa'li:rɐ] M **-s, -**, **Ran|da|lie|re|rin** [-ərɪn] F **-,-nen** hooligan, troublemaker

Rand-: **Rand|aus|gleich** M *(Comput)* justification; **Rand|aus|lö|ser** M margin release; **Rand|be|mer|kung** F *(schriftlich: auf Seite)* note in the margin, marginal note; *(mündlich, fig)* (passing) comment; **etw in einer ~ erwähnen** *(fig)* to mention sth in passing; **Rand|be|zirk** M outlying district

Ran|de ['randə] F **-, -n** *(Sw)* beetroot

Rand|ein|stel|lung F margin setting

rän|deln ['rɛndln] VT *Münze* to mill

rän|dern ['rɛndɐn] VT to edge, to border

Rand-: **Rand|er|schei|nung** F marginal *or* peripheral matter; *(= Nebenwirkung)* side effect; **Rand|fi|gur** F minor figure; **Rand|ge|biet** NT *(Geog)* edge, fringe; *(Pol)* border territory; *(fig)* subsidiary; **rand|ge|näht** [-gənɛ:t] ADJ *Schuhe* welted; **Rand|glos|se** F marginal note; **Rand|grup|pe** F fringe group

-ran|dig [randɪç] ADJ *suf* -edged; **goldrandig** *(Rahmen)* gold-edged; *Tasse* gold-rimmed

Rand-: **rand|los** ADJ *Brille* rimless; *Hut* brimless ADV *(Comput) drucken, bedrucken* without margins; **Rand|no|tiz** F marginal note; **Rand|sport|art** F fringe *or* marginal sport; **Rand|staat** M border state; **die ~en des Mittelmeers** the countries around *or* bordering on the Mediterranean; **die ~en der Nordsee** the North Sea countries; **rand|stän|dig** ADJ *Personen, Position* marginal(ized); *Bevölkerungsgruppen* minority; **Rand|stän|di|ge(r)** [-ʃtɛndɪgə] MF *decl as adj* person marginalized by society; **die ~n der deutschen Gesellschaft** the marginalized in German society; **Rand|stän|dig|keit** F **-**, *no pl* marginality; **Rand|stein** M kerb; **den ~ mitnehmen** *(inf)* to hit the kerb; **Rand|stel|ler** [-ʃtɛlɐ] M **-s, -** margin stop; **rand|voll** ADJ *Glas* full to the brim; *Behälter* full to the top; *Flugzeug, Aktenordner* packed; *(fig) Terminkalender, Programm* packed; (*inf*: *= betrunken*) smashed *(inf)*; **Rand|zo|ne** F peripheral zone *or* area; *(fig)* fringe; **in der ~** on the periphery; **diese Staaten sind vorerst noch ~n der Weltpolitik** these states are still on the periphery *or* perimeter of world politics

Ranft [ranft] M **-(e)s, ⸚e** ['rɛnftə] *(dial)* crust *(Brit)*, heel *(US, Scot)*

rang *pret von* **ringen**

Rang [raŋ] M **-(e)s, ⸚e** ['rɛŋə] **a** *(Mil)* rank; *(in Firma)* position; *(= gesellschaftliche Stellung)* position, rank; *(in Wettbewerb)* place, position; **im ~(e) eines Hauptmanns stehen** to have the rank of captain; **im ~ höher/tiefer stehen** to have a higher/lower rank/position, to rank higher/lower; **einen hohen ~ bekleiden** to hold a high office; *(Mil)* to have a high rank; **ein Mann von ~ und Würden** a man of considerable *or* high standing, a man of status; **ein Mann ohne ~ und Namen** a man without any standing or reputation; **alles, was ~ und Namen hat** everybody who is anybody; **jdm den ~ streitig machen** *(fig)* to challenge sb's position; **jdm den ~ ablaufen** *(fig)* to outstrip sb
b *(= Qualität)* quality, class; **ein Künstler/Wissenschaftler von ~** an artist/scientist of standing, a top artist/scientist; **von hohem ~** high-class; **eine Touristenattraktion ersten ~es** a first-class *or* first-rate tourist attraction; **ein Skandal ersten ~es** a scandal of the highest order; **minderen ~es** low-class, second-rate
c *(Theat)* circle; **erster/zweiter ~** dress/upper circle, first/second circle; **wir sitzen (erster/zweiter) ~ Mitte** *(inf)* we're sitting in the middle of the (dress/upper) circle; **vor leeren/überfüllten Rängen spielen** to play to an empty/a packed house
d Ränge PL *(Sport: = Tribünenränge)* stands *pl*
e *(= Gewinnklasse)* prize category

Rang-: Rang|ab|zei|chen NT *(Mil)* badge of rank, insignia; **Rang|äl|tes|te(r)** MF *decl as adj (Mil)* senior officer

Ran|ge ['raŋə] F **-, -n** urchin

ran+ge|hen ['range:ən] VI *sep irreg aux sein* **a** *(inf)* to get stuck in *(inf)*; **geh ran!** go on! **b** *(sl: = Frau anbaggern)* **der Typ geht schwer ran** that guy's really giving it the chat *(inf)*

Ran|ge|lei [raŋə'lai] F **-, -en** *(inf)* = **Gerangel**

ran|geln ['raŋln] *(inf)* VI to scrap; *(um Sonderangebote auch)* to tussle *(um* for); *(um Posten)* to wrangle *(um* for) VR to sprawl about

Rang-: Rang|fol|ge F order of rank *(esp Mil)* or standing; *(in Sport, Wettbewerb)* order of placing; *(von Problemen, Prioritäten)* order of importance; **nach der ~, der ~ nach** in order of rank *(esp Mil)* or standing; *(in Sport, Wettbewerb)* in order of placing; *(von Problemen, Prioritäten)* in order of importance; **rang|hoch** ADJ senior; *(Mil auch)* high-ranking; **Rang|höchs|te(r)** MF *decl as adj* senior person; *(Mil)* highest-ranking officer

Ran|gier|bahn|hof [rã'ʒi:ɐ-] M marshalling *(Brit)* or marshaling *(US)* yard

ran|gie|ren [rã'ʒi:rən] *ptp* **rangiert** VT **a** *(Rail)* to shunt *(Brit)*, to switch *(US)*
b *(inf: = abschieben)* to shove *(inf)*, to shunt *(inf)*
VI *(inf: = Rang einnehmen)* to rank; **er rangiert gleich hinter** *or* **unter dem Abteilungsleiter** he comes directly beneath the head of department; **seine Familie rangiert in seinem Leben nur am Rande** his family take second place (in his life); **Mathilde rangiert bei mir unter „ferner liefen"** *(inf)* as far as I'm concerned Mathilde is an "also-ran" *(esp Brit)* or "has-been" *(inf)*; **der Intelligenz nach rangiert er ganz vorne** he's quite high up the list as far as intelligence goes; **an erster/letzter Stelle ~** to come first/last, to take first/last place

Ran|gie|rer [rã'ʒi:rɐ] M **-s, -, Ran|gie|re|rin** [-ərın] F **-, -nen** *(Rail)* shunter *(Brit)* or switcher *(US)* driver

Ran|gier-: Ran|gier|gleis NT siding, sidetrack *(US)*; **Ran|gier|lok** F, **Ran|gier|lo|ko|mo|ti|ve** F, **Ran|gier|ma|schi|ne** F shunter *(Brit)*, switcher *(US)*

Rang-: Rang|lis|te F **a** *(Mil)* active list **b** *(Sport, fig)* (results) table; **er steht auf der ~ der weltbesten Boxer** he ranks among the world's top boxers; **Rang|lo|ge** F *(Theat)* box (in the circle); **rang|mä|ßig** ADJ according to rank ADV *höher* in rank; **jdm ~ übergeordnet/untergeordnet sein** to be sb's superior/subordinate; **~ entspricht der Admiral dem General** the rank of admiral corresponds to the rank of general; **~ stehe ich unter ihm** I'm lower than him in rank; **Rang|ord|nung** F hierarchy; *(Mil)* (order of) ranks; **Rang|stu|fe** F rank; **auf der gleichen ~ stehen** to be of *or* to have the same rank; **Rang|un|ter|schied** M social distinction; *(Mil)* difference of rank; **wir machen hier keine ~e** we're not status-conscious here

ran+hal|ten ['ranhaltn] VR *sep irreg (inf)* **a** *(= sich beeilen, sich umtun)* to get a move on *(inf)* **b** *(= schnell zugreifen)* to dig in *(inf)*, to get stuck in *(inf)*

rank [raŋk] ADJ *(liter)* **~ und schlank** slender and supple; *Mädchen auch* slim and sylphlike

Rank [raŋk] M **-(e)s, Ränke** ['rɛŋkə] *(Sw: = Kurve)* curve; **den ~ finden** *(fig: = zurechtkommen)* to cope, to manage; **den ~ zueinander finden** to get on (with each other)

Ran|ke ['raŋkə] F **-, -n** tendril; *(von Brom-, Himbeeren)* branch; *(von Erdbeeren)* stalk; *(von Weinrebe)* shoot

Rän|ke ['rɛŋkə] PL *(liter)* intrigue, cabal *(liter)*; **~ schmieden** to hatch a plot, to intrigue, to cabal *(liter)*

ran|ken ['raŋkn] VR **sich um etw ~** to entwine itself around sth; *(fig: Geschichten etc)* to have grown up around sth VI *aux haben or sein* **an etw** *(dat)* **~** to entwine itself around sth

Ran|ken-: Ran|ken|ge|wächs NT climbing plant, climber; *(= Efeu etc)* creeper; **Ran|ken|werk** NT *(Art)* arabesques *pl*; *(fig)* embellishment

Rän|ke-: Rän|ke|schmied(in) M(F) *(liter)* intriguer; **Rän|ke|spiel** NT *(liter)* intrigue, cabal *(liter)*; **rän|ke|süch|tig, rän|ke|voll** ADJ *(liter)* scheming, caballing *(liter)*

ran|kig ['raŋkıç] ADJ *(Bot)* climbing

Ran|king ['rɛŋkıŋ] NT **-s, -s** *(inf: = Rangordnung)* ranking

ran+klot|zen ['ranklɔtsn] VI *sep (inf)* to get stuck in *(inf)*

ran+kom|men ['rankɔmən] VI *sep irreg aux sein (inf)* **an etw** *(acc)* **~** to get at sth; **an die Helga ist nicht ranzukommen** you won't get anywhere with Helga *(inf)*; **an unseren Chef ist schwer ranzukommen** our boss isn't very easy to get at *(inf)*; **niemanden an sich ~ lassen** to be standoffish *(inf)*, to keep oneself to oneself; **nichts an sich ~ lassen** not to be fazed by anything → *auch* **herankommen, drankommen**

ran+krie|gen ['rankri:gn] VT *sep (inf)* **a** *(= verpflichten)* **jdn ~** *(zur Arbeit)* to make sb knuckle under *(inf)*; *(stärker)* to put sb through the mill *(inf)*; *(zur Mitarbeit)* to make sb pull his *or* her weight *(inf)*; *(zur Verantwortung)* to get sb to take responsibility **b** *(= reinlegen)* **jdn ~** to con sb *(inf)*, to take sb for a ride *(fig)*

Ran|kü|ne [raŋ'ky:nə] F **-,** *no pl (geh, old)* grudge, rancour *(Brit)*, rancor *(US)*

ran+las|sen ['ranlasn] VT *sep irreg (inf)* **jdn ~** *(an Aufgabe etc)* to let sb have a go *(esp Brit) or* a try; **sie lässt jeden ran** *(inf)* she's anybody's *(inf)*, she's an easy lay *(sl)*; **sie lässt keinen mehr (an sich** *acc***) ran** *(inf)* she won't let anybody near her

ran+ma|chen ['ranmaxn] VR *sep (inf)* = **heranmachen**

rann *pret von* **rinnen**

ran+neh|men ['ranne:mən] VT *sep irreg (inf)* **a** *(= fordern)* **jdn ~** to put sb through his *or* her paces; **der neue Lehrer nimmt uns ganz schön ran** the new teacher really gives us a hard time **b** *(= zurechtweisen)* **jdn ~** to let sb have it **c** *(= aufrufen) Schüler* to pick on

rann|te *pret von* **rennen**

Ran|schmei|ße ['ranʃmaisə] F **-,** *no pl (inf)* **er hat den Job durch ~ bekommen** he got the job by being a complete crawler *(Brit inf)* or brown-noser *(esp US sl)*

ran+schmei|ßen ['ranʃmaisn] VR *sep irreg (inf)* **sich an jdn ~** to throw oneself at sb *(inf)*

Ra|nun|kel [ra'nʊŋkl] F **-, -n** *(Bot)* ranunculus

Rän|zel ['rɛntsl] NT OR M **-s, -** *(old, dial)* knapsack, pack; **sein** *or* **das ~ schnüren** *(liter)* to pack up one's belongings

Ran|zen ['rantsn] M **-s, - a** *(= Schulranzen)* satchel **b** *(inf: = Bauch)* belly *(Brit inf)*, gut *(inf)*; **sich** *(dat)* **den ~ vollschlagen** to stuff oneself *(inf)* or one's face *(inf)* **c** *(inf: = Buckel)* hunchback, hump(back); **jdm (ordentlich) den ~ vollhauen, jdm eins auf den ~ geben** to give sb a (good) thrashing

ran|zig ['rantsıç] ADJ rancid ADV **~ schmecken/riechen** to taste/smell rancid

Rap [rɛp] M **-(s), -s** *(Mus)* rap

ra|pid [ra'pi:t], **ra|pi|de** [ra'pi:də] ADJ rapid ADV rapidly

Ra|pier [ra'pi:ɐ] NT **-s, -e** rapier

Rap|pe ['rapə] M **-n, -n** black horse → **Schuster**

Rap|pel ['rapl] M **-s, -** *(inf)* **a** *(= Fimmel)* craze; *(= Klaps)* crazy mood; **seinen ~ kriegen** *or* **bekommen** to go completely crazy; **du hast wohl einen ~!** you must be crazy! **b** *(= Wutanfall)* **einen ~ haben** to be in a foul *or* filthy mood *or* temper; **einen ~ kriegen** *or* **bekommen** to throw a fit; **dabei kann man ja einen ~ kriegen** it's enough to drive you mad *or* up the wall *(inf)*

rap|pel|dürr ['rapl'dʏr] ADJ *(inf)* thin as a rake

rap|pe|lig ['rapəlıç] ADJ *(inf)* **a** *(= verrückt)* crazy, cracked *(inf)*; **bei dem Lärm kann man ja ~ werden** the noise is enough to drive you crazy *(inf)* or round the twist *(Brit inf)* **b** *(= nervös, unruhig)* jumpy *(inf)*

rap|peln ['rapln] VI *(inf)* *(= lärmen)* to rattle; *(Aus: = verrückt sein)* to be crazy; **es rappelt an der Tür** somebody is shaking *or* rattling the door; **bei dir rappelts wohl!** *(inf)* are you crazy?; **bei dem rappelts manchmal** *(inf)* he just flips (out) sometimes *(inf)*

rap|pel|voll ['rapl'fɔl] ADJ *(inf)* jampacked *(inf)*, chock-a-block *(inf)*

rap|pen ['rɛpn] VI *(Mus)* to rap

Rap|pen ['rapn] M **-s, -** *(Sw)* centime

Rap|per ['rɛpɐ] M **-s, -, Rap|pe|rin** [-ərın] F **-, -nen** *(Mus)* rapper; *(= Fan)* rap fan

rapp|lig ['raplıç] ADJ = **rappelig**

Rap|port [ra'pɔrt] M **-(e)s, -e a** report; **sich zum ~ melden** to report; **jdn zum ~ bestellen** to ask sb to present a report **b** *(Psych)* rapport **c** *(Mil old)* report; **sich zum ~ melden** to report; **er ist beim Kommandeur zum ~** he's making a report to the commander

Raps [raps] M **-es, -e** *(Bot)* rape

Raps|öl NT rape(seed) oil

Rap|tus ['raptʊs] M **-, -se** *(Med)* fit, raptus *(spec)*

Ra|pun|zel [ra'pʊntsl] F **-, -n a** *(Bot)* corn salad, lamb's lettuce **b** *(Märchen)* Rapunzel

Ra|pun|zel|sa|lat M corn salad

rar [ra:ɐ] ADJ rare; **sich ~ machen** → **rarmachen**

Ra|ri|tät [rari'tɛ:t] F **-, -en** rarity

Ra|ri|tä|ten-: Ra|ri|tä|ten|händ|ler(in) M(F) dealer in rare objects; **Ra|ri|tä|ten|ka|bi|nett** NT collection of rare objects

rar+ma|chen VR *sep (inf)* to keep *or* stay away; *(= sich zurückziehen)* to make oneself scarce

ra|sant [ra'zant] ADJ **a** *Tempo, Spurt* terrific, lightning *attr (inf)*; *Auto, Fahrer* fast; *Aufstieg, Karriere* meteoric; *Entwicklung, Wachstum, Fortschritt, Abnahme, Zerfall* rapid; **das ist vielleicht ein ~es Auto** this car really can shift *(inf)*; **sie haben das Presto in ~em Tempo gespielt** they really raced *or* rattled *(inf)* through the presto **b** *(= imponierend) Frau* vivacious; *Leistung* terrific **c** *Schuss-, Flugbahn* level, flat ADV **a** *(= sehr schnell)* fast; **sie fuhr ~ die Straße hinunter** she tore *or* raced down the street **b** *(= stürmisch)* dramatically

Ra|sanz [ra'zants] F **-,** *no pl* **a** *(= Geschwindigkeit)* speed; **er jagte mit unheimlicher ~ davon** he tore off at a terrific lick (*Brit inf*) or speed; **er nahm die Kurve mit gekonnter ~** he took the bend with daredevil skill **b** (*= Schwung*) panache

ra̱sch [raʃ] ADJ **a** (*= schnell*) quick, rapid, swift; *Tempo* great **b** (*= übereilt*) rash, (over-)hasty ADV **a** (*= schnell*) quickly, rapidly, swiftly; **nicht so ~!** not so fast *or* quick; **~ machen** to hurry (up), to get a move on (*inf*); **es muss ~ gehen** it's got to be fast; **ich habe so ~ wie möglich gemacht** I was as quick *or* fast as I could be; **ein bisschen ~, bitte!** make it quick, be quick **b** (*= vorschnell*) **mit etw ~ bei der Hand sein** to be rash *or* (over-)hasty about sth, to be too quick off the mark with sth (*inf*)

ra̱|scheln [ˈraʃln] VI to rustle; **es raschelt (im Stroh/Laub)** there's something rustling (in the straw/leaves); **mit etw ~** to rustle sth

Ra̱sch|heit F **-**, *no pl* **a** (*= Schnelligkeit*) rapidity, swiftness **b** (*= Übereiltheit*) rashness, (over) hastiness

ra̱|sen [ˈraːzn] VI **a** (*= wüten, toben*) to rave; (*Sturm*) to rage; **er raste vor Schmerz** he was going wild with pain; **er raste vor Wut** he was mad with rage; **er raste vor Eifersucht** he was half-crazed with jealousy; **die Zuschauer rasten vor Begeisterung** the spectators were wild with excitement

b *aux sein* (*= sich schnell bewegen*) to race, to tear; (*Puls, Herz*) to race; **der Rennwagen raste in die Menge/gegen einen Baum** the racing car crashed *or* smashed into the crowd/a tree; **das Auto raste in den Fluss** the car crashed into the river; **ras doch nicht so!** (*inf*) don't go so fast!; **die Zeit rast** time flies

c *aux sein* (*inf: = herumhetzen*) to race *or* run around

Ra̱|sen [ˈraːzn] M **-s, -** lawn, grass *no indef art, no pl*; (*von Sportplatz*) turf, grass; (*= Sportplatz*) field, pitch; (*Tennis*) court; **einen ~ anlegen** to lay (down) a lawn; **„bitte den ~ nicht betreten"** "please keep off the grass"; **jetzt deckt ihn der kühle** *or* **grüne ~ zu** (*liter*) now he lies beneath the green sward (*liter*); **unter dem grünen ~ ruhen** (*liter*) to be at rest in God's green acre (*liter*)

Ra̱|sen|bank F *pl* **-bänke** grassy bank

ra̱|sen|be|deckt, **ra̱|sen|be|wach|sen** ADJ grassy, grass-covered, covered with grass

ra̱|send ADJ **a** (*= enorm*) terrific; *Eile* terrific, tearing; *Durst* raging, terrific; *Beifall* wild, rapturous; *Eifersucht* burning; *Schmerz* excruciating, terrific; **~e Kopfschmerzen** a splitting headache **b** (*= wütend*) furious, livid, raging; **jdn ~ machen** to make sb furious *or* livid *or* wild (*inf*); **er macht mich noch ~** he'll drive me crazy (*inf*); **ich könnte ~ werden** I could scream; **es ist zum Rasendwerden** it's absolutely infuriating *or* maddening

ADV (*inf*) terrifically, enormously; *schnell* incredibly; *wehtun, sich beeilen, applaudieren* like mad (*inf*) *or* crazy (*inf*); *lieben, verliebt, eifersüchtig sein* madly (*inf*); **~ viel Geld** heaps *or* pots of money (*inf*); **~ gern!** I'd simply love to!

Ra̱|sen|de(r) [ˈraːzndə] MF *decl as adj* madman/-woman, maniac

Ra̱|sen-: **Ra̱|sen|flä|che** F lawn; **Ra̱|sen|mä|her** M, **Ra̱|sen|mäh|ma|schi|ne** F lawn mower; **Ra̱|sen|platz** M (*Ftbl etc*) field, pitch; (*Tennis*) grass court; **Ra̱|sen|spiel** NT (*Sport*) *game played on grass*, outdoor game; **Ra̱|sen|sport** M *sport played on grass*, outdoor sport; **Ra̱|sen|spren|ger** [-ʃprɛŋɐ] M **-s, -** (lawn) sprinkler; **Ra̱|sen|stück** NT patch of grass; **Ra̱|sen|wal|ze** F (lawn) roller

Ra̱|ser [ˈraːzɐ] M **-s, -**, **Ra̱|se|rin** [-ərɪn] F **-, -nen** (*inf*) speed maniac (*esp Brit inf*) *or* merchant (*Brit inf*), speed demon (*US inf*)

Ra|se|rei̱ [razəˈrai] F **-, -en a** (*= Wut*) fury, rage, frenzy **b** (*inf: = schnelles Fahren, Gehen*) mad rush

Ra|si̱er- *in cpds* shaving; **Ra|si̱er|ap|pa|rat** M razor; (*elektrisch auch*) shaver; **Ra|si̱er|creme** F shaving cream

ra|si̱e|ren [raˈziːrən] *ptp* **rasi̱ert** VT **a** *Haare, Kopf, Bart* to shave; **sich ~ lassen** to get a shave; **sie rasiert sich** (*dat*) **die Beine** she shaves her legs **b** (*inf: = streifen*) to scrape VR to (have a) shave; **sich nass ~** to have a wet shave; **sich trocken ~** to use an electric shaver

Ra|si̱e|rer [raˈziːrɐ] M **-s, -** (*inf*) (electric) razor *or* shaver

Ra|si̱er-: **Ra|si̱er|klin|ge** F razor blade; **Ra|si̱er|mes|ser** NT (open) razor, cut-throat razor; **Ra|si̱er|pin|sel** M shaving brush; **Ra|si̱er|scha|le** F shaving mug; **Ra|si̱er|schaum** M shaving foam; **Ra|si̱er|sei|fe** F shaving soap; **Ra|si̱er|was|ser** NT *pl* **-wasser** *or* **-wässer** aftershave (lotion); (*vor der Rasur*) pre-shave (lotion); **Ra|si̱er|zeug** NT *pl* **-zeuge** shaving things *pl or* tackle (*inf*) *or* equipment

Rä|so̱n [rɛˈzõː] F **-**, *no pl* **er will keine ~ annehmen** he refuses to listen *or* won't listen to reason; **jdn zur ~ bringen** to make sb listen to reason, to make sb see reason *or* sense; **jdn zur ~ rufen** to call on sb to see reason *or* sense; **zur ~ kommen** to see reason *or* sense

rä|so|ni̱e|ren [rɛzoˈniːrən] *ptp* **räsoni̱ert** VI (*old*) to grumble

Ra̱s|pel [ˈraspl] F **-, -n a** (*= Holzfeile*) rasp **b** (*Cook*) grater

ra̱s|peln [ˈraspln] VT to grate; *Holz* to rasp → **Süßholz**

rass [ras], **räss** [rɛs] (*S Ger, Sw*) ADJ *Most, Speise* tart; *Witz* earthy; *Pferd* fiery; *Kellnerin* buxom; (*Sw*) *Mensch* wild ADV **~** *or* **räss schmecken** to taste tart

Ra̱s|se [ˈrasə] F **-, -n** (*= Menschenrasse*) race; (*= Tierrasse*) breed; (*fig*) spirit, hot-bloodedness; **das Mädchen hat ~** she's a hot-blooded girl; **das Pferd/der Hund hat ~** that horse/dog has spirit

Ra̱s|se-: **Ra̱s|se|hund** M pedigree *or* thoroughbred dog; **Ra̱s|se|kat|ze** F pedigree cat

Ra̱s|sel [ˈrasl] F **-, -n** rattle

Ra̱s|sel|ban|de F (*dated inf*) mischievous bunch (*inf*)

ra̱s|seln [ˈrasln] VI **a** (*= Geräusch erzeugen*) to rattle; **mit** *or* **an etw** (*dat*) **~** to rattle sth **b** *aux sein* (*inf*) **durch eine Prüfung ~** to flunk an exam (*inf*)

Ra̱s|sen- *in cpds* racial; **Ra̱s|sen|be|wusst|sein** NT racial consciousness; **Ra̱s|sen|dis|kri|mi|nie|rung** F racial discrimination; **Ra̱s|sen|dok|trin** F racial doctrine; **Ra̱s|sen|for|schung** F ethnogeny (*form*), racial research; **Ra̱s|sen|fra|ge** F race *or* racial problem; **Ra̱s|sen|ge|set|ze** PL (*NS*) racial *or* race laws *pl*; **Ra̱s|sen|gleich|heit** F racial equality; **Ra̱s|sen|hass** M race *or* racial hatred; **Ra̱s|sen|hy|gi|e|ne** F (*NS*) eugenics *sing*; **ra̱s|sen|hy|gi|e|nisch** ADJ (*NS*) eugenical; **Ra̱s|sen|kampf** M racial struggle; **Ra̱s|sen|kon|flikt** M racial conflict; **Ra̱s|sen|kra|wall** M race *or* racial riot; **Ra̱s|sen|kreu|zung** F (*von Tieren*) crossbreeding; (*Tier*) crossbreed, crossbred; **Ra̱s|sen|kun|de** F ethnogeny (*form*), study of race; **Ra̱s|sen|merk|mal** NT racial characteristic; **Ra̱s|sen|mi|schung** F mixture of races; (*bei Tieren*) crossbreeding; (*Tier*) crossbreed, crossbred; **Ra̱s|sen|po|li|tik** F racial policy; **Ra̱s|sen|prob|lem** NT race *or* racial problem; **Ra̱s|sen|schan|de** F *Nazi term for sexual relations with a non-Aryan*; **Ra̱s|sen|schran|ke** F racial barrier, barrier of race; (*Farbige betreffend*) colour (*Brit*) *or* color (*US*) bar; **Ra̱s|sen|the|o|rie** F racial theory, theory of race; **Ra̱s|sen|tren|nung** F racial segregation; **Ra̱s|sen|un|ru|hen** PL racial disturbances *pl*; **Ra̱s|sen|vor|ur|teil** NT racial prejudice; **~e haben** to be racially biased

Ra̱s|se-: **Ra̱s|se|pferd** NT thoroughbred (horse); **ra̱s|se|rein** ADJ = **reinrassig**; **Ra̱s|se|rein|heit** F racial purity; **Ra̱s|se|vieh** NT thoroughbred *or* purebred animal(s); **Ra̱s|se|weib** NT (*pej inf*) hot-blooded woman

ra̱s|sig [ˈrasɪç] ADJ *Pferd, Auto* sleek; *Frau* vivacious and hot-blooded; *Erscheinung, Gesichtszüge* sharp, striking; *Wein* spirited, lively; *Sinti or Roma , Südländer* fiery, hot-blooded

ra̱s|sisch [ˈrasɪʃ] ADJ racial ADV racially; **~ anders sein** not to belong to the same race; **jdn ~ verfolgen** to persecute sb because of his/her race

Ras|si̱s|mus [raˈsɪsmʊs] M **-**, *no pl* racialism, racism

Ras|si̱st [raˈsɪst] M **-en, -en**, **Ras|si̱s|tin** [-ˈsɪstɪn] F **-, -nen** racist

ras|si̱s|tisch [raˈsɪstɪʃ] ADJ racist, racialist ADV **sich ~ äußern** to make racist remarks; **sich ~ verhalten** to act like a racist; **~ eingestellt sein** to be a racist; **~ angehauchte Texte** racist sounding texts

Ra̱st [rast] F **-, -en** rest, repose (*liter*); (*auf Autofahrt*) stop (for a rest); **~ machen** to stop (for a rest); (*Mil*) to make a halt; **die schöne Aussicht lädt zur ~** (*liter*) the beautiful view invites repose (*liter*); **er gönnt sich keine ~** he won't rest, he allows himself no respite; **ohne ~ und Ruh** (*liter*) without pause for rest, without respite

Ra̱s|ta [ˈrasta] M **-s, -s**, **Ras|ta|fa̱|ri** [rastaˈfaːri] M **-s, -s** Rasta, Rastafarian

Ra̱s|ta|lo|cken [ˈrasta-] PL dreadlocks *pl*, dreads *pl* (*inf*)

Ra̱s|te [ˈrastə] F **-, -n** notch

ra̱s|ten [ˈrastn] VI to rest; (*Mil*) to make a halt; **er hat nicht gerastet und geruht, bis ...** (*liter*) he did not rest until ...; **wer rastet, der rostet** (*Prov*) a rolling stone gathers no moss (*Prov*)

Ra̱s|ter [ˈrastɐ] NT **-s, -** (*Archit: auf Landkarte*) grid; (*Typ*) halftone *or* raster screen; (*Phot: = Gitter*) screen; (*TV*) raster; (*Comput*) grid; (*fig*) framework; **es passt nicht in das ~, es fällt durch das ~** (*fig*) it doesn't fit into the scheme of things; **ein grobes ~** (*fig*) a rough criterion

Ra̱s|ter-: **Ra̱s|ter|ät|zung** F halftone (engraving); **Ra̱s|ter|bild** NT (*Typ*) halftone picture; (*TV*) frame; **Ra̱s|ter|druck** M *pl* **-drucke** (*Typ*) halftone printing; **Ra̱s|ter|fahn|dung** F computer search; **Ra̱s|ter|li|nie** F grid line

ra̱s|tern [ˈrastɐn] VT (*Typ*) to print in halftone; (*TV*) to scan

Ra̱s|ter|punkt M (*Typ*) (halftone) dot; (*TV*) picture element

Ra̱s|te|rung F **-, -en** (*TV*) scanning

Ra̱st-: **Ra̱st|haus** NT (travellers' (*Brit*) *or* travelers' (*US*)) inn; (*an Autobahn: auch* **Rasthof**) service area (*including motel*); **ra̱st|los** ADJ (*= unruhig*) restless; (*= unermüdlich*) tireless, untiring; *Arbeiten, Bemühen* tireless, ceaseless ADV tirelessly; **~ tätig sein** to work tirelessly *or* ceaselessly; **Ra̱st|lo|sig|keit** F **-, -en** restlessness; **Ra̱st|platz** M resting place, place to rest; (*an Autostraßen*) picnic area; **Ra̱st|stät|te** F (*Mot*) service area, services *pl*

Ra|su̱r [raˈzuːɐ] F **-, -en a** (*= Bartrasur*) shave; (*= das Rasieren*) shaving **b** (*= radierte Stelle*) erasure

Ra̱t ✪ 28.1, 29, 38.3 M [raːt] **-(e)s a** *pl* **Ratschläge** (*= Empfehlung*) [ˈraːtʃlɛːgə] advice *no pl*, counsel *no pl* (*liter*); **ein ~** a piece of advice; **jdm einen ~ geben** to give sb a piece of advice; **jdm den ~ geben, etw zu tun** to advise sb to do sth; **jdn um ~ fragen** *or* **bitten, sich** (*dat*) **bei jdm ~ holen** to ask sb's advice *or* sb for advice; **bei jdm ~ suchen** to seek sb's advice, to seek advice from sb; **~ suchend** seeking advice; **sich ~ suchend an jdn wenden** to turn to sb for advice; **~ Suchende** = **Ratsuchende(r)**; **gegen jds ~ handeln** to go against *or* act against *or* ignore sb's advice; **einem ~ folgen, einen ~ befolgen** to take a piece of advice; **auf jds ~** (*acc*) **(hin)** on *or* following sb's advice; **jdm mit ~ und Tat beistehen** *or* **zur Seite stehen** to support sb *or* back sb up in (both) word and deed; **da ist guter ~ teuer** it's hard to know what to do; **zu ~e**

= **zurate**

b *no pl (liter: = Beratung)* **mit jdm ~ halten** *or* **pflegen** to take counsel with sb *(liter)*

c *no pl (= Abhilfe)* **~ (für etw) wissen** to know what to do (about sth); **sie wusste sich** *(dat)* **keinen ~ mehr** she was at her wits' end; **sich** *(dat)* **keinen ~ mit etw wissen** not to know what to do about sth; **kommt Zeit, kommt ~** *(Prov)* things work themselves out, given time

d *pl* **Räte** *(= Körperschaft)* council; *(= Ratsmitglied)* councillor *(Brit)*, councilor *(US)*, council member; **der ~ der Gemeinde/Stadt** ≈ the district council; [ˈrɛːtə] **der Große ~** *(Sw)* the cantonal parliament; **den ~ einberufen** to call a council meeting; **im ~ sitzen** to be on the council

Rat M **-(e)s, =e, Rä|tin** [ˈrɛːtɪn] F **-, -nen** senior official; *(= Titel)* Councillor *(Brit)*, Councilor *(US)* → **wissenschaftlich**

rät [rɛːt] *3. pers sing pres von* **raten**

Ra|te [ˈraːtə] F **-, -n** **a** *(= Geldbetrag)* instalment *(Brit)*, installment *(US)*; **auf ~n kaufen** to buy in instal(l)ments, to buy on hire purchase *(Brit)* *or* on the installment plan *(US)*; **auf ~n** *(fig)* bit by bit; **Tod auf ~n** slow death; **in ~n zahlen** to pay in instal(l)ments **b** *(= Verhältnis)* rate

ra|ten [ˈraːtn] ✪ 29.1, 29.2 *pret* **riet,** [riːt] *ptp* **geraten** VTI [gəˈraːtn] **a** *(= Ratschläge geben)* to advise; **jdm ~** to advise sb; **jdm gut/richtig/schlecht ~** to give sb good/correct/bad advice; **(jdm) zu etw ~** to recommend sth (to sb); **jdm ~, etw nicht zu tun** to advise sb not to do sth, to advise sb against doing sth; **zu dieser langen Reise kann ich dir nicht ~** I must advise you against making this long journey; **das würde ich dir nicht ~** I wouldn't advise *or* recommend it; **das möchte ich dir nicht ~** *or* **nicht geraten haben** I wouldn't advise *or* recommend it, I wouldn't if I were you; **das möchte ich dir auch geraten haben!** you better had *(inf)*; **was** *or* **wozu ~ Sie mir?** what do you advise *or* recommend?; **lass dir ~!** take some advice, be advised; **ich weiß mir nicht zu ~** *(dated)* I'm at a loss; **wem nicht zu ~ ist, dem ist auch nicht zu helfen** *(prov)* a bit of advice never hurt anybody

b *(= erraten, herausfinden)* to guess; *Kreuzworträtsel etc* to solve, to do; **hin und her ~** to make all sorts of guesses; **rate mal!** (have a) guess; **dreimal darfst du ~** I'll give you three guesses *(auch iro)*; **das rätst du nie!** you'll never guess!; **(gut) geraten!** good guess!; **falsch geraten!** wrong!; **das kann ich nur ~** I can only make a guess, I can only guess at it; **das hab ich nur so geraten** I was only guessing, it was only a guess

Ra|ten-: **Ra|ten|kauf** M *(= Kaufart)* hire purchase *(Brit)*, HP *(Brit inf)*, the installment plan *(US)*; **sie tätigte Ratenkäufe** she bought things on hire purchase *(Brit)* *or* on HP *(Brit inf)* *or* on the installment plan *(US)*; **durch viele Ratenkäufe verschuldet sein** to have hire purchase *(Brit)* *or* installment plan *(US)* debts; **Ra|ten|spar|ver|trag** M *(Fin)* premium-aided saving; **ra|ten|wei|se** ADV in instalments *(Brit)* *or* installments *(US)*; **Ra|ten|zah|lung** F *(= Zahlung einer Rate)* payment of an instalment *(Brit)* *or* installment *(US)*; *(= Zahlung in Raten)* payment by instal(l)ments

Ra|ter [ˈraːtɐ] M **-s, -, Ra|te|rin** [-ərɪn] F **-, -nen** guesser; *(von Rätsel)* solver

Rä|te|re|gie|rung F soviet government

Ra|te|rei [raːtəˈrai] F **-, -en** **a** *(= das Schätzen)* guessing; **lass mal die ~** must we have these guessing games? **b** *(= Rätselraten)* puzzle-solving

Rä|te|re|pub|lik F soviet republic *(esp in Bavaria 1919)*

Ra|te|spiel NT guessing game; *(TV)* quiz; *(Beruferaten etc)* panel game, quiz

Rat-: **Rat|ge|ber** M *(Buch, TV-Sendung etc)* guide; **ein ~ für den Garten** a book of gardening tips; **Rat|ge|ber(in)** M(F) adviser, counsellor *(Brit form)*, counselor *(US form)*; **Rat|haus** NT town hall; *(einer Großstadt)* city hall; **Rat|haus|platz** M town *or* city *(esp US)* hall square; **Rat|haus|saal** M council chamber; **Konzert im ~** concert in the town hall

Ra|ti|fi|ka|ti|on [ratifikaˈtsioːn] F **-, -en** ratification

Ra|ti|fi|ka|ti|ons-: **Ra|ti|fi|ka|ti|ons|klau|sel** F ratification clause; **Ra|ti|fi|ka|ti|ons|ur|kun|de** F ratification document

ra|ti|fi|zie|ren [ratifiˈtsiːrən] *ptp* **ratifiziert** VT to ratify

Ra|ti|fi|zie|rung F **-, -en** ratification

Rä|tin [ˈrɛːtɪn] F → **Rat**

Ra|tio [ˈraːtsio] F **-,** *no pl (geh)* reason; **es ist ein Gebot der ~, zu …** reason demands that …, it's only rational to …

Ra|ti|on [raˈtsioːn] F **-, -en** ration; **jeder bekommt eine bestimmte ~** everyone gets fixed rations

ra|ti|o|nal [ratsioˈnaːl] ADJ rational ADV rationally

ra|ti|o|na|li|sie|ren [ratsionaliˈziːrən] *ptp* **rationalisiert** VTI to rationalize

Ra|ti|o|na|li|sie|rung F **-, -en** rationalization

Ra|ti|o|na|li|sie|rungs-: **Ra|ti|o|na|li|sie|rungs|fach|frau** F, **Ra|ti|o|na|li|sie|rungs|fach|mann** M efficiency expert, time and motion (study) expert; **Ra|ti|o|na|li|sie|rungs|maß|nah|me** F rationalization *or* efficiency measure; **Ra|ti|o|na|li|sie|rungs|schutz** M job protection measures *pl*

Ra|ti|o|na|lis|mus [ratsionaˈlɪsmʊs] M **-,** *no pl* rationalism

Ra|ti|o|na|list [ratsionaˈlɪst] M **-en, -en, Ra|ti|o|na|lis|tin** [-ˈlɪstɪn] F **-, -nen** rationalist

ra|ti|o|na|lis|tisch [ratsionaˈlɪstɪʃ] ADJ rationalist(ic)

Ra|ti|o|na|li|tät [ratsionaliˈtɛːt] F **-,** *no pl* rationality; *(= Leistungsfähigkeit)* efficiency

ra|ti|o|nell [ratsioˈnɛl] ADJ *Methode, Energienutzung etc* efficient ADV efficiently

ra|ti|o|nen|wei|se [raˈtsioːnənvaizə] ADV in rations

ra|ti|o|nie|ren [ratsioˈniːrən] *ptp* **rationiert** VT to ration

Ra|ti|o|nie|rung F **-, -en** rationing

Ra|ti|o|nie|rungs|sys|tem NT rationing system

ra|ti|ons|wei|se [raˈtsioːnsvaizə] ADV = **rationenweise**

rat|los ADJ helpless; **ich bin völlig ~(, was ich tun soll)** I'm at a complete loss (as to what to do), I just don't know what to do; **~e Eltern** parents who are at a loss to know what to do with their children; **sie machte ein ~es Gesicht** she looked helpless *or* at a loss ADV helplessly; **einer Sache** *(dat)* **~ gegenüberstehen** to be at a loss when faced with sth

Rat|lo|sig|keit F **-,** *no pl* helplessness; **in meiner ~ …** not knowing what to do …, being at a loss …

Rä|to|ro|ma|ne [rɛtoroˈmaːnə] M **-n, -n, Rä|to|ro|ma|nin** [-ˈmaːnɪn] F **-, -nen** Rhaetian

rä|to|ro|ma|nisch [rɛtoroˈmaːnɪʃ] ADJ Rhaetian; *Sprache* Rhaeto-Romanic

Rä|to|ro|ma|nisch(e) [rɛtoroˈmaːnɪʃ] NT Rhaeto-Romanic → *auch* **Deutsch(e)**

rat|sam [ˈraːtzaːm] ADJ advisable; **ich halte es für ~, das zu tun** I think it (would be) advisable to do that

Rats|be|schluss M decision of the local council

ratsch [ratʃ] INTERJ rip

Rat|sche [ˈraːtʃə] F **-, -n** *(S Ger, Aus)*, **Rät|sche** [ˈrɛːtʃə] F **-, -n** *(Sw)* rattle

rat|schen [ˈraːtʃn] *(S Ger, Aus)* VI, **rät|schen** [ˈrɛːtʃn] VI *(Sw)* **a** *(mit der Ratsche)* to rattle **b** *(inf: = schwatzen)* to blather *(inf)*

Rat|schlag ✪ 29.2 M piece *or* bit of advice; **Ratschläge** advice; **drei Ratschläge** three pieces of advice; **ein guter ~** a good piece of advice, good advice; **deine klugen Ratschläge kannst du dir sparen** keep your advice for yourself; **jdm einen ~ geben** *or* **erteilen** to give sb a piece of advice *or* some advice; **jds ~** *(dat)* **folgen, jds ~ befolgen** to take sb's advice

rat|schla|gen [ˈraːtʃlaːgn] VI *insep* to deliberate, to consult (together)

Rat|schluss M *(liter)* decision; **Gottes ~** the will of God; **Gottes unerforschlichem ~ hat es gefallen …** it has pleased the Lord in his mysterious wisdom …

Rats|die|ner M *(old)* (town hall) porter

Rät|sel [ˈrɛːtsl] NT **-s, -** **a** riddle; *(= Kreuzworträtsel)* crossword (puzzle); *(= Silbenrätsel, Bilderrätsel etc)* puzzle; **in ~n sprechen** to talk in riddles; **jdm ein ~ aufgeben** to give *or* ask sb a riddle

b *(fig: = Geheimnis)* riddle, mystery, enigma *(um of)*; **die Polizei konnte das ~ lösen** the police have solved the riddle *or* mystery; **vor einem ~ stehen** to be faced with a riddle *or* mystery, to be baffled; **das plötzliche Verschwinden des Zeugen gab der Polizei ~ auf** the sudden disappearance of the witness baffled the police; **es ist mir ein ~, wie …** it's a mystery to me how …, it baffles *or* beats *(inf)* me how …; **er ist mir ein ~** he's a mystery *or* an enigma to me; **(jdm) ein ~ bleiben** to remain a mystery (to sb); **das ist des ~s Lösung!** that's the answer

Rät|sel-: **Rät|sel|ecke** F puzzle corner; **Rät|sel|fra|ge** F *(= Quizfrage)* question; **rät|sel|haft** ADJ mysterious; *Gesichtsausdruck, Lächeln auch* enigmatic; **auf ~e Weise** mysteriously; **es ist mir ~** it's a mystery to me, it baffles me; **Rät|sel|haf|tig|keit** [ˈrɛːtslhaftɪçkait] F **-,** *no pl* mysteriousness; **Rät|sel|heft** NT puzzle book; **Rät|sel|lö|ser** [-løːzɐ] M **-s, -, Rät|sel|lö|se|rin** [-ərɪn] F **-, -nen** puzzle-solver

rät|seln [ˈrɛːtsln] VI to puzzle (over sth), to rack one's brains

Rät|sel-: **Rät|sel|ra|ten** NT **-s,** *no pl* guessing game; *(= Rätseln)* guessing; **rät|sel|voll** ADJ *(geh)* mysterious; **Rät|sel|zei|tung** F puzzle book

Rats-: **Rats|herr(in)** M(F) *(dated)* councillor *(esp Brit)*, councilman *(US)*; **Rats|kel|ler** M rathskeller *(US)*, *restaurant under the town hall*; **Rats|sit|zung** F council meeting; **Rats|stu|be** F *bar/restaurant near the town hall*

rat|su|chend ADJ → **Rat a**

Rat|su|chen|de(r) MF *decl as adj* **~** people *or* those seeking advice

Rats|ver|samm|lung F **a** *(= Sitzung)* council meeting **b** *(= Rat)* council

Rat|tan [ˈratan] NT **-s,** *no pl* rattan

Rat|te [ˈratə] F **-, -n** **a** *(= Tier)* rat; **die ~n verlassen das sinkende Schiff** *(prov)* the rats are deserting the sinking ship → **schlafen** **b** *(inf: = Mensch)* rat *(inf)*; **eine widerliche ~** a dirty rat *(inf)*

Rat|ten-: **Rat|ten|be|kämp|fung** F rat control; **Rat|ten|fän|ger(in)** M(F) rat-catcher; *(Hund)* ratter; *(fig)* rabble-rouser; **der ~ von Hameln** the Pied Piper of Hamelin; **Rat|ten|gift** NT rat poison; **Rat|ten|schwanz** M **a** *(lit)* rat's tail **b** *usu pl (inf: = Zopf)* bunch **c** *(fig inf: = Serie, Folge)* string

rat|tern [ˈratɐn] VI *(als Bewegungsverb: aux sein)* to rattle, to clatter; *(Maschinengewehr)* to chatter

Rat|ze|fum|mel [ˈratsəfʊml] M **-s, -** *(inf: Schülersprache)* rubber *(Brit)*, eraser

rat|ze|kahl [ˈratsəˈkaːl] ADV *(inf)* completely, totally; **alles ~ aufessen** *(Vorräte)* to eat the cupboard bare *(inf)*; *Portion* to polish off the lot *(inf)*; **die Raupen fraßen die Laubbäume ~** the caterpillars ate all the leaves off the trees

rat|zen VI *(dial inf)* to kip *(Brit inf)*, to sleep; **ich hab vielleicht geratzt** I had a really good kip *(Brit inf)* *or* sleep

rat|zen VT to scratch

ratz|fatz [ˈratsˈfats] ADV *(inf: sehr schnell)* in no time, in a flash *(beide nachgestellt)*

rau [rau] ADJ **a** rough; **eine ~e Schale haben** *(fig)* to be a rough diamond; **~e Schale, weicher**

Kern *(fig)* tough exterior, soft centre *(Brit) or* center *(US)*
b *Hals, Kehle* sore; *Stimme* husky; *(= heiser)* hoarse
c *(= nicht mild, streng) Wetter* inclement; *Wind, Luft* raw; *See* rough; *Klima, Winter* harsh, raw; *(= unwirtlich) Gebiet* bleak; *Stadt* tough; **im ~en Norden** in the rugged north; **(die) ~e Wirklichkeit** harsh reality, the hard facts *pl*
d *(= barsch, grob) Benehmen, Wesen* rough; *(= hart) Mann* tough, rugged; *Ton* harsh; *Worte, Behandlung* rough, harsh; **~, aber herzlich** bluff; *Begrüßung, Ton* rough but jovial; **er ist ~, aber herzlich** he's a rough diamond; **in unserer Familie geht es ~, aber herzlich zu** we're a pretty hale and hearty lot in our family; **hier herrschen ja ~e Methoden** their/his *etc* methods are brutal
e *(inf)* **in ~en Mengen** by the ton *(inf)*, galore *(inf)*; **Zucker in ~en Mengen** sugar by the ton *(inf)*, sugar galore *(inf)*

Raub [raup] M **-(e)s** [-bəs], *no pl* **a** *(= das Rauben)* robbery; *(= Diebstahl)* theft; **auf ~ ausgehen** *(Tiere)* to go out hunting *or* on the prowl; *(Räuber)* to go out pillaging; **schwerer ~** aggravated robbery **b** *(= Entführung)* abduction; **der ~ der Sabinerinnen** the rape of the Sabine women **c** *(= Beute)* booty, loot, spoils *pl*; **ein ~ der Flammen werden** *(liter)* to fall victim to the flames

Raub-: **Raub|bau** M, *no pl* overexploitation (of natural resources); *(am Wald)* overfelling; *(an Äckern)* overcropping; *(an Weideland)* overgrazing; *(an Fischbeständen)* overfishing; **~ an etw** *(dat)* **treiben** to overexploit *etc* sth; **am Fischbestand eines Flusses ~ treiben** to overfish a river; **mit seiner Gesundheit ~ treiben** to ruin one's health; **Raub|druck** M *pl* **-drucke** pirate(d) copy; *(= das Drucken)* pirating

Rau-: **Rau|bein** NT *(inf)* rough diamond; **rau|bei|nig** ADJ *(inf)* rough-and-ready

rau|ben ['raubn] **VT** **a** *(= wegnehmen)* to steal; **jdm etw ~** to rob sb of sth **b** *(= entführen)* to abduct, to carry off **c** *(fig)* **jdm etw ~** to rob sb of sth; **das hat uns viel Zeit geraubt** it cost us a lot of time; **jdm einen Kuss ~** to steal a kiss from sb; **jdm den Schlaf/den Verstand ~** to rob sb of his/her sleep/reason; **jdm den Atem ~** to take sb's breath away; **jdm die Unschuld ~** *(obs, iro)* to take sb's virginity; **du raubst mir noch den letzten Nerv!** you'll drive me mad *or* crazy *(inf)* **VI** to rob, to plunder, to pillage

Räu|ber ['rɔybɐ] M **-s, -**, **Räu|be|rin** [-ərɪn] F **-, -nen** robber, brigand *(old)*; *(bei Banküberfall etc)* robber, raider; *(= Wegelagerer)* highwayman; *(inf: = Kind)* rascal *(inf)*; **Ali Baba und die vierzig ~** Ali Baba and the forty thieves; **unter die ~ fallen** *or* **geraten** to fall among thieves; **der Fuchs ist ein ~** the fox is a beast of prey, the fox is a predator; **~ und Gendarm** cops and robbers

Räu|ber|ban|de F robber band, band of robbers; *(pej)* bunch of thieves

Räu|be|rei [rɔybə'rai] F **-, -n** *(inf)* robbery

Räu|ber-: **Räu|ber|ge|schich|te** F **a** story about robbers **b** *(fig)* cock-and-bull story *(inf)*; **Räu|ber|ge|sin|del** NT *(pej)* thieving riffraff; **Räu|ber|haupt|mann** M robber-chief; **Räu|ber|höh|le** F **a** *(lit)* robbers' cave **b** *(fig inf) (= Spelunke)* low dive *(inf)*; *(= Durcheinander)* pigsty

Räu|be|rin [-ərɪn] F → **Räuber**

räu|be|risch ['rɔybərɪʃ] ADJ rapacious, predatory; **~er Diebstahl** *(Jur) theft in which force or the threat of violence is used to remain in possession of the stolen goods*; **~e Erpressung** *(Jur)* armed robbery; **in ~er Absicht** with intent to rob

räu|bern ['rɔybɐn] VI *(inf)* to thieve; **in der Speisekammer ~** to raid the larder

Räu|ber-: **Räu|ber|pis|to|le** F cock-and-bull story *(inf)*; **Räu|ber|zi|vil** NT *(hum inf)* scruffy old clothes *pl (inf)*

Raub-: **Raub|fisch** M predatory fish, predator; **Raub|gier** F *(liter)* rapacity; **raub|gie|rig** ADJ *(liter)* rapacious; **Raub|kat|ze** F (predatory) big cat; **Raub|ko|pie** F pirate(d) copy; **Raub|krieg** M war of conquest; **der ~ gegen unser Land** the rape of our country; **Raub|mord** M robbery with murder; **Raub|mör|der(in)** M(F) robber and murderer; **Raub|pres|sung** F pirate(d) copy; **Raub|rit|ter** M robber baron

Raub|tier NT predator, beast of prey

Raub|tier-: **Raub|tier|haus** NT lion house; **Raub|tier|kä|fig** M lion's/tiger's *etc* cage

Raub-: **Raub|über|fall** M robbery; *(auf Bank etc auch)* raid *(auf on)*; **einen ~ auf jdn begehen** *or* **verüben** to hold sb up; **„Raubüberfall auf Taxifahrer"** "taxi driver attacked and robbed"; **Raub|vo|gel** M bird of prey, predator; **Raub|wild** NT *(Hunt)* predatory game; **Raub|zeug** NT *(Hunt)* vermin *pl*; **Raub|zug** M series *sing* of robberies; *(pej: = Angriffskrieg)* rape *(nach, gegen of)*; *(= Plünderung)* raid *(auf +acc on)*; *(von Tieren)* hunting excursion; **auf ~ gehen** *(Einbrecher)* to commit a series of robberies; *(Tier)* to go hunting *or* on the prowl

Rauch [raux] M **-(e)s**, *no pl* smoke; *(giftig auch)* fumes *pl*; **in ~ und Flammen aufgehen** to go up in smoke *or* flames; **in ~ aufgehen** *(lit, fig)* **sich in ~ auflösen** *(fig)* to go up in smoke; **Würste in den ~ hängen** to hang sausages up to smoke; **kein ~ ohne Feuer** *(Prov)* there's no smoke without fire *(prov)*

Rauch-: **Rauch|ab|zug** M smoke outlet; **rauch|arm** ADJ smokeless; **rauch|bar** ADJ smok(e)able; **hast du was Rauchbares?** have you got anything to smoke?; **Rauch|bil|dung** F production *or* formation of smoke; **mit großer ~ verbrennen** to burn giving off a lot of smoke; **Rauch|bom|be** F smoke bomb

rau|chen ['rauxn] **VI** *(= Rauch abgeben)* to smoke, to give off smoke; **sie sah, dass es aus unserer Küche rauchte** she saw smoke coming from our kitchen; **mir raucht der Kopf** my head's spinning
VTI *(Mensch)* to smoke; **möchten Sie ~?** do you want to smoke?; *(Zigarette anbietend)* would you like a cigarette?; **darf ich ~?** do you mind if I smoke?, may I smoke?; **nach dem Essen rauche ich gern** I like a *or* to smoke after a meal; **eine ~** to have a smoke; **hast du was zu ~?** have you got a smoke?; **„Rauchen verboten"** "no smoking"; **sich** *(dat)* **das Rauchen angewöhnen/abgewöhnen** to take up/give up smoking; **viel** *or* **stark ~** to be a heavy smoker, to smoke a lot; **~ Sie?** do you smoke?

Rauch|ent|wick|lung F production *or* formation of smoke; **mit starker/geringer ~** giving off high/low smoke levels

Rau|cher ['rauxɐ] M **-s, -** *(Rail: = Raucherabteil)* smoker, smoking compartment

Rau|cher ['rauxɐ] M **-s, -**, **Rau|che|rin** [-ərɪn] F **-, -nen** smoker; **sind Sie ~?** do you smoke?, are you a smoker?

Räu|cher|aal ['rɔyçɐ-] M smoked eel

Rau|cher-: **Rau|cher|ab|teil** NT smoking compartment, smoker; **Rau|cherbein** NT hardening of the arteries (in the leg) *(caused by smoking)*; **Rau|cher|ecke** F smokers' corner

Räu|cher-: **Räu|cher|fass** ['rɔyçɐ-] NT *(Eccl)* censer; **Räu|cher|fisch** ['rɔyçɐ-] M smoked fish; **Räu|cher|ge|fäß** ['rɔyçɐ-] NT incense burner; **Räu|cher|he|ring** ['rɔyçɐ-] M kipper, smoked herring

Rau|cher|hus|ten M smoker's cough

Rau|che|rin [-ərɪn] F smoker → *auch* **Raucher**

Räu|cher-: **Räu|cher|kam|mer** ['rɔyçɐ-] F smoking chamber, smokehouse; **Räu|cher|ker|ze** ['rɔyçɐ-] F incense cone; **Räu|cher|lachs** ['rɔyçɐ-] M smoked salmon

Rau|cher|lun|ge F smoker's lung

Räu|cher|männ|chen ['rɔyçɐ-] NT smoking man *(usu wooden figure containing an incense cone)*

räu|chern ['rɔyçɐn] **VT** to smoke **VI** *(inf: mit Weihrauch)* to burn incense

Räu|cher-: **Räu|cher|schin|ken** M smoked ham; **Räu|cher|speck** M ≈ smoked bacon; **Räu|cher|stäb|chen** NT joss stick; **Räu|cher|wa|ren** PL smoked foods *pl*

Rau|cher-: **Rau|cher|zim|mer** NT smoking room; **Rau|cher|zo|ne** F smoking area

Rauch-: **Rauch|fah|ne** F smoke trail, trail of smoke; **Rauch|fang** M **a** *(= Rauchabzug)* chimney hood **b** *(Aus)* chimney; **Rauch|fang|keh|rer** [-keːrɐ] M **-s, -**, **Rauch|fang|keh|re|rin** [-ərɪn] F **-, -nen** *(Aus)* (chimney) sweep; **rauch|far|ben** [-farbn], **rauch|far|big** ADJ smoke-coloured *(Brit)*, smoke-colored *(US)*; **Rauch|fass** NT *(Eccl)* censer; **Rauch|fleisch** NT smoked meat; **rauch|frei** ADJ *Zone* smokeless; *Aufenthaltsraum* no-smoking; **Rauch|ga|se** PL fumes *pl*; **Rauch|gas|ent|schwe|fe|lung** F flue gas desulphurization *(Brit) or* desulfurization *(US)*; **Rauch|gas|ent|schwe|fe|lungs|an|la|ge** F flue gas desulphurization *(Brit) or* desulfurization *(US)* plant; **rauch|ge|schwän|gert** [-gəʃvɛŋɐt] ADJ *Zimmer* smoke-filled; *Luft* heavy with smoke; **rauch|ge|schwärzt** [-gəʃvɛrtst] ADJ blackened by smoke, smoke-blackened; **Rauch|glas** NT smoked glass; **Rauch|glo|cke** F pall of smoke

rau|chig ['rauxɪç] ADJ *Geruch, Geschmack, Stimme* smoky

Rauch-: **rauch|los** ADJ smokeless; **Rauch|mel|der** M smoke alarm *or* detector; **Rauch|pilz** M mushroom cloud; **Rauch|quarz** M smoky quartz, cairngorm; **Rauch|sa|lon** M smoking *or* smoke room; **Rauch|säu|le** F column *or* pillar of smoke; **Rauch|schlei|er** M veil of smoke; **Rauch|schwa|den** PL drifts *pl* of smoke; **Rauch|schwal|be** F swallow; **Rauch|ser|vice** [-zɛrviːs] NT smoker's set; **Rauch|sig|nal** NT smoke signal; **Rauch|ta|bak** M *(form)* tobacco; **Rauch|tisch** M, **Rauch|tisch|chen** NT smoker's table; **Rauch|to|pas** M smoky quartz, cairngorm; **Rauch|uten|si|li|en** PL smoker's requisites *pl*; **Rauch|ver|bot** NT smoking ban, ban on smoking; **hier herrscht ~** smoking is not allowed here, there's no smoking here; **Rauch|ver|gif|tung** F fume poisoning; **eine ~ erleiden** to be overcome by fumes; **Rauch|ver|zeh|rer** [-fɛɐtseːrɐ] M **-s, -** smoke dispeller, *small, often ornamental device for neutralizing tobacco smoke*; **Rauch|vor|hang** M, **Rauch|wand** F smokescreen; **Rauch|wa|ren** PL tobacco (products *pl*); **Rauch|wa|ren** PL *(= Pelze)* furs *pl*; **Rauch|wa|ren|händ|ler(in)** M(F) furrier; **Rauch|wol|ke** F cloud of smoke; **Rauch|zei|chen** NT smoke signal; **Rauch|zim|mer** NT smoking *or* smoke room

Räu|de ['rɔydə] F **-, -n** *(Vet)* mange

räu|dig ['rɔydɪç] ADJ mangy; **du ~er Hund!** *(old inf)* you dirty dog!

rau|en ['rauən] VT to roughen (up); *(Tex) Stoff* to nap

rauf [rauf] ADV *(inf)* **~!** (get) up! → *auch* **herauf, hinauf**

Rau|fa|ser|ta|pe|te F woodchip paper

Rauf|bold ['raufbɔlt] M **-(e)s, -e** [-də] *(dated)* ruffian, roughneck

Rau|fe ['raufə] F **-, -n** hayrack

rau|fen ['raufn] **VT** *Unkraut* to pull up; *Flachs* to pull; **sich** *(dat)* **die Haare ~** to tear (at) one's hair **VIR** to scrap, to fight; **sich um etw ~** to fight over sth

Rau|fe|rei [raufə'rai] F **-, -en** scrap, roughhouse *(inf)*; **nur eine harmlose ~** just a harmless little scrap

Rauf-: **Rauf|han|del** M *(old, form)* affray *(form)*;; **Rauf|lust** F pugnacity; **rauf|lus|tig** ADJ ready for a fight *or* scrap, pugnacious

Rau|fut|ter NT roughage

rauh △ [rau] ADJ → **rau**

Rau|haar|da|ckel M wire-haired dachshund

rau|haa|rig ADJ coarse-haired; *Hund auch* wire-haired; *Fell, Wolle* coarse

Rauh- △: **Rauh|bein** △ NT → **Raubein**; **rauh|bei|nig** △ ADJ → **raubeinig**

Rau|heit ['rauhait] F -, *no pl* **a** roughness **b** *(von Hals, Kehle)* soreness; *(von Stimme)* huskiness; *(= Heiserkeit)* hoarseness **c** *(= Strenge) (von Wind, Luft)* rawness; *(von See)* roughness; *(von Klima, Winter)* harshness; *(von Gegend)* bleakness; **die ~ des schottischen Wetters** the inclement Scottish weather **d** *(= Barschheit, Grobheit)* roughness; *(= Härte)* toughness

rau|hen △ ['rauən] VT → **rauen**

Rauh- △: **Rauh|fa|ser|ta|pe|te** △ F → **Raufasertapete**; **Rauh|fut|ter** △ NT → **Raufutter**; **Rauh|haar|da|ckel** △ M → **Rauhaardackel**; **rauh|haa|rig** △ ADJ → **rauhaarig**; **Rauh|putz** △ M → **Rauputz**; **Rauh|reif** △ M, *no pl* → **Raureif**

Rau|ke ['raukə] F *(Bot)* rocket

Raum [raum] M **-(e)s, Räume** ['rɔymə] **a** *no pl (= Platz)* room, space; *(= Weite)* expanse; **~ schaffen** to make some space *or* room; **~ sparend** = **raumsparend**; **auf engstem ~ leben** to live in a very confined space; **einer Sache** *(dat)* **~ geben** *(geh)* to yield to sth; **eine Frage in den ~ stellen** to pose a question; **eine Frage im ~ stehen lassen** to leave a question unresolved *or* hanging; **den ~ decken** *(Sport)* to cover the area **b** *(= Spielraum)* room, scope **c** *(= Zimmer)* room **d** *(= Gebiet, Bereich)* area; *(größer)* region; *(fig)* sphere; **der ~ Frankfurt** the Frankfurt area; **der mitteleuropäische ~** the Central European region; **im ländlichen ~** in rural areas; **im geistigen ~** in the intellectual sphere; **~ gewinnen** *(Mil, fig)* to gain ground **e** *no pl (Phys, Space)* space *no art*; **der offene** *or* **leere ~** the void → **luftleer**

Raum-: **Raum|an|zug** M spacesuit; **Raum|auf|tei|lung** F floor plan; **Raum|aus|stat|ter** [-lausʃtatɐ] M **-s, -**, **Raum|aus|stat|te|rin** [-ərın] F **-, -nen** interior decorator; **Raum|bild** NT stereoscopic *or* 3-D picture; **Raum|bild|ver|fah|ren** NT stereoscopy

Räum|boot NT minesweeper

Raum|ein|heit F unit of volume

räu|men ['rɔymən] **VT** **a** *(= verlassen) Gebäude, Gebiet, Posten* to vacate; *(Mil: Truppen)* to move out of, to withdraw from; *Wohnung* to vacate, to move out of; *Hotelzimmer* to vacate, to check out of; *Sitzplatz* to vacate, to give up; **wir müssen das Haus bis Mittwoch ~** we have to be out of the house by Wednesday → **Feld** **b** *(= leeren) Gebäude, Straße, Warenlager* to clear *(von* of); **„wir ~"** "clearance sale" **c** *(= woanders hinbringen)* to shift, to move; *(= entfernen) Schnee, Schutt* to clear (away), to shift; *Minen* to clear; *(auf See)* to sweep, to clear; **räum deine Sachen in den Schrank** put your things away in the cupboard; **er hat seine Sachen aus dem Schrank geräumt** he cleared his things out of the cupboard → **Weg**
VI *(= aufräumen)* to clear up; *(= umräumen)* to rearrange things; **in etw** *(dat)* **~** to rummage around in sth

Raum-: **Raum|ent|we|ser** [-lɛntveːzɐ] M **-s, -**, **Raum|ent|we|se|rin** [-ərın] F **-, -nen** *(form)* pest exterminator; **Raum|er|spar|nis** F space-saving; **aus Gründen der ~** to save space, for reasons of space; **Raum|fäh|re** F space shuttle; **Raum|fah|rer(in)** M(F) spaceman/-woman, astronaut; *(russisch)* cosmonaut

Raum|fahrt F space travel *no art or* flight *no art*; **die Ausgaben für die ~ erhöhen** to increase the space budget; **das Zeitalter der ~** the space age; **die bemannte ~** manned space travel *or* flight

Raum|fahrt- *in cpds* space; **Raum|fahrt|be|hör|de** F space authority; **Raum|fahrt|in|ge|ni|eur(in)** M(F) astronautical engineer; **Raum|fahrt|me|di|zin** F space medicine; **Raum|fahrt|pro|gramm** NT space programme; **Raum|fahrt|sta|ti|on** F space station; **Raum|fahrt|tech|nik** F space technology; **Raum|fahrt|zeit|al|ter** NT space age; **Raum|fahrt|zent|rum** NT space centre *(Brit)* or center *(US)*

Raum|fahr|zeug NT spacecraft

Räum|fahr|zeug NT bulldozer; *(für Schnee)* snow-clearer

Raum-: **Raum|flug** M space flight; *(Forschungsflug auch)* space mission; **Raum|for|schung** F space research; **Raum|ge|stal|tung** F interior design; **Raum|ge|winn** M extra space gained; **der ~ war nicht sehr groß** we didn't gain much space; **Raum|git|ter** NT *(Min)* (crystal *or* space) lattice; **Raum|glei|ter** M orbiter; **raum|grei|fend** ADJ far-reaching, extensive; *Schritt* long, lengthy; **eine ~e Skulptur** a sculpture of great presence; **Raum|in|halt** M volume, (cubic) capacity; **Raum|kap|sel** F space capsule; **Raum|klang** M stereophonic sound; **Raum|kli|ma** NT indoor climate, *room temperature and air quality*; **Raum|la|bor** NT space lab; **Raum|leh|re** F geometry

räum|lich ['rɔymlıç] **ADJ** **a** *(= den Raum betreffend)* spatial; **~e Verhältnisse** physical conditions; **~e Nähe** physical closeness, spatial proximity; **~e Entfernung** physical distance **b** *(= dreidimensional)* three-dimensional; **~es Anschauungsvermögen** capacity to think in three dimensions
ADV **a** *(= platzmäßig)* **~ beschränkt sein** to have very little room; **sich ~ beschränken** to make do with very little room; **wir haben ~ keine Probleme** we have no problem with room; **wir wohnen ~ sehr beengt** we live in very cramped conditions; **rein ~ ist das unmöglich** (just) from the point of view of space it's impossible **b** *(= dreidimensional)* **~ sehen** to see in three dimensions, to see three-dimensionally; **Menschen, die auf einem Auge blind sind, können nicht ~ sehen** people who are blind in one eye have no depth perception; **ich kann mir das nicht ~ vorstellen** I can't really picture it

Räum|lich|keit F **-, -en** **a** *no pl* three-dimensionality **b** *(= Zimmer)* room; **~en** *pl* premises *pl*; **dazu fehlen uns die ~en** we don't have the premises for it/them

Raum-: **Raum|man|gel** M lack of space *or* room; **Raum|maß** NT unit of volume; **Raum|me|ter** M OR NT cubic metre *(Brit) or* meter *(US) (of stacked wood)*; **Raum|mis|si|on** F space mission; **Raum|not** F shortage of space; **Raum|ord|nung** F environmental planning; **Raum|ord|nungs|plan** M development plan; **Raum|pfle|ger(in)** M(F) cleaner

Räum|pflug M snowplough *(Brit)*, snowplow *(US)*

Raum-: **Raum|pla|nung** F *(das Planen)* development planning; *(Plan)* development plan; **Raum|schiff** NT spaceship; **Raum|schiff|fahrt** F = **Raumfahrt**; **Raum|son|de** F space probe; **raum|spa|rend** **ADJ** space-saving *attr*; **das ist ~er** that saves more space **ADV** *bauen, einbauen, unterbringen* to save space; **etw ~ stapeln** to stack sth (away) with a minimum use of space; **Raum|sta|ti|on** F space station; **Raum|tei|ler** M room divider; *(dünne Trennwand)* partition; **Raum|tem|pe|ra|tur** F room temperature; **Raum|trans|por|ter** M space shuttle

Räum|trupp M clearance gang *or* workers *pl*

Räu|mung ['rɔymʊŋ] F **-, -en** clearing; *(von Wohnung, Gebäude, Stelle, Posten)* vacation; *(wegen Gefahr etc)* evacuation; *(unter Zwang)* eviction; *(Mil: von besetztem Gebiet)* withdrawal *(gen* from); *(von Lager, Vorräten, Geschäft)* clearance; **„wegen ~ alle Preise radikal herabgesetzt!"** "all prices reduced to clear"

Räu|mungs-: **Räu|mungs|ar|bei|ten** PL clearance operations *pl*; **Räu|mungs|be|fehl** M eviction order; **Räu|mungs|frist** F (period of) notice; **Räu|mungs|kla|ge** F action for eviction; **Räu|mungs|ver|kauf** M clearance sale

Raum|ver|schwen|dung F waste of space

rau|nen ['raunən] VTI *(liter)* to whisper; **es ging ein Raunen durch die Menge** a murmur went through the crowd

raun|zen ['rauntsn] VI *(inf: S Ger, Aus)* to grouse *(Brit inf)*, to grouch *(inf)*

Raun|zer ['rauntsɐ] M **-s, -** *(inf: S Ger, Aus)* grouse(r) *(Brit inf)*, grouch(er) *(inf)*

Rau|pe ['raupə] F **-, -n** **a** caterpillar **b** *(= Planierraupe)* caterpillar®; *(= Kette)* caterpillar® track *or* tread

Rau|pen-: **Rau|pen|fahr|zeug** NT caterpillar® (vehicle); **Rau|pen|ket|te** F caterpillar® track; **Rau|pen|schlep|per** M caterpillar® (tractor)

Rau|putz M roughcast

Rau|reif M hoarfrost, white frost; *(= gefrorener Nebel)* rime

raus [raus] ADV *(inf)* **~!** (get) out! → *auch* **heraus, hinaus**

Rausch [rauʃ] M **-(e)s, Räusche** ['rɔyʃə] **a** *(= Trunkenheit)* intoxication, inebriation; *(= Drogenrausch)* drugged(-up) state, high *(inf)*; **sich** *(dat)* **einen ~ antrinken** to get drunk; **einen ~ haben** to be drunk; **etw im ~ tun/sagen** to do/say sth while under the influence (of alcohol *or* drink); **seinen ~ ausschlafen** to sleep it off **b** *(liter) (= Ekstase)* ecstasy, transport *(liter)*, rapture; *(= Blutrausch, Mordrausch etc)* frenzy; **im ~ der Leidenschaft** inflamed with passion; **im ~ der Gefühle** in an ecstasy of emotion; **der ~ der Geschwindigkeit** the thrill of speed

rausch|arm ADJ *(Rad)* low-noise

Rau|sche|bart M *(inf)* big bushy beard; *(Mann)* man with a big bushy beard, beardy *(hum inf)*

rau|schen ['rauʃn] VI **a** *(Wasser, Meer, Wasserfall)* to roar; *(sanft)* to murmur; *(Brandung)* to boom, to roar; *(Baum, Wald)* to rustle; *(Wind)* to murmur; *(Seide)* to rustle, to swish; *(Korn)* to swish; *(Regen)* to pour down; *(Radio, Lautsprecher etc)* to hiss; *(Muschel)* to sing; *(Applaus)* to resound; **weißes Rauschen** *(Rad)* white noise **b** *aux sein (= sich schnell bewegen) (Bach)* to rush; *(Bumerang, Geschoss)* to whoosh *(inf)*; *(Auto etc)* to whoosh *(inf)*, to whizz *(inf)* **c** *aux sein (inf: Mensch)* to sweep; **sie rauschte in das/aus dem Zimmer** she swept into/out of the room

rau|schend ADJ *Fest* grand; *Beifall, Erfolg* resounding; **im ~en Walde** in the gently murmuring forest; **mit ~en Flügeln** with a swish *or* swoosh of its wings; **eine ~e Ballnacht** a glittering ball

Rau|scher ['rauʃɐ] M **-s, -** *(dial)* sweet cider *(half fermented)*

rausch|frei ADJ *(Rad, Tech)* noiseless

Rausch|gift NT drug, narcotic; *(= Drogen)* drugs *pl*, narcotics *pl*; **~ nehmen** to take drugs; *(regelmäßig auch)* to be on drugs; **mit ~ handeln** to deal in drugs

Rausch|gift-: **Rausch|gift|de|zer|nat** NT narcotics *or* drug squad; **Rausch|gift|fahn|der(in)** M(F) = **Drogenfahnder**; **Rausch|gift|han|del** M drug trafficking; **Rausch|gift|händ|ler(in)** M(F) drug trafficker; **Rausch|gift|sucht** F drug addiction; **rausch|gift|süch|tig** ADJ drug-addicted; **er ist ~** he's addicted to drugs, he's a drug addict; **Rausch|gift|süch|ti|ge(r)** MF *decl as adj* drug addict

Rausch-: **Rausch|gold** NT gold foil; **Rausch|gold|en|gel** M ≈ Christmas tree fairy; **rausch|haft** ADJ *(fig)* ecstatic; **Rausch|mit|tel** NT *(form)* intoxicant *(form)*; **Rausch|zu|stand** M *(form)* state of intoxication, intoxicated state

raus+ekeln ['rausleːkln] VT *sep (inf)* to freeze out *(inf)*

raus+feu|ern ['rausfɔyɐn] VT *sep (inf)* to chuck out *(inf)*, to sling out *(Brit inf)*

raus+flie|gen ['rausfliːgn] VI *sep irreg aux sein (inf)* to be chucked *or* slung out *(inf)*; *(= entlas-*

sen werden auch) to be given the boot *(inf)* or the push *(Brit inf)*

raus+hau|en ['raushauən] VT *sep (fig inf)* = **rauspauken**

raus+krie|gen ['rauskri:gn] VT *sep (inf)* = **herausbekommen**

raus+pau|ken ['rauspaukn] VT *sep (inf)* **jdn ~** to get sb out of trouble, to get sb off the hook *(inf)*; **mein Anwalt hat mich rausgepaukt** my lawyer got me off

räus|pern ['rɔyspɐn] VR to clear one's throat

raus+rei|ßen ['rausraisn] VT *sep irreg (inf)* **jdn ~** to save sb, to save sb's bacon *(Brit inf)*, to get sb out of trouble; **der Torwart/das hat noch alles rausgerissen** the goalkeeper/that saved the day → *auch* **herausreißen**

raus+schmei|ßen ['rausʃmaisn] VT *sep irreg (inf)* to chuck *or* sling *or* kick out (*aus* of) *(all inf)*; *(= entlassen auch)* to give the boot *(inf)*; *(= wegwerfen)* to chuck out *or* away *(inf)*; *Geld* to chuck away *(inf)*, to chuck down the drain *(Brit inf)*; **das ist rausgeschmissenes Geld** that's money down the drain *(inf)*

Raus|schmei|ßer ['rausʃmaisɐ] M *(inf: = letzter Tanz)* last number *or* dance

Raus|schmei|ßer ['rausʃmaisɐ] M **-s, -**, **Raus|schmei|ße|rin** [-ərın] F **-, -nen** *(inf)* bouncer

Raus|schmiss ['rausʃmıs] M *(inf)* booting out *(inf)*; **man drohte uns mit dem ~** they threatened us with the boot *(inf)* or push *(Brit inf)*

Rau|te ['rautə] F **-, -n** **a** *(Bot)* rue **b** *(Math)* rhombus; *(Her)* lozenge

rau|ten|för|mig ADJ rhomboid, diamond-shaped, lozenge-shaped

Rau|ten|mus|ter NT diamond pattern

Rave [re:v] M OR NT **-(s), -s** **a** *(= Party)* rave **b** *no pl (Musikrichtung)* rave (music)

Rave-Par|ty ['re:v-] F rave (party)

Ra|ver ['re:vɐ] M **-s, -**, **Ra|ve|rin** [-ərın] F **-, -nen** raver

Ra|vi|o|li [ravi'o:li] PL ravioli *sing*

Ra|yon [rɛ'jõ:] M **-s, -s** *(Aus)* department; *(old)* region

Raz|zia ['ratsia] F **-, Raz|zien** [-tsiən] raid, swoop *(inf)* (*gegen* on); **eine ~ durchführen** to carry out a raid; **die Polizei machte in ein paar Lokalen ~** the police swooped on *(inf)* or carried out a raid on *or* raided three or four bars

RBB [ɛrbe'be:] M - *abbr von* **Rundfunk Berlin-Brandenburg**

Re [re:] NT **-s, -s** *(Cards)* redouble; **Re ansagen** to redouble

Rea|der ['ri:dɐ] M **-s, -** *(= Lehrbuch)* reader

Re|a|gens [re'a:gɛns, re'la:gɛns] NT **-, Reagenzien** [rea'gɛntsiən], **Re|a|genz** [rea'gɛnts] NT **-es, -ien** [-tsiən] *(Chem)* reagent

Re|a|genz|glas NT, **Re|a|genz|röhr|chen** NT *(Chem)* test tube

re|a|gie|ren [rea'gi:rən] *ptp* **reagiert** VI to react (*auf +acc* to; *mit* with); *(Chem)* to react (*mit* with); **miteinander ~** *(Chem)* to react (together); **auf etw** *(acc)* **verärgert** *or* **mit Verärgerung ~** to react angrily *or* with anger to sth

Re|ak|ti|on [reak'tsio:n] F **-, -en** **a** reaction (*auf +acc* to); *(Chem)* reaction (*mit* with) **b** *(Pol pej)* reaction; **ein Vertreter der ~** a representative of reactionary thinking

re|ak|ti|o|när [reaktsio'nɛ:ɐ] *(Pol pej)* ADJ reactionary ADV **~ denken** to be a reactionary

Re|ak|ti|o|när [reaktsio'nɛ:ɐ] M **-(e)s, -e**, **Re|ak|ti|o|nä|rin** [-'nɛ:rın] F **-, -nen** *(pej)* reactionary

Re|ak|ti|ons-: **Re|ak|ti|ons|fä|hig|keit** F ability to react; *(Chem, Physiol)* reactivity; **Alkohol vermindert die ~** alcohol slows down the *or* one's reactions; **re|ak|ti|ons|freu|dig** ADJ highly reactive; **Re|ak|ti|ons|ge|schwin|dig|keit** F speed of reaction; **re|ak|ti|ons|schnell** ADJ with fast reactions; **~ sein** to have fast reactions ADV **er bremste ~** he reacted quickly and braked; **Re|ak|ti|ons|schnel|lig|keit** F speed of reaction; **re|ak|ti|ons|trä|ge** ADJ of low reactivity; **Re|ak|ti|ons|ver|lauf** M *(Chem)* course of the reaction; **Re|ak|ti|ons|wär|me** F *(Chem)* heat of reaction; **Re|ak|ti|ons|zeit** F reaction time

re|ak|tiv [reak'ti:f] *(geh)* ADJ reactive ADV **er verhält sich nur ~** he doesn't act, he only reacts

re|ak|ti|vie|ren [reakti'vi:rən] *ptp* **reaktiviert** VT *(Sci)* to reactivate; *(Agr, Biol, fig)* to revive; *Kenntnisse, Können* to brush up, to polish up; *Kontakte* to renew, to revive; *Markt* to revive; *Gliedmaßen* to rehabilitate; *(Mil)* to call up again; *Sportler, Beamte* to bring back

Re|ak|ti|vie|rung F **-, -en** *(Sci)* reactivation; *(Agr, Biol, fig)* revival; *(von Kenntnissen, Können)* brushing *or* polishing up; *(von Gliedmaßen)* rehabilitation; *(Mil)* new call-up

Re|ak|tor [re'akto:ɐ] M **-s, Reaktoren** [-'to:rən] reactor

Re|ak|tor-: **Re|ak|tor|block** M *pl* **-blöcke** reactor block; **Re|ak|tor|ge|bäu|de** NT reactor housing *or* dome, concrete sheet; **Re|ak|tor|kern** M reactor core; **Re|ak|tor|si|cher|heit** F reactor safety; **Re|ak|tor|un|glück** NT nuclear disaster

re|al [re'a:l] ADJ real; *(= wirklichkeitsbezogen)* realistic ADV *sinken, steigen* actually; **der ~ existierende Sozialismus** socialism as it exists in reality

Re|al-: **Re|al|bü|ro** NT *(Aus)* estate agency *(Brit)*, real estate agency *(US)*; **Re|al|ein|kom|men** NT real income; **Re|al|en|zyk|lo|pä|die** F specialist encyclopaedia; **Re|al|gym|na|si|um** NT ≈ grammar school *(Brit)*, ≈ high school *(esp US) (stressing modern languages, maths and science)*

Re|a|li|en [re'a:liən] PL realities *pl*, real facts *pl*; *(old Sch)* science and modern languages *pl*

Re|al-: **Re|al|in|dex** M *(dated)* subject index; **Re|al|in|ju|rie** [re'a:lınju:riə] F **-, -n** *(Jur)* ≈ assault

Re|a|li|sa|ti|on [realiza'tsio:n] F **-, -en** (= *Verwirklichung, auch Fin)* realization; *(TV, Rad, Theat)* production

re|a|li|sier|bar ADJ **a** *Idee, Projekt* practicable, feasible, realizable **b** *(Fin)* realizable

Re|a|li|sier|bar|keit [reali'zi:ɐba:ɐkait] F **-**, *no pl* feasibility, practicability

re|a|li|sie|ren [reali'zi:rən] *ptp* **realisiert** VT **a** *Pläne, Ideen, Programm, Projekt* to carry out; *(TV, Rad, Theat)* to produce **b** *(Fin)* to realize; *Verkauf* to make, to conclude **c** *(= erkennen)* to realize

Re|a|li|sie|rung F **-, -en** = **Realisation**

Re|a|lis|mus [rea'lısmʊs] M **-**, *no pl* realism

Re|a|list [rea'lıst] M **-en, -en**, **Re|a|lis|tin** [-'lıstın] F **-, -nen** realist

re|a|lis|tisch [rea'lıstıʃ] ADJ realistic ADV realistically

Re|a|li|tät [reali'tɛ:t] F **-, -en** **a** reality; **der ~** *(dat)* **entsprechen** to correspond to reality *or* the facts; **die ~ anerkennen** to face facts; **die ~en** *pl (= Gegebenheiten)* the realities *pl*, the facts *pl*; **virtuelle ~** virtual reality **b Realitäten** PL *(Aus: = Immobilien)* real estate

Re|a|li|tä|ten|händ|ler(in) M(F), **Re|a|li|tä|ten|ver|mitt|ler(in)** M(F) *(Aus)* estate agent *(Brit)*, realtor *(US)*, real estate agent *(US)*

Re|a|li|täts-: **re|a|li|täts|feind|lich** ADJ *(pej)* **~ sein** to refuse to accept the realities of the situation; **re|a|li|täts|fern** ADJ unrealistic; **Re|a|li|täts|fer|ne** F lack of contact with reality; **re|a|li|täts|fremd** ADJ out of touch with reality; **re|a|li|täts|nah** ADJ realistic; **Re|a|li|täts|nä|he** F contact with reality; **Re|a|li|täts|sinn** M sense of realism; **er hat einen ausgeprägten ~** he has a firm hold on reality; **Re|a|li|täts|ver|lust** M *(Psych)* derealization

re|a|li|ter [re'a:litɐ] ADV *(geh)* in reality, in (point of) fact

Re|a|li|ty|fern|se|hen [ri'ɛlıti-] NT, **Re|a|li|ty-TV** [ri'ɛlıtiti:vi:] NT real-life TV, reality TV *(esp US)*

Re|al-: **Re|al|kanz|lei** F *(Aus)* estate agency *(Brit)*, real estate agency *(US)*; **Re|al|ka|pi|tal** NT physical assets *pl*, non-monetary capital; **Re|al|ka|ta|log** M subject catalogue *(Brit) or* catalog *(US)*; **Re|al|kon|kur|renz** F *(Jur)* **in ~ mit** in conjunction with; **Re|al|kre|dit** [-kre'di:t] M *(Fin)* collateral loan; **Re|al|le|xi|kon** NT specialist dictionary; **Re|al|lohn** M real wages *pl*

Re|a|lo [re'a:lo] M **-s, -s** *(Pol sl)* political realist *(of the Green Party)*

Re|al-: **Re|al|po|li|tik** F political realism, Realpolitik; **Re|al|po|li|ti|ker(in)** M(F) political realist; **re|al|po|li|tisch** ADJ politically realistic, pragmatic; **Re|al|sa|ti|re** F real-life satire; **Re|al|schu|le** F ≈ secondary school, ≈ secondary modern school *(Brit)*; **Re|al|schü|ler(in)** M(F) ≈ secondary modern pupil *(Brit)*, ≈ *student in secondary school (US)*; **Re|al|tei|lung** F *(Jur)* division (of land/property *etc*); **Re|al|wert** M *(Fin)* real value; **Re|al|zins** M *(Fin)* real interest rate

> **REALSCHULE**
>
> A **Realschule** is a type of German secondary school. It normally covers a period of four or six school years and is designed to provide a general education that goes beyond that of a **Hauptschule**. After completing **Realschule** students may try for a **Fachabitur** at a **Fachoberschule** or serve an apprenticeship. If students from a **Realschule** achieve good examination results, they may move up to the eleventh year of a **Gymnasium** and attempt the **Abitur**.
> In Austria the functions of **Realschulen** are performed by **mathematische Realgymnasien** and extended **Hauptschulen**. → ABITUR, GYMNASIUM, HAUPTSCHULE, MITTLERE REIFE

Re|ani|ma|ti|on [relanima'tsio:n] F *(Med)* resuscitation

re|ani|mie|ren [relani'mi:rən] *ptp* **reanimiert** VT *(Med)* to resuscitate

Re|be ['re:bə] F **-, -n** *(= Ranke)* shoot; *(= Weinstock)* vine

Re|bell [re'bɛl] M **-en, -en**, **Re|bel|lin** [-'bɛlın] F **-, -nen** rebel

re|bel|lie|ren [rebɛ'li:rən] *ptp* **rebelliert** VI to rebel, to revolt

Re|bel|li|on [rebɛ'lio:n] F **-, -en** rebellion, revolt

re|bel|lisch [re'bɛlıʃ] ADJ rebellious

Re|ben|saft M *(liter)* wine, juice of the vine *(liter)*, grape *(liter)*

Reb-: **Reb|huhn** ['re:p-, 'rɛp-] NT (common) partridge; **Reb|laus** ['re:p-] F phylloxera *(spec)*, vine pest; **Reb|ling** ['re:plıŋ] M **-s, -e** young vine; **Reb|schnur** ['re:p-] F *(Aus)* rope; **Reb|sor|te** ['re:p-] F type of vine; **Reb|stock** ['re:p-] M vine

Re|bus ['re:bʊs] M OR NT **-, -se** rebus, picture puzzle

Re|chaud [re'ʃo:] M OR NT **-s, -s** hotplate; *(für Tee/Kaffee)* tea/coffee warmer; *(für Fondue)* spirit burner *(Brit)*, ethanol burner *(US)*

re|chen ['rɛçn] VT *(S Ger)* to rake

Re|chen ['rɛçn] M **-s, -** *(S Ger) (= Harke)* rake; *(= Gitter an Bächen, Flüssen)* grill

Re|chen-: **Re|chen|an|la|ge** F computer; **Re|chen|art** F type of calculation; **die vier ~en** the four arithmetical operations; **Re|chen|auf|ga|be** F sum *(esp Brit)*, (arithmetical) problem; **Re|chen|au|to|mat** M (automatic) adding machine, Comptometer® *(Brit)*; **Re|chen|brett** NT abacus; **Re|chen|buch** NT arithmetic book; **Re|chen|exem|pel** NT sum *(esp Brit)*, arithmetical problem; **das ist doch ein ganz einfaches ~** it's a matter of simple arithmetic; **Re|chen|feh|ler** M miscalculation, (arithmetical) error *or* mistake; **Re|chen|funk|ti|on** F *(Comput)* computational function; **Re|chen|ge|schwin|dig|keit** F *(Comput)* processing speed; **Re|chen|heft** NT arithmetic book; **Re|chen|künst|ler(in)** M(F) mathematical genius *or* wizard *(inf)*; **Rẹ|chen|leh|rer(in)** M(F) arithmetic teacher; **Rẹ|chen|ma|schi|ne** F adding machine; **Rẹ|chen|ope|ra|ti|on** F calculation

Rẹ|chen|schaft [ˈrɛçnʃaft] F -, *no pl* account; **jdm über etw** *(acc)* **~ geben** *or* **ablegen** to account to sb for sth, to give *or* render account to sb for sth *(liter)*; **sich** *(dat)* **über etw** *(acc)* **~ ablegen** to account to oneself for sth; **jdm ~ schuldig sein** *or* **schulden** to be accountable to sb, to have to account to sb; **dafür bist du mir ~ schuldig** you owe me an explanation for that; **jdn (für etw) zur ~ ziehen** to call sb to account (for *or* over sth); **(von jdm) ~ verlangen** *or* **fordern** to demand an explanation *or* account (from sb)

Rẹ|chen|schafts-: **Rẹ|chen|schafts|be|richt** M report; **Rẹ|chen|schafts|le|gung** [-leːgʊŋ] F -, *no pl* report; **jdm gegenüber zur ~ verpflichtet sein** to be accountable to sb; **Rẹ|chen|schafts|pflicht** F accountability

Rẹ|chen-: **Rẹ|chen|schie|ber** M slide rule; **Rẹ|chen|schwä|che** F *(Psych)* difficulty in dealing with numbers, dyscalculia *(spec)*; **Rẹ|chen|stab** M slide rule; **Rẹ|chen|stun|de** F arithmetic lesson; **Rẹ|chen|ta|bel|le** F ready reckoner; **Rẹ|chen|ta|fel** F arithmetic slate; *(an der Wand)* (squared) blackboard; **Rẹ|chen|werk** NT *(Comput)* arithmetic unit; **Rẹ|chen|zeit** F *(Comput)* computer time; **Rẹ|chen|zent|rum** NT computer centre *(Brit)* *or* center *(US)*

Re|cher|che [reˈʃɛrʃə, rə-] F -, -n investigation, inquiry; *(in Datenbank, Katalog)* search; **~n anstellen** to make investigations *or* inquiries *(über etw (acc))* about *or* into sth)

Re|cher|chen|jour|na|lis|mus [reˈʃɛrʃən-, rə-] M investigative journalism

re|cher|chie|ren [reʃɛrˈʃiːrən, rə-] *ptp* **recherchiert** VTI to investigate

rech|nen [ˈrɛçnən] VT **a** *(= addieren etc)* to work out, to calculate; *Aufgabe* to work out; **wir ~ gerade Additionen** we're doing addition at the moment; **rund gerechnet** in round figures; **was für einen Unsinn hast du da gerechnet!** how did you get that absurd result?, how did you work that out?

b *(= einstufen)* to count; **jdn/etw zu etw ~, jdn/etw unter etw** *(acc)* **~** to count sb among sth, to class sb/sth as sth; **er wird zu den größten Physikern** *or* **unter die größten Physiker gerechnet** he is rated as one *or* is reckoned to be one of the greatest physicists, he is counted among the greatest physicists

c *(= veranschlagen)* to estimate, to reckon; **wir hatten nur drei Tage gerechnet** we were only reckoning on three days; **für vier Personen rechnet man ca. zwei Pfund Fleisch** for four people you should reckon on about two pounds of meat; **das ist zu hoch/niedrig gerechnet** that's too high/low (an estimate)

d *(= einberechnen)* to include, to count, to take into account; **alles in allem gerechnet** all in all, taking everything into account; **den Ärger/die Unkosten mit dazu gerechnet** what with all the trouble/expense too *or* on top of that

VI **a** *(= addieren etc)* to do *or* make a calculation/calculations; *(esp Sch)* to do sums *(esp Brit)* *or* adding; **falsch ~** to go wrong *or* to make a mistake (in one's calculations); **richtig ~** to calculate correctly; **(da hast du) falsch gerechnet!** you got that wrong; **gut/schlecht ~ können** to be good/bad at arithmetic *or* with figures; *(esp Sch)* to be good/bad at sums *(esp Brit)* *or* adding; **~ lernen** to learn arithmetic; **mit Variablen/Zahlen ~** to do (the) calculations using variables/numbers

b *(= eingestuft werden)* to count; **er rechnet noch als Kind** he still counts as a child

c *(= sich verlassen)* **auf jdn/etw ~** to count on sb/sth

d **mit jdm/etw ~** *(= erwarten, einkalkulieren)* to reckon on *or* with sb/sth; *(= berücksichtigen)* to reckon with sb/sth; **es wird damit gerechnet, dass …** it is reckoned *or* expected that …; **du musst damit ~, dass es regnet** you must reckon on *or* with it raining; **mit ihm/dieser Partei wird man ~ müssen** he/this party will have to be reckoned with; **damit hatte ich nicht gerechnet** I wasn't expecting that, I hadn't reckoned on *or* with that; **mit so etwas muss man ~** you have to reckon on *or* with that sort of thing happening; **er rechnet mit einem Sieg** he reckons he'll win; **mit allem/dem Schlimmsten ~** to be prepared for anything/the worst; **wir hatten nicht mehr mit ihm** *or* **seinem Kommen gerechnet** we hadn't reckoned on him coming any more; **damit ~ müssen, dass …** to have to be prepared for the fact that …, to have to expect that …; **ich rechne morgen fest mit dir** I'll be expecting you tomorrow

e *(inf: = haushalten)* to count the pennies, to be thrifty; **seine Frau kann gut ~** his wife knows how to count the pennies, his wife is thrifty → **Pfennig**

VR to pay off, to turn out to be profitable; **etw rechnet sich/rechnet sich nicht** sth is economical/not economical

Rẹch|nen [ˈrɛçnən] NT -s, *no pl* arithmetic; *(esp Sch)* sums *pl (Brit)*, arithmetic

Rẹch|ner [ˈrɛçnɐ] M -s, - *(= Elektronenrechner)* computer; *(= Taschenrechner)* calculator

Rẹch|ner [ˈrɛçnɐ] M -s, -, **Rẹch|ne|rin** [-ərɪn] F -, -nen arithmetician; **ein guter ~ sein** to be good at arithmetic *or* figures

Rech|ne|rei [rɛçnəˈrai] F -, -en *(inf)* calculation; **das ist eine furchtbare ~** it's incredibly difficult to work out; **die ganze ~ überlasse ich ihm** I leave all the calculations *or* figure-work to him

rẹch|ner-: **rẹch|ner|ge|steu|ert** [-gəʃtɔyɐt] ADJ computer-controlled; **rẹch|ner|ge|stützt** [-gəʃtʏtst] ADJ computer-aided

Rẹch|ne|rin [-ərɪn] F → **Rechner**

rẹch|ne|risch ADJ arithmetical; *(Pol) Mehrheit* numerical; **ein ~es Beispiel** an example with some figures ADV **a** *(= kalkulatorisch)* **~ falsch sein** to be wrongly calculated; **~ richtig** correctly calculated; **rein ~** just on the basis of the figures; **ich bin rein ~ überzeugt, aber …** I'm convinced as far as the figures go but … **b** *(= durch Rechnen)* by *or* through calculation

Rẹch|ner|netz NT *(Comput)* computer network

Rẹch|ner|ver|bund M computer network; **um den ~ zu erleichtern** to make networking easier; **sie arbeiten im ~** they use networking *or* a computer network

Rẹch|nung [ˈrɛçnʊŋ] ✪ 47.5 F -, -en **a** *(= Berechnung)* calculation; *(als Aufgabe)* sum; **die ~ geht nicht auf** *(lit)* the sum doesn't work out; *(fig)* it won't work (out); **eine ~ aufmachen** to work it out → **Strich**

b *(= schriftliche Kostenforderung)* bill *(Brit)*, check *(US)*; *(esp von Firma)* invoice; *(für Kundenkonto)* statement of account; **das geht auf meine ~** I'm paying, this one's on me; **auf ~ kaufen/bestellen** to buy/order on account; **laut ~ vom 5. Juli** as per our invoice of July 5th; **auf** *or* **für eigene ~** on one's own account; **(jdm) etw in ~ stellen** to charge (sb) for sth; **einer Sache** *(dat)* **~ tragen, etw in ~ ziehen** to take sth into account, to bear sth in mind; **auf seine ~ kommen** to get one's money's worth; **mit jdm noch eine ~ offen haben** *(fig)* to have a score to settle with sb; **aber er hatte die ~ ohne den Wirt gemacht** *(inf)* but there was one thing he hadn't reckoned with → **begleichen**

Rẹch|nungs-: **Rẹch|nungs|ab|schluss** M making-up of (the) accounts; **den ~ machen** to do the books, to make up the accounts; **Rẹch|nungs|amt** NT audit office; **Rẹch|nungs|art** F = **Rechenart**; **Rẹch|nungs|be|trag** M → **Rechnung b** (total) amount of a bill *(Brit)* *or* check *(US)*/invoice/account; *(Econ)* invoice amount; **Rẹch|nungs|buch** NT account(s) book *or* ledger; **Rẹch|nungs|ein|heit** F unit of account; **Rẹch|nungs|füh|rer(in)** M(F) chief accountant; **Rẹch|nungs|füh|rung** F accounting; **Rẹch|nungs|hof** M ≈ Auditor General's office *(Brit)*, ≈ audit division *(US)*; *(von EU)* Court of Auditors; **Rẹch|nungs|jahr** NT financial *or* fiscal year; **Rẹch|nungs|le|gung** [-leːgʊŋ] F -, -en tendering of account; **Rẹch|nungs|prü|fer(in)** M(F) auditor; **Rẹch|nungs|prü|fung** F audit; **Rẹch|nungs|sum|me** F amount payable; **Rẹch|nungs|we|sen** NT *(Führung)* accountancy, bookkeeping; *(Prüfung)* auditing

rẹcht [rɛçt] ✪ 36.2 ADJ **a** *(= richtig)* right; **es soll mir ~ sein, mir soll's ~ sein** *(inf)* it's all right *or* OK *(inf)* by me; **ganz ~!** quite right; **ist schon ~!** *(inf)* that's all right, that's OK *(inf)*; **alles, was ~ ist** *(empört)* there is a limit, fair's fair; *(anerkennend)* you can't deny it; **ich will zum Bahnhof, bin ich hier ~?** *(esp S Ger)* I want to get to the station, am I going the right way?; **bin ich hier ~ bei Schmidts?** *(esp S Ger)* is this the Schmidts' place (all right *(inf)*)?; **hier geht es nicht mit ~en Dingen zu** there's something odd *or* not right here; **ich habe keine ~e Lust** I don't particularly feel like it; **ein ~er Narr** *(old)* a real *or* right *(Brit)* fool; **nichts Rechtes** no good; **aus dem Jungen kann nichts Rechtes werden** that boy will come to no good; **aus ihm ist nichts Rechtes geworden** *(beruflich etc)* he never really made it; **er hat nichts Rechtes gelernt** he didn't learn any real trade; **nach dem Rechten sehen** to see that everything's OK *(inf)*; **Tag, ich wollte nur mal nach dem Rechten sehen** hello, I just thought I'd come and see how you're doing *or* how things are; **es ist nicht mehr als ~ und billig** it's only right and proper; **was dem einen ~ ist, ist dem andern billig** *(Prov)* what's sauce for the goose is sauce for the gander *(Brit Prov)*, what's good for the goose is good for the gander *(US Prov)*

b **~ haben/bekommen/behalten/geben** → **Recht d**

ADV **a** *(= richtig)* properly; *(= wirklich)* really; **verstehen Sie mich ~** don't get me wrong *(inf)*, don't misunderstand me; **ich verstehe ihn nicht so ~, wie kann er nur …?** I just don't understand him, how can he …?; **wenn ich Sie ~ verstehe** if I understand you rightly *or* aright *(form)*; **sehe/höre ich ~?** am I seeing/hearing things?; **ich werde daraus nicht ~ klug** I don't really *or* rightly know what to make of it; **das geschieht ihm ~** it serves him right; **nun** *or* **jetzt mache ich es erst ~/erst ~ nicht** now I'm definitely/definitely not going to do it; **du kommst gerade ~, um …** you're just in time to …; **das ist** *or* **kommt mir gerade ~** *(inf)* that suits me fine; **du kommst mir gerade ~** *(iro)* you're all I needed; **gehe ich ~ in der Annahme, dass …?** am I right *or* correct in assuming that …?; **es hat mir nicht mehr ~ gefallen** I didn't really like it any more; **hat es dir gefallen? – nicht so ~** did you like it? – not really; **ich weiß nicht ~** I don't really *or* rightly know; **man kann ihm nichts ~ machen** you can't do anything right for him; **man kann es nicht allen ~ machen** you can't please all of the people all of the time; **ich mache es Ihnen (auch) ~** *(inf)* I'll make it worth your while; **sie versuchte, es ihm immer ~ zu machen** she always tried to do everything right for him; **~ daran tun, zu …** to be *or* do right to …

b *(= ziemlich, ganz)* quite, fairly, pretty *(inf)*; **~ viel** quite a lot

c *(= sehr)* very, right *(Brit dial)*; **~ herzlichen Dank!** thank you very much indeed

Rẹcht [rɛçt] ✪ 38.1, 40.3, 53.6 NT -(e)s, -e **a** *(= Rechtsordnung, sittliche Norm)* law; *(= Gerechtigkeit)* justice; **~ sprechen** to administer *or* dispense justice; **nach geltendem ~** in law; **nach englischem ~** in *or* under *or* according to English law; **~ muss ~ bleiben** *(= Naturrecht)* fair's fair; *(= Gesetz)* the law's the law; **für das ~ kämpfen** to fight for justice; **das Schwurgericht hat für ~ erkannt …** the court has reached the

following verdict *or* has decided …; **von ~s wegen** legally, as of right; (*inf:* = *eigentlich*) by rights *(inf)*
b Rechte PL (*form:* = *Rechtswissenschaft*) jurisprudence; **Doktor der** *or* **beider ~e** Doctor of Laws **c** (= *Anspruch, Berechtigung*) right (*auf +acc* to, *zu* to); **sein ~ fordern** to demand one's rights; **seine ~e geltend machen** to insist on one's rights; **ich nehme mir das ~, das zu tun** I shall make so bold as to do that; **sein ~ bekommen** *or* **erhalten** *or* **kriegen** *(inf)* to get one's rights, to get what is one's by right; **zu seinem ~ kommen** *(lit)* to gain one's rights; *(fig)* to come into one's own; **auch das Vergnügen muss zu seinem ~ kommen** there has to be a place for pleasure too; **der Körper verlangt sein ~ auf Schlaf** the body demands its rightful sleep; **gleiches ~ für alle!** equal rights for all!; **gleiche ~e, gleiche Pflichten** equal rights, equal duties; **das ~ des Stärkeren** the law of the jungle; **mit** *or* **zu ~** rightly, with justification; **und (das) mit ~** and rightly so; **Sie stellen diese Frage ganz zu ~** you are quite right to ask this question; **im ~ sein** to be in the right; **das ist mein gutes ~** it's my right; **es ist unser gutes ~, zu erfahren …** we have every right to know …; **woher nimmt er das ~, das zu sagen?** what gives him the right to say that?; **mit welchem ~?** by what right? → **vorbehalten**
d recht haben to be right; **er hat recht bekommen** he was right; **recht behalten** to be right; **er will immer recht behalten** he always has to be right; **ich hatte recht, und ich habe recht behalten** I was right and I'm still right; **jdm recht geben** to agree with sb, to admit that sb is right

Rech|te ['rɛçtə] F *decl as adj* **a** *(Hand)* right hand; *(Seite)* right(-hand) side; *(Boxen)* right; **zur ~n (des Königs) saß …** to the right (of the king) *or* on the (king's) right sat … **b** *(Pol)* **die ~** the Right

Recht-: **Recht|eck** NT rectangle; **recht|eckig** ADJ rectangular

Rech|te|hand|re|gel F *(Phys)* right-hand rule

rech|ten ['rɛçtn] VI *(geh)* to argue, to dispute

rech|tens ['rɛçtns] ADJ *(form)* **es ist ~/nicht ~, dass er das gemacht hat** he was/was not within his rights to do that; **die Sache war nicht ~** the matter was not right *or (Jur)* legal; **etw für ~ erklären** to declare sth legal

rech|te(r, s) ['rɛçtə] ADJ *attr* **a** right; *Rand, Spur etc auch* right-hand; **auf der ~n Seite** on the right-hand side, on the right; **jds ~ Hand sein** to be sb's right-hand man **b ein ~r Winkel** a right angle **c** (= *konservativ*) right-wing, rightist; **der ~ Flügel** the right wing **d** *(beim Stricken)* plain; **eine ~ Masche stricken** to knit one

rech|ter|seits ['rɛçtezaits] ADV on the right-hand side

recht|fer|ti|gen ['rɛçtfɛrtɪgn] *insep* VT to justify; (= *berechtigt erscheinen lassen auch*) to warrant; **das ist durch nichts zu ~** that can in no way be justified, that is completely unjustifiable VR to justify oneself

Recht|fer|ti|gung F justification; **zu meiner ~** in my defence *(Brit)* or defense *(US)*, in justification of what I did/said *etc*; **etw zur ~ vorbringen** to say sth in one's defence *(Brit)* or defense *(US)*, to say sth to justify oneself

Recht|fer|ti|gungs-: **Recht|fer|ti|gungs|grund** M *(Jur)* justification; **Recht|fer|ti|gungs|schrift** F apologia; **Recht|fer|ti|gungs|ver|such** M attempt at self-justification

Recht-: **recht|gläu|big** ['rɛçtglɔybɪç] ADJ orthodox; **der Rechtgläubige** the orthodox person; **Recht|gläu|big|keit** F orthodoxy; **Recht|ha|ber** ['rɛçthaːbɐ] M **-s, -**, **Recht|ha|be|rin** [-ərɪn] F **-, -nen** *(pej)* know-all *(Brit inf)*, know-it-all *(US inf)*, self-opinionated person; **Recht|ha|be|rei** [rɛçthaːbəˈrai] F **-,** *no pl (pej)* know-all *(Brit inf)* or know-it-all *(US inf)* attitude, self-opinionatedness; **recht|ha|be|risch** ['rɛçthaːbərɪʃ] ADJ know-all *attr (Brit inf)*, know-it-all *attr (US inf)*, self-opinionated; **er ist so ~** he's such a know-all *(Brit inf) or* know-it-all *(US inf)*, he's so self-opinionated ADV **~ bestand er darauf** he insisted on it in his self-opinionated way

recht|lich ['rɛçtlɪç] ADJ **a** (= *gesetzlich*) legal **b** (*old:* = *redlich*) honest, upright, upstanding *(old)* ADV **a** (= *gesetzlich*) legally; **~ verpflichtet** bound by law, legally obliged; **~ zulässig** permissible in law; **~ nicht zulässig** not permissible in law; **~ unmöglich** impossible for legal reasons; **jdn ~ belangen** to take sb to court, to take legal action against sb **b** (*old:* = *redlich*) honestly; **~ denken/handeln** to think/act in an honest *etc* way

Recht-: **recht|los** ADJ **a** without rights **b** *Zustand* lawless; **Recht|lo|se(r)** ['rɛçtloːzə] MF *decl as adj* person with no rights; (= *Vogelfreier*) outlaw; **Recht|lo|sig|keit** F **-,** *no pl* **a** *(von Mensch)* lack of rights; **in völliger ~ leben** to have no rights whatever **b** *(in Land)* lawlessness; **recht|mä|ßig** ADJ (= *legitim*) lawful, legitimate; *Erben, Thronfolger, Besitzer auch* rightful; (= *dem Gesetz entsprechend*) legal, in accordance with the law; **etw für ~ erklären** to legitimize sth; to declare sth legal ADV legally; **jdm etw ~ zuerkennen** to recognize sb's legal right *or* entitlement to sth; **jdm ~ zustehen** to belong to sb legally; **~ gewählt** legally elected, elected in accordance with the law; **Recht|mä|ßig|keit** ['rɛçtmɛːsɪçkait] F **-,** *no pl* (= *Legitimität*) legitimacy; (= *Legalität*) legality

rechts [rɛçts] ADV **a** on the right; **nach ~** (to the) right; **von ~** from the right; **~ von etw** (on *or* to the) right of sth; **~ von jdm** to *or* on sb's right; *(Pol)* to the right of sb; **weiter ~** further to the right; **sich ~ einordnen** to move into *or* take the right-hand lane; **~ vor links** right before left *(rule of the priority system for driving)*; **sich ~ halten** to keep (to the) right; **Augen ~!** *(Mil)* eyes right!; **~ schwenkt, marsch!** *(Mil)* right wheel! *(Brit)*, right about-face! *(US)*; **~ um!** *(Mil)* right about turn!; **~ stehen** *or* **sein** *(Pol)* to be right-wing *or* on the right *or* a right-winger; **~ stehend** right-hand, on the right; *(Pol)* right-wing, on the right; **ich weiß nicht mehr, wo ~ und links ist** *(inf)* I don't know whether I'm coming or going *(inf)*
b ~ stricken to knit (plain); **ein ganz ~ gestrickter Pullover** a pullover knitted in garter stitch; **zwei ~, zwei links** *(beim Stricken)* knit two, purl two, two plain, two purl
PREP *+gen* **~ des Rheins** to *or* on the right of the Rhine

Rechts- *in cpds (Jur)* legal; **Rechts|ab|bie|ger** M **-s, -** (= *Spur*) right-hand turn-off lane; **Rechts|ab|bie|ger** M **-s, -**, **Rechts|ab|bie|ge|rin** [-ərɪn] F **-, -nen** motorist/cyclist/car *etc* turning right; **die Spur für ~** the right-hand turn-off lane; **Rechts|ab|bie|ger|spur** F right-hand turn-off lane; **Rechts|ab|tei|lung** F legal department; **Rechts|ab|weich|ler(in)** M(F) *(Pol inf)* right-wing dissenter; **Rechts|an|ge|le|gen|heit** F legal matter; **Rechts|an|schau|ung** F legal view; **Rechts|an|spruch** M legal right *or* entitlement; **einen ~ auf etw** *(acc)* **haben** to be legally entitled to sth, to have a legal right to sth; **aus etw einen ~ ableiten** to derive a legal right from sth

Rechts|an|walt M, **Rechts|an|wäl|tin** F lawyer, attorney *(US)*; *(als Berater auch)* solicitor *(Brit)*, attorney *(US)*; *(vor Gericht auch)* barrister *(Brit)*, advocate *(Scot)*, attorney *(US)*; **sein ~ behauptete vor Gericht, …** his counsel maintained in court …; **sich** *(dat)* **einen ~ nehmen** to get a lawyer *etc*

Rechts|an|walts-: **Rechts|an|walts|ge|hil|fe** M, **Rechts|an|walts|ge|hil|fin** F legal secretary; **Rechts|an|walts|kam|mer** F Law Society *(Brit)*, Bar Association *(US)*; **Rechts|an|walts|kanz|lei** F lawyer's *or* solicitor's *(Brit)* or attorney's *(US)* office; *(Firma auch)* law firm

Rechts-: **Rechts|auf|fas|sung** F **a** conception of legality **b** (= *Auslegung*) interpretation of the law; **Rechts|aus|kunft** F legal advice; **Rechts|aus|le|ger** M *(Boxen)* southpaw; **Rechts|aus|le|ger(in)** M(F) *(Pol hum)* extreme right-winger (of a party); **Rechts|aus|schuss** M *(Pol)* committee on legal affairs, judiciary committee; **Rechts|au|ßen** [-'ausn] M **-, -** *(Ftbl)* outside-right; *(Pol inf)* extreme right-winger; **Rechts|bei|stand** M legal advice; *(Mensch)* legal adviser; **Rechts|be|leh|rung** F legal information; *(der Geschworenen)* directions *pl*, instruction (of the jury) *(US)*; **Rechts|be|ra|ter(in)** M(F) legal adviser; **Rechts|be|ra|tung** F **a** legal advice **b** (*auch* **Rechtsberatungsstelle**) legal advice office, ≈ citizens' advice bureau *(Brit)*, ≈ ACLU *(US)*; **Rechts|beu|gung** F perversion of the course of justice; **Rechts|bre|cher(in)** M(F) lawbreaker, criminal; **Rechts|bruch** M breach *or* infringement of the law; **rechts|bün|dig** *(Typ)* ADJ ranged *or* flush right *(Brit)*, right-aligned; (*Comput: als Option*) align right ADV flush right *(Brit)*, aligned right

recht|schaf|fen ['rɛçtʃafn] ADJ **a** (= *ehrlich, redlich*) honest, upright **b** (*inf:* = *stark, groß*) **~en Durst/Hunger haben** to be really thirsty/hungry, to be parched *(inf)*/starving *(inf)* ADV **a** (= *redlich*) honestly, uprightly **b** (*inf:* = *sehr*) really; **sich ~ bemühen** to try really hard

Recht|schaf|fen|heit F **-,** *no pl* honesty, uprightness

recht|schrei|ben ['rɛçtʃraibn] VI *infin only* to spell

Recht|schrei|ben ['rɛçtʃraibn] NT spelling

Recht|schreib-: **Recht|schreib|feh|ler** M spelling mistake; **Recht|schreib|hil|fe** F *(Comput)* spelling aid; **Recht|schreib|kon|trol|le** F, **Recht|schreib|prü|fung** F *(Comput)* spell check; (= *Programm*) spellchecker; **Recht|schreib|re|form** F spelling reform

Recht|schrei|bung F spelling

Rechts-: **Rechts|drall** M *(im Gewehrlauf)* clockwise rifling; *(von Geschoss, Billardball)* swerve to the right; *(von Auto, Pferd)* pull to the right; *(Pol inf)* leaning to the right; **einen ~ haben** to swerve/pull/lean to the right; **rechts|dre|hend** ADJ *(Chem)* dextrorotatory *(spec)*; **Rechts|dre|hung** F turn to the right; **Rechts|ein|wand** M objection, demurrer *(spec)*; **Rechts|emp|fin|den** NT sense of justice; **rechts|ext|rem** ADJ right-wing extremist *attr*; **Rechts|ext|re|mis|mus** M right-wing extremism; **Rechts|ext|re|mist(in)** M(F) right-wing extremist; **rechts|ext|re|mis|tisch** ADJ right-wing extremist *attr*; **rechts|fä|hig** ADJ *(Jur)* legally responsible, having legal capacity *(form)*; **Rechts|fä|hig|keit** F *(Jur)* legal responsibility *or* capacity *(form)*; **Rechts|fall** M court case; *(in der Rechtsgeschichte auch)* legal case; **Rechts|form** F legal form; **Rechts|fra|ge** F legal question *or* issue; **rechts|frei** ADJ **~er Raum** unlegislated area; **Rechts|frie|den** M *(Jur)* peace under the law; **Rechts|ge|fühl** NT sense of justice; **rechts|ge|rich|tet** [-gərɪçtət] ADJ *(Pol)* right-wing; **Rechts|ge|schäft** NT legal transaction; **einseitiges/mehrseitiges ~** unilateral/multilateral legal transaction; **~e tätigen** to carry out legal transactions; **Rechts|ge|schich|te** F legal history; (= *Geschichte der Rechtswissenschaft auch*) history of law; **Rechts|ge|win|de** NT right-handed thread; **Rechts|grund** M legal justification; **Rechts|grund|la|ge** F legal basis; **Rechts|grund|satz** M legal maxim; **rechts|gül|tig** ADJ legally valid, legal; *Vertrag auch* legally binding; **Rechts|gül|tig|keit** F legal validity, legality; **~ erlangen** to become legally valid; **Rechts|gut|ach|ten** NT legal report; **Rechts|ha|ken** M *(Boxen)* right hook; **Rechts|hän|der** [-hɛndɐ] M **-s, -**, **Rechts|hän|de|rin** [-ərɪn] F **-, -nen** right-handed person, right-hander *(esp Sport)*; **~ sein** to be right-handed; **rech̨ts|hän|dig** ADJ ADV right-handed; **Rech̨ts|hän|dig|keit** F -, *no pl* right-handedness; **Rech̨ts|hand|lung** F legal act; **rech̨ts|her** ['rɛçtsheːɐ] ADV from the right; **rech̨ts|he|ran** ['rɛçtsheran] ADV over to the right; **rech̨ts|he|rum** ['rɛçtshɛrʊm] ADV (round) to the right; *sich drehen etc auch* clockwise; **Rech̨ts|hil|fe** F (mutual) assistance in law enforcement; **Rech̨ts|hil|fe|ab|kom|men** NT law enforcement treaty; **Rech̨ts|klar|heit** F clear legal principles *pl*; **~ über etw** *(acc)* **schaffen** to clearly define the legal position with regard to sth; **Rech̨ts|kraft** F, *no pl (von Gesetz, Urteil)* legal force, force of law; *(= Gültigkeit: von Vertrag etc)* legal validity; **~ erlangen** *(Gesetz)* to become law, to come into force; *(Urteil)* to come into force; **rech̨ts|kräf|tig** ADJ having the force of law; *Urteil* final; *Vertrag* legally valid; **~ sein/werden** *(Verordnung)* to have the force of law/to become law; *(Urteil)* to be/become final; *(Gesetz)* to be in/come into force ADV **~ verurteilt sein** to be issued with a final sentence; **rech̨ts|kun|dig** ADJ familiar with *or* versed in the law; **Rech̨ts|kur|ve** F *(von Straße)* right-hand bend; *(von Bahn auch)* right-hand curve; **Rech̨ts|la|ge** F legal position; **rech̨ts|las|tig** [-lastɪç] ADJ listing to the right; *Auto auch* down at the right; *(fig)* leaning to the right; **~ sein** to list to/be down at/lean to the right; **rech̨ts|läu|fig** ADJ *Gewinde* right-handed; *Schrift* left-to-right; **Rech̨ts|leh|re** F jurisprudence; **Rech̨ts|miss|brauch** M abuse of the law; **Rech̨ts|mit|tel** NT means *sing* of legal redress; **~ einlegen** to lodge an appeal; **auf ~ verzichten** to relinquish one's right to appeal; **Rech̨ts|mit|tel|be|leh|rung** F statement of rights of redress *or* appeal; **Rech̨ts|nach|fol|ge** F legal succession; **Rech̨ts|nach|fol|ger(in)** M(F) legal successor; **Rech̨ts|nach|teil** M *(Jur)* legal detriment; **Rech̨ts|norm** F legal norm; **Rech̨ts|ord|nung** F **eine ~** a system of laws; **die ~** the law; **die staatliche ~** state laws *pl*; **Rech̨ts|par|tei** F right-wing party; **Rech̨ts|pfle|ge** F administration of justice; **Rech̨ts|pfle|ger(in)** M(F) *official with certain judicial powers*

rech̨t|sei|tig [-zaitɪç] ADJ = **rechtsseitig**

Rech̨t|ser ['rɛçtsɐ] M **-s, -**, **Rech̨t|se|rin** [-ərɪn] F **-, -nen** *(dial)* = **Rechtshänder**

Rech̨ts-: **Rech̨ts|gang** M, *no pl (Jur)* legal procedure; **im ersten ~** at the first court case; **Rech̨ts|gang** M *pl* **-gänge** *(Tech)* right-handed thread; **rech̨ts|gän|gig** ADJ *(Tech)* right-handed; **Rech̨ts|ge|lehr|sam|keit** F *(old)* jurisprudence; **Rech̨ts|ge|lehr|te(r)** MF *decl as adj* jurist, legal scholar; **Rech̨ts|gut** NT something enjoying legal protection, legally protected right; **Rech̨ts|han|del** M *(liter)* lawsuit; **rech̨ts|hän|gig** [-hɛŋɪç] ADJ *(Jur)* sub judice *pred*; **Rech̨ts|hän|gig|keit** F -, *no pl* state of being sub judice; **rech̨ts|hin** ['rɛçtshɪn] ADV *(old)* (to the) right; **Rech̨ts|leh|rer(in)** M(F) *(form)* professor of jurisprudence *(form)*; **Rech̨ts|phi|lo|so|phie** F philosophy of law

Rech̨t|spre|chung ['rɛçtʃprɛçʊŋ] F **-, -en** **a** *(= Rechtspflege)* administration of justice; *(= Gerichtsbarkeit)* jurisdiction **b** *(= richterliche Tätigkeit)* administering *or* dispensation of justice **c** *(= bisherige Urteile)* precedents *pl*

Rech̨ts-: **rech̨ts|ra|di|kal** ADJ radical right-wing; **die Rechtsradikalen** the right-wing radicals ADV **~ eingestellt sein** to be a right-wing radical; **~ klingen** to sound radically right-wing; **Rech̨ts|ra|di|ka|lis|mus** M right-wing radicalism; **Rech̨ts|re|fe|ren|dar(in)** M(F) articled clerk *(Brit)*, legal intern *(US)*; **~ sein** to be under articles *(Brit)*, to be a legal intern *(US)*; **rech̨ts|rhei|nisch** ADJ to *or* on the right of the Rhine; **Rech̨ts|ruck** M, **Rech̨ts|rutsch** M *(Pol)* swing to the right; **rech̨ts|rum** ['rɛçtsrʊm] ADV *(inf)* = **rechtsherum**; **Rech̨ts|sa|che** F legal matter; *(= Fall)* case; **Rech̨ts|schutz** M legal protection; **Rech̨ts|schutz|ver|si|che|rung** F legal costs insurance; **Rech̨ts|schwenk** M *(Pol)* swing to the right; **rech̨ts|sei|tig** [-zaitɪç] ADJ ADV on the right (-hand) side; **~ gelähmt** paralyzed on the right side; **~ blind** blind in the right eye; **er war ~ amputiert worden** his right arm/leg had been amputated; **Rech̨ts|si|cher|heit** F, *no pl* legal certainty; **~ schaffen** to create legal certainty; **Rech̨ts|spra|che** F legal terminology *or* language; **Rech̨ts|spruch** M verdict; **Rech̨ts|staat** M state under the rule of law; **rech̨ts|staat|lich** ADJ of a state under the rule of law; **~e Ordnung** law and order; **seine ~e Gesinnung** his predisposition for law and order; **Rech̨ts|staat|lich|keit** ['rɛçtsʃtaːtlɪçkait] F -, *no pl* rule of law; *(einer Maßnahme)* legality; **Rech̨ts|sta|tus** M legal status; **rech̨ts|ste|hend** ADJ → **rechts ADV a**; **Rech̨ts|stel|lung** F legal position; **Rech̨ts|steu|e|rung** F right-hand drive; **Rech̨ts|streit** M lawsuit; **Rech̨ts|sys|tem** NT judicial system; **Rech̨ts|ti|tel** M legal title

rech̨t|su|chend ADJ *attr* seeking justice

rechts|um ['rɛçts'lʊm] ADV *(Mil)* to the right; **~ (kehrt)!** right about turn!

Rech̨ts-: **Rech̨ts|un|si|cher|heit** F legal uncertainty; **rech̨ts|ver|bind|lich** ADJ legally binding; *Auskunft* legally valid ADV **~ festgelegt** laid down so as to be legally binding; **Rech̨ts|ver|bind|lich|keit** F *(von Auskunft)* legal validity; **Rech̨ts|ver|dre|her** [-fɛɐdreːɐ] M **-s, -**, **Rech̨ts|ver|dre|he|rin** [-ərɪn] F **-, -nen** *(pej)* shyster *(inf)*, Philadelphia lawyer *(US)*; *(hum inf)* legal eagle *(inf)*; **Rech̨ts|ver|glei|chung** F comparative law; **Rech̨ts|ver|hält|nis** NT facts *pl* of the case; **Rech̨ts|ver|kehr** M driving on the right *no def art*; **in Deutschland ist ~** in Germany they drive on the right; **im ~ muss man ...** when driving on the right one must ...; **Rech̨ts|ver|kehr** M *(Jur)* legal dealings *pl*; **Rech̨ts|ver|let|zung** F infringement *or* breach of the law; **Rech̨ts|ver|ord|nung** F ≈ statutory order; **Rech̨ts|ver|tre|ter(in)** M(F) legal representative; **Rech̨ts|vor|schrift** F ≈ legal provision; **Rech̨ts|weg** M legal action; **den ~ beschreiten** *or* **einschlagen** to have recourse to *or* to take legal action, to go to law; **auf dem ~** by recourse to legal action, by taking legal action; **unter Ausschluss des ~es** without possibility of recourse to legal action; **der ~ ist ausgeschlossen** ≈ the judges' decision is final; **rech̨ts|wid|rig** ADJ illegal ADV illegally; **Rech̨ts|wid|rig|keit** F **a** *no pl* illegality **b** *(Handlung)* illegal act, breach of the law; **Rech̨ts|wis|sen|schaft** F jurisprudence

Rech̨t-: **rech̨t|win|ke|lig**, **rech̨t|wink|lig** ADJ right-angled; **rech̨t|zei|tig** ADJ *(= früh genug)* timely; *(= pünktlich)* punctual; **um ~e Anmeldung wird gebeten** you are requested to apply in good time ADV *(= früh genug)* in (good) time; *(= pünktlich)* on time; **gerade noch ~ ankommen** to arrive *or* be just in time; **Rech̨t|zei|tig|keit** ['rɛçttsaitɪçkait] F -, *no pl* timeliness; *(= Pünktlichkeit)* punctuality

Re|ci|tal [riː'saitl] NT **-s, -s** *(Mus)* recital

Reck [rɛk] NT **-(e)s, -e** *(Sport)* horizontal bar

Rę|cke ['rɛkə] M **-n, -n** *(obs)* warrior

rę|cken ['rɛkn] VT **a** *(= aus-, emporstrecken)* to stretch; **den Kopf** *or* **Hals ~** to crane one's neck; **die Glieder ~** to stretch (oneself), to have a stretch; **die Arme in die Höhe ~** to raise one's arms in the air **b** *(dial: = glatt ziehen)* **etw ~** to pull the creases out of sth VR to stretch (oneself); **sich ~ und strecken** to have a good stretch

Reck-: **Reck|stan|ge** F horizontal bar; **Reck|tur|nen** NT bar exercises *pl*

Re|cor|der [re'kɔrdɐ] M **-s, -** → **Rekorder**

re|cy|cel|bar [riː'saikəlbaːɐ] ADJ recyclable

re|cy|celn [riː'saikln] *ptp* **recycelt** [riː'saiklt] VT to recycle

Re|cyc|ling [riː'saiklɪŋ] NT **-s**, *no pl* recycling

Re|cyc|ling-: **Re|cyc|ling|hof** M recycling site; **Re|cyc|ling|pa|pier** NT recycled paper; **Re|cyc|ling|werk** NT recycling plant

Red. **a** *abbr von* **Redakteur** ed **b** *abbr von* **Redaktion**

Re|dak|teur [redak'tøːɐ] M **-s, -e**, **Re|dak|teu|rin** [-'tøːrɪn] F **-, -nen** editor

Re|dak|ti|on [redak'tsioːn] F **-, -en** **a** *(= das Redigieren)* editing; **die ~ dieses Buches hatte ...** this book was edited by ...; **~: XY** editor: XY **b** *(= Personal)* editorial staff **c** *(= Büro)* editorial office(s); **der Reporter rief seine ~ an** the reporter phoned his office *or* paper

re|dak|ti|o|nell [redaktsio'nɛl] ADJ editorial; **die ~e Leitung im Ressort Wirtschaft hat Herr Müller** Mr Müller is the editor responsible for business and finance; **Leserbriefe stellen keine ~en Meinungsäußerungen dar** readers' letters do not necessarily reflect the views of the editor ADV *überarbeiten* editorially; **ein Projekt ~ betreuen** to be the editor of a project; **etw ~ bearbeiten** to edit sth

Re|dak|ti|ons-: **Re|dak|ti|ons|ge|heim|nis** NT press secret; **Re|dak|ti|ons|kon|fe|renz** F editorial conference; **Re|dak|ti|ons|schluss** M time of going to press; *(= Einsendeschluss)* copy deadline; **bei ~** at the time of going to press; **diese Nachricht ist vor/nach ~ eingegangen** this news item arrived before/after the paper went to press *or* bed *(inf)*

Re|dak|tor [re'daktoːɐ] M **-s, Redaktoren** [-'toːrən], **Re|dak|to|rin** [-'toːrɪn] F **-, -nen** *(Sw)* editor

Re|dakt|ri|ce [redak'triːsə] F **-, -n** *(Aus)* editor

Re|de ['reːdə] F **-, -n** **a** speech; *(= Ansprache)* address; **die Kunst der ~** *(form)* the art of rhetoric; **eine ~ halten** *or* **schwingen** *(inf)* to make *or* give a speech; **die ~ des Bundeskanzlers** the Chancellor's speech, the speech given by the Chancellor; **in freier ~** without (consulting) notes; **der langen ~ kurzer Sinn** *(prov)* the long and the short of it **b** *(= Äußerungen, Worte)* words *pl*, language *no pl*; **seine frechen ~n** his cheek *(Brit)* *or* impudence; **große ~n führen** *or* **schwingen** *(inf)* to talk big *(inf)*; **das ist meine ~!** that's what I've always said; **jds stehende ~ sein** to be sb's stock saying; **das ist nicht der ~ wert** it's not worth mentioning; **(es ist) nicht der ~ wert!** don't mention it, it was nothing **c** *(= das Reden, Gespräch)* conversation, talk; **jdm in die ~ fallen** to interrupt sb; **die ~ fiel** *or* **kam auf** *(+acc)* the conversation *or* talk turned to; **die in ~ stehende Person** *(form)* the person in question *or* under discussion; **es war von einer Gehaltserhöhung die ~** there was talk *or* mention of a salary increase; **von Ihnen war eben die ~** we were just talking about you; **aber davon war doch nie die ~** but no-one was ever talking about that; **wovon ist die ~?** what are you/we *etc* talking about?; **von einer Gehaltserhöhung kann keine** *or* **kann nicht die ~ sein** there can be no question of a salary increase; **von Großzügigkeit kann keine** *or* **kann nicht die ~ sein, das war nur ...** there's no question of it being generosity, it was just ...; **davon kann keine** *or* **kann nicht die ~ sein** it's out of the question **d** *(Ling, Liter)* speech; **direkte** *or* **wörtliche/indirekte ~** direct/indirect speech *or* discourse *(US)*; **gebundene ~** verse; **ungebundene ~** prose **e** *(= Gerücht, Nachrede)* rumour *(Brit)*, rumor *(US)*; **kümmere dich doch nicht um die ~n der Leute!** don't worry (about) what people say; **es geht die ~, dass** there's a rumo(u)r that, rumo(u)r has it that; **von ihr geht die ~, dass sie ...** people say *or* it is said (about her) that she ... **f** *(= Rechenschaft)* **(jdm) ~ (und Antwort) stehen** to justify oneself (to sb); **(jdm) für etw ~ und Antwort stehen** to account (to sb) for sth; **jdn zur ~ stellen** to take sb to task

Re|de-: **Re|de|du|ell** NT verbal exchange *or* duel; **Re|de|fi|gur** F *(Liter)* figure of speech; **Re|de|fluss** M flow of words; **er stockte plötzlich in seinem ~** he suddenly stopped in mid-flow; **ich will Ihren ~ nicht unterbrechen, aber …** I don't wish to interrupt your flow but …; **Re|de|frei|heit** F freedom of speech; **Re|de|ga|be** F eloquence; **re|de|ge|wandt** ADJ eloquent; **Re|de|kunst** F **die ~** rhetoric

re|den ['re:dn] VI **a** *(= sprechen)* to talk, to speak; **Reden während des Unterrichts** talking in class; **mit sich selbst/jdm ~** to talk *or* speak to oneself/sb; **wie red(e)st du denn mit deiner Mutter!** that's no way to talk *or* speak to your mother; **so lasse ich nicht mit mir ~!** I won't be spoken to like that!; **sie hat geredet und geredet** she talked and talked; **mit jdm über jdn/etw ~** to talk *or* speak to *or* with sb about sb/sth; **~ wir nicht mehr davon** *or* **darüber** let's not talk *or* speak about it any more, let's drop it *(inf)*; **~ Sie doch nicht!** *(inf)* come off it! *(inf)*; **(viel) von sich ~ machen** to become (very much) a talking point; **das Buch/er macht viel von sich ~** everyone is talking about the book/him; **viel Redens von einer Sache machen** to make a great to-do about sth *(inf)*; **du hast gut** *or* **leicht ~!** it's all very well for you (to talk); **ich habe mit Ihnen zu ~!** I would like to speak *or* talk to you, I would like a word with you; **ich rede gegen eine Wand** *or* **Mauer** it's like talking to a brick wall *(inf)*; **darüber lässt** *or* **ließe sich ~** that's a possibility; *(über Preis, Bedingungen)* I think we could discuss that; **darüber lässt** *or* **ließe sich eher ~** that's more like it, now you're talking; **er lässt mit sich ~** he could be persuaded; *(in Bezug auf Preis)* he's open to offers; *(= gesprächsbereit)* he's open to discussion; **sie lässt nicht mit sich ~** she is adamant; *(bei eigenen Forderungen auch)* she won't take no for an answer; **Reden ist Silber, Schweigen ist Gold** *(Prov)* (speech is silver but) silence is golden *(Prov)*; **das ist ja mein Reden (seit 33)** *(inf)* I've been saying that for (donkey's *(Brit inf)*) years → **Wasserfall**
b *(= klatschen)* to talk *(über +acc* about); **schlecht von jdm ~** to talk *or* speak ill of sb; **in so einem Dorf wird natürlich viel geredet** in a village like that naturally people talk a lot
c *(= eine Rede halten)* to speak; **er redet nicht gerne öffentlich** he doesn't like public speaking; **er kann gut ~** he is a good speaker; **frei ~** to speak extempore, to speak without notes
d *(euph: = gestehen, aussagen)* to talk; **jdn zum Reden bringen** to get sb to talk, to make sb talk; **er will nicht ~** he won't talk
VT **a** *(= sagen)* to talk; *Worte* to say; **einige Worte ~** to say a few words; **kein Wort ~** not to say *or* speak a word; **sich** *(dat)* **etw von der Seele** *or* **vom Herzen ~** to get sth off one's chest
b *(= klatschen)* to say; **es kann dir doch nicht egal sein, was über dich geredet wird** it must matter to you what people say about you; **Schlechtes von jdm** *or* **über jdn ~** to say bad things about sb; **damit die Leute wieder was zu ~ haben** so that people have something to talk about again
VR **sich heiser ~** to talk oneself hoarse; **sich in Zorn** *or* **Wut ~** to talk oneself into a fury

Re|dens|art F *(= Phrase)* hackneyed expression *(Brit)*, cliché; *(= Redewendung)* expression, idiom; *(= Sprichwort)* saying; *(= leere Versprechung)* empty promise; **das ist nur so eine ~** it's just a way of speaking; **bloße ~en** empty talk

Re|den|schrei|ber(in) M(F), **Re|den|ver|fas|ser(in)** M(F) speechwriter

Re|de|rei [re:də'rai] F **-, -en a** *(= Geschwätz)* chattering *no pl*, talking *no pl*; **du mit deiner ~, du bist doch zu feige dazu** you're all talk, you're too scared to do it **b** *(= Klatsch)* gossip *no pl*, talk *no pl*; **zu ~en Anlass geben** to make people talk, to give rise to gossip

Re|de-: **Re|de|schwall** M torrent *or* flood of words; **Re|de|strom** M flow of words; **Re|de|ver|bot** NT ban on speaking; **jdm ~ erteilen** to ban sb from speaking; **(allgemeines) ~!** *(= keine Gespräche erlaubt)* no talking!; **Re|de|wei|se** F style *or* manner (of speaking); **Re|de|wen|dung** F idiom, idiomatic expression

re|di|gie|ren [redi'gi:rən] *ptp* **redigiert** VT to edit

Re|dis|kont|ge|schäft [redɪs'kɔnt-] NT rediscount

Re|dis|kon|tie|rung [redɪskɔn'ti:rʊŋ] F **-, -en** rediscounting

red|lich ['re:tlɪç] ADJ honest ADV **a** *(= ehrlich)* honestly; **~ denken** to be honest; **~ handeln** to be honest, to act honestly; **er meint es ~** he is being honest; **sich** *(dat)* **etw ~ verdient haben** to have really *or* genuinely earned sth; *Geld, Gut* to have acquired sth by honest means; **~ (mit jdm) teilen** to share (things) equally (with sb); **sich ~ durchs Leben schlagen** to make an honest living **b** *(= ziemlich) sich bemühen, sich anstrengen, sich einsetzen* really

Red|lich|keit F **-**, *no pl* honesty

Red|ner ['re:dnɐ] M **-s, -**, **Red|ne|rin** [-ərɪn] F **-, -nen** speaker; *(= Rhetoriker)* orator; **ich bin kein (großer) ~** I'm not much of a speaker

Red|ner-: **Red|ner|büh|ne** F platform, rostrum; **Red|ner|ga|be** F gift of oratory

red|ne|risch ['re:dnərɪʃ] ADJ rhetorical, oratorical; **~e Begabung** talent for public speaking ADV rhetorically; **~ begabt sein** to be a gifted speaker

Red|ner|pult NT lectern

red|se|lig ['re:tze:lɪç] ADJ talkative

Red|se|lig|keit F **-**, *no pl* talkativeness

Re|duk|ti|on [reduk'tsio:n] F **-, -en a** *(= Einschränkung)* reduction (+*gen* in) **b** *(= Zurückführung)* reduction (*auf +acc* to) **c** *(Chem)* reduction

Re|duk|ti|ons-: **Re|duk|ti|ons|mit|tel** NT *(Chem)* reducing agent; **Re|duk|ti|ons|ofen** M *(Metal)* reducing furnace

re|dun|dant [redʊn'dant] ADJ redundant *(auch Comput)* ADV *schreiben* redundantly; **er drückt sich ~ aus** a lot of what he says is redundant; **das ist ~ formuliert** it's redundant

Re|dun|danz [redʊn'dants] F **-, -en** redundancy, redundance *no pl*

Re|dup|li|ka|ti|on [reduplika'tsio:n] F reduplication

re|dup|li|zie|ren [redupli'tsi:rən] *ptp* **redupliziert** VT to reduplicate

re|du|zier|bar, **re|du|zi|bel** [redu'tsi:bl] ADJ reducible (*auf +acc* to)

re|du|zie|ren [redu'tsi:rən] *ptp* **reduziert** VT **a** *(= einschränken)* to reduce **b** *(= zurückführen)* to reduce (*auf +acc* to) **c** *(Chem, Comput)* to reduce VR to decrease, to diminish

Re|du|zie|rung F **-, -en** = **Reduktion**

Ree|de ['re:də] F **-, -n** *(Naut)* roads *pl*, roadstead; **auf der ~ liegen** to be (lying) in the roads

Ree|der ['re:dɐ] M **-s, -**, **Ree|de|rin** [-ərɪn] F **-, -en** shipowner

Ree|de|rei [re:də'rai] F **-, -en** shipping company

Ree|de|rei|flag|ge F house flag

re|ell [re'ɛl] ADJ **a** *(= ehrlich)* honest, straight, on the level *(inf)*; *(Comm) Geschäft, Firma* solid, sound; *Preis* realistic, fair; *Bedienung* good; **das ist etwas Reelles!** it's pretty much on the level! *(inf)* **b** *(= wirklich, echt) Chance* real **c** *(Math) Zahlen* real ADV *(= tatsächlich)* when it comes down to it; *(= nicht betrügerisch)* on the level *(inf)*

Reep [re:p] NT **-(e)s, -e** *(N Ger)* rope

Reet [re:t] NT **-s**, *no pl (N Ger)* reed

Reet-: **Reet|dach** NT thatched roof; **reet|ge|deckt** ADJ thatched

REFA-Fach|frau F, **REFA-Frau** ['re:fa-] F *(inf)* time and motion expert *or* woman

REFA-Fach|mann M, **REFA-Mann** ['re:fa-] M *(inf)* time and motion expert *or* man

Re|fek|to|ri|um [refɛk'to:riʊm] **-s, Refektorien** [-riən] NT *(Eccl)* refectory

Re|fe|rat [refe'ra:t] NT **-(e)s, -e a** *(Univ)* seminar paper; *(Sch)* project; *(= Vortrag)* paper; **ein ~ vortragen** *or* **halten** to give *or* read *or* present a seminar paper/to present a project/to give *or* read *or* present a paper **b** *(Admin: = Ressort)* department

Re|fe|ren|dar [referɛn'da:ɐ] M **-s, -e** trainee (in civil service); *(= Studienreferendar)* student teacher; *(= Gerichtsreferendar)* articled clerk *(Brit)*, legal intern *(US)*

> **REFERENDAR**
>
> **Referendare** are candidates for a higher civil-service post who are doing practical training. They might, for example, be prospective **Gymnasium** teachers who have already taken the first **Staatsexamen** and are now doing two years of teaching practice. At the end of the **Referendar** period they take the second **Staatsexamen**, and only then is their teacher training complete. → GYMNASIUM, STAATSEXAMEN

Re|fe|ren|da|ri|at [referɛnda'ria:t] NT **-(e)s, -e** *probationary training period*

Re|fe|ren|da|rin [-'da:rɪn] F **-, -nen** → **Referendar**

Re|fe|ren|dar|zeit F traineeship; *(= Studienreferendarzeit)* teacher training; *(= Gerichtsreferendarzeit)* time under articles *(Brit)*, legal internship *(US)*

Re|fe|ren|dum [refe'rɛndʊm] NT **-s, Referenden** *or* **Referenda** [-dn, -da] referendum

Re|fe|rent [refe'rɛnt] M **-en, -en**, **Re|fe|ren|tin** [-'rɛntɪn] F **-, -nen** *(= Sachbearbeiter)* consultant, expert; *(= Redner, Berichterstatter)* speaker; *(Univ: = Gutachter)* examiner

Re|fe|renz [refe'rɛnts] F **-, -en** reference *(auch Comput)*; **jdn als ~ angeben** to give sb as a referee

Re|fe|renz|kurs *(Fin)* reference (exchange) rate

re|fe|rie|ren [refe'ri:rən] *ptp* **referiert** VI to (give a) report, to give a review (*über +acc* on)

Reff [rɛf] NT **-(e)s, -e** *(Naut)* reef

ref|fen ['rɛfn] VT *(Naut)* to reef

Re|fi|nan|zie|rung [refinan'tsi:rʊŋ] F financing of financing, rediscounting

Re|flek|tant [reflɛk'tant] M **-en, -en**, **Re|flek|tan|tin** [-'tantɪn] F **-, -nen** *(old)* *(= Kauflustiger)* prospective purchaser; *(= Stellungsbewerber)* applicant

re|flek|tie|ren [reflɛk'ti:rən] *ptp* **reflektiert** VT **a** *(lit, fig: widerspiegeln)* to reflect **b** *(überdenken)* to reflect on, to ponder (on) VI **a** *(Phys)* to reflect **b** *(= nachdenken)* to reflect, to ponder *(über +acc* (up)on) **c** *(= streben nach)* **auf etw** *(acc)* **~** to be interested in sth

Re|flek|tor [re'flɛkto:ɐ] M **-s, Reflektoren** [-'to:rən] reflector

re|flek|to|risch [reflɛk'to:rɪʃ] ADJ **a** *(motorisch)* reflex **b** *(geistig)* reflective ADV by reflex action

Re|flex [re'flɛks] M **-es, -e a** *(Phys)* reflection **b** *(Physiol)* reflex **c** *(Sociol)* reflection

Re|flex|be|we|gung F reflex action

Re|fle|xi|on [reflɛ'ksio:n] F **-, -en a** *(lit, Phys)* reflection **b** *(= Überlegung)* reflection *(über* on); **über etw** *(acc)* **~en anstellen** to reflect on sth

Re|fle|xi|ons|win|kel M *(Phys)* angle of reflection

re|fle|xiv [reflɛ'ksi:f] *(Gram)* ADJ reflexive ADV reflexively

Re|fle|xiv [reflɛ'ksi:f] NT **-s, -e** [-və] reflexive (pronoun/verb)

Re|fle|xiv|pro|no|men NT reflexive pronoun

Re|fle|xi|vum [reflɛ'ksi:vʊm] **-s, Reflexiva** [-va] NT = **Reflexiv**

Re|flex|zo|nen|mas|sa|ge F reflexology

Re|form [re'fɔrm] F **-, -en** reform

Re|for|ma|ti|on [refɔrma'tsio:n] F **-, -en** Reformation

Re|for|ma|ti|ons|tag M Reformation Day

REFORMATIONSTAG

Reformationstag, celebrated on October 31st, is a public holiday in some (predominantly Protestant) regions of Germany. It commemorates Martin Luther's nailing of his 95 theses to the church door at Wittenberg in 1517, an action which marked the beginning of the Reformation.

Re|for|ma|tor [refɔr'ma:toːɐ] M **-s, Reformato|ren** [-'to:rən], **Re|for|ma|to|rin** [-'to:rɪn] F **-, -nen** Reformer

re|for|ma|to|risch [refɔrma'to:rɪʃ] ADJ *(= reformierend)* reforming; *(= aus der Zeit der Reformation)* Reformation *attr*

Re|form-: Re|form|be|darf M need for reform; **re|form|be|dürf|tig** ADJ in need of reform; **Re|form|be|stre|bun|gen** PL striving for *or* after reform; **Re|form|be|we|gung** F reform movement; **Re|form|ei|fer** M reforming zeal

Re|for|mer [re'fɔrmɐ] M **-s, -, Re|for|me|rin** [-ərɪn] F **-, -nen** reformer

re|for|me|risch [re'fɔrmərɪʃ] ADJ reforming

Re|form-: re|form|freu|dig ADJ eager for reform; **Re|form|ge|setz** NT reform bill *or* law; **Re|form|haus** NT health-food shop

REFORMHAUS

Reformhaus sells everything for a healthy diet and lifestyle, including **Reformkost** (natural foodstuffs without chemical additives), health products such as essential oils and natural bath salts, and medicinal herbs. The first **Reformhäuser** were established as early as 1890 with a view to encouraging healthy living. They now compete with **Bioläden.** → BIOLADEN

re|for|mie|ren [refɔr'mi:rən] *ptp* **reformiert** VT to reform

re|for|miert [refɔr'mi:ɐt] ADJ *(Eccl)* Reformed

Re|for|mier|te(r) [refɔr'mi:ɐtə] MF *decl as adj* member of the Reformed Church

Re|for|mis|mus [refɔr'mɪsmʊs] M **-,** *no pl (Pol)* reformism

Re|for|mist [refɔr'mɪst] M **-en, -en, Re|for|mis|tin** [-'mɪstɪn] F **-, -nen** *(Pol)* reformist

re|for|mis|tisch [refɔr'mɪstɪʃ] ADJ *(Pol)* reformist

Re|form-: Re|form|kurs M policy of reform; **einen ~ steuern** to follow a policy of reform; **auf ~ gehen** to embark on a policy of reform; **Re|form|plan** M plan for reform; **Re|form|stau** M *(Pol)* reform bottleneck *or* jam

Ref|rain [rə'frɛ̃:, re-] M **-s, -s** *(Mus)* chorus, refrain

re|frak|tär [refrak'tɛːɐ] ADJ *(Med, liter)* refractory

Re|frak|ti|on [refrak'tsio:n] F **-, -en** *(Phys)* refraction

Re|frak|tor [re'frakto:ɐ] M **-s, Refraktoren** [-'to:rən] *(Phys, Opt)* refractor

Re|fu|gi|um [re'fu:giʊm] NT **-s, Refugien** [-giən] *(geh)* refuge

Re|gal [re'ga:l] NT **-s, -e** **a** *(= Bord)* shelves *pl*; *(Typ)* stand **b** *(Mus) (= tragbare Orgel)* regal; *(Orgelteil)* vox humana

Re|gal NT **-s, -ien** [-liən] *(Jur)* regale *(spec)*

Re|gal-: Re|gal|sys|tem NT shelving system; **Re|gal|wand** F wall unit; *(nur Regale)* wall-to-wall shelving

Re|gat|ta [re'gata] F **-, Regatten** [-tn] regatta

Re|gat|ta|stre|cke F regatta course

Reg. Bez. *abbr von* **Regierungsbezirk**

re|ge ['re:gə] ADJ **a** *(= betriebsam)* active, busy; *Verkehr* busy; *Handel* flourishing; *Briefwechsel* lively; **ein ~s Treiben** a busy to-and-fro, a hustle and bustle; **auf dem Marktplatz herrschte ein ~s Treiben** the market place was bustling with activity *or* life; **Tendenz ~** *(St Ex)* brisk activity; **~ werden** to become active **b** *(= lebhaft)* lively; *Unterhaltung* animated, lively; *Fantasie* vivid; *Interesse auch* avid; **ein ~r Geist** a lively soul; *(= Verstand)* an active mind; **körperlich und geistig ~ sein** to be mentally and physically active, to be active in mind and body; **noch sehr ~ sein** to be very active still; **in ihm wurde der Gedanke ~** *(liter)* the thought stirred within him; **~ Beteiligung** lively participation; *(zahlreich)* good attendance *or* turnout **c** *(= zahlreich)* numerous; *(= häufig)* frequent; **~r Besuch** high attendance ADV *(= lebhaft)* **das Museum wurde nach der Eröffnung ~ besucht** when it opened the museum was very well visited; **sich ~ an etw** *(dat)* **beteiligen** to actively take part in sth; **an etw** *(dat)* **~ Anteil nehmen** to take an active interest in sth

Re|gel ['re:gl] F **-, -n** **a** *(= Vorschrift, Norm)* rule; *(= Verordnung)* regulation; **die ~n der ärztlichen Kunst** the rules of the medical profession; **nach allen ~n der Kunst** *(fig)* thoroughly; **sie überredete ihn nach allen ~n der Kunst, …** she used every trick in the book to persuade him … **b** *(= Gewohnheit)* habit, rule; **sich** *(dat)* **etw zur ~ machen** to make a habit *or* rule of sth; **in der** *or* **aller ~** as a rule; **zur ~ werden** to become a habit **c** *(= Monatsblutung)* period; **die ~ haben/bekommen** to have/get one's period, to menstruate; **sie hat mit zehn ihre ~ bekommen** her periods started when she was ten

Re|gel-: Re|gel|ar|beits|zeit F core working hours *pl*; **re|gel|bar** ADJ *(= steuerbar)* adjustable; *(= klärbar)* easily arranged; **Re|gel|blu|tung** F (monthly) period, monthly cycle; **Re|gel|de|tri** [re:glde'tri:] F **-,** *no pl (Math)* rule of three; **Re|gel|fall** M rule; **im ~** as a rule; **re|gel|mä|ßig** ADJ regular; *Lebensweise auch* well-ordered, orderly ADV **a** *(in gleichmäßiger Folge)* regularly; **das Herz schlägt ~** the heartbeat is normal; **sein Herz schlägt wieder ~er** his heartbeat is more regular now; **etw ~ jeden Tag tun** to do sth every day; **~ spazieren gehen** to take regular walks **b** *(= andauernd)* always; **er kommt ~ zu spät** he's always late; **Re|gel|mä|ßig|keit** ['re:glmɛːsɪçkait] F **-,** *no pl* regularity; **er kommt mit sturer ~ zu spät** he is persistently late; **in** *or* **mit schöner ~** with clockwork regularity, as regular as clockwork

re|geln ['re:gln] VT **a** *(= regulieren) Prozess, Vorgang, Temperatur* to regulate, to control; *Verkehr* to control → *auch* **geregelt** **b** *(= erledigen)* to see to; *(endgültig)* to settle; *Problem etc* to sort out; *(= in Ordnung bringen) Unstimmigkeiten* to settle, to resolve; *Finanzen* to put in order; *Nachlass* to settle; *Finanzierung* to deal with; **das lässt sich ~** that can be arranged; **das werde ich schon ~** I'll see to it **c** *(= festsetzen, einrichten)* to settle; **wir haben die Sache so geregelt …** we have arranged things like this …; **dieses Gesetz regelt …** this law deals with …; **gesetzlich geregelt sein** to be laid down by law VR to sort itself out, to resolve itself

Re|gel-: re|gel|recht ADJ real, proper; *Betrug, Erpressung, Beleidigung etc* downright; **er wollte einen ~en Prozess** he wanted a full-blown trial; **das Spiel artete in eine ~e Schlägerei aus** the match degenerated into a regular brawl ADV really; *unverschämt, beleidigend* downright; *(= buchstäblich)* literally; **Re|gel|schu|le** F ordinary school; **Re|gel|stu|di|en|zeit** F *period of time within which a student should complete his studies*; **Re|gel|tech|nik** F control engineering; **Re|gel|tech|ni|ker(in)** M(F) control engineer

Re|ge|lung ['re:gəlʊŋ] F **-, -en** **a** *(= Regulierung)* regulation, control(ling) **b** *(= Erledigung)* settling, settlement; *(von Unstimmigkeiten)* resolution; *(von Nachlass)* settling, settlement; **ich habe die ~ meiner finanziellen Angelegenheiten meinem Bruder übertragen** I have entrusted my brother with the management of my financial affairs; **ich werde für die ~ dieser Angelegenheit sorgen** I shall see to this matter **c** *(= Abmachung)* arrangement; *(= Bestimmung)* ruling; **gesetzliche ~en** legal *or* statutory regulations; **wir haben eine ~ gefunden** we have come to an arrangement

Re|ge|lungs|tech|nik F control engineering

Re|gel-: Re|gel|ur|laub M ordinary leave; **Re|gel|werk** NT rules *pl* (and regulations *pl*), set of rules; **re|gel|wid|rig** ADJ against the rules; *(= gegen Verordnungen verstoßend)* against the regulations; **~es Verhalten im Verkehr** breaking the traffic regulations; **~e Transaktion** irregular transaction; **ein ~er Einwurf** a foul throw-in; **ein ~er Elfmeter** an improperly taken penalty ADV **~ spielen** to infringe the rules; *(= foulen)* to commit a foul; **Re|gel|wid|rig|keit** F irregularity; *(= Regelverstoß auch)* breach of the rules; *(= Verstoß gegen Verordnungen auch)* breach of regulations

re|gen ['re:gn] VT *(= bewegen)* to move; **keinen Finger (mehr) ~** *(fig)* not to lift a finger (any more) VR *(Mensch, Glied, Baum etc)* to move, to stir; *(Gefühl, Gewissen, Zweifel, Widerstand, Wind etc)* to stir; **unter den Zuhörern regte sich Widerspruch** there were mutterings of disapproval from the audience; **im Bundestag regt sich Widerstand gegen das Gesetz** opposition to the bill is beginning to make itself felt in the Bundestag; **kein Lüftchen regt sich** *(poet)* not a breeze stirs the air; **reg dich!** look lively!; **er kann sich nicht/kaum ~** he is not/hardly able to move; **sich ~ bringt Segen** *(Prov)* hard work brings its own reward

Re|gen ['re:gn] M **-s, -** rain; *(fig: von Schimpfwörtern, Blumen etc)* shower; **in den ~ kommen** to be caught in the rain; **es gibt bald ~** it's going to rain soon; **so ein ~!** what *or* some rain!; **in** *or* **bei strömendem ~** in the pouring rain; **bei ~ entfällt das Konzert** if it rains the concert will be cancelled *(esp Brit) or* canceled *(US)*; **ein warmer ~** *(fig)* a windfall; **jdn im ~ stehen lassen** *(fig)* to leave sb out in the cold; **vom ~ in die Traufe kommen** *(prov)* to jump out of the frying pan into the fire *(prov)*

Re|gen-: re|gen|arm ADJ *Jahreszeit, Gegend* dry; **Re|gen|bö** F rainy squall

Re|gen|bo|gen M rainbow

Re|gen|bo|gen-: Re|gen|bo|gen|fa|mi|lie F *same-sex couple with child or children,* rainbow family; **Re|gen|bo|gen|far|ben** PL colours *pl (Brit) or* colors *pl (US)* of the rainbow; **in allen ~ schillern** to shine like shot silk, to iridesce *(liter)*; **re|gen|bo|gen|far|ben** [-farbn], **re|gen|bo|gen|far|big** ADJ rainbow-coloured *(Brit)*, rainbow-colored *(US)*; **Re|gen|bo|gen|fo|rel|le** F rainbow trout; **Re|gen|bo|gen|haut** F *(Anat)* iris; **Re|gen|bo|gen|haut|ent|zün|dung** F iritis *(spec)*, inflammation of the iris; **Re|gen|bo|gen|pres|se** F trashy *(inf) or* pulp magazines *pl*; **Re|gen|bo|gen|tri|kot** NT *(Sport)* rainbow jersey

Re|gen-: Re|gen|dach NT canopy; *(hum: = Regenschirm)* brolly *(Brit inf)*, bumbershoot *(US inf)*; **re|gen|dicht** ADJ rainproof

Re|ge|ne|ra|ti|on [regenera'tsio:n] F regeneration; *(fig auch)* revitalization

re|ge|ne|ra|ti|ons|fä|hig ADJ capable of regeneration; *(fig auch)* capable of regenerating itself *or* of revitalization

re|ge|ne|ra|tiv [regenera'ti:f] ADJ regenerative

Re|ge|ne|ra|tor [regene'ra:to:ɐ] M *(Tech)* regenerator

re|ge|ne|rie|ren [regene'ri:rən] *ptp* **regeneriert** VR *(Biol)* to regenerate; *(fig)* to revitalize *or* regenerate oneself/itself; *(nach Anstrengung, Schock etc)* to recover VT *(Biol)* to regenerate; *(fig auch)* to revitalize

Re|ge|ne|rie|rung F **-, -en** regeneration; *(fig auch)* revitalization

Re|gen-: Re|gen|fall M *usu pl* (fall of) rain; **ein ~** rain, a shower; **tropische Regenfälle** tropical rains; **heftige Regenfälle** heavy rain; **Re|gen|fass** NT water butt, rain barrel; **Re|gen|flut** F *usu pl* torrential rain *usu sing*, torrent of rain;

re|gen|frei ADJ *Tag* without rain; **Re|gen|guss** M downpour; **Re|gen|haut®** F plastic mac *(Brit inf)* or raincoat; **Re|gen|hut** M waterproof hat, rain hat; **Re|gen|klei|dung** F rainwear; **Re|gen|man|tel** M raincoat, mackintosh *(esp Brit)*, mac *(Brit inf)*; **Re|gen|pfei|fer** M plover; **re|gen|reich** ADJ *Jahreszeit, Region* rainy, wet; **Re|gen|rin|ne** F gutter; **Re|gen|schat|ten** M *(Geog)* rain shadow; **Re|gen|schau|er** M shower (of rain); **Re|gen|schirm** M umbrella → **gespannt**; **re|gen|schwer** ADJ **~e Wolken** black or rain clouds, clouds heavy with rain

Re|gent [re'gɛnt] M **-en, -en**, **Re|gen|tin** [-'gɛntɪn] F **-, -nen** sovereign, reigning monarch; *(= Stellvertreter)* regent

Re|gen-: **Re|gen|tag** M rainy day; **Re|gen|ton|ne** F water butt, rain barrel; **Re|gen|trop|fen** M raindrop

Re|gent|schaft [re'gɛntʃaft] F **-, -en** reign; *(= Stellvertretung)* regency; **die ~ antreten** to ascend the throne; *(als Stellvertreter)* to become regent; **die ~ übernehmen** to take over as regent

Re|gen-: **Re|gen|wahr|schein|lich|keit** F **die ~ liegt bei 80%** there is an 80% chance of rain; **Re|gen|wald** M *(Geog)* rain forest; **Re|gen|was|ser** NT, *no pl* rainwater; **Re|gen|wet|ter** NT rainy weather, rain; **er macht ein Gesicht wie drei** or **sieben Tage ~** *(inf)* he's got a face as long as a month of Sundays *(inf)*; **Re|gen|wol|ke** F rain cloud; **Re|gen|wurm** M earthworm; **Re|gen|zeit** F rainy season, rains *pl*

Reg|gae ['rɛge:] M **-(s)**, *no pl* reggae

Re|gie [re'ʒi:] F **-**, *no pl* **a** *(= künstlerische Leitung)* direction; *(Theat, Rad, TV)* direction, production; **die ~ bei etw haben** or **führen** to direct/produce sth; *(fig)* to be in charge of sth; **die ~ bei diesem Film/dieser Sendung führte** or **hatte Heinz Krüger** this film was directed/this programme *(Brit)* or program *(US)* was produced by Heinz Krüger; **unter der ~ von** directed/produced by; **„Regie: A.G. Meier"** "Director/Producer A.G. Meier"
b *(= Leitung, Verwaltung)* management; **unter jds ~** under sb's control; **etw in eigener ~ führen** to control sth directly or personally; **etw in eigene ~ nehmen** to take or assume direct or personal control of sth; **etw in eigener ~ tun** to do sth oneself

Re|gie-: **Re|gie|an|wei|sung** F (stage) direction; **Re|gie|as|sis|tent(in)** M(F) assistant director; *(Theat, Rad, TV auch)* assistant producer; **Re|gie|be|trieb** M *(Admin)* state-owned factory; **Re|gie|feh|ler** M *(fig)* slip-up; **Re|gie|film** M **sein erster ~** the first film he directed; **Re|gie|pult** NT *(Rad)* control desk *(Brit)* or console

re|gie|ren [re'gi:rən] *ptp* **regiert** VI *(= herrschen)* to rule; *(Monarch auch, fig)* to reign; **der Regierende Bürgermeister von Berlin** the Mayor of Berlin VT *(= beherrschen, lenken) Staat* to rule (over), to govern; *(Monarch auch)* to reign over; *Markt* to control; *(Gram)* to govern; **SPD-regierte Länder** states governed by the SPD → **Geld**

Re|gie|rung [re'gi:rʊŋ] F **-, -en** **a** *(= Kabinett)* government; **die ~ Blair** the Blair government **b** *(= Herrschaft)* government; *(= Zeitabschnitt)* period of government; *(nicht demokratisch)* rule; *(von Monarch)* reign; *(= Führung)* leadership; **an die ~ kommen** to come to power; *(durch Wahl auch)* to come into or take office; **jdn an die ~ bringen** to put sb into power; *(durch Wahl auch)* to put sb into office; **die ~ antreten** to take power; *(nach Wahl auch)* to take office; **die ~ ausüben** to exercise power

Re|gie|rungs-: **Re|gie|rungs|ab|kom|men** NT agreement between governments, international agreement; **re|gie|rungs|amt|lich** ADJ governmental; **Re|gie|rungs|an|hän|ger(in)** M(F) government supporter; **Re|gie|rungs|an|tritt** M coming to power; *(nach Wahl auch)* taking of office; **bei ~** when the government took power/office; **Re|gie|rungs|aus|schuss** M government committee; **Re|gie|rungs|bank** F *pl* **-bänke** government bench; **Re|gie|rungs|be|am|te(r)** M *decl as adj*, **Re|gie|rungs|be|am|tin** F government official; **Re|gie|rungs|be|tei|li|gung** F **a** *(von Partei)* participation in government **b** *(von Regierung an Projekt etc)* government involvement; **Re|gie|rungs|be|zirk** M *primary administrative division of a Land*, ≈ region *(Brit)*, ≈ county *(US)*; **Re|gie|rungs|bil|dung** F formation of a government; **Re|gie|rungs|chef(in)** M(F) head of a/the government; **der belgische ~** the head of the Belgian government; **Re|gie|rungs|di|rek|tor(in)** M(F) senior government official; **Re|gie|rungs|er|klä|rung** F inaugural speech; *(in GB)* King's/Queen's Speech; **re|gie|rungs|fä|hig** ADJ *Partei* able to govern; *Mehrheit* workable; **Re|gie|rungs|fä|hig|keit** F ability to govern; **re|gie|rungs|feind|lich** ADJ anti-government *no adv* ADV **sich ~ verhalten/äußern** to act/speak against the government; **Re|gie|rungs|form** F form or type of government; **re|gie|rungs|freund|lich** ADJ pro-government *no adv* ADV **sich ~ verhalten/äußern** to act/speak in support of the government; **Re|gie|rungs|ge|schäf|te** PL government business *sing*; **Re|gie|rungs|haupt|stadt** F administrative capital; **Re|gie|rungs|ko|a|li|ti|on** F ruling coalition; **Re|gie|rungs|kon|fe|renz** F *(von EU-Regierungschefs etc)* intergovernmental conference; **Re|gie|rungs|krei|se** PL government circles *pl*; **Re|gie|rungs|kri|se** F government(al) crisis; **re|gie|rungs|kri|tisch** ADJ critical of the government ADV **sich ~ äußern** to make statements critical of the government, to speak critically of the government; **Re|gie|rungs|mann|schaft** F government team; **re|gie|rungs|nah** ADJ *Kreise* close to the government; *Zeitung* pro-government; **Re|gie|rungs|par|tei** F ruling or governing party, party in power; **Re|gie|rungs|prä|si|dent(in)** M(F) *chief administrator of a Regierungsbezirk*, ≈ chairman/-woman of the regional council *(Brit)*, ≈ county manager *(US)*; **Re|gie|rungs|prä|si|di|um** NT *highest authority in a Regierungsbezirk*, ≈ regional council *(Brit)* or board *(US)*; **Re|gie|rungs|rat** M *(Sw: Organ)* legislature; **Re|gie|rungs|rat** M, **Re|gie|rungs|rä|tin** F senior civil servant; **Re|gie|rungs|sitz** M seat of government; **Re|gie|rungs|spre|cher(in)** M(F) government spokesperson or spokesman/-woman; **Re|gie|rungs|sys|tem** NT system of government, governmental system; **re|gie|rungs|treu** ADJ loyal to the government; **Re|gie|rungs|um|bil|dung** F cabinet reshuffle; **Re|gie|rungs|vor|la|ge** F government bill; **Re|gie|rungs|wech|sel** M change of government; **Re|gie|rungs|zeit** F rule; *(von Monarch auch)* reign; *(von gewählter Regierung, Präsident)* period or term of office

Re|gime [re'ʒi:m] NT **-s, -s** *(pej)* regime

Re|gime-: **Re|gime|an|hän|ger(in)** M(F) supporter of the regime; **Re|gime|geg|ner(in)** M(F) opponent of the regime; **Re|gime|kri|ti|ker(in)** M(F) critic of the regime, dissident

Re|gi|ment [regi'mɛnt] NT **-(e)s, -e** or *(Einheit)* **-er** **a** *(old: = Herrschaft)* rule; **das ~ führen** *(inf)* to be the boss *(inf)*, to give the orders; **ein strenges** or **straffes ~ führen** *(inf)* to be strict; *(Vorgesetzter etc auch)* to run a tight ship *(inf)*; **der Winter führt ein strenges ~** the winter is harsh and stern **b** *(Mil)* regiment

Re|gi|ments- *in cpds* regimental; **Re|gi|ments|kom|man|deur(in)** M(F) regimental commander

Re|gi|on [re'gio:n] F **-, -en** region → **schweben**

re|gi|o|nal [regio'na:l] ADJ regional ADV regionally; **~ verschieden** or **unterschiedlich sein** to vary from one region to another

Re|gi|o|nal|bahn F *(Rail)* local railway *(Brit)* or railroad *(US)*

re|gi|o|na|li|sie|ren *ptp* **regionalisiert** VT to regionalize

Re|gi|o|na|lis|mus [regiona'lɪsmʊs] M **-, Regionalismen** [-mən] regionalism

Re|gi|o|nal-: **Re|gi|o|nal|li|ga** F regional league *(lower leagues of professional clubs)*; **Re|gi|o|nal|pro|gramm** NT *(TV, Rad)* regional station or *(TV auch)* channel; *(Sendung)* regional programme *(Brit)* or program *(US)*; **Re|gi|o|nal|schnell|bahn** F *(Rail)* high-speed regional railway *(Brit)* or railroad *(US)*; **Re|gi|o|nal|ver|kehr** M regional transport or transportation *(esp US)*; **Re|gi|o|nal|zug** M *(Rail)* local train

Re|gis|seur [reʒɪ'sø:ɐ] M **-s, -e**, **Re|gis|seu|rin** [-'sø:rɪn] F **-, -nen** director; *(Theat, Rad, TV)* producer

Re|gis|ter [re'gɪstɐ] NT **-s, -** **a** *(= amtliche Liste)* register; **ein ~ (über etw** *acc***) führen** to keep a register (of sth); **etw ins ~ (eines Amtes** *etc***) eintragen** to register sth (with an office *etc*) **b** *(= Stichwortverzeichnis)* index **c** *(Mus)* register; *(von Orgel)* stop, register; **alle ~ ziehen** or **spielen lassen** *(fig)* to pull out all the stops; **andere ~ ziehen** *(fig)* to get tough **d** *(fig inf)* **ein langes/altes ~** a tall/an old type *(inf)*

Re|gis|ter-: **Re|gis|ter|kar|te** F *(Comput: bei Dialogfeld)* tab; **Re|gis|ter|ton|ne** F *(Naut)* register ton; **Re|gis|ter|zug** M *(Mus: bei Orgel)* stop

Re|gist|ra|tor [regɪs'tra:to:ɐ] M **-s, Registratoren** [-'to:rən], **Re|gist|ra|to|rin** [-'to:rɪn] F **-, -nen** *(old)* registrar

Re|gist|ra|tur [regɪstra'tu:ɐ] F **-, -en** **a** *(= das Registrieren)* registration **b** *(Büro)* records office **c** *(= Aktenschrank)* filing cabinet **d** *(Mus: bei Orgel)* stops *pl*

Re|gist|rier|bal|lon M *(Met)* sounding balloon

re|gist|rie|ren [regɪs'tri:rən] *ptp* **registriert** VT **a** *(= erfassen)* to register; *(= zusammenzählen)* to calculate; **amtlich registriert** officially registered; **sie ist registriert** *(als Prostituierte)* she is a registered prostitute **b** *(= feststellen)* to note; **sie hat überhaupt nicht registriert, dass ich nicht da war** the fact that I wasn't there didn't register with her at all **c** *(Mus: bei Orgel)* to push the stops; **ein Orgelstück ~** to set the stops for an organ piece VR to register *(bei* with)

Re|gist|rier-: **Re|gist|rier|kas|se** F cash register; **Re|gist|rier|stel|le** F registration office

Re|gist|rie|rung F **-, -en** registration

Reg|le|ment [reglə'mã:] NT **-s, -s** *(old)* rules *pl*, conventions *pl*

reg|le|men|ta|risch [reglemɛn'ta:rɪʃ] ADJ regulation ADV according to (the) regulations; **etw ~ festlegen** to make a regulation about sth

reg|le|men|tie|ren [reglemɛn'ti:rən] *ptp* **reglementiert** VT to regulate; *jdn* to regiment; **staatlich reglementiert** state-regulated

Reg|le|men|tie|rung F **-, -en** regulation

reg|le|ment-: **reg|le|ment|mä|ßig** *(old)* ADJ according to regulation(s) ADV **~ gekleidet sein** to be in regulation dress; **~ grüßen** to give a regulation greeting; **sich ~ verhalten** to behave according to regulation; **reg|le|ment|wid|rig** *(old)* ADJ ADV contrary to regulations

Reg|ler ['re:glɐ] M **-s, -** regulator; *(an Fernseher, Stereoanlage etc)* control; *(von Elektromotor, Fernsteuerung)* control(ler); *(von Benzinmotor)* governor

Reg|let|te [re'glɛtə] F **-, -n** *(Typ)* lead

reg|los ['re:klo:s] ADJ ADV motionless

reg|nen ['re:gnən] VTI *impers* to rain; **es regnet in Strömen** it's pouring (with rain); **es regnet Glückwünsche/Proteste** congratulations/protests are pouring in; **es regnete Vorwürfe** reproaches hailed down → **Bindfaden**

reg|ne|risch ['re:gnərɪʃ] ADJ *Wetter, Tag* rainy

Re|gress [re'grɛs] M **-es, -e** **a** *(Philos)* regress **b** *(Jur)* recourse, redress; **~ anmelden** to seek recourse *or* redress; **einen ~ auf jdn** *or* **an jdn nehmen, jdn in ~ nehmen** to have recourse against sb

Re|gress-: **Re|gress|an|spruch** M *(Jur)* claim for compensation; **Re|gress|for|de|rung** F *(Jur)* recourse demand *or* claim

Re|gres|si|on [regrɛ'sio:n] F **-, -en** regression, retrogression

re|gres|siv [regrɛ'si:f] ADJ *(Biol)* regressive, retrogressive; *(fig)* retrograde, retrogressive ADV **~ verlaufen** *(= abnehmen)* to drop off

Re|gress-: **Re|gress|pflicht** F liability for compensation; **re|gress|pflich|tig** [-pflɪçtɪç] ADJ liable for compensation

reg|sam ['re:kza:m] ADJ active; **geistig ~** mentally active

Reg|sam|keit F activity; **geistige ~** mental activity

re|gu|lär [regu'lɛ:ɐ] ADJ *(= üblich)* normal; *(= vorschriftsmäßig)* proper, regular; *Arbeitszeit* normal, basic, regular; **~e Truppen** regular troops, regulars; **~e Bankgeschäfte** normal banking transactions; **die ~e Spielzeit** *(Sport)* normal time ADV *(= zum normalen Preis)* normally; **etw ~ kaufen/verkaufen** *(= zum normalen Preis)* to buy/sell sth at the normal price; *(= auf normale Weise)* to buy/sell sth in the normal way

Re|gu|la|ti|on [regula'tsio:n] F **-, -en** *(Biol)* regulation

Re|gu|la|ti|ons-: **Re|gu|la|ti|ons|stö|rung** F *(Biol)* malfunction of a regulatory system; **Re|gu|la|ti|ons|sys|tem** NT *(Biol)* regulatory system

re|gu|la|tiv [regula'ti:f] ADJ regulatory, regulative ADV **in etw** *(acc)* **~ eingreifen** to regulate sth

Re|gu|la|tiv [regula'ti:f] NT **-s, -e** [-və] regulating agent; **als ~ wirken, ein ~ bilden** to have a regulating effect

Re|gu|la|tor [regu'la:to:ɐ] M **-s, Regulatoren** [-'to:rən] wall clock

re|gu|lier|bar ADJ regul(at)able, adjustable

re|gu|lie|ren [regu'li:rən] *ptp* **reguliert** VT *(= einstellen)* to regulate; *(= nachstellen)* to adjust VR to regulate itself; **sich (von) selbst ~** to regulate itself

Re|gu|lier|he|bel M *(Tech)* regulating lever

Re|gu|lie|rung F **-, -en** regulation; *(= Nachstellung)* adjustment

Re|gu|lie|rungs|be|hör|de F regulatory body *or* authority

Re|gung ['re:gʊŋ] F **-, -en** *(= Bewegung)* movement; *(des Gefühls, des Gewissens, von Mitleid)* stirring; **ohne jede ~** without a flicker (of emotion); **einer ~ des Herzens folgen** *(liter)* to follow the dictates of one's heart *(liter)*; **zu keiner ~ fähig sein** *(fig)* to be paralyzed; **eine menschliche ~ verspüren** *(hum)* to have to answer a call of nature *(hum)*

re|gungs|los ADJ ADV motionless

Re|gungs|lo|sig|keit F **-**, *no pl* motionlessness

Reh [re:] NT **-s, -e** deer; *(im Gegensatz zu Hirsch etc)* roe deer; **scheu wie ein ~** (as) timid as a fawn

REH *(in Annoncen) abbr von* **Reiheneckhaus**

Re|ha- ['re:ha] *in cpds abbr von* **Rehabilitations-**

Re|ha|bi|li|tand [rehabili'tant] M **-en, -en** [-dn], **Re|ha|bi|li|tan|din** [-'tandɪn] F **-, -nen** *(form)* person undergoing rehabilitation

Re|ha|bi|li|ta|ti|on [rehabilita'tsio:n] F rehabilitation; *(von Ruf, Ehre)* vindication

Re|ha|bi|li|ta|ti|ons-: **Re|ha|bi|li|ta|ti|ons|kli|nik** F rehabilitation clinic; **Re|ha|bi|li|ta|ti|ons|zent|rum** NT rehabilitation centre *(Brit) or* center *(US)*

re|ha|bi|li|tie|ren [rehabili'ti:rən] *ptp* **rehabilitiert** VT to rehabilitate; **das Gericht rehabilitierte ihn** the court overturned his conviction VR to rehabilitate oneself

Re|ha|bi|li|tie|rung F **-, -en** rehabilitation

Reh-: **Reh|bock** M roebuck; **Reh|bra|ten** M roast venison; **reh|braun** ADJ russet; *Augen* hazel; **Reh|geiß** F doe *(of the roe deer)*; **Reh|kalb** NT, **Reh|kitz** NT fawn *or* kid *(of the roe deer)*; **Reh|keu|le** F *(Cook)* haunch of venison; **Reh|le|der** NT deerskin; **reh|le|dern** ADJ deerskin

Reh|ling ['re:lɪŋ] M **-s, -e** *(Bot dial)* chanterelle

Reh-: **Reh|nüss|chen** NT *(Cook)* medallion of venison, venison medallion; **Reh|pos|ten** M *(Hunt: = grober Schrot)* buckshot; **Reh|rü|cken** M *(Cook)* saddle of venison; **Reh|wild** NT *(Hunt)* roe deer

Rei|bach ['raibax] M **-s**, *no pl (inf)* killing *(inf)*; **einen ~** *or* **den großen ~ machen** *(inf)* to make a killing *(inf)*

Rei|be ['raibə] F **-, -n** *(Cook)* grater

Reib|ei|sen NT rasp; *(Cook)* grater; *(fig: = zänkisches Weib)* shrew; **rau wie ein ~** *(inf)* like sandpaper; *Stimme* rasping

Rei|be-: **Rei|be|ku|chen** M *(Cook dial)* ≈ potato fritter; **Rei|be|laut** M *(Ling)* fricative

rei|ben ['raibn] *pret* **rieb** [ri:p], *ptp* **gerieben** [gə'ri:bn] VT **a** *(= frottieren)* to rub; **etw blank ~** to rub sth till it shines; **sich** *(dat)* **die Augen (vor Müdigkeit) ~** to rub one's eyes (because one is tired); **sie rieb dem Kranken die Salbe in die Haut** she rubbed the ointment into the patient's skin; **jdm den Rücken ~** to rub sb's back; **sich** *(dat)* **die Hände ~** *(lit, fig)* to rub one's hands → **Nase a, Schlaf**
b *(= zerkleinern)* to grate
VI **a** *(= frottieren)* to rub; **an etw** *(dat)* **~** to rub sth
b *(= zerkleinern)* to grate
VR to rub oneself *(an +dat* on, against); *(= sich verletzen)* to scrape oneself *(an +dat* on); **ich würde mich ständig an ihm ~** there would always be friction between him and me; **sich an etw** *(dat)* **wund ~** to rub oneself raw on sth; **ich habe mich beim Radfahren wund gerieben** I got chafed cycling → *auch* **gerieben**

Rei|ber|dat|schi M **-s, -** *(S Ger)* potato fritter

Rei|be|rei [raibə'rai] F **-, -en** *usu pl (inf)* friction *no pl*; **(kleinere) ~en** (short) periods of friction; **ihre ständigen ~en** the constant friction between them; **zwischen den beiden Gruppen kam es zu ~en** friction developed between the two groups

Reib|flä|che F *(für Streichholz)* striking surface; *(von Reibe)* scraping surface

Rei|bung ['raibʊŋ] F **-, -en** **a** *(= das Reiben)* rubbing; *(Phys)* friction **b** *(fig)* friction *no pl*; **es kommt zu ~en** friction occurs

Rei|bungs-: **Rei|bungs|elekt|ri|zi|tät** F frictional electricity; **Rei|bungs|flä|che** F *(fig)* source of friction; **(viele) ~n bieten** to be a potential cause of friction; **rei|bungs|los** ADJ frictionless; *(fig inf)* trouble-free ADV *(= problemlos)* smoothly; **~ verlaufen** to go off smoothly *or* without a hitch; **Rei|bungs|ver|lust** M friction(al) loss; **Rei|bungs|wär|me** F *(Phys)* frictional heat; **Rei|bungs|wi|der|stand** M *(Phys)* frictional resistance

reich [raiç] ADJ **a** *(= vermögend, wohlhabend)* rich, wealthy; *Erbschaft* substantial; *Partie, Heirat* good
b *(= kostbar)* costly *no adv*, rich; *Schmuck* costly *no adv*, expensive
c *(= ergiebig, üppig)* rich, copious; *Ernte auch* bountiful, abundant; *Mahl* sumptuous, lavish; **~ an etw** *(dat)* **sein** to be rich in sth; **~ an Fischen/Wild/Steinen** abounding with *or* full of fish/game/stones; **er ist ~ an Erfahrungen** he has had a wealth of experiences; **er ist ~ an guten Einfällen** he is full of good ideas
d *(= groß, vielfältig)* large, copious; *Auswahl* wide, large; *Erfahrungen, Kenntnisse* wide; *Blattwerk, Vegetation* rich, luxuriant; **eine ~e Fülle** a rich abundance; **in ~em Maße vorhanden sein** to abound, to be found in large quantities
ADV **a** *(= wohlhabend)* **~ heiraten** *(inf)* to marry (into) money; **~ begütert** wealthy, affluent
b *(= großzügig)* **jdn ~ belohnen** to reward sb well, to give sb a rich reward; **damit bin ich ~ belohnt** *(fig)* I am richly *or* amply rewarded; **jdn ~ beschenken** to shower sb with presents; **eine mit Kindern ~ beschenkte Familie** a family blessed with many children
c *(= reichhaltig)* richly; **ein ~ ausgestattetes Haus** a richly *or* lavishly furnished house; **eine ~ ausgestattete Bibliothek** a well-stocked library; **~ mit Vorräten ausgestattet** well *or* amply stocked up with supplies; **~ illustriert** richly *or* copiously illustrated; **~ geschmückt** *(Gebäude, Gegenstand)* richly decorated *or* adorned; **~ verziert** richly ornamented

Reich [raiç] NT **-(e)s, -e** **a** *(= Herrschaft(sgebiet), Imperium)* empire; *(= Königreich)* realm, kingdom; **das ~ der aufgehenden Sonne** *(liter)* the land of the rising sun; **das Deutsche ~** the German Reich; *(bis 1918 auch)* the German Empire; **das Dritte ~** the Third Reich; **das ~ der Mitte** the Middle Kingdom; **das himmlische ~** *(liter)* the Kingdom of Heaven, the Heavenly Kingdom; **das ~ Gottes** the Kingdom of God
b *(= Bereich, Gebiet)* realm; **das ~ der Tiere/Pflanzen** the animal/vegetable kingdom; **das ~ der Natur** the world *or* realm of nature; **das ist mein ~** *(fig)* that is my domain; **da bin ich in meinem ~** that's where I'm in my element; **etw ins ~ der Fabel verweisen** to consign sth to the realms of fantasy

reich|be|gü|tert ADJ → **reich ADV a**

rei|chen ['raiçn] ✪ 41 VI **a** *(= sich erstrecken)* to stretch, to extend *(bis zu* to), to reach *(bis zu etw* sth); *(Stimme)* to carry *(bis zu* to), to reach *(bis zu jdm/etw* sb/sth); *(Kleidungsstück)* to reach *(bis zu etw* sth); **sein Swimmingpool reicht bis an mein Grundstück** his swimming pool comes right up to my land; **der Garten reicht bis ans Ufer** the garden stretches *or* extends *or* goes right down to the riverbank; **das Wasser reicht mir bis zum Hals** *(lit)* the water comes up to my neck; **jdm bis zur Schulter ~** to come up to sb's shoulder; **er reicht mit dem Kopf bis zur Decke** his head reaches *or* touches the ceiling; **so weit der Himmel reichte** in the whole sky; **das Spektrum reicht von der Volksmusik bis zum Jazz** the spectrum ranges from folk music to jazz; **so weit ~ meine Beziehungen nicht** my connections are not that extensive; **so weit ~ meine Fähigkeiten nicht** my skills are not that wide-ranging; **... aber sein Arm reichte nicht so weit** ... but his arm wouldn't reach that far; **so weit das Auge reicht** as far as the eye can see
b *(= langen)* to be enough, to suffice *(form)*; **der Saal reicht nicht für so viele Leute** the room isn't big enough *or* won't suffice *(form)* for so many people; **der Zucker reicht nicht** there won't be enough sugar; **reicht mein Geld noch bis zum Monatsende?** will my money last until the end of the month?; **reicht das Licht zum Lesen?** is there enough light to read by?; **dazu reicht meine Geduld nicht** I haven't got enough patience for that; **dazu ~ meine Fähigkeiten nicht** I'm not skilled enough for that; **das muss für vier Leute ~** that will have to be enough *or* to suffice *(form) or* to do *(inf)* for four people; **das sollte eigentlich ~** that should be enough, that should do *(inf)*; **mir reichts** *(inf) (= habe die Nase voll)* I've had enough *(inf)*; *(= habe genug gehabt)* that's enough for me; **als das dann noch passierte, reichte es ihm** when that happened it was just too much for him; **jetzt reichts (mir aber)!** that's the last straw!; *(= Schluss!)* that's enough!; **das reicht ja, um den Geduldigsten aus der Fassung zu bringen!** it's enough to try the patience of a saint!; **es reichte ja schon, dass er faul war** it was bad enough that he was lazy, his being lazy was bad enough
c *(inf)* **mit dem Essen/der Zeit** *etc* **~** to have enough food/time *etc*
VT *(= entgegenhalten)* to hand; *(= geben auch)* to give; *(= herüberreichen, hinüberreichen auch)* to pass (over); *(= anbieten)* to serve; *(Eccl) Abendmahl* to give, to administer; **jdm etw ~** to hand/give/pass sb sth, to hand/give/pass sth to sb;

sie reichte mir die Wange zum Kuss she proffered her cheek for a kiss; **jdm die Hand ~** to hold out one's hand to sb; *(fig)* to extend the hand of friendship to sb; **sich die Hände ~** to join hands; *(zur Begrüßung)* to shake hands; **es wurden Erfrischungen gereicht** refreshments were served

Rei|che(r) ['raiçə] **MF** *decl as adj* rich *or* wealthy man/woman *etc*; **die ~n** the rich *or* wealthy

Reich-: **reich|ge|schmückt** [-gəʃmʏkt] **ADJ** → **reich ADV c**; **reich|hal|tig** **ADJ** extensive; *Auswahl, Angebot auch* wide, large; *Essen* rich; *Informationen* comprehensive; *Programm* varied; **Reich|hal|tig|keit** ['raiçhaltıçkait] **F -,** *no pl* extensiveness; *(von Angebot auch)* wideness; *(von Essen)* richness; *(von Programm etc)* variety; **die ~ der Auswahl** the range of choice

reich|lich ['raiçlıç] **ADJ** **a** *(= sehr viel, groß)* ample, large, substantial; *Vorrat* plentiful, ample, substantial; *Portion, Trinkgeld* generous; *Alkoholgenuss* substantial; *Geschenke* numerous
b *(= mehr als genügend) Zeit, Geld, Platz* ample, plenty of; *Belohnung* ample
c *(inf: = mehr als)* good; **eine ~e Stunde** a good hour
ADV **a** *(= sehr viel) belohnen, sich eindecken* amply; *verdienen* richly; **jdn ~ beschenken** to give sb lots of *or* numerous presents; **~ Trinkgeld geben** to tip generously
b *(= mehr als genügend)* **~ Zeit/Geld haben** to have plenty of *or* ample time/money; **~ vorhanden sein** to abound, to exist in plenty; **mehr als ~ belohnt** more than amply rewarded; **mehr als ~ bezahlt** paid more than enough; **der Mantel ist ~ ausgefallen** the coat is on the big side; **das war ~ gewogen/abgemessen** that was very generously weighed out/measured out; **das ist ~ gerechnet** that's a generous estimate
c *(inf: = mehr als)* **~ 1.000 Euro** a good 1,000 euros
d *(inf: = ziemlich)* pretty

Reichs-: **Reichs|abt** **M** *(Hist) abbot of an abbey under imperial protection*; **Reichs|acht** **F** *(Hist)* outlawry in the Emperor's name; **Reichs|ad|ler** **M** *(Her, Hist)* imperial eagle; **Reichs|ap|fel** **M** *(Her, Hist)* imperial orb; **Reichs|bahn** **F** state railway *(Brit) or* railroad *(US)*; *(DDR)* East German State Railways *(Brit) or* Railroad System *(US)*; **Reichs|ge|biet** **NT** territory of the (German) Reich; **im ~** within the boundaries of the (German) Reich; **Reichs|ge|richt** **NT** *(Hist)* German supreme court *(until 1945)*; **Reichs|gren|ze** **F** border of the empire, prewar German border; **Reichs|grün|dung** **F** foundation of the Reich *or* Prussian Empire; **Reichs|haupt|stadt** **F** *(1933-45)* capital of the Reich; *(vor 1933)* imperial capital; **Reichs|in|sig|ni|en** **PL** *(Hist)* imperial regalia *pl*; **Reichs|kanz|ler** **M** *(bis 1918)* Imperial Chancellor; *(1918-34)* German Chancellor; **Reichs|klein|odi|en** **PL** *(Hist)* imperial regalia *pl*; **Reichs|kon|kor|dat** **NT** Reich Concordat; **Reichs|kris|tall|nacht** **F** *(Hist)* → **Kristallnacht**; **Reichs|mark** **F** *pl* **-mark** *(Hist)* reichsmark, (old) German mark; **Reichs|prä|si|dent** **M** German president *(until 1934)*; **Reichs|re|gie|rung** **F** German government *(until 1945)*; **Reichs|stadt** **F** *(Hist)* free city (of the Holy Roman Empire); **freie ~** free city; **Reichs|stän|de** **PL** *(Hist)* estates of the Empire *pl*; **Reichs|tag** **M** Parliament; *(in Deutschland 1871-1945)* Reichstag; *(in Deutschland vor 1871, in Japan)* Imperial Diet; **Reichs|tags|brand** **M** burning of the Reichstag; **reichs|un|mit|tel|bar** **ADJ** *(Hist)* self-governing under the Kaiser; **Reichs|vogt** **M** *(Hist)* protector; **Reichs|wehr** **F** German army *(1921-35)*

Reich|tum ['raiçtu:m] **M -s, Reichtümer** [-ty:mɐ] **a** wealth *no pl*, richness *no pl*; *(= Besitz)* riches *pl*; **zu ~ kommen** to become rich, to make one's fortune; **Reichtümer erwerben** to gain riches; **die Reichtümer der Erde/des Meeres** the riches of the earth/sea; **der innere** *or* **seelische ~** richness of spirit; **damit kann man keine Reichtümer gewinnen** you won't get rich that way **b** *(fig: = Fülle, Reichhaltigkeit)* wealth, abundance *(an +dat* of); **der ~ an Fischen** the abundance of fish

reich|ver|ziert [-fɛɐtsi:ɐt] **ADJ** *attr* → **reich ADV c**

Reich|wei|te **F** *(von Geschoss, Sender, Tankfüllung, Batterie)* range; *(= greifbare Nähe)* reach; *(fig: = Einflussbereich)* scope; **in ~** within range/reach *(+gen* of); **jd ist in ~** sb is nearby *or* around; **in ~ rücken** *(fig)* to come within reach; **außer ~** out of range/reach *(+gen* of); *(fig)* out of reach; **innerhalb der ~** *(+gen)* within range/the scope of; **außerhalb der ~** *(+gen)* outside the range of/beyond the scope of

reif [raif] **ADJ** **a** *(= voll entwickelt) Früchte, Getreide* ripe; *Mensch, Ei* mature; **der Pickel/das Geschwür ist ~** *(inf)* the spot/abscess has formed a head
b *(= erfahren, älter)* mature; **in ~(er)em Alter, in den ~eren Jahren** in one's mature(r) years; **die ~ere Jugend** those of mellower years; **im ~eren Alter von ...** at the ripe old age of ...
c *(= vorbereitet)* ready, ripe; *(= durchdacht) Urteil, Arbeit, Gedanken* mature; **~ zur Veröffentlichung** ready *or* ripe for publication; **die Zeit ist ~/noch nicht ~** the time is ripe/not yet ripe; **eine ~e Leistung** *(inf)* a brilliant achievement
d **für etw ~ sein** *(inf)* to be ready for sth; **~ sein** *(inf)* to be in for it *(inf)*, to be for the high jump *(inf)*; *(sl: für Geschlechtsverkehr)* to be gagging *(Brit) or* dying for it *(sl)*

Reif [raif] **M -(e)s,** *no pl (= Raureif)* hoarfrost, white frost; *(= gefrorener Nebel)* rime

Reif **M -(e)s, -e** *(old, liter) (= Stirnreif, Diadem)* circlet; *(= Armreif)* bangle; *(= Fingerring)* ring; *(im Rock)* hoop

Rei|fe ['raifə] **F -,** *no pl* **a** *(= das Reifen)* ripening **b** *(= das Reifsein)* ripeness; *(= Geschlechtsreife, von Ei)* maturity; **zur ~ kommen** to ripen; *(geh: Mädchen)* to come to *or* reach maturity; **zur ~ bringen** to ripen **c** *(fig: von Menschen, Gedanken etc)* maturity; **ihm fehlt die (sittliche) ~** he lacks maturity, he's too immature **d** *(Sch)* **Zeugnis der ~** *(form)* = **Reifezeugnis**, → **mittlere(r,s)**

Rei|fe|grad **M** degree of ripeness

rei|fen ['raifn] **VI** *impers* **es reift** there has been/will be a frost

rei|fen **VT** *Obst* to ripen; *jdn* to mature; **das hat ihn zum Manne gereift** *(liter)* that made a man out of him → *auch* **gereift** **VI** *aux sein* **a** *(Obst)* to ripen; *(Mensch, Ei)* to mature → *auch* **gereift** **b** *(fig: Plan, Entscheidung)* to mature; **zur Wirklichkeit ~** to come to fruition, to become reality; **zur Gewissheit ~** to turn into certainty; **die Erkenntnis ist gereift, dass ...** the realization has grown that ...; **langsam reifte in ihm der Entschluss, ...** he slowly reached the decision ...

Rei|fen ['raifn] **M -s, -** tyre *(Brit)*, tire *(US)*; *(= Spielreifen, von Fass, von Rock)* hoop; *(= Armreifen)* bangle; **(den) ~ treiben** *or* **spielen** to bowl *or* roll a hoop

Rei|fen-: **Rei|fen|de|fekt** **M** = **Reifenpanne**; **Rei|fen|druck** **M** *pl* **-drücke** tyre *(Brit) or* tire *(US)* pressure; **Rei|fen|pan|ne** **F** puncture *(Brit)*, flat *(inf)*; *(geplatzt auch)* blowout *(inf)*; **Rei|fen|pro|fil** **NT** tyre *(Brit) or* tire *(US)* tread; **Rei|fen|scha|den** **M** **a** *(= schadhafter Reifen)* faulty tyre *(Brit) or* tire *(US)* **b** = **Reifenpanne**; **Rei|fen|wech|sel** **M** tyre *(Brit) or* tire *(US)* change

Rei|fe-: **Rei|fe|prü|fung** **F** *(Sch)* → **Abitur**; **Rei|fe|zeit** **F** ripening time; *(von Ei)* period of incubation; *(= Pubertät)* puberty *no def art*; **Rei|fe|zeug|nis** **NT** *(Sch) Abitur certificate*, ≈ A Level certificate *(Brit)*, ≈ high school diploma *(US)*

reif|lich ['raiflıç] **ADJ** thorough, careful; **nach ~er Überlegung** after careful consideration, upon mature reflection *(liter)* **ADV** *nachdenken* thoroughly; **sich** *(dat)* **etw ~ überlegen** to consider sth carefully

Reif|rock **M** *(Hist)* farthingale, hoop skirt

Rei|fung ['raifʊŋ] **F -,** *no pl (von Obst)* ripening; *(von Ei)* maturing, maturation; *(von Käse, Bier)* maturing; *(von Mensch)* maturing

Rei|fungs|pro|zess **M** *(von Obst)* ripening process; *(von Ei)* maturation process; *(von Käse, Bier)* maturing process; *(von Mensch)* maturing process

Rei|gen ['raign] **M -s, -** round dance, roundelay *(old)*; *(fig geh)* round; **den ~ eröffnen** *or* **anführen** *(fig geh)* to lead off; **er eröffnete den ~ der Ansprachen** *(geh)* he led off with his speech; **den ~ beschließen** *(fig geh)* to bring up the rear; **ein bunter ~ von Melodien** a varied selection of melodies

Rei|he ['raiə] **F -, -n** **a** *(= geregelte Anordnung)* row, line; *(= Sitzreihe, beim Stricken)* row; **in ~(n) antreten** to line up; *(Mil)* to fall in; **in ~n zu (je) drei antreten/marschieren** to line up/march in rows of three *or* in threes; **sich in einer ~ aufstellen** to line up, to form a row *or* line; **sich in die ~ stellen** to join the row *or* line; **sich in eine ~ stellen** to line up; *(Mil)* to fall in; **in einer ~ stehen** to stand in a row *or* line; **in Reih und Glied antreten** to line up in formation; **sie standen in Reih und Glied vor dem Lehrer** they stood lined up in front of their teacher; **aus der ~ tanzen** *(fig inf)* to be different; *(= gegen Konventionen verstoßen)* to step out of line; **die ~ herumgehen** *(Gegenstand)* to be passed around, to go the rounds; **die ~n schließen** *(Mil)* to close ranks; **die ~n lichten sich** *(fig)* the ranks are thinning; **in den eigenen ~n** within our/their *etc* own ranks; **die ~ eröffnen** *(fig)* to start off; **in einer ~ mit jdm stehen** *(fig)* to be on a par with sb; **sich in eine ~ mit jdm stellen** *(fig)* to put oneself on a par *or* on an equal footing with sb; **in die erste ~ (vor)rücken** *(fig)* to move into the top rank; **in der vordersten ~ stehen** *(fig)* to be in the topmost rank
b *(= Reihenfolge)* **er ist an der ~** it's his turn, he's next; *(beim Spiel etc auch)* it's his go; **die ~ ist an jdm** it's sb's turn; **er kommt an die ~** he's next, it's his turn next, it's him next *(inf)*; **warte, bis du an die ~ kommst** wait till it's your turn/go; **er kommt immer außer der ~** he always comes just when he pleases; **der ~ nach, nach der ~** in order, in turn; **sie sollen der ~ nach hereinkommen** they are to come in one by one *or* one at a time; **erzähl mal der ~ nach, wie alles war** tell us how it was in the order it all happened; **außer der ~** out of order; *(bei Spielen auch)* out of turn; *(= zusätzlich, nicht wie gewöhnlich)* out of the usual way of things; **wenn ich das Auto mal außer der ~ brauche** if I should happen to need the car at a time when I don't normally have it; **es kommt ganz selten vor, dass ich mal außer der ~ da bin** it's very rare for me to be there out of my routine
c *(= Serie, Math, Mus)* series *sing*; *(Biol: = Ordnung)* order
d *(= unbestimmte Anzahl)* number; **in die ~ der Mitgliedsstaaten eintreten** to join the ranks of the member states; **in der ~ der Stars** amongst the ranks of the stars; **eine ganze ~ (von)** a whole lot (of); **eine ganze ~ von Beispielen** a whole string of examples
e *(inf: = Ordnung)* **aus der ~ kommen** *(= in Unordnung geraten)* to get out of order; *(= verwirrt werden)* to lose one's equilibrium; *(gesundheitlich)* to fall ill; **jdn aus der ~ bringen** to muddle *or* confuse sb; **wieder in die ~ kommen** to get one's equilibrium back; *(gesundheitlich)* to get back on form; **nicht in der ~ sein** to be unwell *(esp Brit)*, not to be one hundred per cent *(Brit inf) or* percent *(US inf)*; **in die ~ bringen** to put in order, to put straight; **nicht alle auf der ~ haben** *(sl)* to have a screw loose *(inf)*; **etw auf die ~ kriegen** *(inf)* to handle sth

rei|hen ['raiən] **VT** **a** **Perlen auf eine Schnur ~** to string beads (on a thread); **sie reihte die**

Pilzstücke auf einen Faden she strung the pieces of mushroom up (on a thread) **b** *(Sew)* to tack VR **etw reiht sich an etw** *(acc)* sth follows (after) sth; **eine Enttäuschung reihte sich an die andere** letdown followed letdown

Rei|hen ['raiən] M **-s, -** *(S Ger)* instep

Rei|hen-: **Rei|hen|dorf** NT *village built along a road*, ribbon development *(spec)*; **Rei|hen|eck|haus** NT end terrace *(Brit)*; **Rei|hen|fab|ri|ka|ti|on** F, **Rei|hen|fer|ti|gung** F serial production

Rei|hen|fol|ge F order; *(= notwendige Aufeinanderfolge)* sequence; **der ~ nach** in sequence; **in zwangloser ~** in no particular *or* special order; **in umgekehrter ~** in reverse order; **alphabetische/zeitliche ~** alphabetical/chronological order

Rei|hen-: **Rei|hen|haus** NT terraced house *(Brit)*, town house *(esp US)*; **Rei|hen|(haus)|sied|lung** F estate of terraced houses *(Brit) or* town houses *(esp US)*; **Rei|hen|schal|tung** F *(Elec)* series connection; **in ~** in series; **Rei|hen|un|ter|su|chung** F mass screening; **rei|hen|wei|se** ADV **a** *(= in Reihen)* in rows **b** *(fig: = in großer Anzahl)* by the dozen; **sie sind ~ ohnmächtig geworden** they fainted by the dozen, dozens of them fainted; **Rei|hen|zahl** F *(Math)* member of a series

Rei|her ['raiɐ] M **-s, -** heron

Rei|her-: **Rei|her|fe|der** F heron's feather; *(als Hutschmuck)* aigrette; **Rei|her|horst** M heron's nest

rei|hern ['raiɐn] VI *(sl)* to puke *or* spew (up) *(inf)*

Rei|her|schna|bel M *(Bot)* common storksbill

Reih|garn ['rai-] NT tacking thread

-rei|hig [raiç] ADJ *suf* -rowed; **zweireihige Jacke** double-breasted jacket

reih|um [rai'ʊm] ADV round; **es geht ~** everybody takes their turn; **etw ~ gehen lassen** to pass sth round

Reim [raim] M **-(e)s, -e** rhyme; **ein ~ auf „Hut"** a rhyme for "hat"; **~e bilden** *or* **machen** *or* **drechseln** *(hum) or* **schmieden** *(hum)* to make *or* write rhymes, to versify *(hum)*; **etw in ~e bringen** to make sth rhyme; **sich** *(dat)* **einen ~ auf etw** *(acc)* **machen** *(inf)* to make sense of sth; **ich mache mir so meinen ~ darauf** *(inf)* I can put two and two together *(inf)*; **ich kann mir keinen ~ darauf machen** *(inf)* I can't make head (n)or tail of it, I can see no rhyme (n)or reason in it

Reim|art F type of rhyme

rei|men ['raimən] VT to rhyme (*auf +acc, mit* with); **ich kann das Wort nicht ~** I can't find a rhyme for this word, I can't find anything to rhyme with this word VI to make up rhymes, to rhyme *(liter)*, to versify *(hum)* VR to rhyme (*auf +acc, mit* with); **das reimt sich nicht** *(fig)* it doesn't hang together *or* make sense

Rei|mer ['raimɐ] M **-s, -**, **Rei|me|rin** [-ərɪn] F **-, -nen** *(pej)* rhymester, versifier

Rei|me|rei [raimə'rai] F **-, -en** **a** *(= das Reimen)* versifying **b** *(= Gedicht)* doggerel *no pl*; **eine ~** a piece of doggerel

Reim-: **Reim|le|xi|kon** NT rhyming dictionary; **reim|los** ADJ unrhymed, non-rhyming; **Reim|paar** NT rhyming couplet

Re|im|port [relɪm'pɔrt, 'relɪmpɔrt] M *(Fin, Comm)* reimportation

Reim-: **Reim|sche|ma** NT rhyming pattern, rhyme scheme; **Reim|schmied(in)** M(F) *(hum)* rhymester, versifier; **Reim|wort** NT *pl* **-wörter** rhyme; **ein ~ zu etw finden** to find a rhyme for sth *or* a word to rhyme with sth

rein [rain] ADV *(inf)* = **herein, hinein**

rein ADJ **a** pure; *(= absolut, völlig)* pure, sheer; *Wahrheit* plain, straight, unvarnished; *Gewinn* clear; **das ist die ~ste Freude/der ~ste Hohn** *etc* it's pure *or* sheer joy/mockery *etc*; **er ist der ~ste Künstler/Akrobat** he's a real artist/acrobat; **das Kind ist der ~ste Vater** *(dial)* the child is just like his father; **er ist die ~ste Bestie** he's an absolute *or* downright brute; **mit ihren Kindern hat sie nicht immer die ~ste Freude** she sometimes finds her children a mixed blessing; **die ~e Arbeit kostet ...** the work alone costs ...; **er ist ein Demokrat ~sten Wassers** *or* **von ~stem Wasser** he is the archetypal *or* a pure democrat; **eine ~e Jungenklasse** an all boys' class; **eine ~e Industriestadt** a purely industrial town

b *(= sauber)* clean; *Haut, Teint* clear, pure; **etw ~ machen** to clean sth; **~ Schiff!** *(Naut)* ≈ swab the decks!; **~en Tisch machen** *(fig)* to get things straight, to sort things out; **ich habe ~e Hände** *(fig)* my hands are clean; **die Hände ~ behalten** *(fig)* to keep one's nose clean *(inf)* → **Weste**

c *(= klar, übersichtlich)* **etw ins Reine schreiben** to write out a fair copy of sth, to write sth out neatly; **etw ins Reine bringen** to clear sth up; **die Sache ist ins Reine gekommen** things are cleared up, things have cleared themselves up; **mit sich selbst ins Reine kommen** to get things straight with oneself, to straighten *or* sort things out with oneself; **mit etw ins Reine kommen** to get straight about sth; **mit jdm/sich selbst im Reinen sein** to have got things straightened *or* sorted out with sb/oneself; **mit etw im Reinen sein** to have got sth straightened *or* sorted out; **mit seinem Gewissen im Reinen sein** to have a clear conscience; **er ist mit sich selbst nicht im Reinen** he is at odds with himself

d *(= unschuldig)* pure; *Gewissen* clear; **er ist ~ von Schuld** *(old)* he is free of guilt; **dem Reinen ist alles ~** *(prov)* to the pure all things are pure

ADV **a** *(= ausschließlich)* purely; **~ hypothetisch gesprochen** speaking purely hypothetically

b *(= pur)* pure → **reinleinen, reinseiden, reinwollen**

c *(= sauber)* **~ klingen** to make a pure sound; **~ singen** to have a pure voice

d *(inf: = ganz, völlig)* absolutely; **~ alles/unmöglich** absolutely everything/impossible; **~ gar nichts** absolutely nothing

Rein F **-, -en** *(S Ger, Aus: Cook)* ≈ casserole

rein+bei|ßen VT *sep irreg (inf)* to bite into (*in +acc*); **zum Reinbeißen aussehen** to look scrumptious

Rei|ne|clau|de [rɛːnə'kloːdə] F **-, -n** greengage

Rein|ein|nah|me F net profit(s *pl*) *or* proceeds *pl*

Rei|ne|ke Fuchs ['rainəkə] M **- -** *(Liter)* Reynard the Fox

Rei|ne|ma|che|frau F cleaner, cleaning lady

Rei|ne|ma|chen NT **-s**, *no pl (inf)* cleaning

Rein-: **rein|er|big** ADJ *(Biol)* homozygous *(spec)*; **Rein|er|lös** M, **Rein|er|trag** M net profit(s *pl*) *or* proceeds *pl*

Rei|net|te [re'nɛtə] F **-, -n** rennet

rei|ne|weg ['rainəvɛk] ADV *(inf)* completely, absolutely; **das ist ~ eine Frechheit/erlogen** it's downright cheek *(Brit) or* impudence/a downright lie; **das ist ~ zum Verrücktwerden** it's enough to drive you absolutely mad

Rein|fall M *(inf)* disaster *(inf)*; *(= Pleite auch)* flop *(inf)*; **mit der Waschmaschine/dem Kollegen haben wir einen ~ erlebt** we had real problems with the washing machine/this colleague; **unsere Reise war vielleicht ein ~!** our journey was a real disaster

rein+fal|len ['rainfalən] VI *sep irreg aux sein (inf)* = **hereinfallen, hineinfallen**

Re|in|fek|ti|on [relɪnfɛk'tsioːn] F reinfection

Rein|ge|schmeck|te(r) ['raingəʃmɛktə] MF *decl as adj (S Ger)* outsider

Rein-: **Rein|ge|wicht** NT net(t) weight; **Rein|ge|winn** M net(t) profit; **Rein|hal|tung** F keeping clean; *(von Wasser, Luft auch, von Sprache)* keeping pure; **die ~ des Spielplatzes** keeping the playground clean

rein+hän|gen VR *sep (sl: = sich anstrengen)* to get stuck in *(inf)*

Rein|heit F **-,** *no pl* purity, pureness; *(= Sauberkeit)* cleanness; *(von Haut)* clearness; *(= Unschuld)* purity, pureness; **Rohstoffe in hoher ~** high-purity raw materials

Rein|heits-: **Rein|heits|ge|bot** NT purity law *(regulating the production of beer and various other food and drink items)*; **Rein|heits|grad** M *(Chem)* (degree of) purity

rei|ni|gen ['rainɪgn] VT **a** *(= sauber machen, putzen)* to clean; **etw chemisch ~** to dry-clean sth; **sich** *(dat)* **die Hände ~** to clean one's hands

b *(= säubern)* to purify; *Metall* to refine; *Blut* to purify, to cleanse; **ein ~des Gewitter** *(fig inf)* a row which clears the air

c *(= zensieren) Text* to clean up, to bowdlerize; *Sprache* to purify; **eine Sprache/einen Text von etw ~** to purify *or* purge a language/text of sth

VR to clean itself; *(Mensch)* to cleanse oneself; **normalerweise kann ein Fluss sich von selbst ~** normally a river can cleanse itself *or* keep itself clean; **sich von einer Schuld ~** *(liter)* to cleanse oneself of a sin *(liter)*; **sich von einem Verdacht ~** *(liter)* to clear oneself of suspicion

Rei|ni|ger ['rainɪgɐ] M **-s, -** cleaner

Rei|ni|gung ['rainɪgʊn] F **-, -en** **a** *(= das Saubermachen)* cleaning **b** *(= chemische Reinigung) (Vorgang)* dry cleaning; *(Anstalt)* (dry) cleaner's **c** *(= das Säubern)* purification; *(von Metall)* refining; *(von Blut)* purification, cleansing **d** *(von Text)* cleaning up, bowdlerization; *(von Sprache)* purification **e** *(Rel)* purification

Rei|ni|gungs-: **Rei|ni|gungs|creme** F cleansing cream; **Rei|ni|gungs|milch** F cleansing milk; **Rei|ni|gungs|mit|tel** NT cleansing agent

Re|in|kar|na|ti|on [relɪnkarna'tsioːn] F reincarnation

rein+krie|gen ['rainkriːgn] VT *sep (inf)* = **hereinbekommen**

Rein|kul|tur F *(Biol)* pure culture; **~en der Bierhefe** pure beer-yeast cultures; **Kitsch/Faschismus** *etc* **in ~** *(inf)* pure unadulterated kitsch/fascism *etc*

rein+le|gen ['rainleːgn] VT *sep (inf)* = **hereinlegen, hineinlegen**

rein|lei|nen ADJ pure linen

rein|lich ['rainlɪç] ADJ **a** *(= sauberkeitsliebend)* cleanly **b** *(= ordentlich)* neat, tidy **c** *(= gründlich, klar)* clear ADV **a** *(= sauber)* cleanly **b** *(= genau) trennen, unterscheiden* clearly

Rein|lich|keit F **-,** *no pl* **a** *(= Sauberkeitsliebe)* cleanliness **b** *(= Ordentlichkeit)* neatness, tidiness

Rein-: **Rein|luft|ge|biet** NT pollution-free zone; **Rein|ma|che|frau** ['rainmaxə-] F cleaner, cleaning lady; **rein+ma|chen** VT *sep* → **rein ADJ b**; **rein|ras|sig** ADJ of pure race, pure-blooded; *Tier* purebred, thoroughbred; *(fig) Sportwagen etc* thoroughbred; **Rein|ras|sig|keit** F **-,** *no pl* racial purity; *(von Tier)* pure breeding; **Rein|raum** M clean room; **rein+rei|ten** ['rainraitn] VT *sep irreg* **jdn (ganz schön) ~** *(inf)* to get sb into a (right) mess *(inf)*; **Rein|schiff** NT *(Naut)* **~ machen** ≈ to swab the decks; **rein+schnup|pern** VI *sep (inf)* = **hineinschnuppern**; **Rein|schrift** F writing out a fair copy *no art*; *(Geschriebenes)* fair copy; **etw in ~ schreiben** to write out a fair copy of sth; **Notizen in ~ schreiben** to write up notes; **rein|schrift|lich** ADJ **~es Exemplar** fair copy; **rein|sei|den** ADJ pure silk; **rein+sem|meln** VT *sep (inf)* **jdm eine** *or* **eins ~** *(= schlagen)* to give sb a thump, to land sb one *(inf)*; *(= hereinlegen)* to do the dirty on sb *(inf)*; *(Sport: = Tor/Punkt erzielen)* to get one up on sb *(inf)*

Reinst|raum ['rainst-] M clean room

Rein-: **rein+stres|sen** VR *sep (sl)* to get stressed out *(inf)*; *(= hart arbeiten)* to work like hell *(inf)*; **rein+tun** ['raintuːn] VT *(inf)* **sich** *(dat)* **etw ~** to imagine sth; **das muss man sich mal ~** just imagine that → *auch* **hineintun**; **Rein|ver|dienst** M net earnings *pl*; **Rein|ver|mö|gen** NT net assets *pl*

Re|in|ves|ti|ti|on [reɪnvɛsti'tsio:n] **F -, -en** reinvestment

Rein-: **rein wa|schen** ['rainvaʃn] *irreg* **VT** *(von of)* to clear; *(von Sünden)* to cleanse; *schmutziges Geld* to launder **VR** *(fig)* to clear oneself; *(von Sünden)* to cleanse oneself; **rein|weg** ['rainvɛk] **ADV** = **reineweg**; **rein|wol|len** **ADJ** pure wool; **rein+wür|gen** ['rainvʏrgn] **VT** *(inf) Essen etc* to force down; **jdm einen** *or* **eins ~** to do the dirty on sb *(inf)*; **rein+zie|hen** ['rain-tsi:ən] **VT** *(inf)* **sich** *(dat)* **etw ~** *(Drogen)* to take sth; *Musik* to listen to sth; *Film, Video* to watch sth; *Getränk* to knock sth back *(inf)*; *Essen* to guzzle sth down; *(= vorstellen)* to imagine sth; *(= akzeptieren)* to take sth in → *auch* **hineinziehen**; **Rein|zucht** **F** *(von Tieren)* inbreeding; *(von Bakterien)* cultivation of pure cultures

Reis [rais] **NT -es, -er** [-zɐ] *(old, liter) (= Zweig)* twig, sprig; *(= Pfropfreis)* scion

Reis **M -es, -e** [-zə] rice; **Huhn auf ~** chicken with rice

Reis-: **Reis|auf|lauf** **M** rice pudding; **Reis|bau** **M**, *no pl* rice-growing *no art*, cultivation of rice; **Reis|be|sen** **M** besom; **Reis|brannt|wein** **M** rice spirit; **Reis|brei** **M** ≈ creamed rice; **Reis|bün|del** **NT** bundle of twigs, faggot *(Brit)*

Rei|se ['raizə] **F -, -n** journey, trip; *(= Schiffsreise)* voyage; *(Space)* voyage, journey; *(= Geschäftsreise)* trip; **seine ~n durch Europa** his travels through Europe; **seine ~ nach Spanien** his trip to Spain; **eine ~ mit der Eisenbahn/dem Auto** a train/car journey, a journey by rail/car; **eine ~ zu Schiff** a sea voyage; *(= Kreuzfahrt)* a cruise; **er plant eine ~ durch Afrika** he's planning to travel through Africa; **eine ~ machen** to go on a journey; **wir konnten die geplante ~ nicht machen** we couldn't go away as planned; **er hat in seinem Leben viele interessante ~n gemacht** he has travelled *(Brit) or* traveled *(US)* to a lot of interesting places in his lifetime; **wann machst du die nächste ~?** when are you off (on your travels) again?, when's the next trip?; **ich muss mal wieder eine ~ machen** I must go away again; **die ~ nach Afrika habe ich allein gemacht** I travelled *(Brit) or* traveled *(US)* to Africa by myself; **auf ~n sein** to be away (travelling *(Brit) or* traveling *(US)*); **er ist viel auf ~n** he does a lot of travelling *(Brit) or* traveling *(US)*; **jeden Sommer gehen wir auf ~n** we go away every summer; **er geht viel auf ~n** he travels a lot; **jdn auf die ~ schicken** to see sb off on his/her journey; **etw auf die ~ schicken** *(Brief etc)* to send sth off; **wohin geht die ~?** where are you off to?; **die letzte ~ antreten** *(euph liter)* to enter upon one's last journey *(liter)*; **glückliche** *or* **gute ~!** bon voyage!, have a good journey!; **wenn einer eine ~ tut, so kann er was erzählen** *(prov)* strange things happen when you're abroad; **die ~ nach Jerusalem** *(= Spiel)* musical chairs *sing*; **Gullivers ~n** *(Liter)* Gulliver's Travels

Rei|se-: **Rei|se|an|den|ken** **NT** souvenir; **Rei|se|an|tritt** **M** start of a/the journey; **vor/bei ~** before/at the start of a/the journey; **nach ~** after setting off; **Rei|se|apo|the|ke** **F** first-aid kit; **Rei|se|be|darf** **M** travel requisites *pl*; **Rei|se|be|glei|ter(in)** **M(F)** travelling *(Brit) or* traveling *(US)* companion; *(= Reiseleiter)* courier; *(für Kinder)* chaperon; **Rei|se|be|kannt|schaft** **F** acquaintance made while travelling *(Brit) or* traveling *(US)*; **Rei|se|be|richt** **M** report *or* account of one's journey; *(Buch)* travel story; *(Film)* travel film, travelogue *(Brit)*, travelog *(US)*; *(in Tagebuch)* holiday diary *(Brit)*, travel journal *(US)*; **Rei|se|be|schrän|kun|gen** **PL** travel restrictions *pl*; **Rei|se|be|schrei|bung** **F** description of one's travels; *(Liter)* traveller's *(Brit) or* traveler's *(US)* tale; *(Film)* travelogue *(Brit)*, travelog *(US)*; **Rei|se|bü|ro** **NT** travel agency; **Rei|se|bü|ro|kauf|frau** **F**, **Rei|se|bü|ro|kauf|mann** **M** travel agent; **Rei|se|car** **M** *(Sw)* coach *(Brit)*, bus; **Rei|se|ein|drü|cke** **PL** travel impressions *pl*; **Rei|se|er|leich|te|run|gen** **PL** easing of travel restrictions; **Rei|se|fach|kraft** **F** travel agent; **rei|se|fer|tig** **ADJ** ready (to go *or* leave); **~e Gäste warten bitte in der Hotelhalle** would guests who are ready to leave please wait in the hotel foyer; **Rei|se|fie|ber** **NT** *(fig)* travel nerves *pl*; **Rei|se|flug|hö|he** **F** cruising altitude; **Rei|se|füh|rer** **M** *(Buch)* guidebook; **Rei|se|füh|rer(in)** **M(F)** tour guide, courier; **Rei|se|ge|fähr|te** **M**, **Rei|se|ge|fähr|tin** **F** travelling *(Brit) or* traveling *(US)* companion; **Rei|se|geld** **NT** fare; **Rei|se|ge|neh|mi|gung** **F** travel permit; **Rei|se|ge|päck** **NT** luggage, baggage *(esp US, Aviat)*; **Rei|se|ge|päck|ver|si|che|rung** **F** baggage insurance; **Rei|se|ge|schwin|dig|keit** **F** cruising speed; **Rei|se|ge|sell|schaft** **F** (tourist) party; *(im Bus auch)* coach party; *(inf: = Veranstalter)* tour operator; **eine japanische ~** a party of Japanese tourists; **Rei|se|grup|pe** **F** (tourist) group *or* party; *(im Bus auch)* coach party; **Rei|se|kof|fer** **M** suitcase

Rei|se|kos|ten **PL** travelling *(Brit) or* traveling *(US)* expenses *pl*

Rei|se|kos|ten-: **Rei|se|kos|ten|ab|rech|nung** **F** claim for travelling *(Brit) or* traveling *(US)* expenses; **Rei|se|kos|ten|ver|gü|tung** **F** payment *or* reimbursement of travelling *(Brit) or* traveling *(US)* expenses; **die Firma übernimmt volle ~** the firm will pay all (your) travelling *(Brit) or* traveling *(US)* expenses; **250 Euro ~** 250 euros (in respect of) travelling *(Brit) or* traveling *(US)* expenses

Rei|se-: **Rei|se|kran|ken|ver|si|che|rung** **F** travel health(care) insurance; **Rei|se|krank|heit** **F** travel sickness; **Rei|se|land** **NT** holiday *(esp Brit) or* travel destination; **Rei|se|lei|ter(in)** **M(F)** tour guide, courier; **Rei|se|lei|tung** **F** *(das Leiten)* organization of a/the tourist party; *(= Reiseleiter)* courier(s); **möchten Sie die ~ für eine Englandtour übernehmen?** would you like to take a party for a tour of England?; **wegen schlechter ~** because of the poor way in which the party was run; **Rei|se|lek|tü|re** **F** reading matter (for a journey); **etw als ~ mitnehmen** to take sth to read on the journey; **Rei|se|lust** **F** travel urge, wanderlust; **mich packt die ~** I've got itchy feet *(inf)*, I've got the travel bug *(inf)*; **rei|se|lus|tig** **ADJ** fond of *or* keen on travel *or* travelling *(Brit) or* traveling *(US)*, travel-mad *(Brit inf)*, travel-crazy *(esp US inf)*; **Rei|se|mit|bring|sel** **NT** souvenir

rei|sen ['raizn] **VI** *aux sein* to travel; **in den Urlaub ~** to go away on holiday *(esp Brit) or* vacation *(US)*; **in etw** *(dat)* **~** *(Comm)* to travel in sth; **viel gereist sein** to have travelled *(Brit) or* traveled *(US)* a lot, to be well-travelled *(Brit) or* well-traveled *(US)*

Rei|sen|de(r) ['raizndə] **MF** *decl as adj* traveller *(Brit)*, traveler *(US)*; *(= Fahrgast)* passenger; *(Comm)* (commercial) traveller *(Brit) or* traveler *(US)*, travelling *(Brit) or* traveling *(US)* salesman/-woman

Rei|se-: **Rei|se|ne|ces|saire** **NT** *(für Nagelpflege)* travelling *(Brit) or* traveling *(US)* manicure set; *(= Nähzeug)* travelling *(Brit) or* traveling *(US)* sewing kit; **Rei|se|on|kel** **M** *(hum inf)* globetrotter *(hum)*; **Rei|se|pass** **M** passport; **Rei|se|plan** **M** *usu pl* travel plans *pl*; **meine Mutter schmiedet dauernd irgendwelche Reisepläne** my mother is always planning some journey *or* trip *or* other; **Rei|se|pros|pekt** **M** travel brochure; **Rei|se|pro|vi|ant** **M** food for the journey, provisions *pl (usu hum)*

Rei|se|rei [raizə'rai] **F -, -en** (endless) travelling *(Brit) or* traveling *(US)* around

Rei|se-: **Rei|se|rou|te** **F** route, itinerary; **Rei|se|rück|tritts|ver|si|che|rung** **F** travel *or* holiday *(esp Brit) or* vacation *(US)* cancellation insurance; **Rei|se|ruf** **M** personal message; **Rei|se|scheck** **M** traveller's cheque *(Brit)*, traveler's check *(US)*; **Rei|se|schil|de|rung** **F** = **Reisebericht**; **Rei|se|schreib|ma|schi|ne** **F** portable typewriter; **Rei|se|spe|sen** **PL** travelling *(Brit) or* traveling *(US)* expenses *pl*; **Rei|se|sti|pen|di|um** **NT** travelling *(Brit) or* traveling *(US)* scholarship; **Rei|se|tab|let|te** **F** travel sickness pill; **Rei|se|ta|ge|buch** **NT** travel *or* holiday diary *(Brit)*, travel journal *(US)*; **Rei|se|tan|te** **F** *(hum inf)* globetrotter *(hum)*; **Rei|se|ta|sche** **F** holdall, travelling *(Brit) or* traveling *(US)* bag; **Rei|se|un|ter|la|gen** **PL** travel documents *pl*; **Rei|se|ver|an|stal|ter(in)** **M(F)** tour operator; **Rei|se|ver|kehr** **M** holiday *(esp Brit) or* vacation *(US)* traffic; **Rei|se|ver|si|che|rung** **F** travel insurance; **Rei|se|vor|be|rei|tun|gen** **PL** travel preparations *pl*, preparations *pl* for a/the journey; **Rei|se|we|cker** **M** travelling *(Brit) or* traveling *(US)* alarm clock; **Rei|se|wel|le** **F** (surge of) holiday traffic; **die ~ setzt ein** the holiday season is under way; **die ~ nach Süden** the wave of holiday-makers *(Brit) or* vacationers *(US)* heading south, the surge of holiday-makers *(Brit) or* vacationers *(US)* to the south; **Rei|se|wet|ter** **NT** travelling *(Brit) or* traveling *(US)* weather; **Rei|se|wet|ter|be|richt** **M** holiday *(Brit) or* travel weather forecast; **Rei|se|zeit** **F** *(= günstige Zeit)* time for travelling *(Brit) or* traveling *(US)*; *(= Saison)* holiday *(esp Brit) or* vacation *(US)* period *or* season; *(= Fahrzeit, Fahrtdauer)* travelling *(Brit) or* travel time; **die beste ~ für Ägypten** the best time to go to Egypt; **Rei|se|ziel** **NT** destination

Reis-: **Reis|feld** **NT** paddy field; **Reis|holz** **NT** *(old)* brushwood, twigs *pl*

Rei|sig ['raizɪç] **NT -s,** *no pl* brushwood, twigs *pl*

Rei|sig-: **Rei|sig|be|sen** **M** besom; **Rei|sig|bün|del** **NT** bundle of twigs, faggot *(Brit)*

Reis-: **Reis|korn** **NT** *pl* **-körner** grain of rice; **Reis|mehl** **NT** ground rice; **Reis|pa|pier** **NT** *(Art, Cook)* rice paper

Reis|sa|lat **M** rice salad

Reiß|aus [rais'laus] **M ~ nehmen** *(inf)* to clear off *(Brit inf) or* out *(inf)*, to make oneself scarce *(inf)*

Reiß-: **Reiß|blei** ['rais-] **NT** graphite; **Reiß|brett** ['rais-] **NT** drawing board; **Reiß|brett|stift** ['rais-] **M** drawing pin *(Brit)*, thumb tack *(US)*

Reis-: **Reis|schleim** **M** rice water; **Reis|schnaps** **M** rice spirit

rei|ßen ['raisn] *pret* **riss** [rɪs], *ptp* **gerissen** [gə'rɪsn]

VT **a** *(= zerreißen)* to tear, to rip; **ein Loch ins Kleid ~** to tear *or* rip a hole in one's dress

b *(= abreißen, entreißen, herunterreißen, wegreißen)* to tear, to pull, to rip *(etw von etw* sth off sth); *(= mitreißen, zerren)* to pull, to drag; **jdn zu Boden ~** to pull *or* drag sb to the ground; **jdn/etw in die Tiefe ~** to pull *or* drag sb/sth down into the depths; **der Fluss hat die Brücke mit sich gerissen** the river swept the bridge away; **jdm etw aus den Händen/der Hand ~** to snatch sth from *or* out of sb's hands/hand; **jdn aus der Gefahr ~** to snatch sb from danger; **aus diesem Leben gerissen** snatched from this life; **jdn aus seinen Gedanken ~** to interrupt sb's thoughts; *(= aufmuntern)* to make sb snap out of it; **jdn aus dem Schlaf/seinen Träumen ~** to wake sb from his sleep/dreams; **in etw** *(dat)* **Lücken ~** to make gaps in sth; **jdn ins Verderben ~** to ruin sb; **jdn in den Tod ~** to claim sb's life; *(Flutwelle, Lawine)* to sweep sb to his/her death; **hin und her gerissen werden/sein** *(fig)* to be torn → **Zusammenhang**

c **etw an sich** *(acc)* **~** to seize sth; *Macht auch* to usurp sth; *Unterhaltung* to monopolize sth → **Nagel**

d *(Sport) (Gewichtheben)* to snatch; *(Hochsprung, Pferderennen)* to knock off *or* down

e *(= töten)* to take, to kill

f *(inf: = machen) Witze* to crack *(inf)*; *Possen* to play

g *(Aus sl)* **jdm eine ~** to clout sb (one) *(Brit inf)*, to slap sb; **einen Stern ~** to fall; **damit kannst du nichts ~** that's not going to impress anybody
h *(= Wunde beibringen)* **sich** *(dat)* **eine Wunde an etw** *(dat)* **~** to cut oneself on sth; **sich** *(dat)* **etw blutig ~** to tear sth open
i → **gerissen**
VI a *aux sein (= zerreißen)* to tear, to rip; *(Muskel, Bänder)* to tear; *(Seil)* to tear, to break, to snap; *(= Risse bekommen)* to crack; **mir ist die Kette/der Faden gerissen** my chain/thread has broken *or* snapped; **da riss mir die Geduld** *or* **der Geduldsfaden** then my patience gave out *or* snapped; **es reißt mir in allen Gliedern** *(inf)* I'm aching all over; **wenn alle Stricke** *or* **Stränge ~** *(fig inf)* if the worst comes to the worst, if all else fails
b *(= zerren) (an +dat* at) to pull, to tug; *(wütend)* to tear
c *(Sport) (Gewichtheben)* to snatch; *(Hochsprung)* to knock the bar off *or* down; *(Springreiten)* to knock the bar/top brick(s) *etc* off *or* down
VR a *(= sich verletzen)* to cut oneself *(an +dat* on)
b *(= sich losreißen)* to tear oneself
c *(inf)* **sich um jdn/etw ~** to scramble to get sb/sth

Rei|ßen ['raisn] NT **-s,** *no pl* **a** *(Gewichtheben)* snatch **b** *(inf: = Gliederreißen)* ache

rei|ßend ADJ *Fluss* torrential, raging; *Tier* rapacious; *Schmerzen* searing; *Verkauf, Absatz* massive; **~en Absatz finden** to sell like hot cakes *(inf)*

Rei|ßer ['raisɐ] M **-s, -** *(inf) (Theat, Film, Buch)* thriller; *(Ware)* hot item *(inf) or* line *(inf)*, big seller

rei|ße|risch ['raisərɪʃ] ADJ *Bericht, Titel* sensational ADV sensationally

Reiß-: Reiß|fe|der F *(Art)* (drawing) pen; **reiß|fest** ADJ tear-proof; **Reiß|fes|tig|keit** F (tensile) strength; **Reiß|koh|le** F *(Art)* charcoal; **Reiß|lei|ne** F ripcord; **Reiß|na|gel** M drawing pin *(Brit)*, thumbtack *(US)*; **Reiß|schie|ne** F T-square; **Reiß|stift** M drawing pin *(Brit)*, thumbtack *(US)*; **Reiß|ver|schluss** M zip (fastener) *(Brit)*, zipper *(US)*; **den ~ an etw** *(dat)* **zumachen** *or* **zuziehen** to zip sth up; **den ~ an etw** *(dat)* **aufmachen** *or* **aufziehen** to unzip sth; **Reiß|ver|schluss|prin|zip** NT principle of alternation; **Reiß|wolf** M shredder, shredding machine; **Reiß|wol|le** F shoddy; **Reiß|zahn** M fang, carnassial (tooth) *(spec)*; **Reiß|zeug** NT *pl* **-zeuge** drawing instruments *pl*; **Reiß|zir|kel** M drawing compass(es *pl*); **Reiß|zwe|cke** F drawing pin *(Brit)*, thumbtack *(US)*

Reis-: Reis|tag M day of eating only rice *(as part of a diet)*; **Reis|ter|ras|se** F rice terrace, terraced paddy field; **Reis|wein** M rice wine

Reit-: Reit|an|zug M riding habit; **Reit|bahn** F arena

rei|ten ['raitn] *pret* **ritt** [rɪt], *ptp* **ge|rit|ten** [gə'rɪtn] **VI** *aux sein* **a** *(auf Tier)* to ride; **auf etw** *(dat)* **~** to ride (on) sth; **auf einer Welle ~** *(lit, fig)* to ride (on) a wave; **im Schritt/Trab/Galopp ~** to ride at a walk/trot/gallop; **geritten kommen** to ride up, to come riding up; **das Schiff reitet vor Anker** *(Naut)* the ship is riding at anchor; **auf diesem Messer kann man (nach Köln) ~!** *(inf)* you couldn't cut butter with this knife!
b *(sl: = koitieren)* to ride *(sl)*
VT to ride; **Schritt/Trab/Galopp ~** to ride at a walk/trot/gallop; **ein schnelles Tempo ~** to ride at a fast pace; **sich** *(dat)* **Schwielen ~** to get saddle-sore; **jdn zu Boden** *or* **über den Haufen** *(inf)* **~** to trample sb down; **jdn in die Patsche** *or* **den Schlamassel ~** *(inf)* to get sb into a jam *(inf) or* mess; **Prinzipien ~** *(inf)* to insist on one's principles; **was hat dich denn da geritten, dass du so ausfällig geworden bist?** what was eating you to make you so obnoxious? *(inf)*

rei|tend ADJ mounted; **~e Artillerie** horse artillery

Rei|ter ['raitɐ] M **-s, - a** rider, horseman; *(Mil)* cavalryman; **ein Trupp preußischer ~** a troop of Prussian horse *(Brit) or* horses *(US)* **b** *(an Waage)* rider; *(= Karteireiter)* index tab **c** *(Mil: = Absperrblock)* barrier; **spanische ~** *pl* barbed-wire barricade

Rei|ter-: Rei|ter|an|griff M cavalry charge; **Rei|ter|auf|zug** M cavalcade

Rei|te|rei [raitə'rai] F **-, -en a** *(Mil)* cavalry **b** *(inf: = das Reiten)* riding

Rei|te|rin ['raitərɪn] F **-, -nen** rider, horsewoman

Rei|ter|re|gi|ment NT cavalry regiment

Rei|ters|mann M *pl* **-männer** *(liter)* horseman

Rei|ter|stand|bild NT equestrian statue

Reit-: Reit|ger|te F riding crop; **Reit|ho|se** F riding breeches *pl*; *(Hunt, Sport)* jodhpurs *pl*; **Reit|ja|cke** F riding jacket; **Reit|kleid** NT riding habit; **Reit|knecht** M *(old)* groom; **Reit|kunst** F horsemanship, riding skill; **Reit|peit|sche** F riding whip; **Reit|pferd** NT saddle horse, mount; **Reit|sat|tel** M (riding) saddle; **Reit|schu|le** F riding school; **Reit|sitz** M riding position; *(rittlings)* straddling position; **im ~ sitzen** to sit astride *(auf etw (dat)* sth); **Reit|sport** M (horse-)riding, equestrian sport *(form)*; **Reit|stall** M riding stable; **Reit|stie|fel** M riding boot; **Reit|stun|de** F riding lesson; **Reit|tier** NT mount, animal used for riding; **Reit|tur|nier** NT horse show; *(Geländereiten)* point-to-point; **Reit- und Fahr|tur|nier** NT horse show; **Reit|un|ter|richt** M riding lessons *pl*; **Reit|weg** M bridle path; **Reit|zeug** NT *pl* **-zeuge** riding equipment *or* things *pl*

Reiz [raits] M **-es, -e a** *(Physiol)* stimulus; **einen ~ auf etw** *(acc)* **ausüben** to act as a stimulus on sth
b *(= Verlockung)* attraction, appeal; *(des Unbekannten, Fremdartigen, der Großstadt)* lure, appeal; *(= Zauber)* charm; **der ~ des Neuen/des Verbotenen** the lure *or* appeal of novelty/forbidden fruits; **(auf jdn) einen ~ ausüben** to have *or* hold great attraction(s) (for sb); **das erhöht den ~** it adds to the thrill *or* pleasure; **einen/keinen ~ für jdn haben** to appeal/not to appeal to sb; **diese Idee hat auch ihren ~** this idea also has its attractions; **seinen** *or* **den ~ verlieren** to lose all one's/its charm; **an ~ verlieren** to be losing one's/its charm *or* attraction *or* appeal, to begin to pall; **seine ~e spielen lassen** to display one's charms; **weibliche ~e** feminine charms; **seine ~e zeigen** *(euph iro)* to reveal one's charms

Reiz-: Reiz|aus|lö|ser M stimulant; *(von krankhaftem Zustand)* irritant; **reiz|bar** ADJ *(= empfindlich)* sensitive, touchy *(inf)*; *(Med)* irritable, sensitive; *(= erregbar)* irritable; **leicht ~ sein** to be very sensitive/irritable; *(= ständig erregbar auch)* to be quick-tempered *or* hot-tempered; **~e Schwäche** *(Med)* irritability; *(fig)* sensitive spot *or* point; **Reiz|bar|keit** ['raitsbaːɐkait] F **-,** *no pl (= Empfindlichkeit)* sensitiveness, sensitivity, touchiness *(inf)*; *(Med)* irritability, sensitivity; *(= Erregbarkeit)* irritability; **Reiz|be|hand|lung** F *(Med)* stimulation therapy; **reiz|emp|fäng|lich** ADJ responsive; *(Physiol)* receptive to stimuli; **Reiz|emp|fäng|lich|keit** F responsiveness; *(Physiol)* receptiveness to stimuli

rei|zen ['raitsn] **VT a** *(Physiol)* to irritate; *(= stimulieren)* to stimulate
b *(= verlocken)* to appeal to; **jds Gaumen ~** to make sb's mouth water; **den Gaumen ~** to make one's mouth water; **jds Verlangen ~** to waken *or* rouse sb's desire; **es würde mich ja sehr ~, …** I'd love to …; **es reizt mich, nach Skye zu fahren** I've got an itch to go to Skye; **es hat mich ja immer sehr gereizt, …** I've always had an itch to …; **Ihr Angebot reizt mich sehr** I find your offer very tempting; **sie versteht es, Männer zu ~** she knows how to appeal to men; **was reizt Sie daran?** what do you like about it?
c *(= ärgern)* to annoy; *Tier* to tease, to annoy; *(= herausfordern)* to provoke; **ein gereiztes Nashorn …** a rhinoceros when provoked …; **jds Zorn ~** to arouse sb's anger; **jdn bis aufs Blut ~** to push sb to breaking point; **die Kinder reizten sie bis zur Weißglut** the children really made her see red → *auch* **gereizt**
d *(Skat)* to bid
VI a *(Med)* to irritate; *(= stimulieren)* to stimulate; **auf der Haut** *etc* **~** to irritate the skin *etc*; **der Rauch reizt zum Husten** the smoke makes you cough; **zum Widerspruch ~** to invite contradiction
b *(Cards)* to bid; **hoch ~** *(lit, fig)* to make a high bid

rei|zend ADJ charming, lovely; **es ist ~ (von dir)** it's charming *or* lovely (of you); **das ist ja ~** *(iro)* (that's) charming ADV *einrichten, schmücken* attractively; **~ aussehen** to look charming; **sie haben sich ~ um uns gekümmert** they took such good care of us; **er hat mich ~ umsorgt** he was so considerate to me

Reiz-: Reiz|fi|gur F controversial figure; **er ist eine politische ~** he is a politically controversial figure; **Reiz|gas** NT irritant gas; **Reiz|hus|ten** M chesty *(Brit) or* deep *(US)* cough; *(nervös)* nervous cough

Reiz|ker ['raitskɐ] M **-s, -** *(Bot)* saffron milk cap

Reiz-: Reiz|kli|ma NT bracing climate; *(fig)* charged atmosphere; **reiz|los** ADJ dull, uninspiring; **das ist ja ~** that's no fun; **Reiz|lo|sig|keit** F **-,** *no pl* dullness, uninspiring nature; **Reiz|mit|tel** NT *(Med)* stimulant; **Reiz|schwel|le** F *(Physiol)* stimulus *or* absolute threshold; *(Comm)* sales resistance; **Reiz|stoff** M irritant; **Reiz|the|ma** NT controversial issue; **Reiz|the|ra|pie** F *(Med)* stimulation therapy; **Reiz|über|flu|tung** F overstimulation

Rei|zung ['raitsʊŋ] F **-, -en a** *(Med)* stimulation; *(krankhaft)* irritation **b** *(= Herausforderung)* provocation

Reiz-: reiz|voll ADJ charming, delightful; *Aufgabe, Beruf* attractive; **die Aussicht ist nicht gerade ~** the prospect is not particularly enticing *or* appealing; **es wäre ~, mal dahin zu fahren** it would be lovely to go there some time; **es wäre ~, das ganz anders zu machen** it would be interesting to do it quite differently; **Reiz|wä|sche** F *(inf)* sexy underwear; **Reiz|wort** NT *pl* **-wörter** emotive word

Re|ka|pi|tu|la|ti|on [rekapitula'tsioːn] F recapitulation

re|ka|pi|tu|lie|ren [rekapitu'liːrən] *ptp* **rekapituliert** VT to recapitulate

Re|ke|lei [reːkə'lai] F **-, -en** *(inf)* lolling about *(Brit) or* around *(inf)*

re|keln ['reːkln] VR *(inf) (= sich herumlümmeln)* to loll about *(Brit) or* around *(inf)*; *(= sich strecken)* to stretch; **sich noch ein paar Minuten im Bett ~** to stretch out in bed for a few more minutes; **er rekelte sich im behaglichen Sessel vor dem Feuer** he snuggled down in the comfy chair in front of the fire; **die Katze rekelte sich genüsslich in der Sonne** the cat stretched out contentedly in the sun

Re|kla|ma|ti|on [reklama'tsioːn] F **-, -en** query; *(= Beschwerde)* complaint; **„spätere ~en können nicht anerkannt werden"** "please check your change/money immediately since mistakes cannot be rectified later"

Re|kla|me [re'klaːmə] F **-, -n a** *(= Werbewesen, Werbung)* advertising; **~ für jdn/etw machen** to advertise sb/sth; *(fig)* to do a bit of advertising for sb/sth; **mit jdm ~ machen** *(pej)* to show sb off; **~ mit etw machen** *(pej)* to show off about sth; **das ist keine gute ~ für die Firma** it's not a very good advertisement for the company **b** *(= Einzelwerbung)* advertisement, advert *(Brit inf)*, ad *(inf)*; *(esp TV, Rad)* commercial

Re|kla|me-: Re|kla|me|ar|ti|kel M free gift, sales gimmick *(often pej)*; *(= Probe)* (free) sample; **Re|kla|me|bro|schü|re** F (advertising)

brochure, handout; **~n** advertising literature; **Re|kla|me|feld|zug** M advertising campaign; **Re|kla|me|film** M advertising film, commercial; **Re|kla|me|pla|kat** NT (advertising) poster, advertisement; **Re|kla|me|rum|mel** M *(pej)* advertising frenzy *(inf)*; **Re|kla|me|schild** NT *pl* **-schilder** advertising sign; **Re|kla|me|sen|dung** F *(TV, Rad)* commercial break, commercials *pl*; *(= Postwurfsendung)* mailshot *(Brit)*, mailing; **eine verkappte ~** a disguised commercial; **Re|kla|me|spot** M (advertising) spot, commercial; **Re|kla|me|ta|fel** F hoarding; **Re|kla|me|trick** M sales trick; **Re|kla|me|trom|mel** F **die ~ für jdn/etw rühren** *(inf)* to beat the (big) drum for sb/sth; **Re|kla|me|zet|tel** M (advertising) leaflet, hand-out

re|kla|mie|ren [rekla'mi:rən] *ptp* **reklamiert** VI *(= Einspruch erheben)* to complain, to make a complaint; **bei jdm wegen etw ~** to complain to sb about sth; **die Rechnung kann nicht stimmen, da würde ich ~** the bill can't be right, I would query it VT **a** *(= bemängeln)* to complain about (*etw bei jdm* sth to sb); *(= infrage stellen) Rechnung, Rechnungsposten* to query (*etw bei jdm* sth with sb) **b** *(= in Anspruch nehmen)* to claim; **jdn/etw für sich ~** to lay claim to sb/sth, to claim sb/sth as one's own

re|kom|man|die|ren [rekɔman'di:rən] *ptp* **rekommandiert** VT *(Aus) Brief, Sendung* to register; **einen Brief rekommandiert aufgeben** to register a letter, to send a letter by registered post *(Brit)* or certified mail *(US)* VR *(obs, Aus)* **sich jdm ~** to present one's compliments to sb

Re|kom|pens [rekɔm'pɛns] **-, -en** [-zn] F, *(Aus)* **Re|kom|penz** *(Admin)* [rekɔm'pɛnts] F **-, -en** compensation

re|kon|stru|ie|ren [rekɔnstru'i:rən] *ptp* **rekonstruiert** VT to reconstruct

Re|kon|struk|ti|on [rekɔnstrʊk'tsio:n] F reconstruction

Re|kon|va|les|zent [rekɔnvalɛs'tsɛnt] M **-en, -en**, **Re|kon|va|les|zen|tin** [-'tsɛntɪn] F **-, -nen** convalescent

Re|kon|va|les|zenz [rekɔnvalɛs'tsɛnts] F **-, -en** convalescence

Re|kord [re'kɔrt] M **-s, -e** [-də] record; **einen ~ aufstellen** to set a record; **das Zeitalter der ~e** the age of superlatives; *(des Fortschritts)* the age of achievement

Re|kord- *in cpds* record; **Re|kord|bre|cher(in)** M(F) record breaker

Re|kor|der [re'kɔrdɐ] M **-s, -** (cassette) recorder

Re|kord-: **Re|kord|er|geb|nis** NT record result(s) *pl*; **Re|kord|hal|ter(in)** M(F), **Re|kord|in|ha|ber(in)** M(F) record holder; **Re|kord|lauf** M record(-breaking) run

Re|kord|ler [re'kɔrtlɐ] M **-s, -**, **Re|kord|le|rin** [-ərɪn] F **-, -nen** *(inf)* record holder

Re|kord-: **Re|kord|mar|ke** F *(Sport, fig)* record; **die bisherige ~ im Weitsprung war ...** till now the long-jump record stood at *or* was ...; **auf der ~ (von)** at the record *or (fig)* record level (of); **Re|kord|stand** M record; **Re|kord|tief** NT *(St Ex)* record *or* all-time low; **re|kord|ver|däch|tig** ADJ of seemingly record proportions; *Leistung* which must be a record; **sie ist heute ~** today she can beat the record; **Re|kord|ver|lust** M *(Fin, Comm)* record(-breaking) losses *pl*; **Re|kord|ver|such** M attempt on the/a record; **Re|kord|wert** M record figure *or* level; **~e erreichen** to reach record levels *or* an all-time record; **Re|kord|zeit** F record time

Rek|rut [re'kru:t] M **-en, -en**, **Rek|ru|tin** [-'kru:tɪn] F **-, -nen** *(Mil)* recruit

Rek|ru|ten-: **Rek|ru|ten|aus|bil|dung** F *(Mil)* basic training; **Rek|ru|ten|aus|he|bung** F *(old Mil)* levy *(old)*; **Rek|ru|ten|schu|le** F *(Sw Mil)* recruit school

rek|ru|tie|ren [rekru'ti:rən] *ptp* **rekrutiert** VT *(Mil, fig)* to recruit VR *(fig)* **sich ~ aus** to be recruited *or* drawn from

Rek|ru|tie|rung F **-, -en** recruitment, recruiting

Rek|ru|tie|rungs|stel|le F *(Mil)* recruiting centre *(Brit) or* center *(US)*

Re|kru|tie|rungs|ver|fah|ren NT recruitment process

Rek|ru|tin [-'kru:tɪn] F **-, -nen** *(Mil)* recruit

Rek|ta *pl von* **Rektum**

rek|tal [rɛk'ta:l] ADJ *(Med)* rectal ADV **~ einführen** to insert through the rectum; **die Temperatur ~ messen** to take the temperature rectally

Rek|ti|fi|ka|ti|on [rɛktifika'tsio:n] F **-, -en** **a** *(old)* correction; *(= Berichtigung)* correction, rectification **b** *(Chem, Math)* rectification

rek|ti|fi|zie|ren [rɛktifi'tsi:rən] *ptp* **rektifiziert** VT **a** *(old)* to correct; *(= berichtigen)* to correct, to rectify **b** *(Chem, Math)* to rectify

Rek|ti|on [rɛk'tsio:n] F **-, -en** *(Gram)* government; **die ~ eines Verbs** the case governed by a verb

Rek|tor ['rɛkto:ɐ] M **-s, Rektoren** [-'to:rən], **Rek|to|rin** [-'to:rɪn, 'rɛktorɪn] F **-, -nen** *(Sch)* head teacher, principal *(esp US)*; *(Univ)* vice chancellor *(Brit)*, rector *(US)*; *(von Fachhochschule)* principal; *(von kirchlicher Einrichtung)* rector

Rek|to|rat [rɛkto'ra:t] NT **-(e)s, -e** *(Sch) (= Amt, Amtszeit)* headship, principalship *(esp US)*; *(= Zimmer)* headmaster's/headmistress's study, principal's room *(esp US)*; *(Univ)* vice chancellorship *(Brit)*, rectorship *(US)*; vice chancellor's *(Brit) or* rector's *(US)* office; *(in Fachhochschule)* principalship; principal's office

Rek|to|rats|re|de F *(Univ)* (vice chancellor's *(Brit) or* rector's *(US)*) inaugural address

Rek|tum ['rɛktʊm] NT **-s, Rekta** [-ta] *(form)* rectum

re|kur|rie|ren [rekʊ'ri:rən] *ptp* **rekurriert** VI **a** *(old Jur)* to appeal **b** *(liter. = auf etw zurückkommen)* to return (*auf +acc* to)

Re|kurs [re'kʊrs] M **-es, -e** [-zə] *(old Jur)* appeal

Rel. *abbr von* **Religion**

Re|lais [rə'lɛ:] NT **-, -** [rə'lɛ:s, rə'lɛ:s] *(Elec)* relay

Re|lais|schal|tung [rə'lɛ:-] F *(Elec)* relay circuit *or* connection

Re|lais|sta|ti|on [rə'lɛ:-] F *(Elec)* relay station

Re|la|ti|on [rela'tsio:n] F **-, -en** relation; **in einer/keiner ~ zu etw stehen** to bear some/no relation to sth; **etw in ~ (zu** *or* **mit etw) setzen** to compare sth (to *or* with sth)

re|la|ti|o|nal [relatsio'na:l] *(Comput)* ADJ relational; **~e Datenbank** relational database ADV relationally

re|la|tiv [rela'ti:f] ADJ relative; **~e Mehrheit** *(Parl)* simple majority; **alles ist ~** everything is relative ADV relatively

Re|la|tiv [rela'ti:f] NT **-s, -e** [-və] relative pronoun

Re|la|tiv|ad|verb NT relative adverb

re|la|ti|vie|ren [relati'vi:rən] *ptp* **relativiert** *(geh)* VT *Begriff, Behauptung etc* to qualify VI to see things *or* to think in relative terms VR to become relative

Re|la|ti|vis|mus [relati'vɪsmʊs] M **-**, *no pl* relativism

re|la|ti|vis|tisch [relati'vɪstɪʃ] ADJ relativistic

Re|la|ti|vi|tät [relativi'tɛ:t] F **-**, *no pl* relativity

Re|la|ti|vi|täts|the|o|rie F theory of relativity, relativity theory *no art*

Re|la|tiv-: **Re|la|tiv|pro|no|men** NT relative pronoun; **Re|la|tiv|satz** M relative clause

Re|la|ti|vum [rela'ti:vʊm] NT **-s, Relativa** [-va] *(form)* relative pronoun

Re|launch ['ri:lo:ntʃ] M OR NT **-(e)s, -(e)s** relaunch

re|laxed *(inf)* ADJ *pred* relaxed, laid-back *(inf)*; **(ganz) ~ sein** to feel *or* be (totally) relaxed ADV **~ auf etw** *(acc)* **reagieren** to be laid-back about sth *(inf)*; **an etw** *(acc)* **~ herangehen** to be laid-back *(inf) or* relaxed about tackling sth; **sie ist alles andere als ~ in die Prüfung gegangen** she was anything but relaxed when she went to sit *(Brit) or* take her exam

re|la|xen [ri'lɛksn] *ptp* **relaxt** VI *(inf)* to take it easy *(inf)*, to relax

re|laxt [ri'lɛkst] ADJ *attr (inf)* relaxed, laid-back *(inf)*; **eine ~e Atmosphäre** a relaxed atmosphere ADV **~ auf etw** *(acc)* **reagieren** to be laid-back about sth *(inf)*; **an etw** *(acc)* **~ herangehen** to be laid-back *(inf) or* relaxed about tackling sth; **sie ist alles andere als ~ in die Prüfung gegangen** she was anything but relaxed when she went to sit *(Brit) or* take her exam

Re|le|ga|ti|on [relega'tsio:n] F **-, -en** *(form)* expulsion

re|le|gie|ren [rele'gi:rən] *ptp* **relegiert** VT *(form)* to expel

re|le|vant [rele'vant] ADJ relevant

Re|le|vanz [rele'vants] F **-**, *no pl* relevance

Re|li ['rɛli] F **-**, *no pl (Sch inf: = Religion)* RE

Re|li|ef [reli'ɛf] NT **-s, -s** *or* **-e** relief

Re|li|ef-: **Re|li|ef|druck** M *pl* **-drucke** relief printing; **Re|li|ef|kar|te** F relief map

Re|li|gi|on [reli'gio:n] F **-, -en** *(lit, fig)* religion; *(Schulfach)* religious instruction *or* education, RI, RE; **seine ~ ausüben** to practise *(Brit) or* practice *(US)* one's religion; **~ sehr gut, Kopfrechnen schwach** *(inf)* virtuous but stupid

Re|li|gi|ons-: **Re|li|gi|ons|be|kennt|nis** NT denomination; **Re|li|gi|ons|buch** NT religion *or* religious textbook; **Re|li|gi|ons|er|satz** M substitute for religion; **Re|li|gi|ons|frei|heit** F religious freedom, freedom of worship; **Re|li|gi|ons|frie|de(n)** M religious peace; **Re|li|gi|ons|füh|rer(in)** M(F) religious leader; **Re|li|gi|ons|ge|mein|schaft** F religious community; **Re|li|gi|ons|ge|schich|te** F history of religion; **Re|li|gi|ons|krieg** M religious war, war of religion; **Re|li|gi|ons|leh|re** F religious education *or* instruction; **Re|li|gi|ons|leh|rer(in)** M(F) teacher of religious education, RI *or* RE teacher; **re|li|gi|ons|los** ADJ not religious; *(= bekenntnislos)* nondenominational; **Re|li|gi|ons|stif|ter(in)** M(F) founder of a religion; **Re|li|gi|ons|streit** M religious controversy; **Re|li|gi|ons|stun|de** F religious education *or* instruction lesson, RI *or* RE lesson; **Re|li|gi|ons|un|ter|richt** M religious education *or* instruction; *(Sch)* religious education *or* instruction lesson, RE *or* RI lesson; **Re|li|gi|ons|wis|sen|schaft** F religious studies *pl*; **vergleichende ~** comparative religion; **Re|li|gi|ons|zu|ge|hö|rig|keit** F religious affiliation, religion

re|li|gi|ös [reli'giø:s] ADJ religious ADV **~ motiviert** religiously motivated *or* inspired; **sie werden ~ verfolgt** they are being persecuted because of their religion; **~ erzogen werden** to have *or* receive a religious upbringing

Re|li|gi|o|si|tät [religiozi'tɛ:t] F **-**, *no pl* religiousness; **ein Mensch von tiefer ~** a deeply religious person

Re|likt [re'lɪkt] NT **-(e)s, -e** relic

Re|ling ['re:lɪŋ] F **-, -s** *or* **-e** *(Naut)* (deck) rail

Re|li|qui|ar [relikvi'a:ɐ] NT **-s, -e** reliquary

Re|li|quie [re'li:kviə] F **-, -n** relic

Re|li|qui|en|schrein M reliquary

Re|lo|cate-Funk|ti|on [ri:lo'ke:t-] F relocate function

Rem NT, **rem** [rɛm] NT **-, -** *(= Einheit)* rem

Re|make ['ri:me:k] NT **-s, -s** remake

Re|ma|nenz [rema'nɛnts] F **-**, *no pl (Phys)* remanence, residual magnetism

Rem|bours [rã'bu:ɐ] M **-, -** *(Fin)* reimbursement, payment

Rem|bours|ge|schäft [rã'bu:ɐ-] NT *(Fin)* documentary credit trading; *(Einzelgeschäft)* documentary credit transaction

Re|mig|rant [remi'grant] M **-en, -en**, **Re|mig|ran|tin** [-'grantɪn] F **-, -nen** returned emigrant; *(= Heimkehrender)* returning emigrant

re|mi|li|ta|ri|sie|ren [remilitari'zi:rən] *ptp* **remilitarisiert** VTI to remilitarize

Re|mi|nis|zenz [reminɪs'tsɛnts] F **-, -en** *(geh) (= Erinnerung)* memory (*an +acc* of); *(= Ähnlichkeit)* similarity, resemblance (*an +acc* to); **ich habe**

aus seinem Vortrag ~en an Spengler herausgehört I found his lecture in some ways reminiscent of Spengler

re|mis [rə'mi:] ADJ *inv* drawn; **~ spielen** to draw; **die Partie ist ~** the game has ended in a draw *or* has been drawn; **die Vereine trennten sich ~** the clubs held each other to a draw

Re|mis [rə'mi:] NT **- -** *or* **-en** [rə'mi:s, rə'mi:zn] **a** [rə'mi:s, rə'mi:zn] *(Chess, Sport)* draw; **gegen jdn ein ~ erzielen** to hold sb to a draw **b** *(fig)* stalemate, deadlock; **mit einem ~** in stalemate *or* deadlock

Re|mi|se [rə'mi:zə] F **-, -n** *(old)* shed, outbuilding

Re|mis|si|on [remi'sio:n] F **-, -en** *(Med old: = Erlass)* remission; *(Comm)* remittance

Re|mit|ten|de [remɪ'tɛndə] F **-, -n** *(Comm)* return

Re|mit|tent [remɪ'tɛnt] M **-en, -en**, **Re|mit|ten|tin** [-'tɛntɪn] F **-, -nen** *(Fin)* payee

re|mit|tie|ren [remɪ'ti:rən] *ptp* **remittiert** VT *(Comm) Waren* to return; *Geld* to remit VI *(Med: = nachlassen)* to remit *(form)*

Rem|mi|dem|mi ['rɛmi'dɛmi] NT **-s**, *no pl (inf) (= Krach)* row, rumpus *(inf)*; *(= Trubel)* to-do *(inf)*; **~ machen** to make a row *etc*

Re|mou|la|de [remu'la:də] F **-, -n**, **Re|mou|la|den|so|ße** F *(Cook)* remoulade

Rem|pe|lei [rɛmpə'lai] F **-, -en** *(inf)* barging *(inf)*, jostling, pushing and shoving; *(im Sport)* pushing

rem|peln ['rɛmpln] *(inf)* VT to barge *(jdn into sb) (inf)*, to jostle, to elbow; *(im Sport)* to barge *(jdn into sb) (inf)*; *(= foulen)* to push VI to barge *(inf)*, to jostle; *(Sport)* to barge *(inf)*; *(= foulen)* to push

REM-Pha|se ['rɛm-] F REM sleep

Rem|pler ['rɛmplɐ] M *(inf: = Stoß)* push, shove

Rem(p)|ter ['rɛm(p)tɐ] M **-s, -** *(in Klöstern)* refectory; *(in Burgen)* banquet(ing) hall

Re|mu|ne|ra|ti|on [remunera'tsio:n] F **-, -en** *(Aus) (= Gratifikation)* bonus; *(= Vergütung)* remuneration

Ren [rɛn, re:n] NT **-s, -e** *or* **-s** ['re:nə, rɛns] reindeer

Re|nais|sance [rənɛ'sã:s] F **-, -en** **a** *(Hist)* renaissance **b** *(fig)* revival, rebirth; *(von Kunstformen)* renaissance, revival; **eine ~ erleben** to enjoy *or* experience a revival

Re|nais|sance- *in cpds* renaissance; **Re|nais|sance|mensch** M renaissance man *no art*

Re|na|tu|rie|rung [renatu'ri:rʊŋ] F **-, -en** **die ~ von Flüssen** the restoration of rivers to their natural state

Ren|dez|vous [rãde'vu:, 'rã:devu] NT **-, -** [-'vu:s, -'vu:s] rendezvous *(liter, hum)*, date *(inf)*; *(Space)* rendezvous

Ren|dez|vous|ma|nö|ver [rãde'vu:-] NT *(Space)* rendezvous manoeuvre *(Brit) or* maneuver *(US)*

Ren|di|te [rɛn'di:tə] F **-, -n** *(Fin)* yield, return on capital

Re|ne|gat [rene'ga:t] M **-en, -en**, **Re|ne|ga|tin** [-'ga:tɪn] F **-, -nen** *(Eccl, Pol)* renegade

Re|ne|klo|de [re:nə'klo:də] F **-, -n** greengage

Re|net|te [re'nɛtə] F **-, -n** rennet

re|ni|tent [reni'tɛnt] ADJ refractory, defiant ADV defiantly

Re|ni|tenz [reni'tɛnts] F **-, -en** refractoriness, defiance

Ren|ke ['rɛŋkə] F **-, -n** whitefish

Renn- *in cpds* race; **Renn|bahn** F (race)track; **Renn|boot** NT powerboat

ren|nen ['rɛnən] *pret* **rannte** ['rantə], *ptp* **gerannt** [gə'rant] VI *aux sein* **a** *(= schnell laufen)* to run; *(Sport) (Mensch, Tier)* to run, to race; *(Auto etc)* to race; **um die Wette ~** to have a race; **(aufs Klo) ~** *(inf)* to run (to the loo *(Brit inf)* or bathroom *(US)*); **(mit offenen Augen) ins Verderben** *or* **Unglück ~** to rush into disaster (with one's eyes wide open) **b** *(inf: = hingehen)* to run (off); **sie rennt wegen jeder Kleinigkeit zum Chef** she goes running (off) to the boss at the slightest little thing; **er rennt zu jedem Fußballspiel** he goes to every football match; **sie rennt jeden Tag in die Kirche** she goes running off to church every day **c** *(= stoßen)* **an** *or* **gegen jdn/etw ~** to run *or* bump *or* bang into sb/sth; **er rannte mit dem Kopf gegen ...** he bumped *or* banged his head against ...; **mit dem Kopf durch** *or* **gegen die Wand ~** *(fig)* to bang one's head against a brick wall VT **a** *aux haben or sein (Sport)* to run; **einen neuen Rekord über 100 Meter ~** to set a new record for the 100 metres *(Brit) or* meters *(US)* **b** **jdn zu Boden** *or* **über den Haufen ~** to knock sb down *or* over; **sich** *(dat)* **(an etw) ein Loch in den Kopf ~** to crack one's head (against sth) **c** *(= stoßen) Messer etc* to run

Ren|nen ['rɛnən] NT **-s, -** running; *(Sport) (Vorgang)* racing; *(Veranstaltung)* race; *(fig)* race *(um* for); **totes ~** dead heat; **gehst du zum ~?** *(bei Pferderennen, Hunderennen etc)* are you going to the races?, are you going racing?; *(bei Autorennen etc)* are you going to the racing?; **gut im ~ liegen** *(lit, fig)* to be well-placed; **das ~ ist gelaufen** *(lit)* the race is over; *(fig)* it's all over; **das ~ machen** *(lit, fig)* to win (the race); **aus dem ~ ausscheiden** *(lit, fig)* to drop out; **jdn aus dem ~ werfen** *(lit)* to put sb out of the race; *(fig)* to put sb out of the running; **das ~ aufgeben** *(lit)* to drop out (of the race); *(fig auch)* to throw in the towel

Ren|ner ['rɛnɐ] M **-s, -** *(inf: = Verkaufsschlager)* winner, world-beater *(Brit)*; *(Pferd auch)* flier

Ren|ne|rei [rɛnə'rai] F **-, -en** *(inf) (lit, fig: = das Herumrennen)* running around; *(= Hetze)* mad chase *(inf)*; **die ~, bis ich endlich meinen Pass gekriegt habe** all that running around until I finally got my passport; **nach meinem Umzug hatte ich tagelange ~en** after moving I was running around for days; **diese ~ zum Klo** this running to the loo *(Brit inf) or* bathroom *(US)*

Renn-: **Renn|fah|rer(in)** M(F) *(= Radrennfahrer)* racing cyclist; *(= Motorradrennfahrer)* racing motorcyclist; *(= Autorennfahrer)* racing driver; **Renn|jacht** F racing yacht; **Renn|lei|ter(in)** M(F) race organizer; **Renn|lei|tung** F organization of a race meeting; *(= die Rennleiter)* race organizers *pl*; **Renn|lenk|stan|ge** F drop handlebars *pl*; **Renn|ma|schi|ne** F racer; **Renn|pferd** NT racehorse; **aus einem Ackergaul kann man kein ~ machen** *(prov)* you can't make a silk purse out of a sow's ear *(Prov)*; **Renn|pis|te** F (race)track; **Renn|platz** M racecourse; **Renn|rad** NT racing bicycle *or* bike *(inf)*; **Renn|ro|deln** NT **-s**, *no pl* bob (-sleigh) racing; **Renn|schlit|ten** M bob (-sleigh), bobsled; **Renn|schu|he** PL *(Sport)* spikes *pl*; **Renn|sport** M racing; **Renn|stall** M *(Tiere, Zucht)* stable; *(Rennsport, Radrennen)* team; **Renn|stre|cke** F *(= Rennbahn)* (race)-track; *(= zu laufende Strecke)* course, distance; **eine ~ von 100km** a 100 km course, a distance of 100km; **Renn|tag** M race day; **das Rennen erstreckt sich über drei ~e** the race is a three-day event; **Renn|ver|an|stal|tung** F races *pl*, race meeting; **Renn|wa|gen** M racing car; **Renn|wet|te** F bet (on a race); **Ergebnisse der ~n** betting results

Re|nom|mee [renɔ'me:] NT **-s, -s** reputation, name

Re|nom|mier|club M posh club *(inf)*

re|nom|mie|ren [renɔ'mi:rən] *ptp* **renommiert** VI to show off, to swank *(Brit inf)*; *(= aufschneiden auch)* to brag

Re|nom|mier-: **Re|nom|mier|fi|gur** F famous name; **Re|nom|mier|klub** M posh club *(inf)*; **Re|nom|mier|schu|le** F *(inf)* posh *or* classy school *(inf)*; **Re|nom|mier|stück** NT pride and joy, showpiece

re|nom|miert [renɔ'mi:ɐt] ADJ *(wegen* for) renowned, famed, famous

re|no|vie|ren [reno'vi:rən] *ptp* **renoviert** VT to renovate; *(= tapezieren etc)* to redecorate, to do up *(inf)*

Re|no|vie|rung F **-, -en** renovation

ren|ta|bel [rɛn'ta:bl] ADJ profitable; **es ist nicht ~, das reparieren zu lassen** it is not worth (-while) having it repaired; **das ist eine rentable Sache** *or* **Angelegenheit** it will pay (off) ADV profitably; **~ wirtschaften** *(= gut einteilen)* to spend one's money sensibly; *(= mit Gewinn arbeiten)* to make *or* show a profit; **~ kalkulieren** *(= gut einteilen)* to budget sensibly; *(= Gewinn einplanen)* to think in terms of profit(s), to go for profit(s)

Ren|ta|bi|li|tät [rɛntabili'tɛ:t] F **-, -en** profitability

Ren|ta|bi|li|täts-: **Ren|ta|bi|li|täts|ge|sichts|punk|te** PL profitability point of view; **Ren|ta|bi|li|täts|gren|ze** F limit of profitability; **Ren|ta|bi|li|täts|prü|fung** F investigation into profitability; **Ren|ta|bi|li|täts|rech|nung** F profitability calculation; **Ren|ta|bi|li|täts|schwel|le** F breakeven point

Rent|amt NT *(old Admin)* bursary

Ren|te ['rɛntə] F **-, -n** *(= Altersrente, Invalidenrente)* pension; *(aus Versicherung, = Lebensrente)* annuity; *(aus Vermögen)* income; *(St Ex: = Rentenpapier)* fixed-interest security; **in** *or* **auf** *(inf)* **~ gehen** to start drawing one's pension; **in** *or* **auf** *(inf)* **~ sein** to be on a pension; **jdn in ~ schicken** *(inf)* to pension sb off *(inf)*

Ren|ten-: **Ren|ten|al|ter** NT retirement age; **Ren|ten|an|he|bung** F pension increase; **Ren|ten|an|pas|sung** F tying of pensions to the national average wage; **Ren|ten|an|pas|sungs|ge|setz** NT law tying pensions to the national average wage; **Ren|ten|an|spruch** M pension entitlement; **Ren|ten|ba|sis** F annuity basis; **Ren|ten|bei|trag** M pension contribution; **ständig steigende Rentenbeiträge** *pl* ever-increasing pension contributions *pl*, steady increase in pension contributions; **Ren|ten|be|mes|sungs|grund|la|ge** F basis of calculation of a pension/the pensions; **Ren|ten|be|rech|nung** F calculation of a pension/the pensions; **ren|ten|be|rech|tigt** ADJ entitled to a pension; *Alter* pensionable; **Ren|ten|be|scheid** M notice of the amount of one's pension; **Ren|ten|be|steu|e|rung** F taxation of pensions; **Ren|ten|be|zü|ger(in)** M(F) *(Sw)* pensioner; **Ren|ten|ein|tritts|al|ter** NT retirement age; **gesetzliches/tatsächliches ~** statutory/actual retirement age; **Ren|ten|emp|fän|ger(in)** M(F) pensioner; **Ren|ten|er|hö|hung** F pension increase; **Ren|ten|fi|nan|zie|rung** F financing of pensions; **Ren|ten|fonds** M fixed-income fund; **Ren|ten|for|mel** F *pension formula*; **Ren|ten|kas|se** F pension fund *(paying out pensions)*; *(= Rentenversicherung)* pension scheme *(Brit)*, retirement plan *(US)*; **Milliardenloch in der ~** pension fund announces *or* expects *etc* multibillion deficit; **Ren|ten|mark** F *(Hist)* rentenmark; **Ren|ten|markt** M market in fixed-interest securities; **Ren|ten|ni|veau** NT pensions level; **Ren|ten|op|ti|ons|han|del** M bond option dealing; **Ren|ten|pa|pier** NT fixed-interest security; **ren|ten|pflich|tig** [-pflɪçtɪç] ADJ responsible for paying a pension; **Ren|ten|po|li|tik** F pension policy; **Ren|ten|re|form** F reform of pensions; **Ren|ten|si|che|rung** F safeguarding of pensions; **Ren|ten|sys|tem** NT pensions system; **Ren|ten|ver|si|che|rung** F pension scheme *(Brit)*, retirement plan *(US)*; **Ren|ten|ver|si|che|rungs|bei|trag** M pension scheme *(Brit) or* retirement plan *(US)* contribution; **Ren|ten|ver|si|che|rungs|trä|ger** M provider of a pension scheme *(Brit) or* retirement plan *(US)*; **Ren|ten|wer|te** PL fixed-interest securities *pl*; **Ren|ten|zahl|tag** M pension day

> **RENTENVERSICHERUNG**
>
> Many Germans are provided for in their old age by the state pension **Rentenversicherung**, to which all employees are required to contribute. The **Rentenversicherung** is funded by the contributions of employees and employers, and by a subsidy from the Federal Government. The amount of the pension depends on the period and level of contribution, with allowances made for time spent in education or bringing up children. In addition, many firms pay a **Betriebsrente** (occupational pension) to employees.

Ren|tier [ˈrɛntiːɐ, ˈreːntiːɐ] **NT** *(Zool)* reindeer

Ren|ti|er [rɛnˈtieː] **M -s, -s** *(old)* man of private means, gentleman of leisure; *(mit staatlicher Rente)* pensioner

ren|tie|ren [rɛnˈtiːrən] *ptp* **rentiert** VI to be worthwhile; *(Wertpapier)* to yield a return VR to be worthwhile; *(Geschäft, Unternehmen etc auch, Maschine)* to pay; **es hat sich doch rentiert, dass ich noch ein bisschen dageblieben bin** it was worth(while) staying on a bit; **das rentiert sich nicht** it's not worth it; **ein Auto rentiert sich für mich nicht** it's not worth my having a car

ren|tier|lich [rɛnˈtiːɐlɪç] **ADJ** profitable

Rent|ner [ˈrɛntnɐ] **M -s, -**, **Rent|ne|rin** [-ərɪn] **F -, -nen** pensioner; *(= Altersrentner auch)* senior citizen, old age pensioner *(Brit)*

re|ok|ku|pie|ren [reːɔkuˈpiːrən] *ptp* **reokkupiert** VT *(Mil)* to reoccupy

Re|or|ga|ni|sa|ti|on [reːɔrganizaˈtsioːn] **F**, **Re|or|ga|ni|sie|rung** **F -, -en** reorganization

re|or|ga|ni|sie|ren [reːɔrganiˈziːrən] *ptp* **reorganisiert** VT to reorganize

Rep [rɛp] **M -s, -s(e)** *usu pl (inf) abbr von* **Republikaner** Republican, *member of the right-wing German Republikaner party*

re|pa|ra|bel [repaˈraːbl] **ADJ** repairable

Re|pa|ra|ti|on [reparaˈtsioːn] **F -, -en** *usu pl* reparations *pl*; **~en leisten** *or* **zahlen** to pay *or* make reparations

Re|pa|ra|ti|ons-: **Re|pa|ra|ti|ons|aus|schuss** **M** reparations committee; **Re|pa|ra|ti|ons|zah|lun|gen** **PL** reparations *pl*

Re|pa|ra|tur [reparaˈtuːɐ] **F -, -en** repair; **~en am Auto** car repairs; **~en am Haus vornehmen** *or* **ausführen** to do some repairs on *or* to the house; **in ~** being repaired; **er übernimmt ~en von Schuhen** he does shoe repairs, he mends shoes; **etw in ~ geben** to have sth repaired *or* mended; *Auto, Fahrrad* to have sth repaired

Re|pa|ra|tur-: **re|pa|ra|tur|an|fäl|lig** **ADJ** prone to break down; **Re|pa|ra|tur|ar|bei|ten** **PL** repairs *pl*, repair work *no pl*; **re|pa|ra|tur|be|dürf|tig** **ADJ** in need of repair; **Re|pa|ra|tur|kos|ten** **PL** repair costs *pl*; **Re|pa|ra|tur|set** **NT** repair kit; **Re|pa|ra|tur|werk|statt** **F** workshop; *(= Autowerkstatt)* garage, auto repair shop *(US)*

re|pa|rie|ren [repaˈriːrən] *ptp* **repariert** VT to repair, to mend; *Auto, Fahrrad* to repair; **etw notdürftig ~** to repair sth in a makeshift way

Re|par|tie|rung [reparˈtiːrʊŋ] **F -, -en** *(Fin)* scaling down, allotment

re|pat|ri|ie|ren [repatriˈiːrən] *ptp* **repatriiert** VT **a** *(= wiedereinbürgern)* to renaturalize **b** *(= heimschicken)* to repatriate

Re|pat|ri|ie|rung **F -, -en** *(= Einbürgerung)* renaturalization; *(= Zurückschicken)* repatriation

Re|per|toire [repɛrˈtoaːɐ] **NT -s, -s** repertory, repertoire *(auch fig)*

Re|per|toire-: **Re|per|toire|stück** **NT** repertory *or* stock play; **Re|per|toire|the|a|ter** **NT** repertory theatre *(Brit) or* theater *(US)*, rep *(inf)*

Re|pe|tent [repeˈtɛnt] **M -en, -en**, **Re|pe|ten|tin** [-ˈtɛntɪn] **F -, -nen** *(Aus form) pupil who has to repeat a year*

re|pe|tie|ren [repeˈtiːrən] *ptp* **repetiert** VT **a** *(old) Stoff, Vokabeln* to revise **b** *(= wiederholen)* to repeat; *(Aus form) Klasse* to repeat, to take again; *Jahr* to repeat, to stay down for VI **a** *(old)* to do revision, to revise **b** *(Aus form)* to stay down, to repeat a class

Re|pe|tier|ge|wehr **NT** *(old)* repeating rifle

Re|pe|ti|ti|on [repetiˈtsioːn] **F -, -en** **a** *(old: von Stoff etc)* revision **b** *(= Wiederholung)* repetition

Re|pe|ti|tor [repeˈtiːtoːɐ] **M -s, Repetitoren** [-ˈtoːrən], **Re|pe|ti|to|rin** [-ˈtoːrɪn] **F -, -nen** *(Univ)* coach, tutor, crammer *(esp Brit inf)*

Re|pe|ti|to|ri|um [repetiˈtoːriʊm] **NT -s, Repetitorien** [-riən] *(Buch)* revision book; *(Unterricht)* revision *or* cramming *(Brit inf) or* tutorial *(US)* course

Rep|lik [reˈpliːk] **F -, -en** **a** *(Jur)* replication; *(fig geh)* riposte, reply **b** *(Art)* replica

rep|li|zie|ren [repliˈtsiːrən] *ptp* **repliziert** VT **a** *auch vi (Jur)* to reply; *(fig geh)* to ripost, to reply **b** *(Art)* to make a replica of

Re|port [reˈpɔrt] **M -(e)s, -e** **a** report **b** *(Fin)* contango

Re|por|ta|ge [repɔrˈtaːʒə] **F -, -n** report

Re|por|ter [reˈpɔrtɐ] **M -s, -**, **Re|por|te|rin** [-ərɪn] **F -, -nen** reporter; **Sport-/Wirtschaftsreporter** sports/economics correspondent

Re|port|ge|schäft **NT** *(Fin)* contango

Re|po|si|ti|on [repoziˈtsioːn] **F** *(Med)* resetting

re|prä|sen|ta|bel [reprɛzɛnˈtaːbl] **ADJ** impressive, prestigious; *Frau* (highly) presentable

Re|prä|sen|tant [reprɛzɛnˈtant] **M -en, -en**, **Re|prä|sen|tan|tin** [-ˈtantɪn] **F -, -nen** representative

Re|prä|sen|tan|ten|haus **NT** *(US Pol)* House of Representatives

Re|prä|sen|tanz [reprɛzɛnˈtants] **F -, -en** **a** *(Pol)* representation **b** *(= Geschäftsvertretung)* branch

Re|prä|sen|ta|ti|on [reprɛzɛntaˈtsioːn] **F** **a** *(= Vertretung, Vorhandensein)* representation; *(von Firma)* office **b** *(= Darstellung)* **der ~ dienen** to create a good image, to have good prestige value, to make the right impression; **die Diplomatenfrau fand die Pflichten der ~ sehr anstrengend** the diplomat's wife found her life of official functions very tiring; **die einzige Funktion des Monarchen ist heute die ~** the sole function of the monarch today is that of an official figurehead

re|prä|sen|ta|tiv [reprɛzɛntaˈtiːf] ADJ **a** *(= stellvertretend, typisch)* representative *(für* of); **~e Umfrage** representative survey **b** *Haus, Auto, Ausstattung* prestigious; *Erscheinung* presentable; **die ~en Pflichten eines Botschafters** the social duties of an ambassador; **der ~e Aufwand des Königshauses/der Firma** the expenditure for maintaining the royal household's/company's image; **ein großes Konferenzzimmer für ~e Zwecke** a large conference room to provide a suitable setting for functions ADV *bauen* prestigiously; **sie sind sehr ~ eingerichtet** their decor is very impressive

Re|prä|sen|ta|tiv|um|fra|ge **F** representative survey

re|prä|sen|tie|ren [reprɛzɛnˈtiːrən] *ptp* **repräsentiert** VT to represent VI to perform official duties

Re|pres|sa|lie [reprɛˈsaːliə] **F -, -n** reprisal; **~n anwenden** *or* **ergreifen** to take reprisals

Re|pres|si|on [reprɛˈsioːn] **F -, -en** repression

re|pres|si|ons|frei **ADJ** free of repression

re|pres|siv [reprɛˈsiːf] **ADJ** repressive

Re|pri|se [reˈpriːzə] **F -, -n** **a** *(Mus)* recapitulation; *(TV, Rad)* repeat; *(Film, Theat)* rerun; *(nach längerer Zeit)* revival **b** *(Mil)* recapture

Re|pri|va|ti|sie|rung [reprivatiˈziːrʊŋ] **F** denationalization

Re|pro [ˈreːpro] **F -, -s** *(Typ sl) abbr von* **Reproduktion**

Re|pro|duk|ti|on [reprodʊkˈtsioːn] **F** reproduction; *(Typ auch)* repro *(inf)*

Re|pro|duk|ti|ons-: **Re|pro|duk|ti|ons|fak|tor** **M** *(Econ)* production factor; **Re|pro|duk|ti|ons|me|di|zin** **F** reproductive medicine; **Re|pro|duk|ti|ons|pro|zess** **M** reproductive process; **Re|pro|duk|ti|ons|tech|nik** **F** reproduction technology

re|pro|duk|tiv [reprodʊkˈtiːf] ADJ reproductive ADV **er arbeitet rein ~** he merely reproduces what others have done

re|pro|du|zier|bar **ADJ** reproducible

Re|pro|du|zier|bar|keit [reproduˈtsiːɐbaːɐkait] **F -,** *no pl* reproducibility

re|pro|du|zie|ren [reproduˈtsiːrən] *ptp* **reproduziert** VT to reproduce

re|pro-: **re|pro|fä|hig** ADJ camera-ready ADV **etw ~ ausgeben/vorlegen** to produce camera-ready copy; **Re|pro|film** **M** repro film; **Re|pro|fo|to|gra|fie** **F** repro photography; **Re|pro|gra|fie**, **Re|pro|gra|phie** [reprograˈfiː] **F**, **Re|pro|pho|to|gra|phie -, -n** [-ˈfiːən] *(Typ)* reprography

Rep|til [rɛpˈtiːl] **NT -s, -ien** [-liən] reptile

Rep|ti|li|en|fonds **M** slush fund

Re|pub|lik [repuˈbliːk] **F -, -en** republic

Re|pub|li|ka|ner [republiˈkaːnɐ] **M -s, -**, **Re|pub|li|ka|ne|rin** [-ərɪn] **F -, -nen** republican; *(Pol)* Republican

> **REPUBLIKANER**
>
> Founded in 1983, the **Republikaner** is a far-right political party. The party stands for nationalist values: populist economic policies, repressive law-and-order, and the exclusion of foreigners. Its increasingly aggressive nationalism and xenophobia have led to its being officially classified as a right-wing extremist party hostile to the constitution.

re|pub|li|ka|nisch [republiˈkaːnɪʃ] **ADJ** republican

Re|pub|lik-: **Re|pub|lik|flucht** **F** *(DDR)* illegal crossing of the border; **re|pub|lik|flüch|tig** **ADJ** *(DDR)* illegally emigrated; **~ werden** to cross the border illegally; **Re|pub|lik|flücht|ling** **M** *(DDR)* illegal emigrant

Re|pun|ze [reˈpʊntsə] **F -, -n** hallmark, platemark

Re|pu|ta|ti|on [reputaˈtsioːn] **F -,** *no pl (old)* (good) reputation

re|pu|tier|lich [repuˈtiːɐlɪç] *(old)* ADJ reputable, of good *or* high renown *(old, liter)* ADV **~ leben** to lead a respectable life

Re|qui|em [ˈreːkviɛm] **NT -s, -s** *or (Aus)* **Requien** [-viən] requiem

re|qui|rie|ren [rekviˈriːrən] *ptp* **requiriert** VT *(Mil)* to requisition, to commandeer

Re|qui|sit [rekviˈziːt] **NT -s, -en** equipment *no pl*, requisite *(form)*; **ein unerlässliches ~** an indispensable piece of equipment; **~en** *(Theat)* props, properties *(form)*

Re|qui|si|teur [rekviziˈtøːɐ] **M -s, -e**, **Re|qui|si|teu|rin** [-ˈtøːrɪn] **F -, -nen** *(Theat)* props *or* property manager

Re|qui|si|ti|on [rekviziˈtsioːn] **F -, -en** requisition(ing), commandeering

Re|qui|si|ti|ons|schein **M** *(Mil)* requisition order

resch [rɛʃ] **ADJ** *(Aus) (= knusprig) Brötchen etc* crisp, crunchy, crispy; *(fig: = lebhaft) Frau* dynamic

Re|se|da [reˈzeːda] **F -, Reseden** [-dn], **Re|se|de** [reˈzeːdə] **F -, -n** *(Gattung)* reseda; *(= Gartenreseda)* mignonette

re|ser|vat [rezɛrˈvaːt] **ADJ** *(Aus)* classified

Re|ser|vat [rezɛrˈvaːt] **NT -(e)s, -e** **a** *(= Naturschutzgebiet)* reserve; *(fig)* preserve **b** *(für Indianer, Ureinwohner etc)* reservation **c** *(old: = Sonderrecht)* right, discretionary power; **sich** *(dat)* **das ~ vorbehalten, etw zu machen** to reserve the right to do sth

Re|ser|va|ti|on [rezɛrvaˈtsioːn] **F -, -en** **a** *(old: = Sonderrecht)* = **Reservat a** **b** *(für Indianer, Ureinwohner etc)* reservation

Re|ser|vat|recht [rezɛrˈvaːt-] **NT** discretionary power

Re|ser|ve [reˈzɛrvə] **F -, -n** **a** *(= Vorrat)* reserve(s *pl*) *(an +dat* of); *(= angespartes Geld)* savings *pl*;

(= Kapitalrücklagen) reserve(s *pl*); *(Mil, Sport)* reserves *pl*; **offene ~n** *(Fin)* disclosed reserves; **(noch) etw/jdn in ~ haben** to have sth/sb (still) in reserve; **in ~ liegen** *(Mil)* to stay back in reserve **b** *(= Zurückhaltung)* reserve; *(= Bedenken)* reservation; **jdn aus der ~ locken** to break down sb's reserve, to bring sb out of his shell *(inf)*; **aus der ~ heraustreten** to lose one's reserve, to come out of one's shell *(inf)*

Re|ser|ve-: **Re|ser|ve|bank** F *pl* **-bänke** *(Sport)* substitutes *or* reserves bench; **er saß nur auf der ~** he only sat on the bench; **Re|ser|ve|fonds** M reserve fund; **Re|ser|ve|gut|ha|ben** NT *(Fin, Econ)* reserve holdings *pl*; **Re|ser|ve|ka|nis|ter** M spare can; **Re|ser|ve|mann** M *pl* **-männer** *or* **-leute** *(Sport)* reserve; **Re|ser|ve|of|fi|zier(in)** M(F) reserve officer; **Re|ser|ve|rad** NT spare (wheel); **Re|ser|ve|rei|fen** M spare (tyre *(Brit)* or tire *(US)*); **Re|ser|ve|spie|ler(in)** M(F) *(Sport)* reserve; **Re|ser|ve|tank** M reserve tank; **Re|ser|ve|trup|pen** PL reserves *pl*; **Re|ser|ve|übung** F (army) reserve training *no pl*

re|ser|vie|ren [rezɛrˈviːrən] *ptp* **reserviert** VT to reserve

re|ser|viert [rezɛrˈviːɐt] ADJ *Platz, Mensch* reserved; *(Comput) Speicherplatz auch* allocated

Re|ser|viert|heit F -, *no pl* reserve, reservedness

Re|ser|vie|rung ✪ 48.3 F -, **-en** reservation

Re|ser|vie|rungs|num|mer F reservation number

Re|ser|vist [rezɛrˈvɪst] M **-en, -en**, **Re|ser|vis|tin** [-ˈvɪstɪn] F **-, -nen** reservist

Re|ser|voir [rezɛrˈvoaːɐ] NT **-s, -e** reservoir; *(fig auch)* pool

Re|set|tas|te [riːˈsɛt-] F *(Comput)* reset key

re|si|dent [reziˈdɛnt] ADJ *(Comput)* resident

Re|si|dent [reziˈdɛnt] M **-en, -en**, **Re|si|den|tin** [-ˈdɛntɪn] M **-, -nen** envoy, resident *(rare)*

Re|si|denz [reziˈdɛnts] F **-, -en a** *(= Wohnung)* residence, residency **b** *(= Hauptstadt)* royal seat *or* capital

Re|si|denz|stadt F royal seat *or* capital

re|si|die|ren [reziˈdiːrən] *ptp* **residiert** VI to reside

re|si|du|al [reziˈduaːl] ADJ *(geh)* residual

Re|si|du|um [reˈziːduʊm] NT **-s, Residuen** [-duən] *(geh)* residue, residuum *(form)*

Re|sig|na|ti|on [rezignaˈtsioːn] F -, *no pl (geh)* resignation; **(über etw** *acc***) in ~ verfallen, sich der ~ überlassen** to become resigned (to sth); **in der Partei macht sich ~ breit** a feeling of resignation is spreading through the party

re|sig|na|tiv [rezignaˈtiːf] ADJ resigned

re|sig|nie|ren [reziˈgniːrən] *ptp* **resigniert** VI to give up; **resigniert** resigned; **... sagte er ~d** *or* **resigniert** ... he said with resignation *or* in a resigned way

re|sis|tent [rezɪsˈtɛnt] ADJ *(auch Med)* resistant *(gegen* to)

Re|sis|tenz [rezɪsˈtɛnts] F **-, -en** *(auch Med)* resistance *(gegen* to)

re|sis|tie|ren [rezɪsˈtiːrən] *ptp* **resistiert** VI *(Med)* to resist

re|so|lut [rezoˈluːt] ADJ resolute, determined ADV resolutely, determinedly

Re|so|lut|heit [rezoˈluːthait] F **-, -en** resoluteness; *(= Entschlossenheit)* determination

Re|so|lu|ti|on [rezoluˈtsioːn] F **-, -en** *(Pol) (= Beschluss)* resolution; *(= Bittschrift)* petition

Re|so|nanz [rezoˈnants] F **-, -en a** *(Mus, Phys)* resonance **b** *(fig)* response *(auf +acc* to); **keine/wenig/große ~ finden** to meet with *or* get no/little/a good response; **(bei jdm) auf positive ~ stoßen** to meet with *or* get a positive response (from sb)

Re|so|nanz-: **Re|so|nanz|bo|den** M sounding board; **Re|so|nanz|kas|ten** M soundbox

Re|so|pal® [rezoˈpaːl] NT **-s**, *no pl* ≈ Formica®

re|sor|bie|ren [rezɔrˈbiːrən] *ptp* **resorbiert** VT to absorb

Re|sorp|ti|on [rezɔrpˈtsioːn] F **-, -en** absorption

re|so|zi|a|li|sie|ren [rezotsialiˈziːrən] *ptp* **resozialisiert** VT to rehabilitate

Re|so|zi|a|li|sie|rung F rehabilitation

resp. *abbr von* **respektive**

Res|pekt [reˈspɛkt, rɛsˈpɛkt] ✪ 40.4 M **-s**, *no pl (= Achtung)* respect; *(= Angst)* fear; **jdm ~ einflößen** *(Achtung)* to command *or* inspire respect from sb; *(Angst)* to put the fear of God into sb; **~ einflößend** authoritative; **ein wenig ~ einflößender Mensch** a person who commands *or* inspires little respect; **vor jdm den ~ verlieren** to lose one's respect for sb; **bei allem ~ (vor jdm/etw)** with all due respect (to sb/for sth); **vor jdm/etw ~ haben** *(Achtung)* to respect sb/sth, to have respect for sb/sth; *(Angst)* to be afraid of sb/sth; **~ heischend** demanding respect; **jdn/etw mit ~ behandeln** to treat sb/sth with respect; **jdm mit ~ begegnen** to behave respectfully toward(s) sb, to treat sb with respect; **sich** *(dat)* **~ verschaffen** to make oneself respected; **allen ~!** well done!

res|pek|ta|bel [respɛkˈtaːbl, rɛs-] ADJ respectable

res|pekt-: **res|pekt|ein|flö|ßend** ADJ → **Respekt**; **res|pekt|hei|schend** ADJ → **Respekt**

res|pek|tie|ren [respɛkˈtiːrən, rɛs-] *ptp* **respektiert** VT to respect; *Wechsel* to honour *(Brit)*, to honor *(US)*

res|pek|ti|ve [respɛkˈtiːvə, rɛs-] ADV *(geh, Comm)* **a** *(= jeweils)* and ... respectively; **Fritz und Franz verdienen 100 ~ 150 Euro pro Tag** Fritz and Franz earn 100 and 150 euros per day respectively **b** *(= anders ausgedrückt)* or rather; *(= genauer gesagt)* (or) more precisely **c** *(= oder)* or

Res|pekt-: **res|pekt|los** ADJ disrespectful ADV disrespectfully; **Res|pekt|lo|sig|keit** F **-, -en a** *(no pl: Verhalten)* disrespect(fulness), lack of respect **b** *(Bemerkung)* disrespectful remark *or* comment

Res|pekts|per|son F person to be respected; *(= Beamter etc)* person in authority

Res|pekt-: **Res|pekt|ta|ge** PL *(Comm)* days *pl* of grace; **res|pekt|voll** ADJ respectful ADV respectfully; **res|pekt|wid|rig** ADJ disrespectful, irreverent

Re|spi|ra|ti|on [respiraˈtsioːn, rɛs-] F -, *no pl (form)* respiration

Re|spi|ra|ti|ons|ap|pa|rat M, **Re|spi|ra|tor** [respiˈraːtoːɐ, rɛs-] M **-s, Respiratoren** [-ˈtoːrən] respirator

re|spi|rie|ren [respiˈriːrən, rɛs-] *ptp* **respiriert** VI *(form)* to respire

Res|sen|ti|ment [rɛsãtiˈmãː, rə-] NT **-s, -s** resentment *no pl*, feeling of resentment *(gegen* against)

Res|sort [rɛˈsoːɐ] NT **-s, -s** department; **in das ~ von jdm/etw fallen** to be sb's/sth's department; **das ~ Finanzen** *etc* the finance *etc* department

Res|sort-: **Res|sort|lei|ter(in)** M(F) department head, head of department; **Res|sort|mi|nis|ter(in)** M(F) department minister; **der ~ für die Polizei** the minister responsible for the police

Res|sour|ce [rɛˈsʊrsə] F **-, -n** *(auch Comput)* resource; **erneuerbare ~n** renewable resources

Rest [rɛst] M **-(e)s, -e a** rest; **die ~e einer Kirche/Stadt/Kultur** the remains *or* remnants of a church/city/civilization; **der ~ der Welt** the rest of the world; **90% sind schon fertig, den ~ mache ich** 90% is done, I'll do the rest *or* remainder; **am Anfang hatte ich 25 Schüler, die 3 hier sind noch der ~ (davon)** at the beginning I had 25 pupils, these 3 are what's left *or* all that is left; **der letzte ~** the last bit; **der letzte ~ vom Schützenfest** *(hum)* the last little bit; **bis auf einen ~** except for a little bit *or* a small amount; **dieser kleine ~** this little bit that's left (over); **der kümmerliche** *or* **klägliche** *or* **schäbige ~** *(von meinem Geld)* all that's left, the miserable remains; *(vom Essen)* the sad remnants; **der ~ ist Schweigen** the rest is silence; **der ~ ist für Sie** *(beim Bezahlen)* keep the change; **jdm/einer Sache den ~ geben** *(inf)* to finish sb/sth off; **sich** *(dat)* **den ~ holen** *(inf)* to make oneself really ill *(Brit) or* sick **b Reste** PL *(= Essensreste)* leftovers *pl* **c** *(= Stoffrest)* remnant **d** *(Math)* remainder; **2 ~ 3** 2 and 3 over, 2 remainder 3

Rest- *in cpds* remaining; **Rest|ab|schnitt** M remaining part; **Rest|al|ko|hol** M, *no pl* residual alcohol; **Rest|auf|la|ge** F remainder(ed) stock, remainders *pl*

Res|tant [rɛsˈtant] M **-en, -en** *(Comm: = Ladenhüter)* slow *or* slow-moving line

Res|tant [rɛsˈtant] M **-en, -en**, **Res|tan|tin** [-ˈtantɪn] F **-, -nen** *(Comm: = Schuldner)* defaulter

Res|tau|rant [rɛstoˈrãː] NT **-s, -s** restaurant

Res|tau|ra|teur [rɛstoraˈtøːɐ] M **-s, -e**, **Res|tau|ra|teu|rin** [-ˈtøːrɪn] F **-, -nen** *(old)* restaurateur

Res|tau|ra|ti|on [restoraˈtsioːn, rɛs-] F **-, -en** restoration; **die ~** *(Hist)* the Restoration

Res|tau|ra|ti|on [rɛstoraˈtsioːn] F **-, -en** *(old, Aus)* inn, tavern *(old)*; *(im Bahnhof)* refreshment rooms *pl*

Res|tau|ra|ti|ons-: **Res|tau|ra|ti|ons|be|trieb** M catering business; **Res|tau|ra|ti|ons|zeit** F period of ultraconservatism; **die ~** *(Hist)* the Restoration

Res|tau|ra|tor [restauˈraːtoːɐ, rɛs-] M **-s, Restauratoren** [-ˈtoːrən], **Res|tau|ra|to|rin** [-ˈtoːrɪn] F **-, -nen** restorer

res|tau|rie|ren [restauˈriːrən, rɛs-] *ptp* **restauriert** VT to restore VR *(old)* to partake of some refreshment *(old form)*

Res|tau|rie|rung F **-, -en** restoration

Rest-: **Rest|be|stand** M remaining stock; *(fig)* remnant; **wir haben noch einen kleinen ~ an Bikinis** we still have a few bikinis left; **Rest|be|trag** M balance

Res|te-: **Res|te|es|sen** NT leftovers *pl*; **Res|te|ver|kauf** M remnants sale

Rest|fi|nan|zie|rung F financing of the rest; *(= Betrag)* residual *or* remaining amount

Rest|for|de|rung F residual claim

re|sti|tu|ie|ren [restituˈiːrən, rɛs-] *ptp* **restituiert** VT *(form)* to make restitution of *(form)*

Re|sti|tu|ti|on [restituˈtsioːn, rɛs-] F **-, -en** *(form)* restitution *(form)*

Re|sti|tu|ti|ons-: **Re|sti|tu|ti|ons|edikt** NT Edict of Restitution; **Re|sti|tu|ti|ons|kla|ge** F action for a retrial

Rest|lauf|zeit F *(Fin)* unexpired *or* remaining term, remaining life

rest|lich [ˈrɛstlɪç] ADJ remaining, rest of the ...; **die ~e Welt** the rest of the world; **die ~en** the rest

Rest|lie|fe|rung F *(Comm)* rest of the/a delivery

rest|los ADJ complete, total ADV completely, totally; **ich war ~ begeistert** I was completely bowled over *(inf)*

Rest-: **Rest|men|ge** F residue; **Rest|müll** M non-recyclable waste; **Rest|pos|ten** M **a** *(Comm)* remaining stock; **ein ~** remaining stock; **ein großer ~ Bücher/Zucker** a lot of books/sugar left in stock; **„Restposten"** "reduced to clear" **b** *(Fin: in Bilanz)* residual item

Rest|rik|ti|on [restrɪkˈtsioːn, rɛs-] F **-, -en** *(form)* restriction

Rest|rik|ti|ons|maß|nah|me F restriction, restrictive measure

rest|rik|tiv [restrɪkˈtiːf, rɛs-] *(geh)* ADJ restrictive ADV restrictively; **die Werbebeschränkungen wurden ~ gehandhabt** advertising restrictions were rigorously applied

Rest-: **Rest|ri|si|ko** NT residual risk; **Rest|sum|me** F balance, amount remaining; **Rest|ur|laub** M unused holiday *(esp Brit) or* vacation *(US)*, remaining holiday *(esp Brit) or* vacation *(US, form)* (entitlement); **ich habe noch (10 Tage) ~** I've still got (ten days') holiday owing *or* vacation owed *(US)* to me; **Rest|wär|me** F residual heat; **Rest|wert** M residual;

Rest|zah|lung F final payment, payment of the balance

Re|sul|tan|te [rezʊl'tantə] F -, -n *(Math)* resultant

Re|sul|tat [rezʊl'ta:t] NT -(e)s, -e result; *(von Prüfung auch)* results *pl*; **zu einem ~ kommen** to come to *or* arrive at a conclusion; **gute ~e erzielen** to achieve good results

re|sul|tat|los ADJ fruitless, without result ADV **das Spiel verlief ~** the game was undecided *or* ended in a draw

re|sul|tie|ren [rezʊl'ti:rən] *ptp* **resultiert** VI *(geh)* to result *(in +dat* in); *(Sw: sich ergeben)* to result; **aus etw ~** to be the result of sth, to result from sth; **aus dem Gesagten resultiert, dass ...** from what was said one must conclude that ...; **die daraus ~den ...** the resulting ...; **daraus resultiert ...** the result (of this) is ...

Re|sul|tie|ren|de [rezʊl'ti:rəndə] F *decl as adj (Math)* resultant

Re|sü|mee [rezy'me:] NT -s, -s, *(Aus, Sw)* **Re|su|mé** [rezy'me:] NT -s, -s *(geh)* summary, résumé; *(am Ende einer Rede auch)* recapitulation

re|sü|mie|ren [rezy'mi:rən] *ptp* **resümiert** VTI *(geh)* to summarize, to sum up; *(am Ende einer Rede auch)* to recapitulate

Re|tar|da|ti|on [retarda'tsio:n] F -, -en retardation

re|tar|die|ren [retar'di:rən] *ptp* **retardiert** VT to retard; **ein ~des Moment** a delaying factor *or* element; **retardiert** *(= geistig zurückgeblieben)* retarded

re|ti|rie|ren [reti'ri:rən] *ptp* **retiriert** VI *aux sein (old Mil, hum)* to beat a retreat

Re|tor|te [re'tɔrtə] F -, -n *(Chem)* retort; **aus der ~** *(fig inf)* synthetic; **Baby aus der ~** test-tube baby

Re|tor|ten|ba|by NT test-tube baby

Re|tor|ten|stadt F *(pej inf)* ≈ new town *(Brit)*, purpose-built town

re|tour [re'tu:ɐ] ADV *(Aus dial)* back

Re|tour|bil|lett [re'tu:ɐbɪl'jɛt] NT *(Sw)* return (ticket) *(esp Brit)*, round-trip ticket *(US)*

Re|tou|re [re'tu:rə] F -, -n *usu pl* return

Re|tour-: **Re|tour|gang** M *pl* -gänge *(Aus)* reverse (gear); **Re|tour|kar|te** F *(Aus)* return (ticket) *(esp Brit)*, round-trip ticket *(US)*; **Re|tour|kut|sche** F *(inf) (Worte)* retort; *(Handlung)* retribution

re|tour|nie|ren [retʊr'ni:rən] *ptp* **retourniert** VT *(old, Aus)* to return

Re|tour|spiel [re'tu:ɐ-] NT *(Aus)* return (match)

ret|ro|spek|tiv [retrospɛk'ti:f] *(liter)* ADJ retrospective ADV in retrospect

Ret|ro|spek|ti|ve [retrospɛk'ti:və] F -, -n *(liter)* retrospective

Ret|ro|vi|rus [retro'vi:rʊs] NT OR M retrovirus

ret|ten ['rɛtn] VT to save; *(aus Gefahr auch, = befreien)* to rescue; *(Comput) Datei* to recover; **jdn/etw vor jdm/etw ~** to save sb/sth from sb/sth; **jdm das Leben ~** to save sb's life; **ein ~der Gedanke** a bright idea that saved the situation *or* his/our *etc* bacon *(inf)*; **der Patient/die alte Kirche ist noch/nicht mehr zu ~** the patient/the old church can still be saved *or* is not yet past saving/is past saving; **wir sollten ~, was noch zu ~ ist** we should salvage what we can; **er hat wieder geheiratet? er ist nicht mehr zu ~** he got married again? he's beyond redemption *or* past saving *or* past helping; **bist du noch zu ~?** *(inf)* are you out of your mind?, have you gone completely round the bend? *(Brit inf)*
VR to escape; **sich auf/unter etw** *(acc)***/aus etw ~** to escape onto/under/from sth; **sich vor jdm/etw ~** to escape (from) sb/sth; **sich durch die Flucht ~** to escape; **sich vor etw nicht mehr ~ können** *or* **zu ~ wissen** *(fig)* to be swamped with sth; **rette sich, wer kann!** (it's) every man for himself!

Ret|ter ['rɛtɐ] M -s, -, **Ret|te|rin** [-ərɪn] F -, -nen *(aus Notlage)* rescuer, deliverer *(liter)*; **der ~** *(Rel)* the Saviour *(Brit) or* Savior *(US)*; **ach mein ~!** oh my hero!; **der ~ des Unternehmens/von 1000 Arbeitsplätzen** the saviour *(Brit) or* savior *(US)* of the business/of 1000 jobs → **Not**

Ret|tich ['rɛtɪç] M -s, -e radish

Ret|tung ['rɛtʊŋ] F -, -en *(aus Notlage)* rescue, deliverance *(liter)*; *(= Erhaltung)* saving; *(von Waren)* recovery; *(Rel)* salvation, deliverance; **die ~ und Erhaltung historischer Denkmäler** the saving and preservation of historical monuments; **Gesellschaft zur ~ Schiffbrüchiger** Lifeboat Service; **die ~ kam in letzter Minute** the situation was saved at the last minute; *(für Schiffbrüchige etc)* help came in the nick of time; **auf ~ hoffen** to hope to be saved, to hope for deliverance *(liter)*; **an seine (eigene) ~ denken** to worry about one's own safety; **für den Patienten/unsere Wirtschaft gibt es keine ~ mehr** the patient/our economy is beyond saving, our economy is beyond salvation; **das war meine ~** that saved me, that was my salvation; **es war meine ~, dass ...** I was saved by the fact that ...; **das war meine letzte ~** that was my last hope; *(= hat mich gerettet)* that was my salvation, that saved me

Ret|tungs-: **Ret|tungs|ak|ti|on** F rescue operation; **Ret|tungs|an|ker** M sheet anchor; *(fig)* anchor; **Ret|tungs|arzt** M, **Ret|tungs|ärz|tin** F emergency doctor; **Ret|tungs|bo|je** F life belt; *(= Hosenboje)* breeches buoy; **Ret|tungs|boot** NT lifeboat; **Ret|tungs|dienst** M rescue service; **Ret|tungs|fahr|zeug** NT rescue vehicle; **Ret|tungs|floß** NT life raft; **Ret|tungs|flug|wacht** F air rescue service; **Ret|tungs|flug|zeug** NT rescue aircraft; **Ret|tungs|ge|rät** NT rescue equipment *no pl or* apparatus *no pl*; **Ret|tungs|gür|tel** M life belt; **Ret|tungs|hub|schrau|ber** M rescue helicopter; **Ret|tungs|in|sel** F inflatable life raft; **Ret|tungs|kom|man|do** NT rescue squad; **Ret|tungs|lei|ne** F lifeline; **Ret|tungs|lei|ter** F rescue ladder; **ret|tungs|los** ADJ beyond saving; *Lage* hopeless, irredeemable; *Verlust* irrecoverable ADV *verloren* hopelessly, irretrievably; **er ist ihr ~ verfallen** he is completely under her spell; **Ret|tungs|mann|schaft** F rescue team *or* party; **Ret|tungs|me|dail|le** F lifesaving medal; **Ret|tungs|ring** M life buoy, life belt; *(hum: = Bauch)* spare tyre *(Brit hum)*, spare tire *(US hum)*; **Ret|tungs|sa|ni|tä|ter(in)** M(F) paramedic; **Ret|tungs|schuss** M **finaler ~** fatal shot *(fired by the police)*; **Ret|tungs|schwim|men** NT lifesaving; **Ret|tungs|schwim|mer(in)** M(F) lifesaver; *(an Strand, Pool)* lifeguard; **Ret|tungs|sta|ti|on** F, **Ret|tungs|stel|le** F rescue centre *(Brit) or* center *(US)*; *(für Erste Hilfe)* first-aid post; *(mit Rettungsbooten)* lifeboat *or* coastguard station; **Ret|tungs|trupp** M rescue squad; **Ret|tungs|ver|such** M rescue attempt *or* bid; *(von Arzt etc)* attempt to save sb; **Ret|tungs|wa|che** F rescue station; *(kleiner)* rescue post; **Ret|tungs|wa|gen** M ambulance; **Ret|tungs|we|sen** NT rescue services *pl*

Re|turn|taste F *(Comput)* return key

Re|tu|sche [re'tʊʃə] F -, -n *(Phot)* retouching

Re|tu|scheur [retu'ʃø:ɐ] M -s, -e, **Re|tu|scheu|rin** [-'ʃø:rɪn] F -, -nen retoucher

re|tu|schie|ren [retu'ʃi:rən] *ptp* **retuschiert** VT *(Phot)* to retouch, to touch up *(inf, auch fig)*

Reue ['rɔyə] F -, *no pl* remorse *(über +acc* at, about), repentance *(auch Rel) (über +acc* of), rue *(old, liter) (über +acc* at, of); *(= Bedauern)* regret *(über +acc* at, about)

reue|los ADJ unrepentant

reu|en ['rɔyən] VT *(liter)* **etw reut jdn** sb regrets *or* rues *(liter, old)* sth; **es reut mich, dass ich das getan habe** I regret *or* rue *(liter, old)* having done that

reue|voll ADJ, ADV = **reumütig**

reu|ig ['rɔyɪç] ADJ, ADV *(liter)* = **reumütig**

reu|mü|tig ['rɔymy:tɪç] ADJ *(= voller Reue)* remorseful, repentant; *Sünder* contrite, penitent; *(= betreten, zerknirscht)* rueful ADV *gestehen, bekennen* full of remorse; **du wirst bald ~ zu mir zurückkommen** you'll soon come back to me feeling sorry

Reu|se ['rɔyzə] F -, -n fish trap

re|üs|sie|ren [reły'si:rən] *ptp* **reüssiert** VI *(old)* to succeed, to be successful *(bei, mit* with)

Re|van|che [re'vã:ʃ(ə)] F -, -n **a** *(Sport)* revenge *(für* for); *(= Revanchepartie)* return match *(Brit)*, rematch *(US)*; **du musst ihm ~ geben!** you'll have to let him have *or* get his revenge, you'll have to give him a return match *(Brit) or* a rematch *(US)*; **(für etw) ~ nehmen** to have *or* get one's revenge (for sth) **b** *no pl (= Rache)* revenge, vengeance

Re|van|che-: **Re|van|che|krieg** M war of revenge; **re|van|che|lüs|tern** ADJ revanchist; **Re|van|che|par|tie** F *(Sport)* return match *(Brit)*, rematch *(US)*; **Re|van|che|po|li|tik** F *(pej)* revanchist policy; **Re|van|che|spiel** NT *(Sport)* return match *(Brit)*, rematch *(US)*

re|van|chie|ren [revã'ʃi:rən] *ptp* **revanchiert** VR **a** *(= sich rächen)* to get *or* have one's revenge, to get one's own back *(Brit) (bei jdm für etw* on sb for sth); *(Sport)* to get *or* have one's revenge **b** *(= sich erkenntlich zeigen)* to reciprocate; **ich werde mich bei Gelegenheit mal ~** I'll return the compliment some time; *(für Hilfe)* I'll do the same for you one day, I'll return the favour *(Brit) or* favor *(US)* one day; **das Problem bei Geschenken ist, dass man meint, sich ~ zu müssen** the problem with getting presents is that one always feels one has to give something in return; **sich bei jdm für eine Einladung/seine Gastfreundschaft ~** to return sb's invitation/hospitality

Re|van|chis|mus [revã'ʃɪsmʊs] M -, *no pl* revanchism

Re|van|chist [revã'ʃɪst] M -en, -en, **Re|van|chis|tin** [-'ʃɪstɪn] F -, -nen revanchist

re|van|chis|tisch [revã'ʃɪstɪʃ] ADJ revanchist

Re|ve|renz [reve'rɛnts] F -, -en *(old) (= Hochachtung)* reverence; *(= Geste der Hochachtung)* gesture of respect; *(= Verbeugung)* obeisance, reverence *(old)*; **jdm seine ~ erweisen** to show one's reverence *or* respect for sb; **seine ~en machen** to make one's obeisances *(old)*, to bow

Re|vers [re've:ɐ, re'vɛ:ɐ, rə'-] NT OR (AUS) M -, - [-ɐs, -ɐs] *(an Kleidung)* lapel, revere, revers *(esp US)*

Re|vers [re'vɛrs] M -es, -e [-zə] **a** *(= Rückseite)* reverse **b** *(= Erklärung)* declaration

re|ver|si|bel [revɛr'zi:bl] ADJ reversible

Re|ver|si|on [revɛr'zio:n] F -, -en *(Biol, Psych)* reversion

re|vi|die|ren [revi'di:rən] *ptp* **revidiert** VT to revise; *(Comm)* to audit, to check; **die Wachstumsprognosen wurden nach oben/unten revidiert** the growth forecasts were revised upwards/downwards

Re|vier [re'vi:ɐ] NT -s, -e **a** *(= Polizeidienststelle)* (police) station, station house *(US)*; *(= Dienstbereich)* beat, district, precinct *(US)*, patch *(inf)*; *(von Prostituierter)* beat, patch *(inf)*
b *(Zool: = Gebiet)* territory; **die Küche ist mein ~** the kitchen is my territory *or* preserve
c *(Hunt: = Jagdrevier)* hunting ground, shoot
d *(old: = Gebiet, Gegend)* district, area
e *(Mil: = Krankenrevier)* sickbay; **auf dem** *or* **im ~ liegen** to be in the sickbay
f *(Min: = Kohlenrevier)* (coal) mines *pl*, coalfields *pl*; **im ~ an der Ruhr** in the mines of the Ruhr; **das ~** *(= Ruhrgebiet)* the Ruhr; *(= Saarland)* the Saar

Re|vier-: **Re|vier|förs|ter(in)** M(F) forester, forest ranger *(US)*; **Re|vier|förs|te|rei** F forester's lodge; **re|vier|krank** ADJ *(Mil)* hospitalized, in the sickbay; **Re|vier|wa|che** F duty room; **Re|vier|wacht|meis|ter(in)** M(F) station sergeant

Re|vi|re|ment [revirə'mã:, revir'mã:] NT -s, -s *(Pol)* reshuffle

Re|vi|si|on [revi'zio:n] F -, -en **a** *(von Meinung, Politik etc)* revision; **sich in ~ befinden** to be undergoing revision **b** *(Comm: = Prüfung)* audit

c (*Typ:* = *letzte Überprüfung*) final (proof)read; **~ lesen** to do the final (proof)read **d** (*Jur.* = *Urteilsanfechtung*) appeal (*an +acc* to); **in die ~ gehen, ~ einlegen** to lodge an appeal, to appeal

Re|vi|si|o|nis|mus [revizio'nɪsmʊs] **M -,** *no pl* (*Pol*) revisionism

Re|vi|si|o|nist [revizio'nɪst] **M -en, -en, Re|vi|si|o|nis|tin** [-'nɪstɪn] **F -, -nen** (*Pol*) revisionist

re|vi|si|o|nis|tisch [revizio'nɪstɪʃ] **ADJ** (*Pol*) revisionist

Re|vi|si|ons-: **Re|vi|si|ons|an|trag M** (*Jur*) notice of appeal; **Re|vi|si|ons|bo|gen M** page proof; **Re|vi|si|ons|frist F** time for appeal; **Re|vi|si|ons|ge|richt NT** court of appeal, appeal court; **Re|vi|si|ons|ver|fah|ren NT** (*Jur*) appeal proceedings *pl*; **Re|vi|si|ons|ver|hand|lung F** appeal hearing

Re|vi|sor [re'viːzoːɐ] **M -s, Revisoren** [-'zoːrən], **Re|vi|so|rin** [-'zoːrɪn] **F -, -nen** (*Comm*) auditor; (*Typ*) proofreader

Re|vol|te [re'vɔltə] **F -, -n** revolt

re|vol|tie|ren [revɔl'tiːrən] *ptp* **revoltiert VI** to revolt, to rebel (*gegen* against); (*fig:* *Magen*) to rebel

Re|vo|lu|ti|on [revolu'tsioːn] **F -, -en** (*lit, fig*) revolution; **eine ~ der Moral** a moral revolution, a revolution in morals; **die sanfte/friedliche ~** the velvet/peaceful revolution

re|vo|lu|ti|o|när [revolutsio'nɛːɐ] **ADJ** (*lit, fig*) revolutionary **ADV etw als ~ betrachten** to view sth as revolutionary; **etw als ~ bezeichnen** to call sth revolutionary

Re|vo|lu|ti|o|när [revolutsio'nɛːɐ] **M -s, -e, Re|vo|lu|ti|o|nä|rin** [-'nɛːrɪn] **F -, -nen** revolutionary

re|vo|lu|ti|o|nie|ren [revolutsio'niːrən] *ptp* **revolutioniert VT** to revolutionize

Re|vo|lu|ti|ons- *in cpds* revolutionary; **Re|vo|lu|ti|ons|füh|rer(in) M(F)** revolutionary leader; **Re|vo|lu|ti|ons|re|gie|rung F** revolutionary government

Re|vo|luz|zer [revo'lʊtsɐ] **M -s, -, Re|vo|luz|ze|rin** [-ərɪn] **F -, -nen** (*pej*) would-be revolutionary

Re|vol|ver [re'vɔlvɐ] **M -s, -** revolver, gun

Re|vol|ver-: **Re|vol|ver|blatt NT** (*pej*) scandal sheet; **Re|vol|ver|griff M** butt (of a/the revolver); **Re|vol|ver|held(in) M(F)** (*pej*) gunslinger; **Re|vol|ver|lauf M** barrel (of a/the revolver); **Re|vol|ver|mün|dung F** mouth (of a/the revolver); **plötzlich starrte er in eine ~** he suddenly found himself staring down the barrel of a revolver; **Re|vol|ver|pres|se F** (*pej*) gutter press

Re|vue [rə'vyː] **F -, -n** [-'vyːən] **a** (*Theat*) revue **b** (*rare:* = *Zeitschrift*) review **c** (*old, Mil*) review (*fig*) **etw ~ passieren lassen** to let sth parade before one, to pass sth in review

Re|vue|tän|zer(in) [rə'vyː-] **M(F)** chorus boy/girl

Reyk|ja|vik ['raikjaviːk] **NT -s** Reykjavik

Re|zen|sent [retsɛn'zɛnt] **M -en, -en, Re|zen|sen|tin** [-'zɛntɪn] **F -, -nen** reviewer

re|zen|sie|ren [retsɛn'ziːrən] *ptp* **rezensiert VT** to review

Re|zen|si|on [retsɛn'zioːn] **F -, -en** review, write-up (*inf*)

Re|zen|si|ons|ex|emp|lar NT review copy

re|zent [re'tsɛnt] **ADJ a** (*Biol*) living; (*Ethnologie*) *Kulturen* surviving **b** (*dial:* = *säuerlich, pikant*) tart, sour **c** (*geh:* = *neuerlich*) recent

Re|zept [re'tsɛpt] **NT -(e)s, -e a** (*Med*) prescription; (*fig:* = *Heilmittel*) cure, remedy (*für, gegen* for); **auf ~** on prescription **b** (*Cook, fig:* = *Anleitung*) recipe (*zu* for)

Re|zept-: **Re|zept|block M** *pl* **-blöcke** *or* **-blocks** prescription pad; **re|zept|frei ADJ** available without prescription **ADV** over the counter, without a prescription; **Re|zept|ge|bühr F** prescription charge

Re|zep|ti|on [retsɛp'tsioːn] **F -, -en a** (*liter:* von *Gedankengut, Kultur*) adoption; (*von Buch, Musikstück*) reception **b** (*von Hotel:* = *Empfang*) reception

re|zep|tiv [retsɛp'tiːf] **ADJ** receptive; **der Kritiker als ~er Mensch** the critic as one who assimilates *or* receives ideas

Re|zep|tor [re'tsɛptoːɐ] **M -s, Rezeptoren** (*Biol, Physiol*) receptor

Re|zept-: **Re|zept|pflicht F** prescription requirement; **der ~ unterliegen** *or* **unterstehen** to be available only on prescription; **dafür besteht jetzt keine ~ mehr** you don't need a prescription for it any more; **re|zept|pflich|tig** [-pflɪçtɪç] **ADJ** available only on prescription, ethical (*spec*); **etw ~ machen** to put sth on prescription

Re|zep|tur [retsɛp'tuːɐ] **F -, -en** (*form*) dispensing

Re|zess [re'tsɛs] **M -es, -e** (*Jur*) written settlement *or* agreement

Re|zes|si|on [retsɛ'sioːn] **F -, -en** (*Econ*) recession

re|zes|siv [retsɛ'siːf] **ADJ a** (*Biol*) recessive **b** (*Econ*) recessionary **ADV** (*Biol*) **Erbanlagen, die ~ vorhanden sind** genetic traits which are recessive, recessive genetic traits

Re|zi|pi|ent [retsipi'ɛnt] **M -en, -en, Re|zi|pi|en|tin** [retsipi'ɛntɪn] **F -, -nen a** (*form:* Person) recipient **b** (*Chem, Phys*) recipient

re|zi|pie|ren [retsi'piːrən] *ptp* **rezipiert VT** *Ideen etc* to adopt, to accept; *Text, Buch* to apprehend

re|zip|rok [retsi'proːk] **ADJ** (*Math, Gram*) reciprocal **ADV sich ~ zueinander verhalten** to be in a reciprocal relationship

Re|zi|ta|ti|on [retsita'tsioːn] **F -, -en** recitation

Re|zi|ta|ti|ons|abend M poetry evening

Re|zi|ta|tiv [retsita'tiːf] **NT -s, -e** [-və] (*Mus*) recitative

Re|zi|ta|tor [retsi'taːtoːɐ] **M -s, Rezitatoren** [-'toːrən], **Re|zi|ta|to|rin** [-'toːrɪn] **F -, -nen** reciter

re|zi|tie|ren [retsi'tiːrən] *ptp* **rezitiert VTI** to recite

R-Ge|spräch ['ɛr-] **NT** transfer *or* reverse charge call (*Brit*), collect call (*US*); **ein ~ führen** to make a transfer charge call *etc*, to transfer *or* reverse the charges, to call collect (*US*)

rh [ɛr'haː] *abbr von* **Rhesusfaktor negativ**

Rh [ɛr'haː] *abbr von* **Rhesusfaktor positiv**

RH (*in Annoncen*) *abbr von* **Reihenhaus**

Rha|bar|ber [ra'barbɐ] **M -s,** *no pl* rhubarb

Rha|bar|ber NT -s, *no pl* (*inf:* = *Gemurmel*) rhubarb

Rhap|so|die [rapso'diː, rapzo'diː] **F -, -n** [-'diːən] (*Mus, Liter*) rhapsody

rhap|so|disch [rap'soːdɪʃ, rap'zoːdɪʃ] **ADJ** (*Mus, Liter*) rhapsodic(al)

Rhein [rain] **M -s** Rhine

Rhein-: **rhein|ab(|wärts)** [rain'lap(vɛrts)] **ADV** down the Rhine; **Rhein|ar|mee F** British Army of the Rhine; **rhein|auf(|wärts)** [rain'lauf(vɛrts)] **ADV** up the Rhine; **Rhein|bund M,** *no pl* (*Hist*) Confederation of the Rhine; **Rhein|fall M** Rhine Falls *pl*, Falls *pl* of the Rhine

rhei|nisch ['rainɪʃ] **ADJ** *attr* Rhenish, Rhineland

Rhein-: **Rhein|län|der** ['rainlɛndɐ] **M -s, -** (= *Tanz*) ≈ schottische; **Rhein|län|der** ['rainlɛndɐ] **M -s, -, Rhein|län|de|rin** [-ərɪn] **F -, -nen** Rhinelander; **rhein|län|disch** ['rainlɛndɪʃ] **ADJ** Rhenish, Rhineland; **Rhein|land-Pfalz** ['rainlant'pfalts] **NT** Rhineland-Palatinate; **Rhein|wein M** Rhine wine, Rhenish (wine); (*weißer auch*) hock

Rhe|ni|um ['reːniʊm] **NT -s,** *no pl* (*abbr* **Re**) rhenium

Rhe|sus-: **Rhe|sus|af|fe M** rhesus monkey; **Rhe|sus|fak|tor M** (*Med*) rhesus *or* Rh factor; **Rhesus(faktor) positiv/negativ** rhesus positive/negative

Rhe|to|rik [re'toːrɪk] **F -, -en** rhetoric

Rhe|to|ri|ker [re'toːrikɐ] **M -s, -, Rhe|to|ri|ke|rin** [-ərɪn] **F -, -nen** rhetorician (*form*), master of rhetoric; (= *Redner*) orator

rhe|to|risch [re'toːrɪʃ] **ADJ** rhetorical; **~e Frage** rhetorical question **ADV a** (*als Redner*) rhetorically; **~ begabt sein** to have a gift for rhetoric **b rein ~** rhetorically; **verstehen Sie diese Frage bitte rein ~** of course, you understand this question is purely rhetorical

Rheu|ma ['rɔyma] **NT -s,** *no pl* rheumatism

Rheu|ma|mit|tel NT (*inf*) cure for rheumatism *or* the rheumatics (*inf*)

Rheu|ma|ti|ker [rɔy'maːtikɐ] **M -s, -, Rheu|ma|ti|ke|rin** [-ərɪn] **F -, -nen** rheumatic, rheumatism sufferer

rheu|ma|tisch [rɔy'maːtɪʃ] **ADJ** rheumatic **ADV ~ bedingte Schmerzen** rheumatic pains

Rheu|ma|tis|mus [rɔyma'tɪsmʊs] **M -, Rheumatismen** [-mən] rheumatism

Rheu|ma|to|lo|ge [rɔymato'loːgə] **M -n, -n, Rheu|ma|to|lo|gin** [-'loːgɪn] **F -, -nen** rheumatologist

Rhi|no|ze|ros [ri'noːtserɔs] **NT -(ses), -se** rhinoceros, rhino (*inf*); (*inf:* = *Dummkopf*) fool, twit (*inf*), sap (*inf*)

Rhi|zom [ri'tsoːm] **NT -s, -e** (*Bot*) rhizome

Rho|de|si|en [ro'deːziən] **NT -s** (*Hist*) Rhodesia

Rho|de|si|er [ro'deːziɐ] **M -s, -, Rho|de|si|e|rin** [-iərɪn] **F -, -nen** (*Hist*) Rhodesian

rho|de|sisch [ro'deːzɪʃ] **ADJ** (*Hist*) Rhodesian

Rho|di|um ['roːdiʊm] **NT -s,** *no pl* (*abbr* **Rh**) rhodium

Rho|do|dend|ron [rodo'dɛndrɔn] **M OR NT -s, Rhododendren** [-drən] rhododendron

Rho|dos ['roːdɔs, 'rɔdɔs] **NT -'** Rhodes

Rhom|ben *pl von* **Rhombus**

rhom|bisch ['rɔmbɪʃ] **ADJ** rhomboid(al)

Rhom|bo|id [rɔmbo'iːt] **NT -(e)s, -e** [-də] rhomboid

Rhom|bus ['rɔmbʊs] **M -, Rhomben** [-bn] rhombus, rhomb

Rhön|rad ['røːnraːt] **NT** (*Turnen*) aero wheels *pl*

Rhyth|mik ['rʏtmɪk] **F -, -en** rhythmics *sing*; (*inf:* = *Rhythmus*) rhythm

Rhyth|mi|ker ['rʏtmikɐ] **M -s, -, Rhyth|mi|ke|rin** [-ərɪn] **F -, -nen** rhythmist

rhyth|misch ['rʏtmɪʃ] **ADJ** rhythmic(al); **~e Prosa** rhythmic prose; **~e (Sport)gymnastik** rhythmic gymnastics *sing*, music and movement **ADV** rhythmically; **sie bewegten sich ~ zum Schlagen der Trommeln** they moved to the rhythm of the drums

rhyth|mi|sie|ren [rʏtmi'ziːrən] *ptp* **rhythmisiert VT** to make rhythmic, to put rhythm into; **rhythmisiert** rhythmic

Rhyth|mus ['rʏtmʊs] **M -, Rhythmen** [-mən] (*Mus, Poet, fig*) rhythm

Rhyth|mus|ins|tru|ment NT rhythm instrument

RIAS ['riːas] **M** *abbr von* **Rundfunk im amerikanischen Sektor** broadcasting station in the American sector (of Berlin)

Ri|bi|sel ['riːbiːzl] **F -, -n, Ri|bisl** ['riːbiːzl] **F -, -n** (*Aus:* = *Johannisbeere*) (*rot*) redcurrant; (*schwarz*) blackcurrant

Ri|bo|nuk|le|in|säu|re [ribonukle'iːn-] **F** (*abbr* **RNS**) ribonucleic acid

Ri|bo|se [ri'boːzə] **F -, -n, Ri|bo|som** [ribo'zoːm] **NT -s, -e** ribosome

Richt-: **Richt|an|ten|ne F** directional aerial (*esp Brit*) *or* antenna; **Richt|baum M** *tree used in the topping-out ceremony*; **Richt|beil NT** executioner's axe (*Brit*) *or* ax (*US*); **Richt|blei NT** plumb line, plummet

rich|ten ['rɪçtn] **VT a** (= *lenken*) to direct (*auf +acc* towards), to point (*auf +acc* at, towards); *Augen, Blicke, Aufmerksamkeit, Kamera* to direct, to turn (*auf +acc* towards), to focus (*auf +acc* on); *Pläne, Wünsche, Tun* to direct (*auf +acc* towards); **den Kurs nach Norden/Osten** *etc* **~** to set *or* steer a northerly/easterly *etc* course; **die Augen gen Himmel ~** (*liter*) to raise *or* lift one's eyes heavenwards (*liter*) *or* to heaven (*liter*); **richt euch!** (*Mil*) right dress!; (*Sch*) get in a straight line!; **einen Verdacht gegen jdn ~** to suspect sb → **zugrunde**

b *(= ausrichten)* **etw nach jdm/etw ~** to suit *or* fit sth to sb/sth; *Lebensstil, Verhalten* to orientate sth to sb/sth
c *(= adressieren) Briefe, Anfragen* to address, to send *(an +acc* to); *Bitten, Forderungen, Gesuch* to address, to make *(an +acc* to); *Kritik, Vorwurf* to level, to direct, to aim *(gegen* at, against); **das Wort an jdn ~** to address sb
d *(esp S Ger) (= zurechtmachen)* to prepare, to get ready; *Essen auch* to get, to fix; *(= in Ordnung bringen)* to do, to fix; *(= reparieren)* to fix; *Haare* to do; *Tisch* to lay *(Brit)*, to set; *Betten* to make, to do; **jdm ein Bad ~** *(form, S Ger)* to draw *(form) or* run a bath for sb
e *(= einstellen)* to set; *(S Ger: = gerade biegen)* to straighten (out), to bend straight; **einen Knochenbruch ~** to set a fracture
f *(Aus: = erreichen)* **sichs** *(dat)* **~** to do nicely for oneself *(inf)*
g *(old: = hinrichten)* to execute, to put to death; **sich selbst ~** *(liter)* to find death by one's own hand *(liter)*; **sich von selbst ~** *(fig)* to condemn oneself

VR a *(= sich hinwenden)* to focus, to be focussed *(auf +acc* on), to be directed *(auf +acc* towards); *(Gedanken, Augen, Blick)* to turn, to be directed *(auf +acc* towards); *(Hoffnungen)* to be focussed *(auf +acc* on); *(Protest, Kritik)* to be directed *or* aimed *(gegen* at)
b *(= sich wenden)* to consult *(an jdn* sb); *(Maßnahme, Vorwurf etc)* to be directed *or* aimed *(gegen* at)
c *(= sich anpassen)* to follow *(nach jdm/etw* sb/sth); **sich nach den Vorschriften ~** to go by the rules; **sich nach jds Wünschen ~** to comply with *or* go along with sb's wishes; **mir ist es egal, ob wir früher oder später gehen, ich richte mich nach dir** I don't mind if we go earlier or later, I'll fit in with you *or* I'll do what you do; **wir ~ uns ganz nach unseren Kunden** we are guided entirely by our customers' wishes; **warum sollte die Frau sich immer nach dem Mann ~?** why should the woman always do what the man wants?; **sich nach den Sternen/der Wettervorhersage/dem, was er behauptet, ~** to go by the stars/the weather forecast/what he maintains; **und richte dich (gefälligst) danach!** *(inf)* (kindly) do as you're told
d *(= abhängen von)* to depend *(nach* on)
e *(esp S Ger: = sich zurechtmachen)* to get ready; **für die Party brauchst du dich nicht extra zu ~** you don't have to get specially done up for the party *(inf)*

VI *(liter: = urteilen)* to judge *(über jdn* sb), to pass judgement *(über +acc* on); **milde/streng ~** to be mild/harsh in one's judgement; **richtet nicht, auf dass ihr nicht gerichtet werdet!** *(Bibl)* judge not, that ye be not judged *(Bibl)*

Rich|ter [ˈrɪçtɐ] **M -s, -, Rich|te|rin** [-ərɪn] **F -, -nen** judge; **jdn/einen Fall vor den ~ bringen** *or* **zerren** to bring sb/a case before a judge; **die verfassungsrechtlich verankerte Garantie des gesetzlichen ~s** the constitutional right to a fair trial; **der vorsitzende ~** the presiding judge; **die ~** the Bench, the judiciary, the judges *pl*; **die Karlsruher ~** the judges of the Federal Constitutional Court; **das Buch der ~** *(Bibl)* (the Book of) Judges; **sich zum ~ aufwerfen** *or* **machen** *(fig)* to set (oneself) up in judgement; **der höchste ~** *(liter: = Gott)* the Supreme Judge; **vor dem höchsten ~ stehen** *(liter: = vor Gott)* to stand before the Judgement Seat *or* the Throne of Judgement

Rich|ter-: **Rich|ter|amt** NT judicial office; *(Sw: = Behörde)* court; **das ~ ausüben** to sit on the Bench; **Rich|ter|ge|setz** NT *law defining the functions and powers of judges*; **rich|ter|lich** [ˈrɪçtɐlɪç] ADJ *attr* judicial; **Rich|ter|ro|be** F judge's robe(s *pl*); **Rich|ter|schaft** [ˈrɪçtɐʃaft] F -, **-en** judiciary, Bench

Rich|ter|ska|la [ˈrɪçtɐ-] F *(Geol)* Richter scale

Rich|ter-: **Rich|ter|spruch** M **a** *(Jur)* ≈ judgement **b** *(Sport)* judges' decision; *(Pferderennen)* stewards' decision; **Rich|ter|stuhl** M Bench; *(= Richteramt)* judicial office; **auf dem ~ sitzen** to be on the Bench; **der ~ (Gottes)** the Judgement Seat, the Throne of Judgement

Richt-: **Richt|fest** NT topping-out ceremony; **Richt|feu|er** NT *(Naut)* leading lights *pl*; *(Aviat)* approach lights *pl*

Richt|funk M directional radio

Richt|funk-: **Richt|funk|ba|ke** F *(Naut)* directional radio beacon; **Richt|funk|ver|bin|dung** F microwave link

Richt|ge|schwin|dig|keit F recommended speed

rich|tig [ˈrɪçtɪç] ✪ 38.1, 40.2, 41, 53.6 **ADJ a** right *no comp*; *(= zutreffend)* correct, right; **eine ~e Erkenntnis/Voraussetzung** *etc* a correct realization/presupposition *etc*; **der ~e Mann am ~en Ort** the right man for the job; **ich halte es für ~/das Richtigste, …** I think it would be right/best …; **nicht ganz ~ (im Kopf) sein** *(inf)* to be not quite right (in the head) *(inf)*; **bin ich hier ~ bei Müller?** *(inf)* is this right for the Müllers?; **der Junge ist ~** *(inf)* that boy's all right *(inf) or* OK *(inf)*
b *(= wirklich, echt)* real, proper; **der ~e Vater** the real father; **die ~e Mutter** the real mother; **ein ~er Idiot** a real *or* proper *or* right *(inf)* idiot

ADV a *(= korrekt)* correctly, right; *passen, funktionieren, liegen etc* properly, correctly, right; **ich habe ihn ~ eingeschätzt** I was right about him; **~ gehend** *(Uhr, Waage)* accurate; **die Uhr geht ~** the clock is right *or* correct; **habe ich ~ gehört?** *(iro)* do my ears deceive me?, am I hearing things?; *(Gerücht betreffend)* is it right what I've heard?; **wenn man es ~ nimmt** *(inf)* really, actually, properly speaking; **du kommst gerade ~!** you're just in time; *(iro)* you're just what I need
b *(inf: = ganz und gar)* really, real *(esp US inf)*; *sich schämen, verlegen* thoroughly, really, real *(esp US inf)*
c *(= wahrhaftig)* right, correct; **du bist doch Konrads Schwester – ~!** you're Konrad's sister – (that's) right; **das ist doch Paul! – ach ja, ~** that's Paul – oh yes, so it is; **wir dachten, es würde gleich regnen, und ~, kaum …** we thought it would soon start raining and, sure enough, scarcely …

Rich|ti|ge(r) [ˈrɪçtɪgə] **MF** *decl as adj* right person, right man/woman *etc*; *(zum Heiraten auch)* Mr/Miss Right; **du bist mir der ~!** *(iro)* you're a fine one *(inf)*; **an den ~n/die ~ geraten** *or* **kommen** to come to the right person; **sechs ~ im Lotto** six right in the lottery

Rich|ti|ge(s) [ˈrɪçtɪgə] NT *decl as adj* right thing; **das ist das ~** that's right; **das ist genau das ~** that's just right *or* the thing *or* the job *(inf)*; **das ist auch nicht das ~** that's not right either; **ich habe nichts ~s gegessen** I haven't had a proper meal; **ich habe nichts ~s gelernt** I didn't really learn anything; **ich habe noch nicht das ~ gefunden** I haven't found anything right *or* suitable; **ich habe endlich was ~s gefunden** at last I've found something suitable

rich|tig|ge|hend **ADJ** *attr* **a** *(inf: = regelrecht)* real, regular *(inf)*, proper **b** *(Uhr etc)* → **richtig ADV a ADV** *(inf)* **~ intelligent** really intelligent; **das ist ja ~ Betrug** that's downright deceit

Rich|tig|keit F -, *no pl* correctness, accuracy; *(von Verhalten, Vorgehen, Meinung)* correctness; *(von Entscheidung)* rightness, correctness; **an der ~ von etw zweifeln, bei etw an der ~ zweifeln** *(inf)* to doubt whether sth is correct *or* right; **die ~ einer Abschrift bescheinigen** to certify a copy as being accurate; **damit hat es** *or* **das hat schon seine ~** that's (quite) right; **es wird schon seine ~ haben** it's bound to be right *or* OK *(inf)*

rich|tig-: **rich|tig+lie|gen** *sep irreg (S Ger, Aus, Sw: aux sein)*, **rich|tig lie|gen** △ *irreg (S Ger, Aus, Sw: aux sein)* VI *(inf)* to fit in; *(= recht haben)* to be right; **bei jdm ~** to get on well with sb; **damit liegst du richtig** *(inf)* you're right there; **bei mir liegen Sie richtig (damit)** *(inf)* you've come to the right person (for that); **rich|tig+stel|len** *sep*, **rich|tig stel|len** △ VT to correct; **ich muss Ihre Behauptung ~** I must put you right there; **Rich|tig|stel|lung** F correction

Richt-: **Richt|ka|no|nier(in)** M(F) *(Mil)* gun-layer; **Richt|kranz** M, **Richt|kro|ne** F *(Build) wreath used in the topping-out ceremony*; **Richt|li|nie** F guideline; **Richt|li|ni|en|kom|pe|tenz** F *(Pol)* authority in matters of general policy; **Richt|maß** NT standard measure; *(= Gewicht)* standard weight; *(fig)* standard; **Richt|mik|ro|fon**, **Richt|mik|ro|phon** NT directional microphone *or* mike *(inf)*; **Richt|platz** M place of execution; **Richt|preis** M **(unverbindlicher) ~** recommended price; **Richt|scheit** NT *(Build)* (spirit) level; **Richt|schnur** F **a** *(Build)* guide line; *(senkrecht)* plumb line **b** *(fig: = Grundsatz)* guiding principle; **Richt|spruch** M *(old)* judgement; **Richt|stät|te** F *(old)* place of execution; **Richt|strahl|an|ten|ne** F, **Richt|strah|ler** M beam *or* directional antenna

Rich|tung [ˈrɪçtʊŋ] F **-, -en a** direction; **in ~ Hamburg** towards *(Brit) or* toward *(US)* Hamburg, in the direction of Hamburg; *(auf Autobahn)* towards *(Brit) or* toward *(US)* Hamburg; **in ~ Süden** towards *(Brit) or* toward *(US)* the south, in a southerly direction; *(auf Autobahn)* on the southbound carriageway *(Brit) or* lane; **in nördliche ~** northwards, towards *(Brit) or* toward *(US)* the north, in a northerly direction; **die Autobahn/der Zug ~ Hamburg** the Hamburg autobahn/train; **nach allen ~en, in alle ~en** in all directions; **in umgekehrter ~** in the opposite *or* other direction; **die ~ ändern** *or* **wechseln** to change direction(s); **die ~ anzeigen** to indicate the direction, to point the way; *(mit Fahrzeug)* to indicate which way one is going to turn; **eine ~ nehmen** *or* **einschlagen** to head *or* drive/walk *etc* in a direction; **eine neue ~ bekommen** to change course, to take a new turn *or* direction; **einem Gespräch eine bestimmte ~ geben** to turn a conversation in a particular direction; **in die gleiche ~ gehen** *or* **zielen** *(fig)* to point in the same direction; **er will sich nach keiner ~ hin festlegen** he won't commit himself in any way at all; **ein Schritt in die richtige/falsche ~** a step in the right/wrong direction; **ein Schritt in ~ Frieden und Stabilität** a step toward(s) peace and stability; **in jeder ~** each way, in each direction; *(fig: = in jeder Hinsicht)* in every respect; **irgend etwas in der** *or* **dieser ~** something along those lines
b *(= Tendenz)* trend; *(in der Kunst, einer Partei)* line, trend; *(= die Vertreter einer Richtung)* movement; *(= Denkrichtung, Lehrmeinung)* school of thought; **die herrschende ~** the prevailing trend; **Picasso begann eine völlig neue ~ in der Malerei** Picasso started a completely new direction in painting; **die beiden ~en in der katholischen Kirche** the two lines of thought in the Catholic church; **sie gehören den verschiedensten politischen ~en an** they have the most varied political sympathies; **die ganze ~ passt uns nicht!** that's not the sort of thing we want

rich|tung|ge|bend ADJ pointing the way; *(in der Mode)* trendsetting; **für jdn/etw ~ sein** to set the pattern for sb/sth

Rich|tungs-: **Rich|tungs|än|de|rung** F change of *or* in direction; **Rich|tungs|kampf** M *(Pol)* factional dispute; **rich|tungs|los** ADJ lacking a sense of direction; **Rich|tungs|lo|sig|keit** F -, *no pl* lack of a sense of direction; **Rich|tungs|pfeil** M *(Mot)* lane indication arrow; **Rich|tungs|streit** M *(Pol)* factional dispute; **Rich|tungs|tas|te** F *(Comput)* direction key, arrow key; **Rich|tungs|wech|sel** M *(lit, fig)* change of direction

rich|tung(s)|wei|send ADJ pointing the way; **~ sein** to point the way (ahead)

Richt-: **Richt|waa|ge** F spirit level; **Richt|wert** M guideline; **Richt|zahl** F approximate figure

Ri|cke ['rɪkə] **F -, -n** doe

rieb *pret von* **reiben**

rie|chen ['ri:çn] *pret* **roch** [rɔx], *ptp* **gerochen** [gə'rɔxn] **VT** to smell; **ich rieche Gas** I (can) smell gas; **ich rieche das Gewürz gern** I like the smell of this spice; **Lunte** *or* **den Braten ~** *(inf)* to smell a rat *(inf)*; **ich kann das nicht ~** *(inf)* I can't stand the smell of it; *(fig: = nicht leiden)* I can't stand it; **jdn nicht ~ können** *(inf)* not to be able to stand sb, to hate sb's guts *(inf)*; **das konnte ich doch nicht ~!** *(inf)* how was I (supposed) to know?, I'm not psychic *(inf)* → **Meile**

VI a *(= Geruchssinn haben)* to have a sense of smell, to be able to smell; **nicht mehr ~ können** to have lost one's sense of smell; **Hunde können gut ~** dogs have a good sense of smell

b *(= bestimmten Geruch haben)* to smell; **gut/schlecht ~** to smell good/bad; **nach etw ~** to smell of sth; **aus dem Mund ~** to have bad breath; **das riecht nach Betrug/Verrat** *(fig inf)* that smacks of deceit/treachery

c *(= schnüffeln)* to smell, to sniff; *(Tier)* to sniff; **an jdm/etw ~** to smell sb/sth, to sniff (at) sb/sth; *(Tier)* to sniff (at) sb/sth; **riech mal** have a sniff *or* smell

VI *impers* to smell; **es riecht angebrannt** there's a smell of burning, there's a burning smell; **es riecht nach Gas** there's a smell of gas

Rie|cher ['ri:çɐ] **M -s, -** *(inf)* **einen ~ (für etw) haben** to have a nose (for sth); **einen guten** *or* **den richtigen ~ (für etw) haben** to have a good nose (for sth) *(inf)*; **da habe ich doch den richtigen ~ gehabt!** I knew it all along!

Riech-: **Riech|fläsch|chen** NT (bottle of) smelling salts *pl*; **Riech|kol|ben** M *(inf)* hooter *(Brit inf)*, conk *(Brit inf)*, honker *(US inf)*; **Riech|nerv** M olfactory nerve; **Riech|or|gan** NT organ of smell, olfactory organ; **Riech|salz** NT smelling salts *pl*; **Riech|stoff** M aromatic substance

Ried [ri:t] **NT -s, -e** [-də] **a** *(= Schilf)* reeds *pl* **b** *(S Ger: = Moor)* marsh

Ried|gras NT sedge

rief *pret von* **rufen**

Rie|fe ['ri:fə] **F -, -n** groove, channel; *(in Säulen)* flute

Rie|ge ['ri:gə] **F -, -n** *(Sport)* team, squad; *(fig: = Gruppe)* team

Rie|gel ['ri:gl] **M -s, - a** *(= Verschluss)* bolt; **den ~ an etw** *(dat)* **vorlegen** to bolt sth; **vergiss nicht, den ~ vorzulegen!** don't forget to bolt the door *etc*; **den ~ an etw** *(dat)* **zurückschieben** to unbolt sth; **einer Sache** *(dat)* **einen ~ vorschieben** *or (Sw)* **schieben** *(fig)* to put a stop to sth, to clamp down on sth; **ein ~ gegen aggressive Politik** a restraint on *or* against aggressive policies → **Schloss b b** *(= Schokoladenriegel)* bar; *(= Seifenstück)* cake, bar **c** *(Sew) (= Lasche)* tab; *(von Jackett)* strap; *(für Haken)* eye; *(am Knopfloch)* bar tack

Rie|gel-: **Rie|gel|bau** M *pl* **-bauten** *(Sw)* half-timbering; *(Gebäude)* half-timbered building; **Rie|gel|stel|lung** F *(Mil)* switch line *or* position; **Rie|gel|werk** NT *(dial)* half-timbering

Rie|gen-: **Rie|gen|füh|rer(in)** M(F) team *or* squad leader *or* captain; **rie|gen|wei|se** ADV in teams *or* squads

Riem|chen|schuh ['ri:mçən-] M strap shoe

Rie|men ['ri:mən] **M -s, -** *(= Treibriemen, Gürtel)* belt; *(an Schuhen, Kleidung, Koffer, Gepäck)* strap; *(= Schnürsenkel)* leather shoelace; *(= Peitschenriemen)* thong; **jdn mit einem ~ verdreschen** to strap sb, to give sb the strap *or* belt; **den ~ enger schnallen** *(fig)* to tighten one's belt; **sich am ~ reißen** *(fig inf)* to get a grip on oneself

Rie|men **M -s, -** *(Sport)* oar; **die ~ einlegen** to ship oars; **sich in die ~ legen** *(lit, fig)* to put one's back into it

Rie|men-: **Rie|men|an|trieb** M belt drive; **Rie|men|werk** NT strapping

Ries [ri:s] **NT -es, -e** [-zə] *(Measure)* German ream, ≈ 2 reams

Rie|se ['ri:zə] **das macht nach Adam ~ EUR 3,50** *(hum inf)* the way I learned it at school that makes EUR 3.50

Rie|se **M -n, -n** *(lit, fig)* giant; *(sl Hist: = Tausendmarkschein)* 1000 mark note, big one *(inf)*; **ein böser ~** an ogre; **ein ~ von Mensch** *or* **von einem Menschen** a giant of a man/woman; **roter ~** *(Astron)* red giant

Rie|sel|fel|der PL sewage farm

rie|seln ['ri:zln] **VI** *aux sein (Wasser, Sand)* to trickle; *(Regen)* to drizzle; *(Schnee)* to float *or* flutter down; *(Staub)* to fall down; *(Musik)* to filter; **der Kalk rieselt von der Wand** lime is crumbling off the wall; **Schuppen ~ ihm vom Kopf** dandruff is flaking off his head; **ein angenehmes Lustgefühl rieselte durch seinen Körper** a pleasurable sensation ran *or* thrilled through his body; **ein Schauder rieselte mir über den Rücken/durch alle Glieder** a shiver went down my spine/through me

Rie|sen- PREF gigantic, enormous, colossal; *(Zool, Bot etc auch)* giant; **Rie|sen|amei|se** F carpenter ant; **Rie|sen|ar|beit** F *(= Pensum)* gigantic *etc* job; *(= Anstrengung)* gigantic *etc* effort; **Rie|sen|ba|by** NT *(Kind)* huge baby; *(fig pej inf: = Mann)* (lumbering) hulk *(inf)*; *(= Hund)* huge hound; **Rie|sen|chan|ce** F tremendous chance; **Rie|sen|dumm|heit** F *(inf)* monumental stupidity *or* mistake, mega boo-boo *(US inf)*; **Rie|sen|er|folg** M gigantic *etc* success; *(Theat, Film)* smash hit; **Rie|sen|fräu|lein** NT giantess; **Rie|sen|gar|ne|le** F *(Zool)* king prawn; **Rie|sen|ge|bir|ge** NT *(Geog)* Sudeten Mountains *pl*; **Rie|sen|ge|stalt** F **a** *(Größe)* gigantic *etc* frame **b** *(= Riese)* giant; **Rie|sen|ge|winn** M huge profits *pl*; *(beim Spiel)* huge winnings *pl*; **einen ~ erzielen** to win a fortune; **rie|sen|groß**, **rie|sen|haft** ADJ = **riesig**; **Rie|sen|hai** M basking shark; **Rie|sen|hun|ger** M *(inf)* enormous appetite; **ich habe einen ~** *(inf)* I could eat a horse *(inf)*; **Rie|sen|kraft** F colossal *or* enormous strength *no pl*; **mit Riesenkräften** *(= mit enormer Anstrengung)* with a colossal *or* an enormous effort; **Rie|sen|por|ti|on** F *(inf)* giant portion; **eine ~ Fleisch** a huge piece of meat; **Rie|sen|rad** NT big *or* Ferris wheel; **Rie|sen|sa|la|man|der** M giant salamander; **Rie|sen|schild|krö|te** F giant tortoise; **Rie|sen|schlan|ge** F boa; **Rie|sen|schreck** M **einen ~ kriegen** *(inf)* to get a terrible fright; **ich habe einen ~ gekriegt** I got such a fright; **Rie|sen|schritt** M giant step *or* stride; **wir nähern uns mit ~en dem amerikanischen System** we are moving swiftly toward(s) the American system; **Weihnachten nähert sich mit ~en** Christmas is fast approaching; **einer Sache** *(dat)* **einen ~ näher kommen** to take a giant step *or* stride towards sth; **Rie|sen|sla|lom** M giant slalom; **Rie|sen|tra|ra** NT *(inf)* great fuss *or* to-do *(inf)*; **Rie|sen|werk** NT colossal work; *(= Gesamtwerk)* colossal works *pl*; **Rie|sen|wuchs** M giantism; *(Med auch)* gigantism; **Rie|sen|wut** F **eine ~ (im Bauch) haben** *(inf)* to be wild with rage

rie|sig ['ri:zɪç] **ADJ a** *(= sehr groß, gigantisch)* enormous, huge; *Spaß* tremendous **b** *(inf: = toll)* terrific, fantastic **ADV** *(inf: = sehr, überaus)* tremendously, incredibly

Rie|sin ['ri:zɪn] **F -, -nen** giantess

Ries|ling ['ri:slɪŋ] **M -s, -e** Riesling

riet *pret von* **raten**

Riff [rɪf] **NT -(e)s, -e** *(= Felsklippe)* reef

Riff **M -(e)s, -s** *(Mus)* riff

Rif|fel ['rɪfl] **F -, -n** *(Tex)* (flax) hackle, flax comb

rif|feln ['rɪfln] **VT a** *Flachs* to comb **b** *(Tech)* to groove, to channel; *Säule* to flute

Rigg [rɪg] **NT -s, -s** *(Naut)* rigging

Rig|gung ['rɪgʊŋ] **F -, -en** *(Naut)* rigging

ri|gi|de [ri'gi:də] **ADJ** *(geh)* rigid

Ri|gi|di|tät [rigidi'tɛ:t] **F -**, *no pl (Med, Psych)* rigidity

Ri|gips|plat|te® ['ri:gɪpsplatə] **F** *type of plasterboard*, gypsum wallboard, dry wall *(US)*, ≈ Sheetrock® *(US)*

Ri|go|le [ri'go:lə] **F -, -n** *(Agr)* (drainage) trench

Ri|go|ris|mus [rigo'rɪsmʊs] **M -**, *no pl (geh)* rigour *(Brit)*, rigor *(US)*

ri|go|ris|tisch [rigo'rɪstɪʃ] **ADJ** *(geh)* rigorous

ri|go|ros [rigo'ro:s] **ADJ** rigorous; **ich bleibe dabei, da bin ich ganz ~** I'm sticking to that, I'm adamant **ADV** *ablehnen* rigorously; *kürzen auch* drastically; **~ durchgreifen** to take decisive action

Ri|go|ro|si|tät [rigorozi'tɛ:t] **F -**, *no pl* rigour *(Brit)*, rigor *(US)*

Ri|go|ro|sum [rigo'ro:zʊm] **NT -s, Rigorosa** *or (Aus)* **Rigorosen** [-za, -zn] *(Univ)* (doctoral *or* PhD) viva *(Brit) or* oral

Rik|scha ['rɪkʃa] **F -, -s** rickshaw

Ril|le ['rɪlə] **F -, -n** groove; *(in Säule)* flute

Ril|len-: **ril|len|för|mig** ADJ groove-like; **Ril|len|pro|fil** NT tread

ril|lig ['rɪlɪç] **ADJ** *(rare)* fluted

Ri|mes|se [ri'mɛsə] **F -, -n** *(Fin)* remittance

rin- [rɪn] **PREF** *(dial)* = **herein-, hinein-**

Rind [rɪnt] **NT -(e)s, -er** [-dɐ] **a** *(= Tier)* cow; *(= Bulle)* bull; **~er** cattle *pl*; **10 ~er** 10 head of cattle; **die Inkubationszeit beim ~** the incubation period in cattle **b** *(inf: = Rindfleisch)* beef; **vom ~** beef *attr*; **Hackfleisch vom ~** minced *(esp Brit) or* ground *(US)* beef, mince

Rin|de ['rɪndə] **F -, -n** *(= Baumrinde)* bark; *(= Brotrinde)* crust; *(= Käserinde)* rind; *(Anat)* cortex

rin|den|los ADJ *Baum* barkless; *Käse* rindless

Rin|der-: **Rin|der|bouil|lon** F beef stock *or* bouillon *(form)*; **Rin|der|bra|ten** M *(roh)* joint of beef; *(gebraten)* roast beef *no indef art*; **Rin|der|brem|se** F horsefly; **Rin|der|brü|he** F beef broth; **Rin|der|brust** F brisket (of beef); **Rin|der|fi|let** NT fillet of beef; **Rin|der|her|de** F herd of cattle; **Rin|der|hirt(in)** M(F) cowherd; *(in Nordamerika)* cowboy/-girl; *(in Südamerika)* gaucho; *(in Australien)* drover; **Rin|der|len|de** F beef tenderloin

rin|dern ['rɪndɐn] **VI** *(Kuh)* to be on *(Brit) or* in heat

Rin|der-: **Rin|der|pest** F *(Vet)* rinderpest; **Rin|der|roll|bra|ten** M roast rolled *or* collared beef; **Rin|der|seu|che** F epidemic cattle disease; *(= BSE)* mad cow disease; **Rin|der|talg** M beef tallow; **Rin|der|wahn|(sinn)** M mad cow disease; **Rin|der|zucht** F cattle farming *or* raising; **Rin|der|zun|ge** F ox tongue

Rind-: **Rind|fleisch** NT beef; **Rind|fleisch|brü|he** F beef broth

Rinds- *in cpds (Aus, S Ger)* = **Rinder-**: **Rinds|le|der** NT cowhide; **rinds|le|dern** ADJ *attr* cowhide; **Rinds|stück** NT *(Cook)* joint of beef

Rind|vieh **NT a** *no pl* cattle; **10 Stück ~** 10 head of cattle **b** *pl* **Rindviecher** *(inf: = Idiot)* ass *(inf)*

Ring [rɪŋ] **M -(e)s, -e a** ring; *(= Kettenring)* link; *(= Wurfring)* quoit; *(= Einweckring)* seal, rubber; *(= Rettungsring)* life buoy, life belt; **die ~e tauschen** *or* **wechseln** to exchange rings

b *(= Kreis) (= Jahresring, Rauchring)* ring; *(auf dem Wasser, von Menschen)* circle, ring; *(= Ringstraße)* ring road; **(dunkle) ~e unter den Augen haben** to have (dark) rings under one's eyes

c *(Sport) (= Boxring)* ring; *(von Schießscheibe)* ring, circle; **~e** *(Turnen)* rings; **acht ~e schießen** to score an eight; **~ frei!** seconds out *or* away!; *(fig)* clear the decks!; **in den ~ steigen** *(lit)* to climb into the ring; *(fig)* to enter the lists *or* the fray

d *(Astron, Met, Chem)* ring

e *(= Vereinigung)* circle, group; *(von Großhändlern, Erzeugern)* group; *(= Bande)* ring; *(Theat: = Abonnentenring)* theatre-goers' *(Brit) or* theater-goers' *(US)* group

f *(liter: = Kreislauf)* circle, cycle; **der ~ schließt sich** the circle is completed *or* closed, the wheel comes *or* turns full circle

g (= *Sagenzyklus*) cycle; **der ~ (des Nibelungen)** the Ring (of the Nibelung)
Ring-: **ring|ar|tig** ADJ ring-like; **Ring|bahn** F circle line; **Ring|buch** NT ring binder; **Ring|buch|ein|la|ge** F loose-leaf pad
Rin|gel [ˈrɪŋl] M **-s, -** ring; (= *Locke*) ringlet
Rin|gel|blu|me F marigold
Rin|gel|chen [ˈrɪŋlçən] NT **-s, -** (*inf*) little ring
Rin|gel|gans F Brent goose
rin|ge|lig [ˈrɪŋəlɪç] ADJ ringleted
Rin|gel|lo|cke F ringlet; **~n tragen** to wear one's hair in ringlets, to have ringlets
rin|geln [ˈrɪŋln] VT (*Pflanze*) to (en)twine; *Schwanz etc auch* to curl → *auch* **geringelt** VR to go curly, to curl; (*Rauch*) to curl up(wards); **die Schlange ringelte sich durch das Unterholz** the snake wriggled through the undergrowth; **der Schwanz des Schweins ringelt sich** the pig has a curly tail; **die Schlange ringelte sich um den Baum** the snake coiled *or* curled itself around the tree
Rin|gel-: **Rin|gel|nat|ter** F grass snake; **Rin|gel|pie(t)z** [ˈrɪŋlpiːts] M **-es, -e** (*hum inf*) hop (*inf*); **~ mit Anfassen** hop (*inf*); **Rin|gel|rei|gen** M, **Rin|gel|rei|hen** [-raiən] M **-s, -** ring-a-ring-o' roses; **einen ~ tanzen** to play ring-a-ring-o' roses; **Rin|gel|schwanz** M, **Rin|gel|schwänz|chen** NT (*inf*) curly tail; **Rin|gel|so|cke** F hooped *or* striped sock; **Rin|gel|spiel** NT (*Aus*) merry-go-round, roundabout (*Brit*); **Rin|gel|tau|be** F wood pigeon, ring-dove; **Rin|gel|wurm** M ringed worm, annelid (*spec*)
rin|gen [ˈrɪŋən] *pret* **rang** [raŋ], *ptp* **gerungen** [gəˈrʊŋən] VT **die Hände ~** to wring one's hands; **er rang ihr das Messer aus der Hand** he wrenched *or* wrested the knife from her hand
VI **a** (*lit, fig*: = *kämpfen*) to wrestle (*mit* with); **mit sich/dem Tode ~** to wrestle with oneself/death; **mit den Tränen ~** to struggle *or* fight to keep back one's tears
b (= *streben*) **nach** *or* **um etw ~** to struggle for sth; **er rang um Fassung** he struggled to maintain his composure; **ums Überleben ~** (*liter*) to struggle to survive
VR **ein Schluchzen rang sich aus ihrer Brust** (*liter*) a sob was wrung from her breast (*liter*)
Rin|gen [ˈrɪŋən] NT **-s,** *no pl* (*Sport*) wrestling; (*fig*) struggle
Rin|ger [ˈrɪŋɐ] M **-s, -**, **Rin|ge|rin** [-ərɪn] F **-, -nen** wrestler
Rin|ger|griff M wrestling hold
rin|ge|risch [ˈrɪŋərɪʃ] ADJ *Fähigkeiten* as a wrestler; **mit ~em Geschick** with the skill of a wrestler
Ring-: **Ring|fahn|dung** F dragnet; **Ring|fin|ger** M ring finger; **ring|för|mig** ADJ ring-like; **~e Verbindungen** (*Chem*) cyclic *or* ring compounds ADV in a ring *or* circle; **die Truppen schlossen die Festung ~ ein** the troops surrounded the fortress; **die Straße führt ~ um die Stadt herum** the road encircles the town; **der Wallgraben umschließt die Stadt ~** the rampart rings *or* encircles the town; **Ring|hef|ter** M ring binder; **Ring|kampf** M fight; (*Sport*) wrestling match; **Ring|kämp|fer(in)** M(F) wrestler
Ring|lein [ˈrɪŋlain] NT **-s, -** ring
Ring|lei|tung F (*Elec etc*) ring main
ring|lig [ˈrɪŋlɪç] ADJ ringleted
Rin|glot|te [rɪŋˈglɔtə] F **-, -n** (*Aus*: = *Reneklode*) greengage
Ring-: **Ring|map|pe** ring binder; **Ring|mau|er** F circular wall; **die ~ rund um die Burg** the wall encircling *or* surrounding the castle; **Ring|mus|kel** M sphincter; **Ring|ord|ner** M ring binder; **Ring|pan|zer** M articulated *or* jointed armour (*Brit*) *or* armor (*US*); **Ring|rich|ter(in)** M(F) (*Sport*) referee
rings [rɪŋs] ADV (all) around; **die Stadt ist ~ von Bergen umgeben** the town is completely surrounded *or* encircled by mountains, there are mountains all around the town; **ich bin ~ um die Kirche gegangen** I went all the way (a)round (the outside of) the church; **wir mussten uns alle ~ im Kreis aufstellen** we all had to get into *or* make a circle
Ring-: **Ring|schei|be** F (*Sport*) target (*marked with concentric rings*); **Ring|sen|dung** F (*Rad, TV*) link up (transmission)
rings|he|rum [ˈrɪŋshɛˈrʊm] ADV all (the way) around
Ring|stra|ße F ring road
rings-: **rings|um** [ˈrɪŋsˈlʊm] ADV (all) around; **~ konnte ich nichts sehen** I could see nothing around me; **rings|um|her** [ˈrɪŋslʊmˈheːɐ] ADV around
Ring-: **Ring|tausch** M exchange (*between three or more people*); (*bei Heirat*) exchanging of rings; **Ring|ten|nis** NT (*Sport*) quoits *sing*, deck tennis; **Ring|vor|le|sung** F *series of lectures by different speakers*; **Ring|wall** M = **Ringmauer**
Rin|ne [ˈrɪnə] F **-, -n** (= *Rille*) groove; (= *Furche, Abflussrinne, Fahrrinne*) channel; (= *Dachrinne, inf*: = *Rinnstein*) gutter; (*Geog*) gap
rin|nen [ˈrɪnən] *pret* **rann** [ran], *ptp* **geronnen** [gəˈrɔnən] VI *aux sein* (= *fließen*) to run; **das Blut rann ihm in Strömen aus der Wunde** blood streamed from his wound; **die Zeit rinnt (dahin)** (*liter*) time is slipping away (*liter*); **das Geld rinnt ihm durch die Finger** (*fig*) money slips through his fingers
Rinn-: **Rinn|sal** [ˈrɪnzaːl] NT **-(e)s, -e** rivulet; **Rinn|stein** M (= *Gosse*) gutter; (*old*: = *Ausguss*) drain; **jdn aus dem ~ holen** *or* **auflesen** (*fig*) to pick sb out of the gutter; **im ~ enden** to come to a sorry end
Ripp|chen [ˈrɪpçən] NT **-s, -** (*Cook*) *slightly cured pork rib*
Rip|pe [ˈrɪpə] F **-, -n** **a** (*Anat, Cook*) rib; **bei ihm kann man die ~n zählen** (*inf*) you could play a tune on his ribs (*inf*); **er hat nichts auf den ~n** (*inf*) he's just skin and bones; **… damit du was auf die ~n kriegst** (*inf*) … to put a bit of flesh on you; **ich kann es mir nicht aus den ~n schneiden** (*inf*) **ich kann es doch nicht durch die ~n schwitzen** (*inf*) I can't just produce it from nowhere → **leiern** **b** (*von Blatt, Gewölbe etc, in Stoffmuster*) rib **c** (*von Heizkörper, Kühlaggregat*) fin **d** (*von Apfelsine*) segment; (*von Schokolade*) row (of squares)
rip|pen [ˈrɪpn] VT to rib → *auch* **gerippt**
Rip|pen-: **Rip|pen|bo|gen** M (*Anat*) costal arch; **Rip|pen|bruch** M broken *or* fractured rib; **Rip|pen|fell** NT pleura; **Rip|pen|fell|ent|zün|dung** F pleurisy; **Rip|pen|ge|wöl|be** NT (*Archit*) ribbed vaulting; **Rip|pen|qual|le** F comb jelly, ctenophorane (*spec*); **Rip|pen|shirt** NT ribbed shirt; **Rip|pen|slip** M ribbed briefs *pl*; **Rip|pen|speer** M OR NT (*Cook*) spare rib; **Kass(e)ler ~** *slightly cured pork spare rib*; **Rip|pen|stoß** M nudge, dig (*Brit*) *or* poke in the ribs; (*schmerzhaft*) thump (*inf*) *or* dig (*Brit inf*) *or* poke in the ribs; **ein freundschaftlicher ~** (*fig*) a quiet *or* friendly word; **Rip|pen|strick|pul|li** M ribbed sweater; **Rip|pen|stück** NT (*Cook*) rib cut; **vorderes ~ vom Lamm** rack of lamb
Ripp|li [ˈrɪpli] PL (*Sw*) ribs *pl*
Ripp|speer [ˈrɪp-] M = **Rippenspeer**
rips [rɪps] INTERJ **~, raps!** rip!
Rips [rɪps] M **-es, -e** (*Tex*) rep
Ri|si|ko [ˈriːziko] NT **-s, -s** *or* **Risiken** *or* (*Aus*) **Risken** [ˈriːzikn, ˈrɪskn] risk; **auf eigenes ~** at one's own risk; **bitte, Sie können das machen, aber auf eigenes ~** do it by all means, but on your own head be it; **ohne ~** without risk; **etw ohne ~ tun** to do sth without taking a risk; **es ist nicht ohne ~, das zu tun** there is a risk involved in doing that, doing that is not without risk; **die Sache ist ohne ~** there's no risk involved; **als gutes ~ gelten** to be a good (credit) risk
Ri|si|ko-: **Ri|si|ko|be|reit|schaft** F readiness to take risks; **sie hat eine hohe ~** she is prepared to take big risks; **Ri|si|ko|fak|tor** M risk factor; **Ri|si|ko|freu|de** F readiness to take risks; **ri|si|ko|freu|dig** ADJ prepared to take risks; **sie ist sehr ~** she likes to take risks; **Ri|si|ko|ge|burt** F (*Med*) high-risk birth; **Ri|si|ko|grup|pe** F (high-)risk group; **Ri|si|ko|ka|pi|tal** NT (*Fin*) risk *or* venture capital; **Ri|si|ko|le|bens|ver|si|che|rung** F (renewable) term life insurance; **Ri|si|ko|ma|nage|ment** NT (*Fin, St Ex*) risk management; **Ri|si|ko|pa|ti|ent(in)** M(F) high-risk patient; **ri|si|ko|scheu** ADJ unwilling to take risks; **Ri|si|ko|schwan|ger|schaft** F (*Med*) high-risk pregnancy; **Ri|si|ko|stu|die** F risk analysis; **Ri|si|ko|trä|ger(in)** M(F) (*von Krankheit*) high-risk carrier; (*Insur, Fin*) risk bearer; **~ von Lungenkrebs sein** to be in a high-risk category for lung cancer; **Ri|si|ko|ver|si|che|rung** F term insurance; **Ri|si|ko|vor|sor|ge** F (*auch Econ*) risk provision, provision for risks; **Ri|si|ko|zu|la|ge** F ≈ danger money, ≈ hazard pay (*US*); **Ri|si|ko|zu|schlag** M (*bei Versicherung*) excess, loading
ris|kant [rɪsˈkant] ADJ risky, chancy (*inf*); **das ist mir zu ~** that's too risky *or* chancy (*inf*) for me
ris|kie|ren [rɪsˈkiːrən] *ptp* **riskiert** VT **a** (= *aufs Spiel setzen*) to risk; **etwas/nichts ~** to take risks *or* chances/no risks *or* chances; **seine Stellung/sein Geld ~** to risk losing one's job/money, to put one's job/money at risk; **sein Geld bei etw ~** to risk one's money on sth **b** (= *wagen*) to venture; **traust du dich, hier runterzuspringen? – ja, ich riskiers!** do you think you dare jump down? – yes, I'll risk *or* chance it!; **in Gegenwart seiner Frau riskiert er kein Wort** when his wife is present he dare not say a word → **Lippe**
Ri|sot|to [riˈzɔto] M OR NT **-(s), -s** risotto
Ris|pe [ˈrɪspə] F **-, -n** (*Bot*) panicle
ris|pen|för|mig, **ris|pig** [ˈrɪspɪç] ADJ (*Bot*) panicled, paniculate
riss *pret von* **reißen**
Riss [rɪs] M **-es, -e** **a** (*in Stoff, Papier etc*) tear, rip; (*in Erde, Gestein*) crevice, fissure; (= *Sprung*: *in Wand, Behälter etc*) crack; (= *Hautriss*) chap; (*fig*: = *Kluft*) rift, split; **die Freundschaft hat einen (tiefen) ~ bekommen** a (deep) rift has developed in their friendship; **durch das Volk geht ein tiefer ~** there is a deep split in the people, the people are deeply divided **b** (*Archit*: = *Zeichnung*) sketch, sketch plan **c** (*Hunt*: = *Raubwildbeute*) kill
ris|sig [ˈrɪsɪç] ADJ *Boden, Wand, Leder* cracked; *Haut, Hände, Lippen* chapped
Riss|wun|de F laceration, lacerated wound
Rist [rɪst] M **-(e)s, -e** **a** (*am Fuß*) instep; (*an der Hand*) back (of the hand) **b** (*beim Pferd*) withers *pl*
ri|te [ˈriːtə] ADV (*Univ*) *lowest pass grade in doctoral examinations*
Ri|ten *pl von* **Ritus**
ritsch [rɪtʃ] INTERJ **~, ratsch!** rip!
ritt *pret von* **reiten**
Ritt [rɪt] M **-(e)s, -e** ride; **einen ~ machen** to go for a ride; **in scharfem ~ jagte er über die Felder** he rode furiously across the fields; **ein ~ über den Bodensee** (*fig geh*) a leap in the dark
Ritt|ber|ger [ˈrɪtbɛrgɐ] M **-s, -** (*Eiskunstlauf*) Rittberger
Rit|ter [ˈrɪtɐ] M **-s, -** **a** (*im Mittelalter, im alten Rom*) knight; (= *Kavalier*) cavalier; (*fig, hum*: = *Kämpfer*) champion; **fahrender ~** knight errant; **jdn zum ~ schlagen** to knight sb, to dub sb knight; **der ~ von der traurigen Gestalt** the Knight of the Sorrowful Countenance; **ein ~ ohne Furcht und Tadel** (*lit*) a doughty knight; (*fig*) a knight in shining armour (*Brit*) *or* armor (*US*) **b** (*Adelstitel*) ≈ Sir; **X ~ von Y** ≈ Sir X of Y **c** (= *Ordensträger*) knight **d** (= *Schmetterling*) swallowtail **e** (*Cook*) **arme ~** *pl* ≈ bread-and-butter pudding
Rit|ter-: **Rit|ter|burg** F knight's castle; **Rit|ter|gut** NT ≈ manor; **Rit|ter|guts|be|sit|zer(in)** M(F) ≈ lord/lady of the manor; **rit|-**

ter|haft ADJ = **ritterlich**; **Rit|ter|kreuz** NT *(Mil)* Knight's Cross; ~ **mit Eichenlaub** ≈ Knight's Cross with bar; **Rit|ter|kreuz|trä|ger** M holder of the Knight's Cross; **rit|ter|lich** ['rɪtɐlɪç] ADJ *(lit)* knightly; *(fig)* chivalrous; **Rit|ter|lich|keit** F -, -en chivalry, chivalrousness; **Rit|ter|or|den** M order of knights; **der Deutsche** ~ the Teutonic Order; **Rit|ter|ro|man** M *(Liter)* romance of chivalry; **Rit|ter|rüs|tung** F knight's armour *(Brit)* or armor *(US)*; **Rit|ter|schaft** ['rɪtɐʃaft] F -, -en **a** *(= die Ritter)* knights *pl*, knighthood **b** *(= Ritterehre)* knighthood; **Rit|ter|schlag** M *(Hist)* dubbing; *(fig)* ennoblement; **den ~ empfangen** to be knighted, to be dubbed knight; **(jdm) den ~ erteilen** to confer a knighthood (on sb)

Rit|ters|mann M *pl* **-leute** *(poet)* knight

Rit|ter-: **Rit|ter|sporn** M *pl* **-sporne** *(Bot)* larkspur, delphinium; **Rit|ter|stand** M knighthood; **in den ~ erhoben werden** to be raised to the knighthood, to be knighted; **Rit|ter|tum** ['rɪtɐtu:m] NT -s, *no pl* knighthood; **Rit|ter-und-Räu|ber-Ro|man** M *(Liter)* late eighteenth century sentimental novel about knights and robbers, romance of chivalry; **Rit|ter|we|sen** NT, *no pl* knighthood; **Rit|ter|zeit** F Age of Chivalry

ritt|lings ['rɪtlɪŋs] ADV astride *(auf etw (dat)* sth)

Ritt|meis|ter M *(old Mil)* cavalry captain, captain (of horse)

Ri|tu|al [ri'tua:l] NT -s, -e *or* -ien [-liən] *(lit, fig)* ritual

Ri|tu|a|le [ri'tua:lə] NT -, *no pl (Eccl)* ritual *(book)*; ~ **Romanum** missal

Ri|tu|al|hand|lung F ritual act

Ri|tu|a|li|en PL *(Eccl)* ritual objects *pl*

Ri|tu|al|mord M ritual murder

ri|tu|ell [ri'tuɛl] ADJ *(Rel, fig)* ritual

Ri|tus ['ri:tʊs] M -, **Riten** [-tn] rite; *(fig)* ritual

Ritz [rɪts] M -es, -e **a** *(= Kratzer)* scratch **b** *(= Spalte)* chink, crack

Rit|ze ['rɪtsə] F -, -n *(= Riss, Poritze)* crack; *(= Fuge)* join, gap; **auf der ~ schlafen** *(hum inf)* to sleep in the middle

Rit|zel ['rɪtsl] NT -s, - *(Tech)* pinion

rit|zen ['rɪtsn] VT to scratch; *(= einritzen) Initialen, Namen etc auch* to carve → *auch* **geritzt** VR to scratch oneself

Rit|zer ['rɪtsɐ] M -s, - *(inf)* scratch

Ri|va|le [ri'va:lə] M -n, -n, **Ri|va|lin** [ri'va:lɪn] F -, -nen rival

ri|va|li|sie|ren [rivali'zi:rən] *ptp* **rivalisiert** VI **mit jdm (um etw)** ~ to compete with sb (for sth); **34 ~de Parteien** 34 rival parties

Ri|va|li|tät [rivali'tɛ:t] F -, -en rivalry

Ri|va|ner [ri'va:nɐ] M -s, - *(= Wein)* riesling-silvaner

Ri|vi|e|ra [ri'vie:ra] F - Riviera

Ri|zi|nus ['ri:tsinʊs] M -, - *or* -se **a** *(Bot)* castor-oil plant **b** *(auch* **Rizinusöl)** castor oil

RNS [ɛrlɛn'lɛs] F -, - *abbr von* **Ribonukleinsäure** RNA

Road|die ['ro:dɪ] M -s, -s roadie

Road|show ['ro:dʃo:] F -, -s road show

Roads|ter ['ro:dstɐ] M -s, - roadster

Roast|beef ['ro:stbi:f] NT -s, -s *(roh)* beef; *(gebraten)* roast beef

Rob|be ['rɔbə] F -, -n seal

rob|ben ['rɔbn] VI *aux sein (Mil)* to crawl

Rob|ben-: **Rob|ben|fang** M sealing, seal hunting; **Rob|ben|fän|ger(in)** M(F) sealer, seal hunter; **Rob|ben|jagd** F sealing, seal hunting; **Rob|ben|ster|ben** NT (high number of) seal deaths *pl*; **das ~ an der Nordsee** the high number of seal deaths in the North Sea

Ro|be ['ro:bə] F -, -n **a** *(= Abendkleid)* evening gown; **in großer ~** in evening dress **b** *(= Amtstracht)* (official) robe *or* robes *pl*

Ro|bi|nie [ro'bi:niə] F -, -n robinia

Ro|bin|so|na|de [robɪnzo'na:də] F -, -n Robinsonade; *(Sport)* flying save *(towards attacker)*

Ro|bot|bild ['rɔbɔt-] NT *(Sw)* Identikit® (picture)

Ro|bo|ter ['rɔbɔtɐ] M -s, - **a** robot **b** *(Sport)* ball-feeder

Ro|bo|ter|tech|nik F, **Ro|bo|tik** [ro'bo:tɪk] F -, *no pl* robotics *sing or pl*

ro|bust [ro'bʊst] ADJ *Mensch, Gesundheit, Konjunktur* robust; *Material* tough

Ro|bust|heit F -, *no pl (von Mensch, Gesundheit, Konjunktur)* robustness; *(von Material)* toughness

roch *pret von* **riechen**

Ro|cha|de [rɔ'xa:də, rɔ'ʃa:də] F -, -n *(Chess)* castling; *(Ftbl)* switch-over, change of position; *(fig)* switch; **die kleine** *or* **kurze/große** *or* **lange** ~ castling king's side/queen's side

rö|cheln ['rœçln] VI to groan; *(Sterbender)* to give the death rattle; **~d atmen** to breathe with a rasping sound

Rö|cheln NT -s, *no pl* groan; *(= Todesröcheln)* death rattle; **das ~ der Verletzten** the groans *or* groaning of the wounded

Ro|chen ['rɔxn] M -s, - ray

ro|chie|ren [rɔ'xi:rən, rɔ'ʃi:rən] *ptp* **rochiert** VI to castle; *(Ftbl)* to change *or* switch positions

Rock [rɔk] M -(e)s, ¨-e ['rœkə] **a** *(= Damenrock)* skirt; *(= Schottenrock)* kilt; *(Sw: = Kleid)* dress **b** *(geh: = Herrenrock)* jacket; **der grüne ~ (des Försters)** *(old)* the green coat of a forester; **der schwarze ~ (des Geistlichen)** *(old)* the black gown *or* cassock of a priest; **den bunten ~ anziehen** *(old)* to take the King's/Queen's shilling *(Brit old)*, to enlist in the army; **den bunten ~ ausziehen** *(old)* to come out of the army

Rock M -s, *no pl (Mus)* rock

Rock-: **Rock|auf|schlag** M lapel; **Rock|band** [-bɛnt] F *pl* **-bands** rock band; **Rock|bar|de** M rock poet; **Rock|bar|din** F rock poetess

Röck|chen ['rœkçən] NT -s, - *dim von* **Rock**

Ro|cken ['rɔkn] M -s, - *(Tex)* distaff

ro|cken ['rɔkn] VI *(Mus)* to rock

Ro|cker ['rɔkɐ] M -s, - rocker

Ro|cker-: **Ro|cker|ban|de** F gang of rockers; **Ro|cker|braut** F *(inf)* rocker's moll *(inf)*

Ro|cke|rin [-ərɪn] F -, -nen → **Rocker**

Rock-: **Rock|fal|te** F *(von Damenrock)* inverted pleat; *(von Jackett)* vent; **Rock|fes|ti|val** NT rock festival; **Rock|fut|ter** NT skirt lining; **Rock|grup|pe** F rock band

ro|ckig ['rɔkɪç] ADJ *Musik* which sounds like (hard) rock ADV ~ **klingender Blues** blues which sounds like (hard) rock; **die Band spielt mir zu ~** I don't like this band because their music sounds too much like (hard) rock

Rock-: **Rock|mu|sik** F rock music; **Rock|röh|re** F *(Press sl)* rock singer; **Rock|saum** M hem of a/the skirt; **Rock|schoß** M coat-tail; **an jds Rockschößen hängen** *(inf)* **sich an jds Rockschöße klammern** *(inf)* to cling to sb's coat-tails *(inf)*; **Rock|star** M rock star; **Rock|zip|fel** M **unter ihrem Mantel guckt ein ~ hervor** part of her skirt is hanging down below her coat; **der Mutter am ~ hängen, an Mutters ~ hängen** *(inf)* to be tied to (one's) mother's apron strings *(inf)*; **an jds ~ (dat) hängen** *(inf)* to cling to sb's coat-tails *(inf)*

Ro|de|ha|cke F mattock

Ro|del ['ro:dl] M -s, - *(S Ger, Aus)* F -, -n sledge *(Brit)*, sled *(esp US)*, toboggan, sleigh

Ro|del|bahn F toboggan run

ro|deln ['ro:dln] VI *aux sein or haben* to toboggan *(auch Sport)*, to sledge

Ro|del-: **Ro|del|schlit|ten** M toboggan, sledge *(Brit)*, sled *(esp US)*; **Ro|del|sport** M tobogganing

ro|den ['ro:dn] VT *Wald, Land* to clear; *Kartoffeln* to lift

Ro|deo [ro'de:o, 'ro:deo] M OR NT -s, -s rodeo

Rod|ler ['ro:dlɐ] M -s, -, **Rod|le|rin** [-ərɪn] F -, -nen tobogganer; *(Sport auch)* tobogganist

Ro|dung ['ro:dʊŋ] F -, -en *(= das Roden, Siedlung)* clearing

Ro|gen ['ro:gn] M -s, - roe

Ro|ge|ner ['ro:gənɐ] M -s, - spawner

Ro|gen|stein ['ro:gn-] M *(Geol)* oolite, oolitic limestone

ro|ger ['rɔdʒɐ] ADV **a** *(Rad: = verstanden)* roger **b** *(inf: = einverstanden)* roger, OK; **alles ~!** all agreed!

Rog|gen ['rɔgn] M -s, *no pl* rye

Rog|ner ['ro:gnɐ] M -s, - spawner

roh [ro:] ADJ **a** *(= ungebraten, ungekocht)* raw; *Milch* unpasteurized → **Ei b** *(= unbearbeitet) Bretter, Stein etc* rough; *Diamant* uncut, rough; *Eisen, Metall* crude; *Felle* untreated; **etw aus dem Rohen arbeiten** *(Art)* to work sth from the rough; **die Statue/das Bild/das Manuskript ist im Rohen fertig** the rough shape of the statue/the rough sketch of the picture/the rough draft of the manuscript is finished **c** *(= unkultiviert, brutal)* rough; **~e Gewalt** brute force; **wo ~e Kräfte sinnlos walten ...** *(prov)* brute force does it ADV **a** *(= ungekocht)* raw **b** *(= grob) behauen, zusammen nageln* roughly **c** *(= brutal)* brutally

Roh-: **Roh|bau** M *pl* **-bauten a** *(Bauabschnitt)* shell *or* carcass (of a/the building); **das Haus ist im ~ fertig(gestellt)** the house is structurally complete **b** *(Ind: von Fahrzeug)* shell; **Roh|baum|wol|le** F raw cotton; **Roh|ben|zin** NT naphtha; **Roh|bi|lanz** F trial balance sheet; **Roh|bo|gen** M unbound sheet; **Roh|di|a|mant** M rough *or* uncut *or* unpolished diamond; **Roh|ein|nah|me** F gross proceeds *pl*; **Roh|ei|sen** NT pig iron

Ro|heit △ ['ro:hait] F -, -en → **Rohheit**

Roh-: **Roh|ent|wurf** M rough draft; **Roh|er|trag** M gross proceeds *pl*

ro|her|wei|se ['ro:ɐ'vaizə] ADV roughly

Roh|fa|ser F raw fibre *(Brit)* or fiber *(US)*

Roh|fas|sung F rough draft

Roh|ge|wicht NT gross weight

Roh|gum|mi M OR NT raw rubber

Roh|heit ['ro:hait] F -, -en **a** *no pl (Eigenschaft)* roughness; *(= Brutalität)* brutality **b** *(Tat)* brutality **c** *(= ungekochter Zustand)* rawness

Roh|kost F raw fruit and vegetables *pl*

Roh|köst|ler ['ro:kœstlɐ] M -s, -, **Roh|köst|le|rin** [-ərɪn] F -, -nen *person who prefers fruit and vegetables uncooked*

Roh|le|der NT rawhide, untanned leather

Roh|ling ['ro:lɪŋ] M -s, -e **a** *(= Grobian)* brute, ruffian **b** *(Tech)* blank **c** *(auch* **CD-Rohling)** blank CD

Roh-: **Roh|ma|te|ri|al** NT raw material; **Roh|milch|kä|se** M unpasteurized cheese; **Roh|öl** NT crude oil; **Roh|pro|dukt** NT raw material; **Roh|pro|duk|ten|händ|ler(in)** M(F) scrap dealer *or* merchant

Rohr [ro:ɐ] NT -(e)s, -e **a** *(= einzelnes Schilfrohr)* reed; *(= Röhricht, Schilf)* reeds *pl*; *(= Zuckerrohr)* cane; *(für Stühle etc)* cane, wicker *no pl*; **aus ~ geflochtene Stühle** wicker(work) *or* basketwork *or* cane *(esp Brit)* chairs; **wie ein schwankendes ~ im Wind** *(liter)* like a reed in the wind *(liter)*; **spanisches ~** *(old)* cane **b** *(Tech, Mech)* pipe; *(= Geschützrohr)* (gun) barrel; *(= Blasrohr)* blowpipe; **aus allen ~en feuern** *(lit)* to fire with all its guns; *(fig)* to use all one's fire power; **volles ~** *(inf)* flat out *(Brit)*, at full speed **c** *(S Ger, Aus: = Backröhre)* oven

Rohr-: **Rohr|am|mer** F *(Orn)* reed bunting; **Rohr|blatt** NT *(Mus)* reed; **Rohr|bruch** M burst pipe

Röhr|chen ['rø:ɐçən] NT -s, - tube; *(Chem)* test tube; *(inf: zur Alkoholkontrolle)* Breathalyzer®; **ins ~ blasen** *(inf)* to be breathalyzed

Rohr|dom|mel ['ro:ɐdɔml] F -, -n *(Orn)* bittern

Röh|re ['rø:rə] F -, -n **a** *(= Ofenröhre)* warming oven; *(= Backröhre)* oven; *(= Drainageröhre)* drainage pipe; **in die ~ gucken** *(inf)* to be left out **b** *(= Neonröhre)* (neon) tube *or* strip; *(= Elektronenröhre)* valve *(Brit)*, tube *(US)*; *(= Fernsehröhre)* tube; *(fig: = Fernseher)* telly *(Brit inf)*, box *(esp Brit inf)*, tube *(US inf)*; **in die ~ gucken** *or* **glotzen** *(inf)* to watch telly *(Brit inf)*, to watch the tube *(US inf)*, to sit in front of the box *(esp Brit inf)* **c** *(= Höhlung, Hohlkörper)* tube; *(in Knochen)* cavity; *(von Tunnel, U-Bahn)* tube **d** *(Hunt: = Gang im Tierbau)* gallery

röh|ren ['rø:rən] VI *(Hunt)* to bell; *(Motorrad, Mensch)* to roar; **der ~de Hirsch** *(als Sinnbild)* ≈ the Monarch of the Glen

Röh|ren-: **Röh|ren|blüt|ler** [-bly:tlɐ] PL *(Bot)* tubiflorae *pl (spec)*; **röh|ren|för|mig** ADJ tubular; *Hosenbein* drainpipe *attr*; **Röh|ren|ho|se** F *(inf)* drainpipe trousers *pl (esp Brit)*, drainpipes *pl*; **Röh|ren|kno|chen** M long bone; **Röh|ren|pilz** M boletus

Rohr-: **Rohr|flö|te** F *(Mus)* reed pipe; *(von Orgel)* rohrflöte, rohr flute; *(= Panrohrflöte)* panpipes *pl*; **Rohr|ge|flecht** NT wickerwork, basketwork; **Rohr|kol|ben** M *(Bot)* reed mace, cat's tail; **Rohr|kre|pie|rer** [-krepi:rɐ] M **-s, -** *(Mil sl)* barrel burst; **zum ~ werden** *(fig)* **ein ~ sein** *(fig)* to backfire; **Rohr|le|ger** [-le:gɐ] M **-s, -**, **Rohr|le|ge|rin** [-ərın] F **-, -nen** pipe fitter; **Rohr|lei|tung** F pipe, conduit; **Rohr|lei|tungs|sys|tem** NT network *or* system of pipes

Röh|richt ['rø:rıçt] NT **-s, -e** *(old)* reeds *pl*, reed bed

Röhr|ling ['rø:elıŋ] M **-s, -e** *(Bot)* boletus

Rohr-: **Rohr|mat|te** F rush *or* reed mat; **Rohr|mö|bel** PL cane *(esp Brit) or* wicker furniture *sing*; **Rohr|muf|fe** F *(Tech)* socket; **Rohr|netz** NT network of pipes; **Rohr|pal|me** F calamus; **Rohr|post** F pneumatic dispatch system; **Rohr|sän|ger** M *(Orn)* warbler; **Rohr|spatz** M **schimpfen wie ein ~** *(inf)* to make a fuss; *(= Schimpfwörter gebrauchen)* to curse and swear; **Rohr|stock** M cane; **Rohr|stuhl** M basketwork *or* wickerwork chair; **Rohr|zan|ge** F pipe wrench; **Rohr|zu|cker** M cane sugar

Roh-: **Roh|sei|de** F wild silk; **roh|sei|den** ADJ wild silk

Roh|stoff M raw material; *(St Ex)* commodity

Roh|stoff-: **roh|stoff|arm** ADJ *Land* poor or lacking in raw materials; **Roh|stoff|bör|se** F commodities market; **Roh|stoff|fonds** M commodity fund; **Roh|stoff|man|gel** M shortage of raw materials; **Roh|stoff|markt** M commodities market; **Roh|stoff|preis** M commodity price; **Roh|stoff|quel|le** F source of raw materials; **roh|stoff|reich** ADJ *Land* rich in raw materials; **Roh|stoff|re|ser|ven** PL reserves *pl* of raw materials

Roh-: **Roh|ta|bak** M tobacco; *(ungetrocknet)* uncured tobacco; *(ungeschnitten)* leaf tobacco; **Roh|über|set|zung** F rough translation; **Roh|zu|cker** M crude *or* unrefined sugar; **Roh|zu|stand** M natural state *or* condition; **im ~** *(Denkmal etc)* in its initial stages; *(Übersetzung)* in its first draft

ro|jen ['ro:jən] VTI *(Naut)* to row

Ro|ko|ko ['rɔkoko, ro'kɔko, roko'ko:] NT **-(s)**, *no pl* Rococo period; *(= Stil)* Rococo, rococo

Rolladen △ M → **Rollladen**

Roll-: **Roll|bahn** F *(Aviat)* taxiway; *(= Start-, Landebahn)* runway; **Roll|bal|ken** M *(Comput)* scroll bar; **Roll|bra|ten** M *(Cook)* collared roast meat, collared (roast) beef/pork *etc*; **Roll|brett** NT *(Sport)* skateboard

Röll|chen ['rœlçən] NT **-s, -** little roll; *(von Garn)* reel

Rol|le ['rɔlə] F **-, -n** **a** *(= Zusammengerolltes)* roll; *(= Garnrolle, Zwirnrolle)* reel, bobbin *(spec)*; *(= Papierrolle)* reel; *(= Urkunde)* scroll; **eine ~ Garn/Zwirn** a reel of thread; **eine ~ Bindfaden** a ball of string; **eine ~ Toilettenpapier** a toilet roll, a roll of toilet paper; **eine ~ Drops** a tube of fruit drops; **eine ~ Film** a roll of film; *(im Kino)* a reel of film

b *(= kleines Rad, Walze)* roller; *(an Möbeln, Kisten)* caster, castor; *(an Flaschenzug)* pulley; *(= Gardinenrolle)* runner; **von der ~ sein** *(fig inf)* to have lost it *(inf)*

c *(Sport, Aviat)* roll; **eine ~ machen** to do a roll; **eine ~ vorwärts/rückwärts** a forward/backward roll

d *(Theat, Film, fig)* role, part; *(Sociol)* role; **es war ein Spiel mit vertauschten ~n** *(fig)* it was a situation where the roles were reversed; **ein Stück mit verteilten ~n lesen** to read a play with the parts cast; *(in Schule)* to read a play with the parts given out; **der literarische Kreis liest jeden Dienstag ein Stück mit verteilten ~n** the literary circle has a play-reading every Tuesday; **eine Ehe mit streng verteilten ~n** a marriage with strict allocation of roles; **jds ~ bei** *or* **in etw** *(fig)* sb's role *or* part in sth; **in der ~ von jdm/etw auftreten** to appear in the role of sb/sth; **er gefällt sich** *(dat)* **in der ~ des ...** *(fig)* he likes to think of *or* see himself in the role of the ...; **sich in die ~ eines anderen versetzen** *(fig)* to put oneself in sb else's place; **bei** *or* **in etw** *(dat)* **eine ~ spielen** to play a part in sth; *(Mensch auch)* to play a role in sth; **als Lehrer hat er eine klägliche ~ gespielt** as a teacher he was not up to much *or* he left much to be desired; **etw spielt eine große ~ (bei jdm)** sth is very important (to sb); **es spielt keine ~, (ob) ...** it doesn't matter (whether) ..., it doesn't make any difference (whether) ..., whether ... doesn't come into it; **das spielt hier keine ~** that is irrelevant; **bei ihm spielt Geld keine ~** with him money is no object; **aus der ~ fallen** *(fig)* to do/say the wrong thing; **du bist aber gestern wirklich aus der ~ gefallen!** you really behaved badly yesterday!; **seine ~ ausgespielt haben** *(fig)* to have played one's part

e *(dial: = Wäschemangel)* roller iron

rol|len ['rɔlən] **VI** **a** *aux sein* to roll; *(Flugzeug)* to taxi; **der Stein kommt ins Rollen** *(fig)* the ball has started rolling; **die Ermittlungen sind ins Rollen gekommen** the investigation has gathered momentum; **etw/den Stein ins Rollen bringen** *(fig)* to set *or* start sth/the ball rolling; **es werden einige Köpfe ~** heads will roll; **die Privatisierungswelle rollt** privatizations are in full flow **b** **mit den Augen ~** to roll one's eyes **VT** to roll; *Teig* to roll out; *Teppich, Papier* to roll up; *(dial: = mangeln) Wäsche, Betttücher* to mangle **VR** to curl up; *(Schlange auch)* to curl itself up

Rol|len-: **Rol|len|be|set|zung** F *(Theat, Film)* casting; **Rol|len|bild** NT *(Sociol)* role model; **Rol|len|er|war|tung** F *(Sociol)* role expectation; **Rol|len|fach** NT *(Theat)* character *or* type part; **der jugendliche Liebhaber ist sein ~** he's a character actor specializing in the young lover; **rol|len|för|mig** ADJ cylindrical; **Rol|len|ge|dicht** NT *(Liter)* dramatic monologue *(Brit) or* monolog *(US)*;; **rol|len|ge|la|gert** ADJ mounted on roller bearings; **Rol|len|kon|flikt** M role conflict; **Rol|len|la|ger** NT roller bearings *pl*; **Rol|len-Off|set-Ver|fah|ren** NT rotary offset process; **Rol|len|prüf|stand** M *(Tech)* rolling road dynamometer; **rol|len|spe|zi|fisch** ADJ role-specific; **Rol|len|spiel** NT role play; **Rol|len|tausch** M exchange of roles, role reversal; **Rol|len|ver|hal|ten** NT *(Sociol)* behavioural *(Brit) or* behavioral *(US)* role; **Rol|len|ver|ständ|nis** NT understanding of one's role; **Rol|len|ver|tei|lung** F *(Sociol)* role allocation; **Rol|len|zug** M block and tackle; **Rol|len|zwang** M role constraint(s *pl*)

Rol|ler ['rɔlɐ] M **-s, -** **a** *(= Motorroller, für Kinder)* scooter **b** *(Naut: = Welle)* roller **c** *(Aus: = Rollo)* (roller) blind **d** *(Orn)* **Harzer ~** canary, roller **e** *(= Walze)* roller

Rol|ler|fah|ren NT **-s**, *no pl* riding a scooter

rol|lern ['rɔlɐn] VI *aux sein* to ride one's scooter

Rol|ler|skates ['ro:lɐske:ts] PL rollerskates *pl*

Roll-: **Roll|feld** NT runway; **Roll|film** M roll film; **Roll|fuhr|dienst** M road-rail haulage; **Roll|geld** NT carriage, freight charge; **Roll|gers|te** F *(Agr)* pot barley, hulled barley; **Roll|gut** NT *(Rail)* freight; **Roll|ho|ckey** NT roller-skate hockey

Rol|li ['rɔli] M **-s, -s** *(Fashion inf)* rollneck

rol|lig ['rɔlıç] ADJ *(inf) Katze* on *(Brit) or* in heat; *(sl) Mensch* horny *(inf)*

Roll-: **Roll|kom|man|do** NT raiding party; **Roll|kra|gen** M rollneck, polo neck *(Brit)*, turtleneck *(US)*; **Roll|kra|gen|pul|lo|ver** M polo-neck sweater; **Roll|kunst|lauf** M roller skating; **Roll|kur** F *(Med) treatment for stomach disorders where the patient takes medicine, lies for 5 minutes on his back, 5 minutes on his side, then on his front etc*; **Roll|la|den** M *(an Fenster, Tür etc)* (roller) shutters *pl*; *(von Schreibtisch)* roll top; *(von Schrank)* roll front; **Roll|mops** M rollmops

Rol|lo ['rɔlo, rɔ'lo:] NT **-s, -s** (roller) blind

Roll-: **Roll|schin|ken** M smoked ham; **Roll|schnell|lauf** M speed (roller-)skating; **Roll|schrank** M roll-fronted cupboard

Roll|schuh M roller skate; **~ laufen** to roller-skate

Roll|schuh-: **Roll|schuh|bahn** F roller-skating rink; **Roll|schuh|lau|fen** NT **-s**, *no pl* roller-skating; **Roll|schuh|läu|fer(in)** M(F) roller skater; **Roll|schuh|sport** M roller-skating

Roll-: **Roll|sitz** M *(im Rennboot)* sliding seat; **Roll|splitt** M loose chippings *pl*; **Roll|sport** M roller-skating; **Roll|steg** M travolator, moving pavement *(Brit)*, mobile walkway *(US)*; *(Naut)* gangplank, gangway

Roll|stuhl M wheelchair

Roll|stuhl-: **Roll|stuhl|fah|rer(in)** M(F) wheelchair user; **roll|stuhl|ge|recht** ADJ, ADV suitable *or* accessible for wheelchairs

Roll-: **Roll|ta|bak** M tobacco plug; **Roll|trep|pe** F escalator; **Roll|werk** NT *(Archit)* cartouche, scrollwork

Rom [ro:m] NT **-s** Rome; **~ ist auch nicht an einem Tag erbaut worden** *(prov)* Rome wasn't built in a day *(Prov)*; **viele** *or* **alle Wege führen nach ~** *(Prov)* all roads lead to Rome *(Prov)*; **das sind Zustände wie im alten ~** *(inf) (unmoralisch)* it's disgraceful; *(primitiv)* it's medieval *(inf)*

ROM [rɔm] NT **-s, -s** *(Comput)* ROM

Ro|ma ['ro:ma] PL *(= Zigeuner)* Romanies *pl*

Ro|mag|na-Sa|lat [ro'manja-] M cos *or* romaine *(esp US)* lettuce

Ro|man [ro'ma:n] M **-s, -e** novel; *(höfisch, ritterlich etc auch)* romance; **ich könnte einen ~ schreiben!** *(inf)* I could write a book about it!; **(jdm) einen ganzen ~ erzählen** *(inf)* to give sb a long rigmarole *(inf)*; **erzähl keine ~e!** *(inf)* don't tell stories! *(inf)*

ro|man|ar|tig ADJ novelistic

Ro|ma|na-Sa|lat M cos *or* romaine *(esp US)* lettuce

Ro|man|au|tor(in) M(F), **Ro|man|ci|er** [romã'sie:] M **-s, -s** novelist

Ro|man|die [roman'di:] F **-** *(esp Sw)* **die ~** French-speaking Switzerland

Ro|ma|ne [ro'ma:nə] M **-n, -n**, **Ro|ma|nin** [-'ma:nın] F **-, -nen** person speaking a Romance language

Ro|ma|nen|tum [ro'ma:nəntu:m] NT **-s**, *no pl* Latin nature

Ro|man-: **Ro|man|fi|gur** F character (in a novel); **ro|man|haft** ADJ like a novel; **Ro|man|heft** NT cheap pulp novel, penny dreadful *(dated Brit)*; **Ro|man|held** M hero of a/the novel; **Ro|man|hel|din** F heroine of a/the novel

Ro|ma|nik [ro'ma:nık] F **-**, *no pl (Archit, Art)* Romanesque period; *(Stil)* Romanesque (style)

Ro|ma|nin [-'ma:nın] F → **Romane**

ro|ma|nisch [ro'ma:nıʃ] ADJ *Volk, Sprache* Romance; *(Art, Archit)* Romanesque

Ro|ma|nist [roma'nıst] M **-en, -en**, **Ro|ma|nis|tin** [-'nıstın] F **-, -nen** *(Univ)* student of *or (Wissenschaftler)* expert on Romance languages and literature

Ro|ma|nis|tik [roma'nıstık] F **-**, *no pl (Univ)* Romance languages and literature

ro|ma|nis|tisch [roma'nıstıʃ] ADJ Romance; **~es Institut** *(Univ)* Institute for Romance Languages and Literature

Ro|man-: **Ro|man|le|ser(in)** M(F) novel reader; **Ro|man|li|te|ra|tur** F fiction, novels *pl*; **Ro|man|schrei|ber(in)** M(F) *(inf)* novelist;

(pej) scribbler; **Ro|man|schrift|stel|ler(in)** M(F) novelist

Ro|man|tik [ro'mantɪk] F -, *no pl* **a** *(Liter, Art, Mus)* Romanticism; *(Epoche)* Age of Romanticism, Romantic period **b** *(fig)* romance; *(Gefühl, Einstellung)* romanticism; **keinen Sinn für ~ haben** to have no sense of romance

Ro|man|ti|ker [ro'mantikɐ] M -s, -, **Ro|man|ti|ke|rin** [-ərɪn] F -, -nen *(Liter, Art, Mus)* Romantic; *(fig)* romantic

ro|man|tisch [ro'mantɪʃ] ADJ romantic; *(Liter etc)* Romantic ADV romantically; **~ liegen** to be in a romantic spot; **die Halle war ~ ausgestattet** the hall was decorated to give it a romantic feel

ro|man|ti|sie|ren [romanti'zi:rən] *ptp* **romantisiert** VT to romanticize

ro|mantsch [ro'mantʃ] ADJ = **rätoromanisch**

Ro|man|ze [ro'mantsə] F -, -n *(Liter, Mus, fig)* romance

ro|maun(t)sch [ro'maun(t)ʃ] ADJ = **rätoromanisch**

Rö|mer ['rø:mɐ] M -s, - *wineglass with clear glass bowl and green or brown coiled stem*

Rö|mer M -s **der ~** *town hall of Frankfurt am Main*

Rö|mer ['rø:mɐ] M -s, -, **Rö|me|rin** [-ərɪn] F -, -nen Roman; **die alten ~** the (ancient) Romans

Rö|mer-: **Rö|mer|brief** M Letter *or* Epistle of Paul to the Romans, Romans *sing, no art*; **Rö|mer|reich** NT Roman Empire; **Rö|mer|stra|ße** F Roman road; **Rö|mer|topf®** M *(Cook)* clay casserole dish; **Rö|mer|tum** ['rø:mɐtu:m] NT -s, *no pl* Roman culture *etc*; **die Haupttugenden des ~s** the main virtues of Rome; **das ~ hat zahlreiche griechische Elemente absorbiert** Rome absorbed many elements from Greece

Rom|fah|rer(in) M(F) pilgrim to Rome

rö|misch ['rø:mɪʃ] ADJ Roman; **~ 12** 12 in Roman numerals

rö|misch-ka|tho|lisch ['rø:mɪʃka'to:lɪʃ] ADJ Roman Catholic

Rom|mé [rɔ'me:, 'rɔme] NT -s, -s, **Rom|mee** NT -s, -s rummy

Ron|deau NT -s, -s **a** [rõ'do:] *(Liter, Mus)* rondeau, rondel **b** [rɔn'do:] *(Aus: = Rondell)* circular flowerbed

Ron|dell [rɔn'dɛl] NT -s, -e **a** *(Archit)* round tower **b** circular flowerbed

Ron|do ['rɔndo] NT -s, -s *(Mus)* rondo

rönt|gen ['rœntgn] VT to X-ray; *Körperteil auch* to take an X-ray of

Rönt|gen NT -s, *no pl* X-raying; **er ist gerade beim ~** he's just being X-rayed

Rönt|gen-: **Rönt|gen|ap|pa|rat** M X-ray equipment *no indef art, no pl*; **Rönt|gen|auf|nah|me** F X-ray (plate); **Rönt|gen|au|gen** PL *(hum)* X-ray eyes *pl (hum)*; **Rönt|gen|be|hand|lung** F, **Rönt|gen|be|strah|lung** F radiotherapy, X-ray treatment *or* therapy; **Rönt|gen|bild** NT, **X-ray**; **Rönt|gen|di|ag|nos|tik** F X-ray diagnosis; **Rönt|gen|film** M X-ray film

rönt|ge|ni|sie|ren [rœntgeni'zi:rən] *ptp* **röntgenisiert** VT *(Aus)* to X-ray; *Körperteil auch* to take an X-ray of

Rönt|gen|la|ser M X-ray laser

Rönt|ge|no|gramm [rœntgeno'gram] NT *pl* **-gramme** X-ray (plate), radiograph *(esp US)*

Rönt|ge|no|gra|fie, **Rönt|ge|no|gra|phie** [rœntgenogra'fi:] F -, -n [-'fi:ən] radiography

Rönt|ge|no|lo|ge [rœntgeno'lo:gə] M -n, -n, **Rönt|ge|no|lo|gin** [-'lo:gɪn] F -, -nen radiologist, roentgenologist *(form)*

Rönt|ge|no|lo|gie [rœntgenolo'gi:] F -, *no pl* radiology, roentgenology *(form)*

Rönt|ge|no|sko|pie [rœntgenosko'pi:] F -, -n [-'pi:ən] radioscopy

Rönt|gen-: **Rönt|gen|pass** M X-ray registration card; **Rönt|gen|rei|hen|un|ter|su|chung** F X-ray screening; **Rönt|gen|röh|re** F X-ray tube; **Rönt|gen|strah|len** PL X-rays *pl*; **jdn mit ~ behandeln** to treat sb with X-rays, to give sb X-ray treatment; **Rönt|gen|the|ra|pie** F radiotherapy, X-ray treatment *or* therapy; **Rönt|gen|un|ter|su|chung** F X-ray examination

Ror|schach|test M *(Psych)* Rorschach test

ro|sa ['ro:za] ADJ *inv* pink; **ein ~** *or* **~nes** *(inf)* **Kleid** a pink dress; **die Welt durch eine ~ Brille sehen** to see the world through rose-coloured *(Brit) or* rose-colored *(US) or* rose-tinted glasses; **in ~ Licht** in a rosy light

Ro|sa ['ro:za] NT -s, -s pink

ro|sa|far|ben [-farbn], **ro|sa|far|big** ADJ = **rosa**

ro|sa|rot ADJ = **rosa**

ro|sa|rot+ma|len VT *sep (fig)* **er malt die Zukunft ~** he paints a rosy picture of the future

rösch [rø:ʃ] ADJ *(S Ger: = knusprig) Brot* crusty; *Fleisch* crisp; *Mädchen* bonnie *(esp N Engl, Scot)*, pretty

Rös|chen ['rø:sçən] NT -s, - (little) rose; *(von Broccoli, Blumenkohl)* floret; *(von Rosenkohl)* sprout

Ro|se ['ro:zə] F -, -n **a** *(Blume)* rose; *(Archit)* rose window; **er ist nicht auf ~n gebettet** *(fig)* life isn't a bed of roses for him; **keine ~ ohne Dornen** *(prov)* no rose without a thorn *(prov)* **b** *(Med)* erysipelas *(spec)*, rose **c** *(Hunt: am Hirschgeweih)* burr

ro|sé [ro'ze:] ADJ *inv* pink; **Schuhe in ~** pink shoes

Ro|sé [ro'ze:] M -s, -s rosé (wine)

Ro|sen-: **ro|sen|ar|tig** ADJ rose-like, rosaceous *(spec)*; **Ro|sen|blatt** NT rose petal; **Ro|sen|duft** M scent *or* perfume of roses; **ro|sen|far|ben** [-farbn], **ro|sen|far|big** ADJ rose-coloured *(Brit)*, rose-colored *(US)*, pink, rosy; **Ro|sen|gar|ten** M rose garden; **Ro|sen|ge|wäch|se** PL rosaceae *pl (spec)*; **Ro|sen|holz** NT rosewood; **Ro|sen|kä|fer** M rose chafer, rose beetle; **Ro|sen|knos|pe** F rosebud; **Ro|sen|kohl** M Brussel(s) sprouts *pl*; **Ro|sen|kranz** M *(Eccl)* rosary; **den ~ beten** to say a rosary; **Ro|sen|kreu(t)|zer** [-krɔytsɐ] PL *(Rel)* Rosicrucians *pl*; **Ro|sen|krie|ge** PL *(Hist)* the Wars of the Roses *pl*; **Ro|sen|mon|tag** M *Monday preceding Ash Wednesday*; **Ro|sen|mon|tags|zug** M *Carnival parade which takes place on the Monday preceding Ash Wednesday*

> **ROSENMONTAG**
>
> **Rosenmontag** is the last Monday of **Karneval**. There are processions, with bands playing and carnival club members in costume throwing toffees **(Kamellen)**, sweets and flowers into the crowd. Spectators too wear costumes. There are also big carnival floats which pass comment on the year's events and carry huge papier-mâché figures which poke fun at local and national politicians. → KARNEVAL

Ro|sen-: **Ro|sen|öl** NT attar of roses; **Ro|sen|quarz** M rose quartz; **ro|sen|rot** ADJ *Wangen, Lippen* rosy (red); **Schneeweißchen und Rosenrot** *(Liter)* Snow White and Rose Red; **Ro|sen|stock** M rose (tree); **Ro|sen|strauch** M rosebush; **Ro|sen|was|ser** NT rosewater; **Ro|sen|zucht** F rose-growing; **Ro|sen|züch|ter(in)** M(F) rose-grower

Ro|set|te [ro'zɛtə] F -, -n rosette

Ro|sé|wein M rosé wine

ro|sig ['ro:zɪç] ADJ *(lit, fig)* rosy; *Braten* pink; **etw in ~em Licht sehen** *(inf)* to see sth in a rosy light; **etw in ~en Farben schildern** *(inf)* to paint a glowing *or* rosy picture of sth, to show sth in a rosy light

ro|sig+ma|len VT *sep* **etw ~** *(fig)* to paint a rosy picture of sth

Ro|si|ne [ro'zi:nə] F -, -n raisin; **(große) ~n im Kopf haben** *(inf)* to have big ideas; **sich** *(dat)* **die (besten** *or* **größten) ~n (aus dem Kuchen) herauspicken** *(inf)* to take the pick of the bunch

Ro|si|nen-: **Ro|si|nen|bom|ber** M *(hum) plane which flew food etc into Berlin during the 1948 airlift*; **Ro|si|nen|bröt|chen** NT ≈ currant bun

Rös|lein ['rø:slain] NT -s, - (little) rose

Ros|ma|rin ['ro:smari:n, ro:sma'ri:n] M -s, *no pl* rosemary

Ross [rɔs] NT -es, -e *or (S Ger, Aus, Sw)* **Rösser** ['rœsɐ] *(liter)* steed; *(S Ger, Aus, Sw)* horse; *(inf: = Dummkopf)* dolt *(inf)*; **~ und Reiter nennen** *(fig geh)* to name names; **der Ritter hoch zu ~** *(liter)* the knight astride his steed *(liter)*; **auf dem hohen ~ sitzen** *(fig)* to be on one's high horse; **hoch zu ~** on horseback

Ross-: **Ross|ap|fel** M *(hum inf)* horse droppings *pl*; **Ross|brei|ten** PL *(Naut)* horse latitudes *pl*

Rös|sel ['rœsl] NT -s, - *(Chess)* knight; *(S Ger: = Pferd)* horse

Ros|se|len|ker ['rɔsə-] M *(poet)* reinsman *(liter)*

Rös|sel|sprung M **a** *(Chess)* knight's move **b** *(= Rätsel) type of puzzle in which certain individual letters or syllables make up a phrase or saying*

Ross-: **Ross|haar** NT horsehair; **Ross|haar|mat|rat|ze** F horsehair mattress; **Ross|kä|fer** M dung beetle; **Ross|kas|ta|nie** F horse chestnut; **Ross|kas|ta|ni|en|ex|trakt** M *extract of horse chestnut used as a medicament for varicose veins*; **Ross|kur** F *(hum)* drastic cure, kill-or-cure remedy; **eine ~ (durch)machen** to follow a drastic cure

Rössl [rœsl] NT -s, - *(Chess)* knight; *(S Ger: = Pferd)* horse

Röss|li|spiel ['rœsli-] NT *(Sw)* merry-go-round, roundabout *(Brit)*

Ross-: **Ross|schläch|ter(in)** M(F) horse butcher; **Ross|schläch|te|rei** F horse butchery; **Ross|täu|scher(in)** M(F) *(old, fig)* horse trader; **Ross|täu|sche|rei** [-tɔyʃə'rai] F -, -en *(fig)* horse trading *no pl*

Rost [rɔst] M -(e)s, *no pl (auch Bot)* rust; **~ ansetzen** to start to rust

Rost M -(e)s, -e *(= Ofenrost)* grill; *(= Gitterrost)* grating, grille; *(dial: = Bettrost)* base, frame; **auf dem ~ braten** *(Cook)* to barbecue, to grill over charcoal

Rost-: **Rost|an|satz** M signs *pl* of rust; **rost|be|stän|dig** ADJ rust-resistant; **Rost|bil|dung** F rust formation; **Rost|bra|ten** M *(Cook)* ≈ roast; **Rost|brat|wurst** F barbecue sausage; **rost|braun** ADJ russet; *Haar* auburn

Röst|brot [(*S Ger*) 'rø:st-] NT toast

Rös|te [(*S Ger*) 'rø:stə] [(*N Ger*) 'rœstə] F -, -n *(Metal)* roasting

ros|ten ['rɔstn] VI *aux sein or haben* to rust, to get rusty *(auch fig)*; **alte Liebe rostet nicht** *(Prov)* true love never dies *(prov)* → **rasten**

rös|ten [(*S Ger*) 'rø:stn] VT **a** *Kaffee, Erdnüsse, Kastanien* to roast; *Brot* to toast; **sich in der Sonne ~ lassen** to lie in the sun and bake **b** *Erz* to roast, to calcine

Rös|te|rei [(*S Ger*) rø:stə'rai] F -, -en roast(ing) house; **frisch aus der ~** fresh from the roast, freshly roasted

Rost-: **rost|far|ben**, **rost|far|big** ADJ = **rostbraun**; **Rost|fleck** M spot *or* patch of rust, rust spot *or* patch; **Rost|fraß** M rust corrosion; **rost|frei** ADJ *Stahl* stainless

röst|frisch [(*S Ger*) 'rø:st-] ADJ *Kaffee* freshly roasted

Rös|ti [(*S Ger*) 'rø:sti] PL *fried grated potatoes*

ros|tig ['rɔstɪç] ADJ *(lit, fig)* rusty

Rös|ti|gra|ben M *(esp Sw hum) lack of understanding between the German-speaking and French-speaking Swiss*

Röst|kar|tof|feln [(*S Ger*) 'rø:st-] PL fried *or* sauté potatoes *pl*

Rost-: **Rost|krank|hei|ten** PL *(Bot)* rust diseases *pl*; **Rost|lau|be** F *(hum)* rust-heap *(hum)*; **rost|rot** ADJ rust-coloured *(Brit)*, rust-colored *(US)*, russet; **Rost|schutz** M antirust protection; **Rost|schutz|far|be** F anti-rust paint; **Rost|schutz|mit|tel** NT rust-proofer; **Rost|um|wand|ler** [-ʊmvandlɐ] M -s, - *(Aut)* rust converter

Röst|zwie|beln [*(S Ger)* 'rø:st-] PL fried onions *pl*

rot [ro:t] ADJ *comp* **röter** ['rø:tɐ], *superl* **röteste(r, s)** ['rø:təstə] red *(auch Pol)*; **Rote Bete** *or* **Rüben** beetroot *(Brit)*, beets *pl (US)*; **Rote Karte** *(Ftbl)* red card; **das Rote Kreuz** the Red Cross; **der Rote Halbmond** the Red Crescent; **der Rote Löwe** the Red Lion; **der Rote Platz** Red Square; **das Rote Meer** the Red Sea; **die Rote Armee** the Red Army; **die Roten** *(pej)* the reds; **~e Zahlen schreiben, in den ~en Zahlen stecken** to be in the red; **Gewalt zieht sich wie ein ~er Faden durch die Geschichte** violence runs like a thread through history; **~ werden** to blush, to go red *(inf)*; **bis über beide Ohren ~ werden** to blush furiously, to turn crimson; **~ wie ein Krebs** red as a lobster; **~e Ohren bekommen** *(hum)* **einen ~en Kopf bekommen** *or* **kriegen** *(inf)* to blush, to go red *(inf)*; **~ sein** *(Pol inf)* to be a socialist → **Grütze, rotsehen, Tuch**

ADV *comp* **röter**, *superl* **am rötesten** **a** *(= mit roter Farbe) anmalen* red; *schreiben, unterstreichen, anstreichen* in red; **die Lippen ~ schminken** to use a red lipstick; **sich** *(dat)* **etw ~ (im Kalender) anstreichen** *(inf)* to make sth a red-letter day; **den Tag werde ich mir ~ im Kalender anstreichen** that will be a red-letter day

b *(= in roter Farbe) glühen, leuchten* a bright red; **~ anlaufen** to turn red; **seine Ohren glühten ~** his ears glowed red; **~ gerändert** red-rimmed; **~ glühend** *(Metall)* red-hot; **der ~ glühende Abendhimmel** the red glow of the evening sky; **~ verheulte Augen** eyes red from crying

c *(Pol inf)* **~ angehaucht sein** to have left-wing leanings

Rot [ro:t] NT -s, -s *or* - red; *(= Wangenrot)* rouge; **bei** *or* **auf ~** at red; **bei ~ anhalten!** stop (when the lights are) at red; **die Ampel stand auf ~** the lights were (at) red; **bei ~ über die Ampel fahren/gehen** to jump *(Brit) or* go through the lights/cross at a red light

Röt [rø:t] NT -(e)s, *no pl (Geol)* upper layer of bunter sandstone

Ro|ta|ri|er [ro'ta:riɐ] M -s, -, **Ro|ta|ri|e|rin** [-iərɪn] F -, -nen Rotarian

Rot|ar|mist ['ro:tlarmɪst] M -en, -en, **Rot|ar|mis|tin** [-mɪstɪn] F -, -nen soldier in *or* of the Red Army; **die ~en zogen auf ihrem Vormarsch durch die Stadt** the Red Army advanced through the town

Ro|ta|ry Club ['ro:tari, 'ro:təri, ro'ta:ri] M Rotary Club

Ro|ta|ti|on [rota'tsio:n] F -, -en *(Phys, Pol)* rotation; *(Math auch)* curl

Ro|ta|ti|ons-: **Ro|ta|ti|ons|ach|se** F *(Math, Phys)* axis of rotation; **Ro|ta|ti|ons|druck** M *pl* **-drucke** *(Typ)* rotary (press) printing; **Ro|ta|ti|ons|flä|che** F *(Math, Phys)* surface of revolution; **Ro|ta|ti|ons|ma|schi|ne** F, **Ro|ta|ti|ons|pres|se** F *(Typ)* rotary press; **Ro|ta|ti|ons|prin|zip** NT *(Pol)* rota system; **Ro|ta|ti|ons|sys|tem** NT rotation system, system of rotation

Rot-: **Rot|au|ge** NT *(Zool)* roach; **rot|ba|ckig** [-bakɪç], **rot|bä|ckig** [-bɛkɪç] ADJ rosy-cheeked; **Rot|barsch** M rosefish; **Rot|bart** M red-beard; **Kaiser ~** Emperor Frederick Barbarossa; **rot|bär|tig** ADJ red-bearded; **rot|blond** ADJ *(Männer)haar* sandy; *Mann* sandy-haired; *Frau, Tönung* strawberry blonde; **rot|braun** ADJ reddish brown; **Rot|bu|che** F (common) beech; **Rot|dorn** M *pl* **-dorne** hawthorn

Rö|te ['rø:tə] F -, *no pl* redness, red; *(= Erröten)* blush; **die ~ des Abendhimmels** the red glow of the evening sky; **die ~ stieg ihr ins Gesicht** her face reddened

Ro|te-Ar|mee-Frak|ti|on [ro:təlar'me:-] F Red Army Faction

Ro|te Khmer [kme:ɐ] PL Khmer Rouge *pl*

Rö|tel ['rø:tl] M -s, - red chalk

Rö|teln ['rø:tln] PL German measles *sing*

rö|ten ['rø:tn] VT to redden, to make red; *Himmel* to turn red; **die frische Luft rötete ihre Wangen** the fresh air gave her rosy cheeks *or* made her cheeks (go) red; **ein gerötetes Gesicht** a flushed face; **gerötete Augen** red eyes VR to turn *or* become red

Rot-: **Rot|fil|ter** NT OR M *(Phot)* red filter; **Rot|front** F *(Pol)* red front; **Rot|fuchs** M red fox; *(Pferd)* sorrel *or* bay (horse); *(fig inf)* carrot-top *(inf)*; **Rot|gar|dist(in)** M(F) Red Guard; **rot|ge|färbt** ADJ → **rot ADV b**; **rot|ge|rän|dert** [-gərɛndɐt] ADJ → **rot ADV b**; **rot|ge|sich|tig** [-gəzɪçtɪç] ADJ florid, red-faced; **rot|glü|hend** ADJ → **rot ADV b**; **Rot|glut** F *(Metal)* red heat; **rot-grün** ADJ red-green; **die ~e Koalition** the Red-Green coalition; **ein ~es Bündnis** a Red-Green alliance; **Rot|grün|blind|heit** F red-green colour *(Brit) or* color *(US)* blindness; **Rot|guss** M *(Metal)* red brass; **rot|haa|rig** ADJ red-haired; **Rot|haa|ri|ge(r)** ['ro:tha:rigə] MF *decl as adj* redhead; **Rot|haut** F *(dated hum)* redskin; **Rot|hirsch** M red deer

ro|tie|ren [ro'ti:rən] *ptp* **rotiert** VI *(auch Pol, Comput)* to rotate; *(inf: = hektisch handeln)* to flap *(inf)*; **anfangen zu ~** *(inf)* to get into a flap *(inf)*; **am Rotieren sein** *(inf)* to be in a flap *(inf)*

Rot-: **Rot|ka|bis** M *(Sw)* red cabbage; **Rot|käpp|chen** [-kɛpçən] NT -s, *no pl (Liter)* Little Red Riding Hood; **Rot|kehl|chen** [-ke:lçən] NT -s, - robin; **Rot|kohl** M red cabbage; **Rot|kopf** M *(inf)* redhead; **Rot|kraut** NT *(S Ger, Aus)* red cabbage

Rot|kreuz-: **Rot|kreuz|lot|te|rie** F Red Cross lottery; **Rot|kreuz|samm|lung** F Red Cross appeal *or* collection; **Rot|kreuz|schwes|ter** F Red Cross nurse

Rot|lauf M, *no pl (Vet)* swine erysipelas *(spec)*

röt|lich ['rø:tlɪç] ADJ reddish → **schimmern**

Rot|licht NT red light

Rot|licht-: **Rot|licht|mi|lieu** NT demimonde; **Rot|licht|re|vier** NT, **Rot|licht|vier|tel** NT red-light district

Ro|tor ['ro:to:ɐ] M -s, **Rotoren** [-'to:rən] rotor

Ro|tor|flü|gel M *(Aviat)* rotor blade

Rot-: **rot+schmin|ken** VT *sep* → **rot ADV a**; **Rot|schwanz** M, **Rot|schwänz|chen** NT redstart; **rot+se|hen** ['ro:tze:ən] VI *sep irreg (inf)* to see red *(inf)*; **Rot|se|hen** NT -s, *no pl (Med)* erythropsia *(spec)*; **Rot|specht** M spotted woodpecker; **Rot|stift** M red pencil; **den ~ ansetzen** *(fig)* to cut back drastically; **dem ~ zum Opfer fallen** *(fig)* to be scrapped *or* rejected, to be cancelled *(Brit) or* canceled *(US)*; **Rot|tan|ne** F Norway spruce

Rot|te ['rɔtə] F -, -n gang; *(bei Jugendorganisation)* troop; *(Mil)* rank; *(Mil Aviat, Mil Naut)* pair *(of planes/ships operating together)*; *(von Hunden etc)* pack; *(Hunt: von Sauen)* herd, sounder *(spec)*

rot|ten|wei|se ['rɔtnvaizə] ADV in groups; **die Hunde fielen ~ über das Reh her** packs of dogs attacked the deer

Rott|wei|ler ['rɔtvailɐ] M -s, - Rottweiler

Ro|tun|de [ro'tʊndə] F -, -n *(Archit)* rotunda

Rö|tung ['rø:tʊŋ] F -, -en reddening

Rot-: **rot|ver|heult** ADJ → **rot ADV b**; **rot|wan|gig** [-vaŋɪç] ADJ *Mensch, Apfel* rosy-cheeked; **Rot|wein** M red wine; **rot|welsch** ['ro:tvɛlʃ] ADJ argot, thieves' cant; **Rot|welsch(e)** ['ro:tvɛlʃ] NT argot, thieves' cant → *auch* **Deutsch(e)**; **Rot|wild** NT red deer; **Rot|wurst** F ≈ black pudding

Rotz [rɔts] M -es, *no pl* **a** *(inf)* snot *(inf)*; **~ und Wasser heulen** *(inf)* to blubber; **Baron** *or* **Graf ~** *(inf)* Lord Muck *(Brit inf)*, His Highness *(inf)* **b** *(Vet)* glanders *sing*, farcy; **den ~ haben** to have glanders **c** *(Bot)* soft rot

Rotz|ben|gel M, *(S Ger, Aus)* **Rotz|bub** M *(inf)* snotty-nosed brat *(inf)*

rotz|be|sof|fen ADJ *(sl)* wrecked *(Brit sl)*, wasted *(sl)*

rot|zen ['rɔtsn] VI *(sl: = spucken)* to spit

Rotz-: **Rotz|fah|ne** F *(sl)* snot-rag *(inf)*; **rotz|frech** *(inf)* ADJ cocky *(inf)* ADV **~ antworten** to give a cocky answer *(inf)*; **~ auftreten** to act cocky *(inf)*; **Rotz|gö|re** F *(inf)* **a** *(= kleines Mädchen)* snotty little madam *(inf)* **b** *(= kleines Kind)* snotty-nosed brat *(inf)*

rot|zig ['rɔtsɪç] ADJ **a** *(inf: lit, fig)* snotty *(inf)* **b** *(Vet)* glanderous

Rotz-: **Rotz|jun|ge** M *(inf)* snotty-nosed kid *(inf)*; **Rotz|ko|cher** M *(pej)* pipe; **Rotz|löf|fel** M *(inf)* cheeky *(Brit) or* impudent brat *(inf)*; **Rotz|na|se** F **a** *(inf)* snotty nose *(inf)* **b** *(inf: = Kind)* snotty-nosed brat *(inf)*; **rotz|nä|sig** [-nɛ:zɪç] ADJ *(inf)* **a** snotty-nosed *(inf)* **b** *(= frech)* snotty *(inf)*; **Rotz|ni|gel** ['rɔtsni:gl] M -s, - *(Aus inf)* snotty-nosed brat *(inf)*

Rot|zun|ge F *(Zool)* witch flounder

Rouge [ru:ʒ] NT -s, -s rouge, blusher

Rou|la|de [ru'la:də] F -, -n *(Cook)* ≈ beef olive

Rou|leau [ru'lo:] NT -s, -s (roller) blind

Rou|lett [ru'lɛt] NT -(e)s, -e *or* -s, **Rou|let|te** [ru'lɛtə] NT -s, -s roulette

rou|lie|ren [ru'li:rən] *ptp* **rouliert** VT *(Sew)* to roll

Rou|te ['ru:tə] F -, -n route *(auch Comput)*; **wir sind die ~ über Bremen gefahren** we took the Bremen route

Rou|ter ['ru:tɐ, 'rautɐ] M -s, - *(Comput)* router

Rou|ti|ne [ru'ti:nə] F -, -n **a** *(= Erfahrung)* experience; *(= Gewohnheit, Trott)* routine; **das ist (bei mir) zur ~ geworden** that has become routine (for me) **b** *(Comput)* routine

Rou|ti|ne-: **Rou|ti|ne|an|ge|le|gen|heit** F routine matter; **Rou|ti|ne|ar|beit** F routine (work); **rou|ti|ne|mä|ßig** ADJ routine ADV **ich gehe ~ zum Zahnarzt** I make routine visits to the dentist's; **das wird ~ überprüft** it's checked as a matter of routine; **ich werde das ~ abwickeln** I'll deal with it in the usual way; **Rou|ti|ne|sa|che** F routine matter; **Rou|ti|ne|un|ter|su|chung** F routine examination

Rou|ti|ni|er [ruti'nie:] M -s, -s old hand

rou|ti|niert [ruti'ni:ɐt] ADJ experienced ADV expertly; **die Kunstfertigkeit der Verse wirkt ~** such skilful verse is made to seem effortless

Row|dy ['raudi] M -s, -s hooligan; *(zerstörerisch)* vandal; *(lärmend)* rowdy (type); *(= Verkehrsrowdy)* road hog *(inf)*

Row|dy|tum ['rauditu:m] NT -s, *no pl* hooliganism; *(zerstörerisch)* vandalism; **das ~ im Verkehr bekämpfen** to combat *or* fight road rage

Ro|ya|lis|mus [roaja'lɪsmʊs] M -, *no pl* royalism

Ro|ya|list [roaja'lɪst] M -en, -en, **Ro|ya|lis|tin** [-'lɪstɪn] F -, -nen royalist

ro|ya|lis|tisch [roaja'lɪstɪʃ] ADJ royalist

RTF [ɛrte:'ɛf] *(Comput) abbr von* **rich rext format** RTF

Rub|bel- ['rʊbl-]: **Rub|bel|kar|te** F, **Rub|bel|los** NT scratch card; **Rub|bel|lot|te|rie** F scratch card lottery; **Rub|bel|mas|sa|ge** F body scrub

rub|beln ['rʊbln] VTI to rub; *Los* to scratch

Rüb|chen ['ry:pçən] NT -s, - *dim von* **Rübe** small turnip; **Teltower ~** *(Cook) glazed turnip with bacon*

Rü|be ['ry:bə] F -, -n **a** turnip; **Gelbe ~** *(S Ger, Sw: = Mohrrübe)* carrot; **Rote ~** beetroot *(Brit)*, beet *(US)*; **Weiße ~** white turnip; **jdn über die ~n jagen** *(sl)* to send sb packing *(inf)* → **Kraut b** *(inf: = Kopf)* nut *(inf)*; **nichts in der ~ haben** to have nothing up top *(inf)*; **jdm die ~ abhacken** *(fig)* to have sb's guts for garters *(inf)*; **~ ab!** off with his/her head!

Ru|bel ['ru:bl] M -s, - rouble; **der ~ rollt** *(inf)* the money's rolling in *(inf)*

Rü|ben-: **rü|ben|ar|tig** ADJ turnip-like; **Rü|ben|saft** M, **Rü|ben|kraut** NT sugar beet syrup; **Rü|ben|zu|cker** M beet sugar

rü|ber- *in cpds (inf)* → *auch* **herüber-, hinüber-**: **rü|ber+brin|gen** VT *sep irreg (inf) Botschaft, Feeling* to get across, to communicate; **rü|ber+kom|men** VI *sep* **a** → **herüberkommen** **b** *(inf)* to come across; **sie kam gut rüber** she came across *or* over well; **mit etw ~** to come out with sth; **rü|ber+wach|sen** *sep irreg* VI ~ **lassen** *(inf, Geld etc)* to come up with; **rü|ber+zie|hen** *sep irreg* VTI = **herüberziehen** VT *(inf: = schlagen)* **jdm eine ~** to give sb one *(inf)*, to stick one on sb *(inf)*

Rü|be|zahl ['ry:bətsa:l] M **-s** *spirit of the Sudeten Mountains*

Ru|bi|di|um [ru'bi:diʊm] NT **-s**, *no pl (abbr* **Rb**) rubidium

Ru|bi|kon ['ru:bikɔn] M **-s** Rubicon; **den ~ überschreiten** *(fig geh)* to cross the Rubicon

Ru|bin [ru'bi:n] M **-s, -e** ruby

ru|bin|rot ADJ ruby-red, ruby

Rüb-: **Rüb|kohl** ['ry:pko:l] M kohlrabi; **Rüb|öl** ['ry:plø:l] NT rapeseed oil, rape oil

Rub|rik [ru'bri:k] F **-, -en** **a** *(= Kategorie)* category; **das gehört in die ~ „Militaria"** this belongs under the category *or* heading "military"; **das läuft unter der ~ Spesen** that comes under expenses **b** *(= Zeitungsrubrik)* section; **wir berichteten unter** *or* **in der ~ Frauen und Politik** we ran a report in the Women and Politics section

rub|ri|zie|ren [rubri'tsi:rən] *ptp* **rubriziert** VT to categorize, to put under a heading/headings

Rub|ri|zie|rung F **-, -en** categorization

Rüb|sa|me(n) ['ry:pza:mə(n)] M **-(n)s**, *no pl (Bot)* rape

Ruch [ru:x, rʊx] M **-(e)s, ⸚e** ['ry:çə, 'rʏçə] *(geh)* **jdn/etw in den ~ der Bestechlichkeit bringen** to pin allegations of corruption on sb/sth; **ein ~ von Korruption** the smell *or* whiff of corruption; **in den ~ der Korruption geraten** to become tainted by corruption; **ihm haftet der ~ der Unfehlbarkeit an** he can't shake off his air of infallibility

Ruch-: **ruch|bar** ADJ **~ werden** *(geh)* to become known; **ruch|los** ADJ *(old, liter)* dastardly *(liter)*; **Ruch|lo|sig|keit** F **-, -en** *(old, liter)* dastardliness *(liter)*

ruck [rʊk] INTERJ → **hau ruck, ruck, zuck**

Ruck [rʊk] M **-(e)s, -e** jerk, tug; *(von Fahrzeug)* jolt, jerk; *(Pol)* swing, shift; **auf einen** *or* **mit einem ~** in one go, with one heave; **er stand mit einem ~ auf** he sprang to his feet, he stood up suddenly; **sich** *(dat)* **einen ~ geben** *(inf)* to make an effort, to give oneself a kick up the backside *(Brit inf) or* in the ass *(US sl)*; **etw in einem ~ erledigen** to do sth at one fell swoop; **durch die Gesellschaft muss ein ~ gehen** society needs to be jolted out of its complacency

Rück-: **Rück|an|sicht** F back *or* rear view; **Rück|ant|wort** F reply, answer; **um ~ wird gebeten** please reply; **Telegramm mit ~** reply-paid telegram

ruck|ar|tig ADJ jerky; **das Auto machte einige ~e Bewegungen** the car jerked a few times ADV jerkily; **er stand ~ auf** he shot to his feet; **sie drehte sich ~ um** she turned round jerkily

Rück-: **Rück|äu|ße|rung** F reply, answer; **Rück|be|ru|fung** F recall; **Rück|be|sin|nung** F **eine ~ auf die Werte der Vergangenheit** a return to past values; **rück|be|züg|lich** ADJ *(Gram)* reflexive; **Rück|bil|dung** F *(Ling)* back formation; *(Biol)* degeneration; **Rück|bil|dungs|gym|nas|tik** F *(nach der Geburt)* postnatal exercise(s *pl*); **Rück|blen|de** F flashback; **Rück|blick** M look back *(auf +acc* at); **im ~ auf etw** *(acc)* looking back on sth; **im ~ lässt sich sagen ...** looking back *or* in retrospect one can say ...; **einen ~ auf etw** *(acc)* **werfen** to look back on *or* at sth; **rück|bli|ckend** ADJ retrospective; **ein auf das vergangene Jahr ~er Bericht** a report that looks back at *or* over the last year ADV in retrospect, looking back; **~ lässt sich sagen, dass ...** looking back *or* in retrospect one can say that ...; **rück+da|tie|ren** ['rʏkdati:rən] *ptp* **rückdatiert** VT *sep infin, ptp only* to backdate; **Rück|de|ckungs|ver|si|che|rung** F *(Econ) firm's private pension plan for employees*; **rück|dre|hend** ADJ *(Met) Wind* backing

ru|cken ['rʊkn] VI to jerk; *(Fahrzeug)* to jerk, to jolt; *(Taube)* to coo; **in den Schultern ~** to jerk one's shoulders back

rü|cken ['rʏkn] VI *aux sein* to move; *(= Platz machen)* to move up *or (zur Seite auch)* over; *(= weiterrücken: Zeiger)* to move on *(auf +acc* to); **näher ~** to move *or* come closer; *(Zeit)* to come *or* get closer; **ins Feld ~** *(old)* to take the field; **ins Manöver ~** *(old)* to go off on manoeuvres *(Brit) or* maneuvers *(US)*; **an die Front ~** *(old)* to go up to the front; **mit etw ~** to move sth; **sie rückten ungeduldig mit den Stühlen** they shuffled their chairs about impatiently; **an etw** *(dat)* ~ *(an Uhrzeiger)* to move sth; *an Krawatte* to pull sth (straight); *(= schieben)* to push at sth; *(= ziehen)* to pull at sth; **an jds Seite** *(acc)* ~ to move up close beside sb; **an jds Stelle** *(acc)* ~ to take sb's place; **nicht von der Stelle ~** not to budge an inch *(inf)*; **in weite Ferne ~** *(lit, fig)* to recede into the distance; **in den Vordergrund ~** *(lit)* to move into the foreground; *(fig)* to come to the fore; **in den Mittelpunkt ~** *(lit)* to move into the centre *(Brit) or* center *(US)*; *(fig)* to become the focus of attention; **in den Hintergrund ~** *(lit)* to move into the background; *(fig)* to be pushed into the background; **in greifbare Nähe ~** *(fig)* to come within reach; **jdm auf den Leib** *or* **Pelz** *(inf) or* **Balg** *(inf) or* **die Pelle** *(inf)* ~ *(= zu nahe kommen)* to crowd sb; *(= sich jdn vorknöpfen)* to get on at sb; *(hum: = besuchen)* to move in on sb; **einer Sache** *(dat)* **zu Leibe ~** to have a go at sth *(Brit)*, to tackle sth → **Bude c, Bewusstsein a**

VT to move → **Licht b**

Rü|cken ['rʏkn] M **-s, -** *(= Stuhlrücken, Handrücken, auch Anat, Sew)* back; *(= Nasenrücken)* ridge; *(= Fußrücken)* instep; *(= Messerrücken)* blunt edge, back; *(= Hügelrücken, Bergrücken)* crest; *(= Buchrücken)* spine; **auf dem/den ~** on one's back; **ich bin ja auf den ~ gefallen!** *(fig)* you could have knocked me down with a feather *(inf)*; **den Feind im ~ haben** to have the enemy to one's rear; **die Sonne im ~ haben** to have the sun behind one *or* on one's back; **den Wind im ~ haben** to have a tail *or* following *(Brit)* wind; **er hat doch die Firma des Vaters im ~** but he's got his father's firm behind him; **ich habe nicht gern jemanden im ~** I don't like having somebody sitting/standing right behind my back; **jdm die Hände auf den ~ binden** to tie sb's hands behind his back; **mit dem ~ zur Tür/Wand** with one's back to the door/wall; **mit dem ~ zur Wand stehen** *(fig) (aus Feigheit)* to cover oneself; *(aus Unterlegenheit)* to have one's back to the wall; **der verlängerte ~** *(hum inf)* one's posterior *(hum inf)*; **~ an ~** back to back; **ein schöner ~ kann auch entzücken** *(hum inf)* you've/she's *etc* got a lovely back; **hinter jds ~** *(dat) (fig)* behind sb's back; **jdm/einer Sache den ~ kehren** *(lit, fig) or* **zuwenden** *(lit) or* **wenden** *(fig) or* **zudrehen** *(lit)* to turn one's back on sb/sth *(lit, fig)*; **den ~ wenden** to turn one's back; **jdm in den ~ fallen** *(fig)* to stab sb in the back; *(Mil)* to attack sb from the rear; **den ~ frei haben** *(fig)* to be free of ties; **sich** *(dat)* **den ~ freihalten** *(inf) or* **decken** to cover oneself; **jdm den ~ decken** *(fig inf)* to back sb up *(inf)*; **auf seinen ~ geht viel** *(inf)* he can take it; **die Sparpolitik wird auf dem ~ der Sozialhilfeempfänger ausgetragen** the cost-cutting policy is being carried out at the expense of people on benefit; **jdm den ~ stärken** *or* **steifen** *(fig inf)* to give sb encouragement → **breit ADJ**

Rü|cken-: **Rü|cken|de|ckung** F *(fig)* backing; **jdm ~ geben** to back sb; **Rü|cken|flos|se** F dorsal fin; **Rü|cken|flug** M *(Aviat)* inverted flight; **rü|cken|frei** ADJ *Kleid* backless, low-backed; **Rü|cken|gym|nas|tik** F back exercise(s *pl*); **rü|cken+krau|len** ['rʏknkraulən] VI *sep infin only* to do *or* swim backstroke *or* back crawl; **Rü|cken|krau|len** NT **-s**, *no pl (Sport)* backstroke, back crawl; **Rü|cken|la|ge** F supine position; **er musste 3 Monate in ~ verbringen** he had to spend 3 months lying (flat) on his back *or* lying in a supine position *(form)*; **er schläft in ~** he sleeps on his back; **in der ~ schwimmen** to swim on one's back; **Rü|cken|leh|ne** F back, back rest; **Rü|cken|mark** NT spinal cord; **Rü|cken|mark(s)|ent|zün|dung** F myelitis; **Rü|cken|mus|kel** M back muscle; **Rü|cken|mus|ku|la|tur** F back muscles *pl*, muscles *pl* of the/one's back; **Rü|cken|schmer|zen** PL backache; **ich habe ~** I've got backache, my back aches; **Rü|cken|schu|le** F, *no pl* programme *(Brit) or* program *(US)* of back exercises; **rü|cken+schwim|men** ['rʏknʃvɪmən] VI *sep infin only* to swim on one's back, to do the *or* swim backstroke; **Rü|cken|schwim|men** NT backstroke, swimming on one's back; **Rü|cken|stär|kung** F *(fig)* moral support; **Rü|cken|stück** NT *(Cook) (vom Rind, Schwein)* chine; *(vom Reh, Hammel)* saddle; **ein schönes ~** a nice piece of back; **Rü|cken|tra|ge** F carrying frame

Rück|ent|wick|lung F *(allgemein)* fall-off *(+gen* in); *(Biol)* degeneration

Rü|cken-: **Rü|cken|wind** M tail *or* following wind; **Rü|cken|wir|bel** M dorsal vertebra

Rück-: **Rück|er|in|ne|rung** F memory *(an +acc* of); **rück+er|stat|ten** ['rʏklɛɐʃtatn] *ptp* **rückerstattet** VT *sep infin, ptp only* to refund; *Ausgaben* to reimburse; **Rück|er|stat|tung** F refund; *(von Ausgaben)* reimbursement; **Rück|fahr|kar|te** F, **Rück|fahr|schein** M return ticket, round-trip ticket *(US)*; **Rück|fahr|schein|wer|fer** M *(Aut)* reversing light; **Rück|fahrt** F return journey; **Rück|fall** M *(Med, fig)* relapse; *(Jur)* subsequent offence *(Brit) or* offense *(US)*, repetition of an/the offence *(Brit) or* offense *(US)*; **ein ~ in alte Gewohnheiten** a relapse into one's old habits; **Diebstahl im ~** a repeated case of theft; **rück|fäl|lig** ADJ *(Med, fig)* relapsed; *(Jur)* recidivistic *(form)*; **ein ~er Dieb** a thief who repeats his offence *(Brit) or* offense *(US)*; **~ werden** *(Med)* to have a relapse; *(fig)* to relapse; *(Jur)* to lapse back into crime; **Rück|fäl|li|ge(r)** ['rʏkfɛlɪgə] MF *decl as adj (Med, fig)* person who has relapsed; *(Jur)* subsequent offender, recidivist *(form)*; **Rück|fall|tä|ter(in)** M(F) recidivist *(form)*, recidivistic offender *(form)*; **Rück|fens|ter** NT *(im Auto)* rear window; **Rück|flug** M return flight; **Rück|fluss** M reflux, flowing back; *(von Investitionen, Kapital)* return; **Rück|for|de|rung** F **~ des Geldes/des Buches** demand for the return of the money/the book; **Rück|fracht** F return load; **Rück|fra|ge** F question; **nach ~ bei der Zentrale ...** after querying *or* checking this with the exchange ...; **bei jdm wegen etw ~ halten** to query sth with sb; **auf ~ wurde uns erklärt ...** when we queried this, we were told ...; **rück+fra|gen** ['rʏkfra:gn] VI *sep infin, ptp only* to inquire, to check; **ich habe an der Rezeption rückgefragt** I inquired *or* checked at reception; **ich muss beim Chef ~** I'll have to check with the boss *or* query it with the boss; **Rück|front** F back, rear façade; **Rück|führ|ge|bühr** F *(bei Leihwagen)* drop-off charge; **Rück|füh|rung** F **a** *(= Deduktion)* tracing back; **die ~ der Probleme auf** *(+acc)* tracing the problems back to **b** *(von Menschen)* repatriation, return **c** *(Fin: von Kredit, Schulden)* repayment; *(= Senkung)* reduction **d** *(= Zurückgabe)* restitution; **Rück|ga|be** F return; **Rück|ga|be|recht** NT *(Comm)* right of return; **mit ~ bestellen** to order on a sale or return basis; **Rück|gang** M *pl* **-gänge** fall, drop *(+gen* in); **einen ~ *or* Rückgänge zu verzeichnen haben** to report a drop *or* fall; **rück|gän|gig** ADJ **a** *(= zurückgehend)* declining, falling, dropping **b** **~ machen** *(= widerrufen)* to undo; *Bestellung, Geschäft, Vertrag, Termin* to cancel; *Entscheidung* to go back on; *Verlobung, Hoch-*

zeit to call off; *chemischen Prozess* to reverse; *(Comput)* to undo; **Rück|gän|gig|ma|chung** [ˈrʏkgɛŋɪçmaxʊŋ] F -, -en *(form)* cancellation; *(Chem)* reversal; **Rück|ge|bäu|de** NT rear building; **rück|ge|bil|det** ADJ *(Biol)* degenerate; **Rück|ge|win|nung** F recovery; *(von Land, Gebiet)* reclaiming, reclamation; *(aus verbrauchten Stoffen)* recycling; **Rück|glie|de|rung** F *(Pol)* reintegration

Rück|grat [ˈrʏkgraːt] NT -(e)s, -e spine, backbone; **er ist ein Mensch ohne ~** *(fig)* he's a spineless creature, he's got no backbone; **das ~ der Wirtschaft** the backbone *or* mainstay of the economy; **jdm das ~ stärken** *(fig inf)* to give sb encouragement *or* a boost; **jdm das ~ brechen** *(fig)* to break *or* ruin sb

Rück|grat|ver|krüm|mung F curvature of the spine

Rück-: **Rück|griff** M **a** **durch einen** *or* **unter ~ auf jdn/etw** by reverting to sb/sth; **wenn ein ~ auf vorhandene Reserven nicht möglich ist** if it is not possible to fall back on available resources; **erlauben Sie mir einen ~ auf bereits Gesagtes** allow me to revert to something that has already been said **b** *(Jur)* = **Regress b**; **Rück|halt** M **a** *(= Unterstützung)* support, backing; **an jdm einen ~ haben** to find a support in sb; **keinen/starken ~ haben** to have no/strong support **b** *(= Einschränkung)* **ohne ~** without reservation; **Rück|hal|te|be|cken** NT storage pond; **rück|halt|los** ADJ complete; *Unterstützung auch* unqualified, wholehearted; *Vertrauen auch* implicit ADV completely; *unterstützen auch* wholeheartedly; *ermitteln* thoroughly; **sich ~ zu etw bekennen** to proclaim one's total allegiance to sth; **Rück|hand** F *(Sport)* backhand; **~ spielen** to play backhand; **er kann erstklassig ~ spielen** he has a first-rate backhand; **den Ball (mit der) ~ schlagen** to hit the ball (on one's) backhand; **Rück|hand|schlag** M *(Sport)* backhand (stroke)

ru|cki|zu|cki [ˈrʊkiˈtsʊki] ADV *(inf)* = **ruck, zuck**

Rück|kampf M *(Sport)* return match

Rück|kauf M repurchase

Rück|kaufs-: **Rück|kaufs|recht** NT right of repurchase; **Rück|kaufs|wert** M repurchase value

Rück|kehr [ˈrʏkkeːɐ] F -, *no pl* return; **bei seiner ~** on his return; **jdn zur ~ (nach X/zu jdm) bewegen** to persuade sb to return (to X/to sb)

Rück|kehr-: **Rück|kehr|för|de|rungs|ge|setz** NT, **Rück|kehr|hil|fe|ge|setz** NT *law encouraging the return of immigrants to their native country*; **rück|kehr|wil|lig** ADJ willing to return

Rück-: **rück+kop|peln** [ˈrʏkkɔpln] VTI *sep infin, ptp only (alle Bedeutungen)* to feed back; **Rück|kop|pe|lung** F, **Rück|kopp|lung** F feedback; **Rück|kreu|zung** F backcross; *(Vorgang)* backcrossing; **Rück|kunft** [ˈrʏkkʊnft] F -, *no pl (liter)* return; **Rück|la|ge** F *(Fin: = Reserve)* reserve, reserves *pl*; *(= Ersparnisse auch)* savings *pl*; **Rück|lauf** M, *no pl (Tech)* reverse running; *(von Maschinenteil)* return travel; *(= Gegenströmung)* countercurrent; *(TV)* flyback; *(Naut)* slip; *(beim Tonband)* fast rewind; *(von Schusswaffe)* recoil; *(von Fragebögen, Waren)* returns *pl*; **ein guter ~** a good number of returns; **rück|läu|fig** ADJ declining, falling, dropping; *Tendenz* downward; **eine ~e Entwicklung** a decline, a falling off; **Rück|licht** NT tail-light, rear light; *(bei Fahrrad auch)* back light; **rück|lings** [ˈrʏklɪŋs] ADV *(= rückwärts)* backwards; *(= von hinten)* from behind; *(= auf dem Rücken)* on one's back; **Rück|marsch** M *(Mil)* march back; *(= Rückzug)* retreat

Rück|mel|de-: **Rück|mel|de|frist** F *(Univ)* re-registration period; **Rück|mel|de|ge|büh|ren** PL *(Univ)* re-registration fee

Rück-: **Rück|mel|dung** F **a** *(= Antwort)* response, feedback, reaction **b** *(Univ)* re-registration **c** *(Comput)* response, *(= Echorückmeldung)* reply; **Rück|nah|me** [-naːmə] F -, -n taking back; *(von Verordnung, Gesetz)* revocation, revoking; *(von Geldkürzungen)* reversal; *(= Senkung)* reduction; **die ~ des Gerätes ist unmöglich** it is impossible for us to take this set back; **ich bestehe auf der ~ des Gerätes** I must insist that you take this set back; **Rück|nah|me|preis** M repurchase price; **Rück|pass** M *(Sport)* return pass; **Rück|por|to** NT return postage; **Rück|prall** M rebound; *(von Kugel, Stein etc)* ricochet; **Rück|prä|mie** F *(Fin)* put premium; **Rück|prä|mi|en|ge|schäft** NT *(Fin)* put

Rück|rei|se F return journey

Rück|rei|se-: **Rück|rei|se|ver|kehr** M homebound traffic; **Rück|rei|se|vi|sum** NT return visa; **Rück|rei|se|wel|le** F surge of homebound traffic, rush of returning holidaymakers

Rück-: **Rück|ruf** M **a** *(am Telefon)* **Herr X hat angerufen und bittet um ~** Mr X called and asked you to call (him) back; **automatischer ~** automatic callback **b** *(Jur)* rescission of permission to manufacture under licence *(Brit)* *or* license *(US)* **c** *(von Botschafter, Auto, Waren)* recall; **Rück|ruf|ak|ti|on** F call-back campaign; **Rück|run|de** F *(Sport)* second half of the season; *(= Rückspiel)* return match *or* leg

Ruck|sack [ˈrʊkzak] M rucksack

Ruck|sack|tou|rist(in) M(F) backpacker

Rück-: **Rück|schalt|tas|te** F backspace key; **Rück|schau** F reflection *(auf +acc* on); *(in Medien)* review *(auf +acc* of); **~ halten** to reminisce, to reflect; **auf etw** *(acc)* **~ halten** to look back on sth; **in ~ auf das vergangene Jahr ...** looking back on the past year ...; **Rück|schein** M ≈ recorded delivery slip; **Rück|schlag** M **a** *(von Ball)* rebound; *(von Gewehr)* recoil; *(fig)* setback; *(bei Patient)* relapse **b** *(Biol)* atavism **c** *(Sw: = Defizit)* deficit; **Rück|schlä|ger(in)** M(F) *(Sport)* receiver; **Rück|schlag|ven|til** NT check valve; **Rück|schluss** M conclusion; **den ~ gestatten, dass ...** to admit of the conclusion that ...; **den ~ ziehen, dass ...** to draw the conclusion that ..., to conclude that ...; **Rückschlüsse auf etw** *(acc)* **zulassen** to allow conclusions to be drawn about sth; **Rückschlüsse ziehen** to draw one's own conclusions *(aus* from); **Rück|schritt** M *(fig)* retrograde step, step backwards, retrogression *(form)*; **ein gesellschaftlicher ~** a retrograde *or* retrogressive *(form)* social step, a social step backwards; **rück|schritt|lich** [ˈrʏkʃrɪtlɪç] ADJ reactionary; *Entwicklung* retrograde

Rück|sei|te F back; *(von Blatt Papier, Geldschein auch)* reverse; *(von Planet auch)* far side; *(von Gebäude auch)* rear; *(von Buchseite, Münze)* reverse, verso; *(von Zeitung)* back page; **siehe ~** see over(leaf)

rück|sei|tig [ˈrʏkzaitɪç] ADJ on the back *or* reverse; **die ~en Bemerkungen** the remarks overleaf ADV *(= auf der Rückseite)* on the back; **das Papier soll auch ~ beschrieben werden** you should write on both sides of the paper; **der Garten liegt ~** the garden is at the back

ruck|sen [ˈrʊksn] VI *(Taube)* to coo

Rück|sen|dung F return

Rück|sicht [ˈrʏkzɪçt] F -, -en **a** *(= Schonung, Nachsicht)* consideration; **aus** *or* **mit ~ auf jdn/etw** out of consideration for sb/sth; **ohne ~ auf jdn/etw** with no consideration for sb/sth; **ohne ~ auf Verluste** *(inf)* regardless; **auf jdn/etw ~ nehmen** to consider sb/sth, to show consideration for sb/sth; **er kennt keine ~** he's ruthless; **da kenne ich keine ~!** I can be ruthless **b** **Rücksichten** PL *(= Gründe, Interessen)* considerations *pl*

rück|sicht|lich [ˈrʏkzɪçtlɪç] PREP *+gen (old)* in view of

Rück|sicht|nah|me [-naːmə] F -, *no pl* consideration

Rück|sichts-: **rück|sichts|los** ADJ **a** inconsiderate, thoughtless; *(im Verkehr)* reckless **b** *(= unbarmherzig)* ruthless ADV **a** *(= ohne Nachsicht)* inconsiderately, thoughtlessly; **er verfolgt ~ seine Interessen** he follows his own interests without consideration for others **b** *(= schonungslos)* ruthlessly; **Rück|sichts|lo|sig|keit** F -, -en **a** *(= rücksichtslose Tat)* inconsiderate act; **das ist doch eine ~!** how inconsiderate *or* thoughtless **b** *no pl (= das Rücksichtslossein)* lack of consideration, thoughtlessness; *(= Unbarmherzigkeit)* ruthlessness; **rück|sichts|voll** ADJ considerate, thoughtful *(gegenüber, gegen* towards) ADV considerately, thoughtfully; **behandeln Sie ihn etwas ~er** show him a little more consideration

Rück-: **Rück|sitz** M *(von Fahrrad, Motorrad)* pillion; *(von Auto)* back seat; **Rück|spie|gel** M *(Aut)* rear(-view) *or* driving mirror; *(außen)* outside mirror; **Rück|spiel** NT *(Sport)* return match; **Rück|spra|che** F consultation; **nach ~ mit Herrn Müller ...** after consulting Mr Müller ...; **~ mit jdm halten** *or* **nehmen** to confer with *or* consult (with) sb

Rück|spul|au|to|ma|tik F *(von Kamera, Video etc)* automatic rewind

rück+spu|len [ˈrʏkʃpuːlən] VT *sep infin, ptp only Tonband, Film* to rewind

Rück|spul|knopf M *(von Kamera)* rewind knob

Rück|spul|tas|te F *(von Tonbandgerät etc)* rewind key

Rück|stand [ˈrʏkʃtant] M **a** *(= Überrest)* remains *pl*; *(bei Verbrennung: = Bodensatz)* residue **b** *(= Verzug)* delay; *(bei Aufträgen)* backlog; *(bei Entwicklung)* slow progress; **im ~ sein** to be behind; *(bei Zahlungen auch)* to be in arrears *pl*; **in ~ geraten** to fall behind; *(bei Zahlungen auch)* to get in arrears *pl*; **seinen ~ aufholen** to make up for one's delay; *(bei Aufträgen)* to catch up on a backlog; *(bei Zahlungen)* to catch up on one's payments; *(in Leistungen)* to catch up **c** *(= Außenstände)* arrears *pl*; **wie hoch ist mein ~?** how much are my arrears?; **Rückstände eintreiben/bezahlen** to collect/pay arrears **d** *(Sport)* amount by which one is behind; **mit 0:2 (Toren) im ~ sein** to be 2-0 down; **ihr ~ auf den Tabellenführer beträgt 4 Punkte** they are 4 points behind the leader; **seinen ~ aufholen** to catch up, to close the gap

rück|stän|dig [ˈrʏkʃtɛndɪç] ADJ **a** *(= überfällig) Betrag* overdue; *Mensch* in arrears; **~er Betrag** amount overdue **b** *(= zurückgeblieben) Land, Mensch* backward; *Methoden, Ansichten* backward, antiquated ADV **~ denken** to have antiquated ideas

Rück|stän|dig|keit F -, *no pl* backwardness

rück|stand(s)|frei ADJ residue-free; *Verbrennung auch* clean ADV **ein Diamant verbrennt ~** a diamond burns without leaving any residue; **dieses Öl verbrennt nahezu ~** this oil burns cleanly

Rück-: **Rück|stau** M *(von Wasser)* backwater; *(von Autos)* tailback; *(von Unerledigtem)* backlog; **Rück|stell|tas|te** F *(an Tastatur)* backspace key; **Rück|stel|lung** F *(Fin)* reserve; **Rück|stoß** M repulsion; *(bei Gewehr)* recoil; *(von Rakete)* thrust; **Rück|stoß|an|trieb** M *(Aviat)* reaction propulsion; **rück|stoß|frei** ADJ *Geschütze* recoilless; **Rück|strah|ler** M reflector; **Rück|strom** M *(Elec)* reverse current; *(von Menschen, Fahrzeugen)* return; **der ~ der Urlauber aus Italien** the stream of holiday-makers *(Brit)* *or* vactioners *(US)* returning from Italy; **Rück|ta|bu|la|tor** M *(an Schreibmaschine)* tab left (key); **Rück|tas|te** F *(an Tastatur)* backspace key; **Rück|trans|port** M return transport; *(bei Schreibmaschine)* return

Rück|tritt M **a** *(= Amtsniederlegung)* resignation; *(von König)* abdication; **seinen ~ einreichen** *or* **erklären** to hand in *or* tender *(form)* one's resignation **b** *(Jur) (von Vertrag)* withdrawal *(von* from), rescission *(form) (von* of); **~ vom Versuch** abandonment of intent **c** *(inf: = Bremse)* backpedal *or* coaster brake

Rück|tritt|brem|se F backpedal *or* coaster brake

Rück|tritts-: **Rück|tritts|an|ge|bot** NT offer of resignation; **Rück|tritts|dro|hung** F threat to resign; *(von König)* threat to abdicate; **Rück|tritts|er|klä|rung** F announcement of one's resignation, resignation announcement; *(schriftlich)* letter of resignation; **Rück|tritts|for|de|rung** F demand for his *or* her resignation; **Rück|tritts|frist** F period for withdrawal; **Rück|tritts|ge|such** NT resignation; **das ~ einreichen** to tender one's resignation *(form)*; **Rück|tritts|klau|sel** F withdrawal clause; **Rück|tritts|recht** NT right of withdrawal

Rück|tritts|vor|be|halt M option of withdrawal

Rück-: **rück+über|set|zen** ['rʏkly:bɐzɛtsn] *ptp* **rückübersetzt** VT *sep infin, ptp only* to translate back into the original language; **Rück|über|set|zung** F retranslation into the original language; **Rück|um|schlag** M reply-paid *or* business reply *(US)* envelope; **adressierter und frankierter ~** stamped addressed envelope; **Rück|ver|folg|bar|keit** F (re)traceability; **rück+ver|gü|ten** ['rʏkfɛɐgy:tn] *ptp* **rückvergütet** VT *sep infin, ptp only* to refund *(jdm etw* sb sth); **Rück|ver|gü|tung** F refund; **Rück|ver|si|che|rer** M reinsurer; *(fig)* hedger; **rück+ver|si|chern** ['rʏkfɛɐzɪçɐn] *ptp* **rückversichert** *sep* VTI to reinsure VR to check (up *or* back); **Rück|ver|si|che|rung** F reinsurance; **Rück|ver|si|che|rungs|ver|trag** M *(Hist)* Reinsurance Treaty; **Rück|ver|weis** M reference back; **rück+ver|wei|sen** ['rʏkfɛɐvaizn] *ptp* **rückverwiesen** VTI *sep irreg infin, ptp only* to refer back; **Rück|wand** F *(von Zimmer, Gebäude etc)* back wall; *(von Möbelstück etc)* back; **Rück|wan|de|rer** M, **Rück|wan|de|rin** F returning emigrant, remigrant; **Rück|wan|de|rung** F remigration; **rück|wär|tig** ['rʏkvɛrtɪç] ADJ back; *Tür, Eingang, Ausgang auch* rear; *(Mil)* rear; **~e Verbindungen** *(Mil)* lines of communication

rück|wärts ['rʏkvɛrts] ADV **a** *(= zurück, rücklings)* backwards; **Rolle ~** backward roll; **Salto ~** back somersault; **~ einparken** to back *or* reverse into a parking space → **rückwärtsgewandt** **b** *(Aus: = hinten)* behind, at the back; **von ~** from behind

Rück|wärts-: **Rück|wärts|dre|hung** F reverse turn; **Rück|wärts|fah|ren** NT **-s,** *no pl* reversing; **Rück|wärts|gang** M *pl* **-gänge** *(Aut)* reverse gear; **den ~ einlegen** to change *(Brit) or* shift *(US)* into reverse, to put the car *etc* into reverse; **im ~ fahren** to reverse; **sich im ~ bewegen** *(fig)* to go backwards, to regress *(form)*; **rück|wärts|ge|wandt** ADJ *(fig)* backward-looking, retrogressive

Rück|weg M way back; **auf dem ~ vorbeikommen** to call in on one's way back; **den ~ antreten, sich auf den ~ begeben** to set off back; **sich auf den ~ machen** to head back; **jdm den ~ abschneiden** to cut off sb's line of retreat

ruck|wei|se ['rʊkvaizə] ADV jerkily; **sich ~ bewegen** to jerk, to move jerkily

Rück-: **Rück|wen|dung** F return *(zu, auf +acc* to); **rück|wir|kend** ['rʏkvɪrknt] ADJ *(Jur)* retrospective; *Lohn-, Gehaltserhöhung* backdated ADV **es wird ~ vom 1. Mai bezahlt** it will be backdated to 1st May; **das Gesetz tritt ~ vom** *or* **zum 1. Januar in Kraft** the law is made retrospective to 1st January; **etw ist ~ fällig** sth is backdated; **die Erhöhung der Renten gilt ~ zum 1. Januar** the rise in pensions is backdated to 1st January; **Rück|wir|kung** F repercussion; **~en auf etw** *(acc)* **haben** to have repercussions on sth; **eine Zahlung/Gesetzesänderung mit ~ vom ...** a payment backdated to/an amendment made retrospective to ...; **rück|zahl|bar** ADJ repayable; **Rück|zah|lung** F repayment; **Rück|zie|her** ['rʏktsi:ɐ] M **-s, -** *(inf)* backing down; **einen ~ machen** to back down; **rück|zie|lend** ADJ *(Gram rare)* reflexive

Ruck|zuck ['rʊk'tsʊk] NT **-s,** *no pl (inf)* **etw mit ~ machen** to do sth at the double *(inf)*

ruck, zuck ['rʊk'tsʊk] INTERJ *(beim Ziehen)* heave; *(beim Schieben)* push ADV in a flash; *(Imperativ)* jump to it; **das geht ~** it won't take a second; **wenn er nicht gehorcht, fliegt er raus, das geht ~** if he doesn't obey he'll be out, just like that

Rück|zug M *(Mil)* retreat; *(fig)* withdrawal; **geordneter/ungeordneter ~** *(lit, fig)* orderly/disorderly retreat; **auf dem ~** in the retreat; **den ~ antreten** *(lit, fig)* to retreat, to beat a retreat; **den ~ ins Private antreten** to withdraw into oneself → **blasen VI**

Rück|zugs-: **Rück|zugs|ge|biet** NT retreat; **Rück|zugs|ge|fecht** NT *(Mil, fig)* rearguard action

Ru|co|la ['ru:kola] F *(Bot)* (garden *or* salad) rocket, rucola

rü|de ['ry:də], *(Aus)* **rüd** [ry:t] ADJ impolite; *Antwort* curt, brusque; *Methoden* crude; *Angriff, Foul* rough; **das war sehr ~ von dir** that was very rude of you ADV rudely

Rü|de ['ry:də] M **-n, -n** *(= Männchen)* dog, male; *(= Hetzhund)* hound

Ru|del ['ru:dl] NT **-s, -** *(von Hunden, Wölfen)* pack; *(von Wildschweinen, Hirschen)* herd; *(fig dated)* swarm, horde; **in ~n auftreten** to go (a)round in packs/herds/swarms *or* hordes

ru|del|wei|se ADV → **Rudel** in packs/herds/swarms *or* hordes

Ru|der ['ru:dɐ] NT **-s, -** *(von Ruderboot, Galeere etc)* oar; *(Naut, Aviat: = Steuerruder)* rudder; *(fig: = Führung)* helm; **das ~ fest in der Hand haben** *(fig)* to be in control of the situation; **am ~ sein** *(lit, fig)* to be at the helm; **ans ~ kommen** *or* **das ~ übernehmen** *(lit, fig)* to take over (at) the helm; **sich in die ~ legen** *(lit, fig)* to put one's back into it; **sich für etw in die ~ legen** *(fig)* to put one's back into sth; **das ~ herumwerfen** *or* **herumreißen** *(fig)* to change course *or* tack; **aus dem ~ laufen** *(fig)* to get out of hand

Ru|der-: **Ru|der|bank** F *pl* **-bänke** rowing seat; *(in Galeere)* rowing bench; **Ru|der|blatt** NT (oar) blade; **Ru|der|boot** NT rowing boat *(Brit)*, rowboat *(US)*; **Ru|der|dol|le** F rowlock

Ru|de|rer ['ru:dərɐ] M **-s, -** oarsman, rower

Ru|der|gän|ger [-gɛŋɐ] M **-s, -**, **Ru|der|gän|ge|rin** [-ərɪn] F **-, -nen** *(Naut)* helmsman/woman

Ru|der|haus NT *(Naut)* wheelhouse, pilot house

Ru|de|rin ['ru:dərɪn] F oarswoman, rower

ru|dern ['ru:dɐn] VI **a** *aux haben or sein* to row **b** *(Schwimmvögel)* to paddle; *(fig)* to struggle; **mit den Armen ~** *(fig)* to flail *or* wave one's arms about VT to row

Ru|der-: **Ru|der|pin|ne** F tiller; **Ru|der|re|gat|ta** F rowing regatta; **Ru|der|schlag** M stroke; **Ru|der|sport** M rowing *no def art*; **Ru|der|stan|ge** F tiller

Ru|di|ment [rudi'mɛnt] NT **-(e)s, -e** rudiment

ru|di|men|tär [rudimɛn'tɛ:ɐ] ADJ rudimentary; *(Biol) Organ auch* vestigial ADV rudimentarily; **~ ausgebildet** rudimentary; **~ vorhanden sein** to be vestigial

Rud|rer ['ru:drɐ] M **-s, -**, **Rud|re|rin** [-ərɪn] F **-, -nen** = **Ruderer, Ruderin**

Ruf [ru:f] M **-(e)s, -e** **a** *(= Ausruf, Vogelruf, fig: = Aufruf)* call *(nach* for); *(lauter)* shout; *(= gellender Schrei)* cry; **ein ~ ertönte** a cry rang out; **in den ~ „...“ ausbrechen** to burst into cries *or* shouts of "..."; **der ~ des Muezzins** the call of the muezzin; **der ~ der Wildnis** the call of the wild; **dem ~ des Herzens/Gewissens folgen** *(fig)* to obey the voice of one's heart/conscience; **der ~ nach Freiheit/Gerechtigkeit** *(fig)* the call for freedom/justice; **der ~ zu den Waffen** the call to arms; **der ~ zur Ordnung** *(fig)* the call to order

b *(= Ansehen, Leumund)* reputation; **einen guten ~ haben** *or* **genießen, sich eines guten ~es erfreuen** *(geh)* to have *or* enjoy a good reputation; **einen schlechten ~ haben** to have a bad reputation; **dem ~ nach** by reputation; **eine Firma von ~** a firm with a good reputation, a firm of high repute, a firm with a good name; **sich** *(dat)* **einen ~ als etw erwerben** to build up a reputation for oneself as sth, to make a name for oneself as sth; **seinem ~ (als etw) gerecht werden** to live up to one's reputation (as sth); **ein Mann von schlechtem ~** a man with a bad reputation, a man with a bad name; **von üblem** *or* **zweifelhaftem ~** with a bad reputation; **von üblem** *or* **zweifelhaftem ~ sein** to have a bad reputation; **jdn/etw in schlechten ~ bringen** to give sb/sth a bad name; **jdn bei jdm in schlechten ~ bringen** to bring sb into disrepute with sb; **sie/das ist besser als ihr/sein ~** she/it is better than she/it is made out to be, she/it is not as black as she/it is painted; **ist der ~ erst ruiniert, lebt man völlig ungeniert** *(prov)* you live freely if you haven't a reputation to lose

c *(Univ: = Berufung)* offer of a chair *or* professorship; **er hat einen ~ nach Mainz erhalten** he has been offered a chair *or* professorship at Mainz

d *(= Fernruf)* telephone number; **„Ruf: 2785“** "Tel 2785"

Ru|fe ['ru:fə] F **-, -n**, **Rü|fe** ['ry:fə] F **-, -n** *(Sw)* **a** *(= Steinlawine)* rock fall; *(= Erdrutsch)* landslide **b** *(auch S Ger: auf Wunde)* scab

ru|fen ['ru:fn] *pret* **rief** [ri:f], *ptp* **gerufen** [gə'ru:fn] VI to call; *(Mensch: = laut rufen)* to shout; *(Gong, Glocke, Horn etc)* to sound *(zu* for); **um Hilfe ~** to call *or* cry for help; **die Pflicht ruft** duty calls; **die Arbeit ruft** my/your *etc* work is waiting; **nach jdm/etw ~** to call for sb/sth

VI *impers* **es ruft eine Stimme** a voice is calling; **es hat gerufen** somebody called

VT *(= laut sagen)* **a** to call; *(= ausrufen)* to cry; *(Mensch: = laut rufen)* to shout; **jdm etw in Erinnerung** *or* **ins Gedächtnis ~** to bring back (memories of) sth to sb; **sich** *(dat)* **etw in Erinnerung** *or* **ins Gedächtnis ~** to recall sth; **jdn zur Ordnung ~** to call sb to order; **jdn zur Sache ~** to bring sb back to the point; **jdn zu den Waffen ~** to call sb to arms; **bravo/da capo ~** to shout hooray *(Brit) or* bravo/encore; **sich heiser ~** to shout oneself hoarse

b *(= kommen lassen)* to send for; *Arzt, Polizei* to send for, to call; *Taxi* to call; **jdn zu sich ~** to send for sb; **Gott hat sie zu sich gerufen** God has called her to Him; **Sie haben mich ~ lassen?** you called, sir/madam?; **~ Sie ihn bitte!** please send him to me; **jdn zu Hilfe ~** to call on sb to help; **du kommst wie gerufen** you're just the man/woman I wanted; **das kommt mir wie gerufen** that's just what I needed; *(= kommt mir gelegen)* that suits me fine *(inf)*

Ru|fen NT **-s,** *no pl* calling *no indef art*; *(von Mensch: laut)* shouting *no indef art*; **haben Sie das ~ nicht gehört?** didn't you hear him/her *etc* calling/shouting?

Ru|fer ['ru:fɐ] M **-s, - der ~ im Streit** *(liter)* the leader in battle; **der (einsame) ~ in der Wüste** the (lone) voice (crying) in the wilderness

Ru|fe|rei [ru:fə'rai] F **-, -en** *(inf)* = **Rufen**

Rüf|fel ['rʏfl] M **-s, -** *(inf)* telling-off *(inf)*, ticking-off *(Brit inf)*

rüf|feln ['rʏfln] VT *(inf)* to tell *or* tick *(Brit)* off *(inf)*

Ruf-: **Ruf|mord** M character assassination; **Ruf|mord|kam|pag|ne** F smear campaign; **Ruf|na|me** M forename (by which one is generally known); **Ruf|num|mer** F (tele)phone number; *(bei Modems auch)* number to dial; **Ruf|num|mern|an|zei|ge** F *(von Telefon)* caller display; **Ruf|num|mern|spei|cher** M *(von Telefon)* memory; **Ruf|pro|to|koll** NT *(Comput: für Modems)* call log; **Ruf|säu|le** F *(für Taxi)* telephone; *(Mot: = Notrufsäule)* emergency telephone; **ruf|schä|di|gend** ADJ **~ sein** to be damaging to one's reputation; **Ruf|schä|di|gung** F defamation; **Ruf|um|lei|tung** F *(Telec)* call forwarding *or* diversion; **Ruf|wei|te** F **in ~** within earshot, within calling distance; **außer**

~ out of earshot; **Ruf|zei|chen** NT **a** *(Telec)* call sign; *(von Telefon)* ringing tone **b** *(Aus)* exclamation mark

Rug|by ['rakbi] NT -, *no pl* rugby, rugger *(Brit inf)*

Rug|by|spiel ['rakbi-] NT *(Veranstaltung)* rugby match; **das ~** *(Sportart)* rugby

Rü|ge ['ry:gə] F -, -n *(= Verweis)* reprimand, rebuke *(für jdn* for sb); *(= Kritik)* criticism *no indef art*; *(= scharfe Kritik)* censure *no indef art*; **jdm eine ~ erteilen** to reprimand *or* rebuke/criticize/censure sb *(für, wegen* for)

rü|gen ['ry:gn] VT *(form)* jdn to reprimand *(wegen, für* for); *etw* to reprehend; **ich muss dein Verhalten ~** I must reprimand you for your behaviour *(Brit) or* behavior *(US)*

rü|gens|wert ADJ reprehensible

Ru|he ['ru:ə] F -, *no pl* **a** *(= Schweigen, Stille)* quiet, silence; **~!** quiet!, silence!; **~, bitte!** quiet, please; **gebt ~!** be quiet!; **ihr sollt ~ geben!** once and for all: (will you) be quiet!; **jdn zur ~ ermahnen** to tell sb to be quiet; **sich** *(dat)* **~ verschaffen** to get quiet *or* silence; **es herrscht ~** all is silent, silence reigns *(liter)*; *(fig: = Disziplin, Frieden)* all is quiet; **~ halten** *(lit, fig)* to keep quiet *or* silent; **die ~ der Natur** the stillness of nature; **himmlische ~** heavenly peace; **~ und Frieden** peace and quiet; **in ~ und Abgeschiedenheit** in peaceful seclusion; **die ~ vor dem Sturm** *(fig)* the calm before the storm
b *(= Ungestörtheit, Frieden)* peace, quiet; *(= Ruhestätte)* resting place; **~ ausstrahlen** to radiate a sense of calm; **in ~ und Frieden leben** to live a quiet life; **~ und Ordnung** law and order; **nach tagelangen Krawallen ist wieder ~ eingekehrt** after days of rioting, order *or* calm has returned; **~ ist die erste Bürgerpflicht** *(prov)* the main thing is to keep calm; **die ~ wiederherstellen** to restore order; **ich brauche meine ~** I need a bit of peace; **lass mich in ~!** leave me in peace, stop bothering me; **ich will meine ~ haben!** leave *or* let me alone *or* be; **dann hat die liebe Seele Ruh** *(prov)* then perhaps we'll get a bit of peace; **vor jdm ~ haben wollen** to want a rest from sb; *(endgültig)* to want to get *or* be rid of sb; **jdm keine ~ lassen** *or* **gönnen** *(Mensch)* not to give sb any peace; **keine ~ geben** to keep on and on; **das lässt ihm keine ~** he can't stop thinking about it; **zur ~ kommen** to get some peace; *(= solide werden)* to settle down; **jdn zur ~ kommen lassen** to give sb a chance to rest; **keine ~ finden (können)** to know no peace, not to be able to find any peace of mind; **jdn zur letzten** *or* **ewigen ~ betten** *(liter)* to lay sb to rest *(liter)*; **die letzte ~ finden** *(liter)* to be laid to rest *(liter)*
c *(= Erholung)* rest, repose *(liter)*; *(= Ruhestand)* retirement; *(= Stillstand)* rest; **der Patient braucht viel ~** the patient needs a great deal of rest; **das Pendel befindet sich in ~** the pendulum is stationary; **jdm keine ~ gönnen** not to give sb a minute's rest; **sich zur ~ begeben** *(form)* **zur ~ gehen** to retire (to bed) *(form)*; **angenehme ~!** sleep well!; **sich zur ~ setzen** to retire
d *(= Gelassenheit)* calm(ness); *(= Disziplin)* quiet, order; **die ~ weghaben** *(inf)* to be unflappable *(inf)*; **~ bewahren** to keep calm; **die ~ selbst sein** to be calmness itself; **jdn aus der ~ bringen** to throw sb *(inf)*; **sich nicht aus der ~ bringen lassen, nicht aus der ~ zu bringen sein** not to (let oneself) get worked up; **in aller ~** calmly; **er trank noch in aller ~ seinen Kaffee** he drank his coffee as if he had all the time in the world; **überlege es dir in (aller) ~** take your time and think about it; **sich** *(dat)* **etw in ~ ansehen** to look at sth in one's own time; **immer mit der ~** *(inf)* don't panic

Ru|he-: **Ru|he|bank** F *pl* **-bänke** bench, seat; **Ru|he|be|dürf|nis** NT need for rest; **ru|he|be|dürf|tig** ADJ in need of rest; **Ru|he|bett** NT bed; **Ru|he|ge|halt** NT *(form)* superannuation *(Brit)*, retirement pension; **Ru|he|geld** NT *(form)*, *(Aus)* **Ru|he|ge|nuss** M pension; **Ru|he|kis|sen** NT bolster → **Gewissen**; **Ru|he|la|ge** F *(von Mensch)* reclining position; *(Med: bei Bruch)* immobile position; *(Tech) (von Maschine)* resting position; *(von Zeiger)* neutral position; *(= Unbeweglichkeit)* immobility; **sich in ~ befinden** *(Mensch, Maschine)* to be at rest; *(Wein)* to be kept still; *(= unbeweglich sein)* to be immobile; **ru|he|lie|bend** ADJ fond of peace and quiet; **ru|he|los** ADJ restless; **eine ~e Zeit** a time of unrest; **Ru|he|lo|sig|keit** F -, *no pl* restlessness; **Ru|he|mas|se** F *(Phys)* rest mass

ru|hen ['ru:ən] VI **a** *(= ausruhen)* to rest; **nach dem Essen soll man ruhn oder tausend Schritte tun** *(Prov)* after a meal one should either rest or take some exercise; **ich möchte etwas ~** I want to take a short rest, I want to rest a little; **nicht (eher) ~** *or* **nicht ~ und rasten, bis ...** *(fig)* not to rest until ...; **ich wünsche wohl zu ~!** *(form)* I wish you a good night *(form)*; **(ich) wünsche, wohl geruht zu haben!** *(form)* I trust that you slept well *(form)*
b *(geh: = liegen)* to rest *(an or auf +dat* on); *(Gebäude)* to be supported *(auf +dat* by), to rest *(auf +dat* on); *(Fluch)* to lie *(auf +dat* on); **unsere Hoffnung ruht auf ...** *(dat)* our hopes rest on ...; **möge Gottes Segen auf dir ~** may God's blessing be with you; **auf ihm ruht ein Verdacht** suspicion hangs over him *(liter)*
c *(= stillstehen)* to stop; *(Maschinen)* to stand idle; *(Arbeit)* to stop, to cease; *(Verkehr)* to be at a standstill; *(Waffen)* to be laid down; *(= unterbrochen sein: Verfahren, Verhandlung, Vertrag)* to be suspended; **lass die Arbeit jetzt ~** *(geh)* leave your work now
d *(= tot und begraben sein)* to lie, to be buried; **„hier ruht (in Gott) ..."** "here lies ..."; **„ruhe in Frieden!"** "Rest in Peace"; **„ruhe sanft!"** "rest eternal"
VR *impers* **hier ruht es sich gut** this is good to rest on

ru|hend ADJ resting; *Kapital* dormant; *Maschinen* idle; *Verkehr* stationary; **~e Venus** Venus reclining → **Pol**

ru|hen+las|sen VT *ptp* **ruhenlassen** *or (rare)* **ruhengelassen** *sep irreg* = **ruhen lassen b**

ru|hen las|sen VT *ptp* **ruhen lassen** *or (rare)* **ruhen gelassen** *irreg* **a** *Teig* to allow to rest **b** *(fig) Vergangenheit, Angelegenheit* to let rest; *Verhandlungen, Prozess* to adjourn; *Amt* to leave temporarily vacant

Ru|he-: **Ru|he|pau|se** F break; *(wenig Betrieb, Arbeit)* slack *or* quiet period; **eine ~ einlegen** to take *or* have a break; **Ru|he|platz** M resting place; **Ru|he|pos|ten** M sinecure; **Ru|he|punkt** M place of rest; **Ru|he|raum** M rest room; **Ru|he|sitz** M *(Haus)* retirement home; **er hat seinen ~ in Ehlscheid aufgeschlagen** he has retired to Ehlscheid; **Ru|he|stand** M retirement; **im ~ sein** *or* **leben** to be retired; **er ist Bankdirektor im ~** he is a retired bank director; **in den ~ treten** *or* **gehen** to retire, to go into retirement; **jdn in den ~ versetzen** to retire sb; **er wurde in den ~ verabschiedet** a retirement ceremony was held for him; **Ru|he|ständ|ler** [-ʃtɛndlɐ] M -s, -, **Ru|he|ständ|le|rin** [-ərɪn] F -, -nen retired person; **Ru|he|stands|be|am|te(r)** M *decl as adj*, **Ru|he|stands|be|am|tin** F retired civil servant; **Ru|he|statt** F *pl* **-stätten** [-ʃtɛtn], **Ru|he|stät|te** F resting place; **letzte Ruhestätte** last *or* final resting place; **Ru|he|stel|lung** F *(von Körper)* resting position; *(von beweglichem Gegenstand)* resting point; *(von Maschinen)* off position; **der Arm muss in ~ bleiben** the arm must not be moved; **ru|he|stö|rend** ADJ **~er Lärm** *(Jur)* disturbance of the peace; **Ru|he|stö|rer(in)** M(F) disturber of the peace; **Ru|he|stö|rung** F *(Jur)* disturbance of the peace; **Ru|he|tag** M rest day, day off; *(von Geschäft etc)* closing day; **einen ~ einlegen** to have a day's rest, to take a day off; **„Mittwoch ~"** "closed (on) Wednesdays"; **Ru|he|zeit** F rest period; *(= Nebensaison)* off season; **Ru|he|zu|stand** M state of rest; *(Tech)* idle state; **im ~** (when) at rest; *(Tech)* when idle

ru|hig ['ru:ɪç] ADJ **a** *(= still)* quiet; *Wetter, Meer* calm; **seid ~!** be quiet!; **ihr sollt ~ sein!** (will you) be quiet!
b *(= geruhsam)* quiet; *Urlaub, Feiertage, Leben* quiet, peaceful; *Farbe* restful; *(= ohne Störung) Überfahrt, Verlauf* smooth; *(Tech)* smooth; **gegen 6 Uhr wird es ~er** it quietens *(Brit) or* quiets *(US)* down around 6 o'clock; **alles geht seinen ~en Gang** everything is going smoothly → **Kugel a**
c *(= gelassen)* calm; *Gewissen* easy; **nur ~ (Blut)!** keep calm, take it easy *(inf)*; **bei ~er Überlegung** on (mature) consideration; **du wirst auch noch ~er!** you'll calm down one day; **du kannst/Sie können ganz ~ sein** I can assure you → **Blut**
d *(= sicher) Hand, Blick* steady
e *(= teilnahmslos)* calm
ADV **a** *(= still) sitzen, stehenbleiben, dastehen* still; **sitz doch ~!** sit still!
b *(= untätig)* **etw ~ mitansehen** to stand by and watch sth; **~ dabeistehen** just to stand by; **ich kann doch nicht ~ mit ansehen, wie er so etwas tut** I can't just stand there and watch him do a thing like that; **sich ~ verhalten** to keep calm
c *(inf)* **du kannst ~ hierbleiben** feel free to stay here, you're welcome to stay here if you want; **ihr könnt ~ gehen, ich passe schon auf** you just go and I'll look after things; **man kann ~ behaupten/sagen/annehmen, dass ...** *(= mit Recht)* one may well assert/say/assume that ..., one need have no hesitation in *or* about asserting/saying/assuming that ...; **die können ~ etwas mehr zahlen** *(= leicht)* they could easily pay a little more; **wir können ~ darüber sprechen** we can talk about it if you want; **du könntest ~ mal etwas für mich tun!** it's about time you did something for me!
d *(= ohne Turbulenzen) laufen* very quietly; **das Flugzeug liegt ~ in der Luft** the plane is flying smoothly; **ihr Leben verläuft sehr ~** she leads a very quiet life
e *(= gelassen)* **wenn du etwas ~er überlegen würdest** if you took more time to think things over; **lass uns ~ nachdenken** let's think things over calmly
f *(= beruhigt) schlafen* peacefully; **du kannst ~ ins Kino gehen** go ahead, go to the cinema; **jetzt kann ich ~ in Urlaub fahren** now I can go on holiday *(esp Brit) or* vacation *(US)* with an easy mind

ru|hig+stel|len VT *sep* **a** *(Med) Patienten (bei Knochenbruch etc)* to immobilize; *(mit Drogen)* to sedate **b** *(fig: = beruhigen)* to pacify, to calm

ru|hig stel|len VT *(Med) Bein etc* to immobilize

Ruhm [ru:m] M -(e)s, *no pl* glory; *(= Berühmtheit)* fame; *(= Lob)* praise; **des ~es voll sein** to be full of praise *(über +acc* for); **jds ~ begründen** to establish *or* make sb's name, to make sb famous; **zu ~ gelangen** to find fame, to become famous; **mit etw keinen ~ ernten** *(inf)* not to win any medals with *or* for sth; **sich in seinem ~ sonnen** to rest on one's laurels → **bekleckern VR**

ruhm|be|deckt ADJ covered with glory

rüh|men ['ry:mən] VT *(= preisen, empfehlen)* to praise, to sing the praises of; *Tugenden, Schönheit auch* to extol; **jdn ~d erwähnen** to give sb an honourable *(Brit) or* honorable *(US)* mention; **etw ~d hervorheben** to single sth out for *or* give sth special praise VR **sich einer Sache** *(gen)* **~** *(= prahlen)* to boast about sth; *(= stolz sein)* to pride oneself on sth; **sich einer Sache** *(gen)* **~ können** to be able to boast of sth; **die Stadt rühmt sich eines eigenen Schwimmbads** *(iro)* the town boasts its own swimming pool; **ohne mich zu ~** without wishing to boast

rüh|mens|wert ADJ praiseworthy, laudable

Ruh|mes-: **Ruh|mes|blatt** NT *(fig)* glorious chapter; **Ruh|mes|hal|le** F hall of fame; **Ruh|mes|tag** M glorious day; **Ruh|mes|tat** F glorious deed

rühm|lich [ˈryːmlɪç] ADJ praiseworthy, laudable; *Ausnahme* notable; **kein ~es Ende finden** *or* **nehmen** to meet a bad end; **sich ~ hervortun** to distinguish oneself

Ruhm-: **ruhm|los** ADJ inglorious; **ruhm|reich** ADJ *(liter)* glorious; **Ruhm|sucht** F thirst for glory; **ruhm|süch|tig** ADJ thirsting for glory; **ruhm|voll** ADJ glorious

Ruhr [ruːɐ] F - *(Geog)* Ruhr

Ruhr F -, *no pl (Krankheit)* dysentery

Rühr|ei [ˈryːɐlai] NT scrambled egg; *(als Gericht)* scrambled eggs *pl*

rüh|ren [ˈryːrən] VI **a** *(= umrühren)* to stir; **sie rührte in ihrem Kaffee** she stirred her coffee
b an etw *(acc or dat)* ~ *(= anfassen)* to touch sth; *(fig: = erwähnen)* to touch on sth; **daran wollen wir nicht ~** let's not go into it; *(in Bezug auf Vergangenes)* let sleeping dogs lie; **rühret nicht daran!** *(liter)* let us not dwell on that; **die Sache rührte an ihren Herzen** the matter touched their hearts
c von etw ~ to stem from sth; **das rührt daher, dass ...** that is because ...; **daher rührt sein Misstrauen!** so that is the reason for his distrust!
VT **a** *(= umrühren) Teig, Farbe etc* to stir; *(= schlagen) Eier* to beat
b *(= bewegen)* to move; **er rührte kein Glied** he didn't stir at all; **er rührte keinen Finger** *or* **keine Hand, um mir zu helfen** *(inf)* he didn't lift a finger to help me *(inf)*
c *(= Gemüt bewegen)* to move; *Herz* to stir; **das kann mich nicht ~!** that leaves me cold; *(= stört mich nicht)* that doesn't bother me; **jdn zu Tränen ~** to move sb to tears; **sie war äußerst gerührt** she was extremely moved *or* touched
d *(Mus) Trommel* to strike, to beat
e ihn hat der Schlag gerührt *(inf)* he was thunderstruck; **ich glaubte, mich rührt der Schlag** *(inf)* you could have knocked me down with a feather *(inf)* → **Donner**
VR **a** *(= sich bewegen) (Blatt, Mensch)* to stir; *(Körperteil)* to move; *(= sich von der Stelle bewegen)* to move; *(= aktiv sein)* to buck up *(inf)*; *(= sich beeilen)* to bestir oneself, to get a move on *(inf)*; **rührt euch!** *(Mil)* at ease!; **~ lassen** *(Mil)* to give the order to stand at ease; **kein Lüftchen rührte sich** the air was still, there was not the slightest breeze; **er rührt sich nicht mehr** *(inf)* he won't get up again; **hier kann man sich nicht ~** you can't move in here; **sich vor Muskelkater/Kisten kaum ~ können** to be hardly able to move because of stiffness/for boxes; **nichts hat sich gerührt** nothing happened → **Stelle a**
b *(Gewissen, Mitleid, Reue)* to stir, to be awakened; *(inf: = sich melden)* to say something; **sie hat sich schon zwei Jahre nicht gerührt** *(inf)* she hasn't been in touch for two years

Rüh|ren NT -s, *no pl* stirring; **ein menschliches ~ (verspüren)** (to feel) a stirring of human pity; *(hum)* (to have to answer) a *or* the call of nature *(hum)*

rüh|rend ADJ touching; **das ist ~ von Ihnen** that is sweet of you ADV **sie kümmert sich ~ um das Kind** it's touching how she looks after the child

Ruhr|ge|biet NT, *no pl* Ruhr (area)

rüh|rig [ˈryːrɪç] ADJ active

ruhr|krank ADJ suffering from dysentery

Rühr-: **Rühr|ku|chen** M stirred cake; **Rühr|löf|fel** M mixing spoon; **Rühr|ma|schi|ne** F mixer; *(in Bäckerei)* mixing machine; **Rühr|mich|nicht|an** [ˈryːɐmɪçnɪçtlan] NT -, - *(Bot)* touch-me-not

Ruhr|pott M, *no pl (inf)* Ruhr (Basin *or* Valley)

Rühr-: **Rühr|schüs|sel** F mixing bowl; **rühr|se|lig** ADJ *(pej)* touching, tear-jerking *(pej inf)*; *Person* weepy; *Stimmung* sentimental; **Rühr|se|lig|keit** F, *no pl* sentimentality; **Rühr|stück** NT *(Theat)* melodrama; **Rühr|teig** M sponge mixture

Rüh|rung [ˈryːrʊŋ] F -, *no pl* emotion; **vor ~ nicht sprechen können** to be choked with emotion

Ru|in [ruˈiːn] M -s, *no pl* ruin; **vor dem ~ stehen** to be on the brink *or* verge of ruin; **jdn in den ~ treiben** to ruin sb; **seinem/dem ~ entgegengehen** to be on the way to ruin; **das ist mein ~!** that will be my ruin *or* the ruin of me; **du bist noch mein ~!** *(hum inf)* you'll be the ruin of me

Ru|i|ne [ruˈiːnə] F -, -n *(lit, fig)* ruin

Ru|i|nen-: **Ru|i|nen|feld** NT sea of debris; **ru|i|nen|haft** ADJ ruined; **Ru|i|nen|stadt** F ruined city

ru|i|nie|ren [ruiˈniːrən] *ptp* **ruiniert** VT to ruin; **sich ~** to ruin oneself

ru|i|nös [ruiˈnøːs] ADJ *Wettbewerb, Gebäude* ruinous

Rülps [rʏlps] M -es, -e *(dial inf)* belch

rülp|sen [ˈrʏlpsn] VI to belch; **das Rülpsen** belching

Rülp|ser [ˈrʏlpsɐ] M -s, - *(inf)* belch

rum [rʊm] ADV *(inf)* = **herum**

Rum [rʊm, *(S Ger, Aus auch)* ruːm] M -s, -s rum

Ru|mä|ne [ruˈmɛːnə] M -n, -n, **Ru|mä|nin** [-ˈmɛːnɪn] F -, -nen Romanian

Ru|mä|ni|en [ruˈmɛːniən] NT -s Romania

ru|mä|nisch [ruˈmɛːnɪʃ] ADJ Romanian

Ru|mä|nisch(e) [ruˈmɛːnɪʃ] NT Romanian → *auch* **Deutsch(e)**

Rum|ba [ˈrʊmba] F -, -s *or (inf)* m -s, -s rumba; **~ tanzen** to (dance the) rumba

Rum|ba|ku|gel F, **Rum|ba|ras|sel** F maraca

rum+flach|sen [ˈrʊmflaksn] VI *sep (inf)* to have a laugh, to joke around

rum+gam|meln VI *sep (inf)* to loaf *or* bum *(US)* around *or* about *(inf)*

rum+gif|ten VI *sep (sl)* to bitch *(inf)*

rum+gra|ben VI *sep irreg (sl: = Annäherungsversuche machen)* to try it on *(inf)*

rum+gur|ken VI *sep (sl: = herumfahren)* to drive around

rum+hän|gen VI *sep irreg aux haben or sein (inf)* *(in +dat* in) to hang around; **sie hängt zurzeit nur so rum** she's just killing time at the moment; **er hängt ständig mit diesen Typen rum** he's always hanging around with that lot

rum+kom|men [ˈrʊmkɔmən] VI *sep irreg (inf)* **a** = **herumkommen b dabei kommt nichts rum** nothing will come out of it

rum+krie|gen [ˈrʊmkriːgn] VT *sep (inf)* **jdn ~** to talk sb round *(Brit)*, to bring sb around *(US)*

Rum|ku|gel F rum truffle

rum+ma|chen [ˈrʊmmaxn] VI *sep (inf)* to mess about *(Brit) or* around *(mit jdm* with sb, *an etw (dat)* with sth)

Rum|mel [ˈrʊml] M -s, *no pl* **a** *(inf) (= Betrieb)* (hustle and) bustle; *(= Getöse)* racket *(inf)*; *(= Aufheben)* fuss *(inf)*; **der ganze ~** the whole business *or* carry-on *(inf)*; **den ~ kennen** to know all about it; **großen ~ um jdn/etw machen** *or* **veranstalten** to make a great fuss *or* to-do about sb/sth *(inf)* **b** *(= Rummelplatz)* fair; **auf den ~ gehen** to go to the fair

Rum|mel|platz M *(inf)* fairground

rum+mot|zen VI *sep (inf)* to moan

Rum|my [ˈrœmi] NT -s, -s *(Aus)* rummy

rum+nüs|sen [ˈrʊmnʏsn] VI *sep (sl: = Sex haben)* to shag *(sl)*

ru|mo|ren [ruˈmoːrən] *ptp* **rumort** VI to make a noise; *(Mensch)* to rumble about; *(Magen, Vulkan)* to rumble; *(Gewissen)* to play up; *(Gedanke)* to float about; **etw rumort in den Köpfen** sth is going through people's minds VI *impers* **es rumort in meinem Magen** *or* **Bauch** my stomach's rumbling; **es rumort in der Mannschaft** *(fig)* there is growing unrest in the team

rum+or|geln VI *sep (sl: = Sex haben)* to screw *(sl)*

rum|pe|lig [ˈrʊmpəlɪç] ADJ *(inf) Weg, Pflaster* bumpy

Rum|pel|kam|mer F *(inf)* junk room *(inf)*

rum|peln [ˈrʊmpln] VI **a** *(= Geräusch machen)* to rumble; **er fiel ~d die Treppe hinunter** he fell down the stairs with a clatter **b** *aux sein (= sich polternd bewegen)* to rumble; *(Mensch)* to clatter

Rum|pel|stilz|chen [ˈrʊmplʃtɪltsçən] NT -s Rumpelstiltskin

Rumpf [rʊmpf] M -(e)s, ¨-e [ˈrʏmpfə] trunk; *(Sport)* body; *(von geschlachtetem Tier)* carcass; *(von Statue)* torso; *(von Schiff)* hull; *(von Flugzeug)* fuselage; **~ beugt!** *(Sport)* bend; **~ streckt!** *(Sport)* stretch

Rumpf|beu|ge F forward bend

rümp|fen [ˈrʏmpfn] VT **die Nase ~** to turn up one's nose *(über +acc* at)

Rumpf|par|la|ment NT *(Hist)* Rump (Parliament)

rump|lig [ˈrʊmplɪç] ADJ *Weg, Pflaster* bumpy

Rump|steak [ˈrʊmpsteːk] NT rump steak

rums [rʊms] INTERJ bang

rum|sen [ˈrʊmzn] VI *(inf)* to bang

rum+stän|kern VI *sep (inf)* to stir *(inf)*

Rum-: **Rum|topf** M rumpot *(soft fruit in rum)*; **Rum|ver|schnitt** M blended rum

rum+zi|cken [ˈrʊmtsɪkn] VI *sep (sl)* to turn awkward

Run [ran] M -s, -s run *(auf +acc* on)

rund [rʊnt] ADJ round; *Figur, Arme* plump; *Ton, Klang* full; *Wein* mellow; **~e Klammern** *pl* parentheses, round brackets; **du wirst mit jedem Jahr ~er** you're getting bigger *or* plumper every year; **~e 50 Jahre/2000 Euro** a good 50 years/2,000 euros; **ein ~es Dutzend Leute** a dozen or more people; **das Kind machte ~e Augen** the child's eyes grew round; **~er Tisch** round table; **Konferenz am ~en Tisch** round-table talks *pl*; **die Sache wird ~** it all works out; **das ist eine ~e Sache** that's pretty good
ADV **a** *(= herum)* (a)round; **~ um** right (a)round; **~ um die Uhr** right (a)round the clock
b *(= ungefähr)* (round) about, roughly; **~ gerechnet 200** call it 200
c *(fig: = glattweg) abschlagen, ablehnen* flatly
d *(Aut)* **der Motor läuft ~** the engine runs smoothly

Rund-: **Rund|bank** F *pl* -bänke circular bench; **Rund|bau** M *pl* -bauten rotunda; **Rund|blick** M panorama; **Rund|bo|gen** M *(Archit)* round arch; **Rund|brief** M circular; **Rund|bürs|te** F curved brush

Run|de [ˈrʊndə] F -, -n **a** *(= Gesellschaft)* company; *(von Teilnehmern)* circle; **sich zu einer gemütlichen ~ treffen** to meet informally
b *(= Rundgang)* walk, turn; *(von Wachmann)* rounds *pl*; *(von Briefträger etc)* round; **die/seine ~ machen** to do the/one's rounds; *(Gastgeber)* to circulate; *(= herumgegeben werden)* to be passed round; **das Gerücht machte die ~** the rumour did the rounds *(Brit)*, the rumor *(US)* went around; **eine ~ durch die Lokale machen** to go on a pub crawl *(Brit)*, to go bar-hopping *(US)*; **eine ~ machen** to go for a walk; *(mit Fahrzeug)* to go for a ride; **eine ~ um etw machen** to go for a walk (a)round sth, to take a turn (a)round sth; *(mit Fahrzeug)* to ride (a)round sth; **zwei ~n um etw machen** to do two circuits of sth; **eine ~ um den Block machen** to walk around the block
c *(= Gesprächsrunde, Verhandlungsrunde)* round; *(Cards)* game; *(Golf)* round; *(Sport) (bei Rennen)* lap; *(von Turnier, Wettkampf)* round; **noch drei ~n** *(Sport)* three laps to go; **seine ~n drehen** *or* **ziehen** to do one's laps; **über die ~n kommen** *(Sport, fig)* to pull through; **etw über die ~n bringen** *(fig)* to manage sth, to get through sth; **eine ~ schlafen** *(inf)* to have a kip *(Brit inf) or* nap
d *(von Getränken)* round; **(für jdn) eine ~ spendieren** *or* **ausgeben** *or* **schmeißen** *(inf)* to buy *or* stand *(Brit)* (sb) a round
e *(liter: = Umkreis)* surroundings *pl*; **in die/der ~** round about

run|den ['rʊndn] VT *Lippen* to round; *Zahl (= abrunden)* to round down; *(= aufrunden)* to round up; **nach oben/unten ~** *(Math)* to round up/down VR *(lit: = rund werden) (Bauch)* to become round; *(Gesicht auch)* to become full; *(Lippen)* to grow round; *(fig: = konkrete Formen annehmen)* to take shape; **sich zu etw ~** *(fig)* to develop into sth

Rund-: **Rund|er|lass** M circular (directive); **rund+er|neu|ern** ['rʊntlɛɐnɔyɐn] *ptp* **runderneuert** VT *sep infin, ptp only (lit, fig)* to remould *(Brit)*, to remold *(US)*; **runderneuerte Reifen** remoulds *(Brit)*, remolds *(US)*; **Rund|er|neu|e|rung** F remoulding *(Brit)*, remolding *(US)*; **Rund|fahrt** F tour; **eine ~ machen, an einer ~ teilnehmen** to go on a tour; **Rund|flug** M *(= Besichtigungsflug)* sightseeing flight; *(= Reiseroute)* round trip; **Rund|fra|ge** F survey *(an +acc, unter +dat* of)

Rund|funk M broadcasting; *(= Hörfunk)* radio, wireless *(esp Brit dated)*; *(= Organisation)* broadcasting company *or* corporation; **der ~ überträgt etw** sth is broadcast; **im/über ~** on the radio; **~ hören** to listen to the radio; **beim ~ arbeiten** *or* **(tätig) sein** to work *or* be in broadcasting

Rund|funk- *in cpds* radio; **Rund|funk|an|sa|ger(in)** M(F) (radio) announcer; **Rund|funk|an|stalt** F *(form)* broadcasting corporation; **Rund|funk|durch|sa|ge** F special announcement (on the radio); **Rund|funk|emp|fang** M radio reception; **Rund|funk|emp|fän|ger** M radio receiver; **Rund|funk|ge|bühr** F radio licence *(Brit) or* license *(US)* fee; **Rund|funk|ge|rät** NT radio set *(Brit)*, radio; **Rund|funk|ge|sell|schaft** F broadcasting company; **Rund|funk|hö|rer(in)** M(F) (radio) listener; **Rund|funk|or|ches|ter** NT radio orchestra; **Rund|funk|pro|gramm** NT *(= Kanal, inf: = Sendung)* radio programme *(Brit) or* program *(US)*; *(= Sendefolge)* radio programmes *(Brit) or* programs *(US)*; *(= gedrucktes Rundfunkprogramm)* radio programme *(Brit) or* program *(US)* guide; **Rund|funk|sa|tel|lit** M TV satellite; **Rund|funk|sen|der** M **a** *(= Sendeanlage)* radio transmitter **b** *(= Sendeanstalt)* radio station; **Rund|funk|sen|dung** F radio programme *(Brit) or* program *(US)*; **Rund|funk|spre|cher(in)** M(F) radio announcer; **Rund|funk|sta|ti|on** F radio station; **Rund|funk|tech|nik** F radiotechnology; **Rund|funk|tech|ni|ker(in)** M(F) radio engineer; **Rund|funk|teil|neh|mer(in)** M(F) *(form)* owner of a radio set *(Brit) or* radio; **Rund|funk|über|tra|gung** F radio broadcast; **Rund|funk|zeit|schrift** F radio programme *(Brit) or* program *(US)* guide

Rund|gang M *pl* **-gänge a** *(= Spaziergang)* walk; *(zur Besichtigung)* tour *(durch* of); *(von Wachmann)* rounds *pl*; *(von Briefträger etc)* round; **einen ~ machen** to go for a walk; to go on a tour; **seinen ~ machen** to do one's rounds/round **b** *(Archit)* circular gallery

rund+ge|hen ['rʊntgeːən] VI *sep irreg (inf)* **a jetzt gehts rund** this is where the fun starts *(inf)*; **wenn er das erfährt, gehts rund** all hell will break loose when he finds out *(inf)*; **es geht rund, wenn sie zu Besuch kommen** there's never a dull moment when they come to visit; **es geht rund im Büro** there's a lot (going) on at the office **b** *(= herumgehen)* to do the rounds *(Brit)*, to go around; **die Neuigkeit ist schon rundgegangen** the news has already got (a)round

Rund-: **Rund|ge|sang** M *(Mus)* chorus song *(in which a different person sings each verse)*; *(= Kanon)* round; **Rund|hals|pul|lo|ver** M crew-neck sweater; **Rund|heit** F -, *no pl* roundness; **rund|he|raus** ['rʊnthɛ'raus] ADV straight out; *sagen, fragen auch* bluntly; *ablehnen auch* flatly; **~ gesagt** frankly; **rund|he|rum** ['rʊnthɛ'rʊm] ADV all round *(Brit)*, all around; *(fig inf: = völlig)* totally; **Rund|kopf|schrau|be** F round-headed *or* button-head *(US)* screw; **Rund|kurs** M circuit; **rund|lich** ['rʊntlɪç] ADJ *Mensch, Gesicht* plump, chubby; *Form* roundish; **Rund|lich|keit** F -, *no pl (von Mensch)* plumpness; **Rund|ling** ['rʊntlɪŋ] M **-s, -e** *circular village grouped around a green*, nuclear village; **Rund|rei|se** F tour *(durch* of); **Rund|rü|cken** M *(Med)* round shoulders *pl*; **Rund|ruf** M **per ~** with a series of phone calls; **Rund|schä|del** M shorthead; **Rund|schau** F *(Rad, TV)* magazine programme *(Brit)*, news magazine (show) *(US)*; **Rund|schnitt** M round haircut; **Rund|schrei|ben** NT circular; **Rund|sicht** F panorama; **Rund|strick|na|del** F circular needle; **Rund|stück** NT *(N Ger: Brötchen)* roll

rund|um ['rʊnt'lʊm] ADV all around; *(fig)* completely, totally

Rund|um-: **Rund|um|er|neu|e|rung** F general overhaul; **Rund|um|leuch|te** F *(als Warnlicht)* warning beacon; **Rund|um|schlag** M *(lit, fig)* sweeping blow; **Rund|um|sicht** F panoramic view

Run|dung ['rʊndʊŋ] F **-, -en** curve

Rund-: **Rund|wan|der|weg** M circular route; **rund|weg** ['rʊnt'vɛk] ADV = **rundheraus**; **Rund|zan|ge** F round-nosed pliers *pl*

Ru|ne ['ruːnə] F **-, -n** rune

Ru|nen- *in cpds* runic; **Ru|nen|rei|he** F runic alphabet; **Ru|nen|schrift** F runic writing; **Ru|nen|stein** M rune stone; **Ru|nen|zei|chen** NT runic character

Run|ge ['rʊŋə] F **-, -n** stake

Run|kel ['rʊŋkl] F **-, -n** *(Aus)*, **Run|kel|rü|be** F mangelwurzel

Ru|no|lo|ge [runo'loːgə] M **-n, -n**, **Ru|no|lo|gin** [-'loːgɪn] F **-, -nen** runologist

run|ter ['rʊntɐ] ADV *(inf)* = **herunter, hinunter**; **~!** down!

run|ter- PREF *(inf)* down; **run|ter+hau|en** ['rʊntɐhauən] VT *sep (inf)* **a** *(= ohrfeigen)* **jdm eine** *or* **ein paar ~** to give sb a clip round *(Brit) or* a smack on the ear **b** *(= schreiben)* **einen Text ~** to bang out a text *(inf)*; **run|ter+ho|len** ['rʊntɐhoːlən] VT *sep* to get down; **jdm/sich einen ~** *(inf)* to jerk sb/(oneself) off *(sl)* → *auch* **herunterholen**; **run|ter+kom|men** ['rʊntɐkɔmən] VI *sep irreg aux sein (inf: von Drogen/Heroin etc)* **von etw ~** to come off sth → *auch* **herunterkommen**; **run|ter+las|sen** ['rʊntɐlasn] VT *sep irreg* = **herunterlassen**; **die Hosen ~** *(sl)* to come clean *(inf)*

run|ter sein VI *sep irreg aux sein (inf: = erschöpft sein)* to be run down; **von etw ~** *(inf: von Drogen/Heroin etc)* to be off sth; **gesundheitlich ~** to be under the weather *(inf)*, to feel off *(inf)*; **mit den Nerven ~** to be at the end of one's tether *(Brit inf) or* rope *(US inf)*

Run|zel ['rʊntsl] F **-, -n** wrinkle; *(auf Stirn auch)* line; **~n bekommen** *(Mensch)* to get wrinkles; *(Haut)* to get *or* become wrinkled

run|ze|lig ['rʊntsəlɪç] ADJ wrinkled; *Stirn auch* lined

run|zeln ['rʊntsln] VT *Stirn* to wrinkle, to crease; *Brauen* to knit VR to become wrinkled

runz|lig ['rʊntslɪç] ADJ = **runzelig**

Rü|pel ['ryːpl] M **-s, -** lout, yob(bo) *(Brit inf)*

Rü|pe|lei [ryːpə'lai] F **-, -en** *(= rüpelhafte Art)* loutishness; *(= rüpelhafte Handlung/Bemerkung)* loutish act/remark *etc*

rü|pel|haft ADJ loutish ADV **sich ~ benehmen** to behave like a lout

rup|fen ['rʊpfn] VT *Geflügel, Federn* to pluck; *Gras, Unkraut* to pull up; **jdn ~** *(fig inf)* to fleece sb *(inf)*, to take sb to the cleaners *(inf)*; **sie sieht aus wie ein gerupftes Huhn** *(= schlecht frisiert)* she looks as if she's been dragged through a hedge backwards; *(= schlechter Haarschnitt)* she looks like a half-shorn sheep

Rup|fen ['rʊpfn] M **-s, -** *(Tex)* gunny; *(für Wandbehänge)* hessian

Ru|pie ['ruːpiə] F **-, -n** rupee

rup|pig ['rʊpɪç] ADJ *(= grob)* rough; *Antwort* gruff; *Autofahren* reckless; **sein ~es Äußeres** his rough-looking exterior; **~es Benehmen** uncouth behaviour *(Brit) or* behavior *(US)* ADV *behandeln, sagen* gruffly; *Auto fahren* recklessly; **~ spielen** to play rough; **~ antworten** to give a gruff answer; **sich ~ benehmen** to behave in an uncouth way

Rup|pig|keit F **-, -en a** *no pl (= Benehmen)* gruff manner; *(von Antwort)* gruffness; *(von Fahrer)* thuggishness; **die ~ seines Fahrstils** his thuggish driving **b** *(= Handlung)* **~en** *pl* rough behaviour *(Brit) or* behavior *(US)*; **zwischen den beiden kam es zu ~en** things got rough between the two of them

Rup|recht ['ruːprɛçt] M **-s** Rupert → **Knecht c**

Rü|sche ['ryːʃə] F **-, -n** ruche, frill

Rush|hour ['raʃlauɐ] F **-, -s**, **Rush-hour** △ F **-, -s** rush hour

Ruß [ruːs] M **-es**, *no pl* soot; *(von Kerze)* smoke; *(von Petroleumlampe)* lampblack; *(von Dieselmotor)* exhaust particulate *(spec)*

ruß|be|deckt ADJ covered in *or* with soot

Rus|se ['rʊsə] M **-n, -n**, **Rus|sin** ['rʊsɪn] F **-, -nen** Russian

Rüs|sel ['rʏsl] M **-s, -** *(auch inf: = Nase)* snout; *(von Elefant)* trunk; *(von Insekt)* proboscis

rüs|sel|för|mig ADJ → **Rüssel** snoutlike; trunklike; proboscidean *(spec)*

ru|ßen ['ruːsn] VI *(Öllampe, Kerze)* to smoke; *(Ofen)* to produce soot; **es rußt** there's a lot of soot; **eine stark ~de Lampe** a very smoky lamp VT *(Sw, S Ger)* **den Ofen ~** to clean the soot out of the stove; **den Kamin ~** to sweep the chimney

Rus|sen-: **rus|sen|freund|lich** ADJ pro-Russian; **Rus|sen|kit|tel** M smock; **Rus|sen|stie|fel** M Cossack boot

Ruß-: **ruß|far|ben** [-farbn], **ruß|far|big** ADJ soot-black; **Ruß|fil|ter** M *(esp Aut)* particulate filter *(spec)*; **Ruß|fleck** M sooty mark; **Ruß|flo|cke** F soot particle; **ruß|ge|schwärzt** [-gəʃvɛrtst] ADJ soot-blackened

ru|ßig ['ruːsɪç] ADJ sooty

Rus|sin ['rʊsɪn] F **-, -nen** Russian

rus|sisch ['rʊsɪʃ] ADJ Russian; **~es Roulett** Russian roulette; **~e Eier** *(Cook)* egg(s) mayonnaise; **~er Salat** *(Cook)* Russian salad

Rus|sisch|brot NT *(Cook)* alphabet biscuits *pl (Brit) or* cookies *pl (US)*

Rus|sisch(e) ['rʊsɪʃ] NT Russian → *auch* **Deutsch(e)**

Russ|land ['rʊslant] NT **-s** Russia

Russ|land|deut|sche(r) MF *decl as adj ethnic German living in Russia and the Republics*

Ruß|par|ti|kel F soot particle

rüs|ten ['rʏstn] VI *(Mil)* to arm; *(fig)* to arm oneself; **zum Krieg/Kampf ~** to arm for war/battle; **gut/schlecht gerüstet sein** to be well/badly armed; *(fig)* to be well/badly prepared; **um die Wette ~** to be involved in an arms race VR to prepare *(zu* for); *(lit, fig: = sich wappnen)* to arm oneself *(gegen* for); **sich zur Abreise ~** to get ready to leave; **sich zum Fest ~** to prepare for the festival VT **a** *(old: = vorbereiten)* to prepare; *Nachtlager auch* to make ready **b** *(Build) Haus* to scaffold

Rüs|ter ['ryste] F **-, -n** elm

rüs|tern ['rystɐn] ADJ *attr* elm

Rüs|ter(n)|holz NT elm (wood)

rüs|tig ['rʏstɪç] ADJ sprightly; **geistig/körperlich ~** mentally/physically active

Rüs|tig|keit F **-**, *no pl* sprightliness

rus|ti|kal [rʊsti'kaːl] ADJ *Möbel* rustic; *Speisen* country-style, farmhouse *attr* ADV *wohnen* rustically; **sich ~ einrichten** to furnish one's home in a rustic *or* farmhouse style

Rüst|kam|mer F *(Mil, fig)* armoury *(Brit)*, armory *(US)*

Rüs|tung ['rʏstʊŋ] F **-, -en a** *(= das Rüsten)* armament; *(= Waffen)* arms *pl*, weapons *pl* **b** *(= Ritterrüstung)* armour *(Brit)*, armor *(US)*

Rüs|tungs- *in cpds* arms; **Rüs|tungs|aus|ga|ben** PL defence *(Brit) or* defense *(US)* spending *sing*; **Rüs|tungs|be|gren|zung** F arms limitation; **Rüs|tungs|be|gren|zungs|ver|-**

hand|lun|gen PL arms limitation talks *pl*; **Rüs|tungs|be|schrän|kung** F arms limitation; **Rüs|tungs|be|trieb** M, **Rüs|tungs|fab|rik** F armaments *or* ordnance factory; **Rüs|tungs|etat** M defence *(Brit) or* defense *(US)* budget; **Rüs|tungs|ex|por|te** PL export of arms; **Rüs|tungs|geg|ner(in)** M(F) supporter of disarmament; **Rüs|tungs|in|dust|rie** F armaments industry; **Rüs|tungs|kon|trol|le** F arms control; **Rüs|tungs|kon|troll|ver|hand|lun|gen** PL arms control talks *pl*; **Rüs|tungs|pro|duk|ti|on** F arms production; **Rüs|tungs|wett|lauf** M arms race

Rüst|zeug NT, *no pl* **a** *(old: = Handwerkszeug)* tools *pl* **b** *(fig)* skills *pl*

Ru|te ['ru:tə] F -, -n **a** *(= Gerte)* switch; *(= esp Stock zum Züchtigen)* cane, rod; *(= Birkenrute)* birch (rod); *(von Gertenbündel)* birch; **jdn mit einer ~ schlagen** to cane/birch sb, to beat sb with a cane/birch; **mit eiserner ~ regieren** *(fig)* to rule with a rod of iron **b** *(= Wünschelrute)* (divining *or* dowsing) rod; *(= Angelrute)* (fishing) rod; **mit der ~ gehen** to go divining **c** *(Hunt: = Schwanz)* tail **d** *(= Tierpenis)* penis; *(dated sl: von Mann)* cock *(sl)*, prick *(sl)* **e** *(Aus: = Schneebesen)* whisk **f** *(old: Measure)* rod

Ru|ten-: **Ru|ten|bün|del** NT *(Hist)* fasces *pl*; **Ru|ten|gän|ger** [-gɛŋɐ] M -s, -, **Ru|ten|gän|ge|rin** [-ərɪn] F -, -nen diviner, dowser; **Ru|ten|ge|hen** NT dowsing; **Ru|ten|hieb** M stroke (of the birch)

Ru|the|ni|um [ru'te:niʊm] NT -s, *no pl (abbr* **Ru***)* ruthenium

Rüt|li|schwur ['ry:tli-] M, *no pl (Hist) oath taken on the Rütli Mountain by the founders of Switzerland*

rutsch [rʊtʃ] INTERJ whee, whoomph

Rutsch [rʊtʃ] M -es, -e slip, slide, fall; *(= Erdrutsch)* landslide; *(von Steinen)* rock fall; *(fig) (Pol)* shift, swing; *(Fin)* slide, fall; *(inf: = Ausflug)* trip, outing; **guten ~!** *(inf)* have a good New Year!; **in einem ~** in one go

Rutsch|bahn F, **Rut|sche** ['rʊtʃə] F -, -n *(Mech)* chute; *(= Kinderrutschbahn)* slide

rut|schen ['rʊtʃn] VI *aux sein* **a** *(= gleiten)* to slide; *(= ausrutschen, entgleiten)* to slip; *(Aut)* to skid; *(fig) (Preise, Kurse)* to slip; *(Regime, Hierarchie)* to crumble; **auf dem Stuhl hin und her ~** to fidget (around) *or* shift around on one's chair; **ins Rutschen kommen** *or* **geraten** *(lit, fig)* to start to slip; *(Unternehmen)* to start to go downhill
b *(inf: = rücken)* to move *or* shove *(inf)* up; **zur Seite ~** to move *or* shove *(inf)* up *or* over; **ein Stück(chen) ~** to move *or* shove *(inf)* up a bit
c *(= herunterrutschen)* to slip down; *(Essen, Tablette)* to go down
d *(auf Rutschbahn)* to slide; **darf ich mal ~?** can I have a go on the slide?
e *(= rutschend kriechen)* to crawl; **auf den Knien ~** *(lit)* to go along on one's knees; **auf den Knien gerutscht kommen** *(fig inf)* to go down on bended knee

Rut|scher ['rʊtʃɐ] M -s, - *(Aus) (= Abstecher)* small detour; *(= kleine Strecke)* stone's throw

Rutsch-: **rutsch|fest** ADJ nonslip; **Rutsch|ge|fahr** F danger of skidding; **„Rutschgefahr"** "slippery road"

rut|schig ['rʊtʃɪç] ADJ slippery, slippy *(inf)*

Rutsch-: **Rutsch|par|tie** F *(hum inf) (= das Ausrutschen)* slip; *(von Auto)* skid; *(auf Rutschbahn)* slide; **eine ~ machen** *(= ausrutschen)* to slip; *(mit Auto)* to skid; *(auf Rutschbahn)* to slide; **das war eine schöne ~** *(auf vereister Straße)* we were sliding all over the place; **rutsch|si|cher** ADJ nonslip

Rüt|te|lei [rʏtə'lai] F -, *no pl* shaking; *(von Fahrzeug, Zug)* jolting; *(von Fenstern, Türen)* rattling; **die Fahrt war eine einzige ~** we were jolted about the whole way

rüt|teln ['rʏtln] VT to shake (about); *Getreide etc* to riddle, to sieve; **jdn am Arm/an der Schulter ~** to shake sb's arm/shoulder, to shake sb by the arm/shoulder → *auch* **gerüttelt** VI to shake; *(Fahrzeug)* to jolt; *(Fenster, Tür: im Wind)* to rattle; **an etw** *(dat)* **~** *(an Tür, Fenster etc)* to rattle (at) sth; *(fig) an Grundsätzen, Ergebnis etc* to call sth into question; **daran ist nicht zu ~, daran gibt es nichts zu ~** *(inf)* there's no doubt about that

Rüt|tel|sieb NT sieve, riddle

S

S, s [ɛs] NT -, - S, s
s. *abbr von* **siehe** see
S *abbr von* **Süden** S
S. *abbr von* **Seite** p
SA [ɛs'la:] F -, *no pl (NS) abbr von* **Sturmabteilung**
s. a. *abbr von* **siehe auch**
Saal [za:l] M -(e)s, **Säle** ['zɛ:lə] hall; *(für Sitzungen etc)* room; *(= Lesesaal)* reading room; *(= Tanzsaal, Ballsaal)* ballroom; *(für Hochzeiten, Empfänge)* function suite; *(= Theatersaal)* auditorium
Saal-: **Saal|mie|te** F hall hire *or* rental *(US)* charge; **Saal|ord|ner** M usher; **Saal|ord|ne|rin** F usherette; **Saal|schlacht** F *(inf)* brawl, punch-up *(inf)*; **Saal|toch|ter** F *(Sw)* waitress
Saar [za:ɐ] F - Saar
Saar-: **Saar|ge|biet** NT, **Saar|land** NT -s Saarland; **Saar|län|der** ['za:ɐlɛndɐ] M -s, -, **Saar|län|de|rin** [-ərɪn] F -, -nen Saarlander; **saar|län|disch** ['za:ɐlɛndɪʃ] ADJ (of the) Saarland
Saat [za:t] F -, -en **a** *(= das Säen)* sowing **b** *(= Samen, Saatgut)* seed(s) *(auch fig)*; **die ~ ist aufgegangen** *(lit)* the seed has begun to grow; *(fig)* the seeds have borne fruit; **die ~ für etw legen** *(fig)* to sow the seed(s) of sth; **wie die ~, so die Ernte** *(prov)*, **ohne ~ keine Ernte** *(prov)* as you sow, so shall you reap *(Prov)* **c** *(= junges Getreide)* young crop(s *pl*), seedlings *pl*
Saat|beet NT bed of seedlings, seedling bed
Saa|ten|stand M state of the crop(s)
Saat-: **Saat|feld** NT cornfield *(Brit)*, grain field; **Saat|gut** NT, *no pl* seed(s); **Saat|kar|tof|fel** F seed potato; **Saat|korn** NT *pl* **-körner** seed corn; **Saat|krä|he** F rook; **Saat|zeit** F seedtime, sowing time
Sa|ba ['za:ba] NT -s *(Hist)* Sheba; **die Königin von ~** the Queen of Sheba
Sab|bat ['zabat] M -s, -e Sabbath
Sab|bat-: **Sab|bat|jahr** NT sabbatical year; **Sab|bat|schän|der** [-ʃɛndɐ] M -s, -, **Sab|bat|schän|de|rin** [-ərɪn] F -, -nen desecrator of the Sabbath
Sab|bel ['zabl] M -s, *no pl (dial)* slobber, saliva, slaver
sab|beln ['zabln] VTI *(dial)* = **sabbern**
Sab|ber ['zabɐ] M -s, *no pl (dial)* slobber, saliva, slaver
Sab|be|rei [zabə'rai] F -, -en *(inf) (dial)* slobbering; *(fig: = Geschwätz)* drivel *(inf)*
Sab|ber|lätz|chen NT *(dial)* bib
sab|bern ['zabɐn] *(inf)* **VI** to slobber, to slaver; **vor sich hin ~** *(fig)* to mutter away to oneself **VT** to blether *(Brit inf)*, to blather; **dummes Zeug ~** to talk drivel *(inf)*
Sä|bel ['zɛ:bl] M -s, - sabre *(Brit)*, saber *(US)*; *(= Krummsäbel)* scimitar; **jdn auf ~ fordern** to challenge sb to a (sabre *(Brit)* or saber *(US)*) duel; **mit dem ~ rasseln** *(fig)* to rattle the sabre *(Brit)* or saber *(US)*
Sä|bel-: **Sä|bel|bei|ne** PL *(inf)* bow *or* bandy *(Brit)* legs *pl*; **sä|bel|bei|nig** ADJ *(inf)* bow-legged, bandy-legged *(Brit)*; **Sä|bel|fech|ten** NT -s, *no pl* sabre *(Brit)* or saber *(US)* fencing; **Sä|bel|ge|ras|sel** [-gərasl] NT -s, *no pl* sabre-rattling *(Brit)*, saber-rattling *(US)*; **Sä|bel|hieb** M stroke of one's sabre *(Brit)* or saber *(US)*

sä|beln ['zɛ:bln] *(inf)* **VT** to saw away at **VI** to saw away *(an +dat* at)
Sä|bel-: **Sä|bel|ras|seln** NT -s, *no pl* sabre-rattling *(Brit)*, saber-rattling *(US)*; **sä|bel|ras|selnd** ADJ sabre-rattling *(Brit)*, saber-rattling *(US)*; **Sä|bel|rass|ler** [-raslɐ] M -s, -, **Sä|bel|rass|le|rin** [-ərɪn] F -, -nen sabre-rattler *(Brit)*, saber-rattler *(US)*
Sa|bi|ner M -s, -, **Sabinerin** F -, -nen Sabine; **der Raub der ~innen** the rape of the Sabines *or* the Sabine women
Sa|bo|ta|ge [zabo'ta:ʒə] F -, -n sabotage *(an +dat* of); **~ treiben** to perform acts of sabotage
Sa|bo|ta|ge|akt M act of sabotage
Sa|bo|teur [zabo'tø:ɐ] M -s, -e, **Sa|bo|teu|rin** [-'tø:rɪn] F -, -nen saboteur
sa|bo|tie|ren [zabo'ti:rən] *ptp* **sabotiert** VT to sabotage
Sa(c)|cha|rin [zaxa'ri:n] NT -s, *no pl* saccharin
Sach-: **Sach|an|la|ge|ver|mö|gen** NT *(Econ)* tangible fixed assets *pl*; **Sach|aus|ga|ben** PL material costs *pl*; **Sach|be|ar|bei|ter(in)** M(F) specialist; *(= Beamter)* official in charge *(für* of); **der ~ für Anträge ist nicht da** the person who deals with applications isn't here; **Sach|be|reich** M (specialist) area; **Sach|be|schä|di|gung** F damage to property; **sach|be|zo|gen** **ADJ** *Wissen, Fragen, Angaben, Politik* relevant, pertinent **ADV** with reference to the relevant issue/issues; **Sach|be|zü|ge** PL payment *or* contributions *pl* in kind; **Sach|buch** NT nonfiction book; **sach|dien|lich** ADJ *Hinweise* useful; **es ist nicht ~, wenn ...** it won't help the matter if ...
Sa|che ['zaxə] ✪ 33.2 **F** -, -n **a** thing; *(= Gegenstand)* object, thing; *(Jur: = Eigentum)* article of property; **der Mensch wird zur ~** man is reduced to *or* becomes an object; **~n gibts(, die gibts gar nicht)!** *(inf)* would you credit it! *(inf)* **b** **Sachen** **PL** *(inf: = Zeug)* things *pl*; *(Jur)* property; **seine ~n packen** to pack ones bags **c** *(= Angelegenheit)* matter; *(= Rechtsstreit, Fall)* case; *(= Aufgabe)* job; **eine ~ der Polizei/der Behörden** a matter for the police/authorities; **es ist ~ der Polizei/der Behörden, das zu tun** it's up to the police/authorities *or* it's for the police/authorities to do that; **das mit dem Präsidenten war eine unangenehme ~** that was an unpleasant business with the president; **das ist eine ganz tolle/unangenehme ~** it's really fantastic/unpleasant; **die ~ macht sich** *(inf)* things are coming along; **ich habe mir die ~ anders vorgestellt** I had imagined things differently; **das ist eine andere ~** that's a different matter, that's a different kettle of fish *(inf)*, that's a different cup of tea *(US inf)*; **das ist meine/seine ~** that's my/his affair *or* business; **in eigener ~** on one's own account; **in ~n** *or* **in der ~ A gegen B** *(Jur)* in the case (of) A versus B; **das ist nicht jedermanns ~** it's not everyone's cup of tea *(inf)*; **er versteht seine ~** he knows what he's doing *or* what he's about *(inf)*; **er macht seine ~ gut** he's doing very well; *(beruflich)* he's doing a good job; **diese Frage können wir nicht hier mitbesprechen, das ist eine ~ für sich** we can't discuss this question now, it's a separate issue all to itself; **und was hat deine Frau gesagt?/was meinen Sie zu diesen Streiks? – das ist eine ~ für sich** and what did your wife say?/what do you think about these strikes? – that's another story; **das ist so eine ~** *(inf)* it's a bit tricky, it's a bit of a problem; **das ist 'ne ~** *(inf: = prima)* great *(inf)*; **der ~ zuliebe** for the love of it; **die ~ mit der Bank ist also geplatzt** so the bank job fell through; **er ist für illegale ~n nicht zu haben** you won't get him to do anything illegal; **solche ~n liegen mir nicht** I don't like things like that
d *(= Vorfall)* business, affair; **~n** **PL** *(= Vorkommnisse)* things *pl*; **die ~ mit dem verschwundenen Schlüssel** the business *or* affair with the disappearing key; **machst du bei der ~ mit?** are you with us?; **bei der ~ mache ich nicht mit** I'll have nothing to do with it; **was hat die Polizei zu der ~ gesagt?** what did the police say about it *or* about all this business?; **das ist (eine) beschlossene ~** it's (all) settled; **die ~ hat geklappt/ist schiefgegangen** everything *or* it worked/went wrong; **mach keine ~n!** *(inf)* don't be daft *(Brit inf)* or silly!; **was machst du bloß für ~n!** *(inf)* the things you do!; **was sind denn das für ~n?** what's all this? **e** *(= Frage, Problem)* matter, question; *(= Thema)* subject; *(= Ideal, Anliegen)* cause; **eine ~ der Erziehung/des Geschmacks** a matter *or* question of education/taste; **mehr kann ich zu der ~ nicht sagen** that's all I can say on the subject; **um die ~ herumreden** to talk (all) round the subject; **zur ~!** let's get on with it; *(Parl, Jur etc)* come to the point!; **zur ~ kommen** to come to the point; **zur ~ gehen** *(inf)* to come to the crunch *(inf)*; *(Sport)* to get stuck in *(inf)*; **das tut nichts zur ~** that doesn't matter; **sich** *(dat)* **seiner ~ sicher** *or* **gewiss sein** to be sure of one's ground; **bei der ~ sein** to be with it *(inf)*, to be on the ball *(inf)*; **sie war nicht bei der ~** her mind was elsewhere; **bei der ~ bleiben** to keep one's mind on the job; *(bei Diskussion)* to keep to the point
f *(= Sachlage)* things *pl*, *no art*; **so steht die ~ also** so that's the way things are; **die ~ ist die, dass ...** the thing is that ...; **jdm sagen, was ~ ist** *(inf)* to tell sb what's what; **neben der ~ liegen** to be beside the point
g *(= Tempo)* **mit 60/100 ~n** *(inf)* at 60/100
-sa|che F *suf in cpds* a matter of ...; **das ist Ansichtssache/Geschmackssache** that's a matter of opinion/taste
Sach|ein|la|ge F *(Econ)* contribution in kind
Sa|chen|recht NT *(Jur)* law of property
Sa|cher|tor|te ['zaxɐ-] F *rich chocolate cake,* sachertorte
Sach-: **Sach|fahn|dung** F search for lost or stolen property; **Sach|fra|ge** F question regarding the matter itself; **Sach- und Personalfragen** questions relating to work and to personnel matters; **sach|fremd** ADJ irrelevant; **Sach|ge|biet** NT subject area; **sach|ge|mäß, sach|ge|recht** **ADJ** proper; **bei ~er Anwendung** if used properly **ADV** properly; **etw ~ machen** to do sth properly; **Sach|ka|ta|log** M subject index; **Sach|ken|ner(in)** M(F) expert *(in +dat* on); **~ auf einem** *or* **für ein Gebiet sein** to be an expert in a field; **Sach|kennt|nis** F

(in Bezug auf Wissensgebiet) knowledge of the/his subject; *(in Bezug auf Sachlage)* knowledge of the facts; **Sach|kun|de** F, *no pl* **a** = **Sachkenntnis** **b** *(Schulfach)* general knowledge;
sach|kun|dig ADJ (well-)informed; *Beratung, Information* expert; *Erklärung* competent; **sich ~ machen** to inform oneself ADV **~ antworten** to give an informed answer; **jdn ~ beraten** to give sb expert advice; **etw ~ erklären** to give a competent explanation of sth; **Sach|kun|di|ge(r)** [-kʊndɪgə] MF *decl as adj* = **Sachkenner(in)**; **Sach|la|ge** F situation, state of affairs; **Sach|leis|tung** F payment in kind; *(bei Krankenkasse etc)* benefit in kind

sach|lich [ˈzaxlɪç] ADJ **a** *(= faktisch) Irrtum, Angaben* factual; *Unterschied* material, factual; *Grund, Einwand* practical; *(= sachbezogen) Frage, Wissen* relevant **b** *(= objektiv) Kritik, Bemerkung* objective; *(= nüchtern)* unemotional, matter-of--fact; **bleiben Sie mal ~** don't get carried away; *(= nicht persönlich werden)* don't get personal, stay objective **c** *(= schmucklos)* functional, businesslike ADV **a** *(= faktisch) unzutreffend* factually; **die Auskunft war ~ falsch/richtig** the information was wrong/correct; **rein ~ hast du recht** from a purely factual point of view you are right **b** *(= objektiv)* objectively

säch|lich [ˈzɛçlɪç] ADJ *(Gram)* neuter

Sach|lich|keit F -, *no pl* **a** *(= Objektivität: von Kritik, Bemerkung)* objectivity; *(= Nüchternheit)* matter-of-factness; **mit ~ kommt man weiter** you get on better if you stay objective **b** *(= Schmucklosigkeit)* functionality; **die Neue ~** *(Art, Archit)* the new functionalism

Sach-: **Sach|män|gel** PL material defects *pl*; **Sach|män|gel|haf|tung** F liability for material defects; **Sach|mit|tel** PL *(form)* materials *pl*; *(= Zubehör)* equipment *no pl*; **Sach|re|gis|ter** NT subject index; **Sach|scha|den** M damage (to property); **bei dem Unfall hatte ich nur ~** only the car was damaged in the accident; **es entstand ~ in Höhe von ...** there was damage amounting to ...

Sach|se [ˈzaksə] M -n, -n, **Säch|sin** [ˈzɛksɪn] F -, -nen Saxon

säch|seln [ˈzɛksln] VI *(inf) (mit Akzent)* to speak with a Saxon accent; *(in Mundart)* to speak in the Saxon dialect

Sach|sen [ˈzaksn] NT -s Saxony

Sach|sen-An|halt [ˈzaksnˈlanhalt] NT -s Saxony-Anhalt

säch|sisch [ˈzɛksɪʃ] ADJ Saxon; **die Sächsische Schweiz** *area southeast of Dresden known for its health resorts and unusual rock formations*

Säch|sisch(e) [ˈzɛksɪʃ] NT Saxon (dialect) → *auch* **Deutsch(e)**

Sach|spen|de F gift; **wir bitten um Geld- und ~n** we are asking for donations of money and goods

sacht [zaxt], **sach|te** [ˈzaxtə] ADJ *(= leise)* soft; *(= sanft)* gentle; *(= vorsichtig)* cautious, careful; *(= allmählich)* gentle, gradual; **mit ~en Schritten** softly ADV softly, gently; *ansteigen, abfallen* gently; *(= vorsichtig) anfragen* carefully; **~e, ~e!** *(inf)* take it easy!

Sach-: **Sach|ver|halt** [-fɛɐhalt] M -(e)s, -e facts *pl* (of the case); **Sach|ver|stand** M expertise; **Sach|ver|stän|di|gen|aus|schuss** M committee of experts; **Sach|ver|stän|di|gen|gut|ach|ten** NT specialist report; **Sach|ver|stän|di|ge(r)** [-fɛɐʃtɛndɪgə] MF *decl as adj* expert, specialist; *(Jur)* expert witness; **Sach|ver|zeich|nis** NT subject index; **Sach|wal|ter** [ˈzaxvaltɐ] M -s, -, **Sach|wal|te|rin** [-ərɪn] F -, -nen *(geh) (= Verwalter)* agent; *(= Treuhänder)* trustee; *(fig: = Fürsprecher)* champion; **Sach|wert** M real *or* intrinsic value; **~e** *pl* material assets *pl*; **Sach|wör|ter|buch** NT specialist dictionary; **~ der Kunst/Botanik** dictionary of art/botany, art/botanical dictionary; **Sach|zu|sam|men|hang** M factual connection; **Sach|zwang** M practical constraint; **Sachzwängen unterliegen, unter Sachzwängen** *(dat)* **stehen** to be constrained by circumstances

Sack [zak] M -(e)s, ⸚e [ˈzɛkə] **a** sack; *(aus Papier, Plastik)* bag; **drei ~ Kartoffeln/Kohlen** three sacks of potatoes/sacks *or* bags of coal; **in ~ und Asche** in sackcloth and ashes; **in ~ und Tüten sein** *(inf)* to be in the bag *(inf)*, to be all wrapped up *(inf)*; **etw im ~ haben** *(inf)* to have sth in the bag *(inf)*; **mit ~ und Pack** *(inf)* with bag and baggage; **den ~ schlägt man, und den Esel meint man** *(Prov)* to kick the dog and mean the master *(prov)*; **jdn in den ~ stecken** *(fig inf)* to put sb in the shade *(Brit)*, to outdo sb **b** *(Anat, Zool)* sac **c** *(S Ger, Aus: = Hosentasche)* (trouser *(Brit) or* pants *(US)*) pocket; **Geld im ~ haben** to have money in one's pocket **d** *(vulg: = Hoden)* balls *pl (sl)*; **jdm auf den ~ gehen** *(sl)* to get on sb's tits *(sl)* **e** *(inf: = Kerl, Bursche)* sod *(Brit inf)*, bastard *(sl)*, cunt *(vulg)*; **fauler ~** lazy bugger *(Brit inf) or* bastard *(sl)*; **alter ~** old bastard *(sl)*

Sack|bahn|hof M terminus

Säckel [ˈzɛkl] M -s, - *(S Ger) (= Beutel)* bag; *(= Hosentasche)* pocket; *(= Geldsäckel)* money bag; *(old, hum: = Staatssäckel)* national coffers *pl*; **tief in den ~ greifen müssen** to have to dig deep (into one's pockets); **sich** *(dat)* **den ~ füllen** to line one's (own) pockets

sa|cken [ˈzakn], **sä|ckeln** [ˈzɛkln] *(dial)* VT to put into sacks, to sack

sa|cken VI *aux sein (lit, fig)* to sink; *(Flugzeug)* to lose height; *(= durchhängen)* to sag; **in die Knie ~** to sag at the knees; **die Aktienkurse sackten in den Keller** share prices went through the floor *or* hit rock bottom

sa|cker|lot [zakɐˈloːt], **sa|cker|ment** [zakɐˈmɛnt] INTERJ *(old)* stap me *(Brit old)*, upon my soul *(old)*

sä|cke|wei|se [ˈzɛkəvaizə] ADJ ADV → **Sack a** by the sack/bag

Sack-: **sack|för|mig** ADJ like a sack, sack-like ADV like a sack; **Sack|gas|se** F dead end, blind alley, cul-de-sac *(esp Brit)*; *(fig)* dead end; **in eine ~ geraten** *(fig)* to finish up a blind alley; *(Verhandlungen)* to reach an impasse; **in einer ~ stecken** *(fig)* to be (stuck) up a blind alley; *(mit Bemühungen etc)* to have come to a dead end; **die Verhandlungen in die ~ führen** *(fig)* to lead the negotiations into an impasse; **die Verhandlungen aus der ~ führen** *(fig)* to end the impasse in the negotiations; **Sack|hüp|fen** NT -s, *no pl* sack race; **Sack|kar|re** F barrow, handcart; **Sack|kleid** NT sack dress; **Sack|lei|nen** NT, **Sack|lein|wand** F sacking, burlap *(US)*; **Sack|mes|ser** NT *(Sw, S Ger: = Taschenmesser)* pocketknife, penknife; **Sack|pfei|fe** F bagpipes *pl*; **Sack|tuch** NT *pl* **-tü|cher** **a** *(= Sackleinen)* sacking, burlap *(US)* **b** *(S Ger, Aus, Sw: = Taschentuch)* handkerchief; **Sack|wich|ser** M *(sl)* wanker *(vulg)*

Sa|dis|mus [zaˈdɪsmʊs] M -, **Sadismen** [-mən] **a** *no pl* sadism **b** *(Handlung)* sadistic act

Sa|dist [zaˈdɪst] M -en, -en, **Sa|dis|tin** [-dɪstɪn] F -, -nen sadist

sa|dis|tisch [zaˈdɪstɪʃ] ADJ sadistic ADV sadistically

Sa|do|ma|so [zadoˈmaːzo] M -, *no pl (sl)* SM

Sa|do|ma|so|chis|mus [zadomazɔˈxɪsmʊs] M sadomasochism

sä|en [ˈzɛːən] VTI to sow; *(fig)* to sow (the seeds of); **dünn** *or* **spärlich** *or* **nicht dick gesät** *(fig)* thin on the ground, few and far between → **Wind a**

Sa|fa|ri [zaˈfaːri] F -, -s safari; **eine ~ machen** to go on safari

Sa|fa|ri-: **Sa|fa|ri|an|zug** M safari suit; **Sa|fa|ri|look** [-lʊk] M safari look; **Sa|fa|ri|park** M safari park

Safe [zeːf] M OR NT -s, -s safe

Sa|fer Sex [ˈzeːfɐˈzɛks] M - -(es), *no pl*, **Sa|fer|sex** △ M - -(e)s, *no pl* safe sex

Saf|fi|an [ˈzafian, ˈzafiaːn] M -s, *no pl*, **Saf|fi|an|le|der** NT morocco (leather)

Saf|ran [ˈzafraːn, ˈzafran] M -s, -e *(= Krokus, Gewürz)* saffron

saf|ran|gelb ADJ saffron (yellow)

Saft [zaft] M -(e)s, ⸚e [ˈzɛftə] *(= Obstsaft)* (fruit) juice; *(= Pflanzensaft)* sap; *(= Bratensaft, Fleischsaft)* juice; *(= Flüssigkeit)* liquid; *(= Hustensaft etc)* syrup; *(= Magensaft)* juices *pl*; *(old: = Körpersaft)* humour *(Brit old)*, humor *(US old)*; *(inf: = Strom, Benzin)* juice *(inf)*; *(sl: = Sperma)* spunk *(vulg)*; **roter ~** lifeblood; **Blut ist ein ganz besonderer ~** blood is a very special stuff; **der ~ der Reben** the juice of the grape; **voll im ~ stehen** to be full of sap; **die Säfte der Natur** *(liter)* the vital forces of nature; **von ~ und Kraft** *(fig)* dynamic, vital, vibrant; **ohne ~ und Kraft** *(fig)* wishy-washy *(inf)*, effete → **schmoren VI a**

Saft|bra|ten M *(Cook)* roast

Säft|chen [ˈzɛftçən] NT -s, - *dim von* **Saft** *(= Fruchtsäftchen)* juice; *(pej: = Arznei)* mixture, medicine

Saft|fot|ze F *(pej vulg)* cunt *(vulg)*

saf|tig [ˈzaftɪç] ADJ **a** *(= voll Saft) Obst, Fleisch* juicy; *Wiese, Grün* lush **b** *(inf: = kräftig) Witz* juicy *(inf)*; *Rechnung, Strafe, Ohrfeige* hefty *(inf)*; *Brief, Antwort, Ausdrucksweise* potent; **da habe ich ihm einen ~en Brief geschrieben** so I wrote him a pretty potent letter *or* one hell of a letter *(inf)*

Saf|tig|keit F -, *no pl (von Obst, Fleisch, Witz)* juiciness; *(von Wiese etc)* lushness

Saft-: **Saft|kur** F fruit-juice diet; **Saft|la|den** M *(pej inf)* dump *(pej inf)*; **saft|los** ADJ **a** not juicy, juiceless **b** *(fig: = kraftlos)* feeble; **saft- und kraftlos** *(Mensch)* washed-out; *Bild, Gedicht etc* lifeless ADV *(fig)* feebly; **Saft|pres|se** F fruit press; **Saft|sack** M *(inf)* stupid bastard *(sl) or* bugger *(Brit inf)*; **Saft|tag** M juice day; **einen ~ haben/einlegen** to have a day on juices only

Sa|ga [ˈzaːga] F -, -s saga

sag|bar ADJ sayable

Sa|ge [ˈzaːgə] F -, -n legend; *(altnordische)* saga; **es geht die ~, dass ...** legend has it that ...; *(= Gerücht)* rumour *(Brit) or* rumor *(US)* has it that ...

Sä|ge [ˈzɛːgə] F -, -n **a** *(Werkzeug)* saw **b** *(Aus: = Sägewerk)* sawmill

Sä|ge-: **Sä|ge|blatt** NT saw blade; **Sä|ge|bock** M sawhorse; **Sä|ge|fisch** M sawfish; **Sä|ge|ma|schi|ne** F mechanical saw; **Sä|ge|mehl** NT sawdust; **Sä|ge|mes|ser** NT serrated knife; **Sä|ge|müh|le** F sawmill

sa|gen [ˈzaːgn]

TRANSITIVES VERB

a = äußern to say; **wie kannst du so etwas sagen?** how can you say such things?; **wie ich schon sagte** as I said before; **wie gesagt** as I say; **das kann ich Ihnen nicht sagen** I couldn't say; **das kann ich noch nicht sagen** I can't say yet; **das sage ich nicht!** I'm not saying!; **so was sagt man doch nicht!** you can't say things like that!; *(bei Schimpfen, Fluchen)* (mind your) language!; **haben Sie dazu etwas zu sagen?** do you have anything to say (about that)?; **was soll man dazu sagen?** what can you say?; **was sagen Sie dazu?** what do you think about it?; **sich** *(dat)* **etw sagen** to say sth to oneself; **das möchte** *or* **will ich nicht sagen** I wouldn't say that; **um nicht zu sagen ...** not to say ...; **das würde ich (wieder) nicht sagen** I wouldn't say that; **ich sags ja immer ...** I always say ...; **ich möchte fast sagen, ...** I'd almost say ..., one could almost say ...; **wenn ich so sagen darf** if I may say so; **sag, was du willst, ...** *(inf)* say what you like ...; **damit ist alles gesagt** that says it all; **sag bloß!** you don't say!; **was Sie nicht sagen!** you don't say!; **ich sage gar nichts**

mehr! I'm not saying another word!; *(verblüfft)* good heavens!; **das kann man wohl sagen!** you can say that again!; **ich muss schon sagen** I must say; **wie man so sagt** as they say, as the saying goes; **das ist nicht gesagt** that's by no means certain; **leichter gesagt als getan** easier said than done; **gesagt, getan** no sooner said than done; **ich bin, sagen wir, in einer Stunde da** I'll be there in an hour, say; **da soll noch einer sagen, wir Deutschen hätten keinen Humor!** never let it be said that we Germans have no sense of humour *(Brit) or* humor *(US)!*

Das englische Verb *to tell* kann von einem Personalpronomen gefolgt werden, *to say* jedoch nicht.

jdm etw sagen to say sth to sb, to tell sb sth; **was hast du ihm gesagt?** what did you say to him?, what did you tell him?; **könnten Sie mir sagen, was das kosten soll?** could you tell me how much it will cost?; **ich sags ihm** I'll tell him; **ich kann dir sagen …** *(inf)* I can tell you …; **sag mir, was du liest, und ich sage dir, wer du bist** *(prov)* tell me what you read and I'll tell you what kind of person you are; **ich sage, wie es ist** I'm telling you the way it is; **das ist schnell gesagt** I can tell you in two words; **wem sagen Sie das!** you don't need to tell ME that!, tell me about it! *(inf)*; **sag an, …** *(old, liter)* pray tell, … *(old)*
b [= bedeuten, meinen] to mean; **was will er damit sagen?** what does he mean (by that)?; **das hat nichts zu sagen** that doesn't mean anything; **sagt dir der Name etwas?** does the name mean anything to you?; **ich will damit nicht sagen, dass …** I don't mean to imply *or* to say that …; **damit ist nichts gesagt** that doesn't mean anything; **damit ist nicht gesagt, dass …** that doesn't mean (to say) that …; **willst du vielleicht sagen, dass …** are you trying to say that …?; **sein Gesicht sagte alles** it was written all over his face
c [= befehlen] to tell; **jdm sagen, er solle etw tun** to tell sb to do sth; **du hast hier (gar) nichts zu sagen** it's not your job to tell us what to do, you're not the boss; **hat er im Betrieb etwas zu sagen?** does he have a say in the firm?; **das Sagen haben** to be the boss; **hier habe ich das Sagen** I'm the boss here
♦ **sagen lassen ich habe mir sagen lassen, …** *(= ausrichten lassen)* I've been told …; **was ich mir von ihm nicht alles sagen lassen muss!** the things I have to take from him!; **lass dir von mir sagen** *or* **gesagt sein, …** let me tell you …; **lass dir das gesagt sein** let me tell you; **er lässt sich** *(dat)* **nichts sagen** he won't be told, you can't tell him anything; **das lass ich mir von dem nicht sagen** I won't take that from him; **sie ließen es sich** *(dat)* **nicht zweimal sagen** they didn't need to be told twice
d [andere Redewendungen] **das hättest du dir selbst sagen können** *or* **müssen!** you might have known that!; **im Vertrauen gesagt** in confidence; **unter uns gesagt** between you and me; **genauer/deutlicher gesagt** to put it more precisely/clearly; **sag nicht so etwas** *or* **so was!** *(inf)* don't talk like that!; **sag das nicht!** *(inf)* don't you be so sure!; **was ich noch sagen wollte, …** another point I would like to make is that …; **was ich noch sagen wollte, vergiss nicht …** *(inf)* by the way, don't forget …; **dann will ich nichts gesagt haben** in that case forget I said anything; **es ist nicht zu sagen!** it doesn't bear thinking about!; *(entrüstet)* there aren't any words to describe it!; **das muss man sagen** you have to admit that; **sage und schreibe 100 Euro** 100 euros, would you believe it
♦ **sag mal/sagen Sie mal du, Veronika, sag mal, wollen wir …** hey Veronika, listen, shall we …; **sag mal, Peter, kannst du mir fünf Euro leihen?** hey Peter, can you lend me five euros?; **sag mal, willst du nicht endlich Schluss machen?** come on, isn't it time to stop?; **nun sagen Sie/sag mal selber, ist das nicht unpraktisch?** you must admit that's impractical → **offen, Dank, Meinung**

sä|gen ['zɛ:gn] VTI to saw VI *(inf: = schnarchen)* to snore, to saw wood *(US inf)*
Sa|gen-: **Sa|gen|dich|tung** F sagas *pl*; **sa|gen|haft** ADJ **a** *(= nach Art einer Sage)* legendary **b** *(= enorm) Summe* fabulous **c** *(inf: = hervorragend)* fantastic *(inf)*, terrific *(inf)* ADV *(inf: = unglaublich)* unbelievably, incredibly; **Sa|gen|kreis** M group of sagas; **sa|gen|um|wo|ben** [-ʊmvo:bn] ADJ legendary; **Sa|gen|welt** F mythology, legend
Sä|ge|rei [zɛ:gə'rai] F -, -en **a** *(= Sägewerk)* sawmill **b** *no pl (inf: = das Sägen)* sawing
Sä|ge-: **Sä|ge|spä|ne** PL wood shavings *pl*; **Sä|ge|werk** NT sawmill; **Sä|ge|zahn** M sawtooth
Sa|go ['za:go] M OR NT -s, *no pl* sago
Sa|go|pal|me F sago palm
sah *pret von* **sehen**
Sa|ha|ra [za'ha:ra, 'za:hara] F - Sahara (Desert)
Sa|hel [za'he:l, 'za:hɛl] M -(s) Sahel
Sa|hel|zo|ne F Sahel region
Sah|ne ['za:nə] F -, *no pl* cream; **(aller)erste ~ sein** *(inf)* to be top-notch *(inf)*
Sah|ne-: **Sah|ne|bai|ser** NT cream meringue; **Sah|ne|bon|bon** M OR NT toffee; **Sah|ne|eis** NT ice cream; **Sah|ne|häub|chen** NT *(lit)* cream topping; *(fig)* icing on the cake; **als besonderes ~ erzielte er das letzte Tor zum 6:0** the crowning moment was when he scored the final goal to make it 6-0; **Sah|ne|kä|se** M cream cheese; **Sah|ne|meer|ret|tich** M creamy *or* creamed horseradish; **Sah|ne|quark** [-kvark] M creamy quark; **Sah|ne|so|ße** F cream sauce; **Sah|ne|tor|te** F cream gateau
sah|nig ['za:nɪç] ADJ creamy ADV **etw ~ schlagen** to whip *or* beat sth until creamy
Saib|ling ['zaiplɪŋ] M -s, -e char(r)
Sai|son [zɛ'zõ:, zɛ'zɔŋ, *(Aus)* zɛ'zo:n] F -, -s *or (Aus)* **-en** season; **außerhalb der ~, in der stillen** *or* **toten ~** in the off season; **~ haben** *(Obst, Gemüse)* to be in season; *(inf: Konsumgüter)* to be in demand
Sai|son- [zɛ'zõ:, zɛ'zɔŋ, *(Aus)* zɛ'zo:n] *in cpds* seasonal
sai|so|nal [zɛzo'na:l] ADJ seasonal
Sai|son-: **Sai|son|ar|beit** F seasonal work; **Sai|son|ar|bei|ter(in)** M(F) seasonal worker; **sai|son|be|dingt** ADJ seasonal; **Sai|son|be|ginn** M start of the season; **sai|son|be|rei|nigt** [-bərainɪçt] ADJ *Zahlen etc* seasonally adjusted; **Sai|son|be|schäf|ti|gung** F seasonal job; **Sai|son|be|trieb** M *(= Hochsaison)* high season; *(= Saisongeschäft)* seasonal business; **Sai|son|er|öff|nung** F opening of the season; **Sai|son|ge|schäft** NT seasonal business; **Sai|son|ge|wer|be** NT seasonal trade; **Sai|son|in|dust|rie** F seasonal industry; **Sai|son|kenn|zei|chen** NT *(Aut) vehicle number plate valid only for certain months of the year*; **Sai|son|schluss** M end of the season; **Sai|son|schwan|kung** F seasonal fluctuation; **Sai|son|stel|lung** F seasonal job; **in ~ gehen** to take a seasonal job; **Sai|son|wan|de|rung** F *(Econ)* seasonal movement of labour *(Brit) or* labor *(US)*; **Sai|son|zu|schlag** M in-season supplement
Sai|te ['zaitə] F -, -n **a** *(Mus, Sport)* string **b** *(fig liter)* **eine ~ in jdm berühren** *or* **anschlagen, eine ~ in jdm zum Klingen bringen** to strike a chord in sb; **andere ~n aufziehen** *(inf)* to get tough
Sai|ten-: **Sai|ten|in|stru|ment** NT string(ed) instrument; **Sai|ten|klang** M *(liter)* sound of strings; **Sai|ten|spiel** NT, *no pl* playing of a stringed instrument; **Sai|ten|wurst** F *type of frankfurter*
-sai|tig [zaitɪç] ADJ *suf* -string(ed); **eine zwölfsaitige Gitarre** a twelve-string(ed) guitar
Sait|ling ['zaitlɪŋ] M -s, -e sausage skin *(for frankfurters)*

Sak|ko ['zako] M OR NT -s, -s sports jacket *(esp Brit)*, sport coat *(US)*; *(aus Samt etc)* jacket
sak|ra ['zakra] INTERJ *(S Ger, Aus)* good God, my God
sak|ral [za'kra:l] ADJ sacred
Sak|ral-: **Sak|ral|bau** M *pl* **-bauten** sacred building; **~ten** *pl (auch)* ecclesiastical *or* sacred architecture *sing*; **Sak|ral|kunst** F religious art, sacral art
Sak|ra|ment [zakra'mɛnt] NT -(e)s, -e sacrament; **das ~ der Taufe** the sacrament of baptism; **die ~e spenden** to administer the sacraments; **~ (noch mal)!** *(inf)* Jesus Christ! *(sl)*; **Himmel, Herrgott, ~!** *(inf)* Christ Almighty! *(sl)*
sak|ra|men|tal [zakramɛn'ta:l] ADJ sacramental
Sak|ra|ment(s)|häus|chen [-hɔysçən] NT tabernacle
Sak|ri|leg [zakri'le:k] NT -s, -e [-gə] *(geh)* sacrilege
Sak|ri|le|gi|um [zakri'le:giʊm] NT -s, **Sakrilegien** [-giən] *(geh)* = **Sakrileg**
sak|risch ['zakrɪʃ] ADV *(dial inf)* damned *(inf)*; *schreien* like hell *(inf)*
Sak|ris|tei [zakrɪs'tai] F -, -en sacristy
sak|ro|sankt [zakro'zaŋkt] ADJ sacrosanct
sä|ku|lar [zɛku'la:ɐ] ADJ **a** *(= weltlich)* secular **b** *(= zeitüberdauernd)* timeless
Sä|ku|la|ri|sa|ti|on [zɛkulariza'tsio:n] F -, -en secularization
sä|ku|la|ri|sie|ren [zɛkulari'zi:rən] *ptp* **säkularisiert** VT to secularize
Sä|ku|lum ['zɛ:kulʊm] NT -s, **Säkula** [-la] *(geh)* century
Sa|la|man|der [zala'mandɐ] M -s, - salamander
Sa|la|mi [za'la:mi] F -, -s salami
Sa|la|mi|tak|tik F *(inf)* policy of small steps
Sa|lär [za'lɛ:ɐ] NT -s, -e *(old, Sw)* salary
Sa|lat [za'la:t] M -(e)s, -e **a** *(= Pflanze, Kopfsalat)* lettuce **b** *(= Gericht)* salad; **da haben wir den ~!** *(inf)* now we're in a fine mess *or* in a pickle *(inf)*
Sa|lat-: **Sa|lat|be|steck** NT salad servers *pl*; **Sa|lat|dres|sing** [-drɛsɪŋ] NT -s, -s salad dressing; **Sa|lat|gur|ke** F cucumber; **Sa|lat|kar|tof|fel** F potato *(used for potato salad)*; **Sa|lat|kopf** M (head of) lettuce; **Sa|lat|öl** NT salad oil; **Sa|lat|pflan|ze** F **a** *(= Setzling)* lettuce (plant) **b** *(= Sorte)* salad; **Sa|lat|plat|te** F salad; **Sa|lat|schleu|der** F salad drainer *(Brit) or* strainer *(US)*; **Sa|lat|schüs|sel** F salad bowl; **Sa|lat|so|ße** F salad dressing
Sal|ba|de|rei [zalba:də'rai] F -, -en *(pej geh)* sanctimonious prating
sal|ba|dern [zal'ba:dɐn] *ptp* **salbadert** VI to prate
Sal|be ['zalbə] F -, -n ointment
Sal|bei ['zalbai, zal'bai] M -s *or f* -, *no pl* sage
Sal|bei|bon|bon NT sage cough sweet *or* drop *(US)*
sal|ben ['zalbn] VT *(liter)* to anoint; **jdn zum König ~** to anoint sb king
Salb|öl NT consecrated oil
Sal|bung ['zalbʊŋ] F -, -en *(liter)* anointing, unction
sal|bungs|voll *(pej)* ADJ *Worte, Ton* unctuous *(pej)* ADV *sprechen, predigen* unctuously *(pej)*
Sal|chow ['zalço] M -s, -s *(Eiskunstlauf)* salchow
sal|die|ren [zal'di:rən] *ptp* **saldiert** VT *(Comm)* to balance; *(Aus)* to confirm payment
Sal|do ['zaldo] M -s, -s *or* **Saldi** *or* **Salden** [-di, -dn] *(Fin)* balance; **per saldo** *(lit, fig)* on balance; **per saldo bezahlen** *or* **remittieren** to pay off the balance in full; **in saldo bleiben/sein** to stay/be in debt
Sal|do|über|trag M, **Sal|do|vor|trag** M *(Fin)* balance brought forward *or* carried forward
Sä|le *pl von* **Saal**
Sa|li|ne [za'li:nə] F -, -n saltworks *sing or pl*
sa|lisch ['za:lɪʃ] ADJ *(Hist)* Salian, Salic
Sa|li|zyl|säu|re [zali'tsy:l-] F salicylic acid
Salm [zalm] M -(e)s, -e **a** *(= Lachs)* salmon **b** *(inf: = Gerede)* rigmarole *(inf)*

Sal|mi|ak [zal'miak, 'zalmiak] M OR NT -s, *no pl* sal ammoniac, ammonium chloride

Sal|mi|ak-: **Sal|mi|ak|geist** M, *no pl* (liquid) ammonia; **Sal|mi|ak|pas|til|le** F *bitter-tasting lozenge*, liquorice imp® *(Brit)*

Sal|mo|nel|len [zalmo'nɛlən] PL salmonellae *pl*

Sal|mo|nel|len|ver|gif|tung F salmonella (poisoning)

Sal|mo|nel|lo|se [zalmonɛ'lo:zə] F -, -n salmonellosis

Sa|lo|mo(n) ['za:lomo, 'za:lomɔn] M -s *or (geh)* **Salomonis** [zalo'mo:nɪs] Solomon

sa|lo|mo|nisch [zalo'mo:nɪʃ] ADJ of Solomon; *Urteil* worthy of a Solomon; **ein wahrhaft ~es Urteil!** a real judgement of Solomon!

Sa|lon [sa'lõ:, za'lɔŋ, *(Aus)* za'lo:n] M -s, -s **a** *(= Gesellschaftszimmer)* drawing room; *(Naut)* saloon **b** *(= Friseursalon, Modesalon, Kosmetiksalon etc)* salon **c** *(Hist: = literarischer etc Zirkel)* salon **d** *(= Messe, Ausstellung)* show; *(= Messestand)* stand, exhibition stand **e** *(= Kunstsalon)* exhibition room

Sa|lon- [sa'lõ:-, za'lɔŋ-]: **Sa|lon|anar|chist(in)** M(F) *(pej)* drawing-room revolutionary; **Sa|lon|mu|sik** F palm court music; **Sa|lon|wa|gen** M *(Rail)* Pullman (carriage), special coach

Sa|lon-: **sa|lon|fä|hig** ADJ *(iro)* socially acceptable; *Leute, Aussehen* presentable; **ein nicht ~er Witz** an objectionable joke; *(= unanständig auch)* a rude *or* naughty joke; **nicht ~e Ausdrucksweise** uncouth language, not the sort of language to be used in polite society; **Sa|lon|fä|hig|keit** F social acceptability; **Sa|lon|lö|we** M, **Sa|lon|lö|win** F socialite, society man/woman

sa|lopp [za'lɔp] ADJ **a** *(= nachlässig)* sloppy, slovenly; *Manieren* slovenly; *Ausdruck, Sprache* slangy **b** *(= ungezwungen)* casual ADV *sich kleiden, sich ausdrücken* casually; **~ gesagt, ...** to put it crudely ...

Sal|pe|ter [zal'pe:tɐ] M -s, *no pl* saltpetre *(Brit)*, saltpeter *(US)*, nitre *(Brit)*, niter *(US)*

sal|pe|te|rig [zal'pe:tərɪç] ADJ *(Chem) Säure* nitrous

Sal|pe|ter|säu|re F nitric acid

sal|pet|rig [zal'pe:trɪç] ADJ *(Chem) Säure* nitrous

Sal|sa ['zalza] M -, *no pl (Mus)* salsa

Sal|sa|mu|sik F salsa (music)

Sal|to ['zalto] M -s, -s *or* **Sal|ti** [-ti] somersault; *(Turmspringen auch)* turn; **~ vorwärts/rückwärts** forward/backward somersault; **ein anderthalbfacher ~** a one-and-a-half somersault; **dreifacher ~** triple somersault; **~ mortale** *(im Zirkus)* death-defying leap; *(Aviat)* loop; **einen ~ mortale machen** *(im Zirkus)* to perform a death-defying leap; *(Aviat)* to loop the loop; **ein logischer/gedanklicher ~ mortale** a logical/an intellectual leap

Sa|lut [za'lu:t] M -(e)s, -e *(Mil)* salute; **~ schießen** *or* **feuern** to fire a salute; **21 Schuss ~** 21-gun salute

sa|lu|tie|ren [zalu'ti:rən] *ptp* **salutiert** VTI *(Mil)* to salute

Sa|lut|schuss M **man gab** *or* **feuerte fünf Salutschüsse ab** a five-gun salute was fired

Sal|ve ['zalvə] F -, -n salvo, volley; *(= Ehrensalve)* salute; *(fig) (= Lachsalve)* burst of laughter; *(von Applaus)* volley, burst; *(von Vorwürfen)* volley; **eine ~ auf jdn abschießen** *(lit, fig)* to fire a salvo *or* volley at sb

sal|vie|ren [zal'vi:rən] *ptp* **salviert** VT *(geh)* to exculpate

Salz [zalts] NT -es, -e salt; **jodiertes ~** iodized salt; **das ~ der Erde** *(liter)* the salt of the earth; **das ist das ~ in der Suppe** *(fig)* that's what gives it that extra something; **wie eine Suppe ohne ~** *(fig)* like ham *or* bacon without eggs *(hum)*; **er gönnt einem nicht das ~ in der Suppe** he even begrudges you the air you breathe; **in ~ legen** to salt down *or* away → **Wunde**

Salz-: **salz|arm** ADJ *(Cook)* low-salt, with a low salt content ADV **~ essen** to eat low-salt food; **~ leben** to live on a low-salt diet; **~ kochen** to use very little salt in one's cooking; **Salz|berg|werk** NT salt mine; **Salz|bre|zel** F pretzel

sal|zen ['zaltsn] *ptp* **gesalzen** [gə'zaltsn] VT to salt → *auch* **gesalzen**

Salz-: **Salz|fass** NT, **Salz|fäss|chen** NT saltcellar; **Salz|fleisch** NT *(Cook)* salt meat; **salz|frei** ADJ salt-free; *Diät auch* no-salt *attr* ADV **~ essen** not to eat salt; **~ kochen** to cook without salt; **Salz|ge|bäck** NT savoury *(Brit) or* savory *(US)* biscuits *pl*; **Salz|gur|ke** F pickled gherkin, pickle *(US)*; **salz|hal|tig** ADJ *Boden, Luft, Wasser* salty, saline; **Salz|he|ring** M salted herring

sal|zig ['zaltsɪç] ADJ *Speise, Wasser* salty

Sal|zig|keit F -, *no pl* saltiness

Salz-: **Salz|kar|tof|feln** PL boiled potatoes *pl*; **Salz|korn** NT *pl* **-körner** grain of salt; **Salz|la|ke** F brine; **salz|los** ADJ salt-free ADV **~ essen** not to eat salt; **~ kochen** to cook without salt; **Salz|lö|sung** F saline solution; **Salz|man|del** F salted almond; **Salz|säu|le** F **zur ~ erstarren** *(Bibl)* to turn into a pillar of salt; *(fig)* to stand as though rooted to the spot; **Salz|säu|re** F hydrochloric acid; **Salz|see** M salt lake; **Salz|sie|der** [-zi:dɐ] M -s, -, **Salz|sie|de|rin** [-ərɪn] F -, -nen *(Hist)* salt-maker; **Salz|sie|de|rei** [-zi:də'rai] F -, -en *(Hist)* saltworks *sing or pl*; **Salz|so|le** F brine; **Salz|stan|ge** F pretzel stick; **Salz|stock** M salt mine; **Salz|streu|er** [-ʃtrɔyɐ] M -s, - salt shaker, saltcellar; **Salz|teig** M salt dough; **Salz|was|ser** NT, *no pl* salt water; **Salz|wüs|te** F salt desert, salt flat

Sä|mann ['zɛ:man] M *pl* **-männer** *(old liter)* sower

SA-Mann [ɛs'la:-] M *pl* **SA-Leute** storm trooper, SA-man

Sa|ma|ri|ter [zama'ri:tɐ] M -s, - *(Bibl)* Samaritan; **der Barmherzige ~** the good Samaritan

Sa|ma|ri|ter [zama'ri:tɐ] M -s, -, **Sa|ma|ri|te|rin** [-ərɪn] F -, -nen *(fig)* **a** *(= barmherziger Mensch)* Samaritan **b** *(= Sanitäter)* first-aid volunteer

Sa|ma|ri|ter|dienst M **a** act of mercy; **jdm einen ~ erweisen** to be a good Samaritan to sb **b** *(= Sanitätsdienst)* first-aid service

Sa|ma|ri|um [za'ma:riʊm] NT -s, *no pl* (*abbr* **Sm**) samarium

Sam|ba ['zamba] M -s, -s *or f* -, -s samba

Sam|be|si [zam'be:zi] M -(s) Zambezi

Sam|bia ['zambia] NT -s Zambia

Sam|bier ['zambiɐ] M -s, -, **Sam|bie|rin** [-iərɪn] F -, -nen Zambian

sam|bisch ['zambɪʃ] ADJ Zambian

Sa|me ['za:mə] M -ns, -n *(liter)* = **Samen**

Sa|men ['za:mən] M -s, - **a** *(Bot, fig)* seed; **~ tragend** seed-bearing **b** *(= Menschensamen, Tiersamen)* sperm **c** *(liter, Bibl: = Nachkommen)* seed *(liter, Bibl)*

Sa|men-: **Sa|men|an|la|ge** F *(Bot)* ovule; **Sa|men|bank** F *pl* **-banken** sperm bank; **Sa|men|bla|se** F seminal vesicle; **Sa|men|er|guss** M ejaculation, emission of semen, seminal discharge *or* emission; **Sa|men|fa|den** M spermatozoon; **Sa|men|flüs|sig|keit** F semen, seminal fluid; **Sa|men|händ|ler(in)** M(F) seed merchant; **Sa|men|hand|lung** F seed shop; **Sa|men|kap|sel** F seed capsule; **Sa|men|korn** NT *pl* **-körner** seed; **Sa|men|lei|ter** M vas deferens; **Sa|men|spen|der** M sperm donor; **Sa|men|strang** M spermatic cord; **sa|men|tra|gend** ADJ → **Samen a**; **Sa|men|zel|le** F sperm cell; **Sa|men|zwie|bel** F seed onion

Sä|me|rei|en [zɛ:mə'raiən] PL seeds *pl*

sä|mig ['zɛ:mɪç] ADJ *Soße* thick

Sä|misch|le|der ['zɛ:mɪʃ-] NT chamois (leather)

Säm|ling ['zɛ:mlɪŋ] M -s, -e seedling

Sam|mel-: **Sam|mel|al|bum** NT (collector's) album; **Sam|mel|an|schluss** M *(Telec)* private (branch) exchange; *(von Privathäusern)* party line; **Sam|mel|band** [-bant] M *pl* **-bände** anthology; **Sam|mel|be|cken** NT collecting tank; *(Geol)* catchment area; *(fig)* melting pot (*von* for); **Sam|mel|be|griff** M *(Gram)* collective name *or* term; **Sam|mel|be|stel|lung** F joint *or* collective order; **Sam|mel|be|zeich|nung** F collective name *or* term; **Sam|mel|büch|se** F collecting tin *or* box; **Sam|mel|de|pot** NT *(Fin)* collective securities deposit; **Sam|mel|fahr|schein** M, **Sam|mel|kar|te** F *(für mehrere Fahrten)* multi-journey ticket; *(für mehrere Personen)* group ticket; **Sam|mel|kon|to** NT combined account; **Sam|mel|map|pe** F folder

sam|meln ['zamln] VT to collect; *Holz, Ähren, Fakten, Material, Erfahrungen auch* to gather; *Blumen, Pilze etc* to pick, to gather; *Truppen, Anhänger* to gather, to assemble; **neue Kräfte ~** to build up one's energy again; **seine Gedanken ~** to collect one's thoughts; **Punkte ~** *(Sport, fig)* to score points VR **a** *(= zusammenkommen)* to gather, to collect; *(Menschenmenge)* to gather; *(= sich anhäufen: Wasser, Geld etc)* to collect, to accumulate; *(Lichtstrahlen)* to converge, to meet **b** *(= sich konzentrieren)* to collect *or* compose oneself *or* one's thoughts → *auch* **gesammelt** VI to collect (*für* for)

Sam|mel-: **Sam|mel|na|me** M collective name *or* term; **Sam|mel|num|mer** F *(Telec)* private exchange number, switchboard number; **Sam|mel|pass** M group passport; **Sam|mel|platz** M **a** *(= Treffpunkt)* assembly point **b** *(= Lagerplatz)* collecting point; *(= Deponie)* dump; **Sam|mel|punkt** M **a** *(= Treffpunkt)* assembly point **b** *(Opt)* focus **c** *(= Lagerplatz)* collecting point; **Sam|mel|sen|dung** F joint consignment; **Güter als ~ schicken** to send goods part-load; **Sam|mel|ste|cker** M *(Elec)* plugboard; **Sam|mel|stel|le** F = **Sammelplatz**

Sam|mel|su|ri|um [zaml'zu:riʊm] NT -s, **Sammelsurien** [-riən] conglomeration

Sam|mel-: **Sam|mel|tas|se** F ornamental cup, saucer and plate; **Sam|mel|ta|xi** NT share-a-ride taxi; **Sam|mel|trans|port** M *(von Gütern)* general shipment; *(von Personen)* group transport; **Sam|mel|vi|sum** NT collective visa; **Sam|mel|wut** F collecting mania

Sam|met ['zamət] M -s, -e *(obs, Sw)* velvet

Samm|ler ['zamlɐ] M -s, -, **Samm|le|rin** [-ərɪn] F -, -nen collector; *(von Beeren)* picker; *(von Holz)* gatherer → **Jäger a**

Samm|ler|fleiß M collector's enthusiasm; **diese Kollektion ist mit großem ~ zusammengetragen** it has taken a lot of hard work to put this collection together

Samm|lung ['zamlʊŋ] F -, -en **a** collection **b** *(fig: = Konzentration)* composure; **ihm fehlt die innere ~** he lacks composure; **zur ~ (meiner Gedanken)** to collect myself *or* my thoughts

Samm|lungs|be|we|gung F coalition movement

Sa|mos(|wein) ['za:mɔs-] M -, - Samian wine, wine from Samos

Sa|mo|war ['zamova:ɐ, zamo'va:ɐ] M -s, -e samovar

Samp|ler ['zamplɐ] M -s, - *(= Gerät, CD)* sampler

Sams|tag ['zamsta:k] M Saturday → *auch* **Dienstag**

sams|tä|gig ['zamstɛ:gɪç] ADJ Saturday

sams|tags ['zamsta:ks] ADV on Saturdays

Sams|tags|zie|hung F *(im Lotto)* Saturday draw

samt [zamt] PREP +*dat* along *or* together with; **sie kam ~ Katze** *(hum)* she came complete with cat ADV **~ und sonders** the whole lot (of them/us/you), the whole bunch *(inf)*; **die Teilnehmer wurden ~ und sonders verhaftet** all the participants were arrested, the whole lot of them

Samt [zamt] M -(e)s, -e velvet; **in ~ und Seide** *(liter)* in silks and satins; **zart wie ~ und Seide** *(liter)* as soft as silk

Samt- *in cpds* velvet; **samt|ar|tig** ADJ velvety, like velvet; **Samt|band** [-bant] NT *pl* **-bänder** velvet ribbon; **Samt|blu|me** F *(Bot)* marigold

sam|ten ['zamtn] ADJ *(liter)* velvet

Samt|hand|schuh M velvet glove; **jdn mit ~en anfassen** *(inf)* to handle sb with kid gloves *(inf)*

sam|tig ['zamtɪç] ADJ velvety

sämt|lich ['zɛmtlɪç] ADJ *(= alle)* all; *(= vollständig)* complete; **~e Unterlagen waren verschwunden** all the *or* every one of the documents had disappeared, the documents had all disappeared; **Schillers ~e Werke** the complete works of Schiller; **~e Anwesenden** all those present; **sie mussten ~en Besitz zurücklassen** they had to leave all their possessions behind ADV all; **die Unterlagen waren ~ verschwunden** all the *or* every one of the documents had disappeared, the documents had all disappeared

Samt-: **Samt|pföt|chen** NT *(inf)* velvet paw; **~ machen** *(Katze)* to draw in its claws; *(fig)* to go all soft; **wie auf ~ gehen** to tread softly; **Samt|schlei|fe** F velvet bow; **samt|weich** ADJ (as) soft as velvet, velvet-soft, velvety

Sa|na|to|ri|um [zana'to:riʊm] NT **-s, Sanatorien** [-riən] sanatorium *(Brit)*, sanitarium *(US)*

Sand [zant] M **-(e)s, -e** [-də] sand; *(= Scheuersand)* scouring powder; **mit ~ bestreuen** to sand; **das/die gibts wie ~ am Meer** *(inf)* there are heaps of them *(inf)*; **auf ~ laufen** *or* **geraten** to run aground; **auf ~ bauen** *(fig)* to build upon sandy ground; **jdm ~ in die Augen streuen** *(fig)* to throw dust *(Brit) or* dirt *(US)* in sb's eyes; **~ ins Getriebe streuen** to throw a spanner in the works *(Brit)*, to throw a (monkey) wrench into the works *(US)*; **im ~e verlaufen** *(inf)* to peter out, to come to naught *or* nothing; **den Kopf in den ~ stecken** to stick *or* bury *or* hide one's head in the sand; **etw in den ~ setzen** *(inf, Projekt, Prüfung)* to blow sth *(inf)*; *Geld* to squander sth

San|da|le [zan'da:lə] F **-, -n** sandal

San|da|let|te [zanda'lɛtə] F **-, -n** high-heeled sandal

Sand-: **Sand|bank** F *pl* **-bänke** sandbank, sandbar; **Sand|bo|den** M sandy soil; **Sand|burg** F sandcastle; **Sand|dorn** M *pl* **-dorne** *(Bot)* sea buckthorn

San|del|holz ['zandl-] NT sandalwood

san|deln ['zandln] VI *(S Ger, Aus, Sw)* to play in the sand

San|del|öl ['zandl-] NT sandalwood oil

Sand-: **sand|far|ben** [-farbn], **sand|far|big** ADJ sand-coloured *(Brit)*, sand-colored *(US)*; **Sand|förm|chen** NT sand mould *(Brit)*, sand mold *(US)*; **Sand|gru|be** F sandpit *(esp Brit)*, sandbox *(US)*; *(Golf)* bunker, sand trap *(esp US)*; **Sand|hau|fen** M pile *or* heap of sand; *(= Sandkasten)* sandpit *(esp Brit)*, sandbox *(US)*; **Sand|ho|se** F sand column *or* spout, dust devil

san|dig ['zandɪç] ADJ sandy

San|di|nist [zandi'nɪst] M **-en, -en**, **San|di|nis|tin** [-'nɪstɪn] F **-, -nen** Sandinista

Sand-: **Sand|kas|ten** M sandpit *(esp Brit)*, sandbox *(US)*; *(Mil)* sand table; **Sand|kas|ten|spie|le** PL *(Mil)* sand-table exercises *pl*; *(fig)* tactical manoeuvrings *(Brit) or* maneuverings *(US) pl*; **Sand|korn** NT *pl* **-körner** grain of sand; **Sand|ku|chen** M *(Cook)* sand cake *(a Madeira-type cake)*; *(von Kindern)* mud pie; **Sand|mann** M, *no pl*, **Sand|männ|chen** NT, *no pl (in Geschichten)* sandman; **Sand|meer** NT *(geh)* sea of sand; **Sand|pa|pier** NT sandpaper; **Sand|platz** M *(Tennis)* clay court; **Sand|sack** M sandbag; *(Boxen)* punchbag *(Brit)*, punching bag *(US)*

Sand|stein M sandstone; **ein Haus aus rotem ~** a red sandstone house, a brownstone (house) *(US)*

Sand|stein- *in cpds* sandstone; **Sand|stein|fel|sen** M sandstone cliff

Sand-: **Sand|strahl** M jet of sand; **etw mit ~ abblasen** *or* **reinigen** to sandblast sth; **sand|strah|len** *ptp* **gesandstrahlt** *or (spec)* **sandgestrahlt** VTI to sandblast; **Sand|strahl|ge|blä|se** NT sandblasting equipment *no indef art, no pl*; **Sand|strand** M sandy beach; **Sand|sturm** M sandstorm

sand|te *pret von* **senden**

Sand-: **Sand|uhr** F hourglass; *(= Eieruhr)* egg timer; *(Comput: Form des Mauszeigers)* hourglass pointer; **Sand|weg** M dirt road, track

Sand|wich ['zɛntvɪtʃ] NT OR M **-(s), -(e)s** sandwich

Sand|wich-: **Sand|wich|bau|wei|se** F sandwich construction; **Sand|wich|mann** M *pl* **-männer** *(hum)* sandwich man; **Sand|wich|we|cken** M *(Aus) long thin white loaf*, French loaf

Sand|wüs|te F sandy waste; *(Geog)* (sandy) desert

sanft [zanft] ADJ gentle; *Berührung, Stimme, Farbe, Licht, Wind, Regen auch, Haut* soft; *Schlaf, Tod* peaceful; **mit ~er Gewalt** gently but firmly; **mit ~er Hand** with a gentle hand; **von ~er Hand** by a woman's fair hand; **sie schaute das Kind mit ~en Augen an** she looked tenderly at the child; **~ wie ein Lamm** (as) gentle as a lamb; **~er Tourismus** green tourism → **ruhen**
ADV softly; *abfallen, ansteigen, sich winden auch* gently; *lächeln* softly; *tadeln, ermahnen* mildly; *hinweisen* gently; **sie lächelte ~** she smiled softly; **sich ~ anfühlen** to feel soft; **~ mit jdm umgehen** to be gentle with *or* to sb; **~ schlafen** to be sleeping peacefully; **er ist ~ entschlafen** he passed away peacefully, he fell gently asleep *(auch iro)*

Sänf|te ['zɛnftə] F **-, -n** litter; *(esp im 17., 18. Jh. Europas)* sedan chair; *(in Indien)* palanquin; *(auf Elefant)* howdah

Sänf|ten|trä|ger(in) M(F) → **Sänfte** litter bearer; sedan bearer; palanquin bearer

Sanft|heit F **-,** *no pl* gentleness; *(von Stimme, Farbe, Licht auch, von Haut)* softness

sänf|ti|gen ['zɛnftɪgn] VT *(obs)* = **besänftigen**

Sanft|mut ['zanftmu:t] F **-,** *no pl (liter)* gentleness

sanft|mü|tig ['zanftmy:tɪç] ADJ *(liter)* gentle; *(Bibl)* meek

sang *pret von* **singen**

Sang [zaŋ] M **-(e)s, ⸗e** ['zɛŋə] *(old liter) (= Gesang)* song; *(= das Singen)* singing; **mit ~ und Klang** *(lit)* with drums drumming and pipes piping; *(fig iro) durchfallen* disastrously, catastrophically; *entlassen werden* with a lot of hullaballoo; **ohne ~ und Klang** *(inf)* without any ado, quietly; **ohne ~ und Klang verschwinden** to just simply disappear

Sän|ger ['zɛŋɐ] M **-s, -** **a** singer; *(= esp Jazzsänger, Popsänger)* vocalist **b** *(old liter: = Dichter)* bard *(old)*, poet; **da(rüber) schweigt des ~s Höflichkeit** modesty forbids me to say **c** *(= Singvogel)* songbird, songster

Sän|ger-: **Sän|ger|bund** M *pl* **-bünde** choral union; **Sän|ger|fest** NT choral festival

Sän|ge|rin ['zɛŋərɪn] F singer; *(= esp Jazzsängerin, Popsängerin)* vocalist

San|ges-: **San|ges|bru|der** M *(inf)* chorister; **San|ges|freu|de** F, **San|ges|lust** F *(dated)* love of song *or* singing; **san|ges|freu|dig**, **san|ges|lus|tig** ADJ *(dated)* fond of singing, song-loving; **San|ges|schwes|ter** F *(inf)* chorister

Sang|ria [zaŋ'gri:a, 'zaŋgria] F **-, -s** sangria

San|gu|i|ni|ker [zaŋ'gui:nikɐ] M **-s, -**, **San|gu|i|ni|ke|rin** [-ərɪn] F **-, -nen** *(Psych)* sanguine person

san|gu|i|nisch [zaŋ'gui:nɪʃ] ADJ *(Psych)* sanguine

sang- und klang|los ADV *(inf)* without any ado, quietly; **sie ist ~ verschwunden** she just simply disappeared

Sa|ni ['zani] M **-s, -s** *(Mil inf)* medical orderly

sa|nie|ren [za'ni:rən] *ptp* **saniert** VT **a** *(= gesunde Lebensverhältnisse schaffen) Gebäude* to renovate; *Stadtteil, Gelände* to redevelop; *Fluss* to clean up **b** *(Econ) Unternehmen, Wirtschaft* to put (back) on its feet, to rehabilitate; *Haushalt* to turn round VR **a** *(inf: Mensch)* to line one's own pocket *(inf)*; **bei dem Geschäft hat er sich saniert** he made a killing on the deal *(inf)* **b** *(Unternehmen, Wirtschaft, Industrie)* to put itself (back) in good shape

Sa|nie|rung F **-, -en** **a** *(von Gebäude)* renovation; *(von Stadtteil)* redevelopment; *(von Fluss)* cleaning-up **b** *(Econ)* rehabilitation; *(von Rentensystem etc)* modernization; **Maßnahmen zur ~ des Dollars** measures to put the dollar back on an even keel *or* on its feet again **c** *(inf: = Bereicherung)* self-enrichment; **er ist nur auf die eigene ~ bedacht** he is only interested in lining his own pocket *(inf)*

Sa|nie|rungs-: **Sa|nie|rungs|ge|biet** NT redevelopment area; **Sa|nie|rungs|ge|winn** M *profit from property speculation in a redevelopment area*; **Sa|nie|rungs|kos|ten** PL redevelopment costs *pl*; **Sa|nie|rungs|maß|nah|me** F *(für Gebiete etc)* redevelopment measure; *(Econ)* rehabilitation measure; **Sa|nie|rungs|plan** M redevelopment plan *or* scheme; *(Econ)* rehabilitation plan

sa|ni|tär [zani'tɛ:ɐ] ADJ *no pred* sanitary; **~e Anlagen** sanitation (facilities), sanitary facilities ADV **ein Haus ~ ausstatten** to install sanitation in a house

Sa|ni|tär|an|la|gen PL sanitary *or* sanitation facilities *pl*

Sa|ni|tät [zani'tɛ:t] F **-, -en** *(Aus, Sw)* **a** medical service; *(= Krankenpflege)* nursing **b** *(inf: = Krankenwagen)* ambulance

Sa|ni|tä|ter [zani'tɛ:tɐ] M **-s, -**, **Sa|ni|tä|te|rin** [-ərɪn] F **-, -nen** first-aid attendant; *(Mil)* (medical) orderly; *(in Krankenwagen)* ambulanceman/-woman

Sa|ni|täts-: **Sa|ni|täts|au|to** NT ambulance; **Sa|ni|täts|dienst** M *(Mil)* medical duty; *(= Heeresabteilung)* medical corps; **Sa|ni|täts|flug|zeug** NT ambulance plane, air ambulance; **Sa|ni|täts|ge|frei|te(r)** MF *decl as adj* (medical) orderly; **Sa|ni|täts|kas|ten** M first-aid box *(esp Brit) or* kit; **Sa|ni|täts|kom|pa|nie** F medical company; **Sa|ni|täts|of|fi|zier(in)** M(F) *(Mil)* Medical Officer, MO; **Sa|ni|täts|trup|pe** F medical corps; **Sa|ni|täts|wa|gen** M ambulance; **Sa|ni|täts|we|sen** NT *(Mil)* medical service; **Sa|ni|täts|zelt** NT first-aid tent

sank *pret von* **sinken**

San|ka ['zaŋka] M **-s, -s** *(Mil inf)* ambulance

Sankt [zaŋkt] ADJ *inv* saint; **~ Nikolaus** Santa (Claus), Father Christmas; *(Rel)* St *or* Saint Nicholas

Sankt-Flo|ri|ans-Prin|zip [zaŋkt'flo:ria:ns-] NT *(inf)* not-in-my-back-yard attitude

Sankt Gal|len [zaŋkt 'galən] NT **- -s** *(= Kanton, Stadt)* St Gall

Sank|ti|on [zaŋk'tsio:n] F **-, -en** sanction

sank|ti|o|nie|ren [zaŋktsio'ni:rən] *ptp* **sanktioniert** VT to sanction

Sank|ti|o|nie|rung F **-, -en** sanctioning

Sankt-Lo|renz-Strom [zaŋkt'lo:rɛnts-] M St Lawrence river

Sankt-Nim|mer|leins-Tag [zaŋkt'nɪmɐlains-] M *(hum)* never-never day; **ja ja, am ~** yes yes, and pigs might fly *(hum)*; **etw auf den ~ verschieben** to put sth off indefinitely

sann *pret von* **sinnen**

Sann|ya|si [zan'ja:zi] MF **-, -n** sannyasi(n)

San|se|vi|e|ria [zanze'vieria] F **-, Sansevierien**, **San|se|vi|e|rie** [zanze'vie:riə] F **-, -n** *(Bot)* sansevieria

San|si|bar ['zanziba:ɐ, zanzi'ba:ɐ] NT **-s** Zanzibar

Sansk|rit ['zanskrɪt] NT **-s,** *no pl* Sanskrit

San|ya|si [zan'ja:zi] MF **-, -n** sannyasi(n)

Sa|phir ['za:fɪr, 'za:fi:ɐ, za'fi:ɐ] M **-s, -e** sapphire

sap|per|lot [zapɐ'lo:t], **sap|per|ment** [zapɐ'mɛnt] INTERJ *(old)* stap me *(old)*, upon my soul *(old)*

sap|phisch ['zapfɪʃ, 'zafɪʃ] ADJ Sapphic

Sa|ra|ban|de [zara'bandə] F **-, -n** *(Mus)* saraband

Sa|ra|ze|ne [zara'tse:nə] M -n, -n, **Sa|ra|ze|nin** [-'tse:nın] F -, -nen Saracen

sa|ra|ze|nisch [zara'tse:nıʃ] ADJ Saracen

Sa|rde ['zardə] M -n, -n, **Sar|din** ['zardın] F -, -nen Sardinian

Sar|del|le [zar'dɛlə] F -, -n anchovy

Sar|del|len-: **Sar|del|len|but|ter** F anchovy butter; **Sar|del|len|pas|te** F anchovy paste

Sar|din ['zardın] F -, -nen Sardinian

Sar|di|ne [zar'di:nə] F -, -n sardine

Sar|di|nen|büch|se F sardine tin; **wie in einer ~** *(fig inf)* like sardines *(inf)*

Sar|di|ni|en [zar'di:niən] NT -s Sardinia

Sar|di|ni|er [zar'di:niɐ] M -s, -, **Sar|di|ni|e|rin** [-iərın] F -, -nen Sardinian

sar|di|nisch [zar'di:nıʃ], **sar|disch** ['zardıʃ] ADJ Sardinian

sar|do|nisch [zar'do:nıʃ] *(liter)* ADJ sardonic ADV sardonically

Sarg [zark] M -(e)s, ⸚e ['zɛrgə] coffin, casket *(US)*; **ein Nagel zu jds ~ sein** *(hum inf)* to be a nail in sb's coffin; **du kannst dir schon deinen ~ machen lassen** *(hum inf)* you'd better start arranging your funeral

Sarg-: **Sarg|de|ckel** M coffin lid, casket lid *(US)*; **Sarg|na|gel** M coffin nail; *(fig inf auch: = Zigarette)* cancer stick *(hum inf)*; **ein letzter/der letzte ~ für etw sein** to be the final nail in the coffin of sth; **Sarg|tisch|ler(in)** M(F) coffin-maker, casket-maker *(US)*; **Sarg|trä|ger(in)** M(F) pallbearer

Sa|ri ['za:ri] M -(s), -s sari

Sa|rin [za'ri:n] NT -s, *no pl (Chem)* sarin

Sar|kas|mus [zar'kasmʊs] M -, **Sarkasmen** [-mən] **a** *no pl* sarcasm **b** *(= Bemerkung)* sarcastic comment *or* remark

sar|kas|tisch [zar'kastıʃ] ADJ sarcastic ADV sarcastically

Sar|kom [zar'ko:m] NT -s, -e *(Med)* sarcoma

Sar|ko|phag [zarko'fa:k] M -(e)s, -e [-gə] sarcophagus

Sa|rong ['za:rɔŋ] M -(s), -s sarong

SARS NT - *abbr von* **severe acute respiratory syndrome** SARS

saß *pret von* **sitzen**

Sa|tan ['za:tan] M -s, -e *(Bibl, fig)* Satan; **dieses Weib ist ein ~** this woman is a (she-)devil

sa|ta|nisch [za'ta:nıʃ] ADJ satanic ADV satanically

Sa|ta|nis|mus [zata'nısmʊs] M -, *no pl* Satanism

Sa|tans-: **Sa|tans|bra|ten** M *(hum inf)* young devil; **Sa|tans|kult** M satan cult; **Sa|tans|pilz** M Satan's mushroom, boletus satanas *(spec)*

Sa|tel|lit [zatɛ'li:t] M -en, -en *(alle Bedeutungen)* satellite

Sa|tel|li|ten- *in cpds* satellite; **Sa|tel|li|ten|ab|wehr|waf|fe** F antisatellite weapon; **Sa|tel|li|ten|an|ten|ne** F *(TV)* satellite dish; **Sa|tel|li|ten|bahn** F satellite orbit; **Sa|tel|li|ten|bild** NT *(TV)* satellite picture; **Sa|tel|li|ten|emp|fän|ger** M satellite receiver; **Sa|tel|li|ten|fern|se|hen** NT satellite television; **Sa|tel|li|ten|fo|to** NT satellite picture; **Sa|tel|li|ten|schüs|sel** F *(TV inf)* satellite dish; **Sa|tel|li|ten|sen|der** M satellite (TV) station; **Sa|tel|li|ten|staat** M satellite state; **Sa|tel|li|ten|stadt** F satellite town; **Sa|tel|li|ten|sta|ti|on** F space station; **Sa|tel|li|ten|sys|tem** NT satellite system; **Sa|tel|li|ten|über|tra|gung** F *(Rad, TV)* satellite transmission

Sa|tin [za'tɛ̃:] M -s, -s satin; *(= Baumwollsatin)* sateen

sa|ti|nie|ren [zati'ni:rən] *ptp* **satiniert** VT *Papier* to glaze; *(Typ)* to satin-coat

Sa|tin|pa|pier [za'tɛ̃:-] NT glazed paper

Sa|ti|re [za'ti:rə] F -, -n satire *(auf +acc* on)

Sa|ti|ri|ker [za'ti:rikɐ] M -s, -, **Sa|ti|ri|ke|rin** [-ərın] F -, -nen satirist

sa|ti|risch [za'ti:rıʃ] ADJ satirical ADV satirically

Sa|tis|fak|ti|on [zatısfak'tsio:n] F -, -en *(old)* satisfaction; **ich verlange** *or* **fordere ~!** I demand satisfaction

sa|tis|fak|ti|ons|fä|hig ADJ *(old)* capable of giving satisfaction

Sat|rap [za'tra:p] M -en, -en *(Hist)* satrap

satt [zat] ✪ 41 ADJ **a** *(= gesättigt) Mensch* replete *(hum, form)*, full (up) *(inf)*; *Magen, Gefühl* full; **~ sein** to have had enough (to eat), to be full (up) *(inf)*; **~ werden** to have enough to eat; **von so was kann man doch nicht ~ werden** it's not enough to satisfy you *or* to fill you up; **das macht ~** it's filling; **sich (an etw** *dat***) ~ essen** to eat one's fill (of sth); *(= überdrüssig werden auch)* to have had one's fill (of sth); **wie soll sie ihre Kinder ~ kriegen?** *(inf)* how is she supposed to feed her children?; **er ist kaum ~ zu kriegen** *(inf: lit, fig)* he's insatiable; **~ sank er in den Sessel zurück** having eaten his fill he sank back into his chair; **wie ein ~er Säugling** *(inf)* with a look of contentment, like a contented cow *(inf)*
b *(fig)* **jdn/etw ~ sein** to be fed up with sb/sth *(inf)* → **sattbekommen, satthaben** *etc*
c *(= blasiert, übersättigt)* well-fed; *(= selbstgefällig)* smug
d *(= kräftig, voll) Farben, Klang* rich, full; *(inf) Applaus* resounding; *(inf) Mehrheit* comfortable; **~e 10 Prozent/1000 Euro** *(inf)* a cool 10 per cent *(Brit) or* percent *(US)*/1000 euros *(inf)*
e *(inf: = im Überfluss)* **... ~** ... galore, ... in abundance
ADV *(inf) verdienen, da sein* more than enough; **es gab Champagner ~** there was more than enough champagne; **sie haben nicht ~ zu essen** they don't have enough to eat

satt+be|kom|men VT *sep irreg (inf, fig)* **jdn/etw ~** to get fed up with sb/sth *(inf)*

Sat|tel ['zatl] M -s, ⸚ ['zɛtl] **a** saddle; **ohne/mit ~ reiten** to ride bareback *or* without a saddle/with a saddle; **sich in den ~ schwingen** to swing (oneself) into the saddle; *(auf Fahrrad)* to jump onto one's bicycle; **in den ~ steigen** *(= reiten, radfahren)* to ride; **sich im ~ halten** *(lit, fig)* to stay in the saddle; **jdn aus dem ~ heben** *(= herunterhelfen)* to help sb (to) dismount; *(lit, fig: = zu Fall bringen)* to unseat sb; **jdn in den ~ heben** *(lit)* to lift sb into the saddle; *(fig)* to help sb to power; **er ist in allen Sätteln gerecht** *or* **sicher** *(fig)* he can turn his hand to anything; **fest im ~ sitzen** *(fig)* to be firmly in the saddle
b *(= Bergsattel)* saddle; *(= Geigensattel)* nut; *(= Nasensattel)* bridge

Sat|tel-: **Sat|tel|dach** NT saddle roof; **Sat|tel|de|cke** F saddlecloth; **sat|tel|fest** ADJ **~ sein** *(Reiter)* to have a good seat; **in etw** *(dat)* **~ sein** *(fig)* to have a firm grasp of sth; **Sat|tel|gurt** M girth; **Sat|tel|knopf** M pommel

sat|teln ['zatln] VT *Pferd* to saddle (up); **für etw gesattelt sein** *(fig)* to be ready for sth

Sat|tel-: **Sat|tel|na|se** F saddlenose; **Sat|tel|pferd** NT saddle horse; **Sat|tel|platz** M paddock; **Sat|tel|schlep|per** M articulated lorry *(Brit)*, artic *(Brit inf)*, semitrailer *(US)*, semi *(US inf)*; **Sat|tel|ta|sche** F saddlebag; *(= Gepäcktasche am Fahrrad, aus Stroh)* pannier; **Sat|tel|zeug** NT *pl* **-zeuge** saddlery; **Sat|tel|zug** M = **Sattelschlepper**

satt+ha|ben VT *sep irreg (inf, fig)* **jdn/etw ~** to be fed up with sb/sth *(inf)*

Satt|heit F -, *no pl* **a** *(Gefühl)* full feeling, feeling of being full **b** *(von Farben, Klang)* richness, fullness

satt+hö|ren VR *sep (fig, inf)* **sie konnte sich an der Musik nicht ~** she could not get enough of the music

sät|ti|gen ['zɛtıgn] VT **a** *Hunger, Neugier* to satisfy, to satiate; *jdn* to make replete; *(= ernähren)* to feed, to provide with food; **ich bin gesättigt** I am *or* feel replete **b** *(Comm, Chem)* to saturate → *auch* **gesättigt** VI to be filling VR **sich an etw** *(dat) or* **mit etw ~** to eat one's fill of sth

sät|ti|gend ADJ *Essen* filling

Sät|ti|gung F -, -en **a** *(geh: = Sattsein)* repletion; **die ~ der Hungrigen** the feeding of the hungry; **das Essen dient nicht nur der ~** eating does not only serve to satisfy hunger **b** *(Chem, Comm, von Farbe)* saturation

Sät|ti|gungs-: **Sät|ti|gungs|bei|la|ge** F filling vegetables, trimmings *pl (inf)*; **Sät|ti|gungs|grad** M degree of saturation; **Sät|ti|gungs|punkt** M saturation point

satt+krie|gen VT *sep (inf, fig)* = **sattbekommen**

Satt|ler ['zatlɐ] M -s, -, **Satt|le|rin** [-ərın] F -, -nen saddler; *(= Polsterer)* upholsterer

Satt|le|rei [zatlə'rai] F -, -en saddlery; *(= Polsterei)* upholstery; *(= Werkstatt)* saddler's; upholsterer's

Satt|ler|meis|ter(in) M(F) master saddler; *(= Polsterer)* master upholsterer

satt+ma|chen VT *sep* → **satt a**

satt|sam ['zatza:m] ADV amply; *bekannt* sufficiently

satt+se|hen VR *sep irreg (fig, inf)* **er konnte sich an ihr nicht ~** he could not see enough of her

sa|tu|rie|ren [zatu'ri:rən] *ptp* **saturiert** VT *(liter)* to satisfy, to content VR *(geh)* to do well for oneself

sa|tu|riert [zatu'ri:ɐt] *(geh)* ADJ *Markt* saturated; *Klasse* prosperous ADV **~ leben** to prosper, to live prosperously

Sa|turn [za'tʊrn] M -s *(Myth, Astron)* Saturn; **die Ringe des ~s** the rings of Saturn

Sa|tur|na|li|en [zatʊr'na:liən] PL *(Hist)* Saturnalia *pl*

Sa|tyr ['za:tʏr] M -s *or* -n, -n *or* -e satyr

Satz [zats] M -es, ⸚e ['zɛtsə] **a** sentence; *(= Teilsatz)* clause; *(Jur: = Gesetzabschnitt)* clause; **ich kann nur ein paar Sätze Italienisch** I only know a few phrases of Italian; **mitten im ~** in mid-sentence; **abhängiger/selbstständiger ~** subordinate/principal clause; **eingeschobener ~** appositional phrase
b *(= Lehrsatz, auch Philos)* proposition; *(Math)* theorem; **der ~ des Pythagoras** Pythagoras' theorem
c *(Typ) (= das Setzen)* setting; *(= das Gesetzte)* type *no pl*; **etw in ~ geben** to send sth for setting; **in ~ gehen** to go for setting; **das Buch ist im ~** the book is being set
d *(Mus) (= Abschnitt)* movement; *(= Kompositionsweise)* composition
e *(= Bodensatz)* dregs *pl*; *(= Kaffeesatz)* grounds *pl*; *(= Teesatz)* leaves *pl*, dregs *pl*
f *(= Zusammengehöriges)* set; *(Comput: = Datensatz)* record; *(Hunt: = Wurf)* litter
g *(Sport)* set; *(Tischtennis, Badminton)* game
h *(= Tarifsatz)* charge; *(= Spesensatz)* allowance; *(= Zinssatz)* rate
i *(= Sprung)* leap, jump; **einen ~ machen** *or* **tun** to leap, to jump; **mit einem ~** in one leap *or* bound

Satz-: **Satz|aus|sa|ge** F *(Gram)* predicate; **Satz|ball** M *(Sport)* set point; *(Tischtennis)* game point; **Satz|bau** M, *no pl* sentence construction; **Satz|be|fehl** M *(Typ)* typographical command; **Satz|er|gän|zung** F *(Gram)* object; **Satz|feh|ler** M *(Typ)* printer's error; **Satz|fet|zen** M sentence fragment; **Satz|ge|fü|ge** NT *(Gram)* complex sentence; **Satz|ge|gen|stand** M *(Gram)* subject; **Satz|glied** NT part of a/the sentence; **Satz|her|stel|lung** F *(Typ)* typesetting

-sät|zig [zɛtsıç] ADJ *suf (Mus)* in ... movements; **eine dreisätzige Sonate** a sonata in three movements

Satz-: **Satz|leh|re** F *(Gram)* syntax; **Satz|me|lo|die** F *(Phon)* intonation; **Satz|mus|ter** NT *(Ling)* sentence pattern; **Satz|rei|he** F compound sentence; **Satz|spie|gel** M *(Typ)* type area, area of type; **Satz|teil** M part or constituent of a/the sentence

Sat|zung ['zatsʊŋ] F -, -en constitution, statutes *pl*; *(von Verein)* rules *pl*

sat|zungs|ge|mäß ADJ ADV → **Satzung** according to the statutes/rules

Satz-: **Satz|ver|bin|dung** F clause construction; **Satz|ver|lust** M *(Tennis)* loss of a set; **satz|wei|se** ADJ **a** *(Ling)* sentence by sentence **b** *(Tech)* in sets ADV **a** *(Ling)* sentence by sentence; **sprechen Sie mir ~ nach** repeat after me; **eine Sprache lernt man besser ~** you are better to learn a language in phrases **b** *(= in Sets)* in sets; **Satz|zei|chen** NT punctuation mark; **Satz|zu|sam|men|hang** M context of the sentence

Sau [zau] F **-, Säue** *or (Hunt)* **-en** [ˈzɔyə] **a** sow; *(inf: = Schwein)* pig; *(Hunt)* wild boar; **die ~ rauslassen** *(fig inf)* to let it all hang out *(inf)*; **wie eine gestochene ~ bluten** *(sl)* to bleed like a (stuck) pig *(inf)*; **wie eine gesengte ~** *(inf)* **wie die ~** *(inf)* like a maniac *(inf)*
b *(pej inf) (= Schmutzfink)* dirty swine *(inf)*; **du ~!** you dirty swine! *(inf)*; **du alte ~!** *(vulg)* you dirty bastard *(sl)*, you son of a bitch *(sl)*; *(Frau auch)* you dirty bitch *(sl)*; **miese ~** bastard *(sl)*; **dumme ~** stupid cow *(inf)*
c *(fig inf)* **da war keine ~ zu sehen** there wasn't a bloody *(Brit inf)* or goddamn *(inf)* soul to be seen; **das interessiert keine ~** nobody gives a damn about that *(inf)*; **jdn zur ~ machen** to bawl sb out *(inf)*; **unter aller ~** bloody *(Brit inf)* or goddamn *(inf)* awful or lousy; **wie die ~** *(= wie verrückt)* like mad or crazy

Sau-: **Sau|ban|de** F *(inf)* gang of hoodlums *(inf)* or gang-bangers *(US sl)*; **Sau|bär** M *(sl: = gemeiner Typ)* bastard *(sl)*

sau|ber [ˈzaubɐ] ADJ **a** *(= rein, reinlich)* clean; **~ sein** *(Hund etc)* to be house-trained; *(Kind)* to be (potty-)trained
b *(= ordentlich)* neat, tidy; *(Aus, Sw, S Ger: = hübsch) Mädel* pretty; *(= exakt)* accurate
c *(= anständig)* honest, upstanding; **~ bleiben** to keep one's hands clean; **bleib ~!** *(inf)* keep your nose clean *(inf)*
d *(inf: = großartig)* fantastic, great; **~! ~!** that's the stuff! *(inf)*; **du bist mir ja ein ~er Freund!** *(iro)* a fine friend YOU are! *(iro)*; **eine ~e Gesellschaft!** *(iro)* a bunch of crooks; **das ist ja ~!** *(iro)* that's great *(iro)*
ADV **a** *(= rein)* **etw ~ putzen** to clean sth; **~ singen/spielen** to sing/play on key
b *(= sorgfältig)* very thoroughly, well
c *(= genau) analysieren, darstellen* carefully; **etw ~ lösen** to find a neat solution for sth
d *(Aus, S Ger: verstärkend)* really and truly → *auch* **sauber machen**

Sau|ber|frau F *(fig inf)* decent and upstanding sort; *(in Politik etc)* squeaky-clean woman *(inf)*

sau|ber hal|ten VT *irreg* to keep clean

Sau|ber|keit F **-,** *no pl* **a** *(= Hygiene, Ordentlichkeit)* cleanliness; *(= Reinheit) (von Wasser, Luft etc)* cleanness; *(von Tönen)* accuracy **b** *(= Anständigkeit)* honesty, upstandingness; *(im Sport)* fair play

Sau|ber|keits|fim|mel M *(pej)* mania for cleanliness, thing about cleanliness *(inf)*

säu|ber|lich [ˈzɔybɐlɪç] ADJ neat and tidy ADV neatly; *auseinanderhalten, trennen* clearly; **fein ~** neatly and tidily

sau|ber ma|chen , **sau|ber+ma|chen** *sep* VT to clean

Sau|ber|mann M *pl* **-männer** *(fig inf)* decent and upstanding sort; *(in Politik etc)* Mr Clean *(inf)*, squeaky-clean man *(inf)*; **die Saubermänner** the squeaky-clean brigade *(inf)*

säu|bern [ˈzɔybɐn] VT **a** *(= reinigen)* to clean; **er säuberte seinen Anzug von den Blutflecken** he cleaned the bloodstains off his jacket; **das Wasser (von Verschmutzung) ~** to cleanse the water **b** *(fig euph) Partei, Buch* to purge *(von* of); *Saal* to clear *(von* of); *(Mil) Gegend* to clear *(von* of); **eine Region ethnisch ~** to ethnically cleanse a region

Säu|be|rung F **-, -en a** *(= Reinigung)* cleaning; *(von Wasser)* cleansing **b** *(fig: von Partei, Buch)* purging; *(von Gegend)* clearing; *(Pol: Aktion)* purge; **ethnische ~** ethnic cleansing

Säu|be|rungs|ak|ti|on F cleaning-up operation; *(Pol)* purge

Sau-: **sau|blöd, sau|blö|de** *(inf)* ADJ bloody *(Brit inf)* or damn *(inf)* stupid ADV **sich ~ anstellen** to behave like a bloody *(Brit sl)* or damn idiot *(inf)*; **~ fragen** to ask a damn stupid question *(inf)*; **Sau|boh|ne** F broad bean, horse bean

Sau|ce [ˈzoːsə] F **-, -n** sauce; *(= Bratensauce)* gravy

Sau|ci|e|re [zoˈsieːrə, zoˈsiɛːrə] F **-, -n** sauce boat

Sau|di [ˈzaudi, zaˈuːdi] M **-(s), -(s)** *or f* **-, -s** Saudi

Sau|di-: **Sau|di|ara|ber(in)** [ˈzaudiˈlarabɐ, ˈzaudilaˈraːbɐ] M(F) Saudi; **Sau|di-Ara|bi|en** [ˈzaudilaˈraːbiən] NT Saudi Arabia; **sau|di-ara|bisch** ADJ Saudi *attr*, Saudi Arabian

sau|disch ADJ Saudi *attr*, Saudi Arabian

sau|dumm *(inf)* ADJ damn stupid *(inf)* ADV **sich ~ benehmen** to behave like a stupid idiot *(inf)*; **~ fragen** to ask a damn stupid question *(inf)*

sau|en [ˈzauən] VI **a** *(= Ferkel bekommen)* to litter **b** *(inf: = Dreck machen)* to make a mess **c** *aux sein (S Ger inf: = rennen)* to run

sau|er [ˈzauɐ] ADJ **a** *(= nicht süß)* sour, sharp; *Wein* acid(ic); **saure Drops** acid drops → **aufstoßen, Apfel**
b *(= verdorben)* off *pred (Brit)*, bad; *Milch* sour, off *pred (Brit)*; *Geruch* sour, sickly; **~ werden** *(Milch, Sahne)* to go off *(Brit)* or sour, to turn (sour)
c *(= mit Säure zubereitet) Gurke, Hering* pickled; *Sahne* soured
d *(= sumpfig) Wiese, Boden* acidic
e *(Chem)* acid(ic); **saurer Regen** acid rain
f *(inf: = schlecht gelaunt) (auf +acc* with) mad *(inf)*, cross; **eine ~e Miene machen** to look sour or annoyed
g *(= unerfreulich)* **jdm das Leben ~ machen** to make sb's life a misery, to make life miserable for sb
ADV **a** *(= verdorben)* **es roch so ~** there was a sickly smell
b *(Cook)* **~ einlegen** to pickle
c *(Chem)* **~ reagieren** to react acidically
d *(= mühselig)* **das habe ich mir ~ erworben** I got that the hard way; **~ erworbenes Geld** hard-earned money; **mein ~ erspartes Geld** money I had painstakingly saved
e *(inf: = übel gelaunt)* **~ reagieren** to get annoyed; **~ antworten** to give a cross answer

Sau|er-: **Sau|er|amp|fer** M sorrel; **Sau|er|bra|ten** M braised beef (marinaded in vinegar), sauerbraten *(US)*; **Sau|er|brun|nen** M **a** *(= Heilquelle)* acidic spring **b** *(= Wasser)* acidic mineral water

Sau|e|rei [zauəˈrai] F **-, -en** *(inf)* **a** *(= Unflätigkeit)* **~en erzählen** to tell filthy stories; **eine einzige ~** a load of filth **b** *(= Gemeinheit)* **das ist eine ~!, so eine ~!** it's a bloody *(Brit inf)* or downright disgrace or scandal **c** *(= Dreck, Unordnung)* mess; **(eine) ~ machen** to make a mess

Sau|er-: **Sau|er|kir|sche** F sour cherry; **Sau|er|klee** M wood sorrel, oxalis; **Sau|er|kohl** M *(dial)*, **Sau|er|kraut** NT sauerkraut, pickled cabbage

säu|er|lich [ˈzɔyɐlɪç] ADJ *(lit, fig)* sour; *Wein auch* sharp; *Obst auch* sharp, tart ADV **a** *(Cook)* **~ schmecken** to taste a little sour **b** *(= übellaunig)* **~ reagieren** to get peeved *(inf)*; **~ antworten** to answer in a peeved tone

Säu|er|lich|keit F **-,** *no pl (lit, fig)* sourness

Säu|er|ling [ˈzɔyɐlɪŋ] M **-s, -e a** = **Sauerbrunnen b** *(Bot)* = **Sauerampfer**

sau|er+ma|chen VT *sep* → **sauer ADJ g**

Sau|er|milch F sour milk

säu|ern [ˈzɔyɐn] VT *Brot, Teig* to leaven; *Kohl, Gurken* to pickle; *Fisch* to put vinegar/lemon juice on VI to go or turn sour, to sour

Sau|er|rahm M thick sour(ed) cream

Sau|er|stoff M, *no pl (abbr* **O**) oxygen

Sau|er|stoff- *in cpds* oxygen; **Sau|er|stoff|ap|pa|rat** M breathing apparatus; **sau|er|stoff|arm** ADJ low in oxygen; *(zu wenig)* oxygen-deficient; **Sau|er|stoff|ent|zug** M *(Med)* oxygen deficiency; *(Chem)* deoxygenation; **Sau|er|stoff|fla|sche** F oxygen cylinder or *(kleiner)* bottle; **Sau|er|stoff|ge|halt** M oxygen content; **Sauer|stoff|ge|rät** NT breathing apparatus; *(Med) (für künstliche Beatmung)* respirator; *(für Erste Hilfe)* resuscitator; **sau|er|stoff|hal|tig** ADJ containing oxygen; **Sau|er|stoff|man|gel** M lack of oxygen; *(akut)* oxygen deficiency; **Sau|er|stoff|mas|ke** F oxygen mask; **Sau|er|stoff|pat|ro|ne** F oxygen cartridge; **Sau|er|stoff|zelt** NT oxygen tent; **Sau|er|stoff|zu|fuhr** F oxygen supply; **mittels ~** by supplying oxygen

Sau|er-: **sau|er|süß** ADJ, ADV = **süßsauer**; **Sau|er|teig** M sour dough; **Sau|er|topf** M *(old hum)* sourpuss *(inf)*; **sau|er|töp|fisch** [-tœpfɪʃ] ADJ *(old hum)* sour; *Mensch auch* sour-faced

Säu|e|rung F **-, -en** leavening

Sauf-: **Sauf|aus** [ˈzauflaus] M **-, -**, **Sauf|bold** [ˈzaufbɔlt] M **-(e)s, -e** [-də] *(old pej)* sot *(old)*, drunkard; **Sauf|bru|der** M *(pej inf) (= Kumpan)* drinking companion or buddy *(esp US inf)*; *(= Säufer)* soak *(inf)*, boozer *(inf)*

sau|fen [ˈzaufn] *pret* **soff** [zɔf], *ptp* **gesoffen** [gəˈzɔfn] VTI **a** *(Tiere)* to drink **b** *(inf: Mensch)* to booze *(inf)*, to drink; **das Saufen** boozing; **sich zu Tode ~** to drink oneself to death; **wie ein Loch** or **Bürstenbinder** *(dated)* **~** to drink like a fish

Säu|fer [ˈzɔyfɐ] M **-s, -**, **Säu|fe|rin** [-ərɪn] F **-, -nen** *(inf)* boozer *(inf)*, drunkard

Sau|fe|rei [zaufəˈrai] F **-, -en** *(inf)* **a** *(= Trinkgelage)* booze-up *(inf)* **b** *no pl (= Trunksucht)* boozing *(inf)*

Säu|fer-: **Säu|fer|le|ber** F *(inf)* gin-drinker's liver *(inf)*; **Säu|fer|na|se** F boozer's nose; **Säu|fer|wahn|(sinn)** M the DTs *pl (inf)*

Sauf-: **Sauf|ge|la|ge** NT *(pej inf)* drinking bout or binge, booze-up *(inf)*; **Sauf|kum|pan(in)** M(F), **Sauf|kum|pel** M *(pej inf)* drinking pal *(inf)*

säuft [zɔyft] *3. pers sing pres von* **saufen**

Sauf|tour F *(inf)* drinking binge *(inf)*, pub crawl *(esp Brit inf)*, bar hop *(US inf)*; **eine ~ machen** to go on a pub crawl *(esp Brit inf)* or bar hop *(US inf)*

Säug|am|me F *(old)* wet nurse

Saug|bag|ger M suction dredger

sau|gen [ˈzaugn] *pret* **sog** or **saugte** [zoːk, ˈzauktə], *ptp* **gesogen** or **gesaugt** [gəˈzoːgn, gəˈzaukt] VTI to suck; *(Pflanze, Schwamm)* to draw up, to absorb; *(inf: mit Staubsauger)* to vacuum; **an etw** *(dat)* **~** to suck sth; *an Pfeife* to draw on sth → **Finger**

säu|gen [ˈzɔygn] VT to suckle

Sau|ger [ˈzaugɐ] M **-s, - a** *(auf Flasche)* teat *(Brit)*, nipple *(US)*; *(= Schnuller)* dummy *(Brit)*, pacifier *(US)* **b** *(von Krake)* sucker **c** *(inf: = Staubsauger)* vacuum (cleaner)

Säu|ger [ˈzɔygɐ] M **-s, -**, **Säu|ge|tier** NT mammal

Saug-: **saug|fä|hig** ADJ absorbent; **Saug|fä|hig|keit** F absorbency; **Saug|fla|sche** F *(form)* feeding bottle; **Saug|glo|cke** F **a** *(Med)* vacuum extractor, ventouse *(spec)* **b** *(zur Abflussreinigung)* plunger; **Saug|glo|cken|ge|burt** F *(Med)* suction or ventouse *(spec)* delivery; **Saug|kraft** F suction (force)

Säug|ling [ˈzɔyklɪŋ] M **-s, -e** baby, infant *(form)*

Säug|lings- *in cpds* baby, infant *(form)*; **Säug|lings|al|ter** NT babyhood; **das Kind ist noch im ~** the child is still a baby; **Säug|lings|für|sor|ge** F infant welfare; **Säug|lings|heim** NT home for babies; **Säug|lings|nah|rung** F baby food(s *pl*); **Säug|lings|pfle|ge** F babycare; **Säug|lings|schwes|ter** F infant nurse; **Säug|lings|sta|ti|on** F neonatal care unit; **Säug|lings|sterb|lich|keit** F infant mortality

Saug-: **Saug|mas|sa|ge** F suction or vacuum massage; **Saug|napf** M sucker; **Saug|or|gan**

NT suctorial organ *(form)*; **Saug|pum|pe** F suction pump; *(für Brust)* breast pump; **Saug|re|flex** M sucking reflex; **Saug|rohr** NT, **Saug|röhr|chen** NT pipette; **Saug|rüs|sel** M **a** *(Zool)* proboscis **b** *(an Tanksäule) flexible tube fitted around pump nozzle for drawing off fumes*; **Saug|wurm** M trematode *(spec)*

Sau-: **Sau|hatz** F *(Hunt)* wild boar hunt; **Sau|hau|fen** M *(inf)* bunch of layabouts *(Brit inf)* *or* slobs; **Sau|hirt(in)** M(F) *(old)* swineherd *(old)*;; **Sau|hund** M *(dated sl)* bastard *(sl)*; **Sau|jagd** F wild boar hunt; **sau|kalt** ADJ *(inf)* bloody *(Brit inf)* *or* damn *(inf)* cold; **Sau|käl|te** F *(inf)* bloody *(Brit inf)* *or* damn *(inf)* freezing weather; **Sau|kerl** M *(inf)* bastard *(sl)*; **Sau|klaue** F *(inf)* scrawl *(inf)*

Säu|le ['zɔylə] F -, -n column; (= *Rauchsäule, Wassersäule auch, inf:* = *Pfeiler, fig:* = *Stütze*) pillar; **ei|ne/die tragende ~ sein** *(fig)* to be a/the mainstay; **die ~n des Herkules** the Pillars of Hercules

Säu|len-: **Säu|len|ab|schluss** M capital; **Säu|len|bau** M *pl* **-bauten** building with columns; **Säu|len|dia|gramm** NT bar chart; **säu|len|för|mig** ADJ like a column/columns, columnar *(form)*; **Säu|len|fuß** M base; **Säu|len|gang** M *pl* **-gänge** colonnade; *(um einen Hof)* peristyle; **Säu|len|hal|le** F columned hall; **Säu|len|hei|li|ge(r)** MF *decl as adj* stylite; **Säu|len|ord|nung** F order (of columns); **die dorische ~** the Doric Order; **Säu|len|por|tal** NT colonnaded doorway; **Säu|len|rei|he** F row of columns; **Säu|len|schaft** M shaft of a column; **Säu|len|tem|pel** M colonnaded temple

Sau|lus ['zaulʊs] M -' *(Bibl)* Saul; **vom ~ zum Paulus werden** *(fig)* to have seen the light

Saum [zaum] M -(e)s, **Säume** ['zɔymə] (= *Stoffumschlag*) hem; (= *Naht*) seam; *(fig:* = *Waldsaum etc)* edge; **ein schmaler ~ am Horizont** a thin band of cloud *(Brit)* *or* clouds *(US)* on the horizon

sau|mä|ßig ['zaumɛːsɪç] *(inf)* ADJ lousy *(inf)*; *(zur Verstärkung)* hell of a *(inf)* ADV lousily *(inf)*; *(zur Verstärkung)* damn *(inf)*; **das hat er ~ gemacht** he made a real mess of it

säu|men ['zɔymən] VT *(Sew)* to hem; *(fig geh)* to line

säu|men VI *(liter)* to tarry *(liter)*

säu|mig ['zɔymɪç] ADJ *(geh) Schuldner* defaulting; *Zahlung* late, overdue; *Schüler* dilatory; **~ sein/bleiben/werden** to be/remain/get behind

Säum|nis ['zɔymnɪs] F -, -se *(obs)* delay

Säum|nis|ge|bühr F, **Säum|nis|zu|schlag** M late payment charge, extra charge (for late payment)

Saum-: **Saum|pfad** M mule track; **saum|se|lig** ['zaumzeːlɪç] ADJ *(old liter)* dilatory; **Saum|se|lig|keit** F *(old liter)* dilatoriness; **Saum|stich** M hemstitch; **Saum|tier** NT pack animal

Sau|na ['zauna] F -, -s *or* **Saunen** [-nən] sauna

sau|nie|ren [zau'niːrən] *ptp* **sauniert** VI to have a sauna

Sau|pack NT *(pej inf)* scum *(pej inf)*

Sau|preu|ße M, **Sau|preu|ßin** F *(S Ger inf)* Prussian swine

Säu|re ['zɔyrə] F -, -n **a** (= *Magensäure, auch Chem*) acid **b** (= *saurer Geschmack*) sourness; *(von Wein, Bonbons)* acidity, sharpness; *(von Obst)* sharpness; **dieser Wein hat zu viel ~** this wine is too sharp

Säu|re-: **säu|re|arm** ADJ low in acid; **Säu|re|bad** NT acid bath; **säu|re|be|stän|dig**, **säu|re|fest** ADJ acid-resistant; **säu|re|frei** ADJ acid-free; **Säu|re|ge|halt** M acid content

Sau|re|gur|ken|zeit F bad time *or* period; *(in den Medien)* silly season *(Brit)*, off season *(US)*

Säu|re-: **säu|re|hal|tig** ADJ acidic; **säu|re|lös|lich** ADJ acid-soluble

Sau|re(s) ['zaurə] NT *decl as adj* **gib ihm ~s!** *(inf)* let him have it! *(inf)*

Säu|re|schutz|man|tel M *(von Haut)* hydrolipidic film *(spec)*

Säu|re|ver|gif|tung F acid poisoning

Säu|re|zün|der M acid fuse

Sau|ri|er ['zaurie] M -s, - dinosaur, saurian *(spec)*

Saus [zaus] M **in ~ und Braus leben** to live like a lord *(Brit)* *or* king

Sau|se ['zauzə] F -, -n *(inf)* **a** (= *Party*) bash *(inf)* **b** (= *Kneipentour*) pub crawl *(esp Brit inf)*, bar hop *(US inf)*; **eine ~ machen** to go on a pub crawl *(esp Brit inf)* *or* bar hop *(US inf)*

säu|seln ['zɔyzln] VI *(Wind)* to murmur, to sigh; *(Blätter)* to rustle; *(Mensch)* to purr; **mit ~der Stimme** in a purring voice VT to murmur, to purr; *Worte* to murmur

sau|sen ['zauzn] VI **a** *(Ohren, Kopf)* to buzz; *(Wind)* to whistle; *(Sturm)* to roar; **ihr sauste das Blut in den Ohren** *(geh)* the blood pounded in her ears; **mir ~ die Ohren, es saust mir in den Ohren** my ears are buzzing **b** *aux sein (Geschoss, Peitsche)* to whistle **c** *aux sein (inf: Mensch)* to tear *(inf)*, to charge *(inf)*; *(Fahrzeug)* to roar; *(Schlitten, Gegenstand)* to hurtle; **saus mal schnell zum Bäcker** nip round *(Brit)* *or* run round to the baker's; **in den Graben ~** to fly into the ditch

sau|sen las|sen *ptp* **sausen lassen** *or (rare)* **sausen gelassen** *irreg*, **sau|sen+las|sen** *ptp* **sausenlassen** *or (rare)* **sausengelassen** *sep irreg* VT *(inf)* **a** **jdn ~** to drop sb; **etw ~** to let sth go; *Termin* to skip sth; **die Party heute Abend lass ich sausen** I'll not bother going to the party tonight **b** **einen ~** *(inf)* to let off *(inf)*

Sau|ser ['zauze] M -s, - *(S Ger)* fermented apple/grape juice

Sau|se|wind M **a** *(dated inf) (lebhaft)* live wire *(inf)*; *(unstet)* restless person; **wie ein ~** (= *sehr schnell*) like a whirlwind **b** *(baby-talk:* = *Wind)* wind

Sau-: **Sau|stall** M *(inf) (unordentlich)* pigsty *(inf)*; *(chaotisch)* mess; **sau|teu|er** ADJ *(inf)* incredibly expensive

sau|tie|ren [zo'tiːrən] *ptp* **sautiert** VT *(Cook)* to sauté

Sau-: **Sau|wet|ter** NT *(inf)* bloody *(Brit inf)* *or* damn *(inf)* awful weather; **sau|wohl** ADJ *pred (inf)* bloody *(Brit inf)* *or* really good; **mir ist ~, ich fühle mich ~** I feel bloody *(Brit inf)* *or* really good; **Sau|wut** F *(inf)* absolute rage *(inf)*; **eine ~ (im Bauch) haben** to be flaming mad; **eine ~ auf jdn/etw haben** to be flaming mad at sb/sth

Sa|van|ne [za'vanə] F -, -n savanna(h)

sa|ven ['seːvn] VTI *(Comput inf)* to save

Sa|voy|en [za'vɔyən] NT -s Savoy

Sa|xo|fon [zakso'foːn, 'zaksofoːn] NT -(e)s, -e saxophone, sax *(inf)*

Sa|xo|fo|nist [zaksofo'nɪst] M -en, -en, **Sa|xo|fo|nis|tin** [-'nɪstɪn] F -, -nen saxophone player, saxophonist

Sa|xo|phon [zakso'foːn, 'zaksofoːn] *etc* = **Saxofon** *etc*

SB- [ɛs'beː] *in cpds* self-service

S-Bahn ['ɛs-] F *abbr von* **Schnellbahn, Stadtbahn**

S-Bahn|hof ['ɛs-] M suburban line station

S-Bahn-Li|nie ['ɛs-] F suburban rail line

S-Bahn-Netz ['ɛs-] NT suburban rail network

SBB [ɛsbeː'beː] F - *abbr von* **Schweizerische Bundesbahn**

s. Br. *abbr von* **südlicher Breite**

SB-: **SB-Tank|stelle** F self-service petrol *(Brit)* *or* gas *(US)* station; **SB-Wa|ren|haus** NT superstore, hypermarket *(Brit)*

Scam|pi ['skampi] PL scampi *pl*

scan|nen ['skɛnən] VT to scan

Scan|ner ['skɛne] M -s, - *(Med, Comput)* scanner

Scan|ner-Kas|se ['skɛnɐ-] F, **Scan|ner|kas|se** F electronic scanning cash register

sch [ʃ] INTERJ shh; *(zum Fortscheuchen)* shoo

Scha|bau [ʃa'bau] M -s, -s *(dial)* spirits *pl*

Scha|be ['ʃaːbə] F -, -n cockroach

Scha|be|fleisch NT *(Cook dial)* minced steak *(Brit)*, ground beef *(US)* *(often eaten raw)*

Scha|be|mes|ser NT scraping knife, scraper

scha|ben ['ʃaːbn] VT to scrape; *Fleisch* to chop finely; *Leder, Fell* to shave

Scha|ber ['ʃaːbɐ] M -s, - scraper

Scha|ber|nack ['ʃaːbɐnak] M -(e)s, -e **a** prank, practical joke; **jdm einen ~ spielen, mit jdm einen ~ treiben** to play a prank on sb; **allerlei ~ treiben** to get up to all sorts of pranks; **ich bin zu jedem ~ bereit** I'm always ready for a laugh **b** *(Kind)* monkey *(inf)*

schä|big ['ʃɛːbɪç] ADJ **a** (= *unansehnlich*) *Wohnung, Teppich, Aussehen* shabby **b** (= *niederträchtig*) mean, shabby; (= *geizig*) mean, stingy; *Bezahlung* poor, shabby ADV **a** (= *unansehnlich*) shabbily; **~ aussehen** to look shabby **b** (= *gemein*) **jdn ~ behandeln** to treat sb shabbily **c** (= *dürftig*) *bezahlen* poorly

Schä|big|keit F -, -en **a** (= *Unansehnlichkeit*) shabbiness **b** (= *Niederträchtigkeit*) meanness, shabbiness; *(Verhalten)* mean *or* shabby behaviour *(Brit)* *or* behavior *(US)* *no pl*

Schab|lo|ne [ʃa'bloːnə] F -, -n **a** stencil; (= *Muster*) template; *(Comput)* template **b** *(fig pej) (bei Arbeit, Arbeitsweise)* routine, pattern; *(beim Reden)* cliché; **in ~n denken** to think in a stereotyped way; **in ~n reden** to speak in clichés; **nicht in die ~ passen** not to fit the stereotype; **etw in ~n pressen** to stereotype sth; **etw geht nach ~** sth follows the same routine; **der Präsident lächelte, aber das war reine ~** the President smiled but it was just a matter of convention; **das ist alles nur ~** that's all just for show

schab|lo|nen|haft ADJ *(pej) Denken, Vorstellungen, Argumente* stereotyped; *Ausdrucksweise* clichéd ADV in stereotypes/clichés

Schab|mes|ser NT scraping knife, scraper

Schab|ra|cke [ʃa'brakə] F -, -n **a** (= *Satteldecke*) saddlecloth **b** (= *altes Pferd*) nag **c** (= *Querbehang*) pelmet

Schab|sel ['ʃaːpsl] PL shavings *pl*

Schach [ʃax] NT -s, *no pl* chess; (= *Stellung im Spiel*) check; **kannst du ~ (spielen)?** can you play chess?; **~ (dem König)!** check; **~ (und) matt** checkmate; **im ~ stehen** *or* **sein** to be in check; **jdm ~ bieten** *(lit)* to put sb in check, to check sb; *(fig)* to thwart sb; **jdn in ~ halten** *(fig)* to keep sb in check; *(mit Pistole etc)* to cover sb, to keep sb covered

Schach-: **Schach|auf|ga|be** F chess problem; **Schach|brett** NT chessboard; **schach|brett|ar|tig** ADJ chequered *(Brit)*, checkered *(US)* ADV **Platten ~ anlegen** to lay tiles in a chequered *(Brit)* *or* checkered *(US)* pattern *or* like a chessboard; **die Straßen sind ~ angeordnet** the roads are laid out like a grid; **~ gemustert** chequered *(Brit)*, checkered *(US)*; **Schach|brett|mus|ter** NT chequered *(Brit)* *or* checkered *(US)* pattern; **Schach|com|pu|ter** M chess computer

Scha|cher ['ʃaxɐ] M -s, *no pl (pej)* (= *das Feilschen*) haggling *(um* over *or* about); (= *Wucher*) sharp practice; *(fig Pol)* haggling *(um* over *or* about), horse trading *(um* over *or* about); **~ treiben** to indulge in haggling *etc*

Schä|cher ['ʃɛçɐ] M -s, - *(Bibl)* thief

Scha|che|rei [ʃaxə'rai] F -, -en *(pej)* = **Schacher**

Scha|che|rer [ʃaxərɐ] M -s, -, **Scha|che|rin** [-ərɪn] F -, -nen *(pej)* haggler; (= *Wucherer*) sharper; *(Pol)* horse trader

scha|chern ['ʃaxɐn] VI *(pej)* **um etw ~** to haggle over sth

Schach-: **Schach|er|öff|nung** F chess opening; **Schach|feld** NT square (on a chessboard); **Schach|fi|gur** F chesspiece, chessman; *(fig)* pawn; **Schach|groß|meis|ter(in)** M(F) chess grandmaster; **schach|matt** ADJ *(lit)* (check)mated; *(fig:* = *erschöpft*) exhausted, shattered *(Brit inf)*; **~!** (check)mate; **jdn ~ setzen** *(lit)* to (check)mate sb; *(fig)* to snooker sb *(inf)*; **Schach|par|tie** F game of chess; **Schach|prob|lem** NT chess problem; **Schach|spiel** NT (= *Spiel*) game of chess; (= *Spielart*) chess *no art*; (= *Brett und Figuren*) chess set; **Schach|spie|ler(in)** M(F) chess player

Schacht [ʃaxt] M -(e)s, ¨-e [ˈʃɛçtə] shaft; *(= Brunnenschacht)* well; *(= Straßenschacht)* manhole; *(= Kanalisationsschacht)* drain; *(Comput: von Laufwerk)* bay, slot; *(= Druckerschacht)* tray

Schach|tel [ˈʃaxtl] F -, -n **a** box; *(= Zigarettenschachtel)* packet; **eine ~ Streichhölzer/Pralinen** a box of matches/chocolates **b** *(inf: = Frau)* **alte ~** old bag *(inf)* **c** *(Fin: auch* **Schachtelbeteiligung***)* participation in an affiliated company *(minimum of 25%)*

Schach|tel-: **Schach|tel|halm** M *(Bot)* horsetail; **Schach|tel|satz** M complicated *or* multi-clause sentence

schäch|ten [ˈʃɛçtn] VT to slaughter according to religious rites; **das rituelle Schächten von Tieren** the ritual slaughter of animals

Schach-: **Schach|tur|nier** NT chess tournament; **Schach|uhr** F chess clock; **Schach|zug** M *(fig)* move

scha|de [ˈʃaːdə] ✪ 45.3 ADJ *pred* **(das ist aber) ~!** what a pity *or* shame; **es ist (zu) ~, dass ...** it's a (real) pity *or* shame that ...; **es ist ~ um jdn/etw** it's a pity *or* shame about sb/sth; **um ihn ist es nicht ~** he's no great loss; **für etw zu ~ sein** to be too good for sth; **sich** *(dat)* **für etw zu ~ sein** to consider oneself too good for sth; **sich** *(dat)* **für nichts zu ~ sein** to consider nothing (to be) beneath one

Scha|de [ˈʃaːdə] M *(old)* **es soll dein ~ nicht sein** it will not be to your disadvantage

Schä|del [ˈʃɛːdl] M -s, - skull; **ein kahler ~** a bald head; **jdm den ~ einschlagen** to beat sb's skull *or* head in; **jdm den ~ spalten/zertrümmern** to split *or* cleave/crush sb's skull; **sich** *(dat)* **den ~ einrennen** *(inf)* to crack one's skull; **mir brummt der ~** *(inf)* my head is going round and round; *(vor Kopfschmerzen)* my head is throbbing; **einen dicken ~ haben** *(fig inf)* to be stubborn

Schä|del-: **Schä|del|ba|sis|bruch** M fracture at the base of the skull; **Schä|del|bruch** M fractured skull; **Schä|del|de|cke** F top of the skull; **Schä|del-Hirn-Trau|ma** NT *(Med)* head trauma; **Schä|del|la|ge** F vertex presentation; **Schä|del|naht** F suture

scha|den [ˈʃaːdn] VI +*dat* to damage, to harm; *einem Menschen* to harm, to hurt; *jds Ruf* to damage; **das/Rauchen schadet Ihrer Gesundheit/Ihnen** that/smoking is bad for your health/you; **das schadet nichts** it does no harm; *(= macht nichts)* that doesn't matter; **das kann nicht(s) ~** that won't do any harm, it wouldn't hurt; **es kann nicht(s) ~, wenn ...** it would do no harm if ...; **das schadet dir gar nichts** it serves you right; **was schadet es, wenn ...?** what harm can it do if ...?; **mehr ~ als nützen** to do more harm than good VR **sich** *(dat)* **selbst ~** to harm *or* hurt oneself, to do oneself harm

Scha|den [ˈʃaːdn] M -s, ¨- [ˈʃɛːdn] **a** *(= Beschädigung, Zerstörung)* damage *no pl, no indef art* (*durch* caused by, *an +dat* to); *(= Personenschaden)* injury; *(= Verlust)* loss; *(= Unheil, Leid)* harm; **einen ~ verursachen, ~/Schäden anrichten** to cause damage; **den ~ begrenzen** to limit the damage; **ich habe einen ~ am Auto** my car has been damaged; **zu jds ~ gereichen** *(geh)* to be to sb's detriment; **es soll sein ~ nicht sein** it will not be to his disadvantage; **es ist nicht zu deinem ~** it won't do you any harm; **den ~ von etw haben** to suffer for sth; **zu ~ kommen** to suffer; *(physisch)* to be hurt *or* injured; **nicht zu ~ kommen** not to come to any harm; **an etw** *(dat)* **~ nehmen** to damage *or* harm sth; **jdm ~ zufügen** to harm sb; **einer Sache** *(dat)* **~ zufügen** to harm *or* damage sth; **geringe/einige Schäden aufweisen** to have suffered little/some damage; **aus** *or* **durch ~ wird man klug** *(Prov)* you learn by *or* from your mistakes; **wer den ~ hat, braucht für den Spott nicht zu sorgen** *(Prov)* don't mock the afflicted **b** *(= Defekt)* fault; *(= körperlicher Mangel)* defect; **Schäden an der Lunge** lung damage; **Schäden aufweisen** to be defective; *(Organ)* to be damaged; **ein ~ an der Leber** a damaged liver; **du hast wohl 'nen ~!** *(inf)* you're not quite right in the head! *(inf)*

Scha|den-: **Scha|den|er|satz** M = **Schadensersatz**; **Scha|den|fall** M = **Schadensfall**; **Scha|den|fest|stel|lung** F assessment of damage; **Scha|den|frei|heits|ra|batt** M no-claims bonus; **Scha|den|freu|de** F malicious joy, gloating; **... sagte er mit einer gewissen ~** ... he gloated; **scha|den|froh** ADJ gloating ADV with malicious delight; *sagen* gloatingly

Scha|dens-: **Scha|dens|be|gren|zung** F damage limitation; **Scha|dens|bi|lanz** F total damage *or* loss

Scha|dens|er|satz M damages *pl*, compensation; **jdn auf ~ verklagen** to sue sb for damages *or* compensation; **~ leisten** to pay damages *or* compensation

Scha|dens|er|satz-: **Scha|dens|er|satz|an|spruch** M claim for damages *or* compensation; **Scha|dens|er|satz|kla|ge** F action for damages *or* compensation; **scha|dens|er|satz|pflich|tig** [-pflɪçtɪç] ADJ liable for damages *or* compensation

Scha|dens-: **Scha|dens|fall** M *(Insur)* case of damage; **im ~** in the event of damage; **Scha|dens|hö|he** F amount of damages; **Scha|dens|re|gu|lie|rung** F settlement of damages; **Scha|dens|sum|me** amount of damages

schad|haft ADJ *no adv* faulty, defective; *(= beschädigt)* damaged; *(= abgenutzt) Kleidung* worn; *Zähne* decayed; *Gebäude* dilapidated

schä|di|gen [ˈʃɛːdɪgn] VT to damage; *Gesundheit, Umwelt auch* to harm; *jdn* to hurt, to harm; *Firma, Ansehen* to damage, to hurt; **man muss die Firma ~, wo man nur kann** *(iro)* you've got to get what you can out of the firm

Schä|di|gung F -, -en (+*gen* done to) damage; *(von Menschen)* hurt, harm

schäd|lich [ˈʃɛːtlɪç] ADJ harmful; *Wirkung, Einflüsse* detrimental, damaging; **~ für etw sein** to be damaging to sth; **~es Tier** pest

Schäd|lich|keit F -, *no pl* harmfulness

Schäd|ling [ˈʃɛːtlɪŋ] M -s, -e pest

Schäd|lings-: **Schäd|lings|be|fall** M (pest) infestation; **Schäd|lings|be|kämp|fung** F pest control *no art*; **Schäd|lings|be|kämp|fungs|mit|tel** NT pesticide

schad|los ADJ **a sich an jdm/etw ~ halten** to take advantage of sb/sth; **wir halten uns dafür am Bier ~** *(hum)* ... but we'll make up for it on the beer **b** *(= keine Schäden verursachend) Müllbeseitigung etc* without damage to the environment; **etw ~ überstehen** to survive sth unharmed

Scha|dor [ʃaˈdoːɐ] M -s, -s *(= Schleier)* chador

Schad|soft|ware F -, *no pl (Comput)* malware

Schad|stoff M harmful substance

Schad|stoff-: **schad|stoff|arm** ADJ **~ sein** to contain a low level of harmful substances; **ein ~es Auto** a clean-air car; **Schad|stoff|aus|stoß** M noxious emission; *(von Auto)* exhaust emission; **schad|stoff|be|las|tet** ADJ polluted, pollutant-bearing *or* -laden; **Schad|stoff|be|las|tung** F *(von Umwelt)* pollution; **Schad|stoff|ge|halt** M level of harmful substances (+*gen* in); *(der Luft)* pollution content (+*gen* of); **Schad|stoff|kon|zent|ra|ti|on** F concentration of harmful substances; **Schad|stoff|re|du|zie|rung** F reduction *or* limitation of harmful substances

Schaf [ʃaːf] NT -(e)s, -e sheep; *(inf: = Dummkopf)* twit *(Brit inf)*, dope *(inf)*; **das schwarze ~ sein** to be the black sheep (*in +dat, gen* of); **~e zählen** *(fig)* to count sheep → **Bock¹ a**

Schaf|bock M ram

Schäf|chen [ˈʃɛːfçən] NT -s, - lamb, little sheep; *(inf: = Dummerchen)* silly-billy *(inf)*; **~** *pl (= Gemeinde, Anvertraute)* flock *sing*; **sein ~ ins Trockene bringen** *(prov)* to look after *or* take care of number one *(inf)*; **sein ~ im Trockenen haben** to have looked after *or* taken care of number one *(inf)*

Schäf|chen|wol|ken PL cotton wool clouds *pl*, fleecy clouds *pl*

Schä|fer [ˈʃɛːfɐ] M -s, - shepherd

Schä|fer|dich|tung F *(Liter)* pastoral poetry

Schä|fe|rei [ʃɛːfəˈrai] F -, -en **a** *(= Schafhaltung)* sheep rearing, sheep farming **b** *(Betrieb)* sheep farm

Schä|fer|hund M Alsatian (dog) *(Brit)*, German shepherd (dog) *(US)*

Schä|fe|rin [ˈʃɛːfərɪn] F -, -nen shepherdess

Schä|fer-: **Schä|fer|ro|man** M *(Liter)* pastoral novel; **Schä|fer|stünd|chen** NT *(euph hum)* bit of hanky-panky *(hum inf)*

Schaf|fell NT sheepskin

schaf|fen¹ [ˈʃafn] *pret* **schuf** [ʃuːf], *ptp* **geschaffen** [gəˈʃafn] VT **a** *(= hervorbringen)* to create; **die ~de Natur** the creative power of nature; **der ~de Mensch** the creative human being; **dafür ist er wie geschaffen** he's just made for it; **wie ihn Gott geschaffen hatte** as God made him **b** *pret auch* **schaffte** *(= herstellen)* to make; [ˈʃaftə] *Bedingungen, Möglichkeiten, System, Methode, Arbeitsplätze* to create; *(= verursachen) Ärger, Unruhe, Verdruss* to cause, to create; **Raum** *or* **Platz ~** to make room; **Probleme ~** to create problems; **Ruhe ~** to establish order; **Klarheit ~** to provide clarification; **Linderung ~** to bring relief *(für* to) → **Blut**

schaf|fen² VT **a** *(= bewältigen, zustande bringen) Aufgabe, Hürde, Portion etc* to manage; *Prüfung* to pass; **~ wir das zeitlich?** are we going to make it?; **schaffst dus noch?** *(inf)* can you manage?; **wir habens geschafft** we've managed it; *(= Arbeit erledigt)* we've done it; *(= gut angekommen)* we've made it; **so, das hätten wir** *or* **das wäre geschafft!** there, that's done; **das ist nicht zu ~** that can't be done; **das hast du wieder mal geschafft** you've done it again; **wir haben nicht viel geschafft** we haven't managed to do much *or* haven't got much done; **er schafft es noch, dass ich ihn rauswerfe/er rausgeworfen wird** he'll end up with me throwing him out/(by) being thrown out **b** *(inf: = überwältigen) jdn* to see off *(inf)*; **das hat mich geschafft** it took it out of me; *(nervlich)* it got on top of me; **geschafft sein** to be shattered *(Brit inf) or* exhausted **c** *(= bringen)* **etw in etw** *(acc)* **~** to put sth in sth; **wie sollen wir das in den Keller/auf den Berg ~?** how will we manage to get that into the cellar/up the mountain?; **etw aus etw ~** to get sth out of sth; **einen Koffer zum Bahnhof ~** to take a (suit)case to the station; **alte Zeitungen auf den Boden ~** to put old newspapers in the attic; **etw aus der Welt ~** to settle sth (for good); **sich** *(dat)* **jdn/etw vom Hals(e)** *or* **Leib(e) ~** to get sb/sth off one's back → **beiseiteschaffen**

VI **a** *(= tun)* to do; **ich habe damit nichts zu ~** that has nothing to do with me; **ich habe nichts mit ihm zu ~** I don't have anything to do with him; **was haben Sie dort zu ~?** what do you think you're doing (there)?; **sich** *(dat)* **an etw** *(dat)* **zu ~ machen** to fiddle about with sth; **sich mit etw zu ~ machen** to busy oneself with sth **b** *(= zusetzen)* **jdm (sehr** *or* **schwer) zu ~ machen** to cause sb (a lot of) trouble; *(= bekümmern)* to worry sb (a lot); **das macht ihr heute noch zu ~** she still worries about it today **c** *(S Ger: = arbeiten)* to work

Schaf|fen NT -s, *no pl* **die Freude am ~** the joy of creation; **sein musikalisches/künstlerisches ~** his musical/artistic works *pl or* creations *pl*; **der Künstler bei seinem ~** the artist at work; **auf dem Höhepunkt seines ~s** at the peak of his creative powers *or* prowess

Schaf|fens-: **Schaf|fens|drang** M energy; *(von Künstler)* creative urge; **Schaf|fens|freu|de** F (creative) zest *or* enthusiasm; **schaf|fens|freu|dig** ADJ (creatively) enthusiastic; *Künstler* creative; **Schaf|fens|kraft** F creativity

Schaf|fer [ˈʃafɐ] M -s, -, **Schaf|fe|rin** [-ərɪn] F -, -nen (inf) hard worker

Schaff|hau|sen [ʃafˈhauzn] NT -s (Kanton, Stadt) Schaffhausen

Schaf|fleisch NT mutton

Schaff|ner [ˈʃafnɐ] M -s, -, **Schaff|ne|rin** [-ərɪn] F -, -nen **a** (im Bus) conductor/conductress; (Rail) ticket collector; (im Zug) guard (Brit), conductor (US); (im Schlafwagen) attendant; (= Fahrkartenkontrolleur) ticket inspector **b** (old: = Verwalter) steward, estate manager

Schaf|fung [ˈʃafʊŋ] F -, -en creation

Schaf- → auch **Schafs-**: **Schaf|gar|be** F yarrow; **Schaf|her|de** F flock of sheep; **Schaf|hirt** M shepherd; **Schaf|hir|tin** F shepherdess; **Schaf|hür|de** F sheep pen, (sheep)fold; **Schaf|kopf** M, no pl = **Schafskopf b**

Schäf|lein [ˈʃɛːflain] NT -s, - (lit, fig) lamb; (pl fig) flock *sing or pl*

Scha|fott [ʃaˈfɔt] NT -(e)s, -e scaffold

Schaf-: **Schaf|pelz** M sheepskin; **Schaf|sche|rer** [-ʃeːrɐ] M -s, -, **Schaf|sche|re|rin** [-ərɪn] F -, -nen sheepshearer; **Schaf|schur** F sheepshearing

Schafs-: **Schafs|kä|se** M sheep's milk cheese; **Schafs|kopf** M **a** sheep's head; (pej: = Dummkopf) blockhead, dolt, numskull **b** no pl (Cards) *German card game, a simplified version of skat*; **Schafs|milch** F sheep's milk; **Schafs|pelz** M sheepskin → **Wolf**

Schaf|stall M sheepfold

Schaft [ʃaft] M -(e)s, ⸚e [ˈʃɛftə] **a** shaft (auch *Archit*); (von Gewehr) stock; (von Stiefel) leg; (von Schraube, Schlüssel) shank; (Bot) stalk **b** (Sw, S Ger) (= Regal) shelves pl; (= Schrank) cupboard

Schaft|stie|fel PL high boots pl; (Mil) jackboots pl

Schaf-: **Schaf|wei|de** F sheep pasture; **Schaf|wol|le** F sheep's wool; **Schaf|zucht** F sheep breeding *no art*

Schah [ʃaː] M -s, -s Shah

Scha|kal [ʃaˈkaːl] M -s, -e jackal

Schä|ker [ˈʃɛːkɐ] M -s, - (inf) flirt; (= Witzbold) joker

Schä|ke|rei [ʃɛːkəˈrai] F -, -en (inf) flirting; (= Witzelei) fooling around

Schä|ke|rin [ˈʃɛːkərɪn] F -, -nen (inf) flirt, coquette; (= Witzbold) joker

schä|kern [ˈʃɛːkɐn] VI to flirt; (= necken) to play about

schal [ʃaːl] ADJ Getränk flat; Wasser, Geschmack stale; (fig: = geistlos) Witz weak; Leben empty; Gerede vapid, empty

Schal [ʃaːl] M -s, -s or -e scarf; (= Umschlagtuch) shawl

Schäl|chen [ˈʃɛːlçən] NT -s, - dim von **Schale** (small) bowl

Scha|le [ˈʃaːlə] F -, -n bowl; (flach, zum Servieren etc) dish; (von Waage) pan; (= Sektschale) champagne glass; (esp S Ger, Aus: = Tasse) cup

Scha|le F -, -n (von Obst, Gemüse) skin; (abgeschält) peel *no pl*; (= Rinde) (von Käse) rind; (von Nuss, Ei, Muschel, Krebs) shell; (von Getreide) husk, hull; (Hunt) hoof; (fig: = äußeres Auftreten) appearance; **sich in ~ werfen** or **schmeißen** (inf) to get dressed up; (Frau auch) to get dolled up (inf); **in seiner rauen ~ steckt ein guter Kern** beneath that rough exterior (there) beats a heart of gold (prov)

schä|len [ˈʃɛːlən] **VT** to peel; Tomate, Mandel to skin; Erbsen, Eier, Nüsse to shell; Getreide to husk **VR** to peel; **sich aus den Kleidern ~** to peel off (one's clothes); **ich schäle mich auf der Nase** my nose is peeling

Scha|len-: **Scha|len|obst** NT nuts pl; **Scha|len|ses|sel** M shell chair; **Scha|len|sitz** M bucket seat; **Scha|len|tier** NT shellfish; **~e** shellfish pl; **Scha|len|wild** NT hoofed game

Schal|heit F -, no pl (von Getränk) flatness; (von Wasser, Geschmack) staleness

Schal|holz NT shuttering wood

Schalk [ʃalk] M -(e)s, -e or ⸚e [ˈʃɛlkə] joker; **ihm sitzt der ~ im Nacken** he's in a devilish mood; **ihr schaut der ~ aus den Augen** she (always) has a roguish *or* mischievous look on her face

schalk|haft ADJ roguish, mischievous ADV roguishly, mischievously

Schalk|haf|tig|keit [ˈʃalkhaftɪçkait] F -, no pl roguishness, mischievousness

Schal|kra|gen M shawl collar; (mit losen Enden) scarf collar

Schall [ʃal] M -s, -e or ⸚e [ˈʃɛlə] sound; **Ruhm vergeht wie ~ und Rauch** (geh) fame is but a transient shadow; **Name ist ~ und Rauch** (Prov) what's in a name?; **das ist alles ~ und Rauch** it's all hollow words

Schall-: **Schall|be|cher** M (Mus) bell; **Schall|bo|den** M sound(ing) board; **schall|däm|men** VT to soundproof; **schall|däm|mend** ADJ sound-deadening; **Schall|däm|mung** F sound absorption; (= Abdichtung gegen Schall) soundproofing; **schall|dämp|fend** ADJ Wirkung sound-muffling, sound-deadening; Material soundproofing; **Schall|dämp|fer** M sound absorber; (von Auto) silencer (Brit), muffler (US); (von Gewehr etc) silencer; (Mus) mute; **Schall|dämp|fung** F sound absorption; (= Abdichtung gegen Schall) soundproofing; (von Auto etc) silencing; **schall|dicht** ADJ soundproof ADV **~ abgeschlossen sein** to be fully soundproofed

Schalleiter △ M → **Schallleiter**

schal|len [ˈʃalən] VI to sound [ˈʃaltə, ʃɔl]; (Stimme, Glocke, Beifall) to ring (out) [gəˈʃalt, gəˈʃɔlən]; (= widerhallen) to resound, to echo; **das Schlagen der Turmuhr schallte zu uns herüber** we could hear the church clock ring out

schal|lend ADJ Beifall, Ohrfeige resounding; Gelächter ringing ADV **~ lachen** to roar with laughter; **jdn ~ ohrfeigen** to give sb a resounding slap

Schall-: **Schall|ge|schwin|dig|keit** F speed of sound; **Schall|gren|ze** F sound barrier; **Schall|lei|ter** M conductor of sound; **Schall|mau|er** F sound barrier; **Schall|mes|sung** F sound ranging

Schall|plat|te F record

Schall|plat|ten-: **Schall|plat|ten|al|bum** NT record case; **Schall|plat|ten|ar|chiv** NT (gramophone) record archive; **Schall|plat|ten|auf|nah|me** F (gramophone) recording

Schall-: **schall|schlu|ckend** ADJ sound-absorbent; Material soundproofing; **Schall|schutz|fens|ter** NT soundproof window; **schall|si|cher** ADJ soundproof; **schall|tot** ADJ Raum completely soundproof, anechoic (spec); **Schall|trich|ter** M horn; (von Trompeten etc) bell; **Schall|wand** F baffle (of loudspeaker etc); **Schall|wel|le** F sound wave; **Schall|wort** NT pl -wörter onomatopoeic word

Schal|mei [ʃalˈmai] F -, -en shawm

Schal|obst NT nuts pl

Scha|lot|te [ʃaˈlɔtə] F -, -n shallot

schalt pret von **schelten**

Schalt-: **Schalt|an|la|ge** F switchgear; **Schalt|bild** NT circuit diagram, wiring diagram; **Schalt|brett** NT switchboard, control panel

schal|ten [ˈʃaltn] **VT** **a** Gerät to switch, to turn; (= in Gang bringen) to switch or turn on; Leitung to connect; **etw auf „2" ~** to turn or switch sth to "2"; **etw auf die höchste Stufe ~** to turn sth on full, to turn sth full on or up; **in Reihe/parallel ~** (Elec) to connect in series/in parallel; **das Gerät lässt sich schwer ~, das Gerät schaltet sich schwer** this device has a difficult switch (to operate); **das Auto schaltet sich leicht** it's easy to change (esp Brit) or shift (US) gear in this car

b Werbung, Anzeige to place; Hotline to set up; **eine Anzeige ~** to place an advertisement or ad (inf)

VI **a** (Gerät, Ampel) to switch (auf +acc to); (Aut) to change (esp Brit) or shift (US) gear; **in den 2. Gang ~** to change (esp Brit) or shift (US) into 2nd gear; **auf stur ~** (fig) to dig one's heels in

b (fig: = verfahren, handeln) **~ und walten** to bustle around; **frei ~ (und walten) können** to have a free hand (to do as one pleases); **jdn frei ~ und walten lassen** to give sb a free hand, to let sb manage things as he sees fit

c (inf) (= begreifen) to latch on (inf), to get it (inf), to get the message (inf); (= reagieren) to react

Schal|ter [ˈʃaltɐ] M -s, - **a** (Elec etc) switch **b** (in Post®, Bank, Amt) counter; (im Bahnhof) ticket window

Schal|ter-: **Schal|ter|be|am|te(r)** M decl as adj, **Schal|ter|be|am|tin** F counter clerk; (im Bahnhof) ticket clerk; **Schal|ter|dienst** M counter duty; **Schal|ter|hal|le** F (in Post®) hall; (in Bank) (banking) hall; (im Bahnhof) booking or ticket hall; **Schal|ter|leis|te** F (Comput) toolbar; **Schal|ter|raum** M = **Schalterhalle**; **Schal|ter|schluss** M (einer Bank, Behörde) closing time; **~ ist um vier** offices close at four; **nach ~** after hours; **Schal|ter|stun|den** PL hours pl of business, business hours pl

schalt|faul ADJ (inf) reluctant to change (esp Brit) or shift (US) gear; **~es Fahren** driving without changing (esp Brit) or shifting (US) gear

Schalt-: **Schalt|flä|che** F (Comput) button; **Schalt|ge|trie|be** NT manual transmission, stick shift (US); **Schalt|he|bel** M switch lever; (Aut) gear lever (Brit), gear shift (US); **an dem ~ der Macht sitzen** to hold the reins of power; **Schalt|jahr** NT leap year; **alle ~e** (inf) once in a blue moon; **Schalt|kas|ten** M switch box; **Schalt|knüp|pel** M (Aut) gear lever (Brit), gear shift (US); (Aviat) joystick; **Schalt|kreis** M (Tech) (switching) circuit; **Schalt|pau|se** F (TV, Rad) pause (before going over to another region or station); **Schalt|plan** M circuit diagram, wiring diagram; **Schalt|pult** NT control desk; **Schalt|satz** M (Ling) parenthetic clause; **Schalt|schritt** M (von Schreibmaschine) horizontal spacing; **Schalt|skiz|ze** F circuit diagram, wiring diagram; **Schalt|stel|le** F (fig) cordinating point; **Schalt|ta|fel** F switchboard, control panel; **Schalt|tag** M leap day

Schal|tung [ˈʃaltʊŋ] F -, -en switching; (Elec) wiring; (Aut) gear change (Brit), gearshift (US)

Schalt|zent|ra|le F (lit) control centre (Brit) or center (US); (fig) nerve centre (Brit) or center (US)

Scha|lung [ˈʃaːlʊŋ] F -, -en formwork, shuttering

Scha|lup|pe [ʃaˈlʊpə] F -, -n sloop

Schal|wild [ʃaːl-] NT hoofed game

Scham [ʃaːm] F -, no pl **a** shame; **er wurde rot vor ~** he went red with shame; **die ~ stieg ihm ins Gesicht** (old) a blush of shame mounted to his cheeks; **ich hätte vor ~ (in den Boden) versinken können** I wanted the floor to swallow me up or to open up under me; **er versteckte sich vor ~** he hid himself in shame; **aus falscher ~** from a false sense of shame; **nur keine falsche ~!** (inf) no need to feel or be embarrassed!, no need for embarrassment!; **sie hat kein bisschen ~ (im Leibe)** she doesn't have an ounce of shame (in her); **ohne ~** unashamedly; **alle ~ verlieren** to lose all sense of shame

b (geh: = Genitalien) private parts pl; (von Frau) pudenda pl

Scha|ma|ne [ʃaˈmaːnə] M -n, -n, **Scha|ma|nin** [-ˈmaːnɪn] F -, -nen shaman

Scham-: **Scham|bein** NT pubic bone; **Scham|berg** M (geh) mount of Venus, mons veneris (form); **Scham|bo|gen** M pubic arch

schä|men [ˈʃɛːmən] VR to be ashamed; **du solltest dich ~!, du sollst dich was ~** (inf) you ought to be ashamed of yourself!; **sich einer Sache** (gen) or **für etw** or **wegen etw ~** to be ashamed of sth; **sich jds/einer Sache** or **wegen**

jdm/etw *(inf)* ~ to be ashamed of sb/sth; **sich für jdn ~** to be ashamed for sb; **sich vor jdm ~** to be *or* feel ashamed in front of sb; **ich schäme mich so vor ihm** he makes me feel so ashamed; **schäme dich!** shame on you!

Scham-: **Scham|frist** F decent interval; **Scham|fu|ge** F pubic symphysis *(spec)*; **Scham|ge|fühl** NT sense of shame; **ganz ohne ~ sein** to have no (sense of) shame; **Scham|ge|gend** F pubic region; **Scham|gren|ze** F bounds *pl* of what is acceptable; **keine ~ haben** to have no sense of shame; **die ~ überschreiten** to go beyond the bounds of what is acceptable; **da liegt meine ~** – that's going too far for me; **Scham|haar** NT pubic hair; **scham|haft** ADJ modest; *(= verschämt)* bashful, coy; **die heutige Jugend ist nicht sehr ~** today's young people have very little modesty ADV modestly; *(= verschämt)* bashfully, coyly; **Scham|haf|tig|keit** [ˈʃaːmhaftɪçkait] F -, *no pl* modesty; **Scham|hü|gel** M mount of Venus, mons veneris *(form)*; **Scham|lip|pen** PL labia *pl*, lips *pl* of the vulva; **scham|los** ADJ shameless; *(= unanständig auch)* indecent; *(= unverschämt auch)* brazen; *Frechheit, Lüge* brazen, barefaced; **~e Reden führen** to make indecent remarks ADV shamelessly; **sich ~ zeigen** to flaunt oneself brazenly *or* shamelessly; **sich ~ kleiden** to dress indecently; **Scham|lo|sig|keit** F -, -en shamelessness; *(= Unanständigkeit auch)* indecency; *(= Unverschämtheit auch)* brazenness

Scha|mott [ʃaˈmɔt] M -s, *no pl* **a** *(inf)* junk *(inf)*, trash *(inf)*, rubbish **b** *(Aus, S Ger: = Ton)* fireclay

Scha|mot|te [ʃaˈmɔtə] F -, *no pl* fireclay

Scha|mot|te-: **Scha|mot|te|stein** M firestone; **Scha|mot|te|zie|gel** M firebrick

scha|mot|tie|ren [ʃamɔˈtiːrən] *ptp* **schamottiert** VT to line with firebricks

Scham|pus [ˈʃampʊs] M -s, *no pl (dated inf)* champers *sing (dated Brit inf)*, bubbly *(inf)*

Scham-: **scham|rot** ADJ red (with shame); **~ werden** *or* **anlaufen** to turn red *or* to blush *or* flush with shame; **Scham|rö|te** F flush *or* blush of shame; **die ~ stieg ihr ins Gesicht** her face flushed with shame; **Scham|tei|le** PL private parts *pl*, genitals *pl*

schand|bar ADJ shameful, disgraceful ADV **a** *(= schändlich)* shamefully, disgracefully **b** *(dial: = sehr)* awfully; *wehtun* terribly

Schan|de [ˈʃandə] F -, *no pl* disgrace; *(= Unehre auch)* shame, ignominy; **er ist eine ~ für seine Familie** he is a disgrace to his family; **das ist eine (wahre) ~!** this is a(n absolute) disgrace!; **~!** *(euph inf)* sugar! *(euph inf)*, hell! *(inf)*; **es ist doch keine ~, Gefühle zu zeigen** *or* **wenn man Gefühle zeigt** there is no shame *or* disgrace in showing one's feelings; **~ über jdn bringen** to bring disgrace *or* shame upon sb, to disgrace sb; **~ über dich!** *(dated)* shame on you!; **jdm/einer Sache ~ machen** to be a disgrace to sb/sth; **mach mir keine ~** – don't show me up *(inf)*, don't be a disgrace to me; **zu meiner (großen) ~ muss ich gestehen, ...** to my great *or* eternal shame I have to admit that ...; **zu ~n = zuschanden**

schän|den [ˈʃɛndn] VT *Leichnam* to violate, to defile; *Heiligtum, Grab, Friedhof, Denkmal auch* to desecrate; *Sabbat, Sonntag etc* to violate, to desecrate; *Frauen, Kinder* to violate; *Ansehen, Namen* to dishonour *(Brit)*, to dishonor *(US)*, to discredit, to sully

Schand-: **Schand|fleck** M blot *(in +dat* on); *(Gebäude etc auch)* eyesore; **er war der ~ der Familie** he was the disgrace of his family; **Schand|geld** NT ridiculous *or* extortionate price

schänd|lich [ˈʃɛndlɪç] ADJ disgraceful, shameful ADV shamefully; *behandeln* disgracefully; **jdn ~ betrügen** to deceive sb shamefully; **er hat sie ~ verlassen** it was a disgrace the way he left her

Schänd|lich|keit F -, -en shamefulness

Schand-: **Schand|mal** NT *pl* **-male** brand, stigma; **Schand|maul** NT *(pej)* malicious *or* evil tongue; **er ist ein ~** he has a malicious *or* an evil tongue; **Schand|pfahl** M pillory; **Schand|tat** F scandalous *or* disgraceful deed; *(hum)* prank, escapade; **zu jeder ~ bereit sein** *(inf)* to be always ready for mischief *or* a lark *(inf)*

Schän|dung [ˈʃɛndʊŋ] F -, -en *(von Leichnam)* violation, defilement; *(von Heiligtum, Grab, Denkmal auch)* desecration; *(von Sabbat, Frauen, Kindern)* violation; *(von Namen, Ansehen)* dishonouring *(Brit)*, dishonoring *(US)*, discrediting, sullying

schang|hai|en [ʃaŋˈhaiən, ˈʃaŋhaiən] *ptp* **schanghait** VT *(Naut)* to shanghai

Scha|ni [ˈʃaːni] M -s, - *(Aus inf)* **a** *(= Freund)* mate *(inf)*, buddy *(US inf)* **b** *(= Diener)* servant

Scha|ni|gar|ten [ˈʃaːni-] M *(Aus)* pavement café *(Brit)*, sidewalk café *(US)*

Schank [ʃaŋk] F -, -en *(Aus)* bar

Schank-: **Schank|be|trieb** M bar service; **nach 24 Uhr kein ~ mehr** the bar closes at 12 midnight; **Schank|bier** NT draught *(Brit) or* draft *(US)* beer

Schän|ke [ˈʃɛŋkə] F -, -n tavern, inn

Schan|ker [ˈʃaŋkɐ] M -s, - chancre

Schank-: **Schank|er|laub|nis** F licence *(of publican) (Brit)*, excise license *(US)*; **Schank|fräu|lein** NT *(Aus)* barmaid; **Schank|kon|zes|si|on** F licence *(of publican) (Brit)*, excise license *(US)*; **Schank|stu|be** F (public) bar *(esp Brit)*, saloon *(US dated)*; **Schank|tisch** M bar; **Schank|wirt(in)** M(F) *(old)* taverner *(old)*, publican *(Brit)*, saloon keeper *(US dated)*, barkeeper *(US)*; **Schank|wirt|schaft** F *(old, Aus)* tavern *(old)*, public house *(Brit)*, saloon *(US dated)*

Schanz-: **Schanz|ar|beit** F *usu pl* trench digging *no pl*, trench work *no pl*; **Schanz|bau** M, *no pl* construction of fieldwork *or* entrenchments

Schan|ze [ˈʃantsə] F -, -n *(Mil)* fieldwork, entrenchment; *(Naut)* quarterdeck; *(Sport)* (ski) jump; *(für Skateboarder)* ramp; **kleine/große ~** *(Sport)* 90-/120-metre *(Brit) or* meter *(US)* (ski) jump; **sein Leben in die ~ schlagen** *(geh)* to risk one's life, to put one's life at risk *or* in jeopardy

schan|zen [ˈʃantsn] VI *(Mil)* to dig (trenches)

Schan|zen-: **Schan|zen|bau** M, *no pl* construction of fieldwork *or* entrenchments; **Schan|zen|re|kord** M *(Sport)* ski-jump record; **Schan|zen|tisch** M *(Sport: Skispringen)* take-off area

Schanz|werk NT entrenchment

Schar [ʃaːɐ] F -, -en crowd, throng *(liter)*; *(von Vögeln)* flock; *(von Insekten, Heuschrecken etc)* swarm; *(= Reiterschar, Soldatenschar etc)* band, company; *(von Jägern)* party; *(von Pfadfindern)* company, troop; *(von Engeln)* host, band, throng *(liter)*; **~en von Hausfrauen stürzten sich auf die Sonderangebote** hordes *or* crowds of housewives descended on the special offers; **die Fans verließen das Stadion in (hellen) ~en** the fans left the stadium in droves; **der Partei laufen die Mitglieder in ~en davon** members are leaving the party in droves; **die Menschen kamen in (hellen) ~en nach Lourdes** people flocked to Lourdes

Schar F -, -en *(= Pflugschar)* (plough)share *(Brit)*, (plow)share *(US)*

Scha|ra|de [ʃaˈraːdə] F -, -n charade; **~ spielen** to play charades

Schar|bocks|kraut [ˈʃaːɐbɔks-] NT (lesser) celandine

Schä|re [ˈʃɛːrə] F -, -n skerry

scha|ren [ˈʃaːrən] VT **Menschen/Anhänger um sich ~** to gather people/to rally supporters around one VR **sich um jdn/etw ~** to gather around sb/sth; *(Anhänger auch)* to rally around sb/sth

scha|ren|wei|se ADV *(in Bezug auf Menschen)* in droves; **die Heuschrecken/Vögel fielen ~ über die Saat her** swarms of locusts/whole flocks of birds descended on the seedcrop; **~ drängten sich die Leute vor dem Schaufenster** people crowded *or* thronged in front of the shop window

scharf [ʃarf] ADJ *comp* **=er** [ˈʃɛrfɐ], *superl* **=ste(r, s)** [ˈʃɛrfstə] **a** *Messer, Kante, Kurve* sharp; *(= durchdringend) Wind* keen, biting, cutting; *Kälte* biting; *Luft* raw, keen; *Frost* sharp, keen; *Ton* piercing, shrill; **das ~e S** *(Aus inf)* the "scharfes s" *(German symbol ß)*, ess-tset; **ein Messer ~ machen** to sharpen a knife

b *(= stark gewürzt)* hot; *Geruch, Geschmack* pungent, acrid; *Käse* strong, sharp; *Alkohol (= stark)* strong; *(= brennend)* fiery; *(= ätzend) Waschmittel, Lösung* caustic; **~e Sachen** *(inf)* hard stuff *(inf)*

c *(= hart, streng) Mittel, Maßnahmen* tough, severe, drastic; *(inf) Prüfung, Untersuchung* strict, tough; *Lehrer, Polizist* tough; *Bewachung* close, tight; *Hund* fierce

d *(= schonungslos, stark) Worte, Kritik* sharp, biting, harsh; *Widerstand, Konkurrenz* fierce, tough; *Gegner, Protest* strong, fierce; *Auseinandersetzung* bitter, fierce; **eine ~e Zunge haben** to have a sharp tongue, to be sharp-tongued; **jdn/etw in ~er Form kritisieren** to criticize sb/sth in strong terms; **etw in schärfster Form** *or* **aufs Schärfste** *or* **aufs schärfste verurteilen** to condemn sth in the strongest possible terms

e *(= deutlich, klar, genau)* sharp; *Unterschied* sharp, marked; *Brille, Linse* sharply focusing; *Augen* sharp, keen; *Töne* clear, precise; *Verstand, Intelligenz, Gehör* sharp, keen, acute; *Beobachter* keen; **ein ~es Auge für etw haben** *(fig)* to have a keen *or* sharp eye for sth; **mit ~em Blick** *(fig)* with penetrating insight

f *(= heftig, schnell) Ritt, Trab* hard; **ein ~es Tempo fahren** *(inf)* to drive hell for leather *(Brit) or* like a bat out of hell *(inf)*, to drive at quite a lick *(Brit inf)*; **einen ~en Stil fahren** *(inf)* to drive hard

g *(= echt) Munition etc, Schuss* live; **etw ~ machen** to arm sth; **~e Schüsse abgeben** to shoot *or* fire live bullets

h *(inf: = geil)* randy *(Brit inf)*, horny *(inf)*; **jdn ~ machen** to turn sb on *(inf)*; **~ werden** to get turned on *(inf)*, to get randy *(Brit inf) or* horny *(inf)*; **auf jdn/etw ~ sein** to be keen on *(inf) or* hot for *(inf)* sb/sth, to fancy sb/sth *(inf)*; **der Kleine/Alte ist ~ wie Nachbars Lumpi** *or* **tausend Russen** *or* **sieben Sensen** *(dated)* he's a randy *(Brit) or* horny little/old bugger *(inf)* → *auch* **scharfmachen**

ADV *comp* **=er**, *superl* **am =sten** **a** *(= intensiv)* **~ nach etw riechen** to smell strongly of sth; **~ würzen** to season highly, to make hot *(inf)*; **Fleisch ~ anbraten** to sear meat; **sie kocht sehr ~** her cooking is very spicy; **sie hat das Curry ~ zubereitet** she made the curry hot

b *(= schneidend)* **etw ~ schleifen** to sharpen *or* hone sth to a fine edge; **schärfer geschliffen** more finely sharpened; **das „s" wird oft ~ ausgesprochen** "s" is often voiceless, "s" is often pronounced as an "s" and not a "z"

c *(= heftig) attackieren, kritisieren* sharply; *ablehnen* adamantly; *protestieren* emphatically; **etw ~ verurteilen** to criticize sth sharply

d *(= konzentriert) zuhören* closely; **~ beobachten** to be very observant; **etw ~ unter die Lupe nehmen** to examine sth carefully; **etw ~ betrachten** to look at sth intensely; **~ aufpassen** to pay close attention; **~ zuhören** to listen closely; **jdn ~ ansehen** to give sb a scrutinizing look; *(missbilligend)* to look sharply at sb; **~ nachdenken** to have a good *or* long think, to think long and hard

e *(= präzise) analysieren* carefully, in detail; **etw ~ umreißen** *(fig)* to outline sth precisely *or* clearly

f *(= genau)* **etw ~ einstellen** *(Bild, Diaprojektor etc)* to bring sth into focus; *Sender* to tune sth in (properly); ~ **eingestellt**; in (sharp) focus, (properly) tuned in; ~ **sehen/hören** to have sharp eyes/ears

g *(= schnell) fahren, marschieren* fast; ~ **galoppieren** to ride at a full gallop; ~ **reiten** to ride hard

h *(= abrupt) bremsen* sharply, hard; ~ **links abbiegen** to take a hard left; ~ **kehrtmachen** to turn on one's heel

i *(= hart)* ~ **vorgehen/durchgreifen** to take decisive action; **etw ~ bekämpfen** to take strong measures against sth

j *(= streng) bewachen* closely; **jdn ~ kontrollieren** to examine sb thoroughly

k *(= knapp)* ~ **kalkulieren** to reduce one's profit margin; **schärfer kalkulieren** to reduce one's profit margin even more; ~ **rechnen** to figure it out carefully

l *(= fein) hören, sehen* clearly, well

m *(Mil)* **das Gewehr war ~ geladen** the rifle was loaded with live ammunition; ~ **schießen** *(lit) (= mit scharfer Munition)* to shoot with live ammunition; *(= auf den Mann)* to aim to hit; *(fig)* to let fly; **in der Diskussion wurde ziemlich ~ geschossen** *(inf)* the discussion became rather heated, sparks flew in the discussion

Scharf|blick M *(fig)* perspicacity, keen insight, penetration

Schär|fe [ˈʃɛrfə] F -, -n **a** *(von Messer, Kante, Kurve)* sharpness; *(von Wind, Frost)* keenness; *(von Ton)* shrillness
b *(von Essen)* spiciness; *(von Geruch, Geschmack)* pungency; *(von Lösung)* causticity
c *(= Härte, Strenge)* toughness, severity; **mit ~ vorgehen** to take tough *or* severe measures
d *(von Worten, Kritik)* sharpness, harshness; *(von Widerstand, Konkurrenz)* toughness; *(von Protest)* strength; *(von Auseinandersetzung)* bitterness; **ich möchte in aller ~ sagen, dass ...** I'm going to be quite harsh (about this) and say that ...; **etw/jdn in** *or* **mit aller ~ kritisieren** to be sharply critical of sth/sb; **der Konflikt hat an ~ zugenommen** the conflict has become more bitter
e *(= Deutlichkeit)* sharpness; *(von Brille, Linse)* strength; *(von Augen)* sharpness, keenness; *(von Gehör, Verstand)* keenness; *(an Kamera, Fernsehen)* focus; *(an Radio)* tuning; **dem Bild fehlt die ~** the picture lacks sharpness (of focus) *or* definition

Scharf|ein|stel|lung F focusing

schär|fen [ˈʃɛrfn] VT *(lit, fig)* to sharpen

Schär|fen|ein|stel|lung F focusing control

Scharf-: **scharf|kan|tig** ADJ with sharp edges, sharp-edged; **scharf+ma|chen** VT *sep (inf: = aufstacheln)* to stir up, to get up in arms; *(= aufreizen)* to turn on *(inf)*; **Scharf|ma|cher(in)** M(F) *(inf)* rabble-rouser, agitator; **Scharf|ma|che|rei** [-maxəˈrai] F -, -en *(inf)* rabble-rousing, agitation; **Scharf|rich|ter** M executioner; **Scharf|schüt|ze** M marksman; **Scharf|schüt|zin** F markswoman; **scharf|sich|tig** [-zɪçtɪç] ADJ keen-sighted, sharp-sighted; *(fig)* perspicacious, clear-sighted; **Scharf|sinn** M astuteness, acumen, keen perception; **scharf|sin|nig** ADJ *Bemerkung* astute, penetrating; *Detektiv etc* astute, sharp-witted ADV astutely; **wie er ~ bemerkte** as he so astutely remarked

Schär|fung [ˈʃɛrfʊŋ] F -, *no pl (lit, fig)* sharpening

Scha|ria [ʃaˈriːa] F -, *no pl (= islamische Rechtsordnung)* sharia

Schar|lach [ˈʃarlax] M -s, *no pl* **a** *(Farbe)* scarlet
b *(= Scharlachfieber)* scarlet fever

Schar|lach-: **schar|lach|far|ben** [-farbn] ADJ scarlet; **Schar|lach|fie|ber** NT scarlet fever; **schar|lach|rot** ADJ scarlet (red)

Schar|la|tan [ˈʃarlatan] M -s, -e charlatan; *(= Arzt auch)* quack

Schar|la|ta|ne|rie [ʃarlatanəˈriː] F -, -n [-ˈriːən] charlatanism

Schar|müt|zel [ʃaːrˈmʏtsl] NT -s, - skirmish, brush with the enemy

Schar|nier [ʃarˈniːɐ] NT -s, -e, **Schar|nier|ge|lenk** NT hinge

Schär|pe [ˈʃɛrpə] F -, -n sash

schar|ren [ˈʃarən] VTI to scrape; *(Pferd, Hund)* to paw; *(Huhn)* to scratch; *(= verscharren)* to bury (hurriedly); **mit dem Huf ~** to paw the ground; **mit den Füßen ~** to shuffle one's feet

Schar|te [ˈʃartə] F -, -n nick; *(in Bergkamm)* wind gap; *(= Schießscharte)* embrasure; *(in Kampfwagen)* gun-port; **eine ~ auswetzen** *(fig)* to make amends, to patch things up

Schar|te|ke [ʃarˈteːkə] F -, -n *(pej)* (old) hag; *(= Buch)* tattered old volume

schar|tig [ˈʃartɪç] ADJ jagged, notched

schar|wen|zeln [ʃarˈvɛntsln] *ptp* **scharwenzelt** VI *aux sein or haben (inf)* to dance attendance *(um* upon)

Schasch|lik [ˈʃaʃlɪk] NT -s, -s (shish) kebab

schas|sen [ˈʃasn] VT *(inf)* to chuck out *(inf)*, to boot out *(inf)*

Schat|ten [ˈʃatn] M -s, - *(lit, fig)* shadow; *(= schattige Stelle)* shade; *(= Geist)* shade; **im ~ sitzen** to sit in the shade; **40 Grad im ~** 40 degrees in the shade; ~ **geben** *or* **spenden** to give *or* provide shade; ~ **spendend** *(Baum, Dach)* shady; **einen ~ auf etw** *(acc)* **werfen** *(lit)* to cast a shadow on sth; *(fig)* to cast a shadow *or* cloud (up)on sth; **aus dem ~ (ans Licht) treten** *(lit, fig)* to come out of the shadows; **große Ereignisse werfen ihre ~ voraus** great events are often foreshadowed; **in jds ~** *(dat)* **stehen** *(fig)* to stand *or* be in sb's shadow; **im ~ bleiben** *(fig)* to remain in the background *or* shadows; **jdn/etw in den ~ stellen** *(fig)* to put sb/sth in the shade, to overshadow *or* eclipse sb/sth; **jdm wie ein ~ folgen** *(fig)* to follow sb like a shadow; **man kann nicht über seinen eigenen ~ springen** *(fig)* the leopard cannot change his spots *(prov)*; **sich vor seinem eigenen ~ fürchten** *(fig)* to be afraid of one's own shadow; **nur noch ein ~ (seiner selbst) sein** to be (only) a shadow of one's former self; **die ~ des Todes/der Nacht** *(liter)* the shades of death/night *(liter)*; **Reich der ~** *(liter)* realm of shades *(liter)*; **es fiel nicht der leiseste ~ des Verdachts auf ihn** not a shadow of suspicion fell on him; **nicht der ~ eines Beweises** not the slightest proof; ~ **unter den Augen** shadows under the eyes; **du hast ja einen ~** *(sl)* you must be nuts *(inf)* → **Licht a**

Schat|ten-: **Schat|ten|bild** NT silhouette; *(in Schattenspiel)* shadow picture, shadow(graph); **Schat|ten|bo|xen** NT shadow-boxing; **Schat|ten|da|sein** NT shadowy existence; **Schat|ten|druck** M *pl* **-drucke** *(Comput)* shadow printing; **Schat|ten|ein|kom|men** NT *(Pol)* shadow *or* hidden earnings *pl*; **schat|ten|haft** ADJ shadowy, shadow-like; *(fig: = vage)* shadowy, fuzzy, vague ADV *sehen, erkennen* vaguely; *sichtbar* barely; **im Dunkeln zeichneten sich die Umrisse nur ~ ab** the silhouettes were shadowy in the dark; **Schat|ten|ka|bi|nett** NT *(Pol)* shadow cabinet; **schat|ten|los** ADJ shadowless; **Schat|ten|mo|rel|le** [-morɛlə] F -, -n morello cherry; **Schat|ten|par|ker** [-parkɐ] M *(sl: Schimpfwort)* tosser *(sl)*; **schat|ten|reich** ADJ shady; **Schat|ten|reich** NT *(liter)* realm of shadows *(liter) or* shades *(liter)*; **Schat|ten|riss** M silhouette; **Schat|ten|sei|te** F shady side; *(von Planeten)* dark side; *(fig: = Nachteil)* drawback, disadvantage; **die ~(n) des Lebens** the dark side of life, life's dark side; *(in Milieu, Slums etc)* the seamy side of life; **schat|ten|spen|dend** △ ADJ *attr* → **Schatten**; **Schat|ten|spiel** NT shadow play *or* show; *(Art)* contrast, shadow play; **Schat|ten|the|a|ter** NT shadow theatre *(Brit) or* theater *(US)*; **Schat|ten|wirt|schaft** F black economy

schat|tie|ren [ʃaˈtiːrən] *ptp* **schattiert** VT to shade

Schat|tie|rung F -, -en *(lit, fig)* shade; *(= das Schattieren)* shading; **aller politischen ~en** of every political shade; **in allen ~en** *(fig)* of every shade

schat|tig [ˈʃatɪç] ADJ shady

Scha|tul|le [ʃaˈtʊlə] F -, -n casket; *(= Geldschatulle)* coffer; *(pej inf)* bag *(inf)*

Schatz [ʃats] M -es, =e [ˈʃɛtsə] **a** *(lit, fig)* treasure; **Schätze** *pl (= Bodenschätze)* natural resources *pl*; *(= Reichtum)* riches *pl*, wealth *sing*; **nach Schätzen graben** to dig for (buried) treasure; **du bist ein ~!** *(inf)* you're a (real) treasure *or* gem!; **für alle Schätze der Welt** *(fig)* for all the money in the world, for all the tea in China
b *(= Liebling)* sweetheart; *(als Anrede)* sweetheart, darling

Schatz-: **Schatz|amt** NT Treasury; **Schatz|an|wei|sung** F treasury bond

schätz|bar ADJ assessable; **gut/schlecht/schwer ~** easy/hard/difficult to assess *or* estimate

Schätz|chen [ˈʃɛtsçən] NT -s, - darling

schät|zen [ˈʃɛtsn] ✪ 40.4 VT **a** *(= veranschlagen)* to estimate, to assess *(auf +acc* at); *Wertgegenstand, Gemälde etc* to value, to appraise; *(= annehmen)* to reckon, to think; **die Besucherzahl wurde auf 500.000 geschätzt** the number of visitors was estimated at *or* to be 500,000; **wie alt ~ Sie mich denn?** how old do you reckon I am then?, how old would you say I am, then?; **was schätzt du, wie lange/wie viele/wie alt ...?** how long/how many/how old do you reckon *or* would you say ...?; **was/wie viel schätzt du denn?** what/how much do you reckon it is?, what/how much would you say it was?; **ich hätte sie älter geschätzt** I'd have said *or* thought she was older, I'd have thought her older *(esp Brit)* → **hoch 2 e**
b *(= würdigen)* to regard highly, to value; **jdn ~** to think highly of sb, to hold sb in high regard *or* esteem; **mein geschätzter Kollege** *(form)* my esteemed colleague *(form)*; **etw besonders ~** to hold sth in very high esteem; **etw zu ~ wissen** to appreciate sth; **das schätzt er (überhaupt) nicht** he doesn't care for *or* appreciate that (at all); **sich glücklich ~** to consider *or* deem *(form)* oneself lucky
VI *(= veranschlagen, raten)* to guess; **schätz mal** have a guess

schät|zen ler|nen VT to come to appreciate *or* value

schät|zens|wert ADJ estimable

Schät|zer [ˈʃɛtsɐ] M -s, -, **Schät|ze|rin** [-ərɪn] F -, -nen valuer; *(Insur)* assessor

Schatz-: **Schatz|fund** M find *(of treasure)*, treasure-trove *(Jur)*; **Schatz|grä|ber** [-grɛːbɐ] M -s, -, **Schatz|grä|be|rin** [-ərɪn] F -, -nen treasure hunter; **Schatz|kam|mer** F treasure chamber *or* vault; **Schatz|kanz|ler(in)** M(F) *(Pol)* minister of finance, Chancellor of the Exchequer *(Brit)*, Secretary of the Treasury *(US)*; **Schatz|käst|chen** NT, **Schatz|käst|lein** [-kɛstlain] NT -s, - casket, (small) treasure chest; *(fig: als Buchtitel etc)* treasury; **Schatz|meis|ter(in)** M(F) treasurer; **Schatz|ob|li|ga|ti|on** F *(Fin)* treasury bond

Schätz|preis M valuation price

Schatz-: **Schatz|schein** M *(Fin)* treasury note; **Schatz|su|che** F treasure hunt(ing); **auf ~ gehen** to go on a treasure hunt, to go treasure hunting

Schät|zung [ˈʃɛtsʊŋ] F -, -en estimate; *(= das Schätzen)* estimation; *(von Wertgegenstand)* valuation, appraisal; **nach meiner ~ ...** I reckon that ...; *(= ungefähr)* approximately, roughly

schät|zungs|wei|se ADV *(= so vermutet man)* it is estimated *or* thought; *(= ungefähr)* approximately, roughly; *(= so schätze ich)* I think, I reckon; **die Inflationsrate wird sich ~ verdoppeln** it is thought *or* estimated (that) the rate of inflation will double; **es werden ~ 3.000 Zuschauer kommen** an estimated 3,000 spectators will come; **das wird ~ länger dauern** I think *or* reckon (that) that'll take longer; **wann wirst du ~ kommen?** when do you think *or* reckon you'll come?

Schatz|wech|sel M *(Fin)* Treasury bill
Schätz|wert M estimated value
Schau [ʃau] F -, -en **a** *(= Vorführung)* show; *(= Ausstellung)* show, display, exhibition; **etw zur ~ stellen** *(= ausstellen)* to put sth on show, to display *or* exhibit *or* show sth; *(fig)* to make a show of sth, to parade sth; *(= protzen mit)* to show off sth; **zur ~ gestellter Wohlstand** display of wealth; **sich zur ~ stellen** to make a spectacle *or* exhibition of oneself; **etw zur ~ tragen** to display sth
b *(inf)* **eine ~ abziehen** to put on a display *or* show; *(= Theater machen)* to make a big show *(inf)*; **das war eine ~!** that was really great *or* fantastic *(inf)*; **das ist nur ~** it's only show; **er macht nur (eine) ~** he's (only) putting it on; **jdm die ~ stehlen** *or* **klauen** to steal the show from sb
Schau-: **Schau|bild** NT diagram; *(= Kurve)* graph; **Schau|bu|de** F (show) booth; **Schau|büh|ne** F *(old)* theatre *(Brit)*, theater *(US)*; *(fig)* stage, scene
Schau|der [ˈʃaudɐ] M -s, - shudder; *(vor Angst, Kälte auch)* shiver; **~ erregend** = **schaudererregend**; **jdm einen ~ über den Rücken jagen** to send a shudder/shiver down sb's spine; **ein ~ lief mir über den Rücken** a shudder/shiver ran down my spine
schau|der-: **schau|der|er|re|gend** ADJ terrifying, fearsome, horrifying; *Vorstellung, Vision, Geschichte auch* horrific; **schau|der|haft** ADJ *(lit)* horrible, ghastly, terrible; *(fig inf)* terrible, dreadful, awful ADV *verstümmeln* gruesomely; *(fig inf)* horribly, awfully; **er spricht ~ schlecht Italienisch** his Italian is terrible
schau|dern [ˈʃaudɐn] VI *(vor Grauen, Abscheu)* to shudder; *(vor Kälte, Angst auch)* to shiver; *(vor Ehrfurcht)* to tremble, to quiver; **mich schauderte bei dem Anblick/Gedanken** I shuddered/shivered/trembled *or* quivered at the sight/thought (of it); **ihr schaudert vor ihm** he makes her shudder/shiver; **mit Schaudern** with a shudder
schau|en [ˈʃauən] VI *(esp dial)* to look; **verärgert/traurig** *etc* **~** to look angry/sad *etc*; **auf etw** *(acc)* **~** to look at sth; **um sich ~** to look around (one); **die Sonne schaut durch die Wolken** the sun is peeping *or* shining through the clouds *or* from behind the clouds; **jdm (fest) in die Augen ~** to look sb (straight) in the eye; **jdm verliebt in die Augen ~** to gaze adoringly into sb's eyes; **ihm schaut der Ärger/Zorn/Schrecken aus den Augen** annoyance/anger/fright is written all over his face; **nach jdm/etw ~** *(= suchen)* to look for sb/sth; *(= sich kümmern um)* to look after sb/sth; **da schaust du aber!** there, see!, there you are!; **schau, schau!** *(inf)* well, well!, what do you know! *(inf)*, how about that! *(inf)*; **schau, dass du ...** see *or* mind (that) you ...
VT *(geh)* to see, to behold *(old, liter)*; *(= erkennen)* to see; **Gott ~** to see God
Schau|er [ˈʃauɐ] M -s, - **a** *(= Regenschauer)* shower **b** = **Schauder**
Schau|er|ge|schich|te F horror story; *(Liter)* gothic tale *or* story; *(inf: = Lügengeschichte)* horror story
Schau|er|leu|te *pl von* **Schauermann**
schau|er|lich [ˈʃauɐlɪç] ADJ **a** horrific, horrible; *Schrei* bloodcurdling, spine-chilling; *(= gruselig)* eerie, creepy *(inf)* **b** *(inf: = fürchterlich)* terrible, dreadful, awful ADV *entstellt, verstümmelt* horribly; *(fig inf auch)* dreadfully; **sie spricht ~ schlecht Englisch** her English is terrible
Schau|er-: **Schau|er|mann** M *pl* **-leute** docker, longshoreman *(US)*; **Schau|er|mär|chen** NT *(inf)* horror story
schau|ern [ˈʃauɐn] VI *impers* **es schauert** it's just a shower VI = **schaudern**
Schau|er|ro|man M *(lit, fig inf)* horror story; *(Liter auch)* Gothic novel

Schau|fel [ˈʃaufl] F -, -n shovel; *(kleiner: für Mehl, Zucker)* scoop; *(= Kehrichtschaufel)* dustpan; *(von Bagger)* scoop; *(von Schaufelrad)* paddle; *(von Wasserrad, Turbine)* vane; *(= Geweihschaufel)* palm; *(Hunt: von Auerhahn)* fan; **zwei ~n (voll) Sand/Kies** two shovel(ful)s of sand/gravel
Schäu|fe|le [ˈʃɔyfələ] NT -s, - *(S Ger Cook)* cured shoulder of pork; *(gebraten)* roast shoulder of pork
schau|fel|för|mig ADJ shaped like a shovel, shovel-shaped
schau|feln [ˈʃaufln] VTI to shovel; *Grab, Grube* to dig → **Grab**
Schau|fel-: **Schau|fel|rad** NT *(von Dampfer)* paddle wheel; *(von Turbine)* vane wheel, impeller; *(von Bagger)* bucket wheel; **Schau|fel|rad|-damp|fer** M paddle steamer; **schau|fel|wei|se** ADV in shovelfuls
Schau|fens|ter NT display window; *(von Geschäft auch)* shop window; *(fig)* shop window
Schau|fens|ter-: **Schau|fens|ter|aus|la|ge** F window display; **Schau|fens|ter|bum|mel** M window-shopping expedition; **einen ~ machen** to go window-shopping; **Schau|fens|ter|de|-ko|ra|teur(in)** M(F) window-dresser; **Schau|-fens|ter|de|ko|ra|ti|on** F *(= Dekoration)* window decorations *pl*; *(= das Dekorieren)* window dressing; **Schau|fens|ter|front** F shop front, storefront *(US)*; **Schau|fens|ter|ge|stal|tung** F window-dressing; **Schau|fens|ter|krank|-heit** F intermittent claudication; **Schau|-fens|ter|pup|pe** F display dummy, mannequin
Schau-: **Schau|flie|gen** NT -s, *no pl* stunt flying; *(Veranstaltung)* air display; **Schau|flug** M stunt flight; **Schau|ge|schäft** NT show business; **Schau|kampf** M exhibition bout *or* fight; **Schau|kas|ten** M showcase
Schau|kel [ˈʃaukl] F -, -n swing
schau|ke|lig [ˈʃaukəlɪç] ADJ *Brücke* swaying *attr*; *Überfahrt* rough; *Auto, Fahrt* bouncy; **ein ~es Boot** a boat which rocks
schau|keln [ˈʃaukln] VI **a** *(mit Schaukel)* to swing; *(im Schaukelstuhl)* to rock; **die Kinder wollen ~** the children want to play on the swings; **auf** *or* **mit dem Stuhl ~** to swing *or* rock back and forth in one's chair, to tip one's chair back and forth
b *(= sich hin und her bewegen)* to swing *or* sway (to and fro *or* back and forth); *(= sich auf und ab bewegen)* to rock up and down; *(Fahrzeug)* to bounce (up and down); *(Schiff)* to rock, to pitch and toss; *(Aktienkurse)* to go up and down, to fluctuate
c *aux sein (= sich schaukelnd bewegen: Schiff)* to pitch and toss; *(= gemütlich fahren)* to jog along
VT to rock; **jdn durch die Gegend ~** *(inf)* to take sb for a spin round the place *(inf)*; **wir werden das Kind** *or* **die Sache** *or* **das schon ~** *(inf)* we'll manage it
VI *impers* **bei der Überfahrt hat es geschaukelt** the boat pitched and tossed on the way over; **im Auto hat es geschaukelt** it was a bouncy ride
Schau|kel-: **Schau|kel|pferd** NT rocking horse; **Schau|kel|po|li|tik** F seesaw(ing) policy; **Schau|kel|stuhl** M rocking chair
schauk|lig [ˈʃauklɪç] ADJ = **schaukelig**
Schau-: **Schau|lau|fen** NT -s, *no pl* exhibition skating; *(Veranstaltung)* skating display; **schau|-lus|tig** ADJ curious; **Schau|lus|ti|ge** [-lʊstɪgə] PL *decl as adj* (curious) onlookers *pl*, rubbernecks *pl (US inf)*
Schaum [ʃaum] M -s, **Schäume** [ˈʃɔymə] foam, froth; *(= Seifenschaum, Shampooschaum)* lather; *(von Waschmittel)* lather, suds *pl*; *(zum Feuerlöschen)* foam; *(Cook, auf Speisen, Getränken)* froth; *(auf Marmelade, Flüssen, Sümpfen)* scum; *(von Bier)* head, froth; **~ vor dem Mund haben** *(lit, fig)* to froth *or* foam at the mouth; **etw zu ~ schlagen** *(Cook)* to beat *or* whip sth until frothy; **~ schlagen** *(fig inf)* to be all hot air

Schaum-: **Schaum|bad** NT bubble *or* foam bath; **Schaum|bla|se** F bubble
schäu|men [ˈʃɔymən] VI to foam, to froth; *(Seife, Shampoo, Waschmittel)* to lather (up); *(Limonade, Wein)* to bubble; *(inf: = wütend sein)* to foam at the mouth; **das Waschmittel schäumt stark/schwach** it's a high-lather/low-lather detergent; **vor Wut ~** to be foaming at the mouth VT **Kunststoff ~** to produce foam synthetics
Schaum-: **Schaum|fes|ti|ger** M mousse; **Schaum|feu|er|lö|scher** M foam fire-extinguisher; **Schaum|gum|mi** NT OR M foam rubber
schau|mig [ˈʃaumɪç] ADJ foamy, frothy; *Seife, Shampoo* lathery; *Waschmittel* lathery, sudsy; *Speise, Getränk, Bier* frothy; *Marmelade, Fluss, Sumpf* scummy; **ein Ei ~ schlagen** to beat an egg until frothy
Schaum-: **Schaum|ka|no|ne** F foam machine; **Schaum|kel|le** F skimmer; **Schaum|kro|ne** F whitecap, white crest *or* horse; **Schaum|-löf|fel** M skimmer; **Schaum|lö|scher** M, **Schaum|lösch|ge|rät** NT foam extinguisher
Schaum|ma|schi|ne F foam machine
Schäum|mit|tel NT foaming agent
Schaum-: **Schaum|rei|ni|ger** M foam cleaner; **Schaum|schlä|ger(in)** M(F) *(fig inf)* hot-air merchant *(Brit inf)*, person full of hot air *(inf)*; **Schaum|schlä|ge|rei** F *(fig inf)* hot air *(inf)*; **Schaum|stoff** M foam material; **Schaum|-tö|nung** F colour *(Brit)* *or* color *(US)* mousse; **Schaum|wein** M sparkling wine
Schau-: **Schau|platz** M scene; **vom ~ berichten** to give an on-the-spot report; **am ~ sein** to be on *or* at the scene *or* on the spot; **auf dem ~ erscheinen** to appear on the scene; **vom ~ (der Politik) abtreten** to leave the (political) scene *or* arena; **Schau|pro|zess** M show trial
schau|rig [ˈʃaurɪç] ADJ gruesome; *Schrei* spine-chilling, bloodcurdling; *(inf: = sehr schlecht)* dreadful, abysmal *(inf)*, awful ADV *(inf)* terribly, dreadfully; **er spricht ~ schlecht Japanisch** his Japanese is terrible
schau|rig-schön ADJ gruesomely beautiful; *(= unheimlich)* eerily beautiful
Schau|spiel NT **a** *(Theat)* *(= Stück)* drama, play; *(= Theater)* **Leipziger ~** Leipzig Playhouse **b** *(fig)* spectacle; **wir wollen doch den Leuten kein ~ bieten** *or* **geben** let's not make a spectacle of ourselves
Schau|spie|ler M actor, player; *(fig)* (play-)actor
Schau|spie|le|rei F acting; *(fig: = Verstellung)* play-acting
Schau|spie|le|rin F *(lit)* actress; *(fig)* (play-)actress
schau|spie|le|risch ADJ acting *attr*; *Talent* for acting; **eine überzeugende ~e Leistung** a convincing piece of acting ADV as regards acting, as far as (the) acting is/was concerned
schau|spie|lern [ˈʃauʃpiːlɐn] VI *insep* to act; *(fig)* to (play-)act
Schau|spiel-: **Schau|spiel|haus** NT playhouse, theatre *(Brit)*, theater *(US)*; **Schau|-spiel|kunst** F dramatic art, drama; *(in Bezug auf Schauspieler)* acting; **Schau|spiel|schu|le** F drama school; **Schau|spiel|schü|ler(in)** M(F) drama student; **Schau|spiel|un|ter|richt** M acting *or* drama lessons *pl* *or* classes *pl*
Schau-: **Schau|stel|ler** [ˈʃauʃtɛlɐ] M -s, -, **Schau|stel|le|rin** [-ərɪn] F -, -nen showman; **Schau|stück** NT showpiece; **Schau|ta|fel** F *(zur Information)* (notice) board; *(= Schaubild)* diagram; **Schau|tanz** M exhibition dance; **Schau|tur|nen** NT gymnastic display
Scheck [ʃɛk] M -s, -s *or (rare)* -e cheque *(Brit)*, check *(US)*; **einen ~ ausstellen/einlösen** to write out/to cash a cheque *(Brit)* *or* check *(US)*; **mit (einem)** *or* **per ~ bezahlen** to pay by cheque *(Brit)* *or* check *(US)*; **ein ~ auf** *or* **über EUR 200** a cheque *(Brit)* *or* check *(US)* for 200 euros

Scheck-: **Scheck|be|trug** M cheque *(Brit)* or check *(US)* fraud; **Scheck|be|trü|ger(in)** M(F) cheque *(Brit)* or check *(US)* fraud; **Scheck|buch** NT NT chequebook *(Brit)*, checkbook *(US)*

Sche|cke ['ʃɛkə] M -n, -n or f -, -n *(= Pferd)* dappled horse/pony; *(= Rind)* spotted ox/bull/cow

Scheck-: **Scheck|fäl|schung** F cheque *(Brit)* or check *(US)* forgery; **Scheck|heft** NT chequebook *(Brit)*, checkbook *(US)*

sche|ckig ['ʃɛkɪç] ADJ spotted; *Pferd* dappled; *(inf) (= kunterbunt)* gaudy; *(= verfärbt)* blotchy, patchy; **sich ~ lachen** → **scheckiglachen**

sche|ckig+la|chen VR *sep (inf)* to laugh oneself silly *(inf)*

Scheck-: **Scheck|kar|te** F cheque card *(Brit)*, check card *(US)*, banker's card; **Scheck|ver|kehr** M cheque *(Brit)* or check *(US)* transactions *pl*

scheel [ʃe:l] ADJ **a** *(old: = schielend)* cross-eyed **b** *(= missgünstig)* envious, jealous; *(= abschätzig)* disparaging; **ein ~er Blick** a dirty look ADV **jdn ~ ansehen** to give sb a dirty look; *(= abschätzig)* to look askance at sb

Schef|fel ['ʃɛfl] M -s, - *(= Gefäß, Hohlmaß)* ≈ bushel; *(= Flächenmaß) area between 12 and 42 acres*; **sein Licht unter den ~ stellen** *(inf)* to hide one's light under a bushel

schef|feln ['ʃɛfln] VT *Geld* to rake in *(inf)*; *Gold, Orden* to pile up, to accumulate VI **er scheffelt seit Jahren** he's been raking it in for years *(inf)*

schef|fel|wei|se ADV in large quantities, by the sackful; **~ Geld verdienen** to be raking it in *(inf)*

scheib|chen|wei|se ['ʃaipçənvaizə] ADV *(fig)* bit by bit, little by little, a bit or little at a time

Schei|be ['ʃaibə] F -, -n **a** disc *(esp Brit)*, disk; *(= Schießscheibe)* target; *(Eishockey)* puck; *(= Wählscheibe)* dial; *(Tech) (= Unterlegscheibe, Dichtungsscheibe)* washer; *(= Kupplungsscheibe, Bremsscheibe)* disc *(esp Brit)*, disk; *(= Töpferscheibe)* wheel; *(inf: = Schallplatte)* disc *(esp Brit inf)*, disk
b *(= abgeschnittene Scheibe)* slice; *(= Längsscheibe: von Orange etc)* segment; **etw in ~n schneiden** to slice sth (up), to cut sth (up) into slices; **von ihm könntest du dir eine ~ abschneiden** *(fig inf)* you could take a leaf out of his book *(inf)*
c *(= Glasscheibe)* (window)pane; *(= Fenster, auch von Auto)* window; *(inf: = Windschutzscheibe)* windscreen *(Brit)*, windshield *(US)*; *(= Spiegelscheibe)* glass
d *(euph inf)* **~!** sugar! *(euph inf)*

Schei|ben-: **Schei|ben|brem|se** F disc *(esp Brit)* or disk brake; **Schei|ben|ho|nig** M comb honey; **~!** *(euph inf)* sugar! *(euph inf)*; **Schei|ben|kleis|ter** INTERJ *(euph inf)* sugar! *(euph inf)*; **Schei|ben|kupp|lung** F disc *(esp Brit)* or disk or plate clutch; **Schei|ben|schie|ßen** NT -s, *no pl* target shooting; **Schei|ben|wasch|an|la|ge** F windscreen *(Brit)* or windshield *(US)* washers *pl*; **schei|ben|wei|se** ['ʃaibnvaizə] ADV in slices; **Schei|ben|wi|scher** M windscreen *(Brit)* or windshield *(US)* wiper; **Schei|ben|wi|scher|blatt** NT windscreen *(Brit)* or windshield *(US)* wiper blade

Scheich [ʃaiç] M -s, -e sheik(h); *(inf)* bloke *(Brit inf)*, guy *(inf)*

Scheich|tum ['ʃaiçtu:m] NT -s, **Scheichtümer** [-ty:mɐ] sheik(h)dom

Schei|de ['ʃaidə] F -, -n **a** sheath; *(von Schwert)* sheath, scabbard; *(= Vagina)* vagina; **das Schwert aus der ~ ziehen** to unsheathe or draw one's sword; **das Schwert in die ~ stecken** to put up or sheathe one's sword **b** *(obs, fig: = Grenze)* border

Schei|de-: **Schei|de|an|stalt** F separating works *sing* or *pl*; **Schei|de|li|nie** F *(lit)* border(line); *(fig)* dividing line; **Schei|de|mit|tel** NT *(Chem)* separating agent

schei|den ['ʃaidn] *pret* **schied** [ʃi:t], *ptp* **geschieden** [gə'ʃi:dn] VT **a** *(= auflösen) Ehe* to dissolve; *Eheleute* to divorce; **sich ~ lassen** to get divorced, to get a divorce; **er will sich von ihr ~ lassen** he wants to divorce her or to get a divorce (from her); **er lässt sich nicht von ihr ~** he won't give her a divorce → *auch* **geschieden**
b *(geh: = trennen)* to separate; *(Chem)* to separate (out) → **Geist c**
VI *aux sein (liter) (= sich trennen)* to part; *(= weggehen)* to depart; **aus dem Dienst/Amt ~** to retire from service/office; **aus dem Leben ~** to depart this life; **Scheiden tut weh** *(Prov)* parting is such sweet sorrow *(Prov)*
VR *(Wege)* to divide, to part, to separate; *(Meinungen)* to diverge, to part company

Schei|den-: **Schei|den|ab|strich** M vaginal smear *(esp Brit)*, Pap smear; **Schei|den|krampf** M vaginal cramp, vaginismus *(form)*; **Schei|den|vor|fall** M prolapse of the vagina

Schei|de-: **Schei|de|wand** F partition; *(von Nase, Herz)* septum *(spec)*; *(fig)* barrier; **Schei|de|was|ser** NT *pl* **-wässer** *(Chem)* nitric acid, aqua fortis; **Schei|de|weg** M *(fig)* crossroads *sing*; **am ~ stehen** to be at a crossroads

Schei|dung ['ʃaidʊŋ] F -, -en **a** *(= das Scheiden)* separation **b** *(= Ehescheidung)* divorce; **die ~ dieser Ehe** the dissolution of this marriage; **in ~ leben** or **liegen** to be in the middle of divorce proceedings, to be getting a divorce; **die ~ einreichen** to file a petition for divorce

Schei|dungs-: **Schei|dungs|grund** M grounds *pl* for divorce; *(hum: Mensch)* reason for his/her *etc* divorce; **Schei|dungs|kind** NT child of a divorced couple or of a broken home; **Schei|dungs|kla|ge** F petition for divorce; **Schei|dungs|pro|zess** M divorce proceedings *pl*; **Schei|dungs|recht** NT divorce law(s *pl*); **Schei|dungs|rich|ter(in)** M(F) divorce judge; **Schei|dungs|ur|kun|de** F divorce certificate; **Schei|dungs|ur|teil** NT decree of divorce; **Schei|dungs|wai|se** F *(inf)* child of divorced parents

Schein [ʃain] M -(e)s, *no pl* **a** *(= Licht)* light; *(matt)* glow; *(von Gold, Schwert etc)* gleam, glint; **einen (hellen) ~ auf etw** *(acc)* **werfen** to shine (brightly) on sth, to cast a (bright) light on sth **b** *(= Anschein)* appearances *pl*; *(= Vortäuschung)* pretence, sham; **~ und Sein/Wirklichkeit** appearance and reality; **das ist mehr ~ als Sein** it's all (on the) surface; **der ~ trügt** or **täuscht** appearances are deceptive; **dem ~ nach** on the face of it, to all appearances; **den ~ wahren** to keep up appearances; **etw nur zum ~ tun** only to pretend to do sth, to make only a pretence or a show of doing sth

Schein M -(e)s, -e *(= Geldschein)* note, bill *(US)*; *(= Bescheinigung)* certificate; *(Univ)* credit; *(= Fahrschein)* ticket; **~e machen** *(Univ)* to get credits

Schein-: **Schein|an|griff** M feint (attack); **Schein|asy|lant(in)** M(F) bogus asylum-seeker; **schein|bar** ADJ apparent, seeming *attr*; *(= vorgegeben)* feigned, ostensible ADV apparently, seemingly; **er hörte ~ interessiert zu** he listened with apparent or seeming/feigned interest; **Schein|blü|te** F illusory flowering; *(Econ)* illusory boom; **Schein|da|sein** NT phantom existence; **Schein|ehe** F fictitious or sham marriage

schei|nen ['ʃainən] ✪ 33.2, 38.2, 39.2, 41, 53.4, 53.5 *pret* **schien**, [ʃi:n] *ptp* **geschienen** VI [gə'ʃi:nən] **a** *(= leuchten)* to shine
b *auch vi impers (= den Anschein geben)* to seem, to appear; **es scheint, dass .../als (ob) ...** it seems or appears that .../as if ...; **mir scheint, (dass) ...** it seems or appears to me that ...; **wie es scheint** as it seems, as it would appear, apparently; **es scheint nur so** it only seems or appears to be like that; **er kommt scheints nicht mehr** *(dial inf)* it would seem that he won't come now, seemingly he's not coming now; **du hast scheints vergessen, dass ...** *(dial inf)* you seem to have forgotten that ...

Schein-: **Schein|fir|ma** F dummy or fictitious firm; **Schein|frie|de** M phoney peace, peace in name only, semblance *no pl* of peace; **Schein|ge|fecht** NT mock or sham fight; **Schein|ge|schäft** NT bogus transaction; **Schein|grund** M spurious reason; *(= Vorwand)* pretext; **schein|hei|lig** ADJ hypocritical; *(= Arglosigkeit vortäuschend)* innocent ADV *fragen, sagen, grinsen* innocently; **~ tun** to be hypocritical; *(= Arglosigkeit vortäuschen)* to act innocent, to play or act the innocent; **Schein|hei|li|ge(r)** MF *decl as adj* hypocrite; *(Arglosigkeit vortäuschend)* sham; **Schein|hei|lig|keit** F hypocrisy; *(= vorgetäuschte Arglosigkeit)* feigned innocence; **Schein|hei|rat** F sham or bogus marriage; **Schein|hin|rich|tung** F mock execution; **Schein|schwan|ger|schaft** F false pregnancy; **Schein|selbst|stän|di|ge(r)** MF *decl as adj person who has adopted freelance status so that his employer avoids paying social security contributions*; **Schein|selbst|stän|dig|keit** F freelance status *(to avoid employer paying social security contributions)*; **Schein|tod** M apparent death, suspended animation; **schein|tot** ADJ in a state of apparent death or of suspended animation; *(fig) Mensch, Partei* on one's/its last legs; **Schein|to|te(r)** MF *decl as adj* apparent corpse, apparently dead person; **Schein|welt** F illusory world

Schein|wer|fer M *(zum Beleuchten)* floodlight; *(im Theater)* spotlight; *(= Suchscheinwerfer)* searchlight; *(Aut)* (head)light, headlamp

Schein|wer|fer|licht NT floodlight(ing); *(im Theater)* spotlight; *(von Suchscheinwerfer)* searchlight (beam); *(Aut)* light or beam of the headlights or headlamps; *(fig)* limelight; **im ~ (der Öffentlichkeit) stehen** *(fig)* to be in the glare of publicity; **ein Problem ins ~ rücken** to spotlight or highlight a problem

Schein|wi|der|stand M sham resistance; *(Elec)* impedance, apparent resistance

Scheiß [ʃais] M -, *no pl (sl)* shit *(sl)*, crap *(sl)*; **ein ~** a load of shit *(sl)* or crap *(sl)*; **einen ~** *(= nichts)* fuck-all *(vulg)*; **~ machen** *(= herumalbern)* to bugger about *(Brit sl)*, to mess around *(inf)*; *(= Fehler machen)* to make a balls-up *(Brit sl)*, to screw up *(sl)*; **mach keinen ~!** don't do anything so bloody *(Brit inf)* or damn *(inf)* silly; **red doch keinen ~!** don't talk crap! *(esp Brit inf)*, cut (out) the crap! *(inf)*; **was soll der ~?** what the hell's the matter with you/him *etc*? *(inf)*

Scheiß- *in cpds (inf)* **a** *(= verdammt)* damn(ed) *(inf)*, bloody *(Brit sl)*, fucking *(vulg)*; **diese Scheißpolitiker!** those damn(ed) *etc* politicians! **b** *(= miserabel)* awful, crap(py) *(sl)*, shitty *(sl)*; **so ein Scheißwetter!** what awful *etc* weather!

Scheiß|dreck M *(vulg: = Kot)* shit *(sl)*, crap *(sl)*; *(sl) (= blödes Gerede, schlechtes Buch, schlechte Ware etc)* load of shit *(sl)*; *(= unangenehme Sache, Arbeit)* effing thing *(sl)*, bloody thing *(Brit inf)*; *(= Angelegenheiten)* effing business *(sl)*, bloody business *(Brit inf)*; **~!** shit! *(sl)*; **wegen jedem ~** about every effing *(sl)* or bloody *(Brit sl)* little thing; **das geht dich einen ~ an** it's none of your effing *(sl)* or bloody *(Brit inf)* business, it's got bugger all *(Brit inf)* or shit *(US vulg)* to do with you; **einen ~ werd ich tun!** like (bloody *(Brit inf)*) hell I will!; **sich einen ~ um jdn/etw kümmern** not to give a shit *(sl)* or a damn *(inf)* about sb/sth

Schei|ße ['ʃaisə] F -, *no pl (vulg: = Kot)* shit *(sl)*, crap *(sl)*; *(inf: = unangenehme Lage)* shit *(sl)*; *(inf: = Unsinn)* shit *(sl)*, crap *(sl)*; **(echt) ~ sein** *(inf)* to be bloody awful *(Brit inf)* or goddamn *(inf)* awful; *(= ärgerlich)* to be a bloody *(Brit inf)* or goddamn *(inf)* nuisance; **das ist doch alles ~** *(inf)* it's all a bloody mess *(Brit inf)*, it's all shit *(sl)*; *(= Unsinn)* it's all a load of shit *(sl)*; **in der**

~ sitzen *(inf)* to be in the shit *(sl)*, to be up shit creek *(sl)*; **~ bauen** *(inf)* to make a balls-up *(Brit sl)*, to screw up *(sl)* → *auch* **Scheiß**

scheiß|egal [ˈʃaisləˈgaːl] ADJ *(inf)* **das ist mir doch ~!** I don't give a shit *(sl)* *or* a damn *(inf)*

schei|ßen [ˈʃaisn] *pret* **schiss** [ʃɪs], *ptp* **geschissen** [gəˈʃɪsn] VI *(vulg)* to shit *(sl)*, to crap *(sl)*; **auf jdn/etw** *(acc)* **~** *(fig sl)* not to give a shit about sb/sth *(sl)* VR *(vulg)* **sich** *(dat)* **vor Angst in die Hosen ~** to have *or* get the shits *(sl)*, to shit oneself *(sl)*

Schei|ßer [ˈʃaisɐ] M **-s, -, Schei|ße|rin** [-ərɪn] F **-, -nen** *(sl: = Arschloch)* arsehole *(Brit sl)*, asshole *(US sl)*; *(inf: Kosename)* chubby cheeks *sing (hum inf)*

Schei|ße|rei [ʃaisəˈrai] F **-, -en** *(inf)* **die ~** the runs *(inf)*, the shits *(sl)*

Schei|ße|ri|tis [ʃaisəˈriːtɪs] F **-**, *no pl (hum inf)* = **Scheißerei**

Scheiß-: **scheiß|freund|lich** [ˈʃaisˈfrɔyntlɪç] ADJ *(inf)* as nice as pie *(iro inf)*; **Scheiß|haus** NT *(sl)* shithouse *(sl)*; **Scheiß|kerl** M *(inf)* bastard *(sl)*, sod *(Brit inf)*, son of a bitch *(sl)*, mother(fucker) *(US vulg)*; **Scheiß|wut** F *(sl)* **eine ~ (auf jdn/etw) haben** to be mad as hell (with sb/sth) *(inf)*

Scheit [ʃait] M **-(e)s, -e** *or (Aus, Sw)* **-er** log, piece of wood

Schei|tel [ˈʃaitl] M **-s, -** **a** *(= Haarscheitel)* parting *(Brit)*, part *(US)*; *(liter: = Haupthaar)* locks *pl*; **vom ~ bis zur Sohle** *(fig)* through and through **b** *(= höchster Punkt)* vertex

schei|teln [ˈʃaitln] VT to part

Schei|tel-: **Schei|tel|punkt** M vertex; **Schei|tel|wert** M peak (value); **Schei|tel|win|kel** M vertical angle

schei|ten [ˈʃaitn] VT *(Sw) Holz* to chop

Schei|ter|hau|fen [ˈʃaitɐ-] M (funeral) pyre; *(Hist: zur Hinrichtung)* stake; **die Hexe wurde auf dem ~ verbrannt** the witch was burned at the stake

schei|tern [ˈʃaitɐn] VI *aux sein* **a** *(an +dat* because of) *(Mensch, Unternehmen, Versuch)* to fail; *(Plan, Vorhaben auch)* to fall through; *(Verhandlungen, Ehe)* to break down; *(Regierung)* to founder *(an +dat* on); *(Mannschaft)* to be defeated *(an +dat* by); **die Partei scheiterte an der Fünf-Prozent-Hürde** the party fell at the five-percent hurdle → **Existenz b** *(dated: Schiff)* to be wrecked

Schei|tern [ˈʃaitɐn] NT **-s**, *no pl* **a** *(von Menschen, Unternehmen)* failure; *(von Plan, Vorhaben auch)* falling through; *(von Verhandlungen, Ehe)* breakdown; *(von Regierung)* foundering; *(von Mannschaft)* defeat; **das war zum ~ verurteilt** *or* **verdammt** that was doomed to failure; **etw zum ~ bringen** to make sth fail/fall through/break down **b** *(von Schiff)* wrecking

Scheit|holz NT firewood

Schelf [ʃɛlf] M OR NT **-s, -e** *(Geog)* (continental) shelf

Schelf|meer NT shelf sea

Schel|lack [ˈʃɛlak] M **-(e)s, -e** shellac

Schel|le [ˈʃɛlə] F **-, -n** **a** bell; *(dial: = Klingel)* (door)bell **b** *(Tech)* clamp **c** *(= Handschelle)* handcuff **d** *(dial)* = **Ohrfeige** **e** **Schellen** PL *(Cards)* ≈ diamonds *sing or pl (shaped like bells on traditional German cards)*

schel|len [ˈʃɛlən] VI to ring *(nach jdm* for sb); **es hat geschellt** the bell has gone; **bei jdm** *or* **an jds Tür** *(dat)* **~** to ring at sb's door

Schel|len-: **Schel|len|baum** M *(Mus)* Turkish crescent, pavillon chinois; **Schel|len|bu|be** M ≈ jack *or* knave *(Brit)* of diamonds; **Schel|len|ge|läut** NT, **Schel|len|ge|läu|te** NT jingling (of bells); **mit ~(e) fuhr der Pferdeschlitten vorbei** the sleigh passed by with its bells jingling; **Schel|len|kap|pe** F cap and bells, fool's cap; **Schel|len|kö|nig** M ≈ king of diamonds; **Schel|len|ober** M ≈ queen of diamonds *(a man on traditional German cards)*; **Schel|len|un|ter** [-ʊntɐ] M **-s, -** ≈ jack *or* knave *(Brit)* of diamonds

Schell|fisch [ˈʃɛl-] M haddock

Schelm [ʃɛlm] M **-(e)s, -e** *(dated: = Spaßvogel)* joker, wag *(dated)*; *(obs: = Gauner)* knave *(Brit obs)*, scoundrel; *(Liter)* picaro; **den ~ im Nacken haben** to be up to mischief; **ein ~, der Böses dabei denkt** *(prov)* honi soit qui mal y pense *(prov)*, evil to him who evil thinks *(prov)*

Schel|men-: **Schel|men|ge|sicht** NT mischievous face; **Schel|men|ro|man** M picaresque novel; **Schel|men|streich** M *(dated)* roguish prank, dirty trick; **Schel|men|stück** NT *(dated)* knavery *(esp Brit old)*, trickery; *(obs: = Missetat)* villainous deed *(old)*

schel|misch [ˈʃɛlmɪʃ] ADJ *Blick, Lächeln* mischievous ADV mischievously

Schel|te [ˈʃɛltə] F **-, -n** scolding; *(= Kritik)* attack; **er hat ~ bekommen** he got a scolding

schel|ten [ˈʃɛltn] *pret* **schalt** [ʃalt], *ptp* **gescholten** [gəˈʃɔltn] VT to scold, to chide; **jdn einen Dummkopf ~** to call sb an idiot; **(als) faul gescholten werden** to be called lazy VI *(= schimpfen)* to curse; **über** *or* **auf jdn/etw ~** to curse sb/sth, to rail at sb/sth *(old)*; **mit jdm ~** to scold sb

Schelt|wort NT *pl* **-worte** *or* **-wörter** word of abuse; **~e** words of abuse, invective *sing*

Sche|ma [ˈʃeːma] NT **-s, Schemen** *or* **-ta** [-mən, -ta] scheme; *(= Darstellung)* diagram; *(= Ordnung, Vorlage)* plan; *(= Muster)* pattern; *(Philos, Psych)* schema; **nach ~ F** in the same (old) way; **etw nach einem ~ machen** to do sth according to a pattern

sche|ma|tisch [ʃeˈmaːtɪʃ] ADJ schematic; *(= mechanisch)* mechanical ADV **etw ~ darstellen** to show sth schematically; **etw ~ umreißen** to give a general outline of sth; **~ vorgehen** to work methodically; **er arbeitet zu ~** he works too mechanically

sche|ma|ti|sie|ren [ʃematiˈziːrən] *ptp* **schematisiert** VTI to schematize

Sche|ma|tis|mus [ʃemaˈtɪsmʊs] M **-, Schematismen** [-mən] schematism

Sche|mel [ˈʃeːml] M **-s, -** stool

Sche|men [ˈʃeːmən] M **-s, -** silhouette; *(= Gespenst)* spectre

sche|men|haft ADJ shadowy; *Erinnerungen* hazy ADV **etw ~ sehen/erkennen** to see/make out the outlines of sth; **etw ~ zeichnen** to sketch sth; **die Bäume hoben sich ~ gegen den Himmel ab** the trees were silhouetted against the sky

Schen|ke [ˈʃɛŋkə] F **-, -n** tavern, inn

Schen|kel [ˈʃɛŋkl] M **-s, -** **a** *(Anat)* *(= Oberschenkel)* thigh; *(= Unterschenkel)* lower leg; **sich** *(dat)* **auf die ~ schlagen** to slap one's thighs; **dem Pferd die ~ geben** to press a horse on **b** *(von Zirkel)* leg; *(von Zange, Schere)* shank; *(Math: von Winkel)* side

Schen|kel-: **Schen|kel|bruch** M fracture of the thigh(bone) *or* femur; **Schen|kel|hals** M neck of the femur; **Schen|kel|hals|bruch** M fracture of the neck of the femur

schen|ken [ˈʃɛŋkn] VT **a** *(= Geschenk geben)* **jdm etw ~** to give sb sth *or* give sth to sb (as a present *or* gift); **sich** *(dat)* **(gegenseitig) etw ~** to give each other sth (as a present *or* gift); **etw geschenkt bekommen** to get sth as a present *or* gift; **etw zum Geburtstag/zu Weihnachten geschenkt bekommen** to get sth for one's birthday/for Christmas; **zu Weihnachten hat er nichts geschenkt bekommen** he didn't get anything *or* any presents for Christmas; **so was kaufe ich nicht, das lasse ich mir immer ~** I don't buy anything like that, I always like to get these things as presents; **ich möchte nichts geschenkt haben!** *(lit)* I don't want any presents!; *(fig: = bevorzugt werden)* I don't want any special treatment!; **ich nehme nichts geschenkt!** I'm not accepting any presents!; **das ist geschenkt!** *(inf) (= ist ein Geschenk)* it's a present; *(= nicht der Rede wert)* that's no great shakes *(inf)*; *(sl: = nichts wert)* forget it! *(inf)*; **das ist (fast** *or* **glatt) geschenkt!** *(inf: = billig)* that's dirt cheap *(inf)* *or* a giveaway *(inf)*; **das möchte ich nicht mal geschenkt haben!** I wouldn't want it if it was given to me; **einem geschenkten Gaul sieht man nicht ins Maul** *(Prov)* don't look a gift horse in the mouth *(Prov)*

b *(= erlassen)* **jdm etw ~** to let sb off sth; **ihm ist nie etwas geschenkt worden** *(fig)* he never had it easy

c **sich** *(dat)* **etw ~** to skip sth *(inf)*; **deine Komplimente kannst du dir ~!** you can keep your compliments *(inf)*; **sich** *(dat)* **die Mühe ~** to save oneself the trouble; **er hat sich** *(dat)* **nichts geschenkt** he spared no pains; **die beiden haben sich nichts geschenkt** neither was giving anything away

d *(in Verbindung mit n siehe auch dort)* **jdm das Leben ~** *(= begnadigen)* to spare sb's life; **einem Kind das Leben ~** *(geh)* to give birth to a child; **jdm die Freiheit ~** to set sb free; **jdm seine Liebe/seine Aufmerksamkeit** *etc* **~** to give sb one's love/one's attention *etc*; **jdm/einer Sache Glauben/keinen Glauben ~** to give credence/no credence to sb/sth; **jdm Vertrauen ~** to put one's trust in sb

VI to give presents

VR **sich jdm ~** *(liter: Frau)* to give oneself to sb

Schen|kung [ˈʃɛŋkʊŋ] F **-, -en** *(Jur)* gift

Schen|kungs-: **Schen|kungs|steu|er** F gift tax; **Schen|kungs|ur|kun|de** F deed of gift

schep|pern [ˈʃɛpɐn] VI *(dial)* to clatter; **es hat gescheppert** there was a clatter; *(loser Gegenstand)* there was a rattle; *(Autounfall)* there was a bang; *(Ohrfeige)* he/she got a clip round *(Brit)* *or* a slap on *(US)* the ear

Scher [ʃeːɐ] M **-(e)s, -e** *(S Ger, Aus, Sw)* mole

Scher|be [ˈʃɛrbə] F **-, -n** fragment, (broken) piece; *(= Glasscherbe/Porzellanscherbe/Keramikscherbe)* broken piece of glass/china/pottery; *(Archeol)* shard, potsherd; **etw in ~n schlagen** to shatter sth; **in ~n gehen** to break, to shatter; *(fig)* to fall *or* go to pieces; **~n machen** to break something; *(fig)* to put one's foot in it; **die ~n zusammenkehren** to sweep up the (broken) pieces; *(fig)* to pick up the pieces; **es hat ~n gegeben** *(fig)* there was lots of trouble; *(bei Streit)* sparks flew; **die ~n unseres Glücks** the shattered remains of our happiness; **~n bringen Glück** *(Prov)* broken crockery brings you luck

Scher|ben [ˈʃɛrbn] M **-s, -** *(S Ger, Aus)* = **Scherbe**

Scher|ben-: **Scher|ben|ge|richt** NT ostracism; **über jdn ein ~ abhalten** *(geh)* to take sb to task; **Scher|ben|hau|fen** M pile of smashed crockery; **wir stehen vor einem ~** *(fig)* it's all gone to pot *(inf)*, it's all come to nothing; **er stand vor dem ~ seiner Ehe** he was faced with the ruins of his marriage; **einen ~ hinterlassen** *(fig)* to leave behind a complete mess

Sche|re [ˈʃeːrə] F **-, -n** **a** *(Werkzeug) (klein)* scissors *pl*; *(groß)* shears *pl*; *(= Drahtschere)* wire-cutters *pl*; *(fig: = Kluft)* divide; **eine ~** a pair of scissors/shears/wire-cutters **b** *(Zool)* pincer; *(von Hummer, Krebs etc)* claw, pincer **c** *(Turnen, Ringen)* scissors *sing*

sche|ren [ˈʃeːrən] *pret* **schor** [ʃoːɐ], *ptp* **geschoren** [gəˈʃoːrən] VT to clip; *Schaf* to shear; *(Tech)* to shear; *Haare* to crop; *Bart (= rasieren)* to shave; *(= stutzen)* to trim; **er war/seine Haare waren kurz geschoren** his hair was cropped short → **kahl scheren, Kamm a**

sche|ren VTR *(= kümmern)* **sich nicht um jdn/etw ~** not to care *or* bother about sb/sth; **was schert mich das?** what do I care (about that)?, what's that to me?; **er scherte sich nicht im Geringsten darum** he couldn't have cared less about it VR *(inf)* **scher dich (weg)!** scram! *(inf)*, beat it! *(inf)*; **scher dich heim!** go home!; **scher dich ins Bett!** get to bed!; **es ist Zeit, dass du dich nach Hause scherst** it's time you were off (to *(US)*) home → **Teufel b, Kuckuck c**

Sche|ren-: **Sche|ren|fern|rohr** NT binocular periscope; **Sche|ren|git|ter** NT concertina barrier; **Sche|ren|schlag** M scissors kick;

Sche|ren|schlei|fer(in) M(F) scissor(s) grinder, knife grinder; **Sche|ren|schnitt** M silhouette

Sche|re|rei [ʃe:rəˈrai] F -, -en *usu pl (inf)* trouble *no pl*

Scherf|lein [ˈʃɛrflain] NT -s, *no pl (Bibl)* mite; **sein ~ (zu etw) beitragen** *or* **dazu geben** *or* **dazu beisteuern** *(Geld)* to pay one's bit (towards sth); *(fig)* to do one's bit (for sth) *(inf)*

Scher|ge [ˈʃɛrgə] M -n, -n **a** *(geh: = Büttel)* thug **b** *(obs: = Häscher)* henchman

Scher|gen|dienst M dirty work

Scher-: **Scher|kopf** M shaving head; **Scher|maus** F *(Aus, S Ger)* vole; *(Sw)* mole; **Scher|mes|ser** NT shearing knife; **Scher|wind** M *(Met)* wind shear; **Scher|wol|le** F fleece

Scherz [ʃɛrts] M -es, -e joke, jest; *(= Unfug)* tomfoolery *no pl*; **aus** *or* **zum ~** as a joke; **im ~** in jest; **einen ~ machen** to make a joke; *(= Streich)* to play a joke; **mach keine ~e!** *(inf)* you're joking!, you must be kidding! *(inf)*; **mit so etwas macht man keine ~e** you don't joke *or* make jokes about things like that; **zu ~en aufgelegt sein** to be in a joking mood; **seine ~e über jdn/etw machen** to make *or* crack jokes about sb/sth; **seine ~e (mit jdm) treiben** to play jokes; **sich** *(dat)* **(mit jdm) einen (schlechten) ~ erlauben** to play a (dirty) trick (on sb); **... und solche ~e** *(inf)* ... and what have you *(inf)*; **(ganz) ohne ~!** *(inf)* no kidding! *(inf)*; **~ beiseite!** joking aside *or* apart!

Scherz M -es, -e, **Scher|zel** [ˈʃɛrtsl] NT -s, - *(Aus)* hunk of bread; *(= Endstück)* heel

Scherz-: **Scherz|ar|ti|kel** M *usu pl* joke (article); **Scherz|bold** [-bɔlt] M -(e)s, -e *(inf)* joker *(inf)*

scher|zen [ˈʃɛrtsn] VI *(old, geh)* to joke, to jest; *(= albern)* to banter; *(= nicht ernst nehmen)* to trifle *(mit* with*)*; **mir scheint, du scherzt** you can't be serious; **ich scherze nicht** *(old, geh)* I'm not joking; **Sie belieben wohl zu ~!** *(old, geh)* surely you are in jest *(old, liter)*, surely you're joking; **mit jdm/etw ist nicht zu ~** one can't trifle with sb/sth

Scherz-: **Scherz|fra|ge** F riddle; **Scherz|gedicht** NT humorous poem; **scherz|haft** ADJ jocular, jovial; *Angelegenheit* joking; *(= spaßig) Einfall* playful ADV jokingly; **etw ~ sagen** to say sth jokingly *or* as a joke *or* in jest; **etw ~ meinen** to mean sth as a joke; **etw ~ aufnehmen** to take sth as a joke; **Scherz|keks** M *(inf)* joker *(inf)*

Scher|zo [ˈskɛrtso] NT -s, -s *or* **Scherzi** [-tsi] scherzo

Scherz|wort NT *pl* -worte witticism, jocular *or* joking remark

sche|sen [ˈʃe:zn] VI *aux sein (dial)* to rush

scheu [ʃɔy] ADJ *(= schüchtern)* shy; *(= ängstlich) Reh, Tier auch* timid; *(= zaghaft) Versuche, Worte* cautious; **jdn ~ machen** to make sb shy; *(= ängstigen)* to frighten *or* scare sb; **mach doch die Pferde** *or* **Gäule nicht ~** *(fig inf)* keep your hair *(Brit) or* head *(US) or* shirt on *(inf)*; **~ werden** *(Pferd)* to be frightened ADV shyly, timidly

Scheu [ʃɔy] F -, *no pl* fear *(vor +dat* of*)*; *(= Schüchternheit)* shyness; *(von Reh, Tier)* shyness, timidity; *(= Hemmung)* inhibition; *(= Ehrfurcht)* awe; **seine ~ verlieren** to lose one's inhibitions; **ohne jede ~** without any inhibition; *sprechen* quite freely

scheu|chen [ˈʃɔyçn] VT to shoo (away); *(= verscheuchen)* to frighten *or* scare away *or* off; *(= antreiben) Tiere* to drive; *Menschen* to shoo (along)

scheu|en [ˈʃɔyən] VT *Kosten, Arbeit, Vergleich, Konflikt, Risiko* to shy away from; *Menschen, Licht* to shun; **weder Mühe noch Kosten ~** to spare neither trouble nor expense; **keine Mühe(n) ~** to go to endless trouble; **wir brauchen den Vergleich mit ihnen nicht zu ~** we don't have to be afraid of the comparison with them VR **sich vor etw** *(dat)* **~** *(= Angst haben)* to be afraid of sth; *(= zurückschrecken)* to shy away from sth; **sich (davor) ~, etw zu tun** *(= Angst haben)* to be afraid of doing sth; *(= zurückschrecken)* to shrink back from doing sth; **und ich scheue mich nicht, das zu sagen** and I'm not afraid of saying it VI *(Pferd etc)* to shy *(vor +dat* at*)*

Scheu|er [ˈʃɔyɐ] F -, -n barn

Scheu|er-: **Scheu|er|be|sen** M scrubbing *(Brit) or* scrub *(US)* broom; **Scheu|er|bürs|te** F scrubbing *(Brit) or* scrub *(US)* brush; **Scheu|er|frau** F char *(Brit)*, cleaning woman; **Scheu|er|lap|pen** M floorcloth; **Scheu|er|leis|te** F skirting board *(Brit)*, baseboard *(US)*; **Scheu|er|mit|tel** NT scouring agent

scheu|ern [ˈʃɔyɐn] VTI **a** *(= putzen)* to scour; *(mit Bürste)* to scrub **b** *(= reiben)* to chafe; **der Rucksack scheuert mich am Rücken** the rucksack is chafing my back; **der Kragen scheuert am Hals** the collar chafes at the neck VT *(inf)* **jdm eine ~** to smack sb one *(inf)* VR **sich (an etw** *dat***) ~** to rub (against sth); **sich** *(acc)* **(wund) ~** to chafe oneself

Scheu|er-: **Scheu|er|sand** M scouring powder; **Scheu|er|tuch** NT *pl* **-tücher** floor cloth

Scheu|klap|pe F blinker *(Brit)*, blinder *(US)*; **~n haben** *or* **tragen** *(lit, fig)* to be blinkered *(Brit)*, to wear blinkers *(Brit) or* blinders *(US)*; **mit ~n herumlaufen** *or* **durchs Leben laufen** to be wearing blinkers *(Brit) or* blinders *(US)*

scheu+ma|chen VT *sep* → **scheu**

Scheu|ne [ˈʃɔynə] F -, -n barn

Scheu|nen-: **Scheu|nen|dre|scher** M **wie ein ~ fressen** *(inf)* to eat like a horse *(inf)*; **Scheu|nen|tor** NT barn door → **Ochse**

Scheu|re|be [ˈʃɔyre:bə] F -, -n **a** *no pl (Rebsorte)* Scheurebe grape **b** *(Wein)* Scheurebe wine

Scheu|sal [ˈʃɔyza:l] NT -s, -e *or (inf)* **Scheusäler** [-zɛ:lɐ] monster

scheuß|lich [ˈʃɔyslɪç] ADJ dreadful; *(= abstoßend hässlich)* hideous ADV **a** *(= widerlich) kochen* terribly; *speisen* badly; **~ riechen/schmecken** to smell/taste terrible **b** *(= gemein) sich benehmen* dreadfully, terribly **c** *(inf: = furchtbar)* dreadfully; **es hat ~ wehgetan** it hurt dreadfully, it was horribly *or* terribly painful

Scheuß|lich|keit F -, -en **a** *no pl (= das Scheußlichsein)* dreadfulness; *(= Hässlichkeit)* hideousness **b** *(= Greueltat etc)* monstrosity

Schi [ʃi:] M -s, -er *or* - [ˈʃi:ɐ] = **Ski**

Schicht [ʃɪçt] F -, -en **a** *(= Lage)* layer; *(= dünne Schicht)* film; *(Geol, Sci)* layer, stratum; *(= Farbschicht)* coat; *(der Gesellschaft)* level, stratum; **breite ~en der Bevölkerung** large sections of the population; **aus allen ~en (der Bevölkerung)** from all walks of life **b** *(= Arbeitsabschnitt, -gruppe etc)* shift; **er hat jetzt ~** *(inf)* **er ist auf ~** *(inf)* he's on shift; **zur ~ gehen** to go on shift; **er muss ~ arbeiten** he has to work shifts

Schicht-: **Schicht|ar|beit** F shiftwork; **Schicht|ar|bei|ter(in)** M(F) shiftworker; **Schicht|be|trieb** M shift operation; **im ~ arbeiten** to work in shifts; **Schicht|dienst** M shiftwork; **~ haben** to be working shifts

schich|ten [ˈʃɪçtn] VT to layer; *Holz, Steine, Bücher etc* to stack VR *(Geol)* to form layers; *(Gestein)* to stratify

schich|ten|spe|zi|fisch ADJ *(Sociol)* specific to a particular social stratum

Schicht-: **Schicht|kä|se** M *low-fat quark with an interposed layer of high-fat quark*; **Schicht|lohn** M shift(work) rates *pl*; **Schicht|stoff** M laminate; **Schicht|stoff|plat|te** F laminated sheet

Schich|tung [ˈʃɪçtʊŋ] F -, -en layering; *(von Holz, Heu, Büchern etc)* stacking; *(Sociol, Geol, Met)* stratification

Schicht-: **Schicht|un|ter|richt** M teaching in shifts; **Schicht|wech|sel** M change of shifts; **um 6 Uhr ist ~ bei uns** we change *or* switch *(US)* shifts at six o'clock; **schicht|wei|se** ADV in layers; *(Farbe, Lack)* in coats

schick [ʃɪk] ADJ elegant, smart; *Haus, Wohnung auch, Möbel* stylish; *Frauenmode, Kleidung* chic; *Auto* smart; *(inf: = prima)* great *(inf)* ADV stylishly, smartly

Schick [ʃɪk] M -s, *no pl* style; *(von Frauenmode, Frau auch)* chic

schi|cken [ˈʃɪkn] ✪ 48.1, 48.3 VTI to send; **(jdm) etw ~** to send sth (to sb), to send (sb) sth; **jdn einkaufen ~** to send sb to do the shopping; **jdn Bier holen ~** to send sb to fetch some beer *or* for some beer, to send sb on a beer run *(US)*; **(jdn) nach jdm/etw ~** to send (sb) for sb/sth; **jdn in den Ruhestand ~** to pension sb off VR *impers (= sich ziemen)* to be fitting *or* proper; **das schickt sich nicht für ein Mädchen** it does not befit *or* become a girl VR *(old: = sich abfinden)* **sich in etw** *(acc)* **~** to resign *or* reconcile oneself to sth

Schi|cke|ria [ʃɪkəˈri:a] F -, *no pl (iro)* in-crowd *(inf)*

Schi|cki|mi|cki [ʃɪkiˈmɪki] M -(s), -s *(inf)* trendy

schick|lich [ˈʃɪklɪç] ADJ *Kleidung* proper, fitting; *Verhalten* seemly, becoming; **es ist nicht ~ zu pfeifen** it is unseemly *or* unbecoming to whistle ADV properly, as one should

Schick|lich|keit F seemliness; **sobald die ~ es zulässt** as soon as it is seemly to do so

Schick|sal [ˈʃɪkza:l] NT -s, -e fate, destiny; *(= Pech)* fate; **das ~ wollte es, (dass) ...** as fate would have it, ...; **~ spielen** to influence fate; **die ~e der Flüchtlinge** the fate of the refugees; **manche schweren ~e** many a difficult fate; **das sind (schwere) ~e** those are tragic cases; **er hat ein schweres ~ gehabt** *or* **durchgemacht** fate has been unkind to him; **(das ist) ~** *(inf)* that's life; **jdn seinem ~ überlassen** to leave *or* abandon sb to his fate; **sein ~ herausfordern** to tempt fate *or* providence; **dem ~ haben wir es zu verdanken, dass ...** we have to thank our good fortune that ...; **das ~ hat es gut mit uns gemeint** fortune has smiled on us

schick|sal|haft ADJ fateful

Schick|sals-: **schick|sals|er|ge|ben** ADJ resigned to one's fate *pred*; **Schick|sals|fra|ge** F fateful question; **Schick|sals|ge|fähr|te** M, **Schick|sals|ge|fähr|tin** F companion in misfortune; **Schick|sals|ge|mein|schaft** F **wir waren eine ~** we shared a common destiny; **Schick|sals|glau|be** M fatalism; **Schick|sals|göt|tin** F goddess of destiny; **die ~nen** the Fates; *(= Nornen)* the Norns; **Schick|sals|schlag** M great misfortune, stroke of fate; **Schick|sals|tra|gö|die** F tragedy of fate *or* destiny; **Schick|sals|wen|de** F change in fortune

Schick|se [ˈʃɪksə] F -, -n *(pej inf)* floozy *(pej inf)*

Schi|ckung [ˈʃɪkʊŋ] F -, -en *(liter)* act of providence *(esp Brit) or* God

Schie|be-: **Schie|be|büh|ne** F traverser; *(Theat)* sliding stage; **Schie|be|dach** NT sunroof; **Schie|be|fens|ter** NT sliding window

schie|ben [ˈʃi:bn] *pret* **schob** [ʃo:p], *ptp* **geschoben** [gəˈʃo:bn] VT **a** *(= bewegen)* to push, to shove; *Fahrrad, Rollstuhl etc* to push, to wheel; *Auto* to push; *(in den Ofen)* to put; **etw von sich** *(dat)* **~** *(fig)* to put sth aside; *Schuld, Verantwortung* to reject sth; **etw vor sich** *(dat)* **her ~** *(fig)* to put off sth; **etw von einem Tag auf den andern ~** to put sth off from one day to the next; **etw auf jdn/etw ~** to blame sb/sth for sth, to put the blame onto sb/sth; **die Schuld auf jdn ~** to put the blame on sb; **die Verantwortung auf jdn ~** to put the responsibility at sb's door → **beiseiteschieben**
b *(= stecken)* to put; *Hände* to slip, to put; **jdm/sich etw in den Mund ~** to put sth into sb's/one's mouth
c *(inf: = handeln mit)* to traffic in; *Drogen* to push *(inf)*
d *(inf)* **Dienst/Wache ~** to do duty/guard duty → **Kohldampf**
e *(Rail)* to shunt
VI **a** *(= drücken, schubsen)* to push, to shove

b *(inf)* **mit etw ~** to traffic in sth; **mit Drogen ~** to push drugs *(inf)*
c *(inf: = begünstigen)* to wangle *(inf)*; **da wurde viel geschoben** there was a lot of wangling going on *(inf)*
VR a *(mit Anstrengung)* to push, to shove; **sich an die Spitze ~** to push one's way to the front
b *(= sich bewegen)* to move

Schie|ber [ˈʃiːbɐ] **M -s, - a** slide; *(am Ofen etc)* damper; *(= Bettpfanne)* bedpan; *(= Essbesteck für Kinder)* pusher **b** *(inf: = Tanz)* shuffle

Schie|ber [ˈʃiːbɐ] **M -s, -, Schie|be|rin** [-ərɪn] **F -, -nen** *(= Schwarzhändler)* black marketeer; *(= Waffenschieber)* gunrunner; *(= Drogenschieber)* pusher *(inf)*

Schie|be|reg|ler **M** *(Tech)* slide control; *(Comput: in Dialogfeldern)* slider

Schie|be|rei [ʃiːbəˈrai] **F -, -en** *(inf)* **a** *(= Drängelei)* pushing, shoving **b** *(= Begünstigung)* string-pulling *no pl* **c** *(= Schwarzhandel)* black marketeering; *(mit Waffen)* gunrunning

Schie|ber|ge|schäft **NT** shady deal; *(= Schwarzhandel)* black marketeering

Schie|ber|müt|ze **F** flat cap

Schie|be-: **Schie|be|sitz** **M** sliding seat; **Schie|be|tür** **F** sliding door; **Schie|be|wand** **F** sliding partition (wall)

Schieb|leh|re **F** calliper *(Brit)* or caliper *(US)* rule

Schie|bung [ˈʃiːbʊŋ] **F -, -en** *(= Begünstigung)* string-pulling *no pl*; *(Sport)* rigging; *(= Schiebergeschäfte)* shady deals *pl*; **der ~ bezichtigt werden** to be accused of rigging; **das war doch ~** that was rigged, that was a fix; **die Zuschauer riefen „Schiebung!"** the spectators shouted "fix!"

schiech [ʃiːçʃ] **ADJ** *(Aus)* **a** *(= hässlich)* ugly **b** *(= bang)* **jdm wird ~** sb gets scared

schied *pret von* **scheiden**

schied|lich [ˈʃiːtlɪç] **ADV ~ und friedlich** amicably

Schieds-: **Schieds|frau** **F** arbitrator, arbiter; **Schieds|ge|richt** **NT**, **Schieds|ge|richts|hof** **M** court of arbitration; **schieds|ge|richt|lich** **ADJ** arbitral **ADV** by arbitration; **Schieds|ge|richts|bar|keit** **F** arbitral jurisdiction; **Schieds|mann** **M** *pl* **-leute** arbitrator, arbiter; **Schieds|rich|ter(in)** **M(F)** arbitrator, arbiter; *(Fußball, Eishockey, Boxen)* referee; *(Hockey, Tennis, Federball, Kricket, Mil)* umpire; *(= Preisrichter)* judge; **Schieds|rich|ter|ent|schei|dung** **F** *(Sport)* referee's/umpire's decision; **schieds|rich|ter|lich** **ADJ** arbitrational, arbitral; *(bei Hockey, Federball, Kricket, Tennis)* umpiring; *(bei Fußball, Eishockey, Boxen)* refereeing **ADV das muss ~ entschieden werden** the arbitrator/referee *etc* decides; **schieds|rich|tern** [ˈʃiːtsrɪçtɐn] **VI** *insep (inf)* → **Schiedsrichter(in)** to arbitrate/referee/umpire/judge; **Schieds|rich|ter|stuhl** **M** *(Tennis etc)* umpire's chair; **Schieds|spruch** **M** (arbitral) award; **Schieds|stel|le** **F** arbitration service; **Schieds|ver|fah|ren** **NT** arbitration proceedings *pl*

schief [ʃiːf] **ADJ** crooked, not straight *pred*; *(= nach einer Seite geneigt)* lopsided, tilted; *Winkel* oblique; *Blick, Lächeln* wry; *Absätze* worn (-down); *(fig: = unzutreffend)* inappropriate; *Deutung* wide of the mark, inappropriate; *Bild* distorted; **~e Ebene** *(Phys)* inclined plane; **auf die ~e Bahn geraten** or **kommen** *(fig)* to leave the straight and narrow; **einen ~en Mund** or **ein ~es Gesicht ziehen** *(fig inf)* to pull a (wry) face; **der Schiefe Turm von Pisa** the Leaning Tower of Pisa → **Licht**
ADV a *(= schräg) halten, wachsen* crooked; *hinstellen* at an angle; **er hatte den Hut ~ auf** he wore his hat at an angle; **~ laufen** to walk lopsidedly; **das Bild hängt ~** the picture is crooked or isn't straight
b *(= scheel)* **jdn ~ ansehen** *(fig)* to look askance at sb; **sie lächelte ~** she gave me a crooked smile
c *(= unrichtig) übersetzen* badly; **etw ~ schildern/wiedergeben** to give a distorted version of sth; **du siehst die Sache ganz ~!** *(fig)* you're looking at it all wrong!; **~ gewickelt** → **schiefgewickelt**

Schie|fe [ˈʃiːfə] **F -,** *no pl* crookedness; *(= Neigung)* lopsidedness, tilt; *(von Ebene)* inclination; *(von Winkel)* obliqueness

Schie|fer [ˈʃiːfɐ] **M -s, -** *(Gesteinsart)* slate; *(esp Aus: = Holzsplitter)* splinter

Schie|fer-: **Schie|fer|bruch** **M** slate quarry; **Schie|fer|dach** **NT** slate roof; **schie|fer|grau** **ADJ** slate-grey; **Schie|fer|kas|ten** **M** pencil box; **Schie|fer|plat|te** **F** slate; **Schie|fer|stift** **M** slate pencil; **Schie|fer|ta|fel** **F** slate

schief-: **schief+ge|hen** *sep irreg aux sein*, **schief ge|hen** △ *irreg aux sein* **VI** to go wrong; **es wird schon ~!** *(hum)* it'll be OK *(inf)*; **schief|ge|wi|ckelt** [-gəvɪklt] **ADJ** *(fig inf)* on the wrong track; **da bist du ~** you've got a surprise coming to you there *(inf)*; **wenn du das denkst, bist du ~!** if you think that, you're very much mistaken; **schief+la|chen** **VR** *sep (inf)* to kill oneself (laughing) *(inf)*; **Schief|la|ge** **F a** *(lit, auch Geol)* inclined position **b** *(fig)* tricky situation; **in ~** in difficulties; **in eine gefährliche ~ geraten** to get into serious difficulties; **schief+lau|fen** *sep irreg aux sein*, **schief lau|fen** △ *irreg aux sein* **VI** *(inf)* to go wrong; **schief lau|fen** *irreg*, **schief+lau|fen** *sep irreg* **VT = schief treten**; **schief+lie|gen** *sep irreg (S Ger, Aus, Sw: aux sein)*, **schief lie|gen** △ *irreg (S Ger, Aus, Sw: aux sein)* **VI** *(inf)* to be wrong; **mit einer Meinung ~** to be on the wrong track; **schief tre|ten** *irreg*, **schief+tre|ten** *sep irreg* **VT** *Absätze* to wear down; **die Schuhe ~** to wear down the heels of one's shoes; **schief|win|ke|lig**, **schief|wink|lig** **ADJ** oblique-angled

schiel|äu|gig **ADJ** cross-eyed, squint-eyed, boss-eyed *(Brit)*

schie|len [ˈʃiːlən] **VI** to squint, to be cross-eyed or boss-eyed *(Brit)*; **auf** or **mit einem Auge ~** to have a squint in one eye; **auf etw** *(acc)* **~** *(inf)* to steal a glance at sth; **nach jdm/etw ~** *(inf)* to look at sb/sth out of the corner of one's eye; *(begehrlich)* to eye sb/sth up *(Brit)*, to look sb/sth up and down; *(heimlich)* to sneak a look at sb/sth

schien *pret von* **scheinen**

Schien|bein [ˈʃiːnbain] **NT** shin; *(= Schienbeinknochen)* shinbone; **jdm gegen** or **vor das ~ treten** to kick sb on or in *(esp US)* the shin(s)

Schien|bein|scho|ner **M**, **Schien|bein|schutz** **M**, **Schien|bein|schüt|zer** [-ʃʏtsɐ] **M -s, -** shin pad, shin guard

Schie|ne [ˈʃiːnə] **F -, -n a** rail; *(Med)* splint; *(von Lineal)* edge, guide; *(von Winkelmesser)* blade; **auf oberster ~ backen** *(im Backofen)* to bake at the top of the oven **b Schienen PL** *(Rail)* track *sing*, rails *pl*; **aus den ~n springen** to leave or jump the rails; **Verkehr auf die ~(n) verlagern** to transfer traffic onto the rails **c** *(fig)* **auf der politischen ~** along political lines; **ein Problem auf der pragmatischen/politischen ~ lösen** to solve a problem pragmatically/by political means; **auf der emotionalen ~** on an emotional level

schie|nen [ˈʃiːnən] **VT** *Arm, Bein* to put in a splint/splints, to splint; *Bruch* to splint

Schie|nen-: **Schie|nen|bahn** **F a** *(Transportsystem)* track transport **b** *(Fahrzeug)* track vehicle; **Schie|nen|brem|se** **F** slipper brake; **Schie|nen|bus** **M** rail bus; **Schie|nen|er|satz|ver|kehr** **M** *(Rail)* alternative transport(ation) *(when trains or trams are not running)*; **Schie|nen|fahr|zeug** **NT** track vehicle; **schie|nen|gleich** **ADJ ~er Straßenübergang** level crossing *(Brit)*, grade crossing *(US)*; **Schie|nen|netz** **NT** *(Rail)* rail network; **Schie|nen|räu|mer** [-rɔymɐ] **M -s, -** track clearer; **Schie|nen|strang** **M** (section of) track; **Schie|nen|weg** **M** railway *(Brit)* or railroad *(US)* line; **etw auf dem ~ versenden** to send sth by rail

schier [ʃiːɐ] **ADJ** pure; *(fig)* sheer

schier **ADV** *(= beinahe)* nearly, almost

Schier|ling [ˈʃiːɐlɪŋ] **M -s, -e** hemlock

Schier|lings|be|cher **M** (cup of) hemlock

Schieß-: **Schieß|be|fehl** **M** order to fire or shoot; **Schieß|bu|de** **F** shooting gallery; **Schieß|bu|den|fi|gur** **F** target figure or doll; *(fig inf)* clown; **du siehst ja aus wie eine ~** you look like something out of a pantomime; **Schieß|ei|sen** **NT** *(hum inf)* shooting iron *(inf)*

schie|ßen [ˈʃiːsn] *pret* **schoss** [ʃɔs], *ptp* **geschossen** [gəˈʃɔsn] **VT** to shoot; *Kugel, Rakete* to fire *(auf jdn/etw* at sb/sth); *(Ftbl etc)* to kick; *Tor* to score; *(mit Stock, Schläger)* to hit; **jdn in den Kopf ~** to shoot sb in the head; **etw an der Schießbude ~** to win sth at the shooting gallery; **ein paar Bilder ~** *(Phot inf)* to shoot a few pictures, to take a few shots; **eine Filmszene ~** *(inf)* to shoot a film scene; **sie hat ihn zum Krüppel geschossen** she shot and crippled him
VI a *(mit Waffe, Ball)* to shoot; **auf jdn/etw ~** to shoot at sb/sth; **nach etw ~** to shoot at sth; **aufs Tor/ins Netz ~** to shoot or kick at goal/into the net; **es wurde scharf geschossen** there was shooting with live ammunition; **das ist zum Schießen** *(inf)* that's a scream *(inf)*
b *aux sein (= in die Höhe schießen)* to shoot up; *(Bot: = Samenstand entwickeln)* to run *(Brit)* or go to seed; **die Pflanzen/Kinder sind in die Höhe geschossen** the plants/children have shot up; **die Preise schossen in die Höhe** prices rocketed; **(wie Pilze) aus dem Boden ~** *(lit, fig)* to spring or sprout up → **Kraut b**
c *aux sein (inf: = sich schnell bewegen)* to shoot; **er ist** or **kam um die Ecke geschossen** he shot round the corner; **jdm durch den Kopf ~** *(fig)* to flash through sb's mind
d *aux sein (Flüssigkeit)* to shoot; *(= spritzen)* to spurt; **das Blut schoss ihm ins Gesicht** blood rushed or shot to his face; **die Tränen schossen ihr in die Augen** tears flooded her eyes
e *aux sein (S Ger, Aus: = verbleichen)* to fade
VR to have a shoot-out

Schie|ße|rei [ʃiːsəˈrai] **F -, -en** gun battle, shoot-out; *(= das Schießen)* shooting; **bei einer ~ getötet werden** to be killed in a shoot-out

Schieß-: **Schieß|ge|wehr** **NT** *(hum)* gun; **Schieß|hund** **M wie ein ~ aufpassen** *(inf)* to keep a close watch, to watch like a hawk; **Schieß|kunst** **F** marksmanship *no pl*; **Schieß|platz** **M** (shooting or firing) range; **Schieß|prü|gel** **M** *(sl)* iron *(inf)*; **Schieß|pul|ver** **NT** gunpowder; **Schieß|schar|te** **F** embrasure; **Schieß|schei|be** **F** target; **Schieß|sport** **M** shooting; **Schieß|stand** **M** shooting range; *(= Schießbude)* shooting gallery; **Schieß|übung** **F** shooting or target practice *no pl*

Schiet [ʃiːt] **M -s,** *no pl (N Ger inf)* = **Scheiße**

Schiff [ʃɪf] **NT -(e)s, -e a** ship; **das ~ der Wüste** *(geh)* the ship of the desert; **das ~ des Staates** *(geh)* the ship of state → **klar b** *(Archit)* *(= Mittelschiff)* nave; *(= Seitenschiff)* aisle; *(= Querschiff)* transept **c** *(in Kohleherd)* boiler **d** *(Typ: = Setzschiff)* galley

Schiffahrt △ **F** → **Schifffahrt**

Schiff-: **schiff|bar** **ADJ** *Gewässer* navigable; **Schiff|bar|keit** [ˈʃɪfbaːɐkait] **F -,** *no pl* navigability; **Schiff|bar|ma|chung** [ˈʃɪfbaːɐmaxʊŋ] **F -, -en** *(von Fluss)* canalization; **Schiff|bau** **M,** *no pl* shipbuilding; **Schiff|bau|er(in)** **M(F)** *pl* **-bauer(innen)** shipwright; **Schiff|bruch** **M** shipwreck; **~ erleiden** *(lit)* to be shipwrecked; *(fig)* to fail; *(Firma)* to founder; **schiff|brü|chig** **ADJ** shipwrecked; **~ werden** to be shipwrecked; **Schiff|brü|chi|ge(r)** [-brʏçɪgə] **MF** *decl as adj* person who has/had been shipwrecked

Schiff|chen [ˈʃɪfçən] **NT -s, - a** *(zum Spielen)* little boat **b** *(Mil, Fashion)* forage cap **c** *(Tex,*

Sew) shuttle **d** *(Bot)* keel, carina *(spec)* **e** *(für Weihrauch)* boat

schif|fen [ˈʃɪfn] VI **a** *aux sein (old) (= Schiff fahren)* to ship *(old)*, to go by ship; *(= Schiff steuern)* to steer **b** *(sl: = urinieren)* to piss *(sl)* VI *impers (sl: = regnen)* to piss down *(Brit inf)*, to pour down

Schif|fer [ˈʃɪfɐ] M **-s, -, Schif|fe|rin** [-ərɪn] F **-, -nen** boatman, sailor; *(von Lastkahn)* bargee; *(= Kapitän)* skipper

Schif|fer-: **Schif|fer|kla|vier** NT accordion; **Schif|fer|kno|ten** M sailor's knot; **Schif|fer|müt|ze** F yachting cap

Schiff|fahrt F shipping; *(= Schifffahrtskunde)* navigation; **die ~ wurde eingestellt** all shipping movements were halted

Schiff|fahrts-: **Schiff|fahrts|ge|sell|schaft** F shipping company; **Schiff|fahrts|kun|de** F navigation; **Schiff|fahrts|li|nie** F **a** *(= Schiffsweg)* shipping route **b** *(= Unternehmen)* shipping line; **Schiff|fahrts|recht** NT maritime law; **Schiff|fahrts|stra|ße** F, **Schiff|fahrts|weg** M *(= Kanal)* waterway; *(= Schifffahrtslinie)* shipping route *or* lane

Schiffs- *in cpds* ship's; **Schiffs|an|le|ge|stel|le** F ship's berth, ship's mooring point; **Schiffs|arzt** M, **Schiffs|ärz|tin** F ship's doctor; **Schiffs|bauch** M bilge; **Schiffs|be|sat|zung** F ship's company

Schiff|schau|kel F swingboat

Schiffs-: **Schiffs|eig|ner(in)** M(F) *(form)* shipowner; **Schiffs|füh|rer(in)** M(F) *(form)* boatman; *(= Kapitän)* master, skipper; **Schiffs|hy|po|thek** F ship mortgage; **Schiffs|jun|ge** M ship's boy; **Schiffs|ka|pi|tän(in)** M(F) ship's captain; **Schiffs|kar|te** F chart; **Schiffs|koch** M, **Schiffs|kö|chin** F ship's cook; **Schiffs|kör|per** M *(form)* hull; **Schiffs|la|dung** F shipload; **Schiffs|mak|ler(in)** M(F) ship-broker; **Schiffs|mann|schaft** F ship's crew; **Schiffs|mo|dell** NT model ship; **Schiffs|pa|pie|re** PL ship's papers *pl*; **Schiffs|raum** M hold; **Schiffs|re|gis|ter** NT register of shipping; **Schiffs|rumpf** M hull; **Schiffs|schna|bel** M bow; **Schiffs|schrau|be** F ship's propeller; **Schiffs|ta|ge|buch** NT ship's log; **Schiffs|tau** NT (ship's) rope; **Schiffs|tau|fe** F christening *or* naming of a/the ship; **Schiffs|trans|port** M maritime transport; **Schiffs|un|fall** M, **Schiffs|un|glück** NT shipping accident; *(Zusammenstoß)* ship collision; **Schiffs|ver|bin|dung** F connecting boat service; **Schiffs|ver|kehr** M shipping; **Schiffs|werft** F shipyard; **Schiffs|zwie|back** M ship's biscuit

Schi|is|mus [ʃiˈɪsmʊs] M **-**, *no pl* Shiism

Schi|it [ʃiˈiːt] M **-en, -en, Schi|i|tin** [-ˈiːtɪn] F **-, -nen** Shiite

schi|i|tisch [ʃiˈiːtɪʃ] ADJ Shiite

Schi|ka|ne [ʃiˈkaːnə] F **-, -n** **a** harassment; *(von Mitschülern)* bullying *no pl*; **diese neuerlichen ~n an der Grenze** this recent harassment at the border; **das hat er aus reiner ~ gemacht** he did it out of sheer bloody-mindedness *(Brit) or* pig-headedness; **die Schüler brauchen sich nicht alle ~n gefallen zu lassen** the pupils don't have to put up with being messed around *(inf)* **b mit allen ~n** *(inf)* with all the trimmings **c** *(Sport)* chicane

schi|ka|nie|ren [ʃikaˈniːrən] *ptp* **schikaniert** VT to harass, to bully; *Ehepartner, Freundin etc* to mess around; *Mitschüler* to bully; **ich lasse mich nicht weiter von diesem Weibsstück ~** I won't let this female mess me around any more *(inf)*; **er hat mich einmal so schikaniert, dass ...** he once gave me such a rough time that ...

schi|ka|nös [ʃikaˈnøːs] ADJ *Mensch* bloody-minded *(Brit)*, pig-headed; *Maßnahme etc* harassing; *Mitschüler, Ehemann, Vorgesetzter* bullying; **~e Behandlung** harassment; bullying ADV **jdn ~ behandeln** to give sb a rough time, to harass/bully sb

Schi|ko|ree [ˈʃɪkore] F **-** *or m* **-s**, *no pl* chicory

Schild [ʃɪlt] M **-(e)s, -e** [-də] shield; *(= Wappenschild)* escutcheon; *(von Schildkröte)* shell, carapace *(spec)*; **etwas im ~e führen** *(fig)* to be up to something; **nichts Gutes im ~e führen** *(fig)* to be up to no good; **jdn auf den ~ heben** *(fig)* to make sb one's leader

Schild NT **-(e)s, -er** [-dɐ] *(= Aushang, Warenschild, Verkehrsschild)* sign; *(= Wegweiser)* signpost; *(= Namensschild, Türschild)* nameplate; *(= Kennzeichen)* number plate *(Brit)*, license plate *(US)*; *(= Preisschild)* ticket; *(= Etikett: an Käfig, Gepäck etc)* label; *(= Plakette)* badge; *(= Plakat)* placard; *(von Plakatträger)* board; *(an Monument, Haus, Grab)* plaque; *(von Mütze)* peak; **im Fenster stand ein ~** there was a sign *or* notice in the window

Schild|bür|ger(in) M(F) *(Liter)* ≈ Gothamite; *(hum)* fool

Schild|bür|ger|streich M foolish act; **das war ein ~** that was a stupid thing to do

Schild|chen [ˈʃɪltçən] NT **-s, -** → **Schild** small sign; small plate *etc*

Schild|drü|se F thyroid gland; **an der ~ leiden** to have a thyroid complaint

Schild|drü|sen-: **Schild|drü|sen|hor|mon** NT thyroid hormone; **Schild|drü|sen|über|funk|ti|on** F overactive thyroid, hyperthyroidism *(spec)*; **Schild|drü|sen|un|ter|funk|ti|on** F underactive thyroid, hypothyrosis *(spec)*

Schil|de|rer [ˈʃɪldərɐ] M **-s, -, Schil|de|rin** [-ərɪn] F **-, -nen** portrayer

Schil|der|haus NT, **Schil|der|häus|chen** [-hɔysçən] NT sentry box

Schil|der|ma|ler(in) M(F) sign writer

schil|dern [ˈʃɪldɐn] VT *Ereignisse, Situation, Erlebnisse, Vorgänge* to describe; *(= skizzieren)* to outline; *Menschen, Landschaften* to portray; **es ist kaum zu ~** it's almost impossible to describe; **es ist kaum zu ~, wie frech er war** he was indescribably cheeky *(Brit) or* fresh *(US)*; **~ Sie den Verlauf des Unfalls** give an account of how the accident happened → **Farbe a**

Schil|de|rung [ˈʃɪldərʊŋ] F **-, -en** *(= Beschreibung)* description; *(= Bericht: auch von Zeuge)* account; *(= literarische Schilderung)* portrayal

Schil|der|wald M *(hum)* forest *or* jungle of traffic signs

Schild-: **Schild|knap|pe** M *(Hist)* squire, shield-bearer; **Schild|krö|te** F *(= Landschildkröte)* tortoise; *(= Wasserschildkröte)* turtle; **Schild|krö|ten|sup|pe** F turtle soup; **Schild|laus** F scale insect; **Schild|müt|ze** F peaked cap; **Schild|patt** [ˈʃɪltpat] NT **-s**, *no pl* tortoiseshell; **Schild|wa|che** F *(old)* sentry; **~ stehen** to stand sentry

Schilf [ʃɪlf] NT **-(e)s, -e** reed; *(= mit Schilf bewachsene Fläche)* reeds *pl*

Schilf-: **Schilf|dach** NT thatched roof; **Schilf|gras** NT, **Schilf|rohr** NT reed

Schil|ler [ˈʃɪlɐ] M **-s**, *no pl* **a** *(= Schimmer, Glanz)* shimmer **b** *(Wein)* rosé (wine)

Schil|ler-: **Schil|ler|kra|gen** M Byron collar; **Schil|ler|lo|cke** F **a** *(Gebäck)* cream horn **b** *(Räucherfisch)* strip of smoked rock salmon

schil|lern [ˈʃɪlɐn] VI to shimmer

schil|lernd ADJ *Farben, Stoffe* shimmering; *(in Regenbogenfarben)* iridescent; *(fig) Charakter* enigmatic; **~e Seide** shot silk

Schil|ler|wein M rosé (wine)

Schil|ling [ˈʃɪlɪŋ] M **-s, -** *or (bei Geldstücken)* **-e** shilling; *(Hist: Aus)* schilling

schil|pen [ˈʃɪlpn] VI to twitter, to chirp

schilt [ʃɪlt] *3. pers sing pres von* **schelten**

Schi|mä|re [ʃiˈmɛːrə] F **-, -n** chimera

schi|mä|risch [ʃiˈmɛːrɪʃ] ADJ chimerical

Schim|mel [ˈʃɪml] M **-s, -** *(= Pferd)* white horse, grey *(Brit)*, gray *(US)*; **ein weißer ~** *(hum)* a pleonasm

Schim|mel M **-s**, *no pl (auf Nahrungsmitteln)* mould *(Brit)*, mold *(US)*; *(auf Leder, Papier etc)* mildew

Schim|mel|bil|dung F formation of mould *(Brit) or* mould *(US) or* mildew

schim|me|lig [ˈʃɪməlɪç] ADJ *Nahrungsmittel* mouldy *(Brit)*, moldy *(US)*; *Leder, Papier etc* mildewy; **~ riechen** to smell mo(u)ldy; **~ werden** *(Nahrungsmittel)* to go mo(u)ldy; *(Leder, Papier etc)* to become covered with mildew

schim|meln [ˈʃɪmln] VI *aux sein or haben (Nahrungsmittel)* to go mouldy *(Brit) or* moldy *(US)*; *(Leder, Papier etc)* to go mildewy; **die Wand schimmelt** the wall has mould *(Brit) or* mold *(US)* on it

Schim|mel-: **Schim|mel|pilz** M mould *(Brit)*, mold *(US)*; **Schim|mel|rei|ter** M *(Myth)* ghost rider

Schim|mer [ˈʃɪmɐ] M **-s**, *no pl* glimmer, gleam; *(von Licht auf Wasser, von Perlen, Seide)* shimmer; *(von Metall)* gleam; *(im Haar)* sheen; **beim ~ der Lampe/Kerzen** by *or* in the soft glow of the lamp/glimmer of the candles; **keinen (blassen)** *or* **nicht den geringsten ~ von etw haben** *(inf)* not to have the slightest *or* the faintest *(inf)* idea about sth

schim|mern [ˈʃɪmɐn] VI to glimmer, to gleam; *(Licht auf Wasser auch, Perlen, Seide)* to shimmer; *(Metall)* to gleam; **der Stoff/ihr Haar schimmert rötlich** the material/her hair has a tinge of red; **ihre Augen schimmerten feucht** her eyes glistened moistly

schimm|lig [ˈʃɪmlɪç] ADJ = **schimmelig**

Schim|pan|se [ʃɪmˈpanzə] M **-n, -n, Schim|pan|sin** [-ˈpanzɪn] F **-, -nen** chimpanzee, chimp *(inf)*

Schimpf [ʃɪmpf] M **-(e)s**, *no pl (liter)* insult, affront; **mit ~ und Schande** in disgrace

schimp|fen [ˈʃɪmpfn] VI to get angry; *(= sich beklagen)* to moan, to grumble, to bitch *(inf)*; *(= fluchen)* to swear, to curse; *(Vögel, Affen etc)* to bitch *(inf)*; **mit jdm ~** to scold sb, to tell sb off; **heute hat der Lehrer geschimpft, weil ich ...** the teacher told me off today because I ... *(inf)*; **auf** *or* **über jdn/etw ~** to bitch about sb/sth *(inf)*, to curse (about *or* at) sb/sth; **vor sich hin ~** to grumble → **Rohrspatz** VT *(= ausschimpfen)* to tell off, to scold; **jdn einen Idioten ~** to call sb an idiot VR **sich etw ~** *(inf)* to call oneself sth

Schimp|fe|rei [ʃɪmpfəˈrai] F **-, -en** cursing and swearing; *(= Geschimpfe)* scolding; *(= Beschimpfung)* row, set-to *(Brit inf)*, slanging match *(Brit inf)*; *(= das Murren)* moaning, grumbling, bitching *(inf)*; *(von Vögeln, Affen etc)* bitching *(inf)*

Schimpf|ka|no|na|de F barrage of abuse

schimpf|lich [ˈʃɪmpflɪç] *(geh)* ADJ *(= beleidigend)* insulting; *(= schmachvoll)* humiliating ADV **jdn ~ verjagen** to drive sb away in disgrace

Schimpf-: **Schimpf|na|me** M insulting nickname; **Slick Willie war sein ~** they dubbed him Slick Willie; **Schimpf|wort** NT *pl* **-wörter** swearword; **mit Schimpfwörtern um sich werfen** to curse and swear

Schi|na|kel [ʃiˈnaːkl] NT **-s, -(n)** *(Aus inf) (= Ruderboot)* rowing boat; *(= klappriges Fahrzeug)* rattletrap *(inf)*

Schind|an|ger [ˈʃɪntlaŋɐ] M *(old)* knacker's yard *(Brit)*, slaughterhouse

Schin|del [ˈʃɪndl] F **-, -n** shingle

Schin|del|dach NT shingle roof

schin|den [ˈʃɪndn] *pret* **schindete** *or (rare)* **schund** [ˈʃɪndətə, ʃʊnt], *ptp* **geschunden** [gəˈʃʊndn] VT **a** *(= quälen) Gefangene, Tiere* to maltreat; *(= ausbeuten)* to overwork, to drive hard; *Maschine, Motor, Auto* to flog; **jdn zu Tode ~** to work sb to death → *auch* **geschunden** **b** *(inf: = herausschlagen) Zeilen* to pad (out); *Arbeitsstunden* to pile up; **Zeit ~** to play for time; **(bei jdm) Eindruck ~** to make a good impression (on sb), to impress (sb); **Mitleid ~** to get some sympathy **c** *(old: = abdecken) Tier* to flay, to skin VR *(= hart arbeiten)* to struggle; *(= sich quälen)* to strain; **sich mit etw ~** to slave away at sth

Schin|der [ˈʃɪndɐ] M **-s, -, Schin|de|rin** [-ərɪn] F **-, -nen** **a** *(old: = Abdeckerei)* knacker's yard

(Brit), slaughterhouse **b** *(old: = Abdecker)* knacker *(Brit)*, butcher **c** *(fig: = Quäler)* slave-driver

Schin|de|rei [ʃɪndəˈrai] F -, -en **a** *(old: = Abdeckerei)* knacker's yard *(Brit)*, slaughterhouse **b** *(= Plackerei)* struggle; *(= Arbeit)* slavery *no indef art* **c** *(= Quälerei)* maltreatment *no pl*

Schind|lu|der [ˈʃɪntluːdɐ] NT *(inf)* **mit jdm ~ treiben** to make sb suffer; **mit etw ~ treiben** to misuse sth; **mit seiner Gesundheit/seinen Kräften ~ treiben** to abuse one's health/strength

Schind|mäh|re [ˈʃɪntmɛːrə] F *(old)* nag

Schin|ken [ˈʃɪŋkn] M -s, - **a** ham; *(gekocht und geräuchert)* gammon, ham **b** *(pej inf)* hackneyed and clichéd play/book/film; *(= großes Buch)* tome; *(= großes Bild)* great daub *(pej inf)*

Schin|ken-: **Schin|ken|brot** NT ham sandwich; *(offen)* open ham sandwich; **Schin|ken|bröt|chen** NT ham roll; **Schin|ken|nu|deln** PL *noodles pl with (pieces of) ham*; **Schin|ken|röll|chen** NT roll of ham; **Schin|ken|speck** M bacon; **Schin|ken|wurst** F ham sausage

Schinn [ʃɪn] M -s, *no pl*, **Schin|nen** [ˈʃɪnən] PL *(N Ger)* dandruff *no pl*

Schin|to|is|mus [ʃɪntoˈɪsmʊs] M -, *no pl (Rel)* Shintoism

Schip|pe [ˈʃɪpə] F -, -n **a** *(esp N Ger: = Schaufel)* shovel, spade; **jdn auf die ~ nehmen** *(fig inf)* to pull sb's leg *(inf)*; **dem Tod von der ~ springen** *(inf)* to be snatched from the jaws of death **b** **~n** *pl (Cards)* spades *pl*

schip|pen [ˈʃɪpn] VT to shovel; **Schnee ~** to shovel the snow away

schip|pern [ˈʃɪpɐn] VI *aux sein (inf)* to sail

Schi|ri [ˈʃiːri] M -s, -s *(Ftbl inf)* ref *(inf)*

Schirm [ʃɪrm] M -(e)s, -e **a** *(= Regenschirm)* umbrella; *(= Sonnenschirm)* sunshade, parasol; *(von Pilz)* cap **b** *(= Mützenschirm)* peak; **eine Mütze mit ~** a peaked cap **c** *(= Röntgenschirm, Wandschirm, Ofenschirm)* screen; *(= Lampenschirm)* shade **d** *(liter: = Schutz)* umbrella; **unter seinem Schutz und ~** under his protection; **jdm** *or* **jds ~ und Schild sein** to be sb's protector; **der nukleare** *or* **atomare ~ der USA** the nuclear umbrella of the USA **e** *(= Bildschirm)* screen

Schirm-: **Schirm|aka|zie** F umbrella thorn; **Schirm|bild** NT X-ray (picture); **Schirm|bild|auf|nah|me** F *(form)* X-ray; **Schirm|bild|stel|le** F X-ray unit

schir|men [ˈʃɪrmən] VT *(geh)* to shield, to protect *(vor +dat* from, *gegen* against)

Schirm-: **Schirm|fut|te|ral** NT umbrella cover *or* case; **Schirm|herr(in)** M(F) patron; *(Frau auch)* patroness; **Schirm|herr|schaft** F patronage; **unter der ~ von** under the patronage of; *(von Organisation)* under the auspices of; **die ~ übernehmen** to become patron; **Schirm|hül|le** F umbrella cover; **Schirm|müt|ze** F peaked cap; **Schirm|pilz** M parasol mushroom; **Schirm|stän|der** M umbrella stand

Schi|rok|ko [ʃiˈrɔko] M -s, -s sirocco

Schis|ma [ˈʃɪsma, ˈsçɪ-] NT -s, **Schismen** *or (geh)* **-ta** [-mən, -ta] *(Eccl, Pol)* schism

Schis|ma|ti|ker [ʃɪsˈmaːtikɐ, sçɪ-] M(F) -s, -, **Schis|ma|ti|ke|rin** [-ərɪn] F -, -nen *(liter)* schismatic

schis|ma|tisch [ʃɪsˈmaːtɪʃ, sçɪ-] ADJ *(geh)* schismatic

schiss *pret von* **scheißen**

Schiss [ʃɪs] M -es, *no pl (sl)* **(fürchterlichen) ~ haben** to be scared to death *(vor +dat* of) *(inf)*; **~ kriegen** to get scared

schi|zo|phren [ʃitsoˈfreːn, sçi-] ADJ **a** *(Med)* schizophrenic **b** *(pej: = widersinnig)* contradictory, topsy-turvy ADV *(pej)* schizophrenically

Schi|zo|phre|nie [ʃitsofreˈniː, sçi-] F -, *no pl* **a** *(Med)* schizophrenia **b** *(pej: = Widersinn)* contradictoriness; **das ist die reinste ~** that's a flat contradiction

Schlab|be|rei [ʃlabəˈrai] F -, -en *(inf)* slurping, slobbering

Schlab|ber|ho|se F baggy pants *pl or* trousers *pl (esp Brit)*

schlab|be|rig [ˈʃlabərɪç] ADJ *(inf) Brei, Suppe* watery; *Pullover, Hose* baggy; *(= glitschig)* slithery

Schlab|ber-: **Schlab|ber|look** M [-lʊk] *(inf)* baggy look; **Schlab|ber|maul** NT *(inf: von Hund)* slobbery mouth

schlab|bern [ˈʃlabɐn] *(inf)* VI **a** *(geräuschvoll)* to slurp; **er schlabberte beim Essen** he slurped his food **b** *(= kleckern)* to make a mess **c** *(= zu weit sein: Rock, Hose)* to flap **d** *(dial inf: = sich unterhalten)* **mit jdm ~** to blether with sb VT *(= schlürfend essen/trinken)* to slurp

schlabb|rig ADJ *(inf)* = **schlabberig**

Schlacht [ʃlaxt] F -, -en battle; **die ~ bei** *or* **um X** the battle of X; **in die ~ gehen** *or* **ziehen** to go into battle; **jdm eine ~ liefern** to fight sb, to battle with sb; **die Kelten lieferten den Römern eine ~, die ...** the Celts gave the Romans a battle that ... → **schlagen VT f**

Schlacht|bank F **jdn (wie ein Lamm) zur ~ führen** to lead sb (like a lamb) to the slaughter

schlach|ten [ˈʃlaxtn] VT *Schwein, Kuh* to slaughter, to butcher; *Huhn, Kaninchen, Opfertier etc* to slaughter, to kill; *(hum) Sparschwein* to break into; **heilige Kühe ~** *(fig)* to kill *or* slaughter sacred cows VI to do one's slaughtering; **unser Fleischer schlachtet selbst** our butcher does his own slaughtering; **heute wird geschlachtet** we're/they're *etc* slaughtering today

Schlach|ten-: **Schlach|ten|bumm|ler(in)** M(F) *(Sport inf)* visiting *or* away supporter *or* fan; **Schlach|ten|ma|ler(in)** M(F) painter of battle scenes

Schlach|ter [ˈʃlaxtɐ] M -s, -, **Schlach|te|rin** [-ərɪn] F -, -nen *(esp N Ger)* butcher

Schläch|ter [ˈʃlɛçtɐ] M -s, -, **Schläch|te|rin** [-ərɪn] F -, -nen *(dial, fig)* butcher

Schlach|te|rei [ʃlaxtəˈrai] F -, -en *(esp N Ger)* butcher's (shop)

Schläch|te|rei [ʃlɛçtəˈrai] F -, -en **a** *(dial)* butcher's (shop) **b** *(fig: = Blutbad)* slaughter, butchery *no pl*, massacre

Schlacht-: **Schlacht|feld** NT battlefield; **auf dem ~ bleiben** *(lit)* to fall in battle; *(fig) (nach Schlägerei etc)* to be left lying; *(esp Pol)* to be finished; **das ~ räumen** *(= aufräumen)* to clear the (battle)field; *(= verlassen)* to leave the (battle)field; *(fig)* to drop out of contention; **das Zimmer sieht aus wie ein ~** the room looks like a battlefield, the room looks as if a bomb has hit it *(inf)*; **Schlacht|fest** NT *country feast to eat up meat from freshly slaughtered pigs*; **Schlacht|ge|sang** M battle song; **Schlacht|ge|tüm|mel** NT thick of the battle, fray; **Schlacht|ge|wicht** NT dressed weight; **Schlacht|ge|wühl** NT thick of the battle, fray; **Schlacht|haus** NT, **Schlacht|hof** M slaughterhouse, abattoir *(esp Brit)*; **Schlacht|kreu|zer** M battle cruiser; **Schlacht|li|nie** F battle line; **Schlacht|mes|ser** NT butcher's knife; **Schlacht|op|fer** NT sacrifice; *(Mensch)* human sacrifice; **Schlacht|ord|nung** F battle formation; **Schlacht|plan** M battle plan; *(für Feldzug)* campaign plan; *(fig)* plan of action, battle plan; **Schlacht|plat|te** F *(Cook) ham and German sausage made with meat from freshly slaughtered pigs and served with sauerkraut*; **schlacht|reif** ADJ *(lit, fig)* ready for the slaughter; **Schlacht|ross** NT *(liter)* warhorse, charger; *(fig inf)* heavyweight; **Schlacht|ruf** M battle cry; **Schlacht|schiff** NT battleship; **Schlacht|schüs|sel** F *(Cook) selection of boiled pork, pork sausages etc from freshly slaughtered pigs, served with sauerkraut*; **Schlacht|tag** M slaughtering day

Schlach|tung [ˈʃlaxtʊŋ] F -, -en *(von Schwein, Kuh)* slaughter(ing), butchering; *(von Huhn, Kaninchen, Opfertier)* killing

Schlacht|vieh NT, *no pl* animals *pl* for slaughter; *(= Rinder auch)* beef cattle *pl*

Schla|cke [ˈʃlakə] F -, -n *(= Verbrennungsrückstand)* clinker *no pl*; *(= Aschenteile auch)* cinders *pl*; *(Metal)* slag *no pl*; *(Geol)* scoria *pl (spec)*, slag *no pl*; *(Physiol)* waste products *pl*

Schla|cken-: **Schla|cken|bahn** F *(Sport)* cinder track; **schla|cken|frei**, **schla|cken|los** ADJ *(= ohne Verbrennungsrückstand)* non-clinker *attr*, clinker-free; *(= ohne Stoffwechselrückstand)* free of waste products ADV **Anthrazit brennt ~** anthracite burns without clinkering

schla|ckern [ˈʃlakɐn] VI *(inf)* to tremble, to shake; *(vor Angst auch)* to quake; *(Kleidung)* to hang loosely, to be baggy; **mit den Knien ~** to tremble at the knees; **mit den Ohren ~** *(fig)* to be (left) speechless

Schlaf [ʃlaːf] M -(e)s, *no pl* sleep; *(= Schläfrigkeit auch)* sleepiness; **einen leichten/festen/tiefen ~ haben** to be a light/sound/deep sleeper; **keinen ~ finden** to be unable to sleep; **um seinen ~ kommen** *or* **gebracht werden** to lose sleep; *(= überhaupt nicht schlafen)* not to get any sleep; **jdm den ~ rauben** to rob *or* deprive sb of his/her sleep; **jdn um seinen ~ bringen** to keep sb awake; **im ~** *(= während des Schlafens)* while he sleeps/they slept *etc*; **halb im ~e** half asleep; **im ~ reden** to talk in one's sleep; **ein Kind in den ~ singen** to sing a child to sleep; **sich** *(dat)* **den ~ aus den Augen reiben** to rub the sleep out of one's eyes; **in einen unruhigen/tiefen ~ fallen** to fall into a troubled/deep sleep; **in tiefstem ~ liegen** to be sound *or* fast asleep; **aus dem ~ erwachen** *(geh)* to awake, to waken (from sleep); **den ewigen** *or* **letzten ~ schlafen** *(euph)* to sleep one's last sleep; **den Seinen gibts der Herr im ~** *(Prov)* the devil looks after his own; **es fällt mir nicht im ~(e) ein, das zu tun** I wouldn't dream of doing that; **das macht** *or* **tut** *or* **kann er (wie) im ~** *(fig inf)* he can do that in his sleep → **gerecht ADJ a**

Schlaf-: **Schlaf|an|zug** M pyjamas *pl (Brit)*, pajamas *pl (US)*; **schlaf|be|dürf|tig** ADJ **(besonders) ~ sein** to need a lot of sleep; **Kinder sind ~er als Erwachsene** children need more sleep than adults

Schläf|chen [ˈʃlɛːfçən] NT -s, - nap, snooze; **ein ~ machen** to have a nap *or* snooze

Schlaf|couch F studio couch, sofa bed

Schlä|fe [ˈʃlɛːfə] F -, -n temple; **graue ~n** greying *(Brit) or* graying *(US)* temples

schla|fen [ˈʃlaːfn] *pret* **schlief** [ʃliːf], *ptp* **geschlafen** [gəˈʃlaːfn] VI to sleep; *(= nicht wach sein auch)* to be asleep; *(euph: = tot sein)* to be asleep *(euph)*; *(geh: Stadt, Land)* to be quiet, to slumber *(liter)*; *(inf: = nicht aufpassen) (bei bestimmter Gelegenheit)* to be asleep; *(immer)* not to pay attention; **er schläft immer noch** he's still asleep, he's still sleeping; **tief** *or* **fest ~** *(zu diesem Zeitpunkt)* to be fast *or* sound asleep; *(immer)* to be a deep *or* sound sleeper; **~ gehen** to go to bed; **sich ~ legen** to lie down to sleep; **jdn ~ legen** to put sb to bed; **schläfst du schon?** are you asleep?; **jetzt wird (aber) geschlafen!** go to sleep this minute!; **lange ~** to sleep for a long time; *(= spät aufstehen)* to sleep late, to have a long lie (in) *(Brit)*; **schlaf gut** *or (geh)* **wohl** sleep well; **hast du gut geschlafen?** did you sleep well?, did you have a good sleep? *(Brit)*; **mittags** *or* **über Mittag ~** to have an afternoon nap; **~ wie ein Murmeltier** *or* **Bär** *or* **Sack** *or* **Stein** *or* **eine Ratte** *(all inf)* to sleep like a log; **bei jdm ~** to stay overnight with sb; **wir können ruhig ~** *(fig)* we can sleep easy; **er kann nachts nicht mehr ~** *(fig)* he can't sleep nights; **ich konnte die ganze Nacht nicht ~** I couldn't sleep at all last night; **das lässt ihn nicht ~** *(fig)* it preys on his mind, it gives him no peace; **darüber muss ich erst mal ~** *(fig: = überdenken)* I'll have to sleep on it; **mit jdm ~** *(euph)* to sleep with sb; **miteinander ~** *(euph)* to sleep with each other; **sie schläft mit jedem** she sleeps around; **schlaf nicht!** wake up!

VR *impers* **auf dieser Matratze schläft es sich schlecht** this mattress is terrible to sleep on

Schlä|fen|bein NT temporal bone

schla|fend ADJ sleeping; **im ~en Zustand** asleep → **Hund** ADV asleep; **sich ~ stellen** to pretend to be asleep

Schla|fen|ge|hen NT **-s**, *no pl* going to bed; **vor dem ~** before going to bed

Schlä|fen|lo|cke F sidelock

Schla|fens|zeit F bedtime

Schlaf|ent|zug M sleep deprivation

Schlä|fer [ˈʃlɛːfɐ] M **-s, -**, **Schlä|fe|rin** [-ərɪn] F **-, -nen** **a** sleeper; *(fig)* dozy person *(inf)* **b** *(= Terrorist in Wartestellung)* sleeper

schlaff [ʃlaf] ADJ limp; *(= locker) Seil, Segel* loose, slack; *Moral* lax, loose; *Disziplin* lax; *Haut* flabby, loose; *Muskeln* flabby; *(= erschöpft)* worn-out, shattered *(Brit inf)*, exhausted; *(= energielos)* listless, floppy ADV limply; *(bei Seil, Segel)* loosely

Schlaff|heit F **-**, *no pl* limpness; *(von Seil)* looseness, slackness; *(von Haut, Muskeln)* flabbiness; *(= Erschöpftheit)* exhaustion; *(= Energielosigkeit)* listlessness

Schlaf|fi [ˈʃlafi] M **-s, -s** *(inf)* wimp *(inf)*

Schlaf-: **Schlaf|ge|le|gen|heit** F place to sleep; **wir haben ~ für mehrere Leute** we can sleep several people *(Brit)*, we have room for several people to sleep over; **Schlaf|ge|mach** NT *(liter)* bedchamber *(liter)*

Schla|fitt|chen [ʃlaˈfɪtçən] NT **jdn am** *or* **beim ~ nehmen** *or* **kriegen** *(inf)* to take sb by the scruff of the neck; *(= zurechtweisen)* to give sb a dressing down *(esp Brit inf)*, to reprimand sb

Schlaf-: **Schlaf|kam|mer** F *(dial)* bedroom; **Schlaf|krank|heit** F sleeping sickness; **Schlaf|lied** NT lullaby; **schlaf|los** ADJ *(lit, fig)* sleepless; **~ liegen** to lie awake; **jdm ~e Nächte bereiten** to give sb many a sleepless night ADV sleeplessly; **Schlaf|lo|sig|keit** F **-**, *no pl* sleeplessness, insomnia; **sie verbrachte die folgenden Nächte in ~** she spent the following nights unable to sleep; **Schlaf|mit|tel** NT sleeping drug; *(fig iro)* soporific; **diese Zeitung ist das reinste ~** this newspaper just sends you to sleep; **Schlaf|mit|tel|ver|gif|tung** F (poisoning from an) overdose of sleeping pills, ≈ barbiturate poisoning; **Schlaf|mün|zen|ak|ti|on** F *programme to collect old coins before they cease to be legal tender*; **Schlaf|müt|ze** F **a** nightcap **b** *(inf: Person)* dozy devil *(inf)*; *(= jd, der viel schläft)* sleepyhead *(inf)*; **diese ~n im Parlament** that dozy lot in Parliament *(inf)*; **schlaf|müt|zig** [-mʏtsɪç] ADJ *(inf)* dozy *(inf)*, dopey *(inf)*; **Schlaf|müt|zig|keit** F *(inf)* doziness *(inf)*, dopiness *(inf)*; **Schlaf|pil|le** F *(inf)* sleeping pill; **Schlaf|raum** M dormitory, dorm *(inf)*

schläf|rig [ˈʃlɛːfrɪç] ADJ sleepy, drowsy; *(fig: = träge)* sleepy

Schläf|rig|keit F **-**, *no pl* sleepiness, drowsiness; *(fig: = Trägheit)* sleepiness

Schlaf-: **Schlaf|rock** M dressing gown; **Äpfel im ~** baked apples in puff pastry; **Würstchen im ~** ≈ sausage roll; **Schlaf|saal** M dormitory; **Schlaf|sack** M sleeping bag; **Schlaf|sack|tou|rist(in)** M(F) backpacker; **Schlaf|ses|sel** M reclining seat; **Schlaf|so|fa** NT sofa bed, bed-settee *(Brit)*, hideaway bed *(US)*; **Schlaf|stadt** F dormitory town; **Schlaf|stel|le** F place to sleep; **Schlaf|stö|rung** F sleeplessness, insomnia; **Schlaf|stu|be** F *(dial)* bedroom; **Schlaf|sucht** F hypersomnia

schläft [ʃlɛːft] *3. pers sing pres von* **schlafen**

Schlaf-: **Schlaf|tab|let|te** F sleeping pill; **Schlaf|trunk** M *(old)* sleeping draught *(Brit)* *or* draft *(US, old)*; *(hum inf: Alkohol)* nightcap; **schlaf|trun|ken** *(geh)* ADJ drowsy, half asleep ADV drowsily, half-asleep

Schlaf|wa|gen M sleeping car, sleeper

Schlaf|wa|gen-: **Schlaf|wa|gen|kar|te** F sleeper ticket; **Schlaf|wa|gen|platz** M berth; **Schlaf|wa|gen|schaff|ner(in)** M(F) sleeping-car attendant

Schlaf-: **schlaf|wan|deln** VI *insep aux sein or haben* to sleepwalk, to walk in one's sleep, to somnambulate *(form)*; **Schlaf|wand|ler** [-vandlɐ] M **-s, -**, **Schlaf|wand|le|rin** [-ərɪn] F **-, -nen** sleepwalker, somnambulist *(form)*; **schlaf|wand|le|risch** [-vandlərɪʃ] ADJ sleepwalking *attr*, somnambulatory *(form)*; **mit ~er Sicherheit** *(wählen, Fragen beantworten)* intuitively, instinctively; **das Kind lief mit ~er Sicherheit durch den dichten Verkehr** the child ran through the heavy traffic with instinctive assurance; **Schlaf|zim|mer** NT bedroom; **Schlaf|zim|mer|blick** M *(hum inf)* come-to-bed eyes *pl (inf)*; **Schlaf|zim|mer|ein|rich|tung** F bedroom furniture *sing*; *(Garnitur)* bedroom suite; **Schlaf|zim|mer|ge|schich|te** F *(inf)* sexual adventure, bedroom antic *(inf)*

Schlag [ʃlaːk] M **-(e)s, ⸚e** [ˈʃlɛːgə] **a** *(lit, fig)* blow *(gegen* against); *(= Faustschlag auch)* punch; *(mit der Handfläche)* smack, slap; *(leichter)* pat; *(= Handkantenschlag, auch Judo etc)* chop *(inf)*; *(= Ohrfeige)* cuff, clout *(inf)*, slap; *(mit Rohrstock etc)* stroke; *(= Peitschenschlag)* stroke, lash; *(= einmaliges Klopfen)* knock; *(dumpf)* thump, thud; *(= leichtes Pochen)* tap; *(= Glockenschlag)* chime; *(= Standuhrschlag)* stroke; *(von Metronom)* tick, beat; *(= Gehirnschlag, Schlaganfall, Kolbenschlag, Ruderschlag, auch Schwimmen, Tennis)* stroke; *(= Herzschlag, Pulsschlag, Trommelschlag, Wellenschlag)* beat; *(= Blitzschlag)* bolt, stroke; *(= Donnerschlag)* clap; *(= Stromschlag)* shock; *(= Militärschlag)* strike; **man hörte die Schläge des Hammers/der Trommeln** you could hear the clanging of the hammer/beating of the drums; **Schläge kriegen** to get a hiding *or* thrashing *or* beating; **zum entscheidenden ~ ausholen** *(fig)* to strike the decisive blow; **~ auf ~** *(fig)* in quick succession, one after the other; **~ acht Uhr** *(inf)* at eight on the dot *(inf)*, on the stroke of eight; **jdm/einer Sache einen schweren ~ versetzen** *(fig)* to deal a severe blow to sb/sth; **ein ~ ins Gesicht** *(lit, fig)* a slap in the face; **ein ~ ins Kontor** *(dated inf)* a nasty shock *or* surprise; **ein ~ ins Wasser** *(inf)* a washout *(inf)*, a letdown *(inf)*; **ein ~ aus heiterem Himmel** a bolt from the blue; **mit einem** *or* **auf einen ~** *(inf)* all at once; *(= auf einmal, zugleich auch)* in one go; **mit einem ~ berühmt werden** to become famous overnight; **die haben keinen ~ getan** *(inf)* they haven't done a stroke (of work); **einen ~ weghaben** *(sl: = blöd sein)* to have a screw loose *(inf)*; **ihn hat der ~ getroffen** *(Med)* he had a stroke; **ich dachte, mich rührt** *or* **trifft der ~** *(inf)* I was flabbergasted *(inf)* *or* thunderstruck; **ich glaube, mich trifft der ~** I don't believe it; **wie vom ~ gerührt** *or* **getroffen sein** to be flabbergasted *(inf)* *or* thunderstruck *(inf)*

b *(inf: = Wesensart)* type (of person *etc*); **vom ~ der Südländer sein** to be a Southern type; **vom gleichen ~ sein** to be cast in the same mould *(Brit)* *or* mold *(US)*; *(pej)* to be tarred with the same brush; **vom alten ~** of the old school

c *(= Vogelschlag)* song

d *(dated: = Wagenschlag)* door

e *(= Taubenschlag)* cote, pigeon cage

f *(Aus: = Schlagsahne)* cream

g *(inf: = Portion)* helping

h *(= Hosenschlag)* flare; **eine Hose mit ~** flared trousers *pl (esp Brit)* *or* pants *pl (esp US)*, flares *pl (inf)*

Schlag-: **Schlag|ab|tausch** M *(Boxen)* exchange of blows; *(fig)* (verbal) exchange; **offener ~** public exchange (of views); **Schlag|ader** F artery; **Schlag|an|fall** M stroke; **schlag|ar|tig** ADJ sudden, abrupt ADV suddenly; **Schlag|ball** M *(Spiel)* rounders *sing*; *(Ball)* rounders ball; **schlag|bar** ADJ beatable; **diese Mannschaft ist durchaus ~** this team is by no means invincible *or* unbeatable; **Schlag|baum** M barrier; **Schlag|boh|rer** M, **Schlag|bohr|ma|schi|ne** F hammer drill; **Schlag|bol|zen** M firing pin

Schlä|ge *pl von* **Schlag**

Schlä|gel [ˈʃlɛːgl] M **-s, -** **a** *(Min)* (miner's) hammer; **~ und Eisen** crossed hammers *(miner's symbol)* **b** stick; *(= Trommelschlägel)* (drum)stick

schla|gen [ˈʃlaːgn] *pret* **schlug** [ʃluːk], *ptp* **geschlagen** [gəˈʃlaːgn] VTI **a** *(= zuschlagen, prügeln)* to hit; *(= hauen)* to beat; *(= einmal zuschlagen, treffen)* to hit, to strike; *(mit der flachen Hand)* to slap, to smack; *(leichter)* to pat; *(mit der Faust)* to punch; *(mit Schläger)* to hit; *(= treten)* to kick; *(mit Hammer, Pickel etc) Loch* to knock; **die Bombe schlug ein Loch in die Straße** the bomb blew a hole in the road; **jdn bewusstlos ~** to knock sb out *or* unconscious; *(mit vielen Schlägen)* to beat sb unconscious; **etw in Stücke** *or* **kurz und klein ~** to smash sth up *or* to pieces; **nach jdm/etw ~** to hit out *or* lash out at sb/sth; **um sich ~** to lash out; **mit dem Hammer auf den Nagel ~** to hit the nail with the hammer; **mit der Faust an die Tür/auf den Tisch ~** to beat *or* thump on the door/table with one's fist; **gegen die Tür ~** to hammer on the door; **jdm** *or (rare)* **jdn auf die Schulter ~** to slap sb on the back; *(leichter)* to pat sb on the back; **jdm** *or (rare)* **jdn auf den Kopf ~** to hit sb on the head; **jdm ein Buch** *or* **mit einem Buch auf den Kopf ~** to hit sb on the head with a book; **jdm etw aus der Hand ~** to knock sth out of sb's hand; **jdm** *or (rare)* **jdn ins Gesicht ~** to hit/slap/punch sb in the face; **ihm schlug das Gewissen** his conscience pricked *(Brit)* *or* bothered him; **einer Sache** *(dat)* **ins Gesicht ~** *(fig)* to be a slap in the face for sth; **na ja, ehe ich mich ~ lasse!** *(hum inf)* yes, I don't mind if I do, I suppose you could twist my arm *(hum inf)* → **grün, Fass**

b *(= läuten)* to chime; *Stunde* to strike; **die Uhr hat 12 geschlagen** the clock has struck 12; **eine geschlagene Stunde** a full hour; **wissen, was es** *or* **die Uhr** *or* **die Glocke** *or* **die Stunde geschlagen hat** *(fig inf)* to know what's what *(inf)* → **dreizehn**

c *(= heftig flattern)* **mit den Flügeln ~, die Flügel ~** *(liter)* to beat *or* flap its wings

VT **a** *(= besiegen, übertreffen) Gegner, Konkurrenz, Rekord* to beat; **jdn in etw** *(dat)* **~** to beat sb at sth; **unsere Mannschaft schlug den Gegner (mit) 2:1** our team beat their opponents (by) 2-1; **sich geschlagen geben** to admit that one is beaten, to admit defeat

b *Teig, Eier* to beat; *(mit Schneebesen)* to whisk; *Sahne* to whip; **ein Ei in die Pfanne ~** to crack an egg into the pan; **ein Ei in die Suppe ~** to beat an egg into the soup

c *(Chess)* to take, to capture

d *(liter: = treffen)* **das Schicksal schlug sie hart** fate dealt her a hard blow; **ein vom Schicksal geschlagener Mann** a man dogged by fate

e *(Bibl: = bestrafen)* to strike (down), to smite *(Bibl)*; **mit Blindheit geschlagen sein** *(lit, fig)* to be blind; **mit Dummheit geschlagen sein** to be dumb

f *(= fällen)* to fell

g *(= fechten) Mensuren* to fight

h *(liter: = krallen, beißen)* **seine Fänge/Zähne in etw** *(acc)* **~** to sink one's talons/teeth into sth

i *(Hunt: = töten)* to kill

j *(= spielen) Trommel* to beat; *(liter) Harfe, Laute* to pluck, to play; **das Schlagen der Trommeln** the beat(ing) of the drums

k *(dated: = prägen) Münzen etc* to mint, to coin

l *(= hinzufügen)* to add *(auf +acc, zu* to); *Gebiet* to annexe

m *(in Verbindung mit n siehe auch dort) Kreis, Bogen* to describe; *Purzelbaum, Rad* to do; *Alarm, Funken* to raise; *Krach* to make; **Profit aus etw ~** to make a profit from sth; *(fig)* to profit from sth; **eine Schlacht ~** to fight a battle

n **den Kragen nach oben ~** to turn up one's collar; **die Hände vors Gesicht ~** to cover one's face with one's hands

o *(= wickeln)* to wrap

VI a (Herz, Puls) to beat; (heftig) to pound, to throb; sein Puls schlug unregelmäßig his pulse was irregular; ihr Herz schlägt für den FC Bayern she's passionate about FC Bayern → höherschlagen
b aux sein (= auftreffen) mit dem Kopf auf/gegen etw (acc) ~ to hit one's head on/against sth
c aux sein (= gelangen) ein leises Wimmern schlug an sein Ohr he could hear a faint whimpering
d (Regen) to beat; (Wellen) to pound, to beat → Welle a
e aux sein or haben (Flammen) to shoot out (aus of); (Rauch) to pour out (aus of)
f (Blitz) to strike (in etw acc sth)
g (= singen: Nachtigall, Fink) to sing
h aux sein (inf: = ähneln) er schlägt sehr nach seinem Vater he takes after his father a lot → Art a
i (= betreffen) in jds Fach/Gebiet (acc) ~ to be in sb's field/line
j aux sein (esp Med: = in Mitleidenschaft ziehen) auf die Augen/Nieren etc ~ to affect the eyes/kidneys etc; jdm auf die Augen etc ~ to affect sb's eyes etc → Magen
VR a (= sich prügeln) to fight; (= sich duellieren) to duel (auf +dat with); als Schuljunge habe ich mich oft geschlagen I often had fights when I was a schoolboy; sich mit jdm ~ to fight (with) sb, to have a fight with sb; (= duellieren) to duel with sb; sich um etw ~ (lit, fig) to fight over sth; er schlägt sich nicht um die Arbeit he's not too keen on work (Brit), he's not crazy about work (inf)
b (= sich selbst schlagen) to hit or beat oneself
c (= sich bewähren) to do, to fare; sich tapfer or gut ~ to make a good showing
d (= sich begeben) sich nach rechts/links/Norden ~ to strike out to the right/left/for the North; sich auf jds Seite (acc) ~ to side with sb; (= die Fronten wechseln) to go over to sb; sich zu einer Partei ~ to throw in one's lot with a party → Leben a, Busch
e (Mech) sich auf etw (acc) ~ to affect sth

schla|gend ADJ (= treffend) Bemerkung, Vergleich apt, appropriate; (= überzeugend) Beweis striking, convincing → Verbindung, Wetter ADV etw ~ beweisen/widerlegen to prove/refute sth convincingly

Schla|ger [ˈʃlaːgɐ] M -s, - a (Mus) pop song; (erfolgreich) hit song, hit b (inf) (= Erfolg) hit; (= Waren) bargain; (= Verkaufsschlager, Buch) bestseller; der ~ in der Bundesliga the big match in the (German) national league

Schlä|ger [ˈʃlɛːgɐ] M -s, - a (= Tennisschläger, Federballschläger) racquet (Brit), racket (US); (= Hockeyschläger, Eishockeyschläger) stick; (= Golfschläger) club; (= Kricketschläger, Baseballschläger) bat; (= Tischtennisschläger) bat, paddle; (= Poloschläger) mallet b (= Waffe) straight-bladed sabre used by students in duelling bouts

Schlä|ger [ˈʃlɛːgɐ] M -s, -, **Schlä|ge|rin** [-ərɪn] F -, -nen a (= Spieler) (Kricket) batsman; (Baseball) batter b (= Raufbold) thug, ruffian

Schlä|ger|ban|de F gang of thugs

Schlä|ge|rei [ʃlɛːgəˈrai] F -, -en fight, brawl

Schla|ger|mu|sik F pop music

Schlä|ger|müt|ze F cap

Schla|ger-: **Schla|ger|pa|ra|de** F hit parade; **Schla|ger|sän|ger(in)** M(F) pop singer; **Schla|ger|sen|dung** F pop music programme (Brit) or program (US); **Schla|ger|text** M (pop music) lyrics pl; **Schla|ger|tex|ter(in)** M(F) writer of pop music lyrics, pop lyricist

Schlä|ger|trupp M, **Schlä|ger|trup|pe** F (inf) gang of thugs

Schlä|ger|typ M (inf) thug

Schlag-: **schlag|fer|tig** ADJ Antwort quick and clever; er ist ein ~er Mensch he is always ready with a quick (-witted) reply ADV ~ reagieren to give a quick-witted reply; ~ antworten to be quick with an answer; … bemerkte sie ~ … she said smartly; **Schlag|fer|tig|keit** F, no pl (von Mensch) quick-wittedness; (von Antwort) cleverness; **Schlag|ho|se** F flared trousers pl (esp Brit) or pants pl (esp US), flares pl (inf); **Schlag|in|stru|ment** NT percussion instrument; **Schlag|kraft** F (lit, fig) power; (Boxen) punch(ing power); (Mil) strike power; **schlag|kräf|tig** ADJ Boxer, Armee, Argumente powerful; Beweise clear-cut; **Schlag|licht** NT (Art, Phot) highlight; ein ~ auf etw (acc) werfen (lit, fig) to highlight sth; **schlag|licht|ar|tig** ADV etw ~ beleuchten to give a sudden insight into sth; ~ deutlich werden to become clear at a stroke; **Schlag|loch** NT pothole; **Schlag|mann** M pl -männer (Rudern) stroke; (Kricket) batsman; (Baseball) batter; **Schlag|obers** [ˈʃlaːkloːbɐs] NT -, - (Aus), **Schlag|rahm** M (S Ger) (whipping) cream; (geschlagen) whipped cream; **Schlag|ring** M a knuckle-duster b (Mus) plectrum; **Schlag|sah|ne** F (whipping) cream; (geschlagen) whipped cream; **Schlag|schat|ten** M (Art, Phot) shadow (of person or object); **Schlag|sei|te** F (Naut) list; ~ haben (Naut) to be listing, to have a list; (fig) to be one-sided; (hum inf: = betrunken sein) to be half seas over (Brit inf), to be three sheets to the wind (inf); **Schlag|stock** M (form) truncheon, baton, nightstick (US); Schlagstöcke einsetzen to charge with batons; **Schlag|stock|ein|satz** M (form) baton charge

schlägt [ʃlɛːkt] 3. pers sing pres von schlagen

Schlag-: **Schlag|werk** NT striking mechanism (of a clock); **Schlag|wet|ter** NT (Min) firedamp; **Schlag|wort** NT a pl -wörter (= Stichwort) headword b pl -worte (= Parole) catchword, slogan; **Schlag|wort|ka|ta|log** M subject catalogue (Brit) or catalog (US); **Schlag|zei|le** F headline; ~n machen (inf) to hit the headlines; in die ~n geraten to make the headlines; für ~n sorgen to make headlines; etw/jdn aus den ~n bringen to get sth/sb out of the media spotlight; aus den ~n verschwinden not to be big news anymore; **schlag|zei|len** [ˈʃlaːktsailən] VT to headline; **Schlag|zeug** NT pl -zeuge drums pl; (in Orchester) percussion no pl; **Schlag|zeu|ger** [-tsɔygɐ] M -s, -, **Schlag|zeu|ge|rin** [-ərɪn] F -, -nen drummer; (inf: in Orchester) percussionist; **Schlag|zeug|spie|ler(in)** M(F) percussionist

schlak|sig [ˈʃlaːksɪç] (esp N Ger inf) ADJ gangling, gawky ADV in a gangling way, gawkily

Schla|mas|sel [ʃlaˈmasl] M OR NT -s, - (inf) (= Durcheinander) mix-up; (= missliche Lage) mess (inf); der or das ganze ~ (Zeug) the whole lot (inf), the whole (kit and) caboodle (inf); da haben wir den or das ~ now we're in a right mess (inf); im ~ stecken to be in a mess (inf); jdn aus dem ~ ziehen to get sb out of the mess he/she is in (inf); jdn in den ~ bringen or reiten to get sb into a mess (inf)

Schlamm [ʃlam] M -(e)s, -e or =e [ˈʃlɛmə] mud; (= Schlick auch) sludge

Schlamm|bad NT mud bath

schläm|men [ˈʃlɛmən] VT a (= reinigen) Hafenbecken to dredge; Kreide to wash b (= weißen) Wand to whitewash

schlam|mig [ˈʃlamɪç] ADJ muddy; (= schlickig auch) sludgy

Schlämm|krei|de F whiting

Schlamm|la|wi|ne F mudflow, mudslide

Schlamm|schlacht F (inf) mud bath

Schlam|pe [ˈʃlampə] F -, -n (pej inf) slut (inf)

schlam|pen [ˈʃlampn] VI (inf) to be sloppy (in one's work); bei einer Arbeit ~ to do a piece of work sloppily; die Behörden haben wieder einmal geschlampt (once again) the authorities have done a sloppy job

Schlam|per [ˈʃlampɐ] M -s, -, **Schlam|pe|rin** [-ərɪn] F -, -nen (S Ger inf) sloppy person; (unordentlich) untidy person

Schlam|pe|rei [ʃlampəˈrai] F -, -en (inf) sloppiness; (= schlechte Arbeit) sloppy work; (= Unordentlichkeit) untidiness; das ist eine ~! that's a disgrace!

schlam|pig [ˈʃlampɪç], (Aus, S Ger) **schlam|pert** [ˈʃlampɐt] ADJ sloppy, careless; Arbeit auch slipshod; (= unordentlich) untidy; (= liederlich) slovenly ADV (= nachlässig) carelessly, sloppily; (= ungepflegt) slovenly; die Arbeit ist ~ erledigt worden the work has been sloppily or carelessly done, the work has been done in a slipshod manner

Schlam|pig|keit F -, no pl (inf) sloppiness, carelessness; (= Unordentlichkeit) untidiness; (= Liederlichkeit) slovenliness

schlang pret von schlingen , von schlingen

Schlan|ge [ˈʃlaŋə] F -, -n a snake, serpent (liter); (fig: = Frau) Jezebel; die ~ (Astron) Serpens, the Serpent; eine falsche ~ a snake in the grass; sich winden wie eine ~ (fig) to go through all sorts of contortions b (= Menschenschlange, Autoschlange) queue (Brit), line (US); ~ stehen to queue (up) (Brit), to stand in line (US) c (Tech) coil

schlän|ge|lig [ˈʃlɛŋəlɪç] ADJ Weg winding

Schlän|gel|li|nie F wavy line

schlän|geln [ˈʃlɛŋln] VR (Weg, Menschenmenge) to wind (its way), to snake; (Fluss auch) to meander; (Schlange) to wriggle; sich um etw ~ to wind around sth; sich durch etw ~ (fig) to worm one's way or wriggle through sth; eine geschlängelte Linie a wavy line

Schlan|gen-: **schlan|gen|ar|tig** ADJ ADV snake-like; **Schlan|gen|be|schwö|rer** [-bəʃvøːrɐ] M -s, -, **Schlan|gen|be|schwö|re|rin** [-ərɪn] F -, -nen snake charmer; **Schlan|gen|biss** M snakebite; **Schlan|gen|brut** F (old liter) brood of vipers; **Schlan|gen|fraß** M (pej inf) muck no indef art; **Schlan|gen|ge|zücht** NT brood of vipers; **Schlan|gen|gift** NT snake venom or poison; **Schlan|gen|gur|ke** F snake cucumber or gourd; **schlan|gen|haft** ADJ snake-like; **Schlan|gen|haut** F snake's skin; (= Leder) snakeskin; **Schlan|gen|le|der** NT snakeskin; **Schlan|gen|li|nie** F wavy line; (in) ~n fahren to swerve about; **Schlan|gen|mensch** M contortionist

Schlan|ge|ste|hen NT -s, no pl queueing (Brit), standing in line (US)

schlank [ʃlaŋk] ADJ a slim; Hals, Bäume auch slender; ~ werden to slim; ihr Kleid macht sie ~ her dress makes her look slim; Jog(h)urt macht ~ yoghurt is slimming, yoghurt is good for the figure; sich ~ machen (fig) to breathe in → Linie b (fig: = effektiv) lean; ~er Staat (Pol) lean or slimmed-down state

Schlank|heit F -, no pl slimness

Schlank|heits|kur F diet; (Med) course of slimming treatment; eine ~ machen/anfangen to be/go on a diet; eine ~ für den Staat (fig) slimming down the state

schlank+ma|chen VT sep → schlank a

Schlank|ma|cher M slimming agent

schlank|weg [ˈʃlaŋkvɛk] ADV (inf) ablehnen, sagen point-blank, flatly

schlank|wüch|sig [ˈʃlaŋkvyːksɪç] ADJ Person tall and slim, willowy; Baum tall and slender

schlapp [ʃlap] ADJ (inf) (= erschöpft, kraftlos) worn-out, shattered (Brit inf); (= energielos) listless, floppy (inf); (nach Krankheit etc) run-down; (= feige) Haltung, Mensch lily-livered (inf), yellow (inf); (= gering, unbedeutend) measly (inf); sich ~ lachen → schlapplachen; ~e 300 Euro a mere or measly 300 euros

Schläpp|chen [ˈʃlɛpçən] NT -s, - usu pl (für Gymnastik, Ballett) slipper

Schlap|pe [ˈʃlapə] F -, -n (inf) setback; (esp Sport) defeat; eine ~ einstecken (müssen) or erleiden to suffer a setback/defeat; jdm eine ~ beibringen or erteilen to defeat sb

schlap|pen [ˈʃlapn] VI aux sein or haben (inf) (= lose sitzen) to be baggy; (Schuhe) to flap; (= latschen) to slouch VT (Tier) to lap (up)

Schlap|pen [ˈʃlapn] M -s, - (inf) slipper

Schlạpp|heit F -, *no pl (= Erschöpfung)* exhaustion; *(= Energielosigkeit)* listlessness; *(= Feigheit)* cowardice

Schlạpp-: Schlạpp|hut M floppy hat; **schlạpp+la|chen** VR *sep (inf)* to laugh oneself silly; **schlạpp+ma|chen** VI *sep (inf)* to wilt; *(= zusammenbrechen, ohnmächtig werden)* to collapse; **die meisten Manager machen mit 40 schlapp** most managers are finished by the time they're 40; **Leute, die bei jeder Gelegenheit ~, können wir nicht gebrauchen** we can't use people who can't take it *or* who can't stand the pace *(inf)*; **Schlạpp|ohr** NT **a** *(hum: = Kaninchen)* bunny (rabbit) *(inf)* **b Schlappohren** PL floppy ears *pl*; **Schlạpp|schwanz** M *(pej inf)* wimp *(inf)*

Schla|raf|fen|land NT Cockaigne, land of milk and honey

schlau [ʃlau] ADJ clever, smart; *Mensch, Idee auch* shrewd; *(= gerissen)* cunning, crafty, wily; *Sprüche* clever; **er ist ein ~er Kopf** he has a good head on his shoulders; **ein ~er Bursche** a crafty *or* cunning devil *(inf)*; **ein ~es Buch** *(inf)* a clever book; **ich werde nicht ~ aus ihm/dieser Sache** I can't make him/it out → **Fuchs** ADV cleverly; **sie tut immer so ~** she always thinks she's so clever *or* smart; **etw ~ anfangen** *or* **anstellen** to manage sth cleverly → **schlaumachen**

Schlau|be [ʃlaubə] F -, -n *(dial)* skin

Schlau|ber|ger [ʃlaubɛrgɐ] M -s, -, **Schlau|ber|ge|rin** [-ərɪn] F -, -nen *(inf)* clever Dick *(Brit inf)*, smart aleck *(inf)*

Schlau|ber|ge|rei [ʃlaubɛrgə'rai] F -, *no pl (iro inf)* know-all attitude

Schlauch [ʃlaux] M -(e)s, **Schläuche** ['ʃlɔyçə] hose; *(Med)* tube; *(= Gartenschlauch)* hose (pipe); *(= Fahrradschlauch, Autoschlauch)* (inner) tube; *(= Weinschlauch etc)* skin; **das Zimmer ist ein richtiger ~** the room is really narrow; **auf dem ~ stehen** *(inf) (= nicht begreifen)* not to have a clue *(inf)*; *(= nicht weiterkommen)* to be stuck *(inf)*

Schlauch-: schlauch|ar|tig ADJ tube-like, tubular; *Zimmer* narrow; **Schlauch|boot** NT rubber dinghy

schlau|chen [ʃlauxn] VT *(inf) jdn (Reise, Arbeit etc)* to wear out; *(Chef, Feldwebel etc)* to drive hard VI *(inf: = Kraft kosten)* to wear you/one *etc* out, to take it out of you/one *etc (inf)*; **das schlaucht echt!** it really takes it out of you *(inf)*

schlauch|los ADJ *Reifen* tubeless

Schläue ['ʃlɔyə] F -, *no pl* cunning, craftiness, slyness

schlau|er|wei|se [ʃlauɐ'vaizə] ADV cleverly, shrewdly; *(= gerissen)* craftily, cunningly, slyly; **wenn du das wusstest, hättest du mich ~ benachrichtigen können** if you knew about it, you should have had the sense to tell me

Schlau|fe [ʃlaufə] F -, -n *(an Kleidungsstück, Schuh etc)* loop; *(= Aufhänger)* hanger; *(= Strecke)* loop

Schlau|fuchs M → **Schlauberger**

Schlau|heit [ʃlauhait] F -, -en, **Schlau|ig|keit** [ʃlauɪçkait] F -, -en *(rare)* **a** *no pl* cleverness, smartness; *(von Mensch, Idee auch)* shrewdness; *(= Gerissenheit)* cunning, craftiness **b** *(= Bemerkung)* clever remark

Schlau|kopf M, *(S Ger)* **Schlau|le** [ʃlaulə] *(inf)* NT -s, - clever Dick *(Brit inf)*, smart aleck *(inf)*

schlau+ma|chen VR *sep* **sich über etw** *(acc)* **~** *(inf)* to inform oneself about sth

Schlau|mei|er [-maiɐ] M -s, - = **Schlaukopf**

Schla|wi|ner [ʃla'viːnɐ] M -s, - *(hum inf)* villain, rogue

schlẹcht [ʃlɛçt] ADJ **a** bad; *Zustand, Aussprache, Geschmack, Zensur, Leistung* poor, bad; *Qualität* poor, bad, inferior; *Luft* stale, bad; *Zeiten* bad, hard; **das Schlechte in der Welt/im Menschen** the evil in the world/in man; **das ist ein ~er Scherz** that is a dirty trick; **er ist in Latein ~er als ich** he is worse at Latin than I am; **sich zum Schlechten wenden** to take a turn for the worse; **nur Schlechtes von jdm** *or* **über jdn sagen** not to have a good word to say for sb → **Dienst c, Eltern, Licht b**

b *pred (= ungenießbar)* off *pred (Brit)*, bad; **die Milch/das Fleisch ist ~** the milk/meat has gone off *or* is off *(Brit)*, the milk/meat has gone bad *or* is bad; **~ werden** to go off *(Brit) or* bad

c *(gesundheitlich etc) Zustand* poor; *Nieren, Herz* bad; *Durchblutung* bad, poor; **jdm ist (es) ~** sb feels sick *or* ill; **in ~er Verfassung sein** to be in a bad way; **~ aussehen** *(Mensch)* to look bad *or* sick *or* ill; *(Lage)* to look bad; **mit jdm/etw sieht es ~ aus** sb/sth looks in a bad way; **damit sieht es ~ aus** things look bad → **schlecht gehen**

ADV **a** badly; **~ beraten sein** to be ill-advised; **~ bezahlt** *(Person, Job)* low-paid, badly paid; **sich ~ vertragen** *(Menschen)* to get along badly; *(Dinge, Farben etc)* not to go well together; **die beiden können sich ~ leiden** the two of them don't get along (with each other); **an jdm ~ handeln** to do sb wrong, to wrong sb; **~ über jdn sprechen/von jdm denken** to speak/think ill of sb; **~ gelaunt** bad-tempered; **~ gelaunt sein** to be in a bad mood

b *(= mit Schwierigkeiten) hören, sehen* badly; *lernen, begreifen* with difficulty; **er kann ~ nein** *or* **Nein sagen** he finds it hard to say no, he can't say no; **da kann man ~ nein** *or* **Nein sagen** you can hardly say no to that, it's hard to say no to that; **heute geht es ~** today is not very convenient; **das lässt sich ~ machen, das geht ~** that's not really possible *or* on *(inf)*; **er ist ~ zu verstehen** he is hard to understand; **sie kann sich ~ anpassen** she finds it difficult *or* hard to adjust; **das kann ich ~ sagen** it's hard to say, I can't really say; **sie kann es sich ~ leisten, zu ...** she can ill afford to ...; **ich kann sie ~ sehen** I can't see her very well

c *(in festen Redewendungen)* **auf jdn/etw ~ zu sprechen sein** not to have a good word to say for sb/sth; **~ gerechnet** at the very least; **~ und recht** *(hum)* **mehr ~ als recht** *(hum)* after a fashion

d *(inf)* **er hat nicht ~ gestaunt** he wasn't half surprised *(Brit inf)*, he was very surprised

schlẹcht-: schlẹcht|be|ra|ten [-bəraːtn] ADJ *attr* → **schlecht ADV a**; **schlẹcht|be|zahlt** ADJ *attr* → **schlecht ADV a**

schlẹch|ter|dings [ʃlɛçtɐdɪŋs] ADV *(= völlig)* absolutely; *(= nahezu)* virtually

schlẹcht-: schlẹcht ge|hen *impers irreg aux sein*, **schlẹcht+ge|hen** *sep impers irreg aux sein* VI **es geht jdm schlecht** sb is in a bad way; *(finanziell)* sb is doing badly; **wenn er das erfährt, gehts dir schlecht** if he hears about that you'll be for it *(inf)*; **schlẹcht|ge|launt** ADJ *attr* → **schlecht ADV a**; **schlẹcht|ge|stellt** ADJ **~ sein** to be badly off; **schlẹcht|hin** [ʃlɛçt'hɪn] ADV *(= vollkommen)* quite, absolutely; *(= als solches, in seiner Gesamtheit)* as such, per se; **er gilt als** *or* **er ist der romantische Komponist ~** he is the epitome of the Romantic composer; **Studenten/die deutsche Sprache ~** students/the German language as such *or* per se

Schlẹch|tig|keit [ʃlɛçtɪçkait] F -, -en **a** *no pl* badness; *(esp qualitativ)* inferiority **b** *(= schlechte Tat)* misdeed

Schlecht-: schlẹcht+ma|chen *sep*, **schlẹcht ma|chen** △ VT *(= herabsetzen)* to denigrate, to run down; **schlẹcht+ste|hen** *sep irreg (S Ger, Aus, Sw: aux sein)*, **schlẹcht ste|hen** △*irreg (S Ger, Aus, Sw: aux sein)* VR **a** *(= bedient sein)* **sich bei** *or* **mit jdm/etw ~** to be badly off with sb/sth; **mit diesem Billigflug stehst du dich schlecht** this cheap flight isn't a good choice **b** *(= sich verstehen)* **sich mit jdm ~** to get on badly with sb → *auch* **stehen 4**; **schlẹcht+stel|len** VR *sep (finanziell)* to be badly off; **schlẹcht|weg** [ʃlɛçtvɛk] ADV = **schlechthin**; **Schlecht|wẹt|ter** NT bad weather; **Schlecht|wẹt|ter|geld** NT bad-weather money *or* pay; **Schlecht|wẹt|ter|pe|ri|o|de** F spell of bad weather

schlẹ|cken [ʃlɛkn] *(Aus, S Ger)* VT = **lecken** VI *(= Süßigkeiten essen)* to eat sweets *(esp Brit)* *or* candies *(US)*; **Lust auf was zum Schlecken haben** to feel like eating something sweet

Schle|cke|rei [ʃlɛkə'rai] F -, -en *(Aus, S Ger)* **a** *no pl (= das Lecken)* licking **b** *no pl (= das Naschen)* eating sweet things; **die ~ der Kinder** the children eating sweet things **c** *(= Leckerbissen)* delicacy; *(= Süßigkeit)* sweet *(esp Brit)*, sweetie *(Brit inf)*, candy *(US)*

Schlẹ|cker|maul NT *(hum inf)* **sie ist ein richtiges ~** she really has a sweet tooth

Schle|gel [ʃleːgl] M -s, - *(S Ger, Aus: Cook)* leg; *(von Geflügel)* drumstick, leg → *auch* **Schlägel**

Schleh|dorn [ʃleːdɔrn] M *pl* **-dorne** blackthorn, sloe

Schle|he [ʃleːə] F -, -n sloe

Schlei [ʃlai] M -(e)s, -e *(Zool)* tench

schlei|chen [ʃlaiçn] *pret* **schlịch** [ʃlɪç], *ptp* **geschlịchen** [gə'ʃlɪçn] VI *aux sein* to creep; *(heimlich auch)* to sneak, to steal; *(Fahrzeug)* to crawl; *(fig: Zeit)* to crawl (by); **um das Haus ~** to prowl around the house VR **a** *(= leise gehen)* to creep, to sneak, to steal; *(fig: Misstrauen)* to enter; **sich in jds Vertrauen** *(acc)* **~** to worm one's way into sb's confidence; **sich in jds Herz** *(acc)* **~** *(Zweifel etc)* to enter sb's heart **b** *(S Ger, Aus: = weggehen)* to go away; **schleich dich** get lost *(inf)*

schlei|chend ADJ *attr* creeping; *Krankheit, Gift* insidious; *Fieber* lingering

Schlei|cher [ʃlaiçɐ] M -s, -, **Schlei|che|rin** [-ərɪn] F -, -nen hypocrite

Schlei|che|rei [ʃlaiçə'rai] F -, -en hypocrisy, insincerity

Schleich-: Schleich|han|del M illicit trading *(mit* in); **der ~ mit Waffen** gunrunning; **der ~ mit Alkohol** bootlegging; **Schleich|händ|ler(in)** M(F) illicit trader; **Schleich|pfad** M, **Schleich|weg** M secret *or* hidden path; *(= wenig befahrene Straßenverbindung)* short cut *(avoiding traffic)*; **auf Schleichwegen** *(fig)* on the quiet, surreptitiously; **Schleich|wer|bung** F a plug; **~ vermeiden** to avoid making plugs

Schleie [ʃlaiə] F -, -n *(Zool)* tench

Schlei|er [ʃlaiɐ] M -s, - *(lit, fig)* veil; *(von Wolken, Nebel auch)* haze; **das Foto hat einen ~** the photo is foggy *or* fogged; **die Berggipfel waren in ~ von Nebel gehüllt** the mountain tops were veiled in mist; **einen ~ vor den Augen haben, wie durch einen ~ sehen** to have a mist in front of one's eyes; **den ~ (des Geheimnisses) lüften** to lift the veil of secrecy; **einen ~ über etw** *(acc)* **ziehen** *or* **breiten** *(fig)* to draw a veil over sth; **der ~ des Vergessens** the veil of oblivion; **den ~ nehmen** *(liter)* to take the veil

Schlei|er-: Schlei|er|eu|le F barn owl; **Schlei|er|fahn|dung** F (police search involving) spot checks *pl*; **schlei|er|haft** ADJ *(inf)* baffling, mysterious; **es ist mir völlig ~** it's a complete mystery to me; **Schlei|er|kraut** NT *(Bot)* gypsophila; **Schlei|er|schwanz** M goldfish; **Schlei|er|tanz** M veil dance; **Schlei|er|wol|ke** F *usu pl (Met)* cirrostratus *(spec)*

Schleif|bank F *pl* **-bänke** grinding machine

Schlei|fe [ʃlaifə] F -, -n **a** loop *(auch Aviat, Comput, beim Schlittschuhlaufen)*; *(= Flussschleife)* bow, horseshoe bend; *(= Straßenschleife)* twisty bend **b** *(von Band)* bow; *(= Schuhschleife)* bow(knot); *(= Fliege)* bow tie; *(= Kranzschleife)* ribbon

schlei|fen [ʃlaifn] VT **a** *(lit, fig)* to drag; *(= ziehen)* to haul, to drag; *(Mus) Töne, Noten* to slur; **jdn vor Gericht ~** *(fig)* to drag *or* haul sb into court; **jdn ins Konzert ~** *(hum inf)* to drag sb along to a concert **b** *(= niederreißen)* to raze (to the ground) VI **a** *aux sein or haben* to trail, to drag **b** *(= reiben)* to rub; **die Kupplung ~ lassen** *(Aut)* to slip the clutch; **die Zügel ~ lassen** *(lit, fig)* to slacken the reins; **wir haben die Sache ~ lassen** *(fig)* we let things slide

schlei|fen *pret* **schliff** [ʃlɪf], *ptp* **geschliffen** [gə'ʃlɪfn] VT **a** *Rasiermesser, Messer, Schere* to sharpen, to whet; *Beil, Sense* to grind, to whet; *Werkstück, Linse* to grind; *Parkett* to sand; *Edelstein, Glas, Spiegel* to cut → *auch* **geschliffen** **b** (*inf*: = *drillen*) **jdn ~** to drill sb hard

schlei|fen+las|sen VT *ptp* **schleifenlassen** *or* (*rare*) **schleifengelassen** *sep irreg* → **schleifen** VI **b**

Schlei|fer [ˈʃlaifɐ] M **-s, -** (*Mus*) slurred note

Schlei|fer [ˈʃlaifɐ] M **-s, -, Schlei|fe|rin** [-ərɪn] F **-, -nen** **a** grinder; (= *Edelsteinschleifer*) cutter **b** (*Mil sl*) slave-driver

Schlei|fe|rei [ʃlaifəˈrai] F **-, -en** **a** (*Werkstatt*) grinding shop; (*für Edelstein, Glas*) cutting shop **b** (*Mil sl*: = *Drill*) square-bashing (*Brit inf*), drill on barrack square

Schleif-: **Schleif|lack** M (coloured (*Brit*) *or* colored (*US*)) lacquer *or* varnish; **Schleif|lack|mö|bel** PL lacquered furniture *sing*; **Schleif|ma|schi|ne** F grinding machine; **Schleif|mit|tel** NT abrasive (agent); **Schleif|pa|pier** NT abrasive paper; **Schleif|rad** NT, **Schleif|schei|be** F grinding wheel; **Schleif|spur** F *blutig etc* trail; **Schleif|stein** M grinding stone, grindstone; **er sitzt da wie ein Affe auf dem ~** (*dated inf*) he looks a proper idiot *or* a proper Charlie (*Brit inf*) sitting there

Schlei|fung [ˈʃlaifʊŋ] F **-, -en** razing

Schleim [ʃlaim] M **-(e)s, -e** **a** slime; (*Med*) mucus; (*in Atemorganen*) phlegm, mucus; (*Bot*) mucilage **b** (*Cook*) gruel

Schleim-: **Schleim|ab|son|de|rung** F mucous secretion; **Schleim|beu|tel** M (*Physiol*) bursa (*spec*); **Schleim|drü|se** F mucous gland; (*von Schnecken etc*) slime gland

schlei|men [ˈʃlaimən] VI to leave a coating *or* film; (*fig inf*: = *schmeicheln*) to fawn, to crawl (*inf*)

Schlei|mer [ˈʃlaimɐ] M **-s, -, Schlei|me|rin** [-ərɪn] F **-, -nen** (*inf*) crawler (*inf*)

Schleim|haut F mucous membrane

schlei|mig [ˈʃlaimɪç] ADJ **a** slimy; (*Med*) mucous; (*Bot*) mucilaginous **b** (*pej*: = *unterwürfig*) slimy (*inf*)

Schlei|mig|keit F **-**, *no pl* (*pej*) sliminess (*inf*)

Schleim-: **schleim|lö|send** ADJ expectorant; **Schleim|pilz** M slime mould (*Brit*) *or* mold (*US*), slime fungus; **Schleim|schei|ßer(in)** M(F) (*inf*) bootlicker (*inf*), arse licker (*Brit sl*), ass licker (*US sl*); **Schleim|sup|pe** F gruel

Schle|mihl [ʃleˈmiːl, ˈʃleːmiːl] M **-s, -s** (*geh*: = *Pechvogel*) unlucky devil (*inf*), schlemiel (*inf*); (*inf*: = *Schlitzohr*) crafty customer (*inf*)

schlem|men [ˈʃlɛmən] VI (= *üppig essen*) to feast, to have a feast; (= *üppig leben*) to live it up VT to feast on

Schlem|mer [ˈʃlɛmɐ] M **-s, -, Schlem|me|rin** [-ərɪn] F **-, -nen** gourmet, bon vivant

Schlem|me|rei [ʃlɛməˈrai] F **-, -en** feasting; (= *Mahl*) feast

schlem|mer|haft, schlem|me|risch [ˈʃlɛmərɪʃ] ADJ gourmandizing, gluttonous (*pej*)

Schlem|mer|mahl NT feast, banquet

schlen|dern [ˈʃlɛndɐn] VI *aux sein* to stroll, to amble

Schlend|ri|an [ˈʃlɛndriaːn] M **-(e)s**, *no pl* (*inf*) casualness, inefficiency; (= *Trott*) rut

Schlen|ker [ˈʃlɛŋkɐ] M **-s, -** swerve; (= *Abstecher*) detour; **einen ~ machen** to swerve; (= *einen Abstecher machen*) to make a detour

schlen|kern [ˈʃlɛŋkɐn] VTI to swing, to dangle; **mit den Beinen/Armen ~, die Beine/Arme ~** to swing *or* dangle one's legs/arms VI (*Auto*) to swerve, to sway

schlen|zen [ˈʃlɛntsn] VI (*Sport*) to scoop

Schlepp [ʃlɛp] M (*Naut, fig*) **jdn/etw in ~ nehmen** to take sb/sth in tow; **in** *or* **im ~ haben** to have in tow

Schlepp|damp|fer M tug(boat)

Schlep|pe [ˈʃlɛpə] F **-, -n** **a** (*von Kleid*) train **b** (*Hunt*) drag

schlep|pen [ˈʃlɛpn] VT (= *tragen*) *Lasten, Gepäck* to lug, to schlepp (*US sl*); (= *zerren*) to drag, to haul, to schlepp (*US sl*); *Auto, Schiff* to tow; (*fig*) to drag; *Flüchtlinge* to smuggle; **jdn vor den Richter ~** to haul sb (up) before the judge; **etw mit sich ~** (*fig, Verantwortung etc*) to carry sth on one's shoulders, to be burdened with sth VI (*inf*: = *nachschleifen*) to drag, to trail VR to drag or haul oneself; (*Verhandlungen etc*) to drag on

schlep|pend ADJ *Gang* dragging, shuffling; *Bedienung, Abfertigung* sluggish, slow; *Absatz, Nachfrage, Geschäft* slack, sluggish; *Stimme* drawling; *Gesang* dragging, slow; **wehmütig ~e Klänge** melancholy languorous sounds; **nach ein paar Stunden wurde die Unterhaltung immer ~er** after a few hours the conversation began to drag ADV **nur ~ vorankommen** to progress very slowly; **die Unterhaltung kam nur ~ in Gang** conversation was very slow to start *or* started sluggishly

Schlep|pen|trä|ger(in) M(F) trainbearer

Schlep|per [ˈʃlɛpɐ] M **-s, -** **a** (*Aut*) tractor **b** (*Naut*) tug

Schlep|per [ˈʃlɛpɐ] M **-s, -, Schlep|pe|rin** [-ərɪn] F **-, -nen** **a** (*sl*: *für Lokal*) tout **b** (= *Fluchthelfer*) *somebody who smuggles people across borders*

Schlep|per|ban|de F people *or* refugee smuggling ring

Schlep|pe|rei [ʃlɛpəˈrai] F **-**, *no pl* (*inf*) lugging around *or* about

Schlep|per|or|ga|ni|sa|ti|on F, **Schlep|per|ring** M ring *or* syndicate of touts; (= *Fluchthelfer*) people *or* refugee smuggling ring

Schlepp-: **Schlepp|kahn** M lighter, (canal) barge; **Schlepp|lift** M ski tow; **Schlepp|lohn** M (*Naut*) towage; **Schlepp|netz** NT trawl (net); **Schlepp|netz|fahn|dung** F dragnet; **Schlepp|schiff** NT tug(boat); **Schlepp|tau** NT (*Naut*) tow rope; (*Aviat*) dragrope, trail rope; **ein Schiff/jdn ins ~ nehmen** to take a ship/sb in tow

Schle|si|en [ˈʃleːziən] NT **-s** Silesia

Schle|si|er [ˈʃleːziɐ] M **-s, -, Schle|si|e|rin** [-iərɪn] F **-, -nen** Silesian

schle|sisch [ˈʃleːzɪʃ] ADJ Silesian

Schles|wig-Hol|stein [ˈʃleːsvɪçˈhɔlʃtain] NT **-s** Schleswig-Holstein

Schleu|der [ˈʃlɔydɐ] F **-, -n** **a** (*Waffe*) sling; (= *Wurfmaschine*) catapult, onager; (= *Zwille*) catapult (*Brit*), slingshot (*US*) **b** (= *Zentrifuge*) centrifuge; (*für Honig*) extractor; (= *Wäscheschleuder*) spin-dryer

Schleu|der-: **Schleu|der|ball** M (*Sport*) **a** *heavy leather ball with a strap attached, swung round the head and then thrown* **b** *no pl a game using such a ball*; **Schleu|der|gang** M (*bei Waschmaschine*) spin (cycle); **Schleu|der|ge|fahr** F (*Mot*) risk of skidding; **„Achtung ~"** "slippery road ahead"; **Schleu|der|ho|nig** M extracted honey; **Schleu|der|ma|schi|ne** F (= *Wurfmaschine*) catapult, onager; (*für Milch etc*) centrifuge; (*für Honig*) extractor

schleu|dern [ˈʃlɔydɐn] VTI **a** (= *werfen*) to hurl, to sling, to fling; **durch die Luft geschleudert werden** to be flung through the air; **jdm etw ins Gesicht** *or* **an den Kopf ~** (*lit*) to hurl *or* fling sth in sb's face; (*fig*) to throw sth in sb's face; **jdn zu Boden ~** to hurl *or* fling sb to the ground **b** (*Tech*) to centrifuge, to spin; *Honig* to extract; *Wäsche* to spin-dry; **kalt geschleuderter Honig** cold-pressed honey VI *aux sein or haben* (*Aut*) to skid; **ins Schleudern kommen** *or* **geraten** to go into a skid; (*fig inf*) to run into trouble

Schleu|der-: **Schleu|der|preis** M giveaway price, throwaway price; **Schleu|der|sitz** M (*Aviat*) ejection *or* ejector seat; (*fig*) hot seat; **Schleu|der|spur** F skid mark; **Schleu|der|start** M (*Aviat*) catapult start; **Schleu|der|trau|ma** NT (*Med*) whiplash (injury); **Schleu|der|wa|re** F cut-price goods *pl*, cheap goods *pl*; **Schleu|der|wä|sche** F **ist das ~?** are those clothes for spinning?

schleu|nig [ˈʃlɔynɪç] ADJ *attr usu superl* prompt, speedy; *Schritte* quick, rapid; **nur ~stes Eingreifen kann jetzt helfen** only immediate measures can help now

schleu|nigst [ˈʃlɔynɪçst] ADV at once, straight away, immediately; **verschwinde, aber ~!** beat it, on the double!; **ein Bier, aber ~!** a beer, and make it snappy! (*inf*)

Schleu|se [ˈʃlɔyzə] F **-, -n** (*für Schiffe*) lock; (*zur Regulierung des Wasserlaufs*) sluice, floodgate; (*für Abwasser*) sluice; (= *Sicherheitsschleuse*) double door system; **die ~n öffnen** (*fig*) to open the floodgates; **der Himmel öffnete seine ~n** (*liter*) the heavens opened (*fig*), the rain sluiced down

schleu|sen [ˈʃlɔyzn] VT *Schiffe* to pass through a lock, to lock; *Wasser* to channel; (*langsam*) *Menschen* to filter; *Antrag* to channel; (*fig*: *heimlich*) *Flüchtlinge* to smuggle; **er wurde in den Saal geschleust** he was smuggled into the hall

Schleu|sen-: **Schleu|sen|geld** NT lock dues *pl*, lockage; **Schleu|sen|kam|mer** F (lock) basin; **Schleu|sen|meis|ter(in)** M(F) lock keeper; **Schleu|sen|tor** NT (*für Schiffe*) lock gate; (*zur Regulierung des Wasserlaufs*) sluicegate, floodgate; **Schleu|sen|wär|ter(in)** M(F) lock keeper

Schleu|ser [ˈʃlɔyzɐ] M **-s, -, Schleu|se|rin** [-ərɪn] F **-, -nen** = **Schlepper b**

Schleu|sung [ˈʃlɔyzʊŋ] F **-, -en** lockage, locking; (*von Menschen*) smuggling; **bei der ~ größerer Schiffe** when putting bigger ships through the locks

schlich *pret von* **schleichen**

Schlich [ʃlɪç] M **-(e)s, -e** *usu pl* ruse, trick, wile *usu pl*; **alle ~e kennen** to know all the tricks; **jdm auf** *or* **hinter die ~e kommen** to catch on to sb, to get on to sb, to get wise to sb (*inf*)

schlicht [ʃlɪçt] ADJ simple; **die ~e Wahrheit/Tatsache** the plain *or* simple truth/fact; **~ und einfach** plain and simple; **der ~e Menschenverstand** basic common sense; **das geht über den ~en Menschenverstand** this is beyond the normal human mind *or* beyond human comprehension; **diese Gedichte sind ~ und ergreifend** (*iro*) these poems are not exactly brilliant; **unser Abschied war ~ und ergreifend** our parting was short and sweet ADV **a** (= *einfach*) simply **b** (= *glattweg*) *gelogen, erfunden* simply; *falsch* simply, just; *vergessen* completely **c das ist ~ und einfach nicht wahr** that's just simply not true; **er sagte ~ und ergreifend nein** *or* **Nein** he said quite simply no

schlich|ten [ˈʃlɪçtn] VT **a** *Streit* (= *vermitteln*) to mediate, to arbitrate (*esp Ind*); (= *beilegen*) to settle **b** (= *glätten*) *Werkzeug, Leder, Gewebe* to dress; *Holz* to smooth (off) VI to mediate, to arbitrate (*esp Ind*); **zwischen zwei Ländern ~** to mediate between two countries; **er wollte ~d in den Streit eingreifen** he wanted to intervene in the quarrel (to settle it)

Schlich|ter [ˈʃlɪçtɐ] M **-s, -, Schlich|te|rin** [-ərɪn] F **-, -nen** mediator; (*Ind*) arbitrator

Schlich|ter|spruch M (= *Schiedsspruch*) (arbitral) award

Schlicht|fei|le F smooth-cut file

Schlicht|heit F **-**, *no pl* simplicity

Schlicht|ho|bel M smoothing plane

Schlich|tung [ˈʃlɪçtʊŋ] F **-, -en** (= *Vermittlung*) mediation, arbitration (*esp Ind*); (= *Beilegung*) settlement

Schlich|tungs-: **Schlich|tungs|aus|schuss** M arbitration *or* conciliation commission; **Schlich|tungs|stel|le** F arbitration *or* conciliation board; **Schlich|tungs|ver|fah|ren** NT, **Schlich|tungs|ver|hand|lun|gen** PL arbitration (proceedings *pl*); **Schlich|tungs|ver|such** M attempt at mediation *or* arbitration

schlicht|weg [ˈʃlɪçtˈvɛk] ADV → **schlechthin**

Schlick [ʃlɪk] M **-(e)s, -e** silt, ooze; (= *Ölschlick*) slick

schli|ckig [ˈʃlɪkɪç] ADJ muddy, slimy

schlid|dern [ˈʃlɪdɐn] VI *aux haben or sein* (*N Ger*) = **schlittern**

schlief *pret von* **schlafen**

Schlie|re [ˈʃliːrə] F -, -n streak, schlieren *pl (Tech)*

schließ|bar ADJ *(rare)* closable; *(= zuschließbar)* lockable

Schlie|ße [ˈʃliːsə] F -, -n fastening, fastener

schlie|ßen [ˈʃliːsn] *pret* **schloss** [ʃlɔs], *ptp* **ge|schlos|sen** [gəˈʃlɔsn] VT **a** *(= zumachen)* to close, to shut; *(= verriegeln)* to bolt; *(= Betrieb einstellen)* to close *or* shut down; *Stromkreis* to close; **seine Pforten ~** to close its doors; **eine Lücke ~** *(lit)* to close a gap; *(fig auch)* to fill a gap; **die Reihen ~** *(Mil)* to close ranks
b *(= beenden) Versammlung* to close, to conclude, to wind up; *Brief* to conclude, to close; *(Comput) Datei, Programm* to close
c *(= eingehen) Vertrag* to conclude; *Frieden* to make; *Bündnis* to enter into; *Freundschaft* to form; **wo wurde Ihre Ehe geschlossen?** where did your marriage take place?; **wer hat Ihre Ehe geschlossen?** who married you?
d *(geh: = umfassen)* **etw in sich** *(dat)* **~** *(lit, fig)* to contain sth, to include sth; *(indirekt)* to imply sth; **jdn in die Arme ~** to embrace sb; **lass dich in die Arme ~** let me embrace you; **jdn/etw in sein Herz ~** to take sb/sth to one's heart
e *(= befestigen)* **etw an etw** *(acc)* **~** to fasten sth to sth; **daran schloss er eine Bemerkung** he added a remark (to this)
VR *(= zugehen)* to close, to shut; *(Wunde)* to close; *(fig geh: Wunde)* to heal; **daran schließt sich eine Diskussion** this is followed by a discussion; **sich um etw ~** to close around sth
VI **a** *(= zugehen)* to close, to shut; *(= Betrieb einstellen)* to close *or* shut down; *(Schlüssel)* to fit; **die Tür schließt nicht** the door doesn't *or* won't close *or* shut; **„geschlossen"** "closed"
b *(= enden)* to close, to conclude; *(St Ex)* to close; **leider muss ich jetzt ~** *(in Brief)* I'm afraid I must conclude *or* close now; **die Börse schloss fester/schwächer** the market closed stronger/weaker
c *(= schlussfolgern)* to infer; **aus etw auf etw** *(acc)* **~** to infer sth from sth; **auf etw** *(acc)* **lassen** to indicate sth, to suggest sth; **von sich auf andere ~** to judge others by one's own standards → *auch* **geschlossen**

Schlie|ßer [ˈʃliːsɐ] M -s, -, **Schlie|ße|rin** [-ərɪn] F -, -nen *(inf)* jailer, warder *(Brit)*

Schließ-: **Schließ|fach** NT locker; *(= Postschließfach)* post office box, PO box; *(= Bankschließfach)* safe-deposit box, safety-deposit box; **Schließ|korb** M hamper

schließ|lich [ˈʃliːslɪç] ✪ 53.2, 53.5 ADV *(= endlich)* in the end, finally, eventually; *(= immerhin)* after all; **er kam ~ doch** he came after all; **~ und endlich** at long last; **~ und endlich bist du doch kein Kind mehr** after all you're not a child any more

Schließ|mus|kel M *(Anat)* sphincter

Schlie|ßung [ˈʃliːsʊŋ] F -, -en **a** *(= das Schließen)* closing, shutting; *(= Betriebseinstellung)* closure **b** *(= Beendigung) (einer Versammlung)* closing, breaking-up; *(von Debatte etc)* conclusion, closing; *(= Geschäftsschluss)* closing (time); *(Parl)* closure **c** *(= Vereinbarung) (von Frieden, Vertrag, Ehe)* conclusion; *(von Bündnis)* conclusion, forming

schliff *pret von* **schleifen**

Schliff [ʃlɪf] M -(e)s, -e *(von Glas, von Edelstein) (Prozess)* cutting; *(Ergebnis)* cut; *(von Linse)* grinding; *(fig: = Umgangsformen)* refinement, polish; **jdm ~ beibringen** *or* **geben** to give sb some polish *or* refinement; **jdm den letzten ~ geben** *(fig)* to perfect sb; **einer Sache den letzten ~ geben** *(fig)* to put the finishing touch(es) to sth

schlimm [ʃlɪm] ADJ **a** *Mensch* bad, wicked; *(= unartig)* naughty, bad; **es gibt Schlimmere als ihn** there are worse than him; **ein ~er Bösewicht** *(old)* an out-and-out villain; **Sie sind ja ein ganz Schlimmer!** *(hum)* you ARE naughty *or* wicked
b *(inf: = krank, entzündet)* bad
c *(= übel)* bad; *Krankheit* nasty, bad; *Wunde* nasty, bad, ugly; *Nachricht* awful, terrible, bad; **~, ~!** terrible, terrible!; **das war ~** that was awful *or* terrible; **~ genug, dass ...** it is/was bad enough that ...; **das finde ich nicht ~** I don't find that so bad; **eine ~e Geschichte** *(inf)* a nasty state of affairs; **eine ~e Zeit** bad times *pl*; **das ist halb so** *or* **nicht so ~!** that's not so bad!, it doesn't matter!; **zu Anfang war es ~ für ihn** in the beginning he had a hard time of it; **ist es ~** *or* **etwas Schlimmes?** is it bad?; **wenn es nichts Schlimmeres ist!** if that's all it is!; **es gibt Schlimmeres** it *or* things could be worse; **~er kann es nicht mehr werden** things can hardly get any worse; **im ~sten Fall** if (the) worst comes to (the) worst; **das Schlimmste** the worst; **was aber das Schlimmste ist, ...** but the worst of it is that ...; **das Schlimmste liegt hinter uns** the worst (of it) is behind us
ADV **a** *(= gravierend) sich täuschen, sich irren* really
b *(= äußerst schlecht) sich benehmen, zurichten* horribly; *zerstören* totally; **sie haben ~ gehaust** they wreaked *or* created havoc; **mit der neuen Frisur siehst du ~ aus** you look awful with that new hairdo; **es steht ~ (um ihn)** things aren't looking too good (for him)
c *(Med) sich verletzen, entzündet* badly; **~ eitern** to abscess badly
d *(= übel)* **er ist ~ dran** *(inf)* he's in a bad way; **wenn es ganz ~ kommt** if things get really bad; **es hätte ~er kommen können** it *or* things could have been worse; **umso** *or* **desto ~er** all the worse

schlimms|ten|falls [ˈʃlɪmstnfals] ADV at (the) worst; **~ wird er nur sein Geld verlieren** at worst, he will only lose his money; **~ kann ich dir £ 100 leihen** if (the) worst comes to (the) worst I can lend you £100

Schlin|ge [ˈʃlɪŋə] F -, -n loop; *(an Galgen)* noose; *(Med: = Armbinde)* sling; *(= Falle)* snare; **~n legen** to set snares; **den Kopf** *or* **sich aus der ~ ziehen** *(fig)* to get out of a tight spot *(inf)*; **(bei jdm) die ~ zuziehen** *(fig)* to tighten the noose (on sb); **die ~ um seinen Hals zieht sich langsam zu** *(fig)* the noose is slowly tightening on him

Schlin|gel [ˈʃlɪŋl] M -s, - rascal

schlin|gen¹ [ˈʃlɪŋən] *pret* **schlang** [ʃlaŋ], *ptp* **ge|schlun|gen** [gəˈʃlʊŋən] *(geh)* VT *(= binden) Knoten* to tie; *(= umbinden) Schal etc* to wrap *(um +acc* around); **die Arme um jdn ~** to wrap one's arms around sb, to hug sb VR **sich um etw ~** to coil (itself) around sth; *(Pflanze auch)* to twine (itself) around sth

schlin|gen² *pret* **schlang** [ʃlaŋ], *ptp* **ge|schlun|gen** [gəˈʃlʊŋən] VI to gobble, to gulp, to bolt one's food

Schlin|ger|be|we|gung F rolling (motion)

Schlin|ger|kurs M *(fig)* wavering course; *(Pol)* wavering policy; **auf ~** wavering *or* vacillating from one possibility to another; *(Pol)* wavering in his/her *etc* policy; **einen ~ steuern/verfolgen** to steer/follow a wavering course; *(Pol)* to pursue a wavering policy

schlin|gern [ˈʃlɪŋɐn] VI *(Schiff)* to roll; *(Auto etc)* to lurch from side to side; **ins Schlingern geraten** *(Auto etc)* to go into a skid; *(fig)* to run into trouble

Schling|ge|wächs NT, **Schling|pflan|ze** F creeper

Schlips [ʃlɪps] M -es, -e tie, necktie *(US)*; **mit** *or* **in ~ und Kragen** *(inf)* wearing a collar and tie → **treten VI c**

Schlit|ten [ˈʃlɪtn] M -s, - **a** sledge, sled; *(= Pferdeschlitten)* sleigh; *(= Rodelschlitten)* toboggan; *(= Rennschlitten)* bobsleigh; **~ fahren** to go tobogganing; **mit jdm ~ fahren** *(inf)* to have sb on the carpet *(inf)*, to bawl sb out *(inf)* **b** *(Tech) (= Schreibmaschinenschlitten)* carriage; *(zum Stapellauf)* cradle **c** *(inf: = Auto)* big car

Schlit|ten-: **Schlit|ten|bahn** F toboggan run; **Schlit|ten|fah|ren** NT -s, *no pl* sledging; *(= Rodeln)* tobogganing; *(mit Pferdeschlitten etc)* sleighing; **Schlit|ten|fahrt** F sledge ride; *(mit Rodel)* toboggan ride; *(mit Pferdeschlitten etc)* sleigh ride; **Schlit|ten|hund** M sledge *or* sled dog; *(= Eskimohund)* husky; **Schlit|ten|par|tie** F sleigh ride

Schlit|ter|bahn F slide

schlit|tern [ˈʃlɪtɐn] VI **a** *aux sein or haben (absichtlich)* to slide **b** *aux sein (= ausrutschen)* to slide, to slip; *(Wagen)* to skid; *(fig)* to slide, to stumble; **in den Konkurs/Krieg ~** to slide into bankruptcy/war

Schlitt|schuh M (ice) skate; **~ laufen** *or* **fahren** *(inf)* to (ice-)skate

Schlitt|schuh-: **Schlitt|schuh|bahn** F ice rink; **Schlitt|schuh|lau|fen** NT -s, *no pl* (ice) skating; **Schlitt|schuh|läu|fer(in)** M(F) (ice) skater; **Schlitt|schuh|schritt** M skating step

Schlitz [ʃlɪts] M -es, -e slit; *(= Einwurfschlitz)* slot; *(= Hosenschlitz)* fly, flies *pl (Brit)*; *(= Kleiderschlitz)* slit; *(= Jackettschlitz)* vent; **die Augen zu einem ~ zusammenkneifen** to narrow one's eyes to slits

Schlitz-: **Schlitz|au|ge** NT slit *or* slant eye; *(pej: = Chinese)* Chink *(pej)*; **schlitz|äu|gig** ADJ slit-eyed, slant-eyed ADV **er grinste ~** he grinned a slant-eyed *or* slit-eyed grin

schlit|zen [ˈʃlɪtsn] VT to slit

Schlitz-: **Schlitz|ohr** NT *(fig)* sly fox; **schlitz|oh|rig** [-loːrɪç] ADJ *(fig inf)* sly, crafty; **Schlitz|oh|rig|keit** F -, *no pl (fig inf)* slyness, craftiness; **Schlitz|schrau|be** F slotted screw; **Schlitz|ver|schluss** M *(Phot)* focal plane shutter

schloh|weiß [ˈʃloːˈvais] ADJ *Haare* snow-white

schloss *pret von* **schließen**

Schloss [ʃlɔs] NT -es, ⸚er [ˈʃlœsɐ] **a** *(= Gebäude)* castle; *(= Palast)* palace; *(= großes Herrschaftshaus)* mansion, stately home; *(in Frankreich)* château; **~ Nymphenburg** Nymphenburg Palace; **Schlösser und Burgen** castles and stately homes; **Schlösser im Mond** *(fig)* castles in the air, castles in Spain **b** *(= Türschloss, Gewehrschloss etc)* lock; *(= Vorhängeschloss)* padlock; *(an Handtasche etc)* clasp; **ins ~ fallen** to click shut *or* to; **die Tür ins ~ werfen** to slam the door shut; **hinter ~ und Riegel sitzen/bringen** to be/put behind bars

Schloss-: **schloss|ar|tig** ADJ palatial; **Schloss|berg** M castle *etc* hill; **Schloss|be|sit|zer(in)** M(F) owner of a castle *etc*

Schlöss|chen [ˈʃlœsçən] NT -s, - *dim von* **Schloss** small castle *etc*

Schlos|ser [ˈʃlɔsɐ] M -s, -, **Schlos|se|rin** [-ərɪn] F -, -nen fitter, metalworker; *(für Schlösser)* locksmith

Schlos|se|rei [ʃlɔsəˈrai] F -, -en **a** *(= Schlossereihandwerk)* metalworking **b** *(= Schlossereiwerkstatt)* metalworking shop

Schlos|ser|hand|werk NT metalworking

Schlos|ser-: **Schlos|ser|meis|ter(in)** M(F) master fitter; **Schlos|ser|werk|statt** F metalworking shop

Schloss-: **Schloss|gar|ten** M castle *etc* gardens *pl*; **Schloss|herr(in)** M(F) owner of a castle *etc*; *(= Adliger)* lord/lady of the castle; **Schloss|hof** M courtyard; **Schloss|ho|tel** NT castle hotel; *(kleiner)* country house hotel *(Brit)*; **Schloss|hund** M *(obs: = Kettenhund)* watchdog; **heulen wie ein ~** *(inf)* to howl one's head off *(inf)*; **Schloss|ka|pel|le** F castle *etc* chapel; **Schloss|park** M castle *etc* grounds *pl*, estate; **Schloss|platz** M castle *etc* square; **Schloss|vogt** M *(Hist)* castellan; **Schloss|wa|che** F castle *etc* guard

Schlot [ʃloːt] M -(e)s, -e *or (rare)* ⸚e [ˈʃløːtə] **a** *(= Schornstein)* chimney (stack), smokestack; *(Naut, Rail)* funnel, chimney (stack); *(von Vulkan)* chimney; **rauchen** *or* **qualmen wie ein ~** *(inf)* to smoke like a chimney *(inf)* **b** *(inf: = Flegel)* slob *(inf)*, peasant *(inf)*

schlot|te|rig [ˈʃlɔtərɪç] ADJ *(inf)* **a** *(= zitternd)* shivering *attr*; *(vor Angst, Erschöpfung)* trembling *attr* **b** *Kleider* baggy

schlot|tern [ˈʃlɔtɐn] VI **a** (*vor* with) (*= zittern*) to shiver; (*vor Angst, Erschöpfung*) to tremble; **an allen Gliedern ~** to shake all over; **ihm schlotterten die Knie** he was shaking at the knees, his knees were knocking *or* shaking **b** (*Kleider*) to hang loose, to be baggy

schlott|rig [ˈʃlɔtrɪç] ADJ = **schlotterig**

schlot|zen [ˈʃlɔtsn] VTI (*S Ger inf: = lutschen*) to suck; (*= trinken*) to slurp; (*mit Genuss*) to savour (*Brit*), to savor (*US*); **ein Viertele ~** to sip a quarter litre (*Brit*) *or* liter (*US*) of wine

Schlucht [ʃlʊxt] F **-, -en** gorge, ravine

schluch|zen [ˈʃlʊxtsn] VTI (*lit, fig*) to sob

Schluch|zer [ˈʃlʊxtsɐ] M **-s, -** sob

Schluck [ʃlʊk] M **-(e)s, -e** *or* (*rare*) **⸚e** [ˈʃlʏkə] drink; (*= ein bisschen*) drop; (*= das Schlucken*) swallow; (*großer*) gulp; (*kleiner*) sip; **der erste ~ war mir ungewohnt** the first mouthful tasted strange; **er stürzte das Bier in einem ~ herunter** he downed the beer in one gulp *or* in one go; **etw ~ für ~ austrinken** to drink every drop; **einen (kräftigen) ~ nehmen** to take a (long) drink *or* swig (*inf*); **einen ~ aus der Flasche/dem Glas nehmen** to take a drink *or* swig (*inf*) from *or* out of the bottle/the glass; **ein ~ aus der Pulle** (*fig inf*) a fair whack (*inf*)

Schluck|auf [ˈʃlʊklauf] M **-s,** *no pl* hiccups *pl*; **einen/den ~ haben** to have (the) hiccups

Schluck|be|schwer|den PL difficulties *pl* in swallowing

Schlück|chen [ˈʃlʏkçən] NT **-s, -** *dim von* **Schluck** drop; (*von Alkohol auch*) nip

schlück|chen|wei|se ADV in short sips; **~ trinken** to sip

schlu|cken [ˈʃlʊkn] **VT a** (*= hinunterschlucken*) to swallow; (*hastig*) to gulp down; **Alkohol ~** (*sl*) to booze (*inf*); **Pillen ~** (*sl*) to pop pills (*inf*) → **Kröte a b** (*Comm, inf: = absorbieren*) to swallow up; *Benzin, Öl* to guzzle **c** (*inf: = hinnehmen*) *Beleidigung* to swallow, to take **d** (*inf: = glauben*) to swallow (*inf*) **VI** to swallow; (*hastig*) to gulp; **da musste ich erst mal (trocken** *or* **dreimal) ~** (*inf*) I had to take a deep breath, I had to count to ten; **daran hatte er schwer zu ~** (*fig*) he found that difficult to swallow

Schlu|cken [ˈʃlʊkn] M **-s,** *no pl* = **Schluckauf**

Schlu|cker [ˈʃlʊkɐ] M **-s, -** (*inf*) **armer ~** poor devil

Schluck-: **Schluck|imp|fung** F oral vaccination; **Schluck|specht** M (*dated inf*) boozer (*inf*); **schluck|wei|se** ADV in sips

Schlu|der|ar|beit F (*inf*) botched-up *or* sloppy job (*inf*)

Schlu|de|rei [ʃluːdəˈrai] F **-, -en** (*inf*) sloppiness; **das ist eine ~!** how sloppy can you get!

schlu|de|rig [ˈʃluːdərɪç] (*inf*) **ADJ** *Arbeit* sloppy, slipshod *no adv* **ADV** *schreiben, Hausaufgaben machen* sloppily; *arbeiten auch* in a slipshod way

Schlu|de|rig|keit F **-, -en** (*inf*) sloppiness

schlu|dern [ˈʃluːdɐn] (*inf*) **VT** to skimp; **das ist geschludert!** this is a sloppy piece of work! **VI** to do sloppy work, to work sloppily

schlud|rig [ˈʃluːdrɪç] ADJ ADV (*inf*) = **schluderig**

Schlud|rig|keit F **-, -en** (*inf*) sloppiness

schlug *pret von* **schlagen**

Schlum|mer [ˈʃlʊmɐ] M **-s,** *no pl* (*liter*) (light) slumber (*liter*)

Schlum|mer|lied NT (*geh*) cradlesong (*esp Brit*), lullaby

schlum|mern [ˈʃlʊmɐn] VI (*geh*) to slumber (*liter*); (*fig auch*) to lie dormant

Schlum|mer-: **Schlum|mer|rol|le** F bolster; **Schlum|mer|tas|te** F (*an Radiowecker*) snooze button; **Schlum|mer|trunk** M nightcap

Schlumpf [ʃlʊmpf] M **-(e)s, ⸚e** [ˈʃlʏmpfə] (*inf: = komischer Kauz*) odd bod (*Brit inf*), oddball (*inf*); **„die Schlümpfe"** "the Smurfs"

Schlund [ʃlʊnt] M **-(e)s, ⸚e** [ˈʃlʏndə] (*Anat*) pharynx, gullet; (*fig liter*) maw (*liter*)

schlun|zen [ˈʃlʊntsn] VI (*dial*) to do sloppy work, to work sloppily

Schlupf [ʃlʊpf] M **-(e)s,** *no pl* (*Elec, Naut*) slip; (*Tech*) slip, slippage

schlüp|fen [ˈʃlʏpfn] VI *aux sein* to slip; (*Küken*) to hatch (out)

Schlüp|fer [ˈʃlʏpfɐ] M **-s, -** panties *pl*, knickers *pl* (*Brit*)

Schlupf|lid NT hooded (eye)lid

Schlupf|loch NT hole, gap; (*= Versteck*) hideout, lair; (*fig*) loophole; **ein ~ stopfen** (*fig*) to close a loophole

schlüpf|rig [ˈʃlʏpfrɪç] ADJ **a** slippery **b** (*fig*) *Bemerkung* suggestive

Schlüpf|rig|keit F **-, -en a** *no pl* slipperiness; (*fig: von Bemerkung*) suggestiveness **b** (*Bemerkung*) suggestive remark

Schlupf-: **Schlupf|wes|pe** F ichneumon fly *or* wasp; **Schlupf|win|kel** M hiding place; (*fig*) quiet corner

schlur|fen [ˈʃlʊrfn] VI *aux sein* to shuffle

schlür|fen [ˈʃlʏrfn] **VT** to slurp; (*mit Genuss*) to savour (*Brit*), to savor (*US*); **er schlürfte die letzten Tropfen** he slurped up the last drops **VI** to slurp

Schluss [ʃlʊs] M **-es, ⸚e** [ˈʃlʏsə] **a** *no pl* (*= Ende*) end; (*eines Romans, Gedichts, Theaterstücks*) end, ending, conclusion; (*= hinterer Teil*) back, end, rear; **~!** that'll do!, stop!; **~ für heute!** that's it *or* all for today, that'll do for today; **~ damit!** stop it!, that'll do!; **... und damit ~!** ... and that's that!, ... and that's the end of it!; **nun ist aber ~!, ~ jetzt!** that's enough now!; **dann ist ~** that'll be it; **~ folgt** to be concluded; **am/zum ~ des Jahres** at the end of the year; **fünf Minuten vor ~ des Spiels** five minutes before the end of the game; **zum ~ sangen wir ...** at the end we sang ...; **zum ~ hat sies dann doch erlaubt** finally *or* in the end she allowed it after all; **bis zum ~ bleiben** to stay to the end; **zum ~ kommen** to conclude; **zum ~ möchte ich noch darauf hinweisen, dass ...** to conclude *or* in conclusion I would like to point out that ...; **~ machen** (*inf*) (*= aufhören*) to finish, to call it a day (*inf*); (*= zumachen*) to close, to shut; (*= Selbstmord begehen*) to put an end to oneself, to end it all; (*= Freundschaft beenden*) to break *or* call it off; **er hat mit mir ~ gemacht** he dumped me (*inf*); **ich muss ~ machen** (*in Brief*) I'll have to finish off now; (*am Telefon*) I'll have to go now; **mit etw ~ machen** to stop *or* end sth, to finish with sth (*inf*); **mit der Arbeit ~ machen** to stop *or* leave off work

b *no pl* (*= das Schließen*) closing

c (*= Folgerung*) conclusion; **zu dem ~ kommen, dass ...** to come to the conclusion *or* to conclude that ...; **aus etw den ~ ziehen, dass ...** to draw the conclusion *or* to conclude from sth that ...; **aus etw die richtigen/falschen Schlüsse ziehen** to draw the right/wrong conclusions from sth; **ich ziehe meine Schlüsse daraus!** I can draw my own conclusions! → **Weisheit a**

d (*Tech*) **die Tür hat einen guten/schlechten ~** the door is a good/bad fit

e (*Mus*) cadence

f (*St Ex*) minimum amount allowed for dealing

Schluss-: **Schluss|ab|rech|nung** F final statement *or* account; **Schluss|ak|kord** M final chord; **Schluss|akt** M (*lit, fig*) final act; **Schluss|ak|te** F (*Pol*) final agreement; **Schluss|an|spra|che** F closing address *or* speech; **Schluss|be|mer|kung** F final observation, concluding remark; **Schluss|be|stim|mung** F final clause; **Schluss|bi|lanz** F (*lit*) final balance (sheet); (*fig*) final position; **Schluss|di|vi|den|de** F (*St Ex*) final dividend; **Schluss|do|ku|ment** NT final document *or* statement

Schlüs|sel [ˈʃlʏsl] M **-s, -** (*lit, fig*) key (*zu* to); (*= Chiffrenschlüssel auch*) cipher; (*Sch: = Lösungsheft*) key; (*Tech*) spanner (*Brit*), wrench; (*= Verteilungsschlüssel*) ratio (of distribution); (*Mus*) clef

Schlüs|sel-: **Schlüs|sel|an|hän|ger** M keyring pendant; **Schlüs|sel|bart** M bit, ward; **Schlüs|sel|be|griff** M (*= Wort*) keyword; (*= Konzept*) key concept; **Schlüs|sel|bein** NT collarbone, clavicle (*form*); **Schlüs|sel|blu|me** F cowslip; **Schlüs|sel|brett** NT keyboard; **Schlüs|sel|bund** M OR NT *pl* **-bunde** keyring, bunch of keys; **Schlüs|sel|dienst** M key cutting service; **Schlüs|sel|er|leb|nis** NT (*Psych*) crucial experience; **schlüs|sel|fer|tig** ADJ *Neubau* ready for moving into, ready for occupancy; **Schlüs|sel|fi|gur** F key figure; **Schlüs|sel|ge|walt** F (*Jur*) *a wife's power to represent her husband in matters concerning the household* (*Eccl*) power of the keys; **Schlüs|sel|in|dust|rie** F key industry; **Schlüs|sel|kind** NT (*inf*) latchkey kid (*inf*); **Schlüs|sel|loch** NT keyhole; **Schlüs|sel|loch|chi|rur|gie** F keyhole surgery; **Schlüs|sel|po|si|ti|on** F key position; **Schlüs|sel|qua|li|fi|ka|ti|on** F key qualification; **Schlüs|sel|reiz** M (*Psych*) key stimulus; **Schlüs|sel|ring** M keyring; **Schlüs|sel|ro|man** M roman à clef; **Schlüs|sel|stel|lung** F key position; **Schlüs|sel|ta|sche** F key wallet; **Schlüs|sel|wort** NT *pl* **-wörter** keyword; (*für Schloss*) combination, code

Schluss-: **schluss|end|lich** ADV (*geh*) to conclude, in conclusion *or* closing; **Schluss|er|geb|nis** NT final result; **schluss|fol|gern** ✪ 53.4 VI *insep* to conclude, to infer; **Schluss|fol|ge|rung** ✪ 38.1, 53.4 F conclusion, inference; **Schluss|for|mel** F (*in Brief*) complimentary close; (*bei Vertrag*) final clause

schlüs|sig [ˈʃlʏsɪç] **ADJ** *Beweis* conclusive; *Konzept* logical; **sich** (*dat*) **(über etw** *acc*) **~ sein** to have made up one's mind (about sth) **ADV** *begründen* conclusively

Schlüs|sig|keit F **-,** *no pl* conclusiveness

Schluss-: **Schluss|ka|pi|tel** NT concluding *or* final chapter; **Schluss|kom|mu|ni|qué** NT, **Schluss|kom|mu|ni|kee** NT final communiqué; **Schluss|kund|ge|bung** F (*Pol: bei Wahlen*) final (election) rally; **Schluss|kurs** M (*St Ex*) closing prices *pl*; **Schluss|läu|fer(in)** M(F) last runner; (*in Staffel*) anchor(man/-woman); **Schluss|licht** NT rear light (*Brit*), tail-light; (*inf: bei Rennen etc*) tailender (*Brit*), back marker; **~ der Tabelle/in der Klasse sein** to be bottom of the table/class; **das ~ bilden** (*fig*) (*beim Laufen etc*) to bring up the rear; (*in einer Tabelle*) to be bottom of the league; **Schluss|mann** M *pl* **-männer** (*Sport sl*) goalie (*inf*), keeper (*Brit inf*); **Schluss|no|tie|rung** F (*St Ex*) closing quotation; **Schluss|of|fe|ns|ive** F (*Sport*) final assault; **Schluss|pfiff** M final whistle; **Schluss|pha|se** F final stages *pl*; **Schluss|punkt** M **einen ~ unter etw** (*acc*) **setzen** to round off sth; (*bei etwas Unangenehmem*) to write sth off; **Schluss|rech|nung** F **a** (*Comm*) final account *or* settlement **b** (*Math: = Dreisatz*) computation using the rule of three; **Schluss|re|dak|ti|on** F final edit(ing); **Schluss|run|de** F (*Boxen, Golf etc, fig*) final round; (*in Rennsport, Leichtathletik*) final lap; (*bei Ausscheidungskämpfen*) final heat; (*= Endausscheidung*) final(s); **Schluss|run|den|teil|neh|mer(in)** M(F) finalist; **Schluss|satz** M closing *or* concluding sentence; (*Logik*) conclusion; (*Mus*) last *or* final movement; **Schluss|schein** M (*Comm*) contract note; **Schluss|sprung** M standing jump; (*beim Turnen*) finishing jump; **Schluss|stand** M final result; (*von Spiel auch*) final score; (*von Aktienindex etc*) closing price; **Schluss|stein** M (*Archit, fig*) keystone; **Schluss|strich** M (*fig*) final stroke; **einen ~ unter etw** (*acc*) **ziehen** to consider sth finished; **Schluss|tag** M (*St Ex*) settlement day; **Schluss|ver|kauf** M (end-of-season) sale (*Brit*), season close-out sale (*US*); **Schluss|wort** NT *pl* **-worte** closing words *or* remarks *pl*; (*= Schlussrede*) closing *or* concluding speech; (*= Nachwort*) postscript

Schmach [ʃmaːx] F **-,** *no pl* (*geh*) disgrace, ignominy, shame *no indef art*; (*= Demütigung auch*) humiliation; **etw als ~ empfinden** to see sth as a disgrace; to feel humiliated by sth

schmach|ten [ˈʃmaxtn] VI *(geh)* a *(= leiden)* to languish; **vor Durst ~** to be parched; **vor Hunger ~** to starve; **vor Liebeskummer ~** to pine with love b *(= sich sehnen)* **nach jdm/etw ~** to pine *or* yearn for sb/sth

schmach|tend ADJ *Stimme, Blick* yearning, soulful; *Liebhaber* languishing

Schmacht|fet|zen M *(dated hum)* tear-jerker *(inf)*

schmäch|tig [ˈʃmɛçtɪç] ADJ slight, weedy *(pej inf)*

Schmäch|tig|keit F -, *no pl* slightness, weediness *(pej inf)*

Schmacht-: **Schmacht|lap|pen** M *(dated hum)* Romeo *(inf)*;; **Schmacht|lo|cke** F *(dated hum)* kiss curl *(Brit)*, spit curl *(US)*

schmach|voll *(geh)* ADJ *Niederlage* ignominious; *(= demütigend auch) Frieden* humiliating ADV *verlieren* ignominiously

Schma|ckes [ˈʃmakəs] PL *(dial inf)* a *(= Schläge)* **~ kriegen** to get a smacking b *(= Schwung)* **er knallte das Buch mit ~ auf den Tisch** he slammed *or* banged *(inf)* the book down on the table; **das muss man mit ~ machen!** *(= richtig zuschlagen)* give it a good clout *(esp Brit inf)* or bang *(inf)*

schmack|haft ADJ *(= wohlschmeckend)* tasty; *(= appetitanregend)* appetizing; **jdm etw ~ machen** *(fig)* to make sth palatable to sb

Schmack|haf|tig|keit [ˈʃmakhaftɪçkait] F -, *no pl* tastiness

Schmäh [ʃmɛː] M -s, -(s) *(Aus inf)* a *(= Trick)* con *(inf)*, dodge *(inf)*; **jdn am ~ halten** to make a fool out of sb b *(= Scherzhaftigkeit)* jokiness; **einen ~ führen** *(= Witze machen)* to clown around

Schmäh|brief M defamatory *or* abusive letter

schmä|hen [ˈʃmɛːən] VT *(geh)* to abuse, to revile *(liter)*, to vituperate against *(liter)*

schmäh|lich [ˈʃmɛːlɪç] *(geh)* ADJ ignominious, shameful; *(= demütigend)* humiliating ADV shamefully; *versagen* miserably; **~ im Stich gelassen werden** to be left in the lurch in a humiliating way

Schmäh-: **Schmäh|re|de** F *(geh)* invective, diatribe; **~n (gegen jdn) führen** to launch diatribes (against sb); **Schmäh|schrift** F defamatory piece of writing; *(= Satire)* lampoon

Schmä|hung [ˈʃmɛːʊŋ] F -, -en *(geh)* abuse, vituperation *(liter)*; **(gegen jdn) ~en ausstoßen** to hurl abuse (at sb)

Schmäh|wort NT *pl* **-worte** *(liter)* abusive word, term of abuse; **~e** abuse *sing*, invective *sing*

schmal [ʃmaːl] ADJ *comp* **-er** *or* **⸗er** [ˈʃmɛːlɐ], *superl* **-ste(r, s)** *or* **⸗ste(r, s)** [ˈʃmɛːlstə], *adv superl* **am -sten** *or* **⸗sten** a narrow; *Hüfte, Taille* slim, slender, narrow; *Mensch* slim, slender; *Band, Buch* slim; *Gelenke, Lippen* thin; **er ist sehr ~ geworden** he has got *(Brit)* or gotten *(US)* very thin b *(fig: = karg)* meagre *(Brit)*, meager *(US)*, slender; **~e Kost** slender fare; **einen ~en Geldbeutel haben** *(fig)* to have to watch the pennies

schmal|brüs|tig [-brʏstɪç] ADJ narrow-chested; *(fig)* limited

schmä|lern [ˈʃmɛːlɐn] VT to diminish, to reduce, to lessen; *(= heruntermachen)* to detract from, to belittle, to diminish

Schmä|le|rung F -, -en diminishing, reduction, lessening; *(= Schlechtmachen)* detraction, belittlement; **eine ~ seines Ruhms** a detraction from *or* a diminishing of his fame

Schmal-: **Schmal|film** M cine film *(Brit)*, movie film *(US)*; **Schmal|film|ka|me|ra** F cine camera *(Brit)*, movie camera *(US)*; **Schmal|hans** M *(inf)* **bei ihnen/uns ist ~ Küchenmeister** their/our cupboard is nearly always bare; **schmal|lip|pig** [-lɪpɪç] ADJ thin-lipped; *(fig: = schweigsam)* tight-lipped; **schmal|schul|te|rig**, **schmal|schult|rig** ADJ narrow-shouldered; **Schmal|sei|te** F narrow side

Schmal|spur F *(Rail)* narrow gauge

Schmal|spur- *in cpds (Rail)* narrow-gauge; *(pej)* small-time; **Schmal|spur|aka|de|mi|ker(in)** M(F) *(pej)* small-time academic; **Schmal|spur|bahn** F narrow-gauge railway

schmal|spu|rig [-ʃpuːrɪç] ADJ *(Rail) Strecke* narrow-gauge; *(fig) Fachmann* overspecialized ADV *ausgebildet* narrowly; **der Lehrplan ist sehr ~ angelegt** the curriculum is very narrow

Schmalz [ʃmalts] NT **-es, -e** a fat; *(= Schweineschmalz)* lard; *(= Bratenschmalz)* dripping *(Brit)*, drippings *pl (US)* b *(= Ohrenschmalz)* earwax

Schmalz M **-es**, *no pl (pej inf)* schmaltz *(inf)*

schmal|zen [ˈʃmaltsn] VTI to drool; *Lied* to croon

Schmalz-: **Schmalz|fleisch** NT rillettes *pl*, potted meat; **Schmalz|ge|bäck** NT, **Schmalz|ge|ba|cke|ne(s)** [-gəbakənə] NT *decl as adj* deep-fried pastry

schmal|zig [ˈʃmaltsɪç] *(pej inf)* ADJ schmaltzy *(inf)*, slushy *(inf)* ADV **er singt mir zu ~** his songs are too schmaltzy for me *(inf)*; **seine Liebesbriefe sind ziemlich ~ geschrieben** his love letters are pretty schmaltzy *(inf)*

Schmalz|ler [ˈʃmaltslɐ] M -s, - *(S Ger)* snuff

Schmalz|topf M pot of lard; **tief in den ~ greifen** *(fig inf)* to lay on the sentiment with a trowel

Schmand [ʃmant] M -(e)s [-dəs], *no pl* sour(ed) cream

Schman|kerl [ˈʃmaŋkɐl] NT -s, -n *(S Ger, Aus)* a *(= Speise)* delicacy, titbit *(Brit)*, tidbit *(US)* b *(fig)* gem

Schmant [ʃmant] M -(e)s, *no pl (dial)* a *(= Sahne)* cream b *(= Matsch)* muck

schma|rot|zen [ʃmaˈrɔtsn] *ptp* **schmarotzt** VI to sponge, to scrounge *(Brit)*, to freeload *(esp US)* *(bei* on, off); *(Biol)* to be parasitic *(bei* on)

Schma|rot|zer [ʃmaˈrɔtsɐ] M -s, - *(Biol)* parasite

Schma|rot|zer [ʃmaˈrɔtsɐ] M -s, -, **Schma|rot|ze|rin** [-ərɪn] F -, -nen *(fig)* sponger, scrounger *(Brit)*, freeloader *(esp US)*

schma|rot|zer|haft, **schma|rot|ze|risch** [ʃmaˈrɔtsərɪʃ] ADJ *(Biol, fig)* parasitic

Schma|rot|zer|tum [ʃmaˈrɔtsɐtuːm] NT -s, *no pl (Biol, fig)* parasitism

Schmar|re [ˈʃmarə] F -, -n *(dial)* cut, gash; *(= Narbe)* scar

Schmar|ren [ˈʃmarən] M -s, -, **Schmarrn** [ʃmarn] M -s, - a *(S Ger, Aus: Cook) pancake cut up into small pieces* b *(inf: = Quatsch)* rubbish *(Brit)*, tripe *(inf)*; **das geht dich einen ~ an!** that's none of your business!

Schmatz [ʃmats] M -es, -e *(inf: = Kuss)* smacker *(inf)*

schmat|zen [ˈʃmatsn] VI *(beim Essen)* to eat noisily, to smack *(US)*; *(beim Trinken)* to slurp; *(in Morast etc)* to squelch; **er aß ~d seine Suppe** he slurped his soup; **schmatz nicht so!** don't make so much noise when you eat!, don't smack when you eat! *(US)*; **mit den Lippen ~** to smack one's lips; **Oma küsste das Kind ~d** grandma gave the child a real smacker of a kiss *(inf)*

schmau|chen [ˈʃmauxn] VT to puff away at VI to puff away

Schmauch|spur F *usu pl* traces *pl* of powder

Schmaus [ʃmaus] M -es, **Schmäuse** [ˈʃmɔyzə] *(dated)* feast

schmau|sen [ˈʃmauzn] *(geh)* VI to feast VT to feast on

schme|cken [ˈʃmɛkn] VI a *(= Geschmack haben)* to taste *(nach* of); *(= gut schmecken)* to be good, to taste good *or* lovely; *(= probieren)* to taste, to have a taste; **ihm schmeckt es** *(= gut finden)* he likes it; *(= Appetit haben)* he likes his food; **ihm schmeckt es nicht** *(= keinen Appetit haben)* he's lost his appetite, he's off his food *(esp Brit)*; **das schmeckt ihm nicht** *(lit, fig)* he doesn't like it; **diese Arbeit schmeckt ihm nicht** this work doesn't agree with him, he has no taste for this work; **wie schmeckt die Ehe?** how does marriage agree with you?; **nach etw ~** *(fig)* to smack of sth; **das schmeckt nach nichts** it's tasteless; **das schmeckt nach mehr!** *(inf)* it tastes moreish *(Brit hum inf)*, it tastes like I want some more; **schmeckt es (Ihnen)?** do you like it?, is it good?, are you enjoying your food *or* meal? *(esp form)*; **das hat geschmeckt** that was good; **und das schmeckt!** and it tastes so good, and it's so good; **das schmeckt nicht (gut)** it doesn't taste good *or* nice; **es schmeckt mir ausgezeichnet** it is *or* it tastes really excellent; **Hauptsache, es schmeckt** *(inf)* the main thing is it tastes nice; **es sich** *(dat)* **~ lassen** to tuck in; **sich** *(dat)* **etw ~ lassen** to tuck into sth b *(S Ger, Aus, Sw: = riechen)* to smell VT a *(= den Geschmack wahrnehmen von)* to taste; *(= probieren)* to taste, to have a taste of; **etw zu ~ bekommen** *(fig inf)* to have a taste of sth b *(S Ger, Aus, Sw: = riechen)* to smell; *(fig: = ahnen)* to sense

Schmei|che|lei [ʃmaiçəˈlai] F -, -en flattery; *(= Kompliment auch)* flattering remark, compliment; **so eine ~!** such flattery!

schmei|chel|haft ADJ flattering; *Bemerkung auch* complimentary; **wenig ~** not very flattering/complimentary

schmei|cheln [ˈʃmaiçln] VI a **jdm ~** to flatter sb; *(um etw zu erreichen)* to flatter sb, to butter sb up *(Brit inf)*; **es schmeichelt mir, dass ...** it flatters me that ..., I find it flattering that ...; **... sagte sie ~d** ... she wheedled b *(= verschönen)* to flatter; **das Bild ist aber geschmeichelt!** the picture is very flattering VR **sich** *(dat)* **~ ...** *(geh)* to flatter oneself (that) ...

Schmei|chel|wort NT *pl* **-worte** *(geh)* flattery, honeyed word, sweet nothing *usu pl*

Schmeich|ler [ˈʃmaiçlɐ] M -s, -, **Schmeich|le|rin** [-ərɪn] F -, -nen flatterer; *(= Kriecher)* sycophant, fawner

schmeich|le|risch [ˈʃmaiçlərɪʃ] ADJ flattering; *(= lobhudelnd auch)* unctuous, fawning, sycophantic

schmei|ßen [ˈʃmaisn] *pret* **schmiss** [ʃmɪs], *ptp* **geschmissen** [gəˈʃmɪsn] *(inf)* VT a *(= werfen)* to sling *(inf)*, to chuck *(inf)*, to fling; **die Tür (ins Schloss) ~** to slam the door; **Pillen ~** *(sl)* to be a pill-popper *(inf)* b *(inf: = spendieren)* **eine Runde** *or* **Lage ~** to stand a round; **eine Party ~** to throw a party c *(= managen)* **den Laden ~** to run the (whole) show; **die Sache ~** to handle it d *(= aufgeben) Ausbildung, Schule, Job etc* to chuck in *(inf)* VI *(= werfen)* to throw, to chuck *(inf)*; **mit Steinen ~** to throw *or* chuck *(inf)* stones; **mit etw um sich ~** to throw sth about, to chuck sth around *(inf)*; **mit dem Geld (nur so) um sich ~** to throw *or* chuck *(inf)* money around; **mit Fremdwörtern um sich ~** to bandy foreign words about VR **sich auf etw** *(acc)* **~** to throw oneself into sth; **die Kunden schmissen sich auf die Sonderangebote** the customers made a rush for the special offers; **sich jdm an den Hals ~** *(fig)* to throw oneself at sb; **er schmiss sich mutig zwischen die beiden** he courageously flung *or* threw *or* hurled himself between the two

Schmeiß|flie|ge F bluebottle

Schmelz [ʃmɛlts] M -(e)s, -e *(= Glasur)* glaze; *(= Zahnschmelz)* enamel; *(geh, einer Farbe)* lustre *(Brit)*, luster *(US)*, glow; *(= Wohlklang)* melodiousness, mellifluousness

schmelz|bar ADJ fusible, meltable; **Eisen ist leicht ~** iron is easily melted *or* melts easily

Schmelz-: **Schmelz|bar|keit** [ˈʃmɛltsbaːɐ̯kait] F -, *no pl* fusibility

Schmel|ze [ˈʃmɛltsə] F -, -n a *(Metal, Geol)* melt b *(= Schmelzen)* melting; *(Metal: von Erz)* smelting c *(= Schmelzhütte)* smelting plant *or* works *sing or pl*

schmel|zen [ˈʃmɛltsn] *pret* **schmolz** [ʃmɔlts], *ptp* **geschmolzen** [gəˈʃmɔltsn] VI *aux sein (lit, fig: = erweichen)* to melt; *(Reaktorkern)* to melt down;

(*fig*: = *schwinden*) to melt (away); **es ist ihr gelungen, sein hartes Herz zum Schmelzen zu bringen** she succeeded in melting his heart of stone VT *Metall, Fett, Schnee* to melt; *Erz* to smelt

schmel|zend ADJ (*geh*) *Gesang, Ton, Stimme* mellifluous

Schmel|ze|rei [ʃmɛltsəˈrai] F -, -en smelting plant *or* works *sing or pl*

Schmelz-: **Schmelz|far|be** F (*Tech*) vitrifiable pigment *or* colour (*Brit*) *or* color (*US*); **Schmelz|glas** NT enamel; **Schmelz|hüt|te** F smelting plant *or* works *sing or pl*; **Schmelz|kä|se** M cheese spread; **Schmelz|ofen** M melting furnace; (*für Erze*) smelting furnace; **Schmelz|punkt** M melting point; **Schmelz|tie|gel** M (*lit, fig*) melting pot; **Schmelz|wär|me** F (*Metal*) heat of fusion; **Schmelz|was|ser** NT *pl* **-wasser** melted snow and ice; (*Geog, Phys*) meltwater

Schmer [ʃmeːɐ] M OR NT **-s**, *no pl* (*old, dial*) pork fat

Schmer-: **Schmer|bauch** M (*inf*) paunch, potbelly; **schmer|bäu|chig** [-bɔyçɪç] ADJ (*inf*) paunchy, potbellied

Schmer|le [ˈʃmɛrlə] F -, -n loach

Schmerz [ʃmɛrts] M **-es, -en** pain *pl rare*; (= *Kummer auch*) grief *no pl*; **ihre ~en** her pain; **chronische ~en** chronic pain; **dumpfer ~** ache; **stechender ~** stabbing pain; **sie schrie vor ~en** she cried out in pain; **~en haben** to be in pain; **~en in der Nierengegend haben** to have a pain in the kidneys; **~en in den Ohren haben** to have (an (*US*)) earache; **~en im Hals haben** to have a sore throat; **wo haben Sie ~en?** where does it hurt?, where's the pain?; **wenn der Patient wieder ~en bekommt ...** if the patient starts feeling pain again ...; **von ~en geplagt werden** to be racked with pain; **jdm ~en bereiten** to cause sb pain; (*seelisch auch*) to pain sb; **mit ~en** (*fig*) regretfully; **jdn/etw mit ~en erwarten** to wait impatiently for sb/sth; **unter ~en** while in pain; (*fig*) regretfully; **jdn mit ~(en) erfüllen** (*fig*) to grieve *or* hurt sb

Schmerz-: **schmerz|be|täu|bend** ADJ pain-killing; **Schmerz|emp|fin|den** NT sensation *or* experience of pain; **schmerz|emp|find|lich** ADJ *Mensch* sensitive to pain; *Wunde, Körperteil* sensitive, tender; **Schmerz|emp|find|lich|keit** F sensitivity to pain; (*von Wunde*) sensitivity, tenderness

schmer|zen [ˈʃmɛrtsn] (*geh*) VT to hurt, to pain; (*körperlich*) to hurt VI to hurt; (*Kopf, Bauch auch, Wunde*) to be sore, to ache; **mir schmerzt der Kopf** my head aches; **es schmerzt** (*lit, fig*) it hurts; **eine ~de Stelle** a painful spot *or* area

-schmer|zen PL *suf in cpds* -ache; **Bauch-/Kopfschmerzen haben** to have stomach ache/a headache; **Herzschmerzen haben** to have pains in the chest; **ich habe Halsschmerzen** I have a sore throat

Schmer|zens-: **Schmer|zens|geld** NT (*Jur*) damages *pl*; **Schmer|zens|laut** M (*geh*) cry of pain; **Schmer|zens|schrei** M scream of pain

Schmerz-: **schmerz|er|füllt** [-lɛɐfʏlt] ADJ (*geh*) racked with pain; (*seelisch*) grief-stricken; **schmerz|frei** ADJ free of pain; *Operation* painless; **Schmerz|frei|heit** F freedom from pain; **Schmerz|gren|ze** F (*lit, fig*) pain barrier; **schmerz|haft** ADJ (*lit, fig*) painful; **Schmerz|kran|ke(r)** MF *decl as adj person suffering from chronic pains*; **schmerz|lich** [ˈʃmɛrtslɪç] (*geh*) ADJ painful; *Lächeln* sad; **es ist mir sehr ~, Ihnen mitteilen zu müssen, dass ...** it is my painful duty to inform you that ... ADV *entbehren* painfully; **etw/jdn ~ vermissen** to miss sth/sb dreadfully; **schmerz|lin|dernd** ADJ pain-relieving, analgesic (*Med*); **Schmerz|lin|de|rung** F relief *or* alleviation of pain; **schmerz|los** ADJ (*lit, fig*) painless; **~er** less painful → **kurz**; **Schmerz|lo|sig|keit** F -, *no pl* (*lit, fig*) painlessness; **Schmerz|mit|tel** NT pain-killing drug, painkiller, ≈ aspirin (*esp US inf*); **Schmerz|schwel|le** F pain threshold; **schmerz|stil|lend** ADJ pain-killing, pain-relieving, analgesic (*Med*); **~es Mittel** pain-killing drug, painkiller, analgesic (*Med*), ≈ aspirin (*esp US inf*); **Schmerz|tab|let|te** F painkiller, ≈ aspirin (*esp US inf*); **schmerz|un|emp|find|lich** ADJ insensitive to pain; **schmerz|ver|zerrt** [-fɛɐtsɛrt] ADJ *Gesicht* twisted *or* distorted with pain; **mit ~em Gesicht** his/her face twisted with pain; **schmerz|voll** ADJ (*fig*) painful

Schmet|ter|ball M smash

Schmet|ter|ling [ˈʃmɛtɐlɪŋ] M **-s, -e** (*Zool, inf*: *Schwimmart*) butterfly; **kannst du ~ schwimmen?** can you do the butterfly?

Schmet|ter|lings-: **Schmet|ter|lings|blüt|ler** [-blyːtlɐ] M **-s, - die ~** the papilionaceae (*spec*); **ein ~** a member of the papilionaceae family (*spec*); **Schmet|ter|lings|netz** NT butterfly net; **Schmet|ter|lings|stil** M butterfly stroke

schmet|tern [ˈʃmɛtɐn] VT **a** (= *schleudern*) to smash; *Tür* to slam; (*Sport*) *Ball* to smash; **etw in Stücke ~** to smash sth to pieces **b** *Lied, Arie* to bellow out; (*Vogel*) to sing, to warble VI **a** (*Sport*) to smash, to hit a smash (*esp Brit*) **b** (*Trompete etc*) to blare (out); (*Sänger*) to bellow; (*Vogel*) to sing, to warble

Schmied [ʃmiːt] M **-(e)s, -e** [-də], **Schmie|din** [ˈʃmiːdɪn] [ˈʃmiːdɪn] F **-, -nen** (black)smith → **Glück a**

schmied|bar ADJ malleable

Schmie|de [ˈʃmiːdə] F **-, -n** smithy, forge

Schmie|de-: **Schmie|de|ar|beit** F (= *das Schmieden*) forging; (*Gegenstand*) piece of wrought-iron work; **Schmie|de|ei|sen** NT wrought iron; **schmie|de|ei|sern** ADJ wrought-iron; **Schmie|de|ham|mer** M blacksmith's hammer; **Schmie|de|kunst** F skill in wrought-iron work

schmie|den [ˈʃmiːdn] VT (*lit, fig*) to forge (*zu* into); (= *ersinnen*) *Plan, Komplott* to hatch, to concoct; (*hum*) *Verse* to concoct; **geschmiedet sein** (*Gartentür etc*) to be made of wrought iron; **jdn in Ketten ~** (*liter*) to bind sb in chains

Schmie|din [ˈʃmiːdɪn] [ˈʃmiːdɪn] F **-, -nen** (black)smith

schmie|gen [ˈʃmiːgn] VR **sich an jdn ~** to cuddle *or* snuggle up to sb; **sich an/in etw** (*acc*) **~** to nestle *or* snuggle into sth; **die Weinberge/Häuser ~ sich an die sanften Hänge** the vineyards/houses nestle into the gentle slopes; **sich um etw ~** to hang gracefully on sth; (*Haare*) to fall gracefully (a)round sth VT **etw an/in etw** (*acc*) **~** to nestle sth into sth; **etw um etw ~** to wrap sth around sth; **die an den Felsen geschmiegte Kapelle** the chapel nestled *or* nestling in the cliffs

schmieg|sam [ˈʃmiːkzaːm] ADJ supple; *Stoff* soft; (*fig*: = *anpassungsfähig*) adaptable, flexible

Schmie|re [ˈʃmiːrə] F **-, -n a** (*inf*) grease; (= *Salbe*) ointment; (= *feuchter Schmutz*) mud, grease; (*pej*: = *Schminke*) paint; (= *Aufstrich*) spread **b** (*pej*) (= *Wanderbühne*) (troop of) barnstormers *pl*; (= *schlechtes Theater*) fleapit **c** (*inf*) **~ stehen** to be the look-out

schmie|ren [ˈʃmiːrən] VT **a** (= *streichen*) to smear; *Butter, Aufstrich* to spread; *Brot* (*mit Butter*) to butter; *Salbe, Make-up* to rub in (*in +acc* -to); (= *einfetten, ölen*) to grease; (*Tech*) *Achsen, Gelenke etc* to grease, to lubricate; **sie schmierte sich ein Brot** she made herself a sandwich; **es geht** *or* **läuft wie geschmiert** it's going like clockwork; **jdm eine ~** (*inf*) to smack sb one (*inf*) **b** (*pej*: = *schreiben*) to scrawl; (= *malen*) to daub **c** (*inf*: = *bestechen*) **jdn ~** to grease sb's palm (*inf*) **d** (*Cards*) *Ass, Zehn* to discard (*on a trick which one's partner is winning*) VI **a** (*pej*) (= *schreiben*) to scrawl; (= *malen*) to daub **b** (*Stift, Radiergummi, Scheibenwischer*) to smear **c** (*inf*: = *bestechen*) to give a bribe/bribes **d** (*Cards*) *to discard a high-value card on a trick which one's partner is winning*

Schmie|ren-: **Schmie|ren|ko|mö|di|ant(in)** M(F) (*pej*) ham (actor/actress); **Schmie|ren|ko|mö|die** F (*pej*) slapstick farce, pantomime; (*fig*) pantomime, farce; **Schmie|ren|schau|spie|ler(in)** M(F) barnstormer; (*pej*) ham (actor/actress); **Schmie|ren|the|a|ter** NT (*pej*) (troop of) barnstormers *pl*; (= *schlechtes Theater*) fleapit; (*fig*) farce

Schmie|rer [ˈʃmiːrɐ] M **-s, -**, **Schmie|re|rin** [-ərɪn] F **-, -nen** (*pej inf*) scrawler, scribbler; (*von Parolen*) slogan dauber; (*in Toiletten, an Gebäuden*) graffiti writer; (= *Maler*) dauber; (= *Autor, Journalist*) hack, scribbler

Schmie|re|rei [ʃmiːrəˈrai] F **-, -en** (*pej inf*) (= *Geschriebenes*) scrawl, scribble; (= *Parolen etc*) graffiti *pl*; (= *Malerei*) daubing; (= *Schriftstellerei*) scribbling; (= *das Schmieren von Parolen etc*) scrawling, scribbling; (*von Stift, Scheibenwischer etc*) smearing

Schmie|re|ste|hen NT (*inf*) keeping lookout

Schmier-: **Schmier|fett** NT (lubricating) grease; **Schmier|fink** M (*pej*) **a** (= *Autor, Journalist*) hack, scribbler; (= *Skandaljournalist*) muckraker (*inf*) **b** (= *Schüler*) messy writer, scrawler; **Schmier|geld** NT bribe, bribe money

Schmier|geld-: **Schmier|geld|af|fä|re** F bribery case *or* affair; **Schmier|geld|zah|lung** F bribe payment

Schmier|heft NT jotter (*Brit*), rough book (*Brit*), sketchbook

schmie|rig [ˈʃmiːrɪç] ADJ greasy; *Restaurant auch* grimy; (*fig*) (= *unanständig*) dirty, filthy; (= *schleimig*) greasy, smarmy (*Brit inf*)

Schmier-: **Schmier|in|fek|ti|on** F (*Med*) infection (*passed on through touch*); **Schmier|kä|se** M (*dated*) cheese spread; **Schmier|mit|tel** NT lubricant; **Schmier|öl** NT lubricating oil; **Schmier|pa|pier** NT scrap *or* jotting paper (*Brit*), scratch paper (*US*); **Schmier|sei|fe** F soft soap

Schmie|rung [ˈʃmiːrʊŋ] F **-, -en** lubrication

Schmier|zet|tel M piece of rough *or* jotting paper (*Brit*), piece of scratch paper (*US*)

schmilzt [ʃmɪltst] *3. pers sing pres von* **schmelzen**

Schmin|ke [ˈʃmɪŋkə] F **-, -n** make-up

schmin|ken [ˈʃmɪŋkn] VT to make up; **sich** (*dat*) **die Lippen/Augen ~** to put on lipstick/eye make-up VR to make oneself up, to put on make-up; **sich selten ~** to wear make-up rarely; **sich stark ~** to wear a lot of make-up

Schmink-: **Schmink|kof|fer** M vanity case; **Schmink|täsch|chen** [-tɛʃçən] NT make-up bag; **Schmink|tisch** M dressing table

Schmir|gel [ˈʃmɪrgl] M **-s**, *no pl* emery

schmir|geln [ˈʃmɪrgln] VT to sand, to rub down (*esp Brit*) VI to sand

Schmir|gel-: **Schmir|gel|pa|pier** NT sandpaper; **Schmir|gel|schei|be** F sanding disc

schmiss *pret von* **schmeißen**

Schmiss [ʃmɪs] M **-es, -e a** (= *Fechtwunde*) gash, wound; (= *Narbe*) duelling scar **b** (*dated*: = *Schwung*) dash, élan; **~ haben** (*Musik etc*) to go with a swing; (*Mensch*) to have go (*inf*)

schmis|sig [ˈʃmɪsɪç] ADJ (*dated*) dashing (*dated*); *Musik auch* spirited

Schmock [ʃmɔk] M **-(e)s, -e** *or* **-s** (*pej*) hack

Schmok [ʃmoːk] M **-s**, *no pl* (*N Ger*) smoke

schmö|ken [ˈʃmøːkn] VTI (*N Ger*) to smoke

Schmö|ker [ˈʃmøːkɐ] M **-s, -** book (*usu of light literature*); (*dick*) tome

schmö|kern [ˈʃmøːkɐn] (*inf*) VI to bury oneself in a book/magazine *etc*; (= *in Büchern blättern*) to browse VT to bury oneself in

Schmoll|ecke F = **Schmollwinkel**

schmol|len [ˈʃmɔlən] VI to pout; (= *gekränkt sein*) to sulk; **mit jdm ~** to be annoyed with sb

Schmoll-: **Schmoll|mund** M pout; **einen ~ machen** to pout; **Schmoll|win|kel** M (*inf*) **im ~ sitzen** to have the sulks (*Brit inf*), to sulk; **sich in den ~ zurückziehen** to go off into a corner to sulk; **aus dem ~ herauskommen** to stop sulking

schmolz *pret von* **schmelzen**

Schmon|zes [ˈʃmɔntsəs] M **-, -** *(dated)* balderdash *(Brit dated)*, tripe *(inf)*

Schmon|zet|te [ʃmɔnˈtsɛtə] F **-, -n** *(inf)* kitschy film/book *etc*

Schmor-: **Schmor|brand** M smouldering *(Brit) or* smoldering *(US)* fire; **Schmor|bra|ten** M pot roast

schmo|ren [ˈʃmoːrən] VT to braise; *Braten auch* to pot-roast; **geschmorte Kalbshaxe** braised knuckle of veal VI **a** *(Cook)* to braise; *(inf: = schwitzen)* to roast, to swelter; **jdn (im eigenen Saft** *or* **Fett) ~ lassen** to leave sb to stew (in his/her own juice); **in der Hölle ~** to roast in hell **b** *(= unbearbeitet liegen)* to moulder *(Brit)*, to molder *(US)*

schmo|ren+las|sen VT *ptp* **schmorenlassen** *or (rare)* **schmorengelassen** *sep irreg* → **schmoren VI a**

Schmor-: **Schmor|fleisch** NT *(Cook)* braising steak; *(Braten)* pot roast; **Schmor|topf** M casserole

Schmu [ʃmuː] M **-s,** *no pl (inf)* cheating; *(esp mit Geld auch)* fiddling *(inf)*; **das ist ~!** that's cheating *or* fiddling! *(inf)*; **~ machen** to cheat, to fiddle *(inf)*; **bei der Abrechnung ~ machen** to fiddle the expenses; **bei der Prüfung ~ machen** to cheat in the exam

schmuck [ʃmʊk] ADJ *(dated) Haus etc* neat, tidy; *Schiff* neat, trim; *Bursche, Mädel* smart, spruce; *Paar* smart

Schmuck [ʃmʊk] M **-(e)s,** *(rare)* **-e a** *(= Schmuckstücke)* jewellery *(Brit) no pl*, jewelry *(US) no pl* **b** *(= Verzierung)* decoration; *(fig)* embellishment; **der ~ am Christbaum** the decorations on the Christmas tree; **im ~ der Blumen/Fahnen** *(liter)* decked with flowers/flags; **Natürlichkeit ist der schönste ~ eines Mädchens** naturalness is the greatest adornment a girl can have

schmü|cken [ˈʃmʏkn] VT to decorate, to adorn; *Baum* to decorate; *Rede* to embellish; **die mit Blumenkränzen geschmückten Tänzerinnen** the dancers adorned with garlands of flowers; **mit Juwelen geschmückt** bejewelled *(Brit)*, bejeweled *(US)*; **~des Beiwerk/Beiwort** embellishment VR *(zum Fest etc) (Mensch)* to adorn oneself; *(Stadt)* to be decorated; **sich mit etw ~** *(lit, fig)* to adorn oneself with sth; **sich mit Blumenkränzen ~** to garland oneself with flowers → **fremd a**

Schmuck-: **Schmuck|ge|gen|stand** M ornament; *(= Ring etc)* piece of jewellery *(Brit) or* jewelry *(US)*; **Schmuck|kas|set|te** F, **Schmuck|käst|chen** NT, **Schmuck|kas|ten** M jewellery *(Brit) or* jewelry *(US)* box; **ihr Haus war ein Schmuckkästchen** her house was a picture; **schmuck|los** ADJ plain; *Fassade* unadorned; *Einrichtung, Stil* simple, plain; *Prosa* simple, unadorned; **Schmuck|lo|sig|keit** F **-,** *no pl* plainness; *(von Einrichtung, Stil, Prosa)* simplicity; **Schmuck|sa|chen** PL jewellery *(Brit) sing*, jewelry *(US) sing*; **Schmuck|stein** M *(= Edelstein)* precious stone, gem; *(= Halbedelstein)* semiprecious stone; **Schmuck|stück** NT *(= Ring etc)* piece of jewellery; *(= Schmuckgegenstand)* ornament; *(fig: = Prachtstück)* gem; *(fig inf: = Frau)* better half *(hum inf)*; **Schmuck|wa|ren** PL jewellery *(Brit) sing*, jewelry *(US) sing*

Schmud|del [ˈʃmʊdl] M **-s,** *no pl (N Ger inf) (= Schmutz)* mess; *(auf Straße)* dirt, mud

Schmud|de|lei [ʃmʊdəˈlai] F **-, -en** *(inf)* mess *no pl*

schmud|de|lig [ˈʃmʊdəlɪç] ADJ messy; *(= schmutzig auch)* dirty; *(= schmierig, unsauber)* filthy; *(= schlampig) Bedienung* sloppy; *Frau, Schüler* sloppy, slovenly

Schmud|del-: **Schmud|del|kind** NT *(fig)* (street) urchin; **Schmud|del|look** M *(iro)* urchin look *(iro)*; **Schmud|del|wet|ter** NT lousy *or* mucky weather

schmudd|lig [ˈʃmʊdlɪç] ADJ = **schmuddelig**

Schmug|gel [ˈʃmʊgl] M **-s,** *no pl* smuggling; *(= einzelne Schmuggeloperation)* smuggling operation; **~ treiben** to smuggle; **der ~ von Heroin** heroin smuggling

Schmug|ge|lei [ʃmʊgəˈlai] F **-, -en** smuggling *no pl*; **seine kleinen ~en** his small-scale smuggling

schmug|geln [ˈʃmʊgln] VTI *(lit, fig)* to smuggle; **mit etw ~** to smuggle sth

Schmug|geln NT **-s,** *no pl* smuggling

Schmug|gel|wa|re F smuggled goods *pl*, contraband *no pl*

Schmugg|ler [ˈʃmʊglɐ] M **-s, -, Schmugg|le|rin** [-ərɪn] F **-, -nen** smuggler; **~ von Rauschgift** drug smuggler; **~ von Waffen** arms smuggler, gunrunner

Schmugg|ler-: **Schmugg|ler|ban|de** F smuggling ring, ring of smugglers; **Schmugg|ler|pfad** M smugglers' path; **Schmugg|ler|ring** M → **Schmugglerbande**

schmun|zeln [ˈʃmʊntsln] VI to smile

Schmun|zeln NT **-s,** *no pl* smile

Schmus [ʃmuːs] M **-es,** *no pl (inf) (= Unsinn)* nonsense; *(= Schmeicheleien)* soft soap *(Brit inf)*, cajolery; **~ erzählen** to talk nonsense

Schmu|se-: **Schmu|se|de|cke** F *(inf)* comfort blanket; **Schmu|se|kat|ze** F *(fig inf: = Person)* cuddly type; *(= Kind)* cuddly little thing; **Schmu|se|kurs** M *(inf)* friendly overtures *pl*; **mit jdm auf ~ gehen** to cosy up to sb; **der ~ zwischen SPD und Unternehmern** the friendly noises between the SPD and the employers; **sich mit jdm auf ~ begeben** to try to ingratiate oneself with sb; **Schmu|se|me|lo|die** F *(inf)* smoochy ballad *(inf)*

schmu|sen [ˈʃmuːzn] VI *(inf) (= zärtlich sein)* to cuddle; *(mit Freund, Freundin)* to cuddle, to canoodle *(Brit inf)*; **mit jdm ~** to cuddle sb/canoodle *(Brit inf)* with sb

Schmu|se-: **Schmu|se|pup|pe** F *(inf)* cuddly toy; **Schmu|se|tier** NT *(= Stofftier)* cuddly toy *or* animal

Schmu|ser [ˈʃmuːzɐ] M **-s, -, Schmu|se|rin** [-ərɪn] F **-, -nen** *(inf: = zärtlicher Mensch)* affectionate person; **er ist ein kleiner ~** he likes a cuddle

schmu|se|weich ADJ *(inf)* velvet-soft

schmu|sig [ˈʃmuːzɪç] ADJ *(inf)* smoochy *(inf)*

Schmutz [ʃmʊts] M **-es,** *no pl* **a** dirt; *(= Schlamm auch)* mud; **die Handwerker haben viel ~ gemacht** the workmen have made a lot of mess; **sie leben in ~** they live in real squalor; **der Stoff nimmt leicht ~ an** the material dirties easily; **~ abweisend** dirt-repellent; *Kleidung, Teppich etc* stain-resistant **b** *(fig)* filth, dirt, smut; **~ und Schund** obscene *or* offensive material; **jdn/etw in den ~ ziehen** *or* **zerren** to drag sb/sth through the mud → **bewerfen a**

schmutz|ab|wei|send [adj] → **Schmutz a**

Schmutz|blatt NT *(Typ)* half-title (page)

schmut|zen [ˈʃmʊtsn] VI to get dirty

Schmutz-: **Schmutz|fän|ger** M dust trap; **Schmutz|fink** M *(inf) (= unsauberer Mensch)* dirty slob *(inf)*; *(= Kind)* mucky pup *(Brit inf)*, messy thing *(esp US inf)*; *(fig) (= Mann)* dirty old man; *(= Journalist)* muckraker *(inf)*; **Schmutz|fleck** M dirty mark; **Schmutz|fracht** F dirty cargo

schmut|zig [ˈʃmʊtsɪç] ADJ *(= unsauber, unanständig)* dirty; *Geschäft* dirty, sordid; *Witze, Geschichten* smutty, dirty; **sich ~ machen** to get oneself dirty; **Geld ist doch nicht ~** money is money no matter where it comes from; **~e Wäsche (vor anderen Leuten) waschen** to wash *(Brit) or* air *(US)* one's dirty linen in public; **~e Reden führen** to use bad *or* foul language

Schmut|zig|keit F **-, -en a** *no pl (= Unsauberkeit)* dirtiness **b** *(= Witz)* dirty joke; *(= Bemerkung)* dirty remark

Schmutz-: **Schmutz|kam|pag|ne** F smear campaign; **Schmutz|li|te|ra|tur** F dirty *or* smutty literature; **Schmutz|schicht** F layer of dirt; **Schmutz|ti|tel** M *(Typ)* half-title; **Schmutz|wä|sche** F dirty washing; **Schmutz|was|ser** NT *pl* **-wässer** dirty water

Schna|bel [ˈʃnaːbl] M **-s, ¨** [ˈʃnɛːbl] **a** *(= Vogelschnabel)* beak, bill **b** *(von Kanne)* spout; *(von Krug)* lip; *(von Schiff)* prow **c** *(Mus: = Mundstück)* mouthpiece **d** *(inf: = Mund)* mouth; **halt den ~!** shut your mouth *(inf) or* trap! *(inf)*; **mach doch den ~ auf** say something; **reden, wie einem der ~ gewachsen ist** to say exactly what comes into one's head; *(unaffektiert)* to talk naturally

Schnä|be|lei [ʃnɛːbəˈlai] F **-, -en** *(lit, fig)* billing and cooing

Schna|bel|hieb M peck

schnä|beln [ˈʃnɛːbln] VI *(lit, fig)* to bill and coo

Schna|bel-: **Schna|bel|schuh** M pointed shoe (with turned-up toe); **Schna|bel|tas|se** F feeding cup; **Schna|bel|tier** NT duckbilled platypus

schna|bu|lie|ren [ʃnabuˈliːrən] *ptp* **schnabuliert** VI *(inf: = essen)* to nibble

Schnack [ʃnak] M **-(e)s, -s** *(N Ger inf) (= Unterhaltung)* chat; *(= Ausspruch)* silly *or* amusing phrase; **das ist ein dummer ~** that's a silly phrase

schna|ckeln [ˈʃnakln] VI *(S Ger) (Mensch)* to shake; **mit den Fingern ~** to snap *or* click one's fingers; **jdm ~ die Knie** sb's knees are trembling *or* shaking; **es hat (bei jdm) geschnackelt** it's clicked

schna|cken [ˈʃnakn] VI *(N Ger)* to chat

Schna|ckerl [ˈʃnakɐl] M OR NT **-s,** *no pl (Aus)* hiccup; **den ~ haben** to have (the) hiccups

Schna|ke [ˈʃnaːkə] F **-, -n a** *(inf: = Stechmücke)* gnat, midge *(Brit)*, mosquito **b** *(= Weberknecht)* daddy-longlegs

Schna|ken|stich M mosquito bite

Schnal|le [ˈʃnalə] F **-, -n a** *(= Schuhschnalle, Gürtelschnalle)* buckle **b** *(an Handtasche, Buch)* clasp **c** *(Aus, S Ger: = Türklinke)* handle **d** *(sl: = Frau, Mädchen)* bird *(esp Brit inf)*, chick *(esp US inf)* **e** *(vulg: = Vagina)* fanny *(sl)*

schnal|len [ˈʃnalən] VT **a** *(= befestigen)* to strap; *Gürtel* to buckle, to fasten → **Gürtel b** *(inf: = begreifen)* **etw ~** to catch on to sth; **hast du das noch immer nicht geschnallt?** have you still not caught on?

Schnal|len|schuh M buckled shoe

schnal|zen [ˈʃnaltsn] VI **mit der Peitsche ~** to crack one's whip, to give a crack of one's whip; **mit der Zunge ~** to click one's tongue

Schnal|zer [ˈʃnaltsɐ] M **-s, -** *(inf) (mit Zunge)* click; *(von Peitsche)* crack

Schnalz|laut M *(Ling)* click

schnapp [ʃnap] INTERJ snap → **schnipp**

Schnäpp|chen [ˈʃnɛpçən] NT **-s, -** *(inf)* bargain; **ein ~ machen** to get a bargain

Schnäpp|chen|jä|ger(in) M(F) *(inf)* bargain hunter

Schnäpp|chen|preis M *(inf)* bargain price

schnap|pen [ˈʃnapn] VI **a nach jdm/etw ~** to snap at *or* take a snap at sb/sth; *(= greifen)* to snatch at *or* grab at sb/sth → **Luft b b** *aux sein (= sich bewegen)* to spring up; **die Tür schnappt ins Schloss** the door snaps *or* clicks shut VT *(inf)* **a** *(= ergreifen)* to snatch, to grab; **jdn am Arm ~** to grab sb's arm *or* sb by the arm; **sich** *(dat)* **jdn/etw ~** to grab sb/sth *(inf)* → **Luft b** *(= fangen)* to catch, to nab *(inf)*

Schnap|per [ˈʃnapɐ] M **-s, -** *(inf: von Hund etc)* snap

Schnäp|per [ˈʃnɛpɐ] M **-s, -** *(Med)* lancet

Schnapp-: **Schnapp|fe|der** F spring catch; **Schnapp|hahn** M *(Hist)* highwayman; **Schnapp|mes|ser** NT clasp knife; **Schnapp|schloss** NT *(an Tür)* spring lock; *(an Schmuck)* spring clasp; **Schnapp|schuss** M *(= Foto)* snap(shot); **Schnapp|ver|schluss** M snap lock

Schnaps [ʃnaps] M **-es, ¨e** [ˈʃnɛpsə] *(= klarer Schnaps)* schnapps; *(inf) (= Branntwein)* spirits *pl*;

(= Alkohol) drink, booze (inf), liquor (esp US inf)

Schnaps-: **Schnaps|bren|ner(in)** M(F) distiller; **Schnaps|bren|ne|rei** F **a** (Gebäude) distillery **b** no pl (= das Brennen) distilling of spirits or liquor; **Schnaps|bru|der** M (inf) boozer (inf)

Schnäps|chen ['ʃnɛpsçən] NT -s, - (inf) little drink, wee dram (esp Scot)

Schnaps|dros|sel F (inf, hum) boozer (inf), lush (esp US inf)

schnap|sen ['ʃnapsn], (Aus) **schnap|seln** ['ʃnapsln] VI (inf) to booze (inf)

Schnaps-: **Schnaps|fah|ne** F (inf) boozy breath (inf); **Schnaps|fla|sche** F bottle of booze (inf) or spirits or liquor; **Schnaps|glas** NT small glass for spirits; **Schnaps|idee** F (inf) crazy or crackpot idea; **Schnaps|la|den** M off-licence (Brit), liquor store (US); **Schnaps|lei|che** F (inf) drunk; **Schnaps|na|se** F (inf) boozer's nose (inf); **Schnaps|zahl** F (inf) multidigit number with all digits identical

schnar|chen ['ʃnarçn] VI to snore

Schnar|cher ['ʃnarçɐ] M -s, -, **Schnar|che|rin** [-ərın] F -, -nen snorer

Schnar|re ['ʃnarə] F -, -n rattle

schnar|ren ['ʃnarən] VI (Wecker, Radio, Saite etc) to buzz; (Maschine, Spinnrad etc) to clatter; (Uhrwerk) to creak; (Vogel, Frosch) to croak; **mit ~der Stimme** in a rasping or grating voice

Schnat|ter|gans F, **Schnat|ter|lie|se** [-li:zə] F -, -n, **Schnat|ter|maul** NT (all inf) chatterbox (inf)

schnat|tern ['ʃnatɐn] VI (Gans) to gabble; (Ente) to quack; (Affen) to chatter, to gibber; (inf: = schwatzen) to natter (inf); **sie schnattert vor Kälte** her teeth are chattering with (the) cold

schnau|ben ['ʃnaubn] pret **schnaubte** or (old) **schnob** [ʃnauptə, ʃno:p], ptp **geschnaubt** or (old) **geschnoben** [gə'ʃnaupt, gə'ʃno:bn] VI **a** (Tier) to snort **b** (= fauchen) to snort; **vor Wut/Entrüstung ~** to snort with rage/indignation VT **a** (= schnäuzen) **sich** (dat) **die Nase ~** to blow one's nose **b** (= fauchen) to snort; **Unverschämtheit, schnaubte er** disgraceful, he snorted **c** (liter: Pferd etc) to breathe VR **sich ~** to blow one's nose

schnau|fen ['ʃnaufn] VI **a** (= schwer atmen) to wheeze; (= keuchen) to puff, to pant; (fig) (Lokomotive) to puff; (inf: Auto) to struggle **b** (esp S Ger: = atmen) to breathe **c** aux sein (= sich keuchend bewegen) (Auto) to struggle; (Lokomotive) to puff; **ich bin in den fünften Stock geschnauft** (inf) I went puffing and panting up to the fifth floor

Schnau|fer ['ʃnaufɐ] M -s, - (inf) breath; **ein ~ frische Luft** a breath of fresh air; **seinen letzten ~ tun** to breathe one's last, to kick the bucket (inf), to snuff it (Brit inf)

Schnau|ferl ['ʃnaufɐl] NT -s, - or (Aus) -n (hum: = Oldtimer) veteran car

Schnauf|pau|se F (Aus, S Ger) short breather (inf)

Schnauz|bart M walrus moustache (Brit) or mustache (US)

Schnäuz|chen ['ʃnɔytsçən] NT -s, - dim von **Schnauze** nose

Schnau|ze ['ʃnautsə] F -, -n **a** (von Tier) snout, muzzle; **eine feuchte ~ haben** to have a wet nose; **mit einer Maus in der ~** with a mouse in its mouth

b (= Ausguss) (an Kaffeekanne etc) spout; (an Krug etc) lip

c (inf) (von Fahrzeugen) front; (von Flugzeug, Schiff) nose

d (inf) (= Mund) gob (Brit inf), trap (inf); (= respektlose Art zu reden) bluntness; **(halt die) ~!** shut your gob (Brit inf) or trap! (inf); **auf die ~ fallen** (lit) to fall flat on one's face; (fig auch) to come a cropper (Brit inf); **jdm die ~ einschlagen** or **polieren** to smash sb's face in (sl); **die ~ (von jdm/etw) (gestrichen) voll haben** to be fed up (to the back teeth) (with sb/sth) (inf); **eine große ~ haben** to have a big mouth, to be a bigmouth (inf); **die ~ halten** to hold one's tongue; **etw frei nach ~ machen** to do sth any old (Brit) or ole (US) how (inf); **Berliner ~** endearing Berlin bluntness

schnau|zen ['ʃnautsn] VI (inf) to shout; (= jdn anfahren) to snap, to bark

schnäu|zen ['ʃnɔytsn] VR to blow one's nose VT **einem Kind/sich die Nase ~** to blow a child's/one's nose

Schnau|zer ['ʃnautsɐ] M -s, - **a** (= Hundeart) schnauzer **b** (inf: = Schnauzbart) walrus moustache (Brit) or mustache (US)

Schneck [ʃnɛk] M -s, -en (Aus, S Ger) = **Schnecke a, b**

Schne|cke ['ʃnɛkə] F -, -n **a** (Zool, fig) snail; (= Nacktschnecke) slug; (Cook) escargot, snail; **wie eine ~ kriechen** to crawl at a snail's pace; **jdn zur ~ machen** (inf) to give sb a real bawling-out (inf), to bawl sb out (inf) **b** (Anat) cochlea (spec) **c** (Archit: an Säule) volute; (= Treppe) spiral staircase **d** (Tech) (= Schraube) worm, endless screw; (= Förderschnecke) worm or screw conveyor **e** usu pl (Frisur) earphone **f** (Cook: Gebäck) ≈ Chelsea bun **g** (Mus: an Geige etc) scroll

Schne|cken-: **schne|cken|för|mig** ADJ spiral; (Archit) Ornament scroll-shaped; **Schne|cken|ge|häu|se** NT, **Schne|cken|haus** NT snail shell; **sich in sein Schneckenhaus zurückziehen** (fig inf) to retreat into one's shell; **Schne|cken|korn** NT, no pl slug pellets pl; **Schne|cken|mu|schel** F (Zool) conch; **Schne|cken|post** F (inf) snail mail (inf); **du bist wohl mit der ~ gefahren?** you must have crawled your way here; **Schne|cken|tem|po** NT (inf) **im ~** at a snail's pace; **dein ~ kenn ich schon** I know how slowly you do things

Schnee [ʃne:] M -s, no pl **a** (auch TV) snow; **vom ~ eingeschlossen sein** to be snowbound; **im Jahre ~** (Aus) ages ago; **das ist ~ von gestern** (inf) that's old hat **b** (= Eischnee) whisked egg white; **Eiweiß zu ~ schlagen** to whisk the egg white(s) till stiff **c** (inf: = Heroin, Kokain) snow (sl)

Schnee-: **Schnee|an|zug** M snowsuit; **schnee|arm** ADJ Gebiet, Winter with little snow

Schnee|ball M snowball; (Bot) snowball, guelder rose

Schnee|ball-: **Schnee|ball|ef|fekt** M snowball effect; **Schnee|ball|prin|zip** NT snowball effect; **Schnee|ball|schlacht** F snowball fight; **eine ~ machen** to have a snowball fight; **Schnee|ball|sys|tem** NT accumulative process; (Comm) pyramid selling; **ein Gewinnspiel/Geldgeschäft nach dem** or **im ~** a prize game/financial transaction involving a pyramid scheme; **das vermehrt sich nach dem ~** it snowballs

Schnee-: **schnee|be|deckt** ADJ snow-covered; Berg auch snowcapped; **Schnee|be|sen** M (Cook) whisk; **schnee|blind** ADJ snow-blind; **Schnee|blind|heit** F snow blindness; **Schnee|brett** NT windslab (Brit), snow/ice slab (US); **Schnee|brett|ge|fahr** F danger of windslab (Brit) or snow/ice slab (US) avalanches; **Schnee|bril|le** F snow goggles pl; **Schnee|de|cke** F blanket or (Met) covering of snow; **Schnee-Eu|le** F snowy owl; **Schnee|fall** M snowfall, fall of snow; **dichter ~ behindert die Sicht** heavy falling snow is impairing visibility; **Schnee|fall|gren|ze** F snowline; **über/unter der ~** above/below the snowline; **Schnee|flo|cke** F snowflake; **Schnee|frä|se** F snow blower; **schnee|frei** ADJ Gebiet, Bergpass free of snow; **in der ~en Zeit** when there is no snow; **Schnee|gans** F snow goose; **Schnee|ge|stö|ber** NT (leicht) snow flurry; (stark) snowstorm; **Schnee|glät|te** F hard-packed snow no pl; **Schnee|glöck|chen** NT snowdrop; **Schnee|gren|ze** F snow line; **Schnee|ha|se** M blue hare; **Schnee|hemd** NT (Mil) white coat for camouflage in snow; **Schnee|hüt|te** F hut made of snow; **Schnee|ka|no|ne** F snow cannon; **Schnee|ket|te** F (Aut) snow chain; **Schnee|ket|ten|pflicht** F (Aut) obligation to fit snow chains, chain law (US); **Schnee|kö|nig** M **sich freuen wie ein ~** to be as pleased as Punch; **Schnee|kris|tall** M snow crystal; **Schnee|land|schaft** F snowy landscape; **Schnee|mann** M pl **-männer** snowman; **Schnee|matsch** M slush; **Schnee|mensch** M abominable snowman, yeti; **Schnee|mo|bil** [-mobi:l] NT -s, -e snowmobile; **Schnee|pflug** M (Tech, Ski) snowplough (Brit), snowplow (US); **Schnee|rau|pe** F snow cat; **Schnee|re|gen** M sleet; **Schnee|schau|fel** F, **Schnee|schie|ber** M, **Schnee|schip|pe** F snow shovel, snowpusher (US); **Schnee|schlä|ger** M whisk; **Schnee|schmel|ze** F thaw; **Schnee|schuh** M snowshoe; (dated Ski) ski; **schnee|si|cher** ADJ **~e Gebiete** areas that are assured of snow; **Schnee|sturm** M snowstorm; (stärker) blizzard; **Schnee|trei|ben** NT driving snow; **Schnee|ver|hält|nis|se** PL snow conditions pl; **Schnee|ver|we|hung** F snowdrift; **Schnee|wäch|te** △ [-vɛçtə] F -, -n → **Schneewechte**; **Schnee|was|ser** NT, no pl water from melting snow, snowmelt (US); **Schnee|wech|te** [-vɛçtə] F -, -n snow cornice; **Schnee|we|he** F snowdrift; **schnee|weiß** ADJ snow-white, as white as snow; Haare snowy-white; Hände lily-white; Gewissen clear; **Schnee|weiß|chen** [-'vaisçən] NT -s, no pl, **Schnee|witt|chen** [-'vıtçən] NT -s, no pl Snow White

Schneid [ʃnait] M -(e)s (S Ger, Aus) f - [-dəs], no pl (inf) guts pl (inf), nerve, courage; **~/keinen ~ haben** to have/not to have guts (inf); **den ~ verlieren** to lose one's nerve; **jdm den ~ abkaufen** (fig) to knock the stuffing out of sb (inf), to take the fight out of sb

Schneid|bren|ner M (Tech) oxyacetylene cutter, cutting torch

Schnei|de ['ʃnaidə] F -, -n (sharp or cutting) edge; (von Messer, Schwert) blade → **Messer**

Schnei|de|brett NT chopping or cutting board

schnei|den ['ʃnaidn] pret **schnitt** [ʃnıt], ptp **geschnitten** [gə'ʃnıtn] VI to cut; (Med) to operate; (bei Geburt) to do an episiotomy; **jdm ins Gesicht/in die Hand** etc **~** to cut sb on the face/on the hand etc; **der Wind schneidet** the wind is biting; **die Kälte schneidet** it is bitingly cold; **jdm ins Herz** or **in die Seele ~** to cut sb to the quick

VT **a** Papier etc, Haare, Hecke to cut; Getreide to mow, to cut; (= klein schneiden) Schnittlauch, Gemüse etc to chop; (Sport) Ball to slice, to cut; (= schnitzen) Namen, Figuren to carve; (Math) to intersect with, to cut; (Weg) to cross; **eine Kurve ~** to cut a corner; **jdn ~** (beim Überholen) to cut in on sb; (= ignorieren) to cut sb dead (Brit) or off; **sein schön/scharf geschnittenes Gesicht** his clean-cut/sharp features or face; **Gesichter** or **Grimassen ~** to make or pull faces; **die Luft ist zum Schneiden (dick)** (fig inf) the air is very bad; **die Atmosphäre ist zum Schneiden** (fig inf) you could cut the atmosphere with a knife; **weit/eng geschnitten sein** (Sew) to be cut wide/narrow

b Film, Tonband to edit

c (inf: = operieren) to operate on; Furunkel to lance; **jdn ~** to cut sb open (inf); (bei Geburt) to give sb an episiotomy; **geschnitten werden** (bei Geburt) to have an episiotomy

d (fig: = meiden) to cut

VR **a** (Mensch) to cut oneself; **sich in den Finger** etc **~** to cut one's finger etc → **Fleisch a**

b (inf: = sich täuschen) **da hat er sich aber geschnitten!** he's made a big mistake, he's very mistaken

c (Linien, Straßen etc) to intersect

schnei|dend ADJ biting; *Hohn, Bemerkung auch* cutting; *Wind, Kälte auch* piercing, bitter; *Schmerz* sharp, searing; *Stimme, Ton* piercing

Schnei|der [ˈʃnaidɐ] M **-s, -** **a** *(Cards)* **einen ~ machen** to score half (the full) points; **im ~ sein** to have less than half points; **aus dem ~ sein** to have slightly more than half points; *(fig)* to be out of the woods **b** *(Gerät)* cutter; *(inf: für Brot etc)* slicer **c** *(= Schnake)* gnat; *(= Weberknecht)* daddy-longlegs

Schnei|der [ˈʃnaidɐ] M **-s, -**, **Schnei|de|rin** [ˈʃnaidərɪn] F **-, -nen** tailor; *(= Damenschneider auch)* dressmaker → **frieren VI a**

Schnei|de|raum M *(= Filmschneideraum)* cutting room, editing suite

Schnei|de|rei [ʃnaidəˈrai] F **-, -en** **a** *no pl (Handwerk)* tailoring; *(für Damen)* dressmaking **b** *(Werkstatt)* tailor's/dressmaker's

Schnei|der-: **Schnei|der|ge|sel|le** M, **Schnei|der|ge|sel|lin** F → **Schneider** journeyman tailor/dressmaker; **Schnei|der|hand|werk** NT tailoring *no art*; *(für Damenkleidung)* dressmaking *no art*; **Schnei|der|kos|tüm** NT tailored suit; **Schnei|der|krei|de** F tailor's chalk; **Schnei|der|leh|re** F tailoring apprenticeship; *(für Damenmode)* dressmaking apprenticeship; **Schnei|der|lehr|ling** M → **Schneider** tailor's/dressmaker's apprentice; **Schnei|der|meis|ter(in)** M(F) → **Schneider** master tailor/dressmaker

schnei|dern [ˈʃnaidɐn] VI *(beruflich)* to be a tailor; *(Damenschneider)* to be a dressmaker; *(als Hobby)* to do dressmaking VT to make, to sew; *Anzug, Kostüm* to tailor, to make; *(fig) Plan, Programm* to draw up; **jdm (wie) auf den Leib geschneidert sein** *(fig)* to be tailor-made for sb

Schnei|der-: **Schnei|der|pup|pe** F → **Schneider** tailor's/dressmaker's dummy; **Schnei|der|sitz** M **im ~ sitzen** to sit cross-legged; **Schnei|der|werk|statt** F → **Schneider** tailor's/dressmaker's workshop

Schnei|de-: **Schnei|de|tisch** M *(Film)* editing *or* cutting table; **Schnei|de|werk|zeug** NT cutting tool; **Schnei|de|zahn** M incisor

schnei|dig [ˈʃnaidɪç] ADJ *Mensch* dashing; *Musik, Rede* rousing; *Tempo* fast

schnei|en [ˈʃnaiən] VI *impers* to snow VT *impers* **es schneit dicke Flocken** big flakes (of snow) are falling; **es schneite Konfetti** confetti rained down VI *aux sein (fig)* to rain down; **jdm ins Haus ~** *(inf) (Besuch)* to drop in on sb; *(Rechnung, Brief)* to arrive through sb's letter box *(Brit) or* mailbox *(US)*, to arrive in the post *(Brit) or* mail for sb

Schnei|se [ˈʃnaizə] F **-, -n** break; *(= Waldschneise)* aisle, lane; *(= Feuerschneise)* firebreak; *(= Flugschneise)* path; **eine ~ schlagen** *(lit)* to cut a lane; **der Toleranz** *(dat)* **eine ~ schlagen** to pave the way for tolerance

schnell [ʃnɛl] ADJ quick; *Bedienung, Fahrt, Tempo, Läufer auch* fast; *Schritte, Puls, Verbesserung auch* fast, rapid; *Auto, Zug, Verkehr, Fahrer, Strecke* fast; *Abreise, Bote, Hilfe* speedy; *Antwort* quick, speedy, prompt; *Genesung, Besserung* quick, rapid, speedy; **er kam in ~em Lauf dahergerannt** he came running up quickly; **er ist sehr ~ mit seinem Urteil/seiner Kritik** he's very quick to judge/to criticize; **~es Geld (machen)** *(inf)* (to make) a fast buck *(inf)* → **Schnelle, Truppe a**
ADV **a** *(= mit hoher Geschwindigkeit)* quickly, fast; **~er als der Schall fliegen** to fly faster than the speed of sound; **wie ~ ist er die 100 Meter gelaufen?** how fast did he run the 100 metres *(Brit) or* meters *(US)?*; **geh ~er!** hurry up!; **nicht so ~!** not so fast!; **sein Puls ging ~** his pulse was very fast
b *(= zügig) arbeiten, handeln, durchführen, erwärmen* fast, quickly; **das geht ~** *(grundsätzlich)* it doesn't take long; **das mache ich gleich, das geht ~** I'll do that now, it won't take long; **das ging ~** that was quick; **mach ~/~er!** hurry up!; **es ist mit dem Patienten ~ gegangen** it was all over quickly; **mit dicker Wolle geht es ~, einen Pullover zu stricken** knitting a pullover with thick wool is very quick; **an der Grenze ist es ~ gegangen** things went very quickly at the border; **das ging alles viel zu ~** it all happened much too quickly *or* fast; **das werden wir ~ erledigt haben** we'll soon have that finished; **das werden wir ~ sehen** *(= bald)* we'll soon see about that
c *(= leicht)* **das sagt sich so ~** that's easy to say; **sie wird ~ böse, sie ist ~ verärgert** she loses her temper quickly, she is quick to get angry; **das werde ich so ~ nicht vergessen/wieder tun** I won't forget that/do that again in a hurry; **diese dünnen Gläser gehen ~ kaputt** these thin glasses break easily
d *(= kurz)* **ich gehe noch ~ beim Bäcker vorbei** I'll just stop by at the baker's; **kannst du das vorher noch ~ machen?** *(inf)* can you do that quickly first?; **ich muss mir nur noch ~ die Haare kämmen** I must just give my hair a quick comb; **ich rauche ~ noch eine Zigarette** I'll just have a quick cigarette

Schnell-: **Schnell|an|sicht** F *(Comput)* quick view; **Schnelläufer** △ M → **Schnellläufer, Schnellläufer(in)**; **Schnell|bahn** F *(= S-Bahn)* suburban railway *(Brit)*, city railroad *(US)*; **Schnell|bau|wei|se** F high-speed building methods *pl*; **Schnell|boot** NT speedboat; *(Mil)* motor torpedo boat *(Brit)*, PT boat *(US)*; **Schnell|den|ker(in)** M(F) *(inf: = intelligenter Mensch)* bright *or* clever person, brainbox *(Brit inf)*; **Schnell|dienst** M express service; **Schnell|dru|cker** M high-speed printer

Schnel|le [ˈʃnɛlə] F **-, -n** **a** *no pl (= Schnelligkeit)* quickness, speed **b** *(= Stromschnelle)* rapids *pl* **c** **etw auf die ~ machen** to do sth quickly *or* in a rush; **das lässt sich nicht auf die ~ machen** we can't rush that, that will take time; **Sex/ein Bier auf die ~** *(inf)* a quickie *(inf)*

schnellebig △ ADJ → **schnelllebig**

Schnellebigkeit △ F → **Schnelllebigkeit**

schnel|len [ˈʃnɛlən] VI *aux sein (lit, fig)* to shoot; **in die Höhe ~** to shoot up; **ein Gummiband ~ lassen** to flick a rubber band

Schnell|feu|er NT *(Mil)* rapid fire

Schnell|feu|er-: **Schnell|feu|er|ge|schütz** NT automatic rifle; **Schnell|feu|er|ge|wehr** NT automatic pistol; **Schnell|feu|er|waf|fe** F rapid-fire weapon

Schnell-: **schnell|fü|ßig** ADJ *(geh)* fleet-footed *(liter)*, fleet of foot *(liter)*; **Schnell|gast|stät|te** F fast-food restaurant, cafeteria, fast-food store *(US)*; **Schnell|ge|richt** NT **a** *(Jur)* summary court **b** *(Cook)* convenience food; **Schnell|hef|ter** M spring folder

Schnel|lig|keit [ˈʃnɛlɪçkait] F **-, -en** *(von Auto, Verkehr, Abreise)* speed; *(von Bewegung, Tempo auch)* quickness; *(von Schritten, Besserung, Verbesserung, Entwicklung auch, von Puls)* rapidity; *(von Bote, Hilfe)* speediness; *(von Antwort)* speediness, promptness

Schnell-: **Schnell|im|biss** M **a** *(Essen)* (quick) snack **b** *(Raum)* snack bar; **Schnell|koch|plat|te** F high-speed ring; **Schnell|koch|topf** M *(= Dampfkochtopf)* pressure cooker; *(= Wasserkochtopf)* ≈ electric kettle; **Schnell|kraft** F *(von Feder, Sprungbrett)* springiness, resilience; *(von Sportler, Fischen)* ability to jump; **Schnell|kurs** M crash course; **Schnell|läu|fer** M *(Astron)* high-velocity star; *(Tech)* high-speed machine; **Schnell|läu|fer(in)** M(F) *(Sport)* sprinter; **schnell|le|big** [-le:bɪç] ADJ *Zeit, Geschäft, Markt* fast-moving; **Schnell|le|big|keit** [-le:bɪç-] F **-**, *no pl* fast-moving nature; **Schnell|pa|ket** NT express parcel; **Schnell|pres|se** F high-speed printing machine *or* press; **Schnell|rei|ni|gung** F express cleaning service; **Schnell|res|tau|rant** NT fast-food restaurant; **Schnell|rück|lauf** M fast rewind; **Schnell|schrift** F *(Comput)* draft quality; **Schnell|schuss** M *(inf: = vorschnelle Handlung)* hasty reaction; *(Buch, Fernsehsendung etc)* rush job; **einen ~ machen** to react too hastily; **Schnell|start** M *(esp Comput)* quick start

schnells|tens [ˈʃnɛlstns] ADV as quickly as possible

schnellst|mög|lich [ˈʃnɛlst-] ADJ *attr* fastest *or* quickest possible *attr* ADV as quickly as possible

Schnell-: **Schnell|stra|ße** F expressway; **Schnell|such|lauf** M rapid search; **Schnell|ver|fah|ren** NT *(Jur)* summary trial; *(Mil)* summary court martial; **im ~ abgeurteilt werden** to be sentenced by a summary trial/court martial; **Schnell|ver|kehr** M fast-moving traffic; *(im Transportwesen)* express service; **etw im ~ schicken** to send sth express delivery; **Schnell|vor|lauf** M fast forward; **Schnell|zug** M fast train; **Schnell|zug|zu|schlag** M supplementary *or* extra charge for travel on a fast train; *(inf: = Zuschlagkarte)* supplementary ticket

Schnep|fe [ˈʃnɛpfə] F **-, -n** snipe; *(pej inf)* silly cow *(inf)*

schnet|zeln [ˈʃnɛtsln] VT *(S Ger, Sw) Frucht, Gemüse* to slice; *Fleisch* to shred

schneu|zen △ [ˈʃnɔytsn] VTR → **schnäuzen**

Schnick|schnack [ˈʃnɪkʃnak] M **-s**, *no pl (inf) (= Unsinn)* twaddle *(inf) no indef art*, poppycock *(inf) no indef art*; *(= Kinkerlitzchen)* paraphernalia *(inf) no indef art*; **ach ~!** *(dated)* balderdash! *(Brit dated inf)*, fiddlesticks! *(dated inf)*

Schnick|se [ˈʃnɪksə] F **-, -n** *(sl: = Frau, Mädchen)* bird *(esp Brit inf)*, chick *(esp US inf)*

Schnie|del [ˈʃniːdl] M **-s, -**, **Schnie|del|wutz** [ˈʃniːdlwʊts] M **-es, -e** *(hum inf: = Penis)* willy *(Brit hum inf)*, weenie *(US hum inf)*

schnie|fen [ˈʃniːfn] VI *(dial) (bei Schnupfen)* to sniff(le); *(beim Weinen)* to sniffle, to snivel

schnie|geln [ˈʃniːgln] *(inf)* VT *Kleidung, Kinder, Auto* to spruce up VR to get spruced up, to spruce oneself up → *auch* **geschniegelt**

schnie|ke [ˈʃniːkə] ADJ *(N Ger inf: = schick)* swish *(inf)*

schnipp [ʃnɪp] INTERJ snip; **~, schnapp** snip, snip *(Brit)*, snip, snap *(US)*

Schnipp|chen [ˈʃnɪpçən] NT **-s, -** *(inf)* **jdm ein ~ schlagen** to play a trick on sb, to trick sb; **dem Tod ein ~ schlagen** to cheat death

Schnip|pel [ˈʃnɪpl] M OR NT **-s, -** *(inf)* scrap; *(= Papierschnipsel)* scrap *or* bit of paper

schnip|peln [ˈʃnɪpln] *(inf)* VI to snip *(an +dat* at); *(mit Messer)* to hack *(an +dat* at); **an ihr haben die Ärzte schon was geschnippelt!** she has already been hacked about a bit by the doctors *(inf)* VT to snip; *(mit Messer)* to hack; *Gemüse* to chop up

schnip|pen [ˈʃnɪpn] VI **mit den Fingern ~** to snap one's fingers VT **etw (von etw) ~** to flick sth (off *or* from sth)

schnip|pisch [ˈʃnɪpɪʃ] ADJ saucy, pert ADV saucily, pertly

Schnip|sel [ˈʃnɪpsl] M OR NT **-s, -** *(inf)* scrap; *(= Papierschnipsel)* scrap *or* bit of paper

schnip|seln [ˈʃnɪpsln] VTI *(inf)* = **schnippeln**

schnip|sen [ˈʃnɪpsn] VTI *(inf)* = **schnippen**

schnitt *pret von* **schneiden**

Schnitt [ʃnɪt] M **-(e)s, -e** **a** cut; *(= Kerbe)* notch, nick; *(Med)* incision, cut; *(von Heu, Getreide)* crop; **Blumen für den ~** flowers *pl* (suitable) for cutting
b *(= Haarschnitt)* (hair)cut; **einen kurzen ~ bitte** cut it short please
c *(Sew)* cut; *(= Schnittmuster)* pattern
d *(= Form) (von Edelstein)* cut; *(von Gesicht, Augen)* shape; *(von Profil)* line
e *(Film)* editing *no pl*; **der Film ist jetzt beim ~** the film is now being edited *or* cut; **schnelle ~e** quick cutting; **~: L. Schwarz** editor - L. Schwarz
f *(Math) (= Schnittpunkt)* (point of) intersection; *(= Schnittfläche)* section; *(inf: = Durchschnitt)* average; **im ~** on average; **unter/über dem ~** below/above average
g *(= Längsschnitt, Querschnitt)* section; **im ~ gezeichnet** drawn in section

h (inf: = Gewinn) profit
i (Typ) (= das Beschneiden) cut; (= Buchrand) (trimmed) edge; **dann kommt das gebundene Buch zum ~** then the bound book is cut or trimmed
j (Hort: von Bäumen etc) cutting *no indef art*

Schnitt-: **Schnitt|blu|men** PL cut flowers *pl*; (im Garten) flowers *pl* (suitable) for cutting; **Schnitt|boh|nen** PL French or green beans *pl*

Schnit|te [ˈʃnɪtə] F -, -n **a** slice; (belegt) open sandwich; (zusammengeklappt) sandwich; **womit soll ich dir die ~ belegen?** what shall I put on your (slice of) bread? **b** (sl: = Frau, Mädchen) bird (*esp Brit inf*), chick (*esp US inf*)

Schnitt|ebe|ne F (Math) sectional plane

Schnit|ter [ˈʃnɪtɐ] M -s, -, **Schnit|te|rin** [-ərɪn] F -, -nen reaper

Schnitt-: **schnitt|fest** ADJ Tomaten, Käse etc firm; **Schnitt|flä|che** F section

schnit|tig [ˈʃnɪtɪç] ADJ smart; Mann, Auto, Formen auch stylish; Mund, Lippen finely shaped; Tempo auch snappy (*inf*) ADV **er ist ganz schön ~ gefahren** he nipped or zipped along (*inf*)

Schnitt-: **Schnitt|kä|se** M slicing cheese; (= aufgeschnittener Käse) cheese slices *pl*; **Schnitt|lauch** M, *no pl* chives *pl*; **Schnitt|lauch|lo|cken** PL (hum inf) straight hair *no pl*; **Schnitt|li|nie** F (Math) line of intersection; (Sew) cutting line; **Schnitt|men|ge** F (Math) intersection; **Schnitt|mus|ter** NT (Sew) (paper) pattern; **Schnitt|mus|ter|bo|gen** M (Sew) pattern chart; **Schnitt|punkt** M (von Straßen) intersection; (Math auch) point of intersection; (fig) interface; **Schnitt|stel|le** F cut; (Comput, fig) interface; (fig: = Vermittler) go-between; **grafische/serielle ~** graphic(al)/serial (user) interface; **Schnitt|ver|let|zung** F → **Schnittwunde**; **Schnitt|win|kel** M angle of intersection; **Schnitt|wun|de** F cut; (tief) gash

Schnitz [ʃnɪts] M -es, -e (S Ger, Aus) piece; (von Orange auch) segment; (von Apfel auch) slice

Schnitz|ar|beit F (wood)carving

Schnit|zel [ˈʃnɪtsl] NT OR M -s, - **a** (= Papierschnitzel) bit or scrap of paper; (= Holzschnitzel) shaving; (= Fetzen, Karottenschnitzel, Kartoffelschnitzel) shred, sliver **b** **Schnitzel** PL (= Abfälle) scraps *pl*

Schnit|zel NT -s, - (Cook) veal/pork cutlet, schnitzel

Schnit|zel|jagd F paper chase

schnit|zeln [ˈʃnɪtsln] VT Gemüse to shred; Holz to chop (up) (into sticks)

schnit|zen [ˈʃnɪtsn] VTI to carve; **wir haben in der Schule Schnitzen gelernt** we learned woodcarving at school → **Holz a**

Schnit|zer [ˈʃnɪtsɐ] M -s, - (inf) (in Benehmen) blunder, boob (*esp Brit inf*), goof (*US inf*); (= Fauxpas) gaffe, clanger (*Brit inf*); (= Fehler) howler (*Brit inf*), blooper (*US inf*); **ein grober ~** an awful blunder; (= Fauxpas) a real gaffe or clanger (*Brit inf*)

Schnit|zer [ˈʃnɪtsɐ] M -s, -, **Schnit|ze|rin** [ˈʃnɪtsərɪn] F -, -nen woodcarver

Schnit|ze|rei [ʃnɪtsəˈrai] F -, -en (wood)carving

Schnitz-: **Schnitz|kunst** F (art of) woodcarving; **Schnitz|mes|ser** NT woodcarving knife; **Schnitz|werk** NT (wood)carving

schnob (old) pret von **schnauben**

schnöd [ʃnøːt] ADJ ADV = **schnöde**

schnod|de|rig [ˈʃnɔdərɪç], **schnodd|rig** [ˈʃnɔdrɪç] ADJ (inf) Mensch, Bemerkung brash

Schnod|de|rig|keit F -, -en, **Schnodd|rig|keit** F -, -en (inf) brashness

schnö|de [ˈʃnøːdə] ADJ (= niederträchtig) despicable, contemptible, base; Geiz, Verrat base; Gewinn vile; Behandlung, Ton, Antwort contemptuous, disdainful; **~r Mammon, ~s Geld** filthy lucre ADV behandeln despicably; **jdn ~ verlassen** to leave sb in a most despicable fashion; **jdn ~ verraten** to betray sb in a despicable way; **er wurde ~ entlassen** it was despicable the way they fired him

Schnö|dig|keit [ˈʃnøːdɪçkait] F -, -en **a** (= Gemeinheit) baseness; (= Geringschätzung) contempt *no pl*, disdain *no pl* **b** (= gemeine Handlung/Bemerkung) despicable or contemptible thing (to do/say)

Schnor|chel [ˈʃnɔrçl] M -s, - (von U-Boot, Taucher) snorkel; (= Schnorchelmaske) snorkel mask

schnor|cheln [ˈʃnɔrçln] VI to snorkel, to go snorkelling (*Brit*) or snorkeling (*US*)

Schnör|kel [ˈʃnœrkl] M -s, - flourish; (an Möbeln, Säulen) scroll; (fig: = Unterschrift) squiggle (*hum*), signature

schnör|ke|lig [ˈʃnœrkəlɪç] ADJ ornate; Schrift auch full of flourishes; Rede auch flowery

schnör|kel|los ADJ without frills; Eleganz simple; Einfachheit unadorned; Sprache plain, simple

schnor|ren [ˈʃnɔrən] VTI (inf) to cadge (*Brit inf*), to scrounge (*inf*) (bei from)

Schnor|rer [ˈʃnɔrɐ] M -s, -, **Schnor|re|rin** [-ərɪn] F -, -nen (inf) cadger (*Brit inf*), scrounger (*inf*)

Schnö|sel [ˈʃnøːzl] M -s, - (inf) snotty(-nosed) little upstart (*inf*)

schnö|se|lig [ˈʃnøːzəlɪç] (inf) ADJ Benehmen, jugendlicher snotty (*inf*), snotty-nosed (*inf*) ADV sich benehmen snottily

Schnö|se|lig|keit F -, *no pl* (inf) snottiness (*inf*)

Schnu|ckel|chen [ˈʃnʊklçən] NT -s, - (inf) sweetheart, pet, baby (*esp US*)

schnu|cke|lig [ˈʃnʊkəlɪç] (inf) ADJ (= gemütlich) snug, cosy; Wärme cosy; (= niedlich) cute ADV **~ warm** warm and cosy

Schnüf|fe|lei [ʃnʏfəˈlai] F -, -en (inf) **a** (von Hund) snuffling *no pl*, sniffing *no pl*; (von Mensch) sniffing *no pl* **b** (fig: = das Spionieren) snooping *no pl* (*inf*)

schnüf|feln [ˈʃnʏfln] VI **a** (= schnuppern, riechen) to sniff; (Hund) to sniff, to snuffle; **an etw** (dat) **~** to sniff (at) sth **b** (bei Erkältung etc) to sniffle, to snuffle **c** (fig inf: = spionieren) to snoop around (*inf*), to nose around (*inf*) **d** (von Drogen, Klebstoff) to sniff VT Drogen, Klebstoff to sniff

Schnüff|ler [ˈʃnʏflɐ] M -s, -, **Schnüff|le|rin** [-ərɪn] F -, -nen (inf) (fig) snooper (*inf*), nosey parker (*Brit inf*), curious George (*US*); (= Detektiv) sleuth (*inf*), private eye (*inf*); (von Drogen, Klebstoff) glue-sniffer

Schnul|ler [ˈʃnʊlɐ] M -s, - (inf) dummy (*Brit*), pacifier (*US*); (auf Flasche) teat (*Brit*), nipple (*US*)

Schnul|ze [ˈʃnʊltsə] F -, -n (inf) schmaltzy film/book/song (*inf*); **das sind alles ~n** it's all schmaltz (*inf*)

Schnul|zen|sän|ger(in) M(F) (pej inf) crooner (*pej*)

schnul|zig [ˈʃnʊltsɪç] (inf) ADJ slushy, soppy, schmaltzy (*all inf*) ADV schreiben soppily (*inf*); **er singt so ~** his songs are so schmaltzy (*inf*)

schnup|fen [ˈʃnʊpfn] VTI Kokain to snort, to sniff; **Tabak ~** to take snuff; **willst du auch ~?** would you like some snuff too?

Schnup|fen [ˈʃnʊpfn] M -s, - cold, head cold; **(einen) ~ bekommen, sich** (dat) **einen ~ holen** (inf) to catch a cold; **(einen) ~ haben** to have a cold

Schnup|fer [ˈʃnʊpfɐ] M -s, -, **Schnup|fe|rin** [-ərɪn] F -, -nen snuff-taker

Schnupf-: **Schnupf|ta|bak** M snuff; **Schnupf|ta|bak(s)|do|se** F snuffbox; **Schnupf|tuch** NT *pl* **-tücher** (S Ger) handkerchief, hanky (*inf*)

schnup|pe [ˈʃnʊpə] ADJ *pred* (inf) **jdm ~ sein** to be all the same to sb; **das Wohl seiner Angestellten ist ihm völlig ~** he couldn't care less about the welfare of his employees (*inf*)

Schnup|per- in cpds (inf) trial, taster; **Schnup|per|kurs** M (inf) taster course

schnup|pern [ˈʃnʊpɐn] VI to sniff; (Hund auch) to snuffle; **an etw** (dat) **~** to sniff (at) sth; **wir kamen nur zum Schnuppern** (fig inf) we only came to get a taste of it VT to sniff; (fig) Atmosphäre etc to sample

Schnup|per|preis M (inf) (special) introductory price

Schnur [ʃnuːɐ] F -, =e [ˈʃnyːrə] (= Bindfaden) string; (= Kordel, an Vorhang) cord; (= Litze) braid *no indef art, no pl*, piping *no indef art, no pl*; (= Zeltschnur) guy (rope); (= Angelschnur) (fishing) line; (= Kabel) flex, lead

Schnür-: **Schnür|band** [-bant] NT *pl* **-bänder** lace; **Schnür|bo|den** M (Theat) flies *pl*

Schnür|chen [ˈʃnyːɐçən] NT -s, - dim von **Schnur** bit of string; **es läuft** or **geht** or **klappt alles wie am ~** everything's going like clockwork; **etw wie am ~ hersagen** to say or recite sth off pat (*Brit*) or on cue

schnü|ren [ˈʃnyːrən] VT Paket, Strohbündel to tie up; Schuhe auch, Mieder to lace (up); Körper to lace in; (fig) Maßnahmenpaket etc to put together; **Schuhe zum Schnüren** lace-up shoes, lace-ups VI **a** (inf: = eng sein) to be too tight **b** aux sein (Hunt) to run in a straight line VR (Frauen) to lace oneself up or in

Schnur-: **schnur|ge|ra|de** ADJ (dead) straight ADV (perfectly) straight, straight as an arrow; **~ auf jdn/etw zugehen** to make a beeline for sb/sth (*inf*), to go straight up to sb/sth; **Schnur|ke|ra|mik** F (Archeol) string ceramics *sing*

Schnür|leib|chen NT lace-up corset

schnur|los ADJ Telefon, Apparat cordless ADV **~ telefonieren** to use a cordless phone

Schnürl- (Aus): **Schnürl|re|gen** M pouring or streaming rain; **Schnürl|samt** M corduroy

Schnür|mie|der NT lace-up corset

Schnurr|bart M moustache (*Brit*), mustache (*US*)

schnurr|bär|tig ADJ with a moustache (*Brit*) or mustache (*US*), mustachioed (*esp Brit*), mustached (*US*)

Schnur|re [ˈʃnʊrə] F -, -n **a** (= Erzählung) funny story **b** (= Posse) farce

schnur|ren [ˈʃnʊrən] VI (Katze) to purr; (Spinnrad etc) to hum, to whir(r)

Schnurr|haa|re PL whiskers *pl*

Schnür|rie|men M shoelace; (für Stiefel) bootlace

schnur|rig [ˈʃnʊrɪç] ADJ amusing, droll; alter Mann quaint, funny ADV drolly

Schnür-: **Schnür|schuh** M lace-up or laced shoe; **Schnür|sen|kel** M shoelace; (für Stiefel) bootlace; **sich** (dat) **die ~ binden** to tie one's laces; **Schnür|stie|fel** M lace-up or laced boot

schnur|stracks [ˈʃnuːɐˈʃtraks] ADV straight, directly; **du gehst jetzt ~ nach Hause!** you are to go straight home (now), you are to go home directly; **~ auf jdn/etw zugehen** to make a beeline for sb/sth (*inf*), to go straight up to sb/sth

schnurz [ʃnʊrts], **schnurz|(piep)|egal** ADJ (inf) **das ist ihm ~** he couldn't care less (about it) (*inf*), he couldn't give a damn (about it) (*inf*); **das ist ~!** it doesn't matter a damn! (*inf*)

Schnu|te [ˈʃnuːtə] F -, -n (inf) (= Mund) mouth; (= Schmollmund) pout; (pej: = Mundwerk) big mouth (*inf*); **eine ~ ziehen** or **machen** to pout, to pull a face

Scho|ah [ʃoˈaː, ˈʃoːa] F -, *no pl* (= Holocaust) Shoah

schob pret von **schieben**

Scho|ber [ˈʃoːbɐ] M -s, - (S Ger, Aus) **a** (= Scheune) barn **b** (= Heuhaufen) haystack, hayrick

Schock [ʃɔk] NT -(e)s, -e (obs) three score (*old*)

Schock M -(e)s, -s or (rare) -e (= Schreck, elektrisch) shock; **unter ~ stehen** to be in (a state of) shock

Schock-: **Schock|an|ruf** M (per Telefon) nuisance call; **Schock|an|ru|fer(in)** M(F) (am Telefon) nuisance caller

scho|ckant [ʃɔˈkant] (dated) ADJ shocking ADV shockingly

Schock-: **Schock|be|hand|lung** F shock therapy; (elektrisch auch) electroconvulsive therapy; **Schọck|ein|wir|kung** F state of shock; **unter ~ stehen** to be in (a state of) shock

schọ|cken [ˈʃɔkn] VT *(inf)* to shock; **jdn elektrisch ~** *(Med)* to give sb an electric shock, to administer an electric shock to sb *(form)*

Schọ|cker [ˈʃɔkɐ] M **-s, -** *(inf: = Film/Roman)* shock film/novel, film/novel aimed to shock

Schọck|far|be F electric colour *(Brit)* or color *(US)*

scho|ckie|ren [ʃɔˈkiːrən] *ptp* **schockiert** VTI to shock; *(stärker)* to scandalize; **sich leicht ~ lassen** to be easily shocked; **~d** shocking; **schockiert sein** to be shocked *(über +acc* at)

Schọck-: **Schọck|the|ra|pie** F shock therapy; *(elektrisch auch)* electroconvulsive therapy; **schọck|wei|se** ADV *(obs)* by the three score *(old)*

schọ|fel [ˈʃoːfl], **schọ|fe|lig** [ˈʃoːfəlɪç] *(inf)* ADJ *Behandlung, Ausrede* mean, rotten *no adv (inf)*; *Spende, Geschenk, Mahlzeit* miserable ADV miserably

Schọ̈f|fe [ˈʃœfə] M **-n, -n**, **Schọ̈f|fin** [ˈʃœfɪn] F **-, -nen** ≈ juror

Schọ̈f|fen-: **Schọ̈f|fen|amt** NT ≈ jury service; **Schọ̈f|fen|bank** F *pl* **-bänke** ≈ jury bench; **Schọ̈f|fen|ge|richt** NT court *(with jury)*; **einen Fall vor einem ~ verhandeln** ≈ to try a case by jury

Schọ̈f|fin [ˈʃœfɪn] F **-, -nen** ≈ juror

schọf|lig [ˈʃoːflɪç] ADJ ADV *(inf)* = **schofel**

Scho|ko|la|de [ʃokoˈlaːdə] F **-, -n** chocolate

Scho|ko|la|den- *in cpds* chocolate; **scho|ko|la|den|braun** ADJ chocolate-coloured *(Brit)*, chocolate-colored *(US)*; **Scho|ko|la|den|ei** NT chocolate egg; **Scho|ko|la|den|guss** M chocolate icing; **Scho|ko|la|den|ras|pel** F chocolate flake; **Scho|ko|la|den|rie|gel** M chocolate bar; **Scho|ko|la|den|sei|te** F *(fig)* attractive side; **sich von seiner ~ zeigen** to show oneself at one's best; **Scho|ko|la|den|so|ße** F chocolate sauce

Scho|ko|rie|gel [ˈʃoko-] M chocolate bar

Scho|las|tik [ʃoˈlastɪk] F **-,** *no pl* scholasticism

Scho|las|ti|ker [ʃoˈlastikɐ] M **-s, -**, **Scho|las|ti|ke|rin** [-ərɪn] F **-, -nen** scholastic

scho|las|tisch [ʃoˈlastɪʃ] ADJ scholastic

scholl *(old) pret von* **schallen**

Schol|le [ˈʃɔlə] F **-, -n** *(Fisch)* plaice

Schol|le F **-, -n** *(= Eisscholle)* (ice) floe; *(= Erdscholle)* clod (of earth); **mit der ~ verbunden sein** *(fig)* to be a son of the soil

Schol|len|fi|let NT *(= Fisch)* plaice fillet, fillet of plaice

Schol|li [ˈʃɔli] M **mein lieber ~!** *(inf) (drohend)* now look here!; *(erstaunt)* my goodness me!, my oh my!

Schöll|kraut NT *(Bot)* celandine

schon [ʃoːn]

ADVERB

a = bereits already; **Sie kommen erst nächste Woche? aber ich warte doch schon drei Wochen!** you'll come next week? but I've already been waiting three weeks!; **schon vor 100 Jahren kämpften Frauen um das Wahlrecht** 100 years ago women were already fighting for the vote

Im Englischen wird *schon* oft nicht übersetzt.

er ist schon hier! he's (already) here!; **danke, ich habe schon** *(inf)* no thank you, I have (already) got some; **ich habe den Film schon gesehen** I've (already) seen that film; **es ist schon 11 Uhr** it's (already) 11 o'clock; **wie schon erwähnt** as has (already) been mentioned; **ich warte nun schon seit drei Wochen!** I've been waiting three whole weeks!; **ich bin schon drei Jahre alt** I'm THREE (years old); **der Milchmann kommt schon um 6 Uhr!** the milkman comes at 6 o'clock!; **ich finde das Buch toll, ich habe es schon zweimal gelesen!** I love that book, I've read it twice!; **das habe ich dir doch schon hundertmal gesagt** I've told you that a hundred times; **schon vor drei Wochen** three weeks ago; **schon am frühen Morgen** early in the morning; **ich werde schon bedient** I'm being served; **er wollte schon die Hoffnung aufgeben, als …** he was about to give up hope when …; **das haben wir schon gestern** *or* **gestern schon gemacht** we did that yesterday; **schon damals** even then; **schon damals, als …** even when …; **schon früher wusste man …** even in years gone by they knew …; **schon im 13. Jahrhundert** as early as the 13th century; **schon am nächsten Tag** the very next day; **das habe ich schon oft gehört** I've often heard that; **das ist schon längst erledigt** that was done a long time ago; **ich bin schon lange fertig** I've been ready for ages; **wie schon so oft** as ever; **schon immer** always; **ich hatte schon immer dunkle Haare** I've always had dark hair

♦ **schon einmal, schon mal** before; *(= je: in Fragen)* ever; **ich habe das schon mal gehört** I've heard that before; **warst du schon (ein)mal dort?** have you ever been there?; **ich habe Sie schon (ein)mal gesehen** I've seen you before somewhere; **ich habe dir schon (ein)mal gesagt, dass …** I've already told you once that …

♦ **schon wieder** **schon wieder zurück** back already; **da ist sie schon wieder** *(= zum x-ten Male)* there she is again, she's back again; *(= schon zurück)* she's back already; **was, schon wieder?** what - AGAIN?; **was denn nun schon wieder?** what is it NOW?

b = bereits: in Fragen = überhaupt schon ever; *(= je)* ever; **ist er schon hier?** is he here yet?; **warst du schon dort?** have you been there (yet)?; *(= je)* have you (ever) been there?; **musst du schon gehen?** must you go so soon?

In Fragesätzen wird *schon* oft nicht übersetzt.

kommt er schon heute? is he coming today?; **wie lange wartest du schon?** how long have you been waiting?; **wartest du schon lange?** have you been waiting long?

c = allein, bloß just; **der braucht kein Geld, der hat (ohnehin) schon genug** he doesn't need any money, he's got (quite) enough as it is; **allein schon der Gedanke, dass …** just the thought that …; **schon die Tatsache, dass …** just the fact that …; **wenn ich das schon sehe/höre/lese!** if I even see/hear/read that!; **schon deswegen** if only because of that; **schon weil** if only because

d = bestimmt all right; **du wirst schon sehen** you'll see (all right); **das wirst du schon noch lernen** you'll learn that one day; **sie wird es schon machen** (don't worry,) she'll do it; *(= schaffen)* she'll manage (it) all right

e = tatsächlich, allerdings really; **das ist schon eine Frechheit!** that's real impudence!; **das ist schon etwas, (wenn …)** it's really something (if …); **da gehört schon Mut/Geschick** *etc* **dazu** that takes real courage/skill *etc*; **da müssten wir schon großes Glück haben** we'd be very lucky; **du müsstest schon etwas mehr arbeiten** you really ought to work a bit harder; **das ist schon möglich** that's quite possible; **das musst du schon machen!** you really ought to do that!

f ungeduldig **hör schon auf damit!** will you stop that!; **so antworte schon!** come on, answer!; **geh schon** go on; **nun sag schon!** come on, tell me/us *etc*!; **mach schon!** get a move on! *(inf)*; **wenn doch schon …!** if only …!; **ich komme ja schon!** I'm just coming!

g einschränkend **schon** *or* **ja schon, aber …** *(inf)* yes (well), but …; **da haben Sie schon recht, aber …** yes, you're right (there), but …

h in rhetorischen Fragen **was macht das schon, wenn …** what does it matter if …; *(= was hilft das schon)* what(ever) use is it if …; **wer fragt schon danach, ob …** who wants to know if …; **aber wer fragt schon danach** *(resignierend)* but no-one wants to know; **10 Euro, was ist das schon?, was sind heute schon 10 Euro?** what's 10 euros these days?; **die paar Tropfen, was ist das schon, das ist doch kein Regen** a few drops, what are you talking about, that's not rain; **3 Seiten schreiben, was ist das schon?** write 3 pages? that's nothing!

i Füllwort *inf* **schon gut!** all right!, okay! *(inf)*; **ich verstehe schon** I understand; **ich weiß schon** I know; **danke, es geht schon** thank you, I'll/we'll *etc* manage; **so kannst du das schon gar nicht machen!** you CERTAINLY can't do that!; **für Krimis gebe ich kein Geld aus und für Pornoheftchen schon gar nicht** I won't spend money on thrillers and certainly not on pornography

j bedingt → **wenn, wennschon**

schön [ʃøːn] ADJ **a** *(= hübsch anzusehen)* beautiful, lovely; *Mann* handsome; **das Schöne** beauty; **na, ~es Kind** *(inf)* well then, beautiful *(inf)* → **Auge a**

b *(= nett, angenehm)* good; *Erlebnis, Stimme, Musik, Wetter* good, lovely; *Gelegenheit* great, splendid; **die ~en Künste** the fine arts; **die ~e Literatur** belles-lettres *sing*; **das ist ein ~er Tod** that's a good way to die; **eines ~en Tages** one fine day; **(wieder) in ~ster Ordnung** *(nach Krach etc)* back to normal (again); **in ~ster Eintracht** *or* **Harmonie** in perfect harmony; **das Schöne beim Skilaufen ist …** the nice thing about skiing is …; **das Schönste daran ist …** the beauty of it is …, the nicest *or* best thing about it is …; **~e Ferien!, ~en Urlaub!** have a good *or* nice holiday *(esp Brit) or* vacation *(US)*; **~es Wochenende** have a good *or* nice weekend; **~en guten Tag** a very good morning/afternoon/evening to you; **war es ~ im Urlaub?** did you have a nice *or* good holiday *(esp Brit) or* vacation *(US)*?; **war es ~ bei Tante Veronika?** did you have a nice *or* good time at Aunt Veronika's?; **~, dass du gekommen bist** nice of you to come; **es ist ~, dass du wieder da bist** it's good to have you back; **~er, heißer Kaffee** nice hot coffee; **ein ~er frischer Wind** a nice fresh wind

c *(iro) Unordnung* fine, nice, lovely; *Überraschung, Wetter* lovely; *Unsinn, Frechheit* absolute; **da hast du etwas Schönes angerichtet** you've made a fine *or* nice *or* lovely mess; **du bist mir ein ~er Freund/Vater/Held** *etc* a fine friend/father/hero *etc* you are, you're some friend/father/hero *etc*; **du machst** *or* **das sind mir ja ~e Sachen** *or* **Geschichten** here's *or* this is a pretty state of things, here's a pretty kettle of fish *(inf)*; **von dir hört man ~e Sachen** *or* **Geschichten** I've been hearing some nice *or* fine things about you; **das wäre ja noch ~er** *(inf)* that's (just) too much!; **es wird immer ~er** *(inf)* things are going from bad to worse → **Bescherung**

d *(inf: = gut)* nice; **das war nicht ~ von dir** *(inf)* that wasn't very nice of you; **zu ~, um wahr zu sein** *(inf)* too good to be true; **~, ~, (also) ~, sehr ~, na ~** fine, okay, all right; **~ und gut, aber …** (that's) all well and good but …, that's all very well but …

e *(= beträchtlich, groß) Erfolg* great; *Strecke, Stück Arbeit, Alter* good; **ein ~es Stück weiterkommen** to make good progress; **eine ganz ~e Leistung** quite an achievement; **eine ganz ~e Arbeit** quite a lot of work; **eine ganz ~e Menge** quite a lot; **das hat eine ~e Stange Geld gekostet** *(inf)* that cost a pretty penny

ADV **a** *(= hübsch)* **sich ~ anziehen** to get dressed up; **~ machen** *(Kind)* to dress up; *(Wohnung, Straßen)* to decorate; **sich ~ machen** to get dressed up, to dress (oneself) up; *(= sich schminken)* to make (oneself) up

b *(bei Verben) (= gut)* well; *sich waschen, verarbeiten lassen* easily; *scheinen* brightly; *schreiben* beautifully; *(= richtig, genau) ansehen, durchlesen etc* carefully; **es ~ haben** to be well off; *(im Urlaub etc)* to have a good time (of it); **etw am**

~sten machen to do sth best → **danke, bitte**
c *(= angenehm)* ~ **weich/warm/stark** *etc* nice and soft/warm/strong *etc*
d *(bei Wünschen)* **schlaf** ~ sleep well; **amüsiere dich** ~ have a nice *or* good time; **erhole dich** ~ have a good rest → **grüßen**
e *(inf: = brav, lieb)* nicely; **iss mal ~ deinen Teller leer** eat it all up nicely (now), be a good girl/boy and eat it all up; **sag ~ „Guten Tag"** say "hello" nicely; **sei ~ still/ordentlich** *etc (als Aufforderung)* be nice and quiet/tidy *etc*; **sei ~ brav** be a good boy/girl; **fahr ~ langsam** drive nice and slowly → **bleiben lassen**
f *(inf: = sehr, ziemlich)* really; **sich** *(dat)* **~ wehtun** to hurt oneself a lot; **sich ~ täuschen** to make a big mistake; **sich ~ ärgern** to be very angry; **jdn ~ erschrecken** to give sb quite a *or* a real fright; **ganz ~ teuer/kalt** pretty expensive/cold; **(ganz) ~ weit weg** a long *or* good way off, quite a distance away; **ganz ~ lange** quite a while; **(ganz) ~ viel Geld kosten** to cost a pretty penny

Schon|be|zug M *(für Matratzen)* mattress cover; *(für Möbel)* loose cover; *(für Autositz)* seat cover

Schön|druck M *pl* **-drucke** *(Typ)* first printing

Schö|ne [ˈʃøːnə] F *decl as adj (liter, hum: = Mädchen)* beauty, belle *(esp Brit liter, hum)*; **nun, ihr beiden ~n** *(inf)* now, my beauties *(inf)*

scho|nen [ˈʃoːnən] **VT** *Gesundheit, Herz, Körperteil, Buch, Kleider* to look after, to take care of; *Ressourcen, eigene Kraft* to save, to conserve; *Umwelt* to protect, to conserve; *eigene Nerven* to go easy on; *jds Nerven, Gefühle, Kraft* to spare; *Gegner, Kind* to be easy on; *(= nicht stark beanspruchen) Teppich, Schuhsohlen, Füße* to save; *Bremsen, Auto, Batterie* to go easy on; *(iro) Gehirn* to save; *(= schützen)* to protect; **ein Waschmittel, das die Hände/Wäsche schont** a detergent that is kind to your hands/washing; **ein Licht, das die Augen schont** lighting that is easy on the eyes; **sie trägt eine Schürze, um ihre Kleider zu ~** she wears an apron to save her clothes; **er muss den Arm noch ~** he still has to be careful with his arm, he still has to look after his arm; **um seine Nerven/die Nerven seiner Mutter zu ~** for the sake of his/his mother's nerves; **ein Beruf, der die Nerven nicht gerade schont** a job that isn't exactly easy on the nerves; **du brauchst mich nicht zu ~, sag ruhig die Wahrheit** you don't need to spare me *or* my feelings - just tell me the truth
VR to look after oneself, to take care of oneself; *(Patient auch)* to take things easy; **er schont sich für das nächste Rennen** he's saving himself for the next race

schö|nen [ˈʃøːnən] **VT** **a** *Wein* to clarify **b** *Statistik, Zahlen* to dress up

scho|nend **ADJ** gentle; *(= rücksichtsvoll)* considerate; *Waschmittel, Politur* mild; *Nutzung (von Ressourcen etc)* sparing, careful **ADV** **jdm etw ~ beibringen** to break sth to sb gently; **jdn ~ behandeln** to be *or* go easy on sb; *Kranken* to treat sb gently; **etw ~ behandeln** to treat sth with care, to look after sth

Scho|ner [ˈʃoːnɐ] M **-s, -** *(Naut)* schooner

Scho|ner M **-s, -** cover; *(für Rückenlehnen)* antimacassar, chairback; *(= Ärmelschoner)* sleeve-protector

Schön-: **schön+fär|ben** *sep* **VT** *(fig)* to gloss over **VI** to gloss things over; **Schön|fär|ber(in)** M(F) *(fig)* **ein ~ sein** to tend to gloss things over; **Schön|fär|be|rei** F *(fig)* glossing things over

Schon-: **Schon|frist** F period of grace; **eine ~ von 12 Tagen** 12 days' grace; **Schon|gang** M *pl* **-gänge** *(bei Waschmaschine)* gentle action wash

Schön|geist M aesthete

schön|geis|tig ADJ aesthetic; **~e Literatur** belletristic literature

Schön|heit F **-, -en** beauty

Schön|heits-: **Schön|heits|chi|rur|gie** F cosmetic surgery; **Schön|heits|farm** F beauty farm; **Schön|heits|feh|ler** M blemish; *(von Gegenstand)* flaw; **Schön|heits|fleck** M beauty spot; **Schön|heits|ide|al** NT ideal of beauty; **Schön|heits|kö|ni|gin** F beauty queen; **Schön|heits|kon|kur|renz** F beauty contest; **Schön|heits|kor|rek|tur** F correction of an imperfection/imperfections; *(fig)* cosmetic alteration; **Schön|heits|ope|ra|ti|on** F cosmetic operation *(Brit) or* surgery; **Schön|heits|pfläs|ter|chen** [-pflɛstɐçən] NT **-s, -** (artificial) beauty spot; **Schön|heits|pfle|ge** F beauty care; **Schön|heits|sa|lon** M beauty parlour *(Brit) or* parlor *(US)*, beauty salon; **Schön|heits|sinn** M sense of beauty; **Schön|heits|wett|be|werb** M beauty contest

Schon-: **Schon|kaf|fee** M mild coffee; **Schon|kost** F light diet; *(= Spezialdiät)* special diet

Schön|ling [ˈʃøːnlɪŋ] M **-s, -e** *(pej)* pansy *(inf)*, pretty boy *(inf)*

Schön-: **schön+ma|chen** *sep* **VI** *(Hund)* to sit up (and beg) **VTR** → **schön ADV a**; **schön+rech|nen** VT *sep* **etw ~** to make the figures for sth seem better than they are; **schön+re|den** *sep* **VI** to use flattery; **das Schönreden** smooth talking, flattery **VT** **etw ~** to make sth seem better than it is; **Schön|red|ner(in)** M(F) flatterer, smooth-talker; **Schön|schrei|ben** NT, *no pl (Sch)* writing; **Schön|schreib|dru|cker** M letter-quality printer; **Schön|schreib|heft** NT writing book; *(mit vorgedruckten Buchstaben)* copybook; **Schön|schrift** F, *no pl* **a** **in ~** *(= Handschrift)* in one's best (copybook) (hand)writing **b** *(Comput) (of printer)* letter quality

schöns|tens [ˈʃøːnstns] ADV most beautifully; *bitten, fragen* respectfully

Schön-: **Schön|tu|e|rei** [ʃøːntuːəˈrai] F flattery, blandishments *pl*, soft soap *(Brit inf)*; **schön+tun** VI *sep irreg* **jdm ~** *(= schmeicheln)* to flatter sb, to soft-soap sb *(Brit inf)*, to sweet-talk sb *(inf)*; *(= sich lieb Kind machen)* to pay court to sb *(dated)*, to play up to sb, to suck up to sb *(inf)*

Scho|nung [ˈʃoːnʊŋ] F **-, -en** **a** *(= Waldbestand)* (protected) forest plantation area
b *no pl (= das Schonen) (von Gefühlen, Kraft)* sparing; *(von Teppich, Schuhsohlen, Kleider)* saving; *(von Umwelt)* protection, conservation; *(von Ressourcen)* saving, conservation; *(= das Schützen)* protection; **der Patient/Arm braucht noch ein paar Wochen ~** the patient/arm still needs looking after for a few weeks; **zur ~ meiner Gefühle/der Gefühle anderer** to spare my feelings/the feelings of others; **auf ~ seiner Gesundheit Wert legen** to value one's health; **zur ~ des Magens sollten Sie nur Tee trinken** in order not to irritate your stomach you should only drink tea; **zur ~ Ihrer Augen/Waschmaschine** to look after your eyes/washing machine; **zur ~ des Getriebes** to give your gears a longer life
c *no pl (= Nachsicht, Milde)* mercy

Scho|nungs-: **scho|nungs|be|dürf|tig** ADJ in need of care; *(in Bezug auf Gefühle, Nerven)* in need of careful handling; **scho|nungs|los** **ADJ** ruthless, merciless; *Wahrheit* blunt; *Ehrlichkeit, Offenheit* brutal; *Kritik* savage **ADV** ruthlessly; **jdm ~ die Wahrheit sagen** to tell sb the truth with no holds barred; **Scho|nungs|lo|sig|keit** F **-,** *no pl* ruthlessness; *(von Kritik)* savageness; **mit einer solchen ~** so ruthlessly, so mercilessly; so savagely; **scho|nungs|voll** **ADJ** gentle; **~er Umgang mit der Umwelt** treating the environment with care **ADV** gently; **er geht jetzt ~er mit ihr um** he treats her more kindly now

Schon|wald M protected woodland

Schön|wet|ter NT *(lit)* fine weather; **~ machen** *(fig inf)* to smooth things over; **bei jdm um ~ bitten** *(fig inf)* to be as nice as pie to sb *(inf)*

Schön|wet|ter-: **Schön|wet|ter|front** F warm front; **Schön|wet|ter|pe|ri|o|de** F period of fine weather, spell of good weather, sunny spell; **Schön|wet|ter|wol|ke** F *(inf)* cloud that means good weather

Schon|zeit F close season; *(fig)* honeymoon period

Schopf [ʃɔpf] M **-(e)s, ⸚e** [ˈʃœpfə] (shock of) hair; *(von Vogel)* tuft, crest; **jdn beim ~ packen** to grab sb by the hair; **eine Gelegenheit beim ~ ergreifen** *or* **packen** *or* **fassen** to seize *or* grasp an opportunity with both hands

schöp|fen [ˈʃœpfn] VT **a** *auch vi (aus* from) *Wasser* to scoop; *Suppe* to ladle; *Papier* to dip; **Wasser aus einem Boot ~** to bale out a boat **b** *Mut, Kraft* to summon up; *Vertrauen, Hoffnung* to find; **Atem ~** to draw breath, to take a breath; **Verdacht ~** to become suspicious; **Vertrauen/Hoffnung/Mut** *etc* **aus etw ~** to draw confidence/hope/courage *etc* from sth → **voll ADJ a**
c *auch vi (= schaffen) Kunstwerk* to create; *neuen Ausdruck, Wörter* to coin, to create

Schöp|fer [ˈʃœpfɐ] M **-s, -** **a** *(inf: = Schöpflöffel)* ladle **b** *(= Papierschöpfer)* paper maker

Schöp|fer [ˈʃœpfɐ] M **-s, -**, **Schöp|fe|rin** [-ərɪn] F **-, -nen** creator; *(= Gott)* Creator; **seinem ~ danken** to thank one's Maker *or* Creator

Schöp|fer-: **Schöp|fer|geist** M creative spirit; *(Rel)* Holy Spirit; **Schöp|fer|hand** F *(Rel)* Hand of the Creator

schöp|fe|risch [ˈʃœpfərɪʃ] **ADJ** creative; **~er Augenblick** moment of inspiration, creative moment; **~e Pause** *(hum)* pause for inspiration **ADV** creatively; **~ tätig sein** to do creative work; **~ begabt sein** to be creative; **sie ist ~ veranlagt** she is creative; *(= künstlerisch)* she is artistic

Schöp|fer|kraft F creative power, creativity

Schöpf|kel|le F, **Schöpf|löf|fel** M ladle

Schöp|fung [ˈʃœpfʊŋ] F **-, -en** creation; *(= Wort, Ausdruck)* coinage, invention; **die ~** *(Rel)* the Creation; *(= die Welt)* Creation → **Herr a**, **Krone b**

Schöp|fungs-: **Schöp|fungs|be|richt** M, **Schöp|fungs|ge|schich|te** F story of the Creation; **Schöp|fungs|tag** M *(Rel)* day of the Creation

schöp|peln [ˈʃœpln] VTI *(dial)* **(einen) ~** to have a drink

Schop|pen [ˈʃɔpn] M **-s, -** **a** *(old: Flüssigkeitsmaß)* half-litre *(Brit) or* half-liter *(US)* (measure); *(S Ger: = Glas Wein)* glass of wine; *(S Ger: = Glas Bier)* ≈ half-pint of beer, ≈ glass of beer **b** *(dial: = Beisammensein)* **zum ~ gehen** to go for a drink; **sich beim ~ treffen** to meet for *or* over a drink **c** *(S Ger, Sw: = Babyfläschchen)* bottle

Schop|pen|wein M *(dial)* wine by the glass

schop|pen|wei|se ADV *(dial)* by the glass(ful)

Schöps [ʃœps] M **-es, -e** *(Aus)* = **Hammel**

Schöp|ser|ne(s) [ˈʃœpsɐnə] NT *decl as adj (Aus)* mutton

schor *pret von* **scheren**

Schorf [ʃɔrf] M **-(e)s, -e** **a** crust, scaly skin; *(= Wundschorf)* scab **b** *(= Pflanzenkrankheit)* scab

schor|fig [ˈʃɔrfɪç] ADJ **a** *Wunde* that has formed a scab; *Haut* scaly **b** *Pflanzen* scabby

Schor|le [ˈʃɔrlə] **F** **-, -n** *or* **NT** **-s, -s** spritzer

Schorn|stein [ˈʃɔrnʃtain] M chimney; *(von Fabrik auch)* stack; *(von Schiff, Lokomotive)* funnel, (smoke)stack; **etw in den ~ schreiben** *(inf)* to write sth off (as a dead loss *(inf)*); **damit der ~ raucht** *(inf)* to keep body and soul together

Schorn|stein-: **Schorn|stein|brand** M chimney fire; **Schorn|stein|fe|ger** [-feːgɐ] M **-s, -**, **Schorn|stein|fe|ge|rin** [-ərɪn] F **-, -nen**, **Schorn|stein|keh|rer** [-keːrɐ] M **-s, -**, **Schorn|stein|keh|re|rin** [-ərɪn] F **-, -nen** chimney sweep

Scho|se [ˈʃoːzə] F **-, -n** *(dated inf)* = **Chose**

schoss *pret von* **schießen**

Schoss [ʃɔs] M **-es, -e** *(Bot)* shoot

Schoß [ʃoːs] **-es, ⸚e** [ˈʃøːsə] M **a** lap; **die Hände in den ~ legen** *(lit)* to put one's hands in one's lap; *(fig)* to sit back (and take it easy); **das ist ihm nicht in den ~ gefallen** *(fig)* it wasn't handed (to) him on a plate, it didn't just fall into his lap → **Abraham** **b** *(liter) (= Mutterleib)* womb; *(= Scheide)* vagina; **im ~e der Familie/Kirche** in the bosom of one's family/of the church; **im ~ der Erde** in the bowels of the earth; **in den ~ der Familie/Kirche zurückkehren** *(fig)* to return to the bosom of one's family/the church **c** *(an Kleidungsstück)* tail

Schoß [ʃoːs] F -, -en *or* ⸚e [ˈʃøːsə] *(Aus)* skirt

Schö|ß|chen [ˈʃøːsçən] NT -s, - *dim von* **Schoß c**

Schö|ß|chen|ja|cke F peplum jacket

Schoß-: **Schoß|hund** M lapdog; **Schoß|kind** NT spoiled child *(esp Brit)*; **Mamas ~** mummy's *(Brit)* or mamma's *(US)* little boy/girl; **ein ~ des Glücks** *(geh)* a child of Fortune

Schöss|ling [ˈʃœslɪŋ] M -s, -e *(Bot)* shoot

Schot [ʃoːt] F -, -en *(Naut)* sheet

Scho|te [ˈʃoːtə] F -, -n **a** *(Bot)* pod; **~n** *(inf: = Erbsen)* peas (in the pod) **b** *(inf)* yarn, tall story **c** *(Naut)* sheet

Schott [ʃɔt] NT -(e)s, -e(n) *(Naut)* bulkhead; **die ~en dichtmachen** *(inf)* to close up shop

Schot|te [ˈʃɔtə] M -n, -n Scot, Scotsman; **er ist ~** he's a Scot, he's Scottish; **die ~n** the Scots, the Scottish

Schot|ten-: **Schot|ten|ka|ro** NT, **Schot|ten|mus|ter** NT tartan; **Rock mit** *or* **im ~** tartan skirt; **Schot|ten|preis** M *(hum)* rock-bottom price; **Schot|ten|rock** M tartan skirt; *(= Kilt)* kilt

Schot|ter [ˈʃɔtɐ] M -s, - gravel; *(im Straßenbau)* (road) metal; *(Rail)* ballast; *(inf: = Geld)* dough *(inf)*

Schot|ter|de|cke F gravel surface

schot|tern [ˈʃɔtɐn] VT to gravel (over); *(im Straßenbau)* to metal; *(Rail)* to ballast

Schot|ter-: **Schot|ter|stra|ße** F gravel road; **Schot|ter|weg** M gravel path

Schot|tin [ˈʃɔtɪn] F -, -nen Scot, Scotswoman; **sie ist ~** she's a Scot, she's Scottish; **die ~nen** Scottish women, Scotswomen

schot|tisch [ˈʃɔtɪʃ] ADJ Scottish; *Sprache* Scots

Schott|land [ˈʃɔtlant] NT -s Scotland

schraf|fie|ren [ʃraˈfiːrən] *ptp* **schraffiert** VT to hatch

Schraf|fie|rung F -, -en, **Schraf|fur** [ʃraˈfuːɐ] F -, -en hatching

schräg [ʃrɛːk] ADJ **a** *(= schief, geneigt)* sloping; *Schrift* sloping, slanting; *Augen* slanted, slanting; *Kante* bevelled *(Brit)*, beveled *(US)*

b *(= nicht gerade, nicht parallel)* oblique; *Linie* oblique, diagonal

c *(inf: = verdächtig)* suspicious, fishy *(inf)*

d *(inf: = seltsam) Musik, Vorstellungen, Leute* weird; **ein ~er Vogel** a queer fish *(Brit inf)*, a strange bird *(US)*

ADV **a** *(= geneigt)* at an angle; *halten* on the slant, slanting; *(= krumm)* slanting, skewwhiff *(Brit inf)*; **den Hut ~ aufsetzen** to put one's hat on at an angle; **~ stehende Augen** slanting or slanted eyes

b *(= nicht gerade, nicht parallel)* obliquely; *überqueren, gestreift* diagonally; *(Sew)* on the bias; *schneiden* on the cross or bias; **~ gegenüber/hinter** diagonally opposite/behind; **~ rechts/links** diagonally to the right/left; **~ rechts/links abbiegen** *(Auto, Fähre)* to bear or fork right/left; **die Straße biegt ~ ab** the road forks off; **~ gedruckt** in italics; **~ laufend** diagonal, oblique; **den Kopf ~ halten** to hold one's head at an angle or cocked to one side; **~ parken** to park at an angle; **die Sonne schien ~ ins Fenster** the sun slanted in through the window; **jdn ~ ansehen** *or* **angucken** *(lit)* to look at sb out of the corner of one's eye; *(fig)* to look askance at sb; **~ zum Hang queren/fahren** to traverse; **~ zum Fadenlauf** on the bias

Schräg-: **Schräg|band** [-bant] NT *pl* **-bänder** bias binding; **Schräg|bank** F *(in Fitnessstudio)* incline bench; **Schräg|dach** NT *pl* **-dächer** pitched roof

Schrä|ge [ˈʃrɛːgə] F -, -n **a** *(= schräge Fläche)* slope, sloping surface; *(= schräge Kante)* bevel, bevelled *(Brit)* or beveled *(US)* edge **b** *(= Schrägheit)* slant, angle; *(von Dach)* pitch, slope; *(im Zimmer)* sloping ceiling; **eine ~ haben** to be on the slant, to slope, to slant; *(Zimmer)* to have a sloping ceiling

schrä|gen [ˈʃrɛːgn] VT to chamfer; *Kanten* to bevel

Schräg|heck NT *(am Auto)* coupé back; *(= Auto)* coupé

Schräg|heit F -, *no pl* slant, angle; *(von Wand auch)* slope; *(von Dach)* pitch, slope, slant; *(von Schrift, Augen)* slant

Schräg-: **Schräg|kan|te** F bevelled *(Brit)* or beveled *(US)* edge; **Schräg|la|ge** F angle, slant; *(von Flugzeug)* bank(ing); *(im Mutterleib)* oblique position; **etw in ~ bringen/aufbewahren** to put/keep sth at an angle or on the slant; **das Baby ist in ~** the baby is in an oblique position; **schräg|lau|fend** ADJ → **schräg ADV b**; **Schräg|li|nie** F diagonal line, oblique (line); **Schräg|schrift** F *(Handschrift)* slanting hand (-writing) or writing; *(Typ)* italics *pl*; **Schräg|strei|fen** M **a** *(Muster)* diagonal stripe **b** *(Sew)* bias binding; **Schräg|strich** M *(Typ)* (forward) slash, oblique; **umgekehrter ~** backslash; **doppelter umgekehrter ~** double backslash

schrak *(old) pret von* **schrecken**

Schram|me [ˈʃramə] F -, -n scratch

Schram|mel|mu|sik [ˈʃraml-] F *popular Viennese music for violins, guitar and accordion*

Schram|meln [ˈʃramln] PL *(Aus) quartet playing Schrammelmusik*

schram|men [ˈʃramən] VT to scratch; **sich** *(dat)* **den Arm/sich ~** to scratch one's arm/oneself VI **über den Boden ~** to scrape across the floor

Schrank [ʃraŋk] M -(e)s, ⸚e [ˈʃrɛŋkə] cupboard *(Brit)*, closet *(US)*; *(im Wohnzimmer, = Vitrinenschrank, Medizinschrank auch)* cabinet; *(= Küchenschrank)* cupboard; *(= Kleiderschrank)* wardrobe *(Brit)*, closet *(US)*; *(für Bücher)* bookcase; *(= Plattenschrank)* record cabinet; *(= Umkleideschrank, Mil: = Spind)* locker; *(inf: Mann)* giant → **Tasse**

Schrank|bett NT foldaway bed

Schränk|chen [ˈʃrɛŋkçən] NT -s, - *dim von* **Schrank** small cupboard *(Brit)* or closet *(US)*; *(= Arzneischränkchen, im Badezimmer)* cabinet; *(neben dem Bett)* bedside cupboard or cabinet *(Brit)*, night stand *(US)*

Schran|ke [ˈʃraŋkə] F -, -n **a** barrier; *(= Barrikade)* barricade; *(fig) (= Grenze)* limit; *(= Hindernis)* barrier; **die ~ ist zu/auf** *(Rail)* the barrier is down/up; **vor den ~n des Gerichts** before the court; **keine ~n kennen** to know no bounds; *(Mensch)* not to know when to stop; **er kennt keine ~n mehr** there's no restraining him; **sich in ~n halten** to keep or to remain within reasonable limits; **meine Begeisterung hält sich in ~n** I'm not exactly overwhelmed by it; **etw in ~n halten** to keep sth within reasonable limits or bounds; **einer Sache** *(dat)* **(enge) ~n setzen** to put a limit on sth; **seiner Geduld sind keine ~n gesetzt** his patience knows no bounds **b** **Schranken** PL *(Hist)* lists *pl*; **jdn in die ~n fordern** *(fig)* to challenge sb; **jdn in seine** *or* **die ~n (ver)weisen** *(fig)* to put sb in his place

Schran|ken [ˈʃraŋkn] M -s, - *(Aus)* (level-crossing *(Brit)* or grade-crossing *(US)*) barrier

Schran|ken-: **schran|ken|los** ADJ *(fig) Weiten* boundless, unbounded, unlimited; *Egoismus, Glück* unbounded, boundless; *Vertrauen* total; *Verhalten, Forderungen, Ansprüche* unrestrained, unbridled; **Schran|ken|lo|sig|keit** F -, *no pl (fig)* boundlessness; *(von Forderungen etc)* lack of restraint (+*gen* in); **Schran|ken|wär|ter(in)** M(F) attendant *(at level crossing)*

Schrank-: **Schrank|fach** NT shelf; **im obersten ~** on the top shelf; **schrank|fer|tig** ADJ *Wäsche* washed and ironed; **Schrank|kof|fer** M wardrobe *(Brit)* or clothes trunk; **Schrank|spie|gel** M wardrobe *(Brit)* or vanity *(US)* mirror; **Schrank|tür** F cupboard *(Brit)* or closet *(US)* door; *(von Kleiderschrank)* wardrobe door; **Schrank|wand** F wall unit

Schränk|zan|ge [ˈʃrɛŋk-] F saw set pliers *pl*

Schran|ze [ˈʃrantsə] F -, -n *(pej inf)* toady *(inf)*, lackey *(pej)*

Schrap|nell [ʃrapˈnɛl] NT -s, -e *or* -s shrapnel *no pl*

Schrap|per [ˈʃrapɐ] M -s, - scraper

Schrat [ʃraːt] M -(e)s, -e, **Schratt** [ʃrat] M -(e)s, -e forest demon

Schraub|de|ckel M screw(-on) lid

Schrau|be [ˈʃraubə] F -, -n **a** screw; *(ohne Spitze)* bolt; **bei ihr ist eine ~ locker** *(inf)* she's got a screw loose *(inf)* **b** *(Naut, Aviat)* propeller, prop *(inf)* **c** *(Sport)* twist **d** **alte ~** *(pej inf)* old bag *(inf)*

schrau|ben [ˈʃraubn] VTI to screw; **etw höher/niedriger ~** to screw sth in/out; **etw fester ~** to screw sth tighter; **etw in die Höhe ~** *(fig, Preise, Rekorde, Gewinn)* to push sth up; *Ansprüche, Erwartungen* to raise; **das Flugzeug schraubte sich in die Höhe** the plane spiralled *(esp Brit)* or spiraled *(US)* upwards → *auch* **geschraubt, niedrigerschrauben**

Schrau|ben-: **Schrau|ben|bol|zen** M bolt; **Schrau|ben|damp|fer** M propeller-driven steamer; **Schrau|ben|dre|her** M screwdriver; **Schrau|ben|ge|win|de** NT screw thread; **Schrau|ben|kopf** M screw head; **Schrau|ben|mut|ter** F *pl* **-muttern** nut; **Schrau|ben|schlüs|sel** M spanner *(Brit)*, wrench *(US)*; **Schrau|ben|win|dung** F screw thread; *(= Umdrehung)* turn; **Schrau|ben|zie|her** [-tsiːɐ] M -s, - screwdriver

Schraub-: **Schraub|fas|sung** F screw fitting *(on light bulb)*; **Schraub|glas** NT screw-top jar; **Schraub|stock** M vice; **etw wie ein ~ umklammern** *(fig)* to clasp sth in a vicelike grip; **Schraub|ver|schluss** M screw top or cap; **Schraub|zwin|ge** F screw clamp

Schre|ber|gar|ten [ˈʃreːbɐ-] M allotment *(Brit)*, garden plot

Schreck [ʃrɛk] M -s, *(rare)* -e fright, scare; *(= Schreckfigur)* terror; **vor ~** in fright; *zittern* with fright; **zu meinem großen ~(en)** to my great horror or dismay; **einen ~(en) bekommen** to get a fright or scare; **jdm einen ~(en) einjagen** to give sb a fright or scare; **der ~ fuhr mir in die Glieder** *or* **Knochen** my knees turned to jelly *(inf)*; **mir sitzt** *or* **steckt der ~ noch in den** *or* **allen Gliedern** *or* **Knochen** my knees are still like jelly *(inf)*; **auf den ~ (hin)** to get over the fright; **sich vom ersten ~ erholen** to recover from the initial shock; **mit dem ~(en) davonkommen** to get off or escape with no more than a fright; **ach du ~!** *(inf)* (oh) crumbs! *(inf)*, blast! *(inf)*; **(o) ~, lass nach!** *(hum inf)* for goodness sake! *(inf)*, for heaven's sake! *(inf)*

Schreck|bild NT terrible or awful vision, nightmare

schre|cken [ˈʃrɛkn] *pret* **schreckte** [ˈʃrɛktə], *ptp* **geschreckt** [gəˈʃrɛkt] VT **a** *(= ängstigen)* to frighten, to scare; *(stärker)* to terrify; **jdn aus dem Schlaf/aus seinen Träumen ~** to startle sb out of his sleep/dreams **b** *(Cook)* to dip quickly in cold water VI *pret auch (old)* **schrak** [ʃraːk], *ptp auch (old)* **geschrocken** [gəˈʃrɔkn] **a** *aux sein* **aus dem Schlaf ~** to be startled out of one's sleep; **aus den Gedanken ~** to be startled **b** *(Hunt)* to start up

Schre|cken [ˈʃrɛkn] M -s, - **a** *(= plötzliches Erschrecken)* → **Schreck** **b** *(= Furcht, Entsetzen)* terror, horror; **~ erregend** = **schreckenerregend**; **einer Sache** *(dat)* **den ~ nehmen** to make a thing less frightening or terrifying; **er war der ~ der ganzen Lehrerschaft** he was the terror of all the teachers; **das Gleichgewicht des ~s** the balance of terror; **jdn in Angst und ~ versetzen** to frighten and terrify sb; **ein Land in Angst und ~**

versetzen to spread fear and terror throughout a country → **Ende**

schrẹ|cken|er|re|gend [-lɛreːgnt] ADJ terrifying, horrifying

Schrẹckens-: **schrẹ|ckens|blass**, **schrẹ|ckens|bleich** ADJ as white as a sheet *or* ghost; **Schrẹ|ckens|bot|schaft** F terrible *or* alarming piece of news; **Schrẹ|ckens|herr|schaft** F (reign of) terror; **Schrẹ|ckens|kam|mer** F chamber of horrors; **Schrẹ|ckens|mel|dung** F, **Schrẹ|ckens|nach|richt** F shock news *sing*; **Schrẹ|ckens|nacht** F night of horror; **Schrẹ|ckens|tat** F atrocity; **Schrẹ|ckens|vi|si|on** F terrifying *or* terrible vision, nightmare

Schrẹck-: **Schrẹck|ge|spenst** NT nightmare; **das ~ des Krieges/der Inflation** the bogey of war/inflation; **schrẹck|haft** ADJ easily startled; *Mensch auch* jumpy *(inf)*; **Schrẹck|haf|tig|keit** [ˈʃrɛkhaftɪçkait] F -, *no pl* nervousness; *(von Mensch auch)* jumpiness *(inf)*

schrẹck|lich [ˈʃrɛklɪç] **ADJ** terrible, dreadful; *(inf: = sehr, groß auch)* awful; *Freude* great; **er war ~ in seinem Zorn** *(geh)* his wrath was terrible (to behold) *(liter)* **ADV** **a** *(= entsetzlich)* horribly; **~ schimpfen** to swear dreadfully *or* terribly **b** *(inf: = sehr)* terribly; **sich ~ freuen** to be terribly *or* awfully pleased; **~ gerne!** I'd absolutely love to; **~ viel** an awful lot (of); **~ wenig** very little; **~ nett** *(usu iro)* terribly nice

Schrẹck|nis [ˈʃrɛknɪs] NT **-ses, -se** *(old)* horror(s *pl*), terror(s *pl*)

Schrẹck-: **Schrẹck|schrau|be** F *(pej inf)* (old) battle-axe *(Brit inf)* or battle-ax *(US inf)*; *(in Bezug auf Äußeres)* dolled-up old bag *(inf)*; **Schrẹck|schuss** M *(lit)* warning shot; **einen ~ abgeben** *(lit, fig)* to give *or* fire a warning shot; **Schrẹck|schuss|pis|to|le** F blank gun; **Schrẹck|se|kun|de** F moment of shock

Schred|der [ˈʃrɛdɐ] M **-s, -** shredder

Schrei [ʃrai] M **-(e)s, -e** cry, shout; *(brüllender)* yell; *(gellender)* scream; *(kreischender)* shriek; *(von Vogel, von Wild)* cry, call; *(von Esel)* bray; *(von Eule etc)* screech; *(von Hahn)* crow; **einen ~ ausstoßen** to give a cry *or* shout/yell/scream/shriek; **einen ~ unterdrücken** to suppress a cry; **ein spitzer ~** a sharp cry; **der ~ nach Freiheit/Rache** the call for freedom/revenge; **ein ~ der Entrüstung** an (indignant) outcry; **der letzte ~** *(inf)* the latest thing, all the rage *(inf)*; **nach dem letzten ~ gekleidet** *(inf)* dressed in the latest style *or* in the height of fashion

Schreib-: **Schreib|ar|beit** F *(einzeln)* written assignment; *(kollektiv, = Verwaltungsarbeit)* paperwork *no pl*; **Schreib|art** F style; **Schreib|be|darf** M writing materials *pl*, stationery *no pl*; **alles, was Sie für Ihren ~ brauchen** everything you need in the way of stationery *or* writing materials; **Schreib|block** M *pl* **-blöcke** *or* **-blocks** (writing) pad; **Schreib|blo|ckade** F writer's block *no art*; **Schreib|bü|ro** NT typing pool; **Schreib|dich|te** F *(Comput)* **mit hoher ~** high-density *attr*

Schrei|be [ˈʃraibə] F **-, -en** *(inf)* writing

schrei|ben [ˈʃraibn] ✪ 48.1, 48.2 *pret* **schrieb**, [ʃriːp] *ptp* **geschrieben** **VT** [gəˈʃriːbn] **a** *(= schriftlich aufzeichnen)* to write; *(= ausstellen) Scheck* to write (out), to make out; *Rechnung* to make out, to write out; *(mit Schreibmaschine)* to type (out); *Klassenarbeit, Übersetzung, Examen* to do; *(= niederschreiben)* to write (down); **sie schreibt einen guten Stil** she has *or* writes a good style; **jdm** *or* **an jdn einen Brief ~** to write a letter to sb, to write sb a letter; **jdm ein paar Zeilen ~** to write *or* drop sb a few lines, to write a few lines to sb; **schwarze/rote Zahlen ~** *(Comm)* to be in the black/red; **etw auf Diskette ~** to write *(Brit)* or save sth to disk; **sich** *(dat)* **etw von der Seele** *or* **dem Herzen ~** to get sth off one's chest; **wo steht das geschrieben?** where does it say that?; **es steht geschrieben** *(Rel)* it is written; **es steht Ihnen im Gesicht** *or* **auf der Stirn geschrieben** it's written all over your face → **Handschrift a**, **Stern a**

b *(orthografisch)* to spell; **ein Wort falsch ~** to misspell a word, to spell a word wrong(ly); **wie schreibt man das?** how do you spell that?, how is that spelled? → **großschreiben, kleinschreiben**

c *(Datum)* **wir ~ heute den 10. Mai** today is the 10th May; **den Wievielten ~ wir heute?** what is the date today?; **man schrieb das Jahr 1939** the year was 1939, it was (in) 1939

d *(= verbuchen)* **jdm etw auf sein (Bank)konto ~** to credit sth to sb's (bank) account; **jdm etw auf die Rechnung ~** to put sth on sb's bill

VI to write; *(= Schriftsteller sein)* to write, to be a writer; *(= tippen)* to type; *(= berichten)* to say; **jdm ~** to write to sb, to write sb *(US)*; **ich schrieb ihm, dass …** I wrote and told him that …; **er schreibt orthografisch richtig** his spelling is correct; **an einem Roman** *etc* **~** to be working on *or* writing a novel *etc*; **über etw** *(acc)* **~** *(= abhandeln)* to write about sth; *(Univ auch)* to work on sth; **ich kann nicht mit der Maschine ~** I can't type; **wie viel Anschläge schreibt sie pro Minute?** what is her (typing) speed?; **mit Bleistift ~** to write in pencil, to write with a pencil; **mit Tinte ~** to write in ink; **hast du was zum Schreiben?** have you something *or* anything to write with?

VR *impers* to write; **mit diesem Bleistift schreibt es sich gut/schlecht** this pencil writes well/doesn't write properly; **auf diesem Papier schreibt es sich gut/schlecht** this paper is easy *or* good/difficult to write on

VR **a** *(= korrespondieren)* to write (to one another *or* to each other), to correspond; **ich schreibe mich schon lange mit ihm** *(inf)* I've been writing to him for a long time

b *(= geschrieben werden)* to be spelt *(esp Brit)* *or* spelled; **wie schreibt er sich?** how does he spell his name?, how is his name spelled?; **wie schreibt sich das?** how is that spelled?, how do you spell that?

c *(dated: = heißen)* to call oneself; **seit wann schreibst du dich wieder mit deinem Mädchennamen?** how long have you been calling yourself by your maiden name again?

Schrei|ben [ˈʃraibn] NT **-s, -** **a** *no pl* writing **b** *(= Mitteilung)* communication *(form)*; *(= Brief)* letter

Schrei|ber [ˈʃraibɐ] M **-s, -** **a** *(inf: = Schreibgerät)* writing implement; **einen/keinen ~ haben** to have something/nothing to write with **b** *(Tech)* *(= Fahrtenschreiber)* tachograph; *(an Messgerät)* recording instrument, recorder; *(= Fernschreiber)* teleprinter, telex

Schrei|ber [ˈʃraibɐ] M **-s, -**, **Schrei|be|rin** [-ərɪn] F **-, -nen** *(= Verfasser)* writer, author; *(= Briefschreiber)* (letter-)writer; *(Hist)* scribe; *(= Angestellter, Gerichtsschreiber)* clerk/clerkess; *(Sw: = Schriftführer)* secretary; *(pej: = Schriftsteller)* scribbler

Schrei|be|rei [ʃraibəˈrai] F **-, -en** *(inf)* *(= das Schreiben, Geschriebenes)* writing *no indef art*; *(= Schriftverkehr)* paperwork *no indef art, no pl*; *(pej: von Schriftsteller)* scribbling

Schrei|ber|ling [ˈʃraibɐlɪŋ] M **-s, -e** *(pej)* *(= Schriftsteller)* scribbler; *(= kleiner Angestellter)* penpusher

Schreib-: **schreib|faul** ADJ lazy (about letter writing); **ich bin ~** I'm no great letter writer, I'm a poor correspondent; **Schreib|faul|heit** F laziness (about letter writing); **Schreib|fe|der** F (pen) nib; *(= Federhalter)* ink pen; *(= Gänseschreibfeder)* quill (pen); **Schreib|feh|ler** M (spelling) mistake; *(aus Flüchtigkeit)* slip of the pen; *(= Tippfehler)* (typing) mistake *or* error; **Schreib|ge|rät** NT writing implement; *(Tech)* recording instrument, recorder; **schreib|ge|schützt** ADJ *(Comput)* write-protected, read-only; **Schreib|heft** NT exercise book; *(= Schönschreibheft)* copybook; **Schreib|kraft** F typist; **Schreib|krampf** M writer's cramp; **einen ~ (in der Hand) bekommen** to get writer's cramp; **Schreib-/Le|se|kopf** M *(Comput)* read-write head; **Schreib-/Le|se|spei|cher** M *(Comput)* read-write memory; **Schreib|ma|schi|ne** F typewriter; **auf** *or* **mit der ~ schreiben** to type; **mit der ~ geschrieben** typewritten, typed; **Schreib|ma|schi|nen|pa|pier** NT typing paper; **Schreib|ma|te|ri|al** NT writing materials *pl*, stationery *no pl*; **Schreib|pa|pier** NT (typing) paper; *(= Briefpapier)* writing paper, letter paper, notepaper; **Schreib|pult** NT (writing) desk; **Schreib|schrift** F cursive (hand)writing, script; *(Typ)* script; **Schreib|schutz** M *(Comput)* write protection; **schreib|schüt|zen** VT *(Comput)* to write-protect; **Schreib|stel|le** F *(Comput)* (cursor) position; **Schreib|stel|len|mar|ke** F *(Comput: = Cursor)* cursor; **Schreib|stift** M *(auch Comput)* pen; **Schreib|stil** M style of writing; **Schreib|stu|be** F *(Hist)* writing room; *(= Büro)* (typists') office, typing room; *(Mil)* orderly room; **Schreib|ta|fel** F *(Hist)* tablet; *(für Schüler)* slate; *(= Wandtafel)* blackboard; **Schreib|tisch** M desk; **Schreib|tisch|ar|beit** F desk work; **Schreib|tisch|stuhl** M office *or* desk chair; **Schreib|tisch|tä|ter(in)** M(F) *(bei Verbrechen)* mastermind *or* brains *sing* behind the scenes (of a/the crime); *(pej inf)* *(= Beamter)* desktop administrator; **Schreib|übung** F writing exercise

Schrei|bung [ˈʃraibʊŋ] F **-, -en** spelling; **falsche ~ eines Namens** misspelling of a name

Schreib-: **schreib|un|kun|dig** ADJ unable to write; **Schreib|un|ter|la|ge** F pad; *(auf Schreibtisch)* desk pad; **ein Buch als ~ benutzen** to use a book to rest (one's paper) on; **Schreib|wa|ren** PL stationery *sing*, writing materials *pl*; **Schreib|wa|ren|händ|ler(in)** M(F) stationer; **Schreib|wa|ren|hand|lung** F stationer's (shop), stationery shop; **Schreib|wei|se** F *(= Stil)* style; *(= Rechtschreibung)* spelling; **Schreib|werk** NT typing mechanism; **Schreib|zeug** NT *pl* **-zeuge** writing things *pl*; **Schreib|zim|mer** NT *(= Büro)* (typists') office, typing room; *(von Schriftsteller)* study

schrei|en [ˈʃraiən] *pret* **schrie** [ʃriː], *ptp* **geschrien** [gəˈʃriː(ə)n] **VI** to shout, to cry out; *(gellend)* to scream; *(vor Angst, vor Schmerzen)* to cry out/to scream; *(kreischend)* to shriek; *(= brüllen)* to yell; *(inf: = laut reden)* to shout; *(inf: = schlecht und laut singen)* to screech; *(= heulen, weinen: Kind)* to howl; *(= jammern)* to moan; *(Esel)* to bray; *(Vogel, Wild)* to call; *(Eule, Käuzchen etc)* to screech; *(Hahn)* to crow; **vor Lachen ~** to roar *or* hoot with laughter; *(schrill)* to scream with laughter; **es war zum Schreien** *(inf)* it was a scream *(inf)* *or* a hoot *(inf)*; **nach jdm ~** to shout for sb; **nach etw ~** *(fig)* to cry out for sth → **Hilfe a**

VT *Befehle etc* to shout (out); **jdm etw ins Gesicht ~** to shout sth in sb's face; **sich** *(dat)* **die Kehle heiser** *or* **aus dem Hals ~** *(inf)* to shout oneself hoarse, to shout one's head off *(inf)*

VR **sich heiser ~** to shout oneself hoarse; *(Baby)* to cry itself hoarse

schrei|end ADJ *Farben* loud, garish, gaudy; *Unrecht* glaring, flagrant

Schrei|er [ˈʃraiɐ] M **-s, -**, **Schrei|e|rin** [-ərɪn] F **-, -nen** *(inf: = Baby)* bawler *(inf)*; *(= Unruhestifter)* rowdy, noisy troublemaker; *(fig: = Nörgler)* moaner, grouser *(inf)*

Schrei|e|rei [ʃraiəˈrai] F **-, -en** *(inf)* bawling *(inf)* *no pl*, yelling *no pl*

Schrei-: **Schrei|hals** M *(inf)* *(= Baby)* bawler *(inf)*; *(= Unruhestifter)* rowdy, noisy troublemaker; **Schrei|krampf** M screaming fit

Schrein [ʃrain] M **-(e)s, -e** *(geh)* shrine; *(= Reliquienschrein auch)* reliquary; *(old: = Sarg)* coffin, casket *(US)*

Schrei|ner [ˈʃrainɐ] M **-s, -**, **Schrei|ne|rin** [-ərɪn] F **-, -nen** *(esp S Ger)* carpenter

schrei|nern [ˈʃrainɐn] *(esp S Ger)* **VI** to do carpentry; **mein Mann kann gut ~** my husband is good at carpentry *or* woodwork, my husband is a good carpenter **VT** to make

schrei|ten [ˈʃraitn] *pret* **schritt** [ʃrɪt], *ptp* **geschritten** [gəˈʃrɪtn] VI *aux sein (geh)* (= *schnell gehen*) to stride; (= *feierlich gehen*) to walk; (*vorwärts*) to proceed; (= *stolzieren*) to strut, to stalk; **im Zimmer auf und ab ~** to stride *or* pace up and down the room; **zu etw ~** *(fig)* to get down to sth, to proceed with sth; **es wird Zeit, dass wir zur Tat ~** it's time we got down to work *or* action; **zum Äußersten ~** to take extreme measures; **zur Abstimmung/Wahl ~** to proceed *or* go to a vote

schrie *pret von* **schreien**

schrieb *pret von* **schreiben**

Schrieb [ʃriːp] M **-s, -e** [-bə] *(inf)* missive *(hum)*

Schrift [ʃrɪft] F **-, -en** **a** writing; (= *Handschrift*) (hand)writing; (= *Schriftsystem*) script; *(Typ)* type, typeface, font; **gotische ~ schreiben** to write in Gothic script; **er hat eine schlechte ~** he has bad handwriting, he writes *or* has a poor hand **b** (= *Schriftstück*) document; (= *Bericht*) report; (= *Eingabe*) petition **c** (= *Broschüre*) leaflet; (= *Buch*) work; (= *kürzere Abhandlung*) paper; **seine früheren ~en** his early writings *or* works; **Schopenhauers sämtliche ~en** the complete works of Schopenhauer; **die (Heilige) ~** the (Holy) Scriptures *pl*

Schrift-: **Schrift|art** F (= *Handschrift*) script; *(Typ)* font (type), type, typeface; **Schrift|aus|le|gung** F *(Bibl)* interpretation (of the Bible); **Schrift|bild** NT script; **Schrift|da|tei** F *(Comput)* font file; **Schrift|deutsch** NT (*nicht Umgangssprache*) written German; (*nicht Dialekt*) standard German; **Schrift|deu|tung** F graphology

Schrif|ten|nach|weis M, **Schrif|ten|ver|zeich|nis** NT bibliography

Schrift-: **Schrift|form** F *(Jur)* **dieser Vertrag erfordert die ~** this contract must be drawn up in writing; **Schrift|füh|rer(in)** M(F) secretary; (= *Protokollführer auch*) clerk; **Schrift|ge|lehr|te(r)** M *decl as adj (Bibl)* scribe; **Schrift|gie|ßer(in)** M(F) typefounder; **Schrift|grad** M *(Typ)* type size; *(esp Comput)* font size; **Schrift|guss** M typefounding; **Schrift|hö|he** F x-height *(spec)*, height of the type; **Schrift|kunst** F calligraphy; **Schrift|lei|ter(in)** M(F) editor; **Schrift|lei|tung** F (= *Redaktionsstab*) editorial staff *pl*; (= *Redaktionsleitung*) editorship; **Schrift|le|sung** F *(Eccl)* lesson

schrift|lich [ˈʃrɪftlɪç] ADJ written; **in ~er Form** in writing; **auf ~em Wege** in writing; **die ~e Prüfung, das Schriftliche** *(inf)* the written exam; **ich habe nichts Schriftliches darüber** I haven't got anything in writing ADV in writing; **ich bin ~ eingeladen worden** I have had a written invitation; **ich muss mich bei ihm ~ für das Geschenk bedanken** I must write and thank him for the present; **etw ~ festhalten/niederlegen/machen** *(inf)* to put sth down in writing; **das kann ich Ihnen ~ geben** *(fig inf)* I can tell you that for free *(inf)*

Schrift-: **Schrift|li|nie** F *(Typ)* type line; **Schrift|pro|be** F (*von Handschrift*) sample of one's handwriting; *(Typ)* sample (proof); **Schrift|rol|le** F scroll; **Schrift|sach|ver|stän|di|ge(r)** MF *decl as adj* handwriting expert; **Schrift|satz** M **a** *(Jur)* legal document **b** *(Typ)* form(e); **Schrift|schnitt** M *(Typ)* type style; *(esp Comput)* font style; **Schrift|set|zer(in)** M(F) typesetter, compositor, comp *(Typ sl)*; **Schrift|spra|che** F (= *nicht Umgangssprache*) written language; (= *nicht Dialekt*) standard language; **die französische ~** written/(good) standard French; **schrift|sprach|lich** ADJ *Ausdruck, Konstruktion* used in the written language ADV **~ würde man ... sagen** in the written language one would say ...; **~ reden** to speak as it would be written

Schrift|stel|ler [-ʃtɛlɐ] M **-s, -** author, writer

Schrift|stel|le|rei [-ʃtɛləˈrai] F **-,** *no pl* writing

Schrift|stel|le|rin [-ʃtɛlərɪn] F **-, -nen** author (-ess), writer

schrift|stel|le|risch [-ʃtɛlərɪʃ] ADJ *Arbeit, Werk, Talent* literary ADV **~ tätig sein** to write; **er ist ~ begabt** he has literary talent, he has talent as a writer

schrift|stel|lern [-ʃtɛlɐn] VI *insep (inf)* to try one's hand at writing *or* as an author; **der ~de General Patschke** General Patschke, who also writes in his free time

Schrift|stel|ler|na|me M pen name, nom de plume

Schrift-: **Schrift|stück** NT paper; *(Jur)* document; **Schrift|tum** [ˈʃrɪfttuːm] NT **-s,** *no pl* literature; **Schrift|ver|kehr** M, **Schrift|wech|sel** M correspondence; **im ~ stehen** to be in correspondence; **Schrift|zei|chen** NT character; **Schrift|zug** M *usu pl* stroke; (= *Duktus*) hand

schrill [ʃrɪl] ADJ *Ton, Stimme* shrill; *(fig)* () *Misston, Missklang* jarring; *Fest, Musik, Persönlichkeit* brash; *Farbe, Accessoires, Outfit* garish; **er reagierte mit ~en Tönen** his reaction was quite strident ADV shrilly; *gekleidet* loudly; **sie lachte ~ auf** she gave a shriek *or* screech of laughter

schril|len [ˈʃrɪlən] VI to shrill; (*Stimme auch*) to sound shrilly; (*Telefon, Wecker*) to ring shrilly

Schrip|pe [ˈʃrɪpə] F **-, -n** *(dial)* (bread) roll

schritt *pret von* **schreiten**

Schritt [ʃrɪt] M **-(e)s, -e** **a** *(lit, fig)* step (*zu* towards); (*weit ausholend*) stride; (*hörbar*) footstep; **mit schnellen/langsamen ~en** quickly/slowly, with quick/slow steps; **mit schleppenden ~en** dragging one's feet, with dragging feet; **sie näherte sich ihm mit trippelnden ~en** she tripped towards him; **einen ~ zurücktreten** to step back; **einen ~ zur Seite gehen** to step aside *or* to one side; **~ vor ~ setzen** to put one foot in front of the other; **ein paar ~e spazieren gehen** to go for *or* take a short walk *or* stroll; **einen ~ machen** *or* **tun** to take a step; **kleine** *or* **kurze/große** *or* **lange ~e machen** to take small steps/long strides; **ich habe seit Wochen keinen/kaum einen ~ aus dem Haus getan** I haven't/have hardly set foot outside the house for weeks; **die ersten ~e machen** *or* **tun** to take one's first steps; *(fig)* to take the first step; **den ersten ~ tun** *(fig)* to make the first move; (= *etw beginnen*) to take the first step; **den zweiten ~ vor dem ersten tun** *(fig)* to put the cart before the horse; **den ~ tun** *(fig)* to take the plunge; **~e gegen jdn/etw unternehmen** to take steps against sb/sth; **ein großer ~ sein hin zu ...** *(fig)* to be a huge step towards ...; **ich würde sogar noch einen ~ weiter gehen und behaupten ...** I would go even further and maintain ...; **im gleichen ~ und Tritt** *(lit, fig)* in step; **auf ~ und Tritt** *(lit, fig)* wherever *or* everywhere one goes; **~ für** *or* **um ~** step by step; *(fig auch)* little by little, gradually; **Politik der kleinen ~e** step-by-step *or* gradualistic policy; **ein ~ in Richtung Frieden** a step towards peace **b** (= *Gang*) walk, gait; (= *Tempo*) pace; **~ halten** *(lit, fig)* to keep pace, to keep up; **mit der Zeit ~ halten** to keep abreast of the times; **einen schnellen/unwahrscheinlichen ~ am Leib** *(inf) or* **an sich** *(dat)* **haben** to walk quickly/incredibly quickly; **gemessenen/leichten/langsamen ~es** *(geh)* with measured/light/slow step(s) *or* tread; **seinen ~** *or* **seine ~e beschleunigen/verlangsamen** *(geh)* to increase/slow one's pace, to speed up/slow down; **den ~ anhalten** to stop **c** (= *Schrittgeschwindigkeit*) walking pace; **(im) ~ fahren** to go at a crawl, to drive at walking speed; **„Schritt fahren"** "dead slow" *(Brit)*, "slow"; **im ~ reiten/gehen** to go at a walk **d** (*Maßangabe*) ≈ yard; **mit zehn ~ or ~en Abstand** at a distance of ten paces; **sich** *(dat)* **jdn drei ~(e) vom Leib halten** *(inf)* to keep sb at arm's length **e** (= *Hosenschritt*) crotch; (= *Schrittweite*) crotch measurement

Schrittempo △ NT → **Schritttempo**

Schritt-: **Schritt|fol|ge** F (*beim Tanzen*) sequence of steps, step sequence; **Schritt|ge|schwin|dig|keit** F walking pace; **mit ~ fahren** to drive at a walking pace *or* a crawl; **Schritt|kom|bi|na|ti|on** F *(Sport)* combination of steps; **Schritt|län|ge** F length of one's stride; **Schritt|ma|cher** M *(Med)* pacemaker; **Schritt|ma|cher|diens|te** PL *(fig)* **jdm ~ leisten** to smooth the path *or* way for sb; **Schritt|ma|cher(in)** M(F) *(Sport)* pacemaker *(esp Brit)*, pacer; *(fig auch)* pacesetter; **die Universitäten waren ~ der Revolution** the universities were in the vanguard of *or* led the way in the revolution; **Schritt|ma|cher|ma|schi|ne** F *(Sport)* pacemaker *(esp Brit)*, pacer; **Schritt|tem|po** NT walking speed; **im ~ fahren** to crawl along; **„Schritttempo"** "dead slow" *(Brit)*, "slow"; **schritt|wei|se** ADV gradually, little by little ADJ gradual; **Schritt|wei|te** F *(Sew)* (*von Hose*) (waist-to-)crotch measurement; (*von Kleid, Rock*) hemline; **Schritt|zäh|ler** M pedometer

schroff [ʃrɔf] ADJ (= *rau, barsch*) curt, brusque; (= *krass, abrupt*) *Übergang, Bruch* abrupt; (= *steil, jäh*) *Fels, Klippe* precipitous, steep; **das ~e Nebeneinander von Arm und Reich** the stark juxtaposition of rich and poor; **~e Gegensätze** stark *or* sharp contrasts ADV **a** (= *barsch*) curtly, gruffly; *zurückweisen, ablehnen* curtly, brusquely **b** (= *steil*) steeply

Schroff|heit F **-, -en** **a** *no pl* (= *Rauheit, Barschheit*) curtness, brusqueness **b** (= *schroffes Wort*) curt remark

schröp|fen [ˈʃrœpfn] VT (= *Blut absaugen*) to bleed, to cup *(old)*; **jdn ~** *(fig)* to fleece sb *(inf)*, to rip sb off *(inf)*

Schröpf|kopf M *(Med)* cupping glass

Schrot [ʃroːt] M OR NT **-(e)s, -e** **a** grain (*coarsely ground*); (= *Weizenschrot*) ≈ wholemeal *(Brit)*, ≈ whole-wheat *(US)*; **ein Schotte von echtem ~ und Korn** a true Scot; **er ist ein Bauer von echtem ~ und Korn** he is a farmer through and through; **vom alten ~ und Korn** *(fig)* of the old school **b** *(Hunt)* shot; **einem Hasen eine Ladung ~ aufbrennen** *(inf)* to pepper a hare with shot

Schrot-: **Schrot|brot** NT *bread made from coarsely-ground grain* (*aus Weizenschrot*) ≈ wholemeal *(Brit) or* whole-wheat *(US)* bread; **Schrot|büch|se** F *(Hunt)* shotgun; **Schrot|ef|fekt** M *(Elec)* shot effect

schro|ten [ˈʃroːtn] VT *Getreide* to grind coarsely; *Alteisen* to break up

Schrot-: **Schrot|flin|te** F shotgun; **Schrot|korn** NT *pl* **-körner** **a** grain **b** *(Hunt)* pellet; **Schrot|ku|gel** F pellet; **Schrot|la|dung** F round of shot; **Schrot|mehl** NT coarsely-ground flour; (= *Weizenmehl*) ≈ wholemeal *(Brit) or* whole-wheat *(US)* flour; **Schrot|mei|ßel** M blacksmith's chisel; **Schrot|sä|ge** F crosscut saw; **Schrot|schuss** M round of shot *or* pellets

Schrott [ʃrɔt] M **-(e)s,** *no pl* scrap metal; (*aus Eisen auch*) old iron; *(fig)* rubbish *(Brit)*, garbage, trash; (*Comput; inf*) (= *fehlerhafte Daten*) corrupt data; (= *überflüssige Daten*) rubbish data, garbage → **fahren 2 a**

Schrott-: **Schrott|au|to** NT car that is ready for the scrap heap; **Schrott|hal|de** F scrap heap; **Schrott|han|del** M scrap trade; **Schrott|händ|ler(in)** M(F) scrap dealer *or* merchant; **Schrott|hau|fen** M *(lit)* scrap heap; (*fig:* = *Auto*) pile *or* heap of scrap; **Schrott|mö|bel** PL *(fig)* trashy furniture; **Schrott|platz** M scrap yard; **schrott|reif** ADJ ready for the scrap heap, only fit for scrap → **fahren 2 a**; **Schrott|wert** M scrap value

schrub|ben [ˈʃrʊbn] VTI to scrub; **das Deck ~** to swab *or* scrub the deck/decks VR to scrub oneself

Schrub|ber [ˈʃrʊbɐ] M **-s, -** (long-handled) scrubbing *(Brit) or* scrub *(US)* brush

Schrul|le [ˈʃrʊlə] F **-, -n** **a** quirk; **was hast du dir denn da für eine ~ in den Kopf gesetzt?** *(inf)* what strange idea have you got into your head now? **b** (*pej:* = *alte Frau*) old crone

schrul|len|haft ADJ odd, cranky *(Brit)* ADV *sich benehmen* oddly

Schrul|len|haf|tig|keit [ˈʃrʊlənhaftɪçkait] F -, *no pl* oddness, crankiness *(Brit)*

schrul|lig [ˈʃrʊlɪç] ADJ odd, cranky *(Brit)* ADV *sich benehmen* oddly

Schrul|lig|keit F -, -en oddness, crankiness *(Brit)*

Schrum|pel [ˈʃrʊmpl] F -, -n *(dial)* wrinkle

schrum|pe|lig [ˈʃrʊmpəlɪç] ADJ *(inf) Haut, Apfel* wrinkled

schrum|peln [ˈʃrʊmpln] VI *aux sein (inf)* to go wrinkled

schrump|fen [ˈʃrʊmpfn] VI *aux sein* **a** *(lit)* to shrink; *(Leber, Niere)* to atrophy; *(Muskeln)* to waste, to atrophy; *(Metall, Gestein etc)* to contract; *(= runzlig werden)* to get wrinkled **b** *(fig)* to shrink; *(Exporte, Mitgliederschaft, Interesse)* to dwindle; *(Währung)* to depreciate; *(Industriezweig)* to decline

Schrumpf-: **Schrumpf|kopf** M shrunken head; **Schrumpf|le|ber** F cirrhosis of the liver; **Schrumpf|nie|re** F cirrhosis of the kidney

Schrump|fung [ˈʃrʊmpfʊŋ] F -, -en shrinking; *(= Raumverlust)* shrinkage; *(von Fundamenten, Metall)* contraction; *(Med)* atrophy(ing); *(von Kapital, Arbeitskräften, Exporten)* dwindling, diminution; *(von Währung)* depreciation; *(von Industriezweig etc)* decline

schrump|lig [ˈʃrʊmplɪç] ADJ *(inf) Haut, Apfel* wrinkled

Schrund [ʃrʊnt] M -(e)s, ⸚e [ˈʃrʏndə] *(= Bergschrund)* crevasse

Schrun|de [ˈʃrʊndə] F -, -n *(in der Haut)* crack; *(durch Kälte)* chap; *(= Felsschrunde, Gletscherspalte)* crevasse

schrun|dig [ˈʃrʊndɪç] ADJ *Haut, Hände* cracked; *(durch Kälte)* chapped; *Papier* rough; *Weg* creviced

schrup|pen [ˈʃrʊpn] VT **a** *(Tech) (mit Feile)* to rough-file; *(mit Hobel)* to rough-plane; *(mit Maschine)* to rough-machine **b** *(= schrubben)* to scrub

Schrupp-: **Schrupp|fei|le** F rough file; **Schrupp|ho|bel** M jack plane

Schub [ʃuːp] M -(e)s, ⸚e [ˈʃyːbə] **a** *(= Stoß)* push, shove **b** *(Phys) (= Vortriebskraft)* thrust; *(= Scherung)* shear; *(fig: = Impuls, Anstoß)* impetus; **einer Sache neuen ~ geben** *(fig)* to give sth new impetus *or* momentum **c** *(Med)* phase **d** *(= Anzahl)* batch **e** *(= Kegelschub)* throw; **alle neune auf einen ~** a strike; **auf zwei Schübe** in two throws **f** *(inf: = Schubfach)* drawer

schub|bern [ˈʃʊbɐn] VTI *(N Ger)* to scratch

Schu|ber [ˈʃuːbɐ] M -s, - slipcase

Schub-: **Schub|fach** NT drawer; **Schub|haft** F *(Jur)* = **Abschiebehaft**; **Schub|kar|re** F, **Schub|kar|ren** M wheelbarrow; **Schub|kas|ten** M drawer; **Schub|kraft** F *(Phys)* thrust; *(= Scherung)* shearing stress

Schub|la|de [ˈʃuːplaːdə] F -, -n drawer; *(fig)* pigeonhole, compartment; **in der ~ liegen** *(fig)* to be in reserve

Schub|la|den-: **Schub|la|den|den|ken** NT pigeonholing, stereotyped thinking; **Schub|la|den|ge|setz** NT *(Pol pej) law kept in reserve to deal with a special situation*

Schub|lad|kas|ten M *(Aus)* chest of drawers

Schub|leh|re F vernier calliper

Schubs [ʃʊps] M -es, -e *(inf)* shove *(inf)*, push; *(Aufmerksamkeit erregend)* nudge; **jdm einen ~ geben** to give sb a shove *(inf) or* push/nudge; *(fig)* to give sb a prod

Schub|schiff NT tug (boat) *(which pushes)*

schub|sen [ˈʃʊpsn] VTI *(inf)* to shove *(inf)*, to push; *(Aufmerksamkeit erregend)* to nudge

Schub|um|kehr F *(Aviat)* thrust reverser

schub|wei|se ADV in batches; *(Med)* in phases

schüch|tern [ˈʃʏçtɐn] ADJ shy; *(= scheu auch)* bashful; **einen ~en Versuch unternehmen** *(iro)* to make a half-hearted attempt ADV shyly; *(= scheu auch)* bashfully

Schüch|tern|heit F -, *no pl* shyness; *(= Scheu auch)* bashfulness

schu|ckeln [ˈʃʊkln] VI *(dial)* = **wackeln a**

schuf *pret von* **schaffen**

Schu|fa [ˈʃuːfa] F -, *no pl abbr von* **Schutzgemeinschaft für allgemeine Kreditsicherung** ≈ credit investigation company *(Brit)*, ≈ credit bureau *(US)*

Schuft [ʃʊft] M -(e)s, -e heel *(inf)*, cad, blackguard *(old)*

schuf|ten [ˈʃʊftn] VI *(inf)* to graft (away) *(inf)*, to slave away; **wie ein Pferd ~** *(inf)* to work like a Trojan *(Brit) or* a horse

Schuf|te|rei [ʃʊftəˈrai] F -, -en *(inf)* graft *(inf)*, hard work

schuf|tig [ˈʃʊftɪç] ADJ mean, shabby ADV *behandeln* meanly, shabbily; **sich jdm gegenüber ~ verhalten** to behave meanly toward(s) sb

Schuf|tig|keit F -, -en meanness, shabbiness; **das war eine ~ von ihm** that was a mean thing he did, that was mean of him

Schuh [ʃuː] M -(e)s, -e **a** shoe; **jdm etw in die ~e schieben** *(inf)* to lay the blame for sth at sb's door, to put the blame for sth on sb; **wissen, wo jdn der ~ drückt** to know what is bothering *or* troubling sb; **wo drückt der ~?** what's the trouble?, what's bothering you?; **umgekehrt wird ein ~ d(a)raus** *(fig)* exactly the opposite is the case **b** *(= Bremsschuh etc)* shoe

Schuh- *in cpds* shoe; **Schuh|ab|satz** M heel (of a/one's shoe); **Schuh|an|zie|her** [-lantsiːɐ] M -s, - shoehorn; **Schuh|band** [-bant] NT *pl* -**bänder** shoelace; **Schuh|bürs|te** F shoe brush

Schüh|chen [ˈʃyːçən] NT -s, - *dim von* **Schuh**

Schuh-: **Schuh|creme** F shoe polish *or* cream; **Schuh|grö|ße** F shoe size; **Schuh|haus** NT shoe shop; **Schuh|kar|ton** M shoebox; **Schuh|löf|fel** M shoehorn; **Schuh|ma|cher(in)** M(F) shoemaker; *(= Flickschuster)* cobbler; **Schuh|num|mer** F *(inf)* shoe size; **jds ~ sein** *(fig)* to be sb's cup of tea *(inf)*; **ein paar** *or* **mindestens zwei ~n zu groß für jdn** *(fig)* out of sb's league; **Schuh|platt|ler** [-platlɐ] M -s, - *Bavarian folk dance*; **Schuh|put|zer** [-putsɐ] M -s, -, **Schuh|put|ze|rin** [-ərɪn] F -, -nen bootblack, shoeshine boy/girl *(US)*; **jdn wie einen ~ behandeln** to treat sb like dirt; **ich bin doch nicht dein ~!** I'm not your slave!; **Schuh|putz|mit|tel** NT shoe polish; **Schuh|rie|men** M strap (of a/one's shoe); *(= Schnürsenkel)* shoelace; **Schuh|soh|le** F sole (of a/one's shoe); **~n sparen** to save shoe leather; **Schuh|span|ner** M shoetree; **Schuh|wa|ren** PL footwear *sing*; **Schuh|werk** NT, *no pl* footwear; **Schuh|wich|se** F *(inf)* shoe polish; **Schuh|zeug** NT, *no pl* footwear

Schu|ko-® [ˈʃuːko-]: **Schu|ko|steck|do|se®** F safety socket; **Schu|ko|ste|cker®** M safety plug

Schul-: **Schul|ab|gän|ger** [-lapgɛŋɐ] M -s, -, **Schul|ab|gän|ge|rin** [-ərɪn] F -, -nen school-leaver *(Brit)*, graduate *(US)*; **Schul|ab|schluss** M school-leaving qualification, ≈ high school diploma *(US)*; **Schul|al|ter** NT school age; **im ~** of school age; **ins ~ kommen** to reach school age; **Schul|amt** NT education authority; **Schul|an|fang** M beginning of (the *(esp US)*) term; *(= Schuleintritt)* first day at school; **morgen ist ~** school starts tomorrow; **Schul|an|fän|ger(in)** M(F) child just starting school; **Schul|ar|beit** F **a** *usu pl* homework *no pl*, prep *no pl (Brit inf)* **b** *(Aus, S Ger)* test; **Schul|art** F type of school; **Schul|arzt** M, **Schul|ärz|tin** F school doctor; **Schul|auf|ga|ben** PL homework *sing*; **Schul|auf|satz** M class essay; **Schul|auf|sicht** F supervision of schools; **die ~ obliegt dem Kultusministerium** the ministry of education is responsible for schools; **Schul|auf|sichts|be|hör|de** F education authority; **Schul|aus|flug** M school outing *(esp Brit) or* trip, field trip *(US)*; **Schul|aus|ga|be** F school edition; **Schul|bank** F *pl* -**bänke** school desk; **die ~ drücken** *(inf)* to go to school; **Schul|be|ginn** M *(= Schuljahrsbeginn)* beginning of the school year; *(nach Ferien)* beginning of (the *(esp US)*) term; **(der) ~ ist um neun** school starts at nine; **Schul|be|hör|de** F education authority; **Schul|bei|spiel** NT *(fig)* classic example *(für* of); **Schul|be|such** M school attendance; **Schul|bil|dung** F (school) education; **Schul|bub** M *(S Ger, Aus)* schoolboy; **Schul|buch** NT schoolbook, textbook; **Schul|buch|ver|lag** M educational publishing company; **Schul|bus** M school bus

schuld [ʃʊlt] ADJ *pred* **~ sein** to be to blame *(an +dat* for); **er war ~ an dem Streit** the argument was his fault, he was to blame for the argument; **das Wetter/ich war ~ daran, dass wir zu spät kamen** the weather/I was to blame for us being late, it was the fault of the weather/my fault that we were late; **bin ich denn ~, wenn ...?** is it my fault if ...?; **du bist selbst ~** that's your own fault, that's nobody's fault but your own

Schuld [ʃʊlt] ✪ 45.2 F -, -en **a** [-dn] *no pl (= Ursache, Verantwortlichkeit)* **die ~ an etw** *(dat)* **haben** *or* **tragen** *(geh)* to be to blame for sth; **~ haben** to be to blame *(an +dat* for); **er hatte ~ an dem Streit** the argument was his fault, he was to blame for the argument; **du hast selbst ~** that's your own fault, that's nobody's fault but your own; **die ~ auf sich** *(acc)* **nehmen** to take the blame; **jdm die ~ geben** *or* **zuschreiben** to blame sb; **die ~ auf jdn abwälzen** *or* **schieben** to put the blame on sb; **die ~ bei anderen suchen** to try to blame somebody else; **die ~ liegt bei mir** I am to blame (for that); **das ist meine/deine ~** that is my/your fault, I am/you are to blame (for that); **das ist meine eigene ~** it's my own fault, I've nobody but *or* only myself to blame; **durch meine/deine ~** because of me/you; **jdm/einer Sache ~ geben** to blame sb/sth; **er gab ihr ~, dass es nicht klappte** he blamed her for it not working, he blamed her for the fact that it didn't work

b *no pl (= Schuldhaftigkeit, Schuldgefühl)* guilt; *(= Unrecht)* wrong; *(Rel: = Sünde)* sin; *(im Vaterunser)* trespasses *pl*; **die Strafe sollte in einem angemessenen Verhältnis zur ~ stehen** the punishment should be appropriate to the degree of culpability; **sich frei von ~ fühlen** to consider oneself completely blameless; **ich bin mir keiner ~ bewusst** I'm not aware of having done anything wrong; **ich bin mir meiner ~ bewusst** I know that I have done wrong; **ihm konnte seine ~ nicht nachgewiesen werden** his guilt could not be proved; **ihm konnte keine ~ nachgewiesen werden** it couldn't be proved that he had done anything wrong; **~ auf sich** *(acc)* **laden** to burden oneself with guilt; **für seine ~ büßen** to pay for one's sin/sins; **~ und Sühne** crime and punishment; **zu ~en** = **zuschulden**

c *(= Zahlungsverpflichtung)* debt; **ich stehe tief in seiner ~** *(lit)* I'm deeply in debt to him; *(fig)* I'm deeply indebted to him; **~en machen** to run up debts; **~en haben** to be in debt; **EUR 10.000 ~en haben** to have debts totalling *(Brit) or* totaling *(US) or* of 10,000 euros, to be in debt to the tune of 10,000 euros; **in ~en geraten** to get into debt; **mehr ~en als Haare auf dem Kopf haben** *(inf)* **bis über beide Ohren in ~en stecken** *(inf)* to be up to one's ears in debt *(inf)*; **das Haus ist frei von ~en** the house is unmortgaged

Schuld-: **Schuld|an|er|kennt|nis** NT admission of one's guilt; *(= Schuldschein)* promissory note, IOU; **Schuld|be|kennt|nis** NT confession; **schuld|be|la|den** [-bəlaːdn] ADJ burdened with guilt; **Schuld|be|weis** M proof *or* evidence of one's guilt; **schuld|be|wusst** ADJ *Mensch* feeling guilty; *Gesicht, Miene* guilty ADV guiltily; **jdn ~ ansehen** to give sb a guilty look; **~ erröten** to turn red with guilt *(Brit)*, to blush from guilt; **Schuld|be|wusst|sein** NT feelings *pl* of guilt; **Schuld|buch** NT *(Econ)* Debt Register; **Schuld|buch|for|de|rung** F *(Econ)* Debt Register Claims; **Schuld|ein|ge|-ständ|nis** NT admission of guilt

schul|den [ˈʃʊldn] VT to owe; **das schulde ich ihm** I owe him that, I owe it to him; **jdm Dank ~** to owe sb a debt of gratitude

Schul|den-: **Schul|den|berg** M mountain of debts; **Schul|den|dienst** M *(Econ)* debt servicing; **Schul|den|er|lass** M *(Econ)* debt relief, waiving of debts; **Schul|den|fal|le** F debt trap; **schul|den|frei** ADJ free of debt(s); *Besitz* unmortgaged; **Schul|den|kri|se** F debt crisis; **Schul|den|last** F debts *pl*; **Schul|den|ma|-cher(in)** M(F) *(inf)* habitual debtor; **er ist ein notorischer ~** he is notorious for running up debts; **Schul|den|ma|nage|ment** NT debt management; **Schul|den|mas|se** F *(Jur)* aggregate liabilities *pl*; **Schul|den|po|li|tik** F *(Econ)* debt management policy; **Schul|den|til|gung** F discharge of one's debt(s)

Schuld-: **schuld|fä|hig** ADJ *(Jur)* criminally responsible; **voll/vermindert ~** fully/not fully responsible; **Schuld|fä|hig|keit** F *(Jur)* criminal responsibility; **verminderte ~** diminished responsibility; **Schuld|for|de|rung** F claim; **Schuld|fra|ge** F question of guilt; **schuld|-frei** ADJ blameless; **Schuld|ge|fäng|nis** NT *(Hist)* debtors' prison; **Schuld|ge|fühl** NT sense *no pl* or feeling of guilt; **Schuld|ge|-ständ|nis** NT → **Schuldbekenntnis**; **schuld|-haft** *(Jur)* ADJ culpable ADV culpably; **jdm etw ~ nachweisen** to prove sb's culpability for sth; **Schuld|haft** F *(Hist)* imprisonment for debt

Schul-: **Schul|die|ner** M *(old)* school janitor *or* caretaker; **Schul|dienst** M (school)teaching *no art*; **in den ~ treten** *or* **gehen** to go into teaching; **im ~ (tätig) sein** to be a teacher, to be in the teaching profession

schul|dig [ˈʃʊldɪç] ADJ **a** *(= schuldhaft, straffällig, schuldbeladen)* guilty; *(= verantwortlich)* to blame *pred* *(an +dat* for); *(Rel)* sinful; **einer Sache** *(gen)* **~ sein** to be guilty of sth; **jdn einer Tat** *(gen)* **(für) ~ erklären** *or* **befinden** *(Jur)* to find sb guilty of *or* to convict sb of an offence *(Brit)* *or* offense *(US)*; **sich einer Sache** *(gen)* **~ machen** to be guilty of sth; **jdn ~ sprechen** to find *or* pronounce sb guilty, to convict sb; **~ in allen Anklagepunkten** *(Jur)* guilty as charged; **sich ~ bekennen** to admit one's guilt; *(Jur)* to plead guilty; **an jdm ~ werden** *(geh)* to wrong sb

b *(geh: = gebührend)* due; **jdm die ~e Achtung/den ~en Respekt zollen** to give sb the attention/respect due to him/her

c *(= verpflichtet)* **jdm etw** *(acc)* **~ sein** *(lit, fig)* to owe sb sth; **ich muss Ihnen 2 Euro ~ bleiben** I'll have to owe you 2 euros; **was bin ich Ihnen ~?** how much *or* what do I owe you?; **jdm Dank ~ sein** to owe sb a debt of gratitude; **sie blieb mir die Antwort ~** she didn't answer me, she didn't have an answer; **sie blieb mir die Antwort nicht ~** she hit back at me; **er blieb ihr nichts ~** *(fig)* he gave (her) as good as he got

ADV **~ geschieden sein** to be the guilty party in a/the divorce

Schul|di|ge(r) [ˈʃʊldɪgə] MF *decl as adj* guilty person; *(zivilrechtlich)* guilty party

Schul|di|ger [ˈʃʊldɪgɐ] M **-s, -** *(Bibl)* trespasser; **wie auch wir vergeben unseren ~n** as we forgive those who trespass against us

Schul|dig|keit F **-,** *no pl* duty; **seine ~ tun** to do one's duty → **Mohr**

schul|dig+spre|chen VT *sep irreg* → **schuldig a**

Schul|dig|spre|chung [-ʃprɛçʊŋ] F **-, -en** conviction

Schul|di|rek|tor(in) M(F) headteacher *(esp Brit)*, headmaster/headmistress, principal

Schuld-: **Schuld|kom|plex** M guilt complex; **schuld|los** ADJ *(an Verbrechen)* innocent *(an +dat* of); *(an Fehler, Unglück etc)* blameless, free from blame; **er war vollständig ~ an dem Unglück** he was in no way to blame for the accident ADV *in etw geraten* innocently; **~ in einen Unfall verwickelt sein** to be involved in an accident without being at fault; **~ geschieden sein** to be the innocent party in a/the divorce; **Schuld|lo|sig|keit** F **-,** *no pl* innocence

Schuld|ner [ˈʃʊldnɐ] M **-s, -**, **Schuld|ne|rin** [-ərɪn] F **-, -nen** debtor

Schuld|ner-: **Schuld|ner|be|ra|tung** F advisory service for debtors, debt advisory service, credit counseling *(US)*; **Schuld|ner|staat** M debtor nation; **Schuld|ner|ver|zeich|nis** NT *(Jur)* (court) register of outstanding debts

Schuld-: **Schuld|prin|zip** NT *(Jur)* principle of the guilty party; **Schuld|recht** NT *(Jur)* law of contract; **Schuld|schein** M IOU, promissory note; **Schuld|schein|dar|le|hen** F loan against borrower's note; **Schuld|spruch** M verdict of guilty; **Schuld|turm** M *(Hist)* debtors' prison; **Schuld|über|nah|me** F assumption of debt; **schuld|un|fä|hig** ADJ *(Jur)* not criminally responsible; **Schuld|un|fä|hig|keit** F *(Jur)* lack of criminal responsibility; **Schuld|-ver|hält|nis** NT *(Jur)* relationship of debenture; **Schuld|ver|schrei|bung** F *(Fin)* debenture bond; **Schuld|zins** M debt interest; **Schuld|zu|wei|sung** F accusation, assignment of guilt

Schu|le [ˈʃu:lə] F **-, -n** **a** *(= Lehranstalt, Lehrmeinung, künstlerische Richtung)* school; **in die** *or* **zur ~ kommen** to start school; **in die** *or* **zur ~ gehen** to go to school; **er hat nie eine ~ besucht** he has never been to school; **auf** *or* **in der ~** at school; **die ~ wechseln** to change schools; **von der ~ abgehen** to leave school; **die ~ ist aus** school is over, the schools are out; **sie ist an der ~** *(= sie ist Lehrerin)* she is a (school)teacher; **~ des Violinspiels** *(= Lehrwerk)* violin tutor; **er ist bei Brecht in die ~ gegangen** *(fig)* he was greatly influenced by Brecht; *(= wurde von Brecht unterrichtet)* he was a student of Brecht's; **darin hat er bei seinen Eltern eine gute ~ gehabt** his parents have given him a good schooling in that; **durch eine harte ~ gegangen sein** *(fig)* to have learned in a hard school; **~ machen** to become the accepted thing; **aus der ~ plaudern** to tell tales (out of school *(Brit inf)*); **ein Kavalier der alten ~** a gentleman of the old school

b *(Reiten)* school of riding → **hoch 1 f**

schu|len [ˈʃu:lən] VT to train; *Auge, Gedächtnis, Pferd auch* to school; *(Pol)* to give political instruction to

Schul-: **Schul|eng|lisch** NT schoolboy/schoolgirl English; **zwei Jahre ~** two years' English at school; **mein ~** the English I learned at school; **schul|ent|las|sen** ADJ **kaum ~, begann er ...** hardly had he left school when he began ...; **die ~e Jugend** the young people who have recently left school; **Schul|ent|las|se|ne** [-lɛntlasnə] PL *decl as adj* school-leavers *pl (Brit)*, ≈ graduates *pl (US)*; **Schul|ent|las|sung** F **der Tag der ~** the day one leaves *(Brit)* *or* graduates from *(US)* school; **nach seiner/der ~** after leaving *(Brit)* *or* graduating from *(US)* school; **Schul|ent|las|sungs|fei|er** F school-leavers' day *(Brit)*, ≈ graduation day *(US)*

Schü|ler [ˈʃy:lɐ] M **-s, -**, **Schü|le|rin** [-ərɪn] F **-, -nen** schoolboy/-girl; *(einer bestimmten Schule, eines Künstlers)* pupil; *(einer Oberschule)* pupil, student; *(= Jünger)* follower, disciple; **als ~ habe ich ...** when I was at school I ...; **alle ~ und ~innen dieser Stadt** all the schoolchildren of this town; **ein ehemaliger ~ (der Schule)** an old boy *or* pupil (of the school)

Schü|ler-: **Schü|ler|aus|tausch** M school *or* student exchange; **Schü|ler|aus|weis** M (school) student card; **Schü|ler|er|mä|ßi|-gung** F reduction *or* concession for pupils *or* students, student discount *(US)*; **schü|ler|haft** ADJ schoolboyish/-girlish; *(pej)* childish, puerile ADV childishly; **sein Benehmen wirkte ~** his behaviour *(Brit)* *or* behavior *(US)* seemed childish; **Schü|ler|heim** NT (school) boarding house

Schü|le|rin [-ərɪn] F → **Schüler**

Schü|ler-: **Schü|ler|kar|te** F school season ticket; **Schü|ler|lot|se** M, **Schü|ler|lot|sin** F *pupil acting as warden at a crossing*, lollipop man/lady *(Brit inf)*; **Schü|ler|mit|ver|wal|-tung** F school *or* student council; **Schü|ler|-par|la|ment** NT interschool student council; **Schü|ler|schaft** [ˈʃy:lɐʃaft] F **-, -en** pupils *pl*; **Schü|ler|spra|che** F school slang; **Schü|ler|-ver|tre|tung** F pupil *or* student representation; **Schü|ler|zahl** F number of pupils *or* students; **zurückgehende ~en** falling pupil numbers *or* school enrollment *(US)*; **Schü|ler|zei|-tung** F school magazine *or* newspaper

Schul-: **Schul|er|zie|hung** F schooling; **Schul|fach** NT school subject; **Schul|fei|er** F school function; **Schul|fe|ri|en** PL school holidays *pl (Brit)* *or* vacation *(US)*; **Schul|-fern|se|hen** NT schools' *or* educational television; **Schul|fest** NT school function; **Schul|-film** M educational film; **schul|frei** ADJ **ein ~er Nachmittag** an afternoon when one doesn't have to go to school; **an ~en Samstagen** on Saturdays when there's no school; **nächsten Samstag ist ~** there's no school next Saturday; **die Kinder haben morgen ~** the children don't have to go to school tomorrow; **Schul|freund(in)** M(F) schoolfriend; **Schul|-funk** M schools' radio; **Schul|ge|bäu|de** NT school building; **Schul|ge|brauch** M **zum** *or* **für den ~** for use in schools; **Schul|ge|gen|-stand** M *(Aus)* school subject; **Schul|ge|län|-de** NT school grounds *pl*; **Schul|geld** NT school fees *pl*; **Schul|ge|lehr|sam|keit** F *(pej)* book-learning; **Schul|ge|setz** NT education act; **Schul|gram|ma|tik** F (school) grammar book *or* grammar *(inf)*; **Schul|haus** NT schoolhouse; **Schul|heft** NT exercise book; **Schul|hof** M school playground, schoolyard

schu|lisch [ˈʃu:lɪʃ] ADJ *Leistungen, Probleme, Verbesserung* at school; *(= rein akademisch)* scholastic; *Bildung, Einrichtung* school *attr*; **seine ~en Leistungen/Probleme** his progress/problems at school; **~e Angelegenheiten** school matters; **aus ~er Sicht** from the school angle ADV scholastically; **er hat ~ große Fortschritte gemacht** he has improved greatly at school

Schul-: **Schul|jahr** NT school year; *(= Klasse)* year; **ihre ~e** her school days; **Schul|ju|gend** F schoolchildren *pl*; **Schul|jun|ge** M schoolboy; **Schul|ka|me|rad(in)** M(F) schoolmate *(Brit)*, schoolfriend; **Schul|kennt|nis|se** PL knowledge *sing* acquired at school; **Schul|-kind** NT schoolchild; **Schul|kin|der|gar|ten** M *establishment for children whose primary school entry has been delayed for a year*; **Schul|klas|se** F (school) class; **Schul|land|-heim** NT *country house used by school classes for short visits*; **Schul|leh|rer(in)** M(F) schoolteacher; **Schul|lei|ter** M headmaster, principal; **Schul|lei|te|rin** F headmistress, principal; **Schul|lek|tü|re** F book/books read in school; **~ sein** to be read in schools; **Schul|mäd|chen** NT schoolgirl; **Schul|map|pe** F schoolbag; **schul|mä|ßig** ADJ **a** *Unterricht, Kurs, Lehrbuch* didactic **b** *(fig: = wie im Lehrbuch)* textbook *attr*; **ein ~es Tor** a textbook goal ADV *machen* strictly by the book; *gekleidet* for school; *reglementiert* just like in school; **weniger ~ ausgedrückt** to say it less technically *or* formally; **Schul|me|di|zin** F orthodox medicine; **Schul|me|di|zi|ner(in)** M(F) orthodox medical practitioner; **Schul|-mei|nung** F received opinion; **Schul|meis|-ter** M *(old, hum, pej)* schoolmaster; **schul|-meis|ter|lich** *(pej)* ADJ schoolmasterish ADV like a schoolmaster; **sich ~ aufspielen** to play the schoolmaster; **schul|meis|tern** [ˈʃu:lmaistɐn] *insep* VT to lecture (at *or* to) VI to lecture; **Schul|mö|bel** PL school furniture *sing*; **Schul|ord|nung** F school rules *pl*; **Schul|-**

pflicht F compulsory school attendance *no art*; **allgemeine ~** compulsory school attendance for all children; **es besteht ~** school attendance is compulsory; **schul|pflich|tig** [-pflıçtıç] ADJ *Kind* required to attend school; **im ~en Alter** of school age; **Schul|po|li|tik** F education policy; **schul|po|li|tisch** ADJ related to schools *or* educational policy; *Entscheidung etc* affecting schools *or* educational policy; **Schul|psy|cho|lo|ge** M, **Schul|psy|cho|lo|gin** F educational psychologist; **Schul|ran|zen** M (school) satchel; **Schul|rat** M, **Schul|rä|tin** F schools inspector *(Brit)*, ≈ school board superintendent *(US)*; **Schul|re|form** F educational reform; **Schul|rei|fe** F school readiness *(spec)*; **die ~ haben** to be ready to go to school; **Schul|rei|fe|test** M school readiness test; **Schul|sa|chen** PL school things *pl*, things *pl* for school; **seine ~ packen** to get one's things ready for school; **Schul|schiff** NT training ship; **Schul|schluss** M, *no pl* end of school; *(vor den Ferien)* end of term; **~ ist um 13.10** school finishes at 13.10; **kurz nach ~** just after school finishes; **Schul|schwän|zen** NT -s, *no pl* truancy; **Schul|schwän|zer** [-ʃvɛntsɐ] M -s, -, **Schul|schwän|ze|rin** [-ərın] F -, -nen truant; **Schul|se|na|tor(in)** M(F) schools minister *(in Berlin, Hamburg and Bremen)*; **Schul|spei|sung** F free school meals *pl*; **Schul|sport** M school sport; **Schul|spre|cher** M head boy *(Brit)*, school representative; **Schul|spre|che|rin** F head girl *(Brit)*, school representative; **Schul|spren|gel** M *(Aus)* (school) catchment *(Brit) or* service *(US)* area; **Schul|stress** M stress at school; **im ~ sein** to be under stress at school; **Schul|stun|de** F (school) period *or* lesson; **Schul|sys|tem** NT school system; **Schul|tag** M school day; **der erste ~** the/one's first day at school; **Schul|ta|sche** F schoolbag

Schul|ter [ˈʃʊltɐ] F -, -n shoulder; **mit gebeugten/hängenden ~n dastehen** to stand there with sloping/drooping shoulders; *(fig: = niedergeschlagen sein)* to be careworn/downcast; **breite ~n haben** *(lit)* to be broad-shouldered, to have broad shoulders; *(fig)* to have a broad back; **er ließ die ~n hängen** he was slouching; *(niedergeschlagen)* he hung his head; **sich** *(dat)* **den Fotoapparat über die ~ hängen** to sling one's camera over one's shoulder; **sich** *(dat)* **eine Jacke über die ~n hängen** to put a jacket round one's shoulders; **jdm die Hand auf die ~ legen** to put one's hand on sb's shoulder; **jdm auf die ~ klopfen** *or* **schlagen** to give sb a slap on the back, to clap sb on the back; *(lobend)* to pat sb on the back; **sich** *(dat)* **selbst auf die ~ klopfen** *(fig)* to blow one's own trumpet; **jdm** *or* **jdn um die ~ fassen** to put one's arm round sb's shoulders; **~ an ~** *(= dicht gedrängt)* shoulder to shoulder; *(= gemeinsam, solidarisch)* side by side; **die** *or* **mit den ~n zucken** to shrug one's shoulders; **jdn auf die ~ legen** *or* **werfen** to get sb in a shoulder-press; **dem Künstler beim Arbeiten über die ~ sehen** to look over the artist's shoulder while he works; **die Verantwortung ruht auf seinen ~n** the responsibility rests on his shoulders *or* lies at his door; **die Arbeit sollte auf mehr/mehrere ~n verteilt werden** the work should be shared out between more/several people; **etw auf die leichte ~ nehmen** to take sth lightly → **kalt**

Schul|ter-: **Schul|ter|blatt** NT shoulder blade; **schul|ter|frei** ADJ *Kleid* off-the-shoulder; *(ohne Träger)* strapless; *(mit Nackenträger)* halterneck; **sie war/kam ~** her shoulders were bare, she was wearing a dress which left her shoulders bare; **Schul|ter|ge|lenk** NT shoulder joint; **Schul|ter|hö|he** F shoulder height; **in ~** at shoulder level *or* height

-schul|te|rig [ʃʊltərıç] ADJ *suf* -shouldered; **breitschulterig** broad-shouldered; **schmalschulterig** with narrow shoulders

Schul|ter-: **Schul|ter|klap|pe** F *(Mil)* epaulette; **Schul|ter|klop|fen** NT -s, *no pl* slap on the shoulder; *(fig: = Lob)* pat on the shoulder; **schul|ter|lang** ADJ shoulder-length

schul|tern [ˈʃʊltɐn] VT *(lit, fig)* to shoulder; **das Gewehr ~** to shoulder arms

Schul|ter-: **Schul|ter|pols|ter** NT shoulder pad; **Schul|ter|rie|men** M shoulder strap; **Schul|ter|schluss** M, *no pl* shoulder-to--shoulder stance, solidarity; *(= Solidarisierung)* closing of ranks; **Schul|ter|sieg** M *(Sport)* fall; **Schul|ter|stand** M *(Sport)* shoulder stand; **Schul|ter|stück** NT **a** *(Mil)* epaulette **b** *(Cook)* piece of shoulder; **Schul|ter|wurf** M *(Sport)* shoulder-throw; **Schul|ter|zu|cken** NT -s, *no pl* shrug (of the shoulders); **die Antwort war ein ~** he/she answered with a shrug, he/she shrugged in reply

Schult|heiß [ˈʃʊlthais] M -en, -en *(Hist)* mayor

Schul|trä|ger(in) M(F) *(form)* **der ~ (dieser Schule) ist der Staat** the school is supported *or* maintained by the State

-schult|rig [ʃʊltrıç] ADJ *suf* = **-schulterig**

> **SCHULTÜTE**
>
> It is a German custom to give every child a **Schultüte** on their very first day at school. This is a long pointed cone made of cardboard and filled with sweets or small presents. It is intended to help children overcome any fears they may have about starting school.

Schul|typ M type of school

Schu|lung [ˈʃuːlʊŋ] F -, -en *(= Ausbildung, Übung)* training; *(von Auge, Gedächtnis, Pferd auch)* schooling; *(Pol)* political instruction

Schu|lungs-: **Schu|lungs|dis|ket|te** F tutorial diskette; **Schu|lungs|kurs** M training course; **Schu|lungs|la|ger** NT training camp; **Schu|lungs|raum** M training *or* tutorial room

Schul-: **Schul|uni|form** F school uniform; **Schul|un|ter|richt** M school lessons *pl*; **Schul|ver|sa|ger(in)** M(F) failure at school; **Schul|wan|de|rung** F school outing; **Schul|weg** M way to school; *(Entfernung)* distance to school; *(Route)* route to school; **ich habe einen ~ von 20 Minuten** it takes me 20 minutes to get to school; **Schul|weis|heit** F *(pej)* book-learning; **Schul|we|sen** NT school system; **Schul|wis|sen** NT knowledge acquired at school; **Schul|wör|ter|buch** NT school dictionary

Schul|ze [ˈʃʊltsə] M -n, -n *(Hist)* mayor

Schul-: **Schul|zeit** F *(= Schuljahre)* school days *pl*; **nach 13-jähriger ~** after 13 years at school; **seit der ~** since we/they were at school, since our/their school days; **Schul|zei|tung** F school magazine *or* newspaper; **Schul|zent|rum** NT school complex; **Schul|zeug|nis** NT school report; **Schul|zwang** M = **Schulpflicht**; **Schul|zwe|cke** PL **für ~, zu ~n** for school; *(= als geeignetes Lehrmittel)* for use in schools

schum|meln [ˈʃʊmln] VI *(inf)* to cheat; **in Latein/beim Kartenspiel ~** to cheat in Latin/at cards

schum|me|rig [ˈʃʊmərıç], **schumm|rig** [ˈʃʊmrıç] ADJ *Beleuchtung* dim; *Raum* dimly-lit; **bei ~em Licht** in the half-light; **es war schon ~** it was already getting dark

schum|mern [ˈʃʊmɐn] **VI** *impers (N Ger)* **es schummert** dusk is falling **VT** *(Geog)* to shade (in)

Schum|mer|stun|de F *(N Ger)* twilight hour

Schum|me|rung [ˈʃʊmərʊŋ] F -, -en *(Geog)* shading

schumm|rig [ˈʃʊmrıç] ADJ = **schummerig**

schund *(rare) pret von* **schinden**

Schund [ʃʊnt] M -(e)s [-dəs], *no pl (pej)* trash, rubbish *(Brit)*, garbage; **was für ~/einen ~ hast du denn da?** what's that trash/trashy book you're reading? → **Schmutz b**

Schund-: **Schund|li|te|ra|tur** F trash, trashy *or* pulp literature; **Schund|ro|man** M trashy *or* pulp novel

Schun|kel|lied NT German drinking song

schun|keln [ˈʃʊŋkln] VI to link arms and sway from side to side

Schup|fen [ˈʃʊpfn] M -s, - *(esp S Ger)* shed

Schup|fer [ˈʃʊpfɐ] M -s, - *(Aus)* = **Schubs**

Schupf|nu|deln [ˈʃʊpf-] PL *(Cook) finger-shaped potato dumplings*

Schu|po [ˈʃuːpo] F -, *no pl abbr von* **Schutzpolizei**

Schu|po M -s, -s *(dated inf) abbr von* **Schutzpolizist** cop *(inf)*, copper *(esp Brit inf)*

Schup|pe [ˈʃʊpə] F -, -n **a** *(Bot, Zool)* scale; *(von Ritterrüstung, Tierpanzer)* plate; **es fiel mir wie ~n von den Augen** the scales fell from my eyes **b** **Schuppen** PL *(= Kopfschuppen)* dandruff *sing*

schup|pen [ˈʃʊpn] **VT** *Fische* to scale **VR** to flake

Schup|pen [ˈʃʊpn] M -s, - **a** shed; *(= Flugzeugschuppen)* hangar **b** *(inf) (= Haus, Wohnung etc)* joint *(inf)*, hole *(pej inf)*, hovel *(pej)*; *(= übles Lokal)* dive *(inf)* **c** *(sl: = Disko etc)* club

Schup|pen-: **schup|pen|ar|tig** **ADJ** scale-like **ADV** **die Ziegel sind ~ angeordnet** the tiles are arranged so that they overlap; **Schup|pen|bil|dung** F, *no pl* dandruff; **Schup|pen|flech|te** F *(Med)* psoriasis *(spec)*; **schup|pen|för|mig** ADJ ADV = **schuppenartig**; **Schup|pen|pan|zer** M scale armour *(Brit) or* armor *(US)*; **Schup|pen|tier** NT scaly anteater

schup|pig [ˈʃʊpıç] **ADJ** scaly; *(= abblätternd auch)* flaking **ADV** **die Haut löst sich ~ ab** his *etc* skin is flaking (off); **~ abblättern** to scale off

Schups [ʃʊps] M -es, -e = **Schubs**

schup|sen [ˈʃʊpsn] VTI *(inf)* = **schubsen**

Schur [ʃuːɐ] F -, -en *(= das Scheren)* shearing; *(= geschorene Wolle)* clip

Schür|ei|sen NT poker

schü|ren [ˈʃyːrən] VT **a** *Feuer, Glut* to rake, to poke **b** *(fig)* to stir up; *Zorn, Eifersucht, Leidenschaft, Hass* to fan the flames of

schür|fen [ˈʃʏrfn] **VI** *(Min)* to prospect *(nach* for); **tief ~** *(fig)* to dig deep **VT** *Bodenschätze* to mine **VR** to graze oneself; **sich** *(dat)* **die Haut ~, sich ~** to graze oneself *or* one's skin; **sich am Knie ~** to graze one's knee

Schürf-: **Schürf|gru|be** F, **Schürf|loch** NT *(Min)* test pit; **Schürf|recht** NT mining rights *pl*; **Schürf|wun|de** F graze, abrasion

Schür|ha|ken M poker

schu|ri|geln [ˈʃuːriːgln] VT *(inf) (= hart anfahren)* to lay into *(inf)*; *(= schikanieren)* to bully

Schur|ke [ˈʃʊrkə] M -n, -n, **Schur|kin** [ˈʃʊrkın] F -, -nen *(dated)* villain, scoundrel, rogue

Schur|ken|staat M *(Pol)* rogue state *or* nation

Schur|ken|streich M, **Schur|ken|tat** F, **Schur|ke|rei** [ʃʊrkəˈrai] F -, -en *(old)* (piece of) villainy

schur|kisch [ˈʃʊrkıʃ] *(dated)* **ADJ** base, despicable **ADV** despicably

schur|ren [ˈʃʊrən] VI *(dial) (Schlitten)* to grate; **mit den Füßen ~** to shuffle one's feet; *(beim Gehen)* to drag one's feet

Schur|wol|le [ˈʃuːɐ-] F virgin wool; **„reine ~"** "pure new wool"

Schurz [ʃʊrts] M -es, -e loincloth; *(von Schmied, Arbeiter etc, dial)* apron

Schür|ze [ˈʃʏrtsə] F -, -n apron; *(= Frauenschürze, Kinderschürze mit Latz auch)* pinafore, pinny *(Brit inf)*; *(= Kittelschürze)* overall; **sich** *(dat)* **eine ~ umbinden** to put an apron on; **er ist hinter jeder ~ her** *(dated inf)*, **er läuft jeder ~ nach** *(dated inf)* he runs after anything in a skirt *(inf)*

schür|zen [ˈʃʏrtsn] VT **a** *(dated) Rock* to gather (up) **b** *(geh: = schlingen) Knoten* to tie; *Faden* to knot, to tie a knot in **c** *(geh: = aufwerfen)* **die Lippen/den Mund ~** *(zum Pfeifen)* to purse one's lips; *(verführerisch)* to pout; **ihr geschürzter Mund** her pursed lips; her pout

Schür|zen-: **Schür|zen|band** [-bant] NT *pl* **-bänder** = **Schürzenzipfel**; **Schür|zen|jä|ger** M *(inf)* philanderer, one for the girls *(inf)*; **Schür|zen|zip|fel** M apron string; **er hängt der Mutter noch am ~** he's still tied to his mother's apron strings

Schuss [ʃʊs] M **-es, ¨-e** [ˈʃʏsə] **a** shot; *(= Schuss Munition)* round; **sechs ~** or **Schüsse** six shots/rounds; **einen ~ auf jdn/etw abgeben** to fire a shot at sb/sth; **zum ~ kommen** to have a chance to shoot; **ein ~ ins Schwarze** *(lit, fig)* a bull's-eye; **weit (ab) vom ~ sein** *(fig inf)* to be miles from where the action is *(inf)*; **er ist keinen ~ Pulver wert** *(fig)* he is not worth tuppence (*Brit inf*) or two cents (*US inf*); **das war ein (schöner) ~ vor den Bug** *(fig)* that was a warning not to be ignored; **der ~ ging nach hinten los** it backfired; **ein ~ in den Ofen** *(inf)* a complete waste of time
b *(Min: = Sprengung)* blast, charge
c *(Ftbl)* kick; *(esp zum Tor)* shot; **zum ~ kommen** to get the ball; *(zum Tor)* to get a chance to shoot
d *(Ski)* schuss; **im ~ fahren** to schuss
e *(= Spritzer) (von Wein, Essig etc)* dash; *(von Whisky)* shot; *(von Humor, Leichtsinn etc)* touch, dash
f *(Tex: = Querfäden)* weft, woof
g *(inf: mit Rauschgift)* shot; **(sich** *dat*) **einen ~ setzen** to shoot up *(inf)*; **sich** *(dat)* **den goldenen ~ setzen** to OD *(inf)*
h *(inf)* **in ~ sein/kommen** to be in/get into (good) shape; *(Mensch, Sportler auch)* to be on form/get into good form; *(Schüler, Klasse)* to be/get up to the mark *(esp Brit)* or up to snuff; *(Party)* to be going well/get going; **etw in ~ bringen/halten** to knock sth into shape/keep sth in good shape; *Schulklasse* to bring/keep sth up to the mark *(esp Brit)* or up to snuff; *Party* to get/keep sth going
i *(sl)* **einen ~ (an der Waffel) haben** to be off one's nut *(inf)*

Schuss-: **Schuss|be|reich** M (firing) range; **im ~** within range; **schuss|be|reit** ADJ ready to fire; *Gewehr auch* cocked

Schus|sel [ˈʃʊsl] M **-s, -** *(inf)* or f **-, -n** *(inf)* dolt *(inf)*; *(zerstreut)* scatterbrain *(inf)*; *(ungeschickt)* clumsy clot *(inf)*

Schüs|sel [ˈʃʏsl] F **-, -n** bowl; *(= Servierschüssel auch, = Satellitenschüssel)* dish; *(= Waschschüssel)* basin; **vor leeren ~n sitzen** *(nach dem Essen)* to sit staring at the dirty dishes; *(in Notzeit)* to go hungry

schus|se|lig [ˈʃʊsəlɪç] ADJ *(= zerstreut)* scatterbrained *(inf)*, muddleheaded (*Brit inf*); *(= ungeschickt)* clumsy, all thumbs *pred*

Schus|se|lig|keit F **-, -en** *(= Zerstreutheit)* muddleheadedness (*Brit inf*), emptyheadedness; *(= Ungeschick)* clumsiness

schus|seln [ˈʃʊsln] VI *(inf) (= zerstreut sein)* to be scatterbrained *(inf)* or muddle-headed (*Brit inf*); *(= ungeschickt vorgehen)* to be clumsy; *(= sich ungeschickt bewegen)* to bumble *(inf)*

Schus|ser [ˈʃʊsɐ] M **-s, -** *(dial)* marble

Schuss-: **Schuss|fa|den** M *(Tex)* weft thread; **Schuss|fahrt** F *(Ski)* schuss; *(= das Schussfahren)* schussing; **Schuss|feld** NT field of fire; *(= Übungsplatz)* firing range; **schuss|fest** ADJ *Glas, Weste* bulletproof; **schuss|frei** ADJ clear for firing; **Schuss|ge|schwin|dig|keit** F velocity *(of bullet etc)*; **Schuss|ka|nal** M *(Med)* path of a/the bullet through the body

schuss|lig [ˈʃʊslɪç] ADJ *(inf)* = **schusselig**

Schuss|lig|keit F **-, -en** *(inf)* = **Schusseligkeit**

Schuss-: **Schuss|li|nie** F line of fire; *(fig auch)* firing line; **Schuss|rich|tung** F direction of fire; **schuss|si|cher** ADJ *Glas, Weste* bulletproof; **Schuss|ver|let|zung** F bullet wound; **Schuss|waf|fe** F firearm; **Schuss|waf|fen|ge|brauch** M *(form)* use of firearms; **Schuss|wech|sel** M exchange of shots or fire; **Schuss|wei|te** F range (of fire); **in/außer ~** within/out of range; **Schuss|win|kel** M angle of fire; **Schuss|wun|de** F bullet wound; **Schuss|zahl** F *(Tex)* number of weft threads

Schus|ter [ˈʃuːstɐ] M **-s, -**, **Schus|te|rin** [-ərɪn] F **-, -nen** shoemaker; *(= Flickschuster)* cobbler; **auf ~s Rappen** *(hum)* by shanks's pony *(Brit)* or mare *(US)*; **~, bleib bei deinem Leisten!** *(Prov)* cobbler, stick to your last *(Prov)*

Schus|ter-: **Schus|ter|ah|le** F shoemaker's awl; **Schus|ter|draht** M waxed thread

Schus|te|rei [ʃuːstəˈrai] F **-, -en** **a** *(Werkstatt)* shoemaker's; *(von Flickschuster)* cobbler's **b** *(pej inf: = Pfuscherei)* botching *(inf)*

Schus|ter|hand|werk NT shoemaking, cobbling

Schus|te|rin [-ərɪn] F → **Schuster**

Schus|ter|jun|ge M **a** *(old) (= Schusterlehrling)* shoemaker's apprentice; *(= Flickschuster)* cobbler's apprentice **b** *(Typ)* widow

schus|tern [ˈʃuːstɐn] VI *(= Schusterarbeit machen)* to cobble or repair or mend shoes VT *(pej inf: = zusammenpfuschen)* to cobble together *(inf)*

Schus|ter-: **Schus|ter|pech** NT shoemaker's or cobbler's wax; **Schus|ter|pfriem** M, **Schus|ter|pfrie|men** M shoemaker's awl; **Schus|ter|werk|statt** F shoemaker's workshop; *(Flickschuster)* cobbler's workshop

Schu|te [ˈʃuːtə] F **-, -n** **a** *(Naut)* lighter **b** *(= Damenhut)* poke (bonnet)

Schutt [ʃʊt] M **-(e)s,** *no pl (= Trümmer, Bauschutt)* rubble; *(Geol)* debris, detritus *(spec)*; **„Schutt abladen verboten"** "no tipping" *(Brit)*, "no dumping" *(US)*; **eine Stadt in ~ und Asche legen** to reduce a town to rubble; **in ~ und Asche liegen** to be in ruins

Schutt|ab|la|de|platz M tip *(Brit)*, dump

Schütt-: **Schütt|be|ton** M cast concrete; **Schütt|bo|den** M strawloft; *(für Getreide)* granary

Schüt|te [ˈʃʏtə] F **-, -n** **a** *(= Bund)* stock **b** *(Behälter) wall-mounted drawer-like canister for sugar, flour etc*

Schüt|tel-: **Schüt|tel|be|cher** M (cocktail) shaker; **Schüt|tel|frost** M *(Med)* shivering fit, fit of the shivers *(inf)*; **Schüt|tel|läh|mung** F *(Med)* Parkinson's disease

schüt|teln [ˈʃʏtln] VT to shake; *(= rütteln)* to shake about, to jolt (about); **den** or **mit dem Kopf ~** to shake one's head; **von Angst geschüttelt werden** to be gripped with fear; **von Fieber geschüttelt werden** to be racked with fever → **Hand a** VR to shake oneself; *(vor Kälte)* to shiver (*vor* with); *(vor Ekel)* to shudder (*vor* with, in); **sich vor Lachen ~** to shake with laughter

Schüt|tel-: **Schüt|tel|reim** M goat rhyme, *rhyme in which the consonants of the rhyming syllables are transposed in the next line*; **Schüt|tel|rut|sche** F *(Tech)* vibrating chute; **Schüt|tel|sieb** NT riddle

schüt|ten [ˈʃʏtn] VT to tip; *Flüssigkeiten* to pour; *(= verschütten)* to spill VI *impers (inf)* **es schüttet** it's pouring (with rain), it's pouring (down), it's bucketing (down) (*Brit inf*), it's coming down in buckets (*US inf*)

schüt|ter [ˈʃʏtɐ] ADJ *Haar, Schneedecke, Pflanzen* thin; *Gruppe* small and pitiful

Schütt|gut NT, *no pl* bulk goods *pl*

Schutt-: **Schutt|hal|de** F *(= Schutthaufen)* rubble tip *(Brit)* or heap; *(Geol)* scree slope; **Schutt|hau|fen** M pile or heap of rubble; **etw in einen ~ verwandeln** to reduce sth to a pile of rubble; **Schutt|ke|gel** M *(Geol)* cone of scree or debris; **Schutt|mul|de** F skip *(Brit)*, Dumpster® *(US)*; **Schutt|platz** M tip *(Brit)*, dump

Schütt-: **Schütt|stein** M *(S Ger, Sw)* sink; **Schütt|stroh** NT bedding straw

Schutz [ʃʊts] M **-es,** *no pl* protection (*vor +dat, gegen* against, from); *(= Zuflucht auch)* shelter, refuge (*vor +dat, gegen* from); *(der Natur, Umwelt etc)* protection, conservation; *(esp Mil: = Deckung)* cover; **jdn um ~ bitten** to ask sb for protection; **~ suchend** seeking protection; *(nach Obdach)* seeking refuge or shelter; **bei jdm ~ suchen** to look to sb for protection, to seek shelter or refuge with sb; **unter einem Baum ~ suchen** to shelter under a tree, to take or seek refuge under a tree; **im ~(e) der Nacht** or **Dunkelheit/des Artilleriefeuers** under cover of night or darkness/artillery fire; **zum ~ von Leib und Leben** for the protection of life and limb; **jdn/etw als ~ mitnehmen** to take sb/sth with one for protection; **zum ~ der Augen** to protect the eyes; **der ~ der Privatsphäre** respect for privacy; **jdn in ~ nehmen** *(fig)* to take sb's part, to stand up for sb; **etw unter ~ stellen** *(= unter Denkmalschutz, Naturschutz)* to give sth protected status; **zu ~ und Trutz zusammenstehen** *(old, liter)* to stand together

Schutz-: **Schutz|an|strich** M protective coat; **Schutz|an|zug** M protective clothing *no indef art, no pl*; **Schutz|är|mel** M sleeve-protector; **Schutz|auf|sicht** F *(Jur)* supervision by a social worker; **schutz|be|dürf|tig** ADJ in need of protection; **Schutz|be|dürf|tig|keit** F need for protection; **Schutz|be|foh|le|ne(r)** [-bəfoːlənə] MF *decl as adj* protégé; *(= esp Kind)* charge; **Schutz|be|haup|tung** F lie to cover oneself; **Schutz|blech** NT mudguard; **Schutz|brief** M **a** (letter of) safe-conduct **b** = **Auslandsschutzbrief**; **Schutz|bril|le** F protective goggles *pl*; **Schutz|bünd|nis** NT defensive alliance; **Schutz|dach** NT porch; *(an Haltestelle)* shelter; **Schutz|deck** NT shelter deck

Schüt|ze [ˈʃʏtsə] M **-n, -n** **a** marksman; *(= Schießsportler)* rifleman; *(Hunt)* hunter; *(= Bogenschütze)* archer; *(Hist)* bowman, archer; *(Ftbl: = Torschütze)* scorer; **er ist der beste ~** he is the best shot **b** *(Mil) (= Dienstgrad)* private; *(= Maschinengewehrschütze)* gunner **c** *(Astrol, Astron)* Sagittarius *no art*; **sie ist ~** she's Sagittarius or a Sagittarian **d** *(= Weberschiffchen)* shuttle

schüt|zen [ˈʃʏtsn] VT to protect (*vor +dat, gegen* from, against); *Umwelt auch* to conserve; *(= Zuflucht bieten auch)* to shelter (*vor +dat, gegen* from); *(= absichern: Versicherung etc auch)* to safeguard; *(esp Mil: = Deckung geben)* to cover; **urheberrechtlich geschützt** protected by copyright; **gesetzlich geschützt** registered; **patentrechtlich geschützt** patented; **vor Hitze/Sonnenlicht ~!** keep away from heat/sunlight; **vor Nässe ~!** keep dry; **Gott schütze dich!** *(old)* (may) the Lord protect or keep you → *auch* **geschützt**
VI to give or offer protection (*vor +dat, gegen* from, against); *(= Zuflucht bieten auch)* to give or offer shelter (*vor +dat, gegen* from); *(esp Mil: = Deckung geben)* to give cover
VR to protect oneself (*vor +dat, gegen* from, against); *(= sich absichern auch)* to safeguard oneself (*vor +dat, gegen* against); **er weiß sich zu ~** he knows how to look after himself

Schüt|zen [ˈʃʏtsn] M **-s, -** *(Tex)* shuttle

Schüt|zen-: **Schüt|zen|an|ger** M = **Schützenwiese**; **Schüt|zen|bru|der** M member of a rifle club

schüt|zend ADJ protective; **ein ~es Dach** *(gegen Wetter)* a shelter; **ein ~es Dach über sich** *(dat)* **haben** to be under cover; **der ~e Hafen** *(lit)* the protection of the harbour *(Brit)* or harbor *(US)*; *(fig)* a/the safe haven; **seine ~e Hand über jdn halten** or **breiten** to take sb under one's wing ADV protectively

Schüt|zen|fest NT *fair featuring shooting matches*

SCHÜTZENFEST

The **Schützenfest** is celebrated in rural areas, particularly in Austria and Southern Germany. Archery competitions are held and the winners become the **Schützenkönig** and **Schützenkönigin**. Their prize is usually a chain which is placed around their neck and which they keep until the following year. Usually there is also a parade and a small fair.

Schutz|en|gel M guardian angel

Schüt|zen-: **Schüt|zen|ge|sell|schaft** F, **Schüt|zen|gil|de** F rifle *or* shooting club; **Schüt|zen|gra|ben** M trench; **Schüt|zen|haus** NT clubhouse *(of a rifle club)*; **Schüt|zen|hil|fe** F *(fig)* support; **jdm ~ geben** to back sb up, to support sb; **Schüt|zen|ket|te** F *(Mil)* firing line; **Schüt|zen|kö|nig(in)** M(F) *champion rifleman/-woman at a Schützenfest*; **Schüt|zen|li|nie** F *(Mil)* firing line; **Schüt|zen|loch** NT *(Mil)* foxhole; **Schüt|zen|pan|zer|(wa|gen)** M armoured *(Brit) or* armored *(US)* personnel carrier; **Schüt|zen|platz** M = **Schützenwiese**; **Schüt|zen|schwes|ter** F member of a rifle club; **Schüt|zen|ver|ein** M rifle *or* shooting club; **Schüt|zen|wie|se** F *fairground at which a rifle club holds its competitions*; **Schüt|zen|zug** M procession *(Brit) or* parade of riflemen

Schutz-: **Schutz|far|be** F, **Schutz|fär|bung** F *(Biol)* protective *or* adaptive colouring *(Brit) or* coloring *(US)*; **Schutz|film** M protective layer *or* coating; **Schutz|fo|lie** F protective film; **Schutz|frist** F term of copyright; **Schutz|ge|biet** NT *(Pol)* protectorate; **Schutz|ge|bühr** F (token) fee; **Schutz|geist** M *(Myth)* protecting *or* tutelary *(liter)* spirit; **Schutz|ge|län|der** NT guardrail; **Schutz|geld** NT protection money; **Schutz|geld|er|pres|sung** F extortion of protection money; **Schutz|ge|wahr|sam** M *(Jur)* protective custody; **Schutz|git|ter** NT *(um Denkmal etc)* protective barrier; *(vor Maschine, Fenster, Tür)* protective grill(e); *(um Leute zu schützen)* safety barrier/grill(e); *(vor Kamin)* (fire)guard; *(Elec)* screen grid; **Schutz|gott** M *(Myth)* tutelary god *(liter)*; **Schutz|göt|tin** F *(Myth)* tutelary goddess *(liter)*; **Schutz|ha|fen** M port of refuge; *(= Winterhafen)* winter harbour *(Brit) or* harbor *(US)*; **Schutz|haft** F *(Jur)* protective custody; *(Pol)* preventive detention; **Schutz|hand|schuh** M protective glove; **Schutz|hau|be** F protective hood; *(für Schreibmaschine)* cover; **Schutz|haut** F protective covering; **Schutz|hei|li|ge(r)** MF *decl as adj* patron saint; **Schutz|helm** M safety helmet; *(von Bauarbeiter auch)* hard hat *(inf)*; **Schutz|herr** M patron; **Schutz|her|rin** F patron, patroness; **Schutz|herr|schaft** F *(Pol)* protection, protectorate; *(= Patronat)* patronage; **Schutz|hül|le** F protective cover; *(= Buchumschlag)* dust cover *or* jacket; **Schutz|hüt|te** F shelter, refuge; **schutz|imp|fen** *pret* **schutzimpfte**, *ptp* **schutzgeimpft** VT to vaccinate, to inoculate; **Schutz|imp|fung** F vaccination, inoculation

Schüt|zin [ˈʃʏtsɪn] F -, -nen markswoman; *(= Schießsportlerin)* riflewoman; *(Hunt)* huntress; *(= Bogenschützin)* archer; *(Ftbl: = Torschützin)* scorer

Schutz-: **Schutz|kap|pe** F (protective) cap; **Schutz|kar|ton** M cardboard box; *(für Buch)* slipcase; **Schutz|klau|sel** F protective *or* let-out clause; **Schutz|klei|dung** F protective clothing; **Schutz|kon|takt** M *(Elec)* safety contact; **Schutz|kon|takt|(steck)|do|se** F *(Elec)* safety socket; **Schutz|kon|takt|ste|cker** M *(Elec)* safety plug; **Schutz|leis|te** F protective strip; *(bei Maschine)* guardrail

Schütz|ling [ˈʃʏtslɪŋ] M -s, -e protégé; *(esp Kind)* charge

schutz|los ADJ *(= wehrlos)* defenceless *(Brit)*, defenseless *(US)*; *(gegen Kälte etc)* without protection, unprotected ADV **jdm/einer Sache ~ ausgeliefert** *or* **preisgegeben sein** to be at the mercy of sb/sth, to be defenceless *(Brit) or* defenseless *(US)*/without protection against sb/sth

Schutz|lo|sig|keit F -, *no pl* defencelessness *(Brit)*, defenselessness *(US)*

Schutz-: **Schutz|macht** F *(Pol)* protecting power, protector; **Schutz|mann** M *pl* **-leute** policeman, constable *(Brit)*; **Schutz|man|tel** M *(Tech)* protective casing; *(gegen Strahlen)* radiation shield; *(der Haut)* protective layer; **Schutz|mar|ke** F trademark; **Schutz|mas|ke** F (protective) mask; **Schutz|maß|nah|me** F precaution, precautionary measure; *(vorbeugend)* preventive measure; **Schutz|mau|er** F protecting wall; *(von Festung)* defensive wall; **Schutz|me|cha|nis|mus** M *(esp Psych)* protective mechanism; **Schutz|mit|tel** NT means of protection *sing*; *(Substanz)* protective substance, prophylactic *(Med)* *(gegen* for); **Schutz|netz** NT *(im Zirkus)* safety net; *(an Damenfahrrad)* skirt guard; *(gegen Stechmücken etc)* mosquito net; **Schutz|pat|ron** M, **Schutz|pat|ro|nin** F patron saint; **Schutz|po|li|zei** F *(form)* police force, constabulary *(Brit form)*; **Schutz|po|li|zist(in)** M(F) *(form)* police officer, (police) constable *(Brit)*, policeman/-woman; **Schutz|pro|gramm** NT a conservation programme *(Brit) or* program *(US)* b *(Comput) (= Virenschutzprogramm)* antivirus program; *(= Datenschutzprogramm)* privacy and security program; **Schutz|raum** M shelter; **Schutz|schicht** F protective layer; *(= Überzug)* protective coating; **Schutz|schild** M *pl* **-schilde** shield; *(an Geschützen)* gun shield; **Schutz|schirm** M *(Tech)* protective screen; **Schutz|schrift** F *(Jur)* precautionary writing of defence *(Brit) or* defense *(US)*; *(patent law)* caveat; **Schutz|staf|fel** F *(Hist)* SS; **schutz|su|chend** ADJ → **Schutz**; **Schutz|trup|pe** F protection force; *(Hist)* colonial army *or* force; **Schutz|um|schlag** M dust cover *or* jacket; **Schutz-und-Trutz-Bünd|nis** NT *(old)* defensive and offensive alliance; **Schutz|ver|band** M a protective association; **der ~ der ...** *(in Namen)* the Association for the Protection of ... b *(Med)* protective bandage *or* dressing; **Schutz|ver|let|zung** F *(Comput)* protection error *or* fault; **Schutz|vor|rich|tung** F safety device; **Schutz|wald** M barrier woodland; **Schutz|wall** M protective wall *(gegen* to keep out), barrier; **Schutz|weg** M *(Aus)* pedestrian crossing *(Brit)*, crosswalk *(US)*; **Schutz|wes|te** F protective jacket; *(= schusssichere Weste)* bulletproof vest; **schutz|wür|dig** ADJ *Interessen* worth protecting; *Gebäude, Sitten, Status* worth preserving; **Schutz|wür|dig|keit** F **die ~ eines Gebäudes in Frage stellen** to question whether a building is worth preserving; **die ~ des Lebens sollte im Grundgesetz festgeschrieben werden** it should be laid down in the constitution that life must be protected; **Schutz|zoll** M protective duty *or* tariff; **Schutz|zo|ne** F *(= Sicherheitszone, um Gefahrenherd)* safety zone; *(= militärische Schutzzone)* safe haven; *(= Naturschutzzone)* conservation area; *(im Seerecht)* exclusion zone

Schwa [ʃva:] NT -s, *no pl (Ling)* schwa

schwab|be|lig [ˈʃvabəlɪç] ADJ *(inf) Körperteil* flabby; *Gelee* wobbly

schwab|beln [ˈʃvabln] VI *(inf)* to wobble (about)

Schwab|bel|schei|be F *(Tech)* buffing wheel

Schwa|be [ˈʃva:bə] M -n, -n, **Schwä|bin** [ˈʃvɛ:bɪn] F -, -nen Swabian

schwä|beln [ˈʃvɛ:bln] VI *(inf)* to speak Swabian *or* the Swabian dialect; *(mit Akzent)* to speak with a Swabian accent

Schwa|ben [ˈʃva:bn] NT -s Swabia

Schwa|ben|streich M piece of folly

Schwä|bin [ˈʃvɛ:bɪn] F -, -nen Swabian (woman/girl)

schwä|bisch [ˈʃvɛ:bɪʃ] ADJ Swabian; **die Schwäbische Alb** the Swabian mountains *pl*; **das Schwäbische Meer** *(hum)* Lake Constance

schwach [ʃvax] ADJ *comp* **=er** [ˈʃvɛçɐ], *superl* **=ste(r, s)** [ˈʃvɛçstə] weak *(auch Gram)*; *Mensch, Greis, Begründung, Versuch, Aufführung, Alibi, Widerstand auch* feeble; *Konstitution auch* frail; *Gesundheit, Beteiligung, Gedächtnis* poor; *Ton, Anzeichen, Hoffnung, Bewegung* faint, slight; *Gehör* poor, dull; *Stimme* weak, faint; *Licht* poor, dim; *Wind* light; *(Comm) Nachfrage, Geschäft* slack, poor; **~e Augen** weak *or* poor (eye)sight; **das ist ein ~es Bild** *(inf) or* **eine ~e Leistung** *(inf)* that's a poor show *(inf)*; **ein ~es Lob** faint praise; **jds ~e Seite/Stelle** sb's weak point/spot; **ein ~er Trost** cold *or* small comfort; **in einem ~en Augenblick, in einer ~en Stunde** in a moment of weakness, in a weak moment; **jdn ~ machen** → **schwachmachen**; **in etw** *(dat)* **~ sein** to be weak in sth; **auf ~en Beinen** *or* **Füßen stehen** *(fig)* to be on shaky ground; *(Theorie)* to be shaky; **alles, was in meinen ~en Kräften steht** everything within my power; **jdn an seiner ~en** *or* **schwächsten Stelle treffen** to strike at *or* hit sb's weak spot; **mir wird ~** *(lit)* I feel faint; *(fig inf)* it makes me sick *(inf)*; **nur nicht ~ werden!** don't weaken!; **schwächer werden** to grow weaker, to weaken; *(Augen)* to fail, to grow worse; *(Stimme)* to grow fainter; *(Licht)* to (grow) dim; *(Ton)* to fade; *(Nachfrage)* to fall off, to slacken; **die Schwachen** the weak; **der Schwächere** the weaker (person); *(gegenüber Gegner)* the underdog

ADV *comp* **=er**, *superl* **am =sten** a *(= leicht) schlagen* weakly; *vibrieren, radioaktiv* slightly; *spüren, riechen, hören* barely

b *(= spärlich) besucht, bestückt* poorly; **~ besiedelt** *or* **bevölkert** sparsely populated; **das Stadion war nur ~ besetzt** there were only a few people in the stadium

c *(= geringfügig) klatschen* weakly; *sich interessieren* slightly; *sich beteiligen* very little; **sich immer schwächer beteiligen** to participate less and less; **~ aktiv** *(Atommüll etc)* low-level; **~ radioaktiv** with low-level radioactivity; **~ betont** weakly stressed; **~ bewegt** *(Meer)* gently rolling; **schon bei ~ bewegtem Meer werde ich seekrank** as soon as there's the slightest swell I get seasick

d *(= mild) salzen, süßen* slightly; *würzen* lightly; *pfeffern* mildly

schwach-: **schwach|ak|tiv** ADJ → **schwach ADV c**; **schwach|be|sie|delt** ADJ → **schwach ADV b**; **schwach|be|tont** ADJ → **schwach ADV c**; **schwach|be|völ|kert** ADJ → **schwach ADV b**; **schwach|be|wegt** ADJ → **schwach ADV c**; **schwach|brüs|tig** [-brʏstɪç] ADJ *(hum)* feeble

Schwä|che [ˈʃvɛçə] ✪ 34.2 F -, -n a *no pl* weakness; *(von Stimme)* feebleness, faintness; *(von Licht)* dimness; *(von Wind)* lightness; **sie brach vor ~ zusammen** she was so weak she collapsed; **die zunehmende ~ seines Gehörs** his increasing deafness b *(= Schwächeanfall)* feeling of weakness c *(= Nachteil, Fehler)* weakness d *(= Vorliebe)* weakness *(für* for) e *(= Charaktermangel)* weakness, failing; **menschliche ~n** human failings *or* frailties; **jeder Mensch hat seine ~n** we all have our little weaknesses *or* failings

Schwä|che-: **Schwä|che|an|fall** M sudden feeling of weakness; **Schwä|che|ge|fühl** NT feeling of weakness

schwä|cheln [ˈʃvɛçln] VI *(inf)* to weaken slightly; **geistig ~** to begin to go a bit gaga; **der Dollar schwächelt** the dollar is showing signs of weakness

schwä|chen [ˈʃvɛçn] VT *(lit, fig)* to weaken VR to weaken oneself VI **etw schwächt** sth has a weakening effect

Schwä|che-: **Schwä|che|punkt** M low point; **einen ~ erreichen** to reach a low point *or* a low ebb; **Schwä|che|zu|stand** M condition of weakness *or* debility *(spec)*, weak condition

Schwach|heit F -, -en a *no pl (fig)* weakness, frailty; **~, dein Name ist Weib** *(prov)* frailty, thy name is woman! *(prov)* b *no pl (rare)* = **Schwäche a** c *(inf)* **bilde dir nur keine ~en ein!** don't fool *or* kid yourself! *(inf)*

Schwach-: **Schwach|kopf** M *(inf)* dimwit *(inf)*, idiot, thickie *(Brit inf)*; **schwach|köp|fig** *(inf)* ADJ daft *(Brit inf)*, idiotic ADV idiotically

schwäch|lich [ˈʃvɛçlɪç] ADJ weakly; *(= zart auch)* puny

Schwäch|lich|keit F -, *no pl* weakness

Schwäch|ling [ˈʃvɛçlɪŋ] M **-s, -e** *(lit, fig)* weakling

Schwach-: **schwach+ma|chen** VT *sep* **jdn ~** *(inf, fig)* to soften sb up, to talk sb round *(esp Brit)*; **mach mich nicht schwach!** *(inf)* don't say that! *(inf)*; **Schwach|ma|ti|kus** [ʃvaxˈmaːtikʊs] M **-, -se**, **Schwach|ma|ti|ker** [ʃvaxˈmaːtikɐ] M **-s, -** *(hum inf)* weakling; **Schwach|punkt** M weak point; **schwach|ra|dio|ak|tiv** ADJ → **schwach ADV c**; **schwach|sich|tig** [-zɪçtɪç] ADJ *(Med)* poor- or weak-sighted; **Schwach|sich|tig|keit** F **-**, *no pl (Med)* poor vision, amblyopia *(spec)*; **Schwach|sinn** M *(Med)* mental deficiency, feeble-mindedness *(dated)*; *(fig inf)* (= *unsinnige Tat*) idiocy *no indef art*; (= *Quatsch*) rubbish *(Brit inf)*, garbage; **leichter/mittelschwerer/schwerer ~** mild/severe to moderate/profound mental deficiency, moronism/imbecility/idiocy *(Med)*; **schwach|sin|nig** ADJ *(Med)* mentally deficient, feeble-minded *(dated)*; *(fig inf)* daft *(Brit inf)*, idiotic ADV *(fig inf)* idiotically; **Schwach|sin|ni|ge(r)** [ˈʃvaxzɪnɪgə] MF *decl as adj* mental defective; *(fig inf)* moron *(inf)*, imbecile *(inf)*; **Schwach|stel|le** F weak point

Schwach|strom M *(Elec)* low-voltage *or* weak current

Schwach|strom-: **Schwach|strom|lei|tung** F low-voltage (current) line; **Schwach|strom|tech|nik** F *(dated)* communications engineering *or* technology

Schwä|chung [ˈʃvɛçʊŋ] F **-, -en** weakening

schwach+wer|den VI *sep irreg aux sein (fig)* → **schwach ADJ**

schwach|win|dig ADV **morgen ~** *(Met)* light winds tomorrow

Schwa|de [ˈʃvaːdə] F **-, -n** swath(e), windrow *(spec)*

Schwa|den [ˈʃvaːdn] M **-s, - a** *usu pl* (= *Dunst*) cloud **b** (= *Abgemähtes*) swath(e), windrow *(spec)*

Schwad|ron [ʃvaˈdroːn] F **-, -en** *(Mil Hist)* squadron

Schwad|ro|neur [ʃvadroˈnøːɐ] M **-s, -e** blusterer

schwad|ro|nie|ren [ʃvadroˈniːrən] *ptp* **schwadroniert** VI to bluster

Schwa|fe|lei [ʃvafəˈlai] F **-, -en** *(pej inf)* drivel *no pl (inf)*, twaddle *no pl (inf)*; (= *das Schwafeln*) drivelling *(Brit) or* driveling *(US) or* blathering on *(inf)*

schwa|feln [ˈʃvaːfln] *(pej inf)* VI to drivel (on), to blather (on), to talk drivel *(all inf)*; *(in einer Prüfung)* to waffle *(inf)* VT **dummes Zeug ~** to talk drivel *(inf)*; **was schwafelst du da?** what are you drivelling *(Brit) or* driveling *(US) or* blathering on about? *(inf)*

Schwaf|ler [ˈʃvaːflɐ] M **-s, -**, **Schwaf|le|rin** [-ərɪn] F **-, -nen** *(pej inf)* windbag, gasbag, blatherer *(all inf)*

Schwa|ger [ˈʃvaːgɐ] M **-s, ⸚** [ˈʃvɛːgɐ] **a** brother-in-law **b** *(obs: = Postillion)* coachman

Schwä|ge|rin [ˈʃvɛːgərɪn] F **-, -nen** sister-in-law

Schwä|ger|schaft [ˈʃvɛːgɐʃaft] F **-, -en** *(Jur)* relationship by marriage, affinity *(spec)*

Schwai|ge [ˈʃvaigə] F **-, -n** *(S Ger, Aus)* Alpine dairy hut

Schwai|ger [ˈʃvaigɐ] M **-s, -** *(S Ger, Aus)* (Alpine) dairyman

Schwai|ge|rin F **-, -nen** *(S Ger, Aus)* (Alpine) dairymaid

Schwälb|chen [ˈʃvɛlpçən] NT **-s, -** *dim von* **Schwalbe**

Schwal|be [ˈʃvalbə] F **-, -n** swallow; **eine ~ machen** *(Ftbl sl)* to take a dive; **eine ~ macht noch keinen Sommer** *(Prov)* one swallow doesn't make a summer *(Prov)*

Schwal|ben-: **Schwal|ben|nest** NT **a** swallow's nest **b** *(Mil)* (bandsman's) epaulette **c** *(Naut)* sponson **d** *(Cook)* bird's nest soup; **Schwal|ben|nes|ter|sup|pe** F bird's nest soup; **Schwal|ben|schwanz** M **a** *(Zool)* swallowtail (butterfly) **b** *(inf)* (= *Frack*) swallow-tailed coat, swallowtails *pl*, cutaway; (= *Frackschoß*) (swallow)tails *pl* **c** *(Tech)* dovetail; **mit einem ~ verbinden** to dovetail; **Schwal|ben|wurz** [-vʊrts] F **-, -e** *(Bot)* swallowwort

Schwall [ʃval] M **-(e)s, -e** flood, torrent; *(von Worten auch)* effusion

schwal|len [ˈʃvalən] *(sl)* VI to chatter on VT to chatter about

schwamm *pret von* **schwimmen**

Schwamm [ʃvam] M **-(e)s, ⸚e** [ˈʃvɛmə] **a** sponge; **etw mit dem ~ abwischen** to sponge sth (down), to wipe sth with a sponge; **~ drüber!** *(inf)* (let's) forget it! **b** *(dial: = Pilz)* fungus; *(essbar)* mushroom; *(giftig)* toadstool **c** (= *Hausschwamm*) dry rot; **den ~ haben** to have dry rot **d** (= *Feuerschwamm*) touchwood, tinder, punk *all no pl* **e** *(Zool)* sponge

Schwämm|chen [ˈʃvɛmçən] NT **-s, - a** *dim von* **Schwamm b** *(Med)* thrush

Schwam|merl [ˈʃvamɐl] NT **-s, -(n)** *(inf: S Ger, Aus)* = **Schwamm b**

schwam|mig [ˈʃvamɪç] ADJ **a** *(lit)* spongy **b** *(fig) Gesicht, Hände* puffy, bloated; (= *vage*) *Begriff, Gesetz, Regelung* woolly ADV (= *vage*) vaguely

Schwamm|tuch NT *pl* **-tücher** sponge cloth

Schwan [ʃvaːn] M **-(e)s, ⸚e** [ˈʃvɛːnə] swan; **mein lieber ~!** *(inf) (überrascht)* my goodness!; *(drohend)* my boy/girl

schwand *pret von* **schwinden**

schwa|nen [ˈʃvaːnən] VI *impers* **ihm schwante etwas** he had forebodings, he sensed something might happen; **mir schwant nichts Gutes** I don't like it, I've a feeling something bad is going to happen

Schwa|nen-: **Schwa|nen|ge|sang** M *(fig)* swan song; **Schwa|nen|hals** M swan's neck; *(fig)* swanlike neck; *(Tech)* gooseneck, swan neck; **Schwa|nen|jung|frau** F *(Myth)* swan maiden; **Schwa|nen|see** M Swan Lake; **Schwa|nen|teich** M swan pond; **schwa|nen|weiß** ADJ *(geh)* lily-white

schwang *pret von* **schwingen**

Schwang [ʃvaŋ] M **im ~(e) sein** to be in vogue, to be afoot; "in" *(inf)*; (= *in der Entwicklung*) to be afoot; **in ~ kommen** to come into vogue

schwan|ger [ˈʃvaŋɐ] ADJ pregnant; **~ sein** *or* **gehen** to be pregnant; **mit etw ~ gehen** *(fig)* to be big with sth; **mit großen Ideen ~ gehen** *(fig)* to be full of great ideas

Schwan|ge|re [ˈʃvaŋərə] F *decl as adj* pregnant woman

schwän|gern [ˈʃvɛŋɐn] VT to make pregnant, to impregnate *(form)*; **mit etw geschwängert sein** *(fig)* to be impregnated with sth; **die Luft war mit Rauch/Weihrauch geschwängert** the air was thick with smoke/heavy *or* impregnated with incense

Schwan|ger|schaft [ˈʃvaŋɐʃaft] F **-, -en** pregnancy

Schwan|ger|schafts-: **Schwan|ger|schafts|ab|bruch** M termination of pregnancy, abortion; **Schwan|ger|schafts|gym|nas|tik** F antenatal *(esp Brit) or* prenatal exercises *pl*; **Schwan|ger|schafts|kon|flikt|be|ra|tung** F counselling *(Brit) or* counseling *(US)* on pregnancy options; **Schwan|ger|schafts|mo|nat** M month of pregnancy; **im dritten ~ sein** to be three months pregnant; **Schwan|ger|schafts|nach|weis** M pregnancy test; **Schwan|ger|schafts|nar|be** F stretchmark; **Schwan|ger|schafts|strei|fen** M stretchmark; **Schwan|ger|schafts|test** M pregnancy test; **Schwan|ger|schafts|un|ter|bre|chung** F termination of pregnancy; **Schwan|ger|schafts|ver|hü|tung** F contraception; **Schwan|ger|schafts|wo|che** F week of pregnancy

Schwän|ge|rung [ˈʃvɛŋərʊŋ] F **-, -en die ~ einer Frau** making a woman pregnant

schwank [ʃvaŋk] ADJ *(poet)* **~en Schrittes** with faltering steps, shakily, falteringly

Schwank [ʃvaŋk] M **-(e)s, ⸚e** [ˈʃvɛŋkə] *(Liter)* merry *or* comical tale *(esp Brit)*, comical story; *(Theat)* farce; **ein ~ aus der Jugendzeit** *(hum)* a tale of one's youthful exploits

schwan|ken [ˈʃvaŋkn] VI **a** (= *wanken, sich wiegen*) to sway; *(Schiff) (auf und ab)* to pitch; *(seitwärts)* to roll; (= *beben*) to shake, to rock; **der Boden schwankte unter meinen Füßen** *(lit, fig)* the ground rocked beneath my feet **b** *aux sein* (= *gehen*) to stagger, to totter **c** *(Preise, Temperatur, Stimmung etc)* to fluctuate, to vary; *(Gebrauch, Schätzungen, Angaben)* to vary; *(Phys, Math)* to fluctuate; *(Kompassnadel etc)* to swing, to oscillate **d** (= *hin und her gerissen werden*) to vacillate; (= *wechseln*) to alternate; **sie schwankte zwischen Stolz und Mitleid** she alternated between pride and pity **e** (= *zögern*) to hesitate; (= *sich nicht schlüssig sein*) to waver, to vacillate; **~, ob** to hesitate as to whether, to be undecided (as to) whether **f ins Schwanken kommen** *or* **geraten** *(Baum, Gebäude etc)* to start to sway; *(Erde)* to start to shake *or* rock; *(Preise, Kurs, Temperatur etc)* to start to fluctuate *or* vary; *(Autorität, Überzeugung etc)* to begin to waver; *(Institution)* to begin to totter

schwan|kend ADJ **a** (= *wankend, sich wiegend*) swaying; *Schiff (auf und ab)* pitching; *(seitwärts)* rolling; (= *bebend*) shaking, rocking; **auf ~en Füßen stehen** *(fig)* to be shaky; **auf ~em Boden stehen** *(fig)* to be on shaky ground **b** *Mensch* staggering; *Gang* rolling; *Schritt* unsteady **c** *Preise, Temperatur, Stimmung etc* fluctuating *esp attr*; *Gebrauch* varying; *Kompassnadel etc* oscillating **d** (= *unschlüssig*) uncertain, wavering *attr*; (= *zögernd*) hesitant; (= *unbeständig*) vacillating, unsteady; **jdn ~ machen** to make sb waver; **~ werden** to waver; **sie ist sehr ~ in ihren Entschlüssen** she vacillates a lot

Schwan|kung [ˈʃvaŋkʊŋ] F **-, -en a** *(hin und her)* swaying *no pl*; *(auf und ab)* shaking *no pl*, rocking *no pl*; **um die ~en des Turms zu messen** to measure the extent to which the tower sways **b** *(von Preisen, Temperatur, Stimmung etc)* fluctuation, variation (+*gen* in); *(von Kompassnadel etc)* oscillation; **seelische ~en** fluctuations in one's mental state, mental ups and downs *(inf)*

Schwan|kungs|be|reich M range

Schwan|kungs|brei|te F range of variation

Schwanz [ʃvants] M **-es, ⸚e** [ˈʃvɛntsə] **a** *(lit, fig)* tail; *(inf: von Zug)* (tail) end; **den ~ zwischen die Beine klemmen und abhauen** *(lit, fig sl)* to put one's tail between one's legs and run; **den ~ hängen lassen** *(lit)* to let its tail droop; *(fig inf)* to be down in the dumps *(inf)*; **das Pferd** *or* **den Gaul beim** *or* **am ~ aufzäumen** to do things back to front; **kein ~** *(inf)* not a (blessed) soul *(inf)* → **treten VI c b** *(sl: = Penis)* prick *(sl)*, cock *(sl)*

Schwänz|chen [ˈʃvɛntsçən] NT **-s, -** *dim von* **Schwanz**

Schwän|ze|lei [ʃvɛntsəˈlai] F **-**, *no pl (fig pej: von Mensch)* crawling *(inf)*

schwän|zeln [ˈʃvɛntsln] VI **a** *(Hund: = mit dem Schwanz wedeln)* to wag its tail **b** *(fig pej: Mensch)* to crawl *(inf)* **c** *aux sein* (= *geziert gehen*) to sashay *(inf)*

schwän|zen [ˈʃvɛntsn] *(inf)* VT *Stunde, Vorlesung* to skip *(inf)*, to cut *(inf)*; *Schule* to play truant *(esp Brit) or* hooky *(esp US inf)* from, to skive off *(Brit inf)* VI to play truant *(esp Brit)*, to play hooky *(esp US inf)*, to skive *(Brit inf)*

Schwanz-: **Schwanz|en|de** NT end *or* tip of the tail; *(fig)* tail end; *(von Flugzeug)* tail; **Schwanz|fe|der** F tail feather; **Schwanz|flos|se** F tail *or* caudal fin; *(Aviat)* tail fin; **schwanz|ge|steu|ert** ADJ *(vulg pej)* dick-driven *(vulg pej)*; **schwanz|las|tig** [-lastɪç] ADJ *(Aviat)* tail-heavy; **schwanz|los** ADJ tailless *(auch Aviat)*; **Schwanz|lurch** M *(Zool)* caudate *(spec)*, urodele *(spec)*; **Schwanz|lut|**

scher M *(sl)* prick *(sl)*; **Schwanz|mei|se** F *(Orn)* long-tailed tit; **Schwanz|spit|ze** F tip of the/its tail; **Schwanz|sta|chel** M *(Zool)* sting (in the tail); **Schwanz|wir|bel** M *(Anat)* caudal vertebra

schwapp [ʃvap] INTERJ slosh, splash; *(= schwups)* slap, smack

Schwapp [ʃvap] M **-(e)s, -e** slosh, splash

schwap|pen [ˈʃvapn] VI **a** *(Flüssigkeit)* to slosh around **b** *aux sein (= überschwappen)* to splash, to slosh; *(fig)* to spill; **die Modewelle schwappt nach Europa** the fashion spills over into Europe

schwaps [ʃvaps] INTERJ = **schwapp**

Schwaps [ʃvaps] M **-(e)s, -e** slosh, splash

Schwä|re [ˈʃvɛːrə] F *(liter)* abscess, boil

schwä|ren [ˈʃvɛːrən] VI *(liter)* to fester; **eine ~de Wunde** *(lit, fig)* a festering sore

Schwarm [ʃvarm] M **-(e)s, ⸚e** [ˈʃvɛrmə] **a** swarm; *(= Flugzeugformation)* flight **b** *(inf: = Angebeteter)* idol; *(= Schauspieler, Popsänger)* idol, heart-throb *(inf)*; *(= Vorliebe)* passion, big thing *(inf)*; **der neue Englischlehrer ist ihr ~** she's got a crush on the new English teacher *(inf)*

schwär|men [ˈʃvɛrmən] VI **a** *aux sein* to swarm **b** *(= begeistert reden)* to enthuse (von about), to go into raptures (von about); **für jdn/etw ~** *(= außerordentlich angetan sein)* to be mad *or* wild *or* crazy about sb/sth *(inf)*; *(= verliebt sein, verehren auch)* to worship sb/sth, to be smitten with sb/sth *(liter, hum)*; **ins Schwärmen kommen** *or* **geraten** to go *or* fall into raptures; **ich schwärme nicht gerade für ihn** *(iro)* I'm not exactly crazy about him *(inf)*

Schwär|mer [ˈʃvɛrmɐ] M **-s, - a** *(Zool)* hawk moth *(esp Brit)*, sphinx moth *(US)* **b** *(= Feuerwerkskörper)* jumping jack

Schwär|mer [ˈʃvɛrmɐ] M **-s, -, Schwär|me|rin** [-ərɪn] F **-, -nen** *(= Begeisterter)* enthusiast, zealot; *(= Fantast)* dreamer, visionary; *(= sentimentaler Schwärmer)* sentimentalist

Schwär|me|rei [ʃvɛrməˈrai] F **-, -en** *(= Begeisterung)* enthusiasm; *(in Worten ausgedrückt)* effusion *no pl*; *(= Leidenschaft)* passion; *(= Verzückung)* rapture; **sich in ~en über jdn/etw ergehen** to go into raptures over sb/sth; **sich in ~en verlieren** to get *or* become carried away

schwär|me|risch [ˈʃvɛrmərɪʃ] ADJ *(= begeistert)* enthusiastic; *Worte, Übertreibung* effusive; *(= verliebt)* infatuated, gooey *(inf)*; *(= verzückt)* enraptured; *Illusion, Glaube, Gemüt* fanciful; **die Romantiker hatten alle etwas Schwärmerisches** the Romantics were all filled with a great emotional passion ADV enthusiastically; *(verliebt)* infatuated; **seine Stimme klang ~** he sounded captivated

Schwarm-: **Schwarm|geist** M *(= Fantast)* visionary; *(= Eiferer)* zealot; **schwarm|wei|se** ADV in swarms

Schwärm|zeit F swarming time

Schwar|te [ˈʃvartə] F **-, -n a** *(= Speckschwarte)* rind; *(Hunt: = Haut)* skin, hide; *(= Abfallholz)* slab; **arbeiten, dass** *or* **bis die ~ kracht** *(inf) or* **knackt** *(inf)* to work oneself into the ground *(inf)* **b** *(inf) (Buch)* old book, tome *(hum)*; *(Gemälde)* daub(ing) *(pej)*

Schwar|ten|ma|gen M *(Cook)* brawn

schwar|tig [ˈʃvartɪç] ADJ *(rare)* rindy

schwarz [ʃvarts] ADJ *comp* **⸚er** [ˈʃvɛrtsɐ], *superl* **⸚este(r, s)** [ˈʃvɛrtsəstə] **a** *(lit, fig)* black; *(= schmutzig)* dirty, black; *(= stark sonnengebräunt)* deeply tanned, brown; **~e Blattern** *or* **Pocken** smallpox; **~e Diamanten** black diamonds; **der Schwarze Erdteil** the Dark Continent; **der Schwarze Freitag** Black Friday; **~es Gold** *(fig)* black gold; **~er Humor** black humour *(Brit) or* humor *(US)*; **~er Kaffee/Tee** black coffee/tea; **die Schwarze Kunst** *(= Buchdruckerkunst)* (the art of) printing; *(= Magie)* the Black Art; **~e Liste** blacklist; **jdn auf die ~e Liste setzen** to blacklist sb, to put sb on the blacklist; **~es Loch** black hole; **~e Magie** black magic; **der ~e Mann** *(= Schornsteinfeger)* the (chimney) sweep; *(= Kinderschreck)* the bogeyman; **das Schwarze Meer** the Black Sea; **eine ~e Messe** a black mass; **Schwarzer Peter** *(Cards) children's card game*, ≈ old maid; **jdm den ~en Peter zuschieben** *or* **zuspielen** *(fig) (= die Verantwortung abschieben)* to pass the buck to sb *(inf)*, to leave sb holding the baby *(Brit) or* bag *(US)*; *(= etw Unangenehmes abschieben)* to give sb the worst of the deal; **das ~e Schaf (in der Familie)** the black sheep (of the family); **eine ~e Seele** a black *or* evil soul; **~er Star** *(Med)* amaurosis *(spec)*; **ein ~er Tag** a black day; **der ~e Tod** the Black Death; **die Schwarze Witwe** the Black Widow (spider); **etw ~ auf weiß haben** to have sth in black and white; **etw in den schwärzesten Farben** *or* **~ in ~ schildern/darstellen** to describe/present sth in the blackest terms; **~ von Menschen** crowded *or* black with people; **~ wie die Nacht/wie Ebenholz** jet-black; **in den ~en Zahlen sein, ~e Zahlen schreiben** *(Comm)* to be in the black; **sich ~ ärgern** → **schwarzärgern**; **er wurde ~ vor Ärger** his face went black; **mir wurde ~ vor den Augen** everything went black, I blacked out; **~ werden** *(Cards)* to lose every trick, to be whitewashed *(inf)*; **da kannst du warten, bis du ~ wirst** *(inf)* you can wait till the cows come home *(inf)*; **da kannst du schreien, bis du ~ wirst** *(inf)* you can shout until you're blue in the face *(inf)*
b *(inf: = ungesetzlich)* illicit; **der ~e Markt** the black market; **~e Geschäfte machen** to do shady deals; **~es Konto** secret account
c *(pej inf) (= katholisch)* Catholic, Papist *(pej)*; *(Pol: = konservativ)* Conservative
ADV *comp* **⸚er**, *superl* **am ⸚esten a** *(= mit schwarzer Farbe) anstreichen, färben, lackieren* black; *einrichten, sich kleiden* in black; **~ gestreift** with black stripes
b *(= illegal) erwerben, über die Grenze gehen* illegally; **sich** *(dat)* **etw ~ besorgen** to get sth illicitly; *(= auf dem Schwarzmarkt)* to get sth on the black market; **etw ~ verdienen** to earn sth on the side *(inf)*
c *(= konservativ)* **~ wählen** to vote Conservative; **dort wählen alle ~** they all vote Conservative there

Schwarz [ʃvarts] NT **-,** *no pl inv* black; **in ~ gehen** to wear black

Schwarz-: **Schwarz|af|ri|ka** NT Black Africa; **Schwarz|ar|beit** F illicit work, work on the side *(inf)*; *(nach Feierabend)* moonlighting *(inf)*; **schwarz+ar|bei|ten** VI *sep* to do illicit work, to work on the side *(inf)*; *(nach Feierabend)* to moonlight *(inf)*; **Schwarz|ar|bei|ter(in)** M(F) person doing illicit work *or* doing work on the side *(inf)*; *(nach Feierabend)* moonlighter *(inf)*; **schwarz+är|gern** VR *sep* to get extremely annoyed, to get hopping mad *(esp Brit inf)*; **schwarz|äu|gig** ADJ dark-eyed; *Schönheit auch* sloe-eyed *(liter)*; **Schwarz|bee|re** F *(S Ger, Aus: = Heidelbeere)* bilberry *(Brit)*, blueberry *(esp US)*; **schwarz|blau** ADJ bluish black, inky blue; *Tinte* blue-black; **Schwarz|blech** NT black plate; **schwarz|braun** ADJ dark brown; **Schwarz|bren|ner(in)** M(F) illicit distiller, moonshine distiller *(inf)*, moonshiner *(inf)*; **Schwarz|bren|ne|rei** F illicit still, moonshine still *(inf)*; **Schwarz|brot** NT *(braun)* brown rye bread; *(schwarz, wie Pumpernickel)* black bread, pumpernickel; **Schwarz|bun|te** [ˈʃvartsbʊntə] F *decl as adj* Friesian; **Schwarz|dorn** M *pl* **-dorne** *(Bot)* blackthorn; **Schwarz|dros|sel** F blackbird

Schwarze [ˈʃvartsə] F *decl as adj* black woman/lady/girl; *(= Schwarzhaarige)* black-haired woman/girl

Schwär|ze [ˈʃvɛrtsə] F **-, -n a** *(no pl: = Dunkelheit)* blackness **b** *(Farbe)* black dye; *(= Druckerschwärze)* printer's ink

schwär|zen [ˈʃvɛrtsn] VTR to blacken

Schwar|ze(r) [ˈʃvartsə] M *decl as adj* black (person/man), *(in USA auch)* African American; *(= Schwarzhaariger)* dark(-haired) man/boy; *(pej sl: = Katholik)* Catholic, Papist *(pej)*; *(Aus: = schwarzer Mokka)* black (mocha) coffee; **die ~n** *(pej inf)* the Conservatives

Schwarz|er|de F *(Geol)* black earth

Schwar|ze(s) [ˈʃvartsə] NT *decl as adj* black; *(auf Zielscheibe)* bull's-eye; **das kleine ~** *(inf)* the little black dress; **ins ~ treffen** *(lit, fig)* to score a bull's-eye; **jdm nicht das ~ unter den Nägeln gönnen** *(dated)* to begrudge sb the very air he/she breathes

Schwarz-: **schwarz+fah|ren** VI *sep irreg aux sein (ohne zu zahlen)* to travel without paying, to dodge paying the fare *(inf)*; *(ohne Führerschein)* to drive without a licence *(Brit) or* license *(US)*; **Schwarz|fah|rer(in)** M(F) fare dodger *(inf)*; *(ohne Führerschein)* driver without a licence *(Brit) or* license *(US)*; **Schwarz|fahrt** F ride without paying; *(ohne Führerschein)* drive without a licence *(Brit) or* license *(US)*; **sie wurde bei einer ~ geschnappt** she was caught travelling *(Brit) or* traveling *(US)* without a ticket *or* taking a free ride *(inf)*/driving without a licence *(Brit) or* license *(US)*; **Schwarz|fäu|le** F *(Bot)* black rot; **Schwarz|film** M *(Typ)* film; **Schwarz|fil|ter** M *(Phot)* black filter; **Schwarz|geld** NT illegal earnings *pl*; **schwarz|ge|streift** ADJ → **schwarz ADV a**; **schwarz|grau** ADJ grey-black *(Brit)*, gray-black *(US)*, greyish-black *(Brit)*, grayish-black *(US)*; **schwarz|haa|rig** ADJ black-haired; **eine Schwarzhaarige** a black-haired woman/girl; **Schwarz|han|del** M, *no pl* black market; *(= Tätigkeit)* black marketeering; **im ~** on the black market; **Schwarz|händ|ler(in)** M(F) black marketeer; **Schwarz|hem|den** PL *(Hist)* Blackshirts *pl*; **schwarz+hö|ren** VI *sep (Rad)* to use a radio without having a licence *(Brit) or* license *(US)*; **Schwarz|hö|rer(in)** M(F) *(Rad)* radio-owner without a licence *(Brit) or* license *(US)*; **Schwarz|kit|tel** M *(inf)* wild boar; *(pej: = Geistlicher)* priest

Schwarz|kon|to NT secret account

schwärz|lich [ˈʃvɛrtslɪç] ADJ blackish; *Haut* dusky

Schwarz-: **schwarz+ma|len** *sep*, **schwarz ma|len** △ VI to be pessimistic VT to be pessimistic about, to paint a black picture of; **Schwarz|ma|ler(in)** M(F) pessimist; **Schwarz|ma|le|rei** F pessimism; **Schwarz|markt** M black market; **Schwarz|markt|händ|ler(in)** M(F) black marketeer; **Schwarz|markt|preis** M black-market price; **Schwarz|meer|flot|te** F Black Sea fleet; **Schwarz|pap|pel** F black poplar; **Schwarz|pul|ver** NT black (gun)powder; **Schwarz|rock** M *(pej)* priest; **Schwarz-Rot-Gold** NT, **Schwarz|rot|gold** NT **die Farben/Fahne ~** the black-red-and-gold colours *(Brit) or* colors *(US)*/flag *(of Germany)*; **schwarz-rot-gol|den**, **schwarz|rot|gol|den** ADJ *Fahne* black-red-and-gold; **schwarz+schlach|ten** *sep* VI to slaughter pigs *etc* illegally *or* illicitly VT to slaughter illegally *or* illicitly; **schwarz+se|hen** *sep irreg*, **schwarz se|hen** △ *irreg* VT to be pessimistic about VI to be pessimistic; **für jdn/etw ~** to be pessimistic about sb/sth; **schwarz+se|hen** VI *sep irreg (TV)* to watch TV without a licence *(Brit) or* license *(US)*; **Schwarz|se|her(in)** M(F) **a** pessimist **b** *(TV) somebody watching TV without a licence*, (TV) licence-dodger *(Brit inf)*; **Schwarz|se|he|rei** [-zeːəˈrai] F **-,** *no pl* pessimism; **schwarz|se|he|risch** ADJ pessimistic, gloomy; **Schwarz|sen|der** M pirate (radio) station; **Schwarz|specht** M black woodpecker; **Schwarz|storch** M black stork; **Schwarz|tee** M black tea

Schwär|zung [ˈʃvɛrtsʊŋ] F **-, -en** blackening

Schwarz-: **Schwarz|wald** M Black Forest; **Schwarz|wäl|der** [-vɛldɐ] [-vɛldɐ] ADJ *attr* Black Forest; **~ Kirschtorte** Black Forest gateau *(Brit) or* cake *(US)*; **~ Kirschwasser** kirsch; **Schwarz|wäl|der** [-vɛldɐ] [-vɛldɐ] M **-s, -**,

Schwarz|wäl|de|rin [-ərın] F -, -nen person from the Black Forest

schwarz-weiß △, **schwarz|weiß** ADJ black-and-white *attr*, black and white ADV black and white; ~ **gepunktet/gestreift** with black and white polka dots/stripes

Schwarz-Weiß- △: **Schwarz-Weiß-Auf|nah|me** F black-and-white (shot); **Schwarz-Weiß-Emp|fän|ger** M black-and-white *or* monochrome set; **Schwarz-Weiß-Fern|se|hen** NT black-and-white *or* monochrome television; **Schwarz-Weiß-Fern|se|her** M black-and-white *or* monochrome television (set); **Schwarz-Weiß-Film** M black-and-white film; **Schwarz-Weiß-Fo|to** NT black-and-white (photo); **Schwarz-Weiß-Ge|rät** NT black-and-white *or* monochrome set; **Schwarz-Weiß-Gra|fik** F *(Comput: Druckoption)* line art; **schwarz-weiß ma|len** △, **schwarz|weiß ma|len** VTI *(fig)* to depict in black and white (terms); **das kann man doch nicht so ~** it's not as black and white as that; **Schwarz-Weiß-Ma|le|rei** F *(fig)* black-and-white portrayal; **die ~ älterer Geschichtsbücher** the way older history books make everything seem black and white *or* reduce everything to black and white (terms); **schwarz-weiß-rot** △, **schwarz|weiß|rot** ADJ black-white-and-red *(relating to the German imperial flag)*; **Schwarz-Weiß-Rot** NT △, **Schwarz|weiß|rot** NT **die Farben/Fahne ~** the black-white-and-red colours *(Brit)* *or* colors *(US)*/flag; **Schwarz-Weiß-Zeich|nung** F black-and-white (drawing)

Schwarz-: **schwarz+wer|den** VI *sep irreg aux sein (fig)* → **schwarz ADJ a**; **Schwarz|wild** NT wild boars *pl*; **Schwarz|wur|zel** F viper's grass; *(Cook)* salsify; **schwarz+zie|hen** VT *sep irreg Computerprogramme* to pirate

Schwatz [ʃvats] M **-es, -e** *(inf)* chat, chinwag *(Brit inf)*; **auf einen ~ kommen** to come (round *(Brit)* *or* by) for a chat

Schwatz|ba|se F, *(S Ger)* **Schwätz|ba|se** F *(inf)* gossip

Schwätz|chen [ʃvɛtsçən] NT **-s, -** *dim von* **Schwatz**

schwat|zen [ʃvatsn] VI to talk; *(pej) (unaufhörlich)* to chatter; *(über belanglose, oberflächliche Dinge, kindisch)* to prattle; *(= Unsinn reden)* to blather *(inf)*; *(= klatschen)* to gossip; **über Politik ~** to prattle on about politics *(pej)* VT to talk; **dummes Zeug ~** to talk a lot of rubbish *(esp Brit inf)* or drivel *(inf)*

schwät|zen [ʃvɛtsn] VTI *(S Ger, Aus)* = **schwatzen**

Schwät|zer [ʃvɛtsɐ] M **-s, -, Schwät|ze|rin** [-ərın] F **-, -nen** *(pej)* chatterer, chatterbox *(inf)*; *(= Schwafler)* windbag, gasbag, blether *(all inf)*; *(= Klatschmaul)* gossip

Schwät|ze|rei [ʃvɛtsəˈrai] F **-, -en** *(pej) (= Gerede, im Unterricht)* talk, chatter; *(über Belanglosigkeiten, kindisch)* prattle; *(= Unsinn)* drivel *(inf)*; *(= Klatsch)* gossip

schwät|ze|risch [ʃvɛtsərıʃ] ADJ windy *(inf)*, gassy *(inf)*

schwatz|haft ADJ *(= geschwätzig)* talkative, garrulous; *(= klatschsüchtig)* gossipy

Schwatz|haf|tig|keit [ʃvatshaftıçkait] F -, *no pl (= Geschwätzigkeit)* garrulousness, talkativeness; *(= Klatschsucht)* gossipy nature

Schwe|be [ʃveːbə] F -, *no pl* **sich in der ~ halten** *(Ballon)* to hover, to float in the air; *(Waage)* to balance; *(fig)* to hang in the balance; **in der ~ sein/bleiben** *(fig)* to be/remain in the balance, to be/remain undecided; *(Jur, Comm)* to be/remain pending

Schwe|be-: **Schwe|be|bahn** F suspension railway; *(= Seilbahn)* cable railway; **Schwe|be|bal|ken** M, **Schwe|be|baum** M *(Sport)* beam

schwe|ben [ʃveːbn] VI **a** *(= frei im Raum stehen, hängen) (Nebel, Rauch)* to hang; *(in der Luft)* to hang, to float; *(Wolke)* to float; *(in Flüssigkeit)* to float; *(an Seil etc)* to hang, to dangle; *(= sich unbeweglich in der Luft halten: Geier etc)* to hover; *(= nachklingen, zurückbleiben: Klänge, Parfüm)* to linger (on); **und der Geist Gottes schwebte über den Wassern** *(Bibl)* and the Spirit of the Lord moved over the waters *(Bibl)*; **und über allem schwebt ...** and over everything there hangs ...; **ihr war, als ob sie schwebte** she felt she was walking *or* floating on air; **etw schwebt jdm vor Augen** *(fig)* sb envisages sth, sb has sth in mind; *(Bild)* sb sees sth in his mind's eye; **in großer Gefahr ~** to be in great danger; **der Verletzte schwebt in Lebensgefahr** the injured man is in a critical condition; **in höheren Regionen** *or* **Sphären ~, über** *or* **in den Wolken ~** *(fig)* to have one's head in the clouds

b *aux sein (= durch die Luft gleiten)* to float, to sail; *(= hochschweben)* to soar; *(= niederschweben)* to float down; *(an Seil etc)* to swing; *(mit Fahrstuhl)* to soar, to zoom; *(= sich leichtfüßig bewegen)* to glide, to float

c *(= schwanken)* to hover, to waver; *(Angelegenheit)* to hang *or* be in the balance, to be undecided; *(Jur)* to be pending

schwe|bend ADJ *(Tech, Chem)* suspended; *(fig) Fragen etc* unresolved, undecided; *Musik, Rhythmus* floating; *(Jur) Verfahren* pending; *(Comm) Geschäft* pending; *Schulden* floating; *(Poet) Betonung* hovering

Schwe|be-: **Schwe|be|zug** M hovertrain; **Schwe|be|zu|stand** M *(fig)* state of suspense; *(zwischen zwei Stadien)* in-between state

Schweb-: **Schweb|flie|ge** F hover fly, ≈ sweat bee *(US)*; **Schweb|staub** M floating dust; **Schweb|stoff** M suspended matter; *(in Luft)* airborne particles *pl*

Schwe|de [ʃveːdə] M **-n, -n**, **Schwe|din** [ʃveːdın] F **-, -nen** Swede; **alter ~** *(inf)* (my) old fruit *(Brit inf)* or chap *(inf)* or buddy *(esp US inf)*

Schwe|den [ʃveːdn] NT **-s** Sweden

Schwe|den-: **Schwe|den|plat|te** F *(Cook)* smorgasbord; **Schwe|den|punsch** M arrack punch, Swedish punch; **Schwe|den|stahl** M Swedish steel

Schwe|din [ʃveːdın] F **-, -nen** Swede, Swedish woman/girl

schwe|disch [ʃveːdıʃ] ADJ Swedish; **hinter ~en Gardinen** *(inf)* behind bars; **hinter ~e Gardinen kommen** *(inf)* to be put behind bars

Schwe|disch(e) [ʃveːdıʃ] NT Swedish → *auch* **Deutsch(e)**

Schwe|fel [ʃveːfl] M **-s**, *no pl (abbr* **S**) sulphur *(Brit)*, sulfur *(US)*, brimstone *(old, Bibl)*

Schwe|fel- *in cpds* sulphur *(Brit)*, sulfur *(US)*; **schwe|fel|ar|tig** ADJ sulphur(e)ous *(Brit)*, sulfurous *(US)*; **Schwe|fel|blu|me** F, **Schwe|fel|blü|te** F flowers of sulphur *(Brit)* or sulfur *(US)*; **Schwe|fel|di|oxid**, **Schwe|fel|di|oxyd** NT sulphur *(Brit)* *or* sulfur *(US)* dioxide; **schwe|fel|gelb** ADJ sulphurous *(Brit)* *or* sulfurous *(US)* yellow; **schwe|fel|hal|tig** ADJ containing sulphur *(Brit)* *or* sulfur *(US)*, sulphur(e)ous *(Brit)*, sulfurous *(US)*; **Schwe|fel|hölz|chen** NT *(old)* match, lucifer *(old)*

schwe|fe|lig [ʃveːfəlıç] ADJ ADV = **schweflig**

Schwe|fel-: **Schwe|fel|kies** M iron pyrites *sing or pl*; **Schwe|fel|koh|len|stoff** M carbon disulphide *(Brit)* *or* disulfide *(US)*

schwe|feln [ʃveːfln] VT to sulphurize *(Brit)*, to sulfurize *(US)*

schwe|fel|sau|er ADJ *(Chem)* sulphuric *(Brit)*, sulfuric *(US)*; *(in bestimmten Verbindungen auch)* sulphate *(Brit)* or sulfate *(US)* of

Schwe|fel|säu|re F sulphuric *(Brit)* *or* sulfuric *(US)* acid

Schwe|fe|lung F **-, -en** sulphurization *(Brit)*, sulfurization *(US)*

Schwe|fel-: **Schwe|fel|ver|bin|dung** F sulphur *(Brit)* *or* sulfur *(US)* compound; **Schwe|fel|was|ser|stoff** M hydrogen sulphide *(Brit)* *or* sulfide *(US)*, sulphuretted *(Brit)* *or* sulfureted *(US)* hydrogen

schwef|lig [ʃveːflıç] ADJ sulphurous *(Brit)*, sulfurous *(US)* ADV **es roch ~** there was a smell of sulphur *(Brit)* *or* sulfur *(US)*

Schweif [ʃvaif] M **-(e)s, -e** *(auch Astron)* tail

schwei|fen [ʃvaifn] VI *aux sein (lit geh, fig)* to roam, to wander, to rove; **warum in die Ferne ~?** why roam so far afield?; **seine Gedanken in die Vergangenheit ~ lassen** to let one's thoughts roam *or* wander over the past; **seinen Blick ~ lassen** to let one's eyes wonder *(über etw (acc)* over sth) VT *Bretter, Blechgefäß* to curve → *auch* **geschweift**

Schweif-: **Schweif|haar** NT tail hair(s *pl*); **Schweif|sä|ge** F fret saw; **Schweif|stern** M comet

Schwei|fung [ʃvaifʊŋ] F **-, -en** curving; *(= geschweifte Form)* curve

schweif|we|deln [ʃvaifweːdln] VI *insep (Hund)* to wag its tail; *(fig old: = liebedienern)* to fawn

Schwei|ge-: **Schwei|ge|an|ruf** M *telephone call during which the caller remains silent*, silent call; **Schwei|ge|geld** NT hush money; **Schwei|ge|marsch** M silent march (of protest); **Schwei|ge|mi|nu|te** F one minute('s) silence

schwei|gen [ʃvaign] *pret* **schwieg** [ʃviːk], *ptp* **geschwiegen** [gəˈʃviːgn] VI to be silent; *(= still sein auch)* to keep quiet; *(= sich nicht äußern auch)* to remain silent, to say nothing; *(= aufhören: Musik, Geräusch, Wind)* to cease, to stop; **~ Sie!** be silent *or* quiet!; **kannst du ~?** can you keep a secret?; **seit gestern ~ die Waffen** yesterday the guns fell silent; **plötzlich schwieg er** suddenly he fell *or* went silent; **er kann ~ wie ein Grab** he knows how to keep quiet; **auf etw** *(acc)***/zu etw ~** to make no reply to sth; **ganz zu ~ von ..., von ... ganz zu ~** to say nothing of ...

Schwei|gen NT **-s**, *no pl* silence; **jdn zum ~ bringen** to silence sb *(auch euph)*; **(es herrscht) ~ im Walde** (there is) dead silence → **reden VI a**

schwei|gend ADJ silent; **die ~e Mehrheit** the silent majority ADV in silence, silently; **~ verharren** to remain silent; **~ über etw** *(acc)* **hinweggehen** to pass over sth in silence

Schwei|ge|pflicht F pledge of secrecy; *(von Anwalt)* requirement of confidentiality; **die ärztliche ~** medical confidentiality *or* secrecy; **die priesterliche ~** a priest's duty to remain silent; **unter ~ stehen** to be bound to observe confidentiality; **jdn von der ~ entbinden** to release sb from his/her duty of confidentiality

Schwei|ger [ʃvaigɐ] M **-s, -, Schwei|ge|rin** [-ərın] M **-, -nen** man/woman of few words; **der große ~** the strong silent type; *(als Beiname)* the silent

schweig|sam [ʃvaikzaːm] ADJ silent, quiet; *(als Charaktereigenschaft)* silent, taciturn; *(= verschwiegen)* discreet

Schweig|sam|keit F -, *no pl* silence, quietness; *(als Charaktereigenschaft)* silent manner, taciturnity

Schwein [ʃvain] NT **-s, -e** **a** pig, hog *(US)*; *(Fleisch)* pork; **sich wie die ~e benehmen** *(inf)* to behave like pigs *(inf)*; **bluten wie ein ~** *(inf)* to bleed like a stuck pig; **mit jdm (zusammen) ~e gehütet haben** *(hum inf)* to be on familiar terms (with sb); **ich glaub, mein ~ pfeift!** *(dated sl)* blow me down! *(dated inf)*, well kiss my ass! *(US sl)* **b** *(inf: Mensch)* pig *(inf)*, swine; *(= Schweinehund)* swine *(inf)*, bastard *(sl)*; **ein armes/faules ~** a poor/lazy sod *(Brit sl)* *or* bastard *(sl)*; **kein ~** nobody, not one single person **c** *no pl (inf: = Glück)* **~ haben** to be lucky; **~ gehabt!** that's a stroke of luck

Schwein|chen [ʃvainçən] NT **-s, -** *dim von* **Schwein** little pig, piglet; *(baby-talk)* piggy(-wiggy) *(baby-talk)*; *(fig inf: = kleiner Schmutzfink)* mucky pup *(Brit inf)*, messy thing *(esp US inf)*

Schwei|ne-: **Schwei|ne|ar|beit** F *(inf) (schmutzig)* dirty work; *(schwierig)* ghastly job; **Schwei|ne|ba|cke** F *(sl: = Mann)* fat bastard *(sl)*; **Schwei|ne|ban|de** F *(fig inf)* pack;

Schwei|ne|bauch M *(Cook)* belly of pork; **Schwei|ne|bra|ten** M joint of pork; *(gekocht)* roast pork; **Schwei|ne|bucht** F *(Geog)* **die ~** the Bay of Pigs; **Schwei|ne|fett** NT pig fat; **Schwei|ne|fi|let** NT fillet of pork; **Schwei|ne|fleisch** NT pork; **Schwei|ne|fraß** M *(fig inf)* muck *(inf)*; **Schwei|ne|fut|ter** NT pig feed; *(flüssig)* pig swill; **Schwei|ne|geld** NT *(inf)* **ein ~** a packet *(Brit inf)*, a fistful *(US inf)*; **Schwei|ne|hal|tung** F pig-keeping; **Schwei|ne|hirt(in)** M(F), **Schwei|ne|hir|te** M *(esp liter)* swineherd *(esp old, liter)*; **Schwei|ne|hund** M *(inf)* bastard *(sl)*, swine *(inf)*; **den inneren ~ überwinden** *(inf)* to conquer one's weaker self; **Schwei|ne|kerl** M *(inf)* swine *(inf)*, bastard *(sl)*; **Schwei|ne|ko|ben** [-ko:bn] M **-s, -**, **Schwei|ne|ko|fen** [-ko:fn] M **-s, -** pigsty, pigpen *(esp US)*; **Schwei|ne|ko|te|lett** NT pork chop; **Schwei|ne|len|de** F pork tenderloin; **~ in Blätterteig** tenderloin en croute; **Schwei|ne|mast** F pig-fattening; *(Futter)* pig food; **Schwei|ne|mäs|te|rei** F piggery; **Schwei|ne|mett** NT *(N Ger Cook)* minced *(esp Brit)* or ground *(US)* pork; **Schwei|ne|pack** NT *(pej inf)* vermin; **Schwei|ne|pest** F *(Vet)* swine fever; **Schwei|ne|pries|ter** M *(pej inf)* bastard *(sl)*

Schwei|ne|rei [ʃvainəˈrai] F **-, -en** *(inf)* **a** *no pl* mess; **es ist eine ~, wenn ...** it's disgusting if ...; **so eine ~!** how disgusting!; **Fische zu schuppen ist eine ~** scaling fish is a messy business **b** *(= Skandal)* scandal; *(= Gemeinheit)* dirty *or* mean trick *(inf)*; **ich finde es eine ~, wie er sie behandelt** I think it's disgusting the way he treats her; **(so eine) ~!** what a dirty trick! *(inf)* **c** *(= Zote)* smutty *or* dirty joke; *(= unzüchtige Handlung)* indecent act; **~en machen** to do dirty *or* filthy things; **das Buch besteht nur aus ~en** the book is just a lot of dirt *or* filth **d** *(iro: = Leckerbissen)* delicacy

Schwei|ne|ripp|chen NT *(Cook)* cured pork chop

Schwei|ne|roll|bra|ten M roast rolled *or* collared pork

schwei|nern [ˈʃvainɐn] ADJ pork; **Schweinernes** pork

Schwei|ne-: **Schwei|ne|rot|lauf** M *(Vet)* swine erysipelas *(spec)*; **Schwei|ne|rüs|sel** M pig's snout; **Schwei|ne|schmalz** NT dripping *(Brit)*, drippings *pl (US)*; *(als Kochfett)* lard; **Schwei|ne|schnit|zel** NT pork cutlet, escalope of pork; **Schwei|ne|stall** M *(lit, fig)* pigsty, pigpen *(esp US)*; *(= korruptes System)* corrupt shambles *sing*; **Schwei|ne|zucht** F pig-breeding; *(Hof)* pig farm; **Schwei|ne|züch|ter(in)** M(F) pig-breeder

Schwein|igel [ˈʃvainli:gl] M *(inf)* dirty pig *(inf)* or so-and-so *(inf)*

Schwein|ige|lei [ʃvainli:gəˈlai] F **-, -en** *(inf)* *(Witz)* dirty *or* smutty joke; *(Bemerkung)* dirty *or* smutty remark; *(= das Schweinigeln)* dirty *or* smutty jokes *pl*/remarks *pl*

schwein|igeln [ˈʃvainli:gln] VI *insep (inf) (= Witze erzählen)* to tell dirty jokes; *(= Bemerkungen machen)* to make dirty *or* smutty remarks; *(= Schmutz machen)* to make a mess

schwei|nisch [ˈʃvainɪʃ] *(inf)* ADJ *Benehmen* piggish *(inf)*, swinish *(inf)*; *Witz* dirty ADV like a pig; **benimm dich nicht so ~!** stop behaving like a pig!

Schwein|kram M *(inf)* dirt, filth

Schweins-: **Schweins|au|gen** PL, **Schweins|äug|lein** [-ɔyklain] PL *(inf)* piggy eyes *pl (inf)*; **Schweins|bla|se** F pig's bladder; **Schweins|bors|te** F pig's bristle; **Schweins|fü|ße** PL *(Cook dial)* (pig's) trotters *pl*; **Schweins|ga|lopp** M **im ~ davonlaufen** *(hum inf)* to go galumphing *(esp Brit)* or galloping off *(inf)*; **Schweins|ha|xe** F *(S Ger Cook)* knuckle of pork; **Schweins|kopf** M *(Cook)* pig's head; **Schweins|le|der** NT pigskin; **schweins|le|dern** ADJ pigskin; **Schweins|ohr** NT **a** pig's ear; *(Gebäck)* (kidney-shaped) pastry **b** *(Bot) (= Kalla)* calla (lily); *(Pilz)* cantharellus clavatus *(spec)*; **Schweins|stel|ze** F *(Aus)* (pig's) trotters *pl*

Schweiß [ʃvais] M **-es**, *no pl* sweat; *(von Mensch auch)* perspiration; *(Hunt)* blood; **in ~ geraten** *or* **kommen** to break into a sweat, to start sweating/perspiring; **der ~ brach ihm aus allen Poren** he was absolutely dripping with sweat; **der ~ brach ihm aus** he broke out in a sweat; **nass von ~** soaked with perspiration *or* sweat; **kalter ~** cold sweat; **das hat viel ~ gekostet** it was a sweat *(inf)*; **im ~e seines Angesichts** *(Bibl, liter)* in the sweat of his brow *(Bibl)*; **die Früchte seines ~es** *(liter)* the fruits of his toil *or* labour(s) *(Brit) or* labor *(US)*

Schweiß-: **Schweiß|ab|son|de|rung** F perspiration; **Schweiß|ap|pa|rat** M welding equipment *no indef art, no pl*; **Schweiß|aus|bruch** M sweating *no indef art, no pl*; **Schweiß|band** [-bant] NT *pl* **-bänder** sweatband; **schweiß|bar** ADJ *(Tech)* weldable; **schweiß|be|deckt** ADJ covered in sweat; **Schweiß|bläs|chen** [-blɛ:sçən] PL *(Med)* prickly heat *sing*, miliaria *sing (spec)*; **Schweiß|bren|ner** M *(Tech)* welding torch; **Schweiß|bril|le** F *(Tech)* welding goggles *pl*; **Schweiß|draht** M *(Tech)* welding rod *or* wire; **Schweiß|drü|se** F *(Anat)* sweat *or* perspiratory *(form)* gland

schwei|ßen [ˈʃvaisn] VT *(Tech)* to weld VI **a** *(Tech)* to weld **b** *(Hunt)* to bleed

Schwei|ßer [ˈʃvaisɐ] M **-s, -**, **Schwei|ße|rin** [-ərɪn] F **-, -nen** *(Tech)* welder

Schweiß-: **Schweiß|fähr|te** F *(Hunt)* trail of blood, blood track; **Schweiß|flam|me** F welding flame; **Schweiß|fleck** M sweat stain, perspiration mark; **Schweiß|fuß** M sweaty foot; **schweiß|ge|ba|det** [-gəba:dət] ADJ bathed in sweat; *Mensch auch* bathed in perspiration; **Schweiß|ge|ruch** M smell of sweat *or* perspiration; **Schweiß|hand** F sweaty palm; **Schweiß|hund** M *(Hunt)* bloodhound

schwei|ßig [ˈʃvaisɪç] ADJ sweaty; *(Hunt) Tier* bleeding; *Fährte* bloody

Schweiß-: **Schweiß|naht** F *(Tech)* weld, welded joint; **schweiß|nass** ADJ sweaty; **Schweiß|per|le** F bead of perspiration *or* sweat; **Schweiß|ro|bo|ter** M welding robot; **Schweiß|stahl** M welding steel; **Schweiß|stel|le** F weld; **Schweiß|tech|nik** F welding (engineering); **schweiß|trei|bend** ADJ *Tätigkeit* that makes one sweat, sudorific *(spec)*; **~es Mittel** sudorific *(spec)*; **schweiß|trie|fend** ADJ dripping with perspiration *or* sweat; **Schweiß|trop|fen** M drop of sweat *or* perspiration; **Schweiß|tuch** NT *pl* **-tücher** **a** *(obs: = Taschentuch)* handkerchief **b** **das ~ der Veronika** the sudarium, Veronica's veil; **schweiß|über|strömt** [-ly:bɐʃtrø:mt] ADJ streaming *or* running with sweat

Schwei|ßung [ˈʃvaisʊŋ] F **-, -en** welding; *(Naht, Stelle)* weld

Schweiz [ʃvaits] F **- die ~** Switzerland

Schwei|zer [ˈʃvaitsɐ] M **-s, -** **a** *(= Melker)* dairyman **b** *(Eccl: = Pförtner)* beadle, usher **c** *(= päpstlicher Leibgardist)* Swiss Guard ADJ *attr* Swiss; **~ Käse** Swiss cheese

Schwei|zer [ˈʃvaitsɐ] M **-s, -**, **Schwei|ze|rin** [-ərɪn] F **-, -nen** Swiss

Schwei|zer-: **Schwei|zer|de|gen** M *(Typ)* compositor-printer; **schwei|zer|deutsch** ADJ Swiss-German; **Schwei|zer|deutsch(e)** NT Swiss German → *auch* **Deutsch(e)**; **Schwei|zer|fran|ken** M Swiss franc; **Schwei|zer|gar|de** F Swiss Guard

Schwei|ze|rin [-ərɪn] F **-, -nen** Swiss (woman/girl)

schwei|ze|risch [ˈʃvaitsərɪʃ] ADJ Swiss

Schwei|zer|mes|ser NT Swiss army knife

Schwel|brand M smouldering *(Brit) or* smoldering *(US)* fire

schwe|len [ˈʃve:lən] VI *(lit, fig)* to smoulder *(Brit)*, to smolder *(US)* VT *Rasen* to burn off (slowly); *Koks* to carbonize at a low temperature

schwel|gen [ˈʃvɛlgn] VI to indulge oneself *(in +dat* in); **von Schwelgen und Prassen hat er nichts gehalten** he had no time for self-indulgence and feasting; **wir schwelgten in Kaviar und Sekt** we feasted on caviar and champagne; **in Erinnerungen ~** to indulge in reminiscences; **in Farben/Worten ~** to revel in colour *(Brit) or* color *(US)*/in the sound of words; **im Überfluss ~** to live in the lap of luxury; **in Gefühlen** *etc* **~** to revel in one's emotions

Schwel|ge|rei [ʃvɛlgəˈrai] F **-, -en** high living *no pl*, indulgence *no pl*; *(= Schlemmerei)* feasting *no pl*

schwel|ge|risch [ˈʃvɛlgərɪʃ] ADJ *(= üppig) Mahl, Farbe* sumptuous; *Akkorde auch* voluptuous; *(= genießerisch)* self-indulgent

Schwel-: **Schwel|koh|le** F high-bituminous brown coal; **Schwel|koks** M low-temperature coke

Schwel|le [ˈʃvɛlə] F **-, -n** **a** *(= Türschwelle, fig, Psych)* threshold; *(= Stein etc)* sill; *(auf Straße)* ramp, bump; **einen/keinen Fuß über die ~ setzen** to set foot/not to set foot in sb's house; **er darf mir nicht mehr über die ~ kommen, er darf meine ~ nie wieder betreten** he shall *or* may not darken my door again *(liter)*, he may not cross my threshold again *(liter)*; **an der ~ (zu) einer neuen Zeit** on the threshold of a new era; **an der ~ des Grabes** *or* **Todes** at death's door **b** *(Rail)* sleeper *(Brit)*, cross-tie *(US)* **c** *(Geog)* rise

schwel|len [ˈʃvɛlən] VI *pret* **schwoll** [ʃvɔl], *ptp* **geschwollen** [gəˈʃvɔlən] *aux sein* to swell; *(lit: Körperteile auch)* to swell up; **der Wind schwoll zum Sturm** the wind grew into a storm; **ihm schwoll der Kamm** *(inf) (vor Eitelkeit, Übermut)* he got swollen-headed *(esp Brit) or* swell-headed *(esp US)*, he got above himself *(Brit)*; *(vor Wut)* he saw red → *auch* **geschwollen** VT *(geh) Segel* to swell *or* belly (out); *(fig) Brust* to swell

Schwel|len|angst F *(Psych)* fear of entering a place; *(fig)* fear of embarking on something new

schwel|lend ADJ *(geh)* swelling; *Lippen* full

Schwel|len-: **Schwel|len|land** NT fast-developing nation; **Schwel|len|macht** F rising power; **Schwel|len|preis** M *(Econ)* threshold price; **Schwel|len|wert** M *(Phys, Psych)* threshold value

Schwel|ler [ˈʃvɛlɐ] M **-s, -** *(Mus)* swell

Schwell|kör|per M *(Anat)* erectile tissue

Schwel|lung [ˈʃvɛlʊŋ] F **-, -en** swelling; *(von Penis)* tumescence *(spec)*

Schwe|lung [ˈʃve:lʊŋ] F **-, -en** *(Tech)* low-temperature carbonization

Schwemm|bo|den M alluvial land

Schwem|me [ˈʃvɛmə] F **-, -n** **a** *(für Tiere)* watering place **b** *(= Überfluss)* glut *(an +dat* of) **c** *(= Kneipe)* bar, public bar *(Brit)* **d** *(Aus: im Warenhaus)* bargain basement

-schwem|me F *suf in cpds* glut of; **Akademikerschwemme** glut of university graduates

schwem|men [ˈʃvɛmən] VT *(= treiben) Sand etc* to wash; *Vieh* to water; *(= wässern) Felle* to soak; *(Aus: = spülen) Wäsche* to rinse; **etw an(s) Land ~** to wash sth ashore

Schwemm-: **Schwemm|land** NT alluvial land; **Schwemm|sand** M alluvial sand

Schwen|gel [ˈʃvɛŋl] M **-s, -** *(= Glockenschwengel)* clapper; *(= Pumpenschwengel)* handle; *(inf: = Penis)* dong *(US sl)*, tool *(sl)*

Schwenk [ʃvɛŋk] M **-(e)s, -s** *(= Drehung)* wheel; *(Film)* pan, panning shot; *(fig)* about-turn; **einen ~ machen** *(Kolonne)* to swing *or* wheel around

Schwenk-: **Schwenk|arm** M swivel arm; **schwenk|bar** ADJ swivelling *(Brit)*, swiveling *(US)*; *Lampe auch* swivel *attr*; *Geschütz* traversable; **Schwenk|be|reich** M jib range

schwen|ken [ˈʃvɛŋkn] VT **a** *(= schwingen)* to wave; *(= herumfuchteln mit)* to brandish **b** *Lampe etc* to swivel, to swing; *Kran* to swing, to slew; *Geschütz* to traverse, to swivel; *Kamera* to pan **c** *(Cook) Kartoffeln, Nudeln* to toss **d** *Tanzpartnerin* to swing round, to spin (round) **VI** *aux sein* to swing; *(Kolonne von Soldaten, Autos etc)* to wheel; *(Geschütz)* to traverse, to swivel; *(Kamera)* to pan; *(fig)* to swing over, to switch; **links schwenkt!** *(Mil)* left wheel!

Schwen|ker [ˈʃvɛŋkɐ] M **-s, -** balloon glass

Schwenk-: **Schwenk|flü|gel** M *(Tech)* swing-wing; **Schwenk|kar|tof|feln** PL sauté potatoes *pl*; **Schwenk|kran** M swing crane; **Schwenk|so|ckel** M *(Comput)* swivel base

Schwen|kung [ˈʃvɛŋkʊŋ] F **-, -en** swing; *(Mil)* wheel; *(von Kran)* slewing, swing; *(von Geschütz)* traverse; *(von Kamera)* pan(ning); **eine ~ vollziehen** *(Mil)* to wheel; *(fig)* to swing around

schwer [ʃveːɐ] ✪ 33.3, 53.3, 53.6 ADJ **a** *(lit, fig)* heavy; *(= massiv) Gold* solid; **ein 10 kg ~er Sack** a sack weighing 10 kgs, a sack 10 kgs in weight; **die Beine wurden mir ~** my legs grew heavy; **er ist fünf Millionen ~** *(inf)* he is worth five million → **Herz b, Kapee, Magen, Stand a**

b *(= stark) Fahrzeug, Maschine* powerful; *Artillerie, Kavallerie, Wein, Parfüm* heavy; *Zigarre* strong; *(= nährstoffreich) Boden* rich; **~es Wasser** *(Phys)* heavy water → **Geschütz**

c *(= heftig) Sturm, See, Angriff, Artilleriefeuer* heavy; *Winter* hard, severe

d *(= ernst) Sorge, Bedenken, Unrecht, Unfall, Verlust, Krankheit, Beleidigung* serious, grave; *Fehler, Enttäuschung* serious, grave, big; *(Comput) Fehler* fatal, critical; *Zeit, Leben, Schicksal* hard; *Leiden, Belastungsprobe, Strafe, Buße* severe; *Musik* heavy; **~e Verluste** heavy losses; **Schweres erlebt** *or* **durchgemacht haben** to have been through (some) hard times, to have had a hard time (of it); **das war ein ~er Schlag für ihn** it was a hard blow for him → **Stunde, Junge**

e *(= hart, anstrengend) Amt, Aufgabe, Dienst, Arbeit, Tag* hard; *Geburt, Tod* difficult; **es ~ haben** to have a hard time (of it) → **Anfang, Geburt**

f *(= schwierig) Frage, Entscheidung, Übung* hard, difficult, tough

g *(inf: = enorm)* **~es Geld machen** to make a packet *(inf)*

ADV **a** *(= mit schwerer Last) beladen, bepackt, bewaffnet* heavily; **~ auf jdm/etw liegen/lasten** to lie/weigh heavily on sb/sth; **~ an etw** *(dat)* **zu tragen haben** *(sich abschleppen)* to be loaded down with sth; *(fig) an Schuld etc* to be heavily burdened with sth; **an den 50 Sack hast du viel zu ~ zu tragen** these 50 sacks are too much for you to carry; **das Bewusstsein, ihr unrecht getan zu haben, lastet ~ auf ihm** knowing that he did her an injustice is hard for him to bear

b *(= hart) arbeiten, schuften* hard; *bestrafen, tadeln, missbilligen* severely; **~ geprüft sein** to be sorely tried; **~ verdientes Geld** hard-earned money; **es ~ haben** to have a hard time of it; **es mit jdm ~ haben** to have a hard time with sb

c *(= ernstlich) verletzen, verwunden* seriously; *krank* seriously, critically; *beleidigen, kränken, treffen, gekränkt* deeply; **~ behindert** = **schwerbehindert**; **~ beschädigt** = **schwerbeschädigt**; **~ kriegsbeschädigt** seriously disabled *(in war)*; **~ erkältet sein** to have a bad cold; **~ stürzen** to have a bad fall; **~ verunglücken** to have a serious accident

d *(= nicht einfach)* **~ zu sehen/sagen** hard *or* difficult to see/say; **es lässt sich ~ abschätzen/voraussagen** it's hard to estimate/to predict

e *(= mit Mühe)* **sich ~ entschließen können** to find it hard *or* difficult to decide; **er lernt ~** he's a slow learner; **~ hören** to be hard of hearing; **~ löslich** *(attr)* not easily dissoluble; **etw ist ~ löslich** sth is not easy to dissolve; **jd ist ~ erziehbar** sb has behavioural *(Brit)* *or* behavioral *(US)* problems; **ein ~ erziehbares Kind** a maladjusted child; **~ verdaulich** *(Speisen)* indigestible; *(fig auch)* difficult; **etw ist ~ verdaulich** sth is hard to digest; **~ verständlich** difficult *or* hard to understand, incomprehensible; **~ verträglich sein** *(Speise)* to be indigestible; *(Medikament)* to have side effects; *(Klima)* to be unhealthy; **ein ~ verträgliches Medikament** medicine which has side effects

f *(inf: = sehr)* really; **da musste ich ~ aufpassen** I really had to watch out; **~ betrunken** completely drunk, rolling drunk *(Brit inf)*; **~ verdienen** to earn a packet *(Brit inf)* *or* a fistful *(US inf)*; **sich ~ blamieren** to make a proper fool *(Brit)* *or* an ass *(esp US)* of oneself; **ich werde mich ~ hüten** there's no way (I will) *(inf)*; **~ im Irrtum sein** to be badly *or* seriously mistaken; **er ist ~ in Ordnung** he's OK *(inf)*, he's a good bloke *(Brit inf)* *or* guy *(inf)*

Schwer-: **Schwer|ar|beit** F heavy labour *(Brit)* *or* labor *(US)*; **Schwer|ar|bei|ter(in)** M(F) labourer *(Brit)*, laborer *(US)*; **Schwer|ath|let(in)** M(F) weightlifter; boxer; wrestler; **Schwer|ath|le|tik** F *weightlifting sports, boxing, wrestling etc*; **schwer|be|hin|dert** ADJ severely handicapped, severely disabled; **Schwer|be|hin|der|te(r)** MF *decl as adj* severely disabled person; **Schwer|be|hin|der|ten|aus|weis** M disabled pass *or* ID; **schwer|be|la|den** [-bəladn] ADJ → **schwer ADV a**; **Schwer|ben|zin** NT heavy benzene *(Brit)*, naphtha;; **schwer|be|packt** [-bəpakt] ADJ → **schwer ADV a**; **schwer|be|schä|digt** [-bəʃɛːdɪçt] ADJ severely disabled; **Schwer|be|schä|dig|te(r)** MF *decl as adj* severely disabled person; **schwer|be|waff|net** ADJ → **schwer ADV a**; **schwer|blü|tig** ADJ serious, ponderous; **ein ~er Mensch** a ponderous (sort of) person

Schwe|re [ˈʃveːrə] F **-,** *no pl* **a** heaviness **b** *(= Ernsthaftigkeit, von Krankheit)* seriousness, gravity; **die ganze ~ des Gesetzes** the full severity of the law **c** *(= Schwierigkeit)* difficulty; **das hängt von der ~ der Aufgabe ab** it depends on how difficult the task is **d** *(Phys: = Schwerkraft)* gravitation

Schwe|re-: **Schwe|re|feld** NT field of gravity, gravitational field; **schwe|re|los** ADJ weightless; **Schwe|re|lo|sig|keit** F **-,** *no pl* weightlessness; **Schwe|re|nö|ter** [ˈʃveːrənøːtɐ] M **-s, -**, **Schwe|re|nö|te|rin** [-ərɪn] F **-, -nen** *(dated)* philanderer

schwer|er|zieh|bar ADJ *Kind* → **schwer ADV e**

Schwer|er|zieh|ba|re(r) MF *decl as adj* difficult *or* problem child

schwer+fal|len *sep irreg aux sein*, **schwer fal|len** △ *irreg aux sein* VI to be difficult *or* hard (*jdm* for sb); **das dürfte dir doch nicht ~** you shouldn't find that too difficult *or* hard

schwer|fäl|lig ADJ *(= unbeholfen) Gang, Bewegungen* heavy (in one's movements); *(= langsam) Verstand* slow, ponderous; *Stil, Übersetzung* ponderous; *Verwaltung, Staatsapparat* cumbersome; **~ sein** *(Mensch)* to move heavily ADV heavily; *sprechen* ponderously; *sich bewegen* with difficulty; **du bewegst dich so ~** you seem to have so much trouble moving

Schwer|fäl|lig|keit F *(= Unbeholfenheit: von Gang, Bewegungen)* heaviness; *(= Langsamkeit: von Verstand)* slowness, ponderousness; **die ~ seines Stils** his ponderous style

Schwer-: **schwer|ge|prüft** [-gəpryːft] ADJ → **schwer ADV b**; **Schwer|ge|wicht** NT **a** *(Sport, fig)* heavyweight **b** *(= Nachdruck)* stress, emphasis; **das ~ verlagern** to shift the emphasis; **das ~ auf etw** *(acc)* **legen** to put the stress *or* emphasis on sth; **schwer|ge|wich|tig** ADJ *(lit, fig)* heavyweight; **Schwer|ge|wicht|ler** [-gəvɪçtlɐ] M **-s, -**, **Schwer|ge|wicht|le|rin** [-ərɪn] F **-, -nen** *(Sport)* heavyweight; **schwer|hö|rig** ADJ hard of hearing; **du bist wohl ~!** *(inf)* are you deaf? *(inf)*; **Schwer|hö|ri|ge(r)** MF *decl as adj* person with hearing difficulties *or* impaired hearing, hearing-impaired person; **Schwer|hö|rig|keit** F hardness of hearing; **Schwer|in|dust|rie** F heavy industry; **Schwer|in|dust|ri|el|le(r)** MF *decl as adj* industrialist *(in heavy industry)*; **Schwer|kraft** F, *no pl* gravity; **schwer|krank** ADJ → **schwer ADV c**; **Schwer|kran|ke(r)** MF *decl as adj* seriously *or* critically ill patient; **schwer|kriegs|be|schä|digt** ADJ severely war-disabled; **Schwer|kriegs|be|schä|dig|te(r)** MF *decl as adj* seriously disabled ex-serviceman/ex-servicewoman, seriously disabled war veteran *(US)*; **Schwer|last|ver|kehr** M heavy vehicle traffic

schwer|lich [ˈʃveːɐlɪç] ADV hardly, scarcely

Schwer-: **schwer|lös|lich** △ ADJ → **schwer ADV e**; **schwer ma|chen**, **schwer+ma|chen** *sep* VT **a** **jdm das Herz ~** to make sb's heart sad *or* heavy; **jdm das Leben ~** to make life difficult *or* hard for sb **b** **es jdm/sich ~** to make it *or* things difficult *or* hard for sb/oneself; **Schwer|me|tall** NT heavy metal

Schwer|mut [ˈʃveːɐmuːt] F **-,** *no pl* melancholy

schwer|mü|tig [ˈʃveːɐmyːtɪç] ADJ *Mensch, Geschichte, Musik* melancholy

schwer+neh|men *sep irreg*, **schwer neh|men** △ *irreg* VT **etw ~** to take sth hard

Schwer|öl NT heavy oil

Schwer|punkt M *(Phys)* centre *(Brit)* *or* center *(US)* of gravity; *(fig) (= Zentrum)* centre *(Brit)*, center *(US)*, main focus; *(= Hauptgewicht)* main emphasis *or* stress; **politische/thematische ~e** main political/thematic emphases; **er hat Französisch mit ~ Linguistik studiert** he studied French with the main emphasis *or* main stress on linguistics; **den ~ einer Sache** *(gen)* **bilden** to occupy the central position in sth; **den ~ auf etw** *(acc)* **legen** to put the main emphasis *or* stress on sth; **~e setzen** to set priorities

Schwer|punkt-: **Schwer|punkt|bil|dung** F concentration; **Schwer|punkt|in|dust|rie** F main industry; **schwer|punkt|mä|ßig** ADJ **eine ~e Betrachtung** a look at the main points ADV **sich mit etw ~ befassen** to concentrate on sth; **~ konzentrieren wir uns auf ...** principally we concentrate on ...; **Schwer|punkt|pro|gramm** NT programme *(Brit)* *or* program *(US)* *or* plan of main points of emphasis; **Schwer|punkt|streik** M pinpoint strike; **Schwer|punkt|the|ma** NT main (discussion) topic; *(in Prüfung)* special subject; **Schwer|punkt|ver|la|ge|rung** F shift of emphasis; **schwer|reich** ADJ *(inf)* stinking rich *(inf)*; **Schwer|spat** M heavy spar, barite, barytes *sing*

Schwerst-: **Schwerst|ar|bei|ter(in)** M(F) heavy labourer *(Brit)*, hard laborer *(US)*; **schwerst|be|hin|dert** ADJ totally disabled; **Schwerst|be|hin|der|te(r)** MF *decl as adj* totally disabled person

Schwert [ʃveːɐt] NT **-(e)s, -er** **a** sword; **das ~ ziehen** *or* **zücken** to draw one's sword; **sich mit dem ~ gürten** *(liter)* to gird (on) one's sword **b** *(von Segelboot)* centreboard *(Brit)*, centerboard *(US)*

Schwert|adel M *(Hist, fig)* military nobility

Schwer|ter-: **Schwer|ter|ge|klirr** NT *(liter)* ring(ing) *or* clash(ing) of swords; **Schwer|ter|tanz** M sword dance

Schwert-: **Schwert|fisch** M swordfish; **schwert|för|mig** ADJ sword-shaped; *Blatt auch* gladiate *(spec)*; **Schwert|griff** M (sword) hilt; **Schwert|hieb** M sword stroke, stroke *or* blow of the sword; **Schwert|klin|ge** F sword blade; **Schwert|knauf** M (sword) pommel; **Schwert|lei|te** [-laitə] F **-, -n** *(Hist)* accolade; **Schwert|li|lie** F *(Bot)* iris

Schwer|trans|port M *(Ladung)* heavy load; *(= Transporter)* → **Schwertransporter**

Schwer|trans|por|ter M heavy truck *or* lorry *(Brit)*, heavy goods *or* heavy weight *(US)* vehicle *(form)*, HGV *(Brit)*

Schwert-: **Schwert|schlu|cker(in)** M(F) sword-swallower; **Schwert|streich** M sword stroke, stroke *or* blow of the sword; **Schwert|tanz** M sword dance; **Schwert|trä|ger** M *(Zool)* swordtail

schwer+tun *sep irreg*, **schwer tun** △ *irreg* VR *(inf)* **sich** *(acc or dat)* **mit** *or* **bei etw ~** **a** *(= Schwierigkeiten haben)* to have problems with sth **b** *(psychisch)* to make heavy weather of sth *(Brit inf)*, to make a big deal of sth *(inf)*

Schwert|wal M killer whale

Schwer-: **Schwer|ver|bre|cher(in)** M(F) criminal, felon *(esp Jur)*; **schwer|ver|dau|lich** ADJ → **schwer ADV e**; **schwer|ver|dient** ADJ → **schwer ADV b**; **Schwer|ver|kehr** M heavy goods traffic; **Schwer|ver|kehrs|ab|ga|be** F heavy goods vehicle supplement; **schwer|ver|letzt** [-fɛɐlɛtst] ADJ → **schwer ADV c**; **Schwer|ver|letz|te(r)** MF *decl as adj* serious casualty; **schwer|ver|ständ|lich** ADJ → **schwer ADV e**; **schwer|ver|träg|lich** ADJ → **schwer ADV e**; **schwer|ver|wun|det** ADJ *attr* → **schwer ADV c**; **Schwer|ver|wun|de|te(r)** MF *decl as adj* major casualty; **Schwer|was|ser|re|ak|tor** M heavy water reactor; **schwer|wie|gend**, **schwer wie|gend** ADJ *(fig) Fehler, Mängel, Folgen* serious; *(Comput) Fehler* fatal, critical

Schwes|ter [ˈʃvɛstɐ] F **-, -n** sister; *(= Krankenschwester)* nurse; *(= Stationsschwester)* sister; *(= Ordensschwester)* nun, sister; *(= Gemeindeschwester)* district nurse; *(inf: = Schwesterfirma)* sister *or* associate(d) company

Schwes|ter|chen [ˈʃvɛstɐçən] NT **-s, -** little sister, baby sister

Schwes|ter-: **Schwes|ter|fir|ma** F sister *or* associate(d) company; **Schwes|ter|herz** NT *(inf)* (dear) sister, sis *(inf)*

Schwes|ter|lein [ˈʃvɛstɐlain] NT **-s, -** little sister, baby sister

schwes|ter|lich [ˈʃvɛstɐlɪç] ADJ sisterly ADV like sisters; **ich bin ihr ~ verbunden** she's like a sister to me

Schwes|ter|lie|be F sisterly love

Schwes|tern-: **Schwes|tern|heim** NT nurses' home; **Schwes|tern|hel|fer(in)** M(F) nursing auxiliary *(Brit) or* assistant *(US)*; **Schwes|tern|lie|be** F sisterly love; **Schwes|tern|or|den** M sisterhood; **Schwes|tern|paar** NT two sisters *pl*; **Schwes|tern|schaft** [ˈʃvɛstənʃaft] F **-, -en** nursing staff; *(von Orden)* sisterhood; **Schwes|tern|schu|le** F nurses' training college; **Schwes|tern|schü|le|rin** F student nurse; **Schwes|tern|tracht** F nurse's uniform; **Schwes|tern|wohn|heim** NT nurses' home

Schwes|ter-: **Schwes|ter|par|tei** F sister party; **Schwes|ter|schiff** NT sister ship

Schwib|bo|gen [ˈʃvɪpboːgn] M *(Archit)* flying buttress

schwieg *pret von* **schweigen**

Schwie|ger-: **Schwie|ger|el|tern** PL parents-in-law *pl*; **Schwie|ger|leu|te** PL *(inf)* in-laws *pl (inf)*; **Schwie|ger|ma|ma** [-mamaː] F *(inf)*; **Schwie|ger|mut|ter** F *pl* **-mütter** mother-in-law; **Schwie|ger|pa|pa** [-papaː] M *(inf)* father-in-law; **Schwie|ger|sohn** M son-in-law; **Schwie|ger|toch|ter** F daughter-in-law; **Schwie|ger|va|ter** M father-in-law

Schwie|le [ˈʃviːlə] F **-, -n** callus; *(= Vernarbung)* welt

schwie|lig [ˈʃviːlɪç] ADJ *Hände* callused

schwie|me|lig [ˈʃviːməlɪç], **schwiem|lig** [ˈʃviːmlɪç] ADJ *(dial inf)* dizzy

schwie|rig [ˈʃviːrɪç] ADJ difficult; *(= schwer zu lernen etc auch)* hard; **er ist ein ~er Fall** he is a problem ADV **~ zu übersetzen** difficult to translate; **das Gespräch verlief ~** the discussion didn't go well; **die Klärung seiner Identität gestaltete sich ~** it was difficult to identify him

Schwie|rig|keit F **-, -en** difficulty; **in ~en geraten** *or* **kommen** to get into difficulties *or* trouble; **auf ~en stoßen** to meet with difficulties; **jdm ~en machen** to make trouble for sb; **es macht mir überhaupt keine ~en** it won't be at all difficult for me; **warum musst du bloß immer ~en machen!** why must you always be difficult!; **jdn in ~en** *(acc)* **bringen** to create difficulties for sb; **mach keine ~en!** *(inf)* don't be difficult, don't make any trouble; **ohne ~en** without any difficulty; **ohne große ~(en)** without any great difficulty; **~en haben, etw zu tun** to have difficulties doing sth

Schwie|rig|keits|grad M degree of difficulty

schwillt [ʃvɪlt] *3. pers sing pres von* **schwellen**

Schwimm-: **Schwimm|bad** NT swimming pool; *(= Hallenbad)* swimming baths *pl*; **Schwimm|bag|ger** M dredger; **Schwimm|bahn** F lane; **Schwimm|bas|sin** NT, **Schwimm|be|cken** NT (swimming) pool; **Schwimm|be|we|gun|gen** PL swimming action *sing*; *(= Schwimmzüge)* swimming strokes *pl*; **Schwimm|bla|se** F *(Zool)* air bladder; **Schwimm|bril|le** F swimming goggles *pl*; **Schwimm|dock** NT floating dock

schwim|men [ˈʃvɪmən] *pret* **schwamm** [ʃvam], *ptp* **geschwommen** [gəˈʃvɔmən] *aux sein* VI **a** *auch aux haben* to swim; **~ gehen** to go swimming, to go for a swim; **er ist über den Fluss geschwommen** he swam (across) the river

b *(= auf dem Wasser treiben)* to float; **seine Schiffe ~ auf allen Meeren** his ships are afloat on every ocean

c *(inf: = überschwemmt sein, triefen) (Boden)* to be swimming *(inf)*, to be awash; **in Fett** *(dat)* **~** to be swimming in fat; **in seinem Blut ~** to be soaked in blood; **in Tränen ~** to be bathed in tears; **in** *or* **im Geld ~** to be rolling in it *or* in money *(inf)*

d *(fig: = unsicher sein)* to be at sea, to flounder

e es schwimmt mir vor den Augen I feel giddy *or* dizzy, everything's going round

VT *auch aux haben (Sport)* to swim

Schwim|men NT **-s,** *no pl* swimming; **zum ~ gehen** to go swimming; **ins ~ geraten** *or* **kommen** *(fig)* to begin to flounder

schwim|mend ADJ floating; **~es Fett** deep fat; **im ~en Fett aufbraten** to deep-fry

Schwim|mer [ˈʃvɪmɐ] M **-s, -** *(Tech, Angeln)* float

Schwim|mer [ˈʃvɪmɐ] M **-s, -**, **Schwim|me|rin** [-ərɪn] F **-, -nen** swimmer

Schwim|mer|be|cken NT swimmer's pool

Schwimm-: **schwimm|fä|hig** ADJ *Material* buoyant; *Fahrzeug, Flugzeug* amphibious; *Boot, Floß* floatable; **~ sein** to be able to float; *(Material)* to float, to be buoyant; **Schwimm|fest** NT swimming gala; **Schwimm|flos|se** F fin; *(von Taucher auch, von Wal, Robbe)* flipper; **Schwimm|flü|gel** M water wing; **Schwimm|fuß** M webfoot, webbed foot; **Schwimm|gür|tel** M swimming *or* cork belt; **Schwimm|hal|le** F swimming bath(s *pl*), (indoor) swimming pool; **Schwimm|haut** F *(Orn)* web; **Schwimm|hil|fe** F swimming aid; **Schwimm|kä|fer** M diving beetle; **Schwimm|kis|sen** NT water wing; **Schwimm|kran** M floating crane; **Schwimm|kurs** M swimming course *or* lessons *pl*; **Schwimm|la|ge** F swimming position; **Schwimm|leh|rer(in)** M(F) swimming instructor; **Schwimm|nu|del** F *(Sport)* aqua *or* swim *or* water noodle; **Schwimm|rei|fen** M **a** *(zum Schwimmen)* rubber ring **b** *(fig hum: = Hüftspeck)* spare tyre *(Brit) or* tire *(US) (hum)*, love handles *pl (hum)*; **Schwimm|sport** M swimming *no art*; **Schwimm|sta|di|on** NT swimming stadium, international swimming pool; **Schwimm|stil** M stroke; *(= Technik)* (swimming) style; **Schwimm|stoß** M stroke; **Schwimm|übun|gen** PL swimming exercises *pl*; **Schwimm|un|ter|richt** M swimming lessons *pl*; **Schwimm|ver|ein** M swimming club; **Schwimm|ver|such** M *(fig)* **die ersten ~e** the/one's first tentative steps; **Schwimm|vo|gel** M water bird, waterfowl; **Schwimm|wes|te** F life jacket

Schwin|del [ˈʃvɪndl] M **-s,** *no pl* **a** *(= Gleichgewichtsstörung)* dizziness; *(esp nach Drehen)* giddiness; **~ erregend** = **schwindelerregend**

b *(= Lüge)* lie; *(= Betrug)* swindle, fraud; *(= Vertrauensmissbrauch)* con *(inf)*; **die Berichte über das perfekte Haarwuchsmittel sind reiner ~** the reports about this perfect hair-restorer are a complete swindle *or* fraud *or* con *(inf)*; **das ist alles ~, was er da sagt** what he says is all a pack of lies *or* a big con *(inf)*; **glaub doch nicht an diesen ~!** don't be taken in!; **den ~ kenne ich!** *(inf)*, **auf den ~ falle ich nicht herein!** *(inf)* that's an old trick; **mit Subventionen wird viel ~ getrieben** a lot of swindling *or* cheating goes on with subsidies

c *(inf: = Kram)* **der ganze ~** the whole (kit and) caboodle *(inf) or* shoot *(inf)*; **ich will von dem ganzen ~ nichts mehr wissen!** I don't want to hear another thing about the whole damn business *(inf)*

Schwin|del|an|fall M dizzy turn, attack of dizziness

Schwin|de|lei [ʃvɪndəˈlai] F **-, -en** *(inf) (= leichte Lüge)* fib *(inf)*; *(= leichter Betrug)* swindle; **seine ständige ~** his constant fibbing *(inf)*

Schwin|del-: **schwin|del|er|re|gend** ADJ *Höhe* dizzy, vertiginous *(form)*; *Tempo* dizzying; *(inf) Preise* astronomical; **in ~er Höhe** at a dizzy height; **Schwin|del|fir|ma** F bogus firm *or* company; **schwin|del|frei** ADJ **Wendy ist nicht ~** Wendy can't stand heights, Wendy suffers from vertigo; **sie ist völlig ~** she has a good head for heights, she doesn't suffer from vertigo at all; **Schwin|del|ge|fühl** NT feeling of dizziness; *(esp nach Drehen)* feeling of giddiness

schwin|de|lig [ˈʃvɪndəlɪç] ADJ dizzy; *(esp nach Drehen)* giddy; **mir ist** *or* **ich bin ~** I feel dizzy/giddy; **mir wird leicht ~** I get dizzy/giddy easily

schwin|deln [ˈʃvɪndln] VI **a mir** *or* **mich** *(rare)* **schwindelt** I feel dizzy *or (esp vom Drehen)* giddy; **mir schwindelte der Kopf, mein Kopf schwindelte** my head was reeling; **der Gedanke macht mich ~** *(fig)* my head reels *or* I feel dizzy at the thought; **in ~der Höhe** at a dizzy height; **ein ~der Abgrund** a yawning abyss *or* chasm

b *(inf: = lügen)* to fib *(inf)*, to tell fibs *(inf)*

VT *(inf)* **das hat sie geschwindelt** she was fibbing *(inf) or* telling fibs *(inf)*; **das ist alles geschwindelt** it's all lies

VR **sich durch die Kontrollen/in den Saal ~** to con *or* wangle one's way through the checkpoint/into the hall *(inf)*; **sich durchs Leben/durch die Schule ~** to con one's way through life/school

Schwin|del-: **Schwin|del|preis** M astronomical *or* exorbitant price; **Schwin|del|un|ter|neh|men** NT bogus firm *or* company

schwin|den [ˈʃvɪndn] *pret* **schwand** [ʃvant], *ptp* **geschwunden** [gəˈʃvʊndn] VI *aux sein* **a** *(= abnehmen)* to dwindle; *(Schönheit)* to fade, to wane; *(= allmählich verschwinden) (Hoffnung)* to fade away, to dwindle; *(Erinnerung, Angst, Chance, Zeit)* to fade away; *(Kräfte)* to fade, to fail; **im Schwinden begriffen sein** to be dwindling; *(Schönheit)* to be on the wane; **ihm schwand der Mut, sein Mut schwand** his courage failed him; **ihm schwanden die Sinne** *(liter)* he grew faint; **aus den Augen ~** to fade from view; **aus der Erinnerung/dem Bewusstsein ~** to fade from (one's) memory/one's consciousness

b *(= verblassen: Farben)* to fade; *(= leiser werden: Ton)* to fade (away); *(= sich auflösen: Dunkelheit)* to fade away, to retreat *(liter)*

c *(Tech: Holz, Metall, Ton)* to shrink, to contract

Schwind|ler [ˈʃvɪndlɐ] M **-s, -**, **Schwind|le|rin** [-ərɪn] F **-, -nen** swindler; *(= Hochstapler)* con man, con merchant *(Brit inf)*; *(= Lügner)* liar, fibber *(inf)*, fraud

schwind|le|risch [ˈʃvɪndlərɪʃ] ADJ fraudulent

schwind|lig [ˈʃvɪndlɪç] ADJ = **schwindelig**

Schwind|sucht [ˈʃvɪnt-] F *(dated)* consumption; **die (galoppierende) ~ haben** *(dated)* to have galloping consumption; *(fig hum)* to suffer from a sort of wasting disease

schwind|süch|tig ADJ *(dated)* consumptive; *(fig hum)* shrinking, ailing

Schwind|süch|ti|ge(r) MF *decl as adj (dated)* consumptive

Schwing|be|sen M *(Sw Cook)* whisk

Schwing|bo|den M sprung floor

Schwin|ge [ˈʃvɪŋə] **F -, -n** (*liter.* = *Flügel*) wing, pinion (*poet*); **auf den ~n der Poesie/Begeisterung** on wings of poetry/passion

Schwin|gen NT -s, *no pl* (*Sw Sport*) (kind of) wrestling

schwin|gen [ˈʃvɪŋən] *pret* **schwang** [ʃvaŋ], *ptp* **geschwungen** [ɡəˈʃvʊŋən] **VT** *Schläger* to swing; *(drohend) Schwert, Stock etc* to brandish; *Hut, Zauberstab, Fahne* to wave; **die Gläser** *or* **den Becher ~** (*hum*) to quaff a glass (*old, hum*); **Rahm ~** (*Sw*) to whip cream → *auch* **geschwungen, Rede a, Tanzbein, Zepter**
VR sich auf etw (*acc*) **~** to leap *or* jump onto sth, to swing oneself onto sth; **sich über etw** (*acc*) **~** to vault across *or* over sth, to swing oneself over sth; **sich in etw** (*acc*) **~** to vault into sth, to swing oneself into sth; **sich in die Luft** *or* **Höhe ~** (*geh*) to soar (up) into the air; **der Aktienindex schwang sich auf Rekordhöhe** the share index leapt *or* jumped to a record high; **die Brücke schwingt sich elegant über das Tal** the bridge sweeps elegantly over the valley
VI a (= *sich hin- und herbewegen*) to swing
b (= *vibrieren*) (*Brücke, Saite*) to vibrate; (*Wellen*) to oscillate
c (*geh*) (= *nachklingen*) to linger; **in ihren Worten schwang leichte Kritik** her words had a tone of mild criticism
d (*Ski*) to swing

Schwin|ger[1] [ˈʃvɪŋɐ] **M -s, -** (*Boxen*) swing

Schwin|ger[2] [ˈʃvɪŋɐ] **M -s, -, Schwin|ge|rin** [-ərɪn] **F -, -nen** (*Sw*) wrestler

Schwing-: **Schwing|flü|gel M** casement window; **Schwing|he|bel M** (*Aut*) rocker arm; **Schwing|schlei|fer M** (orbital) sander; **Schwing|tür F** swing door

Schwin|gung [ˈʃvɪŋʊŋ] **F -, -en** (*Phys*) vibration; (*von Wellen*) oscillation; (*fig*) vibration; **in ~ kommen** to begin to swing *or* (*Saite*) to vibrate *or* (*Wellen*) to oscillate; **etw in ~(en) versetzen** to set sth swinging; to start sth vibrating; to start sth oscillating

Schwin|gungs-: **Schwin|gungs|dämp|fer M** (*Tech*) vibration damper; **Schwin|gungs|dau|er F** (*Phys*) time of vibration, period (of oscillation); **Schwin|gungs|kreis M** (*Rad*) resonant circuit; **Schwin|gungs|wei|te F** (*Phys*) amplitude; **Schwin|gungs|zahl F** (*Phys*) frequency of oscillation

schwipp [ʃvɪp] **INTERJ ~, schwapp** splish-splash

Schwipp-: **Schwipp|schwa|ger M** (*inf*) sister-in-law's husband; sister-in-law's/brother-in-law's brother; **Schwipp|schwä|ge|rin F** (*inf*) brother-in-law's wife; brother-in-law's/sister-in-law's sister

Schwips [ʃvɪps] **M -es, -e** (*inf*) **einen (kleinen) ~ haben** to be tiddly (*Brit inf*) *or* (slightly) tipsy

schwir|ren [ˈʃvɪrən] **VI** *aux sein* to whizz (*Brit*), to whiz; (*Bienen, Fliegen etc*) to buzz; **unzählige Gerüchte ~ durch die Presse** the press is buzzing with countless rumours (*Brit*) *or* rumors (*US*); **die Gedanken/Zahlen schwirrten mir durch den Kopf** thoughts/figures were whirling around in my head *or* buzzing through my head; **mir schwirrt der Kopf** my head is buzzing

Schwitz|bad NT Turkish bath; (= *Dampfbad*) steam bath

Schwit|ze [ˈʃvɪtsə] **F -, -n** (*Cook*) roux

schwit|zen [ˈʃvɪtsn] **VI** (*lit, fig*) to sweat; (*Mensch auch*) to perspire; (*Fenster*) to steam up; **Gott sei Dank, dass du kommst, wir haben vielleicht geschwitzt!** (*inf*) thank God you've come, we were really in a sweat (*inf*) **VT a** *Harz* to sweat → **Rippe a, Blut b** (*Cook*) *Mehl* to brown in fat **VR sich halb tot ~** (*inf*) to get drenched in sweat; **wir schleppen diese Kisten und ~ uns halb tot** (*inf*) we've been sweating away with these crates (*inf*); **sich nass ~** to get drenched in sweat

Schwit|zen NT -s, *no pl* sweating; (*von Mensch auch*) perspiration; **ins ~ kommen** *or* **geraten** (*lit*) to break out in a sweat; (*fig*) to get into a sweat; **jdn ins ~ bringen** (*lit, fig*) to make sb sweat

schwit|zig [ˈʃvɪtsɪç] **ADJ** = **verschwitzt**

Schwitz-: **Schwitz|kas|ten M** (*Ringen*) headlock; **jdn in den ~ nehmen** to get sb in a headlock, to put a headlock on sb; **Schwitz|kur F** sweating cure; **Schwitz|pa|ckung F** hot pack; **Schwitz|was|ser NT,** *no pl* condensation

Schwof [ʃvoːf] **M -(e)s, -e** (*inf*) hop (*inf*), shindig (*dated inf*), dance

schwo|fen [ˈʃvoːfn] **VI** (*inf*) to dance; **~ gehen** to go to a hop (*inf*)

schwoll *pret von* **schwellen**

schwö|ren [ˈʃvøːrən] *pret* **schwor** [ʃvoːɐ], *ptp* **geschworen** [ɡəˈʃvoːrən] **VT** to swear; *Eid auch* to take; **ich schwöre es(, so wahr mir Gott helfe)** I swear it (so help me God); **er schwor bei Gott/seiner Ehre, nichts davon gewusst zu haben** he swore by God/by *or* on his honour (*Brit*) *or* honor (*US*) that he knew nothing about it; **ich kann darauf ~, dass ...** I could swear to it that ...; **ich hätte ~ mögen** *or* **hätte geschworen, dass ...** I could have sworn that ...; **jdm/sich etw ~** to swear sth to sb/oneself; **ich spreche nie mehr mit ihm, das habe ich mir geschworen** I have sworn never to speak to him again; **er macht das nie wieder, das hat er ihr geschworen** he has sworn to her that he'll never do it again; **aber das hast du mir geschworen!** but you swore ...!; **sie schworen sich** (*dat*) **ewige Liebe** they swore (each other) eternal love
VI to swear; **auf jdn/etw ~** (*fig*) to swear by sb/sth; **auf die Bibel/die Verfassung** *etc* **~** to swear on the Bible/the Constitution *etc*

Schwuch|tel [ˈʃvʊxtl] **F -, -n** (*pej inf*) queen (*sl*); (*sl*: *Schimpfwort*) dick (*sl*)

schwul [ʃvuːl] **ADJ** (*inf*) gay, queer (*pej inf*)

schwül [ʃvyːl] **ADJ** (*lit, fig*) *Wetter, Tag etc* sultry, close, muggy; *Träume, Fantasien* sensuous; *Beleuchtung* murky

Schwü|le [ˈʃvyːlə] **F -,** *no pl* (*lit, fig*) sultriness; (*von Wetter, Tag etc auch*) closeness, mugginess; **in dieser ~** in this sultry weather

Schwu|len- (*inf*): **Schwu|len|bar F** gay bar; **Schwu|len|be|we|gung F** gay rights movement; **Schwu|len|ehe F** gay marriage; **Schwu|len|knei|pe F, Schwu|len|lo|kal NT** gay bar *or* pub (*Brit*); **Schwu|len|strich M** (*inf*) gay *or* queer (*pej inf*) beat (*inf*); **Schwu|len|sze|ne F** gay scene

Schwu|le(r) [ˈʃvuːlə] **MF** *decl as adj* gay

Schwu|li|tät [ʃvuliˈtɛːt] **F -, -en** (*inf*) trouble *no indef art*, difficulty; **in ~en geraten** *or* **kommen** to get in a fix (*inf*); **jdn in ~en bringen** to get sb into trouble *or* hot water (*inf*)

schwul|les|bisch ADJ (*inf*) lesbian-gay

Schwulst [ʃvʊlst] **M -(e)s,** *no pl* (*pej*) (*in der Sprache*) bombast, fustian, pompousness; (*in der Kunst*) bombast, ornateness, floridness

schwuls|tig [ˈʃvʊlstɪç] **ADJ ADV a** = **geschwollen b** (*esp Aus*) = **schwülstig**

schwüls|tig [ˈʃvʏlstɪç] (*pej*) **ADJ** *Stil, Redeweise* bombastic, fustian, pompous **ADV** bombastically, pompously

schwum|me|rig [ˈʃvʊmərɪç], **schwumm|rig** [ˈʃvʊmrɪç] **ADJ** (*inf*) (= *nervös*) uneasy, apprehensive; (*dial*) (= *schwindelig*) dizzy, giddy; (= *unwohl*) funny (*inf*); **mir wird ~** I feel uneasy/dizzy/funny (*inf*)

Schwund [ʃvʊnt] **M -(e)s** [-dəs], *no pl* **a** (= *Abnahme, Rückgang*) decrease (+*gen* in), decline (+*gen* in), dwindling (+*gen* of) **b** (*von Material*) shrinkage; (*Tech*: = *Abfall*) waste; **~ machen** (*inf*) to produce scrap **c** (*Rad*) fading **d** (*Med*) atrophy **e** (*Ling*: *von Vokal etc*) loss

Schwund-: **Schwund|aus|gleich M** (*Rad*) automatic frequency control, anti-fade device; **Schwund|stu|fe F** (*Ling*) zero grade

Schwung [ʃvʊŋ] **M -(e)s, ¨-e** [ˈʃvʏŋə] **a** swing; (= *ausholende Handbewegung*) flourish; (= *Sprung*) leap; **jdm/einer Sache einen ~ geben** to give sb/sth a push; **etw in ~ setzen** to set sth in motion
b *no pl* (*lit*: = *Antrieb*) momentum; (*fig*: = *Elan*) verve, zest; **~ holen** (*lit, fig*) to get up *or* build up momentum; **in ~ kommen** (*lit*: *Schlitten etc*) to gather *or* gain momentum; (*fig auch*) to get going; **an ~ gewinnen/verlieren** (*fig*) to gain/lose momentum; **jdn/etw in ~ bringen** (*lit, fig*) to get sb/sth going; **die Sache** *or* **den Laden in ~ bringen** (*inf*) to get things going; **~ in die Sache** *or* **den Laden bringen** (*inf*) to put a bit of life into things, to liven things up; **jdm/einer Sache ~ geben** *or* **verleihen** (*lit*) to give sb/sth momentum; (*fig auch*) to get sb/sth going; **in ~ sein** (*lit*: *Schlitten etc*) to be going full pelt (*esp Brit inf*) *or* at full speed; (*fig*) to be in full swing; **etw mit ~ tun** (*fig*) to do sth with zest; **voller/ohne ~** (*fig*) full of/lacking life *or* verve *or* zest
c (= *Linienführung*) sweep
d *no pl* (*inf*: = *Menge*) (*Sachen*) stack, pile (*inf*); (*Leute*) bunch

Schwung-: **Schwung|fe|der F** (*Orn*) wing feather; **schwung|haft ADJ** *Handel* flourishing, roaring **ADV sich ~ entwickeln** to grow hand over fist; **Schwung|kraft F** centrifugal force; **schwung|los ADJ** lacking in verve *or* zest, lacking life; *Absatz, Konjunktur* sluggish, slack **ADV** sluggishly, slackly; **im Endspiel wirkte Brasilien ~** Brazil seemed sluggish in the final; **Schwung|rad NT** flywheel

schwung|voll ADJ a *Linie, Bewegung, Handschrift* sweeping **b** (= *mitreißend*) *Rede, Aufführung* lively **ADV a** (= *mit Schwung*) *auf etw zugehen, aufstehen, hereinkommen, sich an die Arbeit machen* energetically; *werfen, schaukeln* powerfully; **etw ~ unterschreiben** to sign sth with a flourish **b** *spielen* with verve *or* zest; **die Aufführung war ~ inszeniert** it was a very lively performance; **etw ~er spielen** to play sth with more verve *or* zest

schwupp [ʃvʊp] **INTERJ** in a flash, as quick as a flash; **~! da ist er hingefallen** bang! down he fell; **und ~ hatte der Zauberer ...** and (hey (*Brit*)) presto, the conjurer had ...

Schwupp [ʃvʊp] **M -s, -e** (*inf*: = *Stoß*) push; **in einem ~** in one fell swoop

schwupp|di|wupp [ˈʃvʊpdiˈvʊp], **schwups** [ʃvʊps] **INTERJ** = **schwupp**

Schwups [ʃvʊps] **M -es, ¨-e** [ˈʃvʏpsə] (*inf*) = **Schwupp**

Schwur [ʃvuːɐ] **M -(e)s, ¨-e** [ˈʃvyːrə] (= *Eid*) oath; (= *Gelübde*) vow

Schwur-: **Schwur|fin|ger PL** *thumb, first finger and second finger, raised in swearing an oath*; **Schwur|ge|richt NT** *court with a jury*; **vor das ~ kommen** to be tried by jury; **Schwur|ge|richts|ver|fah|ren NT** trial by jury *no def art*

Schwyz [ʃviːts] **NT -** (= *Kanton*) Schwyz

Schwy|zer|dütsch [ˈʃviːtsɐdyːtʃ] **NT, Schwy|zer|tütsch** [-tyːtʃ] **NT -(s),** *no pl* (*Sw*) Swiss German

Sci|ence-Fic|tion [ˈsaiənsˈfɪkʃn] **F -, -s** science fiction, sci-fi (*inf*)

Sci|en|to|lo|ge [saiəntoˈloːɡə] **M -n, -n, Sci|en|to|lo|gin** [-ˈloːɡɪn] **F -, -nen** Scientologist

sci|en|to|lo|gisch [saiəntoˈloːɡɪʃ] **ADJ** Scientologist

Sci|en|to|lo|gy® [saiənˈtɔlədʒi] **F -,** *no pl* Scientology®

Sci|en|to|lo|gy-Kir|che F Church of Scientology

Sci|roc|co [ʃiˈrɔko] **M -s, -s** sirocco

Scotch|ter|rier [ˈskɔtʃtɛriɐ] **M** Scotch terrier, Scottie

Screen|shot [ˈskriːnʃɔt] **M -s, -s** (*Comput*) screenshot

Scri|bble [ˈskrɪbl] **NT -s, -s** (*spec*: = *Entwurf*) first draft (*of a publicity visual*)

Scroll|bar [ˈskroːlbaːɐ] **M -s, -s** (*Comput*) scrollbar

scrol|len [ˈskroːlən] **VTI** (*Comput*) to scroll

Scroll-Tas|te [ˈskroːl-] **F** (*Comput*) scroll key

Scro|tum ['skro:tʊm] NT **-s, Scrota** [-ta] *(Med)* scrotum
SCSI [ɛstse:lɛs'li:, 'skazi] NT **-** *abbr von* **small computer system interface** SCSI
SDS [ɛsde:'lɛs] M **-** *(Hist) abbr von* **Sozialistischer Deutscher Studentenbund**
Scyl|la ['stsʏla] F **-**, *no pl (Myth)* = **Szylla**
SD [ɛs'de:] M **-**, *no pl (NS) abbr von* **Sicherheitsdienst** Security Service
SD [ɛs'de:] F **-, -s** *abbr von* **Super Density Disc** SD
SDS [ɛsde:'lɛs] M **-** *abbr von* **Sozialistischer Deutscher Studentenbund**
Seal [si:l] M OR NT **-s, -s** sealskin
Seal|skin ['si:lskɪn] M OR NT **-s, -s** **a** sealskin **b** imitation sealskin
Sé|an|ce [ze'ã:s(ə)] F **-, -n** séance
Se|bor|rhö [zebɔ'rø:] F **-, -en** [-'rø:ən] dandruff, seborrh(o)ea *(spec)*
sec *abbr von* **Sekunde**
sechs [zɛks] NUM six → *auch* **vier**
Sechs- *in cpds* six → *auch* **vier-**; **Sechs|ach|tel|takt** M *(Mus)* six-eight time; **Sechs|eck** NT hexagon; **sechs|eckig** ADJ hexagonal
Sech|ser ['zɛksɐ] M **-s, -** **a** *(obs)* six-kreutzer/ /six-groschen *etc* piece; *(Hist dial inf)* five-pfennig piece; **nicht für einen ~ Verstand haben** not to have a scrap *or* a ha'p'orth *(Brit)* of sense **b** six → *auch* **Vierer**
sech|ser|lei ['zɛksɐ'lai] ADJ *inv* six kinds of → *auch* **viererlei**
Sech|ser|pack [-pak] M **-s, -s** six-pack
Sechs-: **sechs|fach** ADJ sixfold ADV sixfold, six times → *auch* **vierfach**; **Sechs|fü|ßer** [-fy:sɐ] M **-s, -** *(Zool)* hexapod; **sechs|hun|dert** NUM six hundred; **Sechs|kampf** M *gymnastic competition with six events*; **sechs|mal** ADV six times; **Sechs|ta|ge|krieg** M *(Hist)* Six Day War; **Sechs|ta|ge|ren|nen** NT six-day (bicycle) race; **sechs|tä|gig** ADJ six-day; **sechs|tau|send** NUM six thousand; **ein Sechstausender** *a mountain six thousand metres in height*
Sechs|tel ['zɛkstl] NT **-s, -** sixth → *auch* **Viertel**
sechs|tens ['zɛkstns] ADV sixth(ly), in the sixth place
sechs|te(r, s) ['zɛkstə] ADJ sixth; **einen ~n Sinn für etw haben, den ~n Sinn haben** to have a sixth sense (for sth) → *auch* **vierte(r, s)**
Sechs|und|sech|zig ['zɛkslʊnt'zɛçtsɪç] NT **-**, *no pl (Cards)* sixty-six
Sechs|zy|lin|der ['zɛks-] M *(Auto)* six-cylinder car; *(Motor)* six-cylinder engine
sech|zehn ['zɛçtse:n] NUM sixteen → *auch* **vierzehn**
Sech|zehn|tel ['zɛçtse:ntl] NT **-s, -** *(Mus)* semiquaver *(Brit)*, sixteenth note *(US)*
Sech|zehn|tel|no|te F *(Mus)* semiquaver *(Brit)*, sixteenth note *(US)*
sech|zig ['zɛçtsɪç] NUM sixty → *auch* **vierzig**
Sech|zi|ger ['zɛçtsɪgɐ] M **-s, -**, **Sech|zi|ge|rin** [-ərɪn] F **-, -nen** sixty-year-old, sexagenarian
Se|cond|hand- *in cpds* second-hand; **Se|cond|hand|la|den** M second-hand shop
SED [ɛsle:'de:] F **-** *(DDR) abbr von* **Sozialistische Einheitspartei Deutschlands**
Se|da|tiv [zeda'ti:f] NT **-s, -e** [-və], **Se|da|ti|vum** [zeda'ti:vʊm] NT **-s, Sedativa** [-va] *(Pharm)* sedative
Se|dez|for|mat [ze'de:ts-] NT *(Typ)* sextodecimo
se|die|ren [ze'di:rən] *ptp* **sediert** VTI *(Med)* to sedate
Se|di|ment [zedi'mɛnt] NT **-(e)s, -e** *(Geol)* sediment
se|di|men|tär [zedimɛn'tɛ:ɐ] ADJ *(Geol)* sedimentary
Se|di|ment|ge|stein NT *(Geol)* sedimentary rock
See [ze:] F **-, -n** ['ze:ən] sea; **raue** *or* **schwere ~** rough *or* heavy seas; **an der ~** by the sea, at the seaside; **an die ~ fahren** to go to the sea(side); **auf hoher ~** on the high seas; **auf ~** at sea; **in ~ gehen** *or* **stechen** to put to sea; **zur ~ fahren** to be a merchant seaman; **zur ~ gehen** to go to sea
See M **-s, -n** lake; *(in Schottland)* loch; *(= Teich)* pond
See-: **See|aal** M **a** *(Zool)* conger (eel) **b** *(Comm)* dogfish; **See|ad|ler** M sea eagle; **See|al|pen** PL *(Geog)* Maritime Alps *pl*; **See|amt** NT *(Admin)* maritime court; **See|ane|mo|ne** F sea anemone; **See|bad** NT **a** *(= Kurort)* seaside resort **b** *(= Bad im Meer)* bathe *or* swim in the sea; **See|bär** M **a** *(hum inf)* seadog *(inf)* **b** *(Zool)* fur seal; **See|bar|be** F *(Zool)* red mullet; **See|be|ben** NT seaquake; **see|be|schä|digt** [-bəʃɛ:dɪçt] ADJ *(form) Schiff* damaged at sea; **See|blick** M view of the sea/lake; **ein Zimmer mit ~** *(am Meer)* a room with sea view; *(am See)* a room overlooking the lake; **See|bo|den** M bottom *or* bed of a/the lake; *(von Meer)* bottom *or* bed of a/the sea; **der ~ des Loch Ness** the bottom *or* bed of Loch Ness; **See-Ele|fant** M, **See|ele|fant** M sea elephant; **see|er|fah|ren** ADJ *Volk* experienced at navigation *or* seafaring; **see|fah|rend** ADJ *attr Volk* seafaring; **See|fah|rer(in)** M(F) seafarer; **Sindbad der ~** Sinbad the Sailor; **See|fahrt** F **a** *(= Fahrt)* (sea) voyage; *(= Vergnügungsseefahrt)* cruise **b** *(= Schifffahrt)* seafaring *no art*; **ungeeignet für die ~ in ...** unsuited for navigation *or* sailing in ...; **die ~ lernen** to learn to sail; **die Regeln der ~** the rules of the sea
See|fahrts-: **See|fahrts|amt** NT shipping board; **See|fahrts|buch** NT (seaman's) registration book; **See|fahrts|schu|le** F merchant navy *(Brit)* or merchant marine *(US)* training college
See-: **see|fest** ADJ **a** *Mensch* not subject to seasickness; **~ sein** to be a good sailor **b** = **seetüchtig** **c** *Ladung* fit for sea transport; **See|fisch** M saltwater fish; **See|fi|sche|rei** F sea fishing; **See|fracht** F sea freight; **See|fracht|brief** M *(Comm)* bill of lading; **See|frau** F sailor, mariner *(esp liter)*; **See|funk(|dienst)** M shipping radio service; **See|gang** [-gaŋ] M, *no pl* swell; **starker** *or* **hoher ~** heavy *or* rough seas *or* swell; **See|ge|fahr** F *(Comm)* sea risk; **See|ge|fecht** NT sea *or* naval battle; **See|gel|tung** F *(Hist)* naval prestige; **See|ge|mäl|de** NT seascape; **see|ge|stützt** [-gəʃtʏtst] ADJ *(Mil)* sea-based; *Flugkörper auch* sea-launched; **See|gras** NT *(Bot)* eelgrass, sea grass *or* hay; **See|gras|mat|rat|ze** F sea grass mattress; **see|grün** ADJ sea-green; **See|gur|ke** F *(Zool)* sea cucumber; **See|ha|fen** M seaport; **See|han|del** M maritime trade; **See|ha|se** M lumpsucker; **See|herr|schaft** F naval *or* maritime supremacy; **See|hö|he** F sea level; **See|hund** M seal; **See|hunds|fell** NT sealskin; **See|igel** M sea urchin; **See|jung|fer** F *(Zool)* dragonfly; **See|jung|frau** F *(Myth)* mermaid; **See|ka|dett(in)** M(F) *(Mil)* naval cadet; **See|ka|nal** M (maritime) canal; **See|kar|te** F sea *or* nautical chart; **See|kat|ze** F catfish; **see|klar** ADJ ready to sail; **See|kli|ma** NT maritime climate; **see|krank** ADJ seasick; **Paul wird leicht ~** Paul is a bad sailor; **See|krank|heit** F seasickness; **See|krieg** M naval war; **See|kriegs|recht** NT laws *pl* of naval warfare; **See|kuh** F *(Zool)* sea cow, manatee; **See|lachs** M *(Zool)* pollack; *(Cook)* rock salmon; **See|lachs|fi|let** NT *(Cook)* rock salmon fillet
Seel|amt NT *(Sw Eccl)* requiem
See|land ['ze:lant] NT **-s** *(Geog)* **a** *(dänisch)* Zealand, Seeland **b** *(niederländisch)* Zeeland
Seel|chen ['ze:lçən] NT **-s, -** *(inf)* dear soul
See|le ['ze:lə] F **-, -n** **a** *(Rel, fig)* soul; *(= Herzstück, Mittelpunkt)* life and soul; **seine ~ aushauchen** *(euph liter)* to breathe one's last *(liter)*; **in tiefster** *or* **innerster ~** *(geh)* in one's heart of hearts; **mit ganzer ~** with all one's soul; **von ganzer ~** with all one's heart (and soul); **aus tiefster** *or* **innerster ~** with all one's heart and with all one's soul; *danken* from the bottom of one's heart; **jdm aus der ~** *or* **aus tiefster ~ sprechen** to express exactly what sb feels; **das liegt mir auf der ~** it weighs heavily on my mind; **sich** *(dat)* **etw von der ~ reden** to get sth off one's chest; **sich** *(dat)* **die ~ aus dem Leib reden/schreien** *(inf)* to talk/shout until one is blue in the face *(inf)*; **das tut mir in der ~ weh** I am deeply distressed; **zwei ~n und ein Gedanke** *(prov)* two minds with but a single thought; **zwei ~n wohnen in meiner Brust** *(liter)* I am torn; **dann/nun hat die liebe** *or* **arme ~ Ruh** that'll put him/us *etc* out of his/our misery; **meiner Seel!** *(old)* upon my soul! *(old)*
b *(= Mensch)* soul; **eine ~ von Mensch** *or* **von einem Menschen** an absolute dear
c *(von Feuerwaffen)* bore
d *(von Tau)* core
See|len-: **See|len|ach|se** F axis (of the bore); **See|len|adel** M *(liter)* nobility of mind; **See|len|amt** NT *(Eccl)* requiem; **See|len|arzt** M, **See|len|ärz|tin** F *(hum)*, **See|len|dok|tor** M, **See|len|dok|to|rin** F *(hum inf)* head-shrinker *(hum inf)*, shrink *(inf)*, trick cyclist *(Brit hum sl)*; **See|len|dra|ma** NT psychological drama; **See|len|for|scher(in)** M(F) psychologist; **See|len|freund(in)** M(F) *(geh)* soul mate; **See|len|frie|de(n)** M *(geh)* peace of mind; **See|len|grö|ße** F *(geh)* greatness of mind, magnanimity; **see|len|gut** ADJ kind-hearted; **See|len|gü|te** F *(geh)* kind-heartedness; **See|len|heil** NT spiritual salvation, salvation of one's soul; *(fig)* spiritual welfare; **See|len|hirt(in)** M(F), **See|len|hir|te** M *(geh, iro)* pastor; **See|len|klemp|ner(in)** M(F) *(pej inf: = Psychiater)* head shrinker *(hum inf)*, shrink *(inf)*, trick cyclist *(Brit hum sl)*; **See|len|kun|de** F *(dated)* psychology; **See|len|la|ge** F *(von Individuum)* inner state; *(politisch, von Nation, Partei etc auch)* inner feeling; **See|len|land|schaft** F *(inf)* mindset; *(künstlerisch, literarisch)* landscape of the soul; **See|len|le|ben** NT inner life; **er versteht ihr ~ überhaupt nicht** he does not understand her emotions *or* feelings at all; **See|len|leh|re** F *(dated)* psychology; **see|len|los** ADJ soulless; **See|len|mas|sa|ge** F *(hum inf)* gentle persuasion; **See|len|mes|se** F *(Eccl)* requiem mass; **See|len|not** F, **See|len|pein** F, **See|len|qual** F *(geh)* (mental) anguish; **See|len|re|gung** F sign of emotion, emotional reaction *or* response; **See|len|ru|he** F calmness, coolness; **in aller ~** calmly; *(= kaltblütig)* as cool as you please *(Brit)*, as cool as ice; **see|len|ru|hig** ADJ calm; *(= kaltblütig)* as cool as you please, as cool as a cucumber *(inf)* ADV calmly; *(= kaltblütig)* callously; **See|len|strip|tease** M *(inf)* baring one's soul; **See|len|trös|ter** M *(hum: = Schnaps)* pick-me-up *(inf)*; **See|len|trös|ter(in)** M(F) *(Mensch)* comforter; **See|len|ver|käu|fer** M *(Hist)* seller of souls; *(fig pej) (= Heuerbaas)* press-gang officer; *(Schiff)* death trap; **see|len|ver|wandt** ADJ congenial *(liter)*; **sie waren ~** they were kindred spirits; **See|len|ver|wandt|schaft** F affinity, congeniality of spirit *(liter)*; **see|len|voll** ADJ *Blick, Tonfall* soulful ADV soulfully, passionately; **See|len|wan|de|rung** F *(Rel)* transmigration of souls, metempsychosis; **See|len|wär|mer** [-vɛrmɐ] M **-s, -** *(hum: = Schnaps)* pick-me-up *(inf)*; **See|len|zu|stand** M psychological *or* mental state
See-: **See|leu|te** *pl von* **Seemann**; **See|li|lie** F sea lily
see|lisch ['ze:lɪʃ] ADJ *(Rel)* spiritual; *(= geistig) Gesundheit, Gleichgewicht* mental; *Schaden* psychological; *Erschütterung, Belastung* emotional; *Grausamkeit* mental; **~e Kraft zu etw haben** to have the strength of mind for sth; **~e Abgründe** the blackest depths of the human soul ADV psychologically; **~ bedingt sein** to have psychological causes; **~ krank** mentally ill; **jdn ~ misshandeln** to ill-treat sb psychologically

See-: **See|lot|se** M, **See|lot|sin** F pilot; **See|lö|we** M sea lion

Seel|sor|ge ['ze:lzɔrgə] F, *no pl* spiritual welfare; **in der ~ arbeiten** to do spiritual welfare work with a church

Seel|sor|ger [-zɔrgɐ] M **-s, -**, **Seel|sor|ge|rin** [-ərɪn] F **-, -nen** pastor

seel|sor|ge|risch [-zɔrgərɪʃ], **seel|sor|ger|lich**, **seel|sorg|lich** ADJ *Tätigkeit, Betreuung* pastoral ADV **~ tätig sein** to do pastoral work; **jdn ~ betreuen** to be a religious counsellor *(Brit) or* counselor *(US)* to sb

See-: **See|luft** F sea air; **See|macht** F naval *or* sea *or* maritime power

See|mann M *pl* **-leute** sailor, seaman, mariner *(esp liter)*

see|män|nisch [-mɛnɪʃ] ADJ *Ausbildung, Sprache etc* nautical; *Tradition auch* seafaring; **das ist typisch ~** that is typical of sailors ADV nautically; **~ heißen sie ...** in nautical *or* sailors' language they are called ...

See|manns-: **See|manns|amt** NT shipping board; **See|manns|aus|druck** M *pl* **-ausdrücke** nautical *or* sailors' term; **See|manns|brauch** M seafaring custom; **See|manns|gang** [-gaŋ] M, *no pl* sailor's walk *or* swagger; **See|manns|garn** NT, *no pl (inf)* sailor's yarn; **~ spinnen** to spin a yarn; **See|manns|grab** NT watery grave, Davy Jones' *or* Jones's locker; **ein ~ finden** to go to a watery grave; **See|manns|heim** NT sailors' home; **See|manns|lied** NT sea shanty; **See|manns|los** NT a sailor's lot; **See|manns|mis|si|on** F mission to seamen, seamen's mission; **See|manns|spra|che** F nautical *or* sailors' slang; **See|manns|tod** M sailor's death; **den ~ sterben** to die a sailor's death

See-: **see|mä|ßig** ADJ *Verpackung* seaworthy; **See|mei|le** F nautical *or* sea mile; **See|mi|ne** F (sea) mine; **See|mö|we** F seagull; **See|mu|schel** F *(Zool)* conch; **See|nel|ke** F sea anemone

Seen|ge|biet ['ze:ən-] NT, **Seen|land|schaft** F lakeland area

See|not F, *no pl* distress; **in ~ geraten** to get into distress

See|not-: **See|not|kreu|zer** M (motor) lifeboat; **See|not|(ret|tungs)|dienst** M sea rescue service; **See|not|zei|chen** NT nautical distress signal

Seen|plat|te ['ze:ən-] F *lowland plain full of lakes*

See-: **See|nym|phe** F mermaid; **See|ot|ter** M sea otter; **See|pferd** NT, **See|pferd|chen** [-pfe:ɐtçən] NT **-s, -** sea horse; **See|räu|ber(in)** M(F) pirate; *(in Mittelamerika im 17., 18. Jh. auch)* buccaneer; **See|räu|be|rei** F piracy; **See|räu|ber|schiff** NT pirate (ship); buccaneer; **See|recht** NT maritime law; **See|rei|se** F (sea) voyage; *(= Kreuzfahrt)* cruise; **See|ro|se** F water lily; **See|sack** M seabag, sailor's kitbag *(Brit)*; **See|salz** NT sea salt; **See|sand** M sea sand; **See|scha|den** M damage at sea, average *(spec)*; **See|schiff** NT seagoing *or* ocean-going ship *or* vessel; **See|schiff|fahrt** F maritime *or* ocean shipping; **See|schild|krö|te** F sea turtle; **See|schlacht** F naval *or* sea battle; **See|schlan|ge** F sea snake; *(Myth)* sea serpent; **See|schwal|be** F tern; **See|sieg** M naval victory; **See|sper|re** F naval blockade; **See|stadt** F seaside town; **See|stern** M *(Zool)* starfish; **See|stra|ße** F sea route, shipping lane; **See|stra|ßen|ord|nung** F rules *pl* of the road (at sea), international regulations *pl* for preventing collisions at sea *(form)*; **See|streit|kräf|te** PL naval forces *pl*, navy; **See|stück** NT *(Art)* seascape; **See|tang** M seaweed; **See|tau|cher** M *(Orn)* grebe; **See|teu|fel** M *(Zool)* angler, allmouth; *(am Meeresboden lebend)* monkfish; **See|trans|port** M shipment *or* transport by sea, sea transport; **see|tüch|tig** ADJ seaworthy; **See|tüch|tig|keit** F seaworthiness; **See|ufer** NT lakeside; *(von großem See auch)* (lake) shore; **See|un|ge|heu|er** NT sea monster; **see|un|tüch|tig** ADJ unseaworthy; **See|ver|kehr** M maritime traffic; **See|ver|si|che|rung** F marine insurance; **See|vo|gel** M sea bird; **See|volk** NT *(Nation)* seafaring nation *or* people; *(inf: = Seeleute)* seafaring people *pl*; **See|wal|ze** F *(Zool)* sea cucumber; **see|wärts** ['ze:vɛrts] ADV *(= in Richtung Meer)* seaward(s), toward(s) the sea; *(= in Richtung (Binnen)see)* toward(s) the lake; **See|was|ser** NT, *no pl (= Meerwasser)* sea water; *(= Wasser eines Sees)* lake water; **See|weg** M sea route; **auf dem ~ reisen** to go *or* travel by sea; **See|we|sen** NT maritime affairs *pl*, *no art*; **See|wet|ter|dienst** M meteorological service, Met Office (*Brit inf*); **See|wind** M sea breeze, onshore wind; **See|wolf** M *(Zool)* wolffish; **See|zei|chen** NT navigational aid; **See|zun|ge** F sole

Se|gel ['ze:gl] NT **-s, -** sail; **die ~ setzen** to set the sails; **mit vollen ~n** under full sail *or* canvas; *(fig)* with gusto; **unter ~ gehen** *(Naut)* to set sail; **die ~ streichen** *(Naut)* to strike sail; *(fig)* to give in → **Wind a**

Se|gel-: **Se|gel|boot** NT sailing boat *(Brit)*, sailboat *(US)*; **Se|gel|fahrt** F sail; **se|gel|flie|gen** VI *infin only* to glide; **~ gehen** to go gliding; **Se|gel|flie|gen** NT **-s**, *no pl* gliding; **Se|gel|flie|ger(in)** M(F) glider pilot; **Se|gel|flie|ge|rei** F gliding; **Se|gel|flug** M *(no pl: = Segelfliegerei)* gliding; *(= Flug)* glider flight; **Se|gel|flug|platz** M gliding field; **Se|gel|flug|zeug** NT glider; *(leichter gebaut auch)* sailplane; **Se|gel|jacht** F (sailing) yacht, sailboat *(US)*; **Se|gel|kar|te** F chart; **se|gel|klar** ADJ *pred* ready to sail; **Se|gel|klas|se** F *(Sport)* (yacht) class; **Se|gel|klub** M sailing club; **Se|gel|ma|cher(in)** M(F) sailmaker

se|geln ['ze:gln] VTI *aux haben or sein (lit, fig)* to sail; **eine Strecke ~** to sail a course; **eine Regatta ~** to sail in a regatta; **als junger Mensch hat** *or* **ist er viel gesegelt** in his younger days he did a lot of sailing *or* he sailed a lot; **~ gehen** to go for a sail VI *aux sein (inf)* **durch eine Prüfung ~** to flop in an exam (*Brit inf*), to fail an exam

Se|geln NT **-s**, *no pl* sailing

Se|gel-: **Se|gel|oh|ren** PL *(hum)* flappy ears *pl (inf)*; **Se|gel|par|tie** F sail, sailing trip; **Se|gel|re|gat|ta** F sailing *or* yachting regatta; **Se|gel|schiff** NT sailing ship *or* vessel; **Se|gel|schu|le** F sailing school; **Se|gel|schul|schiff** NT training sailing ship; **Se|gel|sport** M sailing *no art*; **Se|gel|törn** M cruise (on a yacht *etc*); **Se|gel|tuch** NT *pl* **-tuche** canvas

Se|gen ['ze:gn] M **-s, -** **a** *(lit, fig)* blessing; *(Eccl: = Gnadengebet)* blessing, benediction; **es ist ein ~, dass ...** it is a blessing that ...; **über jdn/etw den ~ sprechen** to give sb/sth one's blessing; *(Eccl auch)* to pronounce one's blessing upon sb/sth; **jdm den ~ erteilen** *or* **spenden** to give sb one's blessing *or* benediction; **~ spendend** beneficent; **jdm/einer Sache seinen ~ erteilen** *or* **geben** *(fig)* to give sb/sth one's blessing; **meinen ~ hat er, er hat meinen ~** he has my blessing
b *(= Heil, Erfolg)* blessing, boon, godsend; **das bringt keinen ~** no good will come of it; **~ bringend** beneficent; **ein wahrer ~** a real blessing *or* boon; **zum ~ der Menschheit werden** to be for *or* to redound to *(liter)* the benefit of mankind; **zum ~ des Unternehmens handeln** to act for the good of the company; **jdm zum ~ gereichen** to be a blessing *or* boon *or* godsend to sb
c *(liter: = Ertrag, Lohn)* fruits *pl*
d *(inf)* **der ganze ~** the whole lot *or* shoot *(inf)*

Se|gen-: **se|gen|brin|gend** ADJ → **Segen b**; **Se|gen|er|tei|lung** F *(Eccl)* benediction, blessing; **se|gen|spen|dend** ADJ → **Segen a**

Se|gens-: **se|gens|reich** ADJ beneficial; *Tätigkeit* beneficent; **Se|gens|wunsch** M *(liter)* blessing; **herzliche Segenswünsche** congratulations and best wishes

Seg|ler ['ze:glɐ] M **-s, -** **a** *(= Schiff)* sailing vessel **b** *(Orn)* swift

Seg|ler ['ze:glɐ] M **-s, -**, **Seg|le|rin** [-ərɪn] F **-, -nen** *(= Segelsportler)* yachtsman/-woman, sailor

Seg|ler|müt|ze F sailor's cap

Seg|ment [zɛ'gmɛnt] NT **-(e)s, -e** segment

seg|men|tal [zɛgmɛn'ta:l] ADJ segmental

seg|men|tär [zɛgmɛn'tɛ:ɐ] ADJ segmentary

seg|men|tie|ren [zɛgmɛn'ti:rən] *ptp* **segmentiert** VT to segment

Seg|men|tie|rung F **-, -en** segmentation

seg|nen ['ze:gnən] VT *(Rel)* to bless; **~d die Hände erheben** to raise one's hands in blessing → *auch* **gesegnet**

Seg|nung F **-, -en** *(Rel)* blessing, benediction

Seg|re|ga|ti|on [zegrega'tsio:n] F **-, -en** *(Sociol)* segregation

seh|be|hin|dert ADJ partially sighted

Seh|be|hin|de|rung F impaired vision *or* sight

se|hen ['ze:ən]

pret **sah** [za:], *ptp* **gesehen** [gə'ze:ən]

1 TRANSITIVES VERB
2 REFLEXIVES VERB
3 INTRANSITIVES VERB

1 – TRANSITIVES VERB

a [= mit den Augen wahrnehmen] to see; *(= ansehen)* to look at, to see; **siehst du irgendwo mein Buch?** can you see my book anywhere?; **Sie sehen jetzt eine Direktübertragung ...** we now bring you a live broadcast ...; **Sie sahen eine Direktübertragung ...** that was a live broadcast ...; **ich sehe was, was du nicht siehst** *(= Spiel)* I spy (with my little eye *(Brit)*); **gut zu sehen sein** to be clearly visible; **schlecht zu sehen sein** to be difficult to see; **sieht man das?** does it show?; **das kann man sehen** you can see that; **von ihm war nichts mehr zu sehen** he was no longer to be seen; **da gibt es nichts zu sehen** there is nothing to see; **darf ich das mal sehen?** can I have a look at that?; **jdn kommen/weggehen sehen** to see sb coming/leaving; **jdn/etw zu sehen bekommen** to get to see sb/sth; **sich/jdn als etw sehen** to see oneself/sb as sth; **etw in jdm sehen** to see sb as sth; **Sie sah in ihm ihren Nachfolger** she saw him as her successor; **das Kind sah in ihm den Beschützer** the child saw him as a protector; **ich kann den Mantel/Mann nicht mehr sehen** *(= nicht mehr ertragen)* I can't stand the sight of that coat/the man any more; **das muss man gesehen haben** it has to be seen to be believed; *(= lässt sich nicht beschreiben)* you have to see it for yourself; **den möchte ich sehen, der ...** I'd like to meet the man who ...; **hat man so was schon gesehen!** *(inf)* did you ever see anything like it!

♦ **sich sehen lassen** to put in an appearance; **er hat sich schon lange nicht mehr zu Hause sehen lassen** he hasn't put in an appearance at home for a long time; **er lässt sich kaum noch bei uns sehen** he hardly ever comes to see us now, we hardly ever see him these days; **lassen Sie sich doch mal wieder sehen!** do come again!; **er kann sich in dieser Gegend nicht mehr sehen lassen** he can't show his face in the area any more; **kann ich mich in diesem Anzug sehen lassen?** do I look all right in this suit?; **mit diesem eleganten Kostüm kann sie sich überall sehen lassen** she'd look fine anywhere in this smart suit; **mit diesem Mann kannst du dich doch nirgends sehen lassen!** you don't want to be seen with this man!; **mit diesem Ergebnis kann sich die Mannschaft sehen lassen** the team can be proud of this result

b [= treffen] to see; **sich** *or* **einander sehen** to see each other; **ich freue mich, Sie zu sehen!** nice to see you!; **also, wir sehen uns morgen** right, I'll see you tomorrow; **sie sehen sich in letzter**

Zeit oft they've been seeing a lot of each other lately

c (= feststellen) to see; **das wird man noch sehen** we'll see; **ob er tatsächlich kommt, das wird man noch sehen** we'll see if he actually comes; **das wollen wir (doch) erst mal sehen!** we'll see about that!; **das wollen wir (doch) erst mal sehen, ob …** we'll see if …; **das müssen wir erst mal sehen** that remains to be seen; **da sieht man es mal wieder!** that's typical!; **das sehe ich noch nicht** *(inf)* I still don't see that happening

d (= beurteilen) to see; *(= deuten, interpretieren)* to look at, to see; **wie siehst du das?** how do you see it?; **das sehe ich anders, so sehe ich das nicht** that's not how I see it; **du hast wohl keine Lust, oder wie sehe ich das?** *(inf)* you don't feel like it, do you?; **das darf man nicht so sehen** that's not the way to look at it; **du siehst das/ihn nicht richtig** you've got it/him wrong; **seit dieser Unterhaltung sehe ich sie anders** since this conversation I see her differently; **rein menschlich/wirtschaftlich gesehen** from a purely personal/economic point of view; **so gesehen** looked at in this way

2 – REFLEXIVES VERB

♦ **sich sehen sich betrogen/getäuscht sehen** to see oneself cheated/deceived; **sich enttäuscht sehen** to feel disappointed; **sich genötigt** *or* **veranlasst sehen, zu …** to find it necessary to …; **sich gezwungen sehen, zu …** to find oneself obliged to …; **sich in der Lage sehen, zu …** *(form)* to find oneself in a position to … *(form)*

3 – INTRANSITIVES VERB

a (mit den Augen) to see; **er sieht gut/schlecht** he can/cannot see very well; **er sieht nur mit einem** *or* **auf einem Auge** he only has sight in one eye; **seit diesem Unfall sehe ich doppelt** I've been seeing double *or* I've had double vision since the accident; **nichts mehr sehen** *(sl: = betrunken sein)* to be wrecked *(Brit)* *or* wasted *(sl)*; **durchs Schlüsselloch sehen** to look through the keyhole; **jdm tief in die Augen sehen** to look deep into sb's eyes; **jdm über die Schulter sehen** to look over sb's shoulder; **siehe oben/unten** see above/below; **sieh(e) da!** *(liter)* behold! *(liter)*; **siehst du (wohl)!, siehste!** *(inf)* you see!; **sieh doch!** look (here)!; **sehen Sie mal!** look!; **siehe!, sehet!** *(old, liter, Bibl)* lo! *(Bibl)*, behold! *(Bibl)*; **willst du mal sehen?** do you want to have a look?; **lass mal sehen** let me see, let me have a look; **sehenden Auges** *(geh)* with one's eyes open; **das Boot sah kaum aus dem Wasser** the boat hardly showed above the water

b (= feststellen) **na siehst du** (there you are,) you see?; **wie ich sehe …** I see that …; **wie ich sehe, hast du schon angefangen** I see you have already started; **Sie sind beschäftigt, wie ich sehe** I can see you're busy; **ich sehe schon, du willst nicht** I can see you don't want to; **wir werden schon sehen** we'll see; **da kann man mal sehen, da kannste mal sehen** *(inf)* that just goes to show *(inf)*; **wir wollen sehen** we'll have to see; **mal sehen, ob …** *(inf)* let's see if …; **mal sehen!** *(inf)* we'll see; **jeder muss sehen, wo er bleibt** (it's) every man for himself; **sieh, dass du …** make sure you…, see (that) you …

♦ **auf etw** *(acc)* **sehen** *(= hinsehen)* to look at sth; *(= achten)* to consider sth important; **auf die Uhr sehen** to look at one's watch; **jdm auf den Mund sehen** to watch sb's lips; **das Fenster sieht auf den Garten** the window looks onto the garden; **darauf sehen, dass …** to make sure (that) …; **er sieht auf Pünktlichkeit** he's a stickler for punctuality; **er sieht auf gute Umgangsformen** he thinks good manners are important; **er sieht nur auf seinen eigenen Vorteil** he only cares about what's good for him

♦ **sehen nach nach jdm sehen** *(= betreuen)* to look after sb; *(= besuchen)* to go to see sb; **nach etw sehen** to look after sth; **ich muss nur mal eben nach den Kartoffeln sehen** I've just got to have a look at the potatoes; **nach der Post sehen** to see if there are any letters

Se|hen NT **-s,** *no pl* seeing; *(= Sehkraft)* sight, vision; **als Fotograf muss man richtiges, bewusstes ~ lernen** as a photographer one has to learn to see correctly and consciously; **ich kenne ihn nur vom ~** I only know him by sight

se|hen+las|sen VT *ptp* **sehenlassen** *or (rare)* **sehengelassen** *sep irreg (fig)* → **sehen 1 a**

se|hens|wert, se|hens|wür|dig ADJ worth seeing; **ein ~es Schloss** a castle (which is) worth seeing

Se|hens|wür|dig|keit [-vʏrdɪçkait] F **-, -en** sight; **dieses Gebäude ist wirklich eine ~!** that building is really (a sight) worth seeing!; **die ~en (einer Stadt) besichtigen** to go sightseeing (in a city), to see the sights (of a city)

Se|her [ˈzeːɐ] M **-s, -** *(Hunt)* eye

Se|her [ˈzeːɐ] M **-s, -, Se|he|rin** [-ərɪn] F **-, -nen** *(liter)* seer

Se|her-: Se|her|blick M *(geh)* prophetic eye; **den ~ haben** to have a prophetic eye; **Se|her|ga|be** F *(geh)* gift of prophecy, prophetic gift

se|he|risch [ˈzeːərɪʃ] ADJ *attr Fähigkeit* prophetic

Seh-: Seh|feh|ler M visual *or* sight defect; **Seh|feld** NT field of vision, visual field; **Seh|hil|fe** F seeing aid; **Seh|kraft** F, *no pl* (eye)sight; **Seh|kreis** M = **Gesichtskreis**; **Seh|loch** NT *(Opt)* pupil

Seh|ne [ˈzeːnə] F **-, -n** **a** *(Anat)* tendon, sinew **b** *(= Bogensehne)* string **c** *(Math)* chord

seh|nen [ˈzeːnən] VR **sich nach jdm/etw ~** to long *or* yearn *(liter)* for sb/sth; *(schmachtend)* to pine for sb/sth; **mit ~dem Verlangen** *(geh)* with longing *or* yearning

Seh|nen NT **-s,** *no pl* = **Sehnsucht**

Seh|nen-: Seh|nen|re|flex M tendon reflex; **Seh|nen|schei|den|ent|zün|dung** F tendinitis, tendonitis; **Seh|nen|zer|rung** F pulled tendon

Seh|nerv M optic nerve

seh|nig [ˈzeːnɪç] ADJ *Gestalt, Mensch* sinewy, wiry; *Fleisch* stringy

sehn|lich [ˈzeːnlɪç] ADJ *Wunsch* ardent; *Erwartung* eager; **sein ~ster Wunsch** his fondest *or* most ardent *(liter)* wish ADV *hoffen, wünschen* ardently; **sich** *(dat)* **etw ~(st) wünschen** to long for sth with all one's heart; **wir alle hatten sie ~(st) erwartet** we had all been (most) eagerly awaiting her

Sehn|sucht [ˈzeːnzʊxt] F longing, yearning *(nach* for); *(schmachtend)* pining; **~ haben** to have a longing *or* yearning

sehn|süch|tig ADJ longing, yearning; *Verlangen, Wunsch etc* ardent; *Erwartung, Ungeduld* eager; *Brief* full of longing *or* yearning; **der dritte Satz hat etwas seltsam Sehnsüchtiges** the third movement has a strangely yearning quality ADV *hoffen, wünschen* ardently; **~ auf jdn warten** to yearn for sb; **~ auf etw** *(acc)* **warten** to long for sth

sehn|suchts|voll ADJ longing, yearning; *Blick, Augen, Brief, Schilderung, Musik* wistful ADV *betrachten, denken* longingly; *singen* yearningly; **~ auf etw** *(acc)* **warten** to long for sth

Seh|or|gan NT visual organ

sehr [zeːɐ] ADV *comp* **(noch) mehr** [meːɐ], *superl* **am meisten** [ˈmaistn] **a** *(mit adj, adv)* very; **~ verbunden!** *(dated form)* much obliged; **er ist ~ dafür** he is very much in favour *(Brit) or* favor *(US)* of it, he is all for it; **er ist ~ dagegen** he is very much against it; **hat er ~ viel getrunken?** did he drink very much?; **er hat ~ viel getrunken** he drank a lot; **~ zu meiner Überraschung** very much to my surprise; **es geht ihm ~ viel besser** he is very much better; **wir haben ~ viel Zeit/Geld** we have plenty of time/money, we have a lot of time/money, we have lots of time/money; **wir haben nicht ~ viel Zeit/Geld** we don't have very much time/money **b** *(mit vb)* very much, a lot; **so ~** so much; **jdn so ~ schlagen/zusammenschlagen, dass …** to hit sb so hard that/to beat sb up so much *or* so badly that …; **sich über etw** *(acc)* **so ~ ärgern/freuen, dass …** to be so (very) annoyed/pleased about sth that …; **~ verwurzelt sein** to be very deeply rooted; **wie ~** how much; **wie ~ er sich auch …** however much he …; **sich ~ vorsehen** to be very careful, to be very much on the lookout; **sich** *(dat)* **etw ~ überlegen** to consider sth very carefully; **sich ~ anstrengen** to try very hard; **es lohnt sich ~** it's very *or* well worthwhile; **~ weinen** to cry a lot *or* a great deal; **hat sie ~ geweint?** did she cry very much *or* a lot?; **es regnet ~** it's raining hard *or* heavily; **regnet es ~?** is it raining very much?, is it raining a lot?; **freust du dich? – ja, ~!** are you pleased? – yes, very; **freust du dich darauf? – ja, ~** are you looking forward to it? – yes, very much; **tut es weh? – ja, ~/nein, nicht ~** does it hurt? – yes, a lot/no, not very much *or* not a lot; **~ sogar!** yes, very much so (in fact); **zu ~** too much; **man sollte sich nicht zu ~ ärgern** one shouldn't get too annoyed

seh|ren [ˈzeːrən] VT *(old, dial)* = **verletzen**

Seh-: Seh|rohr NT periscope; **Seh|schär|fe** F keenness of sight, visual acuity; **Seh|schlitz** M slit; *(von Panzer etc)* observation slit; **Seh|schwä|che** F poor eyesight; **Seh|stö|rung** F visual defect; **wenn ~en auftreten** when the vision becomes disturbed; **Seh|test** M eye test; **Seh|ver|mö|gen** NT powers *pl* of vision; **Seh|wei|te** F = **Sichtweite**

sei [zai] *imper sing, 1. and 3. pers sing subjunc von* **sein**

sei|bern [ˈzaibɐn] VI *(dial)* = **sabbern**

Seich [zaiç] M **-(e)s,** *no pl,* **Sei|che** [ˈzaiçə] F **-,** *no pl* **a** *(dial sl)* piss *(sl)* **b** *(inf: = Geschwätz)* claptrap *(inf)*

sei|chen [ˈzaiçn] VI **a** *(dial sl)* to piss *(sl)* **b** *(inf)* = **schwafeln**

seicht [zaiçt] ADJ *(lit, fig)* shallow; *Unterhaltung, TV-Programm* trivial; **die ~e Stelle** the shallows *pl*

Seicht|heit F **-, -en** *(lit, fig)* shallowness

seid [zait] *2. pers pl pres, imper pl von* **sein**

Sei|de [ˈzaidə] F **-, -n** silk

Sei|del [ˈzaidl] NT **-s, -** **a** *(Gefäß)* stein, (beer) mug **b** *(S Ger. altes Maß)* half-litre *(Brit)*, half-liter *(US)*, ≈ pint

Sei|del|bast M *(Bot)* daphne

sei|den [ˈzaidn] ADJ *attr (= aus Seide)* silk, silken *(liter)*

Sei|den- *in cpds* silk; **sei|den|ar|tig** ADJ silky, silk-like; **Sei|den|at|las** M *pl* **-se** silk satin; **Sei|den|band** [-bant] NT *pl* **-bänder** silk ribbon; **Sei|den|fa|den** M, **Sei|den|garn** NT silk thread; **Sei|den|ge|we|be** NT silk fabric; **Sei|den|glanz** M silky *or* silken sheen; **Sei|den|ma|le|rei** F silk painting; **sei|den|matt** ADJ *Foto* semi-matt; **Sei|den|pa|pier** NT tissue paper; *(Phot)* satin-finished paper; **Sei|den|rau|pe** F silkworm; **Sei|den|rau|pen|zucht** F silkworm breeding; **Sei|den|schwanz** M *(Orn)* waxwing; **Sei|den|spin|ner** M *(Zool)* silk(worm) moth; **Sei|den|spin|ner(in)** M(F) silk spinner; **Sei|den|spin|ne|rei** F **a** silk spinning **b** *(Betrieb)* silk mill; **Sei|den|stoff** M silk cloth *or* fabric; **Sei|den|stra|ße** F *(Hist)* silk road; **Sei|den|strumpf** M silk stocking; **Sei|den|tuch** NT silk scarf; **sei|den|weich** ADJ soft as silk, silky soft

sei|dig [ˈzaidɪç] ADJ *(= wie Seide)* silky, silken

Sei|en|de(s) [ˈzaiəndə] NT *decl as adj (Philos)* being *no art*

Sei|fe [ˈzaifə] F **-, -n** **a** soap **b** *(Geol)* alluvial deposit

sei|fen [ˈzaifn] VT **a** *(= einseifen, abseifen)* to soap **b** *(Min)* to wash

Sei|fen-: Sei|fen|bla|se F soap bubble; *(fig)* bubble; **~n machen** to blow (soap) bubbles; **Sei|fen|flo|cken** PL soap flakes *pl*; **Sei|fen|-**

kis|ten|ren|nen NT soapbox derby; **Sei|fen|lau|ge** F (soap)suds *pl*; **Sei|fen|napf** M shaving mug; **Sei|fen|oper** F *(inf)* soap (opera); **Sei|fen|pul|ver** NT soap powder; **Sei|fen|scha|le** F soap dish; **Sei|fen|schaum** M lather; **Sei|fen|spen|der** M soap dispenser; **Sei|fen|was|ser** NT, *no pl* soapy water

sei|fig ['zaifɪç] ADJ soapy; *(fig)* soppy

Sei|ger|schacht ['zaige-] M *(Min)* perpendicular shaft

Sei|he ['zaiə] F -, -n = **Seiher**

sei|hen ['zaiən] VT *(= sieben)* to sieve; *(S Ger, Aus: = Flüssigkeit abgießen von)* to strain

Sei|her ['zaiɐ] M -s, - *(esp S Ger, Aus)* strainer, colander

Seih|tuch NT *pl* **-tücher** (muslin) cloth

Seil [zail] NT **-(e)s, -e** rope; *(= Kabel)* cable; *(= Hochseil)* tightrope, high wire; **auf dem ~ tanzen** *(fig)* to be walking a tightrope

Seil-: **Seil|bahn** F cable railway; *(= Bergseilbahn auch)* funicular; **Seil|brü|cke** F rope bridge

Sei|ler ['zailɐ] M -s, -, **Sei|le|rin** [-ərɪn] F -, -nen ropemaker

Sei|ler|bahn F ropewalk

Sei|le|rei [zailə'rai] F -, -en **a** *(= Seilerhandwerk)* ropemaking **b** *(= Seilerwerkstatt)* ropewalk, ropery *(rare)*

Sei|ler|wa|ren PL rope goods *pl*

Seil-: **Seil|fäh|re** F cable ferry; **seil+hüp|fen** VI *sep aux sein, usu infin or ptp* to skip; **Seil|schaft** ['zailʃaft] F -, -en *(Bergsteigen)* rope, roped party; *(fig: in Politik, Industrie etc)* clique, coterie; **Seil|schwe|be|bahn** F cable railway; *(= Bergseilbahn auch)* funicular; **seil+sprin|gen** VI *sep aux sein, usu infin or ptp* to skip; **Seil|tanz** M tightrope *or* high-wire act; **seil+tan|zen** VI *sep, usu infin or ptp* to walk the tightrope *or* high wire; **Seil|tän|zer(in)** M(F) tightrope walker, high-wire performer; **Seil|win|de** F winch; **Seil|zie|hen** NT tug-of-war; **Seil|zug** M *(Tech)* cable control

Seim [zaim] M **-(e)s, -e** viscous *or* glutinous substance

sei|mig ['zaimɪç] ADJ viscous, glutinous

sein [zain] *pres* **ist** [ɪst], *pret* **war** [vaːɐ], *ptp* **gewesen** [gə'veːzn] *aux sein* VI **a** *(= in einem Zustand sein, sich befinden)* to be; **wir waren** we were; **wir sind gewesen** we have been, we've been; **sei (mir)/seien Sie (mir) nicht böse, aber ...** don't be angry (with me) but ...; **sei/seid so nett und ...** be so kind as to ...; **du bist wohl verrückt!** *(inf)* you must be crazy *(inf)*; **ist das heiß/kalt!** that's really hot/cold!, is that hot/cold! *(inf)*; **das wäre gut** that would *or* that'd *(inf)* be a good thing; **es wäre schön gewesen** it would *or* it'd *(inf)* have been nice; **die Arbeit will sofort erledigt ~** *(geh)* this work must be done immediately; **er ist Lehrer/Inder/ein Verwandter/der Chef** he is a teacher/(an) Indian/a relative/the boss; **was sind Sie (beruflich)?** what do you do?; **er ist immer noch nichts** he still hasn't become anything; **wir sind wieder wer** we're somebody again; **Liverpool ist Fußballmeister/eine große Stadt** Liverpool are football champions/is a large town; **in der Küche sind noch viele** there's *(inf) or* there are still plenty in the kitchen; **drei und vier ist** *or* **sind sieben** three and four is *or* are seven; **x sei 4** let x be *or* equal 4; **wenn ich Sie/er wäre** if I were *or* was you/him *or* he *(form)*; **er war es nicht** it wasn't him; **niemand will es gewesen ~** nobody admits that it was him/her *or* them *(inf)*; **ich will mal nicht so ~ und ...** I don't want to be awkward and ...; **das kann schon ~** that may well be; **und das wäre?** and what would *or* might that be?; **das wärs!** that's all, that's it; **wie war das noch?** what was that again?; **wie war das noch mit dem Witz?** how did that joke go now?; **bist du/ist ers?** is that you/him?; **wer ist da?** who's there?; **ist da jemand?** is (there) anybody there?; **er ist aus Genf/aus guter Familie** he is *or* comes from Geneva/a good family; **morgen bin ich im Büro/in Rom** I'll *or* I will *or* I shall be in the office/in Rome tomorrow; **waren Sie (schon) mal in Rom?** have you ever been to Rome?; **wir waren baden/essen** we went swimming/out for a meal; **wo warst du so lange?** where have you been all this time?, what kept you?; **er war vier Jahre hier, bevor er ...** he had been here for four years before he ...; **es ist über zwanzig Jahre her, dass ...** it is more than twenty years since ...; **was nicht ist, kann ja noch werden** anything can happen, things can change → *auch* **gewesen**

b *(mit infin +zu)* **du bist nicht zu sehen** you cannot be seen; **das war ja vorauszusehen** that was to be expected; **das war nicht vorauszusehen** we couldn't have known that; **der Brief ist persönlich abzugeben** the letter is to be delivered by hand; **wie ist das zu verstehen?** how is that to be understood?; **er ist nicht zu ersetzen** he cannot be replaced; **ein eigener Garten ist nicht zu unterschätzen** a garden of one's own is not to be underestimated; **mit ihr ist ja nicht zu sprechen** you can't talk to her

c **was ist?** what's the matter?, what is it?, what's up *(inf)*; **ist was?** what is it?; *(= passt dir was nicht)* is something the matter?; **was ist mit dir/ihm?** what *or* how about you/him?; *(= was hast du/hat er?)* what's wrong *or* the matter *or* up *(inf)* with you/him?; **das kann nicht ~** that can't be (true); **wie wäre es mit ...?** how about ...?, what about ...?; **sei es, dass ..., sei es, dass ...** whether ... or ...; **es sei denn ...** unless ...; **nun, wie ist es?** well, how *or* what about it?; **wie wäre es, wenn wir ihn besuchen würden?** what about *or* how about going to see him?, why don't we go to see him?; **das brauchte nicht zu ~** *(= hätte nicht passieren müssen)* it need not *or* it need never have happened *or* have been *(Brit dial, liter)*, it didn't have to happen

d *(= da sein, existieren)* to be; **wenn du nicht gewesen wärest ...** if it hadn't been for you ...; **er ist nicht mehr** *(euph)* he is no more *(euph liter)*; **alles, was (bis jetzt/damals) war** all that has/had been *(liter)*

e *(in unpersönlicher Konstruktion)* **mir ist schlecht** *or* **übel** I feel ill; **mir ist kalt** I'm cold; **was ist Ihnen?** what's the matter with you?; **mir ist, als wäre ich zehn Jahre jünger** I feel ten years younger; **mir ist, als hätte ich ihn früher schon einmal gesehen** I have a feeling I've seen him before

V AUX to have; **er ist/war jahrelang krank gewesen** he has/had been *or* he's/he'd been ill for years; **sie ist gestern nicht zu Hause gewesen** she was not *or* wasn't at home yesterday; **er ist verschwunden** he has *or* he's disappeared; **er ist gestern verschwunden** he disappeared yesterday; **er ist eben nach Hause gekommen** he has just come home; **er ist gestern nach Hause gekommen** he came home yesterday; **er ist geschlagen worden** he has been beaten

sein POSS PRON **a** *(adjektivisch) (bei Männern)* his; *(bei Dingen, Abstrakta)* its; *(bei Mädchen)* her; *(bei Tieren)* its, his/her; *(bei Ländern, Städten)* its, her; *(bei Schiffen)* her, its; *(auf „man" bezüglich)* one's, his *(US)*, your; **wenn man ~ Leben betrachtet** when one looks at one's *or* his *(US)* life, when you look at your life; **jeder hat ~e Probleme** everybody has his *or* their *(inf)* problems; **~e komische Frau** that peculiar wife of his, his peculiar wife; **mein und ~ Freund** my friend and his; **~e zwanzig Zigaretten** his/her/one's twenty cigarettes; **er wiegt gut ~e zwei Zentner** *(inf)* he weighs a good two hundred pounds; **er ist gut ~e zwei Meter** *(inf)* he's a good two metres *(Brit) or* meters *(US)*

b *(old: substantivisch)* his

PERS PRON *gen von* **er** *von* **es** *(old, poet)* **ich werde ewig ~ gedenken** I shall remember him forever

Sein [zain] NT **-s**, *no pl* being *no art*; *(Philos) (= Existenz, Dasein auch)* existence *no art*; *(= Wesen, Sosein)* essence, suchness; **~ und Schein** appearance and reality; **~ oder Nichtsein** to be or not to be

sei|ner ['zainɐ] PERS PRON *gen von* **er, es** *(geh)* **gedenke ~** remember him; **er war ~ nicht mächtig** he was not in command of himself

sei|ne(r, s) ['zainə] POSS PRON *(substantivisch)* his; **der/die/das ~** *or* **Seine** *(geh)* his; **das ~** *or* **Seine tun** *(geh)* to do one's *or* his *(US)* bit; **er hat das ~** *or* **Seine getan** *(geh)* he did his bit; **jedem das ~** *or* **Seine** each to his own *(Brit)*, to each his own; **sie ist die ~** *or* **Seine geworden** *(geh)* she has become his *(liter)*; **die ~n** *or* **Seinen** *(geh)* his family, his people; *(auf „man" bezüglich)* one's *or* his *(US)* family *or* people; **das ~** *or* **Seine** *(geh: = Besitz)* what is his; *(auf „man" bezüglich)* what is one's own *or* his *(US)* → **Schlaf**

sei|ner-: **sei|ner|seits** ['zainɐ'zaits] ADV *(= von ihm)* on his part; *(= er selbst)* for his part; **sei|ner|zeit** ['zainɐtsait] ADV at that time; *(rare: künftig)* one day; **sei|ner|zei|tig** ['zainɐtsaitɪç] ADJ *attr (Aus)* then *attr*

sei|nes ['zainəs] POSS PRON → **seine(r, s)**

sei|nes|glei|chen ['zainəs'glaiçn] PRON *inv* *(gleichgestellt)* his equals *pl*; *(auf „man" bezüglich)* one's *or* his *(US)* equals; *(gleichartig)* his kind *pl*; of one's own kind; *(pej)* the likes of him *pl*; **jdn wie ~ behandeln** to treat sb as an equal *or* on equal terms; **das hat nicht** *or* **das sucht ~** it is unparalleled; *(Kunstwerk auch)* it has no equal

sei|net-: **sei|net|hal|ben** ['zainət'halbn] *(dated)* ADV = **seinetwegen**; **sei|net|we|gen** ['zainət'veːgn] ADV **a** *(= wegen ihm)* because of him, on account of him, on his account; *(= ihm zuliebe)* for his sake; *(= um ihn)* about him; *(= für ihn)* on his behalf **b** *(= von ihm aus)* as far as he is concerned; **sei|net|wil|len** ['zainət'vɪlən] ADV **um ~** for his sake, for him

sei|ni|ge ['zainɪgə] POSS PRON **der/die/das ~** *or* **Seinige** *(form, old)* → **seine(r, s)**

sein las|sen *ptp* **sein lassen** *or (rare)* **sein gelassen** *irreg*, **sein+las|sen** *ptp* **seinlassen** *or (rare)* **seingelassen** *sep irreg* VT **etw ~** *(= aufhören)* to stop sth/doing sth; *(= nicht tun)* to drop sth, to leave sth; **jdn/etw ~** to leave sb/sth alone, to let sb/sth be; **lass das sein!** stop that!; **du hättest es ~ sollen** you should have left well (enough *(US)*) alone; **sie kann es einfach nicht ~** she just can't stop herself

seins [zains] POSS PRON his

Seins|leh|re F *(Philos)* ontology

seis|misch ['zaismɪʃ] ADJ seismic

Seis|mo|graf [zaismo'graːf] M **-en, -en** seismograph

Seis|mo|gramm [zaismo'gram] NT *pl* **-gramme** seismogram

Seis|mo|graph [zaismo'graːf] M **-en, -en** seismograph

Seis|mo|lo|ge [zaismo'loːgə] M **-n, -n**, **Seis|mo|lo|gin** [-'loːgɪn] F **-, -nen** seismologist

Seis|mo|lo|gie [zaismolo'giː] F -, *no pl* seismology

seit [zait] PREP *+dat (in Bezug auf Zeitpunkt)* since; *(in Bezug auf Zeitdauer)* for, in *(esp US)*; **~ wann?** since when?; **~ Jahren** for years; **ich habe ihn ~ Jahren nicht gesehen** I haven't seen him for *or* in *(esp US)* years; **ich bin ~ zwei Jahren hier** I have been here for two years; **schon ~ zwei Jahren nicht mehr** not for two years, not since two years ago; **wir warten schon ~ zwei Stunden** we have been *or* we've been waiting (for) two hours; **~ etwa einer Woche** since about a week ago, for about a week CONJ since

seit|dem [zait'deːm] ADV since then; **~ ist die Strecke nicht mehr in Betrieb** the line has been closed down since then CONJ since

Sei|te ['zaitə] F -, -n **a** *(= auch Abstammungslinie, Charakterzug)* side; **die hintere/vordere ~** the back/front; **zu** *or* **auf beiden ~n des Fensters/des Hauses/der Straße** on both sides of the window/house/street; **mit der ~ nach vorn** sideways on; **~ an ~** side by side; **an jds ~** *(dat)*

gehen to walk at *or* by sb's side, to walk beside sb; **halt dich an meiner ~!** stay by my side; **er ging** *or* **wich uns nicht von der ~** he never left our side; **ich kann mich nicht an Ihrer ~ zeigen** I can't be seen with you; **jdn von der ~ ansehen** to give sb a sidelong glance; **auf die** *or* **zur ~ gehen** *or* **treten** to step aside; **an der ~ (einer Reihe) sitzen** to sit at the end (of a row); **zur ~ sprechen/sehen** to speak/look to one side; **zur ~** *(Theat)* aside; **die ~n wechseln** *(Sport)* to change ends *or* over; *(fig)* to change sides; **jdn auf seine ~ bringen** *or* **ziehen** *(fig)* to get sb on one's side; **auf einer ~ gelähmt sein** to be paralyzed down one side; **die Hände in die ~n gestemmt** with arms akimbo, with one's hands on one's hips; **jedes Ding** *or* **alles hat zwei ~n** there are two sides to everything; **jdm zur ~ stehen** *(fig)* to stand by sb's side; **jdn jdm an die ~ stellen** *(= gleichstellen)* to put sb on a level with sb; *(zur Unterstützung)* to put sb alongside sb; **auf jds** *(dat)* **~ stehen** *or* **sein** *(fig)* to be on sb's side; **das Recht ist auf ihrer ~** she has right on her side; **etw auf die ~ legen** *(lit, fig)* to put sth on one side, to put sth aside; *(= umkippen)* to put sth on its side; **etw zur ~** *or* **auf die ~ schaffen** *(inf)* to help oneself to sth; **jdn zur ~** *or* **auf die ~ schaffen** *(inf)* to get rid of sb; **jdn zur ~ nehmen** to take sb aside *or* on one side; **auf der einen ~..., auf der anderen (~) ...** on the one hand ..., on the other (hand) ...; **jds starke ~** sb's forte, sb's strong point; **jds schwache ~** sb's weakness, sb's weak spot; **sich von seiner besten ~ zeigen** to show oneself at one's best; **neue ~n an jdm/etw entdecken** to discover new sides to sb/sth; **von dieser ~ kenne ich ihn gar nicht** I didn't know that side of him; **einer Sache** *(dat)* **die beste ~ abgewinnen** to make the best of sth

b *(= Richtung)* **von allen ~n** *(lit, fig)* from all sides; **nach allen ~n auseinandergehen** to scatter in all directions; **sich nach allen ~n umsehen** to look around on all sides; **sich nach allen ~n vergewissern** to check up on all sides; **das habe ich von einer anderen ~ erfahren** *(fig)* I heard it from another source *or* from elsewhere; **er erfuhr es von dritter ~** *(fig)* he heard it from a third party; **bisher wurden von keiner ~ Einwände erhoben** so far no objections have been voiced from any quarter; **die Behauptung wurde von keiner ~ bestritten** nobody challenged the claim; **die Behauptung wurde von allen/beiden ~n bestritten** the claim was challenged by all/both parties; **von meiner ~ aus** *(fig)* on my part; **von kirchlicher ~ (aus)** on the part of the church; **auf ~n** *+gen* = **aufseiten**; **von ~n** *+gen* = **vonseiten**

c *(= Buchseite, Zeitungsseite)* page; **die erste/letzte ~** the first/last page; *(von Zeitung)* the front/back page

Sei|ten- *in cpds* side; *(esp Tech, Sci etc)* lateral; **Sei|ten|air|bag** M *(Aut)* side-impact airbag; **Sei|ten|al|tar** M side altar; **Sei|ten|an|ga|be** F page reference; **Sei|ten|an|sicht** F side view; *(Tech)* side elevation; *(Comput)* page preview; *(zum Drucken)* print preview; **Sei|ten|arm** M branch, feeder; *(von Fluss)* branch; **Sei|ten|auf|prall|schutz** M *(Aut)* side impact protection system, SIPS; **Sei|ten|aus|gang** M side exit; **Sei|ten|be|schrei|bungs|spra|che** F *(Comput)* page description language; **Sei|ten|blick** M sidelong glance; **mit einem ~ auf** *(+acc) (fig)* with one eye on; **Sei|ten|ein|gang** M side entrance; **Sei|ten|ein|stei|ger(in)** M(F) *(fig)* person who comes in through the back door; **Sei|ten|flä|che** F *(Tech)* lateral face *or* surface; **Sei|ten|flos|se** F *(Aviat)* fin; **Sei|ten|flü|gel** M side wing; *(von Altar)* wing; **Sei|ten|gang** M *pl* **-gänge** *(Naut)* side strake; *(Rail)* (side) corridor; **Sei|ten|gas|se** F side street, backstreet; **Sei|ten|ge|bäu|de** NT side building; *(auf Hof)* outhouse; *(= Anbau)* annex(e); **Sei|ten|ge|wehr** NT bayonet; **Sei|ten|hal|bie|ren|de** [-halbi:rəndə] F *decl as adj* *(Math)* median; **Sei|ten|hieb** M *(Fechten)* side cut; *(fig)* sideswipe; **Sei|ten|kan|te** F lateral edge; **Sei|ten|la|ge** F side position; **in ~ schlafen** to sleep on one's side; **stabile ~** recovery position; **sei|ten|lang** ADJ several pages long, going on for pages ADV **darstellen** over pages and pages; **etw ~ beschreiben** to devote pages to describing sth; **sich ~ über etw** *(acc)* **auslassen** to go on for pages about sth; **sie hat mir ~ geschrieben** she wrote me a long letter; **Sei|ten|län|ge** F length of a/the side; **ein gleichseitiges Dreieck mit der ~ 4,5 cm** an equilateral triangle whose sides are 4.5 cm long; **Sei|ten|lay|out** NT *(Typ)* page layout; **Sei|ten|leh|ne** F arm(rest); **Sei|ten|leit|werk** NT *(Aviat)* rudder (assembly); **Sei|ten|li|nie** F **a** *(Rail)* branch line **b** *(von Fürstengeschlecht)* collateral line **c** *(Tennis)* sideline; *(Ftbl etc)* touchline *(Brit)*, sideline; **Sei|ten|mo|rä|ne** F *(Geol)* lateral moraine; **Sei|ten|pfad** M bypath; **Sei|ten|rand** M margin; **Sei|ten|riss** M *(Tech)* side elevation; **Sei|ten|ru|der** NT *(Aviat)* rudder

sei|tens ['zaitns] PREP *+gen (form)* on the part of

Sei|ten-: **Sei|ten|schei|tel** M side parting *(Brit)*, side part *(US)*; **Sei|ten|schiff** NT *(Archit)* (side) aisle; **Sei|ten|schnei|der** M side cutters *pl*, cutting pliers *pl*; **Sei|ten|schwel|ler** M *(Aut)* side skirt; **Sei|ten|spie|gel** M *(Aut)* wing mirror; **Sei|ten|sprung** M *(fig)* bit on the side *(inf)* *no pl*, (little) infidelity; **die Versuchung, Seitensprünge zu machen** the temptation to have a bit on the side *(inf)*; **Sei|ten|ste|chen** NT, *no pl* stitch; **~ haben/bekommen** to have/get a stitch; **Sei|ten|sti|che** PL = **Seitenstechen**; **Sei|ten|stra|ße** F side street, side road; **Sei|ten|strei|fen** M verge; *(der Autobahn)* hard shoulder *(Brit)*, shoulder *(US)*; **„Seitenstreifen nicht befahrbar"** "soft verges" *(Brit)*, "soft shoulder" *(US)*; **Sei|ten|tal** NT valley; **Sei|ten|ta|sche** F side pocket; **Sei|ten|teil** M OR NT side; **Sei|ten|um|bruch** M **a** *(Typ)* page make-up **b** *(Comput)* page break; **einen ~ einfügen** to insert a page break; **Sei|ten|ver|hält|nis** NT *(Comput etc)* aspect ratio; **sei|ten|ver|kehrt** ADJ ADV the wrong way round; **Sei|ten|vor|schub** M *(beim Drucker)* form feed; **Sei|ten|wa|gen** M sidecar; **Sei|ten|wand** F side wall; *(von Schiff)* side; **Seitenwände** *pl (Theat)* wings *pl*; **Sei|ten|wech|sel** M **a** *(Sport)* changeover **b** *(Comput)* page break; **Sei|ten|weg** M side road, byway, back road; **~e gehen** *(fig)* to indulge in clandestine activities; **sei|ten|wei|se** ADV *(viele Seiten)* pages (and pages) of; **~ vorgehen** *(= Seite für Seite vorgehen)* to proceed a page at a time; **Sei|ten|wind** M crosswind; **Sei|ten|zahl** F **a** page number **b** *(= Gesamtzahl)* number of pages

seit|her [zait'he:ɐ] ADV since then

seit|he|rig [zait'he:rɪç] ADJ = **bisherig**

seit|lich ['zaitlɪç] ADJ lateral *(esp Sci, Tech)*, side *attr*; **die ~e Begrenzung der Straße wird durch einen weißen Streifen markiert** the side of the road is marked by a white line; **bei starkem ~en Wind** in a strong crosswind ADV at the side; *(= von der Seite)* from the side; **~ von** at the side of; **~ stehen** to stand sideways on; **etw/sich ~ stellen** to put sth/stand sideways on; **die Kisten sind ~ grün bemalt** the sides of the boxes are painted green; **er ist mir ~ ins Auto gefahren** he crashed into the side of my car PREP *+gen* to *or* at the side of

seit|lings ['zaitlɪŋs] ADV *(obs) (= zur Seite)* sideways; *(= auf der Seite)* on one's side

seit|wärts ['zaitvɛrts] ADV sideways; **sich ~ halten** → **seitwärtshalten**

seit|wärts+halten VR *sep irreg* to keep to the side

Sek., **sek.** *abbr von* **Sekunde** sec

Se|kans ['ze:kans] M **-, -** *or* **Sekanten** [ze'kantn], **Se|kan|te** [ze'kantə] F **-, -n** *(Math)* secant

Se|kond [ze'kɔnt] F **-, -en** [-dn] *(Fechten)* seconde

Se|kret [ze'kre:t] NT **-(e)s, -e** *(Physiol)* secretion

Se|kret F **-,** *no pl (Eccl)* secret (of the mass)

Se|kre|tär [zekre'tɛ:ɐ] M **-s, -e** **a** *(= Schreibschrank)* bureau *(Brit)*, secretaire *(Brit)*, secretary desk *(US)* **b** *(Orn)* secretary bird

Se|kre|tär [zekre'tɛ:ɐ] M **-s,-e**, **Se|kre|tä|rin** [-'tɛ:rɪn] F **-, -nen** secretary

Se|kre|ta|ri|at [zekreta'ria:t] NT **-(e)s, -e** office

Se|kre|ti|on [zekre'tsio:n] F **-, -en** *(Physiol)* secretion

Sekt [zɛkt] M **-(e)s, -e** sparkling wine, champagne

Sek|te ['zɛktə] F **-, -n** sect

Sekt|emp|fang M champagne reception

Sek|ten-: **Sek|ten|be|auf|trag|te(r)** MF *decl as adj* religious sects adviser; **Sek|ten|füh|rer(in)** M(F) sect leader; **Sek|ten|we|sen** NT sectarianism

Sekt-: **Sekt|früh|stück** NT champagne breakfast; **Sekt|glas** NT champagne glass

Sek|tie|rer [zɛk'ti:rɐ] M **-s, -**, **Sek|tie|re|rin** [-ərɪn] F **-, -nen** sectarian

sek|tie|re|risch [zɛk'ti:rərɪʃ] ADJ sectarian ADV in a sectarian way; **~ denken** to think in a sectarian way

Sek|tie|rer|tum [zɛk'ti:rɐtu:m] NT **-s,** *no pl* sectarianism

Sek|ti|on [zɛk'tsio:n] F **-, -en** **a** section; *(= Abteilung)* department **b** *(= Obduktion)* postmortem (examination), autopsy

Sek|ti|ons-: **Sek|ti|ons|be|fund** M postmortem *or* autopsy findings *pl*; **Sek|ti|ons|chef(in)** M(F) *(von Abteilung)* head of department; **Sek|ti|ons|saal** M dissection room; **sek|ti|ons|wei|se** ADV in sections

Sekt-: **Sekt|kelch** M champagne flute; **Sekt|kor|ken** M champagne cork; **Sekt|küh|ler** M champagne bucket *or* cooler

Sek|tor ['zɛkto:ɐ] M **-s, Sektoren** [-'to:rən] sector *(auch Comput)*; *(= Sachgebiet)* field

Sek|to|ren|gren|ze F sector boundary

Sekt|scha|le F champagne glass

Se|kund [ze'kʊnt] F **-, -en** [-dn] *(Mus)* second

Se|kun|da [ze'kʊnda] F **-, Sekunden** [-dn] *(dated Sch) sixth and seventh year of German secondary school*

Se|kund|ak|kord M *(Mus)* third inversion (of the seventh chord)

Se|kun|da|ner [zekʊn'da:nɐ] M **-s, -**, **Se|kun|da|ne|rin** [-ərɪn] F **-, -nen** *(dated Sch) pupil in sixth and seventh year of German secondary school*

Se|kun|dant [zekʊn'dant] M **-en, -en**, **Se|kun|dan|tin** [-'dantɪn] F **-, -nen** second

se|kun|där [zekʊn'dɛ:ɐ] ADJ secondary ADV secondarily; **nur ~ von Bedeutung sein** to be of secondary importance; **nur ~ eine Rolle spielen** to play only a secondary role

Se|kun|där- *in cpds* secondary; **Se|kun|där|ener|gie** F secondary energy; **Se|kun|där|kreis|lauf** M *(in Atomkraftwerk)* secondary circuit

Se|kun|dar|leh|rer(in) [zekʊn'da:ɐ-] M(F) *(Sw)* secondary *or* high *(esp US)* school teacher

Se|kun|där|li|te|ra|tur F secondary literature

Se|kun|där|markt M *(Econ)* aftermarket; *(Fin)* secondary market

Se|kun|dar-: **Se|kun|dar|schu|le** F *(Sw)* secondary school; **Se|kun|dar|stu|fe** F secondary *or* high *(esp US)* school level

Se|kun|de [ze'kʊndə] F **-, -n** *(auch Mus, Math)* second; **eine ~, bitte!** just a *or* one second, please; **auf die ~ genau** to the second

Se|kun|den *pl von* **Sekunda** *von* **Sekunde**

Se|kun|den-: **Se|kun|den|bruch|teil** M split second, fraction of a second; **se|kun|den|ge|nau** ADJ **~e Abrechnung** *(Telec)* per second billing; **Se|kun|den|ge|schwin|dig|keit** F **in ~** in a matter of seconds; **Se|kun|den|kle|ber** M superglue, instant glue; **se|kun|den|lang** ADJ of a few seconds ADV for a few seconds;

Se|kun|den|schlaf M *(am Steuer)* momentary nodding off, microsleep *(spec)*; **se|kun|den|schnell** ADJ *Reaktion, Entscheidung* split-second *attr*, lightning *attr*; *Antwort* quick-fire *attr* ADV **sich ~ entscheiden müssen** to have to make a snap decision; **alles ging ~** it all happened in a matter of seconds; **Se|kun|den|schnel|le** F **in ~** in a matter of seconds; **Se|kun|den|tod** M *(Med)* sudden death, sudden adult death syndrome; **Se|kun|den|zei|ger** M second hand

se|kun|die|ren [zekʊn'di:rən] *ptp* **sekundiert** VI *+dat* to second; *(= unterstützen auch)* to back up; **jdm (bei einem Duell) ~** to act as *or* be sb's second (in a duel)

se|kund|lich [ze'kʊntlɪç], **se|künd|lich** [ze'kʏntlɪç] ADJ *(rare) Abstand* one-second ADV every second

Se|ku|rit® [zeku'ri:t] NT **-s,** *no pl* ≈ Triplex®

sel. *abbr von* **selig**

Se|la ['ze:la] NT **-s, -s** *(Bibl)* selah

sel|ber ['zɛlbɐ] DEM PRON = **selbst DEM PRON**

sel|be(r, s) ['zɛlbə] PRON → **derselbe, dieselbe, dasselbe**

Sel|ber|ma|chen NT **-s,** *no pl* do-it-yourself, DIY *(inf)*; *(von Kleidern etc)* making one's own; **Möbel zum ~** do-it-yourself furniture; **Spielzeug zum ~** build-it-yourself toy

sel|big ['zɛlbɪç] PRON *(obs, Bibl)* the same

selbst [zɛlpst] DEM PRON **a** **ich ~** I myself; **er ~** he himself; **Sie ~** *(sing)* you yourself; *(pl)* you yourselves; **sie ~** she herself; **das Haus ~** the house itself; **die Katze ~** the cat itself; **wir ~** we ourselves; **sie ~** they themselves; **die Häuser ~** the houses themselves; **er ist gar nicht mehr er ~** he's not himself any more; **du Esel! – ~ einer** *(inf)* you idiot! – same to you *(inf)*; **sie ist die Güte/Tugend ~** she's kindness/virtue itself; **~ ist der Mann/die Frau!** self-reliance is the name of the game *(inf)*; **er wäscht seine Wäsche ~** he does his washing himself, he does his own washing; **was man von sich ~ hält** what one thinks of oneself; **zu sich ~ kommen** to collect one's thoughts; **eine Sache um ihrer ~ willen tun** to do sth for its own sake; **sie tut mir ~ leid** I feel very sorry for her myself

b *(= ohne Hilfe)* alone, by oneself/himself/yourself *etc*, on one's/his/your *etc* own

c **von ~** by myself/yourself/himself/itself/ourselves *etc*; **das funktioniert von ~** it works by itself, it works automatically; **das regelt sich alles von ~** it'll sort itself out (by itself); **er kam ganz von ~** he came of his own accord, he came off his own bat *(Brit inf)*; **das hat er ganz von ~ entschieden** he decided that all by himself

ADV **a** *(= eigen)* **~ ernannt** self-appointed; *(in Bezug auf Titel)* self-styled; **~ gebacken** home-baked, home-made; **~ gebastelt** home-made; **~ gebaut** home-made; *(Haus)* self-built; **~ gebraut** *(Bier)* home-brewed; **~ gemacht** home-made; **~ gesponnen** homespun; **~ gestrickt** *(Pullover etc)* hand-knitted; *(pej inf)* home-made; **ist das ~ gestrickt?** did you knit it yourself?; **~ gezogen** *(Rosen etc)* home-cultivated; *(Kerzen)* home-made; **~ verdientes Geld** money one has earned oneself; **sein ~ verdientes Motorrad** the motorbike he bought with the money he earned; **~ verfasst** of one's own composition; **alle seine Reden sind ~ verfasst** he writes all his speeches himself; **~ verschuldet** *(Unfälle, Notlagen)* for which one is oneself responsible or to blame; **der Unfall war ~ verschuldet** the accident was his/her own fault; **wenn der Unfall/Verlust ~ verschuldet ist** if the claimant is himself/herself responsible *or* to blame for the accident/loss

b *(= sogar)* even; **~ der Minister/Gott** even the Minister/God (himself); **~ wenn** even if

Selbst [zɛlpst] NT **-,** *no pl* self

Selbst-: **Selbst|ab|ho|ler** [-lapho:lɐ] M **-s, -,** **Selbst|ab|ho|le|rin** [-ərɪn] F **-, -nen ~ sein** to collect one's own mail; **Selbst|ach|tung** F self-respect, self-esteem; **Selbst|ana|ly|se** F self-analysis

selb|stän|dig ['zɛlpʃtɛndɪç] ADJ ADV = **selbstständig**

Selb|stän|di|ge(r) ['zɛlpʃtɛndɪgə] MF *decl as adj* = **Selbstständige(r)**

Selb|stän|dig|keit F **-,** *no pl* = **Selbstständigkeit**

Selbst-: **Selbst|an|kla|ge** F self-accusation; **Selbst|an|zei|ge** F **a** *(steuerlich)* voluntary declaration **b ~ erstatten** to come forward oneself; **Selbst|auf|ga|be** F surrender of one's identity, self-abnegation; **Selbst|auf|op|fe|rung** F self-sacrifice; **Selbst|aus|kunft** F (one's own) personal details *pl*; **Selbst|aus|lö|ser** M *(Phot)* delayed-action shutter release, delay timer; **Selbst|be|die|nung** F self-service; *(fig: finanziell)* helping oneself to funds; **Selbst|be|die|nungs|la|den** M self-service shop *(esp Brit)* or store; **Selbst|be|die|nungs|men|ta|li|tät** F self-service mentality; **Selbst|be|fle|ckung** F *(old, Rel)* self-abuse; **Selbst|be|frei|ung** F self-liberation; *(Jur)* prison escape without outside assistance; **Selbst|be|frie|di|gung** F masturbation; *(fig auch)* self-gratification; **Selbst|be|fruch|tung** F *(Biol)* self-fertilization; **Selbst|be|halt** [-bəhalt] M **-(e)s, -e** **a** *(Insur: = Selbstbeteiligung)* (percentage) excess **b** *(= Medikamentenzuzahlung)* patient's contribution; **Selbst|be|haup|tung** F self-assertion; **Selbst|be|herr|schung** F self-control; **die ~ wahren/verlieren** to keep/lose one's self-control *or* temper; **Selbst|be|kennt|nis** NT confession; **Selbst|be|kös|ti|gung** F *(dated)* self-catering; **Selbst|be|ob|ach|tung** F self-observation; **Selbst|be|schei|dung** [-bəʃaidʊŋ] F **-,** *no pl (geh)* self-denial; **Selbst|be|sin|nung** F self-contemplation; **zur ~ kommen** to reflect; **hier ist es unmöglich, zur ~ zu kommen** that there is no opportunity (afforded) here for self-contemplation; **Selbst|be|spie|ge|lung** [-bəʃpi:gəlʊŋ] F **-, -en** *(pej)* self-admiration; **Selbst|be|stä|ti|gung** F self-affirmation; **das empfand er als ~** it boosted his ego; **man braucht ab und zu eine ~** now and then you need something to boost your ego; **Lob dient der ~ der Kinder** praise boosts the children's confidence; **Selbst|be|stäu|bung** F *(Bot)* self-pollination; **selbst|be|stimmt** ADJ self-determined; **~ leben** to be independent, to live an independent life; **sein Wunsch nach ~em Sterben** his desire to determine his own death; **Selbst|be|stim|mung** F self-determination; **Selbst|be|stim|mungs|recht** NT right of self-determination; **Selbst|be|tei|li|gung** F *(Insur)* (percentage) excess; **Selbst|be|trug** M self-deception; **Selbst|be|weih|räu|che|rung** [-bəvairɔyçərʊŋ] F **-, -en** *(pej)* self-congratulation, self-promotion, self-admiration; **Selbst|be|wun|de|rung** F self-admiration; **selbst|be|wusst** ADJ **a** *(= selbstsicher)* self-assured, self-confident; *(= eingebildet)* self-important **b** *(Philos)* self-aware, self-conscious ADV self-confidently; **Selbst|be|wusst|sein** NT **a** self-assurance, self-confidence; *(= Einbildung)* self-importance **b** *(Philos)* self-awareness, self-consciousness; **selbst|be|zo|gen** ADJ self-centred *(Brit)*, self-centered *(US)*, egocentric *(geh)*; **Selbst|bild** NT *(Psych)* self-image; **sein ~** the way he sees himself; **Selbst|bild|nis** NT self-portrait; **Selbst|bräu|ner** [-brɔynɐ] M **-s, -** self-tanning lotion; **Selbst|bu|cher** [-bu:xɐ] M **-s, -,** **Selbst|bu|che|rin** [-ərɪn] F **-, -nen** *(Post) person/firm etc with own franking machine*; **Selbst|dar|stel|lung** F **a** *(= Selbstpräsentation)* self-presentation; *(= Selbstbeweihräucherung)* self-promotion **b** *(= Selbstbildnis)* self-portrait; **Selbst|dis|zip|lin** F self-discipline; **Selbst|ein|schät|zung** F self-assessment; **eine gesunde ~** a healthy self-awareness; **Selbst|ent|fal|tung** F self-development; *(Philos)* unfolding; **Selbst|ent|lei|bung** [-lɛntlaibʊŋ] F **-, -en** *(liter)* suicide; **Selbst|ent|zün|dung** F spontaneous combustion; **Selbst|er|fah|rung** F self-awareness; **Selbst|er|fah|rungs|grup|pe** F encounter group; **Selbst|er|hal|tung** F self-preservation, survival; **Selbst|er|hal|tungs|trieb** M survival instinct, instinct of self-preservation; **Selbst|er|kennt|nis** F self-knowledge; **~ ist der erste Schritt zur Besserung** *(prov)* self-knowledge is the first step toward(s) self-improvement; **selbst|er|nannt** [-lɛɐnant] ADJ → **selbst ADV a**; **Selbst|er|nied|ri|gung** F self-abasement; **Selbst|er|zie|hung** F self-discipline; **~ zur Pünktlichkeit** teaching oneself to be punctual; **Selbst|fah|rer** M *(= Krankenfahrstuhl)* self-propelling wheelchair; **Selbst|fah|rer(in)** M(F) *(Aut) person who rents a car and drives it himself*; **Autovermietung für ~** self-drive car hire *(Brit)*, car rental; **wir vermieten nur an ~** we only have self-drive *(Brit)*; **Selbst|fahr|la|fet|te** F *(Mil)* self-propelled gun; **selbst|fi|nan|zie|rend** ADJ self-financing; **Selbst|fi|nan|zie|rung** F self-financing; **in** *or* **durch ~** with one's own resources *or* means; **Selbst|fin|dung** [-fɪndʊŋ] F **-,** *no pl* finding one's self; **Selbst|gän|ger** [-gɛŋɐ] M **-s, -** *(inf, fig)* **a** *(= etwas, das von alleine funktioniert)* **Existenzgründungen in der Internetbranche sind keine ~ mehr** Internet start-ups no longer generate automatic success without any hitches; **ich halte Bayern München nicht für einen ~** I don't think Bayern München is hooked on success forever; **keine Unternehmensgemeinschaft ist ein ~** no merger runs that smoothly; **sind diese bevorzugten Industriestandorte nicht ~?** are these preferred industrial locations not self-perpetuating?; **ein ~ wird die neue Saison bestimmt nicht** we can't expect the new season to become a sweeping success (without a great deal of effort on our part); **Beach Volleyball ist kein ~ mehr** beach volleyball is no longer a popular game that easily attracts crowds; **für Sven als Legastheniker ist die Schule kein ~** Sven being dyslexic, going to school is no mean feat for him **b** *(= etwas Selbstverständliches)* **sein fünfter WM-Titel sei keinesfalls ein ~ gewesen** his fifth world title was by no means to be taken for granted; **glückliche Ehen sind heute nicht unbedingt ~** happy marriages aren't necessarily a matter of course nowadays; **es ist ein ~, dass die bestehenden Gesetze auch anzuwenden sind** it is self-evident that existing laws have to be applied; **erfolgreiche Öffentlichkeitsarbeit ist kein ~** successful PR work is by no means a self-fulfilling prophecy; **wir dachten, die Liebe wäre ein ~** we thought love would stay forever **c** *(= etwas, das sich notgedrungen ergeben muss)* **das war doch ein ~** *(bei schwacher gegnerischer Mannschaft etc)* they were a walk-over **d** *(= etwas, das logischerweise zu erwarten ist)* **das zu erwartende Urteil wäre ein ~** the judgement would be the sort one would have expected; **Nein, das ist kein ~** *(bei Rückgängigmachung einer Schiedsrichterentscheidung etc)* No, I don't think this can be taken for granted **e** *(= etwas, das sich leicht erfolgreich vermarkten lässt)* **ein ~ in Sachen Unterhaltung** an instant success in terms of entertainment; **unser neues Versicherungspaket ist konkurrenzlos - ein ~** our new insurance package is unrivalled: sure seller; **wie die Soap „Big Brother" zum ~ wurde** how the soap opera "Big Brother" became a regular feature on TV; **ein US-College-Radio-~** a piece of music very often played by US college radio stations **f** *(= etwas, das nicht viel Können erfordert)* **das Gelände war für die Radsportler dennoch kein ~** nevertheless, the terrain wasn't that easy to tackle for the cyclists; **bei Hobby-Zauberkünstlern kommen oft ~ zum Einsatz** amateur magicians often use tricks that don't really afford much skill and are nevertheless impressive **g** *(= ein Muss)* **diese Punk-Jazz-Nummer ist ein ~ für Musikfreaks** this punkjazz piece is a must for music-lovers; **selbst|ge|ba|cken** ADJ → **selbst** ADV a; **selbst|ge|bas|telt** ADJ → **selbst** ADV a; **selbst|ge|baut** ADJ → **selbst** ADV a; **selbst|ge|braut** [-gəbraut] ADJ → **selbst** ADV a; **Selbst|ge|dreh|te** [-gədreːtə] F *decl as adj* roll-up *(inf)*; **~ rauchen** to roll one's own; **selbst|ge|fäl|lig** ADJ self-satisfied, smug, complacent ADV smugly, complacently; **Selbst|ge|fäl|lig|keit** F self-satisfaction, smugness, complacency; **Selbst|ge|fühl** NT self-esteem; **ein übertriebenes ~ besitzen** to have an exaggerated opinion of oneself, to have an oversized ego *(inf)*; **selbst|ge|macht** ADJ → **selbst** ADV a; **selbst|ge|nüg|sam** ADJ **a** *(= bescheiden)* modest (in one's demands) **b** *(= sich selbst genug)* self-sufficient; **Selbst|ge|nüg|sam|keit** F modesty (in one's demands); **selbst|ge|recht** ADJ self-righteous ADV self-righteously; **Selbst|ge|rech|tig|keit** F self-righteousness; **selbst|ge|spon|nen** ADJ → **selbst** ADV a; **Selbst|ge|spräch** NT **~e führen** *or* **halten** to talk to oneself; **selbst|ge|strickt** [-gəʃtrɪkt] ADJ → **selbst** ADV a; **selbst|ge|zo|gen** ADJ → **selbst** ADV a; **Selbst|hass** M self-hate, self-hatred; **Selbst|hei|lungs|kraft** F self-healing power; **selbst|herr|lich** *(pej)* ADJ **a** *(= eigenwillig)* high-handed **b** *(= selbstgefällig, selbstgerecht)* arrogant ADV **a** *(= eigenwillig)* high-handedly **b** *(= selbstgefällig)* arrogantly; **Selbst|herr|lich|keit** F *(pej)* **a** *(= Eigenwilligkeit)* high-handedness **b** *(= Selbstgerechtigkeit)* arrogance; **Selbst|herr|schaft** F *(rare)* autocracy; **Selbst|herr|scher(in)** M(F) *(rare)* autocrat; **Selbst|hil|fe** F self-help; **zur ~ greifen** to take matters into one's own hands; **Selbst|hil|fe|grup|pe** F self-help group; **Selbst|in|sze|nie|rung** F self-promotion, self-glorification; **ihr Auftreten ist eine gigantische ~** the way she carries on is all one great act of self-promotion; **Selbst|in|ter|pre|ta|ti|on** F image of oneself, self-image; **Selbst|iro|nie** F self-mockery, self-irony

selbs|tisch ['zɛlbstɪʃ] ADJ *(geh)* selfish

Selbst-: **Selbst|iso|lie|rung** F self-isolation; **Selbst|jus|tiz** F arbitrary law; **~ üben** to take the law into one's own hands; **Selbst|kle|be|eti|kett** NT self-adhesive label; **selbst|kle|bend** ADJ self-adhesive; **Selbst|kon|trol|le** F check on oneself; *(von Computer)* automatic check; **zur ~** to keep a check on oneself; **der Computer hat ~** the computer is self-checking, the computer has an automatic check

Selbst|kos|ten PL *(Econ)* prime costs *pl*

Selbst|kos|ten-: **Selbst|kos|ten|be|tei|li|gung** F *(Insur)* excess; **Selbst|kos|ten|preis** M cost price; **zum ~** at cost

Selbst-: **Selbst|kri|tik** F self-criticism; **selbst|kri|tisch** ADJ self-critical ADV self-critically; **Selbst|la|der** [-laːdɐ] M **-s, -** self-loader, semiautomatic weapon *or* firearm; **Selbst|läu|fer** M *(inf)* **a** *(= eigenständiger Erfolg)* sure-fire success *(inf)* **b** → **Selbstgänger**; **Selbst|laut** M vowel; **selbst|lau|tend** ADJ vocalic; **Selbst|ler|ner(in)** M(F) autodidact *(form)*; **er ist ~** he is self-taught; **dies Buch ist geeignet für ~** this book is suitable for people teaching themselves; **Selbst|lob** NT self-importance, vaingloriousness; **selbst|los** ADJ *Mensch, Liebe, Motiv* selfless ADV selflessly; **Selbst|lo|sig|keit** F **-,** *no pl* selflessness; **Selbst|me|di|ka|ti|on** [-medikatsioːn] F **-,** *no pl* self-medication; **Selbst|mit|leid** NT self-pity

Selbst|mord M *(lit, fig)* suicide

Selbst|mord|an|schlag M suicide attack

Selbst|mord|at|ten|tä|ter(in) M(F) suicide attacker

Selbst|mör|der(in) M(F) suicide; **ich bin doch kein ~!** *(inf)* I have no desire to commit suicide

selbst|mör|de|risch ADJ *(lit, fig)* suicidal; **in ~er Absicht** intending to commit suicide

Selbst|mord-: **Selbst|mord|ge|dan|ken** PL suicidal thoughts *pl*; **sich mit ~ tragen** to contemplate suicide; **selbst|mord|ge|fähr|det** ADJ suicidal; **Selbst|mord|kom|man|do** NT suicide squad; **Selbst|mord|ver|such** M suicide attempt, attempted suicide

Selbst-: **Selbst|pflü|cker(in)** M(F) *usu pl* customer who picks his/her own; **Selbst|port|rät** NT self-portrait; **selbst|quä|le|risch** ADJ self-tormenting; **selbst|re|dend** ADV of course, naturally; **Selbst|re|gie|rung** F self-government; **Selbst|rei|ni|gungs|kraft** F self-purifying power; **Selbst|schuld|ner(in)** M(F) *(Jur)* directly suable guarantor; **selbst|schuld|ne|risch** [-ʃʊldnərɪʃ] ADJ *(Jur) Bürgschaft* directly enforceable; *Bürge* directly suable; **Selbst|schuss** M set gun, spring gun; **Selbst|schutz** M self-protection; **selbst|si|cher** ADJ self-assured, self-confident ADV self-confidently; **Selbst|si|cher|heit** F self-assurance, self-confidence; **selbst|stän|dig** ['zɛlpstʃtɛndɪç] ADJ independent; *(beruflich)* self-employed; *(rare: = getrennt)* separate; **~ sein** *(beruflich)* to be self-employed, to have set up on one's own; **sich ~ machen** *(beruflich)* to set up on one's own, to start one's own business; *(hum)* to go off on its own; *(= verschwinden)* to grow legs *(hum)* ADV independently, on one's own; **~ denken** to think for oneself; **das entscheidet er ~** he decides that on his own *or* by himself *or* independently; **Selbst|stän|di|ge(r)** ['zɛlpstʃtɛndɪgə] MF *decl as adj* self-employed person; **die ~n** the self-employed; **Selbst|stän|dig|keit** F **-,** *no pl* independence; *(beruflich)* self-employment; **in großer ~ handeln** *(beruflich)* to act on one's own (initiative); **~ im Denken lernen** to learn to think for oneself; **Selbst|stu|di|um** NT private study; **etw im ~ lernen** to learn sth by studying on one's own; **Selbst|sucht** F, *no pl* egoism; **selbst|süch|tig** ADJ egoistic; **selbst|tä|tig** ADJ **a** *(= automatisch)* automatic, self-acting **b** *(= eigenständig)* independent ADV *(= automatisch)* automatically; **damit sich nicht ~ ein Schuss lösen kann** so that a gun can't fire by itself; **Selbst|täu|schung** F self-deception; **Selbst|test** M *(von Maschine)* self-test; **Selbst|tor** NT own goal; **Selbst|tö|tung** F suicide; **Selbst|über|schät|zung** F overestimation of one's abilities; **das ist eine ~, wenn er meint ...** he's overestimating himself *or* his abilities if he thinks ...; **Selbst|über|win|dung** F willpower; **das war echte ~** that shows real willpower; **selbst bei der größten ~ könnte ich das nicht tun** I simply couldn't bring *or* force myself to do it; **Selbst|ver|ach|tung** F self-contempt; **selbst|ver|ant|wort|lich** ADJ autonomous, independent ADV **etw ~ entscheiden/leiten** to be personally responsible for a decision on sth/in charge of sth; **Selbst|ver|ant|wor|tung** F **in ~** *(entscheiden)* on one's own responsibility; **Selbst|ver|brau|cher** M **Verkauf nur an ~** goods not for resale; **Selbst|ver|bren|nung** F **sich durch ~ töten** to burn oneself to death; **„zwei ~en in einem Monat"** "two people burn themselves to death in one month"; **selbst|ver|dient** ADJ → **selbst** ADV a; **selbst|ver|fasst** [-fɛɐfast] ADJ → **selbst** ADV a; **selbst|ver|ges|sen** ADJ absent-minded; *Blick* faraway ADV **~ dasitzen** to sit there lost to the world; **Selbst|ver|ges|sen|heit** F absent-mindedness; **in seinem Blick lag völlige ~** he looked totally lost to the world; **Selbst|ver|göt|te|rung** F self-glorification; **Selbst|ver|lag** M **im ~ erschienen** published oneself, published at one's own expense; **Selbst|ver|leug|nung** F self-denial; **selbst|ver|liebt** ADJ narcissistic ADV narcissistically; **Selbst|ver|liebt|heit** F self-love, narcissism; **Selbst|ver|nich|tung** F self-destruction; **Selbst|ver|pfle|ger** [-fɛɐpfleːgɐ] M **-s, -**, **Selbst|ver|pfle|ge|rin** [-ərɪn] F **-, -nen** self-caterer; **Ferien für ~** self-catering holiday(s); **Selbst|ver|pfle|gung** F self-catering; **Selbst|ver|schul|den** NT one's own fault; **wenn ~ vorliegt ...** if the claimant is himself at fault ...; **selbst|ver|schul|det** [-fɛɐʃʊldət] ADJ → **selbst** ADV a; **Selbst|ver|si|che|rung** F personal insurance; **Selbst|ver|sor|ger(in)** M(F) **a ~ sein** to be self-sufficient *or* self-reliant **b** *(im Urlaub etc)* sb who is self-catering *(Brit) or* self-sufficient; **Appartements für ~** self-catering apartments *(Brit)*, condominiums *(US)*; **Selbst|ver|sor|gung** F self-sufficiency, self-reliance; *(in Urlaub etc)* self-catering *(Brit)*, self-sufficiency; **selbst|ver|ständ|lich** ADJ *Freundlichkeit* natural; *Wahrheit* self-evident; **das ist doch ~!** that goes without saying, that's obvious; **vielen Dank für Ihre Hilfe – aber das ist doch ~** thanks for your help – it's no more than anybody would have done; **kann ich mitkommen? – aber das ist doch ~** can I come too? – but of course; **es war für uns ~, dass Sie ...** we took it for granted that you ...; **das ist keineswegs ~** it's by no means a matter of course, it cannot be taken for granted; **etw für ~ halten, etw als ~ annehmen** to take sth for granted ADV of course; **wie ~** as if it were the most natural thing in the world; **Selbst|ver|ständ|lich|keit** [-fɛɐʃtɛntlɪçkait] F **-, -en** naturalness; *(= Unbefangenheit)* casualness *no indef art*; *(von Wahrheit)* self-evidence; *(= selbstverständliche Wahrheit etc)* self-evident truth *etc*; **nichts zu danken, das war doch eine ~** think nothing of it, it was no more than anyone would have done; **das war doch eine ~, dass wir ...** it was only natural that we ...; **etw für eine ~ halten** to take sth as a matter of course; **Meinungsfreiheit ist für uns eine ~** we take freedom of speech for granted; **das sind heute ~en** those are things we take for granted today; **mit der größten ~** as if it were the most natural thing in the world; **Selbst|ver|ständ|nis** NT **jds ~** the way sb sees himself/herself; **nach seinem eigenen ~** as he sees himself; **Selbst|ver|stüm|me|lung** F self-inflicted wound; *(= das Verstümmeln)* self-mutilation; **Selbst|ver|such** M experiment on oneself; **Selbst|ver|tei|di|gung** F self-defence *(Brit)*, self-defense *(US)*; **Selbst|ver|trau|en** NT self-confidence; **Selbst|ver|wal|tung** F self-administration; *(Verwaltungskörper)* self-governing body; **Selbst|ver|wirk|li|chung** F self-realization; **Selbst|vor|wurf** M self-reproach; **Selbst|wähl|fern|dienst** M *(Telec)* automatic dialling *(Brit) or* dialing *(US)* service, subscriber trunk dialling *(Brit)*, STD *(Brit)*; **Selbst|wähl|fern|ver|kehr** M *(Telec)* automatic dialling *(Brit) or* dialing *(US)*, STD system *(Brit)*; **Selbst|wahr|neh|mung** F self-perception; **Selbst|wert|ge|fühl** NT feeling of one's own worth *or* value, self-esteem; **Selbst|zer|flei|schung** [-tsɛɐflaiʃʊŋ] F **-, -en** self-destruction; **selbst|zer|stö|re|risch** ADJ self-destructive ADV self-destructively; **Selbst|zer|stö|rung** F self-destruction; **selbst|zu|frie|den** ADJ self-satisfied ADV complacently, smugly; **Selbst|zu|frie|den|heit** F self-satisfaction; **selbst|zün|dend** ADJ self-igniting; **Selbst|zün|der** M *(Aut inf, Motor, Fahrzeug)* diesel; **Selbst|zweck** M end in itself; **als ~** as an end in itself; **Selbst|zwei|fel** M *usu pl* self-doubt *no pl*

sel|chen ['zɛlçn] VTI *(S Ger, Aus) Fleisch* to smoke

Sel|cher ['zɛlçɐ] M **-s, -**, **Sel|che|rin** [-ərɪn] F **-, -nen** *(S Ger, Aus)* (pork) butcher

Selch|fleisch NT *(S Ger, Aus)* smoked meat

se|lek|tie|ren [zelɛk'tiːrən] *ptp* **selektiert** VT to select

Se|lek|ti|on [zelɛk'tsioːn] F **-, -en** selection

Se|lek|ti|ons|leh|re F, **Se|lek|ti|ons|the|o|rie** F theory of natural selection

se|lek|tiv [zelɛk'tiːf] ADJ selective ADV selectively

Se|lek|ti|vi|tät [zelɛktivi'tɛːt] F **-,** *no pl (Rad, Biol, Psych)* selectivity; *(fig)* selectiveness

Se|len [ze'le:n] NT **-s**, *no pl* (*abbr* **Se**) selenium
Se|len|zel|le F (*Phot*) selenium cell
Self|made|man ['sɛlfme:dmən] M **-s, Self-mademen** self-made man
se|lig ['ze:lɪç] ADJ **a** (*Rel*) blessed; (*old*: = *verstorben*) late; ~ **(sind) die Armen im Geiste, denn …** (*Bibl*) blessed are the poor in spirit, for … (*Bibl*); **bis an mein ~es Ende** (*old, hum*) until the day I die; **mein Vater ~** (*old*), **mein ~er Vater** (*old*) my late father → **Angedenken, glauben** **b** (= *überglücklich*) overjoyed; *Lächeln* blissful, beatific (*liter*); *Stunden* blissful; (*inf*: = *beschwipst*) tipsy (*inf*), merry (*Brit inf*) ADV **a** (*Rel*) ~ **entschlafen** (*liter*) departed this life; **Gott hab ihn ~** (*old*) God rest his soul **b** (= *glücklich*) blissfully; ~ **schlafen** to sleep blissfully
Se|li|ge(r) ['ze:lɪgə] MF *decl as adj* **a** (*Eccl*) blessed (*inf*); **die ~n** the Blessed **b** (*old*) **mein/Ihr ~r** my/your late husband
Se|lig|keit F **-, -en a** *no pl* (*Rel*) salvation; **ewige ~** eternal salvation **b** (= *Glück*) (supreme) happiness, bliss
Se|lig-: **se|lig+prei|sen** *sep irreg*, **se|lig prei|sen** △ *irreg* VT **a** (*Bibl*) to bless **b** (*liter*: = *verherrlichen*) to glorify VR to thank one's lucky stars; **Se|lig|prei|sung** [-praizʊŋ] F **-, -en** (*Bibl*) Beatitude; (*liter*) glorification; **se|lig+spre|chen** *sep irreg*, **se|lig spre|chen** △ *irreg* VT (*Eccl*) to beatify; **Se|lig|spre|chung** ['ze:lɪçʃprɛçʊŋ] F **-, -en** (*Eccl*) beatification
Sel|le|rie ['zɛləri:] M **-s, -(s)** *or f* **-, -** celeriac; (= *Stangensellerie*) celery
sel|ten ['zɛltn] ADJ rare; (= *kaum vorkommend auch*) scarce; **du bist ja in letzter Zeit ein ~er Gast** you're a stranger here these days → **Erde, Vogel** ADV (= *nicht oft*) rarely, seldom; (= *besonders*) exceptionally; **nur/höchst ~** very/extremely rarely *or* seldom; ~ **so gelacht!** (*inf*) what a laugh! (*inf*)
Sel|ten|heit F **-, -en a** *no pl* (= *seltenes Vorkommen*) rareness, rarity **b** (= *seltene Sache*) rarity; **das ist keine ~ bei ihr** it's nothing unusual with her
Sel|ten|heits|wert M rarity value
Sel|ters ['zɛltɐs] NT **-, -** (*inf*), **Sel|ter(s)|was|ser** NT *pl* **-wässer** soda (water)
selt|sam ['zɛltza:m] ADJ strange; (= *komisch auch*) odd, peculiar ADV strangely; ~ **berührt** strangely moved; ~ **klingen/aussehen/schmecken/riechen** to sound/look/taste/smell strange; **es schimmerte ~ grünlich** it had a strange green shimmer to it
selt|sa|mer|wei|se ['zɛltza:mɐ'vaizə] ADV strangely enough
Selt|sam|keit F **-, -en a** *no pl* (= *Sonderbarkeit*) strangeness **b** (= *seltsame Sache*) oddity
Se|man|tik [ze'mantɪk] F **-,** *no pl* semantics *sing*
se|man|tisch [ze'mantɪʃ] ADJ semantic ADV semantically
Se|ma|phor [zema'fo:ɐ] NT OR M **-s, -e** (*Naut, Rail*) semaphore
Se|ma|sio|lo|gie [zemaziolo'gi:] F **-,** *no pl* (*Ling*) semasiology
Se|mes|ter [ze'mɛstɐ] NT **-s, -** (*Univ*) semester (*esp US*), term (*of a half-year's duration*); **im 7./8. ~ sein** to be in one's 4th year; **die älteren ~** the older *or* senior students; **ein älteres ~** a senior student; (*hum*) an old boy/girl; **sie ist auch schon ein älteres ~** she's no spring chicken (*inf*)
Se|mes|ter- (*Univ*): **Se|mes|ter|be|ginn** M **zu ~** at the beginning of term *or* semester (*esp US*); **Se|mes|ter|en|de** NT **zu ~** at the end of term *or* semester (*esp US*); **Se|mes|ter|fe|ri|en** PL vacation *sing*; **se|mes|ter|lang** ADJ ADV for years; **Se|mes|ter|schluss** M end of term, end of the semester (*esp US*); **Se|mes|ter|ti|cket** NT student ticket (*valid during term*); **Se|mes|ter|zeug|nis** NT (*Aus Sch*) interim *or* end-of-term report
-se|mest|rig [zemɛstrɪç] ADJ *suf* **ein acht-/zehnsemestriges Studium** a four-/five-year course

Se|mi-, se|mi- ['zemi] *in cpds* semi-; **Se|mi|fi|na|le** ['ze:mi-] NT (*Sport*) semifinal(s); **Se|mi|ko|lon** [zemi'ko:lɔn] NT **-s, -s** *or* **Semikola** [-la] semicolon
Se|mi|nar [zemi'na:ɐ] NT **-s, -e** *or* (*Aus*) **-rien** [-iən] **a** (*Univ*) department; (= *Seminarübung*) seminar **b** (= *Priesterseminar*) seminary **c** (= *Lehrerseminar, Studienseminar*) teacher training college, college of education
Se|mi|nar- (*Univ*): **Se|mi|nar|ap|pa|rat** M seminar course books *pl*; **Se|mi|nar|ar|beit** F seminar paper
Se|mi|na|rist [zemina'rɪst] M **-en, -en**, **Se|mi|na|ris|tin** [-'rɪstɪn] F **-, -nen** (*Eccl*) seminarist
se|mi|na|ris|tisch [zemina'rɪstɪʃ] ADJ **a** (*Univ*) *Struktur* departmental; **~e Ausbildung** (= *in Gruppen*) training through seminars **b** (*Eccl*) seminary
Se|mi|nar- (*Univ*): **Se|mi|nar|rei|he** F series of seminars; **Se|mi|nar|schein** M *certificate of attendance for one semester or half-year*; **Se|mi|nar|übung** F seminar
Se|mio|lo|gie [zemiolo'gi:] F **-,** *no pl* semiology
Se|mi|o|tik [zemi'o:tɪk] F **-,** *no pl* semiotics *sing*
se|mi|per|me|a|bel ADJ semipermeable
Se|mit [ze'mi:t] M **-en, -en**, **Se|mi|tin** [-'mi:tɪn] F **-, -nen** Semite
se|mi|tisch [ze'mi:tɪʃ] ADJ Semitic
Se|mi|tist [zemi'tɪst] M **-en, -en**, **Se|mi|tis|tin** [-'tɪstɪn] F **-, -nen** Semitist
Se|mi|tis|tik [zemi'tɪstɪk] F **-,** *no pl* Semitics *sing*
Se|mi|vo|kal ['ze:mi-] M semivowel
Sem|mel ['zɛml] F **-, -n** (*dial*) roll; **geriebene ~** breadcrumbs *pl*
Sem|mel-: **sem|mel|blond** ADJ (*dated*) flaxen-haired; **Sem|mel|brö|sel(n)** [-brø:zl(n)] PL breadcrumbs *pl*; **Sem|mel|kloß** M = **Semmelknödel**; **Sem|mel|knö|del** M (*S Ger, Aus*) bread dumpling; **Sem|mel|mehl** NT breadcrumbs *pl*
sen. *abbr von* **senior** sen.
Se|nat [ze'na:t] M **-(e)s, -e a** (*Pol, Univ*) senate **b** (*Jur*) Supreme Court
Se|na|tor [ze'na:to:ɐ] M **-s, Senatoren** [-'to:rən], **Se|na|to|rin** [-'to:rɪn] F **-, -nen** senator
Se|nats- *in cpds* of the senate; **Se|nats|aus|schuss** M senate committee; **se|nats|ei|gen** ADJ belonging to the senate; **Se|nats|prä|si|dent(in)** M(F) chairman/-woman of the senate; **Se|nats|wah|len** PL elections *pl* to the senate
Send-: **Send|bo|te** M (*Hist*) emissary, ambassador (*old*); **Send|brief** M (*liter*) circular letter
Sen|de-: **Sen|de|an|la|ge** F transmitting installation; **Sen|de|an|stalt** F broadcasting organization *or* station; **Sen|de|an|ten|ne** F transmitting aerial (*esp Brit*) *or* antenna (*US*); **Sen|de|be|reich** M transmission range; **Sen|de|ein|rich|tung** F transmitting facility; **Sen|de|fol|ge** F **a** (= *Sendung in Fortsetzungen*) series *sing*; (= *einzelne Folge*) episode **b** (= *Programmfolge*) programmes *pl* (*Brit*), programs *pl* (*US*); **Sen|de|ge|biet** NT transmission area; **Sen|de|lei|ter(in)** M(F) producer; **Sen|de|mast** M radio *or* transmitter mast, broadcasting tower (*US*)
sen|den ['zɛndn] ✪ 50.2 *pret* **sandte** *or* **sendete**, ['zantə, 'zɛndətə] *ptp* **gesandt** *or* **gesendet** VT [gə'zant, gə'zɛndət] to send (*an* +*acc* to); **jdm etw ~** to send sb sth, to send sth to sb VI **nach jdm ~** to send for sb
sen|den VTI (*Rad, TV*) to broadcast; *Signal etc* to transmit
Sen|de|pau|se F interval; (*fig inf*) deathly silence; **danach tritt eine ~ bis 6 Uhr ein** afterwards we shall be going off the air until 6 o'clock; **auf meine Frage hin herrschte ~** my question was met by deathly silence
Sen|der ['zɛndɐ] M **-s, -** transmitter; (= *Senderkanal*) (*Rad*) station; (*TV*) channel (*esp Brit*), station (*esp US*); **der ~ Prag** Radio Prague; **über den ~ gehen** to go on the air

Sen|de-: **Sen|de|raum** M studio; **Sen|de|rei|he** F (radio/television) series
Sen|der-: **Sen|der|ein|stel|lung** F tuning; **Sen|der-Emp|fän|ger** M transceiver; **Sen|der|such|lauf** M search tuning
Sen|de-: **Sen|de|saal** M studio; **Sen|de|schluss** M (*Rad, TV*) close-down, end of broadcasts; **und nun bis ~** and now until we close down; **Sen|de|turm** M radio tower; **Sen|de|zei|chen** NT call sign; **Sen|de|zeit** F broadcasting time; **und damit geht unsere heutige ~ zu Ende** and that concludes our programmes (*Brit*) *or* programs (*US*) for today; **in der besten ~** in prime time
Send|schrei|ben NT (*liter*) circular letter
Sen|dung ['zɛndʊŋ] F **-, -en a** *no pl* (= *das Senden*) sending **b** (= *Postsendung*) letter; (= *Päckchen*) packet; (= *Paket*) parcel; (*Comm*) consignment **c** (*TV*) programme (*Brit*), program (*US*); (*Rad*) broadcast, programme (*Brit*), program (*US*); (= *das Senden*) broadcasting; (*von Signal etc*) transmission; **auf ~ gehen/sein** to go/be on the air **d** (*liter*: = *Aufgabe*) mission
Sen|dungs|be|wusst|sein NT sense of mission
Se|ne|gal ['ze:negal] M **-(s) der ~** the Senegal (River)
Se|ne|gal NT **-s** Senegal
Se|ne|ga|ler [zene'ga:lɐ] M **-s, -**, **Se|ne|ga|le|rin** [-ərɪn] F **-, -nen**, **Se|ne|ga|le|se** [zenega'le:zə] M **-n, -n**, **Se|ne|ga|le|sin** [-'le:zɪn] F **-, -nen** Senegalese
se|ne|ga|le|sisch [zenega'le:zɪʃ], **se|ne|ga|lisch** [zene'ga:lɪʃ] ADJ Senegalese
Se|ne|schall ['ze:nəʃal] M **-s, -e** (*Hist*) seneschal
Se|nes|zenz [zenɛs'tsɛnts] F **-,** *no pl* (*Med*) senescence
Senf [zɛnf] M **-(e)s, -e** mustard; **seinen ~ dazugeben** (*inf*) to get one's three ha'p'orth (*Brit*) *or* two cents (*US*) in (*inf*), to have one's say
Senf-: **senf|far|ben** [-farbn], **senf|far|big** ADJ mustard(-coloured) (*Brit*), mustard(-colored) (*US*); **Senf|gas** NT (*Chem*) mustard gas; **Senf|gur|ke** F *gherkin pickled with mustard seeds*; **Senf|korn** NT *pl* **-körner** mustard seed; **Senf|mehl** NT flour of mustard; **Senf|pa|ckung** F (*Med*) mustard poultice; **Senf|pflas|ter** NT (*Med*) mustard plaster; **Senf|so|ße** F, **Senf|tun|ke** F (*dial*) mustard sauce; **Senf|um|schlag** M (*Med*) mustard poultice
Sen|ge ['zɛŋə] PL (*dated inf*) **~ kriegen** to get a good hiding
sen|gen ['zɛŋən] VT to singe VI to scorch; **~d und brennend** (*old liter*) with fire and sword
se|nil [ze'ni:l] ADJ (*pej*) senile
Se|ni|li|tät [zenili'tɛ:t] F **-,** *no pl* senility
se|ni|or ['ze:nio:ɐ] ADJ **Franz Schulz ~** Franz Schulz senior
Se|ni|or ['ze:nio:ɐ] M **-s, Senioren** [ze'nio:rən], **Se|ni|o|rin** [ze'nio:rɪn] F **-, -nen a** (*auch* **Seniorchef(in)**) boss; **kann ich mal den ~ sprechen?** can I speak to Mr X senior? **b** (*Sport*) senior player; **die ~en** the seniors, the senior team **c Senioren** PL senior citizens *pl*; (*hum*) old folk *pl*
Se|ni|o|ren-: **Se|ni|o|ren|ho|tel** NT hotel for the elderly; **Se|ni|o|ren|kar|te** F pensioner's ticket, senior citizen's ticket; **Se|ni|o|ren|mann|schaft** F senior team; **Se|ni|o|ren|pass** M senior citizen's travel pass; **Se|ni|o|ren|tel|ler** M dish for senior citizens; **Se|ni|o|ren|wohn|an|la|ge** F housing development for the elderly; (*betreut auch*) sheltered housing development, assisted living development; **Se|ni|o|ren|(wohn)|haus** NT, **Se|ni|o|ren|(wohn)|heim** NT old people's home
Se|ni|o|rin [ze'nio:rɪn] F → **Senior**
Se|ni|or|part|ner(in) M(F) senior partner
Senk|blei NT plumb line; (= *Gewicht*) plummet
Sen|ke ['zɛŋkə] F **-, -n** valley
Sen|kel ['zɛŋkl] M **-s, - a** (= *Schnürsenkel*) lace; **jdm auf den ~ gehen** (*fig: inf*) to get on sb's wick (*Brit inf*) *or* nerves **b** (= *Senklot*) plumb

line; *(= Gewicht)* plummet; **jdn in den ~ stellen** *(fig inf)* to put sb in his/her place

sen|ken ['zɛŋkn] VT to lower; *Lanze, Fahne* to dip; *Kopf* to bow; *Preis, Steuern, Kosten* to decrease, to lower; *(Tech) Schraube, Loch, Schacht* to sink; *(Hort) Schösslinge, Wurzeln etc* to plant; **den Blick ~** to lower one's gaze VR to sink; *(Grab, Haus, Boden, Straße auch)* to subside; *(Wasserspiegel auch)* to go down, to fall; *(Decke)* to sag; *(Flugzeug)* to descend; *(Stimme)* to drop; *(liter: Nacht, Nebel)* to fall, to descend *(über, auf +acc* on); **dann senkte sich ihr Blick** then she looked down, then she lowered her eyes *or* her gaze *(liter)*

Senk-: **Senk|fuß** M *(Med)* fallen arches *pl*; **Senk|fuß|ein|la|ge** F arch support; **Senk|gru|be** F cesspit; **Senk|kas|ten** M caisson; **Senk|kopf|schrau|be** F countersunk screw; **Senk|lot** NT plumb line; *(= Gewicht)* plummet

senk|recht ['zɛŋkrɛçt] ADJ vertical; *(Math)* perpendicular; *(in Kreuzworträtsel)* down; **immer schön ~ bleiben!** *(inf)* keep your end up *(inf)* ADV vertically, perpendicularly; *aufsteigen, in die Höhe steigen* straight up; **sie stehen ~ aufeinander** they are perpendicular to each other

Senk|rech|te ['zɛŋkrɛçtə] F *decl as adj* vertical; *(Math)* perpendicular

Senk|recht|star|ter M *(Aviat)* vertical takeoff aircraft

Senk|recht|star|ter(in) M(F) *(fig inf)* whiz(z) kid *(inf)*

Sen|kung ['zɛŋkʊŋ] F -, -en **a** sinking; *(von Boden, Straße)* subsidence; *(von Wasserspiegel)* fall (+*gen* in), drop (+*gen* in); *(als Maßnahme)* lowering; *(von Decke)* sag(ging); *(von Stimme)* lowering; *(von Preisen, Steuern)* lowering *(von* of), decrease *(von* in); *(von Arbeitslosigkeit)* fall, drop *(von* in) **b** *(= Vertiefung)* hollow, valley **c** *(Poet)* thesis **d** *(Med)* = **Blutsenkung**

Sen|kungs|ge|schwin|dig|keit F *(Med)* rate of sedimentation

Senk|waa|ge F hydrometer

Senn [zɛn] [zɛn] M -(e)s, -e, **Sen|ne** ['zɛnə] M -n, -n *(S Ger, Aus)* Alpine dairyman

Sen|ne ['zɛnə] F -, -n *(S Ger, Aus)* Alpine pasture

Sen|ner ['zɛnɐ] M -s, - *(S Ger, Aus)* Alpine dairyman

Sen|ne|rei [zɛnə'rai] F -, -en *(S Ger, Aus, Gebäude)* Alpine dairy; *(Wirtschaftsform)* Alpine dairy farming

Sen|ne|rin ['zɛnərɪn] F -, -nen *(S Ger, Aus)* Alpine dairymaid

Sen|nes|blät|ter ['zɛnəs-] PL senna leaves *pl*

Senn|hüt|te F Alpine dairy hut

Sen|sa|ti|on [zɛnza'tsio:n] F -, -en sensation

sen|sa|ti|o|nell [zɛnzatsio'nɛl] ADJ sensational ADV sensationally; **er wurde ~ Dritter** he came a sensational third; **~ schnell** incredibly fast

Sen|sa|ti|ons-: **Sen|sa|ti|ons|be|dürf|nis** NT need for sensation; **Sen|sa|ti|ons|blatt** NT sensational paper; **Sen|sa|ti|ons|gier** F *(pej)* sensation-seeking; **aus ~** for the sheer sensation; **Sen|sa|ti|ons|lust** F desire for sensation; **sen|sa|ti|ons|lüs|tern** ADJ sensation-seeking; **sen|sa|ti|ons|lus|tig** ADJ sensation-loving; **Sen|sa|ti|ons|ma|che** F *(inf)* sensationalism; **Sen|sa|ti|ons|mel|dung** F, **Sen|sa|ti|ons|nach|richt** F sensational news *sing*; **eine Sensationsnachricht** a sensation, a scoop, a sensational piece of news; **Sen|sa|ti|ons|pres|se** F sensational papers *pl*, yellow press; **Sen|sa|ti|ons|pro|zess** M sensational trial

Sen|se ['zɛnzə] F -, -n **a** scythe **b** *(inf)* **jetzt/dann ist ~!** that's the end!; **es ist nichts mehr da, ~!** there's none left, all gone!

Sen|sen|mann M *pl* **-männer der ~** the Grim Reaper

sen|si|bel [zɛn'zi:bl] ADJ sensitive; *(= heikel auch)* problematic, delicate ADV *schildern* sensitively; **~ auf etw** *(acc)* **reagieren** to be sensitive to sth; **~ mit jdm umgehen** to treat sb sensitively

Sen|si|bel|chen [zɛn'zi:blçən] NT -s, - *(inf, usu pej)* sensitive soul

Sen|si|bi|li|sa|tor [zɛnzibili'za:to:ɐ] M -s, **Sensibilisatoren** [-'to:rən] *(Phot)* sensitizer

sen|si|bi|li|sie|ren [zɛnzibili'zi:rən] *ptp* **sensibilisiert** VT to sensitize

Sen|si|bi|li|sie|rung F -, -en sensitization

Sen|si|bi|li|tät [zɛnzibili'tɛ:t] F -, *no pl* sensitivity; *(= Feingefühl auch)* sensibility

sen|si|tiv [zɛnzi'ti:f] ADJ *(geh, Comput)* sensitive

Sen|si|ti|vi|tät [zɛnzitivi'tɛ:t] F -, *no pl (geh, Comput)* sensitivity

Sen|sor ['zɛnzo:ɐ] M -s, **Sensoren** [-'zo:rən] sensor

sen|so|ri|ell [zɛnzo'riɛl] ADJ ADV = **sensorisch**

Sen|so|ri|en [zɛn'zo:riən] PL sensoria *pl*

sen|so|risch [zɛn'zo:rɪʃ] ADJ sensory ADV *aktivieren, steuern* by a sensor; **~ gestört sein** to have a sensory disability

Sen|sor|tas|te F touch-sensitive button

Sen|su|a|lis|mus [zɛnzua'lɪsmʊs] M -, *no pl (Philos)* sensualism, sensationalism

Sen|su|a|li|tät [zɛnzuali'tɛ:t] F -, *no pl* sensuality

sen|su|ell [zɛn'zuɛl] ADJ sensory

Sen|tenz [zɛn'tɛnts] F -, -en aphorism

sen|ten|zi|ös [zɛntɛn'tsiø:s] ADJ sententious

Sen|ti|ment [zãti'mã:] NT -s, -s *(liter)* feeling

sen|ti|men|tal [zɛntimɛn'ta:l] ADJ sentimental ADV sentimentally; **~ klingen** to sound sentimental; **sich jdm gegenüber ~ verhalten** to be sentimental about sb; **der Brief war ~ angehaucht** the letter had a sentimental tone to it

Sen|ti|men|ta|li|tät [zɛntimɛntali'tɛ:t] F -, -en sentimentality

se|pa|rat [zepa'ra:t] ADJ separate; *(= in sich abgeschlossen) Wohnung, Zimmer* self-contained ADV separately

Se|pa|rat-: **Se|pa|rat|(ab)|druck** M *pl* **-drucke** offprint; **Se|pa|rat|frie|de(n)** M separate peace

Se|pa|ra|tis|mus [zepara'tɪsmʊs] M -, *no pl (Pol)* separatism

Se|pa|ra|tist [zepara'tɪst] M -en, -en, **Se|pa|ra|tis|tin** [-'tɪstɪn] F -, -nen *(Pol)* separatist

se|pa|ra|tis|tisch [zepara'tɪstɪʃ] ADJ *(Pol)* separatist

Se|pa|ra|to|ren|fleisch NT mechanically recovered meat

Sé|pa|ree [zepa're:] NT -s, -s, **Se|pa|rée** NT -s, -s private room; *(= Nische)* private booth

se|pa|rie|ren [zepa'ri:rən] *ptp* **separiert** VT *(rare)* to separate; *(= isolieren)* to isolate

se|pa|riert [zepa'ri:ɐt] ADJ *(esp Aus) Zimmer* self-contained

se|pia ['ze:pia] ADJ *inv* sepia

Se|pia ['ze:pia] F -, **Sepien** [-piən] **a** *(Zool)* cuttlefish **b** *no pl (Farbstoff)* sepia (ink)

Se|pia-: **Se|pia|scha|le** F cuttlefish shell; **Se|pia|zeich|nung** F sepia (drawing)

Se|pi|en ['ze:piən] *pl von* **Sepia**

Sepp [zɛp] M -s *(S Ger) abbr von* **Josef**

Sep|pel-: **Sep|pel|ho|se** ['zɛpl-] F *(inf)* lederhosen *pl*, leather shorts *pl*; **Sep|pel|hut** ['zɛpl-] M *(inf) traditional Bavarian hat*

Sep|sis ['zɛpsɪs] F -, **Sepsen** ['zɛpsn] *(Med)* sepsis

Sep|tem|ber [zɛp'tɛmbɐ] M -(s), - September → *auch* **März**

Sep|tett [zɛp'tɛt] NT -(e)s, -e *(Mus)* septet(te)

Sep|ti|me [zɛp'ti:mə] F -, -n, *(Aus)* **Sep|tim** [zɛp'ti:m] F -, -en *(Mus)* seventh

sep|tisch ['zɛptɪʃ] ADJ *(Med)* septic

Sep|tu|a|gin|ta [zɛptua'gɪnta] F - *(Eccl)* Septuagint

se|quen|ti|ell [zekvɛn'tsiɛl] ADJ, ADV = **sequenziell**

Se|quenz [ze'kvɛnts] F -, -en sequence; *(Cards auch)* flush, run

Se|quen|zer ['zi:kvɛntsɐ] M -s, - *(Tech)* sequencer

se|quen|zi|ell [zekvɛn'tsiɛl] ADJ sequential ADV sequentially

se|quest|rie|ren [zekvɛs'tri:rən] *ptp* **sequestriert** VT *(Jur)* to sequester, to sequestrate

Se|ra *pl von* **Serum**

Se|rail [ze'ra:j, ze'rai(l)] NT -s, -s seraglio

Se|raph ['ze:raf] M -s, -e *or* -im [-fi:m] seraph

Ser|be ['zɛrbə] M -n, -n, **Ser|bin** ['zɛrbɪn] F -, -nen Serbian

Ser|bi|en ['zɛrbiən] NT -s Serbia

Ser|bin ['zɛrbɪn] F -, -nen Serbian (woman/girl)

ser|bisch ['zɛrbɪʃ] ADJ Serbian

Ser|bo|kro|a|tisch(e) [zɛrbokro'a:tɪʃ] NT Serbo-Croat → *auch* **Deutsch(e)**

Se|ren PL *von* **Serum**

Se|re|na|de [zere'na:də] F -, -n serenade

Ser|geant [zɛr'ʒant] M -en, -en *(dated Mil)* sergeant

Se|rie ['ze:riə] F -, -n series *sing*; *(von Waren auch)* line; *(Billard)* break; **13 Siege in ~** 13 wins in a row; **in ~ gehen** to go into production, to go onto the production line; **in ~ hergestellt werden** to be mass-produced; **das Gesetz der ~** the law of averages; **in ~ schalten** *(Elec)* to connect in series

se|ri|ell [ze'riɛl] ADJ *Herstellung* series *attr*; *(Comput)* serial; **~e Musik** serial music ADV serially; **~ hergestellt werden** to be mass-produced

Se|ri|en-: **Se|ri|en|au|to** NT mass-produced car; **Se|ri|en|brief** M *(Comput)* mail-merge letter, form letter; **Se|ri|en|brief|er|stel|lung** F *(Comput)* mail merge; **Se|ri|en|fab|ri|ka|ti|on** F, **Se|ri|en|fer|ti|gung** F, **Se|ri|en|her|stel|lung** F series production; **Se|ri|en|fax** NT mail-merge fax; **se|ri|en|mä|ßig** ADJ *Autos* production *attr*; *Ausstattung* standard; *Herstellung* series *attr* ADV *herstellen* in series; **das wird ~ eingebaut** it's a standard fitting; **Se|ri|en|mör|der(in)** M(F) serial killer; **Se|ri|en|num|mer** F serial number; **Se|ri|en|pro|duk|ti|on** F series production; **in ~ gehen** to go into production, to go onto the production line; **se|ri|en|reif** ADJ *(esp Aut)* ready to go into production; **Se|ri|en|rei|fe** F readiness for production; **etw zur ~ entwickeln** to develop sth so that it is ready for production; **Se|ri|en|schal|tung** F *(Elec)* series connection; **Se|ri|en|tä|ter(in)** M(F) serial offender; **se|ri|en|wei|se** [-vaizə] ADV *produzieren* in series; *(inf: = in Mengen)* wholesale

Se|ri|fe [ze'ri:fə] F -, -n *(Typ)* serif

se|ri|fen|los ADJ *(Typ)* sanserif

Se|ri|gra|fie, **Se|ri|gra|phie** [zerigra'fi:] F -, -n [-'fi:ən] **a** *(Verfahren)* silk-screen printing, serigraphy *(spec)* **b** *(Bild)* silk-screen print, serigraph *(spec)*

se|ri|ös [ze'riø:s] ADJ serious; *(= anständig)* respectable; *Firma* reputable ADV **~ auftreten** to appear respectable; **~ wirken** to give the impression of being respectable; **~ klingen** to sound serious

Se|ri|o|si|tät [zeriozi'tɛ:t] F -, *no pl* seriousness; *(= Anständigkeit)* respectability; *(von Firma)* integrity; **von zweifelhafter ~** of doubtful reputation

Ser|mon [zɛr'mo:n] M -s, -e *(pej)* sermon, lecture

Se|ro|di|ag|nos|tik [zero-] F serodiagnosis

Se|ro|lo|gie [zerolo'gi:] F -, *no pl* serology

se|ro|lo|gisch [zero'lo:gɪʃ] ADJ serological

se|ro|ne|ga|tiv [zero-] ADJ HIV negative, seronegative *(spec)*

se|ro|po|si|tiv ADJ HIV positive, seropositive *(spec)*

Ser|pen|tin [zɛrpɛn'ti:n] M -s, -e *(Miner)* serpentine

Ser|pen|ti|ne [zɛrpɛn'ti:nə] F -, -n winding road, zigzag; *(= Kurve)* double bend; **die Straße führt in ~n den Berg hinauf** the road winds *or* zigzags its way up the mountain

Ser|pen|ti|nen|stra|ße F winding *or* serpentine road

Se|rum ['ze:rʊm] NT -s, **Seren** *or* **Sera** ['ze:rən, 'ze:ra] serum

Se|rum|be|hand|lung F, **Se|rum|the|ra|pie** F serotherapy, serum therapy

Ser|ver ['zœrvɐ] M **-s, -** *(Comput)* server

Ser|vice [zɛr'vi:s] NT **-(s), -** [-'vi:səs, -'vi:sə] *(= Essgeschirr)* dinner service; *(= Kaffee-/Teeservice)* coffee/tea service; *(= Gläserservice)* set

Ser|vice ['sø:ɐvɪs, 'zœrvɪs] M OR NT **-, -s** *(Comm)* service; *(Sport)* service, serve

Ser|vice-: **Ser|vice|leis|tung** ['zœrvɪs-, 'sø:ɐvɪs-] F service; **Ser|vice|pro|vi|der** ['zœrvɪsprɔ'vaidɐ, 'sø:ɐvɪs-] M **-s, -** *(für Mobilfunk, Internet)* service provider; **Ser|vice|te|le|fon** ['zœrvɪs-, 'sø:ɐvɪs-] NT customer service hotline

Ser|vice|wüs|te F *(inf)* service-free zone

Ser|vier|brett [zɛr'vi:ɐ-] NT tray

ser|vie|ren [zɛr'vi:rən] *ptp* **serviert** VT to serve *(jdm etw* sb sth, sth to sb); *(inf: = anbieten)* to serve up *(inf) (jdm* for sb); *(Tennis)* to serve; **jdm etw auf dem Silbertablett ~** *(fig)* to hand sth to sb on a plate *(Brit)* or on a silver platter; **jdm den Ball ~** *(Ftbl etc)* to pass the ball to sb; *(Tennis)* to hit the ball right to sb; **er bekam den Ball toll serviert** the ball was beautifully set up for him VI **a** to serve; **nach 24 Uhr wird nicht mehr serviert** there is no waiter service after midnight; **es ist serviert!** lunch/dinner *etc* is served **b** *(Tennis)* to serve

Ser|vie|re|rin [zɛr'vi:rərɪn] F **-, -nen** waitress

Ser|vier-: **Ser|vier|tisch** M serving table; **Ser|vier|toch|ter** F *(Sw)* waitress; **Ser|vier|vor|schlag** M *(auf Verpackungen)* serving suggestion; **Ser|vier|wa|gen** M trolley

Ser|vi|et|te [zɛr'vietə] F **-, -n** serviette *(Brit)*, napkin

Ser|vi|et|ten-: **Ser|vi|et|ten|knö|del** M *(Cook)* *dumpling cooked in a napkin*; **Ser|vi|et|ten|ring** M serviette *(Brit)* or napkin ring

ser|vil [zɛr'vi:l] *(geh)* ADJ servile ADV servilely

Ser|vi|li|tät [zɛrvili'tɛ:t] F **-,** *no pl (geh)* servility

Ser|vo- *(Tech)*: **Ser|vo|brem|se** F power brake, servo(-assisted) brake; **Ser|vo|len|kung** F power steering, servo(-assisted) steering; **Ser|vo|mo|tor** M servomotor

ser|vus ['zɛrvʊs] INTERJ *(Aus, S Ger) (beim Treffen)* hello; *(beim Abschied)* goodbye, so long *(inf)*, cheerio *(Brit inf)*, see ya *(esp US inf)*

Se|sam ['ze:zam] M **-s, -s** sesame; **~, öffne dich!** open Sesame!

Se|sam|bröt|chen NT sesame roll

Se|sam|stra|ße® F, *no pl (TV: Kindersendung)* Sesame Street®

Ses|sel ['zɛsl] M **-s, -** easy chair; *(= Polstersessel)* armchair; *(Aus: = Stuhl)* chair; **am ~ kleben** *(fig)* to cling to one's position; **seinen ~ räumen** *(fig)* to clear one's desk

Ses|sel-: **Ses|sel|leh|ne** F (chair) arm; **Ses|sel|lift** M chairlift

sess|haft ADJ settled; *(= ansässig)* resident; **~ werden, sich ~ machen** to settle down

Sess|haf|tig|keit ['zɛshaftɪçkait] F **-,** *no pl* settled existence; *(von Lebensweise mit festem Wohnsitz)* settledness; **die sprichwörtliche ~ der Holsteiner** the Holsteiners' proverbial lack of wanderlust

Ses|si|on [zɛ'sio:n] F **-, -en** *(Parl)* session; *(Jur)* term

Set [zɛt, sɛt] M OR NT **-s, -s** **a** *(Tennis: = Satz)* set **b** *(= Deckchen)* place mat, table mat

Set M **-(s), -s** *(TV, Film)* set

Set|ter ['zɛtɐ] M **-s, -** setter

Set-up ['zɛtap] NT **-s, -** *(Comput)* setup

Set-up-Da|tei ['zɛtap-] F *(Comput)* setup file

Setz|ei ['zɛtslai] NT fried egg

set|zen ['zɛtsn] VT **a** *(= hintun, hinbringen)* to put, to place, to set; *(= sitzen lassen)* to sit, to place, to put; **etw auf die Rechnung/Speisekarte** *etc* **~** to put sth on the bill/menu *etc*; **etw an den Mund/die Lippen ~** to put sth to one's mouth/lips; **jdn an Land ~** to put *or* set sb ashore; **jdn über den Fluss ~** to take sb across the river; **Fische in einen Teich ~** to stock a pond with fish; **ein Stück auf den Spielplan ~** to put on a play; **etw auf die Tagesordnung ~** to put sth on the agenda; **etw in die Zeitung ~** to put sth in the paper; **jdn über jemanden anders/andere ~** to put *or* set sb above somebody else/others; **sich** *(dat)* **etw in den Kopf** *or* **Schädel ~** *(inf)* to take sth into one's head; **dann setzt es was** *or* **Hiebe** *or* **Prügel** *(all inf)* there'll be trouble; **seine Hoffnung/sein Vertrauen in jdn/etw ~** to put *or* place one's hopes/trust in sb/sth; **seine Ehre in etw** *(acc)* **~** to make sth a point of honour *(Brit)* or honor *(US)*; **seinen Ehrgeiz in etw** *(acc)* **~** to make sth one's goal; **sein Leben an etw** *(acc)* **~** *(geh)* to devote one's life to sth → **Druck a**

b *(Hort: = pflanzen)* to set, to plant; *(= aufziehen) Ständer, Laternen* to put up; *(Naut) Segel* to set; *(Typ)* to set; *(geh: = formulieren) Worte* to choose; **ein Gedicht/einen Text in Musik ~** to set a poem/words to music

c *Preis, Summe* to put *(auf +acc* on); *(bei Gesellschaftsspielen: = spielen, ziehen) Stein, Figur* to move; **Geld auf ein Pferd ~** to put *or* place *or* stake money on a horse; **auf seinen Kopf sind 100.000 Dollar gesetzt** there's 100,000 dollars on his head

d *(= errichten, aufstellen)* to build; *Denkmal auch* to erect, to put *or* set up; *(fig) Norm etc* to set; **jdm ein Grabmal/Denkmal ~** to put *or* set up *or* build a monument to sb; **sich** *(dat)* **ein Denkmal ~** *(fig)* to ensure that one will not be forgotten

e *(= schreiben) Komma, Punkt* to put; **seinen Namen unter etw** *(acc)* **~** to put one's signature to sth

f *(= bestimmen) Ziel, Grenze, Termin, Preis, Prioritäten etc* to set; **jdm/sich ein Ziel/eine Frist ~** to set sb/oneself a goal/deadline; **den Fall ~** to make the assumption

g **jdm eine Spritze ~** to give sb an injection; **sich** *(dat)* **einen Schuss ~** *(inf)* to shoot up *(inf)*

h *(= einstufen) Sportler* to place; *(Tennis)* to seed; **sie wurde auf Platz zwei gesetzt** she was placed/seeded second; **der an Nummer eins/zwei gesetzte Spieler** *(Tennis)* the top/second seed, the top-seeded/second-seeded player

i *(Hunt: = gebären)* to bear, to produce

j → **gesetzt**

VR **a** *(= Platz nehmen)* to sit down; *(Vogel)* to perch, to alight; **sich auf einen Stuhl/seinen Platz ~** to sit down on a chair/at one's place; **sich ins Auto ~** to get into the car; **sich in die Sonne/ins Licht ~** to sit in the sun/light; **sich jdm auf den Schoß ~** to sit on sb's lap; **sich zu jdm ~** to sit with sb; **wollen Sie sich nicht zu uns ~?** won't you join us?; **darf ich mich zu Ihnen ~?** may I join you?; **bitte ~ Sie sich** please sit down, please take a seat, please be seated *(form)*; **setz dich doch** sit yourself down *(inf)*

b *(Kaffee, Tee, Lösung)* to settle

c *(= sich festsetzen: Staub, Geruch, Läuse)* to get *(in +acc* into)

VI **a** *(bei Glücksspiel, Wetten)* to bet; **auf ein Pferd ~** to bet on *or* to place a bet on *or* to back a horse; **auf jdn/etw ~** *(lit, fig)* to put one's money on sb/sth, to back sb/sth; **hoch/niedrig ~** to play for high/low stakes

b *(Typ)* to set

c *(= springen) (Pferd, Läufer)* to jump; *(Mil)* to cross; **über einen Graben/Zaun/ein Hindernis ~** to jump (over) *or* clear a ditch/fence/hurdle; **über einen Fluss ~** to cross a river

Set|zer ['zɛtsɐ] M **-s, -**, **Set|ze|rin** [-ərɪn] F **-, -nen** *(Typ)* typesetter

Set|ze|rei [zɛtsə'rai] F **-, -en** *(= Firma)* typesetter's

Setz-: **Setz|feh|ler** M *(Typ)* printer's error, literal; **Setz|ha|se** M *(Hunt)* doe hare; **Setz|kas|ten** M case; **Setz|lat|te** F *(Surv)* aligning pole; **Setz|ling** ['zɛtslɪŋ] M **-s, -e** **a** *(Hort)* seedling **b** *(= Fisch)* fry; **Setz|ma|schi|ne** F typesetting machine, typesetter; **Setz|schiff** NT *(Typ)* galley; **Setz|waa|ge** F spirit level

Seu|che ['zɔyçə] F **-, -n** epidemic; *(fig pej)* scourge

Seu|chen-: **seu|chen|ar|tig** ADJ epidemic ADV **sich ~ ausbreiten** to spread like an epidemic; **Seu|chen|be|kämp|fung** F epidemic control; **Seu|chen|ge|biet** NT epidemic *or* infested area *or* zone; **Seu|chen|ge|fahr** F danger of epidemic; **Seu|chen|herd** M centre *(Brit)* or center *(US)* of an/the epidemic

seuf|zen ['zɔyftsn] VTI to sigh

Seuf|zer ['zɔyftsɐ] M **-s, -** sigh

Seuf|zer|brü|cke F Bridge of Sighs

Sex [zɛks] M **-(es),** *no pl* sex; **sie hat viel ~** she's very sexy

Sex-: **sex|ak|tiv** ADJ sexually active; **Sex-Ap|peal** [-lə'pi:l] M **-s,** *no pl* sex appeal; **sex|be|ses|sen** ADJ sex-obsessed; **Sex|bom|be** F *(inf)* sex bomb *(inf)*; **Sex|film** M sex film, skin flick *(inf)*; **Sex|fo|to** NT sexy photo

Se|xis|mus [zɛ'ksɪsmʊs] M **-, Sexismen** [-mən] sexism

Se|xist [zɛ'ksɪst] M **-en, -en**, **Se|xis|tin** [-'ksɪstɪn] F **-, -nen** sexist

se|xis|tisch [zɛ'ksɪstɪʃ] ADJ sexist ADV **~ eingestellt sein** to be sexist; **sich ~ verhalten** to act in a sexist way; **sich ~ geben** to give the impression of being sexist; **~ klingen** to sound sexist

Sex-: **Sex|kon|trol|le** F sex check; **Sex|ma|ga|zin** NT sex magazine; **Sex|muf|fel** M *(hum inf)* sexless person; **Sex|ob|jekt** NT sex object

Se|xo|lo|ge [zɛkso'lo:gə] M **-n, -n**, **Se|xo|lo|gin** [-'lo:gɪn] F **-, -nen** sexologist

Se|xo|lo|gie [zɛksolo'gi:] F **-,** *no pl* sexology

Sex-: **Sex|protz** M *(hum inf)* sexual athlete; **Sex|shop** ['zɛksʃɔp] M **-s, -s** sex shop

Sex|ta ['zɛksta] F **-, Sexten** [-tn] *(dated Sch) first year in a secondary school (Aus Sch) top year in a secondary school*

Sex|ta|ner [zɛks'ta:nɐ] M **-s, -**, **Sex|ta|ne|rin** [-ərɪn] F **-, -nen** *(dated Sch) pupil in the first year of a secondary school (Aus Sch) pupil in the top year of a secondary school*

Sex|ta|ner|bla|se F *(hum inf)* weak *or* Chinese *(hum sl)* bladder

Sex|tant [zɛks'tant] M **-en, -en** *(Naut)* sextant

Sex|te ['zɛkstə] F **-, -n** *(Mus)* sixth

Sex|ten *pl von* **Sexta**

Sex|tett [zɛks'tɛt] NT **-(e)s, -e** *(Mus)* sextet(te)

Sex|til|li|on [zɛkstɪ'lio:n] F **-, -en** sextillion *(Brit)*, undecillion *(US)*

Sex-: **Sex|tou|ris|mus** M sex tourism; **Sex|tou|rist(in)** M(F) sex tourist

se|xu|al [zɛ'ksua:l] ADJ *(rare)* sexual

Se|xu|al-: **Se|xu|al|at|las** M illustrated sex handbook; **Se|xu|al|emp|fin|den** NT sexual feeling; **Se|xu|al|er|zie|hung** F sex education; **Se|xu|al|ethik** F sexual ethics *pl*; **Se|xu|al|for|scher(in)** M(F) sexologist; **Se|xu|al|for|schung** F sexology; **Se|xu|al|hor|mon** NT sex hormone; **Se|xu|al|hy|gi|e|ne** F sex(ual) hygiene

se|xu|a|li|sie|ren [zɛksuali'zi:rən] *ptp* **sexualisiert** VT to eroticize

Se|xu|a|li|sie|rung F **-, -en** eroticization

Se|xu|a|li|tät [zɛksuali'tɛ:t] F **-,** *no pl* sexuality

Se|xu|al-: **Se|xu|al|kun|de** F *(Sch)* sex education; **Se|xu|al|le|ben** NT sex life; **Se|xu|al|lock|stoff** M pheromone; **Se|xu|al|mo|ral** F sexual morals *pl*; **Se|xu|al|mord** M sex murder; **Se|xu|al|mör|der(in)** M(F) sex murderer; **Se|xu|al|neu|ro|se** F sex neurosis; **Se|xu|al|ob|jekt** NT sex object; **Se|xu|al|pä|da|go|gik** F sex education; **Se|xu|al|part|ner(in)** M(F) sexual partner; **Se|xu|al|prak|tik** F sexual practice *usu pl*; **Se|xu|al|straf|tä|ter** M, **Se|xu|al|tä|ter** M sex offender; **Se|xu|al|trieb** M sex(ual) drive; **Se|xu|al|ver|bre|chen** NT sex(ual) offence *(Brit)* or offense *(US)*; **Se|xu|al|ver|hal|ten** NT sexual behaviour *(Brit)* or behavior *(US)*; **Se|xu|al|ver|kehr** M sexual intercourse; **Se|xu|al|wis|sen|schaft** F sexology

se|xu|ell [zɛ'ksuɛl] ADJ sexual ADV sexually

Se|xus ['zɛksʊs] M **-, -** ['zɛksu:s] *(geh)* sexuality

se|xy ['zɛksi] **ADJ** *inv (inf)* sexy *(inf)*, dishy *(inf)*

Sey|chel|len [ze'ʃɛlən] **PL** *(Geog)* Seychelles *pl*

Se|zes|si|on [zetsɛ'sio:n] **F -, -en** secession

Se|zes|si|o|nist [zetsɛsio'nɪst] **M -en, -en, Se|zes|si|o|nis|tin** [-'nɪstɪn] **F -, -nen** secessionist

se|zes|si|o|nis|tisch [zetsɛsio'nɪstɪʃ] **ADJ** secessionist

Se|zes|si|ons|krieg **M** American Civil War

se|zie|ren [ze'tsi:rən] *ptp* **seziert** **VTI** *(lit, fig)* to dissect

Se|zier|saal **M** dissecting room

SFB [ɛslɛf'be:] **M -** *(Hist) abbr von* **Sender Freies Berlin**

SFOR, Sfor ['ɛsfɔ:ɐ] **F** *abbr von* **Stabilization Force** SFOR

S-för|mig ['ɛs-] **ADJ** S-shaped

sfr *abbr von* **Schweizer Franken** sfr

SGML *abbr (Comput, Internet) von* **standard generalized markup language** SGML

Sgraf|fi|to [sgra'fi:to] **NT -s, -s** *or* **Sgraffiti** [-ti] *(Art)* sgraffito

Shag [ʃɛk] **M -s, -s** *(= Tabak)* shag

Shake|hands ['ʃe:khɛndz] **NT -, -** *(inf)* handshake; **~ machen** to shake hands, to press the flesh *(hum inf)*

Shake|speare|büh|ne ['ʃe:kspi:ɐ-] **F** Elizabethan stage

shake|spea|resch ['ʃe:kspi:rɛʃ], **shake|spea|risch** ['ʃe:kspi:rɪʃ] **ADJ** Shakespearean

Sham|poo [ʃampu:, 'ʃampo:] **NT -s, -s, Sham|poon** [ʃam'po:n, ʃɛm'pu:n] **NT -s, -s** shampoo

sham|poo|nie|ren [ʃampo'ni:rən, ʃampu'ni:rən] *ptp* **shampooniert** **VT** to shampoo

Shan|ty ['ʃɛnti, 'ʃanti] **NT -s, -s** shanty

Share|ware ['ʃɛ:ɐvɛ:ɐ] **F -,** *no pl (Comput)* shareware

Share|ware-Pro|gramm ['ʃɛ:ɐvɛ:ɐ-] **NT** shareware program

Shell [ʃɛl] **M -, -s** *(Comput)* shell

She|riff ['ʃɛrɪf] **M -s, -s** sheriff

Sher|pa ['ʃɛrpa] **M -s, -s** Sherpa

Sher|ry ['ʃɛri] **M -s, -s** sherry

Shet|land-: **Shet|land|in|seln** **PL** Shetland Islands *pl*, Shetlands *pl*; **Shet|land|po|ny** **NT** Shetland pony; **Shet|land|wol|le** **F** Shetland wool

Shift|tas|te ['ʃɪft-] **F** *(Comput)* shift key

Shin|to|is|mus [ʃɪnto'ɪsmʊs] **M -,** *no pl (Rel)* Shintoism, Shinto

shin|to|is|tisch [ʃɪnto'ɪstɪʃ] **ADJ** Shinto, Shintoistic

Shit [ʃɪt] **NT -s,** *no pl (sl: = Haschisch)* dope *(inf)*

sho|cking ['ʃɔkɪŋ] **ADJ** *pred* shocking

Shoo|ting|star ['ʃu:tɪŋ'sta:ɐ] **M** shooting star, whiz(z) kid *(inf)*

Shop-Bot **M -(s), -s** *(Internet: = elektronischer Einkaufshelfer)* shop bot

shop|pen ['ʃɔpn] **VI** to shop; **~ gehen** to go shopping

Shop|ping ['ʃɔpɪŋ] **NT -s,** *no pl* shopping *(for luxury items)*; **~ gehen** *or* **machen** *(inf)* to go shopping *(for luxury items)*

Shop|ping|cen|ter ['ʃɔpɪŋsɛnte] **NT -s, -** shopping centre *(Brit) or* center *(US)*

Shop|ping|sen|der **M** *(TV)* shopping channel

Short|cut ['ʃɔ:ɐtkat, 'ʃɔrt-] **M -(s), -s** *(Comput)* shortcut, short cut

Shorts [ʃo:ɐts, ʃɔrts] **PL** (pair of) shorts *pl*

Shor|ty ['ʃo:ɐti, 'ʃɔrti] **NT -s, -s** shorty pyjamas *pl (Brit) or* pajamas *pl (US)*

Show [ʃo:] **F -, -s** show; **eine ~ abziehen** *(inf)* to put on a show *(inf)*

Show-: **Show|down** ['ʃo:daun] **M OR NT -(s), -s, Show-down** **M OR NT -(s), -s** showdown; **Show|ein|la|ge** ['ʃo:-] **F** entertainment section *(of a programme)*; **Show|ge|schäft** ['ʃo:-] **NT** show business; **Show|man** ['ʃo:mən] **M -s, -men** showman; **Show|mas|ter** ['ʃo:ma:stɐ] **M -s, -, Show|mas|te|rin** [-ərɪn] **F -, -nen** compère, emcee *(US)*

Shred|der ['ʃrɛdɐ] **M -s, -, Shred|der|an|la|ge** **F** shredder, shredding machine

Shunt [ʃant] **M -s, -s** *(Med)* shunt

Shut|tle ['ʃatl] **M -s, -s** *(Aut, Aviat, Space)* shuttle

Shut|tle-Bus **M** shuttle bus

Shut|tle-Flug ['ʃatl-] **M** *(Space)* shuttle flight

Si|am ['zi:am] **NT -s** *(Hist)* Siam

Si|a|me|se [zia'me:zə] **M -n, -n, Si|a|me|sin** [-'me:zɪn] **F -, -nen** *(Hist)* Siamese

si|a|me|sisch [zia'me:zɪʃ] **ADJ** **a** *(Hist)* Siamese **b** **~e Katze** Siamese cat; **~e Zwillinge** Siamese twins

Si|am|kat|ze **F** Siamese (cat)

Si|bi|ri|en [zi'bi:riən] **NT -s** Siberia

si|bi|risch [zi'bi:rɪʃ] **ADJ** Siberian; **~e Kälte** Siberian *or* arctic conditions *pl*

Si|byl|la [zi'bʏla] **F -, Sibyllen, Si|byl|le** [zi'bʏlə] **F -, Sibyllen** sibyl

si|byl|li|nisch [zibʏ'li:nɪʃ] *(geh)* **ADJ** sibylline, sibyllic **ADV** prophetically; *sich ausdrücken* mysteriously; *(= drohend)* ominously

sich [zɪç] **REFL PRON** **a** *(acc) (+infin, bei „man")* oneself; *(3. pers sing)* himself; herself; itself; *(Höflichkeitsform sing)* yourself; *(Höflichkeitsform pl)* yourselves; *(3. pers pl)* themselves
b *(dat) (+infin, bei „man")* to oneself; *(3. pers sing)* to himself; to herself; to itself; *(Höflichkeitsform sing)* to yourself; *(Höflichkeitsform pl)* to yourselves; *(3. pers pl)* to themselves; **~ die Haare waschen/färben** *etc* to wash/dye *etc* one's hair; **er hat ~ das Bein gebrochen** he has broken his leg; **sie hat ~ einen Pulli gekauft/gestrickt** she bought/knitted herself a pullover, she bought/knitted a pullover for herself; **wann hat sie ~ das gekauft?** when did she buy that?
c *acc, dat (mit prep) (+infin, bei „man")* one; *(3. pers sing)* him, her, it; *(Höflichkeitsform)* you; *(3. pers pl)* them; **wenn man keinen Pass bei ~** *(dat)* **hat** if one hasn't a passport with one *or* him *(US)*, if you haven't got a passport with you; **nur an ~** *(acc)* **denken** to think only of oneself; **wenn er jemanden zu ~** *(dat)* **einlädt** if he invites somebody round to his place
d *(= einander)* each other, one another; **sie schreiben ~ schon viele Jahre** they have been writing to each other *or* to one another for many years
e *(impers)* **hier sitzt/singt es ~ gut** it's good to sit/sing here; **diese Wolle strickt ~ gut** this wool knits well; **dieses Auto fährt ~ gut** this car drives well

Si|chel ['zɪçl] **F -, -n** sickle; *(= Mondsichel)* crescent

Si|chel|zel|len|anä|mie **F** *(Med)* sickle cell anaemia *(Brit) or* anemia *(US)*

si|cher ['zɪçɐ] ✪ 42.1, 43.1, 53.6 **ADJ** **a** *(= gewiss)* certain, sure; **der ~e Tod/Sieg** certain death/victory; **(sich** *dat)* **einer Sache** *(gen)* **~ sein** to be sure *or* certain of sth; **sich** *(dat)* **jds/seiner selbst ~ sein** to be sure of sb/oneself; **(sich** *dat)* **seiner Sache** *(gen)* **~ sein** to be sure of what one is doing/saying; **so viel ist ~** this much is certain; **ist das ~?** is that certain?; **man weiß nichts Sicheres** we don't know anything certain; **das ist uns ~** that is for sure; **mit der guten Zeit ist uns der zweite Platz ~** with such a good time we're sure *or* certain of second place → **Leben a**
b *(= geschützt, gefahrlos)* safe; *(= geborgen)* secure; *Investition* secure, safe; **vor jdm/etw ~ sein** to be safe from sb/sth; **~ ist ~** you can't be too sure
c *(= zuverlässig)* reliable; *Methode* reliable, sure-fire *attr (inf)*; *Verhütungsmethode* safe, reliable; *Fahrer, Schwimmer* safe; *(= fest) Gefühl, Zusage* certain, definite; *Hand, Einkommen, Job* steady; *Stellung* secure; **ein ~er Schütze** a sure shot; **~ auf den Beinen sein** to be steady on one's legs; **mit ~em Instinkt** with a sure instinct
d *(= selbstbewusst)* (self-)confident, (self-)assured
ADV **a** *fahren, aufbewahren etc* safely; **~ wirkend** reliable; **~ leben** to live *or* lead a secure life; **~ schießen** to be a reliable shot; **sehr ~ Ski fahren** to ski extremely well
b *(= selbstbewusst)* **~ wirken/auftreten** to give an impression of (self-)confidence *or* (self-)assurance
c *(= natürlich)* of course; **~!** of course, sure *(esp US)*
d *(= bestimmt)* **das wolltest du ~ nicht sagen** surely you didn't mean that; **du hast dich ~ verrechnet** you must have counted wrong; **das weiß ich ganz ~** I know that for certain *or* for sure; **das ist ganz ~ das Beste** it's quite certainly the best; **aber er kommt ~ noch** I'm sure *or* certain he'll come; **das hat er ~ vergessen** I'm sure he's forgotten it; *(= garantiert)* he's sure to have forgotten it; **er kommt ~ auch mit** he's bound *or* sure *or* certain to want to come too

si|cher+ge|hen **VI** *sep irreg aux sein* to be sure; *(= sich vergewissern auch)* to make sure

Si|cher|heit ✪ 42.1, 43.1 **F -, -en** **a** *no pl (= Gewissheit)* certainty; **sich** *(dat)* **~ darüber verschaffen, dass ...** to assure oneself that ...; **verschaffen Sie sich persönlich ~ darüber** you have to make certain for yourself; **woher nimmst du die ~, ...?** how can you be so sure ...?; **mit an ~ grenzender Wahrscheinlichkeit** almost certainly, probably if not certainly; **das ist mit ~ richtig** that is definitely right; **das lässt sich nicht mit ~ sagen/beweisen** that cannot be said/proved with any degree of certainty
b *no pl (= Schutz, das Sichersein)* safety; *(als Aufgabe von Sicherheitsbeamten etc)* security; **~ und Ordnung** law and order; **die öffentliche ~** public safety *or* security; **innere ~** internal security; **die ~ der Bevölkerung** the safety *or* security of the people; **soziale ~** social security; **jdn/etw in ~ bringen** to get sb/sth to safety; **sich in ~ bringen** to get (oneself) to safety; **es gelang mir in letzter Minute, mich im Keller in ~ zu bringen** at the last minute I managed to get to the safety of the cellar; **~ im Straßen-/Flugverkehr** road/air safety; **in ~ sein, sich in ~ befinden** to be safe; **sich in ~ wiegen** *or* **wähnen** to think oneself safe; **jdn in ~ wiegen** to lull sb into a (false) sense of security; **jdn in ~ wähnen** to think sb safe; **der ~** *(geh)* **halber** in the interests of safety; *(= um sicherzugehen)* to be on the safe side; **schnallen Sie sich zu Ihrer ~ an** fasten your seat belt for your own safety
c *no pl (= Zuverlässigkeit) (von Mittel, Methode, Geschmack, Instinkt)* reliability, sureness; *(= Festigkeit) (von Hand, beim Balancieren etc)* steadiness; *(von Fahrer, Schwimmer)* competence; *(von Hand, Job, Einkommen)* steadiness; *(von Stellung)* security; **mit tödlicher ~** with deadly accuracy
d *(= Treffsicherheit im Umgang mit Sprache)* sureness
e *no pl (= Selbstsicherheit)* (self-)confidence, (self-)assurance; **~ im Auftreten** self-confident *or* self-assured manner
f *(Comm, Fin)* security; *(= Pfand)* surety; **~ leisten** *(Comm, Fin)* to offer security; *(Jur)* to stand *or* go bail; **etw als ~ hinterlegen** *(Comm, Fin)* to deposit *or* lodge sth as security; *(Jur)* to put up sth as bail

Si|cher|heits-: **Si|cher|heits|ab|stand** **M** safe distance; **Si|cher|heits|au|to** **NT** safe car; **Si|cher|heits|be|am|te(r)** **M** *decl as adj*, **Si|cher|heits|be|am|tin** **F** security officer; *(Pol auch)* security agent; **Si|cher|heits|be|häl|ter** **M** *(von Atomreaktor)* containment dome; **Si|cher|heits|be|hör|de** **F** security service; **Si|cher|heits|be|ra|ter(in)** **M(F)** safety adviser; **Si|cher|heits|be|stim|mun|gen** **PL** safety regulations *pl*; *(betrieblich, Pol etc)* security controls *pl or* regulations *pl*; **Si|cher|heits|bin|dung** **F** *(Ski)* safety binding; **Si|cher|heits|bü|gel** **M** *(an Sessellift)* safety bar; **Si|cher|heits|ex|per|te** **M, Si|cher|heits|ex|per|tin** **F** security expert; **Si|cher|heits|fak|tor** **M** security factor; **Si|cher|heits|ga|ran|tie** **F** safety guarantee; **Si|cher|heits|glas** **NT** safety glass; **Si|cher|heits|gurt** **M** *(in Flugzeug)* seat belt; *(in Auto auch)* safety belt; **si|cher|heits|hal|ber** **ADV** to be on the safe side; **Si|cher|heits|hül|le** F *(von Atomreaktor)* shell; **Si|cher|heits|ket|te** F safety chain; **Si|cher|heits|kon|trol|le** F security check; **Si|cher|heits|ko|pie** F *(Comput)* backup copy; **Si|cher|heits|kräf|te** PL security forces *pl*; **Si|cher|heits|la|ge** F security situation; **Si|cher|heits|lam|pe** F *(Min)* safety lamp; **Si|cher|heits|leis|tung** F *(Comm)* surety; *(Jur)* bail; **Si|cher|heits|lü|cke** F security gap; **Si|cher|heits|maß|nah|me** F safety precaution *or* measure; *(betrieblich, Pol etc)* security measure; **Si|cher|heits|na|del** F safety pin; **Si|cher|heits|phi|lo|so|phie** F attitude to security; **Si|cher|heits|rat** M security council; **Si|cher|heits|ri|si|ko** NT security risk; **Si|cher|heits|schleu|se** F security door system; **Si|cher|heits|schloss** NT safety *or* Yale® lock; **Si|cher|heits|schlüs|sel** M special key *(for safety locks)*, Yale® key; **Si|cher|heits|seil** NT safety rope; **Si|cher|heits|stan|dard** M standard of security; **Si|cher|heits|tech|nik** F security technology; *(im Verkehr etc)* safety technology; **Si|cher|heits|trup|pen** PL security troops *pl*; **si|cher|heits|über|prü|fen** VT *ptp* **sicherheitsüberprüft** *Bedienstete, Mitarbeiter* to vet; **Si|cher|heits|über|prü|fung** F **a** *(Tech)* safety check **b** *(von Bediensteten, Mitarbeitern)* vetting; **Si|cher|heits|ven|til** NT safety valve; **Si|cher|heits|ver|schluss** M safety catch; **Si|cher|heits|vor|keh|rung** F safety precaution; *(betrieblich, Pol etc)* security precaution; **die ~en waren sehr gut** security was *or* the security precautions were very good

si|cher|lich [ˈzɪçɐlɪç] ADV = **sicher ADV c, d**

si|chern [ˈzɪçɐn] VT **a** *(gegen, vor +dat* against) to safeguard; *(= absichern)* to protect; *(= sicher machen) Tür, Wagen, Fahrrad, Unfallstelle* to secure; *Bergsteiger etc* to belay, to secure; *(Mil)* to protect, to cover; *(Comput) Daten* to save, *(mittels Sicherungskopie)* to back up; **eine Feuerwaffe ~** to put the safety catch of a firearm on; **den Frieden ~** to maintain the peace

b **jdm/sich etw ~** to get *or* secure sth for sb/oneself; **diese beiden Flaschen habe ich extra für mich gesichert** I've made sure of *or* I've set aside these two bottles for myself

VR to protect oneself; *(Bergsteigen)* to belay *or* secure oneself; **sich vor etw** *(dat)* *or* **gegen etw ~** to protect oneself against sth, to guard against sth

VI *(Hunt)* to scent

si|cher+stel|len VT *sep* **a** *(= in Gewahrsam nehmen) Waffen, Drogen* to take possession of; *Beweismittel* to secure; **das Tatfahrzeug wurde sichergestellt** the vehicle used in the crime was found (and taken in) **b** *(= garantieren)* to guarantee

Si|cher|stel|lung F **a** *(von Waffen, Drogen)* taking possession; *(= Auffinden, von Fahrzeug)* finding **b** *(= Garantie)* guarantee

Si|che|rung [ˈzɪçərʊŋ] F **-, -en** **a** *no pl (= das Sichern) (gegen, vor +dat* against) safeguarding; *(= Absicherung)* protection; *(von Tür, Wagen, Fahrrad)* securing **b** *(= Schutz)* safeguard **c** *(Elec)* fuse; *(von Waffe)* safety catch; **da ist (bei) ihm die ~ durchgebrannt** *(fig inf)* he blew a fuse *(inf)* **d** *(Comput) (von Datei)* backup

Si|che|rungs-: **Si|che|rungs|ko|pie** F *(Comput)* backup copy; **Si|che|rungs|über|eig|nung** F *(Jur)* transfer of ownership as security on a debt; **Si|che|rungs|ver|kauf** M *(Fin)* hedge selling; **Si|che|rungs|ver|wah|rung** F *(Jur)* preventive detention

Sicht [zɪçt] F **-,** *no pl* **a** *(= Sehweite)* visibility; **die ~ betrug teilweise nur 20 Meter** at times visibility was down to 20 metres *(Brit) or* meters *(US)*; **eine ~ von 30 Metern** 30 metres' *(Brit) or* meters' *(US)* visibility; **in ~ sein/kommen** to be in/come into sight; **aus meiner/seiner** *etc* **~** *(fig)* as I see/he sees it, from my/his point of view; **aus heutiger ~** from today's standpoint *or* perspective; **auf lange/kurze ~** *(fig)* in the long/short term; *planen* for the long/short term; **auf lange ~ ausgebucht** fully booked for a long time ahead → **Land a**

b *(= Ausblick)* view

c *(Comm)* **auf** *or* **bei ~** at sight; **acht Tage nach ~** one week after sight

sicht|bar ADJ *(lit, fig)* visible; **etw ~ machen** to make sth visible; *(fig)* to make sth clear; **~ werden** *(fig)* to become apparent; **allmählich wurden Fortschritte ~** it could gradually be seen that progress was being made ADV *altern* visibly; *Fortschritte machen* obviously; *sich verändern* noticeably; *sich verbessern, sich verschlechtern* clearly; **sie hat ~ abgenommen/zugenommen** it's obvious that she's lost/gained weight

Sicht|bar|keit [ˈzɪçtbaːɐkait] F **-,** *no pl* visibility

Sicht|bar|wer|den [ˈzɪçtbaːɐveːɐdn] NT **-s,** *no pl (lit, fig)* appearance; **um das ~ früherer Fehler zu verhindern** to prevent earlier mistakes from becoming apparent

Sicht-: **Sicht|be|ton** M exposed concrete; **Sicht|ein|la|ge** F *(Fin)* sight *(esp Brit) or* demand deposit

sich|ten [ˈzɪçtn] VT **a** *(= erblicken)* to sight **b** *(= durchsehen)* to look through, to examine, to inspect; *(= ordnen)* to sift through

Sicht-: **Sicht|feld** NT field of view *or* vision; **Sicht|fens|ter** NT window; **Sicht|flug** M contact flight; **Sicht|ge|rät** NT monitor; *(Comput)* VDU, (visual) display unit; **Sicht|gren|ze** F visibility limit; **Sicht|kar|tei** F visible card index; **Sicht|kon|takt** M eye contact

sicht|lich [ˈzɪçtlɪç] ADJ obvious ADV obviously; *beeindruckt* visibly

Sicht|schutz M privacy fence *or* screen

Sich|tung [ˈzɪçtʊŋ] F **-, -en** sighting; *(= Prüfung)* examination, inspection

Sicht-: **Sicht|ver|hält|nis|se** PL visibility *sing*; **Sicht|ver|merk** M endorsement; *(im Pass)* visa stamp; **Sicht|wech|sel** M *(Fin)* bill payable on demand; **Sicht|wei|se** F view (of things); **Sicht|wei|te** F visibility *no art*; **außer ~** out of sight

Si|cker|gru|be F soakaway

si|ckern [ˈzɪkɐn] VI *aux sein* to seep; *(dickere Flüssigkeit auch)* to ooze; *(in Tropfen)* to drip; *(fig)* to leak out; **in die Presse ~** to be leaked to the press

Si|cker|was|ser NT, *no pl* water seeping through the ground

Side|board [ˈsaidbɔːɐd] NT **-s, -s** sideboard

si|de|risch [ziˈdeːrɪʃ] ADJ *(Astron)* sidereal

sie [ziː] PERS PRON 3. *pers* **a** *sing gen* **ihrer** [ˈiːrɐ], *dat* **ihr** [iːɐ], *acc* **sie** *(von Frau, weiblichem Tier) (nom)* she; *(acc)* her; *(von Dingen)* it; *(von Behörde, Polizei) (nom)* they *pl*; *(acc)* them *pl*; **wenn ich ~ wäre ...** if I were her *or* she *(form)* ...; **~ ist es** it's her, it is she *(form)*; **wer hat das gemacht? – ~** who did that? – she did *or* her!; **wer ist der Täter? – ~** who is the culprit? – she is *or* her!; **~ war es nicht, ich wars** it wasn't her, it was me; **~ und du** you and she; **~ und ich** she and I; **unser Hund ist eine ~** our dog is a she

b *pl gen* **ihrer** [ˈiːrɐ], *dat* **ihnen** [ˈiːnən], *acc* **sie** *(nom)* they; *(acc)* them; **~ sind es** it's them; **~ sind es, die ...** it's them *or* it is they *(form)* who ...; **wer hats zuerst bemerkt? – ~** who noticed it first? – they did *or* them *(inf)*

c *(obs: als Anrede)* **Sie** *(sing)* you, thee *(obs)*; *(pl)* you

Sie [ziː] PERS PRON 2. *pers sing or pl with 3. pers pl vb gen* **Ihrer** [ˈiːrɐ], *dat* **Ihnen** [ˈiːnən], *acc* **Sie** you; *(im Imperativ: nicht übersetzt)* **beeilen ~ sich!** hurry up!; **he, ~!** *(inf)* hey, you!; **~, wissen ~ was ...** *(inf)* do you know what ... NT **-s,** *no pl* polite *or* "Sie" form of address; **jdn per** *or* **mit ~ anreden** to use the polite form of address to sb, to call sb "Sie"

Sieb [ziːp] NT **-(e)s, -e** [-bə] sieve; *(für Erde auch)* riddle; *(für Korn, Gold auch)* screen; *(= Teesieb)* strainer; *(= Gemüsesieb)* colander; **ein Gedächtnis wie ein ~ haben** to have a memory like a sieve

Sieb-: **Sieb|bein** NT *(Anat)* ethmoid (bone); **Sieb|druck** M *pl* **-drucke** (silk-)screen print; *(= Siebdruckverfahren)* (silk-)screen printing

sie|ben [ˈziːbn] VT to pass through a sieve; *Korn, Gold* to screen; *(Cook)* to sift, to sieve; **gesiebte Luft atmen** *(inf: = im Gefängnis sein)* to do time *(inf)*, to be inside *(inf)* VI *(fig inf)* **solche Unternehmen ~ sehr** organizations like that pick and choose very carefully *or* are very selective; **es wird stark gesiebt** they pick and choose, they are very selective; **bei der Prüfung wird stark gesiebt** the exam will weed a lot of people out

sie|ben NUM seven; **die Sieben Weisen** the Seven Sages; **die ~ freien Künste** the humanities, the (seven) liberal arts; **die ~ Todsünden** *or* **Hauptsünden** the seven deadly sins; **die ~ fetten und die ~ mageren Jahre** *(Bibl)* the seven fat and the seven lean years → *auch* **vier**

Sie|ben [ˈziːbn] F **-, -** *or* **-en** seven → **Vier**

sie|ben-, **Sie|ben-** *in cpds* → *auch* **Vier-**; **sie|ben|ar|mig** ADJ *Leuchter* seven-armed; **Sie|ben|bür|gen** [ziːbnˈbʏrgn] NT **-s** *(Geog)* Transylvania; **Sie|ben|eck** NT heptagon; **Sie|ben|ge|stirn** NT *(Astron)* Pleiades *pl*; **Sie|ben|hü|gel|stadt** F city of the seven hills; **sie|ben|hun|dert** [ˈziːbnˈhʊndɐt] NUM seven hundred; **sie|ben|jäh|rig** ADJ seven-year-old; *(= sieben Jahre dauernd)* seven-year *attr*; **der Siebenjährige Krieg** the Seven-Years' War; **sie|ben|mal** [ˈziːbnmaːl] ADV seven times; **Sie|ben|mei|len|stie|fel** PL *(Liter)* seven-league boots *pl*; **Sie|ben|me|ter** M *(Sport)* penalty; **Sie|ben|mo|nats|kind** NT seven-month baby; **Sie|ben|sa|chen** PL *(inf)* belongings *pl*, things *pl*; **seine ~ packen** to pack one's bits and pieces; **Sie|ben|schlä|fer** M **a** *(Zool)* edible *or* fat dormouse; **Gemeiner ~** common dormouse **b** 27th June *(day which is said to determine the weather for the next seven weeks)*; **sie|ben|tau|send** [ˈziːbnˈtauznt] NUM seven thousand

Sie|ben|tel [ˈziːbntl] NT **-s, -**, **Sieb|tel** [ˈziːptl] NT **-s, -** seventh

sie|ben|tens [ˈziːbntəns], **sieb|tens** [ˈziːptns] ADV seventh(ly), in seventh place

sie|ben|te(r, s) [ˈziːbntə] ADJ = **siebte(r, s)**

sieb|te(r, s) [ˈziːptə] ADJ seventh; **einen ~n Sinn haben** *(inf)* to have a sixth sense → *auch* **vierte(r, s)**

sieb|zehn [ˈziːptseːn] NUM seventeen; **Siebzehn und Vier** *(Cards)* pontoon → *auch* **vierzehn**

17-Zöl|ler M **-s, -** *(Comput)* 17-inch *or* 17" monitor

sieb|zig [ˈziːptsɪç] NUM seventy → *auch* **vierzig**

Sieb|zi|ger [ˈziːptsɪgɐ] M **-s, -**, **Sieb|zi|ge|rin** [-ərɪn] F **-, -nen**, **Sieb|zig|jäh|ri|ge(r)** [-jɛːrɪgə] MF *decl as adj* seventy-year-old, septuagenarian

siech [ziːç] ADJ *(liter)* infirm; *(fig) Wirtschaft, Unternehmen* ailing

sie|chen [ˈziːçn] VI *(rare)* = **dahinsiechen**

Siech|tum [ˈziːçtuːm] NT **-s,** *no pl (liter)* infirmity; *(fig: von Wirtschaft, Unternehmen)* ailing state

Sie|del|land NT settlement area

sie|deln [ˈziːdln] VI to settle

sie|den [ˈziːdn] *pret* **siedete** *or* **sott** [ˈziːdətə, zɔt], *ptp* **gesiedet** *or* **gesotten** [gəˈziːdət, gəˈzɔtn] VI *(Wasser, Zucker etc)* to boil; *(Aus, S Ger: = köcheln)* to simmer; **Scandium siedet bei 2830°C** scandium boils at 2830°C; **da siedet einem das Blut** it makes your blood boil; **~d heiß** boiling *or* scalding hot; *(von Klima auch)* swelteringly hot; **~de Hitze** boiling *or* scalding heat; *(von Klima auch)* sweltering heat VT *Seife, Leim* to produce by boiling; *(Aus, S Ger: = köcheln lassen)* to simmer → *auch* **gesotten**

Sie|de-: **Sie|de|punkt** M *(Phys, fig)* boiling point; **Sie|de|was|ser|re|ak|tor** M boiling-water reactor

Sied|ler [ˈziːdlɐ] M **-s, -**, **Sied|le|rin** [-ərɪn] F **-, -nen** settler; *(= Bauer)* smallholder

Sied|lung [ˈziːdlʊŋ] F **-, -en** **a** *(= Ansiedlung)* settlement **b** *(= Siedlerstelle)* smallholding **c**

(= Wohnsiedlung) housing scheme *(Brit) or* estate *or* development *(US)*

Sied|lungs-: **Sied|lungs|dich|te** F population density; **Sied|lungs|haus** NT *house in a housing scheme*

Sieg [ziːk] M **-(e)s, -e** [-gə] victory *(über +acc* over); *(in Wettkampf auch)* win *(über +acc* over); **um den ~ kämpfen** to fight for victory; **den ~ davontragen** *or* **erringen** to be victorious; *(in Wettkampf auch)* to be the winner; **einer Sache** *(dat)* **zum ~ verhelfen** to help sth to triumph; **von ~ zu ~ schreiten** *(geh)* to heap victory upon victory

Sieg|chan|ce F chance of victory *or* winning; **seine ~ verspielen** to throw away one's chance of winning

Sie|gel [ˈziːgl] NT **-s, -** seal; **unter dem ~ der Verschwiegenheit** under the seal of secrecy → **Buch a, Brief a**

Sie|gel|lack M sealing wax

sie|geln [ˈziːgln] VT *Urkunde* to affix a/one's seal to; *(= versiegeln) Brief* to seal

Sie|gel-: **Sie|gel|ring** M signet ring; **Sie|gel|wachs** NT sealing wax

sie|gen [ˈziːgn] VI *(Mil)* to be victorious; *(fig auch)* to triumph; *(in Wettkampf)* to win; **über jdn/etw ~** *(Mil)* to vanquish sb/sth; *(fig)* to triumph over sb/sth; *(in Wettkampf)* to beat sb/sth, to win against sb/sth; **ich kam, sah und siegte** I came, I saw, I conquered

Sie|ger [ˈziːgɐ] M **-s, -**, **Sie|ge|rin** [-ərɪn] F **-, -nen** victor; *(in Wettkampf)* winner; **zweiter ~** runner-up; **~ werden** to be the winner, to win; **als ~ hervorgehen** to emerge victorious

Sie|ger-: **Sie|ger|eh|rung** F *(Sport)* presentation ceremony; **Sie|ger|kranz** M victor's laurels *pl*; **im ~** crowned with the victor's laurels; **Sie|ger|macht** F *usu pl (Pol)* victorious power; **Sie|ger|po|dest** NT *(Sport)* winners' podium *or* rostrum; **Sie|ger|po|se** F victory pose; **Sie|ger|stra|ße** F road to victory; **Sie|ger|trepp|chen** NT winners' rostrum *(Brit) or* podium; **Sie|ger|ur|kun|de** F *(Sport)* winner's certificate

Sie|ges-: **sie|ges|be|wusst** ADJ confident of victory; **Sie|ges|bot|schaft** F news *sing* of victory; **Sie|ges|denk|mal** NT victory monument; **Sie|ges|fei|er** F victory celebrations *pl*; *(Sport)* victory celebration; **Sie|ges|ge|schrei** NT *(pej)* shouts *pl* of victory; **sie|ges|ge|wiss** ADJ certain *or* sure of victory; **sie|ges|ge|wohnt** ADJ = **sieggewohnt**; **Sie|ges|göt|tin** F goddess of victory; **Sie|ges|kranz** M victor's laurels *pl*; **Sie|ges|pal|me** F palm (of victory); **Sie|ges|preis** M winner's prize; *(Boxen)* winner's purse; **Sie|ges|säu|le** F victory column; **Sie|ges|se|rie** F series *sing* of victories; *(bei Wettkämpfen auch)* series *sing* of wins; **sie|ges|si|cher** ADJ certain *or* sure of victory ADV confidently; **Sie|ges|tau|mel** M triumphant euphoria; **im ~** euphoric with their *etc* victory *or* triumph; **Sie|ges|tor** NT **a** *(= Bauwerk)* triumphal arch **b** *(Sport)* winning goal; **sie|ges|trun|ken** ADJ *(liter)* drunk with victory; **Sie|ges|zug** M triumphal march

sieg-: **sieg|ge|wohnt** ADJ used to victory; *(bei Wettkämpfen auch)* used to winning; **sieg|haft** ADJ = **siegesbewusst**; **sieg|reich** ADJ victorious, triumphant; *(in Wettkampf)* winning *attr*, successful ADV triumphantly, victoriously

sieh [ziː], **sie|he** [ˈziːə] *imper sing von* **sehen**

siehs|te [ˈziːstə] *(inf) 2. pers sing pres von* **sehen** *(inf)* (you) see

sieht [ziːt] *(inf) 3. pers sing pres von* **sehen**

Siel [ziːl] NT OR M **-(e)s, -e** *(= Schleuse)* sluice; *(= Abwasserkanal)* sewer

Sie|le [ˈziːlə] F **-, -n** trace; **in den ~n sterben** *(fig)* to die in harness

sie|len [ˈziːlən] VR *(dial)* to wallow

si|e|na [ˈzieːna] ADJ *inv* sienna

Si|er|ra [siˈɛra] F **-, -s** *or* **Sierren** [siˈɛrən] *(Geog)* sierra

Si|es|ta [ziˈɛsta] F **-, -s** *or* **Siesten** [ziˈɛstn] siesta, afternoon nap *or* snooze *(inf)*; **~ halten** to have a siesta *or* an afternoon nap *or* snooze *(inf)*

Sie|vert [ˈziːvɐt] NT **-, -** *(Phys) (abbr* **Sv***)* sievert

sie|zen [ˈziːtsn] VT **jdn/sich ~** to use the formal term of address to sb/each other, to address sb/each other as "Sie" → *auch* **duzen**

Siff [zɪf] M **-s**, *no pl*, **Sif|fe** [ˈzɪfə] F **-**, *no pl (pej sl) (= Dreck)* filth; *(= Zustand)* mess

sif|fen [ˈzɪfn] VI *(pej sl: = Dreck machen)* to make a filthy mess

sif|fig [ˈzɪfɪç] ADJ *(pej sl)* filthy

Si|gel [ˈziːgl] NT **-s, -**, **Sigle** [ˈziːgl] F **-, -n** short form, grammalogue *(spec)*

Sight|see|ing [ˈsaitsiːɪŋ] NT **-**, *no pl* sightseeing; **~ machen** to do some sightseeing

Sig|nal [zɪˈgnaːl] NT **-s, -e** *(auch Rail, Comput))* signal; **(ein) ~ geben** to give a signal; **mit der Hupe (ein) ~ geben** to hoot (as a signal); **~e setzen** *(fig)* to blaze a trail; **falsche ~e setzen** *(fig)* to point in the wrong direction

Sig|nal|an|la|ge F signals *pl*, set of signals

Sig|na|le|ment [zɪgnaləˈmãː, -ˈmɛnt] NT **-s, -s** *(Sw)* (personal) description

Sig|nal-: **Sig|nal|far|be** F striking colour *(Brit) or* color *(US)*; **Sig|nal|flag|ge** F signal flag; **Sig|nal|gast** M signalman; **Sig|nal|horn** NT *(Hunt)* (hunting) horn; *(Mil)* bugle

sig|na|li|sie|ren [zɪgnaliˈziːrən] *ptp* **signalisiert** VT *(lit, fig)* to signal

Sig|nal-: **Sig|nal|kel|le** F signalling *(Brit) or* signaling *(US)* disc; **Sig|nal|lam|pe** F, **Sig|nal|la|ter|ne** F signalling *(Brit) or* signaling *(US)* lamp; *(installiert)* signal lamp; **Sig|nal|mast** M signal mast; **Sig|nal|pfei|fe** F whistle; **Sig|nal|pis|to|le** F Very® pistol; **Sig|nal|tech|nik** F signalling *(Brit)*, signaling *(US)*; **Sig|nal|wir|kung** F signal; **davon ging eine ~ aus** this acted as a signal

Sig|na|tar [zɪgnaˈtaːɐ] M **-s, -e**, **Sig|na|ta|rin** [-ˈtaːrɪn] F **-, -nen** *(form)* signatory *(+gen* to)

Sig|na|tar|mäch|te PL signatory powers *pl*

Sig|na|tur [zɪgnaˈtuːɐ] F **-, -en** **a** *(= Unterschrift, Buchsignatur)* signature **b** *(auf Landkarten)* symbol **c** *(= Bibliothekssignatur)* shelf mark **d** *(Comput)* signature

Sig|na|tur|da|tei F *(Comput)* signature file

Sig|net [zɪˈgneːt, zɪˈgnɛt, zɪnˈjeː] NT **-s, -s** *(Typ)* publisher's mark

sig|nie|ren [zɪˈgniːrən] *ptp* **signiert** VT to sign; *(mit Anfangsbuchstaben auch)* to initial

Sig|nie|rung F **-, -en** signing; *(mit Anfangsbuchstaben)* initialling

sig|ni|fi|kant [zɪgnifiˈkant] *(geh)* ADJ significant ADV significantly

Sig|ni|fi|kanz [zɪgnifiˈkants] F **-**, *no pl (geh)* significance

Sikh [ziːk] M **-(s), -s** Sikh

Si|la|ge [ziˈlaːʒə] F **-**, *no pl (Agr)* silage

Sil|be [ˈzɪlbə] F **-, -n** syllable; **~ für ~** *(fig)* word for word; **er hat es mit keiner ~ erwähnt/verraten** he didn't say/breathe a word about it

Sil|ben-: **Sil|ben|rät|sel** NT *word game in which the answers are obtained by combining syllables from a given list*; **Sil|ben|schrift** F syllabary; **Sil|ben|trenn|pro|gramm** NT *(Typ, Comput)* hyphenation program; **Sil|ben|tren|nung** F syllabification; *(Typ, Comput)* hyphenation; **sil|ben|wei|se** ADV in syllables; **Sil|ben|zahl** F number of syllables

Sil|ber [ˈzɪlbɐ] NT **-s**, *no pl (abbr* **Ag***)* silver; *(= Tafelbesteck auch)* silverware; *(Her)* argent; **aus ~** made of silver → **reden VI a**

Sil|ber- *in cpds* silver; **Sil|ber|ar|beit** F silverwork *no pl*; **Sil|ber|be|steck** NT silver(ware), silver cutlery; **Sil|ber|blick** M *(inf)* squint; **Sil|ber|dis|tel** F carline thistle; **sil|ber|far|ben** [-farbn], **sil|ber|far|big** ADJ silver(-coloured) *(Brit)*, silver(-colored) *(US)*; *(Her)* argent; **Sil|ber|fisch|chen** [-fɪʃçən] NT **-s, -** silverfish; **Sil|ber|fo|lie** F silver foil; **Sil|ber|fuchs** M silver fox; **Sil|ber|ge|halt** M silver content; **Sil|ber|geld** NT silver; **Sil|ber|ge|schirr** NT silver(ware); **Sil|ber|glanz** M *(Miner, Chem)* silver glance, argentite, silver sulphide *(Brit) or* sulfide *(US)*; *(poet)* silvery gleam; **sil|ber|grau** ADJ silver(y)-grey *(Brit)*, silver(y)-gray *(US)*; **Sil|ber|haar** NT *(poet)* silver(y) hair; *(von Mann auch)* hoary head *(poet)*; **sil|ber|hal|tig** ADJ silver-bearing, argentiferous *(spec)*; **sil|ber|hell** ADJ *Stimme, Lachen* silvery ADV **~ lachen** to give a silvery laugh; **Sil|ber|hoch|zeit** F silver wedding (anniversary); **Sil|ber|hüt|te** F silverworks *sing or pl*

sil|be|rig [ˈzɪlbərɪç] ADJ ADV = **silbrig**

Sil|ber-: **Sil|ber|klang** M *(poet)* silvery sound; **Sil|ber|ling** [ˈzɪlbɐlɪŋ] M **-s, -e** *(Bibl)* piece of silver; **Sil|ber|lö|we** M puma *(esp Brit)*, mountain lion; **Sil|ber|me|dail|le** F silver medal; **Sil|ber|mö|we** F herring gull

sil|bern [ˈzɪlbɐn] ADJ silver; *(liter) Licht, Stimme, Haare* silvery *(liter)*, silvern *(poet)*; **~e Hochzeit** silver wedding (anniversary) ADV **~ schimmern** to have a silvery gleam

Sil|ber-: **Sil|ber|pa|pier** NT tin foil, silver paper *(esp Brit)*; **Sil|ber|pap|pel** F white poplar; **Sil|ber|schmied(in)** M(F) silversmith; **Sil|ber|schmuck** M silver jewellery *(Brit) or* jewelry *(US)*; **Sil|ber|sti|cke|rei** F *(Kunst)* silver embroidery; *(Produkt)* silver-embroidered garment/cushion *etc*; **Sil|ber|streif** [-ʃtraif] M **-en, -en**, **Sil|ber|strei|fen** M *(fig)* **es zeichnete sich ein ~(en) am Horizont ab** you/they *etc* could see light at the end of the tunnel; **das war wie ein ~(en) am Horizont** that was a ray of sunshine; **Sil|ber|stück** NT silver coin; **Sil|ber|tan|ne** F noble fir; **Sil|ber|wäh|rung** F currency based on the silver standard; **Sil|ber|wa|ren** PL silver *sing*; **sil|ber|weiß** ADJ silvery white; **Sil|ber|zeug** NT, *no pl* silver *sing*

-sil|big [zɪlbɪç] ADJ *suf* **fünfsilbig/zehnsilbig sein** to have five/ten syllables; **ein sechssilbiges Wort** a word with six syllables

silb|rig [ˈzɪlbrɪç] ADJ silvery ADV **~ schimmern/glänzen** to shimmer/gleam like silver; **~ weißes Haar** silvery white hair

Sil|hou|et|te [ziˈluɛtə] F **-, -n** silhouette; **sich als ~ gegen etw abheben** *or* **abzeichnen** to be silhouetted against sth

Si|li|cat [ziliˈkaːt] NT **-(e)s, -e** *(spec)*, **Si|li|kat** [ziliˈkaːt] NT **-(e)s, -e** silicate

Si|li|kon [ziliˈkoːn] NT **-s, -e** silicone

Si|li|ko|se [ziliˈkoːzə] F **-, -n** *(Med)* silicosis

Si|li|zi|um [ziˈliːtsiʊm] NT **-s**, *no pl (abbr* **Si***)* silicon

Si|li|zi|um|schei|be F silicon chip

Si|lo [ˈziːlo] M **-s, -s** silo

Si|lur [ziˈluːɐ] NT **-s**, *no pl (Geog)* Silurian

Sil|va|ner [zɪlˈvaːnɐ] M **-s, -** *(= Traubensorte)* Sylvaner (grape); *(= Wein)* Sylvaner (wine)

Sil|ves|ter [zɪlˈvɛstɐ] M OR NT **-s, -** New Year's Eve, Hogmanay *(esp Scot)*

> **SILVESTER**
>
> December 31st is known as **Silvester** after the saint commemorated on that day. The old year is seen out with friends, often with a special **Silvester** meal. At midnight people drink **Sekt** and let off fireworks to welcome the New Year. There is also the custom of **Bleigießen,** when people melt small amounts of lead and drop them into cold water. The resulting shapes are used as the basis for prophecies about the coming year. In some parts of Switzerland the old year is seen out with noisy processions in which the participants wear traditional masks.

Sil|ves|ter-: **Sil|ves|ter|abend** M New Year's Eve, Hogmanay *(esp Scot)*; **Sil|ves|ter|fei|er** F New Year's Eve party, New Year party, Hogmanay party *(esp Scot)*; **Sil|ves|ter|nacht** F night of New Year's Eve *or* Hogmanay *(esp Scot)*

Sim|bab|we [zɪm'bapvə] **NT -s** Zimbabwe
SIM-Kar|te **F** *(Telec)* SIM card
Sim|mer|ring® ['zɪmerɪŋ] **M** *(Tech)* shaft seal
Si|mo|nie [zimo'ni:] **F -, -n** [-'ni:ən] simony
sim|pel ['zɪmpl] **ADJ** simple; *Mensch auch* simple-minded; *(= vereinfacht)* simplistic **ADV** simply
Sim|pel ['zɪmpl] **M -s, -** *(inf)* simpleton
Sim|plex ['zɪmplɛks] **NT -, -e** *or* **Simplizia** [zɪm'pli:tsia] *(Gram)* simplex
Simp|li|fi|ka|ti|on [zɪmplifika'tsio:n] **F -, -en** *(geh)* simplification
simp|li|fi|zie|ren [zɪmplifi'tsi:rən] *ptp* **simplifiziert** **VT** *(geh)* to simplify
Simp|li|zi|tät [zɪmplitsi'tɛ:t] **F -,** *no pl (geh)* simplicity
Sims [zɪms] **M OR NT -es, -e** [-zə] *(= Fenstersims)* (window)sill; *(außen auch)* (window) ledge; *(= Gesims)* ledge; *(= Kaminsims)* mantlepiece
sim|sen ['zɪmzn] **VTI** *(Telec: inf)* to text *(inf)*, to send a text message/text messages
Si|mu|lant [zimu'lant] **M -en, -en**, **Si|mu|lan|tin** [-'lantɪn] **F -, -nen** malingerer
Si|mu|la|ti|on [zimula'tsio:n] **F -, -en** simulation
Si|mu|la|tor [zimu'la:to:ɐ] **M -s, Simulatoren** [-'to:rən] *(Sci)* simulator
si|mu|lie|ren [zimu'li:rən] *ptp* **simuliert** **VI** *(= sich krank stellen)* to feign illness; **er simuliert nur** he's shamming; *(um sich zu drücken auch)* he's malingering **VT** **a** *(Sci, Tech, Comput)* to simulate **b** *(= vorgeben) Krankheit* to feign, to sham; *Empörung, Frohsinn* to feign
si|mul|tan [zimʊl'ta:n] **ADJ** simultaneous **ADV** simultaneously
Si|mul|tan-: **Si|mul|tan|dol|met|schen** **NT -s,** *no pl* simultaneous translation; **Si|mul|tan|dol|met|scher(in)** **M(F)** simultaneous translator
Si|mul|ta|ne|i|tät [zimʊltanei'tɛ:t] **F -, -en**, **Si|mul|ta|ni|tät** [zimʊltani'tɛ:t] **F -, -en** *(geh)* simultaneity
sin. *abbr von* **Sinus**
Si|nai ['zi:nai] **M -(s)**, **Si|nai|halb|in|sel** **F** Sinai (Peninsula)
sind [zɪnt] *1. and 3. pers pl, with Sie sing and pl pres von* **sein**
Si|ne|ku|re [zine'ku:rə] **F -, -n** *(liter)* sinecure
si|ne tem|po|re ['zi:nə'tɛmpore] **ADV** *(abbr* **s. t.**) *(Univ)* punctually
Sin|fo|nie [zɪnfo'ni:] **F -, -n** [-'ni:ən] symphony
Sin|fo|nie-: **Sin|fo|nie|kon|zert** **NT** symphony concert; **Sin|fo|nie|or|ches|ter** **NT** symphony orchestra
Sin|fo|ni|ker [zɪn'fo:nikɐ] **M -s, -**, **Sin|fo|ni|ke|rin** [-ərɪn] **F -, -nen** member of a symphony orchestra; **die Bamberger ~** the Bamberg Symphony Orchestra
sin|fo|nisch [zɪn'fo:nɪʃ] **ADJ** symphonic; **~e Dichtung** symphonic poem
Sing|aka|de|mie **F** choral society
Sin|ga|pur ['zɪŋgapu:ɐ] **NT -s** Singapore
Sing-: **sing|bar** **ADJ** singable; **schwer ~ sein** to be hard to sing; **Sing|dros|sel** **F** song thrush
sin|gen ['zɪŋən] *pret* **sang** [zaŋ], *ptp* **gesungen** [gə'zʊŋən] **VI** **a** *(lit, fig)* to sing; *(esp Eccl: eintönig, feierlich)* to chant; *(Dynamo)* to hum; *(Telegrafendrähte)* to hum, to sing; **zur Gitarre/Mandoline ~** to sing to the guitar/mandoline; **ein ~der Tonfall** a lilt, a lilting accent; **singe, wem Gesang gegeben** *(dated prov)* if God gave you a good voice you should use it → **Alte(r)**
b *(inf: = gestehen)* to squeal *(inf)*, to sing *(inf)*, to talk
VT *(lit, fig)* to sing; *(esp Eccl) Psalmen, Kanon* to chant; **jdn in den Schlaf** *or* **Schlummer** *(liter)* **~** to sing sb to sleep; **das kann ich schon ~** *(inf)* I know it backwards *(Brit)*, I know it backwards and forwards *(US)*
VR **sich heiser/in den Schlaf ~** to sing oneself hoarse/to sleep; **sich müde ~** to sing until one is tired; **das Lied singt sich leicht** it's an easy song to sing
Sin|gen **NT -s,** *no pl* singing *(auch Sch)*; *(eintönig, feierlich)* chanting; *(von Dynamo, Telegrafendrähten)* humming
Sin|ge|rei [zɪŋə'rai] **F -, -en** *(inf)* singing
Sin|gha|le|se [zɪŋga'le:zə] **M -n, -n**, **Sin|gha|le|sin** [-'le:zɪn] **F -, -nen** Sin(g)halese
sin|gha|le|sisch [zɪŋga'le:zɪʃ] **ADJ** Sin(g)halese
Sin|gle ['sɪŋgl] **F -, -(s)** *(= Schallplatte)* single
Sin|gle **NT -, -(s)** *(Tennis etc)* singles *sing*
Sin|gle **M -s, -s** *(= Alleinlebender)* single; **Urlaub für ~s** singles' holiday *(Brit)*, vacation for singles *(US)*
Sin|gle-: **Sin|gle|bar** **F** singles' bar; **Sin|gle|da|sein** **NT** singledom, singlehood; **Sin|gle|haus|halt** **M** single(-person) household, one-person houshold; **Sin|gle|woh|nung** **F** apartment *or* flat *(Brit)* for single occupation
Sing-: **Sing|sang** ['zɪŋzaŋ] **M -s, -s** **a** *(= Liedchen)* ditty **b** *(= Gesang)* monotonous singing **c** *(= singende Sprechweise)* singsong; **Sing|spiel** **NT** lyrical drama; **Sing|stim|me** **F** vocal part
Sin|gu|lar ['zɪŋgula:ɐ] **M -s, -e** *(Gram)* singular; **im ~ stehen** to be (in the) singular; **den ~ zu etw bilden** to form the singular of sth
sin|gu|lär [zɪŋgu'lɛ:ɐ] **ADJ** *(geh)* unique
sin|gu|la|risch [zɪŋgu'la:rɪʃ] **ADJ** *(Gram)* singular
Sin|gu|la|ri|tät [zɪŋgulari'tɛ:t] **F -,** *no pl (geh)* uniqueness
Sing-: **Sing|vo|gel** **M** songbird; **Sing|wei|se** **F** way of singing
si|nis|ter [zi'nɪstɐ] **ADJ** *(geh)* sinister
sin|ken ['zɪŋkn] *pret* **sank** [zaŋk], *ptp* **gesunken** [gə'zʊŋkn] **VI** *aux sein* **a** *(Mensch, Gegenstand)* to sink; *(Schiff)* to sink, to go down; *(Ballon)* to descend; *(Nebel)* to come down, to descend *(liter)*; **auf den Grund ~** to sink to the bottom; **auf einen Stuhl/zu Boden ~** to sink into a chair/to the ground; **ins Bett ~** to fall into bed; **in Schlaf ~** to sink into a sleep; **an jds Brust** *(acc)* *or* **jdm an die Brust ~** *(liter)* to fall upon sb's breast; **in Ohnmacht ~** *(geh)* to swoon *(old)*, to fall into a faint *(esp Brit)*, to faint; **ich hätte in die Erde ~ mögen** I wished that the earth would (open and) swallow me up; **sein Stern ist im** *or* **am Sinken** *(geh)* his star is waning; **die Arme/den Kopf ~ lassen** to let one's arms/head drop
b *(Boden, Gebäude)* to subside, to sink; *(Fundament)* to settle; **das Haus war ein Meter tiefer gesunken** the house had sunk one metre *(Brit)* *or* meter *(US)*; **in Staub** *or* **Trümmer ~** *(geh)* to fall into ruin(s); **in Schutt und Asche ~** *(geh)* to be reduced to a pile of rubble
c *(= niedriger werden: Wasserspiegel, Temperatur, Preise etc)* to fall, to drop
d *(= schwinden) (Ansehen, Vertrauen)* to diminish; *(Einfluss)* to wane, to decline, to diminish; *(Hoffnung, Stimmung)* to sink; **den Mut/die Hoffnung ~ lassen** to lose courage/hope
e *(moralisch)* to sink; **tief gesunken sein** to have sunk low; **in jds Meinung/Achtung** *(dat)* **~** to go down in sb's estimation
Sinn [zɪn] **M -(e)s, -e** **a** *(= Wahrnehmungsfähigkeit)* sense; **die ~e** *(= sinnliche Begierde)* one's desires; **seiner ~e** *(gen)* **nicht mehr mächtig sein, nicht mehr Herr seiner ~e** *(gen)* **sein** to have lost all control over oneself → **fünf, sechste(r, s), siebte(r, s)**
b **Sinne** **PL** *(= Bewusstsein)* senses *pl*, consciousness; **er war von ~en, er war nicht bei ~en** he was out of his senses *or* mind; **wie von ~en** like one demented; **bist du noch bei ~en?** have you taken leave of your senses? **c** *(= Gedanken, Denkweise)* mind; **sich** *(dat)* **jdn/etw aus dem ~ schlagen** to put (all idea of) sb/sth out of one's mind, to forget all about sb/sth; **es kommt** *or* **geht** *or* **will mir nicht aus dem ~** *(geh)* I can't get it out of my mind; **es kam** *or* **fuhr mir plötzlich in den ~** it suddenly came to me; **das will mir einfach nicht in den ~** I just can't understand it; **jdm durch den ~ gehen** to occur to sb; **etw im ~ haben** to have sth in mind; **mit etw nichts im ~ haben** to want nothing to do with sth; **anderen ~es werden** *(geh)* to change one's mind; **(mit jdm) eines ~es sein** *(geh)* to be of the same mind (as sb)
d *(= Wunsch)* inclination; **ihr ~ ist auf ...** *(acc)* **gerichtet** *(geh)* her inclination is for ...; **danach steht ihm der ~** *(geh)* that is his wish; **mir steht der ~ nach Tanzen** *(geh)* I feel like dancing
e *(= Verständnis, Empfänglichkeit)* feeling; **dafür fehlt ihm der ~** he has no feeling for that sort of thing; **~ für Proportionen/Gerechtigkeit** *etc* **haben** to have a sense of proportion/justice *etc*; **~ für Kunst/Literatur/das Höhere haben** to appreciate art/literature/higher things
f *(= Geist)* spirit; **im ~e des Gesetzes** according to the spirit of the law; **in jds ~e** *(dat)* **handeln** to act as sb would have wished; **im ~e des Verstorbenen** in accordance with the wishes of the deceased; **das ist nicht in meinem/seinem ~e** that is not what I myself/he himself would have wished; **das wäre nicht im ~e unserer Kunden** it would not be in the interests of our customers; **das ist nicht im ~e des Erfinders** *(inf)* that's not what was originally intended
g *(= Zweck)* point; **das ist nicht der ~ der Sache** that is not the point, that is not the object of the exercise; **~ und Zweck einer Sache** *(gen)* the (aim and) object of sth; **~ und Unsinn dieser Maßnahmen/des Geschichtsunterrichts** reasoning or lack of it behind these measures/behind history teaching; **der ~ des Lebens** the meaning of life; **ohne ~ und Verstand sein** to make no sense at all; **das hat keinen ~** there is no point *or* sense in that; **was hat denn das für einen ~?** what's the point of *or* in that?, what's the sense in that?
h *(= Bedeutung)* meaning; *(von Wort, Ausdruck)* sense, meaning; **im übertragenen/weiteren ~** in the figurative/broader sense; **~ machen** to make sense; **das macht keinen/wenig ~** that makes no/little sense; **der Satz (er)gibt** *or* **macht keinen ~** the sentence doesn't make sense; **~ stiftend** = **sinnstiftend**
Sinn-: **sinn|be|tö|rend** **ADJ** *(liter)* sensuously intoxicating; **Sinn|bild** **NT** symbol; **sinn|bild|lich** **ADJ** symbolic(al) **ADV** symbolically
sin|nen ['zɪnən] *pret* **sann** [zan], *ptp* **gesonnen** [gə'zɔnən] *(geh)* **VI** **a** *(= nachdenken)* to meditate, to ponder, to muse; *(= grübeln)* to brood; **über etw** *(acc)* to reflect on sth; *(= grübeln)* to brood over sth **b** *(= planen)* **auf etw** *(acc)* **~** to devise sth, to think sth up, to think of sth; **auf Abhilfe ~** to think up *or* devise a remedy; **auf Verrat/Rache ~** to plot treason/revenge; **all sein Sinnen und Trachten** all his mind and energies
→ *auch* **gesonnen** **VT** *(old liter) Verrat, Rache* to plot
Sin|nen-: **Sin|nen|freu|de** **F** enjoyment of the pleasures of life; **sin|nen|freu|dig**, **sin|nen|froh** **ADJ** **ein ~er Mensch** a person who enjoys the pleasures of life; **Sin|nen|ge|nuss** **M** sensual pleasure; **Sin|nen|lust** **F** *(liter)* sensuality; **Sin|nen|mensch** **M** sensuous person; **Sin|nen|rausch** **M** *(liter)* sensual passion
sinn-: **sinn|ent|leert** [-lɛntle:ɐt] **ADJ** bereft of content; **sinn|ent|stel|lend** **ADJ** **~ sein** to distort the meaning **ADV** **~ übersetzt** translated so that the meaning is/was distorted; **etw ~ zitieren** to quote sth in a way that distorts the meaning
Sin|nen|welt **F** *(liter)* material world
Sin|nes-: **Sin|nes|än|de|rung** **F** change of mind *or* heart; **Sin|nes|art** **F** *(geh)* = **Gesinnung**; **Sin|nes|ein|druck** **M** sensory impression, impression on the senses; **Sin|nes|nerv** **M** sensory nerve; **Sin|nes|or|gan** **NT** sense organ; **Sin|nes|reiz** **M** sensory stimulus; **Sin|nes|stö|rung** **F** sensory disorder; **Sin|nes|täu|schung** **F** hallucination; **Sin|nes|wahr|neh|mung** **F** sensory perception *no pl*; **Sin|nes|wan|del** **M** change of mind *or* heart

Sinn-: **sinn|fäl|lig** ADJ *Beispiel, Symbol* manifest, obvious; **Sinn|fra|ge** F question of the meaning *or* purpose of life; **Sinn|ge|bung** [-geːbʊŋ] F -, -en *(geh)* giving meaning (+*gen* to); *(= Sinn)* meaning; **Sinn|ge|dicht** NT epigram; **sinn|ge|mäß** ADJ **a** *(= inhaltlich)* **eine ~e Zusammenfassung** a summary which gives the gist (of it) **b** *(esp Jur: = analog)* corresponding, analogous ADV **a** *(= dem Sinn nach)* **etw ~ wiedergeben** to give the gist of sth **b** *(Jur)* **etw ~ anwenden** to apply sth by analogy; **sinn|ge|treu** ADJ *Übersetzung* faithful (to the sense *or* meaning) ADV **etw ~ übersetzen** to do a faithful translation of sth

sin|nie|ren [zɪ'niːrən] *ptp* **sinniert** VI to brood (*über +acc* over), to ruminate (*über +acc* about)

sin|nig ['zɪnɪç] ADJ apt; *Vorrichtung* practical; *(iro: = wenig sinnvoll)* clever

sin|ni|ger|wei|se ADV *(iro)* naturally *(iro)*

Sinn|kri|se F identity crisis

sinn|lich ['zɪnlɪç] ADJ **a** *(Philos) Empfindung, Eindrücke* sensory, sensorial; **die ~e Welt** the material world; **~e Anschauung** perception (by the senses) **b** *(= vital, sinnenfroh)* sensuous; *(= erotisch)* sensual; **~e Liebe** sensual love ADV **a** *(= sexuell)* sexually **b** *(= mit den Sinnen)* **~ wahrnehmbar** perceptible by the senses; **Menschen können diesen Ton nicht ~ wahrnehmen** this tone is not perceptible to humans

Sinn|lich|keit F -, *no pl* **a** *(Philos)* sensory *or* sensorial nature **b** *(= Vitalität, Sinnenfreude)* sensuousness; *(= Erotik)* sensuality

sinn|los ADJ **a** *(= unsinnig) Redensarten, Geschwätz* meaningless; *Verhalten, Töten* senseless **b** *(= zwecklos)* pointless, futile, senseless; *Hoffnung* forlorn; **es ist/wäre ~, zu …** it is/would be pointless *or* futile to …; **das ist völlig ~** there's no sense in that, that's completely pointless **c** *Wut* blind; *Hast* desperate ADV **a** *(= ohne Sinn) zerstören, morden* senselessly; **ich habe mich ~ bemüht, ihm das beizubringen** I tried in vain to teach him that **b** *(= äußerst)* **~ betrunken** blind drunk; **sich ~ betrinken** to get blind drunk

Sinn|lo|sig|keit F -, -en **a** *(= Unsinnigkeit) (von Redensart, Geschwätz)* meaninglessness; *(von Verhalten, Töten)* senselessness **b** *(= Zwecklosigkeit)* pointlessness, futility, senselessness; *(von Hoffnung)* forlornness

Sinn-: **sinn|reich** ADJ *Deutung* meaningful; *(= zweckdienlich) Einrichtung, Erfindung* useful; **Sinn|spruch** M epigram; **sinn|stif|tend** ADJ *(geh)* meaningful; **sinn|ver|wandt** ADJ synonymous; **~e Wörter** synonyms; **Sinn|ver|wandt|schaft** F synonymity; **sinn|voll** ADJ **a** *Satz* meaningful **b** *(fig) (= vernünftig)* sensible; *(= nützlich)* useful ADV **sein Geld ~/~er anlegen** to invest one's money sensibly/more sensibly; **seine Zeit ~/~er nutzen** to do something sensible/more constructive with one's time; **seine Fähigkeiten ~ einsetzen** to use one's capabilities intelligently; **sein Geld ~ verwenden** to use one's money for something useful; **sinn|wid|rig** ADJ nonsensical, absurd; **Sinn|wid|rig|keit** F absurdity

Si|no|lo|ge [zino'loːgə] M -n, -n, **Si|no|lo|gin** [-'loːgɪn] F -, -nen Sinologist

Si|no|lo|gie [zinolo'giː] F -, *no pl* Sinology

sin|te|mal ['zɪntə'maːl] CONJ *(obs, hum)* because, since

Sin|ter ['zɪntɐ] M -s, - *(Miner)* sinter

sin|tern ['zɪntɐn] VTI to sinter

Sint|flut ['zɪntfluːt] F *(Bibl)* Flood; **nach mir/uns die ~** *(inf)* it doesn't matter what happens when I've/we've gone

sint|flut|ar|tig ADJ **~e Regenfälle** torrential rain

Sin|to ['zɪnto] M -, **Sinti** ['zɪnti] *usu pl* Sinto (gypsy); **Sinti und Roma** Sinti and Romanies

Si|nus ['ziːnʊs] M -, -se *or* - [-nuːs] **a** *(Math)* sine **b** *(Anat)* sinus

Si|nus-: **Si|nus|kur|ve** F sine curve; **Si|nus|satz** M sine theorem

Si|oux ['ziːʊks] M -, - Sioux

Si|phon ['ziːfõ, zi'fõː, zi'foːn] M -s, -s siphon; *(Aus inf)* soda (water)

Sip|pe ['zɪpə] F -, -n (extended) family, kinship group *(spec)*; *(inf: = Verwandtschaft)* family, clan *(inf)*; *(Zool)* species *sing*

Sip|pen-: **Sip|pen|äl|tes|te(r)** MF *decl as adj* head of the family; **Sip|pen|for|schung** F genealogy, genealogical research; **Sip|pen|haft** F *(inf)*, **Sip|pen|haf|tung** F *(Jur)* liability of all the members of a family for the crimes of one member; **Sip|pen|ver|band** M kinship group

Sipp|schaft ['zɪpʃaft] F -, -en *(pej inf) (= Familie)* tribe *(inf)*; *(= Bande, Gesindel auch)* bunch *(inf)*

Sire [siːr] INTERJ *(old liter)* Sire *(old)*

Si|re|ne [zi'reːnə] F -, -n *(Myth, Tech, fig)* siren; *(Zool)* sirenian

Si|re|nen-: **Si|re|nen|ge|heul** NT wail of a/the siren/sirens; **Si|re|nen|ge|sang** M siren song

Si|ri|us ['ziːriʊs] M - *(Astron)* Sirius

sir|ren ['zɪrən] VI = **surren**

Si|rup ['ziːrʊp] M -s, -e syrup; *(schwarz, aus Zuckerrohr auch)* treacle

Si|sal(hanf) ['ziːzal-] M -s sisal (hemp)

Si|sal|tep|pich M sisal mat

sis|tie|ren [zɪs'tiːrən] *ptp* **sistiert** VT *(Jur) Verdächtigen* to detain; *Verfahren* to adjourn

Si|sy|phus|ar|beit ['ziːzyfʊs-] F Sisyphean task *(liter)*, never-ending task

Site [sait] F -, -s *(=Website)* site

Sit-in [sɪt'lɪn] NT -(s), -s sit-in; **ein ~ machen** to have *or* stage *or* hold a sit-in

Sit|te ['zɪtə] F -, -n **a** *(= Brauch)* custom; *(= Mode)* practice; **~ sein** to be the custom/the practice; **~n und Gebräuche** customs and traditions; **was sind denn das für ~n?** what's all this?; **hier reißen ja ~n ein!** *(inf)* the things people have started doing! **b** *usu pl (= gutes Benehmen)* manners *pl*; *(= Sittlichkeit)* morals *pl*; **gegen die (guten) ~n verstoßen, ~ und Anstand verletzen** to offend common decency; **gute ~n** good manners *pl*; **was sind denn das für ~n?** what sort of a way is that to behave! **c** *(sl: = Sittenpolizei)* vice squad

Sit|ten-: **Sit|ten|apos|tel** M *(pej)* moralizer; **Sit|ten|bild** NT *(Art)* genre picture; **Sit|ten|de|zer|nat** NT vice squad; **Sit|ten|ge|mäl|de** NT genre picture; **Sit|ten|ge|schich|te** F **~ Roms** history of Roman life and customs; **Sit|ten|ge|setz** NT moral law; **Sit|ten|ko|dex** M moral code; **Sit|ten|leh|re** F ethics *sing*; **sit|ten|los** ADJ immoral; **Sit|ten|lo|sig|keit** F -, *no pl* immorality; **Sit|ten|po|li|zei** F vice squad; **Sit|ten|pre|di|ger(in)** M(F) moralist, sermonizer; **Sit|ten|rich|ter(in)** M(F) judge of public morals; **sit|ten|streng** ADJ highly moral; **Sit|ten|stren|ge** F strict morality; **Sit|ten|strolch** M *(Press inf)* sex fiend; **Sit|ten|ver|fall** M decline *or* drop in moral standards; **Sit|ten|wäch|ter(in)** M(F) *(iro)* guardian of public morals; **sit|ten|wid|rig** ADJ *(form)* immoral; **Sit|ten|wid|rig|keit** F *(form)* immorality

Sit|tich ['zɪtɪç] M -s, -e parakeet

sitt|lich ['zɪtlɪç] ADJ moral; **ihm fehlt der ~e Halt** he lacks moral fibre *(Brit)* *or* fiber *(US)*; **ihm fehlt die ~e Reife** he's morally immature; **er verlor jeden ~en Halt** he became morally unstable; **das Sittliche** morality

Sitt|lich|keit F -, *no pl* morality

Sitt|lich|keits-: **Sitt|lich|keits|de|likt** NT sexual offence *(Brit)* *or* offense *(US)*; **Sitt|lich|keits|ver|bre|chen** NT sex crime; **Sitt|lich|keits|ver|bre|cher(in)** M(F) sex offender

sitt|sam ['zɪtzaːm] ADJ demure ADV demurely

Sitt|sam|keit F -, *no pl* demureness

Si|tu|a|ti|on [zitua'tsioːn] F -, -en situation; *(= persönliche Lage auch)* position

Si|tu|a|ti|ons-: **Si|tu|a|ti|ons|be|richt** M report on the situation; **Si|tu|a|ti|ons|ko|mik** F comicalness *or* comedy of the situation/situations; *(= Art der Komik)* situation comedy, sitcom *(inf)*

si|tu|iert [zitu'iːɐt] ADJ **a gut ~** *(attr)* well-off; **gut/schlecht ~ sein** to be well/poorly situated financially **b** *(S Ger, esp Aus: = sich befindend)* situated

Sit|-up M -(s), -s sit-up, crunch; **Sit-ups machen** to do sit-ups

Sitz [zɪts] M -es, -e **a** *(= Sitzplatz, Parl)* seat; **~ und Stimme haben** to have a seat and a vote **b** *(von Regierung, Herrscher, Universität, fig)* seat; *(= Wohnsitz)* residence, domicile *(form)*; *(von Firma, Verwaltung)* headquarters *pl*; **die Welthandelsorganisation hat ihren ~ in Genf** the World Trade Organization has its headquarters in Geneva **c** *no pl (Tech, von Kleidungsstück)* sit; *(von der Größe her)* fit; **einen guten ~ haben** to sit/fit well; **einen schlechten ~ haben** to sit/fit badly **d** *no pl (von Reiter)* seat

Sitz-: **Sitz|bad** NT sitz *or* hip *(esp Brit)* bath; **Sitz|ba|de|wan|ne** F sitz *or* hip *(esp Brit)* bath; **Sitz|bank** F *pl* **-bänke** bench; **Sitz|blo|cka|de** F sit-in; **Sitz|de|monst|rant(in)** M(F) sit-down demonstrator; **Sitz|ecke** F corner seating unit

sit|zen ['zɪtsn] *pret* **saß** [zaːs], *ptp* **gesessen** [gə'zɛsn] VI *aux haben or (Aus, S Ger, Sw) sein* **a** *(Mensch, Tier)* to sit; *(Vogel)* to perch; **~ Sie bequem?** are you comfortable?; **hier sitzt man sehr bequem** it's very comfortable sitting here; **auf der Toilette ~** to be on *(inf)* *or* in the toilet; **etw im Sitzen tun** to do sth sitting down; **beim Frühstück/Mittagessen ~** to be having breakfast/lunch; **beim Wein/Schach ~** to sit over a glass of wine/a game of chess; **an einer Aufgabe/über den Büchern/über einer Arbeit ~** to sit over a task/one's books/a piece of work → *auch* **sitzen bleiben**

b *(= Modell sitzen)* to sit (*jdm* for sb)

c *(= seinen Sitz haben) (Regierung, Gericht etc)* to sit; *(Firma)* to have its headquarters

d *(= Mitglied sein) (im Parlament)* to have a seat (*in +dat* in); *(im Vorstand, Aufsichtsrat etc)* to be *or* sit (*in +dat* on)

e *(inf: = im Gefängnis sitzen)* to be inside *(inf)*; **gesessen haben** to have done time *(inf)*, to have been inside *(inf)*; **er musste zwei Jahre ~** he had to do two years *(inf)*

f *(= sein)* to be; **er sitzt in Bulgarien/im Kultusministerium** *(inf)* he's in Bulgaria/the ministry of culture; **er sitzt in der Äußeren Mongolei (und kann nicht weg)** *(inf)* he's stuck in outer Mongolia *(inf)*; **er sitzt im Gefängnis** *(inf)* he's in prison; **die Verfolger saßen uns auf den Fersen** our pursuers were hard on our heels; **auf der Bank ~** *(Sport)* to be *or* sit on the bench

g *(= angebracht sein: Deckel, Schraube etc)* to sit; **der Deckel sitzt fest** the lid is on tightly; **die Schraube sitzt fest** the screw is in tightly; **locker ~** to be loose

h *(= stecken)* to be (stuck); **fest ~** to be stuck tight(ly); **der Splitter saß fest in meinem Fuß** the splinter was stuck in my foot

i *(= im Gedächtnis sitzen)* to have sunk in

j *(= seinen Herd haben) (Infektion, Schmerz)* to be; *(fig: Übel, Hass, Schmerz)* to lie, to be

k *(Kleid, Frisur)* to sit; **deine Krawatte sitzt nicht richtig** your tie isn't straight; **sein Hut saß schief** his hat was (on) crooked

l *(inf: = treffen)* to hit home; **das saß!, das hat gesessen!** that hit home

m einen ~ haben *(inf)* to have had one too many *(inf)*

sit|zen+blei|ben VI *sep irreg aux sein (inf, fig)* = **sitzen bleiben b, c, e**

sit|zen blei|ben VI *irreg aux sein* **a** *(= nicht aufstehen)* to remain seated; **bleiben Sie bitte sitzen!, bitte bleiben Sie sitzen!** please don't get up **b** *(Sch) (inf)* to stay down (a year), to have to repeat a year **c** *(inf)* **auf einer Ware ~** to be left with a product **d** *(Mädchen) (beim Tanz)* to be left sitting **e** *(inf) (= nicht heiraten)* to be left on the shelf *(inf)*

Sit|zen|blei|ber [-blaibɐ] M **-s, -**, **Sit|zen|blei|be|rin** [-ərın] F **-, -nen** (inf) *pupil who has to repeat a year*

sit|zend ADJ *attr Lebensweise etc* sedentary ADV sitting down, seated; **er hat mich ~ begrüßt** he greeted me without getting up; **ich verbringe die meiste Zeit ~** I sit most of the time

sit|zen las|sen *ptp* **sitzen lassen** *or (rare)* **sitzen gelassen** *irreg*, **sit|zen+las|sen** *ptp* **sitzenlassen** *or (rare)* **sitzengelassen** *sep irreg* VT (inf) **a** (*Sch:* = *nicht versetzen*) to keep down (a year) **b** (= *hinnehmen*) **eine Beleidigung** *etc* **auf sich** (dat) **~** to stand for *or* take an insult *etc* **c** **jdn ~** (= *im Stich lassen*) to leave sb in the lurch; (= *warten lassen*) to leave sb waiting; *Freund(in)* (*durch Nichterscheinen*) to stand sb up; (*für immer*) to walk out on sb **d** (= *nicht heiraten*) to jilt, to walk out on

-sit|zer [zıtsɐ] M *suf* **-s, -** *in cpds* -seater; **ein Zweisitzer** a two-seater

Sit|ze|rei [zıtsə'rai] F **-**, *no pl* (inf) sitting about

Sitz-: **Sitz|fleisch** NT (inf) ability to sit still; **~ haben** to be able to sit still; (*hum: Besucher*) to stay a long time; **Sitz|gar|ni|tur** F living-room suite; (*dreiteilig auch*) three-piece suite; **Sitz|ge|le|gen|heit** F seats *pl*, seating (accommodation); **eine ~ suchen** to look for somewhere to sit, to look for a seat; **Sitz|hei|zung** F (Aut) seat heating; **Sitz|kis|sen** NT (floor) cushion; **Sitz|ord|nung** F seating plan; **Sitz|pink|ler** [-pıŋklɐ] M **-s, -** (*sl: Schimpfwort*) tosser (*sl*); **Sitz|platz** M seat; **Sitz|rei|he** F row of seats; **Sitz|rie|se** M (*hum*) *short person with a long body who looks tall when sitting down*; **Sitz|streik** M sit-down strike

Sit|zung ['zıtsʊŋ] F **-, -en** **a** (= *Konferenz*) meeting; (*Jur:* = *Gerichtsverhandlung*) session; (= *Parlamentssitzung*) sitting **b** (= *Einzelsitzung*) (*bei Künstler*) sitting; (*bei Zahnarzt*) visit; (*inf:* = *Toilettenbesuch*) session; **spiritistische ~** séance **c** (*Comput*) session

Sit|zungs-: **Sit|zungs|be|richt** M minutes *pl*; **Sit|zungs|geld** NT (*Parl*) attendance allowance; **Sit|zungs|ma|ra|thon** M (*inf*) marathon session *or* meeting; **Sit|zungs|pe|ri|o|de** F (*Parl*) session; (*Jur*) term; **Sit|zungs|saal** M conference hall; (*Jur*) courtroom; **Sit|zungs|zim|mer** NT conference room

six|ti|nisch [zıks'ti:nıʃ] ADJ Sistine

Si|zi|li|a|ner [zitsi'lia:nɐ] M **-s, -**, **Si|zi|li|a|ne|rin** [-ərın] F **-, -nen** Sicilian

si|zi|li|a|nisch [zitsi'lia:nıʃ] ADJ Sicilian

Si|zi|li|en [zi'tsi:liən] NT **-s** Sicily

Skai® [skai] NT **-(s)**, *no pl* imitation leather

Ska|la ['ska:la] F **-, Skalen** *or* **-s** ['ska:lən] (= *Gradeinteilung, auch Mus*) scale; (= *Reihe gleichartiger Dinge*) range; (*fig*) gamut, range

Ska|lar [ska'la:ɐ] M **-s, -e** (*Math*) scalar

Ska|lar|pro|dukt NT (*Math*) scalar product

Skal|de ['skaldə] M **-n, -n** skald

Skal|den|dich|tung F skaldic poetry

Skalp [skalp] M **-s, -e** scalp

Skal|pell [skal'pɛl] NT **-s, -e** scalpel

skal|pie|ren [skal'pi:rən] *ptp* **skalpiert** VT to scalp

Skan|dal [skan'da:l] M **-s, -e** scandal; (*inf:* = *Krach*) to-do (*inf*), fuss; **einen ~ machen** to create *or* cause a scandal; to make a to-do (*inf*) *or* fuss; **das ist ein ~!** it's scandalous *or* a scandal

Skan|dal-: **Skan|dal|blatt** NT (*pej*) scandal sheet; **skan|dal|ge|plagt** ADJ *Partei, Unternehmen* scandal-plagued; **Skan|dal|ge|schich|te** F (bit *or* piece of) scandal; **Skan|dal|nu|del** F (*hum*) **sie ist eine richtige ~** she's always involved in some scandal or other

skan|da|lös [skanda'lø:s] ADJ scandalous ADV scandalously

Skan|dal-: **Skan|dal|pres|se** F (*pej*) gutter press (*Brit*), tabloids *pl*; **Skan|dal|pro|zess** M sensational trial *or* case; **skan|dal|süch|tig** ADJ (*pej*) *Publikum, Leser* fond of scandal; *Klatschtante, Presse etc auch* scandalmongering *attr*; **skan|dal|träch|tig** ADJ potentially scandalous; **skan|dal|um|wit|tert** ADJ (*Press*) surrounded by scandal

skan|die|ren [skan'di:rən] *ptp* **skandiert** VTI to scan

Skan|di|na|vi|en [skandi'na:viən] NT **-s** Scandinavia

Skan|di|na|vi|er [skandi'na:viɐ] M **-s, -**, **Skan|di|na|vi|e|rin** [-iərın] F **-, -nen** Scandinavian

skan|di|na|visch [skandi'na:vıʃ] ADJ Scandinavian

Skan|di|um ['skandiʊm] NT **-s**, *no pl* (*abbr* **Sc**) scandium

Ska|ra|bä|us [skara'bɛ:ʊs] M **-**, **Skarabäen** [-'bɛ:ən] scarab

Skat [ska:t] M **-(e)s, -e** (*Cards*) skat; **~ spielen** *or* **dreschen** (*inf*) *or* **kloppen** (*sl*) to play skat

> **SKAT**
>
> **Skat** is a card game that is extremely popular in Germany. It is played amongst friends at regular **Skatrunden** or **Skatabende** and requires a pack of 32 German or French cards. There are also **Skat** competitions between clubs which have been organized into leagues, with the German championship being decided every year. Since 1927 **Skat** has had its own special panel in Altenburg for settling disputes.

Skat|brü|der PL (*inf*) fellow skat players *pl*

Skate|board ['ske:tbɔ:ɐd] NT **-s, -s** skateboard rink

Skate|board|bahn ['ske:tbɔ:ɐdba:n] F skateboard rink

Skate|boar|den ['ske:tbɔ:ɐdn] NT **-s**, *no pl* skateboarding

Skate|board|fah|rer(in) ['ske:tbɔ:ɐd-] M(F) skateboarder

ska|ten ['ska:tn] VI (*inf*) to play skat

Skat|spie|ler(in) M(F) skat player

Ske|le|ton ['skɛlətn, 'skɛletɔn] M **-s, -s** (*Sport*) skeleton

Ske|lett [ske'lɛt] NT **-(e)s, -e** (*lit, fig*) skeleton; **er war bis aufs ~ abgemagert, er war nur noch ein ~** he was like a skeleton

Skep|sis ['skɛpsıs] F **-**, *no pl* scepticism (*Brit*), skepticism (*US*); **mit** *or* **voller ~** sceptically (*Brit*), skeptically (*US*)

Skep|ti|ker ['skɛptikɐ] M **-s, -**, **Skep|ti|ke|rin** [-ərın] F **-,-nen** sceptic (*Brit*), skeptic (*US*)

skep|tisch ['skɛptıʃ] ADJ sceptical (*Brit*), skeptical (*US*) ADV sceptically (*Brit*), skeptically (*US*); **das Ergebnis muss ~ stimmen** the results must make you sceptical (*Brit*) *or* skeptical (*US*)

Skep|ti|zis|mus [skɛpti'tsısmʊs] M **-**, *no pl* (*esp Philos*) scepticism (*Brit*), skepticism (*US*)

skep|ti|zis|tisch [skɛpti'tsıstıʃ] ADJ (*esp Philos*) sceptic(al) (*Brit*), skeptic(al) (*US*)

Sketch [skɛtʃ] M **-(es), -e(s)** (*Art, Theat*) sketch

Ski [ʃi:] M **-s, -** *or* **-er** ['ʃi:ɐ] ski; **~ laufen** *or* **fahren** to ski

Ski- *in cpds* ski; **Ski|an|zug** M ski suit; **Ski|aus|rüs|tung** F skiing gear; **eine komplette ~** a complete set of skiing gear; **Ski|bin|dung** F ski binding; (*pl auch*) ski fittings *pl*; **Ski|bob** M skibob; **Ski|bril|le** F ski goggles *pl*

Ski|er *pl von* **Ski**

Ski-: **Ski|fah|rer(in)** M(F) skier; **Ski|flie|gen** NT **-s**, *no pl*, **Ski|flug** M ski flying; **Ski|ge|biet** NT ski(ing) area; **Ski|ge|län|de** NT ski(-ing) area; **Ski|gym|nas|tik** F skiing exercises *pl*; **Ski|ha|se** M, **Ski|ha|serl** [-ha:zɐl] NT **-s, -n** (*hum inf*) girl skier; **Ski|ho|se** F (pair of) ski pants *pl*; **Ski|hüt|te** F ski hut *or* lodge (*US*); **Ski|kurs** M skiing course; **Ski|lang|lauf** M → **Langlauf**; **Ski|lauf** M skiing; **Ski|lau|fen** NT skiing; **zum ~ fahren** to go skiing; **Ski|läu|fer(in)** M(F) skier; **Ski|leh|rer** M ski instructor; **Ski|lift** M ski lift

Skin [skın] M **-s, -s** (*inf*) skin (*inf*)

Skin|head ['skınhɛd] M **-s, -s** skinhead

Ski-: **Ski|pass** M ski pass; **Ski|pis|te** F ski run; **Ski|schan|ze** F ski jump; **Ski|schuh** M ski boot; **Ski|schu|le** F ski school; **Ski|sport** M skiing; **Ski|sprin|gen** NT ski jumping; **Ski|sprin|ger(in)** M(F) ski jumper; **Ski|stie|fel** M ski boot; **Ski|stock** M ski stick; **Ski|trä|ger** M (*Aut*) ski rack, ski roof carrier (*US*); **Ski|ur|laub** M skiing holiday (*esp Brit*) *or* vacation (*US*); **Ski|zir|kus** M ski circus

Skiz|ze ['skıtsə] F **-, -n** sketch; (*fig:* = *Grundriss*) outline, plan

Skiz|zen-: **Skiz|zen|block** M *pl* **-blöcke** *or* **-blocks** sketchpad; **Skiz|zen|buch** NT sketchbook; **skiz|zen|haft** ADJ *Zeichnung etc* roughly sketched; *Beschreibung etc* (given) in broad outline ADV **etw ~ zeichnen** to sketch sth roughly; **etw ~ beschreiben** to describe sth in broad outline

skiz|zie|ren [skı'tsi:rən] *ptp* **skizziert** VT to sketch; (*fig*) *Plan etc* to outline

Skiz|zie|rung F **-, -en** sketching; (*fig: von Plan etc*) outlining

Skla|ve ['skla:və, 'skla:fə] M **-n, -n**, **Skla|vin** ['skla:vın, 'skla:fın] F **-, -nen** slave; **~ einer Sache** (*gen*) **sein** (*fig*) to be a slave to sth; **jdn zum ~n machen** to make a slave of sb; (*fig*) to enslave sb, to make sb one's slave

Skla|ven-: **Skla|ven|ar|beit** F slavery; (= *Arbeit von Sklaven*) work of slaves; **Skla|ven|dienst** M slavery; **Skla|ven|ga|lee|re** F slave galley; **Skla|ven|hal|ter(in)** M(F) slaveholder, slave owner; **Skla|ven|hal|ter|ge|sell|schaft** F slave-owning society; **Skla|ven|han|del** M slave trade; **~ betreiben** to deal in slaves; **Skla|ven|händ|ler(in)** M(F) slave-trader, slaver (*esp Brit*); **Skla|ven|markt** M slave market; **Skla|ven|trei|ber(in)** M(F) (*lit, fig*) slave-driver

Skla|ve|rei [skla:və'rai, skla:fə'rai] F **-**, *no pl* (*lit, fig*) slavery *no art*; **jdn in die ~ führen** to take sb into slavery

Skla|vin ['skla:vın, 'skla:fın] F (*lit, fig*) slave → *auch* **Sklave**

skla|visch ['skla:vıʃ, 'skla:fıʃ] ADJ slavish ADV slavishly

Skle|ro|se [skle'ro:zə] F **-, -n** (*Med*) sclerosis

Sko|li|o|se [skoli'o:zə] F **-, -n** (*Med*) scoliosis

skon|tie|ren [skɔn'ti:rən] *ptp* **skontiert** VT **jdm etw ~** to give sb a cash discount on sth

Skon|to ['skɔnto] NT OR M **-s, -s** *or* **Skonti** [-ti] cash discount; **bei Barzahlung 3% ~** 3% discount for cash; **jdm ~ geben** *or* **gewähren** (*form*) to give *or* allow sb a cash discount *or* a discount for cash

Skor|but [skɔr'bu:t] M **-(e)s**, *no pl* scurvy

Skor|pi|on [skɔr'pio:n] M **-s, -e** (*Zool*) scorpion; (*Astrol*) Scorpio

Skri|bent [skri'bɛnt] M **-en, -en**, **Skri|ben|tin** [-'bɛntın] F **-, -nen** (*dated pej*) hack, scribbler

Skript [skrıpt] NT **-(e)s, -en** **a** *pl usu* **-s** (*Film*) (film) script **b** (*Univ*) (set of) lecture notes *pl*; **ein ~ anfertigen** to take lecture notes

Skript|girl ['skrıpt-] NT script girl

Skrip|tum ['skrıptʊm] NT **-s, Skripten** *or* **Skripta** [-tn, -ta] (*esp Aus Univ*) (set of) lecture notes *pl*; **ein ~ anfertigen** to take lecture notes

Skro|tum ['skro:tʊm] NT **-s, Skrota** [-ta] (*Med*) scrotum

Skru|pel ['skru:pl] M **-s, -** *usu pl* scruple; **keine ~ haben** *or* **kennen** to have no scruples; **er hatte keine ~, das zu tun** he didn't scruple to do it; **ohne (jeden) ~** without (the slightest) scruple

Skru|pel-: **skru|pel|los** ADJ unscrupulous ADV unscrupulously; **Skru|pel|lo|sig|keit** F **-**, *no pl* unscrupulousness

skru|pu|lös [skrupu'lø:s] (*geh*) ADJ scrupulous ADV scrupulously

Skull|boot ['skʊlbo:t] NT sculling boat

skul|len ['skʊlən] VI (*Sport*) to scull

Skulp|tur [skʊlp'tu:ɐ] F **-, -en** sculpture

Skunk [skʊŋk] M **-s, -s** *or* **-e** skunk

skur|ril [skʊ'ri:l] ADJ (*geh*) droll, comical

Skur|ri|li|tät [skʊrili'tɛːt] F -, -en *(geh)* drollery
S-Kur|ve ['ɛs-] F S-bend
Sky|bea|mer M skybeam
Skye|ter|ri|er ['skaitɛriɐ] M Skye terrier
Sky-Mar|shal M -s, -s sky marshal
Sky|sur|fing ['skai-] NT, *no pl* sky surfing
Sla|lom ['slaːlɔm] M -s, -s slalom; **(im) ~ fahren** *(fig inf)* to drive a crazy zigzag course *(inf)*
Slang [slɛŋ] M -s, *no pl* slang
Slap|stick ['slɛpstɪk] M -s, -s slapstick
Slash [slɛʃ] M -, -es ['slɛʃɪz] *(= Schrägstrich)* slash
S-Laut ['ɛs-] M *(stimmlos)* 's'-sound; *(stimmhaft)* 'z'-sound
Sla|we ['slaːvə] M -n, -n, **Sla|win** ['slaːvɪn] F -, -nen Slav
sla|wisch ['slaːvɪʃ] ADJ Slavonic, Slavic
Sla|wist [sla'vɪst] M -en, -en, **Sla|wis|tin** [-'vɪstɪn] F -, -nen Slavonicist, Slavist
Sla|wis|tik [sla'vɪstɪk] F -, *no pl* Slavonic studies *sing*
Sli|bo|witz ['sliːbovɪts] M -(e)s, -e slivovitz
Slip [slɪp] M -s, -s (pair of) briefs *pl*; *(= Damenslip auch)* (pair of) panties *pl*
Slip|ein|la|ge F panty liner
Slip|per ['slɪpɐ] M -s, - slip-on shoe
Slo|gan ['sloːgn] M -s, -s slogan
Slot [slɔt] M -s, -s *(Comput, Aviat)* slot
Slo|wa|ke [slo'vaːkə] M -n, -n, **Slo|wa|kin** [-'vaːkɪn] F -, -nen Slovak
Slo|wa|kei [slova'kai] F - **die ~** Slovakia
slo|wa|kisch [slo'vaːkɪʃ] ADJ Slovakian, Slovak
Slo|wa|kisch(e) NT Slovak → *auch* **Deutsch(e)**
Slo|we|ne [slo'veːnə] M -n, -n, **Slo|we|nin** [-'veːnɪn] F -, -nen Slovene
Slo|we|ni|en [slo'veːniən] NT -s Slovenia
slo|we|nisch [slo'veːnɪʃ] ADJ Slovenian, Slovene
Slo|we|nisch(e) NT Slovene, Slovenian → *auch* **Deutsch(e)**
Slow|fox ['sloːfɔks] M -(es), -e slow foxtrot
Slum [slam] M -s, -s slum
sm *abbr von* **Seemeile**
SM [ɛs'lɛm] M -(s) *abbr von* **Sadomasochismus** SM
S. M. *abbr von* **seine(r) Majestät** HM
Small Talk ['smɔːltɔːk] M -(s), *no pl*, **Small|talk** M -(s), *no pl* small talk
Sma|ragd [sma'rakt] M -(e)s, -e [-də] emerald
sma|ragd|grün ADJ emerald-green
smart [smaːɐt, smart] *(inf)* ADJ smart ADV *gekleidet* smartly; **~ klingen** to sound smart
Smart|card F -, -s, **Smart Card** ['smaːɐtkaːɐd] F - -, - -s *(inf)* smart card
Smi|ley ['smaili] NT -s, -s *(Comput)* smiley
Smi|ley ['smaili] M -s, -s *(pej: = ständig lächelnder Mensch)* grinner, smiler
Smog [smɔk] M -(s), -s smog
Smog-: **Smog|alarm** M smog alert; **Smog|alarm|stu|fe** F **~ 1** smog warning level 1; **Smog|ge|fahr** F danger of smog; **Smog|ver|ord|nung** F smog regulations *pl*
Smok|ar|beit F *(Sew)* smocking
smo|ken ['smoːkn] VTI *(Sew)* to smock
Smo|king ['smoːkɪŋ] M -s, -s dinner jacket, dj *(inf)*, tuxedo *(esp US)*, tux *(esp US inf)*
SMS [ɛslɛm'lɛs] F -, - *abbr von* **Short Message Service** text message; **jdm eine ~ schicken** to text sb
SMSen ['zɪmzn] VTI → **simsen**
Smut|je ['smʊtjə] M -s, -s *(Naut)* ship's cook
SMV [ɛslɛm'fau] -, *no pl abbr von* **Schülermitverwaltung** *or* **-mitverantwortung** school council
Smyr|na|tep|pich ['smyrna-] M Smyrna (carpet)
Snack [snɛk] M -s, -s snack (meal)
snif|fen ['snɪfn] VI *(sl) (von Drogen)* to sniff; *(von Kokain auch)* to snort
Snob [snɔp] M -s, -s snob
Sno|bis|mus [sno'bɪsmʊs] M -, **Snobismen** [-mən] **a** *no pl* snobbery, snobbishness **b** *(= Bemerkung)* snobbish remark *or* comment
sno|bis|tisch [sno'bɪstɪʃ] ADJ snobbish

Snow-: **Snow|board** ['snoːbɔːɐd] NT -s, -s snowboard; **Snow|boar|den** ['snoːbɔːɐdn] NT -s, *no pl*, **Snow|boar|ding** ['snoːbɔːɐdɪŋ] NT -s, *no pl* snowboarding; **Snow|boar|der** ['snoːbɔːɐdɐ] M -s, -, **Snow|boar|de|rin** [-ərɪn] F -, -nen snowboarder; **Snow|mo|bil** ['snoːmobiːl] NT -s, -e snowmobile; **Snow|raf|ting** ['snoːraːftɪŋ] NT -s, *no pl* snow rafting

so [zoː] ADV **a** *(mit adj, adv)* so; *(mit vb: = so sehr)* so much; **so groß** *etc* so big *etc*; **eine so große Frau** such a big woman; **es ist gar nicht so einfach** it's really not so easy; **so groß** *etc* **wie ...** as big *etc* as ...; **so groß** *etc*, **dass ...** so big *etc* that ...; **sie hat ihn so geschlagen, dass ...** she hit him so hard that ...; **er ist so gelaufen** he ran so fast; **ich habe so gearbeitet** I worked so hard; **so gut es geht** as best *or* well as I/he *etc* can; **er ist nicht so dumm, das zu glauben** he's not so stupid as to believe that, he's not stupid enough to believe that; **sie hat sich so gefreut** she was so *or* really pleased; **das hat ihn so geärgert, dass ...** that annoyed him so much that ...; **ich wusste nicht, dass es ihn so ärgern würde** I didn't know that it would annoy him so *or* that much; **ich freue mich so sehr, dass du kommst** I'm so pleased you're coming
b *(= auf diese Weise, von dieser Art)* like this/that, this/that way, thus *(form)*; **mach es nicht so, sondern so** don't do it like this but like that; **du sollst es so machen, ...** do it like this ..., do it this way ...; **mach es so, wie er es vorgeschlagen hat** do it the way *or* as *or* like *(inf)* he suggested; **ist es dort tatsächlich so?** is it really like that there?; **ist das tatsächlich so?** is that really so?; **so ist sie nun einmal** that's the way she is, that's what she's like; **sei doch nicht so** don't be like that; **so ist es nicht gewesen** it wasn't like that, that's not how it was; **es ist vielleicht besser so** perhaps it's better like that *or* that way; **so IST das!** that's the way things are, that's how it is; **(ach) so ist das!** I see!; **ist das so?** is that so?; **so oder** *or* **und so** either way; **und so weiter (und so fort)** and so on (and so forth); **gut so!** fine!, good!; **das ist gut so** that's fine; **das ist auch gut so!** (and) a good thing too!; **mir ist (es) so, als ob ...** it seems to me as if ...; **so geht es, wenn ...** that's what happens if ...; **... und so ist es also geschehen** ... and so that is what happened; **das kam so ...** this is what happened ..., it happened like this ...; **es verhält sich so ...** the facts are thus *(form) or* are as follows ...; **das habe ich nur so gesagt** I didn't really mean it; **so genannt** = **sogenannt**
c *(= etwa)* about, or so; **ich komme so um 8 Uhr** I'll come at about 8, I'll come at 8 or so *or* or thereabouts; **sie heißt doch Malitzki oder so** she's called Malitzki or something
d *(inf: = umsonst)* for nothing
e *(als Füllwort: nicht übersetzt)* **so dann und wann** now and then; **so bist du also gar nicht dort gewesen?** *(geh)* so you weren't there after all?; **so beeil dich doch!** do hurry up!; **so mancher** a number of people *pl*, quite a few people *pl*
f *(= solch)* **so ein Gebäude/Fehler** a building/mistake like that, such a building/mistake; **so ein guter Lehrer/schlechtes Bild** *etc* such a good teacher/bad picture *etc*; **so ein Idiot!** what an idiot!; **hast du so etwas schon einmal gesehen?** have you ever seen anything like it?; **so (et)was ist noch nie vorgekommen** nothing like that has ever happened; **sie ist doch Lehrerin oder so was** she's a teacher or something like that; **na so was!** well I never!, no!; **so etwas Schönes** something as beautiful as that, such a beautiful thing; **so einer wie ich/er** somebody like *or* a person such as myself *or* me/him; **er ist so einer wie ich** he's like me → **umso, viel, weit, wenig**
CONJ **a** **so dass** so that
b **so wie es jetzt ist** as *or* the way things are at the moment
c **so klein er auch sein mag** however small he may be; **so wahr ich lebe** as true as I'm standing here
d **kaum hatte er ..., so ...** scarcely had he ... when ...
e *(old: = falls)* if, provided that; **so (der Herr-) Gott will, sehen wir uns wieder** God willing, we shall see one another again
INTERJ so; *(= wirklich)* oh, really; *(abschließend)* well, right; **er ist schon da – so?** he's here already – is he? *or* oh! *or* really?; **ich kann nicht mitkommen – so?** I can't come with you – can't you? *or* oh!; **so, das wärs für heute** well *or* right *or* so, that's it for today; **so, jetzt habe ich die Nase voll** I've had enough; **so, so!** well well → **ach**
SO *abbr von* **Südosten** SE
s. o. *abbr von* **siehe oben**
so|bald [zo'balt] CONJ as soon as
Söck|chen ['zœkçən] NT -s, - *dim von* **Socke**
So|cke ['zɔkə] F -, -n sock; **sich auf die ~n machen** *(inf)* to get going *(inf)*; **von den ~n sein** *(inf)* to be flabbergasted *(inf)*, to be knocked for six *(Brit inf)*
So|ckel ['zɔkl] M -s, - base; *(von Denkmal, Statue)* plinth, pedestal, socle *(spec)*; *(Elec)* socket; *(für Birne)* holder
So|ckel-: **So|ckel|be|trag** M basic sum; **So|ckel|ren|te** F basic pension
So|cken ['zɔkn] M -s, - *(S Ger, Aus)* sock
So|cken|hal|ter M (sock) suspender *(Brit)*, garter
So|da ['zoːda] F -, *no pl or nt* -s, *no pl* soda
so|dann [zo'dan] ADV *(old)* thereupon *(old, form)*, then
so|dass [zo'das] CONJ so that
So|da|was|ser NT *pl* **-wässer** soda water
Sod|bren|nen ['zoːtbrɛnən] NT -s, *no pl* heartburn
So|de ['zoːdə] F -, -n *(= Rasenstück, Torfscholle)* turf, sod
So|dom ['zoːdɔm] NT -s Sodom; **~ und Gomorrha** *(lit, fig)* Sodom and Gomorrah
So|do|mie [zodo'miː] F -, *no pl* buggery, bestiality
so|do|mi|tisch [zodo'miːtɪʃ] ADJ bestial
so|eben [zo'leːbn] ADV just (this moment); **~ hören wir** *or* **haben wir gehört ...** we have just (this moment) heard ...; **~ erschienen** just out *or* published
So|fa ['zoːfa] NT -s, -s sofa, settee *(esp Brit)*
So|fa-: **So|fa|bett** NT bed-settee *(Brit)*, sofa bed, hideaway bed *(US)*; **So|fa|ecke** F corner of the/a sofa; **So|fa|kis|sen** NT sofa cushion
so|fern [zo'fɛrn] CONJ provided (that); **~ ... nicht** if ... not
soff *pret von* **saufen**
So|fia ['zɔfia, 'zoːfia] NT -s *(Geog)* Sofia
So|fi|o|ter [zo'fioːtɐ] M -s, -, **So|fi|o|te|rin** [-ərɪn] F -, -nen Sofian
so|fort [zo'fɔrt] ADV immediately, straight *or* right away, at once; **~ nach ...** immediately after ...; **komm hierher, aber ~** *or* **und zwar ~!** come here this instant *or* at once!; **(ich) komme ~!** (I'm) just coming!; *(Kellner etc)* I'll be right with you
So|fort-: **So|fort|bild|ka|me|ra** F Polaroid® camera, instant camera; **So|fort|hil|fe** F emergency relief *or* aid
so|for|tig [zo'fɔrtɪç] ADJ immediate, instant
So|fort|maß|nah|me F immediate measure
Soft|drink ['zɔftdrɪŋk] M -s, -s, **Soft Drink** M - -s, - -s soft drink
Soft|eis ['zɔftlais] NT soft ice cream
Sof|tie ['zɔfti] M -s, -s *(inf)* caring type
Soft|ware ['sɔftwɛːɐ] F -, -s *(Comput)* software
Soft|ware-: **Soft|ware|ent|wick|ler(in)** ['sɔftwɛːɐ-] M(F) software developer; **Soft|ware|pa|ket** ['sɔftwɛːɐ-] NT software package; **Soft|ware|un|ter|neh|men** ['sɔftwɛːɐ-] NT software company *or* firm
sog *pret von* **saugen**

Sog [zo:k] M -(e)s, -e [-gə] *(= saugende Kraft)* suction; *(bei Schiff)* wake; *(bei Flugzeug, Fahrzeug)* slipstream; *(von Strudel)* vortex; *(von Brandungswelle)* undertow; *(fig)* maelstrom

sog. *abbr von* **sogenannt**

so|gar [zo'ga:ɐ] ADV even; **er kam ~** he even came; **jedes Getränk, ja ~ schon ein kleines Bier, kostet sehr viel** every drink, even a small glass of beer *or* a small glass of beer, even, costs a lot; **schön, ~ sehr schön** beautiful, in fact very beautiful; **ich kann sie gut leiden, ich finde sie ~ sehr nett** I like her, in fact I think she's very nice; **ich habe sie nicht nur gesehen, sondern ~ geküsst** I didn't just see her, I actually kissed her (as well)

so|ge|nannt ['zo:gənant] ADJ *attr* as it/he *etc* is called; *(= angeblich)* so-called

so|gleich [zo'glaiç] ADV = **sofort**

Sog|wir|kung F suction; *(fig)* knock-on effect

Soh|le ['zo:lə] F -, -n **a** *(= Fußsohle etc)* sole; *(= Einlage)* insole; **auf leisen ~n** *(poet)* softly, noiselessly; **mit nackten ~n** barefoot; **es brennt ihm unter den ~n** he has itchy feet *(inf)*, his feet are itching *(inf)*; **eine kesse ~ aufs Parkett legen** *(inf hum)* to put up a good show on the dance floor → **heften VR b**, **Scheitel a** **b** *(= Boden)* bottom; *(= Talsohle)* floor, bottom **c** *(Min)* *(= Grubenboden)* floor; *(= Stollen)* level

soh|len ['zo:lən] VT to sole

Soh|len|le|der NT, **Sohl|le|der** NT sole leather

Sohn [zo:n] M -(e)s, ¨-e ['zø:nə] *(lit, fig)* son; **Gottes ~** *(Bibl)* **der ~ Gottes** *(Bibl)* the Son of God; **des Menschen ~** *(Bibl)* the Son of Man; **na, mein ~** well, son *or* sonny → **verloren**

Söhn|chen ['zø:nçən] NT -s, - *dim von* **Sohn**

Soh|ne|mann ['zo:nəman] M *pl* **-männer** *(dial inf)* son, sonny

Söhn|lein ['zø:nlain] NT -s, - *dim von* **Sohn**

soig|niert [soan'ji:ɐt] ADJ *(geh)* elegant; *Frau auch* soignée; *Mann auch* soigné

Soi|ree [soa're:] F -, -n [-'re:ən] soirée

So|ja ['zo:ja] F -, **Sojen** ['zo:jən] soya *(esp Brit)*, soy

So|ja-: **So|ja|boh|ne** F soya bean *(esp Brit)*, soybean; **So|ja|boh|nen|kei|me** PL → **Sojasprossen**; **So|ja|so|ße** F soya *(esp Brit) or* soy sauce; **So|ja|spros|sen** PL soya bean *(esp Brit) or* soybean sprouts *pl*

So|ko ['zo:ko] F -, -s *abbr von* **Sonderkommission**

Sok|ra|tes ['zo:kratɛs] M -' Socrates

sok|ra|tisch [zo'kra:tɪʃ] ADJ Socratic

so|lang [zo'laŋ], **so|lan|ge** [zo'laŋə] CONJ as *or* so long as

So|lar- *in cpds* solar; **So|lar|an|la|ge** F solar power plant; **So|lar|an|trieb** M solar drive; **so|lar|be|trie|ben** ADJ solar-powered, driven by solar power *pred*; **So|lar|ener|gie** F solar energy

So|la|ri|um [zo'la:riʊm] NT -s, **Solarien** [-riən] solarium

So|lar|mo|bil NT solar-powered vehicle

So|lar|ple|xus [zola:ɐ'plɛksʊs] M -, - *(Anat)* solar plexus

So|lar-: **So|lar|strom** M, *no pl* solar electricity; **So|lar|zel|le** F solar cell

Sol|bad ['zo:lba:t] NT *(= Bad)* saltwater *or* brine bath; *(= Badeort)* saltwater spa

solch [zɔlç] ADJ *inv*, **sol|che(r, s)** ['zɔlçə] ADJ such; **ein ~er Mensch, ~ ein Mensch** such a person, a person like that; **~e Menschen** people like that, such people; **~es Wetter/Glück** such weather/luck; **wir haben ~en Durst/~e Angst** we're so thirsty/afraid; **~ langer Weg** such a long way; **der Mensch als ~er** man as such; **~es** that kind of thing; **~e** *(Leute)* such people; **Experten und ~e, die es werden wollen** experts and people who would like to be experts; **Rechtsanwälte gibt es ~e und ~e** there are lawyers and lawyers; **ich hätte gern ~e und ~e (Bonbons)** I'd like some of those (sweets) and some of those

sol|cher-: **sol|cher|art** ['zɔlçɐla:ɐt] ADJ *attr inv* *(geh)* such; **sol|cher|ge|stalt** ['zɔlçɐgə'ʃtalt] ADV *(geh)* = **dergestalt**; **sol|cher|lei** ['zɔlçɐ'lai] ADJ *attr inv* *(geh)* such; **sol|cher|ma|ßen** ['zɔlçɐ'ma:sn] ADV to such an extent, so; **~ ermutigt, wagten wir ...** thus emboldened, we ventured ...

Sold [zɔlt] M -(e)s [-dəs], *no pl (Mil)* pay; **in jds ~** *(dat)* **stehen** *(old)* to be in sb's employ; *(pej)* to be in sb's pay

Sol|dat [zɔl'da:t] M -en, -en, **Sol|da|tin** [-'da:tɪn] F -, -nen soldier; **bei den ~en sein** *(dated)* to be in the army, to be a soldier; **zu den ~en kommen** *(dated)*, **~ werden** to join the army, to join up *(inf)*, to become a soldier; **~ spielen** to play soldiers → **Grabmal**

Sol|da|ten-: **Sol|da|ten|fried|hof** M military cemetery; **Sol|da|ten|ge|setz** NT military regulations *pl, no art*; **Sol|da|ten|lied** NT army *or* soldier's song; **Sol|da|ten|rat** M soldiers' council; *(= Sowjet)* soldiers' soviet; **Sol|da|ten|rock** M *(old)* military *or* soldier's uniform; **Sol|da|ten|spra|che** F military *or* soldier's slang; **Sol|da|ten|stie|fel** M army *or* soldier's *(esp Brit)* boot; **Sol|da|ten|tum** [zɔl'da:tntu:m] NT -s, *no pl* soldiership *no art*, soldiery *no art*; *(Tradition)* military tradition

Sol|da|tes|ka [zɔlda'tɛska] F -, **Soldatesken** [-'tɛskn] *(pej)* band of soldiers

Sol|da|tin [-'da:tɪn] F -, -nen soldier → *auch* **Soldat**

sol|da|tisch [zɔl'da:tɪʃ] ADJ *(= militärisch)* military; *(= soldatengemäß)* soldierly ADV *sich verhalten* like a soldier; **~ stramm stehen** to stand up straight like a soldier; **~ grüßen** to salute

Sold|buch NT *(Hist)* military passbook

Söld|ner ['zœldnɐ] M -s, -, **Söld|ne|rin** [-ərɪn] F -, -nen mercenary

Söld|ner|heer NT army of mercenaries, mercenary army

Söld|ner|trup|pe F mercenary force

So|le ['zo:lə] F -, -n brine, salt water

Sol|ei ['zo:llai] NT pickled egg

So|li *pl von* **Solo**

So|li ['zo:li] M -s, *no pl (inf)* = **Solidaritätszuschlag**

so|lid [zo'li:t] ADJ ADV = **solide**

So|li|dar-: **So|li|dar|bei|trag** M *(von Interessengemeinschaft)* supportive contribution *(to public funds, social services etc)*; **So|li|dar|ge|mein|schaft** F (mutually) supportive society; *(= Beitragszahler)* contributors *pl*; **der ~ zur Last fallen** to be a burden on the social security system

so|li|da|risch [zoli'da:rɪʃ] ADJ showing solidarity; **sich mit jdm ~ erklären** to declare one's solidarity with sb; **eine ~e Haltung zeigen** to show (one's) solidarity; **in ~er Übereinstimmung** in complete solidarity; **sich mit jdm ~ fühlen** to feel solidarity with sb ADV in/showing solidarity; **~ mit jdm handeln** to act in solidarity with sb

so|li|da|ri|sie|ren [zolidari'zi:rən] *ptp* **solidarisiert** VR **sich ~ mit** to show (one's) solidarity with

So|li|da|ri|tät [zolidari'tɛ:t] F -, *no pl* solidarity; **~ üben** to show solidarity

So|li|da|ri|täts-: **So|li|da|ri|täts|ad|res|se** F message of solidarity; **So|li|da|ri|täts|ak|ti|on** F solidarity campaign; **So|li|da|ri|täts|bei|trag** M solidarity contribution; **So|li|da|ri|täts|be|kun|dung** F *usu pl* declaration of solidarity; **So|li|da|ri|täts|fonds** M solidarity fund; **So|li|da|ri|täts|ge|fühl** NT feeling of solidarity; **So|li|da|ri|täts|prin|zip** NT principle of solidarity; **So|li|da|ri|täts|streik** M sympathy strike; **So|li|da|ri|täts|zu|schlag** M *(Fin)* solidarity surcharge on income tax *(for the reconstruction of eastern Germany)*

SOLIDARITÄTSZUSCHLAG

The **Solidaritätszuschlag** (colloquially known as the **Soli**) is a supplementary tax to which everyone in paid employment in Germany and every German firm must pay. It is designed to help cover the huge costs associated with re-unification and the economic development of the former East Germany. As soon as the **Aufbau Ost** is concluded, there should be no further need for the **Soli**. → AUFBAU OST

So|li|dar|pakt [zoli'da:ɐ-] M solidarity pact *or* agreement

So|li|dar|zu|schlag M = **Solidaritätszuschlag**

so|li|de [zo'li:də] ADJ *Haus, Möbel etc* solid, sturdy; *Arbeit, Wissen, Mechaniker, Politik, Basis, Finanzen* sound; *Ausbildung* sound, solid; *Mensch, Leben, Lokal* respectable; *Firma, Mehrheit* solid; *Preise* reasonable ADV **a** *(= untadelig)* **~ leben** to lead a well-ordered life **b** *(= stabil)* **~ gebaut** solidly built; **~ konstruiert** well-constructed **c** *(= gründlich) arbeiten* thoroughly; **~ ausgebildet** well-trained **d** *(= überzeugend) begründen* solidly; **~ argumentieren** to have well-founded arguments

So|li|di|tät [zolidi'tɛ:t] F -, *no pl (von Haus, Möbeln etc)* solidness, sturdiness; *(von Arbeit, Wissen, Finanzen)* soundness; *(von Firma)* solidness

So|lip|sis|mus [zolɪ'psɪsmʊs] M -, *no pl (Philos)* solipsism

So|list [zo'lɪst] M -en, -en, **So|lis|tin** [-'lɪstɪn] F -, -nen *(Mus)* soloist

so|lis|tisch [zo'lɪstɪʃ] ADJ ADV solo

So|li|tär [zoli'tɛ:ɐ] M -s, -e solitaire; *(= Diamant)* diamond solitaire, solitaire diamond

Soll [zɔl] NT -(s), -(s) **a** *(= Schuld)* debit; *(= Schuldseite)* debit side; **~ und Haben** debit and credit **b** *(Comm: = Planaufgabe)* target

Soll|bruch|stel|le F *(Tech)* predetermined breaking point

sol|len ['zɔlən]

28.1, 29, 30, 37.2, 41, 43.1, 43.2, 47.1, 53.2, 53.6

1 HILFSVERB
2 INTRANSITIVES VERB
3 TRANSITIVES VERB

1 – HILFSVERB

pret **sollte**, ['zɔltə] *ptp* **sollen**

a Befehl, Verpflichtung, Plan **was soll ich/er tun?** what shall *or* should I/should he do?; *(= was sind meine/seine Aufgaben auch)* what do I/does he have to do?; **kannst du mir helfen? – klar, was soll ich tun?** can you help me? – of course, what shall I do?; **soll ich Ihnen helfen?** can I help you?; **soll ich dir mal sagen, wie ...?** shall *or* will I tell you how ...?; **soll ich (gehen/singen)? – ja, du sollst (gehen/singen)** shall I (go/sing)? – yes, do; **du weißt, dass du das nicht tun sollst** you know that you're not supposed to do that; **er weiß nicht, was er tun soll** he doesn't know what to do; *(= kennt seine Aufgaben nicht auch)* he doesn't know what he's meant to do; **sie sagte ihm, er solle draußen warten** she told him (that he was) to wait outside; **er wurde wütend, weil er draußen warten sollte** he was livid that he had to wait outside; **sie sagte mir, was ich tun sollte/was ich alles tun soll** she told me what to do *or* what I should do/everything I should do; **was ich (nicht) alles tun/wissen soll!** the things I'm meant *or* supposed to do/know!; **es soll nicht wieder vorkommen** it won't happen again; **er soll reinkommen** tell him to come in; **der soll nur kommen!** just let him come!; **und da soll man nicht böse werden/nicht lachen!** and then they expect you/me *etc* not to get cross/not to laugh; **niemand soll sagen, dass ...** let no-one say that ...; **ich soll Ihnen sagen, dass ...** I've been asked to tell you that ...; **ich soll dir schöne Grüße von Renate bestellen** Renate asked me to give you her best wishes; **du sollst nicht töten** *(Bibl)* thou shalt not kill; **so soll es sein** that's how it should be; **das Haus soll nächste Woche gestrichen werden** the house is to be painted next week; **das Gebäude soll ein Museum werden** the building is (meant) to become a museum

b konjunktivisch **was sollte ich/er deiner Meinung nach tun?** what do you think I/he should do *or* ought to do?; **so etwas sollte man nicht tun** one shouldn't do that, one oughtn't to do that *(esp Brit)*; **das hättest du nicht tun sollen** you shouldn't have *or* oughtn't to have *(esp Brit)* done that; **das hättest du sehen sollen!** you should have seen it!; **er hätte (gehen/singen) sollen** he should have (gone/sung); **du solltest lieber etwas früher kommen/zu Hause bleiben** it would be better if you came early/stayed at home

c konditional **sollte das passieren, …** if that should happen …, should that happen …; **sollte ich unrecht haben, tut es mir leid** I'm sorry if I am wrong

d Vermutung, Erwartung to be supposed *or* meant to; **er soll heute kommen** he should come today, he is supposed *or* meant to come today; **sie soll krank/verheiratet sein** apparently she's ill/married; **er soll angeblich sehr reich sein** he's supposed to be very rich; **Xanthippe soll zänkisch gewesen sein** Xanthippe is supposed to have been quarrelsome; **das soll gar nicht so einfach sein** they say it's not that easy; **was soll das heißen?** what's that supposed to mean?; **wer soll das sein?** who is that supposed *or* meant to be?

e = können, mögen **gut, Sie sollen recht haben!** all right, have it your own way *(inf)*, all right, whatever you say; **mir soll es gleich sein** it's all the same to me; **so etwas soll es geben** these things happen; **man sollte glauben, dass …** you would think that …; **sollte das möglich sein?** is that possible?

f in Prophezeihung *geh* **er sollte sie nie wiedersehen** he was never to see her again; **es hat nicht sollen sein** it wasn't to be; **Jahre sollten vergehen, bevor …** years were to pass before …; **es sollte nicht lange dauern, bis …** it was not to be long until …

2 – INTRANSITIVES VERB

pret **sollte** ['zɔltə], *ptp* **gesollt** [gə'zɔlt]

(= *bewirken, bedeuten, in Fragen* [gə'zɔlt]) **was soll das?** what's all this?; (= *warum denn das*) what's that for?; **was solls!** *(inf)* what the hell! *(inf)*; **was soll der Quatsch** *or* **Mist?** *(inf)* what's this stupid nonsense? *(inf)*; **was soll ich dort?** what would I do there?

3 – TRANSITIVES VERB

pret **sollte** ['zɔltə], *ptp* **gesollt** [gə'zɔlt]

das sollst/solltest du nicht you shouldn't do that; **das hast du nicht gesollt** you shouldn't have done that; **was man nicht alles soll** *or* **sollte!** *(inf)* the things you're expected to do!

Söl|ler ['zœlɐ] M **-s, -** balcony

Soll-: **Soll|sei|te** F *(Fin)* debit side; **Soll|stär|ke** F required *or* authorized strength; **Soll|zin|sen** PL *(Fin)* interest owing *sing*

so|lo ['zo:lo] ADV *(Mus)* solo; *(fig inf)* on one's own, alone

So|lo ['zo:lo] NT **-s, Soli** ['zo:li] *(alle Bedeutungen)* solo

So|lo- *in cpds* solo; **So|lo|auf|tritt** M *(auf Bühne etc)* solo performance *or* appearance; **So|lo|ge|sang** M solo; **So|lo|ge|schäft** NT *(St Ex)* outright transaction; **So|lo|in|stru|ment** NT solo instrument; **So|lo|kar|ri|e|re** F career as a soloist; **So|lo|künst|ler(in)** M(F) solo artist; **So|lo|stim|me** F (= *Stimme*) solo voice; (= *Part*) solo part; **So|lo|tän|zer(in)** M(F) solo dancer; *(im Ballett)* principal dancer

So|lo|thurn ['zo:lotʊrn] NT **-s** (= *Kanton, Stadt*) Solothurn

sol|vent [zɔl'vɛnt] ADJ *(Fin)* solvent

Sol|venz [zɔl'vɛnts] F **-, -en** *(Fin)* solvency

So|ma|li [zo'ma:li] M **-(s), -(s)** *or f* **-, -s** Somali

So|ma|lia [zo'ma:lia] NT **-s** Somalia

So|ma|li|er [zo'ma:liɐ] M **-s, -**, **So|ma|li|e|rin** [-iərɪn] F **-, -nen** Somali

So|ma|li|halb|in|sel F, **So|ma|li|land** NT **-(e)s** Somaliland

so|ma|lisch [zo'ma:lɪʃ] ADJ Somali

so|ma|tisch [zo'ma:tɪʃ] *(Med)* ADJ somatic ADV *krank* somatically; **~ bedingt sein** to have a somatic cause

Somb|re|ro [zɔm'bre:ro] M **-s, -s** sombrero

so|mit [zo'mɪt, 'zo:mɪt] ADV consequently, therefore

Som|me|li|er [zɔmə'lie:] M **-s, -s**, **Som|me|li|e|re** [zɔmə'lie:rə] F **-, -n** wine waiter *(Brit)*, wine server *(US)*

Som|mer ['zɔmɐ] M **-s, -** summer; **im ~, des ~s** *(geh)* in (the) summer; **im nächsten ~** next summer; **im ~ (des Jahres) 1951** in the summer of 1951; **~ wie** *or* **und Winter** all year round

Som|mer- *in cpds* summer; **Som|mer|abend** M summer('s) evening; **Som|mer|an|fang** M beginning of summer; **Som|mer|fahr|plan** M summer timetable; **Som|mer|fell** NT *(Zool)* summer coat; **Som|mer|fe|ri|en** PL summer holidays *pl (Brit) or* vacation *(US)*; *(Jur, Parl)* summer recess; **in die ~ fahren** to go away for the *or* one's summer holidays *(Brit) or* vacation *(US)*; **in die ~ gehen** to begin one's summer holidays *(Brit) or* vacation *(US)*; *(Sch auch)* to break up for the summer (holidays) *(Brit)*; *(Univ)* to go down for the summer; *(Jur, Parl)* to go into the summer recess; **Som|mer|fest** NT summer party; **Som|mer|flug|plan** M summer flight schedule; **Som|mer|fri|sche** F *(dated)* **a** *no pl* (= *Sommerurlaub*) summer holiday *(esp Brit) or* vacation *(US) or* break; **in die ~ gehen** to go away for a summer holiday *etc* **b** *(Ort)* summer resort; **Som|mer|frisch|ler** [-frɪʃlɐ] M **-s, -**, **Som|mer|frisch|le|rin** [-ərɪn] F **-, -nen** *(dated)* summer holiday-maker *(Brit) or* vacationist *(US)*; **Som|mer|gast** M summer guest; **Som|mer|gers|te** F spring barley; **Som|mer|ge|trei|de** NT spring cereal; **Som|mer|halb|jahr** NT summer semester, ≈ summer term *(Brit)*; **Som|mer|haus** NT holiday home *(esp Brit)*; **Som|mer|kleid** NT **a** *(Kleidungsstück)* summer dress **b** (= *Sommerfell*) summer coat; *(von Vögeln)* summer plumage; **Som|mer|klei|dung** F summer clothing; *(esp Comm)* summerwear

som|mer|lich ['zɔmɐlɪç] ADJ (= *sommerartig, heiter*) summery; (= *Sommer-*) summer *attr* ADV **es ist ~ warm** it's as warm as it is in summer; **~ heiße Temperaturen** hot summery temperatures; **~ gekleidet sein** to be in summer clothes

Som|mer-: **Som|mer|loch** NT *(inf)* silly *(Brit) or* off *(US)* season; **Som|mer|mo|nat** M summer month; **Som|mer|nacht** F summer('s) night; **Som|mer|olym|pi|a|de** F Summer Olympics *pl*; **Som|mer|pau|se** F summer break; *(Jur, Parl)* summer recess; **Som|mer|rei|fen** M normal tyre *(Brit) or* tire *(US)*

som|mers ['zɔmɐs] ADV *(geh)* in summer; **~ wie winters** all year round

Som|mer-: **Som|mer|sai|son** F summer season; **Som|mer|schluss|ver|kauf** M summer sale; **Som|mer|se|mes|ter** NT *(Univ)* summer semester, ≈ summer term *(Brit)*; **Som|mer|sitz** M summer residence; **Som|mer|son|nen|wen|de** F summer solstice; **Som|mer|spie|le** PL Summer Games *pl*; **die Olympischen ~** the Summer Olympics, the Summer Olympic Games; **Som|mer|spros|se** F freckle; **som|mer|spros|sig** [-ʃprɔsɪç] ADJ freckled

som|mers|über ['zɔmɐsly:bɐ] ADV during summer

Som|mer-: **Som|mer|tag** M summer's day; **Som|mer|the|a|ter** NT open-air theatre *(Brit) or* theater *(US)*; **Som|mer|wei|zen** M spring wheat; **Som|mer|woh|nung** F holiday flat *(Brit)*, vacation apartment *(US)*; **Som|mer|wet|ter** NT summer weather; **Som|mer|zeit** F summer time *no art*; *(geh:* = *Sommer)* summertime, summertide *(liter)*; **zur ~** *(geh)* in summertime

som|nam|bul [zɔmnam'bu:l] ADJ *(spec)* somnambulary

Som|nam|bu|le(r) [zɔmnam'bu:lə] MF *decl as adj (spec)* somnambulist

Som|nam|bu|lis|mus [zɔmnambu'lɪsmʊs] M **-**, *no pl (spec)* somnambulism

so|nach [zo'na:x, 'zo:na:x] ADV *(old)* = **somit**

So|nar [zo'na:ɐ] NT **-s, -e** sonar

So|nar|ge|rät NT sonar (device)

So|na|te [zo'na:tə] F **-, -n** sonata

So|na|ti|ne [zona'ti:nə] F **-, -n** sonatina

Son|de ['zɔndə] F **-, -n** *(Space, Med: zur Untersuchung)* probe; *(Med: zur Ernährung)* tube; *(Met)* sonde

son|der ['zɔndɐ] PREP *+acc (obs)* without

Son|der- *in cpds* special; **Son|der|ab|druck** M *(Typ)* offprint; **Son|der|ab|fall** M hazardous *or* special waste; **Son|der|ab|ga|be** F special tax, special impost *(spec)*; **Son|der|ab|schrei|bung** F *(von Steuern)* special depreciation allowance; **Son|der|an|fer|ti|gung** F special model; **eine ~ sein** to have been made specially; **Son|der|an|ge|bot** NT special offer; **im ~ sein** to be on special offer; **Son|der|aus|bil|dung** F specialist *or* special training; **Son|der|aus|füh|rung** F special model *or* version; *(Auto auch)* custom-built model; **Son|der|aus|ga|be** F **a** special edition **b** **Sonderausgaben** PL *(Fin)* additional *or* extra expenses *pl*; **Son|der|aus|stel|lung** F special exhibition

son|der|bar ADJ strange, peculiar, odd ADV strangely; **~ klingen** to sound strange; **sich ~ benehmen** to act strangely *or (esp US)* strange

son|der|ba|rer|wei|se ['zɔndɐba:rɐ'vaizə] ADV strangely enough, strange to say

Son|der-: **Son|der|be|auf|trag|te(r)** MF *decl as adj (Pol)* special emissary; **Son|der|be|richt|er|stat|ter(in)** M(F) *(Press)* special correspondent; **Son|der|bot|schaf|ter(in)** M(F) ambassador/ambassadress extraordinary; **Son|der|druck** M *pl* **-drucke** offprint; **Son|der|ein|satz** M special action; **Son|der|er|laub|nis** F special permission; (= *Schriftstück*) special permit; **Son|der|er|mitt|ler(in)** M(F) special investigator; **Son|der|fahrt** F special excursion *or* trip; **„Sonderfahrt"** *(auf Schild)* "special"; **Son|der|fall** M special case; (= *Ausnahme*) exception; **Son|der|ge|neh|mi|gung** F special permission; *(Schein)* special permit; **Son|der|ge|richt** NT special court; **son|der|glei|chen** ['zɔndɐglaiçn] ADJ *inv* **eine Geschmacklosigkeit ~** the height of bad taste; **mit einer Arroganz ~** with unparalleled arrogance; **Son|der|klas|se** F special class; *(von Obst etc)* top grade; **Son|der|kom|man|do** NT special unit; **Son|der|kom|mis|si|on** F special commission; **Son|der|kon|to** NT special account

son|der|lich ['zɔndɐlɪç] ADJ *attr* particular, especial, special; **ohne ~e Begeisterung** without any particular enthusiasm, without much enthusiasm ADV particularly, especially

Son|der|ling ['zɔndɐlɪŋ] M **-s, -e** eccentric

Son|der-: **Son|der|mar|ke** F special issue (stamp); **Son|der|ma|schi|ne** F special plane *or* aircraft; **Son|der|mel|dung** F *(Rad, TV)* special announcement; **Son|der|müll** M hazardous waste; **Son|der|müll|de|po|nie** F hazardous waste depot

son|dern ['zɔndɐn] CONJ but; **~?** where/who/what *etc* then?; **wir fahren nicht nach Spanien, ~ nach Frankreich** we're not going to Spain, we're going to France, we're not going to Spain but to France; **nicht nur …, ~ auch** not only … but also

son|dern VT *(old, geh)* to separate *(von* from) → *auch* **gesondert**

Son|der-: **Son|der|num|mer** F *(Press)* special edition *or* issue; **Son|der|pä|da|go|gik** F remedial *or* special education; **Son|der|par|tei|tag** M special party conference *or* convention;

Son|der|preis M special reduced price; **Son|der|recht** NT (special) privilege; **Son|der|re|ge|lung** F special provision

son|ders ['zɔndɐs] ADV → **samt**

Son|der-: **Son|der|schicht** F special shift; *(zusätzlich)* extra shift; **Son|der|schu|le** F special school; **Son|der|schul|leh|rer(in)** M(F) teacher at a special school

SONDERSCHULE

A **Sonderschule** is a school for disabled and special-needs children. It aims to develop their abilities and help to compensate for their disability. Opportunities also exist for children to move to a conventional school at a later stage. There are different kinds of **Sonderschulen** catering for visually-impaired children, children with learning difficulties, and those with physical disabilities.

Son|der-: **Son|der|sen|dung** F special broadcast; **Son|der|sit|zung** F special session; *(von Vorstand)* special meeting; **Son|der|stel|lung** F special position; **Son|der|stem|pel** M *(bei der Post®)* special postmark; **Son|der|ur|laub** M *(Mil)* special leave; *(für Todesfall etc)* compassionate leave; **Son|der|voll|macht** F emergency powers *pl*; **Son|der|wirt|schafts|zo|ne** F special economic area; **Son|der|wün|sche** PL special requests *pl*; **Son|der|zah|lung** F special payment; **Son|der|zei|chen** NT *(Comput)* special character; **Son|der|zie|hungs|rech|te** PL *(Fin)* special drawing rights *pl*; **Son|der|zug** M special train; **Son|der|zu|la|ge** F special bonus

son|die|ren [zɔn'di:rən] *ptp* **sondiert** VT to sound out; **das Terrain** *or* **Gelände ~** to spy out the land; **die Lage ~** to find out how the land lies VI to sound things out; **~, ob …** to try to sound out whether …

Son|die|rung F -, -en sounding out *no pl*; **die ~ des Terrains** spying out the land; **ohne gründliche ~** without sounding things out thoroughly

Son|die|rungs|ge|spräch NT exploratory discussion *or* talk

So|nett [zo'nɛt] NT -(e)s, -e sonnet

Song [sɔŋ] M -s, -s song

Sonn|abend ['zɔnla:bnt] M Saturday → *auch* **Dienstag**

sonn|abends ['zɔnla:bnts] ADV on Saturdays, on a Saturday → *auch* **dienstags**

Son|ne ['zɔnə] F -, -n **a** sun; *(= Sonnenlicht)* sun(light); **die liebe ~** *(poet, inf)*, **Frau ~** *(poet)* the sun; **unter der ~** *(fig geh)* under the sun; **an** *or* **in die ~ gehen** to go out in the sun(shine); **er kommt viel/wenig an die ~** he gets/doesn't get a lot of sun, he goes/doesn't go out in the sun a lot; **geh mir aus der ~!** *(inf)* stop blocking my view!, get out of the way!; *(= aus dem Licht)* get out of the *or* my light!; **das Zimmer hat wenig ~** the room doesn't get much sun(light); **die ~ bringt es an den Tag** *(prov)* truth will out *(prov)*; **keine ~ sehen** *(inf)* not to have a hope in hell *(inf)*; **das Reich** *or* **Land der aufgehenden ~** the Land of the Rising Sun **b** *(= Heizsonne)* electric fire

son|nen ['zɔnən] VT *Betten* to put out in the sun VR to sun oneself; **sich in etw** *(dat)* **~** *(fig)* to bask in sth

Son|nen-: **Son|nen|an|be|ter(in)** M(F) *(lit, fig)* sun worshipper; **Son|nen|auf|gang** M sunrise, sunup *(inf)*; **den ~ abwarten** to wait for the sun to rise; **Son|nen|bad** NT sunbathing *no pl*; **ein fünfstündiges ~** five hours in the sun, five hours' sunbathing; **ein ~ nehmen** to sunbathe, to bask in the sun; **son|nen+ba|den** VI *sep infin, ptp only* to sunbathe; **Son|nen|bahn** F sun's path; **Son|nen|ball** M *(liter)* fiery orb *(liter)*; **Son|nen|bank** F *pl* **-bänke** sun bed; **Son|nen|blen|de** F *(Aut)* sun visor; *(Phot)* lens hood

Son|nen|blu|me F sunflower

Son|nen|blu|men-: **Son|nen|blu|men|kern** M sunflower seed; **Son|nen|blu|men|öl** NT sunflower oil

Son|nen-: **Son|nen|brand** M sunburn *no art*; **Son|nen|bräu|ne** F suntan; **Son|nen|bril|le** F (pair of) sunglasses *pl*, shades *pl* *(esp US inf)*; **Son|nen|creme** F suntan cream *or* lotion; **Son|nen|dach** NT awning, sun blind; *(Aut dated)* sun *or* sunshine *(Brit)* roof; **Son|nen|deck** NT *(Naut)* sun deck; **son|nen|durch|flu|tet** [-durçflu:tət] ADJ *(geh)* sunny, with the sun streaming in; **Son|nen|ein|strah|lung** F solar radiation; **Son|nen|ener|gie** F solar energy; **Son|nen|fer|ne** F *(Astron)* aphelion; **Son|nen|fins|ter|nis** F solar eclipse, eclipse of the sun; **Son|nen|fleck** M *(Astron)* sunspot; **son|nen|ge|bräunt** ADJ suntanned; **Son|nen|ge|flecht** NT *(Physiol)* solar plexus; **Son|nen|gel** NT suntan gel; **Son|nen|ge|ne|ra|tor** M *(an Satellit)* solar generator; **son|nen|ge|trock|net** sun-dried; **Son|nen|glanz** M *(poet)*, **Son|nen|glut** F *(geh)* blazing heat of the sun; **Son|nen|gott** M sun-god; **Son|nen|gür|tel** M *(der Erde)* Torrid Zone; **son|nen|halb** ['zɔnənhalp] ADV *(Sw)* = **sonnseitig**; **son|nen|hell** ADJ sunny, sunlit; **Son|nen|hit|ze** F heat of the sun; **son|nen|hung|rig** ADJ hungry for the sun; **Son|nen|hung|ri|ge** [-hʊŋrɪgə] PL *decl as adj* sun-seekers *pl*; **Son|nen|hut** M sunhat; **Son|nen|jahr** NT *(Astron)* solar year; **son|nen|klar** ADJ *(inf)* clear as daylight, crystal-clear; **Son|nen|kol|lek|tor** M solar panel; **Son|nen|kö|nig** M *(Hist)* Sun King, Roi Soleil; **Son|nen|kraft|werk** NT solar power station; **Son|nen|kult** M sun cult; **Son|nen|licht** NT sunlight; **Son|nen|milch** F suntan lotion; **Son|nen|nä|he** F *(Astron)* perihelion; **Son|nen|öl** NT suntan oil; **Son|nen|pad|del** NT *(inf: = Sonnengenerator)* solar paddle *(inf)*; **Son|nen|rad** NT *(Hist)* (representation of the) sun; **Son|nen|rol|lo** NT sun blind; **Son|nen|schein** M sunshine; **bei ~** in the sunshine; **bei strahlendem ~** in brilliant sunshine; **Son|nen|schirm** M sunshade; *(für Frauen auch)* parasol; **Son|nen|schutz** M protection against the sun; **Son|nen|schutz|fak|tor** M protection factor; **Son|nen|schutz|mit|tel** NT sunscreen; **Son|nen|se|gel** NT **a** *(= Schutzdach)* awning **b** *(bei Raumfahrzeug)* solar sail; **Son|nen|sei|te** F side facing the sun, sunny side *(auch fig)*; **Son|nen|stand** M position of the sun; **Son|nen|stich** M heatstroke *no art*, sunstroke *no art*; **du hast wohl einen ~!** *(inf)* you must have been out in the sun too long!; **Son|nen|strahl** M sunbeam, ray of sunshine; *(esp Astron, Phys)* sun ray; **Son|nen|stu|dio** NT tanning salon *(esp US)* *or* studio, solarium; **Son|nen|sys|tem** NT solar system; **Son|nen|tag** M sunny day; *(Met auch)* day of sunshine; *(Astron)* solar day; **Son|nen|ter|ras|se** F sun terrace *or* deck *(US)*; **Son|nen|uhr** F sundial; **Son|nen|un|ter|gang** M sunset, sundown; **den ~ abwarten** to wait for the sun to set; **son|nen|ver|brannt** ADJ *Vegetation* scorched; *Mensch* sunburnt; **Son|nen|wen|de** F solstice; **Son|nen|wend|fei|er** F = **Sonnwendfeier**; **Son|nen|wind** M *(Phys)* solar wind

son|nig ['zɔnɪç] ADJ *(lit, fig)* sunny

Sonn-: **Sonn|sei|te** F *(Aus)* side facing the sun, sunny side *(auch fig)*; **sonn|sei|tig** ['zɔnzaitɪç] ADV *(Aus)* **~ gelegen** facing the sun

Sonn|tag ['zɔnta:k] M Sunday → *auch* **Dienstag**

sonn|tä|gig ['zɔntɛ:gɪç] ADJ *attr* Sunday; **die gestrigen ~en Verhandlungen …** the negotiations yesterday, Sunday …

sonn|täg|lich ['zɔntɛ:klɪç] ADJ Sunday *attr* ADV **~ gekleidet** dressed in one's Sunday best; **~ ruhig** as quiet as a Sunday

sonn|tags ['zɔnta:ks] ADV on Sundays, on a Sunday → *auch* **dienstags**

Sonn|tags- *in cpds* Sunday; **Sonn|tags|ar|beit** F Sunday working; **Sonn|tags|aus|flug** M Sunday trip; **Sonn|tags|bei|la|ge** F Sunday supplement; **Sonn|tags|bra|ten** M Sunday roast; **Sonn|tags|dienst** M *(von Polizist etc)* Sunday duty; **~ haben** *(Apotheke)* to be open on Sundays; **Sonn|tags|fah|rer(in)** M(F) *(pej)* Sunday driver; **Sonn|tags|fahr|ver|bot** NT Sunday driving ban; **Sonn|tags|fra|ge** F *(inf)* question about voting intentions; **Sonn|tags|kind** NT *(lit)* Sunday's child; **ein ~ sein** *(fig)* to have been born under a lucky star; **Sonn|tags|klei|dung** F Sunday clothes *pl*; **Sonn|tags|ma|ler(in)** M(F) Sunday painter; **Sonn|tags|re|de** F *(iro)* **~n halten** to make sunshine speeches; **Sonn|tags|red|ner(in)** M(F) *(iro)* person who makes sunshine speeches; **Sonn|tags|ru|he** F **die ~ stören/einhalten** to contravene the observance of/to observe Sunday as a day of rest; **Sonn|tags|schu|le** F Sunday school; **Sonn|tags|staat** M *(hum)* Sunday best; **in vollem ~** in one's Sunday best; **Sonn|tags|zei|tung** F Sunday paper

Sonn- und Fei|er|ta|ge PL Sundays and public holidays *pl*

sonn- und fei|er|tags ['zɔnlunt'faiɐta:ks] ADV on Sundays and public holidays

Sonn|wend-: **Sonn|wend|fei|er** F *(im Sommer)* midsummer celebrations *pl*; *(im Winter)* midwinter celebrations *pl*; **Sonn|wend|feu|er** NT *bonfire at midsummer/midwinter celebrations*

Son|ny|boy ['zɔnibɔy] M -s, -s *(inf)* blue-eyed boy *(inf)*

So|no|gra|fie, **So|no|gra|phie** [zonogra'fi:] F -, -n [-'fi:ən] *(Med)* sonography

so|nor [zo'no:ɐ] ADJ sonorous

So|no|ri|tät F -, *no pl* sonority *(form)*, sonorousness

sonst [zɔnst] ADV **a** *(= außerdem) (mit pron, adv)* else; *(mit n)* other; **~ keine Besucher/Zeitungen** *etc* no other visitors/papers *etc*; **~ noch Fragen?** any other questions?; **wer/wie** *etc* **(denn) ~?** who/how *etc* else?; **bringst du all deine Freunde mit? – was denn ~** are you bringing all your friends? – of course; **~ niemand** *or* **keiner/(noch) jemand** *or* **wer** *(inf)* nobody/somebody else; **das kannst du ~ jemandem** *or* **wem** *(inf)* **erzählen** tell that to the marines *(Brit inf)* *or* to the judge *(US)*; **der Text ist von Handke oder ~ jemandem** *or* **wem** *(inf)* the text is by Handke or somebody; **da kann ~ wer kommen, wir machen keine Ausnahme** *(inf)* it doesn't matter who it is, we're not making any exceptions; **das kannst du ~ wem schenken** *(inf)* you can give that to some other sucker *(inf)* *or* to somebody else; **es könnte ~ wer kommen** *(inf)* anybody might come; **ich will weder dich noch ~ jemanden** *or* **wen** *(inf)* **sehen** I don't want to see you or anyone else; **er und ~ keiner** nobody else but he, he and nobody else, he and he alone; **wenn du ~ irgendjemanden kennst** if you know somebody else *or* anybody else *or* any other person; **~ wann** *(inf)* some other time; **wenn du ~ irgendwann mal kommen kannst** if you can come some *or* any other time; **er denkt, er ist ~ wer** *(inf)* he thinks he's somebody special, he thinks he's the bee's knees *(Brit inf)* *or* the cat's whiskers *(Brit inf)* *or* the cat's meow *(US inf)*; **~ nichts/noch etwas** nothing/something else; **da kann ja ~ was passieren** *(inf)* anything could happen; **von mir aus kannst du ~ was machen** *(inf)* as far as I'm concerned you can do whatever you like; **ich habe ~ was versucht** *(inf)* I've tried everything; **ich werde weder das tun noch ~ was** *(inf)* I won't do that or anything else; **~ noch etwas?** is that all?, anything else?; *(in Geschäft auch)* will there be anything else?, will that be all?; **ja ~ noch was?** *(iro inf)* that'd be right! *(inf)*; **~ wie** *(inf)* (in) some other way; *(= sehr)* like mad *(inf)* *or* crazy *(inf)*; **~ wo** *(inf)* somewhere else; **~ wo, nur nicht hier** anywhere (else) but here; **~ wohin** *(inf)* somewhere else; **wo soll ich hingehen? – von mir aus ~ wohin** where should I go? – (as far as I'm concerned,) anywhere you like; **das kannst du dir ~ wohin stecken!** *(inf)* you can stuff that! *(inf)*, you know where you can put that! *(inf)*; **~ bist du gesund?** *(iro inf)* **~ gehts dir gut?** *(iro inf)* are you feeling okay? *(inf)*; **~ willst du nichts?** *(iro inf)* anything else you'd like?; **und wer weiß was ~ noch alles** and goodness knows what else; **wo warst du ~ überall?** where else were you?

b *(= andernfalls, im übrigen)* otherwise; **wie gehts ~?** how are things otherwise *or* apart from that?

c *(= in anderer Hinsicht)* in other ways; **wenn ich Ihnen ~ noch behilflich sein kann** if I can help you in any *or* some other way

d *(= gewöhnlich)* usually; **genau wie es ~ ist** just as it usually is; **genau wie ~** the same as usual; **anders als ~** different from usual; **mehr/weniger als ~** more/less than usual; **der ~ so mürrische Herr Grün war heute direkt freundlich** Mr Grün, who is usually so grumpy, was really friendly today

e *(= früher)* **alles war wie ~** everything was as it always used to be; **war das auch ~ der Fall?** was that always the case?; **wenn er ~ zu Besuch hier war** when he has visited us before

CONJ otherwise, or (else)

sons|tig ['zɔnstɪç] ADJ *attr* other; *Fragen, Auskünfte etc* further; **aber ihr ~es Verhalten ist/ihre ~en Leistungen sind verhältnismäßig gut** but her behaviour *(Brit)* or behavior *(US)*/performance otherwise is quite good; **„Sonstiges"** "other"

sonst-: **sonst|je|mand** △ INDEF PRON *(inf)* → **sonst** ADV **a**; **sonst|wann** △ ADV → **sonst** ADV **a**; **sonst|was** △ INDEF PRON → **sonst** ADV **a**; **sonst|wer** △ INDEF PRON → **sonst** ADV **a**; **sonst|wie** △ ADV → **sonst** ADV **a**; **sonst|wo** △ ADV → **sonst** ADV **a**; **sonst|wo|hin** △ ADV → **sonst** ADV **a**

so|oft [zo'ɔft] CONJ whenever

Soor [zoːɐ] M **-(e)s, -e** *(Med)* thrush *no art*

So|phis|mus [zo'fɪsmʊs] M **-, Sophismen** [-mən] sophism

So|phist [zo'fɪst] M **-en, -en**, **So|phis|tin** [-'fɪstɪn] F **-, -nen** sophist

So|phis|te|rei [zofɪstə'rai] F **-, -en** sophistry

So|phis|tik [zo'fɪstɪk] F **-**, *no pl* sophistry

So|phok|les ['zoːfokles] M **-'** Sophocles

So|pran [zo'praːn] M **-s, -e** soprano; *(= Knabensopran, Instrumentensopran auch)* treble; *(Chorstimmen)* sopranos *pl*/trebles *pl*

So|pra|nist [zopra'nɪst] M **-en, -en** treble

So|pra|nis|tin [zopra'nɪstɪn] F **-, -nen** soprano

Sor|be ['zɔrbə] M **-n, -n**, **Sor|bin** ['zɔrbɪn] F **-, -nen** Sorb

Sor|bet [zɔr'beː] M OR NT **-s, -s**, **Sor|bett** [zɔr'bɛt] M OR NT **-(e)s, -e** *(Cook)* sorbet

Sor|bin|säu|re [zɔr'biːn-] F sorbic acid

sor|bisch ['zɔrbɪʃ] ADJ Sorbian

Sor|bisch(e) ['zɔrbɪʃ] NT *decl as adj (Ling)* Sorbian → **Deutsch(e)**

So|re ['zoːrə] F **-**, *no pl (sl)* loot, swag *(hum)*

Sor|ge ['zɔrgə] F **-, -n** **a** worry; *(= Ärger)* trouble; *(= Kummer)* care, worry; **frei von ~n** free of care *or* worries; **keine ~!** *(inf)* don't (you) worry!; **~ haben, ob/dass ...** to be worried whether/that ...; **wir betrachten diese Entwicklung mit ~** we view this development with concern; **~n haben** to have problems; **nichts als ~n haben** to have nothing but problems *(inf)*; **ich habe solche ~** I'm so worried; **du hast ~n!** *(iro)* **deine ~n möchte ich haben!** *(inf)* you think you've got problems!; **~n haben die Leute!** the worries people have!; **mit ihm/damit haben wir nichts als ~n** we've had nothing but trouble with him/that; **ich habe andere ~n, als ...** I have other things to worry about than ...; **jdm ~n machen** *or* **bereiten** *(= Kummer bereiten)* to cause sb a lot of worry; *(= beunruhigen)* to worry sb; **es macht mir ~n, dass ...** it worries me that ...; **in ~** *(dat)* **sein** to be worried; **sich** *(dat)* **~n machen** to worry; **wir haben uns solche ~n gemacht** we were so worried; **machen Sie sich deshalb keine ~n** don't worry about that; **seien Sie ohne ~!** *(geh)* do not fear *(liter) or* worry; **lassen Sie das meine ~ sein** let me worry about that; **das ist nicht meine ~** that's not my problem; **für etw ~ tragen** *(geh)* to attend *or* see to sth, to take care of sth; **dafür ~ tragen, dass ...** *(geh)* to see to it that ...

b *(= Fürsorge, auch Jur)* care

Sor|ge-: **sor|ge|be|rech|tigt** ADJ **~ sein** to have custody; **Sor|ge|be|rech|tig|te(r)** [-bərɛçtɪçtə] MF *decl as adj* person having custody

sor|gen ['zɔrgn] VR to worry; **sich ~ um** to be worried about, to worry about

VI **~ für** *(= sich kümmern um)* to take care of, to look after; *(= betreuen auch)* to care for; *(= vorsorgen für)* to provide for; *(= herbeischaffen) Proviant, Musik* to provide; *(= bewirken)* to ensure; *Aufregung* to cause; **dafür ~, dass ...** to see to it that ..., to make sure that ...; **für Schlagzeilen ~** to make headlines; **für Wirbel ~** to cause a commotion; **für Ruhe/einen reibungslosen Ablauf ~** to make sure that things are quiet/go smoothly; **für Aufsehen ~** to cause a sensation; **das reichlich fließende Bier sorgte für Stimmung** the plentiful supply of beer made sure that things went with a swing; **dafür ist gesorgt** that's taken care of

Sor|gen-: **Sor|gen|fal|te** F worry line; **sor|gen|frei** ADJ free of care; *(= heiter, sich keine Sorgen machend)* carefree ADV **~ leben** to live a carefree life; **Sor|gen|kind** NT *(inf)* problem child; *(fig auch)* biggest headache *(inf)*; **Aktion ~** *(dated) charity for people with disabilities*; **Sor|gen|last** F *(geh)* burden of one's cares; **sor|gen|los** ADJ, ADV = **sorgenfrei**; **Sor|gen|püpp|chen** NT worry doll; **sor|gen|schwer** ADJ *Stimme, Blick* troubled; *Leben* full of cares; **Sor|gen|te|le|fon** NT helpline; **sor|gen|voll** ADJ *Blick, Miene* worried; *Leben* full of worries ADV *sagen* worried, with worry; **~ seufzen** to give a worried sigh; **..., seufzte er ~** ..., he said with a worried sigh; **etw ~ betrachten** to view sth with concern; **einer Sache ~ entgegensehen** to await sth with concern

Sor|ge|recht NT *(Jur)* custody

Sorg|falt ['zɔrkfalt] F **-**, *no pl* care; **ohne ~ arbeiten** to work carelessly; **viel ~ auf etw** *(acc)* **verwenden** to take a lot of care over sth

sorg|fäl|tig ['zɔrkfɛltɪç] ADJ careful ADV carefully

Sorg|falts|pflicht F *(Jur)* duty of care to a child; **Verletzung der ~** negligence of one's duties as a parent *or (als Vormund)* as a guardian

sorg|los ADJ *(= unbekümmert)* carefree; *(= leichtfertig, nachlässig)* careless ADV carelessly; in a carefree way; **jdm ~ vertrauen** to trust sb implicitly; **sie geht ganz ~ mit den Kindern um** she gets along with the children so easily

Sorg|lo|sig|keit F **-**, *no pl (= Unbekümmertheit)* carefreeness; *(= Leichtfertigkeit)* carelessness

sorg|sam ['zɔrkzaːm] ADJ careful ADV carefully; **ein ~ gehütetes Geheimnis** a well-guarded secret

Sor|te ['zɔrtə] F **-, -n** **a** sort, type, kind; *(von Waren)* variety, type; *(= Qualität, Klasse)* grade; *(= Marke)* brand; **beste** *or* **erste ~** top quality *or* grade; **diese Psychiater sind eine ganz komische ~** these psychiatrists are quite a peculiar bunch *(inf)* **b** *(Fin) usu pl* foreign currency

Sor|ten-: **Sor|ten|ge|schäft** NT, **Sor|ten|han|del** M *(Fin)* foreign currency trading; **Sor|ten|kurs** M *(Fin)* exchange rate *(for notes and coins)*

sor|ten|rein ADJ *Materialien* unmixed ADV *Materialien* **~ trennen** to separate out materials

Sor|ter ['zɔrtɐ] M **-s, -** sorting machine, sorter

sor|tie|ren [zɔr'tiːrən] *ptp* **sortiert** VT to sort *(auch Comput)*; *(beim Drucken) Kopien* to collate; *Waren (nach Qualität, Größe auch)* to grade; **etw in einen Schrank/ein Regal** *etc* **~** to sort sth and put it in a cupboard/bookcase *etc*

Sor|tie|rer [zɔr'tiːrɐ] M **-s, -**, **Sor|tie|re|rin** [-ərɪn] F **-, -nen** sorter

Sor|tier-: **Sor|tier|feld** NT *(Comput)* sort field; **Sor|tier|lauf** M *(Comput)* sort run; **Sor|tier|ma|schi|ne** F sorting machine, sorter; **Sor|tier|pro|gramm** M *(Comput)* sort(ing) program; **Sor|tier|rei|hen|fol|ge** F *(Comput)* sorting order; **Sor|tier|schlüs|sel** M *(Comput)* sort key

Sor|tie|rung [zɔr'tiːrʊŋ] F **-, -en** sorting; *(Comput: von Daten)* sort

Sor|tier-: **Sor|tier|vor|gang** M *(Comput)* sort; **Sor|tier|wert** M *(Comput)* sort value

Sor|ti|ment [zɔrti'mɛnt] NT **-(e)s, -e** **a** assortment; *(von Waren)* range, assortment; *(= Sammlung)* collection; **etw ins ~ nehmen** to add sth to one's range; **etw aus dem ~ nehmen** to drop sth from one's range **b** *(= Buchhandel)* retail book trade

Sor|ti|men|ter [zɔrti'mɛntɐ] M **-s, -**, **Sor|ti|men|te|rin** [-ərɪn] F **-, -nen** retail bookseller, book retailer

Sor|ti|ments-: **Sor|ti|ments|buch|han|del** M retail book trade; **Sor|ti|ments|buch|händ|ler(in)** M(F) retail bookseller, book retailer; **Sor|ti|ments|buch|hand|lung** F retail bookshop *(esp Brit) or* bookstore *(esp US)*

SOS [ɛsloː'lɛs] NT **-, -** SOS; **~ funken** to put out an SOS

so|sehr [zo'zeːɐ] CONJ however much, no matter how much

So|sein ['zoːzain] NT *(Philos)* essence

SOS-Kin|der|dorf NT *children's home organized into family units*

so|so [zo'zoː] ADV *(inf: = einigermaßen)* so-so *(inf)*, middling *(inf)* INTERJ **~!** I see!; *(indigniert, iro auch)* really!; *(interessiert-gelassen auch)* oh yes?; *(erstaunt)* well well!; *(drohend)* well!

SOS-Ruf M *(lit)* SOS (call), Mayday; *(fig)* SOS

So|ße ['zoːsə] F **-, -n** sauce; *(= Bratensoße)* gravy; *(pej inf)* gunge *(Brit inf)*, goo *(US inf)*; *(sl: = Sperma)* spunk *(sl)*, come *(sl)*

So|ßen|löf|fel M gravy spoon

sott *pret von* **sieden**

Soub|ret|te [zu'brɛtə] F **-, -n** soubrette

Souff|lé [zu'fleː] NT **-s, -s**, **Souff|lee** NT **-s, -s** *(Cook)* soufflé

Souff|leur [zu'fløːɐ] M **-s, -e** *(Theat)* prompter

Souff|leur|kas|ten [zu'fløːɐ-] M *(Theat)* prompt box

Souff|leu|se [zu'fløːzə] F **-, -n** *(Theat)* prompter

souff|lie|ren [zu'fliːrən] *ptp* **souffliert** VTI *(Theat)* to prompt; **jdm (den Text) ~** to prompt sb

Soul [soːl] M **-s**, *no pl (Mus)* soul

Sound [saund] M **-s, -s** *(inf)* sound

Sound|kar|te F *(Comput)* sound card, sound board

so|und|so ['zoːluntzoː] ADV **~ lange** for such and such a time; **~ groß/breit** of such and such a size/width; **~ oft** n (number of) times; **~ viele** so and so many; **Paragraf ~** article such-and--such *or* so-and-so; **er sagte, mach das ~** he said, do it in such and such a way

So|und|so ['zoːluntzoː] M **-s, -s** *or f* **-, -s der ~** whatshisname; **die ~** whatshername; **Herr/Frau ~** Mr/Mrs So-and-so; **eine Margot ~ hat gesagt ...** a Margot Something-or-other said ...

so|und|so|viel|te(r, s) ['zoːluntzofiːltə] ADJ umpteenth; **am/bis zum Soundsovielten** *(Datum)* on/by such and such a date; **er ist der Soundsovielte, der ...** he's the umpteenth person who ... *(inf)*

Sound|track ['saundtrɛk] M **-s, -s** *(inf)* soundtrack (music)

Sou|per [zu'peː] NT **-s, -s** *(geh)* dinner

sou|pie|ren [zu'piːrən] *ptp* **soupiert** VI *(geh)* to dine

Sou|ta|ne [zu'taːnə] F **-, -n** *(Eccl)* cassock

Sou|ter|rain [zutɛ'rɛ̃ː, 'zuːtɛrɛ̃] NT **-s, -s** basement

Sou|ve|nir [zuvə'niːɐ] NT **-s, -s** souvenir

Sou|ve|nir-: **Sou|ve|nir|jä|ger(in)** M(F) *(inf)* souvenir hunter; **Sou|ve|nir|la|den** M souvenir shop

sou|ve|rän [zuvə'rɛːn] ADJ sovereign *no adv*; *(fig)* supremely good; *(= überlegen)* (most) superior *no adv*; *Sieg* commanding; **das Land wurde ~** the country became a sovereign state ADV **a ~ regieren** to rule as (the) sovereign, to have sovereign power, to be sovereign **b** *(= überlegen) handhaben* supremely well; **etw ~ meistern** to resolve sth masterfully; **~ siegen** to win a commanding victory; **sein Gebiet ~ beherrschen** to have a commanding knowledge of one's field; **die Lage ~ beherrschen** to be in full command of the situation; **eine Sprache ~ beherrschen** to have a superb command of a language; **er ist ganz ~ darüber hinweggegangen** he blithely ignored it

Sou|ve|rän [zuvə'rɛːn] M **-s, -e** sovereign; *(= Parlament, Organisation)* sovereign power

Sou|ve|rä|ni|tät [zuvərɛni'tɛːt] F **-,** *no pl* sovereignty; *(fig)* *(= Überlegenheit)* superiority; *(= Leichtigkeit)* supreme ease

so|viel [zo'fiːl] ADV △ → **viel a** CONJ as *or* so far as; **~ ich weiß, nicht!** not as *or* so far as I know; **~ ich auch ...** however much I ...

so|viel|mal [zo'fiːlmaːl] ADV so many times CONJ **~ ... auch ...** no matter how many times ..., however many times ...

so|weit [zo'vait] ADV △ → **weit 1 b 2 f** CONJ as *or* so far as; *(= insofern)* in so far as; **~ ich sehe** as *or* so far as I can tell *or* see

so|we|nig [zo'veːnɪç] ADV △ → **wenig ADJ a** CONJ however little, little as; **~ ich auch ...** however little I ...

so|wie [zo'viː] CONJ **a** *(= sobald)* as soon as, the moment *(inf)* **b** *(= und auch)* as well as

so|wie|so [zovi'zoː] ADV anyway, anyhow, in any case; **wir sind ~ nicht gegangen** we didn't go anyway *or* anyhow *or* in any case; **das ~!** obviously!, of course!, that goes without saying

Sow|jet [zɔ'vjɛt, 'zɔvjɛt] M *(Hist)* **-s, -s** Soviet

Sow|jet|ar|mee F *(Hist)* Soviet Army

Sow|jet|bür|ger(in) M(F) *(Hist)* Soviet citizen

sow|je|tisch [zɔ'vjɛtɪʃ, zɔ'vjeːtɪʃ] ADJ *(Hist)* Soviet

Sow|jet- *(Hist)*: **Sow|jet|macht** F Soviet power *no art*; **Sow|jet|mensch** M Soviet citizen; **Sow|jet|re|pub|lik** F Soviet Republic; **Union der Sozialistischen ~en** Union of Soviet Socialist Republics; **Sow|jet|rus|se** M, **Sow|jet|rus|sin** F Soviet Russian; **Sow|jet|staat** M Soviet State; **Sow|jet|stern** M Soviet star, star of the Soviets; **Sow|jet|uni|on** F Soviet Union; **Sow|jet|zo|ne** F *(Hist)* Soviet zone

so|wohl [zo'voːl] CONJ **~ ... als** *or* **wie (auch)** both ... and, ... as well as

So|zi ['zoːtsi] M **-s, -s** *(pej inf)* Socialist

So|zia ['zoːtsia] F **-, -s a** *(= Partner)* partner **b** *(usu hum: = Beifahrerin)* pillion rider *or* passenger

so|zi|al [zo'tsiaːl] ADJ social; *(= sozial bewusst)* socially conscious; *(= an das Gemeinwohl denkend)* public-spirited; **die ~en Berufe** the caring professions; **~e Dienste** social services; **~er Wohnungsbau** ≈ council *(Brit)* or public *(US)* housing; **~es Jahr** *year spent by young person as voluntary assistant in hospitals, with social services etc*; **~e Indikation** *(bei Abtreibung)* social factor; **~er Friede** social harmony; **~e Marktwirtschaft** social market economy; **~e Medien** social media; **~es Netzwerk** social network; **~e Sicherheit** social security *(as a concept)*; **ich habe heute meinen ~en Tag!** *(inf)* I'm feeling charitable today ADV **~ eingestellt sein** to be public-spirited; **~ handeln** to act for the good of all; **~ denken** to be socially minded

So|zi|al-: **So|zi|al|ab|bau** M, *no pl* cuts *pl* in social services; **So|zi|al|ab|ga|ben** PL social security *(Brit) or* social welfare *(US)* contributions *pl*; **So|zi|al|amt** NT social security *(Brit) or* social welfare *(US)* office; **So|zi|al|ar|beit** F social work; **So|zi|al|ar|bei|ter(in)** M(F) social worker; **So|zi|al|aus|ga|ben** PL public spending *sing*; **So|zi|al|aus|schuss** M social committee; **So|zi|al|bei|trä|ge** PL social security *(Brit) or* social welfare *(US)* contributions *pl*; **So|zi|al|be|richt** M *(Parl)* welfare report; **So|zi|al|be|ruf** M caring profession; **So|zi|al|bin|dung** F social obligation scheme *(restricting rents etc to a socially acceptable level)*, rent control regulations *pl*; **unter die ~ fallen** to come under the social obligation scheme *or* under rent control regulations; **So|zi|al|dar|wi|nis|mus** M social Darwinism; **So|zi|al|de|mo|krat(in)** M(F) social democrat; **So|zi|al|de|mo|kra|tie** F social democracy; **so|zi|al|de|mo|kra|tisch** ADJ social democratic ADV **die ~ regierten Bundesländer** the states controlled by the Social Democrats; **~ wählen** to vote for the Social Democrats; **der ~ orientierte Flügel** the Social Democratic wing; **So|zi|al|de|mo|kra|tis|mus** [-demokratɪsmʊs] M **-,** *no pl (pej)* social democracy; **So|zi|al|ein|rich|tun|gen** PL social facilities *pl*; **So|zi|al|ethik** F social ethics *sing*; **so|zi|al|ethisch** ADJ social-ethical; **So|zi|al|ex|per|te** M, **So|zi|al|ex|per|tin** F social affairs expert; **So|zi|al|fall** M hardship case; **So|zi|al|fa|schis|mus** M socialist fascism; **So|zi|al|fonds** M social capital; **So|zi|al|for|schung** F social research; **So|zi|al|für|sor|ge** F *(dated)* income support *(Brit)*, welfare (aid) *(US)*; **So|zi|al|ge|fü|ge** NT social fabric; **So|zi|al|ge|richt** NT (social) welfare tribunal; **So|zi|al|ge|schich|te** F social history; **So|zi|al|ge|setz|ge|bung** F social welfare legislation; **So|zi|al|hil|fe** F income support *(Brit)*, welfare (aid) *(US)*; **So|zi|al|hil|fe|emp|fän|ger(in)** M(F) person receiving income support *(Brit) or* welfare (aid) *(US)*; **So|zi|al|hy|gi|e|ne** F public health *or* hygiene; **So|zi|al|im|pe|ri|a|lis|mus** M social imperialism

So|zi|a|li|sa|ti|on [zotsializa'tsioːn] F **-,** *no pl (Psych, Sociol)* socialization

so|zi|a|li|sie|ren [zotsiali'ziːrən] *ptp* **sozialisiert** VT *(Psych, Sociol, Ind)* to socialize; *(Pol: = verstaatlichen)* to nationalize

So|zi|a|li|sie|rung F **-, -en** socialization; *(= Verstaatlichung)* nationalization

So|zi|a|lis|mus [zotsia'lɪsmʊs] M **-, Sozialismen** [-mən] socialism

So|zi|a|list [zotsia'lɪst] M **-en, -en**, **So|zi|a|lis|tin** [-'lɪstɪn] F **-, -nen** socialist

so|zi|a|lis|tisch [zotsia'lɪstɪʃ] ADJ socialist ADV socialistically

So|zi|al-: **So|zi|al|kun|de** F *(Schulfach)* social studies *pl*; **So|zi|al|leis|tun|gen** PL employers' contribution *(sometimes including pension scheme payments)*; **So|zi|al|neid** M social envy; **so|zi|al|öko|no|misch** ADJ socio-economic; **So|zi|al|ord|nung** F social order; **So|zi|al|pä|da|go|ge** M, **So|zi|al|pä|da|go|gin** F social education worker; **So|zi|al|pä|da|go|gik** F social education; **So|zi|al|part|ner** PL unions and management *pl*; **wenn einer der ~ ...** if either unions or management ...; **So|zi|al|plan** M redundancy payments scheme; **So|zi|al|po|li|tik** F social policy; **so|zi|al|po|li|tisch** ADJ socio-political; **So|zi|al|pres|ti|ge** NT social standing; **So|zi|al|pro|dukt** NT national product; **So|zi|al|psy|cho|lo|gie** F social psychology; **So|zi|al|recht** NT social legislation; **So|zi|al|re|form** F social reform; **So|zi|al|ren|te** F social security pension; **So|zi|al|staat** M welfare state; **So|zi|al|sta|ti|on** F health and advice centre *(Brit) or* center *(US)*; **So|zi|al|struk|tur** F social structure; **So|zi|al|sys|tem** NT social system; **So|zi|al|ta|rif** M subsidized rate; **so|zi|al|ver|si|chert** ADJ covered by national insurance *(Brit) or* social security *(US)*; **So|zi|al|ver|si|che|rung** F national insurance *(Brit)*, social security *(US)*; **So|zi|al|ver|si|che|rungs|aus|weis** M ≈ national insurance card *(Brit)*, ≈ social security card *(US)*; **so|zi|al|ver|si|che|rungs|frei** ADJ exempt from social insurance *or* national insurance *(Brit) or* social security *(US) pred*; **so|zi|al|ver|si|che|rungs|pflich|tig** ADJ liable for social insurance *or* national insurance *(Brit) or* social security *(US) pred*; **So|zi|al|ver|si|che|rungs|trä|ger** M ≈ Department of Social Security

> **SOZIALVERSICHERUNGSAUSWEIS**
>
> The **Sozialversicherungsausweis** is a document that must be produced by every employee starting a new job, even when the pay is too low for social security contributions to be payable. The **Sozialversicherungsausweis** is issued by the cardholder's pension scheme and shows the name of the insured person as well as a 12-digit insurance number. The system is designed to discourage illegal work and the misappropriation of social security benefits.

So|zi|al-: **so|zi|al|ver|träg|lich** ADJ socially acceptable; **So|zi|al|wahl** F *election to the representative bodies of the state pension and health insurance schemes*; **So|zi|al|we|sen** NT social services *pl*; **So|zi|al|wis|sen|schaf|ten** PL social sciences *pl*; **So|zi|al|wis|sen|schaft|ler(in)** M(F) social scientist; **so|zi|al|wis|sen|schaft|lich** ADJ *attr* social science; **So|zi|al|woh|nung** F ≈ council flat *(Brit)*, state-subsidized apartment; **So|zi|al|zu|la|ge** F (welfare) allowance

> **SOZIALWOHNUNG**
>
> A **Sozialwohnung** is a flat for people with special social needs, such as families with low incomes or with a large number of children. The construction of **Sozialwohnungen** is subsidized by public money, which means that the rent can be kept artificially low for several years. The right to rent such a flat has to be established by means of a certificate obtained from the social security office. If the tenants' income increases, then they must either pay a surcharge or move out.

So|zi|e|tät [zotsie'tɛːt] F **-, -en a** *(von Anwälten, Ärzten etc)* joint practice **b** *(Sociol: Gruppe)* social group, (branch of) society

so|zio- PREF socio-

So|zio-: **So|zio|gra|fie**, **So|zio|gra|phie** [zotsiogra'fiː] F **-,** *no pl* sociography; **So|zio|gramm** [zotsio'gram] NT *pl* **-gramme** sociogram; **so|zio|kul|tu|rell** [sotsiokʊltu'rɛl] ADJ socio-cultural ADV socio-culturally; **So|zio|lekt** [zotsio'lɛkt] M **-(e)s, -e** sociolect; **So|zio|lin|gu|is|tik** [zotsiolɪŋ'guɪstɪk] F sociolinguistics *sing*; **so|zio|lin|gu|is|tisch** [zotsiolɪŋ'guɪstɪʃ] ADJ sociolinguistic

So|zio|lo|ge [zotsio'loːgə] M **-n, -n**, **So|zio|lo|gin** [-'loːgɪn] F **-, -nen** sociologist

So|zio|lo|gie [zotsiolo'giː] F **-,** *no pl* sociology

so|zio|lo|gisch [zotsio'loːgɪʃ] ADJ sociological ADV sociologically; **~ gesehen/betrachtet** from a sociological point of view

So|zio-: **So|zio|met|rie** [zotsiome'triː] F **-,** *no pl* sociometry; **so|zio|öko|no|misch** [zotsiøko'noːmɪʃ] ADJ socioeconomic ADV socioeconomically; **sein Sozialismus ist eher religiös als ~ fundiert** religious conviction rather than socioeconomic principle underpins his socialism

So|zi|us ['zoːtsiʊs] M **-, -se a** *(= Partner)* partner **b** *(= Beifahrer)* pillion rider *or* passenger **c** *(inf: = Soziussitz)* pillion (seat)

So|zi|us|sitz M pillion (seat)

so|zu|sa|gen [zoːtsu'zaːgn, 'zoːtsuzaːgn] ADV so to speak, as it were

Space-Tas|te ['spe:s-] F *(Comput)* space bar
Spach|tel ['ʃpaxtl] M **-s, -** *or f* **-, -n** **a** *(Werkzeug)* spatula **b** *(spec: = Spachtelmasse)* filler
Spach|tel|mas|se F filler
spach|teln ['ʃpaxtln] VT *Mauerfugen, Ritzen* to fill (in), to smooth over, to stop VI to do some filling; *(inf: = essen)* to tuck in *(inf)*, to dig in *(US inf)*
Spa|gat [ʃpa'ga:t] M OR NT **-(e)s, -e** *(lit)* splits *pl*; *(fig)* balancing act; **~ machen** to do the splits
Spa|gat M **-(e)s, -e** *(S Ger, Aus: = Bindfaden)* string
Spa|get|ti [ʃpa'gɛti, sp-] *etc* = **Spaghetti** *etc*
Spa|ghet|ti [ʃpa'gɛti, sp-] PL spaghetti *sing*
Spa|ghet|ti M **-(s), -s**, **Spa|ghet|ti|fres|ser** M **-s, -**, **Spa|ghet|ti|fres|se|rin** F **-, -nen** *(pej inf: = Italiener)* wop *(pej sl)*, Eyetie *(Brit pej sl)*, dago *(pej sl)*
Spa|ghet|ti|trä|ger M *(Fashion)* shoestring *(Brit)* or spaghetti strap
Spa|ghet|ti|wes|tern M *(inf)* spaghetti western
spä|hen ['ʃpɛ:ən] VI to peer; *(durch Löcher etc auch)* to peep; *(vorsichtig auch)* to peek; *(old Mil)* to reconnoitre *(Brit)*, to reconnoiter *(US)*, to scout; **nach jdm/etw ~** to look out for sb/sth
Spä|her ['ʃpɛ:ɐ] M **-s, -**, **Spä|he|rin** [-ərɪn] F **-, -nen** *(old Mil)* scout; *(= Posten)* lookout
Späh|trupp M *(Mil)* reconnaissance *or* scouting party *or* patrol
spa|kig ['ʃpa:kɪç] ADJ *(N Ger) Bettwäsche, Matratze* mildewed
Spa|lier [ʃpa'li:ɐ] NT **-s, -e** **a** trellis; **am ~ ziehen** to trellis, to train on a trellis **b** *(von Menschen)* row, line; *(zur Ehrenbezeigung)* guard of honour *(Brit)*, honor guard *(US)*; **~ stehen/ein ~ bilden** to form a guard of honour *(Brit)* or honor guard *(US)*
Spa|lier|obst NT wall fruit
Spalt [ʃpalt] M **-(e)s, -e** **a** *(= Öffnung)* gap, opening; *(= Riss)* crack; *(= Felsspalt)* crevice, fissure; **die Tür stand einen ~ (breit) offen** the door was slightly ajar; **die Tür/Augen einen ~ (breit) öffnen** to open the door/one's eyes slightly **b** *(fig: = Kluft)* split
spalt|bar ADJ *(Phys) Material* fissile
Spalt|bar|keit ['ʃpaltba:ɐkait] F **-**, *no pl (Phys)* fissionability
spalt|breit ADJ **ein ~er Schlitz** a narrow crack
Spalt|breit ['ʃpaltbrait] M **etw einen ~ öffnen** *etc* to open *etc* sth slightly; **die Tür stand einen ~ offen** the door was slightly ajar
Spal|te ['ʃpaltə] F **-, -n** **a** *(esp Geol)* fissure; *(= esp Felsspalte)* cleft, crevice; *(= Gletscherspalte)* crevasse; *(in Wand)* crack; *(sl: = Vagina)* hole *(sl)* **b** *(Comput, Typ, Press)* column
spal|ten ['ʃpaltn] *ptp auch* **gespalten** [gə'ʃpaltn] VT *(lit, fig)* to split; *(Chem) Öl* to crack *(spec)*; *Holz* to chop → **Schädel** VR to split; *(Meinungen)* to be split → *auch* **gespalten**
Spalt|en|brei|te F column width
Spalt-: **Spalt|ma|te|ri|al** NT fissile material; **Spalt|pilz** M *(old) usu pl* bacterium; **Spalt|pro|dukt** NT fission product
Spal|tung ['ʃpaltʊŋ] F **-, -en** *(lit, fig)* splitting; *(von Atomkernen auch)* fission; *(von Öl)* cracking *(spec)*; *(in Partei etc)* split; *(eines Landes)* split, division; **die ~ der Persönlichkeit/des Bewusstseins** the split in his *etc* personality/mind
Spam M [spɛm] *(Internet)* spam; *(= Spam-Mails auch)* spam mails *pl*; *(= einzelne Spam-Mail auch)* spam mail
Spam|fil|ter, **Spam-Fil|ter** M *(Internet)* (anti)-spam filter
Spam|ming ['spɛmɪŋ] NT **-(s)**, *no pl (Internet)* spamming
Spam|schutz, **Spam-Schutz** ['spɛm-] M *(Internet)* spam protection
Span [ʃpa:n] M **-(e)s, =e** ['ʃpɛ:nə] *(= Hobelspan)* shaving; *(= Bohrspan auch)* boring; *(zum Feueranzünden)* piece of kindling; *(= Metallspan)* filing; **arbeiten, dass die Späne fliegen** to work furiously
spä|nen ['ʃpɛ:nən] VT *Holzboden* to scour with steel wool
Span|fer|kel NT sucking pig
Span|ge ['ʃpaŋə] F **-, -n** clasp; *(= Haarspange)* hair slide *(Brit)*, barrette *(US)*; *(= Schuhspange)* strap, bar; *(= Schnalle)* buckle; *(= Armspange)* bangle, bracelet
Span|gen|schuh M bar shoe
Spa|ni|el ['ʃpa:niəl] M **-s, -s** spaniel
Spa|ni|en ['ʃpa:niən] NT **-s** Spain
Spa|ni|er ['ʃpa:niɐ] M **-s, -**, **Spa|ni|e|rin** [-iərɪn] F **-, -nen** Spaniard; **die ~** the Spanish, the Spaniards; **stolz wie ein ~ sein** *(prov)* to be (very) proud
spa|nisch ['ʃpa:nɪʃ] ADJ Spanish; **Spanische Fliege** Spanish fly; **~e Wand** (folding) screen; **das kommt mir ~ vor** *(inf)* that seems odd to me
Spa|nisch(e) ['ʃpa:nɪʃ] NT Spanish → *auch* **Deutsch(e)**
Span|korb M chip basket
spann *pret von* **spinnen**
Spann [ʃpan] M **-(e)s, -e** instep
Spann-: **Spann|be|ton** M prestressed concrete; **Spann|bett|tuch** NT fitted sheet
Span|ne ['ʃpanə] F **-, -n** *(altes Längenmaß)* span; *(geh: = Zeitspanne)* while; *(= Verdienstspanne)* margin; **eine ~ Zeit** *(geh)* a space *or* span of time
span|nen ['ʃpanən] VT **a** *Saite, Seil, Geigenbogen* to tighten, to tauten; *Bogen* to draw; *Feder* to tension; *Muskeln* to tense, to flex; *Strickteile, Wolle* to stretch; *Gewehr, Abzugshahn, Kameraverschluss* to cock; **einen Tennisschläger ~** to put a tennis racket in a/the press
b *(= straff befestigen) Werkstück* to clamp; *Wäscheleine* to put up; *Netz, Plane, Bildleinwand* to stretch; **einen Bogen in die Schreibmaschine ~** to insert *or* put a sheet in the typewriter
c *Zugtier* to hitch up (an *+acc*, vor *+acc* to); **sich vor jds Karren ~ lassen** *(fig)* to let oneself be used by sb
d *(fig)* **seine Erwartungen zu hoch ~** to set one's expectations too high; **die Ausstellung spannt einen weiten thematischen Bogen** the exhibition spans *or* covers a wide range of themes → **Folter**
e → **gespannt**
f *(S Ger, Aus inf: = merken)* to catch on to *(inf)*, to get wise to *(inf)*
VR **a** *(Haut)* to go *or* become taut; *(Muskeln)* to tense
b **sich über etw** *(acc)* **~** *(Regenbogen, Brücke)* to span sth; *(Haut)* to stretch over sth
VI **a** *(Kleidung)* to be (too) tight; *(Haut)* to be taut
b *(= Gewehr spannen)* to cock; *(= Kamera spannen)* to cock the shutter
span|nend ADJ exciting; *(stärker)* thrilling; *(inf: = interessant)* fascinating; **machs nicht so ~!** *(inf)* don't keep me/us in suspense ADV full of suspense; **der Bericht liest sich ~** the report is thrilling to read; **er kann ~ erzählen** his stories are thrilling
Span|ner ['ʃpanɐ] M **-s, -** **a** *(für Tennisschläger)* press; *(= Hosenspanner)* hanger; *(= Schuhspanner)* shoetree; *(= Stiefelspanner)* boot tree **b** *(Zool)* geometer moth; *(= Raupe)* looper **c** *(inf: = Voyeur)* peeping Tom
-spän|ner [ʃpɛnɐ] M *suf* **-s, -** *in cpds* **Vierspänner** *etc* four-in-hand *etc*
Span|ne|rin ['ʃpanərɪn] F **-, -nen** *(inf: = Voyeurin)* female peeping Tom
-spän|nig [ʃpɛnɪç] ADJ *suf* **vierspännig fahren** to drive a four-inhand
Spann-: **Spann|kraft** F *(von Feder, Bremse)* tension; *(von Muskel)* tone, tonus *(spec)*; *(fig)* vigour *(Brit)*, vigor *(US)*; **spann|kräf|tig** ADJ *(fig)* vigorous
Span|nung ['ʃpanʊŋ] F **-, -en** **a** *no pl (von Seil, Feder, Muskel etc)* tension, tautness; *(Mech: = innerer Druck)* stress; **wegen der zu großen ~ riss das Seil** the rope broke because the strain (on it) was too great
b *(Elec)* voltage, tension; **unter ~ stehen** to be live
c *no pl (fig)* excitement; *(= Spannungsgeladenheit)* suspense, tension; **mit großer/atemloser ~** with great/breathless excitement; **in erwartungsvoller ~** full of excited anticipation, full of excitement; **etw mit ~ erwarten** to await sth full of suspense; **seine mit ~ erwarteten Memoiren sind endlich erschienen** his eagerly awaited memoirs have appeared at last
d *no pl (= innerliche, nervliche Anspannung)* tension
e *usu pl (= Feindseligkeit)* tension *no pl*
Span|nungs-: **Span|nungs|ab|fall** M voltage drop; **Span|nungs|feld** NT *(lit)* electric field; *(fig)* area of conflict; **span|nungs|frei** ADJ *(lit) Metall, Glas* unstressed; *(fig)* relaxed; **Span|nungs|ge|biet** NT *(Pol)* flash point, area of tension; **Span|nungs|kopf|schmerz** M *usu pl* tension headache; **Span|nungs|mes|ser** M **-s, -** *(Elec)* voltmeter; **Span|nungs|mo|ment** NT *(fig)* suspense-creating factor; **Span|nungs|prü|fer** M voltage detector; **Span|nungs|reg|ler** M voltage regulator; **Span|nungs|stoß** M surge; **Span|nungs|ver|hält|nis** NT tense *or* strained relationship; *(Pol auch)* tense *or* strained relations *pl*
Spann|wei|te F *(Math)* range; *(Archit)* span; *(Aviat)* (wing)span; *(von Vogelflügeln)* wingspread, (wing)span
Span-: **Span|plat|te** F chipboard; **Span|schach|tel** F *small box made from very thin strips of wood*
Spant [ʃpant] NT **-(e)s, -en** *(Naut)* rib
Spant M **-(e)s, -en** *(Aviat)* frame
Spar-: **Spar|brief** M *(Fin)* savings certificate; **Spar|buch** NT savings book; *(bei Bank auch)* bankbook; **Spar|büch|se** F, **Spar|do|se** F piggy bank; **Spar|eck|zins** M basic savings rate; **Spar|ein|la|ge** F savings deposit
spa|ren ['ʃpa:rən] VT to save; *Energie auch* to conserve; **dadurch habe ich (mir) viel Geld/Zeit/Arbeit gespart** I saved (myself) a lot of money/time/work that way; **keine Kosten/Mühe ~** to spare no expense/effort; **spar dir deine guten Ratschläge!** *(inf)* you can keep your advice!; **diese Mühe/diese Kosten/das hätten Sie sich** *(dat)* **~ können** you could have saved *or* spared yourself the trouble/this expense/the bother; **diese Bemerkung hätten Sie sich** *(dat)* **~ können!** you should have kept that remark to yourself!
VI to save; *(= sparsam sein, Haus halten)* to economize, to make savings; **an etw** *(dat)* **~** to be sparing with sth; *(= mit etw Haus halten)* to economize *or* save on sth; **bei etw ~** to save on sth; **er hatte nicht mit Lob gespart** he was unstinting *or* lavish in his praise; **für** *or* **auf etw** *(acc)* **~** to save up for sth; **am falschen Ort ~** to make false economies, to make savings in the wrong place; **spare in der Zeit, so hast du in der Not** *(Prov)* waste not, want not *(Prov)*
Spa|rer ['ʃpa:rɐ] M **-s, -**, **Spa|re|rin** [-ərɪn] F **-, -nen** *(bei Bank etc)* saver
Spa|rer|frei|be|trag M *(Steuern)* savers' tax-free amount, allowance on savings
Spar|flam|me F low flame; *(= Zündflamme)* pilot light; **auf ~** *(fig inf)* just ticking over *(Brit inf)* or coming along *(US)*; **auf ~ kochen** *(fig)* to soft-pedal *(inf)*, to go easy
Spar|gel ['ʃpargl] M **-s, -** *or (Sw) f* **-, -n** asparagus
Spar|gel|creme|sup|pe F cream of asparagus soup
Spar|gel|der PL savings *pl*
Spar|gel|spit|ze F asparagus tip
Spar-: **Spar|gro|schen** M nest egg; **Spar|gut|ha|ben** NT savings account; **Spar|kas|se** F savings bank; **Spar|kas|sen|buch** NT savings book, bankbook; **Spar|kon|to** NT savings *or* deposit account; **Spar|kurs** M economy drive *(Brit)*, budget *(US)*; **auf ~ gehen** to start an

economy drive *(Brit) or* a budget *(US)*; **einen strikten ~ einhalten** to be on a strict economy drive *(Brit) or* strict budget *(US)*

spär|lich [ˈʃpɛːrlɪç] ADJ sparse; *Ausbeute, Reste, Einkünfte, Kenntnisse* sketchy, scanty; *Beleuchtung* poor; *Kleidung* scanty, skimpy; *Mahl* meagre *(Brit)*, meager *(US)*; *Nachfrage* poor, low ADV *bevölkert* sparsely, thinly; *beleuchtet, besucht* poorly; *eingerichtet* sparsely; **~ bekleidet** scantily clad *or* dressed; **die Geldmittel fließen nur ~** the money is only coming slowly *or* in dribs and drabs

Spär|lich|keit F -, *no pl* sparseness; *(von Nachfrage)* low level; **die ~ meiner Kenntnisse auf dem Gebiet** my sketchy *or* scanty knowledge in this area

Spar-: **Spar|maß|nah|me** F economy *(Brit) or* budgeting *(US)* measure; **Spar|pa|ckung** F economy size (pack); **Spar|pa|ket** NT savings package; *(Pol)* package of austerity measures; **Spar|pfen|nig** M *(fig)* nest egg; **Spar|po|li|tik** F cost-cutting policy; **Spar|prä|mie** F savings premium; **Spar|preis** M economy price; **Spar|quo|te** F, **Spar|ra|te** F rate of saving

Spar|ren [ˈʃparən] M -s, - rafter; **du hast ja einen ~ (zu viel im Kopf)** *(inf)* you must have a screw loose *(inf)*

Spar|ring [ˈʃparɪŋ, ˈsp-] NT -s, *no pl (Boxen)* sparring

Spar|rings-: **Spar|rings|kampf** M sparring bout; **Spar|rings|partner(in)** M(F) sparring partner

spar|sam [ˈʃpaːrzaːm] ADJ *Mensch* thrifty; *(= haushälterisch, wirtschaftlich) Hausfrau, Motor, Verbrauch* economical; **~ im Verbrauch** economical; **von einer Möglichkeit nur ~en Gebrauch machen** to make little use of an opportunity ADV *leben, essen* economically; *verwenden* sparingly; **~ wirtschaften** to keep expenses as low as possible; **~er wirtschaften** to spend less money; **mit etw ~ umgehen** *or* **sein** to be economical *or* sparing with sth; **von etw nur ~ Gebrauch machen** to make little use of sth

Spar|sam|keit F -, *no pl* thrift; *(= sparsames Haushalten)* economizing; **~ im Verbrauch** economy

Spar|schwein NT piggy bank

Spar|strumpf M money sock

Spar|ta|ki|a|de [ʃpartaˈkiaːdə, sp-] F -, -n Spartakiad

Spar|ta|kus|bund [ˈʃpartakʊs-, ˈsp-] M, *no pl* Spartacus league

Spar|ta|ner [ʃparˈtaːnɐ, sp-] M -s, -, **Spar|ta|ne|rin** [-ərɪn] F -, -nen Spartan

spar|ta|nisch [ʃparˈtaːnɪʃ, sp-] ADJ *(lit)* Spartan; *(fig auch)* spartan ADV spartanly; **~ leben** to lead a Spartan *or* spartan life

Spar|ta|rif M discount price; *(bei Strom, Gas etc)* economy rate; *(Telec)* reduced rate, off-peak rate; **zum ~ einkaufen** to shop at discount prices

Spar|te [ˈʃpartə] F -, -n **a** *(Comm) (= Branche)* line of business; *(= Teilgebiet)* branch, area **b** *(= Rubrik)* column, section

Spar|ten|ka|nal M *(TV)* specialist channel

Spar-: **Spar|ver|trag** M savings agreement; **Spar|vo|lu|men** NT targeted savings figure; **Spar|zins** M interest *no pl* (on a savings account); **Spar|zu|la|ge** F savings bonus

spas|misch [ˈʃpasmɪʃ, ˈsp-], **spas|mo|disch** [ʃpasˈmoːdɪʃ, sp-] ADJ *(Med)* spasmodic, spasmic

Spaß [ʃpaːs] M -es, ≃e [ˈʃpɛːsə], **Spass** *Aus* [ʃpas] M -es, ≃e [ˈʃpɛsə] *(no pl: = Vergnügen)* fun; *(= Scherz)* joke; *(= Streich)* prank, lark *(Brit inf)*; **lass die dummen Späße!** stop fooling around!; **~ beiseite** joking apart; **viel ~!** have fun! *(auch iro)*, have a good time!, enjoy yourself/yourselves!; **wir haben viel ~ gehabt** we had a lot of fun, we had a really good time, we enjoyed ourselves a lot; **an etw** *(dat)* **~ haben** to enjoy sth; **er hat viel ~ an seinem Garten** his garden gives him a lot of pleasure; **es macht mir ~/keinen ~ (, das zu tun)** it's fun/no fun (doing it), I enjoy *or* like/don't enjoy *or* like (doing) it; **wenns dir ~ macht** if you want to, if it turns you on *(inf)*; **Hauptsache, es macht ~** the main thing is to have fun *or* to enjoy yourself; **~/keinen ~ machen** to be fun/no fun; **ich hab doch nur ~ gemacht!** I was only joking *or* kidding *(inf)!*, it was only (in *(Brit) or* for) fun; **(nur so,) zum** *or* **aus ~** (just) for fun, (just) for the fun *or* hell of it *(inf)*; **etw aus** *or* **im** *or* **zum ~ sagen** to say sth as a joke *or* in *(Brit) or* for fun; **das sage ich nicht bloß zum ~** I'm not saying that for the fun of it, I kid you not *(hum inf)*; **aus ~ an der Freude** (just) for the fun of it; **da hört der ~ auf, das ist kein ~ mehr** that's going beyond a joke; **aus (dem) ~ wurde Ernst** the fun turned deadly earnest; **~ muss sein** there's no harm in a joke; *(als Aufheiterung)* all work and no play (makes Jack a dull boy) *(prov)*; **es war ein ~, ihm bei der Arbeit zuzusehen** it was a joy to see him at work; **sich** *(dat)* **einen ~ daraus machen, etw zu tun** to get enjoyment *or* a kick *(inf)* out of doing sth; **seinen ~ mit jdm treiben** to make fun of sb; *(= sich mit jdm vergnügen)* to have one's fun with sb; **lass** *or* **gönn ihm doch seinen** *or* **den ~!** let him enjoy himself, let him have his fun; **er versteht keinen ~** he has no sense of humour *(Brit) or* humor *(US)*; *(= er lässt nicht mit sich spaßen)* he doesn't stand for any nonsense; **da verstehe ich keinen ~!** I won't stand for any nonsense; **das war ein teurer ~** *(inf)* that was an expensive business *(inf)*

Spaß|bad NT leisure pool

Späß|chen [ˈʃpɛːsçən] NT -s, - *dim von* **Spaß** little joke

spa|ßen [ˈʃpaːsn] VI *(dated)* to joke, to jest; **mit Blutvergiftung ist nicht zu ~** blood poisoning is no joke *or* no joking matter; **mit radioaktivem Material ist nicht zu ~** radioactive material is no joke; **mit der aufgebrachten Menge ist nicht zu ~** an angry mob is not to be trifled with; **mit ihm ist nicht zu ~, er lässt nicht mit sich ~** he doesn't stand for any nonsense

spa|ßes|hal|ber ADV for the fun of it, for fun

spaß|haft, spa|ßig [ˈʃpaːsɪç] ADJ funny, droll

Späß|lein [ˈʃpɛːslain] NT -s, - little joke

Spaß-: **Spaß|ma|cher(in)** M(F) *(= Spaßvogel)* joker; *(im Zirkus)* clown; **Spaß|ver|der|ber** [-fɛɐdɛrbɐ] M -s, -, **Spaß|ver|der|be|rin** [-ərɪn] F -, -nen spoilsport, wet blanket *(inf)*, killjoy; **Spaß|vo|gel** M joker

Spas|ti [ˈʃpasti] M -s, -s *(sl)* spastic *(sl)*

Spas|ti|ker [ˈʃpastikɐ, ˈsp-] M -s, -, **Spas|ti|ke|rin** [-ərɪn] F -, -nen spastic

spas|tisch [ˈʃpastɪʃ, ˈsp-] ADJ spastic ADV *sich bewegen* spastically; **~ gelähmt** suffering from spastic paralysis

Spat [ʃpaːt] M -(e)s, -e **a** *(Miner)* spar **b** *no pl (Vet)* spavin

spät [ʃpɛːt] ADJ late; *Reue, Ruhm, Glück* belated; **am ~en Nachmittag** in the late afternoon; **im ~en 18. Jahrhundert** in the late 18th century; **die Werke des ~en Shakespeare, die ~en Werke Shakespeares** the works of the late(r) Shakespeare, Shakespeare's late(r) works; **ein ~es Mädchen** *(inf)* an old maid ADV late; **~ in der Nacht/am Tage** late at night/in the day; **es ist schon ~** it is late; **es wird schon ~** it is getting late; **heute Abend wird es ~** it'll be a late night tonight; *(nach Hause kommen)* I/he *etc* will be late this evening; **gestern ist es (bei der Arbeit) ~ geworden** I worked late yesterday; **wir hatten gestern eine Party und da ist es ziemlich ~ geworden** we had a party yesterday and it went on fairly late; **wie ~ ist es?** what's the time?; **zu ~** too late; **er kommt morgens regelmäßig fünf Minuten zu ~** he's always five minutes late in the mornings; **der Zug ist zu ~ angekommen** the train arrived late; **wir sind ~ dran** we're late; **er hat erst ~ mit dem Schreiben angefangen** he only started writing late in life; **besser ~ als nie** *(prov)* better late than never *(prov)* → *auch* **später**

Spät- *in cpds* late; **Spät|auf|ste|her(in)** [-laufʃteːɐ, -ərɪn] M(F) late riser; **Spät|aus|sied|ler(in)** M(F) *emigrant of German origin from Eastern European state*; **Spät|bur|gun|der** M *(= Rebsorte)* pinot noir; **~ Rotwein/Weißherbst** *(= Wein)* red/rosé wine made from pinot noir grapes

Spa|tel [ˈʃpaːtl] M -s, - spatula

Spa|ten [ˈʃpaːtn] M -s, - spade

Spa|ten|stich M cut of the spade; **den ersten ~ tun** to turn the first sod

Spät|ent|wick|ler(in) M(F) late developer

spä|ter [ˈʃpɛːtɐ] *comp von* **spät** ADJ later; *(= zukünftig)* future; **in der ~en Zukunft** further on in the future; **die Späteren** *(liter)* posterity *sing* ADV later (on); **das werden wir ~ erledigen** we'll settle that later (on); **ein paar Minuten ~** a few minutes later; **~ als** later than; **das war viel ~ als Augustus** that was much later (on) than Augustus; **was will er denn ~ (einmal) werden?** what does he want to do later (on)?; **an ~ denken** to think of the future; **bis ~!, also dann, auf ~!** see you later!

spä|ter|hin [ˈʃpɛːtɐˈhɪn] ADV *(liter)* later (on)

spä|tes|tens [ˈʃpɛːtəstns] ADV at the latest; **~ morgen/in einer Stunde** tomorrow/in one hour at the latest; **~ um 8 Uhr** not later than 8 o'clock, by 8 o'clock at the latest; **bis ~ in einer Woche** in one week at the latest

Spät-: **Spät|fol|ge** F *usu pl* late effect; **Spät|ge|bä|ren|de** [-gəbɛːrəndə] F *decl as adj* woman having her (first) child around forty, elderly prim *(Brit inf)*; **Spät|ge|burt** F late birth; **Spät|go|tik** F late Gothic; **Spät|heim|keh|rer(in)** M(F) late returnee *(from a prisoner-of-war camp)*; **Spät|herbst** M late autumn, late fall *(US)*; **Spät|jahr** NT *(liter)* autumn, fall *(US)*; **Spät|ka|pi|ta|lis|mus** M late capitalism; **Spät|le|se** F late vintage; **Spät|nach|mit|tag** M late afternoon; **Spät|nach|rich|ten** PL late(-night) news *sing*; **Spät|scha|den** M *usu pl* long-term damage; **Spät|schicht** F late shift; **Spät|som|mer** M late summer; **Spät|vor|stel|lung** F late show

Spatz [ʃpats] M -en, -en **a** sparrow; **wie ein ~ essen** to peck at one's food; **besser ein ~ in der Hand als eine Taube auf dem Dach** *(Prov)* a bird in the hand is worth two in the bush *(Prov)* → **pfeifen b** *(inf: = Kind)* tot, mite *(Brit)*, halfpint *(US inf)*; *(= Anrede)* darling, honey

Spätz|chen [ˈʃpɛtsçən] NT -s, - *dim von* **Spatz** little sparrow; *(inf: = Kind)* tot, mite *(Brit)*, halfpint *(US inf)*; *(= Anrede)* honeybun *(inf)*, sweetie pie *(inf)*

Spat|zen|hirn NT *(pej)* birdbrain *(inf)*

Spätz|le [ˈʃpɛtslə] PL *(S Ger Cook)* spaetzle *(sort of pasta)*

Spät-: **Spät|zün|der(in)** M(F) *(hum inf)* **~ sein** *(= schwer von Begriff sein)* to be slow on the uptake; *(= spät im Leben mit etw anfangen)* to be a late starter; **Spät|zün|dung** F retarded ignition; **~ haben** *(inf)* to be slow on the uptake

spa|zie|ren [ʃpaˈtsiːrən] *ptp* **spaziert** VI *aux sein* to stroll; *(= stolzieren)* to strut; **wir waren ~** we went for a walk *or* stroll

spa|zie|ren fah|ren *irreg* VI *aux sein (im Auto)* to go for a drive *or* ride *or* run; *(mit Fahrrad, Motorrad)* to go for a ride; **ich will nur ein bisschen ~** I just want to go for a little drive *or* ride *or* run VT **jdn ~** to take sb for a drive *or* ride *or* run; **das Baby (im Kinderwagen) ~** to take the baby for a walk (in the pram *(Brit) or* baby carriage *(US)*)

spa|zie|ren füh|ren VT **jdn ~** to take sb for a walk; **sie hat ihr neues Kleid/ihren Fotoapparat spazieren geführt** *(inf)* she paraded her new dress/her camera

spa|zie|ren ge|hen VI *irreg aux sein* to go for a walk *or* stroll; **ich gehe jetzt ein bisschen**

spazieren I'm going to go for a little walk *or* stroll now

Spa|zier-: **Spa|zier|fahrt** F *(im Auto)* ride, drive, run; *(mit Fahrrad, Motorrad)* ride; **eine ~ machen** to go for a ride *etc*; **Spa|zier|gang** M *pl* **-gänge** walk, stroll; *(fig)* child's play *no art*, doddle *(Brit inf)*; *(Match)* walkover; **einen ~ machen** to go for a walk *or* stroll; **~ im All** space walk, walk in space; **Spa|zier|gän|ger** [-gɛŋɐ] M **-s, -**, **Spa|zier|gän|ge|rin** [-ərɪn] F **-, -nen** stroller; **Spa|zier|ritt** M ride; **Spa|zier|stock** M walking stick; **Spa|zier|weg** M path, walk

SPD [ɛspeː'deː] F **-** *abbr von* **Sozialdemokratische Partei Deutschlands**

> **SPD**
>
> Re-founded in 1945, the **SPD (Sozialdemokratische Partei Deutschlands)** is one of the large political parties in Germany. It is traditionally a workers' party and supports social justice within a social market economy.

Specht [ʃpɛçt] M **-(e)s, -e** woodpecker

Speck [ʃpɛk] M **-(e)s, -e** *(= Schweinespeck)* bacon fat; *(= Schinkenspeck, durchwachsener Speck)* bacon; *(= Walspeck)* blubber; *(inf: bei Mensch)* fat, flab *(inf)*; **mit ~ fängt man Mäuse** *(Prov)* you have to use a sprat to catch a mackerel *(prov)*; **~ ansetzen** *(inf)* to get fat, to put on weight, to put it on *(inf)*; **~ auf den Knochen haben** *(inf)* **~ draufhaben** *(inf)* to be fat; *(an Hüften)* to be broad in the beam *(inf)*; **ran an den ~** *(inf)* let's get stuck in *(inf)*

Speck-: **Speck|bauch** M *(inf)* potbelly *(inf)*, paunch; **speck|bäu|chig** [-bɔyçɪç] ADJ *(inf)* potbellied *(inf)*; **Speck|gür|tel** M *(fig: um Stadt) affluent areas outside city boundaries*, (ring of) suburban sprawl

spe|ckig ['ʃpɛkɪç] ADJ *Kleidung, Haar* greasy

Speck-: **Speck|na|cken** M fat neck; **speck|na|ckig** ADJ fat-necked; **Speck|schei|be** F (bacon) rasher; **Speck|schwar|te** F bacon rind; **wie eine ~ glänzen** *(inf)* to shine greasily; **Speck|sei|te** F side of bacon; **Speck|stein** M *(Miner)* soapstone, steatite

Spe|di|teur [ʃpedi'tøːɐ] M **-s, -e**, **Spe|di|teu|rin** [-'tøːrɪn] F **-, -nen** carrier, haulier, haulage contractor; *(= Zwischenspediteur)* forwarding agent; *(von Schiffsfracht)* shipper, shipping agent; *(= Umzugsfirma)* furniture remover

Spe|di|ti|on [ʃpedi'tsioːn] F **-, -en** **a** *(= das Spedieren)* carriage, transporting; *(auf dem Wasserweg)* shipping **b** *(= Firma)* haulage contractor; *(= Zwischenspedition)* forwarding agency; *(= Schiffskontor)* shipping agency; *(= Umzugsfirma)* removal firm; *(= Versandabteilung)* forwarding department

Spe|di|ti|ons-: **Spe|di|ti|ons|bran|che** F haulage business; **Spe|di|ti|ons|fir|ma** F, **Spe|di|ti|ons|ge|schäft** NT haulage contractor; *(= Zwischenspediteur)* forwarding agency; *(= Schiffskontor)* shipping agency; *(= Umzugsfirma)* removal firm; **Spe|di|ti|ons|kauf|frau** F, **Spe|di|ti|ons|kauf|mann** M forwarding agent; **Spe|di|ti|ons|kos|ten** PL haulage (costs *pl*)

Speed [spiːd] NT **-s, -s** *(inf: = Droge)* speed *(inf)*

Speed [spiːd] M **-s, -s** *(Sport: = Spurt)* burst of speed

Speer [ʃpeːɐ] M **-(e)s, -e** spear; *(Sport)* javelin

Speer-: **Speer|spit|ze** F *(lit, fig)* spearhead; **Speer|wer|fen** NT **-s**, *no pl (Sport)* **das ~** the javelin, throwing the javelin; **im ~** in the javelin; **Speer|wer|fer(in)** M(F) *(Sport)* javelin thrower

Spei|che ['ʃpaiçə] F **-, -n** **a** spoke; **dem Schicksal in die ~n greifen** *or* **fallen** *(fig)* to try to stop the wheel of fate **b** *(Anat)* radius

Spei|chel ['ʃpaiçl] M **-s**, *no pl* saliva, spittle

Spei|chel-: **Spei|chel|drü|se** F salivary gland; **Spei|chel|fluss** M salivation; **Spei|chel|le|cker** [-lɛkɐ] M **-s, -**, **Spei|chel|le|cke|rin** [-ərɪn] F **-, -nen** *(pej)* lickspittle, toady, bootlicker *(inf)*; **Spei|chel|le|cke|rei** F *(pej inf)* toadying, bootlicking *(inf)*

Spei|cher ['ʃpaiçɐ] M **-s, -** *(= Lagerhaus)* storehouse; *(im Haus)* loft, attic; *(= Wasserspeicher)* tank, reservoir; *(Comput)* memory, store; **auf dem ~** in the loft *or* attic; **virtueller ~** *(Comput)* virtual memory

Spei|cher-: **Spei|cher|ab|zug** M *(Comput)* dump; **Spei|cher|ad|res|se** F *(Comput)* memory address; **Spei|cher|bat|te|rie** F storage battery, accumulator *(Brit)*; **Spei|cher|be|cken** NT reservoir; **Spei|cher|be|reich** M *(Comput)* memory are aor range; **Spei|cher|chip** M *(Comput)* memory chip; **Spei|cher|dich|te** F *(Comput)* storage density; **Spei|cher|ein|heit** F *(Comput) (= Gerät)* storage device; *(= Einheit)* storage unit; **Spei|cher|er|wei|te|rung** F *(Comput)* memory expansion; **Spei|cher|funk|ti|on** F *(Comput)* memory function; **Spei|cher|ka|pa|zi|tät** F storage capacity; *(Comput auch)* memory capacity, disk space; **Spei|cher|kar|te** F *(Comput)* memory card; **Spei|cher|kraft|werk** NT storage power station; **Spei|cher|me|di|um** NT *(Comput)* storage medium; **Spei|cher|mo|dul** [-moduːl] NT *(Comput)* memory module

spei|chern ['ʃpaiçɐn] VT *Vorräte, Energie, Daten* to store; *(Comput: = abspeichern)* to save; *(fig) Gefühle* to store up; **Dateien auf der Festplatte ~** *(Comput)* to save files on the hard disk; **~ unter ...** *(Comput)* save as ... VR to accumulate

Spei|cher-: **Spei|cher|ofen** M storage heater; **Spei|cher|ort** M *(Comput)* location; **Spei|cher|plat|te** F *(Comput)* storage disk; **Spei|cher|platz** M *(Comput)* storage space, disk space; **~ schaffen** to free up memory; **spei|cher|re|si|dent** ADJ *(Comput)* memory-resident; **Spei|cher|schreib|ma|schi|ne** F memory typewriter; **Spei|cher|schutz** M *(Tech)* memory protection

Spei|che|rung ['ʃpaiçərʊŋ] F **-, -en** storing, storage

Spei|cher|ver|wal|tung F *(Comput)* memory management

spei|en ['ʃpaiən] *pret* **spie** [ʃpiː], *ptp* **gespien** [gə'ʃpiː(ə)n] VT to spit, to expectorate *(spec)*; *Lava, Feuer* to spew (forth); *Wasser* to spout; *Flammen, Dämpfe* to belch (forth *or* out); *(= erbrechen)* to vomit; **der Drache spie Feuer** the dragon breathed fire → **Gift** VI *(= sich übergeben)* to vomit

Speis [ʃpais] M **-es** [-zəs] *no pl (S Ger: = Mörtel)* mortar

Spei|se ['ʃpaizə] F **-, -n** **a** *(geh: = Nahrung)* food, fare *(liter)*; *(= Gericht)* dish; *(= Süßspeise)* sweet *(Brit)*, dessert; **~n und Getränke** meals and beverages; **vielen Dank für Speis und Trank** *(hum)* many thanks for the meal; **kalte und warme ~n** hot and cold meals; **erlesene ~n** choice dishes **b** *no pl (= Mörtel)* mortar **c** *(Metal)* speiss; *(= Glockenspeise)* bell metal

Spei|se-: **Spei|se|brei** M chyme; **Spei|se|eis** NT ice cream; **Spei|se|fett** NT cooking *or* edible fat; **Spei|se|kam|mer** F larder *(esp Brit)*, pantry; **Spei|se|kar|te** F menu; **Spei|se|lei|tung** F *(Elec)* feeder, supply main; **Spei|se|lo|kal** NT restaurant

spei|sen ['ʃpaizn] *ptp auch (hum)* **gespiesen** [gə'ʃpiːzn] VI *(geh)* to eat, to dine *(form)*; **zu Abend ~** to have dinner, to dine (in the evening) *(form)*; **zu Mittag ~** to have lunch; **wünsche wohl zu ~** I hope you enjoy your meal VT **a** *(= essen)* to eat, to dine on *(form)*; **was wünschen Sie zu ~?** what do you wish to eat, sir/madam? **b** *(liter, Tech)* to feed; *(old) Gast* to dine VR **sich aus etw ~** *(= seinen Ursprung haben)* to have its source in sth; *(= finanziert werden)* to be financed by sth

Spei|sen-: **Spei|sen|auf|zug** M dumb waiter, service lift; **Spei|sen|fol|ge** F order of the menu *or* the courses

Spei|se-: **Spei|se|öl** NT salad oil; *(zum Braten)* cooking *or* edible oil; **Spei|se|plan** M today's/this week's *etc* menu; **Spei|se|quark** [-kvark] M quark; **Spei|se|res|te** PL leftovers *pl*; *(zwischen den Zähnen)* food particles *pl*; **Spei|se|röh|re** F *(Anat)* gullet; **Spei|se|saal** M dining hall; *(in Hotel etc)* dining room; *(auf Schiffen)* dining saloon; **Spei|se|salz** NT table salt; **Spei|se|schrank** M larder *(esp Brit)*, pantry; **Spei|se|stär|ke** F cornflour *(Brit)*, cornstarch *(US)*; **Spei|se|wa|gen** M *(Rail)* dining car, restaurant car, diner *(esp US)*; **Spei|se|wär|mer** [-vɛrmɐ] M **-s, -** hotplate; **Spei|se|zet|tel** M menu; **Spei|se|zim|mer** NT dining room

Spei|sung ['ʃpaizʊŋ] F **-, -en** *(geh)* feeding; *(Tech auch)* supply; **die ~ der fünftausend** the feeding of the five thousand

spei|übel ['ʃpailyːbl] ADJ **mir ist ~** I think I'm going to be sick *or* to throw up *(inf)*; **da kann einem ~ werden, wenn man das sieht** the sight of that is enough to make you feel sick

Spek|ta|bi|li|tät [ʃpɛktabili'tɛːt, sp-] F **-, -en** *(dated Univ)* (Mr) Dean

Spek|ta|kel [ʃpɛk'taːkl] M **-s, -** *(inf)* row, rumpus *(inf)*; *(= Aufregung)* fuss, palaver *(inf)*

Spek|ta|kel [ʃpɛk'taːkl, sp-] NT **-s, -** *(old)* spectacle, show

spek|ta|ku|lär [ʃpɛktaku'lɛːɐ, sp-] ADJ spectacular ADV spectacularly

Spek|tra *pl von* **Spektrum**

Spek|tral-: **Spek|tral|ana|ly|se** F spectrum analysis; **Spek|tral|far|be** F colour *(Brit)* *or* color *(US)* of the spectrum

Spek|tren *pl von* **Spektrum**

Spek|tro|skop [ʃpɛktro'skoːp, sp-] NT **-s, -e** spectroscope

Spek|trum ['ʃpɛktrʊm, 'sp-] NT **-s, Spektren** *or* **Spektra** [-trən, -tra] spectrum

Spe|ku|lant [ʃpeku'lant] M **-en, -en**, **Spe|ku|lan|tin** [-'lantɪn] F **-, -nen** speculator

Spe|ku|la|ti|on [ʃpekula'tsioːn] F **-, -en** **a** *(Fin)* speculation *(mit* in); **~ mit Grundstücken** property speculation **b** *(= Vermutung)* speculation *(über* about); **das ist reine ~** that is pure *or* mere speculation; **~en anstellen** to speculate

Spe|ku|la|ti|ons-: **Spe|ku|la|ti|ons|ge|schäft** NT speculative transaction *or* operation; **es war ein ~, aber es hat sich gelohnt** it was a gamble but it was worth it; **Spe|ku|la|ti|ons|ge|winn** M speculative gains *pl or* profit; **Spe|ku|la|ti|ons|ob|jekt** NT object of speculation; **Spe|ku|la|ti|ons|steu|er** F windfall tax, tax on speculative profits

Spe|ku|la|ti|us [ʃpeku'laːtsiʊs] M **-, -** spiced biscuit *(Brit) or* cookie *(US)*

spe|ku|la|tiv [ʃpekula'tiːf, sp-] ADJ speculative

spe|ku|lie|ren [ʃpeku'liːrən] *ptp* **spekuliert** VI **a** *(Fin)* to speculate *(mit* in) → **Baisse, Hausse** **b** *(= Vermutungen anstellen)* to speculate; **auf etw** *(acc)* **~** *(inf)* to have hopes of sth

Spell|che|cker ['spɛltʃɛkɐ] M **-s, -** *(Comput)* spellchecker

Spe|lun|ke [ʃpe'lʊŋkə] F **-, -n** *(pej inf)* dive *(inf)*

Spelz [ʃpɛlts] M **-es, -e** *(Agr)* spelt

Spel|ze ['ʃpɛltsə] F **-, -n** *(Bot)* husk; *(von Gras)* glume

spen|da|bel [ʃpɛn'daːbl] ADJ *(inf)* generous, open-handed

Spen|de ['ʃpɛndə] F **-, -n** donation; *(= Beitrag)* contribution; **eine ~ geben** *or* **machen** to give a donation/contribution, to donate/contribute something; **bitte eine kleine ~!** please give *or* donate *or* contribute something (for charity)

spen|den ['ʃpɛndn] VT *Lebensmittel, Blut, Geld, Hilfsgüter* to donate, to give; *(= beitragen) Geld* to contribute; *Abendmahl, Segen* to administer; *Schatten* to afford, to offer; *Trost* to give → **Beifall, Lob** VI to donate; *(= Geld beitragen)* to contribute; **bitte ~ Sie für das Rote Kreuz!** please donate/contribute something to *or* for the Red Cross

Spen|den-: **Spen|den|af|fä|re** F donations scandal; **Spen|den|ak|ti|on** F fund-raising *or* charity drive, fund-raiser; **Spen|den|auf|kom|men** NT revenue from donations; **Spen|den|auf|ruf** M charity appeal; **Spen|den|be|reit|schaft** F readiness to donate money; **Spen|den|be|schaf|fung** F procuring of donations; **Spen|den|be|schei|ni|gung** F charitable donation certificate; **spen|den|freu|dig** ADJ keen *or* eager *(US)* to donate money; **die Deutschen sind sehr ~** the Germans are very generous donors; **Spen|den|freu|dig|keit** F keenness *or* eagerness *(US)* to donate money; **Spen|den|kam|pag|ne** F fund-raising campaign; **Spen|den|kon|to** NT donations account; **Spen|den|samm|ler(in)** M(F) fundraiser; **Spen|den|wasch|an|la|ge** F *(Pol)* donation-laundering scheme

Spen|der [ˈʃpɛndɐ] M **-s, -** *(= Seifenspender etc)* dispenser

Spen|der [ˈʃpɛndɐ] M **-s, -**, **Spen|de|rin** [-ərɪn] F **-, -nen** donator; *(= Beitragsleistender)* contributor; *(Med)* donor; **wer war der edle ~?** *(inf)* to whom am I indebted?

Spen|der- *in cpds (Med)* donor; **Spen|der|aus|weis** M donor card; **Spen|der|blut** NT donor blood; **Spen|der|herz** NT donor heart

spen|die|ren [ʃpɛnˈdiːrən] *ptp* **spendiert** VT to buy, to get *(jdm etw* sb sth, sth for sb); **spendierst du mir einen?** *(inf)* are you going to buy *or* stand *(esp Brit)* me a drink?; **lass mal, das spendiere ich** forget it, it's on me

Spen|dier|ho|sen PL *(inf)* **seine ~ anhaben** to be in a generous mood, to be feeling generous

Speng|ler [ˈʃpɛŋlɐ] M **-s, -**, **Speng|le|rin** [-ərɪn] F **-, -nen** *(dial: = Klempner)* plumber

Spen|zer [ˈʃpɛntsɐ] M **-s, -** long-sleeved vest; *(= kurze Jacke)* short jacket

Sper|ber [ˈʃpɛrbɐ] M **-s, -** sparrowhawk

Spe|renz|chen [ʃpeˈrɛntsçən] PL *(inf)* **~ machen** to make trouble, to be difficult

Spe|ren|zi|en [ʃpeˈrɛntsiən] PL *(inf)* = **Sperenzchen**

Sper|ling [ˈʃpɛrlɪŋ] M **-s, -e** sparrow

Sper|ma [ˈʃpɛrma, ˈsp-] NT **-s, Spermen** *or* **-ta** [-mən, -ta] sperm

Sper|mio|gramm [ʃpɛrmioˈgram, sp-] NT *pl* **-gramme** spermiogram

sper|mi|zid [ʃpɛrmiˈtsiːt, sp-] ADJ spermicidal

Sper|mi|zid [ʃpɛrmiˈtsiːt, sp-] NT **-(e)s, -e** [-də] spermicide

Sperrad △ NT → **Sperrrad**

Sperr-: **sperr|an|gel|weit** [ˈʃpɛrˈlaŋlˈvait] ADV *(inf)* **~ offen** wide open; **Sperr|bal|lon** M *(Mil)* barrage balloon; **Sperr|be|zirk** M no-go area, prohibited area; **Sperr|dif|fe|ren|zi|al** NT *(Aut)* locking differential

Sper|re [ˈʃpɛrə] F **-, -n** **a** *(= Hindernis, Schlagbaum, Bahnsteigsperre etc)* barrier; *(= Polizeisperre)* roadblock; *(Mil)* obstacle; *(Tech)* locking device **b** *(= Verbot, auch Sport)* ban; *(= Blockierung)* blockade; *(Comm)* embargo; *(= Nachrichtensperre)* (news) blackout **c** *(Psych)* mental block; **eine psychologische/emotionale ~** a mental/emotional block

sper|ren [ˈʃpɛrən] VT **a** *(= schließen) Grenze, Hafen, Straße, Brücke, Tunnel etc* to close; *Platz, Gegend* to close (off); *(Tech)* to lock; **Tunnel gesperrt!** tunnel closed; **etw für jdn/etw ~** to close sth to sb/sth

b *(Comm) Konto, Gelder* to block, to freeze; *Scheck, Kreditkarte* to stop; *(Comput) Datensätze, Zugriff* to lock

c *(Sport: = ausschließen)* to ban

d *(Sport: = behindern) Gegner* to obstruct, to block

e *(= verbieten) Einfuhr, Ausfuhr* to ban; **jdm das Gehalt ~** to stop sb's salary; **jdm den Ausgang ~** *(Mil)* to confine sb to barracks

f *(= abstellen) Gas, Strom, Telefon* to cut off, to disconnect; **jdm den Strom/das Telefon ~** to cut off *or* disconnect sb's electricity/telephone

g *(= einschließen)* **jdn in etw** *(acc)* **~** to shut *or* lock sb in sth

h *(Typ)* to space out

VR **sich (gegen etw) ~** to ba(u)lk *or* jib (at sth); **jetzt lass dir doch auch einmal etwas schenken und sperr dich nicht so** can't you just accept a present for once and not be so ungracious

VI **a** *(= nicht schließen: Tür, Fenster)* to stick, to jam; *(= blockiert sein: Räder)* to lock **b** *(Sport)* to obstruct; **Sperren ist nicht zulässig** obstruction is not allowed

Sperr-: **Sperr|feu|er** NT *(Mil, fig)* barrage; **sein Vorschlag geriet ins ~ der Kritik** his suggestion came in for a barrage of criticism; **Sperr|frist** F waiting period *(auch Jur)*; *(Sport)* (period of) suspension; **Sperr|ge|biet** NT no-go area, prohibited area *or* zone; **Sperr|ge|trie|be** NT locking mechanism; **Sperr|gut** NT, *no pl* bulky freight *or* goods *pl*; **Sperr|holz** NT plywood

sper|rig [ˈʃpɛrɪç] ADJ bulky; *(= unhandlich)* unwieldy; *(fig) Slogan, Sprache* unwieldy, clumsy; *Text, Musik* unwieldy; *Thema, Charakter* awkward; **sich ~ zeigen** to be awkward

Sperr-: **Sperr|ket|te** F chain; *(an Haustür)* safety chain; **Sperr|klau|sel** F exclusion clause; **Sperr|klin|ke** F pawl; **Sperr|kon|to** NT blocked account; **Sperr|kreis** M *(Rad)* wave trap; **Sperr|mau|er** F wall; **Sperr|mi|no|ri|tät** F *(Fin)* blocking minority; **Sperr|müll** M bulky refuse; **Sperr|müll|ab|fuhr** F removal of bulky refuse; **Sperr|rad** NT ratchet wheel; **Sperr|schrift** M *(Typ)* spaced type; **Sperr|sitz** M *(im Kino)* back seats *pl*; *(im Zirkus)* front seats *pl*; *(old: im Theater)* stalls *pl*, orchestra; **Sperr|stück** M *(Fin)* blocked security; **Sperr|stun|de** F closing time

Sper|rung [ˈʃpɛrʊŋ] F **-, -en** **a** *(= Schließung)* closing; *(von Platz, Gegend)* closing off; *(Tech)* locking; *(von Konto)* blocking; *(von Scheck)* stopping; *(Sport: = Ausschluss)* banning, barring; *(= Verbot)* banning; *(von Urlaub, Gehalt)* stopping, stoppage; *(von Strom, Gas, Telefon)* cutting off, disconnection, disconnecting; *(Typ)* spacing **b** = **Sperre b**

Sperr-: **Sperr|ver|merk** M *(in Dokumenten)* restricted notice; **Sperr|ver|trag** M *(Pol)* blocking treaty; **Sperr|zoll** M prohibitive tariff; **Sperr|zo|ne** F no-go area, prohibited area *or* zone

Spe|sen [ˈʃpeːzn] PL *(auch Fin)* expenses *pl*; **auf ~ reisen/essen** to travel/eat on expenses; **außer ~ nichts gewesen** nothing doing, no joy *(esp Brit inf)*

Spe|sen-: **Spe|sen|ab|rech|nung** F calculation of expenses; **spe|sen|frei** ADJ free of charge; **Spe|sen|kon|to** NT expense account; **Spe|sen|rech|nung** F statement of expenses; **Spe|sen|rit|ter** M *(inf)* expense-account type *(inf)*

Spe|ze|rei [ʃpeːtsəˈrai] F **-, -en** *usu pl (old)* spice; *(= Delikatesse)* exotic delicacy

Spe|zi [ˈʃpeːtsi] M **-s, -s** *(S Ger inf)* pal *(inf)*, mate *(Brit inf)*, buddy *(esp US inf)*

Spe|zi® NT **-s, -s** *(Getränk) mixture of cola and orangeade*

Spe|zi|al-: **Spe|zi|al|arzt** M, **Spe|zi|al|ärz|tin** F specialist; **Spe|zi|al|aus|bil|dung** F specialized training; **Spe|zi|al|aus|füh|rung** F special model *or* version; **ein Modell in ~** a special version; **Spe|zi|al|be|reich** M **a** special field *or* area **b** *(= Thema)* special topic; **Spe|zi|al|dis|zip|lin** F special discipline; **Spe|zi|al|ef|fekt** M special effect; **Spe|zi|al|ein|heit** F special unit, special task force; **Spe|zi|al|fach** NT special subject; **Spe|zi|al|fahr|zeug** NT special-purpose vehicle; **Spe|zi|al|fall** M special case; **Spe|zi|al|fra|ge** F **a** special question **b** *(Aus Sch)* question from a special(ist) field; **Spe|zi|al|ge|biet** NT **a** special field *or* area **b** *(= Thema)* special topic; **Spe|zi|al|ge|schäft** NT specialist shop; **ein ~ für Sportkleidung** a sportswear specialist's

spe|zi|a|li|sie|ren [ʃpetsialiˈziːrən] *ptp* **spezialisiert** VR **sich (auf etw** *acc*) **~** to specialize (in sth) VT *(old: = spezifizieren)* to specify, to itemize

Spe|zi|a|li|sie|rung F **-, -en** specialization

Spe|zi|a|list [ʃpetsiaˈlɪst] M **-en, -en**, **Spe|zi|a|lis|tin** [-ˈlɪstɪn] F **-, -nen** specialist *(für* in)

Spe|zi|a|lis|ten|tum [ʃpetsiaˈlɪstntuːm] NT **-s**, *no pl* specialization

Spe|zi|a|li|tät [ʃpetsialiˈtɛːt] F **-, -en** **a** speciality *(Brit)*, specialty *(US)* **b** **Spezialitäten** PL *(Cook)* specialities *pl*; **~ des Hauses** *(auf Speisekarte)* speciality *(Brit) or* specialty *(US)* of the house

Spe|zi|a|li|tä|ten|res|tau|rant NT speciality *(Brit) or* specialty *(US)* restaurant

Spe|zi|al-: **Spe|zi|al|sla|lom** M special slalom; **Spe|zi|al|voll|macht** F special authorization

spe|zi|ell [ʃpeˈtsiɛl] ADJ special; **auf Ihr (ganz) Spezielles!** (to) your good health!; **er ist mein ganz ~er Freund** he's a very special friend of mine *(auch iro)* ADV (e)specially

Spe|zi|es [ˈʃpeːtsiɛs, ˈsp-] F **-, -** *(Biol)* species *sing*; **die ~ Mensch** the human species

Spe|zi|fi|ka|ti|on [ʃpetsifikaˈtsioːn, sp-] F **-, -en** specification; *(= Aufgliederung)* classification

Spe|zi|fi|kum [ʃpeˈtsiːfikʊm] NT **-s, Spezifika** [-ka] *(geh: = Besonderheit)* specific feature; *(Med)* specific

spe|zi|fisch [ʃpeˈtsiːfɪʃ, sp-] ADJ specific ADV specifically; *(= typisch)* typically

spe|zi|fi|zie|ren [ʃpetsifiˈtsiːrən, sp-] *ptp* **spezifiziert** VT to specify; *(= einzeln aufführen auch)* to itemize

Spe|zi|fi|zie|rung [ʃpetsifiˈtsiːrʊŋ, sp-] F **-, -en** specification, specifying; *(= Einzelaufführung auch)* itemization, itemizing

Sphä|re [ˈsfɛːrə] F **-, -n** *(lit, fig)* sphere → **schweben a**

Sphä|ren-: **Sphä|ren|har|mo|nie** F harmony of the spheres; **Sphä|ren|mu|sik** F music of the spheres

sphä|risch [ˈsfɛːrɪʃ] ADJ spherical; *Klänge, Musik* celestial

Sphinx [sfɪŋks] F **-, -e** sphinx

Spick-: **Spick|aal** M smoked eel; **Spick|bra|ten** M larded *(esp Brit) or* basted roast

spi|cken [ˈʃpɪkn] VT *(Cook) Braten* to lard *(esp Brit)*, to baste; *(inf: = bestechen)* to bribe, to square *(Brit inf)*; **eine (gut) gespickte Brieftasche** a well-lined wallet; **mit Zitaten gespickt** larded *(esp Brit) or* peppered with quotations; **mit Fehlern gespickt** peppered with mistakes VI *(Sch inf)* to copy, to crib *(Brit inf)* *(bei* off, from)

Spi|cker [ˈʃpɪkɐ] M **-s, -** *(inf)*, **Spick|zet|tel** M crib *(Brit)*, cheat sheet *(US)*

spie *pret von* **speien**

Spie|gel [ˈʃpiːgl] M **-s, -** **a** mirror, glass *(old)*; *(Med)* speculum; *(fig)* mirror; **in den ~ schauen** *or* **sehen** to look in the mirror; **glatt wie ein ~** like glass; **im ~ der Öffentlichkeit** *or* **der öffentlichen Meinung** as seen by the public, as reflected in public opinion; **jdm den ~ vorhalten** *(fig)* to hold up a mirror to sb

b *(= Wasserspiegel, Alkoholspiegel, Zuckerspiegel)* level; *(= Wasseroberfläche)* surface

c *(= Aufschlag)* lapel; *(Mil: = Kragenspiegel)* tab

d *(Archit: von Decke, Tür)* panel

e *(Hunt) (bei Rotwild)* escutcheon; *(bei Vögeln)* speculum

f *(Liter: = Sammlung von Regeln, Gesetzen etc)* code

g *(Typ)* type area

Spie|gel-: **Spie|gel|bild** NT *(lit, fig)* reflection; *(= seitenverkehrtes Bild)* mirror image; **die Schrift im ~** the mirror image of the writing; **spie|gel|bild|lich** ADJ *(lit, fig)* mirror image; **~ dazu ...** as a direct contrast, ... ADV **~ schreiben** to do mirror writing; **~ gleich sein** *(zwei Dinge)* to be the mirror image of each other; **spie|gel|blank** ADJ glossy, shining ADV **etw**

~ putzen/polieren/reiben/wienern to polish sth until it shines

Spie|gel|ei [ˈʃpiːglˈai] NT fried egg

Spie|gel-: **Spie|gel|fech|te|rei** [-fɛçtəˈrai] F -, -en *(fig)* *(= Scheingefecht)* shadow-boxing; *(= Heuchelei, Vortäuschung)* sham, bluff; **Spie|gel|fern|rohr** NT reflector (telescope); **Spie|gel|fo|lie** F mirror foil; **spie|gel|frei** ADJ *Brille, Bildschirm etc* nonreflecting; **Spie|gel|glas** NT mirror glass; **spie|gel|glatt** ADJ *Fahrbahn, Meer etc* like glass *pred*, glassy; **spie|gel|gleich** ADJ symmetrical; **Spie|gel|gleich|heit** F symmetry; **Spie|gel|heck** NT *(Naut)* square stern; **Spie|gel|karp|fen** M mirror carp

spie|geln [ˈʃpiːgln] VI *(= reflektieren)* to reflect (the light); *(= glitzern)* to gleam, to shine VT to reflect, to mirror VR to be mirrored *or* reflected; *(= sich betrachten)* to look at one's reflection

Spie|gel-: **Spie|gel|re|flex|ka|me|ra** F reflex camera; **Spie|gel|schrift** F mirror writing; **etw in ~ schreiben** to write sth backwards

Spie|ge|lung [ˈʃpiːgəlʊŋ] F -, -en reflection; *(= Luftspiegelung)* mirage

spie|gel|ver|kehrt ADJ back-to-front, backward *(US)*; **~e Abbildung** mirror image ADV *abbilden* in mirror image

Spie|ker [ˈʃpiːkɐ] M -s, - **a** *(N Ger. = Nagel)* nail; *(Naut)* spike **b** *(N Ger. = Speicher)* storehouse

Spiel [ʃpiːl] NT -(e)s, -e **a** *(= Unterhaltungsspiel, Glücksspiel, Sport, Tennis)* game; *(= Wettkampfspiel, Fußballspiel)* game, match; *(Theat: = Stück)* play; *(fig: = eine Leichtigkeit)* child's play *no art*; **ein ~ spielen** *(lit, fig)* to play a game; **im ~ sein** *(lit)* to be in the game; *(fig)* to be involved *or* at work; **die Kräfte, die hier mit im ~ waren** the forces which were at play here; **das Leben ist kein ~** life is not a game; **das ~ verloren geben** to give the game up for lost; *(fig)* to throw in the towel; **machen Sie ihr ~!** place your bets!, faites vos jeux; **das ~ machen** *(Sport)* to make the play; **jdn ins ~ schicken** *(Sport)* to send sb on; **jdn aus dem ~ nehmen** *(Sport)* to take sb off
b *(= das Spielen, Spielweise)* play(ing); *(Mus, Theat)* playing; *(Sport)* play; *(bei Glücksspielen)* gambling; **das ~ ist für die Entwicklung des Kindes wichtig** play(ing) is important for children's development; **stör die Kinder nicht beim ~** don't disturb the children while they're playing *or* at play; **stummes ~** miming
c *(= Bewegung, Zusammenspiel)* play; **~ der Hände** hand movements; **das (freie) ~ der Kräfte** the (free) (inter)play of forces; **~ der Lichter** play of lights; **das ~ der Wellen** the play of the waves
d **ein ~ des Schicksals** *or* **Zufalls** a whim of fate
e *(= Spielzubehör)* game; *(Cards)* deck, pack; *(= Satz)* set; **führen Sie auch ~e?** do you have games?; **das Monopolyspiel ist nicht mehr vollständig** the Monopoly® set has something missing
f *(von Stricknadeln)* set
g *(Tech)* (free) play; *(= Spielraum)* clearance
h *(Hunt)* tail
i *(fig)* **das ist ein ~ mit dem Feuer** that's playing with fire; **leichtes ~ (mit** *or* **bei jdm) haben** to have an easy job of it (with sb); **bei den einfachen Bauern hatten die Betrüger leichtes ~** the simple peasants were easy prey for the swindlers; **das ~ ist aus** the game's up; **die Hand** *or* **Finger im ~ haben** to have a hand in it; **jdn/etw aus dem ~ lassen** to leave *or* keep sb/sth out of it; **aus dem ~ bleiben** to stay *or* keep out of it; **jdn/etw ins ~ bringen** to bring sb/sth into it; **etw aufs ~ setzen** to put sth at stake *or* on the line *(inf)*, to risk sth; **auf dem ~(e) stehen** to be at stake; **sein ~ mit jdm treiben** to play games with sb

Spiel-: **Spiel|al|ter** NT playing stage; **Spiel|an|zug** M playsuit, rompers *pl*; **Spiel|art** F variety; **Spiel|au|to|mat** M gambling *or* gaming machine; *(zum Geldgewinnen)* fruit machine, one-armed bandit *(hum inf)*; **Spiel|bahn** F *(Golf)* fairway; **Spiel|ball** M *(Volleyball)* match ball, game ball *(US)*; *(Tennis)* game point; *(Billard)* cue ball; *(fig)* plaything; **ein ~ der Wellen sein** *(geh)* to be at the mercy of the waves, to be tossed about by the waves; **Spiel|bank** F *pl* **-banken** casino; **spiel|bar** ADJ playable; *Theaterstück* actable; **Spiel|be|ginn** M start of play; **gleich nach ~** just after the start of play; **Spiel|bein** NT free leg; **spiel|be|reit** ADJ ready to play; **Spiel|brett** NT board; *(Basketball)* backboard

Spiel|chen [ˈʃpiːlçən] NT -s, - *(inf)* little game

Spiel|com|pu|ter M *(für Computerspiele)* games computer; *(= Lerncomputer)* educational computer

Spiel|do|se F musical box *(Brit)*, music box

Spie|le|com|pu|ter M = **Spielcomputer**

Spie|le|kon|so|le F *(Comput)* game(s) console, play console

spie|len [ˈʃpiːlən] VT to play; **Klavier/Flöte ~** to play the piano/the flute; **was wird heute im Theater/Kino gespielt?** what's on at the theatre *(Brit) or* theater *(US)*/cinema today?, what's playing at the theatre *(Brit) or* theater *(US)*/what's showing at the cinema today?; **sie ~ einen Film von ...** they're showing a film by ...; **das Stück war sehr gut gespielt** the play was very well acted *or* performed *or* done; **wir haben die Mutter Courage in Stuttgart gespielt** we played Mother Courage in Stuttgart; **den Unschuldigen ~** to play the innocent; **den Beleidigten ~** to act all offended; **sie spielt die große Dame** she's playing *or* acting the grand lady *or* the grand old dame *(US)*; **am Sonntag musste ich mal wieder Klempner ~** on Sunday I had to do my plumber's act again; **was wird hier gespielt?** *(inf)* what's going on here? → **Herr c**, **Schicksal**
VI to play; *(Theat) (Schauspieler)* to act, to play; *(Stück)* to be on, to be playing; *(Film)* to be on, to be showing; *(beim Glücksspiel)* to gamble; **die Mannschaft hat gut/schlecht** *etc* **gespielt** the team had a good/bad *etc* game, the team played well/badly *etc*; **bei ihm spielt das Radio den ganzen Tag** he has the radio on all day; **seine Beziehungen ~ lassen** to bring one's connections to bear *or* into play; **seine Muskeln ~ lassen** to ripple one's muscles; **wie das Leben so spielt** life's funny like that; **in der Hauptrolle spielt X** X is playing the lead; **das Stück spielt im 18. Jahrhundert/in Italien** the play is set in the 18th century/in Italy; **nervös spielte er mit dem Bleistift** he played *or* toyed nervously with the pencil; **mit dem Gedanken ~, etw zu tun** to toy *or* play with the idea of doing sth; **mit jdm/jds Liebe/Gefühlen ~** to play (around) with sb/sb's affections/feelings; **ein Lächeln spielte um ihre Lippen** a smile played about her lips; **ihr Haar spielt ins Rötliche** her hair has a reddish tinge
VR **sich müde ~** to tire oneself out playing; **sich warm ~** to warm up; **sich in den Vordergrund ~** to push oneself into the foreground; **auf nassem Boden spielt es sich schlecht** *(Sport)* wet ground isn't very good to play on → *auch* **gespielt**

spie|lend ADJ playing ADV easily; **das ist ~ leicht** that's very easy

Spiel|en|de [ˈʃpiːlˈɛndə] NT end of play; **kurz vor ~** just before the end of play

spie|len+las|sen VT *ptp* **spielenlassen** *or (rare)* **spielengelassen** *sep irreg (fig)* → **spielen VI**

Spie|ler [ˈʃpiːlɐ] M -s, -, **Spie|le|rin** [-ərɪn] F -, -nen player; *(Theat auch)* actor/actress; *(= Glücksspieler)* gambler

Spie|le|rei [ʃpiːləˈrai] F -, -en **a** *no pl (= das Spielen)* playing; *(beim Glücksspiel)* gambling; *(= das Herumspielen)* playing *or* fooling *or* fiddling *(inf)* about *(Brit) or* around; *(= Kinderspiel)* child's play *no art*, doddle *(Brit inf)*; **das ist nur ~** I am/he is *etc* just playing *or* fooling about *(Brit) or* around; **hör mit der ~ am Fernseher auf!** stop playing *or* fooling *or* fiddling *(inf)* about *(Brit) or* around with the TV! **b** *(= Gegenstand)* frivolity; *(= Gerät)* gadget

spie|le|risch [ˈʃpiːlərɪʃ] ADJ **a** *(= verspielt) Geste, Katze etc* playful **b** **mit ~er Leichtigkeit** with the greatest of ease, with consummate ease **c** *(Sport)* playing; *(Theat)* acting; **~es Können** playing/acting ability; **die ~e Leistung** the playing/acting ADV **a** *(= verspielt)* playfully **b** *(= mit Leichtigkeit)* with the greatest of ease, with consummate ease **c** *(Sport)* in playing terms; *(Theat)* in acting terms **d** *(= im Spiel)* **etw ~ lernen** to learn sth through play(ing)

Spie|ler-: **Spie|ler|na|tur** F gambler; **Spie|ler|wech|sel** M substitution

Spiel-: **Spiel|feld** NT field, pitch *(Brit)*; *(Tennis, Squash, Basketball)* court; **Spiel|feld|hälf|te** F half (of the field *or* pitch *(Brit)*); *(Tennis, Squash, Basketball)* half (of the court); **Spiel|feld|rand** M touchline; **Spiel|fest** NT *(für Kinder)* games party, party with organized games; **Spiel|fi|gur** F piece; **Spiel|film** M feature film; **Spiel|flä|che** F playing area; *(bei Gesellschaftsspielen)* playing surface; **Spiel|fol|ge** F *(Sport)* order of play; *(Theat)* programme *(Brit)*, program *(US)*; **spiel|frei** ADJ *(Theat, Sport)* **~er Tag** rest day; **die ~e Zeit** the close season; **der Sonntag ist ~** there is no performance on Sundays; *(Sport)* there is no game on Sundays; **spiel|freu|dig** ADJ keen, enthusiastic; **Spiel|füh|rer(in)** M(F) (team) captain; **Spiel|ge|fähr|te** M, **Spiel|ge|fähr|tin** F playmate, playfellow *(Brit)*; **Spiel|geld** NT **a** *(= Einsatz)* stake **b** *(= unechtes Geld)* play money, toy money *(Brit)*; **Spiel|ge|nos|se** M, **Spiel|ge|nos|sin** F playmate, playfellow *(Brit)*; **Spiel|ge|sche|hen** NT *(Sport)* play, action; **das gesamte ~** all of the play *or* action; **Spiel|ge|stal|ter** [-gəʃtaltɐ] M -s, -, **Spiel|ge|stal|te|rin** [-ərɪn] F -, -nen *(Sport)* key player; **Spiel|hal|le** F amusement arcade *(Brit)*, arcade; **Spiel|höl|le** F gambling den; **Spiel|ka|me|rad(in)** M(F) playmate, playfellow *(Brit)*; **Spiel|kar|te** F playing card; **Spiel|ka|si|no** NT (gambling) casino; **Spiel|klas|se** F division; **Spiel|kon|so|le** F *(Comput)* game(s) console, play console; **Spiel|lei|den|schaft** F passion for gambling, gambling mania; **Spiel|lei|ter(in)** M(F) **a** *(= Regisseur)* director; *(Theat, Rad, TV auch)* producer *(Brit)* **b** *(Sport)* organizer **c** *(= Conférencier)* master of ceremonies, emcee *(esp US inf)*; **Spiel|ma|cher(in)** M(F) key player; **Spiel|mann** M *pl* **-leute** *(Hist)* Minstrel; *(= Mitglied eines Spielmannszuges)* bandsman; **Spiel|manns|zug** M (brass) band; **Spiel|mar|ke** F chip, counter; **Spiel|ma|te|ri|al** NT *(von Brettspielen etc)* game components *pl*; *(fig: = Spielzeug)* plaything; **Spiel|mi|nu|te** F minute (of play)

Spie|lo|thek [ʃpiːloˈteːk] F -, -en amusement arcade *(Brit)*, arcade

Spiel-: **Spiel|plan** M *(Theat, Film)* programme *(Brit)*, program *(US)*; **ein Stück vom ~ absetzen** to drop a play (from the programme *(Brit) or* program *(US)*); **Spiel|platz** M *(für Kinder)* playground; *(Sport)* playing field; **Spiel|raum** M room to move; *(fig)* scope; *(zeitlich)* time; *(bei Planung etc)* leeway; *(Tech)* clearance, (free) play; **jedes Kind braucht einen gewissen ~, um sich frei entwickeln zu können** all children need a certain amount of scope to be able to develop freely; **Spiel|rausch** M gambling fever; **Spiel|re|gel** F *(lit, fig)* rule of the game; **sich an die ~n halten** *(lit, fig)* **die ~n beachten** *(lit, fig)* to stick to the rules of the game, to play the game; **gegen die ~n verstoßen** *(lit, fig)* to break the rules, not to play the game; **Spiel|run|de** F round; **Spiel|saal** M gambling hall; **Spiel|sa|chen** PL toys *pl*, playthings *pl*; **Spiel|sai|son** F *(Theat, Sport)* season; **Spiel|show** F game show; **Spiel|schuld** F gambling debt; **Spiel|stand** M score; **bei einem ~ von …** with the score (standing) at …; **Spiel|stät|te** F play area; **Spiel|stra|ße** F **a** (= *verkehrsberuhigte Zone*) play street **b** (*auf Kinderfest*) play area; **Spiel|sucht** F compulsive gambling; **Spiel|süch|ti|ge(r)** MF *decl as adj* compulsive gambler; **Spiel|tag** M (*Ftbl etc*) day; **Spiel|teu|fel** M gambling urge *or* bug (*inf*); **vom ~ besessen sein** (*inf*) to have the gambling bug (*inf*); **Spiel|tisch** M games table; (*beim Glückspiel*) gaming *or* gambling table; **Spiel|trieb** M play instinct; **Spiel|uhr** F musical box (*Brit*), music box; **Spiel|ver|bot** NT (*Sport*) ban; **~ haben** to be banned; **Spiel|ver|der|ber** [-fɛɐdɛrbɐ] M **-s, -**, **Spiel|ver|der|be|rin** [-ərɪn] F **-, -nen** spoilsport; **du bist ein alter ~!** you're an old killjoy!; **Spiel|ver|län|ge|rung** F extra time (*Brit*), overtime (*US*); (*wegen Verletzung auch*) injury time (*Brit*); **es gab eine ~ (von 30 Minuten)** (30 minutes') extra time *etc* was played; **Spiel|ver|lauf** M action, play; **Spiel|wa|ren** PL toys *pl*; **Spiel|wa|ren|ge|schäft** NT, **Spiel|wa|ren|hand|lung** F toy shop (*esp Brit*) or store (*esp US*); **Spiel|wei|se** F way of playing; **offensive/defensive/unfaire ~** attacking/defensive/unfair play; **Spiel|werk** NT musical mechanism; **Spiel|wie|se** F playing field; **Spiel|zeit** F **a** (= *Saison*) season **b** (= *Spieldauer*) playing time; **die normale ~** (*Sport*) normal time; **die reguläre ~ ist abgelaufen** (*Ftbl*) the ninety minutes are up; **nach dreimonatiger ~ wurde das Stück abgesetzt** the play was taken off after a three-month run

Spiel|zeug NT *pl* **-zeuge** toys *pl*, playthings *pl*; (*einzelnes*) toy; **er hat viel ~** he has a lot of toys

Spiel|zeug- *in cpds* toy; **Spiel|zeug|ei|sen|bahn** F (toy) train set

Spiel|zim|mer NT playroom

Spie|re [ˈʃpiːrə] F **-, -n** (*Naut*) spar, boom

Spier|ling [ˈʃpiːɐlɪŋ] M **-s, -e** (= *Eberesche*) service tree

Spieß [ʃpiːs] M **-es, -e** M **-es, -e** **a** (= *Stich- und Wurfwaffe*) spear; (= *Bratspieß*) spit; (*kleiner*) skewer; **am ~ gebraten** roasted on the spit, spit-roast(ed); **Lamm am ~** spit-roast(ed) lamb; **wie am ~(e) schreien** (*inf*) **schreien als ob man am ~ steckt** (*inf*) to squeal like a stuck pig; **den ~ umkehren** *or* **umdrehen** (*fig*) to turn the tables → **brüllen** **b** (*Mil sl*) sarge (*inf*) **c** (*Hunt*) spike **d** (*Typ*) spacing mark, work-up (*US*)

Spieß-: **Spieß|bock** M (*Hunt*) brocket, spike buck; **Spieß|bra|ten** M joint roasted on a spit; **Spieß|bür|ger(in)** M(F) (*pej*) (petit) bourgeois; **ihre Eltern sind richtige ~** her parents are typically middle-class; **spieß|bür|ger|lich** (*pej*) ADJ middle-class, (petit) bourgeois ADV *denken, sich benehmen, leben* in a middle-class *or* bourgeois way; **Spieß|bür|ger|tum** NT (*pej*) (petit-)bourgeois conformism, middle-class values *pl*

spie|ßen [ˈʃpiːsn] VT **etw auf etw** (*acc*) **~** (*auf Pfahl etc*) to impale sth on sth; (*auf Gabel etc*) to skewer sth on sth; (*auf größeren Bratspieß*) to spit sth on sth; (*auf Nadel*) to pin sth on sth

Spie|ßer[1] [ˈʃpiːsɐ] M **-s, -** (*Hunt*: = *Spießbock*) brocket, spike buck

Spie|ßer[2] [ˈʃpiːsɐ] M **-s, -**, **Spie|ße|rin** [-ərɪn] F **-, -nen** (*pej*) = **Spießbürger(in)**

Spieß|ge|sel|le M (*old*) companion; (*hum*: = *Komplize*) crony (*inf*)

spie|ßig [ˈʃpiːsɪç] ADJ ADV (*pej*) = **spießbürgerlich**

Spieß|ru|te F switch; **~n laufen** (*fig*) to run the gauntlet

Spieß|ru|ten|lauf M (*fig*) running the gauntlet; **für ihn wird jeder Gang durch die Stadt zum ~** every time he walks through town it's like running the gauntlet

Spikes [ʃpaiks, sp-] PL (= *Sportschuhe, Stifte*) spikes *pl*; (= *Autoreifen*) studded tyres *pl* (*Brit*) *or* tires *pl* (*US*); (= *Stifte an Reifen*) studs *pl*

Spill [ʃpɪl] NT **-(e)s, -e** (*Naut*) capstan

spil|le|rig [ˈʃpɪlərɪç] ADJ (*N Ger*) spindly

spi|nal [ʃpiˈnaːl, sp-] ADJ (*Med*) spinal; **~e Kinderlähmung** poliomyelitis; **~er Muskelschwund** spinal muscular atrophy

Spi|nat [ʃpiˈnaːt] M **-(e)s,** *no pl* spinach

Spi|nat|wach|tel F (*pej inf*) old cow (*inf*) *or* baggage (*inf*)

Spind [ʃpɪnt] M OR NT **-(e)s, -e** [-də] (*Mil, Sport*) locker; (*old*: = *Vorratskammer*) cupboard

Spin|del [ˈʃpɪndl] F **-, -n** spindle; (= *Treppenspindel*) newel

spin|del|dürr ADJ (*pej*) spindly, thin as a rake (*Brit*) *or* rail (*US*); **~e Beine** spindleshanks (*inf*), spindly legs

spin|del|för|mig ADJ spindle-shaped

Spi|nett [ʃpiˈnɛt] NT **-s, -e** (*Mus*) spinet

Spin|na|ker [ˈʃpɪnakɐ] M **-s, -** (*Naut*) spinnaker

Spin|ne [ˈʃpɪnə] F **-, -n** spider; (= *Wäschespinne*) rotary clothesline

spin|ne|feind ADJ, **Spin|ne|feind** △ M (*inf*) **sich** *or* **einander** (*dat*) **~ sein** to be deadly enemies

spin|nen [ˈʃpɪnən] *pret* **spann** [ʃpan], *ptp* **gesponnen** [gəˈʃpɔnən] VT to spin; (*old liter*: = *ersinnen*) *Verrat, Ränke* to plot; *Lügen* to concoct, to invent; *Geschichte* to spin; **ein Netz von Lügen ~, ein Lügengewebe ~** to weave a web of lies; **das ist alles gesponnen** (*inf*) it's all fairy tales; **Fäden ~** (*fig*) to create a network of contacts → **Garn a**

VI **a** (*lit*) to spin

b (*inf*) (= *leicht verrückt sein*) to be crazy *or* nutty *or* screwy (*all inf*); (= *Unsinn reden*) to talk rubbish (*Brit inf*) *or* garbage (*inf*); (= *Lügengeschichten erzählen*) to make it up, to tell tall stories; **stimmt das oder spinnst du?** is that true, or are you having me on (*inf*) *or* putting me on (*US inf*)?; **sag mal, spinn ich, oder …?** am I imagining things or …?; **ich denk ich spinn** I don't believe it; **ich spinn doch nicht** no way (*inf*); **spinn doch nicht!** come off it! (*inf*); **du spinnst wohl!, spinnst du?** you must be crazy!, are you crazy!; **ich dein Auto waschen?, du spinnst wohl!** me clean your car?, you've got to be joking *or* kidding! (*inf*)

Spin|nen-: **Spin|nen|fa|den** M spider's thread; **Spin|nen|ge|we|be** NT, **Spin|nen|netz** NT cobweb, spider's web

Spin|ner[1] [ˈʃpɪnɐ] M (*Zool*) silkworm moth

Spin|ner[2] [ˈʃpɪnɐ] M **-s, -**, **Spin|ne|rin** [-ərɪn] F **-, -nen** **a** (*Tex*) spinner **b** (*inf*) nutcase (*inf*), screwball (*esp US inf*); **du ~, das stimmt doch nicht!** are you crazy? that's not true at all!

Spin|ne|rei [ʃpɪnəˈrai] F **-, -en** **a** (= *das Spinnen*) spinning **b** (= *Spinnwerkstatt*) spinning mill **c** (*inf*) crazy behaviour (*Brit*) *or* behavior (*US*) *no pl*, crazy thing; (= *Unsinn*) rubbish (*Brit inf*), garbage (*inf*); **das ist doch eine ~, so was zu machen** it's crazy to do that; **deine ~en glaubt dir doch kein Mensch!** nobody's going to believe all that rubbish (*Brit inf*) *or* garbage (*inf*)

spin|nert [ˈʃpɪnɐt] (*S Ger, Aus*: *inf*) ADJ crazy (*inf*) ADV crazily; **~ daherreden** to talk daft (*Brit inf*) *or* crazy (*US inf*)

Spinn-: **Spinn|fa|ser** F spinning fibre (*Brit*) *or* fiber (*US*); **Spinn|ge|we|be** NT cobweb, spider's web; **Spinn|ma|schi|ne** F spinning machine; **Spinn|rad** NT spinning wheel; **Spinn|ro|cken** [-rɔkn] M **-s, -** distaff; **Spinn|stu|be** F spinning room; **Spinn|we|be** [-veːbə] F **-, -n**, (*Aus, S Ger*) **Spinn|web** [-veːp] NT OR M **-(e)s, -e** [-bə] cobweb, spider's web

spi|nös [ʃpiˈnøːs, sp-] ADJ crackpot *attr* (*inf*)

spin|ti|sie|ren [ʃpɪntiˈziːrən] *ptp* **spintisiert** VI (*inf*) to ruminate, to muse

Spi|on[1] [ʃpioːn] M **-s, -e** (*inf*) (= *Guckloch*) spyhole, peephole; (= *Fensterspiegel*) window mirror

Spi|on[2] [ʃpioːn] M **-s, -e**, **Spi|o|nin** [ˈʃpioːnɪn] F **-, -nen** spy

Spi|o|na|ge [ʃpioˈnaːʒə] F **-,** *no pl* spying, espionage; **~ treiben** to spy, to carry on espionage; **unter dem Verdacht der ~ für …** on suspicion of spying for …

Spi|o|na|ge-: **Spi|o|na|ge|ab|wehr** F counterintelligence *or* counterespionage (service); **Spi|o|na|ge|dienst** M (*inf*) secret service; **Spi|o|na|ge|netz** NT spy network; **Spi|o|na|ge|ring** M spy ring; **Spi|o|na|ge|sa|tel|lit** M spy satellite; **Spi|o|na|ge|soft|ware** F **-s,** *no pl* (*Comput*) spyware

spi|o|nie|ren [ʃpioˈniːrən] *ptp* **spioniert** VI to spy; (*fig inf*: = *nachforschen*) to snoop *or* poke about (*inf*)

Spi|o|nin [ˈʃpioːnɪn] F **-, -nen** spy

Spi|ral|block F *pl* **-blöcke** *or* **-blocks** spiral notebook

Spi|ra|le [ʃpiˈraːlə] F **-, -n** spiral; (*geometrisch, Sci auch*) helix; (*Med*) coil

Spi|ral-: **Spi|ral|fe|der** F coil spring; **spi|ral|för|mig** ADJ spiral ADV in a spiral; **das Flugzeug schraubte sich ~ in den Himmel hinauf** the plane spiralled (*Brit*) *or* spiraled (*US*) up into the sky

spi|ra|lig [ʃpiˈraːlɪç] ADJ (*rare*) spiral, helical

Spi|ral|ne|bel M (*Astron*) spiral nebula

Spi|rans [ˈʃpiːrans, ˈsp-] F **-, Spiranten** [-ˈrantn], **Spi|rant** [ʃpiˈrant, sp-] M **-en, -en** (*Ling*) fricative, spirant

Spi|ri|tis|mus [ʃpiriˈtɪsmʊs, sp-] M **-,** *no pl* spiritualism, spiritism

Spi|ri|tist [ʃpiriˈtɪst, sp-] M **-en, -en**, **Spi|ri|tis|tin** [-ˈtɪstɪn] F **-, -nen** spiritualist

spi|ri|tis|tisch [ʃpiriˈtɪstɪʃ, sp-] ADJ **~e Sitzung** seance

Spi|ri|tu|al [ˈspɪrɪtjʊəl] M OR NT **-s, -s** (negro) spiritual

Spi|ri|tu|a|lis|mus [ʃpiritualˈɪsmʊs, sp-] M **-,** *no pl* spiritualism

spi|ri|tu|a|lis|tisch [ʃpiritualˈɪstɪʃ, sp-] ADJ spiritualist

spi|ri|tu|ell [ʃpiriˈtuɛl, sp-] ADJ spiritual ADV spiritually

Spi|ri|tu|o|sen [ʃpiriˈtuoːzn, sp-] PL spirits *pl*

Spi|ri|tus M **-,** *no pl* **a** [ˈʃpiːrɪtʊs] (= *Alkohol*) spirit; **mit ~ kochen** to cook with *or* on a spirit stove; **etw in ~ legen** to put sth in alcohol **b** [ˈspiːrɪtʊs] (*Ling*) spiritus

Spi|ri|tus-: **Spi|ri|tus|ko|cher** M spirit stove; **Spi|ri|tus|lam|pe** F spirit lamp

Spi|tal [ʃpiˈtaːl] NT **-s, Spitäler** [-ˈtɛːlɐ] (*old, Aus, Sw*: = *Krankenhaus*) hospital, spital (*obs*); (*rare*: = *Altersheim*) old people's home

spitz [ʃpɪts] ADJ **a** (= *mit einer Spitze*) pointed; (= *nicht stumpf*) *Bleistift, Nadel etc* sharp; (*Math*) *Winkel* acute; **die Feder dieses Füllhalters ist nicht ~ genug** the nib on this fountain pen is too broad; **~e Schuhe** pointed shoes, winkle-pickers (*Brit hum inf*), elf-shoes (*US hum inf*); **~e Klammern** angle brackets; **mit dem ~en Bleistift rechnen** (*fig*) to work everything out (down) to the last penny; **etw mit ~en Fingern anfassen** (*inf*) to pick sth up gingerly; **über einen ~en Stein stolpern** (*hum*) *to pronounce "sp" and "st" as in English*

b (= *gehässig*) *Bemerkung* pointed, barbed; *Zunge* sharp → **Feder b**

c (= *kränklich*) *Aussehen, Gesicht* pinched, haggard, peaky

d (*sl*: = *lüstern*) randy (*Brit inf*), horny (*inf*); **~ wie Nachbars Lumpi** *or* **wie ein Turnschuh** *or* **wie Rettich** as randy (*Brit*) *or* horny as (*Frau*) a bitch in heat *or* (*Mann*) an old goat (*all inf*); **jdn ~ machen** to turn sb on (*inf*)

ADV **a** *feilen, zuhauen* to a point

b (= *V-förmig*) *zulaufen, vorstehen, abgehen* to a point, sharply; **der Ausschnitt des Kleides lief unten ~ zu** the dress had a V-shaped neckline

c (= *spitzzüngig*) *bemerken, kontern, antworten* sharply

d (= *knapp*) **~ kalkulieren** *or* **rechnen** to calculate very carefully

Spitz [ʃpɪts] M **-es, -e** (*Hunderasse*) spitz, pomeranian

Spitz-: **Spitz|bart** M goatee; **spitz|bär|tig** ADJ with a goatee, goateed; **Spitz|bauch** M potbelly *(inf)*; **spitz+be|kom|men** *ptp* **spitzbekommen** VT *sep irreg (inf)* **etw ~** to cotton *(Brit) or* catch on to sth *(inf)*, to get wise to sth *(inf)*; **~, dass ...** to cotton *(Brit) or* catch on *or* get wise to the fact that ... *(inf)*; **Spitz|bo|gen** M pointed arch, ogive *(spec)*; **Spitz|bub** M, **Spitz|bu|be** M, **Spitz|bü|bin** [-by:bɪn] F **-, -nen** *(old)* villain, rogue; *(dial inf: = Schlingel)* scamp *(inf)*, scallywag *(inf)*; **Spitz|bu|ben|ge|sicht** NT *(old)* villainous *or* roguish face; **Spitz|bu|ben|streich** M *(dated)* nasty *or* knavish *(Brit old)* trick; **spitz|bü|bisch** ADJ roguish, mischievous ADV roguishly, mischievously; **Spitz|dach** NT *(Archit)* pointed roof

spit|ze ADJ *(inf: (= prima))* great *(inf)* → *auch* **Spitze**

Spit|ze [ˈʃpɪtsə] F **-, -n** **a** *(= Schwertspitze, Nadelspitze, Pfeilspitze, Bleistiftspitze, Kinnspitze)* point; *(= Schuhspitze)* toe; *(= Fingerspitze, Nasenspitze, Bartspitze, Spargelspitze)* tip; *(= Zigarrenspitze, Haarspitze)* end; *(= Bergspitze, Felsspitze)* peak, top; *(= Baumspitze, Turmspitze, Giebelspitze)* top; *(= Pyramidenspitze)* top, apex *(form)*; *(= Dreiecksspitze)* top, vertex *(form)*; **auf der ~ stehen** to be upside down; **etw auf die ~ treiben** to carry sth too far *or* to extremes; **einer Sache** *(dat)* **die ~ abbrechen** *or* **nehmen** *(fig)* to take the sting out of sth

b *(fig) (= Höchstwert)* peak; *(inf: = Höchstgeschwindigkeit)* top speed; **dieser Sportwagen fährt 200 ~** *(inf)* ≈ this sports car has a top speed of 125

c *(= Führung)* head; *(= vorderes Ende)* front; *(esp Mil: von Kolonne etc)* head; *(= Tabellenspitze)* top; **die ~n der Gesellschaft** the leading lights of society; **an der ~ stehen** to be at the head; *(auf Tabelle)* to be (at the) top (of the table); **an der ~ liegen** *(Sport, fig)* to be in front, to be in the lead; **Ruritanien liegt im Lebensstandard an der ~** Ruritania has the highest standard of living; **die ~ halten** *(Sport, fig)* to keep the lead; **sich an die ~ setzen** to put oneself at the head; *(in Wettbewerb etc, Sport)* to go into *or* take the lead; *(auf Tabelle)* to go to the top (of the table); *(im Pferderennen)* to take up the running; **er wurde an die ~ des Unternehmens gestellt** he was put at the top *or* head of the company

d *(= Zigaretten-/Zigarrenhalter)* (cigarette/cigar) holder

e *(fig: = Stichelei)* dig *(esp Brit)*, cut *(US)*; **das ist eine ~ gegen Sie** that's a dig *(esp Brit) or* cut *(US)* at you, that's directed at you; **die ~ zurückgeben** to give tit for tat

f *(Comm: = Überschuss)* surplus

g *(Gewebe)* lace; **Höschen mit ~n** panties with lace borders

h das war einsame *or* **absolute ~!** *(inf)* that was really great! *(inf)* → *auch* **spitze**

Spit|zel [ˈʃpɪtsl] M **-s, -** *(= Informant)* informer; *(= Spion)* spy; *(= Schnüffler)* snooper; *(= Polizeispitzel)* police informer, nark *(inf)*

Spit|zel|diens|te PL informing *no pl*; **für jdn ~ leisten** to act as an informer for sb

spit|zeln [ˈʃpɪtsln] VI to spy; *(= Spitzeldienste leisten)* to act as an informer

spit|zen [ˈʃpɪtsn] VT *(= spitz machen) Bleistift* to sharpen; *Lippen, Mund* to purse; *(zum Küssen)* to pucker (up); *Ohren (lit, fig)* to prick up; **spitzt doch die Ohren, dann versteht ihr auch, was ich sage!** open your ears and then you'll understand what I'm saying! VIR *(inf)* **(sich) auf etw** *(acc)* **~** to look forward to sth VI *(dial inf) (= aufpassen)* to keep a lookout, to keep one's eyes peeled *(inf)*; *(= heimlich spähen)* to peek

Spit|zen- *in cpds* top; *(= aus Spitze)* lace; **Spit|zen|an|ge|bot** NT top-of-the-range *or* top-of-the-line *(US)* offer; **Spit|zen|be|darf** M peak demand; **Spit|zen|be|las|tung** F peak (load); **die Zeit der ~** the peak period; **Spit|zen|be|satz** M lace trimming; **Spit|zen|blu|se** F lace blouse; **Spit|zen|deck|chen** NT, **Spit|zen|de|cke** F lace doily; **Spit|zen|ein|kom|men** NT top income; **Spit|zen|er|geb|nis** NT outstanding result; **Spit|zen|er|zeug|nis** NT top(-quality) product; **Spit|zen|feld** NT *(Sport)* leaders *pl*, leading group; **im ~** amongst the leaders, in the leading group; **Spit|zen|funk|ti|o|när(in)** M(F) top official; **Spit|zen|gar|ni|tur** F set of lace underwear; **Spit|zen|ge|halt** NT top salary; **Spit|zen|ge|schwin|dig|keit** F top speed; **Spit|zen|ge|spräch** NT top-level talks *pl*; *(Pol: = Gipfel)* summit (meeting); **Spit|zen|gre|mi|en** PL leading *or* top committees *pl*; **Spit|zen|grup|pe** F top group; *(Sport: = Spitzenfeld)* leading group; **Spit|zen|hös|chen** [-høːsçən] NT lace panties *pl*; **Spit|zen|jahr|gang** M *(von Wein)* top-quality *or* outstanding(ly good) vintage; **Spit|zen|kan|di|dat(in)** M(F) top candidate; **Spit|zen|klas|se** F top class; **Sekt/ein Auto etc der ~** top-class champagne/a top-class car etc; **~!** *(inf)* great! *(inf)*; **Spit|zen|kön|ner(in)** M(F) ace, first-rate *or* top-class talent; **Spit|zen|kra|gen** M lace collar; **Spit|zen|leis|tung** F top performance; *(von Maschine, Auto)* peak performance; *(bei der Herstellung von Produkten, Energie)* peak output; *(fig: = ausgezeichnete Leistung)* top-class *or* first-rate performance; *(Sport: = Rekord)* record (performance); **Spit|zen|lohn** M top wage(s *pl*); **spit|zen|mä|ßig** *(inf)* ADJ fantastic *(inf)*, great *(inf)* ADV fantastically *(inf)*; **Spit|zen|mo|dell** NT top model; **Spit|zen|or|ga|ni|sa|ti|on** F leading organization *or* group; **Spit|zen|po|si|ti|on** F leading *or* top position; **Spit|zen|prei|se** PL *(Comm)* top prices *pl*; **Spit|zen|qua|li|tät** F top quality; **Spit|zen|rei|ter** M *(Ware)* top seller; *(Film, Stück etc)* hit; *(= Schlager)* top of the pops, number one; **Spit|zen|rei|ter(in)** M(F) *(Sport)* leader; *(fig: Kandidat)* frontrunner; **Spit|zen|sport|ler(in)** M(F) top(-class) sportsman/-woman; **Spit|zen|stel|lung** F leading position; **Spit|zen|steu|er|satz** M top rate of income tax; **Spit|zen|sti|cke|rei** F lace embroidery; **Spit|zen|tanz** M dance on points, toe dance *(US)*; **Spit|zen|tech|no|lo|gie** F state-of-the-art technology; **Spit|zen|tref|fen** NT summit meeting; **Spit|zen|tuch** NT *pl* **-tücher** lace cloth, piece of lace; *(= Taschentuch)* lace handkerchief; **Spit|zen|ver|band** M leading organization *or* group; **Spit|zen|ver|die|ner(in)** M(F) top earner; **Spit|zen|ver|kehrs|zeit** F peak period; **Spit|zen|ver|tre|ter(in)** M(F) *usu pl (der Wirtschaft etc)* leading representative; **Spit|zen|wein** M top-quality wine; **Spit|zen|wert** M peak; **Spit|zen|zeit** F *(Sport)* record time

Spit|zer [ˈʃpɪtsɐ] M **-s, -** *(inf)* (pencil) sharpener

Spitz-: **Spitz|fei|le** F taper file; **spitz|fin|dig** ADJ over(ly)-subtle, over(ly)-precise; *(= haarspalterisch auch)* hairsplitting, nit-picking *(inf)*; *Unterschied auch* over(ly)-nice ADV in an over(ly)-subtle way; **er argumentiert immer sehr ~** he always splits hairs; **Spitz|fin|dig|keit** [ˈʃpɪtsfɪndɪçkait] F **-, -en** over-subtlety, over-precision *no pl*; *(= Haarspalterei auch)* hairsplitting *no pl*, nit-picking *no pl (inf)*; **zu behaupten, dass das Wort hier seine Bedeutung ändert, ist eine ~** it's splitting hairs *or* it's nit-picking *(inf)* to claim that the word changes its meaning here; **spitz|gie|b(e)|lig** ADJ with pointed gables; **spitz+ha|ben** VT *sep irreg (inf)* **etw ~** to have cottoned *(Brit) or* caught on to sth *(inf)*, to have got wise to sth *(inf)*; **~, dass ...** to have cottoned *(Brit) or* caught on to *or* to have got wise to the fact that ... *(inf)*; **Spitz|ha|cke** F pickaxe *(Brit)*, pickax *(US)*

spit|zig [ˈʃpɪtsɪç] ADJ ADV *(old, dial)* = **spitz**

Spitz-: **Spitz|keh|re** F *(Rail)* switchback turn; *(Ski)* kick turn; **Spitz|kopf** M pointed head; **spitz+krie|gen** VT *sep (inf)* = **spitzbekommen**; **Spitz|küh|ler** M *(Aut)* pointed *or* V-shaped radiator; *(hum inf)* potbelly *(inf)*; **Spitz|mar|ke** F *(Typ)* sidehead; **Spitz|maus** F shrew; **du bist eine richtige ~ geworden** *(inf)* you've got *(Brit) or* gotten *(US)* so thin; **Spitz|na|me** M nickname; **mit dem ~n** nicknamed; **Spitz|we|ge|rich** M ribwort; **spitz|win|ke|lig, spitz|wink|lig** ADJ *(Math) Dreieck* acute-angled; *Gasse* sharp-cornered, angular ADV *abzweigen, auslaufen* at a sharp angle; **spitz|zün|gig** [-tsʏŋɪç] ADJ sharp-tongued; *Bemerkung* sharp ADV *antworten* sharply

Spleen [ʃpliːn] M **-s, -s** *(inf) (= Angewohnheit)* strange *or* crazy habit, eccentricity, quirk (of behaviour *(Brit) or* behavior *(US)*); *(= Idee)* crazy idea *or* notion; *(= Fimmel)* obsession; **die Psychologen haben doch alle irgendeinen ~!** these psychologists are all quacks!; **du hast ja einen ~!** you're round the bend *(Brit inf)*, you're off your head *(Brit inf) or* rocker *(inf)*

splee|nig [ˈʃpliːnɪç] ADJ *(inf)* crazy, nutty *(inf)*

splei|ßen [ˈʃplaisn] *pret* **spliss** [ʃplɪs], *ptp* **gesplissen** [gəˈʃplɪsn] VT **a** *(dial, old) Holz* to split **b** *(Naut) Taue, Leinen* to splice

splen|did [ʃplɛnˈdiːt, sp-] ADJ *(geh)* generous; *Behandlung etc auch* handsome

Splint [ʃplɪnt] M **-(e)s, -e** cotter (pin), split pin

Splin|ten|trei|ber M pin punch

spliss *pret*

Spliss [ʃplɪs] M **-es, -e** **a** *(dial: = Splitter)* splinter **b** *no pl (= gespaltene Haarspitzen)* split ends *pl*

splis|sig [ˈʃplɪsɪç] ADJ **~e (Haar)spitzen** split ends

Splitt [ʃplɪt] M **-(e)s, -e** stone chippings *pl*; *(= Streumittel)* grit

Split|ter [ˈʃplɪtɐ] M **-s, -** *(= Holzsplitter, Metallsplitter, Knochensplitter)* splinter; *(= Glassplitter auch, Granatsplitter)* fragment; **der ~ in deines Bruders Auge** *(Bibl)* the mote that is in thy brother's eye *(Bibl)*

Split|ter-: **Split|ter|bom|be** F *(Mil)* fragmentation bomb; **split|ter|fa|ser|nackt** ADJ *(inf)* stark-naked, starkers *pred (Brit hum inf)*; **Split|ter|frak|tur** F *(Med)* splintered *or* comminuted *(spec)* fracture; **split|ter|frei** ADJ *Glas* shatterproof; **Split|ter|gra|ben** M *(Mil)* slit trench; **Split|ter|grup|pe** F *(Pol)* splinter group

split|te|rig [ˈʃplɪtərɪç] ADJ splintering

split|tern [ˈʃplɪtɐn] VI *aux sein or haben (Holz, Glas, Knochen)* to splinter

split|ter|nackt ADJ = **splitterfasernackt**

Split|ter|par|tei F *(Pol)* splinter party

Split|ting [ˈʃplɪtɪŋ, ˈsp-] NT **-s, -s** **a** *(von Aktien)* splitting **b** *(Pol: bei Wahlen) distribution of first and second votes among the parties* **c** *(Fin)* → **Splittingsystem**

Split|ting|sys|tem [ˈʃplɪtɪŋ-, ˈsp-] NT *(Fin) tax system in which husband and wife each pay income tax on half the total of their combined incomes*

splitt|rig [ˈʃplɪtrɪç] ADJ splintering

SPÖ [ɛspeːˈøː] F - *abbr von* **Sozialdemokratische Partei Österreichs**

Spoi|ler [ˈʃpɔylɐ, ˈsp-] M **-s, -** spoiler

Spö|ken|kie|ker [ˈʃpøːknkiːkɐ] M **-s, -**, **Spö|ken|kie|ke|rin** [-ərɪn] F **-, -nen** *(N Ger)* psychic, clairvoyant, person who has second sight

spon|sern [ˈʃpɔnzɐn, ˈsp-] VT to sponsor

Spon|si|on [ʃpɔnˈzioːn] F *(Aus: Univ) academic degree ceremony in which the title of Magister is awarded*

Spon|sor [ˈʃpɔnzɐ, ˈsp-] M **-s, Sponsoren** [-ˈzoːrən], **Spon|so|rin** [-ˈzoːrɪn] F **-, -nen** sponsor

Spon|so|ren|geld NT sponsorship (money)

Spon|so|ring [ˈʃpɔnzorɪŋ, ˈsp-] NT **-s,** *no pl* sponsorship

spon|tan [ʃpɔnˈtaːn, sp-] ADJ spontaneous ADV spontaneously

Spon|ta|ne|i|tät [ʃpɔntaneiˈtɛːt, sp-] F **-,** *no pl* spontaneity

Spon|tan|hei|lung F *(Med)* spontaneous recovery

Spon|tan|kauf M impulse buy *or* purchase; **Spontankäufe** *pl (regelmäßig)* impulse buying *no pl*

Spon|ti [ˈʃpɔnti] M **-s, -s** *(Pol sl) member of alternative movement rejecting traditional procedures*

Spoo|ler [ˈspuːlɐ] M **-s, -** *(Comput)* spooler

spo|ra|disch [ʃpoˈraːdɪʃ, sp-] ADJ sporadic ADV sporadically

Spo|re [ˈʃpoːrə] F **-, -n** *(Biol)* spore

Spo|ren *pl von* **Sporn, Spore**

spo|ren|klir|rend ADV *(old)* with a clatter of spurs

Spo|ren|tier|chen PL *(Biol)* sporozoa *pl*

Sporn [ʃpɔrn] M **-(e)s, Sporen** [ˈʃpoːrən] *usu pl (auch Zool, Bot)* spur; *(Naut auch)* ram; *(am Geschütz)* trail spade; *(Aviat: = Gleitkufe)* tailskid; *(Rad)* tail wheel; **einem Pferd die Sporen geben** to spur a horse, to give a horse a touch of the spurs; **sich** *(dat)* **die (ersten) Sporen verdienen** *(fig)* to win one's spurs

spor|nen [ˈʃpɔrnən] VT *(geh)* to spur; *(fig)* to spur on → **gestiefelt b**

sporn|streichs [ˈʃpɔrnʃtraiçs] ADV *(old)* posthaste, straight away

Sport [ʃpɔrt] M **-(e)s,** *(rare)* **-e** sport; *(= Zeitvertreib)* hobby, pastime; **treiben Sie ~?** do you do any sport?; **er treibt viel ~** he goes in for *or* he does a lot of sport; **etw aus** *or* **zum ~ betreiben** to do sth as a hobby *or* for fun; **sich** *(dat)* **einen ~ aus etw machen** *(inf)* to get a kick out of sth *(inf)*

Sport-: **Sport|ab|zei|chen** NT sports certificate; **Sport|ang|ler(in)** M(F) angler; **Sport|an|la|ge** F sports complex; **Sport|an|zug** M sports clothes *pl*; *(= Trainingsanzug)* tracksuit; **Sport|art** F (kind of) sport; **Sport|ar|ti|kel** M **a** *(pl)* sports equipment *with sing vb*; **ein ~** a piece of sports equipment **b** *(inf: = Sportbericht)* sports report; **Sport|arzt** M, **Sport|ärz|tin** F sports physician; **sport|be|geis|tert** ADJ keen on sport, sports-mad *(Brit inf)*, crazy about sports *(US inf)*; **ein Sportbegeisterter** a sports enthusiast *or* fan; **Sport|bei|la|ge** F sports section *or* page(s *pl*); **Sport|be|richt** M sports report; **Sport|be|richt|er|stat|tung** F sports reporting; **Sport-BH** M sports bra; **Sport|club** M sports club

spor|teln [ˈʃpɔrtln] VI *(inf)* to do a bit of sport(s), to dabble in sport(s)

Sport-: **Sport|er|eig|nis** NT sporting event; **Sport|fech|ten** NT **-s,** *no pl* fencing; **Sport|feld** NT sports ground; **Sport|fest** NT sports festival; **Sport|flie|ger(in)** M(F) amateur pilot; **Sport|flug|zeug** NT sporting aircraft; **Sport|freund(in)** M(F) sport(s) fan; **Sport|geist** M sportsmanship; **Sport|ge|rät** NT piece of sports equipment; **~e** sports equipment; **Sport|ge|schäft** NT sports shop, sporting goods store *(US)*; **Sport|ge|tränk** NT sports drink; **Sport|hal|le** F sports hall; **Sport|hemd** NT casual *or* sports shirt; **Sport|hoch|schu|le** F college of physical education

spor|tiv [spɔrˈtiːf, ʃp-] ADJ *Mensch, Kleidung, Auto* sporty

Sport-: **Sport|ja|ckett** NT sports jacket *or* coat; **Sport|kar|re** F *(N Ger)* pushchair *(Brit)*, (baby) stroller *(US)*; **Sport|klei|dung** F sportswear; **Sport|klub** M sports club; **Sport|leh|rer(in)** M(F) sports instructor; *(Sch)* PE *or* physical education teacher

Sport|ler [ˈʃpɔrtlɐ] M **-s, -** sportsman, athlete

Sport|ler|herz NT athlete's heart

Sport|le|rin [ˈʃpɔrtlərɪn] F **-, -nen** sportswoman, (woman) athlete

sport|lich [ˈʃpɔrtlɪç] ADJ **a** *(= den Sport betreffend) Veranstaltung, Wettkampf, Leistung, Erfolg* sporting **b** *Mensch* sporty; *(= durchtrainiert)* athletic **c** *(= fair)* sporting, sportsmanlike *no adv* **d** *Kleidung* casual; *(= sportlich-schick)* natty *(inf)*, snazzy *(inf)*, smart but casual; *(= wie Sportkleidung aussehend)* sporty; **eine ~e Note** a sporty touch **e** *Auto* sporty ADV **a sich ~ betätigen, ~ aktiv sein** to do sport; **~ gesehen, ...** from a sporting point of view ... **b** *(= fair)* sportingly; **er hat sich ihr gegenüber nicht besonders ~ verhalten** he wasn't particularly sporting in his behaviour *(Brit) or* behavior *(US)* toward(s) her **c** *(= leger)* casually; **~ gekleidet** casually dressed; wearing smart but casual clothes, smartly but casually dressed **d** *(= rasant) fahren* fast

Sport|lich|keit F **-,** *no pl* **a** *(von Menschen)* sportiness **b** *(= Fairness)* sportsmanship **c** *(von Auto)* sportiness

Sport-: **Sport|man|tel** M casual coat; **sport|mä|ßig** ADJ, ADV = **sportsmäßig**; **Sport|me|di|zin** F sports medicine; **Sport|mel|dung** F, **Sport|nach|richt** F, **Sport|nach|rich|ten** PL sports news *with sing vb or* reports *pl*; **eine wichtige ~** *or* **Sportnachricht** an important piece of sports news; **Sport|platz** M sports field; *(in der Schule)* playing field(s *pl*); **Sport|rad** NT sports cycle *or* bike *(inf)*; **Sport|re|dak|teur(in)** M(F) sports editor; **Sport|re|por|ta|ge** F sports reporting; *(= Bericht)* sports report; **die ~ über die Weltmeisterschaft** the coverage of the world championships; **Sport|schlit|ten** M racing toboggan; **Sport|schuh** M casual shoe

Sports-: **Sports|frau** F sportswoman; **Sports|freund(in)** M(F) *(fig inf)* buddy *(inf)*; **wenn der ~ da ...** if this guy ... *(inf)*; **Sports|ka|no|ne** F *(inf)* sporting ace *(inf)*; **Sports|mann** M *pl* **-männer** *or* **-leute** *(dated)* sportsman; *(inf, als Anrede)* sport *(esp Austral inf)*, mate *(Brit inf)*, buddy *(inf)*; **sports|mä|ßig** ADJ sporty ADV **sich ~ betätigen** to do sport; **wie siehts denn dort ~ aus?** what sort of sporting facilities are there?

Sport-: **Sport|un|fall** M sporting accident; **Sport|ver|an|stal|tung** F sporting event; **Sport|ver|ein** M sports club; **Sport|ver|let|zung** F sports injury; **Sport|wa|gen** M sports car; *(für Kind)* pushchair *(Brit)*, (baby) stroller *(US)*; **Sport|zei|tung** F sports paper; **Sport|zeug** NT, *no pl (inf)* sport(s) things *pl (Brit) or* stuff

Spot [spɔt, ʃpɔt] M **-s, -s** commercial, advertisement, ad *(inf)*

Spot-: **Spot|ge|schäft** NT *(Fin)* spot transaction; **Spot|light** [ˈspɔtlait] NT **-s, -s** spotlight; **Spot|markt** M *(Fin)* spot market

Spott [ʃpɔt] M **-(e)s,** *no pl* mockery; *(höhnisch auch)* ridicule, derision; **jdn dem ~ preisgeben** to hold sb up to ridicule; **dem ~ preisgegeben sein** to be held up to ridicule, to be made fun of; **seinen ~ mit jdm treiben** to make fun of sb; **Gegenstand des allgemeinen ~es** object of general ridicule, laughing stock; **zum ~ der Nachbarn werden** to become the laughing stock of the neighbourhood *(Brit) or* neighborhood *(US)* → **Schaden a**

Spott-: **Spott|bild** NT *(fig)* travesty, mockery; **das ~ eines Präsidenten** a travesty *etc* of a president; **spott|bil|lig** *(inf)* ADJ dirt-cheap *(inf)* ADV **das habe ich ~ gekauft** I bought it for a song *(inf) or* for practically nothing, I bought it dirt-cheap *(inf)*; **Spott|dros|sel** F mockingbird; *(dated fig: = Spötter)* tease, mocker

Spöt|te|lei [ʃpœtəˈlai] F **-, -en** *(= das Spotten)* mocking; *(= ironische Bemerkung)* mocking remark

spöt|teln [ˈʃpœtln] VI to mock *(über jdn/etw* sb/sth), to poke gentle fun *(über jdn/etw* at sb/sth)

spot|ten [ˈʃpɔtn] VI **a** *(= sich lustig machen)* to mock, to poke fun; *(= höhnen)* to mock, to ridicule, to be derisive; **über jdn/etw ~** to mock sb/sth, to poke fun at sb/sth, to ridicule sb/sth; *(höhnisch auch)* to deride sb/sth, to ridicule sb/sth; **du hast leicht ~!, spotte (du) nur!** it's easy for you to mock *or* laugh!, it's all very well for you to mock; **..., spottete er** ..., he mocked **b** *+gen (old, liter: = Hohn sprechen)* to mock; *(geh: = missachten) der Gefahr* to be contemptuous of, to scorn; **das spottet jeder Beschreibung** that simply defies *or* beggars description

Spöt|ter [ˈʃpœtɐ] M **-s, -, Spöt|te|rin** [-ərɪn] F **-, -nen** *(= satirischer Mensch)* wit, satirist; *(= jd, der über etw spottet)* mocker

Spott-: **Spott|fi|gur** F joke figure, ludicrous character; **eine ~ sein** to be a figure of fun, to be an object of ridicule; **Spott|ge|burt** F *(liter)* freak, monstrosity; **Spott|ge|dicht** NT satirical poem, lampoon; **Spott|ge|läch|ter** NT mocking laughter

spöt|tisch [ˈʃpœtɪʃ] ADJ *Blick, Lächeln, Bemerkung* mocking; *(höhnisch auch)* derisive ADV mockingly

Spott-: **Spott|lied** NT satirical song; **Spott|lust** F love of mockery, inclination to mock; **spott|lus|tig** ADJ given to mockery, inclined to mock; **Spott|na|me** M derisive nickname; **Spott|preis** M ridiculously *or* ludicrously low price; **für einen ~** for a song *(inf)*; **Spott|re|de** F satirical *or* lampooning speech; **~n führen** to make satirical *or* lampooning speeches; **Spott|sucht** F, *no pl* compulsive mocking; **spott|süch|tig** ADJ **~ sein** to delight in (constant) mockery; **Spott|vers** M satirical verse

sprach *pret von* **sprechen**

Sprach-: **Sprach|at|las** M linguistic atlas; **Sprach|aus|ga|be|sys|tem** NT *(Comput)* audio response system; **Sprach|au|to|no|mie** F *(Pol)* linguistic autonomy; **Sprach|bar|ri|e|re** F language barrier; **Sprach|bau** M, *no pl* linguistic structure; **sprach|be|gabt** ADJ good at languages, linguistically talented *or* gifted; **Sprach|be|ga|bung** F talent for languages, linguistic talent; **Sprach|com|pu|ter** M computer with speech synthesizer; *(= Taschenübersetzer)* pocket electronic dictionary; **Sprach|denk|mal** NT linguistic monument

Spra|che [ˈʃpraːxə] F **-, -n** language; *(= das Sprechen)* speech; *(= Sprechweise)* speech, way of speaking; *(= Fähigkeit, zu sprechen)* power *or* faculty of speech; **eine/die ~ sprechen** to (be able to) speak a language/the language *or* lingo *(inf)*; **die ~ analysieren** to analyze language; **die ~ der Musik** the language of music; **in französischer** *etc* **~** in French *etc*; **die gleiche ~ sprechen** *(lit, fig)* to speak the same language; **das spricht eine klare** *or* **deutliche ~** *(fig)* that speaks for itself, it's obvious what that means; **er spricht jetzt eine ganz andere ~** *(fig)* he's changed his tune now; **mit der ~ herausrücken** to come out with it; **heraus mit der ~!** *(inf)* come on, out with it!; **die ~ auf etw** *(acc)* **bringen** to bring the conversation (a)round to sth; **zur ~ kommen** to be mentioned *or* brought up, to come up; **etw zur ~ bringen** to bring sth up, to mention sth; **die ~ verlieren** to lose the power of speech; **hast du die ~ verloren?** have you lost your tongue?, has the cat got your tongue? *(inf)*; **die ~ wiederfinden** to be able to speak again; **es raubt** *or* **verschlägt einem die ~** it takes your breath away; **mir blieb die ~ weg** I was speechless

Sprach-: **Sprach|ei|gen|tüm|lich|keit** F linguistic peculiarity *or* idiosyncrasy; **Sprach|ein|heit** F **a** *(Ling)* linguistic unit **b** *(= Einheitlichkeit)* linguistic unity

Spra|chen-: **Spra|chen|ge|wirr** NT babel of tongues *(usu hum)*, mixture *or* welter of languages; **Spra|chen|schu|le** F language school; **Spra|chen|zent|rum** NT *(Univ)* language centre *(Brit) or* center *(US)*

Sprach-: **Sprach|er|ken|nung** F *(Comput)* speech *or* voice recognition; **Sprach|er|ken|nungs|pro|gramm** NT *(Comput)* speech *or* voice recognition program; **Sprach|er|werb** M language acquisition; **Sprach|er|zie|hung** F *(form)* language education; **Sprach|fa|mi|lie** F family of languages, language family;

Sprach|feh|ler M speech defect *or* impediment; **Sprach|for|scher(in)** M(F) linguist(ic researcher); *(= Philologe)* philologist; **Sprach|for|schung** F linguistic research; *(= Philologie)* philology; **Sprach|füh|rer** M phrase book; **Sprach|ge|biet** NT language area; **ein französisches** *etc* **~** a French-speaking *etc* area; **Sprach|ge|brauch** M (linguistic) usage; **moderner deutscher ~** modern German usage; **Sprach|ge|fühl** NT feeling for language; **Sprach|ge|lehr|te(r)** MF *decl as adj* linguist; **Sprach|ge|mein|schaft** F speech community; **Sprach|ge|nie** NT linguistic genius; **Sprach|ge|schich|te** F, *no pl* linguistic history; **die ~ des Mongolischen** the history of the Mongolian language; **Sprach|ge|set|ze** PL linguistic laws *pl*; **sprach|ge|steu|ert** [-gəʃtɔyɐt] ADJ *(Comput)* voice-controlled, speech-driven; **Sprach|ge|walt** F power of expression, eloquence; **sprach|ge|wal|tig** ADJ eloquent; **ein ~er Redner** a powerful speaker; **sprach|ge|wandt** ADJ articulate, fluent; **Sprach|gren|ze** F linguistic *or* language boundary; **Sprach|gut** NT, *no pl* linguistic heritage; **ein Wörterbuch kann nicht das gesamte ~ widerspiegeln** a dictionary cannot reflect the whole wealth of a language

-spra|chig [ʃpraːxɪç] ADJ *suf* **a** *(= in einer Sprache)* -language; *(= sprechend)* -speaking; **englischsprachig** *(Film, Buch)* English-language; *Mensch* English-speaking **b** *Wörterbuch, Mensch* -lingual; **einsprachig** monolingual; **zweisprachig** bilingual; **mehrsprachig** multilingual

Sprach-: **Sprach|in|sel** F linguistic enclave *or* island; **Sprach|kennt|nis|se** PL knowledge *sing* of languages/the language/a language; **mit englischen ~n** with a knowledge of English; **haben Sie irgendwelche ~?** do you know any languages?; **~ erwünscht** (knowledge of) languages desirable; **Sprach|kom|pe|tenz** F linguistic competence; **Sprach|kri|tik** F linguistic criticism; **sprach|kun|dig** ADJ *(in mehreren Sprachen)* proficient in *or* good at (foreign) languages; *(in einer bestimmten Sprache)* linguistically proficient; **es ist schwer, sich in diesem Land zurechtzufinden, wenn man nicht ~ ist** it's very difficult to get along in this country if you don't know the language *or* if you are not familiar with the language; **Sprach|kurs** M, **Sprach|kur|sus** M language course; **Sprach|la|bor** NT language laboratory *or* lab *(inf)*; **Sprach|läh|mung** F paralysis of the organs of speech *or* the speech organs; **Sprach|land|schaft** F linguistic geography; **Sprach|leh|re** F *(= Grammatik, Grammatikbuch)* grammar; **Sprach|leh|rer(in)** M(F) language teacher; **Sprach|lehr|gang** M language course

sprach|lich [ʃpraːxlɪç] ADJ *Eigenheit, Kommunikation, Minderheit* linguistic; *Unterricht, Schwierigkeiten* language *attr*; *Fehler* grammatical ADV linguistically; **~ hatten die Einwanderer keine Schwierigkeiten** the immigrants had no language difficulties; **~ falsch/richtig** ungrammatical/grammatical, grammatically incorrect/correct; **eine intelligente Analyse, auch ~ gut** an intelligent analysis, well written too

sprach|los ADJ *(= ohne Sprache)* speechless; *(= erstaunt)* speechless, dumbfounded; **ich bin ~!** I'm speechless; **da ist man (einfach) ~** *(inf)* that's quite *or* really something *(inf)*

Sprach|lo|sig|keit F -, *no pl* speechlessness

Sprach-: **Sprach|me|lo|die** F intonation, speech melody; **Sprach|miss|brauch** M misuse of language; **Sprach|mitt|ler(in)** M(F) translator and interpreter; **Sprach|mo|dul** [-moduːl] NT *(Comput) (in Textverarbeitung)* language module; *(zur Umwandlung in Gesprochenes)* speech synthesizer; **Sprach|pfle|ge** F concern for the purity of language; **aktive ~ betreiben** to be actively concerned with the purity of a language; **Sprach|phi|lo|so|phie** F philosophy of language; **Sprach|psy|cho|lo|gie** F psychology of language; **Sprach|raum** M = **Sprachgebiet**; **Sprach|re|gel** F grammatical rule, rule of grammar; *(für Aussprache)* pronunciation rule; *(Ling)* linguistic rule, rule of language; **die einfachsten ~n des Lateinischen** the most elementary rules of Latin; **Sprach|re|ge|lung** F **a** *(= Bestimmung)* linguistic ruling **b** *(= Version)* **offizielle ~** official version; **Sprach|reg|ler(in)** M(F) linguistic arbiter; **Sprach|rein|heit** F linguistic purity; **Sprach|rei|se** F language(-learning) holiday *(esp Brit) or* trip; **Sprach|rohr** NT *(= Megafon)* megaphone; *(fig)* mouthpiece; **sich zum ~ einer Sache/Gruppe machen** to become the spokesperson for *or* mouthpiece *(usu pej)* of sth/a group; **Sprach|schatz** M *(geh)* vocabulary; **dem englischen ~ fehlt ein Wort für …** the English language has no word for …; **Sprach|schön|heit** F linguistic beauty, beauty of language; **die ~ Rimbauds** the beauty of Rimbaud's language; **Sprach|schöp|fer(in)** M(F) linguistic innovator; **sprach|schöp|fe|risch** ADJ innovatory, (linguistically) creative; **Sprach|schöp|fung** F linguistic innovation; **Sprach|schu|le** F language school; **Sprach|sil|be** F syllable; **Sprach|so|zio|lo|gie** F sociology of language; **Sprach|stamm** M (language) stock; **Sprach|steu|e|rung** *(Comput)* voice control; **Sprach|stil** M style, way one uses language; **Sprach|stö|rung** F speech disorder; **Sprach|struk|tur** F linguistic structure; **Sprach|stu|di|um** NT study of languages/a language, linguistic *or* language studies *pl*; **Sprach|ta|lent** NT talent *or* gift for languages; **Sprach|the|o|rie** F theory of language; **Sprach|übung** F linguistic *or* language exercise; **Sprach|un|ter|richt** M language teaching *or* instruction; **der französische ~** French teaching, the teaching of French; **~/französischen ~ erteilen** to give language lessons/French lessons; **Sprach|ur|laub** M language-learning holiday *(esp Brit) or* trip; **Sprach|ver|ar|bei|tung** F *(Comput)* speech *or* voice processing; **Sprach|ver|ein** M language society; **Sprach|ver|fall** M decay of language; **Sprach|ver|glei|chung** [-fɛɐglaiçʊŋ] F -, -en comparative analysis (of languages); **Sprach|ver|mö|gen** NT faculty of language; **Sprach|ver|wandt|schaft** F linguistic relationship *or* kinship; **Sprach|ver|wir|rung** F confused mixture of languages, confusion of tongues *(Bibl)* → **babylonisch**; **Sprach|wis|sen|schaft** F linguistics *sing*; *(= Philologie)* philology; **vergleichende ~en** comparative linguistics/philology; **Sprach|wis|sen|schaft|ler(in)** M(F) linguist; *(= Philologe)* philologist; **sprach|wis|sen|schaft|lich** ADJ linguistic ADV linguistically; **~ interessierte Menschen** people interested in linguistics; **Sprach|zent|rum** NT *(Univ)* language centre *(Brit) or* center *(US)*; **Sprach|zweig** M (language) branch

sprang *pret von* **springen**

Spray [ʃpreː, spreː] M OR NT -s, -s spray

Spray|do|se [ʃpreː-, ˈspreː-] F aerosol (can), spray

spra|yen [ʃpreːən, ˈsp-] VTI to spray

Spra|yer [ʃpreːɐ, ˈsp-] M -s, -, **Spra|ye|rin** [-ərɪn] F -, -nen sprayer

Spread|sheet [ˈsprɛtʃiːt] NT -s, -s *(Comput: = Kalkulationstabelle)* spreadsheet

Sprech-: **Sprech|akt** M *(Ling)* speech act; **Sprech|an|la|ge** F intercom; **Sprech|bla|se** F balloon; **Sprech|büh|ne** F theatre *(Brit)*, theater *(US)*, stage; **Sprech|chor** M chorus; *(fig)* chorus of voices; **im ~ rufen** to shout in unison, to chorus; **Sprech|ein|heit** F *(Telec)* unit

spre|chen [ʃprɛçn] ✪ 27, 28.1, 46.2, 53.2, 53.3, 53.6 *pret* **sprach**, [ʃpraːx] *ptp* **gesprochen** VI [gəˈʃprɔxn] to speak *(über +acc, von* about, of*)*; *(= reden, sich unterhalten)* to talk, to speak *(über +acc, von* about*)*; **viel ~** to talk a lot; **frei ~** to extemporize, to speak off the cuff *(inf)*; **er spricht wenig** he doesn't say *or* talk very much; **sprich!** *(liter)* speak! *(liter)*; **~ Sie!** *(form)* speak away!; **sprich doch endlich!** *(geh)* say something; **also sprach …** *(liter, Bibl)* thus spoke …, thus spake … *(liter, Bibl)*; **im Traum** *or* **Schlaf ~** to talk in one's sleep; **gut/schön ~** to speak well/beautifully; **im Rundfunk/Fernsehen ~** to speak on the radio/on television; **es spricht …** the speaker is …; **es ~ …** the speakers are …; **die Vernunft ~ lassen** to listen to reason, to let the voice of reason be heard; **sein Herz ~ lassen** to follow the dictates of one's heart; **schlecht** *or* **nicht gut auf jdn/etw zu ~ sein** not to have a good thing to say about sb/sth; **mit jdm ~** to speak *or* talk with *or* to sb; **mit sich selbst ~** to talk to oneself; **ich muss mit dir ~** I must talk *or* speak to you; **ich habe mit dir zu ~** I want to have a word *or* a few words with you; **wie sprichst du mit mir?** who do you think you're talking to?; **so spricht man nicht mit seinem Großvater** that's no way to talk *or* speak to your grandfather; **sie spricht nicht mit jedem** she doesn't speak *or* talk to just anybody; **wir ~ nicht mehr miteinander** we are no longer on speaking terms, we're not speaking any more; **mit wem spreche ich?** to whom am I speaking, please?; **~ wir nicht mehr darüber!** let's not talk about that any more, let's drop the subject; **darüber spricht man nicht** one doesn't talk about *or* speak of such things; **ich weiß nicht, wovon Sie ~** I don't know what you're talking about; **~ wir von etwas anderem** let's talk about something else, let's change the subject; **wir haben gerade von dir gesprochen** we were just talking about you; **es wird kaum noch von ihm gesprochen** he's hardly mentioned now; **auf jdn/etw zu ~ kommen** to get to talking about sb/sth; **für jdn/etw ~** to speak for sb/sth, to speak on behalf of sb/sth; **gegen jdn/etw ~** to speak against sb/sth; **es spricht für jdn/etw(, dass …)** it says something for sb/sth (that …), it speaks well for sb/sth (that …); **das spricht für ihn** that's a point in his favour *(Brit) or* favor *(US)*, that says something for him; **es spricht nicht für die Firma, dass so was passieren konnte** it doesn't say much for the firm that something like that could happen; **das spricht für sich (selbst)** that speaks for itself; **es spricht vieles dafür/dagegen** there's a lot to be said for/against it; **es spricht vieles dafür, dass …** there is every reason to believe that …; **was spricht dafür/dagegen?** what is there to be said for/against it?; **aus seinen Worten sprach Verachtung/Hoffnung** his words expressed contempt/hope; **er sprach vor den Studenten/dem Ärztekongress** he spoke to the students/the medical conference; **ganz allgemein gesprochen** generally speaking

VT **a** *(= sagen)* to say, to speak; *eine Sprache, Mundart* to speak; *(= aufsagen) Gebet* to say; *Gedicht* to say, to recite; **es wurde viel gesprochen** a lot of talking was done; **alles, was er sprach …** everything he said …; **~ Sie Japanisch?** do you speak Japanese?; **hier spricht man Spanisch** Spanish spoken, we speak Spanish → **Sprache**

b *Urteil* to pronounce → **Recht a, schuldig ADJ a**

c *(= mit jdm reden)* to speak to; **kann ich bitte Herrn Kurz ~?** may I speak to Mr Kurz, please?; **er ist nicht zu ~** he can't see anybody; **ich bin für niemanden zu ~** I can't see anybody, I'm not available; **ich hätte gern Herrn Bremer gesprochen** could I speak to Mr Bremer?; **kann ich Sie einen Augenblick** *or* **kurz ~?** can I see you for a moment?, can I have a quick word?; **für Sie bin ich jederzeit zu ~** I'm always at your disposal; **wir ~ uns noch!** you haven't heard the last of this!

spre|chend ADJ *Augen, Gebärde* eloquent

spre|chen+las|sen VT *ptp* **sprechenlassen** *or (rare)* **sprechengelassen** *sep irreg* → **sprechen VI**

Spre|cher [ˈʃprɛçɐ] M -s, -, **Spre|che|rin** [-ərɪn] F -, -nen speaker; *(= Nachrichtensprecher)* newscaster, newsreader; *(für Dokumentarfilme, Stücke etc)* narrator; *(= Ansager)* announcer; *(= Wortführer)* spokesperson; **sich zum ~ von jdm/etw machen** to become the spokesperson for sb/sth

Sprech-: **Sprech|er|zie|hung** F speech training, elocution; **sprech|faul** ADJ taciturn; **sei doch nicht so ~!** haven't you got a tongue in your head!; **morgens ist sie besonders ~** she's not exactly talkative in the mornings; **Sprech|feh|ler** M slip of the tongue; **Sprech|fens|ter** NT grille; **Sprech|funk** M radiotelephone system; **Sprech|funk|ge|rät** NT radiotelephone; *(tragbar auch)* walkie-talkie; **Sprech|funk|ver|kehr** M local radio traffic; **den ~ unterbrechen** to interrupt radiotelephone communications; **Sprech|ge|bühr** F *(Telec)* call *(Brit)* or calling *(US)* charge; **Sprech|ge|sang** M *(Mus)* speech song, sprechgesang; **Sprech|kun|de** F study of speech; **Sprech|me|lo|die** F intonation, speech melody; **Sprech|mu|schel** F *(Telec)* mouthpiece; **Sprech|or|gan** NT organ of speech, speech organ; **Sprech|plat|te** F spoken-word record; **Sprech|pro|be** F voice trial; **Sprech|pup|pe** F talking *or* speaking doll; **Sprech|rol|le** F speaking part; **Sprech|schu|lung** F voice training; **Sprech|sil|be** F *(Ling)* (phonetic) syllable; **Sprech|stim|me** F speaking voice; *(Mus)* sprechstimme, speech voice; **Sprech|stun|de** F consultation (hour); *(von Arzt)* surgery *(Brit)*, consultation *(US)*; **~n** consultation hours; *(von Arzt)* surgery *(Brit)* or consulting hours; **~ halten** to hold surgery *(Brit)*; **Sprech|stun|den|hil|fe** F *(neg!)* (doctor's) receptionist; **Sprech|tas|te** F "talk" button *or* switch; **Sprech|the|a|ter** NT theatre *(Brit)* or theater *(US)* of the spoken word, straight theatre *(Brit)* or theater *(US)*; **Sprech|übung** F speech exercise; **Sprech|un|ter|richt** M elocution lessons *pl*; **Sprech|wei|se** F way of speaking; **Sprech|werk|zeu|ge** PL organs *pl* of speech, speech organs *pl*; **Sprech|zeit** F **a** *(= Sprechstunde)* consulting time; *(von Arzt)* surgery time *(Brit)* **b** *(= Besuchszeit: in Gefängnis, Kloster)* visiting time **c** *(Telec)* call time; **Sprech|zim|mer** NT consulting room

Sprei|ßel [ˈʃpraisl] NT -s, - *(Aus: zum Feuermachen)* kindling *no pl*

Sprei|ßel M -s, - *(esp S Ger: = Splitter)* splinter

Sprei|te [ˈʃpraitə] F -, -n (leaf) blade

Spreiz|dü|bel M cavity plug

Sprei|ze [ˈʃpraitsə] F -, -n **a** *(Build)* strut **b** *(Sport)* straddle

sprei|zen [ˈʃpraitsn] VT *Flügel, Gefieder* to spread; *Finger, Zehen auch* to splay (out); *Beine auch* to open; *(Sport)* to straddle → *auch* **gespreizt** VR *(= sich sträuben)* to kick up *(inf)*; *(= sich aufplustern)* to give oneself airs, to put on airs; **sich wie ein Pfau ~** to puff oneself up, to put on airs; **sich gegen etw ~** to kick against sth

Spreiz-: **Spreiz|fuß** M splayfoot; **Spreiz|schritt** M *(Sport)* straddle; **im ~ stehen** to stand with one's legs apart

Spreng-: **Spreng|ar|bei|ten** PL blasting operations *pl*; **„Sprengarbeiten"** "blasting"; **Spreng|bom|be** F high-explosive bomb

Spren|gel [ˈʃprɛŋl] M -s, - *(= Kirchspiel)* parish; *(= Diözese)* diocese

spren|gen [ˈʃprɛŋən] VT **a** *(mit Sprengstoff)* to blow up; *Fels* to blast; **etw in die Luft ~** to blow sth up **b** *Türschloss, Tor* to force (open); *Tresor* to break open; *Bande, Fesseln* to burst, to break; *Eisdecke, Versammlung* to break up; *(Spiel)bank* to break; **die Grenzen von etw ~** *(fig)* to go beyond the boundaries of sth → **Rahmen b** **c** *(= bespritzen)* to sprinkle; *Beete, Rasen* to water; *Wäsche* to sprinkle (with water); *(= verspritzen) Wasser* to sprinkle, to spray VI **a** *(= Sprengarbeiten vornehmen)* to blast **b** *aux sein (liter: = kraftvoll reiten)* to thunder

Spreng-: **Spreng|kam|mer** F demolition chamber; **Spreng|kap|sel** F detonator; **Spreng|kom|man|do** NT demolition squad; *(zur Bombenentschärfung)* bomb disposal squad; **Spreng|kopf** M warhead; **Spreng|kör|per** M explosive device; **Spreng|kraft** F explosive force; **Spreng|la|dung** F explosive charge; **Spreng|meis|ter(in)** M(F) *(in Steinbruch)* blaster; *(bei Abbrucharbeiten)* demolition expert; *(zur Bombenentschärfung)* bomb disposal expert; **Spreng|satz** M explosive device

Spreng|stoff M explosive; *(fig)* dynamite

Spreng|stoff|an|schlag M, **Spreng|stoff|at|ten|tat** NT bomb attack; *(erfolgreich auch)* bombing; **auf ihn wurde ein ~ verübt** he was the subject of a bomb attack; **auf das Haus wurde ein ~ verübt** there was a bomb attack on the house

Spren|gung [ˈʃprɛŋʊŋ] F -, -en **a** blowing-up; *(von Felsen)* blasting **b** *(von Tür, Schloss)* forcing (open); *(von Tresor)* breaking open; *(von Fesseln)* bursting, breaking; *(von Eisdecke, Versammlung)* breaking-up **c** *(= Bespritzen)* sprinkling; *(von Beeten, Rasen)* watering

Spreng-: **Spreng|wa|gen** M water(ing) cart, street sprinkler; **Spreng|we|del** M *(Eccl)* aspergillum; **Spreng|wir|kung** F explosive effect

Spren|kel [ˈʃprɛŋkl] M -s, - **a** *(= Tupfen)* spot, speckle **b** *(= Vogelschlinge)* snare

spren|keln [ˈʃprɛŋkln] VT *Farbe* to sprinkle spots of → *auch* **gesprenkelt**

Spreu [ʃprɔy] F -, *no pl* chaff; **wie (die) ~ im Wind** *(Bibl)* like chaff in the wind *(Bibl)*; **die ~ vom Weizen trennen** *or* **sondern** *(fig)* to separate the wheat from the chaff

spricht [ʃprɪçt] *3. pers sing pres von* **sprechen**

Sprich|wort NT *pl* **-wörter** proverb

sprich|wört|lich ADJ *(lit, fig)* proverbial

sprie|ßen [ˈʃpriːsn] *pret* **spross** *or* **sprießte** [ʃprɔs, ˈʃpriːstə], *ptp* **gesprossen** [gəˈʃprɔsn] VI *aux sein (aus der Erde)* to come up, to spring up; *(Knospen, Blätter)* to shoot; *(fig geh: Liebe, Zuneigung)* to burgeon *(liter)* → **Pilz a**

Spriet [ʃpriːt] NT -(e)s, -e *(Naut)* sprit

Spring|brun|nen M fountain

sprin|gen [ˈʃprɪŋən] *pret* **sprang** [ʃpraŋ], *ptp* **gesprungen** [gəˈʃprʊŋən] VI *aux sein* **a** *(lit, fig, Sport, bei Brettspielen)* to jump; *(esp mit Schwung)* to leap, to spring; *(beim Stabhochsprung)* to vault; *(Raubtier)* to pounce; *(= sich springend fortbewegen)* to bound; *(= hüpfen, seilhüpfen)* to skip; *(= auf einem Bein hüpfen)* to hop; *(Ball etc)* to bounce; *(Wassersport)* to dive; *(S Ger inf: = eilen)* to nip *(Brit inf)*, to pop *(inf)*; **tanzen und ~** to dance and leap about; **jdm an den Hals** *or* **die Kehle** *or* **die Gurgel** *(inf)* **~** to leap *or* fly at sb's throat; *(fig)* to fly at sb, to go for sb; **ich hätte ihm an die Kehle ~ können** I could have strangled him; **aus dem Gleis** *or* **aus den Schienen ~** to jump the rails; **ins Aus ~** *(Sport)* to go out (of play) → **Auge a, Bresche, Klinge, Schatten**

b **etw ~ lassen** *(inf)* to fork out for sth *(inf)*; *Runde* to stand sth; *Geld* to fork out sth *(inf)*; **für jdn etw ~ lassen** *(inf)* to treat sb to sth; **das hat der Chef ~ lassen!** *(inf)* that was on the boss! *(inf)*

c *(geh: = hervorsprudeln)* to spring; *(Wasserstrahl, Quelle)* to spring, to spurt; *(Blutstrahl)* to spurt; *(Funken)* to leap

d *(Glas, Porzellan, Saite)* to break; *(= Risse bekommen)* to crack; *(= sich lösen: Knopf)* to come off *(von etw* sth)

e *(geh: = aufplatzen)* to burst (forth)

VT *aux haben* **einen (neuen) Rekord ~** *(Sport)* to make a record jump

Sprin|gen NT -s, - *(Sport)* jumping; *(= Stabhochspringen)* vaulting; *(Wassersport)* diving

sprin|gend ADJ **der ~e Punkt** the crucial point

sprin|gen+las|sen VT *ptp* **springenlassen** *or (rare)* **springengelassen** *sep irreg* → **springen VI b**

Sprin|ger [ˈʃprɪŋɐ] M -s, - *(Chess)* knight

Sprin|ger [ˈʃprɪŋɐ] M -s, -, **Sprin|ge|rin** [-ərɪn] F -, -nen **a** jumper; *(= Stabhochspringer)* vaulter; *(Wassersport)* diver **b** *(Ind)* stand-in

Sprin|ger|stie|fel PL Doc Martens® (boots) *pl*

Spring-: **Spring|flut** F spring tide; **Spring|form** F *(Cook)* springform

Spring|ins|feld [ˈʃprɪŋlɪnsfɛlt] M -(e)s, -e [-də] madcap

Spring-: **Spring|kraut** NT, *no pl (Bot)* touch-me-not; **spring|le|ben|dig** ADJ lively, full of beans *(esp Brit inf)*, antsy *(US)* ADV in a lively manner, full of beans *(esp Brit inf)*; **Spring|pferd** NT jumper; **Spring|rei|ten** NT -s, *no pl* show jumping; **Spring|rol|lo** NT roller blind; **Spring|seil** NT skipping-rope *(Brit)*, jump rope *(US)*; **über ein ~ springen** *(= seilspringen)* to skip; **Spring|tur|nier** NT show jumping competition

Sprink|ler [ˈʃprɪŋklɐ] M -s, - sprinkler

Sprink|ler|an|la|ge F sprinkler system

Sprint [ʃprɪnt] M -s, -s sprint

sprin|ten [ˈʃprɪntn] VTI *aux sein* to sprint

Sprin|ter [ˈʃprɪntɐ] M -s, -, **Sprin|te|rin** [-ərɪn] F -, -nen sprinter

Sprint|stre|cke F sprint distance

Sprit [ʃprɪt] M -(e)s, -e *(inf: = Benzin)* gas *(inf)*, juice *(inf)*; *(= Rohspiritus)* neat spirit *(Brit)*, pure alcohol

Spritz-: **Spritz|be|steck** NT **a** *(Med)* (set of) instruments *pl* for giving injections **b** *(für Drogen)* needles *pl*; **Spritz|beu|tel** M icing *or* piping bag; **Spritz|dü|se** F nozzle; *(Tech)* jet

Sprit|ze [ˈʃprɪtsə] F -, -n syringe; *(= Feuerspritze, Gartenspritze)* hose; *(= Injektion)* injection, jab *(Brit inf)*; **eine ~ bekommen** to have an injection *or* a jab *(Brit inf)*

sprit|zen [ˈʃprɪtsn] VT **a** *Flüssigkeit* to spray; *(in einem Strahl) Wasser* to squirt, to spray; *(Cook) Zuckerguss etc* to pipe; *(= verspritzen) Wasser, Schmutz etc* to splash; *(Fahrzeug)* to spray, to spatter; **die Feuerwehr spritzte Wasser in das brennende Gebäude** the firemen directed their hoses into the burning building; **das vorbeifahrende Auto spritzte mir Wasser ins Gesicht** the passing car sprayed *or* spattered water in my face

b *(= lackieren) Auto, Gegenstand* to spray

c *Wein* to dilute with soda water; **er trinkt Rotwein gespritzt** he drinks red wine and soda → **Gespritzte(r)**

d *(= injizieren) Serum etc* to inject; *Heroin etc* to inject, to shoot (up) *(inf)*; *(= eine Injektion geben)* to give injections/an injection; **wir müssen (dem Kranken) Morphium ~** we have to give (the patient) a morphine injection; **sich** *(dat)* **Heroin ~** to inject (oneself with) heroin, to shoot (up) heroin *(inf)*

VI **a** *aux haben or sein (Wasser, Schlamm)* to spray, to splash; *(heißes Fett)* to spit; *(Blut)* to spray; *(in einem Strahl)* to spurt; *(aus einer Tube, Wasserpistole etc)* to squirt; **es spritzte gewaltig, als er ins Wasser plumpste** there was an enormous splash when he fell into the water; **die Feuerwehr spritzte in das brennende Gebäude** the firemen directed their hoses into the burning building

b *(= lackieren)* to spray

c *(= sich injizieren)* to inject oneself; **er spritzt seit einem Jahr** *(inf)* he has been shooting (up) *or* mainlining for a year *(sl)*; *(Diabetiker)* he has been injecting himself for a year

d *aux sein (inf: = eilen)* to dash, to nip *(Brit inf)*

Sprit|zen-: **Sprit|zen|haus** NT fire station; **Sprit|zen|wa|gen** M *(old)* fire engine

Sprit|zer [ˈʃprɪtsɐ] M -s, - *(= Farbspritzer, Wasserspritzer)* splash; *(von Parfüm, Mineralwasser auch)* dash

Spritz-: **Spritz|fahrt** F *(inf)* spin *(inf)*; **eine ~ machen** to go for a spin *(inf)*; **Spritz|ge|bäck**

NT (Cook) ≈ Viennese whirl/whirls pl; **Spritz|guss** M injection moulding (Brit) or molding (US); (Metal) die-casting

sprit|zig [ˈʃprɪtsɪç] ADJ Wein tangy; Auto lively, nippy (Brit inf), zippy (inf); Aufführung, Dialog etc sparkling, lively; (= witzig) witty; **das Kabarett war ~ und witzig** the cabaret was full of wit and sparkle ADV aufführen, darstellen with sparkle; schreiben racily; (= witzig) wittily

Sprit|zig|keit F liveliness; **aufgrund seiner ~ eignet sich dieser Wein besonders für ...** its tangy flavour (Brit) or flavor (US) means this wine goes especially well with ...

Spritz-: **Spritz|ku|chen** M (Cook) cruller; **Spritz|lack** M spray paint; **Spritz|la|ckie|rung** F spraying; **Spritz|pis|to|le** F spray gun; **Spritz|schutz** M guard; **Spritz|tour** F = **Spritzfahrt**; **Spritz|tül|le** F nozzle

spröd [ʃprøːt], **sprö|de** [ˈʃprøːdə] ADJ Glas, Stein, Haar brittle; Haut rough; Stimme thin; (fig) Material obdurate, recalcitrant; (= abweisend) Mensch aloof, standoffish (inf); Charakter aloof; Sprache, Worte offhand; Atmosphäre, Stimmung chilly; Charme austere; Text, Musik etc unwieldy

spross pret von **sprießen**

Spross [ʃprɔs] M **-es, -e** shoot; (fig: = Nachkomme) scion (liter)

Spros|se [ˈʃprɔsə] F **-, -n** (lit, fig) rung; (= Fenstersprosse) (senkrecht) mullion; (waagerecht) transom; (= Geweihsprosse) branch, point, tine

spros|sen [ˈʃprɔsn] VI aux sein (liter) = **sprießen**

Spros|sen-: **Spros|sen|fens|ter** NT lattice window; **Spros|sen|wand** F (Sport) wall bars pl

Spröss|ling [ˈʃprœslɪŋ] M **-s, -e** shoot; (fig hum) offspring pl

Sprot|te [ˈʃprɔtə] F **-, -n** sprat

Spruch [ʃprʊx] M **-(e)s, ¨-e** [ˈʃprʏçə] **a** saying; (= Sinnspruch) saying, aphorism; (= Maxime) adage, maxim; (= Wahlspruch) motto; (= Bibelspruch) quotation, quote; (Poet: = Gedicht) medieval lyric poem; **die Sprüche Salomos** (Bibl) (the Book of) Proverbs; **Sprüche** (inf: = Gerede) patter no pl (inf); **flotte Sprüche** wisecracks; **Sprüche klopfen** (inf) to talk fancy (Brit inf); (= angeben) to talk big (inf); (Verkäufer) to give one's patter (Brit inf) or spiel (inf); **mach keine Sprüche!** (inf) come off it! (inf); **das sind doch nur Sprüche!** that's just talk
b (= Richterspruch) judgement; (= Freispruch/Schuldspruch) verdict; (= Strafurteil) sentence; (= Schiedsspruch) ruling

Spruch|band [-bant] NT pl **-bänder** banner

Spruch|dich|tung F (Poet) medieval lyric poetry

Sprü|che|klop|fer(in) M(F) (inf) patter merchant (Brit inf), smooth talker (esp US inf); (= Angeber) big talker (inf)

Sprüch|lein [ˈʃprʏçlain] NT **-s, -** dim von **Spruch**; **sein ~ hersagen** to say one's (little) piece

spruch|reif ADJ (inf) **die Sache ist noch nicht ~** it's not definite yet so we'd better not talk about it; **die Sache wird erst ~, wenn ...** we can only start talking about it definitely when ...; **es gibt noch keine ~e Lösung** there is still no solution to speak of

Spru|del [ˈʃpruːdl] M **-s, -** (= saurer Sprudel) mineral water; (= süßer Sprudel) fizzy drink

Spru|del|bad NT whirlpool (bath), jacuzzi

spru|deln [ˈʃpruːdln] VI **a** (= schäumen) (Wasser, Quelle) to bubble; (Sekt, Limonade) to effervesce, to fizz; (fig: vor Freude, guten Ideen etc) to bubble **b** aux sein (= hervorsprudeln) (Wasser etc) to bubble; (fig) (Worte) to pour out; (Steuern, Einnahmen) to pour in VT (Aus: = quirlen) to whisk

spru|delnd ADJ (lit) Getränke fizzy, effervescent; Quelle bubbling; (fig) Temperament, Witz bubbly, effervescent; Geldquelle, Gewinne inexhaustible

Spru|del|tab|let|te F effervescent tablet

Sprud|ler [ˈʃpruːdlɐ] M **-s, -** (Aus) whisk

Sprüh-: **Sprüh|ak|ti|on** F slogan-spraying operation; **Sprüh|do|se** F spray (can); (unter Druck stehend auch) aerosol (can)

sprü|hen [ˈʃpryːən] VI **a** aux haben or sein to spray; (Funken) to fly **b** (fig) (vor Witz, Ideen etc) to bubble over (vor +dat with); (Augen) (vor Freude etc) to sparkle (vor +dat with); (vor Zorn etc) to flash (vor +dat with) VT to spray; (fig: Augen) to flash; **er sprühte Lack auf die beschädigte Stelle** he sprayed the damaged spot with paint

sprü|hend ADJ Laune, Temperament etc bubbly, effervescent; Energie bubbly; Witz sparkling, bubbly

Sprüh-: **Sprüh|flug|zeug** NT crop-spraying plane; **Sprüh|ne|bel** M mist; **Sprüh|re|gen** M drizzle, fine rain

Sprung [ʃprʊŋ] M **-(e)s, ¨-e** [ˈʃprʏŋə] **a** jump; (schwungvoll, fig: = Gedankensprung) leap, jump; (= Hüpfer) skip; (auf einem Bein) hop; (= Satz) bound; (von Raubtier) pounce; (= Stabhochsprung) vault; (Wassersport) dive; **einen ~ machen** to jump; **einen kleinen ~ machen** to do a small jump; **zum ~ ansetzen** (lit) to get ready to jump etc; (fig) to get ready to pounce; **sie wagte den ~ (ins kalte Wasser) nicht** (fig) she didn't dare (to) take the plunge; **ein großer ~ nach vorn** (fig) a great leap forward; **damit kann man keine großen Sprünge machen** (inf) you can't exactly live it up on that (inf); **auf dem ~ sein** or **stehen, etw zu tun** to be about to do sth; **immer auf dem ~ sein** (inf) to be always on the go (inf); (= aufmerksam) to be always on the ball (inf); **jdm auf die Sprünge helfen** (wohlwollend) to give sb a (helping) hand; (drohend) to show sb what's what
b (inf: = kurze Strecke) stone's throw (inf); **bis zum Postamt ist es nur ein ~** the post office is only a stone's throw from here (inf); **auf einen ~ bei jdm vorbeikommen/-gehen** to drop in to see sb (inf)
c (= Riss) crack; (= Kratzer) scratch; **einen ~ haben** to be cracked/scratched; **einen ~ bekommen** to crack; **einen ~ in der Schüssel haben** (fig inf: = verrückt sein) to be off one's rocker (inf)
d (Geol) fault
e (Hunt: = Rudel) herd
f (Agr: = Begattung) mounting; **dieser Hengst eignet sich nicht zum ~** this stallion isn't suitable for stud purposes; **es kam nicht zum ~** they didn't mate

Sprung-: **Sprung|bein** NT **a** (Anat) anklebone **b** (Sport) takeoff leg; **sprung|be|reit** ADJ ready to jump; Katze ready to pounce; (fig hum) ready to go; **Sprung|brett** NT (lit, fig) springboard; **Sprung|de|ckel** M spring lid; **Sprung|fe|der** F spring; **Sprung|fe|der|mat|rat|ze** F spring mattress; **Sprung|ge|lenk** NT ankle joint; (von Pferd) hock; **Sprung|gru|be** F (Sport) (landing) pit; **sprung|haft** ADJ **a** Mensch, Charakter volatile; Denken disjointed **b** (= rapide) Aufstieg, Entwicklung, Zunahme etc rapid; Preisanstieg sharp, rapid ADV ansteigen, entwickeln by leaps and bounds; **Sprung|haf|tig|keit** [ˈʃprʊŋhaftɪçkait] F **-,** no pl **a** (von Mensch) volatility **b** (von Entwicklung etc) rapidity, rapidness; **Sprung|kraft** F (Sport) takeoff power, leg power; **Sprung|lauf** M (Ski) ski-jumping; **Sprung|netz** NT (jumping) net, life net (US), safety net; **Sprung|schan|ze** F (Ski) ski jump; **Sprung|stab** M (vaulting) pole; **Sprung|tuch** NT pl **-tücher** jumping sheet or blanket, life net (US), safety net; **Sprung|turm** M diving platform; **sprung|wei|se** ADV in bounds or jumps; (fig) by leaps and bounds

Spu|cke [ˈʃpʊkə] F **-,** no pl (inf) spittle, spit; **da bleibt einem die ~ weg!** (inf) it's flabbergasting (inf); **als ich das hörte, blieb mir die ~ weg** when I heard that I was flabbergasted (inf), when I heard that you could have knocked me down with a feather (inf); **mit Geduld und ~** (hum inf) with blood, sweat and tears (hum)

spu|cken [ˈʃpʊkn] VT to spit; (inf: = erbrechen) to throw or bring up (inf); Lava, Flammen to spew (out) VI to spit; (inf: = sich übergeben) to throw up (inf), to be sick; (inf: Motor, Maschine etc) to give the occasional hiccup (inf); **in die Hände ~** (lit) to spit on one's hands; (fig) to roll up one's sleeves

Spuck|napf M spittoon

Spuck|tü|te F (inf: esp Aviat) sick bag

Spuk [ʃpuːk] M **-(e)s, -e** **a** (= Geistererscheinung) **der ~ fing um Mitternacht an** the ghosts started to walk at midnight; **ich glaube nicht an diesen ~** I don't believe the place is haunted **b** (fig) (= Lärm) din, racket (inf); (= Aufheben) fuss, to-do (inf), palaver (inf)

spu|ken [ˈʃpuːkn] VI to haunt; **an einem Ort/in einem Schloss ~** to haunt or walk a place/castle; **es spukt auf dem Friedhof/im alten Haus** etc the cemetery/old house etc is haunted; **hier spukt es** this place is haunted; **durch den Film spukten wunderliche Gestalten/eigenartige Ideen** the film was haunted by weird and wonderful apparitions/strange ideas; **das spukt noch immer in den Köpfen** or **durch die Köpfe** that still has a hold on people's minds

Spuk-: **Spuk|ge|schich|te** F ghost story; **spuk|haft** ADJ eerie; **Spuk|schloss** NT haunted castle

Spül-: **Spül|au|to|mat** M (automatic) dishwasher; **Spül|bad** NT rinse; **Spül|be|cken** NT sink; **Spül|bürs|te** F washing-up (Brit) or dishwashing (US) brush

Spu|le [ˈʃpuːlə] F **-, -n** **a** spool, reel; (= Nähmaschinenspule, Ind) bobbin; (Elec) coil **b** (= Federkiel) quill

Spü|le [ˈʃpyːlə] F **-, -n** sink

spu|len [ˈʃpuːlən] VT to spool, to reel; (= aufspulen auch) to wind onto a spool or reel or (auf Nähmaschinespule, Ind) bobbin

spü|len [ˈʃpyːlən] VT **a** (= ausspülen, abspülen) Mund to rinse; Wunde to wash; Darm to irrigate; Vagina to douche; (= abwaschen) Geschirr to wash up **b** (Wellen etc) to wash; (fig) Menschen to bring; **etw an Land ~** to wash sth ashore; **Geld in die Kassen ~** to bring money pouring into the coffers VI (Waschmaschine) to rinse; (= Geschirr spülen) to wash up; (auf der Toilette) to flush; **du spülst und ich trockne ab** you wash and I'll dry; **vergiss nicht zu ~** don't forget to flush the toilet

Spü|ler [ˈʃpyːlɐ] M **-s, -**, **Spü|le|rin** [-ərɪn] F **-, -nen** dishwasher, washer-up (inf)

Spül|icht [ˈʃpyːlɪçt] NT **-s, -e** (old) dishwater

Spül-: **Spül|kas|ten** M cistern; **Spül|klo|sett** NT flush toilet, water closet (dated); **Spül|lap|pen** M dishcloth; **Spül|ma|schi|ne** F (automatic) dishwasher; **spül|ma|schi|nen|fest** ADJ dishwasher-proof; **Spül|mit|tel** NT washing-up liquid; **Spül|pro|gramm** NT wash programme (Brit) or program (US); (von Waschmaschine) rinse cycle

Spul|rad NT bobbin winder

Spül-: **Spül|schüs|sel** F washing-up bowl; **Spül|tisch** M sink (unit); **Spül|tuch** NT pl **-tücher** dishcloth

Spü|lung [ˈʃpyːlʊŋ] F **-, -en** rinsing; (= Mundspülung) rinse; (= Wasser-, Toilettenspülung) flush; (= Spülkasten) cistern, tank (esp US); (= Haarspülung) conditioner; (Med) (= Darm-, Nasenspülung etc) irrigation; (= Vaginalspülung) douche; (Aut) scavenging

Spül|was|ser NT pl **-wässer** (beim Abwaschen) dishwater, washing-up water; (beim Wäschewaschen) rinsing water

Spul|wurm M roundworm, ascarid (Med)

Spund [ʃpʊnt] M **-(e)s, ¨-e** [ˈʃpʏndə] bung (Brit), stopper, spigot; (Holztechnik) tongue

Spund [ʃpʊnt] M **-(e)s, -e** [-də] **junger ~** (dated inf) young pup (dated inf)

spun|den [ˈʃpʊndn] VT Fass to bung (Brit), to stop up

Spund-: **Spund|loch** NT bunghole (Brit), cork hole; **Spund|wand** F (Build) bulkhead

Spur [ʃpuːɐ] F **-, -en** **a** (= Abdruck im Boden etc) track; (Hunt) track, spoor no pl; (= hinterlassenes Zeichen) trace, sign; (= Bremsspur) skidmarks pl;

(= Blutspur, Schleimspur etc, Fährte zur Verfolgung) trail; **von den Tätern fehlt jede ~** there is no clue as to the whereabouts of the persons responsible; **der Täter hat keine ~en hinterlassen** the culprit left no traces *or* marks; **jds ~ aufnehmen** to take up sb's trail; **auf der richtigen/falschen ~ sein** *(lit, fig)* to be on the right/wrong track; **jdn auf jds ~ bringen** to put sb onto sb's trail *or* onto sb; **jdn auf die richtige ~ bringen** *(fig)* to put sb on(to) the right track; **jdm/einer Sache auf der ~ sein/auf die ~ kommen** to be/get onto sb/sth; **die Polizei ist ihm jetzt auf der ~** the police are onto him now; **auf** *or* **in jds ~en wandeln** *(fig)* to follow in sb's footsteps; **(seine) ~en hinterlassen** *(fig)* to leave its mark; **~en hinterlassen** *(fig)* to leave one's/its mark; **ohne ~(en) an jdm vorübergehen** to have no effect on sb; **nicht ohne ~(en) an jdm vorübergehen** to leave its mark on sb

b *(fig: = kleine Menge, Überrest)* trace; *(von Pfeffer, Paprika etc)* touch, soupçon; *(von Vernunft, Anstand, Talent etc)* scrap, ounce; **von Anstand/Takt keine ~** *(inf)* no decency/tact at all; **von Liebe keine ~** *(inf)* love doesn't/didn't come into it; **keine ~!** *(inf)* not at all; **keine ~ davon ist wahr** *(inf)* there's not a scrap *or* an ounce of truth in it; **wir hatten nicht die ~ einer Chance** we didn't have a ghost of a chance *(inf)*; **eine ~ zu laut/grell** a shade *or* a touch too loud/garish

c *(= Fahrbahn)* lane; **auf der linken ~ fahren** to drive in the left-hand lane; **in der ~ bleiben** to keep in lane; **die ~ wechseln** to change lanes

d *(Aut: = gerade Fahrtrichtung)* tracking; **~ halten** *(beim Bremsen etc)* to hold its course; *(nach Unfall)* to track properly; **aus der ~ geraten** *or* **kommen** *(durch Seitenwind etc)* to go off course; *(beim Bremsen etc)* to skid

e *(= Spurweite) (Rail)* gauge; *(Aut)* track

f *(Comput)* track

spür|bar ADJ noticeable, perceptible ADV noticeably, perceptibly

Spur|brei|te F *(Rail)* gauge

Spur|bus M guided bus *(which travels on road and rails)*

spu|ren [ˈʃpuːrən] VT *(Ski) Loipe* to make, to lay VI *(Ski)* to make *or* lay a track; *(Aut)* to track; *(inf)* to obey; *(= sich fügen)* to toe the line; *(= funktionieren: Maschine, Projekt)* to run smoothly, to go well; **jetzt wird gespurt!** *(inf)* I want a little obedience; **bei dem Lehrer wird gespurt** *(inf)* he makes you obey, that teacher

spü|ren [ˈʃpyːrən] VT to feel; *(= intuitiv erfassen) jds Hass, Zuneigung, Unwillen etc auch* to sense; **sie spürte, dass der Erdboden leicht bebte** she felt the earth trembling underfoot; **sie ließ mich ihr Missfallen ~** she made no attempt to hide her displeasure, she let me know that she was displeased; **etw in allen Gliedern ~** *(lit, fig)* to feel sth in every bone of one's body; **davon ist nichts zu ~** there is no sign of it, it's not noticeable; **etw zu ~ bekommen** *(lit)* to feel sth; *(fig)* to feel the (full) force of sth; *jds Spott, Anerkennung etc* to meet with sth; *(= bereuen)* to suffer for sth, to regret sth; **es zu ~ bekommen, dass ...** to feel the effects of the fact that ...; **ihr werdet es noch zu ~ bekommen, dass ihr so faul seid** some day you'll regret being so lazy; **sie bekamen es deutlich zu ~, dass sie Weiße waren** they were made very conscious *or* aware of the fact that they were whites

VTI *(Hunt)* **(nach) etw ~** to track sth, to follow the scent of sth

Spu|ren-: **Spu|ren|ele|ment** NT trace element; **Spu|ren|gas** NT trace gas; **Spu|ren|si|che|rung** F securing of evidence; **die Leute von der ~** the forensic people

Spür|hund M tracker dog; *(inf: Mensch)* sleuth

spur|los ADJ ADV without trace; **~ verschwinden** to disappear *or* vanish without trace, to vanish into thin air; **~ an jdm vorübergehen** to have no effect on sb; *(Ereignis, Erfahrung etc auch)* to wash over sb; **das ist nicht ~ an ihm vorübergegangen** it left its mark on him

Spür|na|se F *(Hunt)* nose; **eine ~ für etw haben** *(fig inf)* to have a (good) nose for sth

Spür|pan|zer M *(Mil)* NBC *(nuclear, biological, and chemical)* reconnaissance system

Spur|ril|le F *(Mot)* rut

Spür|sinn M, *no pl (Hunt, fig)* nose; *(fig: = Gefühl)* feel

Spurt [ʃpʊrt] M **-s, -s** *or* **-e** spurt; *(= Endspurt, fig)* final spurt; **zum ~ ansetzen** *(lit, fig)* to make a final spurt

spur|ten [ˈʃpʊrtn] VI *aux sein (Sport)* to spurt; *(= zum Endspurt ansetzen)* to make a final spurt; *(inf: = rennen)* to sprint, to dash

Spur|wech|sel M *(Mot)* lane change; **ein ~ war unmöglich** it was impossible to change lanes

Spur|wei|te F *(Rail)* gauge; *(Aut)* track

spu|ten [ˈʃpuːtn] VR *(old, dial)* to hurry, to make haste *(old, liter)*

Sput|nik [ˈʃpʊtnɪk, ˈsp-] M **-s, -s** sputnik

Squash [skvɔʃ] NT **-,** *no pl* squash

Squash-: **Squash|hal|le** F squash courts *pl*; **Squash|schlä|ger** M squash racket

SR M **-s,** *no pl abbr von* **Saarländischer Rundfunk**

> **SRG**
>
> **SRG** is the **Schweizerische Radio- und Fernsehgesellschaft**, founded in 1931. It is a private company but is non-profit-making. Altogether it transmits ten radio and three television channels in the four national languages of German, French, Italian and Rhaeto-Romanic. **SRG** is funded by licence fees and television advertising and aims to provide balanced and diverse political and cultural broadcasting.

Sri Lan|ka [ˈsriː ˈlaŋka] NT **- -s** Sri Lanka

Sri Lan|ker [sriːˈlaŋkɐ] M **-s, -,** **Sri Lan|ke|rin** [-ərɪn] F **-, -nen** Sri Lankan

sri-lan|kisch [sriːˈlaŋkɪʃ] ADJ Sri Lankan

SS [ɛsˈlɛs] NT **-, -** *(Univ) abbr von* **Sommersemester**

SS [ɛsˈlɛs] F **-,** *no pl (NS) abbr von* **Schutzstaffel** SS

SSO *abbr von* **Südsüdost** SSE

SSV [ɛslɛsˈfau] M **-s, -s** *abbr von* **Sommerschlussverkauf**

SSW *abbr von* **Südsüdwest** SSW

st INTERJ *(Aufmerksamkeit erregend)* psst; *(Ruhe gebietend)* shh

s. t. [ɛsˈteː] ADV *abbr von* **sine tempore**

St. *abbr von* **Stück** *abbr von* **Sankt** St

Staat [ʃtaːt] M **-(e)s, -en** **a** state; *(= Land)* country; **die ~en** *(inf)* the States *(inf)*; **im deutschen ~** in Germany; **die beiden deutschen ~en** *(Hist)* the two Germanies *or* German states; **ein ~ im ~e** a state within a state; **von ~s wegen** on a governmental level; **im Interesse des ~es** in the national interest, in the interests of the state; **zum Wohl des ~es** for the good of the nation; **beim ~ arbeiten** *or* **sein** *(inf)* to be employed by the government *or* state; **so wenig ~ wie möglich** minimal government; **der schlanke ~** the slimmed-down *or* lean state; **~ ist ~** the state's the state; **der ~ bin ich** *(prov)* l'État, c'est moi

b *(= Ameisenstaat, Bienenstaat)* colony

c *(fig) (= Pracht)* pomp; *(= Kleidung, Schmuck)* finery; **in vollem ~** in all one's finery; *(Soldaten)* in full dress; *(Würdenträger)* in full regalia; **(großen) ~ machen (mit etw)** to make a show (of sth); **damit ist kein ~ zu machen, damit kann man nicht gerade ~ machen** that's nothing to write home about *(inf)*; **ohne großen ~ damit zu machen** without making a big thing about it *(inf)*

Staa|ten-: **Staa|ten|bund** M *pl* **-bünde** confederation (of states); **Staa|ten|ge|mein|schaft** F community of states; **staa|ten|los** ADJ stateless; **Staa|ten|lo|se(r)** [ˈʃtaːtnloːzə] MF *decl as adj* stateless person; **Staa|ten|lo|sig|keit** F **-,** *no pl* statelessness

staatl. gepr. *abbr von* **staatlich geprüft**

staat|lich [ˈʃtaːtlɪç] ADJ state *attr*; *Gelder, Unterstützung etc auch* government *attr*; *(= staatseigen) Betrieb, Güter auch* state-owned; *(= staatlich geführt)* state-run ADV by the state; **~ subventioniert** subsidized by the state, state-subsidized; **~ anerkannt** state-approved; **~ geprüft** state-certified

staat|li|cher|seits [ˈʃtaːtlɪçɐzaits] ADV on the part of the state

Staats-: **Staats|ab|ga|ben** PL (government) taxes *pl*; **Staats|af|fä|re** F **a** *(lit)* affair of state **b** *(fig)* major operation; **Staats|akt** M *(lit)* state occasion; *(fig inf)* song and dance *(inf)*; **er wurde in** *or* **mit einem feierlichen ~ verabschiedet** his farewell was a state occasion; **Staats|ak|ti|on** F major operation; **Staats|amt** NT public office; **Staats|an|ge|hö|ri|ge(r)** MF *decl as adj* national; *(einer Monarchie auch)* subject; **Staats|an|ge|hö|rig|keit** [-langəhøːrɪçkait] F **-, -en** nationality; **Staats|an|ge|hö|rig|keits|nach|weis** M proof of nationality; **Staats|an|ge|le|gen|heit** F state affair; **Staats|an|lei|he** F government bond; **Staats|an|walt** M, **Staats|an|wäl|tin** F district attorney *(US)*, public prosecutor *(esp Brit)*; **der ~ forderte ...** the prosecution called for ...; **Staats|an|walt|schaft** F district attorney's office *(US)*, public prosecutor's office *(esp Brit)*; *(= Anwälte)* district attorneys *pl (US)*, public prosecutors *pl (esp Brit)*; **Staats|ap|pa|rat** M apparatus of state; **Staats|ar|chiv** NT state archives *pl*; **Staats|aus|ga|ben** PL public spending *sing or* expenditure *sing*; **Staats|bahn** F state-owned *or* national railway(s *pl*) *(Brit)*, state-owned *or* national railroad(s *pl*) *(US)*;; **Staats|bank** F *pl* **-banken** national *or* state bank; **Staats|bank|rott** M national bankruptcy; **Staats|be|am|te(r)** M *decl as adj*, **Staats|be|am|tin** F public servant; **Staats|be|gräb|nis** NT state funeral; **Staats|be|sitz** M state property; **(in) ~ sein** to be state-owned; **Staats|be|such** M state visit; **Staats|be|trieb** M state-owned *or* nationalized enterprise; **Staats|bib|lio|thek** F national library; **Staats|bür|ger(in)** M(F) citizen; **Staats|bür|ger|kun|de** F *(Sch)* civics *sing*; **staats|bür|ger|lich** ADJ *attr Pflicht* civic; *Rechte* civil; **Staats|bür|ger|schaft** F nationality; **doppelte ~** dual nationality; **Staats|chef(in)** M(F) head of state; **Staats|die|ner(in)** M(F) public servant; **Staats|dienst** M civil service; **staats|ei|gen** ADJ state-owned; **Staats|ei|gen|tum** NT state property *no art*, property of the state; **Staats|ein|nah|men** PL public revenue *sing*; **Staats|emp|fang** M state reception; **staats|er|hal|tend** ADJ conducive to the wellbeing of the state; **Staats|exa|men** NT state exam(ination), ≈ first degree, *university degree required for the teaching profession*

> **STAATSEXAMEN**
>
> The **Staatsexamen**, or **Staatsprüfung** (its official name), is set by state-run examination boards. It has to be taken by everyone trying to get into certain professions, such as those of lawyer, teacher, doctor, pharmacist or nurse. The first **Staatsexamen** is followed by a two- to three-year period of practical training and the second **Staatsexamen** or, in the case of doctors and pharmacists, the **Approbation**.

Staats-: **Staats|fei|er|tag** M national holiday; **Staats|feind(in)** M(F) enemy of the state; **staats|feind|lich** ADJ *Person, Gruppe* hostile to the state; *Tätigkeit, Hetze* against the state ADV **sich ~ betätigen** to engage in activities hostile to the state; **Staats|fi|nan|zen** PL public finances *pl*; **Staats|flag|ge** F national flag; **Staats|form** F type of state; **Staats|ge|biet** NT national territory *no art*; **staats|ge|fähr|-**

dend ADJ threatening the security of the state; **Staats|ge|fähr|dung** F threat to the security of the state; **Staats|ge|heim|nis** NT *(lit, fig hum)* state secret; **Staats|gel|der** PL public funds *pl*; **Staats|ge|richts|hof** M constitutional court; **Staats|ge|walt** F authority of the state; **Staats|gren|ze** F state frontier *or* border; **Staats|haus|halt** M national budget; **Staats|ho|heit** F sovereignty; **Staats|idee** F conception of a state; **Staats|in|te|res|se** NT interests *pl* of (the) state; **Staats|kanz|lei** F state chancellery; **Staats|ka|pi|ta|lis|mus** M state capitalism; **Staats|ka|ros|se** F state carriage; **Staats|kas|se** F treasury, public purse; **Staats|kir|che** F state church; **Staats|klug|heit** F *(liter)* statesmanship; **Staats|kne|te** F *(inf)* public money; **Staats|kom|mis|sar(in)** M(F) state commissioner; **Staats|kos|ten** PL public expenses *pl*; **auf ~** at the public expense; **Staats|kunst** F *(liter)* statesmanship, statecraft; **Staats|leh|re** F political science; **Staats|lot|te|rie** F national *or* state lottery; **Staats|macht** F state power; **Staats|mann** M *pl* **-männer** statesman; **staats|män|nisch** [-mɛnɪʃ] ADJ statesmanlike ADV in a statesmanlike manner; **Staats|mi|nis|ter(in)** M(F) state minister; **Staats|mo|no|pol** NT state monopoly; **Staats|ober|haupt** NT head of state; **Staats|ord|nung** F system of government; **Staats- und Gesellschaftsordnung** social system and system of government; **Staats|or|gan** NT organ of the state; **Staats|par|tei** F official party; **staats|po|li|tisch** ADJ political; **Staats|po|li|zei** F ≈ FBI *(US)*, ≈ Special Branch *(Brit)*; **die Geheime ~** *(Hist)* the Gestapo; **Staats|prä|si|dent(in)** M(F) president; **Staats|prü|fung** F *(form)* = **Staatsexamen**; **Staats|rai|son** [-rɛzõ:] F -, *no pl*, **Staats|rä|son** F reasons of state; **Staats|rat** M council of state; *(Sw)* cantonal government; **Staats|rat** M, **Staats|rä|tin** F councillor *(Brit) or* councilor *(US)* of state; *(Sw)* member of the cantonal government; **Staats|rats|vor|sit|zen|de(r)** MF *decl as adj (DDR)* head of state; **Staats|recht** NT, *no pl* **a** national law **b** *(= Verfassungsrecht)* constitutional law; **staats|recht|lich** ADJ **a** *Entscheidung, Überlegung* of national law **b** *(= verfassungsrechtlich)* constitutional ADV according to national law; *(= verfassungsrechtlich)* constitutionally; **~ unterscheiden sich ...** in national law there are differences between ...; **Staats|re|gie|rung** F state government; **Staats|re|li|gi|on** F state religion; **Staats|ren|te** F state *or* government pension; **Staats|ru|der** NT *(geh)* helm of (the) state; **Staats|sä|ckel** M *(old, hum)* national coffers *pl*; **Staats|schatz** M national treasury; **Staats|schiff** NT *(liter)* ship of state; **Staats|schuld** F *(Fin)* national debt; **Staats|sek|re|tär(in)** M(F) *(= Beamter)* ≈ permanent secretary *(Brit)*, ≈ undersecretary *(US)*; **Staats|si|cher|heit** F national *or* state security; **Staats|si|cher|heits|dienst** M *(DDR)* national *or* state security service; **Staats|so|zi|a|lis|mus** M state socialism; **Staats|streich** M coup (d'état); **Staats|the|a|ter** NT state theatre *(Brit) or* theater *(US)*; **staats|tra|gend** ADJ *Politiker* representing the interests of the state; *Partei* established; *Rede* statesmanlike ADV **~ ausgedrückt** expressed in a statesmanlike manner; **Staats|trau|er|tag** M national day of mourning; **Staats|un|ter|neh|men** NT state-owned enterprise; **Staats|ver|bre|chen** NT political crime; *(fig)* major crime; **Staats|ver|dros|sen|heit** F dissatisfaction *or* disenchantment with the state; **Staats|ver|fas|sung** F (national) constitution; **Staats|ver|leum|dung** F slander *or (schriftlich)* libel of the state; **Staats|ver|mö|gen** NT national *or* public assets *pl*; **Staats|ver|schul|dung** F national debt; **Staats|ver|trag** M international treaty; **Staats|ver|wal|tung** F administration of the state; **Staats|wald** M state-owned forest; **Staats|we|sen** NT, *no pl* state; **Staats|wis|sen|schaft** F, **Staats|wis|sen|schaf|ten** PL *(dated)* political science; **Staats|wohl** NT public welfare; **Staats|zu|schuss** M state *or* government grant

Stab [ʃta:p] M **-(e)s, ¨-e** [ˈʃtɛ:bə] **a** rod; *(= Gitterstab)* bar; *(= Spazierstock, Wanderstab)* stick; *(= Bischofsstab)* crosier; *(= Hirtenstab)* crook; *(= Marschallstab, Dirigentenstab, für Staffellauf, von Majorette etc)* baton; *(als Amtzeichen)* mace; *(für Stabhochsprung, = Zeltstab)* pole; *(= Messstab)* (measuring) rod *or* stick; *(Aut)* dipstick; *(= Zauberstab)* wand; **den ~ über jdn brechen** *(fig)* to condemn sb; **den ~ führen** *(Mus geh)* to conduct **b** *(= Mitarbeiterstab, Mil)* staff; *(von Experten)* panel; *(Mil: = Hauptquartier)* headquarters *sing or pl*

Stäb|chen [ˈʃtɛ:pçən] NT **-s, -** *dim von* **Stab** *(= Essstäbchen)* chopstick; *(= Kragenstäbchen)* (collar) stiffener; *(= Korsettstäbchen)* bone; *(Anat: der Netzhaut)* rod; *(beim Häkeln)* treble; *(inf: = Zigarette)* cig *(esp US)*, ciggy *(inf)*

Stab-: **stab|för|mig** ADJ rod-shaped; **Stab|füh|rung** F *(Mus)* conducting; **unter der ~ von** conducted by, under the baton of; **Stab|heu|schre|cke** F stick insect; **Stab|hoch|sprin|ger(in)** M(F) pole-vaulter; **Stab|hoch|sprung** M pole vault

stabil [ʃtaˈbi:l, st-] ADJ *Möbel, Schuhe, Kind* sturdy, robust; *Währung, Beziehung, Charakter* stable; *Gesundheit* sound; *(euph: = korpulent)* well-built, solid ADV *gebaut* solidly, sturdily

Sta|bi|li|sa|ti|on [ʃtabilizaˈtsio:n, st-] F **-, -en** stabilization

Sta|bi|li|sa|tor [ʃtabiliˈza:to:ɐ, st-] M **-s, Stabilisatoren** [-ˈto:rən] stabilizer

sta|bi|li|sie|ren [ʃtabiliˈzi:rən, st-] *ptp* **stabilisiert** VT to stabilize VR to stabilize, to become stable

Sta|bi|li|tät [ʃtabiliˈtɛ:t, st-] F **-**, *no pl (von Währung, Land, Situation)* stability

Sta|bi|li|täts|pakt [ʃtabiliˈtɛ:ts-, st-] M *(Pol, Econ)* stability pact

Stab-: **Stab|kir|che** F stave church; **Stab|lam|pe** F (electric) torch, flashlight; **Stab|mag|net** M bar magnet; **Stab|mi|xer** M hand blender; **Stab|reim** M alliteration

Stabs-: **Stabs|arzt** M, **Stabs|ärz|tin** F *(Mil)* captain in the medical corps; **Stabs|chef(in)** M(F) *(Mil inf)* Chief of Staff; **Stabs|feld|we|bel(in)** M(F) *(Mil)* warrant officer class II *(Brit)*, master sergeant *(US)*; **Stabs|of|fi|zier(in)** M(F) *(Mil)* staff officer; *(Rang)* field officer; **Stabs|stel|le** F specialist team; *(Mil)* staff

Stab|wech|sel M *(Sport)* baton change, changeover

Stac|ca|to [staˈka:to, ʃt-] NT **-s, -s** *or* **Staccati** [-ti] staccato

stach *pret von* **stechen**

Sta|chel [ˈʃtaxl] M **-s, -n** *(von Rosen, Ginster etc)* thorn, prickle; *(von Kakteen, Stachelhäutern, Igel)* spine; *(von Stachelschwein)* quill, spine; *(auf Stacheldraht)* barb; *(zum Viehantrieb)* goad; *(= Giftstachel: von Bienen etc)* sting; *(fig liter) (von Ehrgeiz, Neugier etc)* spur; *(von Vorwurf, Hass)* sting; **seinen ~ verlieren** *(fig)* to lose its sting; **Tod, wo ist dein ~?** *(Bibl)* Death where now thy sting?; **der ~ des Fleisches** *(liter)* the urges *pl* of the body; **ein ~ im Fleisch** *(liter)* a thorn in the flesh *or* side → **löcken**

Sta|chel-: **Sta|chel|bee|re** F gooseberry; **Sta|chel|beer|strauch** M gooseberry bush

Sta|chel|draht M barbed wire

Sta|chel|draht-: **Sta|chel|draht|ver|hau** M barbed-wire entanglement; **Sta|chel|draht|zaun** M barbed-wire fence

Sta|chel-: **Sta|chel|flos|ser** [-flɔsɐ] M **-s, -** *(Zool)* spiny-finned fish; **sta|chel|för|mig** ADJ spiky; *(Biol)* spiniform *no adv*; **Sta|chel|hals|band** NT spiked (dog) collar; **Sta|chel|häu|ter** [-hɔytɐ] M **-s, -** *(Zool)* echinoderm *(spec)*

sta|che|lig [ˈʃtaxəlɪç] ADJ *Rosen, Ginster etc* thorny; *Kaktus, Igel etc* spiny; *(= sich stachelig anfühlend)* prickly; *Kinn, Bart* bristly; *Draht* spiky, barbed

sta|cheln [ˈʃtaxln] VT = **anstacheln**

Sta|chel-: **Sta|chel|ro|chen** M stingray; **Sta|chel|schne|cke** F murex; **Sta|chel|schwein** NT porcupine

stach|lig [ˈʃtaxlɪç] ADJ = **stachelig**

Sta|del [ˈʃta:dl] M **-s, -** *(S Ger, Aus, Sw)* barn

Sta|di|on [ˈʃta:diɔn] NT **-s, Stadien** [-diən] stadium

Sta|di|um [ˈʃta:diʊm] NT **-s, Stadien** [-diən] stage; **im vorgerückten/letzten ~** *(Med)* at an advanced/terminal stage; **er hat Krebs im vorgerückten/letzten ~** he has advanced/terminal cancer

Stadt [ʃtat] F **-, ¨-e** [ˈʃtɛ:tə, ˈʃtɛtə] **a** town; *(= Großstadt)* city; **die ~ Paris** the city of Paris; **Mexiko-~** Mexico City; **~ und Land** town and country; **in ~ und Land** throughout the land, the length and breadth of the land; **die ganze ~ spricht davon** it's all over town, the whole town is talking about it, it's the talk of the town; **in die ~ gehen** to go into town **b** *(= Stadtverwaltung)* (town) council; *(von Großstadt)* (city) council; **bei der ~ angestellt sein** to be working for the council; **die ~ Ulm** Ulm City Council; **die ~ Güstrow** Güstrow Town Council

städt. *abbr von* **städtisch**

Stadt-: **Stadt|adel** M town nobility; **stadt|aus|wärts** ADV out of town; **für den Verkehr ~ gesperrt** closed to traffic going out of town; **Stadt|au|to|bahn** F urban motorway *(Brit) or* freeway *(US)*; **Stadt|bad** NT municipal baths *pl (Brit) or* swimming pool; **Stadt|bahn** F suburban railway *(Brit)*, city railroad *(US)*; **Stadt|be|hör|de** F municipal authority; **stadt|be|kannt** ADJ well-known, known all over town; **Stadt|be|sich|ti|gung** F town/city (sightseeing) tour, tour of a/the town/city; **Stadt|be|woh|ner(in)** M(F) town dweller *(esp Brit) or* resident; *(von Großstadt)* city dweller *(esp Brit) or* resident; **~** *pl* townspeople *pl*; *(von Großstadt)* city people *pl*; **Stadt|be|zirk** M municipal district; **Stadt|bild** NT urban features *pl*, townscape; cityscape; **das ständig wechselnde ~ Bonns** the constantly changing face of Bonn; **Stadt|bü|che|rei** F → **Stadt a** municipal *or* town/city (lending) library, public library; **Stadt|bum|mel** M stroll in the *or* through town

Städt|chen [ˈʃtɛ:tçən, ˈʃtɛtçən] NT **-s, -** *dim von* **Stadt** small town

Stadt-: **Stadt|chro|nik** F → **Stadt a** town/city chronicles *pl*; **Stadt|di|rek|tor(in)** M(F) → **Stadt a** town clerk *(Brit)*, town/city manager *(US)*

Städ|te-: **Städ|te|bau** M, *no pl* urban development; **städ|te|bau|lich** ADJ *Entwicklung* of urban building; *Maßnahme* for urban development; *Veränderungen* in urban development ADV as regards urban development

stadt|ein|wärts ADV into town; **für den Verkehr ~ gesperrt** closed to traffic going into town

Städ|te-: **Städ|te|part|ner|schaft** F town twinning *(Brit)*, sister city agreement *(US)*; **Städ|te|pla|nung** F town *or* urban planning

Städ|ter [ˈʃtɛ:tɐ, ˈʃtɛtɐ] M **-s, -**, **Städ|te|rin** [-ərɪn] F **-, -nen** town dweller *(Brit) or* resident; *(= Großstädter)* city dweller *(Brit) or* resident

Städ|te|tag M convention *or* congress of municipal authorities

Stadt-: **Stadt|ex|press** M *(Rail)* city express; **Stadt|fahrt** F → **Stadt a** journey within a/the town/city; **Stadt|flucht** F exodus from the cities; **Stadt|füh|rung** F guided tour of a/the town/city; **Stadt|gas** NT, *no pl* town gas; **Stadt|ge|biet** NT municipal area; *(von Großstadt auch)* city zone; **Stadt|ge|mein|de** F municipality; **Stadt|ge|spräch** NT **a** **(das) ~ sein** to be the talk of the town **b** *(Telec)* local call; **Stadt|gren|ze** F → **Stadt a** town/city boundary; **Stạdt|gue|ril|la** F urban guerrilla; **Stạdt|haus** NT townhouse

städ|tisch [ˈʃtɛːtɪʃ, ˈʃtɛtɪʃ] ADJ municipal, town *attr*; *(= einer Großstadt auch)* city *attr*; *(= nach Art einer Stadt)* urban; **die ~e Bevölkerung** the town/city *or* urban population; **die ~e Lebensweise** the urban way of life, town/city life

Stạdt-: **Stạdt|käm|me|rer** M, **Stạdt|käm|me|rin** F → **Stadt a** town/city treasurer; **Stạdt|kas|se** F → **Stadt a** town/city treasury; **Stạdt|kern** M → **Stadt a** town/city centre *(Brit) or* center *(US)*; **Stạdt|kind** NT → **Stadt a** town/city kid *(inf)*; **Stạdt|kom|man|dant(in)** M(F) → **Stadt a** military governor (of a town/city); **Stạdt|kreis** M → **Stadt a** town/city borough; **Stạdt|land|schaft** F → **Stadt a** town/city landscape, townscape/cityscape; **Stạdt|luft** F → **Stadt a** town/city air; **~ macht frei** *(Hist) principle whereby a serf became a freeman if he stayed in a town/city for a year and a day*; **Stạdt|ma|ga|zin** NT listings magazine, entertainment and events guide; **Stạdt|mau|er** F city wall; **Stạdt|mensch** M → **Stadt a** town/city person; **Stạdt|mis|si|on** F city mission; **Stạdt|mit|te** F → **Stadt a** town/city centre *(Brit) or* center *(US)*; **Stạdt|ober|haupt** NT → **Stadt a** head of a/the town/city; **Stạdt|park** M → **Stadt a** town/city *or* municipal park; **Stạdt|par|la|ment** NT city council; **Stạdt|plan** M → **Stadt a** (street) map (of a/the town/city); *(Archit)* town/city plan; **Stạdt|pla|nung** F town planning; **Stạdt|ra|dio** NT city radio; **Stạdt|rand** M → **Stadt a** outskirts *pl* (of a/the town/city); **am nördlichen ~** on the (of the town/city); **am nördlichen ~** on the northern edge of town; **Stạdt|rand|sied|lung** F suburban housing scheme; **Stạdt|rat** M → **Stadt a** (town/city) council; **Stạdt|rat** M, **Stạdt|rä|tin** F → **Stadt a** (town/city) councillor *(Brit) or* councilor *(US)*; **Stạdt|recht** NT *(Hist)* town charter; **Stạdt|rund|fahrt** F → **Stadt a** (sightseeing) tour of a/the town/city; **eine ~ machen** to go on a (sightseeing) tour of a/the town/city; **Stạdt|rund|gang** M → **Stadt a** walking tour of a/the town/city, town/city walking tour; **Stạdt|schrei|ber(in)** M(F) *(obs, Sw)* town clerk; **Stạdt|staat** M city state; **Stạdt|strei|cher** [-ʃtraiçɐ] M **-s, -**, **Stạdt|strei|che|rin** [-ərɪn] F **-, -nen** → **Stadt a** (town/city) tramp; **Stạdt|strei|che|rei** [-ʃtraiçəˈrai] F **-**, *no pl* urban vagrancy; **Stạdt|teil** M → **Stadt a** district, part of town/city; **Stạdt|the|a|ter** NT municipal theatre *(Brit) or* theater *(US)*; **Stạdt|tor** NT → **Stadt a** town/city gate; **Stạdt|vä|ter** PL *(old, hum)* city fathers *pl or* elders *pl*; **Stạdt|ver|kehr** M → **Stadt a** **a** *(= Straßenverkehr)* town/city traffic **b** *(= örtlicher Nahverkehr)* local town/city transport; **Stạdt|ver|ord|ne|te(r)** [-fɛɐ̯ɔrdnətə] MF *decl as adj* → **Stadt a** town/city councillor *(Brit) or* councilor *(US)*; **Stạdt|ver|wal|tung** F → **Stadt a** (town/city) council; **Stạdt|vier|tel** NT → **Stadt a** district, part of town/city; **Stạdt|wap|pen** NT municipal coat of arms; **Stạdt|wer|ke** PL → **Stadt a** town's/city's department of works; **Stạdt|woh|nung** F → **Stadt a** town/city apartment *or* flat *(Brit)*; **Stạdt|zent|rum** NT → **Stadt a** town/city centre *(Brit) or* center *(US)*

Sta|fẹt|te [ʃtaˈfɛtə] F **-, -n** *(Hist)* courier, messenger

Staf|fa|ge [staˈfaːʒə] F **-, -n** *(Art: = Beiwerk)* staffage; *(fig)* window-dressing

Stạf|fel [ˈʃtafl] F **-, -n** **a** *(= Formation) (Mil, Naut, Aviat)* echelon; *(Aviat: = Einheit)* squadron; **~ fliegen** to fly in echelon formation **b** *(Sport)* relay (race); *(= Mannschaft)* relay team; *(fig)* relay; **~ laufen/schwimmen** to run/swim in a relay (race) **c** *(= Stufe, Sprosse)* rung; *(S Ger: = Steintreppe)* stone steps *pl* **d** *(TV: = neue Folgen einer TV-Serie)* season, series

Stạf|fe|lei [ʃtafəˈlai] F **-, -en** easel

Stạf|fel-: **Stạf|fel|lauf** M relay (race); **Stạf|fel|mie|te** F graduated rent

stạf|feln [ˈʃtafln] VT **a** *Gehälter, Tarife, Fahrpreise* to grade, to graduate; *Anfangszeiten, Startplätze* to stagger; **nach Dienstalter gestaffelte Gehälter** salaries graded according to years of service; **die Gehaltserhöhung wird zeitlich gestaffelt** the salary increase is being phased (over a period of time); **diese Zahlungen werden sozial gestaffelt** these payments are graded according to need; **die Startplätze gestaffelt anordnen** to stagger the starting places **b** *(= in Formation bringen)* to draw up in an echelon; **gestaffelte Formation** *(Aviat)* echelon formation

Stạf|fel-: **Stạf|fel|schwim|men** NT relay swimming; **Stạf|fel|ta|rif** M graduated *or* differential tariff

Stạf|fe|lung [ˈʃtafəlʊŋ] F **-, -en**, **Stạff|lung** [ˈʃtaflʊŋ] F **-, -en** **a** *(von Gehältern, Tarifen, Preisen)* grading, graduating; *(von Zeiten, Startplätzen)* staggering **b** *(in Formation)* drawing up in an echelon

Stạf|fel|zins M *(Fin)* graduated interest *sing*

Stag [ʃtaːk] NT **-(e)s, -e(n)** [-gə, -gn] *(Naut)* stay

Stag|fla|ti|on [ʃtakflaˈtsioːn, st-] F **-, -en** *(Econ)* stagflation

Stag|na|ti|on [ʃtagnaˈtsioːn, st-] F **-, -en** stagnation, stagnancy; **es kam zu einer ~** there was a period of stagnation *or* stagnancy

stag|nie|ren [ʃtaˈgniːrən, st-] *ptp* **stagniert** VI to stagnate

Stag|nie|rung F **-, -en** = **Stagnation**

stahl *pret von* **stehlen**

Stahl [ʃtaːl] M **-(e)s, -e** *or* **Stähle** [ˈʃtɛːlə] steel; *(old liter: = Schwert auch)* blade; **Nerven aus** *or* **wie ~** nerves of steel

Stahl- *in cpds* steel; **Stahl|bau** M *pl* **-bauten** steel-girder construction; **Stahl|be|ton** M reinforced concrete; **stahl|blau** ADJ steel-blue; **Stahl|blech** NT sheet steel; *(Stück)* steel sheet; **Stahl|bram|me** [-bramə] F **-, -n** steel girder

stäh|len [ˈʃtɛːlən] VT *Körper, Muskeln, Nerven, Charakter* to harden, to toughen; **seinen Mut ~** to steel oneself VR to toughen *or* harden oneself; *(= sich wappnen)* to steel oneself

stäh|lern [ˈʃtɛːlɐn] ADJ *Waffen, Ketten* steel; *(fig) Muskeln, Wille* of iron, iron *attr*; *Nerven* of steel; *Blick* steely

Stahl-: **Stahl|fe|der** F steel nib; **Stahl|ge|rüst** NT tubular steel scaffolding; *(= Gerippe)* steel-girder frame; **stahl|grau** ADJ steel-grey *(Brit)*, steel-gray *(US)*; **stahl|hart** ADJ *Mensch, Muskeln* (as) hard as steel; *Blick* steely; **Stahl|helm** M *(Mil)* steel helmet; **Stahl|helm-Frak|ti|on** F *(Pol)* hawks *pl*, hardliners *pl*; **Stahl|in|dus|trie** F, *no pl* steel industry; **Stahl|kam|mer** F strongroom; **Stahl|ko|cher(in)** M(F) steelworker; **Stahl|man|tel|ge|schoss** NT steel jacket bullet; **Stahl|rohr** NT tubular steel; *(Stück)* steel tube; **Stahl|rohr|mö|bel** PL tubular steel furniture *sing*; **Stahl|ross** NT *(hum)* bike *(inf)*, velocipede *(form, hum)*; **Stahl|stich** M *(Art)* steel engraving; **Stahl|trä|ger** M steel girder; **Stahl|wa|ren** PL steel goods *pl*, steelware *sing*; **Stahl|werk** NT steelworks *sing or pl*; **Stahl|wol|le** F steel wool

stak *(geh) pret von* **stecken VI**

Sta|ke [ˈʃtaːkə] F **-, -n** *(N Ger)* (barge)pole; *(für Stechkahn)* (punt) pole

sta|ken [ˈʃtaːkn] VTI *(N Ger) (vi: aux sein)* to pole; *Stechkahn auch* to punt; *(fig)* to stalk

Sta|ken [ˈʃtaːkn] M **-s, -** *(N Ger)* = **Stake**

Sta|ket [ʃtaˈkeːt] NT **-(e)s, -e**, **Sta|ke|ten|zaun** M paling, picket fence

Stak|ka|to [ʃtaˈkaːto, st-] NT **-s, -s** *or* **Stakkati** [-ti] staccato

stak|sen [ˈʃtaːksn] VI *aux sein (inf)* to stalk; *(unsicher)* to teeter; *(steif)* to hobble; **mit ~den Schritten gehen** to stalk/teeter/hobble

stak|sig [ˈʃtaːksɪç] ADJ *Beine* spindly; *(= unbeholfen)* gawky ADV **~ gehen** *(= steif)* to hobble; *(= unsicher)* to teeter; **jdm ~ entgegenkommen** to teeter toward(s) sb

Sta|lag|mit [stalaˈgmiːt, ʃt-, -mɪt] M **-en** *or* **-s, -en** stalagmite

Sta|lak|tit [stalakˈtiːt, ʃt-, -tɪt] M **-en** *or* **-s, -en** stalactite

Sta|li|nis|mus [staliˈnɪsmʊs, ʃt-] M **-**, *no pl* Stalinism

Sta|li|nist [staliˈnɪst, ʃt-] M **-en, -en**, **Sta|li|nis|tin** [-ˈnɪstɪn] F **-, -nen** Stalinist

sta|li|nis|tisch [staliˈnɪstɪʃ, ʃt-] ADJ Stalinist ADV *geführt* along Stalinist lines; in a Stalinist way; **~ klingend** Stalinist sounding; **~ gesinnt** Stalinist; **~ beeinflusst** influenced by (the teachings of) Stalin

Sta|lin|or|gel [ˈstaːlin-, ˈʃt-] F multiple rocket launcher

Stall [ʃtal] M **-(e)s, ⸚e** [ˈʃtɛlə] **a** *(= Pferdestall, Gestüt, Aut: = Rennstall, fig)* stable; *(= Kuhstall)* cowshed, (cow) barn *(US)*, byre *(Brit)*; *(= Hühnerstall)* henhouse, coop; *(= Kaninchenstall)* hutch; *(= Schafstall)* (sheep)cote; *(= Schweinestall)* (pig)sty, (pig)pen *(US)*; **den ~ ausmisten** to clean out the stable *etc*; *(fig)* to clean out the Augean stables; **ein (ganzer) ~ voll Kinder** *(inf)* a (whole) pack of children **b** *(inf: = Hosenschlitz)* flies *pl (Brit)*, fly

Stallaterne △ F → **Stalllaterne**

Stall-: **Stall|bur|sche** M = **Stallknecht**; **Stall|dung** M, **Stall|dün|ger** M farmyard manure; **Stall|ge|ruch** M farmyard smell; *(fig: = Merkmale)* characteristics *pl*; **Stall|ha|se** M rabbit; **Stall|knecht** M farm hand; *(für Pferde)* stableman, stable lad *or* hand; *(für Kühe)* cowhand; **Stall|la|ter|ne** F stable lamp; **Stall|magd** F farm girl; *(für Pferde)* stable maid; *(= Kuhmagd)* milkmaid; **Stall|meis|ter(in)** M(F) stable boy, equerry; **Stall|mist** M farmyard manure; **Stall|pflicht** F *(für Tiere)* ≈ a ban on keeping livestock outdoors; **es herrscht ~ für Geflügel** poultry are required to be kept indoors

Stal|lung [ˈʃtalʊŋ] F **-, -en**, **Stal|lun|gen** PL stables *pl*

Stall|wa|che F *(fig)* watchdog

Stamm [ʃtam] M **-(e)s, ⸚e** [ˈʃtɛmə] **a** *(= Baumstamm)* trunk → **Apfel**
b *(Ling)* stem
c *(= Volksstamm)* tribe; *(= Abstammung)* line; *(Biol)* phylum; *(= Bakterienstamm)* strain; **der ~ der Massai** the Masai tribe; **der ~ der Bourbonen** the house of Bourbon; **aus königlichem ~** of royal blood *or* stock *or* lineage; **aus dem ~e Davids** of the line of David, of David's line; **vom ~e Nimm sein** *(hum)* to be one of the takers of this world
d *(= Kern, fester Bestand)* regulars *pl*; *(= Kunden)* regular customers *pl*; *(von Mannschaft)* regular team members *pl*; *(= Arbeiter)* regular *or* permanent workforce; *(= Angestellte)* permanent staff *pl*; **ein fester ~ von Kunden** regular customers, regulars; **zum ~ gehören** to be one of the regulars *etc*
e *usu pl (St Ex)* ordinary *or* common share
f *(Comput)* root

Stamm-: **Stamm|ak|tie** F *(St Ex)* ordinary *or* common share; **Stamm|baum** M family *or* genealogical tree; *(Biol)* phylogenetic tree; *(von Zuchttieren)* pedigree; *(Ling)* tree; **einen guten ~ haben** *(lit, hum)* to have a good pedigree; **Stamm|be|leg|schaft** F permanent *or* regular workforce; *(= Angestellte)* regular staff *pl*; **Stamm|buch** NT **a** *book recording family events with some legal documents* **b** *(fig)* **jdm etw ins ~ schreiben** to make sb take note of sth; **Stamm|burg** F ancestral castle; **Stamm|da|tei** F *(Comput)* master file; **Stamm|da|ten** PL *(Comput)* master data; **Stamm|ein|la|ge** F *(Fin)* capital investment in ordinary shares *or* in common stock *(US)*

stam|meln [ˈʃtamln] VTI to stammer

Stamm|el|tern PL progenitors *pl*

stam|men [ˈʃtamən] VI to come *(von, aus* from); *(zeitlich)* to date *(von, aus* from); *(Gram)* to be derived *(von, aus* from), to come *(von, aus* from); **woher ~ Sie?** where do you come from (originally)?; **die Bibliothek/Uhr stammt von seinem Großvater** the library/watch originally belonged to his grandfather

Stam|mes- *in cpds* tribal; **Stam|mes|be|wusst|sein** NT tribal spirit; **Stam|mes|füh|rer** M, **Stam|mes|fürst** M (tribal) chieftain; **Stam|mes|ge|nos|se** M, **Stam|mes|ge|nos|sin** F member of a/the tribe, tribesman/-woman; **Stam|mes|ge|schich|te** F *(Biol)* phylogeny; **stam|mes|ge|schicht|lich** ADJ *(Biol)* phylogenetic; **Stam|mes|kun|de** F *(Hist)* ethnology; **Stam|mes|zu|ge|hö|rig|keit** F tribal membership

Stamm-: **Stamm|form** F base form; **Stamm|gast** M regular; **Stamm|ge|richt** NT standard meal; **Stamm|gut** NT *pl* **-güter** family estate; **Stamm|hal|ter** M son and heir; **Stamm|haus** NT *(Comm)* parent branch; *(= Muttergesellschaft)* parent company; *(= Fabrik)* parent factory; **Stamm|hirn** NT *(Anat)* brainstem; **Stamm|holz** NT trunk wood

stäm|mig [ˈʃtɛmɪç] ADJ *(= gedrungen)* stocky, thickset *no adv*; *(= kräftig)* sturdy

Stamm-: **Stamm|ka|pi|tal** NT *(Fin)* ordinary share *or* common stock *(US)* capital; **Stamm|knei|pe** F *(inf)* local *(Brit inf)*, local bar; **Stamm|kun|de** M, **Stamm|kun|din** F regular (customer); **Stamm|kund|schaft** F regulars *pl*, regular customers *pl*; **Stamm|land** NT place of origin

Stamm|ler [ˈʃtamlɐ] M **-s, -**, **Stamm|le|rin** [-ərɪn] F **-, -nen** stammerer

Stamm-: **Stamm|lo|kal** NT favourite *(Brit) or* favorite *(US)* café/restaurant *etc*; *(= Kneipe)* local *(Brit inf)*, local bar; **Stamm|mut|ter** F *pl* **-mütter** progenitrix *(form)*; **Stamm|per|so|nal** NT permanent staff *pl*; **Stamm|platz** M usual *or* regular seat; **Stamm|pub|li|kum** NT *(im Theater)* regular audience; *(im Lokal)* regulars *pl*, regular customers *pl*; **Stamm|rol|le** F *(Mil)* muster roll; **Stamm|sil|be** F radical, root syllable; **Stamm|sitz** M *(von Firma)* headquarters *sing or pl*; *(von Geschlecht)* ancestral seat; *(im Theater etc)* regular seat; **Stamm|ta|fel** F genealogical table; **Stamm|tisch** M *(= Tisch in Gasthaus)* table reserved for the regulars; *(= Stammtischrunde)* group of regulars; **er hat mittwochs seinen ~** Wednesday is his night for meeting his friends at the pub; **Stamm|tisch|po|li|ti|ker(in)** M(F) *(pej)* armchair politician; **Stamm|tisch|run|de** F group of regulars

> **STAMMTISCH**
>
> The **Stammtisch** is a table in a pub that is reserved for regulars. The gathering round the table is also known as a **Stammtisch**. Since it was mostly simple folk who originally met at a **Stammtisch**, the word has become a synonym for **Volkes Stimme** (popular opinion). People talk of **Stammtischpolitik** (armchair politics) when politicians seize upon policies in a populist way solely in order to win votes.

Stammutter △ F *pl* **-mütter** → **Stammmutter**

Stamm-: **Stamm|va|ter** M progenitor *(form)*; **stamm|ver|wandt** ADJ related; *Wörter* cognate, derived from the same root; **Stamm|ver|zeich|nis** NT *(Comput)* root directory; **Stamm|vo|kal** M radical *or* root vowel; **Stamm|wäh|ler(in)** M(F) *(Pol)* staunch supporter, loyal voter; **Stamm|wür|ze** F original wort; **Stamm|zel|le** F stem cell; **adulte/embryonale ~** adult/embryonic stem cell; **Stamm|zel|len|for|schung** F stem cell research

Sta|mo|kap [ˈʃtaːmokap] M **-s,** *no pl (Pol) abbr von* **staatsmonopolistischer Kapitalismus**

Stam|per [ˈʃtampɐ] M **-s, -**, **Stam|perl** [ˈʃtampɐl] NT **-s, -n** *(S Ger, Aus) stemless schnapps glass*

stamp|fen VI **a** *(= laut auftreten)* to stamp; *(= auf und nieder gehen: Maschine)* to pound; **mit dem Fuß ~** to stamp one's foot; **mit den Hufen ~** to paw *(Brit) or* stamp *(US)* the ground (with its hooves) **b** *aux sein (= gehen) (mit schweren Schritten)* to tramp; *(wütend)* to stamp; *(= stapfen)* to trudge **c** *aux haben or sein (Schiff)* to pitch, to toss VT **a** *(= festtrampeln) Lehm, Sand* to stamp; *Trauben* to press; *(mit den Füßen)* to tread → **Boden a b** *(mit Stampfer)* to mash; *(im Mörser)* to pound

Stampf|fer [ˈʃtampfɐ] M **-s, -** *(= Stampfgerät)* pounder; *(= Saugkolben)* plunger; *(pej inf: = Bein)* tree trunk *(inf)*

Stampf|kar|tof|feln PL *(dial)* mashed potato(es *pl*)

stand *pret von* **stehen**

Stand [ʃtant] M **-(e)s, ⸗e** [ˈʃtɛndə] **a** *no pl (= das Stehen)* standing position; *(= Standfläche)* place to stand; *(für Gegenstand)* stand; **aus dem ~** from a standing position; **ein Sprung/Start aus dem ~** a standing jump/start; **bei jdm** *or* **gegen jdn/bei etw einen schweren ~ haben** *(fig)* to have a hard time with sb/in sth; **aus dem ~ (heraus)** *(fig inf)* off the cuff

b *(= Marktstand etc)* stand; *(= Taxistand)* stand, rank

c *no pl (= Lage)* state; *(= Niveau, Fin: = Kurs)* level; *(= Zählerstand, Thermometerstand, Barometerstand etc)* reading, level; *(= Kassenstand, Kontostand)* balance; *(von Gestirnen)* position; *(Sport: = Spielstand)* score; **beim jetzigen ~ der Dinge** the way things stand *or* are at the moment; **nach letztem ~ der Dinge** from the way things stood *or* were when we *etc* last heard; **der neueste ~ der Forschung** the latest developments in research; **etw auf den neuesten ~ bringen** to bring sth up to date; **jdn auf den neuesten ~ bringen** to bring sb up to speed *(inf)*; **auf dem neuesten ~ der Technik sein** *(Gerät)* to be state-of-the-art technology; **im ~ der Sklaverei/Knechtschaft** in a state of slavery/bondage; **~ November 1997** as at November 1997; **außer ~e = außerstande**; **im ~e = imstande**; **in ~ = instand**; **zu ~e = zustande**

d *(= soziale Stellung)* station, status; *(= Klasse)* rank, class; *(= Beruf, Gewerbe)* profession; *(= Reichsstand)* estate; **Name und ~** *(old)* name and profession; **die niederen/vornehmen** *or* **höheren Stände** *(old)* the lower/upper classes; **ein Mann von (hohem) ~** *(old)* a man of (high) rank; **in den ~ der Ehe treten** *(geh)* to enter into the state of matrimony

Stan|dard [ˈʃtandart, ˈst-] M **-s, -s** standard; *(Comput: = Voreinstellung)* default; *(Typ) (von Schriftschnitt)* regular

Stan|dard- *in cpds* standard; **Stan|dard|aus|stat|tung** F standard equipment; **Stan|dard|brief** M standard *or* regular *(US)* letter (size); **Stan|dard|dru|cker** M *(Comput)* default printer; **Stan|dard|ein|stel|lung** F *(Comput)* default

stan|dar|di|sie|ren [ʃtandardiˈziːrən, st-] *ptp* **standardisiert** VT to standardize

Stan|dar|di|sie|rung F **-, -en** standardization

Stan|dard-: **Stan|dard|ob|jek|tiv** NT *(Phot)* standard lens; **Stan|dard|schalt|flä|che** F *(Comput)* standard button; **Stan|dard|si|tu|a|ti|on** F *(esp Ftbl)* set piece; **Stan|dard|tanz** M standard dance; **Stan|dard|wert** M *(Tech, Comput)* default (value); **Stan|dard|werk** NT standard work

Stan|dar|te [ʃtanˈdartə] F **-, -n** **a** *(Mil, Pol)* standard **b** *(Hunt)* brush

Stand-: **Stand|bein** NT *(Sport)* pivot leg; *(Art)* standing leg; *(fig)* pillar; **Stand|bild** NT statue; *(TV)* freeze frame

Stand-by- *in cpds* standby; **Stand-by-Be|trieb** M *(Comput)* standby; **Stand-by-Mo|dus** M *(Comput)* standby mode; **„~ beenden"** "resume"; **Stand-by-Ti|cket** NT *(Aviat)* standby ticket

Ständ|chen [ˈʃtɛntçən] NT **-s, -** serenade; **jdm ein ~ bringen** to serenade sb

Stän|de-: **Stän|de|ord|nung** F system of estates; **Stän|de|or|ga|ni|sa|ti|on** F professional organization; **Stän|de|par|la|ment** NT parliament of estates

Stan|der [ˈʃtandɐ] M **-s, -** pennant

Stän|der [ˈʃtɛndɐ] M **-s, -** *(= Hutständer, Notenständer, Kartenständer etc)* stand; *(= Pfeifenständer, Schallplattenständer etc auch)* rack; *(= Pfeiler)* upright; *(Elec)* stator; *(inf: = Erektion)* hard-on *(sl)*, stiffy *(inf)*

Stän|de|rat M *(Sw Parl)* upper chamber

Stän|de|rat M, **Stän|de|rä|tin** F *(Sw Parl)* member of the upper chamber

> **STÄNDERAT**
>
> The **Ständerat** is one of the two chambers of the **Bundesversammlung** and is the federal body of Switzerland. Each canton sends two representatives to it and each demi-canton sends one, making a total of 46 members. These are elected for a period of four years.
>
> → BUNDESVERSAMMLUNG

Stan|des-: **Stan|des|amt** NT registry office *(Brit), official building where civil marriages take place*; **auf dem ~** at the registry office *(Brit)*; **stan|des|amt|lich** ADJ **~e Trauung** registry office *(Brit) or* civil wedding ADV **sich ~ trauen lassen** to get married in a registry office *(Brit)*, to have a registry office *(Brit) or* civil wedding; **Stan|des|be|am|te(r)** M *decl as adj*, **Stan|des|be|am|tin** F registrar; **Stan|des|be|wusst|sein** NT status consciousness; **Stan|des|dün|kel** M snobbishness, snobbery; **Stan|des|ehe** F marriage between people of the same rank; **Stan|des|eh|re** F honour *(Brit) or* honor *(US)* as a nobleman *etc*; *(von Ärzten, Handwerkern etc)* professional honour *(Brit) or* honor *(US)*; **stan|des|ge|mäß** ADJ befitting one's rank *or* station *(dated)* ADV in a manner befitting one's rank *or* station *(dated)*; **Stan|des|hei|rat** F marriage between people of the same rank; **Stan|des|herr** M *(Hist)* mediatized prince; **Stan|des|or|ga|ni|sa|ti|on** F professional association; **Stan|des|per|son** F *(old)* person of quality *(old)*; **Stan|des|pri|vi|leg** NT class privilege; **Stan|des|tracht** F (official) robes *pl*; **Stan|des|un|ter|schied** M class difference; **stan|des|wid|rig** ADJ socially degrading; *(beruflich)* unprofessional; **~es Verhalten** *(im Beruf)* unprofessional conduct ADV **sich ~ verhalten** to behave unprofessionally

Stän|de|staat M *(Hist)* corporate *or* corporative state

Stand-: **stand|fest** ADJ *Tisch, Leiter* stable, steady; *(fig)* steadfast; **Stand|fes|tig|keit** F stability *(auch Sci)*; *(fig)* steadfastness; **Stand|fo|to** NT still (photograph); **Stand|gas** NT *(Aut)* idling mixture; **Stand|geld** NT stallage; **Stand|ge|richt** NT *(Mil)* drumhead court martial; **vor ein ~ gestellt werden** *or* **kommen** to be summarily court-martialled *(Brit) or* court-martialed *(US)*; **stand|haft** ADJ steadfast, strong ADV **etw ~ verteidigen** *or* **vertreten** to defend sth staunchly; **er weigerte sich ~, er lehnte ~ ab** he staunchly *or* steadfastly refused; **Stand|haf|tig|keit** [ˈʃtanthaftɪçkait] F **-,** *no pl* steadfastness; **stand+hal|ten** [ˈʃtanthaltn] ✪ 32.3, 53.3, 53.6 VI *sep irreg (Mensch)* to stand firm; *(Gebäude, Brücke etc)* to hold; **jdm ~** to stand up to sb; **einer Sache** *(dat)* **~** to withstand sth; **der Versuchung** *(dat)* **~** to resist temptation; **einer/der Prüfung ~** to stand up to *or* bear close examination; **Stand|hei|zung** F *(Aut)* stationary heating

stän|dig [ˈʃtɛndɪç] ADJ **a** *(= dauernd)* permanent; *Praxis, Regel* established; *Korrespondent (von Zeitung)* resident; *Mitglied* permanent; *Einkommen* regular; **~er Ausschuss** standing committee **b** *(= unaufhörlich)* constant, continual ADV **a** *(= andauernd)* constantly; **müssen Sie mich ~ unterbrechen?** must you keep (on) interrupting me?, must you continually *or* constantly interrupt me?; **sie kommt ~ zu spät** she's constantly *or* always late; **sie beklagt sich ~** she's forever *or* always complaining; **sie ist ~ krank** she's always ill; **passiert das oft? – ~** does it happen often? – always *or* all the time **b** *(= permanent) wohnen* permanently; **sich ~ niederlassen** to settle (down)

stän|disch [ˈʃtɛndɪʃ] ADJ corporate, corporative

Stand|lei|tung F *(Telec)* dedicated line

Stand|licht NT sidelights *pl*; **mit ~ fahren** to drive on sidelights

Stand|mie|te F *(auf Messe)* stand rent

Stand|ort M *pl* **-orte** location; *(von Schütze, Schiff etc)* position; *(Mil)* garrison; *(Bot)* habitat; *(von Pflanzungen, Industriebetrieb)* site; *(fig)* position; **den ~ der Schule in der Gesellschaft bestimmen** to define the position *or* place of the school in society; **die Division hat ihren ~ in ...** the division is based *or* garrisoned in ...

Stand|ort-: **Stand|ort|äl|tes|te(r)** MF *decl as adj (Mil)* senior officer *(of a garrison)*, post senior officer *(US)*; **Stand|ort|ana|ly|se** F *(Comm)* location study; **Stand|ort|be|din|gung** F *usu pl* local conditions *pl*; **Stand|ort|be|stim|mung** F *(fig)* definition of the position; **Stand|ort|de|bat|te** F; **Stand|ort|dis|kus|si|on** F debate on (industrial) location(s); **Stand|ort|fak|tor** M *usu pl (Econ)* locational factor; **Stand|ort|ka|ta|log** M shelf catalogue *(Brit) or* catalog *(US)*, shelf list; **Stand|ort|nach|teil** M *(Comm)* locational disadvantage; **Stand|ort|si|che|rung** F *(Comm)* investment incentives *pl (provided by government to attract business to an area)*; **Stand|ort|vor|teil** M *(Comm)* locational advantage; **Stand|ort|wahl** F *(Comm)* choice of site *or* location; **Stand|ort|zei|chen** NT shelf mark

Stand-: **Stand|pau|ke** F *(inf)* lecture *(inf)*, telling-off *(esp Brit inf)*; **jdm eine ~ halten** to give sb a lecture *(inf) or* telling-off *(esp Brit inf)*, to tell sb off *(inf)*; **Stand|platz** M stand; *(für Taxis)* rank *(Brit)*, stand; **Stand|punkt** M **a** *(rare: = Beobachtungsplatz)* vantage point, viewpoint **b** *(= Meinung)* point of view, standpoint; **auf dem ~ stehen** *or* **den ~ vertreten** *or* **sich auf den ~ stellen, dass ...** to take the view that ...; **jdm seinen ~ klarmachen** to make one's point of view clear to sb; **von meinem ~ aus** from my point of view; **das ist vielleicht ein ~!** *(iro)* what kind of attitude is that!; **Stand|quar|tier** NT *(Mil)* base; **Stand|recht** NT, *no pl (Mil)* military law *(invoked in times of emergency)*; **~ verhängen** to impose military law *(über +acc* on); **stand|recht|lich** ADJ **eine ~e Erschießung** an on-the-spot execution ADV **~ erschießen** to put straight before a firing squad; **stand|si|cher** ADJ *Gebäude, Konstruktion* stable; *Mensch* steady; **Stand|si|cher|heit** F *(von Gebäude, Konstruktion)* stability; *(von Mensch)* steadiness; **Stand|spur** F *(Aut)* hard shoulder *(Brit)*, shoulder *(US)*; **Stand|uhr** F grandfather clock; **Stand|vo|gel** M non-migratory bird

Stan|ge [ˈʃtaŋə] F **-, -n a** *(= langer, runder Stab)* pole; *(= Querstab)* bar; *(= Ballettstange)* barre; *(= Kleiderstange, Teppichstange)* rail; *(= Gardinenstange, Leiste für Treppenläufer)* rod; *(= Vogelstange)* perch; *(= Hühnerstange)* perch, roost; *(= Gebissstange)* bit; *(Hunt) (= Schwanz)* brush; *(= Geweihteil)* branch (of antlers); *(fig: = dünner Mensch)* beanpole *(inf)*
b *(= länglicher Gegenstand)* stick; **eine ~ Zigaretten** a carton of 200 cigarettes
c *(= zylinderförmiges Glas)* tall glass
d *(Redewendungen)* **ein Anzug von der ~** a suit off the peg *(Brit) or* rack *(US)*; **von der ~ kaufen** to buy off the peg *(Brit) or* rack *(US)*; **jdn bei der ~ halten** *(inf)* to keep *or* hold sb; **bei der ~ bleiben** *(inf)* to stick at it *(inf)*; **jdm die ~ halten** *(inf)* to stick up for sb *(inf)*, to stand up for sb; **eine (schöne** *or* **ganze) ~ Geld** *(inf)* a tidy sum *(inf)*

Stän|gel [ˈʃtɛŋl] M **-s, -** stem, stalk; **vom ~ fallen** *(inf) (= Schwächeanfall haben)* to collapse; *(= überrascht sein)* to be staggered *(inf)*; **fall nicht vom ~!** *(inf)* prepare yourself for a shock!; **er fiel fast vom ~** *(inf)* he almost fell over backwards *(inf)*

stän|gel|los ADJ stemless

Stan|gen-: **Stan|gen|boh|ne** F runner *(Brit) or* pole *(US)* bean; **Stan|gen|brot** NT French bread; *(= Laib)* French loaf; **Stan|gen|sel|le|rie** M OR F celery; **Stan|gen|spar|gel** M asparagus spears *pl*

stank *pret von* **stinken**

Stän|ker [ˈʃtɛŋkɐ] M **-s, -** *(inf)* grouser

Stän|ke|rei [ʃtɛŋkəˈrai] F **-, -en** *(inf)* grousing

Stän|ke|rer [ˈʃtɛŋkərɐ] M **-s, -**, **Stän|ke|rin** [-ərɪn] F **-, -nen** *(inf)* grouser

stän|kern [ˈʃtɛŋkɐn] VI *(inf)* **a** *(= Unfrieden stiften)* to stir things up *(inf)* **b** *(= Gestank verbreiten)* to make a stink *(inf)*

Stan|ni|ol [ʃtaˈnioːl, st-] NT **-s, -e** silver foil

Stan|ni|ol|pa|pier NT silver paper

stan|te pe|de [ˈstantə ˈpeːdə] ADV *(geh, Jur)* instanter

Stan|ze [ˈʃtantsə] F **-, -n a** *(für Prägestempel, Bleche)* die, stamp; *(= Lochstanze)* punch **b** *(Poet)* eight-line stanza

stan|zen [ˈʃtantsn] VT to press; *(= prägen)* to stamp, to emboss; *Löcher* to punch

Stan|zer [ˈʃtantsɐ] M **-s, -**, **Stan|ze|rin** [-ərɪn] F **-, -nen** press worker

Sta|pel [ˈʃtaːpl] M **-s, - a** *(= geschichteter Haufen, fig: = Vorrat)* stack, pile **b** *(Comm) (= Stapelplatz)* store, depot; *(= Handelsplatz)* trading centre *(Brit) or* center *(US)*, emporium **c** *(Naut: = Schiffsstapel)* stocks *pl*; **auf ~ legen** to lay down; **auf ~ liegen** to be on the stocks; **vom ~ laufen** to be launched; **vom ~ lassen** to launch; *(fig)* to come out with *(inf)* **d** *(von Wolle, Baumwolle)* staple **e** *(Comput)* stack

Sta|pel-: **Sta|pel|box** F stacking box; **Sta|pel|da|tei** F *(Comput)* batch file; **Sta|pel|feh|ler** *(Comput)* stack fault; **Sta|pel|kas|ten** M crate; **Sta|pel|lauf** M *(Naut)* launching

sta|peln [ˈʃtaːpln] VT to stack *(auch Comput)*; *(= lagern)* to store VR to pile up

Sta|pel-: **Sta|pel|platz** M store, depot; **Sta|pel|stuhl** M stackable chair

Sta|pe|lung [ˈʃtaːpəlʊŋ] F **-, -en** stacking; *(= Lagerung)* storing

Sta|pel-: **Sta|pel|ver|ar|bei|tung** F *(Comput)* batch processing; **Sta|pel|ver|ar|bei|tungs|da|tei** F *(Comput)* batch file; **Sta|pel|wa|re** F staple commodity; **sta|pel|wei|se** ADV in piles; **bei ihm liegen ~ die Computerhefte herum** he's got piles *or* stacks of computer magazines lying around

Stap|fe [ˈʃtapfə] F **-, -n**, **Stap|fen** [ˈʃtapfn] M **-s, -** footprint

stap|fen [ˈʃtapfn] VI *aux sein* to trudge, to plod

Star [ʃtaːɐ] M **-(e)s, -e** *(Orn)* starling

Star [ʃtaːɐ] M **-(e)s, -e** *(Med)* **grauer ~** cataract; **grüner ~** glaucoma; **schwarzer ~** amaurosis *(spec)*; **jdm den ~ stechen** *(fig)* to tell sb some home truths

Star [ʃtaːɐ, staːɐ] M **-s, -s** *(Film etc)* star; *(fig auch)* leading light; **er trat wie ein ~ auf** he put on a big star act

Star-: **Star|al|lü|ren** [ˈʃtaːɐ-, ˈstaːɐ-] PL *(inf)* airs and graces *pl*; **~ an den Tag legen** to put on *or* to give oneself airs and graces; **Star|an|walt** [ˈʃtaːɐ-, ˈstaːɐ-] M; **Star|an|wäl|tin** F *(inf)* star *or* top lawyer *or* attorney *(US)*, rainmaker *(US sl)*; **Star|ar|chi|tekt(in)** M(F) big-name *or* top architect; **Star|auf|ge|bot** [ˈʃtaːɐ-, ˈstaːɐ-] NT *(Film, Ereignis)* gathering of stars; **mit einem riesigen ~** with a whole galaxy of stars

starb *pret von* **sterben**

Star|be|set|zung [ˈʃtaːɐ-, ˈstaːɐ-] F star cast

Star|bril|le [ˈʃtaːɐ-] F (pair of) glasses *pl* fitted with cataract lenses

Sta|ren|kas|ten M **a** nesting box (for starlings) **b** *(Aut inf: = Überwachungsanlage)* police camera

Star- *(Press)*: **Star|ga|ge** F top fee; **Star|gast** M star guest

stark [ʃtark] ADJ *comp* **=er** [ˈʃtɛrkɐ], *superl* **=ste(r, s)** [ˈʃtɛrkstə] **a** *(= kräftig, konzentriert)* strong *(auch Gram)*; *(= mächtig) Stimme, Staat, Partei* strong, powerful; **~ bleiben** to be strong; *(im Glauben)* to hold firm; **den ~en Mann spielen** *or* **markieren** *or* **mimen** *(all inf)* to play the big guy *(inf)*; **das ist seine ~e Seite** that is his strong point *or* his forte; **das ist ~** *or* **ein ~es Stück!** *(inf)* that's a bit much!; *(= eine Unverschämtheit auch)* that's a bit thick! *(inf)* → **starkmachen**
b *(= dick)* thick; *(euph: = korpulent) Dame, Herr* large, well-built *(euph)*; *Arme, Beine* large, strong *(euph)*; **Kostüme für stärkere Damen** suits for the fuller figure
c *(= beträchtlich, heftig) Schmerzen, Kälte* intense; *Frost* severe, heavy; *Regen, Schneefall, Verkehr, Raucher, Trinker, Druck* heavy; *Sturm* violent; *Erkältung* bad, heavy; *Wind, Strömung, Eindruck* strong; *Appetit, Esser* hearty; *Beifall* hearty, loud; *Fieber, Nachfrage* high; *Trauer, Schmerz* deep; *Übertreibung, Widerhall, Bedenken* considerable, great; **~e Abneigung** strong dislike
d *(= leistungsfähig) Motor* powerful; *Sportler* able; *Mannschaft, Brille, Arznei* strong; **er ist in Englisch nicht sehr ~** he's quite weak in English
e *(= zahlreich) Auflage, Gefolge* large; *Nachfrage* great, big; **wir hoffen auf ~e Beteiligung** we are hoping that a large number of people will take part; **zehn Mann ~** ten strong; **das Buch ist 300 Seiten ~** the book is 300 pages long
f *(inf: = hervorragend) Leistung, Werk* great *(inf)*; **Meatloafs stärkstes Album** Meatloaf's greatest album *(inf)*
ADV *comp* **=er** [ˈʃtɛrkɐ], *superl* **am =sten a** *(mit vb)* a lot; *(mit adj, ptp)* very; *applaudieren* loudly; *pressen, drücken, ziehen* hard; *regnen* heavily; *rauchen* a lot, heavily; *beeindrucken* greatly; *vertreten, dagegen sein* strongly; *abgenutzt, beschmutzt, beschädigt, entzündet etc* badly; *bluten* profusely; *vergrößert, verkleinert* greatly; **es hat ~ gestürmt** there was a severe storm; **es hat ~ gedonnert** there was a loud clap of thunder; **es donnert nicht mehr so ~** the thunder is not as loud now; **~ wirken** to have a strong effect; **~ wirkend** *(Medikament, Alkohol)* potent; **~ gesalzen** very salty; **~ gewürzt** highly spiced; **~ verschuldet** heavily *or* deeply in debt; **~ behaart sein** to be very hairy; **stärker befahrene Straßen** busier roads; **die Ausstellung wurde ~ besucht** the exhibition was well attended; **das Auto zieht ~ nach links** the car is pulling badly to the left; **er ist ~ erkältet** he has a bad *or* heavy cold; **er hat das Schmerzmittel zu ~ dosiert** the painkillers he prescribed were too strong; **Frauen sind stärker vertreten** there are more women; **der Artikel wird immer stärker verkauft** sales of this product continue to increase
b *(inf: = hervorragend)* really well; **die singt unheimlich ~** she's a really great singer *(inf)*, she sings really well

Star|kas|ten M = **Starenkasten**

Stark|bier NT strong beer

Stär|ke [ˈʃtɛrkə] F **-, -n a** strength *(auch fig)*; *(von Stimme, Land, Regierung)* power
b *(= Dicke, Durchmesser)* thickness
c *(= Heftigkeit) (von Strömung, Wind, Einfluss)* strength; *(von Eindruck, Leid, Kälte, Schmerzen, Druck)* intensity; *(von Regen, Verkehr)* heaviness; *(von Sturm, Abneigung)* violence; *(von Erkältung)* severity; *(von Appetit)* heartiness
d *(= Leistungsfähigkeit) (von Motor)* power; *(von Sportmannschaft, Arznei, Brille)* strength
e *(= Anzahl) (von Gefolge, Heer, Mannschaft)* size, strength; *(von Klasse)* size; *(von Beteiligung, Nachfrage)* level; *(= Auflage)* size
f *(fig: = starke Seite)* strength, strong point

Stär|ke F **-, -n** *(Chem)* starch

Stär|ke|mehl NT *(Cook)* thickening agent, ≈ cornflour *(Brit)*, ≈ cornstarch *(US)*

stär|ken ['ʃtɛrkn] **VT** **a** *(= kräftigen) (lit, fig)* to strengthen; *Selbstbewusstsein* to boost, to increase; *Gesundheit* to improve; **gestärkt** *(Mensch)* strengthened → **Rückgrat** **b** *(= erfrischen)* to fortify **c** *Wäsche* to starch **VI** to be fortifying; **das stärkt** it fortifies you; **~des Mittel** tonic **VR** to fortify oneself

Stär|ke|zu|cker M glucose

stark|glied|rig [-gli:drɪç], **stark|kno|chig** ADJ heavy-boned

stark+ma|chen VR *sep* **sich für etw ~** *(inf)* to stand up for sth

Stark|strom M *(Elec)* heavy current

Stark|strom- *in cpds* power; **Stark|strom|ka|bel** NT power cable; **Stark|strom|lei|tung** F power line; *(= Kabel)* power lead; **Stark|strom|tech|nik** F *branches of electrical engineering not connected with telecommunications*

Star|kult ['ʃta:ɐ-, 'sta:ɐ-] M star cult

Stär|kung ['ʃtɛrkʊŋ] F **-, -en** **a** strengthening *(auch fig)*; *(des Selbstbewusstseins)* boosting; **das dient der ~ der Gesundheit** it is beneficial to the health **b** *(= Erfrischung)* refreshment; **eine ~ zu sich nehmen** to take *or* have some refreshment

Stär|kungs|mit|tel NT *(Med)* tonic

stark-: **stark|wan|dig** ADJ *Schiff* thick-walled; **stark|wir|kend** ADJ *attr* → **stark ADV a**

Star|let ['ʃta:ɐlɛt, 'st-] NT **-s, -s** *(Film)* starlet

Star|ope|ra|ti|on F cataract operation

starr [ʃtar] **ADJ** **a** stiff; *(= unbeweglich)* rigid; **~ vor Frost** stiff with frost; **meine Finger sind vor Kälte ganz ~** my fingers are frozen stiff *or* are stiff with cold

b *(= unbewegt) Augen* glassy; *Blick* fixed

c *(= regungslos)* paralyzed; **~ vor Schrecken/Entsetzen** paralyzed with fear/horror; **~ vor Staunen** dumbfounded

d *(= nicht flexibel) Regelung, Prinzip* inflexible, rigid; *Haltung* inflexible, intransigent

ADV **a** *(= unbeweglich)* **~ miteinander verbunden** joined rigidly; **~ abstehen** to stand up stiffly

b *(= bewegungslos) lächeln* stiffly; **jdn ~ ansehen** to stare at sb

c *(= rigide)* **~ an etw** *(dat)* **festhalten** to cling to sth

Star|re ['ʃtarə] F **-**, *no pl* stiffness, rigidity

star|ren ['ʃtarən] VI **a** *(= starr blicken)* to stare *(auf +acc* at); **ins Leere ~** to stare *or* gaze into space; **jdm ins Gesicht ~** to stare sb in the face; **vor sich** *(acc)* **hin ~** to stare straight ahead; **was ~ Sie so?** what are you staring at? → **Loch** **b** **von Gewehren ~** to bristle with guns **c** *(= steif sein)* to be stiff *(von, vor +dat* with); **Moskau starrt vor Kälte** Moscow is in the grip of the cold; **vor Dreck ~** to be thick *or* covered with dirt; *(Kleidung)* to be stiff with dirt **d** *(= aufragen)* to jut up

Starr|flüg|ler [-fly:glɐ] M **-s, -** *(Aviat)* fixed-wing aircraft

Starr|heit F **-**, *no pl* **a** *(von Gegenstand)* rigidity **b** *(= Sturheit)* inflexibility, rigidity; *(von Haltung auch)* intransigence

Starr-: **Starr|kopf** M *(= Mensch)* stubborn *or* obstinate mule; **einen ~ haben** to be stubborn *or* obstinate; **starr|köp|fig** **ADJ** stubborn, obstinate **ADV** stubbornly, obstinately; **Starr|köp|fig|keit** [-kœpfɪçkait] F **-**, *no pl* stubbornness, obstinacy; **Starr|krampf** M *(Med)* tetanus, lockjaw; **Starr|sinn** M, *no pl* stubbornness, mulishness; **starr|sin|nig** **ADJ** stubborn, mulish **ADV** stubbornly, mulishly; **Starr|sin|nig|keit** [-zɪnɪçkait] F **-**, *no pl* stubbornness, mulishness; **Starr|sucht** F *(Med)* catalepsy

Start [ʃtart] M **-s, -s** **a** *(lit, fig)* start; **das Zeichen zum ~ geben** to give the starting signal; **einen guten/schlechten ~ haben** to get (off to) a good/bad start **b** *(= Startplatz, Startlinie)* start(ing line); *(bei Pferderennen)* start(ing post); *(bei Autorennen)* (starting) grid; **am ~ sein, an den ~ gehen** to be at the start/on *or* at the starting line/at the start(ing post)/on the (starting) grid; *(Läufer)* to be on their blocks **c** *(Aviat)* takeoff; *(= Raketenstart)* launch; *(= Startplatz)* runway; **der Maschine den ~ freigeben** to clear the plane for takeoff

Start-: **Start|ab|bruch** M *(Aviat)* aborted takeoff; **Start|auf|la|ge** F *(Press)* initial (print) run; **Start|au|to|ma|tik** F *(Aut)* automatic choke; **Start|bahn** F *(Aviat)* runway; **Start- und Landebahn** runway; **start|be|rech|tigt** ADJ *(Sport)* eligible (to enter); **start|be|reit** ADJ *(Sport, fig)* ready to start *or* go, ready for (the) off *(inf)*; *(Aviat)* ready for takeoff; *(Space)* ready for liftoff; **Start|block** M *pl* **-blöcke** *(Sport)* starting block

star|ten ['ʃtartn] **VI** *aux sein* to start; *(Aviat)* to take off; *(= zum Start antreten)* to take part; to run; to swim; *(bei Pferde-/Autorennen)* to race; *(inf: = abreisen)* to set off; **in die letzte Runde ~** to go into *or* enter the last lap **VT** *Satelliten, Rakete* to launch; *Unternehmen, Kampagne auch, Motor, Computer, Programm, Versuch, Rennen* to start; *Expedition* to get under way; **neu ~** *(Comput)* to restart, to reboot

Star|ter ['ʃtartɐ] M **-s, -** *(Aut)* starter

Star|ter ['ʃtartɐ] M **-s, -**, **Star|te|rin** [-ərɪn] F **-, -nen** *(Sport)* starter

Star|ter|klap|pe F *(Aut)* choke

Start-: **Start|er|laub|nis** F *(Sport)* permission to take part; *(Aviat)* clearance for takeoff; **Start|flag|ge** F starting flag; **Start|frei|ga|be** F clearance for takeoff; **Start|geld** NT *(Sport)* entry fee; **Start|ge|rät** NT *(für Raketen)* launcher; **Start|gut|ha|ben** NT *(bei Prepaidhandy)* initial (free) credit; **Start|hil|fe** F *(Aviat)* rocket-assisted takeoff; *(fig)* initial aid; **im Winter braucht mein Auto ~** my car won't start on its own in winter; **jdm ~ geben** to help sb get off the ground; **Start|hil|fe|ka|bel** NT jump leads *pl (Brit)*, jumper cables *pl (US)*; **Start|ka|pi|tal** NT starting capital; **start|klar** ADJ *(Aviat)* clear(ed) for takeoff; *(Sport, fig)* ready to start, ready for the off; **Start|kom|man|do** NT *(Sport)* starting signal; *(Aviat)* takeoff command; **Start|li|nie** F *(Sport)* starting line; **Start|loch** NT *(Sport)* starting hole; **in den Startlöchern** on their marks; **Start|ma|schi|ne** F *(Sport)* starting gate; **Start|me|nü** NT *(Comput)* start menu; **Start|num|mer** F number; **Start|platz** M *(Sport)* starting place; *(für Läufer)* marks *pl*; *(Autorennen)* starting grid; **Start|po|si|ti|on** F starting position; *(bei Autorennen)* grid position; **Start|ram|pe** F *(Space)* launch(ing) pad; **Start|schleu|der** F *(Aviat)* catapult; **Start|schuss** M *(Sport)* starting signal; *(fig)* signal *(zu* for); **vor dem ~** before the gun; **den ~ geben** to fire the (starting) pistol; *(fig)* to open the door; *(= Erlaubnis geben)* to give the go-ahead; **Start|schwie|rig|kei|ten** PL *(Sport)* difficulties *pl* at the start; *(Aviat)* difficulties *pl* during takeoff; *(fig)* teething troubles *pl*; **Start|sei|te** F *(Internet)* home page, start(up) page; *(von Browser)* start page; **Start|sprung** M racing dive; **Start|ver|bot** NT *(Aviat)* ban on takeoff; *(Sport)* ban; **~ bekommen** to be banned *or* barred; **Start-Ziel-Sieg** M *(Sport)* runaway victory

Sta|si ['ʃta:zi] M **-**, *no pl (DDR) abbr von* **Staatssicherheitsdienst** Stasi

> **STASI**
>
> The **Stasi** – short for **Staatssicherheitsdienst** – was the secret service of the former East Germany. The **Ministerium für Staatssicherheit** (or MfS) was established in 1950 and disbanded in 1989 before re-unification, as it was the most hated institution in the land and was regarded as the embodiment of a repressive regime. The **Stasi** built up a vast network of both full-time and unofficial collaborators (**IMs**), some of whom held prominent positions in West Germany. With their help the **Stasi** compiled dossiers on over 6 million people. → IM

Sta|si-Un|ter|la|gen-Ge|setz NT Stasi Records Act

State|ment ['ste:tmənt] NT **-s, -s** statement; **ein ~ abgeben** to issue a statement

Sta|tik ['ʃta:tɪk, 'st-] F **-**, *no pl* **a** *(Sci)* statics *sing* **b** *(Build)* structural engineering

Sta|ti|ker ['ʃta:tikɐ, 'st-] M **-s, -**, **Sta|ti|ke|rin** [-ərɪn] F **-, -nen** *(Tech)* structural engineer

Sta|tin NT **-s, -e** *(Med)* statin

Sta|ti|on [ʃta'tsio:n] F **-, -en** **a** station; *(= Haltestelle)* stop; *(fig: = Abschnitt) (von Reise)* stage; *(von Leben)* phase; **~ machen** to stop off **b** *(= Krankenstation)* ward; **er liegt/arbeitet auf ~ drei** he is in/works on ward three

sta|ti|o|när [ʃtatsio'nɛ:ɐ] **ADJ** *(Astron, Comput, Sociol)* stationary; *(Med) Behandlung, Pflegeeinrichtungen* inpatient *attr*; **~er Patient** inpatient **ADV** *entbinden* in hospital; **jdn ~ behandeln** to treat sb in hospital *or* as an inpatient; **er liegt ~ bei Dr. Weiß** he is being treated by Dr Weiß as an inpatient; **jdn ~ einweisen** to hospitalize sb; **jdn ~ aufnehmen** to admit sb to hospital

sta|ti|o|nie|ren [ʃtatsio'ni:rən] *ptp* **stationiert** VT *Truppen, Beobachter* to station; *Atomwaffen etc* to deploy

Sta|ti|o|nie|rung F **-, -en** *(von Truppen)* stationing; *(von Atomwaffen etc)* deployment

Sta|ti|o|nie|rungs|ab|kom|men NT agreement on the stationing of troops

Sta|ti|o|nie|rungs|kos|ten PL stationing costs *pl*

Sta|ti|ons-: **Sta|ti|ons|arzt** M, **Sta|ti|ons|ärz|tin** F ward doctor; **Sta|ti|ons|schwes|ter** F ward sister *(Brit)*, senior nurse *(in a ward)*; **Sta|ti|ons|vor|steher(in)** M(F) *(Rail)* stationmaster; **Sta|ti|ons|wahl|tas|te** F tuning button

sta|tisch ['ʃta:tɪʃ, 'st-] **ADJ** *(lit, fig)* static; *Gesetze* of statics **ADV** **das Gebäude ist ~ einwandfrei** the building is structurally sound; **die Brücke ist ~ falsch berechnet** the design of this bridge is structurally unsound; **etw ~ berechnen** to do the structural design work for sth; **meine Haare haben sich ~ aufgeladen** my hair is full of static electricity

Sta|tist [ʃta'tɪst] M **-en, -en**, **Sta|tis|tin** [-'tɪstɪn] F **-, -nen** *(Film)* extra; *(Theat)* supernumerary; *(fig)* cipher; **er war nur ein kleiner ~** *(fig)* he only played a minor role

Sta|tis|ten|rol|le F *(lit, fig)* minor role; *(Film, Theat)* walk-on part, bit part

Sta|tis|te|rie [ʃtatɪstə'ri:] F **-, -n** [-'ri:ən] *(Film)* extras *pl*; *(Theat)* supernumeraries *pl*

Sta|tis|tik [ʃta'tɪstɪk] F **-, -en** statistics *sing*; **eine ~** a set of statistics; **die ~en** the statistics *pl*

Sta|tis|ti|ker [ʃta'tɪstikɐ] M **-s, -**, **Sta|tis|ti|ke|rin** [-ərɪn] F **-, -nen** statistician

Sta|tis|tin [-'tɪstɪn] F → **Statist**

sta|tis|tisch [ʃta'tɪstɪʃ] **ADJ** statistical; **~es Amt** statistics office **ADV** statistically; **~ gesehen** statistically → **erfassen**

Sta|tiv [ʃta'ti:f] NT **-s, -e** [-və] tripod

statt [ʃtat] **PREP** *+gen or (old, inf, wenn kein Artikel) +dat* instead of; **~ meiner/seiner/ihrer** *etc* in my/his/her *etc* place, instead of me/him/her *etc*; **~ Urlaub(s)** in lieu of *or* instead of holiday *(Brit)*, instead of vacation *(US)*; **~ Karten** *heading of an announcement expressing thanks for condolences in place of individual replies*; **an meiner/seiner/ihrer ~** in my/his/her stead *(form) or* place; **an Kindes ~ annehmen** *(Jur)* to adopt; **an Zahlungs ~** *(Comm)* in lieu of payment → **Eid, stattdessen**

CONJ instead of; **~ zu bleiben** instead of staying; **~ zu bleiben, wollte ich lieber ...** rather than stay I wanted to ...

statt|des|sen ADV instead

Stät|te ['ʃtɛtə] F **-, -n** place; **eine bleibende ~** a permanent home

Statt-: **statt+fin|den** ['ʃtatfɪndn] VI *sep irreg* to take place; *(Veranstaltung, Wahlen auch)* to be held; *(Ereignis auch)* to occur; **statt+ge|ben**

[ˈʃtatgeːbn] VI sep irreg +dat (form) to grant → **Einspruch**; **statt|haft** [ˈʃtathaft] ADJ pred permitted, allowed; **Statt|hal|ter(in)** M(F) governor; **Statt|hal|ter|schaft** [ˈʃtathaltəʃaft] F -, no pl governorship

statt|lich [ˈʃtatlɪç] ADJ **a** (= hochgewachsen, groß) Tier magnificent; Bursche strapping, powerfully built; (= eindrucksvoll) Erscheinung, Fünfziger imposing; (= ansehnlich) Gebäude, Anwesen, Park magnificent, splendid; **ein ~er Mann** a fine figure of a man **b** (= umfangreich) Sammlung impressive; Familie large; (= beträchtlich) Summe, Anzahl, Einnahmen handsome, considerable

Statt|lich|keit F -, no pl (= Größe) magnificence; (= Eindrücklichkeit) imposing appearance; (= Ansehnlichkeit) (von Gebäude) splendour (Brit), splendor (US); (von Mann) imposing presence; **die ~ seiner Erscheinung** his imposing appearance

Sta|tue [ˈʃtaːtuə, ˈst-] F -, -n statue

sta|tu|en|haft ADJ statuesque; (= unbeweglich) like a statue, statue-like ADV like statues/a statue

Sta|tu|et|te [ʃtatuˈɛtə, st-] F -, -n statuette

sta|tu|ie|ren [ʃtatuˈiːrən, st-] ptp **statuiert** VT **a ein Exempel an jdm ~** to make an example of sb; **ein Exempel mit etw ~** to use sth as a warning; **um ein Exempel zu ~** as an example or warning to others; **wir müssen da ein Exempel ~** we will have to make an example of somebody **b** (= festlegen) to lay down

Sta|tur [ʃtaˈtuːɐ] F -, **Staturen** build

Sta|tus [ˈʃtaːtʊs, ˈst-] M -, - [-tuːs] status (auch Comput); (Comput: = Verarbeitungsstatus) progress; **~ quo** status quo; **~ quo ante** status quo

Sta|tus-: **Sta|tus|be|reich** M (Comput) status area; **Sta|tus|leis|te** F (Comput) status bar; **Sta|tus|sym|bol** NT status symbol; **Sta|tus|zei|le** F (Comput) status line

Sta|tut [ʃtaˈtuːt, st-] NT -(e)s, -en statute

sta|tu|ta|risch [ʃtatuˈtaːrɪʃ, st-] ADJ statutory ADV **das ist ~ nicht möglich** that is excluded by statute

Stau [ʃtau] M -(e)s, -e or -s **a** (= Wasserstauung) build-up; (= Windstau) barrier effect; (= Verkehrsstauung) traffic jam; **ein ~ von 3 km** a 3km tailback (Brit), a 3km backup (of traffic) (US) **b** = **Stauung**

Stau|ab|ga|be F congestion charge

Stau|an|la|ge F dam

Staub [ʃtaup] M -(e)s, -e or **Stäube** [-bə, ˈʃtɔybə] dust; (Bot) pollen; **~ saugen** to vacuum, to hoover® (Brit); **~ wischen** to dust; **zu ~ werden** (liter) to turn to dust; (wieder) to return to dust (liter); **sich vor jdm in den ~ werfen** to throw oneself at sb's feet; **vor jdm im ~ kriechen** (lit, fig) to grovel before sb, to grovel at sb's feet; **sich aus dem ~(e) machen** (inf) to clear off (inf); **den ~ (eines Ortes/Landes) von den Füßen schütteln** (liter) to shake the dust (of a place/country) off one's feet → **aufwirbeln**

Staub- in cpds dust; **Staub|beu|tel** M **a** (Bot) anther **b** (von Staubsauger) dustbag; **Staub|blatt** NT (Bot) stamen

Stäub|chen [ˈʃtɔypçən] NT -s, - speck or particle of dust

Stau|be|cken NT reservoir

stau|ben [ˈʃtaubn] VI to be dusty; (= Staub machen, aufwirbeln) to make or create a lot of dust; **bei Trockenheit staubt es mehr** there's a lot more dust around when it's dry

stäu|ben [ˈʃtɔybn] VT **Mehl/Puder** etc **auf etw** (acc) **~** to dust sth with flour/powder etc (esp Brit), to sprinkle flour/powder etc on sth VI aux sein (rare) (= zerstieben) to scatter; (Wasser) to spray

Stau|be|ra|ter(in) M(F) traffic problem adviser

Staub-: **Staub|fa|den** M (Bot) filament; **Staub|fän|ger** M (inf) dust collector; **die vielen Bücher sind bloß ~** all those books just lie around collecting dust; **Staub|fet|zen** M (Aus) duster; **Staub|flo|cke** F piece of fluff; **Staub|ge|bo|re|ne(r)** [-gəboːrənə] MF decl as adj (old, liter) mortal (being); **Staub|ge|fäß** NT (Bot) stamen

stau|big [ˈʃtaubɪç] ADJ dusty

Staub-: **Staub|kamm** M fine-tooth comb; **Staub|korn** NT pl **-körner** speck of dust, dust particle; **Staub|lap|pen** M duster; **Staub|lun|ge** F (Med) dust on the lung; (von Kohlenstaub) black lung, silicosis; **staub+sau|gen** [ˈʃtaupzaugn] ptp **staubgesaugt** [ˈʃtaupgəzaukt] VI insep to vacuum, to hoover® (Brit); **Staub|sau|ger** M vacuum cleaner, Hoover® (Brit); **Staub|sau|ger|ver|tre|ter(in)** M(F) vacuum cleaner salesman/-woman; (pej) door-to-door salesman/-woman; **Staub|schicht** F layer of dust; **staub|tro|cken** ADJ **a** (lit) Lack etc ≈ touch-dry; Landschaft etc parched **b** (fig inf) dry as dust pred; **Staub|tuch** NT pl **-tücher** duster; **Staub|we|del** M feather duster; **Staub|wol|ke** F cloud of dust

stau|chen [ˈʃtauxn] VT **a** (= zusammendrücken) to compress (auch Tech), to squash (inf); (rare: = verstauchen) to sprain **b** (inf: = zusammenstauchen) to give a dressing-down (inf)

Stau|damm M dam

Stau|de [ˈʃtaudə] F -, -n (Hort) herbaceous perennial (plant); (= Busch) shrub; (= Bananenstaude, Tabakstaude, Rosenkohlstaude) plant

stau|en [ˈʃtauən] VT **a** Wasser, Fluss to dam (up); Blut to stop or stem the flow of **b** (Naut) to stow (away) VR (= sich anhäufen) to pile up; (= ins Stocken geraten) to get jammed; (Verkehr) to build up; (Wasser, fig) to build up; (Menschen) to form a crowd; (Blut) to accumulate; (durch Abbinden) to be cut off; **die Menschen stauten sich in den Gängen** people were jamming the corridors; **der Verkehr staute sich** or **die Autos stauten sich über eine Strecke von 2 km** there was a 2km tailback (Brit) or backup (of traffic) (US)

Stau|en|de NT (Mot) end of the tailback (Brit) or backup (US)

Stau|er [ˈʃtauɐ] M -s, -, **Stau|e|rin** [-ərɪn] F -, -nen (Naut) stevedore

Stau-: **Stau|ge|bühr** F congestion charge; **Stau|ge|fahr** F risk of congestion; **„Staugefahr"** "delays likely"; **Stau|mau|er** F dam wall; **Stau|mel|dung** F (Mot) congestion or traffic report

stau|nen [ˈʃtaunən] VI to be astonished or amazed (über +acc at); **~d** in astonishment or amazement; **ich staune(, ich staune)!** (inf) well, I never!, well well!; **man staunt, wie ...** it's amazing how ...; **da kann man nur noch ~** it's just amazing; **da staunst du, was?** (inf) you didn't expect that, did you!; **da hat er nicht schlecht gestaunt** (inf) he was flabbergasted (inf) → **Bauklotz**

Stau|nen NT -s, no pl astonishment, amazement (über +acc at); **jdn in ~ versetzen** to amaze or astonish sb

stau|nens|wert ADJ astonishing, amazing ADV astonishingly, amazingly

Stau|pe [ˈʃtaupə] F -, -n (Vet) distemper

Stau-: **Stau|raum** M storage space; **Stau|see** M reservoir, artificial lake; **Stau|stu|fe** F (in Flüssen) barrage (forming one of a series)

Stau|ung [ˈʃtauʊŋ] F -, -en **a** (= Stockung) pile-up; (in Lieferungen, Post etc) hold-up; (von Menschen) jam; (von Verkehr) tailback (Brit), backup (US); **bei einer ~ der Schiffe im Hafen** when the harbour (Brit) or harbor (US) gets congested; **eine ~ des Verkehrs** a traffic jam **b** (von Wasser) build-up (of water); **ein durch ~ geschaffener See** a lake created by damming a river; **~en sind hier sehr häufig** the water often builds up here; **zur ~ eines Flusses** to dam a river **c** (= Blutstauung) congestion no pl; **bei ~(en) (des Blutes) in den Venen** when the veins become congested, when blood becomes congested in the veins

Stau|war|nung F warning of traffic congestion

Std. abbr von **Stunde** hr

stdl. abbr von **stündlich**

Steak [steːk, ʃteːk] NT -s, -s steak

Ste|a|rin [ʃteaˈriːn, st-] NT -s, -e stearin

Stech-: **Stech|ap|fel** M (Bot) thorn apple; **Stech|be|cken** NT (Med) bedpan; **Stech|bei|tel** M chisel

ste|chen [ˈʃtɛçn] pret **stach** [ʃtaːx], ptp **gestochen** [gəˈʃtɔxn] VI **a** (Dorn, Stachel etc) to prick; (Wespe, Biene) to sting; (Mücken, Moskitos) to bite; (mit Messer etc) to (make a) stab (nach at); (Sonne) to beat down; (mit Stechkarte) (bei Ankunft) to clock in or on; (bei Weggang) to clock out or off; **die Sonne sticht in die Augen** the sun hurts one's eyes; **der Geruch sticht in die Nase** the smell stings one's nose; **mit etw in etw** (acc) **~** to stick sth in(to) sth; **jdm durch die Ohrläppchen ~** to pierce sb's ears

b (Cards) to trump

c (Sport) to have a play-off; (bei Springreiten) to have a jump-off

d (Farbe: = spielen) **die Farbe sticht ins Rötliche** the colour (Brit) or color (US) has a tinge of red or a reddish tinge

VT **a** (Dorn, Stachel etc) to prick; (Wespe, Biene) to sting; (Mücken, Moskitos) to bite; (mit Messer etc) to stab; Löcher to pierce; **die Kontrolluhr ~** to clock on or in; (beim Hinausgehen) to clock out or off

b (Cards) to trump

c (= ausschneiden, herauslösen) Spargel, Torf, Rasen to cut

d (= abstechen) Schwein, Kalb to stick, to kill; (Angeln) Aale to spear

e (= gravieren) to engrave → auch **gestochen**

VR to prick oneself (an +dat on, mit with); **sich** (acc or dat) **in den Finger ~** to prick one's finger

VTI impers **es sticht** it is prickly; **es sticht mir** or **mich im Rücken** I have a sharp pain in my back

Ste|chen [ˈʃtɛçn] NT -s, - **a** (Sport) play-off; (bei Springreiten) jump-off **b** (= Schmerz) sharp pain

ste|chend ADJ piercing; Sonne scorching; (= durchdringend) Augen, Blick piercing, penetrating; (= jäh) Schmerz sharp; (= beißend) Geruch pungent ADV **jdn ~ ansehen** to give sb a piercing look; **~ heiß** burning hot

Ste|cher [ˈʃtɛçɐ] M -s, - (sl: = Freund) shagging partner (sl)

Stech-: **Stech|flie|ge** F stable fly; **Stech|gins|ter** M (Bot) gorse; **Stech|kahn** M punt; **Stech|kar|te** F clocking-in card; **Stech|mü|cke** F gnat, midge (Brit), mosquito; **Stech|pal|me** F holly; **Stech|schritt** M (Mil) goose step; **Stech|uhr** F time clock; **Stech|zir|kel** M (pair of) dividers

Steck-: **Steck|brief** M "wanted" poster; (fig) personal description; **steck|brief|lich** ADV **jdn ~ verfolgen** to put up "wanted" posters for sb; **~ gesucht werden** to be wanted, to be on the wanted list; **Steck|brü|cke** F (Comput) jumper; **Steck|do|se** F (Elec) (wall) socket

ste|cken [ˈʃtɛkn] VI pret **steckte** or (geh) **stak** [ˈʃtɛktə, ʃtaːk], ptp [gəˈʃtɛkt] **gesteckt a** (= festsitzen) to be stuck; (= an- or eingesteckt sein) to be; (Nadel, Splitter etc) to be (sticking); (Brosche, Abzeichen etc) to be (pinned); **eine Blume im Knopfloch ~ haben** to have a flower in one's buttonhole; **einen Ring am Finger ~ haben** to have a ring on one's finger; **der Stecker steckt in der Dose** the plug is in the socket; **er steckte in einem neuen Anzug** (hum) he was all done up in a new suit (inf); **der Schlüssel steckt** the key is in the lock

b (= verborgen sein) to be (hiding); **wo steckt er?** where has he got to?; **wo hast du die ganze Zeit gesteckt?** where have you been (hiding) all this time?; **darin steckt viel Mühe** a lot of work or trouble has gone into that or has been put into that; **da steckt etwas dahinter** (inf) there's something behind it; **in ihm steckt etwas** he certainly has it in him; **zeigen, was in**

einem steckt to show what one is made of, to show one's mettle
c *(= strotzen vor)* **voll** *or* **voller Fehler/Nadeln/Witz** *etc* ~ to be full of mistakes/pins/wit *etc*
d *(= verwickelt sein in)* **in Schwierigkeiten** ~ to be in difficulties; **tief in Schulden** ~ to be deep(ly) in debt; **in einer Krise** ~ to be in the throes of a crisis; **in der Pubertät** ~ to be an adolescent
VT *pret* **steckte**, *ptp* [gəˈʃtɛkt] **gesteckt** **a** *(= hineinstecken)* to put; *Haare* to put up; *Brosche* to pin *(an +acc* onto); **die Hände in die Taschen** ~ to put *or* stick *(inf)* one's hands in one's pockets; **das Hemd in die Hose** ~ to tuck one's shirt in (one's trousers *(esp Brit) or* pants *(esp US))*; **jdn ins Bett** ~ *(inf)* to put sb to bed *(inf)*; **jdn ins Gefängnis** ~ *(inf)* to stick sb in prison *(inf)*, to put sb away *or* inside *(inf)*; **jdn in Uniform** ~ *(inf)* to put sb in uniform; **etw in den Backofen/Kasten** ~ to put *or* stick *(inf)* sth in the oven/box
b *(Sew)* to pin; **den Saum eines Kleides** ~ to pin up the hem of a dress
c *(inf: = investieren) Geld, Mühe* to put *(in +acc* into); *Zeit* to devote *(in +acc* to)
d *(sl: = aufgeben)* to jack in *(Brit inf)*, to chuck *(inf)*
e **jdm etw** ~ *(inf)* to tell sb sth; **es jdm** ~ *(inf)* to give sb a piece of one's mind
f *(= pflanzen)* to set

Ste|cken [ˈʃtɛkn] **M -s, -** stick

Ste|cken-: **ste|cken+blei|ben** **VI** *sep irreg aux sein (fig)* → **stecken bleiben b**; **ste|cken blei|ben** **VI** *irreg aux sein* **a** to stick fast, to get stuck; *(Kugel)* to be lodged **b** *(in der Rede)* to falter; *(beim Gedichtaufsagen etc)* to get stuck; **etw bleibt jdm im Halse stecken** *(lit, fig)* sth sticks in sb's throat; **ste|cken+las|sen** *ptp* **steckenlassen** *or (rare)* **steckengelassen** **VT** *sep irreg (fig)* → **stecken lassen b**; **ste|cken las|sen** *ptp* **stecken lassen** *or (rare)* **stecken gelassen** **VT** *irreg* **a** to leave; **den Schlüssel** ~ to leave the key in the lock **b** **lass dein Geld stecken!** leave your money where it is!, leave your money in your pocket!; **Ste|cken|pferd** **NT** *(lit, fig)* hobbyhorse; **sein** ~ **reiten** *(fig)* to be on one's hobbyhorse

Ste|cker [ˈʃtɛkɐ] **M -s, -** *(Elec)* plug

Steck-: **Steck|kar|te** **F** *(Comput)* expansion card; **Steck|kis|sen** **NT** papoose; **Steck|kon|takt** **M** *(Elec)* plug

Steck|ling [ˈʃtɛklɪŋ] **M -s, -e** *(Hort)* cutting

Steck|na|del **F** pin; **etw mit ~n befestigen** to pin sth *(an +dat* to); **keine** ~ **hätte zu Boden fallen können** *(fig)* there wasn't room to breathe; **man hätte eine** ~ **fallen hören können** *(fig)* you could have heard a pin drop; **jdn/etw wie eine** ~ **suchen** *(fig)* to hunt high and low for sb/sth; **eine** ~ **im Heuhaufen** *or* **Heuschober suchen** *(fig)* to look for a needle in a haystack

Steck|na|del|kis|sen **NT** pincushion

Steck-: **Steck|platz** **M** *(Comput)* (expansion) slot; **Steck|reis** **NT** *(Hort)* cutting; **Steck|rü|be** **F** swede, rutabaga *(US)*; **Steck|schach** **NT** travelling *(Brit) or* traveling *(US)* chess set; **Steck|schloss** **NT** bicycle lock; **Steck|schlüs|sel** **M** box spanner; **Steck|schuss** **M** bullet lodged in the body; **Steck|tuch** **NT** *pl* **-tücher** *(esp Aus)* breast-pocket handkerchief; **Steck|zi|ga|ret|te** **F** *(cigarette formed out of a) ready-made paper tube into which one inserts tobacco*; **Steck|zwie|bel** **F** bulb

Ste|fan [ˈʃtɛfan] **M -s** Stephen

Steg [ʃteːk] **M -(e)s, -e** [-gə] **a** *(= Brücke)* footbridge; *(= Landungssteg)* landing stage; *(old: = Pfad)* path **b** *(Mus: = Brillensteg)* bridge; *(Tech: an Eisenträgern)* vertical plate, web **c** *(= Hosensteg)* stirrup **d** *(Typ)* furniture

Steg|ho|se **F** stirrup pants *pl*

Steg|reif [ˈʃteːkraif] **M** **aus dem** ~ **spielen** *(Theat)* to improvise, to ad-lib; **eine Rede aus dem** ~ **halten** to make an impromptu *or* off-the-cuff *or* ad-lib speech; **etw aus dem** ~ **tun** to do sth just like that

Steg|reif-: **Steg|reif|dich|ter(in)** **M(F)** extempore poet; **Steg|reif|ko|mö|die** **F** improvised comedy; **Steg|reif|re|de** **F** impromptu speech; **Steg|reif|spiel** **NT** *(Theat)* improvisation; **Steg|reif|vor|trag** **M** impromptu lecture

Steh- *in cpds* stand-up

Steh|auf|männ|chen [ˈʃteːlauf-] **NT** *(Spielzeug)* tumbler; *(fig)* somebody who always bounces back; **er ist ein richtiges** ~ he always bounces back, you can't keep a good man down *(prov)*

Steh-: **Steh|aus|schank** **M** stand-up bar; **Steh|ca|fé** **NT** stand-up café; **Steh|emp|fang** **M** stand-up reception

ste|hen [ˈʃteːən]
pret **stand** [ʃtant], *ptp* **gestanden** [gəˈʃtandn] *aux haben or (S Ger, Aus, Sw) sein*

1 INTRANSITIVES VERB	3 REFLEXIVES VERB
2 TRANSITIVES VERB	4 UNPERSÖNLICHES VERB

1 – INTRANSITIVES VERB

a [= in aufrechter Stellung sein] to stand; *(= warten)* to wait; *(Penis)* to be erect; **fest/sicher stehen** to stand firm(ly)/securely; *(Mensch)* to have a firm/safe foothold; **unter der Dusche stehen** to be in the shower; **an der Bushaltestelle stehen** to stand *or* wait at the bus stop; **vor der Tür stand ein Fremder** there was a stranger (standing) at the door; **neben jdm zu stehen kommen** *(Mensch)* to end up beside sb; **ich kann nicht mehr stehen** I can't stay on my feet any longer; **so wahr ich hier stehe** as sure as I'm standing here; **hier stehe ich, ich kann nicht anders!** *(prov)* here I stand, I can do no other; **mit jdm/etw stehen und fallen** to depend on sb/sth; **mit ihm steht und fällt die Firma** he's the kingpin of the organization; **sein Hemd steht vor Dreck** *(inf)* his shirt is stiff with dirt; **der Kaffee ist so stark, dass der Löffel drin steht** the coffee's so strong a spoon will stand up in it; **der Weizen steht gut** the wheat is growing well; **er hat einen stehen** *(inf)* he has a hard-on *(sl)*

b [= sich befinden] to be; **die Vase/Tasse steht auf dem Tisch** the vase/cup is on the table; **meine alte Schule steht noch** my old school is still standing; **auf der Fahrbahn stand Wasser** there was water on the road; **ihm steht der Schweiß auf der Stirn** his forehead is covered in sweat; **am Himmel stehen** to be in the sky; **der Mond steht am Himmel** the moon is shining; **die Sonne steht abends tief/im Westen** in the evening the sun is low/in the west; **kurz vor dem Krieg stehen** to be on the brink of war; **im 83. Lebensjahr stehen** to be in one's 83rd year; **unter Schock stehen** to be in a state of shock; **unter Drogen/Alkohol stehen** to be under the influence of drugs/alcohol; **man muss wissen, wo man steht** you have to know where you stand; **vor einer Entscheidung stehen** to be faced with a decision; **die Frage steht vor der Entscheidung** the question is about to be decided; **ich tue, was in meinen Kräften/meiner Macht steht** I'll do everything I can/in my power; **das steht zu erwarten/fürchten** *(geh)* that is to be expected/feared → **Leben a**

c [= geschrieben, gedruckt sein] to be; **was steht da/in dem Brief?** what does it/the letter say?; **es stand im „Kurier"** it was in the "Courier"; **das steht bei Nietzsche** Nietzsche says that; **das steht in der Bibel (geschrieben)** it says that in the Bible; **es steht geschrieben** *(Bibl)* it is written *(Bibl)*; **das steht im Gesetz** that is what the law says; **darüber steht nichts im Gesetz** the law says nothing about that

d [= angehalten haben] to have stopped; **meine Uhr steht** my watch has stopped; **der ganze Verkehr steht** traffic is at a complete standstill; **wo stehen Sie?** *(inf: = geparkt)* where are *or* have you parked?

e [= bewertet werden] *Währung, Kurs* to be *or* stand *(auf +dat* at); **wie steht das Pfund?** what's the exchange rate for the pound?; **das Pfund steht auf EUR 1,40** the pound stands at EUR 1.40; **am besten steht der Schweizer Franken** the Swiss franc is strongest

f [= in bestimmter Position sein] *Rekord* to stand *(auf +dat* at); *(Mannschaft etc)* to be *(auf +dat* in); **der Pegel des Rheins ist stark gestiegen und steht inzwischen auf 3,84 m** the level of the Rhein has risen sharply and now stands at 3.48 m; **der Zeiger steht auf 4 Uhr** the clock says 4 (o'clock); **die Kompassnadel steht auf** *or* **nach Norden** the compass needle is pointing north; **wie steht das Spiel?** what is the score?; **es steht 2:1 für München** the score is *or* it is 2--1 to Munich

g [= passen zu] **jdm stehen** to suit sb; **Gelb/dieses Kleid steht ihr (gut)** yellow/this dress suits her; **ich finde, diese Farbe steht mir gar nicht** I don't think this colour *(Brit) or* color *(US)* suits me

h [grammatikalisch bei Satzstellung] to come; *(bei Zeit, Fall, Modus)* to be; *(= gefolgt werden von)* to take; **das Adjektiv steht im Deutschen vor dem Substantiv** in German the adjective comes before the noun; **dieses Verb steht im Perfekt** this verb is in the perfect; **nach „in" steht der Akkusativ oder der Dativ** "in" takes the accusative or the dative; **mit dem Dativ/Akkusativ stehen** to take the dative/accusative

i [Belohnung, Strafe] **auf Betrug steht Gefängnis** *or* **eine Gefängnisstrafe** fraud is punishable by imprisonment; **auf sachdienliche Hinweise steht eine Belohnung** there is a reward for useful information

j → **gestanden**

k [Redewendungen] **das/die Sache steht** *(inf)* that/the whole business is settled; **es/die Sache steht mir bis hier (oben)** *(inf)* I've had it up to here with it *(inf)*; **für etw stehen** to stand for sth; **hinter jdm/etw stehen** to be behind sb/sth; **das steht (ganz) bei Ihnen** *(form)* that is (entirely) up to you; **auf jdn/etw stehen** *(inf)* to be mad about sb/sth *(inf)*

♦ **stehen zu** **zu jdm stehen** to stand *or* stick by sb; **zu seinem Versprechen stehen** to stand by one's promise; **zu seinen Behauptungen/seiner Überzeugung stehen** to stand by what one says/by one's convictions; **zu dem, was man gesagt hat, stehen** to stick to what one has said; **zum Sozialismus stehen** to be a staunch socialist; **wie stehen Sie dazu?** what are your views on that?, what is your opinion on that?

2 – TRANSITIVES VERB

Posten stehen to stand guard; **Wache stehen** to mount watch; **Spalier stehen** to form a guard of honour *(Brit)*, to form an honor guard *(US)*; **sich müde stehen, sich** *(dat)* **die Beine in den Bauch stehen** *(inf)* to stand until one is ready to drop

3 – REFLEXIVES VERB

♦ **sich stehen**
a [unpersönlich] **hier steht es sich nicht gut** this isn't a very good place to stand
b → **gutstehen, schlechtstehen**

4 – UNPERSÖNLICHES VERB

wie stehts? how are *or* how's things?; **so steht es also!** so that's how it is!; **wie steht es damit?** how about it?; **wie steht es mit ...?** what's the state of play with ...?; **es steht schlecht/gut/besser um jdn** *(bei Aussichten)* things look *or* it looks bad/good/better for sb; *(gesundheitlich, finanziell)* sb is doing badly/well/better; **es steht schlecht/gut/besser um etw** things look *or* it looks bad/good/better for sth, sth is doing badly/well/better

Ste|hen NT -s, *no pl* **a** standing; **das viele ~** all this standing; **etw im ~ tun** to do sth standing up **b** *(= Halt)* stop, standstill; **zum ~ bringen** to stop; *Lokomotive, LKW, Verkehr, Produktion auch* to bring to a standstill *or* halt *or* stop; *Heer, Vormarsch auch* to halt; **zum ~ kommen** to stop; *(Lokomotive, LKW, Verkehr, Produktion auch)* to come to a standstill *or* halt *or* stop

ste|hen+blei|ben VI *sep irreg aux sein (fig)* *(Produktion, Uhr, Zeit, Vorwurf etc)* → **stehen bleiben**

ste|hen blei|ben VI *irreg aux sein* **a** *(= anhalten)* to stop; *(Zug, LKW, Verkehr, Produktion)* to stop, to come to a standstill *or* halt *or* stop; *(Aut: Motor)* to cut out, to stop; **~!** stop!; *(Mil)* halt!
b *(= nicht weitergehen) (Mensch, Tier)* to stay; *(Uhr, Entwicklung)* to stop; *(Zeit)* to stand still; *(Auto, Zug)* to stand
c *(= vergessen/zurück gelassen werden)* to be left (behind); **mein Regenschirm muss im Büro stehen geblieben sein** I must have left my umbrella in the office
d *(= unverändert bleiben)* to be left (in); **soll das so ~?** should that stay *or* be left as it is?; **im Raum ~** *(Vorwurf etc)* to be left hanging in the air

ste|hend ADJ *attr Fahrzeug* stationary; *Wasser, Gewässer* stagnant; *(= ständig) Heer* standing, regular; *Start (Radfahren)* standing; **~e Redensart** stock phrase; **~en Fußes** *(liter)* without delay; **~es Gut** *(Naut)* standing rigging

ste|hen las|sen *ptp* **stehen lassen** *or (rare)* **stehen gelassen** *irreg*, **ste|hen+las|sen** *ptp* **stehenlassen** *or (rare)* **stehengelassen** *sep irreg* VT to leave; *(= zurücklassen, vergessen auch)* to leave behind; *(Cook)* to let stand; *Essen, Getränk* to leave (untouched); *Fehler* to leave (in); **lasst das (an der Tafel) stehen** leave it (on the board); **alles stehen und liegen lassen** to drop everything; *(Flüchtlinge etc)* to leave everything behind; **jdn einfach ~** to leave sb standing (there), to walk off and leave sb; **sich** *(dat)* **einen Bart ~** to grow a beard; **jdn vor der Tür/in der Kälte ~** to leave sb standing outside/in the cold; **das Auto ~ und zu Fuß gehen** to leave the car behind and walk → **Regen**

Ste|her [ˈʃteːɐ] M -s, - *(Pferderennen, fig)* stayer

Ste|her [ˈʃteːɐ] M -s, -, **Ste|he|rin** [-ərɪn] F -, -nen *(Radfahren)* motor-paced rider

Ste|her|ren|nen NT *(Radfahren)* motor-paced race

Steh-: **Steh|gei|ger(in)** M(F) café violinist; **Steh|im|biss** M stand-up snack bar; **Steh|knei|pe** F stand-up bar; **Steh|kon|vent** M *(hum)* stand-up do *(inf)*; **Steh|kra|gen** M stand-up collar; *(von Geistlichen auch)* dog collar; *(= Vatermörder)* wing collar; **Steh|lam|pe** F standard lamp; **Steh|lei|ter** F stepladder

steh|len [ˈʃteːlən] *pret* **stahl** [ʃtaːl], *ptp* **gestohlen** [gəˈʃtoːlən] VTI to steal; **hier wird viel gestohlen** there's a lot of stealing around here; **jdm die Ruhe ~** to disturb sb; **jdm die Zeit ~** to waste sb's time → **Elster, Schau b** VR to steal; **sich in das/aus dem Haus ~** to steal into/out of the house; **sich aus der Verantwortung ~** to evade one's responsibility; **die Sonne stahl sich durch die Wolken** *(liter)* the sun stole forth from behind the clouds *(liter)* → *auch* **gestohlen**

Steh|ler [ˈʃteːlɐ] M -s, -, **Steh|le|rin** [-ərɪn] F -, -nen → **Hehler(in)**

Stehl|gut NT *(form)* stolen goods *pl*

Steh-: **Steh|lo|kal** NT stand-up café; **Steh|par|ty** F buffet party; **Steh|platz** M **ich bekam nur noch einen ~** I had to stand; **ein ~ kostet 8 Euro** a ticket for standing room costs 8 euros, it costs 8 euros to stand; **Stehplätze** standing room *sing*; **zwei Stehplätze, bitte** two standing, please; **die Anzahl der Stehplätze ist begrenzt** only a limited number of people are allowed to stand; **Steh|pult** NT high desk; **Steh|satz** M *(Typ)* standing *or* line type; **Steh|ver|mö|gen** NT staying power, stamina

Stei|er|mark [ˈʃtaiɐmark] F - Styria

steif [ʃtaif] ADJ **a** stiff; *Grog* stiff, strong; *Penis* hard, stiff, erect; **~ vor Kälte** stiff *or* numb with cold; **eine ~e Brise** a stiff breeze; **ein ~er Hals** a stiff neck; **ein ~er Hut** a homburg (hat); *(= Melone)* a bowler (hat), a derby *(US)*; **sich ~ (wie ein Brett) machen** to go rigid; **ein Steifer** *(inf: = Erektion)* a stiffy *(inf)*, a hard-on *(sl)*; *(sl: = Toter)* a stiff *(inf)*
b *(= gestärkt)* starched
c *(= förmlich)* stiff; *Empfang, Konventionen, Begrüßung, Abend* formal
ADV **a** *(= hart)* **das Eiweiß ~ schlagen** to beat the egg white until stiff; **~ und fest auf etw** *(dat)* **beharren** to insist stubbornly *or* obstinately on sth; **sie behauptete ~ und fest, dass …** she insisted that …; **etw ~ und fest glauben** to be convinced of sth
b *(= förmlich)* stiffly; **~ lächeln** to smile stiffly; **jdn ~ behandeln** to be standoffish to sb

Stei|fe [ˈʃtaifə] F -, -n **a** *no pl* stiffness **b** *(= Stärkemittel)* starch

stei|fen [ˈʃtaifn] VT to stiffen; *Wäsche* to starch → **Nacken**

Steiff|tier® [ˈʃtaif-] NT soft toy (animal)

Steif|heit F -, *no pl* stiffness; *(= Förmlichkeit auch)* formality

Steif|lei|nen NT buckram

steif+schla|gen VT *sep irreg* → **steif ADV a**

Steig [ʃtaik] M -(e)s, -e [-gə] steep track

Steig|bü|gel M stirrup; **jdm den ~ halten** *(fig)* to help sb on

Steig|bü|gel|hal|ter(in) M(F) *(esp Pol pej)* **jds ~ sein** to help sb to come to power

Stei|ge [ˈʃtaigə] F -, -n *(dial)* **a** *(= Steig)* steep track **b** *(= Treppe)* (narrow) staircase **c** *(= Lattenkiste)* crate

Steig|ei|sen NT climbing iron *usu pl*; *(Bergsteigen)* crampon; *(an Mauer)* rung (in the wall)

stei|gen [ˈʃtaign] *pret* **stieg** [ʃtiːk], *ptp* **gestiegen** [gəˈʃtiːgn] *aux sein* VI **a** *(= klettern)* to climb; **auf einen Berg/Turm/Baum/eine Leiter ~** to climb (up) a mountain/tower/tree/ladder; **aufs Fahrrad ~** to get on(to) the/one's bicycle; **aufs Pferd ~** to get on(to) *or* mount the/one's horse; **ins Bett/in die Straßenbahn ~** to get into bed/on the tram; **in die Badewanne ~** to climb *or* get into the bath; **in die Kleider ~** *(inf)* to put on one's clothes; **vom Fahrrad/Pferd ~** to get off *or* dismount from the/one's bicycle/horse; **aus dem Wasser/der Badewanne/dem Bett ~** to get out of the water/the bath/bed; **aus dem Zug/Bus/Flugzeug ~** to get off the train/bus/plane; **in den Zug/Bus ~** to get on the train/bus; **wer hoch steigt, fällt tief** *(Prov)* the bigger they come the harder they fall *(prov)*
b *(= sich aufwärtsbewegen)* to rise; *(Vogel)* to rise, to soar; *(Flugzeug, Straße)* to climb; *(= sich erhöhen) (Preis, Zahl, Gehalt etc)* to increase, to go up, to rise; *(Fieber)* to go up; *(= zunehmen) (Chancen, Misstrauen, Ungeduld etc)* to increase; *(Spannung)* to increase, to mount; *(= sich aufbäumen: Pferd)* to rear; *(= sich auflösen: Nebel)* to lift; **Drachen ~ lassen** to fly kites; **der Gestank/Duft stieg ihm in die Nase** the stench/smell reached his nostrils; **das Blut stieg ihm in den Kopf/das Gesicht** the blood rushed to his head/face; **in jds Achtung** *(dat)* **~** to rise in sb's estimation; **die allgemeine Stimmung stieg** the general mood improved; **meine Stimmung stieg** my spirits rose
c *(inf: = stattfinden)* to be; **steigt die Demo/Prüfung oder nicht?** is the demo/exam on or not?; **bei Helga steigt Sonnabend eine Party** Helga's having a party on Saturday
VT *Treppen, Stufen* to climb (up)

Stei|ger [ˈʃtaigɐ] M -s, - *(Min)* pit foreman

Stei|ge|rer [ˈʃtaigərɐ] M -s, -, **Stei|ge|rin** [-ərɪn] F -, -nen bidder

stei|gern [ˈʃtaigɐn] VT **a** *(= erhöhen)* to increase (*auf +acc* to, *um* bei); *Wirkung* to increase, to heighten; *(= verschlimmern) Übel, Zorn* to aggravate; *(= verbessern) Leistung* to improve **b** *(Gram) Adjektiv* to compare **c** *(= ersteigern)* to buy at an auction VI to bid (*um* for) VR **a** *(= sich erhöhen)* to increase; *(Zorn, Übel)* to be aggravated, to worsen; **sein Ärger steigerte sich zu Zorn** his annoyance turned into rage; **seine Schmerzen steigerten sich ins Unerträgliche** his pain became unbearable **b** *(= sich verbessern)* to improve **c** *(= hineinsteigern)* **sich in etw** *(acc)* **~** to work oneself (up) into sth

Stei|ge|rung [ˈʃtaigərʊŋ] F -, -en **a** *(= das Steigern)* increase (+*gen* in); *(von Wirkung auch)* heightening; *(von Farbe)* intensification, heightening; *(= Verschlimmerung)* aggravation; *(= Verbesserung)* improvement **b** *(Gram)* comparative

Stei|ge|rungs-: **stei|ge|rungs|fä|hig** ADJ improvable; **Stei|ge|rungs|form** F *(Gram)* *(= Komparativ)* comparative form; *(= Superlativ)* superlative form; **Stei|ge|rungs|stu|fe** F *(Gram)* degree of comparison

Steig-: **Steig|fä|hig|keit** F, *no pl (Aut)* hill-climbing *or* pulling capacity; *(Aviat)* climbing capacity; **~ beweisen** to pull well; **Steig|flug** M *(Aviat)* climb, ascent; **Steig|ge|schwin|dig|keit** F rate of climb *or* ascent; **Steig|rie|men** M stirrup leather

Stei|gung [ˈʃtaigʊŋ] F -, -en *(= Hang)* slope; *(von Hang, Straße, Math)* gradient *(Brit)*, grade *(esp US)*; *(= Gewindesteigung)* pitch; **eine ~ von 10%** a gradient *(Brit) or* grade *(esp US)* of one in ten, a gradient *(Brit) or* grade *(esp US)* of 10%

Stei|gungs-: **Stei|gungs|grad** M gradient *(Brit)*, grade *(esp US)*; **Stei|gungs|win|kel** M angle of gradient *(Brit) or* grade *(esp US)*

steil [ʃtail] ADJ **a** *Abhang, Treppe* steep; *(fig) Anstieg, Rückgang* steep, rapid; **eine ~e Karriere** *(fig)* a rapid rise **b** *(= senkrecht)* upright **c** *(Sport)* **~e Vorlage, ~er Pass** through ball **d** *(dated sl)* super *(inf)*, smashing *(inf)*; **ein ~er Zahn** *(inf)* a smasher *(inf)* ADV steeply; **sich ~ aufrichten** to sit/stand up straight

Steil-: **Steil|hang** M steep slope; **Steil|heck** NT hatchback; **Steil|heit** F, *no pl* steepness; **Steil|küs|te** F steep coast; *(= Klippen)* cliffs *pl*; **Steil|pass** M, **Steil|vor|la|ge** F *(Sport)* through ball; **Steil|wand** F steep face; **Steil|wand|fah|rer(in)** M(F) wall-of-death rider; **Steil|wand|zelt** NT frame tent

Stein [ʃtain] M -(e)s, -e **a** *(auch Bot, Med)* stone; *(= Feuerstein)* flint; *(= Edelstein)* jewel, stone; *(in Uhr)* jewel; *(= Spielstein)* piece; **heißer ~** *(Cook)* hot stone; **der ~ der Weisen** *(lit, fig)* the philosophers' stone; **es blieb kein ~ auf dem anderen** everything was smashed to pieces; *(bei Gebäuden, Mauern)* not a stone was left standing; **das könnte einen ~ erweichen** that would move the hardest heart to pity; **mir fällt ein ~ vom Herzen!** *(fig)* that's a load off my mind!; **bei jdm einen ~ im Brett haben** *(fig inf)* to be well in with sb *(inf)*; **jdm einen ~ aus dem Weg räumen** *(fig)* to remove an obstacle from sb's path; **den ersten ~ (auf jdn) werfen** *(fig)* to cast the first stone (at sb) → **Anstoß c, rollen VI a**
b *(= Baustein, Naturstein)* stone; *(groß, esp Hohlblock)* block; *(kleiner, esp Ziegelstein)* brick
c *no pl (Material)* stone; **ein Haus aus ~** a house made of stone, a stone house; **ein Herz aus ~** *(fig)* a heart of stone; **es friert ~ und Bein** *(fig inf)* it's freezing cold outside; **~ und Bein schwören** *(fig inf)* to swear blind *(Brit inf)*, to swear to God *(inf)*; **zu ~ erstarren** *or* **werden** to turn to stone; *(fig)* to be as if turned to stone

Stein-: **Stein|ad|ler** M golden eagle; **stein|alt** ADJ ancient, as old as the hills; **Stein|bau** M **a** *no pl* building in stone *no art* **b** *pl* **-bauten** *(= Gebäude)* stone building; **Stein|bock** M **a** *(Zool)* ibex **b** *(Astrol)* Capricorn; **Stein|bo|den** M stone floor; **Stein|bohr|rer** M masonry drill; *(= Gesteinsbohrer)* rock drill; **Stein|bruch** M quarry; **Stein|bruch|ar|bei|ter(in)** M(F) quarry worker; **Stein|butt** M *(Zool)* turbot; **Stein|druck** M *pl* **-drucke** *(Typ)* lithography; **Stein|dru|cker(in)** M(F) lithographer; **Stein|ei|che** F holm oak, holly oak

stei|nern [ˈʃtainɐn] ADJ stone; *(fig)* stony; **ein ~es Herz** a heart of stone

Stein-: **Stein|er|wei|chen** NT **zum ~ weinen** to cry heartbreakingly; **stein|er|wei|chend** ADJ heart-rending, heartbreaking ADV heart--rendingly, heartbreakingly; **Stein|fraß** M stone erosion; **Stein|frucht** F stone fruit; **Stein|fuß|bo|den** M stone floor; **Stein|gar|ten** M rockery, rock garden; **Stein|geiß** F female ibex; **stein|grau** ADJ stone-grey *(Brit)*, stone-gray *(US)*; **Stein|gut** NT, *no pl* stoneware; **Stein|ha|gel** M hail of stones

Stein|hä|ger® [-hɛːgɐ] M **-s, -** Steinhäger®, *type of schnapps*

stein|hart ADJ (as) hard as a rock, rock hard

stei|nig [ˈʃtainɪç] ADJ stony; **ein ~er Weg** *(fig)* a path of trial and tribulation

stei|ni|gen [ˈʃtainɪgn] VT to stone

Stei|ni|gung F **-, -en** stoning

Stein|koh|le F hard coal

Stein|koh|len-: **Stein|koh|len|berg|bau** M coal mining; **Stein|koh|len|berg|werk** NT coal mine, colliery; **Stein|koh|len|re|vier** NT coal-mining area

Stein-: **Stein|krug** M *(= Kanne)* stoneware jug; *(= Becher)* earthenware/stoneware mug; *(für Bier)* stein; **Stein|lei|den** NT *(= Nieren-/Blasensteine)* kidney/bladder stones *pl*; *(= Gallensteine)* gallstones *pl*; **ein ~ haben** to suffer from kidney *etc* stones; **Stein|mei|ßel** M stone chisel; **Stein|metz** [-mɛts] M **-en, -en**, **Stein|met|zin** [-mɛtsɪn] F **-, -nen** stonemason; **Stein|obst** NT stone fruit; **Stein|pilz** M boletus edulis *(spec)*; **Stein|plat|te** F stone slab; *(zum Pflastern)* flagstone; **stein|reich** ADJ *(inf)* stinking rich *(Brit inf)*, rolling in it *(inf)*; **Stein|salz** NT rock salt; **Stein|schlag** M **a** rockfall; **„Achtung ~"** "danger falling stones" **b** *no pl (= Schotter)* broken stone; *(zum Straßenbau)* (road) metal; **Stein|schlag|ge|fahr** F danger of rockfall(s); **Stein|schleu|der** F catapult *(Brit)*, slingshot *(US)*; **Stein|schnei|der(in)** M(F) gem cutter; **Stein|schnitt** M **a** cut (gem)stone **b** *no pl (Verfahren)* gem cutting; **Stein|ta|fel** F stone tablet; **Stein|topf** M stoneware pot; **Stein|wild** NT *(Hunt)* ibexes *pl*; **Stein|wurf** M **a** *(fig)* stone's throw **b** *(lit)* **mit einem ~** by throwing a stone; **Stein|wüs|te** F stony desert; *(fig)* concrete jungle; **Stein|zeit** F *(lit, fig)* Stone Age; **stein|zeit|lich** ADJ Stone Age *attr*; **Stein|zeug** NT, *no pl* stoneware

Stei|rer [ˈʃtairɐ] M **-s, -**, **Stei|re|rin** [-ərɪn] F **-, -nen** Styrian

stei|risch [ˈʃtairɪʃ] ADJ Styrian

Steiß [ʃtais] M **-es, -e** *(Anat)* coccyx; *(hum inf)* tail *(inf)*, behind

Steiß-: **Steiß|bein** NT *(Anat)* coccyx; **Steiß|ge|burt** F *(Med)* breech birth *or* delivery; **Steiß|la|ge** F *(Med)* breech presentation

Ste|le [ˈsteːlə, ˈʃt-] F **-, -n** *(Bot, Archeol)* stele

Stel|la|ge [ʃtɛˈlaːʒə] F **-, -n** *(inf: = Gestell)* rack, frame; *(dial inf: = Beine)* legs *pl*, pins *pl (inf)*

stel|lar [ʃtɛˈlaːɐ, st-] ADJ *(Astron)* stellar

Stell|dich|ein [ˈʃtɛldɪçlain] NT **-(s), -(s)** *(dated)* rendezvous, tryst *(old)*; **sich** *(dat)* **ein ~ geben** *(fig)* to come together

Stel|le [ˈʃtɛlə] ✪ 28.1, 28.2, 29.1, 29.2, 46.1, 46.5, 46.6, 53.2 F **-, -n** **a** place, spot; *(= Standort)* place; *(= Fleck: rostend, nass, faul etc)* patch; **an dieser ~** in this place, on this spot; **eine gute ~ zum Parken/Picknicken** a good place *or* spot to park/for a picnic; **legen Sie das an eine andere ~** put it in a different place; **diese ~ muss repariert werden** this bit needs repairing, it needs to be repaired here; **eine kahle ~ am Kopf** a bald patch on one's head; **eine entzündete ~ am Finger** an inflammation on one's finger, an inflamed finger; **Salbe auf die wunde/aufgeriebene ~ auftragen** apply ointment to the affected area; **eine empfindliche ~** *(lit)* a sensitive spot *or* place; *(fig)* a sensitive point; **eine schwache ~** a weak spot; *(fig auch)* a weak point; **auf der ~ laufen** to run on the spot; **auf der ~ treten** *(lit)* to mark time; *(fig)* not to make any progress *or* headway; **auf der ~** *(fig: = sofort)* on the spot; *kommen, gehen* straight *or* right away; **nicht von der ~ kommen** not to make any progress *or* headway; *(fig auch)* to be bogged down; **etw nicht von der ~ kriegen** *(inf)* to be unable to move *or* shift sth; **sich nicht von der ~ rühren** *or* **bewegen, nicht von der ~ weichen** to refuse to budge *(inf) or* move; **zur ~ sein** to be on the spot; *(= bereit, etw zu tun)* to be at hand; **X zur ~!** *(Mil)* X reporting!; **sich bei jdm zur ~ melden** *(Mil)* to report to sb → **Ort a**

b *(in Buch etc)* place; *(= Abschnitt)* passage; *(= Textstelle, esp beim Zitieren)* reference; *(= Bibelstelle)* verse; *(Mus)* passage; **an dieser ~** here; **an anderer ~** elsewhere, in another place

c *(= Zeitpunkt)* point; **an dieser ~** at this point *or* juncture; **an anderer ~** on another occasion; **an früherer/späterer ~** earlier/later; *(= an anderem Tag auch)* on an earlier/a later occasion; **an passender ~** at an appropriate moment

d *(in Reihenfolge, Ordnung, Liste)* place; *(in Tabelle, Hierarchie)* place, position; **an erster ~** in the first place, first; **an erster/zweiter ~ geht es um ...** in the first instance *or* first/secondly it's a question of ...; **(bei jdm) an erster/letzter ~ kommen** to come first/last (for sb); **an erster/zweiter** *etc* **~ stehen** to be first/second *etc*, to be in first/second *etc* place; *(in Bezug auf Wichtigkeit)* to come first/second *etc*; **an führender/einflussreicher ~ stehen** to be in *or* have a leading/an influential position

e *(Math)* figure, digit; *(hinter Komma)* place; **drei ~n hinter dem Komma** three decimal places; **eine Zahl mit drei ~n** a three-figure number

f *(= Lage, Platz, Aufgabenbereich)* place; **an ~ von** in place of, instead of; **an jds ~** *(acc)***/an die ~ einer Sache** *(gen)* **treten** to take sb's place/the place of sth; **das erledige ich an deiner ~** I'll do that for you; **ich gehe an deiner ~** I'll go in your place; **ich möchte jetzt nicht an seiner ~ sein** I wouldn't like to be in his position *or* shoes now; **an deiner ~ würde ich ...** in your position I would ..., if I were you I would ... → *auch* **anstelle**

g *(= Posten)* job; *(= Ausbildungsstelle)* place; **eine freie** *or* **offene ~** a vacancy; **ohne ~** without a job; **wir haben zurzeit keine ~n zu vergeben** we haven't any vacancies at present

h *(= Dienststelle)* office; *(= Behörde)* authority; **da bist du bei mir/uns an der richtigen ~!** *(inf)* you've come to the right place; **bei ihm/ihnen bist du an der richtigen ~!** *(inf)* you went to the right place; **sich an höherer ~ beschweren** to complain to somebody higher up, to complain to a higher authority

stel|len [ˈʃtɛlən] VT **a** *(= hinstellen)* to put; *(= an bestimmten Platz legen)* to place, to put; **jdm etw auf den Tisch ~** to put sth on the table for sb; **jdn über/unter jdn ~** *(fig)* to put *or* place sb above/below sb; **auf sich** *(acc)* **selbst** *or* **allein gestellt sein** *(fig)* to have to fend for oneself

b *(= in senkrechte Position bringen)* to stand; **die Ohren ~** to prick up its ears; **du solltest es ~, nicht legen** you should stand it up, not lay it down

c *(= Platz finden für)* **etw nicht ~ können** *(= unterbringen)* not to have room *or* space for sth; **etw gut ~ können** to have a good place for sth

d *(= anordnen)* to arrange; **das sollten Sie anders ~** you should put it in a different position

e *(= erstellen)* **(jdm) eine Diagnose ~** to provide (sb with) a diagnosis, to make a diagnosis (for sb); **jdm sein Horoskop ~** to draw up *or* cast sb's horoscope

f *(= arrangieren) Szene* to arrange; *Aufnahme* to pose; **gestellt** *(Bild, Foto)* posed; **die Szene war gestellt** they posed for the scene; **eine gestellte Pose** a pose

g *(= beschaffen, aufbieten)* to provide; **die CDU stellt zwei Minister** the CDU has two ministers

h *(= einstellen)* to set *(auf +acc* at); *Uhr etc* to set *(auf +acc* for); **das Radio lauter/leiser ~** to turn the radio up/down; **die Heizung höher/kleiner ~** to turn the heating up/down

i *(finanziell)* → **bessergestellt, gutgestellt, schlechtgestellt**

j *(= erwischen)* to catch; *(fig inf)* to corner → **Rede f**

k *(in Verbindung mit n siehe auch dort) Aufgabe, Thema, Bedingung, Termin* to set *(jdm* sb); *Frage* to put *(jdm, an jdn* to sb); *Antrag, Forderung* to make

l *(in Redewendungen)* **etw in jds Belieben** *or* **Ermessen** *(acc)* **~** to leave sth to sb's discretion, to leave sth up to sb; **jdn unter jds Aufsicht** *(acc)* **~** to place *or* put sb under sb's care; **jdn vor ein Problem/eine Aufgabe** *etc* **~** to confront sb with a problem/task *etc*; **jdn vor eine Entscheidung ~** to put sb in the position of having to make a decision

VR **a** *(= sich hinstellen)* to (go and) stand *(an +acc* at, by); *(= sich aufstellen, sich einordnen)* to position oneself; *(= sich aufrecht hinstellen)* to stand up; **sich auf (die) Zehenspitzen ~** to stand on tiptoe; **sich auf den Standpunkt ~, ...** to take the view ...; **sich gegen jdn/etw ~** *(fig)* to oppose sb/sth; **sich hinter jdn/etw ~** *(fig)* to support *or* back sb/sth, to stand by sb/sth; **sich jdm in den Weg ~** *(lit, fig)* to stand in sb's way; **sich jdm vor die Nase ~** to stand right in front of sb

b *(Gegenstand, Körperteil)* **sich senkrecht ~** to stand *or* come up; **sich in die Höhe ~** to stand up; *(Ohren)* to prick up

c *(fig: = sich verhalten)* **sich positiv/anders zu etw ~** to have a positive/different attitude toward(s) sth; **wie stellst du dich zu ...?** how do you regard ...?, what do you think of ...?; **sich gut mit jdm ~** to put oneself on good terms with sb

d *(inf: finanziell)* → **gutstellen, schlechtstellen**

e *(= sich einstellen: Gerät etc)* to set itself *(auf +acc* at); **die Heizung stellt sich von selbst kleiner** the heating turns itself down

f *(= sich ausliefern)* to give oneself up, to surrender *(jdm* to sb); **sich der öffentlichen Kritik ~** to lay oneself open to public criticism; **sich den Journalisten ~** to make oneself available to the reporters; **sich den Fragen der Journalisten ~** to be prepared to answer reporters' questions; **sich einer Herausforderung ~** to take up a challenge; **sich einem Herausforderer ~** to take on a challenger; **sich (jdm) zum Kampf ~** to be prepared to do battle (with sb), to announce one's readiness to fight (sb)

g *(= sich verstellen)* **sich krank/schlafend** *etc* **~** to pretend to be ill/asleep *etc* → **dumm, taub**

h *(fig: = entstehen)* to arise *(für* for); **es stellten sich uns** *(dat)* **allerlei Probleme** we were faced *or* confronted with all sorts of problems; **es stellt sich die Frage, ob ...** the question arises whether ...

Stel|len-: **Stel|len|ab|bau** M staff cuts *pl or* reductions *pl*, reduction(s *pl*) in staff; **Stel|len|an|ge|bot** NT offer of employment *(Brit)*, job offer; **„Stellenangebote"** "situations vacant", "vacancies"; **Stel|len|an|zei|ge** F, **Stel|len|aus|schrei|bung** F job advertisement *or* ad *(inf)*; **Stel|len|be|schrei|bung** F job description; **Stel|len|be|set|zung** F appointment, filling a/the position *no art*; **Stel|len|ein|spa|rung** F *usu pl* job cut; **Stel|len|ge|such** NT advertisement seeking employment, "employment wanted" advertisement; **„Stellengesuche"** "situations wanted" *(Brit)*, "employment wanted"; **Stel|len|markt** M employment *(Brit) or* job market; *(in Zeitung)* appointments section; **Stel|len|nach|weis** M, **Stel|len|ver|mitt|lung** F employment bureau *(Brit)*, employment centre *(Brit) or* center *(US)*; *(privat auch)* employment agency; **Stel|-**

len|strei|chun|gen PL job cuts *pl*; **stel|len|wei|se** ADV in places, here and there; **~ Schauer** scattered showers, showers in places; **Stel|len|wert** M *(Math)* place value; *(fig)* status; **einen hohen ~ haben** to play an important role

Stell|flä|che F area; **10.000 Quadratmeter ~** an area of 10,000 square metres *(Brit)* *or* meters *(US)*; **der Drucker benötigt nur eine kleine ~** the printer does not take up much space

-stel|lig [ʃtɛlɪç] ADJ *suf (bei Zahlen)* -figure, -digit; *(hinter Komma)* -place; **ein dreistelliger Dezimalbruch** a number with three decimal places

Stell- [ʃtɛl-]: **Stell|ma|che|rei** [ʃtɛlmaxəˈrai] F -, -en → **Stellmacher(in)** cart-making; *(Werkstatt)* cartwright's/wheelwright's (work)shop; **Stell|ma|cher(in)** M(F) *(N Ger)* (= *Wagenbauer)* cartwright; *(esp von Wagenrädern)* wheelwright

Stell-: **Stell|platz** M *(für Auto)* parking space; **Stell|pro|be** F *(Theat)* blocking rehearsal; **Stell|schrau|be** F *(Tech)* adjusting *or* set screw

Stel|lung [ʃtɛlʊŋ] F -, -en **a** *(lit, fig, Mil)* position; **in ~ bringen/gehen** to bring/get into position, to place in position/take up one's position; **die ~ halten** *(Mil)* to hold one's position; *(hum)* to hold the fort; **~ beziehen** *(Mil)* to move into position; *(fig)* to declare one's position, to make it clear where one stands; **zu etw ~ nehmen** *or* **beziehen** to give one's opinion on sth, to comment on sth; **ich möchte dazu nicht ~ nehmen** I would rather not comment on that; **für jdn ~ nehmen** *or* **beziehen** to come out in favour *(Brit)* *or* favor *(US)* of sb; (= *verteidigen)* to take sb's part; **für etw ~ nehmen** *or* **beziehen** to defend sth; **gegen jdn/etw ~ nehmen** *or* **beziehen** to come out against sb/sth **b** (= *Rang)* position; **in führender/untergeordneter ~** in a leading/subordinate position; **in meiner ~ als ...** in my capacity as ...; **die rechtliche ~ des Mieters** the legal status of the tenant; **gesellschaftliche ~** social status *or* standing; **eine marktbeherrschende ~ innehaben** to occupy a dominant position in the market **c** (= *Posten)* position, post *(esp Brit)*, situation *(dated, form)*; **bei jdm in ~ sein** to be in sb's employment *(Brit)* *or* employ *(form)*; **ohne ~ sein** to be without employment, to be unemployed

Stel|lung|nah|me [-naːmə] F -, -n statement *(zu* on); **eine ~ zu etw abgeben** to make a statement on sth; **sich** *(dat)* **seine ~ vorbehalten, sich einer ~** *(gen)* **enthalten** to decline to comment; **was ist Ihre ~ dazu?** what is your position on this?

Stel|lungs-: **Stel|lungs|be|fehl** M *(Mil)* call-up *(Brit)*, draft papers *pl (US)*; **Stel|lungs|feh|ler** M *(Sport)* positional error; **Stel|lungs|krieg** M positional warfare *no indef art*; **stel|lungs|los** ADJ without employment, unemployed; **Stel|lungs|spiel** NT *(Sport)* positional play *no indef art*; **Stel|lungs|su|che** F search for employment; **auf ~ sein** to be looking for employment *or* a position; **Stel|lungs|wech|sel** M change of employment *(esp Brit)*, change of job

stellv. *abbr von* **stellvertretend**

Stell-: **stell|ver|tre|tend** ADJ *(von Amts wegen)* deputy *attr*; (= *vorübergehend)* acting *attr* ADV **~ für jdn** for sb; *(Rechtsanwalt)* on behalf of sb; **ich bin ~ für ihn da** I'm here in his place; **~ für jdn handeln** to deputize *or* act for sb; **~ für etw stehen** to stand in place of sth; **Stell|ver|tre|ter(in)** M(F) (acting) representative; *(von Amts wegen)* deputy; *(von Arzt)* locum; **der ~ Christi (auf Erden)** the Vicar of Christ; **Stell|ver|tre|tung** F (= *Stellvertreter)* representative; *(von Amts wegen)* deputy; *(von Arzt)* locum; **die ~ für jdn übernehmen** to represent sb; *(von Amts wegen)* to stand in *or* deputize for sb; **in ~** *(+gen)* for, on behalf of; **Stell|wand** F partition wall; **Stell|werk** NT *(Rail)* signal box *(Brit)*, signal *or* switch tower *(US)*

stelz|bei|nig ADJ *(fig)* (= *steif)* stiff ADV **er kam ~ auf uns zu** he came towards *(Brit)* *or* toward *(US)* us with long lanky strides; **der Storch stolzierte ~ durch den Sumpf** the stork paraded on long thin legs through the swamp

Stel|ze [ʃtɛltsə] F -, -n **a** stilt; *(inf:* = *Bein)* leg, pin *(inf)*; **auf ~n gehen** to walk on stilts; *(fig: Lyrik etc)* to be stilted **b** *(Orn)* wagtail **c** *(Aus:* = *Schweinsstelze)* pig's trotter

stel|zen [ʃtɛltsn] VI *aux sein (inf)* to stalk → *auch* **gestelzt**

Stel|zen|lau|fen NT -s, *no pl* walking *no art* on stilts; **~ lernen** to learn to walk on stilts

Stelz-: **Stelz|fuß** M wooden leg, peg *(inf)*, peg leg *(inf)*; *(Mensch)* peg leg *(inf)*; **Stelz|vo|gel** M *(Orn)* wader

Stemm|bo|gen M *(Ski)* stem turn

Stemm|ei|sen NT crowbar

stem|men [ʃtɛmən] VT **a** (= *stützen)* to press; *Ellenbogen* to prop; **die Arme in die Seiten** *or* **Hüften gestemmt** with arms akimbo; **die Arme** *or* **die Hände in die Hüften ~** to put one's hands on one's hips; **er hatte die Arme in die Hüften gestemmt** he stood with arms akimbo **b** (= *hochstemmen)* to lift (above one's head); **einen ~** *(inf)* to have a few *(inf)*; **Gewichte ~** to lift weights **c** (= *meißeln)* to chisel; *(kräftiger) Loch* to knock *(in +acc* in) VR **sich gegen etw ~** to brace oneself against sth; *(fig)* to set oneself against sth, to oppose sth VI *(Ski)* to stem

Stemm|schwung M *(Ski)* stem turn

Stem|pel [ʃtɛmpl] M -s, - **a** (= *Gummistempel)* (rubber) stamp **b** (= *Abdruck)* stamp; (= *Poststempel)* postmark; (= *Viehstempel)* brand, mark; *(auf Silber, Gold)* hallmark; **jdm/einer Sache** *(dat)* **einen/seinen ~ aufdrücken** *or* **aufprägen** *(fig)* to make a/one's mark on sb/sth; **jds ~/den ~ einer Sache** *(gen)* **tragen** to bear the stamp of sb/sth **c** *(Tech)* (= *Prägestempel)* die; *(stangenförmig,* = *Lochstempel)* punch **d** *(Tech: von Druckpumpe etc)* piston, plunger **e** *(Min)* prop **f** *(Bot)* pistil

Stem|pel-: **Stem|pel|far|be** F stamping ink; **Stem|pel|geld** NT *(inf)* dole (money) *(Brit inf)*, welfare *(US)*; **Stem|pel|kar|te** F punch card; **Stem|pel|kis|sen** NT ink pad

stem|peln [ʃtɛmpln] VT to stamp; *Brief* to postmark; *Briefmarke* to frank; *Gold, Silber* to hallmark; **jdn zum Lügner/Verbrecher ~** *(fig)* to brand sb (as) a liar/criminal; **jdn zum Sündenbock ~** *(fig)* to make a scapegoat of sb VI *(inf)* **a ~ gehen** (= *arbeitslos sein)* to be on the dole *(Brit inf)*, to be on welfare *(US)*; (= *sich arbeitslos melden)* to go on the dole *(Brit inf)* *or* on welfare *(US)* **b** (= *Stempeluhr betätigen) (beim Hereinkommen)* to clock on *or* in; *(beim Hinausgehen)* to clock off *or* out

Stem|pel-: **Stem|pel|schnei|der(in)** M(F) punch cutter; **Stem|pel|stän|der** M rubber-stamp holder; **Stem|pel|uhr** F time clock

Stem|pe|lung [ʃtɛmpəlʊŋ] F -, -en stamping; *(von Brief)* postmarking; *(von Briefmarke)* franking; *(von Gold, Silber)* hallmarking

Sten|gel △ [ʃtɛŋl] M -s, - → **Stängel**

sten|gel|los △ ADJ → **stängellos**

Ste|no [ʃteːno] F -, *no pl (inf)* shorthand

Ste|no-: **Ste|no|block** M *pl* **-blöcke** *or* **-blocks** shorthand pad; **Ste|no|graf** [ʃtenoˈgraːf] M -en, -en, **Ste|no|gra|fin** [-ˈgraːfɪn] F -, -nen *(im Büro)* shorthand secretary; *(esp in Gericht, bei Konferenz etc)* stenographer; **Ste|no|gra|fie** [ʃtenograˈfiː] F -, *no pl* shorthand, stenography *(dated, form)*; **ste|no|gra|fie|ren** [ʃtenograˈfiːrən] *ptp* **stenografiert** VT to take down in shorthand VI to take shorthand; **können Sie ~?** can you take shorthand?; **ste|no|gra|fisch** [ʃtenoˈgraːfɪʃ] ADJ shorthand *attr* ADV **etw ~ notieren** to take sth down in shorthand; **Ste|no|gramm** [ʃtenoˈgram] NT *pl* **-gramme** text in shorthand; (= *Diktat)* shorthand dictation; **ein ~ aufnehmen** to take shorthand; **Ste|no|gramm|block** M *pl* **-blöcke** *or* **-blocks** shorthand pad; **Ste|no|graph** [ʃtenoˈgraːf] *etc* = **Stenograf** *etc*; **Ste|no|stift** M shorthand pencil; **Ste|no|ty|pist** [ʃtenotyˈpɪst] M -en, -en, **Ste|no|ty|pis|tin** [-ˈpɪstɪn] F -, -nen shorthand typist

Sten|tor|stim|me [ˈʃtɛntoːɐ-, ˈst-] F *(geh)* stentorian voice

Stenz [ʃtɛnts] M -es, -e *(dated)* dandy

Step △ [ʃtɛp, st-] M -s, -s → **Stepp**

Step|ei|sen △ NT → **Steppeisen**

Ste|phan [ˈʃtɛfan] M -s, **Ste|phen** [ˈʃtɛfn] M -s Stephen, Steven

Stepp [ʃtɛp, st-] M -s, -s tap dance; **~ tanzen** to tap-dance

Stepp|ano|rak M quilted anorak *(Brit)* *or* jacket

Stepp|de|cke F quilt

Step|pe [ˈʃtɛpə] F -, -n steppe

Stepp|ei|sen NT tap *(on tap-dancing shoes)*

step|pen [ˈʃtɛpn] VTI to (machine-)stitch; *wattierten Stoff* to quilt

step|pen [ˈʃtɛpn, ˈst-] VI to tap-dance

Step|pen-: **Step|pen|brand** M steppe fire; **Step|pen|kä|se** M *low-fat (hard) cheese*; **Step|pen|wolf** M *(Zool)* prairie wolf, coyote

Step|per M *(in Fitnessstudio)* stepper

Stepp-: **Stepp|fuß** M foot; **Stepp|ja|cke** F quilted jacket

Stepp|ke [ˈʃtɛpkə] M -(s), -s *(N Ger inf)* nipper *(Brit inf)*, whippersnapper *(US)*, (little) laddie *(Brit inf)*

Stepp-: **Stepp|naht** F *(Sew)* backstitch seam; *(mit Maschine)* lockstitch seam; **Stepp|stich** M *(Sew)* backstitch; *(mit Maschine)* lockstitch; **Stepp|tanz** [ˈʃtɛp-, ˈst-] M tap dance; **Stepp|tän|zer(in)** M(F) tap-dancer

Ster [ʃteːɐ] NT -s, -s *or* -e stere

Ster|be-: **Ster|be|al|ter** NT age of death; **was war sein ~?** what was his age at the time of his death?; **Ster|be|be|glei|tung** F terminal care; **Ster|be|bett** NT deathbed; **auf dem ~ liegen** to be on one's deathbed; **Ster|be|buch** NT register of deaths; **Ster|be|da|tum** NT date of death; **Ster|be|fall** M death; **Ster|be|geld** NT death benefit; **Ster|be|glo|cke** F funeral bell; **das Läuten der ~** the death knell; **Ster|be|hemd** NT (burial) shroud; **Ster|be|hil|fe** F **a** death benefit **b** (= *Euthanasie)* euthanasia; **jdm ~ geben** *or* **gewähren** to administer euthanasia to sb *(form)*; **Ster|be|kas|se** F death benefit fund; **Ster|be|kli|nik** F hospice; **Ster|be|la|ger** NT *(geh)* deathbed

ster|ben [ʃtɛrbn] *pret* **starb** [ʃtarp], *ptp* **gestorben** [gəˈʃtɔrbn] VTI *aux sein* to die; **jung/als Christ ~** to die young/a Christian; **einen schnellen Tod ~** to die quickly; **einen leichten Tod ~** to have an easy death; **eines natürlichen/gewaltsamen Todes ~** to die a natural/violent death; **an einer Krankheit/Verletzung ~** to die of an illness/from an injury; **daran wirst du nicht ~!** *(hum)* it won't kill you!; **vor Angst/Durst/Hunger ~** to die of fright/thirst/hunger *(auch fig)*; **er stirbt vor Angst** *(fig)* he's frightened to death, he's scared stiff *(inf)*; **vor Langeweile/Neugierde ~** to die of boredom/curiosity; **tausend Tode ~** to die a thousand deaths; **so leicht stirbt man nicht!** *(hum)* you'll/he'll *etc* survive!; **gestorben sein** to be dead, to be deceased *(Jur, form)*; *(fig: Projekt)* to be over and done with; **gestorben!** *(Film sl)* print it!, I'll buy it! *(Brit)*, it's a wrap! *(inf)*; **er ist für mich gestorben** *(fig inf)* he might as well be dead *or* he doesn't exist as far as I'm concerned; **und wenn sie nicht gestorben sind, so leben sie noch heute** and they lived happily ever after

Ster|ben NT -s, *no pl* death; **Angst vor dem ~** fear of death *or* dying; **wenn es ans ~ geht** when it comes to dying; **im ~ liegen** to be dying; **zum ~ langweilig** *(inf)* deadly boring *or* dull, deadly *(Brit inf)*; **zum Leben zu wenig, zum ~ zu viel** barely enough to keep body and soul together

Ster|bens-: **Ster|bens|angst** F *(inf)* mortal fear; **ster|bens|elend** ADJ *(inf)* wretched, ghastly; **ich fühle mich ~** I feel wretched *or*

ghastly, I feel like death *(inf)*; **ster|bens|krank** ADJ mortally ill; **ster|bens|lang|wei|lig** ADJ *(inf)* deadly boring *or* dull, deadly *(Brit inf)*; **Ster|bens|wort** NT, **Ster|bens|wört|chen** NT *(inf)* **er hat kein ~ gesagt** *or* **verraten** he didn't say a (single) word; **ich werde kein ~ davon sagen** I won't breathe a word

Ster|be-: **Ster|be|ort** M *pl* **-orte** place of death; **Ster|be|ra|te** F death rate; **Ster|be|sak|ra|men|te** PL last rites *pl or* sacraments *pl*; **Ster|be|stun|de** F last hour, dying hour; **Ster|be|ur|kun|de** F death certificate; **Ster|be|zif|fer** F mortality *or* death rate; **Ster|be|zim|mer** NT death chamber *(liter, form)*; **Goethes ~** the room where Goethe died

sterb|lich [ˈʃtɛrplɪç] ADJ mortal; **jds ~e Hülle** *or* **(Über)reste** sb's mortal remains *pl* ADV *(inf)* terribly *(inf)*, dreadfully *(inf)*

Sterb|li|che(r) [ˈʃtɛrplɪçə] MF *decl as adj* mortal

Sterb|lich|keit F -, *no pl* mortality; *(Zahl)* mortality (rate), death rate

ste|reo [ˈʃteːreo, ˈst-] ADV (in) stereo

Ste|reo [ˈʃteːreo, ˈst-] NT **-s, -s in ~** in stereo

Ste|reo- *in cpds* stereo; *(= stereoskopisch)* stereoscopic; **Ste|reo|an|la|ge** F stereo unit *or* system, stereo *(inf)*; **Ste|reo|auf|nah|me** F stereo recording; **Ste|reo|box** F speaker; **ste|reo|fon** [ʃtereoˈfoːn, st-] ADJ stereophonic ADV stereophonically; **Ste|reo|fo|nie** [ʃtereofoˈniː, st-] F -, *no pl* stereophony; **ste|reo|fo|nisch** [ʃtereoˈfoːnɪʃ, st-] ADJ stereophonic ADV stereophonically; **Ste|reo|ge|rät** NT stereo unit; **Ste|reo|ka|me|ra** F stereoscopic camera; **Ste|reo|met|rie** [ʃtereomeˈtriː, st-] F -, *no pl* stereometry, solid geometry; **ste|reo|phon** [ʃtereoˈfoːn, st-] ADJ ADV = **stereofon**; **Ste|reo|pho|nie** [ʃtereofoˈniː, st-] F -, *no pl* = **Stereofonie**; **ste|reo|pho|nisch** [ʃtereoˈfoːnɪʃ, st-] ADJ ADV = **stereofonisch**; **Ste|reo|skop** [ʃtereoˈskoːp, st-] NT **-s, -e** stereoscope; **Ste|reo|sko|pie** [ʃtereoskoˈpiː, st-] F -, *no pl* stereoscopy; **ste|reo|sko|pisch** [ʃtereoˈskoːpɪʃ, st-] ADJ stereoscopic; *(= dreidimensional)* 3-D, three-dimensional; **Ste|reo|turm** M hi-fi stack; **ste|reo|typ** [ʃtereoˈtyːp, st-] ADJ *(fig)* stereotyped, stereotypical; *Lächeln (= gezwungen)* stiff; *(= unpersönlich)* impersonal ADV in stereotyped fashion; **~ darstellen** to represent as stereotypes; **Ste|reo|typ** NT *(Psych)* stereotype; **Ste|reo|typ|druck** M *pl* **-drucke** stereotype; **Ste|reo|ty|pie** [ʃtereotyˈpiː, st-] F **-, -n** [-ˈpiːən] *(Psych)* stereotypy; *(Typ auch)* stereotype printing; *(Werkstatt)* stereotype printing shop

ste|ril [ʃteˈriːl, st-] ADJ *(lit, fig)* sterile

Ste|ri|li|sa|ti|on [ʃteriliza'tsioːn, st-] F **-, -en** sterilization

ste|ri|li|sie|ren [ʃteriliˈziːrən, st-] *ptp* **sterilisiert** VT to sterilize

Ste|ri|li|tät [ʃteriliˈtɛːt, st-] F -, *no pl (lit, fig)* sterility

Ster|ling [ˈʃtɛrlɪŋ, ˈst-] M **-s, -e** sterling; **30 Pfund ~** 30 pounds sterling

Stern [ʃtɛrn] M **-(e)s, -e** **a** star; **mit ~en übersät** star-spangled *attr*; *Himmel auch* starry *attr*; **in den ~en lesen** *(Astrol)* to read the stars; **in den ~en (geschrieben) stehen** *(fig)* to be (written) in the stars; **das steht (noch) in den ~en** *(fig)* it's in the lap of the gods; **nach den ~en greifen** *(fig)* to reach for the stars; **er wollte die ~e vom Himmel holen** he wanted the moon (and the stars), he wanted the stars in the sky; **für sie holt er die ~e vom Himmel** he would do anything for her, he would go to the ends of the earth and back again for her; **der ~ der Weisen** *(Bibl)* the Star of Bethlehem; **sein ~ geht auf** *or* **ist im Aufgehen/sinkt** *or* **ist im Sinken** his star is in the ascendant/on the decline; **mein guter ~** my lucky star; **unter einem guten** *or* **glücklichen** *or* **günstigen ~ geboren sein** to be born under a lucky star; **unter einem guten** *or* **glücklichen** *or* **günstigen ~ stehen** to be blessed with good fortune; **unter einem unglücklichen ~ stehen** to be ill-starred *or* ill-fated; **mit ihr ging am Theaterhimmel ein neuer ~ auf** with her coming a new star was born in the theatrical world; **~e sehen** *(inf)* to see stars *(inf)*

b *(= Abzeichen, auch an Uniform)* star; **ein Hotel/Cognac mit drei ~en** a three-star hotel/brandy; **ein Vier-~e-General** a four-star general

Stern [ʃtɛrn] M **-(e)s, -e** **a** star; **dieser ~** *(poet: = die Erde)* this earth *or* orb *(poet)*; **mit ~en übersät** star-spangled *attr*; *Himmel auch* starry *attr*; **unter fremden ~en sterben** *(poet)* to die in foreign climes *(liter)*; **in den ~en lesen** *(Astrol)* to read the stars; **in den ~en (geschrieben) stehen** *(fig)* to be (written) in the stars; **das steht (noch) in den ~en** *(fig)* it's in the lap of the gods; **nach den ~en greifen** *(fig)* to reach for the stars; **er wollte die ~e vom Himmel holen** he wanted the moon (and the stars), he wanted the stars in the sky; **für sie holt er die ~e vom Himmel** he would do anything for her, he would go to the ends of the earth and back again for her; **der ~ der Weisen** *(Bibl)* the Star of Bethlehem; **sein ~ geht auf** *or* **ist im Aufgehen/sinkt** *or* **ist im Sinken** his star is in the ascendant/on the decline; **mein guter ~** my lucky star; **unter einem guten** *or* **glücklichen** *or* **günstigen ~ geboren sein** to be born under a lucky star; **unter einem guten** *or* **glücklichen** *or* **günstigen ~ stehen** to be blessed with good fortune; **unter einem unglücklichen ~ stehen** to be ill-starred *or* ill-fated; **mit ihr ging am Theaterhimmel ein neuer ~ auf** with her coming a new star was born in the theatrical world; **~e sehen** *(inf)* to see stars *(inf)*

b *(= Abzeichen, auch an Uniform)* star; **ein Hotel/Cognac mit drei ~en** a three-star hotel/brandy; **ein Vier-Sterne-General** a four-star general

Stern M **-s, -e** *(Naut)* stern

Stern-: **Stern|anis** M star aniseed; **stern|be|deckt** ADJ starry, star-spangled; **Stern|bild** NT *(Astron)* constellation; *(Astrol)* sign (of the zodiac)

Stern|chen [ˈʃtɛrnçən] NT **-s, -** *dim von* **Stern** **a** little star **b** *(Typ)* asterisk *(Brit)* **c** *(Film)* starlet

Stern-: **Stern|deu|te|rei** [-dɔytəˈrai] F -, *no pl* astrology, stargazing *(hum)*; **Stern|deu|ter(in)** M(F) astrologer, stargazer *(hum)*; **Stern|deu|tung** F astrology, stargazing *(hum)*

Ster|ne-: **Ster|ne|koch** M, **Ster|ne|kö|chin** F *(Cook)* (Michelin-)starred chef; **Ster|ne|lo|kal** NT, **Ster|ne|res|tau|rant** NT *(Cook)* (Michelin-)starred restaurant

Ster|nen-: **Ster|nen|ban|ner** NT Star-Spangled Banner, Stars and Stripes *sing*; **ster|nen|be|deckt** ADJ starry, star-covered; **Ster|nen|ge|wöl|be** NT *(poet)* starry vault *(poet)*; **Ster|nen|glanz** M *(poet)* starshine *(liter)*; **der Himmel erstrahlte im ~** the heavens shone with the light of the stars *(liter)*; **Ster|nen|him|mel** M starry sky; **Veränderungen am ~** changes in the star formation; **ster|nen|klar** ADJ *Himmel, Nacht* starry *attr*, starlit; **Ster|nen|krieg** M *(Pol)* Star Wars *pl*; **ster|nen|los** ADJ starless; **Ster|nen|zelt** NT *(poet)* starry firmament *(liter)*

Stern-: **Stern|fahrt** F *(Mot, Pol)* rally *(where participants commence at different points)*; **eine ~ nach Ulan Bator** a rally converging on Ulan Bator; **stern|för|mig** ADJ star-shaped, stellate *(spec)* ADV **~ angelegte Straßen, die vom Platz wegführen** streets radiating out from the square; **~ angelegte Gebäudekomplexe** buildings laid out like the spokes of a wheel; **~ vernetzt** *(Comput)* in a star-type network; **Stern|for|scher(in)** M(F) astronomer; **Stern|frucht** F star fruit, carambola; **Stern|ge|wöl|be** NT *(Archit)* stellar vault; **Stern|gu|cker** [-gʊkɐ] M **-s, -**, **Stern|gu|cke|rin** [-ərɪn] F **-, -nen** *(hum)* stargazer *(hum)*; **stern|ha|gel|voll** [ˈʃtɛrnˈhaːglˈfɔl] ADJ *(inf)* roaring drunk *(inf)*, blotto *pred (Brit sl)*; **Stern|hau|fen** M *(Astron)* star cluster; **stern|hell** ADJ starlit, starry *attr*; **Stern|jahr** NT sidereal year; **Stern|kar|te** F *(Astron)* celestial chart, star *or* stellar map *or* chart; **stern|klar** ADJ *Himmel, Nacht* starry *attr*, starlit; **Stern|kons|tel|la|ti|on** F (stellar) constellation; **Stern|kun|de** F astronomy; **Stern|marsch** M *(Pol) protest march with marchers converging on assembly point from different directions*; **Stern|mo|tor** M radial engine; **Stern|schnup|pe** [-ʃnʊpə] F **-, -n** shooting star; **Stern|sin|ger** PL carol singers *pl*; **Stern|stun|de** F great moment; **das war meine ~** that was a great moment in my life; **Stern|sys|tem** NT galaxy; **Stern|tag** M *(Astron)* sidereal day; **Stern|war|te** F observatory; **Stern|zei|chen** NT *(Astrol)* sign of the zodiac; **im ~ der Jungfrau** under the sign of Virgo; **Stern|zeit** F *(Astron)* sidereal time

Ste|ro|id [ʃteroˈiːt] NT **-(e)s, -e** [-də] steroid

Stert [ʃteːɐt] M **-(e)s, -e** *(N Ger)* = **Sterz**

Sterz [ʃtɛrts] M **-es, -e** **a** *(= Schwanzende)* tail; *(Cook)* parson's nose *(inf)* **b** *(= Pflugsterz)* handle

stet [ʃteːt] ADJ *attr* constant; *Fleiß auch* steady; *Arbeit, Wind auch* steady, continuous; **~er Tropfen höhlt den Stein** *(Prov)* constant dripping wears away the stone

Ste|tho|skop [ʃtetoˈskoːp, st-] NT **-s, -e** stethoscope

ste|tig [ˈʃteːtɪç] ADJ steady; *(Math) Funktion* continuous; **~es Meckern** constant moaning ADV *wachsen, sinken etc* steadily; **~ steigende Bedeutung** ever-increasing *or* steadily increasing importance

Ste|tig|keit F -, *no pl* steadiness; *(Math, von Funktion)* continuity; **er arbeitet mit bewundernswerter ~** you have to admire how consistently he works

stets [ʃteːts] ADV always; **~ zu Ihren Diensten** *(form)* always *or* ever *(form)* at your service; **~ der Ihre** *(old form)* yours ever

Steu|er [ˈʃtɔyɐ] NT **-s, -** *(Naut)* helm, tiller; *(Aut)* (steering) wheel; *(Aviat)* control column, controls *pl*; **am ~ stehen** *(Naut) or* **sein** *(fig)* to be at the helm; **am ~ sitzen** *or* **sein, hinter dem ~ sitzen** *(inf) (Aut)* to be at *or* behind the wheel, to drive; *(Aviat)* to be at the controls; **jdn ans ~ lassen** *(Aut)* to let sb drive, to let sb take the wheel; **das ~ übernehmen** *(lit, fig)* to take over; *(lit auch)* to take (over) the helm/wheel/controls; *(fig auch)* to take the helm; **das ~ fest in der Hand haben** *(fig)* to be firmly in control, to have things firmly under control; **das ~ herumwerfen** *or* **herumreißen** *(fig)* to turn the tide of events

Steu|er F **-, -n** **a** *(= Abgabe)* tax; *(an Gemeinde)* council tax *(Brit)*, local tax *(US)*; *(von Firmen)* rates *pl (Brit)*, corporate property tax *(US)*; **~n** tax; *(= Arten von Steuern)* taxes; **~n zahlen** to pay tax; **ich bezahle 35% ~n** I pay 35% tax; **in Schweden zahlt man hohe ~n** in Sweden tax is very high, in Sweden people are highly taxed; **die ~n herabsetzen** to reduce taxation, to cut tax *or* taxes; **der ~ unterliegen** *(form)* to be liable *or* subject to tax, to be taxable; **Gewinn vor/nach ~n** pre-/after-tax profit, profit before/after tax

b *(inf: = Steuerbehörde)* **die ~** the tax people *pl (inf) or* authorities *pl*, the Inland Revenue *(Brit)*, the Internal Revenue Service *(US)*

Steu|er-: **Steu|er|auf|kom|men** NT tax revenue, tax yield; **Steu|er|aus|fall** M *(Fin)* tax *or* revenue loss; **Steu|er|aus|gleich** M *(Fin)* tax equalization

steu|er|bar ADJ **a** *(= versteuerbar)* taxable, liable *or* subject to tax **b** *(= lenkbar, bedienbar)* controllable; *Schiff, Auto* steerable; *Flugzeug* flyable; **leicht/schwer ~** easy/difficult to control/steer/fly

Steu|er-: **Steu|er|be|am|te(r)** M *decl as adj*, **Steu|er|be|am|tin** F tax officer *or* official; **steu|er|be|güns|tigt** [-bəgʏnstɪçt] ADJ *Investitionen, Hypothek, Spende* tax-deductible; *Waren* taxed at a lower rate; **~es Sparen** *form of sav-*

ing entitling the saver to tax relief; **Investitionen sind ~** you get tax relief on investments; **Steu|er|be|güns|ti|gung** F tax concession (+*gen* on); **Steu|er|be|hör|de** F tax authorities *pl*, Inland Revenue *(Brit)*, Internal Revenue Service *(US)*; **Steu|er|be|mes|sungs|grund|la|ge** F *(Fin)* basis of tax assessment, tax base; **Steu|er|be|ra|ter(in)** M(F) tax consultant; **Steu|er|be|scheid** M tax assessment; **Steu|er|be|trug** M tax evasion *or* dodging; **Steu|er|be|voll|mäch|tig|te(r)** MF *decl as adj* tax expert *or* consultant; **Steu|er|bord** [ˈʃtɔyɐbɔrt] NT **-s,** *no pl (Naut)* starboard; **steu|er|bord(s)** [ˈʃtɔyɐbɔrt(s)] ADV *(Naut)* to starboard; **steu|er|ehr|lich** ADJ **~ sein** to be honest in tax matters; **Steu|er|ehr|lich|keit** F honesty in tax matters; **Steu|er|ein|heit** F *(Comput)* control unit; **Steu|er|ein|nah|men** PL revenue from taxation; **Steu|er|ein|neh|mer(in)** M(F) *(Hist)* tax collector; **Steu|er|ent|las|tung** F tax relief; **Steu|er|er|hö|hung** F tax increase; **Steu|er|er|klä|rung** F tax return, tax declaration *(Brit)*; **Steu|er|er|lass** M tax exemption; **Steu|er|er|leich|te|rung** F *usu pl* tax relief *no pl*; **Steu|er|er|mä|ßi|gung** F tax allowance *or* relief; **Steu|er|er|stat|tung** F tax rebate; **Steu|er|fahn|dung** F investigation of (suspected) tax evasion; *(Behörde)* commission for investigation of suspected tax evasion; **Steu|er|flucht** F tax evasion *(by leaving the country)*; **Steu|er|flücht|ling** M tax exile; **Steu|er|frau** F *(Rudern)* cox(swain); **steu|er|frei** ADJ tax-free, exempt from tax ADV tax-free; **Abfindungen können ~ vereinnahmt werden** settlements are tax-free; **er hat den Nebenverdienst ~ kassiert** he didn't pay taxes on his additional earnings; **Steu|er|frei|be|trag** M tax-free allowance; **Steu|er|frei|heit** F tax exemption, exemption from tax; **~ genießen** to be exempt from tax; **Steu|er|gel|der** PL tax money, taxes *pl*; **warum soll das aus ~n finanziert werden?** why should it be paid for with taxpayers' money?, why should the taxpayer have to pay for it?; **Veruntreuung von ~n** tax embezzlement; **Steu|er|ge|rät** NT tuner-amplifier; *(Comput)* control unit; **Steu|er|har|mo|ni|sie|rung** F harmonization of taxes; **Steu|er|hin|ter|zie|hung** F tax evasion; **Steu|er|ho|heit** F right to levy tax(es); **Steu|er|in|spek|tor(in)** M(F) tax inspector; **Steu|er|jahr** NT tax year; **Steu|er|kar|te** F *notice of pay received and tax deducted*; **Steu|er|ket|te** F *(an Motorrad)* timing chain; **Steu|er|ket|ten|span|ner** M timing chain tightener; **Steu|er|klas|se** F tax bracket *or* group; **Steu|er|knüp|pel** M control column; *(Aviat auch)* joystick; **Steu|er|last** F tax burden

steu|er|lich [ˈʃtɔyɐlɪç] ADJ tax *attr*; **~e Belastung** tax burden; **aus ~en Überlegungen** for tax reasons ADV **es ist ~ günstiger ...** for tax purposes it is better ...; **das wirkt sich ~ ganz günstig aus** from the tax point of view *or* taxwise it works out very well; **das ist ~ vorteilhaft** that's a good way to save on taxes; **~ abzugsfähig** tax-deductible; **~ stark belastet werden** *(Mensch)* to pay high taxes; **~ entlastet werden** *(Mensch)* to get a tax reduction *or* break; **etw wird ~ berücksichtigt** sth is tax-deductible

steu|er|los ADJ rudderless, out of control; *(fig)* leaderless

Steu|er-: **Steu|er|mann** M *pl* **-männer** *or* **-leute** helmsman; *(als Rang)* (first) mate; *(Rudern)* cox (-swain); **Zweier mit/ohne ~** coxed/coxless pairs; **Steu|er|manns|pa|tent** NT *(Naut)* mate's ticket *(inf)* or certificate; **Steu|er|mar|ke** F revenue *or* tax stamp; *(für Hunde)* dog licence disc *(Brit)*, dog tag *(US)*; **steu|er|min|dernd** ADJ tax-reducing ADV **etw (als) ~ geltend machen** to offset sth against tax; **sich ~ auswirken** to have the effect of reducing tax; **Steu|er|mit|tel** PL tax revenue(s *pl*); **etw aus ~n finanzieren** to finance sth out of public funds; **Steu|er|mo|ral** F honesty in tax matters

steu|ern [ˈʃtɔyɐn] VT **a** *Schiff* to steer, to navigate; *Flugzeug* to pilot, to fly; *Auto* to steer; *(fig) Wirtschaft, Politik* to run, to control, to manage; *(Comput)* to control; **staatlich gesteuert** state-controlled, under state control; **einen Kurs ~** *(lit, fig)* to steer a course; *(fig auch)* to take *or* follow a line; **eine Diskussion/die Wirtschaft in eine bestimmte Richtung ~** to steer a discussion/the economy in a certain direction

b *(= regulieren)* to control

VI **a** *aux sein* to head; *(Aut)* to drive, to head; *(Naut)* to make *or* head for, to steer; **wohin steuert die Wirtschaft?** where is the economy heading *or* headed (for)?

b *(= am Steuer sein) (Naut)* to be at the helm; *(Aut)* to be at the wheel; *(Aviat)* to be at the controls

Steu|er-: **Steu|er|nach|zah|lung** F additional tax payment; **Steu|er|num|mer** F tax(payer's) reference number; **Steu|er|oa|se** F, **Steu|er|pa|ra|dies** NT tax haven; **Steu|er|pflicht** F liability to tax; *(von Person auch)* liability to pay tax; **der ~ unterliegen** to be liable to tax, to be taxable; **steu|er|pflich|tig** [-pflɪçtɪç] ADJ *Einkommen* taxable, liable to tax; *Person auch* liable to (pay) tax; **Steu|er|pflich|ti|ge(r)** [-pflɪçtɪgə] MF *decl as adj* taxpayer; **Steu|er|po|li|tik** F tax *or* taxation policy; **steu|er|po|li|tisch** ADJ relating to tax policy; **~e Maßnahmen der Regierung** government tax measures; **aus ~en Gründen** for tax *or* taxation reasons ADV **es wäre ~ unklug ...** it would be unwise tax policy ...; **sich ~ profilieren wollen** to try and make a good impression with tax policy; **~ notwendige Maßnahmen** tax policies; **Steu|er|pro|gres|si|on** F progressive taxation; **Steu|er|prü|fer(in)** M(F) tax inspector, tax auditor *(esp US)*; **Steu|er|prü|fung** F tax inspector's investigation *(Brit)*, tax audit *(esp US)*; **Steu|er|rad** NT *(Aviat)* control wheel; *(Aut)* (steering) wheel; **Steu|er|recht** NT tax law; **steu|er|recht|lich** ADJ relating to tax law; **~e Änderungen** changes in the tax laws; **ein ~er Fachmann** a tax expert ADV **das ist ~ unmöglich** the tax laws make that impossible; **er ist ~ versiert** he is familiar with tax law; **~ bedenkliche Maßnahmen** *(von Person)* dubious accounting practices; *(von Staat)* dubious tax policies; **~ zulässig** allowed by tax law; **Steu|er|re|form** F tax reform; **Steu|er|rück|zah|lung** F tax rebate; **Steu|er|ru|der** NT rudder; **Steu|er|sa|che** F tax matter; **Helfer in ~n** tax consultant; **Steu|er|satz** M rate of taxation; **Steu|er|schät|zung** F tax estimate; **Steu|er|schlupf|loch** NT tax loophole; **steu|er|scho|nend** ADJ tax-saving; **Steu|er|schrau|be** F **die ~ anziehen** to put the screws on the taxpayer, to squeeze the taxpayer; **Steu|er|schuld** F tax (-es *pl*) owing *no indef art*, tax liability; **Steu|er|sen|kung** F tax cut; **Steu|er|spar|mo|dell** NT tax relief scheme; **Steu|er|sün|der(in)** M(F) tax evader; **Steu|er|sys|tem** NT tax system; **Steu|er|tas|te** F *(Comput)* navigation key, arrow key; **steu|er|un|ehr|lich** ADJ **~ sein** to be dishonest in tax matters

Steu|e|rung [ˈʃtɔyərʊŋ] F **-, -en** **a** *no pl (= das Steuern) (von Schiff)* steering, navigation; *(von Flugzeug)* piloting, flying; *(fig) (von Politik, Wirtschaft)* running, control, management; *(Comput)* control; *(= Regulierung)* control, regulation; *(= Bekämpfung)* control **b** *(= Steuervorrichtung) (Aviat)* controls *pl*; *(Tech)* steering apparatus *or* mechanism; *(elektronisch)* control; **automatische ~** *(Aviat)* automatic pilot, autopilot; *(Tech)* automatic steering (device)

Steu|e|rungs-: **Steu|e|rungs|fä|hig|keit** F *(Psych)* ability to control oneself; **Steu|e|rungs|tas|te** F *(Comput)* control key; **Steu|e|rungs|zei|chen** NT *(Comput)* control character

Steu|er-: **Steu|er|ver|an|la|gung** F tax assessment; **Steu|er|ver|ge|hen** NT tax evasion *or* dodging *no pl*; **Steu|er|ver|güns|ti|gung** F tax break *or* concession; **~en** *pl (auch)* tax relief; **Steu|er|vor|teil** M tax advantage *or* benefit; **Steu|er|werk** NT *(Comput)* control unit; **Steu|er|zah|ler(in)** M(F) taxpayer; **Steu|er|zei|chen** NT *(Comput)* control character

Ste|ven [ˈʃteːvn] M **-s, -** *(Naut) (= Vordersteven)* prow; *(= Achtersteven)* stern

Ste|ward [ˈstjuːɐt, ˈʃt-] M **-s, -s** *(Naut, Aviat)* steward

Ste|war|dess [ˈstjuːɐdɛs, stjuːɐˈdɛs, ʃt-] F **-, -en** stewardess

StGB [ɛsteːgeːˈbeː] NT **-s** *abbr von* **Strafgesetzbuch**

sti|bit|zen [ʃtiˈbɪtsn] *ptp* **stibitzt** VT *(dated hum)* to swipe *(inf)*, to pinch *(inf)*

stich [ʃtɪç] *imper sing von* **stechen**

Stich [ʃtɪç] M **-(e)s, -e** **a** *(= das Stechen) (= Insektenstich)* sting; *(= Mückenstich)* bite; *(= Nadelstich)* prick; *(= Messerstich)* stab

b *(= Stichwunde) (von Messer etc)* stab wound; *(von Insekten)* sting; *(von Mücken)* bite; *(= Einstichloch)* prick

c *(= stechender Schmerz)* piercing *or* shooting *or* stabbing pain; *(= Seitenstich)* stitch; *(fig)* pang; **~e haben** to have a stitch; **es gab mir einen ~ (ins Herz)** I was cut to the quick *(esp Brit) or* to the heart *(US)*

d *(Sew)* stitch

e *(= Kupferstich, Stahlstich)* engraving

f *(= Schattierung)* tinge, shade *(in +acc* of); *(= Tendenz)* hint, suggestion *(in +acc* of); **ein ~ ins Rote** a tinge of red, a reddish tinge; **ein ~ ins Gewöhnliche/Vulgäre** a hint *or* suggestion of commonness/vulgarity

g *(Cards)* trick; **einen ~ machen** *or* **bekommen** to get a trick

h **jdn im ~ lassen** to let sb down; *(= verlassen)* to abandon *or* desert sb, to leave sb in the lurch; **etw im ~ lassen** to abandon sth

i **~ halten** to hold water, to be valid *or* sound

j **einen ~ haben** *(Esswaren)* to be off *(Brit) or* bad, to have gone off *(Brit) or* bad; *(Butter auch)* to be *or* have gone rancid; *(Milch)* to be *or* have gone off *(Brit) or* sour; *(inf: Mensch: = verrückt sein)* to be nuts *(inf)*, to be round the bend *(Brit inf)*

Stich-: **Stich|bahn** F *(Rail)* branch terminal line; **Stich|blatt** NT **a** *(von Degen)* guard **b** *(Cards)* trump (card)

Sti|chel [ˈʃtɪçl] M **-s, -** *(Art)* gouge

Sti|che|lei [ʃtɪçəˈlai] F **-, -en** **a** *(= Näherei)* sewing **b** *(pej inf: = boshafte Bemerkung)* snide *or* sneering remark, gibe, dig; **deine ständigen ~en kannst du dir sparen** stop getting at me *(Brit)*, stop making digs *(Brit) or* pokes *(US)* at me

sti|cheln [ˈʃtɪçln] VI **a** *(= nähen)* to sew; *(= sticken)* to embroider **b** *(pej inf: = boshafte Bemerkungen machen)* to make snide *or* sneering remarks; **gegen jdn ~** to make digs *(Brit) or* pokes *(US)* at sb

Stich-: **Stich|ent|scheid** M *(Pol)* result of a/the runoff *(US)*, final ballot; *(Sport)* result of a/the play-off; **stich|fest** ADJ → **hiebfest**; **Stich|flam|me** F tongue of flame; **stich+hal|ten** [ˈʃtɪçhaltn] VI *sep irreg (Aus)* → **Stich i**; **stich|hal|tig**, *(Aus)* **stich|häl|tig** ✪ 53.3 ADJ *Argument, Grund* sound, valid; *Erklärung* valid; *Beweis* conclusive; **sein Alibi ist nicht ~** his alibi doesn't hold water ADV conclusively; **Stich|hal|tig|keit** [ˈʃtɪçhaltɪçkait] F **-,** *no pl (von Argument, Grund)* soundness, validity; *(von Erklärung)* validity; *(von Beweis)* conclusiveness; **Stich|kampf** M *(Sport)* play-off

Stich|ling [ˈʃtɪçlɪŋ] M **-s, -e** *(Zool)* stickleback

Stich|pro|be F spot check; *(Sociol)* (random) sample survey; **~n machen** to carry out *or* make spot checks; *(Sociol)* to carry out a (random) sample survey; **bei der ~ wurde festgestellt, dass ...** the spot check/sampling revealed that ...

Stich|pro|ben-: **Stich|pro|ben|er|he|bung** F *(Sociol)* (random) sample survey; **stich|pro|**

ben|wei|se ADV on a random basis; **es werden nur ~ Kontrollen gemacht** only spot checks are made

Stich-: **Stich|punkt** M *(= Schlüsselbegriff)* key word *or* point; **~e** *pl (als Gedächtnisstütze für Vortrag etc.)* notes *pl*; **sich** *(dat)* **ein paar ~e machen** to jot down a few notes; **Stich|sä|ge** F fret saw; **Stich|stra|ße** F cul-de-sac

sticht [ʃtɪçt] *3. pers sing pres von* **stechen**

Stich-: **Stich|tag** M qualifying date; **Stich|ver|let|zung** F stab wound, knife wound; **Stich|waf|fe** F stabbing weapon; **Stich|wahl** F *(Pol)* final ballot, runoff *(US)*

Stich|wort NT **a** *pl* **-wörter** *(in Nachschlagewerken)* headword; *(Comput)* keyword **b** *pl* **-worte** *(Theat, fig)* cue **c** *pl* **-worte** *usu pl* notes *pl*; *(bei Nacherzählung etc)* key words *pl*

Stich|wort-: **stich|wort|ar|tig** ADJ abbreviated, shorthand; **eine ~e Gliederung** an outline ADV **etw ~ zusammenfassen** to summarize the main points of sth; **etw ~ wiedergeben** to recount sth in a shorthand *or* an abbreviated fashion; **jdn ~ über etw** *(acc)* **informieren** to give sb a brief outline of sth; **Stich|wort|ge|ber(in)** M(F) *(Theat)* stooge; *(fig)* person raising issues/the issue; **Stich|wort|ka|ta|log** M classified catalogue *(Brit) or* catalog *(US)*; **Stich|wort|ver|zeich|nis** NT index

Stich|wun|de F stab wound

Stick|ar|beit F embroidery; **sie saß gerade an einer ~** she was sitting embroidering

sti|cken [ˈʃtɪkn] VTI to embroider

Sti|cker [ˈʃtɪkɐ, ˈst-] M **-s, -** *(inf: = Aufkleber)* sticker

Sti|cke|rei [ʃtɪkəˈrai] F **-, -en a** *no pl (= das Sticken)* embroidery, embroidering **b** *(Gegenstand)* embroidery

Sti|cke|rin [ˈʃtɪkərɪn] F **-, -nen** embroideress, embroiderer

Stick|garn NT embroidery thread *or* silk

sti|ckig [ˈʃtɪkɪç] ADJ *Luft, Zimmer* stuffy, close; *Klima* sticky, humid; *(fig) Atmosphäre* stifling, oppressive

Stick-: **Stick|ma|schi|ne** F embroidery machine; **Stick|mus|ter** NT embroidery pattern; **Stick|na|del** F embroidery needle; **Stick|oxid, Stick|oxyd** [ˈʃtɪklɔksiːt] NT nitric oxide; **Stick|rah|men** M embroidery frame

Stick|stoff [ˈʃtɪkʃtɔf] M *(abbr* **N***)* nitrogen

Stick|stoff-: **Stick|stoff|dün|ger** M nitrogen fertilizer; **stick|stoff|hal|tig** ADJ containing nitrogen, nitrogenous *(spec)*

stie|ben [ˈʃtiːbn] *pret* **stob** *or* **stiebte** [ʃtoːp, ˈʃtiːptə], *ptp* **gestoben** *or* **gestiebt** [gəˈʃtoːbn, gəˈʃtiːpt] VI *(geh)* **a** *aux haben or sein (= sprühen) (Funken, Staub etc)* to fly; *(Schnee)* to spray, to fly; *(Wasser)* to spray **b** *aux sein (= jagen, rennen)* to flee; *(= auseinanderstieben)* to scatter

Stief|bru|der [ˈʃtiːf-] M stepbrother

Stie|fel [ˈʃtiːfl] M **-s, - a** boot; **der italienische ~** the Italian boot, the boot of Italy; **das sind zwei Paar ~** *(fig)* they are two completely different things; **jdm die ~ lecken** *(fig)* to lick sb's boots **b** *(inf)* **seinen (alten) ~ arbeiten** *or* **weitermachen** to carry on as usual, to carry on in the same old way; **einen ~ zusammenreden** to talk a lot of nonsense *or* a load of rubbish *(Brit inf)* **c** *(= Trinkgefäß)* large, boot-shaped beer glass holding 2 litres; **einen (ordentlichen) ~ vertragen** *(inf)* to be able to take one's drink *(Brit) or* hold one's liquor

Stie|fel-: **Stie|fel|ab|satz** M (boot) heel; **Stie|fel|an|zie|her** [-lantsiːɐ] M **-s, -** boot hook

Stie|fe|let|te [ʃtifəˈlɛtə] F **-, -n** *(= Frauenstiefelette)* bootee; *(= Männerstiefelette)* half-boot

Stie|fel|knecht M bootjack

stie|feln [ˈʃtiːfln] VI *aux sein (inf)* to hoof it *(inf)* → **gestiefelt**

Stie|fel|schaft M bootleg, leg of a/the boot

Stief|el|tern [ˈʃtiːf-] PL step-parents *pl*

Stie|fel|wich|se F *(dated)* boot polish, boot-blacking

Stief-: **Stief|ge|schwis|ter** PL stepbrother(s *pl*) and sister(s *pl*); **Stief|kind** NT stepchild; *(fig)* poor cousin; **sie fühlt sich immer als ~ des Glücks** she always feels that fortune never smiles upon her; **Stief|mut|ter** F *pl* **-mütter** stepmother; **Stief|müt|ter|chen** NT *(Bot)* pansy; **stief|müt|ter|lich** ADV *(fig)* **jdn/etw ~ behandeln** to pay little attention to sb/sth, to put sb/sth in second place; **die Natur hat ihn ~ behandelt** Nature has not been kind to him; **Stief|schwes|ter** F stepsister; **Stief|sohn** M stepson; **Stief|toch|ter** F stepdaughter; **Stief|va|ter** M stepfather

stieg *pret von* **steigen**

Stieg [ʃtiːk] M **-(e)s, -e** [-gə] steep track

Stie|ge [ˈʃtiːgə] F **-, -n a** *(= schmale Treppe)* (narrow) flight of stairs, (narrow) staircase **b** *(old: = 20 Stück)* score; **eine ~ Eier** a score of eggs **c** *(= Lattenkiste)* crate

Stie|gen|haus NT *(S Ger, Aus)* staircase

Stieg|litz [ˈʃtiːglɪts] M **-es, -e** goldfinch

stiehlt [ʃtiːlt] *3. pers sing pres von* **stehlen**

stie|kum [ˈʃtiːkʊm] ADV *(N Ger: = heimlich)* on the sly *(inf) or* fly *(inf)*

Stiel [ʃtiːl] M **-(e)s, -e a** *(= Griff)* handle; *(= Pfeifenstiel, Glasstiel)* stem **b** *(= Stängel)* stalk; *(= Blütenstiel)* stalk, stem, peduncle *(spec)*; *(= Blattstiel)* leafstalk, petiole *(spec)*

Stiel|au|gen PL *(fig inf)* **~ machen** *or* **kriegen** to gawk *(inf)*, to gawp *(Brit inf)*, to goggle *(inf)*; **er machte ~** his eyes (nearly) popped out of his head

Stiel-: **Stiel|glas** NT stemmed glass; **Stiel|kamm** M tail comb; **stiel|los** ADJ *Gerät* handleless, without a handle; *Pflanze, Blatt* stalkless; *Glas* stemless; **Stiel|pfan|ne** F frying pan with a (long) handle; **Stiel|topf** M long-handled pan

stier [ʃtiːɐ] ADJ **a** *(= stumpfsinnig) Blick* vacant, blank **b** *(inf: Aus, Sw) Geschäft* slack, slow; *Mensch* broke *(inf)* ADV *starren* vacantly; **~ blicken** to have a blank stare

Stier [ʃtiːɐ] M **-(e)s, -e a** bull; *(= junger Stier)* bullock; **wütend wie ein ~ (sein)** (to be) beside oneself with rage *or* fury; **wie ein ~ brüllen** to bawl one's head off *(inf)*, to bellow like a bull; **den ~ bei den Hörnern packen** *or* **fassen** *(prov)* to take the bull by the horns *(prov)* **b** *(Astrol)* Taurus *no art*; **ich bin (ein) ~** I'm (a) Taurus

stie|ren [ˈʃtiːrən] VI *(auf +acc* at) to stare; *(neugierig auch)* to gape; **(lüstern) auf jdn ~** to ogle sb *(inf)*, to eye sb up *(Brit)*; **sein Blick stierte ins Leere** he stared vacantly into space

Stier-: **Stier|kampf** M bullfight; **Stier|kampf|are|na** F bullring; **Stier|kämp|fer(in)** M(F) bullfighter; **Stier|na|cken** M neck like a bull, thick neck; **stier|na|ckig** ADJ bull-necked; **Stier|op|fer** NT sacrifice of a bull

Stie|sel [ˈʃtiːzl] M **-s, -** *(inf)* boor, lout *(inf)*

stie|se|lig [ˈʃtiːzəlɪç], **sties|lig** [ˈʃtiːzlɪç] *(inf)* ADJ boorish, loutish *(inf)* ADV **sich ~ benehmen** to behave like a boor *or* lout

Stie|se|lig|keit [ˈʃtiːzəlɪçkait] F **-,** *no pl*, **Sties|lig|keit** [ˈʃtiːzlɪçkait] F **-,** *no pl (inf)* boorishness, loutishness *(inf)*

stieß *pret von* **stoßen**

Stift [ʃtɪft] M **-(e)s, -e a** *(= Metallstift)* pin; *(= Holzstift)* peg, pin; *(= Nagel)* tack **b** *(= Bleistift)* pencil; *(= Buntstift)* pencil, crayon; *(= Filzstift)* felt-tip, felt-tipped pen; *(= Kugelschreiber)* ballpoint (pen), Biro® *(Brit)*; *(Comput)* pen **c** *(inf) (= Lehrling)* apprentice (boy); *(= Knirps)* nipper *(Brit inf)*, whippersnapper *(US inf)*

Stift NT **-(e)s, -e** *(= Domstift)* cathedral chapter; *(= Theologiestift)* seminary

stif|ten [ˈʃtɪftn] VT **a** *(= gründen) Kirche, Universität* to found, to establish; *(= spenden, spendieren)* to donate; *Geld, Summe* to put up, to donate; *Preis, Stipendium etc* to endow **b** *Verwirrung* to cause; *Unfrieden, Unheil* to cause, to bring about; *Identität* to create; *Frieden* to bring about; *Ehe* to arrange; **Gutes/Schaden ~** to do good/damage

stif|ten ge|hen VI *irreg aux sein (inf)* to hop it *(Brit inf)*, to move it *(US inf)*

Stif|ten|kopf [ˈʃtɪftn-] M *(dated inf)* crew cut; *(Mensch)* person with a crew cut

Stif|ter [ˈʃtɪftɐ] M **-s, -**, **Stif|te|rin** [-ərɪn] F **-, -nen** *(= Gründer)* founder; *(= Spender)* donator

Stif|ter|re|li|gi|on F *religion founded by a particular person eg Buddha, Jesus*

Stifts-: **Stifts|da|me** F *(Eccl)* canoness; **Stifts|herr** M *(Eccl)* canon; **Stifts|hüt|te** F *(Bibl)* Tabernacle; **Stifts|kir|che** F collegiate church

Stif|tung [ˈʃtɪftʊŋ] F **-, -en a** *(= Gründung)* foundation, establishment; *(= Schenkung)* donation; *(von Universität, Stipendium etc)* endowment **b** *(= Organisation)* foundation

Stif|tungs-: **Stif|tungs|fest** NT Founder's Day celebration; **Stif|tungs|ini|ti|a|ti|ve** F **die ~ „Erinnerung, Verantwortung und Zukunft"** the Remembrance, Responsibility and Future Foundation; **Stif|tungs|ur|kun|de** F foundation charter

Stift|zahn M post crown

Stig|ma [ˈʃtɪgma, st-] NT **-s, -ta** [-ta] *(Biol, Rel, fig)* stigma

stig|ma|ti|sie|ren [ʃtɪgmatiˈziːrən, st-] *ptp* **stigmatisiert** [-ˈziːɐt] VT *(Rel, auch fig)* to stigmatize *(als* as), to brand *(als* as) *(fig)*

Stig|ma|ti|sier|te(r) [ʃtɪgmatiˈziːɐtə, st-] MF *decl as adj (Biol, Rel)* stigmatic; *(fig)* stigmatized person

Stil [ʃtiːl, stiːl] M **-(e)s, -e** style; *(= Eigenart)* way, manner; **in großem ~, im großen ~, großen ~s** in a big way; **... alten ~s** old-style ...; **schlechter ~** bad style; **das ist schlechter ~** *(fig)* that is bad form; **~ haben** *(fig)* to have style; **er fährt einen rücksichtslosen ~** he drives recklessly *or* in a reckless manner; **er schreibt einen sehr schwerfälligen ~** his writing style is very clumsy

Stil-: **Stil|ana|ly|se** F *(Art, Liter)* stylistic analysis; **stil|bil|dend** ADJ **(für jdn) ~ sein** to improve sb's style; **~ sein/wirken** *(einen Stil kreieren)* to help set a style; **Stil|blü|te** F *(hum)* stylistic howler *(Brit inf) or* blooper *(US inf)*; **Stil|bruch** M stylistic incongruity *or* inconsistency; *(in Roman etc)* abrupt change in style; **das ist ein glatter ~** *(inf)* that is really incongruous; **Stil|ebe|ne** F *(Liter, Ling)* style level; **stil|echt** ADJ authentic(-style); *Möbel* period *attr* ADV in an authentic style; **~ eingerichtet** with period furniture; **Stil|ele|ment** NT stylistic element; **Stil|emp|fin|den** NT feeling for style, sense of style

Sti|lett [ʃtiˈlɛt, st-] NT **-s, -e** stiletto

Stil-: **Stil|feh|ler** M stylistic lapse; **Stil|fi|gur** F stylistic device; **Stil|ge|fühl** NT feeling for style, sense of style; **stil|ge|recht** ADJ appropriate to *or* in keeping with a/the style; **stil|ge|treu** ADJ true to *or* in the original style

sti|li|sie|ren [ʃtiliˈziːrən, st-] *ptp* **stilisiert** VT to stylize

Sti|li|sie|rung F **-, -en** stylization

Sti|list [ʃtiˈlɪst, st-] M **-en, -en**, **Sti|lis|tin** [-ˈlɪstɪn] F **-, -nen** stylist

Sti|lis|tik [ʃtiˈlɪstɪk, st-] F **-, -en** *(Liter)* stylistics *sing*; *(= Handbuch)* guide to good style

sti|lis|tisch [ʃtiˈlɪstɪʃ, st-] ADJ stylistic ADV **ich muss meine Vorlesung ~ überarbeiten** I must go over my lecture from the point of view of style; **etw ~ ändern/verbessern** to change/improve the style of sth; **~ gesehen** *or* **betrachtet ist der Artikel brillant** the style of this article is brilliant

Stil|kun|de F stylistics *sing*; *(= Handbuch)* guide to good style

still [ʃtɪl] ADJ **a** *(= ruhig)* quiet, silent; *(= lautlos) Seufzer* quiet; *Gebet* silent; *(= schweigend) Vorwurf, Beobachter* silent; **~ werden** to go quiet, to fall silent; **im Saal wurde es ~, der Saal wurde ~** the room fell silent; **um ihn/darum ist es ~ geworden** you don't hear anything about him/it any more; **es blieb ~** there was no sound, silence reigned; **Stille Nacht** Silent Night; **in ~em Gedenken** in silent tribute; **in ~em Schmerz/in**

~er Trauer in silent suffering/grief; **im Stillen** without saying anything, quietly; **ich dachte mir im Stillen** I thought to myself; **die Stillen im Lande** the quiet ones; **sei doch ~!** be *or* keep quiet; **~e Messe** silent mass

b *(= unbewegt) Luft* still; *See* calm, still; *(= ohne Kohlensäure) Mineralwasser* still; **der Stille Ozean** the Pacific (Ocean); **~e Wasser sind tief** *(Prov)* still waters run deep *(Prov)*; **er ist ein ~es Wasser** he's a deep one, he's a dark horse

c *(= einsam, abgeschieden) Dorf, Tal, Straße* quiet; **ein ~es Eckchen** a quiet corner; **ein ~es Plätzchen** a quiet spot

d *(= heimlich)* secret; **im Stillen** in secret; **er ist dem ~en Suff ergeben** *(inf)* he drinks on the quiet, he's a secret drinker

e *(Comm) Gesellschafter, Teilhaber* sleeping *(Brit)*, silent *(US)*; *Reserven, Rücklagen* secret, hidden; **~e Beteiligung** sleeping partnership *(Brit)*, non-active interest

ADV **a** *(= leise) weinen, arbeiten, nachdenken* quietly; *leiden* in silence; *auseinandergehen, weggehen* silently; **~ lächeln** to give a quiet smile

b *(= unbewegt) daliegen, dasitzen, liegen bleiben* still; **~ halten** to keep *or* hold still; **~ sitzen** to sit *or* keep still; **den Kopf/die Hände/Füße ~ halten** to keep one's head/hands/feet still; **ein Glas/Tablett ~ halten** to hold a glass/tray steady; **vor uns lag ~ die Ägäis** before us lay the calm waters of the Aegean → *auch* **stillhalten**

c *(= ohne viel Trubel) vor sich hin leben, arbeiten* quietly; **ganz ~ und leise** *(etw erledigen)* discreetly; **er hat sich ~ und leise aus dem Staub gemacht** he just disappeared

Still-BH [ˈʃtılbeːhaː] **M** nursing bra

stil|le [ˈʃtılə] **ADJ, ADV** *(old)* = **still**

Stil|le [ˈʃtılə] **F -,** *no pl* **a** *(= Ruhe)* quiet(ness), peace(fulness); *(= Schweigen)* silence; **in der ~ der Nacht** in the still of the night; **in aller ~** quietly, calmly; **die Beerdigung fand in aller ~ statt** it was a quiet funeral; **jdn in aller ~ begraben** to give sb a quiet burial **b** *(= Unbewegtheit)* calm(ness); *(der Luft)* stillness **c** *(= Einsamkeit, Abgeschiedenheit)* quiet, seclusion **d** *(= Heimlichkeit)* secrecy; **in aller ~** in secret, secretly

Stilleben △ **NT** → **Stillleben**

stillegen △ **VT** → **stilllegen**

Stillegung △ **F -, -en** → **Stilllegung**

Stil|leh|re **F** stylistics *sing*

Still|ein|la|ge **F** *(für BH)* nursing pad

stil|len [ˈʃtılən] **VT** **a** *(= zum Stillstand bringen) Tränen* to stop; *Schmerzen* to ease, to relieve, to allay; *Blutung* to staunch, to stop **b** *(= befriedigen) Neugier, Begierde, Verlangen, Hunger* to satisfy, to still *(liter)*; *Durst* to quench **c** *Säugling* to breast-feed, to nurse **VI** to breast-feed; **~de Mutter** nursing mother

Still|geld **NT** nursing mothers' allowance

still|ge|stan|den **INTERJ** *(Mil)* halt

Still|grup|pe **F** mothers' group

Still|hal|te|ab|kom|men **NT** *(Fin, fig)* moratorium

still+hal|ten **VI** *sep irreg (fig)* to keep quiet → *auch* **still ADV b**

Still|hal|ter(in) **M(F)** *(St Ex)* taker of an option

stilliegen △ **VI** → **stillliegen**

Still-: **Still|le|ben** **NT** still life; **still+le|gen** **VT** *sep* to close down, to shut down; *Schiff* to lay up; **stillgelegtes Bergwerk** disused *or* abandoned mine; **Still|le|gung** [-leːgʊŋ] **F -, -en** closure, shutdown; *(von Schiff)* laying-up; **still+lie|gen** **VI** *sep irreg aux sein or haben* **a** *(= außer Betrieb sein)* to be closed down, to be shut down **b** *(= lahmliegen)* to be at a standstill, to have been brought to a standstill, to have come to a halt

stil|los **ADJ** lacking in style; *(= fehl am Platze)* incongruous; **eine völlig ~e Zusammenstellung von Möbelstücken** a collection of furniture completely lacking (in) any sense of style **ADV** with no sense of style; **völlig ~ servierte sie Hummersuppe in Teetassen** showing absolutely no sense of style she served up lobster soup in tea cups

Stil|lo|sig|keit **F -, -en** lack of style *no pl*; **solche ~en ist man von ihr gewohnt** we're used to her having no sense of style

still+schwei|gen **VI** *sep irreg* to remain silent; **zu etw ~** to remain silent in the face of sth; **schweig still!** be silent *or* quiet

Still|schwei|gen **NT** silence; **auf sein ~ kann man sich verlassen** one can rely on his keeping silent; **jdm ~ auferlegen, jdn zum ~ verpflichten** to swear sb to silence; **beide Seiten haben ~ vereinbart** both sides have agreed not to say anything; **über etw** *(acc)* **~ bewahren** to observe *or* maintain silence about sth; **etw mit ~ übergehen** to pass over sth in silence

still|schwei|gend **ADJ** silent; *Einverständnis* tacit **ADV** tacitly; **über etw** *(acc)* **~ hinweggehen** to pass over sth in silence; **etw ~ hinnehmen** to accept sth silently *or* without protest

still+sit|zen **VI** *sep irreg aux sein or haben* → **still ADV b**

Still|stand **M** standstill; *(von Betrieb, Produktion, Verhandlungen etc auch)* stoppage; *(vorübergehend)* interruption; *(in Entwicklung)* halt; **bei ~ der Maschine ...** when the machine is stopped ...; **ein ~ des Herzens** a cardiac arrest; **Hauptsache ist, dass kein ~ in der Produktion eintritt** the main thing is that production is not interrupted; **zum ~ kommen** *(Verkehr)* to come to a standstill *or* stop; *(Produktion auch, Maschine, Motor, Herz, Blutung)* to stop; *(Wirtschaft)* to come to a standstill *or* halt; *(Prozess, Entwicklung)* to come to a halt; **etw zum ~ bringen** *(Verkehr)* to bring sth to a standstill *or* stop; *Produktion auch, Maschine, Motor* to stop sth; *Blutung* to stop *or* check sth; *Prozess, Entwicklung* to bring sth to a halt; **~ ist Rückgang** *(prov)* if you don't go forwards, you go backwards

still+ste|hen **VI** *sep irreg aux sein or haben* **a** *(Produktion, Handel etc)* to be at a standstill; *(Fabrik, Maschine)* to be *or* stand idle; *(Verkehr)* to be stopped, to be at a standstill; *(Herz)* to have stopped; **die Zeit schien stillzustehen** time seemed to stand still *or* to stop; **alle Räder stehen still** *(fig)* everything has ground to a halt **b** *(= stehen bleiben)* to stop; *(Maschine)* to stop working; **keinen Moment ~** not to stop for a moment; **mein Herz stand still vor Schreck** I was so frightened my heart stood still

still|ver|gnügt **ADJ** contented **ADV** happily, contentedly

Still|zeit **F** lactation period

Stil-: **Stil|merk|mal** **NT** stylistic feature; **Stil|mit|tel** **NT** stylistic device; **Stil|mö|bel** **PL** period furniture *sing*; **Stil|pro|be** **F** specimen *or* sample of written work; **stil|rein** **ADJ** stylistically correct; **Stil|rich|tung** **F** style; **stil|si|cher** **ADJ** stylistically confident **ADV** **~ schreiben** to write with a good consistent style; **sich ~ ausdrücken** to be a stylistically confident speaker

Stil-: **Stil|übung** **F** exercise in stylistic composition; **stil|voll** **ADJ** *Einrichtung, Ambiente* stylish **ADV** stylishly; **stil|wid|rig** **ADJ** (stylistically) incongruous *or* inappropriate; **Stil|wör|ter|buch** **NT** dictionary of correct usage

Stimm-: **Stimm|ab|ga|be** **F** voting; **sie kommen zur ~** they come to vote *or* cast their votes; **Stimm|auf|wand** **M** vocal effort; **Stimm|band** [-bant] **NT** *pl* **-bänder** *usu pl* vocal chord; **seine Stimmbänder strapazieren** to strain one's voice; *(fig)* to talk one's head off; **stimm|be|rech|tigt** **ADJ** entitled to vote; **Stimm|be|rech|tig|te(r)** [-bərɛçtıçtə] **MF** *decl as adj* person entitled to vote; **Stimm|be|zirk** **M** constituency; **Stimm|bil|dung** **F** **a** voice production **b** *(= Ausbildung)* voice training; **Stimm|bruch** **M** = **Stimmwechsel**; **Stimm|bür|ger(in)** **M(F)** voter, elector

Stim|me [ˈʃtımə] **F -, -n** **a** voice; *(Mus: = Part)* part; *(= Orgelstimme)* register; *(fig) (= Meinungsäußerung)* voice; *(= Sprachrohr)* mouthpiece, voice; *(liter: = Ruf)* call; **mit leiser/lauter ~** in a soft/loud voice; **gut/nicht bei ~ sein** to be in good/bad voice; **erste/zweite/dritte ~** *(in Chor)* first/second/third part; **bei einem Lied die erste/zweite ~ singen** to sing the top part *or* melody of/the descant to a song; **die ~n mehren sich, die ...** there is a growing body of (public) opinion that ..., there is a growing number of people calling for ...; **die ~(n) der Glocken/Geigen** *(liter)* the sound of the bells/violins; **die ~ der Öffentlichkeit** *(geh)* public opinion; **die ~ des Volkes** *(geh)* the voice of the people; **die ~ der Wahrheit** the voice of truth; **eine ~ aus dem Dunkel/Exil** a voice out of the darkness/from exile; **der ~ der Natur folgen** *(euph hum) (= seine Notdurft verrichten)* to answer the call of nature; *(= dem Geschlechtstrieb nachgeben)* to give way to a natural urge; **der ~ des Gewissens folgen** to act on *or* according to one's conscience; **der ~ des Herzens folgen** to follow the leanings *or* dictates of one's heart; **der ~ der Vernunft folgen** to be guided by reason, to listen to the voice of reason

b *(= Wahlstimme, Votum)* vote; **eine ~ haben** to have the vote; *(= Mitspracherecht)* to have a say *or* voice; **keine ~ haben** not to be entitled to vote; *(= Mitspracherecht)* to have no say *or* voice; **seine ~ abgeben** to cast one's vote, to vote; **jdm/einer Partei seine ~ geben** to vote for sb/a party; **die abgegebenen ~n** the votes cast; **40% der ~n erhalten** to receive 40% of the vote(s) → **enthalten VR b**

stim|men [ˈʃtımən] ✪ 38.1 **VI** **a** *(= richtig sein)* to be right *or* correct; **stimmt es, dass ...?** is it true that ...?; **das stimmt nicht** that's not right, that's wrong; **hier stimmt was nicht!** there's something wrong here; **mit ihr stimmt etwas nicht** there's something wrong *or* the matter with her; **das stimmt schon, aber ...** that's true, but ...; **stimmts, oder hab ich recht?** *(hum, inf)* am I right or am I right? *(hum)*; **stimmt so!** that's all right, keep the change

b *(= zusammenpassen)* to go (together)

c *(= wählen, sich entscheiden)* to vote; **für/gegen jdn/etw ~** to vote for/against sb/sth

VT *Instrument* to tune; **etw höher/niedriger ~** to raise/lower the pitch of sth, to tune sth up/down, to sharpen/flatten sth; **jdn froh/traurig ~** to make sb (feel) cheerful/sad; **jdn gegen etw ~** *(geh)* to prejudice *or* turn sb against sth → *auch* **gestimmt**

Stim|men-: **Stim|men|aus|zäh|lung** **F** count (of votes); **Stim|men|fang** **M** *(inf)* canvassing, vote-getting *(inf)*; **auf ~ sein/gehen** to be/go canvassing; **Stim|men|ge|wirr** **NT** babble of voices; **Stim|men|gleich|heit** **F** tie, tied vote; **bei ~** in the event of a tie *or* tied vote; **Stim|men|hö|ren** **NT** *(Psych, Med)* hearing voices; **Stim|men|kauf** **M** vote-buying, buying votes; **Stim|men|mehr|heit** **F** majority (of votes); **Stim|men|split|ting** [-ʃplıtıŋ, -sp-] **NT -s,** *no pl (Pol)* splitting one's vote

Stimm|ent|hal|tung **F** abstention

Stim|men|wer|bung **F** canvassing

Stim|mer [ˈʃtımɐ] **M -s, -, Stim|me|rin** [-ərın] **F -, -nen** *(Mus)* tuner

Stimm-: **Stimm|ga|bel** **F** tuning fork; **stimm|ge|wal|tig** **ADJ** *(geh)* with a strong *or* powerful voice; **stimm|haft** *(Ling)* **ADJ** voiced **ADV** **~ ausgesprochen werden** to be voiced

stim|mig [ˈʃtımıç] **ADJ** *Umfeld* ordered; *Argumente* coherent

Stim|mig|keit **F -,** *no pl* coherence

Stimm|la|ge **F** *(Mus)* voice, register

stimm|lich [ˈʃtımlıç] **ADJ** vocal; **ihre ~en Qualitäten** the quality of her voice **ADV** **~ hat er nicht viel zu bieten** he doesn't have much of a voice; **sie hat ~ nachgelassen** the quality of her voice has declined

Stimm-: **Stimm|lis|te** **F** voting list; **stimm|los** *(Ling)* **ADJ** voiceless, unvoiced **ADV** **~ ausgesprochen werden** not to be voiced; **Stimm|-**

recht NT right to vote; **Stimm|rit|ze** F glottis; **Stimm|schlüs|sel** M *(Mus)* tuning hammer *or* key; **Stimm|um|fang** M vocal range

Stim|mung [ˈʃtɪmʊŋ] F -, -en **a** *(= Gemütszustand)* mood; *(= Atmosphäre)* atmosphere; *(bei der Truppe, unter den Arbeitern)* morale; **in (guter) ~** in a good mood; **in gehobener ~** in high spirits; **in schlechter ~** in a bad mood; **wir hatten eine tolle ~** we were in a tremendous mood; **in ~ kommen** to liven up; **für ~ sorgen** to make sure there is a good atmosphere; **in ~ sein** to be in a good mood; **ich bin nicht in der ~ zum Tanzen** I'm not in the mood for dancing; **sehr von ~en abhängig sein** to be moody, to be subject to mood swings; **~!** enjoy yourselves!, have a good time!
b *(= Meinung)* opinion; **~ gegen/für jdn/etw machen** to stir up (public) opinion against/in favour *(Brit) or* favor *(US)* of sb/sth
c *(St Ex)* mood
d *(Mus) (= das Stimmen)* tuning; *(= das Gestimmtsein)* pitch

Stim|mungs-: **Stim|mungs|ba|ro|me|ter** NT *(esp Pol)* barometer of public opinion; **Stim|mungs|bild** NT atmospheric picture; **dieser Bericht gibt ein eindrucksvolles ~** this report conveys the general atmosphere extremely well; **stim|mungs|för|dernd** ADJ **~es Mittel** anti-depressant (drug); **Stim|mungs|ka|no|ne** F *(inf)* life and soul of the party; **eine richtige ~** the life and soul of the party; **Stim|mungs|ka|pel|le** F band which plays light music; **Stim|mungs|la|ge** F atmosphere; **Stim|mungs|ma|che** F, *no pl (pej)* cheap propaganda; **Stim|mungs|mensch** M moody person; **Stim|mungs|mu|sik** F light music; **Stim|mungs|tief** NT *(auch St Ex, Econ)* depressed mood; *(einer Person)* low; **er steckt in einem ~, he's going through a low (patch)**; **Stim|mungs|um|schwung** M change of atmosphere; *(Pol)* swing (in public opinion); *(St Ex)* change in trend; **stim|mungs|voll** ADJ *Bild* idyllic; *Atmosphäre* tremendous; *Gedicht, Musikstück, Beschreibung* full of atmosphere, atmospheric; **Stim|mungs|wan|del** M, **Stim|mungs|wech|sel** M change of atmosphere; *(Pol)* change *or* shift in (public) opinion

Stimm-: **Stimm|ver|zer|rer** [-fɛɐtsɛrɐ] M -s, - voice distorter; **Stimm|vieh** NT *(pej)* gullible voters *pl*; **Stimm|volk** NT voters *pl*, electorate; **Stimm|wech|sel** M **nach dem ~** after one's voice has broken; **er ist im ~** his voice is breaking; **Stimm|werk|zeu|ge** PL vocal organs *pl*; **Stimm|zet|tel** M ballot paper

Sti|mu|lans [ˈʃtiːmulans, ˈst-] NT -, **Stimulantia** *or* **Stimulanzien** [ʃtimuˈlantsia, ʃtimuˈlantsiən, st-] *(Med, fig)* stimulant

Sti|mu|la|ti|on [ʃtimulaˈtsioːn, st-] F -, -en *(Med, fig)* stimulation

Sti|mu|li *pl von* **Stimulus**

sti|mu|lie|ren [ʃtimuˈliːrən, st-] *ptp* **stimuliert** VT *(Med, fig)* to stimulate

Sti|mu|lie|rung F -, -en *(Med, fig)* stimulation

Sti|mu|lus [ˈʃtiːmulʊs, ˈst-] M -, **Stimuli** [-li:] *(Psych)* stimulus; *(fig auch)* stimulant

Stin|ka|do|res [ʃtɪŋkaˈdoːrɛs] F -, - *(inf)* smelly cigar

Stink-: **Stink|bom|be** F stink bomb; **Stink|drü|se** F *(Zool)* scent gland

Stin|ke|fin|ger M *(inf)* finger *(inf) (held up as rude gesture)*, bird *(US inf)*; **jdm den ~ zeigen** to give sb the finger *(inf) or* the bird *(US inf)*

stin|ken [ˈʃtɪŋkn] *pret* **stank** [ʃtaŋk], *ptp* **gestunken** [gəˈʃtʊŋkn] VI **a** *(nach* of) to stink, to reek, to pong *(Brit inf)*; **er stinkt nach Kneipe** he smells of drink; **wie ein Bock** *or* **Wiedehopf** *or* **eine Wachtel** *or* **die Pest ~** *(inf)* to stink to high heaven *(inf)*
b *(fig inf)* **er stinkt nach Geld** he's stinking rich *(inf)*; **er stinkt vor Faulheit** he's bone idle; **das stinkt zum Himmel** it's an absolute scandal, it's absolutely appalling; **an der Sache stinkt etwas** there's something fishy about it *(inf)*; **das stinkt nach Verrat** that smells of treachery; **die Sache stinkt mir** *(inf)*, **mir stinkts (gewaltig)!** *(inf)* I'm fed up to the back teeth (with it) *(Brit inf) or* to the back of my throat (with it) *(US inf)*

stin|kend ADJ stinking, foul-smelling

stink|faul ADJ *(inf)* bone idle *(Brit)*, extremely lazy

stin|kig [ˈʃtɪŋkɪç] ADJ *(inf)* stinking *(inf)*; *(= verärgert)* pissed off *(sl)*

Stink-: **stink|lang|wei|lig** ADJ *(inf)* deadly boring *or* dull; **Stink|lau|ne** F *(inf)* stinking *(inf) or* foul mood; **Stink|mor|chel** F *(Bot)* stinkhorn; **stink|nor|mal** ADJ *(inf)* boringly normal *or* ordinary; **stink|reich** ADJ *(inf)* stinking rich *(Brit inf)*, rolling in it *(inf)*; **stink|sau|er** ADJ *(sl)* pissed off *(inf)*; **Stink|stie|bel** [ˈʃtɪŋkʃtiːbl] M -s, - *(dial, inf)*, **Stink|stie|fel** M *(inf)* stinking pig *(inf)*; *(hum: = Kumpel)* mate *(inf)*; **Stink|tier** NT skunk; **stink|vor|nehm** *(inf)* ADJ posh *(inf)*, swanky *(inf)*; *Lokal* posh *(inf)*, swish *(Brit inf)* ADV *speisen, wohnen* regally; **sie tut so ~** she acts so posh *(inf)*; **Stink|wut** F *(inf)* raging temper; **eine ~ (auf jdn) haben** to be livid (with sb)

Stint [ʃtɪnt] M -(e)s, -e *(Zool)* smelt, sparling

Sti|pen|di|at [ʃtipɛnˈdiaːt] M -en, -en, **Sti|pen|di|a|tin** [-ˈdiaːtɪn] F -, -nen → **Stipendium** scholarship holder, person receiving a scholarship/grant

Sti|pen|di|um [ʃtiˈpɛndiʊm] NT -s, **Stipendien** [-diən] *(als Auszeichnung etc erhalten)* scholarship; *(zur allgemeinen Unterstützung des Studiums)* grant

Stip|pe [ˈʃtɪpə] F -, -n *(dial)* sauce

stip|pen [ˈʃtɪpn] VTI *(dial)* to dip, to dunk

Stipp|vi|si|te [ˈʃtɪp-] F *(inf)* flying visit

Sti|pu|la|ti|on [ʃtipulaˈtsioːn, st-] F -, -en *(Jur)* stipulation

sti|pu|lie|ren [ʃtipuˈliːrən, st-] *ptp* **stipuliert** VT to stipulate; **von Arbeitgeberseite wurden neue Verhandlungen stipuliert** the employers insisted on new talks

stirbt [ʃtɪrpt] *3. pers sing pres von* **sterben**

Stirn [ʃtɪrn] F -, -en forehead, brow *(esp liter)*; **die ~ runzeln** to wrinkle one's brow; **sich/jdm das Haar aus der ~ streichen** to brush one's/sb's hair out of one's/his/her face; **den Hut in die ~ drücken** to pull one's hat down over one's eyes; **es steht ihm auf der ~ geschrieben** it is written all over his face; **die ~ haben** *or* **besitzen, zu ...** to have the effrontery *or* nerve *or* gall to ...; **jdm/einer Sache die ~ bieten** *(geh)* to stand up to sb/sth, to defy sb/sth → **eisern ADJ b**

Stirn-: **Stirn|ader** F vein in the/one's temple; **Stirn|au|ge** NT *(Zool)* ocellus; **Stirn|band** [-bant] NT *pl* **-bänder** headband; **Stirn|bein** NT frontal bone; **Stirn|fal|te** F wrinkle (on one's forehead); **Stirn|glat|ze** F receding hairline; **Stirn|höh|le** F frontal sinus; **Stirn|höh|len|ka|tarr(h)** M, **Stirn|höh|len|ver|ei|te|rung** F sinusitis; **Stirn|la|ge** F *(Med)* brow presentation; **Stirn|lo|cke** F quiff *(Brit)*, cowlick; **Stirn|rad** NT *(Tech)* spur wheel; **Stirn|re|flek|tor** M *(Med)* forehead mirror; **Stirn|rie|men** M brow band; **Stirn|run|zeln** NT -s, *no pl* frown; **Stirn|sei|te** F end wall, gable end; **Stirn|spie|gel** M *(Med)* forehead mirror; **Stirn|wand** F end wall

Stoa [ˈʃtoːa, ˈst-] F -, *no pl (Philos)* Stoics *pl*, Stoic school

stob *pret von* **stieben**

stö|bern [ˈʃtøːbɐn] VI to rummage *(in +dat* in, *durch* through)

Sto|cher|kahn M punt

sto|chern [ˈʃtɔxɐn] VI to poke *(in +dat* at); *(im Essen)* to pick *(in +dat* at); **er stocherte mit einem Schürhaken im Feuer** he poked the fire; **sich** *(dat)* **in den Zähnen ~** to pick one's teeth

Stock [ʃtɔk] M -(e)s, **=e** [ˈʃtœkə] **a** stick; *(= Rohrstock)* cane; *(= Taktstock)* baton; *(= Zeigestock)* pointer; *(= Billardstock)* cue; **er stand da (steif) wie ein ~** *or* **als ob er einen ~ verschluckt hätte** he stood there as stiff as a poker; **am ~ gehen** to walk with (the aid of) a stick; *(fig inf)* to be in a bad way *or* in bad shape; *(nach viel Arbeit)* to be dead beat *(Brit inf) or* dead *(US inf)*; *(finanziell)* to be in difficulties; **~ und Hut** *(dated)* hat and stick
b *(= Wurzelstock)* roots *pl*; **über ~ und Stein** up hill and down dale *(Brit)*, over stick and stone *(US)*
c *(Pflanze) (= Rebstock)* vine; *(= Rosenstock)* rose bush; *(Bäumchen)* rose tree; *(= Blumenstock)* pot plant
d *(= Bienenstock)* hive
e *(Geol: = Gesteinsmasse)* massif, rock mass
f *(Hist)* stocks *pl*; **jdn in den ~ legen** to put sb in the stocks
g *pl* - *(= Stockwerk)* floor, storey *(Brit)*, story *(US)*; **das Haus hat drei ~** *or* **ist drei ~ hoch** the house is three storeys *(Brit) or* three stories *(US)* high; **im ersten ~** on the first floor *(Brit)*, on the second floor *(US)*
h *(Sw: = Kartoffelbrei)* mashed potato(es *pl*)

Stock [stɔk] M -s, -s *(Econ)* stock

Stock-: **stock|be|sof|fen**, **stock|be|trun|ken** ADJ *(inf)* dead drunk *(inf)*, plastered *(inf)*; **ein Stockbesoffener** a drunk; **Stock|bett** NT bunk bed; **stock|blind** ADJ *(inf)* as blind as a bat, completely blind

Stöck|chen [ˈʃtœkçən] NT -s, - *dim von* **Stock a, c**

stock-: **stock|dumm** ADJ *(inf)* thick (as two short planks) *(Brit inf)*, dumb as a doorknob *(US inf)*; **stock|dun|kel** ADJ *(inf)* pitch-dark; **im Stockdunkeln** in the pitch dark

Stö|ckel [ˈʃtœkl] M -s, - *(inf)* stiletto

Stö|ckel NT -s, - *(Aus)* outhouse, outbuilding

Stö|ckel|ab|satz M stiletto heel

stö|ckeln [ˈʃtœkln] VI *aux sein (inf)* to trip, to mince

Stö|ckel|schuh M stiletto, stiletto-heeled shoe

sto|cken [ˈʃtɔkn] VI **a** *(Herz, Puls)* to miss *or* skip a beat; *(Gedanken, Worte)* to falter; *(= nicht vorangehen) (Arbeit, Entwicklung)* to make no progress; *(Unterhaltung, Gespräch)* to flag; *(Verhandlungen)* to grind to a halt; *(Konjunktur, Geschäfte, Handel)* to stagnate; *(Verkehr)* to be held up *or* halted; **ihm stockte das Herz/der Puls** his heart/pulse missed *or* skipped a beat; **ihm stockte der Atem** he caught his breath; **ins Stocken geraten** *or* **kommen** *(Unterhaltung, Gespräch)* to begin to flag; *(Entwicklung)* to make no progress; *(Verhandlungen)* to grind to a halt; *(Konjunktur etc)* to stagnate
b *(= innehalten) (in der Rede)* to falter; *(im Satz)* to break off, to stop short; **ihre Stimme stockte** she *or* her voice faltered
c *(= gerinnen) (Blut)* to thicken; *(S Ger, Aus: Milch)* to curdle, to go sour; **das Blut stockte ihm in den Adern** *(geh)* the blood froze in his veins
d *(= stockig werden) (Wäsche, Papier, Bücher)* to become mildewed, to go mouldy *(Brit) or* moldy *(US)*

sto|ckend ADJ *Stimme, Deutsch* faltering, hesitant; *Konjunktur, Verhandlungen* faltering; *Verkehr* stop-go ADV *sprechen* haltingly; **der Verkehr kam nur ~ voran** traffic was stop and go

Stock|en|te F mallard

Stock-: **stock|fins|ter** ADJ *(inf)* pitch-dark, pitch-black; **Stock|fisch** M dried cod; *(pej: Mensch)* dull old stick *(Brit)*, stick-in-the-mud *(pej inf)*; **Stock|fleck** M *mark caused by mould or mildew*; **stock|fle|ckig** ADJ mouldy *(Brit)*, moldy *(US)*, mildewed; **Stock|haus** NT *(Hist)* gaol; **Stock|hieb** M blow (from a stick); *(mit Rohrstock)* stroke of the cane

Stock|holm [ˈʃtɔkhɔlm] NT -s Stockholm

Stock|hol|mer [ˈʃtɔkhɔlmɐ] ADJ Stockholm *attr*

Stock|hol|mer [ˈʃtɔkhɔlmɐ] M **-s, -**, **Stock|hol|me|rin** [-ərɪn] F **-, -nen** native of Stockholm; *(Einwohner)* inhabitant of Stockholm

sto|ckig [ˈʃtɔkɪç] ADJ *Geruch, Luft* musty; *Papier, Wäsche* mildewed, mouldy *(Brit)*, moldy *(US)*

-stö|ckig [ʃtœkɪç] ADJ *suf* -storey *attr (Brit)*, -storeyed *(Brit)*, -story *attr (US)*, -storied *(US)*; **ein zweistöckiges Haus** a two-stor(e)y house

Stock-: **stock|ka|tho|lisch** ADJ *(inf)* Catholic through and through; **stock|kon|ser|va|tiv** ADJ *(inf)* archconservative; **stock|nüch|tern** ADJ *(inf)* stone-cold sober *(inf)*; **stock|sau|er** ADJ *(inf)* pissed off *(inf)*; **Stock|schirm** M walking-length umbrella; **Stock|schlag** M blow (from a stick); *(mit Rohrstock)* stroke of the cane; **Stock|schnup|fen** M permanent cold; **stock|steif** *(inf)* ADJ as stiff as a poker ADV as stiff as a statue; **sie bewegt sich ~** she moves very stiffly; **stock|taub** ADJ *(inf)* as deaf as a post

Sto|ckung [ˈʃtɔkʊŋ] F **-, -en** **a** *(= vorübergehender Stillstand)* interruption, holdup *(+gen, in +dat* in); *(= Verkehrsstockung)* congestion, traffic jam, hold-up; **der Verkehr läuft wieder ohne ~en** traffic is flowing smoothly again **b** *(von Verhandlungen)* breakdown *(+gen* of, in); *(von Geschäften, Handel)* slackening *or* dropping off *(+gen* in) **c** *(= Pause, Unterbrechung) (im Gespräch)* break, lull; *(in der Rede)* pause, hesitation **d** *(= Gerinnung)* thickening; *(von Milch)* curdling

Stock|werk NT floor, storey *(Brit)*, story *(US)*; **im 5. ~** on the 5th *(Brit) or* 6th *(US)* floor; **ein Haus mit vier ~en** a four-storeyed *(Brit) or* four-storied *(US)* building

Stock|zahn M *(Aus)* molar (tooth)

Stoff [ʃtɔf] M **-(e)s, -e** **a** material, fabric; *(als Materialart)* cloth
b *(no pl: = Materie)* matter; **~ und Form** *(Philos)* matter and form
c *(= Substanz, Chem)* substance; *(= Papierstoff)* pulp; **tierische ~e** animal substance; **pflanzliche ~e** vegetable matter; **radioaktive ~e** radioactive substances; **aus härterem ~ gemacht sein** *(fig)* to be made of sterner stuff
d *(= Gegenstand, Thema)* subject (matter); *(= Unterhaltungsstoff, Diskussionsstoff)* topic, subject; *(= Material)* material; **~ für ein** *or* **zu einem Buch sammeln** to collect material for a book; **der Vortrag bot reichlich ~ für eine Diskussion** the lecture provided plenty of material or topics for discussion; **~ zum Lesen** reading matter; **~ zum Nachdenken** food for thought
e *(inf: = Rauschgift)* dope *(inf)*, stuff *(inf)*

Stoff-: **Stoff|bahn** F length of material; **Stoff|bal|len** M roll *or* bolt of material *or* cloth; **stoff|be|spannt** [-bəʃpant] ADJ fabric-covered

Stof|fel [ˈʃtɔfl] M **-s, -** *(pej inf)* lout *(inf)*, boor

stof|fe|lig [ˈʃtɔfəlɪç] *(pej inf)* ADJ uncouth, boorish ADV *sich benehmen* uncouthly

Stoff-: **Stoff|fet|zen** M scrap of cloth; **Stoff|fül|le** F wealth of material; **Stoff|ge|biet** NT *(Sch)* subject area; **Stoff|hand|schuh** M fabric glove

stoff|lich [ˈʃtɔflɪç] ADJ **a** *(Philos, Chem)* material; **~e Verwertung** use of materials **b** *(= den Inhalt betreffend)* as regards subject matter ADV **a** *(Chem)* **etw ~ (wieder)verwerten** to (re)use the materials in sth **b** *(von der Materie her)* **ein ~ hochinteressanter Bericht** a report with a very interesting subject matter

Stoff|lich|keit F **-**, *no pl (Philos)* materiality

stoff|lig ADJ ADV *(pej inf)* = **stoffelig**

Stoff-: **Stoff|pup|pe** F rag doll; **Stoff|rest** M remnant; **Stoff|samm|lung** F *(zu einem Buch etc)* gathering of material; **Stoff|tier** NT soft toy

Stoffülle △ F → **Stofffülle**

Stoff|wahl F choice of subject

Stoff|wech|sel M metabolism

Stoff|wech|sel-: **Stoff|wech|sel|krank|heit** F metabolic disease *or* disorder; **Stoff|wech|sel|stö|rung** F metabolic disturbance

Stoff|zu|ga|be F extra material

stöh|nen [ˈʃtøːnən] VI to groan; *(= klagen auch)* to moan; **~d** with a groan

Stöh|nen NT **-s**, *no pl (lit, fig)* groaning *no pl*; *(= Stöhnlaut)* groan

Sto|i|ker [ˈʃtoːikɐ, st-] M **-s, -**, **Sto|i|ke|rin** [-ərɪn] F **-, -nen** *(Philos)* Stoic (philosopher); *(fig)* stoic

sto|isch [ˈʃtoːɪʃ, st-] ADJ *(Philos)* Stoic; *(fig)* stoic(al) ADV *(fig)* stoically

Sto|i|zis|mus [ʃtoiˈtsɪsmʊs, st-] M **-**, *no pl (Philos)* Stoicism; *(fig)* stoicism

Sto|la [ˈʃtoːla, ˈst-] F **-, Stolen** [-lən] stole

Stol|le [ˈʃtɔlə] F **-, -n** *(Cook)* fruit loaf *(eaten at Christmas)*, stollen

Stol|len [ˈʃtɔlən] M **-s, -** **a** *(Min, Mil)* gallery, tunnel **b** *(Cook)* fruit loaf *(eaten at Christmas)*, stollen **c** *(= Zapfen) (an Hufeisen)* calk(in); *(= Schuhstollen)* stud **d** *(Poet)* stollen, *one of the two equal sections forming the "Aufgesang" in "Minnesang"*

> **STOLLEN**
>
> **Stollen**, or **Christstollen**, is a baked Christmas loaf made from a heavy yeast dough mixed with a lot of butter, dried fruit and almonds. There are also varieties which use marzipan or quark. The best-known **Stollen** comes from Dresden, where it has been baked since the early Middle Ages.

Stol|per|draht M tripwire; *(fig)* stumbling block

stol|pe|rig [ˈʃtɔlpərɪç] ADJ *Gang* stumbling; *Weg* uneven, bumpy

stol|pern [ˈʃtɔlpɐn] VI *aux sein* to stumble, to trip *(über +acc* over); *(fig: = zu Fall kommen)* to come a cropper *(Brit inf)*, to fall flat on one's face *(inf)*, to come unstuck *(esp Brit inf)*; **ins Stolpern geraten** *or* **kommen** to come a cropper *(Brit inf)*, to fall flat on one's face *(inf)*; *(fig auch)* to slip up; **jdn zum Stolpern bringen** *(lit)* to trip sb up, to make sb trip; *(fig)* to be sb's downfall; **über einen Hinweis ~** *(fig)* to stumble upon a clue; **über einen Bekannten ~** *(fig)* to bump *or* run into an acquaintance; **über einen Strohhalm ~** *(fig)* to come to grief over a trifle

Stol|per|stein M *(fig)* stumbling block

stolp|rig [ˈʃtɔlprɪç] ADJ = **stolperig**

stolz [ʃtɔlts] ADJ **a** proud *(auf +acc* of); **~ wie ein Pfau** as proud as a peacock; **warum so ~?** why so proud?; *(bei Begegnung)* don't you know me any more?; **darauf kannst du ~ sein** that's something to be proud of; **der ~e Besitzer** the proud owner **b** *(= imposant) Bauwerk, Schiff* majestic, impressive; *(iro: = stattlich) Preis, Summe* princely ADV proudly; **~ erhebt sich die Burg über der kleinen Stadt** the castle rises proudly above the little town

Stolz [ʃtɔlts] M **-es**, *no pl* pride; **sein Garten/Sohn** *etc* **ist sein ganzer ~** his garden/son *etc* is his pride and joy; **voller ~ auf etw** *(acc)* **sein** to be very proud of sth; **ich habe auch meinen ~** I do have my pride; **aus falschem/verletztem ~ handeln** to act out of false/wounded pride; **seinen ~ in etw** *(acc)* **setzen** to take a pride in sth

stol|zie|ren [ʃtɔlˈtsiːrən] *ptp* **stolziert** VI *aux sein* to strut, to swagger; *(hochmütig, beleidigt)* to stalk

stop [ʃtɔp, st-] INTERJ stop; *(auf Verkehrsschild auch)* halt *(esp Brit)*

Stop-and-go-Ver|kehr [stɔpəndˈgoː-] M stop-and-go traffic, slow-moving traffic

Stopf-: **Stopf|büch|se** F, **Stopf|buch|se** F *(Tech)* stuffing box; **Stopf|ei** [ˈʃtɔpflai] NT ≈ darning mushroom

stop|fen [ˈʃtɔpfn] VT **a** *(= ausstopfen, füllen)* to stuff; *Pfeife, Loch, Wurst* to fill; *(inf) Taschen* to stuff, to cram; **jdm den Mund** *(inf) or* **das Maul** *(inf)* **~** to silence sb
b *(= hineinstopfen)* to stuff; *Korken auch* to ram; **sich** *(dat)* **Watte in die Ohren ~** to plug one's ears with cotton wool *(Brit) or* cotton *(US)*, to put cotton-wool *(Brit) or* cotton *(US)* plugs in one's ears; **gierig stopfte er alles in sich hinein, was man ihm auftischte** he greedily stuffed down everything they served up
c *(= verstopfen) Trompete etc* to mute; *(mit Stöpsel)* to plug, to stop
d *(= ausbessern, flicken) Loch, Strümpfe etc* to darn, to mend; *(fig) Haushaltslöcher etc* to plug → *auch* **gestopft**
VI **a** *(Speisen) (= verstopfen)* to cause constipation, to constipate; *(= sättigen)* to be filling
b *(inf: = gierig essen)* to bolt *or* wolf (down) one's food, to stuff oneself *(inf)*
c *(= flicken)* to darn, to do darning

Stop|fen [ˈʃtɔpfn] M **-s, -** *(dial)* stopper; *(= Korken)* cork

Stop|fer [ˈʃtɔpfɐ] M **-s, -** *(= Pfeifenstopfer)* tamper

Stopf-: **Stopf|garn** NT darning cotton *or* thread; **Stopf|na|del** F darning needle; **Stopf|pilz** M *(Sew)* darning mushroom

stopp [ʃtɔp] INTERJ stop

Stopp [ʃtɔp] M **-s, -s** stop, halt; *(= Lohnstopp)* freeze

Stopp|ball M *(Tennis etc)* dropshot

Stop|pel [ˈʃtɔpl] F **-, -n** *(= Getreidestoppel, Bartstoppel)* stubble

Stop|pel M **-s, -** *(Aus)* = **Stöpsel**

Stop|pel-: **Stop|pel|bart** M stubbly beard, stubble; **Stop|pel|feld** NT stubble field; **Stop|pel|haar** NT bristly hair

stop|pe|lig [ˈʃtɔpəlɪç] ADJ *Bart* stubbly; *Kinn auch* bristly

stop|pen [ˈʃtɔpn] VT **a** *(= anhalten, aufhalten)* to stop; *(Ftbl) Ball* to trap, to stop **b** *(= Zeit abnehmen)* to time; **er hat die Laufzeit/Zeit genau gestoppt** he timed exactly how long it took VI **a** *(= anhalten)* to stop **b** **ihr beide lauft und ich stoppe** you two run and I'll time you

Stop|per [ˈʃtɔpɐ] M **-s, -** **a** *(Naut)* stopper **b** *(an Gardinenstange)* curtain stop, end piece

Stop|per [ˈʃtɔpɐ] M **-s, -**, **Stop|pe|rin** [-ərɪn] F **-, -nen** **a** *(Ftbl)* centre *(Brit) or* center *(US)* half **b** *(= Zeitnehmer)* timekeeper

Stopp|licht NT stoplight, red light; *(Aut)* brake light

stopp|lig [ˈʃtɔplɪç] ADJ = **stoppelig**

Stopp-: **Stopp|schild** NT *pl* **-schilder** stop *or* halt *(esp Brit)* sign; **Stopp|stra|ße** F *road with stop signs*, secondary road, stop street *(US)*; **Stopp|uhr** F stopwatch

Stop|sel [ˈʃtɔpsl] M **-s, -** *(Aus)* stopper; *(= Korken)* cork

Stöp|sel [ˈʃtœpsl] M **-s, -** *(von Waschbecken, Badewanne etc)* plug; *(Telec auch)* jack; *(= Pfropfen)* stopper; *(= Korken)* cork; *(inf: = Knirps)* little fellow

stöp|seln [ˈʃtœpsln] VTI *(Telec)* to connect

Stop|sel|zie|her [-tsiːɐ] M **-s, -** *(Aus)* corkscrew

Stör [ʃtøːɐ] M **-(e)s, -e** *(Zool)* sturgeon

Stör F *(Aus)* **in** *or* **auf die ~ gehen** to work at the customer's home

Stör-: **Stör|ak|ti|on** F disruptive action *no pl*; **stör|an|fäl|lig** ADJ *Technik, Bauteil, Kraftwerk* susceptible to faults; *Gerät, Verkehrsmittel* liable to break down; *Zündung, Lenkung etc* unreliable; *(fig) Verhältnis* shaky; **Stör|an|fäl|lig|keit** F *(von Technik, Bauteil, Kraftwerk)* susceptibility to faults; *(von Gerät, Verkehrsmittel)* liability to break down; *(von Zündung, Lenkung etc)* unreliability; *(fig: von Verhältnis)* shakiness

Storch [ʃtɔrç] M **-(e)s, ⸗e** [ˈʃtœrçə] stork; **wie der ~ im Salat gehen** *(inf)* to pick one's way carefully; **der ~ hat sie ins Bein gebissen** *(dated hum)* she's expecting a little stranger *(hum)*

Stor|chen|nest NT stork's nest

Stör|chin [ˈʃtœrçɪn] F **-, -nen** female stork

Storch|schna|bel M **a** *(Bot)* cranesbill **b** *(Tech)* pantograph

Store [ʃtoːɐ, stoːɐ] M **-s, -s** *usu pl* net curtain; *(Sw)* shutters *pl*

stö|ren [ˈʃtøːrən] ✪ 27.7, 36.1 VT **a** *(= beeinträchtigen) Schlaf, öffentliche Ordnung, Frieden etc* to disturb; *Verhältnis, Harmonie, Gesamteindruck etc* to spoil; *Rundfunkempfang* to interfere with; *(absichtlich)* to jam; **jds Pläne ~** to interfere with sb's plans → *auch* **gestört**
b *Handlungsablauf, Prozess, Vorlesung, Feier* to disrupt
c *(= unangenehm berühren)* to disturb, to bother; **was mich an ihm/daran stört** what I don't like about him/it; **entschuldigen Sie, wenn ich Sie störe** I'm sorry to bother you, I'm sorry if I'm disturbing you; **störe mich jetzt nicht!** don't bother *or* disturb me now!; **lassen Sie sich nicht ~!** don't let me disturb you, don't mind me; **stört es Sie, wenn ich rauche?** do you mind if I smoke?, does it bother you if I smoke?; **würden Sie bitte aufhören zu rauchen, es stört mich** would you mind not smoking, I find it annoying; **das stört mich nicht** that doesn't bother me, I don't mind; **sie stört uns nicht** she doesn't bother us, we don't mind her; **sie lässt sich durch nichts ~** she doesn't let anything bother her
VR **sich an etw** *(dat)* **~** to be bothered about sth; **ich störe mich an seiner Unpünktlichkeit** I take exception to his unpunctuality
VI **a** *(= lästig sein, im Weg sein)* to get in the way; *(= unterbrechen)* to interrupt; *(= Belästigung darstellen: Musik, Lärm etc)* to be disturbing; **bitte nicht ~!** please do not disturb!; **ich möchte nicht ~** I don't want to be in the way *or* to be a nuisance, I don't want to interrupt; *(in Privatsphäre etc)* I don't want to intrude; **störe ich?** am I disturbing you?; **wenn ich nicht störe** if I'm not in the way, if I'm not disturbing you; **stört das sehr, wenn ich jetzt fernsehe?** would it disturb you if I watch television?; **etw als ~d empfinden** to find sth bothersome; **sich ~d bemerkbar machen** to be all too noticeable *or* obvious; **ein ~der Lärm** a disturbing noise; **ein ~der Umstand** a nuisance, an annoyance; **eine ~de Begleiterscheinung** a troublesome side effect; **ein ~der Besucher** an unwelcome visitor
b *(= unangenehm auffallen)* to spoil the effect, to stick out; **ein hübsches Gesicht, aber die große Nase stört doch etwas** a pretty face, though the big nose does spoil the effect

Stö|ren|fried [-friːt] M **-(e)s, -e** [-də], **Stö|rer** [ˈʃtøːrɐ] M **-s, -**, **Stö|re|rin** [-ərɪn] F **-, -nen** troublemaker

Stör-: **Stör|fak|tor** M source of friction, disruptive factor; **Stör|fall** M *(in Kernkraftwerk etc)* malfunction, accident; **stör|frei** ADJ free from interference; **Stör|ge|räusch** NT *(Rad, TV)* interference; **Stör|ma|nö|ver** NT disruptive action

Stor|ni *pl von* **Storno**

stor|nie|ren [ʃtɔrˈniːrən, st-] ✪ 47.4, 48.3 *ptp* **storniert** VTI *(Comm) Auftrag, Reise, Flug* to cancel; *Buchungsfehler* to reverse

Stor|no [ˈʃtɔrno, ˈst-] M OR NT **-s, Storni** [-ni] *(Comm) (von Buchungsfehler)* reversal; *(von Auftrag)* cancellation

Stor|no|ge|bühr F *(Comm)* cancellation fee *or* charge

stör|risch [ˈʃtœrɪʃ], **störrig** *(rare)* [ˈʃtœrɪç] ADJ stubborn, obstinate; *Kind* unmanageable, disobedient; *Pferd* restive, refractory; *Haare* unmanageable → **Esel** ADV **sich ~ verhalten** *or* **anstellen** to act stubborn

Stör|sen|der M *(Rad)* jamming transmitter, jammer

Stö|rung [ˈʃtøːrʊŋ] F **-, -en a** disturbance
b *(von Ablauf, Verhandlungen etc)* disruption; **die Demonstranten beschlossen die ~ der Parlamentssitzung** the demonstrators decided to disrupt the parliamentary session
c *(= Verkehrsstörung)* holdup; **es kam immer wieder zu ~en des Verkehrs** there were continual holdups (in the traffic), the traffic was continually held up
d *(Tech)* fault, trouble *no indef art*; **eine ~** trouble, a fault; **in der Leitung muss eine ~ sein** there must be a fault on the line
e *(Astron)* perturbation
f *(Met)* disturbance
g *(Rad)* interference; *(absichtlich)* jamming; **atmosphärische ~en** atmospherics *pl*
h *(Med)* disorder; **gesundheitliche/psychische ~en** physical/mental disorders; **nervöse ~en** nervous disorders, nervous trouble

Stö|rungs-: **Stö|rungs|an|zei|ge** F fault indicator; **Stö|rungs|feu|er** NT *(Mil)* harassing fire; **stö|rungs|frei** ADJ trouble-free; *(Rad)* free from interference; **der Verkehr ist** *or* **läuft wieder ~** the traffic is moving freely again; **Stö|rungs|stel|le** F *(Telec)* faults service

Sto|ry [ˈstoːri, ˈstɔri] F **-, -s** story; *(inf: von Verkäufer etc)* spiel *(inf)*

Stoß [ʃtoːs] M **-es, ⸚e** [ˈʃtøːsə] **a** push, shove *(inf)*; *(leicht)* poke; *(mit Faust)* punch; *(mit Fuß)* kick; *(mit Ellbogen)* nudge, dig; *(mit Kopf, Hörnern)* butt; *(= Dolchstoß etc)* stab, thrust; *(Kugelstoßen)* put, throw; *(Fechten)* thrust; *(= Schwimmstoß)* stroke; *(= Atemstoß)* gasp; *(= Koitusbewegung)* thrust; **einen ~ vertragen können** *(lit, fig)* to be able to take a knock (or two); **sich** *(dat)* *or* **seinem Herzen einen ~ geben** to pluck up *or* take courage; **das gab ihm den letzten ~** *(fig)* that was the last straw *or* final blow (for him)
b *(= Anprall)* impact; *(= Erdstoß)* tremor; *(eines Wagens)* jolt, bump
c *(Med)* intensive course of drugs
d *(= Stapel)* pile, stack
e *(Rail: = Schienenstoß)* (rail) joint
f *(Sew: = Stoßband)* selvage; *(Tech: = Kante)* butt joint; **auf ~** edge to edge
g *(Mil: = Feuerstoß)* volley, burst of fire; *(Mil: = Angriff)* strike; *(= Trompetenstoß etc)* blast, blow (in *+acc* on)
h *(Min)* stope, face
i *(Hunt)* tail feathers *pl*

Stoß-: **stoß|ar|tig** ADJ *Bewegung, Fahrt* jerky; *Lachen* staccato; *(= spasmodisch)* spasmodic ADV *fahren* in starts and stops; *sich fortbewegen* jerkily; **~ atmen** to gasp for breath; **Stoß|band** [-bant] NT *pl* **-bänder** *(Sew)* selvage; **Stoß|dämp|fer** M *(Aut)* shock absorber; **stoß|emp|find|lich** ADJ susceptible *or* sensitive to shock; *Obst* easily damaged; **diese Uhr ist ~** this watch is not shockproof

Stö|ßel [ˈʃtøːsl] M **-s, -** pestle; *(Aut: = Ventilstößel)* tappet

sto|ßen [ˈʃtoːsn] *pret* **stieß** [ʃtiːs], *ptp* **gestoßen** [gəˈʃtoːsn] VT **a** *(= einen Stoß versetzen)* to push, to shove *(inf)*; *(leicht)* to poke; *(mit Faust)* to punch; *(mit Fuß)* to kick; *(mit Ellbogen)* to nudge, to dig *(Brit)*, to poke; *(mit Kopf, Hörnern)* to butt; *(= stechen) Dolch* to plunge, to thrust; *(vulg)* to fuck *(vulg)*, to shag *(Brit sl)*, to poke *(sl)*; **sich** *(dat)* **den Kopf** *etc or* **sich** *(acc)* **an den Kopf** *etc* **~** to hit one's head *etc*; **jdm** *or* **jdn in die Seite ~** to nudge sb, to dig *(Brit) or* poke sb in the ribs; **jdn von sich ~** to push sb away; *(fig)* to cast sb aside; **jdn/etw zur Seite ~** to push sb/sth aside; *(mit Fuß)* to kick sb/sth aside *or* to one side; **er stieß den Ball mit dem Kopf ins Tor** he headed the ball into the goal *(Brit)*, he hit the ball into the goal with his head; **ein Loch ins Eis ~** to make *or* bore a hole in the ice
b *(= werfen)* to push; *(Sport) Kugel* to put; **jdn von der Treppe/aus dem Zug ~** to push sb down the stairs/out of *or* off the train; **jdn aus dem Haus ~** *(fig)* to throw *or* turn sb out (of the house); **jdn ins Elend ~** *(liter)* to plunge sb into misery
c *(= zerkleinern) Zimt, Pfeffer, Zucker* to pound
d *(Sw: = schieben, drücken)* to push
VR to bump *or* bang *or* knock oneself; **sich an etw** *(dat)* **~** *(lit)* to bump *etc* oneself on *or* against sth; *(fig)* to take exception to sth, to disapprove of sth; **er stößt sich daran, wenn Männer Ohrringe tragen** he takes exception to men wearing earrings
VI **a** *aux sein (= treffen, prallen)* to run *or* bump into *(auch fig)*; *(= herabstoßen: Vogel)* to swoop down *(auf +acc* on); **an etw** *(acc)* **~** to bump into *or* hit sth; *(= grenzen)* to border on sth; **gegen etw ~** to run into sth; **zu jdm ~** to meet up with sb, to join sb; **auf jdn ~** to bump *or* run into sb; **auf etw** *(acc)* **~** *(Straße)* to lead into *or* onto sth; *(Schiff)* to hit sth, to run into *or* against sth; *(fig: = entdecken)* to come upon *or* across sth; **auf Erdöl ~** to strike oil; **auf Grundwasser ~** to discover underground water; **auf Widerstand ~** to meet with *or* encounter resistance; **auf Ablehnung/Zustimmung ~** to meet with disapproval/approval; **an seine Grenzen ~** to reach one's limits
b *(mit den Hörnern)* to butt *(nach* at)
c *(Tech)* to butt *(an +acc* against)
d *(Gewichtheben)* to jerk
e *(old: = blasen)* to blow, to sound → **Horn b**

Stoß-: **stoß|fest** ADJ shockproof; **Stoß|ge|bet** NT quick prayer; **ein ~ zum Himmel schicken** to say a quick prayer; **Stoß|ge|schäft** NT business with short periods of peak activity; *(= Saisonarbeit)* seasonal business; **Stoß|kar|ret|te** F *(Sw: = Schubkarre)* wheelbarrow; **Stoß|kraft** F force; *(von Aufprall)* impact; *(Mil)* combat strength; **Stoß|rich|tung** F *(Mil, fig)* thrust; **die ~ seines Angriffs ging auf ...** *(fig)* the main thrust of his attack was aimed at ...; **Stoß|seuf|zer** M deep sigh; **stoß|si|cher** ADJ shockproof; **Stoß|stan|ge** F *(Aut)* bumper

stößt [ʃtøːst] *3. pers sing pres von* **stoßen**

Stoß-: **Stoß|the|ra|pie** F *(Med)* intensive course of drug treatment; **Stoß|trupp** M *(Mil)* raiding party; **Stoß|ver|kehr** M rush-hour (traffic); **Stoß|waf|fe** F thrust weapon; **stoß|wei|se** ADV **a** *(= ruckartig)* spasmodically, by fits and starts; **~ atmen** to pant; **die Autoschlange bewegte sich ~ vorwärts** the line of cars moved forward by fits and starts **b** *(= stapelweise)* by the pile; **Stoß|zahl** F *(Phys)* impact coefficient; **Stoß|zahn** M tusk; **Stoß|zeit** F *(im Verkehr)* rush hour; *(in Geschäft etc)* peak period, busy time

Stot|te|rei [ʃtɔtəˈrai] F **-, -en** *(inf)* stuttering; *(fig)* stuttering and stammering

Stot|te|rer [ˈʃtɔtərɐ] M **-s, -**, **Stot|te|rin** [-ərɪn] F **-, -nen** stutterer

stot|tern [ˈʃtɔtɐn] VTI to stutter; *(Motor)* to splutter; **leicht/stark ~** to have a slight/bad stutter, to stutter slightly/badly; **ins Stottern kommen** to start stuttering

Stot|zen [ˈʃtɔtsn] M **-s, -** *(esp S Ger)* **a** *(= Baumstumpf)* (tree) stump **b** *(= Bottich)* tub, vat

Stöv|chen [ˈʃtøːfçən] NT **-s, -** (teapot *etc*) warmer

StPO [ɛsteːpeːˈloː] F - *abbr von* **Strafprozessordnung**

Str. *abbr von* **Straße** St

Stra|ban|zer [ʃtraˈbantsɐ] M **-s, -**, **Stra|ban|ze|rin** [-ərɪn] F **-, -nen** *(Aus inf: = Strolch, Nichtsnutz)* loafer *(inf)*

stracks [ʃtraks] ADV straight

Straf-: **Straf|an|dro|hung** F threat of punishment; **unter ~** on *or* under threat of penalty; **Straf|an|stalt** F penal institution, prison; **Straf|an|trag** M action, legal proceedings *pl*; **~ stellen** to institute legal proceedings; **einen ~ zurückziehen** to withdraw an action; **Straf|an|tritt** M commencement of (prison) sentence; **sein ~** the commencement of his (prison) sentence; **Straf|an|zei|ge** F **~ gegen jdn erstatten** to bring a charge against sb; **Straf|ar|beit** F *(Sch)* punishment; *(schriftlich)* lines *pl*; **Straf|auf|he|bungs|grund** M *(Jur)* ground for exemption from punishment; **Straf|auf|schub** M *(Jur)* suspension of sentence; *(von Todesstrafe)* reprieve; **Straf|aus|schlie|ßungs|grund** M *(Jur)* ground for exemption from punishment; **Straf|aus|set|zung** F *(Jur)* suspension of sentence; **~ zur Bewährung** proba-

tion; **Straf|bank** F *pl* **-bänke** *(Sport)* penalty bench, sin bin *(inf)*

straf|bar ADJ *Vergehen* punishable; **~e Handlung** punishable offence *(Brit) or* offense *(US)*; **das ist ~!** that's an offence *(Brit) or* offense *(US)*; **sich ~ machen** to commit an offence *(Brit) or* offense *(US)*

Straf|bar|keit [ˈʃtraːfbaːɐ̯kait] F -, *no pl* **er war sich** *(dat)* **der ~ seines Verhaltens nicht bewusst** he didn't realize that what he was doing was a punishable offence *(Brit) or* offense *(US)*

Straf-: **Straf|ba|tail|lon** NT *(Mil)* punishment battalion; **Straf|be|fehl** M *(Jur)* order of summary punishment; **~ ergeht gegen ...** ... is being prosecuted; **Straf|be|scheid** M *(Jur)* notification of penalty for a tax offence *(Brit) or* offense *(US)*; **Straf|be|stim|mung** F *(Jur)* penal laws *pl*, legal sanction

Stra|fe [ˈʃtraːfə] F -, **-n** punishment; *(Jur, Sport)* penalty; *(= Geldstrafe)* fine; *(= Gefängnisstrafe)* sentence; **etw bei ~ verbieten** to make sth punishable by law, to prohibit sth by law; **... bei ~ verboten** ... forbidden; **es ist bei ~ verboten, ...** it is a punishable *or* prosecutable offence *(Brit) or offense (US)* ...; **etw unter ~ stellen** to make sth a punishable offence *(Brit) or* offense *(US)*; **unter ~ stehen** to be a punishable offence *(Brit) or* offense *(US)*; **bei ~ von** on pain *or* penalty of; **seine ~ abbüßen** *or* **absitzen** *or* **abbrummen** *(inf)* to serve one's sentence, to do one's time *(inf)*; **eine ~ von drei Jahren Gefängnis** a three-year prison sentence; **~ zahlen** to pay a fine; **100 Dollar ~ zahlen** to pay a 100 dollar fine, to be fined 100 dollars; **zur ~** as a punishment; **~ muss sein!** discipline is necessary; **seine verdiente** *or* **gerechte ~ bekommen** to get one's just deserts, to be duly punished; **die ~ folgte auf dem Fuße** punishment was swift to come; **das ist die (gerechte) ~ dafür(, dass du gelogen hast)** that's your punishment (for lying), that's what you get (for lying); **etw als ~ empfinden** *(= als lästig)* to find sth a bind *(Brit inf) or* chore; *(= als Bestrafung)* to see sth as a punishment; **es ist eine ~, ihr zuhören zu müssen** it's a pain in the neck having to listen to her *(inf)*; **dieses Kind/Wetter ist eine ~** this child/weather is a pain (in the neck) *(inf)*

stra|fen [ˈʃtraːfn] VT *(= bestrafen)* to punish; **jdn (für etw/mit etw) ~** to punish sb (for sth/with sth); **mit etw gestraft sein** to be cursed with sth; **mit seinen Kindern ist er wirklich gestraft** his children are a real trial to him; **mit dieser Arbeit ist er wirklich gestraft** his work is a real bind *(Brit inf) or* a chore; **sie ist vom Schicksal gestraft** she is cursed by Fate, she has the curse of Fate upon her; **er ist gestraft genug** he has been punished enough → **Verachtung, Lüge**

VI to punish; **orientalische Richter ~ hart** oriental judges give severe sentences; **das Strafen** punishment

stra|fend ADJ *attr* punitive; *Blick, Worte* reproachful; **die ~e Gerechtigkeit** *(liter)* avenging justice ADV **jdn ~ ansehen** to give sb a reproachful look

Straf-: **Straf|ent|las|se|ne(r)** [-lɛntlasənə] MF *decl as adj* ex-convict, discharged prisoner; **Straf|ent|las|sung** F discharge, release (from prison); **Straf|er|lass** M remission (of sentence); **straf|er|schwe|rend** ADJ *Umstand* aggravating ADV **(als) ~ kam hinzu, dass ...** the offence *(Brit) or* offense *(US)* was compounded by the fact that ...; **als ~ wurde gewertet, dass der Täter keine Reue gezeigt hat** the accused's lack of remorse led to the passing of a heavier sentence; **straf|ex|er|zie|ren** *ptp* **strafexerziert** VI *insep (Mil)* to do punishment drill; **Straf|ex|pe|di|ti|on** F punitive expedition

straff [ʃtraf] ADJ *Seil* tight, taut; *Haut* smooth; *Busen* firm; *Haltung, Gestalt* erect; *(= straff sitzend) Hose etc* tight, close-fitting; *(fig: = streng) Disziplin, Organisation* strict, tight; *Politik* strict; *Zeitplan* tight ADV *(= stramm)* tightly; *(= streng) organisieren, reglementieren* strictly; **~ sitzen** to fit tightly, to be close-fitting *or* tight; **etw ~ spannen** *or* **ziehen** to tighten sth; *Decke, Laken etc* to pull sth tight; **die Leine muss ~ gespannt sein** the line has to be tight; **das Haar ~ zurückstecken** to tie one's hair back tightly

straf|fäl|lig ADJ **~ werden** to commit a criminal offence *(Brit) or* offense *(US)*; **wenn Sie wieder ~ werden ...** if you commit a further offence *(Brit) or* offense *(US)* ...

Straf|fäl|li|ge(r) [ˈʃtraːffɛlɪgə] MF *decl as adj* offender

straf|fen [ˈʃtrafn] VT to tighten; *(= spannen) Seil, Leine auch* to tauten; *(= raffen) Handlung, Darstellung* to make more taut, to tighten up; **sich** *(dat)* **die Gesichtshaut ~ lassen** to have a face-lift; **sich** *(dat)* **den Busen ~ lassen** to have one's breasts lifted; **die Zügel ~** *(fig)* to tighten the reins VR to tighten, to become taut; *(Haut)* to become smooth; *(Busen)* to become firm; *(= sich aufrichten)* to stiffen

Straff|heit F -, *no pl (von Haut)* smoothness; *(von Busen)* firmness; *(fig: = Strenge)* strictness

Straf-: **straf|frei** ADJ ADV not subject to prosecution; **~ bleiben** *or* **ausgehen** to go unpunished; **Straf|frei|heit** F immunity from prosecution; **Straf|ge|bühr** F surcharge; **Straf|ge|fan|ge|ne(r)** MF *decl as adj* detainee, prisoner; **Straf|geld** NT fine; **Straf|ge|richt** NT criminal court; **ein ~ abhalten** to hold a trial; **das göttliche** *or* **himmlische ~** divine judgement; **das ~ Gottes** *or* **des Himmels** *(liter)* the judgement of God; **ein ~ brach über ihn herein** *(fig)* the wrath of God descended upon him; **Straf|ge|richts|bar|keit** F criminal jurisdiction; **Straf|ge|setz** NT criminal *or* penal law; **Straf|ge|setz|buch** NT Criminal *or* Penal Code; **Straf|ge|setz|ge|bung** F penal legislation; **Straf|ge|walt** F legal authority; **Straf|jus|tiz** F criminal justice *no art*; **Straf|kam|mer** F division for criminal matters (of a court); **Straf|ko|lo|nie** F penal colony; **Straf|kom|pa|nie** F *(Mil)* punishment battalion; **Straf|la|ger** NT disciplinary *or* punishment camp

sträf|lich [ˈʃtrɛːflɪç] ADJ *(lit, fig)* criminal ADV *vernachlässigen etc* criminally; **sich ~ blamieren** to make a terrible fool of oneself, to make a proper charlie of oneself *(Brit inf)*

Sträf|ling [ˈʃtrɛːflɪŋ] M **-s, -e** prisoner

Sträf|lings|klei|dung F prison clothing

Straf-: **straf|los** ADJ ADV = **straffrei**; **Straf|man|dat** NT ticket; **Straf|maß** NT sentence; **das höchste ~** the maximum penalty *or* sentence; **straf|mil|dernd** ADJ extenuating, mitigating; **Straf|mil|de|rung** F mitigation *or* commutation of the/a sentence; **Straf|mi|nu|te** F *(Sport)* penalty minute; **straf|mün|dig** ADJ of the age of criminal responsibility; **ein kleines Kind ist nicht ~** a small child is under the age of criminal responsibility; **Straf|mün|dig|keit** F age of criminal responsibility; **Straf|nach|lass** M remission; **Straf|por|to** NT excess postage; **Straf|pre|digt** F reprimand, dressing-down *(inf)*; **jdm eine ~ halten** to give sb a lecture *or* dressing-down *(inf)*; **Straf|pro|zess** M criminal proceedings *pl*, criminal action *or* case; **Straf|pro|zess|ord|nung** F code of criminal procedure; **Straf|punkt** M *(Sport)* penalty point; **Straf|rah|men** M range of sentences; **Straf|raum** M *(Sport)* penalty area *or (Ftbl auch)* box; **Straf|recht** NT criminal law; **Straf|recht|ler** [-rɛçtlɐ] M **-s, -**, **Straf|recht|le|rin** [-ərɪn] F **-, -nen** expert in criminal law, penologist; **straf|recht|lich** ADJ criminal; **das ist aber kein ~es Problem** but that is not a problem of criminal law ADV **jdn/etw ~ verfolgen** *or* **belangen** to prosecute sb/sth; **Straf|rechts|pfle|ge** F criminal justice; **Straf|re|de** F reprimand, dressing-down *(inf)*; **Straf|re|gis|ter** NT police *or* criminal records *pl*; *(hum inf)* record; **ein Eintrag im ~** an entry in the police *or* criminal records *pl*; **einen Eintrag im ~ haben** to have a record; **er hat ein langes ~** he has a long (criminal) record; *(hum inf)* he's got a bad record; **Straf|rich|ter(in)** M(F) criminal judge *(Brit)*, judge who hears criminal cases; **Straf|sa|che** F criminal matter; **Straf|schuss** M *(Sport)* penalty (shot); **Straf|se|nat** M criminal division *(of the Court of Appeal and Federal Supreme Court)*; **Straf|stoß** M *(Ftbl etc)* penalty (kick); *(Hockey etc)* penalty (shot); **Straf|tat** F criminal offence *(Brit) or* offense *(US)*, criminal act; **Straf|tat|be|stand** M *(Jur)* **das erfüllt den ~ der Verleumdung** *etc* that constitutes calumny *or* libel *etc*; **Straf|tä|ter(in)** M(F) offender, criminal; **Straf|um|wand|lung** F *(Jur)* commutation of a/the penalty; **Straf|ur|teil** NT *(Jur)* conviction and sentence, penal judgement; **Straf|ver|bü|ßung** F serving of a sentence; **nach seiner ~** after serving his sentence; **Straf|ver|fah|ren** NT criminal proceedings *pl*, criminal action *or* case; **Straf|ver|fol|gung** F criminal prosecution; **Straf|ver|fü|gung** F *(Jur)* ticket; **straf|ver|schär|fend** ADJ ADV = **straferschwerend**; **Straf|ver|schär|fung** F increase in the severity of the/a penalty *or* sentence; **das führte zu einer ~** this led to the passing of a heavier sentence; **straf|ver|set|zen** *ptp* **strafversetzt** VT *insep Beamte* to transfer for disciplinary reasons; **Straf|ver|set|zung** F (disciplinary) transfer; **Straf|ver|tei|di|ger(in)** M(F) counsel for the defence *(Brit) or* defense *(US)*, defence *(Brit) or* defense *(US)* counsel *or* lawyer; **Straf|voll|stre|ckung** F execution of the/a sentence; **Straf|voll|zug** M penal system; **offener ~** non-confinement; **Straf|voll|zugs|an|stalt** F *(form)* penal institution; **straf|wür|dig** ADJ *(form)* punishable; **Straf|wurf** M *(Sport)* penalty throw; **Straf|zet|tel** M *(Jur)* ticket

Strahl [ʃtraːl] M **-(e)s, -en** **a** *(lit, fig)* ray; *(= Lichtstrahl)* ray or shaft *or* beam (of light); *(= Sonnenstrahl)* shaft of light; *(= Radiostrahl, Laserstrahl etc)* beam; *(poet: = das Leuchten)* light; **im ~ einer Taschenlampe** by the light *or* in the beam of a torch; **ein ~ der Hoffnung** *(liter)* a ray of hope **b** *(= Wasserstrahl, Luftstrahl)* jet

Strahl|an|trieb M *(Aviat)* jet propulsion

Strah|le|mann M *pl* **-männer** *(inf)* golden boy *(inf)*

strah|len [ˈʃtraːlən] VI **a** *(Sonne, Licht etc)* to shine; *(Sender)* to beam; *(= glühen)* to glow *(vor +dat* with); *(Heizofen etc)* to radiate; *(radioaktiv)* to give off radioactivity **b** *(= leuchten)* to gleam, to sparkle; *(fig) (Gesicht)* to beam; *(Augen)* to shine; **der Himmel strahlte** the sky was bright; **das ganze Haus strahlte vor Sauberkeit** the whole house was sparkling clean; **was strahlst du so?** what are you beaming about?, what are you so happy about?; **er strahlte vor Freude** he was beaming with happiness; **er strahlte (übers ganze Gesicht)** he was beaming all over his face → **strahlend**

sträh|len [ˈʃtrɛːlən] VT *(S Ger, Sw)* to comb

Strah|len-: **Strah|len|be|hand|lung** F *(Med)* ray treatment; **Strah|len|be|las|tung** F radiation; **Strah|len|bio|lo|gie** F radiobiology; **Strah|len|bre|chung** F refraction; **Strah|len|bün|del** NT pencil of rays

strah|lend ADJ radiant; *Gesicht auch* beaming; *Wetter, Tag* bright, glorious; *Farben* brilliant, bright; *(= radioaktiv)* radioactive; **~es Lachen** beaming smile, beam; **mit ~en Augen** with bright *or* shining eyes; **mit ~em Gesicht** with a beaming face; *(von Frau, Kind auch)* with a radiant face ADV **jdn ~ ansehen** *(= lächelnd)* to beam at sb; *(= glücklich)* to look at sb, beaming *or* radiant with happiness; **der Tag war ~ schön, es war ein ~ schöner Tag** it was a glorious day

Strah|len-: **Strah|len|do|sis** F dose of radiation; **strah|len|för|mig** ADJ radial ADV **sich ~ ausbreiten** to radiate out; **~ von etw wegführen** to radiate from sth; **strah|len|ge|schä|digt**

[-gəʃɛːdɪçt] ADJ suffering from radiation damage; *Organ* damaged by radiation; **die Strahlengeschädigten** the radiation victims; **Strahlenheilkunde** F radiotherapy; **strahlenkrank** ADJ radiation sick; **Strahlenkranke(r)** MF *decl as adj* person suffering from radiation sickness; **Strahlenkrankheit** F radiation sickness; **Strahlenopfer** NT radiation victim; **Strahlenpilz** M ray fungus; **Strahlenquelle** F source of radiation; **Strahlenschäden** PL radiation injuries *pl*; *(von Organ auch)* radiation damage *sing*; **Strahlenschutz** M radiation protection; **Strahlenschutzraum** M fall-out shelter; **Strahlentherapie** F radiotherapy; **Strahlentierchen** NT radiolarian; **Strahlentod** M death through radiation; **strahlenverseucht** [-fɛɐzɔyçt] ADJ contaminated (with radiation); **Strahlenwaffe** F laser weapon

Strahler [ˈʃtraːlɐ] M **-s, -** *(= Lampe)* spotlight

strahlig [ˈʃtraːlɪç] ADJ *(Bot)* radial

-strahlig ADJ *suf* **ein zweistrahliges/vierstrahliges Düsenflugzeug** a two-engined/four-engined jet plane

Strahl-: **Strahlkraft** F radiation intensity; *(fig) (von Stimme, Begriff)* force, power; *(von Mensch)* charisma; **Strahlmaterial** NT radioactive material; **Strahltriebwerk** NT jet engine; **Strahlturbine** F turbojet

Strahlung [ˈʃtraːlʊŋ] F **-, -en** radiation

Strahlungs-: **strahlungsarm** ADJ *Bildschirm, Monitor* low-radiation; **Strahlungsenergie** F radiation *or* radiant energy; **Strahlungsgürtel** M Van Allen belt; **der ~ der Erde** the Van Allen belt; **Strahlungsintensität** F dose of radiation; **Strahlungswärme** F radiant heat

Strahlverfahren NT (jet-)blasting

Strähnchen [ˈʃtrɛːnçən] NT **-s, -** streak

Strähne [ˈʃtrɛːnə] F **-, -n**, *(Aus)* **Strähn** [ʃtrɛːn] M **-(e)s, -e** *(= Haarsträhne)* strand; *(Längenmaß, = Wollsträhne, Garnsträhne)* skein, hank; **ich habe schon eine weiße ~** I already have a white streak

strähnig [ˈʃtrɛːnɪç] ADJ *Haar* straggly ADV **das Haar fiel ihr ~ auf die Schultern** her hair straggled down over her shoulders

Stramin [ʃtraˈmiːn] M **-s, -e** even-weave (embroidery) fabric

stramm [ʃtram] ADJ *(= straff) Seil, Hose* tight; *Seil auch* taut; *(= schneidig) Haltung, Soldat* erect, upright; *(= kräftig, drall) Mädchen, Junge* strapping; *Junge, Beine* sturdy; *Brust* firm; *(inf) (= tüchtig) Marsch, Arbeit* strenuous, tough, hard; *Tag, Programm* packed; *Leistung* solid; *Tempo* brisk; *(= überzeugt)* staunch; *(dated inf: = betrunken)* tight *(inf)*; **~e Haltung annehmen** to stand to attention; **~er Max** *open sandwich of boiled ham and fried egg (mit Hackfleisch) open sandwich of seasoned raw minced pork with egg and onion*

ADV *binden* tightly; **~ sitzen** to be tight *or* close-fitting, to fit tightly; **~ arbeiten** *(inf)* to work hard, to get down to it *(inf)*; **~ marschieren** *(inf)* to march hard; **~ an etw** *(dat)* **festhalten** to stick to sth; **~ konservativ** *(inf)* staunchly conservative, true blue *(Brit)*; **das Land wird ~ kommunistisch regiert** *(inf)* the country has a staunchly communist government; **die Politiker sind weiter ~ auf Atomkurs** *(inf)* the politicians are continuing to support nuclear power unreservedly

stramm-: **stramm+stehen** VI *sep irreg (Mil inf)* to stand to attention; **stramm ziehen** *irreg*, **stramm+ziehen** *sep irreg* VT *Seil, Hose* to pull tight, to tighten; *Socken* to pull up; **jdm den Hosenboden** *or* **die Hosen ~** *(inf)* to give sb a good hiding *(inf)*

Strampelanzug M romper suit

Strampelhöschen [-høːsçən] NT rompers *pl*

strampeln [ˈʃtramplṇ] VI **a** *(mit Beinen)* to flail *or* thrash about; *(Baby)* to thrash about; **das Baby strampelte mit Armen und Beinen** the baby was kicking its feet and waving its arms about **b** *aux sein (inf: = Rad fahren)* to pedal **c** *(inf: = sich abrackern)* to (sweat and) slave

Strampelsack M *(für Säuglinge)* carry-nest *(Brit)*, pup sack *(US)*

Strampler [ˈʃtramplɐ] M romper suit

Strand [ʃtrant] M **-(e)s, ⸚e** [ˈʃtrɛndə] *(= Meeresstrand)* beach, strand *(poet)*; *(= Seeufer)* shore; *(poet: = Flussufer)* bank; **am ~** *(= am Meer)* on the beach; *(= am Seeufer)* on the shore; **auf ~ geraten** *or* **laufen** to run aground; **auf ~ setzen** to beach

Strand-: **Strandanzug** M beach suit; **Strandbad** NT (seawater) swimming pool; *(= Badeort)* bathing resort; **Stranddistel** F sea holly

stranden [ˈʃtrandn̩] VI *aux sein* to run aground, to be stranded; *(fig)* to fail

Strand-: **Strandgerste** F sea barley; **Strandgut** NT, *no pl (lit, fig)* flotsam and jetsam; **Strandhafer** M marram (grass); **Strandhaubitze** F **blau** *or* **voll wie eine ~** *(inf)* as drunk as a lord *(Brit inf) or* a sailor *(US inf)*, rolling drunk *(inf)*; **Strandhotel** NT seaside hotel; **Strandkiefer** F *(Bot)* maritime pine, cluster pine; **Strandkleidung** F beachwear; **Strandkorb** M wicker beach chair with a hood; **Strandlaken** NT beach towel; **Strandläufer** M *(Orn)* sandpiper; **Strandpromenade** F promenade; **Strandraub** M beachcombing; **Strandräuber(in)** M(F) beachcomber; **Strandrecht** NT right of salvage; **Strandtuch** NT beach towel

Strandung [ˈʃtrandʊŋ] F **-, -en** running aground

Strand-: **Strandvogt** M beach warden *(Brit)*; **Strandwache** F lifeguard; *(= Dienst)* lifeguard duty; **Strandwächter(in)** M(F) lifeguard; **Strandweg** M beach path

Strang [ʃtraŋ] M **-(e)s, ⸚e** [ˈʃtrɛŋə] *(= Nervenstrang, Muskelstrang)* cord; *(= DNA-Strang)* strand; *(= Strick)* rope; *(= Wollstrang, Garnstrang)* hank, skein; *(am Pferdegeschirr)* trace, tug; *(Rail: = Schienenstrang)* track; **jdn zum Tod durch den ~ verurteilen** to sentence sb to be hanged; **der Tod durch den ~** death by hanging; **an einem** *or* **am gleichen** *or* **an demselben ~ ziehen** *(fig)* to pull together; **über die Stränge schlagen** *or* **hauen** *(inf)* to run riot *or* wild *(inf)*, to get carried away *(inf)* → **reißen VI a**

Strangulation [ʃtraŋgulaˈtsioːn, st-] F **-, -en** strangulation

strangulieren [ʃtraŋguˈliːrən, st-] *ptp* **stranguliert** VT to strangle

Strapaze [ʃtraˈpaːtsə] F **-, -n** strain

strapazfähig ADJ *(Aus)* = **strapazierfähig**

strapazieren [ʃtrapaˈtsiːrən] *ptp* **strapaziert** VT to be a strain on, to take a lot out of; *Schuhe, Kleidung* to be hard on, to give a lot of hard wear to; *(fig inf) Redensart, Begriff* to flog (to death) *(inf)*; *Nerven* to strain, to try; *Geduld* to try; **er sah strapaziert aus** he looked worn out *or* exhausted VR to tax oneself

strapazierfähig ADJ *Schuhe, Kleidung, Material* hard-wearing, durable; *(fig inf) Nerven* strong

Strapazierfähigkeit F durability; **das übersteigt die ~ meiner Nerven** that's more than my nerves can stand

strapaziös [ʃtrapaˈtsiøːs] ADJ *(lit, fig)* wearing, exhausting

Straps [ʃtraps] M **-es, -e** suspender belt *(Brit)*, garter belt *(US)*

Strass [ʃtras] M **-** *or* **-es**, *no pl* paste

straßauf [ʃtraːsˈlauf] ADV **~, straßab** up and down the street

Straßburg [ˈʃtraːsbʊrk] NT **-s** Strasbourg, Strassburg

Sträßchen [ˈʃtrɛːsçən] NT **-s, -** *dim von* **Straße**

Straße [ˈʃtraːsə] F **-, -n** **a** road; *(in Stadt, Dorf)* street, road; *(= kleine Landstraße)* lane; **an der ~** by the roadside; **auf die ~ gehen** *(lit)* to go out on the street; *(als Demonstrant)* to take to the streets, to go out into the streets; *(als Prostituierte)* to go on *or* walk the streets; **auf der ~ liegen** *(fig inf)* to be out of work; *(als Wohnungsloser)* to be on the streets; *(als Faulenzer, Asozialer etc)* to hang around the streets, to hang around street corners; *(Kraftfahrer)* to have broken down; **auf die ~ gesetzt werden** *(inf)* to be turned out (onto the streets); *(als Arbeiter)* to be sacked *(Brit inf)*, to get the sack *(Brit inf)*, to be *or* get fired *(inf)*; **über die ~ gehen** to cross (the road/street); **er wohnt drei ~n weiter** he lives three blocks further on; **mit etw auf die ~ gehen** to take to the streets about sth; **er ist aus unserer ~** he's from our street; **davon spricht die ganze ~** the whole street's talking about it; **die ~n der Großstadt** the city streets; **Verkauf über die ~** takeaway *(Brit) or* takeout *(US)* sales; *(von Getränken)* off-licence sales *pl (Brit)*, package store sales *pl (US)*; **etw über die ~ verkaufen** to sell sth to take away *(Brit) or* to take out *(US)*; **das Geld liegt auf der ~** money is there for the asking; **das Geld liegt nicht auf der ~** money doesn't grow on trees; **ein Mädchen von der ~** a lady of pleasure; **der Mann auf der ~** *(fig)* the man in the street

b *(= Meerenge)* strait(s *pl*); **die ~ von Dover/Gibraltar/Messina** *etc* the Straits of Dover/Gibraltar/Messina *etc*

c *(= Mob, Pöbel)* **die ~** the masses *pl*, the rabble; **die Herrschaft der ~** mob rule

d *(Tech) (= Fertigungsstraße)* (production) line; *(= Walzstraße)* train

Straßen-: **Straßenanzug** M lounge suit *(Brit)*, business suit *(US)*; **Straßenarbeiten** PL roadworks *pl*; **Straßenarbeiter(in)** M(F) roadworker; **Straßenatlas** M road atlas; *(von Stadt)* street atlas; **Straßenausbau** M road improvement

Straßenbahn F *(= Wagen)* tram *(esp Brit)*, streetcar *(US)*; *(= Netz)* tramway(s) *(esp Brit)*, streetcar system *(US)*; **mit der ~** by tram *(esp Brit) or* streetcar *(US)*

Straßenbahner [-baːnɐ] M **-s, -**, **Straßenbahnerin** [-ərɪn] F **-, -nen** *(inf)* tramway *(esp Brit) or* streetcar *(US)* employee

Straßenbahn-: **Straßenbahnfahrer(in)** M(F), **Straßenbahnführer(in)** M(F) tram *(esp Brit) or* streetcar *(US)* driver; **Straßenbahnhaltestelle** F tram *(esp Brit) or* streetcar *(US)* stop; **Straßenbahnlinie** F tramline *(esp Brit)*, tram route *(esp Brit)*, streetcar line *(US)*; **mit der ~ 11 fahren** to take the number 11 tram *(esp Brit) or* streetcar *(US)*; **Straßenbahnschaffner(in)** M(F) tram *(esp Brit) or* streetcar *(US)* conductor/conductress; **Straßenbahnschiene** F tramline *(esp Brit)*, tram *(esp Brit) or* streetcar *(US)* rail; **Straßenbahnwagen** M tram *(esp Brit)*, streetcar *(US)*

Straßen-: **Straßenbau** M, *no pl* road construction; **Straßenbauamt** NT highways *or* *(städtisch)* roads department, ≈ Department of Transportation *(US)*; **Straßenbauarbeiten** PL roadworks *pl*; **Straßenbekanntschaft** F passing *or* nodding acquaintance; **Straßenbelag** M road surface; **Straßenbeleuchtung** F street lighting; **Straßenbenutzungsgebühr** F (road) toll; **Straßenbild** NT street scene; **Straßenböschung** F embankment; **Straßenbreite** F width of a/the road; **Straßencafé** NT pavement café *(Brit)*, sidewalk café *(US)*; **Straßendecke** F road surface; **Straßendirne** F *(dated, form)* common prostitute, streetwalker; **Straßendorf** NT linear village; **Straßenecke** F street corner; **ein paar ~n weiter** a few blocks further; **Straßeneinmündung** F road junction; **Straßenfeger** [-feːgɐ] M **-s, -**, **Straßenfegerin** [-ərɪn] F **-, -nen** road sweeper; **Straßenfest** NT street party; **Straßenführung** F route; **Straßengabelung** F fork (in a/the road); **Straßenglätte** F slippery road surface; **Straßengraben** M ditch; **Stra|ßen|han|del** M street trading; **Stra|ßen|händ|ler(in)** M(F) street trader; *(mit Obst, Fisch etc auch)* costermonger *(Brit)*; **Stra|ßen|jun|ge** M *(pej)* street urchin, street Arab *(Brit liter)*; **Stra|ßen|kampf** M street fighting *no pl*; **ein ~** a street fight *or* battle; **Stra|ßen|kämp|fer(in)** M(F) street fighter; **Stra|ßen|kar|te** F road map; **Stra|ßen|keh|rer** [-keːrɐ] M **-s, -**, **Stra|ßen|keh|re|rin** [-ərɪn] F **-, -nen** road sweeper; **Stra|ßen|klei|dung** F streetwear; **Stra|ßen|kon|trol|le** F (road) checkpoint; **Stra|ßen|kreu|zer** M *(inf)* limo *(inf)*, limousine; **Stra|ßen|kreu|zung** F crossroads *sing or pl*, intersection *(US)*; **Stra|ßen|kri|mi|na|li|tät** F street crime; **Stra|ßen|la|ge** F *(Aut)* road holding; **dieses Auto hat eine gute ~** this car holds the road well, this car has good road holding; **Stra|ßen|lärm** M street noise; **Stra|ßen|la|ter|ne** F streetlamp; **Stra|ßen|mäd|chen** NT streetwalker, prostitute; **Stra|ßen|meis|te|rei** [-maistəˈrai] F **-, -en** road maintenance department *(Brit)*, ≈ City Road Maintenance Office *(US)*; **Stra|ßen|mu|si|kant(in)** M(F) street musician; **Stra|ßen|na|me** M street name; **Stra|ßen|netz** NT road network *or* system; **Stra|ßen|rand** M roadside; **Stra|ßen|raub** M mugging *(inf)*, street robbery; *(durch Wegelagerer)* highway robbery; **Stra|ßen|räu|ber(in)** M(F) mugger *(inf)*, thief; *(= Wegelagerer)* highwayman; **Stra|ßen|rei|ni|gung** F street cleaning; **Stra|ßen|ren|nen** NT road race; **Stra|ßen|samm|lung** F street collection; **Stra|ßen|sän|ger** M street singer; **Stra|ßen|schä|den** PL damage *sing* to the road surface; **„Achtung ~"** "uneven road surface"; **Stra|ßen|schild** NT *pl* **-schilder** street sign; **Stra|ßen|schlacht** F street battle; **Stra|ßen|schuh** M outdoor *or* walking shoe; **Stra|ßen|sei|te** F side of a/the road; **Stra|ßen|sper|re** F roadblock; **Stra|ßen|sper|rung** F closing (off) of a/the road; **eine ~ vornehmen** to close (off) the road; **Stra|ßen|strich** M *(inf)* walking the streets, streetwalking; *(Gegend)* red-light district; **auf den ~ gehen** to walk the streets; **Stra|ßen|the|a|ter** NT street theatre *(Brit) or* theater *(US)*; **Stra|ßen|tun|nel** M (road) tunnel; **Stra|ßen|über|füh|rung** F footbridge, pedestrian bridge; **Stra|ßen|un|ter|füh|rung** F underpass, subway; **Stra|ßen|ver|hält|nis|se** PL road conditions *pl*; **Stra|ßen|ver|kauf** M street trading; *(= Außerhausverkauf)* takeaway *(Brit) or* takeout *(US)* sales *pl*; *(von alkoholischen Getränken)* off-licence sales *pl (Brit)*, package store sales *pl (US)*; *(= Verkaufsstelle)* takeaway *(Brit)*, takeout *(US)*; *(für alkoholische Getränke)* off-licence *(Brit)*, package store *(US)*; **Zeitungen werden im ~ angeboten** newspapers are sold on the streets; **Stra|ßen|ver|käu|fer(in)** M(F) street seller *or* vendor; *(von Obst, Fisch etc)* street seller *or* vendor, costermonger *(Brit)*; **Stra|ßen|ver|kehr** M traffic; **Stra|ßen|ver|kehrs|ord|nung** F ≈ Highway Code *(Brit)*, traffic rules and regulations *pl*; **Stra|ßen|ver|zeich|nis** NT index of street names; *(in Buchform auch)* street directory; **Stra|ßen|wacht** F road patrol; **Stra|ßen|wal|ze** F roadroller, steamroller; **Stra|ßen|zoll** M road toll; **Stra|ßen|zug** M street; **Stra|ßen|zu|stand** M road conditions *pl*; **Stra|ßen|zu|stands|be|richt** M road report

Sträß|lein [ˈʃtrɛːslain] NT **-s, -** *dim von* **Straße**

Strass|schmuck [ˈʃtras-] M paste jewellery *(Brit) no pl*, paste jewelry *(US) no pl*

Stra|te|ge [ʃtraˈteːgə, st-] M **-n, -n**, **Stra|te|gin** [-ˈteːgɪn] F **-, -nen** strategist; **na, alter ~** *(fig inf)* well, you old fox *(inf)*

Stra|te|gie [ʃtrateˈgiː, st-] F **-, -n** [-ˈgiːən] strategy

Stra|te|gie|pa|pier NT *(Pol)* strategy document

stra|te|gisch [ʃtraˈteːgɪʃ, st-] ADJ strategic ADV strategically

Stra|ti|fi|ka|ti|on [ʃtratifikaˈtsioːn, st-] F **-, -en** stratification

stra|ti|fi|zie|ren [ʃtratifiˈtsiːrən, st-] *ptp* **stratifiziert** VT *(Geol, Agr)* to stratify

Stra|to|sphä|re [ʃtratoˈsfɛːrə, st-] F, *no pl* stratosphere

stra|to|sphä|risch [ʃtratoˈsfɛːrɪʃ, st-] ADJ stratospheric

Stra|tus [ˈʃtraːtʊs, ˈst-] M **-, Strati** [-ti], **Stra|tus|wol|ke** F *(Met)* stratus (cloud)

sträu|ben [ˈʃtrɔybn] VR **a** *(Haare, Fell)* to stand on end; *(Gefieder)* to become ruffled; **der Katze sträubt sich das Fell** *(aggressiv)* the cat raises its hackles; **da ~ sich einem die Haare** it's enough to make your hair stand on end **b** *(fig)* to resist *(gegen etw* sth); **die Feder/die Zunge sträubt sich, das zu schildern** *(geh)* one hesitates to put it down on paper/to say it; **es sträubt sich alles in mir, das zu tun** I am most reluctant to do it VT *Gefieder* to ruffle VI *aux sein (rare) (= zerstieben)* to scatter; *(Wasser)* to spray

Strauch [ʃtraux] M **-(e)s, Sträucher** [ˈʃtrɔyçɐ] bush, shrub

Strauch|dieb(in) M(F) *(old)* footpad *(old)*, thief

strau|cheln [ˈʃtrauxln] VI *aux sein* **a** *(geh: = stolpern)* to stumble, to trip **b** *(fig) (= auf die schiefe Bahn geraten)* to transgress; *(moralisch)* to go astray; **ins Straucheln kommen** *or* **geraten** *(fig)* to come to grief; **an etw** *(dat)* **~** to come to grief over sth; **die Gestrauchelten** the reprobates

Strauch-: **Strauch|rit|ter** M *(old)* footpad *(old)*, thief; **Strauch|to|ma|te** F vine-ripened tomato, tomato ripened on the vine; **Strauch|werk** NT, *no pl (= Gebüsch)* bushes *pl*, shrubs *pl*; *(= Gestrüpp)* undergrowth

Strauß [ʃtraus] M **-es, -e** ostrich; **wie der Vogel ~** like an ostrich

Strauß M **-es, Sträuße** [ˈʃtrɔysə] **a** bunch; *(= Blumenstrauß)* bunch of flowers; *(als Geschenk)* bouquet, bunch of flowers; *(= kleiner Strauß, Biedermeierstrauß)* posy; **einen ~ binden** to make up a bouquet **b** *(old: = Kampf, auch fig)* struggle, battle; **mit jdm einen harten ~ ausfechten** *(lit, fig)* to have a hard struggle *or* fight with sb

Sträuß|chen [ˈʃtrɔysçən] NT **-s, -** *dim von* **Strauß**

Strau|ßen|fe|der F ostrich feather *or* plume

Strau|ßen|wirt|schaft F *(S Ger, Aus) private bar opened by wine-growers at certain times*

Strauß|vö|gel PL struthionidae *pl (spec)*, struthioids *pl (spec)*

Strauß|wirt|schaft F = **Straußenwirtschaft**

Strea|mer [ˈstriːmɐ] M **-s, -** *(Comput)* streamer

Streb [ʃtreːp] M **-(e)s, -e** [-bə] *(Min)* coalface; **im ~ arbeiten** to work at the coalface

Stre|be [ˈʃtreːbə] F **-, -n** brace, strut; *(= Deckenstrebe)* joist; *(von Flugzeug)* strut

Stre|be-: **Stre|be|bal|ken** M diagonal brace *or* strut; **Stre|be|bo|gen** M flying buttress

stre|ben [ˈʃtreːbn] VI *(geh)* **a** *(= den Drang haben, sich bemühen)* to strive *(nach, an +acc, zu* for); *(Sch pej)* to swot *(inf)*; **danach ~, etw zu tun** to strive to do sth; **die Pflanze strebt nach dem Licht** the plant seeks the light; **der Fluss strebt zum Meer** the river flows towards *(Brit) or* toward *(US)* the sea; **in die Ferne ~** to be drawn to distant parts; **sich ~d bemühen** to strive one's hardest **b** *aux sein (= sich bewegen)* **nach** *or* **zu etw ~** to make one's way to sth; *(Armee)* to push toward(s) sth; **aus etw ~** to make one's way out of sth **c** *aux sein* **in die Höhe** *or* **zum Himmel ~** to rise *or* soar aloft

Stre|ben [ˈʃtreːbn] NT **-s**, *no pl* **a** *(= Drängen, Sinnen)* striving *(nach* for); *(nach Ruhm, Geld)* aspiration *(nach* to); *(= Bemühen)* efforts *pl* **b** *(= Tendenz)* shift, movement

Stre|be|pfei|ler M buttress

Stre|ber [ˈʃtreːbɐ] M **-s, -**, **Stre|be|rin** [-ərɪn] F **-, -nen** *(pej inf)* pushy person; *(Sch)* swot *(Brit inf)*, grind *(US inf)*

Stre|be|rei [ʃtreːbəˈrai] F **-**, *no pl (pej inf)* pushiness *(inf)*; *(Sch)* swotting *(Brit inf)*, cramming *(inf)*

Stre|ber-: **Stre|ber|na|tur** F *(pej)* pushy nature; *(Mensch)* pushy person; *(Sch)* swot *(Brit inf)*, grind *(US inf)*; **Stre|ber|tum** [ˈʃtreːbɐtuːm] NT **-s**, *no pl* pushiness *(inf)*; *(Sch)* swotting *(Brit inf)*, cramming *(inf)*

streb|sam [ˈʃtreːpzaːm] ADJ assiduous, industrious

Streb|sam|keit F **-**, *no pl* assiduity, industriousness

Stre|bung [ˈʃtreːbʊŋ] F **-, -en** *(esp Psych)* tendency

Streck|bett NT *(Med)* orthopaedic *(Brit) or* orthopedic *(US)* bed *(with traction facilities)*

Stre|cke [ˈʃtrɛkə] F **-, -n** **a** *(= Entfernung zwischen zwei Punkten, Sport)* distance; *(Math)* line *(between two points)*; **eine ~ zurücklegen** to cover a distance; **eine ziemliche** *or* **gute ~ entfernt sein** *(lit, fig)* to be a long way away; **bis zum Ende des Projekts ist es noch eine ziemliche** *or* **lange ~** there is still quite a good way to go until the end of the project **b** *(= Abschnitt) (von Straße, Fluss)* stretch; *(von Bahnlinie)* section **c** *(= Weg, Route, Flugstrecke)* route; *(= Straße)* road; *(= Bahnlinie, Sport: = Bahn)* track; *(fig: = Passage)* passage; **welche ~ bist du gekommen?** which way *or* route did you come?; **für die ~ London-Glasgow brauchen wir 5 Stunden** the journey from London to Glasgow will take us 5 hours; **auf der ~ sein** to be in the race; **auf** *or* **an der ~ Paris-Brüssel** on the way from Paris to Brussels; **die ~ Wien-München führt durch ...** the road/track *etc* between Vienna and Munich goes through ...; **in einer ~** in one go *(inf)*, without stopping; **auf freier** *or* **offener ~** *(esp Rail)* on the open line, between stations; **auf weite ~n (hin)** *(lit, fig)* for long stretches; **auf der ~ bleiben** *(bei Rennen)* to drop out of the running; *(in Konkurrenzkampf)* to fall by the wayside **d** *(Hunt) (= Jagdbeute)* bag, kill; **zur ~ bringen** to bag, to kill; *(fig) Verbrecher* to hunt down **e** *(Min)* gallery

stre|cken [ˈʃtrɛkn] VT **a** *Arme, Beine, Oberkörper* to stretch; *Hals* to crane; *(Sch: um sich zu melden) Finger, Hand* to raise, to put up; **die Zunge aus dem Mund ~** to stick out one's tongue; **den Kopf aus dem Fenster/durch die Tür ~** to stick one's head out of the window/through the door; **jdn zu Boden ~** to knock sb to the floor → **Waffe** **b** *(im Streckverband) Bein, Arm* to straighten **c** *(Metal) Blech, Eisen* to hammer out **d** *(inf: = absichtlich verlängern) Vorräte, Geld* to eke out, to stretch; *Arbeit* to drag out *(inf)*; *Essen, Suppe* to make go further; *(= verdünnen)* to thin down, to dilute **e** → **gestreckt** VR **a** *(= sich recken)* to have a stretch, to stretch; *(inf: = wachsen)* to shoot up *(inf)*; **sich ins Gras/aufs Bett ~** to stretch out on the grass/the bed **b** *(= sich hinziehen)* to drag on

Stre|cken-: **Stre|cken|ab|schnitt** M *(Rail)* section of the line *or* track, track section; **Stre|cken|ar|bei|ter(in)** M(F) *(Rail)* platelayer; **Stre|cken|be|ge|hung** F *(Rail)* track inspection; **Stre|cken|füh|rung** F *(Rail)* route; **Stre|cken|netz** NT rail network; **Stre|cken|pos|ten** M *(Sport)* (race) marshal; *(= Kontrollstelle)* checkpoint control; *(= Verpflegungsposten)* supply station; **Stre|cken|re|kord** M *(Sport)* track record; **Stre|cken|still|le|gung** F *(Rail)* line closure; **Stre|cken|wär|ter(in)** M(F) *(Rail)* track inspector; **stre|cken|wei|se** ADV in parts *or* places

Stre|cker [ˈʃtrɛkɐ] M **-s, -**, **Streck|mus|kel** M *(Anat)* extensor (muscle)

Streck|ver|band M *(Med) bandage used in traction*

Street|ball ['striːtbɔːl] M **-s**, *no pl* streetball

Street|wor|ker ['striːtwøːɐkɐ, -wœrkɐ] M **-s, -**, **Street|wor|ke|rin** [-ərɪn] F **-, -nen** (*= Sozialarbeiter*) outreach worker

Streich [ʃtraiç] M **-(e)s, -e** **a** (*= Schabernack*) prank, trick; **jdm einen ~ spielen** (*lit*) to play a trick on sb; (*fig: Gedächtnis etc*) to play tricks on sb; **immer zu ~en aufgelegt sein** to be always up to pranks *or* tricks **b** (*old, liter*) blow; (*mit Rute, Peitsche*) stroke, lash; **jdm einen ~ versetzen** to strike sb; **auf einen** *or* **mit einem ~** (*lit*) with one blow; (*fig*) in one blow

Strei|chel|ein|hei|ten PL (*= Zärtlichkeit*) tender loving care *sing*; (*= Lob, Anerkennung*) words *pl* of praise; **~ für sein Ego brauchen** to need one's ego stroked

strei|cheln ['ʃtraiçln] VTI to stroke; (*= liebkosen*) to caress; **jdm die Wange/das Haar ~** to stroke/caress sb's cheek/hair

Strei|chel|zoo M petting zoo

strei|chen ['ʃtraiçn] *pret* **strich** [ʃtrɪç], *ptp* **gestrichen** [gə'ʃtrɪçn] VT **a** (*mit der Hand*) to stroke; **etw glatt ~** to smooth sth (out); **sich** (*dat*) **die Haare aus dem Gesicht/der Stirn ~** to push one's hair back from one's face/forehead

b (*= auftragen*) *Butter, Marmelade etc* to spread; *Salbe, Farbe etc* to apply, to put on; **sich** (*dat*) **ein Brot (mit Butter) ~** to butter oneself a slice of bread; **sich ~ lassen** (*Butter etc*) to spread easily

c (*= anstreichen: mit Farbe*) to paint; **frisch gestrichen!** wet (*Brit*) *or* fresh (*US*) paint; **gestrichenes Papier** coated paper

d *Geige, Cello* to bow

e (*= tilgen*) *Zeile, Satz* to delete, to cross out, to strike; *Auftrag, Plan, Zug, freier Tag etc* to cancel; *Schulden* to write off; *Zuschuss, Gelder, Arbeitsplätze etc* to cut; **etw aus dem Protokoll ~** to delete *or* strike sth from the minutes; **jdn/etw von** *or* **aus der Liste ~** to take sb/sth off the list, to delete *or* strike sb/sth from the list; **etw aus seinem Gedächtnis ~** (*geh*) to erase sth from one's memory

f (*Naut*) *Segel, Flagge, Ruder* to strike

g → **gestrichen**

VI **a** (*= über etw hinfahren*) to stroke; **mit der Hand über etw** *acc* **~** to stroke sth (with one's hand); **sie strich ihm über die Hand/das Haar** she stroked his hand/hair

b *aux sein* (*= streifen*) to brush past (*an +dat* sth); (*Wind*) to waft; **um/durch etw ~** (*= herumstreichen*) to prowl around/through sth; **die Katze strich mir um die Beine** the cat rubbed against my legs; **durch den Wald/die Felder ~** (*old, geh*) to ramble *or* wander through the woods/fields

c *aux sein* (*Vögel*) to sweep (*über +acc* over)

d (*= schmieren*) to spread

e (*= malen*) to paint

Strei|cher ['ʃtraiçɐ] PL (*Mus*) strings *pl*

Streich-: **streich|fä|hig** ADJ *Butter* spreadable, easy to spread; **streich|fer|tig** ADJ ready to use *or* apply; **Streich|holz** NT match; **Streich|holz|schach|tel** F matchbox; **Streich|in|stru|ment** NT string(ed) instrument; **die ~e** the strings; **Streich|kä|se** M cheese spread; **Streich|mu|sik** F music for strings; **Streich|or|ches|ter** NT string orchestra; **Streich|quar|tett** NT string quartet; **Streich|quin|tett** NT string quintet; **Streich|rie|men** M strop

Strei|chung ['ʃtraiçʊŋ] F **-, -en** (*= Tilgung*) (*von Zeile, Satz*) deletion; (*= Kürzung*) cut; (*von Auftrag, Plan, Zug, freiem Tag etc*) cancellation; (*von Schulden*) writing off; (*von Zuschüssen, Arbeitsplätzen etc*) cutting; **die drastischen ~en bei den Subventionen** the drastic cuts in subsidies

Streich|wurst F sausage for spreading, ≈ meat paste

Streif|band ['ʃtraifbant] NT *pl* **-bänder** wrapper; **im** *or* **unter** (*Sw*) **~** *posted in a wrapper at reduced rate*

Streif|band-: **Streif|band|de|pot** NT (*Fin*) individual safe-deposit *or* safety-deposit box room; **Streif|band|zei|tung** F *newspaper sent at printed paper rate*

Strei|fe ['ʃtraifə] F **-, -n** **a** (*= Patrouille*) patrol; **auf ~ gehen/sein** to go/be on patrol; **seine ~ machen** to do one's rounds, to patrol; **ein Polizist auf ~** a policeman on his beat **b** (*Hunt*) = **Streifjagd**

strei|fen ['ʃtraifn] VT **a** (*= flüchtig berühren*) to touch, to brush (against); (*Kugel*) to graze; (*Billardkugel*) to kiss; (*Auto*) to scrape; **jdn an der Schulter ~** to touch sb on the shoulder; **jdn mit einem Blick ~** to glance fleetingly at sb; **ein flüchtiger Blick streifte mich** he/she glanced fleetingly at me

b (*fig: = flüchtig erwähnen*) to touch (up)on

c (*= abstreifen, überziehen*) **die Butter vom Messer ~** to scrape the butter off the knife; **die Schuhe von den Füßen ~** to slip one's shoes off; **den Ring vom Finger ~** to slip *or* take the ring off one's finger; **sich** (*dat*) **die Handschuhe über die Finger ~** to pull on one's gloves; **er streifte sich** (*dat*) **den Pullover über den Kopf** (*= an-/ausziehen*) he slipped the pullover over his head; **die Blätter von den Zweigen ~** to strip the leaves from the twigs; **die Ärmel in die Höhe ~** to pull up one's sleeves

VI (*geh*) **a** *aux sein* (*= wandern*) to roam, to wander; (*Fuchs*) to prowl; **(ziellos) durch das Land/die Wälder ~** to roam the country/the forests

b *aux sein* (*= flüchtig berühren: Blick etc*) **sie ließ ihren Blick über die Menge ~** she scanned the crowd; **sein Blick streifte über seine Besitztümer** he gazed at his possessions

c (*fig: = grenzen*) to border (*an +acc* on)

Strei|fen ['ʃtraifn] M **-s, -** **a** (*= Stück, Band, Landstreifen*) strip; (*= Speckstreifen*) rasher; **ein ~ Land/Speck** a strip of land/bacon **b** (*= Strich*) stripe; (*= Farbstreifen*) streak **c** (*= Lochstreifen, Klebestreifen etc*) tape **d** (*= Tresse*) braid; (*Mil*) stripe **e** (*Film*) film; (*= Abschnitt*) strip of film **f** (*= Linie*) line

Strei|fen-: **Strei|fen|dienst** M patrol duty; **Strei|fen|kar|te** F multi-journey ticket; **Strei|fen|mus|ter** NT stripy design *or* pattern; **ein Anzug mit ~** a striped suit; **Strei|fen|po|li|zei** F patrol police (*Brit*) *or* officers (*US*); **Strei|fen|po|li|zist(in)** M(F) policeman/-woman on patrol; **Strei|fen|wa|gen** M patrol car

strei|fig ['ʃtraifɪç] ADJ streaky

Streif-: **Streif|jagd** F walk-up, *hunt where beaters and guns walk together flushing out game*; **Streif|licht** NT (*fig*) highlight; **ein ~ auf etw** (*acc*) **werfen** to highlight sth; **Streif|schuss** M graze; **Streif|zug** M raid; (*= Bummel*) expedition; (*fig: = kurzer Überblick*) brief survey (*durch* of)

Streik [ʃtraik] M **-(e)s, -s** *or* (*rare*) **-e** strike; **zum ~ aufrufen** to call a strike; **jdn zum ~ aufrufen** to call sb out on strike; **in (den) ~ treten** to come out on *or* go on strike

Streik-: **Streik|auf|ruf** M strike call; **Streik|bre|cher** [-brɛçɐ] M **-s, -**, **Streik|bre|che|rin** [-ərɪn] F **-, -nen** strikebreaker, blackleg (*pej*), scab (*pej*)

strei|ken ['ʃtraikn] VI to be on strike, to strike; (*= in Streik treten*) to come out on *or* go on strike, to strike; (*hum inf*) (*= nicht funktionieren*) to pack up (*inf*); (*Magen*) to protest; (*Gedächtnis*) to fail; **die Waschmaschine/das Auto streikt schon wieder** (*inf*) the washing machine/car has packed up again (*inf*); **als er noch einen Schnaps eingoss, habe ich gestreikt** (*inf*) when he poured out another schnapps I refused it; **wenn ich heute abwaschen soll, streike ich** (*inf*) if I have to do the washing-up today, I'll go on strike (*inf*); **da streike ich** (*inf*) I refuse!, count me out (*inf*)

Strei|ken|de(r) ['ʃtraikndə] MF *decl as adj* striker

Streik-: **Streik|geld** NT strike pay; **Streik|kas|se** F strike fund; **Streik|pos|ten** M picket; **~ aufstellen** to put up pickets; **~ stehen** to picket; **Streik|recht** NT right *or* freedom to strike; **Streik|wel|le** F wave *or* series of strikes

Streit [ʃtrait] M **-(e)s, -e** **a** argument (*um, über +acc* about, over); (*leichter*) quarrel, squabble; (*zwischen Eheleuten, Kindern*) fight, argument; (*= Fehde*) feud; (*= Auseinandersetzung*) dispute; **~ haben** to be arguing *or* quarrelling (*Brit*) *or* quarreling (*US*); **wegen etw mit jdm (einen) ~ haben** to argue with sb about sth, to have an argument with sb about sth; **die Nachbarn haben seit Jahren ~** the neighbours (*Brit*) *or* neighbors (*US*) have been arguing *or* fighting for years; **wegen einer Sache ~ bekommen** to get into an argument over sth; **~ anfangen** to start an argument; **~ suchen** to be looking for an argument *or* a quarrel; **in ~ liegen** (*Gefühle*) to conflict; **mit jdm in ~ liegen** to be at loggerheads with sb → **Zaun**

b (*old, liter: = Kampf*) battle; **zum ~(e) rüsten** to arm oneself for battle

Streit|axt F (*Hist*) battle-axe (*Brit*), battle-ax (*US*); **die ~ begraben** (*fig*) to bury the hatchet

streit|bar ADJ **a** (*= streitlustig*) pugnacious **b** (*old: = tapfer*) valiant

strei|ten ['ʃtraitn] *pret* **stritt** [ʃtrɪt], *ptp* **gestritten** [gə'ʃtrɪtn] VI **a** (*= eine Auseinandersetzung haben*) to argue (*um, über +acc* about, over); (*leichter*) to quarrel, to squabble; (*Eheleute, Kinder*) to fight, to argue; (*Jur: = prozessieren*) to take legal action; **mit Waffen/Fäusten ~** to fight with weapons/one's fists; **Scheu und Neugier stritten in ihr** she had conflicting feelings of shyness and curiosity; **die Streitenden** the arguers, the people fighting; **es wird immer noch gestritten, ob ...** the argument about whether ... is still going on

b (*= debattieren*) **über** *or* **um etw** (*acc*) **~** to dispute *or* argue about *or* over sth; (*Jur*) to go to court over sth; **darüber kann man** *or* **lässt sich ~** that's a debatable *or* moot point; **die ~den Parteien** (*Jur*) the litigants

c (*old, liter*) (*= kämpfen*) to fight; (*in Wettbewerb*) to compete (*um* for)

VR to argue; (*leichter*) to quarrel, to squabble; (*Eheleute, Kinder auch*) to fight, to argue; **habt ihr euch schon wieder gestritten?** have you been fighting again?; **wir wollen uns deswegen nicht ~!** don't let's fall out over that!; **man streitet sich, ob ...** there is argument as to whether ...

Strei|ter ['ʃtraitɐ] M **-s, -**, **Strei|te|rin** [-ərɪn] F **-, -nen** (*geh*) fighter (*für* for); (*für Prinzip etc auch*) champion (*für* of)

Strei|te|rei [ʃtraitə'rai] F **-, -en** (*inf*) arguing *no pl*, quarrelling *no pl* (*Brit*), quarreling *no pl* (*US*); (*zwischen Eheleuten, Kindern auch*) fighting *no pl*; **eine ~** an argument

Streit-: **Streit|fall** M dispute, conflict; (*Jur*) case; **im ~** in case of dispute *or* conflict; **im ~ Müller gegen Braun** in the case of Müller versus Braun; **Streit|fra|ge** F dispute; **Streit|ge|gen|stand** M matter in dispute; (*= strittiger Punkt*) matter of dispute; **Streit|ge|spräch** NT debate, discussion; (*Liter, Univ auch*) disputation; **Streit|grund** M cause of the/an argument; **Streit|hahn** M (*inf*) squabbler; **Streit|ham|mel** M, (*S Ger, Aus*) **Streit|han|sel** [-hanzl] M **-s, -** (*inf*) quarrelsome person

strei|tig ['ʃtraitɪç] ADJ **jdm das Recht auf etw** (*acc*) **~ machen** to dispute sb's right to sth; **jdm das Geschäft/den ersten Platz ~ machen** to vie (*form*) *or* compete with sb for business/for first place; **das/seine Kompetenz kann man ihm nicht ~ machen** that/his competence is indisputable

Strei|tig|kei|ten PL quarrels *pl*, squabbles *pl*

Streit-: **Streit|kräf|te** PL forces *pl*, troops *pl*; **Streit|kul|tur** F culture of debate; **eine ~ entwickeln** to debate things in a civilized manner; **Streit|lust** F (*liter*) argumentative disposition;

(= Aggressivität) aggressive disposition; **Streit|lus|tig** ADJ *(geh)* argumentative; *(= aggressiv)* aggressive; **Streit|macht** F armed forces *pl*; **Streit|ob|jekt** NT matter in dispute; *(= strittiger Punkt)* matter of dispute; **Streit|punkt** M contentious issue; **Streit|ross** NT warhorse; **Streit|sa|che** F dispute; *(Jur)* case; **Streit|schrift** F polemic; **Streit|sucht** F quarrelsomeness; **streit|süch|tig** ADJ quarrelsome; **Streit|wa|gen** M *(Hist)* chariot; **Streit|wert** M *(Jur)* amount in dispute

streng [ʃtrɛŋ] ✪ 36.3, 46.5 ADJ **a** strict; *Regel, Kontrolle* strict, stringent; *Maßnahmen* stringent; *Bestrafung* severe; *Anforderungen* rigorous; *Ausdruck, Blick, Gesicht* stern; *Sitten, Disziplin* rigid, strict; *Stillschweigen, Diskretion* absolute; *Mode, Schnitt* severe; *Kritik, Urteil* harsh, severe; *Richter* severe, stern; *Lebensführung, Schönheit, Form* austere; *Examen* stiff; **~ gegen sich selbst sein** to be strict *or* severe on *or* with oneself; **~ aber gerecht** severe but just → **Regiment a**
b *(= durchdringend) Geruch, Geschmack* pungent; *Frost, Kälte, Winter* intense, severe
c *(= strenggläubig) Katholik, Moslem etc* strict
ADV **a** *(= unnachgiebig) befolgen, einhalten* strictly, rigidly; *tadeln, bestrafen* severely; *vertraulich, wissenschaftlich* strictly; **~ genommen** strictly speaking; *(= eigentlich)* actually; **~ gegen jdn/etw vorgehen** to deal severely with sb/sth; **~ durchgreifen** to take rigorous *or* stringent action; **~ geheim** top secret; **~ nach Vorschrift** strictly according to regulations; **~(stens) verboten!** strictly prohibited; **sie kleidet sich sehr ~** she wears very severe clothes
b *(= intensiv)* **~ riechen/schmecken** to have a pungent smell/taste; **der Käse schmeckt mir zu ~** this cheese tastes too strong for me
c *(Sw)* **es ~ haben** to be under a lot of pressure

Stren|ge [ˈʃtrɛŋə] F -, *no pl* **a** strictness; *(von Regel, Kontrolle, Maßnahmen)* stringency; *(von Bestrafung)* severity; *(von Ausdruck, Blick)* sternness; *(von Kritik, Urteil)* harshness, severity; *(von Richter)* severity, sternness; **mit ~ regieren** to rule strictly **b** *(= Schärfe) (von Geruch, Geschmack)* pungency; *(von Kälte)* intensity; *(von Frost, Winter)* severity

streng-: **streng|ge|nom|men** ADV → **streng** ADV **a**; **streng|gläu|big** ADJ strict; **streng neh|men** VT *sep irreg* to take seriously; **es mit etw ~** to be strict about sth; **wenn man es streng nimmt** strictly speaking

Strep|to|kok|ken [ʃtrɛptoˈkɔkn, st-] PL *(Med)* streptococci *pl*

Strep|to|my|cin [ʃtrɛptomyˈtsiːn, st-] NT -s, *no pl (Med)* streptomycin

Stre|se|mann [ˈʃtreːzaman] M -s, *no pl formal, dark suit with striped trousers*

Stress [ʃtrɛs, st-] M -es, -e *(alle Bedeutungen)* stress; **der tägliche ~ im Büro** the daily stress *or* hassle *(inf)* in the office; **(voll) im ~ sein** *or* **stehen** to be under (a lot of) stress; **ich bin heute im ~** I'm feeling hassled today *(inf)*

Stress|ball M stress ball

Stress|be|wäl|ti|gung F stress management

stres|sen [ˈʃtrɛsn] VT to put under stress; **gestresst sein** to be under stress

stress-: **stress|frei** ADJ stress-free; **stress|ge|plagt** [-gəplaːkt] ADJ under stress; **~e Manager** highly stressed executives, executives suffering from stress; **Stress|hor|mon** NT stress hormone

stres|sig [ˈʃtrɛsɪç] ADJ *(inf)* stressful

Stress-: **Stress|krank|heit** F stress disease; **Stress|si|tu|a|ti|on** F stress situation

Stretch-: **Stretch|cord|ho|se** F stretch cords *pl or* corduroys *pl*; **Stretch|ho|se** F stretch trousers *pl*

Stret|ching [ˈstrɛtʃɪŋ] NT -s, *no pl (Gymnastik)* stretching exercises *pl*

Stretch-: **Stretch|li|mo** F *(inf)*, **Stretch|li|mou|si|ne** F stretch limo; **Stretch|stoff** [ˈstrɛtʃ-] M stretch fabric

Streu [ʃtrɔy] F -, *no pl* straw; *(aus Sägespänen)* sawdust

Streu-: **Streu|be|sitz** M *(St Ex)* widely spread shareholdings *pl*, widely held stock; **Streu|dienst** M *(im Winter)* (road-)gritting service, (road) maintenance crew *(US)*; **„kein ~!"** "untreated road"

streu|en [ˈʃtrɔyən] VT *Futter, Samen* to scatter; *Blumen auch* to strew; *Dünger, Stroh, Sand, Kies* to spread; *Gewürze, Zucker etc* to sprinkle; *Straße, Gehweg etc (mit Sand)* to grit; *(mit Salz)* to salt; *(fig) Gerüchte etc* to spread; *Aktien* to make widely available; **die Regierung ließ ~, dass ...** the government gave reason to believe that ... VI **a** *(= Streumittel anwenden)* to grit; to put down salt **b** *(Salzstreuer etc)* to sprinkle **c** *(Linse, Gewehr etc)* to scatter

Streu|er [ˈʃtrɔyɐ] M -s, - shaker; *(= Salzstreuer)* cellar; *(= Pfefferstreuer)* pot

Streu-: **Streu|fahr|zeug** NT gritter; **Streu|gut** NT, *no pl* (road) grit

streu|nen [ˈʃtrɔynən] VI **a** *(= nicht sesshaft sein)* to roam about, to wander about *or* around; *(Hund, Katze)* to stray **b** *aux sein* **durch etw/in etw** *(dat)* **~** to roam *or* wander through/around sth

Streu|ner [ˈʃtrɔynɐ] M -s, - *(= Tier)* stray; *(= Person)* tramp, vagrant

Streu-: **Streu|obst|wie|se** F meadow orchard; **Streu|pflicht** F *obligation on householder to keep area in front of house gritted in icy weather*; **Streu|pul|ver** NT grit *or (Salz)* salt *(for icy roads)*; **Streu|salz** NT salt *(for icy roads)*; **Streu|sand** M sand; *(für Straße)* grit

Streu|sel [ˈʃtrɔyzl] NT -s, - *(Cook)* crumble *(Brit) or* crumb *(US)* (mixture)

Streu|sel|ku|chen M *thin sponge cake with crumble topping*

Streu|ung [ˈʃtrɔyʊŋ] F -, -en *(Statistik)* mean variation; *(Phys)* scattering

Streu-: **Streu|ver|lust** M *(Phys)* loss of intensity due to scattering; *(fig)* loss due to a scattershot approach; **Streu|wa|gen** M (road) gritter; **Streu|zu|cker** M *(grob)* granulated sugar; *(fein)* castor sugar

strich *pret von* **streichen**

Strich [ʃtrɪç] M -(e)s, -e **a** line; *(= Querstrich)* dash; *(= Schrägstrich)* oblique, slash; *(= Federstrich, Pinselstrich)* stroke; *(von Land)* stretch; **etw mit wenigen ~en skizzieren** *or* **zeichnen** *(lit, fig)* to sketch *or* outline sth with a few brief strokes; **jdm einen ~ durch die Rechnung/einen Plan machen** to thwart sb's plans/plan; **einen ~ (unter etw** *acc***) machen** *or* **ziehen** *(fig)* to forget sth; **unterm ~ sein** *(inf)* not to be up to scratch *(Brit) or* up to snuff *(US)*; **unterm ~** at the final count; **er kann noch auf dem ~ gehen** *(inf)* he can still walk along a straight line; **dünn wie ein ~** *(inf)* as thin as a rake *(Brit inf) or* rail *(US inf)*; **sie ist nur noch ein ~ (in der Landschaft** *hum***)** *(inf)* she's as thin as a rake *(Brit) or* rail *(US)* now *(inf)*; **keinen ~ tun** *(inf)* not to do a stroke (of work)
b *no pl (= Kompassstrich)* point
c *(von Teppich)* pile; *(von Samt)* pile, nap; *(von Gewebe)* nap; *(von Fell, Haar)* direction of growth; **gegen den ~ bürsten** *(lit)* to brush the wrong way; **es geht (mir) gegen den ~** *(inf)* it goes against the grain; **nach ~ und Faden** *(inf)* good and proper *(inf)*, thoroughly; **jdn nach ~ und Faden versohlen** *(inf)* to give sb a thorough or good hiding *(inf)*
d *(Mus: = Bogenstrich)* stroke, bow; **einen harten/weichen ~ haben** to bow heavily/lightly
e *(inf) (= Prostitution)* prostitution *no art*; *(= Bordellgegend)* red-light district; **auf den ~ gehen** to be on the game *(Brit inf)*, to be a prostitute
f *(von Schwalben etc)* flight

Strich-: **Strich|ät|zung** F *(Typ)* line etching; **Strich|code** M barcode *(Brit)*, universal product code *(US)*

stri|cheln [ˈʃtrɪçln] VI to sketch it in; *(= schraffieren)* to hatch VT to sketch in; to hatch; **eine gestrichelte Linie** a broken line

Stri|cher [ˈʃtrɪçɐ] M -s, - *(pej inf)* rent boy *(Brit)*, boy prostitute

Stri|che|rin [ˈʃtrɪçərɪn] F -, -nen *(pej inf)* tart *(inf)*, hooker *(esp US inf)*

Strich-: **Strich|jun|ge** M *(inf)* rent boy *(Brit)*, boy prostitute; **Strich|kode** M = **Strichcode**; **Strich|lis|te** F check list; **eine ~ führen** *(auch fig)* to keep a careful record *or* account *(über +acc* of); **Strich|mäd|chen** NT *(inf)* tart *(inf)*, hooker *(esp US inf)*; **Strich|männ|chen** NT matchstick man, stick man; **Strich|punkt** M semicolon; **strich|wei|se** ADV *(auch Met)* here and there; **~ Regen** rain in places; **Strich|zeich|nung** F line drawing

Strick [ʃtrɪk] M -(e)s, -e **a** rope; *(dünner, als Gürtel)* cord; **jdm aus etw einen ~ drehen** to use sth against sb; **zum ~ greifen** *(inf)* to hang oneself; **dann kann ich mir einen ~ nehmen** *or* **kaufen** *(inf)* I may as well pack it all in *(inf)*; **am gleichen** *or* **an einem ~ ziehen** *(fig)* to pull together → **reißen VI a b** *(inf: = Schelm)* rascal; **fauler ~** lazybones *sing (inf)*, lazy so-and-so *(inf)*

Strick NT -(e)s, *no pl (inf)* knitwear

Strick-: **Strick|ar|beit** F knitting *no pl*; **eine ~** a piece of knitting; **Strick|beu|tel** M knitting bag

stri|cken [ˈʃtrɪkn] VTI to knit; *(fig)* to construct; **an etw** *(dat)* **~** *(lit, fig)* to work on sth; **mit der heißen Nadel gestrickt** *(pej inf)* thrown together; **er ist einfach gestrickt** *(inf)* he's a simple soul *(inf)*

Stri|cker [ˈʃtrɪkɐ] M -s, -, **Stri|cke|rin** [-ərɪn] F -, -nen knitter

Stri|cke|rei [ʃtrɪkəˈrai] F -, -en **a** knitting *no indef art, no pl* **b** *(Betrieb)* knitwear factory

Strick-: **Strick|garn** NT knitting wool; **Strick|hand|schu|he** PL knitted gloves *pl*; **Strick|ja|cke** F cardigan; **Strick|kleid** NT knitted dress; **Strick|lei|ter** F rope ladder; **Strick|ma|schi|ne** F knitting machine; **Strick|mus|ter** NT *(lit)* knitting pattern; *(fig)* pattern; **Strick|na|del** F knitting needle; **Strick|wa|ren** PL knitwear *sing*; **Strick|wes|te** F knitted waistcoat; *(mit Ärmeln)* cardigan; **Strick|wol|le** F knitting wool; **Strick|zeug** NT, *no pl* knitting

Strie|gel [ˈʃtriːgl] M -s, - currycomb

strie|geln [ˈʃtriːgln] VT **a** *Tier* to curry(comb); *(fig inf: = kämmen)* to comb → *auch* **gestriegelt b** *(inf: = hart behandeln)* **jdn ~** to put sb through the hoop *(inf)* VR *(inf)* to spruce oneself up

Strie|me [ˈʃtriːmə] F -, -n, **Strie|men** [ˈʃtriːmən] M -s, - weal

strie|mig [ˈʃtriːmɪç] ADJ *Haut* marked with weals

Strie|zel [ˈʃtriːtsl] M -s, - *(dial Cook)* plaited Danish pastry

strikt [ʃtrɪkt, st-] ADJ strict; *Ablehnung* categorical ADV strictly; *ablehnen* categorically; **~ gegen etw sein** to be totally opposed to sth

String-
String|slip M G-string, thong
String|tan|ga M string tanga

strin|gent [ʃtrɪŋˈgɛnt, st-] *(geh)* ADJ stringent; *Politik, Entscheidungen, Konzept* rigorous; *Schlussfolgerung* compelling; *Handlung* tight ADV *argumentieren, durchführen* stringently; **etw ~ nachweisen** to provide compelling proof for sth

Strip [ʃtrɪp, st-] M -s, -s *(inf)* strip(tease)

Strip|pe [ˈʃtrɪpə] F -, -n *(inf)* **a** *(= Bindfaden)* string; **die ~n ziehen** *(fig)* to pull the strings **b** *(= Telefonleitung)* phone, blower *(Brit inf)*; **an der ~ hängen** to be on the phone *or* blower *(Brit sl)*; **sich an die ~ hängen** to get on the phone *or* blower *(Brit sl)*; **jdn an der ~ haben** to have sb on the line *or* phone *or* blower *(Brit sl)*

strip|pen ['ʃtrɪpn, 'st-] VI to strip, to do a striptease act

Strip|pen|zie|her ['ʃtrɪpəntsiːɐ] M **-s, -, Strip|pen|zie|he|rin** [-ərɪn] F (inf) **er war der ~** he was the one pulling the strings

Strip|per ['ʃtrɪpɐ, 'st-] M **-s, -, Strip|pe|rin** [-ərɪn] F **-, -nen** (inf) stripper

Strip|tease ['ʃtrɪptiːs, 'st-] M OR NT **-,** no pl striptease

Strip|tease|tän|zer(in) ['ʃtrɪptiːs-, st-] M(F) stripper

stritt pret von **streiten**

strit|tig ['ʃtrɪtɪç] ADJ contentious, controversial; **noch ~** still in dispute

Striz|zi ['ʃtrɪtsi] M **-s, -s** (Aus inf) pimp

Stro|bo|skop [ʃtrobo'skoːp, st-] NT **-s, -e** stroboscope

Stro|bo|skop|blitz M stroboscopic light

stro|bo|sko|pisch [ʃtrobo'skoːpɪʃ, st-] ADJ stroboscopic

Stro|bo|skop|lam|pe F strobe light

Stroh [ʃtroː] NT **-(e)s,** no pl straw; (= Dachstroh) thatch; **~ im Kopf haben** (inf) to have sawdust between one's ears (inf) → **dreschen VT a**

Stroh-: **Stroh|bal|len** M bale of straw; **stroh|blond** ADJ Mensch flaxen-haired; Haare flaxen, straw-coloured (Brit), straw-colored (US); **Stroh|blu|me** F strawflower; **Stroh|bund** NT pl **-bunde** bundle of straw; **Stroh|dach** NT thatched roof; **stroh|dumm** ADJ thick (inf); **stroh|far|ben** [-farbn] ADJ straw-coloured (Brit), straw-colored (US); Haare auch flaxen; **Stroh|feu|er** NT **ein ~ sein** (fig) to be a passing fancy; **Stroh|frau** F (fig) front woman; **stroh|ge|deckt** ADJ thatched; **stroh|gelb** ADJ straw-coloured; Haare auch flaxen; **Stroh|halm** M straw; **sich an einen ~ klammern, nach einem ~ greifen** to clutch at straws; **Stroh|hut** M straw hat; **Stroh|hüt|te** F thatched hut

stro|hig ['ʃtroːɪç] ADJ Gemüse tough; Orangen etc dry; Haar dull and lifeless

Stroh-: **Stroh|kopf** M (inf) blockhead (inf); **Stroh|la|ger** NT pallet, straw mattress; **Stroh|mann** M pl **-männer** (= Strohpuppe) scarecrow; (fig) front man; (Cards) dummy; **Stroh|mat|te** F straw mat; **Stroh|pup|pe** F scarecrow; **Stroh|sack** M palliasse; **heiliger ~!** (dated inf) good(ness) gracious (me)!; **stroh|tro|cken** ADJ very dry; (fig: = langweilig) (as) dry as dust; **Stroh|wit|we** F grass widow; **Stroh|wit|wer** M grass widower

Strolch [ʃtrɔlç] M **-(e)s, -e** (dated pej) rogue, rascal

strol|chen ['ʃtrɔlçn] VI aux sein to roam about; **durch etw/in etw** (dat) **~** to roam through/around sth

Strom [ʃtroːm] M **-(e)s, ¨-e** ['ʃtrøːmə] **a** (large) river; (= Strömung) current; (von Schweiß, Blut) river; (von Besuchern, Flüchen etc) stream; **ein reißender ~** a raging torrent; **Ströme und Flüsse Europas** rivers of Europe; **ein ~ von Tränen** (geh) floods of tears pl; **in dem** or **im ~ der Vergessenheit versinken** (geh) to sink or pass into oblivion; **es regnet in Strömen** it's pouring (with rain); **der Wein floss in Strömen** the wine flowed like water; **der ~ seiner Rede** (geh) the torrent or flood of his words; **der ~ der Zeit** (geh) the flow of time; **der ~ der Geschichte** (geh) the course of history; **mit dem/gegen den ~ schwimmen** (lit) to swim with/against the current; (fig) to swim or go with/against the tide **b** (Elec) **(elektrischer) ~** current; (= Elektrizität) electricity; **~ führen** to be live; **~ führend** (Elec, Leitung) live; **unter ~ stehen** (lit) to be live; (fig) to be high (inf); **mit ~ heizen** to have electric heating; **der ~ ist ausgefallen** the power or electricity is off

Strom-: **strom|ab** [ʃtroːm'lap] ADV downstream; **Strom|ab|neh|mer** M (Rail etc) pantograph; **Strom|ab|neh|mer(in)** M(F) (= Verbraucher) user or consumer of electricity; **strom|ab|wärts** [ʃtroːm'lapvɛrts] ADV downstream; **Strom|an|bie|ter** M electricity supplier or provider; **Strom|an|schluss** M **~ haben** to be connected to the electricity mains; **strom|auf|(wärts)** [ʃtroːm'lauf(vɛrts)] ADV upstream; **Strom|aus|fall** M power failure; **Strom|bett** NT riverbed

strö|men ['ʃtrøːmən] VI aux sein to stream; (Blut auch, Gas) to flow; (Menschen) to pour (in into, aus out of); **bei ~dem Regen** in (the) pouring rain

Stro|mer ['ʃtroːmɐ] M **-s, -, Stro|me|rin** [-ərɪn] F **-, -nen** (inf) rover; (= Landstreicher) tramp, hobo (esp US)

stro|mern ['ʃtroːmɐn] VI aux sein (inf) to roam or wander about

Strom-: **Strom|er|zeu|ger** M (electricity) generator; **Strom|er|zeu|gung** F electricity production or generation; **strom|füh|rend** ADJ attr → **Strom b**; **Strom|ka|bel** NT electric or power cable; **Strom|kreis** M (electrical) circuit; **Strom|lei|tung** F electric cables pl; **Strom|li|ni|en|form** F streamlined design; (von Auto auch) streamlined body; **strom|li|ni|en|för|mig** ADJ (lit, fig) streamlined ADV (fig) **sich ~ verhalten** to be a conformist; **Parteimitglieder, die ~ denken** party members who think exactly along party lines; **sich einer Sache** (dat) **~ anpassen, sich ~ in etw** (acc) **einfügen** to adapt (oneself) to sth; **Strom|mes|ser** M **-s, -** (Elec) ammeter; **Strom|netz** NT electricity or power supply system; **Strom|preis** M electricity price; **Strom|pro|duk|ti|on** F electricity production or generation; **Strom|quel|le** F source of power or electricity; **Strom|schie|ne** F (Rail) live or conductor rail; **Strom|schlag** M electric shock; **Strom|schnel|le** F rapids pl; **Strom|span|nung** F voltage; **Strom|spei|cher** M (storage) battery; **Strom|sper|re** F power cut; **Strom|stär|ke** F strength of the/an electric current; **Strom|stoß** M electric shock; **Strom|ta|rif** M tariff of electricity charges; (einzelner) electricity rate

Strö|mung ['ʃtrøːmʊŋ] F **-, -en** current; (fig auch) trend

Strö|mungs|leh|re F (von Flüssigkeiten) hydrodynamics sing; (von Luft und Gasen) aerodynamics sing

Strom-: **Strom|ver|brauch** M electricity or power consumption; **Strom|ver|sor|ger(in)** M(F) electricity supplier; **Strom|ver|sor|gung** F electricity or power supply; **Strom|wen|der** [-vɛndɐ] M **-s, -** commutator; **Strom|zäh|ler** M electricity meter

Stron|ti|um ['ʃtrɔntsiʊm, 'st-] NT **-s,** no pl (abbr **Sr**) strontium

Stro|phe ['ʃtroːfə] F **-, -n** verse; (in Gedicht auch) stanza

-stro|phig [ʃtroːfɪç] ADJ suf **dreistrophig/vierstrophig sein** (Gedicht) to have three/four stanzas or verses; (Lied) to have three/four verses

stro|phisch ['ʃtroːfɪʃ] ADJ stanzaic ADV in stanzas

strot|zen ['ʃtrɔtsn] VI to be full (von, vor +dat of), to abound (von, vor +dat with); (von Kraft, Gesundheit, Lebensfreude) to be bursting (von with); (vor Ungeziefer) to be teeming or crawling (vor +dat with); (von Waffen) to be bristling (von with); **von Schmutz ~** to be thick or covered with dirt

strub|be|lig ['ʃtrʊbəlɪç] ADJ (inf) Haar, Fell tousled

Strub|bel|kopf ['ʃtrʊbl-] M (inf) tousled hair; (Mensch) tousle-head; **einen ~ haben, ein ~ sein** to have tousled hair

strubb|lig ['ʃtrʊblɪç] ADJ (inf) Haar, Fell tousled

Stru|del ['ʃtruːdl] M **-s, -** **a** (lit, fig) whirlpool; (von Ereignissen, Vergnügen) whirl **b** (Cook) strudel

stru|deln ['ʃtruːdln] VI to whirl, to swirl

Stru|del|teig M (esp S Ger, Aus: Cook) strudel pastry

Struk|tur [ʃtrʊk'tuːɐ, st-] F **-, -en** structure; (von Stoff etc) texture; (= Webart) weave

Struk|tu|ra|lis|mus [ʃtrʊktura'lɪsmʊs, st-] M **-,** no pl structuralism

struk|tu|ra|lis|tisch [ʃtrʊktura'lɪstɪʃ, st-] ADJ structuralist ADV **etw ~ interpretieren** to interpret sth according to structuralist methods

Struk|tur|ana|ly|se F structural analysis

struk|tu|rell [ʃtrʊktu'rɛl, st-] ADJ Probleme, Veränderungen structural; **~e Arbeitslosigkeit** structural unemployment ADV **~ bedingt** structurally; **~ gesehen** looking at the infrastructure; **sich ~ auswirken** to have an effect on the infrastructure; **ein ~ schwaches Gebiet** a region with a weak infrastructure

Struk|tur|fonds M structural fund (to assist infrastructually weak regions of the EU)

Struk|tur|for|mel F (Chem) structural formula

struk|tu|rie|ren [ʃtrʊktu'riːrən, st-] ptp **strukturiert** VT to structure

Struk|tu|rie|rung F **-, -en** structuring

Struk|tur-: **Struk|tur|kri|se** F structural crisis; **Struk|tur|po|li|tik** F structural policy; **Struk|tur|prob|lem** NT structural problem; **Struk|tur|re|form** F structural reform; **struk|tur|schwach** ADJ lacking in infrastructure; **die ~en Gebiete Bayerns** the parts of Bavaria with less well-developed infrastructure; **Struk|tur|schwä|che** F lack of infrastructure; **Struk|tur|wan|del** M structural change (+gen in)

strul|lern ['ʃtrʊlɐn] VI (sl: = pinkeln) to have a slash (Brit inf), to take a leak (inf)

Strumpf [ʃtrʊmpf] M **-(e)s, ¨-e** ['ʃtrʏmpfə] **a** sock; (= Damenstrumpf) stocking; **ein Paar Strümpfe** a pair of socks/stockings; **auf Strümpfen** in one's stockinged feet **b** (= Sparstrumpf) **sein Geld im ~ haben** ≈ to keep one's money under the mattress **c** (= Glühstrumpf) mantle

Strumpf-: **Strumpf|band** [-bant] NT pl **-bänder** garter; **Strumpf|fab|rik** F hosiery factory; **Strumpf|ge|schäft** NT hosiery shop (esp Brit) or store (esp US); **Strumpf|hal|ter** M suspender (Brit), garter (US); **Strumpf|hal|ter|gür|tel** M suspender belt (Brit), garter belt (US); **Strumpf|ho|se** F tights pl (esp Brit), pantihose; **eine ~** a pair of tights (esp Brit) or pantihose; **Strumpf|mas|ke** F stocking mask; **Strumpf|wa|ren** PL hosiery sing; **Strumpf|wir|ker** [-vɪrkɐ] M **-s, -, Strumpf|wir|ke|rin** [-ərɪn] F **-, -nen** hosiery worker

Strunk [ʃtrʊŋk] M **-(e)s, ¨-e** ['ʃtrʏŋkə] stalk

strup|pig ['ʃtrʊpɪç] ADJ unkempt; Tier shaggy

Struw|wel|kopf ['ʃtrʊvl-] M (inf) = **Strubbelkopf**

Struw|wel|pe|ter ['ʃtrʊvl-] M tousle-head; **der ~** (Liter) shock-headed Peter, Struwwelpeter

Strych|nin [ʃtrʏç'niːn, st-] NT **-s,** no pl strychnine

Stub|ben ['ʃtʊbn] M **-s, -** (N Ger) tree stump

Stüb|chen ['ʃtyːpçən] NT **-s, -** dim von **Stube** little room

Stu|be ['ʃtuːbə] F **-, -n** (dated, dial) room; (dial: = Wohnzimmer) lounge; (in Kaserne) barrack room (Brit), quarters; (Sch) study; (= Schlafsaal) dormitory; **auf der ~** (Mil) in one's barrack room (Brit), in one's quarters; (Sch) in one's study/dormitory; **die gute ~** the parlour (dated Brit) or parlor (dated US); **(immer) herein in die gute ~!** (hum inf) come right in!; **in der ~ hocken** (inf) to sit around indoors

Stü|bel ['ʃtyːbl] NT **-s, -** (Aus) small room

Stu|ben-: **Stu|ben|äl|tes|te(r)** MF decl as adj → **Stube** (Mil) senior soldier in a/the barrack room (Brit) or in the quarters; (Sch) study/dormitory prefect; **Stu|ben|ap|pell** M → **Stube** (Mil) barrack-room inspection (Brit), inspection of quarters; (Sch) study/dormitory inspection; **Stu|ben|ar|rest** M confinement to one's room or (Mil) quarters; **~ haben** to be confined to one's room/quarters; **Stu|ben|dienst** M → **Stube** (Mil) fatigue duty, barrack-room duty

(Brit); *(Sch)* study/dormitory cleaning duty; **~ haben** to be on fatigue duty *etc*; **Stu|ben|flie|ge** F (common) housefly; **Stu|ben|ge|lehr|te(r)** MF *decl as adj (pej)* armchair scholar; **Stu|ben|ho|cker** [-hɔkɐ] M **-s, -, Stu|ben|ho|cke|rin** [-ərɪn] F **-, -nen** *(pej inf)* stay-at--home; **er ist ein richtiger ~** he sits at home all the time; **Stu|ben|ka|me|rad(in)** M(F) *(esp Mil)* roommate *(Brit)*, bunkmate *(US)*; **Stu|ben|kü|cken** NT *(Cook)* young chick *(six to eight weeks old)*; **Stu|ben|mäd|chen** NT *(dated)* chambermaid; **stu|ben|rein** ADJ *Katze, Hund* house-trained; *(hum) Witz* clean

Stü|berl [ˈʃtyːbɐl] NT **-s, -** *(Aus)* small room

Stuck [ʃtʊk] M **-(e)s,** *no pl* stucco; *(zur Zimmerverzierung)* moulding *(Brit)*, molding *(US)*

Stück [ʃtʏk] NT **-(e)s, -e** *or (nach Zahlenangaben)* **-** **a** piece; *(von Vieh, Wild)* head; *(von Zucker)* lump; *(= Ausstellungsstück)* item, piece; *(= Seifenstück)* bar, cake; *(= abgegrenztes Land)* plot; **ich nehme fünf ~** I'll take five; **12 ~ (Eier)** twelve *or* a dozen (eggs); **20 ~ Vieh** 20 head of cattle; **sechs ~ von diesen Apfelsinen** six of these oranges; **12 ~, ~er 12** *(hum)* 12 all told; **10 Cent das ~, pro ~ 10 Cent** 10 cents each; **im** *or* **am ~** in one piece; *Käse, Wurst auch* unsliced; **etw nach ~ verkaufen** to sell sth by the piece; **aus einem ~** in one piece; **~ für ~** *(= ein Exemplar nach dem andern)* one by one; **nach ~ bezahlt werden** *(Stücklohn erhalten)* to do piecework; **das größte/beste ~ (Fleisch** *etc***)** the biggest/best piece (of meat *etc*); **ein ~ Garten** a patch of garden; **das ist unser bestes ~** *(hum)* that is our pride and joy
b *(= Teil, Abschnitt)* piece, bit; *(von Buch, Rede, Reise etc)* part; *(von Straße etc)* stretch; **ich möchte nur ein kleines ~** I only want a little bit *or* a small piece; **~ für ~** *(= einen Teil um den andern)* bit by bit; **in ~e gehen/zerspringen** to be broken/smashed to pieces; **etw in ~e schlagen** to smash sth to pieces; **etw in ~e reißen** to tear sth to pieces *or* shreds; **sich für jdn in ~e reißen lassen** to do anything for sb; **ein ~ Heimat** a piece of home; **in allen ~en** on every matter; *übereinstimmen auch* in every detail; **ich komme ein ~ (des Weges) mit** I'll come some *or* part of the way with you
c ein ~ spazieren gehen to go for a walk; **ein gutes ~ weiterkommen** to make considerable progress *or* headway; **ein schweres ~ Arbeit** a tough job; **ein schönes ~ Geld** *(inf)* a tidy sum, a pretty penny *(inf)*; **das ist (doch) ein starkes ~!** *(inf)* that's a bit much *(inf)*; **große ~e auf jdn halten** to think much *or* highly of sb, to have a high opinion of sb; **große ~e auf etw** *(acc)* **halten** to be very proud of sth; **aus freien ~en** of one's own free will
d *(Fin)* share
e *(= Bühnenstück)* play; *(= Musikstück)* piece
f *(inf: Mensch)* beggar *(esp Brit inf)*, so-and-so *(inf)*; **mein bestes ~** *(hum inf)* my pride and joy; **ein ~ Dreck** *(inf) (Frau)* a bitch *(sl)*, a cow *(inf)*; *(Mann)* a bastard *(sl)*

Stück|ak|kord M piecework

Stuck|ar|beit F stucco work *no pl*; *(in Zimmer)* moulding *(Brit)*, molding *(US)*

Stück|ar|beit F piecework

Stu|cka|teur [ʃtʊkaˈtøːɐ] M **-s, -e, Stu|cka|teu|rin** [-ˈtøːrɪn] F **-, -nen** plasterer *(who works with stucco)*

Stu|cka|tur [ʃtʊkaˈtuːɐ] F **-, -en** stucco (work), ornamental plasterwork

Stück|chen [ˈʃtʏkçən] NT **-s, -** *dim von* **Stück a, b, e**

Stuck|de|cke F stucco(ed) ceiling

stü|ckeln [ˈʃtʏkln] VT to patch VI to patch it together

Stü|cke|lung F **-, -en** *(= Aufteilung)* splitting up; *(von Geld, Aktien)* denomination; **in kleiner ~** *(Geldbetrag)* in small denominations

stu|cken [ˈʃtʊkn] VI *(Aus inf)* to swot *(Brit inf)*, to cram *(inf)*

Stü|cke|schrei|ber(in) M(F) dramatist, playwright

Stück-: Stück|fass NT *(Weinmaß) measure of wine containing 1,200 litres*; **Stück|gut** NT *(Rail)* parcel service; **etw als ~ schicken** to send sth as a parcel *(Brit) or* package; **Stück|kos|ten** PL unit cost *sing*; **Stück|leis|tung** F production capacity; **Stück|lohn** M piece(work) rate; **Stück|no|tie|rung** F quotation per unit; **Stück|preis** M unit price; **stück|wei|se** ADV bit by bit, little by little; **~ verkaufen** to sell individually; **Stück|werk** NT, *no pl* incomplete *or* unfinished work; **~ sein/bleiben** to be/remain incomplete *or* unfinished; **Stück|zahl** F number of pieces *or* items; **Stück|zeit** F production time per piece *or* item; **Stück|zins** M *(Fin)* accrued interest

stud. *abbr von* **studiosus**; **~ med./phil.** *etc* student of medicine/humanities *etc*

Stu|dent [ʃtuˈdɛnt] M **-en, -en** student; *(Aus: = Schüler)* schoolboy; *(einer bestimmten Schule)* pupil → *auch* **Studentin**

Stu|den|ten-: Stu|den|ten|aus|weis M student (ID) card; **Stu|den|ten|be|we|gung** F student movement; **Stu|den|ten|blu|me** F French marigold; **Stu|den|ten|bu|de** F *(inf)* student digs *pl (Brit) or* housing; **Stu|den|ten|fut|ter** NT nuts and raisins *pl*; **Stu|den|ten|ge|mein|de** F student religious society; **Stu|den|ten|heim** NT hall of residence *(Brit)*, student hostel, dormitory *(US)*; **Stu|den|ten|le|ben** NT student life; **Stu|den|ten|lie|be** F student romance; **Stu|den|ten|lied** NT student song; **Stu|den|ten|lo|kal** NT students' pub; **Stu|den|ten|pfar|rer(in)** M(F) university/college chaplain; **Stu|den|ten|ra|batt** M student discount; **Stu|den|ten|re|vol|te** F student revolt; **Stu|den|ten|schaft** [ʃtuˈdɛntn̩ʃaft] F **-, -en** students *pl*, student body; **Stu|den|ten|spra|che** F student slang; **Stu|den|ten|ver|bin|dung** F students' society *or* association; *(für Männer auch)* fraternity *(US)*; *(für Frauen auch)* sorority *(US)*; **Stu|den|ten|werk** NT student administration; **Stu|den|ten|wohn|heim** NT hall of residence *(Brit)*, student hostel, dormitory *(US)*

Stu|den|tin [ʃtuˈdɛntɪn] F **-, -nen** student; *(Aus: = Schülerin)* schoolgirl; *(einer bestimmten Schule)* pupil

stu|den|tisch [ʃtuˈdɛntɪʃ] ADJ *attr* student *attr*; **~e Hilfskraft** student assistant

Stu|die [ˈʃtuːdiə] F **-, -n** study *(über +acc* of); *(= Entwurf auch)* sketch; *(= Abhandlung)* essay *(über +acc* on)

Stu|dien-: Stu|di|en|ab|bre|cher(in) M(F) dropout, *student who fails to complete his/her course of study*; **Stu|di|en|ab|schluss** M completion of a course of study; **Volkswirtschaftler mit ~** graduate economist; **die Universität ohne ~ verlassen** to leave university without graduating; **Stu|di|en|an|fän|ger(in)** M(F) first year (student), freshman *(US)*, fresher *(Brit)*; **Stu|di|en|an|ge|bot** NT range of (degree) courses, (degree) courses on offer; **Stu|di|en|as|ses|sor(in)** M(F) *graduate teacher who has recently completed his/her training*; **Stu|di|en|auf|ent|halt** M study visit; **Stu|di|en|aus|ga|be** F *(= Buch)* student's edition; **Stu|di|en|be|ra|tung** F course guidance service; **Stu|di|en|buch** NT *book in which the courses one has attended are entered*; **Stu|di|en|di|rek|tor(in)** M(F) *(von Fachschule)* principal; *(in Gymnasium)* ≈ deputy *or* vice principal; **Stu|di|en|fach** NT subject; **Stu|di|en|fahrt** F study trip; *(Sch)* educational trip; **Stu|di|en|för|de|rung** F study grant; *(an Universität)* university grant; **Stu|di|en|freund(in)** M(F) university/college friend; **Stu|di|en|gang** M *pl* **-gänge** course of studies; **Stu|di|en|ge|büh|ren** PL tuition fees *pl*; **stu|di|en|hal|ber** ADV for the purpose of study *or* studying; **Stu|di|en|in|hal|te** PL course contents *pl*; **Stu|di|en|jahr** NT academic year; **Stu|di|en|jah|re** PL university/college years *pl*; **Stu|di|en|plan** M course of study; **Stu|di|en|platz** M university/college place; **ein ~ in Medizin** a place (at university/college) to study medicine; **Stu|di|en|rat** M, **Stu|di|en|rä|tin** F teacher at a secondary school; **Stu|di|en|re|fe|ren|dar(in)** M(F) student teacher; **Stu|di|en|re|form** F university/college reform; **Stu|di|en|rei|se** F study trip; *(Sch)* educational trip; **Stu|di|en|se|mi|nar** NT teacher training course; **sie ist im ~ in Essen** she is doing her teacher training in Essen; **Stu|di|en|zeit** F **a** student days *pl* **b** *(= Dauer)* duration of a/one's course of studies; **Stu|di|en|zeit|be|gren|zung** F limitation on the length of courses of studies; **Stu|di|en|zeit|ver|kür|zung** F shortening of the period of study; **Stu|di|en|zweck** M **für ~e, zu ~en** for the purposes of study, for study purposes

stu|die|ren [ʃtuˈdiːrən] *ptp* **studiert** VI to study; *(= Student sein)* to be a student, to be at university/college, to be at school *(US inf)*; **ich studiere an der Universität Bonn** I am (a student) at Bonn University; **nicht jeder kann ~** not everyone can go to university/college; **wo haben Sie studiert?** what university/college did you go to?; **bei jdm ~** to study under sb; **jdn ~ lassen** to send sb to university/college VT to study; *(an Uni auch)* to read; *(= genau betrachten)* to scrutinize; **sie hat vier Semester Jura studiert** she has studied law for two years

Stu|die|ren|de(r) [ʃtuˈdiːrəndə] MF *decl as adj* student

stu|diert [ʃtuˈdiːɐt] ADJ *(inf)* **~ sein** to have been to university/college

Stu|dier|te(r) [ʃtuˈdiːɐtə] MF *decl as adj* university-educated person; **er ist ein ~r** he is university-educated; *(pej inf)* he's an intellectual

Stu|dier|zim|mer NT study

Stu|dio [ˈʃtuːdio] NT **-s, -s** studio

Stu|dio|büh|ne F studio theatre *(Brit) or* theater *(US)*

Stu|di|o|sus [ʃtuˈdioːzʊs] M **-, Studiosi** [-zi] *(old, hum)* student

Stu|di|um [ˈʃtuːdiʊm] NT **-s, Studien** [-diən] study; *(= Hochschulstudium)* studies *pl*; *(= genaue Betrachtung)* scrutiny, study; **sein ~ beginnen** *or* **aufnehmen** *(form)* to begin one's studies, to go to university/college; **das ~ hat fünf Jahre gedauert** the course (of study) lasted five years; **das ~ ist kostenlos/teuer** studying (at university) is free/expensive; **während seines ~s** while he is/was *etc* a student *or* at university/college; **er ist noch im ~** he is still a student; **das ~ der Mathematik, das mathematische ~** the study of mathematics, mathematical studies *pl*; **archäologische/psychologische Studien betreiben** to study archaeology/psychology; **er war gerade beim ~ des Börsenberichts, als ...** he was just studying the stock exchange report when ...; **seine Studien zu etw machen** to study sth

Stu|di|um ge|ne|ra|le [ˈʃtuːdiʊm genəˈraːlə, ˈst-] NT **- -,** *no pl* general course of studies; **ein ~ machen** to do a general degree

Stu|fe [ˈʃtuːfə] F **-, -n a** step; *(= Geländestufe auch)* terrace; *(Mus: = Tonstufe)* degree; *(an Rock, Kleid etc)* tier; *(zum Kürzen)* tuck; *(im Haar)* layer; *(von Rakete)* stage; **mehrere ~n auf einmal nehmen** to run up the stairs two or three at a time; **Vorsicht ~!** mind *or* watch the step!
b *(fig) (= Phase)* stage; *(= Niveau)* level; *(= Rang)* grade; *(Gram: = Steigerungsstufe)* degree; **eine ~ höher als ...** a step up from ...; **die höchste ~** the height *or* pinnacle; **die tiefste ~** the depths *pl*; **mit jdm auf gleicher ~ stehen** to be on a level with sb; **jdn/sich mit jdm/etw auf die gleiche** *or* **eine ~ stellen** to put *or* place sb/oneself on a level *or* on a par with sb/sth

stu|fen [ˈʃtuːfn] VT *Schüler, Preise, Gehälter* to grade; *Haare* to layer; *Land etc* to terrace → *auch* **gestuft**

Stu|fen-: Stu|fen|bar|ren M asymmetric bar; **Stu|fen|dach** NT stepped roof; **stu|fen|för|-**

mig ADJ (lit) stepped; *Landschaft* terraced; (fig) gradual ADV (lit) in steps; *angelegt* in terraces; (fig) in stages, gradually; **Stu|fen|füh|rer|schein** M (graded) motorcycle licence (Brit) or license (US); **Stu|fen|heck** NT **ein Auto mit ~** a saloon car; **Stu|fen|lei|ter** F (fig) ladder (+gen to); **stu|fen|los** ADJ *Schaltung, Regelung* infinitely variable; (fig: = *gleitend*) smooth; **Stu|fen|ord|nung** F successive order; **Stu|fen|plan** M step-by-step plan (*zu* for); **Stu|fen|ra|ke|te** F multi-stage rocket; **Stu|fen|schal|ter** M (Elec) sequence switch; **Stu|fen|schnitt** M (*von Haaren*) layered cut; **Stu|fen|ta|rif** M (Econ) graduated tariff; **Stu|fen|ta|rif|ver|trag** M graduated wage agreement; **stu|fen|wei|se** ADV step by step, gradually ADJ *attr* gradual

stu|fig [ˈʃtuːfɪç] ADJ stepped; *Land etc* terraced; *Haar* layered ADV **das Haar ~ schneiden** to layer sb's hair

-stu|fig ADJ *suf* -stage *attr*; **dreistufig** (*Rakete, Plan, Verfahren*) three-stage *attr*

Stu|fung [ˈʃtuːfʊŋ] F **-, -en** gradation

Stuhl [ʃtuːl] M **-(e)s, ¨-e** [ˈʃtyːlə] **a** chair; **ist dieser ~ noch frei?** is this chair taken?, is this somebody's chair?; **sich zwischen zwei Stühle setzen** (fig) **zwischen zwei Stühlen sitzen** (fig) to fall between two stools; **ich wäre fast vom ~ gefallen** (inf) I nearly fell off my chair (inf); **jdm den ~ vor die Tür setzen** (fig) to kick sb out (inf)

b (= *Königsstuhl*) throne; **der Apostolische** or **Heilige** or **Päpstliche ~** the Apostolic or Holy or Papal See; **der ~ Petri** the See of Rome; **vor Gottes ~ gerufen werden** to be called before one's Maker

c (= *Lehramt*) chair (+gen of, *für* of, in)

d (= *Stuhlgang*) bowel movement; (= *Kot*) stool; **~/keinen ~ haben** to have had/not to have had a bowel movement

Stuhl-: **Stuhl|bein** NT chair leg; **Stuhl|drang** M, *no pl* (*form*) urgent need to empty the bowels; **Stuhl|ent|lee|rung** F (*form*) evacuation of the bowels; **Stuhl|gang** [-gaŋ] M, *no pl* bowel movement; **regelmäßig ~ haben** to have regular bowels; **~/keinen ~ haben** to have had/not to have had a bowel movement; **Stuhl|leh|ne** F back of a chair; **Stuhl|rei|he** F row of chairs; **Stuhl|ver|hal|tung** F (*form*) retention of faeces (Brit) or feces (US)

Stu|ka [ˈʃtuːka, ˈʃtʊka] M **-s, -s** *abbr von* **Sturzkampfflugzeug** stuka, dive bomber

Stuk|ka|teur △ [ʃtʊkaˈtøːɐ] M **-s, -e**, **Stuk|ka|teu|rin** △ [-ˈtøːrɪn] F **-, -en** → **Stuckateur**

Stuk|ka|tur △ [ʃtʊkaˈtuːɐ] F **-, -en** → **Stuckatur**

Stul|le [ˈʃtʊlə] F **-, -n** (*N Ger*) slice of bread and butter; (= *Doppelstulle*) sandwich

Stul|pe [ˈʃtʊlpə] F **-, -n** cuff; (*von Handschuh*) gauntlet

stül|pen [ˈʃtʏlpn] VT **den Kragen nach oben ~** to turn up one's collar; **etw auf/über etw** (acc) **~** to put sth on/over sth; **etw nach innen/außen ~** to turn sth to the inside/outside; **sich** (dat) **den Hut auf den Kopf ~** to put on one's hat

Stul|pen-: **Stul|pen|hand|schuh** M gauntlet; **Stul|pen|stie|fel** M top boot

Stülp|na|se F snub or turned-up nose

stumm [ʃtʊm] ADJ **a** (*lit, fig*) dumb; **die ~e Kreatur** (*geh*) the dumb creatures *pl*; **~ vor Schmerz** in silent agony; **~ vor Zorn** speechless with anger; **~er Diener** (= *Servierwagen*) dumbwaiter; (= *Kleiderständer*) valet **b** (= *schweigend*) mute; *Anklage, Blick, Gebet* silent; **~ bleiben** to stay silent → **Fisch c** (*Gram*) mute, silent **d** *Rolle* nonspeaking; *Film, Szene* silent ADV (= *schweigend*) mutely, silently; **sie sah mich ~ an** she looked at me without saying a word or without speaking

Stum|mel [ˈʃtʊml] M **-s, - a** (= *Zigarettenstummel, Zigarrenstummel*) end, stub, butt; (= *Kerzenstummel*) stub; (*von Gliedmaßen, Zahn*) stump **b** (= *Stummelschwanz*) dock

Stum|mel|pfei|fe F short-stemmed pipe

Stum|me(r) [ˈʃtʊmɐ] MF *decl as adj* dumb or mute person; **die ~n** the dumb

Stumm|film M silent film

Stumm|film|zeit F silent film era

Stum|pen [ˈʃtʊmpn] M **-s, -** cheroot

Stüm|per [ˈʃtʏmpɐ] M **-s, -**, **Stüm|pe|rin** [-ərɪn] F **-, -nen** (*pej*) **a** amateur **b** (= *Pfuscher*) bungler

Stüm|pe|rei [ʃtʏmpəˈrai] F **-, -en** (*pej*) **a** amateur work **b** (= *Pfuscherei*) bungling; (= *stümperhafte Arbeit*) botched (inf) or bungled job

stüm|per|haft (*pej*) ADJ (= *nicht fachmännisch*) amateurish; (= *schlecht auch*) botched (inf), bungled ADV *ausführen, malen* crudely; *arbeiten* poorly; *übersetzen* clumsily, crudely; **~ vorgehen** to be clumsy

stüm|pern [ˈʃtʏmpɐn] VI (*auf Klavier, bei Schach etc*) to play in an amateurish way (*auf +dat* on); **bei einer Arbeit ~** to do a job in an amateur way; **er stümpert nur** he's just an amateur; (= *pfuschen*) he's just a bungler

stumpf [ʃtʊmpf] ADJ **a** *Messer* blunt; *Nase* snub, turned-up; **Rhabarber macht die Zähne ~** rhubarb sets the teeth on edge **b** (*fig*) *Haar, Farbe, Mensch* dull; *Blick, Sinne* dulled, dull; **einer Sache gegenüber ~ sein** to remain impassive about sth **c** (*Math*) *Winkel* obtuse; *Kegel etc* truncated **d** (*Poet*) *Reim* masculine ADV *ansehen* dully; **~ vor sich hin brüten** to sit brooding impassively

Stumpf [ʃtʊmpf] M **-(e)s, ¨-e** [ˈʃtʏmpfə] stump; (= *Bleistiftstumpf*) stub; **etw mit ~ und Stiel ausrotten** to eradicate sth root and branch

Stumpf|heit F **-**, *no pl* bluntness; (*fig*) dullness

Stumpf-: **Stumpf|sinn** M, *no pl* mindlessness; (= *Langweiligkeit*) monotony, tedium; **das ist doch ~** that's a tedious business; **stumpf|sin|nig** ADJ mindless; (= *langweilig*) monotonous, tedious; **Stumpf|sin|nig|keit** [ˈʃtʊmpfzɪnɪkkait] F **-**, *no pl* = **Stumpfsinn**; **stumpf|win|ke|lig**, **stumpf|wink|lig** ADJ (*Math*) *Winkel, Dreieck* obtuse

Stünd|chen [ˈʃtʏntçən] NT **-s, -** *dim von* **Stunde**; **ein paar ~** an hour or so

Stun|de [ˈʃtʊndə] F **-, -n a** hour; **eine viertel ~** a quarter of an hour; **eine halbe ~** half an hour; **eine ganze/gute ~** a whole/good hour; **eine knappe ~** barely an hour; **eine halbe ~ Pause** a half-hour break, a break of half an hour; **drei ~n lang** for three hours; **eine ~ entfernt** an hour away; **eine Reise von zwei ~n** a two-hour journey; **jede ~** every hour; **~ um ~, ~n um ~n** hour after hour; **von ~ zu ~** hourly, from hour to hour; **sein Befinden wird von ~ zu ~ schlechter** his condition is becoming worse hour by hour or worse every hour; **130 Kilometer in der ~** 130 kilometres (Brit) or kilometers (US) per or an hour → *auch* **Achtstundentag**

b (= *Augenblick, Zeitpunkt*) time; **zu dieser ~** at this/that time; **zu jeder ~** at any time; **zu später ~** at a late hour; **zur ~** at the present moment or time, at present; **bis zur ~** up to the present moment, as yet; **von Stund an** (old) from henceforth; **die ~ X** (*Mil*) the impending onslaught; **sich auf die ~ X vorbereiten** (*fig*) to prepare for the inevitable; **eine schwache ~** a moment of weakness; **eine schwere ~** a time of difficulty; **seine ~ kommen** or **nahen fühlen** (*geh*: = *Tod*) to feel one's hour (of death) approaching; **seine ~ hat geschlagen** (*fig*) his hour has come; **seine schwerste ~** his darkest hour; **die ~ der Entscheidung/Wahrheit** the moment of decision/truth

c (= *Unterricht*) lesson; (= *Unterrichtsstunde*) class, period, lesson; **sonnabends haben wir vier ~n** on Saturday we have four lessons; **in der zweiten ~ haben wir Latein** in the second period we have Latin; **~n geben/nehmen** to give/have or take lessons

stun|den [ˈʃtʊndn] VT **jdm etw ~** to give sb time to pay sth; **jdm etw zwei Wochen/bis Mittwoch ~** to give sb two weeks/until Wednesday to pay sth

Stun|den-: **Stun|den|buch** NT (*Hist Liter*) book of hours; **Stun|den|ge|bet** NT *prayer said at any of the canonical hours eg matins, vespers*; **Stun|den|ge|schwin|dig|keit** F speed per hour; **eine ~ von 90 km** a speed of 90 km per hour; **Stun|den|glas** NT hourglass; **Stun|den|ho|tel** NT *hotel where rooms are rented by the hour*; **Stun|den|ki|lo|me|ter** PL kilometres *pl* (Brit) or kilometers *pl* (US) per or an hour; **stun|den|lang** ADJ lasting several hours; **eine ~e Verspätung** a delay of several hours; **nach ~em Warten** after hours of waiting ADV for hours; **Stun|den|lohn** M hourly wage; **~ bekommen** to be paid by the hour; **Stun|den|plan** M (*Sch*) timetable; **Stun|den|satz** M (= *Bezahlung*) hourly rate; **Stun|den|schlag** M striking of the hour; **Stun|den|takt** M hourly frequency; **im ~** at hourly intervals; **stun|den|wei|se** ADV (= *pro Stunde*) by the hour; (= *stündlich*) every hour; **Kellner ~ gesucht** part-time waiters required; **der Patient darf ~ aufstehen** the patient may get up for an hour at a time; **Wasser gibt es nur ~** water is only available for a few hours at a time; **Stun|den|wie|der|ho|lung** F (*Sch*) *repetition of the subject matter of previous lesson(s)*; **Stun|den|zei|ger** M hour hand

-stün|dig [ʃtʏndɪç] ADJ *suf* **eine halbstündige/zweistündige Fahrt** a half-hour/two-hour journey, a journey of half an hour/two hours

Stünd|lein [ˈʃtʏntlain] NT **-s, - ein ~** a short while; **sein letztes ~ hat geschlagen** (= *er stirbt*) his last hour has come; (*fig inf*) he's had it (inf)

stünd|lich [ˈʃtʏntlɪç] ADJ hourly ADV hourly, every hour

-stünd|lich ADV *suf* **zweistündlich/dreistündlich** every two/three hours

Stun|dung [ˈʃtʊndʊŋ] F **-, -en** deferment of payment

Stunk [ʃtʊŋk] M **-s**, *no pl* (*inf*) stink (inf), row (inf); **~ machen** to kick up a stink (inf); **dann gibt es ~** then there'll be a stink (inf)

Stunt [stant] M **-s, -s** stunt

Stunt|man [ˈstantmən] M **-s, Stuntmen** [-mən] stunt man

Stunt|wo|man [ˈstantvʊmən] F **-, Stuntwomen** [-vɪmɪn] stunt woman

stu|pend [ʃtuˈpɛnt, st-] ADJ (*geh*) astounding, tremendous

stu|pid [ʃtuˈpiːt, st-], **stu|pi|de** [ʃtuˈpiːdə, st-] ADJ (*geh*) mindless

Stu|pi|di|tät F (*geh*) mindlessness

Stups [ʃtʊps] M **-es, -e** nudge

stup|sen [ˈʃtʊpsn] VT to nudge

Stups|na|se F snub nose

stur [ʃtuːɐ] ADJ pig-headed, stubborn; *Nein, Arbeiten* dogged; **sich ~ stellen** (inf) **auf ~ stellen** or **schalten** (inf) to dig one's heels in; **ein ~er Bock** (inf) a pig-headed fellow ADV *beharren, bestehen* stubbornly; **~ weitermachen/weiterreden/weitergehen** to carry on regardless or doggedly; **er fuhr ~ geradeaus/in der Mitte der Straße** he just carried straight on/carried on driving in the middle of the road

Stur|heit F **-**, *no pl* pig-headedness, stubbornness

Sturm [ʃtʊrm] M **-(e)s, ¨-e** [ˈʃtʏrmə] **a** (*lit, fig*) storm; **in ~ und Regen** in wind and rain; **das Barometer steht auf ~** (*lit*) the barometer is indicating stormy weather; (*fig*) there's a storm brewing; **die Ruhe** or **Stille vor dem ~** the calm before the storm; **ein ~ im Wasserglas** (*fig*) a storm in a teacup (Brit), a tempest in a teapot (US); **~ läuten** to keep one's finger on the doorbell; (= *Alarm schlagen*) to ring or sound the alarm bell; **die Stürme des Lebens** the storms of life, the ups and downs of life; **ein ~ der Begeisterung/Entrüstung** a wave of enthusiasm/indignation; **im ~ der Leidenschaft** (*geh*) in the throes of passion; **~ und Drang** (*Liter*) Storm and Stress, Sturm und Drang; (*fig*) emotion

b (= *Angriff*) attack (*auf* on); (*Mil*) assault, attack; (*Sport*: = *Stürmerreihe*) forward line; **etw im**

~ nehmen *(Mil, fig)* to take sth by storm; **zum ~ blasen** *(Mil, fig)* to sound the attack; **gegen etw ~ laufen** *(fig)* to be up in arms against sth; **ein ~ auf die Banken/Aktien** a run on the banks/shares; **ein ~ auf die Karten/Plätze** a rush for tickets/seats; **der ~ auf die Festung/Bastille** the storming of the stronghold/Bastille → **erobern**

Sturm-: **Sturm|ab|tei|lung** F *(NS)* Storm Troopers *pl*; **Sturm|an|griff** M *(Mil)* assault *(auf +acc* on); **sturm|be|wegt** ADJ stormy, storm-tossed *(liter)*; **Sturm|bö** F squall; **Sturm|bock** M *(Mil)* battering ram; **Sturm|boot** NT *(Mil)* assault boat; **Sturm|deck** NT hurricane deck

stür|men [ˈʃtʏrmən] VI **a** *(Meer)* to rage; *(Wind auch)* to blow; *(Mil)* to attack, to assault *(gegen etw* sth) **b** *(Sport) (= als Stürmer spielen)* to play forward; *(= angreifen)* to attack **c** *aux sein (= rennen)* to storm VI *impers* to be blowing a gale VT *(Mil, fig)* to storm; *Bank etc* to make a run on

Stür|mer [ˈʃtʏrmɐ] M **-s, -**, **Stür|me|rin** [-ərɪn] F **-, -nen** *(Sport)* forward; *(Ftbl auch)* striker; *(fig: = Draufgänger)* go-getter *(inf)*; **~ und Dränger** *(Liter)* writer of the Storm and Stress *or* Sturm und Drang period; *(fig)* ≈ angry young man

sturm|er|probt ADJ *(fig geh)* battle-tried

Stür|mer|rei|he F *(Sport)* forward line

Sturm-: **Sturm|fah|ne** F warning flag; *(Mil Hist)* standard; **sturm|fest** ADJ *(lit)* stormproof; *(fig)* steadfast; **Sturm|flut** F storm tide; **sturm|frei** ADJ *(lit)* storm-free; *(Mil)* unassailable; **bei mir ist heute Abend ~e Bude** *(inf)* it's open house at my place tonight; **ich habe eine ~e Bude** *(inf)* where I live I can do as I please; **Sturm|ge|päck** NT combat *or* light pack; **sturm|ge|peitscht** [-gəpaitʃt] ADJ *(geh)* storm-lashed *(liter)*; **Sturm|ge|wehr** NT submachine gun; **Sturm|hau|be** F **a** *(Hist)* helmet, morion **b** *(Zool)* whelk shell; **Sturm|hut** M *(Bot)* aconite

stür|misch [ˈʃtʏrmɪʃ] ADJ **a** *Meer, Überfahrt* rough, stormy; *Wetter, Tag* blustery; *(mit Regen)* stormy **b** *(fig)* tempestuous; *(= aufregend) Zeit, Jugend* stormy, turbulent; *Entwicklung, Wachstum* rapid; *Liebhaber* passionate, ardent; *Jubel, Beifall* tumultuous, frenzied; **nicht so ~** take it easy ADV enthusiastically; **jdn ~ bejubeln/feiern** to give sb a tumultuous reception

Sturm-: **Sturm|la|ter|ne** F hurricane lamp; **Sturm|lauf** M trot; **im ~** at a trot; **Sturm|lei|ter** F scaling ladder; **sturm|reif** ADJ *(Mil)* **~ sein** to be ripe for attack *(für* by); **etw ~ schießen** *(Mil)* to weaken sth in preparation for an attack; *(fig)* to undermine sth and expose it to attack; **Sturm|scha|den** M storm damage *no pl*; **Sturm|schritt** M *(Mil, fig)* double-quick pace; **im ~** at the double; **Sturm|se|gel** NT storm sail; **Sturm|spit|ze** F *(Mil, Sport)* spearhead; **sturm|stark** ADJ *(Sport)* **eine ~e Mannschaft** a team with a strong forward line; **Sturm|tief** NT *(Met)* deep depression; **Sturm|trupp** M *(Mil)* assault troop; **Sturm-und-Drang-Zeit** F *(Liter)* Storm and Stress *or* Sturm und Drang period; **Sturm|vo|gel** M petrel; *(= Albatros)* albatross; **Sturm|war|nung** F gale warning; **Sturm|wind** M whirlwind

Sturz [ʃtʊrts] M **-es, ⸚e** [ˈʃtʏrtsə] **a** *(von* from, off) *(aus* out of) fall; **einen ~ tun** to have a fall **b** *(in Temperatur, Preis)* drop, fall; *(von Börsenkurs)* slump **c** *(von Regierung, Minister)* fall; *(durch Coup, von König)* overthrow **d** *(Archit)* lintel **e** *(= Radsturz)* camber **f** *(S Ger, Aus: = Glassturz)* cover

Sturz-: **Sturz|acker** M *(Agr)* newly ploughed *(Brit) or* plowed *(US)* field; **Sturz|bach** M *(lit)* fast-flowing stream; *(fig)* stream, torrent; **sturz|be|sof|fen** *(inf)*, **sturz|be|trun|ken** *(inf)* ADJ pissed as a newt *(Brit inf)*, drunk as a sailor *(US inf)*

stür|zen [ˈʃtʏrtsn] VI *aux sein* **a** *(= fallen)* to fall *(von* from, off); *(geh: = steil abfallen)* to plunge; *(= hervorstürzen)* to stream; **ins Wasser ~** to plunge into the water; **vom Pferd ~** to fall off a/one's horse; **zu Boden ~** to crash to the ground; **zu Tode** *or* **in den Tod ~** to fall to one's death; **er ist schwer** *or* **heftig/unglücklich gestürzt** he had a heavy/bad fall; **die Tränen stürzten ihm aus den Augen** *(geh)* tears streamed from his eyes **b** *(fig: = abgesetzt werden)* to fall **c** *(= rennen)* to rush, to dash; **sie kam ins Zimmer gestürzt** she burst *or* came bursting into the room; **jdm in die Arme ~** to fling oneself into sb's arms

VT **a** *(= werfen)* to fling, to hurl; **jdn aus dem Fenster ~** to fling *or* hurl sb out of the window; **jdn ins Unglück** *or* **Verderben ~** to bring disaster to sb; **jdn/etw in eine Krise ~** to plunge sb/sth into a crisis **b** *(= kippen)* to turn upside down; *Pudding* to turn out; **„nicht ~!"** "this side up"; **etw über etw** *(acc)* **~** to put sth over sth **c** *(= absetzen) Regierung, Minister* to bring down; *(durch Coup)* to overthrow; *König* to depose

VR **sich zu Tode ~** to fall to one's death; *(absichtlich)* to jump to one's death; **sich auf jdn/etw ~** to pounce on sb/sth; *auf Essen* to fall on sth; *auf Zeitung etc* to grab sth; *auf den Feind* to attack sb/sth; **sich ins Wasser ~** to fling *or* hurl oneself into the water; *(= sich ertränken)* to drown oneself; **sich in die Arbeit ~** to throw oneself into one's work; **sich in Schulden ~** to plunge into debt; **sich ins Unglück/Verderben ~** to plunge headlong into disaster/ruin; **sich ins Vergnügen ~** to fling oneself into a round of pleasure; **sich in Unkosten ~** to go to great expense

Sturz-: **Sturz|flug** M (nose) dive; **etw im ~ angreifen** to dive and attack sth; **Sturz|ge|burt** F *(Med)* precipitate delivery; **Sturz|gut** NT *(form)* goods unloaded by tipping; **Sturz|helm** M crash helmet; **Sturz|kampf|flug|zeug** NT dive bomber; **Sturz|see** F *(Naut)* breaker

Stuss [ʃtʊs] M **-es**, *no pl (inf)* nonsense, rubbish *(Brit inf)*, codswallop *(Brit inf)*; **was für ein ~** what a load of nonsense *etc (inf)*; **~ lallen** *(sl)* to talk shite *(Brit sl) or* crap *(inf)*

Stut|buch [ˈʃtuːt-] NT studbook

Stu|te [ˈʃtuːtə] F **-, -n** mare

Stu|ten-: **Stu|ten|foh|len** NT, **Stu|ten|fül|len** NT filly; **Stu|ten|zucht** F stud farm; *(= Züchtung)* stud farming

Stutz [ʃtʊts] M **-es, Stütze** [ˈʃtʏtsə] *(Sw inf: = Franken)* (Swiss) franc

Stütz-: **Stütz|ap|pa|rat** M calliper *(Brit)*, caliper *(US)*, brace; *(für Kopf)* collar; **Stütz|bal|ken** M beam; *(in Decke)* joist; *(quer)* crossbeam

Stüt|ze [ˈʃtʏtsə] F **-, -n** **a** support; *(= Pfeiler)* pillar; *(für Wäscheleine etc)* prop; *(= Buchstütze)* rest **b** *(= Halt)* support; *(= Fußstütze)* footrest **c** *(fig) (= Hilfe)* help, aid *(für* to); *(= Beistand)* support; *(= wichtiger Mensch)* mainstay; *(dated: = Hausgehilfin)* (domestic) help; **als ~ für seinen Kreislauf** as an aid for *or* to aid his circulation; **die ~n der Gesellschaft** the pillars of society **d** *(inf: = Arbeitslosengeld)* dole *(Brit inf)*, welfare *(US)*; **~ bekommen** to be on the dole *(Brit inf)*, to be on welfare *(US)*

stut|zen [ˈʃtʊtsn] VI to stop short; *(= zögern)* to hesitate

stut|zen VT to trim; *Baum auch* to prune; *Flügel, Ohren, Hecke* to clip; *Schwanz* to dock

Stut|zen [ˈʃtʊtsn] M **-s, -** **a** *(= Gewehr)* carbine **b** *(= Rohrstück)* connecting piece; *(= Endstück)* nozzle **c** *(= Strumpf)* woollen *(Brit) or* woolen *(US)* gaiter

stüt|zen [ˈʃtʏtsn] VT *(= Halt geben)* to support; *Gebäude, Mauer* to shore up; *Währung* to back, to support; *(fig: = untermauern)* to back up, to support; **einen Verdacht durch etw ~** to back up *or* support a suspicion with sth; **einen Verdacht auf etw** *(acc)* **~** to base *or* found a suspicion on sth; **die Ellbogen auf den Tisch ~** to prop *or* rest one's elbows on the table; **den Kopf in die Hände ~** to hold one's head in one's hands

VR **sich auf jdn/etw ~** *(lit)* to lean on sb/sth; *(fig)* to count on sb/sth; *(Beweise, Verteidigung, Theorie etc)* to be based on sb/sth; **können Sie sich auf Fakten ~?** can you produce facts to bear out what you're saying?; **er konnte sich auf eigene Erfahrungen ~** he had his own experiences to fall back on; **in seiner Dissertation stützte er sich weitgehend auf diese Theorie** he based his thesis closely on this theory

Stut|zer [ˈʃtʊtsɐ] M **-s, -** **a** *(dated pej)* fop *(dated)*, dandy **b** *(= Mantel)* three-quarter length coat

stut|zer|haft ADJ *(dated pej)* foppish *(dated)*, dandified ADV *gekleidet, sich kleiden* foppishly *(dated)*

Stutz|flü|gel M baby grand (piano)

Stütz|ge|we|be NT *(Med)* stroma *(spec)*

stut|zig [ˈʃtʊtsɪç] ADJ *pred* **~ werden** *(= argwöhnisch)* to become *or* grow suspicious; *(= verwundert)* to begin to wonder; **jdn ~ machen** to make sb suspicious; **das hat mich ~ gemacht** that made me wonder; *(= argwöhnisch)* that made me suspicious

Stütz-: **Stütz|kor|sett** NT support corset; **Stütz|kurs** M *(Sch)* extra classes *pl*; **Stütz|mau|er** F retaining wall; **Stütz|pfei|ler** M supporting pillar *or* column; *(von Brücke auch)* pier; **Stütz|preis** M *(Econ)* support price; **Stütz|punkt** M *(Mil, fig)* base; *(= Ausbildungsstätte)* centre; **Stütz|rad** NT *(an Fahrrad)* stabilizer; **Stütz|stan|ge** F supporting pole; **Stütz|strumpf** M support stocking

Stüt|zung [ˈʃtʏtsʊŋ] F **-, -en** support

Stüt|zungs-: **Stüt|zungs|käu|fe** PL *purchases to support share prices, currency rate etc*; **Stüt|zungs|maß|nah|me** F supporting measure

Stütz|ver|band M support bandage

StVO [ɛsteːfauˈoː] *abbr von* **Straßenverkehrsordnung**

sty|len [ˈstailən] VT *Wagen, Wohnung* to design; *Frisur* to style; *Kleidung* to design, to style; *jdn* to do up VR to do oneself up

Sty|ling [ˈstailɪŋ] NT **-s**, *no pl* styling

Sty|ro|por® [ʃtyroˈpoːɐ, st-] NT **-s** ≈ polystyrene

Styx [ʃtʏks, st-] M **-** *(Myth)* Styx

SU [ɛsˈuː] F **-** *abbr von* **Sowjetunion**

s. u. *abbr von* **siehe unten**

Su|a|da [ˈzuaːda] F **-, Suaden** [-dn], **Su|a|de** [ˈzuaːdə] F **-, -n** *(liter)* torrent of words

Su|a|he|li [zuaˈheːli] M **-(s), -(s)** *or f* **-, -(s)** Swahili

Su|a|he|li NT **-(s)**, *no pl (Ling)* Swahili

Sub-, sub- *in cpds* sub-; **sub|al|tern** [zʊpalˈtɛrn] ADJ *(pej) Stellung, Beamter* subordinate; *Gesinnung* obsequious, subservient; *(= unselbstständig)* unselfreliant; **sub|ato|mar** [zʊpatoˈmaːɐ] ADJ *(Phys)* subatomic; **Sub|do|mi|nan|te** [zʊpdomiˈnantə, ˈzʊp-] F *(Mus)* subdominant

Sub|jekt [zʊpˈjɛkt, ˈzʊp-] NT **-(e)s, -e** **a** subject **b** *(pej: = Mensch)* customer *(inf)*, character *(inf)*

sub|jek|tiv [zʊpjɛkˈtiːf, ˈzʊp-] ADJ subjective ADV subjectively

Sub|jek|ti|vis|mus [zʊpjɛktiˈvɪsmʊs] M **-**, *no pl (Philos)* subjectivism

Sub|jek|ti|vi|tät [zʊpjɛktiviˈtɛːt] F **-**, *no pl* subjectivity

Sub|jekt|satz M *(Gram)* noun clause as subject

Sub-: **Sub|kon|ti|nent** M subcontinent; **Sub|kul|tur** F subculture; **sub|ku|tan** [zʊpkuˈtaːn] *(Med)* ADJ subcutaneous ADV *spritzen* subcutaneously

sub|lim [zuˈbliːm] ADJ *(geh)* sublime, lofty; *Einfühlungsvermögen, Charakter* refined; *Interpretation* eloquent

Sub|li|mat [zubliˈmaːt] NT **-(e)s, -e** *(Chem)* **a** *(= Niederschlag)* sublimate **b** *(= Quecksilberverbindung)* mercuric chloride

Sub|li|ma|ti|on [zublima'tsio:n] F -, -en *(Chem)* sublimation
sub|li|mie|ren [zubli'mi:rən] *ptp* **sublimiert** VT **a** *(Psych)* to sublimate **b** *(Chem)* to sublimate, to sublime
Sub|li|mie|rung F -, -en sublimation
sub|ma|rin [zupma'ri:n] ADJ submarine, underwater
Sub|or|di|na|ti|on [zuplɔrdina'tsio:n] F subordination
sub|op|ti|mal ADJ *(inf)* less than ideal; **das ist ~** it leaves something to be desired
Sub|si|di|a|ri|tät [zupzidiari'tɛ:t] F -, -en *(Pol)* subsidiarity
Sub|si|di|a|ri|täts|prin|zip NT *(Pol)* subsidiarity principle
Sub|sis|tenz|wirt|schaft [zupzıs'tɛnts-] F subsistence farming
Sub|skri|bent [zupskri'bɛnt] M -en, -en, **Sub|skri|ben|tin** [-'bɛntın] F -, -nen subscriber
sub|skri|bie|ren [zupskri'bi:rən] *ptp* **subskribiert** VTI **(auf) etw** *(acc)* ~ to subscribe to sth
Sub|skrip|ti|on [zupskrıp'tsio:n] F -, -en subscription (+*gen*, *auf* +*acc* to)
Sub|skrip|ti|ons|preis M subscription price
sub|stan|ti|ell [zupstan'tsiɛl] ADJ = **substanziell**
Sub|stan|tiv ['zupstanti:f] NT -s, -e *or (rare)* -a [-və, -va] noun
sub|stan|ti|vie|ren [zupstanti'vi:rən] *ptp* **substantiviert** VT to nominalize
sub|stan|ti|visch ['zupstanti:vıʃ] ADJ nominal ADV *verwenden* nominally, as a noun/as nouns
Sub|stanz [zup'stants] F -, -en **a** substance; *(= Wesen)* essence; **die ~ des Volkes** the (essential) character of the people; **etw in seiner ~ treffen** to affect the substance of sth **b** *(Fin)* capital assets *pl*; **von der ~ zehren** *or* **leben** to live on one's capital
sub|stan|zi|ell [zupstan'tsiɛl] ADJ **a** *(Philos) (= stofflich)* material; *(= wesenhaft)* essential **b** *(fig geh: = bedeutsam, inhaltlich)* fundamental **c** *(= nahrhaft)* substantial, solid ADV *(= wesentlich)* substantially; **die Aussagen waren ~ verschieden** the essence of the statements was completely different; **~ an etw** *(dat)* **beteiligt sein** to own a substantial part of sth
Sub|stanz-: **sub|stanz|los** ADJ insubstantial; **sub|stanz|reich** ADJ solid; *Aufsatz auch* meaty *(inf)*; **Sub|stanz|ver|lust** M loss of volume; *(= Gewichtsverlust)* loss of weight; *(fig)* loss of significance *or* importance
sub|sti|tu|ie|ren [zupstitu'i:rən] *ptp* **substituiert** VT *(geh)* **A durch B ~** to substitute B for A, to replace A with B
Sub|sti|tut [zupsti'tu:t] M -en, -en, **Sub|sti|tu|tin** [-'tu:tın] F -, -nen deputy *or* assistant departmental manager
Sub|sti|tu|ti|on [zupstitu'tsio:n] F -, -en *(geh)* **die ~ von A durch B** the substitution of B for A, the replacement of A by B
Sub|strat [zup'stra:t] NT -(e)s, -e substratum
sub|su|mie|ren [zupzu'mi:rən] *ptp* **subsumiert** VT to subsume (*unter* +*dat* to)
sub|til [zup'ti:l] *(geh)* ADJ subtle ADV subtly; **es wird ~ unterschieden zwischen ...** there is a subtle difference between ...
Sub|ti|li|tät [zuptili'tɛ:t] F -, -en *(geh)* subtlety
Sub|tra|hend [zuptra'hɛnt] M -en, -en [-dn] *(Math)* subtrahend
sub|tra|hie|ren [zuptra'hi:rən] *ptp* **subtrahiert** VTI to subtract
Sub|trak|ti|on [zuptrak'tsio:n] F -, -en subtraction
Sub|trak|ti|ons|zei|chen NT subtraction sign
Sub|tro|pen PL subtropics *pl*
sub|tro|pisch ADJ subtropical
Sub|un|ter|neh|mer(in) M(F) subcontractor
Sub|ven|ti|on [zupvɛn'tsio:n] F -, -en subsidy; *(von Regierung, Behörden auch)* subvention
sub|ven|ti|o|nie|ren [zupvɛntsio'ni:rən] *ptp* **subventioniert** VT to subsidize
Sub|ven|ti|o|ni|tis [zupvɛntsio'ni:tıs] F -, *no pl (hum)* compulsive subsidization
Sub|ven|ti|ons|ab|bau M cutback on subsidies
Sub|ver|si|on [zupvɛr'zio:n] F -, -en *(Pol)* subversion
sub|ver|siv [zupvɛr'zi:f] ADJ subversive ADV **sich ~ betätigen** to engage in subversive activities
Such-: **Such|ak|ti|on** F search operation; **Such|an|zei|ge** F missing person/dog *etc* report; **eine ~ aufgeben** to report sb/sth missing; **Such|be|fehl** M *(Comput)* search command; **Such|be|griff** M *(Comput)* search item; **Such|bild** NT *(form)* searching image; *(= Rätsel)* picture puzzle; **Such|dau|er** F *(Comput)* search time; **Such|dienst** M missing persons tracing service
Su|che ['zu:xə] F -, *no pl* search (*nach* for); **auf die ~ nach jdm/etw gehen, sich auf die ~ nach jdm/etw machen** to go in search of sb/sth; **auf der ~ nach etw sein** to be looking for sth
-su|che F *suf in cpds* **auf ...suche sein** to be looking for a ...
su|chen ['zu:xn] VT **a** *(um zu finden)* to look for; *(stärker, intensiv)* to search for *(auch Comput)*; **Abenteuer ~** to go out in search of adventure; **die Gefahr ~** to look for *or* seek danger; **sich** *(dat)* **einen Mann/eine Frau ~** to look for a husband/wife (for oneself); **Verkäufer(in) gesucht** sales person wanted; **gesucht!** wanted (*wegen* for); **er wurde mit** *or* **per Haftbefehl gesucht** there was a warrant out for his arrest; **Streit/Ärger (mit jdm) ~** to be looking for trouble/a quarrel (with sb); **Schutz vor etw** *(dat)* **~** to seek shelter from sth; **Zuflucht ~ bei jdm** to seek refuge with sb; **etw zu tun ~** *(geh)* to seek *or* strive to do sth; **was suchst du hier?** what are you doing here?; **du hast hier nichts zu ~** you have no business being here; **seinesgleichen ~** to be unparalleled → *auch* **gesucht**
b *(= wünschen, streben nach)* to seek; *(= versuchen)* to strive, to try; **er sucht die tragischen Erlebnisse zu vergessen** he is trying to forget the tragic events; **sein Recht/seinen Vorteil ~** to be out for one's rights/one's own advantage; **ein Gespräch ~** to try to have a talk
VI to search, to hunt; **nach etw ~** to look for sth; *(stärker)* to search *or* hunt for sth; **nach Worten ~** to search for words; *(= sprachlos sein)* to be at a loss for words; **Suchen und Ersetzen** *(Comput)* search and replace; **such!** *(zu Hund)* seek!, find!; **suchet, so werdet ihr finden!** *(Bibl)* seek and ye shall find *(Bibl)*
Su|cher ['zu:xɐ] M -s, - *(Phot)* viewfinder; *(Astron)* finder
Su|cher ['zu:xɐ] M -s, -, **Su|che|rin** [-ərın] F -, -nen *(geh)* seeker
Su|che|rei [zu:xə'rai] F -, -en *(inf)* searching
Such-: **Such|er|geb|nis** NT *(Internet)* search result; **Such|for|mu|lar** NT *(Comput)* search form; **Such|funk|ti|on** F *(Comput)* search function; **Such|lauf** M *(TV, Comput etc)* search; **Such|lauf|funk|ti|on** F search function; **Such|mann|schaft** F search party; **Such|ma|schi|ne** F *(Comput)* search engine; **Such|mas|ke** F *(Comput)* search panel; **Such|mel|dung** F SOS message; *(von Suchdienst)* missing person announcement; **Such|mo|dus** M *(Comput)* search mode; **Such|pro|gramm** NT *(Comput)* search program; **Such|rich|tung** F *(Comput)* direction (of the search); **~ abwärts/aufwärts** search down/up; **Such|schein|wer|fer** M searchlight
Sucht [zʊxt] F -, **=e** ['zʏçtə] addiction (*nach* to); *(fig)* obsession (*nach* with); **~ erzeugend** addictive; **eine krankhafte ~ haben, etw zu tun** *(fig)* to be obsessed with doing sth; **das kann zur ~ werden** you'll get *or* become addicted to that; **das Trinken ist bei ihm zur ~ geworden** he has become addicted to drink; **an einer ~ leiden** to be an addict
-sucht F, *no pl suf in cpds* **Drogensucht** addiction to drugs; **Trinksucht** addiction to drink
Sucht-: **Sucht|be|auf|trag|te(r)** MF *decl as adj* anti-drugs coordinator; **Sucht|be|ra|ter(in)** M(F) addiction counsellor *(Brit) or* counselor *(US)*; **Sucht|dro|ge** F addictive drug; **sucht|er|zeu|gend** ADJ → **Sucht**; **Sucht|for|scher(in)** M(F) addiction researcher; **Sucht|ge|fahr** F danger of addiction
süch|tig ['zʏçtıç] ADJ addicted (*nach* to); **von** *or* **nach etw ~ werden/sein** to get *or* become/be addicted to sth; **~ machen** *(Droge)* to be addictive; **davon wird man nicht ~** that's not addictive
Süch|ti|ge(r) ['zʏçtıgə] MF *decl as adj* addict
Süch|tig|keit F -, *no pl* addiction (*nach* to)
Sucht-: **Sucht|kli|nik** F detox(ification) centre *(Brit) or* center *(US)*; **Sucht|kran|ke(r)** MF *decl as adj* addict; **Sucht|krank|heit** F addictive illness; **Sucht|mit|tel** NT addictive drug; **Sucht|mit|tel|miss|brauch** M drug abuse; **Sucht|prä|ven|ti|on** F prevention of addiction
Such|vor|gang M *(Comput)* search
Sud [zu:t] M -(e)s, -e [-də] liquid; *(esp von Fleisch, für Suppe)* stock; **der ~ des Gemüses** the vegetable water
Süd [zy:t] M -(e)s, *(rare)* -e [-də] **a** *(Naut, Met, liter)* south; **aus** *or* **von/nach ~** from/to the south **b** *(liter: Wind)* south wind, southerly (wind)
Süd- *in cpds (in Ländernamen, politisch)* South; *(geografisch auch)* the South of ..., Southern; **Süd|af|ri|ka** NT South Africa; **Süd|ame|ri|ka** NT South America
Su|dan [zu'da:n, 'zu:dan] M -s **der ~** the Sudan
Su|da|ner [zu'da:nɐ] M -s, -, **Su|da|ne|rin** [-ərın] F -, -nen, **Su|da|ne|se** [zuda'ne:zə] M -n, -n, **Su|da|ne|sin** [-'ne:zın] F -, -nen Sudanese
su|da|ne|sisch [zuda'ne:zıʃ], **su|da|nisch** [zu'da:nıʃ] ADJ Sudanese
Süd-: **süd|deutsch** ADJ South German; *Dialekt, Spezialität, Mentalität auch* Southern German; **die Süddeutschen** the South Germans; **Süd|deutsch|land** NT South(ern) Germany, the South of Germany
Su|del ['zu:dl] M -s, - *(Sw: = Kladde)* draft, rough outline; **im ~** in draft (form)
Su|de|lei [zu:də'lai] F -, -en *(geschrieben)* scrawling; *(gezeichnet)* daubing; *(an Mauern etc)* graffiti
su|deln ['zu:dln] VTI *(= schreiben)* to scrawl; *(= zeichnen)* to daub
Sü|den ['zy:dn] M -s, *no pl* south; *(von Land)* South; **aus dem ~, vom ~ her** from the south; **gegen** *or* **gen** *(liter) or* **nach ~** south(wards), to the south; **nach ~ hin** to the south; **im ~ der Stadt/des Landes** in the south of the town/country; **im tiefen ~** in the deep *or* far south; **weiter** *or* **tiefer im ~** further south; **im ~ Frankreichs** in southern France
Süd|eng|land NT the South of England
Su|de|ten [zu'de:tn] PL *(Geog)* **die ~** the Sudeten(land)
Su|de|ten|land NT **das ~** the Sudetenland
Süd-: **Süd|eu|ro|pa** NT Southern Europe; **Süd|frank|reich** NT the South of France; **Süd|früch|te** PL citrus and tropical fruit(s *pl*); **Süd|halb|ku|gel** F southern hemisphere; **auf der ~** in the southern hemisphere
Sud|haus ['zu:t-] NT *(in Brauerei)* brewing room
Süd-: **Süd|ita|li|en** NT Southern Italy; **Süd|je|men** M South Yemen; **Süd|ko|rea** NT South Korea; **Süd|küs|te** F south(ern) coast; **die ~ Englands** the south coast of England; **Süd|la|ge** F southern aspect; **Süd|län|der** ['zy:tlɛndɐ] M -s, -, **Süd|län|de|rin** [-ərın] F -, -nen southerner; *(= Italiener, Spanier etc)* Mediterranean *or* Latin type; **süd|län|disch** [-lɛndıʃ] ADJ southern; *(= italienisch, spanisch etc)* Mediterranean, Latin; *Temperament* Latin ADV **~ aussehen** to look Mediterranean
süd|lich ['zy:tlıç] ADJ **a** southern; *Kurs, Wind, Richtung* southerly; **der ~e Polarkreis** the Antarctic Circle; **der ~e Wendekreis** the Tropic of

Capricorn; **52 Grad ~er Breite** 52 degrees south; **~es Eismeer** Antarctic Ocean **b** *(= mediterran)* Mediterranean, Latin; *Temperament* Latin ADV (to the) south; ~ **von Wien (gelegen)** (to the) south of Vienna; **es liegt ~er** *or* **weiter** ~ it is further (to the) south PREP *+gen* (to the) south of

Süd-: Süd|licht NT, *no pl* southern lights *pl*, aurora australis; *(fig hum: Mensch)* Southerner; **Süd-Nord-Gefäl|le** NT North-South divide

Süd|ost [zy:t'ɔst] M **a** **-en**, *no pl (Met, Naut, liter)* southeast, sou'-east *(Naut)*; **aus** *or* **von** ~ from the southeast; **nach** ~ to the southeast, southeast(wards) **b** **-(e)s, -e** *(liter: Wind)* southeast(erly) (wind), sou'-easterly *(Naut)*

Süd|ost- *in cpds* southeast; *(bei Namen)* South-east

Süd|os|ten [zy:t'ɔstn] M southeast; *(von Land)* South East; **aus** *or* **von** ~ from the southeast; **nach** ~ to the southeast, southeast(wards)

Süd|ost|eu|ro|pa NT Southeast(ern) Europe

süd|öst|lich [zy:t'œstlɪç] ADJ *Gegend* southeastern; *Wind* southeast(erly) ADV (to the) southeast (*von* of) PREP *+gen* (to the) southeast of

Süd-: Süd|pol M South Pole; **Süd|po|lar|ge|biet** NT Antarctic (region), area of the South Pole; **Süd|po|lar|meer** NT Antarctic Ocean; **Süd|pol|ex|pe|di|ti|on** F South Pole *or* Antarctic expedition; **Süd|see** ['zy:tze:] F South Seas *pl*, South Pacific; **Süd|see|in|su|la|ner(in)** M(F) South Sea Islander; **Süd|sei|te** F south(ern) side; *(von Berg)* south(ern) face; **Süd|staat** M southern state; **die ~en** *(US)* the Southern States; **Süd|staat|ler** ['zy:tʃta:tlɐ] M **-s, -**, **Süd|staat|le|rin** [-ərɪn] F **-, -nen** *(US)* Southerner; *(US Hist)* Confederate

Süd|süd-: Süd|süd|ost M **a** *(Naut, Met, liter)* south-southeast, sou'-sou'-east *(Naut)* **b** *(liter: Wind)* sou'-sou'-easterly; **Süd|süd|os|ten** M south-southeast, sou'-sou'-east *(Naut)*; **süd|süd|öst|lich** ADJ south-southeast(erly), sou'-sou'-east(erly) *(Naut)*; **Süd|süd|west** M **a** *(Naut, Met, liter)* south-southwest, sou'-sou'-west *(Naut)* **b** *(liter: Wind)* sou'-sou'-westerly; **Süd|süd|wes|ten** M south-southwest, sou'-sou'-west *(Naut)*; **süd|süd|west|lich** ADJ south-southwest(erly), sou'-sou'-west(erly) *(Naut)*

Süd-: Süd|ti|rol NT South(ern) Tyrol; **Süd|ti|ro|ler(in)** M(F) South Tyrolean; **Süd|vi|et|nam** NT *(Hist)* South Vietnam; **Süd|wand** F *(von Berg)* south face

süd|wärts ['zy:tvɛrts] ADV south(wards) → **südwärtsdrehen**

süd|wärts+dre|hen VI *sep* **der Wind dreht** ~ the wind is moving round to the south

Süd|wein M Mediterranean wine

Süd|west M **a** *(Naut, Met, liter)* southwest; **aus** ~ from the southwest **b** *(liter: = Wind)* southwest(erly) wind, southwester(ly), sou'-wester *(Naut)*

Süd|west- *in cpds* south-west; *(bei Namen)* South-west; **Süd|west|af|ri|ka** NT South-West Africa

Süd|wes|ten [zy:t'vɛstn] M southwest; *(von Land)* South West; **aus** *or* **von** ~ from the southwest; **nach** ~ to the southwest, southwest(-wards)

Süd|wes|ter [zy:t'vɛstɐ] M **-s, -** *(Hut)* sou'wester

süd|west|lich ADJ *Gegend* southwestern; *Wind* southwest(erly) ADV (to the) southwest (*von* of) PREP *+gen* (to the) southwest of

Süd|wind M south wind

Su|es|ka|nal ['zu:ɛs-] M Suez Canal

Suff [zʊf] M **-(e)s**, *no pl (inf)* **dem** ~ **verfallen** to hit the bottle *(inf)*; **dem** ~ **ergeben** *or* **verfallen sein** to be on the bottle *(inf)*; **im** ~ while under the influence *(inf)*; **im** ~ **ist er unberechenbar** there's no knowing what he'll do when he's had a few *(inf)*

süf|feln ['zʏfln] VI *(inf)* to tipple *(inf)*

süf|fig ['zʏfɪç] ADJ *Wein, Bier* drinkable, that goes down well; *Melodie, Ballade* lovely

Süf|fi|sance [zyfi'zã:s] F **-**, *no pl (geh)* smugness, complacency

süf|fi|sant [zyfi'zant] ADJ smug ADV smugly

Suf|fix [zʊ'fɪks, 'zʊfɪks] NT **-es, -e** suffix

Suff|ra|get|te [zʊfra'gɛtə] F **-, -n** suffragette

Su|fi ['zu:fi] M **-(s), -s** Sufi

Su|fis|mus [zu'fɪsmʊs] M **-**, *no pl* Sufism

sug|ge|rie|ren [zʊge'ri:rən] *ptp* **suggeriert** VT to suggest; **jdm etw** ~ to influence sb by suggesting sth; **jdm ~, dass ...** to get sb to believe that ...; **jdm Zweifel an seinen Fähigkeiten** ~ to get sb to doubt his own abilities

sug|ges|ti|bel [zʊgɛs'ti:bl] ADJ suggestible

Sug|ges|ti|bi|li|tät F suggestibility

Sug|ges|ti|on [zʊgɛs'tio:n] F **-, -en** suggestion

sug|ges|tiv [zʊgɛs'ti:f] ADJ suggestive ADV suggestively

Sug|ges|tiv|fra|ge F leading question

Suh|le ['zu:lə] F **-, -n** muddy pool

suh|len ['zu:lən] VR *(lit, fig)* to wallow

Süh|ne ['zy:nə] F **-, -n** *(Rel, geh)* atonement; *(von Schuld)* expiation; **als** ~ **für etw** to atone for sth; **das Verbrechen fand seine** ~ the crime was atoned for; ~ **leisten** to atone (*für* for) → **Schuld**

süh|nen ['zy:nən] VT *Unrecht, Verbrechen* to atone for; **seine Schuld** ~ to expiate one's guilt *or* sins, to atone for one's sins VI to atone

Süh|ne-: Süh|ne|op|fer NT *(Rel)* expiatory sacrifice; **Süh|ne|ter|min** M *(Jur)* conciliatory hearing

Sui|te ['svi:tə, 'zui:tə] F **-, -n** suite; *(= Gefolge)* retinue

Su|i|zid [zui'tsi:t] M OR NT **-(e)s, -e** [-də] *(form)* suicide

su|i|zi|dal [zuitsi'da:l] ADJ *(form)* suicidal

Su|i|zid-: Su|i|zid|ge|fahr F risk of suicide; **su|i|zid|ge|fähr|det** ADJ suicidal; **Su|i|zid|ge|fähr|de|te(r)** [-gəfɛ:ɐdətə] MF *decl as adj* suicidal man/woman; **die ~n** the suicidal; **Su|i|zid|tä|ter(in)** M(F) *(form)* suicide; **Su|i|zid|ver|such** M suicide attempt

Su|jet [sy'ʒe:] NT **-s, -s** *(geh)* subject

Suk|ka|de [zʊ'ka:də] F **-, -n** candied peel

suk|zes|siv [zʊktsɛ'si:f], **suk|zes|si|ve** [zʊktsɛ'si:və] ADJ gradual ADV gradually

Sul|fat [zʊl'fa:t] NT **-(e)s, -e** sulphate *(Brit)*, sulfate *(US)*

Sul|fid [zʊl'fi:t] NT **-(e)s, -e** [-də] sulphide *(Brit)*, sulfide *(US)*

Sul|fit [zʊl'fi:t] NT **-s, -e** sulphite *(Brit)*, sulfite *(US)*

Sul|fo|na|mid [zʊlfona'mi:t] NT **-(e)s, -e** [-də] sulphonamide *(Brit)*, sulfonamide *(US)*

Sul|ky ['zʊlki, 'zalki] NT **-s, -s** sulky

Süll [zʏl] M OR NT **-(e)s, -e**, **Süll|bord** M, **Süll|rand** M *(Naut)* coaming

Sul|tan ['zʊlta:n] M **-s, -e** sultan

Sul|ta|nat [zʊlta'na:t] NT **-(e)s, -e** sultanate

Sul|ta|nin ['zʊltanɪn, zʊl'ta:nɪn] F **-, -nen** sultana

Sul|ta|ni|ne [zʊlta'ni:nə] F **-, -n** *(= Rosine)* sultana

Sulz [zʊlts] F **-, -en** *(esp S Ger, Aus, Sw)* brawn

Sül|ze ['zʏltsə] F **-, -n** brawn

sül|zen ['zʏltsn] VT **a** *(sl)* to go on and on about *(inf)* **b** *(Cook)* to pickle in aspic VI *(sl)* to go on and on *(inf)*

sul|zig ['zʊltsɪç] ADJ *Schnee* slushy

Sülz|ko|te|lett NT cutlet in aspic

Su|mat|ra [zu'ma:tra, 'zu:matra] NT **-s** Sumatra

Su|mat|ra F **-, -s** *mild cigar originally from Sumatra*

Su|me|rer [zu'me:rɐ] M **-s, -**, **Su|me|re|rin** [-ərɪn] F **-, -nen** *(Hist)* Sumerian

su|me|risch [zu'me:rɪʃ] ADJ *(Hist)* Sumerian

summ [zʊm] INTERJ buzz; ~ **machen** to buzz

sum|ma cum lau|de ['zʊma kʊm 'laudə] ADV *(Univ)* summa cum laude *(US)*, with distinction

Sum|mand [zʊ'mant] M **-en, -en** [-dn] *(Math)* summand

sum|ma|risch [zʊ'ma:rɪʃ] ADJ *(auch Jur)* summary; *Zusammenfassung* summarizing ADV **etw** ~ **zusammenfassen** to summarize sth; ~ **lässt sich sagen, dass ...** to summarize, we can say that ...

sum|ma sum|ma|rum ['zʊma zʊ'ma:rʊm] ADV *(geh)* all in all, on the whole

Sümm|chen ['zʏmçən] NT **-s, -** *dim von* **Summe**; **ein nettes** ~ *(hum)* a tidy sum *(inf)*, a pretty penny *(inf)*

Sum|me ['zʊmə] F **-, -n** sum; *(= Gesamtsumme auch)* total; *(fig)* sum total; **die** ~ **aus etw ziehen** to sum up *or* evaluate sth

sum|men ['zʊmən] VT *Melodie etc* to hum VI to buzz; *(Mensch, Motor, Gerät)* to hum VI *impers* **es summt** there is a buzzing/humming noise

Sum|mer ['zʊmɐ] M **-s, -** buzzer

sum|mie|ren [zʊ'mi:rən] *ptp* **summiert** VT to sum up VR to mount up; **das summiert sich** it (all) adds *or* mounts up

Summ|ton M *pl* **-töne**, **Summ|zei|chen** NT buzz, buzzing sound

Su|mo ['zu:mo] NT **-**, *no pl* sumo

Su|mo|rin|gen NT sumo wrestling

Su|mo|rin|ger M sumo wrestler

Sumpf [zʊmpf] M **-(e)s, ¨-e** ['zʏmpfə] marsh; *(= Morast)* mud; *(in tropischen Ländern)* swamp; *(fig)* morass; **im ~ der Großstadt** in the squalor and corruption of the big city

Sumpf-: Sumpf|blü|te F *sb who or sth which flourishes in a decaying society*; **Sumpf|bo|den** M marshy ground; **Sumpf|dot|ter|blu|me** F marsh marigold

sump|fen ['zʊmpfn] VI *(inf)* to live it up *(inf)*

Sumpf-: Sumpf|fie|ber NT malaria; **Sumpf|huhn** NT moorhen; *(inf: = unsolider Mensch)* fast-liver *(inf)*

sump|fig ['zʊmpfɪç] ADJ marshy, swampy

Sumpf-: Sumpf|land NT marshland; *(in tropischen Ländern)* swampland; **Sumpf|ot|ter** M mink; **Sumpf|pflan|ze** F marsh plant; **Sumpf|vo|gel** M wader; **Sumpf|zyp|res|se** F deciduous cypress

Sund [zʊnt] M **-(e)s, -e** [-də] sound, straits *pl*

Sün|de ['zʏndə] F **-, -n** sin; **eine** ~ **begehen** to sin, to commit a sin; **jdm seine ~n vergeben** to forgive sb his sins; **es ist eine** ~ **und Schande** *(inf)* it's a crying shame; **ökologische ~n** ecological sins *or* crimes

Sün|den-: Sün|den|ba|bel [-ba:bl] NT **-s, -** hotbed of vice; **Sün|den|be|kennt|nis** NT confession of one's sins; *(Gebet)* confession (of sins); **Sün|den|bock** M *(inf)* scapegoat, whipping boy; **jdn zum ~ machen** to make sb one's scapegoat; **Sün|den|fall** M *(Rel)* Fall (of Man); *(fig)* sin; **sün|den|frei** ADJ free from sin, without sin; **Sün|den|pfuhl** M den of iniquity; **Sün|den|re|gis|ter** NT *(fig)* list of sins; **jds ~ vorhalten** to list all sb's sins; **jdm ein langes/sein ~ vorhalten** to list all sb's sins; **Sün|den|ver|ge|bung** F forgiveness *or* remission of sins

Sün|der ['zʏndɐ] M **-s, -**, **Sün|de|rin** [-ərɪn] F **-, -nen** sinner; **armer** ~ *(Eccl)* miserable sinner; *(old) criminal under sentence of death (fig)* poor wretch; **na, alter ~!** *(dated inf)* well, you old rogue! *(inf)*

Sün|der|mie|ne F shamefaced expression; **jdn mit einer** ~ **ansehen** to look at sb shamefaced(ly)

Sünd|flut F, *no pl* = **Sintflut**

sünd|haft ADJ *(lit)* sinful; *(fig inf) Preise* wicked; **ein ~es Geld** *(inf)* a ridiculous amount of money ADV *(inf)* ~ **teuer** wickedly expensive

Sünd|haf|tig|keit ['zʏnthaftɪçkait] F **-**, *no pl* sinfulness

sün|dig ['zʏndɪç] ADJ sinful; ~ **werden** to sin (*an +dat* against)

sün|di|gen ['zʏndɪgn] VI to sin (*an +dat* against); *(hum)* to indulge; **gegen Gott** ~ to sin against God; **gegen die Natur** ~ to commit a crime against nature; **gegen seine Gesundheit** ~ to jeopardize one's health

sünd|teu|er ADJ *(Aus)* wickedly expensive

Sun|nit [zʊ'ni:t] M **-en, -en**, **Sun|ni|tin** [zʊ'ni:tɪn] F **-, -nen** Sunnite

su|per ['zu:pɐ] *(inf)* ADJ *inv* super, smashing, great *(all inf)* ADV *(mit adj)* really, incredibly *(inf)*; *(mit vb)* really *or* incredibly *(inf)* well; **sie haben sich (gleich) ~ miteinander verstanden** they got on like a house on fire (right from the start)

Su|per ['zu:pɐ] NT **-s**, *no pl (= Benzin)* ≈ four-star (petrol) *(Brit)*, ≈ premium *(US)*

Su|per- *in cpds* super-; *(= sehr)* ultra-; **Su|per-8-Film** [zu:pɐ'laxt-] M Super 8 film

su|perb [zu'pɛrp], **sü|perb** [zy'pɛrp] *(dated geh)* ADJ splendid, superb, superlative ADV superbly; **~ schmecken** to taste superb; **sich ~ unterhalten** to have a splendid time

Su|per-: **Su|per|ben|zin** NT = **Super**; **Su|per-CD** F super CD; **Su|per|chip** M *(Comput)* superchip; **su|per|fein** ADJ *Qualität* top *attr*; *Esswaren etc* top-quality; *(inf)* posh *(inf)*; **Su|per|frau** F superwoman; **Su|per-G** ['zu:pɐdʒi:] M **-(s), -(s)** *(Ski)* super G; **Su|per-GAU** M ultimate MCA; *(fig)* total meltdown; **Su|per|in|ten|dent** [zupɐlɪntɛn'dɛnt, 'zu:pɐ-] M **-en, -en**, **Su|per|in|ten|den|tin** [-'dɛntɪn] F **-, -nen** *(Eccl)* superintendent

Su|pe|ri|or [zu'pe:rio:ɐ] M **-s, Superioren** [-'rio:rən], **Su|pe|ri|o|rin** [-'rio:rɪn] F **-, -nen** superior

Su|pe|ri|o|ri|tät [zuperiori'tɛ:t] F **-**, *no pl (geh)* superiority

su|per|klug ADJ *(iro inf)* brilliant; **du bist ein Superkluger** *(= Besserwisser)* you are a (real) know-all *(Brit inf)* or know-it-all *(US inf)*; *(= Dummkopf)* you're brilliant, you are *(iro)*; *(= das ist nichts Neues)* you're not telling us anything new

Su|per|la|tiv ['zu:pɐlati:f] M **-s, -e** [-və] *(Gram, fig)* superlative

su|per|la|ti|visch ['zu:pɐlati:vɪʃ] ADJ *(Gram)* superlative; *(fig)* grand; **ins Superlativische geraten** to assume massive proportions, to snowball in a big way *(inf)*; **er bedient sich einer ~en Ausdrucksweise** his speech is full of superlatives

Su|per-: **su|per|leicht** ADJ *(inf) Zigaretten* extra mild; *(= kinderleicht)* dead easy *(Brit inf)*, very easy; *(= wenig wiegend)* ultralight; **Su|per|macht** F superpower; **Su|per|mann** M *pl* **-männer** superman; **Su|per|markt** M supermarket; **Su|per|mi|nis|ter(in)** M(F) *(inf)* super minister *(inf, who takes on several different portfolios)*; **su|per|mo|dern** [-modɛrn] *(inf)* ADJ ultramodern ADV ultramodernly; **sich ~ ausdrücken** to use ultramodern expressions; **Su|per|no|va** [zupɐ'no:va] F **-, Supernovä** [-'no:vɛ] supernova; **su|per|schnell** *(inf)* ADJ ultrafast ADV incredibly fast *(inf)*; **Su|per|schnell|zug** M high-speed train; **Su|per|star** M *(inf)* superstar; **su|per|stark** ADJ *(inf)* brilliant

Süpp|chen ['zʏpçən] NT **-s, -** *dim von* **Suppe**; **sein eigenes ~ kochen** *(fig)* to do one's own thing *(inf)*; **sein ~ am Feuer anderer kochen** *(fig)* to exploit *or* use other people

Sup|pe ['zʊpə] F **-, -n** soup; *(sämig mit Einlage)* broth; *(= klare Brühe)* bouillon; *(fig inf: = Nebel)* peasouper *(Brit inf)*, dense fog; **klare ~** consommé; **jdm ein schöne ~ einbrocken** *(fig inf)* to get sb into a pickle *(inf)* or nice mess; **du musst die ~ auslöffeln, die du dir eingebrockt hast** *(inf)* you've made your bed, now you must lie on it *(prov)*; **jdm die ~ versalzen** *(inf)* **jdm in die ~ spucken** *(inf)* to put a spoke in sb's wheel *(inf)*, to queer sb's pitch *(Brit inf)*; **du siehst aus, als ob dir jemand in die ~ gespuckt hätte** you look as though you've lost a pound and found sixpence *(Brit)*, you look as though you've lost your best friend *(US)* → **Haar c**, **Salz**

Sup|pen- *in cpds* soup; **Sup|pen|fleisch** NT meat for making soup; *(= gekochtes Rindfleisch)* boiled beef; **Sup|pen|ge|mü|se** NT vegetables *pl* for making soup; **Sup|pen|grün** NT herbs and vegetables *pl* for making soup; **Sup|pen|huhn** NT boiling fowl; **Sup|pen|kas|par** [-kaspar] M **-s, -e**, **Sup|pen|kas|per** M *(inf)* poor eater; *(= Suppenfreund)* soup fan *(inf)*; **Sup|pen|kel|le** F soup ladle; **Sup|pen|kü|che** F soup kitchen; **Sup|pen|löf|fel** M soup spoon; **Sup|pen|nu|del** F vermicelli *pl*, noodles *pl*; **Sup|pen|schüs|sel** F tureen; **Sup|pen|tas|se** F soup bowl; **Sup|pen|tel|ler** M soup plate; **Sup|pen|wür|fel** M stock cube; **Sup|pen|wür|ze** F soup seasoning

Sup|ple|ment [zʊple'mɛnt] NT **-(e)s, -e** *(geh)* supplement

Sup|ple|ment-: **Sup|ple|ment|band** [-bant] M *pl* **-bände** supplementary volume; **Sup|ple|ment|win|kel** M supplementary angle

Sup|port [sə'po:ɐt, sə'pɔrt] M **-s**, *no pl (Comput etc)* support

Sup|po|si|to|ri|um [zʊpozi'to:riʊm] **-s, Suppositorien** [-riən] NT *(Med)* suppository

Sup|ra- ['zu:pra-]: **sup|ra|lei|tend** ADJ *(Phys)* superconductive; **Sup|ra|lei|ter** M *(Phys)* superconductor; **Sup|ra|lei|tung** F *(Phys)* superconductivity; **sup|ra|na|ti|o|nal** [zupranatio'na:l, 'zu:pra-] ADJ supranational ADV supranationally; **Sup|ra|na|tu|ra|lis|mus** [zupranatura'lɪsmʊs, 'zu:pra-] M supernaturalism

Sup|re|mat [zupre'ma:t] M OR NT **-(e)s, -e**, **Sup|re|ma|tie** [zuprema'ti:] F **-, -n** [-'ti:ən] *(geh)* supremacy

Su|re ['zu:rə] F **-, -n** *(im Koran)* sura(h)

Surf|brett ['zø:ɐf-, 'zœrf-, s-] NT surfboard

sur|fen ['zø:ɐfn, 'zœrfn, s-] VI to surf; **im Internet ~** to surf the Internet

Sur|fer ['zø:ɐfɐ, 'zœrfɐ, s-] M **-s, -**, **Sur|fe|rin** [-ərin] F **-, -nen** surfer

Sur|fing ['zø:ɐfɪŋ, 'zœr-, s-] NT **-s**, *no pl (Sport)* surfing

Su|ri|nam [zuri'nam] NT **-s** Dutch Guiana

sur|re|al ['zʊrea:l, 'zʏ-] ADJ surreal

Sur|re|a|lis|mus [zʊrea'lɪsmʊs, zʏ-] M, *no pl* surrealism

sur|re|a|lis|tisch [zʊrea'lɪstɪʃ, zʏ-] ADJ surrealist(ic)

sur|ren ['zʊrən] VI **a** *(Projektor, Computer)* to hum; *(Motor)* to hum, to whir(r); *(Ventilator, Kamera)* to whir(r) **b** *aux sein (= sich bewegen: Insekt)* to buzz

Sur|ro|gat [zʊro'ga:t] NT **-(e)s, -e** surrogate

Su|se ['zu:zə] F **-s**, **Su|si** ['zu:zi] F **-s** *contr von* **Susanne**

Su|shi NT **-s, -s** sushi

sus|pekt [zʊs'pɛkt] ADJ suspicious; **jdm ~ sein** to seem suspicious to sb

sus|pen|die|ren [zʊspɛn'di:rən] *ptp* **suspendiert** VT to suspend *(von* from)

Sus|pen|si|on [zʊspɛn'zio:n] F **-, -en** *(alle Bedeutungen)* suspension

sus|pen|siv [zʊspɛn'zi:f] ADJ *(Jur)* suspensory

Sus|pen|so|ri|um [zʊspɛn'zo:riʊm] NT **-s, Suspensorien** [-riən] *(Med)* suspensory

süß [zy:s] ADJ *(lit, fig)* sweet; **etw ~ machen** to sweeten sth; *Tee, Kaffee (mit Zucker)* to sugar sth; **sie ist eine Süße** *(inf) (= isst gerne süß)* she has a sweet tooth; *(= ist nett)* she's a sweetie(-pie) *(inf)*; **das ~e Leben** the good life; **es auf die ~e Tour versuchen, es auf die Süße versuchen** *(inf)* to turn on the charm; **(mein) Süßer, (meine) Süße** *(inf)* my sweetheart; *(als Anrede auch)* my sweet, sweetie(-pie) *(inf)* → **Geheimnis, Rache** ADV *sich bedanken, sagen* sweetly; **gern ~ essen** to have a sweet tooth, to be fond of sweet things; **den Kaffee ~ trinken** to put sugar in one's coffee; **etw sehr ~ zubereiten** to make sth very sweet; **~ duften** to smell sweet; **~ aussehen** to look sweet; **sie haben uns ganz ~ betreut** *(inf)* they were so sweet to us

Sü|ße ['zy:sə] F **-**, *no pl (lit, fig)* sweetness

sü|ßen ['zy:sn] VT to sweeten; *(mit Zucker) Tee, Kaffee* to sugar VI **mit Honig** *etc* **~** to use honey *etc* as a sweetener

Süß|holz NT liquorice *(Brit)*, licorice *(US)*; **~ raspeln** *(fig)* to turn on the blarney; **du kannst aufhören, ~ zu raspeln** you can stop sucking up to *or* soft-soaping *(Brit)* me/him *etc (inf)*

Süß|holz|rasp|ler [-rasplɐ] M **-s, -**, **Süß|holz|rasp|le|rin** [-ərɪn] F **-, -nen** *(hum)* soft-soaper *(Brit inf)*, sweet-talker

Sü|ßig|keit ['zy:sɪçkait] F **-, -en** **a** *no pl (lit, fig)* sweetness **b** **Süßigkeiten** PL sweets *pl (Brit)*, candy *(US)*

Süß-: **Süß|kar|tof|fel** F sweet potato; **Süß|kir|sche** F sweet cherry; **Süß|klee** M hedysarum *(spec)*

süß|lich ['zy:slɪç] ADJ **a** *Geruch, Geschmack (= leicht süß)* sweetish, slightly sweet; *(= unangenehm süß)* sickly (sweet), cloying **b** *(fig) Töne, Miene, Worte* sweet; *Lächeln, Schlager* sugary; *Farben, Modegeschmack* pretty-pretty *(Brit inf)*, overly pretty; *(= kitschig)* mawkish, tacky

Süß-: **Süß|most** M unfermented fruit juice; **Süß|rahm|but|ter** F creamery butter; **süß|sau|er** ADJ sweet-and-sour; *Gurken etc* pickled; *(fig: = gezwungen freundlich) Lächeln* forced; *Miene* artificially friendly; **Ente ~** sweet-and-sour duck ADV *würzen, einlegen* in a sweet-and-sour sauce; **~ schmecken** to taste sweet-and-sour; **~ lächeln** to give a bittersweet smile; **Süß|spei|se** F sweet dish; **Süß|stoff** M sweetener; **Süß|wa|ren** PL confectionery *sing*; **Süß|wa|ren|ge|schäft** NT sweetshop *(Brit)*, candy store *(US)*, confectioner's; **Süß|was|ser** NT *pl* **-wasser** freshwater; **Süß|was|ser|fisch** M freshwater fish; **Süß|wein** M dessert wine

Su|ta|ne [zu'ta:nə] F **-, -n** *(Eccl)* cassock

Süt|ter|lin|schrift ['zʏtɐli:n-] F *old-fashioned style of German handwriting*

SV [ɛs'fau] M **-** *abbr von* **Sportverein** SC; **der SV Mannheim** Mannheim SC

SVGA *abbr von* **super video graphics array** SVGA

SVP [ɛsfau'pe:] F **-** *abbr von* **Schweizerische Volkspartei**

SW *abbr von* **Südwesten** SW

Swap [svɔp] M **-s, -s** *(Fin)* swap

Swa|si|land ['sva:zilant] NT **-s** Swaziland

Swas|ti|ka ['svastika] F **-, Swastiken** [-kn] swastika

Sweat|shirt ['svɛtʃœrt, -ʃø:ɐt] NT **-s, -s** sweatshirt

Swim|ming|pool ['svɪmɪŋpu:l] M **-s, -s** swimming pool

Swin|egel ['svi:nle:gl] M **-s, -** *(dial)* hedgehog

Swing [svɪŋ] M **-s**, *no pl (Mus, Fin)* swing

swin|gen ['svɪŋən] VI *(Mus)* to swing

Swin|ger|club ['svɪŋɐ-] M *(inf)* = **Swingerklub**

Swin|ger|klub ['svɪŋɐ-] M *(inf)* swingers' bar *(inf)*

SWR [ɛsve:'lɛr] M **-** *abbr von* **Südwestrundfunk**

syl|la|bisch [zʏ'la:bɪʃ] ADJ syllabic

Syl|lo|gis|mus [zʏlo'gɪsmʊs] M **-, Syllogismen** [-mən] *(Philos)* syllogism

Syl|phe ['zʏlfə] M **-n, -n** *or f* **-, -n** *(Myth)* sylph

Sylt [zʏlt] NT **-s** Sylt

Syl|va|ner [zʏl'va:nɐ] M **-s, -** *(= Traubensorte)* Sylvaner (grape); *(= Wein)* Sylvaner (wine)

Syl|ves|ter [zʏl'vɛstɐ] NT **-s, -** = **Silvester**

Sym|bi|o|se [zʏm'bio:zə] F **-, -n** symbiosis

sym|bi|o|tisch [zʏm'bio:tɪʃ] ADJ symbiotic ADV **~ zusammenleben** to have a symbiotic relationship; *(Menschen)* to live together symbiotically

Sym|bol [zʏm'bo:l] NT **-s, -e** symbol; *(Comput)* (toolbar) icon

Sym|bol-: **Sym|bol|fi|gur** F symbol, symbolic figure; **Sym|bol|ge|halt** M symbolic content; **sym|bol|haft** ADJ symbolic(al)

Sym|bo|lik [zʏm'bo:lɪk] F **-**, *no pl* symbolism

sym|bo|lisch [zʏm'bo:lɪʃ] ADJ symbolic(al) *(für* of) ADV symbolically

sym|bo|li|sie|ren [zʏmboli'zi:rən] *ptp* **symbolisiert** VT to symbolize

Sym|bo|lis|mus [zʏmbo'lɪsmʊs] M **-**, *no pl* symbolism

Sym|bo|list [zʏmbo'lɪst] M **-en, -en**, **Sym|bo|lis|tin** [-'lɪstɪn] F **-, -nen** symbolist

sym|bo|lis|tisch [zʏmbo'lɪstɪʃ] ADJ symbolist(ic)

Sym|bol-: **Sym|bol|kraft** F symbolic force *or* power; **sym|bol|kräf|tig** ADJ strongly *or* richly symbolic; **Sym|bol|leis|te** F *(Comput)* toolbar; **sym|bol|träch|tig** ADJ heavily symbolic, full of symbolism; **Sym|bol|un|ter|schrift** F *(Comput)* text label

Sym|met|rie [zyme'tri:] F -, -n [-'tri:ən] symmetry

Sym|met|rie-: **Sym|met|rie|ach|se** F axis of symmetry; **Sym|met|rie|ebe|ne** F plane of symmetry

sym|met|risch [zy'me:trɪʃ] ADJ symmetric(al) ADV symmetrically

Sym|pa|thie [zympa'ti:] F -, -n [-'ti:ən] *(= Zuneigung)* liking; *(= Mitgefühl, Solidaritätsgefühl)* sympathy; **für jdn/etw ~ haben** to have a liking for/ a certain amount of sympathy with sb/sth; **jdm große** *or* **viel ~ entgegenbringen** to have a lot of sympathy for sb; **diese Maßnahmen haben meine volle ~** I sympathize completely with these measures; **durch seine Unverschämtheit hat er meine ~/hat er sich** *(dat)* **alle ~(n) verscherzt** he has turned me/everyone against him with his rudeness; **~n gewinnen** to win favour *(Brit) or* favor *(US)*; **seine ~n gelten nicht der extremen Rechten** he isn't sympathetic to the extreme right

Sym|pa|thie-: **Sym|pa|thie|äu|ße|rung** F expression of support; **Sym|pa|thie|kund|ge|bung** F demonstration of support; **Sym|pa|thie|streik** M sympathy strike; **in ~ (mit jdm) treten** to come out in sympathy (with sb); **Sym|pa|thie|trä|ger(in)** M(F) popular figure; **Sym|pa|thie|wer|bung** F campaign for greater popularity; *(von Politiker etc auch)* charm offensive; **Sym|pa|thie|wer|te** PL popularity rating *sing*

Sym|pa|thi|kus [zym'pa:tikʊs] M -, *no pl (Physiol)* sympathetic nerve

Sym|pa|thi|sant [zympati'zant] M **-en, -en**, **Sym|pa|thi|san|tin** [-'zantɪn] F **-, -nen** sympathizer

sym|pa|thisch [zym'pa:tɪʃ] ADJ **a** pleasant, nice, simpatico *(esp US inf)*; **er/es ist mir ~** I like him/it; **er/es war mir gleich ~** I liked him/it at once, I took to him/it at once, I took an immediate liking to him/it; **das ist mir gar nicht ~** I don't like it at all **b** *(Anat, Physiol)* sympathetic

sym|pa|thi|sie|ren [zympati'zi:rən] *ptp* **sympathisiert** VI to sympathize *(mit* with)

Sym|pho|nie [zymfo'ni:] F -, -n [-'ni:ən] = **Sinfonie**

Sym|pho|nie- *in cpds* = **Sinfonie-**

Sym|pho|ni|ker [zym'fo:nikɐ] M **-s, -**, **Sym|pho|ni|ke|rin** [-ərɪn] F **-, -nen** = **Sinfoniker**

sym|pho|nisch [zym'fo:nɪʃ] ADJ = **sinfonisch**

Sym|po|si|on [zym'po:ziɔn] NT **-s, Symposien** [-ziən], **Sym|po|si|um** [zym'po:ziʊm] NT **-s, Symposien** [-ziən] symposium

Symp|tom [zymp'to:m] NT **-s, -e** symptom

symp|to|ma|tisch [zympto'ma:tɪʃ] ADJ symptomatic *(für* of)

Sy|na|go|ge [zyna'go:gə] F -, -n synagogue

Sy|nap|se [zy'napsə, zʏn'lapsə] F -, -n *(Anat, Physiol)* synapse

Syn|äs|the|sie [zynɛste'zi:, zʏnlɛs-] F -, -n *(Med, Psych, Liter)* synaesthesia *(Brit)*, synesthesia *(US)*

syn|chron [zʏn'kro:n] ADJ synchronous; *(Ling)* synchronic ADV synchronologically

Syn|chron|ge|trie|be NT *(Aut)* synchromesh gearbox

Syn|chro|ni|sa|ti|on [zʏnkroniza'tsio:n] F -, **-en** *(Film, TV)* synchronization; *(= Übersetzung)* dubbing

syn|chro|ni|sie|ren [zʏnkroni'zi:rən] *ptp* **synchronisiert** VT to synchronize; *(= übersetzen) Film* to dub

Syn|chron-: **Syn|chron|schwim|men** NT synchronized swimming; **Syn|chron|spre|cher(in)** M(F) dubbing artist; **Syn|chron|uhr** F synchronous *or* mains-synchronized clock; **Syn|chron|ver|schluss** M *(Phot)* flash-synchronized shutter

Syn|di|ka|lis|mus [zʏndika'lɪsmʊs] M -, *no pl* syndicalism

syn|di|ka|lis|tisch [zʏndika'lɪstɪʃ] ADJ syndicalist(ic)

Syn|di|kat [zʏndi'ka:t] NT **-(e)s, -e** *(= Kartell)* syndicate

Syn|di|kus ['zʏndikʊs] M -, **Syndiken** *or* **Syndizi** [-kn, -tsi] *(= Geschäftsführer)* syndic; *(= Justitiar)* (company *etc)* lawyer

Syn|drom [zʏn'dro:m] NT **-s, -e** syndrome

Sy|ner|gie [zynɛr'gi:, zʏnlɛr'gi:] F -, *no pl* synergy

Sy|ner|gie|ef|fekt M *(Chem, Phys)* synergistic effect; *(fig)* synergy effect

Syn|ko|pe F -, -n **a** ['zʏnkopə] syncope, syncopation **b** [zʏn'ko:pə] *(Mus)* syncopation

syn|ko|pie|ren [zʏnko'pi:rən] *ptp* **synkopiert** VT to syncopate

syn|ko|pisch [zʏn'ko:pɪʃ] ADJ syncopic, syncopated *(esp Mus)*

Syn|kre|tis|mus [zʏnkre'tɪsmʊs] M -, *no pl* syncretism

Sy|no|da|le(r) [zyno'da:lə] MF *decl as adj (Eccl)* synod member

Sy|no|de [zy'no:də] F -, -n *(Eccl)* synod

sy|no|nym [zyno'ny:m], **sy|no|ny|misch** [zyno'ny:mɪʃ] ADJ synonymous

Sy|no|nym [zyno'ny:m] NT **-s, -e** synonym

Sy|no|nym|wör|ter|buch NT dictionary of synonyms, thesaurus

Sy|nop|se [zy'nɔpsə, zʏn'lɔpsə] F -, -n, **Sy|nop|sis** [zy'nɔpsɪs, 'zʏnlɔpsɪs] F -, **Synopsen** [-sn] synopsis; *(Bibl)* synoptic Gospels *pl*, Synoptics *pl*

Sy|nop|ti|ker [zy'nɔptikɐ, zʏn'lɔptikɐ] PL *(Bibl)* Synoptics *pl*; *(= Apostel)* Synoptists *pl*

Syn|tag|ma [zʏn'tagma] NT **-s, Syntagmen** *or* **-ta** [-mən, -ta] *(Ling)* syntactic construction

syn|tak|tisch [zʏn'taktɪʃ] ADJ syntactic(al) ADV **das ist ~ korrekt/falsch** the syntax (of this) is correct/wrong; **~ schwierige Übersetzungen** translations with difficult syntax

Syn|tax ['zʏntaks] F -, **-en** syntax

Syn|tax|feh|ler M *(Comput)* syntax error

Syn|the|se [zʏn'te:zə] F -, -n synthesis

Syn|the|si|zer ['zʏntəsaizɐ] M **-s, -** synthesizer

Syn|the|tik [zʏn'te:tɪk] F -, *no pl* **a** *(Math)* synthesis **b** *(= Kunstfaser)* synthetic fibre *(Brit) or* fiber *(US)*

syn|the|tisch [zʏn'te:tɪʃ] ADJ synthetic; *Stoff, Faser auch* man-made ADV **etw ~ herstellen** to make *or* produce sth synthetically

syn|the|ti|sie|ren [zʏnteti'zi:rən] *ptp* **synthetisiert** VT to syntheticize

Sy|phi|lis ['zy:filɪs] F -, *no pl* syphilis

sy|phi|lis|krank ADJ syphilitic, suffering from syphilis; **~ sein** to have syphilis

Sy|phi|li|ti|ker [zyfi'li:tikɐ] M **-s, -**, **Sy|phi|li|ti|ke|rin** [-ərɪn] F **-, -nen** syphilitic

sy|phi|li|tisch [zyfi'li:tɪʃ] ADJ syphilitic

Sy|ra|kus [zyra'ku:s] NT -' Syracuse

Sy|rer ['zy:rɐ] M **-s, -**, **Sy|re|rin** [-ərɪn] F **-, -nen** Syrian

Sy|ri|en ['zy:riən] NT **-s** Syria

Sy|ri|er ['zy:riɐ] M **-s, -**, **Sy|ri|e|rin** [-iərɪn] F **-, -nen** Syrian

sy|risch ['zy:rɪʃ] ADJ Syrian

Sy|risch(e) ['zy:rɪʃ] NT Syriac → *auch* **Deutsch(e)**

Sys|tem [zʏs'te:m] NT **-s, -e** system *(auch Comput)*; *(= Ordnung, Ordnungsprinzip auch)* method; **etw mit ~ machen** to do sth systematically; **etw mit einem ~ machen** to do sth according to a system; **hinter dieser Sache steckt ~** there's method behind it; **~ in etw** *(acc)* **bringen** to get *or* bring some system into sth; **Apparate verschiedener ~e** machinery of different designs; **ein ~ von Straßen/Kanälen** a road/canal system

Sys|tem-: **Sys|tem|ab|sturz** M *(Comput)* system crash; **gelegentlich treten Systemabstürze auf** occasionally the system crashes; **Sys|tem|ad|mi|ni|stra|tor(in)** M(F) *(Comput)* system administrator; **Sys|tem|ana|ly|se** F systems analysis; **Sys|tem|ana|ly|ti|ker(in)** M(F) systems analyst

Sys|te|ma|tik [zʏste'ma:tɪk] F -, *no pl* **a** *(= systematisches Ordnen)* system **b** *(= Lehre, Klassifikation)* systematology

Sys|te|ma|ti|ker [zʏste'ma:tikɐ] M **-s, -**, **Sys|te|ma|ti|ke|rin** [-ərɪn] F **-, -nen** systematist; *(fig)* systematic person

sys|te|ma|tisch [zʏste'ma:tɪʃ] ADJ systematic ADV systematically

sys|te|ma|ti|sie|ren [zʏstemati'zi:rən] *ptp* **systematisiert** VT to systematize

Sys|tem-: **sys|tem|be|dingt** ADJ determined by the system; **Sys|tem|be|treu|er(in)** M(F) *(Comput)* systems administrator; **Sys|tem|da|tei** F *(Comput)* system file; **Sys|tem|dis|ket|te** F systems disk; **Sys|tem|feh|ler** M *(Comput)* system error; **sys|tem|ge|recht** ADJ ADV in accordance with the system; **sys|tem|im|ma|nent** ADJ inherent in the system; **dem Kapitalismus ~ sein** to be inherent in the capitalist system; **Sys|tem|in|for|ma|ti|o|nen** PL *(Comput)* system information

sys|te|misch [zʏs'te:mɪʃ] ADJ systemic

Sys|tem-: **sys|tem|kon|form** ADJ in conformity with the system ADV **sich ~ verhalten** to conform to the system; **sich ~ geben** to give the impression of conforming to the system; **Sys|tem|kri|ti|ker(in)** M(F) critic of the system; **sys|tem|kri|tisch** ADJ critical of the system ADV **sich ~ äußern** to make remarks critical of the system; **~ eingestellt sein** to be critical of the system; **~ schreiben** to write critically about the system; **sys|tem|los** ADJ unsystematic ADV unsystematically; **Sys|tem|ma|na|ger** M *(Comput: = Programm)* system manager program; **Sys|tem|me|nü** NT *(Comput)* control *or* system menu; **Sys|tem|pro|gramme** PL *(Comput)* system tools; **Sys|tem|soft|ware** F systems software; **Sys|tem|spe|zi|a|list(in)** M(F) *(Comput)* systems specialist; **Sys|tem|steu|e|rung** F system control, control panel; **Sys|tem|tech|ni|ker(in)** M(F) *(Comput)* systems engineer; **Sys|tem|treue** F loyalty to the system; **Sys|tem|ver|än|de|rer** [-fɛɐlɛndərɐ] M **-s, -**, **Sys|tem|ver|än|de|rin** [-ərɪn] F **-, -nen** *(Pol pej)* **die Partei besteht aus lauter ~n** the whole party is just a bunch of people out to change the system; **Sys|tem|ver|än|de|rung** F change in the system; **Sys|tem|vo|raus|set|zung** F *usu pl* systems requirement *usu pl*; **Sys|tem|wech|sel** M change of system; **Sys|tem|zwang** M obligation to conform to the system

Sys|to|le ['zʏstolə, -'to:lə] F -, -n *(Med)* systole

Sze|nar [stse'na:ɐ] NT **-s, -e** = **Szenario**

Sze|na|rio [stse'na:rio] NT **-s, -s**, **Sze|na|ri|um** [stse'na:riʊm] NT **-s, Szenarien** [-riən] scenario

Sze|ne ['stse:nə] F -, -n **a** *(Theat, fig)* scene; *(Theat: = Bühnenausstattung)* set; *(sl: = Drogenszene etc)* scene *(inf)*; *(sl: = Milieu)* subculture; *(sl: der Leute, die in sind)* in places *pl (inf)*; **Beifall auf offener ~** applause during the performance; **hinter der ~** backstage; *(fig)* behind the scenes; **in ~** *(acc)* **gehen** to be staged; **etw in ~ setzen** *(lit, fig)* to stage sth; **sich in ~ setzen** *(fig)* to play to the gallery; **die ~ beherrschen** *(fig)* to dominate the scene (+*gen* in); *(= meistern)* to control things; **sich in der ~ auskennen** *(inf)* to know the scene *(inf)*; **die rechte/linke ~** *(inf)* the right-/left-wing scene

b *(fig: = Zank, Streit)* scene; **jdm eine ~ machen** to make a scene in front of sb; **mach bloß keine ~** don't go making a scene, I don't want a scene

-sze|ne F *suf in cpds (inf)* scene *(inf)*; **die Drogenszene** the drugs *(Brit) or* drug scene

Sze|ne- *in cpds (inf)* in-; **ein Szenekenner** somebody who knows the in places *(inf)*

Sze|ne|knei|pe F *(inf)* hip bar *(inf)*, *bar fashionable with a certain clique*

Sze|nen- *in cpds*: **Sze|nen|ap|plaus** M spontaneous applause; **Sze|nen|bild** NT (stage) set, stage setting; **Sze|nen|fol|ge** F sequence of scenes; **Sze|nen|wech|sel** M scene change

Sze|ne|rie [stsenəˈriː] F -, -n [-ˈriːən] *(Theat, fig)* scenery

sze|nisch [ˈstseːnɪʃ] ADJ *(Theat)* scenic; *Lesung, Aufführung* staged ADV **etw ~ aufführen** to act sth out; **etw ~ umsetzen** to adapt sth for the stage

Szep|ter [ˈstsɛptɐ] NT -s, - *(dated, Aus)* sceptre *(Brit)*, scepter *(US)*

Szil|la [ˈstsɪla] F -, **Szillen** [-lən] *(Bot)* scilla

Szin|ti-: **Szin|ti|graf** [stsɪntiˈgraːf] M -en, -en scintigraph; **Szin|ti|gra|fie** [stsɪntigraˈfiː] F -, -n [-ˈfiːən] scintigraphy; **Szin|ti|gramm** [stsɪntiˈgram] NT *pl* **-gramme** scintigram; **Szin|ti|graph** [stsɪntiˈgraːf] *etc* = **Szintigraf** *etc*

Szyl|la [ˈstsʏla] F - *(Myth)* Scylla; **zwischen ~ und Charybdis** *(liter)* between Scylla and Charybdis

T

T, t [te:] NT **-, -** T, t
t [te:] *abbr von* **Tonne**
Tab [tɛb] M **-s, -s** tab
Ta|bak ['ta:bak, 'tabak, (*Aus*) ta'bak] M **-s, -e** tobacco; (*= Schnupftabak*) snuff
Ta|bak- *in cpds* tobacco; **Ta|bak|beu|tel** M tobacco pouch; **Ta|bak|do|se** F tobacco tin; (*für Schnupftabak*) snuffbox; **Ta|bak|ge|nuss** M (tobacco) smoking; **Ta|bak|händ|ler(in)** M(F) (*im Großhandel*) tobacco merchant; (*im Einzelhandel*) tobacconist; **Ta|bak|kon|zern** M tobacco group; **Ta|bak|la|den** M tobacconist's, tobacco shop; **Ta|bak|mi|schung** F blend (of tobaccos), (tobacco) mixture; **Ta|bak|mo|no|pol** NT tobacco monopoly, monopoly on tobacco; **Ta|bak|pfei|fe** F pipe; **Ta|bak|qualm** M (*pej*) fug; **Ta|bak|rauch** M tobacco smoke
Ta|baks-: **Ta|baks|beu|tel** M tobacco pouch; **Ta|baks|do|se** F tobacco tin; (*für Schnupftabak*) snuffbox; **Ta|baks|pfei|fe** F pipe
Ta|bak-: **Ta|bak|steuer** F duty on tobacco; **Ta|bak|tra|fik** [ta'bak-] F (*Aus*) tobacconist's, tobacco shop; **Ta|bak|tra|fi|kant(in)** [ta'bak-] M(F) (*Aus*) tobacconist; **Ta|bak|wa|ren** PL tobacco; **Ta|bak|wa|ren|la|den** M tobacconist's
Ta|ba|ti|e|re [taba'tie:rə] F **-, -n** (*Aus*) tobacco tin; (*old*: = *Schnupftabakdose*) snuffbox
ta|bel|la|risch [tabɛ'la:rɪʃ] **ADJ** tabular; **bitte fügen Sie einen ~en Lebenslauf bei** please write out your curriculum vitae (*Brit*) *or* résumé (*US*) in tabular form **ADV** in tabular form, in tables/a table
ta|bel|la|ri|sie|ren [tabɛlari'zi:rən] *ptp* **tabellarisiert** VT to tabulate
Ta|bel|le [ta'bɛlə] F **-, -n** table (*auch Comput*); (*= Diagramm*) chart; (*von Tabellenkalkulation*) sheet; (*Sport*) (league) table
Ta|bel|len-: **Ta|bel|len|en|de** NT (*Sport*) bottom of the league *or* table; **am ~ stehen** to be at the bottom of the league *or* table, to be cellar-dwelling (*US inf*); **Ta|bel|len|form** F **in ~** in tabular form, in tables/a table; (*Diagramm*) as a chart, in chart form; **ta|bel|len|för|mig** **ADJ** tabular, in tabular form, in the form of a table; (*= als Diagramm*) as a chart, in chart form **ADV** in a table; as a chart; **Ta|bel|len|füh|rer(in)** M(F) (*Sport*) league leaders *pl*; **~ sein** to be at the top of the (league) table; **Ta|bel|len|füh|rung** F (*Sport*) league leadership, position at the top of the table; **die ~ abgeben/verteidigen/zurückerobern** to give up/defend/regain the lead; **Ta|bel|len|ge|stal|tung** F (*an Schreibmaschine*) tabulation; **Ta|bel|len|kal|ku|la|ti|on** F (*Comput*) spreadsheet; **Ta|bel|len|kal|ku|la|ti|ons|pro|gramm** NT (*Comput*) spreadsheet (program); **Ta|bel|len|platz** M (*Sport*) place *or* position in the league; **auf den letzten ~ fallen** to drop to the bottom of the table; **Ta|bel|len|spit|ze** F (*Sport*) top position in the (league) table, top of the league *or* table; **an der ~ stehen** to be at the top of the league *or* table; **Ta|bel|len|stand** M (*Sport*) league situation; **~ auf Seite 15** league tables on page 15
Ta|ber|na|kel [tabɛr'na:kl] NT OR M **-s, -** tabernacle
Tab|lett [ta'blɛt] NT **-(e)s, -s** *or* **-e** tray; **jdm etw auf einem silbernen ~ servieren** (*fig*: = *einfach machen*) to hand sb sth on a plate (*Brit*) *or* on a silver platter; **muss man dir alles auf einem silbernen ~ servieren?** do you have to have everything done for you?
Tab|let|te [ta'blɛtə] F **-, -n** tablet, pill
Tab|let|ten-: **Tab|let|ten|form** F **in ~** in tablet form; **Tab|let|ten|miss|brauch** M pill abuse; **Tab|let|ten|röh|re** F tube of tablets *or* pills; **Tab|let|ten|sucht** F addiction to pills, compulsive pill-taking; **tab|let|ten|süch|tig** ADJ addicted to pills; **Tab|let|ten|süch|ti|ge(r)** MF *decl as adj* pill addict, pill-popper (*inf*)
ta|bu [ta'bu:, 'ta:bu] ADJ *pred* taboo
Tab|stopp ['tɛp-] M **-s, -s** (*Comput*) tab stop
Tab|tas|te ['tɛp-] F (*Comput*) tab key
Ta|bu [ta'bu:, 'ta:bu] NT **-s, -s** taboo
ta|bu|ie|ren [tabu'i:rən] *ptp* **tabuiert** VT to make taboo, to taboo
ta|bu|i|sie|ren [tabui'zi:rən] *ptp* **tabuisiert** VT to make taboo, to taboo
Ta|bu|i|sie|rung F **-, -en** taboo(ing)
Ta|bu|la ra|sa ['tabula 'ra:za] F **- -,** *no pl* (*Philos*) tabula rasa; **~ machen** (*inf*) to make a clean sweep
Ta|bu|la|tor [tabu'la:to:ɐ] M **-s, Tabulatoren** [-'to:rən] tabulator, tab (*inf*)
Ta|bu|la|tor|tas|te F tab key
Ta|bu-: **ta|bu|los** ADJ taboo-free; **Ta|bu|schran|ke** F taboo; **Ta|bu|wort** NT *pl* **-wörter** taboo word *or* expression
Ta|che|les ['taxələs] *no art* (*inf*) **(mit jdm) ~ reden** to have a talk (with sb); **nun wollen wir beide mal ~ reden** let's do some straight talking, let's talk turkey (*dated US inf*)
ta|chi|nie|ren [taxi'ni:rən] *ptp* **tachiniert** VI (*Aus inf*) to laze *or* loaf about (*inf*)
Ta|chi|nie|rer [taxi'ni:rɐ] M **-s, -**, **Ta|chi|nie|re|rin** [-ərɪn] F **-, -nen** (*Aus inf*) layabout (*Brit inf*), loafer (*inf*), do-nothing (*US inf*)
Ta|cho ['taxo] M **-s, -s** (*inf*) speedo (*Brit inf*), speedometer
Ta|cho|me|ter [taxo'me:tɐ] M OR NT **-s, -** speedometer
Ta|cho|me|ter|stand M, **Ta|cho|stand** M (*inf*) mileage, number of kilometres (*Brit*) *or* kilometers (*US*)/miles on the clock; **beim ~ von 10.000 km** at 10,000 km, after clocking up 10,000 km
Ta|cker ['takɐ] M **-s, -** (*inf*) stapler
Ta|del ['ta:dl] M **-s, -** (*= Verweis*) reprimand; (*= Vorwurf*) reproach; (*= Kritik*) criticism, censure; (*geh*: = *Makel*) blemish, taint; (*Sch*: = *Eintragung ins Klassenbuch*) black mark; **ein Leben ohne jeden ~** (*geh*) an unblemished *or* spotless *or* blameless life; **ihn trifft kein ~** (*geh*) he is above *or* beyond reproach
ta|del|los **ADJ** perfect; *Deutsch etc auch* faultless; *Benehmen, Haltung auch* faultless, irreproachable; *Leben* blameless; (*inf*) splendid, first-class **ADV** perfectly; *sprechen auch* faultlessly; *sich benehmen auch* irreproachably; *gekleidet* immaculately
ta|deln ['ta:dln] VT *jdn* to rebuke, to reprimand; *jds Benehmen* to criticize, to express one's disapproval of
ta|delnd ADJ *attr* reproachful; **ein ~er Blick** a reproachful look, a look of reproach
ta|delns|wert, **ta|delns|wür|dig** ADJ (*geh*) reprehensible, blameworthy
Ta|dels|an|trag M (*Parl*) motion of censure, censure motion
Ta|fel ['ta:fl] F **-, -n** **a** (*= Platte*) slab; (*= Holztafel*) panel; (*= Tafel Schokolade etc*) bar; (*= Gedenktafel*) plaque; (*= Wandtafel*) (black)board; (*= Schiefertafel*) slate; (*Elec*: = *Schalttafel*) control panel, console; (*= Anzeigetafel*) board; (*= Verkehrstafel*) sign **b** (*= Bildseite*) plate **c** (*form*: = *festlicher Speisetisch*) table; (*= Festmahl*) meal; (*mittags*) luncheon (*form*); (*abends*) dinner; **jdn zur ~ bitten** to ask sb to table; **die ~ aufheben** to officially end the meal
Ta|fel-: **Ta|fel|ap|fel** M eating apple; **Ta|fel|auf|satz** M centrepiece (*Brit*), centerpiece (*US*); **Ta|fel|berg** M (*Geog*) table mountain; **Ta|fel|be|steck** NT (best) silver; **Ta|fel|bild** NT panel; **Ta|fel|dienst** M (*Sch*) **wer hat ~?** who's the blackboard monitor?, who's in charge of the board?; **ta|fel|fer|tig** ADJ ready to serve; **ta|fel|för|mig** ADJ slab-like; *Hochplateau* table-shaped; **Ta|fel|freu|den** PL (*geh*) delicacies *pl*, culinary delights *pl*; (*= Freude am Essen*) pleasures *pl* of the table; **Ta|fel|ge|schäft** NT (*Fin*) counter transactions *pl*; **Ta|fel|ge|schirr** NT tableware; **Ta|fel|glas** NT sheet glass, plate glass; **Ta|fel|land** NT plateau, tableland; **Ta|fel|lap|pen** M (blackboard) duster; **Ta|fel|ma|le|rei** F panel painting; **Ta|fel|mu|sik** F musical entertainment
ta|feln ['ta:fln] VI (*geh*) to feast; **mit jdm ~** to dine with sb
tä|feln ['tɛ:fln] VT *Wand* to wainscot; *Decke, Raum* to panel, to line with wooden panels
Ta|fel-: **Ta|fel|obst** NT (dessert) fruit; **Ta|fel|öl** NT cooking oil; (*= Salatöl*) salad oil; **Ta|fel|run|de** F company (at table); (*Liter*) Round Table; **die ganze ~ applaudierte** the whole table applauded; **eine festliche ~ saß beisammen** a festive banquet was in progress; **Ta|fel|salz** NT table salt; **Ta|fel|sil|ber** NT silver; **Ta|fel|spitz** M (*Cook*) soured boiled rump
Tä|fe|lung ['tɛ:fəlʊŋ] F **-, -en** (*von Wand*) wainscoting; (*von Decke*) (wooden) panelling (*Brit*) *or* paneling (*US*)
Ta|fel-: **Ta|fel|was|ser** NT *pl* **-wässer** mineral water, table water; **Ta|fel|wein** M table wine
Täf|lung ['tɛ:flʊŋ] F **-, -en** = **Täfelung**
Taft [taft] M **-(e)s, -e** taffeta
taf|ten ['taftn] ADJ taffeta
Tag [ta:k] M **-(e)s, -e** [-gə] **a** day; **am ~(e) des/der ...** (on) the day of ...; **am ~** during the day; **alle ~e** (*inf*) **jeden ~** every day; **am vorigen ~(e), am ~(e) vorher** the day before, the previous day; **auf den ~ (genau)** to the day; **auf ein paar ~e** for a few days; **auf seine alten ~e** at his age; **bis auf seine letzten ~e** to his dying day, right up to the very end; **bei ~ und Nacht** night and day, day and night; **bis in unsere ~e** up to the present day; **in den letzten ~en** in the last few days, in recent days; **bis die ~e!** (*inf*) so long (*inf*), cheerio (*Brit inf*), see ya (*inf*); **diese** (*inf*) *or* **dieser ~e** (*= bald*) in the next few days; **den ganzen ~ (lang)** (*lit, fig*) all day long, the whole day; **eines ~es** one day; **eines ~es wirst du ...** one day *or* one of these days you'll ...; **eines**

schönen *or* **guten ~es** one fine day; **sich** *(dat)* **einen schönen/faulen ~ machen** to have a nice/lazy day; **~ für** *or* **um ~** day by day; **in unseren ~en, in den heutigen ~en** these days, nowadays; **unter ~s** *(dial)* during the daytime; **von ~ zu ~** from day to day, every day; **~ der Arbeit** Labour Day *(Brit)*, Labor Day *(US)*; **~ der Republik/Befreiung** *(DDR)* Republic/Liberation Day; **der ~ des Herrn** *(Eccl)* the Lord's Day; **welcher ~ ist heute?** what day is it today?, what's today?; **ein ~ wie jeder andere** a day like any other; **guten ~!** hello *(inf)*, good day *(dated form)*; *(vormittags auch)* good morning; *(nachmittags auch)* good afternoon; *(esp bei Vorstellung)* how-do-you-do; **~!** *(inf)* hello, hi *(inf)*; morning *(inf)*; afternoon *(inf)*; **ich wollte nur Guten** (*or* **guten**) **~ sagen** I just wanted to have a chat; **zweimal am ~(e)** *or* **pro ~** twice daily *or* a day; **von einem ~ auf den anderen** overnight; **der Lärm des ~es** the bustle of the world; **der ~ X** D-Day *(fig)*; **er erzählt** *or* **redet viel, wenn der ~ lang ist** *(inf)* he'll tell you anything if you let him; **seinen guten/schlechten ~ haben** to have a good/bad *or* off day, to have one of one's good/bad *or* off days; **das war heute wieder ein ~!** *(inf)* what a day!; **das Ereignis/Thema des ~es** the event/talking point of the day; **Sie hören jetzt die Nachrichten des ~es** and now the *or* today's news; **in den ~ hinein leben** to take each day as it comes, to live from day to day; **~ und Nacht** night and day, day and night; **das ist ein Unterschied wie ~ und Nacht** they are as different as chalk and cheese *(Brit)* *or* night and day *(US)*; **~ und Stunde bestimmen** to fix a precise time → **Abend a**

b *(= Tageslicht)* **bei ~(e)** *(ankommen)* while it's light; *arbeiten, reisen* during the day; **es wird schon ~** it's getting light already; **es ist ~** it's light; **solange (es) noch ~ ist** while it's still light; **an den ~ kommen** *(fig)* to come to light; **etw an den ~ bringen** to bring sth to light; **er legte großes Interesse an den ~** he showed great interest; **zu ~e = zutage**

c *(inf: = Menstruation)* **meine/ihre ~e** my/her period; **sie hat ihre ~e (bekommen)** it's her time of the month *(Brit)*, she has her period *(US)*

d *(Min)* **über ~e arbeiten** to work above ground, to work on *or* at the surface; **unter ~e arbeiten** to work underground *or* below ground, to work below the surface; **etw unter ~e abbauen** to mine sth; **etw über ~e abbauen** to quarry *(esp Brit)* *or* excavate sth

Tag [tɛk] **M -s, -s** *(Comput)* tag

-tag M *suf in cpds (= Konferenz)* conference; **Weltfrauentag** International Women's Conference

Tag- *(S Ger, Aus, Sw) in cpds* = **Tage-**

tag|ak|tiv ADJ *(Zool)* diurnal *(spec)*

tag|aus [ta:k'laus] **ADV** → **tagein**

Tag|blatt NT = **Tageblatt**

Tag|chen ['taxçən] **INTERJ** *(hum)* hello there, hi(ya) *(inf)*

Tag|dienst M = **Tagesdienst**

Ta|ge-: **Ta|ge|bau M** *pl* **-baue** *(Min)* opencast mining; **Ta|ge|blatt NT** daily (news)paper; **Göttinger ~** Göttingen Daily News; **Ta|ge|buch NT** diary, journal *(liter, form)*; **(über etw** *acc***) ~ führen** to keep a diary (of sth); **Ta|ge|dieb(in) M(F)** *(dated)* idler *(Brit)*, wastrel *(liter)*, loafer *(inf)*; **Ta|ge|geld NT** daily allowance

tag|ein [ta:k'lain] **ADV ~, tagaus** day in, day out, day after day

Ta|ge-: **ta|ge|lang ADJ** lasting for days; **nach ~er Unterbrechung** after an interruption of several days, after an interruption lasting several days; **~e Regenfälle** several days' rain **ADV** for days; **Ta|ge|lohn M** *(dated)* daily wage(s); **im ~ arbeiten** *or* **stehen** to be paid by the day; **Ta|ge|löh|ner** [-lø:nɐ] **M -s, -, Ta|ge|löh|ne|rin** [-ərɪn] **F -, -nen** *(dated)* day labourer *(Brit)* *or* laborer *(US)*, temporary worker

ta|gen ['ta:gn] **VI** *impers (geh)* **es tagt** day is breaking *or* dawning; **es begann schon zu ~** day was breaking *or* dawning, (the) dawn was breaking **VI** *(Parlament, Rat, Gericht)* to sit; *(Minister, Leiter)* to meet; **wir haben noch bis in den frühen Morgen getagt** *(fig inf)* we stayed up enjoying ourselves until the early hours

Ta|ge|rei|se F day's journey

Ta|ges-: **Ta|ges|ab|lauf M** day; **Ta|ges|an|bruch M** daybreak, dawn; **Ta|ges|ar|beit F** day's work; **Ta|ges|auf|trag M** *(St Ex)* day order; **Ta|ges|aus|flug M** day trip *or* excursion, day's outing; **Ta|ges|be|darf M** daily requirement; **Ta|ges|be|fehl M** *(Mil)* order of the day; **Ta|ges|creme F** day cream; **Ta|ges|de|cke F** bedspread; **Ta|ges|dienst M** day duty; **~ haben** to be on day shift; **Ta|ges|ein|nah|men PL** day's takings *pl*; **Ta|ges|er|eig|nis NT** event of the day; **Ta|ges|fest|preis M** fixed daily rate; **Ta|ges|form F** *(Sport etc)* form of the day; **Ta|ges|fra|gen PL** issues *pl* of the day, day-to-day matters *pl*; **Ta|ges|geld NT** *(Fin)* overnight money; **Ta|ges|ge|schäft NT** *(Econ, Comm)* routine business, day-to-day business; *(= Einzeltransaktion)* day order; **Ta|ges|ge|sche|hen NT** events *pl* of the day; **Ta|ges|ge|spräch NT** talk of the town; **Ta|ges|hälf|te F** half of the day; **Ta|ges|höchst|tem|pe|ra|tur F** (day's) maximum temperature; *(an bestimmtem Tag)* highest temperature (of the day); **Ta|ges|kar|te F a** *(= Speisekarte)* menu of the day *(Brit)*, specialties *pl* of the day *(US)* **b** *(= Fahr-, Eintrittskarte)* day ticket; **Ta|ges|kas|se F a** *(Theat)* box office **b** *(Econ)* day's takings *pl*; **Ta|ges|kli|nik F** day clinic; **Ta|ges|kurs M** *(St Ex) (von Effekten)* current price; *(von Devisen)* current rate; **Ta|ges|lauf M** day; **Ta|ges|leis|tung F** daily workload; *(von Maschine, Schriftsteller etc)* daily output; *(von Milchkuh)* daily yield; *(Sport)* performance of the day; **Ta|ges|licht NT**, *no pl* daylight; **ans ~ kommen** *(fig)* to come to light; **das ~ scheuen** to be a creature of the night, to shun the daylight; **Ta|ges|licht|pro|jek|tor M** overhead projector; **Ta|ges|lohn M** day's wages; **Ta|ges|lo|sung F** *(Mil)* password of the day; **Ta|ges|marsch M** day's march; **zwei Tagesmärsche entfernt** two days' march away; **Ta|ges|me|nü NT** menu of the day *(Brit)*, specialties *pl* of the day *(US)*; **Ta|ges|mut|ter F** *pl* **-mütter** child minder *(Brit)*, nanny; **Ta|ges|nach|rich|ten PL** (today's) news *sing*; **die wichtigsten ~** the (main) headlines; **Ta|ges|ord|nung F** agenda, order of the day *(form)*; **zur ~!** keep to the agenda!; **etw auf die ~ setzen** to put sth on the agenda; **auf der ~ stehen** to be on the agenda; **zur ~ übergehen** to proceed to the agenda; *(= an die Arbeit gehen)* to get down to business; *(= wie üblich weitermachen)* to carry on as usual; **an der ~ sein** *(fig)* to be the order of the day; **Ta|ges|ord|nungs|punkt M** item on the agenda; **Ta|ges|pau|scha|le F** fixed daily amount; **Ta|ges|pfle|ge F** day care, daycare *(US)*; **Ta|ges|preis M** *(Comm)* current price; **gestern betrug der ~ …** yesterday's price was …; **Tages- und Abendpreise** daytime and nighttime prices; **Ta|ges|pres|se F** daily (news)papers *pl* *or* press; **Ta|ges|ra|ti|on F** daily rations *pl*; **Ta|ges|raum M** day room; **Ta|ges|rei|se F a** *(= Entfernung)* day's journey **b** *(= Ausflug)* day trip; **Ta|ges|satz M** daily rate; **Ta|ges|schau F** *(TV)* news *sing*; **Ta|ges|stät|te F** *(für Kinder)* daycare centre *(Brit)* *or* center *(US)*; **Ta|ges|sup|pe F** soup of the day; **Ta|ges|tour F** day trip; **Ta|ges|um|satz M** *(= Durchschnittswert)* daily turnover; *(des aktuellen Tages)* day's turnover; **Ta|ges|ver|lauf M** course of the day; **im ~** *(auch)* as the day went on; **Ta|ges|zeit F** time (of day); **zu jeder Tages- und Nachtzeit** at all hours of the day and night; **zu dieser ~ kommst du nach Hause?!** what sort of time do you call this to come home!; **Ta|ges|zei|tung F** daily (paper)

Ta|ge|tes [ta'ge:tɛs] **F -, -** *(Bot)* tagetes *(spec)*, marigold

Ta|ge-: **ta|ge|wei|se** ['ta:gəvaizə] **ADV** for a few days at a time; **Ta|ge|werk NT** *(geh)* day's work

Tag|fahrt F *(Min)* ascent

tag|gen ['tɛgn] **VT** *(Comput)* to tag

Tag|ging ['tɛgɪŋ] **NT -s,** *no pl (Comput)* tagging

tag|hell ADJ (as) bright as day; **es war schon ~** it was already broad daylight **ADV etw ~ erleuchten** to light sth up very brightly; **der Blitz erhellte die Nacht ~** the lightning lit up the night sky

-tä|gig [tɛ:gɪç] **ADJ** *suf* -day; **eine dreitägige Konferenz** a three-day conference

tägl. *abbr von* **täglich**

täg|lich ['tɛ:glɪç] **ADJ** daily; *(attr: = gewöhnlich)* everyday; **~e Gelder** *(Comm)* call money; **~e Zinsen** *(Comm)* daily interest; **das reicht gerade fürs ~e Leben** it's just about enough to get by on; **sein ~(es) Brot verdienen** to earn a living; **das ist unser ~(es) Brot** *(fig: Ärger etc)* it is our stock in trade; **das ist so wichtig wie das ~e Brot** it's as important as life itself; **unser ~ Brot gib uns heute** *(Bibl)* give us this day our daily bread **ADV** every day; **einmal ~** once a day, once daily

-täg|lich ADJ *suf* **sechstäglich** every six days

Tag|mem [ta'gme:m] **NT -s, -e** *(Ling)* tagmeme

tags [ta:ks] **ADV a ~ zuvor** the day before, the previous day; **~ darauf** *or* **danach** the next *or* following day **b** *(= bei Tag)* in the daytime, by day

Tag|schicht F day shift; **~ haben** to be on (the) day shift

tags|über ['ta:ksly:bɐ] **ADV** during the day

Tag-: **tag|täg|lich ADJ** daily **ADV** every (single) day; **Tag|traum M** daydream; **Tag|träu|mer(in) M(F)** daydreamer; **Tag|und|nacht|glei|che** ['ta:klunt'naxtglaiçə] **F** *decl as adj* equinox

Ta|gung ['ta:gʊŋ] **F -, -en** conference; *(von Ausschuss)* sitting, session

Ta|gungs-: **Ta|gungs|ort M** *pl* **-orte** venue (of a/the conference); **Ta|gungs|raum M** conference room; *(größer auch)* conference hall; **Ta|gungs|stät|te F** → **Tagungsort**; **Ta|gungs|teil|nehmer(in) M(F)** conferee, person attending a conference; **Ta|gungs|zent|rum NT** conference centre *(Brit)* *or* center *(US)*

Tag-: **Tag|wa|che F** *(Aus, Sw: Mil)* **a** reveille **b ~!** rise and shine!; **Tag|wa|che F, Tag|wacht F** *(Aus, Sw)* day guard

Ta|hi|ti [ta'hi:ti] **NT -s** Tahiti

Ta|hi|ti|a|ner [tahi:'tia:nɐ] **M -s, -, Ta|hi|ti|a|ne|rin** [-ərɪn] **F -, -nen, Ta|hi|ti|er** [ta'hi:tiɐ] **M -s, -, Ta|hi|ti|e|rin** [-iərɪn] **F -, -nen** Tahitian

ta|hi|tisch [ta'hi:tɪʃ] **ADJ** Tahitian

Tai-Chi (Chu|an) ['tai 'tʃi: ('tʃuan)] **NT -,** *no pl* t'ai chi (ch'uan)

Tai|fun [tai'fu:n] **M -s, -e** typhoon

Tai|ga ['taiga] **F -,** *no pl* taiga

Tail|le ['taljə] **F -, -n** waist; *(bei Kleidungsstücken auch)* waistline; **auf seine ~ achten** to watch one's waistline; **in der ~ zu eng** too tight at the waist; **ein Kleid auf ~** a fitted dress

Tail|len|wei|te ['taljən-] **F** waist measurement

tail|lie|ren [ta(l)'ji:rən] *ptp* **tailliert VT** to fit (at the waist)

tail|liert [ta(l)'ji:ɐt] **ADJ** waisted, fitted; *Hemd auch* slim-fit

Tai|wan ['taivan, tai'va(:)n] **NT -s** Taiwan

Tai|wa|ne|se [taiva'ne:zə] **M -n, -n, Tai|wa|ne|sin** [-'ne:zɪn] **F -, -nen** Taiwanese

tai|wa|ne|sisch [taiva'ne:zɪʃ] **ADJ** Taiwan(ese)

Take [te:k] **NT OR M -, -s** *(Film, TV)* take

Ta|kel ['ta:kl] **NT -s, -** *(Naut)* tackle

Ta|ke|la|ge [takə'la:ʒə] **F -, -n** *(Naut)* rigging, tackle

ta|keln ['ta:kln] **VT** *(Naut)* to rig

Ta|ke|lung ['ta:kəlʊŋ] **F -, -en** rigging

Takt [takt] **M -(e)s, -e a** *(= Einheit) (Mus)* bar; *(Phon, Poet)* foot; **mit jdm ein paar ~e reden** *(inf:*

= *die Meinung sagen)* to give sb a good talking-to *(inf)*

b *(= Rhythmus)* time; **den ~ schlagen** to beat time; **(den) ~ halten** to keep time; **im ~ bleiben** to stay in time; **den ~ verlieren** to lose the beat; **den ~ wechseln** to change the beat, to change (the) time; **im ~ singen/tanzen** to sing/dance in time (to *(Brit)* or with the music); **gegen den ~** out of time (with the music); **im/gegen den ~ marschieren** to be in/out of step; **den ~ angeben** *(lit)* to give the beat or time; *(fig)* to call the tune; **im ~ der Musik** in time to *(Brit)* or with music; **das Publikum klatschte den ~ dazu** the audience clapped in time to the music; **wenn alle Kolben im ~ arbeiten** if all the pistons are in phase

c *(Aut)* stroke

d *(Ind)* phase

e *no pl (= Taktgefühl)* tact; **mit dem ihm eigenen ~** with his great tact(fulness); **er hat keinen ~ im Leibe** *(inf)* he hasn't an ounce of tact in him

f *(= Taktverkehr)* regular service; **im ~ fahren** to go at regular intervals; **alle Linien verkehren im Einstundentakt** there is an hourly service on all routes

g *(Comput)* (clock) pulse or signal

Takt|be|zeich|nung F time signature

tak|ten ['taktn] VT *(Comput)* to clock; **ein mit 60 MHz getakteter Prozessor** a processor with a clock speed of 60 MHz

Takt-: **Takt|fahr|plan** M *(Rail)* fixed-interval timetable; **takt|fest** ADJ **a** *(Mus)* able to keep time **b** *(inf) (gesundheitlich)* fighting fit *(Brit inf)*, in fighting shape *(US)*; *(sicher)* sure of his etc stuff *(inf)*; **Takt|fol|ge** F *(form)* sequence; **Takt|fre|quenz** F *(Comput)* clock speed; **Takt|ge|fühl** NT **a** sense of tact **b** *(rare: Mus)* sense of rhythm or time

tak|tie|ren [tak'ti:rən] *ptp* **taktiert** VI **a** *(= Taktiken anwenden)* to manoeuvre *(Brit)*, to maneuver *(US)*; **so kann man nicht ~** you can't use those tactics **b** *(rare: Mus)* to beat time

Tak|tik ['taktɪk] F -, -en tactics *pl*; **eine ~** tactics *pl*, a tactical approach; **man muss mit ~ vorgehen** you have to use tactics; **~ der verbrannten Erde** *(Mil)* scorched earth policy

Tak|ti|ker ['taktikɐ] M -s, -, **Tak|ti|ke|rin** [-ərɪn] F -, -nen tactician

tak|tisch ['taktɪʃ] ADJ tactical ADV tactically; **~ vorgehen** to use tactics; **~ klug** good tactics

Takt-: **takt|los** ADJ tactless ADV tactlessly; **Takt|lo|sig|keit** F -, -en tactlessness; **es war eine ~ sondergleichen** it was a particularly tactless thing to do/say; **Takt|maß** NT *(Mus)* time; **Takt|mes|ser** M -s, - *(Mus)* metronome; **Takt|stock** M baton; **den ~ schwingen** *(inf)* to wield the baton; **Takt|strich** M *(Mus)* bar (line); **Takt|ver|kehr** M *(Rail etc)* regular service; **die Züge fahren im ~** the trains go at regular intervals; **einstündiger ~** hourly service; **takt|voll** ADJ tactful ADV tactfully; **benimm dich bitte ~er** please be more tactful; **Takt|wech|sel** M *(Mus)* change of time, time change

Tal [ta:l] NT -(e)s, ⸗er ['tɛ:lɐ] valley, vale *(poet)*; **zu ~e** into the valley

tal|ab|(wärts) [ta:l'lap(vɛrts)] ADV **a** down into the valley **b** *(= flussabwärts)* downriver, downstream

Ta|lar [ta'la:ɐ] M -s, -e *(Univ)* gown; *(Eccl auch)* cassock; *(Jur)* robe(s *pl*)

tal|auf|(wärts) ADV **a** up the valley **b** *(= flussaufwärts)* upriver, upstream

Tal-: **Tal|brü|cke** F bridge over a valley; **Tal|en|ge** F narrow part of a/the valley, gorge

Ta|lent [ta'lɛnt] NT -(e)s, -e **a** *(= Begabung)* talent (*zu* for); **ein großes ~ haben** to be very talented; **sie hat viel ~ zum Singen/zur Schauspielerin** she has a great talent or gift for singing/acting; **da saß** or **stand er nun mit seinem ~** *(inf)* he was left looking a right charlie *(Brit inf)* **b** *(= begabter Mensch)* talented person; **junge ~e** young talent; **er ist ein großes ~** he is very talented **c** *(Hist: = Geld)* talent

ta|len|tiert [talɛn'ti:ɐt] ADJ talented, gifted; **die Mannschaft lieferte ein ~es Spiel** the team played a game of great skill or a brilliant game

Ta|lent-: **ta|lent|los** ADJ untalented; **Ta|lent|pro|be** F audition; **Ta|lent|scout** [-skaut] M -(s), -s talent scout; **Ta|lent|su|che** F search for talent; **wir sind auf ~** we are looking for new talent; **ta|lent|voll** ADJ talented; **das war nicht sehr ~** *(inf)* that wasn't very clever or bright

Ta|ler ['ta:lɐ] M -s, - *(Hist)* T(h)aler; *(inf)* euro, ≈ quid *(Brit inf)*, ≈ buck *(US inf)*

Tal|fahrt F *(bergabwärts)* descent; *(flussabwärts)* downriver trip; *(fig)* decline

Talg [talk] M -(e)s, -e [-gə] tallow; *(Cook)* suet; *(= Hautabsonderung)* sebum

Talg|drü|se F *(Physiol)* sebaceous gland

Ta|li|ban [tali'ba:n] F -, - Taliban, Taleban

Ta|lis|man ['ta:lɪsman] M -s, -e talisman, (lucky) charm; *(= Maskottchen)* mascot

Tal|je ['taljə] F -, -n *(Naut)* block and tackle

Talk [talk] M -(e)s, *no pl* talc(um)

tal|ken ['tɔ:kn] VI *(inf)* to talk

Tal|kes|sel M basin, hollow

Talk|mas|ter ['tɔ:kma:stɐ] M -s, -, **Talk|mas|te|rin** [-ərɪn] F -, -nen talk show or chat show *(Brit)* host

Talk|pu|der M OR NT talcum powder

Talk|show ['tɔ:kʃo:] F *(TV)* talk show, chat show *(Brit)*

Tal|kum ['talkʊm] NT -s, *no pl* **a** *(= Talk)* talc(um) **b** *(= Puder)* talc, talcum powder

Tal|land|schaft F valley; *(mit mehreren Tälern)* valleys *pl*

Tal|mi ['talmi] NT -s, *no pl (geh)* pinchbeck; *(fig)* rubbish *(Brit inf)*, trash *(inf)*; **~-Religion** sham religion

Tal|mi|gold NT pinchbeck gold

Tal|mud ['talmu:t] M -(e)s, -e [-də] Talmud

Tal|mul|de F basin, hollow

Ta|lon [ta'lõ:] M -s, -s *(St Ex)* renewal coupon

Tal-: **Tal|schaft** ['ta:lʃaft] F -, -en *(Sw, Aus)* valley inhabitants *pl* or dwellers *pl* or folk; **Tal|sen|ke** F hollow (of a/the valley); **Tal|soh|le** F bottom of a/the valley, valley bottom; *(fig)* rock bottom; **in der ~** *(fig)* at rock bottom, in the doldrums; **Tal|sper|re** F dam; **Tal|sta|ti|on** F base camp; *(von Skilift etc)* station at the bottom of a ski lift *etc*; **tal|wärts** ['ta:lvɛrts] ADV down to the valley

Ta|ma|rin|de [tama'rɪndə] F -, -n tamarind

Ta|ma|ris|ke [tama'rɪskə] F -, -n tamarisk

Tam|bour ['tambu:ɐ] M -s, -e drummer

Tam|bour|ma|jor ['tambu:ɐ-] M drum major

Tam|bu|rin [tambu'ri:n, 'tam-] NT -s, -e tambourine

Ta|mi|le [ta'mi:lə] M -n, -n, **Ta|mi|lin** [-'mi:lɪn] F -, -nen Tamil

ta|mi|lisch [ta'mi:lɪʃ] ADJ Tamil

Ta|mi|lisch(e) NT Tamil → *auch* **Deutsch(e)**

Tamp [tamp] M -s, -e, **Tam|pen** ['tampn] M -s, - *(Naut)* rope end

Tam|pon ['tampɔn, tam'po:n] M -s, -s tampon; *(für Wunde auch)* plug

tam|po|nie|ren [tampo'ni:rən] *ptp* **tamponiert** VT to plug, to tampon

Tam|tam [tam'tam, 'tam-] NT -s, -s *(Mus)* tom-tom; *(inf) (= Wirbel)* fuss, to-do *(inf)*, ballyhoo *(Brit inf)*; *(= Lärm)* row, din *(inf)*; **der Faschingszug zog mit großem ~ durch die Straßen** the Fasching procession paraded loudly through the streets

Tand [tant] M -(e)s [-dəs], *no pl (liter)* trinkets *pl*, knick-knacks *pl*; **alles Menschenwerk ist doch nur ~** all human works are but dross *(liter)*

Tän|de|lei [tɛndə'lai] F -, -en *(liter) (= Spielerei)* (dilly-)dallying, trifling *(Brit)*, lallygagging *(US)*; *(= Liebelei)* dalliance *(liter)*

Tan|del|markt ['tandl-] M *(Aus)*, **Tän|del|markt** ['tɛndl-] M *(dial)* flea market

tän|deln ['tɛndln] VI *(liter) (= liebeln)* to dally *(liter)*; *(= trödeln)* to (dilly-)dally, to trifle *(Brit)*, to lallygag *(US)*

Tan|dem ['tandɛm] NT -s, -s tandem

Tand|ler ['tandlɐ] M -s, -, **Tand|le|rin** [-ərɪn] F -, -nen *(Aus)* **a** *(= Trödler)* second-hand dealer **b** *(= langsamer Mensch)* slowcoach *(Brit inf)*, slowpoke *(US inf)*

Tang [taŋ] M -(e)s, -e seaweed

Tan|ga ['taŋga] M -s, -s tanga, thong *(US)*

Tan|gan|ji|ka [taŋgan'ji:ka] NT -s Tanganyika

Tan|ga-Slip M, **Tan|ga|slip** M tanga, thong *(US)*

Tan|gens ['taŋgɛns] M -, - *(Math)* tan(gent)

Tan|gens|kur|ve F *(Math)* tan wave

Tan|gen|te [taŋ'gɛntə] F -, -n *(Math)* tangent; *(= Straße)* ring road *(Brit)*, expressway, beltway *(US)*

tan|gen|ti|al [taŋgɛn'tsia:l] ADJ tangential

Tan|ger ['taŋɐ, 'tandʒɐ] NT -s Tangier(s)

tan|gie|ren [taŋ'gi:rən] *ptp* **tangiert** VT **a** *(Math)* to be tangent to **b** *(= berühren) Problem* to touch on; *Stadt, Gebiet* to skirt; **das tangiert das Problem nur** that is merely tangential or peripheral to the problem **c** *(= betreffen)* to affect; *(inf: = kümmern)* to bother

Tan|go ['taŋgo] M -s, -s tango

Tank [taŋk] M -(e)s, -s or -e *(= Behälter, Panzer)* tank

Tank-: **Tank|an|zei|ge** F fuel gauge; **Tank|de|ckel** M filler cap *(Brit)*, gas cap *(US)*

tan|ken ['taŋkn] **VI** *(Autofahrer)* to get petrol *(Brit)* or gas *(US)*; *(Rennfahrer, Flugzeug)* to refuel; **wo kann man hier ~?** where can I get petrol *(Brit)* or gas *(US)* (a)round here?; **hier kann man billig ~** you can get cheap petrol *(Brit)* or gas *(US)* here; **ich muss noch ~** I have to get some petrol *(Brit)* or gas *(US)*; **wir hielten an, um zu ~** we stopped for petrol *(Brit)* or gas *(US)*; **ich tanke nur für 20 Euro** I'll just put 20 euros' worth in; **hast du getankt?** have you filled up or tanked up?, have you put petrol *(Brit)* or gas *(US)* in?

VT **a** *Super, Diesel* to get; **ich tanke bleifrei** I use unleaded; **ich habe 30 Liter getankt** I put 30 litres *(Brit)* or liters *(US)* in (the tank)

b *(fig inf) frische Luft* to get, to fill one's lungs with; *Sonne, Selbstvertrauen, neue Kräfte* to get

c *(inf: = viel trinken)* **er hat einiges** or **ganz schön getankt** he's had a few, he's really tanked up *(inf)*

Tan|ker ['taŋkɐ] M -s, - *(Naut)* tanker

Tan|ker|flot|te F tanker fleet, fleet of tankers

Tan|ker|un|glück NT (oil) tanker disaster

Tank-: **Tank|fahr|zeug** NT *(Aut)* tanker; **Tank|füll|men|ge** F tank capacity; **Tank|fül|lung** F tankful; **mit einer ~ komme ich bis nach München** I can get to Munich on a tankful or on one tank; **Tank|in|halt** M contents *pl* of the tank; **der ~ beträgt ...** the tank holds ..., the tank capacity is ... *(form)*

Tan|ki|ni M -s, -s *(= Badeanzug)* tankini

Tank-: **Tank|la|ger** NT oil or petrol *(Brit)* or gas *(US)* depot; **Tank|las|ter** M, **Tank|last|zug** M tanker; **Tank|mög|lich|keit** F **letzte ~ vor ...** last petrol *(Brit)* or gas *(US)* station before ...; **Tank|säu|le** F petrol pump *(Brit)*, gas(oline) pump *(US)*; **Tank|schiff** NT tanker; **Tank|stel|le** F filling or petrol *(Brit)* or gas(oline) *(US)* station; **Tank|stut|zen** M filler pipe; **Tank|uhr** F fuel gauge; **Tank|ver|schluss** M petrol *(Brit)* or gas *(US)* cap; **Tank|wa|gen** M tanker; *(Rail)* tank wagon or car; **Tank|wart(in)** M(F) petrol pump *(Brit)* or gas station *(US)* attendant; **Tank|zug** M tanker

Tann [tan] M -(e)s, -e *(poet)* forest

Tänn|chen ['tɛnçən] NT -s, - *dim von* **Tanne**

Tan|ne ['tanə] F -, -n fir; *(Holz)* pine, deal; **sie ist schlank wie eine ~** she is as slender as a reed

Tan|nen-: **Tan|nen|baum** M **a** fir tree **b** *(= Weihnachtsbaum)* Christmas tree; **Tan|nen|na|del** F fir needle; **Tan|nen|wald** M fir forest;

Tan|nen|we|del M fir(-twig) broom; **Tan|nen|zap|fen** M fir cone; **Tan|nen|zweig** M fir branch; *(kleiner)* sprig of fir

Tan|nin [ta'ni:n] NT -s, *no pl* tannin

Tann|zap|fen M fir cone

Tan|sa|nia [tanza'ni:a, tan'za:nia] NT -s Tanzania

Tan|sa|ni|er [tan'za:niɐ] M -s, -, **Tan|sa|ni|e|rin** [-iərɪn] F -, -nen Tanzanian

tan|sa|nisch [tan'za:nɪʃ] ADJ Tanzanian

Tan|tal ['tantal] NT -s, *no pl (abbr* **Ta**) tantalum

Tan|ta|lus|qua|len ['tantalʊs-] PL *(geh)* torments *pl* of Tantalus *(liter)*; **ich litt ~** it was tantalizing, I suffered torments *(liter)*; **jdm ~ bereiten** to tantalize sb

Tant|chen ['tantçən] NT -s, - *(inf)* **a** *(Verwandte)* auntie, aunty **b** *(= alte Dame)* old dear *(Brit inf)* or lady

Tan|te ['tantə] F -, -n **a** *(Verwandte)* aunt, aunty, auntie **b** *(pej inf: = Frau)* woman *(inf)*, old dear *(Brit inf)* or lady **c** *(baby-talk) (= Frau)* lady; *(= Kindergartenschwester etc)* teacher; *(= Krippenschwester)* nurse; **~ Schneider/Monika** aunty or auntie Schneider/Monika

Tan|te-Em|ma-La|den [tantə'lɛma-] M *(inf)* corner shop

tan|ten|haft ADJ **a** *(inf)* old-maidish **b** *(pej: = betulich) Ausdruck(sweise)* twee ADV **sie benimmt sich so richtig ~** she acts like a real old maid or maiden aunt *(Brit)*

Tan|ti|e|me [tã'tie:mə, -'tie:mə] F -, -n percentage (of the profits); *(für höhere Angestellte)* director's fee; *(für Künstler)* royalty

Tant|ra ['tantra] NT -(s), *no pl* Tantra

Tanz [tants] M -es, ⸚e ['tɛntsə] **a** dance; **dort ist heute Abend ~** there's a dance or *(für Jugendliche)* disco there this evening; **im Goldenen Ochsen ist neuerdings auch ~** they now have dancing too at the Golden Ox; **zum ~ aufspielen** *(dated)* to strike up a dance (tune) *(dated)*; **jdn zum ~ auffordern** to ask sb to dance or for a dance → **golden ADJ**
b *(fig geh: von Licht, Schatten)* play; **der ~ der Boote auf den Wellen** the boats' dancing *(liter)* or bobbing on the waves; **ein ~ auf dem Vulkan** *(fig)* living on the edge
c *(inf: = Aufheben)* fuss; **einen ~ um jdn machen** to make a fuss of *(esp Brit)* or over sb

Tanz-: **Tanz|abend** M dance; **Tanz|bar** F bar with dancing; **Tanz|bär** M dancing bear; **Tanz|bein** NT **(mit jdm) das ~ schwingen** *(hum)* to trip the light fantastic (with sb) *(hum)*; **Tanz|bo|den** M *(= Tanzfläche)* dance floor; *(= Saal)* dance hall; *(dated: Veranstaltung)* dance; **Tanz|ca|fé** NT restaurant with dancing

Tänz|chen ['tɛntsçən] NT -s, - *dim von* **Tanz** *(dated hum)* dance; **ein ~ wagen** to venture onto the floor

Tanz|die|le F *(dated) (Raum)* dance hall; *(= Tanzfläche)* dance floor

tän|zeln ['tɛntsln] VI *aux haben or (bei Richtungsangabe) sein* to mince *(Brit)*, to sashay *(esp US)*, to trip; *(Boxer)* to skip; *(Pferd)* to step delicately

tan|zen ['tantsn] VI *aux haben or (bei Richtungsangabe) sein* to dance; *(Boot auch)* to bob; *(Kreisel)* to spin; *(hüpfen)* to hop; **~ gehen, zum Tanzen gehen** to go dancing → **Pfeife a, Reihe a** VT *Walzer, Tango etc* to dance; **er hat mit mir einen Walzer getanzt** he danced or did a waltz with me

Tän|zer ['tɛntsɐ] M -s, -, **Tän|ze|rin** [-ərɪn] F -, -nen dancer; *(= Tanzpartner)* (dancing) partner; *(= Balletttänzer)* ballet dancer

Tan|ze|rei [tantsə'rai] F -, -en **a** dancing; *(pej)* prancing about **b** *(Aus)* dancing party

tän|ze|risch ['tɛntsərɪʃ] ADJ *Grazie, Beschwingtheit etc* dance-like; **eine große ~e Leistung** a tremendous piece of dancing; **~e Darbietungen** dance acts; **sein ~es Können** his dancing ability ADV **~ veranlagt sein** to have a talent for dancing; **~ ausgebildet** trained as a dancer; **~ gestaltete Gymnastik** gymnastics done in a dance-like way or as a dance; **die Darsteller waren ~ hervorragend** the dancing was excellent; **die Kür war ~ miserabel** the dance technique in the free section was terrible

Tanz-: **Tanz|flä|che** F dance floor; **Tanz|grup|pe** F dance group; *(bei Revue, TV-Show auch)* chorus; **Tanz|ka|pel|le** F dance band; **Tanz|kunst** F art of dancing, dance; **Tanz|kurs** M dancing course; **Tanz|kur|sus** M = **Tanzkurs**; **Tanz|leh|rer(in)** M(F) dancing teacher; **Tanz|lied** NT dance tune; **Tanz|lo|kal** NT café with dancing; **tanz|lus|tig** ADJ fond of or keen on dancing; **einige ~e Paare blieben noch** a few couples who wanted to dance stayed on; **Tanz|mu|sik** F dance music; **Tanz|or|ches|ter** NT dance orchestra; **Tanz|part|ner(in)** M(F) dancing partner; **Tanz|plat|te** F record of dance music; **Tanz|platz** M (open-air) dance floor; **Tanz|saal** M dance hall; *(in Hotel etc)* ballroom; **Tanz|schritt** M (dance) step; **Tanz|schuh** M dancing shoe; **Tanz|schu|le** F dancing or dance school, school of dancing; **Tanz|sport** M competitive dancing; **Tanz|spra|che** F *(Zool)* dance language; **Tanz|stun|de** F dancing lesson or class; **sie haben sich in der ~ kennengelernt** they met at dancing lessons or classes; **Tanz|tee** M thé dansant, tea dance; **Tanz|the|a|ter** NT dance theatre *(Brit)* or theater *(US)*; **Tanz|tur|nier** NT dancing or dance contest or competition; **Tanz|ver|an|stal|tung** F, **Tanz|ver|gnü|gen** NT dance

Ta|o|is|mus [tao'ɪsmʊs, tau-] M -, *no pl* Taoism

Ta|per|greis(in) M(F) *(pej inf)* old dodderer *(pej inf)*

ta|pe|rig ['ta:pərɪç] ADJ *(pej inf)* doddering, doddery

ta|pern ['ta:pɐn] VI *(inf)* to totter

Ta|pet [ta'pe:t] NT *(inf)* **etw aufs ~ bringen** to bring sth up; **aufs ~ kommen** to be brought up, to come up

Ta|pe|te [ta'pe:tə] F -, -n wallpaper; **ohne ~n** without wallpaper; **die ~n wechseln** *(fig inf)* to have a change of scenery or surroundings

Ta|pe|ten-: **Ta|pe|ten|bahn** F strip of wallpaper; **Ta|pe|ten|rol|le** F roll of wallpaper; **Ta|pe|ten|tür** F concealed door; **Ta|pe|ten|wech|sel** M *(inf)* change of scenery or surroundings

Ta|pe|zier [tape'tsi:ɐ] M -s, -e, **Ta|pe|zie|rin** [-'tsi:ərɪn] F -, -nen *(esp S Ger)* = **Tapezierer**

Ta|pe|zier-: **Ta|pe|zier|ar|beit** F wallpapering; **Ta|pe|zier|bürs|te** F wallpaper brush

ta|pe|zie|ren [tape'tsi:rən] *ptp* **tapeziert** VT to (wall)paper; *(inf: mit Bildern)* to plaster *(inf)*; **neu ~** to repaper

Ta|pe|zie|rer [tape'tsi:rɐ] M -s, -, **Ta|pe|zie|re|rin** [-ərɪn] F -, -nen **a** paperhanger, decorator **b** *(= Polsterer)* upholsterer

Ta|pe|zier-: **Ta|pe|zier|na|gel** M tack; **Ta|pe|zier|tisch** M trestle table

tap|fer ['tapfɐ] ADJ brave, courageous; *Soldat, Versuch auch* bold; *(= wacker)* steadfast ADV bravely, courageously; **wir marschierten immer ~ weiter, ohne zu merken ...** we marched on blithely, not realizing ...; **halt dich** or **bleib ~!** *(inf)* be brave; **sich ~ schlagen** *(inf)* to put on a brave show

Tap|fer|keit F -, *no pl* bravery, courage; *(von Soldat auch)* boldness

Tap|fer|keits|me|dail|le F medal for bravery

Ta|pi|o|ka [ta'pio:ka] F -, *no pl* tapioca

Ta|pir ['ta:pi:ɐ] M -s, -e *(Zool)* tapir

Ta|pis|se|rie [tapɪsə'ri:] F -, -n [-'ri:ən] **a** tapestry **b** *(old, Sw)* drapery

tapp [tap] INTERJ tap

tap|pen ['tapn] VI **a** *aux sein (= tapsen)* to go falteringly; *(Bär)* to lumber, to lollop *(Brit inf)*; *(dial: = gehen)* to wander; **~de Schritte** faltering steps; **er ist in eine Pfütze getappt** *(inf)* he walked smack into a puddle *(inf)*; **in eine Falle ~** *(fig)* to walk or fall into a trap **b** *(= tasten)* **nach etw ~** to grope for sth; **im Finstern** or **Dunkeln ~** *(fig)* to grope in the dark

täp|pisch ['tɛpɪʃ], **täp|pig** ['tɛpɪç] *(dial)* ADJ awkward, clumsy ADV **sich ~ anstellen** to act awkwardly or clumsily

tap(p)|rig ['taprɪç] ADJ *(dial)* = **taperig**

Taps [taps] M -es, -e *(dial)* clumsy oaf *(inf)*; **kleiner ~** little bundle

tap|sen ['tapsn] VI *aux sein (inf) (Kind)* to toddle; *(Bär)* to lumber, to lollop *(Brit inf)*; *(Kleintier)* to waddle

tap|sig ['tapsɪç] *(inf)* ADJ awkward, clumsy ADV awkwardly, clumsily

Ta|ra ['ta:ra] F -, **Taren** [-rən] *(Comm)* tare

Ta|ran|tel [ta'rantl] F -, -n tarantula; **wie von der ~ gestochen** as if stung by a bee, as if bitten by a snake

Ta|ran|tel|la [taran'tɛla] F -, -s or **Tarantellen** [-'tɛlən] tarantella

ta|rie|ren [ta'ri:rən] *ptp* **tariert** VT to tare

Ta|rif [ta'ri:f] M -(e)s, -e rate; *(= Wassertarif, Gastarif etc auch)* tariff; *(= Gebühr auch)* charge; *(= Fahrpreis)* fare; **die ~e für Telefonanschlüsse** telephone line rental; **neue ~e für Löhne/Gehälter** new wage rates/salary scales; **die Gewerkschaft hat die ~e für Löhne und Gehälter gekündigt** the union has put in a new wage claim; **nach/über/unter ~ bezahlen** to pay according to/above/below the (union) rate(s)

Ta|rif-: **Ta|rif|ab|schluss** M wage settlement; **Ta|rif|aus|ei|nan|der|set|zung** F wage dispute; **Ta|rif|au|to|no|mie** F (right to) free collective bargaining; **Ta|rif|er|hö|hung** F **a** *(= Gebührenerhöhung)* increase in rates or charges, rate or charge increase; *(= Fahrpreiserhöhung)* fare(s) increase or hike *(US)* **b** *(= Lohnerhöhung)* increase in pay rates, (across-the-board) pay increase, pay rise *(Brit)* or raise *(US)*; **Ta|rif|ge|halt** NT union rates *pl*; **Ta|rif|ge|mein|schaft** F **a** *(Econ)* tariff community **b** *(in Verkehrsverbund)* fare(s) cooperative; **Ta|rif|grup|pe** F grade; **Ta|rif|kom|mis|si|on** F joint working party on pay; **Ta|rif|kon|flikt** M wage dispute

ta|rif|lich [ta'ri:flɪç] ADJ *Arbeitszeit, Regelung* agreed; **der ~e Mindestlohn** the agreed minimum wage ADV **die Gehälter sind ~ festgelegt** there are fixed rates for salaries; **etw ~ festschreiben** to include sth in the labour *(Brit)* or labor *(US)* contract; **~ vereinbart sein** to be in the labour *(Brit)* or labor *(US)* contract

Ta|rif-: **Ta|rif|lohn** M standard wage; **ta|rif|los** ADJ **~er Zustand** period when new rates are being negotiated; **ta|rif|mä|ßig** ADJ ADV = **tariflich**; **Ta|rif|ord|nung** F *(für Löhne)* wage scale; *(für Gehälter)* salary scale; **Ta|rif|par|tei** F party to a wage agreement; **die ~en** unions and management; **Ta|rif|part|ner(in)** M(F) party to the wage or *(für Gehälter)* salary agreement; **die ~** union and management; *(= Sozialpartner)* both sides of industry; **Ta|rif|po|li|tik** F tariff policy; *(bei Lohnforderungen)* wage policy; **Ta|rif|run|de** F pay round; **Ta|rif|ver|hand|lun|gen** PL negotiations *pl* on pay; *(für Löhne auch)* wage negotiations *pl*; *(für Gehälter auch)* salary negotiations *pl*; **Ta|rif|ver|trag** M pay agreement; *(für Löhne auch)* wage agreement; **Ta|rif|zo|ne** F fare zone; **Ta|rif|zwang** M binding nature of a/the wage agreement; **wir haben ~** our wage agreements are binding

Tarn-: **Tarn|an|strich** M camouflage; **Tarn|an|zug** M *(Mil)* camouflage battledress

tar|nen ['tarnən] VT to camouflage; *(fig) Absichten, Identität etc* to disguise; **Saunas sind oft getarnte Bordelle** saunas are often a cover for brothels; **als Polizist getarnt** disguised as a policeman VR *(Tier)* to camouflage itself; *(Mensch)* to disguise oneself

Tarn-: **Tarn|far|be** F camouflage colour *(Brit)* or color *(US)*; *(Anstrich)* camouflage paint; **Tarn|kap|pe** F magic hat; **Tarn|kap|pen|bom|ber** M Stealth bomber; **Tarn|kleid** NT *(Zool)* protective camouflage; **Tarn|na|me** M cover name; **Tarn|netz** NT *(Mil)* camouflage netting

Tar|nung ['tarnʊŋ] F -, -en camouflage; *(von Agent etc)* disguise; **die Arztpraxis ist nur eine ~** the doctor's practice is just a cover; **er fuhr zur ~ erst eine Station mit der U-Bahn** as a cover he first went one stop on the subway

Ta|rock [ta'rɔk] M OR NT -s, -s tarot

Ta|rot [ta'ro:] NT OR M -s, -s tarot

Tar|tan|bahn ['tartan-] F *(Sport)* tartan track

Tar|tar [tar'ta:ɐ] NT -(s), *no pl*, **Tar|tar|beef|steak** NT steak tartare

Tar|tar [tar'ta:ɐ] M -en, -en, **Tar|ta|rin** [-'ta:rɪn] F -, -nen Tartar

Tar|tar|so|ße tartare sauce

Täsch|chen ['tɛʃçən] NT -s, - *dim von* **Tasche**

Ta|sche ['taʃə] F -, -n **a** *(= Handtasche)* bag *(Brit)*, purse *(US)*; *(= Reisetasche etc)* bag; *(= Backentasche)* pouch; *(= Aktentasche)* case **b** *(bei Kleidungsstücken, = Billardtasche)* pocket; **sich** *(dat)* **die ~n füllen** *(fig)* to line one's own pockets; **in die eigene ~ arbeiten** *or* **wirtschaften** to line one's own pockets; **etw in der ~ haben** *(inf)* to have sth in the bag *(inf)*; **die Hand auf die ~ halten** *(dated inf)*, **die ~ zuhalten** *(dated inf)* to keep a tight grip on the purse strings; **jdm das Geld aus der ~ locken** *or* **ziehen** *or* **lotsen** to get sb to part with his money; **etw aus der eigenen ~ bezahlen** to pay for sth out of one's own pocket; **etw in die eigene ~ stecken** *(fig)* to put sth in one's own pocket, to pocket sth; **sich** *(dat)* **etwas in die ~ lügen** *(inf)* to kid oneself *(inf)*; **jdm auf der ~ liegen** *(inf)* to live off sb, to live at sb's expense; **die Hände in die ~n stecken** *(lit)* to put one's hands in one's pockets; *(fig)* to stand idly by; **jdn in die ~ stecken** *(inf)* to put sb in the shade *(inf)*; **jdm in die ~ greifen** *(fig)* to get money out of sb → **tief ADV a**

Ta|schel|zie|her ['taʃltsi:ɐ] M -s, -, **Ta|schel|zie|he|rin** [-ərɪn] F -, -nen *(Aus inf: = Taschendieb)* pickpocket

Ta|schen-: **Ta|schen|aus|ga|be** F pocket edition; **Ta|schen|buch** NT paperback (book); **Ta|schen|buch|aus|ga|be** F paperback (edition); **Ta|schen|com|pu|ter** M pocket *or* handheld computer; **Ta|schen|dieb(in)** M(F) pickpocket; **Ta|schen|dieb|stahl** M pickpocketing; **Ta|schen|fahr|plan** M (pocket) timetable; **Ta|schen|fei|tel** M *(Aus inf)* penknife, pocketknife; **Ta|schen|for|mat** NT pocket size; **Transistorradio im ~** pocket-size(d) transistor (radio); **Ta|schen|geld** NT pocket money; **Ta|schen|ka|len|der** M pocket diary; **Ta|schen|kamm** M pocket comb; **Ta|schen|krebs** M edible crab; **Ta|schen|lam|pe** F torch, flashlight; **Ta|schen|mes|ser** NT pocketknife, penknife; **wie ein ~ zusammenklappen** *(inf)* to double up; **Ta|schen|rech|ner** M pocket calculator; **Ta|schen|schirm** M collapsible umbrella; **Ta|schen|spie|gel** M pocket mirror; **Ta|schen|spie|ler(in)** M(F) conjurer *(esp Brit)*, magician; **Ta|schen|spie|le|rei** F sleight of hand *no pl*; **Ta|schen|spie|ler|trick** M *(fig)* sleight of hand *no indef art, no pl*; **Ta|schen|tuch** NT *pl* **-tücher** handkerchief, hanky *(inf)*; **Ta|schen|uhr** F pocket watch; **Ta|schen|vei|tel** [-faitl] M -s, - *(Aus inf)* penknife, pocketknife; **Ta|schen|wör|ter|buch** NT pocket dictionary

Tasch|ner ['taʃnɐ] M -s, -, **Tasch|ne|rin** [-ərɪn] F -, -nen, **Täsch|ner** ['tɛʃnɐ] M -s, -, **Täsch|ne|rin** [-ərɪn] F -, -nen bag-maker *(Brit)*, purse-maker *(US)*

Task|leis|te F *(Comput)* task bar

Tas|ma|ni|en [tas'ma:niən] NT -s Tasmania

Tas|ma|ni|er [tas'ma:niɐ] M -s, -, **Tas|ma|ni|e|rin** [-iərɪn] F -, -nen Tasmanian

tas|ma|nisch [tas'ma:nɪʃ] ADJ Tasmanian

Täss|chen ['tɛsçən] NT -s, - *dim von* **Tasse** (little) cup; **ein ~ Tee** a quick cup of tea

Tas|se ['tasə] F -, -n cup; *(mit Untertasse)* cup and saucer; *(= Henkeltasse)* mug; *(= Suppentasse)* bowl; **eine ~ Kaffee** a cup of coffee; **er hat nicht alle ~n im Schrank** *(inf)* he's a sandwich short of a picnic *(Brit inf)*, he's one card shy of a full deck *(US inf)*; **eine trübe ~** *(inf)* a wet blanket *(inf)*; **hoch die ~n!** *(inf)* bottoms up *(inf)*

Tas|ta|tur [tasta'tu:ɐ] F -, -en keyboard

tast|bar ADJ palpable; **eine ~e Beule** a raised bump

Tas|te ['tastə] F -, -n key; *(= Knopf an Gerät auch)* button; **in die ~n greifen** *(inf)* to play the piano; **auf die ~n hauen** *or* **hämmern** *(inf)* to hammer away at the keyboard; **„Taste drücken"** "push button"

Tast-: **Tast|emp|fin|den** NT sense of touch; **Tast|emp|fin|dung** F tactual sensation

tas|ten ['tastn] VI to feel; **nach etw ~** *(lit, fig)* to feel *or* grope for sth; **vorsichtig ~d** feeling *or* groping one's way carefully; **~de Schritte** *(lit, fig)* tentative steps VR to feel *or* grope one's way VT *(= drücken)* to press, to punch; *Nummer auch* to punch out; *Telex etc* to key; *(Typ: = setzen)* to key(board)

Tas|ten-: **Tas|ten|an|schlag** M, **Tas|ten|druck** M *(Comput)* keystroke; **Tas|ten|feld** NT *(Comput)* keypad, keys *pl*; **Tas|ten|in|stru|ment** NT *(Mus)* keyboard instrument; **Tas|ten|kom|bi|na|ti|on** F *(Comput)* (keyboard) shortcut; **Tas|ten|te|le|fon** NT push-button telephone

Tas|ter ['tastɐ] M -s, - **a** *(Zool)* organ of touch, tactile organ **b** *(Typ: = Tastatur)* keyboard

Tast-: **Tast|or|gan** NT organ of touch, tactile organ; **Tast|sinn** M sense of touch; **Tast|werk|zeug** NT organ of touch, tactile organ; **Tast|zir|kel** M (outside) callipers *pl (Brit) or* calipers *pl (US)*

tat *pret von* **tun**

Tat [ta:t] F -, -en *(= das Handeln)* action; *(= Einzeltat auch)* act; *(= Heldentat, Untat)* deed; *(= Leistung)* feat; *(= Verbrechen)* crime; **ein Mann der ~** a man of action; **keine Worte, sondern ~en** not words but deeds *or* actions; **seinen Worten ~en folgen lassen** to follow up one's words with actions, to suit the action to the word *(liter)*; **eine ~ der Verzweiflung/Nächstenliebe** an act of desperation/charity; **als er sah, was er mit dieser ~ angerichtet hatte** when he saw what he had done by this; **eine geschichtliche/verbrecherische ~** an historic/a criminal act *or* deed; **eine gute/böse ~** a good/wicked deed; **eine eindrucksvolle ~ vollbringen** to do something impressive; **Leben und ~en des ...** the life and exploits of ...; **etw in die ~ umsetzen** to put sth into action; **zur ~ schreiten** to proceed to action; *(hum)* to get on with it; **in der ~** indeed; *(wider Erwarten, erstaunlicherweise etc)* actually

Ta|tar [ta'ta:ɐ] NT -(s), *no pl*, **Ta|tar|beef|steak** NT steak tartare

Ta|tar [ta'ta:ɐ] M -en, -en, **Ta|ta|rin** [-'ta:rɪn] F -, -nen Tartar

Tat-: **Tat|be|stand** M *(Jur)* facts *pl* (of the case); *(= Sachlage)* facts *pl* (of the matter); **den ~ des Betrugs erfüllen** *(Jur)* to constitute fraud; **Tat|ein|heit** F *(Jur)* **in ~ mit** concomitantly with

Ta|ten-: **Ta|ten|drang** M thirst for action, energy; **Ta|ten|durst** M *(old, hum)* thirst for action; **ta|ten|durs|tig** ADJ *(old, hum)* eager for action; **ta|ten|froh** *(dated)* ADJ enthusiastic ADV enthusiastically; **ta|ten|los** ADJ idle ADV **~ herumstehen** to stand idly by, to stand by and do nothing; **~ abwarten** to sit idly and wait; **wir mussten ~ zusehen** we could only stand and watch; **Ta|ten|lo|sig|keit** F -, *no pl* inaction

Tä|ter ['tɛ:tɐ] M -s, -, **Tä|te|rin** [-ərɪn] F -, -nen culprit; *(Jur)* perpetrator *(form)*; **als ~ verdächtigt werden** to be a suspect; **als ~ in Frage kommen** to be a possible suspect; **nach dem ~ wird noch gefahndet** the police are still searching for the person responsible *or* the person who committed the crime; **wer war der ~?** who did it?; **unbekannte ~** person or persons unknown; **jugendliche ~** young offenders

Tä|ter|pro|fil NT suspect *or* criminal profile; **psychologisches ~** psychological profile of the offender *or* of the wanted person

Tä|ter|schaft ['tɛ:tɐʃaft] F -, -en guilt; **die Frage (nach) der ~** *(form)* the question of who was responsible *or* of who committed the crime; **die ~ leugnen/zugeben** to deny/admit one's guilt; *(vor Gericht)* to plead not guilty/guilty

Tat-: **Tat|form** F *(Gram)* active (voice); **tat|froh** ADJ, ADV = **tatenfroh**; **Tat|her|gang** M sequence of events; *(bei Verbrechen auch)* particulars *pl*

tä|tig ['tɛ:tɪç] ADJ **a** *attr* active; **dadurch hat er ~e Reue bewiesen** he showed his repentance in a practical way; **~e Nächstenliebe** practical charity; **in einer Sache ~ werden** *(form)* to take action in a matter **b** *(= arbeitend)* **~ sein** to work; **als was sind Sie ~?** what do you do?; **er ist im Bankwesen ~** he's in banking

tä|ti|gen ['tɛ:tɪgn] VT *(Comm)* to conclude, to effect; *Geschäft auch* to transact; *(geh) Einkäufe* to carry out; *(geh) Anruf* to make

Tä|tig|keit ['tɛ:tɪçkait] F -, -en activity; *(= Beschäftigung)* occupation; *(= Arbeit)* work; *(= Beruf)* job; **während meiner ~ als Lehrer** while I was working as a teacher; **zurzeit übt er eine andere ~ aus** at present he has a different occupation; **auf eine langjährige ~ (als ...) zurückblicken** to look back on many years of active life (as ...); **in ~ treten** to come into operation; *(Mensch)* to act, to step in; **in ~ sein** *(Maschine)* to be operating *or* running; **in ~ setzen** *(Maschine)* to set going *or* in motion; *Alarmanlage* to activate; **außer ~ setzen** *(Maschine)* to stop; *Alarmanlage* to put out of action

Tä|tig|keits-: **Tä|tig|keits|be|reich** M field of activity; **Tä|tig|keits|be|richt** M progress report; **Tä|tig|keits|be|schrei|bung** F job description; **Tä|tig|keits|form** F *(Gram)* active (voice); **Tä|tig|keits|merk|ma|le** PL job characteristics *pl*; **Tä|tig|keits|wort** NT *pl* **-wörter** *(Gram)* verb

Tä|ti|gung ['tɛ:tɪgʊŋ] F -, *rare* **-en** conclusion, effecting; *(von Geschäft auch)* transaction; *(von Einkäufen)* carrying out; *(von Anruf)* making

Tat-: **Tat|kraft** F, *no pl* energy, vigour *(Brit)*, vigor *(US)*, drive; **tat|kräf|tig** ADJ energetic; *Hilfe* active ADV actively; **etw/jdn ~ unterstützen** to actively support sth/sb

tät|lich ['tɛ:tlɪç] ADJ violent; **~e Beleidigung** *(Jur)* assault (and battery); **~ werden** to become violent; **gegen jdn ~ werden** to assault sb ADV **jdn ~ angreifen** to attack sb physically, to assault sb

Tät|lich|keit F violent act, act of violence; **~en** violence *sing*; **es kam zu ~en** there was violence

Tat-: **Tat|mensch** M man/woman of action; **Tat|mo|tiv** NT motive (for the crime); **Tat|ort** M *pl* **-orte** scene of the crime

tä|to|wie|ren [tɛto'vi:rən] *ptp* **tätowiert** VT to tattoo; **sich ~ lassen** to have oneself tattooed

Tä|to|wie|rung F -, -en **a** *no pl (= das Tätowieren)* tattooing **b** *(= Darstellung)* tattoo

Tat|sa|che ✪ 44.1 F fact; **~ ist aber, dass ...** but the fact of the matter *or* but the truth is that ...; **~?** *(inf)* really?, no!; **das stimmt, ~!** *(inf)* it's true, really; **das ist ~** *(inf)* that's a fact; **nackte ~n** *(inf)* the hard facts; *(hum)* girlie pictures; **vollendete ~n schaffen** to create a fait accompli; **jdn vor vollendete ~n stellen** to present sb with a fait accompli; **vor der vollendeten ~ stehen** to be faced with a fait accompli; **(unter) Vorspiegelung falscher ~n** (under) false pretences *(Brit) or* pretenses *(US)*

Tat|sa|chen-: **Tat|sa|chen|be|haup|tung** F allegation; **Tat|sa|chen|be|richt** M documentary (report); **Tat|sa|chen|ma|te|ri|al** NT facts *pl*

tat|säch|lich ['ta:tzɛçlɪç, ta:t'zɛçlɪç] ADJ *attr* real, actual ADV **a** *(= in Wirklichkeit, objektiv)* actually, really, in fact; ~ **war es aber ganz anders** in (actual) fact *or* actually *or* really it was quite different **b** *(= sage und schreibe)* really, actually; **willst du das ~ tun?** are you really *or* actually going to do it?; **~?** really?; **~!** oh yes, so it/he *etc* is/was *etc*; **da kommt er! – ~!** here he comes! – so he does!

tät|scheln ['tɛtʃln] **VT** to pat

tat|schen ['tatʃn] **VI** *(pej inf)* **auf etw** *(acc)* ~ to paw sth

Tat|ter|greis(in) ['tatɐ-] **M(F)** *(pej inf)* old dodderer, doddering old man/woman *(pej)*

Tat|te|rich ['tatərɪç] **M -(e)s,** *no pl (inf)* **den ~ haben/bekommen** to have/get the shakes *(inf)*

tat|te|rig ['tatərɪç], **tatt|rig** ['tatrɪç] **ADJ** *(inf) Mensch* doddering, doddery; *Hände, Schriftzüge* shaky, quivery

ta|tü|ta|ta [ta'ty:ta'ta:] **INTERJ ~! die Feuerwehr ist da!** da-da-da-da! here comes the fire engine!; **das Tatütata des Polizeiautos** the (wailing) siren of the police car

Tat-: **Tat|ver|dacht M** suspicion *(of having committed a crime)*; **unter ~ stehen** to be under suspicion; **tat|ver|däch|tig ADJ** suspected; **Tat|ver|däch|ti|ge(r) MF** *decl as adj* suspect; **Tat|waf|fe F** weapon (used in the crime); *(= bei Mord)* murder weapon

Tat|ze ['tatsə] **F -, -n** *(lit, fig)* paw

Tat-: **Tat|zeit F** time of the incident *or* crime; **Tat|zeu|ge M, Tat|zeu|gin F** witness (to the incident *or* crime)

Tau [tau] **M -(e)s,** *no pl* dew; **vor ~ und Tag** *(poet)* at break of day *(poet)*

Tau NT -(e)s, -e *(= Seil)* rope; *(Naut auch)* hawser

taub [taup] **ADJ** deaf; *Glieder* numb; *Gestein* dead; *Metall* dull; *Ähre* unfruitful; *Nuss* empty; **sich ~ stellen** to pretend not to hear; **gegen** *or* **für etw ~ sein** *(fig)* to be deaf to sth → **Ohr, Nuss**

Täub|chen ['tɔypçən] **NT -s, -** *dim von* **Taube**; **mein ~!** my little dove

Tau|be ['taubə] **F -, -n a** *(Zool)* pigeon; *(= Turteltaube)* dove, pigeon; **hier fliegen einem die gebratenen ~n nicht ins Maul** *(prov)* this isn't exactly the land of milk and honey **b** *(fig, als Symbol)* dove; **~n und Falken** *(Pol inf)* hawks and doves

Tau|ben-: **tau|ben|blau ADJ** blue-grey *(Brit)*, blue-gray *(US)*; **Tau|ben|ei** ['taubnlai] **NT** → **Taube a** pigeon's/dove's egg; **tau|ben|ei|groß ADJ** the size of a golf ball

tau|be|netzt [-bənɛtst] **ADJ** *(liter)* dewy, dew-covered

Tau|ben-: **tau|ben|grau ADJ** dove grey *(Brit) or* gray *(US)*; **Tau|ben|haus NT** dovecot(e); *(für Brieftauben)* pigeon loft; **Tau|ben|post F mit der ~** by pigeon post *(esp Brit)*; **Tau|ben|schie|ßen NT -s,** *no pl (Sport)* pigeon shooting; **Tau|ben|schlag M a** *(lit)* = **Taubenhaus b** *(fig)* **hier geht es zu wie im ~** it's mobbed here *(inf)*; **Tau|ben|sport M** pigeon racing; **Tau|ben|zucht F** pigeon fancying *(Brit) or* breeding

Tau|be(r) ['taubə] **MF** *decl as adj* deaf person *or* man/woman *etc*; **die ~n** the deaf

Tau|ber ['taubɐ] **M -s, -, Täu|ber** ['tɔybɐ] **M -s, -, Täu|be|rich** ['tɔybərɪç] **M -s, -e** cock pigeon

Taub|heit F -, *no pl* **a** deafness **b** *(von Körperteil)* numbness

Täub|ling ['tɔyplɪŋ] **M -s, -e** *(Bot)* russula (toadstool)

Taub-: **Taub|nes|sel F** dead-nettle; **taub|stumm ADJ** deaf and dumb, deaf-mute *attr*; **Taub|stum|men|spra|che F** sign language; **Taub|stum|me(r)** [-ʃtʊmə] **MF** *decl as adj* deaf-mute; **Taub|stumm|heit F -,** *no pl* deaf-mutism

Tauch|boot NT submersible

tau|chen ['tauxn] **VI a** *aux haben or sein* to dive *(nach* for); *(= kurz tauchen)* to duck under; *(= unter Wasser sein)* to stay under water; *(U-Boot)* to submerge, to dive **b** *aux sein (fig)* to disappear *(in +acc* into); *(Boxen: = abducken)* to duck; **die Sonne tauchte langsam ins Meer/hinter den Horizont** the sun sank slowly into the sea/beneath the horizon **VT** *(= kurz tauchen)* to dip; *Menschen, Kopf* to duck; *(= eintauchen, auch bei Taufe)* to immerse; **in Licht getaucht** *(geh)* bathed in light

Tau|chen NT -s, *no pl* diving

Tau|cher ['tauxɐ] **M -s, -, Tau|che|rin** [-ərɪn] **F -, -nen** diver

Tau|cher-: **Tau|cher|an|zug M** diving *(Brit) or* dive *(US)* suit; **Tau|cher|aus|rüs|tung F** diving *(Brit) or* dive *(US)* equipment *or* gear; **Tau|cher|bril|le F** diving *(Brit) or* dive *(US)* goggles *pl*; **Tau|cher|flos|se F** (diving *(Brit) or* dive *(US)*) flipper; **Tau|cher|glo|cke F** diving *(Brit) or* dive *(US)* bell; **Tau|cher|helm M** diving *(Brit) or* dive *(US)* helmet, diver's helmet

Tau|che|rin [-ərɪn] **F -, -nen** diver

Tauch-: **Tauch|gang M** dive; **Tauch|mas|ke F** *pl* **-gänge** diving *(Brit) or* dive *(US)* mask; **Tauch|sie|der** [-zi:dɐ] **M -s, -** immersion coil *(for boiling water)*; **Tauch|sport M** (skin) diving; **Tauch|sta|ti|on F auf ~ gehen** *(U-Boot)* to dive; *(hum: in Schützengraben etc)* to duck, to get one's head down; *(fig: = sich verstecken)* to make oneself scarce; **auf ~ sein** *(U-Boot)* to be submerged; **Tauch|tie|fe F** depth; *(Naut: von Fluss)* navigable depth

tau|en ['tauən] **VTI** *(vi: aux haben or sein) (Eis, Schnee)* to melt, to thaw; **es taut** it is thawing; **der Schnee taut von den Bergen/Dächern** the snow on the mountains/roofs is melting *or* thawing

tau|en VT *(N Ger, Naut)* to tow

Tau|en|de ['taulɛndə] **NT** *(Naut)* end of a piece of rope

Tauf-: **Tauf|akt M** baptism *or* christening (ceremony); **Tauf|be|cken NT** font; **Tauf|buch NT** baptismal register

Tau|fe ['taufə] **F -, -n** baptism; *(christliche auch, esp von Kindern)* christening; *(= Schiffstaufe)* launching (ceremony); **die ~ empfangen** to be baptized *or* christened; **jdm die ~ spenden** to baptize *or* christen sb; **ein Kind aus der ~ heben** *(old)* to stand sponsor to a child *(old)*; **etw aus der ~ heben** *(hum, Verein, Firma)* to start sth up; *Zeitung, Projekt* to launch sth

tau|fen ['taufn] **VT** to baptize; *(bei Äquatortaufe)* to duck; *(= nennen) Kind, Schiff, Hund etc* to christen; **sich ~ lassen** to be baptized; **jdn auf den Namen Rufus ~** to christen sb Rufus

Täu|fer ['tɔyfɐ] **M -s, - Johannes der ~** John the Baptist; **die ~** *(Eccl)* the Baptists

tau|feucht ADJ dewy, wet with dew

Tauf-: **Tauf|for|mel F** baptism formula; **Tauf|ge|lüb|de NT** baptismal vows *pl*; **Tauf|ka|pel|le F** baptistry; **Tauf|kleid NT** christening robe

Täuf|ling ['tɔyflɪŋ] **M -s, -e** child/person to be baptized

Tauf-: **Tauf|na|me M** Christian name; **Tauf|pa|te M** godfather; **Tauf|pa|tin F** godmother; **Tauf|re|gis|ter NT** baptismal register

tau|frisch ADJ *(geh)* dewy; *(fig)* fresh; *(= fit für sein Alter)* sprightly

Tauf-: **Tauf|schein M** certificate of baptism; **Tauf|stein M** (baptismal) font; **Tauf|zeu|ge M, Tauf|zeu|gin F** godparent

tau|gen ['taugn] **VI a** *(= geeignet sein)* to be suitable *(zu, für* for); **wozu soll denn das ~?** what is that supposed to be for?; **er taugt zu gar nichts** he is useless; **er taugt nicht zum Arzt** he wouldn't make a good doctor; **in der Schule taugt er nichts** he's useless *or* no good at school; **er taugt nicht zu harter Arbeit** he's not much good at hard work; *(wegen Faulheit)* he's not keen on hard work **b** *(= wert sein)* **etwas ~** to be good *or* all right; **nichts** *or* **nicht viel ~** to be not much good *or* no good *or* no use; **taugt der Neue etwas?** is the new bloke any good *or* use?; **der Bursche taugt nicht viel/gar nichts** that bloke is a (real) bad lot *(inf)*; **als Mensch taugt er gar nichts** he is worthless as a person

Tau|ge|nichts ['taugənɪçts] **M -(es), -e** *(dated)* good-for-nothing, ne'er-do-well *(old)*

taug|lich ['tauklɪç] **ADJ** *Kandidat, Bewerber, Material* suitable *(zu* for); *(Mil)* fit *(zu* for); **jdn für ~ erklären** *(Mil)* to declare *or* certify sb fit for service

Taug|lich|keit F -, *no pl* suitability; *(Mil)* fitness (for service)

Taug|lich|keits|grad M *(Mil)* physical fitness rating (for military service)

Tau|mel ['tauml] **M -s,** *no pl (geh: = Schwindel)* (attack of) dizziness *or* giddiness; *(liter: = Rausch)* frenzy; **im ~ der Ereignisse sein** *(liter)* to be caught up in the whirl of events; **im ~ des Glücks** *(liter)* in a transport of happiness *(liter)*; **im ~ der Sinne** *or* **Leidenschaft** *(liter)* in the fever of his/her *etc* passion; **wie im ~** *(geh)* in a daze

tau|me|lig ['tauməlɪç] **ADJ** dizzy, giddy

tau|meln ['taumln] **VI** *aux sein* to stagger; *(zur Seite)* to sway

taum|lig ['taumlɪç] **ADJ** = **taumelig**

Tau-: **Tau|per|le F** *(liter)* dewdrop; **Tau|punkt M** dew point

Tausch [tauʃ] **M -(e)s, -e** exchange, swap; *(= Tauschhandel)* barter; **im ~ gegen** *or* **für etw** in exchange for sth; **etw in ~ geben** to exchange *or* swap/barter sth; *(bei Neukauf)* to give sth in part exchange; **jdm etw zum ~ für etw anbieten** to offer to exchange *or* swap sth for sth; **etw in ~ nehmen** to take sth in exchange; **einen guten/schlechten ~ machen** to get a good/bad deal

Tausch|bör|se F barter exchange, bartering centre *(Brit) or* center *(US)*; *(im Internet)* online exchange service

tau|schen ['tauʃn] **VT** to exchange, to swap; *Güter* to barter; *(= austauschen) Briefmarken, Münzen etc* to swap; *Geschenke* to exchange; *Geld* to change *(in +acc* into); *(inf: = umtauschen) Gekauftes* to change; **einen Blick mit jdm ~** *(geh)* to exchange glances with sb; **die Rollen ~** to swap roles; **Küsse ~** *(geh)* to kiss; **wollen wir die Plätze ~?** shall we change *or* swap places? **VI** to swap; *(in Handel)* to barter; **wollen wir ~?** shall we swap (places *etc*)?; **wir haben getauscht** we swapped, we did a swap; **ich möchte nicht mit ihm ~** I wouldn't like to change places with him

täu|schen ['tɔyʃn] **VT** to deceive; **mit dieser Fälschung täuschte er sogar die Experten** he even deceived *or* fooled the experts with this forgery; **man kann ihn nicht ~** you can't fool him; **er wurde in seinen Erwartungen/Hoffnungen getäuscht** his expectations/hopes were disappointed; **wenn mich mein Gedächtnis nicht täuscht** if my memory serves me right; **wenn mich nicht alles täuscht** unless I'm completely wrong; **sie lässt sich leicht/nicht ~** she is easily/not easily fooled *(durch* by)

VR to be wrong *or* mistaken *(in +dat, über +acc* about); **darin ~ Sie sich** you are mistaken there, that's where you're wrong; **dann hast du dich getäuscht!** then you are mistaken; **so kann man sich ~!** it shows how wrong you can be

VI a *(= irreführen) (Aussehen etc)* to be deceptive; *(Sport)* to feint; **das täuscht** that is deceptive; **wenn (mich) nicht alles täuscht, …** unless I'm very much mistaken, …; **der Eindruck täuscht** things are not what they seem **b** *(Sch form: = betrügen)* to cheat

täu|schend ADJ *Nachahmung* remarkable; *Ähnlichkeit auch* striking; **eine ~e Ähnlichkeit mit jdm haben** to look remarkably like sb **ADV sich** *(dat)* **~ ähnlich sehen/sein** to look/be remarkably alike, to look/be almost identical; **jdm ~ ähnlich sehen** to look remarkably like sb, to be the spitting image of sb; **eine ~ echte Fälschung/Nachahmung** a remarkably convincing fake/imitation

Täu|scher ['tɔyʃɐ] M **-s, -**, **Täu|sche|rin** [-ərɪn] F **-, -nen** phoney *(inf)*

Tau|sche|rei [tauʃə'rai] F **-, -en** *(inf)* exchanging, swapping

Tausch-: **Tausch|ge|schäft** NT exchange, swap; *(= Handel)* barter (deal); **mit etw ein ~ machen** to exchange/barter sth; **Tausch|ge|sell|schaft** F barter society; **Tausch|han|del** M barter; **~ treiben** to barter; **Tausch|mit|tel** NT medium of exchange; **Tausch|ob|jekt** NT barter *no pl*, barter object; **Tausch|part|ner(in)** M(F) **~ für 2-Zimmer-Wohnung gesucht** exchange *or* swap wanted for two-room(ed) flat *(Brit)* or apartment

Täu|schung ['tɔyʃʊŋ] F **-, -en** **a** *(= das Täuschen)* deception; **das tat er zur ~** he did that in order to deceive **b** *(= Irrtum)* mistake, error; *(= Irreführung)* deceit; *(= falsche Wahrnehmung)* illusion; *(= Selbsttäuschung)* delusion; **er gab sich einer ~** *(dat)* **hin** he was deluding himself; **darüber darf man sich keiner ~** *(dat)* **hingeben** one must not delude oneself (about that)

Täu|schungs-: **Täu|schungs|ab|sicht** F intention to deceive; **Täu|schungs|ma|nö|ver** NT *(Sport)* feint; *(inf)* ploy; **Täu|schungs|ver|such** M attempted deception

Tausch-: **Tausch|wert** M *(Sociol)* exchange value, value in exchange; **Tausch|wirt|schaft** F, *no pl (Econ)* barter economy

tau|send ['tauznt] NUM a *or* one thousand; **~ Dank/Grüße/Küsse** a thousand thanks/greetings/kisses → *auch* **hundert**

Tau|send ['tauznt] F **-, -en** [-dn] *(Zahl)* thousand

Tau|send NT **-s, -e** [-də] thousand; **vom ~** in a *or* per thousand; **ei der ~!** *(obs)* zounds! *(obs)* → *auch* **Hundert**

Tau|sen|der ['tauzndɐ] M **-s, -** **a** *(= Zahl)* **ein ~** a figure in the thousands; **die ~** the thousands **b** *(= Geldschein)* thousand (euro/dollar *etc* note *or* bill)

tau|sen|der|lei ['tauzndɐ'lai] ADJ *inv* a thousand kinds of

Tau|send-: **Tau|send|fü|ßer** [-fy:sɐ] M **-s, -** *(form)*, **Tau|send|füß|ler** [-fy:slɐ] M **-s, -** centipede; **die ~** the myriapods *(spec)*; **Tau|send|jahr|fei|er** F millenary; **tau|send|jäh|rig** ADJ *attr* thousand-year-old; *(= tausend Jahre lang)* thousand-year(-long); **nach mehr als ~er Unterdrückung** after more than a thousand years of oppression; **das ~e Reich** *(Bibl)* the millennium; **Hitlers „tausendjähriges Reich"** Hitler's "thousand-year empire"; **Tau|send|künst|ler(in)** M(F) jack of all trades; **tau|send|mal** ADV a thousand times; **ich bitte ~ um Entschuldigung** a thousand pardons; **viel ~** *(old)* times without number → *auch* **hundertmal**; **Tau|send|sa|sa** ['tauzntsasa] M **-s, -(s)**, **Tau|send|sas|sa** ['tauzntsasa] M **-s, -(s)** *(dated inf)* hell of a chap *(Brit dated inf)* or guy *(inf)*; **Tau|send|schön** ['tauzntʃø:n] NT **-s, -e**, **Tau|send|schön|chen** [-ʃø:nçən] NT **-s, -** daisy

Tau|sends|tel ['tauzntstl] NT **-s, -** thousandth

tau|sends|te(r, s) ['tauzntstə] ADJ thousandth → *auch* **hundertste(r, s)**

Tau|send-: **tau|send|und|ei|ne(r, s)** ['tauzntlunt'lainə] ADJ a thousand and one; **Märchen aus Tausendundeiner Nacht** Tales of the Thousand and One Nights, the Arabian Nights; **tau|send|(und)|eins** ['tauznt(lunt)'lains] NUM one thousand and one

Tau|to|lo|gie [tautolo'gi:] F **-, -n** [-'gi:ən] tautology

tau|to|lo|gisch [tauto'lo:gɪʃ] ADJ tautological, tautologous ADV *sich ausdrücken, formulieren* tautologically

Tau-: **Tau|trop|fen** M dewdrop; **Tau|werk** NT, *no pl (Naut)* rigging; **Tau|wet|ter** NT thaw; *(fig auch)* relaxation; **wir haben** *or* **es ist ~** it is thawing; **bei ~** during a thaw, when it thaws; **es herrschte ein kulturelles/politisches ~** there was a period of cultural/political relaxation; **Tau|zie|hen** NT **-s**, *no pl (lit, fig)* tug-of-war

Ta|ver|ne [ta'vɛrnə] F **-, -n** *(old)* tavern *(old)*, inn; *(in Italien)* taverna

Ta|xa|me|ter [taksa'me:tɐ] M **-s, -** taximeter, clock *(inf)*

Ta|xa|tor [ta'ksa:to:ɐ] M **-s, Taxatoren** [-'to:rən], **Ta|xa|to|rin** [-'to:rɪn] F **-, -nen** *(Comm)* valuer

Ta|xe ['taksə] F **-, -n** **a** *(= Schätzung)* valuation, estimate **b** *(= Gebühr)* charge; *(= Kurtaxe etc)* tax; *(= Gebührenordnung)* scale of charges **c** *(dial)* = **Taxi**

Ta|xi ['taksi] NT **-s, -s** taxi, cab, taxicab *(form)*; **sich** *(dat)* **ein ~ nehmen** to take a taxi, to go by taxi; **~ fahren** to drive a taxi; *(als Fahrgast)* to go by taxi

Ta|xi|chauf|feur(in) M(F) taxi *or* cab driver

ta|xie|ren [ta'ksi:rən] *ptp* **taxiert** VT **a** *Preis, Wert* to estimate *(auf +acc* at); *Haus, Gemälde etc* to value *(auf +acc* at); **etw zu hoch ~** to overestimate/overvalue sth; **etw zu niedrig ~** to underestimate/undervalue sth; **er hat mich richtiggehend taxiert** he looked me up and down **b** *(geh: = einschätzen) Situation* to assess

Ta|xi-: **Ta|xi|fah|rer(in)** M(F) taxi *or* cab driver, cabby *(inf)*; **Ta|xi|fahrt** F taxi ride; **Ta|xi|stand** M taxi rank *(Brit) or* stand

Tax|kurs ['taks-] M rate of taxation

Tax|ler ['takslɐ] M **-s, -**, **Tax|le|rin** [-ərɪn] F **-, -nen** *(Aus inf)* cabby *(inf)*

Tax|preis ['taks-] M estimated price *(according to valuation)*

Ta|xus ['taksʊs] M **-, -** yew (tree)

Tax|wert ['taks-] M estimated value

Tb(c) [te:(')be:'tse:] F **-, -s** *abbr von* **Tuberkulose** TB

Tb(c)-krank [te:(')be:'tse:-] ADJ **~ sein** to have TB; **die ~en Patienten** patients with TB, TB patients *or* cases

Teak|holz ['ti:k-] NT teak; **ein Tisch aus ~** a teak table

Team [ti:m] NT **-s, -s** team

Team-: **Team|ar|beit** F teamwork; **etw in ~ machen** to do sth as a team *or* through teamwork; **das wird in ~ gemacht** it's done through teamwork; **team|fä|hig** ADJ able to work in a team; **sie ist nicht ~** she's not a team player; **Team|fä|hig|keit** F ability to work in a team; **Team|geist** M team spirit; **Team|work** ['ti:mwø:ɐk, -wœrk] NT **-s**, *no pl* = **Teamarbeit**

Tech|ne|ti|um [tɛç'ne:tsiʊm] NT **-s**, *no pl (abbr* **Tc**) technetium

Tech|nik ['tɛçnɪk] F **-, -en** **a** *(no pl: = Technologie)* technology; *(esp als Studienfach)* engineering; **der Mensch und die ~** man and technology; **das Zeitalter der ~** the technological age, the age of technology; **verfluchte ~!** stupid technology! **b** *(= Arbeitsweise, Verfahren)* technique; **jdn mit der ~ von etw vertraut machen** to familiarize sb with the techniques *or* skills of sth; **die ~ des Dramas/der Musik** dramatic/musical techniques **c** *(no pl: = Funktionsweise und Aufbau) (von Auto, Motor etc)* mechanics *pl* **d** *(Sch: = Schulfach) (= Haushaltslehre)* home economics; *(= Werken)* technical studies **e** *(inf: = technische Abteilung)* technical department, back-room boys *pl (inf)* **f** *(Aus inf: = Technische Hochschule)* institute of technology

tech|nik|be|geis|tert ADJ technology-mad *(Brit inf)*, techno-crazy *(US inf)*

tech|nik|be|ses|sen ADJ obsessed with new technology

Tech|ni|ker ['tɛçnikɐ] M **-s, -**, **Tech|ni|ke|rin** [-ərɪn] F **-, -nen** engineer; *(= Beleuchtungstechniker, Labortechniker)* technician; *(fig: = Fußballspieler, Künstler)* technician; **ich bin kein ~, ich verstehe das nicht** I am not technically minded, I don't understand that; **er ist mehr Theoretiker als ~** he is more concerned with theoretical than practical matters

tech|nik|feind|lich ADJ hostile to new technology, technophobic

Tech|nik|feind|lich|keit F hostility to new technology, technophobia

Tech|nik|fol|gen|ab|schät|zung F, **Tech|nik|fol|gen-Ab|schät|zung** F technology assessment

tech|nik|freund|lich ADJ receptive to new technology

Tech|ni|kum ['tɛçnikʊm] NT **-s, Technika** [-ka] college of technology

tech|nisch ['tɛçnɪʃ] ADJ **a** *(= technologisch)* technological; *Studienfach* technical; **~e Hochschule/Universität** technological university, Institute of (Science and) Technology; **~e Chemie/Medizin** chemical/medical engineering; **das ~e Zeitalter** the technological age, the age of technology; **Technisches Hilfswerk** → **THW** **b** *(= die Ausführung betreffend) Schwierigkeiten, Gründe* technical; *(= mechanisch)* mechanical; **~er Zeichner** engineering draughtsman *(Brit) or* draftsman *(US)*; **~er Leiter** technical director; **~e Einzelheiten** *(fig)* technicalities, technical details; **~e Daten** specifications ADV technically; **er ist ~ begabt** he is technically minded; **~ versiert sein** to have technical skills; **~ sehr anspruchsvoll** technically very demanding; **~ machbar** technically feasible *or* possible; **das ist ~ unmöglich** it is technically impossible; *(inf: = das geht nicht)* it is absolutely impossible

tech|ni|sie|ren [tɛçni'zi:rən] *ptp* **technisiert** VT to mechanize

Tech|ni|sie|rung F **-, -en** mechanization

Tech|no ['tɛçno] M **-**, *no pl (Mus)* techno

Tech|no|krat [tɛçno'kra:t] M **-en, -en**, **Tech|no|kra|tin** [-'kra:tɪn] F **-, -nen** technocrat

Tech|no|kra|tie [tɛçnokra'ti:] F **-**, *no pl* technocracy

tech|no|kra|tisch [tɛçno'kratɪʃ] ADJ technocratic ADV technocratically

Tech|no|lo|ge [tɛçno'lo:gə] M **-n, -n**, **Tech|no|lo|gin** [-'lo:gɪn] F **-, -nen** technologist

Tech|no|lo|gie [tɛçnolo'gi:] F **-, -n** [-'gi:ən] technology

Tech|no|lo|gie-: **tech|no|lo|gie|las|tig** ADJ technology-dominated; **Tech|no|lo|gie|park** M technology park; **Tech|no|lo|gie|trans|fer** M technology transfer; **Tech|no|lo|gie|wer|te** PL *(St Ex)* technology *or* tech stocks *pl*; **Tech|no|lo|gie|zent|rum** NT technology park

Tech|no|lo|gin [-'lo:gɪn] F **-, -nen** technologist

tech|no|lo|gisch [tɛçno'lo:gɪʃ] ADJ technological ADV technologically; **eine ~ führende Nation** a leading technological nation

Tech|no|mu|sik F F techno music

Tech|no|par|ty F F techno party

Tech|tel|mech|tel [tɛçtl'mɛçtl] NT **-s, -** *(inf)* affair, carry-on *(inf)*; **mit jdm ein ~ haben** to be carrying on with sb *(inf)*

Te|ckel ['tɛkl] M **-s, -** dachshund

Ted [tɛt] M **-(s), -s** *(inf: Mensch)* ted *(inf)*

TED [tɛt] M **-(s)** *abbr von* **Teledialog** *computer used to work out results of telephone polls*

Ted|dy ['tɛdi] M **-s, -s** **a** *(auch* **Teddybär**) teddy (bear) **b** *(auch* **Teddystoff**) fur fabric

Ted|dy|fut|ter NT fleecy *or* fur-fabric lining

Te|de|um [te'de:ʊm] NT **-s, -s** Te Deum

Tee [te:] M **-s, -s** tea; **einen im ~ haben** *(inf)* to be tipsy *(inf)*; **einen ~ geben** *(dated)* to give a tea party

TEE [te:le:'le:] M **-, -(s)** *(Rail) abbr von* **Trans-Europ(a)-Express**

Tee-: **Tee|beu|tel** M tea bag; **Tee|blatt** NT tea leaf; **Tee-Ei** NT, **Tee|ei** NT (tea) infuser *(esp Brit)*, tea ball *(esp US)*; **Tee|fil|ter** M tea filter; **Tee|ge|bäck** NT, *no pl* sweet biscuits *pl (Brit)*, cookies *pl (esp US)*; **Tee|glas** NT tea glass; **Tee|hau|be** F tea cosy *(Brit) or* cozy *(US)*; **Tee|haus** NT teahouse; **Tee|kan|ne** F teapot; **Tee|kes|sel** M **a** kettle **b** *(= Gesellschaftsspiel) guessing game based on puns*; **Tee|kü|che** F kitchenette; **Tee|licht** NT tea light (candle); **Tee|löf|fel** M teaspoon; *(Men-*

ge) teaspoonful; **tee|löf|fel|wei|se** ADV by the teaspoonful; **Tee|ma|schi|ne** F tea urn; **Tee|mi|schung** F blend of tea

Teen [ti:n] M **-s, -s** *(Press sl)* teenager

Teen|ager ['ti:ne:dʒɐ] M **-s, -** teenager

Tee|netz NT tea filter

Tee|nie, Tee|ny ['ti:ni] M **-s, -s** *(inf)* teenybopper *(inf)*

Tee|pau|se F tea break

Teer [te:ɐ] M **-(e)s, -e** tar

Teer-: **Teer|dach|pap|pe** F (bituminous) roofing felt; **Teer|de|cke** F tarred (road) surface

tee|ren ['te:rən] VT to tar; **~ und federn** to tar and feather

Teer-: **Teer|far|ben** PL, **Teer|farb|stof|fe** PL aniline dyes *pl*; **Teer|ge|halt** M tar content; **teer|hal|tig** ADJ **eine wenig/stark ~e Zigarette** a low/high tar cigarette; **~ sein** to contain tar

Tee|ro|se F tea rose

Teer-: **Teer|pap|pe** F (bituminous) roofing felt; **Teer|stra|ße** F tarred road

Tee|rung ['te:rʊŋ] F **-, -en** tarring

Tee-: **Tee|ser|vice** [-zɛrvi:s] NT tea set; **Tee|sieb** NT tea strainer; **Tee|sor|te** F (type *or* sort of) tea; **Tee|strauch** M tea bush; **Tee|strumpf** M tea filter; **Tee|stu|be** F tearoom; **Tee|stun|de** F afternoon tea (time) *(Brit)*; **Tee|tas|se** F teacup; **Tee|wa|gen** M tea trolley; **Tee|wär|mer** [-vɛrmɐ] M **-s, -** tea cosy *(Brit) or* cozy *(US)*; **Tee|was|ser** NT **das ~ aufsetzen** to put the water *or* kettle *(Brit)* on for (some) tea; **Tee|wurst** F *smoked German sausage for spreading*

Tef|lon® ['tɛflo:n, tɛf'lo:n] NT **-s** Teflon®, *eingetragene Marke von DuPont*

Te|he|ran ['te:həra:n, tehə'ra:n] NT **-s** Teh(e)ran

Teich [taiç] M **-(e)s, -e** pond; **der große ~** *(dated inf)* the (herring) pond *(hum)*

Teich-: **Teich|molch** M smooth newt; **Teich|ro|se** F yellow water lily

Teig [taik] M **-(e)s, -e** [-gə] *(= Hefeteig, Knetteig, Nudelteig)* dough; *(= Mürbteig, Blätterteig etc)* pastry; *(= Pfannkuchenteig)* batter

tei|gig ['taigɪç] ADJ doughy; *(= voller Teig) Hände* covered in dough/pastry

Teig-: **Teig|mas|se** F → **Teig** *(Cook)* dough; pastry; batter; mixture; **Teig|schüs|sel** F mixing bowl; **Teig|ta|sche** F pastry case; **Teig|wa|ren** PL *(= Nudeln)* pasta *sing*

Teil [tail] M **-(e)s, -e** **a** part; *(von Strecke)* stretch, part; *(von Stadt)* part, district, area; *(von Gebäude)* part, area, section; *(von Zeitung)* section; **der Bau/das Projekt ist zum ~ fertig** the building/project is partly finished; **wir hörten zum ~ interessante Reden** some of the speeches we heard were interesting; **200 Menschen wurden zum ~ schwer verletzt** 200 people were injured, some of them badly; **zum ~ …, zum ~ …** partly …, partly …; **zum größten/größten ~** for the most part, mostly; **er hat die Bücher darüber zum großen/größten ~ gelesen** he has read many/most of the books about that; **die Studenten wohnen zum größten ~ bei ihren Eltern** for the most part the students live with their parents; **der größere ~ ihres Einkommens** the bulk of her income; **ein großer ~ stimmte dagegen** a large number (of people) voted against it; **der dritte/vierte/fünfte** *etc* **~** *(= ein Drittel/Viertel/Fünftel etc)* a third/quarter/fifth *etc (von* of); **in zwei ~e zerbrechen** to break in two *or* half

b *(Jur: = Partei, Seite)* party

c *auch nt (= Anteil)* share; **ein gut ~ Arbeit** *(dated)* quite a bit of work; **ein gut ~ der Leute** *(dated)* many *or* a lot of people; **zu gleichen ~en erben** to get an equal share of an inheritance; **zu gleichen ~en beitragen** to make an equal contribution; **er hat sein(en) ~ dazu beigetragen** he did his bit *or* share; **er hat sein(en) ~ bekommen** *or* **weg** *(inf)* he has (already) had his due; **sich** *(dat)* **sein(en) ~ denken** *(inf)* to draw one's own conclusions

d *auch nt* **ich für mein(en) ~** for my part, I …, I, for my part …

Teil NT **-(e)s, -e** **a** part; *(= Bestandteil)* component, part; *(= Ersatzteil)* spare, (spare) part; *(sl: = Ding)* thing; **etw in seine ~e zerlegen** *(Tier, Leiche)* to cut sth up; *Motor, Möbel etc* to take sth apart *or* to bits *or* to pieces **b** → **Teil c d**

Teil-: **Teil|ab|kom|men** NT partial agreement; **Teil|an|sicht** F partial view; **Teil|as|pekt** M aspect, part; **teil|bar** ADJ divisible, which can be divided *(durch* by); **Teil|bar|keit** ['tailba:ɐkait] F **-,** *no pl* divisibility; **Teil|be|reich** M part; *(in Abteilung)* section; **Teil|be|trag** M part (of an amount); *(auf Rechnung)* item; *(= Rate)* instalment; *(= Zwischensumme)* subtotal

Teil|chen ['tailçən] NT **-s, -** particle; *(dial: = Gebäckstück)* cake

Teil|chen-: **Teil|chen|be|schleu|ni|ger** M *(Phys)* particle accelerator; **Teil|chen|phy|sik** F particle physics *sing*

Tei|le|fer|ti|gung F *(Ind)* manufacture of parts *or* components

tei|len ['tailən] **VT** **a** *(= zerlegen, trennen)* to divide (up); *(Math)* to divide *(durch* by); *(Comput) Bildschirm, Fenster* to split; **27 lässt sich durch 9 ~** 27 can be divided by 9; **27 geteilt durch 9** 27 divided by 9; **etw in drei Teile ~** to divide sth in(to) three (parts); **der Fluss teilt das Land in der Mitte** the river divides the country down the middle; **(politisch) geteilter Meinung sein** to have different (political) opinions; **darüber sind die Meinungen geteilt** opinions differ on that; **darüber kann man geteilter Meinung sein** one can disagree about that; **das Schiff teilte die Wellen** *or* **Wogen** *(liter)* the ship forged its way through the waves

b *(= aufteilen)* to share (out) *(unter +dat* amongst); **etw mit jdm ~** to share sth with sb

c *(= an etw teilhaben)* to share; **sie haben Freud und Leid miteinander geteilt** they shared the rough and the smooth *(Brit) or* the good and bad times; **geteilte Freude ist doppelte Freude** *(prov)* a joy shared is a joy doubled *(prov)*; **geteilter Schmerz ist halber Schmerz** *(prov)* a trouble shared is a trouble halved *(prov)*; **sie teilten unser Schicksal** *or* **Los** they shared the same fate as us; **sie teilten das Zimmer mit ihm** they shared the room with him

VR **a** *(in Gruppen)* to split up

b *(Straße, Fluss)* to fork, to divide; *(Vorhang)* to part

c **sich** *(dat)* **etw ~** to share *or* split sth; **teilt euch das!** share *or* split that between you; **sich in etw** *(acc)* **~** *(geh)* to share sth

d *(fig: = auseinandergehen)* **in diesem Punkt ~ sich die Meinungen** opinion is divided on this

VI to share; **er teilt nicht gern** he doesn't like sharing

Tei|ler ['tailɐ] M **-s, -** *(Math)* factor

Teil-: **Teil|er|folg** M partial success; **Teil|er|geb|nis** NT partial result; **einige ~se sind schon bekannt** we already know some of the results; **Teil|er|rich|tungs|ge|neh|mi|gung** F restricted planning permission; **Teil|fab|ri|kat** NT component; **Teil|fra|ge** F part (of a question); **Teil|ge|biet** NT **a** *(= Bereich)* branch **b** *(räumlich)* area; **Teil|ge|neh|mi|gung** F partial permission; **Teil|ge|ständ|nis** NT partial confession, partial admission of guilt; **Teil|ha|be** F *(liter)* participation, sharing *(an +dat* in); *(esp an Gott)* communion *(an +dat* with); **teil+ha|ben** VI *sep irreg (geh) (an +dat* in) *(= mitwirken)* to have a part, to participate; *(liter: = teilnehmen)* to share; **Teil|ha|ber** ['tailha:bɐ] M **-s, -**, **Teil|ha|be|rin** [-ərɪn] F **-, -nen** *(Comm)* partner; **Teil|ha|ber|schaft** ['tailha:bɐʃaft] F **-, -en** *(Comm)* partnership; **teil|haf|tig** ADJ *(old)* **eines großen Glücks/einer großen Ehre** *etc* **~ werden** to be blessed with great good fortune/a great honour *(Brit) or* honor *(US) etc (liter)*

-tei|lig [tailɪç] ADJ *suf (von Kleidung, Geschirr etc)* -piece; **ein zweiteiliges Kostüm** a two-piece suit; **ein dreiteiliges Fernsehspiel** a three-part TV drama

Teil|kas|ko-: **teil|kas|ko|ver|si|chert** [-fɛɐzɪçɐt] ADJ **~ sein** to be insured third party, fire and theft; **Teil|kas|ko|ver|si|che|rung** F third party, fire and theft

Teil-: **Teil|men|ge** F *(Math)* subset; **teil|möb|liert** [-møbli:ɐt] ADJ partially furnished

Teil|nah|me [-na:mə] F **-, -n** **a** *(= Anwesenheit)* attendance *(an +dat* at); *(= Beteiligung an Wettbewerb etc)* participation *(an +dat* in); **seine ~ absagen** to withdraw; **jdn zur ~ an etw** *(dat)* **aufrufen** to urge sb to take part *or* participate in sth; **~ am Straßenverkehr** *(form)* road use **b** *(= Interesse)* interest *(an +dat* in); *(= Mitgefühl)* sympathy; **jdm seine herzliche** *or* **aufrichtige ~ aussprechen** to offer sb one's heartfelt condolences

Teil|nah|me-: **teil|nah|me|be|rech|tigt** ADJ eligible; **Teil|nah|me|be|rech|ti|gung** F eligibility; **von der ~ ausgeschlossen sein** to be ineligible, not to be eligible; **Teil|nah|me|kar|te** F slip *or* voucher *(for use in a competition)*

Teil|nahms-: **teil|nahms|los** **ADJ** *(= gleichgültig)* indifferent, apathetic; *(= stumm leidend)* listless **ADV** indifferently, apathetically; *(= stumm leidend)* listlessly; **Teil|nahms|lo|sig|keit** F **-,** *no pl* indifference, apathy; **teil|nahms|voll** **ADJ** compassionate, sympathetic **ADV** compassionately, sympathetically

teil+neh|men VI *sep irreg* **a** **an etw** *(dat)* **~** *(= sich beteiligen)* to take part *or* participate in sth; *(= anwesend sein)* to attend sth; *an Wettkampf, Preisausschreiben etc* to take part in sth, to enter sth, to go in for sth; **er hat nicht teilgenommen** he did not take part *etc*; **an einem Ausflug ~** to go on an outing; **am Krieg ~** to fight in the war; **am Unterricht ~** to attend classes; **lebhaft am Unterricht ~** to take an active part in the lessons; **an einem Kurs ~** to do a course; **an den Wahlen ~** *(Partei, Kandidat)* to stand in the elections; *(Wähler)* to vote in the elections **b** *(= Anteil nehmen)* to share *(an +dat* in)

teil|neh|mend ADJ compassionate, sympathetic; **~e Beobachtung** *(Sociol)* participatory observation

Teil|neh|mer ['tailne:mɐ] M **-s, -**, **Teil|neh|me|rin** [-ərɪn] F **-, -nen** **a** *(= Beteiligter bei Kongress etc)* participant; *(= Kriegsteilnehmer)* combatant; *(bei Wettbewerb, Preisausschreiben etc)* competitor, contestant; *(= Kursteilnehmer)* student; *(bei Ausflug etc)* member of a party; **alle ~ an dem Ausflug** all those going on the outing **b** *(Telec)* subscriber; **der ~ meldet sich nicht** there is no reply

Teil|neh|mer|lis|te F list of participants; *(Sport auch)* list of entrants

Teil|neh|mer|zahl F attendance

Teil|netz NT *(Comput)* subnet

Teil|pe|rü|cke F toupee; *(für Damen)* hairpiece

teils [tails] ADV partly; **~ … ~ …** partly … partly …; *(inf: = sowohl … als auch)* both … and …; **die Demonstranten waren ~ Arbeiter, ~ Studenten** some of the demonstrators were workers and the others were students; **~ heiter, ~ wolkig** cloudy with sunny periods; **~, ~** *(als Antwort)* half and half; *(inf)* sort of *(inf)*; **wie geht es dir? – ~, ~** how are you? – so-so *(inf)*

Teil-: **Teil|schuld|ver|schrei|bung** F *(Fin)* bond (forming part of a loan issue); **Teil|staat** M region, state; **Teil|stre|cke** F stretch (of road/railway *etc*); *(bei Reise)* stage; *(bei Rennen)* leg, stage; *(bei öffentlichen Verkehrsmitteln)* (fare) stage; **Teil|strich** M secondary graduation line; **Teil|stück** NT part; *(= Teilstrecke auch)* stretch

Tei|lung ['tailʊŋ] F **-, -en** division; *(Comput: von Bildschirm, Fenster)* split

Tei|lungs-: **Tei|lungs|ar|ti|kel** M *(Gram)* partitive article; **Tei|lungs|zei|chen** NT *(Math)* division sign

Teil|ver|lust M partial loss

teil|wei|se ['tailvaizə] ADV partly; *(= manchmal)* sometimes; **nicht alle Schüler sind so faul, ~ sind sie sehr interessiert** not all the pupils are so lazy, some of them are very interested; **der Film war ~ gut** the film was good in parts; **~ bewölkt** cloudy in parts; **morgen tritt ~ eine Wetterbesserung ein** there will be a partial improvement in the weather tomorrow ADJ *attr* partial

Teil|zah|lung F hire-purchase *(Brit)*, installment plan *(US)*; *(= Rate)* instalment *(Brit)*, installment *(US)*; **auf ~** on hire-purchase *(Brit)* *or* (an) installment plan *(US)*

Teil|zah|lungs-: **Teil|zah|lungs|ge|schäft** NT hire purchase business, credit selling; *(= Transaktion)* hire purchase *or* credit transaction; **Teil|zah|lungs|kauf** M hire purchase *(Brit)*, installment plan *(US)*; **Teil|zah|lungs|preis** M hire-purchase price *(Brit)*

Teil|zeit F **~ arbeiten** to work part time

Teil|zeit-: **Teil|zeit|ar|beit** F part-time work; *(= Stelle)* part-time job; **Teil|zeit|ar|beits|platz** M part-time job; **Teil|zeit|ba|sis** F **auf ~** on a part-time basis; **auf ~ arbeiten** to work part time; **teil|zeit|be|schäf|tigt** ADJ employed part time; **Teil|zeit|be|schäf|tig|te(r)** MF *decl as adj* part-time employee; **Teil|zeit|be|schäf|ti|gung** F part-time work; *(= Stelle)* part-time job; **Teil|zeit|job** M *(inf)* part-time job; **Teil|zeit|kraft** F part-time worker; **Teil|zeit|re|ge|lung** F part-time working arrangements *pl*

Teint [tɛ̃:] M **-s, -s** complexion

T-Ei|sen ['te:-] NT t-iron, tee-iron

Tek|to|nik [tɛk'to:nɪk] F **-,** *no pl (Archit, Geol)* tectonics *pl*

tek|to|nisch [tɛk'to:nɪʃ] ADJ tectonic

Tel. *abbr von* **Telefon**

Te|le-: **Te|le|ar|beit** F telecommuting, teleworking; **Te|le|ar|bei|ter(in)** M(F) telecommuter, teleworker; **Te|le|ar|beits|platz** M job for telecommuters *or* teleworkers; **Te|le|ban|king** [-bɛŋkɪŋ] NT **-s,** *no pl* telebanking; **Te|le|brief** M telemessage, mailgram *(US)*; **Te|le|dia|log** M telephone poll; **Te|le|fax** NT *(= Kopie, Gerät)* fax; **te|le|fa|xen** VTI *insep* to fax; **Te|le|fax|ge|rät** NT fax machine; **Te|le|fax|teil|neh|mer(in)** M(F) fax subscriber

Te|le|fon [tele'fo:n, 'te:lefo:n] NT **-s, -e** (tele)phone; **am ~ (verlangt werden)** (to be wanted) on the phone; **~ haben** to be on the phone; **jdn ans ~ rufen** to get sb (to come) to the phone; **ans ~ gehen** to answer the phone

Te|le|fon- *in cpds* (tele)phone → *auch* **Fernsprech-**; **Te|le|fon|an|ruf** M (tele)phone call; **Te|le|fon|an|sa|ge** F telephone information service; **Te|le|fon|an|schluss** M telephone connection, telephone line; *(= Nebenanschluss)* extension (line); **Te|le|fon|ap|pa|rat** M telephone

Te|le|fo|nat [telefo'na:t] NT **-(e)s, -e** (tele)phone call

Te|le|fon-: **Te|le|fon|aus|kunft** F directory inquiries *pl (Brit) or* assistance *(US)*, information *(US)*; **Te|le|fon|ban|king** [-bɛŋkɪŋ] NT **-s,** *no pl* telephone banking, telebanking; **Te|le|fon|buch** NT (tele)phone book; **Te|le|fon|buch|se** F telephone socket; **Te|le|fon|draht** M telephone line; **Te|le|fon|ge|bühr** F call charge; *(= Grundgebühr)* telephone rental; **Te|le|fon|ge|spräch** NT (tele)phone call; *(= Unterhaltung)* telephone conversation; **Te|le|fon|haupt|an|schluss** M telephone line; **Te|le|fon|häus|chen** [-hɔysçən] NT *(inf)* phone box *(Brit) or* booth; **Te|le|fon|hö|rer** M (telephone) receiver

Te|le|fo|nie F **-,** *no pl* telephony

te|le|fo|nie|ren [telefo'ni:rən] *ptp* **telefoniert** VI to make a (tele)phone call; **wir haben stundenlang telefoniert** we talked *or* were on the phone for hours; **mit jdm ~** to speak to sb on the phone; **miteinander ~** to speak (to each other) on the phone; **bei jdm ~** to use sb's phone; **es wird entschieden zu viel telefoniert** the phones are definitely used too much; **ins Ausland ~** to make an international call; **am Ort ~** to make a local call; **nach Amerika/Hamburg ~** to call America/Hamburg; **er telefoniert den ganzen Tag** he is on the phone all day long

VT *(inf, Sw)* to phone, to ring (up) *(Brit)*, to call; **jdm etw ~** to call *or* phone and tell sb sth

te|le|fo|nisch [tele'fo:nɪʃ] ADJ telephonic; **~e Auskunft/Beratung** telephone information/advice service; **eine ~e Mitteilung** a (tele)phone message; **die ~e Zeitangabe** the Speaking Clock *(Brit)*, TIME *(US)* ADV *Auskunft geben* over the phone; *beraten, erpressen, bedrohen* on the phone; **jdm etw ~ mitteilen** to tell sb sth over the phone; **~ anfragen** to call to ask; **er hat sich ~ entschuldigt** he phoned to apologize; **jdn ~ belästigen** to make crank phone calls to sb; **ich bin ~ erreichbar** *or* **zu erreichen** I can be contacted by phone; **bitte melden Sie sich ~ unter …** please phone on …

Te|le|fo|nist [telefo'nɪst] M **-en, -en, Te|le|fo|nis|tin** [-'nɪstɪn] F **-, -nen** telephonist; *(in Betrieb auch)* switchboard operator

Te|le|fo|ni|tis [telefo'ni:tɪs] F **-,** *no pl (hum inf)* **die ~ haben** to be telephone-mad *(Brit inf) or* a telephone addict *(inf)*

Te|le|fon-: **Te|le|fon|kar|te** F phonecard; **Te|le|fon|ket|te** F telephone tree; **Te|le|fon|kon|fe|renz** F telephone conference, teleconference; **Te|le|fon|kun|de** M, **Te|le|fon|kun|din** F telephone customer; **Te|le|fon|lei|tung** F telephone line; **Te|le|fon|mar|ke|ting** NT telemarketing; **Te|le|fon|netz** NT telephone network; **Te|le|fon|num|mer** F (tele)phone number; **Te|le|fon|rech|nung** F (tele)phone bill; **Te|le|fon|sa|tel|lit** M telecommunications satellite; **Te|le|fon|seel|sor|ge** F ≈ Samaritans *pl (Brit)*, ≈ advice hotline *(US)*; **Te|le|fon|sex** M telephone sex; **Te|le|fon|ter|ror** M telephone harassment; *(bedrohlicher)* threatening phone calls *pl*; **Te|le|fon|über|wa|chung** F telephone tapping, wiretapping; **Te|le|fon|ver|bin|dung** F telephone line; *(zwischen Orten)* telephone link → *auch* **Verbindung c**; **Te|le|fon|ver|kauf** M telephone sales *pl*; **Te|le|fon|ver|stär|ker** M telephone amplifier; **Te|le|fon|ver|zeich|nis** NT telephone directory; **Te|le|fon|wer|bung** F telephone advertising; *(im Wahlkampf)* telephone canvassing; **Te|le|fon|zel|le** F (tele)phone box *(Brit) or* booth; **Te|le|fon|zent|ra|le** F (telephone) switchboard

te|le|gen [tele'ge:n] ADJ telegenic

Te|le|graf [tele'gra:f] M **-en, -en** telegraph

Te|le|gra|fen-: **Te|le|gra|fen|amt** NT (telegraph) office; **Te|le|gra|fen|ap|pa|rat** M telegraph; **Te|le|gra|fen|bü|ro** NT *(dated)* news agency; **Te|le|gra|fen|mast** M telegraph pole

Te|le|gra|fie [telegra'fi:] F **-,** *no pl* telegraphy

te|le|gra|fie|ren [telegra'fi:rən] *ptp* **telegrafiert** VTI to send a telegram, to cable, to wire

te|le|gra|fisch [tele'gra:fɪʃ] ADJ telegraphic ADV **jdm ~ Geld überweisen** to wire sb money

Te|le|gramm [tele'gram] NT *pl* **-gramme** telegram; *(= Auslandstelegramm auch)* cable

Te|le|gramm-: **Te|le|gramm|ad|res|se** F telegraphic address; **Te|le|gramm|bo|te** M, **Te|le|gramm|bo|tin** F telegram boy/girl; **Te|le|gramm|for|mu|lar** NT telegram form; **Te|le|gramm|stil** M staccato *or* telegram style, telegraphese

Te|le|graph *etc* M = **Telegraf** *etc*

Te|le|gra|phie [telegra'fi:] *etc* = **Telegrafie** *etc*

Te|le-: **Te|le|ki|ne|se** [teleki'ne:zə] F **-,** *no pl* telekinesis; **te|le|ki|ne|tisch** [teleki'ne:tɪʃ] ADJ telekinetic ADV *bewegen* telekinetically, through telekinesis; **Te|le|kol|leg** ['te:lə-] NT ≈ Open University *(esp Brit)*, ≈ Distance Education *(US)*

Te|le|kom ['te:lekɔm] F **-,** *no pl* **die ~** *German telecommunications service*

Te|le-: **Te|le|kom|mu|ni|ka|ti|on** F telecommunications *pl or (als Fachgebiet) sing*; **Te|le|kom|mu|ni|ka|ti|ons|ser|vice** M telecommunications service; **Te|le|kon|fe|renz** F teleconference; **Te|le|ko|pie** F fax; **Te|le|ko|pie|rer** M fax machine

Te|le|mark ['te:ləmark] M **-s, -s** *(Ski)* telemark

Te|le|ma|tik F **-,** *no pl (= Wissenschaft)* telematics *sing*

Te|le|me|di|zin F telemedicine

Te|le|no|ve|la ['te:lənovɛla] F **-, s** *(Philos) (TV)* telenovela

Te|le|ob|jek|tiv ['te:lə-] NT *(Phot)* telephoto lens

Te|leo|lo|gie [teleolo'gi:] F **-,** *no pl (Philos)* teleology

te|leo|lo|gisch [teleo'lo:gɪʃ] ADJ *(Philos)* teleological

Te|le|or|dern ['te:lə-] NT **-s,** *no pl* teleordering

Te|le|path [tele'pa:t] M **-en, -en, Te|le|pa|thin** [-'pa:tɪn] F **-, -nen** telepathist

Te|le|pa|thie [telepa'ti:] F **-,** *no pl* telepathy

te|le|pa|thisch [tele'pa:tɪʃ] ADJ telepathic ADV telepathically

Te|le|phon *etc* NT = **Telefon** *etc*

Te|le|promp|ter® ['te:leprɔmptɐ] M **-s, -** ≈ Autocue® *(Brit)*, Teleprompter® *(US)*

Te|le|shop|ping ['te:lə-] NT teleshopping

Te|le|skop [tele'sko:p] NT **-s, -e** telescope

Te|le|skop|au|ge NT telescope eye

te|le|sko|pisch [tele'sko:pɪʃ] ADJ telescopic

Te|le-: **Te|le|spiel** ['te:lə-] NT video game; **Te|le|tex** ['te:lətɛks] NT **-,** *no pl* teletex; **Te|le|vi|si|on** [televi'zio:n] F, *no pl* = **Fernsehen**

Te|lex ['te:lɛks] NT **-, -e** telex

Te|lex|an|schluss M telex link

te|le|xen ['te:lɛksn] VTI to telex

Tel|ler ['tɛlɐ] M **-s, -** **a** plate; **ein ~ Suppe** a plate of soup **b** *(sl: = Plattenteller)* turntable **c** *(Ski)* basket

Tel|ler-: **Tel|ler|ei|sen** NT *(Hunt)* steel trap; **Tel|ler|fleisch** NT *(Cook)* boiled beef/pork (pieces); **tel|ler|för|mig** ADJ plate-shaped; **Tel|ler|ge|richt** NT *(Cook)* one-course meal; **Tel|ler|mi|ne** F *(Mil)* flat antitank mine; **Tel|ler|rand** M rim *or* edge of a/the plate; **nicht zum Blick über den ~ fähig sein** *(fig)* to be unable to see beyond the end of one's own nose; **Tel|ler|wär|mer** [-vɛrmɐ] M **-s, -** plate warmer; **Tel|ler|wä|scher(in)** M(F) dishwasher; **Tel|ler|wä|scher|kar|ri|e|re** F *(inf)* rags-to-riches career

Tel|lur [tɛ'lu:ɐ] NT **-s,** *no pl (abbr* **Te**) tellurium

Tel|net ['tɛlnɛt] NT **-,** *no pl (Comput)* telnet

Tem|pel ['tɛmpl] M **-s, -** temple *(auch fig)*

Tem|pel-: **Tem|pel|bau** M *pl* **-bauten** *(Gebäude)* temple; **Tem|pel|herr** M, **Tem|pel|rit|ter** M *(Hist)* (Knight) Templar; **Tem|pel|schän|dung** F desecration of a temple; **Tem|pel|tanz** M temple dance; **Tem|pel|tän|ze|rin** F temple dancer

Tem|pe|ra ['tɛmpera] F **-, -s** tempera (colour *(Brit) or* color *(US)*)

Tem|pe|ra-: **Tem|pe|ra|far|be** F tempera (colour *(Brit) or* color *(US)*); **Tem|pe|ra|ma|le|rei** F *(= Maltechnik)* painting in tempera; *(= Gemälde)* tempera painting(s *pl*)

Tem|pe|ra|ment [tɛmpəra'mɛnt] NT **-(e)s, -e** **a** *(= Wesensart)* temperament; **die vier ~e** *(old)* the four humours *(Brit old) or* humors *(US old)*; **ein hitziges ~ haben** to be hot-tempered **b** *no pl (= Lebhaftigkeit)* vitality, vivacity; **viel/kein ~ haben** to be very/not to be vivacious *or* lively; **sein ~ ist mit ihm durchgegangen** he lost his temper; **sie konnte ihr ~ nicht mehr zügeln** she could control herself *or* her temper no longer

Tem|pe|ra|ment-: **tem|pe|ra|ment|los** ADJ lifeless, spiritless ADV listlessly; **Tem|pe|ra|ment|lo|sig|keit** F **-,** *no pl* lifelessness

Tem|pe|ra|ments|aus|bruch M temperamental fit *or* outburst

tem|pe|ra|ment|voll ADJ vivacious, lively; *Aufführung auch* spirited; *Auto, Fahrer* nippy *(Brit* *inf*), speedy (*US inf*) ADV exuberantly; **ein Lied ~ vortragen** to give a spirited rendering of a song

Tem|pe|ra|tur [tɛmpəra'tuːɐ] F -, -en temperature; **erhöhte ~ haben** to have a *or* be running a temperature; **die ~en sind angestiegen/gesunken** the temperature has risen/fallen; **bei diesen/solchen ~en** in these/such temperatures; **bei ~en von bis zu 42 Grad Celsius** in temperatures of up to 42°C

Tem|pe|ra|tur-: **Tem|pe|ra|tur|ab|fall** M drop *or* fall in temperature; **Tem|pe|ra|tur|an|stieg** M rise in temperature; **tem|pe|ra|tur|be|stän|dig** ADJ temperature-resistant; **Tem|pe|ra|tur|reg|ler** M thermostat; **Tem|pe|ra|tur|rück|gang** M fall in temperature; **Tem|pe|ra|tur|schwan|kung** F variation in temperature; **Tem|pe|ra|tur|ska|la** F temperature scale; **Tem|pe|ra|tur|sturz** M sudden drop *or* fall in temperature

Tem|pe|renz|ler [tɛmpə'rɛntslɐ] M -s, -, **Tem|pe|renz|le|rin** [-ərɪn] F -, -nen member of a/the temperance league

tem|pe|rie|ren [tɛmpə'riːrən] *ptp* **temperiert** VT **etw ~** (*= auf die richtige Temperatur bringen*) to make sth the right temperature; (*= anwärmen*) to warm sth up; **der Raum ist angenehm temperiert** the room is at a pleasant temperature, the room is pleasantly warm; **Rotwein leicht temperiert trinken** to drink red wine at room temperature

Temp|ler ['tɛmplɐ] M -s, - (Knight) Templar

Temp|ler|or|den M Order of the Knights Templar

Tem|po ['tɛmpo] NT -s, -s **a** (*= Geschwindigkeit*) speed; (*= Arbeitstempo, Schritttempo*) pace, speed; **~!** (*inf*) hurry up!; **bei jdm ~ (dahinter** *or* **hinter etw** *acc*) **machen** (*inf*) to make sb get a move on (with sth) (*inf*); **nun mach mal ein bisschen ~!** (*inf*) get a move on! (*inf*); **~ 100** speed limit (of) 100 km/h; **mit vollem/hohem ~** at full/a high speed; **im ~ zulegen** to speed up; **im ~ nachlassen** to slow down; **aufs ~ drücken** (*inf*) to step on the gas (*inf*) **b** (*Mus*) *pl* **Tempi** ['tɛmpi] tempo; **das ~ halten** to keep time; **das ~ angeben** to set the tempo; (*fig*) to set the pace **c** ~® (*inf*: *= Taschentuch*) paper handkerchief, tissue, ≈ Kleenex®

Tem|po-30-Zo|ne [tɛmpo'draisɪç-] F ≈ 20 mph zone

Tem|po|li|mit NT speed limit

Tem|po|mat [tɛmpo'maːt] M -en, -en (*Aut*) cruise control

Tem|po|ra *pl von* **Tempus**

tem|po|ral [tɛmpo'raːl] ADJ (*Gram*) temporal

Tem|po|ral|satz M temporal clause

tem|po|rär [tɛmpo'rɛːɐ] (*geh*) ADJ temporary (*auch Datei*) ADV temporarily

Tem|po-: **Tem|po|sün|der(in)** M(F) person caught for speeding; **Tem|po|ta|schen|tuch®** NT paper handkerchief, tissue, ≈ Kleenex®; **Tem|po|über|schrei|tung** [-lyːbɐʃraitʊŋ] F -, -en speeding

Tem|pus ['tɛmpʊs] NT -, **Tempora** ['tɛmpora] (*Gram*) tense

Ten|denz [tɛn'dɛnts] F -, -en trend (*auch St Ex*); (*= Neigung*) tendency; (*= Absicht*) intention; (*no pl*: *= Parteilichkeit*) bias, slant; **die ~ haben, zu ...** to tend to ..., to have a tendency to ...; **die ~ zeigen, zu ...** to show a tendency to ...; **er hat nationalistische ~en** he has nationalist leanings; **vier Millionen Menschen sind arbeitslos, ~ steigend** the number of people out of work is four million and rising

ten|den|zi|ell [tɛndɛn'tsiɛl] ADJ **eine ~e Veränderung** a change in direction ADV **~ ist Ruritanien ein faschistischer Staat** Ruritania is a country which shows fascist tendencies; **die Ziele der beiden Parteien unterscheiden sich ~ kaum voneinander** the aims of the two parties are broadly similar (in direction)

ten|den|zi|ös [tɛndɛn'tsiøːs] ADJ tendentious ADV tendentiously; **etw ist ~ gefärbt** sth has a tendentious cast to it

Ten|denz-: **Ten|denz|stück** NT tendentious play; **Ten|denz|wen|de** F change of direction; (*= Wendepunkt*) turning point

Ten|der ['tɛndɐ] M -s, - (*Naut, Rail*) tender

ten|die|ren [tɛn'diːrən] *ptp* **tendiert** VI **a** **dazu ~, etw zu tun** (*= neigen*) to tend to do sth; (*= beabsichtigen*) to be moving toward(s) doing sth; **zum Kommunismus/Katholizismus ~** to have leanings toward(s) communism/Catholicism, to have communist/Catholic leanings *or* tendencies; **zu Erkältungen/Wutausbrüchen ~** to tend to get colds/fits of anger; **seine Begabung tendiert mehr ins Künstlerische** his talents tend more toward(s) the artistic **b** (*Fin, St Ex*) to tend; **freundlich/fester/schwächer ~** to show a favourable (*Brit*) *or* favorable (*US*)/stronger/weaker tendency

Te|ne|rif|fa [tene'rɪfa] NT -s Tenerife

Ten|ne ['tɛnə] F -, -n, (*Sw*) **Tenn** [tɛn] M -s, -e threshing floor

Ten|nis ['tɛnɪs] NT -, *no pl* tennis

Ten|nis- *in cpds* tennis; **Ten|nis|arm** M tennis elbow; **Ten|nis|ball** M tennis ball; **Ten|nis|hal|le** F indoor tennis centre (*Brit*) *or* center (*US*); **Ten|nis|platz** M tennis court; **Ten|nis|schlä|ger** M tennis racquet (*esp Brit*) *or* racket; **Ten|nis|schuh** M tennis shoe; **Ten|nis|spie|ler(in)** M(F) tennis player; **Ten|nis|zir|kus** M tennis circus

Ten|no ['tɛno] M -s, -s Emperor of Japan

Te|nor ['teːnoːɐ] M -s, *no pl* tenor

Te|nor [te'noːɐ] M -s, =e [-'nøːrə] (*Mus*) tenor

Te|no|rist [teno'rɪst] M -en, -en tenor (singer)

Te|nor|schlüs|sel [te'noːɐ-] M tenor clef

Ten|sid [tɛn'ziːt] NT -(e)s, -e [-də] (*Chem*) surfactant

Ten|ta|kel [tɛn'takl] M OR NT -s, - tentacle

Te|nu|is ['teːnuɪs] F -, **Tenues** ['teːnueːs] (*Phon*) tenuis

Tep|pich ['tɛpɪç] M -s, -e **a** carpet (*auch fig*); (*inf*: *= Brücke auch*) rug; (*= Gobelin*) tapestry; (*inf*: *= Wandbehang*) wall hanging; (*= Ölteppich*) (oil) slick; **etw unter den ~ kehren** *or* **fegen** (*lit, fig*) to sweep sth under the carpet; **bleib auf dem ~!** (*inf*) be realistic!, be reasonable!; **den roten ~ ausrollen** to bring out the red carpet **b** (*dial inf*: *= Decke*) blanket; (*kleiner*) rug

Tep|pich-: **Tep|pich|bo|den** M carpet(ing); **das Zimmer ist mit ~ ausgelegt** the room has wall-to-wall carpeting *or* a fitted carpet; **Tep|pich|flie|se** F carpet tile; **Tep|pich|keh|rer** [-keːrɐ] M -s, -, **Tep|pich|kehr|ma|schi|ne** F carpet-sweeper; **Tep|pich|klop|fer** M carpet-beater; **Tep|pich|schnee** M carpet foam; **Tep|pich|stan|ge** F *frame for hanging carpets over for beating*

Ter|bi|um ['tɛrbiʊm] NT -s, *no pl* (*abbr* **Tb**) terbium

Term [tɛrm] M -s, -e (*Math, Phys, Ling*) term

Ter|min [tɛr'miːn] M -s, -e date; (*für Fertigstellung*) deadline; (*Comm*: *= Liefertag*) delivery date; (*bei Arzt, Besprechung etc*) appointment; (*Sport*) fixture; (*Jur*: *= Verhandlung*) hearing; **der letzte ~** the deadline, the last date; (*bei Bewerbung etc*) the closing date; **sich** (*dat*) **einen ~ geben lassen** to make an appointment; **sich** (*dat*) **einen ~ in der Autowerkstatt geben lassen** to book one's car/van *etc* into the garage; **schon einen anderen ~ haben** to have a prior engagement

Ter|min|ab|spra|che F (*= Frist*) negotiation of a/the deadline, deadline negotiation(s *pl*); (*= Zeitpunkt*) agreeing (on) a date *or* time

Ter|mi|nal ['tøːɐminəl, 'tœr-] NT OR M -s, -s (*Aviat etc*) terminal

Ter|mi|nal NT -s, -s (*Comput*) terminal

Ter|min-: **Ter|min|bör|se** F futures market, forward exchange (*Brit*); **Ter|min|druck** M time pressure, deadline pressure; **unter ~ stehen** (*= Zeitdruck haben*) to have a very tight schedule; (*= Termin einhalten müssen*) to have to meet a (strict) deadline; **Ter|min|ein|la|ge** F (*Fin*) time deposit; **Ter|min|geld** NT fixed-term deposit; **ter|min|ge|mäß, ter|min|ge|recht** ADJ, ADV on schedule, according to schedule; **Ter|min|ge|schäft** NT deal on the forward (*Brit*) *or* futures market; **~e** futures; **Ter|min|grund** M **aus Termingründen** because of problems with one's schedule

Ter|mi|ni *pl von* **Terminus**

Ter|min|ka|len|der M (appointments *or* engagements) diary

Ter|min|kon|trakt [-kɔntrakt] M -(e)s, -e (*St Ex*) futures contract

ter|min|lich [tɛr'miːnlɪç] ADJ **aus ~en Gründen absagen** to cancel because of problems with one's schedule; **~e Verpflichtungen** commitments; **ich habe schon zu viele ~e Verpflichtungen** I have too many prior commitments ADV **etw ~ einrichten** to fit sth in (to one's schedule); **~ in Anspruch genommen sein** to have a full schedule; **diese Woche bin ich ~ zu** *or* **voll** (*inf*) this week I'm booked up; **das ist ~ zu schaffen** the scheduling is no problem

Ter|min|markt M (*St Ex*) forward (*Brit*) *or* futures market

ter|min|mä|ßig ADJ ADV = **terminlich**

Ter|mi|no|lo|gie [tɛrminolo'giː] F -, -n [-'giːən] terminology

ter|mi|no|lo|gisch [tɛrmino'loːgɪʃ] ADJ terminological ADV terminologically; **~ arbeiten** to work in terminology; **sich ~ abstimmen** to agree on the terminology one is using; **das ist ~ nicht sauber** the terms here are not used correctly

Ter|min-: **Ter|min|pla|nung** F time scheduling; **Ter|min|schwie|rig|kei|ten** PL scheduling difficulties *pl*

Ter|min|treue F adherence to deadlines

Ter|mi|nus ['tɛrminʊs] M -, **Termini** [-ni] term; **~ technicus** technical term

Ter|min-: **Ter|min|ver|ein|ba|rung** F agreement on a deadline/on deadlines, deadline agreement; (*für Zeitpunkt*) agreement on a time/date; (*für Termin*) agreed deadline, agreed time/date; **Ter|min|ver|schie|bung** F postponement

Ter|mi|te [tɛr'miːtə] F -, -n termite, white ant

Ter|mi|ten-: **Ter|mi|ten|hü|gel** M termites' nest, termitarium (*form*); **Ter|mi|ten|staat** M colony of termites

Ter|pe|ne [tɛr'peːnə] PL terpenes *pl*

Ter|pen|tin [tɛrpɛn'tiːn] NT OR (AUS) M -s, -e turpentine; (*inf*: *= Terpentinöl*) turps (*inf*)

Ter|pen|tin|öl NT oil of turpentine, turps *sing* (*inf*)

Terr. (*in Annoncen*) *abbr von* **Terrasse**

Ter|rain [tɛ'rɛ̃ː] NT -s, -s land, terrain; (*fig*) territory; **das ~ sondieren** (*Mil*) to reconnoitre (*Brit*) *or* reconnoiter (*US*) the terrain; (*fig*) to see how the land lies; **sich auf neuem ~ bewegen** to be exploring new ground; **sich auf unsicheres ~ begeben** to get onto shaky ground; **verlorenes ~ (wieder)gutmachen** *or* **zurückerobern** (*lit, fig*) to regain lost ground

Ter|ra|kot|ta [tɛra'kɔta] F -, **Terrakotten** [-tn] terracotta

Ter|ra|ri|um [tɛ'raːriʊm] NT -s, **Terrarien** [-riən] terrarium

Ter|ras|se [tɛ'rasə] F -, -n **a** (*Geog*) terrace **b** (*= Veranda*) terrace, patio; (*= Dachterrasse*) roof garden

Ter|ras|sen-: **ter|ras|sen|ar|tig, ter|ras|sen|för|mig** ADJ terraced ADV in terraces; **Ter|ras|sen|gar|ten** M terraced garden; **Ter|ras|sen|haus** NT *house built on a terraced slope* (*modern*) split-level house

Ter|raz|zo [tɛ'ratso] M -s, **Terrazzi** [-tsi] terrazzo

ter|rest|risch [tɛ'rɛstrɪʃ] ADJ terrestrial

Ter|rier ['tɛriɐ] M -s, - terrier

Ter|ri|ne [tɛ'riːnə] F -, -n tureen

ter|ri|to|ri|al [tɛrito'riaːl] ADJ territorial

Ter|ri|to|ri|al-: **Ter|ri|to|ri|al|ar|mee** F territorial army; **Ter|ri|to|ri|al|ge|wäs|ser** PL territorial waters *pl*; **Ter|ri|to|ri|al|ho|heit** F territorial sovereignty

Ter|ri|to|ri|um [terito'ri̯ʊm] NT **-s, Territorien** [-ri̯ən] territory

Ter|ror ['tɛroːɐ] M **-s,** *no pl* terror; *(= Terrorismus)* terrorism; *(= Terrorherrschaft)* reign of terror; *(= brutale Einschüchterung)* intimidation; *(= Belästigung)* menace; **die Stadt steht unter dem ~ der Mafia** the town is being terrorized by the Mafia; **blutiger ~** terrorism and bloodshed; **organisierter ~** organized terrorism/intimidation; **~ machen** *(inf)* to raise hell *(inf)*

Ter|ror-: **Ter|ror|akt** M act of terrorism, terrorist act; **Ter|ror|an|griff** M terrorist raid; **Ter|ror|an|schlag** M terrorist attack; **Ter|ror|be|dro|hung** F terrorist threat; **Ter|ror|be|kämp|fung** F fighting terrorism, battle against terrorism; **Ter|ror|ge|fahr** F terrorist threat; **Ter|ror|herr|schaft** F reign of terror

ter|ro|ri|sie|ren [terori'ziːrən] *ptp* **terrorisiert** VT to terrorize; *Untergebene etc auch* to intimidate

Ter|ro|ris|mus [tero'rɪsmʊs] M **-,** *no pl* terrorism

Ter|ro|ris|mus-: **Ter|ro|ris|mus|be|kämp|fung** F counterterrorism; **Ter|ro|ris|mus|ex|per|te** M, **Ter|ro|ris|mus|ex|per|tin** F expert on terrorism

Ter|ro|rist [tero'rɪst] M **-en, -en, Ter|ro|ris|tin** [-'rɪstɪn] F **-, -nen** terrorist

ter|ro|ris|tisch [tero'rɪstɪʃ] ADJ terrorist *attr*; **eine ~e Gruppierung** a terrorist group

Ter|ror-: **Ter|ror|jus|tiz** F brutal, intimidatory justice; **Ter|ror|or|ga|ni|sa|ti|on** F terrorist organization

Ter|tia ['tɛrtsi̯a] F **-, Tertien** [-tsi̯ən] **a** *(dated Sch) (= Unter-/Obertertia) fourth/fifth year of German secondary school* **b** *no pl (Typ)* 16 point type

Ter|ti|a|ner [tɛrtsi'aːnɐ] M **-s, -, Ter|ti|a|ne|rin** [-ərɪn] F **-, -nen** → **Tertia a** *(dated Sch) pupil in fourth/fifth year of German secondary school*

ter|ti|är [tɛr'tsi̯ɛːɐ] ADJ tertiary

Ter|ti|är [tɛr'tsi̯ɛːɐ] NT **-s,** *no pl (Geol)* tertiary period

Ter|ti|är|be|reich M tertiary education

Ter|ti|en *pl von* **Tertia**

Terz [tɛrts] F **-, -en** *(Mus)* third; *(Fechten)* tierce; **große/kleine ~** *(Mus)* major/minor third

Ter|zett [tɛr'tsɛt] NT **-(e)s, -e** *(Mus)* trio

Ter|zi|ne [tɛr'tsiːnə] F **-, -n** *(Poet)* tercet

Te|sa|film® ['teːza-] M ≈ Sellotape® *(Brit)*, ≈ Scotch tape® *(esp US)*

Tes|sin [tɛ'siːn] NT **-s das ~** Ticino

Test [tɛst] M **-(e)s, -s** *or* **-e** test

Tes|ta|ment [tɛsta'mɛnt] NT **-(e)s, -e** **a** *(Jur)* will; *(fig)* legacy; **das ~ eröffnen** to read the will; **sein ~ machen** to make one's will; **du kannst dein ~ machen!** *(inf)* you'd better make your will! *(inf)*; **ohne Hinterlassung eines ~s** intestate **b** *(Bibl)* Testament; **Altes/Neues ~** Old/New Testament

tes|ta|men|ta|risch [tɛstamɛn'taːrɪʃ] ADJ testamentary; **eine ~e Verfügung** an instruction in the will ADV in one's will; **etw ~ festlegen** *or* **verfügen** to write sth in one's will; **~ festgelegt** (written) in the will; **jdm etw ~ vermachen** to will sth to sb

Tes|ta|ments-: **Tes|ta|ments|er|öff|nung** F reading of the will; **Tes|ta|ments|voll|stre|cker(in)** M(F) executor; *(Frau auch)* executrix

Test|an|ruf M *(Telec)* mystery call

Test|an|ru|fer(in) M(F) *(Telec)* mystery caller

Tes|tat [tɛs'taːt] NT **-(e)s, -e** *(Univ)* certificate *(awarded for successful completion of a course)*

Tes|ta|tor [tɛs'taːtoːɐ] M **-s, Testatoren** [-'toːrən], **Tes|ta|to|rin** [-'toːrɪn] F **-, -nen** *(= Erblasser)* testator

Test-: **Test|be|su|cher(in)** M(F) mystery visitor; **Test|be|trieb** M trial (operation); *(Comput)* test mode; **Test|bild** NT *(TV)* test card; **Test|bo|gen** M test paper

tes|ten ['tɛstn] VT to test *(auf +acc* for); **jdn auf seine Intelligenz ~** to test sb's intelligence

Tes|ter ['tɛstɐ] M **-s, -, Tes|te|rin** [-ərɪn] F **-, -nen** tester

Test-: **Test|er|geb|nis** NT result(s *pl*) of a/the test; **Test|fah|rer(in)** M(F) test driver; **Test|fall** M test case; **Test|fra|ge** F test question

tes|tie|ren [tɛs'tiːrən] *ptp* **testiert** VT **a** *(= bescheinigen)* to certify; **sich** *(dat)* **etw ~ lassen** to get oneself a certificate of sth; **jdm etw ~** to certify sth for sb **b** *(Jur: = letztwillig verfügen)* to will

Tes|ti|kel [tɛs'tiːkl] M **-s, -** testicle

Test-: **Test|kauf** M mystery shopping; **Test|käu|fer(in)** M(F) mystery shopper; **Test|lauf** M trial (run); *(Comm)* pre-launch trial

Tes|tos|te|ron [tɛstoste'roːn] NT **-s** testosterone

Test-: **Test|per|son** F subject (of a test); **Test|pi|lot(in)** M(F) test pilot; **Test|pro|gramm** NT *(Comput)* test program; **Test|rei|he** F, **Test|se|rie** F series of tests; **Test|stopp** M test ban; **Test|stopp|ab|kom|men** NT test ban treaty *or* agreement; **Test|ver|fah|ren** NT method of testing; **Test|wahl** F *(inf)* test election; **Kommunalwahlen kann man häufig als ~en ansehen** local elections can often be regarded as a test of electoral feeling

Te|ta|nus ['teːtanʊs, 'tɛtanʊs] M **-,** *no pl* tetanus

Te|te ['teːtə, 'tɛːtə] F **-, -n** *(Mil)* head of a column

Tête-à-tête [tɛːta'tɛːt] NT **-, -s, Tete-a-tete** NT **-, -s** **a** *(hum: = Schäferstündchen)* **ein ~** a bit of hanky-panky *(hum inf)* **b** tête-à-tête *(esp Brit)*, private conversation between two people

Tet|ra-: **Tet|ra|eder** [tetra'leːdɐ] NT **-s, -** *(Math)* tetrahedron; **Tet|ra|gon** [tetra'goːn] NT **-s, -e** *(Math)* tetragon; **Tet|ra|lo|gie** [tetralo'giː] F **-, -n** [-'giːən] tetralogy

teu|er ['tɔyɐ] ADJ expensive, dear *usu pred*; *(fig)* dear; **etw für teures Geld kaufen** to pay good money for sth; **teurer werden** to go up (in price); **Brot wieder teurer!** bread up again; **in Tokio ist das Leben ~** life is expensive in Tokyo, Tokyo is expensive; **~ aber gut** expensive but well worth the money; **das ist mir (lieb und) ~** *(liter)* that's very dear *or* precious to me; **mein Teurer** *or* **Teuerster, meine Teure** *or* **Teuerste** *(old, hum)* my dearest; *(von Mann zu Mann)* my dearest friend → **Vergnügen, Spaß, Pflaster b**

ADV *anbieten, speisen* expensively; **etw ~ kaufen/verkaufen** to buy/sell sth for *or* at a high price; **etw zu ~ kaufen** to pay too much for sth; **in Tokio lebt man ~** life is expensive in Tokyo; **das wird ihn ~ zu stehen kommen** *(fig)* that will cost him dear; **einen Sieg ~ erkaufen** to pay dearly for victory; **~ erkauft** dearly bought; **etw ~ bezahlen** *(fig)* to pay a high price for sth; **sich** *(dat)* **etw ~ bezahlen lassen** to charge a high price for sth

Teu|e|rung ['tɔyərʊŋ] F **-, -en** rise in prices, rising prices *pl*

Teu|e|rungs-: **Teu|e|rungs|aus|gleich** M adjustment for inflation; **Teu|e|rungs|ra|te** F rate of price increases; **Teu|e|rungs|wel|le** F wave *or* round of price increases; **Teu|e|rungs|zu|la|ge** F cost of living bonus *or* supplement; **Teu|e|rungs|zu|schlag** M surcharge

Teu|fel ['tɔyfl] M **-s, -** **a** *(lit, fig)* devil; **den ~ durch Beelzebub austreiben** to replace one evil with another; **den ~ im Leib haben** to be possessed by the devil; **der ~ der Eifersucht** *etc* a jealous *etc* devil; **ein ~ von einem Mann/einer Frau** *(old)* a devil of a man/woman

b *(inf)* **~ (noch mal** *or* **aber auch)!** damn it (all)! *(inf)*, confound it! *(inf)*; **~ auch** *(bewundernd)* well I'll be damned *(inf) or* blowed *(Brit inf)*, I'll be a sun-of-a-gun *(US inf)*; **scher dich** *or* **geh zum ~, hol dich der ~!** go to blazes *(inf) or* hell!; **der ~ soll ihn/es holen!, hol ihn/es der ~** damn *(inf) or* blast *(inf)* him/it!, to hell with him/it *(inf)*; **jdn zum ~ wünschen** to wish sb in hell; **jdn zum ~ jagen** *or* **schicken** to send sb packing *(inf)*; **zum ~!** damn! *(inf)*, blast! *(inf)*; **wer zum ~?** who the devil *(inf) or* the hell?; **zum ~ mit dem Ding!** damn *or* blast the thing! *(inf)*, to hell with the thing! *(inf)*; **zum ~ sein** *(= kaputt sein)* to have had it *(inf)*; *(= verloren sein)* to have gone west *(Brit inf)*, to have gone to the devil *(inf)*; **den ~ an die Wand malen** *(= schwarzmalen)* to think *or* imagine the worst; *(= Unheil heraufbeschwören)* to tempt fate *or* providence; **wenn man vom ~ spricht(, dann ist er nicht weit)** *(prov)* talk *(Brit) or* speak of the devil (and he's sure to appear) *(inf)*; **das müsste te schon mit dem ~ zugehen** that really would be a stroke of bad luck; **ihn muss der ~ geritten haben** he must have had a devil in him; **welcher ~ reitet ihn denn?** what's got into him?; **dann kommst** *or* **gerätst du in ~s Küche** then you'll be in a hell of a mess *(inf)*; **wie der ~** like hell *(inf)*, like the devil *(inf)*; **er ist hinter dem Geld her wie der ~ hinter der armen Seele** he's money mad *(Brit inf)*, he loves money like the devil loves souls *(US)*; **jdn/etw fürchten wie der ~ das Weihwasser** to be absolutely terrified of sb/sth; **jdn/etw meiden wie der ~ das Weihwasser** to avoid sb/sth like the plague; **auf ~ komm raus** like crazy *(inf)*; **ich mache das auf ~ komm raus** I'll do that come hell or high water; **da ist der ~ los** all hell's been let loose *(inf)*; **bist du des ~s?** *(old)* have you taken leave of your senses?; **sich den ~ um etw kümmern** *or* **scheren** not to give a damn *(inf) or* a fig *(Brit inf)* about sth; **den ~ werde ich (tun)!** I'll be damned if I will! *(inf)*, like hell I will! *(inf)*; **der ~ steckt im Detail** the devil is *or* lies in the detail

Teu|fe|lei [tɔyfə'lai] F **-, -en** *(inf)* devilish trick; *(= Streich)* piece of devilry

Teu|fels-: **Teu|fels|aus|trei|bung** F casting out *no pl* of devils, exorcism; **Teu|fels|be|schwö|rung** F exorcism; *(Anrufen)* invocation of the devil; **Teu|fels|bra|ten** M *(old inf)* devil; **Teu|fels|brut** F *(old)* devil's *or* Satan's brood; **Teu|fels|kerl** M *(inf)* daredevil; **Teu|fels|kir|sche** F *(Bot)* deadly nightshade, belladonna; **Teu|fels|kreis** M vicious circle; **Teu|fels|kult** M devil worship; **Teu|fels|mes|se** F black mass; **Teu|fels|weib** NT *(dated)* devil of a woman

teuf|lisch ['tɔyflɪʃ] ADJ fiendish, devilish, diabolical ADV fiendishly, devilishly, diabolically

Teu|to|ne [tɔy'toːnə] M **-n, -n, Teu|to|nin** [-'toːnɪn] F **-, -nen** Teuton

teu|to|nisch [tɔy'toːnɪʃ] ADJ Teutonic

Text [tɛkst] M **-(e)s, -e** text; *(einer Urkunde auch, eines Gesetzes)* wording; *(von Lied)* words *pl*; *(von Schlager)* lyrics *pl*; *(von Film, Hörspiel, Rede etc)* script; *(Mus: = Operntext)* libretto; *(unter Bild)* caption; *(auf Plakat)* words *pl*; **weiter im ~** *(inf)* (let's) get on with it; **ein Telegramm mit folgendem ~ ...** a telegram which said *or* read ...

Text-: **Text|auf|ga|be** F problem; **Text|aus|rich|tung** F *(Comput, Typ)* text alignment, justification; **Text|bau|stein** M *(Comput)* template; **Text|buch** NT script; *(für Lieder)* songbook; **Text|dich|ter(in)** M(F) *(von Liedern)* songwriter; *(bei Oper)* librettist; **Text|edi|tor** M *(Comput)* text editor

tex|ten ['tɛkstn] VT to write VI → **Texter** to write songs/copy

Tex|ter ['tɛkstɐ] M **-s, -, Tex|te|rin** [-ərɪn] F **-, -nen** *(für Schlager)* songwriter; *(für Werbesprüche)* copywriter

Text|er|fas|ser [-lɛɐfasɐ] M **-s, -, Text|er|fas|se|rin** [-ərɪn] F **-, -nen** keyboarder

Text|feld NT *(Comput)* text box

Tex|til- *in cpds* textile; **Tex|til|ar|bei|ter(in)** M(F) textile worker; **Tex|til|bran|che** F textile trade; **Tex|til|fab|rik** F textile factory; *(für Textilien aus Naturfasern auch)* textile mill

Tex|ti|li|en [tɛks'tiːli̯ən] PL *linen, clothing, fabrics etc (Ind)* textiles *pl*

Tex|til-: **Tex|til|in|dust|rie** F textile industry; **Tex|til|wa|ren** PL textiles *pl*

Text-: **Text|kri|tik** F textual criticism; **Text|lin|gu|is|tik** F *(Ling)* text linguistics *sing*; **Text|mo|dus** M *(Comput)* text mode; **Text|rah|men** M *(Comput)* text frame; **Text|se|man|tik** F *(Ling)* textual semantics *sing*; **Text|spei|cher** M *(Comput)* memory; **Text|stel|le** F passage; **Text|sys|tem** NT *(Comput)* word processor, word processing system; **Text|um|bruch** M *(Comput: in Textverarbeitung)* wordwrap

Tex|tur [tɛks'tuːɐ] F **-, -en** texture

Text|ver|ar|bei|tung F word processing

Text|ver|ar|bei|tungs-: **Text|ver|ar|bei|tungs|an|la|ge** F word processor, word processing system; **Text|ver|ar|bei|tungs|pro|gramm** NT word processor, word processing program; **Text|ver|ar|bei|tungs|sys|tem** NT word processor, word processing system

Te|zett ['teːtsɛt, te'tsɛt] NT *(inf)* **jdn/etw bis ins** *or* **zum ~ kennen** to know sb/sth inside out *(inf)*

TG *(in Annoncen) abbr von* **Tiefgarage**

TH [teː'haː] F **-, -s** *abbr von* **Technische Hochschule**

Thai [tai] M **-(s), -(s)** Thai

Thai [tai] F **-, -** Thai

Thai [tai] NT **-**, *no pl (Ling)* Thai

Thai|land ['tailant] NT **-s** Thailand

Thai|län|der ['tailɛndɐ] M **-s, -**, **Thai|län|de|rin** [-ərɪn] F **-, -nen** Thai

thai|län|disch ['tailɛndɪʃ] ADJ Thai

Tha|las|so|the|ra|pie [talaso-] F *(Med)* thalassotherapy

Thal|li|um ['taliʊm] NT **-s**, *no pl (abbr* **Tl**) thallium

The|a|ter [te'aːtɐ] NT **-s, - a** theatre *(Brit)*, theater *(US)*; *(= Schauspielbühne)* theatre *(Brit)* or theater *(US)* company; *(= Zuschauer)* audience; **beim** *or* **am ~ arbeiten** to work in the theatre *(Brit)* or theater *(US)*; **er ist** *or* **arbeitet beim Ulmer ~** he's with the Ulm theatre *(Brit)* or theater *(US)* company; **heute Abend wird im ~ „Othello" gezeigt** *or* **gegeben** "Othello" is on *or* is playing at the theatre *(Brit)* or theater *(US)* tonight; **das ~ fängt um 8 Uhr an** the performance begins at 8 o'clock; **zum ~ gehen** to go on the stage; **ins ~ gehen** to go to the theatre *(Brit)* or theater *(US)*; **das französische ~** French theatre *(Brit)* or theater *(US)*; **~ spielen** *(lit)* to act; *(= Stück aufführen)* to put on a play; *(fig)* to put on an act, to play-act; **jdm ein ~ vormachen** *or* **vorspielen** *(fig)* to put on an act for sb's benefit; **das ist doch alles nur ~** *(fig)* it's all just play-acting

b *(fig)* to-do *(inf)*, fuss; **das war vielleicht ein ~, bis ich ...** what a palaver *or* performance *or* carry-on I had to ... *(inf)*; **das ist (vielleicht) immer ein ~, wenn er kommt** there's always a big fuss when he comes; **(ein) ~ machen** *(= Umstände)* to make a (big) fuss *(mit jdm* of sb); *(= Szene auch)* to make a song and dance *(inf)* or a scene

The|a|ter- *in cpds* theatre *(Brit)*, theater *(US)*; **The|a|ter|abon|ne|ment** NT theatre subscription; **The|a|ter|auf|füh|rung** F stage production; *(= Vorstellung, Darbietung)* performance; **The|a|ter|be|such** M visit to the theatre; **The|a|ter|be|su|cher(in)** M(F) theatregoer *(Brit)*, theatergoer *(US)*; **The|a|ter|dich|ter(in)** M(F) dramatist, playwright; **The|a|ter|fes|ti|val** NT drama festival; **The|a|ter|ge|bäu|de** NT theatre; **The|a|ter|kar|te** F theatre ticket; **The|a|ter|kas|se** F theatre box office; **The|a|ter|kri|ti|ker(in)** M(F) theatre *or* drama critic; **The|a|ter|pro|be** F rehearsal; **The|a|ter|pro|duk|ti|on** F dramatic *or* theatrical production; **The|a|ter|stück** NT (stage) play; **The|a|ter|tref|fen** NT **Berliner ~** Berlin Theatre *(Brit)* or Theater *(US)* Meeting; **The|a|ter|vor|stel|lung** F (stage) performance; **The|a|ter|wis|sen|schaft** F theory of drama; *(= Studienfach)* theatre *(Brit)* or theater *(US)* studies *pl*

the|at|ra|lisch [tea'traːlɪʃ] ADJ theatrical, histrionic ADV theatrically

The|is|mus [te'ɪsmʊs] M **-**, *no pl* theism

The|ke ['teːkə] F **-, -n** *(= Schanktisch)* bar; *(= Ladentisch)* counter

T-Hel|fer-Zel|le ['teː-] F T helper cell

The|ma ['teːma] NT **-s, Themen** *or* **-ta** [-mən, -ta] *(= Gegenstand)* subject, topic; *(= Leitgedanke, auch Mus)* theme; **interessant vom ~ her** interesting as far as the subject matter is concerned; **beim ~ bleiben** to stick to the subject *or* point; **vom ~ abschweifen** to stray from *or* wander off the subject *or* point; **das ~ wechseln** to change the subject; **ein/kein ~ sein** to be/not to be an issue; **Geld ist für sie kein ~** money is no object for her; **aus etw ein ~ machen** to make an issue of sth; **zum ~ werden** to become an issue; **wir wollen das ~ begraben** *(inf)* let's not talk about it any more, let's forget the whole subject; **das ~ ist (für mich) erledigt** *(inf)* as far as I'm concerned the matter's closed

The|ma|ta *pl von* **Thema**

The|ma|tik [te'maːtɪk] F **-, -en** topic

the|ma|tisch [te'maːtɪʃ] ADJ thematic; *(= vom Thema her)* as regards subject matter; **~es Verzeichnis** subject index ADV **~ interessant sein** to be an interesting subject; **der Aufsatz ist ~ unbedeutend** the subject of this essay is trivial; **~ geordnet** arranged according to subject

the|ma|ti|sie|ren [temati'ziːrən] *ptp* **thematisiert** VT *(geh)* to pick out as a central theme

The|ma|wech|sel M change of subject; **~: ...** moving on *or* switching to another subject now ...

The|men *pl von* **Thema**

The|men-: **The|men|abend** M *(TV etc)* theme evening; **The|men|be|reich** M, **The|men|kreis** M topic; **in den ~ „Tiere" gehören** to come under the heading of "animals"; **The|men|park** M theme park; **The|men|stel|lung** F subject; **The|men|wahl** F choice of subject *or* topic; **The|men|wech|sel** M → **Themawechsel**

Them|se ['tɛmzə] F **- die ~** the Thames

Theo|lo|ge [teo'loːgə] M **-n, -n**, **Theo|lo|gin** [-'loːgɪn] F **-, -nen** theologian

Theo|lo|gie [teolo'giː] F **-**, *no pl* theology; **Doktor der ~** Doctor of Divinity *(Brit)*, Doctor of Theology *(US)*

theo|lo|gisch [teo'loːgɪʃ] ADJ theological ADV theologically; **sich ~ gut auskennen** to know quite a bit about theology; **~ interessiert sein** to be interested in theology; **eine ~ interessante Frage** a question which is interesting from a theological point of view; **sich ~ weiterbilden** to learn more about theology

The|o|rem [teo'reːm] NT **-s, -e** theorem

The|o|re|ti|ker [teo'reːtikɐ] M **-s, -**, **The|o|re|ti|ke|rin** [-ərɪn] F **-, -nen** theorist, theoretician

the|o|re|tisch [teo'reːtɪʃ] ADJ theoretical ADV theoretically; **~ gesehen** in theory, theoretically

the|o|re|ti|sie|ren [teoreti'ziːrən] *ptp* **theoretisiert** VI to theorize

The|o|rie [teo'riː] F **-, -n** [-'riːən] theory → **grau**

Theo|so|phie [teozo'fiː] F **-, -n** [-'fiːən] theosophy

The|ra|peut [tera'pɔyt] M **-en, -en**, **The|ra|peu|tin** [-'pɔytɪn] F **-, -nen** therapist

The|ra|peu|tik [tera'pɔytɪk] F **-**, *no pl* therapeutics *sing*

the|ra|peu|tisch [tera'pɔytɪʃ] ADJ therapeutic(al) ADV therapeutically; **~ umstrittene Methoden** controversial therapeutic methods

The|ra|pie [tera'piː] F **-, -n** [-'piːən] therapy *(auch fig)*, treatment; *(= Behandlungsmethode)* (method of) treatment *(gegen* for)

The|ra|pie|er|folg M success of *or* with a therapy, therapeutic success

The|ra|pie|platz M place in therapy

the|ra|pie|ren [tera'piːrən] *ptp* **therapiert** VT to give therapy to, to treat

The|ra|pie|zen|trum NT treatment centre *(Brit)* or center *(US)*

Ther|mal-: **Ther|mal|bad** NT thermal bath; *(Gebäude)* thermal baths *pl*; *(= Badeort)* spa, watering place *(old)*; **jdm Thermalbäder verschreiben** to prescribe hydrotherapy for sb; **Ther|mal|quel|le** F thermal spring

Ther|me ['tɛrmə] F **-, -n** *(= Quelle)* thermal *or* hot spring; **die ~n** the thermals; *(Hist)* the (thermal) baths

Ther|mik ['tɛrmɪk] F **-**, *no pl (Met)* thermal activity, thermals *pl*

ther|misch ['tɛrmɪʃ] ADJ *attr (Phys)* thermal

Ther|mo- *in cpds* thermo-; **Ther|mo|che|mie** F thermochemistry; **Ther|mo|dru|cker** M thermal printer; **Ther|mo|dy|na|mik** F thermodynamics *sing*; **ther|mo|dy|na|misch** ADJ thermodynamic; **ther|mo|elek|trisch** ADJ thermoelectric(al); **Ther|mo|ho|se** F thermal trousers *pl (esp Brit)* or pants *pl (esp US)*; **Ther|mo|kan|ne** F ≈ Thermos® jug *or* container

Ther|mo|me|ter NT **-s, -** thermometer

Ther|mo|me|ter|stand M temperature; **bei ~ 60°** when the temperature reaches 60°, when the thermometer reads 60°

ther|mo|nuk|le|ar ADJ thermonuclear

Ther|mo|pa|pier NT thermal paper

Ther|mos|fla|sche® F Thermos® (flask *or* bottle *(US)*), ≈ vacuum flask *or* bottle *(US)*

Ther|mos|tat [tɛrmo'staːt] M **-(e)s, -e** thermostat

the|sau|rie|ren [tezau'riːrən] VT *(Econ, St Ex)* to accumulate; **~der Fonds** accumulated fund

The|sau|rie|rung F **-, -en** *(Econ, St Ex)* accumulation

The|sau|rus [te'zaurʊs] M **-, Thesauri** *or* **Thesauren** [-ri, -rən] thesaurus

The|se ['teːzə] ✪ 53.2 F **-, -n** hypothesis, thesis; *(inf: = Theorie)* theory; **Luthers 95 ~n** Luther's 95 propositions

The|sen|pa|pier NT *(Sch, Univ)* academic *or* research paper; *(= Zusammenfassung)* synopsis (of a lecture)

Thing [tɪŋ] NT **-(e)s, -e** *(Hist)* thing

Thing|platz M *(Hist)* thingstead

Tho|ra ['toːra] F **-**, *no pl (Rel)* Torah

Tho|ra-: **Tho|ra|rol|le** F *(Rel)* Torah scroll; **Tho|ra|schrein** M *(Rel)* ark of the Law

Tho|ri|um ['toːriʊm] NT **-s**, *no pl (abbr* **Th**) thorium

Thril|ler ['θrɪlɐ] M **-s, -** thriller

Throm|bo|se [trɔm'boːzə] F **-, -n** thrombosis

Throm|bo|se|strumpf M compression stocking

throm|bo|tisch [trɔm'boːtɪʃ] ADJ thrombotic

Thron [troːn] M **-(e)s, -e** throne; *(hum inf: = Nachttopf)* pot; **von seinem ~ herabsteigen** *(fig)* to come down off one's high horse

Thron-: **Thron|an|wär|ter(in)** M(F) claimant to the throne; *(= Thronfolger)* heir apparent; **Thron|be|stei|gung** F accession (to the throne)

thro|nen ['troːnən] VI *(lit: = auf dem Thron sitzen)* to sit enthroned; *(fig: = in exponierter Stellung sitzen)* to sit in state; *(liter: = überragen)* to stand in solitary splendour *(Brit)* or splendor *(US)*

Thron-: **Thron|er|be** M, **Thron|er|bin** F heir to the throne; **Thron|fol|ge** F line of succession; **die ~ antreten** to succeed to the throne; **Thron|fol|ger** [-fɔlgɐ] M **-s, -**, **Thron|fol|ge|rin** [-ərɪn] F **-, -nen** heir to the throne, heir apparent; **Thron|him|mel** M canopy; **Thron|räu|ber(in)** M(F) usurper; **Thron|re|de** F King's/Queen's speech at the opening of parliament; **Thron|saal** M throne room

Thu|ja ['tuːja] F **-, Thujen** [-jən] arbor vitae, thuja

Thu|li|um ['tuːliʊm] NT **-s**, *no pl (abbr* **Tm**) thulium

Thun|fisch ['tuːn-] M tuna (fish)

Thur|gau ['tuːɐgau] M **-s der ~** the Thurgau

Thü|rin|gen ['tyːrɪŋən] NT **-s** Thuringia

Thü|rin|ger ['tyːrɪŋɐ] ADJ Thuringian; **der ~ Wald** the Thuringian Forest

Thü|rin|ger ['ty:rɪŋɐ] M **-s, -**, **Thü|rin|ge|rin** [-ərɪn] F **-, -nen** Thuringian
thü|rin|gisch ['ty:rɪŋɪʃ] ADJ Thuringian
Thus|nel|da [tʊs'nɛlda] F **-, -s** *(inf)* bird *(esp Brit inf)*, chick *(inf)*
THW [te:ha:'ve:] *abbr von* **Technisches Hilfswerk**

THW

THW – short for **Technisches Hilfswerk** – was founded in 1950, under the organizational control of the Ministry of the Interior. It provides technical assistance in response to cases of civil defence, major accidents and natural disasters both in Germany and abroad. It also supports humanitarian relief work outside the country. It has about 80,000 voluntary workers.

Thy|mi|an ['ty:mia:n] M **-s, -e** thyme
Thy|mus|drü|se ['ty:mʊs-] F thymus (gland)
Ti|a|ra ['tia:ra] F **-, Tiaren** [-rən] tiara, triple crown
Ti|bet ['ti:bɛt, ti'be:t] NT **-s** Tibet
Ti|be|ta|ner [tibe'ta:nɐ] M **-s, -**, **Ti|be|ta|ne|rin** [-ərɪn] F **-, -nen** Tibetan
ti|be|ta|nisch [tibe'ta:nɪʃ], **ti|be|tisch** [ti'be:tɪʃ] ADJ Tibetan
tick [tɪk] INTERJ tick; **~ tack!** ticktock!
Tick [tɪk] M **-(e)s, -s** **a** *(Med)* tic; **nervöser ~** nervous tic **b** *(inf: = Schrulle)* quirk *(inf)*; **Uhren sind sein ~** he has a thing about clocks *(inf)*; **einen ~ haben** *(inf)* to be crazy; **er hat einen ~ mit seiner Ordnung** he has this thing about tidiness *(inf)*; **einen ~ besser/schneller** *etc* **sein** *(inf)* to be a shade better/faster *etc*
-tick M *suf in cpds (inf)* **ein Autotick** a thing about cars *(inf)*
ti|cken ['tɪkn] VI to tick (away); **anders ~** *(fig inf)* to have a different mentality; **du tickst ja nicht richtig** *(inf)* you're off your rocker! *(inf)* VT *(Press sl: = zusammenschlagen)* to bash *(inf)*
Ti|cker ['tɪkɐ] M **-s, -** *(inf)* telex (machine), ticker *(US)*
ti|ckern ['tɪkɐn] *(inf)* VI **aus dem Fernschreiber ~** to come out of the telex VT to telex
Ti|cket ['tɪkət] NT **-s, -s** (plane) ticket
Ti|de ['ti:də] F **-, -n** *(N Ger)* tide
Ti|den|hub M *(N Ger)* tidal range
Tie|break M **-s, -s**, **Tie-Break** ['taibre:k] M **-s, -s** *(Tennis)* tie-break *(esp Brit)*, tie-breaker
tief [ti:f] ADJ **a** *(= weitreichend) Tal, Wasser, Wurzeln, Schnee, Wunde, Seufzer* deep; *Verbeugung, Ausschnitt* low; **~er Teller** soup plate; **ein ~er Eingriff in jds Rechte** *(acc)* a gross infringement of sb's rights; **die ~eren Ursachen** the underlying causes; **aus ~stem Herzen** from the bottom of one's heart; **aus ~ster Seele** from the depths of one's soul
b *(= sehr stark, groß) Ohnmacht, Schlaf, Erröten, Gefühl* deep; *Schmerz* intense; *Not* dire; *Verlassenheit, Einsamkeit, Elend* utter; **bis in den ~sten Winter, bis ~ in den Winter** (till) well into winter; **bis in die ~ste Nacht, bis ~ in die Nacht hinein** (till) late into the night
c *auch adv (= mitten in etwas liegend)* **er wohnt ~ in den Bergen** he lives deep in the mountains; **~ im Wald, im ~en Wald** deep in the forest, in the depths of the forest; **~ im Winter, im ~en Winter** in the depths of winter; **~ in der Nacht, in der ~en Nacht** at dead of night; **~ in Afrika, im ~sten Afrika** in darkest Africa; **~ im Innern, im ~sten Innern** in one's heart of hearts
d *(= tiefgründig)* deep, profound; **der ~ere Sinn** the deeper meaning
e *(= niedrig) Lage, Stand, Temperatur* low
f *(= dunkel) Farbton, Stimme* deep; *(Mus)* low; *Ton* low
ADV **a** *(= weit nach unten, innen, hinten)* a long way; *bohren, graben, eindringen, tauchen* deep; *sich bücken* low; *untersuchen* in depth; **~ in etw** *(acc)* **einsinken** to sink deep into sth, to sink down a long way into sth; **3 m ~ fallen** to fall 3 metres *(Brit)* or meters *(US)*; **~ gehend** *(lit, fig)* deep; *Schmerz* extreme, acute; *Kränkung* extreme; **~ sinken** *(fig)* to sink low; **~ fallen** *(fig)* to go downhill; **~ liegend** *(Augen)* deep-set; *(nach Krankheit)* sunken; *(fig) Gefühl, Problem* deep-seated, deep-rooted; **bis ~ in etw** *(acc)* **hinein** *(örtlich)* a long way down/deep into sth; **(ganz) ~ unter uns** a long way below us, far below us; **seine Augen liegen ~ in den Höhlen** his eyes are like hollows in his face; **~ verschneit** deep with snow; **~ in Gedanken (versunken)** deep in thought; **~ in Schulden stecken** to be deep in debt; **jdm ~ in die Augen sehen** to look deep into sb's eyes; **~ in die Tasche** *or* **den Beutel greifen müssen** *(inf)* to have to reach *or* dig deep in one's pocket; **das geht bei ihm nicht sehr ~** *(inf)* it doesn't go very deep with him → **Schuld c, blicken**
b *(= sehr stark) verletzen, atmen, erröten, schockieren, erschüttern, betrübt, bewegt, erschüttert, empfunden* deeply; *schlafen* soundly, deeply; *fühlen, empfinden* acutely, deeply; *bedauern* deeply, profoundly; *erschrecken* terribly; **~ greifend** *(Reform, Veränderung)* far-reaching; *sich verändern* significantly; *reformieren* thoroughly; **die Gesellschaft hat sich ~ greifend gewandelt** society has done a basic turnaround; **~ erschüttert** deeply disturbed
c *(= tiefgründig) nachdenken* deeply; **etw ~er begründen** to find a deeper reason for sth; **~ blickend** *(fig)* perceptive, astute; **~ schürfend** → **tiefschürfend**
d *(= niedrig)* low; **ein Stockwerk ~er** one floor down *or* lower, on the floor below; **Hanau liegt ~er als Schlüchtern** Hanau is lower-lying than Schlüchtern; **das Haus liegt ~er als die Straße** the house lies below (the level of) the road; **~ liegend** *(Gegend, Häuser)* low-lying; **im Winter steht die Sonne ~er** the sun is lower (in the sky) in winter
e *(= mit tiefer Stimme) sprechen* in a deep voice; **so ~ kann ich nicht singen** I can't sing that low; **~er singen** to sing lower; **etw zu ~ singen** to sing sth flat; **~er spielen** to play in a lower key, to play lower; **~er stimmen** to tune down
Tief [ti:f] NT **-(e)s, -e** **a** *(Met)* depression; *(im Kern, fig)* low; **ein moralisches ~** *(fig)* a low **b** *(Naut: = Rinne)* deep *(spec)*, channel
Tief-: **Tief|bau** M, *no pl* civil engineering *(excluding the construction of buildings)* → **Hoch- und Tiefbau**; **tief|be|trübt** ADJ *attr* → **tief ADV b**; **tief|be|wegt** ADJ *attr* → **tief ADV b**; **tief|blau** ADJ *attr* deep blue; **tief|bli|ckend** ADJ *attr* → **tief ADV c**
Tief|druck M **a** *no pl (Met)* low pressure **b** *pl* **-drucke** *(Typ)* gravure
Tief|druck-: **Tief|druck|ge|biet** NT *(Met)* area of low pressure, depression; **Tief|druck|keil** M *(Met)* trough of low pressure; **Tief|druck|rin|ne** F *(Met)* depression
Tie|fe ['ti:fə] F **-, -n** **a** *(= Ausdehnung nach unten)* depth; *(von Verbeugung, Ausschnitt)* lowness; **unten in der ~** far below; **in die ~ blicken** to look down into the depths *or* a long way; **in der ~ versinken** to sink into the depths; **das U-Boot ging auf ~** the submarine dived; **in 450 Metern ~** at a depth of 450 metres *(Brit)* or meters *(US)*; **aus der ~ meines Herzens** from the depths of my heart
b *(= Intensität)* deepness; *(von Schmerz)* intensity; *(von Not)* direness; *(von Elend)* depths *pl*
c *(von Wald)* depths *pl*
d *(= Tiefgründigkeit)* deepness, profundity
e *(= niedriger Stand)* lowness
f *(von Farbton, Stimme)* deepness; *(von Ton)* lowness
g *(Art, Phot)* depth
Tief-: **Tief|ebe|ne** F lowland plain; **die Oberrheinische ~** the Upper Rhine Valley; **tief|emp|fun|den** ADJ *attr* → **tief ADV b**
Tie|fen-: **Tie|fen|be|strah|lung** F deep ray therapy; **Tie|fen|ge|stein** NT plutonic rock, pluton; **Tie|fen|psy|cho|lo|ge** M, **Tie|fen|psy|cho|lo|gin** F depth psychologist; **Tie|fen|psy|cho|lo|gie** F depth psychology; **Tie|fen|rausch** M *(Med)* rapture(s *pl*) of the deep; **Tie|fen|schär|fe** F *(Phot)* depth of field; **Tie|fen|wir|kung** F deep action; *(Art, Phot)* effect of depth
Tief-: **tief|er|schüt|tert** [-lɛɐʃytɐt] ADJ *attr* → **tief ADV b**; **Tief|flie|ger** M low-flying aircraft, hedgehopper *(inf)*; **geistiger ~** *(pej inf)* numskull *(inf)*, dummy *(inf)*; **Tief|flug** M low-level *or* low-altitude flight; **er überquerte den Kanal im ~** he crossed low over the Channel; **Tief|flug|übung** F low-flying exercise; **Tief|gang** [-gaŋ] M, *no pl (Naut)* draught *(Brit)*, draft *(US)*; *(fig inf)* depth; **Tief|ga|ra|ge** F underground car park *(Brit)*, underground parking garage *(esp US)*; **tief|ge|frie|ren** VT *irreg* to (deep-)freeze; **tief|ge|fro|ren** ADJ (deep) -frozen ADV **Spinat ~ kaufen** to buy frozen spinach; **~ halten Erdbeeren ein Jahr** frozen strawberries can be stored for a year; **tief|ge|hend** ADJ → **tief ADV a**; **tief|ge|kühlt** ADJ *(= gefroren)* frozen; *(= sehr kalt)* chilled ADV **Spinat ~ kaufen** to buy frozen spinach; **~ halten Erdbeeren ein Jahr** frozen strawberries can be stored for a year; **~ servieren** to serve frozen; **Tief|ge|schoss** ; **Tief|ge|schoß** *(Aus)* NT basement; **tief|ge|stellt** ADJ *Ziffer* subscript; **~es Zeichen** subscript; **tief|grei|fend** ADJ → **tief ADV a**; **tief|grün|dig** [-grʏndɪç] ADJ profound, deep; *(= durchdacht)* well-grounded
Tief|kühl-: **Tief|kühl|fach** NT freezer compartment; **Tief|kühl|kost** F frozen food; **Tief|kühl|tru|he** F (chest) freezer
Tief-: **Tief|la|der** [-la:dɐ] M **-s, -**, **Tief|la|de|wa|gen** M low-loader; **Tief|land** NT lowlands *pl*; **tief|lie|gend** ADJ *attr* → **tief ADV a, d**; **Tief|punkt** M low; **Tief|schlaf** M deep sleep; **sich im ~ befinden** to be in a deep sleep, to be fast asleep; **Tief|schlag** M *(Boxen, fig)* hit below the belt; **jdm einen ~ verpassen** *(lit, fig)* to hit sb below the belt; **das war ein ~** *(lit, fig)* that was below the belt; **Tief|schnee** M deep powder, deep (powder) snow; **tief|schür|fend** ADJ profound
Tief|see F deep sea
Tief|see- *in cpds* deep-sea; **Tief|see|gra|ben** M ocean *or* deep-sea trench; **Tief|see|tau|cher(in)** M(F) deep-sea diver
Tief-: **Tief|sinn** M profundity; **tief|sin|nig** ADJ profound; **Tief|sin|nig|keit** ['ti:fzɪnɪçkait] F **-**, *no pl* profundity; **Tief|stand** M low; **Tief|sta|pe|lei** [-ʃta:pə'lai] F **-, -en** understatement; *(auf eigene Leistung bezogen)* modesty; **tief+sta|peln** VI *sep* to understate the case; to be modest; **Tief|start** M crouch start
Tiefst-: **Tiefst|preis** M lowest price; **„Tiefstpreise"** "rock bottom prices"; **Tiefst|tem|pe|ra|tur** F lowest temperature; **Tiefst|wert** M lowest value
tief|trau|rig ADJ very sad
Tie|gel ['ti:gl] M **-s, -** *(zum Kochen)* (sauce)pan; *(in der Chemie)* crucible; *(= Tiegeldruckpresse)* platen (press)
Tier [ti:ɐ] NT **-(e)s, -e** animal; *(= großes Tier auch)* beast; *(= Haustier auch)* pet; *(inf: = Ungeziefer)* bug *(inf)*; *(inf: = Mensch) (grausam)* brute; *(grob)* animal; *(gefräßig)* pig *(inf)*; **großes** *or* **hohes ~** *(inf)* big shot *(inf)*; **das ~ im Menschen** the beast in man; **da wird der Mensch zum ~** it brings out man's bestiality; **sich wie die ~e benehmen** to behave like animals
Tier- *in cpds* animal; *(Med)* veterinary; *(für Haustiere)* pet; **Tier|arzt** M, **Tier|ärz|tin** F vet, veterinary surgeon *(form)*, veterinarian *(US)*; **Tier|asyl** NT (animal) pound
Tier|chen ['ti:ɐçən] NT **-s, -** *dim von* **Tier** little animal; **ein niedliches ~** a sweet little creature → **Pläsierchen**
Tier-: **Tier|fab|rik** F *(pej)* animal factory; **Tier|freund(in)** M(F) animal lover; *(von Haustier auch)* pet lover; **Tier|fut|ter** NT animal food *or* fodder; *(für Haustiere)* pet food; **Tier|gar|ten** M zoo; **Tier|hal|ter(in)** M(F) *(von Haustieren)* pet

owner; *(von Nutztieren)* livestock owner; **Tier|hand|lung** F pet shop; **Tier|heil|kun|de** F veterinary medicine; **Tier|heim** NT animal home

tie|risch ['ti:rɪʃ] ADJ animal *attr; (fig) Rohheit, Grausamkeit* bestial; *(= unzivilisiert) Benehmen, Sitten* animal *attr; (fig inf: = unerträglich)* deadly *(inf)*, terrible; **~er Ernst** *(inf)* deadly seriousness ADV *(inf: = ungeheuer)* horribly *(inf); wehtun, nerven* like hell *(inf); ernst* deadly; *gut* incredibly; **ich habe mich ~ geärgert** I got really furious; **~ schaffen** to work like a dog/like dogs; **~ schwitzen** to sweat like a pig/like pigs *(inf)*; **~ wenig verdienen** to earn practically nothing

Tier-: **Tier|kämp|fe** PL animal fights *pl*; **Tier|kör|per|be|sei|ti|gungs|an|stalt** F carcass disposal plant; **Tier|kreis** M zodiac; **Tier|kreis|zei|chen** NT sign of the zodiac; **im ~ des Skorpions geboren sein** to be born under Scorpio; **Tier|kun|de** F zoology; **tier|lieb** ADJ animal-loving *attr*, fond of animals *pred*; **~ sein** to like animals; *(stärker)* to love animals; **Tier|lie|be** F love of animals; **tier|lie|bend** ADJ fond of animals, animal-loving *attr; (= Haustiere liebend)* pet-loving *attr*; **Tier|me|di|zin** F veterinary medicine; **Tier|mehl** NT meat and bone meal; **Tier|park** M zoo; **Tier|pen|si|on** F boarding establishment for pets; *(für Hunde auch)* boarding kennels *pl or (US)* kennel; *(für Katzen auch)* (boarding) cattery; **Tier|pfle|ger(in)** M(F) zoo keeper; **Tier|quä|ler** [-kvɛːlɐ] M **-s, -**, **Tier|quä|le|rin** [-ərɪn] F **-, -nen** person who is cruel to animals; **ein ~ sein** to be cruel to animals; **Tier|quä|le|rei** F cruelty to animals; *(fig inf)* cruelty to dumb animals; **Tier|reich** NT animal kingdom; **Tier|schutz** M protection of animals; **Tier|schüt|zer** [-ʃʏtsɐ] M **-s, -**, **Tier|schüt|ze|rin** [-ərɪn] F **-, -nen** animal conservationist; **Tier|schutz|ver|ein** M society for the prevention of cruelty to animals; **Tier|trans|port** M transportation of animals *or* livestock; **Tier|ver|such** M animal experiment; **Tier|welt** F animal kingdom; **Tier|zucht** F stockbreeding

TIFF [tɪf] *abbr von* **tagged image file format** *(Comput)* TIFF

Ti|ger ['tiːgɐ] M **-s, -** tiger → *auch* **Tigerin**

Ti|ger-: **Ti|ger|au|ge** NT tiger's-eye; **Ti|ger|fell** NT tiger skin

Ti|ge|rin ['tiːgərɪn] F **-, -nen** tigress

ti|gern ['tiːgɐn] VT → **getigert** VI *aux sein (inf)* to mooch (about *(Brit)*)

Ti|ger|staat M tiger economy

Tig|ris ['tiːgrɪs] M **-'** Tigris

Til|de ['tɪldə] F **-, -n** tilde

tilg|bar ADJ *Schulden* repayable

til|gen ['tɪlgn] VT *(geh)* **a** *Schulden* to pay off **b** *(= beseitigen) Sünde, Unrecht, Spuren* to wipe out; *Erinnerung, Druckfehler* to erase; *Strafe* to remove; *Posten (Typ, Ling)* to delete; **ein Volk von der Erde** *or* **vom Erdboden ~** to wipe a nation off the face of the earth

Til|gung ['tɪlgʊŋ] F **-, -en** **a** *(von Schulden)* repayment **b** *(fig) (von Sünde, Unrecht, Spuren)* wiping out; *(von Erinnerung, Druckfehler)* erasure; *(von Strafe)* removal; *(Typ, Ling)* deletion

Til|gungs-: **til|gungs|frei** ADJ redemption-free; **Til|gungs|ra|te** F redemption instalment *(Brit) or* installment *(US)*; **Til|gungs|zeit|raum** M repayment period

Til|si|ter ['tɪlzɪtɐ] M **-s, -** Tilsit cheese

Timb|re ['tɛ̃ːbrə, 'tɛ̃ːbɐ] NT **-s, -s** *(geh)* timbre

ti|men ['taimən] VT to time

Ti|mer ['taimɐ] M **-s, -** timer

Time|sha|ring ['taimʃɛːrɪŋ] NT **-(s), -s** time sharing

Ti|ming ['taimɪŋ] NT **-**, *no pl* timing

Tim|pa|ni ['tɪmpani] PL *(Mus)* timpani *pl*

tin|geln ['tɪŋln] VI *(inf)* to appear in small nightclubs/theatres *(Brit) or* theaters *(US) etc*

Tin|gel|tan|gel ['tɪŋltaŋl] NT OR M **-s, -** *(dated) (Veranstaltung)* hop *(inf)*; *(Lokal)* second-rate nightclub

Tink|tur [tɪŋk'tuːɐ] F **-, -en** tincture

Tin|nef ['tɪnəf] M **-s**, *no pl (inf)* rubbish *(Brit inf)*, trash *(inf)*

Tin|ni|tus ['tɪnitʊs] M **-, -** *(Med)* tinnitus

Tin|te ['tɪntə] F **-, -n** ink; **in der ~ sitzen** *(inf)* to be in the soup *(inf)*; **~ gesoffen haben** *(inf)* to be off one's rocker *(inf)*, to have a screw loose *(inf)*

Tin|ten-: **Tin|ten|fass** NT inkpot; *(eingelassen)* inkwell; **Tin|ten|fisch** M cuttlefish; *(= Kalmar)* squid; *(achtarmig)* octopus; **Tin|ten|fleck** M *(auf Kleidung)* ink stain; *(auf Papier)* ink blot; **Tin|ten|kar|tu|sche** F ink cartridge; **Tin|ten|kil|ler** M *(inf)* correction pen; **Tin|ten|klecks** M ink blot; **Tin|ten|pat|ro|ne** F ink cartridge; **Tin|ten|pilz** M ink-cap; **Tin|ten|stift** M indelible pencil; **Tin|ten|strahl|dru|cker** M ink-jet (printer)

Tipp [tɪp] M **-s, -s** (= *Empfehlung, Sport, St Ex*) tip; *(= Andeutung)* hint; *(an Polizei)* tip-off; **ich gebe dir einen ~, wie du ...** I'll give you a tip how to ...; **ich gebe dir einen ~, was du mir schenken kannst** I'll give you a hint as to what you could give me; **unser ~ für diesen Sommer ...** this summer we recommend ...; **unser Garten-~ für August** our gardening tip for August

Tip|pel|bru|der M *(dated inf)* gentleman of the road

tip|peln ['tɪpln] VI *aux sein (inf) (= gehen)* to foot it *(inf)*; *(mit kurzen Schritten)* to trip; *(auf Zehenspitzen)* to tiptoe; *(Maus, Kinder)* to patter

tip|pen ['tɪpn] VT **a** *(inf: = schreiben)* to type **b** *(= wetten auf)* **eine bestimmte Zahl ~** to put a particular number on one's coupon **c** *(= klopfen)* **jdn auf die Schulter ~** to tap sb on the shoulder VI **a** *(= klopfen)* **an/auf/gegen etw** *(acc)* ~ to tap sth; **an** *or* **auf etw** *(acc)* ~ *(= zeigen)* to touch sth; **jdn** *or* **jdm auf die Schulter ~** to tap sb on the shoulder; **sich** *(dat)* **an die Stirn ~** to tap one's forehead **b** *(inf: auf der Schreibmaschine, am Computer)* to type **c** *(= wetten)* to fill in one's coupon; *(esp im Toto)* to do the pools; **im Lotto ~** to do *(Brit) or* play the lottery **d** *(inf: = raten)* to guess; **auf jdn/etw ~** to put one's money on sb/sth *(inf)*; **ich tippe darauf, dass ...** I bet (that) ...; **auf jds Sieg** *(acc)* ~ to back sb to win *(inf)*

Tip|per ['tɪpɐ] M **-s, -**, **Tip|pe|rin** [-ərɪn] F **-, -nen** *(im Lotto)* lottery player; *(im Fußballtoto)* person who does the pools

Tipp-Ex® ['tɪpɛks] NT **-**, *no pl* Tipp-Ex®, ≈ whiteout *(US)*; **etw mit ~ entfernen** to Tipp-Ex® sth out *(Brit)*, to white sth out *(US)*

Tipp-: **Tipp|feh|ler** M *(inf)* typing mistake *or* error; **Tipp|fräu|lein** NT *(inf)* typist; **Tipp|ge|ber(in)** M(F) person who gives a/the tip-off; **Tipp|ge|mein|schaft** F *(im Lotto)* lottery syndicate; *(im Fußballtoto)* pools syndicate

Tipp|se ['tɪpsə] F **-, -n** *(pej)* typist

tipp|tapp ['tɪp'tap] INTERJ pitter-patter

tipp|topp ['tɪp'tɔp] *(inf)* ADJ immaculate; *(= prima)* first-class, tip-top *(dated inf)* ADV immaculately; *(= prima)* really well; **~ sauber** spotless

Tipp|zet|tel M *(im Toto)* football *or* pools coupon; *(im Lotto)* lottery coupon

Ti|ra|de [ti'raːdə] F **-, -n** tirade, diatribe

Ti|ra|na [ti'raːna] NT **-s** Tirana

ti|ri|lie|ren [tiri'liːrən] *ptp* **tiriliert** VI *(geh)* to warble, to trill

Ti|rol [ti'roːl] NT **-s** Tyrol

Ti|ro|ler [ti'roːlɐ] M **-s, -**, **Ti|ro|le|rin** [-ərɪn] F **-, -nen** Tyrolese, Tyrolean

Ti|ro|ler|hut M Tyrolean hat

Tisch [tɪʃ] M **-(e)s, -e** table; *(= Schreibtisch)* desk; *(= Werktisch)* bench; *(= Mahlzeit)* meal; **bei ~** at (the) table; **vom ~ aufstehen** to leave the table; **sich an den** *or* **zu ~ setzen** to sit down at the table; **die Gäste zu ~ bitten** to ask the guests to take their places; **bitte zu ~!** lunch/dinner is served!; **vor/nach ~** before/after the meal; **bei ~** at the table; **zu ~ sein** to be having one's lunch/dinner; **Herr Kleinhaus ist zu ~** Mr Kleinhaus is out at lunch; **zu ~ gehen** to go to lunch/dinner; **er zahlte bar auf den ~** he paid cash down *or* cash on the nail *(Brit inf) or* on the barrelhead *(US)*; **etw auf den ~ bringen** *(inf)* to serve sth (up); **die Beine** *or* **Füße unter jds ~ strecken** *(inf)* to eat at sb's table; **getrennt von ~ und Bett leben** to be separated; **unter den ~ fallen** *(inf)* to go by the board; **jdn unter den ~ trinken** *or* **saufen** *(inf)* to drink sb under the table; **es wird gegessen, was auf den ~ kommt!** you'll eat what you're given; **auf den ~ kommen** *(fig: Vorschlag etc)* to be put forward; **vom ~ sein** *(fig)* to be cleared out of the way; **vom ~ müssen** *(fig)* to have to be cleared out of the way; **auf dem ~ liegen** *(fig, Vorschlag etc)* to be on the table; **etw auf den ~ legen** *(fig, Geld, Vorschlag etc)* to put sth on the table; **etw vom ~ wischen** *(fig)* to dismiss sth; **zwei Parteien an einen ~ bringen** *(fig)* to get two parties (a)round the conference table; **an einem ~ sitzen** *(fig: = verhandeln)* to sit (together) (a)round a table; **mit jdm am ~ sitzen** *(fig)* to sit at the same table as sb; **jdn über den ~ ziehen** *(fig inf)* to take sb to the cleaners *(inf)* → **rund ADJ**, **grün**, **rein ADJ b**

Tisch- *in cpds* table; **Tisch|bein** NT table leg; **Tisch|be|sen** M crumb brush; **Tisch|da|me** F dinner partner; **Tisch|de|cke** F tablecloth; **Tisch|en|de** NT end of a/the table; **am oberen/unteren ~ sitzen** to sit at the head/the foot of the table; **Tisch|feu|er|zeug** NT table lighter; **Tisch|fuß|ball** NT table football *or* soccer, foozball; **Tisch|ge|bet** NT grace; **Tisch|ge|sell|schaft** F dinner party; **Tisch|ge|spräch** NT table talk; **Tisch|grill** M table grill; **Tisch|herr** M dinner partner; **Tisch|kan|te** F edge of a/the table; **Tisch|kar|te** F place card; **Tisch|lam|pe** F table lamp; **Tisch|läu|fer** M table runner

Tisch|lein|deck|dich [tɪʃlain'dɛkdɪç] NT **-(s)** **ein ~ gefunden haben** *(fig)* to be on to a good thing *(inf)*

Tisch|ler ['tɪʃlɐ] M **-s, -**, **Tisch|le|rin** [-ərɪn] F **-, -nen** joiner, carpenter; *(= Möbeltischler)* cabinet-maker

Tisch|le|rei [tɪʃlə'rai] F **-, -en** **a** *(Werkstatt)* joiner's *or* carpenter's workshop; *(= Möbeltischlerei)* cabinet-maker's workshop **b** *no pl (inf) (= Handwerk)* joinery, carpentry; *(von Möbeltischler)* cabinet-making

Tisch|ler|hand|werk NT joinery, carpentry; *(von Möbeltischler)* cabinet-making

tisch|lern ['tɪʃlɐn] *(inf)* VI to do woodwork VT *Tisch, Regal etc* to make

Tisch|ler|werk|statt F = **Tischlerei a**

Tisch-: **Tisch|nach|bar(in)** M(F) neighbour *(Brit) or* neighbor *(US)* (at table); **Tisch|ord|nung** F seating plan; **Tisch|plat|te** F tabletop; **Tisch|rech|ner** M desk calculator; **Tisch|re|de** F after-dinner speech; *(= Unterhaltung)* table talk; **Tisch|red|ner(in)** M(F) after-dinner speaker; **Tisch|schmuck** M table decoration(s *pl*); **Tisch|te|le|fon** NT table telephone *(in nightclub)*

Tisch|ten|nis NT table tennis

Tisch|ten|nis- *in cpds* table-tennis; **Tisch|ten|nis|plat|te** F table-tennis table; **Tisch|ten|nis|schlä|ger** M table-tennis bat

Tisch-: **Tisch|tuch** NT *pl* **-tücher** tablecloth; **Tisch|wä|sche** F table linen; **Tisch|wein** M table wine; **Tisch|zeit** F mealtime; **zur ~** at mealtimes

Ti|tan [ti'taːn] M **-en, -en** *(Myth)* Titan

Ti|tan NT **-s**, *no pl (abbr* **Ti**) titanium

ti|ta|nen|haft, ti|ta|nisch [ti'taːnɪʃ] ADJ titanic

Ti|tel ['tiːtl, 'tɪtl] M **-s, -** **a** title; **jdn mit ~ ansprechen** to address sb by his/her title, to give sb his/her title; **unter dem ~** under the title;

(*fig:* = *Motto*) under the slogan **b** (= *Titelblatt*) title page **c** (*von Gesetz, Etat*) section

Ti|tel-: **Ti|tel|an|wär|ter(in)** M(F) (main) contender for the title; **Ti|tel|bild** NT cover (picture); **Ti|tel|blatt** NT title page

Ti|te|lei [ti:tə'lai, tɪtə'lai] F **-, -en** (*Typ*) prelims *pl* (*esp Brit*), front matter

Ti|tel-: **Ti|tel|fi|gur** F → **Titelheld(in)**; **Ti|tel|ge|schich|te** F lead, cover story; **Ti|tel|held(in)** M(F) eponymous hero/heroine, hero/heroine (*mentioned in the title*); **Ti|tel|kampf** M (*Sport*) finals *pl*; (*Boxen*) title fight; **Ti|tel|leis|te** F (*Comput*) title bar; **Ti|tel|me|lo|die** F (*von Film*) theme tune *or* music

ti|teln ['ti:tln, 'tɪtln] VT (*Zeitung*) to give as its headline; **„Clinton am Ende", titelte „Bild"** "Bild"'s headline was "Clinton finished"

Ti|tel-: **Ti|tel|rol|le** F title role; **Ti|tel|schutz** M copyright (*of a title*); **Ti|tel|sei|te** F cover, front page; **Ti|tel|sto|ry** F cover story; **Ti|tel|trä|ger(in)** M(F) person with a title; **Ti|tel|ver|tei|di|ger(in)** M(F) title holder; **Ti|tel|zei|le** F title line

Tit|te ['tɪtə] F **-, -n** (*sl*) tit (*sl*), boob (*inf*), knocker (*inf*)

Ti|tu|lar|bi|schof [titu'la:ɐ-] M titular bishop

Ti|tu|la|tur [titula'tu:ɐ] F **-, -en** title, form of address

ti|tu|lie|ren [titu'li:rən] *ptp* **tituliert** VT *Buch, Werk etc* to entitle (*mit etw* sth); *jdn* to call (*mit etw* sth), to address (*mit* as)

ti|zi|an|rot ['ti:tsia:n-, 'ti:tsia:n-] ADJ *Haare* titian (red) ADV **sich** (*dat*) **die Haare ~ färben** to dye one's hair titian red

tja [tja, tja:] INTERJ well

TL *abbr von* **Teelöffel** tsp

T-Lym|pho|zyt ['te:-] M (*Med, Biol*) T-lymphocyte

Toast [to:st] M **-(e)s, -e** **a** (= *Brot*) toast; **ein ~** a slice *or* piece of toast **b** (= *Trinkspruch*) toast; **einen ~ auf jdn ausbringen** to propose a toast to sb

Toast|brot ['to:st-] NT *sliced white bread for toasting*

toas|ten ['to:stn] VI to drink a toast (*auf +acc* to) VT *Brot* to toast

Toas|ter ['to:stɐ] M **-s, -** toaster

Toast|stän|der ['to:st-] M toast rack

To|bak ['to:bak] M **das ist starker ~!** (*inf*) that's a bit much! (*inf*) → **anno**

to|ben ['to:bn] VI **a** (= *wüten*) (*Sturm, Elemente, Leidenschaften, Kämpfe etc*) to rage; (*Mensch*) to throw a fit; (*vor Wut, Begeisterung etc*) to go wild (*vor* with) **b** (= *ausgelassen spielen*) to rollick (about) **c** *aux sein* (*inf:* = *laufen*) to charge about

To|be|rei [tobə'rai] F **-, -en** (*inf*) rollicking about

Tob|sucht ['to:pzʊxt] F (*bei Tieren*) madness; (*bei Menschen*) maniacal rage

tob|süch|tig ADJ mad; *Mensch auch* raving mad

Tob|suchts|an|fall M (*inf*) fit of rage; **einen ~ bekommen** to blow one's top (*inf*), to go stark raving mad (*inf*)

Toch|ter ['tɔxtɐ] F **-, ⸚** ['tœçtɐ] daughter; (= *Tochterfirma*) subsidiary; (*Sw:* = *Bedienstete*) girl; **die ~ des Hauses** (*form*) the daughter *or* young lady of the house; **das Fräulein ~** (*iro, form*) mademoiselle → **höher**

Töch|ter|chen ['tœçtɐçən] NT **-s, -** baby daughter

Toch|ter-: **Toch|ter|fir|ma** F subsidiary (firm); **Toch|ter|ge|schwulst** F secondary growth *or* tumour; **Toch|ter|ge|sell|schaft** F subsidiary (company)

töch|ter|lich ['tœçtɐlɪç] ADJ *attr* daughterly; *Pflicht, Gehorsam, Liebe* filial

Toch|ter|un|ter|neh|men NT → **Tochterfirma**

Tod [to:t] ✪ 51.4 M **-(e)s, -e** death [-də]; **ein früher ~** an early *or* premature death; **der ~ als Schnitter** the Grim Reaper; **der Schwarze ~** (= *die Pest*) the Black Death, the plague; **~ durch Erschießen/Ersticken/Erhängen** death by firing squad/suffocation/hanging; **eines natürlichen/gewaltsamen ~es sterben** to die of natural causes/a violent death; **er ist des ~es** (*geh*) he is doomed; **er muss des ~es sterben** (*geh*) he will have to die; **sich zu ~e fallen** to fall to one's death; **sich zu ~e trinken** to drink oneself to death; **sich** (*dat*) **den ~ holen** to catch one's death (of cold); **den ~ finden, zu ~e kommen** to die; **in den ~ gehen** to go to one's death; **für jdn in den ~ gehen** to die for sb; **bis in den ~** until death; **jdn in den ~ treiben** to drive sb to his/her death; **jdm in den ~ folgen** to follow sb; **~ und Teufel!** (*old*) by the devil! (*old*); **weder ~ noch Teufel werden mich davon abhalten!** I'll do it, come hell or high water!; **jdn/etw auf den ~ nicht leiden** *or* **ausstehen können** (*inf*) to be unable to abide *or* stand sb/sth; **etw zu ~e hetzen** *or* **reiten** (*fig*) to flog sth to death; **sich zu ~(e) langweilen** to be bored to death; **sich zu ~(e) schämen** to be utterly ashamed; **zu ~e betrübt sein** to be in the depths of despair → **Leben a, bleich, Schippe a**

tod-: **tod|brin|gend** ADJ (*geh*) *Gift* deadly, lethal; *Krankheit* fatal; **tod|elend** ADJ (*inf*) as miserable as sin (*inf*), utterly miserable; **tod|ernst** (*inf*) ADJ deadly serious; **es ist mir ~ (damit)** I'm deadly serious (about it) ADV **jdn ~ ansehen** to give sb a deadly serious look; **und das alles sagte er ~** and the way he said it all was deadly serious

To|des-: **To|des|angst** F mortal agony; **eine ~ haben** (*inf*) **Todesängste ausstehen** (*inf*) to be scared to death (*inf*); **To|des|an|zei|ge** F (*als Brief*) letter announcing sb's death; (= *Annonce*) obituary (notice); **„Todesanzeigen"** "Deaths"; **To|des|art** F death, way to die; **To|des|dro|hung** F death threat; **~en erhalten** to receive death threats; **To|des|fall** M death; (*bei Unglück auch*) fatality; (*in der Familie auch*) bereavement; **To|des|fol|ge** F (*Jur*) **schwere Körperverletzung mit ~** grievous bodily harm resulting in death; **To|des|furcht** F fear of death; **To|des|ge|fahr** F mortal danger; **To|des|jahr** NT year of sb's death; **To|des|kampf** M death throes *pl*; **To|des|kan|di|dat(in)** M(F) condemned man/woman *etc*; **To|des|kom|man|do** NT death squad; **to|des|mu|tig** ADJ absolutely fearless ADV (absolutely) fearlessly; **To|des|nach|richt** F news *sing* of sb's death; **To|des|not** F mortal anguish; **in Todesnöten sein** (*fig*) to be in a desperate situation; **To|des|op|fer** NT death, casualty, fatality; **To|des|qua|len** PL final *or* mortal agony; **~ ausstehen** (*fig*) to suffer agony *or* agonies; **To|des|schuss** M fatal shot; **der ~ auf jdn** the shot which killed sb; **To|des|schüt|ze** M, **To|des|schüt|zin** F person who fires/fired the fatal shot; (= *Attentäter*) assassin; **To|des|schwad|ron** F death squad; **To|des|spi|ra|le** F death spiral; **To|des|stoß** M deathblow; **jdm/einer Sache den ~ geben** *or* **versetzen** (*lit, fig*) to deal sb the deathblow/deal the deathblow to sth; **To|des|stra|fe** F death penalty; **To|des|strei|fen** M (*an Grenze*) no-man's-land; **To|des|stun|de** F hour of death; **To|des|tag** M day of sb's death; (= *Jahrestag*) anniversary of sb's death; **To|des|trieb** M death wish; **To|des|ur|sa|che** F cause of death; **To|des|ur|teil** NT death sentence; **To|des|ver|ach|tung** F (*inf*) **mit ~** with utter disgust *or* repugnance; **jdn mit ~ strafen** to scorn to notice sb; **To|des|zel|le** F death cell (*Brit*), cell on Death Row (*US*)

Tod-: **Tod|feind(in)** M(F) deadly *or* mortal enemy; **tod|ge|weiht** [-gəvait] ADJ *Mensch, Patient* doomed; **tod|krank** ADJ (= *sterbenskrank*) dangerously *or* critically ill; (= *unheilbar krank*) terminally ill

töd|lich ['tø:tlɪç] ADJ *Unfall, Verletzung, Schuss, Schlag* fatal; *Gefahr* mortal, deadly; *Gift, Waffe* deadly, lethal; *Dosis* lethal; (*inf*) *Langeweile, Ernst, Sicherheit* deadly; *Beleidigung* mortal ADV **a** (*mit Todesfolge*) **~ verunglücken** to be killed in an accident; **~ abstürzen** to die in a fall **b** (*inf:* = *äußerst*) horribly (*inf*); *langweilen* to death

Tod-: **tod|mü|de** ADJ (*inf*) dead tired (*inf*); **tod|schick** (*inf*) ADJ dead smart (*inf*) ADV *gekleidet* ravishingly; *eingerichtet* exquisitely; **er hat sich ~ zurechtgemacht** he was dressed to kill (*inf*); **sie wohnen ~ in einer Villa in Cannes** they live in an exquisite villa in Cannes; **tod|si|cher** (*inf*) ADJ dead certain (*inf*); *Methode, Tipp* sure-fire (*inf*); **eine ~e Angelegenheit** *or* **Sache** a dead cert (*Brit inf*), a cinch (*esp US inf*), a done deal (*inf*); **das ist doch ~, dass ...** it's a dead cert (*Brit*) *or* a done deal that ... (*inf*) ADV for sure *or* certain; **Tod|sün|de** F mortal *or* deadly sin; **tod|un|glück|lich** ADJ (*inf*) desperately unhappy

Toe|loop ['to:lu:p] M **-s, -s** (*Eiskunstlauf*) toe loop

To|fu ['to:fu] NT **-,** *no pl* tofu

To|ga ['to:ga] F **-, Togen** [-gn] toga

To|go ['to:go] NT **-s** Togo

To|go|er ['to:goɐ] M **-s, -**, **To|go|e|rin** [-ərɪn] F **-, -nen** Togolese

to|go|isch ['to:goɪʃ] ADJ, **to|go|le|sisch** [togo'le:zɪʃ] ADJ Togolese

To|go|le|se [togo'le:zə] M **-n, -n**, **To|go|le|sin** [-'le:zɪn] F **-, -nen** Togolese

to|go|le|sisch [togo'le:zɪʃ] ADJ Togolese

To|hu|wa|bo|hu [to:huva'bo:hu] NT **-(s), -s** chaos *no pl*; **das war ein ~** it was utter *or* complete chaos

To|i|let|te [toa'lɛtə] F **-, -n** **a** (= *Abort*) toilet, lavatory (*esp Brit*), bathroom (*esp US*); **öffentliche ~** public conveniences *pl* (*Brit*), rest stop (*US*), comfort station (*US*); **auf die ~ gehen** to go to the toilet; **auf der ~ sein** to be in the toilet **b** *no pl* (*geh:* = *Ankleiden, Körperpflege*) toilet; **~ machen** to do one's toilet (*old*) **c** (*geh:* = *Kleidung*) outfit; **in großer ~** in full dress

To|i|let|ten- *in cpds* toilet; **To|i|let|ten|ar|ti|kel** M *usu pl* toiletry; **To|i|let|ten|beu|tel** M sponge (*Brit*) *or* toilet bag; **To|i|let|ten|frau** F toilet *or* lavatory (*esp Brit*) *or* restroom (*US*) attendant; **To|i|let|ten|gar|ni|tur** F **a** toilet (*Brit*) *or* bathroom set **b** (*für Toilettentisch*) dressing table set (*Brit*), vanity set; **To|i|let|ten|mann** M *pl* **-männer** toilet *or* lavatory (*esp Brit*) *or* restroom (*US*) attendant; **To|i|let|ten|pa|pier** NT toilet paper; **To|i|let|ten|schrank** M bathroom cabinet; **To|i|let|ten|sei|fe** F toilet soap; **To|i|let|ten|sitz** M toilet *or* lavatory (*esp Brit*) seat; **To|i|let|ten|ta|sche** F toilet bag; **To|i|let|ten|tisch** M dressing table (*Brit*), vanity (*US*); **To|i|let|ten|wa|gen** M mobile toilet unit; **To|i|let|ten|was|ser** NT *pl* **-wässer** toilet water

toi, toi, toi ['tɔy 'tɔy 'tɔy] INTERJ (*inf*) (*vor Prüfung etc*) good luck; (*unberufen*) touch wood (*Brit*), knock on wood (*US*)

To|kai|er(wein) ['to:kaiɐ-] M **-s, -** Tokay

To|kio ['to:kio] NT **-s** Tokyo

To|ki|o|ter [to'kio:tɐ] ADJ *attr* Tokyo

To|ki|o|ter [to'kio:tɐ] M **-s, -**, **To|ki|o|te|rin** [-ərɪn] F **-, -nen** native of Tokyo; (*Einwohner*) inhabitant of Tokyo

Tö|le ['tø:lə] F **-, -n** (*dial pej*) cur

to|le|rant [tole'rant] ADJ tolerant (*gegen* of)

To|le|ranz [tole'rants] F **-, -en** tolerance (*gegen* of)

To|le|ranz-: **To|le|ranz|be|reich** M range of tolerance, tolerance range; **To|le|ranz|do|sis** F tolerance dose; **To|le|ranz|gren|ze** F limit of tolerance; **To|le|ranz|schwel|le** F tolerance level *or* threshold

to|le|rie|ren [tole'ri:rən] *ptp* **toleriert** VT to tolerate

To|le|rie|rung F **-, -en** toleration

To|le|rie|rungs|ab|kom|men NT (*Pol*) toleration agreement

To|le|rie|rungs|po|li|tik F policy of toleration

toll [tɔl] ADJ **a** (= *wild, ausgelassen*) wild; *Streiche, Gedanken, Treiben* wild, mad; **die (drei) ~en**

Tage (the last three days of) Fasching
b *(inf: = verrückt)* mad, crazy; **das war ein ~es Ding** that was mad *or* madness
c *(inf: = schlimm)* terrible
d *(inf: = großartig)* fantastic *(inf)*, great *(inf) no adv*
e *(old: = irr, tollwütig)* mad
ADV **a** *(inf: = großartig)* fantastically; *schmecken* fantastic; **~ aussehen** to look fab *(inf)*
b *(= wild, ausgelassen)* **es ging ~ her** *or* **zu** things were pretty wild *(inf)*
c *(inf: = verrückt)* **(wie) ~ regnen** to rain like mad *(inf) or* crazy *(inf)*; **(wie) ~ fahren** *etc* to drive *etc* like a madman *or* maniac
d *(inf: = schlimm)* **es kommt noch ~er!** there's more *or* worse to come; **es zu ~ treiben** to go too far

toll|dreist ADJ bold, (as) bold as brass

Tol|le ['tɔlə] F -, -n quiff *(Brit)*, pompadour *(US)*

tol|len ['tɔlən] VI **a** *(= herumtollen)* to romp *or* rollick about **b** *aux sein (= laufen)* to rush about

Tol|le|rei [tɔlə'rai] F -, -en *(inf, von Kindern)* romping around; *(von Jugendlichen)* charging about *or* around; *(= Späße)* high jinks *pl (inf)*; **aus lauter Jux und ~** from sheer high spirits *or* sheer exuberance

Toll-: **Toll|haus** NT *(old)* bedlam *(old)*, madhouse; *(fig)* madhouse, bear garden *(Brit)*; **hier geht es zu wie im ~** it's like a bear garden *(Brit) or* madhouse here; **Toll|heit** F -, -en **a** *no pl (old)* madness **b** *(Tat)* mad act; *(Idee)* mad idea; **Toll|kir|sche** F deadly nightshade, belladonna; **toll|kühn** ADJ *Person, Plan, Fahrt* daredevil *attr*, daring ADV daringly; *fahren* like a real daredevil; **Toll|kühn|heit** F daring; **in seiner ~** daringly; **Toll|patsch** ['tɔlpatʃ] M -s, -e *(inf)* clumsy *or* awkward creature; **toll|pat|schig** ['tɔlpatʃɪç] ADJ awkward, ungainly, clumsy ADV clumsily; **Toll|wut** F rabies *sing*; **Toll|wut|ge|fahr** F danger of rabies; **toll|wü|tig** ADJ rabid

Tol|patsch △ ['tɔlpatʃ] M -es, -e → **Tollpatsch**

tol|pat|schig △ ['tɔlpatʃɪç] ADJ ADV → **tollpatschig**

Töl|pel ['tœlpl] M -s, - *(inf)* fool

töl|pel|haft ADJ foolish, silly ADV foolishly

To|lu|ol [to'luo:l] NT -s, *no pl* toluol, toluene

To|ma|hawk ['tɔmaha:k, -ho:k] M -s, -s tomahawk

To|ma|te [to'ma:tə] F -, -n tomato; **du treulose ~!** *(inf)* you're a fine friend!

To|ma|ten- *in cpds* tomato; **To|ma|ten|mark** NT, **To|ma|ten|pü|ree** NT tomato puree

Tom|bo|la ['tɔmbola] F -, -s *or* **Tombolen** [-lən] tombola *(Brit)*, raffle *(US)*

Tom|my ['tɔmi] M -s, -s *(inf)* tommy *(Brit inf)*, British soldier

To|mo|graf [tomo'gra:f] M -en, -en *(Med)* tomograph

To|mo|gra|fie [tomogra'fi:] F -, -n [-'fi:ən] tomography

To|mo|gramm [tomo'gram] NT *pl* **-gramme** *(Med)* tomogram

To|mo|graph [tomo'gra:f] M -en, -en = **Tomograf**

To|mo|gra|phie [tomogra'fi:] F -, -n [-'fi:ən] = **Tomografie**

Ton [to:n] M -(e)s, -e *(= Erdart)* clay

Ton M -(e)s, ¨-e ['tø:nə] **a** *(= Laut)* sound *(auch Rad, Film, Comput)*; *(von Zeitzeichen, im Telefon)* pip; *(= Klangfarbe)* tone; *(Mus)* tone; *(= Note)* note; **halber ~** semitone; **ganzer ~** tone; **den ~ angeben** *(lit)* to give the note; *(fig) (Mensch)* to set the tone; *(Thema, Farbe etc)* to be predominant; **keinen ~ herausbringen** *or* **hervorbringen** not to be able to say a word; **keinen ~ sagen** *or* **von sich geben** not to make a sound; **er hat keinen ~ von sich hören lassen** *(fig)* we haven't heard a word *or* a peep *(inf)* from him; **keinen ~ (über etw** *acc***) verlauten lassen** *(fig)* not to say a word (about sth); **aus dem Regierunglager kamen kritische Töne** criticism came from the government camp; **hast du** *or* **hat der Mensch Töne!** *(inf)* did you ever! *(inf)*; **dicke** *or* **große Töne spucken** *or* **reden** *(inf)* to talk big; **jdn in (den) höchsten Tönen loben** *(inf)* to praise sb to the skies, to praise sb highly; **~ aus** *(Comput)* mute
b *(= Betonung)* stress; *(= Tonfall)* intonation; *(im Chinesischen etc)* tone
c *(= Redeweise, Umgangston)* tone; *(= Atmosphäre)* atmosphere; **den richtigen ~ finden** to strike the right note; **ich verbitte mir diesen ~** I will not be spoken to like that; **er hat einen unverschämten ~ am Leib(e)** *or* **am Hals** *(inf)* he's very cheeky *(Brit) or* fresh *(US)*; **einen anderen ~ anschlagen** to change one's tune; **der ~ macht die Musik** *(prov)* it's not what you say but the way that *or* how you say it; **der gute ~** good form
d *(= Farbton)* tone; *(= Nuance)* shade

Ton|ab|neh|mer M cartridge, pick-up

to|nal [to'na:l] ADJ tonal

To|na|li|tät F tonality

Ton-: **ton|an|ge|bend** ADJ who/which sets the tone; **~ sein** to set the tone; **Ton|arm** M pick-up arm; **Ton|art** F *(Mus)* key; *(fig: = Tonfall)* tone; **eine andere ~ anschlagen** to change one's tune; **Ton|as|sis|tent(in)** M(F) sound operator; **Ton|as|sis|tenz** F sound; **Ton|ate|lier** NT recording studio; **Ton|aus|fall** M *(TV)* loss of sound; *(kurz)* (sound) dropout

Ton|band [-bant] NT *pl* **-bänder** tape *(mit* of); *(inf: = Gerät)* tape recorder

Ton|band-: **Ton|band|auf|nah|me** F tape recording; **Ton|band|ge|rät** NT tape recorder

Ton-: **Ton|blen|de** F tone control; **Ton|dich|ter(in)** M(F) composer; **Ton|dich|tung** F tone poem

to|nen ['to:nən] VT *(Phot)* to tone

tö|nen ['tø:nən] VI *(lit, fig: = klingen)* to sound; *(= schallen auch)* to resound; *(= großspurig reden)* to boast; **nach etw ~** *(fig)* to contain (over)tones of sth; **von unten tönten Kinderstimmen** children's voices could be heard from below

tö|nen VT to tint; **sich** *(dat)* **die Haare ~** to tint one's hair; **die Sonne hat ihre Haut schon goldbraun getönt** the sun has bronzed her skin; **der Herbst tönt alle Blätter** autumn makes all the leaves change colour *(Brit)*, fall makes all the leaves change color *(US)*; **etw leicht rot** *etc* **~** to tinge sth (with) red *etc* → *auch* **getönt**

To|ner ['to:nɐ] M -s, - toner

Ton|er|de F aluminium oxide → **essigsauer**

tö|nern ['tø:nɐn] ADJ *attr* clay; **auf ~en Füßen stehen** *(fig)* to be shaky

Ton-: **Ton|fall** M tone of voice; *(= Intonation)* intonation; **Ton|film** M sound film, talkie *(dated inf)*; **Ton|fol|ge** F sequence of sounds; *(Mus)* sequence of notes; *(bei Film)* sound sequence; **Ton|fre|quenz** F audio frequency; **Ton|ge|fäß** NT earthenware vessel; **Ton|ge|schirr** NT earthenware; **Ton|ge|schlecht** NT scale; **ton|hal|tig** ADJ clayey, argillaceous *(spec)*, argilliferous *(spec)*; **Ton|hö|he** F pitch

To|ni|ka ['to:nika] F -, **Toniken** [-kn] *(Mus)* tonic

To|ni|kum ['to:nikʊm] NT -s, **Tonika** [-ka] tonic

Ton-: **Ton|in|ge|ni|eur(in)** M(F) sound engineer; **Ton|ka|bi|ne** F sound booth; **Ton|ka|me|ra** F sound camera; **Ton|kopf** M recording head; **Ton|la|ge** F pitch (level); *(= Tonumfang)* register; **eine ~ höher** one note higher; **Ton|lei|ter** F scale; **ton|los** ADJ toneless; *Stimme auch* flat ADV in a flat voice; **Ton|ma|le|rei** F *(Mus)* tone painting; **Ton|meis|ter(in)** M(F) sound mixer

Ton|na|ge [tɔ'na:ʒə] F -, -n *(Naut)* tonnage

Tönn|chen ['tœnçən] NT -s, - little barrel, tub; *(fig hum, Mensch)* roly-poly *(inf)*, dumpling *(inf)*

Ton|ne ['tɔnə] F -, -n **a** *(= Behälter)* barrel, cask; *(aus Metall)* drum; *(= Mülltonne)* bin *(Brit)*, trash can *(US)*; *(inf: Mensch)* fatty *(inf)*; **gelbe ~** yellow bin *(Brit) or* trash can *(US, for recyclable material)*; **grüne ~** green bin *(Brit) or* trash can *(US, for paper)*; **braune ~** brown bin *(Brit) or* trash can *(US, for biodegradable waste)* **b** *(= Gewicht)* metric ton(ne) **c** *(= Registertonne)* (register) ton **d** *(Naut: = Boje)* buoy

Ton|nen-: **Ton|nen|ge|wöl|be** NT *(Archit)* barrel vaulting; **ton|nen|wei|se** ADV by the ton, in tons; **~ Fische fangen** *(fig)* to catch tons (and tons) of fish

Ton-: **Ton|set|zer(in)** M(F) *(geh)* composer; **Ton|sig|nal** NT sound signal, audible signal; **Ton|sil|be** F tonic *or* stressed syllable; **Ton|spra|che** F tone language; **Ton|spur** F soundtrack; **Ton|stö|rung** F sound interference; **Ton|strei|fen** M soundtrack; **Ton|stu|dio** NT recording studio

Ton|sur [tɔn'zu:ɐ] F -, -en tonsure

Ton-: **Ton|tau|be** F clay pigeon; **Ton|tau|ben|schie|ßen** NT -s, *no pl* clay pigeon shooting; **Ton|tech|ni|ker(in)** M(F) sound technician; **Ton|trä|ger** M sound carrier; **Ton|um|fang** M register

To|nung ['to:nʊŋ] F -, -en *(Phot)* toning

Tö|nung ['tø:nʊŋ] F -, -en *(= Haartönung)* hair colour *(Brit) or* color *(US)*; *(= das Tönen)* tinting; *(= Farbton)* shade, tone

To|nus ['to:nʊs] M -, **Toni** **a** *(Physiol)* tone, tonus, tonicity *(spec)* **b** *(Mus)* whole tone

Ton-: **Ton|wa|ren** PL earthenware *sing*; **Ton|zie|gel** M brick; *(= Dachziegel)* tile

Tool|box F -, -en *(Comput)* toolbox

Top [tɔp] NT -s, -s *(Fashion)* top

TOP *abbr von* **Tagesordnungspunkt**

Top-, top- ['tɔp] *in cpds* top; **Top|agent(in)** M(F) top agent; **top|ak|tu|ell** ADJ up-to-the--minute; *Nachrichten auch* latest

To|pas [to'pa:s] M -es, -e [-zə] topaz

Topf [tɔpf] M -(e)s, ¨-e ['tœpfə] pot; *(= Kochtopf auch)* (sauce)pan; *(= Nachttopf)* potty *(inf)*; *(inf: = Toilette)* loo *(Brit inf)*, john *(US inf)*; **alles in einen ~ werfen** *(fig)* to lump everything together; **jeder ~ findet seinen Deckel** *(prov)* every Jack will find his Jill *(prov)*

Top-Fa|vo|rit(in) M(F) top favourite *(Brit) or* favorite *(US)*

Topf|blu|me F potted flower

Töpf|chen ['tœpfçən] NT -s, - *dim von* **Topf**

Topf|de|ckel M *(von Kochtopf)* saucepan lid; *(von Behälter)* pot *or* jar lid

Top|fen ['tɔpfn] M -s, - *(Aus, S Ger)* quark

Töp|fer ['tœpfɐ] M -s, -, **Töp|fe|rin** [-ərɪn] F -, -nen potter; *(dial: = Ofensetzer)* stove fitter

Töp|fe|rei [tœpfə'rai] F -, -en pottery

Töp|fer|hand|werk NT potter's trade

töp|fern ['tœpfɐn] VI to do pottery VT to make (in clay); **wir sahen zu, wie er auf der Scheibe eine Vase töpferte** we watched him throwing a vase

Töp|fer-: **Töp|fer|ofen** M kiln; **Töp|fer|schei|be** F potter's wheel; **Töp|fer|wa|ren** PL pottery *sing*; *(irden)* earthenware *sing*

Topf|hand|schuh M oven glove *(Brit) or* mitt

top|fit ADJ *pred* in top form; *(gesundheitlich)* as fit as a fiddle

Topf-: **Topf|ku|chen** M gugelhupf; **Topf|lap|pen** M oven cloth; *(kleiner)* pan holder; **Topf|markt** M *market where pots and pans are sold*

Top|form F **in ~ sein** *(inf)* to be in top form

Topf|pflan|ze F potted plant

To|pi|nam|bur [topinam'bu:ɐ] M -s, -s *or* -e, *or* *f* -, -en Jerusalem artichoke

Top-: **Top|la|der** ['tɔpla:dɐ] M -s, - top loader; **Top|ma|nage|ment** NT *(= das Management)* top management; *(= die Manager)* chief executives *pl*; **Top|mo|dell** NT *(Fashion, Tech)* top model

To|po|graf [topo'gra:f] M -en, -en, **To|po|gra|fin** [-'gra:fɪn] F -, -nen topographer

To|po|gra|fie [topogra'fi:] F -, -n [-'fi:ən] topography

to|po|gra|fisch [topo'gra:fɪʃ] ADJ topographic(al) ADV *vermessen* topographically; **das Land ist topographisch und klimatisch ungeeignet**

the topography and the climate of this country are ill suited

To|po|graph [topo'gra:f] *etc* = **Topograf** *etc*

To|po|lo|gie [topolo'gi:] F -, *no pl (Math)* topology

To|pos ['to:pɔs, 'tɔpɔs] M -, **Topoi** ['to:pɔy] *(Liter)* topos

topp [tɔp] INTERJ done, it's a deal

Topp [tɔp] M -s, -e *or* -s *(Naut)* masthead; **über die ~en geflaggt sein** *or* **haben** to be dressed overall

top|pen VT to top, to beat; **das ist schwer zu ~** it's hard to top *or* beat

Topp|se|gel NT topsail

Tor [to:ɐ] M -en, -en *(old, liter)* fool

Tor NT -(e)s, -e **a** *(lit, fig: = Himmelstor, Höllentor)* gate; *(= Durchfahrt, fig: zum Glück etc)* gateway; *(= Torbogen)* archway; *(von Garage, Scheune)* door; *(= Felsentor)* arch in the rock; *(= Gletschertor)* mouth (of glacier); **jdm das ~ zu etw öffnen** to open sb's eyes to sth; *zu Karriere etc* to open the door to sth for sb → **Tür b** *(Sport)* goal; *(bei Skilaufen)* gate; **im ~ stehen** to be in goal, to be the goalkeeper

Tor-: **Tor|ab|stoß** M *(Ftbl)* goal kick; **Tor|aus** NT *(Ftbl)* **der Ball geht ins ~** the ball goes behind the goal line; **Tor|aus|li|nie** F *(Ftbl)* goal line; **Tor|bo|gen** M arch, archway; **Tor|chan|ce** F *(Sport)* chance (to score), scoring opportunity, opening; **eine ~ herausspielen** to create an opening; **eine ~ nutzen/vergeben** to take/to waste a scoring opportunity; **Tor|dif|fe|renz** F *(Sport)* goal difference; **Tor|ein|fahrt** F entrance gate

To|re|ro [to're:ro] M -(s), -s torero

To|res|schluss M = **Torschluss**

Torf [tɔrf] M -(e)s, *no pl* peat

Torf-: **Torf|bo|den** M peat; **Torf|er|de** F peat; **Torf|feu|e|rung** F peat fire(s *pl*)

tor|fig ['tɔrfɪç] ADJ peaty

Tor|flü|gel M gate *(of a pair of gates)*

Torf-: **Torf|moor** NT peat bog *or (trocken)* moor; **Torf|moos** NT sphagnum (moss); **Torf|mull** M (loose) garden peat

Tor|frau F goalkeeper, goalie *(inf)*

Torf-: **Torf|ste|cher** [-ʃtɛçɐ] M -s, -, **Torf|ste|che|rin** [-ərɪn] F -, -nen peat-cutter; **Torf|stich** M patch *or* plot of peat

tor|ge|fähr|lich ADJ *Spieler* dangerous, potent

Tor|heit ['to:ɐhait] F -, -en *(geh)* foolishness, stupidity; *(= törichte Handlung)* foolish *or* stupid act; **er hat die ~ begangen, zu ...** he was foolish *or* stupid enough to ...

Tor|hü|ter(in) M(F) goalkeeper

tö|richt ['tø:rɪçt] *(geh)* ADJ foolish, stupid; *Wunsch, Hoffnung* idle ADV foolishly, stupidly

tö|rich|ter|wei|se ['tø:rɪçtə'vaizə] ADV foolishly, stupidly

Tor|jä|ger(in) M(F) (goal)scorer

tor|keln ['tɔrkln] VI *aux sein* to stagger, to reel

Tor-: **Tor|lat|te** F crossbar; **Tor|lauf** M slalom; **Tor|li|nie** F goal line; **tor|los** ADJ goalless; **das Spiel blieb ~, das Spiel ging ~ aus** it was a goalless draw, there was no score; **Tor|mann** M *pl* **-männer** goalkeeper, goalie *(inf)*

Törn [tœrn] M -s, -s *(Naut)* cruise

Tor|na|do [tɔr'na:do] M -s, -s tornado

Tor|nis|ter [tɔr'nɪstɐ] M -s, - *(Mil)* knapsack; *(dated: = Schulranzen)* satchel

tor|pe|die|ren [tɔrpe'di:rən] *ptp* **torpediert** VT *(Naut, fig)* to torpedo

Tor|pe|do [tɔr'pe:do] M -s, -s torpedo

Tor|pe|do|boot NT torpedo boat

Tor-: **Tor|pfos|ten** M gatepost; *(Sport)* goalpost; **Tor|raum** M *(Sport)* goalmouth; **Tor|schluss** M, *no pl (fig)* **kurz vor ~** at the last minute, at the eleventh hour; **nach ~** too late; **Tor|schluss|pa|nik** F *(inf)* last minute panic; *(von Unverheirateten)* fear of being left on the shelf; **Tor|schüt|ze** M, **Tor|schüt|zin** F (goal)scorer; **Tor|schüt|zen|kö|nig(in)** M(F) top goalscorer

Tor|si|on [tɔr'zio:n] F -, -en torsion

Tor|si|ons-: **Tor|si|ons|fes|tig|keit** F torsional strength; **Tor|si|ons|stab** M torsion bar

Tor|so ['tɔrzo] M -s, -s *or* **Torsi** ['tɔrzi] torso; *(fig)* skeleton

Tor|sze|ne F action *no pl* in the goal area

Tort [tɔrt] M -(e)s, *no pl (geh)* wrong, injustice; **jdm etw zum ~ tun** to do sth to vex sb

Tört|chen ['tœrtçən] NT -s, - *dim von* **Torte** (small) tart, tartlet

Tor|te ['tɔrtə] F -, -n gâteau; *(= Obsttorte)* flan

Tor|te|lett [tɔrtə'lɛt] NT -s, -s, **Tor|te|let|te** [tɔrtə'lɛtə] F -, -n (small) tart, tartlet

Tor|ten-: **Tor|ten|bo|den** M flan case *or (ohne Seiten)* base; **Tor|ten|dia|gramm** NT pie chart; **Tor|ten|guss** M glaze; **Tor|ten|he|ber** [-he:bɐ] M -s, - cake slice; **Tor|ten|plat|te** F cake plate; **Tor|ten|schau|fel** F cake slice; **Tor|ten|schlacht** F *(in Film)* custard-pie battle; **Tor|ten|stück** NT slice of cake; *(fig inf)* big draw *(inf)*

Tor|tur [tɔr'tu:ɐ] F -, -en torture; *(fig auch)* ordeal

Tor-: **Tor|ver|hält|nis** NT score; **Tor|wäch|ter(in)** M(F), **Tor|wart** [-vart] M -(e)s, -e, **Tor|war|tin** [-vartɪn] F -, -nen goalkeeper

to|sen ['to:zn] VI **a** *(Wasserfall, Wellen, Verkehr)* to roar, to thunder; *(Wind, Sturm)* to rage; **~der Beifall** thunderous applause **b** *aux sein (mit Ortsangabe)* to thunder

tot [to:t] ADJ **a** *(= gestorben) (lit, fig)* dead; *(inf: = erschöpft)* beat *(inf)*, whacked *(Brit inf)*; **mehr ~ als lebendig** *(fig inf)* more dead than alive; **~ geboren** stillborn; **~ geboren werden** to be stillborn; **ein ~ geborenes Kind sein** *(fig)* to be doomed (to failure); **~ umfallen, ~ zu Boden fallen** to drop dead; **ich will ~ umfallen, wenn das nicht wahr ist** cross my heart and hope to die (if it isn't true) *(inf)*; **~ zusammenbrechen** to collapse and die; **er war auf der Stelle ~** he died instantly; **den ~en Mann machen** *(inf)* to float on one's back; **ein ~er Mann sein** *(fig inf)* to be a goner *(inf)*; **den ~en Mann spielen** *or* **markieren** to play dead

b *(= leblos) Ast, Pflanze, Geschäftszeit, Sprache, Leitung* dead; *Augen* sightless, blind; *Haus, Stadt* deserted; *Landschaft etc* bleak; *Wissen* useless; *Vulkan* extinct, dead; *Farbe* dull, drab; *(Rail) Gleis* disused; **~er Flussarm** backwater; *(= Schleife)* oxbow (lake); **ein ~er Briefkasten** a dead letter box; **~er Winkel** blind spot; *(Mil)* dead angle; **das Tote Meer** the Dead Sea; **~er Punkt** *(= Stillstand)* standstill, halt; *(in Verhandlungen)* deadlock; *(= körperliche Ermüdung)* low point; **ich habe im Moment meinen ~en Punkt** I'm at a low ebb just now; **den ~en Punkt überwinden** to break the deadlock; *(körperlich)* to get one's second wind

c *(= nutzlos) Last, Gewicht, Kapital* dead; **ein ~es Rennen** *(lit, fig)* a dead heat; **~er Gang** *(Tech)* play

d *(Min)* **ein ~er Mann** *a worked-out part of a mine*

to|tal [to'ta:l] ADJ total; *Staat* totalitarian ADV totally

To|tal|an|sicht F complete view

To|tal|aus|ver|kauf M clearance sale

To|ta|le F -, -n *(Film, Phot)* wide shot

To|ta|li|sa|tor [totali'za:to:ɐ] M -s, **Totalisatoren** [-'to:rən] totalizator, tote *(inf)*

to|ta|li|tär [totali'tɛ:ɐ] ADJ totalitarian ADV in a totalitarian way

To|ta|li|ta|ris|mus [totalita'rɪsmʊs] M -s, *no pl* totalitarianism

To|ta|li|tät [totali'tɛ:t] F -, -en totality, entirety

To|tal-: **To|tal|ope|ra|ti|on** F extirpation; *(von Gebärmutter)* hysterectomy; *(mit Eierstöcken)* hysterosaphorectomy; **To|tal|scha|den** M write-off; **~ machen** *(inf)* to write a car *etc* off; **To|tal|ver|wei|ge|rer** M *(= Kriegsdienstverweigerer)* conscientious objector *(to both military service and civilian alternative)*

tot-: **tot+ar|bei|ten** VR *sep (inf)* to work oneself to death; **tot+är|gern** VR *sep (inf)* to be/become livid

To|tem ['to:tɛm] NT -s, -s totem

To|te|mis|mus [tote'mɪsmʊs] M -, *no pl* totemism

To|tem|pfahl M totem pole

tö|ten ['tø:tn] VTI *(lit, fig)* to kill; *Zahnnerv* to deaden → **Blick a**

To|ten-: **To|ten|acker** M *(liter)* graveyard; **To|ten|amt** NT requiem mass; **To|ten|be|stat|tung** F burial of the dead; **To|ten|bett** NT deathbed; **to|ten|blass** ADJ deathly pale, pale as death; **To|ten|bläs|se** F deathly pallor; **to|ten|bleich** ADJ = **totenblass**; **To|ten|fei|er** F funeral *or* burial ceremony; **To|ten|fle|cke** PL postmortem *or* cadaveric *(spec)* lividity *sing*; **To|ten|glo|cke** F (death) knell; **To|ten|grä|ber(in)** M(F) gravedigger; **To|ten|hemd** NT shroud; **To|ten|kla|ge** F lamentation of the dead; *(Liter)* dirge, lament; **To|ten|kopf** M **a** skull; *(als Zeichen)* death's-head; *(auf Piratenfahne, Arzneiflasche etc)* skull and crossbones **b** *(Zool)* death's-head moth; **To|ten|kult** M cult of the dead; **To|ten|mas|ke** F death mask; **To|ten|mes|se** F requiem mass; **To|ten|reich** NT *(Myth)* kingdom of the dead; **To|ten|schein** M death certificate; **To|ten|sonn|tag** M *Sunday before Advent, on which the dead are commemorated*; **To|ten|stadt** F necropolis; **To|ten|star|re** F rigor mortis; **to|ten|still** ADJ deathly silent *or* quiet; **To|ten|stil|le** F deathly silence *or* quiet; **To|ten|tanz** M dance of death, danse macabre; **To|ten|wa|che** F wake

To|te(r) ['to:tə] MF *decl as adj* dead person, dead man/woman; *(bei Unfall etc)* fatality, casualty; *(Mil)* casualty; **die ~n** the dead; **es gab 3 ~** 3 people died *or* were killed; **das ist ein Lärm, um ~ aufzuwecken** the noise is enough to wake(n) the dead

Tot-: **Tot|er|klär|te(r)** ['to:tlɛɐklɛ:ɐtə] MF *decl as adj* person *or* man/woman *etc* declared to be dead; **tot+fah|ren** VT *sep irreg (inf)* to knock down and kill; **tot|ge|bo|ren** ADJ *attr* → **tot a**; **Tot|ge|burt** F stillbirth; *(= Kind)* stillborn child *or* baby; **Tot|ge|glaub|te(r)** [-gəglauptə] MF *decl as adj* person *or* man/woman *etc* believed to be dead; **tot|ge|sagt** ADJ declared dead; *(fig)* written off; **Tot|ge|sag|te(r)** [-gəza:ktə] MF *decl as adj* person *or* man/woman *etc* said to be dead; **~ leben länger!** there's life in the old dog yet *(iro)*; **tot+krie|gen** VT *sep (inf)* **nicht totzukriegen sein** to go on for ever; **tot+la|chen** VR *sep (inf)* to kill oneself (laughing) *(Brit inf)*, to die laughing; **es ist zum Totlachen** it is hilarious; **tot+lau|fen** VR *sep irreg (inf)* to peter out; **tot+ma|chen** *sep (inf)* VT to kill VR *(fig)* to kill oneself

To|to ['to:to] M OR (INF, AUS, SW) NT -s, -s (football) pools *pl (Brit)*; **(im) ~ spielen** to do the pools *(Brit)*; **etw im ~ gewinnen** to win sth on the pools *(Brit)*; **im ~ gewinnen** *(Hauptgewinn)* to win the pools *(Brit)*; **er hat vier Richtige im ~** four of his matches came up

To|to- *in cpds* pools *(Brit)*; **To|to|schein** M, **To|to|zet|tel** M pools coupon *(Brit)*

Tot-: **tot+schie|ßen** VT *sep irreg (inf)* to shoot dead; **Tot|schlag** M *(Jur)* manslaughter → **Mord**; **Tot|schlag|ar|gu|ment** NT *(inf)* knock-out argument; **tot+schla|gen** VT *sep irreg (lit, fig)* to kill; *(inf) Menschen auch* to beat to death; **du kannst mich ~, ich weiß es nicht** for the life of me I don't know; **Tot|schlä|ger** M cudgel, club; **tot+schwei|gen** VT *sep irreg* to hush up *(inf)*; **tot stel|len** VR to pretend to be dead, to play dead; *(Mensch auch)* to play possum *(inf)*; **tot+tre|ten** VT *sep irreg* to trample to death; *Insekt etc* to tread on and kill

Tö|tung ['tø:tʊŋ] F -, -en killing; **fahrlässige ~** manslaughter (through culpable negligence *(esp Brit)*)

Tö|tungs-: **Tö|tungs|ab|sicht** F intention to kill; **Tö|tungs|ver|such** M attempted murder

Touch [tatʃ] M **-s, -s** *(= Atmosphäre)* air, tone, flavour *(Brit)*, flavor *(US)*; *(= Flair)* touch; *(= Tendenz)* leanings *pl*

tou|chie|ren [tu'ʃiːrən] *ptp* **touchiert** VT **a** *(esp Sport)* to touch, to brush, to bump **b** *(Med) (= austasten)* to palpate; *(= abätzen)* to cauterize

Touch|screen ['tatʃskriːn] M **-s, -s** *(Comput)* touch screen

Tou|pet [tu'peː] NT **-s, -s** toupée

tou|pie|ren [tu'piːrən] *ptp* **toupiert** VT to backcomb

Tour [tuːɐ] F **-, -en** **a** *(= Fahrt)* trip, outing; *(= Ausflugstour)* tour; *(= Spritztour) (mit Auto)* drive; *(mit Rad)* ride; *(= Wanderung)* walk, hike; *(= Bergtour)* climb; *(= Tournee)* tour; **auf ~ gehen** to go on *or* for a trip *or* an outing/on a tour/for a drive/ride/walk *or* hike/climb
b *(= Umdrehung)* revolution, rev *(inf)*; *(beim Tanz)* figure; *(beim Stricken)* two rows; *(mit Rundnadeln)* round; **auf ~en kommen** *(Auto)* to reach top speed; *(fig inf)* to get into top gear; *(= sich aufregen)* to get worked up *(inf)*; **ich komme heute aber auch gar nicht auf ~en** I can't get going at all today; **jdn/etw auf ~en bringen** *(fig)* to get sb/sth going; **auf vollen ~en laufen** *(lit)* to run at full *or* top speed; *(fig)* to be in full swing; **in einer ~** *(inf)* incessantly, the whole time
c *(inf: = Art und Weise)* ploy; **mit der ~ brauchst du mir gar nicht zu kommen** don't try that one on me; **auf die krumme** *or* **schiefe** *or* **schräge ~** by dishonest means; **etw auf die weiche** *or* **sanfte ~ versuchen** to try using soft soap *(Brit)* *or* sweet talk to get sth *(inf)*; **jdm die ~ vermasseln** *(inf)* to put a spoke *(Brit)* *or* wrench *(US)* in sb's wheel *(inf)*, to put paid to sb's plans

Tour de Force [turdə'fɔrs] F **-,** *no pl (geh)* tour de force

Tour d'Ho|ri|zon [turdɔri'zõː] F **- -, -s -** *(geh)* tour d'horizon *(liter)*, broad survey

tou|ren ['tuːrən] VI *(inf: = reisen, auf Tournee sein)* to tour; **durch ein Land ~** to tour (through *or* across) a country

Tou|ren-: **Tou|ren|fah|rer(in)** M(F) long-distance driver; **Tou|ren|rad** NT tourer; **Tou|ren|ski** M cross-country ski; **Tou|ren|wa|gen** M *(im Motorsport)* touring car; **Tou|ren|zahl** F number of revolutions *or* revs *pl (inf)*; **Tou|ren|zäh|ler** M rev counter

Tou|ri ['tuːri] M **-(s), -s** *usu pl (inf pej: = Tourist)* grockle *(Brit inf)*, shoobie *(US sl)*

Tou|ris|mus [tu'rɪsmʊs] M **-,** *no pl* tourism

Tou|ris|mus|in|dust|rie F tourist industry

Tou|rist [tu'rɪst] M **-en, -en**, **Tou|ris|tin** [-'rɪstɪn] F **-, -nen** tourist

Tou|ris|ten|at|trak|ti|on F tourist attraction

Tou|ris|ten|klas|se F tourist class

Tou|ris|tik [tu'rɪstɪk] F **-,** *no pl* tourism, tourist industry

Tou|ris|tik|un|ter|neh|men NT tour company

Tou|ris|tin [-'rɪstɪn] F **-, -nen** tourist

Tour|ne|dos [tʊrnə'doː] NT **-, -** [-'doːs] *usu pl (Cook)* tournedos

Tour|nee [tʊr'neː] F **-, -s** *or* **-n** [-'neːən] tour; **auf ~ gehen** to go on tour; **auf ~ sein** to be on tour, to be touring

tour-re|tour [tuːɐre'tuːɐ] ADV *(Aus)* return

To|wer ['tauɐ] M **-s, -** **a** *(Aviat)* control tower **b** *(Comput)* tower

To|xi|ko|lo|ge [tɔksiko'loːgə] M **-n, -n**, **To|xi|ko|lo|gin** [-'loːgɪn] F **-, -nen** toxicologist

to|xi|ko|lo|gisch [tɔksiko'loːgɪʃ] ADJ toxicological ADV toxicologically; **etw ~ untersuchen** to do a toxicological analysis of sth; **~ unbedenklich** nontoxic

to|xisch ['tɔksɪʃ] ADJ toxic ADV toxically; **~ wirken** to be toxic

To|xi|zi|tät [tɔksitsi'tɛːt] F **-,** *no pl* toxicity

To|xo|plas|mo|se [tɔksoplas'moːzə] F **-, -n** toxoplasmosis

Trab [traːp] M **-(e)s** [-bəs], *no pl* trot; **im ~** at a trot; **(im) ~ reiten** to trot; **sich in ~ setzen** *(inf)* to get going *or* cracking *(inf)*; **auf ~ sein** *(inf)* to be on the go *(inf)*; **jdn in ~ halten** *(inf)* to keep sb on the go *(inf)*; **jdn auf (den) ~ bringen** *(inf)* to make sb get a move on *(inf)*

Tra|bant [tra'bant] M **-en, -en** **a** *(Astron)* satellite **b** *(Hist)* bodyguard; *(fig)* satellite **c** *usu pl (dated inf)* kiddie-wink *(Brit inf)*, kiddie *(inf)*

Trabant® M **-s, -s** *most popular make of East German car*

Tra|ban|ten|stadt F satellite town

Trab|bi ['trabi] M **-s, -s** *(inf) abbr von* **Trabant**

tra|ben ['traːbn] VI **a** *aux haben or sein* to trot; **mit dem Pferd ~** to trot one's horse **b** *aux sein (inf: = laufen)* to trot; **ich musste noch einmal in die Stadt ~** I had to go traipsing back into town

Tra|ber ['traːbɐ] M **-s, -** trotter

Tra|bi ['traːbi] M **-s, -s** *(inf) abbr von* **Trabant**

Trab-: **Trab|renn|bahn** F trotting course; **Trab|ren|nen** NT trotting; *(Veranstaltung)* trotting race

Tracht [traxt] F **-, -en** **a** *(= Kleidung)* dress, garb; *(= Volkstracht etc)* costume; *(= Schwesterntracht)* uniform **b** *(obs: = Traglast)* load; **jdm eine ~ Prügel verabfolgen** *or* **verabreichen** *(inf)* to give sb a beating *or* thrashing

trach|ten ['traxtn] VI *(geh)* to strive *(nach* for, after); **danach ~, etw zu tun** to strive *or* endeavour *(Brit)* *or* endeavor *(US)* to do sth; **jdm nach dem Leben ~** to be after sb's blood

Trach|ten-: **Trach|ten|fest** NT *festive occasion where traditional/national costume is worn*; **Trach|ten|grup|pe** F *group dressed in traditional/national costume*; **Trach|ten|ja|cke** F *traditionally styled jacket made of thick woollen material (von Volkstracht) jacket worn as part of traditional/national costume*; **Trach|ten|kos|tüm** NT *suit made of thick woollen material*

träch|tig ['trɛçtɪç] ADJ *(lit) Tier* pregnant; *(fig geh)* laden *(von* with); *Gedanke etc* meaningful, significant

Träch|tig|keit F *(von Tier)* pregnancy

Track [trɛk] M **-s, -s** **a** *(auf CD, Band)* track **b** *(= Route)* route; *(= Bergwanderung)* mountain hike *or* walk

Track|ball ['trɛkbɔːl] M **-s, -s** *(Comput)* trackball

tra|die|ren [tra'diːrən] *ptp* **tradiert** VT *(geh)* to hand down

Tra|di|ti|on [tradi'tsioːn] F **-, -en** tradition; **(bei jdm) ~ haben** to be a tradition (for sb)

Tra|di|ti|o|na|lis|mus [traditsiona'lɪsmʊs] M **-,** *no pl* traditionalism

Tra|di|ti|o|na|list [traditsiona'lɪst] M **-en, -en**, **Tra|di|ti|o|na|lis|tin** [-'lɪstɪn] F **-, -nen** traditionalist

tra|di|ti|o|na|lis|tisch [traditsiona'lɪstɪʃ] ADJ traditionalistic, traditionalist ADV **~ veranlagt sein** to be traditionally-minded

tra|di|ti|o|nell [traditsio'nɛl] ADJ *usu attr* traditional ADV traditionally

Tra|di|ti|ons-: **tra|di|ti|ons|be|wusst** ADJ tradition-conscious; **Tra|di|ti|ons|be|wusst|sein** NT consciousness of tradition; **tra|di|ti|ons|ge|bun|den** ADJ bound by tradition; **tra|di|ti|ons|ge|mäß** ADV traditionally, according to tradition; **tra|di|ti|ons|reich** ADJ rich in tradition

traf *pret von* **treffen**

Tra|fik [tra'fɪk] F **-, -en** *(Aus)* tobacconist's (shop)

Tra|fi|kant [trafi'kant] M **-en, -en**, **Tra|fi|kan|tin** [-'kantɪn] F **-, -nen** *(Aus)* tobacconist

Tra|fo ['traːfo] M **-(s), -s** *(inf)* transformer

träg [trɛːk] ADJ ADV = **träge**

Trag-: **Trag|bah|re** F stretcher; **trag|bar** ADJ **a** *Apparat, Gerät* portable; *Kleid* wearable **b** *(= annehmbar)* acceptable *(für* to); *(= erträglich)* bearable

Tra|ge ['traːgə] F **-, -n** *(= Bahre)* litter; *(= Tragkorb)* pannier

trä|ge ['trɛːgə] ADJ **a** sluggish; *Mensch, Handbewegung etc* lethargic; *(= faul)* lazy, idle; **geistig ~** mentally lazy **b** *(Phys) Masse* inert ADV *sich bewegen* sluggishly; *sich rekeln* lethargically

Tra|ge|gurt M (carrying) sling, harness

tra|gen ['traːgn] *pret* **trug** [truːk], *ptp* **getragen** [gə'traːgn] VT **a** *(= befördern, dabeihaben)* to carry; *(= an einen Ort bringen)* to take; *(Wellen etc)* to bear, to carry; *(fig) Gerücht etc* to pass on, to spread; **etw mit** *or* **bei sich ~** to carry sth with one; **den Brief zur Post® ~** to take the letter to the post office; **den Arm in der Schlinge ~** to have one's arm in a sling
b *(= am Körper tragen) Kleid, Brille, Rot etc, Perücke* to wear; *Bart, Gebiss* to have; *Waffen* to carry; **wie trägt sie zurzeit ihre Haare?** how is she wearing her hair now?; **getragene Kleider** second-hand clothes; *(= abgelegt)* castoffs *(Brit)*, throwouts *(US)* → **Trauer**
c *(= stützen, halten)* to support → **tragend**
d *(= aushalten, Tragfähigkeit haben)* to take (the weight of), to carry
e *(= hervorbringen) Zinsen* to yield; *Ernte* to yield, to produce; *(lit, fig) Früchte* to bear; **der Baum trägt viele Früchte** the tree produces a good crop of fruit; *(in dieser Saison)* the tree is full of fruit
f *(= trächtig sein)* to be carrying
g *(= ertragen) Schicksal, Leid etc* to bear, to endure; *Kreuz* to bear
h *(= übernehmen) Verluste* to defray; *Kosten* to bear, to carry; *Risiko* to take; *Folgen* to take, to bear; **die Verantwortung für etw ~** to be responsible for sth; **die Schuld für etw ~** to be to blame for sth
i *(= unterhalten) Verein, Organisation* to support, to back
j *(= haben) Titel, Namen, Aufschrift etc* to bear, to have; *Vermerk* to contain; *Etikett* to have; **der Brief trägt das Datum vom ...** the letter is dated ... → **getragen**
VI **a** *(Baum, Acker etc)* to crop, to produce a crop; **gut/schlecht ~** to crop well/badly, to produce a good/bad crop; *(in dieser Saison)* to have a good/bad crop
b *(= trächtig sein)* to be pregnant
c *(= reichen: Geschütz, Stimme)* to carry
d *(Eis)* to take weight; **das Eis trägt noch nicht** the ice won't take anyone's weight yet
e schwer an etw *(dat)* **~** to have a job carrying *or* to carry sth; *(fig)* to find sth hard to bear; **schwer zu ~ haben** to have a lot to carry; *(fig)* to have a heavy cross to bear
f zum Tragen kommen to come to fruition, to bear fruit, to take effect, to bring results; *(= nützlich werden)* to come in useful; **etw zum Tragen bringen** to bring sth to bear *(in +dat* on)
VR **a sich gut** *or* **leicht/schwer** *or* **schlecht ~** to be easy/difficult *or* hard to carry; **schwere Lasten ~ sich besser auf dem Rücken** it is better to carry heavy loads on one's back
b *(Kleid, Stoff)* to wear
c sich mit etw ~ *(geh)* to contemplate sth
d *(= ohne Zuschüsse auskommen)* to be self-supporting

tra|gend ADJ **a** *(= stützend) Säule, Bauteil, Chassisteil* weight-bearing, load-bearing; *(fig: = bestimmend) Bedeutung, Idee, Motiv* fundamental, basic **b** *(Theat) Rolle* major, main **c** *Stimme* resonant **d** *(= trächtig)* pregnant

Trä|ger ['trɛːgɐ] M **-s, -** **a** *(an Kleidung)* strap; *(= Hosenträger)* braces *pl (Brit)*, suspenders *pl (US)* **b** *(Build) (= Holzträger, Betonträger)* (supporting) beam; *(= Stahlträger, Eisenträger)* girder **c** *(Tech: = Stütze von Brücken etc)* support **d** *(= Flugzeugträger)* carrier **e** *(Biol: von Gen)* carrier **f** *(von Sozialeinrichtung)* provider **g** *(= Kostenträger)* funding provider

Trä|ger ['trɛːgɐ] M **-s, -**, **Trä|ge|rin** [-ərɪn] F **-, -nen** **a** *(von Lasten)* bearer, porter; *(von Namen)* bearer; *(von Orden, Amt, Titel)* bearer, holder; *(von Kleidung)* wearer; *(eines Preises)* winner; *(von Krankheit, Gen)* carrier **b** *(fig) (der Kultur, Staatsgewalt etc)* representative; *(einer Bewegung, Entwicklung)* upholder, supporter; *(einer Veranstal-*

tung) sponsor; *(Mittel)* vehicle; **~ einer Einrichtung sein** to be in charge of an institution

Trä|ger-: **Trä|ger|flug|zeug** NT carrier plane; **Trä|ger|ho|se** F trousers *pl (esp Brit) or* pants *pl (esp US)* with straps; **Trä|ger|kleid** NT pinafore dress *(Brit)*, jumper *(US)*; *(sommerlich)* sundress; **Trä|ger|lohn** M porterage; **trä|ger|los** ADJ *Kleidungsstück* strapless; **Trä|ger|ma|te|ri|al** NT base material, carrier material; **Trä|ger|ra|ke|te** F carrier rocket; **Trä|ger|rock** M pinafore dress *(Brit)*, jumper *(US)*; *(für Kinder)* skirt with straps; **Trä|ger|schür|ze** F pinafore; **Trä|ger|sys|tem** NT *(Mil)* carrier system; **Trä|ger|waf|fe** F carrier weapon

Tra|ge-: **Tra|ge|ta|sche** F carrier bag; **Tra|ge|tü|te** F carrier bag; **Tra|ge|zeit** F gestation period

Trag-: **trag|fä|hig** ADJ able to take a weight; *(fig) Kompromiss, Konzept, Lösung* workable; **Trag|fä|hig|keit** F, *no pl* weight-bearing capacity; *(von Brücke)* maximum load; *(fig)* workability; **Trag|flä|che** F wing; *(von Boot)* hydrofoil; **Trag|flä|chen|boot** NT hydrofoil; **Trag|flü|gel** M wing; *(von Boot)* hydrofoil; **Trag|flü|gel|boot** NT hydrofoil

Träg|heit F -, -en sluggishness; *(von Mensch)* lethargy; *(= Faulheit)* laziness; *(Phys)* inertia

Träg|heits-: **Träg|heits|ge|setz** NT law of inertia; **Träg|heits|mo|ment** NT moment of inertia

Trag|him|mel M canopy, baldachin

Tra|gik ['tra:gɪk] F -, *no pl* tragedy; **das ist die ~ der Sache, dass ...** what's tragic about it is that ...

Tra|gi|ker ['tra:gikɐ] M -s, -, **Tra|gi|ke|rin** [-ərɪn] F -, -nen tragedian

Tra|gi-: **Tra|gi|ko|mik** [tragi'ko:mɪk, 'tra:gi-] F tragicomedy; **tra|gi|ko|misch** [tragi'ko:mɪʃ, 'tra:gi-] ADJ tragicomical; **Tra|gi|ko|mö|die** [tragiko'mø:diə, 'tra:gi-] F tragicomedy

tra|gisch ['tra:gɪʃ] ADJ tragic; **das ist nicht so ~** *(inf)* it's not the end of the world ADV tragically; **~ umkommen** to die tragically; **etw ~ nehmen** *(inf)* to take sth to heart

Trag-: **Trag|korb** M pannier; **Trag|kraft** F, *no pl* weight-bearing capacity; *(von Brücke)* maximum load; **Trag|last** F load; *(= Gepäck)* heavy luggage *(esp Brit) or* baggage; **Trag|luft|hal|le** F air hall

Tra|gö|de [tra'gø:də] M -n, -n tragedian → *auch* **Tragödin**

Tra|gö|die [tra'gø:diə] F -, -n *(Liter, fig)* tragedy; **es ist eine ~ mit ihm/dieser Maschine** he/this machine is a disaster

Tra|gö|di|en-: **Tra|gö|di|en|dar|stel|ler(in)** M(F) tragedian/tragedienne; **Tra|gö|di|en|dich|ter(in)** M(F) tragedian

Tra|gö|din [tra'gø:dɪn] F -, -nen tragedienne

Trag-: **Trag|pfei|ler** M weight-bearing *or* load-bearing pillar; *(von Brücke)* support; **Trag|rie|men** M strap; *(von Gewehr)* sling; **Trag|schicht** F base course; **Trag|ses|sel** M sedan chair

trägt [trɛ:kt] *3. pers sing pres von* **tragen**

Trag-: **Trag|wei|te** F *(von Geschütz etc)* range; *(fig)* consequences *pl*; *(von Gesetz)* scope; **sind Sie sich der ~ dieses Schritts/Ihres Handelns bewusst?** are you aware of the possible consequences *or* of the implications of this step/of your action?, are you aware of what this step/your action could mean?; **von großer ~ sein** to have far-reaching consequences *or* implications; **Trag|werk** NT *(Aviat)* wing assembly

Trai|ler ['tre:lɐ] M -s, - **a** *(Aut: = Anhänger)* trailer **b** *(= Filmwerbung)* trailer

Trai|ner ['trɛ:nɐ, 'tre:nɐ] M -s, - *(Sw: = Trainingsanzug)* tracksuit

Trai|ner ['trɛ:nɐ, 'tre:nɐ] M -s, -, **Trai|ne|rin** [-ərɪn] F -, -nen trainer; *(von Rennpferd)* trainer; *(von Schwimmer, Tennisspieler)* coach; *(bei Fußball)* manager

Trai|ner|bank ['trɛ:nɐ-, 'tre:nɐ-] F *pl* **-bänke** bench

trai|nie|ren [trɛ'ni:rən, tre-] *ptp* **trainiert** VT to train; *Mannschaft, Sportler auch* to coach; *Sprung, Übung, Sportart* to practise *(Brit)*, to practice *(US)*; *Muskel, Kreislauf* to exercise; **Fußball/Tennis ~** to do some football/tennis practice; **ein (gut) trainierter Sportler** an athlete who is in training; **auf etw** *(acc)* **trainiert sein** to be trained to do sth; **jdn auf** *or* **für etw** *(acc)* **~** to train *or* coach sb for sth

VI *(Sportler)* to train; *(Rennfahrer)* to practise *(Brit)*, to practice *(US)*; *(= Übungen machen)* to exercise; *(= üben)* to practise *(Brit)*, to practice *(US)*; **auf** *or* **für etw** *(acc)* **~** to train/practise *(Brit) or* practice *(US)* for sth; **da musst du schon noch etwas ~** you'll have to practise *(Brit) or* practice *(US)* that a bit more

VR to train *(auf +acc* for); *(= üben)* to practise *(Brit)*, to practice *(US)*; *(um fit zu werden)* to get some exercise, to get into training

Trai|ning ['trɛ:nɪŋ, 'tre:-] NT -s, -s training *no pl*; *(= Fitnesstraining)* workout; *(bei Autorennen)* practice; *(fig: = Übung)* practice; **er geht jeden Abend zum ~** he goes for a workout every evening; **ein 2-stündiges ~** a 2-hour training session; *(= Fitnesstraining)* a 2-hour workout; **er übernimmt das ~ der Mannschaft** he's taking over the training *or* coaching of the team; **im ~ stehen** to be in training; **durch regelmäßiges ~ lernen die Schüler ...** by regular practice the pupils learn ...

Trai|nings-: **Trai|nings|an|zug** M tracksuit; **Trai|nings|ho|se** F tracksuit trousers *pl (esp Brit) or* bottoms *pl or* pants *pl (esp US)*; **Trai|nings|ja|cke** F tracksuit top; **Trai|nings|la|ger** NT training camp; **Trai|nings|me|tho|de** F training method; **Trai|nings|mög|lich|keit** F training facilities *pl*; **Trai|nings|run|de** F practice lap; **Trai|nings|schuh** M training shoe; **Trai|nings|zeit** F practice time

Tra|keh|ner [tra'ke:nɐ] M -s, - *type of riding horse from Prussia*

Trakt [trakt] M -(e)s, -e *(= Gebäudeteil)* section; *(= Flügel)* wing; *(von Autobahn)* stretch, section

trak|tan|die|ren [traktan'di:rən] *ptp* **traktandiert** VT *(Sw: = auf die Tagesordnung setzen)* to put on the agenda; **traktandiert sein** to be on the agenda

Trak|tat [trak'ta:t] M OR NT -(e)s, -e **a** *(= Abhandlung)* treatise; *(= Flugschrift, religiöse Schrift)* tract **b** *(obs: = Vertrag)* treaty

Trak|tät|chen [trak'tɛ:tçən] NT -s, - *(pej)* tract

trak|tie|ren [trak'ti:rən] *ptp* **traktiert** VT *(inf) (= schlecht behandeln)* to maltreat; *Menschen auch* to give a rough time; *(= quälen) kleine Schwester, Tier etc* to torment; **jdn mit Vorwürfen ~** to keep on at sb *(inf)*; **er hat ihn mit Fäusten/Füßen/Schlägen traktiert** he punched/kicked/hit him

Trak|ti|on [trak'tsio:n] F -, -en *(Aut)* traction

Trak|tor ['trakto:ɐ] M -s, **Traktoren** [-'to:rən] tractor; *(Comput)* tractor feed

Trak|to|rist [trakto'rɪst] M -en, -en, **Trak|to|ris|tin** [-'rɪstɪn] F -, -nen *(dial)* tractor driver

Trak|tor|zu|fuhr F *(Comput) (von Drucker)* tractor feed

träl|lern ['trɛlɐn] VTI to warble; *(Vogel auch)* to trill; **vor sich hin ~** to warble away to oneself

Tram [tram] F -, -s *(dial, Sw)*, **Tram|bahn** F *(S Ger)* = **Straßenbahn**

Tramp [trɛmp, tramp] M -s, -s tramp

Tram|pel ['trampl] M OR NT -s, - *or f* -, -n clumsy clot *(inf) or* oaf *(inf)*; **~ vom Land** (country) bumpkin *or* cousin

tram|peln ['trampln] VI **a** *(= mit den Füßen stampfen)* to stamp; **die Zuschauer haben getrampelt** the audience stamped their feet **b** *aux sein (= schwerfällig gehen)* to stamp *or* tramp along; **über die Wiese/das Gras ~** to tramp across the meadow/grass VT **a** *(= mit Füßen bearbeiten) Weg* to trample; **jdn zu Tode ~** to trample sb to death **b** *(= abschütteln)* to stamp *(von* from)

Tram|pel-: **Tram|pel|pfad** M track, path; **Tram|pel|tier** NT **a** *(Zool)* (Bactrian) camel **b** *(inf)* clumsy oaf *(inf)*

tram|pen ['trɛmpn, 'tram-] VI *aux sein* to hitch-hike, to hitch *(Brit inf)*

Tram|per ['trɛmpɐ] M -s, -, **Tram|pe|rin** [-ərɪn] F -, -nen hitchhiker, hitcher *(Brit inf)*

Tramp|fahrt ['trɛmp-, 'tramp-] F **a** *(Naut)* tramp voyage; **auf ~ sein** to be tramping **b** *(= Reise per Anhalter)* hitchhiking tour; **auf ~ sein** to be away hitchhiking

Tram|po|lin [trampo'li:n, 'tram-] NT -s, -e trampoline

Tram|po|lin|sprin|gen NT -s, *no pl* trampolining

Tramp- ['tramp-]: **Tramp|schiff** NT tramp (ship); **Tramp|schiff|fahrt** F tramp shipping

Tram|way ['tramvai] F -, -s *(Aus)* = **Straßenbahn**

Tran [tra:n] M -(e)s, -e **a** *(von Fischen)* train oil **b** *(inf)* **im ~** dop(e)y *(inf)*; *(= leicht betrunken)* tipsy, merry *(inf)*; **ich lief wie im ~ durch die Gegend** I was running around in a dream *or* a daze; **das habe ich im ~ ganz vergessen** it completely slipped my mind

Tran|ce ['trã:s(ə)] F -, -n trance

Tran|ce-: **tran|ce|ar|tig** ADJ trancelike; **Tran|ce|zu|stand** M (state of) trance

Tran|che ['trã:ʃ(ə)] F -, -n **a** *(St Ex)* tranche of a bond issue; *(= Anleihe)* quota share **b** *(= Abschnitt)* tranche

Tran|chier|be|steck [trã'ʃi:ɐ-] NT carving set, set of carvers

tran|chie|ren [trã'ʃi:rən] *ptp* **tranchiert** VT to carve

Tran|chier-: **Tran|chier|ga|bel** F carving fork; **Tran|chier|mes|ser** NT carving knife

Trä|ne ['trɛ:nə] F -, -n tear; *(= einzelne Träne)* tear(drop); *(inf: Mensch)* drip *(inf)*; **den ~n nahe sein** to be near to *or* on the verge of tears; **ich bin zu ~n gerührt** I am moved to tears; **unter ~n lächeln** to smile through one's tears; **unter ~n gestand er seine Schuld/Liebe** in tears he confessed his guilt/love; **ihm kamen die ~n** tears welled (up) in his eyes; **mir kommen die ~n** *(iro)* my heart bleeds for him/her *etc*; **~n lachen** to laugh till one cries, to laugh till the tears run down one's cheeks; **deswegen vergieße ich keine ~n** *(fig)* I'll shed no tears over that; **die Sache/der Mann ist keine ~ wert** the matter/man isn't worth crying over; **bittere ~n weinen** to shed bitter tears; **jdm/sich die ~n trocknen** *or* **abwischen** to dry sb's/one's eyes, to wipe away sb's/one's tears

trä|nen ['trɛ:nən] VI to water

Trä|nen-: **Trä|nen|drü|se** F lachrymal gland; **der Film drückt sehr auf die ~n** the film is a real tear-jerker *(inf)*; **im Schlussakt drückt der Autor kräftig auf die ~n** *(inf)* the author has written a real tear-jerker of a final act *(inf)*; **trä|nen|feucht** ADJ wet with tears; *Augen* tear-filled; **Trä|nen|fluss** M flood of tears; **Trä|nen|gas** NT tear gas; **Trä|nen|ka|nal** M tear duct; **trä|nen|reich** ADJ tearful ADV tearfully; **~ enden** to end in tears; **Trä|nen|sack** M lachrymal sac; **Trä|nen|schlei|er** M blur of tears

Tran|fun|sel F, **Tran|fun|zel** F *(inf)* slowcoach *(Brit inf)*, slowpoke *(US inf)*

tra|nig ['tra:nɪç] ADJ like train oil; *(inf)* slow, sluggish ADV *schmecken* oily; *(inf) sich bewegen* sluggishly; *fahren, arbeiten* slowly

trank *pret von* **trinken**

Trank [traŋk] M -(e)s, ⸗e ['trɛŋkə] *(liter)* drink, draught *(Brit liter)*, draft *(US liter)*, potion *(liter)*

Trän|ke ['trɛŋkə] F -, -n drinking trough

trän|ken ['trɛŋkn] VT **a** *Tiere* to water **b** *(= durchnässen)* to soak; **seine Antwort war mit Hohn getränkt** *(geh)* his answer was awash with scorn

Trans- *in cpds* trans-

Trans|ak|ti|on [translak'tsio:n] F transaction

trans|at|lan|tisch [translat'lantɪʃ] ADJ transatlantic
Tran|schier- *(Aus)* = **Tranchier-**
Trans-Eu|ro|pa-Ex|press [transl ɔy'ro:pa-] M Trans-Europe Express
trans|eu|ro|pä|isch [translɔyro'pɛ:ɪʃ] ADJ trans-European
Trans|fer [trans'fe:ɐ] M **-s, -s** transfer; *(Psych)* transference
trans|fe|rie|ren [transfe'ri:rən] *ptp* **transferiert** VT to transfer
Trans|fer|leis|tung F *(Psych)* transfer effect; *(Econ)* transfer
Trans|for|ma|ti|on [transfɔrma'tsio:n] F transformation
Trans|for|ma|ti|ons-: **Trans|for|ma|ti|ons|gram|ma|tik** F transformational grammar; **Trans|for|ma|ti|ons|re|gel** F transformation rule
Trans|for|ma|tor [transfɔr'ma:to:ɐ] M **-s, Transformatoren** [-'to:rən] transformer
Trans|for|ma|to|ren|häus|chen NT transformer
trans|for|mie|ren [transfɔr'mi:rən] *ptp* **transformiert** VT to transform
Trans|fu|si|on [transfu'zio:n] F transfusion
trans|gen [trans'ge:n] ADJ transgenic
Tran|sis|tor [tran'zɪsto:ɐ] M **-s, Transistoren** [-'to:rən] transistor
Tran|sis|tor|ra|dio NT transistor (radio)
Tran|sit ['tranzi:t, tran'zi:t, 'tranzɪt] M **-s, -e** transit
Tran|sit-: **Tran|sit|ab|kom|men** NT transit agreement; **Tran|sit|hal|le** F *(Aviat)* transit area; **Tran|sit|han|del** M transit trade
tran|si|tiv ['tranziti:f, tranzi'ti:f] *(Gram)* ADJ transitive ADV *gebrauchen* transitively
Tran|sit-: **Tran|sit|raum** M *(Aviat)* transit lounge; **Tran|sit|rei|sen|de(r)** MF *decl as adj (Aviat)* transit passenger; ~ **nach ...** transit passengers bound for *or* continuing their flight to ...; **Tran|sit|sper|re** F, **Tran|sit|ver|bot** NT transit ban *(prohibiting goods or people from passing through a country)*; **Tran|sit|ver|kehr** M transit traffic; *(= Transithandel)* transit trade; **Passagiere im ~** transit passengers *pl*; **Tran|sit|vi|sum** NT transit visa
tran|skri|bie|ren [transkri'bi:rən] *ptp* **transkribiert** VT to transcribe; *(Mus)* to arrange
Tran|skrip|ta|se [transkrɪp'ta:zə] F **-, -n** transcriptase; **reverse ~** reverse transcriptase
trans|kul|tu|rell ADJ transcultural
Trans|mis|si|on [transmɪ'sio:n] F *(Mech)* transmission
Trans|oze|an- *in cpds* transoceanic; **Trans|oze|an|flug** M transoceanic flight
trans|pa|rent [transpa'rɛnt] ADJ transparent; *(fig geh) Argument* lucid
Trans|pa|rent [transpa'rɛnt] NT **-(e)s, -e** *(= Reklameschild etc)* neon sign; *(= Durchscheinbild)* transparency; *(= Spruchband)* banner
Trans|pa|rent|pa|pier NT waxed tissue paper; *(zum Pausen)* tracing paper
Trans|pa|renz [transpa'rɛnts] F **-,** *no pl* transparency; *(fig geh: von Argument)* lucidity; **sie fordern mehr ~ bei allen Vorgängen in der Politik** they demand more openness in political matters
trans|per|so|nal [transpɛrzo'na:l] ADJ *(Psych)* transpersonal
Tran|spi|ra|ti|on [transpira'tsio:n] F **-,** *no pl (geh)* perspiration; *(von Pflanze)* transpiration
tran|spi|rie|ren [transpi'ri:rən] *ptp* **transpiriert** VI *(geh)* to perspire; *(Pflanze)* to transpire
Trans|plan|tat [transplan'ta:t] NT **-(e)s, -e** *(Haut)* graft; *(Organ)* transplant
Trans|plan|ta|ti|on [transplanta'tsio:n] F **-, -en** **a** *(Med)* transplant; *(von Haut)* graft; *(Vorgang)* transplantation; *(von Haut)* grafting **b** *(Bot)* grafting
Trans|plan|ta|ti|ons|me|di|zin F transplant *or* transplantation medicine
trans|plan|tie|ren [transplan'ti:rən] *ptp* **transplantiert** VTI **a** *(Med) Organ, Gen* to transplant; *Haut* to graft **b** *(Bot)* to graft
Trans|pon|der [trans'pɔndɐ] M **-s, -** transponder
trans|po|nie|ren [transpo'ni:rən] *ptp* **transponiert** VT *(Mus)* to transpose
Trans|port [trans'pɔrt] M **-(e)s, -e** **a** *(= das Transportieren)* transport; **ein ~ auf dem Landweg** road transport; **ein ~ des Kranken ist ausgeschlossen** moving the patient is out of the question; **beim** *or* **auf dem ~ beschädigte/verloren gegangene Waren** goods damaged/lost in transit **b** *(= Fracht)* consignment, shipment; *(von Soldaten etc)* load, transport; *(von Gefangenen)* transport
trans|por|ta|bel [transpɔr'ta:bl] ADJ *Fernseher, Computer etc* portable
Trans|port-: **Trans|port|ar|bei|ter(in)** M(F) transport worker; **Trans|port|band** [-bant] NT *pl* **-bänder** conveyor belt; **Trans|port|be|häl|ter** M container
Trans|por|ter [trans'pɔrtɐ] M **-s, -** *(Schiff)* cargo ship; *(Flugzeug)* transport plane; *(Auto)* van; *(= Autotransporter)* transporter
Trans|por|teur [transpɔr'tø:ɐ] M **-s, -e** **a** *(an Nähmaschine)* fabric guide, feed dog **b** *(= Winkelmesser)* protractor
Trans|por|teur [transpɔr'tø:ɐ] M **-s, -e, Trans|por|teu|rin** [-'tø:rɪn] F **-, -nen** haulier *(Brit)*, hauler *(US)*
Trans|port-: **trans|port|fä|hig** ADJ *Patient* moveable; **Trans|port|flug|zeug** NT transport plane *or* aircraft
trans|por|tie|ren [transpɔr'ti:rən] *ptp* **transportiert** VT to transport; *Güter auch* to carry; *Patienten* to move; *Film* to wind on; *(Nähmaschine)* to feed VI *(Förderband)* to move; *(Nähmaschine)* to feed; *(Kamera)* to wind on
Trans|port-: **Trans|port|kos|ten** PL carriage *sing*; **Trans|port|mit|tel** NT means *sing* of transport; **Trans|port|scha|den** M damage in transit; **Trans|port|schiff** NT cargo ship; *(Mil)* transport ship; **Trans|port|un|ter|neh|men** NT haulier *(Brit)*, hauler *(US)*, haulage firm; **Trans|port|ver|si|che|rung** F *(Insur)* transport insurance; *(Versicherer)* transport insurance company; **Trans|port|we|sen** NT transport
Trans|po|son [transpo'zo:n] NT **-s, -s** *or* **-en** transposon
Trans|ra|pid® [transra'pi:t] M **-,** *no pl (Rail)* Transrapid maglev (train)
Trans|se|xu|el|le(r) [transzɛ'ksuɛlə] MF *decl as adj* transsexual
Tran|su|se ['tra:nzu:zə] F **-, -n** *(inf)* slowcoach *(Brit inf)*, slowpoke *(US inf)*
Trans|ves|tis|mus [transvɛs'tɪsmʊs] M **-,** *no pl* transvestism
Trans|ves|tit [transvɛs'ti:t] M **-en, -en** transvestite
trans|zen|dent [transtsɛn'dɛnt] ADJ transcendent(al); *(Math)* transcendental
trans|zen|den|tal [transtsɛndɛn'ta:l] ADJ transcendental
Trans|zen|denz [transtsɛn'dɛnts] F **-,** *no pl* transcendency, transcendence
Tran|tü|te F *(inf)* slowcoach *(Brit inf)*, slowpoke *(US inf)*
Tra|pez [tra'pe:ts] NT **-es, -e** **a** *(Math)* trapezium **b** *(von Artisten)* trapeze
Tra|pez-: **Tra|pez|akt** M trapeze act; **tra|pez|för|mig** ADJ trapeziform; **Tra|pez|künst|ler(in)** M(F) trapeze artist
Tra|pe|zo|e|der [trapetso'le:dɐ] NT **-s, -** trapezohedron
Tra|pe|zo|id [trapetso'i:t] NT **-(e)s, -e** [-də] trapezoid
trap|peln ['trapln] VI *aux sein* to clatter; *(Pony)* to clip-clop
trapp, trapp ['trap 'trap] INTERJ *(von Kindern etc)* clitter-clatter; *(von Pferd)* clip-clop
Trap|pist [tra'pɪst] M **-en, -en, Trap|pis|tin** [-'pɪstɪn] F **-, -nen** *(Eccl)* Trappist
trap|sen ['trapsn] VI *aux sein (inf)* to galumph *(inf)* → **Nachtigall**
Tra|ra [tra'ra:] NT **-s, -s** *(von Horn)* tantara; *(fig inf)* hullabaloo *(inf)*, to-do *(inf)* *(um* about)
Tras|sant [tra'sant] M **-en, -en, Tras|san|tin** [-'santɪn] F **-, -nen** *(Fin)* drawer
Tras|sat [tra'sa:t] M **-en, -en, Tras|sa|tin** [-'sa:tɪn] M **-, -nen** *(Fin)* drawee
Tras|se ['trasə] F **-, -n** *(Surv)* marked-out route
Tras|sen|füh|rung F route
trat *pret von* **treten**
Tratsch [tra:tʃ] M **-(e)s,** *no pl (inf)* gossip, scandal, tittle-tattle *(esp Brit inf)*
trat|schen ['tra:tʃn] VI *(inf)* to gossip
Trat|sche|rei [tra:tʃə'rai] F **-, -en** *(inf)* gossip(-ing) *no pl*, scandalmongering *no pl*
Tratsch|maul NT, **Tratsch|tan|te** F *(pej inf)* scandalmonger, gossip
Trat|te ['tratə] F **-, -n** *(Fin)* draft
Trau|al|tar M altar
Trau|be ['traubə] F **-, -n** *(einzelne Beere)* grape; *(ganze Frucht)* bunch of grapes; *(= Blütenstand)* raceme *(spec)*; *(fig) (von Bienen)* cluster; *(= Menschentraube)* bunch, cluster; **~n** *(Fruchtart)* grapes
Trau|ben-: **Trau|ben|le|se** F grape harvest; **Trau|ben|saft** M grape juice; **Trau|ben|zu|cker** M glucose, dextrose
trau|en ['trauən] VI +*dat* to trust; **einer Sache** *(dat)* **nicht ~** to be wary of sth; **ich traute meinen Augen/Ohren nicht** I couldn't believe my eyes/ears; **ich traue dem Frieden nicht** (I think) there must be something afoot, it's too good to be true → **Weg a** VR to dare; **sich** *(acc or (rare) dat)* **~, etw zu tun** to dare (to) do sth; **ich trau mich nicht** I daren't, I dare not; **sich auf die Straße/nach Hause/zum Chef ~** to dare to go out/home/to one's boss VT to marry; **sich standesamtlich/kirchlich ~ lassen** to get married in a registry office *(Brit)* or in a civil ceremony/in church
Trau|er ['trauɐ] ✪ 51.4 F **-,** *no pl (= das Trauern, Trauerzeit, Trauerkleidung)* mourning; *(= Schmerz, Leid)* sorrow, grief; **~ haben/tragen** to be in mourning; **in tiefer ~ ...** (much loved and) sadly missed by ...
Trau|er-: **Trau|er|an|zei|ge** F obituary, death notice; **Trau|er|ar|beit** F, *no pl (Psych)* grieving; **Trau|er|bin|de** F black armband; **Trau|er|bot|schaft** F sad news *sing, no indef art*; **Trau|er|brief** M letter announcing sb's death; **Trau|er|fall** M bereavement, death; **Trau|er|fei|er** F funeral service; **Trau|er|flor** M black ribbon; **Trau|er|ge|fol|ge** NT funeral procession; **Trau|er|ge|mein|de** F mourners *pl*; **Trau|er|haus** NT house of mourning; **Trau|er|jahr** NT year of mourning; **Trau|er|kar|te** F card announcing sb's death; **Trau|er|klei|dung** F mourning; **Trau|er|kloß** M *(inf)* wet blanket *(inf)*; **Trau|er|man|tel** M *(Zool)* Camberwell beauty; **Trau|er|marsch** M funeral march; **Trau|er|mie|ne** F *(inf)* long face
trau|ern ['trauɐn] VI to mourn *(um jdn* (for) sb, *um etw* sth); *(= Trauerkleidung tragen)* to be in mourning; **die ~den Hinterbliebenen** his/her bereaved family
Trau|er-: **Trau|er|nach|richt** F sad news *sing, no indef art*; **Trau|er|par|te** [-partə] F **-, -n** *(Aus)* obituary, death notice; **Trau|er|rand** M black edge *or* border; **Trauerränder** *(inf)* dirty fingernails; **Trau|er|schlei|er** M black *or* mourning veil; **Trau|er|spiel** NT tragedy; *(fig inf)* fiasco; **es ist ein ~ mit ihm** he's really pathetic; **es ist ein ~ mit dem Projekt** the project is in a bad way *(inf)* or in bad shape; **Trau|er|wei|de** F weeping willow; **Trau|er|zeit** F (period of) mourning; **Trau|er|zug** M funeral procession
Trau|fe ['traufə] F **-, -n** eaves *pl* → **Regen**
träu|feln ['trɔyfln] VT to dribble VI *aux haben or sein (old, geh: Wasser)* to trickle
Trau|for|mel F marriage vows *pl*

trau|lich ['traulɪç] ADJ cosy *(Brit)*, cozy *(US)* ADV ~ **zusammenleben** to live together harmoniously *or* in harmony

Trau|lich|keit F -, *no pl* cosiness *(Brit)*, coziness *(US)*

Traum [traum] M -(e)s, **Träume** ['trɔymə] *(lit, fig)* dream; *(= Tagtraum auch)* daydream, reverie; **sie lebt wie im** ~ she is living (as if) in a dream *or (nach Schock)* daze; **er fühlte sich wie im** ~ he felt as if he were dreaming; **es war immer sein** ~, **ein großes Haus zu besitzen** he had always dreamed of owning a large house; **aus der** ~**!, der** ~ **ist aus!** it's all over; **aus der** ~ **vom neuen Auto** that's put paid to your/my *etc* dreams of a new car; **dieser** ~ **ist ausgeträumt** this dream is over; **der** ~ **meiner schlaflosen Nächte** *(hum inf)* the man/woman of my dreams; **Träume sind Schäume** *(prov)* dreams are but shadows → **einfallen a**

Trau|ma ['trauma] NT -s, **Traumen** *or* -ta [-mən, -ta] *(Med, Psych)* trauma; *(fig auch)* nightmare

Traum|ar|beit F, *no pl (Psych)* dreaming

trau|ma|tisch [trau'ma:tɪʃ] ADJ *(Psych)* traumatic; *(fig auch)* nightmarish

trau|ma|ti|sie|ren [traumati'zi:rən] *ptp* **traumatisiert** VT to traumatize, to have a traumatizing effect on VI to have a traumatizing effect

Traum-: **Traum|be|ruf** M dream job, job of one's dreams; **Traum|bild** NT vision; **Traum|deu|ter(in)** M(F) interpreter of dreams; **Traum|deu|tung** F dream interpretation, interpretation of dreams

Trau|men *pl von* **Trauma**

träu|men ['trɔymən] VI to dream; *(= tagträumen auch)* to daydream; *(inf: = nicht aufpassen)* to (day)dream, to be in a dream; **von jdm/etw** ~ to dream about sb/sth; *(= sich ausmalen)* to dream of sb/sth; **mir träumte, dass ...** I dreamed that ...; **träum(e) süß!** sweet dreams!; **vor sich hin** ~, **mit offenen Augen** ~ to daydream; **du träumst wohl!** *(inf)* you must be joking!, dream on! *(inf)*; **das hätte ich mir nicht** ~ **lassen** I'd never have thought it possible VT to dream; *Traum* to have; **etwas Schönes/Schreckliches** ~ to have a pleasant/an unpleasant dream

Träu|mer ['trɔymɐ] M -s, -, **Träu|me|rin** [-ərɪn] F -, -nen (day)dreamer; *(= Fantast)* dreamer, visionary

Träu|me|rei [trɔymə'rai] F -, -en **a** *no pl (= das Träumen)* (day)dreaming **b** *(= Vorstellung)* daydream, reverie

träu|me|risch ['trɔymərɪʃ] ADJ dreamy; *(= schwärmerisch)* wistful

Traum-: **Traum|fab|rik** F *(pej)* dream factory; **Traum|frau** F *(inf)* dream woman; **die** ~ the woman of one's dreams; **eine absolute** ~ the perfect *or* one's ideal woman; **traum|haft** ADJ *(= fantastisch)* fantastic; *(= wie im Traum)* dreamlike ADV *(= fantastisch)* fantastically; ~ **aussehen** to look fantastic; ~ **schönes Wetter** fantastic weather; ~ **leere Strände** fantastic deserted beaches

Trau|mi|net ['trauminɛt] M -s, -e *(Aus inf)* coward

Traum-: **Traum|job** M ideal job, plum job *(inf)*; **Traum|mann** M *(inf)* dream man; **der Traummaunn** the man of one's dreams; **ein absoluter** ~ the perfect *or* one's ideal man; **Traum|paar** NT perfect couple; **Traum|rei|se** F trip of a lifetime, dream holiday *(esp Brit) or* vacation *(US)*; **Traum|tän|zer(in)** M(F) dreamer; **traum|tän|ze|risch** ADJ dreamy, idealistic; **traum|ver|lo|ren** ADJ dreamy ADV dreamily, as if in a dream; **traum|wand|le|risch** [-vandlərɪʃ] ADJ somnambulistic; **mit** ~**er Sicherheit** with instinctive certainty ADV ~ **sicher** instinctively certain

Trau|re|de F marriage sermon; *(im Standesamt)* marriage address

trau|rig ['traurɪç] ADJ sad; *(= unglücklich) Verhältnisse, Leben auch* unhappy; *Blick auch* sorrowful; *(= beklagenswert) Zustand* sad, sorry; *Leistung, Erfolg, Rekord* pathetic, sorry; *Wetter* miserable; *Berühmtheit* notorious; **die** ~**e Realität** *or* **Wirklichkeit** the sad reality; **die** ~**e Bilanz** the tragic toll; **das ist doch** ~, **was er da geleistet hat** what he's done is pathetic; **das sind ja** ~**e Verhältnisse, wenn ...** it is a sorry *or* sad state of affairs when ...; **es ist** ~, **wenn** it is sad if ... ADV sadly; *(= tief betrübt)* sorrowfully; ~ **weggehen** to go away sadly *or* feeling sad; **mit meinen Finanzen/der Wirtschaft sieht es sehr** ~ **aus** my finances are/the economy is in a very sorry state; ~, ~ dear, dear; **wie sieht es damit aus? –** ~**(,** ~**)** what are the prospects for that? – pretty bad *or* not at all good; **um meine Zukunft sieht es** ~ **aus** my future doesn't look too bright

Trau|rig|keit F -, -en sadness; **allgemeine** ~ a general feeling of sadness → **Kind**

Trau-: **Trau|ring** M wedding ring; **Trau|schein** M marriage certificate

traut [traut] ADJ *(liter, hum) (= gemütlich)* cosy *(Brit)*, cozy *(US)*; *Harmonie* sweet; *(= vertraut)* familiar; *Freund* close; **im** ~**en Kreise** among one's family and friends; **ein Abend im** ~**en Heim** an evening at home; ~**es Heim, Glück allein** *(Prov)* home sweet home

Trau|te ['trautə] F ~ **haben** *(inf)* to have the guts *(inf)*; **keine** ~ **haben** *(inf)* not to have the guts *(inf)*

Trau|ung ['trauʊŋ] F -, -en wedding, wedding *or* marriage ceremony

Trau|zeu|ge M, **Trau|zeu|gin** F witness *(at marriage ceremony)*

Tra|ves|tie [travɛs'ti:] F -, -n [-'ti:ən] travesty

tra|ves|tie|ren [travɛs'ti:rən] *ptp* **travestiert** VT to travesty, to make a travesty of

Tre|be ['tre:bə] F *(inf)* **auf** ~ **gehen** to run away from home; **auf** ~ **sein** to be a runaway

Tre|ber ['tre:bɐ] PL *(= Biertreber)* spent hops *pl (Brit)*, hop pulp *(US)*; *(= Weintreber)* marc *sing*; *(= Fruchttreber)* pomace *sing*

Treck [trɛk] M -s, -s trek, trail; *(= Leute)* train; *(= Wagen etc)* wagon train

Tre|cker ['trɛkɐ] M -s, - tractor

Tre|cking ['trɛkɪŋ] NT -s, *no pl* → **Trekking**

Treff [trɛf] NT -s, -s *(Cards)* club; **die** ~**sieben** the seven of clubs; **das** ~**ass** the ace of clubs

Treff M -s, -s *(inf) (= Treffen)* meeting, get-together *(inf)*; *(= Treffpunkt)* haunt, rendezvous, meeting place

tref|fen ['trɛfn] *pret* **traf** [tra:f], *ptp* **getroffen** [gə'trɔfn] VT **a** *(durch Schlag, Schuss etc)* to hit *(an/in +dat* on, *in +acc* in); *(Blitz, Faust)* to strike, to hit; *(Unglück)* to strike; **auf dem Foto bist du gut getroffen** *(inf)* that's a good photo or picture of you → **Schlag a**

b *(fig: = kränken)* to hurt

c *(= betreffen)* to hit, to affect; **es trifft immer die Falschen** it's always the wrong people who are hit *or* affected; **ihn trifft keine Schuld** he's not to blame

d *(= finden)* to hit upon, to find; *(lit, fig) Ton* to hit; **du hasts getroffen** *(mit Antwort)* you've hit the nail on the head; *(mit Geschenk)* that's the very thing → *auch* **Nerv**

e *(= jdm begegnen, mit jdm zusammenkommen)* to meet; *(= antreffen)* to find

f es gut/schlecht ~ to be fortunate *or* lucky/unlucky *(mit* with); **es mit dem Wetter/der Unterkunft gut/schlecht** ~ to have good/bad weather/accommodation; **ich hätte es schlechter** ~ **können** it could have been worse

g *Vorbereitungen, Anstalten etc* to make; *Vereinbarung* to reach; *Entscheidung* to make, to take; *Vorsorge, Maßnahmen* to take

VI **a** *(Schlag, Schuss etc)* to hit; **der Schuss/er hat getroffen** the shot/he hit it/him etc; **tödlich getroffen** *(von Schuss, Pfeil etc)* fatally wounded; **nicht** ~ to miss; **gut/schlecht** ~ to aim well/badly; **getroffen!** a hit → **Schwarze(s)**

b *aux sein (= stoßen)* **auf jdn/etw** ~ to meet sb/sth

c *(= verletzen)* to hurt; **sich getroffen fühlen** to feel hurt; *(= auf sich beziehen)* to take it personally

VR *(= zusammentreffen)* to meet; **unsere Interessen** ~ **sich im Sport** we are both/all interested in sport

VR *impers* **es trifft sich, dass ...** it (just) happens that ...; **das trifft sich gut/schlecht, dass ...** it is convenient/inconvenient that ...

Tref|fen ['trɛfn] NT -s, - meeting; *(Sport, Mil)* encounter; **ins** ~ **führen** *(Mil)* to send into battle; *(fig)* to put forward

tref|fend ADJ *Beispiel, Bemerkung* apt, apposite *(form)*; *Ähnlichkeit* striking ADV aptly, appropriately; **jdn** ~ **nachahmen** to do a brilliant imitation of sb; ~ **bemerken** to remark aptly; **etw** ~ **darstellen** to describe sth perfectly; **man hätte es nicht** ~**er vergleichen können** you couldn't have made a more apt comparison

Tref|fer ['trɛfɐ] M -s, - hit; *(= Tor)* goal; *(fig) (= Erfolg)* hit; *(= Gewinnlos)* winner; **das Geschenk/das Auto war ein** ~ the present/car was just right; **einen** ~ **erzielen** *or* **landen** *(inf)* to score a hit; *(Ftbl)* to score a goal

Tref|fer|quo|te F hit rate; *(Ftbl)* number of goals scored; *(bei Ratespiel etc)* score

treff|lich ['trɛflɪç] *(liter)* ADJ splendid, excellent ADV splendidly, excellently

Treff-: **Treff|punkt** M rendezvous, meeting place; **einen** ~ **ausmachen** to arrange where *or* somewhere to meet; **treff|si|cher** ADJ *Stürmer etc* accurate; *(fig) Bemerkung* apt; *Urteil* sound, unerring; **Treff|si|cher|heit** F *(von Stürmer etc)* accuracy; *(von Bemerkung)* aptness; *(von Urteil)* soundness

Treib-: **Treib|an|ker** M sea anchor, drag anchor; **Treib|eis** NT drift ice

trei|ben ['traibn] *pret* **trieb** [tri:p], *ptp* **getrieben** [gə'tri:bn] VT **a** *(lit, fig)* to drive; *(auf Treibjagd) Wild* to beat; *Teig* to make rise; *(fig: = drängen)* to rush; *(= antreiben)* to push; **jdn zum** *or* **in den Wahnsinn/zur** *or* **in die Verzweiflung/zum** *or* **in den Selbstmord** ~ to drive sb mad/to despair/to (commit) suicide; **jdn zur Eile/Arbeit** ~ to make sb hurry (up)/work; **jdn zum Äußersten** ~ to push sb too far; **die Preise (in die Höhe)** ~ to push *or* drive prices up; **die** ~**de Kraft bei etw sein** to be the driving force behind sth

b *(= Reaktion erzeugen)* to bring; **jdm den Schweiß/das Blut ins Gesicht** ~ to make sb sweat/blush; **der Wind treibt mir Tränen in die Augen** the wind makes my eyes water; **der Gedanke treibt mir Tränen in die Augen** the thought brings tears to my eyes

c *(= einschlagen) Nagel, Pfahl etc* to drive

d *(= bearbeiten, formen) Metall* to beat

e *(= ausüben, betreiben) Handel, Geschäfte* to do; *Studien, Politik* to pursue; *Gewerbe* to carry on; *Sport* to do; *(= machen)* to do; *Schabernack, Unfug, Unsinn* to be up to; *Spaß* to have; *Aufwand* to make, to create; *Unzucht* to commit; **was treibst du?** what are you up to?; **Missbrauch mit etw** ~ to abuse sth; **Handel mit etw/jdm** ~ to trade in sth/with sb; **Wucher** ~ to profiteer

f wenn du es weiter so treibst ... if you go *or* carry on like that ...; **es toll** ~ to have a wild time; **es zu toll** ~ to overdo it; **es schlimm** ~ to behave badly; **es zu bunt** *or* **weit** ~ to go too far; **er treibt es noch so weit, dass er hinausgeworfen wird** if he goes on like that, he'll get thrown out; **es mit jdm** ~ *(inf)* to have it off with sb *(Brit inf)*, to get it on with sb *(US sl)*, to have sex with sb

g *(= hervorbringen) Blüten, Knospen etc* to sprout, to put forth; *(im Treibhaus)* to force → **Blüte a**

VI **a** *aux sein (= sich fortbewegen)* to drift; **sich** ~ **lassen** *(lit, fig)* to drift; **sich von der Stimmung** ~ **lassen** to let oneself be carried along by the mood; **die Dinge** ~ **lassen** to let things go

b *(= wachsen)* to sprout

c *(Bier, Kaffee, Medizin etc)* to have a diuretic effect; *(Hefe)* to make dough *etc* rise; ~**de Medikamente** diuretics

Trei|ben ['traibn] NT -s, - **a** *(= Getriebe)* hustle and bustle; *(von Schneeflocken)* swirling; **ich be-**

obachte dein ~ schon lange I've been watching what you've been (getting) up to for a long time **b** = **Treibjagd**

trei|ben+las|sen *ptp* **treibenlassen** *or (rare)* **treibengelassen** *sep irreg* VTR → **treiben VI a**

Trei|ber ['traibɐ] M **-s, -** *(Comput)* driver

Trei|ber ['traibɐ] M **-s, -**, **Trei|be|rin** [-ərɪn] F **-, -nen** *(= Viehtreiber)* drover; *(Hunt)* beater

Treib-: **Treib|gas** NT *(bei Sprühdosen)* propellant; **Treib|gut** NT flotsam and jetsam *pl*

Treib|haus NT hothouse

Treib|haus-: **Treib|haus|ef|fekt** M *(Met)* greenhouse effect; **Treib|haus|gas** NT greenhouse gas; **Treib|haus|luft** F **a** hothouse *or* greenhouse air **b** *(fig)* hot, humid atmosphere; **Treib|haus|pflan|ze** F hothouse *or* greenhouse plant; **Treib|haus|tem|pe|ra|tur** F hothouse *or* greenhouse temperature; **hier herrscht die reinste ~!** it's like a greenhouse here

Treib-: **Treib|holz** NT driftwood; **Treib|jagd** F battue *(spec)*, shoot *(in which game is sent up by beaters)*; **Treib|mit|tel** NT *(in Sprühdosen)* propellant; *(Cook)* raising agent; **Treib|netz** NT drift net; **Treib|sand** M quicksand; **Treib|schlag** M *(Sport)* drive; **Treib|stoff** M fuel; *(= Raketentreibstoff auch)* propellant

trei|deln ['traidln] VT to tow

Trek|king ['trɛkɪŋ] NT **-s**, *no pl* trekking

Trek|king|rad NT hybrid bike

Tre|ma ['tre:ma] NT **-s, -s** *or* **-ta** [-ta] dieresis

tre|mo|lie|ren [tremo'li:rən] *ptp* **tremoliert** VI to quaver

Tre|mo|lo ['tre:molo] NT **-s, -s** *or* **Tremoli** [-li] tremolo

Trench|coat ['trɛntʃko:t] M **-(s), -s** trench coat

Trend [trɛnt] M **-s, -s** trend; **voll im ~ liegen** to follow the trend

Trend-: **Trend|mel|dung** F *(Pol)* report on voting trends *or* patterns; *(fig)* projection; **Trend|scout** ['trɛntskaut] M **-(s), -s** trend spotter *or* forecaster; **Trend|set|ter** ['trɛntsɛtɐ] M **-s, -**, **Trend|set|te|rin** [-ərɪn] F **-, -nen** trendsetter; **Trend|wen|de** F new trend

tren|dy *(inf)* ADJ trendy **~ gewandet und beschuht** trendily turned out, the last word in trendiness

trenn|bar ADJ separable; **ein nicht ~es Wort** an inseparable word

Trenn|blatt NT divider

tren|nen ['trɛnən] VT **a** *(= entfernen) Mensch, Tier* to separate *(von* from); *(Tod)* to take away *(von* from); *(= in Teile teilen, abtrennen)* to separate; *Kopf, Glied etc* to sever; *(= abmachen)* to detach *(von* from); *Aufgenähtes* to take off, to remove; **zwei Teile voneinander ~** to separate two parts; **etw in zwei Hälften ~** to divide *or* split sth into two halves

b *(= aufspalten, scheiden) Bestandteile, Eier, Raufende* to separate; *Partner, Freunde* to split up; *(Comput, Telec) Verbindung* to disconnect; *(räumlich)* to separate; *Begriffe* to differentiate, to distinguish (between); *(nach Rasse, Geschlecht)* to segregate; **voneinander getrennt werden** to be separated; **Ursache und Folge ~** to make *or* draw a distinction between cause and results; **Gut von Böse ~** to distinguish between good and evil, to differentiate *or* distinguish good from evil; **uns trennt zu vieles** we have too little in common; **jetzt kann uns nichts mehr ~** now nothing can ever come between us; **alles Trennende (zwischen uns/den beiden)** all our/their differences; **das Radio trennt die Sender gut/schlecht** the radio has good/bad selectivity → *auch* **getrennt**

c *(= in Bestandteile zerlegen) Kleid* to take to pieces; *(Ling) Wort* to divide, to split up; *(Chem) Gemisch* to separate (out)

VR **a** *(= auseinandergehen)* to separate; *(Partner, Eheleute etc)* to split up, to separate; *(= Abschied nehmen)* to part; **sich von jdm/der Firma ~** to leave sb/the firm; **die Firma trennte sich von ihrem Geschäftsführer** the firm parted company with its managing director; **die zwei Mannschaften trennten sich 2:0** the final score was 2-0; **sich im Guten/Bösen ~** to part on good/bad terms

b *(= weggeben, verkaufen etc)* **sich von etw ~** to part with sth; **er konnte sich davon nicht ~** he couldn't bear to part with it; *(von Plan)* he couldn't give it up; *(von Anblick)* he couldn't take his eyes off it

c *(= sich teilen) (Wege, Flüsse)* to divide; **hier ~ sich unsere Wege** *(fig)* now we must go our separate ways

VI *(zwischen Begriffen)* to draw *or* make a distinction

Trenn-: **Trenn|kost** F food combining, Hay diet; **Trenn|mes|ser** NT *(Sew)* unpicker; **Trenn|punkt** M *(Ling)* dieresis; **trenn|scharf** ADJ **~ sein** to have good selectivity; **Trenn|schär|fe** F selectivity

Trenn|strich M *(Typ)* hyphen

Tren|nung ['trɛnʊŋ] F **-, -en** **a** *(= Abschied)* parting **b** *(= Getrenntwerden, Getrenntsein)* separation; *(in Teile)* division; *(von Begriffen)* distinction; *(von Sender)* selectivity; *(von Wort)* division; *(= Rassentrennung, Geschlechtertrennung)* segregation; **die Partner entschlossen sich zu einer ~** the partners decided to split up *or* separate; **in ~ leben** to be separated; **~ von Tisch und Bett** judicial separation

Tren|nungs-: **Tren|nungs|ent|schä|di|gung** F, **Tren|nungs|geld** NT separation allowance, alimony *(dated)*; **Tren|nungs|schmerz** M pain of parting; **Tren|nungs|strich** M hyphen; **einen ~ ziehen** *(fig)* to make a clear distinction *(zwischen* between); **Tren|nungs|wand** F partition (wall); **Tren|nungs|zei|chen** NT hyphen

Trenn|wand F partition (wall)

Trenn|zei|chen NT hyphen; *(Comput) (zwischen Datenwerten)* delimiter; *(in per Tags strukturierten Daten)* separator

Tren|se ['trɛnzə] F **-, -n** snaffle

trepp|auf [trɛp'lauf] ADV **~, treppab** up and down stairs

Trep|pe ['trɛpə] F **-, -n** **a** *(= Aufgang)* (flight of) stairs *pl*, staircase; *(im Freien)* (flight of) steps *pl*; **eine ~** a staircase, a flight of stairs/steps; **wir haben die ~** *(inf)* **wir sind mit der ~ an der Reihe** *(inf)* it's our turn to clean *or* do the stairs; **die ~ hinaufgehen/hinuntergehen** to go up/down the stairs, to go upstairs/downstairs; **du bist wohl die ~ hinuntergefallen!** *(fig inf)* what's happened to your hair? → **hinauffallen** **b** *(inf: = Stufe)* step; **~n steigen** to climb stairs **c** *(inf: = Stockwerk)* floor

Trep|pen-: **Trep|pen|ab|satz** M half landing; **Trep|pen|ge|län|der** NT banister; **Trep|pen|haus** NT stairwell; **im ~** on the stairs; **Trep|pen|stu|fe** F step, stair; **Trep|pen|witz** M **ein ~ der Weltgeschichte** an irony of history

Tre|sen ['tre:zn] M **-s, -** *(= Theke)* bar; *(= Ladentisch)* counter

Tre|sor [tre'zo:ɐ] M **-s, -e** *(= Raum)* strongroom, vault; *(= Schrank)* safe

Tre|sor|kna|cker M, **Tre|sor|kna|cke|rin** [-ərɪn] F **-, -nen** *(inf)* safe-breaker

Tre|sor|raum M strongroom

Tres|se ['trɛsə] F **-, -n** braid

Tres|ter ['trɛstɐ] PL *(= Biertrester)* spent hops *pl (Brit)*, hop pulp *(US)*; *(= Weintrester)* marc *sing*; *(= Fruchttrester)* pomace *sing*

Tret-: **Tret|au|to** NT pedal car; **Tret|boot** NT pedal boat, pedalo *(Brit)*; **Tret|ei|mer** M pedal bin

tre|ten ['tre:tn] *pret* **trat** [tra:t], *ptp* **getreten** [gə'tre:tn] VI **a** *(= ausschlagen, mit Fuß anstoßen)* to kick *(gegen etw* sth, *nach* out at)

b *aux sein (mit Raumangabe)* to step; **hier kann man nicht mehr ~** there is no room to move here; **vom Schatten ins Helle ~** to move out of the shadow into the light; **näher an etw** *(acc)* **~** to move *or* step closer to sth; **vor die Kamera ~** *(im Fernsehen)* to appear on TV; *(im Film)* to appear in a film *or* on the screen; **in den Vordergrund/Hintergrund ~** to step forward/back; *(fig)* to come to the forefront/to recede into the background; **an jds Stelle ~** to take sb's place → **nahe ADV a**

c *aux sein or haben (in Loch, Pfütze, auf Gegenstand etc)* to step, to tread; **jdm auf den Fuß ~** to step on sb's foot, to tread *(esp Brit) or* step on sb's toe; **jdm auf die Füße ~** *(fig)* to tread *(esp Brit) or* step on sb's toes; **jdm auf den Schlips** *(inf) or* **Schwanz** *(sl)* **~** to tread on sb's toes; **sich auf den Schlips** *(inf) or* **Schwanz** *(sl)* **getreten fühlen** to feel offended, to be put out → **Stelle a**

d *aux sein or haben (= betätigen)* **in die Pedale ~** to pedal hard; **aufs Gas(pedal) ~** *(= Pedal betätigen)* to press the accelerator; *(= schnell fahren)* to put one's foot down *(inf)*, to step on it *(inf)*; **auf die Bremse ~** to brake, to put one's foot on the brake

e *aux sein (= hervortreten, sichtbar werden)* **Wasser trat aus allen Ritzen und Fugen** water was coming out of every nook and cranny; **der Schweiß trat ihm auf die Stirn** sweat appeared on his forehead; **Tränen traten ihr in die Augen** tears came to her eyes, her eyes filled with tears; **der Fluss trat über die Ufer** the river overflowed its banks; **der Mond trat aus den Wolken** the moon appeared from behind the clouds; **es trat plötzlich wieder in mein Bewusstsein** it suddenly came back to me

f *aux sein (Funktionsverb) (= beginnen)* to start, to begin; *(= eintreten)* to enter; **in jds Leben** *(acc)* **~** to come into *or* enter sb's life; **ins Leben ~** to come into being; **in den Ruhestand ~** to retire; **in den Streik** *or* **Ausstand ~** to go on strike; **in den Staatsdienst/Stand der Ehe** *or* **Ehestand ~** to enter the civil service/into the state of matrimony; **mit jdm in Verbindung ~** to get in touch with sb; **in die entscheidende Phase ~** to enter the crucial phase → **Erscheinung a**, **Kraft d**

VT **a** *(= einen Fußtritt geben, stoßen)* to kick; *(Sport) Ecke, Freistoß* to take; **jdn ans Bein ~** to kick sb's leg, to kick sb on *or* in the leg; **jdn mit dem Fuß ~** to kick sb; **sich** *(dat)* **in den Hintern ~** *(fig inf)* to kick oneself

b *(= mit Fuß betätigen) Spinnrad, Nähmaschine, Webstuhl, Blasebalg* to operate *(using one's foot)*; **die Bremse ~** to brake, to put on the brakes; **die Pedale ~** to pedal

c *(= trampeln) Pfad, Weg, Bahn* to tread; **sich** *(dat)* **einen Splitter in den Fuß ~** to get a splinter in one's foot → **Wasser c**

d *(fig) (= schlecht behandeln)* to shove around *(inf)*; **jdn ~** *(inf: = antreiben)* to get at sb

e *(= begatten)* to tread, to mate with

Tre|ter ['tre:tɐ] M **-s, -** *(inf)* comfortable shoe

Tret-: **Tret|mi|ne** F *(Mil)* (antipersonnel) mine; **Tret|müh|le** F *(lit, fig)* treadmill; **in der ~ sein** to be in a rut *(inf)*; **die tägliche ~** the daily grind; **Tret|rad** NT treadmill; **Tret|rol|ler** M scooter

treu [trɔy] ADJ *Freund, Sohn, Kunde etc* loyal; *Diener auch* devoted; *Seele auch, Hund, Gatte etc* faithful; *Abbild* true; *Gedenken* respectful; *(= treuherzig)* trusting; *Miene* innocent; **jdm in ~er Liebe verbunden sein** to be bound to sb by loyalty and love; **jdm ~ sein/bleiben** to be/remain faithful to sb; *(= nicht betrügen auch)* to be/remain true to sb; **sich** *(dat)* **selbst ~ bleiben** to be true to oneself; **seinen Grundsätzen ~ bleiben** to stick to *or* remain true to one's principles; **der Erfolg ist ihr ~ geblieben** success kept coming her way; **das Glück ist ihr ~ geblieben** her luck held (out); **~ wie Gold** faithful and loyal; *(Diener etc auch)* faithful as a dog; **dein ~er Freund** *(old)* yours truly; **jdm etw zu ~en Händen übergeben** to give sth to sb for safekeeping

ADV faithfully; *dienen auch* loyally; *sorgen* devotedly; *(= treuherzig)* trustingly; *ansehen* innocently; **~ ergeben** devoted, loyal, faithful; **jdm ~ ergeben sein** to be loyally devoted to sb; **~**

sorgend devoted; ~ **und brav** *(Erwachsener)* dutifully; *(Kind)* like a good boy/girl, as good as gold

Treu-: **Treu|bruch** M breach of faith; **treu|brü|chig** ADJ faithless, false; **(jdm) ~ werden** to break faith (with sb); **treu|deutsch** ADJ truly German; *(pej)* typically German; **treu|doof** *(inf)* ADJ stupidly naive ADV stupidly and naively

Treue ['trɔyə] F -, *no pl (von Freund, Sohn, Kunde etc)* loyalty; *(von Diener auch)* devotion, devotedness; *(von Hund)* faithfulness; *(= eheliche Treue)* faithfulness, fidelity; **der Flagge ~ geloben** to pledge allegiance to the flag; **sie gelobten einander ewige ~** they vowed to be eternally faithful to one another; **jdm die ~ halten** to keep faith with sb; *Ehegatten etc* to remain faithful to sb; **auf Treu und Glauben** in good faith; **in alter ~** for old times' sake; **in alter ~, Dein Franz** Yours (as) ever, Franz → **brechen VT a**

Treu|eid M oath of allegiance

Treue-: **Treue|pflicht** F loyalty *(owed by employee to employer and vice versa)*; **Treue|prä|mie** F long-service bonus; **Treue|punkt** M *(zur Anrechnung für Kundenkarte etc)* reward *or* loyalty point

treu|er|ge|ben ADJ *attr* **treu ADV**

Treue|schwur M oath of allegiance; *(von Geliebtem etc)* vow to be faithful

Treu|hän|der [-hɛndɐ] M -s, -, **Treu|hän|de|rin** [-ərɪn] F -, -nen trustee, fiduciary *(form)*

Treu|hand|ge|sell|schaft F trust *or* fiduciary *(form)* company

Treu-: **treu|her|zig** ADJ innocent, trusting ADV innocently, trustingly; **Treu|her|zig|keit** ['trɔyhɛrtsɪçkait] F -, *no pl* innocence; **treu|los** ADJ disloyal, faithless; **du ~es Stück** *(inf)* you wretch → **Tomate** ADV disloyally, faithlessly; **~ an jdm handeln** to fail sb; **Treu|lo|sig|keit** F -, *no pl* disloyalty, faithlessness; **treu|sor|gend** ADJ *attr* → **treu ADV**

Tri|a|de [tri'a:də] F -, -n **a** *(Rel, Liter, Math)* triad; *(Rel, fig auch)* trinity **b** *(= Verbrecherorganisation)* triad

Tri|a|ge [tri'a:ʒə] F -, -n **a** *(Med)* triage **b** *(Comm)* lower grade goods *pl*

Tri|an|gel ['tri:aŋl] M OR (AUS) NT -s, - triangle

Tri|as ['tri:as] F -, *no pl* Triassic (Period)

Tri|ath|lon ['tri:atlɔn] M -, -e *(Sport)* triathlon

Tri|ba|lis|mus [triba'lɪsmʊs] M -, *no pl* tribalism

Tri|bun [tri'bu:n] M -s *or* -en, -e(n), **Tri|bu|nin** [-'bu:nɪn] F -, -nen tribune

Tri|bu|nal [tribu'na:l] NT -s, -e tribunal

Tri|bu|nat [tribu'na:t] NT -(e)s, -e tribunate

Tri|bü|ne [tri'by:nə] F -, -n *(= Rednertribüne)* platform, rostrum; *(= Zuschauertribüne, Zuschauer)* stand; *(= Haupttribüne)* grandstand

Tri|bu|nin [-'bu:nɪn] F -, -nen tribune

Tri|but [tri'bu:t] M -(e)s, -e *(Hist)* tribute, dues *pl*; *(fig)* tribute; *(= Opfer)* toll; **jdm ~ entrichten** *or (fig)* **zollen** to pay tribute to sb

tri|but|pflich|tig [-pflɪçtɪç] ADJ tributary *(rare)*, obliged to pay tribute

Tri|chi|ne [trɪ'çi:nə] F -, -n trichina

Tri|chi|nen-: **tri|chi|nen|hal|tig** ADJ trichinous; **Tri|chi|nen|schau** F meat inspection *(to check for trichinae)*; **Tri|chi|nen|schau|er** [-ʃauɐ] M -s, -, **Tri|chi|nen|schau|e|rin** [-ərɪn] F -, -nen meat inspector

Trich|ter ['trɪçtɐ] M -s, - funnel; *(= Schüttgutbehälter)* hopper; *(= Bombentrichter)* crater; *(von Grammofon)* horn; *(von Trompete, Megafon etc)* bell; *(von Hörgerät)* trumpet; *(von Lautsprecher)* cone; **jdn auf den ~ bringen** *(inf)* to give sb a clue; **auf den ~ kommen** *(inf)* to catch *(Brit) or* cotton on *(inf)* → **Nürnberg**

trich|ter|för|mig ADJ funnel-shaped, funnel-like

Trick [trɪk] M -s, -s *or (rare)* -e trick; *(betrügerisch auch, raffiniert)* ploy, dodge; *(= Tipp, Rat)* tip; **ein fauler/gemeiner ~** a mean *or* dirty trick; **keine faulen ~s!** no funny business! *(inf)*; **das ist der ganze ~** that's all there is to it; **den ~ raushaben, wie man etw macht** *(inf)* to have got the knack of doing sth; **der ~ dabei ist, ...** the trick is to ...; **da ist doch ein ~ dabei** there is a trick to (doing) it; **jdm einen ~ verraten** to give sb a tip

Trick-: **Trick|be|trug** M confidence trick *(esp Brit) or* game *(US)*; **Trick|be|trü|ger(in)** M(F), **Trick|dieb(in)** M(F) confidence trickster; **Trick|film** M trick film; *(= Zeichentrickfilm)* cartoon (film); **Trick|kis|te** F *(von Zauberer)* box of tricks; *(fig inf)* bag of tricks; **trick|reich** *(inf)* ADJ tricky; *(= raffiniert)* clever ADV *erschwindeln, abgaunern* through various tricks; **~ vorgehen, sich ~ verhalten** to be very tricky

trick|sen ['trɪksn] *(inf)* VI to fiddle *(inf)*; *(Sport)* to feint; **fantastisch, wie er mit den Karten trickst** it's amazing what he can do with cards VT to fiddle *(inf)*

Trick|ser ['trɪksɐ] M -s, - *(inf)* tricky customer, trickster *(inf)*; *(Sport auch)* deceptive *or* inventive player

Trick|ski NT trick skiing, hot dogging *(esp US)*

Trick|tas|te F trick *or* superimpose button

trieb *pret von* **treiben**

Trieb [tri:p] M -(e)s, -e [-bə] **a** *(= Naturtrieb, auch Psych)* drive; *(= Drang)* urge; *(= Verlangen)* desire, urge; *(= Neigung, Hang)* inclination; *(= Selbsterhaltungstrieb, Fortpflanzungstrieb)* instinct; **sie ist von ihren ~en beherrscht** she is ruled completely by her physical urges *or* desires; **einen ~ zum Verbrechen haben** to have criminal urges **b** *(Bot)* shoot **c** *(Tech)* drive

Trieb-: **Trieb|ab|fuhr** F *(Psych)* = **Triebbefriedigung**; **trieb|ar|tig** ADJ *attr Verhalten* instinctive; *(von Sexualverbrecher etc)* compulsive; **Trieb|be|frie|di|gung** F gratification of a physical urge; *(sexuell)* gratification of sexual urges; **Trieb|fe|der** F *(fig)* motivating force (+*gen* behind); **trieb|haft** ADJ *Handlungen* compulsive; **ein ~er Instinkt** an instinctive urge; **sie hat ein sehr ~es Wesen, sie ist ein ~er Mensch** she is ruled by her physical urges *or* desires; **Trieb|haf|tig|keit** ['tri:phaftɪçkait] F -, *no pl* domination by one's physical urges; **Trieb|hand|lung** F act motivated by one's physical urges; **Trieb|kraft** F *(Mech)* motive power; *(Bot)* germinating power; *(fig)* driving force; **Trieb|le|ben** NT physical activities *pl*; *(= Geschlechtsleben)* sex life; **Trieb|mensch** M creature of instinct; **Trieb|mit|tel** NT *(Cook)* raising agent; *(in Sprühdosen)* propellant; **Trieb|rad** NT driving wheel *(Brit)*, gear wheel; **Trieb|sand** M quicksand; **Trieb|stau** M *(Psych)* build-up of physical urges; *(sexuell)* build-up of sexual urges; **Trieb|tä|ter(in)** M(F), **Trieb|ver|bre|cher(in)** M(F) sexual offender; **Trieb|wa|gen** M *(Rail)* railcar; **Trieb|werk** NT power plant; *(in Uhr)* mechanism

Trief-: **Trief|au|ge** NT *(Med)* bleary eye; **~n** *(pej)* watery eyes; *(von Mensch)* sheeplike eyes; **trief|äu|gig** ADJ watery-eyed ADV **er schaute mich ~ an** *(pej)* he looked at me with dumb devotion

trie|fen ['tri:fn] *pret* **triefte** *or (geh)* **troff** ['tri:ftə, trɔf], *ptp* **getrieft** *or (rare)* **getroffen** [gə'tri:ft, gə'trɔfn] VI to be dripping wet; *(Nase)* to run; *(Auge)* to water; **~ vor** to be dripping with; *(fig pej)* to gush with; **~d vor Nässe, ~d nass** dripping wet, wet through; **~d** soaking (wet)

Trief|na|se F *(inf)* runny nose *(inf)*

trief|nass ADJ *(inf)* dripping *or* soaking wet, wet through; **du bist ja ~!** (but) you're soaking wet!

trie|zen ['tri:tsn] VT *(inf)* **jdn ~** to pester sb; *(= schuften lassen)* to drive sb hard

trifft [trɪft] *3. pers sing pres von* **treffen**

Trift [trɪft] F -, -en *(= Weide)* pasture; *(= Weg)* cattle/sheep track

trif|tig ['trɪftɪç] ADJ convincing; *Entschuldigung, Grund auch* good ADV convincingly

Tri|go|no|met|rie [trigonome'tri:] F -, *no pl* trigonometry

tri|go|no|met|risch [trigono'me:trɪʃ] ADJ trigonometric(al)

Tri|ko|lo|re [triko'lo:rə] F -, -n tricolour *(Brit)*, tricolor *(US)*

Tri|kot [tri'ko:, 'trɪko] M OR NT -s, *no pl (= Trikotstoff)* cotton jersey

Tri|kot NT -s, -s *(= Hemd)* shirt, jersey; **das Gelbe ~** *(bei Tour de France)* the yellow jersey

Tri|ko|ta|ge [triko'ta:ʒə] F -, -n cotton jersey underwear *no pl*

Tri|kot|wer|bung [tri'ko:-] F shirt advertising

Tril|ler ['trɪlɐ] M -s, - *(Mus)* trill; *(von Vogel auch)* warble

tril|lern ['trɪlɐn] VTI to warble, to trill; **du trillerst wie eine Lerche** you sing like a lark

Tril|ler|pfei|fe F (pea) whistle

Tril|li|on [trɪ'lio:n] F -, -en trillion *(Brit)*, quintillion *(US)*

Tri|lo|gie [trilo'gi:] F -, -n [-'gi:ən] trilogy

Tri|ma|ran [trima'ra:n] M OR NT -s, -e *(Naut)* trimaran

Tri|mes|ter [tri'mɛstɐ] NT -s, - term

Trimm-: **Trimm|ak|ti|on** F keep-fit campaign; **Trimm-dich-Ge|rät** NT keep-fit apparatus; **Trimm-dich-Pfad** M keep-fit trail

trim|men ['trɪmən] VT *Hund, Schiff, Flugzeug* to trim; *(inf) Mensch, Tier* to teach, to train; *Funkgerät* to tune; **den Motor/das Auto auf Höchstleistung ~** *(inf)* to soup up the engine/car *(inf)*; **jdn auf tadelloses Benehmen ~** to teach *or* train sb to behave impeccably; **etw auf alt ~** to make sth look old; **auf alt getrimmt** done up to look old; **ein auf rustikal getrimmtes Restaurant** a rustic restaurant; **jdn auf einen bestimmten Typ ~** to make *or* mould *(Brit) or* mold *(US)* sb into a certain type VR to do keep-fit (exercises); **trimm dich durch Sport** keep fit with sport

Trimm-: **Trimm|ge|rät** NT keep-fit apparatus; **Trimm|pfad** M keep-fit trail

Tri|ni|tät [trini'tɛ:t] F -, *no pl (geh)* trinity

Trink-: **trink|bar** ADJ drinkable; **Trink|brun|nen** M *(in öffentlichen Gebäuden)* drinking fountain; **Trink|ei** NT new-laid egg

trin|ken ['trɪŋkn] *pret* **trank** [traŋk], *ptp* **getrunken** [gə'trʊŋkn] VT to drink; *ein Bier, Tasse Tee, Flasche Wein auch* to have; **alles/eine Flasche leer ~** to finish off all the drink/a bottle; **ich habe nichts zu ~ im Haus** I haven't any drink in the house; **er trinkt gern einen** *(inf)* he likes his drink; **(schnell) einen ~ gehen** *(inf)* to go for a (quick) drink → **Tisch**

VI to drink; **jdm zu ~ geben** to give sb a drink, to give sb something to drink; **lass mich mal ~** let me have a drink; **auf jds Wohl/jdn/etw ~** to drink sb's health/to sb/to sth; **er trinkt** *(= ist Alkoholiker)* he's a drinker

VR **sich satt ~** to drink one's fill → **volltrinken**; **sich arm ~** to drink one's money away

VR *impers* **es trinkt sich gut/schlecht daraus** it is easy/difficult to drink from; **dieser Wein trinkt sich gut** this is a pleasant *or* palatable wine

Trin|ker ['trɪŋkɐ] M -s, -, **Trin|ke|rin** [-ərɪn] F -, -nen drinker; *(= Alkoholiker)* alcoholic

Trin|ker|heil|an|stalt F *(old)* detoxification centre *(Brit) or* center *(US)*

Trink-: **trink|fest** ADJ **so ~ bin ich nicht** I can't hold my drink *(Brit) or* liquor *(esp US)* very well; **seine ~en Freunde** his hard-drinking friends; **Trink|fes|tig|keit** F ability to hold one's drink *(Brit) or* liquor *(esp US)*; **trink|freu|dig** ADJ fond of drinking; **Trink|ge|fäß** NT drinking vessel; **Trink|ge|la|ge** NT drinking session; **Trink|geld** NT tip; **jdm ~ geben** to tip sb, to give sb a tip; **jdm zu viel** *or* **ein zu hohes ~ geben** to over-tip sb; **Trink|glas** NT (drinking) glass; **Trink|hal|le** F *(in Heilbädern)* pump room; *(= Kiosk)* refreshment kiosk; **Trink|halm** M drinking straw; **Trink|lied** NT drinking song; **Trink|milch** F milk; **Trink|scha|le** F drinking bowl; **Trink|scho|ko|la|de** F drinking chocolate; **Trink|spruch** M toast

Trink|was|ser NT *pl* **-wässer** drinking water; **„kein ~"** "not for drinking", "do not drink"

Trink|was|ser-: **Trink|was|ser|brun|nen** M drinking fountain; **Trink|was|ser|ver|ord|nung** F water quality regulation(s *pl*); **Trink|was|ser|ver|sor|gung** F provision of drinking water

Trio [tri:o] NT **-s, -s** trio

Tri|o|le [tri'o:lə] F **-, -n** *(Mus)* triplet

Tri|o|lett [trio'lɛt] NT **-(e)s, -e** triolet

Trip [trɪp] M **-s, -s** *(inf)* trip

trip|peln ['trɪpln] VI *aux haben or (bei Richtungsangabe) sein* to trip *(esp Brit)*, to skip; *(Kind, alte Dame)* to toddle; *(geziert)* to mince *(Brit)*, to sashay *(esp US)*; *(Boxer)* to dance around; *(Pferd)* to prance

Trip|pel|schritt M short *or* little step; **~e** *pl (von Kleinkind)* toddle *sing*, toddling steps *pl*

Trip|per ['trɪpɐ] M **-s, -** gonorrhoea *no art (Brit)*, gonorrhea *no art (US)*; **sich** *(dat)* **den ~ holen** *(inf)* to get a dose (of the clap) *(inf)*

Trip|ty|chon ['trɪptyçɔn] NT **-s, Triptychen** *or* **Triptycha** *(Art)* triptych

trist [trɪst] ADJ dreary, dismal; *Farbe* dull; *Aussichten* dismal

Tris|te ['trɪstə] F **-, -n** *(Aus)* haystack

Tris|tesse F dreariness; *(= Traurigkeit)* sadness

Tri|ti|um ['tri:tsiʊm] NT **-s**, *no pl (abbr* **T***)* tritium

tritt [trɪt] *3. pers sing pres von* **treten**

Tritt [trɪt] M **-(e)s, -e** **a** *(= Schritt)* step; *(= Gang)* step, tread; **einen falschen ~ machen** to take a wrong step; **ich hörte ~e** I heard footsteps; **(wieder) ~ fassen** *(lit, fig)* to find one's/its feet (again)
b *(= Gleichschritt)* step; **im ~ marschieren, ~ halten** to march in step, to keep in step
c *(= Fußtritt)* kick; **jdm einen ~ geben** *or* **versetzen** to give sb a kick, to kick sb; *(fig) (= entlassen etc)* to kick sb out *(inf)*; *(inf: = anstacheln)* to give sb a kick in the pants *(inf) or* up the backside *(inf)*; **einen ~ in den Hintern kriegen** *(inf)* to get a kick in the pants *(inf) or* up the backside *(inf)*; *(fig)* to get kicked out *(inf)*
d *(bei Trittleiter, Stufe)* step; *(= Gestell)* steps *pl*; *(= Trittbrett)* step; *(an Auto)* running board
e *(= Fußspur)* footprint; *(von Tier)* track
f *(Hunt: = Fuß)* foot

Tritt-: **Tritt|brett** NT step; *(an Auto)* running board; *(an Nähmaschine)* treadle; **Tritt|brett|fah|rer(in)** M(F) *(inf)* fare dodger; *(fig)* copycat *(inf)*; **Tritt|lei|ter** F stepladder; **Tritt|rol|ler** M scooter; **Tritt|schall|däm|mung** F *(Archit)* footstep silencing measures *pl*

Tri|umph [tri'ʊmf] M **-(e)s, -e** triumph; **im ~** in triumph; **~e feiern** to be a great success, to be very successful

tri|um|phal [triʊm'fa:l] ADJ triumphant ADV triumphantly

Tri|umph-: **Tri|umph|bo|gen** M triumphal arch; **Tri|umph|ge|schrei** NT triumphant cheer, cheer of triumph

tri|um|phie|ren [triʊm'fi:rən] *ptp* **triumphiert** VI *(= frohlocken)* to rejoice, to exult; **über jdn/etw ~** *(geh)* to triumph over sb/sth, to overcome sb/sth

tri|um|phie|rend ADJ triumphant ADV triumphantly

Tri|umph|zug M triumphal procession

Tri|um|vi|rat [triʊmvi'ra:t] NT **-(e)s, -e** triumvirate

tri|vi|al [tri'via:l] ADJ trivial; *Gespräch auch* banal ADV trivially; **sich ~ unterhalten** to have a trivial conversation

Tri|vi|a|li|tät [triviali'tɛ:t] F **-, -en** triviality; *(von Gespräch auch)* banality; *(= triviale Bemerkung)* banality

Tri|vi|al|li|te|ra|tur F *(pej)* light fiction

Tri|zeps ['tri:tsɛps] M **-(es), -e** triceps

Tro|chä|us [trɔ'xɛ:ʊs] M **-, Trochäen** [-'xɛ:ən] *(Poet)* trochee

tro|cken ['trɔkn] ADJ **a** dry; *Gebiet* arid *(form)*, dry; *Gedeck* without wine *etc*; *(inf) Alkoholiker* dry, off the bottle, on the wagon *(inf)*; **~er Dunst** *(Met)* haze; **~ werden** to dry; *(Brot)* to go *or* get *or* become dry; **noch ~ nach Hause kommen** to get home dry *or* without getting wet; **ins Trockene kommen/gehen** to come/go into the dry *(esp Brit) or* out of the rain; **im Trockenen sein** to be somewhere dry *or* sheltered; **~en Auges** *(liter)* dry-eyed; **~en Fußes** *(liter)* without getting one's feet wet; **~ Brot essen** *(liter)* to eat dry bread; **auf dem Trockenen sitzen** *(inf)* to be in a tight spot *(inf) or* in difficulties → **Schäfchen, Ohr**
b *(= langweilig)* dry
c *(= herb) Sekt, Sherry* dry
d *(fig) Humor, Art etc* dry
ADV *aufbewahren, lagern* in a dry place; **das Schiff liegt ~** the ship is high and dry; **sich ~ rasieren** to use an electric razor; **die Haare ~ schneiden** to cut one's/sb's hair dry

Tro|cken-: **Tro|cken|au|to|mat** M tumble dryer; **Tro|cken|bat|te|rie** F dry-cell battery; **Tro|cken|bee|ren|aus|le|se** F *wine made from choice grapes left on the vine to dry out at the end of the season*; **Tro|cken|blu|me** F dried flower; **Tro|cken|bo|den** M drying room *(in attic)*; **tro|cken bü|geln** △, **tro|cken+bü|geln** *sep* VT to iron dry; **Tro|cken|dock** NT dry dock; **Tro|cken|ei** NT dried egg; **Tro|cken|eis** NT dry ice; **Tro|cken|fut|ter** NT dried *or* dehydrated food; **Tro|cken|ge|biet** NT arid region; **Tro|cken|ge|stell** NT drying rack; **Tro|cken|hau|be** F (salon) hairdryer; **Tro|cken|he|fe** F dried yeast; **Tro|cken|heit** F **-, -en** *(lit, fig)* dryness; *(von Gebiet auch)* aridness *(form)*; *(= Trockenperiode)* drought; **Tro|cken|kurs** M *(Ski, fig) course in which a beginner learns the basic techniques without actually putting them into practice*; **einen ~ machen** to learn the basics; **tro|cken+le|gen** VT *sep* **a** *Sumpf, Gewässer* to drain **b** *Baby* to change; *(inf) Trinker* to dry out; **Tro|cken|le|gung** [-le:gʊŋ] F **-, -en** draining; **Tro|cken|maß** NT dry measure; **Tro|cken|mas|se** F dry matter; **30% Fett in der ~** fat content 30% dry weight; **Tro|cken|milch** F dried milk; **Tro|cken|platz** M drying area; **Tro|cken|ra|sie|rer** [-razi:rɐ] M **-s, -** *(inf)* user of electric shaver *or* razor; *(= Rasierapparat)* electric shaver *or* razor; **Tro|cken|ra|sur** F dry *or* electric shave; *(= das Rasieren)* shaving with an electric razor *no art*; **tro|cken rei|ben** *irreg*, **tro|cken+rei|ben** *sep irreg* VT to rub dry; **Tro|cken|sham|poo** NT dry shampoo; **tro|cken+sit|zen** *sep irreg (S Ger, Aus, Sw: aux sein)*, **tro|cken sit|zen** △ *irreg (S Ger, Aus, Sw: aux sein)* VI **die Gäste ~ lassen** to leave one's guests without a drink; **Tro|cken|spi|ri|tus** [-ʃpi:ritʊs] M solid fuel *(for camping stove etc)*; **Tro|cken|star|re** F aestivation *(Brit)*, estivation *(US)*; **tro|cken+ste|hen** *sep irreg (S Ger, Aus, Sw: aux sein)*, **tro|cken ste|hen** △ *irreg (S Ger, Aus, Sw: aux sein)* VI *(Kuh)* to be dry; **Tro|cken|übung** F *(Sport)* dry ski *etc* exercise; *(= Schwimmübung auch)* land drill; *(fig inf)* dry run; **Tro|cken|wä|sche** F dry weight (of washing); **Tro|cken|zeit** F **a** *(= Jahreszeit)* dry season **b** *(von Wäsche etc)* drying time

trock|nen ['trɔknən] VT to dry VI *aux sein* to dry

Trock|ner ['trɔknɐ] M **-s, -** *(inf)* dryer, drier

Trod|del ['trɔdl] F **-, -n** tassel

Trö|del ['trø:dl] M **-s**, *no pl (inf)* junk

Trö|de|lei [trø:də'lai] F **-, -en** *(inf)* dawdling

Trö|del-: **Trö|del|kram** M junk; **Trö|del|la|den** M junk shop; **Trö|del|markt** M fleamarket

trö|deln ['trø:dln] VI to dawdle

Tröd|ler ['trø:dlɐ] M **-s, -**, **Tröd|le|rin** [-ərɪn] F **-, -nen** **a** *(= Händler)* junk dealer **b** *(inf: = langsamer Mensch)* dawdler, slowcoach *(Brit inf)*, slowpoke *(US inf)*

troff *pret von* **triefen**

trog *pret von* **trügen**

Trog [tro:k] M **-(e)s, ⸚e** ['trø:gə] trough; *(= Waschtrog)* tub

Trog|tal NT glaciated *or* U-shaped valley

Tro|ja ['tro:ja] NT Troy

Tro|ja|ner [tro'ja:nɐ] M **-s, -** *(Comput, Internet)* Trojan (horse)

Tro|ja|ner [tro'ja:nɐ] M **-s, -**, **Tro|ja|ne|rin** [-ərɪn] F **-, -nen** Trojan

tro|ja|nisch [tro'ja:nɪʃ] ADJ Trojan; **Trojanisches Pferd** *(Myth)* Trojan Horse; **~es Pferd** *(Comput, Internet)* Trojan Horse

trö|len ['trø:lən] VI *(Sw)* to dawdle

Troll [trɔl] M **-s, -e** troll

Troll|blu|me F globe flower, trollius

trol|len ['trɔlən] VR *(inf)* to push off *(inf)*

Trom|mel ['trɔml] F **-, -n** **a** *(Mus)* drum; **die ~ rühren** *(fig inf)* to drum up (some) support **b** *(Tech) (in Maschine)* drum; *(in Revolver)* revolving breech

Trom|mel-: **Trom|mel|brem|se** F drum brake; **Trom|mel|fell** NT eardrum; **da platzt einem ja das ~** *(fig)* the noise is earsplitting; **mir platzte fast das ~** my eardrums almost burst; **Trom|mel|feu|er** NT drumfire, heavy barrage

trom|meln ['trɔmln] VI to drum; *(Regen)* to bear (down); **gegen die Tür ~** to bang on the door; **gegen die Brust ~** to beat one's chest; **mit den Fingern ~** to drum one's fingers; **der Regen trommelt gegen die Fensterscheiben** the rain is beating against the window panes VT *Marsch, Lied* to play on the drum/drums, to drum; *Rhythmus* to beat out; **jdn aus dem Schlaf ~** to knock sb up *(Brit inf)*, to wake sb up (by banging on the door)

Trom|mel-: **Trom|mel|re|vol|ver** M revolver; **Trom|mel|schlag** M drum beat; *(= das Trommeln)* drumming; **Trom|mel|schlä|gel** M drumstick; **Trom|mel|spra|che** F bush telegraph; **Trom|mel|stock** M drumstick; **Trom|mel|wasch|ma|schi|ne** F drum washing machine; **Trom|mel|wir|bel** M drum roll

Tromm|ler ['trɔmlɐ] M **-s, -**, **Tromm|le|rin** [-ərɪn] F **-, -nen** drummer

Trom|pe|te [trɔm'pe:tə] F **-, -n** trumpet → **Pauke**

trom|pe|ten [trɔm'pe:tn] *ptp* **trompetet** VI to trumpet; *(= sich schnäuzen)* to blow one's nose loudly VT *Marsch* to play on the trumpet

Trom|pe|ten|baum M trumpet tree, common catalpa *(spec)*

Trom|pe|ter [trɔm'pe:tɐ] M **-s, -**, **Trom|pe|te|rin** [-ərɪn] F **-, -nen** trumpeter

Tro|pen ['tro:pn] PL tropics *pl*

Tro|pen- *in cpds* tropical; **Tro|pen|an|zug** M tropical suit; **Tro|pen|fie|ber** NT malaria; **Tro|pen|helm** M pith helmet, topee; **Tro|pen|holz** NT wood from tropical forests; **Tro|pen|ins|ti|tut** NT institute for tropical diseases; **Tro|pen|kli|ma** NT tropical climate; **Tro|pen|kol|ler** M tropical madness; **Tro|pen|krank|heit** F tropical disease; **Tro|pen|me|di|zin** F tropical medicine; **Tro|pen|tag** M scorcher *(inf)*; **Tro|pen|taug|lich|keit** F *fitness for service in the tropics*

tropf [trɔpf] INTERJ drip

Tropf [trɔpf] M **-(e)s, ⸚e** ['trœpfə] *(inf)* **a** *(= Schelm)* rogue, rascal; **einfältiger ~** twit *(inf)*, dummy *(inf)*; **armer ~** poor bugger *(inf) or* devil **b** *no pl (= Infusion)* drip *(inf)*; **am ~ hängen** to be on a drip; *(fig inf: finanziell)* to be on a drip-feed

Tröpf|chen-: **Tröpf|chen|in|fek|ti|on** F airborne infection; **tröpf|chen|wei|se** ADV in dribs and drabs

tröpf|feln ['trœpfln] VI **a** *(Leitung, Halm)* to drip; *(Nase)* to run **b** *aux sein (Flüssigkeit)* to drip VI *impers* **es tröpfelt** it is spitting VT to drip

trop|fen ['trɔpfn] VI to drip; *(Nase)* to run; **es tropft durch die Decke** there is water dripping through the ceiling; **es tropft von den Bäumen** the rain is dripping from the trees; **es tropft**

aus der Leitung the pipe is dripping VT to drop, to drip

Trop|fen ['trɔpfn] M **-s, -** a drop; *(= Schweißtropfen auch)* bead; *(= einzelner Tropfen: an Kanne, Nase etc)* drip; *(inf: = kleine Menge)* drop; **ein guter** *or* **edler ~** *(inf)* a good wine; **bis auf den letzten ~** to the last drop; **ein ~ auf den heißen Stein** *(fig inf)* a drop in the ocean → **stet** b **Tropfen** PL *(= Medizin)* drops *pl*

-trop|fen PL *suf in cpds (Med)* drops *pl*; **Augentropfen** eye drops

Trop|fen|fän|ger M drip-catcher

trop|fen|wei|se ADV drop by drop

Tropf-: **Tropf|in|fu|si|on** F intravenous drip; **tropf|nass** ['trɔpf'nas] ADJ dripping wet; **Tropf|stein** M dripstone; *(an der Decke)* stalactite; *(am Boden)* stalagmite; **Tropf|stein|höh|le** F dripstone cave

Tro|phäe [tro'fɛ:ə] F **-, -n** trophy

tro|pisch ['tro:pɪʃ] ADJ tropical ADV tropically; **~ wuchernde** *or* **wachsende Vegetation** tropical growth

Tro|po-: **Tro|po|pau|se** [tropo'pauzə] F *(Met)* tropopause; **Tro|po|sphä|re** [tropo'sfɛ:rə] F *(Met)* troposphere

Tross [trɔs] M **-es, -e** *(old)* baggage train; **er gehört zum ~** *(fig)* he's a hanger-on; *(= hat untergeordnete Rolle)* he's an underling

Tros|se ['trɔsə] F **-, -n** cable, hawser

Trost [tro:st] M **-(e)s,** *no pl* consolation, comfort; **jdm ~ zusprechen/bringen** to console *or* comfort sb; **das Kind war ihr einziger ~** the child was her only comfort; **~ im Alkohol/in der Religion suchen** to seek solace in alcohol/religion; **zum ~ kann ich Ihnen sagen, dass ...** it may comfort you to know that ...; **zum** *or* **als ~ gab es ein kleines Geschenk** there was a small consolation prize; **das ist ein schwacher** *or* **schlechter ~** that's pretty cold comfort; **das ist ein schöner ~** *(iro)* some comfort that is!; **du bist wohl nicht ganz** *or* **recht bei ~!** *(inf)* you must be out of your mind!

trös|ten ['trø:stn] VT to comfort; *(= Trost zusprechen auch)* to console; **jdn/sich mit etw ~** to console sb/oneself with sth; **sich über etw** *(acc)* **~** to get over sth; **jdn über etw** *(acc)* **~** to help sb to get over sth; **~ Sie sich!** never mind; **tröste dich, ihm ist es auch nicht besser ergangen** console yourself with the thought that he didn't fare any better

Trös|ter ['trø:stɐ] M **-s, -**, **Trös|te|rin** [-ərɪn] F **-, -nen** comforter

tröst|lich ['trø:stlɪç] ADJ cheering, comforting; **das ist ja sehr ~** *(iro)* that's some comfort

trost|los ADJ hopeless; *Jugend, Verhältnisse* miserable, wretched; *(= verzweifelt)* inconsolable; *(= öde, trist)* dreary; **~ langweilig** desperately boring

Trost|lo|sig|keit F **-,** *no pl* hopelessness; *(von Verhältnissen)* wretchedness; *(= Ödheit, Tristesse)* dreariness

Trost-: **Trost|pflas|ter** NT consolation; **als ~** by way of consolation; **Trost|preis** M consolation prize; **trost|reich** ADJ comforting; **Trost|run|de** F *(Sport)* consolation round; **Trost|wor|te** PL words *pl* of consolation

Trös|tung ['trø:stʊŋ] F **-, -en** comfort; *(= das Trösten)* comforting

Trott [trɔt] M **-s,** *no pl* (slow) trot; *(fig)* routine; **im ~** at a (slow) trot; **aus dem alten ~ herauskommen** to get out of one's rut

Trot|tel ['trɔtl] M **-s, -** *(inf)* idiot, dope *(inf)*

trot|te|lig ['trɔtəlɪç] *(inf)* ADJ stupid, dopey *(inf)*, goofy *(US inf)* ADV stupidly, goofily *(US inf)*

trot|ten ['trɔtn] VI *aux sein* to trot along; *(Pferd)* to trot slowly

Trot|teur [trɔ'tø:ɐ] M **-s, -s** casual (shoe)

Trot|toir [trɔ'toa:ɐ] NT **-s, -s** *or* **-e** *(dated, S Ger)* pavement *(Brit)*, sidewalk *(US)*

trotz [trɔts] PREP *+gen (geh) or +dat (inf)* in spite of, despite; **~ allem** *or* **alledem** in spite of everything, for all that

Trotz [trɔts] M **-es,** *no pl* defiance; *(= trotziges Verhalten)* contrariness; **jdm/einer Sache zum ~** in defiance of sb/sth; **jdm/einer Sache ~ bieten** *(geh)* to defy *or* flout sb/sth

Trotz|al|ter NT defiant age; **sich im ~ befinden, im ~ sein** to be going through a defiant phase; **ins ~ kommen** to get to *or* reach a defiant age

trotz|dem ['trɔtsde:m, 'trɔts'de:m] ADV nevertheless; **(und) ich mache das ~!** I'll do it all the same CONJ *(strictly incorrect)* even though

trot|zen ['trɔtsn] VI a *+dat* to defy; *der Gefahr auch* to brave; *der Kälte, dem Klima etc* to withstand; **Wind und Wetter ~** to defy the elements b *(= trotzig sein)* to be awkward *or* difficult *or* contrary

trot|zig ['trɔtsɪç] ADJ defiant; *Kind etc* difficult, awkward; *(= widerspenstig)* contrary ADV defiantly

Trotz|kis|mus [trɔts'kɪsmʊs] M **-,** *no pl* Trotskyism

Trotz|kist [trɔts'kɪst] M **-en, -en**, **Trotz|kis|tin** [-'kɪstɪn] F **-, -nen** Trotskyite, Trotskyist

Trotz-: **Trotz|kopf** M *(inf) (Einstellung)* defiant streak; *(widerspenstig)* contrary streak; *(Mensch)* contrary so-and-so *(inf)*; **sei doch nicht so ein ~** don't be so difficult; **seinen ~ haben** to be in a defiant/contrary mood; **trotz|köp|fig** ADJ *Kind* contrary; **Trotz|pha|se** F phase of defiance; **Trotz|re|ak|ti|on** F act of defiance; **das war eine reine ~** he/she just reacted like that out of defiance

Trou|ba|dour ['tru:badu:ɐ, truba'du:ɐ] M **-s, -s** *or* **-e** troubadour

Trou|ble ['trabl] M **-s,** *no pl (inf)* trouble; **~ machen** to make trouble; **~ haben** to have problems

Trou|ble|shoo|ter ['trablʃu:tɐ] M **-s, -** troubleshooter

trüb [try:p], **trü|be** ['try:bə] ADJ a *(= unklar) Flüssigkeit* cloudy; *(= glanzlos, matt) Glas, Augen, Himmel, Tag* dull; *Sonne, Mond, Licht* dim; **in ~en Wassern fischen, im Trüben fischen** *(inf)* to fish in troubled waters b *(fig: = bedrückend, unerfreulich)* cheerless; *Zeiten, Zukunft* bleak; *Stimmung, Gedanken, Aussichten, Vorahnung, Miene* gloomy; *Erfahrung* grim; **es sieht ~ aus** things are looking pretty bleak; **~e Tasse** *(inf)* drip *(inf)*; *(= Spielverderber)* wet blanket *(inf)*

Tru|bel ['tru:bl] M **-s,** *no pl* hurly-burly

trü|ben ['try:bn] VT a *Flüssigkeit* to make cloudy, to cloud; *Glas, Metall* to dull; *Himmel* to overcast; *Wasseroberfläche* to ruffle; *Augen, Blick* to dull, to cloud; **getrübt** *(Flüssigkeit, Himmel)* cloudy; *Spiegel, Metall* dull; *Verstand* dulled; *Stimmung, Laune* dampened; **sie sieht aus, als könnte sie kein Wässerchen ~** *(inf)* she looks as if butter wouldn't melt in her mouth; **kein Wölkchen trübte den Himmel** there wasn't a cloud in the sky

b *(fig) Glück, Freude, Verhältnis, Bild* to spoil, to mar; *Beziehungen* to strain; *Laune* to dampen; *Bewusstsein, Erinnerung* to dull, to dim; *(geh) Verstand* to dull; *Urteilsvermögen* to dim, to cloud over

VR *(Flüssigkeit)* to go cloudy; *(Spiegel, Metall)* to become dull; *(geh) (Verstand)* to become dulled; *(Augen)* to dim, to cloud; *(Himmel)* to cloud over; *(fig) (Stimmung, Laune)* to be dampened; *(Beziehungen, Verhältnis)* to become strained; *(Glück, Freude)* to be marred → *auch* **getrübt**

Trüb-: **Trüb|heit** F **-,** *no pl (von Flüssigkeit)* cloudiness; *(= Glanzlosigkeit, Mattheit)* dullness; **Trüb|sal** ['try:pza:l] F **-, -e** *(liter)* afflictions *pl*; *(no pl: = Stimmung)* sorrow; **~ blasen** *(inf)* to mope; **trüb|se|lig** ADJ gloomy; *Gegend* bleak; *Behausung* depressing; **Trüb|se|lig|keit** F gloominess; *(von Landschaft)* bleakness; **Trüb|sinn** M, *no pl* gloom, melancholy; **trüb|sin|nig** ADJ gloomy, melancholy

Trü|bung ['try:bʊŋ] F **-, -en** a *(von Flüssigkeit)* clouding; *(von Glas, Metall)* dulling; *(von Himmel)* overcasting; *(von Wasseroberfläche)* ruffling b *(fig) (von Glück, Freude, Verhältnis)* spoiling, marring; *(von Beziehungen)* straining; *(von Laune)* dampening; *(von Verstand)* dulling

tru|deln ['tru:dln] VI a *aux sein or haben (Aviat)* to spin; *(fig)* to slide; **ins Trudeln kommen** *or* **geraten** to go into a spin; *(fig)* to go into a tailspin b *(dial: = würfeln)* to play dice

True-Type-Schrift ['tru:taip-] F *(Comput)* True Type font

Trüf|fel ['trʏfl] F **-, -n** *or (inf) m* **-s, -** a *(= Pilz)* truffle b *(= Praline)* truffle

trug *pret von* **tragen**

Trug [tru:k] M **-(e)s** [-gəs], *no pl (liter)* deception; *(der Sinne)* illusion; *(der Fantasie)* delusion → **Lug**

Trug|bild NT delusion; *(der Sinne)* illusion

trü|gen ['try:gn] *pret* **trog** [tro:k], *ptp* **getrogen** [gə'tro:gn] VT to deceive; **wenn mich nicht alles trügt** unless I am very much mistaken VI to be deceptive

trü|ge|risch ['try:gərɪʃ] ADJ *(liter) (= betrügerisch)* deceitful, false; *(= irreführend)* deceptive; *Hoffnung* false

Trug|schluss M fallacy, misapprehension; **einem ~ unterliegen** to be labouring *(Brit) or* laboring *(US)* under a misapprehension

Tru|he ['tru:ə] F **-, -n** chest

Trumm [trʊm] NT **-(e)s, Trümmer** ['trʏmɐ] *(inf: = großer, schwerer Gegenstand)* whopper *(inf)*, humdinger *(inf)*; **ein ~ von einem Buch** a great tome of a book; **ein ~ von einem Kerl** a great hulk; **er ist ein ~ von einem Kerl** *(auch)* he's huge, a giant of a man; **so ein ~ (von einem Steak** *etc***)** such a whopper (of a steak *etc*)

Trüm|mer ['trʏmɐ] PL rubble *sing*; *(= Ruinen, fig: von Glück etc)* ruins *pl*; *(von Schiff, Flugzeug etc)* wreckage *sing*; *(= Überreste)* remnants *pl*; *(inf: von Essen)* remains *pl*; **in ~n liegen** to be in ruins; **in ~ gehen** to be ruined *(auch fig)*; *(Schiff, Flugzeug)* to be wrecked; **etw in ~ schlagen** to smash sth to pieces *or* up

Trüm|mer-: **Trüm|mer|feld** NT expanse of rubble; *(= Ruinen)* expanse of ruins; *(fig)* scene of devastation *or* destruction; **Trüm|mer|frau** F *woman who clears away rubble after bombing*; **Trüm|mer|hau|fen** M heap of rubble

Trumpf [trʊmpf] M **-(e)s, ⸗e** ['trʏmpfə] *(Cards) (= Trumpfkarte)* trump (card); *(= Farbe)* trumps *pl*; *(fig)* trump card; **~ sein** to be trumps; *(fig inf: = modisch sein)* to be in *(inf)*; **~ spielen** *(Cards)* to play trumps; **einen ~ ausspielen** *(fig)* to play one's trump card; **alle Trümpfe in der Hand haben** *(fig)* to hold all the trump cards; **alle Trümpfe aus der Hand geben** *(fig)* to throw away *or* waste the advantage; **noch einen ~ in der Hand haben** *(fig)* to have an ace up one's sleeve; **jdm die Trümpfe aus den Händen nehmen** *(fig)* to trump sb

Trumpf|ass NT ace of trumps

trump|fen ['trʊmpfn] VT to trump VI to play a trump (card); **mit dem König ~** to play the king of trumps

Trumpf-: **Trumpf|far|be** F trumps *pl*; **Trumpf|kar|te** F trump (card); **Trumpf|stich** M trick

Trunk [trʊŋk] M **-(e)s, ⸗e** ['trʏŋkə] a *(old, liter)* draught *(Brit old, liter)*, draft *(US old, liter)*; *(= Zaubertrunk auch)* potion; *(= das Trinken)* drink; **jdm etw/das Glas zum ~ reichen** to pass sb sth to drink/a glass *or* a drink b *(= Trunksucht)* **dem ~ ergeben** *or* **verfallen sein** to have taken to drink

trun|ken ['trʊŋkn] *(liter)* ADJ *(von Alkohol)* inebriated, intoxicated; *(vor Freude, Glück etc)* drunk (*vor +dat* with) ADV drunkenly

Trun|ken-: **Trun|ken|bold** ['trʊŋknbɔlt] M **-(e)s, -e** [-də] *(pej)* drunkard; **Trun|ken|heit** F **-,** *no pl* intoxication; **~ am Steuer** drunk *or* drink *(Brit)* driving

Trunk-: **Trunk|sucht** F alcoholism; **trunk|süch|tig** ADJ alcoholic; **~ werden** to become an alcoholic; **Trunk|süch|ti|ge(r)** MF *decl as adj* alcoholic

Trupp [trʊp] M **-s, -s** bunch; *(= Einheit)* group; *(Mil)* squad; *(esp beritten)* troop

Trup|pe ['trʊpə] F -, -n **a** no pl (Mil) army, troops pl; (= Panzertruppe etc) corps sing; **zur ~ zurückkehren** to report back; **von der (ganz) schnellen ~ sein** (inf) to be a fast mover (inf); **nicht von der schnellen ~ sein** (inf) to be slow **b Truppen** PL troops **c** (= Künstlertruppe) troupe, company

Trup|pen-: **Trup|pen|ab|zug** M withdrawal of troops; **Trup|pen|arzt** M, **Trup|pen|ärz|tin** F (army) medical officer; **Trup|pen|auf|marsch** M deployment of troops; (= Massierung) buildup of troops; **Trup|pen|be|we|gung** F usu pl troop movement; **Trup|pen|ein|heit** F unit; (bei der Kavallerie) troop; **Trup|pen|ein|satz** M (Mil) deployment of troops; **Trup|pen|füh|rer(in)** M(F) unit/troop commander; **Trup|pen|gat|tung** F corps sing; **Trup|pen|pa|ra|de** F military parade or review; **Trup|pen|schau** F troop inspection; **Trup|pen|stär|ke** F troop or military strength, number of troops; **Trup|pen|sta|ti|o|nie|rung** F stationing of troops; **Trup|pen|teil** M unit; **Trup|pen|übung** F field exercise; **Trup|pen|übungs|platz** M military training area; **Trup|pen|ver|band** M unit, formation; (mit besonderem Auftrag) task force

trupp|wei|se ADV → **Trupp** in bunches/groups; (Mil) in squads/troops

Trust [trast] M -(e)s, -s or -e trust

Trut-: **Trut|hahn** M turkey (cock); **Trut|hen|ne** F turkey (hen)

Trutz [trʊts] M -es, no pl (obs) = **Schutz**

Trutz|burg F (Hist) castle built in order to lay siege to another castle

trut|zen ['trʊtsn] VI (obs) to defy

Tschad [tʃat, tʃa:t] M - der ~ Chad

tscha|disch ['tʃadɪʃ, 'tʃa:dɪʃ] ADJ Chad attr

Tscha|dor [tʃa'do:ɐ] M -s, -s chador

Tschap|perl ['tʃapɐl] NT -s, -n (Aus) dolt (inf); **armes ~** poor devil (inf)

tschau [tʃau] INTERJ (inf) cheerio (Brit inf), so long (inf), ciao (inf)

Tsche|che ['tʃɛçə] M -n, -n, **Tsche|chin** ['tʃɛçɪn] F -, -nen Czech

Tsche|chei [tʃɛ'çai] F - die ~ (Hist) (neg!) Czechoslovakia

Tsche|chi|en ['tʃɛçiən] NT -s the Czech Republic

tsche|chisch ['tʃɛçɪʃ] ADJ Czech; **die Tschechische Republik** the Czech Republic

Tsche|chisch(e) ['tʃɛçɪʃ] NT Czech → auch **Deutsch(e)**

Tsche|cho|slo|wa|ke [tʃɛçoslo'va:kə] M, **Tsche|cho|slo|wa|kin** [-'va:kɪn] F (Hist) Czechoslovak

Tsche|cho|slo|wa|kei [tʃɛçoslova'kai] F (Hist) **die ~** Czechoslovakia

tsche|cho|slo|wa|kisch [tʃɛçoslo'va:kɪʃ] ADJ (Hist) Czechoslovak(ian)

Tschick [tʃɪk] M -s, - (Aus) (inf: = Stummel) fag end (Brit inf), butt (inf); (sl: = Zigarette) fag (Brit inf), smoke (US sl)

tschil|pen ['tʃɪlpn] VI to chirp

Tschi|nel|le [tʃi'nɛlə] F -, -n (Aus Mus) cymbal

tschüs [tʃʏs] INTERJ = **tschüss**

Tschusch [tʃu:ʃ] M -en, -en (Aus pej) ≈ wog (Brit pej sl), chink (US pej sl)

tschüss [tʃʏs] INTERJ (inf) cheerio (Brit inf), bye (inf), so long (inf)

Tsd. abbr von **Tausend**

Tse|tse|flie|ge ['tse:tse-, 'tsɛtse-] F tsetse fly

T-Shirt ['ti:ʃœrt, -ʃø:ɐt] NT -s, -s T-shirt, tee shirt

T-Shirt-BH ['ti:ʃœrt-, 'ti:ʃø:ɐt-] M T-shirt bra, tee shirt bra

TSV [te:lɛs'fau] M -(s), -s abbr von **Turn- und Sportverein** SC; **~ 1860 München** ≈ 1860 Munich Sports Club

T-Trä|ger ['te:-] M T-bar, T-girder

TU [te:'lu:] F - abbr von **technische Universität**

Tu|ba ['tu:ba] F -, **Tuben** [-bn] **a** (Mus) tuba **b** (Anat) tube

Tu|be ['tu:bə] F -, -n tube; **auf die ~ drücken** (inf) to get a move on (inf); (im Auto auch) to put one's foot down (inf)

Tu|ber|kel [tu'bɛrkl] M -s, - or (Aus auch) f -, -n tubercle

Tu|ber|kel|ba|zil|lus M tuberculosis bacillus

tu|ber|ku|lös [tubɛrku'lø:s] ADJ tubercular, tuberculous

Tu|ber|ku|lo|se [tubɛrku'lo:zə] F -, -n tuberculosis

Tu|ber|ku|lo|se-: **tu|ber|ku|lo|se|krank** ADJ tubercular, tuberculous; **Tu|ber|ku|lo|se|kran|ke(r)** MF decl as adj TB case, TB sufferer

Tuch [tu:x] NT -(e)s, ¨er ['ty:çɐ] **a** (= Stück Stoff) cloth; (= Tischtuch) cloth; (= Halstuch, Kopftuch) scarf; (= Schultertuch) shawl; (= Handtuch) towel; (= Geschirrtuch) cloth, towel; (= Taschentuch) handkerchief; (zum Abdecken von Möbeln) dustsheet (Brit), dust cover; **das rote ~ (des Stierkämpfers)** the bullfighter's cape; **heiße Tücher wurden gereicht** we etc were offered hot towels; **das wirkt wie ein rotes ~ auf ihn** it makes him see red, it's like a red rag to a bull (to him) **b** pl -e (old: = Stoff) cloth, fabric

Tuch-: **Tuch|art** F type of cloth or fabric; **Tuch|fab|rik** F textile factory or mill; **Tuch|füh|lung** F physical or body contact; **in ~** in physical contact; (Mil) shoulder to shoulder; (fig) cheek by jowl; **er blieb mit den Führenden in** or **auf ~** (Sport) he stayed with the leaders; **~ haben** to be in physical contact (with sb); (fig) to be close to sb; **auf ~ gehen** to move closer (to sb/together); **Tuch|händ|ler(in)** M(F) cloth merchant; **Tuch|ma|cher(in)** M(F) clothworker

tüch|tig ['tʏçtɪç] ADJ **a** (= fähig) capable, competent (in +dat at); (= fleißig) efficient; Arbeiter good; **etwas Tüchtiges lernen/werden** (inf) to get a proper training/job; **~, ~!** not bad! **b** (inf: = groß) Portion big, huge; Stoß, Schlag hard; Appetit, Esser big; **eine ~e Tracht Prügel** a good hiding (inf); **eine ~e Portion Arroganz** etc a fair amount of arrogance etc
ADV **a** (= fleißig, fest) hard; essen heartily; **hilf ~ mit** lend or give us a hand
b (inf: = sehr) good and proper (inf); **~ regnen** to pelt (inf); **jdm ~ die Meinung sagen** to give sb a piece of one's mind; **~ ausschimpfen** to scold thoroughly; **~ zulangen** to tuck in (inf); **jdn ~ anschmieren** or **betrügen** to take sb for a ride (inf); **jdn ~ belügen** to tell sb a pack of lies; **sich ~ ausruhen** to have a good rest

Tüch|tig|keit F -, no pl (= Fähigkeit) competence; (von Arbeiter etc) efficiency

Tuch|wa|ren PL cloth goods pl

Tü|cke ['tʏkə] F -, -n **a** (no pl: = Bosheit) malice, spite; (= böswillige Handlung) malicious or spiteful action **b** (= Gefahr) danger, peril; (von Krankheit) perniciousness; **voller ~n stecken** to be difficult; (= gefährlich) to be dangerous or (Berg, Fluss auch) treacherous; **das ist die ~ des Objekts** these things have a will of their own!; **seine ~n haben** (Maschine etc) to be temperamental; (= schwierig sein) to be difficult; (= gefährlich sein) to be dangerous or (Berg, Fluss auch) treacherous → **List c** (des Glücks etc) vagary usu pl; (des Schicksals) fickleness no pl

tu|ckern ['tʊkɐn] VI aux haben or (bei Richtungsangabe) sein to put-put, to chug

tü|ckisch ['tʏkɪʃ] ADJ (= boshaft) Mensch, Blick, Lächeln malicious, spiteful; Zufall unhappy; (= bösartig, gefährlich) Berge, Strom etc treacherous; Krankheit pernicious

tü|de|lig ['ty:dəlɪç] ADJ (N Ger inf) doddery

tu(e) [tu:(ə)] imper sing von **tun**

Tu|e|rei [tu:ə'rai] F -, -en (inf) antics pl

Tuff [tʊf] M -s, -e, **Tuff|stein** M tuff

Tüf|tel|ar|beit F (inf) fiddly (esp Brit) or finicky job

Tüf|te|lei [tʏftə'lai] F -, -en (inf) fiddly (esp Brit) or finicky job; **das ist eine ~** that's fiddly (esp Brit) or finicky

tüf|te|lig ['tʏftəlɪç] ADJ (inf) fiddly (esp Brit), finicky

tüf|teln ['tʏftln] VI (inf) to puzzle; (= basteln) to fiddle about (inf); **an etw** (dat) **~** to fiddle about with sth; (geistig) to puzzle over sth; **er tüftelt gern** he likes doing fiddly (esp Brit) or finicky things

Tüft|ler ['tʏftlɐ] M -s, -, **Tüft|le|rin** [-ərɪn] F -, -nen (inf) person who likes doing finicky things (= Erfinder) inventor

Tu|gend ['tu:gnt] F -, -en [-dən] virtue; **seine ~ bewahren** to remain virtuous; (= Unschuld auch) to keep one's virtue → **Not d**

Tu|gend-: **Tu|gend|bold** ['tu:gntbɔlt] M -(e)s, -e [-də]; **Tu|gend|bol|din** [-dɪn] F -, -nen (pej) paragon of virtue; **tu|gend|haft** ADJ virtuous ADV virtuously; **Tu|gend|haf|tig|keit** ['tu:gnthaftɪçkait] F -, no pl virtuousness; **tu|gend|sam** ['tu:gntza:m] ADJ virtuous ADV virtuously; **Tu|gend|wäch|ter(in)** M(F) (iro) guardian of his/her etc virtue

Tu|kan ['tu:kan, tu'ka:n] M -s, -e toucan

Tüll [tʏl] M -s, -e tulle; (für Gardinen) net

Tül|le ['tʏlə] F -, -n spout; (= Spritzdüse) pipe

Tüll|gar|di|ne F net curtain

Tul|pe ['tʊlpə] F -, -n **a** (Bot) tulip **b** (= Glas) tulip glass

Tul|pen|zwie|bel F tulip bulb

tumb [tʊmp] ADJ (obs, hum) stupid, dim

Tumb|ler ['tamblɐ] M -s, - (Sw: = Wäschetrockner) tumble dryer

tum|meln ['tʊmln] VR **a** (Hunde, Kinder etc) to romp (about) **b** (= sich beeilen) to hurry (up)

Tum|mel|platz ['tʊml-] M play area; (fig) hotbed

Tümm|ler ['tʏmlɐ] M -s, - (bottlenose) dolphin

Tu|mor ['tu:mo:ɐ, tu'mo:ɐ] M -s, **Tumoren** [tu'mo:rən] tumour (Brit), tumor (US)

Tu|mor-Nek|ro|se-Fak|tor [tu:mo:ɐnɛ'kro:zə-] M, **Tu|mor|nek|ro|se|fak|tor** M (Med) tumour (Brit) or tumor (US) necrosis factor

Tüm|pel ['tʏmpl] M -s, - pond

Tu|mult [tu'mʊlt] M -(e)s, -e commotion; (= Aufruhr auch) disturbance; (der Gefühle) tumult, turmoil

tun [tu:n]
pret **tat** [ta:t], *ptp* **getan** [gə'ta:n]

1 TRANSITIVES VERB	3 REFLEXIVES VERB
2 HILFSVERB	4 INTRANSITIVES VERB

1 – TRANSITIVES VERB

a = machen

In Verbindungen mit Substantiv siehe auch Eintrag für das jeweilige Substantiv.

to do; **er tut nichts als faulenzen/unsere Zeit vergeuden** he does nothing but laze around/ waste our time; **so etwas tut man nicht!** that is just not done!, you just can't do that sort of thing!; **so etwas tut man als anständige Frau nicht!** a decent woman doesn't do such things; **was tut man in dieser Situation?** what should one do in this situation?; **wir haben getan, was wir konnten** we did what we could; **... aber er tut es einfach nicht** ... but he just won't (do it); **sie wusste nicht, was tun** or **was sie tun sollte** she didn't know what to do; **was tun?** what can be done?; **mal sehen, was sich (für Sie) tun lässt** let's see what we can do (for you); **was kann ich für Sie tun?** what can I do for you?; **etw aus Liebe/Bosheit** etc **tun** to do sth out of love/malice etc; **jdm etw zu tun geben** to give sb sth to do; **etwas/nichts gegen etw tun** to do something/nothing about sth; **du kannst tun und lassen, was du willst** you can do what you like; **er bestimmt, was wir zu tun und zu lassen haben** he tells us what to do and what not to do; **tu, was du nicht lassen kannst** well, if you have to; **damit ist es noch nicht getan** and that's not all; **was tut das Buch unterm Bett?** (inf) what is the book doing under the bed?; **was tust DU denn hier?** *(inf)* what are YOU doing here?; **seine Arbeit/Pflicht tun** to do one's job/duty; **einen Schrei tun** to cry (out) → *auch* **getan**

♦ **jdm etwas tun** to do something to sb; *(stärker)* to hurt sb; **der Hund tut dir schon nichts** the dog won't hurt you; **jdm Böses** *or* **ein Leid** *(old)* **tun** to harm sb; **jdm einen Gefallen tun** to do sb a favour *(Brit)* or favor *(US)*; **was du nicht willst, dass man dir tu, das füg auch keinem andern zu** *(Prov)* do as you would be done by *(prov)*

♦ **es tun** *(inf)* **es mit jdm tun** *(euph inf)* to do it with sb *(inf)*; **die Uhr/das Auto tut es** *or* **tuts nicht mehr** the watch/car has had it *(inf)*; **das tuts für heute** that'll do for today; **unser Auto muss es noch ein Weilchen tun** we'll have to make do with our car a bit longer

♦ **mit jdm/etw zu tun haben das hat etwas/nichts mit ihm/damit zu tun** that's something/nothing to do with him/it; **das hat doch damit gar nichts zu tun** that's got nothing to do with it; **mit ihm/damit habe ich nichts zu tun/will ich nichts zu tun haben** I have/want nothing to do with him/it; **er hat es mit der Leber/dem Herzen** *etc* **zu tun** *(inf)* he has liver/heart *etc* trouble; **ich habe mit mir selbst zu tun** I have problems myself *or* of my own

♦ **es mit jdm zu tun bekommen** *or* **kriegen** *(inf)* to get into trouble with sb

b [= ausmachen] **was tuts?** what does it matter?; **das tut nichts** it doesn't matter; **das tut dir/ihm nichts** it won't do you/him any harm; **das tut nichts zur Sache** that's beside the point; **darum ist es mir sehr getan** *or* **zu tun** *(geh)* I am very concerned about it

c [= an einen bestimmten Ort legen etc] *inf* to put; **wohin hast du den Brief getan?** where have you put the letter?; **jdn in eine andere Schule tun** to put sb in a different school

2 – HILFSVERB

a [zur Betonung] *(inf)* **sie tun jetzt essen** *(inf)* they're eating; **und dann tut er schwimmen** *(inf)* and then he goes swimming

b [zur Bildung der Vergangenheit] *(old)* **dann tat er sich waschen** then he washed himself

3 – REFLEXIVES VERB

♦ **sich tun**

a [= geschehen] **es tut sich etwas/nichts** there is something/nothing happening, something/nothing is happening; **hier hat sich einiges getan** there have been some changes here; **hat sich bei euch etwas getan?** have things changed (with you)?; **hat sich in dieser Hinsicht schon etwas getan?** has anything been done about this?

b [mit Adjektiv]

♦ **sich schwer tun** → **schwertun**

♦ **sich leicht tun** → **leichttun**

4 – INTRANSITIVES VERB

a [= vorgeben] **so tun, als ob ...** to pretend that ...; **tu doch nicht so** stop pretending; **tust du nur so dumm?** are you just acting stupid?; **sie tut nur so** she's only pretending

b [andere Wendungen]

♦ **zu tun haben** *(= beschäftigt sein)* to have things to do; **in der Stadt zu tun haben** to have things to do in town; **auf dem Finanzamt zu tun haben** to have business at the tax office; **ich hatte zu tun, das wieder in Ordnung zu bringen** I had my work cut out putting *or* to put it back in order; **mit jdm zu tun haben** to have dealings with sb

♦ **daran tun Sie täten gut daran, früh zu kommen** you would do well to come early; **Sie haben recht daran getan** you did right

---

Tun [tu:n] **NT -s,** *no pl* conduct; **sein ganzes ~, sein ~ und Lassen, sein ~ und Treiben** everything he does; **heimliches/verbrecherisches ~** secret/criminal actions

Tün|che ['tʏnçə] **F -, -n** whitewash; *(getönt)* distemper, wash; *(fig)* veneer; *(inf: = Schminke)* make-up

tün|chen ['tʏnçn] **VT** to whitewash; *(mit getönter Farbe)* to distemper

Tund|ra ['tʊndra] **F -, Tundren** [-drən] tundra

Tu|nell [tu'nɛl] **NT -s, -e** *(dial, S Ger, Aus)* tunnel

tu|nen ['tju:nən] **VT** to tune

Tu|ner ['tju:nɐ] **M -s, -** tuner

Tu|ne|si|en [tu'ne:ziən] **NT -s** Tunisia

Tu|ne|si|er [tu'ne:ziɐ] **M -s, -, Tu|ne|si|e|rin** [-iərɪn] **F -, -nen** Tunisian

tu|ne|sisch [tu'ne:zɪʃ] **ADJ** Tunisian

Tunfisch [tu:n-] **M** tuna (fish)

Tu|nicht|gut ['tu:nɪçtgu:t] **M -(e)s, -e** *(dated)* ne'er-do-well *(old)*, good-for-nothing

Tu|ni|ka ['tu:nɪka] **F -, Tuniken** [-kn] tunic

Tu|ning ['tju:nɪŋ] **NT -s,** *no pl* tuning

Tun|ke ['tʊŋkə] **F -, -n** sauce; *(= Bratentunke)* gravy

tun|ken ['tʊŋkn] **VT** to dip; *(= stippen auch)* to dunk *(inf)*; *jdn* to duck

tun|lich ['tu:nlɪç] **ADJ** possible, feasible; *(= ratsam)* advisable

tun|lichst ['tu:nlɪçst] **ADV** **a** *(= möglichst)* if possible; **~ bald** as soon as possible; **ich werde es ~ vermeiden, ihm meine Meinung zu sagen** I'll do my best to avoid telling him what I think **b** *(= gefälligst)* **das wirst du ~ bleiben lassen** you'll do nothing of the kind *or* sort

Tun|nel ['tʊnl] **M -s, -** *or* **-s** tunnel

Tun|te ['tʊntə] **F -, -n** **a** *(dated)* sissy *(inf)* **b** *(inf: = Homosexueller)* fairy *(pej inf)* **c** *(sl: Schimpfwort)* poof(ter) *(Brit inf)*, fag(got) *(US inf)*

tun|ten|haft **ADJ** *(inf)* fussy; *Homosexueller etc* effeminate, camp *(esp Brit inf)*

tun|tig ['tʊntɪç] **ADJ** *(inf)* **a** *(dated: = albern, zimperlich)* sissy *(inf)* **b** *(= weibisch)* effeminate, camp *(esp Brit inf)*

Tupf [tʊpf] **M -(e)s, -e** *(Aus)* spot; *(klein)* dot

Tüp|fel ['tʏpfl] **M OR NT -s, -, Tüp|fel|chen** ['tʏpflçən] **NT -s, -** dot

tüp|feln ['tʏpfln] **VT** to spot; **getüpfelt** spotted; *(= mit kleinen Tupfen)* dotted

tup|fen ['tʊpfn] **VT** to dab; **getupft** spotted

Tup|fen ['tʊpfn] **M -s, -** spot; *(klein)* dot

Tup|fer ['tʊpfɐ] **M -s, -** swab

Tür [ty:ɐ] **F -, -en** door; *(= Gartentür)* gate; **in der ~** in the doorway; **~ an ~ mit jdm wohnen** to live next door to sb; **an die ~ gehen** to answer the door, to go to the door; **vor der ~ stehen** *(fig: Ereignis)* to be on the doorstep; **Weihnachten steht vor der ~** Christmas is just (a)round the corner; **jdn vor die ~ setzen** *(inf)* to throw *or* kick *(inf)* sb out; **jdm die ~ weisen** to show sb the door; **jdm die ~ vor der Nase zumachen/zuschlagen** *(inf)* to shut/slam the door in sb's face; **ein jeder kehre vor seiner ~** *(prov)* everyone should set his own house in order; **jdm mit etw die ~ einrennen** *(= jdn bestürmen)* to bombard sb with sth; **die Leute haben ihm fast die ~ eingerannt** *(nach Anzeige etc)* he was snowed under with replies; **offene ~en einrennen** to preach to the converted; **mit der ~ ins Haus fallen** *(inf)* to blurt it out; **die ~ für etw offen halten** *or* **nicht zuschlagen** *(fig)* to keep the way open for sth; **zwischen ~ und Angel** in passing; **einer Sache** *(dat)* **~ und Tor öffnen** *(fig)* to open the way to sth; **ach, du kriegst die ~ nicht zu!** *(inf)* well I never!

Tür|an|gel **F** (door) hinge

Tur|ban ['tʊrba:n] **M -s, -e** turban

Tür|be|schlag **M** (ornamental) mounting (on a door)

Tur|bi|ne [tʊr'bi:nə] **F -, -n** turbine

Tur|bi|nen-: **Tur|bi|nen|an|trieb** **M** turbine drive; *(an Flugzeug)* turbojet propulsion; **Tur|bi|nen|flug|zeug** **NT** turbojet; **Tur|bi|nen|trieb|werk** **NT** turbine engine; *(an Flugzeug)* turbojet, jet turbine engine

Tur|bo-: **Tur|bo|die|sel** **M** *(Aut)* turbo-diesel engine; **Tur|bo|ge|ne|ra|tor** **M** turbogenerator; **Tur|bo|la|der** [-la:dɐ] **M -s, -** *(Aut)* turbocharger; **Tur|bo|mo|tor** **M** turbo-engine; **Tur|bo-Prop-Flug|zeug** **NT** turboprop aircraft

tur|bu|lent [tʊrbu'lɛnt] **ADJ** turbulent, tempestuous **ADV** turbulently; **auf der Versammlung ging es ~ zu** the meeting was turbulent; **dort gehts ~ zu** things are in turmoil there

Tur|bu|lenz [tʊrbu'lɛnts] **F -, -en** **a** *no pl* turbulence, turmoil **b** *(= turbulentes Ereignis)* excitement, turmoil *no pl* **c** *(= Wirbel, Luftstrom)* turbulence *no pl*

Tür|chen ['ty:ɐçən] **NT -s, -** small door

Tür|drü|cker **M** *(= Knauf)* doorknob; *(inf: = Öffner)* buzzer *(for opening the door)*

Tü|re ['ty:rə] **F -, -n** *(dial)* = **Tür**

Turf [tʊrf] **M -s, -s** **a** *(= Rennbahn)* racecourse **b** *(no pl: = Sportart)* turf

Tür-: **Tür|flü|gel** **M** door *(of a pair of doors)*; **Tür|fül|lung** **F** door panel; **Tür|griff** **M** door handle; **Tür|hü|ter(in)** **M(F)** *(obs)* doorkeeper

-tü|rig [ty:rɪç] **ADJ** *suf* **eintürig/zweitürig** *etc* with one door/two doors *etc*; **ein viertüriges Auto** a four-door car

Tür|ke ['tʏrkə] **M -n, -n** Turk; **einen ~n bauen** *(inf: = etwas vortäuschen)* to fiddle the figures *(inf)* → *auch* **Türkin**

Tür|kei [tʏr'kai] **F -** **die ~** Turkey

tür|ken ['tʏrkn] **VT** *(inf) etw* to fiddle *(inf)*; **die Statistik ~** to massage the figures; **Belege ~** to falsify documents

Tür|ken ['tʏrkn] **M -s,** *no pl (Aus inf)* maize, corn

Tür|ken|bund **M** *pl* **-bünde** *(Bot)* Turk's cap lily

Tür|ket|te **F** (door) chain

Tür|kin ['tʏrkɪn] **F -, -nen** Turk, Turkish woman/girl

tür|kis [tʏr'ki:s] **ADJ** turquoise

Tür|kis [tʏr'ki:s] **M -es, -e** [-zə] *(= Edelstein)* turquoise

Tür|kis **NT -,** *no pl (= Farbe)* turquoise

tür|kisch ['tʏrkɪʃ] **ADJ** Turkish; **~er Honig** nougat

Tür|kisch(e) ['tʏrkɪʃ] **NT** Turkish → *auch* **Deutsch(e)**

tür|kis|far|ben [-farbn], **tür|kis|grün** **ADJ** turquoise(-coloured) *(Brit)*, turquoise(-colored) *(US)*

Tür-: **Tür|klin|ke** **F** door handle; **Tür|klop|fer** **M** doorknocker

Tur|ko|lo|ge [tʊrko'lo:gə] **M -n, -n, Tur|ko|lo|gin** [-'lo:gɪn] **F -, -nen** specialist in Turkic studies

Tur|ko|lo|gie [tʊrkolo'gi:] **F -,** *no pl* Turkic studies *pl*

Turm [tʊrm] **M -(e)s, ¨-e** ['tʏrmə] **a** tower; *(= spitzer Kirchturm)* spire; *(im Schwimmbad)* diving *(Brit)* or dive *(US)* tower **b** *(Chess)* castle, rook

Tur|ma|lin [tʊrma'li:n] **M -s, -e** *(Miner)* tourmaline

Turm|bau **M,** *no pl (= das Bauen)* building a tower; **der ~ zu Babel** the building of the Tower of Babel

Türm|chen ['tʏrmçən] **NT -s, -** *dim von* **Turm** turret

tür|men ['tʏrmən] **VT** to pile (up) **VR** to pile up; *(Wolken)* to build up, to bank; *(Wellen)* to tower up **VI** *aux sein (inf: = davonlaufen)* to skedaddle *(inf)*, to take to one's heels, to run off

Turm-: **Turm|fal|ke** **M** kestrel; **turm|hoch** **ADJ** towering, lofty **ADV** **~ über jdm stehen, jdm ~ überlegen sein** to stand head and shoulders above sb; **Turm|schwal|be** **F** swift; **Turm|spit|ze** **F** spire; **Turm|sprin|gen** **NT** high diving; **Turm|uhr** **F** clock (on a/the tower); *(von Kirche)* church clock

Turn-: **Turn|an|zug** **M** leotard; **Turn|beu|tel** **M** gym bag

tur|nen ['tʊrnən] **VI** **a** *(an Geräten)* to do gymnastics; *(Sch)* to do gym *or* PE; **am Reck/an den Ringen/auf der Matte** *etc* **~** to work on *or* do exercises on the horizontal bar/rings/mat *etc*; **sie**

kann gut ~ she is good at gym *or* PE **b** *aux sein (= herumklettern)* to climb about; *(Kind)* to romp **VT** *Reck etc* to work on, to do exercises on; *Übung* to do

Tur|nen NT **-s,** *no pl* gymnastics *sing*; *(inf: = Leibeserziehung)* gym, PE *(inf)*

Tur|ner ['tʊrnɐ] M **-s, -, Tur|ne|rin** [-ərɪn] F **-, -nen** gymnast

Tur|ne|rei [tʊrnə'rai] F **-, -en** *(inf)* sporting activities *pl*; *(fig)* acrobatics *pl*

tur|ne|risch ['tʊrnərɪʃ] **ADJ** gymnastic **ADV** *sein Bestes geben* gymnastically; ~ **hervorragend** *(Mensch)* excellent at gymnastics; *Übung* excellent gymnastically; **sie hat ~ nicht überzeugt** her gymnastic performance was not up to standard

Tur|ner|schaft ['tʊrnɐʃaft] F **-, -en** **a** *(= die Turner)* gymnasts *pl*; *(= Vereinigung der Turnvereine)* gymnastic association **b** *(= Studentenverbindung)* student organization

Turn-: **Turn|fest** NT gymnastics display *or* festival; *(von Schule)* sports day; **Turn|ge|rät** NT *(= Reifen, Ball etc)* (piece of) gymnastic equipment; *(= Reck, Barren etc)* (piece of) gymnastic apparatus; **Turn|hal|le** F gym(nasium); *(Gebäude auch)* sports hall; **Turn|hemd** NT gym *or* PE shirt; **Turn|ho|se** F gym *or* PE shorts *pl*

Tur|nier [tʊr'niːɐ] NT **-s, -e** *(= Ritterturnier, sportliche Veranstaltung)* tournament; *(= Tanzturnier)* competition; *(= Reitturnier)* show

Tur|nier-: **Tur|nier|pferd** NT show *or* competition horse; **Tur|nier|rei|ter(in)** M(F) show *or* competition rider; **Tur|nier|sieg** M tournament win; **Tur|nier|spiel** NT tournament match; **Tur|nier|tanz** M (competition) ballroom dance *or (Tanzform)* dancing

Turn-: **Turn|klei|dung** F gym *or* PE clothes *pl or* kit *(Brit)*; **Turn|kunst** F gymnastic skills *pl*; **Turn|leh|rer(in)** M(F) gym *or* PE teacher; **Turn|rie|ge** F gymnastics team

Turn|schuh M gym shoe, sneaker *(US)*

Turn|schuh- *in cpds (inf)* unconventional, unorthodox

Turn-: **Turn|stun|de** F gym *or* PE lesson; *(im Verein)* gymnastics lesson; **Turn|übung** F gymnastic exercise; **Turn|un|ter|richt** M gymnastic instruction; *(= Turnstunde)* gym, PE

Tur|nus ['tʊrnʊs] M **-, -se** **a** rota *(Brit)*, roster; **im (regelmäßigen) ~** in rotation **b** *(Aus) (= Arbeitsschicht)* shift; *(Med)* housemanship *(Brit)*, internship *(US)*

Turn-: **Turn|va|ter** M **~ Jahn** Jahn, the father of gymnastics; **Turn|ver|ein** M gymnastics club; **Turn|wart** [-vart] M **-s, -e, Turn|war|tin** [-vartɪn] F **-, -nen** gymnastics supervisor; **Turn|zeug** NT, *no pl* gym *or* PE things *pl or* kit *(Brit)*, gym gear *(inf)*

Tür-: **Tür|öff|ner** M **elektrischer ~** buzzer *(for opening the door)*; **Tür|öff|ner(in)** M(F) *(im Hotel)* commissionaire; *(Mann auch)* doorman; **Tür|pfos|ten** M doorpost; **Tür|rah|men** M doorframe; **Tür|schild** NT *pl* **-schilder** doorplate; **Tür|schloss** NT door lock; **Tür|schnal|le** F *(Aus)* door handle; **Tür|schwel|le** F threshold; **Tür|spalt** M crack (of a/the door); **Tür|sprech|an|la|ge** F entry phone; **Tür|ste|her** [-ʃteːɐ] M **-s, -, Tür|ste|he|rin** [-ərɪn] F **-, -nen** bouncer; *(Mann auch)* doorman; **Tür|stock** M *(S Ger, Aus)* doorframe; **Tür|stop|per** M doorstop(per); **Tür|sturz** M lintel

tur|teln ['tʊrtln] VI to bill and coo; *(Liebespaar auch)* to whisper sweet nothings

Tur|tel|tau|be F turtledove; **~n** *(inf: = Verliebte)* lovebirds, turtledoves

Tür|vor|le|ger M doormat

Tusch [tʊʃ] M **-es, -e** **a** *(Mus)* flourish; *(esp von Blasinstrumenten)* fanfare **b** *(Aus: = Tusche)* Indian ink

Tu|sche ['tʊʃə] F **-, -n** *(= Ausziehtusche)* Indian ink; *(= Tuschfarbe)* watercolour *(Brit)*, watercolor *(US)*; *(= Wimperntusche)* mascara

tu|scheln ['tʊʃln] VTI to whisper; **hinter seinem Rücken über jdn ~** to say things *(inf) or* to talk behind sb's back

tu|schen ['tʊʃn] VT *(mit Farbe)* to paint in watercolour(s) *(Brit) or* watercolor(s) *(US)*; *(mit Ausziehtusche)* to draw in Indian ink; **sich** *(dat)* **die Wimpern ~** to put one's mascara on

Tusch-: **Tusch|far|be** F watercolour *(Brit)*, watercolor *(US)*; **Tusch|kas|ten** M paintbox; **ihr Gesicht sieht aus wie ein ~** *(fig inf)* she's made up to the eyeballs *(inf)*; **Tusch|zeich|nung** F pen-and-ink drawing

Tus|si ['tʊsi] F **-, -s** *(inf)*, **Tuss** [tʊs] F **-, -en** *(sl)* female *(inf)*

tut [tuːt] INTERJ toot

Tü|te ['tyːtə] F **-, -n** *(aus Papier, Plastik)* bag; *(= Eistüte)* cornet, cone; *(von Suppenpulver etc)* packet; *(inf: für Alkoholtest)* Breathalyzer®; *(inf: Mensch)* drip *(inf)*; **in die ~ blasen** *(inf)* to be breathalyzed, to blow in the bag *(inf)*; **~n kleben** *(inf)* to be in clink *(inf)*; **das kommt nicht in die ~!** *(inf)* no way! *(inf)*

tu|ten ['tuːtn] VI to toot; *(Schiff)* to sound its hooter *or (mit Nebelhorn)* foghorn; **von Tuten und Blasen keine Ahnung haben** *(inf)* not to have a clue *(inf)*

Tü|ten|sup|pe F instant soup

Tu|tor ['tuːtoːɐ] M **-s, Tutoren** [-'toːrən], **Tu|to|rin** [-'toːrɪn] F **-, -nen** tutor

TÜV [tʏf] M **-s, -s** *abbr von* **Technischer Überwachungs-Verein** ≈ MOT *(Brit)*, ≈ inspection *(US inf)*; **das Auto ist durch den ~ gekommen** ≈ the car got through *or* passed its MOT *(Brit) or* inspection *(US)*

> **TÜV**
>
> The **TÜV** – short for **Technischer Überwachungs-Verein** – tests the safety of technical installations, machinery and motor vehicles. All vehicles over three years old must have a **TÜV** test every two years. If the vehicle fails, it must be deregistered and taken off the road. The **TÜV** also carries out safety tests on a wide range of other products. If they pass the test, products are permitted to carry the **GS (Geprüfte Sicherheit)** seal. The independence of the **TÜV** means that this seal is regarded as a guarantee of good quality and reliability.

TÜV-ge|prüft ADJ ≈ (TÜV) safety tested

TÜV-Pla|ket|te F *disc displayed on number plate showing that a car has passed the TÜV*, ≈ MOT certificate *(Brit)*, ≈ inspection certificate *(US)*

Tu|wort NT *pl* **-wörter** doing-word

TV [teː'fau] **a** *abbr von* **Television** **b** *abbr von* **Turnverein**

TV- *in cpds* TV; **TV-Du|ell** NT TV debate *or* duel; **TV-Mo|de|ra|tor** M, **TV-Mo|de|ra|to|rin** F TV presenter; **TV-Pro|gramm** NT TV programmes *(Brit) or* programs *(US) pl*; **TV-Sen|dung** F TV broadcast

Tweed [tviːt] M **-s, -s** *or* **-e** [-də] tweed

Twen [tvɛn] M **-(s), -s** *person in his/her twenties*

Twill|ho|se F twill trousers *pl*, twills *pl*

Twin|set ['tvɪnzɛt] NT OR M **-(s), -s** twinset *(Brit)*, sweater-set *(US)*

Twist[1] [tvɪst] M **-es, -e** *(Garn)* twist

Twist[2] M **-s, -s** *(Tanz)* twist

twis|ten ['tvɪstn] VI to twist, to do the twist

Twit|ter® ['twɪtɐ] *no art* Twitter®

Ty|coon [tai'kuːn] M **-s, -s** *or* **-e** tycoon

Tym|pa|non ['tympanɔn] NT **-s, Tympana** [-na] *(Archit)* tympanum

Typ [tyːp] M **-s, -en** **a** *(= Modell)* model **b** *(= Menschenart)* type; **er ist nicht mein ~** *(inf)* he's not my type *(inf)* **c** *(inf: = Mensch)* person, character; *(sl: = Mann, Freund)* man *(inf)*, bloke *(Brit inf)*, guy *(inf)*; **dein ~ wird verlangt** *(inf)* you're wanted; **dein ~ ist nicht gefragt** *(inf)* you're not wanted (a)round here

Ty|pe ['tyːpə] F **-, -n** **a** *(Typ) (= Schreibmaschinentype)* type bar; *(= Druckbuchstabe)* character; **~n** *(= Schrift)* type *sing*; **~n gießen** to set type **b** *(inf: = Mensch)* character **c** *(bei Mehl)* grade

Ty|pen *pl von* **Typus, Type**

Ty|pen|rad NT daisy wheel

Ty|pen|rad|dru|cker M daisy wheel (printer)

Ty|phus ['tyːfʊs] M **-,** *no pl* typhoid (fever)

Ty|phus-: **Ty|phus|epi|de|mie** F typhoid (fever) epidemic; **Ty|phus|imp|fung** F typhoid inoculation; **Ty|phus|kran|ke(r)** MF *decl as adj* typhoid case

ty|pisch ['tyːpɪʃ] **ADJ** typical *(für* of); **(das ist ein) ~er Fall von denkste!** *(inf)* no such luck! *(inf)* **ADV** **~ deutsch/Mann/Frau** typically German/male/female; **ein ~ deutsches Gericht** a typical German dish; **~ Claire** that's so typical of Claire

ty|pi|sie|ren [typi'ziːrən] *ptp* **typisiert** VT *Charakter* to stylize; *Erzeugnisse etc* to standardize

Ty|po|gra|fie [typogra'fiː] F **-, -n** [-'fiːən] typography

ty|po|gra|fisch [typo'graːfɪʃ] **ADJ** typographic(al) **ADV** typographically

Ty|po|gra|phie [typogra'fiː] *etc* = **Typografie** *etc*

Ty|po|lo|gie [typolo'giː] F **-, -n** [-'giːən] typology

Ty|po|skript [typo'skrɪpt] NT **-(e)s, -e** *(Typ)* typescript

Ty|pus ['tyːpʊs] M **-, Typen** ['tyːpn] type

Ty|rann [ty'ran] M **-en, -en, Ty|ran|nin** [-'ranɪn] F **-, -nen** *(lit, fig)* tyrant

Ty|ran|nei [tyra'nai] F **-, -en** tyranny

Ty|ran|nen-: **Ty|ran|nen|mord** M tyrannicide; **Ty|ran|nen|mör|der(in)** M(F) tyrannicide

Ty|ran|nin [-'ranɪn] F **-, -nen** tyrant

ty|ran|nisch [ty'ranɪʃ] **ADJ** tyrannical **ADV** tyrannically

ty|ran|ni|sie|ren [tyrani'ziːrən] *ptp* **tyrannisiert** VT to tyrannize

tyr|rhe|nisch [ty'reːnɪʃ] ADJ **Tyrrhenisches Meer** Tyrrhenian Sea

Tz ['teːtsɛt, te'tsɛt] NT **bis ins** *or* **zum Tz** completely, fully → *auch* **Tezett**

T-Zel|le ['teː-] F *(Med, Biol)* T-cell

U

U, u [uː] NT -, - U, u → **X**
u. *abbr von* **und**
u. a. *abbr von* **und andere(s), unter anderem/anderen**
U. A. w. g. [uːlaːveːˈgeː] *abbr von* **Um Antwort wird gebeten** RSVP
UB [uːˈbeː] F -, -s *abbr von* **Universitätsbibliothek**
U-Bahn [ˈuː-] F underground, subway *(US)*; *(in London)* tube
U-Bahn|hof [ˈuː-] M underground *or* subway *(US)* station; *(in London)* tube station
U-Bahn-Netz [ˈuː-] M underground *or* subway *(US)* system
U-Bahn-Sta|ti|on [ˈuː-] F underground *or* subway *(US)* station; *(in London)* tube station
übel [ˈyːbl] ADJ **a** *(= schlimm, unangenehm)* bad; *Kopfweh, Erkältung etc* nasty, bad; **er war übler Laune** he was in a bad *or* nasty mood; **das ist gar nicht so ~** that's not so bad at all
b *(= moralisch, charakterlich schlecht)* wicked, bad; *Eindruck, Ruf* bad; *Tat* wicked, evil; **ein übler Bursche** *or* **Kunde** *(inf)* a nasty piece of work *(inf)*, a bad lot *(inf)*; **das ist eine üble Sache!** it's a bad business; **ein übler Streich** a nasty trick; **auf üble** *or* **in der ~sten Weise, in übler** *or* **~ster Weise** in a most unpleasant way; **jdm Übles antun** *(geh)* to be wicked to sb, to do wicked things to sb
c *(= physisch schlecht, eklig) Geschmack, Geruch, Gefühl* nasty; **mir wird ~** I feel ill *or* sick; **es kann einem ~ werden** it's enough to make you feel ill *or* sick
d *(= verkommen, übel beleumdet) Stadtviertel* evil, bad; *Kaschemme* evil, low
ADV **a** *(= schlimm, unangenehm, schlecht)* badly; **etw ~ aufnehmen** to take sth badly; **das ist ihm ~ bekommen** it did him no good at all; **~ dran sein** to be in a bad way; **~ beraten** *(geh)* ill-advised; **~ gelaunt** ill-humoured *(Brit)*, ill-humored *(US)*, sullen, morose; **~ gesinnt** *(geh)* ill-disposed; **~ riechend** foul-smelling, evil-smelling; **jd ist ~ gelaunt** sb is in a bad mood; **jdm ~ gesinnt sein** to be ill-disposed to sb; **etw riecht ~** sth smells bad; **es steht ~ mit ihm** he's in a bad way *or* in bad shape; **das schmeckt gar nicht so ~** it doesn't taste so bad; **wie gehts? – danke, nicht ~** how's things? – not bad, thanks; **ich hätte nicht ~ Lust, jetzt nach Paris zu fahren** I wouldn't mind going to Paris now
b *(= moralisch, charakterlich schlecht)* badly; **über jdn ~ reden** to say bad things about sb; **jdm etw ~ vermerken** to hold sth against sb; **~ beleumdet** disreputable, of ill repute
c *(= physisch schlecht)* ill, poorly; **das Essen ist ihm ~ bekommen** the food disagreed with him
Übel [ˈyːbl] NT -s, - **a** *(geh: = Krankheit, Leiden)* illness, malady *(old)* **b** *(= Missstand)* ill, evil; **ein notwendiges/das kleinere** *or* **geringere ~** a necessary/the lesser evil; **das alte ~** the old trouble; **der Grund allen ~s ist, dass ...** the cause *or* root of all the trouble is that ...; **die Gleichgültigkeit ist die Wurzel alles** *or* **allen ~s** indifference is the root of all evil; **das ~ bei der Sache** the trouble **c** *(= Plage, Schaden)* evil; **von ~ sein** to be a bad thing, to be bad; **zu allem ~ ...** to make matters worse ...; **ein ~ kommt selten allein** *(Prov)* misfortunes seldom come alone
übel-: **übel|be|leum|det** ADJ *attr* → **übel ADV b**; **übel|be|ra|ten** ADJ *attr* → **übel ADV a**; **übel|ge|launt** ADJ *attr* → **übel ADV a**; **übel|ge|sinnt** ADJ *attr* → **übel ADV a**
Übel|keit F -, -en *(lit, fig)* nausea; **eine plötzliche ~** a sudden feeling of nausea; **~ erregen** to cause nausea
Übel-: **übel|lau|nig** ADJ ill-tempered, cantankerous; **Übel|lau|nig|keit** F ill temper; **übel neh|men** *irreg*, **übel+neh|men** *sep irreg* VT to take amiss *(Brit)* *or* badly; **jdm etw ~** to hold sth against sb; **bitte nehmen Sie es (mir) nicht übel, aber ...** please don't take offence *(Brit)* *or* offense *(US)*, but ...; **ich habe ihm gar nicht einmal übel genommen, dass er gelogen hat, aber ...** I didn't even mind him lying but ...; **übel|neh|me|risch** [ˈyːblneːmərɪʃ] ADJ *(= schnell beleidigt)* touchy; *(= nachtragend)* resentful; **übel|rie|chend** ADJ → **übel ADV a**; **Übel|sein** NT nausea; **Übel|stand** M (social) evil *or* ill; **Übel|tat** F *(dated, liter)* evil *or* wicked act *or* deed, misdeed; **Übel|tä|ter(in)** M(F) *(geh)* wrongdoer; **übel+tun** *sep irreg*, **übel tun** △ *irreg* VI *(dated, liter)* **jdm ~** to be wicked to sb; **übel+wol|len** *sep irreg*, **übel wol|len** △ *irreg* VI *(geh)* **jdm ~** to wish sb harm *or* ill, to be ill-disposed toward(s) sb
üben [ˈyːbn] VT **a** *(= praktisch erlernen) Aussprache, Musik, Sport* to practise *(Brit)*, to practice *(US)*; *(Mil)* to drill; **Geige/Klavier ~** to practise *(Brit)* *or* practice *(US)* the violin/piano
b *(= schulen, trainieren) Gedächtnis, Muskeln etc* to exercise → *auch* **geübt**
c *(= tun, erkennen lassen)* to exercise; **Gerechtigkeit ~** *(geh)* to be just *(gegen* to), to show fairness *(gegen* to); **Kritik an etw** *(dat)* **~** to criticize sth; **Geduld ~** to be patient → **Barmherzigkeit**
VR **sich in etw** *(dat)* **~** to practise *(Brit)* *or* practice *(US)* sth; **sich in Geduld** *(dat)* **~** *(geh)* to have patience, to possess one's soul in patience
VI *(= praktisch lernen)* to practise *(Brit)*, to practice *(US)*
über [ˈyːbɐ] PREP **a** *+acc (räumlich)* over; *(= quer über)* across; *(= weiter als)* beyond; **etw ~ etw hängen/stellen** to hang/put sth over *or* above sth; **es wurde ~ alle Sender ausgestrahlt** it was broadcast over all transmitters; **er lachte ~ das ganze Gesicht** he was beaming all over his face
b *+dat (räumlich) (Lage, Standort)* over, above; *(= jenseits)* over, across; **zwei Grad ~ null** two degrees (above zero); **~ der Stadt lag dichter Nebel** a thick mist hung over the town; **~ uns lachte die Sonne** the sun smiled above us; **er trug den Mantel ~ dem Arm** he was carrying his coat over his arm; **~ jdm stehen** *or* **sein** *(fig)* to be over *or* above sb; **er steht ~ der Situation** *(fig)* he is above it all
c *+dat (zeitlich: = bei, während)* over; **~ der Arbeit einschlafen** to fall asleep over one's work; **etw ~ einem Glas Wein besprechen** to discuss sth over a glass of wine; **~ all der Aufregung/unserer Unterhaltung habe ich ganz vergessen, dass ...** in all the *or* what with all the excitement/what with all this chatting I quite forgot that ...; **~ Mittag geht er meist nach Hause** he usually goes home at lunch *or* at midday
d *+acc* **Cäsars Sieg ~ die Gallier** Caesar's victory over the Gauls; **Gewalt ~ jdn haben** to have power over sb; **es kam plötzlich ~ ihn** it suddenly came over him; **sie liebt ihn ~ alles** she loves him more than anything; **das geht mir ~ den Verstand** that's beyond my understanding; **Fluch ~ dich!** *(obs)* a curse upon you! *(obs)*
e *+acc (= vermittels, auf dem Wege über)* via; **die Nummer erfährt man ~ die Auskunft** you'll get the number from *or* through *or* via information; **wir sind ~ die Autobahn gekommen** we came by *or* via the autobahn; **nach Köln ~ Aachen** to Cologne via Aachen; **Zug nach Frankfurt ~ Wiesbaden und Mainz** train to Frankfurt via *or* stopping at *or* calling at *(Brit)* Wiesbaden and Mainz
f *+acc (zeitlich) (= innerhalb eines Zeitraums, länger als)* over; **~ Weihnachten** over Christmas; **bis ~ Ostern** until after Easter; **den ganzen Sommer ~** all summer long; **~ Wochen (ausgedehnt)** for weeks on end; **die ganze Zeit ~** all the time; **das ganze Jahr ~** all through the year, all year round; **~ kurz oder lang** sooner or later; **es ist ~ vierzehn Tage her, dass ...** it's over fourteen days since ...
g *+acc (bei Zahlenangaben) (= in Höhe von)* for; *(= mehr als)* over; **ein Scheck ~ 20 Euro** a cheque *(Brit)* *or* check *(US)* for 20 euros; **eine Rechnung von ~ £ 100** a bill for over *or* of over £100; **Kinder ~ 14 Jahre** children over 14 years *or* of 14 (years of age) and over; **Städte ~ 50.000 Einwohner** towns of over 50,000 inhabitants; **Pakete ~ 10 kg** parcels *(esp Brit)* *or* packages over 10 kgs
h *+acc (= wegen)* over; *(= betreffend)* about; **ein Buch/Film/Vortrag** *etc* **~ ...** a book/film/lecture *etc* about *or* on ...; **was wissen Sie ~ ihn?** what do you know about him?; **~ welches Thema schreiben Sie Ihr neues Buch?** what's the subject of your new book?, what's your new book about?; **~ Politik/Wörterbücher/Fußball** *etc* **reden** to talk (about) politics/dictionaries/football *etc*; **~ jdn/etw lachen** to laugh about *or* at sb/sth; **sich ~ etw freuen/ärgern** to be pleased/angry about *or* at sth
i *+acc (steigernd)* upon; **Fehler ~ Fehler** mistake upon *or* after mistake, one mistake after another
ADV **~ und ~** all over; **er wurde ~ und ~ rot** he went red all over; **ich stecke ~ und ~ in Schulden** I am up to my ears in debt; **(das) Gewehr ~!** *(Mil)* shoulder arms!; **jdm in etw** *(dat)* **~ sein** *(inf)* to be better than sb at sth
über|ak|tiv ADJ hyperactive, overactive
Über|ak|ti|vi|tät F hyperactivity
über|all [yːbɐˈlal] ADV everywhere; **ich habe dich schon ~ gesucht** I've been looking everywhere *or* all over *(inf)* for you; **~ herumliegen** to be lying all over the shop *(Brit inf)* *or* place; **~ in London/der Welt** everywhere in *or* all over London/the world; **~ wo** wherever; **~ Bescheid wissen** *(wissensmäßig)* to have a wide-ranging knowledge; *(in Stadt etc)* to know one's way

around; **sie ist ~ zu gebrauchen** she can do everything; **es ist ~ dasselbe** it's the same wherever you go; **so ist es ~** it's the same everywhere; **~ und nirgends zu Hause sein** to be at home everywhere and nowhere; **er ist immer ~ und nirgends, den erreichst du nie** he's always here, there and everywhere, you'll never find him

über|all-: **über|all|her** [y:bɐlal'heːɐ, y:bɐ'lal'heːɐ, y:bɐ'lalheːɐ] ADV from all over; **über|all|hin** [y:bɐlal'hɪn, y:bɐ'lal'hɪn, y:bɐ'lalhɪn] ADV everywhere

Über-: **über|al|tert** [y:bɐ'altɐt] ADJ **a** *(Sociol)* having a disproportionate number of *or* having too high a percentage of old people **b** = **veraltet**; **Über|al|te|rung** F *(Sociol)* increase in the percentage of old people; **Über|an|ge|bot** NT surplus (*an +dat* of); **über|ängst|lich** ADJ overanxious; **über|an|stren|gen** [y:bɐ-'anʃtrɛŋən] *ptp* **überanstrengt** *insep* VT to overstrain, to overexert; *Kräfte* to overtax; *Augen* to strain VR to overstrain *or* overexert oneself; **überanstrenge dich nicht!** *(iro)* don't strain yourself! *(iro)*; **Über|an|stren|gung** F overexertion; **eine ~ der Nerven/Augen** a strain on the *or* one's nerves/eyes; **über|ant|wor|ten** [y:bɐ'antvɔrtn] *ptp* **überantwortet** VT *insep (geh)* **jdm etw ~** to hand sth over to sb, to place sth in sb's hands; **etw dem Feuer ~** *(liter)* to commit sth to the flames; **über|ar|bei|ten** [y:bɐ'larbaitn] *ptp* **überarbeitet** *insep* VT to rework, to go over; **in einer überarbeiteten Fassung** in a revised edition VR to overwork; **Über|ar|bei|tung** F **-, -en a** *(Vorgang)* reworking; *(Ergebnis)* revision, revised version **b** *no pl (= Überanstrengung)* overwork; **über|aus** ['y:bɐlaus, y:bɐ'laus, 'y:bɐ'laus] ADV extremely, exceedingly; **über|ba|cken** [y:bɐ'bakn] *ptp* **überbacken** VT *insep irreg (im Backofen)* to put in the oven; *(im Grill)* to put under the grill; **mit Käse ~** au gratin; **~e Käseschnitten** cheese on toast; **Über|bau** M *pl* **-baue** *or (Build auch)* **-bauten** *(Build, Philos)* superstructure; **über|bau|en** [y:bɐ'bauən] *ptp* **überbaut** VT *insep* to build over; *(mit einem Dach)* to roof over, to build a roof over; **über|be|an|spru|chen** *ptp* **überbeansprucht** VT *insep* **a** *Menschen, Körper* to overtax, to make too many demands on; **(arbeitsmäßig) überbeansprucht sein** to be overworked **b** *Einrichtungen, Dienste* to overburden **c** *Maschine, Auto etc* to overtax, to overstrain **d** *Werkstoffe, Materialien* to overstrain; *(esp durch Gewicht)* to overload; **Über|be|an|spru|chung** F **a** *(von Menschen)* overtaxing; *(arbeitsmäßig)* overworking **b** *(von Einrichtungen, Diensten)* overburdening **c** *(von Maschine, Auto etc)* overtaxing, overstraining **d** *(von Werkstoffen, Material)* overstraining; *(esp durch Gewicht)* overloading; **über+be|hal|ten** *ptp* **überbehalten** VT *sep irreg (inf)* **a** *(= übrig behalten)* to have left over **b** *(= nicht ausziehen) Mantel etc* to keep on; **Über|bein** NT *(an Gelenk)* ganglion; **über+be|kom|men** *ptp* **überbekommen** VT *sep irreg (inf)* **jdn/etw ~** to get sick of *or* fed up with sb/sth *(inf)*; **über|be|las|ten** *ptp* **überbelastet** VT *insep* = **überlasten**; **Über|be|las|tung** F = **Überlastung**; **über|be|le|gen** *ptp* **überbelegt** VT *insep usu ptp* to overcrowd; *Kursus, Fach etc* to oversubscribe; **Über|be|le|gung** F overcrowding; *(von Kursus, Fach etc)* oversubscription; **über|be|lich|ten** *ptp* **überbelichtet** VT *insep (Phot)* to overexpose; **Über|be|lich|tung** F *(Phot)* overexposure; **Über|be|schäf|ti|gung** F overemployment; **über|be|setzt** ADJ *Behörde, Abteilung* overstaffed; **über|be|to|nen** *ptp* **überbetont** VT *insep (fig)* to overstress, to overemphasize; *Hüften, obere Gesichtshälfte etc* to overaccentuate, to overemphasize; **über|be|trieb|lich** ADJ industry-wide ADV industry-wide, for the entire industry; **Über|be|völ|ke|rung** F overpopulation; **über|be|wer|ten** *ptp* **überbewertet** VT *insep (lit)* to overvalue; *(fig auch)* to overrate; *Schulleistung etc* to mark too high; **wollen wir doch eine so vereinzelte Äußerung nicht ~** let's not attach too much importance to such an isolated remark; **Über|be|wer|tung** F *(lit)* overvaluing; *(fig auch)* overrating; **die ~ einer einzelnen Äußerung** attaching too much importance to an isolated statement; **diese Eins ist eine klare ~** this grade one is clearly too high; **Über|be|zah|lung** F overpayment

über|biet|bar ADJ *(fig)* **kaum noch ~ sein** to take some beating; **ein an Vulgarität nicht mehr ~er Pornofilm** a porn film of unsurpassed *or* unsurpassable vulgarity

über|bie|ten [y:bɐ'biːtn] *ptp* **überboten** [y:bɐ-'boːtn] *insep irreg* VT *(bei Auktion)* to outbid (*um* by); *(fig)* to outdo; *Leistung, Rekord* to beat; **das ist kaum noch zu ~** *(fig)* it's outrageous; **diese Geschichte ist an Peinlichkeit kaum noch zu ~** the incident could scarcely have been more embarrassing VR **sich in etw** *(dat)* **(gegenseitig) ~** to vie with one another *or* each other in sth; **sich (selber) ~** to surpass oneself

Über|bie|tung F **-, -en** *(fig)* outdoing; *(von Leistung, Rekord)* beating; **eine ~ dieses Rekordes** to beat this record

über-: **über+bin|den** VT *sep irreg (Mus)* to join up; **über|bla|sen** [y:bɐ'blaːzn] *ptp* **überblasen** VT *insep irreg (Mus)* to overblow; **über|blät|tern** [y:bɐ'blɛtɐn] *ptp* **überblättert** VT *insep Buch* to leaf *or* flick *or* glance through; *Stelle* to skip over *or* past, to miss; **über+blei|ben** VI *sep irreg aux sein (inf)* = **übrigbleiben, übrig bleiben**

Über|bleib|sel ['y:bɐblaipsl] NT **-s, -** remnant; *(= Speiserest)* leftover *usu pl*, remains *pl*; *(= Brauch, Angewohnheit etc)* survival, hangover; *(= Spur)* trace

über+blen|den ['y:bɐblɛndn] VI *sep (Film, Rad: Szene etc)* to fade; *(Film auch)* to dissolve; *(plötzlich)* to cut

über|blen|den [y:bɐ'blɛndn] *ptp* **überblendet** VT *insep (= ausblenden)* to fade out; *(= überlagern)* to superimpose

Über|blen|dung F *(Film, Rad)* fade; *(Film auch)* dissolve; *(plötzlich)* cut

Über|blen|dung F *(= das Ausblenden)* fading out; *(= Überlagerung)* superimposition

Über|blick M *(über +acc* of) **a** *(= freie Sicht)* view **b** *(= Einblick)* perspective, overall *or* broad view, overview; **er hat keinen ~, ihm fehlt der ~, es fehlt ihm an ~** he lacks an overview, he has no overall picture; **den ~ verlieren** to lose track (of things) **c** *(= Abriss)* survey; *(= Übersicht, Zusammenhang)* synopsis, summary; **sich** *(dat)* **einen ~ verschaffen** to get a general idea; **Weltgeschichte im ~** compendium of world history

über|bli|cken [y:bɐ'blɪkn] *ptp* **überblickt** VT *insep* **a** *(lit) Platz, Stadt, Gebiet* to overlook, to have *or* command a view of **b** *(fig)* to see; **die Entwicklung lässt sich leicht ~** the development can be seen at a glance; **bis ich die Lage besser überblicke** until I have a better view of the situation; **das lässt sich noch nicht ~** I/we *etc* cannot tell *or* say as yet

über-: **über|bor|den** [y:bɐ'bɔrdn] *ptp* **überbordet** VI *insep aux haben or sein (fig geh)* to be overextravagant; **~de Metaphern** overextravagant metaphors; **~de Selbstgewissheit** excessive self-assurance; **über|bra|ten** [y:bɐ'braːtn] *ptp* **überbraten** VT *insep irreg (Cook)* to fry lightly; **über+bra|ten** ['y:bɐbraːtn] VT *sep irreg* **jdm eins ~** *(inf)* to land sb one *(Brit inf)*, to hit sb

Über|brei|te F excess width; **Vorsicht, ~!** caution, wide load

über|brin|gen [y:bɐ'brɪŋən] *ptp* **überbracht** [y:bɐ'braxt] VT *insep irreg* **jdm etw ~** to bring sb sth, to bring sth to sb; *Brief etc auch* to deliver sth to sb

Über|brin|ger [y:bɐ'brɪŋɐ] M **-s, -, Über|brin|ge|rin** [-ərɪn] F **-, -nen** bringer, bearer; *(von Scheck etc)* bearer

über|brück|bar ADJ *Gegensätze* reconcilable; *Distanz* bridgeable; **schwer ~e Gegensätze** differences which are difficult to reconcile

über|brü|cken [y:bɐ'brʏkn] *ptp* **überbrückt** VT *insep* **a** *(old) Fluss* to bridge (over) **b** *(fig) Kluft, Zeitraum* to bridge; *Krisenzeiten* to get over *or* through; *Gegensätze* to reconcile; **die Gegensätze zwischen … ~** to bridge the gap between …

Über|brü|ckung F **-, -en** *(fig)* bridging; *(von Krisenzeiten)* getting over *or* through; *(von Gegensätzen)* reconciliation; **100 Euro zur ~** 100 euros to tide me/him *etc* over

Über|brü|ckungs-: **Über|brü|ckungs|bei|hil|fe** F, **Über|brü|ckungs|geld** NT interim aid, money to tide one over; **Über|brü|ckungs|kre|dit** [-krediːt] M bridging loan

Über-: **über|bu|chen** [y:bɐ'buːxn] *ptp* **überbucht** VT *insep* to overbook; **über|bür|den** [y:bɐ'bʏrdn] *ptp* **überbürdet** VT *insep (geh)* to overburden; **Über|dach** NT roof; **über|da|chen** [y:bɐ'daxn] *ptp* **überdacht** VT *insep* to roof over, to cover over; **überdachte Fahrradständer/Bushaltestelle** covered bicycle stands/bus shelter; **Über|dach|ung** F *(= Überdach)* roof(ing); *(= das Überdachen)* roofing over; **über|dau|ern** [y:bɐ'dauɐn] *ptp* **überdauert** VT *insep* to survive; **Über|de|cke** F bedspread, bedcover, counterpane; **über+de|cken** ['y:bɐdɛkn] VT *sep* to cover up *or* over; *(inf: = auflegen) Tischtuch* to put on; **über|de|cken** [y:bɐ'dɛkn] *ptp* **überdeckt** *insep* VT *Riss, Geschmack, Schwächen* to cover up, to conceal VR *(= sich überschneiden)* to overlap; **über|deh|nen** [y:bɐ'deːnən] *ptp* **überdehnt** VT *insep Sehne, Muskel etc* to strain; *Gummi, Begriff* to overstretch; **über|den|ken** [y:bɐ'dɛŋkn] *ptp* **überdacht** VT *insep irreg* to think over, to consider; **etw noch einmal ~** to reconsider sth; **über|deut|lich** ADJ all too obvious ADV **es ist mir ~ klar geworden** it has become perfectly clear to me; **jdm etw ~ zu verstehen geben** to make sth perfectly clear to sb; **er hat sein Missfallen ~ formuliert** the way he phrased it made it perfectly clear that he was displeased

über|dies [y:bɐ'diːs] ADV *(geh)* **a** *(= außerdem)* moreover, furthermore, what is more **b** *(= ohnehin)* in any case, anyway

Über-: **über|di|men|si|o|nal** ADJ colossal, huge, oversize(d); **über|do|sie|ren** *ptp* **überdosiert** VT *insep* **dieses Mittel wird oft überdosiert** an excessive dose of this medicine is often given; **nicht ~** do not exceed the dose; **Über|do|sis** F overdose, OD *(inf)*; *(= zu große Zumessung)* excessive amount; **sich** *(dat)* **eine ~ Heroin spritzen** to overdose *or* OD *(inf)* on heroin; **über|dre|hen** [y:bɐ'dreːən] *ptp* **überdreht** VT *insep Uhr etc* to overwind; *Motor* to overrev; *Gewinde, Schraube* to strip

über|dreht [y:bɐ'dreːt] ADJ *(inf)* overexcited; *(ständig)* highly charged, hyped(-up) *(inf)*; *(= verrückt)* weird; **ein ~er Typ** a weirdo *(inf)*

Über|druck M *pl* **-drucke** overprint

Über|druck M *pl* **-drücke** *(Tech)* excess pressure *no pl*

über|dru|cken [y:bɐ'drʊkn] *ptp* **überdruckt** VT *insep* to overprint

Über|druck-: **Über|druck|ka|bi|ne** F *(Aviat)* pressurized cabin; **Über|druck|ven|til** NT pressure relief valve, blow-off valve

Über|druss ['y:bɐdrʊs] M **-es,** *no pl (= Übersättigung)* surfeit, satiety *(liter)* (*an +dat* of); *(= Widerwille)* aversion (*an +dat* to), antipathy (*an +dat* to); **bis zum ~** ad nauseam; **er aß Kaviar bis zum ~** he ate caviar until he wearied of it *or* had had a surfeit of it; **~ am Leben** weariness of living *or* life

über|drüs|sig ['y:bɐdrʏsɪç] ADJ **jds/einer Sache** *(gen)* **~ sein** to be weary of sb/sth; **jds/einer Sache** *(gen)* **~ werden** to (grow) weary of sb/sth

Über-: **über|dün|gen** [y:bɐ'dʏŋən] *ptp* **überdüngt** VT *sep* to over-fertilize; **Über|dün|gung** F over-fertilization; **über|durch|-**

schnitt|lich ADJ above-average ADV exceptionally, outstandingly; **er arbeitet ~ gut** his work is above average; **sie verdient ~ gut** she earns more than the average, she has an above-average salary; **über|eck** [y:bɐˈlɛk] ADV at right angles (to each other *or* to one another); **Über|ei|fer** M overzealousness; (*pej*: = *Wichtigtuerei*) officiousness; **über|eif|rig** ADJ overzealous; (*pej*: = *wichtigtuerisch*) officious; **über|eig|nen** [y:bɐˈlaignən] *ptp* **übereignet** VT *insep (geh)* **jdm etw ~** to make sth over to sb, to transfer sth to sb; **Über|eig|nung** F *(geh)* transference; **Über|ei|le** F haste; **über|ei|len** [y:bɐˈlailən] *ptp* **übereilt** *insep* VT to rush; **~ Sie nichts!** don't rush things! VR to rush; **übereil dich bloß nicht!** *(iro)* don't rush yourself *(iro)*; **über|eilt** [y:bɐˈlailt] ADJ overhasty, precipitate ADV overhastily, precipitately

über|ei|nan|der [y:bɐlaiˈnandɐ] ADV **a** *(räumlich)* on top of each other *or* one another, one on top of the other; *aufhängen* one above the other **b** *reden etc* about each other *or* one another

über|ei|nan|der-: **über|ei|nan|der+hän|gen** *sep*, **über|ei|nan|der hän|gen** △ VT to hang one above the other VI *irreg* to hang one above the other; **über|ei|nan|der+le|gen** *sep*, **über|ei|nan|der le|gen** △ VT to put *or* lay one on top of the other, to put *or* lay on top of each other *or* one another; **über|ei|nan|der+lie|gen** *sep irreg*, **über|ei|nan|der lie|gen** △ *irreg* VI to lie one on top of the other, to lie on top of each other *or* one another; **über|ei|nan|der+schla|gen** *sep irreg*, **über|ei|nan|der schla|gen** △ *irreg* VT **die Beine ~** to cross one's legs; **die Arme ~** to fold one's arms; **über|ei|nan|der+woh|nen** *sep*, **über|ei|nan|der woh|nen** △ VI **wir wohnen übereinander** we live one above the other, we live on top of each other

über|ein+kom|men [y:bɐˈlain-] VI *sep irreg aux sein* to agree; **wir sind darin übereingekommen, dass ...** we have agreed that ...

Über|ein|kom|men [y:bɐˈlainkɔmən] NT, **Über|ein|kunft** [y:bɐˈlainkʊnft] F -, ¨-e [-kʏnftə] arrangement, understanding, agreement; (= *Vertrag*) agreement; **ein ~** *or* **eine Übereinkunft treffen** to enter into *or* make an agreement; **ein ~** *or* **eine Übereinkunft erzielen** to come to *or* reach an agreement, to reach agreement

über|ein+stim|men [y:bɐˈlain-] VI *sep* to agree, to concur *(form)*; *(Meinungen)* to tally, to concur *(form)*; *(Angaben, Messwerte, Rechnungen etc)* to correspond, to tally, to agree; (= *zusammenpassen*: *Farben, Stile etc*) to match; *(Gram)* to agree; *(Dreiecke)* to be congruent; **mit jdm in etw** *(dat)* **~** to agree with sb on sth; **wir stimmen darin überein, dass ...** we agree *or* are agreed that ...

über|ein|stim|mend ADJ corresponding; *Meinungen, Vermutungen etc* concurring, concurrent; *Farben etc* matching; **nach ~en Angaben/Meldungen** according to all accounts/reports; **nach ~en Zeugenaussagen** according to mutually corroborative testimonies ADV **alle erklärten ~, dass ...** everybody agreed that ..., everybody unanimously stated that ...; **wir sind ~ der Meinung, dass ...** we are unanimously of the opinion that ..., we unanimously agree that ...; **sie bestritten ~, dass ...** they are in agreement in denying that ...; **~ mit** in agreement with **allen Beteiligten ~** all parties involved are agreed on that; **in ~ mit jdm** in agreement with sb; **in ~ mit etw** in accordance with sth

Über|ein|stim|mung F **a** (= *Einklang, Gleichheit*) correspondence, agreement; **sein Handeln steht nicht mit seiner Theorie in ~** there's a disparity *or* no correspondence between his actions and his theory; **bei den Zeugenaussagen gab es nur in zwei Punkten ~** the testimonies only agreed *or* corresponded *or* tallied in two particulars; **zwei Dinge in ~ bringen** to bring two things into line; **es besteht** *or* **herrscht keine ~ zwischen X und Y** X and Y do not agree **b** *(von Meinung)* agreement; **darin besteht bei** **c** *(Gram)* agreement

Über-: **über|emp|find|lich** ADJ *(gegen* to) oversensitive, hypersensitive *(auch Med)* ADV **~ auf etw** *(acc)* **reagieren** to be oversensitive to sth; **meine Haut reagiert ~ auf dieses Waschmittel** I get an allergic reaction from that detergent; **Über|emp|find|lich|keit** F *(gegen* to) oversensitivity, hypersensitivity *(auch Med)*; **über|er|fül|len** *ptp* **übererfüllt** VT *insep Norm, Soll, Plan* to exceed *(um* by); **Über|er|fül|lung** F *(no pl*: = *das Übererfüllen)* exceeding; **bei ~ des Plansolls werden Sonderprämien gezahlt** anyone who exceeds the target *or* quota is paid special premiums; **über|er|näh|ren** *ptp* **überernährt** VT *insep* to overfeed; **Über|er|näh|rung** F *(no pl*: = *das Überernähren)* overfeeding; *(Krankheit)* overeating; **über+es|sen** [ˈy:bɐlɛsn] VT *sep irreg* **sich** *(dat)* **etw ~** to grow sick of sth; **Spargel kann ich mir gar nicht ~** I can't eat enough asparagus; **über|es|sen** [y:bɐˈlɛsn] *pret* **überaß** [y:bɐˈla:s], *ptp* **übergessen** [y:bɐˈgɛsn] VR *insep* to overeat; **ich habe mich an Käse übergessen** I've eaten too much cheese

über+fah|ren [ˈy:bɐfa:rən] *sep irreg* VT *(mit Boot etc)* to take *or* ferry across VI *aux sein* to cross over

über|fah|ren [y:bɐˈfa:rən] *ptp* **überfahren** VT *insep irreg* **a** *jdn, Tier* to run over, to knock down **b** (= *hinwegfahren über*) to go *or* drive over; *Fluss etc* to cross (over) **c** (= *übersehen und weiterfahren*) *Ampel etc* to go through **d** *(inf*: = *übertölpeln)* **jdn ~** to railroad sb into it **e** (= *plötzlich über einen kommen)* to come over

Über|fahrt F crossing

Über|fall M **a** (= *Angriff*) attack *(auf +acc* on); *(esp auf offener Straße)* mugging *(auf +acc* of); *(auf Bank etc)* raid *(auf +acc* on), hold-up; *(auf Land)* invasion *(auf +acc* of); **einen ~ auf jdn/etw verüben** *or* **ausführen** to carry out an attack *etc* on sb/sth; **dies ist ein ~, keine Bewegung!** this is a hold-up *or* stick-up *(esp US inf)*, freeze! **b** *(hum*: = *unerwartetes Erscheinen)* invasion; **er hat einen ~ auf uns vor** he's planning to descend on us

über|fal|len [y:bɐˈfalən] *ptp* **überfallen** VT *insep irreg* **a** (= *angreifen*) to attack; *(esp auf offener Straße)* to mug; *Bank etc* to raid, to hold up, to stick up *(esp US inf)*; *Land, Stadt* to invade, to attack; *(Mil) Hauptquartier, Lager* to raid **b** *(fig geh)* (= *überkommen*: *Gefühle, Schlaf, Müdigkeit, Krankheit etc)* to come over *or* upon; (= *überraschen*: *Nacht*) to overtake, to come upon suddenly; **plötzlich überfiel ihn heftiges Fieber** he suddenly came down with a bad fever **c** *(fig inf)* (= *überraschend besuchen*) to descend (up)on; (= *bestürmen*) to pounce upon; **jdn mit Fragen/Wünschen ~** to bombard sb with questions/requests

Über-: **über|fäl|lig** ADJ overdue *usu pred*; **seit einer Woche ~ sein** to be a week overdue; **Über|fall|kom|man|do** NT, **Über|falls|kom|man|do** *(Aus)* NT flying squad, riot squad; **über|fei|nert** [y:bɐˈfainɐt] ADJ overrefined; **Über|fei|ne|rung** [y:bɐˈfainərʊŋ] F -, -en overrefinement; **über|fi|schen** [y:bɐˈfɪʃn] *ptp* **überfischt** VT *insep* to overfish; **Über|fi|schung** F -, -en overfishing; **über|flie|gen** [y:bɐˈfli:gn] *ptp* **überflogen** [y:bɐˈflo:gn] VT *insep irreg* **a** *(lit)* to fly over **b** *(fig)* **ein Lächeln/eine leichte Röte überflog ihr Gesicht** a smile/a faint blush flitted across her face **c** (= *flüchtig ansehen*) *Buch etc* to take a quick look at, to glance through *or* at *or* over; **Über|flie|ger(in)** M(F) *(fig)* high-flyer; **über+flie|ßen** [ˈy:bɐfli:sn] VI *sep irreg aux sein* **a** *(Gefäß)* to overflow; *(Flüssigkeit)* to run over, to overflow **b** **ineinander ~** *(Farben)* to run **c** *(fig*: *vor Dank, Höflichkeit etc)* to overflow, to gush *(vor +dat* with); **über|flie|ßen** [y:bɐˈfli:sn] *ptp* **überflossen** [y:bɐˈflɔsn] VT *insep irreg (rare)* to inundate, to flood; **Über|flug** M overflight; **einem Flugzeug den ~ verweigern** to refuse to allow an aircraft to fly over one's territory; **über|flü|geln** [y:bɐˈfly:gln] *ptp* **überflügelt** VT *insep* to outdistance, to outstrip; *(in Leistung, bei Wahl)* to outdo; *Erwartungen etc* to surpass

Über|flug|rech|te PL *(Mil)* overfly rights *pl*; **jdm ~ gewähren** to grant sb overfly rights

Über|fluss M, *no pl* **a** (super)abundance *(an +dat* of); (= *Luxus*) affluence; **Arbeit/Geld im ~** plenty of work/money, an abundance of work/money; **das Land des ~es** the land of plenty; **im ~ leben** to live in luxury; **im ~ vorhanden sein** to be in plentiful supply; **~ an etw** *(dat)* **haben, etw im ~ haben** to have plenty *or* an abundance of sth, to have sth in abundance **b** **zu allem** *or* **zum ~** (= *unnötigerweise*) superfluously; (= *obendrein*) to top it all *(inf)*, into the bargain; **zu allem** *or* **zum ~ fing es auch noch an zu regnen** and then, to top it all, it started to rain *(inf)*, and then it started to rain into the bargain

Über|fluss|ge|sell|schaft F affluent society

über|flüs|sig ADJ superfluous; (= *frei, entbehrlich*) spare; (= *unnötig*) unnecessary; (= *zwecklos*) futile, useless; **~ zu sagen, dass ...** it goes without saying that ... → **Kropf b**

über|flüs|si|ger|wei|se [ˈy:bɐflʏsɪgɐˈvaizə] ADV superfluously

Über-: **über+flu|ten** [ˈy:bɐflu:tn] VI *sep aux sein* (= *über die Ufer treten*) to overflow; **über|flu|ten** [y:bɐˈflu:tn] *ptp* **überflutet** VT *insep (lit, fig)* to flood; *(fig auch)* to inundate; **Über|flu|tung** [y:bɐˈflu:tʊŋ] F -, -en **a** *(lit)* flood; (= *das Überfluten*) flooding *no pl* **b** *(fig)* flooding *no pl*, inundation; **über|for|dern** [y:bɐˈfɔrdɐn] *ptp* **überfordert** VT *insep* to overtax; *jdn auch* to ask *or* expect too much of; **damit ist er überfordert** that's asking *or* expecting too much of him; **als Abteilungsleiter wäre er doch etwas überfordert** being head of department would be too much for him *or* would stretch him too far; **Über|for|de|rung** F excessive demand(s *pl*) *(für* on); *(no pl*: = *das Überfordern)* overtaxing; **Über|fracht** F excess freight; **über|frach|ten** [y:bɐˈfraxtn] *ptp* **überfrachtet** VT *insep (fig)* to overload; **ein mit Emotionen überfrachteter Begriff** a concept fraught with emotions, an emotionally loaded concept; **über|fragt** [y:bɐˈfra:kt] ADJ *pred* stumped (for an answer); **da bin ich ~** there you've got me, there you have me, that I don't know; **über|frem|den** [y:bɐˈfrɛmdn] *ptp* **überfremdet** *(neg!)* VT *insep* to infiltrate with too many foreign influences; *(Econ)* to swamp; **überfremdet werden** *(Land)* to be swamped by foreigners; **Über|frem|dung** F -, -en *(neg!)* foreign infiltration; *(Econ)* swamping; **über|fres|sen** [y:bɐˈfrɛsn] *ptp* **überfressen** VR *insep irreg (inf)* to overeat, to eat too much; **sich an etw** *(dat)* **~** to gorge oneself on sth; **über|frie|ren** [y:bɐˈfri:rən] *ptp* **überfroren** [y:bɐˈfro:rən] VI *insep irreg* to freeze over; **Glatteisgefahr durch ~de Nässe** slippery roads due to black ice; **Über|fuhr** [ˈy:bɐfu:ɐ] F -, -en *(Aus)* ferry; **über+füh|ren** [ˈy:bɐfy:rən] VT *sep* to transfer; *Leichnam* to transport; *Wagen* to drive; **über|füh|ren** [y:bɐˈfy:rən] *ptp* **überführt** VT *insep* **a** = **überführen** **b** *Täter* to convict (*+gen* of), to find guilty (*+gen* of); **ein überführter Verbrecher** a convicted criminal **c** (= *überbauen*) **einen Fluss mit einer Brücke ~** to build a bridge over a river; **Über|füh|rung** F **a** transportation **b** *no pl (Jur)* conviction **c** (= *Brücke über Straße etc*) bridge *(auch Rail)*, overpass; (= *Fußgängerüberführung*) footbridge; **Über|fül|le** F profusion, superabundance; **über|fül|len** [y:bɐˈfʏlən] *ptp* **überfüllt** VT *insep Glas* to overfill; **sich** *(dat)* **den Magen ~** to eat too much; **über|füllt** [y:bɐˈfʏlt] ADJ overcrowded; *Kurs* oversubscribed; *(Comm) Lager* overstocked, overfilled; **Über|fül|lung** F, *no pl* overcrowding; *(von Kursus, Vorlesung)* oversubscription; **Über|funk|ti|on** F hyperactivity, hyperfunction(ing); **über|füt|tern** [y:bɐˈfʏtɐn] *ptp* **überfüttert** VT *insep* to overfeed; **Über|füt|te|rung** F overfeeding

Über|ga|be F handing over *no pl*; *(von Neubau)* opening; *(Mil)* surrender; **die ~ der Zeugnisse findet am Ende des Schuljahres statt** reports are handed out at the end of the school year; **die ~ des neuen Schwimmbads an die Öffentlichkeit wird durch den Bürgermeister vorgenommen** the mayor will open the new swimming pool to the public

Über|gang M *pl* **-gänge** **a** *(= das Überqueren)* crossing **b** *(= Fußgängerübergang)* crossing, crosswalk *(US)*; *(= Brücke)* footbridge; *(= Bahnübergang)* level crossing *(Brit)*, grade crossing *(US)* **c** *(= Grenzübergangsstelle)* checkpoint **d** *(fig: = Wechsel, Überleitung)* transition, changeover **e** *(zum Internet)* gateway

Über|gangs-: **Über|gangs|be|stim|mung** F interim *or* temporary regulation; **Über|gangs|er|schei|nung** F temporary phenomenon; **Über|gangs|fi|nan|zie|rung** F gap financing; **Über|gangs|frist** F transitional period; **Über|gangs|geld** NT interim payment *or* allowance; **über|gangs|los** ADJ ADV without a transition; *(zeitlich auch)* without a transitional period; **Über|gangs|lö|sung** F interim *or* temporary solution; **Über|gangs|man|tel** M between-seasons coat; **Über|gangs|maß|nah|me** F transitional measure; **Über|gangs|pha|se** F transitional phase; **Über|gangs|re|ge|lung** F interim arrangement; **Über|gangs|re|gie|rung** F caretaker *or* transitional government; **Über|gangs|sta|di|um** NT transitional stage; **Über|gangs|zeit** F **a** transitional period, period of transition **b** *(zwischen Jahreszeiten)* in-between season; **Über|gangs|zu|stand** M transitional state

Über|gar|di|ne F curtain, drape *(US)*

über|ge|ben [y:bɐˈge:bn] *ptp* **übergeben** *insep irreg* **VT** **a** *(= überreichen)* to hand over; *Dokument, Zettel, Einschreiben* to hand *(jdm* sb); *Diplom etc* to hand over *(jdm* to sb), to present *(jdm* to sb); *(= vermachen)* to bequeath *(jdm* to sb); *(Mil)* to surrender, to hand over; **ein Gebäude der Öffentlichkeit/eine Straße dem Verkehr ~** to open a building to the public/a road to traffic; **eine Angelegenheit einem Rechtsanwalt ~** to place a matter in the hands of a lawyer

b *(= weiterreichen, verleihen) Amt, Macht* to hand over

c **einen Leichnam der Erde/dem Wasser ~** *(liter)* to commit a body to the earth/water

VR *(= sich erbrechen)* to vomit, to be sick; **ich muss mich ~** I'm going to be sick

über+ge|hen [ˈy:bɐge:ən] VI *sep irreg aux sein* **a** **in etw** *(acc)* **~** *(in einen anderen Zustand)* to turn *or* change into sth; *(Farben)* to merge into sth; **in jds Besitz** *(acc)* **~** to become sb's property; **in andere Hände/in Volkseigentum ~** to pass into other hands/into public ownership **b** **auf jdn ~** *(= geerbt, übernommen werden)* to pass to sb **c** **zu etw ~** to go over to sth; **wir sind dazu übergegangen, Computer zu benutzen** we went over to (using) computers *(esp Brit)*, we went to using computers *(esp US)*

über|ge|hen [y:bɐˈge:ən] *ptp* **übergangen** [y:bɐˈgaŋən] VT *insep irreg* to pass over; *Kapitel, Abschnitt etc auch* to skip; *Einwände etc auch* to ignore

Über-: **über|ge|nau** ADJ overprecise, pernickety *(Brit inf)*, persnickety *(US inf)*; **über|ge|nug** ADV more than enough; **über|ge|ord|net** ADJ **a** *Behörde, Dienststelle, Recht* higher; **die uns ~e Behörde** the next authority above us **b** *(Gram) Satz* superordinate; *(Ling, Philos) Begriff* generic **c** *(fig)* **von ~er Bedeutung sein** to be of overriding importance **d** *(Comput) Ordner etc* parent → *auch* **überordnen**; **Über|ge|päck** NT *(Aviat)* excess baggage; **über|ge|scheit** ADJ *(iro)* know-all *(Brit)*, know-it-all *(US)*, smart-ass *(sl) all attr*; **so ein Übergescheiter** some clever Dick *(Brit inf) or* smart-ass *(sl)*, some know-all *(Brit) or* know-it-all *(US)*; **über|ge|schnappt** ADJ *(inf)* crazy → *auch* **überschnappen**; **Über|ge|wicht** NT overweight; *(fig)* predominance; **~ haben** *(Paket etc)* to be overweight; **an ~ leiden, ~ haben** *(Mensch)* to be overweight; **5 Gramm ~** 5 grammes excess weight; **das ~ bekommen** *(fig)* to become predominant; **das ~ haben** *(fig)* to predominate; **wenn sie das militärische ~ bekommen** if they gain military dominance; **über|ge|wich|tig** ADJ overweight; **über+gie|ßen** [ˈy:bɐgi:sn] VT *sep irreg* **jdm etw ~** to pour sth over sb; **über|gie|ßen** [y:bɐˈgi:sn] *ptp* **übergossen** [y:bɐˈgɔsn] VT *insep irreg* to pour over; *jdn* to douse; *Braten* to baste; **jdn/sich mit etw ~** to pour sth over sb/oneself; *(absichtlich auch)* to douse sb/oneself with sth; **über|glück|lich** ADJ overjoyed; **über+grei|fen** VI *sep irreg* **a** *(beim Klavierspiel)* to cross one's hands (over) **b** *(auf Rechte etc)* to encroach *or* infringe *(auf +acc* on); *(Feuer, Streik, Krankheit etc)* to spread *(auf +acc* to); **ineinander ~** to overlap; **über|grei|fend** ADJ *(fig) Gesichtspunkte, Überlegungen, Problem* general; *Ziel auch* overall; **Über|griff** M *(= Einmischung)* infringement *(auf +acc* of), encroachment *(auf +acc* on), interference *no pl (auf +acc* with *or* in); *(Mil)* attack *(auf +acc* upon), incursion *(auf +acc* into); *(= Ausschreitung)* excess; **über|groß** ADJ oversize(d), huge, enormous; *Mehrheit* overwhelming, huge; **Über|grö|ße** F *(bei Kleidung etc)* outsize; **62 ist eine ~** 62 is outsize; **über+ha|ben** VT *sep irreg (inf)* **a** *(= satthaben)* to be sick (and tired) of *(inf)*, to be fed up of *or* with *(inf)* **b** *(= übrig haben)* to have left (over); **für etw nichts ~** not to like sth **c** *Kleidung* to have on

über|hand+neh|men [y:bɐˈhantne:mən] *sep irreg*, **über|hand neh|men** △ [y:bɐˈhantne:mən] *irreg* VI to get out of control *or* hand; *(schlechte Sitten, Laxheit etc auch)* to become rife *or* rampant; *(Meinungen, Ideen etc)* to become rife *or* rampant, to gain the upper hand

Über-: **Über|hang** M **a** *(= Felsüberhang)* overhang, overhanging rock; *(= Baumüberhang)* overhanging branches *pl* **b** *(= Vorhang)* pelmet *(Brit)*, valance *(US)*; *(von Bettdecke etc)* valance **c** *(= Überschuss)* surplus *(an +dat* of); **über+hän|gen** *sep* **VI** *irreg aux haben or sein* to overhang; *(= hinausragen auch)* to jut out **VT** **sich** *(dat)* **ein Gewehr ~** to sling a rifle over one's shoulder; **sich** *(dat)* **einen Mantel ~** to put *or* hang a coat round *or* over one's shoulders; **Über|hang|man|dat** NT *(Pol) seat gained as a result of votes for a specific candidate over and above the seats to which a party is entitled by the number of votes cast for the party*; **über|has|ten** [y:bɐˈhastn] *ptp* **überhastet** VT *insep* to rush; **über|has|tet** [y:bɐˈhastət] **ADJ** overhasty, hurried **ADV** overhastily, hurriedly; **~ sprechen** to speak too fast; **über|häu|fen** [y:bɐˈhɔyfn] *ptp* **überhäuft** VT *insep jdn* to overwhelm, to inundate; *Schreibtisch etc* to pile high; **jdn mit Geschenken/Glückwünschen/Titeln ~** to heap presents/congratulations/titles (up)on sb; **ich bin völlig mit Arbeit überhäuft** I'm completely snowed under *or* swamped (with work); **jdn mit Vorwürfen ~** to heap reproaches (up)on sb('s head)

über|haupt [y:bɐˈhaupt] ADV **a** *(= sowieso, im Allgemeinen)* in general; *(= überdies, außerdem)* anyway, anyhow; **und ~, warum nicht?** and after all *or* anyway, why not?; **er sagt ~ immer sehr wenig** he never says very much anyway *or* anyhow *or* at the best of times; **nicht nur Rotwein, sondern Wein ~ mag ich nicht** it's not only red wine I don't like, I don't like wine at all *or* full stop *(esp Brit) or* period

b *(in Fragen, Verneinungen)* at all; **~ nicht** not at all; **ich denke ~ nicht daran mitzukommen** I've (absolutely) no intention whatsoever of coming along; **~ nie** never (ever), never at all; **~ kein Grund** no reason at all *or* whatsoever; **hast du denn ~ keinen Anstand?** have you no decency at all?; **das habe ich ja ~ nicht gewusst** I had no idea at all; **ich habe ~ nichts gehört** I didn't hear anything at all, I didn't hear a thing; **das steht in ~ keinem Verhältnis zu ...** that bears no relationship at all *or* whatsoever to ...

c *(= erst, eigentlich)* **dann merkt man ~ erst, wie schön ...** then you really notice for the first time how beautiful ...; **waren Sie ~ schon in dem neuen Film?** have you actually been to the latest film?; **da fällt mir ~ ein, ...** now I remember ...; **wenn ~** if at all; **wie ist das ~ möglich?** how is that possible?; **gibt es das ~?** is there really such a thing?, is there really any such thing?; **was wollen Sie ~ von mir?** *(herausfordernd)* what do you want from me?; **wer sind Sie ~?** who do you think you are?; **wissen Sie ~, wer ich bin?** do you realize who I am?

Über-: **über|he|ben** [y:bɐˈhe:bn] *ptp* **überhoben** [y:bɐˈho:bn] VR *insep irreg (lit)* to (over)strain oneself; *(fig: finanziell)* to overreach oneself; *(fig geh: = hochmütig sein)* to be arrogant; **sich über jdn ~** to consider oneself superior to sb; **über|heb|lich** [y:bɐˈhe:plıç] ADJ arrogant; **Über|heb|lich|keit** F -, *no pl* arrogance; **Über|he|bung** F *(fig geh)* presumption; **über|hei|zen** [y:bɐˈhaitsn] *ptp* **überheizt** VT *insep* to overheat; **über|hit|zen** [y:bɐˈhıtsn] *ptp* **überhitzt** VT *insep* to overheat; **über|hitzt** [y:bɐˈhıtst] ADJ *(fig) Konjunktur, Markt* overheated; *Gemüter, Diskussion* very heated *pred*; *Fantasie* overheated; **Über|hit|zung** F overheating; *(Tech)* superheating; **Über|hit|zungs|schutz** M cutout switch *(to prevent overheating)*; **über|hö|hen** [y:bɐˈhø:ən] *ptp* **überhöht** VT *insep Preise* to raise *or* increase excessively; *Kurve* to bank, to superelevate *(spec)*; **über|höht** [y:bɐˈhø:t] ADJ *Kurve* banked, superelevated *(spec)*; *Forderungen, Preise* exorbitant, excessive; *Geschwindigkeit* excessive

über|ho|len [y:bɐˈho:lən] *ptp* **überholt** *insep* **VT** **a** *Fahrzeug* to overtake *(esp Brit)*, to pass; *(fig: = übertreffen)* to overtake **b** *(Tech) Maschine, Motor etc* to overhaul **VI** to overtake

über+ho|len [ˈy:bɐho:lən] *sep* **VTI** *(old)* to ferry; **hol über!** ferry! **VI** *(Naut: Schiff)* to keel over

Über|hol|ma|nö|ver NT *(Aut)* overtaking *or* passing manoeuvre *(Brit)*, passing maneuver *(US)*

Über|hol|spur F *(Aut)* overtaking *(esp Brit) or* fast lane

über|holt [y:bɐˈho:lt] ADJ out-dated

Über|hol-: **Über|hol|ver|bot** NT restriction on overtaking *(esp Brit) or* passing; *(als Schild etc)* no overtaking *(esp Brit)*, no passing; **auf dieser Strecke besteht ~** no overtaking *(esp Brit) or* passing on this stretch; **nach der nächsten Kurve ist das ~ wieder aufgehoben** the restriction on overtaking *(esp Brit) or* passing ends after the next bend; **Über|hol|vor|gang** M *(form)* overtaking *(esp Brit)*, passing; **vor Beginn des ~es** before starting *or* beginning to overtake *(esp Brit) or* pass; **der ~ war noch nicht abgeschlossen, als das Fahrzeug ...** the vehicle had not finished overtaking *(esp Brit) or* passing when it ...

über|hö|ren [y:bɐˈhø:rən] *ptp* **überhört** VT *insep* not to hear; *(= nicht hören wollen)* to ignore; **das möchte ich überhört haben!** (I'll pretend) I didn't hear that!

über+hö|ren [ˈy:bɐhø:rən] VT *sep* **sich** *(dat)* **etw ~** to be tired *or* sick *(inf)* of hearing sth

Über-Ich, Über|ich NT *(Psych)* superego

über|in|ter|pre|tie|ren *ptp* **überinterpretiert** VT *insep* to overinterpret

Über-: **über|ir|disch** **ADJ** **a** *Wesen, Schönheit* celestial, heavenly **b** *(= oberirdisch)* above ground **ADV** **a** **~ schön** heavenly **b** *(= oberirdisch)* above ground; **über|kan|di|delt** ADJ *(inf)* eccentric; **Über|ka|pa|zi|tät** F *usu pl* overcapacity; **über|kauft** [y:bɐˈkauft] ADJ *(Comm)* saturated; **über+kip|pen** VI *sep aux sein* to topple *or* keel over; *(Stimme)* to crack; **über|kle|ben** [y:bɐˈkle:bn] *ptp* **überklebt** VT *insep* **die Kiste ~** to stick something over the box; **etw mit Papier ~** to stick paper over sth; **über+kle|ben** [ˈy:bɐkle:bn] VT *sep* **etwas ~** to stick something over it; **über|klug** ADJ *(pej)* too clever by half *(Brit)*, know-all *attr (Brit)*, know-it-all *attr (US)*, smart-ass *attr (sl)*; **sei doch nicht so ~!** don't be so clever, don't be such a know-all *(Brit) or* know-it-all *(US)*; **über+ko|chen** VI *sep aux sein (lit, fig)* to boil over

über|kom|men [y:bɐˈkɔmən] *ptp* **überkommen** *insep irreg* VT *(= überfallen, ergreifen)* to come over; **ein Gefühl der Verlassenheit überkam ihn** a feeling of desolation came over him, he was overcome by a feeling of desolation; **Furcht** *etc* **überkam ihn** he was overcome with fear *etc*; **was überkommt dich denn?** what's come over you? VI *aux sein ptp only (= überliefern)* **es ist uns** *(dat)* **~** *(old)* it has come down to us, it has been handed down to us

über+kom|men [ˈy:bɐkɔmən] VT *sep irreg (Sw)* to get handed down

Über-: **Über|kom|pen|sa|ti|on** F overcompensation; **über|kom|pen|sie|ren** *ptp* **überkompensiert** VT *insep* to overcompensate for; **über|kreu|zen** [y:bɐˈkrɔytsn] *ptp* **überkreuzt** VT *(= überqueren)* to cross VR *(= sich überschneiden: Linien etc)* to intersect; **über+krie|gen** VT *sep (inf)* **a** *(= überdrüssig werden)* to get tired *or* sick (and tired) *(inf)* of, to get fed up of *or* with *(inf)*, to get browned off with *(Brit inf)* **b** **eins ~** to get landed one *(Brit inf)*, to get hit; **über|kri|tisch** ADJ overcritical, overly critical; **über|krus|ten** [y:bɐˈkrustn] *ptp* **überkrustet** VT *insep* to cover (with a layer *or* crust of); **über|küh|len** [y:bɐˈky:lən] *ptp* **überkühlt** VT *insep (Aus Cook)* to cool down; **über|la|den** [y:bɐˈla:dn] *ptp* **überladen** VT *insep irreg (= zu stark belasten)* to overload; *(mit Arbeit auch)* to overburden; *(= zu voll packen) Schreibtisch, Wand etc auch* to clutter, to cover; *(= zu stark verzieren auch)* to clutter; *(= reichlich geben)* to shower; **über|la|den** [y:bɐˈla:dn] ADJ *Wagen* overloaded, overladen; *(fig) Stil* over-ornate, flowery; *Bild* cluttered; **über|la|gern** [y:bɐˈla:gɐn] *ptp* **überlagert** *insep* VT **a** **diese Schicht wird von einer anderen überlagert** another stratum overlies this one; **am Abend ist dieser Sender von einem anderen überlagert** in the evenings this station is blotted out by another one **b** *Thema, Problem, Konflikt etc* to eclipse **c** *(= zu lange lagern)* to store for too long VR *(= sich überschneiden)* to overlap; **Über|la|ge|rung** F *(von Themen, Problemen etc)* eclipsing; *(= Überschneidung)* overlapping

Über|land-: **Über|land|bus** M country bus, coach; **Über|land|lei|tung** F *(Elec)* overhead power line *or* cable; **Über|land|stra|ße** F road *(heading across country)*; **Über|land|zent|ra|le** F *(Elec)* rural power station

Über-: **über|lang** ADJ *Oper, Stück etc* overlength; *Arme, Mantel, Netze, Schnüre etc* too long; **Über|län|ge** F excessive length; **~ haben** to be overlength; **über|lap|pen** [y:bɐˈlapn] *ptp* **überlappt** VIR *insep* to overlap; **über|lap|pend** ADJ *(Comput: Anordnung von Fenstern)* cascade; **Über|lap|pung** F **-, -en** *(= das Überlappen) (auch Comput)* overlapping; *(= überlappte Stelle) (auch Comput)* overlap

über|las|sen [y:bɐˈlasn] *ptp* **überlassen** VT *insep irreg* **a** *(= haben lassen, abgeben)* **jdm etw ~** to let sb have sth **b** *(= anheimstellen)* **es jdm ~, etw zu tun** to leave it (up) to sb to do sth; **das bleibt (ganz) Ihnen ~** that's (entirely) up to you; **das müssen Sie schon mir ~** you must leave that to me; **es bleibt Ihnen ~, zu ...** it's up to you to ...; **jdm die Initiative/Wahl ~** to leave the initiative/choice (up) to sb **c** *(= in Obhut geben)* **jdm etw ~** to leave sth with sb *or* in sb's care, to entrust sth to sb's care; **sich** *(dat)* **selbst ~ sein** to be left to one's own devices, to be left to oneself; **jdn sich** *(dat)* **selbst ~** to leave sb to his/her own devices **d** *(= preisgeben)* **sich seinem Schmerz/seinen Gedanken/Gefühlen ~** to abandon oneself to one's pain/thoughts/feelings; **jdn seinem Schicksal ~** to leave *or* abandon sb to his fate; **jdn seinem Kummer ~** to offer sb no comfort in his/her grief

über+las|sen [ˈy:bɐlasn] VT *sep irreg (inf: = übrig lassen)* to leave (*jdm* for sb)

Über|las|sung [y:bɐˈlasʊŋ] F **-, -en** *(von Recht, Anspruch)* surrender

über|las|ten [y:bɐˈlastn] *ptp* **überlastet** VT *insep* to put too great a strain on; *jdn* to overtax; *(Elec, durch Gewicht) Telefonnetz, Brücke* to overload; **überlastet sein** to be under too great a strain; *(= überfordert sein)* to be overtaxed; *(Elec etc)* to be overloaded

Über|las|tung F **-, -en** *(von Mensch)* overtaxing; *(= Überlastetsein)* strain; *(Elec, durch Gewicht)* overloading; **bei ~ der Leber** when there is too much strain on the liver

Über|lauf M overflow

Über|lauf|an|zei|ge F *(beim Taschenrechner)* decimal cutoff symbol

über|lau|fen [y:bɐˈlaufn] *ptp* **überlaufen** VT *insep irreg* **a** *Gegner, Abwehr* to overrun **b** *(fig: = ergreifen: Angst etc)* to seize; **es überlief ihn heiß** he felt hot under the collar; **es überlief ihn kalt** a cold shiver ran down his back *or* up and down his spine; **es überlief mich heiß und kalt** I went hot and cold all over

über+lau|fen [ˈy:bɐlaufn] VI *sep irreg aux sein* **a** *(Wasser, Gefäß)* to overflow; *(= überkochen)* to boil over; **ineinander ~** *(Farben)* to run (into one another); **zum Überlaufen voll** full to overflowing; **jetzt läuft das Maß über** *(fig)* my patience is at an end → **Galle** **b** *(Mil, fig: = überwechseln)* to desert; **zum Feind ~** to go over *or* desert to the enemy

über|lau|fen [y:bɐˈlaufn] ADJ overcrowded; *(mit Touristen)* overrun

Über|läu|fer(in) M(F) *(Mil)* deserter, turncoat; *(Pol)* turncoat

Über|lauf|rohr NT overflow pipe

über|laut ADJ **a** *(= zu laut)* overloud **b** *(= aufdringlich) Mensch* obtrusive, loud; *Farben* loud, garish; *(= flegelhaft) Benehmen* brash, loud ADV too loudly

über|le|ben [y:bɐˈle:bn] *ptp* **überlebt** *insep* VT **a** *Unglück, Operation, Anschlag, schwierige Lage etc* to survive; *die Nacht* to last, to survive, to live through; **das überlebe ich nicht!** *(inf)* it'll be the death of me *(inf)*; **du wirst es ~** *(iro)* (it won't kill you), you'll survive; **ums Überleben kämpfen** to fight for survival **b** *(= länger leben als)* to outlive, to survive *(um* by)

VI to survive

VR **das hat sich überlebt** that's had its day; **das wird sich ganz schnell überlebt haben** that will very soon have had its day; **diese Mode überlebt sich ganz schnell** this fashion will soon be a thing of the past → *auch* **überlebt**

Über|le|ben NT **-s**, *no pl* survival; **ums ~ kämpfen** to fight for survival

Über|le|ben|de(r) [y:bɐˈle:bndə] MF *decl as adj* survivor

Über|le|bens|chan|ce F chance of survival

über|le|bens|fä|hig ADJ *pred* capable of surviving *or* survival *pred*

über|le|bens|groß ADJ *Denkmal etc* larger-than-life

Über|le|bens|grö|ße F **in ~** larger than life

Über|le|bens|kampf M fight *or* struggle for survival

Über|le|bens|künst|ler M survivor

Über|le|bens|trai|ning NT survival training

über|le|bens|wich|tig ADJ vital, important for survival

über|lebt [y:bɐˈle:pt] ADJ outmoded, out-of--date → *auch* **überleben**

über|le|gen [y:bɐˈle:gn] ✪ 29.3 *ptp* **überlegt** *insep* VI *(= nachdenken)* to think; **überleg doch mal!** think!; **hin und her ~** to deliberate; **ich habe hin und her überlegt** I've thought about it a lot; **ohne zu ~** without thinking; *(= ohne zu zögern)* without thinking twice VT *(= überdenken, durchdenken)* to think over *or* about, to consider; **das werde ich mir ~** I'll think it over, I'll (have a) think about it, I'll give it some thought; **ich habe es mir anders überlegt** I've changed my mind (about it); **ich habe es mir noch mal überlegt** I've had second thoughts (about it); **wollen Sie es sich** *(dat)* **nicht noch einmal ~?** won't you think it over again?, won't you reconsider?; **das muss ich mir noch sehr ~** I'll have to think it over *or* consider it very carefully; **das hätten Sie sich** *(dat)* **vorher ~ müssen** you should have thought of that before *or* sooner; **es wäre zu ~** it should be considered; **wenn man es sich recht überlegt** if you really think about it

über+le|gen [ˈy:bɐle:gn] *sep* VT **jdm etw ~** to put *or* lay sth over sb VR *(= sich zur Seite legen)* to lean over, to tilt

über|le|gen [ˈy:bɐle:gn] ADJ superior; *(= hochmütig auch)* supercilious; **jdm ~ sein** to be superior to sb; **das war ein ~er Sieg** that was a good *or* convincing victory ADV in a superior manner *or* fashion; **Bayern München hat ~ gesiegt** Bayern Munich won convincingly

Über|le|gen|heit F **-**, *no pl* superiority; *(= Hochmut auch)* superciliousness

über|legt [y:bɐˈle:kt] ADJ (well-)considered ADV in a considered way

Über|le|gung [y:bɐˈle:gʊŋ] F **-, -en** **a** *(= Nachdenken)* consideration, thought, reflection; **bei näherer ~** on closer examination; **bei nüchterner ~** on reflection; **das wäre wohl einer ~ wert** that would be worth thinking about *or* over, that would be worth considering, that would be worthy of consideration; **ohne ~** without thinking → **anstellen VT e, reiflich** **b** *(= Bemerkung)* observation; **~en anstellen** to make observations (*zu* about *or* on); **~en vortragen** to give one's views (*zu* on *or* about)

über+lei|ten *sep* VT *(Thema, Abschnitt etc)* to link up (*in +acc* to, with) VI **zu etw ~** to lead up to sth; **in eine andere Tonart ~** *(Mus)* to change key

Über|lei|tung F connection; *(zur nächsten Frage, Mus)* transition

über|le|sen [y:bɐˈle:zn] *ptp* **überlesen** VT *insep irreg* **a** *(= flüchtig lesen)* to glance through *or* over *or* at **b** *(= übersehen)* to overlook, to miss

über|lie|fern [y:bɐˈli:fɐn] *ptp* **überliefert** VT *insep Brauch, Tradition, Lied* to hand down; **das Manuskript ist nur als Fragment überliefert** the manuscript has only come down to us in fragmentary form; **etw der Nachwelt ~** to preserve sth for posterity

Über|lie|fe|rung F **a** tradition; **schriftliche ~en** (written) records **b** *(= Brauch)* tradition, custom; **an der ~ festhalten** to hold on to tradition; **nach alter ~** according to tradition

über|lis|ten [y:bɐˈlɪstn] *ptp* **überlistet** VT *insep* to outwit

überm [ˈy:bɐm] *contr von* **über dem**

über|ma|chen [y:bɐˈmaxn] *ptp* **übermacht** VT *insep (old: = vermachen)* to make over (*+dat* to)

Über|macht F, *no pl* superior strength *or* might; *(fig: von Gefühlen, Ideologie etc)* predominance; **in der ~ sein** to have the greater strength

über|mäch|tig ADJ *Gewalt, Stärke* superior; *Feind, Opposition* powerful, strong; *Wunsch, Bedürfnis* overpowering; *(fig) Institution, Rauschgift* all-powerful

über+ma|len [ˈy:bɐma:lən] VT *sep* to paint over

über|ma|len [y:bɐˈma:lən] *ptp* **übermalt** VT *insep* to paint over, to paint on top of

über|man|nen [y:bɐˈmanən] *ptp* **übermannt** VT *insep (geh)* to overcome

Über|maß NT, *no pl* excess, excessive amount (*an +acc* of); **im ~** to *or* in excess; **er hat Zeit im ~** he has more than enough time

über|mä|ßig ADJ **a** excessive; *Schmerz, Sehnsucht* violent; *Freude* intense; **das war nicht ~** that was not too brilliant **b** *(Mus)* **~es Intervall** augmented interval ADV excessively; *essen, trinken auch* to excess; **sich ~ anstrengen** to overdo things; **er hat sich nicht ~ bemüht** he didn't exactly overexert himself

Über|mensch M **a** *(Philos)* superman **b** *(fig inf)* superman; superwoman; **ich bin doch kein ~** I'm not superman/superwoman

über|mensch|lich ADJ superhuman; **Übermenschliches leisten** to perform superhuman feats

über|mit|teln [y:bɐˈmɪtln] *ptp* **übermittelt** VT *insep* to convey (*jdm* to sb); *(telefonisch etc) Meldung* to transmit, to send; *Daten* to transmit

Über|mitt|lung [y:bɐˈmɪtlʊŋ] F **-, -en** conveyance; *(telefonisch etc, von Meldung)* transmission, sending

über|mor|gen ADV the day after tomorrow; **~ Abend/früh** the day after tomorrow in the evening/morning

über|mü|den [y:bɐˈmy:dn] *ptp* **übermüdet** VT *insep usu ptp* to overtire; *(= erschöpfen auch)* to overfatigue

Über|mü|dung F **-,** *no pl* overtiredness; *(= Erschöpfung auch)* overfatigue

Über|mü|dungs|er|schei|nung F sign of overtiredness *or (Erschöpfung auch)* fatigue

Über|mut M high spirits *pl*; **vor lauter ~ wussten die Kinder nicht, was sie tun sollten** the children were so full of high spirits that they didn't know what to do with themselves; **~ tut selten gut** *(Prov)* pride goes before a fall *(Prov)*; *(zu Kindern)* it'll all end in tears

über|mü|tig [ˈy:bɐmy:tɪç] ADJ **a** *(= ausgelassen)* high-spirited, boisterous **b** *(= zu mutig)* cocky *(inf)*; **werd bloß nicht ~!** don't be cocky *(inf)* **c** *(dated: = überheblich)* arrogant ADV *(= ausgelassen)* boisterously

Über|mut|ter F *pl* **-mütter** mother figure

übern [ˈy:bɐn] *contr von* **über den**

über|nächs|te(r, s) ADJ *attr* next ... but one; **das ~ Haus** the next house but one; **die ~ Woche** the week after next; **am ~n Tag war er ...** two days later he was ..., the next day but one he was ...; **er kommt ~n Freitag** he's coming a week on Friday *or* (on) Friday week

über|nach|ten [y:bɐˈnaxtn] *ptp* **übernachtet** VI *insep* to sleep; *(in Hotel, Privathaus etc auch)* to stay; *(eine Nacht)* to spend *or* stay the night; **bei jdm ~** to stay with sb, to sleep *or* stay at sb's place; **wie viele Leute können bei dir ~?** how many people can you put up?

über|näch|tigt [y:bɐˈnɛçtɪçt], *(esp Aus)* **über|näch|tig** [ˈy:bɐnɛçtɪç] ADJ bleary-eyed

Über|nach|tung [y:bɐˈnaxtʊŋ] F **-, -en** overnight stay; **~ und Frühstück** bed and breakfast

Über|nach|tungs|mög|lich|keit F overnight accommodation *no pl*; **sich nach einer ~ umsehen** to look for somewhere to stay the night

Über|nah|me [ˈy:bɐna:mə] F **-, -n** **a** takeover *(auch Comm, Fin)*; *(= das Übernehmen)* taking over; *(von Ausdruck, Ansicht)* adoption; *(von Zitat, Wort)* borrowing; **seit der ~ des Geschäfts durch den Sohn** since the son took over the business; **freundliche/feindliche ~** *(Comm)* friendly/hostile takeover **b** *(von Amt)* assumption; *(von Verantwortung)* assumption, acceptance; **durch ~ dieser Aufgabe** by taking on *or* undertaking this task; **er hat sich zur ~ der Kosten/Hypothek verpflichtet** he has undertaken to pay the costs/mortgage; **bei ~ einer neuen Klasse** *(Sch)* when taking charge of a new class; **er konnte Rechtsanwalt Mayer zur ~ seines Falles bewegen** he persuaded Mr Mayer, the barrister, to take (on) his case

Über|nah|me-: Über|nah|me|an|ge|bot NT, **Über|nah|me|of|fer|te** F takeover bid; **Über|nah|me|ver|trag** M takeover agreement

Über|nahms|stel|le F *(Aus)* = **Annahmestelle**

über|na|ti|o|nal ADJ supranational ADV supranationally

über|na|tür|lich ADJ supernatural

über|neh|men [y:bɐˈne:mən] ✪ 47.3 *ptp* **übernommen** [y:bɐˈnɔmən] *insep irreg* VT **a** *(= annehmen)* to take; *Aufgabe, Arbeit* to take on, to undertake; *Funktion* to take on; *Verantwortung* to take on, to assume, to accept; *Kosten, Hypothek* to agree to pay; *(Jur) Fall* to take (on); *jds Verteidigung* to take on; *(= kaufen)* to buy; **den Befehl** *or* **das Kommando ~** to take command *or* charge; **die Führung ~** *(von Organisation etc)* to take charge *(gen* of); *(Sport)* to take over the lead; **seit er das Amt übernommen hat** since he assumed office; **er übernimmt Ostern eine neue Klasse** *(Sch)* he's taking charge of a new class at Easter; **lassen Sie mal, das übernehme ich!** let me take care of that; **es ~, etw zu tun** to take on the job of doing sth, to undertake to do sth

b *(stellvertretend, ablösend)* to take over *(von* from); *Ausdruck, Ansicht* to adopt; *Zitat, Wort* to take, to borrow; *(Comput) Einstellungen* to apply

c *Geschäft, Praxis etc* to take over

d *(Aus inf: = übertölpeln)* to put one over on *(inf)*

VR to take on *or* undertake too much; *(= sich überanstrengen)* to overdo it; *(beim Essen)* to overeat; **~ Sie sich nur nicht!** *(iro)* don't strain yourself! *(iro)*

über+neh|men [ˈy:bɐne:mən] VT *sep irreg Cape etc* to put on; **das Gewehr ~** *(Mil)* to slope arms

über|ner|vös ADJ highly strung

über+ord|nen VT *sep* **a** **jdn jdm ~** to put *or* place *or* set sb over sb → *auch* **übergeordnet** **b** **etw einer Sache** *(dat)* **~** to give sth precedence over sth; **einer Sache** *(dat)* **übergeordnet sein** to have precedence over sth, to be superordinate to sth

über|par|tei|lich ADJ nonparty *attr*; *(= unvoreingenommen)* nonpartisan; *(Parl) Problem* all-party *attr*, cross-bench *attr (Brit)*; *Amt, Präsident etc* above party politics ADV *handeln, denken* in a nonpartisan way; **ein ~ inszenierter Wahlkampf** a nonpartisan election campaign; **eine ~ organisierte Veranstaltung** a nonparty event; **ein ~ zusammengesetztes Komitee** a nonpartisan committee

Über|par|tei|lich|keit F **die ~ des Ausschusses ist gewährleistet** the committee must be nonpartisan

über+pin|seln [ˈy:bɐpɪnzln] VT *sep (inf) Wand* to paint over

über|pin|seln [y:bɐˈpɪnzln] *ptp* **überpinselt** VT *insep Fleck* to paint over

Über|preis M exorbitant price; **zu ~en** at exorbitant prices

Über|pro|duk|ti|on F overproduction

über|prüf|bar ADJ checkable

Über|prüf|bar|keit [y:bɐˈpry:fba:ɐkait] F **-,** *no pl* means *sing* of checking; **aufgrund der mangelnder ~** because there is no means of checking

über|prü|fen [y:bɐˈpry:fn] *ptp* **überprüft** VT *insep (auf +acc* for) to check; *Gepäck auch, Maschine, Waren* to inspect, to examine; *(Fin) Bücher* to inspect, to examine; *Entscheidung, Lage, Frage* to examine, to review; *Ergebnisse, Teilnehmer etc* to scrutinize; *(Pol) jdn* to screen; **etw erneut ~** to recheck sth; to re-examine sth; to scrutinize sth again; **die Richtigkeit von etw ~** to check (the correctness of) sth

Über|prü|fung F **a** *no pl (= das Überprüfen)* checking; *(von Maschinen, Waren, Fin: von Büchern)* inspection, examination; *(von Entscheidung)* review; *(Pol)* screening; **nach ~ der Lage** after reviewing the situation, after a review of the situation **b** *(= Kontrolle)* check, inspection

Über|prü|fungs|ver|fah|ren NT **a** *(Pol)* vetting process **b** *(Tech)* inspection process

über|qua|li|fi|ziert ADJ overqualified

über+quel|len VI *sep irreg aux sein* to overflow *(von, mit* with); *(Cook) (Teig)* to rise over the edge; *(Reis, Brei)* to boil over; **die Augen quollen ihm über** his eyes grew as big as saucers; **vor Freude/Dankbarkeit ~** to be overflowing with joy/gratitude

über|que|ren [y:bɐˈkve:rən] *ptp* **überquert** VT *insep* to cross

Über|que|rung F **-, -en** crossing

über|ra|gen [y:bɐˈra:gn] *ptp* **überragt** VT *insep* **a** *(lit: = größer sein)* to tower above **b** *(fig: = übertreffen)* to outshine *(an +dat, in +dat* in)

über+ra|gen [ˈy:bɐra:gn] VI *sep (= hervorstehen) (senkrecht)* to protrude; *(waagerecht)* to jut out, to project

über|ra|gend ADJ *(fig)* outstanding; *Bedeutung auch* paramount ADV outstandingly well

über|ra|schen [y:bɐˈraʃn] ✪ 42.2 *ptp* **überrascht** VT *insep* to surprise; **jdn ~** *(= überrumpeln)* to surprise sb, to catch *or* take sb unawares, to take sb by surprise; **einen Einbrecher ~** to surprise *or* disturb a burglar; **jdn bei etw ~** to surprise *or* catch sb doing sth; **von einem Gewitter überrascht werden** to be caught in a storm; **lassen wir uns ~!** let's wait and see! → *auch* **überrascht**

über|ra|schend ADJ surprising; *Besuch* surprise *attr*; *Tod, Weggang* unexpected; **eine ~e Wendung nehmen** to take an unexpected turn ADV unexpectedly; **das kam (für uns) völlig ~** that came as a complete surprise *or (Sterbefall etc)* shock (to us)

über|ra|schen|der|wei|se [y:bɐˈraʃndɐˈvaizə] ADV surprisingly

über|rascht [y:bɐˈraʃt] ADJ surprised *(über +dat* at); **da bin ich aber ~!** that's quite a surprise ADV with surprise; **jdn ~ ansehen** to look at sb in surprise; **sich von etw (nicht) ~ zeigen** to show (no) surprise at sth → *auch* **überraschen**

Über|ra|schung [y:bɐˈraʃʊŋ] F **-, -en** surprise; **zu meiner (größten) ~** to my (great) surprise, much to my surprise; **Mensch, ist das eine ~!** *(inf)* well, that's a surprise (and a half *(inf)*)!; **jdm eine kleine ~ kaufen** to buy a little something for sb as a surprise; **für eine ~ sorgen** to have a surprise in store; **sie ist immer für eine ~ gut** she never ceases to amaze *or* surprise; **mit ~ musste ich sehen** *or* **feststellen, dass ...** I was surprised to see that ...

Über|ra|schungs-: Über|ra|schungs|an|griff M surprise attack; **Über|ra|schungs|ef|fekt** M shock effect; **Über|ra|schungs|er|folg** M unexpected success; **Über|ra|schungs|gast** M surprise guest *(auch TV)*; **Über|ra|schungs|hit** M surprise hit; **Über|ra|schungs|mo|ment** NT moment of surprise; **Über|ra|schungs|sie|ger(in)** M(F) *(Sport)* surprise winner

über|re|a|gie|ren *ptp* **überreagiert** VI *insep* to overreact

Über|re|ak|ti|on F overreaction

über|re|den [y:bɐˈre:dn] *ptp* **überredet** VT *insep* to persuade, to talk round *(Brit) or* around *(US)*; **jdn ~, etw zu tun** to persuade sb to do sth, to talk sb into doing sth; **jdn zu etw ~** to talk sb into sth; **ich habe mich zum Kauf ~ lassen** I let myself be talked *or* persuaded into buying it/them; **lass dich nicht ~** don't (let yourself) be talked into anything

Über|re|dung F **-,** *(rare)* **-en** persuasion

Über|re|dungs|kunst F persuasiveness; **all ihre Überredungskünste** all her powers of persuasion

über|re|gi|o|nal ADJ *(= national)* national, nationwide ADV nationally

über|reich ADJ lavish, abundant; *(= zu reich)* overabundant; **~ an etw** *(dat)* overflowing with sth ADV lavishly; *testamentarisch bedenken* generously; **jdn ~ beschenken** to lavish presents on sb

über|rei|chen [y:bɐ'raiçn] *ptp* **überreicht** VT *insep* **(jdm) etw ~** to hand sth over (to sb); *(feierlich)* to present sth (to sb)

über|reich|lich ADJ ample, abundant; *(= zu reichlich)* overabundant; **in ~em Maße** in abundance ADV *Gebrauch machen* excessively; **~ essen/trinken** to eat/drink more than enough; **eine ~ bemessene Dosierung** an extremely high dose; **~ angebotene Informationen** an overabundance of information

Über|rei|chung F -, -en presentation

über|reif ADJ overripe; **die Zeit ist ~ für ...** it is high time for ...

Über|rei|fe F overripeness

über|rei|zen [y:bɐ'raitsn] *ptp* **überreizt** *insep* VT to overtax; *Fantasie* to overexcite; *Nerven, Augen* to overstrain VTR *(Cards)* to overbid

über|reizt [y:bɐ'raitst] ADJ overtaxed; *Augen* overstrained; *(nervlich)* overwrought; *(= zu erregt)* overexcited

Über|rei|zung F, *no pl* overtaxing; *(von Fantasie)* overexcitement, overstimulation; *(von Nerven, Augen)* overstraining

über|ren|nen [y:bɐ'rɛnən] *ptp* **überrannt** [y:bɐ'rant] VT *insep irreg* to run down; *(Mil)* to overrun; *(fig)* to overwhelm

über|re|prä|sen|tiert ADJ overrepresented

Über|rest M remains *pl*; *(= letzte Spur: von Ruhm, Selbstachtung etc auch)* remnant, vestige; **ein Häufchen Asche war der klägliche ~** the only remains were a sorry heap of ashes

über|rie|seln [y:bɐ'ri:zln] *ptp* **überrieselt** VT *insep Wiese* to water, to spray; **ein Schauer überrieselte ihn** a shiver ran down his spine; **es überrieselt mich kalt, wenn ...** it makes my blood run cold when ..., it sends a shiver down my spine when ...

Über|rock M *(dated: = Mantel)* greatcoat, overcoat; *(old: = Gehrock)* frock coat

Über|roll|bü|gel M *(Aut)* rollbar

über|rol|len [y:bɐ'rɔlən] *ptp* **überrollt** VT *insep* to run down; *(Mil, fig)* to overrun; **wir dürfen uns von ihnen nicht ~ lassen** we mustn't let them steamroller us

über|rum|peln [y:bɐ'rʊmpln] *ptp* **überrumpelt** VT *insep (inf)* to take by surprise, to take *or* catch unawares; *(= überwältigen)* to overpower; **jdn mit einer Frage ~** to throw sb with a question

Über|rum|pe|lung [y:bɐ'rʊmpəlʊŋ] F -, -en surprise attack; *(= Überwältigung)* overpowering; **durch ~** with a surprise attack

Über|rum|pe|lungs|tak|tik F surprise tactics *pl*

Über|rump|lung [y:bɐ'rʊmplʊŋ] F -, -en = **Überrumpelung**

über|run|den [y:bɐ'rʊndn] *ptp* **überrundet** VT *insep (Sport)* to lap; *(fig)* to outstrip

übers ['y:bɐs] **a** *contr von* **über das b** *(old)* **~ Jahr** in a year

über|sä|en [y:bɐ'zɛ:ən] *ptp* **übersät** VT *insep* to strew; *(mit Abfall etc auch)* to litter; **übersät** strewn; *(mit Abfall etc auch)* littered; *(mit Sternen) Himmel* studded; *(mit Narben etc)* covered; **ein mit Fehlern übersäter Aufsatz** an essay strewn *or* littered with mistakes

über|satt ADJ more than full *or* replete *(von* with)

über|sät|ti|gen [y:bɐ'zɛtɪgn] *ptp* **übersättigt** VT *insep* to satiate; *Markt* to glut, to oversaturate; *(Chem)* to supersaturate; **übersättigt sein** *(Menschen)* to be sated with luxuries; **das reizt ihn nicht mehr, er ist schon übersättigt** that doesn't hold any attraction for him any more, he has had a surfeit

Über|sät|ti|gung F satiety; *(des Marktes)* glut, oversaturation; *(Chem)* supersaturation

Über|säu|e|rung F -, -en *(Med, von Magen, Blut)* excessive acidity; *(von Gewässer, Boden)* overacidification

Über|schall- *in cpds* supersonic; **Über|schall|flug|zeug** NT supersonic aircraft, SST *(esp US)*; **Über|schall|ge|schwin|dig|keit** F supersonic speed; **mit ~ fliegen** to fly supersonic; **Über|schall|knall** M sonic boom

über|schat|ten [y:bɐ'ʃatn] *ptp* **überschattet** VT *insep (lit, fig)* to overshadow; *(fig: = trüben)* to cast a shadow *or* cloud over

über|schät|zen [y:bɐ'ʃɛtsn] *ptp* **überschätzt** VT *insep* to overrate, to overestimate; *Entfernung, Zahl etc* to overestimate VR **sich (selbst) ~** to overestimate oneself

Über|schät|zung F overestimation

Über|schau F *(geh)* overview *(über +acc* of)

über|schau|bar ADJ *Plan, Gesetzgebung etc* easily understandable; *Grenzen, Größenordnung, Kundenkreis* manageable; *Zeitraum* reasonable; **damit die Abteilung ~ bleibt** so that one can keep a general overview of *or* keep track of *(inf)* the department; **die Folgen sind noch nicht ~** the consequences cannot yet be clearly seen

Über|schau|bar|keit [y:bɐ'ʃauba:ɐkait] F -, *no pl* comprehensibility; **zum Zwecke der besseren ~** to give (you) a better idea

über|schau|en [y:bɐ'ʃauən] *ptp* **überschaut** VT *insep* = **überblicken**

über+schäu|men VI *sep aux sein* to froth *or* foam over; *(fig)* to brim *or* bubble (over) *(vor +dat* with); *(vor Wut)* to seethe; **~de Begeisterung** *etc* exuberant *or* effervescent *or* bubbling enthusiasm *etc*

Über|schicht F *(Ind)* extra shift

über|schläch|tig [-ʃlɛçtɪç] ADJ *Wasserrad* overshot

über|schla|fen [y:bɐ'ʃlafn] *ptp* **überschlafen** VT *insep irreg Problem etc* to sleep on

Über|schlag M **a** *(= Berechnung)* (rough) estimate **b** *(= Drehung)* somersault *(auch Sport)*; *(Aviat: = Looping)* loop; **einen ~ machen** to turn *or* do a somersault; *(Aviat)* to loop the loop

über|schla|gen [y:bɐ'ʃla:gn] *ptp* **überschlagen** *insep irreg* VT **a** *(= auslassen)* to skip, to miss **b** *(= berechnen) Kosten etc* to estimate (roughly) VR **a** *(Mensch)* to somersault; *(Auto)* to turn over; *(fig: Ereignisse)* to come thick and fast; *(= sich gegenseitig übertreffen)* **sich vor Hilfsbereitschaft** *(dat)***/mit Vorschlägen ~** to fall over oneself to be helpful/to make suggestions; **nun überschlag dich mal nicht!** don't get carried away **b** *(Stimme)* to crack

über+schla|gen ['y:bɐʃla:gn] *sep irreg* VT *Beine* to cross; *Arme* to fold; *Decke* to fold *or* turn back; **mit übergeschlagenen Beinen/Armen** with one's legs crossed/arms folded VI *aux sein* **a** *(Wellen)* to break **b** *(Stimmung etc)* **in etw** *(acc)* **~** to turn into sth

über|schla|gen [y:bɐ'ʃla:gn] ADJ *Flüssigkeit* lukewarm, tepid; *Zimmer* slightly warm

Über-: **über|schlä|gig** [-ʃlɛ:gɪç] ADJ, ADV = **überschläglich**; **Über|schlag|la|ken** NT top sheet; **über|schläg|lich** [-ʃlɛ:klɪç] ADJ rough, approximate ADV roughly, approximately; **über|schlank** ADJ too thin; **über|schlau** ADJ *(inf)* too clever by half *(Brit)*, clever-clever *(Brit inf)*, smart-aleck *attr (inf)*

über+schnap|pen VI *sep aux sein* **a** *(Riegel etc)* to clip *or* snap on **b** *(Stimme)* to crack, to break; *(inf: Mensch)* to crack up *(inf)* → *auch* **übergeschnappt**

über|schnei|den [y:bɐ'ʃnaidn] *ptp* **überschnitten** [y:bɐ'ʃnɪtn] VR *insep irreg (Linien)* to intersect; *(Flächen, fig: Themen, Interessen, Ereignisse etc)* to overlap; *(völlig)* to coincide; *(unerwünscht)* to clash

Über|schnei|dung F -, -en *(von Linien)* intersection; *(von Flächen, fig)* overlap *no pl*; *(unerwünscht)* clash

über|schnell ADJ overhasty ADV overhastily

über|schrei|ben [y:bɐ'ʃraibn] *ptp* **überschrieben** [y:bɐ'ʃri:bn] VT *insep irreg* **a** *(= betiteln)* to head **b** *(= übertragen)* **etw jdm** *or* **auf jdn ~** to make *(esp Brit) or* sign sth over to sb **c** *(Computer) Daten, Datenträger* to overwrite; *Text* to overtype, to type over

Über|schreib|mo|dus M *(Comput)* overwrite *or* overtype mode

über|schrei|en [y:bɐ'ʃraiən] *ptp* **überschrie(e)n** [y:bɐ'ʃri:(ə)n] VT *insep irreg* to shout down

über|schrei|ten [y:bɐ'ʃraitn] *ptp* **überschritten** [y:bɐ'ʃrɪtn] VT *insep irreg* to cross; *(fig)* to exceed; *Höhepunkt, Alter* to pass; **„Überschreiten der Gleise verboten"** "do not cross the line"; **die Grenze des Erlaubten/des Anstands ~** to go beyond what is permissible/decent

Über|schrei|tung F -, -en crossing *(+gen* of); *(fig)* overstepping; *(Jur: = Verletzung)* violation, contravention *(geh)*; **~ der zulässigen Geschwindigkeit** exceeding *or* breaking the speed limit

Über|schrift F heading; *(= Schlagzeile)* headline

Über|schuh M overshoe, galosh *usu pl*

über|schul|det [y:bɐ'ʃʊldət] ADJ *Person, Unternehmen* heavily in debt; *Grundstück* heavily mortgaged

Über|schul|dung [y:bɐ'ʃʊldʊŋ] F -, -en excessive debts *pl*; *(von Grundstück)* heavy mortgaging

Über|schuss M surplus *(an +dat* of); **seinen ~ an Kraft austoben** to work off one's surplus energy

Über|schuss|be|tei|li|gung F surplus sharing

über|schüs|sig [-ʃʏsɪç] ADJ *Energie, Fett* surplus

Über|schuss-: **Über|schuss|land** NT country producing a surplus; **Über|schuss|pro|duk|ti|on** F surplus production

über|schüt|ten [y:bɐ'ʃʏtn] *ptp* **überschüttet** VT *insep* **a** *(= bedecken)* **jdn/etw mit etw ~** to tip sth onto sb/sth, to cover sb/sth with sth; *mit Flüssigkeit* to pour sth onto sb/sth **b** *(= überhäufen)* **jdn mit etw ~** to shower sb with sth, to heap sth on sb; *mit Lob, Vorwürfen* to heap sth on sb

Über|schwang [-ʃvaŋ] M **-(e)s**, *no pl* exuberance; **im ~ der Freude** in one's joyful exuberance; **im ~ der Gefühle** in exuberance; **im ersten ~** in the first flush of excitement

über|schwäng|lich ['y:bɐʃvɛŋlɪç] ADJ effusive, gushing *(pej)* ADV effusively

Über|schwäng|lich|keit F -, -en effusiveness

über+schwap|pen VI *sep aux sein* to splash over; *(aus Tasse etc auch)* to slop over; *(= sich ausbreiten)* to spill over; **die von Amerika nach Europa ~de Drogenwelle** the drug wave spilling over from America into Europe

über|schwem|men [y:bɐ'ʃvɛmən] *ptp* **überschwemmt** VT *insep (lit, fig)* to flood; *(Touristen) Land etc auch* to overrun, to inundate *usu pass*; *(Angebote, Anträge) Inserenten, Behörde etc auch* to inundate *usu pass*, to deluge *usu pass*, to swamp; *Verbraucher, Leser etc* to swamp

Über|schwem|mung F -, -en *(lit)* flood; *(= das Überschwemmen)* flooding *no pl*; *(fig)* inundation; *(von Verbrauchern, Lesern)* swamping; **es kam zu ~en** there was a lot of flooding, there were a lot of floods

Über|schwem|mungs-: **Über|schwem|mungs|ge|biet** NT *(= überschwemmtes Gebiet)* flood area; *(Geog)* flood plain; **Über|schwem|mungs|ge|fahr** F danger of flooding; **Über|schwem|mungs|ka|ta|stro|phe** F flood disaster

über|schweng|lich △ ['y:bɐʃvɛŋlɪç] ADJ ADV → **überschwänglich**

Über|schweng|lich|keit △ F -, -en → **Überschwänglichkeit**

Über|see *no art* **in/nach ~** overseas; **aus/von ~** from overseas; **Briefe nach ~** overseas letters, letters to overseas destinations; **Besitzungen in ~ haben** to have overseas territories *or* territories overseas

Über|see-: **Über|see|damp|fer** M ocean liner; **Über|see|ha|fen** M international port; **Über|see|han|del** M overseas trade

über|see|isch ['y:bɐze:ɪʃ] ADJ overseas *attr*

Über|see-: **Über|see|ka|bel** NT transoceanic cable; *(im Atlantik)* transatlantic cable; **Über|see|kof|fer** M trunk; **Über|see|ver|kehr** M overseas traffic

über|seh|bar ADJ **a** *(lit) Gegend etc* visible; **das Tal ist von hier schlecht ~** you don't get a good view of the valley from here **b** *(fig) (= erkennbar) Folgen, Zusammenhänge etc* clear; *(= abschätzbar) Kosten, Dauer etc* assessable; **dieses Fachgebiet ist nicht mehr ~** it is no longer possible to have an overall view of this subject; **die Folgen sind klar/schlecht ~** the consequences are quite/not very clear; **der Schaden ist noch gar nicht ~** the damage cannot be assessed yet **c solche Druckfehler sind leicht ~** misprints like that are easily overlooked *or* are easy to overlook *or* miss

über|se|hen [y:bɐˈze:ən] *ptp* **übersehen** VT *insep irreg* **a** *(lit) Gegend etc* to look over, to have a view of
b *(= erkennen, Bescheid wissen über) Folgen, Zusammenhänge, Sachlage* to see clearly; *Fachgebiet* to have an overall view of; *(= abschätzen) Schaden, Kosten, Dauer* to assess; **dieses Fach ist nicht mehr zu ~** it is no longer possible to have an overall view of this subject
c *(= ignorieren, nicht erkennen)* to overlook; *(= nicht bemerken)* to miss, to fail to see *or* notice; **~, dass …** to overlook the fact that …; **dieses Problem ist nicht mehr zu ~** this problem cannot be overlooked any longer; **etw stillschweigend/geflissentlich ~** to quietly/conveniently ignore sth

über+se|hen [ˈy:bɐze:ən] VT *sep irreg* **sich** *(dat)* **etw ~** to get *or* grow tired *or* to tire of seeing sth

über sein VI *irreg aux sein (inf)* **jdm ist etw über** sb is fed up with sth *(inf)*; **mir ist diese Arbeit schon lange über** I've been fed up with this work for a long time *(inf)*

über|sen|den [y:bɐˈzɛndn] *ptp* **übersandt** *or* **übersendet** [y:bɐˈzant, y:bɐˈzɛndət] VT *insep irreg* to send; *Geld auch* to remit *(form)*; **hiermit ~ wir Ihnen …** please find enclosed …

Über|sen|dung F sending; *(von Geld)* remittance *(form)*

über|setz|bar ADJ translatable; **leicht/schwer ~** easy/hard to translate

über|set|zen [y:bɐˈzɛtsn] *ptp* **übersetzt** VT *insep* **a** *auch vi (in andere Sprachen)* to translate; **aus dem** *or* **vom Englischen ins Deutsche ~** to translate from English into German; **ein Buch aus dem Englischen ~** to translate a book from (the) English; **etw falsch ~** to mistranslate sth; **sich leicht/schwer ~ lassen** to be easy/hard to translate; **sich gut/schlecht ~ lassen** to translate well/badly **b** *(Tech) (= umwandeln)* to translate; *(= übertragen)* to transmit

über+set|zen [ˈy:bɐzɛtsn] *sep* VT **a** *(mit Fähre)* to take *or* ferry across **b den Fuß ~** to put one's leg over VI *aux sein* to cross (over)

Über|set|zer(in) M(F) translator

Über|set|zung [y:bɐˈzɛtsʊŋ] F **-, -en a** translation **b** *(Tech) (= Umwandlung)* translation; *(= Übertragung)* transmission; *(= Herabübersetzung, Heraufübersetzung)* change in the gear ratio; *(= Übersetzungsverhältnis)* gear ratio

Über|set|zungs-: **Über|set|zungs|bü|ro** NT translation bureau *or* agency; **Über|set|zungs|feh|ler** M translation error, error in translation; **Über|set|zungs|ver|hält|nis** NT *(Tech)* gear ratio

Über|sicht F **-, -en a** *no pl (= Überblick)* overall view; **die ~ verlieren** to lose track of things *or* of what's going on **b** *(= Abriss, Resümee)* survey; *(= Tabelle)* table

über|sicht|lich ADJ *Gelände etc* open; *(= erfassbar) Darstellung etc* clear; **eine Bibliothek muss ~ sein** a library should be clearly laid out ADV clearly; **~ angelegt** *or* **geplant** clearly laid out; **~ gegliederte Einträge** well-structured entries

Über|sicht|lich|keit F **-,** *no pl (von Gelände etc)* openness; *(= Verständlichkeit: von Darstellung etc)* clarity

Über|sichts|kar|te F general map

Über|sichts|plan M general plan

über+sie|deln [y:bɐˈzi:dln] [ˈy:bɐzi:dln] *sep*, **über|sie|deln** [y:bɐˈzi:dln] [ˈy:bɐzi:dln] *ptp* **übersiedelt** *insep* VI *aux sein* to move (*von* from, *nach, in +acc* to)

Über|sie|de|lung [y:bɐˈzi:dəlʊŋ, ˈy:bɐ-] F **-, -en** *(= das Übersiedeln)* moving; *(= Umzug)* move, removal *(form)*

Über|sied|ler(in) M(F) migrant

Über|sied|lung [y:bɐˈzi:dlʊŋ, ˈy:bɐ-] F = **Übersiedelung**

über|sinn|lich ADJ supersensory; *(= übernatürlich)* supernatural

über|span|nen [y:bɐˈʃpanən] *ptp* **überspannt** VT *insep* **a** *(Brücke, Decke etc)* to span; **etw mit Leinwand/Folie** *etc* **~** to stretch canvas/foil *etc* over sth, to cover sth with canvas/foil *etc* **b** *(= zu stark spannen)* to put too much strain on; *(fig) Forderungen* to push too far → **Bogen c**

über|spannt [y:bɐˈʃpant] ADJ *Ideen, Forderungen* wild, extravagant; *(= exaltiert)* eccentric; *(= hysterisch)* hysterical; *Nerven* overexcited

Über|spannt|heit F **-, -en** *(von Ideen, Forderungen)* wildness, extravagance; *(= Exaltiertheit)* eccentricity; *(= Hysterie)* hysteria

Über|span|nung F *(Elec)* overload

Über|span|nungs|schutz M *(Elec)* overvoltage *or* surge *(US)* protection

über|spie|len [y:bɐˈʃpi:lən] *ptp* **überspielt** VT *insep* **a** *(= verbergen)* to cover (up) **b** *(= übertragen) Aufnahme* to transfer; **eine CD (auf Kassette) ~** to tape a CD **c** *(Sport)* to pass; *(= ausspielen, klar besiegen)* to outplay

über|spit|zen [y:bɐˈʃpɪtsn] *ptp* **überspitzt** VT *insep* to carry too far, to exaggerate; *Argument* to overstate

über|spitzt [y:bɐˈʃpɪtst] ADJ *Formulierungen (= zu spitzfindig)* oversubtle *(Brit)*, overly subtle *(esp US)*, fiddly *(Brit inf)*; *(= übertrieben)* exaggerated; *Argument* overstated ADV *(= übertrieben)* in an exaggerated fashion; **~ argumentieren** to overstate one's argument(s) *or* case

über|spre|chen [y:bɐˈʃprɛçn] *ptp* **übersprochen** [y:bɐˈʃprɔxn] VT *insep irreg* to speak over

über|sprin|gen [y:bɐˈʃprɪŋən] *ptp* **übersprungen** [y:bɐˈʃprʊŋən] VT *insep irreg* **a** *Hindernis, Höhe* to jump, to clear; **die Fünfprozenthürde ~** to clear the five-percent hurdle **b** *(= weiter springen als)* to jump more than; **die 2-Meter-Marke ~** to jump more than 2 metres *(Brit) or* meters *(US)* **c** *(= auslassen) Klasse, Kapitel, Lektion* to miss (out), to skip; *(Comput)* to skip

über+sprin|gen [ˈy:bɐʃprɪŋən] VI *sep irreg aux sein (lit, fig: = sich übertragen)* to jump *(auf +acc* to); *(Begeisterung)* to spread quickly *(auf +acc* to) → **Funke a**

über+spru|deln VI *sep aux sein (lit, fig)* to bubble over (*vor* with); *(beim Kochen)* to boil over; **~d** *(fig)* bubbling, effervescent

über|spü|len [y:bɐˈʃpy:lən] *ptp* **überspült** VT *insep* to flood; *(Wellen auch)* to wash over; **überspült sein** to be awash

über|staat|lich ADJ supranational

über|ste|hen [y:bɐˈʃte:ən] *ptp* **überstanden** VT *insep irreg (= durchstehen)* to come *or* get through; *(= überleben)* to survive; *(= überwinden)* to overcome; *Unwetter* to weather, to ride out; *Krankheit* to get over, to recover from; **etw lebend ~** to survive sth, to come out of sth alive; **das Schlimmste ist jetzt überstanden** the worst is over now; **nach überstandener Gefahr** when the danger was past; **das wäre überstanden!** thank heavens that's over; **er hat es überstanden** *(euph: = er ist gestorben)* he has gone to rest *(euph)*, he has passed away *(euph)*

über+ste|hen [ˈy:bɐʃte:ən] VI *sep irreg aux haben or sein (= hervorstehen)* to jut *or* stick out, to project; **um 10 cm ~** to jut out *etc* 10 cm

über|stei|gen [y:bɐˈʃtaign] *ptp* **überstiegen** [y:bɐˈʃti:gn] VT *insep irreg* **a** *(= klettern über)* to climb over **b** *(= hinausgehen über)* to exceed, to go beyond; *(Philos, Liter: = transzendieren)* to transcend → **Fassungsvermögen**

über|stei|gern [y:bɐˈʃtaigɐn] *ptp* **übersteigert** *insep* VT *Preise, Tempo* to force up; *Forderungen* to push too far VR to get carried away

über|stei|gert [y:bɐˈʃtaigɐt] ADJ excessive; **an einem ~en Selbstbewusstsein leiden** to have an inflated view of oneself

Über|stei|ge|rung F *(von Emotionen)* excess; *(von Forderungen)* pushing too far

über|stel|len [y:bɐˈʃtɛlən] *ptp* **überstellt** VT *insep (Admin)* to hand over

Über|stel|lung F **-, -en** *(Admin)* handing over

über|stem|peln [y:bɐˈʃtɛmpln] *ptp* **überstempelt** VT *insep* to stamp over; **ein überstempeltes Passbild** a passport photograph which has been stamped (over)

über|steu|ern [y:bɐˈʃtɔyɐn] *ptp* **übersteuert** *insep* VI *(Aut)* to oversteer *(Brit)*, to overcorrect VT *(Elec)* to overmodulate

über|stim|men [y:bɐˈʃtɪmən] *ptp* **überstimmt** VT *insep* to outvote; *Antrag* to vote down

über|strah|len [y:bɐˈʃtra:lən] *ptp* **überstrahlt** VT *insep (lit)* to illuminate; *(fig)* to outshine

über|stra|pa|zie|ren *ptp* **überstrapaziert** *insep* VT to wear out; *Ausrede etc* to wear thin; **überstrapaziert** worn out; thin; **jds Geduld ~** to really try sb's patience VR to wear oneself out

über|strei|chen [y:bɐˈʃtraiçn] *ptp* **überstrichen** VT *insep irreg* to paint over; *(mit Lack)* to varnish over

über+strei|fen VT *sep* **sich** *(dat)* **etw ~** to slip sth on

über|strö|men [y:bɐˈʃtrø:mən] *ptp* **überströmt** VT *insep (= überfluten)* to flood; **von Schweiß/Blut überströmt sein** to be streaming *or* running with sweat/blood

über+strö|men [ˈy:bɐʃtrø:mən] VI *sep aux sein* **a** *(lit, fig: = überlaufen)* to overflow; **er sprach mit ~der Freude/Dankbarkeit** he spoke in a voice overflowing with joy/gratitude **b** *(= hinüberströmen)* to spread, to communicate itself *(auf +acc* to)

über+stül|pen VT *sep* **sich** *(dat)* **etw ~** to put sth on; **jdm/einer Sache etw ~** to put sth on sb/sth

Über|stun|de F hour of overtime; **~n** overtime *sing*; **~n/zwei ~n machen** to do *or* work overtime/two hours overtime

Über|stun|den|zu|schlag M overtime allowance; **der ~ beträgt 50%** overtime is paid at time and a half

über|stür|zen [y:bɐˈʃtʏrtsn] *ptp* **überstürzt** *insep* VT to rush into; *Entscheidung auch* to rush; **man soll nichts ~, nur nichts ~!** look before you leap *(Prov)* VR *(Ereignisse etc)* to happen in a rush; *(Nachrichten)* to come fast and furious; *(Worte)* to come tumbling out; **sich beim Sprechen ~** to speak all in a rush

über|stürzt [y:bɐˈʃtʏrtst] ADJ overhasty, precipitate ADV precipitately, rashly

Über|stür|zung [y:bɐˈʃtʏrtsʊŋ] F **-,** *no pl (= das Überstürzen)* rushing (+*gen* into); *(= Hast)* rush

über|süß ADJ too sweet, oversweet; *Kuchen etc auch* sickly

über|ta|rif|lich ADJ ADV above the agreed *or* union rate

über|teu|ern [y:bɐˈtɔyɐn] *ptp* **überteuert** VT *insep Waren* to overcharge for; *Preis* to inflate, to force up

über|teu|ert [y:bɐˈtɔyɐt] ADJ overexpensive; *Preise, Mieten* inflated, excessive

Über|teu|e|rung F **a** *(= das Überteuern)* overcharging (+*gen* for); *(von Preisen)* forcing up, (over)inflation **b** *(= Überteuertsein)* expensiveness; excessiveness

über|tip|pen [y:bɐˈtɪpn] *ptp* **übertippt** VT *insep* to type over

Über|ti|tel M *(bei Opernaufführung)* surtitle

über|töl|peln [y:bɐˈtœlpln] *ptp* **übertölpelt** VT *insep* to take in, to dupe

Über|töl|pe|lung [y:bɐˈtœlpəlʊŋ] F -, -en taking-in

über|tö|nen [y:bɐˈtø:nən] *ptp* **übertönt** VT *insep* to drown

Über|topf M cachepot

Über|trag [ˈy:bɐtra:k] M -(e)s, ⸚e [-trɛ:gə] amount carried forward *(esp Brit)* or over *(esp US)*

über|trag|bar ADJ transferable *(auch Jur, Comput)*; *Methode, Maßstab* applicable *(auf +acc* to); *Ausdruck* translatable *(in +acc* into); *Krankheit* communicable *(form)* *(auf +acc* to), infectious; *(durch Berührung)* contagious

Über|trag|bar|keit [y:bɐˈtra:kba:ɐkait] F -, *no pl* transferability *(auch Jur, Comput)*; *(von Krankheit)* infectiousness; *(durch Berührung)* contagiousness

über|tra|gen [y:bɐˈtra:gn] *ptp* **übertragen** *insep irreg* VT **a** *(= an eine andere Stelle bringen, an jdn übergeben)* to transfer *(auch Jur, Psych, Comput)*; *Krankheit* to pass on *(auf +acc* to), to transmit *(auf +acc* to); *(Tech) Bewegung, Kraft* to transmit

b *(= an eine andere Stelle schreiben)* to transfer; *(= kopieren)* to copy (out); *(= transkribieren)* to transcribe

c *(TV, Rad)* to broadcast, to transmit; **etw im Fernsehen ~** to televise sth, to broadcast sth on television; **via** *or* **durch Satelliten ~ werden** to be broadcast *or* sent by satellite

d *(= übersetzen) Text* to render *(in +acc* into); **einen Roman aus dem Englischen ins Deutsche ~** to render *or* translate an English novel into German; **... aus dem Englischen ~ von ...** ... translated from the English by ...

e *(= anwenden) Methode, Maßstab* to apply *(auf +acc* to)

f etw auf Band ~ to tape sth, to record sth (on tape); **eine CD auf Kassette ~** to tape a CD

g *(= verleihen) Auszeichnung, Würde* to confer *(jdm* on sb); *Vollmacht, Verantwortung, Amt* to give *(jdm* sb)

h *(= auftragen) Aufgabe, Mission* to assign *(jdm* to sb)

VR *(Eigenschaft, Krankheit etc)* to be passed on *or* communicated *or* transmitted *(auf +acc* to); *(Tech)* to be transmitted *(auf +acc* to); *(Heiterkeit etc)* to communicate itself, to spread *(auf +acc* to); **seine Fröhlichkeit hat sich auf uns ~** we were infected by his happiness

über|tra|gen [y:bɐˈtra:gn] ADJ **a** *(Bedeutung etc)* figurative **b** *(Aus)* worn; *(= gebraucht)* second-hand, used ADV *(= figurativ)* figuratively

Über|trä|ger(in) M(F) *(Med)* carrier

Über|tra|gung F -, -en **a** *(= Transport)* transference, transfer *(auch Comput)*; *(von Krankheit)* passing on, transmission, communication **b** *(schriftlich)* transference; *(= das Kopieren)* copying (out); *(= Transkription)* transcription **c** *(TV, Rad) (= Vorgang)* broadcasting, transmission; *(= Sendung)* broadcast, transmission **d** *(= Übersetzung)* rendering, translation **e** *(= Anwendung)* application **f „Übertragung auf andere Tonträger verboten"** "recording forbidden in any form" **g** *(von Auszeichnung, Würde)* conferral; *(von Vollmacht, Verantwortung)* giving **h** *(von Aufgabe, Mission)* assignment

Über|tra|gungs-: **Über|tra|gungs|feh|ler** M *(Comput)* transmission error; **Über|tra|gungs|ge|schwin|dig|keit** F *(Comput)* transmission speed, transfer rate; **Über|tra|gungs|ra|te** F *(Comput)* transmission *or* transfer rate; **Über|tra|gungs|rech|te** PL *(TV)* broadcasting rights *pl*; **Über|tra|gungs|wa|gen** M outside broadcast unit; **Über|tra|gungs|weg** M *(Comput)* transmission path; **Über|tra|gungs|zeit** F *(Comput)* transfer time

über|trai|niert ADJ overtrained

über|tref|fen [y:bɐˈtrɛfn] *ptp* **übertroffen** [y:bɐˈtrɔfn] *insep irreg* VT to surpass *(an +dat* in); *(= mehr leisten als auch)* to do better than, to outdo, to outstrip; *(= übersteigen auch)* to exceed; *Rekord* to break; **jdn an Intelligenz/Schönheit** *etc* **~** to be more intelligent/beautiful *etc* than sb; **jdn um vieles** *or* **bei Weitem ~** to surpass sb by far; *(bei Leistung auch)* to do far better than sb, to outstrip sb by a long way; **alle Erwartungen ~** to exceed *or* surpass all expectations; **er ist nicht zu ~** he is unsurpassable VR **sich selbst ~** to surpass *or* excel oneself

über|trei|ben [y:bɐˈtraibn] *ptp* **übertrieben** [y:bɐˈtri:bn] VT *insep irreg* **a** *auch vi (= aufbauschen)* to exaggerate; **ohne zu ~** without exaggerating, without any exaggeration **b** *(= zu weit treiben)* to overdo, to take too far *or* to extremes; **es mit der Sauberkeit ~** to take cleanliness too far; **man kann es auch ~** you can overdo things, you can go too far → *auch* **übertrieben**

Über|trei|bung F -, -en **a** exaggeration; **man kann ohne ~ sagen ...** it's no exaggeration to say ... **b ihre ~ der Sparsamkeit/Sauberkeit** the way she carries economy/cleanliness too far *or* to extremes; **etw ohne ~ tun** to do sth without overdoing it *or* carrying it too far *or* to extremes

über+tre|ten [ˈy:bɐtre:tn] VI *sep irreg aux sein* **a** *(Fluss)* to break its banks, to flood **b** *(zu anderer Partei etc)* to go over *(zu* to); *(in andere Schule)* to move *(in +acc* to); **zum christlichen Glauben ~** to convert to Christianity **c** *(im Sport)* to overstep

über|tre|ten [y:bɐˈtre:tn] *ptp* **übertreten** VT *insep irreg Grenze etc* to cross; *(fig) Gesetz, Verbot* to break, to infringe, to violate

Über|tre|tung [y:bɐˈtre:tʊŋ] F -, -en *(von Gesetz etc)* violation, infringement; *(Jur. = strafbare Handlung)* misdemeanour *(Brit)*, misdemeanor *(US)*

über|trie|ben [y:bɐˈtri:bn] ADJ exaggerated; *(= zu stark, übermäßig) Vorsicht, Training* excessive ADV *(= übermäßig)* excessively → *auch* **übertreiben**

Über|tritt M *(über Grenze)* crossing *(über +acc* of); *(zu anderem Glauben)* conversion; *(von Abtrünnigen, esp zu anderer Partei)* defection; *(in andere Schule)* move *(in +acc* to); **die Zahl der ~e zur demokratischen Partei** the number of people going over to the democratic party

Über|tritts|zeug|nis NT *(für andere Schule)* transfer report, *report with the average mark required to enter a school of a higher academic standard*

über|trock|nen [y:bɐˈtrɔknən] *ptp* **übertrocknet** VI *insep aux sein (Aus)* to dry

über|trump|fen [y:bɐˈtrʊmpfn] *ptp* **übertrumpft** VT *insep (Cards)* to overtrump; *(fig)* to outdo

über+tun [ˈy:bɐtu:n] VT *sep irreg* **sich** *(dat)* **einen Mantel** *etc* **~** *(inf)* to put a coat *etc* on; **jdm einen Schal** *etc* **~** to put a scarf *etc* on sb

über|tun [y:bɐˈtu:n] *ptp* **übertan** [y:bɐˈta:n] VR *insep irreg (dial)* to overdo it *(inf)*

über|tün|chen [y:bɐˈtʏnçn] *ptp* **übertüncht** VT *insep* to whitewash; *(mit Farbton)* to distemper; *(fig)* to cover up

über+tün|chen [ˈy:bɐtʏnçn] VT *sep* to whitewash (over); *(mit Farbton)* to distemper (over)

über|über|mor|gen ADV *(inf)* in three days, the day after the day after tomorrow

Über|va|ter M father figure

über|ver|si|chern *ptp* **überversichert** VT *insep* to overinsure

Über|ver|si|che|rung F overinsurance

Über|ver|sor|gung F oversupply *(mit* of)

über|völ|kern [y:bɐˈfœlkɐn] *ptp* **übervölkert** VT *insep* to overpopulate

Über|völ|ke|rung F -, -en overpopulation

über|voll ADJ overfull *(von* with), too full; *(von Menschen, Sachen auch)* crammed *(von* with); *Glas* full to the brim *or* to overflowing

über|vor|sich|tig ADJ overcautious

über|vor|tei|len [y:bɐˈfɔrtailən] *ptp* **übervorteilt** VT *insep* to cheat, to do down *(inf)*

Über|vor|tei|lung F cheating

über|wach ADJ (too) wide-awake; *(fig)* alert

über|wa|chen [y:bɐˈvaxn] *ptp* **überwacht** VT *insep (= kontrollieren)* to supervise; *(= beobachten)* to keep a watch on, to observe; *Verdächtigen* to keep under surveillance, to keep a watch on, to watch; *(auf Monitor, mit Radar, fig)* to monitor

Über|wa|chung F -, -en supervision; *(= Beobachtung)* observation; *(von Verdächtigen)* surveillance; *(auf Monitor, mit Radar, fig)* monitoring

Über|wa|chungs|ka|me|ra F surveillance camera

Über|wa|chungs|staat F Big Brother state

über|wäl|ti|gen [y:bɐˈvɛltɪgn] *ptp* **überwältigt** VT *insep* **a** *(lit)* to overpower; *(zahlenmäßig)* to overwhelm; *(= bezwingen)* to overcome **b** *(fig) (Schlaf, Mitleid, Angst etc)* to overcome; *(Musik, Schönheit etc)* to overwhelm

über|wäl|ti|gend ADJ *Mehrheit, Sieg* overwhelming; *Gestank, Gefühl auch* overpowering; *Schönheit* stunning; *Erfolg* phenomenal, spectacular; **nicht gerade ~** nothing to write home about *(inf)*

Über|wäl|ti|gung F -, -en overpowering; *(= Bezwingung)* overcoming

über|wäl|zen [y:bɐˈvɛltsn] *ptp* **überwälzt** VT *insep (esp Aus)* = **abwälzen**

über+wech|seln VI *sep aux sein* to move *(in +acc* to); *(zu Partei etc)* to go over *(zu* to); *(Wild)* to cross over

Über|weg M **~ für Fußgänger** pedestrian crossing

über|wei|sen [y:bɐˈvaizn] ✪ 47.5 *ptp* **überwiesen** VT [y:bɐˈvi:zn] *insep irreg Geld* to transfer *(an +acc, auf +acc* to); *(= weiterleiten) Vorschlag etc, Patienten* to refer *(an +acc* to); **mein Gehalt wird direkt auf mein Bankkonto überwiesen** my salary is paid directly into my bank account

Über|wei|sung F *(= Geldüberweisung)* (credit) transfer, remittance; *(von Patient)* referral

Über|wei|sungs-: **Über|wei|sungs|auf|trag** M (credit) transfer order; **Über|wei|sungs|for|mu|lar** NT (credit) transfer form; **Über|wei|sungs|schein** M *(von Arzt)* letter of referral; *(für Bank)* (credit) transfer form

über|weit ADJ loose-fitting, too big

Über|wei|te F large size; **Kleider in ~(n)** outsize *(esp Brit)* or oversize *(esp US)* dresses, dresses in larger sizes

über|wer|fen [y:bɐˈvɛrfn] *ptp* **überworfen** [y:bɐˈvɔrfn] VR *insep irreg (= zerstreiten)* **sich (mit jdm) ~** to fall out (with sb)

über+wer|fen [ˈy:bɐvɛrfn] VT *sep irreg* to put over; *Kleidungsstück* to put on; *(sehr rasch)* to throw on

Über|we|sen NT preterhuman being

über|wie|gen [y:bɐˈvi:gn] *ptp* **überwogen** [y:bɐˈvo:gn] *insep irreg* VT to outweigh VI *(= das Übergewicht haben)* to be predominant, to predominate; *(= das Übergewicht gewinnen)* to prevail

über|wie|gend ADJ predominant; *Mehrheit* vast; **der ~e Teil** *(+gen)* the majority (of); **zum ~en Teil** for the most part ADV predominantly, mainly

über|wind|bar ADJ *Schwierigkeiten, Hindernis* surmountable; **diese Angst ist nur schwer ~** it is hard to overcome this fear

über|win|den [y:bɐˈvɪndn] *ptp* **überwunden** [y:bɐˈvʊndn] *insep irreg* VT to overcome; *Schwierigkeiten, Hindernis auch* to surmount, to get over; *Enttäuschung, Angst, Scheu auch* to get over; *(= hinter sich lassen)* to outgrow; **überwunden** *(Standpunkt, Haltung etc)* of the past; *Angst* conquered; *Krise, Rezession* that has been overcome; **ein bis heute noch nicht überwundenes Vorurteil** a prejudice which is still prevalent today VR to overcome one's inclinations; **sich ~, etw zu tun** to force oneself to do sth; **ich konnte mich nicht dazu ~** I couldn't bring myself to do it

Über|win|dung F, *no pl* overcoming; *(von Schwierigkeiten, Hindernis auch)* surmounting; *(=*

Selbstüberwindung) will power; **das hat mich viel ~ gekostet** that was a real effort of will for me, that took me a lot of will power; **selbst bei der größten ~ könnte ich das nicht tun** I simply couldn't bring myself to do it

über|win|tern [y:bɐ'vɪntɐn] *ptp* **überwintert** VI *insep* to (spend the) winter; *(Pflanzen)* to overwinter; *(inf: = Winterschlaf halten)* to hibernate

Über|win|te|rung F -, -en wintering, spending the winter; *(von Pflanzen)* overwintering; *(inf: = Winterschlaf)* hibernation

über|wöl|ben [y:bɐ'vœlbn] *ptp* **überwölbt** VT *insep* to vault

über|wu|chern [y:bɐ'vu:xɐn] *ptp* **überwuchert** VT *insep* to overgrow, to grow over; *(fig)* to obscure

Über|wurf M *(Kleidungsstück)* wrap; *(Ringen)* shoulder throw; *(Aus: = Bettüberwurf)* bedspread, counterpane

Über|zahl F, *no pl* **in der ~ sein** to be in the majority; *(Feind)* to be superior in number; **die Frauen waren in der ~** the women outnumbered the men, the women were in the majority

über|zah|len [y:bɐ'tsa:lən] *ptp* **überzahlt** VT *insep Waren* to pay too much for; **das Auto ist überzahlt** you/he *etc* paid too much for the car, the car cost too much

über|zäh|lig ADJ *(= überschüssig)* surplus; *(= überflüssig)* superfluous; *(= übrig)* spare

über|zeich|nen [y:bɐ'tsaiçnən] *ptp* **überzeichnet** VT *insep* **a** *(Fin) Aktie, Anleihe* to oversubscribe **b** *(fig: = übertrieben darstellen)* to exaggerate, to overdraw

Über-: **Über|zeit** F *(Sw)* overtime; **Über|zelt** NT fly sheet

über|zeu|gen [y:bɐ'tsɔygn] ✪ 28.1, 33.2, 42.1, 43.1, 53.6 *ptp* **überzeugt** *insep* VT to convince; *(= umstimmen auch)* to persuade; *(Jur)* to satisfy; **er ließ sich nicht ~** he would not be convinced *or* persuaded, there was no convincing *or* persuading him; **ich bin davon überzeugt, dass ...** I am convinced *or* certain that ...; **Sie dürfen überzeugt sein, dass ...** you may rest assured *or* be certain that ...; **er ist sehr von sich überzeugt** he is very sure of himself → *auch* **überzeugt**

VI to be convincing, to carry conviction; **er konnte nicht ~** he wasn't convincing, he was unconvincing

VR **sich (selbst) ~** to convince oneself *(von* of), to satisfy oneself *(von* as to); *(mit eigenen Augen)* to see for oneself; **~ Sie sich selbst!** see for yourself!

über|zeu|gend ADJ convincing ADV convincingly; **~ klingen** to sound convincing; **die deutsche Mannschaft hat ~ gespielt** the German team gave a convincing performance

über|zeugt [y:bɐ'tsɔykt] ADJ *attr Anhänger, Vegetarier etc* dedicated, convinced; *Christ, Moslem* devout, convinced → *auch* **überzeugen**

Über|zeu|gung F **a** *(= das Überzeugen)* convincing **b** *(= das Überzeugtsein)* conviction; *(= Prinzipien)* convictions *pl*, beliefs *pl*; **meiner ~ nach ..., nach meiner ~ ...** I am convinced (that) ..., it is my conviction that ...; **aus ~** out of principle; **ich bin der festen ~, dass ...** I am firmly convinced that ..., I am of the firm conviction that ...; **zu der ~ gelangen** *or* **kommen, dass ..., die ~ gewinnen, dass ...** to become convinced that ..., to arrive at the conviction that ... → **Brustton**

Über|zeu|gungs-: **Über|zeu|gungs|ar|beit** F, *no pl* efforts *pl* at persuasion; **einige/viel ~ leisten** to do some/a lot of convincing *or* persuading; **Über|zeu|gungs|kraft** F persuasiveness, persuasive power; **Über|zeu|gungs|tä|ter(in)** M(F) **~ sein** to commit an offence *(Brit) or* offense *(US)* for political/religious *etc* reasons

über|zie|hen [y:bɐ'tsi:ən] *ptp* **überzogen** [y:bɐ'tso:gn] *insep irreg* VT **a** *(= bedecken)* to cover; *(mit Schicht, Belag)* to coat; *(mit Metall)* to plate; *(mit Zuckerguss)* to ice *(Brit)*, to frost *(US)*; **Polstermöbel neu ~ lassen** to have furniture re-covered; **von Rost überzogen** covered in *or* coated with rust; **mit Gold/Silber überzogen** gold-/silver-plated **b** *Konto* to overdraw; **er hat sein Konto (um 500 Euro) überzogen** he has overdrawn his account (by 500 euros), he is (500 euros) overdrawn **c** *(geh: = heimsuchen, befallen)* **das Land mit Krieg ~** to inflict war on the country; **jdn mit Vorwürfen ~** to heap criticism on sb **d** *Redezeit etc* to overrun **e** *(= übertreiben)* to overdo → *auch* **überzogen**

VI **a** *(Fin)* to overdraw one's account **b** *(Redner, Moderator)* to overrun

VR **a** *(= sich bedecken: Himmel)* to cloud over, to become overcast; **der Himmel ist überzogen** the sky is overcast **b** *(mit Schicht etc)* to become covered *or* coated

über+zie|hen ['y:bɐtsi:ən] VT *sep irreg* **a** *(= anziehen)* **(sich** *dat*) **etw ~** to put sth on **b** *(inf: = schlagen)* **jdm eins ~** to give sb a clout *(Brit inf) or* a smack *(inf)*, to clout *(Brit) or* smack *or* clobber sb *(inf)*

Über|zie|her ['y:bɐtsi:ɐ] M -s, - *(dated)* **a** *(= Mantel)* greatcoat **b** *(inf: = Kondom)* sheath, French letter *(Brit inf)*, rubber *(US inf)*

Über|zie|hungs-: **Über|zie|hungs|kre|dit** [y:bɐ'tsi:ʊŋs-] M overdraft provision; **Über|zie|hungs|zins** [y:bɐ'tsi:ʊŋs-] M overdraft interest rate

über|zo|gen [y:bɐ'tso:gn] ADJ *(= übertrieben)* excessive; **sein Benehmen wirkte ~** his behaviour *(Brit) or* behavior *(US)* seemed over the top *(inf) or* exaggerated → *auch* **überziehen**

über|züch|ten [y:bɐ'tsʏçtn] *ptp* **überzüchtet** VT *insep* to overbreed; *Motor* to overdevelop

über|zu|ckern [y:bɐ'tsʊkɐn] *ptp* **überzuckert** VT *insep* **a** *(= mit Zucker überstreuen)* to (sprinkle with) sugar **b** *(= zu stark zuckern)* to put too much sugar in/on

Über|zug M **a** *(= Beschichtung)* coat(ing); *(aus Metall)* plating; *(für Kuchen, esp aus Zuckerguss)* icing *(Brit)*, frosting *(US)* **b** *(= Bettüberzug, Sesselüberzug etc)* cover

Üb|le(s) ['y:blə] NT *decl as adj* → **übel ADJ b**

üb|lich ['y:plɪç] ADJ usual; *(= herkömmlich)* customary; *(= typisch, normal)* normal; **wie ~** as usual; **es ist bei uns/hier ~** *or* **das Übliche, dass ...** it's usual for us/here to ..., it's the custom with us/here that ...; **das ist bei ihm so ~** that's usual for him; **allgemein ~ sein** to be common practice; **die allgemein ~en Bedingungen/Methoden** the usual conditions/methods

üb|li|cher|wei|se ['y:plɪçɐ'vaizə] ADV usually, generally, normally

Üb|li|che(s) ['y:plɪçə] NT *decl as adj* **das ~** the usual

U-Bo|gen ['u:-] M *loop which some Germans write over "u"*

U-Boot ['u:-] NT submarine, sub *(inf)*; *(esp Hist: der deutschen Marine)* U-boat

U-Boot-: **U-Boot-Aus|schnitt** ['u:-] M *(Fashion)* boat neck; **U-Boot-ge|stützt** ['u:bo:tgəʃtʏtst] ADJ submarine-based; **U-Boot-Krieg** ['u:-] M submarine warfare *no art*

üb|rig ['y:brɪç] ADJ **a** *attr (= verbleibend)* rest of, remaining; *(= andere)* other; **meine/die ~en Sachen** the rest of my/the things; **alle ~en Bücher** all the rest of the books, all the other *or* remaining books; **der ~e Teil des Landes** the rest of *or* remaining part of the country, the remainder of the country **b** *pred* left, left over, over; *(= zu entbehren)* spare; **etw ~ haben** to have sth left/to spare; **haben Sie vielleicht eine Zigarette (für mich) ~?** could you spare (me) a cigarette? → **übrighaben** **c** *(substantivisch)* **das Übrige** the rest, the remainder; **alles Übrige** all the rest, everything else; **die/alle Übrigen** the/all the rest *or* others; **im Übrigen** incidentally, by the way; **ein Übriges tun** *(geh)* to do one more thing

üb|rig-: **üb|rig be|hal|ten** VT *irreg* to have left over; **üb|rig+blei|ben** VI *sep irreg aux sein* = **übrig bleiben b**; **üb|rig blei|ben** ✪ 37.1 VI *irreg aux sein* **a** to be left over, to remain; **wie viel ist übrig geblieben?** how much is left? **b** *(fig)* **da wird ihm gar nichts anderes ~** he won't have any choice *or* any other alternative; **was blieb mir anderes übrig als ...?** what choice did I have but ...?, there was nothing left for me but to ...

üb|ri|gens ['y:brɪgns] ADV incidentally, by the way

üb|rig-: **üb|rig+ha|ben** VT *sep irreg (= mögen)* **für jdn/etw wenig ~** not to have much time for sb/sth; **für jdn/etw nichts ~** to have no time for sb/sth; **für jdn/etw etwas ~** to have a soft spot for *or* to be fond of sb/sth, to have a liking for sb/sth; **für jdn/etw viel ~** to be very fond of sb/sth, to have a great liking for sb/sth → *auch* **übrig b**; **üb|rig+las|sen** VI *sep irreg (fig)* = **übrig lassen b**; **üb|rig las|sen** VT *irreg* **a** to leave *(jdm* for sb) **b** **(einiges)/viel zu wünschen ~** *(inf)* to leave something/a lot to be desired

Übung ['y:bʊŋ] F -, -en **a** *no pl (= das Üben, Geübtsein)* practice; **das macht die ~, das ist alles nur ~** it's a question of practice, it comes with practice; **aus der ~ kommen** to get out of practice; **aus der** *or* **außer ~ sein** to be out of practice; **in ~ bleiben** to keep in practice, to keep one's hand in *(inf)*; **zur ~** for *or* as practice; **(richtig) ~ in etw** *(dat)* **haben/bekommen** to have/get (quite) a bit of practice in sth; **~ macht den Meister** *(Prov)* practice makes perfect *(Prov)* **b** *(Veranstaltung)* practice; *(Mil, Sport, Sch)* exercise; *(= Feueralarmübung)* exercise, drill; *(Univ: = Kurs)* seminar

Übungs-: **Übungs|ar|beit** F *(Sch)* practice *or* mock test; **Übungs|auf|ga|be** F *(Sch)* exercise; **Übungs|buch** NT *(Sch)* book of exercises; **Übungs|flug** M practice flight; **übungs|hal|ber** ADV for practice; **Übungs|heft** NT *(Sch)* exercise book; **Übungs|lei|ter(in)** M(F) *(im Sportverein)* trainer, coach; **Übungs|mu|ni|ti|on** F blank ammunition; **Übungs|platz** M training area *or* ground; *(= Exerzierplatz)* drill ground; **Übungs|raum** M *(für Musiker etc)* practice room; **Übungs|stück** NT *(Sch, Mus)* exercise

u. E. *abbr von* **unseres Erachtens**

UdSSR [u:de:lɛslɛs'lɛr] F - *(Hist) abbr von* **Union der Sozialistischen Sowjetrepubliken** USSR

UEFA-Cup [u:'le:fa:kap] M *(Ftbl)* UEFA cup

U-Ei|sen ['u:-] NT U-iron

Ufer ['u:fɐ] NT -s, - *(= Flussufer)* bank; *(= Seeufer)* shore; *(= Küstenlinie)* shoreline; **direkt am ~ gelegen** right on the water's edge *or* waterfront; **etw ans ~ spülen** to wash sth ashore; **der Fluss trat über die ~** the river broke *or* burst its banks; **das sichere** *or* **rettende ~ erreichen** to reach dry land *or* terra firma; **zu neuen ~n aufbrechen** *(fig)* to try something completely new; **auf zu neuen ~n!** on to pastures new!

Ufer-: **Ufer|be|fes|ti|gung** F bank reinforcement; **Ufer|bö|schung** F embankment; **Ufer|land** NT, **Ufer|land|schaft** F shoreland; **ufer|los** ADJ *(= endlos)* endless; *(= grenzenlos)* boundless; **ins Uferlose gehen** *(Debatte etc)* to go on forever *or* interminably, to go on and on; *(Kosten)* to go up and up; **sonst geraten wir ins Uferlose** otherwise things will get out of hand; **ans Uferlose grenzen** *(Verleumdungen etc)* to go beyond all bounds; **Ufer|mau|er** F sea wall; **Ufer|pro|me|na|de** F esplanade; *(am Meer auch)* promenade; *(an See)* lakeside path; *(an Fluss)* riverside path; **Ufer|re|gi|on** F shore area; **Ufer|stra|ße** F *(an See)* lakeside road; *(an Fluss)* riverside road; **Ufer|zo|ne** F shore area

uff [ʊf] INTERJ *(inf)* phew; **~, das wäre geschafft!** phew, that's that done!

Uffz. [ʊfts] M -, -e *abbr von* **Unteroffizier** NCO

UFO, Ufo ['u:fo] **NT -(s), -s** UFO, Ufo

Ufo|lo|ge [ufo'lo:gə] **M -n, -n, Ufo|lo|gin** [-'lo:gɪn] **F -, -nen** ufologist

u-för|mig ['u-] ADJ U-shaped ADV in the shape of a U; **~ gebogen** with a U-shaped bend, bent into a U; **die Straße verläuft ~** the street forms a U

Ugan|da [u'ganda] **NT -s** Uganda

Ugan|der [u'gandɐ] **M -s, -, Ugan|de|rin** [-ərɪn] **F -, -nen** Ugandan

ugan|disch [u'gandɪʃ] **ADJ** Ugandan

uh [u:] **INTERJ** oh; *(angeekelt)* ugh, yuck *(inf)*

U-Haft ['u:-] **F** *(inf)* custody

U-Ha|ken ['u:-] **M** U-shaped hook

Uhl [u:l] **F -, -en** *(N Ger.* = *Eule)* owl

Uh|len|spie|gel M *(N Ger)* = **Eulenspiegel**

Uhr [u:ɐ] **F -, -en a** clock; *(= Armbanduhr, Taschenuhr)* watch; *(= Anzeigeinstrument)* gauge, dial, indicator; *(= Wasseruhr, Gasuhr)* meter; **nach der** *or* **auf die** *or* **zur ~ sehen** to look at the clock *etc*; **Arbeiter, die ständig auf die** *or* **nach der ~ sehen** clock-watchers; **nach meiner ~** by my watch; **wie nach der ~** *(fig)* like clockwork; **rund um die ~** round the clock; **seine ~ ist abgelaufen** *(fig geh)* the sands of time have run out for him; **die innere ~** the body clock; **ein Rennen gegen die ~** a race against the clock **b** *(bei Zeitangaben)* **um drei (~)** at three (o'clock); **ein ~ dreißig, 1.30 ~** half past one, 1.30 *(ausgesprochen "one-thirty")*; **zwei ~ morgens** *or* **nachts/nachmittags** two o'clock in the morning/afternoon; **wie viel ~ ist es?** what time is it?, what's the time?; **um wie viel ~?** (at) what time?

Uhr|(arm)|band [-bant] **NT** *pl* **-bänder** watch strap; *(aus Metall)* watch bracelet

Ühr|chen ['y:ɐçən] **NT -s, -** *dim von* **Uhr** little clock *etc*

Uh|ren-: **Uh|ren|in|dust|rie F** watch-and--clock(making) industry; **Uh|ren|ver|gleich M** → **Uhr a** comparison of clock/watch times; **einen ~ machen** to check *or* synchronize watches

Uhr-: **Uhr|fe|der F** watch spring; **Uhr|glas NT** *(auch Sci)* watch-glass; **Uhr|ket|te F** watch chain, fob (chain); **Uhr|ma|cher|hand|werk NT** → **Uhr a** clockmaking, horology *(form)*; watchmaking; **Uhr|ma|cher(in) M(F)** → **Uhr a** clockmaker, horologist *(form)*; watchmaker; **Uhr|werk NT** → **Uhr a** clockwork mechanism *(auch fig)*, works *pl* (of a clock/watch), movements *pl*; **Uhr|zei|ger M** → **Uhr a** (clock/watch) hand; **Uhr|zei|ger|sinn M im ~** clockwise; **entgegen dem ~** anticlockwise, counterclockwise; **Uhr|zeit F** time (of day); **haben Sie die genaue ~?** do you have the correct time?

Uhu ['u:hu] **M -s, -s** eagle owl

Ukas ['u:kas] **M -ses, -se** *(Hist, pej)* ukase

Uk|ra|i|ne [ukra'i:nə, u'krainə] **F - die ~** the Ukraine

Uk|ra|i|ner [ukra'i:nɐ, u'krainɐ] **M -s, -, Uk|ra|i|ne|rin** [-ərɪn] **F -, -nen** Ukrainian

uk|ra|i|nisch [ukra'i:nɪʃ, u'krainɪʃ] **ADJ** Ukrainian

Uk|ra|i|nisch(e) NT *(Ling)* Ukrainian → *auch* **Deutsch(e)**

Uku|le|le [uku'le:lə] **F -, -n** ukulele

UKW [u:ka:'ve:] *abbr von* **Ultrakurzwelle** VHF

UKW-: **UKW-Emp|fän|ger M** VHF receiver; **UKW-Sen|der M** VHF station; *(= Apparat)* VHF transmitter

Ul [u:l] **F -, -en** *(N Ger.* = *Eule)* owl

Ulan [u'la:n] **M -en, -en** *(Hist)* u(h)lan

Ulen|sp(i)e|gel M = **Eulenspiegel**

Ulk [ʊlk] **M -(e)s, -e** *(inf)* lark *(Brit inf)*, hoax *(US inf)*; *(= Streich)* trick, practical joke; *(= Spaß)* fun *no pl, no indef art*; **~ machen** to clown *or* play about *(Brit) or* around; **etw aus ~ sagen/tun** to say/do sth as a joke *or* in fun; **mit jdm seinen ~ treiben** *(= Spaß machen)* to have a bit of fun with sb; *(= Streiche spielen)* to play tricks on sb

ul|ken ['ʊlkn] **VI** *(inf)* to joke, to clown around; **über ihn wurde viel geulkt** they often had a bit of fun with him

ul|kig ['ʊlkɪç] **ADJ** *(inf)* funny; *(= seltsam auch)* odd, peculiar

Ulk|nu|del F *(inf)* joker *(inf)*

Ul|kus ['ʊlkʊs] **NT -, Ulzera** ['ʊltsera] *(Med)* ulcer

Ul|me ['ʊlmə] **F -, -n** elm

Ul|men|krank|heit F, Ul|men|ster|ben NT Dutch elm disease

Ul|ti|ma ['ʊltima] **F -, Ultimä** *or* **Ultimen** [-mɛ, -mən] *(Ling)* final syllable

Ul|ti|ma Ra|tio ['ʊltima 'ra:tsio] **F - -,** *no pl (geh)* final *or* last resort

Ul|ti|ma|ten *pl von* **Ultimatum**

ul|ti|ma|tiv [ʊltima'ti:f] ADJ **a** *Forderung etc* given as an ultimatum **b** *(inf:* = *beste) Film, Buch* ultimate *(inf)* ADV **wir fordern ~ eine Lohnerhöhung von 9%** we demand a pay rise of 9% and this is an ultimatum; **jdn ~ zu etw auffordern** to give sb an ultimatum to do sth

Ul|ti|ma|tum [ʊlti'ma:tʊm] **NT -s, -s** *or* **Ultimaten** [-tn] ultimatum; **jdm ein ~ stellen** to give sb an ultimatum

Ul|ti|men *pl von* **Ultima**

Ul|ti|mo ['ʊltimo] **M -s, -s** *(Comm)* last (day) of the month; **per ~** by the end of the month; **bis ~** *(fig)* till the last minute

Ul|ti|mo-: **Ul|ti|mo|ab|rech|nung F** *(Comm)* end-of-month settlement; **Ul|ti|mo|geld NT** *(Comm)* end-of-month settlement loan

Ult|ra ['ʊltra] **M -s, -s** *(pej)* extremist

Ult|ra-, **ult|ra-** ['ʊltra] *in cpds* ultra; **ult|ra|hoch|er|hitzt ADJ** *Milch* long-life *attr*; **ult|ra|kurz ADJ** *(Phys)* ultrashort

Ult|ra|kurz|wel|le [ʊltra'kʊrts-] **F** *(Phys)* ultrashort wave; *(Rad)* ≈ very high frequency, ≈ frequency modulation

Ult|ra|kurz|wel|len-: **Ult|ra|kurz|wel|len|emp|fän|ger M** VHF receiver; **Ult|ra|kurz|wel|len|sen|der M** VHF station; *(= Apparat)* VHF transmitter

Ult|ra-: **ul|tra|lin|ke(r, s) ADJ** *attr (Pol)* extreme left-wing; **Ult|ra|ma|rin** [ʊltrama'ri:n] **NT -s,** *no pl* ultramarine; **ult|ra|ma|rin(blau)** [ʊltrama'ri:n-] **ADJ** ultramarine; **ult|ra|mo|dern** [-modɛrn] ADJ ultramodern ADV ultramodernly; **ult|ra|mon|tan** [ʊltramɔn'ta:n] **ADJ** *(pej geh)* papist *(pej)*; **ul|tra|rech|te(r, s) ADJ** *attr (Pol)* extreme right-wing; **ult|ra|rot ADJ** infrared

Ult|ra|schall M *(Phys)* ultrasound

Ult|ra|schall- *in cpds* ultrasound; **Ult|ra|schall|auf|nah|me F** scan *(Brit)*, ultrasound (picture); **Ult|ra|schall|bild NT** ultrasound picture; **Ult|ra|schall|di|ag|nos|tik F** ultrasound diagnosis; **Ult|ra|schall|ge|rät NT** ultrasound scanner; **Ult|ra|schall|un|ter|su|chung F** scan *(Brit)*, ultrasound; **Ult|ra|schall|wel|len PL** ultrasonic waves *pl*

Ult|ra-: **Ult|ra|strah|lung F** *(Phys)* cosmic radiation; **ult|ra|vi|o|lett ADJ** ultraviolet

Ul|ze|ra *pl von* **Ulkus**

um [ʊm] PREP +*acc* **a um ... (herum)** round *(Brit)*, around; *(unbestimmter:* = *in der Gegend von)* around, about; **er hat gern Freunde um sich** he likes to have friends around him **b** *(= nach allen Seiten)* **um sich schauen** to look around (one) *or* about one; **um sich schlagen** to hit out in all directions; **etw um sich werfen** to throw sth around *or* about **c** *(zur ungefähren Zeitangabe)* **um ... (herum)** around about; *(bei Uhrzeiten auch)* at about; **die Tage um die Sommersonnenwende (herum)** the days either side of the summer solstice; **um Weihnachten/Ostern** *etc* around Christmas/Easter *etc* **d** *(zur genauen Angabe der Uhrzeit)* at; **bitte kommen Sie (genau) um acht** please come at eight (sharp) **e** *(= betreffend, über)* about; **es geht um das Prinzip** it's a question of principles, it's the principle of the thing; **es geht um alles** it's all or nothing; **es steht schlecht um seine Gesundheit** his health isn't very good **f** *(= für, Ergebnis, Ziel bezeichnend)* for; **der Kampf um die Stadt/den Titel** the battle for the town/the title; **um Geld spielen** to play for money; **um etw rufen/bitten** *etc* to cry/ask *etc* for sth **g** *(= wegen)* **die Sorge um die Zukunft** concern for *or* about the future; **(es ist) schade um das schöne Buch** (it's a) pity *or* shame about that nice book; **sich um etw sorgen** to worry about sth; **es tut mir leid um ihn** I'm sorry for him **h** *(bei Differenzangaben)* by; **um 10% teurer** 10% more expensive; **er ist um zwei Jahre jünger als sie** he is two years younger than she is, he is younger than her by two years; **um vieles besser** far better, better by far; **um einiges besser** quite a bit better; **um nichts besser/teurer** *etc* no better/dearer *etc* → **umso**; **etw um 4 cm verkürzen** to shorten sth by 4 cm **i** *(bei Verlust)* **jdn um etw bringen** to deprive sb of sth; **um etw kommen** to be deprived of sth, to miss out on sth **j** *(= nach)* after, upon; **Stunde um Stunde** hour after *or* upon hour; **einer um den anderen, eine um die andere** one after the other; **einen Tag um den anderen** day after day

PREP +*gen* **um ... willen** for the sake of; **um Gottes willen!** for goodness' *or (stärker)* God's sake!

CONJ **um ... zu** *(final)* (in order) to; **er spart jeden Cent, um sich später ein Haus kaufen zu können** he is saving every cent in order to be able to buy a house later; **intelligent genug/zu intelligent, um ... zu** intelligent enough/too intelligent to ...; **der Fluss schlängelt sich durch das enge Tal, um dann in der Ebene zu einem breiten Strom anzuwachsen** the stream winds through the narrow valley and then broadens out into a wide river in the plain; **er studierte jahrelang Jura, um dann Taxifahrer zu werden** he studied law for several years only to become a taxi driver

ADV **a** *(= ungefähr)* **um (die) 30 Schüler** *etc* about *or* (a)round about 30 pupils *etc*, 30 pupils *etc* or so **b** *(rare)* **um und um** all around

um+ad|res|sie|ren *ptp* **umadressiert VT** *sep* to readdress; *(und nachschicken)* to redirect

um+än|dern VT *sep* to alter; *(= modifizieren auch)* to modify

um+ar|bei|ten VT *sep* to alter; *Buch etc* to revise, to rewrite, to rework; *Metall etc* to rework; **einen Roman zu einem Drama/Drehbuch ~** to adapt a novel for the stage/screen

Um|ar|bei|tung F -, -en alteration; *(von Buch etc)* revision, rewriting, reworking; *(zu Drama etc)* adaptation; *(von Metall)* reworking

um|ar|men [ʊm'armən] *ptp* **umarmt VT** *insep* to embrace *(auch euph)*, to hug

Um|ar|mung F -, -en embrace *(auch euph)*, hug

um+ar|ran|gie|ren *ptp* **umarrangiert VT** *sep* to rearrange

Um|bau M *pl* **-bauten a** *(von Gebäude)* rebuilding, renovation; *(zu etwas anderem)* conversion *(zu* into); *(= Umänderung)* alterations *pl*; *(von Maschine)* modification; *(von Organisation)* reorganization; *(von Kulisse)* changing; **das Gebäude befindet sich im ~** the building is being renovated **b** *(= Gebäude)* renovated/converted building

Um|bau|ar|bei|ten PL renovation work *no pl*; *(zu etwas Neuem)* conversion work *no pl*; *(= bauliche Veränderung)* alteration work *no pl*, alterations *pl*

um+bau|en ['ʊmbauən] *sep* VT *Gebäude (= gründlich renovieren)* to rebuild, to renovate; *(zu etw anderem)* to convert *(zu* into); *(= umändern)* to alter; *Maschine etc* to modify; *(fig) Organisation, Firma* to restructure, to reorganize; *(Theat) Kulissen* to change VI to rebuild

um|bau|en [ʊm'bauən] *ptp* **umbaut VT** *insep* to enclose; **der Dom ist völlig umbaut** the cathedral is completely surrounded by buildings; **umbauter Raum** enclosed *or* interior area

um+be|hal|ten *ptp* **umbehalten** VT *sep irreg Schal etc* to keep on

um+be|nen|nen *ptp* **umbenannt** VT *sep irreg* to rename (*in etw* sth)

Um|be|nen|nung F renaming

um+be|set|zen *ptp* **umbesetzt** VT *sep (Theat)* to recast; *Mannschaft* to change, to reorganize; *Posten, Stelle* to find someone else for, to reassign

Um|be|set|zung F *(Theat)* recasting; *(von Mannschaft)* change, reorganization; *(von Posten, Stelle)* reassignment; **eine ~ vornehmen** *(Theat)* to alter the cast; **~en vornehmen** *(Theat)* to recast roles; **~en im Kabinett vornehmen** to reshuffle *(Brit) or* shake up *(US)* the cabinet

um+be|stel|len *ptp* **umbestellt** *sep* VI to change one's order VT *Patienten etc* to give another *or* a new appointment to

um+bet|ten VT *sep Kranken* to move *or* transfer (to another bed); *Leichnam* to rebury, to transfer; *Fluss* to rechannel

um+bie|gen *sep irreg* VT to bend VI *aux sein (Weg)* to bend, to turn; *(= zurückgehen)* to turn round *or* back

um+bil|den VT *sep (fig)* to reorganize, to reconstruct; *(Pol) Kabinett* to reshuffle *(Brit)*, to shake up *(US)*

Um|bil|dung F reorganization, reconstruction; *(Pol)* reshuffle *(Brit)*, shake up *(US)*

um+bin|den [ˈʊmbɪndn] VT *sep irreg* to put on; *(mit Knoten auch)* to tie on; **sich** *(dat)* **einen Schal ~** to put a scarf on

um|bin|den [ʊmˈbɪndn] *ptp* **umbunden** [ʊmˈbʊndn] VT *insep irreg* = **umwickeln**

um+bla|sen VT *sep irreg* to blow down

um+blät|tern VTI *sep* to turn over

um+bli|cken VR *sep* to look round; **sich nach jdm/etw ~** to turn (a)round to look at sb/sth

Um|bra [ˈʊmbra] F -, *no pl (Astron)* umbra; *(Farbe)* umber

Umb|ral|glas® [ʊmˈbraːl-] NT photochrom(at)ic glass

um|bran|den [ʊmˈbrandn] *ptp* **umbrandet** VT *insep* to surge around; **von der See umbrandet** surrounded by the surging sea

um|brau|sen [ʊmˈbrauzn] *ptp* **umbraust** VT *insep* to surge around; **vom Sturm umbraust** buffeted by the storm

um+bre|chen [ˈʊmbrɛçn] *sep irreg* VT **a** *(= umknicken)* to break down **b** *(= umpflügen) Erde* to break up VI *aux sein* to break

um|bre|chen [ʊmˈbrɛçn] *ptp* **umbrochen** [ʊmˈbrɔxn] VTI *insep irreg (Typ)* to make up

um+brin|gen *sep irreg* VT to kill *(auch fig)*, to murder; **das ist nicht umzubringen** *(fig inf)* it's indestructible; **das bringt mich noch um!** *(inf)* it'll be the death of me! *(inf)* VR to kill oneself; **bringen Sie sich nur nicht um!** *(fig inf)* you'll kill yourself (if you go on like that)!; **er bringt sich fast um vor Höflichkeit** *(inf)* he falls over himself to be polite

Um|bruch M **a** radical change **b** *(Typ)* make-up **c** *(Agr)* ploughing *(Brit) or* plowing *(US)* up

Um|bruch|pha|se F *(= Veränderung)* period of upheaval

um+bu|chen *sep* ✪ 48.3 VT **a** *Reise, Flug, Termin* to alter one's booking for **b** *(Fin) Betrag* to transfer VI **a** *(= Reisetermin ändern)* to alter one's booking *(auf +acc* for) **b** *(Fin)* to transfer *(auf +acc* to)

Um|bu|chung F **a** *(von Reise, Termin)* rebooking **b** *(Fin)* transfer

um+co|die|ren *ptp* **umcodiert** VT *sep (Comput)* to recode

um+den|ken VI *sep irreg* to change one's ideas *or* views; **darin müssen wir ~** we'll have to rethink that

um+deu|ten VT *sep* to change the meaning of; *(Liter)* to reinterpret, to give a new interpretation to

um+dich|ten VT *sep* to rework, to recast

um+di|ri|gie|ren *ptp* **umdirigiert** VT *sep* to redirect

um+dis|po|nie|ren *ptp* **umdisponiert** VI *sep* to change one's arrangements *or* plans

um|drän|gen [ʊmˈdrɛŋən] *ptp* **umdrängt** VT *insep* to throng *or* crowd around; *(stärker)* to mob; **sie wurde so umdrängt, dass ...** there was such a crowd around her that ...

um+dre|hen *sep* VT **a** *(= auf andere Seite drehen)* to turn over; *(auf den Kopf)* to turn up (the other way); *(mit der Vorderseite nach hinten)* to turn (a)round, to turn back to front; *(von innen nach außen) Strumpf etc* to turn inside out; *Tasche* to turn (inside) out; *(von außen nach innen)* to turn back the right way; *(um die Achse)* to turn (a)round; *Schlüssel* to turn → **Pfennig, Spieß**

b einem Vogel/jdm den Hals ~ to wring a bird's/sb's neck

c *(= verrenken)* **jdm den Arm ~** to twist sb's arm → **Wort b**

VR to turn (a)round *(nach* to look at); *(im Bett etc)* to turn over; **dabei drehte sich ihm der Magen um** *(inf)* it turned his stomach → **Grab**

VI to turn (a)round *or* back

Um|dre|hung F turn; *(Phys)* revolution, rotation; *(Mot)* revolution, rev

Um|dre|hungs|zahl F (number of) revolutions *pl* (per minute/second)

um|düs|tern [ʊmˈdyːstɐn] *ptp* **umdüstert** VR *insep (liter)* to become melancholy, to become sombre *(Brit) or* somber *(US)*

um|ei|nan|der ADV about each other *or* one another; *(räumlich)* (a)round each other

um+er|zie|hen *ptp* **umerzogen** VT *sep irreg (Pol euph)* to re-educate *(zu* to become)

Um|er|zie|hungs|la|ger NT *(Pol euph)* re-education centre *(Brit) or* center *(US)*

um|fä|cheln [ʊmˈfɛçln] *ptp* **umfächelt** VT *insep (geh)* to fan; *(Luftzug auch)* to caress *(liter)*

um+fah|ren [ˈʊmfaːrən] VT *sep irreg (= überfahren)* to run over *or* down, to knock down *(esp Brit)* VI *aux sein (inf)* to go out of one's way *(by mistake)*; **er ist 5 Kilometer umgefahren** he went 5 kilometres *(Brit) or* kilometers *(US)* out of his way

um|fah|ren [ʊmˈfaːrən] *ptp* **umfahren** VT *insep irreg (= fahren um)* to travel *or* go (a)round; *(mit dem Auto)* to drive (a)round; *(auf Umgehungsstraße)* to bypass; *(= ausweichen)* to make a detour (a)round, to detour; *Kap* to round, to double; *die Welt* to sail (a)round, to circumnavigate

Um|fah|rung [ʊmˈfaːrʊŋ] F -, -en **a** travelling round *(Brit)*, traveling around *(US)*; *(mit dem Auto)* driving (a)round; *(von Kap)* rounding, doubling; *(= Umsegelung)* sailing (around), circumnavigation **b** *(Aus: = Umgehungsstraße)* bypass, beltway *(US)*

Um|fah|rungs|stra|ße F *(Aus)* bypass, beltway *(US)*

Um|fall M *(Pol inf)* turnaround *(inf)*

um+fal|len VI *sep irreg aux sein (Mensch)* to fall over *or* down; *(Baum, Gegenstand)* to fall (down); *(= vornüberkippen)* to fall *or* topple over; *(inf: = ohnmächtig werden)* to pass out, to faint; *(fig inf: = nachgeben)* to give in; **vor Müdigkeit fast ~, zum Umfallen müde sein** to be (almost) dead on one's feet *(inf)*, to be fit *(Brit) or* ready to drop; **wir arbeiteten bis zum Umfallen** we worked until were were ready to drop; **vor Schreck fast ~** *(inf)* to almost die with fright, to almost have a heart attack *(inf)*; **~ wie die Fliegen** *(inf)* to drop like flies → **tot a**

um+fal|zen VT *sep* to fold over

Um|fang M **a** *(von Kreis etc)* perimeter, circumference *(auch Geom)*; *(von Baum)* circumference; *(= Bauchumfang)* girth

b *(= Fläche)* area; *(= Rauminhalt)* capacity; *(= Größe)* size; *(von Gepäck etc)* amount; **das Buch hat einen ~ von 800 Seiten** the book contains *or* has 800 pages

c *(fig) (= Ausmaß)* extent; *(= Reichweite)* range; *(= Stimmumfang)* range, compass; *(von Untersuchung, Arbeit etc)* scope; *(von Verkehr, Verkauf etc)* volume; **in großem ~** on a large scale; **in vollem ~** fully, entirely, completely; **größeren/erschreckenden ~ annehmen** to assume greater/alarming proportions; **das hat einen solchen ~ angenommen, dass ...** it has assumed such proportions that ...; **etw in vollem ~ übersehen können** to be able to see the full extent of sth

um|fan|gen [ʊmˈfaŋən] *ptp* **umfangen** VT *insep irreg (geh)* **a jdn mit seinen Blicken ~** *(fig)* to fix one's eyes upon sb **b** *(fig: = umgeben)* to envelop **c** *(= umarmen)* to embrace

um|fäng|lich [ˈʊmfɛŋlɪç], **um|fang|reich** ADJ extensive; *(fig: = breit) Wissen etc auch* wide; *(= geräumig)* spacious; *Buch* thick

um+fär|ben VT *sep* to dye a different colour *(Brit) or* color *(US)*

um|fas|sen [ʊmˈfasn] *ptp* **umfasst** VT *insep* **a** *(= herumgreifen um)* to grasp, to clasp; *(= umarmen)* to embrace; **ich konnte den Baum nicht mit den Armen ~** I couldn't get my arms (a)round the tree; **er hielt sie umfasst** he held her close *or* to him, he held her in an embrace **b** *(Mil)* to encircle, to surround **c** *(fig) (= einschließen) Zeitperiode* to cover; *(= enthalten)* to contain, to include; *Seiten* to contain

um|fas|send ADJ *(= umfangreich, weitreichend)* extensive; *(= vieles enthaltend)* comprehensive; *Vollmachten, Maßnahmen* sweeping, extensive; *Vorbereitung* thorough; *Geständnis* full, complete ADV comprehensively; **~ gestehen** to give a complete *or* full confession

Um|fas|sung F *(Mil)* encirclement

Um|feld NT surroundings *pl*; *(fig)* sphere; **zum ~ von etw gehören** to be associated with sth; **Personen aus dem ~ dieser terroristischen Vereinigung** people associated with this terrorist organization

um+fir|mie|ren *ptp* **umfirmiert** *sep* VT *Unternehmen (= Namen ändern)* to change the name of; *(= Rechtsform ändern)* to change the legal status of VI *(von Unternehmen)* to change one's name/legal status

Um|fir|mie|rung [ˈʊmfɪrmiːrʊŋ] F -, -en change of name

um|flech|ten [ʊmˈflɛçtn] *ptp* **umflochten** [ʊmˈflɔxtn] VT *insep irreg* **eine Flasche** *etc* **mit etw ~** to weave sth around a bottle *etc*; **eine umflochtene Flasche** a raffia-covered bottle

um|flie|gen [ʊmˈfliːgn] *ptp* **umflogen** [ʊmˈfloːgn] VT *insep irreg (= fliegen um)* to fly (a)round

um+flie|gen [ˈʊmfliːgn] VI *sep irreg aux sein (inf)* to go flying *(inf)*

um|flie|ßen [ʊmˈfliːsn] *ptp* **umflossen** [ʊmˈflɔsn] VT *insep irreg (lit, fig)* to flow around; *(fig poet: Licht)* to flood around; **von einem Strom umflossen sein** to be surrounded by a river

um|flort [ʊmˈfloːɐt] ADJ *(liter) Augen* misty, misted over

um|flu|ten [ʊmˈfluːtn] *ptp* **umflutet** VT *insep* to surge around

um+for|ma|tie|ren *ptp* **umformatiert** VT *sep (Comput) Datenträger* to reformat

um+for|men VT *sep* **a** *(= andere Form geben)* to remodel, to reshape *(in +acc* into) **b** *(Elec)* to convert **c** *(Ling)* to transform

Um|for|mer [ˈʊmfɔrmɐ] M -s, - *(Elec)* converter

Um|for|mung F remodelling *(Brit)*, remodeling *(US)*, reshaping; *(Elec)* conversion; *(Ling)* transformation

Um|fra|ge F **a** *(Sociol)* survey; *(esp Pol)* (opinion) poll; **eine ~ halten** *or* **machen** *or* **veranstalten** to carry out *or* hold a survey/a poll *or* an opinion poll **b ~ halten** to ask around

Um|fra|ge-: **Um|fra|ge|er|geb|nis** NT → **Umfrage a** survey/poll result(s *pl*); **Um|fra|ge|wer|te** PL opinion poll results *pl*

um|frie|den [ʊmˈfriːdn] *ptp* **umfriedet** VT *insep (geh)* to enclose; *(mit Zaun auch)* to fence in; *(mit Mauer auch)* to wall in

Um|frie|dung F -, -en **a** *(= das Umfrieden)* **die ~ der Burg dauerte Jahrzehnte** enclosing *or (mit Mauer)* walling in the castle took years **b** *(= Zaun/Mauer etc)* enclosing fence/wall *etc;* **als ~ für den Park dient eine Hecke** the park is enclosed by a hedge

um+fri|sie|ren *ptp* **umfrisiert** VT *sep (inf)* **a** **sich** *(dat)* **die Haare ~ lassen** to have one's hair restyled **b** *(= abändern)* = **frisieren VT b c** *Auto* = **frisieren VT c**

um+fül|len VT *sep* to transfer into another bottle/container *etc*

um+funk|ti|o|nie|ren *ptp* **umfunktioniert** VT *sep* to change *or* alter the function of; **etw in etw** *(acc) or* **zu etw ~** to change *or* turn sth into sth; **die Kinder haben das Wohnzimmer umfunktioniert** *(hum)* the children have done a conversion job on the living room *(hum)*

Um|funk|ti|o|nie|rung [ˈʊmfʊŋktsioniːrʊŋ] F -, -en **die ~ einer Sache** *(gen)* changing the function of sth; **die ~ der Versammlung zu einer Protestkundgebung** changing the function of the meeting and making a protest rally out of it

Um|gang [-gaŋ] M, *no pl* **a** *(= gesellschaftlicher Verkehr)* contact, dealings *pl;* *(= Bekanntenkreis)* acquaintances *pl*, friends *pl;* **schlechten ~ haben** to keep bad company; **das liegt an seinem ~** that's because of the company he keeps; **~ mit jdm haben** *or* **pflegen** to associate with sb; **~ mit einer Gruppe haben** to associate *or* mix with a group; **keinen/so gut wie keinen ~ mit jdm haben** to have nothing/little to do with sb; **sie hat nur ~ mit den besten gesellschaftlichen Kreisen** she only mixes in the best social circles; **er ist kein ~ für dich** he's not fit company *or* no company for you **b** **im ~ mit Tieren/Jugendlichen/Vorgesetzten muss man ...** in dealing with animals/young people/one's superiors one must ...; **durch ständigen ~ mit Autos/Büchern/Kindern** through having a lot to do with cars/books/children; **an den ~ mit Tieren/Kindern gewöhnt sein** to be used to animals/children; **an den ~ mit Büchern/Nachschlagewerken gewöhnt sein** to be used to having books around (one)/to using reference books; **der ~ mit Tieren/Kindern muss gelernt sein** you have to learn how to handle animals/children

Um|gang M *pl* **-gänge** **a** *(Archit: = Säulenumgang)* ambulatory **b** *(= Feldumgang, Flurumgang)* procession

um|gäng|lich [ˈʊmgɛŋlɪç] ADJ affable, pleasant-natured

Um|gäng|lich|keit F -, *no pl (= entgegenkommende Art)* affability, pleasant nature

Um|gangs-: **Um|gangs|for|men** PL manners *pl;* **Um|gangs|recht** NT, *no pl* (right of) access; *(mit to);* **Um|gangs|spra|che** F colloquial language *or* speech; **die deutsche ~** colloquial German; **um|gangs|sprach|lich** ADJ colloquial; **Um|gangs|ton** M *pl* **-töne** tone, way of speaking; **hier herrscht ein rüder/höflicher ~** people talk brusquely/politely here

um|gar|nen [ʊmˈgarnən] *ptp* **umgarnt** VT *insep* to ensnare, to beguile

um|gau|keln [ʊmˈgaukln] *ptp* **umgaukelt** VT *insep (geh)* to flutter about *or* around; *(fig: mit Schmeicheleien etc)* to ensnare, to beguile

um|ge|ben [ʊmˈgeːbn] *ptp* **umgeben** *insep irreg* **VT** to surround *(auch fig);* **mit einer Mauer/einem Zaun ~ sein** to be walled/fenced in, to be surrounded by a wall/fence; **das von Weinbergen ~e Stuttgart** the town of Stuttgart, surrounded by vineyards **VR** **sich mit jdm/etw ~** to surround oneself with sb/sth

Um|ge|bung F -, -en *(= Umwelt)* surroundings *pl;* *(von Stadt auch)* environs *pl*, surrounding area; *(= Nachbarschaft)* vicinity, neighbourhood *(Brit)*, neighborhood *(US);* *(Comput)* environment; *(= gesellschaftlicher Hintergrund)* background; *(= Freunde, Kollegen etc)* people *pl* about one; **Hamburg und ~** Hamburg and the Hamburg area, Hamburg and its environs *or* the surrounding area; **in der näheren ~ Münchens** on the outskirts of Munich; **in der weiteren ~ Münchens** in the area around Munich, in the Munich area; **zu jds (näherer) ~ gehören** *(Menschen)* to be one of the people closest to sb

Um|ge|bungs|va|ri|ab|le F *(Comput)* environment variable

Um|ge|gend F surrounding area; **die ~ von London** the area around London

um+ge|hen [ˈʊmgeːən] VI *sep irreg aux sein* **a** *(Gerücht etc)* to circulate, to go about *(Brit) or* (a)round; *(Grippe)* to be going about *(Brit) or* around; *(Gespenst)* to walk; **in diesem Schloss geht ein Gespenst um** this castle is haunted (by a ghost); **es geht die Furcht um, dass ...** it is feared that ... **b** **mit jdm/etw ~ können** *(= behandeln, handhaben)* to know how to handle *or* treat sb/sth; *mit Geld* to know how to handle sth; *(= mit jdm/etw verfahren)* to know how to deal with *or* handle sb/sth; **mit jdm grob/behutsam ~** to treat sb roughly/gently; **wie der mit seinen Sachen umgeht!** you should see how he treats his things!; **sorgsam/verschwenderisch mit etw ~** to be careful/lavish with sth; **mit dem Gedanken ~, etw zu tun** to be thinking about doing sth **c** *(dial, inf: = Umweg machen)* to go out of one's way (by mistake)

um|ge|hen [ʊmˈgeːən] *ptp* **umgangen** [ʊmˈgaŋən] VT *insep irreg* **a** *(= herumgehen um)* to go (a)round; *(= vermeiden)* to avoid; *(Straße)* to bypass; *(Mil)* to outflank **b** *(fig: = vermeiden)* to avoid; *Schwierigkeit* to avoid, to get (a)round; *Gesetz* to circumvent, to get (a)round, to bypass; *Frage* to avoid, to evade; **die Antwort auf etw** *(acc)* **~** to avoid answering sth

um|ge|hend ADJ immediate, prompt; **mit ~er Post** *(dated)* by return (of post *(Brit))*, by return mail *(US)* ADV immediately

Um|ge|hung [ʊmˈgeːʊŋ] F -, -en **a** *(= Vermeidung)* avoidance; *(durch Straßenführung)* bypassing; *(Mil)* outflanking; *(von Gesetz)* circumvention, getting (a)round; *(von Frage)* evasion; **die ~ des Geländes** going (a)round the grounds; **unter ~ der Vorschriften** by getting (a)round *or* circumventing the regulations **b** *(inf: = Umgehungsstraße)* bypass, beltway *(US)*

Um|ge|hungs|stra|ße F bypass, beltway *(US)*

um|ge|kehrt [ˈʊmgəkeːɐt] ADJ reversed; *Reihenfolge* reverse; *(Math) Vorzeichen* opposite; *(= gegenteilig)* opposite, contrary; *(= andersherum)* the other way (a)round; **in die ~e Richtung fahren** to go in the opposite direction; **nein, ~!** no, the other way (a)round; **gerade** *or* **genau ~!** quite the contrary!, just the opposite!; **die Sache war genau ~ und nicht so, wie er sie erzählte** the affair was exactly the reverse of what he said; **im ~en Verhältnis zu etw stehen** *or* **sein** to be in inverse proportion to sth ADV *(= andersherum)* the other way (a)round; *(am Satzanfang: = dagegen)* conversely; *proportional* inversely; **... und/oder ~** ... and/or vice versa; **~ als** *or* **wie** *(inf)* the other way (a)round to what ...; **es kam ~** *(inf)* the opposite happened

um+ge|stal|ten *ptp* **umgestaltet** VT *sep* to alter; *(= reorganisieren)* to reorganize; *(= umbilden)* to remodel; *(= umordnen)* to rearrange; **etw in etw** *(acc) or* **zu etw ~** to redesign sth as sth; *Werk, Buch* to rewrite *or* recast sth as sth

Um|ge|stal|tung F alteration; *(= Reorganisation)* reorganization; *(= Umbildung)* remodelling *(Brit)*, remodeling *(US);* *(= Umordnung)* rearrangement

um+ge|wöh|nen *ptp* **umgewöhnt** VR *sep* to re-adapt

um+gie|ßen VT *sep irreg* **a** *(in anderen Behälter)* to transfer *(in +acc* into); *(= verschütten)* to spill **b** *(Metal)* to recast

um|glän|zen [ʊmˈglɛntsn] *ptp* **umglänzt** VT *insep (poet) (Sonne etc)* to bathe in light; **von der Morgensonne umglänzt** bathed in the morning sunlight; **von Ruhm umglänzt** resplendent with glory

um+gra|ben VT *sep irreg* to dig over; *Erde* to turn (over)

um|gren|zen [ʊmˈgrɛntsn] *ptp* **umgrenzt** VT *insep* to bound, to surround; *(= umschließen auch)* to enclose; *(fig)* to delimit, to define

Um|gren|zung F -, -en **a** boundary **b** *(= das Umgrenzen) (mit Mauer etc)* enclosing; *(fig)* delimitation, definition

um+grup|pie|ren *ptp* **umgruppiert** VT *sep Möbel etc* to rearrange; *Mitarbeiter* to redeploy; *(= auf andere Gruppen verteilen)* to regroup; *(Mil) Truppen* to regroup

Um|grup|pie|rung F rearrangement; *(von Mitarbeitern)* redeployment; *(= Aufteilung in andere Gruppen, Mil)* regrouping

um+gu|cken VR *sep* = **umsehen**

um+gür|ten [ˈʊmgʏrtn] VT *sep* to fasten *(+dat* around)

um|gür|ten [ʊmˈgʏrtn] *ptp* **umgürtet** VR *insep* **sich mit einem Schwert ~** *(liter)* to gird on a sword *(liter)*

um+ha|ben VT *sep irreg (inf)* to have on

um|hal|sen [ʊmˈhalzn] *ptp* **umhalst** VT *sep* **jdn ~** *(inf)* to throw one's arms around sb's neck

Um|hang M cape; *(länger)* cloak; *(= Umhängetuch)* shawl, wrap *(esp US)*

um|hän|gen VT *sep* **a** *Rucksack etc* to put on; *Jacke, Schal etc* to drape (a)round; *Gewehr* to sling on; **sich** *(dat)* **etw ~** to put sth on; to drape sth (a)round one; **jdm etw ~** to put sth on sb; to drape sth (a)round sb **b** *Bild* to re-hang

Um|hän|ge|ta|sche F shoulder bag

um|hau|en VT *sep irreg* **a** *Baum* to chop *or* cut down, to fell **b** *(inf: = umwerfen)* to knock flying *(inf) or* over **c** *(inf) (= erstaunen)* to bowl over *(inf);* *(Gestank etc)* to knock out

um|he|gen [ʊmˈheːgn] *ptp* **umhegt** VT *insep (geh)* to look after lovingly, to care for lovingly

um|her [ʊmˈheːɐ] ADV around, about *(Brit);* **weit ~** all around

um|her- PREF → *auch* **herum-, rum-** around, about *(Brit);* **um|her+fah|ren** *sep irreg* VT *(mit Auto)* to drive about *(Brit) or* around; *(in Kinderwagen)* to walk about *(Brit) or* around VI *aux sein* to travel about *(Brit) or* around; *(mit Auto)* to drive about *(Brit) or* around; *(mit Kinderwagen)* to walk about *(Brit) or* around; **um|her+ge|hen** VI *sep irreg aux sein* to walk about *(Brit) or* around; **im Zimmer/Garten ~** to walk (a)round the room/garden; **um|her|ge|trie|ben** ADJ *(liter)* wandering *attr;* **Um|her|ge|trie|be|ne(r)** [-gətriːbənə] MF *decl as adj (liter)* wanderer, wandering soul *(liter);* **um|her+ir|ren** VI *sep aux sein (in etw (dat)* sth) to wander about *(Brit) or* around; *(Blick, Augen)* to roam about; **ängstlich irrte ihr Blick im Zimmer umher** her eyes anxiously scanned the room; **nach langen Jahren des Umherirrens** after many years of wandering (around); **um|her+ja|gen** VTI *sep (vi: aux sein)* to chase about *(Brit) or* around; **um|her+lau|fen** VI *sep irreg aux sein* to walk about *(Brit) or* around; *(= rennen)* to run about *(Brit) or* around; **im Garten ~** to walk/run about *(Brit) or* around the garden; **um|her+schlen|dern** VI *sep aux sein* to stroll about *(Brit) or* around *(in etw (dat)* sth); **um|her+spä|hen** VI *sep* to look about *(Brit) or* around; **um|her+strei|fen** VI *sep aux sein* to wander *or* roam around *(in etw (dat)* sth); **um|her+streu|nen** VI *sep aux sein (geh)* to prowl around; **um|her+wan|dern** VI *sep aux sein* to wander *or* roam about *(Brit) or* around *(in etw (dat)* sth); **um|her+zie|hen** *sep irreg* VI *aux sein* to move *or* travel around *(in etw (dat)* sth) VT to pull about *(Brit) or* around

um|hin+kön|nen [ʊmˈhɪn-] VI *sep irreg* **ich/er** *etc* **kann nicht umhin, das zu tun** I/he *etc* can't avoid doing it; *(einem Zwang folgend)* I/he *etc* can't help doing it; **ich konnte nicht umhin** I couldn't avoid it; I couldn't help it; **..., so dass**

sie einfach nicht umhinkonnten, mir zu glauben ... so that they simply couldn't help but believe me

um+hö|ren VR *sep* to ask around; **sich unter seinen Kollegen ~** to ask (around) one's colleagues

um|hül|len [ʊm'hʏlən] *ptp* **umhüllt** VT *insep* to wrap (up) (*mit* in); **von einem Geheimnis umhüllt** shrouded in secrecy *or* mystery

um+in|ter|pre|tie|ren *ptp* **uminterpretiert** VT *sep* to interpret differently; *(Liter)* to reinterpret

um|ju|beln [ʊm'ju:bln] *ptp* **umjubelt** VT *insep* to cheer; **ein umjubelter Popstar** a wildly acclaimed pop idol

um|kämp|fen [ʊm'kɛmpfn] *ptp* **umkämpft** VT *insep Stadt, Gebiet* to fight over; *Entscheidung* to dispute; *Wahlkreis, Sieg* to contest; **ein hart umkämpfter Markt** a hotly contested market

Um|kehr ['ʊmke:ɐ] F -, *no pl* **a** *(lit)* turning back; **jdn zur ~ zwingen** to force sb to turn back **b** *(fig geh)* (= *Änderung*) change; *(zur Religion etc)* changing one's ways; **zur ~ bereit sein** to be ready to change one's ways

Um|kehr|an|stalt F *(Phot)* reversal film processing laboratory

um|kehr|bar ADJ reversible

um+keh|ren *sep* VI *aux sein* to turn back; (= *auf demselben Weg zurückgehen*) to retrace one's steps; *(fig)* to change one's ways

VT *Kleidungsstück (von innen nach außen)* to turn inside out; *(von außen nach innen)* to turn the right way out; *Tasche* to turn (inside) out; *Reihenfolge, Trend* to reverse; *Verhältnisse* (= *umstoßen*) to overturn; (= *auf den Kopf stellen*) to turn upside down, to invert; *(Gram, Math, Mus, Comput)* to invert; **das ganze Zimmer ~** *(inf)* to turn the whole room upside down *(inf)* → *auch* **umgekehrt**

VR *(Verhältnisse)* to become inverted *or* reversed; **dabei kehrt sich mir der Magen um** it turns my stomach; **mein Inneres kehrt sich um, wenn ...** my gorge rises when ...

Um|kehr-: **Um|kehr|film** M *(Phot)* reversal film; **Um|kehr|lin|se** F inverting lens; **Um|kehr|schluss** M inversion of an argument; **im ~ bedeutet das ...** to turn the argument on its head, it means ...

Um|keh|rung ['ʊmke:rʊŋ] F -, **-en** *(von Gesagtem, Reihenfolge etc)* reversal, inversion *(auch Gram, Math, Mus)*; **das ist eine ~ dessen, was ich gesagt habe** that's the opposite *or* reverse of what I said

um+kip|pen *sep* VT (= *umwerfen*) to tip over, to upset; *Auto, Boot* to overturn, to turn over; *Leuchter, Vase* to knock over; *volles Gefäß* to upset VI *aux sein* **a** (= *zur Seite fallen*) to tip *or* fall over; *(Auto, Boot)* to overturn, to turn over; *(volles Gefäß, Bier)* to be spilled *or* upset **b** *(inf* = *ohnmächtig werden)* to pass out **c** *(inf* = *aufgeben)* to back down **d** (= *sich umwandeln*) to tip over (*in +acc* into); **plötzlich kippte seine Fröhlichkeit in Depression um** suddenly his cheerfulness turned to depression **e** *(Fluss, See)* to become polluted

um|klam|mern [ʊm'klamɐn] *ptp* **umklammert** VT *insep* to wrap one's arms/legs around; (= *umarmen auch)* to hug, to embrace; *(mit Händen)* to clasp; (= *festhalten)* to cling to; *(Ringen)* to hold, to clinch; *(Mil)* to trap in a pincer movement; **sie hielt ihn/meine Hand umklammert** she held him/my hand tight, she clung (on) to him/my hand; **einander** *or* **sich ~** *(Ringen)* to go into a clinch

Um|klam|me|rung F -, **-en** clutch; (= *Umarmung)* embrace; *(Ringen)* clinch; *(Mil)* pincer movement

um|klapp|bar ADJ *Rücksitz, Lehne* fold-down *attr*

um+klap|pen *sep* VT to fold down VI *aux sein* *(inf)* to pass out

Um|klei|de F *(inf)* → **Umkleideraum**

Um|klei|de|ka|bi|ne F changing cubicle; *(in Kleidungsgeschäft auch)* changing *or* fitting room

um+klei|den ['ʊmklaidn] VR *sep* to change (one's clothes); **sie ist noch nicht umgekleidet** she hasn't changed yet

um|klei|den [ʊm'klaidn] *ptp* **umkleidet** VT *insep* to cover; **die Wahrheit mit schönen Worten ~** *(fig)* to gloss over *or* varnish the truth

Um|klei|de|raum M changing room; *(esp mit Schließfächern)* locker room; *(Theat)* dressing room

um+kni|cken *sep* VT *Ast, Mast* to snap; *Baum* to break; *Gras, Strohhalm* to bend over; *Papier* to fold (over) VI *aux sein (Ast)* to snap; *(Gras, Strohhalm)* to get bent over; **mit dem Fuß ~** to twist one's ankle

um+ko|die|ren *ptp* **umkodiert** VT *sep (Comput)* to recode

um+kom|men VI *sep irreg aux sein* **a** (= *sterben)* to die, to be killed, to perish *(liter)*; **vor Lange(r)weile ~** *(inf)* to be bored to death *(inf)*, to nearly die of boredom; **da kommt man ja um!** *(inf) (vor Hitze)* the heat is killing *(inf)*; *(wegen Gestank)* it's enough to knock you out *(inf)* **b** *(inf: = verderben: Lebensmittel)* to go off *(Brit) or* bad

um|krän|zen [ʊm'krɛntsn] *ptp* **umkränzt** VT *insep (liter)* to wreathe, to garland

Um|kreis M (= *Umgebung)* surroundings *pl*; (= *Gebiet)* area; (= *Nähe)* vicinity; *(Math)* circumcircle; **im näheren ~** in the vicinity; **im ~ von 20 Kilometern** within a radius of 20 kilometres *(Brit) or* kilometers *(US)*

um|krei|sen [ʊm'kraizn] *ptp* **umkreist** VT *insep* to circle (around); *(Astron)* to orbit, to revolve around; *(Space)* to orbit

Um|krei|sung F -, **-en** *(Space, Astron)* orbiting; **drei ~en der Erde** three orbits of the Earth; **die ~ des Feindes** circling the enemy

um+krem|peln VT *sep* **a** *Ärmel, Hosenbein* to turn up; *(mehrmals)* to roll up **b** (= *umwenden)* to turn inside out; *(inf) Zimmer* to turn upside down *(inf)*; *Betrieb, System* to shake up *(inf)*; **jdn ~** *(fig inf)* to change sb *or* sb's ways

um+ku|cken VR *sep (N Ger inf)* = **umsehen**

um+la|den VT *sep irreg* to transfer, to reload; *(Naut)* to transship

Um|la|dung F transfer, reloading; *(Naut)* transshipping

Um|la|ge F **eine ~ machen** to split the cost; **sie beschlossen eine ~ der Kosten** they decided to split the costs

um|la|gern [ʊm'la:gɐn] *ptp* **umlagert** VT *insep* (= *einkreisen)* to surround; (= *sich drängen um, auch Mil)* to besiege, to beleaguer

um+la|gern ['ʊmla:gɐn] VT *sep* (= *anderswo lagern)* to transfer (*in +acc* into); (= *in anderes Lager bringen) Waren etc* to re-store; *Patienten* to move

Um|la|ge|ver|fah|ren NT assessment system

Um|land NT, *no pl* surrounding countryside

Um|land|ge|mein|de F *usu pl* (small) community in the surrounding area

Um|lauf M **a** *(von Erde etc)* revolution; *(Sport, auf Parcours etc)* round; (= *das Kursieren)* circulation *(auch fig)*; **im ~ sein** to be circulating, to be in circulation; **in ~ bringen** *or* **setzen** to circulate; *Geld auch* to put in circulation; *Gerücht auch* to put about, to spread **b** (= *Rundschreiben)* circular **c** *(Med: = Fingerentzündung)* whitlow

Um|lauf|bahn F orbit; **die ~ um den Mond/die Erde** lunar/earth orbit; **auf der ~ um die Erde sein** to be orbiting the earth

um+lau|fen ['ʊmlaufn] *sep irreg* VT to (run into and) knock over VI *aux sein* to circulate

um|lau|fen [ʊm'laufn] *ptp* **umlaufen** VT *insep irreg* to orbit

Um|lauf-: **Um|lauf|ge|schwin|dig|keit** F *(Fin: des Geldes)* turnover rate; *(Astron)* orbiting speed; **Um|lauf|ren|di|te** F *(Fin)* current yield; *(Econ)* yields *pl* on bonds outstanding; **Um|lauf|schrei|ben** NT circular; **Um|lauf|ver|mö|gen** NT *(Fin)* current assets *pl*; **Um|lauf|zeit** F *(Astron)* period; *(Space)* orbiting time

Um|laut M **a** *no pl* umlaut, vowel mutation *(esp Brit)* **b** *(Laut)* vowel with umlaut, mutated vowel *(esp Brit)*

um+lau|ten VT *sep* to mutate *(esp Brit)*, to modify (*zu* into)

um+le|gen *sep* VT **a** (= *umhängen, umbinden)* to put round; **jdm/sich eine Stola ~** to put a stole (a)round sb's/one's shoulders

b *Mauer, Baum* to bring down; *(sl: = zu Boden schlagen) Gegner* to knock down, to floor

c (= *umklappen)* to tilt (over); *Kragen* to turn down; *Manschetten* to turn up; *(Cards)* to turn (over); *Hebel* to turn; (= *kürzen) Hose, Rock etc* to take up

d (= *verlegen) Kranke* to transfer, to move; *Leitung* to re-lay

e *Termin* to change (*auf +acc* to)

f (= *verteilen)* **die 200 Euro wurden auf uns fünf umgelegt** the five of us each had to pay a contribution toward(s) the 200 euros

g *(inf: = ermorden)* to do in *(inf)*, to bump off *(inf)*

VR *(Boot)* to capsize, to turn over; *(Getreide)* to be flattened

Um|le|gung F **a** *(von Grundstücken etc)* distribution; *(eines Patienten)* moving **b** *(Fin: von Kosten)* division **c** *(eines Termins)* changing

um+lei|ten VT *sep* to divert

Um|lei|tung F diversion; *(Strecke auch)* detour

Um|lei|tungs-: **Um|lei|tungs|schild** NT diversion *or* detour sign; **Um|lei|tungs|stre|cke** F detour

um+ler|nen VI *sep* to retrain; *(fig)* to change one's ideas

um|lie|gend ADJ surrounding

um|lo|dern [ʊm'lo:dɐn] *ptp* **umlodert** VT *insep (liter)* to light up; **von Fackeln umlodert** lit (up) *or* lighted by blazing torches

Um|luft F *(Tech)* circulating air

Um|luft|herd M fan(-assisted) oven, convection oven *(US)*

um|man|teln [ʊm'mantln] *ptp* **ummantelt** VT *insep (Tech)* to coat

Um|man|te|lung F *(Tech)* casing, sheath

um|mau|ern [ʊm'mauɐn] *ptp* **ummauert** VT *insep* to wall in (*mit* by)

um+mel|den VTR *sep* **jdn/sich ~** to notify (the police of) a change in sb's/one's address

Um|mel|dung F notification of (one's) change of address

um|mi ['ʊmi] ADV *(Aus inf)* = **hinüber**

um+mo|deln VT *sep (inf)* to change

um+mün|zen VT *sep (fig)* to turn (*in +acc* into); **eine Niederlage in einen Sieg ~** to make a defeat look like a victory

um|nach|tet [ʊm'naxtət] ADJ *(geh) Geist* clouded over *pred*; **geistig ~** mentally deranged

Um|nach|tung [ʊm'naxtʊŋ] F -, **-en geistige ~** mental derangement; **da muss ich in geistiger ~ gewesen sein** *(hum)* I must have had a brainstorm

um+nä|hen VT *sep Saum* to stitch up

um|ne|beln [ʊm'ne:bln] *ptp* **umnebelt** *insep* VT *(mit Tabakrauch)* to surround with smoke; *(fig) jdn* to muddle; *jds Geist* to cloud VR *(Blick)* to cloud *or* mist over; **mit umnebeltem Blick** with misty eyes

um+neh|men VT *sep irreg Mantel, Schal etc* to put on

um+nie|ten VT *sep (sl: = töten)* to blow away *(inf)*

um+num|me|rie|ren *ptp* **umnummeriert** VT *sep* to renumber

um+ord|nen VT *sep* to rearrange; (= *in andere Reihenfolge bringen auch)* to reorder

Um|or|ga|ni|sa|ti|on F reorganization

um+or|ga|ni|sie|ren *ptp* **umorganisiert** VT *sep* to reorganize

um+ori|en|tie|ren *ptp* **umorientiert** VR *sep (fig)* to reorientate oneself

Um|ori|en|tie|rung F reorientation

um+pa|cken VT *sep* to repack

um+pflan|zen [ˈʊmpflantsn] VT *sep (= woanders pflanzen)* to transplant; *Topfpflanze* to repot

um|pflan|zen [ʊmˈpflantsn] *ptp* **umpflanzt** VT *insep* **einen Platz mit Bäumen ~** to plant trees around a square

um+pflü|gen VT *sep* to plough *(Brit) or* plow *(US)* up

um+po|len VT *sep (Elec)* to reverse the polarity of; *(inf: = ändern)* to convert *(auf +acc* to)

um+quar|tie|ren *ptp* **umquartiert** VT *sep* to move; *Truppen (in andere Kaserne etc)* to requarter; *(in anderes Privathaus)* to rebillet

um|rah|men [ʊmˈraːmən] *ptp* **umrahmt** VT *insep* to frame; **die Ansprache war von musikalischen Darbietungen umrahmt** the speech was accompanied by musical offerings (before and after)

um+rah|men [ˈʊmraːmən] VT *sep* to reframe

Um|rah|mung [ʊmˈraːmʊŋ] F **-, -en** setting (+*gen, von* for); *(= das Umrahmen)* framing; **mit musikalischer ~** with music before and after

um|ran|den [ʊmˈrandn] *ptp* **umrandet** VT *insep* to edge, to border; **tragen Sie die Adresse in das stark umrandete Feld ein** write the address in the area marked in bold outline

um|rän|dert [ʊmˈrɛndɐt] ADJ *Augen* red-rimmed

Um|ran|dung F **-, -en** border, edging

um|ran|ken [ʊmˈraŋkn] *ptp* **umrankt** VT *insep* to climb *or* twine (a)round; **von** *or* **mit Efeu umrankt** twined around with ivy

um+räu|men *sep* VT *(= anders anordnen)* to rearrange, to change (a)round; *(= an anderen Platz bringen)* to shift, to move VI to change the furniture (a)round, to rearrange the furniture

um+rech|nen VT *sep* to convert *(in +acc* into)

Um|rech|ner M *(in Taschenrechner etc)* converter

Um|rech|nung F conversion

Um|rech|nungs-: **Um|rech|nungs|kurs** M exchange *or* conversion rate, rate of exchange; **Um|rech|nungs|ta|bel|le** F conversion table

um+rei|ßen [ˈʊmraisn] VT *sep irreg (= zu Boden reißen)* to tear down; *(= umwerfen)* to knock over

um|rei|ßen [ʊmˈraisn] *ptp* **umrissen** [ʊmˈrɪsn] VT *insep irreg (= skizzieren)* to outline; **scharf umrissen** clear-cut, well defined; *Züge auch* sharply defined

um+ren|nen VT *sep irreg* to (run into and) knock down

um|rin|gen [ʊmˈrɪŋən] *ptp* **umringt** VT *insep* to surround, to gather around; *(drängend)* to throng *or* crowd around; **von neugierigen Passanten umringt** surrounded/thronged by curious passers-by

Um|riss M outline; *(= Kontur)* contour(s *pl*); **etw in ~en zeichnen/erzählen** to outline sth, to draw/tell sth in outline; **„Geschichte in ~en"** "History - A Brief Outline"

um|riss|haft ADJ, ADV in outline

Um|riss|zeich|nung F outline drawing

um+rüh|ren VT *sep* to stir; **etw unter ständigem Umrühren kochen** to boil sth stirring constantly *or* continually

um+run|den *ptp* **umrundet** VT *sep* to go (a)round; *(zu Fuß)* to walk (a)round; *(mit Fahrzeug)* to drive (a)round

um+rüs|ten VT *sep* **a** *(Tech)* to adapt; **etw auf etw** *(acc)* **~** to adapt *or* convert sth to sth **b** *(Mil)* to re-equip

ums [ʊms] *contr von* **um das**

um+sat|teln *sep* VT *Pferd* to resaddle VI *(inf) (beruflich)* to change jobs; *(Univ)* to change courses; **von etw auf etw** *(acc)* **~** to switch from sth to sth

Um|satz M *(Comm)* turnover; **5000 Euro ~ machen** *(inf)* to do 5000 euros' worth of business

Um|satz-: **Um|satz|an|stieg** M increase in turnover; **Um|satz|be|tei|li|gung** F commission; **Um|satz|ein|bruch** M, **Um|satz|ein|bu|ße** F *(Comm)* drop in turnover; **Um|satz|ent|wick|lung** F *(Comm)* sales trend; **Um|satz|er|war|tung** F *(Comm)* estimated sales *pl*; **Um|satz|mi|nus** NT *(Comm)* → **Umsatzrückgang**; **Um|satz|plus** NT *(Comm)* increase in turnover *or* sales, upturn in sales *(esp US)*; **Um|satz|rück|gang** M drop in turnover; **Um|satz|stei|ge|rung** NT → **Umsatzplus**; **Um|satz|steu|er** F sales tax; **Um|satz|wachs|tum** NT *(Comm)* growth in sales; **Um|satz|zahl** NT *usu pl (Comm)* sales figure

um+säu|men [ˈʊmzɔymən] VT *sep Stoffrand* to hem

um|säu|men [ʊmˈzɔymən] *ptp* **umsäumt** VT *insep* to line; *(Sew)* to edge; **von Bäumen umsäumt** tree-lined

um+schal|ten *sep* VT *(auf +acc* to) *Schalter* to flick; *Hebel* to turn; *Strom* to convert; *Gerät* to switch over; **den Schalter auf „heiß" ~** to put the switch to "hot" VI to flick the/a switch; *(auf anderen Sender)* to turn *or* change over *(auf +acc* to); *(im Denken, = sich gewöhnen)* to change *(auf +acc* to); *(Ampel)* to change; **„wir schalten jetzt um nach Hamburg"** "and now we go over *or* we're going over to Hamburg"

Um|schal|ter M *(Elec)* (changeover) switch; *(von Schreibmaschine)* shift key

Um|schalt-: **Um|schalt|flä|che** F *(Comput)* toggle button; **Um|schalt|pau|se** F *(Rad, TV)* intermission, break *(before going over to somewhere else)*; **Um|schalt|tas|te** F *(Comput)* shift key

Um|schal|tung F *(auf +acc* to) changeover; *(im Denken, = Umgewöhnung)* change

um|schat|ten [ʊmˈʃatn] *ptp* **umschattet** VT *insep (geh)* **seine Augen waren umschattet** he had shadows *or* rings under his eyes

Um|schau F, *no pl (fig)* review; *(TV, Rad)* magazine programme *(Brit)*, news magazine (show) *(US)*; **~ halten** to look around *(nach* for)

um+schau|en VR *sep (esp dial)* = **umsehen**

um+schich|ten *sep* VT to restack; *Gelder* to reallocate VR *(Sociol)* to restructure itself

um|schich|tig [ˈʊmʃɪçtɪç] ADV on a shift basis ADV **~ arbeiten** to work in shifts

Um|schich|tung F **a** restacking **b** *(Sociol)* restructuring; **soziale ~** change of social stratification, social regrouping *or* restructuring

um+schie|ßen VT *sep irreg* to (shoot at and) knock over

um|schif|fen [ʊmˈʃɪfn] *ptp* **umschifft** VT *insep* to sail (a)round; *Kap auch* to round, to double *(spec)*; *Erde auch* to circumnavigate → **Klippe**

um+schif|fen [ˈʊmʃɪfn] VT *sep* to transfer; *Fracht auch* to transship

Um|schif|fung [ʊmˈʃɪfʊŋ] F **-, -en** sailing (a)round; *(von Kap auch)* rounding, doubling *(spec)*; *(von Erde auch)* circumnavigation; **die ~ einer gefährlichen Klippe** *(fig)* getting over a dangerous obstacle

Um|schif|fung [ˈʊmʃɪfʊŋ] F transfer; *(von Fracht auch)* transshipping, transshipment

Um|schlag M **a** *(= Veränderung)* (sudden) change (+*gen* in, *in +acc* into) **b** *(= Hülle)* cover; *(= Briefumschlag)* envelope; *(als Verpackung)* wrapping; *(= Buchumschlag)* jacket **c** *(Med)* compress; *(= Packung)* poultice; **jdm heiße/kalte Umschläge machen** to put hot poultices/cold compresses on sb **d** *(= Ärmelumschlag)* cuff; *(= Hosenumschlag)* turn-up *(Brit)*, cuff *(US)* **e** *(= umgeschlagene Gütermenge)* volume of traffic; **einen hohen ~ an Baumwolle** *etc* **haben** to handle a lot of cotton *etc* **f** *(= Umladung) (auf +acc* to) transfer, transshipment

um+schla|gen *sep irreg* VT **a** *Seite etc* to turn over; *Ärmel, Hosenbein, Saum* to turn up; *Teppich, Decke* to fold *or* turn back; *Kragen* to turn down **b** *(um die Schultern) Schal* to put on **c** *(= umladen) Güter* to transfer, to transship; **etw vom Schiff auf die Bahn ~** to unload sth from the ship onto the train **d** *(= absetzen) Güter* to handle VI *aux sein* **a** *(= sich ändern)* to change (suddenly); *(Wind)* to veer; *(Stimme)* to break, to crack; **in etw** *(acc)* **~** to change *or* turn into sth; **ins Gegenteil ~** to become the opposite **b** *(= sauer werden)* to go off *(Brit) or* bad; *(Milch)* to go off *(Brit) or* sour, to turn *(esp Brit)*

Um|schlag-: **Um|schlag|ent|wurf** M jacket design; **Um|schlag|ha|fen** M port of transshipment; **Um|schlag|klap|pe** F jacket flap *(of book)*; **Um|schlag|platz** M trade centre *(Brit) or* center *(US)*; **Um|schlag|tuch** NT *pl* **-tücher** shawl, wrap *(esp US)*

um|schlei|chen [ʊmˈʃlaiçn] *ptp* **umschlichen** [ʊmˈʃlɪçn] VT *insep irreg* to creep *or* prowl around

um|schlie|ßen [ʊmˈʃliːsn] *ptp* **umschlossen** [ʊmˈʃlɔsn] VT *insep irreg* to surround *(auch Mil)*, to enclose; *(mit den Armen)* to embrace; *(fig: Plan, Entwurf etc)* to include, to encompass

um|schlin|gen [ʊmˈʃlɪŋən] *ptp* **umschlungen** [ʊmˈʃlʊŋən] VT *insep irreg* **a** *(Pflanze)* to twine (a)round **b** *(geh)* **jdn (mit den Armen) ~** to enfold *(liter) or* clasp sb in one's arms, to embrace sb

um|schlun|gen [ʊmˈʃlʊŋən] ADJ **eng ~** with their *etc* arms tightly (a)round each other

Um|schluss M *(in Strafanstalt)* recreation

um|schmei|cheln [ʊmˈʃmaiçln] *ptp* **umschmeichelt** VT *insep* to flatter; *(fig)* to caress

um+schmei|ßen VT *sep irreg* **a** *(= umwerfen)* to knock flying *(inf) or* over **b** *(= erstaunen)* to bowl over *(inf)*; *(Gestank etc)* to knock out **c das schmeißt meine Pläne um** that messes my plans up *(inf)*

um+schmel|zen VT *sep irreg* to recast

um+schnal|len VT *sep* to buckle on

um+schrei|ben [ˈʊmʃraibn] VT *sep irreg* **a** *Text etc* to rewrite; *(in andere Schrift)* to transcribe *(auch Phon)*, to transliterate; *(= bearbeiten) Theaterstück etc* to adapt *(für* for) **b** *(= umbuchen)* to alter, to change *(auf +acc* for) **c** *Hypothek etc* to transfer; **etw auf jdn ~/~ lassen** to transfer sth/have sth transferred to sb *or* sb's name

um|schrei|ben [ʊmˈʃraibn] *ptp* **umschrieben** [ʊmˈʃriːbn] VT *insep irreg* **a** *(= mit anderen Worten ausdrücken)* to paraphrase; *(= darlegen)* to outline, to describe; *(= abgrenzen)* to circumscribe; *(= verhüllen) Sachverhalt* to refer to obliquely, to skate around *(inf)* **b** *(Ling) Verneinung* to construct

Um|schrei|bung [ˈʊmʃraibʊŋ] F **a** *(von Text etc)* rewriting; *(in andere Schrift)* transcription *(auch Phon)*, transliteration; *(von Theaterstück etc)* adaptation *(für* for) **b** *(= Umbuchung)* altering, changing *(auf +acc* for) **c** *(von Hypothek etc)* transfer

Um|schrei|bung [ʊmˈʃraibʊŋ] F **a** *no pl (= das Umschreiben)* paraphrasing; *(= das Abgrenzen)* circumscribing, circumscription; *(von Sachverhalt)* oblique reference (+*gen* to) **b** *(= das Umschriebene)* paraphrase; *(= Darlegung)* outline, description; *(= Abgrenzung)* circumscription; *(verhüllend)* oblique reference (+*gen* to), circumlocution **c** *no pl (Gram: von Verneinung)* construction

Um|schrift F **a** *(auf Münze)* inscription, circumscription **b** *(Ling: = Transkription)* transcription *(auch Phon)*, transliteration

um+schul|den VT *sep (Comm) Kredit* to convert, to fund; **ein Unternehmen ~** to change the terms of a firm's debt(s)

Um|schul|dung [ˈʊmʃʊldʊŋ] F **-, -en** funding *no pl*

um+schu|len VT *sep* **a** *(beruflich)* to retrain; *(Pol euph)* to re-educate **b** *(auf andere Schule)* to transfer (to another school)

Um|schü|ler(in) M(F) student for retraining

Um|schu|lung F retraining; *(Pol euph)* re-education; *(auf andere Schule)* transfer; **berufliche ~** vocational retraining

um+schüt|ten VT *sep* to spill, to upset; **etw aus einer Dose in eine Kanne ~** to pour sth from a can into a jug

um|schwär|men [ʊmˈʃvɛrmən] *ptp* **umschwärmt** VT *insep* to swarm (a)round; *(Menschen auch)* to flock (a)round; *(= verehren)* to idolize; **von Ver-**

ehrern umschwärmt werden *(fig)* to be besieged *or* surrounded by admirers; **eine umschwärmte Schönheit** a much-courted beauty

Um|schwei|fe [ˈʊmʃvaifə] PL **ohne ~** straight out, plainly; **mach keine ~!** don't beat about *(Brit) or* around the bush, come (straight) to the point

um+schwen|ken VI *sep* **a** *aux sein or haben (Anhänger, Kran)* to swing out; *(fig)* to do an about-face *(US) or* about-turn *(Brit)*; **der Kran schwenkte nach rechts um** the crane swung to the right **b** *(Wind)* to veer

um|schwir|ren [ʊmˈʃvɪrən] *ptp* **umschwirrt** VT *insep (lit, fig)* to buzz (a)round

Um|schwung M **a** *(Gymnastik)* circle **b** *(fig) (= Veränderung)* drastic change; *(ins Gegenteil)* reversal, about-turn; **ein ~ zum Besseren** a drastic change for the better

um|se|geln [ʊmˈzeːgln] *ptp* **umsegelt** VT *insep* to sail (a)round; *Kap auch* to round, to double *(spec)*; *Erde auch* to circumnavigate

Um|se|ge|lung [ʊmˈzeːgəlʊŋ] F **-, -en, Um|seg|lung** [ʊmˈzeːglʊŋ] F **-, -en** sailing (a)round; *(von Kap auch)* rounding, doubling *(spec)*; *(von Erde auch)* circumnavigation

um+se|hen VR *sep irreg* to look around (*nach* for); *(rückwärts)* to look (a)round *or* back; **sich in der Stadt ~** to have a look (a)round the town; **sich in der Welt ~** to see something of the world; **ich möchte mich nur mal ~** *(in Geschäft)* I'm just looking, I just wanted to have a look (around); **ohne mich wird er sich noch ~** *(inf)* he's not going to find it easy without me

um sein VI *irreg aux sein (Frist, Zeit)* to be up

Um|sei|te F *(Press)* page two; **auf der ~** on page two

um|sei|tig [ˈʊmzaitɪç] ADJ overleaf; **die ~e Abbildung** the illustration overleaf ADV overleaf

um|setz|bar ADJ *(= realisierbar)* practicable; **schwer/nicht ~** *(Plan)* difficult/impossbile to implement

um+set|zen *sep* VT **a** *Pflanzen* to transplant; *Topfpflanze* to repot; *Schüler etc* to move (to another seat) **b** *Waren, Geld* to turn over **c** *(Typ)* to reset **d etw in etw** *(acc)* **~** to convert sth into sth; *(Mus: = transponieren)* to transpose sth into sth; *(in Verse etc)* to render *or* translate sth into sth; **sein Geld in Briefmarken/Alkohol ~** to spend all one's money on stamps/alcohol; **etw in die Tat ~** to translate sth into action VR *(Schüler etc)* to change seats *or* places; **sich in etw** *(acc)* **~** to be converted into sth

Um|set|zung F **-, -en a** *(= Realisierung)* realization; *(eines Plans)* implementation; **wir haben gute Ideen, aber es mangelt noch an der ~** we have some good ideas but we still haven't put them into practice **b** *(= Umwandlung)* conversion (*in +acc* into)

Um|set|zungs|ta|bel|le F *(Comput)* translation table

Um|sich|grei|fen [ʊmˈzɪçgraifn] NT **-s,** *no pl (von Krankheit, Inflation)* spread; *(von Wohnungsnot)* escalation

Um|sicht F **-,** *no pl* circumspection, prudence; *(von Handeln etc auch)* judiciousness

um|sich|tig [ˈʊmzɪçtɪç] ADJ circumspect, prudent; *Handlungsweise etc auch* judicious ADV circumspectly, prudently

um+sie|deln VTI *sep (vi: aux sein)* to resettle; **von einem Ort an einen anderen ~** to move from one place and settle in another

Um|sie|de|lung [ˈʊmziːdəlʊŋ] F **-, -en** resettlement

Um|sied|ler(in) M(F) resettler

Um|sied|lung [ˈʊmziːdlʊŋ] F resettlement

um+sin|ken VI *sep irreg aux sein (geh)* to sink to the ground; **vor Müdigkeit ~** to drop with exhaustion

um|so [ˈʊmzoː] CONJ *(= desto)* **~ besser/schlimmer!** so much the better/worse!, all the better/that's even worse!; **je mehr … ~ weniger/eher kann man …** the more … the less/sooner one can …; **~ mehr, als …** all the more considering *or* as; **unser Aufenthalt ist sehr kurz, ~ besser muss er geplant werden** as our stay is so short, we have to plan it all the better

um|so|mehr △ ADV → **umso**

um|sonst [ʊmˈzɔnst] ADV **a** *(= unentgeltlich)* free, for nothing, free of charge *(esp Comm)*; **~ sein** to be free (of charge); **das hast du nicht ~ getan!** you'll pay for that, I'll get even with you for that; **~ ist nur der Tod(, und der kostet das Leben)** *(prov)* you don't get anything for nothing in this world **b** *(= vergebens)* in vain, to no avail; *(= erfolglos)* without success **c** *(= ohne Grund)* for nothing; **nicht ~** not for nothing, not without reason

um|sor|gen [ʊmˈzɔrgn] *ptp* **umsorgt** VT *insep* to care for, to look after

um|so|we|ni|ger △ ADV → **umso**

um|span|nen [ʊmˈʃpanən] *ptp* **umspannt** VT *insep* **a etw mit beiden Armen/der Hand ~** to get both arms/one's hand (all the way) (a)round sth **b** *(fig) Bereich* to encompass, to embrace

um+span|nen [ˈʊmʃpanən] VT *sep* **a** *Pferde* to change **b** *(Elec)* to transform

Um|span|ner M *(Elec)* transformer

Um|spann|sta|ti|on F, **Um|spann|werk** NT *(Elec)* transformer (station)

um|spie|len [ʊmˈʃpiːlən] *ptp* **umspielt** VT *insep* **a** *(geh) (Rock etc)* to swirl around; *(Lächeln)* to play around; *(Wellen)* to lap at **b** *(Ftbl)* to dribble (a)round, to take out *(inf)*

Um|spring|bild NT *(Psych)* dual-aspect picture

um+sprin|gen [ˈʊmʃprɪŋən] VI *sep irreg aux sein* **a** *(Wind)* to veer (*nach* to), to change; *(Bild)* to change **b** *(Ski)* to jump-turn **c mit jdm grob** *etc* **~** *(inf)* to treat sb roughly *etc*, to be rough *etc* with sb; **so kannst du nicht mit ihr ~!** *(inf)* you can't treat her like that!

um|sprin|gen [ʊmˈʃprɪŋən] *ptp* **umsprungen** [ʊmˈʃprʊŋən] VT *insep irreg* to jump about *(Brit) or* around, to leap around

um+spu|len VT *sep* to rewind

um|spü|len [ʊmˈʃpyːlən] *ptp* **umspült** VT *insep* to wash (a)round

Um|stand ✪ 31 M **a** circumstance; *(= Tatsache)* fact; **ein unvorhergesehener ~** something unforeseen, unforeseen circumstances *pl*; **den Umständen entsprechend** much as one would expect (under the circumstances); **es geht ihm den Umständen entsprechend (gut)** he is as well as can be expected (under the circumstances); **nähere/die näheren Umstände** further details; **in anderen Umständen sein** to be expecting, to be in the family way; **unter diesen/keinen/anderen Umständen** under these/no/any other circumstances; **unter Umständen** possibly; **unter allen Umständen** at all costs → **mildern VT**

b Umstände PL *(= Mühe, Schwierigkeiten)* bother *sing*, trouble *sing*; *(= Förmlichkeit)* fuss *sing*; **ohne (große) Umstände** without (much) fuss, without a (great) fuss; **das macht gar keine Umstände** it's no bother *or* trouble at all; **jdm Umstände machen** *or* **bereiten** to cause sb bother *or* trouble, to put sb out; **machen Sie bloß keine Umstände!** please don't go to any bother *or* trouble, please don't put yourself out; **einen ~ machen** to make a fuss (*mit* over)

um|stän|de|hal|ber [ˈʊmʃtɛndəhalbɐ] ADV owing to circumstances; **„umständehalber zu verkaufen"** "forced to sell"

um|ständ|lich [ˈʊmʃtɛntlɪç] ADJ *Arbeitsweise, Methode* (awkward and) involved; *(= langsam und ungeschickt)* ponderous; *Vorbereitung* elaborate; *Begriff, Erklärung, Übersetzung, Titel, Anleitung* long-winded; *Abfertigung* laborious, tedious; *Arbeit, Reise* awkward; **sei doch nicht so ~!** don't make such heavy weather of everything! *(Brit)*, don't make everything twice as hard as it really is!; **er ist fürchterlich ~** he always makes everything seem twice as hard; **das ist vielleicht ~** what a lot of bother *or* trouble; **das ist mir zu ~** that's too much bother *or* trouble ADV *erklären, fragen, formulieren* in a roundabout way; *arbeiten, vorgehen* awkwardly; **etw ~ machen** to make heavy weather of doing sth *(Brit)*, to make doing sth seem twice as hard; **etw ~ erzählen/erklären** *etc* to tell/explain *etc* sth in a roundabout way

Um|ständ|lich|keit F **-, -en** *(von Arbeitsweise, Methode)* involvedness; *(von Erklärung etc)* long-windedness; **ihre ~** the way she makes such heavy weather of everything *(Brit)*, the way she makes everything seem twice as hard

Um|stands-: **Um|stands|be|stim|mung** F adverbial phrase; **Um|stands|kleid** NT maternity dress; **Um|stands|klei|dung** F maternity wear; **Um|stands|krä|mer(in)** M(F) *(inf)* fusspot *(inf)*, fussbudget *(US inf)*; **Um|stands|mo|den** PL maternity fashions *pl*; **Um|stands|wort** NT *pl* **-wörter** adverb

um+ste|cken VT *sep* **a** *(Elec) Kontakt etc* to move; *Gerät etc* to plug into another socket **b** *Kleid, Saum* to pin up **c** *Pflanzen* to transplant

um|ste|hen [ʊmˈʃteːən] *ptp* **umstanden** [ʊmˈʃtandn] VT *insep irreg* to surround, to stand (a)round; **ein von Bäumen umstandener Teich** a pond surrounded by trees

um|ste|hend ADJ *attr* **a** *(= in der Nähe stehend)* standing nearby; **die Umstehenden** the bystanders, the people standing nearby **b** *(= umseitig)* overleaf; **die ~e Erklärung** the explanation overleaf; **im Umstehenden** overleaf ADV overleaf

Um|stei|ge-: **Um|stei|ge|bahn|hof** M interchange (station); **Um|stei|ge|fahr|schein** M transfer ticket; **Um|stei|ge|mög|lich|keit** F **dort haben Sie ~** you can change there (*nach* for)

um+stei|gen VI *sep irreg aux sein* **a** *(in anderes Verkehrsmittel)* to change (*nach* for); *(in Bus, Zug etc)* to change (buses/trains *etc*); **bitte hier ~ nach Eppendorf** (all) change here for Eppendorf; **in ein anderes Auto ~, von einem Auto ins andere ~** to change *or* switch cars; **bitte beim Umsteigen beeilen!** will those passengers changing here please do so quickly **b** *(fig inf)* to change over, to switch (over) (*auf +acc* to)

Um|stei|ger M *(inf)* transfer (ticket)

um+stel|len [ˈʊmʃtɛlən] *sep* VT **a** *Möbel, Wörter* to rearrange, to change (a)round; *(Gram) Subjekt und Prädikat* to transpose

b *(= anders einstellen) Hebel, Telefon, Fernsehgerät, Betrieb* to switch over; *Radio* to tune *or* switch to another station; *Uhr* to alter, to put back/forward; *Währung* to change over; **etw auf Computer ~** to computerize sth; **der Betrieb wird auf die Produktion von Turbinen umgestellt** the factory is switching over to producing turbines

VI **auf etw** *(acc)* **~** *(Betrieb)* to go *or* switch over to sth; *auf Erdgas etc* to convert *or* be converted to sth

VR to move *or* shift about *(Brit) or* around; *(fig)* to get used to a different lifestyle; **sich auf etw** *(acc)* **~** to adapt *or* adjust to sth

um|stel|len [ʊmˈʃtɛlən] *ptp* **umstellt** VT *insep (= einkreisen)* to surround

Um|stel|lung [ˈʊm-] F **a** *(von Möbel, Wörtern)* rearrangement, changing (a)round; *(Gram, von Subjekt und Prädikat)* transposition **b** *(von Hebel, Telefon, Fernsehgerät, Betrieb)* switch-over; *(von Radio)* tuning to another station; *(von Uhr)* alteration, putting back/forward; *(von Währung)* changeover; **~ auf Erdgas** conversion to natural gas; **~ auf Computer** computerization **c** *(fig: = das Sichumstellen)* adjustment (*auf +acc* to); **das wird eine große ~ für ihn sein** it will be a big change for him

um+steu|ern [ˈʊmʃtɔyɐn] VT *sep Satelliten etc* to alter the course of VI to change course

um|steu|ern [ʊmˈʃtɔyɐn] *ptp* **umsteuert** VT *insep Hindernis* to steer (a)round

um+stim|men VT *sep* **a** *Instrument* to tune to a different pitch, to retune **b jdn ~** to change sb's mind; **er war nicht umzustimmen, er ließ sich nicht ~** he was not to be persuaded

um+sto|ßen VT *sep irreg Gegenstand* to knock over; *(fig) (Mensch) Plan, Testament, Bestimmung etc* to change; *(Umstände etc) Plan, Berechnung* to upset

um|strah|len [ʊmˈʃtraːlən] *ptp* **umstrahlt** VT *insep (liter)* to shine around; **von einem Heiligenschein umstrahlt** surrounded *or* illuminated by a halo

um|strit|ten [ʊmˈʃtrɪtn] ADJ *(= fraglich)* controversial; *(= wird noch debattiert)* disputed

um+struk|tu|rie|ren *ptp* **umstrukturiert** VT *sep* to restructure

Um|struk|tu|rie|rung F restructuring

um+stül|pen VT *sep* to turn upside down; *Tasche* to turn out; *Manschetten etc* to turn up *or* back; *Seite* to turn over

Um|sturz M coup (d'état), putsch

Um|sturz|be|we|gung F subversive movement

um+stür|zen *sep* VT to overturn; *Puddingform etc* to turn upside down; *(fig) Regierung, Staat, Verfassung* to overthrow; *Demokratie* to destroy; **~de Veränderungen** revolutionary changes VI *aux sein* to fall; *(Möbelstück, Wagen etc)* to overturn

Um|stürz|ler [ˈʊmʃtʏrtslɐ] M **-s, -**, **Um|stürz|le|rin** [-ərɪn] F **-, -nen** subversive

um|stürz|le|risch [ˈʊmʃtʏrtslərɪʃ] ADJ subversive ADV **sich ~ betätigen** to engage in subversive activities

Um|sturz|ver|such M attempted coup *or* putsch

um|tan|zen [ʊmˈtantsn] *ptp* **umtanzt** VT *insep* to dance (a)round

um+tau|fen VT *sep* to rebaptize; *(= umbenennen)* to rename, to rechristen

Um|tausch M exchange; **diese Waren sind vom ~ ausgeschlossen** these goods cannot be exchanged; **beim ~ bitte den Kassenzettel vorlegen** please produce the receipt when exchanging goods

um|tausch|bar ADJ exchangeable

um+tau|schen VT *sep* to (ex)change; *Geld, Aktien* to change, to convert *(form)* (*in +acc* into)

Um|tausch-: **Um|tausch|frist** F *(für neu gekaufte Waren)* exchange *or* return period; **Um|tausch|recht** NT right to return *or* exchange goods

um+top|fen VT *sep Blumen etc* to repot

um|tost [ʊmˈtoːst] ADJ *(liter)* buffeted (*von* by)

Um|trie|be PL machinations *pl*; **umstürzlerische ~** subversive activities

um|trie|big [ˈʊmtriːbɪç] ADJ *(= betriebsam)* go-getting

Um|trie|big|keit F (extreme) busyness; *(Eigenschaft)* bustling nature

Um|trunk M drink

um+tun VR *sep irreg (inf)* to look around (*nach* for)

U-Mu|sik [ˈuː-] F *abbr von* **Unterhaltungsmusik**

Um|ver|pa|ckung F external packaging

um+ver|tei|len *ptp* **umverteilt** VT *sep or insep* to redistribute

Um|ver|tei|lung F redistribution

um|wach|sen [ʊmˈvaksn] *ptp* **umwachsen** VT *insep irreg* to grow around; **ein von Bäumen ~er Teich** a pond with trees growing all (a)round it

Um|wal|lung F ramparts *pl*

Um|wälz|an|la|ge F circulating plant

um+wäl|zen VT *sep Luft, Wasser* to circulate; *(fig)* to change radically, to revolutionize

um|wäl|zend ADJ *(fig) Bedeutung, Entwicklung* radical; *Veränderungen auch* sweeping; *Ereignisse* revolutionary

Um|wälz|pum|pe F circulating pump

Um|wäl|zung [ˈʊmvɛltsʊŋ] F **-, -en** *(Tech)* circulation; *(fig)* radical change

um|wan|del|bar ADJ (*in +acc* to) convertible; *Strafe* commutable

um+wan|deln [ˈʊmvandln] *sep* VT to change (*in +acc* into); *(Comm, Fin, Sci)* to convert (*in +acc* to); *(Jur) Strafe* to commute (*in +acc* to); *(fig)* to transform (*in +acc* into); **er ist wie umgewandelt** he's a changed man, he's a (completely) different person VR to be converted (*in +acc* into)

um|wan|deln [ʊmˈvandln] *ptp* **umwandelt** VT *insep (liter)* to walk (a)round

Um|wand|lung [ˈʊm-] F change; *(Comm, Fin, Sci)* conversion; *(von Strafe)* commutation; *(fig)* transformation

um|we|ben [ʊmˈveːbn] *ptp* **umwoben** [ʊmˈvoːbn] VT *insep irreg (liter)* to envelop; **viele Sagen umwoben das alte Schloss** many legends had been woven around the old castle; **ein von Sagen umwobener Ort** a place around which many legends have been woven

um+wech|seln VT *sep Geld* to change (*in +acc* to, into)

Um|wechs|lung [ˈʊmvɛksluŋ] F **-, -en** exchange (*in +acc* for)

Um|weg [ˈʊmveːk] M detour; *(fig)* roundabout way; **einen ~ machen/fahren** to go a long way round *(Brit)* or around; *(absichtlich auch)* to make a detour; **wenn das für Sie kein ~ ist** if it doesn't take you out of your way; **auf ~en (ans Ziel kommen)** (to get there) by a roundabout *or* circuitous route; *(fig)* (to get there) in a rather roundabout way; **auf dem ~ über jdn** *(fig)* indirectly via sb; **etw auf ~en erfahren** *(fig)* to find sth out indirectly

Um|weg|fi|nan|zie|rung F indirect financing

um|we|hen [ʊmˈveːən] *ptp* **umweht** VT *insep* to fan, to blow around; **sich vom Wind ~ lassen** to be fanned by the breeze

um+we|hen [ˈʊmveːən] VT *sep* to blow over

Um|welt F, *no pl* environment

Um|welt- *in cpds* environmental; **Um|welt|alarm** M environmental alarm; **Um|welt|al|ler|gie** F environmental allergy; **Um|welt|as|pekt** M environmental consideration; **Um|welt|auf|la|ge** F *(Admin)* environmental requirement; **Um|welt|au|to** NT environmentally friendly car; **um|welt|be|dingt** ADJ caused by the environment; *Faktoren, Einflüsse* determined by the environment; **Um|welt|be|hör|de** F environmental authority; **um|welt|be|las|tend** ADJ causing environmental pollution; **Um|welt|be|las|tung** F ecological damage, damage to the environment; **um|welt|be|wusst** ADJ *Person* environmentally aware; *Verhalten, Produkt* environmentally friendly, ecofriendly *(Brit)* ADV in an environmentally friendly way; **Um|welt|be|wusst|sein** NT environmental awareness; **Um|welt|bun|des|amt** NT ≈ Department of the Environment *(Brit)*, ≈ Environmental Protection Agency *(US)*; **Um|welt|ein|flüs|se** PL environmental influences *pl*; **Um|welt|en|gel** M **der blaue ~** *symbol attached to a product guaranteeing environmental friendliness*; **Um|welt|ent|las|tung** F environmental relief; **Um|welt|er|zie|hung** F education in environmental problems; **Um|welt|ex|per|te** M, **Um|welt|ex|per|tin** F environmental expert, expert on the environment; **um|welt|feind|lich** ADJ ecologically harmful, environmentally damaging; **um|welt|freund|lich** ADJ environmentally friendly, ecofriendly *(Brit)*; **Um|welt|freund|lich|keit** F ecofriendliness *(Brit)*, environmental friendliness; **um|welt|ge|fähr|dend** ADJ harmful to the environment; **Um|welt|ge|fähr|dung** F endangering of the environment; **um|welt|ge|recht** ADJ environmentally compatible, compatible with the environment ADV in an ecologically desirable *or* environmentally sound way; **um|welt|ge|schä|digt** [-gəʃɛːdɪçt] ADJ suffering from an environmental illness; **wir sind Umweltgeschädigte** our health is affected by the environment; **Um|welt|ge|setz** NT environmental law; **Um|welt|ge|setz|ge|bung** F environmental legislation; **um|welt|ge|stört** ADJ *(Psych)* maladjusted *(due to adverse social factors)*; **Um|welt|gift** NT environmental pollutant; **Um|welt|gip|fel** M environment(al) summit; **Um|welt|kar|te** F *cheap ticket to encourage use of public transport*; **Um|welt|ka|ta|stro|phe** F ecological disaster; **Um|welt|krank|hei|ten** PL environmental illnesses *pl*; **Um|welt|kri|mi|na|li|tät** F environmental crimes *pl*; **Um|welt|kri|se** F ecological crisis; **Um|welt|ma|nage|ment** NT management of environmental resources; **Um|welt|me|di|zin** F environmental medicine; **Um|welt|mi|nis|te|ri|um** NT ≈ Ministry of the Environment *(Brit)*, ≈ Environment and Natural Resources Division *(US)*; **Um|welt|mo|bil** [-mobiːl] NT **-s, -e** environmental information bus; **Um|welt|norm** F environmental standard; **Um|welt|or|ga|ni|sa|ti|on** F environmental organization; **um|welt|o|ri|en|tiert** ADJ environmentally concerned *or* conscious; **Um|welt|pa|pier** NT recycled paper; **Um|welt|pfen|nig** M *(fig)* levy on petrol *(Brit) or* gas *(US) (used to improve the environment)*; **Um|welt|pla|nung** F ecological planning; **Um|welt|po|li|tik** F environmental policy; **um|welt|po|li|tisch** ADJ relating to environmental policy; **~er Sprecher** environment spokesman ADV in terms of environmental policy; **~ umstrittene Gesetzesvorlagen** (draft) bills which are controversial in terms of environmental policy; **Um|welt|pro|gramm** NT *(von UNO etc)* environmental programme *(Brit) or* program *(US)*; **Um|welt|pro|jekt** NT environmental project; **Um|welt|qua|li|tät** F quality of the environment; **Um|welt|recht** NT environmental law; **um|welt|re|le|vant** ADJ relevant to the environment; **Um|welt|scha|den** M damage to the environment; **um|welt|schäd|lich** ADJ ecologically harmful, harmful to the environment ADV in a way which is harmful to the environment; **um|welt|scho|nend** ADJ environmentally friendly, ecofriendly *(Brit)* ADV in an environmentally friendly way

Um|welt|schutz M conservation, environmental protection *no art*

Um|welt|schutz|auf|la|ge F environmental restriction

Um|welt|schüt|zer(in) M(F) conservationist, environmentalist

Um|welt|schutz-: **Um|welt|schutz|ge|setz** NT conservation law; **Um|welt|schutz|or|ga|ni|sa|ti|on** F environmentalist group; **Um|welt|schutz|pa|pier** NT recycled paper; **Um|welt|schutz|tech|nik** F conservation technology

Um|welt-: **Um|welt|steu|er** F ecology tax; **Um|welt|sün|der(in)** M(F) *(inf)* polluter; **Um|welt|tech|nik** F environmental technology; **Um|welt|to|xi|ko|lo|ge** M, **Um|welt|to|xi|ko|lo|gin** F environmental toxicologist; **Um|welt|to|xi|ko|lo|gie** F environmental toxicology; **Um|welt|ver|schmut|zung** F pollution (of the environment); **Um|welt|ver|seu|chung** F contamination of the environment; **Um|welt|ver|stö|ße** PL environmental offences *(Brit) or* offenses *(US) pl*; **um|welt|ver|träg|lich** ADJ *Produkte, Stoffe* not harmful to the environment ADV in a way which is not harmful to the environment; **Um|welt|ver|träg|lich|keit** F ecofriendliness *(Brit)*, environmental friendliness; **Um|welt|ver|träg|lich|keits|prü|fung** F environmental compatibility assessment, environmental audit; **Um|welt|wär|me** F ambient heat; **Um|welt|zer|stö|rung** F destruction of the environment

um+wen|den *sep irreg* VT to turn over VR to turn ((a)round) (*nach* to)

um|wer|ben [ʊmˈvɛrbn] *ptp* **umworben** [ʊmˈvɔrbn] VT *insep irreg* to court

um+wer|fen VT *sep irreg* **a** *Gegenstand* to knock over; *Möbelstück etc* to overturn **b** *(fig: = ändern)* to upset; *Strategie, Vorstellungen* to throw over **c** *jdn (körperlich)* to knock down; *(Ringen)* to throw down; *(fig inf)* to stun, to bowl over; **ein Whisky wirft dich nicht gleich um** one whisky won't knock you out **d** **sich**

(dat) **etw ~** to throw *or* put sth (a)round one's shoulders
um|wer|fend ADJ fantastic; **von ~er Komik** hilarious, a scream *(inf)* ADV fantastically
Um|wer|tung F re-evaluation
um|wi|ckeln [ʊmˈvɪkln] *ptp* **umwickelt** VT *insep* to wrap (a)round; *(mit Band, Verband auch)* to swathe *(liter)* *(mit* in); *(mit Schnur, Draht etc)* to wind (a)round; **etw mit Stoff/Draht ~** to wrap cloth/wind wire (a)round sth
um+wi|ckeln [ˈʊmvɪkln] VT *sep* to wrap (a)round; *Garn etc* to rewind; **jdm/sich etw ~** to wrap sth (a)round sb/oneself
um+wid|men VT *sep* to redesignate *(in* as)
Um|wid|mung F redesignation
um|win|den [ʊmˈvɪndn] *ptp* **umwunden** [ʊmˈvʊndn] VT *insep irreg (geh)* to wind (a)round *(mit* with); **etw mit Blumen ~** to entwine sth with flowers
um|wit|tert [ʊmˈvɪtɐt] ADJ *(geh)* surrounded *(von* by); **von Geheimnissen ~** shrouded in mystery
um|wo|gen [ʊmˈvoːgn] *ptp* **umwogt** VT *insep (liter)* to wash (a)round
um|woh|nend ADJ neighbouring *(Brit)*, neighboring *(US)*; **die Umwohnenden** the local residents
um|wöl|ken [ʊmˈvœlkn] *ptp* **umwölkt** VR *insep (geh)* to cloud over; *(Sonne, Mond auch)* to become veiled in cloud *(Brit liter)* or clouds *(US liter)*, to darken; *(Berggipfel)* to become shrouded in cloud *(Brit)* or clouds *(US)*; *(fig: Stirn)* to cloud
um|zäu|nen [ʊmˈtsɔynən] *ptp* **umzäunt** VT *insep* to fence (a)round
Um|zäu|nung F -, -en *(= das Umzäunen)* fencing (a)round; *(= Zaun)* fence, fencing
um+zie|hen [ˈʊmtsiːən] *sep irreg* VI *aux sein (= Wohnung wechseln)* to move, to move house *(Brit)*; *(Firma etc)* to move; **nach Köln ~** to move to Cologne VT a **die Kinder ~** to get the children changed b *(hum: = den Umzug für jdn durchführen)* to move VR to change, to get changed
um|zie|hen [ʊmˈtsiːən] *ptp* **umzogen** [ʊmˈtsoːgn] *insep irreg (geh)* VT to surround VR *(Himmel)* to cloud over *(auch fig)*, to become overcast *or* cloudy
um|zin|geln [ʊmˈtsɪŋln] *ptp* **umzingelt** VT *insep* to surround, to encircle
Um|zin|ge|lung [ʊmˈtsɪŋəlʊŋ] F -, -en encirclement
Um|zug [ˈʊmtsuːk] M a *(= Wohnungsumzug)* move, removal; **wann soll euer ~ sein?** when are you moving? b *(= Festzug)* procession; *(= Demonstrationszug)* parade
Um|zugs-: Um|zugs|kar|ton M packing case; **Um|zugs|kos|ten** PL removal *or* moving *(US)* costs *pl*
UN [uːˈlɛn] PL UN *sing*, United Nations *sing*
un|ab|än|der|lich [ʊnlapˈlɛndɐlɪç] ADJ a *(= unwiderruflich)* unalterable; *Entschluss, Urteil* irrevocable, irreversible; *Niedergang, Verlust* irreversible; **etw als ~ hinnehmen** to accept sth as an unalterable fact b *(= ewig) Gesetze, Schicksal, Wahrheit* immutable ADV **~ feststehen** to be absolutely certain; **etw ist ~ passiert** sth is irreversible
Un|ab|än|der|lich|keit F -, *no pl (von Entschluss, Urteil)* irrevocability, irreversibility
un|ab|ding|bar [ʊnlapˈdɪŋbaːɐ, ˈʊn-] ADJ *Voraussetzung, Forderung* indispensable; *Recht* inalienable; *Notwendigkeit* absolute; **etw für ~ halten** to consider sth (to be) indispensable
Un|ab|ding|bar|keit F -, *no pl (von Voraussetzung, Forderung)* indispensability
un-: un|ab|ding|lich [ʊnlapˈdɪŋlɪç, ˈʊn-] ADJ = **unabdingbar**; **un|ab|ge|legt** [ˈʊnlapgəleːkt] ADJ unfiled; **un|ab|ge|schlos|sen** ADJ *(= nicht verschlossen)* unlocked; *(= nicht fertiggestellt)* unfinished
un|ab|hän|gig ADJ independent *(von* of); *Journalist* freelance; **das ist ~ davon, ob/wann** *etc* that does not depend on *or* is not dependent on whether/when *etc*; **~ davon, was Sie meinen** irrespective of *or* regardless of what you think; **sich ~ machen** to go one's own way; **sich von jdm/etw ~ machen** to become independent of sb/sth
Un|ab|hän|gig|keit F, *no pl* independence; **ein Land in die ~ entlassen** to grant a country independence
Un|ab|hän|gig|keits-: Un|ab|hän|gig|keits|be|stre|bung F *usu pl* drive *no pl* for independence; **Un|ab|hän|gig|keits|be|we|gung** F independence movement; **Un|ab|hän|gig|keits|er|klä|rung** F declaration of independence; **Un|ab|hän|gig|keits|krieg** M war of independence; **Un|ab|hän|gig|keits|tag** M *(in den USA)* Independence Day, Fourth of July
un|ab|kömm|lich ADJ *(geh)* busy, engaged *pred (form)*; *(= unverzichtbar) Person, Gegenstand* indispensable
un|ab|läs|sig [ʊnlapˈlɛsɪç, ˈʊn-] ADJ continual; *Regen, Lärm etc auch* incessant; *Versuche, Bemühungen auch* unremitting, unceasing ADV continually; **~ für den Frieden kämpfen** to fight unceasingly for peace
un|ab|seh|bar ADJ a *(fig) Folgen etc* unforeseeable; *Schaden* incalculable, immeasurable; **der Schaden/die Zahl der Toten ist noch ~** the amount of damage/the number of dead is not yet known; **auf ~e Zeit** for an indefinite period b *(lit)* interminable; *Weite* boundless; **in ~er Weite** boundlessly; **in ~er Ferne** in the far, far distance ADV *sich verzögern* to an unforeseeable extent; **~ lang sein** to seem to be interminable
Un|ab|seh|bar|keit [ʊnlapˈzeːbaːɐkait] F -, *no pl* unforeseeable nature
Un-: un|ab|sicht|lich ADJ unintentional; *(= aus Versehen auch)* accidental ADV unintentionally; **un|ab|wähl|bar** ADJ **er ist ~** he cannot be voted out of office; **un|ab|weis|bar** [ʊnlapˈvaisbaːɐ, ˈʊn-], **un|ab|weis|lich** [ʊnlapˈvaislɪç, ˈʊn-] ADJ irrefutable; *Notwendigkeit* absolute; **un|ab|wend|bar** ADJ inevitable; **Un|ab|wend|bar|keit** [ʊnlapˈvɛntbaːɐkait, ˈʊn-] F -, *no pl* inevitability; **un|acht|sam** ADJ *(= unaufmerksam)* inattentive; *(= nicht sorgsam)* careless; *(= unbedacht)* thoughtless ADV carelessly; *wegwerfen* thoughtlessly; **benimm dich nicht so ~** don't be so careless; **~ über die Straße laufen** to cross the road without paying attention; **Un|acht|sam|keit** F *(= Unaufmerksamkeit)* inattentiveness; *(= Sorglosigkeit)* carelessness; *(= Unbedachtheit)* thoughtlessness
un|ähn|lich ADJ dissimilar; **einer Sache** *(dat)* **~ sein** to be unlike sth, to be dissimilar to sth; **einander ~** unlike each other, dissimilar
Un|ähn|lich|keit F dissimilarity
un-: un|ak|zep|ta|bel ADJ unacceptable; **un|an|fecht|bar** ADJ *Urteil, Entscheidung, Gesetz* unchallengeable, incontestable; *Argument etc* unassailable; *Beweis* irrefutable; **un|an|ge|bracht** ADJ *Bescheidenheit, Bemerkung* uncalled-for; *Sorge, Sparsamkeit, Bemühungen auch* misplaced; *(für Kinder, Altersstufe etc)* unsuitable; *(= unzweckmäßig) Maßnahmen* inappropriate; **un|an|ge|foch|ten** [ˈʊnlangəfɔxtn] ADJ unchallenged; *Urteil, Entscheidung* undisputed, uncontested; *Testament, Wahlkandidat* uncontested ADV *behaupten, an der Spitze liegen* unchallenged; **Liverpool führt ~ die Tabelle an** Liverpool are unchallenged at the top of the league; **un|an|ge|mel|det** [ˈʊnlangəmɛldət] ADJ unannounced *no adv*; *Besucher* unexpected; *Patient etc* without an appointment ADV unannounced; *besuchen* without letting sb know; *(in Bezug auf Patient)* without an appointment
un|an|ge|mes|sen ADJ *(= zu hoch)* unreasonable, out of all proportion; *(= unzulänglich)* inadequate; **einer Sache** *(dat)* **~ sein** to be inappropriate to sth; **dem Ereignis ~ sein** to be unsuitable for *or* inappropriate to the occasion, to ill befit the occasion ADV *hoch, niedrig, teuer* unreasonably; *gekleidet, sich verhalten* inappropriately; **sich ~ äußern** to make inappropriate remarks
un|an|ge|nehm ADJ unpleasant; *Mensch, Arbeit, Geschmack, Geruch auch* disagreeable; *(= peinlich) Situation auch* awkward, embarrassing; *Frage* awkward; *Zwischenfall, Begegnung* embarrassing; **das ist mir immer so ~** I never like that, I don't like that at all; **es war mir ~, das tun zu müssen** I didn't like having to do it; **es ist mir ~, dass ich Sie gestört habe** I feel bad about having disturbed you; **mein ständiges Husten war mir ~** I felt bad *or* embarrassed about coughing all the time; **er kann ~ werden** he can get quite nasty
ADV unpleasantly; **jdn ~ berühren** to embarrass sb; **~ berührt sein** to be embarrassed *(von* by); **~ schmecken/riechen** to taste/smell unpleasant
un-: un|an|ge|passt ADJ nonconformist; **un|an|ge|tas|tet** [ˈʊnlangətastət] ADJ untouched; **~ bleiben** *(Rechte)* not to be violated; **un|an|greif|bar** ADJ *Macht, Herrscher* unassailable; *Argument auch* irrefutable, unchallengeable; *Festung, Land* impregnable; **un|an|nehm|bar** ADJ unacceptable
Un|an|nehm|lich|keit F *usu pl* trouble *no pl*; *(= lästige Mühe auch)* bother *no pl*; **~en haben/bekommen** *or* **kriegen** to be in/to get into trouble; **jdm ~en bereiten** to cause trouble for sb; **damit hast du nichts als ~en** you'll have nothing but trouble with it; **das macht mir nicht die geringsten ~en** it's no trouble *or* bother at all (to me); **mit etw ~en haben** to have a lot of trouble with sth; **mit den Behörden ~en haben** to get into trouble with the authorities
un|an|sehn|lich ADJ unsightly; *Frau etc* plain; *Tapete, Möbel* shabby; *Nahrungsmittel* unappetizing
un|an|stän|dig ADJ a *(= unkultiviert, unerzogen)* ill-mannered, bad-mannered; *(= frech, unverschämt)* rude; *(= charakterlich minderwertig)* unprincipled; **so was Unanständiges!** how rude! b *(= obszön, anstößig)* dirty; *Witz, Lied* dirty, rude; *Wörter* rude; *(= vulgär) Kleidung* indecent; **~e Wörter gebrauchen** to use four-letter words; **~e Reden führen** to talk smut ADV a *(= rüpelhaft)* in an ill-mannered fashion, in a rude way b *(= obszön)* in a dirty *or* rude way
Un|an|stän|dig|keit F a *(= Unkultiviertheit, Unerzogenheit)* bad *or* ill manners *pl*; *(= Unverschämtheit)* rudeness *no pl* b *(= Obszönität)* obscenity; **~en erzählen** to tell dirty jokes/stories
Un-: un|an|tast|bar [ʊnlanˈtastbaːɐ, ˈʊn-] ADJ sacrosanct; *Rechte* inviolable; **Un|an|tast|bar|keit** F -, *no pl* sanctity; *(von Rechten, Staat, Grenze, Wohnung)* inviolability; **un|ap|pe|tit|lich** ADJ *(lit, fig)* unappetizing
Un|art F bad habit; *(= Ungezogenheit)* rude habit
un|ar|tig ADJ naughty
Un|ar|tig|keit F a *no pl (= Unartigsein)* naughtiness b *(= Handlungsweise)* naughty behaviour *(Brit)* or behavior *(US)* *no pl*, naughty trick
Un-: un|ar|ti|ku|liert [ˈʊnlartikuliːɐt] ADJ inarticulate; *(= undeutlich)* unclear, indistinct ADV inarticulately; **un|äs|the|tisch** ADJ unappetizing; **un|at|trak|tiv** ADJ unattractive ADV unattractively; **auf mich wirkt er ~** I don't find him attractive; **un|auf|dring|lich** ADJ unobtrusive; *Parfüm auch, Geste* discreet; *Mensch* unassuming ADV discreetly
un|auf|fäl|lig ADJ inconspicuous; *(= unscheinbar, schlicht)* unobtrusive; **die Narbe/sein Hinken ist ziemlich ~** the scar/his limp isn't very noticeable; **er ist ein ziemlich ~er junger Mann** he's not the kind of young man you notice particularly ADV unobtrusively, discreetly → **folgen**
Un|auf|fäl|lig|keit F -, *no pl* inconspicuousness; *(= Schlichtheit)* unobtrusiveness
un|auf|find|bar ADJ nowhere to be found; *Verbrecher, vermisste Person* untraceable
un|auf|ge|for|dert [ˈʊnlaufgəfɔrdɐt] ADJ unsolicited *(esp Comm)* ADV without being asked; **~ anfallende Arbeiten erledigen können** to be

able to work on one's own initiative; **jdm ~ Prospekte zuschicken** to send sb unsolicited brochures; **~ zugesandte Manuskripte** unsolicited manuscripts

Un-: un|auf|ge|klärt ADJ **a** unexplained; *Verbrechen* unsolved **b** *Mensch* ignorant; *(sexuell)* ignorant of the facts of life; **Un|auf|ge|klärt|heit** F *(von Mensch)* ignorance; *(sexuell)* ignorance of the facts of life; **un|auf|ge|räumt** ADJ untidy; **un|auf|ge|regt** ADJ calm; *Mensch auch* unexcited; *Erzählstil* sober; *Musik* unobtrusive ADV calmly; **un|auf|halt|bar** [ʊnlaufˈhaltbaːɐ, ˈʊn-] ADJ unstoppable ADV *weitergehen, sich fortentwickeln* unstoppably; **un|auf|halt|sam** [ʊnlaufˈhaltzaːm, ˈʊn-] ADJ **a** *(= unaufhaltbar)* unstoppable **b** *(= unerbittlich)* inexorable ADV **a** *(= unaufhaltbar)* unstoppably **b** *(= unerbittlich)* inexorably; **un|auf|hör|lich** [ʊnlaufˈhøːɐlɪç, ˈʊn-] ADJ continual, constant, incessant ADV continually, constantly, incessantly; **un|auf|lös|bar** [ʊnlaufˈløːsbaːɐ, ˈʊn-], **un|auf|lös|lich** [ʊnlaufˈløːslɪç, ˈʊn-] ADJ *Konflikt, Widersprüche* unresolvable; *Ehe* indissoluble; **Un|auf|lös|bar|keit** F -, *no pl*, **Un|auf|lös|lich|keit** F -, *no pl (von Ehe)* indissolubility; **un|auf|merk|sam** ADJ inattentive; *(= flüchtig) Leser etc* unobservant; **da war ich einen Augenblick ~** I didn't pay attention for a moment; **Un|auf|merk|sam|keit** F inattentiveness; **un|auf|rich|tig** ADJ insincere; **Un|auf|rich|tig|keit** F insincerity; **un|auf|schieb|bar** [ʊnlaufˈʃiːpbaːɐ, ˈʊn-] ADJ urgent; **es ist ~** it can't be put off *or* delayed *or* postponed; **un|aus|bleib|lich** [ʊnlausˈblaiplɪç, ˈʊn-] ADJ inevitable, unavoidable; **un|aus|denk|bar** [ʊnlausˈdɛŋkbaːɐ, ˈʊn-] ADJ unimaginable, unthinkable; **un|aus|führ|bar** ADJ impracticable, unfeasible; **un|aus|ge|füllt** [ˈʊnlausgəfʏlt] ADJ **a** *Formular etc* blank **b** *Leben, Mensch* unfulfilled

un|aus|ge|gli|chen ADJ unbalanced; *Verhältnis auch, Vermögensverteilung etc* unequal; *Stil auch* disharmonious; *Mensch (= launisch)* changeable, up-and-down *(inf)*; **ein Mensch mit ~em Wesen** a person of uneven temper

Un|aus|ge|gli|chen|heit F imbalance; *(von Verhältnis auch)* inequality; *(von Stil auch)* disharmony; *(von Mensch)* changeable moods *pl*; **die ~ seines Wesens** the unevenness of his temper

Un-: un|aus|ge|go|ren ADJ immature; *Idee, Plan auch* half-baked *(inf)*; *Jüngling auch* callow; **un|aus|ge|schla|fen** [ˈʊnlausgəʃlaːfn] ADJ tired; **er ist ~** he hasn't had enough sleep ADV without having had enough sleep; *sich anhören* sleepy; **er kam ziemlich ~ ins Büro** he obviously hadn't had enough sleep when he turned up in the office; **er sieht ~ aus** he looks as if he hasn't had enough sleep; **un|aus|ge|setzt** [ˈʊnlausgəzɛtst] ADJ incessant, constant ADV incessantly, constantly; **un|aus|ge|spro|chen** ADJ unsaid *pred*, unspoken; **un|aus|ge|wo|gen** ADJ unbalanced; **Un|aus|ge|wo|gen|heit** F imbalance; **un|aus|lösch|lich** [ʊnlausˈlœʃlɪç, ˈʊn-] *(geh)* ADJ indelible ADV indelibly; **un|aus|rott|bar** [ʊnlausˈrɔtbaːɐ, ˈʊn-] ADJ *Unkraut* indestructible; *(fig) Vorurteile, Vorstellung etc* ineradicable

un|aus|sprech|lich [ʊnlausˈʃprɛçlɪç, ˈʊn-] ADJ **a** *Wort, Laut* unpronounceable **b** *Schönheit, Leid etc* inexpressible **c** *(liter. = ungeheuerlich) Tat, Verbrechen* unspeakable **d die Unaussprechlichen** *(hum)* one's unmentionables *(Brit inf)*, underwear ADV *(enorm) schön* indescribably; *grausam, leiden* unspeakably; **er verehrt sie ~** he absolutely worships her

Un-: un|aus|steh|lich [ʊnlausˈʃteːlɪç, ˈʊn-] ADJ intolerable; *Mensch, Art, Eigenschaft auch* insufferable; **un|aus|weich|lich** [ʊnlausˈvaiçlɪç, ˈʊn-] ADJ unavoidable, inevitable; *Folgen auch* inescapable ADV unavoidably, inevitably; **Un|aus|weich|lich|keit** F -, *no pl* inevitability; *(= Dilemma)* dilemma

un|bän|dig [ˈʊnbɛndɪç] ADJ **a** *(= ausgelassen, ungestüm) Kind* boisterous **b** *(= ungezügelt) Freude, Lust, Hass, Zorn* unrestrained *no adv*, unbridled *no adv*; *Ehrgeiz, Fleiß* boundless; *Hunger* enormous ADV **a** *(= ungestüm) herumtoben* boisterously; **führt euch nicht so ~ auf** don't be so wild **b** *(= enorm)* enormously; **sie freuten sich ~** they were dancing around (with joy)

Un-: un|bar *(Comm)* ADJ **~e Zahlungsweise** non-cash payment ADV **etw ~ bezahlen** not to pay sth in cash, to pay sth by cheque *(Brit) or* check *(US)*/credit card *etc*; **un|barm|her|zig** ADJ merciless; *Mensch auch* pitiless ADV mercilessly; **Un|barm|her|zig|keit** F mercilessness; *(von Mensch auch)* pitilessness; **un|be|ab|sich|tigt** [ˈʊnbəlapzɪçtɪçt] ADJ unintentional ADV unintentionally

un|be|ach|tet [ˈʊnbəlaxtət] ADJ unnoticed; *Warnung, Vorschläge* unheeded; **~ bleiben** to go unnoticed/unheeded; **jdn/etw ~ lassen** not to take any notice of sb/sth; **wir sollten die weniger wichtigen Punkte zunächst ~ lassen** let's leave the less important points aside for the time being; **das dürfen wir nicht ~ lassen** we mustn't overlook that, we mustn't leave that out of account ADV unnoticed; *daliegen* completely ignored; *sterben* in obscurity

Un-: un|be|acht|lich ADJ insignificant; **un|be|an|stan|det** [ˈʊnbəlanʃtandət] ADJ not objected to; **etw ~ lassen** to let sth pass *or* go ADV without objection; **das Paket wurde ~ weitergeleitet** the parcel *(esp Brit) or* package got through without any problems; **un|be|ant|wor|tet** [ˈʊnbəlantvɔrtət] ADJ, ADV unanswered; **un|be|baut** [ˈʊnbəbaut] ADJ *Land* undeveloped; *Grundstück* vacant; *Feld* uncultivated; **un|be|dacht** ADJ *(= hastig)* rash; *(= unüberlegt)* thoughtless ADV rashly; **Un|be|dacht|heit** F -, **-en** *(= Hast)* rashness; *(= Unüberlegtheit)* thoughtlessness; **un|be|dacht|sam** ADJ, ADV = **unbedacht**; **un|be|darft** [ˈʊnbədarft] ADJ *(inf)* simple-minded; *Mensch (auf bestimmtem Gebiet)* green *(inf)*, clueless *(inf)*; *(= dumm)* dumb *(inf)*; **Un|be|darft|heit** F *(inf)* simple-mindedness; *(= Dummheit)* dumbness *(inf)*; **un|be|deckt** ADJ bare; **~en Hauptes** *(geh)* **mit ~em Haupt** *(geh)* bare-headed

un|be|denk|lich ADJ *(= ungefährlich)* completely harmless, quite safe; *(= sorglos)* thoughtless ADV *(= ungefährlich)* quite safely, without coming to any harm; *(= ohne zu zögern)* without thinking (twice *inf*)

Un|be|denk|lich|keit F *(= Ungefährlichkeit)* harmlessness

Un|be|denk|lich|keits-: Un|be|denk|lich|keits|be|schei|ni|gung F *(Jur) document certifying that one has no taxes, loans etc outstanding*; **Un|be|denk|lich|keits|er|klä|rung** F *(Med) official declaration that a substance etc is harmless*

un|be|deu|tend ADJ *(= unwichtig)* insignificant, unimportant; *(= geringfügig) Rückgang, Änderung etc* minor, minimal ADV *(= geringfügig)* slightly

un|be|dingt ✪ 29.2, 37.1, 37.3, 53.3 ADJ *attr* *(= absolut, bedingungslos) Ruhe, Verschwiegenheit Voraussetzung, Vorrang* absolute; *Gehorsam, Treue auch* implicit, unconditional; *Anhänger etc* unreserved; *Reflex* unconditioned ADV *(= auf jeden Fall)* really; *nötig, erforderlich* absolutely; **ich muss ~ mal wieder ins Kino gehen** I really must go to the cinema again; **ich musste sie ~ sprechen** I really *or* absolutely had to speak to her; *(äußerst wichtig)* it was imperative that I spoke to her; **müsst ihr denn ~ in meinem Arbeitszimmer spielen?** do you HAVE to play in my study?; **das ist nicht meine Schuld, du wolltest ja ~ ins Kino gehen!** it's not my fault, you were (hell)bent on going to the cinema; **er wollte ~ mit Renate verreisen** he was (hell)bent on going away with Renate; **~!** of course!, I should say so!; **nicht ~** not necessarily; **nicht ~ nötig** not absolutely *or* strictly necessary

Un|be|dingt|heit F *(= Bedingungslosigkeit)* unconditionality

Un-: un|be|ei|digt [ˈʊnbəlaidɪçt] ADJ *(Jur)* unsworn *usu attr*, not on oath; **un|be|ein|druckt** [ʊnbəˈlaindrʊkt, ˈʊn-] ADJ, ADV unimpressed *(von* by); **un|be|ein|fluss|bar** ADJ *Entwicklung* unalterable; *Mensch* unswayable, unable to be influenced; **un|be|ein|flusst** [ˈʊnbəlainflʊst] ADJ uninfluenced *(von* by); **un|be|fahr|bar** ADJ *Straße, Weg* impassable; *Gewässer* unnavigable; **un|be|fah|ren** ADJ *Straße, Fluss* unused; **un|be|fan|gen** ADJ **a** *(= unvoreingenommen)* impartial, unbiased *no adv*, objective **b** *(= natürlich)* natural; *(= ungehemmt)* uninhibited ADV **a** *(= unvoreingenommen)* impartially, objectively **b** *(= ungehemmt)* naturally, without inhibition; **Un|be|fan|gen|heit** F **a** *(= unparteiische Haltung)* impartiality, objectiveness **b** *(= Natürlichkeit)* naturalness; *(= Ungehemmtheit)* uninhibitedness; **un|be|fes|tigt** ADJ *Straße* unsurfaced; **un|be|fleckt** ADJ *(liter)* spotless, unsullied, untarnished; *Jungfrau* undefiled; **die Unbefleckte Empfängnis** the Immaculate Conception; **un|be|frie|di|gend** ADJ unsatisfactory ADV unsatisfactorily; **un|be|frie|digt** ADJ *(= frustriert)* unsatisfied; *(= unerfüllt auch)* unfulfilled; *(= unzufrieden)* dissatisfied; **un|be|fris|tet** ADJ *Arbeitsverhältnis, Vertrag* for an indefinite period; *Aufenthaltserlaubnis, Visum* permanent ADV indefinitely, for an indefinite period; **etw ~ verlängern** to extend sth indefinitely *or* for an indefinite period; **un|be|fruch|tet** [ˈʊnbəfrʊxtət] ADJ unfertilized; **un|be|fugt** ADJ unauthorized; **Eintritt für Unbefugte verboten, kein Zutritt für Unbefugte** no admittance to unauthorized persons ADV without authorization; **un|be|gabt** ADJ untalented, ungifted; **für etw ~ sein** to have no talent for sth; **er ist handwerklich völlig ~** he's no handyman; **Un|be|gabt|heit** F -, *no pl* lack of talent; **un|be|gli|chen** [ˈʊnbəglɪçn] ADJ unpaid, unsettled

un|be|greif|lich ADJ *(= unverständlich)* incomprehensible; *Leichtsinn, Irrtum, Dummheit* inconceivable; *(= unergründlich) Menschen, Länder* inscrutable; **es wird mir immer ~ bleiben, wie/dass ...** I shall never understand how/why ...; **es ist uns allen ~, wie das passieren konnte** none of us can understand how it happened; **das Unbegreifliche** *(Rel)* the Unknowable

un|be|greif|li|cher|wei|se [ˈʊnbəgraiflɪçəˈvaizə] ADV inexplicably

un|be|grenzt ADJ unlimited; *Möglichkeiten, Energie, Vertrauen etc auch* limitless, boundless, infinite; *Land, Meer etc* boundless; *Zeitspanne, Frist* indefinite; **zeitlich ~** indefinite; **auf ~e Zeit** indefinitely; **er hat ~e Zeit** he has unlimited time; **in ~er Höhe** of an unlimited *or* indefinite amount; **es ist nach oben ~** there's no upper limit (on it) ADV indefinitely; **„unbegrenzt haltbar"** "will keep indefinitely"

un|be|grün|det ADJ *Angst, Verdacht, Zweifel* unfounded, groundless, without foundation; *Maßnahme* unwarranted; **eine Klage als ~ abweisen** to dismiss a case

un|be|haart ADJ hairless; *(auf dem Kopf)* bald

Un|be|ha|gen NT (feeling of) uneasiness *or* disquiet, uneasy feeling; *(= Unzufriedenheit)* discontent *(an +dat* with); *(körperlich)* discomfort

un|be|hag|lich ADJ uncomfortable; *Gefühl auch* uneasy ADV **sich in jds Gesellschaft** *(dat)* **~ fühlen** to feel uncomfortable *or* ill at ease in sb's company

Un-: un|be|hau|en [ˈʊnbəhauən] ADJ unhewn; **un|be|haust** [ˈʊnbəhaust] ADJ *(liter)* homeless; **un|be|hel|ligt** [ʊnbəˈhɛlɪçt, ˈʊn-] ADJ *(= unbelästigt)* unmolested; *(= unkontrolliert)* unchecked; **jdn ~ lassen** to leave sb alone; *(Polizei etc)* not to stop sb ADV *(= unkontrolliert)* unchecked; *(= ungestört)* undisturbed, in peace; **un|be|herrscht** ADJ *Reaktion, Handlung, Bewegung* uncontrolled; *Mensch* lacking self-control; *(= gierig)* greedy ADV *essen* greedily; **sich ~ verhalten**

to lose control; **~ reagieren** to react in an uncontrolled way *or* without any self-control; **brüll nicht so ~** pull yourself together; **Un|be|herrscht|heit** F **-, -en** **a** *no pl (von Mensch)* lack of self-control; *(= Gier)* greediness **b** *(= unbeherrschte Handlung)* **diese ~ hat ihn seinen Job gekostet** losing his self-control just once cost him his job; **un|be|hin|dert** [ʊnbəˈhɪndɐt, ˈʊn-] ADJ unhindered, unimpeded; *Sicht* clear, uninterrupted; **~er Zugang** unrestricted access ADV unimpeded, without hindrance

un|be|hol|fen [ˈʊnbəhɔlfn] ADJ clumsy, awkward; *(= hilflos)* helpless; *(= plump) Annäherungsversuch* clumsy ADV clumsily, awkwardly; **mit seinem verletzten Bein geht er sehr ~** he walks very awkwardly with his injured leg

Un|be|hol|fen|heit F **-,** *no pl* clumsiness, awkwardness; *(= Hilflosigkeit)* helplessness; *(= Plumpheit)* clumsiness

un-: **un|be|irr|bar** [ʊnbəˈɪrbaːɐ, ˈʊn-] ADJ unwavering ADV unwaveringly; **un|be|irrt** [ʊnbəˈɪrt, ˈʊn-] ADJ unwavering ADV *glauben, festhalten* unwaveringly; *weiterreden, weitermachen* undeterred

un|be|kannt ADJ unknown; *Gesicht auch* unfamiliar; *Flugzeug, Flugobjekt etc* unidentified; **eine (mir) ~e Stadt/Stimme** a town/voice I didn't know, a town/voice unknown to me; **das war mir ~** I didn't know that, I was unaware of that; **dieser Herr/diese Gegend ist mir ~** I don't know *or* I'm not acquainted with this gentleman/area; **Angst ist ihm ~** he doesn't know what fear is *or* the meaning of (the word) fear; **es wird Ihnen nicht ~ sein, dass …** you will no doubt be aware that …; **~e Größe** *(Math, fig)* unknown quantity; **aus ~er Ursache** for some unknown reason; **nach ~ verzogen** moved – address unknown; **ich bin hier ~** *(inf)* I'm a stranger here; **~e Täter** person or persons unknown; **Strafanzeige gegen ~** charge against person or persons unknown

Un|be|kann|te F *decl as adj (Math)* unknown

Un|be|kann|te(r) MF *decl as adj* stranger; **der große ~** *(hum)* the mystery man/person *etc*

un|be|kann|ter|wei|se [ˈʊnbəkantɐˈvaizə] ADV **grüße sie/ihn ~ von mir** give her/him my regards although I don't know her/him

un|be|klei|det ADJ bare; **sie war ~** she had nothing *or* no clothes on, she was naked ADV without any clothes on

un|be|küm|mert [ʊnbəˈkʏmɐt, ˈʊn-] ADJ **a** *(= unbesorgt)* unconcerned; **sei ganz ~** don't worry **b** *(= sorgenfrei)* carefree ADV **a** *(= unbesorgt)* without worrying; **das kannst du ~ tun** you needn't worry about doing that **b** *(= sorglos)* without a care in the world; *lachen* happily

Un|be|küm|mert|heit F **-,** *no pl* **a** *(= Unbesorgtheit)* lack of concern **b** *(= Sorgenfreiheit)* carefreeness

un|be|las|tet [ˈʊnbəlastət] ADJ **a** *(= ohne Last)* unloaded, unladen; **das linke Bein ~ lassen** to keep one's weight off one's left leg **b** *(= ohne Schulden)* unencumbered **c** *(Pol: = ohne Schuld)* guiltless **d** *(= ohne Sorgen)* free from care *or* worries; **von Hemmungen/Ängsten** *etc* **~** free from inhibitions/fears *etc* **e** *(= schadstofffrei) Erdreich, Grundwasser etc* unpolluted ADV *(= ohne Sorgen)* without any worries; *(= unvoreingenommen)* neutrally, impartially

Un-: **un|be|lebt** ADJ *Straße, Gegend* quiet; **die ~e Natur** the inanimate world, inanimate nature; **un|be|leckt** [ˈʊnbəlɛkt] ADJ **~ von aller Kultur sein** *(inf)* to be completely uncultured; **un|be|lehr|bar** ADJ fixed in one's views; *Rassist etc* dyed-in-the-wool *attr*; **er ist ~** you can't tell him anything; **wenn du so ~ bist** if you won't be told; **Un|be|lehr|bar|keit** [ʊnbəˈleːɐbaːɐkait] F **-,** *no pl* **seine ~** the fact that you just can't tell him anything; **un|be|le|sen** ADJ unread, unlettered; **un|be|leuch|tet** [ˈʊnbəlɔyçtət] ADJ *Straße, Weg* unlit; *Fahrzeug* without lights; **un|be|lich|tet** [ˈʊnbəlɪçtət] ADJ *(Phot)* unexposed; **un|be|liebt** ADJ unpopular (*bei* with); **sich ~ machen** to make oneself unpopular; **Un|be|liebt|heit** F unpopularity *(bei* with); **un|be|mannt** [ˈʊnbəmant] ADJ *Raumflug, Station, U-Boot* unmanned; *Fahrzeug* driverless; *Flugzeug* pilotless; *(inf: = ohne Mann)* without a man *or* husband; **un|be|merk|bar** ADJ imperceptible; **un|be|merkt** [ˈʊnbəmɛrkt] ADJ, ADV unnoticed; *(= nicht gesehen auch)* unobserved; **~ bleiben** to escape attention, to go unnoticed; **un|be|mit|telt** ADJ without means; **~e Studenten erhalten vom Staat eine Beihilfe** students without (any) means of their own receive state aid; **un|be|nom|men** [ʊnbəˈnɔmən, ˈʊn-] ADJ *pred (form)* **es bleibt** *or* **ist Ihnen ~, zu …** you are (quite) free *or* at liberty to …; **das bleibt** *or* **ist dir ~** you're quite free *or* at liberty to do so; **un|be|nutz|bar** [ʊnbəˈnʊtsbaːɐ, ˈʊn-] ADJ unusable; **un|be|nutzt** [ˈʊnbənʊtst] ADJ, ADV unused; **un|be|o|bach|tet** [ˈʊnbəloːbaxtət] ADJ unobserved, unnoticed; **in einem ~en Moment** when nobody was looking; **wenn er sich ~ fühlt …** when he thinks nobody is looking …

un|be|quem ADJ *(= ungemütlich)* uncomfortable; *(= lästig) Mensch, Frage, Situation* awkward; *Aufgabe* unpleasant; *(= mühevoll)* difficult; **diese Schuhe sind mir zu ~** these shoes are too uncomfortable; **der Regierung/den Behörden** *etc* **~ sein** to be an embarrassment to the government/authorities *etc*

Un|be|quem|lich|keit F **a** *no pl (= Ungemütlichkeit)* lack of comfort; *(von Situation)* awkwardness **b** *usu pl* inconvenience

Un-: **un|be|re|chen|bar** ADJ unpredictable; **Un|be|re|chen|bar|keit** F unpredictability; **un|be|rech|tigt** ADJ *Sorge, Zweifel etc* unfounded; *Kritik, Forderung* unjustified; *(= unbefugt)* unauthorized ADV *(= unbefugt)* without authorization; *kritisieren* unjustifiably; *in Anspruch nehmen, kassieren* without entitlement; **un|be|rech|tig|ter|wei|se** [ˈʊnbərɛçtɪçtɐˈvaizə] ADV *kritisieren, sich sorgen* without reason; *(= unbefugt)* without authority; *in Anspruch nehmen, kassieren* without entitlement

un|be|rück|sich|tigt [ʊnbəˈrʏkzɪçtɪçt, ˈʊn-] ADJ unconsidered; **etw ~ lassen** not to consider sth, to leave sth out of consideration; **die Frage ist ~ geblieben** this question has not been considered; **ein bisher ~er Punkt** a point which has not yet been considered

un|be|ru|fen ADJ *(= unaufgefordert, unberechtigt)* uncalled-for, unwarranted ADV **~ (toi, toi, toi)!** touch wood! *(Brit)*, knock on wood! *(US)*; **sich ~ einmischen** to interfere without good reason

un|be|rühr|bar [ʊnbəˈryːɐbaːɐ, ˈʊn-] ADJ untouchable; **die Unberührbaren** the untouchables

un|be|rührt [ˈʊnbəryːɐt] ADJ **a** untouched; *(fig) Wald etc* virgin; *Natur* unspoiled; **~ sein** *(Mädchen)* to be a virgin **b** *(= mitleidlos)* unmoved; **das kann ihn nicht ~ lassen** he can't help but be moved by that **c** *(= unbetroffen)* unaffected ADV **a** *(= unangetastet)* **~ in die Ehe gehen** to be a virgin when one marries; **das Essen ~ stehen lassen** to leave one's food untouched **b** *(= unbewegt)* unmoved

Un|be|rührt|heit F **-,** *no pl (von Mädchen)* virginity; **wo finden Sie sonst noch diese ~ der Natur?** where else will you find nature so completely unspoiled?

un-: **un|be|scha|det** [ʊnbəˈʃaːdət, ˈʊn-] PREP *+gen (form)* regardless of; **~ dessen, dass …** regardless of the fact that …; **un|be|schä|digt** [ˈʊnbəʃɛdɪçt] ADJ, ADV undamaged; *Geschirr, Glas etc auch* intact, unbroken; *Siegel* unbroken; *(inf) Mensch* intact *(inf)*, unharmed, in one piece *(inf)*; **~ bleiben** not to be damaged/broken; *(seelisch etc)* to emerge unscathed; **un|be|schäf|tigt** ADJ *(= müßig)* idle; *(= arbeitslos)* not working

un|be|schei|den ADJ *Mensch, Plan* presumptuous; **darf ich mir die ~e Frage erlauben, …?** I hope you don't think me impertinent but might I ask …?

Un|be|schei|den|heit F presumptuousness; *(von Mensch auch)* presumption

Un-: **un|be|schol|ten** [ˈʊnbəʃɔltn] ADJ *(geh)* respectable; *Ruf* spotless; *(Jur)* with no previous convictions; **Un|be|schol|ten|heit** F **-,** *no pl (geh)* respectability; *(von Ruf)* spotlessness; *(Jur)* lack of previous convictions; **un|be|schrankt** ADJ *Bahnübergang* without gates, unguarded

un|be|schränkt ADJ unrestricted; *Freiheit, Vollmacht auch* limitless; *Macht* absolute; *Geldmittel, Haftung, Zeit, Geduld* unlimited; *Vertrauen* unbounded, boundless; **wie viel darf ich mitnehmen? – ~** how much can I take? – there's no limit *or* restriction; **jdm ~e Vollmacht geben** to give sb carte blanche

un|be|schreib|lich [ʊnbəˈʃraiplɪç, ˈʊn-] ADJ indescribable; *Frechheit* tremendous, enormous ADV *schön, gut etc* indescribably; **~ zunehmen** *(zahlenmäßig)* to show a staggering increase

un-: **un|be|schrie|ben** [ˈʊnbəʃriːbn] ADJ blank → **Blatt**; **un|be|schwert** [ˈʊnbəʃveːɐt] ADJ **a** *(= sorgenfrei)* carefree; *Melodien* light; *Unterhaltung, Lektüre* light-hearted **b** *(= ohne Gewicht)* unweighted ADV *(= sorgenfrei)* carefree; **er konnte das Leben ~ genießen** he could enjoy a carefree life; **un|be|seelt** [ˈʊnbəzeːlt] ADJ *(liter)* = **unbelebt**; **un|be|se|hen** [ʊnbəˈzeːən, ˈʊn-] ADV indiscriminately; *(= ohne es anzusehen)* without looking at it/them; **das glaube ich dir ~** I believe it if you say so; **das glaube ich dir nicht ~** I'll believe that when I see it; **un|be|setzt** ADJ vacant; *Stuhl, Platz auch* unoccupied; *Bus, Zug* empty; *Schalter* closed; **un|be|sieg|bar** ADJ *Armee etc* invincible; *Mannschaft, Sportler etc auch* unbeatable; **Un|be|sieg|bar|keit** [ʊnbəˈziːkbaːɐkait, ˈʊn-] F **-,** *no pl* invincibility; **un|be|siegt** [ˈʊnbəziːkt] ADJ undefeated; **un|be|son|nen** ADJ rash ADV rashly; **Un|be|son|nen|heit** F rashness

un|be|sorgt ADJ unconcerned; **Sie können ganz ~ sein** you can set your mind at rest *or* ease ADV without worrying; **das können Sie ~ tun** you don't need to worry about doing that

Un-: **un|be|stän|dig** ADJ *Wetter* changeable; *(zu bestimmtem Zeitpunkt auch)* unsettled; *Mensch* unsteady; *(in Leistungen)* erratic; *Liebhaber* inconstant; *Liebe, Gefühl* transitory; **Un|be|stän|dig|keit** F *(von Wetter)* changeability; *(von Mensch)* unsteadiness; *(in Leistungen)* erratic behaviour *(Brit) or* behavior *(US)*; *(von Liebhaber)* inconstancy; *(von Gefühl, Liebe)* transitory nature; **un|be|stä|tigt** [ˈʊnbəʃtɛːtɪçt, ʊnbəˈʃtɛːtɪçt] ADJ unconfirmed; **un|be|stech|lich** ADJ **a** *Mensch* incorruptible **b** *Urteil, Blick* unerring; **Un|be|stech|lich|keit** F **a** *(von Mensch)* incorruptibility **b** *(von Urteil, Blick)* **die ~ seines Urteils/Blicks** his unerring judgement/eye; **un|be|stimm|bar** ADJ indeterminable; **un|be|stimmt** ADJ **a** *(= ungewiss)* uncertain; *(= unentschieden)* undecided **b** *(= unklar, undeutlich) Gefühl, Erinnerung etc* vague; **etw ~ lassen** to leave sth open; **auf ~e Zeit** for an indefinite period, indefinitely **c** *(Gram)* indefinite; **Un|be|stimmt|heit** F, *no pl (= Ungewissheit)* uncertainty; **un|be|streit|bar** ✪ 42.1, 53.6 ADJ *Tatsache* indisputable; *Verdienste, Fähigkeiten* unquestionable ADV *richtig* indisputably; *fähig* unquestionably; **un|be|strit|ten** [ˈʊnbəʃtrɪtn, ʊnbəˈʃtrɪtn] ADJ undisputed, indisputable; **es ist ja ~, dass …** nobody denies *or* disputes that … ADV indisputably; **un|be|tei|ligt** ADJ **a** *(= uninteressiert)* indifferent; *(bei Diskussion)* uninterested **b** *(= nicht teilnehmend)* uninvolved *no adv (an +dat, bei* in); *(Jur, Comm)* disinterested; **es kamen auch Unbeteiligte zu Schaden** innocent bystanders were also injured; **un|be|tont** ADJ unstressed; **un|be|trächt|lich** ADJ insignificant; *Unannehmlichkeiten etc* minor; *Aufpreis, Verbilligung* slight; **nicht ~** not inconsiderable; **un|beug|sam** [ʊnˈbɔykzaːm, ˈʊn-] ADJ uncompromising, unbending; *Wille* unshakeable; **un|be|wacht** ['ʊnbəvaxt] ADJ, ADV *(lit, fig)* unguarded; *Parkplatz* unattended; **un|be|waff|net** ADJ unarmed; **un|be|wäl|tigt** ['ʊnbəvɛltɪçt, ʊnbə'vɛltɪçt] ADJ unconquered, unmastered; **Deutschlands ~e Vergangenheit** the past with which Germany has not yet come to terms

un|be|weg|lich ADJ **a** *(= nicht zu bewegen)* immovable; *(= steif)* stiff; *(geistig)* rigid, inflexible; **ohne Auto ist man ziemlich ~** you're not very mobile *or* you can't get around much without a car; **~e Güter** *(Jur)* immovable property **b** *(= bewegungslos)* motionless ADV **~ dastehen/daliegen** to stand/lie there motionless *or* without moving

Un|be|weg|lich|keit F immovability; *(= Steifheit)* stiffness; *(geistig)* rigidity, inflexibility

un-: un|be|wegt ADJ *(= bewegungslos)* motionless, unmoving; *Meer* unruffled; *(fig: = unberührt) Miene, Gesicht* impassive ADV *(= unberührt)* impassively; **un|be|weibt** ['ʊnbəvaipt] ADJ *(inf)* unmarried, wifeless *(inf)*; **un|be|wie|sen** ADJ unproven; **un|be|wohn|bar** ADJ uninhabitable; **un|be|wohnt** ADJ *Gegend, Insel, Planet* uninhabited; *Wohnung, Haus* unoccupied, empty; **un|be|wusst** ADJ unconscious; *Reflex* involuntary; **das Unbewusste** *(Psych)* the unconscious ADV unconsciously; **un|be|zahl|bar** ADJ **a** *(lit: = zu teuer)* prohibitively expensive, impossibly dear *(Brit)*; *Miete* prohibitively high; *Luxusartikel* absolutely unaffordable **b** *(fig) (= praktisch, nützlich)* invaluable; *(= komisch)* priceless; **un|be|zahlt** ADJ *Urlaub* unpaid; *Rechnung, Schuld etc auch* unsettled, outstanding; **sein noch ~es Auto** the car he hasn't finished paying for yet; **un|be|zähm|bar** [ʊnbə'tsɛːmbaːɐ, 'ʊn-] ADJ **a** *Optimismus, heiteres Gemüt, Neugier etc* irrepressible, indomitable; *Verlangen, Lust, Kraft* uncontrollable; *Hunger* insatiable; *Durst* unquenchable **b** *(= unbesiegbar)* invincible; **un|be|zwei|fel|bar** ADJ undeniable; *Tatsache auch* unarguable ADV undeniably; **un|be|zwing|bar** [ʊnbə'tsvɪŋbaːɐ], **un|be|zwing|lich** [ʊnbə'tsvɪŋlɪç, 'ʊn-] ADJ unconquerable; *Gegner* invincible; *Festung* impregnable; *Drang* uncontrollable

Un|bil|den ['ʊnbɪldn] PL *(liter)* **a** *(des Wetters)* rigours *pl (Brit)*, rigors *pl (US)* **b** *(einer schweren Zeit etc)* trials *pl*, (trials and) tribulations *pl*

Un|bil|dung F, *no pl* lack of education

Un|bill ['ʊnbɪl] F -, *no pl (old, liter)* injustice, wrong

un|bil|lig ADJ *(Jur: = ungerecht)* unjust; *(= unangemessen)* unreasonable; **~e Härte** *(Jur)* undue hardship

Un|bil|lig|keit F *(Jur: = Ungerechtigkeit)* injustice; *(= Unangemessenheit)* unreasonableness

Un-: un|blu|tig ADJ *Sieg, Umsturz etc* bloodless; *(Med)* non-operative ADV without bloodshed; **un|bot|mä|ßig** ADJ *(geh) (= undiszipliniert)* insubordinate; *(= rebellisch)* rebellious; **un|brauch|bar** ADJ *(= nutzlos)* useless, (of) no use *pred*; *(= nicht zu verwenden)* unusable; **Un|brauch|bar|keit** F *(= Nutzlosigkeit)* uselessness; **un|bü|ro|kra|tisch** ADJ unbureaucratic ADV without a lot of red tape, unbureaucratically; **un|christ|lich** ADJ unchristian; **eine ~e Zeit** *(inf)* an ungodly hour ADV in an unchristian way; **un|cool** ADJ *(inf)* uncool *(inf)*

und [ʊnt] CONJ **a** and; **~?** well?; **~ dann?** (and) what then *or* then what?; *(= danach)* and then?, and after that?; **~ Ähnliches** and things like that, and suchlike; **~ anderes** and other things; **er kann es nicht, ~ ich auch nicht** he can't do it, (and) nor *or* neither can I; **ich ~ ihm Geld leihen?** *(inf)* me, lend him money?; **du ~ tanzen können?** *(inf)* you dance?; **immer zwei ~ zwei** two at a time; **Gruppen zu fünf ~ fünf** groups of five; **er aß ~ aß** he ate and ate, he kept on (and on) eating; **er konnte ~ konnte nicht aufhören** he simply couldn't stop; **Unfälle, Staus, ~ ~ ~** accidents, traffic jams etc etc etc

b *(konzessiv)* even if; **..., ~ wenn ich selbst bezahlen muss** ... even if I have to pay myself; **..., ~ wenn du auch noch so bettelst** ... no matter how much you beg; **~ selbst** even; **~ selbst dann** even then

Un|dank M ingratitude; **~ ernten** to get little thanks; **~ ist der Welt Lohn** *(Prov)* never expect thanks for anything

un|dank|bar ADJ **a** *Mensch* ungrateful **b** *(= unerfreulich) Aufgabe, Arbeit etc* thankless ADV **sich jdm gegenüber ~ zeigen** *or* **erweisen** to be ungrateful to sb

Un|dank|bar|keit F **a** *(von Mensch)* ingratitude, ungratefulness **b** *(von Aufgabe, Arbeit etc)* thanklessness

un-: un|da|tiert ['ʊndatiːɐt] ADJ undated; **un|de|fi|nier|bar** ADJ *Begriff, Aroma, Art* indefinable; **das Essen war ~** nobody could say what the food was; **un|dehn|bar** ADJ inelastic; **un|de|kli|nier|bar** ADJ *(Gram)* indeclinable; **un|de|mo|kra|tisch** ADJ undemocratic ADV undemocratically

un|denk|bar ADJ unthinkable, inconceivable; **es/diese Möglichkeit ist nicht ~** it/the possibility is not inconceivable

un|denk|lich [ʊn'dɛŋklɪç] ADJ **seit ~en Zeiten** *(geh)* since time immemorial

Un|der|dog M -s, -s *(inf)* underdog; **zu den ~s halten** to stick up for the underdogs

un|deut|lich ADJ indistinct; *(wegen Nebel etc auch)* hazy; *Foto auch* blurred; *Erinnerung auch* vague, hazy; *Schrift* illegible; *Ausdrucksweise, Erklärung* unclear, muddled ADV **~ sprechen** to speak indistinctly, to mumble; **ich konnte es nur ~ verstehen** I couldn't understand it very clearly; **bemüh dich mal, nicht so ~ zu schreiben** try to write more clearly; **Sie drücken sich sehr ~ aus** you don't express yourself very clearly; **sie/es war nur ~ erkennbar** *or* **zu erkennen** you couldn't see her/it at all clearly

un|deutsch ADJ un-German

un|dicht ADJ *(= luftdurchlässig)* not airtight; *(= wasserdurchlässig)* not watertight; *Dach* leaky, leaking; **das Rohr ist ~** the pipe leaks; **das Fenster ist ~** the window lets in a draught *(Brit) or* draft *(US)*; **es/er/sie muss eine ~e Stelle haben** *(Rohr etc)* it must have a leak in it; *(Reifen etc)* it must have a hole in it; *(Flasche etc)* the seal must be broken; **in der Regierung muss eine ~e Stelle sein** the government must have a leak somewhere

un|dif|fe|ren|ziert ADJ simplistic; *(= nicht analytisch)* indiscriminate ADV simplistically; *behandeln* in an over-generalized way; *Begriffe verwenden* indiscriminately

Un|ding NT, *no pl* absurdity; **es ist ein ~, zu ...** it is preposterous *or* absurd to ...

Un-: un|dip|lo|ma|tisch ADJ undiplomatic ADV undiplomatically; **un|dis|zip|li|niert** ADJ undisciplined ADV in an undisciplined way; **Un|dis|zip|li|niert|heit** F -, **-en** **a** *no pl* lack of discipline **b** *(= undisziplinierte Handlung)* undisciplined behaviour *(Brit) or* behavior *(US) no pl*; **un|dra|ma|tisch** *(fig)* ADJ undramatic, unexciting ADV undramatically; **un|duld|sam** ADJ intolerant *(gegen* of); **Un|duld|sam|keit** F intolerance *(gegen* of); **un|durch|dring|bar** [ʊndʊrç'drɪŋbaːɐ, 'ʊn-], **un|durch|dring|lich** [ʊndʊrç'drɪŋlɪç, 'ʊn-] ADJ *Gebüsch, Urwald* impenetrable; *Gesicht, Miene* inscrutable; **un|durch|führ|bar** ADJ impracticable, unworkable; **Un|durch|führ|bar|keit** F impracticability, unworkability; **un|durch|läs|sig** ADJ impermeable, impervious *(gegen* to); *Grenze* closed; **Un|durch|läs|sig|keit** F impermeability, imperviousness; **un|durch|schau|bar** ADJ unfathomable; *Exot, Volk etc* inscrutable; **er ist ein ~er Typ** *(inf)* you never know what game he's playing *(inf)*; **Un|durch|schau|bar|keit** [ʊndʊrç'ʃaubaːɐkait, 'ʊn-] F -, *no pl* unfathomability; **un|durch|sich|tig** ADJ **a** *Fenster, Papier, Stoff* opaque **b** *(fig pej) Mensch, Methoden* devious; *Motive* obscure; *Vorgänge, Geschäfte* dark; **es ist eine ganze ~e Angelegenheit** you can't tell what's going on in that business; **Un|durch|sich|tig|keit** F, *no pl* **a** *(von Fenster, Papier, Stoff)* opacity **b** *(fig pej) (von Mensch, Methoden)* deviousness; *(von Motiven)* obscureness

Und-Zei|chen NT *(Typ)* **a** *(= Pluszeichen)* plus sign **b** *(= Et-Zeichen)* ampersand

un|eben ADJ **a** *Oberfläche, Fußboden, Wand etc* uneven; *Straße* bumpy, uneven; *Gelände* rough, bumpy **b** *(dial inf)* bad

Un|eben|heit F *(von Oberfläche etc)* unevenness; *(von Straße auch)* bumpiness; *(von Gelände)* roughness; **kleine ~en** uneven patches

Un-: un|echt ADJ false; *(= vorgetäuscht)* fake; *Schmuck, Edelstein, Blumen etc* artificial, fake *(usu pej)*; *Bruch* improper ADV **~ klingen** to sound false; **~ wirken** to seem false; **un|edel** ADJ **a** *Metalle* base **b** *(fig) Mensch, Gesinnung* base; **un|ef|fek|tiv** ADJ, ADV → **ineffektiv**; **un|ehe|lich** ADJ illegitimate ADV **~ geboren sein** to be illegitimate, to have been born out of wedlock *(old, form)*; **Un|ehe|lich|keit** F illegitimacy; **Un|eh|re** F, *no pl* dishonour *(Brit)*, dishonor *(US)*; **jdm ~ machen, jdm zur ~ gereichen** *(geh)* to disgrace sb; **un|eh|ren|haft** ADJ dishonourable *(Brit)*, dishonorable *(US)* ADV dishonourably *(Brit)*, dishonorably *(US)*; **~ (aus der Armee) entlassen werden** to be given a dishonourable *(Brit) or* dishonorable *(US)* discharge; **un|ehr|er|bie|tig** ADJ disrespectful; **un|ehr|lich** ADJ dishonest; **auf ~e Weise** by dishonest means ADV dishonestly; **~ spielen** to cheat; **Un|ehr|lich|keit** F dishonesty; **un|eid|lich** ADJ **~e Falschaussage** *(Jur)* false statement made while not under oath; **un|ei|gen|nüt|zig** ADJ unselfish, selfless ADV unselfishly, selflessly; **Un|ei|gen|nüt|zig|keit** F unselfishness, selflessness; **un|ei|gent|lich** ADJ **a** *(Math)* improper **b** *(= übertragen)* figurative; **un|ein|ge|la|den** ['ʊnlaingəlaːdn] ADJ uninvited ADV **~ kommen** to come uninvited, to come without an invitation; **~ erscheinen** to gate-crash *(bei etw* sth); **un|ein|ge|löst** ['ʊnlaingəløːst] ADJ *Gutschein* unredeemed; *Wechsel* dishonoured *(Brit)*, dishonored *(US)*; *Versprechen etc* unfulfilled

un|ein|ge|schränkt ADJ absolute, total; *Freiheit, Rechte* unlimited, unrestricted; *Annahme, Zustimmung* unqualified; *Vertrauen* absolute; *Lob* unreserved; *Handel* free, unrestricted; *Vollmachten* plenary ADV absolutely, totally; *beanspruchen* without limitation *or* restriction; *zustimmen, akzeptieren* without qualification; *loben, vertrauen* without reservation, unreservedly; *Handel treiben* freely, without restriction

Un-: un|ein|ge|weiht ['ʊnlaingəvait] ADJ uninitiated; **für Uneingeweihte** for the uninitiated; **un|ein|heit|lich** ADJ nonuniform; *Öffnungszeiten, Arbeitszeiten, Systeme, Reaktion* varied; *(= nicht für alle gleich) Arbeitszeiten, Schulferien* different; *Qualität* inconsistent; *Börse* irregular; *Preise* unsteady; **~ sein** to vary ADV *gekleidet, beurteilen* differently; *sich entwickeln* in different ways; *(St Ex)* irregularly; **die New Yorker Börse hat am Donnerstag ~ tendiert** on Thursday shares on the New York Stock Exchange were mixed; **~ verlaufen** to vary; **un|ei|nig** ADJ **a** *(= verschiedener Meinung)* in disagreement; **über etw** *(acc)* **~ sein** to disagree about sth, to be in disagreement about sth; **ich bin mit mir selbst noch ~** I haven't made up my mind yet **b** *(= zerstritten)* divided; **Un|ei|nig|keit** F disagreement *(+gen* between); **~ in der Partei** disagreement *or* division within the party; **un|ein|nehm|bar** [ʊnlain'neːmbaːɐ, 'ʊn-] ADJ impregnable; **un|eins** ADJ *pred* disagreed; *(= zerstritten)* divided; **(mit jdm) ~ sein/werden** to disagree with sb; **ich bin mit mir selbst ~** I cannot make up my mind; **die Mitglieder sind (untereinander) ~** the members are divided amongst themselves; **un|ele|gant** ADJ inelegant ADV *gekleidet, sich ausdrücken, formulieren* inelegantly; **un|emp|fäng|lich** ADJ *(für* to) insusceptible, unsusceptible;

(für Eindrücke auch, Atmosphäre) insensitive; **Un|emp|fäng|lich|keit** F insusceptibility, unsusceptibility; *(für Eindrücke etc)* insensitiveness

un|emp|find|lich ADJ *(gegen* to) insensitive; *(durch Übung, Erfahrung)* inured; *(gegen Krankheiten, Bazillen etc)* immune; *Pflanze* hardy; *Baustoff* which weathers well; *Textilien, Teppich* hard-wearing and stain-resistant; **gegen Kälte ~e Pflanzen** plants which aren't sensitive to the cold

Un|emp|find|lich|keit F, *no pl* *(gegen* to) insensitiveness, insensitivity; *(gegen Krankheiten, Bazillen etc)* immunity; *(von Pflanzen)* hardiness; *(von Textilien)* practicality; **dieser Baustoff ist wegen seiner ~ gegen Witterungseinflüsse besonders gut geeignet** this building material is particularly suitable because it weathers so well

un|end|lich ADJ infinite; *(zeitlich)* endless; *Universum* infinite, boundless; **das Unendliche** infinity; **im Unendlichen** at infinity; **(bis) ins Unendliche** *(lit, Math)* to infinity; **auf ~ einstellen** *(Phot)* to focus on infinity; **~e Mal** endless times ADV endlessly; infinitely; *(fig: = sehr)* terribly; **~ lange diskutieren** to argue endlessly; **~ viele Dinge/Leute** *etc* no end of things/people *etc*

un|end|li|che|mal △ [ʊn'lɛntlɪçəma:l] ADV = **unendlich ADJ**

Un|end|lich|keit F infinity; *(zeitlich)* endlessness; *(von Universum)* boundlessness; **~ von Raum und Zeit** infinity of time and space

Un|end|lich|keits|zei|chen NT *(Math)* infinity symbol

un|end|lich|mal [ʊn'lɛntlɪçma:l] ADV endless times

Un-: **un|ent|behr|lich** ADJ indispensable; *Kenntnisse auch* essential; **Un|ent|behr|lich|keit** F -, *no pl* indispensability; **er scheint von seiner ~ überzeugt zu sein** he seems to think he's indispensable; **wir haben uns über die ~ gewisser Haushaltsgeräte unterhalten** we discussed how one can't do without certain household appliances; **un|ent|deckt** ['ʊnlɛnt-dɛkt] ADJ undiscovered; **un|ent|gelt|lich** [ʊnlɛnt'gɛltlɪç, 'ʊn-] ADJ free of charge ADV free of charge; *arbeiten* without pay, for nothing; **etw ~ tun** to do sth free of charge; **un|ent|rinn|bar** [ʊnlɛnt'rɪnba:ɐ, 'ʊn-] ADJ *(geh)* inescapable

un|ent|schie|den ADJ *(= nicht entschieden)* undecided; *(= entschlusslos)* indecisive; *(Sport)* drawn; **ein ~es Rennen** a dead heat ADV **das Spiel steht immer noch 2:2 ~** the score is still level *(Brit)* or even *(US)* at 2 all; **~ enden** or **ausgehen** to end in a draw or tie; **~ spielen, sich ~ trennen** to draw, to tie

Un|ent|schie|den ['ʊnlɛntʃi:dn] NT **-s, -** *(Sport)* draw; **mit einem ~ enden** to end in a draw

un|ent|schlos|sen ADJ *(= nicht entschieden)* undecided; *(= entschlusslos) Mensch* indecisive, irresolute; **ich bin noch ~** I haven't decided yet, I haven't made up my mind yet ADV *sich verhalten* indecisively; **~ stand er vor dem Haus** he stood hesitating in front of the house

Un|ent|schlos|sen|heit F (= *Entschlusslosigkeit: von Mensch)* indecisiveness, indecision

un|ent|schuld|bar ADJ inexcusable

un|ent|schul|digt ['ʊnlɛntʃʊldɪçt] ADJ unexcused; **~es Fernbleiben** or **Fehlen von der Arbeit** absenteeism; **~es Fernbleiben** or **Fehlen von der Schule** truancy ADV without an excuse

un|ent|wegt [ʊnlɛnt've:kt, 'ʊn-] ADJ *(mit Ausdauer)* continuous, constant; *(= ohne aufzuhören auch)* incessant; *Kämpfer* untiring; **einige Unentwegte** a few stalwarts ADV constantly; incessantly; without tiring; **~ weitermachen** to continue unceasingly

un-: **un|ent|wirr|bar** ADJ *Knäuel, Geflecht* which can't be disentangled; *Zusammenhänge, Verstrickungen* involved, complex, inextricable ADV inextricably; **un|ent|zünd|bar** ADJ noninflammable, nonflammable; **un|er|ach|tet** [ʊnlɛɐ'laxtət, 'ʊn-] PREP *+gen (old)* = **ungeachtet**

un|er|bitt|lich [ʊnlɛɐ'bɪtlɪç] ADJ *Kampf* relentless; *Härte* unyielding; *Mensch auch* inexorable, pitiless ADV *(= hartnäckig)* obstinately, stubbornly; *(= gnadenlos)* ruthlessly; **er besteht ~ auf Erfüllung des Vertrags** he stubbornly insists that the contract be fulfilled; **die Polizei wird ~ gegen diese Drogenhändler vorgehen** the police will proceed ruthlessly against these drug dealers; **~ auf jdn einschlagen** to beat sb pitilessly or mercilessly

Un|er|bitt|lich|keit F -, *no pl* relentlessness

Un-: **un|er|fah|ren** ADJ inexperienced; **Un|er|fah|re|ne(r)** ['ʊnlɛɐfa:rənə] MF *decl as adj* inexperienced person/man/woman *etc*; **Un|er|fah|ren|heit** F inexperience, lack of experience; **un|er|find|lich** [ʊnlɛɐ'fɪntlɪç, 'ʊn-] ADJ incomprehensible; *Grund* obscure; **aus ~en Gründen** for some obscure reason; **un|er|forsch|bar** [ʊnlɛɐ'fɔrʃba:ɐ, 'ʊn-], **un|er|forsch|lich** [ʊnlɛɐ'fɔrʃlɪç, 'ʊn-] ADJ *Ratschluss, Grund, Wille* unfathomable; **un|er|freu|lich** ADJ unpleasant; **Unerfreuliches** *(= schlechte Nachrichten)* bad news *sing*; *(= Übles)* bad things *pl* ADV *ausgehen, enden, verlaufen* unpleasantly; **un|er|füll|bar** [ʊnlɛɐ'fʏlba:ɐ, 'ʊn-] ADJ unrealizable; *Wunsch, Ziel auch* unattainable; **un|er|füllt** ['ʊnlɛɐfʏlt] ADJ unfulfilled; **un|er|gie|big** ADJ *Quelle, Thema* unproductive; *Boden, Ernte, Nachschlagewerk* poor; *Kaffee, Trauben* uneconomical; **un|er|gründ|bar** [ʊnlɛɐ'grʏntba:ɐ, 'ʊn-], **un|er|gründ|lich** [ʊnlɛɐ'grʏntlɪç, 'ʊn-] ADJ unfathomable; **un|er|heb|lich** ADJ *(= geringfügig)* insignificant; *(= unwichtig auch)* unimportant, irrelevant; **nicht ~** not inconsiderable ADV *(= geringfügig)* insignificantly; **nicht ~ verbessert** considerably or significantly improved; **un|er|hofft** ['ʊnlɛɐhɔft] ADJ unexpected

un|er|hört ['ʊnlɛɐ'hø:ɐt] ADJ *attr* *(= ungeheuer, gewaltig)* enormous; *(= empörend)* outrageous; *Frechheit* incredible; **das ist ja ~!** that's quite outrageous ADV incredibly; **~ viel** a tremendous amount (of); **~ viel wissen** to know a tremendous amount; **~ viel arbeiten** to work tremendously hard; **wir müssen uns ~ beeilen** we really have to hurry; **~ aufpassen** to watch very carefully

un|er|hört ['ʊnlɛɐhø:ɐt] ADJ *Bitte, Gebet* unanswered; *Liebe* unrequited; *Liebhaber* rejected

un-: **un|er|kannt** ['ʊnlɛɐkant] ADJ unrecognized; **~ bleiben** not to be recognized ADV without being recognized; **die Täter konnten ~ entkommen** the culprits managed to escape without being recognized; **un|er|kenn|bar** ADJ unrecognizable; **un|er|klär|bar, un|er|klär|lich** ADJ inexplicable; **das ist mir ~** or **unerklärlich** I can't understand it; **un|er|klärt** ADJ *Phänomen, Sachverhalt* unexplained; *Krieg, Liebe* undeclared; **un|er|läss|lich** [ʊnlɛɐ'lɛslɪç, 'ʊn-] ADJ essential

un|er|laubt ['ʊnlɛɐlaupt] ADJ forbidden; *Betreten, Parken* unauthorized; *(= ungesetzlich)* illegal; **~e Handlung** *(Jur)* tort; **~er Waffenbesitz** illegal possession of firearms → **Entfernung** ADV *betreten, verlassen* without permission or authorization; **etw ~ tun** to do sth without permission → **entfernen**

un|er|laub|ter|wei|se ['ʊnlɛɐlauptə'vaizə] ADV without permission

un|er|le|digt ADJ unfinished; *Post* unanswered; *Rechnung* outstanding; *Auftrag* unfulfilled; *(= schwebend)* pending; **„unerledigt"** "pending" ADV *liegen bleiben* without being dealt with; **etw ~ lassen** not to deal with sth; **während sie krank war, blieb ihre Arbeit ~ liegen** when she was ill her work was left undone

un-: **un|er|mess|lich** [ʊnlɛɐ'mɛslɪç, 'ʊn-] ADJ *Reichtum, Schaden, Leid* untold *attr*, immense; *Weite, Himmel, Ozean* vast ADV *reich, groß* immensely, beyond measure; **un|er|müd|lich** [ʊnlɛɐ'my:tlɪç, 'ʊn-] ADJ *Mensch, Bestrebungen, Kampf, Fleiß* untiring, tireless; *Versuche* unceasing ADV tirelessly; **un|ernst** ADJ frivolous; **un|er|probt** ['ʊnlɛɐpro:pt] ADJ untested, untried; **un|er|quick|lich** ADJ *(= unerfreulich)* unedifying; *(= nutzlos)* unproductive, fruitless; **un|er|reich|bar** ADJ *Ziel, Leistung, Qualität* unattainable; *Ort, Ferne* inaccessible; *(telefonisch)* unobtainable; **seine Beförderung war in ~e Ferne gerückt** promotion was now right out of his reach; **un|er|reicht** [ʊnlɛɐ'raiçt, 'ʊn-] ADJ unequalled *(Brit)*, unequaled *(US)*; *Ziel* unattained

un|er|sätt|lich [ʊnlɛɐ'zɛtlɪç, 'ʊn-] ADJ insatiable; *Wissensdurst auch* inexhaustible

Un|er|sätt|lich|keit [ʊnlɛɐ'zɛtlɪçkait, 'ʊn-] F -, *no pl* insatiability; *(von Wissensdurst auch)* inexhaustibility

Un-: **un|er|schlos|sen** ADJ *Land* undeveloped; *Boden* unexploited; *Vorkommen, Markt, Erdöllager* untapped; **un|er|schöpf|lich** [ʊnlɛɐ'ʃœpflɪç, 'ʊn-] ADJ inexhaustible; **un|er|schro|cken** ADJ intrepid, courageous ADV *für etw eintreten* courageously; *kämpfen auch* intrepidly; **Un|er|schro|cken|heit** F -, *no pl* intrepidity; **un|er|schüt|ter|lich** [ʊnlɛɐ'ʃʏtɐlɪç, 'ʊn-] ADJ unshakeable; *Ruhe* imperturbable ADV steadfastly; **sie glaubt ~ an ...** *(acc)* she has an unshakeable belief in ...; **un|er|schwing|lich** ADJ exorbitant, prohibitive; **für jdn ~ sein** to be beyond sb's means; **ein für uns ~er Luxus** a luxury beyond our means; **~ (teuer) sein** to be prohibitively expensive, to be prohibitive; **un|er|setz|bar** [ʊnlɛɐ'zɛtsba:ɐ, 'ʊn-], **un|er|setz|lich** [ʊnlɛɐ'zɛtslɪç, 'ʊn-] ADJ irreplaceable; *Mensch auch* indispensable; **un|er|sprieß|lich** ADJ *(= unerfreulich)* unedifying; *(= nutzlos)* unproductive, fruitless; **un|er|träg|lich** ADJ unbearable ADV *heiß, laut* unbearably; **er hat sich gestern ~ benommen** his behaviour *(Brit)* or behavior *(US)* was unbearable yesterday; **un|er|wähnt** ['ʊnlɛɐvɛ:nt] ADJ unmentioned; **~ bleiben** not to be mentioned; **un|er|war|tet** ['ʊnlɛɐvartət, ʊnlɛɐ'vartət] ADJ unexpected ADV unexpectedly; **un|er|wi|dert** ['ʊnlɛɐvi:dɐt] ADJ *Brief, Behauptung* unanswered; *Liebe* unrequited; *Sympathie* one-sided; **un|er|wünscht** ADJ *Kind* unwanted; *Besuch, Effekt* unwelcome; *Eigenschaften* undesirable; **du bist hier ~** you're not welcome here; **~e Personen** undesirables; **ein ~er Ausländer** *(Pol)* an undesirable alien; **un|er|zo|gen** ['ʊnlɛɐtso:gn] ADJ ill-bred, ill-mannered; *Kind auch* badly brought up

UNESCO [u'nɛsko] F **- die ~** UNESCO

un|fach|ge|mäß, un|fach|män|nisch ADJ unprofessional ADV unprofessionally, inexpertly

un|fä|hig ✪ 43.4 ADJ **a** *attr* incompetent **b** **~ sein, etw zu tun** to be incapable of doing sth; *(vorübergehend)* to be unable to do sth; **einer Sache** *(gen)* or **zu etw ~ sein** to be incapable of sth

Un|fä|hig|keit F **a** *(= Untüchtigkeit)* incompetence **b** *(= Nichtkönnen)* inability

Un-: **un|fair** ADJ unfair *(gegenüber* to) ADV unfairly; **Un|fair|ness** F unfairness

Un|fall ['ʊnfal] M accident; **er ist bei einem ~ ums Leben gekommen** he died in an accident; **gegen ~ versichert** insured against accidents

Un|fall-: **Un|fall|arzt** M, **Un|fall|ärz|tin** F specialist for accident injuries; **Un|fall|be|tei|lig|te(r)** MF *decl as adj* person/man/woman *etc* involved in an/the accident; **Un|fall|bi|lanz** F accident figures *pl* or statistics *pl*; **Un|fall|fah|rer(in)** M(F) driver at fault in an/the accident; **Un|fall|fahr|zeug** NT accident vehicle, vehicle involved in an accident; **Un|fall|flucht** F failure to stop after an accident; *(nicht melden)* failure to report an accident; *(esp bei Verletzung von Personen)* hit-and-run driving; **~ begehen** to fail to stop after an accident/to fail to report an accident/to commit a hit-and-run offence *(Brit)* or offense *(US)*; **un|fall|flüch|tig** ADJ *Fahrer* who fails to stop after an accident; *(ohne Unfallmeldung)* who fails to report an accident; *(esp bei Verletzung von Personen)* hit-and-run *attr*; **~ werden** to fail to stop after an accident/to fail to report an accident/to commit a hit-and-run offence *(Brit)* or offense *(US)*; **Un|fall|flüch|ti|ge** PL *decl as adj* → **Unfallflucht** drivers *pl* who fail to stop after an accident/who fail to report an accident/hit-and-run drivers *pl*; **Un|fall|fol|ge** F result of an/the accident; **un|fall|frei** ADJ accident-free ADV without an accident; **Un|fall|ge|fahr** F danger *or* risk of accidents, hazard; **es besteht erhöhte ~** there is an increased risk of accidents (occurring); **Un|fall|geg|ner(in)** M(F) plaintiff for damages; **Un|fall|hil|fe** F help at the scene of an/the accident; *(= Erste Hilfe)* first aid; **Un|fall|kli|nik** F, **Un|fall|kran|ken|haus** NT accident hospital, ≈ emergency room *(US)*; **Un|fall|op|fer** NT casualty; **Un|fall|ort** M *pl* **-orte** scene of an/the accident; **Un|fall|quo|te** F, **Un|fall|ra|te** F accident rate; **Un|fall|ren|te** F accident benefits *pl*; **Un|fall|ri|si|ko** NT accident risk; **Un|fall|scha|den** M damages *pl*; **Un|fall|schutz** M *(Versicherung)* accident insurance; *(Maßnahmen)* accident prevention; **Un|fall|schwer|punkt** M accident black spot; **Un|fall|se|rie** F series of accidents; **un|fall|si|cher** ADJ accident-proof; **Un|fall|skiz|ze** F diagram *or* sketch of an/the accident; **Un|fall|sta|ti|on** F accident *or* emergency ward *(Brit)*, emergency room *(US)*; **Un|fall|sta|tis|tik** F accident statistics *pl*; **Un|fall|stel|le** F scene of an/the accident; **Un|fall|tod** M accidental death; **bei ~** in the event of death by misadventure; **Un|fall|to|te(r)** MF *decl as adj* = **Verkehrstote(r)**; **un|fall|träch|tig** ADJ accident-prone; **Un|fall|ur|sa|che** F cause of an/the accident; **Un|fall|ver|hü|tung** F accident prevention; **Un|fall|ver|letz|te(r)** MF *decl as adj* casualty; **Un|fall|ver|si|che|rung** F accident insurance; **Un|fall|wa|gen** M car involved in an/the accident; *(inf: = Rettungswagen)* ambulance; **der Wagen ist so billig, weil es ein ~ ist** the car is so cheap because it has been involved in an accident; **Un|fall|zahl** F number of accidents; **steigende ~en** rising accident rates; **Un|fall|zeu|ge** M, **Un|fall|zeu|gin** F witness to an/the accident; **Un|fall|zif|fer** F = **Unfallzahl**

un|fass|bar, **un|fass|lich** ADJ incomprehensible; **es ist mir** *or* **für mich ~, wie …** I (simply) cannot understand how …

Un-: **un|fehl|bar** ADJ infallible; *Instinkt* unerring ADV without fail; **Un|fehl|bar|keit** [ʊn-ˈfeːlbaːɐkait, ˈʊn-] F -, *no pl* infallibility; **un|fein** ADJ unrefined *no adv*, indelicate; **das ist ~** that's bad manners; **das ist mehr als ~** that's most ungentlemanly/unladylike ADV *sich ausdrücken* in an unrefined way; *sich benehmen* in an ill-mannered way; **un|fern** *(geh)* PREP *+gen* not far from, near ADV **~ von** not far from, near; **un|fer|tig** ADJ *(= unvollendet)* unfinished; *(= nicht vollständig)* incomplete; *(= unreif) Mensch* immature; **Un|flat** [ˈʊnflaːt] M -(e)s, *no pl (lit old)* feculence *(form)*; *(fig geh)* vituperation; **jdn mit ~ bewerfen** *(fig)* to inveigh against sb, to vituperate sb; **un|flä|tig** [ˈʊnflɛːtɪç] ADJ offensive ADV **sich ~ ausdrücken** to use obscene language; **Un|flä|tig|keit** F -, **-en** offensiveness; *(von Ausdrucksweise)* obscenity; **un|flek|tiert** [ˈʊnflɛktiːɐt] ADJ *(Gram)* uninflected; **un|fle|xi|bel** [ˈʊnflɛksiːbl] ADJ *(lit, fig)* inflexible; **un|flott** ADJ *(inf)* not nice; **das ist gar nicht so ~** that's not bad; **er/sie ist gar nicht so ~** he's/she's a bit of all right *(inf)*; **un|folg|sam** ADJ disobedient; **un|for|ma|tiert** [ˈʊnfɔrmatiːɐt] ADJ *(Comput)* unformatted

un|för|mig ADJ *(= formlos)* shapeless; *Möbel, Auto* inelegant; *(= groß)* cumbersome; *Füße, Gesicht* unshapely

Un|för|mig|keit F -, *no pl (= Formlosigkeit)* shapelessness; *(von Möbeln, Auto)* inelegance; *(= Größe)* awkward size; *(von Füßen, Gesicht)* unshapeliness

un-: **un|förm|lich** ADJ informal; **un|fran|kiert** [ˈʊnfraŋkiːɐt] ADJ unstamped ADV *abschicken, einwerfen* unstamped; **un|frau|lich** ADJ unfeminine ADV in an unfeminine way

un|frei ADJ **a** *(politisch, Hist: = leibeigen)* not free; **~ sein** *(Hist)* to be a bondman *or* in bondage *or* a serf **b** *(= befangen, eingeengt)* constrained, uneasy **c** *Brief etc* unfranked ADV **a** *(= gehemmt) sich benehmen* in an inhibited way **b** *(= nicht frankiert)* unfranked

Un|freie(r) MF *decl as adj (Hist)* serf

Un|frei|heit F lack of freedom; *(Hist)* bondage, serfdom

un|frei|wil|lig ADJ **a** *(= gezwungen)* compulsory; **ich war ~er Zeuge** I was an unwilling witness **b** *(= unbeabsichtigt) Witz, Fehler* unintentional ADV involuntarily, against one's will; **ich musste ~ zuhören** I was forced to listen

un|freund|lich ADJ unfriendly *(zu, gegen* to); *Wetter* inclement; *Landschaft, Zimmer, Farbe* cheerless; **ein ~er Akt** *(Pol)* a hostile act ADV in an unfriendly way; **jdn ~ behandeln** to be unfriendly to sb; **jdn ~ begrüßen/ansehen** to give sb an unfriendly welcome/look; **~ reagieren** to react in an unfriendly way

Un|freund|lich|keit F **a** unfriendliness; *(von Wetter)* inclemency **b** *(= unfreundliche Bemerkung)* unpleasant remark

Un|frie|de(n) M strife; **in Unfrieden (mit jdm) leben** to live in conflict (with sb)

un-: **un|fri|siert** [ˈʊnfriziːɐt] ADJ *(lit) Haare* uncombed; *Mensch* with one's hair in a mess; *(fig inf) (= nicht verfälscht)* undoctored; *Auto* not souped-up *(inf)* ADV *(lit: = ungekämmt)* unkempt; **völlig ~ machte sie mir die Tür auf** she opened the door to me looking completely unkempt; **un|fromm** ADJ impious

un|frucht|bar ADJ infertile; *Boden auch* barren; *Frau* infertile, barren *(old, liter)*; *(fig) Debatte etc* sterile; *Schaffenszeit* unproductive; **~ machen** to sterilize; **die ~en Tage** *(Med)* the days of infertility

Un|frucht|bar|keit F infertility; *(von Boden auch)* barrenness; *(fig: von Debatte etc)* sterility

Un|fug [ˈʊnfuːk] M -s, *no pl* nonsense; **~ treiben** *or* **anstellen** *or* **machen** to get up to mischief; **lass den ~!** stop that nonsense!; **diese Idee ist grober ~** this idea is utter nonsense; **grober ~** *(Jur)* public nuisance

un-: **un|fun|diert** ADJ unfounded; **un|ga|lant** *(geh)* ADJ discourteous, ungentlemanly *no adv*; **un|gar** [ˈʊngaːɐ] ADJ underdone

Un|gar [ˈʊŋgar] M -n, -n, **Un|ga|rin** [ˈʊŋgarɪn] F -, -nen Hungarian

un|ga|risch [ˈʊŋgarɪʃ] ADJ Hungarian

Un|ga|risch(e) [ˈʊŋgarɪʃ] NT Hungarian → *auch* **Deutsch(e)**

Un|garn [ˈʊŋgarn] NT -s Hungary

Un-: **un|gast|lich** ADJ inhospitable ADV inhospitably; **wir wurden sehr ~ empfangen** we were given a very inhospitable welcome; **Un|gast|lich|keit** F **der Ort hat die ~ einer Bahnhofshalle** the place is about as hospitable as a railway station; **un|ge|ach|tet** [ˈʊngəlaxtət, ʊngəˈlaxtət] PREP *+gen* in spite of, despite; **~ dessen, dass es regnet** in spite of it raining, in spite of the fact that it is raining; **~ aller Ermahnungen, aller Ermahnungen ~** despite all warnings; **er ist sehr stark, ~ dessen, dass er so klein ist** he's very strong, in spite of being so small; **un|ge|ahn|det** [ˈʊngəlaːndət, ʊngəˈlaːndət] ADJ *(Jur)* unpunished; **un|ge|ahnt** [ˈʊngəlaːnt, ʊngəˈlaːnt] ADJ undreamt-of; **un|ge|ba|cken** ADJ unbaked; **un|ge|bär|dig** [ˈʊngəbeːɐdɪç] ADJ unruly; **un|ge|be|ten** ADJ uninvited ADV **er kam ~** he came uninvited *or* unasked *or* without an invitation; **un|ge|beugt** ADJ **a** unbent, unbowed **b** *(Gram)* uninflected; **un|ge|bil|det** ADJ uncultured; *(= ohne Bildung)* uneducated; **Ungebildete** uneducated *or* uncultured people; **un|ge|bleicht** [ˈʊngəblaiçt] ADJ unbleached; **un|ge|bo|ren** ADJ unborn; **un|ge|brannt** ADJ *Kaffee* unroasted; *Ton etc* unfired; **un|ge|bräuch|lich** ADJ uncommon; **un|ge|braucht** ADJ, ADV unused; **un|ge|bro|chen** ADJ **a** *(fig) Rekord, Wille* unbroken; *Widerstand* unyielding; *Popularität* undiminished **b** *(Phys) Licht* unrefracted ADV *weiterkämpfen, weitermachen* unbroken, undiminished

Un|ge|bühr F, *no pl (old, form)* impropriety; **~ vor Gericht** contempt of court

un|ge|bühr|lich ADJ improper ADV **a** *(= ungehörig)* improperly, inappropriately **b** *(= über Gebühr)* excessively; **sich ~ aufregen** to get unduly excited

un|ge|bun|den ADJ **a** *Buch* unbound; *Blumen* loose **b** **in ~er Rede** in prose **c** *(= unabhängig) Leben* (fancy-)free; *(= unverheiratet)* unattached; *(Pol)* independent; *(Comm) Kredit* untied; **frei und ~** footloose and fancy-free; **parteipolitisch ~** (politically) independent, not attached to any political party

Un|ge|bun|den|heit F independence

Un-: **un|ge|deckt** ADJ **a** *(= schutzlos) Schachfigur etc* unprotected, unguarded; *(Sport) Tor* undefended; *Spieler* unmarked, uncovered; *Scheck, Kredit* uncovered **b** *Tisch* unlaid *(Brit)*, not set *pred*; **un|ge|dient** ADJ *(dated Mil)* with no prior service; **Un|ge|dien|te(r)** [ˈʊngədiːntə] M *decl as adj (dated, Mil)* person/man with no prior service; **un|ge|druckt** ADJ unprinted; *(= nicht veröffentlicht)* unpublished

Un|ge|duld F impatience; **vor ~** with impatience; **voller ~** impatiently

un|ge|dul|dig ADJ impatient ADV impatiently

un|ge|eig|net ADJ unsuitable; *(für Beruf, Stellung auch)* unsuited *(für* to, for)

un|ge|fähr [ˈʊngəfɛːɐ, ʊngəˈfɛːɐ] ADJ *attr* approximate, rough; **nach ~en Schätzungen** at a rough guess *or* estimate

ADV roughly; *(bei Zahlen-, Maßangaben auch)* approximately; **(so) ~ dreißig** about *or* approximately thirty; **~ 12 Uhr** about *or* approximately 12 o'clock; **von ~** from nowhere; *(= zufällig)* by chance; **das kommt nicht von ~** it's no accident; **diese Bemerkung kommt doch nicht von ~** he *etc* didn't make this remark just by chance; **wo ~?** whereabouts?; **wie ~?** approximately how?; **so ~!** more or less!; **können Sie mir (so) ~ sagen, wie viel das kosten soll/wie Sie sich das vorgestellt haben?** can you give me a rough idea of *or* tell me roughly how much it will cost/how you imagined it?; **~ (so) wie** a bit like; **können Sie den Mann ~ beschreiben?** can you give me/us *etc* a rough description of the man?; **etw (so) ~ wissen** to know sth roughly, to have a rough idea of sth; **dann weiß ich ~ Bescheid** then I've got a rough idea; **so ~ habe ich mir das gedacht** I thought it would be something like this; **so ~, als wären wir kleine Kinder** a bit as if we were little children; **das hat sich ~ so abgespielt** it happened something like this

Un-: **un|ge|fähr|det** ADJ **a** safe **b** *(Sport) Sieg* assured ADV *spielen, sich aufhalten* safely; **~ siegen** to win comfortably; **un|ge|fähr|lich** ADJ safe; *Tier, Krankheit, Arzneimittel etc* harmless; **nicht ganz ~** not altogether safe/harmless; *Expedition* not altogether without its dangers; **Un|ge|fähr|lich|keit** F safeness; *(von Tier, Krankheit, Arzneimittel etc)* harmlessness; **un|ge|fäl|lig** ADJ *Mensch* unobliging; **un|ge|färbt** ADJ *Haare, Stoff* undyed, natural; *Lebensmittel* without (added) colouring *(Brit)* or coloring *(US)*; **un|ge|fe|dert** ADJ *Fahrzeug* springless, without springs; **un|ge|fil|tert** [ˈʊngəfɪltɐt] ADJ unfiltered; **un|ge|formt** [ˈʊngəfɔrmt] ADJ unformed; *(= gestaltlos)* amorphous; **un|ge|fragt** ADV unasked; **un|ge|füt|tert** [ˈʊngəfʏtɐt] ADJ *Tier* unfed; **un|ge|füt|tert** ADJ *Kleidung, Briefumschlag* unlined; **un|ge|gerbt** [ˈʊngəgɛrpt] ADJ untanned; **un|ge|glie|dert** ADJ *Körper, Stengel* unjointed; *(fig)* disjointed; *Satz, Aufsatz etc* unstructured

un|ge|hal|ten ADJ indignant *(über +acc* about) ADV indignantly

Un|ge|hal|ten|heit [ˈʊngəhaltnhait] F -, *no pl* indignation

un-: **un|ge|här|tet** [ˈʊngəhɛrtət] ADJ *Stahl* untempered; **un|ge|hei|ßen** ADV *(geh)* voluntarily; **un|ge|heizt** [ˈʊngəhaitst] ADJ unheated; **un|ge|hemmt** ADJ unrestrained ADV without inhibition; **sich ~ benehmen** to behave in an uninhibited way

un|ge|heu|er [ˈʊngəhɔyɐ, ʊngəˈhɔyɐ] ADJ **a** → **ungeheuerlich** **b** *(= riesig)* enormous, immense; *(in Bezug auf Länge, Weite)* vast; **sich ins Ungeheuere steigern** to take on enormous dimensions **c** *(= genial, kühn)* tremendous **d** *(= frevelhaft, vermessen)* outrageous, dreadful ADV *(= sehr)* enormously, tremendously; *(negativ)* terribly, awfully; **~ groß** tremendously big; **~ viele Menschen** an enormous number of people

Un|ge|heu|er [ˈʊngəhɔyɐ] NT **-s, -** monster; *(fig auch)* ogre

un|ge|heu|er|lich [ʊngəˈhɔyɐlɪç, ˈʊn-] ADJ monstrous; *Tat auch* atrocious; *Verleumdung* outrageous; *Verdacht, Dummheit* dreadful; *Leichtsinn* outrageous, appalling

Un|ge|heu|er|lich|keit F **-, -en** **a** *(von Tat)* atrocity, atrociousness; *(von Verleumdung)* outrageousness; **so eine ~!** how outrageous! **b** **Ungeheuerlichkeiten** PL *(= Verbrechen etc)* atrocities; *(= Behauptungen etc)* outrageous claims

Un-: **un|ge|hin|dert** [ˈʊngəhɪndɐt] ADJ unhindered ADV without hindrance; **un|ge|ho|belt** [ˈʊngəhoːblt, ʊngəˈhoːblt] ADJ *Brett etc* unplaned; *Mensch, Benehmen* boorish; **un|ge|hö|rig** ADJ impertinent ADV impertinently; **Un|ge|hö|rig|keit** F **-, -en** impertinence; **un|ge|hor|sam** ADJ disobedient; **Un|ge|hor|sam** M disobedience; *(Mil)* insubordination; **ziviler ~** civil disobedience; **un|ge|hört** [ˈʊngəhøːɐt] ADV unheard; **~ verhallen** *(fig)* to fall on deaf ears; **Un|geist** M, *no pl (geh)* demon; **un|geis|tig** ADJ unintellectual; **un|ge|kämmt** [ˈʊngəkɛmt] ADJ *Haar* uncombed ADV **~ aussehen** to look unkempt; **un|ge|klärt** [ˈʊngəklɛːɐt] ADJ **a** *Abwasser etc* untreated **b** *Frage, Verbrechen* unsolved; *Ursache* unknown; **unter ~en Umständen** in mysterious circumstances; **die Finanzierung des Projekts ist ~** the financing of the project has not been settled ADV **Abwässer ~ einleiten** to discharge effluents in an untreated state; **un|ge|kocht** [ˈʊngəkɔxt] ADJ raw; *Flüssigkeit* unboiled; *Obst etc* uncooked; **un|ge|krönt** [ˈʊngəkrøːnt] ADJ uncrowned; **un|ge|kühlt** ADJ, ADV unchilled; **un|ge|kün|digt** [ˈʊngəkʏndɪçt] ADJ **in ~er Stellung** not under notice (to leave); **un|ge|küns|telt** ADJ natural, genuine; *Sprechweise* unaffected ADV naturally; *sprechen* unaffectedly; **un|ge|kürzt** [ˈʊngəkʏrtst] ADJ not shortened; *Buch* unabridged; *Film* uncut; *Ausgaben* not cut back ADV *veröffentlichen* unabridged; *(Film)* uncut; **der Artikel wurde ~ abgedruckt** the article was printed in full; **un|ge|la|den** ADJ **a** *Kamera, Gewehr etc* unloaded **b** *Gäste etc* uninvited; **un|ge|läu|fig** ADJ unfamiliar

un|ge|le|gen ADJ inconvenient ADV **komme ich (Ihnen) ~?** is this an inconvenient time for you?; **etw kommt jdm ~** sth is inconvenient for sb; **das kam (mir) gar nicht so ~** that was really rather convenient

Un|ge|le|gen|hei|ten PL inconvenience *sing*; **jdm ~ bereiten** *or* **machen** to inconvenience sb

un-: **un|ge|legt** [ˈʊngəleːkt] ADJ → **Ei**; **un|ge|leh|rig** ADJ unteachable; **un|ge|lenk** ADJ awkward; *Bewegungen auch* clumsy ADV awkwardly, clumsily; **un|ge|len|kig** ADJ not supple, stiff; *(fig inf: = nicht flexibel)* inflexible, unbending; **un|ge|lernt** ADJ *attr* unskilled; **un|ge|le|sen** ADJ unread; **un|ge|liebt** ADJ unloved; **un|ge|lo|gen** ADV honestly; **un|ge|löst** ADJ unsolved; *(Chem)* undissolved; **un|ge|lüf|tet** [ˈʊngəlʏftət] ADJ unaired; *(fig) Geheimnis* undisclosed

Un|ge|mach [ˈʊngəmaːx] NT **-s,** *no pl (liter)* hardship

un-: **un|ge|macht** ADJ *Bett* unmade; **un|ge|mah|len** ADJ unground

un|ge|mein ADJ immense, tremendous ADV *schwer, vielseitig etc* extraordinarily; **das freut mich ~** I'm really really pleased

un-: **un|ge|mil|dert** [ˈʊngəmɪldɐt] ADJ undiminished ADV **~ fortbestehen** to continue undiminished; **un|ge|mus|tert** ADJ plain

un|ge|müt|lich ADJ uncomfortable; *Wohnung, Zimmer* not very cosy; *Mensch* awkward; *Land, Wetter, Wochenende* unpleasant; **mir wird es hier ~** I'm getting a bit uncomfortable *or* uneasy; **er kann ~ werden** he can get nasty; **ich kann auch ~ werden** I can be very unpleasant if I choose; **hier kann es gleich sehr ~ werden** things could get very nasty here in a moment ADV uncomfortably; **seine Wohnung wirkt sehr ~** his apartment has a very uncomfortable feel about it

un|ge|nannt ADJ **a** *Mensch* anonymous; **~ bleiben** to remain anonymous **b** *Zahl, Summe* unspecified; **Beträge in ~er Höhe** unspecified amounts

un|ge|nau ADJ *(= nicht fehlerfrei)* inaccurate; *(= nicht wahrheitsgetreu)* inexact; *(= vage)* vague; *(= ungefähr)* rough, approximate ADV *formulieren* imprecisely; *arbeiten, messen* inaccurately; *rechnen* roughly

Un|ge|nau|ig|keit F inaccuracy; *(= Vagheit)* vagueness

un|ge|neigt ADJ disinclined

un|ge|niert [ˈʊnʒeniːɐt] ADJ *(= frei, ungehemmt)* unembarrassed, free and easy; *(= bedenkenlos, taktlos)* uninhibited ADV openly; *(= bedenkenlos, taktlos)* without any inhibition; **greifen Sie bitte ~ zu** please feel free to help yourself/yourselves

Un|ge|niert|heit F **-,** *no pl* lack of embarrassment; *(= Taktlosigkeit)* lack of inhibition

un|ge|nieß|bar ADJ *(= nicht zu essen)* inedible; *(= nicht zu trinken)* undrinkable; *(= unschmackhaft)* unpalatable; *(inf) Mensch* unbearable

un|ge|nü|gend ADJ inadequate, insufficient; *(Sch)* unsatisfactory; **ein Ungenügend** an "unsatisfactory", the lowest mark ADV inadequately, insufficiently

Un-: **un|ge|nutzt** [ˈʊngənʊtst], **un|ge|nützt** [ˈʊngənʏtst] ADJ unused; *Energien* unexploited; **eine Chance ~ lassen** to miss an opportunity ADV unused; **eine Chance ~ vorübergehen lassen** to miss an opportunity; **un|ge|öff|net** [ˈʊngəlœfnət] ADJ, ADV unopened; **un|ge|ord|net** ADJ *Bücher, Papiere etc* untidy, disordered; *(fig)* disordered; *Zuwanderung* uncontrolled ADV untidily; **~ herumliegen** to lie (about) in disorder *or* disarray; **un|ge|pflas|tert** [ˈʊngəpflastɐt] ADJ unpaved; **un|ge|pflegt** ADJ *Mensch* untidy, unkempt; *Park, Rasen, Hände etc* neglected ADV *(= unordentlich)* untidy; **der Garten sieht ~ aus** the garden looks neglected; **sich ~ ausdrücken** to talk in a common way; **un|ge|prüft** [ˈʊngəpryːft] ADJ untested; *Vorwürfe* unchecked ADV without testing, without checking; **etw ~ übernehmen** to accept sth without testing it; *Bilanz* to accept sth without checking it; *(unkritisch)* to accept sth at face value; **un|ge|putzt** [ˈʊngəpʊtst] ADJ uncleaned; *Zähne* unbrushed; *Schuhe* unpolished; **un|ge|rächt** [ˈʊngərɛçt] ADJ unavenged; **un|ge|ra|de** ADJ odd; **un|ge|ra|ten** ADJ *Kind* ill-bred; **un|ge|rech|net** [ˈʊngərɛçnət] PREP *+gen* not including, excluding; **un|ge|recht** ADJ unjust, unfair ADV unjustly, unfairly; **un|ge|rech|ter|wei|se** [ˈʊngərɛçtɐˈvaizə] ADV unjustly, unfairly; **un|ge|recht|fer|tigt** ADJ unjustified; *Behauptung auch* unwarranted ADV unjustly, unduly; **Un|ge|rech|tig|keit** F injustice; **so eine ~!** the injustice of it!, how unjust!; **un|ge|re|gelt** ADJ **a** *Zeiten* irregular; *Leben* disordered **b** *(Tech) Katalysator* open-loop; **un|ge|reimt** [ˈʊngəraimt] ADJ *Verse* unrhymed; *(fig)* inconsistent; **~e Verse** blank verse *sing*; **Un|ge|reimt|heit** F **-, -en** inconsistency

un|gern ADV reluctantly; **(höchst) ~!** if I/we really have to!; **etw höchst ~ tun** to do sth very reluctantly, to do sth with the greatest reluctance; **das tue ich gar nicht ~** I don't mind doing that at all

un-: **un|ge|ru|fen** ADJ uncalled, without being called ADV without being called; **un|ge|rührt** [ˈʊngəryːɐt] ADJ, ADV unmoved; **un|ge|sagt** [ˈʊngəzaːkt] ADJ unsaid; **etw ~ machen** to pretend sth has never been said; **un|ge|sal|zen** ADJ unsalted; **un|ge|sat|telt** [ˈʊngəzatlt] ADJ unsaddled; **un|ge|sät|tigt** ADJ *Hunger etc* unsatisfied; *(Chem) Fettsäuren etc* unsaturated; **un|ge|säu|ert** [ˈʊngəzɔyɐt] ADJ *Brot* unleavened; **un|ge|schält** [ˈʊngəʃɛːlt] ADJ *Obst, Gemüse* unpeeled; *Getreide, Reis* unhusked; **ein ~es Ei** a boiled egg in its shell ADV **einen Apfel ~ essen** to eat an unpeeled apple; **un|ge|sche|hen** ADJ **etw ~ machen** to undo sth

Un|ge|schick NT **-s,** *no pl*, **Un|ge|schick|lich|keit** F clumsiness

un|ge|schickt ADJ clumsy, awkward; *(= unbedacht)* careless, undiplomatic ADV clumsily, awkwardly

Un|ge|schickt|heit F clumsiness; **das war eine ~ von mir** that was clumsy of me; **deine ~en** your clumsiness

Un-: **un|ge|schlacht** [ˈʊngəʃlaxt] ADJ *(pej)* hulking (great); *Sitten* barbaric; **un|ge|schla|gen** ADJ *(= unbesiegt)* undefeated, unbeaten; **sie sind seit Jahren ~** they have remained undefeated for years; **un|ge|schlecht|lich** ADJ asexual ADV *sich vermehren* asexually; **un|ge|schlif|fen** ADJ *Edelstein, Glas* uncut; *Messer etc* blunt; *(fig) Benehmen, Mensch* uncouth; **Un|ge|schlif|fen|heit** F *(fig)* uncouthness; **un|ge|schmä|lert** [ˈʊngəʃmɛːlɐt] ADJ undiminished; **un|ge|schmei|dig** ADJ *Stoff, Leder* rough; *Haar* coarse;; **un|ge|schminkt** [ˈʊngəʃmɪŋkt] ADJ without make-up; *(fig) Wahrheit* unvarnished ADV *(= ohne Schminke)* without make-up; *(= unverblümt)* bluntly; **etw ~ berichten** to give an unvarnished report of sth; **du solltest ihr ~ die Wahrheit sagen** you should tell her the whole truth; **un|ge|scho|ren** ADJ unshorn; *(fig)* spared; **jdn ~ lassen** *(inf)* to spare sb; *(= ungestraft)* to let sb off (scot-free) ADV **~ davonkommen** *(inf)* to escape unscathed; *(Verbrecher)* to get off (scot-free); **un|ge|schrie|ben** ADJ *attr* unwritten; **un|ge|schult** [ˈʊngəʃuːlt] ADJ *Aushilfe, Auge etc* untrained; **un|ge|schützt** ADJ unprotected *(auch Jur)*; *Schachfigur auch* unguarded; *(Mil) Einheit* exposed; *Anlagen* undefended; *(Sport) Tor* undefended ADV without protection; **das Haus ist völlig ~ Wind und Wetter ausgesetzt** the house is completely exposed to the elements; **~ (mit jdm) Geschlechtsverkehr haben** to have unprotected sex (with sb); **un|ge|se|hen** ADJ unseen; **un|ge|sel|lig** ADJ unsociable; *Tier* non-gregarious; **Un|ge|sel|lig|keit** F unsociableness; **un|ge|setz|lich** ADJ unlawful, illegal; **Un|ge|setz|lich|keit** F illegality; **un|ge|si|chert** ADJ unsecured, not secured; *Kredit* unsecured; *Schusswaffe* cocked, with the safety catch off; **un|ge|sit|tet** ADJ uncivilized ADV *sich benehmen, sich aufführen* in an uncivilized manner; **un|ge|stalt** [ˈʊngəʃtalt] ADJ *(geh) Mensch* misshapen, deformed; **un|ge|stem|pelt** [ˈʊngəʃtɛmplt] ADJ unstamped; *Briefmarke* unfranked; *(für Sammler)* mint; **un|ge|stillt** [ˈʊngəʃtɪlt] ADJ *Durst* unquenched; *Hunger* unappeased; *Blutung* unstaunched; *Schmerz* unrelieved; *Verlangen* unfulfilled; *Neugier* unsatisfied; **un|ge|stört** ADJ undisturbed; *(Rad, TV etc)* without interference; **hier sind wir ~** we won't be disturbed here ADV *arbeiten, spielen, sprechen* without being interrupted, undisturbed; **un|ge|straft** [ˈʊngəʃtraːft] ADV with impunity

un|ge|stüm [ˈʊngəʃtyːm] ADJ impetuous ADV impetuously

Un|ge|stüm [ˈʊngəʃtyːm] NT **-(e)s,** *no pl* impetuousness

un-: **un|ge|sühnt** [ˈʊngəzyːnt] ADJ unexpiated, unatoned; **un|ge|sund** ADJ unhealthy; (= *schädlich*) harmful ADV unhealthily; **sie lebt sehr ~** she has a very unhealthy lifestyle; **un|ge|süßt** [ˈʊngəzyːst] ADJ unsweetened; **un|ge|tan** ADJ undone; **etw ~ machen** to undo sth; **un|ge|tauft** [ˈʊngətauft] ADJ unchristened, unbaptized; (*inf: = unverwässert*) undiluted ADV without being christened *or* baptized; **das Baby ist ~ gestorben** the baby died unchristened *or* unbaptized; **un|ge|teilt** [ˈʊngətailt] ADJ undivided; *Beifall* universal; **un|ge|tilgt** [ˈʊngətɪlkt] ADJ *Schulden* uncleared; **un|ge|tra|gen** ADJ *Kleidung* new, unworn; **un|ge|treu** ADJ (*liter*) disloyal, faithless (*liter*); *Ehepartner* unfaithful; **un|ge|trübt** ADJ clear; *Glück, Freude* perfect, unspoilt

Un|ge|tüm [ˈʊngətyːm] NT **-(e)s, -e** monster

un-: **un|ge|übt** ADJ unpractised (*Brit*), unpracticed (*US*); *Mensch* out of practice; **un|ge|wandt** ADJ awkward; **un|ge|wa|schen** ADJ, ADV unwashed

un|ge|wiss ADJ uncertain; (= *vage*) vague; **ein Sprung/eine Reise ins Ungewisse** (*fig*) a leap/a journey into the unknown; **jdn (über etw** *acc*) **im Ungewissen lassen** to leave sb in the dark (about sth); **im Ungewissen bleiben/sein** to stay/be in the dark

Un|ge|wiss|heit F uncertainty

Un|ge|wit|ter NT (*obs*) = **Unwetter**

un|ge|wöhn|lich ADJ unusual ADV unusually; (= *äußerst auch*) exceptionally

Un|ge|wöhn|lich|keit F unusualness

un|ge|wohnt ADJ (= *fremdartig*) strange, unfamiliar; (= *unüblich*) unusual; **das ist mir ~** I am unaccustomed *or* not used to it

un|ge|wollt ADJ unintentional ADV unintentionally; **er musste ~ lachen** he couldn't help laughing

un-: **un|ge|würzt** [ˈʊngəvʏrtst] ADJ unseasoned; **un|ge|zählt** [ˈʊngətsɛːlt] ADJ (= *unzählbar*) countless; (= *nicht gezählt*) uncounted; **un|ge|zähmt** [ˈʊngətsɛːmt] ADJ untamed; (*fig*) uncurbed; **un|ge|zeich|net** ADJ unsigned

Un|ge|zie|fer [ˈʊngətsiːfɐ] NT **-s**, *no pl* pests *pl*, vermin; (*old fig*) vermin

un|ge|zielt ADJ unaimed ADV **~ schießen** to shoot without taking aim

un|ge|zo|gen ADJ ill-mannered ADV badly; (*in Bezug auf Kinder*) naughtily

Un|ge|zo|gen|heit F **-, -en** **a** *no pl* unmannerliness **b** (= *ungezogene Handlung*) bad manners *no indef art*; **so eine ~ von dir!** what manners!; **noch mehr solche ~en, und es setzt was!** just you mind your manners!

Un-: **un|ge|zü|gelt** [ˈʊngətsyːglt] ADJ (= *unbeherrscht*) unbridled; (= *ausschweifend*) dissipated ADV without restraint; **un|ge|zwun|gen** ADJ casual, informal; *Benehmen* natural, unaffected ADV casually, informally; *sich benehmen* naturally, unaffectedly; **Un|ge|zwun|gen|heit** F casualness, informality; **un|gif|tig** ADJ non-poisonous

Un|glau|be M unbelief, lack of faith; (*esp Philos*) scepticism (*Brit*), skepticism (*US*)

un|glaub|haft ADJ incredible, unbelievable ADV implausibly

un|gläu|big ADJ unbelieving; (*Rel*) infidel; (= *zweifelnd*) doubting, disbelieving; **~er Thomas** (*Bibl, fig*) doubting Thomas ADV doubtingly, doubtfully, in disbelief

Un|gläu|bi|ge(r) MF *decl as adj* unbeliever

un|glaub|lich ADJ unbelievable, incredible; **das grenzt ans Unglaubliche** that's almost incredible ADV unbelievably, incredibly; **~ attraktiv sein** to be incredibly attractive

un|glaub|wür|dig ADJ implausible; *Dokument* dubious; *Mensch* unreliable ADV *sich benehmen, sich verhalten* implausibly, unreliably; **sich ~ machen** to lose credibility; **diese Regierung wirkt völlig ~** this government lacks credibility

Un|glaub|wür|dig|keit F implausibility; (*von Mensch*) unreliability

un|gleich ADJ (= *nicht gleichartig*) *Charaktere* dissimilar, unalike *pred*; *Größe, Farbe* different; (= *nicht gleichwertig, nicht vergleichbar*) *Mittel, Waffen, Kampf* unequal; *Partner* very different; (*Math*) not equal; **fünf plus fünf ~ neun** five plus five does not equal nine; **sie sind ein ~es Paar** they are very different; **das Zeichen für ~** the not-equals (*Brit*) *or* inequality (*US*) sign ADV **a** (*unterschiedlich*) unequally, differently **b** (*vor Komparativ*) much, incomparably

Un|gleich-: **Un|gleich|be|hand|lung** F, *no pl* discrimination; **Un|gleich|ge|wicht** NT (*fig*) imbalance

Un|gleich|heit F (= *Ungleichartigkeit*) (*von Charakteren*) dissimilarity; (*von Größe, Farbe*) difference; (*von Mitteln, Waffen, Kampf*) inequality

Un|gleich|heits|zei|chen NT (*Math*) not-equals sign (*Brit*), inequality sign (*US*)

Un|gleich-: **un|gleich|mä|ßig** ADJ uneven; *Atem, Gesichtszüge, Puls* irregular ADV unevenly, irregularly; **~ lang** of uneven length; **Un|gleich|mä|ßig|keit** F unevenness; (*von Atem, Puls, Gesichtszügen*) irregularity; **un|gleich|na|mig** ADJ (*Math*) of different denominations; (*Phys*) *Pole* opposite; **un|gleich|sei|tig** ADJ (*Math*) *Vieleck* irregular

Un|glei|chung F (*Math*) inequation (*Brit*), (expression of) inequality

Un|glück NT **-(e)s, -e** (= *Unfall, Vorfall*) accident; (= *Missgeschick auch*) mishap; (= *Schicksalsschlag*) disaster, tragedy; (= *Unheil*) misfortune; (= *Pech: im Aberglauben, bei Glücksspiel*) bad luck; (= *Unglücklichsein*) unhappiness; **~ bringend** (*geh*) ominous, unpropitious; **in sein ~ rennen** to head for disaster; **sich ins ~ stürzen** to rush headlong into disaster; **du stürzt mich noch ins ~!** you'll be my undoing!; **das ist auch kein ~** that is not a disaster; **so** *or* **welch ein ~!** what a disaster!; **er hat im Leben viel ~ gehabt** he has experienced a great deal of misfortune in life; **es ist ein ~, dass ...** it is bad luck that ...; **das ~ wollte es, dass ...** as (bad) luck would have it, ...; **das bringt ~** that brings bad luck, that's unlucky; **zum ~, zu allem ~** to make matters worse; **ein ~ kommt selten allein** (*prov*) it never rains but it pours (*Brit prov*), when it rains, it pours (*US prov*); **~ im Spiel, Glück in der Liebe** (*prov*) unlucky at cards, lucky in love → **Glück, Häufchen**

un|glück|brin|gend ADJ → **Unglück**

un|glück|lich ✪ 45.3 ADJ **a** (= *traurig*) *Mensch, Gesicht etc* unhappy; *Liebe* unrequited; *Liebesgeschichte* unhappy **b** (= *bedauerlich*) sad, unfortunate; **eine ~e Figur abgeben** to cut a sorry figure ADV **a** (*traurig*) unhappily; **~ verliebt sein** to be crossed in love **b** (*ungünstig*) sadly, unfortunately; **~ enden** *or* **ausgehen** to turn out badly, to end in disaster **c** *stürzen, fallen* awkwardly, badly

Un|glück|li|che(r) [ˈʊnglʏklɪçə] MF *decl as adj* unhappy person, unhappy man/woman *etc*; **ich ~(r)!** poor me!; **der ~!** the poor man!

un|glück|li|cher|wei|se [ˈʊnglʏklɪçɐˈvaizə] ADV unfortunately

Un|glücks-: **Un|glücks|bo|te** M, **Un|glücks|bo|tin** F bringer of bad tidings; **Un|glücks|bot|schaft** F bad tidings *pl*

Un|glück-: **un|glück|se|lig** ADJ (*liter*) **a** (= *Unglück habend*) unfortunate, hapless; (= *armselig*) miserable; (= *bedauernswert*) lamentable **b** (= *Unglück bringend*) disastrous; **Un|glück|se|li|ge(r)** MF *decl as adj* (*liter*) (poor) wretch; **ich ~(r)** woe is me! (*liter*); **un|glück|se|li|ger|wei|se** [ˈʊnglʏkzeːlɪgɐˈvaizə] ADV (*liter*) unfortunately

Un|glücks-: **Un|glücks|fah|rer(in)** M(F) driver who caused an/the accident; **Un|glücks|fall** M accident, mishap; **ein tragischer ~** a tragic accident; **Un|glücks|kind** NT, **Un|glücks|mensch** M unlucky person, unlucky man/woman *etc*; **ich war schon immer ein ~** I've always been unlucky; **Un|glücks|nach|richt** F (= *schlechte Nachricht*) piece of bad news; (= *Nachricht vom Unglück*) news of an/the accident *or* a/the disaster; **Un|glücks|ort** M scene of the accident; **Un|glücks|ra|be** M (*inf*) unlucky thing (*inf*); **Un|glücks|tag** M fateful day; **Un|glücks|vo|gel** M (*inf*) unlucky thing (*inf*); **Un|glücks|wurm** M (*inf*) poor soul; **Un|glücks|zahl** F unlucky number

Un|gna|de F disgrace, disfavour (*Brit*), disfavor (*US*); **bei jdm in ~ fallen** to fall out of favour (*Brit*) *or* favor (*US*) with sb

un|gnä|dig ADJ ungracious; (*hum*) unkind, harsh ADV ungraciously; (*hum*) unkindly, harshly; **etw ~ aufnehmen** to take sth with bad grace

un-: **un|gram|ma|tisch** ADJ ungrammatical ADV ungrammatically; **un|gra|zi|ös** ADJ ungraceful, inelegant ADV ungracefully, inelegantly

Un|gu|la|ten [ʊnguˈlaːtn] PL (*Zool*) ungulates *pl*

un|gül|tig ADJ (= *nicht gültig*) invalid; (*Comput auch*) bad; (= *nicht mehr gültig*) no longer valid; (= *nichtig*) void; *Stimmzettel* spoiled; (*Sport*) *Tor* disallowed; **„ungültig"** (*in Pass*) "cancelled"; **~ werden** (*Pass*) to expire; **~er Sprung** no-jump; **etw für ~ erklären** to declare sth null and void; **eine Ehe für ~ erklären** to annul a marriage

Un|gül|tig|keit F (*von Pass, Visum*) invalidity; (*von Ehe*) nullity; **die ~ einer Wahl** an election's being null and void; **die angebliche ~ einer Entscheidung** the fact that a decision is said to be null and void

Un|gül|tig|ma|chung [-maxʊŋ] F **-, -en** (*Admin*) invalidation

Un|gunst F (*liter*) disfavour (*Brit*), disfavor (*US*); (*von Umständen, Lage*) adversity; (*von Witterung*) inclemency; **zu jds ~en** to sb's disadvantage

un|güns|tig ADJ unfavourable (*Brit*), unfavorable (*US*); *Auswirkungen, Entwicklung* undesirable; *Termin* inconvenient; *Augenblick, Wetter* bad; *Licht* unflattering; **im ~sten Fall** if (the) worst comes to (the) worst

un|güns|tigs|ten|falls ADV if (the) worst comes to (the) worst

un|gut ADJ bad; *Verhältnis auch* strained; *Erinnerungen auch* unpleasant; **ein ~es Gefühl haben** to have an uneasy *or* bad feeling; **nichts für ~!** no offence (*Brit*) *or* offense (*US*)!

un-: **un|halt|bar** ✪ 53.3 ADJ *Zustand* intolerable; *Vorwurf, Behauptung etc* untenable; *Torschuss* unstoppable; **un|hand|lich** ADJ unwieldy; **un|har|mo|nisch** ADJ unharmonious

Un|heil NT disaster; **~ stiften** *or* **anrichten** to do damage; **~ bringend** fateful, ominous; **~ verkündend** (*liter*) ominous, fateful

un|heil|bar ADJ incurable ADV incurably, terminally; **~ krank sein** to have a terminal illness, to be terminally ill

un|heil-: **un|heil|brin|gend** ADJ → **Unheil**; **un|heil|dro|hend, un|heil|schwan|ger** ADJ (*liter*) portentous

Un|heils|pro|phet(in) M(F) prophet of doom

Un|heil|stif|ter(in) M(F) mischief-maker

un|heil-: **un|heil|ver|kün|dend** ADJ → **Unheil**; **un|heil|voll** [ˈʊnhailfɔl] ADJ disastrous

un|heim|lich [ˈʊnhaimlɪç, ʊnˈhaimlɪç] ADJ **a** (= *Angst erregend*) frightening, eerie, sinister; **~e Begegnung** (= *übernatürlich etc*) close encounter; **das/er ist mir ~** it/he gives me the creeps (*inf*); **mir ist ~ (zumute** *or* **zu Mute)** it is uncanny **b** (*inf*) tremendous (*inf*) ADV (*inf: = sehr*) incredibly (*inf*); **~ viel Geld/viele Menschen** a tremendous (*inf*) *or* an incredible (*inf*) amount of money/number of people

Un-: **un|heiz|bar** ADJ unheatable; **un|his|to|risch** ADJ unhistoric; **un|höf|lich** ADJ impolite ADV impolitely; **Un|höf|lich|keit** F impoliteness; **deine ~en** your impoliteness; **es war eine ~ von dir** that was not polite of you

Un|hold [ˈʊnhɔlt] M **-(e)s, -e** [-də] **a** (*old: = Böser*) fiend **b** (*Press sl*) monster, fiend

un-: **un|hör|bar** ADJ silent; *Frequenzen* inaudible; **un|hy|gi|e|nisch** ADJ unhygienic

uni [y'niː] ADJ *pred* self-coloured *(Brit)*, self-colored *(US)*, plain; **in Uniblau** in plain blue

Uni ['ʊni] F -, -s *(inf)* uni *(inf)*, varsity *(dated Brit inf)*, U *(US inf)*, university → *auch* **Universität**

UNICEF ['uːnitsɛf] F - (die) ~ UNICEF

UNICEF-Bot|schaf|ter(in) ['uːnitsɛf-] M(F) UNICEF ambassador

Uni|code-For|mat ['juːnikoːt-] NT *(Comput)* Unicode format

un-: **un|ide|a|lis|tisch** ADJ unidealistic; **un|idi|o|ma|tisch** ADJ unidiomatic ADV unidiomatically

uniert [u'niːɐt] ADJ *(Eccl) Kirche* Uniate

Unier|te(r) [u'niːɐtə] MF *decl as adj (Eccl)* member of a Uniate church

uni|far|ben [y'niːfarbn] ADJ = **uni**

uni|form [uni'fɔrm] ADJ uniform

Uni|form [uni'fɔrm, 'ʊnifɔrm, 'uːnifɔrm] F -, -en uniform

uni|for|mie|ren [unifɔr'miːrən] *ptp* **uniformiert** VT **a** *(= mit Uniform ausstatten)* to uniform **b** *(= einheitlich machen)* to make uniform

uni|for|miert [unifɔr'miːɐt] ADJ uniformed

Uni|for|mier|te(r) [unifɔr'miːɐtə] MF *decl as adj* person/man/woman in uniform

Uni|for|mi|tät [unifɔrmi'tɛːt] F -, *no pl* uniformity

Uni|form|rock M tunic

Uni|kat [uni'kaːt] NT -(e)s, -e unique specimen; **ein ~ sein** to be unique

Uni|kli|nik F *(inf)*

Uni|kli|ni|kum NT university hospital

Uni|kum ['uːnikʊm] NT -s, -s *or* **Unika** [-ka] **a** *(= Einmaliges)* unique thing *etc*; **ein ~** a curiosity; *(= Seltenheit)* a rarity **b** *(inf)* real character

uni|la|te|ral [unilate'raːl] ADJ unilateral ADV unilaterally

un-: **un|in|tel|li|gent** ADJ unintelligent; **~e Datenstation** *(Comput)* dumb terminal; **un|in|te|res|sant** ADJ uninteresting; **sein Angebot ist für uns ~** his offer is of no interest to us; **das ist doch völlig ~** that's of absolutely no interest; **un|in|te|res|siert** ADJ *(= neutral)* disinterested; *(= nicht interessiert)* uninterested ADV uninterested; **die meisten Zuhörer starrten ~ zur Decke** most of the audience stared uninterested at the ceiling

Uni|on [u'nioːn] F -, -en union; **die ~** *(Pol)* the CDU and CSU

Uni|ons|par|tei|en PL *(Ger Pol)* CDU and CSU parties *pl*

uni|so|no [uni'zoːno] ADV *(Mus, fig)* in unison

Uni|so|no [uni'zoːno] NT -s, -s *or* **Unisoni** [-ni] *(Mus)* unison

Uni|ta|ri|er [uni'taːriɐ] M -s, -, **Uni|ta|ri|e|rin** [-iərɪn] F -, -nen Unitarian

Uni|ta|ris|mus [unita'rɪsmʊs] M -, *no pl* Unitarianism

Uni|tät [uni'tɛːt] F -, -en **a** *(= Einheit)* unity **b** *(= Einzigkeit)* uniqueness **c** *(hum: = Universität)* uni *(inf)*, varsity *(dated Brit inf)*, U *(US inf)*, university

Univ. *abbr von* **Universität**

uni|ver|sal [univɛr'zaːl] ADJ universal ADV universally

Uni|ver|sal- *in cpds* all-purpose, universal; *(Mech)* universal; *Bildung etc* general; **Uni|ver|sal|ent|wick|ler** M *(Phot)* universal developer; **Uni|ver|sal|er|be** M, **Uni|ver|sal|er|bin** F universal successor, sole heir/heiress; **Uni|ver|sal|ge|nie** NT universal genius; **Uni|ver|sal|ge|schich|te** F world history

Uni|ver|sa|li|en [univɛr'zaːliən] PL *(Philos, Ling)* universals *pl*

Uni|ver|sa|li|tät [univɛrzali'tɛːt] F -, *no pl* universality

Uni|ver|sal-: **Uni|ver|sal|mit|tel** NT universal remedy, cure-all; **Uni|ver|sal|rei|ni|ger** M general-purpose cleaner

uni|ver|sell [univɛr'zɛl] ADJ universal ADV universally

uni|ver|si|tär ADJ *attr* university- *attr*

Uni|ver|si|tät [univɛrzi'tɛːt] F -, -en university; **die ~ Freiburg, die Freiburger ~** the University of Freiburg, Freiburg University; **an der ~ Heidelberg studieren** to study at the University of Heidelberg; **auf die ~ gehen, die ~ besuchen** to go to university; **die ~ verlassen** to leave university; *(das Gebäude)* to leave the university; **an eine ~ berufen werden** to be appointed to a professorship, to be given a chair

Uni|ver|si|täts- *in cpds* university → *auch* **Hochschul-**; **Uni|ver|si|täts|ab|schluss** M university degree; **Uni|ver|si|täts|bib|lio|thek** F university library; **Uni|ver|si|täts|buch|hand|lung** F university bookshop *(Brit) or* bookstore *(esp US)*; **Uni|ver|si|täts|do|zent(in)** M(F) senior lecturer *(Brit)*, associate professor *(US)*; **Uni|ver|si|täts|ge|län|de** NT university campus; **Uni|ver|si|täts|in|sti|tut** NT university institute; **Uni|ver|si|täts|kli|nik** F university clinic *or* hospital; **Uni|ver|si|täts|lauf|bahn** F university career; **Uni|ver|si|täts|pro|fes|sor(in)** M(F) university professor; **Uni|ver|si|täts|stadt** F university town; **Uni|ver|si|täts|stu|di|um** NT *(Ausbildung)* university training; **dazu ist ein ~ erforderlich** you need a degree for that; **Uni|ver|si|täts|zeit** F university years *pl*

Uni|ver|sum [uni'vɛrzʊm] NT -s, *no pl* universe

Unix® ['juːnɪks] NT -, *no pl (Comput)* Unix®

un|ka|me|rad|schaft|lich ADJ uncomradely; *Schüler, Verhalten* unfriendly ADV in an uncomradely way

un|ka|putt|bar ADJ *(inf)* indestructible

Un|ke ['ʊŋkə] F -, -n toad; *(inf: = Schwarzseher)* Jeremiah

un|ken ['ʊŋkn] VI *(inf)* to foretell gloom

un|kennt|lich ADJ unrecognizable; *Inschrift etc* indecipherable

Un|kennt|lich|keit F -, *no pl* **bis zur ~** beyond recognition

Un|kennt|nis F, *no pl* ignorance; **jdn in ~ über etw** *(acc)* **lassen** to leave sb in ignorance about sth; **in ~ über etw** *(acc)* **sein** to be ignorant about sth; **aus ~** out of ignorance; **~ schützt nicht vor Strafe** *(prov)* ignorance is no excuse

Un|ken|ruf M *(fig)* prophecy of doom; **allen ~en zum Trotz** in defiance of all prophecies of doom

Un-: **un|keusch** ADJ unchaste; **Un|keusch|heit** F unchastity; **un|kind|lich** ADJ unchildlike ADV in an unchildlike manner

un|klar ADJ *(= unverständlich)* unclear; *(= ungeklärt)* unclarified; *(= undeutlich)* blurred, indistinct; *Wetter* hazy; **es ist mir völlig ~, wie das geschehen konnte** I (just) can't understand how that could happen; **ich bin mir darüber noch im Unklaren** I'm not quite clear about that yet; **über etw** *(acc)* **völlig im Unklaren sein** to be completely in the dark about sth; **jdn über etw** *(acc)* **im Unklaren lassen** to leave sb in the dark about sth ADV *sich ausdrücken, formulieren* unclearly; **nur ~ zu erkennen sein** not to be easily discernible, not to be easy to make out

Un|klar|heit F **a** lack of clarity; *(über Tatsachen)* uncertainty; **darüber herrscht noch ~** this is still uncertain *or* unclear **b** *(= unklarer Punkt)* unclear point

Un-: **un|kleid|sam** ADJ unflattering; **un|klug** ADJ unwise, imprudent, ill-advised ADV unwisely, imprudently; **un|kol|le|gi|al** ADJ uncooperative, inconsiderate ADV uncooperatively; **sich ~ verhalten** to behave uncooperatively *(towards one's colleagues)*; **un|kom|pli|ziert** ADJ *Person, Bedienung, Methode etc* straightforward, uncomplicated; **~er** more straightforward, less complicated ADV in a straightforward way, in an uncomplicated way; **Un|kom|pli|ziert|heit** F straightforwardness; **un|kon|trol|lier|bar** ADJ uncontrollable; **~ werden** *(Missbrauch etc)* to get out of hand; **un|kon|trol|liert** ['ʊnkɔntrɔliːɐt] ADJ, ADV unchecked; **un|kon|ven|ti|o|nell** ADJ unconventional ADV unconventionally; **un|kon|zent|riert** ADJ lacking in concentration; **er ist so ~** he can't concentrate ADV without concentrating; **~ arbeiten** to lack concentration in one's work; **Un|kon|zent|riert|heit** F lack of concentration; **un|ko|or|di|niert** ADJ *Bewegungen, Planung etc* uncoordinated; **un|kor|rekt** ADJ **a** *(nicht formgerecht)* improper **b** *(unrichtig)* incorrect ADV *sich verhalten* improperly; *darstellen, wiedergeben* incorrectly; **Un|kor|rekt|heit** F impropriety

Un|kos|ten PL costs *pl*; *(= Ausgaben)* expenses *pl*; **die ~ (für etw) tragen** to bear the cost(s) (of sth), to pay the expenses (for sth); **das ist mit großen ~ verbunden** that involves a great deal of expense; **(mit etw) ~ haben** to incur expense (from sth); **sich in ~ stürzen** *(inf)* to go to a lot of expense

Un|kos|ten-: **Un|kos|ten|bei|trag** M → **Unkosten** contribution toward(s) costs/expenses; **Un|kos|ten|be|tei|li|gung** F share in the cost(s); **Un|kos|ten|ver|gü|tung** F reimbursement of expenses

Un|kraut NT weed; **Unkräuter** weeds; **~ vergeht nicht** *(Prov)* it would take more than that to finish me/him *etc* off! *(hum)*

Un|kraut-: **Un|kraut|be|kämp|fung** F weed control; **Un|kraut|be|kämp|fungs|mit|tel** NT weed killer, herbicide *(form)*; **Un|kraut|ver|nich|tung** F, **Un|kraut|ver|til|gung** F weed killing; **Un|kraut|ver|til|gungs|mit|tel** NT weedkiller, herbicide *(form)*

Un-: **un|krie|ge|risch** ADJ unwarlike; **un|kri|tisch** ADJ uncritical ADV uncritically; **un|kul|ti|viert** ADJ uncultivated; *Mensch auch* uncultured ADV in an uncultivated *or* uncultured manner; **Un|kul|tur** F *(geh)* lack of culture; **un|künd|bar** ADJ *Beamter, Mitarbeiter* permanent; *Vertrag* binding, not terminable; *Anleihe* irredeemable; **in ~er Stellung** in a permanent position; **Un|künd|bar|keit** F *(von Mitarbeiter)* permanent status

un|kun|dig ADJ ignorant (+*gen* of); **einer Sprache ~ sein** to be unacquainted with a language, to have no knowledge of a language; **des Lesens/Schreibens ~ sein** to be illiterate, not to be able to read/write

un-: **un|künst|le|risch** ADJ unartistic; **un|längst** ADV *(geh)* recently; **un|lau|ter** ADJ dishonest; *Wettbewerb* unfair; **un|leid|lich** ADJ disagreeable, unpleasant; **un|lenk|bar** ADJ uncontrollable; *Fahrzeug* unsteerable; **un|les|bar** ADJ *Buch, Diskette, Speicher* unreadable; *Handschrift auch* illegible; **un|le|ser|lich** ADJ *Handschrift etc* illegible, unreadable; **un|leug|bar** [ʊn'lɔykbaːɐ, 'ʊnlɔykbaːɐ] ADJ undeniable, indisputable ADV undeniably, indisputably; **un|lieb** ADJ **es ist mir nicht ~, dass ...** I am quite glad that ...; **un|lie|bens|wür|dig** ADJ not very pleasant ADV in an unpleasant manner

un|lieb|sam ['ʊnliːpzaːm] ADJ unpleasant; *Konkurrent* irksome; **das ist mir noch in ~er Erinnerung** that's still an unpleasant memory ADV *auffallen* unpleasantly, badly; **er ist dem Lehrer ~ aufgefallen** his behaviour *(Brit) or* behavior *(US)* made a bad impression on the teacher

Un-: **un|li|niert** ['ʊnliniːɐt] ADJ *Papier* unruled, unlined; **Un|lo|gik** F illogicality, lack of logic; **un|lo|gisch** ADJ illogical ADV illogically; **un|lös|bar** ADJ **a** *(fig) (= untrennbar)* indissoluble; *(= nicht lösbar) Problem etc* insoluble; *Widerspruch* irreconcilable **b** *(lit) (Chem)* insoluble; *Knoten etc* inextricable; **un|lös|lich** ADJ *(Chem)* insoluble

Un|lust F, *no pl* **a** *(= Widerwille)* reluctance; **etw mit ~ tun** to do sth reluctantly *or* with reluctance **b** *(= Lustlosigkeit, Langeweile)* listlessness; *(St Ex)* slackness

un|lus|tig ADJ *(= gelangweilt)* bored; *(= widerwillig)* reluctant; **ich bin heute ausgesprochen ~** I just can't work up any enthusiasm today

un-: **un|mag|ne|tisch** ADJ nonmagnetic; **un|ma|nie|riert** ADJ *(liter)* unmannered *(liter)*, unaffected; **un|ma|nier|lich** *(dated)* ADJ unmannerly ADV *sich benehmem, sich aufführen* in an unmannerly fashion; **un|männ|lich** ADJ unmanly; **un|mas|kiert** ADJ *Ballbesucher etc* undisguised; *Bankräuber etc* unmasked

Un|mas|se F *(inf)* load *(inf)*; **eine ~ Leute/Bücher** *or* **an Büchern, ~n von Leuten/Büchern** a load of people/books *(inf)*, loads *or* masses of people/books *(inf)*

un|maß|geb|lich ADJ *(= nicht entscheidend) Urteil* not authoritative; *(= unwichtig) Äußerung, Mensch* inconsequential, of no consequence; **nach meiner ~en Meinung** *(hum)* in my humble opinion *(hum)* ADV insignificantly; **nicht ~** to a significant degree

un|mä|ßig ADJ excessive, immoderate ADV *essen, trinken* to excess; *rauchen* excessively; **er hat gestern ~ getrunken** he drank far too much *or* an excessive amount yesterday

Un|mä|ßig|keit F excessiveness, immoderateness; **~ im Essen/Trinken** excessive eating/drinking

un-: **un|ma|te|ri|a|lis|tisch** ADJ unmaterialistic; **un|me|lo|disch** ADJ unmelodious

Un|men|ge F vast number; *(bei unzählbaren Mengenbegriffen)* vast amount; **~n von Leuten, eine ~ Leute** a vast number *or* vast numbers of people; **~n essen** to eat an enormous amount, to eat masses *(inf)*

Un|mensch M brute, monster; **ich bin ja kein ~** I'm not an ogre

un|mensch|lich ADJ **a** *Verhalten, Behandlung* inhuman, appalling **b** *(inf: = unerträglich)* terrible ADV **a** *behandeln, foltern* in an inhuman way, appallingly **b** *heiß, kalt, schwül* unbearably

Un|mensch|lich|keit F inhumanity; **~en** inhumanity, inhuman behaviour *(Brit) or* behavior *(US)*

un-: **un|merk|lich** ADJ imperceptible ADV imperceptibly; **un|mess|bar** ADJ unmeasurable; **un|me|tho|disch** ADJ unmethodical ADV in an unmethodical way; **er arbeitet zu ~** he doesn't work methodically enough; **un|mi|li|tä|risch** ADJ unmilitary

UN-Mis|si|on [u:ˈlɛn-] F *(Pol, Mil)* UN mission

un-: **un|miss|ver|ständ|lich** ADJ unequivocal, unambiguous ADV unequivocally, unambiguously; **jdm etw ~ zu verstehen geben** to tell sb sth in no uncertain terms; **un|mit|tel|bar** ADJ *Nähe, Nachbarschaft etc* immediate; *(= direkt)* direct; *(Jur) Besitz, Besitzer* direct, actual; **aus ~er Nähe schießen** to fire at close range ADV immediately; *(= ohne Umweg)* directly; **~ danach** *or* **darauf** immediately *or* straight afterwards; **~ vor** *(+dat) (zeitlich)* immediately before; *(räumlich)* right *or* directly in front of; **das berührt mich ~** it affects me directly; **Un|mit|tel|bar|keit** [ˈʊnmɪtlbaːɐkait] F *(= Direktheit)* directness; **un|möb|liert** [ˈʊnmøbliːɐt] ADJ *Zimmer* unfurnished ADV *mieten, vermieten* unfurnished; **~ wohnen** to live in unfurnished accommodation; **un|mo|dern** [-mɔdɛrn] ADJ old-fashioned; **~ werden** to go out of fashion ADV *eingerichtet, gekleidet* in an old-fashioned way; **un|mo|disch** ADJ unfashionable ADV *gekleidet, sich kleiden* unfashionably

un|mög|lich ✪ 39.2, 39.3, 43.3, 43.4 ADJ impossible; *(pej inf: = unpassend auch)* ridiculous; **das ist mir ~** that is impossible for me; **Unmögliches, das Unmögliche** the impossible; **etw ~ machen** to make sth impossible; **jdm etw ~ machen** to make it impossible for sb to do sth; **das Unmögliche möglich machen** to do the impossible; **jdn/sich ~ machen** to make sb/oneself look ridiculous, to make sb look (like) a fool/to make a fool of oneself
ADV *(= keinesfalls)* not possibly; *(pej inf: = unpassend)* impossibly; *sich anziehen* ridiculously; **ich kann es ~ tun** I cannot possibly do it; **~ aussehen** *(inf)* to look ridiculous

Un|mög|lich|keit F impossibility; **das ist ein Ding der ~!** that's quite impossible!

Un-: **Un|mo|ral** F immorality; **un|mo|ra|lisch** ADJ immoral; **un|mo|ti|viert** [ˈʊnmotiviːɐt] ADJ unmotivated ADV without motivation; **un|mün|dig** ADJ under-age; *(fig: = geistig unselbstständig)* sheep-like; **Un|mün|di|ge(r)** [ˈʊnmʏndɪgə] MF *decl as adj* minor; **Un|mün|dig|keit** F minority; *(fig: = geistige Unselbstständigkeit)* mental immaturity; **un|mu|si|ka|lisch** ADJ unmusical; **Un|mu|si|ka|li|tät** F lack of musicality

Un|mut [ˈʊnmuːt] M ill humour *(Brit) or* humor *(US)*; *(= Unzufriedenheit)* displeasure *(über +acc* at)

un|mu|tig [ˈʊnmuːtɪç] ADJ ill-humoured *(Brit)*, ill-humored *(US)*; *(= unzufrieden)* displeased *(über +acc* at) ADV with displeasure

Un|muts-: **Un|muts|äu|ße|rung** F expression of annoyance, angry remark; **Un|muts|fal|te** F frown

Un-: **un|nach|ahm|lich** [ʊnnaːxlaːmlɪç, ʊnnaːxˈlaːmlɪç] ADJ inimitable; **un|nach|gie|big** ADJ *Material etc* inflexible; *(fig) Haltung, Mensch auch* intransigent, unyielding ADV inflexibly, obstinately; **sich ~ verhalten** to be obstinate *or* adamant; **Un|nach|gie|big|keit** F *(von Material etc)* inflexibility; *(fig: von Haltung, Mensch auch)* intransigence; **un|nach|sich|tig** ADJ severe; *(stärker)* merciless, pitiless; *Strenge* unrelenting ADV *hinrichten, verfolgen* mercilessly, pitilessly; *bestrafen* severely; **Un|nach|sich|tig|keit** F severity; *(stärker)* mercilessness, pitilessness; **un|nah|bar** ADJ *Mensch* unapproachable, inaccessible; **Un|nah|bar|keit** [ʊnˈnaːbaːɐkait, ˈʊn-] F -, *no pl* inaccessibility; **un|na|tür|lich** ADJ unnatural; *Tod* violent; *(= abnorm)* abnormal ADV unnaturally, abnormally; **er isst ~ viel** he eats an abnormal amount; **Un|na|tür|lich|keit** F unnaturalness; **un|nenn|bar** ADJ *(liter)* unspeakable, unutterable *(liter)*; **un|nor|mal** ADJ abnormal; **un|nö|tig** ADJ unnecessary, needless ADV unnecessarily, needlessly; **sich ~ aufregen** to get unnecessarily *or* needlessly excited; **un|nö|ti|ger|wei|se** [ˈʊnnøːtɪgɐˈvaizə] ADV unnecessarily, needlessly

un|nütz [ˈʊnnʏts] ADJ useless; *Geschwätz* idle; *(= umsonst)* pointless, useless ADV uselessly, pointlessly; *sich Sorgen machen* unnecessarily; **~ Geld ausgeben** to spend money unnecessarily *or* needlessly

un|nüt|zer|wei|se [ˈʊnnʏtsɐˈvaizə] ADV unnecessarily, needlessly

UNO [ˈuːno] F -, *no pl* **die ~** the UN *sing*

UNO-Bot|schaf|ter(in) [ˈuːno-] M(F) UN ambassador, ambassador to the UN

un|öko|no|misch ADJ uneconomic; *Fahrweise, Konsumverhalten* uneconomical

UNO-Mit|glied [ˈuːno-] NT member of the UN, UN member

Un-: **un|or|dent|lich** ADJ untidy; *Lebenswandel* disorderly ADV untidily; **Un|or|dent|lich|keit** F untidiness

Un|ord|nung F disorder *no indef art*; *(in Zimmer etc auch)* untidiness *no indef art*; *(= Durcheinander)* muddle *(esp Brit)*, mess; **in ~ geraten** to get into (a state of) disorder, to become untidy, to get into a muddle *(esp Brit) or* mess; **etw in ~ bringen** to get sth in a mess, to mess sth up; **~ in etw bringen** *(in Leben, System)* to bring disorder to sth; **~ machen** *or* **schaffen** to put *or* throw everything into disorder, to turn everything upside down

Un-: **un|or|ga|nisch** ADJ inorganic; **un|or|ga|ni|siert** ADJ **a** disorganized **b** → **nicht a** ADV in a disorganized fashion *or* way; **un|or|tho|dox** ADJ unorthodox ADV in an unorthodox way

UNO-Trup|pen [ˈuːno-] PL UN troops *pl*

UNO-Voll|ver|samm|lung [ˈuːno-] F UN assembly

Un-: **Un|paar|hu|fer** PL *(Zool)* odd-toed ungulates *pl*; **un|paa|rig** ADJ unpaired; *(Med)* azygous *(spec)*; **un|pä|da|go|gisch** ADJ educationally unsound; *Lehrer etc* bad (as a teacher); **un|par|la|men|ta|risch** ADJ unparliamentary

un|par|tei|isch ADJ impartial, neutral; *Meinung, Richter, Urteil* impartial, unbiased ADV impartially

Un|par|tei|ische(r) [ˈʊnpartaiɪʃə] MF *decl as adj* impartial *or* neutral person; **die Meinung eines ~n einholen** to seek an impartial opinion; **der ~** *(Sport)* the referee

Un-: **un|par|tei|lich** ADJ *(esp Pol)* neutral; **Un|par|tei|lich|keit** F neutrality; **un|pas|send** ADJ *(= unangebracht)* unsuitable, inappropriate; *Zeit auch* inconvenient; *Bemerkung* inappropriate; *Augenblick* inconvenient, inopportune; **un|pas|sier|bar** ADJ impassable

un|päss|lich [ˈʊnpɛslɪç] ADJ *(geh)* indisposed *(form)*, unwell *(auch euph)*; **sich ~ fühlen** to be indisposed/feel unwell

Un|päss|lich|keit F -, **-en** *(geh)* indisposition *(form)*; **sie musste die Vorstellung wegen ~ leider absagen** unfortunately she had to cancel the performance because she was indisposed

Un-: **un|pat|ri|o|tisch** ADJ unpatriotic ADV *sich verhalten* unpatriotically; **Un|per|son** F *(Pol)* unperson; **un|per|sön|lich** ADJ impersonal *(auch Ling)*; *Mensch* distant, aloof; **Un|per|sön|lich|keit** F impersonality; **un|pfänd|bar** ADJ *(Jur)* unseizable; **un|po|e|tisch** ADJ unpoetic(al); **un|po|li|tisch** ADJ unpolitical; **un|po|pu|lär** ADJ unpopular; **un|prak|ti|ka|bel** ADJ impracticable; **un|prak|tisch** ADJ *Mensch* unpractical; *Maschine, Lösung* impractical; **un|prä|ten|ti|ös** ADJ *(geh)* unpretentious; **un|prä|zis, un|prä|zi|se** ADJ imprecise ADV *sich ausdrücken, formulieren* imprecisely; **un|prob|le|ma|tisch** ADJ *(= ohne Probleme)* unproblematic; *(= einfach, leicht)* uncomplicated; **das wird nicht ganz ~ sein** it won't be without its problems ADV without any problems; **un|pro|duk|tiv** ADJ unproductive; *Kapital auch* idle; **un|pro|fes|si|o|nell** ADJ unprofessional; **un|pro|por|ti|o|niert** ADJ out of proportion, disproportionate; *Körper* out of proportion, ill-proportioned

un|pünkt|lich ADJ *Mensch* unpunctual; *Zug* not on time; **er ist immer ~** he's never punctual *or* on time ADV late; **~ kommen/abfahren** to come/leave late; **die Züge fahren immer ~** the trains never run to *(Brit) or* on time; **die Zahlung erfolgte ~** payment was made late *or* was not made on time

Un|pünkt|lich|keit F unpunctuality; **er kommt wegen der ~ der Züge oft zu spät** he's often late because the trains are late

un-: **un|qua|li|fi|ziert** ADJ *Arbeitskraft* unqualified; *Arbeiten, Jobs* unskilled; *Äußerung* incompetent ADV *sich äußern, sich auslassen* incompetently; **un|quit|tiert** [ˈʊnkvitiːɐt] ADJ unreceipted; **un|ra|siert** [ˈʊnraziːɐt] ADJ unshaven → **fern**

Un|rast F, *no pl (geh)* restlessness

Un|rat [ˈʊnraːt] M **-(e)s**, *no pl (geh)* refuse; *(fig)* filth; **~ wittern** to suspect something

un-: **un|ra|ti|o|nell** ADJ inefficient ADV inefficiently; **un|rat|sam** ADJ inadvisable, unadvisable; **un|re|a|lis|tisch** ADJ unrealistic ADV unrealistically

un|recht ADJ wrong; **auf ~e Gedanken kommen** *(dated)* to get naughty *or* wicked ideas; **das ist mir gar nicht so ~** I don't really mind ADV **~ handeln** to do wrong

Un|recht NT, *no pl* wrong, injustice; **zu ~** *(verdächtigt)* wrongly, unjustly; **diese Vorurteile bestehen ganz zu ~** these prejudices are quite unfounded; **nicht zu ~** not without good reason; **im ~ sein** to be wrong; **jdn/sich ins ~ setzen** to put sb/oneself in the wrong *(Brit)*; **ihm ist im Leben viel ~ geschehen** he has suffered many injustices in life, he has often been wronged in life; **unrecht bekommen** to be shown to be wrong; **unrecht haben** to be wrong; **jdm unrecht geben** to contradict sb; **unrecht tun** to do wrong; **ein ~ begehen** to commit a wrong; **jdm ein ~ tun** to do sb an injustice, to do sb a wrong; **Sie haben nicht ganz unrecht** you're not entirely wrong

Un|recht-: **un|recht|mä|ßig** ADJ unlawful, illegal; *Thronfolger* wrongful ADV *besitzen* unlawfully, illegally; **sich etw ~ aneignen** to misappropriate sth; **un|recht|mä|ßi|ger|wei|se** [ˈʊnrɛçtmɛːsɪgɐˈvaizə] ADV unlawfully, illegally; **Un|recht|mä|ßig|keit** F -, -en **a** *no pl* illegality, unlawfulness **b** *(= Handlung)* illegality

Un|rechts-: **Un|rechts|be|wusst|sein** NT awareness of wrongdoing; **Un|rechts|re|gime** [-reʒiːm] NT *(Pol)* tyrannical regime; **Un|rechts|staat** M ≈ police state; **Un|rechts|tat|be|stand** M illegality; **Un|rechts|ur|teil** NT travesty of justice; **Un|rechts|ver|ein|ba|rung** F agreement to break the law

Un-: **un|red|lich** ADJ dishonest; **Un|red|lich|keit** F dishonesty; **un|re|ell** ADJ unfair; *(= unredlich)* dishonest; *Preis, Geschäft* unreasonable; **un|re|flek|tiert** [ˈʊnreflɛktiːɐt] ADJ *Strahlen* unreflected; *Bemerkung* spontaneous ADV **etw ~ wiedergeben** to repeat sth without thinking

un|re|gel|mä|ßig ADJ irregular *(auch Ling)*; *Zähne, Gesicht, Handschrift auch* uneven ADV irregularly; **~ essen/schlafen** not to eat/sleep regularly

Un|re|gel|mä|ßig|keit F irregularity *(auch Ling)*; *(von Zähnen, Gesichtszügen, Handschrift auch)* unevenness; **ihm wurden (finanzielle) ~en vorgeworfen** he was accused of (financial) irregularities

Un-: **un|reif** ADJ *Obst* unripe; *Mensch, Plan, Gedanke, Verhalten, Werk* immature ADV *ernten, verarbeiten* before becoming ripe; **Un|rei|fe** F *(von Mensch, Werk)* immaturity

un|rein ADJ *(= schmutzig)* not clean, dirty; *Klang, Ton* impure; *Atem, Haut* bad; *(Rel) Speise, Tier, Mensch* unclean; *Gedanken, Taten* unchaste, impure; **etw ins Unreine sprechen** to say sth off the record; **etw ins Unreine schreiben** to write sth out in rough

Un|rein|heit F *(= Schmutzigkeit)* dirtiness; *(von Klang, Ton)* impurity; *(von Atem)* unpleasantness; *(Rel)* uncleanness; *(von Gedanken, Taten)* unchasteness, impurity; **die ~ ihrer Haut** her bad skin

Un-: **un|rein|lich** ADJ not clean; **Un|rein|lich|keit** F uncleanliness; **un|ren|ta|bel** ADJ unprofitable ADV unprofitably

UN-Re|so|lu|ti|on [uːˈʔɛn-] F *(Pol)* UN resolution

un|rett|bar [ʊnˈrɛtbaːɐ, ˈʊn-] ADV **~ verschuldet** hopelessly in debt; **~ verloren** irretrievably lost; *(wegen Krankheit)* beyond all hope; **die ~ Verdammten** those damned beyond redemption *or* salvation

Un-: **un|rich|tig** ADJ incorrect; *Vorwurf* false; *(Admin) Angaben etc* false ADV incorrectly; **un|rich|ti|ger|wei|se** [ˈʊnrɪçtɪgɐˈvaizə] ADV incorrectly; falsely; **Un|rich|tig|keit** F incorrectness; *(Admin: von Angaben etc)* falseness; *(= Fehler)* error, mistake; **un|ro|man|tisch** ADJ unromantic

Un|ruh [ˈʊnruː] F -, -en *(von Uhr)* balance spring

Un|ru|he F -, -n **a** *no pl* restlessness; *(= Nervosität)* agitation; *(= Besorgnis)* agitation, disquiet; **in ~ sein** to be restless; *(= besorgt)* to be agitated *or* uneasy **b** *no pl (= Lärm)* noise, disturbance; *(= Geschäftigkeit)* (hustle and) bustle **c** *no pl (= Unfrieden)* unrest *no pl*, trouble; **~ stiften** to create unrest; *(in Familie, Schule)* to make trouble **d (politische) ~n** (political) disturbances *or* unrest *no pl*

Un|ru|he-: **Un|ru|he|herd** M trouble spot; **Un|ru|he|po|ten|ti|al** NT = **Unruhepotenzial**; **Un|ru|he|po|ten|zi|al** NT potential (for) unrest; **Un|ru|he|stif|ter(in)** M(F) troublemaker

un|ru|hig ADJ restless; *(= nervös auch)* fidgety *no adv*; *(= laut, belebt)* noisy; *Schlaf* troubled *no adv*, fitful, uneasy; *Zeit etc* troubled, uneasy; *Bild, Muster* busy; *Meer* troubled; **ein ~er Geist** *(inf)* a restless creature ADV *schlafen* restlessly, fitfully; *(ungleichmäßig)* unevenly; **ihr Herz schlägt zu ~** her heart is beating too irregularly

un|rühm|lich ADJ inglorious; **ein ~es Ende nehmen** to have an inglorious end ADV ingloriously

uns [ʊns] PERS PRON *acc, dat von* **wir** us; *(dat auch)* to us; **bei ~** *(= zu Hause, im Betrieb etc)* at our place; *(= in unserer Beziehung)* between us; *(= in unserem Land)* in our country; **bei ~ zu Hause** at our house; **bei ~ im Garten** in our garden; **einer von ~** one of us; **ein Freund von ~** a friend of ours; **das gehört ~** that is ours, that belongs to us; **viele Grüße von ~ beiden/allen** best wishes from both/all of us

REFL PRON *acc, dat* ourselves; *(= einander)* each other, one another; **wir freuten ~** we were glad; **wir wollen ~ ein neues Auto kaufen** we want to buy (ourselves) a new car; **~ selbst** ourselves; **wann sehen wir ~ wieder?** when will we see each other again?; **unter ~ gesagt** between ourselves, between you and me; **mitten unter ~** in our midst; **hier sind wir unter ~** we are alone here; **das bleibt unter ~** it won't go any further

un|sach|ge|mäß ADJ improper ADV improperly; **ein Gerät ~ behandeln** to put an appliance to improper use

un|sach|lich ADJ **a** *(= nicht objektiv)* unobjective **b** *(= unangebracht)* uncalled-for; **~ werden** to get personal

Un|sach|lich|keit F lack of objectivity; **diese Bemerkung zeugt von ~** this remark was uncalled-for

un|sag|bar, un|säg|lich [ʊnˈzɛːklɪç, ˈʊn-] *(geh)* ADJ unspeakable, unutterable *(liter)* ADV unspeakably, unutterably

un|sanft ADJ rough; *Druck* ungentle; *(= unhöflich)* rude ADV rudely; *durchrütteln* roughly; **~ aus dem Schlaf gerissen werden** to be rudely awakened

un|sau|ber ADJ **a** *(= ungewaschen, schmutzig)* dirty, not clean **b** *(= unordentlich) Handschrift, Arbeit* untidy; *(= nicht exakt) Schuss, Schlag, Schnitt* inaccurate; *Ton, Klang* impure **c** *(= unmoralisch)* shady, underhand; *Spielweise* dirty *(inf)*, unfair ADV *(= unordentlich)* untidily, carelessly

un|schäd|lich ADJ harmless; *Genussmittel, Medikament auch* safe, innocuous; **eine Bombe ~ machen** to make a bomb safe; *(= entschärfen)* to defuse a bomb; **jdn ~ machen** *(inf)* to take care of sb *(inf)*

Un|schäd|lich|keit F harmlessness; **die ~ einer Chemikalie beweisen** to prove that a chemical is safe

un|scharf ADJ **a** blurred, fuzzy; *Foto* blurred, out of focus; *Justierung* unsharp; *(Rad)* indistinct, unclear; *Erinnerung, Vorstellung* indistinct, hazy **b** *Munition* blank; *Bomben etc* unprimed ADV unclearly, indistinctly; **der Sender/das Radio ist ~ eingestellt** the station/the radio is not tuned clearly

Un|schär|fe F fuzziness; *(von Erinnerung, Vorstellung)* haziness; **begriffliche ~** lack of conceptual clarity

Un|schär|fe|re|la|ti|on F *(Phys)* uncertainty principle

un|schätz|bar ADJ *Wert, Verlust* incalculable, inestimable; *Hilfe, Vorteil* invaluable; **von ~em Wert** invaluable; *Schmuck etc* priceless

un|schein|bar ADJ inconspicuous; *(= unattraktiv) Aussehen, Mensch* unprepossessing

un|schick|lich ADJ unseemly, improper; **es ist ~ für eine junge Dame, das zu tun** it doesn't become a young lady *or* it is unseemly *or* improper for a young lady to do that ADV in an unseemly manner, improperly

Un|schick|lich|keit F -, -en **a** *no pl* unseemliness, impropriety **b** *(= unschickliche Handlung)* impropriety

un|schlag|bar ADJ unbeatable

Un|schlag|bar|keit [ʊnˈʃlaːkbaːɐkait, ˈʊn-] F -, *no pl* **er war überzeugt von der ~ seines Teams** he was convinced his team was unbeatable

un|schlüs|sig ADJ *(= unentschlossen)* undecided; *(= zögernd)* irresolute, hesitant; **sich** *(dat)* **~ (über etw** *acc*) **sein** to be undecided (about sth); to be hesitant (about sth) ADV *(= unentschlossen)* undecided; *(= zögernd)* hesitantly; **er blieb ~ stehen** he stopped, uncertain what to do

Un|schlüs|sig|keit F *(= Unentschlossenheit)* indecision; *(= Zögern)* irresoluteness, hesitancy

un|schön ADJ *(= hässlich)* unsightly; *(stärker)* ugly; *Gesicht* plain; *Bilder* unattractive; *(= unangenehm)* unpleasant; *Streit, Auseinandersetzung, Szenen* ugly

Un|schuld F, *no pl* **a** *(= Schuldlosigkeit)* innocence **b** *(= Jungfräulichkeit)* virginity **c** *(= Naivität, Unverdorbenheit)* innocence; *(fig: = Mädchen)* innocent; **die ~ vom Lande** *(inf)* a real innocent; **in aller ~** in all innocence

un|schul|dig ADJ **a** *(= nicht schuldig)* innocent; **an etw** *(dat)* **~ sein** not to be guilty of sth; **er war völlig ~ an dem Unfall** he was completely without blame in the accident, he was in no way responsible for the accident; **sind Sie schuldig oder ~? – ~** how do you plead, guilty or not guilty? – not guilty

b *(= jungfräulich)* innocent, virginal; **er/sie ist noch ~** he/she is still a virgin

c *(= harmlos, unverdorben)* innocent; **~ tun** to act the innocent

ADV **a** *(Jur)* when innocent; **jdn ~ verurteilen** to convict sb when he is innocent; **er sitzt ~ im Gefängnis** he is being held, an innocent man, in prison

b *(= arglos) fragen, sagen* innocently

Un|schul|di|ge(r) MF *decl as adj* innocent person/man/woman/child *etc*; **die ~n** the innocent

un|schul|di|ger|wei|se [ʊnʃʊldɪgɐˈvaizə] ADV unjustly, despite one's innocence

Un|schulds-: **Un|schulds|be|teu|e|rung** F protest of innocence; **Un|schulds|be|weis** M proof of (sb's) innocence; **Un|schulds|en|gel** M *(inf)*, **Un|schulds|lamm** NT *(inf)* little innocent; **Un|schulds|mie|ne** F innocent face *or* expression; **mit ~** with an air of innocence; **Un|schulds|ver|mu|tung** F presumption of innocence; **un|schulds|voll** ADJ innocent; **mit ~er Miene** with an air of innocence

un|schwer ADV easily, without difficulty; **das dürfte ja wohl ~ zu erraten sein** that shouldn't have been too hard to guess

Un|se|gen M *(= Unglück)* misfortune; *(= Fluch)* curse (*für* (up)on)

un|selbst|stän|dig, **un|selb|stän|dig** ADJ *Denken, Handeln* lacking in independence; *Mensch auch* dependent, unable to stand on one's own two feet; **eine ~e Tätigkeit ausüben** to work as an employee; **Einkünfte aus ~er Arbeit** income from (salaried) employment; **manche Menschen bleiben ihr Leben lang ~** some people never manage to stand on their own two feet; **sei doch nicht immer so ~!** show a bit of independence once in a while! ADV *(= mit fremder Hilfe)* not independently; **diese Schularbeit ist ~ angefertigt worden** this exercise was not done independently

Un|selbst|stän|di|ge(r) MF *decl as adj*, **Un|selb|stän|di|ge(r)** MF *decl as adj (Fin)* employed person

Un|selbst|stän|dig|keit F, **Un|selb|stän|dig|keit** F lack of independence, dependence

un|se|lig ADJ *(= unglücklich)* unfortunate; *(= verhängnisvoll)* ill-fated; **Zeiten ~en Angedenkens!** unhappy memories!; **ich Unseliger!** *(old liter)* oh unhappy wretch! *(old liter)*, woe is me! *(old liter)*

un|sen|si|bel ADJ insensitive

un|ser [ˈʊnzɐ] POSS PRON **a** *(adjektivisch)* our; **~e** *or* **unsre Bücher** our books **b** *(old: substantivisch)* ours PERS PRON *gen von* **wir** *(old, Bibl, geh)* of us; **~ beider gemeinsame Zukunft** our common future; **Herr, erbarme dich ~** Lord, have mercy upon us; **~ aller heimlicher Wunsch** the secret wish of all of us

un|ser|ei|ner ['ʊnzɐlainɐ], **un|ser|eins** ['ʊnzɐlains] INDEF PRON *(inf)* the likes of us *(inf)*

un|se|re(r, s) ['ʊnzərə] POSS PRON *(substantivisch)* ours; **der/die/das ~** *or* **Unsere** *(geh)* ours; **wir tun das ~** *or* **Unsere** *(geh)* we are doing our bit; **die ~n** *or* **Unseren** *(geh)* our family; **das ~** *or* **Unsere** *(geh: = Besitz)* what is ours

un|se|rer|seits ['ʊnzərɐ'zaits] ADV *(= auf unserer Seite)* for our part; *(= von unserer Seite)* from *or* on our part; **den Vorschlag haben wir ~ gemacht** we made the suggestion ourselves

un|se|res|glei|chen ['ʊnzərəs'glaiçn] INDEF PRON people like us *or* ourselves; **Menschen ~** people like us *or* ourselves

un|se|res|teils ['ʊnzərəs'tails] ADV = **unsererseits**

un|se|ri|ge(r, s) ['ʊnzərɪgə] POSS PRON *(old, geh)* **der/die/das ~** *or* **Unserige** ours; **die ~n** *or* **Unserigen** our families; **das ~** *or* **Unserige** *(= Besitz)* what is ours; **wir haben das ~** *or* **Unserige getan** we have done our part

un|se|ri|ös ADJ *Mensch* slippery, not straight; *Auftreten, Aussehen, Kleidung, Bemerkung* frivolous; *Methoden* shady, underhand(ed); *Firma, Bank* untrustworthy, shady; *Zeitung* not serious; *Verlag* lowbrow; *Schriftsteller, Wissenschaftler* not to be taken seriously, not serious, frivolous; *Gutachten, Angaben* untrustworthy; *Angebot* not serious; **das Geschäft war keineswegs ~** the deal was strictly above board

un|ser|seits ['ʊnzɐ'zaits] ADV = **unsererseits**

un|sers|glei|chen ['ʊnzɐs'glaiçn] INDEF PRON = **unseresgleichen**

un|sert|hal|ben ['ʊnzɐt'halbn] ADV = **unsertwegen**

un|sert|we|gen ['ʊnzɐt've:gn] ADV *(= wegen uns)* because of us, on our account; *(= uns zuliebe auch)* for our sake; *(= um uns)* about us; *(= für uns)* on our behalf

un|sert|wil|len ['ʊnzɐt'vɪlən] ADV **um ~** for our sake

Un|ser|va|ter ['ʊnzɐfa:tɐ] NT **-s, -** *(Sw)* Lord's Prayer

un|si|cher ADJ **a** *(= gefährlich)* dangerous, unsafe; **die Gegend ~ machen** *(fig inf)* to hang out *(inf)*; **sich ~ fühlen** to feel unsafe
b *(= nicht selbstbewusst, verunsichert)* insecure, unsure (of oneself); **jdn ~ machen** to make sb feel unsure of himself/herself
c *(= ungewiss, zweifelhaft)* unsure, uncertain; *(= unstabil)* uncertain, unstable, unsettled
d *(= ungeübt, ungefestigt)* unsure; *Hand* unsteady; *Kenntnisse* shaky; **mit ~er Hand** with an unsteady hand; **~ auf den Beinen sein** to be unsteady on one's feet
ADV **a** *(= schwankend)* unsteadily
b *(= nicht selbstsicher)* uncertainly; **sie blickte ~ im Kreise umher** she looked around timidly

Un|si|cher|heit F *(= Gefahr)* danger; *(= mangelndes Selbstbewusstsein)* insecurity; *(= Ungewissheit)* uncertainty; *(= Instabilität)* instability

Un|si|cher|heits|fak|tor M element of uncertainty

un|sicht|bar ADJ *(lit, fig)* invisible

Un|sicht|bar|keit F, *no pl* invisibility

Un|sinn M, *no pl* nonsense *no indef art*, rubbish *no indef art (Brit)*; **~ machen** *or* **treiben** to do silly things; **~ reden** to talk nonsense; **lass den ~!** stop fooling about!; **mach keinen ~, Hände hoch!** *(inf)* no funny stuff - put your hands up! *(inf)*; **wirklich? mach keinen ~!** *(inf)* really? - stop messing about *(Brit)* or around! *(inf)* → **Sinn**

un|sin|nig ADJ *(= sinnlos)* nonsensical, foolish; *(= ungerechtfertigt)* unreasonable; *(stärker)* absurd ADV nonsensically, foolishly; *(= ungerechtfertigterweise)* unreasonably; *(stärker)* absurdly; **~ viel** *(inf)* an incredible amount *(inf)*; **~ hohe Preise** *(inf)* ridiculously high prices *(inf)*

Un|sin|nig|keit F **-**, *no pl (= Sinnlosigkeit)* foolishness; *(= Absurdität)* absurdity

Un|sit|te F *(= schlechte Gewohnheit)* bad habit; *(= dummer Brauch)* silly custom

un|sitt|lich ADJ immoral; *(in sexueller Hinsicht)* indecent ADV indecently; **er hat sich ihr ~ genähert** he made indecent advances to her

un|so|lid, un|so|li|de ADJ *Mensch* free-living; *(= unredlich) Firma, Angebot, Geschäftsmann* unreliable; *Politik* without a solid basis; **~(e) leben** to have an unhealthy lifestyle; **ein ~es Leben führen** to be free-living; **an dem Angebot war nichts Unsolides** the offer was strictly above board ADV *(etwas ausschweifend)* dissolutely

un|so|li|da|risch ADJ lacking in solidarity ADV **sich ~ verhalten** to show a lack of solidarity

Un-: un|sor|tiert ['ʊnzɔrti:ɐt] ADJ unsorted; **un|so|zi|al** ADJ *Verhalten, Mensch* antisocial; *Maßnahmen, Politik* unsocial ADV antisocially; **un|spek|ta|ku|lär** ADJ unspectacular; **un|spe|zi|fisch** ADJ nonspecific; **un|sport|lich** ADJ **a** *(= ungelenkig)* unsporty **b** *(= unfair)* unsporting; **Un|sport|lich|keit** F **a** *(= Unfairness)* unsporting behaviour *(Brit) or* behavior *(US) no art, no pl* **b** *(= Ungelenkigkeit)* **und das bei deiner ~!** and you being so unathletic!

uns|re ['ʊnzrə] PRON → **unser**

uns|rer|seits ['ʊnzrɐ'zaits] ADV = **unsererseits**

uns|res|glei|chen ['ʊnzrəs'glaiçn] INDEF PRON = **unseresgleichen**

uns|res|teils ['ʊnzrəs'tails] ADV = **unseresteils**

uns|ret|we|gen ['ʊnzrət've:gn] ADV = **unsertwegen**

uns|ret|wil|len ['ʊnzrət'vɪlen] ADV = **unsertwillen**

uns|ri|ge(r, s) ['ʊnzrɪgə] POSS PRON = **unserige(r, s)**

Un-: un|sta|bil ADJ unstable; **un|statt|haft** ADJ *(form)* inadmissible; *(= ungesetzlich)* illegal; *(Sport)* not allowed

un|sterb|lich ADJ immortal; *Liebe* undying; **jdn ~ machen** to immortalize sb ADV *(inf)* utterly; **sich ~ blamieren** to make an utter fool *or* a complete idiot of oneself; **~ verliebt sein** to be head over heels *or* madly in love *(inf)*

Un|sterb|li|che(r) MF *decl as adj* immortal

Un|sterb|lich|keit F immortality; **die ~ seiner Liebe** his undying love

Un|sterb|lich|keits|glau|be M belief in immortality

Un|stern M, *no pl (liter)* unlucky star; **die Liebe der beiden stand unter einem ~** their love was followed by an unlucky star

un|stet ADJ *Glück, Liebe* fickle; *Mensch* restless; *(= wankelmütig)* changeable; *Entwicklung* unsteady; *Leben* unsettled

Un|ste|te ['ʊnʃte:tə] F **-**, *no pl* = **Unstetigkeit**

un|ste|tig ADJ *(Math)* discontinuous, not continuous

Un|ste|tig|keit F *(von Glück, Liebe)* fickleness; *(von Mensch)* restlessness; *(von Entwicklung)* unsteadiness; *(Math)* discontinuity

Un-: un|still|bar [ʊn'ʃtɪlba:ɐ, 'ʊn-] ADJ **a** *Durst, Wissensdurst* unquenchable; *Verlangen, Sehnsucht, Hunger* insatiable **b** *Blutstrom* uncontrollable; **un|stim|mig** ADJ *Aussagen etc* at variance, differing *attr*; **in einem Punkt sind wir noch ~** we still disagree *or* differ on one point; **Un|stim|mig|keit** F *(= Ungenauigkeit, Fehler)* discrepancy, inconsistency; *(= Streit)* difference; **un|stoff|lich** ADJ immaterial; *Seele auch* incorporeal; **un|strei|tig** ADJ indisputable, incontestable ADV indisputably, incontestably; **un|strit|tig** ADJ indisputable ADV indisputably, unquestionably; **Un|sum|me** F vast sum; **un|sym|met|risch** ADJ asymmetric(al)

un|sym|pa|thisch ADJ unpleasant, disagreeable; **er ist ~** he's unpleasant *or* a disagreeable type; **das/er ist mir ~** I don't like that/him; **am ~sten an diesen Leuten ist mir …** what I find most unpleasant about *or* what I like least about these people is …

un|sys|te|ma|tisch ADJ unsystematic ADV unsystematically

un|ta|de|lig ['ʊnta:dəlɪç, ʊn'ta:dəlɪç], **un|tad|lig** ['ʊnta:dlɪç, ʊn'ta:dlɪç] ADJ impeccable; *Verhalten auch* irreproachable; *Mensch* beyond reproach ADV *sich verhalten* impeccably, irreproachably; **~ gekleidet sein** to be dressed impeccably

un|ta|len|tiert ADJ untalented

Un|tat F atrocity, atrocious deed; **~en begehen** *(im Krieg etc)* to commit atrocities

un|tä|tig ADJ *(= müßig)* idle; *(= nicht handelnd)* passive; *Vulkan* inactive, dormant ADV idly, inactively; **sie sah ~ zu, wie er verblutete** she stood idly by as he bled to death

Un|tä|tig|keit F *(= Müßiggang)* idleness; *(= Passivität)* passivity

Un-: un|taug|lich ADJ *(zu, für* for) unsuitable; *(für Wehrdienst)* unfit; **Un|taug|lich|keit** F unsuitability; *(für Wehrdienst)* unfitness; **un|teil|bar** ADJ indivisible; **Un|teil|bar|keit** F indivisibility

un|ten ['ʊntn] ADV *(= im unteren Teil, am unteren Ende, in Rangfolge)* at the bottom; *(= tiefer, drunten)* (down) below; *(= an der Unterseite)* underneath; *(in Gebäude)* (down) below, downstairs; *(inf: geografisch)* down south; *(= flussab)* downstream; *(= tiefer gelegen)* down there/here; **von ~** from below; **die Frau von ~ war gekommen** the woman from downstairs *or* down below had come; **nach ~** down; **die Säule wird nach ~ hin breiter** the column broadens out toward(s) the base *or* bottom; **bis ~** to the bottom; **der Schneefall kam nicht bis ~ ins Tal** the snow did not reach as far down as the valley; **~ am Berg** at the bottom of the hill; **~ am Fluss** down by the river(side); **~ im Tal/Wasser/Garten** down in the valley/water/garden; **~ im Glas** at the bottom of the glass; **~ auf dem Bild** at the bottom of the picture; **~ auf der Straße** down on the street; **dort** *or* **da/hier ~** down there/here; **weiter ~** further down; **~ bleiben** to stay down; **~ erwähnt, ~ genannt** mentioned below; **der/die ~ Erwähnte** *or* **Genannte** the undermentioned (person) *(form)*, the person mentioned below; **bitte lesen Sie auch das ~ Erwähnte** please see below; **rechts/links ~** down on the right/left; **siehe ~** see below; **er ist bei mir ~ durch** *(inf)* I'm through *or* I've finished with him *(inf)*; **ich weiß schon nicht mehr, was** *or* **wo oben und ~ ist** *(inf)* I don't know whether I'm coming or going *(inf)*; **~ stehend** following; *(lit)* standing below; **im ~ Stehenden** given below; **~ Stehendes** the following; **das ~ Stehende** what follows; **~ wohnen** to live downstairs

Un|ten-: un|ten|an ['ʊntn'lan] ADV *(= am unteren Ende)* at the far end; *(in Reihenfolge: lit, fig)* at the bottom; **(bei jdm) ~ stehen** *(fig)* not to be a priority (with sb), to be at the bottom of sb's list; **un|ten|drun|ter** ['ʊntn'drʊntɐ] ADV *(inf)* underneath; **un|ten|durch** ['ʊntn'dʊrç] ADV *(inf)* through; **bei uns ist sie ~** we're through *or* done with her, we've finished with her; **un|ten|er|wähnt** [-lɛɐvɛ:nt], **un|ten|ge|nannt** ADJ *attr* → **unten**; **Un|ten|er|wähn|te(r)** MF *decl as adj*, **Un|ten|ge|nann|te(r)** MF *decl as adj* **der/die ~** *or* **Untengenannte** the undermentioned (person) *(form)*, the person mentioned below; **Un|ten|er|wähn|te(s)** NT *decl as adj* **bitte lesen Sie auch das ~** please see below also; **un|ten|he|rum** ['ʊntnhɛ'rʊm] ADV *(inf)* down below *(inf)*; **un|ten|ste|hend** ADJ → **unten**; **Un|ten|ste|hen|de(s)** NT *decl as adj* **im ~n** given below; **~s** the following; **das ~** what follows

un|ter ['ʊntɐ] PREP **a** +dat *(= unterhalb von)* under; *(= drunter)* underneath, below; *(Unterordnung ausdrückend)* under; *(= zwischen, innerhalb)* among(st); *(= weniger, geringer als)* under, below; **~ 18 Jahren/EUR 50** under 18 years (of age)/50 euros; **~ dem Durchschnitt** below average; **Temperaturen ~ 25 Grad** temperatures below 25 degrees; **Städte ~ 10.000 Einwohner(n)** towns with a population of under *or* below 10,000; **~**

sich *(dat)* **sein** to be by themselves; **jdn ~ sich haben** to have sb under one; **~ etw leiden** to suffer from sth; **~ Mittag** *(dial)* in the morning; **~ der Woche** *(dial)* within the (working) week; **~ anderem** among other things, inter alia *(form)*

b *+acc* under; **bis ~ das Dach voll mit ...** full to bursting with ...; **~ Verbrecher geraten** to fall in with criminals

Un|ter-: **Un|ter|ab|tei|lung** F subdivision; **Un|ter|an|ge|bot** NT lack *(an +dat* of); **Un|ter|arm** M forearm; **Un|ter|arm|ta|sche** F clutch bag; **Un|ter|art** F *(esp Biol)* subspecies; **Un|ter|aus|schuss** M subcommittee; **Un|ter|bau** M *pl* **-bauten** *(von Gebäude)* foundations *pl*; *(von Brücke, Bahnstrecke, fig)* substructure; *(bei Straßen)* (road)bed; **Un|ter|be|griff** M member of a conceptual class, subsumable concept; **un|ter|be|legt** ADJ *Hotel, Schule etc* not full; *Fortbildungskurs* undersubscribed; **das Hotel ist ziemlich ~** the hotel is not very full; **Un|ter|be|le|gung** F *(eines Hotels, Krankenhauses etc)* underoccupancy; *(eines Kurses)* undersubscription; **un|ter|be|lich|ten** *ptp* **unterbelichtet** VTI *insep (Phot)* to underexpose; **un|ter|be|lich|tet** [ˈʊntɐbəlɪçtət] ADJ *(Phot)* underexposed; **geistig ~ sein** *(hum)* to be a bit dim *(inf)*; **un|ter|be|mannt** [-bəmant] ADJ undermanned; **Un|ter|be|schäf|ti|gung** F *(Econ)* underemployment; **un|ter|be|setzt** ADJ understaffed; **Un|ter|be|set|zung** F understaffing; **Un|ter|bett** NT feather bed; **un|ter|be|wer|ten** *ptp* **unterbewertet** VT *insep* to underrate, to undervalue; **Un|ter|be|wer|tung** F underrating *no pl*, undervaluation; **un|ter|be|wusst** ADJ subconscious; **das Unterbewusste** the subconscious ADV subconsciously; **Un|ter|be|wusst|sein** NT subconscious; **im ~** subconsciously; **un|ter|be|zah|len** *ptp* **unterbezahlt** VT *insep* to underpay; **un|ter|be|zahlt** ADJ underpaid; **Un|ter|be|zah|lung** F underpayment; **un|ter|bie|ten** *ptp* **unterboten** VT *insep irreg Konkurrenten, Preis* to undercut; *(fig)* to surpass; **sich gegenseitig ~** to undercut each other; **eine kaum noch zu ~de Leistung** an unsurpassable achievement *(iro)*; **Un|ter|bi|lanz** F deficit balance; **un|ter|bin|den** [ʊntɐˈbɪndn] *ptp* **unterbunden** [ʊntɐˈbʊndn] VT *insep irreg* to stop, to prevent; *(Med) Blutung* to ligature; **un|ter+bin|den** [ˈʊntɐbɪndn] VT *sep irreg* to tie (on) underneath; **Un|ter|bin|dung** [-ˈbɪndʊŋ] F, *no pl* ending; *(Med)* ligature; **un|ter|blei|ben** [ʊntɐˈblaibn] *ptp* **unterblieben** [ʊntɐˈbliːbn] VI *insep irreg aux sein* **a** *(= aufhören)* to cease, to stop; **das hat zu ~** that will have to cease *or* stop **b** *(= nicht geschehen)* not to occur *or* happen; **das wäre besser unterblieben** *(Vorfall)* it would have been better if it had never happened; *(Bemerkung)* it would have been better left unsaid **c** *(= versäumt werden)* to be omitted; **Un|ter|bo|den** M *(Geog)* subsoil; *(Mot)* underside; *(Archit)* subfloor, underfloor; **Un|ter|bo|den|schutz** M *(Mot)* underseal *(Brit)*, protective undercoating; **un|ter|bre|chen** [ʊntɐˈbrɛçn] *ptp* **unterbrochen** [ʊntɐˈbrɔxn] *insep irreg* VT to interrupt; *Stille, Reise, Eintönigkeit, Langeweile* to break; *(langfristig)* to break off; *Telefonverbindung* to disconnect; *Spiel* to suspend, to stop; *Schwangerschaft* to terminate; **entschuldigen Sie bitte, wenn ich Sie unterbreche** forgive me for interrupting; **wir sind unterbrochen worden** *(am Telefon)* we've been cut off VR to break off; **Un|ter|bre|cher** [ʊntɐˈbrɛçɐ] M **-s, -** *(Elec)* interrupter; *(Aut)* contact breaker; **Un|ter|bre|cher|kon|takt** M *(Elec, Aut)* (contact-breaker) point; **Un|ter|bre|chung** F interruption; *(von Stille, Reise, Langeweile)* break (+*gen* in); *(von Telefonverbindung)* disconnection; *(von Spiel)* stoppage; **bei ~ der Reise** when breaking the journey; **ohne ~** without a break; **nach einer kurzen ~** *(Rad, TV)* after a short break *or* intermission; **mit ~en** with a few breaks in between; **Un|ter|bre|chungs|be|fehl** M *(Comput)* break command; **Un|ter|bre|chungs|funk|ti|on** F *(Comput)* interrupt function; **Un|ter|bre|chungs|tas|te** F *(Comput)* break key; **un|ter|brei|ten** [ʊntɐˈbraitn] *ptp* **unterbreitet** VT *insep Plan* to present; **(jdm) einen Vorschlag/ein Angebot ~** to make a proposal/an offer (to sb); **Un|ter|brei|tung** F *(eines Vorschlags)* submission (+*gen* of)

un|ter+brin|gen VT *sep irreg* **a** *(= verstauen, Platz geben)* to put; *(in Heim, Krankenhaus etc)* to put; *Arbeitslose etc* to fix up *(bei* with); *Zitat (in Text etc)* to get in *(in etw (acc)* sth); **ich kann in meinem Auto noch einen ~** I can get one more in my car, I have room for one more in my car; **das Krankenhaus kann keine neuen Patienten mehr ~** the hospital cannot accommodate any new patients; **etw bei jdm ~** to leave sth with sb; **ich kenne ihn, aber ich kann ihn nirgends ~** *(inf)* I know him, but I just can't place him

b *(= Unterkunft geben) Menschen* to accommodate; *Ausstellung, Sammlung* to house; **gut/schlecht untergebracht sein** to have good/bad accommodation; *(= versorgt werden)* to be well/badly looked after; **die Hochzeitsgäste wurden im Hotel untergebracht** the wedding guests were put up in the hotel; **wie sind Sie untergebracht?** what's your accommodation like? *(Brit)*, what are your accommodations like? *(US)*

Un|ter|brin|gung F **-, -en** accommodation *(Brit)*, accommodations *pl (US)*

Un|ter|brin|gungs|mög|lich|kei|ten PL accommodation *sing (Brit)*, accommodations *pl (US)*, accommodation options *pl*

Un|ter|bruch M *(Sw)* = **Unterbrechung**

un|ter+but|tern VT *sep (inf: = unterdrücken)* to ride roughshod over; *(= opfern)* to sacrifice; **er wird von ihr untergebuttert** she dominates him; **lass dich nicht ~!** don't let them push you around

Un|ter|deck NT *(Naut)* lower deck; **im ~** below deck

Un|ter|de|ckung F *(Fin)* insufficient cover

un|ter|der|hand △ [ʊntɐdeːɐˈhant] ADV → **Hand d**

un|ter|des(sen) [ʊntɐˈdɛs(n)] ADV (in the) meantime, meanwhile

Un|ter|druck M *pl* **-drücke** *(Phys)* below atmospheric pressure; *(Med)* low blood pressure, hypotension *(spec)*

un|ter|drü|cken [ʊntɐˈdrʏkn] *ptp* **unterdrückt** VT *insep* **a** *(= beherrschen) Volk, Sklaven* to oppress, to repress; *Freiheit, Meinung* to suppress; *Revolution* to suppress, to put down; **die Unterdrückten** the oppressed **b** *(= zurückhalten) Neugier, Gähnen, Lachen, Gefühle* to suppress; *Tränen, Antwort, Bemerkung* to hold back

Un|ter|drü|cker [ʊntɐˈdrʏkɐ] M **-s, -**, **Un|ter|drü|cke|rin** [-ərɪn] F **-, -nen** oppressor

Un|ter|druck|schleu|se F vacuum lock

Un|ter|drü|ckung F **-, -en a** *(von Volk, Sklaven)* oppression, repression; *(von Freiheit, Revolution)* suppression **b** *(von Neugier, Gähnen, Lachen, Gefühlen)* suppression; *(von Tränen, Antwort, Bemerkung)* holding back

un|ter|durch|schnitt|lich ADJ below average ADV below the average; **er verdient ~** he has a below average income, he earns below the average

un|ter|ei|nan|der [ʊntɐlaiˈnandɐ] ADV **a** *(= gegenseitig)* each other; *(= miteinander)* among ourselves/themselves *etc*; **Familien, die ~ heiraten** families that intermarry **b** *(räumlich)* one below *or* underneath the other

Un|ter-: **un|ter|ent|wi|ckelt** [-lɛntvɪklt] ADJ underdeveloped; *(inf: = geistig unterentwickelt)* thick *(inf)*; **Un|ter|ent|wick|lung** F underdevelopment

un|te|re(r, s) [ˈʊntərə] ADJ *superl* **unterste(r, s)** [ˈʊntɐstə] lower

Un|ter-: **un|ter|er|nährt** [-lɛɐnɛːɐt] ADJ undernourished, suffering from malnutrition; **Un|ter|er|näh|rung** F malnutrition

un|ter|fan|gen [ʊntɐˈfaŋən] *ptp* **unterfangen** VR *insep irreg (geh)* to dare, to venture

Un|ter|fan|gen [ʊntɐˈfaŋən] NT **-s, -** *(geh)* venture, undertaking; **ein schwieriges ~** a difficult undertaking

un|ter+fas|sen VT *sep* **jdn ~** to take sb's arm; **sie gingen untergefasst** they walked along arm in arm *or* with arms linked

un|ter|for|dern *ptp* **unterfordert** VT **jdn ~** to make too few demands on sb, to not stretch sb enough; **sich unterfordert fühlen** to feel one is not being stretched *or* challenged; **eine Klasse ~** *(Sch)* to ask too little of a class

Un|ter|fran|ken NT *(Geog)* Lower Franconia

Un|ter|füh|rung F **a** underpass; *(für Fußgänger)* subway, underpass **b** *(Typ etc)* ditto (mark)

Un|ter|füh|rungs|zei|chen NT *(Typ)* ditto (mark)

Un|ter-: **Un|ter|funk|ti|on** F insufficient function *no indef art*, hypofunction *(spec)*; **(eine) ~ der Schilddrüse** thyroid insufficiency, hypothyroidism *(spec)*; **Un|ter|fut|ter** NT interfacing; **un|ter|füt|tern** [ʊntɐˈfʏtɐn] *ptp* **unterfüttert** VT *insep* to interface

Un|ter|gang M *pl* **-gänge a** *(von Schiff)* sinking **b** *(von Gestirn)* setting **c** *(= das Zugrundegehen) (allmählich)* decline; *(völlig)* destruction; *(der Welt)* end; *(von Individuum)* downfall, ruin; **die Propheten des ~s** the prophets of doom; **dem ~ geweiht sein** to be doomed; **du bist noch mal mein ~!** you'll be the death of me! *(inf)*

Un|ter|gangs|stim|mung F feeling of doom

Un|ter-: **un|ter|gä|rig** [-gɛːrɪç] ADJ *Bier* bottom-fermented; *Hefe* bottom-fermenting; **Un|ter|gat|tung** F subgenus

un|ter|ge|ben [ʊntɐˈgeːbn] ADJ subordinate

Un|ter|ge|be|ne(r) [ʊntɐˈgeːbənə] MF *decl as adj* subordinate; *(pej: = Subalterner auch)* underling

un|ter|ge|gan|gen ADJ *Schiff* sunken; *Gestirn* set; *Volk etc* extinct; *Zivilisation, Kultur* extinct, lost; *Epoche* lost; **die ~e DDR** the defunct GDR

un|ter+ge|hen VI *sep irreg aux sein* **a** *(= versinken)* to sink; *(fig: im Lärm etc)* to be submerged *or* drowned **b** *(Gestirn)* to set; **sein Stern ist im Untergehen** his star is waning *or* on the wane **c** *(= zugrunde gehen) (Kultur) (allmählich)* to decline; *(völlig)* to be destroyed; *(Welt)* to come to an end; *(Individuum)* to perish; **dort muss man sich durchsetzen, sonst geht man unter** you've got to assert yourself there or you'll go under

Un|ter-: **un|ter|ge|ord|net** ADJ *Dienststelle, Stellung* subordinate; *Rolle auch* secondary; *Bedeutung* secondary; **~er Ordner** *(Comput)* subfolder → *auch* **unterordnen**; **Un|ter|ge|schoss** NT basement; **Un|ter|ge|stell** NT **a** base; *(Mot)* subframe **b** *(inf: = Beine)* pins *pl (inf)*; **Un|ter|ge|wicht** NT underweight; **~ haben** to be underweight; **un|ter|ge|wich|tig** ADJ underweight; **un|ter|glie|dern** [ʊntɐˈgliːdɐn] *ptp* **untergliedert** VT *insep* to subdivide; **Un|ter|glie|de|rung** F subdivision; **un|ter|gra|ben** [ʊntɐˈgraːbn] *ptp* **untergraben** VT *insep irreg (= zerstören)* to undermine; **un|ter+gra|ben** [ˈʊntɐgraːbn] VT *sep irreg (in Erde)* to dig in

Un|ter|gren|ze F lower limit; **~ des Verdienstes** *(Fin)* lower earnings limit *or* level

Un|ter|grund M, *no pl* **a** *(Geol)* subsoil **b** *(= Farbschicht)* undercoat; *(= Hintergrund)* background **c** *(Liter, Pol etc)* underground; **er lebt seit Jahren im ~** he's been living underground for years; **in den ~ gehen** to go underground

Un|ter|grund- *in cpds (Liter, Pol)* underground; **Un|ter|grund|bahn** F underground *(Brit)*, subway *(US)*; **Un|ter|grund|be|we|gung** F underground movement; **Un|ter|grund|kämp|fer(in)** M(F) guerrilla, guerilla, resistance fighter

Un|ter-: **Un|ter|grup|pe** F subgroup; **un|ter+ha|ben** VT *sep irreg (inf)* to have (on) underneath; **un|ter+ha|ken** *sep* VT **jdn ~** to link arms with sb VR **sich bei jdm ~** to link arms with sb; **untergehakt gehen** to walk arm in arm

un|ter|halb [ˈʊntɐhalp] PREP *+gen* below; *(bei Fluss auch)* downstream from ADV below; *(bei Fluss auch)* downstream; **~ von** below; *(bei Fluss auch)* downstream from

Un|ter|halt M, *no pl* **a** *(= Lebensunterhalt)* maintenance *(Brit esp Jur)*, alimony; **für jds ~ aufkommen** to pay for sb's keep; **für seine Kinder ~ zahlen** to pay maintenance *(Brit) or* child support for one's children; **für seine Ex-Ehefrau ~ zahlen** to pay maintenance *(Brit) or* alimony to one's ex-wife; **seinen ~ verdienen** to earn one's living **b** *(= Instandhaltung)* upkeep

un|ter|hal|ten [ʊntɐˈhaltn] *ptp* **unterhalten** *insep irreg* VT **a** *(= versorgen, ernähren)* to support; *Angestellten* to maintain
b *(= halten, betreiben) Geschäft, Gaststätte* to keep, to run; *Konto* to have; *Kfz* to run
c *(= instand halten) Gebäude, Fahrzeug etc* to maintain
d *(= pflegen, aufrechterhalten) Kontakte, Beziehungen* to maintain
e *Gäste, Publikum* to entertain
VR **a** *(= sprechen)* to talk *(mit* to, with); **man kann sich mit ihm gut/schlecht/glänzend ~** he's easy/not easy/really easy to talk to; **man kann sich mit ihm nicht ~** he's impossible to talk to, you can't talk to him; **sich mit jdm (über etw** *acc)* **~** to (have a) talk *or* chat with sb (about sth); **Herr Schmidt, ich hätte mich mal gerne mit Ihnen ein bisschen ~** Herr Schmidt, I would like (to have) a little talk *or* chat with you; **wir ~ uns noch!** *(drohend, begütigend)* we'll talk about that later
b *(= sich vergnügen)* to enjoy oneself, to have a good time; **habt ihr euch gut ~?** did you enjoy yourselves?, did you have a good time?; **sich mit etw ~** to amuse *or* entertain oneself with sth

un|ter+hal|ten [ˈʊntɐhaltn] VT *sep irreg* to hold underneath; **ein Tuch ~** to hold a cloth underneath

Un|ter|hal|ter [ʊntɐˈhaltɐ] M **-s, -**, **Un|ter|hal|te|rin** [-ərɪn] F **-, -nen** **a** entertainer; *(= unterhaltsamer Mensch)* conversationalist **b** *(= Verdiener)* breadwinner

un|ter|halt|sam [ʊntɐˈhaltza:m] ADJ entertaining

Un|ter|halts-: **Un|ter|halts|an|spruch** M maintenance claim *(Brit)*, alimony claim; **un|ter|halts|be|rech|tigt** ADJ entitled to maintenance *(Brit) or* alimony; **Un|ter|halts|geld** NT maintenance *(Brit)*, alimony; **Un|ter|halts|kla|ge** F action for maintenance *(Brit)*, lawsuit for alimony *(esp US)*; **(gegen jdn) ~ erheben** to file a suit for maintenance *(Brit) or* alimony (against sb); **Un|ter|halts|kos|ten** PL *(von Gebäude, Anlage)* maintenance *(Brit) or* alimony (costs *pl*); *(von Kfz)* running costs *pl*; **Un|ter|halts|leis|tung** F payment of maintenance *(Brit) or* alimony; **Un|ter|halts|pflicht** F obligation to pay maintenance *(Brit) or* alimony; **un|ter|halts|pflich|tig** [-pflɪçtɪç] ADJ under obligation to pay maintenance *(Brit) or* alimony; **Un|ter|halts|pflich|ti|ge(r)** [-pflɪçtɪgə] MF *decl as adj* person legally responsible for paying maintenance *(Brit) or* alimony; **Un|ter|halts|zah|lung** F maintenance *(Brit) or* alimony payment

Un|ter|hal|tung [ʊntɐˈhaltʊŋ] F **a** *(= Gespräch)* talk, chat, conversation; **eine ~ (mit jdm) führen** to have a talk *or* conversation (with sb); **hier kann man keine ~ führen** we can't talk here **b** *(= Amüsement)* entertainment; **wir wünschen gute** *or* **angenehme ~** we hope you enjoy the programme *(Brit) or* program *(US)* **c** *no pl (= Instandhaltung)* upkeep; *(von Kfz, Maschinen)* maintenance

Un|ter|hal|tungs-: **Un|ter|hal|tungs|elekt|ro|nik** F *(= Industrie)* consumer electronics *sing*; *(= Geräte)* audio systems *pl*; **Un|ter|hal|tungs|film** M light entertainment film; **Un|ter|hal|tungs|in|dust|rie** F, *no pl* entertainment industry; **Un|ter|hal|tungs|kos|ten** PL = **Unterhaltskosten**; **Un|ter|hal|tungs|lek|tü|re** F light reading; **Un|ter|hal|tungs|li|te|ra|tur** F light fiction; **Un|ter|hal|tungs|mu|sik** F light music; **Un|ter|hal|tungs|pro|gramm** NT light entertainment programme *(Brit) or* program *(US)*; **Un|ter|hal|tungs|ro|man** M light novel; **Un|ter|hal|tungs|sen|dung** F light entertainment programme *(Brit) or* program *(US)*; **Un|ter|hal|tungs|wert** M, *no pl* entertainment value

Un|ter|händ|ler(in) M(F) negotiator

Un|ter|hand|lung F negotiation

Un|ter|haus NT Lower House, House of Commons *(Brit)*, Commons *sing (Brit)*; **Mitglied des ~es** member of parliament, MP

Un|ter|haus-: **Un|ter|haus|ab|ge|ord|ne|te(r)** MF *decl as adj*, **Un|ter|haus|mit|glied** NT member of parliament, MP; **Un|ter|haus|sit|zung** F session of the House; **Un|ter|haus|wahl** F Commons vote *(Brit)*, Lower House vote

Un|ter|haut F *(Anat)* subcutis

un|ter+he|ben VT *sep (Cook)* to stir in (lightly)

Un|ter|hemd NT vest *(Brit)*, undershirt *(US)*

Un|ter|hit|ze F *(Cook)* bottom heat

un|ter|höh|len [ʊntɐˈhø:lən] *ptp* **unterhöhlt** VT *insep* **a** *(= aushöhlen)* to hollow out **b** *(fig)* to undermine

Un|ter|holz NT, *no pl* undergrowth

Un|ter|ho|se F *(= Herrenunterhose)* (pair of) underpants *pl*, (pair of) pants *pl (Brit)*, briefs *pl*; *(= Damenunterhose)* (pair of) pants *pl (Brit) or* panties *pl (esp US) or* briefs *pl*; **lange ~n** long johns *pl*

un|ter|ir|disch ADJ **a** *Parkhaus etc, Atomversuche* underground; *Fluss etc auch* subterranean **b** *(sl)* extremely bad ADV **a** underground; **~ verlaufen** to run underground **b** *(sl)* **~ schlecht** extremely bad

un|ter|jo|chen [ʊntɐˈjɔxn] *ptp* **unterjocht** VT *insep* to subjugate

Un|ter|jo|chung F **-, -en** subjugation

un|ter+ju|beln VT *sep (inf)* **a** *(= andrehen)* **jdm etw ~** to palm sth off on sb *(inf)* **b** *(= anlasten)* **jdm etw ~** to pin sth on sb *(inf)*

un|ter|ka|pi|ta|li|siert [ˈʊntɐkapitalizi:ɐt] ADJ *(Fin)* undercapitalized

un|ter|kel|lern [ʊntɐˈkɛlɐn] *ptp* **unterkellert** VT *insep* to build with a cellar *(Brit) or* basement; **das Haus ist nicht unterkellert** the house doesn't have a cellar *(Brit) or* basement; **ein ganz/teilweise unterkellertes Haus** a house with a cellar *(Brit) or* basement underneath the whole of it/underneath part of it

Un|ter-: **Un|ter|kie|fer** M lower jaw; **Un|ter|klas|se** F **a** subclass **b** *(Sociol)* lower class; **Un|ter|kleid** NT full-length slip *or* petticoat; **Un|ter|klei|dung** F underwear, underclothes *pl*

un|ter+kom|men VI *sep irreg aux sein* **a** *(= Unterkunft finden)* to find accommodation; *(inf: = Stelle finden)* to find a job *(als* as, *bei* with, at); **bei jdm ~** to stay at sb's (place) **b** *(inf)* **so etwas ist mir noch nie untergekommen!** I've never come across anything like it!

Un|ter|kom|men NT **-s, -** *(= Obdach)* accommodation *no pl (Brit)*, accommodations *pl (US)*; **bei jdm ein ~ finden** to be put up at sb's (place)

Un|ter-: **Un|ter|kör|per** M lower part of the body; **un|ter+krie|chen** VI *sep irreg aux sein (inf)* to shack up *(bei jdm* with sb) *(inf)*; **un|ter+krie|gen** VT *sep (inf)* to bring down; *(= deprimieren)* to get down; **sich nicht ~ lassen** not to let things get one down; **lass dich von ihnen nicht ~** don't let them get you down; **un|ter|küh|len** [ʊntɐˈky:lən] *ptp* **unterkühlt** VT *insep* *Flüssigkeit, Metall, Gas* to supercool, to undercool *(Brit)*; *Körper* to expose to subnormal temperatures; **un|ter|kühlt** [ʊntɐˈky:lt] ADJ *Flüssigkeit, Metall, Gas* supercooled, undercooled *(Brit)*; *Körper* affected by hypothermia; *(fig) Atmosphäre* chilly; *Mensch* cool; *Musik, Spielweise* subdued, reserved; **Un|ter|küh|lung** F, *no pl* *(von Flüssigkeit, Metall, Gas)* supercooling, undercooling *(Brit)*; *(im Freien)* exposure; *(Med)* hypothermia

Un|ter|kunft [ˈʊntɐkʊnft] F **-, Unterkünfte** [-kʏnftə] **a** accommodation *no pl (Brit)*, accommodations *pl (US)*, lodging; **eine ~ suchen** to look for accommodation *(Brit) or* accommodations *(US) or* lodging; **~ und Verpflegung** board and lodging **b** *(von Soldaten etc)* quarters *pl*; *(esp in Privathaus)* billet

Un|ter|kunfts-: **Un|ter|kunfts|mög|lich|keit** F accommodation *no pl (Brit)*, accommodations *pl (US)*; **habt ihr dort eine ~?** have you any accommodation *(Brit) or* accommodations *(US)* there?, have you somewhere to stay there?; **Un|ter|kunfts|raum** M quarters *pl*

Un|ter|la|ge F **a** *(für Teppich)* underlay; *(im Bett)* draw sheet; **du brauchst eine ~** you need to put something underneath; *(zum Schreiben)* you need something to rest on; *(zum Schlafen)* you need something to lie on **b** *usu pl (= Belege, Urkunden, Papiere)* document, paper **c** *(Hort)* rootstock

Un|ter-: **Un|ter|land** NT, *no pl* lowland; **Un|ter|län|der** [ˈʊntɐlɛndɐ] M **-s, -**, **Un|ter|län|de|rin** [-ərɪn] F **-, -nen** lowlander; **un|ter|län|disch** [ˈʊntɐlɛndɪʃ] ADJ *attr* lowland; **Un|ter|län|ge** F tail (of letters), descender *(spec)*; **Un|ter|lass** M **ohn(e) ~** *(old)* incessantly, continuously; *arbeiten auch* without respite

un|ter|las|sen [ʊntɐˈlasn] *ptp* **unterlassen** VT *insep irreg (= nicht tun)* to refrain from; *(= nicht durchführen)* not to carry out; *(= auslassen)* to omit; *Bemerkung, Zwischenrufe* to refrain from making; *etwas Dummes etc* to refrain from doing; *Trinken* to abstain from; **keine Anstrengung** *or* **nichts ~** to spare no effort; **~ Sie das!** don't do that!, stop that!; **er hat es ~, mich zu benachrichtigen** he failed *or* omitted to notify me; **warum wurde das ~?** why was it not done?; **~e Hilfeleistung** *(Jur)* failure to give assistance

Un|ter|las|sung F **-, -en** **a** *(= Versäumnis)* omission (of sth), failure (to do sth); **bei ~ (der Zahlung)** in case of default (of payment); **auf ~ klagen** *(Jur)* to ask for an injunction **b** *(Gram)* **~ der Deklination** non-declension

Un|ter|las|sungs-: **Un|ter|las|sungs|de|likt** NT *(Jur)* failure to act; **Un|ter|las|sungs|fall** M *(Admin)* case of default; **im ~e** in case of default; **Un|ter|las|sungs|kla|ge** F *(Jur)* injunction suit; **Un|ter|las|sungs|straf|tat** F *(Jur)* (offence *(Brit) or* offense *(US)* of) default; **Un|ter|las|sungs|sün|de** F sin of omission; **Un|ter|las|sungs|ur|teil** NT injunction

Un|ter|lauf M lower reaches *pl* (of a river)

un|ter|lau|fen [ʊntɐˈlaufn] *ptp* **unterlaufen** *insep irreg* VI *+dat aux sein (Fehler, Irrtum, Versehen)* to occur; **mir ist ein Fehler ~** I made a mistake VT *Bestimmungen, Maßnahmen* to get (a)round; *Steuergesetze* to avoid; *(= umgehen)* to circumvent; *(= zuvorkommen)* to anticipate; *(= unterminieren)* to undermine; **jdn ~** *(Sport)* to slip under sb's guard

un|ter|lau|fen [ʊntɐˈlaufn] ADJ suffused with blood; **ein mit Blut ~es Auge** a bloodshot eye

Un|ter|le|der NT sole leather

un|ter+le|gen [ˈʊntɐle:gn] VT *sep* to put underneath; *(fig)* to attribute, to ascribe; **einer Sache** *(dat)* **einen anderen Sinn ~** to put a different interpretation *or* construction on sth, to read another meaning into sth

un|ter|le|gen [ʊntɐˈle:gn] *ptp* **unterlegt** VT *insep* to underlay; *(mit Stoff, Watte etc)* to line; *(mit Watte)* to pad; **einer Melodie** *(dat)* **einen Text ~** to put *or* set words to a tune

un|ter|le|gen [ʊntɐˈleːgn] ADJ inferior; *(= besiegt)* defeated; **jdm ~ sein** to be inferior to sb, to be sb's inferior; **zahlenmäßig ~ sein** to be outnumbered, to be numerically inferior → *auch* **unterliegen**

Un|ter|le|ge|ne(r) [ʊntɐˈleːgənə] MF *decl as adj* underdog; **der ~ sein** to be in the weaker position

Un|ter|le|gen|heit F -, *no pl* inferiority

Un|ter|leg|schei|be F *(Tech)* washer

Un|ter|leib M abdomen; *(im engeren Sinne: = Geschlechtsorgane)* lower abdomen

Un|ter|leibs- *in cpds* abdominal; *(in Bezug auf weibliche Geschlechtsorgane)* gynaecological *(Brit)*, gynecological *(US)*; **Un|ter|leibs|krebs** M cancer of the abdomen; *(bei Frau)* cancer of the womb; **Un|ter|leibs|or|gan** NT abdominal organ; **Un|ter|leibs|schmer|zen** PL abdominal pains *pl*

Un|ter-: **Un|ter|leut|nant** M *(Mil)* second lieutenant; **Un|ter|lid** NT lower lid

un|ter|lie|gen [ʊntɐˈliːgn] *ptp* **unterlegen** [ʊntɐˈleːgn] VI *insep irreg aux sein* **a** *(= besiegt werden)* to be defeated (+*dat* by), to lose (+*dat* to); *(fig) einer Versuchung etc* to succumb (+*dat* to), to give away (+*dat* to) **b** +*dat (= unterworfen sein)* to be subject to; *einer Gebühr, Steuer* to be liable to; **es unterliegt keinem Zweifel, dass ...** it is not open to any doubt that ... → *auch* **unterlegen**

Un|ter|lip|pe F bottom *or* lower lip

un|term [ˈʊntɐm] *contr von* **unter dem**

un|ter|ma|len [ʊntɐˈmaːlən] *ptp* **untermalt** VT *insep* **a** *(Art) Bild* to prime **b** *(mit Musik)* to provide with background *or* incidental music; *Film* to provide a soundtrack for; *(fig)* to underlie; **eine Ansage mit leiser Musik ~** to play soft background music with an announcement

Un|ter|ma|lung F -, -en **a** *(Art)* preparatory *or* priming coat **b** *(= Musikuntermalung)* background music

un|ter|mau|ern [ʊntɐˈmauɐn] *ptp* **untermauert** VT *insep (Build)* to underpin; *(fig auch) Behauptung, Theorie* to back up, to substantiate, to support

Un|ter|mau|e|rung F -, -en *(Build)* underpinning; *(fig)* support; **zur ~ seiner These** in support of his thesis, to back up *or* substantiate his thesis

Un|ter|men|ge F *(Math)* subset

un|ter+men|gen VT *sep* to mix in, to add

Un|ter|mensch M *(esp NS)* subhuman creature

Un|ter|me|nü NT *(Comput)* submenu

Un|ter|mie|te F subtenancy; **bei jdm zur** *or* **in ~ wohnen** to be sb's tenant; *(als Zimmerherr etc auch)* to lodge *(Brit) or* room *(US)* with sb, to rent a room from sb

Un|ter|mie|ter(in) M(F) lodger *(esp Brit)*, subtenant

Un|ter|miet|zim|mer NT *(Aus)* sublet room

un|ter|mi|nie|ren [ʊntɐmiˈniːrən] *ptp* **unterminiert** VT *insep (lit, fig)* to undermine

Un|ter|mi|nie|rung F -, -en undermining

un|ter+mi|schen VT *sep* to mix in, to add

un|tern [ˈʊntɐn] *contr von* **unter den**

un|ter|neh|men [ʊntɐˈneːmən] *ptp* **unternommen** [ʊntɐˈnɔmən] VT *insep irreg* to do; *(= durchführen auch)* to undertake; *Versuch, Vorstoß, Reise* to make; **einen Ausflug ~** to go on an outing; **Schritte ~** to take steps; **etwas/nichts gegen jdn/etw ~** to do something/nothing about sb/sth, to take some/no action against sb/sth; **zu viel ~** to do too much, to take on too much

Un|ter|neh|men [ʊntɐˈneːmən] NT -s, - **a** *(= Firma)* business, concern, enterprise **b** *(= Aktion, Vorhaben)* undertaking, enterprise, venture; *(Mil)* operation

un|ter|neh|mend ADJ enterprising

Un|ter|neh|mens-: **Un|ter|neh|mens|be|ra|ter(in)** M(F) management consultant; **Un|ter|neh|mens|be|wer|tung** F *(Econ)* business appraisal; *(vor Kauf)* due diligence; **Un|ter|neh|mens|form** F form *or* type of enterprise; **Un|ter|neh|mens|füh|rung** F management (of a/the company); **Un|ter|neh|mens|grün|dung** F *(Comm)* setting up (of) a business, business start-up; **Un|ter|neh|mens|lei|tung** F management; **die Herren in der ~** the management; **Un|ter|neh|mens|phi|lo|so|phie** F company philosophy *or* policy; **Un|ter|neh|mens|pla|nung** F business planning; **Un|ter|neh|mens|spit|ze** F top management; **Un|ter|neh|mens|struk|tur** F corporate structure; **Un|ter|neh|mens|vor|stand** M board of directors

Un|ter|neh|mer-: **Un|ter|neh|mer|geist** M entrepreneurial spirit; **Un|ter|neh|mer|ge|winn** M (business) profit

Un|ter|neh|mer(in) M(F) employer; *(alten Stils)* entrepreneur; *(= Industrieller)* industrialist; **die ~** the employers

un|ter|neh|me|risch [ʊntɐˈneːmərɪʃ] ADJ entrepreneurial ADV *denken, handeln* in an entrepreneurial *or* businesslike way

Un|ter|neh|mer-: **Un|ter|neh|mer|krei|se** PL **in/aus ~n** in/from business circles; **Un|ter|neh|mer|or|ga|ni|sa|ti|on** F employers' association; **Un|ter|neh|mer|tum** [ʊntɐˈneːmɐtuːm] NT -s, *no pl (= die Unternehmer)* management *no art*, employers *pl*; *(= Unternehmergeist)* entrepreneurship; **ein freies/das freie ~** free enterprise; **Un|ter|neh|mer|ver|band** M employers' association

Un|ter|neh|mung [ʊntɐˈneːmʊŋ] F -, -en **a** = **Unternehmen b** *(= Transaktion)* undertaking

Un|ter|neh|mungs-: **Un|ter|neh|mungs|geist** M, *no pl* enterprise; **Un|ter|neh|mungs|lust** F, *no pl* enterprise; **un|ter|neh|mungs|lus|tig** ADJ *(= tatendurstig)* enterprising; *(= abenteuerlustig auch)* adventurous

Un|ter|of|fi|zier(in) M(F) **a** *(= Rang)* noncommissioned officer, NCO; **~ vom Dienst** duty NCO **b** *(= Dienstgrad) (bei der Armee)* sergeant; *(bei der Luftwaffe)* corporal *(Brit)*, airman first class *(US)*

Un|ter|of|fi|ziers-: **Un|ter|of|fi|ziers|an|wär|ter(in)** M(F) NCO candidate; **Un|ter|of|fi|ziers|rang** M noncommissioned rank

Un|ter-: **un|ter+ord|nen** *sep* VT to subordinate (+*dat* to) → *auch* **untergeordnet** VR to subordinate oneself (+*dat* to); **un|ter|ord|nend** ADJ *(Gram) Konjunktion* subordinating; **Un|ter|ord|nung** F **a** *no pl* subordination **b** *(Biol)* suborder; **Un|ter|or|ga|ni|sa|ti|on** F subsidiary organization

Un|ter|pfand NT *(old, liter)* pledge

un|ter+pflü|gen VT *sep* to plough *(Brit) or* plow *(US)* under *or* in

Un|ter|pri|ma F *(dated Sch) eighth year of German secondary school*, ≈ lower sixth *(Brit)*, ≈ twelfth grade *(US)*

Un|ter|pri|ma|ner(in) M(F) *(dated Sch) pupil in eighth year of German secondary school*, ≈ sixth-former *(Brit)*, ≈ twelfth-grader *(US)*

un|ter|pri|vi|le|giert [-privileˈgiːɐt] ADJ underprivileged; **Unterprivilegierte** underprivileged people; **die Unterprivilegierten** the underprivileged

Un|ter|pro|duk|ti|on F underproduction

Un|ter|pro|gramm NT *(Comput)* subroutine

Un|ter|punkt M *(eines Themas)* subordinate point

Un|ter|putz|lei|tung F *(Elec)* concealed cable

un|ter|que|ren [ʊntɐˈkveːrən] *ptp* **unterquert** VT *insep* to underrun

un|ter|re|den [ʊntɐˈreːdn] *ptp* **unterredet** VR *insep* **sich (mit jdm) ~** to confer (with sb), to have a discussion (with sb)

Un|ter|re|dung F -, -en discussion; *(Pol auch)* talks *pl*

un|ter|re|prä|sen|tiert [-reprɛzɛntiːɐt] ADJ underrepresented

Un|ter|richt [ˈʊntɐrɪçt] M -(e)s, *no pl* lessons *pl*, classes *pl*; **theoretischer/praktischer ~** theoretical/practical instruction *or* classes; **~ in Fremdsprachen** foreign language teaching; **~ in Mathematik/Englisch** maths/English lessons *or* classes; **heute fällt der ~ in Englisch aus** there will be no English lesson today; **(jdm) ~ geben** *or* **erteilen** to teach (sb) *(in etw (dat)* sth); **(bei jdm) ~ nehmen** *or* **haben** to take *or* have lessons (with sb); **am ~ teilnehmen** to attend classes; **zu spät zum ~ kommen** to be late for class; **im ~ aufpassen** to pay attention in class; **den ~ vorbereiten** to prepare one's lessons; **der ~ beginnt um 8 Uhr** lessons *or* classes start at 8 o'clock

un|ter|rich|ten [ʊntɐˈrɪçtn] *ptp* **unterrichtet** *insep* VT **a** *(= Unterricht geben) Schüler, Klasse, Fach* to teach; **jdn in etw** *(dat)* **~** to teach sb sth **b** *(= informieren)* to inform *(von, über +acc* about) VI to teach VR **sich über etw** *(acc)* **~** to obtain information about sth, to inform oneself about sth; **sich von jdm über etw** *(acc)* **~ lassen** to be informed by sb about sth

un|ter|rich|tet [ʊntɐˈrɪçtət] ADJ informed; **gut ~e Kreise** well-informed circles; **wie aus gut ~en Kreisen verlautet, ...** according to well-informed sources ...

Un|ter|richts-: **Un|ter|richts|an|ge|bot** NT subjects *pl* taught; **Un|ter|richts|aus|fall** M cancellation of a class/classes; **es gibt zu viele Unterrichtsausfälle** too many classes are being cancelled; **Un|ter|richts|be|ginn** M *(am Morgen)* school starting time; *(für einzelnes Fach)* class starting time; **~ ist um 8.00** school *or* the first lesson starts at 8.00 *or* 8:00 *(US)*; **Un|ter|richts|be|trieb** M, *no pl* lessons *pl*, classes *pl*; *(= Unterrichtsroutine)* teaching *no art*; **Un|ter|richts|ein|heit** F teaching unit; **Un|ter|richts|fach** NT subject; **Geschichte ist ~** history is on the curriculum; **Un|ter|richts|film** M educational film; **un|ter|richts|frei** ADJ *Stunde, Tag* free; **der Montag ist ~** there are no classes on Monday; **Un|ter|richts|ge|gen|stand** M **a** topic, subject **b** *(Aus)* = **Unterrichtsfach**; **Un|ter|richts|ma|te|ri|al** NT teaching materials *pl*; **Un|ter|richts|me|tho|de** F teaching method; **Un|ter|richts|mi|nis|te|ri|um** NT Ministry of Education; **Un|ter|richts|mit|tel** NT teaching aid; **Un|ter|richts|raum** M teaching room, classroom; **Un|ter|richts|soft|ware** F educational software; **Un|ter|richts|spra|che** F language in which lessons are conducted; **Un|ter|richts|stoff** M subject matter, teaching subject; **Un|ter|richts|stun|de** F lesson, period; **während der ~n** during lessons; **Un|ter|richts|ver|an|stal|tung** F lesson; *(Univ)* lecture; **Un|ter|richts|vor|be|rei|tung** F teaching preparation; **Un|ter|richts|we|sen** NT educational system; **Un|ter|richts|zeit** F teaching time; **Un|ter|richts|ziel** NT teaching objective; **Un|ter|richts|zwe|cke** PL **zu ~n** for teaching purposes

Un|ter|rich|tung F, *no pl (= Belehrung)* instruction; *(= Informierung)* information

Un|ter|rock M underskirt, slip

un|ter+rüh|ren VT *sep* to stir *or* mix in

un|ters [ˈʊntɐs] *contr von* **unter das**

un|ter|sa|gen [ʊntɐˈzaːgn] *ptp* **untersagt** VT *insep* to forbid, to prohibit; **jdm etw ~** to forbid sb sth, to prohibit sb from doing sth; **(das) Rauchen (ist hier) strengstens untersagt** smoking (is) strictly prohibited *or* forbidden (here); **jdm etw gerichtlich ~** to enjoin sb to do sth

Un|ter|satz M **a** mat; *(für Gläser, Flaschen etc)* coaster *(esp Brit)*; *(für Blumentöpfe etc)* saucer; **etw als ~ verwenden** to use sth to put underneath → **fahrbar b** *(Philos)* minor premise

Un|ter|schall-: **Un|ter|schall|flug** M subsonic flight; **Un|ter|schall|ge|schwin|dig|keit** F subsonic speed

un|ter|schät|zen [ʊntɐˈʃɛtsn] *ptp* **unterschätzt** VT *insep* to underestimate

Un|ter|schät|zung F underestimation

un|ter|scheid|bar ADJ distinguishable

un|ter|schei|den [ʊntɐˈʃaidn] ✪ 32.1 *ptp* **unterschieden** *insep irreg* [ʊntɐˈʃiːdn] VT *(= einen*

Unterschied machen, trennen) to distinguish; *(= auseinanderhalten auch)* to tell apart; **A nicht von B ~ können** to be unable to tell the difference between A and B, to be unable to tell A from B; **zwei Personen (voneinander) ~** to tell two people apart; **kannst du die beiden ~?** can you tell which is which/who is who?; **das ~de Merkmal** the distinguishing feature; **nach verschiedenen Merkmalen ~** to classify *or* divide according to various characteristics
VI to differentiate, to distinguish
VR **sich von etw/jdm ~** to differ from sth/sb; **worin unterscheidet sich eine Amsel von einer Drossel?** what is the difference between a blackbird and a thrush?

Un|ter|schei|dung F differentiation; *(= Unterschied)* difference, distinction; **eine ~ treffen** to make a distinction

Un|ter|schei|dungs-: Un|ter|schei|dungs|merk|mal NT distinctive *or* distinguishing feature; **Un|ter|schei|dungs|ver|mö|gen** NT discernment; **das ~** the power of discernment

Un|ter|schen|kel M lower leg

Un|ter|schicht F *(Sociol)* lower stratum *(Sociol)*, underclass

un|ter|schie|ben [ʊntɐˈʃiːbn] *ptp* **unterschoben** [ʊntɐˈʃoːbn] VT *insep irreg (inf: = unterstellen)* **jdm etw ~** to insinuate *or* imply that sb has done/said sth; **du unterschiebst mir immer, dass ich schwindle** you're always accusing me of cheating; **einer Äußerung einen ganz falschen Sinn ~** to twist the meaning of a statement completely

un|ter+schie|ben [ˈʊntɐʃiːbn] VT *sep irreg* **a** *(lit: = schieben unter)* to push underneath; **etw unter etw** *(acc)* **~** to push sth under(neath) sth **b** *(fig)* **jdm etw ~** *(= anlasten)* to palm sth off on sb; **er wehrte sich dagegen, dass man ihm das Kind ~ wollte** he defended himself against the charge that the child was his **c** = **unterschieben**

Un|ter|schie|bung [ʊntɐˈʃiːbʊŋ, ˈʊntɐ-] F **a** *(= Unterstellung)* imputation, attribution **b** *(= Anhängen)* foisting

Un|ter|schied [ˈʊntɐʃiːt] ✪ 32.1, 32.4, 53.5 M **-(e)s, -e** difference [-də] *(auch Math)*; *(= Unterscheidung auch)* distinction; **einen ~ (zwischen zwei Dingen) machen** to make a distinction (between two things); **es besteht ein ~ (zwischen ...)** there's a difference *or* distinction (between ...); **das macht keinen ~** that makes no difference; **es ist ein (großer) ~, ob ...** it makes a (big) difference whether ...; **ein feiner ~** a slight difference, a fine distinction; **zum ~ von (jdm/etw)** *(rare)*, **im ~ zu (jdm/etw)** in contrast to (sb/sth), unlike (sb/sth); **mit dem ~, dass ...** with the difference that ...; **alle ohne ~ halfen mit** everyone without exception lent a hand; **es wurden alle ohne ~ getötet** everyone was killed indiscriminately; **das ist ein gewaltiger ~!** there's a vast difference!; **der kleine ~** *(hum)* the difference between the sexes; *(inf: = Penis)* willie *(Brit inf)*, weenie *(US inf)*

un|ter|schied|lich [ˈʊntɐʃiːtlɪç] ADJ different; *(= veränderlich)* variable; *(= gemischt)* varied, patchy; **das ist sehr ~** it varies a lot ADV differently; **~ gut/lang** of varying quality/length; **sie haben ~ reagiert** their reactions varied

Un|ter|schied|lich|keit F **-, -en** difference; *(= Veränderlichkeit)* variability

un|ter|schieds|los ADJ *(= undifferenziert)* indiscriminate; *(= gleichberechtigt)* equal ADV *(= undifferenziert)* indiscriminately; *(= gleichberechtigt)* equally

un|ter|schläch|tig [-ʃlɛçtɪç] ADJ *Wasserrad* undershot

un|ter|schla|gen *ptp* **unterschlagen** VT *insep irreg Geld* to embezzle, to misappropriate; *Brief, Beweise, Tatsachen* to withhold, to suppress; *(inf) Neuigkeit, Nachricht, Wort etc* to keep quiet about; **das hast du mir die ganze Zeit ~** and you've kept quiet about it all this time

un|ter+schla|gen [ˈʊntɐʃlaːgn] VT *sep irreg* **a** *(= verschränken) Beine* to cross; **mit untergeschlagenen Beinen dasitzen** to sit cross-legged **b** *Betttuch* to tuck in

Un|ter|schla|gung [ʊntɐˈʃlaːgʊŋ] F **-, -en** *(von Geld)* embezzlement, misappropriation; *(von Briefen, Beweisen etc)* withholding, suppression

Un|ter|schlupf [ˈʊntɐʃlʊpf] M **-(e)s, Unterschlüpfe** [-ʃlʏpfə] *(= Obdach, Schutz)* cover, shelter; *(= Versteck)* hiding place, hide-out

un|ter+schlüp|fen *(dial)*, **un|ter+schlup|fen** [ˈʊntɐʃlʊpfn] VI *sep aux sein (inf) (= Obdach oder Schutz finden)* to take cover *or* shelter; *(= Versteck finden)* to hide out *(inf)* *(bei jdm* at sb's)

Un|ter|schnei|dung [ʊntɐˈʃnaidʊŋ] F **-, -en** *(Comput, Typ)* kerning

un|ter|schrei|ben [ʊntɐˈʃraibn] *ptp* **unterschrieben** [ʊntɐˈʃriːbn] *insep irreg* VT to sign; **der Brief ist mit „Müller" unterschrieben** the letter is signed "Müller"; **das kann** *or* **würde ich ~!** *(fig)* I'll subscribe to that!, I'll buy that! *(inf)* VI to sign; **mit vollem Namen ~** to sign one's full name

un|ter|schrei|ten [ʊntɐˈʃraitn] *ptp* **unterschritten** [ʊntɐˈʃrɪtn] VT *insep irreg* to fall short of; *Temperatur, Zahlenwert* to fall below

Un|ter|schrei|tung F falling short; *(eines Betrags)* shortfall

Un|ter|schrift F **a** signature; **seine ~/fünf ~en leisten** to give one's signature/one's signature five times; **eigenhändige ~** personal signature; **seine ~ unter etw** *(acc)* **setzen** to put one's signature to sth, to sign sth **b** *(= Bildunterschrift)* caption

Un|ter|schrif|ten-: Un|ter|schrif|ten|ak|ti|on F petition; **eine ~ durchführen** to get up a petition; **Un|ter|schrif|ten|lis|te** F list of signatures; **Un|ter|schrif|ten|map|pe** F signature folder; **Un|ter|schrif|ten|samm|lung** F collection of signatures

un|ter|schrift|lich ADJ ADV by signature

Un|ter|schrifts-: un|ter|schrifts|be|rech|tigt ADJ authorized to sign; **Un|ter|schrifts|be|rech|tig|te(r)** [-bərɛçtɪçtə] MF *decl as adj* authorized signatory; **Un|ter|schrifts|fäl|schung** F forging of a/the signature; **Un|ter|schrifts|leis|tung** F signing of a/the document *etc*; **Un|ter|schrifts|pro|be** F specimen signature; **un|ter|schrifts|reif** ADJ *Vertrag* ready to be signed

un|ter|schwel|lig [-ʃvɛlɪç] ADJ subliminal ADV subliminally

Un|ter|see|boot NT submarine; *(ehemaliges deutsches auch)* U-Boot

un|ter|see|isch [-zeːɪʃ] ADJ underwater, undersea, submarine

Un|ter-: Un|ter|sei|te F underside; *(von Topf, Teller, Kuchen auch)* bottom; *(von Blatt)* undersurface; **an der ~** on the underside/bottom/undersurface; **Un|ter|se|kun|da** F *(dated Sch)* sixth year of German secondary school; **Un|ter|se|kun|da|ner(in)** M(F) *(dated Sch)* pupil in sixth year of German secondary school; **un|ter+set|zen** VT *sep* to put underneath; **Un|ter|set|zer** M = **Untersatz**

un|ter|setzt [ʊntɐˈzɛtst] ADJ stocky

un|ter|spü|len [ʊntɐˈʃpyːlən] *ptp* **unterspült** VT *insep* to undermine, to wash away the base of

Un|ter-: Un|ter|staats|sek|re|tär(in) M(F) Undersecretary of State; **Un|ter|stadt** F lower part of a/the town; **Un|ter|stand** M shelter; *(Mil)* dugout; **un|ter|stän|dig** ADJ *(Bot)* inferior, hypogynous *(spec)*; **un|ter|stands|los** ADJ *(Aus)* homeless

un|ter|ste|hen [ʊntɐˈʃteːən] *ptp* **unterstanden** [ʊntɐˈʃtandn] *insep irreg* VI +*dat* *(= unterstellt sein)* to be under (the control of); *jdm* to be subordinate to; *einer Behörde, dem Ministerium* to come under (the jurisdiction of); *dem Gesetz* to be subject to; *(in Firma)* to report to; **jds Aufsicht** *(dat)* **~** to be under sb's supervision; **dem Verkaufsdirektor ~ sechs Abteilungsleiter** the sales director is in charge of six departmental heads VR *(= wagen)* to dare, to have the audacity; **untersteh dich (ja nicht)!** (don't) you dare!; **was ~ Sie sich!** how dare you!

un|ter+ste|hen [ˈʊntɐʃteːən] VI *sep irreg (bei Regen etc)* to take shelter *or* cover

un|ter|stel|len [ʊntɐˈʃtɛlən] *ptp* **unterstellt** *insep* VT **a** *(= unterordnen)* to (make) subordinate (+*dat* to); *Abteilung, Ministerium etc auch* to put under the control (+*dat* of); **jdm unterstellt sein** to be under sb, to be answerable to sb; *(in Firma)* to report to sb; **ihm sind vier Mitarbeiter unterstellt** he is in charge of four employees, he has four employees subordinate to him; **jdm etw ~** to put sb in charge of sth; *(Mil)* to put sth under the command of sb, to put sth under sb's command **b** *(= annehmen)* to assume, to suppose; **einmal unterstellt, es sei so gewesen** supposing *or* let us suppose (that) it was so **c** *(= unterschieben)* **jdm etw ~** to insinuate *or* imply that sb has done/said sth; **jdm Nachlässigkeit ~** to insinuate that sb has been negligent; **ihm wurde unterstellt, gesagt zu haben, ...** he was purported to have said ... VR to subordinate oneself (+*dat* to)

un|ter+stel|len [ˈʊntɐʃtɛlən] *sep* VT *(= abstellen, unterbringen)* to keep; *Möbel* to store VR to take shelter *or* cover

Un|ter|stel|lung [-ˈʃtɛlʊŋ] F **a** *(= falsche Behauptung)* misrepresentation; *(= Andeutung)* insinuation; *(= Annahme)* assumption, presumption **b** *no pl (= Unterordnung)* subordination *(unter +acc* to)

un|ters|te(r, s) [ˈʊntɐstə] ADJ *superl von* **untere(r, s)** lowest; *(= tiefste auch)* bottom; *(rangmäßig)* lowest; *(= letzte)* last; **das Unterste zuoberst kehren** to turn everything upside down

un|ter|steu|ern [ʊntɐˈʃtɔyɐn] *ptp* **untersteuert** VI *insep* to understeer

un|ter|steu|ert [ʊntɐˈʃtɔyɐt] ADJ *Auto* with understeer

un|ter|strei|chen [ʊntɐˈʃtraiçn] *ptp* **unterstrichen** [ʊntɐˈʃtrɪçn] VT *insep irreg (lit, fig)* to underline; *(fig: = betonen auch)* to emphasize

Un|ter|strei|chung F underlining; *(fig: = Betonung auch)* emphasizing

Un|ter|strich M *(Typ)* underscore, underline

Un|ter|strö|mung F *(lit, fig)* undercurrent

Un|ter|stu|fe F *(Sch)* lower school, lower grade *(US)*

un|ter|stüt|zen [ʊntɐˈʃtʏtsn] ✪ 38.1, 38.2, 39.1, 53.2, 53.6 *ptp* **unterstützt** VT *insep* to support *(auch fig, Comput)*; *(aus öffentlichen Mitteln auch)* to subsidize; *(= finanziell fördern auch)* to back, to sponsor; **jdn (moralisch) ~** to give sb (moral) support

Un|ter|stüt|zung ✪ 38.2 F **a** *no pl (Tätigkeit, auch Comput)* support *(zu, für* for); **zur ~ seiner Behauptung** in support of his statement **b** *(= Zuschuss)* assistance, aid; *(inf: = Arbeitslosenunterstützung)* (unemployment) benefit; **staatliche ~** state aid; **~ beziehen** to be on social security *(Brit)*, to be on welfare *(US)*

Un|ter|stüt|zungs-: un|ter|stüt|zungs|be|dürf|tig ADJ needy; **die Unterstützungsbedürftigen** the needy; **Un|ter|stüt|zungs|emp|fän|ger(in)** M(F) person receiving benefit *(Brit) or* on welfare *(US)*

Un|ter|such [ʊntɐˈzuːx] M **-s, -e** *(Sw)* = **Untersuchung**

un|ter|su|chen [ʊntɐˈzuːxn] *ptp* **untersucht** VT *insep* **a** *(= inspizieren, prüfen)* to examine *(auf* +*acc* for); *(= erforschen)* to look into, to investigate; *(genau) Dokumente etc* to scrutinize; *(statistisch, soziologisch etc)* to sound (out), to survey; *(chemisch, technisch etc)* to test *(auf* +*acc* for); **sich ärztlich ~ lassen** to have a medical (examination) *or* a checkup; **etw gerichtlich ~** to try sth (in court); **etw chemisch ~** to test *or* analyze sth (chemically) **b** *(= nachprüfen)* to check, to verify

Un|ter|su|chung [ʊntɐˈzuːxʊŋ] ✪ 53.2, 53.6 F **-, -en** **a** *(= das Untersuchen)* examination *(auf*

+*acc* for); (= *Erforschung*) investigation (+*gen*, *über* +*acc* into); (= *genaue Prüfung*) scrutiny; (*chemisch, technisch*) test (*auf* +*acc* for); (*ärztlich*) examination, checkup **b** (= *Nachprüfung*) check, verification

Un|ter|su|chungs-: **Un|ter|su|chungs|aus|schuss** M investigating *or* fact-finding committee; (*nach Unfall etc*) committee of inquiry; **Un|ter|su|chungs|be|fund** M (*Med*) result of an/the examination; (= *Bericht*) examination report; **Un|ter|su|chungs|er|geb|nis** NT (*Jur*) findings *pl*; (*Med*) result of an/the examination; (*Sci*) test result; **Un|ter|su|chungs|ge|fan|ge|ne(r)** MF *decl as adj* prisoner awaiting trial; **Un|ter|su|chungs|ge|fäng|nis** NT prison (*for people awaiting trial*); **Un|ter|su|chungs|haft** F custody, (period of) imprisonment *or* detention while awaiting trial; **in ~ sein** *or* **sitzen** (*inf*) to be in prison *or* detention awaiting trial; **jdn in ~ nehmen** to commit sb for trial; **Un|ter|su|chungs|häft|ling** M prisoner awaiting trial; **Un|ter|su|chungs|kom|mis|si|on** F investigating *or* fact-finding committee; (*nach schwerem Unfall etc*) board of inquiry; **Un|ter|su|chungs|me|tho|de** F examination method; (*wissenschaftlich*) research method; **Un|ter|su|chungs|rich|ter(in)** M(F) examining magistrate; **Un|ter|su|chungs|zim|mer** NT (*Med*) examination room; (*in Praxis*) surgery

Un|ter|tag-, **Un|ter|ta|ge-** [ʊntɐˈta:gə] *in cpds* underground; **Un|ter|ta|ge|ar|bei|ter(in)** M(F) (coal)face worker (*Brit*), below-ground worker (*US*); **Un|ter|ta|ge|bau** M, *no pl* underground mining; **Un|ter|ta|ge|de|po|nie** F underground dump

un|ter|tags [ʊntɐˈta:ks] ADV (*Aus dial*) = **tagsüber**

un|ter|tan [ˈʊntɐta:n] ADJ (*pred* +*dat* to) subject; (= *dienstbar, hörig*) subservient; **sich** (*dat*) **ein Volk ~ machen** to subjugate a nation; **macht euch die Erde ~** (*Bibl*) subdue the earth *Bibl*

Un|ter|tan [ˈʊntɐta:n] M **-en, -en**, **Un|ter|ta|nin** [-nɪn] F **-, -nen** (*old*: = *Staatsbürger*) subject; (*pej*) underling (*pej*)

Un|ter|ta|nen|geist M, **Un|ter|ta|nen|ge|sin|nung** F servile *or* subservient spirit

un|ter|tä|nig [ˈʊntɐtɛ:nɪç] **ADJ** subservient, submissive; *Ergebenheit* humble; **Ihr ~ster Diener** (*obs*) your most obedient *or* humble servant **ADV** **jdn ~st bitten** to ask sb most humbly

Un|ter|tä|nig|keit F -, *no pl* subservience, submissiveness

Un|ter|ta|nin [-nɪn] F → **Untertan**

Un|ter-: **un|ter|ta|rif|lich** ADJ, ADV *Bezahlung* below an/the agreed rate; **~ bezahlt werden** to be paid less than the agreed rate; **Un|ter|tas|se** F saucer; **fliegende ~** flying saucer

un|ter+tau|chen *sep* **VI** *aux sein* to dive (under); (*U-Boot auch*) to submerge; (*fig*) to disappear **VT** to immerse; *jdn* to duck

Un|ter|teil NT OR M bottom *or* lower part

un|ter|tei|len [ʊntɐˈtailən] *ptp* **unterteilt** VT *insep* to subdivide (*in* +*acc* into)

Un|ter|tei|lung F subdivision (*in* +*acc* into)

Un|ter-: **Un|ter|tel|ler** M saucer; **Un|ter|tem|pe|ra|tur** F low (body) temperature; **Un|ter|ter|tia** F (*dated Sch*) *fourth year of German secondary school*; **Un|ter|ter|ti|a|ner(in)** M(F) (*dated Sch*) *pupil in fourth year of German secondary school*; **Un|ter|ti|tel** M subtitle; (*für Bild*) caption; **un|ter|ti|teln** [ʊntɐˈti:tln, -ˈtɪtln] *ptp* **untertitelt** VT *insep Film* to subtitle; *Bild* to caption; **Un|ter|ton** M *pl* **-töne** (*Mus, fig*) undertone; **un|ter|tou|rig** [-tu:rɪç] **ADJ** with low revs **ADV** **~ fahren** to drive with low revs; **un|ter|trei|ben** [ʊntɐˈtraibn] *ptp* **untertrieben** [ʊntɐˈtri:bn] *insep irreg* **VT** to understate **VI** to play things down; **Un|ter|trei|bung** F **-, -en a** understatement **b** (= *das Untertreiben*) playing things down *no art*; **un|ter|tun|neln** [ʊntɐˈtʊnln] *ptp* **untertunnelt** VT *insep* to tunnel under; *Berg auch* to tunnel through; **Un|ter|tun|ne|lung** [ʊntɐˈtʊnəlʊŋ] F **-, -en** tunnelling (*Brit*), tunneling (*US*); **un|ter|ver|mie|ten** *ptp* **untervermietet** VTI *insep* to sublet, to sublease; **Un|ter|ver|mie|tung** F subletting; **un|ter|ver|si|chert** [-fɛɐzɪçɐt] ADJ underinsured; **Un|ter|ver|si|che|rung** F underinsurance; **un|ter|ver|sorgt** ADJ undersupplied; **Un|ter|ver|sor|gung** F inadequate provision; **Un|ter|ver|zeich|nis** NT (*Comput*) subdirectory

Un|ter|wal|den [ˈʊntɐvaldn] NT **-s** Unterwalden

un|ter|wan|dern [ʊntɐˈvandɐn] *ptp* **unterwandert** VT *insep* to infiltrate

Un|ter|wan|de|rung F infiltration

un|ter|wärts [ˈʊntɐvɛrts] ADV (*dial*) underneath

Un|ter|wä|sche F **a** *no pl* underwear *no pl* **b** (*für Autos*) underbody cleaning

Un|ter|was|ser-: **Un|ter|was|ser|be|hand|lung** F (*Med*) underwater treatment; **Un|ter|was|ser|fo|to|gra|fie** F underwater photography; **Un|ter|was|ser|gym|nas|tik** F underwater exercises *pl*; **Un|ter|was|ser|jagd** F scuba fishing; **Un|ter|was|ser|jä|ger(in)** M(F) spear fisherman, underwater fisherman; **Un|ter|was|ser|ka|me|ra** F underwater camera; **Un|ter|was|ser|la|bor** NT underwater laboratory, sea lab; **Un|ter|was|ser|mas|sa|ge** F (*Med*) underwater massage; **Un|ter|was|ser|pho|to|gra|phie** F = **Unterwasserfotografie**; **Un|ter|was|ser|sta|ti|on** F (= *Labor*) underwater laboratory, sea lab

un|ter|wegs [ʊntɐˈve:ks] ADV on the *or* one's/its way (*nach, zu* to); (= *auf Reisen*) away; **eine Karte von ~ schicken** to send a card while one is away; **bei denen ist wieder ein Kind ~** they've got another child on the way; **bei ihr ist etwas (Kleines) ~** she's expecting

un|ter|wei|sen [ʊntɐˈvaizn] *ptp* **unterwiesen** [ʊntɐˈvi:zn] VT *insep irreg* (*geh*) to instruct (*in* +*dat* in)

Un|ter|wei|sung F (*geh*) instruction

Un|ter|welt F (*lit, fig*) underworld

un|ter|wer|fen [ʊntɐˈvɛrfn] *ptp* **unterworfen** [ʊntɐˈvɔrfn] *insep irreg* **VT a** *Volk, Land* to subjugate, to conquer **b** (= *unterziehen*) to subject (+*dat* to); **einer Sache** (*dat*) **unterworfen sein** to be subject to sth **VR** (*lit, fig*) **sich jdm/einer Sache ~** to submit to sb/sth

Un|ter|wer|fung F **-, -en a** (*von Volk, Land*) subjugation, conquest **b** (= *das Sichunterwerfen*) submission

un|ter|wor|fen [ʊntɐˈvɔrfn] ADJ **der Mode/dem Zeitgeschmack ~ sein** to be subject to fashion/prevailing tastes

un|ter|wür|fig [ʊntɐˈvʏrfɪç, ˈʊntɐ-] ADJ (*pej*) obsequious

Un|ter|wür|fig|keit [ʊntɐˈvʏrfɪçkait, ˈʊntɐ-] F **-**, *no pl* (*pej*) obsequiousness

Un|ter|zahl F, *no pl* (*Sport*) **in ~** with a player/two players *etc* short; (*Ftbl*) with only ten/nine *etc* men

un|ter|zeich|nen [ʊntɐˈtsaiçnən] *ptp* **unterzeichnet** VT *insep* (*form*) to sign

Un|ter|zeich|ner(in) M(F) signatory

Un|ter|zeich|ner|staat M signatory state

Un|ter|zeich|ne|te(r) [ʊntɐˈtsaiçnətə] MF *decl as adj* (*form*) **der/die ~** the undersigned; **der rechts/links ~** the right/left signatory

Un|ter|zeich|nung F signing

Un|ter|zeug NT, *no pl* (*inf*) underclothes *pl*

un|ter|zie|hen [ʊntɐˈtsi:ən] *ptp* **unterzogen** [ʊntɐˈtso:gn] *insep irreg* **VR** (= *unterwerfen*) **sich einer Sache** (*dat*) **~ (müssen)** to (have to) undergo sth; **sich einer Operation** (*dat*) **~** to undergo *or* have an operation; **sich einer Prüfung** (*dat*) **~** to take an examination; **sich der Mühe** (*dat*) **~, etw zu tun** (*geh*) to take the trouble to do sth **VT** to subject (+*dat* to); **jdn/etw einer Prüfung ~** to subject sb/sth to an examination; **jdn einer Operation ~** to perform an operation on sb

un|ter+zie|hen [ˈʊntɐtsi:ən] VT *sep irreg* **a** *Unterwäsche, Kleidung* to put on underneath; **sich** (*dat*) **etw ~** to put sth on underneath **b** (*Cook*) *Eischnee, Sahne* to fold in

un|ter|zu|ckert ADJ (*Med*) hypoglycaemic (*Brit*), hypoglycemic (*US*); **er ist ~** (*auch*) his blood sugar is low

Un|ter|zu|cke|rung [-ˈtsʊkərʊŋ] F **-, -en** (*Med*) hypoglycaemia (*Brit*), hypoglycemia (*US*)

Un|tie|fe F **a** (= *seichte Stelle*) shallow, shoal **b** (*liter*: = *große Tiefe*) depth

Un|tier NT monster

un|tilg|bar ADJ (*geh*) (= *nicht rückzahlbar*) irredeemable; (*fig*) indelible

Un|to|te(r) MF *decl as adj* **die ~n** the undead

Un-: **un|trag|bar** ADJ *Zustände, Belastung* intolerable, unbearable; *Risiko* unacceptable; **er ist politisch ~ geworden** he has become a political liability; **Un|trag|bar|keit** [ʊnˈtra:kba:ɐkait, ˈʊn-] F **-**, *no pl* **die ~ des hohen Haushaltsdefizits** the intolerably high budget deficit; **un|trai|niert** [ˈʊntrɛni:ɐt, -tre-] ADJ untrained; **un|trenn|bar** **ADJ** inseparable **ADV** **~ zusammengesetzte Verben** inseparable verbs; **mit etw ~ verbunden sein** (*fig*) to be inextricably linked with sth

un|treu ADJ *Liebhaber etc* unfaithful; (*einem Prinzip etc*) disloyal (+*dat* to); **sich** (*dat*) **selbst ~ werden** to be untrue to oneself; **jdm ~ werden** to be unfaithful to sb

Un|treue F **a** (*von Liebhaber etc*) unfaithfulness **b** (*Jur*) embezzlement

un|trink|bar ADJ undrinkable

un|tröst|lich ADJ inconsolable (*über* +*acc* about); **er war ~, dass er es vergessen hatte** he was inconsolable about having forgotten it

un|trüg|lich [ʊnˈtry:klɪç, ˈʊn-] ADJ *Gedächtnis, Instinkt, Gespür* infallible; *Zeichen* unmistakable

un|tüch|tig [ˈʊntʏçtɪç] ADJ (= *unfähig*) incapable, incompetent (*in* +*dat* at); (= *nicht fleißig*) inefficient

Un|tu|gend F (= *Laster*) vice; (= *schlechte Angewohnheit*) bad habit; (= *Schwäche*) weakness

un|tun|lich ADJ (*dated*) (= *unzweckmäßig*) impractical; (= *unklug*) imprudent

un|ty|pisch ADJ atypical (*für* of); *Person auch* out of character (*für* for); **es ist ~ für sie** (*auch*) it's not like her

Un-: **un|übel** ADJ **(gar) nicht (so) ~** not bad (at all); **un|über|biet|bar** ADJ *Preis, Rekord etc* unbeatable; *Leistung* unsurpassable; *Frechheit, Virtuosität, Eifer* unparalleled; **un|über|brück|bar** ADJ (*fig*) *Gegensätze etc* irreconcilable; *Kluft* unbridgeable; **un|über|dacht** [ˈʊnly:bɐdaxt] ADJ open, uncovered; **un|über|legt** **ADJ** *Mensch* rash; *Entschluss, Maßnahmen etc auch* ill-considered **ADV** rashly; **~ entscheiden** to make a rash decision; **~ handeln** to act rashly; **Un|über|legt|heit** F **-, -en** rashness; (= *unüberlegte Handlung*) rash act; **un|über|schau|bar** ADJ **a** (= *groß*) immense, vast **b** (= *nicht vorhersehbar*) *Folgen etc* incalculable **c** (*fig*) (= *unklar*) unclear; (= *verworren*) confusing; **un|über|seh|bar** ADJ **a** (= *nicht abschätzbar*) *Schaden, Schwierigkeiten, Folgen* inestimable, incalculable; (= *nicht übersehbar*) *Menge, Häusermeer etc* vast, immense **b** (= *auffällig*) *Fehler etc* obvious, conspicuous; **un|über|setz|bar** ADJ untranslatable; **un|über|sicht|lich** ADJ **a** *Gelände* broken; *Kurve, Stelle* blind **b** (= *durcheinander*) *System, Plan* confused; **un|über|treff|lich** **ADJ** matchless, unsurpassable; *Rekord* unbeatable **ADV** superbly, magnificently; **un|über|trof|fen** [ʊnly:bɐˈtrɔfn, ˈʊn-] ADJ unsurpassed; **un|über|wind|bar** (*rare*), **un|über|wind|lich** [ʊnly:bɐˈvɪntlɪç, ˈʊn-] ADJ *Gegner, Heer* invincible; *Festung* impregnable; *Hindernis, Schwierigkeit, Gegensätze, Abneigung etc* insuperable, insurmountable; **un|üb|lich** **ADJ** not usual, not customary **ADV** unusually; **es ist ~ schnell gegangen mit dem Antrag** the application was dealt with unusually quickly

un|um|gäng|lich [ʊnlʊmˈgɛŋlɪç, ˈʊn-] ADJ essential, absolutely necessary; (= *unvermeidlich*) inevitable; *Notwendigkeit* absolute; **~ notwendig**

werden to become absolutely essential/quite inevitable
un|um|kehr|bar ADJ irreversible
un|um|schränkt [ʊnlʊm'ʃrɛŋkt, 'ʊn-] ADJ unlimited; *Freiheit, Gewalt, Macht auch, Herrscher* absolute ADV ~ **herrschen** to have absolute rule
un|um|stöß|lich [ʊnlʊm'ʃtøːslɪç, 'ʊn-] ADJ *Tatsache, Wahrheit* irrefutable, incontrovertible; *Entschluss* irrevocable ADV ~ **feststehen** to be absolutely definite
Un|um|stöß|lich|keit F -, *no pl (von Tatsache)* irrefutability, incontrovertibility; *(von Entschluss)* irrevocability
un-: un|um|strit|ten ADJ indisputable, undisputed ADV indisputably, undoubtedly; **un|um|wun|den** ['ʊnlʊmvʊndn, ʊnlʊm'vʊndn] ADV frankly; **un|un|ter|bro|chen** ['ʊnlʊntɐbrɔxn, ʊnlʊntɐ'brɔxn] ADJ **a** *(= nicht unterbrochen)* unbroken, uninterrupted; **~e Tätigkeit** *(in Firma)* continuous employment **b** *(= unaufhörlich)* incessant, continuous ADV *(= unaufhörlich)* incessantly, continuously
un|ver|än|der|lich [ʊnfɛɐ'lɛndɐlɪç, 'ʊn-] ADJ *(= gleichbleibend)* unchanging, invariable; *(= unwandelbar)* unchangeable; **eine ~e Größe** *(Math)* **eine Unveränderliche** *(Math)* a constant, an invariable
Un|ver|än|der|lich|keit F unchanging nature
un|ver|än|dert ['ʊnfɛɐlɛndɐt, ʊnfɛɐ'lɛndɐt] ADJ unchanged; **unsere Weine sind immer von ~er Güte** our wines are consistently good ADV always, consistently; **er ist immer ~ freundlich** he is always friendly; **du siehst ~ jung aus** you look just as young as ever; **das Wetter wird bis auf Weiteres ~ heiter bleiben** the weather will remain fine for the time being
Un-: un|ver|ant|wort|lich [ʊnfɛɐ'lantvɔrtlɪç, 'ʊn-] ADJ irresponsible ADV irresponsibly; **er hat sich ~ intensiv der Sonne ausgesetzt** he spent so much time in the sun, it was irresponsible; **du trinkst ~ viel** you're acting irresponsibly by drinking so much; **sie ist ~ schnell gefahren** she drove dangerously fast; **Un|ver|ant|wort|lich|keit** F irresponsibility; **un|ver|ar|bei|tet** ['ʊnfɛɐlarbaitət, ʊnfɛɐ'larbaitət] ADJ *Material* unprocessed, raw; *(fig) Eindruck* raw, undigested ADV in a raw state; **un|ver|äu|ßer|lich** [ʊnfɛɐ'lɔysɐlɪç, 'ʊn-] ADJ **a** *Rechte* inalienable **b** *Besitz* unmarketable, unsaleable; **un|ver|bes|ser|lich** [ʊnfɛɐ'bɛsɐlɪç, 'ʊn-] ADJ incorrigible; **un|ver|bil|det** ['ʊnfɛɐbɪldət] ADJ *Charakter, Wesen* unspoilt
un|ver|bind|lich ['ʊnfɛɐbɪntlɪç, ʊnfɛɐ'bɪntlɪç] ADJ **a** *(= nicht bindend) Angebot, Preisangabe, Richtlinie* not binding; *Besichtigung* free **b** *(= vage, allgemein)* noncommittal; *(= nicht entgegenkommend)* abrupt, curt ADV *(= nicht bindend)* noncommittally; **sich** *(dat)* **etw ~ schicken lassen** to have sth sent without obligation; **jdm Preise ~ bestätigen** to give sb unconfirmed prices; **etw ~ ausrechnen** to give a nonbinding estimate for sth
Un|ver|bind|lich|keit F **a** *no pl (= Vagheit, Allgemeinheit)* vagueness **b** *(= unverbindliche Äußerung)* noncommittal remark
un-: un|ver|bleit ADJ lead-free, unleaded; **un|ver|blümt** [ʊnfɛɐ'blyːmt, 'ʊn-] ADJ blunt; *Drohung* undisguised; **das kommt einer ~en Erpressung gleich!** that's downright blackmail! ADV bluntly; **un|ver|braucht** ['ʊnfɛɐbrauxt] ADJ *(fig)* unspent; **un|ver|brenn|bar** ADJ incombustible; **un|ver|brüch|lich** [ʊnfɛɐ'brʏçlɪç, 'ʊn-] *(geh)* ADJ steadfast ADV ~ **zu etw stehen** to stand by sth unswervingly; **un|ver|bürgt** [ʊnfɛɐ'bʏrkt, 'ʊn-] ADJ unconfirmed
un|ver|däch|tig ['ʊnfɛɐdɛçtɪç, ʊnfɛɐ'dɛçtɪç] ADJ unsuspicious; *(= nicht unter Verdacht stehend)* unsuspected, above suspicion; **das ist doch völlig ~** there's nothing suspicious about that ADV **sich möglichst ~ benehmen** to arouse as little suspicion as possible; **benimm dich möglichst ~!** act as normally as possible

Un-: un|ver|dau|lich ['ʊnfɛɐdaulɪç, ʊnfɛɐ'daulɪç] ADJ *(lit, fig)* indigestible; **un|ver|daut** ['ʊnfɛɐdaut, ʊnfɛɐ'daut] ADJ undigested; *(fig auch)* unassimilated ADV undigested; **un|ver|derb|lich** ADJ unperishable, nonperishable; **un|ver|dient** ['ʊnfɛɐdiːnt, ʊnfɛɐ'diːnt] ADJ undeserved ADV undeservedly, unjustly, unduly; **un|ver|dien|ter|ma|ßen, un|ver|dien|ter|wei|se** ADV undeservedly, unjustly; **un|ver|dor|ben** ADJ *(lit, fig)* unspoilt, pure; **Un|ver|dor|ben|heit** F *(fig)* purity; **un|ver|dros|sen** ['ʊnfɛɐdrɔsn, ʊnfɛɐ'drɔsn] ADJ *(= nicht entmutigt)* undeterred; *(= unermüdlich)* untiring, indefatigable; *(= unverzagt)* undaunted ADV *(= unverzagt)* undauntedly; *weitermachen* untiringly; **un|ver|dünnt** ['ʊnfɛɐdʏnt] ADJ undiluted ADV *anwenden, auftragen* undiluted; **Spirituosen ~ trinken** to drink spirits neat *or* straight *(Brit)*, to drink alcohol straight *(esp US)*; **un|ver|ehe|licht** ADJ *(old, form)* unwedded, unwed; **„unverehelicht"** *(auf Urkunde) (Frau)* "spinster"; *(Mann)* "bachelor"; **die ~e Eleanor X** Eleanor X, spinster; **un|ver|ein|bar** [ʊnfɛɐ'lainbaːɐ, 'ʊn-] ADJ incompatible; **miteinander ~ sein** to be incompatible; **Un|ver|ein|bar|keit** F incompatibility; **un|ver|fälscht** ['ʊnfɛɐfɛlʃt, ʊnfɛɐ'fɛlʃt] ADJ *(lit, fig)* unadulterated; *Dialekt* pure; *Natürlichkeit* unaffected; *Natur* unspoilt; **un|ver|fäng|lich** ['ʊnfɛɐfɛŋlɪç, ʊnfɛɐ'fɛŋlɪç] ADJ harmless; **das ist ~** it doesn't commit you to anything; **Un|ver|fäng|lich|keit** F harmlessness
un|ver|fro|ren ['ʊnfɛɐfroːrən, ʊnfɛɐ'froːrən] ADJ insolent
Un|ver|fro|ren|heit F -, -en insolence
un|ver|gäng|lich ['ʊnfɛɐgɛŋlɪç, ʊnfɛɐ'gɛŋlɪç] ADJ *Kunstwerk, Werte, Worte, Ruhm* immortal; *Eindruck, Erinnerung, Reiz* everlasting
Un|ver|gäng|lich|keit F *(= Unsterblichkeit)* immortality; *(von Eindruck, Erinnerung)* everlastingness
un|ver|ges|sen ADJ unforgotten; **Roland wird (uns allen) ~ bleiben** we'll (all) remember Roland
un|ver|gess|lich [ʊnfɛɐ'gɛslɪç, 'ʊn-] ADJ unforgettable; *Erlebnis auch* memorable; **das wird mir ~ bleiben, das bleibt mir ~** I'll always remember that, I'll never forget that
Un-: un|ver|gleich|bar [ʊnfɛɐ'glaiçbaːɐ, 'ʊn-] ADJ incomparable; **Un|ver|gleich|bar|keit** F incomparability; **un|ver|gleich|lich** [ʊnfɛɐ'glaiçlɪç, 'ʊn-] ADJ unique, incomparable ADV incomparably, immeasurably; **un|ver|go|ren** ['ʊnfɛɐgoːrən] ADJ unfermented; **un|ver|hält|nis|mä|ßig** ['ʊnfɛɐhɛltnɪsmɛːsɪç, ʊnfɛɐ'hɛltnɪsmɛːsɪç] ADV disproportionately; *(= übermäßig)* excessively ADJ disproportionate; *(= übermäßig)* excessive; **Un|ver|hält|nis|mä|ßig|keit** F disproportion; *(= Übermäßigkeit)* excessiveness; **ihm wurde ~ der Strafe vorgeworfen** he was accused of imposing an excessive punishment; **un|ver|hei|ra|tet** ADJ unmarried, single; **un|ver|hofft** ['ʊnfɛɐhɔft, ʊnfɛɐ'hɔft] ADJ unexpected ADV unexpectedly; **das kam völlig ~** it was quite unexpected, it came out of the blue; **~ Besuch bekommen** to get an unexpected visit; **~ kommt oft** *(Prov)* what you least expect often happens; **un|ver|hoh|len** ['ʊnfɛɐhoːlən, ʊnfɛɐ'hoːlən] ADJ open, unconcealed ADV openly, obviously; **un|ver|hüllt** ['ʊnfɛɐhʏlt] ADJ **a** *Tatsachen, Wahrheit* undisguised, naked **b** *(liter, iro: = nackt)* unclad **c** = **unverhohlen**; **un|ver|jähr|bar** [ʊnfɛɐ'jɛːɐbaːɐ, 'ʊn-] ADJ *(Jur)* not subject to a statute of limitations; **un|ver|käuf|lich** ['ʊnfɛɐkɔyflɪç, ʊnfɛɐ'kɔyflɪç] ADJ unmarketable, unsaleable; **~es Muster** free sample; **„unverkäuflich"** "not for sale"; **un|ver|kenn|bar** [ʊnfɛɐ'kɛnbaːɐ, 'ʊn-] ADJ unmistak(e)able; **un|ver|krampft** ADJ *(lit, fig)* relaxed ADV *(fig)* in a relaxed manner; **un|ver|langt** ['ʊnvɛɐlaŋkt] ADJ unsolicited ADV **~ eingesandte Manuskripte** unsolicited manuscripts; **das Gedicht, das er ~ an die Zeitung schickte** the poem he sent unsolicited to the newspaper; **un|ver|läss|lich** ADJ unreliable; **un|ver|letz|bar** [ʊnfɛɐ'lɛtsbaːɐ, 'ʊn-] ADJ *(lit, fig)* invulnerable; **Un|ver|letz|bar|keit** F *(lit, fig)* invulnerability; **un|ver|letz|lich** [ʊnfɛɐ'lɛtslɪç, 'ʊn-] ADJ **a** *(fig) Rechte, Grenze* inviolable **b** *(lit)* invulnerable; **Un|ver|letz|lich|keit** F *(fig)* inviolability; *(lit)* invulnerability; **un|ver|letzt** ['ʊnfɛɐlɛtst] ADJ uninjured, unhurt, unharmed; *Körperteil* undamaged; *Siegel* unbroken; **~ davonkommen** to walk away unhurt; **un|ver|mählt** ['ʊnfɛɐmɛːlt] ADJ *(geh)* unwedded, unwed; **un|ver|meid|bar** [ʊnfɛɐ'maitbaːɐ, 'ʊn-] ADJ inevitable; **Un|ver|meid|bar|keit** F inevitability; *(= Unumgänglichkeit)* unavoidability; **un|ver|meid|lich** [ʊnfɛɐ'maitlɪç, 'ʊn-] ADJ inevitable; *(= nicht zu umgehen)* unavoidable; **der ~e Herr Braun** the inevitable Mr Braun; **Un|ver|meid|lich|keit** F -, -en inevitability; **un|ver|min|dert** ['ʊnfɛɐmɪndɐt] ADJ ADV undiminished; **un|ver|mischt** ['ʊnfɛɐmɪʃt] ADJ separate, unmixed; *(= rein)* pure; *Tee, Wein etc* pure, unadulterated
un|ver|mit|telt ['ʊnfɛɐmɪtlt] ADJ **a** *(= plötzlich)* sudden, unexpected **b** *(Philos)* immediate ADV suddenly
Un|ver|mö|gen NT, *no pl* inability; *(= Machtlosigkeit)* powerlessness
un|ver|mö|gend ADJ **a** *(= arm)* without means **b** *(old, liter. = unfähig)* helpless; **~ sein, etw zu tun** not to be able to do sth
un|ver|mu|tet ['ʊnfɛɐmuːtət] ADJ unexpected ADV unexpectedly
Un|ver|nunft F *(= Torheit)* stupidity; *(= mangelnder Verstand)* irrationality; *(= Uneinsichtigkeit)* unreasonableness
un|ver|nünf|tig ADJ *(= töricht)* stupid; *(aus mangelnder Vernunft)* irrational; *(= uneinsichtig)* unreasonable; **das war sehr ~ von ihr** it was very stupid *or* unwise of her
un-: un|ver|öf|fent|licht ['ʊnfɛɐlœfntlɪçt] ADJ unpublished; **un|ver|packt** ['ʊnfɛɐpakt] ADJ unpackaged, loose; **un|ver|putzt** ['ʊnfɛɐpʊtst] ADJ unplastered
un|ver|rich|tet ['ʊnfɛɐrɪçtət] ADJ **~er Dinge** *or* **Sache** without having achieved anything, empty-handed
un|ver|rich|te|ter|din|ge △ ['ʊnfɛɐrɪçtətɐ'dɪŋə], **un|ver|rich|te|ter|sa|che** △ [-'zaxə] ADV → **unverrichtet**
un|ver|rück|bar [ʊnfɛɐ'rʏkbaːɐ, 'ʊn-] ADJ *(fig)* unshakeable, unalterable; *Entschluss auch* firm, definite; *Gewissheit* absolute ADV ~ **feststehen** to be absolutely definite
un|ver|schämt ADJ outrageous; *Lüge, Verleumdung etc auch* blatant, barefaced; *Mensch, Frage, Benehmen etc* impudent, impertinent; *(inf) Preis* outrageous; **~es Glück** unbelievable luck ADV **a** *(= dreist) grinsen* impudently; *lügen* shamelessly, blatantly; **grins nicht so ~!** take that impudent grin off your face!; **lüg nicht so ~!** don't tell such barefaced lies! **b** *(inf: = unerhört) teuer, hoch* outrageously
Un|ver|schämt|heit F -, -en **a** *no pl* outrageousness; *(von Mensch, Frage, Benehmen etc)* impudence, impertinence; **die ~ besitzen, etw zu tun** to have the impertinence *or* impudence to do sth **b** *(Bemerkung)* impertinence; *(Tat)* outrageous thing; **das ist eine ~!** it's outrageous!
un-: un|ver|schlei|ert ADJ **a** *Frau* unveiled **b** *(fig) Wahrheit* unvarnished; **un|ver|schlos|sen** ['ʊnfɛɐʃlɔsn, ʊnfɛɐ'ʃlɔsn] ADJ open; *(= nicht abgeschlossen)* unlocked; *Briefumschlag* unsealed; **un|ver|schlüs|selt** ['ʊnfɛɐʃlʏslt] ADJ, ADV *Daten* uncoded; *TV* free to air, without blackouts *pred (US)*
un|ver|schul|det ['ʊnfɛɐʃʊldət, ʊnfɛɐ'ʃʊldət] ADJ **a ein ~er Unfall** an accident which was not his/her *etc* fault **b** *(= ohne Schulden)* free from *or* of debt ADV ~ **in eine Notlage geraten** to get into difficulties through no fault of one's own
un|ver|schul|de|ter|ma|ßen ['ʊnfɛɐʃʊldətɐ'maːsn], **un|ver|schul|de|ter|wei|se**

[ˈʊnfɛɐ̯ʃʊldətɐˈvaizə] ADV through no fault of one's own

un|ver|se|hens [ˈʊnfɛɐ̯zeːəns, ʊnfɛɐ̯ˈzeːəns] ADV all of a sudden, suddenly; *(= überraschend)* unexpectedly

Un-: **un|ver|sehrt** [ˈʊnfɛɐ̯zeːɐt] ADJ *Mensch (lit, fig)* unscathed; *(= unbeschädigt)* intact *pred*; **Un|ver|sehrt|heit** F -, *no pl (= ohne Beschädigung)* intactness; **körperliche ~** freedom from bodily harm; **sie haben die ~ der Geiseln bestätigt** they have confirmed that the hostages are uninjured; **seine seelische ~** the fact that he was mentally unscathed; **un|ver|sieg|bar** [ʊnfɛɐ̯ˈziːkbaːɐ, ˈʊn-] ADJ inexhaustible; **un|ver|sie|gelt** [ˈʊnfɛɐ̯ziːglt] ADJ unsealed; **un|ver|sieg|lich** [ʊnfɛɐ̯ˈziːklɪç, ˈʊn-] ADJ inexhaustible; **un|ver|söhn|lich** [ˈʊnfɛɐ̯zøːnlɪç, ʊnfɛɐ̯ˈzøːnlɪç] ADJ *Standpunkte etc* irreconcilable; **Un|ver|söhn|lich|keit** F -, *no pl* irreconcilability; **un|ver|sorgt** [ˈʊnfɛɐ̯zɔrkt] ADJ *Familie, Kinder* unprovided-for; *Patient, Verletzter* uncared-for

Un|ver|stand M lack of judgement; *(= Torheit)* folly, foolishness; **etw im ~ tun** to do sth to excess

un|ver|stan|den [ˈʊnfɛɐ̯ʃtandn] ADJ not understood; *(= missverstanden)* misunderstood; **er fühlt sich ~** he feels that nobody understands him

un|ver|stän|dig ADJ lacking understanding, ignorant

un|ver|ständ|lich ADJ *(= nicht zu hören)* inaudible; *(= unbegreifbar)* incomprehensible

Un|ver|ständ|nis NT, *no pl* lack of understanding; *(= Nichterfassen, für Kunst etc)* lack of appreciation

un-: **un|ver|stellt** [ˈʊnfɛɐ̯ʃtɛlt, ʊnfɛɐ̯ˈʃtɛlt] ADJ **a** *Stimme* undisguised **b** *(= echt)* unfeigned, genuine; **un|ver|steu|ert** [ˈʊnfɛɐ̯ʃtɔyɐt, ʊnfɛɐ̯ˈʃtɔyɐt] ADJ untaxed; **un|ver|sucht** [ˈʊnfɛɐ̯zuːxt, ʊnfɛɐ̯ˈzuːxt] ADJ **nichts ~ lassen** to try everything

un|ver|träg|lich [ˈʊnfɛɐ̯trɛːklɪç, ʊnfɛɐ̯ˈtrɛːklɪç] ADJ **a** *(= streitsüchtig)* cantankerous **b** *(= unverdaulich)* indigestible; *(Med)* intolerable; *(mit anderer Substanz etc)* incompatible

Un|ver|träg|lich|keit F, *no pl (= Streitsucht)* cantankerousness

un|ver|wandt ADJ **~en Blickes** *(liter)* with a steadfast gaze ADV fixedly, steadfastly

Un-: **un|ver|wech|sel|bar** [ʊnfɛɐ̯ˈvɛkslbaːɐ, ˈʊn-] ADJ unmistak(e)able, distinctive; **Un|ver|wech|sel|bar|keit** [ʊnfɛɐ̯ˈvɛkslbaːɐkait, ˈʊn-] F -, *no pl* distinctiveness; **un|ver|wehrt** [ˈʊnfɛɐ̯veːɐt, ʊnfɛɐ̯ˈveːɐt] ADJ **das sei dir ~** *(old, geh)* you are at liberty to do this *(form)*; **un|ver|wes|lich** [ˈʊnfɛɐ̯veːslɪç, ʊnfɛɐ̯ˈveːslɪç] ADJ imperishable; **un|ver|wind|bar** [ʊnfɛɐ̯ˈvɪntbaːɐ, ˈʊn-] ADJ insurmountable; **un|ver|wirk|licht** [ˈʊnfɛɐ̯vɪrklɪçt] ADJ unrealized; **un|ver|wisch|bar** [ʊnfɛɐ̯ˈvɪʃbaːɐ, ˈʊn-] ADJ *(lit, fig)* indelible; **un|ver|wund|bar** ADJ *(lit, fig)* invulnerable; **Un|ver|wund|bar|keit** F *(lit, fig)* invulnerability

un|ver|wüst|lich [ʊnfɛɐ̯ˈvyːstlɪç, ˈʊn-] ADJ indestructible; *Stoff, Teppich etc auch* tough, durable; *Gesundheit* robust; *Humor, Mensch* irrepressible

un-: **un|ver|zagt** ADJ undaunted ADV undaunted(ly); **un|ver|zeih|bar** [ʊnfɛɐ̯ˈtsaibaːɐ, ˈʊn-] ADJ *(rare)*, **un|ver|zeih|lich** [ʊnfɛɐ̯ˈtsailɪç, ˈʊn-] ADJ unpardonable, unforgivable; **un|ver|zerrt** [ˈʊnfɛɐ̯tsɛrt] ADJ *Fernsehbild etc* undistorted; *(fig: = objektiv)* undistorted; **un|ver|zicht|bar** [ʊnfɛɐ̯ˈtsɪçtbaːɐ, ˈʊn-] ADJ *attr Recht* inalienable; *Anspruch* undeniable, indisputable; *Bedingung, Bestandteil* indispensable; **un|ver|zins|lich** [ʊnfɛɐ̯ˈtsɪnslɪç, ˈʊn-] ADJ interest-free; **un|ver|zollt** [ˈʊnfɛɐ̯tsɔlt] ADJ duty-free

un|ver|züg|lich [ʊnfɛɐ̯ˈtsyːklɪç, ˈʊn-] ADJ immediate, prompt ADV immediately, without delay, at once

un|voll|en|det [ˈʊnfɔlɛndət, ˈʊnfɔlɛndət, ʊnfɔlˈlɛndət] ADJ unfinished; **Die „Unvollendete" von Schubert** Schubert's Unfinished (Symphony)

un|voll|kom|men [ˈʊnfɔlkɔmən, ʊnfɔlˈkɔmən] ADJ *(= unvollständig)* incomplete; *(= fehlerhaft, mangelhaft)* imperfect ADV partially; *wiedergeben* incompletely; **er kann zwar Englisch, aber doch recht ~** he can speak English, but his knowledge is rather limited; **er konnte seine Gefühle nur ~ beschreiben** he could only describe his feelings to a certain degree

Un|voll|kom|men|heit F **a** *no pl (= Unvollständigkeit)* incompleteness; *(= Mangelhaftigkeit)* imperfection **b** *(= Fehler, Mangel)* imperfection

un|voll|stän|dig [ˈʊnfɔlʃtɛndɪç, ʊnfɔlˈʃtɛndɪç] ADJ incomplete; *(Gram) Hilfsverb* defective ADV incompletely, partially; **er hat das Formular ~ ausgefüllt** he didn't fill the form out properly *or* correctly

Un|voll|stän|dig|keit F incompleteness

Un-: **un|vor|be|rei|tet** [ˈʊnfoːɐbəraitət] ADJ unprepared (*auf +acc* for); **eine ~e Rede halten** to make an impromptu speech, to speak off the cuff ADV *reden, unterrichten* unprepared, without preparation; **der Tod des Vaters traf sie ~** her father's death came unexpectedly; **un|vor|denk|lich** [ˈʊnfoːɐdɛŋklɪç] ADJ **seit ~en Zeiten** *(liter)* from time immemorial; **un|vor|ein|ge|nom|men** ADJ unbiased, unprejudiced, impartial ADV impartially; **Un|vor|ein|ge|nom|men|heit** F impartiality; **un|vor|her|ge|se|hen** [ˈʊnfoːɐheːɐgəzeːən] ADJ unforeseen; *Besuch* unexpected; **wir bekamen ~en Besuch** we had visitors unexpectedly, we had unexpected visitors ADV unexpectedly; **un|vor|her|seh|bar** ADJ unforeseeable; **~es Programmende** *(Comput)* unwanted program closure; **un|vor|schrifts|mä|ßig** ADJ not in keeping with the regulations ADV improperly; **ein ~ geparktes Fahrzeug** an improperly parked vehicle; **un|vor|sich|tig** ADJ careless; *(= voreilig)* rash ADV carelessly; *(= unbedacht)* rashly; **un|vor|sich|ti|ger|wei|se** [ˈʊnfoːɐzɪçtɪgɐˈvaizə] ADV carelessly; *(= voreilig)* rashly; **Un|vor|sich|tig|keit** F carelessness; *(= Voreiligkeit)* rashness; **so eine ~ von dir!** how reckless *or* rash of you!; **un|vor|stell|bar** [ʊnfoːɐˈʃtɛlbaːɐ, ˈʊn-] ✪ 43.3 ADJ inconceivable ADV *heiß, kalt* incredibly; *brutal, grausam* inconceivably; **un|vor|teil|haft** ADJ unfavourable *(Brit)*, unfavorable *(US)*, disadvantageous; *Kleid, Frisur etc* unbecoming ADV *gekleidet, geschminkt* unbecomingly; **sie ist ~ frisiert** the way she wears her hair is unbecoming; **~ aussehen** not to look one's best

un|wäg|bar [ʊnˈvɛːkbaːɐ, ˈʊn-] ADJ *Umstand, Unterschied* imponderable; *Risiko* incalculable, inestimable

Un|wäg|bar|keit [ʊnˈvɛːkbaːɐkait, ˈʊn-] F -, -en **a** *no pl (von Umstand, Unterschied)* imponderability; *(von Risiko)* incalculability **b ~en** *(= Risiken)* imponderables *pl*

Un-: **un|wahr** ADJ untrue; **un|wahr|haf|tig** ADJ untruthful; *Gefühle* insincere; **Un|wahr|heit** F **a** *no pl (von Äußerung)* untruthfulness **b** *(= unwahre Äußerung)* untruth; **die ~ sagen** not to tell the truth

un|wahr|schein|lich ✪ 43.2 ADJ *(= nicht zu erwarten, kaum denkbar)* unlikely, improbable; *(= unglaubhaft)* implausible, improbable; *(inf: = groß)* incredible *(inf)* ADV *(inf)* incredibly *(inf)*; **wir haben uns ~ beeilt** we hurried as much as we possibly could; **er gab sich ~ Mühe** he took an incredible amount of trouble *(inf)*

Un|wahr|schein|lich|keit F unlikeliness, improbability

un|wan|del|bar [ʊnˈvandlbaːɐ, ˈʊn-] ADJ *(geh)* **a** *(= unveränderlich)* unalterable, immutable **b** *Treue, Liebe* unwavering, steadfast

un|weg|sam ADJ *Gelände etc* rough

Un|weg|sam|keit F -, *no pl* roughness

un|weib|lich ADJ unfeminine

un|wei|ger|lich [ʊnˈvaigɐlɪç, ˈʊn-] ADJ *attr Folge* inevitable ADV inevitably; *(= fraglos)* undoubtedly; *(= grundsätzlich)* invariably

un|weit PREP *+gen* ADV not far from

un|wert ADJ *(rare)* = **unwürdig**

Un|wert M, *no pl* **a** = **Unwürdigkeit b** demerits *pl*; **über Wert und ~ einer Sache diskutieren** to discuss the merits and demerits of sth

Un|wert|ur|teil NT condemnation

Un|we|sen NT, *no pl (= übler Zustand)* terrible state of affairs; **das ~ (der Rauschgiftsucht) bekämpfen** to combat the problem (of drug addiction); **sein ~ treiben** to be up to mischief; *(Landstreicher etc)* to make trouble; *(Gespenst)* to walk abroad; *(Vampir etc)* to strike terror into people's hearts

un|we|sent|lich ADJ *(= nicht zur Sache gehörig)* irrelevant; *(= unwichtig)* unimportant, insignificant ADV *erhöhen, verringern* insignificantly, minimally; *sich unterscheiden* only slightly, negligibly, marginally; *verändern* only slightly, barely; *mehr, weniger, jünger, besser* just slightly; **zu einer Sache nicht/nur ~ beitragen** to make a not insignificant/only an insignificant contribution to sth

Un|wet|ter NT (thunder)storm; **ein ~ brach los** a storm broke

Un|wet|ter|scha|den M *usu pl* storm damage

Un-: **un|wich|tig** ADJ unimportant, insignificant; *(= belanglos)* irrelevant; *(= verzichtbar)* nonessential; **Un|wich|tig|keit** F unimportance, insignificance; *(= Belanglosigkeit)* irrelevance; **un|wi|der|leg|bar, un|wi|der|leg|lich** [ʊnviːdɐˈleːklɪç, ˈʊn-] ADJ irrefutable; **un|wi|der|ruf|lich** [ʊnviːdɐˈruːflɪç, ˈʊn-] ADJ irrevocable ADV definitely; **die ~ letzte Vorstellung** positively *or* definitely the last *or* final performance; **es steht ~ fest, dass ...** it is absolutely definite that ...; **un|wi|der|spro|chen** [ʊnviːdɐˈʃprɔxn, ˈʊn-] ADJ uncontradicted; *Behauptung auch* unchallenged; **das darf nicht ~ bleiben** we can't let this pass unchallenged; **un|wi|der|steh|lich** [ʊnviːdɐˈʃteːlɪç, ˈʊn-] ADJ irresistible; **un|wie|der|bring|lich** [ʊnviːdɐˈbrɪŋlɪç, ˈʊn-] *(geh)* ADJ irretrievable ADV irretrievably

Un|wil|le(n) M, *no pl* displeasure, indignation (*über +acc* at); *(= Ungeduld)* irritation; **jds Unwillen erregen** to incur sb's displeasure; **seinem Unwillen Luft machen** to give vent to one's indignation

un|wil|lig ADJ indignant (*über +acc* about); *(= widerwillig)* unwilling, reluctant ADV *(= widerwillig)* unwillingly; *(= ungern)* reluctantly

Un|wil|lig|keit F indignation; *(= Widerwilligkeit)* unwillingness, reluctance

un|will|kom|men ADJ unwelcome

un|will|kür|lich [ˈʊnvɪlkyːɐlɪç, ʊnvɪlˈkyːɐlɪç] ADJ spontaneous; *(= instinktiv)* instinctive; *(Physiol, Med)* involuntary ADV *zusammenzucken* instinctively; **ich musste ~ lachen/grinsen** I couldn't help laughing/smiling

Un-: **un|wirk|lich** ADJ unreal; **Un|wirk|lich|keit** F unreality; **un|wirk|sam** ADJ *(= wirkungslos, auch Med)* ineffective; *Vertrag, Rechtsgeschäft* inoperative; *(= nichtig)* null, void; *(Chem)* inactive; **Un|wirk|sam|keit** F *(= Wirkungslosigkeit)* ineffectiveness; *(Jur)* (the fact of) not being operative; **un|wirsch** [ˈʊnvɪrʃ] ADJ *Mensch, Benehmen, Bemerkung* surly, gruff; *Bewegung* brusque ADV gruffly, brusquely; **un|wirt|lich** [ˈʊnvɪrtlɪç] ADJ inhospitable; **Un|wirt|lich|keit** F -, *no pl (von Ort)* inhospitable feel; *(von Klima)* inhospitable nature; **un|wirt|schaft|lich** ADJ uneconomic ADV uneconomically; **Un|wirt|schaft|lich|keit** F **die ~ dieser Methode** because this method is/was uneconomic; **Un|wis|sen** NT ignorance; **un|wis|send** ADJ ignorant; *(= ahnungslos)* unsuspecting; *(= unerfahren)* inexperienced; **Un|wis|sen|heit** F -, *no pl* ignorance; *(= Unerfahrenheit)* inexperience; **~ schützt nicht vor Strafe** *(prov)* ignorance is no excuse *or (Jur)* is no defence *(Brit) or* defense *(US)* in law; **un|wis|sen|schaft|lich** ADJ unscientific; *Textausgabe* unscholarly; *Essay, Aus-*

drucksweise unacademic; **un|wis|sent|lich** ADV unwittingly, unknowingly

un|wohl ADJ *(= unpässlich)* unwell, indisposed *(form)*; *(= unbehaglich)* uneasy; **mir ist ~, ich fühle mich ~** I don't feel well; **in ihrer Gegenwart fühle ich mich ~** I'm ill at ease *or* I feel uneasy in her presence

Un|wohl|sein NT indisposition; *(= unangenehmes Gefühl)* unease; **von einem (plötzlichen) ~ befallen werden** to be taken ill suddenly

Un-: **un|wohn|lich** ADJ *Zimmer etc* uncomfortable, cheerless; **Un|wort** NT *pl* **-wörter** taboo word, non-word; **das ~ des Jahres** the ugliest *or* worst word of the year; **un|wür|dig** ADJ unworthy (+*gen* of); *Verhalten* undignified; *(= schmachvoll)* degrading, shameful; **Un|wür|dig|keit** F unworthiness; *(= Schmach)* degradation, shame

Un|zahl F **eine ~ von** a host of

un|zähl|bar ADJ innumerable, countless; *(Ling)* uncountable ADV **~ viele** huge numbers; **~ viele Bücher/Mädchen** innumerable books/girls

un|zäh|lig [ʊn'tsɛːlɪç, 'ʊn-] ADJ innumerable, countless; **~e Mal(e)** countless times, time and again ADV **~ viele** huge numbers; **~ viele Bücher/Mädchen** innumerable books/girls

un|zäh|li|ge|mal △ ADV → **unzählig**

un-: **un|zähm|bar** [ʊn'tsɛːmbaːɐ, 'ʊn-] ADJ untamable; *(fig auch)* indomitable; **un|zart** ADJ ungentle ADV roughly; **sie machte mich ~ auf mein Alter aufmerksam** she commented bluntly on my age

Un|ze ['ʊntsə] F **-, -n** ounce

Un|zeit F **zur ~** *(geh)* at an inopportune moment, inopportunely

un-: **un|zeit|ge|mäß** ADJ *(= altmodisch)* old-fashioned, outmoded; *(= nicht in die Zeit passend)* anachronistic; *(= der Jahreszeit nicht entsprechend)* unseasonal; **un|zen|siert** ['ʊntsɛnziːɐt] ADJ uncensored; *(Sch)* ungraded; **un|zer|brech|lich** [ʊntsɛɐ'brɛçlɪç, 'ʊn-] ADJ unbreakable; *(fig) Treue, Bündnis etc* steadfast; **un|ze|re|mo|ni|ell** ADJ unceremonious ADV *empfangen, verabschieden* unceremoniously; **un|zer|kaut** ['ʊntsɛɐkaut] ADJ unchewed ADV without chewing; *hinunterschlucken* whole; **un|zer|reiß|bar** [ʊntsɛɐ'raisbaːɐ, 'ʊn-] ADJ untearable; **un|zer|stör|bar** [ʊntsɛɐ'ʃtøːɐbaːɐ, 'ʊn-] ADJ indestructible; **un|zer|trenn|lich** [ʊntsɛɐ'trɛnlɪç, 'ʊn-] ADJ inseparable

Un|zi|a|le [ʊn'tsiaːlə] F **-, -n** *(Typ)* **a** *(Schrift)* uncial (writing) **b** *(Buchstabe)* uncial (letter)

Un-: **un|zie|mend** ['ʊntsiːmənt] *(old)* ADJ, ADV = **unziemlich**; **un|ziem|lich** ADJ unseemly, unbecoming, indecorous ADV *sich benehmen* in an unseemly manner *or* way; **Un|ziem|lich|keit** F **-, -en a** *no pl* unseemliness **b** *(Benehmen)* impropriety; **un|zi|vi|li|siert** ADJ *(lit, fig)* uncivilized ADV *sich benehmen* in an uncivilized manner

Un|zucht F, *no pl (esp Jur)* sexual offence *(Brit) or* offense *(US)*; **das gilt als ~** that's regarded as a sexual offence *(Brit) or* offense *(US)*; **~ treiben** to fornicate; **~ mit Abhängigen/Kindern/Tieren** *(Jur)* illicit sexual relations with dependants/children/animals; **gewerbsmäßige ~** prostitution; **widernatürliche ~** unnatural sexual act(s *pl*); **~ mit jdm treiben** to fornicate with sb; *(Jur)* to commit a sexual offence *(Brit) or* offense *(US)* with sb; **jdn zur ~ missbrauchen** to abuse sb (for sexual purposes)

un|züch|tig ADJ *(esp Jur)* indecent; *Reden, Schriften* obscene; **~e Handlungen** obscene acts; *(Jur)* illicit sexual acts ADV **~ leben** to live licentiously

Un|züch|tig|keit F *(esp Jur)* indecency; *(von Reden, Schriften)* obscenity

Un-: **un|zu|frie|den** ADJ dissatisfied, discontented; *(= missmutig)* unhappy; **manche Leute sind immer ~** some people are never content *or* happy; **Un|zu|frie|den|heit** F, *no pl* dissatisfaction, discontent; *(= Missmut)* unhappiness; **un|zu|gäng|lich** ADJ *Gegend, Gebäude etc* inaccessible; *Charakter, Mensch* unapproachable; *(= taub, unaufgeschlossen)* deaf, impervious (+*dat* to); **Un|zu|gäng|lich|keit** F *(von Gegend, Gebäude etc)* inaccessibility; *(von Charakter, Mensch)* unapproachability; **un|zu|kömm|lich** ['ʊntsuːkœmlɪç] ADJ *(Aus)* insufficient, inadequate; *(= nicht zukommend)* undue; **Un|zu|kömm|lich|keit** F **-, -en** *(Aus)* unpleasantness; *(= Unzulänglichkeit)* inadequacy; **un|zu|läng|lich** ADJ *(= nicht ausreichend)* insufficient; *(= mangelhaft)* inadequate ADV inadequately; **~ unterstützt werden** to get inadequate support; **Un|zu|läng|lich|keit** F **a** *no pl* insufficiency; *(= Mangelhaftigkeit)* inadequacy **b ~en** shortcomings *pl*; **un|zu|läs|sig** ADJ *(auch Jur)* inadmissible; *Gebrauch* improper; *Beeinflussung* undue; *Belastung, Geschwindigkeit* excessive; **für ~ erklären** *(Jur)* to rule out; **un|zu|mut|bar** ADJ *Bedingungen, Zustände* unreasonable; **un|zu|rech|nungs|fä|hig** ADJ not responsible for one's actions, of unsound mind; **jdn für ~ erklären lassen** *(Jur)* to have sb certified (insane); **geistig ~** non compos mentis *(Jur)*, of unsound mind; **Un|zu|rech|nungs|fä|hig|keit** F unsoundness of mind; **~ geltend machen** to put forward *(Brit) or* to enter a plea of insanity; **un|zu|rei|chend** ['ʊntsuːraiçnt] ADJ insufficient, inadequate ADV insufficiently; **un|zu|sam|men|hän|gend** ADJ incoherent, disjointed; **un|zu|stän|dig** ADJ *(Admin, Jur)* incompetent, not competent; **sich für ~ erklären** to disclaim competence; **un|zu|stell|bar** ADJ undeliverable; *Postsendung* dead; **falls ~ bitte zurück an Absender** if undelivered, please return to sender; **Un|zu|stell|bar|keit** ['ʊntsuːʃtɛlbaːɐkait] F **-,** *no pl* **bei ~ geht die Sendung an den Absender zurück** if undelivered the consignment is returned to sender; **un|zu|träg|lich** ADJ *(= nachteilig)* harmful, detrimental; *(gesundheitlich)* unhealthy; **jdm ~ sein** to be harmful *or* detrimental to sb; **jdm (gesundheitlich) *or* jds Gesundheit ~ sein** not to agree with sb, to be bad for sb's health; **un|zu|tref|fend** ADJ inappropriate, inapplicable; *(= unwahr)* incorrect; **Unzutreffendes bitte streichen** delete as applicable; **un|zu|ver|läs|sig** ADJ unreliable; **Un|zu|ver|läs|sig|keit** F unreliability; **un|zweck|mä|ßig** ADJ *(= nicht ratsam)* inexpedient; *(= unpraktisch)* impractical; *(= ungeeignet)* unsuitable, inappropriate; **un|zwei|deu|tig** ADJ unambiguous, unequivocal; *(fig: = unanständig)* explicit ADV explicitly; **jdm ~ zu verstehen geben, dass ...** to make it quite clear to sb that ...; **un|zwei|fel|haft** ADJ undoubted, indubitable, unquestionable ADV without doubt, undoubtedly, indubitably

Up|date ['apdeːt] NT **-s, -s** *(Comput)* update (*auf* +*acc or zu* to)

up|da|ten ['apdeːtn] *ptp* **upgedatet** VTI *insep (Comput)* to update

Up|grade ['apgreːt] NT **-s, -s** *(Comput)* upgrade (*auf* +*acc or zu* to)

up|gra|den ['apgreːdn] *ptp* **upgegradet** VTI *insep (Comput)* to upgrade

Up|load ['aploːt] **-s, -s** M *(Comput)* upload

up|loa|den ['aploːdn] *ptp* **upgeloadet** VTI *insep (Comput)* to upload

üp|pig ['ʏpɪç] ADJ *Wachstum* luxuriant; *Vegetation auch* lush; *Haar* thick; *Mahl, Ausstattung* sumptuous, opulent; *Rente, Gehalt* lavish; *Figur, Frau, Formen* voluptuous; *Busen* ample; *Leben* luxurious; *Fantasie* rich; **nun werd mal nicht zu ~!** *(inf)* let's have no more of your cheek *(Brit) or* impudence! *(inf)* ADV **die ~ ausfallenden Dividenden** the generous *or* lavish dividends; **ihre Bezüge sind sehr ~ bemessen** her earnings are very generously figured; **mit ~ gepolsterten Sitzen** with opulently *or* luxuriantly upholstered seats; **~ wucherndes Gestrüpp** thick *or* lush verdant undergrowth; **die ~ grünen Hügel** the lush green hills; **350 ~ illustrierte Seiten** 350 lavishly illustrated pages; **~ leben** to live in style; **~ wuchernde Vegetation** lush vegetation

Üp|pig|keit F **-,** *no pl (von Wachstum)* luxuriance; *(von Vegetation auch)* lushness; *(von Haar)* thickness; *(von Mahl, Ausstattung)* sumptuousness, opulence; *(von Figur, Frau, Formen)* voluptuousness

up|si|zen VTI *sep (Comput)* to upsize

up to date ['ap tuː 'deːt] ADJ *pred (inf)* up to date; *Kleidung* modern

Ur [uːɐ] M **-(e)s, -e** *(Zool)* aurochs

Ur- *in cpds (= erste)* first, prime; *(= ursprünglich)* original; **Ur|ab|stim|mung** F ballot; **Ur|adel** M ancienne noblesse, ancient nobility; **Ur|ahn** M, **Ur|ah|ne** M *(= Vorfahr)* forefather, forebear; *(= Urgroßvater)* great-grandfather; **Ur|ah|ne** F *(= Vorfahrin)* forebear; *(= Urgroßmutter)* great-grandmother

Ural [u'raːl] M **-s** *(Geog)* **a** *(Fluss)* Ural **b** *(Gebirge)* **der ~** the Urals *pl*, the Ural mountains *pl*

ur|alt ADJ ancient; *Problem, Brauch auch* age-old; **seit ~en Zeiten** from time immemorial; **aus ~en Zeiten** from long (long) ago

Uran [u'raːn] NT **-s,** *no pl (abbr* **U***)* uranium

Uran|bren|ner M uranium pile

Ur-: **Ur|an|fang** M first beginning; **Ur|angst** F primeval fear; **Ur|an|la|ge** F genetic predisposition; **ur|auf|füh|ren** ['uːɐlauffyːrən] *ptp* **uraufgeführt** ['uːɐlaufgəfyːɐt] VT to give the first performance (of), to play for the first time; *Film* to premiere *usu pass*

Ur|auf|füh|rung F premiere; *(von Theaterstück etc auch)* first night *or* performance; *(von Film auch)* first showing

Ur|auf|füh|rungs|(film)|the|a|ter NT, **Ur|auf|füh|rungs|ki|no** NT premiere cinema

Ur|aus|ga|be F first edition

ur|ban [ʊr'baːn] ADJ *(geh)* urbane

ur|ba|ni|sie|ren [ʊrbani'ziːrən] *ptp* **urbanisiert** VTR *(Sociol)* to urbanize

Ur|ba|ni|sie|rung F **-, -en** *(Sociol)* urbanization

Ur|ba|ni|tät [ʊrbani'tɛːt] F **-,** *no pl (geh)* urbanity

ur|bar ['uːɐbaːɐ] ADJ **einen Wald ~ machen** to clear a forest; **die Wüste ~ machen** to reclaim the desert; **Land ~ machen** to cultivate land

ur|ba|ri|sie|ren [ʊrbari'ziːrən] *ptp* **urbarisiert** VT *(Sw)* = **urbar machen**

Ur|ba|ri|sie|rung F **-, -en** *(Sw)*, **Ur|bar|ma|chung** [-maxʊŋ] F **-, -en** *(von Wald)* clearing; *(von Wüste)* reclamation; *(von Ackerland)* cultivation

Ur-: **Ur|ba|yer(in)** M(F) *(inf)* typical Bavarian; **Ur|be|deu|tung** F *(Ling)* original meaning; **Ur|be|ginn** M very beginning; **seit ~, von ~ an** from the beginning(s) of time; **Ur|be|völ|ke|rung** F natives *pl*, original inhabitants *pl*; *(in Australien)* Aborigines *pl*; **Ur|be|woh|ner(in)** M(F) native, original inhabitant; *(in Australien)* Aborigine; **Ur|bild** NT prototype, archetype; *(Philos)* idea

ur|chig ['ʊrçɪç] ADJ *(Sw)* = **urwüchsig**

Ur-: **Ur|chris|ten** PL *(Eccl Hist)* early Christians *pl*; **Ur|chris|ten|tum** NT early Christianity; **ur|christ|lich** ADJ early Christian; **ur|deutsch** ADJ essentially German

Ur|du ['ʊrdu] NT **-(s)** *(Ling)* Urdu

Ur-: **ur|ei|gen** ['uːɐlaign] ADJ very own; **es liegt in seinem ~sten Interesse** it's in his own best interests; **ein dem Menschen ~er Hang** an inherent human quality; **Ur|ein|woh|ner(in)** M(F) native, original inhabitant; *(in Australien)* Aborigine; **Ur|el|tern** PL *(= Vorfahren)* forebears *pl*; *(= Urgroßeltern)* great-grandparents *pl*; **Ur|en|kel** M great-grandchild, great-grandson; **Ur|en|ke|lin** F great-granddaughter; **Ur|fas|sung** F original version; **Ur|feh|de** F *(Hist)* oath of truce; **~ schwören** to abjure all vengeance; **Ur|form** F prototype; **Ur|ge|mein|de** F *(Eccl Hist)* early Christian community; **ur|ge|müt|lich** ADJ *(inf) Wohnung, Lokal, Atmosphäre* really cosy *(Brit) or* cozy *(US)*; *Mensch* really easy-going → *auch* **gemütlich**; **ur|ger|ma|nisch** ADJ *(Ling)* Proto-Germanic; *(fig)* essentially

Germanic; **das Urgermanische** Proto-Germanic; **Ur|ge|schich|te** F prehistory; **Ur|ge|sell|schaft** F primitive society; **Ur|ge|stalt** F prototype; **Ur|ge|stein** NT prehistoric rock, primitive rocks *pl*; **politisches ~** *(fig)* a dyed-in-the--wool politician; **Ur|ge|walt** F elemental force

ur|gie|ren [ʊrˈgiːrən] *ptp* **urgiert** *(Aus form)* VT *(= dringend nachsuchen)* to request *sth* VI *(= um schnelle(re) Erledigung bitten)* to ask *for sth* to be done (more) quickly; *(bei Entscheidung)* to ask for a speedy decision

Ur|groß-: **Ur|groß|el|tern** PL great-grandparents *pl*; **Ur|groß|mut|ter** F great-grandmother; **Ur|groß|va|ter** M great-grandfather

Ur|grund M very basis, source

Ur|he|ber [ˈuːɐheːbɐ] M **-s, -**, **Ur|he|be|rin** [-ərɪn] F **-, -nen** originator; *(liter. = Schöpfer)* creator; *(Jur. = Verfasser)* author; **der geistige ~** the spiritual father

Ur|he|ber-: **Ur|he|ber|ge|bühr** F copyright fee; **Ur|he|ber|recht** NT copyright *(an +dat* on); **ur|he|ber|recht|lich** ADJ ADV on copyright *attr*; **~ geschützt** copyright(ed); **Ur|he|ber|schaft** [ˈuːɐheːbɐʃaft] F **-, -en** authorship; **Ur|he|ber|schutz** M copyright

Ur|hei|mat F original home(land)

Uri [ˈuːri] NT **-s** Uri

urig [ˈuːrɪç] ADJ *(inf) Mensch* earthy; *Lokal etc* ethnic

Urin [uˈriːn] M **-s, -e** urine; **etw im ~ haben** *(dated inf)* to have a gut feeling about sth *(inf)*

Uri|nal [uriˈnaːl] NT **-s, -e** *(Med)* urinal

uri|nie|ren [uriˈniːrən] *ptp* **uriniert** VI to urinate

Urin|pro|be F urine sample *or* specimen

Ur-: **Ur|ins|tinkt** [ˈuːɐlɪnstɪŋkt] M primary *or* basic instinct; **Ur|kan|ton** M *(Sw)* original canton; **Ur|kir|che** F early Church; **Ur|knall** M *(Astron)* big bang; **ur|ko|misch** ADJ *(inf)* screamingly funny *(inf)*; **Ur|kraft** F elemental force

Ur|kun|de [ˈuːɐkʊndə] F **-, -n** document; *(= Kaufurkunde)* deed, title deed; *(= Gründungsurkunde etc)* charter; *(= Siegerurkunde, Diplomurkunde, Bescheinigung etc)* certificate; **eine ~ (über etw** *acc*) **ausstellen** *or* **ausfertigen** *(Jur)* to draw up a document about sth; **eine ~ bei jdm hinterlegen** to lodge a document with sb

Ur|kun|den|fäl|schung F forgery *or* falsification of a/the document/documents

ur|kund|lich [ˈuːɐkʊntlɪç] ADJ documentary ADV **~ verbürgt** *or* **bestätigt** authenticated; **~ beweisen** *or* **belegen** to give documentary evidence; **~ erwähnt** mentioned in a document

Ur|kunds|be|am|te(r) M *decl as adj*, **Ur|kunds|be|am|tin** F, **Ur|kunds|per|son** F registrar

URL [uːlɛrˈlɛl] F **-, -s** *(Comput) abbr von* **uniform resource locator** URL

URL-Ad|res|se F *(Comput)* URL address

Ur|land|schaft F primitive *or* primeval landscape

Ur|laub [ˈuːɐlaup] M **-(e)s, -e** [-bə] *(= Ferien)* holiday(s *pl*) *(esp Brit)*, vacation *(US)*; *(esp Mil)* leave (of absence), furlough *(US)*; **~ haben** to have a holiday *(esp Brit) or* vacation *(US)*; *(esp Mil)* to have leave; **in** *or* **im** *or* **auf** *(inf)* **~ sein** to be on holiday *(esp Brit) or* vacation *(US)*/on leave; **er macht zurzeit ~** he's on holiday *(esp Brit) or* he's vacationing *(US)* at the moment; **in ~ fahren** to go on holiday *(esp Brit) or* vacation *(US)*/on leave; **zwei Wochen ~** two weeks' holiday *(esp Brit) or* vacation *(US)*/leave; **(sich** *dat*) **einen Tag ~ nehmen** to take a day off, to take a day's holiday *(esp Brit) or* vacation *(US)*; **~ bis zum Wecken** *(Mil)* night leave; **bezahlter/unbezahlter ~** paid/unpaid holiday *(esp Brit) or* vacation *(US)*

ur|lau|ben [ˈuːɐlaubn] VI *(inf)* to holiday *(esp Brit)*, to vacation *(US)*

Ur|lau|ber [ˈuːɐlaubɐ] M **-s, -**, **Ur|lau|be|rin** [-ərɪn] F **-, -nen** holiday-maker *(Brit)*, vacationist *(US)*; *(Mil)* soldier on leave

Ur|laubs-: **Ur|laubs|an|spruch** M holiday *(esp Brit) or* vacation *(US)* entitlement; **Ur|laubs|an|trag** M request for time off *or* leave; **Ur|laubs|be|kannt|schaft** F holiday *(esp Brit) or* vacation *(US)* acquaintance; **Ur|laubs|fo|to** NT holiday *(esp Brit) or* vacation *(US)* snap(shot); **Ur|laubs|ge|biet** NT holiday *(esp Brit) or* vacation *(US)* area; **Ur|laubs|geld** NT holiday pay *or* money *(Brit)*, vacation pay *or* money *(US)*; **Ur|laubs|land** NT holiday *(esp Brit) or* vacation *(US)* country, tourist destination; **mein liebstes ~** my favourite *(Brit) or* favorite *(US)* country for a holiday *(esp Brit) or* vacation *(US)*; **Ur|laubs|ort** M holiday *(esp Brit) or* vacation *(US)* resort; **Ur|laubs|plan** M *usu pl* holiday *(esp Brit) or* vacation *(US)* plan; **ur|laubs|reif** ADJ *(inf)* ready for a holiday *(esp Brit) or* vacation *(US)*; **Ur|laubs|rei|se** F holiday *(esp Brit) or* vacation *(US)* trip; **eine ~ machen** to go on a trip; **Ur|laubs|schein** M *(Mil)* pass; **Ur|laubs|sper|re** F *(Mil)* ban on leave; **Ur|laubs|stim|mung** F holiday mood; **Ur|laubs|tag** M (one day of) holiday *(esp Brit) or* vacation *(US)*; **die ersten drei ~e hat es geregnet** it rained on the first three days of the/my/his *etc* holiday *(esp Brit) or* vacation *(US)*; **ich habe noch drei ~e gut** I've still got three days' holiday *(esp Brit) or* vacation *(US)* to come; **Ur|laubs|ver|tre|tung** F temporary replacement; **ich mache ~ für Frau Schumm** I'm filling in while Mrs Schumm is on holiday *(esp Brit) or* is vacationing *(US)*; **Ur|laubs|wo|che** F (one week of) holiday *(esp Brit) or* vacation *(US)*; **Ur|laubs|zeit** F holiday *(esp Brit) or* vacation *(US)* period *or* season; **Ur|laubs|ziel** NT holiday *(esp Brit) or* vacation *(US)* spot; *(Land auch)* tourist destination

Ur-: **Ur|laut** M elemental cry; **Ur|mensch** M primeval man; *(inf)* caveman *(inf)*; **Ur|me|ter** NT, *no pl* standard metre *(Brit) or* meter *(US)*; **Ur|mund** M *(Biol)* blastopore; **Ur|mut|ter** F *pl* **-mütter** first mother

Ur|ne [ˈʊrnə] F **-, -n** urn; *(= Losurne)* box; *(= Wahlurne)* ballot box; **zur ~ gehen** to go to the polls; **die Wähler wurden an die ~n gerufen** the voters were asked to go to the polls

Ur|nen-: **Ur|nen|feld** NT *(Archeol)* urnfield, urnsite; **Ur|nen|fried|hof** M urn cemetery, cinerarium; **Ur|nen|gang** M *pl* **-gänge** *(Pol)* going to the polls *no art*; **Ur|nen|grab** NT urn grave

Uro|ge|ni|tal- *(Anat)*: **Uro|ge|ni|tal|sys|tem** NT urogenital system; **Uro|ge|ni|tal|trakt** M urogenital tract

Uro|lo|ge [uroˈloːgə] M **-n, -n**, **Uro|lo|gin** [-ˈloːgɪn] F **-, -nen** urologist

Uro|lo|gie [uroloˈgiː] F **-**, *no pl* urology

uro|lo|gisch [uroˈloːgɪʃ] ADJ urological

Ur-: **Ur|oma** F *(inf)* great-granny *(inf)*; **Ur|opa** M *(inf)* great-grandpa *(inf)*; **Ur|pflan|ze** F primordial plant; **ur|plötz|lich** *(inf)* ADJ *attr* very sudden ADV all of a sudden; **Ur|quell** M, **Ur|quel|le** F *(geh)* primary source, fountainhead

Ur|sa|che [ˈuːɐzaxə] F cause *(auch Philos)*; *(= Grund)* reason; *(= Beweggrund)* motive; *(= Anlass)* occasion; **~ und Wirkung** cause and effect; **kleine ~, große Wirkung** *(prov)* big oaks from little acorns grow *(prov)*; **keine ~!** *(auf Dank)* don't mention it!, you're welcome!; *(auf Entschuldigung)* that's all right; **ohne (jede) ~** for no reason (at all); **aus nichtiger ~** for a trifling reason/trifling reasons; **aus unbekannter ~** for no apparent reason; **aus ungeklärter ~** for reasons unknown; **jdm ~ geben, etw zu tun** to give sb cause to do sth; **ich habe alle ~ anzunehmen, dass ...** I have every reason to suppose that ...; **alle/keine ~ zu etw haben** to have every/no reason for sth; **alle/keine ~ haben, etw zu tun** to have every/no reason to do sth; **die ~ einer Sache** *(gen) or* **für etw sein** to be the cause of/reason for sth

Ur|sa|chen|for|schung F *(Philos)* aetiology *(Brit)*, etiology *(US)*; **wir müssen etwas ~ betreiben** *(= nach den Ursachen forschen)* we need to do some research into the causes of this

ur|säch|lich [ˈuːɐzɛçlɪç] ADJ *(esp Philos)* causal; **~ für etw sein** to be the cause of sth; **in ~em Zusammenhang stehen** to be causally related

Ur|säch|lich|keit F *(esp Philos)* causality

Ur-: **Ur|schlamm** M primeval mud; **Ur|schleim** M protoplasm; **Ur|schrei** M *(Psych)* primal scream; **Ur|schrift** F original (text *or* copy); **ur|schrift|lich** ADJ original ADV in the original; **ur+sen|den** [ˈuːɐzɛndn] VT *sep infin, ptp only (Rad)* to broadcast for the first time; **das wurde im April urgesendet** that was first broadcast in April; **Ur|sen|dung** F *(Rad)* first broadcast

urspr. *abbr von* **ursprünglich**

Ur|spra|che F **a** proto-language **b** *(bei Übersetzungen)* original (language), source language

Ur|sprung [ˈuːɐʃprʊŋ] M **a** origin; *(= Anfang auch)* beginning; *(= Abstammung)* extraction; **er ist keltischen ~s** he is of Celtic extraction; **dieses Wort ist keltischen ~s** this word is Celtic in origin *or* is of Celtic origin; **seinen ~ in etw** *(dat)* **haben, einer Sache** *(dat)* **seinen ~ verdanken** to originate in sth, to have its origins in sth; **seinen ~ in etw** *(dat)* **nehmen** to originate in sth **b** *(old: lit, fig) (= Quelle)* source

ur|sprüng|lich [ˈuːɐʃprʏŋlɪç, uːɐˈʃp-] ADJ **a** *attr* original; *(= anfänglich)* initial, first **b** *(= urwüchsig)* natural; *Natur* unspoilt ADV originally; *(= anfänglich)* initially, at first, in the beginning

Ur|sprüng|lich|keit F **-**, *no pl* naturalness

Ur|sprungs-: **Ur|sprungs|be|zeich|nung** F *(Comm)* designation of origin; **kontrollierte ~** registered designation of (country of) origin; *(bei Wein)* appellation contrôlée; **Ur|sprungs|land** NT *(Comm)* country of origin

Ur|ständ [ˈuːɐʃtɛnt] F **(fröhliche) ~ feiern** *(hum)* to come back with a vengeance, to come to life again

Ur|strom|tal NT *(Geol, Geog)* glacial valley *(in North Germany)*

Ur|sup|pe F primeval soup

Ur|teil [ˈʊrtail] NT **-s, -e** **a** judgement *(auch Philos)*; *(= Entscheidung)* decision; *(= Meinung)* opinion; **nach meinem ~** in my judgement/opinion; **ich kann darüber kein ~ abgeben** I am no judge of this; **sich** *(dat)* **ein ~ über jdn/etw erlauben, ein ~ über jdn/etw fällen** to pass judgement on sb/sth; **sich** *(dat)* **kein ~ über etw** *(acc)* **erlauben können** to be in no position to judge sth; **nach dem ~ von Sachverständigen** according to expert opinion; **jdn in seinem ~ bestärken** to strengthen sb in his opinion; **(sich) mit seinem ~ zurückhalten** to reserve judgement; **zu dem ~ kommen, dass ...** to come to the conclusion that ...; **sich** *(dat)* **ein ~ über jdn/etw bilden** to form an opinion about sb/sth

b *(Jur) (= Gerichtsurteil)* verdict; *(= Richterspruch)* judgement; *(= Strafmaß)* sentence; *(= Schiedsspruch)* award; *(= Scheidungsspruch)* decree; **das ~ über jdn sprechen** *(Jur)* to pass *or* to pronounce judgement on sb; **jdm/sich selber sein ~ sprechen** *(fig)* to pronounce sb's/one's own sentence

ur|tei|len [ˈʊrtailən] VI to judge *(nach* by); **über etw** *(acc)* **~** to judge sth; *(= seine Meinung äußern)* to give one's opinion on sth; **hart über jdn ~** to judge sb harshly; **abfällig über jdn ~** to be disparaging about sb; **nach seinem Aussehen zu ~** judging by *or* to judge by his appearance; **vorschnell ~** to make a hasty judgement

Ur|teils-: **Ur|teils|be|grün|dung** F *(Jur)* opinion; **ur|teils|fä|hig** ADJ competent *or* able to judge; *(= umsichtig)* discerning, discriminating; **dazu ist er ~ genug** his judgement is sound enough for that; **Ur|teils|fä|hig|keit** F competence *or* ability to judge; *(= Umsichtigkeit)* discernment, discrimination; **Ur|teils|fin|dung** [-fɪndʊŋ] F **-, -en** *(Jur)* reaching a verdict *no* *art;* **Ur|teils|kraft** F, *no pl* power *or* faculty of judgement; *(= Umsichtigkeit)* discernment, discrimination; **„Kritik der ~"** "Critique of Judgement"; **Ur|teils|schel|te** F attack on a/the court's ruling; **Ur|teils|spruch** M *(Jur)* judgement; *(von Geschworenen)* verdict; *(von Strafgericht)* sentence; *(von Schiedsgericht)* award; **Ur|teils|ver|kün|dung** F *(Jur)* pronouncement of judgement; **Ur|teils|ver|mö|gen** NT faculty of judgement; *(= Umsichtigkeit)* discernment, discrimination; **Ur|teils|voll|stre|ckung** F *(Jur)* execution of a/the sentence

Ur-: **Ur|text** M original (text); **Ur|tie|fe** F *(liter)* depth(s *pl*); **Ur|tier** NT, **Ur|tier|chen** NT protozoon *(esp Brit)*, protozoan; *(in der Morphologie)* primordial animal; **Ur|trieb** M basic drive *or* instinct; **ur|tüm|lich** ['u:ɐty:mlɪç] ADJ = **urwüchsig**; **Ur|typ** M, **Ur|ty|pus** M prototype

Uru|guay ['u:rugvai, 'ʊr-, uru'guai] NT **-s** Uruguay

Ur|ur- *in cpds* great-great-; **Ur|ur|groß|mut|ter** F great-great-grandmother; **Ur|ur|groß|va|ter** M great-great-grandfather

Ur-: **Ur|va|ter** M forefather; **Ur|vä|ter|zeit** ['u:ɐfɛ:tɐtsait] F olden times *pl*; **seit ~en** from time immemorial; **schon zur ~** even in olden times; **Ur|ver|trau|en** NT basic trust, primal sense of trust; **ur|ver|wandt** ADJ *Wörter, Sprachen* cognate; **Ur|viech** NT, **Ur|vieh** NT *(inf)* real character; **Ur|vo|gel** M archaeopteryx; **Ur|volk** NT first people; **Ur|wahl** F *(Pol)* primary (election); **Ur|wäh|ler(in)** M(F) *(Pol)* primary elector *(Brit) or* voter; **Ur|wald** M primeval forest; *(in den Tropen)* jungle; **Ur|wald|lau|te** PL *(inf)* jungle noises *pl*; **Ur|weib** NT *(inf)* real woman; **Ur|welt** F primeval world; **ur|welt|lich** ADJ primeval; **ur|wüch|sig** ['u:ɐvy:ksɪç] ADJ *(= unverbildet, naturhaft)* natural; *Natur* unspoilt; *(= urweltlich) Flora, Fauna* primeval; *(= ursprünglich)* original, native; *(= bodenständig)* rooted in the soil; *(= unberührt) Land etc* untouched; *(= urgewaltig) Kraft* elemental; *(= derb, kräftig)* sturdy; *Mensch* rugged; *Humor, Sprache* earthy; **Ur|zeit** F primeval times *pl*; **seit ~en** since primeval times; *(inf)* for donkey's years *(Brit inf)*, for aeons *(Brit inf) or* eons *(US inf)*; **vor ~en** in primeval times; *(inf)* ages ago; **ur|zeit|lich** ADJ primeval; **Ur|zel|le** F *(Biol)* primordial cell; **Ur|zeu|gung** F abiogenesis; **Ur|zu|stand** M primordial *or* original state

USA [u:lɛs'la:] PL **die ~** the USA *sing*; **in die ~ fahren** to travel to the USA

Usam|ba|ra|veil|chen [uzam'ba:ra-] NT African violet

US-ame|ri|ka|nisch [u:'lɛs-] ADJ American

Usance [y'zã:s] F **-, -n** usage, custom; *(Comm)* practice

USB *abbr von* **universal serial bus** *(Comput)* USB

USB-Stick [u:lɛs'be:stɪk] M **-s, -s** *(Comput)* USB flash drive

Use|net ['ju:snet] NT **-s, -s** *(Comput)* Usenet

User ['ju:zɐ] M **-s, -**, **Use|rin** ['ju:zərɪn] F **-, -nen** *(Comput)* user

User-ID ['ju:zɐlai̯di:] F **-, -s** *(Comput)* user ID

usf. *abbr von* **und so fort**

Usur|pa|ti|on [uzʊrpa'tsio:n] F **-, -en** *(liter)* usurpation

Usur|pa|tor [uzʊr'pa:to:ɐ] M **-s, Usurpatoren** [-'to:rən], **Usur|pa|to|rin** [-'to:rɪn] F **-, -nen** *(liter)* usurper

usur|pa|to|risch [uzʊrpa'to:rɪʃ] ADJ *(liter)* usurpatory, usurpative

usur|pie|ren [uzʊr'pi:rən] *ptp* **usurpiert** VT *(liter)* to usurp

Usus ['u:zʊs] M **-s**, *no pl* custom; **das ist hier so ~** it's the custom here

USV *abbr von* **unterbrechungsfreie Stromversorgung** UPS

usw. *abbr von* **und so weiter** etc

Uten|sil [utɛn'zi:l] NT **-s, -ien** [-liən] utensil, implement

Ute|rus ['u:terʊs] M **-, Uteri** [-ri] uterus

Uti|li|ta|ris|mus [utilita'rɪsmʊs] M **-**, *no pl* Utilitarianism

Uti|li|ta|rist [utilita'rɪst] M **-en, -en**, **Uti|li|ta|ris|tin** [-'rɪstɪn] F **-, -nen** Utilitarian

uti|li|ta|ris|tisch [utilita'rɪstɪʃ] ADJ utilitarian

Uto|pia [u'to:pia] NT **-s, -s** Utopia

Uto|pie [uto'pi:] F **-, -n** [-'pi:ən] utopia; *(= Wunschtraum)* utopian dream

uto|pisch [u'to:pɪʃ] ADJ utopian; *(= von Utopia)* Utopian

Uto|pis|mus [uto'pɪsmʊs] M **-**, *no pl* utopianism

Uto|pist [uto'pɪst] M **-en, -en**, **Uto|pis|tin** [-'pɪstɪn] F **-, -nen** utopian

uto|pis|tisch [uto'pɪstɪʃ] ADJ *(pej)* utopian

u. U. *abbr von* **unter Umständen**

UV [u:'fau] *abbr von* **ultraviolett**

UV- [u:'fau] *in cpds* ultraviolet

u. v. a. (m.) *abbr von* **und vieles andere (mehr)**

U. v. D. [u:fau'de:] M **-s, -s** *(Mil) abbr von* **Unteroffizier vom Dienst**

UV-: **UV-Fil|ter** [u:'fau-] M UV *or* ultraviolet filter; **UV-Schutz** M UV block *or* screen; **UV-Strah|len** [u:'fau-] PL ultraviolet rays *pl*

Ü-Wa|gen ['y:-] M *(Rad, TV)* outside broadcast vehicle

Uz ['u:ts] M **-es, -e** *usu sing (inf)* tease *sing (inf)*, leg-pull *(inf)*, joke

uzen ['u:tsn] VTI *(inf)* to tease, to kid *(inf)*

Uze|rei [u:tsə'rai] F **-, -en** *(dial, inf)* teasing, kidding *(inf)*

Uz|na|me M *(inf)* nickname

V

V, v [fau] **NT -, -** V, v

V *abbr von* **Volt, Volumen**

va banque [va'bã:k] **ADV, Vabanque ~ spielen** *(geh)* to play vabanque; *(fig)* to put everything at stake

Va|banque|spiel [va'bã:k-] **NT** *(fig)* dangerous game

Va|duz [fa'dʊts, va'du:ts] **NT -'** Vaduz

vag [va:k] **ADJ = vage**

Va|ga|bund [vaga'bʊnt] **M -en, -en** [-dn], **Va|ga|bun|din** [-'bʊndɪn] **F -, -nen** vagabond

Va|ga|bun|den|le|ben **NT** vagabond life; *(fig auch)* roving life

va|ga|bun|die|ren [vagabʊn'di:rən] *ptp* **vagabundiert** **VI** **a** *(= als Landstreicher leben)* to live as a vagabond/as vagabonds; **das Vagabundieren** vagabondage; **ein ~des Volk** a nomadic people **b** *aux sein (= umherziehen)* to rove around, to lead a vagabond life; **durch die Welt ~** to rove *or* wander all over the world

va|ge ['va:gə] **ADJ** vague **ADV** vaguely; **etw ~ andeuten** to give a vague indication of sth; **drück dich nicht so ~ aus!** don't be so vague!

Vag|heit ['va:khait] **F -, -en** vagueness

Va|gi|na [va'gi:na] **F -, Vaginen** [-nən] vagina

va|gi|nal [vagi'na:l] **ADJ** vaginal **ADV** vaginally; *ertasten* through the vaginal canal; **~ untersucht werden** to have a vaginal examination

va|kant [va'kant] **ADJ** *(old, form)* vacant

Va|kanz [va'kants] **F -, -en** *(old, form: = Stelle)* vacancy; *(old, dial: = Ferien)* vacation

Va|kat ['va:kat] **NT -(s), -s** *(Typ)* blank (page)

Va|ku|um ['va:kuʊm] **NT -s, Vakuen** *or* **Vakua** [-kuən, -kua] *(lit, fig)* vacuum; **unter/im ~** in a vacuum

Va|ku|um-, va|ku|um- *in cpds* vacuum; **Va|ku|um|pum|pe** **F** vacuum pump; **Va|ku|um|röh|re** **F** vacuum tube; **va|ku|um|ver|packt** [-fɛɐpakt] **ADJ** vacuum-packed; **Va|ku|um|ver|pa|ckung** **F** vacuum pack; *(das Verpacken)* vacuum packaging; **va|ku|um|ver|sie|gelt** [-fɛɐzi:glt] **ADJ** vacuum-sealed

Va|len|tins|tag ['va:lɛnti:ns-] **M** (St) Valentine's Day

Va|lenz [va'lɛnts] **F -, -en** valency

va|li|die|ren [vali'di:rən] *ptp* **validiert** **VTI** *(Comput) Dokument* to validate

Va|li|die|rung [vali'di:rʊŋ] **F -, -en** *(Comput: von Dokument)* validation

val|le|ri, val|le|ra [falə'ri:, falə'ra:] **INTERJ** falderal *(esp Brit)*, folderol

Va|lo|ren [va'lo:rən] **PL** *(Sw Fin)* securities *pl*

Va|lu|ta [va'lu:ta] **F -, Valuten** [-tn] **a** *(= Währung)* foreign currency **b** *(im Zahlungsverkehr)* value; *(= Datum)* value date

Va|lu|ta-: **Va|lu|ta|ge|schäft** **NT** *(Fin)* currency draft; **Va|lu|ta|klau|sel** **F** *(Fin)* exchange clause

Vamp [vɛmp] **M -s, -s** vamp

Vam|pir [vam'pi:ɐ] **M -s, -e** vampire; *(Zool)* vampire (bat)

Vam|pi|ris|mus [vampi'rɪsmʊs] **M -,** *no pl* vampirism

Va|na|din [vana'di:n] **NT -s,** *no pl,* **Va|na|di|um** [va'na:diʊm] **NT -s,** *no pl (abbr* **V**) vanadium

Van-Al|len-Gür|tel [vɛn'ɛlɪn-] **M** Van Allen belt

Van|da|le [van'da:lə] **M -n, -n, Van|da|lin** [-'da:lɪn] **F -, -nen** vandal; *(Hist)* Vandal → **hausen**

Van|da|lis|mus [vanda'lɪsmʊs] **M -,** *no pl* vandalism

Va|nil|le [va'nɪljə, va'nɪlə] **F -,** *no pl* vanilla

Va|nil|le-: **Va|nil|le|eis** **NT** vanilla ice cream; **Va|nil|le|ge|schmack** **M** vanilla flavour *(Brit) or* flavor *(US)*; **mit ~** vanilla-flavoured *(Brit)*, vanilla-flavored *(US)*; **Va|nil|le|kip|ferl** **NT** *(Aus) small crescent-shaped biscuit made with almond pastry and sprinkled with vanilla sugar*; **Va|nil|le|pud|ding** **M** ≈ vanilla blancmange; **Va|nil|le|sau|ce** **F** custard; **Va|nil|le|stan|ge** **F** vanilla pod; **Va|nil|le|zu|cker** **M, Va|nil|lin|zu|cker** [vanɪ'li:n-] **M** vanilla sugar

Va|nil|lin [vanɪ'li:n] **NT -,** *no pl (Chem)* vanillin

va|ri|a|bel [va'ria:bl] **ADJ** variable **ADV ~ verzinsliche Anleihen** loans at a variable interest rate

Va|ri|a|bi|li|tät [variabili'tɛ:t] **F -,** *no pl* variability

Va|ri|ab|le [va'ria:blə] **F** *decl as adj* variable

Va|ri|an|te [va'riantə] **F -, -n** variant *(zu* on)

Va|ri|a|ti|on [varia'tsio:n] **F -, -en** *(alle Bedeutungen)* variation; **~en zu einem Thema** variations on a theme

Va|ri|a|ti|ons-: **va|ri|a|ti|ons|fä|hig** **ADJ** capable of variation; **Va|ri|a|ti|ons|mög|lich|keit** **F** possibility of variation

Va|ri|e|tät [varie'tɛ:t] **F -, -en** *(auch Bot, Zool)* variety

Va|ri|e|té, Va|ri|e|tee [varie'te:] **NT -s, -s** **a** variety (entertainment), vaudeville *(esp US)* **b** *(= Theater)* variety theatre *(Brit) or* theater *(US)*, music hall *(Brit)*, vaudeville theater *(US)*

va|ri|ie|ren [vari'i:rən] *ptp* **variiert** **VTI** to vary

Va|sall [va'zal] **M -en, -en** *(Hist, fig)* vassal

Va|sal|len-: **Va|sal|len|pflicht** **F** *(Hist)* vassalage, feudal service; **Va|sal|len|staat** **M** *(Hist)* vassal state; *(fig)* client *or* satellite state; **Va|sal|len|tum** [va'zaləntu:m] **NT -s,** *no pl* vassalage

Väs|chen ['vɛ:sçən] **NT -s, -** little vase

Va|se ['va:zə] **F -, -n** vase

Va|sek|to|mie [vazɛkto'mi:] **F -, -n** [-'mi:ən] *(spec)* vasectomy

Va|se|lin [vaze'li:n] **NT -s,** *no pl,* **Va|se|li|ne** [vaze'li:nə] **F -,** *no pl* Vaseline®

va|so|mo|to|risch [vazomo'to:rɪʃ] **ADJ** vasomotor *attr*, vasomotory **ADV ~ gestört sein** to have a vasomotory disorder

Va|ter ['fa:tɐ] **M -s, =** ['fɛ:tɐ] *(lit, fig)* father; *(Gott, bei Namen)* Father; *(von Zuchttieren)* sire; **~ von zwei Kindern sein** to be the father of two children; **~ unser** *(Rel)* Our Father; **unsere Väter** *pl (geh: = Vorfahren)* our (fore)fathers, our forebears; **wie der ~, so der Sohn** *(prov)* like father, like son *(prov)*; **er ist ganz der ~** he's very like his father; **~ werden ist nicht schwer, ~ sein dagegen sehr** *(prov)* becoming a father is easy, being one is a different matter; **wer war der ~ dieses Gedankens?** whose idea was that?; **ach du dicker ~!** *(inf)* oh my goodness!, oh heavens!; **~ Staat** *(hum)* the State

Vä|ter|chen ['fɛ:tɐçən] **NT -s, -** *dim von* **Vater** *(= Vater)* dad(dy) *(inf)*; *(= alter Mann)* grandad *(inf)*; **~ Staat** *(hum)* the State

Va|ter-: **Va|ter|fi|gur** **F** father figure; **Va|ter|freu|den** **PL** joys *pl* of fatherhood; **Va|ter|haus** **NT** parental home

Va|ter|land **NT** native country; *(esp Deutschland)* Fatherland; **dem ~ dienen** to serve one's country; **sein ~ lieben** to love one's country

va|ter|län|disch [-lɛndɪʃ] **ADJ** *(= national)* national; *(= patriotisch)* patriotic; **(Großer) Vaterländischer Krieg** (Great) Patriotic War

Va|ter|lands-: **Va|ter|lands|lie|be** **F** patriotism, love of one's country; **va|ter|lands|lie|bend** **ADJ** patriotic; **va|ter|lands|los** **ADJ** without a native land *(esp poet)*; *(= staatenlos)* stateless; **Va|ter|lands|ver|rä|ter(in)** **M(F)** traitor to one's country; *(in Deutschland auch)* traitor to the Fatherland

vä|ter|lich ['fɛ:tɐlɪç] **ADJ** *(= vom Vater)* paternal; *(= wie ein Vater auch)* fatherly **ADV** like a father; **er klopfte ihm ~ auf die Schulter** he gave him a fatherly pat on the shoulder

vä|ter|li|cher|seits **ADV** on one's father's side; **meine Großeltern ~** my paternal grandparents

Vä|ter|lich|keit **F -,** *no pl* fatherliness

Va|ter-: **Va|ter|lie|be** **F** paternal *or* fatherly love; **~ ist unersetzbar** a father's love is irreplaceable; **va|ter|los** **ADJ** fatherless; **~ aufwachsen** to grow up without a father; **Va|ter|mord** **M** patricide; **Va|ter|mör|der** **M** *(hum, Kragen)* stand-up collar, choker *(dated)*; **Va|ter|mör|der(in)** **M(F)** patricide, father-killer *(inf)*; **Va|ter|recht** **NT** patriarchy

Va|ter|schaft ['fa:tɐʃaft] **F -, -en** fatherhood *no art*; *(esp Jur)* paternity; **gerichtliche Feststellung der ~** *(Jur)* affiliation

Va|ter|schafts-: **Va|ter|schafts|be|stim|mung** **F** determination of paternity; **Va|ter|schafts|kla|ge** **F** paternity suit; **Va|ter|schafts|nach|weis** **M** proof of paternity; **Va|ter|schafts|pro|zess** **M** paternity suit; **Va|ter|schafts|test** **M** paternity test

Vä|ter|sit|te **F** tradition of one's forefathers

Va|ter(s)|na|me **M** *(old)* surname

Va|ter-: **Va|ter|stadt** **F** home town; **Va|ter|stel|le** **F bei jdm ~ vertreten** to act *or* be a father to sb; **bei jdm an ~ stehen** to take the place of sb's father; **Va|ter|tag** **M** Father's Day; **Va|ter|un|ser** ['fa:tɐ'ʊnzɐ, fa:tɐ'ʊnzɐ] **NT -s, -** Lord's Prayer

Va|ti ['fa:ti] **M -s, -s** *(inf)* dad(dy) *(inf)*

Va|ti|kan [vati'ka:n] **M -s** Vatican

va|ti|ka|nisch [vati'ka:nɪʃ] **ADJ** *attr* Vatican; **Vatikanisches Konzil** Vatican Council

Va|ti|kan|staat **M,** *no pl* Vatican State

Va|ti|kan|stadt **F,** *no pl* Vatican City

V-Aus|schnitt ['fau-] **M** V-neck; **ein Pullover mit ~** a V-neck jumper *(Brit) or* pullover

v. Chr. *abbr von* **vor Christus** BC

VDE [faude:'le:] **M -s,** *no pl abbr von* **Verband Deutscher Elektrotechniker**

VEB [faule:'be:] **M -s, -s** *(DDR) abbr von* **Volkseigener Betrieb**

Ve|du|te [ve'du:tə] **F -, -n** *(Art)* veduta

Ve|ga|ner [ve'ga:nɐ] **M -s, -, Ve|ga|ne|rin** [-ərɪn] **F -, -nen** vegan

Ve|ge|ta|bi|le(r) [vegeta'bi:lə] MF *decl as adj* vegetarian

Ve|ge|ta|ri|er [vege'ta:riɐ] M **-s, -, Ve|ge|ta|ri|e|rin** [-iərɪn] F **-, -nen** vegetarian

ve|ge|ta|risch [vege'ta:rɪʃ] ADJ vegetarian ADV **~ leben** to be a vegetarian; **sich ~ ernähren** to live on a vegetarian diet; **~ kochen** to cook vegetarian meals

Ve|ge|ta|ris|mus [vegeta'rɪsmʊs] M **-,** *no pl* vegetarianism

Ve|ge|ta|ti|on [vegeta'tsio:n] F **-, -en** vegetation

Ve|ge|ta|ti|ons|pe|ri|o|de F vegetation period

ve|ge|ta|tiv [vegeta'ti:f] ADJ *(= pflanzlich)* vegetative; *Nervensystem* autonomic ADV *(Bot)* vegetatively, asexually; **~ bedingt** *(Med)* caused by the autonomic nervous system

ve|ge|tie|ren [vege'ti:rən] *ptp* **vegetiert** VI to vegetate; *(= kärglich leben)* to eke out a bare *or* miserable existence

ve|he|ment [vehe'mɛnt] *(geh)* ADJ vehement ADV vehemently

Ve|he|menz [vehe'mɛnts] F **-,** *no pl (geh)* vehemence

Ve|hi|kel [ve'hikl] NT **-s, -** **a** *(pej inf) (= Fahrrad)* boneshaker *(Brit inf)*, old bike *(inf)*; *(= Auto)* jalopy *(inf)* **b** *(Pharm, fig geh)* vehicle

Veil|chen ['failçən] NT **-s, -** violet; *(inf: = blaues Auge)* shiner *(inf)*, black eye; **sie ist bescheiden wie ein ~, das im Verborgenen blüht** she is modesty itself; **blau wie ein** *or* **tausend ~** *(inf)* drunk as a lord *(Brit inf)* or a sailor *(US inf)*, roaring drunk *(inf)*

veil|chen|blau ADJ violet; *(inf: = betrunken)* roaring drunk *(inf)*

Veits|tanz ['faits-] M *(Med)* St Vitus's dance; **einen ~ aufführen** *(fig inf)* to jump *or* hop about *(Brit) or* around like crazy *(inf)*

Vek|tor ['vɛkto:ɐ] M **-s, Vektoren** [-'to:rən] vector

Vek|tor-: **Vek|tor|raum** M *(Math)* vector space; **Vek|tor|rech|nung** F *(Math)* vector analysis

Ve|lar(|laut) [ve'la:ɐ-] M **-s, -e** velar (sound)

Ve|lo ['ve:lo] NT **-s, -s** *(Sw)* bicycle, bike *(inf)*; *(motorisiert)* moped

Ve|lour [və'lu:ɐ, ve'lu:ɐ] [və'lu:ɐ, ve'lu:ɐ] NT **-s, -s** *or* **-e, Ve|lours** [və'lu:ɐ, ve'lu:ɐ] NT **-, -** *(auch* **Veloursleder***)* suede

Ve|lours M **-, -** *(Tex)* velour(s)

Ve|lours|tep|pich [və'lu:ɐ-, ve'lu:ɐ-] M velvet carpet

Ven|det|ta [vɛn'dɛta] F **-, Vendetten** [-tn] vendetta

Ve|ne ['ve:nə] F **-, -n** vein

Ve|ne|dig [ve'ne:dɪç] NT **-s** Venice

Ve|nen|ent|zün|dung F phlebitis

Ve|nen|lei|den NT varicose veins *pl*

ve|ne|risch [ve'ne:rɪʃ] ADJ *(Med)* venereal

Ve|ne|ro|lo|gie [venerolo'gi:] F **-,** *no pl (Med)* venereology

Ve|ne|zi|a|ner [vene'tsia:nɐ] M **-s, -, Ve|ne|zi|a|ne|rin** [-ərɪn] F **-, -nen** Venetian

ve|ne|zi|a|nisch [vene'tsia:nɪʃ] ADJ Venetian

Ve|ne|zo|la|ner [venetso'la:nɐ] M **-s, -, Ve|ne|zo|la|ne|rin** [-ərɪn] F **-, -nen** Venezuelan

ve|ne|zo|la|nisch [venetso'la:nɪʃ] ADJ Venezuelan

Ve|ne|zu|e|la [vene'tsue:la] NT **-s** Venezuela

Ve|nia Le|gen|di ['ve:niale'gɛndi] F **- -,** *no pl (Univ)* authorization to teach at a university

ve|nös [ve'nø:s] ADJ venous

Ven|til [vɛn'ti:l] NT **-s, -e** *(Tech, Mus)* valve; *(fig)* outlet

Ven|ti|la|ti|on [vɛntila'tsio:n] F **-, -en** ventilation; *(Anlage)* ventilation system

Ven|ti|la|tor [vɛnti'la:to:ɐ] M **-s, Ventilatoren** [-'to:rən] ventilator

ven|ti|lie|ren [vɛnti'li:rən] *ptp* **ventiliert** VT *(geh)* to ventilate; *(fig) (= äußern)* to air; *(= erwägen)* to examine, to consider carefully

Ve|nus ['ve:nʊs] F **-',** *no pl (Myth, Astron)* Venus

Ve|nus-: **Ve|nus|hü|gel** M *(Anat)* mons veneris *(spec)*; **Ve|nus|mu|schel** F *(Zool)* hard *or* round clam

ver|ab|fol|gen [fɛɐ'lapfɔlgn] *ptp* **verabfolgt** VT *(form) Medizin etc* to administer *(form)* *(jdm* to sb); *(= verordnen)* to prescribe *(jdm* for sb)

ver|ab|re|den [fɛɐ'lapre:dn] *ptp* **verabredet** VT to arrange; *Termin auch* to fix, to agree upon; *Maßnahmen* to agree; *Straftat* to collude in; *Mord* to conspire in; **es war eine verabredete Sache** it was arranged beforehand; **ein vorher verabredetes Zeichen** a prearranged signal; **zum verabredeten Zeitpunkt** at the agreed time; **am verabredeten Ort** at the agreed place; **wir haben verabredet, dass wir uns um 5 Uhr treffen** we have arranged to meet at 5 o'clock; **wie verabredet** as arranged; **schon verabredet sein** to have a previous *or* prior engagement *(esp form)*, to have something else on *(inf)*; **mit jdm verabredet sein** to have arranged to meet sb; *(geschäftlich, formell)* to have an appointment with sb; *(esp mit Freund/Freundin)* to have a date with sb

VR **sich mit jdm ~** to arrange to meet sb; *(geschäftlich, formell)* to arrange an appointment with sb; *(esp mit Freund/Freundin)* to make a date with sb; *(Jur)* to collude with sb; **sich miteinander ~** to arrange to meet; *(geschäftlich, formell)* to arrange an appointment; *(esp mit Freund/Freundin)* to make a date; *(Jur)* to collude

Ver|ab|re|dung F **-, -en** *(= Vereinbarung)* arrangement, agreement; *(= Treffen)* engagement *(form)*; *(geschäftlich, formell)* appointment; *(esp mit Freund/Freundin)* date; *(Jur)* collusion; *(von Mord, Hochverrat, Meuterei)* conspiracy; **ich habe eine ~** I'm meeting somebody; **~ einer Straftat** *(Jur)* collusion/conspiracy to commit a criminal offence *(Brit) or* offense *(US)*

ver|ab|rei|chen [fɛɐ'lapraiçn] *ptp* **verabreicht** VT *Tracht Prügel etc* to give; *Arznei, Droge auch* to administer *(form)* *(jdm* to sb); *(= verordnen)* to prescribe *(jdm* for sb); *(old) Speise* to serve

Ver|ab|rei|chung F **-, -en** *(form) (von Tracht Prügel)* giving; *(von Arznei)* administering; *(= Verordnung)* prescription; *(old: von Speisen)* serving

ver|ab|säu|men [fɛɐ'lapzɔymən] *ptp* **verabsäumt** VT *(form)* to neglect, to omit

ver|ab|scheu|en [fɛɐ'lapʃɔyən] *ptp* **verabscheut** VT to detest, to abhor, to loathe

ver|ab|scheu|ens|wert ADJ detestable, abhorrent, loathsome

Ver|ab|scheu|ung F **-,** *no pl* detestation, abhorrence, loathing

ver|ab|scheu|ungs|wür|dig ADJ = **verabscheuenswert**

ver|ab|schie|den [fɛɐ'lapʃi:dn] *ptp* **verabschiedet** VT to say goodbye to; *(= Abschiedsfeier veranstalten für)* to hold a farewell ceremony for; *(= entlassen) Beamte, Truppen* to discharge; *(Pol) Haushaltsplan* to adopt; *Gesetz, Erklärung* to pass; **wie bist du von deinen Kollegen/bei deiner Stelle verabschiedet worden?** what sort of a farewell did your colleagues arrange for you/did you receive at work?

VR **sich (von jdm) ~** to say goodbye (to sb), to take one's leave (of sb) *(form)*, to bid sb farewell *(liter)*; **er ist gegangen, ohne sich zu ~** he left without saying goodbye; **sich von etw ~** *(fig)* to turn one's back on sth; **sich aus etw ~** *(fig)* to withdraw from sth

Ver|ab|schie|dung F **-, -en** *(von Beamten etc)* discharge; *(Pol) (von Gesetz)* passing; *(von Haushaltsplan)* adoption

ver|ab|so|lu|tie|ren [fɛɐlapzolu'ti:rən] *ptp* **verabsolutiert** VT to make absolute

ver|ach|ten *ptp* **verachtet** VT to despise; *jdn auch* to hold in contempt; *(liter) Tod, Gefahr* to scorn; **nicht zu ~** *(inf)* not to be despised, not to be scoffed at, not to be sneezed at *(inf)*; **einen guten Whisky hat er nie verachtet** *(inf)* he never said no to a good drop of whisky

ver|ach|tens|wert ADJ despicable, contemptible

Ver|äch|ter [fɛɐ'lɛçtɐ] M **-s, -, Ver|äch|te|rin** [-ərɪn] F **-, -nen kein ~ von etw sein** to be quite partial to sth

ver|ächt|lich [fɛɐ'lɛçtlɪç] ADJ contemptuous, scornful; *(= verachtenswert)* despicable, contemptible; **jdn/etw ~ machen** to run sb down/belittle sth ADV contemptuously, scornfully

Ver|ach|tung F, *no pl* contempt *(von* for); **jdn mit ~ strafen** to treat sb with contempt

ver|ach|tungs|voll ADJ contemptuous, disdainful

ver|al|bern [fɛɐ'lalbɐn] *ptp* **veralbert** VT *(inf)* to make fun of; **du willst mich wohl ~** are you pulling my leg? *(inf)*

ver|all|ge|mei|nern [fɛɐlalgə'mainɐn] *ptp* **verallgemeinert** VTI to generalize

Ver|all|ge|mei|ne|rung F **-, -en** generalization

ver|al|ten [fɛɐ'laltn] *ptp* **veraltet** VI *aux sein* to become obsolete; *(Ansichten, Methoden)* to become antiquated; *(Mode)* to go out of date

ver|al|tet [fɛɐ'laltət] ADJ obsolete; *Ansichten* antiquated; *Mode* out-of-date

Ve|ran|da [ve'randa] F **-, Veranden** [-dn] veranda, porch

ver|än|der|bar ADJ changeable

Ver|än|der|bar|keit F **-, -en** changeability, changeableness

ver|än|der|lich [fɛɐ'lɛndɐlɪç] ADJ variable; *Wetter, Mensch* changeable

Ver|än|der|lich|keit F **-, -en** variability

ver|än|dern *ptp* **verändert** VT to change VR to change; *(= Stellung wechseln)* to change one's job; *(= Wohnung wechseln)* to move; **sich zu seinem Vorteil/Nachteil ~** *(im Aussehen)* to look better/worse; *(charakterlich)* to change for the better/worse; **verändert aussehen** to look different

Ver|än|de|rung F change; **eine berufliche ~** a change of job

ver|ängs|ti|gen *ptp* **verängstigt** VT *(= erschrecken)* to frighten, to scare; *(= einschüchtern)* to intimidate

ver|an|kern *ptp* **verankert** VT *(Naut, Tech)* to anchor *(in +dat* in); *(fig) Rechte etc (in Gesetz)* to establish, to ground; *Gedanken (in Bewusstsein)* to embed, to fix; **gesetzlich verankert** established in law

Ver|an|ke|rung [fɛɐ'laŋkərʊŋ] F **-, -en** *(Naut, Tech) (= das Verankern)* anchoring; *(= das Verankertsein)* anchorage; *(fig) (von Rechten)* (firm) establishment; *(von Gedanken)* embedding, fixing

ver|an|la|gen [fɛɐ'lanla:gn] *ptp* **veranlagt** VT to assess *(mit* at)

ver|an|lagt [fɛɐ'lanla:kt] ADJ **melancholisch/tuberkulös ~ sein** to have a melancholy/tubercular disposition; **technisch/mathematisch/praktisch ~ sein** to be technically/mathematically/practically minded; **künstlerisch/musikalisch ~ sein** to have an artistic/a musical bent; **zu** *or* **für etw ~ sein** to be cut out for sth; **er ist so ~, dass ...** it's his nature to ...; **er ist eben so ~** that's just the way he is, that's just his nature

Ver|an|la|gung F **-, -en** **a** *(körperlich, esp Med)* predisposition; *(charakterlich)* nature, disposition; *(= Hang)* tendency; *(= allgemeine Fähigkeiten)* natural abilities *pl*; *(= künstlerisches, praktisches etc Talent)* bent; **eine ~ zum Dickwerden haben** to have a tendency to put on weight; **eine ~ zur Kriminalität haben** to have criminal tendencies **b** *(von Steuern)* assessment

ver|an|las|sen [fɛɐ'lanlasn] *ptp* **veranlasst** VT **a etw ~** *(= in die Wege leiten)* to arrange for sth, to see to it that sth is done; *(= befehlen)* to order sth; **eine Maßnahme ~** to arrange for/order a measure to be taken; **ich werde das Nötige ~** I will see (to it) that the necessary steps are taken; **wir werden alles Weitere ~** we will take care of *or* see to everything else **b** *auch vi (= bewirken)* to give rise *(zu* to); **jdn zu etw ~** *(Ereignis etc)* to lead sb to sth; *(Mensch)* to cause sb to do sth; **jdn (dazu) ~, etw zu tun** *(Ereignis etc)* to lead sb to do sth; *(Mensch)* to cause sb to do sth; **das veranlasst zu der An-**

nahme, dass ... that leads one to assume that ...; **sich (dazu) veranlasst fühlen, etw zu tun** to feel compelled *or* obliged to do sth

Ver|an|las|sung F -, -en cause, reason; **auf ~ von** *or* *+gen* at the instigation of; **keine ~ zu etw haben** to have no cause *or* reason for sth; **keine ~ haben, etw zu tun** to have no cause *or* reason to do sth *or* for doing sth; **~ zu etw geben** to give cause for sth

ver|an|schau|li|chen [fɛɐ̯'anʃaulɪçn] ✪ 53.5 *ptp* **veranschaulicht** VT to illustrate (*+dat* to, *an +dat, mit* with); **sich** *(dat)* **etw ~** to picture sth (to oneself), to visualize sth; **sich** *(dat)* **~, dass ...** to see *or* realize that ...

Ver|an|schau|li|chung F -, -en illustration; **zur ~** as an illustration, to illustrate sth

ver|an|schla|gen *ptp* **veranschlagt** VT to estimate (*auf +acc* at); **etw zu hoch ~** to overestimate sth; **etw zu niedrig ~** to underestimate sth

Ver|an|schla|gung [fɛɐ̯'anʃla:gʊŋ] F -, -en estimate; *(= das Veranschlagen)* estimation

ver|an|stal|ten [fɛɐ̯'anʃtaltn] *ptp* **veranstaltet** VT to organize, to arrange; *Wahlen* to hold; *Umfrage* to do; *(kommerziell) Wettkämpfe, Konzerte etc* to promote; *Party etc* to hold, to give; *(inf) Szene* to make

Ver|an|stal|ter [fɛɐ̯'anʃtaltɐ] M -s, -, **Ver|an|stal|te|rin** [-ərɪn] F -, -nen organizer; *(Comm: von Wettkämpfen, Konzerten etc)* promoter

Ver|an|stal|tung [fɛɐ̯'anʃtaltʊŋ] F -, -en **a** event *(von* organized by); *(feierlich, öffentlich)* function **b** *no pl (= das Veranstalten)* organization

Ver|an|stal|tungs-: **Ver|an|stal|tungs|be|ginn** M start (of the event); *(= Kursbeginn)* start of the course; **~: 8 Uhr** start: 8 pm *or* P.M. *(US)*; **Ver|an|stal|tungs|ka|len|der** M calendar of events; **Ver|an|stal|tungs|ort** M venue, location *(esp US)*; **Ver|an|stal|tungs|pro|gramm** NT programme *(Brit) or* program *(US)* of events; **Ver|an|stal|tungs|rei|he** F series of events; *(= Kursreihe)* series of courses; **Ver|an|stal|tungs|ter|min** M date of the event; *(= Kurstermin)* date of the course

ver|ant|wor|ten *ptp* **verantwortet** VT to accept (the) responsibility for; *die Folgen auch, sein Tun* to answer for (*vor +dat* to); **(es) ~, dass jd etw tut** to accept the responsibility for sb doing sth; **wie könnte ich es denn ~, ...?** it would be most irresponsible of me ...; **ein weiterer Streik/eine solche Operation wäre nicht zu ~** another strike/such an operation would be irresponsible; **eine nicht zu ~de Fahrlässigkeit/Schlamperei** inexcusable negligence/sloppiness; **etw sich selbst gegenüber ~** to square sth with one's own conscience
VR **sich für** *or* **wegen etw ~** to justify sth (*vor +dat* to); *für Missetaten etc* to answer for sth (*vor +dat* before); **sich vor Gericht/Gott** *etc* **~ müssen** to have to answer to the courts/God *etc* *(für, wegen* for)

ver|ant|wort|lich [fɛɐ̯'antvɔrtlɪç] ADJ responsible (*für* for); *(= haftbar)* liable; **jdm (gegenüber) ~ sein** to be responsible *or* answerable *or* accountable to sb; **jdn für etw ~ machen** to hold sb responsible for sth; **für etw ~ zeichnen** *(form) (lit)* to sign for sth; *(fig)* to take responsibility for sth; **der ~e Leiter des Projekts** the person in charge of the project

Ver|ant|wort|li|che(r) [fɛɐ̯'antvɔrtlɪçə] MF *decl as adj* person responsible; **die ~n** *pl* those responsible

Ver|ant|wort|lich|keit F -, -en responsibility; *(= Haftbarkeit)* liability

Ver|ant|wor|tung [fɛɐ̯'antvɔrtʊŋ] F -, -en responsibility (*für* for); **auf eigene ~** on one's own responsibility; **auf deine ~!** you take the responsibility!, on your own head be it! *(Brit)*, it's your ass! *(US inf)*; **die ~ übernehmen** to take *or* accept *or* assume *(esp form)* responsibility; **die ~ (für etw) tragen** to take responsibility (for sth); **jdn zur ~ ziehen** to call sb to account; **sich aus der ~ stehlen** to avoid *or* shirk (one's) responsibility

Ver|ant|wor|tungs-: **Ver|ant|wor|tungs|be|reich** M area of responsibility; **ver|ant|wor|tungs|be|wusst** ADJ responsible ADV responsibly, conscientiously; **Ver|ant|wor|tungs|be|wusst|sein** NT sense of responsibility; **ver|ant|wor|tungs|freu|dig** ADJ willing to take responsibility; **Ver|ant|wor|tungs|ge|fühl** NT sense of responsibility; **ver|ant|wor|tungs|los** ADJ irresponsible ADV irresponsibly; **Ver|ant|wor|tungs|lo|sig|keit** F -, *no pl* irresponsibility; **ver|ant|wor|tungs|voll** ADJ responsible ADV responsibly

ver|äp|peln [fɛɐ̯'ɛpln] *ptp* **veräppelt** VT *(inf)* **jdn ~** to make fun of sb; *(= auf den Arm nehmen)* to pull sb's leg *(inf)*

ver|ar|beit|bar ADJ workable; *(Comput)* processable; **leicht/schwer ~** easy/hard to work

ver|ar|bei|ten *ptp* **verarbeitet** VT to use (*zu etw* to make sth); *(Tech, Biol etc)* to process; *Gold etc* to work; *(= verbrauchen)* to consume; *(= verdauen)* to digest; *(fig)* to use (*zu* for); *Stoff* to treat; *Daten* to process; *Erlebnis etc* to assimilate, to digest; *(= bewältigen)* to overcome; **~de Industrie** processing industries *pl*; **etw geistig ~** to assimilate *or* digest sth

ver|ar|bei|tet [fɛɐ̯'arbaitət] ADJ **a** *Materialien, Lebensmittel* processed; **gut/schlecht ~** *(Rock etc)* well/badly finished **b** *(dial: = abgearbeitet)* worn

Ver|ar|bei|tung [fɛɐ̯'arbaitʊŋ] F -, -en **a** use, using; *(Tech, Biol, Comput)* processing; *(von Ton, Gold)* working; *(= Verdauen)* digestion; *(fig) (von Stoff)* treating; *(von Erlebnis etc)* assimilation, digestion; *(= Bewältigung)* overcoming **b** *(= Aussehen)* finish; *(= Qualität)* workmanship *no indef art*

Ver|ar|bei|tungs-: **Ver|ar|bei|tungs|ge|schwin|dig|keit** F *(Comput)* processing speed; **Ver|ar|bei|tungs|ge|wer|be** NT manufacturing *or* processing trade

ver|ar|gen [fɛɐ̯'argn] *ptp* **verargt** VT **jdm etw ~** to hold sth against sb; **jdm ~, dass ...** to hold it against sb that ...; **ich kann es ihm nicht ~, wenn er ...** I can't blame him if he ...

ver|är|gern *ptp* **verärgert** VT **jdn ~** to annoy sb; *(stärker)* to anger sb

ver|är|gert [fɛɐ̯'ɛrgɐt] ADJ annoyed; *(stärker)* angry; **~ über jdn/etw** annoyed/angry with *or* at sb/about sth ADV *reagieren* angrily

Ver|är|ge|rung [fɛɐ̯'ɛrgərʊŋ] F -, -en annoyance; *(stärker)* anger

ver|ar|men [fɛɐ̯'armən] *ptp* **verarmt** VI *aux sein* *(lit, fig)* to become impoverished

ver|armt [fɛɐ̯'armt] ADJ impoverished

Ver|ar|mung F -, -en impoverishment

ver|ar|schen [fɛɐ̯'arʃn, -'la:ɐʃn] *ptp* **verarscht** VT *(inf)* to take the piss out of *(Brit sl)*, to make fun of; *(= für dumm verkaufen)* to mess *or* muck *(Brit)* around *(inf)*

ver|arz|ten [fɛɐ̯'a:ɐtstn, -'artstn] *ptp* **verarztet** VT *(inf)* to fix up *(inf)*; *(mit Verband)* to patch up *(inf)*; *(fig hum)* to sort out *(inf)*

ver|äs|teln [fɛɐ̯'ɛstln] *ptp* **verästelt** VR to branch out; *(fig)* to ramify

ver|äs|telt [fɛɐ̯'ɛstlt] ADJ *Baum* branched; *(fig) Organisation etc* complex

Ver|äs|te|lung [fɛɐ̯'ɛstəlʊŋ] F -, -en branching; *(fig)* ramifications *pl*

ver|aus|ga|ben [fɛɐ̯'ausga:bn] *ptp* **verausgabt** VR to overexert *or* overtax oneself; *(finanziell)* to overspend; **ich habe mich total verausgabt** *(finanziell)* I've badly overspent

ver|aus|la|gen [fɛɐ̯'ausla:gn] *ptp* **verauslagt** VT *(Comm)* to lay out, to disburse *(form)*

ver|äu|ßer|lich ADJ *(form: = verkäuflich)* saleable, for sale

ver|äu|ßer|li|chen [fɛɐ̯'ɔysɐlɪçn] *ptp* **veräußerlicht** VT to trivialize VI *aux sein* to become superficial

ver|äu|ßern *ptp* **veräußert** VT *(form: = verkaufen)* to dispose of; *Rechte, Land* to alienate *(form)*

Ver|äu|ße|rung F *(form)* disposal; *(von Rechten, Land)* alienation *(form)*

Ver|äu|ße|rungs|ge|winn M *(Fin)* gain on sale *or* disposal, capital gain

Verb [vɛrp] NT -s, -en [-bn] verb

ver|bal [vɛr'ba:l] ADJ verbal *(auch Gram)* ADV verbally

Ver|bal|in|ju|rie [vɛr'ba:lɪnju:riə] F *(Jur)* verbal injury

ver|ball|hor|nen [fɛɐ̯'balhɔrnən] *ptp* **verballhornt** VT to parody; *(unabsichtlich)* to get wrong

Ver|ball|hor|nung F -, -en parody; *(unabsichtlich)* ≈ spoonerism

Ver|band [fɛɐ̯'bant] M -(e)s, ¨-e [-'bɛndə] **a** *(Med)* dressing; *(mit Binden)* bandage **b** *(= Bund)* association **c** *(Mil)* unit; **im ~ fliegen** to fly in formation **d** *(Archit)* bond

ver|ban|deln [fɛɐ̯'bandln] *ptp* **verbandelt** VI *(inf)* to get together *(inf)*; **miteinander verbandelt sein** to be an item *(inf)*; **er ist jetzt mit der Dagmar verbandelt** he's now going out with Dagmar

Ve|rband|sfunk|ti|o|när(in) M(F) association official

Ver|band(s)-: **Ver|band(s)|kas|ten** M first-aid box; **Ver|band(s)|ma|te|ri|al** NT dressing material; **Ver|band(s)|päck|chen** NT gauze bandage; **Ver|band(s)|stoff** M dressing; **Ver|band(s)|wat|te** F surgical cotton wool *(Brit)*, absorbent cotton *(US)*, cotton batting *(US)*; **Ver|band(s)|zeug** NT *pl* **-zeuge** dressing material

ver|ban|nen *ptp* **verbannt** VT to banish *(auch fig)*, to exile (*aus* from, *auf* to)

Ver|bann|te(r) [fɛɐ̯'bantə] MF *decl as adj* exile

Ver|ban|nung [fɛɐ̯'banʊŋ] F -, -en banishment *no art*, exile *no art*; *(= das Verbannen)* banishment, exiling

Ver|ban|nungs|ort M *pl* **-orte** place of exile

ver|bar|ri|ka|die|ren *ptp* **verbarrikadiert** VT to barricade VR to barricade oneself in (*in etw (dat)* sth)

ver|ba|seln [fɛɐ̯'ba:zln] *ptp* **verbaselt** VT *(dial)* to mislay; *Termin, Verabredung* to forget

ver|bau|en *ptp* **verbaut** VT **a** *(= versperren)* to obstruct, to block; **sich** *(dat)* **alle Chancen/die Zukunft ~** to spoil one's chances/one's prospects for the future; **jdm die Möglichkeit ~, etw zu tun** to ruin *or* spoil sb's chances of doing sth **b** *(= verbrauchen) Holz etc* to use in building; *Geld* to use for building **c** *(= schlecht bauen)* to construct badly **d** *(inf: = verderben) Text, Arbeit etc* to botch *(inf)*

ver|be|am|ten [fɛɐ̯bə'lamtn] *ptp* **verbeamtet** VT to give the status of civil servant to

Ver|be|am|tung F appointment as a civil servant; **~ auf Lebenszeit** bestowing of the status of civil servant for life

ver|bei|ßen *ptp* **verbissen** *irreg* VT *(fig inf)* **sich** *(dat)* **etw ~** *(Zorn etc)* to stifle sth, to suppress sth; *Bemerkung* to bite back sth; *Schmerz* to hide sth; **sich** *(dat)* **das Lachen ~** to keep a straight face VR **sich in etw** *(acc)* **~** *(lit)* to bite into sth; *(Hund)* to sink its teeth into sth; *(fig)* to become set *or* fixed on sth → *auch* **verbissen**

ver|ber|gen *ptp* **verborgen** [fɛɐ̯'bɔrgn] *irreg* VT (*+dat, vor +dat* from) *(lit, fig)* to hide, to conceal; *(vor der Polizei auch)* to harbour *(Brit)*, to harbor *(US)*; *(Comput) Fenster etc* to hide; **sein Gesicht in den Händen ~** to bury one's face in one's hands; **jdm etw ~** *(= verheimlichen)* to keep sth from sb VR to hide (oneself), to conceal oneself → *auch* **verborgen**

ver|bes|sern *ptp* **verbessert** VT **a** *(= besser machen)* to improve; *Leistung, Bestzeit, Rekord* to improve (up)on, to better; *die Welt* to reform; **eine neue, verbesserte Auflage** a new revised edition **b** *(= korrigieren)* to correct VR **a** *(Lage etc)* to improve, to get better; *(Mensch) (in Leistungen)* to improve, to do better; *(beruflich, finanziell)* to better oneself; **sich (notenmäßig) ~** *(Sch)* to improve one's grade *or* mark **b** *(= sich korrigieren)* to correct oneself

Ver|bes|se|rung F -, -en **a** improvement *(von* in); *(von Leistung, Bestzeit)* improvement *(von* on); *(von Buch)* revision; *(= berufliche, finanzielle Verbesserung)* betterment **b** *(= Berichtigung)* correction

Ver|bes|se|rungs-: **ver|bes|se|rungs|be|dürf|tig** ADJ *pred* in need of improvement; **ver|bes|se|rungs|fä|hig** ADJ capable of improvement; **Ver|bes|se|rungs|vor|schlag** M suggestion for improvement; **ver|bes|se|rungs|wür|dig** ADJ *pred* in need of improvement *pred*

ver|beu|gen *ptp* **verbeugt** VR to bow *(vor +dat* to)

Ver|beu|gung F bow; **eine ~ vor jdm machen** to (make a) bow to sb

ver|beu|len *ptp* **verbeult** VT to dent

ver|bie|gen *ptp* **verbogen** *irreg* VT to bend (out of shape); *(fig) Idee, Wahrheit* to distort; *Mensch* to corrupt; **verbogen** bent; *Rückgrat* curved; *(fig)* twisted, warped VR to bend; *(Holz)* to warp; *(Metall)* to buckle

ver|bies|tern [fɛɐ'bi:stɐn] *ptp* **verbiestert** *(inf)* VT *(= verstören)* to throw *(inf)*; *(= störrisch machen)* to make pig-headed *(inf)* VR **sich in etw** *(acc)* **~** to become fixed on sth

ver|bies|tert [fɛɐ'bi:stɐt] ADJ *(inf) (= missmutig)* crotchety *(inf)*; *(= verstört)* disturbed *no adv*

ver|bie|ten ✪ 36.3, 37.4 *ptp* **verboten** *irreg* [fɛɐ'bo:tn] VT to forbid; *(amtlich auch)* to prohibit; *Zeitung, Partei, Organisation etc* to ban, to prohibit; **jdm ~, etw zu tun** to forbid sb to do sth; *(amtlich auch)* to prohibit sb from doing sth; **jdm das Rauchen/den Zutritt/den Gebrauch von etw ~** to forbid sb to smoke/to enter/the use of sth; *(amtlich auch)* to prohibit sb from smoking/entering/using sth; **mein Taktgefühl/die Höflichkeit verbietet mir eine derartige Bemerkung** tact/politeness prevents me from making such a remark VR **das verbietet sich von selbst** that has to be ruled out → *auch* **verboten**

ver|bil|den *ptp* **verbildet** VT *(fig) jdn* to bring up badly, to miseducate; *Geschmack, Charakter* to spoil, to deform

ver|bild|li|chen [fɛɐ'bɪldlɪçn] *ptp* **verbildlicht** VT = **veranschaulichen**

ver|bil|li|gen *ptp* **verbilligt** VT to reduce the cost of; *Kosten, Preis* to reduce; **verbilligte Waren** reduced goods; **verbilligte Karten** tickets at reduced prices; **verbilligte Darlehen** reduced-rate loans; **etw verbilligt abgeben** to sell sth at a reduced price VR to get *or* become cheaper; *(Kosten, Preise auch)* to go down

ver|bim|sen *ptp* **verbimst** VT *(inf)* to bash up *(inf)*

ver|bin|den ✪ 27 *ptp* **verbunden** *irreg* [fɛɐ'bʊndn] VT **a** *(Med)* to dress; *(mit Binden)* to bandage; **jdm die Augen ~** to blindfold sb; **mit verbundenen Augen** blindfold(ed)

b *(= verknüpfen, in Kontakt bringen) (lit, fig)* to connect, to link; *Punkte* to join (up)

c *(Telec)* **jdn (mit jdm) ~** to put sb through (to sb); **ich verbinde!** I'll put you through, I'll connect you; **(Sie sind hier leider) falsch verbunden!** (I'm sorry, you've got the) wrong number!; **mit wem bin ich verbunden?** who am I speaking to?

d *(= gleichzeitig haben or tun, anschließen)* to combine

e *(= assoziieren)* to associate

f *(= mit sich bringen)* **mit etw verbunden sein** to involve sth; **die damit verbundenen Kosten/Gefahren** *etc* the costs/dangers *etc* involved

g *(emotional) Menschen* to unite, to join together; **freundschaftlich/in Liebe verbunden sein** *(geh)* to be united *or* joined together in friendship/love

VR **a** *(= zusammenkommen)* to combine *(auch Chem)* *(mit* with, *zu* to form), to join (together); *(= sich zusammentun)* to join forces; **sich ehelich/in Liebe/Freundschaft ~** *(geh)* to join together in marriage/love/friendship; **in ihrer Person ~ sich Klugheit und Schönheit** she combines both intelligence and beauty

b *(= assoziiert werden)* to be associated; *(= hervorgerufen werden)* to be evoked *(mit* by)

VI *(emotional)* to form a bond

ver|bind|lich [fɛɐ'bɪntlɪç] ✪ 47.3, 48.3 ADJ **a** obliging; **~sten Dank!** *(form)* thank you kindly!, I/we thank you! **b** *(= verpflichtend)* obligatory, compulsory; *Regelung, Zusage* binding; *(= verlässlich) Auskunft* reliable ADV **a** *(= bindend)* **etw ~ vereinbart haben** to have a binding agreement (regarding sth); **etw ~ reservieren** to make a confirmed reservation for sth; **etw ~ erklären** to officially state sth; **~ zusagen** to accept definitely **b** *(= freundlich)* **~ lächeln** to give a friendly smile; **etwas ~er auftreten** to act a little more friendly

Ver|bind|lich|keit F -, -en **a** *(= Entgegenkommen)* obliging ways *pl*; *(= höfliche Redensart)* civility *usu pl*, courtesy *usu pl*, polite word(s *pl*) **b** *no pl (= verpflichtender Charakter)* obligatory *or* compulsory nature; *(von Regelung, Zusage)* binding nature; *(= Verlässlichkeit: von Auskunft)* reliability; **von absoluter ~** completely compulsory/absolutely binding **c Verbindlichkeiten** PL *(Comm, Jur)* obligations *pl*, commitments *pl*; *(finanziell auch)* liabilities *pl*; **seine ~en erfüllen** to fulfil one's obligations *or* commitments; to meet one's liabilities; **~en gegen jdn haben** to have (financial) commitments to sb

Ver|bin|dung ✪ 27.7, 46.4 F **a** connection; *(= Kontakt)* contact *(zu, mit* with); **in ~ mit** *(= zusammen mit)* in conjunction with; *(= im Zusammenhang mit)* in connection with; **jdn/etw mit etw in ~ bringen** to connect sb/sth with sth; *(= assoziieren)* to associate sb/sth with sth; **er/sein Name wurde mit dem Mord/der Affäre in ~ gebracht** he/his name was mentioned in connection with the murder/the affair; **seine ~en spielen lassen** to use one's connections, to pull a few strings *(inf)*; **~en anknüpfen** *or* **aufnehmen** to get contacts; **~ mit jdm aufnehmen** to contact sb; **die ~ aufrechterhalten** to maintain contact; *(esp zwischen Freunden)* to keep in touch *or* contact; **mit jdm in ~ bleiben** to stay in touch *or* contact with sb; **neue ~ erstellen** *(Comput: Option)* make new connection; **sich (mit jdm) in ~ setzen, (mit jdm) in ~ treten** to get in touch *or* contact (with sb), to contact sb; **mit jdm in ~ stehen, mit jdm ~ haben** to be in touch *or* contact with sb; **mit etw in ~ stehen** to be connected with sth

b *(= Verkehrsverbindung)* connection *(nach* to); **die ~ von Berlin nach Warschau** the connections *pl* from Berlin to Warsaw; **es besteht direkte ~ nach München** there is a direct connection to Munich

c *(Telec: = Anschluss)* line; **telefonische ~** telephonic communication; **~ durch Funk** radio communication; **eine ~ (zu einem Ort) bekommen** to get through (to a place); **die ~ ist sehr schlecht** the line is very poor; **unsere ~ wurde unterbrochen** we were cut off; **eine ~ zwischen zwei Rechnern aufbauen** *or* **herstellen** *(Comput)* to connect two computers

d *(Mil)* contact; *(durch Funk etc)* communication; *(= Zusammenarbeit)* liaison; **~ aufnehmen** to make contact, to establish communication

e *(= Kombination)* combination

f *(= Vereinigung, Bündnis)* association; *(ehelich)* union; *(Univ)* society; *(für Männer auch)* ≈ fraternity *(US)*; *(für Frauen auch)* ≈ sorority *(US)*; **eine ~ mit jdm eingehen** to join together with sb; **eine schlagende/nicht schlagende ~** *(Univ)* a duelling *(Brit) or* dueling *(US)*/nonduelling *(Brit) or* nondueling *(US)* fraternity

g *(Chem) (= Prozess)* combination; *(= Ergebnis)* compound *(aus* (formed out) of); **eine ~ mit etw eingehen** to form a compound with sth, to combine with sth

Ver|bin|dungs- *in cpds (esp Tech, Archit)* connecting; **Ver|bin|dungs|ab|bruch** M *(Telec, Comput)* disconnection; **Ver|bin|dungs|auf|bau** M *(Telec, Comput)* connecting; **Ver|bin|dungs|frau** F → **Verbindungsmann**; **Ver|bin|dungs|haus** NT *house belonging to a student society which provides members with accommodation and is used as a meeting-place*, ≈ fraternity house *(US)*; **Ver|bin|dungs|mann** M *pl* **-leute** *or* **-männer** intermediary; *(= Agent)* contact; **Ver|bin|dungs|of|fi|zier(in)** M(F) liaison officer; **Ver|bin|dungs|stel|le** F *(von Gleisen, Kabeln)* junction (point); *(von Rohren, Geklebtem etc)* join; *(Amt)* liaison office; **Ver|bin|dungs|stra|ße** F connecting road; **Ver|bin|dungs|stück** NT connecting piece; **Ver|bin|dungs|stu|dent** M ≈ member of a fraternity *(US), member of a society of male university or college students*; **Ver|bin|dungs|stu|den|tin** F ≈ member of a sorority *(US), member of a society of female university or college students*; **Ver|bin|dungs|tür** F connecting door

Ver|biss M *(Hunt)* biting off of young shoots

ver|bis|sen [fɛɐ'bɪsn] ADJ *Arbeiter* dogged, determined; *Kampf* dogged; *Gesicht, Miene* determined; *Hartnäckigkeit* grim ADV determinedly; *kämpfen* doggedly; **du solltest das nicht so ~ sehen** you shouldn't take things so seriously → *auch* **verbeißen**

Ver|bis|sen|heit F -, *no pl (von Arbeiter, Kampf)* doggedness; *(von Gesicht, Miene)* determination

ver|bit|ten *ptp* **verbeten** [fɛɐ'be:tn] VT *irreg* **sich** *(dat)* **etw (schwer** *or* **sehr** *etc*) **~** to refuse (absolutely) to tolerate sth; **das verbitte ich mir!, das will ich mir verbeten haben!** I won't have it!

ver|bit|tern [fɛɐ'bɪtɐn] *ptp* **verbittert** VT to embitter, to make bitter; **jdm das Leben ~** to make sb's life a misery VI *aux sein* to become embittered *or* bitter

ver|bit|tert [fɛɐ'bɪtɐt] ADJ embittered, bitter ADV bitterly; **sich ~ verhalten** to act embittered *or* bitter

Ver|bit|te|rung F -, *(rare)* **-en** bitterness, embitterment

ver|bla|sen ADJ *(pej: = verschwommen, unklar)* woolly *(Brit)*, wooly *(US)*, vague

ver|blas|sen [fɛɐ'blasn] *ptp* **verblasst** VI *aux sein (lit, fig)* to fade; *(Mond)* to pale; **alles andere verblasst daneben** *(fig)* everything else pales into insignificance beside it

ver|bläu|en [fɛɐ'blɔyən] *ptp* **verbläut** VT *(inf)* to bash up *(inf)*

Ver|bleib [fɛɐ'blaip] M **-(e)s** [-bəs], *no pl (form)* whereabouts *pl*

ver|blei|ben *ptp* **verblieben** [fɛɐ'bli:bn] VI *irreg aux sein* to remain; **etw verbleibt jdm** sb has sth left; **... verbleibe ich Ihr ...** *(form)* ... I remain, Yours sincerely *(Brit) or* Sincerely (yours) *(US)* ...; **wir sind so verblieben, dass wir ...** we agreed *or* arranged to ..., it was agreed *or* arranged that we ...; **sein Verbleiben in dieser Position ist unmöglich geworden** it has become impossible for him to remain in this position

ver|blei|chen [fɛɐ'blaiçn] *pret* **verblich** [fɛɐ'blɪç], *ptp* **verblichen** [fɛɐ'blɪçn] VI *aux sein (lit, fig)* to fade; *(Mond)* to pale; *(liter: = sterben)* to pass away, to expire *(liter)*

ver|blei|en [fɛɐ'blaiən] *ptp* **verbleit** VT **a** *Benzin* to lead, to put a lead additive in **b** *(= mit Blei überziehen)* to lead-coat, to coat with lead

ver|bleit [fɛɐ'blait] ADJ *Benzin* leaded

ver|blen|den *ptp* **verblendet** VT **a** *(fig)* to blind; **verblendet sein** to be blind **b** *(Archit)* to face

Ver|blen|dung F **a** *(fig)* blindness **b** *(Archit)* facing

ver|bleu|en △ [fɛɐ'blɔyən] VT → **verbläuen**

ver|blich *pret von* **verbleichen**

ver|bli|chen *ptp von* **verbleichen**

Ver|bli|che|ne(r) [fɛɐ'blɪçənə] MF *decl as adj (liter)* deceased

ver|blö|den [fɛɐ'blø:dn] *ptp* **verblödet** VI *aux sein (inf)* to become a zombi(e) *(inf)*

Ver|blö|dung F -, *no pl (inf)* stupefaction; **diese Arbeit führt noch zu meiner völligen ~** this job will turn me into a zombi(e) *(inf)*; **die dauern-**

de Reklame führt noch zu unserer völligen ~ the long-term effect of advertising is to make us totally uncritical

ver|blüf|fen [fɛɐ'blʏfn] *ptp* **verblüfft** VT *(= erstaunen)* to stun, to amaze; *(= verwirren)* to baffle; **sich durch** *or* **von etw ~ lassen** to be taken in by sth

ver|blüf|fend [fɛɐ'blʏfnt] ADJ *(= erstaunlich)* amazing, astonishing, incredible ADV amazingly, incredibly; **~ gut Bescheid wissen** to be incredibly well informed; **eine ~ einfache Lösung** an incredibly simple solution

ver|blüfft [fɛɐ'blʏft] ADJ amazed; **sei nicht so ~!** don't look so amazed!; **~e Miene** astounded expression; **du hättest meine ~e Chefin sehen sollen** you should have seen how amazed my boss was ADV *aufsehen, schauen* perplexed; *sich umdrehen* in surprise; **~ reagieren** to be amazed

Ver|blüf|fung F -, *no pl (= Erstaunen)* amazement; *(= Verwirrung)* bafflement

ver|blü|hen *ptp* **verblüht** VI *aux sein (lit, fig)* to fade; **der Baum ist verblüht** the blossom has fallen from the tree; **sie sieht verblüht aus** her beauty has faded

ver|blümt [fɛɐ'bly:mt] ADJ oblique ADV **etw/sich ~ ausdrücken** to say sth/express oneself in a roundabout way

ver|blu|ten *ptp* **verblutet** VI *aux sein* to bleed to death VR *(fig)* to spend oneself

Ver|blu|tung F fatal haemorrhage *(Brit)* or hemorrhage *(US)*; *(= das Verbluten)* bleeding to death

ver|bo|cken *ptp* **verbockt** VT *(inf) (= verpfuschen)* to botch *(inf)*, to bungle *(inf)*; *(= anstellen)* to get up to *(inf)*

ver|bockt [fɛɐ'bɔkt] ADJ *(inf)* pig-headed *(inf)*; *Kind* headstrong

ver|boh|ren *ptp* **verbohrt** VR *(inf)* **sich in etw** *(acc)* **~** to become obsessed with sth; *(= unbedingt wollen)* to become (dead) set on sth *(inf)*

ver|bohrt [fɛɐ'bo:ɐt] ADJ *Haltung* stubborn, obstinate; *Politiker auch, Meinung* inflexible

Ver|bohrt|heit F -, *no pl* inflexibility

ver|bor|gen [fɛɐ'bɔrgn] *ptp* **verborgt** VT to lend out *(an +acc* to)

ver|bor|gen ADJ hidden; **etw ~ halten** to hide sth; **sich ~ halten** to hide; **im Verborgenen leben** to live hidden away; **so manches große Talent blüht im Verborgenen** great talents flourish in obscurity; **im Verborgenen wachsen/blühen** *(lit)* to grow/bloom in places hard to find; **im Verborgenen liegen** to be not yet known → *auch* **verbergen**

Ver|bor|gen|heit F -, *no pl* seclusion

Ver|bot [fɛɐ'bo:t] NT **-(e)s, -e** ban *(+gen* on); **er ging trotz meines ~s** he went even though I had forbidden him to do so; **trotz des ärztlichen ~es** against doctor's orders, in spite of doctor's orders; **gegen ein ~ verstoßen** to ignore a ban; **das ~ der Eltern, zu rauchen/einen Freund mitzubringen** the parents' ban on smoking/on bringing a friend; **ich bin gegen das ~ irgendeiner Partei/Zeitung** I'm opposed to a ban on *or* to banning any party/newspaper

ver|bo|ten [fɛɐ'bo:tn] ADJ forbidden; *(amtlich)* prohibited; *(= gesetzeswidrig) Handel* illegal; *Zeitung, Partei, Buch etc* banned; **jdm ist etw ~** sb is forbidden to do sth; **Rauchen/Parken ~** no smoking/parking; **er sah ~ aus** *(inf)* he was a real sight *(inf)* → *auch* **verbieten**

ver|bo|te|ner|wei|se [fɛɐ'bo:tnɐ'vaizə] ADV against orders; *(= gesetzeswidrig)* illegally; **er hat ~ geraucht** he smoked even though it was forbidden *or (amtlich)* prohibited

Ver|bots|schild NT *pl* **-schilder, Ver|bots|ta|fel** F *(allgemein)* notice *or* sign (prohibiting something); *(im Verkehr)* prohibition sign

ver|brä|men [fɛɐ'brɛ:mən] *ptp* **verbrämt** VT *(geh) Kleidungsstück* to trim; *(fig) Rede* to pad; *Wahrheit* to gloss over; *Kritik* to veil *(mit* in)

ver|bra|ten *ptp* **verbraten** VT *irreg* **a** *Fleisch etc* to overcook **b** *(inf: = verschwenden) Geld, Zeit, Energie* to fritter away, to squander; *(für* on) **c** *(inf: = äußern)* to come out with

Ver|brauch [fɛɐ'braux] M **-(e)s**, *no pl* consumption *(von, an +dat* of); *(von Geld)* expenditure; *(von Kräften)* drain *(von, an +dat* on); **im Winter ist der ~ an Kalorien/Energie höher** we use up more calories/energy in winter; **sparsam im ~** economical; **zum baldigen ~ bestimmt** to be used immediately; **der ~ von öffentlichen Geldern** public expenditure

ver|brau|chen *ptp* **verbraucht** VT **a** *(= aufbrauchen)* to use; *Benzin, Wasser, Nahrungsmittel etc* to consume, to use; *Energie, Strom etc* to consume; *Vorräte* to use up; **der Wagen verbraucht 10 Liter Benzin auf 100 km** the car does 10 kms to the litre *(Brit)* or liter *(US)*, ≈ the car does 24 miles to the gallon **b** *(= abnützen) Kräfte etc* to exhaust; *Kleidung etc* to wear out; **verbrauchte Luft** stale *or* stuffy air; **sie ist schon völlig verbraucht** she is already completely spent VR to wear oneself out

Ver|brau|cher [fɛɐ'brauxɐ] M **-s, -, Ver|brau|che|rin** [-ərɪn] F **-, -nen** consumer

Ver|brau|cher- *in cpds* consumer; **Ver|brau|cher|be|ra|tung** F consumer advice centre *(Brit)* or center *(US)*; **ver|brau|cher|feind|lich** ADJ anti-consumer; **~ sein** not to be in the interest of the consumer; **ver|brau|cher|freund|lich** ADJ consumer-friendly ADV **~ verpackt** in consumer-friendly packaging; **Ver|brau|cher|ge|nos|sen|schaft** F consumer cooperative

Ver|brau|che|rin [-ərɪn] F **-, -nen** consumer

Ver|brau|cher-: Ver|brau|cher|markt M hypermarket *(Brit)*, large supermarket; **Ver|brau|cher|preis** M consumer price; **Ver|brau|cher|schutz** M consumer protection; **Ver|brau|cher|ver|band** M consumer council; **Ver|brau|cher|zent|ra|le** F consumer advice centre *(Brit) or* center *(US)*

Ver|brauchs-: Ver|brauchs|gü|ter PL consumer goods *pl*; **Ver|brauchs|ma|te|ri|al** NT *(Comput etc)* consumables *pl*; **Ver|brauchs|steu|er** F excise

ver|bre|chen [fɛɐ'brɛçn] *ptp* **verbrochen** [fɛɐ'brɔçn] VT *irreg* **a** *Straftat, Greueltat* to commit; **etwas ~** to commit a crime **b** *(inf: = anstellen)* **etwas ~** to be up to something *(inf)*; **was habe ich denn jetzt schon wieder verbrochen?** what on earth have I done now? **c** *(hum inf) Gedicht, Kunstwerk, Übersetzung etc* to be the perpetrator of *(hum)*

Ver|bre|chen [fɛɐ'brɛçn] NT **-s, -** *(lit, fig)* crime *(gegen, an +dat* against)

Ver|bre|chens|be|kämp|fung F combating crime *no art*

Ver|bre|cher [fɛɐ'brɛçɐ] M **-s, -, Ver|bre|che|rin** [-ərɪn] F **-, -nen** criminal

Ver|bre|cher-: Ver|bre|cher|al|bum NT rogues' gallery *(hum)*; **Ver|bre|cher|ban|de** F gang of criminals; **Ver|bre|cher|ge|sicht** NT *(pej)* criminal face

Ver|bre|che|rin [-ərɪn] F **-, -nen** criminal

ver|bre|che|risch [fɛɐ'brɛçərɪʃ] ADJ criminal; **in ~er Absicht** with criminal intent ADV *verraten, im Stich lassen* vilely, villainously

Ver|bre|cher-: Ver|bre|cher|jagd F chase after a/the criminal/criminals; **Ver|bre|cher|kar|tei** F criminal records *pl*; **Ver|bre|cher|tum** [fɛɐ'brɛçetu:m] NT **-s**, *no pl* criminality; **Ver|bre|cher|vier|tel** NT *(pej inf)* shady part of town; **Ver|bre|cher|vi|sa|ge** F *(pej inf)* criminal face; **Ver|bre|cher|welt** F underworld

ver|brei|ten [fɛɐ'braitn] *ptp* **verbreitet** VT to spread; *Ideen, Lehre auch* to disseminate; *Zeitung* to distribute, to circulate; *(= ausstrahlen) Wärme* to radiate; *Licht* to shed; *Ruhe* to radiate; **eine (weit) verbreitete Ansicht** a widely *or* commonly held opinion; **eine verbreitete Zeitung** a newspaper with a large circulation *or* a wide distribution VR **a** *(= sich ausbreiten)* to spread **b sich über ein Thema ~** to expound on *or* hold forth on a subject

ver|brei|tern *ptp* **verbreitert** VT to widen VR to get wider, to widen out

Ver|brei|te|rung F **-, -en** widening

Ver|brei|tung [fɛɐ'braitʊŋ] F -, *no pl* spreading; *(von Lehre, Ideen auch)* dissemination; *(von Zeitung)* distribution, circulation

ver|brenn|bar ADJ combustible

ver|bren|nen *ptp* **verbrannt** [fɛɐ'brant] *irreg* VT **a** *(mit Feuer)* to burn; *Müll* to burn, to incinerate; *(= einäschern) Tote* to cremate; *(= verbrauchen) Gas, Kerzen* to burn; *Treibstoff, Kalorien* to burn, to use; **verbrannt** burned; **verbrannte Erde** *(fig)* scorched earth **b** *(= versengen)* to scorch; *Finger, Haut etc* to burn; *Haar* to singe; *(= verbrühen)* to scald; **sich** *(dat)* **die Zunge/den Mund ~** *(lit)* to burn one's tongue/mouth; **sich** *(dat)* **den Mund** *or* **Schnabel** *(inf)* **~** *(fig)* to open one's big mouth *(inf)* → **Finger**

VR to burn oneself; *(= sich verbrühen)* to scald oneself

VI *aux sein* to burn; *(Mensch, Tier)* to burn (to death); *(= niederbrennen: Haus etc)* to burn down; *(durch Sonne, Hitze)* to be scorched; **das Fleisch ~ lassen** to burn the meat; **alles verbrannte, alles war verbrannt** everything was destroyed in the fire

Ver|bren|nung [fɛɐ'brɛnʊŋ] F **-, -en a** *no pl (= das Verbrennen)* burning; *(von Müll)* burning, incineration; *(von Treibstoff)* combustion; *(von Leiche)* cremation **b** *(= Brandwunde)* burn; *(= Verbrühung)* scald; **starke/leichte ~en davontragen** to be badly/not seriously burned → **Grad**

Ver|bren|nungs-: Ver|bren|nungs|an|la|ge F incineration plant; **Ver|bren|nungs|kraft|ma|schi|ne** F internal combustion vehicle; **Ver|bren|nungs|mo|tor** M internal combustion engine; **Ver|bren|nungs|ofen** M furnace; *(für Müll)* incinerator; **Ver|bren|nungs|pro|dukt** NT waste product (of combustion); **Ver|bren|nungs|wär|me** F heat of combustion

ver|brie|fen [fɛɐ'bri:fn] *ptp* **verbrieft** VT to document; **verbriefte Rechte/Sicherheit** attested rights/security

ver|brin|gen *ptp* **verbracht** [fɛɐ'braxt] VT *irreg* **a** *Zeit etc* to spend; **eine tolle** *or* **fantastische Zeit ~** to have a fabulous *or* fab *(inf)* time **b** *(obs, Jur: = bringen)* to take

ver|brü|dern [fɛɐ'bry:dɐn] *ptp* **verbrüdert** VR to swear eternal friendship *(mit* to); *(politisch)* to ally oneself *(mit* to, with); **Menschen aller Rassen sollten sich ~** people of all races should be brothers

Ver|brü|de|rung F **-, -en** avowal of friendship; *(politisch)* alliance

ver|brü|hen *ptp* **verbrüht** VT to scald VR to scald oneself

Ver|brü|hung [fɛɐ'bry:ʊŋ] F **-, -en** *(no pl: = das Verbrühen)* scalding; *(= Wunde)* scald

ver|bu|chen *ptp* **verbucht** VT to enter (up) (in a/the book); **einen Betrag auf ein Konto ~** to credit a sum to an account; **einen Erfolg (für sich) ~** to notch up *or* chalk up a success *(inf)*; **etw für sich** *or* **auf sein Konto ~ können** *(fig)* to be able to credit oneself with sth

Ver|bu|chung F entering (up)

ver|bud|deln *ptp* **verbuddelt** VT *(inf)* to bury

Ver|bum ['vɛrbʊm] NT **-s, Verba** [-ba] *(geh)* verb

ver|bum|meln *ptp* **verbummelt** *(inf)* VT *(= verlieren)* to lose; *(= vertrödeln, vergeuden) Nachmittag, Wochenende, Zeit* to waste, to fritter away; *(= verpassen) Verabredung* to miss VI *aux sein* **a** *(= herunterkommen)* to go to seed **b** *(= faul werden)* to get lazy; **verbummelt sein** to be lazy

Ver|bund M **-(e)s**, *no pl (Econ)* combine; **im ~ arbeiten** to cooperate

Ver|bund|bau M *pl* **-bauten** composite (method of) building

ver|bun|den [fɛɐ̯ˈbʊndn] *ptp von* **verbinden** **ADJ** *(form: = dankbar)* **jdm (für etw) ~ sein** to be obliged to sb (for sth)

ver|bün|den [fɛɐ̯ˈbʏndn] *ptp* **verbündet** **VR** to ally oneself *(mit* to); *(Staaten)* to form an alliance; **alle haben sich gegen mich verbündet** everyone is against me, everyone has sided against me; **verbündet sein** to be allies, to be allied

Ver|bun|den|heit **F -,** *no pl (von Völkern)* solidarity; *(von Menschen) (mit Menschen, Natur)* closeness *(mit* to); *(mit Land, Tradition)* attachment *(mit* to); **in tiefer ~, ...** very affectionately yours, ...

Ver|bün|de|te(r) [fɛɐ̯ˈbʏndətə] **MF** *decl as adj* ally

Ver|bund-: **Ver|bund|fahr|aus|weis** **M** travel pass *(valid for all forms of public transport)*; **Ver|bund|glas** **NT** laminated glass; **Ver|bund|kar|te** **F** *(= Eintrittskarte)* integrated ticket; *(Mot)* travel pass *(valid for all forms of public transport)*; **Ver|bund|ma|te|ri|al** **NT** composite (material); **Ver|bund|netz** **NT** *(Elec)* (integrated) grid system; **Ver|bund|plat|te** **F** sandwich panel; **Ver|bund|stahl** **M** laminated steel; **Ver|bund|stoff** **M** composite (material); **Ver|bund|sys|tem** **NT** integrated system; **Ver|bund|wer|bung** **F** joint advertising; **Ver|bund|werk|stoff** **M** composite (material); **Ver|bund|wirt|schaft** **F** integrated economy

ver|bür|gen *ptp* **verbürgt** **VR** **sich für jdn/etw ~** to vouch for sb/sth; **ich will mich nicht dafür ~, dass das stimmt** I cannot guarantee that this is correct **VT** **a** *(= gewährleisten) Freiheit, Recht, Unterstützung* to guarantee; **ein verbürgtes Recht** an established right **b** *(Fin: = bürgen für) Kredit, Mietausfälle* to guarantee **c** *(= dokumentieren)* **eine verbürgte Nachricht** a confirmed report; **historisch verbürgt sein** to be historically documented; **dokumentarisch verbürgt sein** to be backed up by documentary evidence

ver|bür|ger|li|chen [fɛɐ̯ˈbʏrgəlɪçn] *ptp* **verbürgerlicht** **VI** *aux sein* to become bourgeois

ver|bü|ßen *ptp* **verbüßt** **VT** to serve

Ver|bü|ßung [fɛɐ̯ˈbyːsʊŋ] **F -,** *no pl* serving; **zur ~ einer Haftstrafe von zwei Jahren verurteilt werden** to be sentenced to serve two years in prison

ver|chro|men [fɛɐ̯ˈkroːmən] *ptp* **verchromt** **VT** to chromium-plate

Ver|chro|mung **F -, -en** chromium-plating

Ver|dacht [fɛɐ̯ˈdaxt] **M -(e)s, -e** *or* **⸚e** [-ˈdɛçtə] suspicion; *(hum: = Vermutung)* hunch; **jdn in** *or* **im ~ haben** to suspect sb; **im ~ stehen, etw getan zu haben** to be suspected of having done sth; **jdn in ~ bringen** to make sb look guilty; **den ~ auf jdn lenken** to throw *or* cast suspicion on sb; **jdn wegen ~s einer Sache** *(gen)* **festnehmen** to arrest sb on suspicion of sth; **(gegen jdn) ~ schöpfen** to become suspicious (of sb); **~ erregen** to arouse suspicion; **es besteht ~ auf Krebs** *(acc)* cancer is suspected; **bei ~ auf Krebs** in the case of suspected cancer; **etw auf ~ tun** *(inf)* to do sth on spec *(inf)*

ver|däch|tig [fɛɐ̯ˈdɛçtɪç] **ADJ** suspicious; *(= verdächtig aussehend)* suspicious-looking; **sich ~ machen** to arouse suspicion; **die drei ~en Personen** the three suspects; **einer Sache** *(gen)* **~ sein** to be suspected of sth **ADV** suspiciously; *schnell* unbelievably; **~ aussehen** to look suspicious

ver|däch|ti|gen [fɛɐ̯ˈdɛçtɪgn] *ptp* **verdächtigt** **VT** to suspect (*+gen* of); **ich will niemanden ~, aber ...** I don't want to cast suspicion on anyone, but ...; **er wird verdächtigt, gestohlen zu haben, er wird des Diebstahls verdächtigt** he is suspected of theft

Ver|däch|ti|ge(r) [fɛɐ̯ˈdɛçtɪgə] **MF** *decl as adj* suspect

Ver|däch|ti|gung **F -, -en** suspicion; **die ~ eines so integren Mannes käme mir nie in den Sinn** it would never occur to me to suspect a man of his integrity

Ver|dachts-: **Ver|dachts|grund** **M** grounds *pl* for suspicion; **Ver|dachts|mo|ment** **NT** suspicious circumstance

ver|dam|men [fɛɐ̯ˈdamən] *ptp* **verdammt** **VT** *(esp Rel: = verfluchen)* to damn; *(= verurteilen)* to condemn → *auch* **verdammt, Scheitern**

ver|dam|mens|wert **ADJ** damnable, despicable

Ver|damm|nis [fɛɐ̯ˈdamnɪs] **F -, -se** *(Rel)* damnation *no art*

ver|dammt [fɛɐ̯ˈdamt] *(inf)* **ADJ** damned *(inf)*, bloody *(Brit inf)*; **~er Mist!** sod it! *(Brit inf)*, screw it! *(esp US sl)*; **~e Scheiße!** *(sl)* shit! *(sl)* → *auch* **verdammen** **ADV** damn *(inf)*; **das tut ~ weh** that hurts like hell *(inf)*; **~ viel Geld** a hell of a lot of money *(inf)*; **mir gehts ~ gut** I'm on top of the world *(inf)*; **mir gehts ~ schlecht** I'm in a bad way **INTERJ** **~!** damn *or* blast (it) *(inf)*; **~ noch mal!** bloody hell *(Brit sl)*, damn it all *(inf)*; **du wirst dich ~ noch mal entschuldigen!** apologize, damn you! *(inf)*

Ver|damm|te(r) [fɛɐ̯ˈdamtə] **MF** *decl as adj (Rel)* **die ~n** the damned *pl*

Ver|dam|mung **F -, -en** condemnation; *(Rel)* damnation

ver|damp|fen *ptp* **verdampft** **VTI** *(vi: aux sein)* to vaporize; *(Cook)* to boil away

Ver|damp|fer **M** vaporizer

Ver|damp|fung [fɛɐ̯ˈdampfʊŋ] **F -, -en** vaporization

ver|dan|ken *ptp* **verdankt** **VT** **jdm etw ~** to owe sth to sb; **es ist jdm/einer Sache zu ~(, dass ...)** it is thanks *or* due to sb/sth (that ...); **das verdanke ich dir** *(iro)* I've got you to thank for that

Ver|dan|kung [fɛɐ̯ˈdaŋkʊŋ] **F -,** *no pl (Sw)* **unter ~ seiner Verdienste** grateful thanks for his contribution

ver|darb *pret von* **verderben**

ver|da|ten [fɛɐ̯ˈdaːtn] *ptp* **verdatet** **VT** **jdn ~** to store sb's details on computer

ver|dat|tert [fɛɐ̯ˈdatɐt] **ADJ ADV** *(inf: = verwirrt)* flabbergasted *(inf)*

ver|dau|en [fɛɐ̯ˈdauən] *ptp* **verdaut** **VT** *(lit, fig)* to digest **VI** *(Mensch)* to digest (one's food); *(Magen etc)* to digest the food

ver|dau|lich [fɛɐ̯ˈdaulɪç] **ADJ** *(lit, fig)* digestible; **leicht ~** easily digestible, easy to digest; **schwer ~** hard to digest

Ver|dau|lich|keit **F -,** *no pl* digestibility

Ver|dau|ung [fɛɐ̯ˈdauʊŋ] **F -, -en** digestion; **eine gute/schlechte ~ haben** to have good/poor digestion

Ver|dau|ungs-: **Ver|dau|ungs|ap|pa|rat** **M** digestive system; **Ver|dau|ungs|be|schwer|den** **PL** digestive trouble *sing*; **Ver|dau|ungs|ka|nal** **M** alimentary canal, digestive tract; **Ver|dau|ungs|or|gan** **NT** digestive organ; **Ver|dau|ungs|saft** **M** gastric juice; **Ver|dau|ungs|spa|zier|gang** **M** constitutional; **Ver|dau|ungs|stö|rung** **F** *usu pl* indigestion *no pl*; **Ver|dau|ungs|trakt** **M** digestive *or* alimentary tract

Ver|deck [fɛɐ̯ˈdɛk] **NT -(e)s, -e** **a** *(= Dach) (von Kutsche, Kinderwagen)* hood *(Brit)*, canopy; *(von Auto)* soft top, hood *(Brit)*; *(hart)* roof; *(von Flugzeug)* canopy **b** *(von Passagierdampfer)* sun deck; *(von Doppeldeckerbus)* open top deck

ver|de|cken *ptp* **verdeckt** **VT** to hide, to conceal; *(= zudecken)* to cover (up); *Sicht* to block; *(fig) Absichten, Widerspruch, Symptome* to conceal; *Unterschlagungen etc* to conceal, to cover up; **eine Wolke verdeckte die Sonne** a cloud hid *or* covered the sun; **sie verdeckte ihr Gesicht mit den Händen** she covered her face with her hands, she hid her face in her hands → **Karte**

ver|deckt [fɛɐ̯ˈdɛkt] **ADJ** concealed; *Widerspruch* hidden; *Ermittler, Einsatz* undercover **ADV** **~ agieren** to operate undercover; **~ ermitteln** to investigate undercover

ver|den|ken *ptp* **verdacht** [fɛɐ̯ˈdaxt] **VT** *irreg* **jdm etw ~** to hold sth against sb; **ich kann es ihm nicht ~(, dass er es getan hat)** I can't blame him (for doing it)

Ver|derb [fɛɐ̯ˈdɛrp] **M -(e)s** [-bəs], *no pl (geh: = Untergang)* ruin; **sein ~** his ruin, the ruin of him → **Gedeih**

ver|der|ben [fɛɐ̯ˈdɛrbn] *pret* **verdarb** [fɛɐ̯ˈdarp], *ptp* **verdorben** [fɛɐ̯ˈdɔrbn] **VT** to spoil; *Plan auch* to wreck; *(stärker)* to ruin; *Luft* to pollute; *jdn (moralisch)* to corrupt; *(sittlich)* to deprave, to corrupt; *(= verwöhnen)* to spoil; **jdm etw ~** *(Abend, Urlaub)* to spoil *or* ruin sth for sb; *Chancen, Leben, Witz* to ruin sth for sb; **sich** *(dat)* **das Leben ~** to ruin one's life; **sich** *(dat)* **den Magen ~** to give oneself an upset stomach; **sich** *(dat)* **den Appetit ~** to spoil one's appetite; **sich** *(dat)* **die Augen/Stimme/Lungen ~** to ruin *or* damage one's eyes *or* eyesight/voice/lungs; **die Preise ~** *(= verbilligen)* to force prices down; *(= verteuern)* to force prices up; **jdm das Geschäft ~** to damage sb's business; **jds Laune ~, jdm die Laune ~** to put sb in a bad mood; **jdm die Freude** *or* **den Spaß/die Lust an etw** *(dat)* **~** to spoil sb's enjoyment of sth; **es (sich** *dat***) mit jdm ~** to fall out with sb

VI *aux sein (Material)* to become spoiled/ruined; *(Nahrungsmittel)* to go off *(Brit) or* bad; *(Ernte)* to be ruined; *(Mensch)* to become depraved *or* corrupted; **da** *or* **daran ist nichts mehr zu ~** it *or* things couldn't get any worse; **an dem Kuchen/Hemd ist nichts mehr zu ~** the cake/shirt is absolutely ruined anyway → *auch* **verdorben**

Ver|der|ben [fɛɐ̯ˈdɛrbn] **NT -s,** *no pl* **a** *(= Untergang, Unglück)* undoing, ruin; **in sein ~ rennen** to be heading for disaster; **jdn ins ~ stürzen** to bring ruin *or* disaster (up)on sb **b** *(von Material)* spoiling, ruining; *(von Nahrungsmittel)* going off *(Brit) or* bad; *(von Luft, Wasser)* pollution

ver|derb|lich [fɛɐ̯ˈdɛrplɪç] **ADJ** pernicious; *Einfluss auch* corrupting; *Lebensmittel* perishable

Ver|derb|nis [fɛɐ̯ˈdɛrpnɪs] **F -,** *no pl* corruption, depravity; *(= Verderbtheit)* corruptness, depravity

ver|derbt [fɛɐ̯ˈdɛrpt] **ADJ** **a** *(dated: moralisch)* corrupt(ed), depraved **b** *(Typ)* corrupt

Ver|derbt|heit **F -,** *no pl (dated)* corruptness, depravity

ver|deut|li|chen [fɛɐ̯ˈdɔytlɪçn] *ptp* **verdeutlicht** **VT** to show clearly; *(= deutlicher machen)* to clarify, to elucidate; *(= erklären)* to explain; **er versuchte, seinen Standpunkt an einem Beispiel zu ~** he tried to clarify his position by means of an example; **sich** *(dat)* **etw ~** to think sth out for oneself; **etw besser/näher ~** to clarify sth further

Ver|deut|li|chung **F -, -en** clarification; **zur ~ seiner Absichten** in order to show his intentions clearly

ver|deut|schen [fɛɐ̯ˈdɔytʃn] *ptp* **verdeutscht** **VT** to translate into German; *(fig inf)* to translate (into normal language)

ver.di **F -,** *no pl abbr von* **vereinigte Dienstleistungsgewerkschaft** *trade union representing the service industries*

ver|dich|ten *ptp* **verdichtet** **VT** *(Phys)* to compress; *(fig: = komprimieren)* to condense; *Gefühle* to intensify, to heighten **VR** to thicken; *(Schneetreiben)* to worsen; *(Gas)* to become compressed; *(fig: = häufen)* to increase; *(Verdacht, Eindruck)* to deepen; **die Handlung verdichtet sich** the plot thickens; **der Verdacht verdichtet sich, dass ...** the suspicion that ... is growing; **es ~ sich die Hinweise, dass ...** there is growing evidence that ...; **mein Eindruck verdichtete sich zur Gewissheit** my impression hardened into certainty

Ver|dich|ter [fɛɐ̯ˈdɪçtɐ] **M -s, -** *(Tech)* compressor

Ver|dich|tung **F** **a** *(Phys)* compression; *(fig: = Komprimierung)* condensing; *(von Gefühlen)* intensification, heightening **b** *(= das Dichterwerden)* thickening; *(von Gas)* compression; *(= Häu-*

fung) increase (*+gen* in); *(von Verdacht, Eindruck)* deepening

ver|di|cken [fɛɐ'dɪkn] *ptp* **verdickt** VT to thicken; *Blut* to coagulate; *(= verbreitern)* to widen; *(= gelieren lassen)* to make set; *(= verstärken)* to strengthen VR to thicken; *(Gelee)* to set; *(Blut)* to coagulate; *(Milch)* to curdle; *(= weiter werden)* to become thicker; *(Rohr, Flasche)* to become wider, to widen out; *(= anschwellen)* to swell

Ver|di|ckung F -, -en *(= das Verdicken)* thickening; *(von Blut)* coagulation; *(von Gelee)* setting; *(von Milch)* curdling; *(von Rohr, Flasche)* widening; *(= Schwellung)* swelling; *(= Verstärkung)* strengthening; *(= verdickte Stelle)* bulge

ver|die|nen ✪ 38.2, 40.2, 46.2, 53.2 *ptp* **verdient** VT **a** *(= einnehmen)* to earn; *(= Gewinn machen)* to make; **sein Brot** *or* **seinen Unterhalt ~** to earn *or* make one's living; **er hat an dem Auto 500 Euro verdient** he made 500 euros on the car; **dabei ist nicht viel zu ~** there's not much money in that; **sich** *(dat)* **etw ~** to earn the money for sth; **sich** *(dat)* **das Studium ~** to pay for *or* finance one's own studies **b** *(fig) Lob, Strafe* to deserve; **sich** *(dat)* **etw (redlich) verdient haben** to deserve sth, to have earned sth; *Schläge auch* to have had sth coming to one *(inf)*; **er verdient es nicht anders/besser** he doesn't deserve anything else/any better; **eine Reform, die diesen Namen verdient** a reform which lives up to its name → *auch* **verdient**
VI to earn; *(= Gewinn machen)* to make (a profit) *(an +dat* on); **in dieser Familie ~ drei Personen** there are three wage earners in this family; **er verdient gut/besser** he earns a lot/more; **er verdient schlecht** he doesn't earn much; **am Krieg ~** to profit from war

Ver|die|ner [fɛɐ'diːnɐ] M -s, -, **Ver|die|ne|rin** [-ərɪn] F -, -nen wage earner; **der einzige ~** the sole breadwinner

Ver|dienst [fɛɐ'diːnst] M -(e)s, -e *(= Einkommen)* income, earnings *pl*; *(= Profit)* profit; **einen besseren ~ haben** to earn more

Ver|dienst NT -(e)s, -e **a** *(= Anspruch auf Anerkennung)* merit; *(= Dank)* credit; **es ist sein ~/das ~ der Wissenschaftler(, dass ...)** it is thanks to him/the scientists (that ...); **nach ~** on merit; **das ~ gebührt ihm allein** the credit is entirely his; **sich** *(dat)* **etw als** *or* **zum ~ anrechnen** to take the credit for sth
b *usu pl (= Leistung)* contribution; *(national)* service; **ihre ~e um die Wissenschaft** *or* **als Wissenschaftlerin** her services *or* contribution to science; **seine ~e um das Vaterland/die Stadt** his services to his country/town; **seine ~e um die Dichtung/den Weltfrieden** his contribution to poetry/world peace; **hohe ~e erwerben** to make a great contribution *(um* to); **er hat sich** *(dat)* **große ~e um das Vaterland erworben** he has rendered his country great service

Ver|dienst-: **Ver|dienst|ab|rech|nung** F salary statement; *(= Lohnstreifen)* pay slip; **Ver|dienst|adel** M ≈ life peerage; *(= Adlige)* ≈ life peers *pl*; **Ver|dienst|aus|fall** M loss of earnings; **Ver|dienst|aus|fall|ent|schä|di|gung** F compensation for loss of earnings; **Ver|dienst|be|schei|ni|gung** F certificate of earnings; **Ver|dienst|kreuz** NT *highest decoration awarded for military or other service*; **ver|dienst|lich** ADJ commendable; **Ver|dienst|mög|lich|keit** F opportunity for earning money; **Ver|dienst|or|den** M order of merit; **Ver|dienst|span|ne** F profit margin; **ver|dienst|voll** ADJ commendable

ver|dient [fɛɐ'diːnt] ADJ **a** *Lohn, Strafe* rightful; *Ruhe, Lob* well-deserved **b** *Wissenschaftler, Künstler, Politiker, Sportler* of outstanding merit; **sich um etw ~ machen** to render outstanding services to sth ADV *gewinnen, siegen* deservedly → *auch* **verdienen**

ver|dien|ter|ma|ßen [fɛɐ'diːntɐ'maːsn], **ver|dien|ter|wei|se** [fɛɐ'diːntɐ'vaizə] ADV deservedly

Ver|dikt [vɛr'dɪkt] NT -(e)s, -e *(geh)* verdict

ver|din|gen [fɛɐ'dɪŋən] *pret* **verdingte** [fɛɐ'dɪŋktə], *ptp* **verdungen** *or* **verdingt** [fɛɐ'dʊŋən, fɛɐ'dɪŋkt] *(old)* VT *jdn* to put into service *(bei* with); *Arbeit* to give VR **sich (bei jdm) ~** to enter service (with sb)

ver|ding|li|chen [fɛɐ'dɪŋlɪçn] *ptp* **verdinglicht** VT *(= konkretisieren)* to put into concrete terms, to concretize; *(Philos) Ideen* to reify; *Menschen* to objectify

Ver|ding|li|chung F -, *no pl* concretization; *(von Ideen)* reification; *(von Menschen)* objectification

ver|dirbt [fɛɐ'dɪrpt] *3. pers sing pres von* **verderben**

ver|dol|met|schen *ptp* **verdolmetscht** VT to interpret

ver|don|nern *ptp* **verdonnert** VT *(inf: zu Haft etc)* to sentence, to condemn *(zu* to); **jdn zu etw ~, jdn dazu ~, etw zu tun** to order sb to do sth as a punishment; **jdn zu einer Geldstrafe von ... ~** to fine sb ...; **jdn zu einer Gefängnisstrafe ~** to sentence sb to a term of imprisonment

ver|dop|peln *ptp* **verdoppelt** VT to double; *(fig) Anstrengung etc* to redouble VR to double

Ver|dop|pe|lung [fɛɐ'dɔpəlʊŋ] F -, -en, **Ver|dopp|lung** [fɛɐ'dɔplʊŋ] F -, -en doubling; *(von Anstrengung)* redoubling

ver|dor|ben [fɛɐ'dɔrbn] *ptp von* **verderben** ADJ **a** *Lebensmittel* bad, off *pred*; *Wasser, Luft* polluted; *Magen* upset **b** *Stimmung, Urlaub, Freude* spoiled, ruined **c** *(moralisch)* corrupt; *(sittlich)* depraved; *(= verzogen) Kind* spoiled

Ver|dor|ben|heit F -, *no pl* depravity

ver|dor|ren *ptp* **verdorrt** VI *aux sein* to wither

ver|dö|sen *ptp* **verdöst** VT *(inf)* to doze away

ver|drah|ten *ptp* **verdrahtet** VT to wire (up); **fest verdrahtet** *(Comput)* hard-wired

ver|drän|gen *ptp* **verdrängt** VT *jdn* to drive out; *Gegner auch* to oust; *(= ersetzen)* to supersede, to replace; *(Phys) Wasser, Luft* to displace; *(Met)* to drive; *(fig) Sorgen, Angst* to dispel, to drive away; *(Psych)* to repress, to suppress; **er hat sie aus seinem Herzen verdrängt** he has forced himself to forget her; **jdn aus dem Amt/von der Macht ~** to oust sb (from office/power); **das habe ich völlig verdrängt** *(hum: = vergessen)* it completely slipped my mind *(inf)*; **jdn/etw aus dem Bewusstsein ~** to repress *or* suppress all memory of sb/sth

Ver|drän|gung [fɛɐ'drɛŋʊŋ] F -, -en driving out; *(von Gegner auch)* ousting; *(= Ersetzung)* superseding, replacing; *(Phys)* displacement; *(Met)* driving; *(von Sorgen)* dispelling; *(Psych)* repression, suppression

Ver|drän|gungs|kampf M fight for survival

Ver|drän|gungs|wett|be|werb M fierce competition *no indef art*

ver|dre|cken [fɛɐ'drɛkn] *ptp* **verdreckt** VTI *(vi: aux sein) (inf)* to get dirty *or* filthy; **verdreckt** filthy (dirty)

ver|dre|hen *ptp* **verdreht** VT to twist; *Gelenk auch* to wrench; *(= anders einstellen) Radio, Regler, Lampe* to adjust; *(= verknacksen)* to sprain; *Hals* to crick; *Augen* to roll; *jds Worte, Tatsachen* to distort, to twist; **das Recht ~** to pervert the course of justice; **sich** *(dat)* **den Hals ~** *(fig inf)* to crane one's neck → **Kopf d**

ver|dreht [fɛɐ'dreːt] ADJ *(inf)* crazy *(inf)*; *Bericht* confused, garbled

Ver|dreht|heit F -, *no pl (inf)* craziness

Ver|dre|hung F twisting; *(von Worten, Tatsachen)* distortion; *(von Recht)* perversion

ver|drei|fa|chen [fɛɐ'draifaxn] *ptp* **verdreifacht** VTR to treble *(esp Brit)*, to triple

Ver|drei|fa|chung F -, -en trebling *(esp Brit)*, tripling

ver|dre|schen *ptp* **verdroschen** [fɛɐ'drɔʃn] VT *irreg (inf)* to beat up; *(als Strafe)* to thrash

ver|drie|ßen [fɛɐ'driːsn] *pret* **verdross** [fɛɐ'drɔs], *ptp* **verdrossen** [fɛɐ'drɔsn] VT *jdn* to irritate, to annoy; **sich** *(dat)* **den Abend durch etw nicht ~ lassen** not to let sth spoil one's evening; **lassen Sie es sich nicht ~!** don't be put off *or* worried by it → **verdrossen**

ver|drieß|lich [fɛɐ'driːslɪç] ADJ morose; *Arbeit, Angelegenheit* irksome

ver|dross *pret von* **verdrießen**

ver|dros|sen [fɛɐ'drɔsn] *ptp von* **verdrießen** ADJ *(= schlecht gelaunt)* morose; *(= unlustig) Mensch, Gesicht* unwilling, reluctant ADV *(= schlecht gelaunt)* morosely; *(= unlustig)* unwillingly, reluctantly

Ver|dros|sen|heit F -, *no pl (= schlechte Laune)* moroseness; *(= Lustlosigkeit)* unwillingness, reluctance; *(über Politik etc)* dissatisfaction *(über +acc* with); **mit ~ arbeiten** to work unwillingly *or* reluctantly

ver|dru|cken *ptp* **verdruckt** *(inf)* VR to make a misprint VT to misprint

ver|drü|cken *ptp* **verdrückt** VT **a** *(inf) Essen* to polish off *(inf)*; **der kann was ~** he's got some appetite *(inf)* **b** *Kleider* to crumple **c** *(dial: = zerdrücken)* to crush, to squash VR *(inf)* to beat it *(inf)*; **sich heimlich ~** to slip away (unnoticed)

ver|druckst [fɛɐ'drʊkst] ADJ *(inf: = zaghaft)* hesitant

Ver|drü|ckung [fɛɐ'drʏkʊŋ] F -, -en *(inf: = Bedrängnis)* distress; **in ~ geraten** *or* **kommen** to get into difficulties; **jdn in ~ bringen** to put sb under pressure

Ver|druss [fɛɐ'drʊs] M -es, -e frustration; **~ mit jdm haben** to get frustrated with sb; **zu jds ~** to sb's annoyance; **jdm ~ bereiten** to cause annoyance to sb; **etw jdm zum ~ tun** to do sth to spite sb

ver|duf|ten *ptp* **verduftet** VI *aux sein* **a** *(= seinen Duft verlieren)* to lose its smell; *(Parfüm)* to lose its scent; *(Tee, Kaffee)* to lose its aroma **b** *(inf: = verschwinden)* to beat it *(inf)*

ver|dum|men [fɛɐ'dʊmən] *ptp* **verdummt** VT **jdn ~** *(= für dumm verkaufen)* to make sb out to be stupid; *(= dumm machen)* to dull sb's mind VI *aux sein* to stultify, to become stultified

Ver|dum|mung F -, -en **a** *(= Verblödung)* dulling (of the mind) **b** *(= das Dummwerden)* stultification

ver|dun|gen *ptp von* **verdingen**

ver|dun|keln *ptp* **verdunkelt** VT to darken; *Bühne auch* to black out; *Farbe auch* to deepen, to make darker; *(im Krieg)* to black out; *(fig) Zusammenhänge, Motive etc* to obscure; *jds Glück* to cloud; *jds Ruf* to damage, to harm; **Tatbestände ~** to suppress evidence; **die Sonne ~** *(Mond)* to eclipse the sun; *(Wolken)* to obscure the sun VR to darken; *(Himmel auch)* to grow darker; *(Verstand)* to become dulled

Ver|dun|ke|lung [fɛɐ'dʊŋkəlʊŋ] F -, -en **a** *(= das Dunkelmachen)* darkening; *(von Bühne auch, im Krieg)* blacking out; *(fig)* obscuring; *(von Glück)* clouding; **die ~ nicht einhalten** not to keep to the blackout **b** *(= das Dunkelwerden)* darkening **c** *(inf) (= Vorhang)* curtain; *(= Jalousie)* blind *usu pl* **d** *(Jur)* suppression of evidence

Ver|dun|ke|lungs|ge|fahr F, *no pl (Jur)* danger of suppression of evidence

Ver|dunk|lung [fɛɐ'dʊŋklʊŋ] F -, -en = **Verdunkelung**

ver|dün|nen [fɛɐ'dʏnən] *ptp* **verdünnt** VT to thin (down); *(mit Wasser)* to water down; *Lösung* to dilute; *Gas* to rarefy; **den Teig mit Wasser ~** to add water to the dough; **verdünnte Luft** rarefied air VR *(Lösung)* to become diluted; *(Luft)* to become rarefied; *(Vegetation)* to become thinner; *(= schmaler werden)* to become thinner; *(Rohr)* to become narrower

Ver|dün|ner [fɛɐ'dʏnɐ] M -s, - thinner

ver|dün|ni|sie|ren [fɛɐdʏni'ziːrən] *ptp* **verdünnisiert** VR *(hum inf)* to beat a hasty retreat

Ver|dün|nung F -, -en **a** thinning; *(von Lösung)* dilution; *(mit Wasser)* watering down; *(von Luft)* rarefaction *(form)*; *(= Verengung)* narrowing **b** *(= Flüssigkeit zum Verdünnen)* thinner

Ver|dün|nungs|mit|tel NT thinner, thinning agent
ver|duns|ten *ptp* **verdunstet** VI *aux sein* to evaporate
Ver|duns|ter [fɛɐˈdʊnstɐ] M **-s, -** humidifier
Ver|duns|tung [fɛɐˈdʊnstʊŋ] F **-, -en** evaporation
Ver|duns|tungs|röhr|chen NT aromatherapy tube *(hung over radiator in order to allow contents to slowly evaporate)*
ver|durs|ten *ptp* **verdurstet** VI *aux sein* to die of thirst
ver|dus|seln [fɛɐˈdʊsln] *ptp* **verdusselt** VT *(inf)* **etw ~** to forget all about sth
ver|düs|tern [fɛɐˈdyːstɐn] *ptp* **verdüstert** VTR to darken
ver|dut|zen [fɛɐˈdʊtsn] *ptp* **verdutzt** VT *(inf)* to take aback, to nonplus; *(= verwirren)* to baffle
ver|dutzt [fɛɐˈdʊtst] ADJ ADV *(inf)* taken aback, nonplussed; *(= verwirrt)* baffled
Ver|dutzt|heit F **-,** *no pl (inf)* bafflement
ver|eb|ben [fɛɐˈlɛbn] *ptp* **verebbt** VI *aux sein* to subside
ver|edeln [fɛɐˈleːdln] *ptp* **veredelt** VT *Metalle, Erdöl* to refine; *Fasern* to finish; *(Bot)* to graft; *Boden, Geschmack* to improve; *jdn, Charakter* to ennoble
Ver|ede|lung [fɛɐˈleːdəlʊŋ] F **-, -en, Ver|ed|lung** [fɛɐˈleːdlʊŋ] F **-, -en** *(von Metallen, Erdöl)* refining; *(von Fasern)* finishing; *(Bot)* grafting; *(von Boden, Geschmack)* improving; *(von Mensch, Charakter)* ennoblement
ver|ehe|li|chen *ptp* **verehelicht** VR *(form)* **sich (mit jdm) ~** to marry (sb)
ver|ehe|licht [fɛɐˈleːəlɪçt] ADJ *(form)* married; **Eva Schmidt, ~e Meier** Eva Meier née Schmidt; **seine Verehelichte** his wife
Ver|ehe|li|chung [fɛɐˈleːəlɪçʊŋ] F **-, -en** *(form)* marriage
ver|eh|ren *ptp* **verehrt** VT **a** *(= hoch achten)* to admire; *Gott, Maria, Heiligen* to honour; *(= ehrerbietig lieben)* to worship, to adore → *auch* **verehrt b** *(= schenken)* **jdm etw ~** to give sb sth
Ver|eh|rer [fɛɐˈleːrɐ] M **-s, -, Ver|eh|re|rin** [-ərɪn] F **-, -nen** admirer
ver|ehrt [fɛɐˈleːɐt] ADJ *(in Anrede)* **(sehr) ~e Anwesende/Gäste/~es Publikum** Ladies and Gentlemen; **(sehr) ~e gnädige Frau** *(in Brief)* (dear) Madam; **mein Verehrtester** *(iro, form)* (my) dear Sir; **meine Verehrteste** *(iro, form)* (my) dear Madam → *auch* **verehren**
Ver|eh|rung F *(= Hochachtung)* admiration; *(von Heiligen)* worship; *(= Liebe)* adoration
ver|eh|rungs-: ver|eh|rungs|voll ADV *(geh)* reverentially, in reverence; **ver|eh|rungs|wür|dig** ADJ *(geh) Mensch, Güte* commendable, praiseworthy; *Künstlerin* admirable
ver|ei|di|gen [fɛɐˈlaidɪgn] *ptp* **vereidigt, ver|ei|den** [fɛɐˈlaidn] *ptp* **vereidet** *(dated)* VT to swear in; **jdn auf etw** *(acc)* **~** to make *or* have sb swear on sth; **vereidigter Übersetzer** *etc* sworn translator *etc*
Ver|ei|di|gung F **-, -en** swearing in
Ver|ein [fɛɐˈlain] M **-(e)s, -e** organization; *(= esp Tierverein, Landschaftsschutzverein etc auch)* society; *(kulturell auch)* association; *(= Sportverein)* club; *(inf)* crowd; **ein wohltätiger ~** a charity; **eingetragener ~** registered society *or (wohltätig)* charity; **im ~ mit** in conjunction with; **im ~ rufen** to shout *or* chant in unison; **ihr seid vielleicht ein ~!** *(inf)* what a bunch you are! *(inf)* → **gemeinnützig**
ver|ein|bar ADJ compatible; *Aussagen* consistent; **nicht (miteinander) ~** incompatible; *Aussagen* inconsistent; **eine mit meinem Gewissen nicht ~e Tat** a deed which I cannot reconcile with my conscience
ver|ein|ba|ren [fɛɐˈlainbaːrən] ✪ 53.4 *ptp* **vereinbart** VT **a** *(= miteinander absprechen)* to agree; *Zeit, Treffen, Tag* to arrange; **(es) ~, dass ...** to agree/arrange that ... **b etw mit etw ~** to reconcile sth with sth; **Arbeit und Familie miteinander ~** to reconcile the demands of work and family; **sich mit etw ~ lassen** to be compatible with sth; **mit etw zu ~ sein** to be compatible with sth; *(Aussagen)* to be consistent with sth; *(Ziele, Ideale)* to be reconcilable with sth
Ver|ein|bar|keit [fɛɐˈlainbaːɐkait] F **-,** *no pl* compatibility; *(von Aussagen)* consistency
Ver|ein|ba|rung F **-, -en** *(= das Vereinbaren)* agreeing; *(von Zeit, Treffen, Tag)* arranging, arrangement; *(= Abmachung)* agreement; **laut ~** as agreed; **nach ~** by arrangement
ver|ein|ba|rungs|ge|mäß ADV as agreed
ver|ei|nen [fɛɐˈlainən] *ptp* **vereint** VT to unite; *(= miteinander vereinbaren) Ideen, Prinzipien* to reconcile; **eine Familie wieder ~** to reunite a family; **sich nicht mit etw ~ lassen** to be irreconcilable with sth; **sie vereint Tugend und Schönheit in sich** *(dat)* she combines virtue and beauty → *auch* **vereint** VR to join together; **in ihr ~ sich Schönheit und Tugend** she combines beauty and virtue
ver|ein|fa|chen [fɛɐˈlainfaxn] *ptp* **vereinfacht** VT to simplify; *(Math)* to reduce; **etw vereinfacht darstellen** to portray sth in simplified terms
Ver|ein|fa|chung F **-, -en** simplification; *(Math)* reduction
ver|ein|heit|li|chen [fɛɐˈlainhaitlɪçn] *ptp* **vereinheitlicht** VT to standardize
Ver|ein|heit|li|chung F **-, -en** standardization
ver|ei|ni|gen *ptp* **vereinigt** VT to unite; *Kräfte auch* to combine; *Eigenschaften* to bring together; *(Comm) Firmen* to merge (zu into); *Kapital* to pool; **etw mit etw ~** *(= vereinbaren)* to reconcile sth with sth; **Schönheit mit Intelligenz (in sich** *dat***) ~** to combine beauty with intelligence; **die beiden Standpunkte lassen sich nicht ~** the two points of view are incompatible; **in einer Hand vereinigt sein** to be held by the same person; **Freunde um sich ~** to gather friends around one; **alle Stimmen auf sich** *(acc)* **~** to collect all the votes
VR to unite; *(= sich verbünden auch)* to join forces; *(Firmen)* to merge; *(= zusammenkommen)* to combine; *(Töne)* to blend; *(Flüsse)* to meet; *(Zellen etc)* to fuse; *(= sich versammeln)* to assemble; *(geh: geschlechtlich)* to come together; **sich zu einem harmonischen Ganzen ~** to merge into a harmonious whole; **sich zu einer Koalition ~** to form a coalition
ver|ei|nigt ADJ united; **Vereinigtes Königreich** United Kingdom; **Vereinigte Staaten** United States; **Vereinigte Arabische Emirate** United Arab Emirates
Ver|ei|ni|gung F **a** *(= das Vereinigen)* uniting; *(von Kräften auch)* combining; *(von Eigenschaften)* bringing together; *(von Firmen)* merging; *(von Kapital)* pooling; *(Math, geh: = körperliche, eheliche Vereinigung)* union; **die deutsche ~** *(Pol)* German unification, the unification of Germany **b** *(= Organisation)* organization
Ver|ei|ni|gungs-: Ver|ei|ni|gungs|frei|heit F freedom of association; **Ver|ei|ni|gungs|kir|che** F *(= Mun-Sekte)* Unification Church; **Ver|ei|ni|gungs|kri|mi|na|li|tät** F *crime connected with the reunification of Germany*; **Ver|ei|ni|gungs|men|ge** F *(Math)* union *or* join of sets
ver|ein|nah|men [fɛɐˈlainnaːmən] *ptp* **vereinnahmt** VT *(form)* to take; **etw für sich ~** to claim sth for oneself; **jdn ~** *(fig)* to make demands on sb; *(Beruf)* to occupy sb; **sie versucht, ihn völlig zu ~** she wants him all to herself; **sich von jdm ~ lassen** to allow oneself to be monopolized by sb
Ver|ein|nah|mung F **-, -en** taking, collecting; *(fig)* monopolizing
ver|ein|sa|men [fɛɐˈlainzaːmən] *ptp* **vereinsamt** VI *aux sein* to become lonely *or* isolated; **vereinsamt sterben** to die lonely
Ver|ein|sa|mung F **-,** *no pl* loneliness, isolation
Ver|eins-: Ver|eins|far|be NT *usu pl* club colour *(Brit)*, club color *(US)*; **Ver|eins|haus** NT, **Ver|eins|heim** NT clubhouse; **ver|eins|in|tern** ADJ *Termin, Frage, Turnier* internal club *or* society ADV within a/the club *or* society; **Ver|eins|ka|me|rad(in)** M(F) fellow club member; **Ver|eins|lei|tung** F → **Verein a** *(= Amt)* chairmanship of an organization/a society/an association/a club **b** *(= Personen)* club *etc* committee; **Ver|eins|mei|er** [-maiɐ] M **-s, -, Ver|eins|mei|e|rin** [-ərɪn] F **-, -nen** *(inf)* club freak *(inf)*; **er ist ein richtiger ~** all he thinks about is his club; **Ver|eins|mei|e|rei** F **-,** *no pl (inf)* **seine ~ geht mir auf die Nerven** his obsession with his club is getting on my nerves; **diese ewige ~!** all this club nonsense!; **Ver|eins|meis|ter(in)** M(F) club champion; **Ver|eins|meis|ter|schaft** F club championship; **Ver|eins|mit|glied** NT club member; **Ver|eins|re|gis|ter** NT official register of societies and associations; **Ver|eins|sport** M club sport; **Ver|eins|we|sen** NT, *no pl* clubs, organizations and societies *pl*
ver|eint [fɛɐˈlaint] ADJ united; **Vereinte Nationen** United Nations *sing* ADV together, in unison; **~ rufen** to shout in unison; **~ handeln** to act together *or* as one → *auch* **vereinen**
ver|ein|zeln [fɛɐˈlaintsln] *ptp* **vereinzelt** VT *(Agr)* to thin (out)
ver|ein|zelt [fɛɐˈlaintslt] ADJ occasional; *(Met auch)* isolated; *Schauer auch* scattered; **die Faulheit ~er Schüler** the laziness of the occasional *or* odd pupil ADV occasionally; *(zeitlich auch)* now and then; *(örtlich auch)* here and there; **... ~ bewölkt** ... with cloudy patches
Ver|ein|ze|lung [fɛɐˈlaintsəlʊŋ] F **-, -en** *(von Menschen)* isolation; *(Agr)* thinning out
ver|ei|sen *ptp* **vereist** VT *(Med)* to freeze VI *aux sein* to freeze; *(Straße)* to freeze *or* ice over; *(Fensterscheibe)* to ice over; *(Tragfläche auch)* to ice up, to freeze over
ver|eist [fɛɐˈlaist] ADJ *Straßen, Fenster* icy; *Bäche* frozen; *Türschloss, Tragfläche, Piste* iced-up; *Land* covered in ice
Ver|ei|sung [fɛɐˈlaizʊŋ] F **-, -en a** *(Med)* freezing **b** *(= das Vereisen)* freezing; *(von Straße)* freezing *or* icing over; *(von Tragfläche)* icing (up)
ver|ei|teln [fɛɐˈlaitln] *ptp* **vereitelt** VT *Plan etc* to thwart, to foil; *Versuch auch* to frustrate; *Verbrechen, Attentat* to foil, to prevent
Ver|ei|te|lung [fɛɐˈlaitəlʊŋ] F **-, -en** thwarting, foiling; *(von Verbrechen)* prevention; *(von Versuch)* frustration
ver|ei|tern *ptp* **vereitert** VI *aux sein* to go septic; *(Wunde auch)* to fester; **vereitert sein** to be septic; **vereiterte Wunde** septic wound; **vereiterter Zahn** abscess; **vereiterte Mandeln haben** to have tonsillitis
Ver|ei|te|rung [fɛɐˈlaitərʊŋ] F **-, -en** sepsis; **~ der Wunde** septic wound; **~ des Zahns** dental sepsis; **~ der Mandeln** tonsillitis
Ver|eit|lung [fɛɐˈlaitlʊŋ] F **-, -en** = **Vereitelung**
ver|ekeln *ptp* **verekelt** VT *(inf)* **jdm etw ~** to put sb off sth *(inf)*
ver|elen|den [fɛɐˈleːlɛndn] *ptp* **verelendet** VI *aux sein* to become impoverished *or (Mensch auch)* destitute
Ver|elen|dung F **-, -en** impoverishment
ver|en|den *ptp* **verendet** VI *aux sein* to perish, to die
ver|en|gen [fɛɐˈlɛŋən] *ptp* **verengt** VR to narrow, to become narrow; *(Gefäße, Pupille)* to contract; *(Kleid, Taille)* to go in; *(fig: Horizont)* to narrow VT to make narrower; *Blutgefäß, Pupille etc* to make contract; *Kleid* to take in; *Horizont* to narrow
ver|en|gern [fɛɐˈlɛŋɐn] *ptp* **verengert** VT **a** *Kleidung* to take in **b** = **verengen VT** VR **a** *(Ärmel, Hose)* to go in; *(= spitz zulaufen)* to become narrower **b** = **verengen VR**
Ver|en|gung F **-, -en a** narrowing; *(von Pupille, Gefäß)* contraction **b** *(= verengte Stelle)* narrow part (in +*dat* of); *(in Adern)* stricture (in +*dat* of)
ver|erb|bar ADJ **a** *Anlagen, Krankheit* hereditary **b** *Besitz* heritable

ver|e̱r|ben *ptp* **vere̱rbt** VT **a** *Besitz* to leave, to bequeath (*+dat, an +acc* to); *(hum)* to hand on *(jdm* to sb), to bequeath *(jdm* sb) **b** *Anlagen, Eigenschaften* to pass on (*+dat, auf +acc* to); *Krankheit* to transmit VR to be passed on/transmitted *(auf +acc* to)

ver|e̱rb|lich [fɛɐ'lɛrplɪç] ADJ = **vererbbar**

Ver|e̱r|bung [fɛɐ'lɛrbʊŋ] F -, *no pl* **a** *(= das Vererben) (von Besitz)* leaving, bequeathing; *(von Anlagen)* passing on; *(von Krankheit)* transmission **b** *(Lehre)* heredity; **das ist ~** *(inf)* it's hereditary

Ver|e̱r|bungs-: **Ver|e̱r|bungs|for|schung** F genetics *sing*; **Ver|e̱r|bungs|leh|re** F genetics *sing*

ver|e̱wi|gen [fɛɐ'le:vɪgn] *ptp* **vere̱wigt** VT to immortalize; *Zustand, Verhältnisse* to perpetuate; **seine schmutzigen Finger auf der Buchseite ~** to leave one's dirty fingermarks on the page for posterity VR *(lit, fig)* to immortalize oneself

Verf. *abbr von* **Verfasser**

Ver|fa̱h|ren [fɛɐ'fa:rən] NT **-s, -** *(= Vorgehen)* actions *pl*; *(= Verfahrensweise)* procedure; *(Tech)* process; *(= Methode)* method; *(Jur)* proceedings *pl*; **ein ~ gegen jdn anhängig machen** *or* **einleiten** to take *or* initiate legal proceedings against sb

ver|fa̱h|ren [fɛɐ'fa:rən] *ptp* **verfahren** VI *irreg aux sein (= vorgehen)* to act, to proceed; **mit jdm/etw streng/schlecht ~** to deal strictly/badly with sb/sth

ver|fa̱h|ren *ptp* **verfa̱hren** *irreg* VT *(= verbrauchen) Geld, Zeit* to spend in travelling *(Brit) or* traveling *(US)*; *Benzin* to use up VR *(= sich verirren)* to lose one's way

ver|fa̱h|ren [fɛɐ'fa:rən] ADJ *Angelegenheit, Situation* muddled; **eine ~e Sache** a muddle

Ver|fa̱h|rens-: **Ver|fa̱h|rens|be|schleu|ni|gung** F speeding up the procedure; *(Jur)* speeding up the proceedings; **zur ~** to speed up the procedure; *(Jur)* to speed up the proceedings; **Ver|fa̱h|rens|dau|er** F length of the procedure; *(Jur)* length of the proceedings; **Ver|fa̱h|rens|feh|ler** M *(Jur)* procedural error; **Ver|fa̱h|rens|kos|ten** PL *(Jur)* procedural costs *pl*; **ver|fa̱h|rens|recht|lich** ADJ *(form)* procedural; **Ver|fa̱h|rens|tech|nik** F process engineering; **Ver|fa̱h|rens|wei|se** F procedure, modus operandi

Ver|fall M, *no pl* **a** *(= Zerfall)* decay; *(von Gebäude)* dilapidation; *(gesundheitlich, geistig)* decline; **etw dem ~ preisgeben** to let sth go to (rack and) ruin; **in ~ geraten** *(Gebäude)* to become dilapidated; *(stärker)* to fall into ruins **b** *(= Niedergang) (von Kultur, der Sitten, sittlich)* decline; *(des Römischen Reichs)* fall; *(von Reichtum, Vermögen)* fall *(von* in) **c** *(= das Ungültigwerden) (von Schuldansprüchen, Rechnung etc)* lapsing; *(von Scheck, Karte)* expiry

ver|fa̱l|len *ptp* **verfa̱llen** VI *irreg aux sein* **a** *(= zerfallen)* to decay; *(Bauwerk)* to fall into disrepair, to become dilapidated; *(Zellen)* to die; *(körperlich und geistig)* to deteriorate; *(Sitten, Kultur, Reich)* to decline; **der Patient verfällt zusehends** the patient has gone into a rapid decline **b** *(= ungültig werden) (Briefmarken, Geldscheine, Gutschein)* to become invalid; *(Scheck, Fahrkarte)* to expire; *(Strafe, Recht, Termin, Anspruch, Patent)* to lapse **c** *(= in jds Besitz übergehen)* to be forfeited; **jdm ~** to be forfeited to sb, to become the property of sb **d** *(= abhängig werden)* **jdm/einer Sache ~/~ sein** to become/be a slave to sb/sth; *dem Alkohol etc* to become/be addicted to sth; *dem Wahnsinn* to fall/have fallen victim to; *jds Zauber etc* to become/be enslaved by sth; **jdm völlig ~ sein** to be completely under sb's spell; **einem Irrtum ~** to make a mistake, to be mistaken **e auf etw** *(acc)* **~** to think of sth; *(aus Verzweiflung)* to resort to sth; **auf abstruse Gedanken ~** to start having abstruse thoughts; **wer ist denn bloß auf diesen Gedanken ~?** whoever thought this up?; **wie sind Sie bloß darauf ~?** whatever gave you that idea? **f in etw** *(acc)* **~** to sink into sth; **in einen tiefen Schlaf ~** to fall into a deep sleep; **in einen ganz anderen Ton ~** to adopt a completely different tone; **in einen Fehler ~** to make a mistake; **in Panik ~** to get into a panic

ver|fa̱l|len [fɛɐ'falən] ADJ *Gebäude* dilapidated, ruined; *Mensch (körperlich)* emaciated; *(geistig)* senile; *(= abgelaufen) Karten, Briefmarken* invalid; *Strafe* lapsed; *Scheck* expired

Ver|fa̱lls-: **Ver|fa̱lls|da|tum** NT expiry date; *(der Haltbarkeit)* best-before date, use-by date; **Ver|fa̱lls|er|schei|nung** F symptom of decline *(+gen* in); **Ver|fa̱lls|tag** M expiry date; *(von Strafe etc)* date of lapsing; **Ver|fa̱lls|ter|min** M expiry date; *(der Haltbarkeit)* best-before date, use-by date

ver|fä̱l|schen *ptp* **verfälscht** VT to distort; *Wahrheit, Aussage auch, Daten* to falsify; *Lebensmittel, Wein, Geschmack* to adulterate

Ver|fä̱l|schung F distortion; *(von Wahrheit, Aussage auch, von Daten)* falsification; *(von Lebensmitteln, Geschmack)* adulteration

ver|fa̱n|gen *ptp* **verfa̱ngen** *irreg* VR to get caught; **sich in Lügen ~** to get entangled in a web of lies; **sich in Widersprüchen ~** to contradict oneself VI to be accepted; *(Argument, Slogan)* to catch on; **bei jdm nicht ~** not to cut any ice with sb *(inf)*; **die Masche verfing** the trick worked; **dieser Trick verfängt bei mir nicht** that ploy won't work with me

ver|fä̱ng|lich [fɛɐ'fɛŋlɪç] ADJ *Situation* awkward, embarrassing; *Aussage, Beweismaterial, Blicke, Andeutungen* incriminating; *(= gefährlich)* dangerous; *Angewohnheit* insidious; *Frage* tricky

ver|fä̱r|ben *ptp* **verfä̱rbt** VT to discolour *(Brit)*, to discolor *(US)*; **etw rot ~** to turn sth red; **wenn der Herbst die Blätter verfärbt** when autumn *(esp Brit) or* fall *(US)* turns the leaves VR to change colour *(Brit) or* color *(US)*; *(Blätter auch)* to turn; *(Metall, Wäsche, Stoff)* to discolour *(Brit)*, to discolor *(US)*; **sich grün/rot ~** to turn *or* go green/red; **sie verfärbte sich** she went red/white

Ver|fä̱r|bung F change in colour *(Brit) or* color *(US)*; *(von Blättern auch)* turning; *(von Metall, Wäsche, Stoff)* discolouring *(Brit)*, discoloring *(US)*

ver|fa̱s|sen *ptp* **verfa̱sst** VT to write; *Gesetz, Urkunde* to draw up

Ver|fa̱s|ser [fɛɐ'fasɐ] M **-s, -**, **Ver|fa̱s|se|rin** [-ərɪn] F **-, -nen** writer; *(von Buch, Artikel etc auch)* author

Ver|fa̱s|ser|schaft [fɛɐ'fasɐʃaft] F -, *no pl* authorship

Ver|fa̱s|sung F **a** *(Pol)* constitution; **gegen die ~ handeln** to act unconstitutionally **b** *(körperlich)* state (of health); *(seelisch)* state of mind; **sie ist in guter/schlechter ~** she is in good/bad shape; **seine seelische ~ ist gut/schlecht** he is in good/poor spirits; **sie ist nicht in der ~ zu arbeiten** she is in no fit state *(Brit) or* in no shape to work **c** *(= Zustand)* state; **die Firma/Wirtschaft ist in guter ~** the company/economy is in good shape

ver|fa̱s|sung|ge|bend ADJ *attr Versammlung* constituent

Ver|fa̱s|sungs-: **Ver|fa̱s|sungs|än|de|rung** F constitutional amendment; **Ver|fa̱s|sungs|auf|trag** M **der ~ der Regierung** the governmental tasks resulting from the constitution; **im ~ handeln** to act according to the principles stated in the constitution; **Ver|fa̱s|sungs|be|schwer|de** F *complaint about infringement of the constitution*; **Ver|fa̱s|sungs|ent|wurf** M *draft of a/the constitution*; **Ver|fa̱s|sungs|feind(in)** M(F) enemy of the constitution *(being declared as such disbars sb from working in the public service)*; **ver|fa̱s|sungs|feind|lich** ADJ anticonstitutional; **ver|fa̱s|sungs|ge|mäß** ADJ ADV in accordance with the constitution; **Ver|fa̱s|sungs|ge|richt** NT, **Ver|fa̱s|sungs|ge|richts|hof** M constitutional court; **Oberstes ~** supreme constitutional court; *(in den USA)* Supreme Court; **Ver|fa̱s|sungs|kla|ge** F constitutional challenge; **ver|fa̱s|sungs|kon|form** ADJ in conformity with the constitution *pred (nachgestellt)*, constitutional *(US)*; **nicht ~** not in conformity with the constitution *pred (nachgestellt)*, unconstitutional *(US)*; **ver|fa̱s|sungs|mä|ßig** ADJ constitutional; **etw ~ garantieren** to guarantee sth in the constitution; **eine ~e Ordnung** a constitutional law; **Ver|fa̱s|sungs|recht** NT constitutional law; **Ver|fa̱s|sungs|rich|ter(in)** M(F) constitutional judge; **Ver|fa̱s|sungs|schutz** M *(Aufgabe)* defence *(Brit) or* defense *(US)* of the constitution; *(Organ, Amt) office responsible for defending the constitution*; **ver|fa̱s|sungs|treu** ADJ loyal to the constitution; **Ver|fa̱s|sungs|treue** F loyalty to the constitution; **Ver|fa̱s|sungs|ur|kun|de** F constitution, constitutional charter; **ver|fa̱s|sungs|wid|rig** ADJ unconstitutional; **Ver|fa̱s|sungs|wid|rig|keit** F unconstitutionality; **Ver|fa̱s|sungs|wirk|lich|keit** F constitutional reality

ver|fau̱|len *ptp* **verfau̱lt** VI *aux sein* to decay; *(Fleisch, Gemüse, Obst auch)* to rot; *(Körper, organische Stoffe)* to decompose; *(fig)* to degenerate

ver|fau̱lt [fɛɐ'fault] ADJ decayed; *Fleisch, Obst etc* rotten; *Zähne* bad, rotten; *Körper* decomposed; *Mensch (innerlich)* degenerate

ver|fe̱ch|ten *ptp* **verfo̱chten** [fɛɐ'fɔxtn] VT *irreg* to defend; *Lehre* to advocate, to champion; *Meinung* to maintain

Ver|fe̱ch|ter [fɛɐ'fɛçtɐ] M **-s, -**, **Ver|fe̱ch|te|rin** [-ərɪn] F **-, -nen** advocate, champion

Ver|fe̱ch|tung [fɛɐ'fɛçtʊŋ] F **-, -en** defence *(Brit)*, defense *(US)*; *(von Lehre)* advocacy, championing; *(von Meinung)* maintaining

ver|fe̱h|len *ptp* **verfe̱hlt** VT **a** *(= verpassen, nicht treffen)* to miss; **seine Worte hatten ihre Wirkung verfehlt/nicht verfehlt** his words had missed/hit their target; **den Zweck ~** not to achieve its purpose; **das Thema ~** to be completely off the subject **b** *(= versäumen)* **nicht ~, etw zu tun** not to fail to do sth

ver|fe̱hlt [fɛɐ'fe:lt] ADJ *(= unangebracht)* inappropriate; *(= misslungen) Leben, Angelegenheit, Planung, Politik* unsuccessful; **es ist ~, das zu tun** you are mistaken in doing that

Ver|fe̱h|lung [fɛɐ'fe:lʊŋ] F **-, -en a** *(des Ziels)* missing; **bei ~ des Themas bekommt der Schüler ...** if the essay is off the subject the pupil will get ... **b** *(= Vergehen)* misdemeanour *(Brit)*, misdemeanor *(US)*; *(= Sünde)* transgression

ver|fei̱n|den [fɛɐ'faindn] *ptp* **verfei̱ndet** VR to quarrel; **sich mit jdm ~** to make an enemy of sb; *mit Nachbarn* to quarrel with sb; **verfeindet sein** to have quarrelled *(Brit) or* quarreled *(US)*; *(Familie etc)* to be estranged; *(Staaten)* to be on bad terms; **die verfeindeten Schwestern** the estranged sisters; **die verfeindeten Staaten** the enemy states; **verfeindete Volksgruppen** rival ethnic groups VT **warum versucht sie, ihren Mann und seine Familie zu ~?** why is she trying to set her husband against his family?

ver|fei̱|nern [fɛɐ'fainɐn] *ptp* **verfei̱nert** VT to improve; *Methode, Geschmack auch* to refine VR to improve; *(Methoden auch)* to become refined

ver|fei̱|nert [fɛɐ'fainɐt] ADJ *Methode, Geräte, Essen* sophisticated

Ver|fei̱|ne|rung F **-, -en** improvement; *(von Methode auch)* refining; **die zunehmende ~ technischer Geräte** the increasing sophistication of technical equipment

ver|fe̱|men [fɛɐ'fe:mən] *ptp* **verfe̱mt** VT *(Hist)* to outlaw; *(fig) jdn* to ostracize; *Künstler, Ideologie, Methode, Kunstrichtung* to condemn

Ver|fe̱m|te(r) [fɛɐ'fe:mtə] MF *decl as adj (Hist)* outlaw; *(fig)* persona non grata

ver|fe̱r|ti|gen *ptp* **verfe̱rtigt** VT to manufacture, to produce; *Liste* to draw up; *(usu iro) Brief, Aufsatz* to compose

ver|fe̱s|ti|gen *ptp* **verfe̱stigt** VT to harden; *Flüssigkeit* to solidify; *(= verstärken)* to strengthen, to reinforce **VR** to harden; *(Flüssigkeit)* to solidify; *(fig) (Hass, Feindschaft)* to harden; *(Kenntnisse)* to be reinforced; *(Ideen, Gewohnheiten)* to become fixed *or* set; *(Demokratie, Strukturen)* to be strengthened *or* reinforced

ver|fet|ten *ptp* **verfettet** **VI** *aux sein (Med)* to become fat; *Mensch auch* to become obese; *(Herz, Leber)* to become fatty *or* adipose *(spec)*

Ver|fet|tung [fɛɐˈfɛtʊŋ] **F -, -en** *(Med) (von Körper)* obesity; *(von Organ, Muskeln)* fatty degeneration, adiposity *(spec)*

ver|feu|ern **verfeuert** **VT** to burn; *Munition* to fire; **die ganze Munition/das ganze Öl ~** to use up all the ammunition/oil

ver|fil|men *ptp* **verfilmt** **VT** *Buch, Geschichte* to make a film of

Ver|fil|mung [fɛɐˈfɪlmʊŋ] **F -, -en** *(= das Verfilmen)* filming; *(= Film)* film (version)

ver|fil|zen *ptp* **verfilzt** **VI** *aux sein (Wolle, Pullover, Teppich)* to become felted; *(Haare)* to become matted; *(fig: Pol etc)* to become corrupt **VR** to become matted

ver|filzt [fɛɐˈfɪltst] **ADJ** *Wolle, Pullover* felted; *Haare* matted

ver|fins|tern [fɛɐˈfɪnstɐn] *ptp* **verfinstert** **VT** to darken; *Sonne, Mond* to eclipse **VR** *(lit, fig)* to darken

Ver|fins|te|rung **F -, -en** darkening; *(von Sonne etc)* eclipse

ver|fit|zen [fɛɐˈfɪtsn] *ptp* **verfitzt** *(inf)* **VT** to tangle **VR** to become tangled

ver|fla|chen [fɛɐˈflaxn] *ptp* **verflacht** **VI** *aux sein* to flatten *or* level out; *(fig: Diskussion, Gespräch, Mensch)* to become superficial *or* trivial **VR** *(Gelände)* to flatten *or* level out

Ver|fla|chung **F -, -en** flattening out, levelling *(esp Brit) or* leveling *(US)* out; *(fig)* superficiality; **um einer ~ der Diskussion vorzubeugen** to stop the conversation becoming superficial *or* trivial

ver|flech|ten *ptp* **verflochten** [fɛɐˈflɔxtn] *irreg* **VT** to interweave, to intertwine; *Bänder* to interlace; *(auch fig) Methoden* to combine; *Firmen* to interlink; **eng mit etw verflochten sein** *(fig)* to be closely connected *or* linked with sth; **jdn in etw** *(acc)* **~** *(in Gespräch, Unternehmen)* to involve sb in sth; *in dunkle Geschäfte* to entangle *or* embroil sb in sth **VR** to interweave, to intertwine; *(Bänder)* to interlace; *(= sich verwirren)* to become entangled (*mit* in); *(Themen)* to interweave; *(Methoden)* to combine; **sich mit etw ~** to become linked *or* connected with sth

Ver|flech|tung [fɛɐˈflɛçtʊŋ] **F -, -en** **a** *(= das Verflechten)* interweaving, intertwining; *(von Bändern)* interlacing; *(in dunkle Geschäfte)* entanglement; *(von Methoden)* combining **b** *(= das Verflochtensein)* interconnection (*+gen* between); *(Pol, Econ)* integration

ver|fleckt [fɛɐˈflɛkt] **ADJ** *(inf)* stained

ver|flie|gen *ptp* **verflogen** [fɛɐˈflo:gn] *irreg* **VI** *aux sein* **a** *(fig) (Stimmung, Zorn etc)* to blow over *(inf)*, to pass; *(Heimweh, Kummer, Hoffnung etc)* to vanish **b** *(= sich verflüchtigen)* to vanish; *(Alkohol)* to evaporate; *(Duft)* to fade (away); *(Zeit)* to fly **VR** to stray; *(Pilot, Flugzeug)* to lose one's/its bearings

ver|flie|ßen *ptp* **verflossen** [fɛɐˈflɔsn] **VI** *irreg aux sein* **a** *(geh: = vergehen)* to go by, to pass → *auch* **verflossen** **b** *(= verschwimmen) (Farben)* to run; *(fig)* to become blurred

ver|flixt [fɛɐˈflɪkst] *(inf)* **ADJ** blessed *(inf)*, darned *(inf)*; *(= kompliziert)* tricky; **du ~er Kerl!** you devil; **das ~e siebte Jahr** ≈ the seven-year itch **ADV** darned *(inf)* **INTERJ** **~!** blow! *(Brit inf)*, darn! *(US inf)*

Ver|floch|ten|heit [fɛɐˈflɔxtnhait] **F -, -en** *(fig)* interconnections *pl* (*von* between)

ver|flos|sen [fɛɐˈflɔsn] **ADJ** **a** *Jahre, Tage* bygone; *(= letzte)* last **b** *(inf: = ehemalig)* one-time *attr (inf)*, former *attr* → *auch* **verfließen**

Ver|flos|se|ne(r) [fɛɐˈflɔsənə] **MF** *decl as adj (inf)* ex *(inf)*; *(= Mann)* ex-boyfriend; *(nach Scheidung)* ex-husband; *(= Frau)* ex-girlfriend; *(nach Scheidung)* ex-wife

ver|flu|chen *ptp* **verflucht** **VT** to curse; **sei verflucht** curses on you

ver|flucht [fɛɐˈflu:xt] *(inf)* **ADJ** damn *(inf)*, bloody *(Brit inf)*; **~ (noch mal)!** damn (it) *(inf)*; **diese ~e Tat** *(liter)* this cursed deed; **~e Tat!** damn! *(inf)* **ADV** *(bei englischem adj, n)* damn *(inf)*, bloody *(Brit inf)*; *(bei englischem vb)* like hell *(inf)*; **ich habe mich ~ vertan** I made one hell of a mistake *(inf)*

ver|flüch|ti|gen [fɛɐˈflʏçtɪgn] *ptp* **verflüchtigt** **VT** to evaporate **VR** *(Alkohol, Kohlensäure etc)* to evaporate; *(Duft)* to disappear; *(Gase)* to volatilize; *(fig) (Bedenken, Ärger)* to be dispelled; *(hum) (Mensch, Gegenstand, Hoffnungen etc)* to vanish; *(Geld)* to go up in smoke *(inf)*

Ver|flüch|ti|gung **F -, -en** evaporation; *(von Duft)* disappearance; *(von Gasen)* volatilization

ver|flüs|si|gen [fɛɐˈflʏsɪgn] *ptp* **verflüssigt** **VTR** to liquefy

Ver|flüs|si|gung **F -, -en** liquefaction

Ver|folg [fɛɐˈfɔlk] **M -s,** *no pl (form) (= Ausübung)* pursuance; *(= Verlauf)* course; **im ~ des Schreibens vom ...** further to our letter of ...

ver|fol|gen *ptp* **verfolgt** **VT** *Ziel, Idee, Interessen, Karriere, Straftat* to pursue; *jdn auch* to follow; *(= jds Spuren folgen) jdn* to trail; *Tier* to track; *(mit Hunden etc)* to hunt; *Unterricht, Entwicklung, Geschichte, Spur* to follow; *Vorschlag, Gedanken* to follow up; *(Comput) Änderungen* to track; *(politisch, religiös)* to persecute; *(Gedanke, Erinnerung etc) jdn* to haunt; **vom Unglück/Schicksal** *etc* **verfolgt werden** *or* **sein** to be dogged by ill fortune/by fate *etc*; **jdn politisch ~** to persecute sb for political reasons; **jdn gerichtlich ~** to prosecute sb; **jdn mit den Augen** *or* **Blicken ~** to follow sb with one's eyes; **jdn mit Bitten/Forderungen ~** to badger sb with requests/demands; **jdn mit Hass ~** to pursue sb in hate; **welche Absicht verfolgt er?** what is his intention? → **strafrechtlich**

Ver|fol|ger [fɛɐˈfɔlgɐ] **M -s, -,** **Ver|fol|ge|rin** [-ərɪn] **F -, -nen** **a** pursuer **b** *(politisch, wegen Gesinnung)* persecutor

Ver|folg|te(r) [fɛɐˈfɔlktə] **MF** *decl as adj* quarry; *(politisch, wegen Gesinnung)* victim of persecution

Ver|fol|gung [fɛɐˈfɔlgʊŋ] **F -, -en** *(von Ziel, Idee, Karriere, Verbrecher, Fahrzeug)* pursuit; *(= Spurensuche)* trailing; *(von Tier)* tracking; *(= politische Verfolgung)* persecution *no pl*; **die ~ aufnehmen** to take up the chase; **gerichtliche ~** court action; **strafrechtliche ~** prosecution; **bei der weiteren ~ der Frage** when this question was/is pursued further; **~ eines Ziels** pursuance of an aim

Ver|fol|gungs-: **Ver|fol|gungs|jagd** **F** chase, pursuit; **Ver|fol|gungs|ren|nen** **NT** *(Sport)* pursuit race; **Ver|fol|gungs|wahn** **M** persecution mania

ver|for|men *ptp* **verformt** **VT** to make go out of shape, to distort (*zu* into); *(= umformen)* to work; **verformt sein** to be out of shape; *(Mensch, Gliedmaßen)* to be deformed **VR** to go out of shape

Ver|for|mung **F** **a** distortion **b** *(= veränderte Form)* distortion; *(von Mensch, Gliedmaßen)* deformity

ver|frach|ten [fɛɐˈfraxtn] *ptp* **verfrachtet** **VT** *(Comm)* to transport; *(Naut)* to ship; *(inf) jdn* to bundle off *(inf)*; **etw in den Keller/eine Kiste ~** *(inf)* to dump sth in the cellar/a crate

Ver|frach|ter [fɛɐˈfraxtɐ] **M -s, -,** **Ver|frach|te|rin** [-ərɪn] **F -, -nen** transport agent; *(Naut)* shipper

Ver|frach|tung **F -, -en** transporting; *(Naut)* shipping

ver|fran|zen [fɛɐˈfrantsn] *ptp* **verfranzt** **VR** *(inf)* to lose one's way; *(Aviat sl)* to lose one's bearings; *(fig)* to get in a muddle *or* tangle

ver|frem|den [fɛɐˈfrɛmdn] *ptp* **verfremdet** **VT** *Thema, Stoff* to make unfamiliar, to defamiliarize; *Werkstoffe* to use in an unusual way

Ver|frem|dung **F -, -en** defamiliarization; *(Theat, Liter)* alienation, distancing; **die ~ vertrauter Formen** using familiar forms in an unfamiliar way

Ver|frem|dungs|ef|fekt **M** distancing effect; *(Theat, Liter)* alienation *or* estrangement effect

ver|fres|sen *ptp* **verfressen** **VT** *irreg (inf)* to spend *or* blow *(inf)* on food

ver|fres|sen [fɛɐˈfrɛsn] **ADJ** *(inf)* greedy

ver|frie|ren *ptp* **verfroren** [fɛɐˈfro:rən] **VI** *irreg aux sein (dial)* = **erfrieren**

ver|fro|ren [fɛɐˈfro:rən] **ADJ** *(inf)* sensitive to cold; *(= durchgefroren)* frozen, freezing cold; **~ sein** *(= kälteempfindlich)* to feel the cold

ver|frü|hen [fɛɐˈfry:ən] *ptp* **verfrüht** **VR** *(Winter, Entwicklung, Zug)* to come *or* arrive early; *(Gäste)* to be *or* come too early

ver|früht [fɛɐˈfry:t] **ADJ** *(= zu früh)* premature; *(= früh)* early; **solche Aufgaben sind für dieses Alter ~** exercises like this are too advanced for this age group

ver|füg|bar **ADJ** available

Ver|füg|bar|keit **F** availability

ver|fu|gen *ptp* **verfugt** **VT** to fit flush; *Fliesen* to grout

ver|fü|gen ✪ 46.2 *ptp* **verfügt** **VI** **über etw** *(acc)* **~** to have sth at one's disposal; *(= besitzen)* to have sth; **über jdn/etw ~** *(= bestimmen über)* to be in charge of sb/sth; **die Art und Weise, wie er über seine Untergebenen verfügt** the way in which he orders his inferiors around; **Gott verfügt über das Schicksal der Menschen** God determines man's fate; **du kannst über mein Auto ~, wenn ich nicht da bin** you can use my car while I'm away; **du kannst doch nicht über meine Zeit ~** you can't tell me how to spend my time; **du kannst doch nicht über deinen Bruder ~** you can't tell your brother what to do; **über etw** *(acc)* **frei ~ können** to be able to do as one wants with sth; **~ Sie über mich** I am at your disposal

VT to order; *(gesetzlich)* to decree → **letztwillig**

VR *(form)* to proceed *(form)*

Ver|fü|gung ✪ 46.4 **F** **a** *no pl (= das Verfügen)* possession; **freie ~** *(Jur)* free disposal (*über +acc* of); **jdm etw zur ~ stellen** to put sth at sb's disposal; *(= leihen)* to lend sb sth; **jdm zur ~ stehen, zu jds ~ stehen** to be at sb's disposal; **(jdm) zur ~ stehen** *(= verfügbar sein)* to be available (to sb); **sich zur ~ halten** to be available (to sb); **halte dich ab 7 Uhr zur ~** be ready from 7 o'clock; **etw zur ~ haben** to have sth at one's disposal **b** *(behördlich)* order; *(von Gesetzgeber)* decree; *(testamentarisch)* provision; *(= Anweisung)* instruction → **letztwillig, einstweilig**

Ver|fü|gungs-: **Ver|fü|gungs|be|fug|nis** **F** right of disposal (*über +acc* of); **Ver|fü|gungs|ge|walt** **F** *(Jur)* right of disposal; **die ~ über Atomwaffen** the power to use atomic weapons; **Ver|fü|gungs|rah|men** **M** *(Fin)* credit limit; **Ver|fü|gungs|recht** **NT** *(Jur)* right of disposal (*über +acc* of)

ver|führ|bar **ADJ** temptable; *(esp sexuell)* seducible; **sie sind ~** they can be tempted; *(sexuell)* they can be seduced

ver|füh|ren *ptp* **verführt** **VT** to tempt; *(esp sexuell)* to seduce; *die Jugend, das Volk etc* to lead astray; **jdn zu etw ~, jdn ~, etw zu tun** to encourage sb to do sth; **ich lasse mich gern ~** you can twist my arm *(inf)*; **diese offenen Kisten ~ ja direkt zum Diebstahl** these open boxes are an encouragement *or* invitation to steal

Ver|füh|rer **M** seducer

Ver|füh|re|rin **F** seductress, temptress

ver|füh|re|risch [fɛɐˈfy:rərɪʃ] **ADJ** seductive; *(= verlockend)* tempting **ADV** seductively; *duften, riechen, aussehen* seductive, tempting

Ver|füh|rung **F** seduction; *(von Jugend, Volk)* tempting; *(= Verlockung)* enticement, temptation

Ver|füh|rungs|kunst F seductive manner; *(von Werbung)* persuasiveness; **ein Meister der ~** a master of seduction/persuasion; **Verführungskünste** seductive/persuasive charms *or* ways

ver|fül|len *ptp* **verfüllt** VT *(mit Erde, Beton etc)* to fill in

ver|fünf|fa|chen [fɛɐ'fʏnffaxn] *ptp* **verfünffacht** VT *Zahl* to multiply by five, to quintuple *(form)* VR to increase five times *or* fivefold; *(Zahl auch)* to multiply by five

ver|fut|tern *ptp* **verfuttert** VT *(inf)* to spend on food

ver|füt|tern *ptp* **verfüttert** VT to use as animal/bird food; *(= aufbrauchen)* to feed *(an +acc* to); **etw an die Schweine/Vögel ~** to feed sth to the pigs/birds

Ver|füt|te|rung F **-,** *(rare)* **-n** *(an Tiere)* feeding; **die ~ von Küchenabfällen an Schweine** feeding kitchen waste to pigs

Ver|ga|be F **-,** *(rare)* **-n** *(von Arbeiten)* allocation; *(von Stipendium, Auftrag etc)* award

Ver|ga|be|pra|xis F *(von Arbeiten)* allocation procedure; *(von Stipendium, Auftrag etc)* award procedure

Ver|ga|be|stel|le F *(für Studienplätze)* central universities admissions council

ver|gack|ei|ern [fɛɐ'gaklaiɐn] *ptp* **vergackeiert** VT *(inf)* **jdn ~** to pull sb's leg *(inf)*, to have sb on *(inf)*

ver|gaf|fen *ptp* **vergafft** VR *(dated inf)* **sich in jdn ~** to fall for sb *(inf)*

ver|gagt [fɛɐ'gɛ(:)kt] ADJ *(inf)* gimmicky *(inf)*

ver|gäl|len [fɛɐ'gɛlən] *ptp* **vergällt** VT *Alkohol* to denature; *(fig) jdn* to embitter, to sour; *Freude* to spoil; *Leben etc* to sour; **jdm die Freude ~** to spoil sb's fun; **jdm das Leben ~** to sour sb's life

ver|ga|lop|pie|ren *ptp* **vergaloppiert** VR *(inf)* *(= sich irren)* to be on the wrong track; *(= übers Ziel hinausschießen)* to go too far

ver|gam|meln *ptp* **vergammelt** *(inf)* VI *aux sein* **a** *(= verderben)* to get spoiled; *(Speisen)* to go bad; **vergammeltes Obst** mouldy *(Brit) or* moldy *(US)* fruit **b** *(= verlottern)* to go to the dogs *(inf)*; *Gebäude* to become run down; **vergammelt aussehen** to look scruffy; **vergammelte Studenten** scruffy(-looking) students; **eine vergammelte Kneipe** a seedy pub *(Brit) or* bar VT to waste; **ich möchte mal wieder einen Tag ~** I'd like to have a day doing nothing

ver|gan|gen [fɛɐ'gaŋən] ADJ **a** *(= letzte)* last **b** *Jahre* past; *Zeiten, Bräuche* bygone, former; *Größe* past, former; **das Vergangene** the past; **das ist alles ~ und vergessen** that is all in the past now → *auch* **vergehen**

Ver|gan|gen|heit F **-, -en** past; *(von Stadt, Staat etc auch)* history; *(Gram)* past (tense); **die erste** *or* **einfache/zweite** *or* **vollendete/dritte ~** *(Gram)* the simple past/perfect/pluperfect (tense); **eine Frau mit ~** a woman with a past; **der ~ angehören** to be a thing of the past

Ver|gan|gen|heits-: **Ver|gan|gen|heits|be|wäl|ti|gung** F process of coming to terms with the past; **Ver|gan|gen|heits|form** F *(Gram)* past tense

ver|gäng|lich [fɛɐ'gɛŋlɪç] ADJ transitory

Ver|gäng|lich|keit F **-,** *no pl* transitoriness

ver|gä|ren [fɛɐ'gɛ:rən] *ptp* **vergoren** *or* **vergärt** [fɛɐ'go:rən, fɛɐ'gɛ:ɐt] *irreg* VI *aux sein* to ferment VT to ferment *(zu* into)

ver|ga|sen [fɛɐ'ga:zn] *ptp* **vergast** VT *(Tech: in Motor)* to carburet; *Kohle* to gasify; *(= durch Gas töten) jdn, Ungeziefer* to gas

Ver|ga|sen NT **-s,** *no pl* gassing

Ver|ga|ser [fɛɐ'ga:zɐ] M **-s, -** *(Aut)* carburettor *(Brit)*, carburetor *(US)*

Ver|ga|ser-: **Ver|ga|ser|brand** M fire in the carburettor *(Brit) or* carburetor *(US)*; **Ver|ga|ser|mo|tor** M carburettor *(Brit) or* carburetor *(US)* engine

ver|gaß *pret von* **vergessen**

Ver|ga|sung F **-, -en** *(Tech)* carburation; *(von Kohle)* gasification; *(= Tötung)* gassing; **etw bis zur ~ diskutieren** *(inf neg!)* to discuss sth ad nauseum

ver|gat|tern [fɛɐ'gatɐn] *ptp* **vergattert** VT **a** *Garten etc* to fence off; *Tiere* to fence in **b** *(Mil)* to instruct **c** *(inf)* to punish; **jdn zu etw ~** to order sb to do sth

ver|ge|ben *ptp* **vergeben** *irreg* VT **a** *(= weggeben) Auftrag, Stipendium, Preis* to award *(an +acc* to); *Plätze, Studienplätze, Stellen* to allocate; *Kredit* to give out; *Karten* to give away; *Arbeit* to assign; *(fig) Chance, Möglichkeit* to throw away; **ein Amt an jdn ~** to appoint sb to an office; **zu ~ sein** to be available; *(Stelle auch)* to be open; **~ sein** *(Gewinn)* to have been awarded *or* won; *(Wohnung, Karten, Plätze)* to have been taken; *(Stelle)* to have been filled; **er/sie ist schon ~** *(inf)* he/she is already spoken for *(inf) or (verheiratet auch)* married; **ich bin heute Abend schon ~** *(inf)* I've got something else on this evening; **mein Herz ist schon ~** *(liter)* my heart belongs to another *(liter)*; **der nächste Tanz ist schon ~** I've already promised the next dance **b** *(= verzeihen)* to forgive; *Sünde* to forgive, to pardon; **jdm etw ~** to forgive sb (for) sth; **das ist ~ und vergessen** that is over and done with, that is forgiven and forgotten **c sich** *(dat)* **etwas/nichts ~** to lose/not to lose face; **was vergibst du dir, wenn du ein bisschen netter bist?** what have you got to lose by being a bit friendlier? VR *(Cards)* to misdeal

ver|ge|bens [fɛɐ'ge:bns] ADJ *pred* in vain, to no avail ADV in vain, vainly

ver|geb|lich [fɛɐ'ge:plɪç] ADJ futile; *Bitten, Mühe auch* vain *attr*; **alle Bitten/Versuche waren ~** all requests/attempts were in vain *or* to no avail ADV in vain

Ver|geb|lich|keit F **-,** *no pl* futility

Ver|ge|bung [fɛɐ'ge:bʊŋ] F **-, -en** forgiveness

ver|ge|gen|ständ|li|chen [fɛɐ'ge:gnʃtɛntlɪçn] *ptp* **vergegenständlicht** VT to concretize; *(Philos)* to reify, to hypostatize

ver|ge|gen|wär|ti|gen [fɛɐge:gn'vɛrtɪgn, fɛɐ'ge:gnvɛrtɪgn] *ptp* **vergegenwärtigt** VT **sich** *(dat)* **etw ~** *(= vor Augen rufen)* to visualize sth; *(= sich vorstellen)* to imagine sth; *(= erinnern)* to recall sth; **vergegenwärtige dir doch einmal die Folgen** think of the consequences

Ver|ge|gen|wär|ti|gung [fɛɐge:gn'vɛrtɪgʊŋ, fɛɐ'ge:gnvɛrtɪgʊŋ] F **-, -en** visualization; *(= Vorstellung)* imagination

ver|ge|hen *ptp* **vergangen** [fɛɐ'gaŋən] *irreg* VI *aux sein* **a** *(= vorbeigehen)* to pass; *(Liebe, Leidenschaft)* to die; *(Zeit, Jahre etc auch)* to go by, to pass; *(Hunger, Schmerzen)* to wear off, to pass; *(Schönheit, Glück)* to fade; *(Duft)* to go, to wear off; **wie doch die Zeit vergeht** how time flies; **mir ist die Lust/Laune dazu vergangen** I don't feel like it any more; **mir ist der Appetit vergangen** I have lost my appetite; **das vergeht wieder** that will pass; **es werden noch Monate ~, ehe …** it will be months before …; **damit die Zeit vergeht** in order to pass the time → *auch* **vergangen, Hören, Lachen b vor etw** *(dat)* **~** to be dying of sth; **vor Angst ~** to be scared to death; **vor Hunger ~** to be dying of hunger, to be starving; **vor Kälte ~** to be frozen; **vor Sehnsucht ~** to pine away; **sie wollte vor Scham ~** she nearly died of shame VR **sich an jdm ~** to do sb wrong; *(unsittlich)* to assault sb indecently; **sich an Gott ~** to go against God; **sich an der Natur ~** to defile nature; **sich gegen das Gesetz ~** to violate the law; **sich gegen die guten Sitten/die Moral ~** to violate *or* outrage propriety/morality

Ver|ge|hen [fɛɐ'ge:ən] NT **-s, - a** *(= Verstoß)* offence *(Brit)*, offense *(US)*, misdemeanour *(Brit)*, misdemeanor *(US)*; **~ im Amt** professional misconduct *no pl*; **das ist doch kein ~, oder?** that's not a crime, is it? **b** *no pl (geh: = Schwinden)* passing; *(von Zeit)* passage, passing; *(von Schönheit, Glück)* fading

ver|gei|gen *ptp* **vergeigt** VT *(inf)* to botch up *(inf)*

ver|geis|tigt [fɛɐ'gaistɪçt] ADJ cerebral, spiritual

Ver|geis|ti|gung [fɛɐ'gaistɪgʊŋ] F **-, -en** spiritualization

ver|gel|ten *ptp* **vergolten** [fɛɐ'gɔltn] VT *irreg* to repay; **jdm etw ~** to repay sb for sth; **vergelts Gott** *(old, dial)* God bless you → **gleich 1**

Ver|gel|tung F *(= Rache)* retaliation; **~ üben** to take revenge *(an jdm* on sb)

Ver|gel|tungs-: **Ver|gel|tungs|ak|ti|on** F retaliatory operation *or* action *no art*; *(= Vergeltungsschlag)* retaliatory strike; **Ver|gel|tungs|maß|nah|me** F reprisal, retaliatory measure; **Ver|gel|tungs|schlag** M act of reprisal; **Ver|gel|tungs|waf|fen** PL retaliatory weapons *pl*

ver|ge|sell|schaf|ten [fɛɐgə'zɛlʃaftn] *ptp* **vergesellschaftet** VT *(Pol)* to nationalize; *Privatbesitz* to take into public ownership; *(= ins Arbeitereigentum überführen)* to hand over to the workers; *(rare: Sociol)* to socialize

Ver|ge|sell|schaf|tung F **-, -en** *(Pol)* nationalization; *(von Privatbesitz)* taking into public ownership

ver|ges|sen [fɛɐ'gɛsn] ✪ 31, 53.6 *pret* **vergaß**, [fɛɐ'ga:s] *ptp* **vergessen** VT to forget; *(= liegen lassen)* to leave (behind); **… und nicht zu ~ seine Ehrlichkeit** … and not forgetting his honesty; **dass ich es nicht vergesse, ehe ich es vergesse** before I forget; **das werde ich dir nie ~** I will never forget that; **das kannst du (voll) ~!** *(inf)* forget it!; **er vergisst noch mal seinen Kopf** *(inf)* he'd forget his head if it wasn't screwed on *(inf)* VI to forget; **auf jdn/etw ~** *(Aus)* to forget sb/sth VR *(Mensch)* to forget oneself; **Zahlen ~ sich leicht** numbers are easy to forget, numbers are easily forgotten

Ver|ges|sen|heit ✪ 53.1 F **-,** *no pl* oblivion; **in ~ geraten, der ~ anheimfallen** *(geh)* to vanish *or* sink into oblivion; **etw aus der ~ hervorholen** to rescue sth from oblivion

ver|gess|lich [fɛɐ'gɛslɪç] ADJ forgetful

Ver|gess|lich|keit F **-,** *no pl* forgetfulness

ver|geu|den [fɛɐ'gɔydn] *ptp* **vergeudet** VT to waste; *Geld, Talente auch* to squander

Ver|geu|dung F **-, -en** wasting; *(von Geld, Talenten auch)* squandering; **das ist die reinste ~** that is (a) sheer waste; **diese ~!** what a waste!

ver|ge|wal|ti|gen [fɛɐgə'valtɪgn] *ptp* **vergewaltigt** VT to rape; *(fig) Sprache etc* to murder, to mutilate; *Volkswillen* to violate VR to force oneself

Ver|ge|wal|ti|ger [fɛɐgə'valtɪgɐ] M **-s, -** rapist

Ver|ge|wal|ti|gung F **-, -en** rape; *(fig) (von Sprache)* murder(ing), mutilation; *(von Volkswillen)* violation

ver|ge|wis|sern [fɛɐgə'vɪsɐn] *ptp* **vergewissert** VR to make sure; **sich einer Sache** *(gen) or* **über etw** *(acc)* **~** to make sure of sth

ver|gie|ßen *ptp* **vergossen** [fɛɐ'gɔsn] VT *irreg Kaffee, Wasser* to spill; *Blut auch, Tränen* to shed; **ich habe bei der Arbeit viel Schweiß vergossen** I sweated blood over that job

ver|gif|ten *ptp* **vergiftet** VT *(lit, fig)* to poison; *Luft auch* to pollute VR to poison oneself *(mit, durch, an +dat* with)

Ver|gif|tung [fɛɐ'gɪftʊŋ] F **-, -en** poisoning *no pl*; *(der Luft)* pollution; **bei ~en wird der Magen ausgepumpt** the stomach is pumped in cases of poisoning; **an einer ~ sterben** to die of poisoning

Ver|gif|tungs|er|schei|nung F symptom of poisoning

ver|gil|ben *ptp* **vergilbt** VI *aux sein* to go *or* become yellow; **vergilbt** yellowed

ver|giss [fɛɐ'gɪs] IMPER *sing von* **vergessen**

Ver|giss|mein|nicht [fɛɐ'gɪsmainnɪçt] NT **-(e)s, -(e)** forget-me-not

ver|git|tern [fɛɐ'gɪtɐn] *ptp* **vergittert** VT to put a grille on/over; *(mit Stangen)* to put bars on/over; **vergitterte Fenster** windows with grilles over them; *(mit Stangen)* barred windows

Ver|git|te|rung F -, -en (= *Gitter*) grille, grating; (= *Stangen*) bars *pl*; **die ~ der Fenster** putting grilles/bars on the windows

ver|gla|sen [fɛɐ̯'gla:zn] *ptp* **verglast** VT to glaze

ver|glast [fɛɐ̯'gla:st] ADJ *Kuppel etc* glazed

Ver|gla|sung F -, -en glazing

Ver|gleich [fɛɐ̯'glaiç] ✪ 32.1, 32.3, 53.5 M -(e)s, -e **a** comparison; (*Liter*) simile; **~e ziehen** *or* **anstellen** to make *or* draw comparisons; **im ~ zu** *or* **mit** in comparison with, compared with *or* to; **das ist doch gar kein ~!** there is no comparison; **in keinem ~ zu etw stehen** to be out of all proportion to sth; (*Leistungen*) not to compare with sth; **dem ~ mit jdm/etw standhalten, den ~ mit jdm/etw aushalten** to stand *or* bear comparison with sb/sth; **sie hält den ~ mit ihrer Vorgängerin nicht aus** she doesn't compare with her predecessor; **der ~ hinkt** the comparison is misleading **b** (*Jur*) settlement; **einen gütlichen ~ schließen** to reach an amicable settlement; **einen außergerichtlichen ~ schließen** to settle out of court

ver|gleich|bar ✪ 32.5 ADJ comparable

Ver|gleich|bar|keit [fɛɐ̯'glaiçba:ɐ̯kait] F -, *no pl* comparability

ver|glei|chen ✪ 32, 53.5 *ptp* **verglichen** *irreg* [fɛɐ̯'glıçn] VT to compare; **etw mit etw ~** (*prüfend*) to compare sth with sth; (= *einen Vergleich herstellen zwischen*) to compare *or* liken sth to sth; **verglichen mit** compared with; **vergleiche oben** compare above; **sie sind nicht (miteinander) zu ~** they cannot be compared (to one another); **die kann man nicht (miteinander) ~** they cannot be compared (with one another), they are not comparable VR **a sich mit jdm ~** to compare oneself with sb; **wie könnte ich mich mit ihm ~?** how could I compare myself to him? **b** (*Jur*) to reach a settlement, to settle (*mit* with)

ver|glei|chend ADJ comparative

Ver|gleichs-: **Ver|gleichs|an|trag** M (*Jur*) application for the initiation of composition proceedings; **Ver|gleichs|form** F (*Gram*) comparative form; **Ver|gleichs|gläu|bi|ger(in)** M(F) *creditor in insolvency proceedings*; **Ver|gleichs|jahr** NT base year; **Ver|gleichs|mie|te** F comparable rent; **ortsübliche ~** local comparable rent; **Ver|gleichs|satz** M (*Gram*) comparative clause; **Ver|gleichs|schuld|ner(in)** M(F) *debtor in insolvency proceedings*; **Ver|gleichs|ver|fah|ren** NT insolvency proceedings *pl*; **Ver|gleichs|ver|wal|ter(in)** M(F) (*Jur*) trustee in composition proceedings; **Ver|gleichs|vor|schlag** M (*Jur*) offer of a settlement, settlement offer; **Ver|gleichs|weg** M (*Jur*) **auf dem ~** by reaching a settlement; **ver|gleichs|wei|se** ADV comparatively; **Ver|gleichs|wert** M comparative *or* comparable value; **Ver|gleichs|zahl** F *usu pl* comparative figure; **Ver|gleichs|zeit|raum** M comparative period

ver|glet|schern [fɛɐ̯'gletʃɐn] *ptp* **vergletschert** VI *aux sein* to become glaciated

Ver|glet|sche|rung F -, -en glaciation

ver|glim|men *ptp* **verglimmt** *or* **verglommen** [fɛɐ̯'glɔmən] VI *irreg aux sein* (*Zigarette*) to go out; (*Licht, Feuer auch*) to die out *or* away; (*fig liter*) (*Leben*) to be extinguished; (*Hoffnung, Liebe, Tageslicht*) to fade; **~de Kohle** dying cinders

ver|glü|hen *ptp* **verglüht** VI *aux sein* (*Feuer, Feuerwerk*) to die away; (*Draht*) to burn out; (*Raumkapsel, Meteor etc*) to burn up; (*liter. Leidenschaft*) to fade (away), to die down

ver|gnü|gen [fɛɐ̯'gny:gn] *ptp* **vergnügt** VT to amuse VR to enjoy oneself; **sich mit jdm/etw ~** to amuse oneself with sb/sth; **sich mit Lesen/Tennis ~** to amuse *or* entertain oneself by reading/playing tennis; **sich an etw** (*dat*) **~** to be amused *or* entertained by sth → *auch* **vergnügt**

Ver|gnü|gen [fɛɐ̯'gny:gn] ✪ 52.1 NT -s, - **a** (= *Freude, Genuss*) pleasure; (= *Spaß*) fun *no indef art*; (= *Erheiterung*) amusement; **~ an etw** (*dat*) **finden** to find enjoyment *or* pleasure in (doing) sth; **das macht** *or* **bereitet mir ~** I enjoy it, it gives me pleasure; **sich** (*dat*) **ein ~ aus etw machen** to get pleasure from (doing) sth; **für ihn ist es ein ~, nachts durch die menschenleeren Straßen zu wandern** he enjoys wandering around the empty streets at night; **ich laufe jeden Tag eine halbe Stunde nur zum ~** I run for half an hour each day just for pleasure *or* for the fun of it; **das war ein teures ~** (*inf*) that was an expensive bit of fun; **ich höre ihn mit großem ~ singen** it gives me great pleasure to hear him sing; **mit ~** with pleasure; **mit großem ~** with great pleasure; **mit größtem** *or* **dem größten ~** with the greatest of pleasure; **(na dann) viel ~!** (*auch iro*) enjoy yourself/yourselves!; **hinein ins ~!** let the fun begin!; **er hat mir viel ~ gewünscht** he said he hoped I would enjoy myself; **wir wünschen Ihnen bei der Show viel ~** we hope you enjoy the show; **mit wem habe ich das ~?** (*form*) with whom do I have the pleasure of speaking? (*form*); **es ist mir ein ~** it is a pleasure for me **b** (*dated*: *Veranstaltung*) entertainment

ver|gnüg|lich [fɛɐ̯'gny:klıç] ADJ enjoyable; *Stunden auch* pleasurable; (= *erheiternd*) amusing

ver|gnügt [fɛɐ̯'gny:kt] ADJ *Abend, Stunden* enjoyable; *Mensch, Gesichter, Gesellschaft, Lachen, Stimmung* cheerful; **über etw** (*acc*) **~ sein** to be pleased *or* happy about sth ADV happily, cheerfully; **~ aussehen** to look cheerful; **~ lachen** to laugh happily → *auch* **vergnügen**

Ver|gnü|gung F -, -en pleasure; (= *Veranstaltung*) entertainment

Ver|gnü|gungs-: **Ver|gnü|gungs|be|trieb** M **a** *no pl* (= *Unterhaltung*) entertainment **b** (= *Vergnügungsstätte*) bar providing *or* with entertainment, nightclub; **Ver|gnü|gungs|damp|fer** M pleasure steamer; **Ver|gnü|gungs|fahrt** F pleasure trip; **Ver|gnü|gungs|in|dust|rie** F entertainment industry; **Ver|gnü|gungs|park** M amusement park; **Ver|gnü|gungs|rei|se** F pleasure trip; **Ver|gnü|gungs|steu|er** F entertainment tax; **Ver|gnü|gungs|sucht** F craving for pleasure; **ver|gnü|gungs|süch|tig** ADJ pleasure-craving, sybaritic (*liter pej*); **Ver|gnü|gungs|vier|tel** NT entertainments district

ver|gol|den [fɛɐ̯'gɔldn] *ptp* **vergoldet** VT (= *mit Gold bemalen*) *Nüsse etc* to paint gold; (*mit Blattgold*) *Statue, Buchkante* to gild; (= *mit Gold überziehen*) *Schmuck* to gold-plate; (*liter. Sonne, Schein*) to bathe in gold, to turn golden; (*fig*: = *verschönern*) *Zeit, Alter, Erinnerung* to enhance; **der Herbst vergoldet die Natur** autumn turns nature golden; **sich** (*dat*) **etw ~ lassen** (*fig*) to accept a financial inducement to do sth; **er ließ sich seinen Rücktritt ~** he accepted a financial inducement to resign VR (*liter*) to turn to gold

Ver|gol|der [fɛɐ̯'gɔldɐ] M -s, -, **Ver|gol|de|rin** [-ərın] F -, -nen gilder

ver|gol|det [fɛɐ̯'gɔldət] ADJ *Nüsse* gold-painted; *Buchseiten* gilt; *Schmuck* gold-plated; *Kuppeln, Spitzen* gilded; *Natur, Stadt, Erinnerung etc* golden

Ver|gol|dung F -, -en (*von Nüssen*) painting gold; (*von Buchseiten*) gilding; (*von Schmuck*) gold-plating; (= *Überzug*) (*auf Nüssen*) gold paint; (*auf Buchseiten*) gilt; (*auf Schmuck*) gold plate

ver|gön|nen *ptp* **vergönnt** VT (*geh*) **jdm etw ~** not to begrudge sb sth; **es war ihr noch vergönnt, das zu sehen** she was granted the privilege of seeing it; **diese Freude war ihm noch/nicht vergönnt** fate granted/did not grant him this pleasure

ver|göt|tern [fɛɐ̯'gœtɐn] *ptp* **vergöttert** VT to idolize

Ver|göt|te|rung F -, -en idolization

ver|gra|ben *ptp* **vergraben** *irreg* VT to bury VR (*Maulwurf etc*) to bury oneself; (*fig*: = *zurückgezogen leben*) to hide oneself (away); **sich hinter seinen Büchern/in Arbeit ~** to bury oneself in one's books/in work

ver|grä|men *ptp* **vergrämt** VT **a** (= *verärgern, beleidigen*) to antagonize; (= *vertreiben*) to alienate; (= *verletzen*) to grieve; **jdm das Leben ~** to make life a misery for sb **b** (*Hunt*) *Wild* to frighten, to scare

ver|grämt [fɛɐ̯'grɛ:mt] ADJ (= *kummervoll, bitter*) *Gesicht etc* troubled; (= *verärgert*) angered

ver|grät|zen [fɛɐ̯'grɛtsn] *ptp* **vergrätzt** VT (*inf*) to vex

ver|grau|len *ptp* **vergrault** VT (*inf*) to put off; (= *vertreiben*) to scare off

ver|grei|fen *ptp* **vergriffen** [fɛɐ̯'grıfn] VR *irreg* **a** (= *danebengreifen*) to make a mistake; (*Sport*: *bei Gerät*) to miss one's grip; **sich im Ton ~** (*fig*) to adopt the wrong tone; **sich im Ausdruck ~** (*fig*) to use the wrong expression → *auch* **vergriffen** **b sich an etw** (*dat*) **~** (*an fremdem Eigentum*) to misappropriate sth; (*euph*: = *stehlen*) to help oneself to sth (*euph*); (*an Heiligem*) to desecrate *or* profane sth; **sich an jdm ~** (= *angreifen*) to lay hands on sb; (= *geschlechtlich missbrauchen*) to assault sb (sexually)

ver|grei|sen [fɛɐ̯'graizn] *ptp* **vergreist** VI *aux sein* (*Bevölkerung*) to age; (*Mensch*) to become senile; **Deutschland vergreist immer mehr** the German population is getting older and older; **vergreist** aged; senile

Ver|grei|sung F -, *no pl* (*von Bevölkerung*) ageing; (*von Organismen*) senescence; (*von Mensch*) senility

ver|grif|fen [fɛɐ̯'grıfn] ADJ unavailable; *Buch* out of print → *auch* **vergreifen**

ver|grö|bern [fɛɐ̯'grø:bɐn] *ptp* **vergröbert** VT to coarsen VR to become coarse

ver|grö|ßern [fɛɐ̯'grø:sɐn] *ptp* **vergrößert** VT (*räumlich*) *Raum, Gebäude, Fläche, Gebiet* to extend; *Abstand auch, Vorsprung* to increase; (*größenmäßig, umfangmäßig*) *Maßstab, Wissen* to enlarge, to increase; *Bekanntenkreis* to enlarge, to extend; *Firma, Absatzmarkt* to expand; *Produktion* to increase; *Vollmachten* to extend; (*zahlenmäßig*) *Kapital, Mitgliederzahl, Anzahl* to increase; (= *verstärken*) *Einfluss, Not, Probleme, Schmerz etc* to increase; *Fotografie* to enlarge, to blow up; (*Lupe, Brille*) to magnify VR (*räumlich*) to be extended; (*Abstand, Vorsprung*) to increase; (*größenmäßig, umfangmäßig*) (*Maßstab*) to be enlarged, to increase; (*Wissen*) to increase, to expand; (*Bekanntenkreis*) to be enlarged, to be extended; (*Firma, Absatzmarkt*) to expand; (*Produktion*) to increase; (*Vollmachten*) to be extended; (*zahlenmäßig*) to increase; (= *sich verstärken*) to increase; (*Pupille, Gefäße*) to dilate; (*Organ*) to become enlarged; **wir wollen uns ~** (*inf*) we want to move to a bigger place VI (*Lupe, Brille*) to magnify; (*Fotograf*) to do enlarging

Ver|grö|ße|rung F -, -en **a** (*räumlich*) extension; (*von Abstand, umfangmäßig, zahlenmäßig*) increase; (*von Maßstab, Wissen, Fotografie, Bekanntenkreis*) enlargement; (*von Firma, Absatzmarkt*) expansion; (*mit Lupe, Brille*) magnification; (= *Verstärkung*: *von Einfluss, Not, Problemen*) increase; **in 1.000-facher ~** magnified 1,000 times **b** (*von Pupille, Gefäß*) dilation; (*von Organ*) enlargement **c** (= *vergrößertes Bild*) enlargement

Ver|grö|ße|rungs-: **Ver|grö|ße|rungs|ap|pa|rat** M enlarger; **ver|grö|ße|rungs|fä|hig** ADJ *Gebäude* extendable; *Firma, Absatzmarkt* expandable, able to expand; *Bekanntenkreis* able to be enlarged; *Kapital, Produktion* able to be increased; **Ver|grö|ße|rungs|ge|rät** NT enlarger; **Ver|grö|ße|rungs|glas** NT magnifying glass

ver|gu|cken *ptp* **verguckt** VR (*inf*) to see wrong (*inf*); **da hab ich mich verguckt** I didn't see it properly; **sich in jdn/etw ~** to fall for sb/sth (*inf*)

ver|gül|den [fɛɐ̯'gʏldn] *ptp* **vergüldet** VT (*poet*) = **vergolden**

ver|güns|ti|gen [fɛɐ̯'gʏnstıgn] *ptp* **vergünstigt** VT *Lage* to improve VR (*Lage*) to improve; (*Preise*) to come down

ver|gụ̈ns|tigt [fɛɐ'gʏnstɪçt] ADJ *Lage* improved; *Preis* reduced ADV **etw ~ kaufen** to buy sth at a reduced price

Ver|gụ̈ns|ti|gung F -, -en (= *Vorteil*) privilege; (= *Preisermäßigung*) reduction; **besondere ~en für Rentner** special rates for pensioners

ver|gụ̈|ten [fɛɐ'gy:tn] *ptp* **vergütet** VT **a jdm etw ~** (*Unkosten*) to reimburse sb for sth; *Preis* to refund sb sth; *Schaden* to compensate sb for sth; *Arbeit, Leistung* to pay *or* recompense (*form*) sb for sth **b** (*Tech*: = *verbessern*) *Stahl* to temper; *Linse* to coat

Ver|gụ̈|tung F -, -en **a** (*von Unkosten*) reimbursement; (*von Preis*) refunding; (*für Verlust, Schaden*) compensation; (*für Arbeit, Leistung*) payment, recompense **b** (*Tech*: = *Verbesserung*) (*von Stahl*) tempering; (*von Linse*) coating

Ver|gụ̈|tungs|grup|pe F salary bracket

verh. *abbr von* **verheiratet**

ver|hạck|stü|cken [fɛɐ'hakʃtʏkn] *ptp* **verhạckstückt** VT (*inf*) (= *kritisieren*) to tear apart, to rip to pieces (*inf*); *Musikstück* to murder (*inf*)

ver|hạf|ten *ptp* **verhạftet** VT to arrest; **unschuldig verhaftet werden** to be arrested and later proved innocent; **Sie sind verhaftet!** you are under arrest!

ver|hạf|tet [fɛɐ'haftət] ADJ (*geh*) **einer Sache** (*dat*) *or* **mit etw ~ sein** to be (closely) attached to sth; **einem Irrtum ~ sein** to be under a misapprehension

Ver|hạf|te|te(r) [fɛɐ'haftətə] MF *decl as adj* **der ~ wurde abgeführt** the arrested man was taken away; **die zehn ~n** the ten people under arrest

Ver|hạf|tung F arrest

Ver|hạf|tungs|wel|le F wave of arrests

ver|ha̱|geln *ptp* **verha̱gelt** VI *aux sein* to be damaged by hail; **er sieht verhagelt aus** (*inf*) he looks rather the worse for wear

ver|ha̱|ken *ptp* **verha̱kt** VT to hook up VR to get caught; (*fig: in Streit etc*) to get caught up in

ver|hạl|len *ptp* **verhạllt** VI *aux sein* (*Geräusch etc*) to die away; **ihr Ruf/ihre Warnung verhallte ungehört** (*fig*) her call/her warning went unheard *or* unheeded

Ver|hạl|ten [fɛɐ'haltn] NT -s, *no pl* (= *Benehmen*) behaviour (*Brit*), behavior (*US*); (= *Vorgehen*) conduct; (*Chem*) reaction; **falsches Parken ist rechtswidriges ~** unauthorized parking is an offence (*Brit*) *or* offense (*US*); **faires ~** fair conduct

ver|hạl|ten *ptp* **verhạlten** *irreg* VT (*geh*) (= *zurückhalten, unterdrücken*) *Atem* to hold; *Tränen, Urin* to hold back; *seine Schritte* to curb; *Zorn* to restrain; *Lachen* to contain; *Schmerz* to control VI to stop; **im Laufen/Sprechen ~** to stop running/speaking

VR **a** (= *sich benehmen: Mensch, Maschine, Preise etc*) to behave; (= *handeln*) to act; **wie ~ Sie sich dazu?** what is your attitude to that?; **sich ruhig ~** to keep quiet; (= *sich nicht bewegen*) to keep still; **sich rechtswidrig ~** to commit an offence (*Brit*) *or* offense (*US*); **wie man sich bei Hof verhält** how one conducts oneself at court

b (*Sachen, Marktlage*) to be; (*Chem*) to react; **wie verhält sich die Sache?** how do things stand?; **2 verhält sich zu 4 wie 1 zu 2** 2 is to 4 as 1 is to 2

VR *impers* **wie verhält es sich damit?** (= *wie ist die Lage?*) how do things stand?; (= *wie wird das gehandhabt?*) how do you go about it?; **anders/ähnlich verhält es sich mit** *or* **bei ...** the situation is different/the same with regard to ...; **mit den anderen verhält es sich genauso** (= *die anderen denken auch so*) the others feel exactly the same; **wenn sich das so verhält, ...** if that is the case ...

ver|hạl|ten [fɛɐ'haltn] ADJ restrained; *Stimme* muted; *Atem* bated; *Wut* suppressed; *Interesse, Optimismus* guarded; *Tempo, Schritte, Rhythmus* measured; *Aufschwung* limited ADV *sprechen* in a restrained manner; *kritisieren, sich äußern, lachen, weinen* with restraint; *laufen* at a measured pace

Ver|hạl|ten|heit F -, *no pl* restraint; **die ~ des Rhythmus** the measured rhythm

Ver|hạl|tens-: **ver|hạl|tens|auf|fäl|lig** ADJ (*Psych*) displaying behavioural (*Brit*) *or* behavioral (*US*) problems; **Ver|hạl|tens|auf|fäl|lig|keit** F (*Psych*) behavioural (*Brit*) *or* behavioral (*US*) problems *pl*; **Ver|hạl|tens|for|scher(in)** M(F) behavioural (*Brit*) *or* behavioral (*US*) scientist; **Ver|hạl|tens|for|schung** F behavioural (*Brit*) *or* behavioral (*US*) research; **ver|hạl|tens|ge|stört** ADJ disturbed; **Ver|hạl|tens|ko|dex** M code of conduct; **Ver|hạl|tens|maß|re|gel** F rule of conduct; **Ver|hạl|tens|merk|mal** NT behavioural (*Brit*) *or* behavioral (*US*) trait *or* characteristic; **Ver|hạl|tens|mus|ter** NT behaviour (*Brit*) *or* behavior (*US*) pattern; **Ver|hạl|tens|psy|cho|lo|gie** F behavioural (*Brit*) *or* behavioral (*US*) psychology; **Ver|hạl|tens|re|gel** F rule of etiquette *or* conduct; **~n** *pl* (*auch*) code *sing* of conduct; **Ver|hạl|tens|stö|rung** F behavioural (*Brit*) *or* behavioral (*US*) disturbance; **Ver|hạl|tens|wei|se** F behaviour (*Brit*), behavior (*US*)

Ver|hạ̈lt|nis [fɛɐ'hɛltnɪs] NT -ses, -se **a** (= *Proportion*) proportion; (*Math*: = *Mischungsverhältnis*) ratio; **im ~ zu** in relation *or* proportion to; **im ~ zu früher** (= *verglichen mit*) in comparison with earlier times; **im ~ 2 zu 4** in the ratio of 2 to 4; **in einem ~ zu etw stehen** to be in proportion to sth; **in keinem ~ zu etw stehen** to be out of all proportion to sth, to bear no relation to sth; **das ist im ~ wenig** (= *im Vergleich mit anderem*) this is proportionately very little; (= *relativ wenig*) that is comparatively *or* relatively little

b (= *Beziehung*) relationship (*mit jdm/etw* with sb/to sth); relations *pl* (*zu* with); (*zwischen Ländern, innerhalb einer Gruppe*) relations *pl* (*zu* with); (= *Einstellung*) attitude (*zu* to); **ein freundschaftliches ~ zu jdm haben, mit jdm in freundschaftlichem ~ stehen** to be on friendly terms with sb; **sie hat ein gestörtes ~ zur Wirklichkeit** her grasp on reality is distorted; **zu jdm/etw kein ~ finden können** not to be able to relate to sb/sth

c (= *Liebesverhältnis*) affair; (*inf*) (= *Geliebte*) lady friend (*inf*); (= *Geliebter*) friend; **ein ~ mit jdm haben** to have an affair with sb

d Verhältnisse PL (= *Umstände, Bedingungen*) conditions *pl*; (*finanzielle*) circumstances *pl*; **unter** *or* **bei normalen ~sen** under normal circumstances; **so wie die ~se liegen ...** as things stand ...; **die akustischen ~se** the acoustics *pl*; **in ärmlichen ~sen leben** to live in poor conditions; **aus ärmlichen ~sen kommen** to come from a poor background; **über seine ~se leben** to live beyond one's means; **das geht über meine ~se** that is beyond my means; **ich bin für klare ~se** I want to know how we stand; **für klare ~se sorgen, klare ~se schaffen** to get things straight → **räumlich**

Ver|hạ̈lt|nis-: **ver|hạ̈lt|nis|mä|ßig** ADJ **a** (= *proportional*) proportional; (*esp Jur*: = *angemessen*) proportionate, commensurate **b** (= *relativ*) comparative, relative; (*inf*: = *ziemlich*) reasonable ADV **a** (= *proportional*) proportionally **b** (= *relativ, inf*: = *ziemlich*) relatively; **Ver|hạ̈lt|nis|mä|ßig|keit** F **die ~ der Mittel** the appropriateness of the means; **der Grundsatz der ~** the principle of proportionality; **Ver|hạ̈lt|nis|wahl** F proportional representation *no art*; **jdn durch ~ ermitteln** to elect sb by proportional representation; **eine ~ abhalten** to hold a proportional election; **Ver|hạ̈lt|nis|wahl|recht** NT (system of) proportional representation; **Ver|hạ̈lt|nis|wort** NT *pl* **-wörter** preposition; **Ver|hạ̈lt|nis|zahl** F (*Statistik*) ratio

ver|hạn|deln *ptp* **verhạndelt** VT **a** (= *aushandeln*) to negotiate **b** (*Jur*) *Fall* to hear VI **a** (= *Verhandlungen führen*) to negotiate (*über +acc* about); (*inf*: = *diskutieren*) to argue; **da gibts doch nichts zu ~** (*inf*) there's nothing to argue about; **über den Preis lässt sich ~** (*inf*) we can discuss the price **b** (*Jur*) to hear a/the case; **gegen jdn ~** to hear sb's case; **in einem Fall ~** to hear a case

Ver|hạnd|lung F **a** negotiations *pl*; (= *das Verhandeln*) negotiation; **die zur ~ stehende Frage** the question under negotiation; **mit jdm ~en (über etw** *acc*) **aufnehmen** to start negotiations with sb (about sth); **mit jdm in ~(en) stehen** to be negotiating with sb, to be engaged in negotiations with sb; **(mit jdm) in ~(en) treten** to enter into negotiations (with sb); **~en führen** to negotiate; **ich lasse mich auf keine ~(en) ein** (*inf*) I don't propose to enter into any long debates **b** (*Jur*) hearing; (= *Strafverhandlung*) trial

Ver|hạnd|lungs-: **Ver|hạnd|lungs|ba|sis** F basis for negotiation(s); **~ EUR 2.500** (price) EUR 2,500 or near(est) offer; **ver|hạnd|lungs|be|reit** ADJ ready *or* prepared to negotiate; **Ver|hạnd|lungs|be|reit|schaft** F readiness to negotiate; **die mangelnde ~ der Regierung** the government's reluctance to negotiate; **ver|hạnd|lungs|fä|hig** ADJ (*Jur*) able to stand trial; **Ver|hạnd|lungs|fä|hig|keit** F (*Jur*) ability to stand trial; **Ver|hạnd|lungs|füh|rer(in)** M(F) chief negotiator; **Ver|hạnd|lungs|ge|gen|stand** M issue, object of negotiation; **Ver|hạnd|lungs|grund|la|ge** F basis for negotiation(s); **Ver|hạnd|lungs|part|ner(in)** M(F) negotiating party; **Ver|hạnd|lungs|spiel|raum** M room to negotiate, scope for negotiation; (*finanziell*) negotiating range; **Ver|hạnd|lungs|tisch** M negotiating table; **ver|hạnd|lungs|un|fä|hig** ADJ (*Jur*) unable to stand trial; **Ver|hạnd|lungs|un|fä|hig|keit** F (*Jur*) inability to stand trial

ver|hạn|gen [fɛɐ'haŋən] ADJ *Himmel, Tag, Blick* overcast

ver|hạ̈n|gen *ptp* **verhạ̈ngt** VT **a** *Embargo, Strafe, Hausarrest etc* to impose (*über +acc* on); *Ausnahmezustand, Notstand* to declare (*über +acc* in); (*Sport*) *Elfmeter etc* to award, to give **b** (= *zuhängen*) to cover (*mit* with); *Kruzifix, Statue* to veil; **mit verhängtem Zügel, mit verhängten Zügeln** at full speed

Ver|hạ̈ng|nis [fɛɐ'hɛŋnɪs] NT -ses, -se (= *schlimmes Schicksal*) undoing; (= *Katastrophe*) disaster; **jdm zum ~ werden, jds ~ werden** to prove *or* be sb's undoing; **er entging seinem ~ nicht** he could not escape his fate

ver|hạ̈ng|nis|voll ADJ disastrous; *Irrtum, Fehler auch, Zögern, Entschlusslosigkeit* fatal; *Tag* fateful

Ver|hạ̈n|gung [fɛɐ'hɛŋʊŋ] F -, -en (*einer Strafe, eines Verbots etc*) imposition

ver|hạrm|lo|sen [fɛɐ'harmlo:zn] *ptp* **verhạrmlost** VT to play down

Ver|hạrm|lo|sung [fɛɐ'harmlo:zʊŋ] -, -en playing down; (= *Bagatellisierung*) minimizing, minimization

ver|hạ̈rmt [fɛɐ'hɛrmt] ADJ *Mensch, Gesicht* careworn; *Ausdruck* worried

ver|hạr|ren *ptp* **verhạrrt** VI *aux haben or sein* to pause; (*in einer bestimmten Stellung*) to remain; **auf einem Standpunkt/in** *or* **bei einem Entschluss ~** to adhere to a viewpoint/to a decision; **in seinem Stillschweigen ~** to maintain one's silence; (*hartnäckig*) to persist in one's silence

ver|hạr|schen [fɛɐ'harʃn] *ptp* **verhạrscht** VI *aux sein* (*Schnee, Piste*) to crust

ver|hạ̈r|ten *ptp* **verhạ̈rtet** VTR (*alle Bedeutungen*) to harden; **sich** *or* **sein Herz gegen jdn/etw ~** to harden one's heart against sb/sth

Ver|hạ̈r|tung [fɛɐ'hɛrtʊŋ] F -, -en **a** (= *Verhärten*) hardening **b** (*im Gewebe*) lump, knot

ver|has|peln *ptp* **verhaspelt** VR (*inf*) to get into a muddle *or* tangle

ver|hasst [fɛɐ'hast] ADJ hated; *Arbeit auch, Pflicht* hateful; **sich ~ machen** to make oneself hated (*bei* by); **das ist ihm ~** he hates that

ver|hạ̈t|scheln *ptp* **verhạ̈tschelt** VT to spoil, to pamper

Ver|hau [fɛɐ'hau] M -(e)s, -e (*zur Absperrung*) barrier; (= *Käfig*) coop; (= *Bretterbude etc*) shack; (*inf*: = *Unordnung*) mess

ver|hau|en *pret* **verhaute**, *ptp* **verhauen** *(inf)* VT **a** *(= verprügeln)* to beat up; *(zur Strafe)* to beat **b** *Klassenarbeit, Prüfung etc* to make a mess of *(inf)* VR **a** *(= sich verprügeln)* to have a fight **b** *(= Fehler machen)* to make a mistake; *(= sich irren)* to slip up *(inf)*

ver|he|ben *ptp* **verhoben** [fɛɐ'ho:bn] VR *irreg* to hurt oneself lifting something; *(fig)* to overstretch oneself

ver|hed|dern [fɛɐ'hɛdɐn] *ptp* **verheddert** VR *(inf)* to get tangled up; *(beim Sprechen)* to get in a muddle *or* tangle

ver|hee|ren [fɛɐ'he:rən] *ptp* **verheert** VT to devastate; *(Truppen auch)* to lay waste

ver|hee|rend ADJ **a** *Sturm, Folgen, Niederlage, Katastrophe* devastating, disastrous; *Anblick* ghastly **b** *(inf: = schrecklich)* frightful, fearful, ghastly *(all inf)* ADV *(inf: = schrecklich)* frightfully *(inf)*

Ver|hee|rung F -, -en devastation *no pl*; **~(en) anrichten** to cause devastation

ver|heh|len [fɛɐ'he:lən] *ptp* **verhehlt** VT to conceal, to hide; **jdm etw ~** to conceal *or* hide sth from sb; **ich möchte Ihnen nicht ~, dass …** I have no wish to conceal the fact that …

ver|hei|len *ptp* **verheilt** VI *aux sein (Wunde, Bruch)* to heal (up); *(fig)* to heal

ver|heim|li|chen [fɛɐ'haimlɪçn] *ptp* **verheimlicht** VT to keep secret, to conceal *(jdm* from sb); **es lässt sich nicht ~, dass …** it is impossible to conceal the fact that …; **ich habe nichts zu ~** I have nothing to hide

Ver|heim|li|chung F -, -en concealment; *(von Tatsache)* suppression

ver|hei|ra|ten *ptp* **verheiratet** VT to marry *(mit, an +acc* to) VR to get married, to marry; **sich mit jdm ~** to marry sb, to get married to sb

ver|hei|ra|tet [fɛɐ'hairatət] ADJ married; **glücklich ~ sein** to be happily married; **mit jdm/etw ~ sein** *(hum inf)* to be married to sb/sth

Ver|hei|ra|tung [fɛɐ'hairatʊŋ] F -, -en marriage

ver|hei|ßen *ptp* **verheißen** VT *irreg* to promise; **jdm eine große Karriere ~** to predict a great career for sb; **seine Miene verhieß nichts Gutes** his expression did not augur well; **das verheißt schönes Wetter** that heralds good weather

Ver|hei|ßung [fɛɐ'haisʊŋ] F -, -en promise; **das Land der ~** the Promised Land

ver|hei|ßungs|voll ADJ promising; *Anfang auch* auspicious; *Blicke* alluring; **wenig ~** unpromising; **mit ~en Worten** with promises ADV *anfangen* promisingly, auspiciously; *klingen, sich anhören* promising

ver|hei|zen *ptp* **verheizt** VT to burn, to use as fuel; *(fig inf) Sportler* to burn out; *Minister, Untergebene* to crucify; **Soldaten im Kriege ~** *(inf)* to send soldiers to the slaughter

ver|hel|fen *ptp* **verholfen** [fɛɐ'hɔlfn] VI *irreg* **jdm zu etw ~** to help sb to get sth; **jdm zu seinem Glück ~** to help to make sb happy; **jdm zum Sieg ~** to help sb to victory

ver|herr|li|chen [fɛɐ'hɛrlɪçn] *ptp* **verherrlicht** VT *Gewalt, Krieg, Taten, Regime, jdn* to glorify; *Gott* to praise; *Tugenden* to extol; *(in Gedichten)* to celebrate

Ver|herr|li|chung F -, -en glorification; *(von Gott)* praising; *(von Tugenden)* extolment; *(in Gedichten)* celebration

ver|het|zen *ptp* **verhetzt** VT to stir up, to incite (to violence *etc*)

Ver|het|zung [fɛɐ'hɛtsʊŋ] F -, -en incitement, stirring up

ver|heult [fɛɐ'hɔylt] ADJ *Augen, Gesicht* puffy, swollen from crying; **du siehst so ~ aus** you really look as if you have been crying

ver|he|xen *ptp* **verhext** VT to bewitch; *(Fee, Zauberer etc auch)* to cast a spell over; *(inf) Maschine etc* to put a jinx on *(inf)*; **jdn in etw** *(acc)* **~** to turn sb into sth (by magic); **der verhexte Prinz** the enchanted prince; **das verhexte Schloss** the bewitched castle; **heute ist alles wie verhext** *(inf)* there's a jinx on everything today *(inf)*; **das ist doch wie verhext** *(inf)* it's maddening *(inf)*

ver|hin|dern *ptp* **verhindert** VT to prevent; *Unglück auch* to avert; *Versuch, Plan* to foil, to stop; **ich konnte es nicht ~, dass er die Wahrheit erfuhr** I couldn't prevent him from finding out the truth; **das lässt sich leider nicht ~** it can't be helped, unfortunately; **er war an diesem Abend (dienstlich** *or* **geschäftlich) verhindert** he was unable to come that evening (for reasons of work); **ein verhinderter Politiker** *(inf)* a would-be politician

Ver|hin|de|rung F prevention; *(von Unglück auch)* averting; *(von Versuch, Plan)* foiling, stopping; **im Falle seiner ~** if he is unable to come

ver|hoh|len [fɛɐ'ho:lən] ADJ concealed, secret; *Gelächter, Schadenfreude auch, Gähnen* suppressed; **kaum ~** barely concealed/suppressed

ver|höh|nen *ptp* **verhöhnt** VT to mock, to deride

ver|hoh|ne|pi|peln [fɛɐ'ho:nəpi:pln] *ptp* **verhohnepipelt** VT *(inf) (= verspotten)* to send up *(inf)*; *(= zum Besten haben)* to have on *(inf)*

Ver|hoh|ne|pi|pe|lung [fɛɐ'ho:napi:pəlʊŋ] F -, -en send-up *(inf)*

Ver|höh|nung [fɛɐ'hø:nʊŋ] F -, -en mocking, ridiculing; *(Bemerkung)* gibe

ver|hö|kern *ptp* **verhökert** VT *(inf)* to get rid of *(inf)*

ver|ho|len *ptp* **verholt** VT *(Naut)* to haul away

ver|hol|zen *ptp* **verholzt** VI *aux sein (Bot)* to lignify

Ver|hör [fɛɐ'hø:ɐ] NT -(e)s, -e questioning, interrogation; *(bei Gericht)* examination; **jdn ins ~ nehmen** to question sb, to interrogate sb; *(bei Gericht)* to examine sb; *(inf)* to take sb to task; **jdn einem ~ unterziehen** *(form)* to subject sb to questioning *or* interrogation/examination

ver|hö|ren *ptp* **verhört** VT to question, to interrogate; *(bei Gericht)* to examine; *(inf)* to quiz *(inf)* VR to mishear, to hear wrongly; **du musst dich verhört haben** you must have misheard, you must have heard it wrong

ver|hornt [fɛɐ'hɔrnt] ADJ *Haut* horny

ver|hu|deln *ptp* **verhudelt** VT *(inf)* to botch

ver|hül|len *ptp* **verhüllt** VT to veil; *Haupt, Körperteil, Gebäude* to cover; *(fig)* to mask, to disguise VR *(Frau)* to veil oneself; *(Berge etc)* to become veiled

ver|hül|lend ADJ *Ausdruck* euphemistic

Ver|hül|lung [fɛɐ'hʏlʊŋ] F -, -en **a** *(= das Verhüllen)* veiling; *(von Haupt, Körperteil)* covering; *(fig)* masking, disguising **b** *(= Bedeckung)* veil; *(von Haupt, Körperteil)* cover; *(fig)* mask, disguise **c** *(= Ausdruck)* euphemism

ver|hun|dert|fa|chen [fɛɐ'hʊndɐtfaxn] *ptp* **verhundertfacht** VTR to increase a hundredfold

ver|hun|gern *ptp* **verhungert** VI *aux sein* to starve, to die of starvation; *(inf: = Hunger haben)* to be starving *(inf)*; **er sah völlig verhungert aus** he looked half-starved; *(inf)* he looked absolutely famished *(inf)*; **ich bin am Verhungern** *(inf)* I'm starving *(inf)*; **jdn ~ lassen** *(lit)* to let sb starve (to death); *(beim Spielen)* to leave sb out of the game

Ver|hun|gern|de(r) [fɛɐ'hʊŋɐndə] MF *decl as adj* starving person/man/woman

Ver|hun|ger|te(r) [fɛɐ'hʊŋɐtə] MF *decl as adj* person/man/woman *etc* who has starved to death

ver|hun|zen [fɛɐ'hʊntsn] *ptp* **verhunzt** VT *(inf)* to ruin; *Sprache, Lied auch* to murder

ver|hurt [fɛɐ'hu:ɐt] ADJ *(pej)* whorish; *Mann* loose-living

ver|huscht [fɛɐ'hʊʃt] ADJ *(inf)* timid; **~ aussehen** to look shy *or* timid

ver|hü|ten *ptp* **verhütet** VT to prevent; **das verhüte Gott!** God forbid!; **möge Gott ~, dass …** God forbid that …; **~de Maßnahmen** preventive measures; *(zur Empfängnisverhütung)* precautions VI *(= Empfängnisverhütung betreiben)* to take precautions

Ver|hü|ter|li [fɛɐ'hy:tɐli] NT -(s), - *(Sw: = Verhütungsmittel)* contraceptive; *(hum inf: = Kondom)* johnny *(Brit inf)*, rubber *(esp US inf)*

ver|hüt|ten [fɛɐ'hʏtn] *ptp* **verhüttet** VT to smelt

Ver|hüt|tung F -, -en smelting

Ver|hü|tung [fɛɐ'hy:tʊŋ] F -, -en prevention; *(= Empfängnisverhütung)* contraception

Ver|hü|tungs|mit|tel NT contraceptive

ver|hut|zelt [fɛɐ'hʊtslt] ADJ *Gesicht, Männlein* wizened; *Haut auch* wrinkled; *Obst* shrivelled *(esp Brit)*, shriveled *(US)*

Ve|ri|fi|ka|ti|on [verifika'tsio:n] F -, -en verification

ve|ri|fi|zier|bar [verifi'tsi:ɐba:ɐ] ADJ verifiable

ve|ri|fi|zie|ren [verifi'tsi:rən] *ptp* **verifiziert** VT to verify

ver|in|ner|li|chen [fɛɐ'ɪnɐlɪçn] *ptp* **verinnerlicht** VT to internalize; *jdn* to spiritualize

ver|in|ner|licht [fɛɐ'ɪnɐlɪçt] ADJ *Normen, Werte* internalized; *Wesen, Gesichtsausdruck* spiritualized

Ver|in|ner|li|chung F -, -en internalization; *(von Mensch, in Literatur)* spiritualization

ver|ir|ren *ptp* **verirrt** VR to get lost, to lose one's way; *(fig)* to go astray; *(Tier, Kugel)* to stray; **ein verirrtes Schaf** *(lit, fig)* a lost sheep; **hierhin ~ sich die Touristen nur selten** *(fig)* tourists don't venture out here very often

Ver|ir|rung F losing one's way *no art*; *(fig)* aberration

ve|ri|ta|bel ADJ *(geh) attr* veritable *attr*

ver|ja|gen *ptp* **verjagt** VT *(lit, fig)* to chase away; *trübe Gedanken, Kummer auch* to dispel

ver|jäh|ren *ptp* **verjährt** VI *aux sein* to come under the statute of limitations; *(Anspruch)* to be in lapse; **verjährtes Verbrechen** statute-barred crime; **Totschlag verjährt nach 20 Jahren** the statute of limitations for manslaughter is 20 years; **Mord verjährt nie** there is no statute of limitations for murder; **das ist schon längst verjährt** *(inf)* that's all over and done with

Ver|jäh|rung [fɛɐ'jɛ:rʊŋ] F -, -en limitation; *(von Anspruch)* lapse

Ver|jäh|rungs|frist F limitation period

ver|jaz|zen [fɛɐ'dʒɛsn, -'jatsn] *ptp* **verjazzt** VT to jazz up

ver|ju|beln *ptp* **verjubelt** VT *(inf) Geld* to blow *(inf)*

ver|jün|gen [fɛɐ'jʏŋən] *ptp* **verjüngt** VT to rejuvenate; *(= jünger aussehen lassen)* to make look younger; *Baumbestand* to regenerate; **eine Mannschaft/das Personal ~** to build up a younger team/staff; **die neue Stelle hat ihn um Jahre verjüngt** the new job gave him a new lease of life; **er kam (um Jahre) verjüngt von der Gesundheitsfarm zurück** he came back from the health farm looking (years) younger VR **a** *(= jünger werden)* to become younger; *(Haut, Erscheinung)* to become rejuvenated; *(= jünger aussehen)* to look younger; **du hast dich verjüngt** *(inf)* you look (much) younger **b** *(= dünner werden)* to taper; *(Tunnel, Rohr)* to narrow

Ver|jün|gung F -, -en **a** rejuvenation; *(von Baumbestand)* regeneration **b** *(= das Dünnerwerden)* tapering; *(von Tunnel, Rohr)* narrowing

Ver|jün|gungs|kur F rejuvenation cure

ver|ju|xen *ptp* **verjuxt** VT *(inf) Geld* to blow *(inf)*

ver|ka|beln *ptp* **verkabelt** VT *(Telec)* to link up to the cable network

Ver|ka|be|lung [fɛɐ'ka:bəlʊŋ] F -, -en *(Telec)* linking up to the cable network

ver|ka|cken *ptp* **verkackt** VT *(vulg)* **a** → **verscheißen b** *Arbeit, Prüfung etc* to fuck up *(vulg)*; **er hat die Englischprüfung voll verkackt** he totally fucked up (on) the English test

ver|kal|ken *ptp* **verkalkt** VI *aux sein (Arterien)* to harden; *(Gewebe)* to calcify; *(Kessel, Wasserleitung etc)* to fur up, to become furred; *(inf: Mensch)* to become senile

ver|kalkt [fɛɐ'kalkt] ADJ *(inf)* senile

ver|kal|ku|lie|ren *ptp* **verkalkuliert** VR to miscalculate

Ver|kal|kung [fɛɐ'kalkʊŋ] F -, -en *(von Arterien)* hardening; *(von Gewebe)* calcification; *(von Kessel, Wasserleitung etc)* furring; *(inf)* senility

Ver|kal|kungs|er|schei|nung F *(inf: bei alten Menschen)* sign of senility

ver|käl|ten [fɛɐ'kɛltn] *ptp* **verkältet** VR *(dial)* = **erkälten**

ver|kannt [fɛɐ'kant] ADJ unrecognized → *auch* **verkennen**

ver|kan|ten [fɛɐ'kantn] *ptp* **verkantet** VT *(= schräg stellen)* to tilt; *(Skier)* to edge; **sich ~** *(= sich verklemmen)* to get wedged (in); *(Skier)* to edge over

ver|kappt [fɛɐ'kapt] ADJ *attr* hidden; *Lungenentzündung* undiagnosed; **ein ~er Fanatiker/Sozialist** *etc* a closet fanatic/socialist *etc*; **~er Nebensatz** *(Gram)* *subordinate clause without an introductory word*

ver|kap|seln [fɛɐ'kapsln] *ptp* **verkapselt** VR *(Med) (Bakterien)* to become encapsulated; *(Parasit)* to become encysted

Ver|kap|se|lung [fɛɐ'kapsəlʊŋ] F -, -en *(Med) (von Bakterien)* encapsulation; *(von Parasit)* encystment

ver|kars|ten [fɛɐ'karstn] *ptp* **verkarstet** VI *aux sein* to develop to karst *(spec)*

Ver|kars|tung F -, -en karst development *(spec)*

ver|ka|tert [fɛɐ'ka:tɐt] ADJ *(inf)* hung over *usu pred (inf)*; **einen ~en Eindruck machen** to look hung over *(inf)*

Ver|kauf M **a** sale; *(= das Verkaufen)* selling; **zum ~ stehen** to be up for sale; **beim ~ des Hauses** when selling the house → **Straße b** *(= Abteilung)* sales *sing, no art*

ver|kau|fen *ptp* **verkauft** VTI *(lit, fig)* to sell *(für, um* for); **„zu ~"** "for sale"; **jdm etw ~, etw an jdn ~** to sell sb sth, to sell sth to sb; **sie haben ihr Leben so teuer wie möglich verkauft** they sold their lives as dearly as possible; **er würde sogar seine Großmutter ~** he'd even sell his own grandmother → **Straße, verraten, dumm**

VR **a** *(Ware)* to sell; *(Mensch)* to sell oneself; **er hat sich ganz und gar an die Partei verkauft** he is committed body and soul to the party

b *(= einen schlechten Kauf machen)* to make a bad buy; **damit habe ich mich verkauft** that was a bad buy

c *(fig: = sich anpreisen)* to sell oneself

Ver|käu|fer(in) M(F) seller; *(in Geschäft)* sales or shop assistant, salesperson; *(im Außendienst)* salesman/saleswoman/salesperson; *(Jur: von Grundbesitz etc)* vendor

ver|käuf|lich ADJ sal(e)able, marketable; *(= zu verkaufen)* for sale; **leicht** *or* **gut/schwer ~** easy/hard to sell

Ver|käuf|lich|keit F, *no pl* sal(e)ability, marketability

Ver|kaufs- *in cpds* sales; **Ver|kaufs|ab|tei|lung** F sales department; **Ver|kaufs|agen|tur** F sales (promotion) agency; **Ver|kaufs|ak|ti|on** F sales campaign, sales drive *(US)*; **Ver|kaufs|ar|gu|ment** NT *(für Produkt)* selling point; *(von Verkäufer)* sales pitch; **Ver|kaufs|aus|stel|lung** F sales exhibition; **Ver|kaufs|au|to|mat** M vending machine; **Ver|kaufs|be|din|gun|gen** PL conditions *pl* of sale; **Ver|kaufs|be|ra|ter(in)** M(F) sales consultant; **Ver|kaufs|bü|ro** NT sales office; **Ver|kaufs|er|lös** M proceeds *pl* (from the sale); **Ver|kaufs|flä|che** F sales area; **Ver|kaufs|för|de|rung** F sales promotion; *(= Abteilung)* sales promotion department; **Ver|kaufs|ge|nie** NT **ein ~ sein** to be a genius at selling things; **Ver|kaufs|ge|spräch** NT sales consultation; *(zur Überzeugung)* sales talk *no art*; **Ver|kaufs|lei|ter(in)** M(F) sales manager; **ver|kaufs|of|fen** ADJ open for business; **~er Samstag** *Saturday on which the shops are open all day*; **Ver|kaufs|op|ti|on** F *(Fin)* selling option; *(St Ex)* put option; **Ver|kaufs|per|so|nal** NT sales personnel *or* staff; **Ver|kaufs|preis** M retail price; **Ver|kaufs|schla|ger** M big seller; **Ver|kaufs|ver|pa|ckung** F packaging; **Ver|kaufs|zah|len** PL sales figures *pl*

Ver|kehr [fɛɐ'ke:ɐ] M -(e)s, *no pl* **a** traffic; *(= Beförderung, Verkehrsmittel)* transport, transportation *(US)*; **für den ~ freigeben, dem ~ übergeben** *(Straße etc)* to open to traffic; *Transportmittel* to bring into service; **den ~ regeln** to regulate the (flow of) traffic

b *(= Verbindung)* contact, communication; *(= Umgang)* company; *(= Geschlechtsverkehr)* intercourse; **in brieflichem ~ stehen** to correspond; **in seinem ~ mit Menschen** in his dealings with people; **den ~ mit jdm pflegen** *(form)* to associate with sb; **den ~ mit jdm abbrechen** to break off relations *or* contact with sb

c *(= Geschäftsverkehr, Handelsverkehr)* trade; *(= Umsätze, Zahlungsverkehr)* business; *(= Postverkehr)* service; *(= Umlauf)* circulation; **etw in (den) ~ bringen** to put sth into circulation; **etw aus dem ~ ziehen** *(Banknoten)* to take sth out of circulation; *schadhafte Produkte, Fahrzeuge* to withdraw sth; *altes Schiff* to take sth out of commission; *Blutkonserven, medizinische Präparate* to remove sth; **jdn aus dem ~ ziehen** *(= entfernen, betrunkene Autofahrer)* to ban; *Politiker, Dealer* to remove; *(inf: = ins Gefängnis werfen)* to put sb in jug *(Brit inf)* *or* in the slammer *(inf)*

ver|keh|ren *ptp* **verkehrt** VI **a** *aux haben or sein (= fahren)* to run; *(Flugzeug)* to fly; **der Bus/das Flugzeug verkehrt regelmäßig zwischen A und B** the bus runs *or* goes *or* operates regularly/the plane goes *or* operates regularly between A and B

b *(= Gast sein, Kontakt pflegen)* **bei jdm ~** to frequent sb's house, to visit sb (regularly); **mit jdm ~** to associate with sb; **in einem Lokal ~** to frequent a pub; **in Künstlerkreisen ~** to move in artistic circles, to mix with artists; **mit jdm brieflich** *or* **schriftlich ~** *(form)* to correspond with sb; **mit jdm (geschlechtlich) ~** to have (sexual) intercourse with sb

VT to turn *(in +acc* into); **etw ins Gegenteil ~** to reverse sth → *auch* **verkehrt**

VR to turn *(in +acc* into); **sich ins Gegenteil ~** to become reversed

Ver|kehrs- *in cpds* traffic; **Ver|kehrs|ab|wick|lung** F traffic handling; **Ver|kehrs|ader** F artery, arterial road; **Ver|kehrs|am|pel** F traffic lights *pl*; **Ver|kehrs|amt** NT *(= Verkehrsbüro)* tourist information office; **Ver|kehrs|an|bin|dung** F transport links *pl*; **die Stadt hat eine gute ~** the town has good transport links; **ver|kehrs|arm** ADJ *Zeit, Straße* quiet; **ein ~es Gebiet** an area with little traffic; **Ver|kehrs|auf|kom|men** NT volume of traffic; **Ver|kehrs|be|hin|de|rung** F *(Jur)* obstruction (of traffic); **Ver|kehrs|be|las|tung** F burden of traffic; **ver|kehrs|be|ru|higt** [-bəru:ɪçt] ADJ traffic-calmed; **Ver|kehrs|be|ru|hi|gung** F traffic calming; **Ver|kehrs|be|trie|be** PL transport services *pl*; **Ver|kehrs|bü|ro** NT tourist information office; **Ver|kehrs|cha|os** NT chaos on the roads; **Ver|kehrs|de|likt** NT traffic offence *(Brit)* *or* offense *(US)*; **Ver|kehrs|dich|te** F volume of traffic, traffic density; **Ver|kehrs|durch|sa|ge** F traffic announcement; **Ver|kehrs|er|zie|hung** F road safety training; **Ver|kehrs|flug|ha|fen** M (commercial) airport; **Ver|kehrs|flug|zeug** NT commercial aircraft; **Ver|kehrs|füh|rung** F traffic management system; **Ver|kehrs|funk** M radio traffic service; **ver|kehrs|ge|fähr|dend** ADJ dangerous; **Ver|kehrs|ge|fähr|dung** F *(Jur: = verkehrswidriges Fahren)* dangerous driving; **eine ~ darstellen** to be a hazard to other traffic; **ver|kehrs|güns|tig** ADJ *Lage* convenient; *Ort, Viertel* conveniently situated ADV *liegen* conveniently; *wohnen* in a convenient location *or* situation; **Ver|kehrs|hin|der|nis** NT (traffic) obstruction; **ein ~ sein** to cause an obstruction; **Ver|kehrs|hin|weis** M traffic announcement; **Ver|kehrs|in|farkt** M total gridlock; **Ver|kehrs|in|fra|struk|tur** F transport *(Brit)* *or* transportation *(US)* infrastructure; **Ver|kehrs|in|sel** F traffic island; **Ver|kehrs|kno|ten|punkt** M traffic junction; **Ver|kehrs|kol|laps** M total gridlock; **Ver|kehrs|kon|trol|le** F traffic check; **bei jdm eine ~ machen** *(Polizei)* to stop sb; **verstärkte ~n machen** to increase traffic checks; **Ver|kehrs|krei|sel** M roundabout *(Brit)*, traffic circle *(US)*; **Ver|kehrs|la|ge** F situation on the roads, traffic situation; **Ver|kehrs|lärm** M traffic noise; **Ver|kehrs|leit|sys|tem** NT traffic guidance system, traffic management system, TMS; **Ver|kehrs|mel|dung** F traffic announcement; **~en** traffic news *sing*; **Ver|kehrs|mi|nis|ter(in)** M(F) minister of transport; **Ver|kehrs|mi|nis|te|ri|um** NT ministry of transport *(Brit)*, department of transportation *(US)*; **Ver|kehrs|mit|tel** NT means *sing* of transport; **öffentliche/private ~** public/private transport; **Ver|kehrs|mo|ral** F *(im Straßenverkehr)* driving ethics *pl*; **Ver|kehrs|netz** NT traffic network; **Ver|kehrs|op|fer** NT road casualty; **Ver|kehrs|ord|nung** F ≈ Highway Code *(Brit)*, traffic rules and regulations *pl*; **Ver|kehrs|pla|nung** F traffic engineering; **Ver|kehrs|po|li|zei** F traffic police *pl*; **Ver|kehrs|po|li|zist(in)** M(F) traffic policeman/-woman; **Ver|kehrs|re|gel** F traffic regulation; **Ver|kehrs|re|ge|lung** F traffic control; **ver|kehrs|reich** ADJ *Straße, Gegend, Flughafen* busy; **~e Zeit** peak (traffic) time; **Ver|kehrs|row|dy** M, **Ver|kehrs|rü|pel** M road hog *(inf)*; **Ver|kehrs|schild** NT *pl* **-schilder** road sign; **ver|kehrs|schwach** ADJ *Zeit* off-peak; *Gebiet* with little traffic; **die Nachmittagsstunden sind sehr ~** there is very little traffic in the afternoons; **ver|kehrs|si|cher** ADJ *Fahrzeug* roadworthy; *Straße, Brücke* safe (for traffic); **Ver|kehrs|si|cher|heit** F *(von Fahrzeug)* roadworthiness; *(von Straße, Brücke)* safety; **Ver|kehrs|spra|che** F lingua franca; **Ver|kehrs|stau** M, **Ver|kehrs|stau|ung** F traffic jam; **Ver|kehrs|sto|ckung** F traffic hold-up *(Brit)* *or* jam; **Ver|kehrs|stra|ße** F road open to traffic; **Ver|kehrs|strom** M flow of traffic; **Ver|kehrs|sün|der(in)** M(F) *(inf)* traffic offender *(Brit)* *or* violator *(US)*; **Ver|kehrs|sün|der|kar|tei** F *(inf)* *central index of road traffic offenders*; **Ver|kehrs|teil|neh|mer(in)** M(F) road user; **Ver|kehrs|to|te(r)** MF *decl as adj* road casualty; **die Zahl der ~n** the number of deaths on the road; **ver|kehrs|tüch|tig** ADJ *Fahrzeug* roadworthy; *Mensch* fit to drive; **Ver|kehrs|tüch|tig|keit** F *(von Fahrzeug)* roadworthiness; *(von Mensch)* fitness to drive, driving ability; **Ver|kehrs|über|wa|chung** F traffic control *or* surveillance; **Ver|kehrs|un|fall** M road accident; *(hum inf)* accident; **Ver|kehrs|un|ter|neh|men** NT transport company; **Ver|kehrs|un|ter|richt** M traffic instruction; **ver|kehrs|un|tüch|tig** ADJ *Fahrzeug* unroadworthy; *Mensch* unfit to drive; **Ver|kehrs|ver|bin|dung** F link; *(= Anschluss)* connection; **Ver|kehrs|ver|bund** M integrated transport system; **Ver|kehrs|ver|ein** M *local organization concerned with upkeep of tourist attractions, facilities etc*; **Ver|kehrs|ver|hält|nis|se** PL traffic situation *sing*; *(= Straßenzustand)* road conditions *pl*; **Ver|kehrs|ver|stoß** M motoring offence *(Brit)*, traffic violation *(US)*; **Ver|kehrs|vo|lu|men** NT volume of traffic; **Ver|kehrs|vor|schrift** F (road) traffic regulation; **Ver|kehrs|wacht** F traffic patrol; **Ver|kehrs|weg** M highway; **Ver|kehrs|wert** M *(Fin)* current market value; **Ver|kehrs|we|sen** NT, *no pl* transport and communications *no art*; **ver|kehrs|wid|rig** ADJ contrary to road traffic regulations ADV **sich ~ verhalten** to break the road traffic regulations; **Ver|kehrs|zäh|lung** F traffic census; **Ver|kehrs|zei|chen** NT road sign; **Ver|kehrs|zent|ral-**

kar|tei F, **Ver|kehrs|zent|ral|re|gis|ter** NT *central index of traffic offenders*

ver|kehrt [fɛɐ'ke:ɐt] ADJ wrong; *Vorstellung auch, Welt* topsy-turvy; **das ist gar nicht (so) ~** *(inf)* that can't be bad *(inf)*; **der ist gar nicht (so) ~** *(inf)* he's not such a bad sort; **das Verkehrte** the wrong thing; **das Verkehrteste, was du tun könntest** the worst thing you could do; **der/die Verkehrte** the wrong person; **eines Tages wirst du an den Verkehrten geraten** one day you'll get your fingers burned → **Adresse**
ADV wrongly; **etw ~ (herum) anhaben** *(= linke Seite nach außen)* to have sth on inside out; *(= vorne nach hinten)* to have sth on back to front; **etw ~ halten** to hold sth wrongly; *(= falsch herum)* to hold sth the wrong way (a)round; *(= oben nach unten)* to hold sth upside down; **die Möbel alle ~ stellen** *(= an den falschen Platz)* to put all the furniture in the wrong place; **er ist ~ herum** *(inf: homosexuell)* he's bent *(inf)* → *auch* **verkehren**

Ver|keh|rung [fɛɐ'ke:rʊŋ] F -, -en reversal; *(von Rollen auch)* switching; **eine ~ ins Gegenteil** a complete reversal

ver|kei|len *ptp* **verkeilt** VT **a** *(= festmachen)* to wedge tight **b** *(inf: = verprügeln)* to thrash VR to become wedged together

ver|ken|nen *ptp* **verkannt** [fɛɐ'kant] VT *irreg Lage, jdn etc* to misjudge; *(= unterschätzen auch)* to underestimate; **ein Dichter, der zeit seines Lebens verkannt wurde** a poet who remained unrecognized in his lifetime; **ich will nicht ~, dass ...** I would not deny that ...; **es ist nicht zu ~, dass ...** it is undeniable that ..., it cannot be denied that ...; **seine schlechte Laune/seine Absicht war nicht zu ~** his bad temper/his intention was obvious → *auch* **verkannt**

Ver|ken|nung F misjudgement; *(= Unterschätzung auch)* underestimation; *(von Genie, Künstler)* failure to appreciate *(jds* sb); **in ~ der wahren Sachlage ...** misjudging the real situation ...

ver|ket|ten *ptp* **verkettet** VT *(lit)* to chain (up); *Tür, Kiste* to put chains/a chain on; *(fig)* to link VR to become interlinked, to become bound up together; **verkettet sein** *(fig)* to be interlinked, to be bound up (together)

Ver|ket|tung [fɛɐ'kɛtʊŋ] F -, -en *(= das Verketten)* chaining; *(= Ketten)* chains *pl*; *(fig)* interconnection

ver|ket|zern [fɛɐ'kɛtsɐn] *ptp* **verketzert** VT to denounce

ver|kit|schen [fɛɐ'kɪtʃn] *ptp* **verkitscht** VT *(inf)* **a** *Gemälde, Literatur* to make kitschy; *Lied* to sentimentalize **b** *(dial: = verkaufen)* to flog *(Brit inf)*, to sell

ver|kit|ten *ptp* **verkittet** VT to cement; *Fenster* to put putty (a)round

ver|kla|gen *ptp* **verklagt** VT to sue *(wegen* for), to take proceedings against *(wegen* for); **jdn auf etw** *(acc)* **~** to take sb to court for sth; **die verklagte Partei, der/die Verklagte** the defendant

ver|klam|mern *ptp* **verklammert** VT to staple together; *(Med) Wunde* to apply clips to; *(Tech) Bauteile* to brace, to put braces (a)round; *(fig)* to link VR *(Menschen)* to embrace; *(Hände)* to interlock

Ver|klam|me|rung [fɛɐ'klamərʊŋ] F -, -en **a** *(= das Verklammern)* stapling; *(Med)* applying of clips (+*gen* to); *(von Bauteilen)* bracing; *(fig)* linking **b** *(= die Klammern)* staples *pl*; *(Med)* clips *pl*; *(Tech)* braces *pl*; *(fig)* links *pl*

ver|klap|pen *ptp* **verklappt** VT *Abfallstoffe* to dump

Ver|klap|pung [fɛɐ'klapʊŋ] F -, -en *(von Abfallstoffen)* dumping

ver|kla|ren [fɛɐ'kla:rən] *ptp* **verklart** VT *(inf)* **jdm etw ~** to spell sth out for sb

ver|klä|ren *ptp* **verklärt** VT to transfigure VR to become transfigured

ver|klärt [fɛɐ'klɛ:ɐt] ADJ transfigured

Ver|kla|rung F -, -en *(Naut)* ship's protest

Ver|klä|rung F transfiguration

ver|klat|schen *ptp* **verklatscht** VT *(inf)* **a** *(= verpetzen)* to tell on *(inf)* **b** *Zeit* to spend chatting

ver|klau|seln [fɛɐ'klauzln] *ptp* **verklauselt**, **ver|klau|su|lie|ren** [fɛɐklauzu'li:rən] *ptp* **verklausuliert** *(rare)* VT *Vertrag* to hedge in *or* around with (restrictive) clauses; **der Vertrag ist zu verklausuliert** the contract has too many qualifying clauses

ver|kle|ben *ptp* **verklebt** VT *(= zusammenkleben)* to stick together; *(= zukleben)* to cover *(mit* with); *Tapeten* to stick; *Plakate* to stick up; *Haare, Verband* to make sticky; *Wunde (mit Pflaster)* to put a plaster on; *(= verbrauchen)* to use up VI *aux sein (Wunde, Eileiter)* to close; *(Augen)* to get gummed up; *(Mehl, Briefmarken, Bonbons)* to stick together; *(Haare)* to become matted; **mit etw ~** to stick to sth

ver|klebt [fɛɐ'kle:pt] ADJ *Verband, Wunde* sticky; *Augen* gummed up; *Haare* matted; *Eileiter* blocked

ver|kle|ckern *ptp* **verkleckert** VT *(inf)* to spill; *(fig) Zeit, Energie, Geld* to waste

ver|klei|den *ptp* **verkleidet** VT **a** *jdn* to disguise; *(= kostümieren)* to dress up, to put into fancy dress; *(fig) Ideen, Absicht* to disguise, to mask; **alle waren verkleidet** everyone was dressed up, everyone was in fancy dress **b** *(= verschalen) Wand, Schacht, Tunnel* to line; *(= vertäfeln)* to panel; *(= bedecken)* to cover; *(= ausschlagen, auslegen) Kiste etc* to line; *(= verdecken) Heizkörper* to cover, to mask VR to disguise oneself; *(= sich kostümieren)* to dress (oneself) up; **muss man sich ~?** do you have to wear fancy dress?

Ver|klei|dung F **a** *(= das Verkleiden von Menschen)* disguising; *(= Kostümierung)* dressing up, putting into fancy dress; *(= Kleidung)* disguise; *(= Kostüm)* fancy dress **b** *(= das Verkleiden, Material)* lining; *(mit Holz)* panelling *(Brit)*, paneling *(esp US)*; *(= das Bedecken)* covering; *(= das Verdecken)* masking

ver|klei|nern [fɛɐ'klainɐn] *ptp* **verkleinert** VT to reduce; *Raum, Gebiet, Firma* to make smaller; *(Linse, Brille)* to make smaller; *Fotografie* to reduce (in size); *Maßstab* to scale down; *Abstand* to decrease; *Not, Probleme, Schuld* to minimize; *jds Leistungen, Verdienste* to belittle; *Wort* to form the diminutive of
VR to be reduced; *(Raum, Gebiet, Firma)* to become smaller; *(Maßstab)* to be scaled down; *(Abstand)* to decrease; *(Not, Probleme, Schuld)* to become less; **durch den großen Schrank verkleinert sich das Zimmer** the big cupboard makes the room (seem) smaller; **wir haben uns verkleinert** *(wohnungsmäßig)* we have moved into a smaller flat *(Brit) or* apartment
VI *(Linse etc)* to make everything seem smaller

Ver|klei|ne|rung F -, -en **a** *(= das Verkleinern)* reduction; *(von Gebiet, Firma, durch Linse, Brille)* making smaller; *(von Fotografie)* reduction (in size); *(von Maßstab)* scaling down; *(von Abstand)* decreasing; *(von Not, Problemen, Schuld)* minimizing; *(von Leistungen, Verdiensten)* belittling; *(Gram)* formation of the diminutive **b** *(= das Kleinerwerden)* reduction; *(von Raum, Gebiet, Firma)* becoming smaller; *(von Maßstab)* scaling down; *(von Abstand)* decreasing; *(von Not, Problemen, Schuld)* lessening **c** *(= Bild)* reduced size reproduction; *(= Foto)* reduction; *(= Wort)* diminutive (form); *(Mus)* diminution

Ver|klei|ne|rungs|form F diminutive form

ver|kleis|tern *ptp* **verkleistert** VT *(= zusammenkleben)* to stick together; *(= zukleben)* to cover; *(inf) (= mit Kleister beschmieren)* to get glue on; *(fig: = vertuschen)* to cover up

ver|klem|men *ptp* **verklemmt** VR to get *or* become stuck

ver|klemmt [fɛɐ'klɛmt] ADJ *(inf) Mensch* inhibited

Ver|klemmt|heit F -, -en *(inf)*, **Ver|klem|mung** F -, -en inhibitions *pl*; **Sex ohne ~** uninhibited sex

ver|kli|ckern *ptp* **verklickert** VT *(inf)* **jdm etw ~** to make sth clear to sb

ver|klin|gen *ptp* **verklungen** [fɛɐ'klʊŋən] VI *irreg aux sein* to die *or* fade away; *(fig: Begeisterung, Interesse)* to fade

ver|klop|fen *ptp* **verklopft**, **ver|klop|pen** *ptp* **verkloppt** VT *(inf)* **a jdn ~** to give sb what-for *(inf)* **b** *(= verkaufen)* to flog *(Brit inf)*, to sell

ver|klum|pen *ptp* **verklumpt** VI *aux sein* to get lumpy

ver|kna|cken *ptp* **verknackt** VT *(inf)* **jdn zu zwei Jahren ~** to do sb for two years *(inf)*, to give sb two years; **jdn zu einer Geldstrafe ~** to stick a fine on sb *(inf)*; **verknackt werden** to be done *(inf)*

ver|knack|sen [fɛɐ'knaksn] *ptp* **verknackst** VT **(sich** *dat***) den Knöchel** *or* **Fuß ~** to twist one's ankle

ver|knal|len *ptp* **verknallt** *(inf)* VR **sich (in jdn) ~** to fall for sb *(inf)*; **ich war damals unheimlich (in ihn) verknallt** I was head over heels in love (with him) then VT *Feuerwerkskörper* to let off; *Munition* to use up; *Geld (mit Feuerwerkskörpern)* to waste on fireworks

ver|knap|pen [fɛɐ'knapn] *ptp* **verknappt** VT to cut back; *Rationen* to cut down (on) VR to run short

Ver|knap|pung F -, -en *(Comm)* shortage, scarcity

ver|knaut|schen *ptp* **verknautscht** VT to crush, to crumple VIR *(vi: aux sein)* to crease

ver|knei|fen *ptp* **verkniffen** [fɛɐ'knɪfn] VT *irreg (inf)* **sich** *(dat)* **etw ~** to stop oneself (from) saying/doing *etc* sth; *Lächeln* to keep back sth; *Bemerkung* to bite back sth; **ich konnte mir das Lachen nicht ~** I couldn't help laughing; **das kann ich mir ~** I can manage without that *(iro)* → *auch* **verkniffen**

ver|kne|ten *ptp* **verknetet** VT to knead together

ver|knif|fen [fɛɐ'knɪfn] ADJ *Gesicht, Miene (= angestrengt)* strained; *(= verbittert)* pinched; *Ansichten* narrow-minded ADV **etw ~ sehen** to take a narrow view of sth → *auch* **verkneifen**

ver|knit|tern [fɛɐ'knɪtɐn] *ptp* **verknittert** VT → **zerknittern**

ver|knit|tert [fɛɐ'knɪtɐt] ADJ → **zerknittert**

ver|knö|chern [fɛɐ'knœçɐn] *ptp* **verknöchert** VI *aux sein (lit, fig)* to ossify; **verknöchert** *(fig)* ossified, fossilized

ver|knor|peln [fɛɐ'knɔrpln] *ptp* **verknorpelt** VI *aux sein* to become cartilaginous

ver|kno|ten *ptp* **verknotet** VT to tie, to knot; *(inf) Paket* to tie up VR to become knotted

ver|knüp|fen *ptp* **verknüpft** VT **a** *(= verknoten)* to knot *or* tie (together); *(Comput)* to integrate **b** *(fig)* to combine; *(= in Zusammenhang bringen)* to link, to connect; *Gedanken, Geschehnisse* to associate; **etw mit Bedingungen ~** to attach conditions to sth; **mit diesem Ort sind für mich schöne Erinnerungen verknüpft** this place has happy memories for me; **ein Hauskauf ist immer mit großen Ausgaben verknüpft** buying a house always involves a lot of expense

Ver|knüp|fung [fɛɐ'knʏpfʊŋ] F -, -en *(von Bändern, Schnur)* knotting *or* tying (together); *(Comput) (auf Desktop zu Programm)* shortcut; *(bei Hypertext)* link; *(fig)* combining, combination; *(= Assoziieren)* linking, connecting; *(von Gedanken, Geschehnissen)* association; **ungültige ~** *(Comput)* broken shortcut

ver|knu|sen [fɛɐ'knu:zn] *ptp* **verknust** VT *(inf)* **ich kann ihn/das nicht ~** I can't stick him/that *(inf)*

ver|ko|chen *ptp* **verkocht** VI *aux sein (Flüssigkeit)* to boil away; *(Kartoffeln, Gemüse)* to overcook VT *Gemüse* to overcook

ver|koh|len *ptp* **verkohlt** VI *aux sein* to char, to become charred; *(Braten)* to burn to a cinder *(Brit) or* crisp VT **a** *Holz* to char; *(Tech)* to carbonize **b** *(inf)* **jdn ~** to have sb on *(Brit inf)*, to pull sb's leg *(inf)*

Ver|koh|lung [fɛɐ'koːlʊŋ] F -, -en carbonization

ver|ko|ken [fɛɐ'koːkn] *ptp* **verkokt** VT to carbonize

Ver|ko|kung F -, -en carbonization

ver|kom|men [fɛɐ'kɔmən] *ptp* **verkommen** VI *irreg aux sein* **a** *(Mensch)* to go to pieces; *(moralisch)* to become dissolute, to go to the bad *(Brit)*; *(Kind)* to run wild; **zu etw** ~ to degenerate into sth **b** *(Gebäude, Auto)* to become dilapidated, to fall to pieces; *(Stadt, Land)* to become run-down; *(Gelände, Anlage etc)* to run wild **c** *(= nicht genutzt werden: Lebensmittel, Begabung, Fähigkeiten etc)* to go to waste; *(= verderben: Lebensmittel)* to go bad **d** *(Sw: = übereinkommen)* to agree **e** *(Aus inf: = verschwinden)* to clear off *(inf)*

ver|kom|men ADJ *Mensch* depraved; *Auto, Gebäude* dilapidated; *Garten* wild; **der sprachlich ~e Gewaltbegriff** the linguistically debased concept of violence

Ver|kom|men|heit F -, *no pl (von Mensch)* depravity; *(von Auto, Gebäude)* dilapidation, dilapidated state; *(von Garten)* wildness

ver|kom|pli|zie|ren *ptp* **verkompliziert** VT *(inf)* to complicate; **etw** ~ *(auch)* to make sth more complicated than it is; **warum musst du immer alles ~?** why do you always have to complicate matters?

ver|kon|su|mie|ren *ptp* **verkonsumiert** VT *(inf)* to get through; *Essen, Getränke auch* to consume

ver|kopft ADJ overly cerebral

ver|kop|peln *ptp* **verkoppelt** VT to connect, to couple; *(Space)* to link (up)

Ver|kop|pe|lung F, **Ver|kopp|lung** F connection, coupling; *(Space)* linkup

ver|kor|ken [fɛɐ'kɔrkn] *ptp* **verkorkt** VT to cork (up)

ver|kork|sen [fɛɐ'kɔrksn] *ptp* **verkorkst** VT *(inf)* to make a mess *or* cockup *(Brit inf)* of, to mess up *(inf)*, to screw up *(inf)*; *Kind* to screw up *(inf)*; **sich** *(dat)* **den Magen** ~ to upset one's stomach; **jdm etw** ~ to mess *or* screw sth up for sb *(inf)*, to wreck sth for sb

ver|korkst [fɛɐ'kɔrkst] ADJ *(inf)* messed-up *(inf)*, ruined; *Magen* upset; *Kind, Mensch* screwed up *(inf)*; **eine völlig ~e Sache** a real mess

ver|kör|pern [fɛɐ'kœrpɐn] *ptp* **verkörpert** VT to embody, to personify; *(Theat)* to play (the part of), to portray; **jener Staat verkörperte die Idee der Demokratie** that state was the embodiment of the democratic idea

Ver|kör|pe|rung F -, -en embodiment; *(Mensch auch)* personification; *(Theat)* playing, portrayal

ver|kos|ten *ptp* **verkostet** VT to taste

ver|kös|ti|gen [fɛɐ'kœstɪgn] *ptp* **verköstigt** VT to feed

Ver|kös|ti|gung F -, -en feeding

Ver|kos|tung F -, -en *(von Wein)* tasting

ver|kra|chen *ptp* **verkracht** VR *(inf)* **sich (mit jdm)** ~ to fall out (with sb)

ver|kracht [fɛɐ'kraxt] ADJ *(inf) Leben* ruined; *Typ, Mensch* dead beat *(inf)*; *(= zerstritten) Nachbarn, Freunde* who have fallen out with each other → **Existenz**

ver|kraf|ten [fɛɐ'kraftn] *ptp* **verkraftet** VT to cope with; *(finanziell)* to afford, to manage; *(inf: = essen, trinken können)* to manage; **Straßen, die das Verkehrsvolumen nicht** ~ streets which can't cope with the volume of traffic

ver|kral|len *ptp* **verkrallt** VR *(Katze, Raubtier)* to dig *or* sink its claws in; *(Hände)* to clench up; **sich in etw** *(dat)* ~ *(Katze)* to dig *or* sink its claws into sth; *(Mensch)* to dig *or* sink one's fingers into sth; **sich in ein Problem** ~ *(fig)* to get stuck into a problem

ver|kra|men *ptp* **verkramt** VT *(inf)* to mislay

ver|kramp|fen *ptp* **verkrampft** VR to become cramped; *(Hände)* to clench up; *(Mensch)* to go tense, to tense up; **verkrampft** *(fig)* tense

Ver|kramp|fung [fɛɐ'krampfʊŋ] F -, -en *(lit, fig)* tenseness, tension; **seelische** ~ mental tension

ver|krat|zen *ptp* **verkratzt** VT to scratch, to scrape; **verkratzt** scratched; **völlig verkratzt sein** to be scratched all over

ver|krie|chen *ptp* **verkrochen** [fɛɐ'krɔxn] VR *irreg* to creep away; *(fig)* to hide (oneself away); **sich unter den** *or* **dem Tisch** ~ to crawl *or* creep under the table; **sich ins Bett** ~ *(inf)* to run off to bed, to retreat to one's bed; **vor ihm brauchst du dich nicht zu** ~ *(inf)* you don't have to worry about him; **am liebsten hätte ich mich vor Scham verkrochen** I wanted the ground to open up and swallow me

ver|krü|meln *ptp* **verkrümelt** VR *(inf)* to disappear VT to crumble

ver|krüm|men *ptp* **verkrümmt** VT to bend VR to bend; *(Rückgrat)* to become curved; *(Holz)* to warp; *(Baum, Pflanze)* to grow crooked

ver|krümmt [fɛɐ'krʏmt] ADJ bent; *Wirbelsäule* curved; *Finger, Knochen, Bäume* crooked; *Holz* warped

Ver|krüm|mung F bend (*+gen* in), distortion *(esp Tech)*; *(von Holz)* warp; *(von Fingern, Knochen, Bäumen)* crookedness *no pl*; **~ der Wirbelsäule** curvature of the spine; **~ der Hornhaut** *(nach innen)* incurvation of the cornea; *(nach außen)* excurvation of the cornea

ver|krum|peln [fɛɐ'krʊmpln] *ptp* **verkrumpelt** *(dial)* VT to crumple up VI *aux sein* to get crumpled up

ver|krüp|peln [fɛɐ'krʏpln] *ptp* **verkrüppelt** VT to cripple VI *aux sein* to become crippled; *(Zehen, Füße)* to become deformed; *(Baum etc)* to grow stunted

Ver|krüp|pe|lung [fɛɐ'krʏpəlʊŋ] F -, -en, **Ver|krüpp|lung** [fɛɐ'krʏplʊŋ] F -, -en crippling; *(von Zehen, Füßen)* deformity; *(von Baum etc)* stunted growth

ver|krus|ten [fɛɐ'krʊstn] *ptp* **verkrustet** VIR *(vi: aux sein)* to become encrusted

ver|krus|tet [fɛɐ'krʊstət] ADJ *Wunde* scabby; *Strukturen, Ansichten* decrepit

Ver|krus|tung F -, -en *(von Wunde)* scab formation; *(von Strukturen etc)* decrepitude; *(von Partei, Organisation etc)* archaic *or* fossilized structure

ver|küh|len *ptp* **verkühlt** *(inf)* VR to catch a cold, to get a chill VT **sich** *(dat)* **die Nieren** ~ to get a chill on the kidneys *(Brit)*, to get a kidney infection *(resulting from a chill)*

Ver|küh|lung F *(inf)* chill; **~ der Blase** chill on the bladder *(Brit)*, bladder infection *(resulting from a chill)*

ver|küm|meln [fɛɐ'kʏmln] *ptp* **verkümmelt** VT *(inf)* to sell off, to flog *(Brit inf)*

ver|küm|mern *ptp* **verkümmert** VI *aux sein (Glied, Organ)* to atrophy; *(= eingehen: Pflanze)* to die; *(Talent)* to go to waste; *(Schönheitssinn, Interesse etc)* to wither away; *(Mensch)* to waste away; **emotionell/geistig** ~ to become emotionally/intellectually stunted; **wenn die natürlichen Instinkte im Menschen** ~ if man's natural instincts become stunted

Ver|küm|me|rung [fɛɐ'kʏmərʊŋ] F -, -en *(von Organ, Muskel, Glied etc)* atrophy; *(fig) (von Talent)* wasting away, atrophy; *(von Gerechtigkeitssinn, Instinkten etc)* atrophy

ver|kün|den *ptp* **verkündet** VT to announce; *Urteil* to pronounce; *Evangelium* to preach; *Gesetz* to promulgate; *nichts Gutes, Unwetter etc* to forebode, to presage *(liter)*; *Frühling, neue Zeit* to herald

Ver|kün|der(in) M(F) **ein ~ des Evangeliums** a preacher of the gospel; **der ~ einer Friedensbotschaft** a harbinger *or* herald of peace

ver|kün|di|gen *ptp* **verkündigt** VT to proclaim; *Evangelium auch* to preach; *(iro)* to announce; **ich verkündige euch große Freude** *(Bibl)* I bring you tidings of great joy *(Bibl)*

Ver|kün|di|ger [fɛɐ'kʏndɪgɐ] M -s, -, **Ver|kün|di|ge|rin** [-ərɪn] F -, -nen → **Verkünder(in)**

Ver|kün|di|gung F proclamation; *(von Evangelium, von christlicher Lehre auch)* preaching, propagation; **Mariä** ~ the Annunciation; *(Tag)* Lady Day *(Brit)*, the Annunciation

Ver|kün|dung [fɛɐ'kʏndʊŋ] F -, -en announcement; *(von Urteil)* pronouncement; *(von Evangelium)* preaching; *(von Gesetz)* promulgation

ver|küns|teln [fɛɐ'kʏnstln] *ptp* **verkünstelt** VR *(inf)* to overdo it, to go to town *(inf)*; **sich an etw** *(dat)* ~ to go to town on sth *(inf)*, to overdo sth

ver|kup|fern [fɛɐ'kʊpfɐn] *ptp* **verkupfert** VT to copper(-plate); **verkupfert** copper-plated

ver|kup|peln *ptp* **verkuppelt** VT *(pej)* to pair off; **jdn an jdn** ~ *(Zuhälter)* to procure sb for sb

Ver|kup|pe|lung F, *no pl*, **Ver|kupp|lung** F, *no pl* pairing off; *(durch Zuhälter)* procuring

ver|kür|zen *ptp* **verkürzt** VT to shorten; *Arbeitszeit, Fahrzeit* to reduce, to cut down; *Lebenserwartung auch* to reduce; *Strecke, Weg etc auch* to cut; *Abstand, Vorsprung* to narrow; *Aufenthalt* to cut short; *(Art)* to foreshorten; *Haltbarkeit* to reduce; *Schmerzen, Leiden* to end, to put an end to; **den Spielstand** ~ to narrow the gap (between the scores); **sich** *(dat)* **die Zeit** ~ to pass the time, to make the time pass more quickly; **jdm die Zeit** ~ to help sb pass the time; **verkürzte Arbeitszeit** shorter working hours; **verkürzter Nebensatz** *(Gram)* elliptical subordinate clause

VR to be shortened; *(Strecke, Zeit auch)* to be cut; *(Art)* to become foreshortened; *(Abstand)* to be narrowed; *(Muskel)* to contract; *(Haltbarkeit)* to be reduced; *(Leiden)* to be ended; *(Urlaub, Aufenthalt)* to be cut short

Ver|kür|zung F *(= das Verkürzen)* shortening; *(von Zeit, Lebenserwartung auch)* reduction; *(von Abstand, Vorsprung)* narrowing; *(von Aufenthalt)* cutting short; *(Art)* foreshortening; *(von Haltbarkeit)* reduction; *(von Schmerzen, Leiden)* ending

Verl. *abbr von* **Verlag, Verleger**

ver|la|chen *ptp* **verlacht** VT to ridicule, to deride, to laugh at

Ver|la|de-: **Ver|la|de|bahn|hof** M loading station; **Ver|la|de|brü|cke** F loading bridge, gantry

ver|la|den *ptp* **verladen** VT *irreg* **a** *Güter, Menschen* to load; *(Mil) (in Eisenbahn)* to entrain; *(auf Schiff)* to embark; *(in Flugzeug)* to emplane *(Brit)*, to enplane; **die Güter vom Eisenbahnwaggon aufs Schiff** ~ to offload the goods from the train onto the ship **b** *(fig inf: = betrügen, für dumm verkaufen)* to con *(inf)*, to dupe

Ver|la|de|ram|pe F loading platform

Ver|la|dung F loading; *(Mil) (in Eisenbahn)* entrainment; *(auf Schiff)* embarkation; *(in Flugzeug)* emplaning *(Brit)*, enplaning *(US)*

Ver|lag [fɛɐ'laːk] M -(e)s, -e [-gə] **a** *(= Buchverlag)* publishing house *or* company; *(= Zeitungsverlag)* newspaper publisher's *sing*; **~ HarperCollins** HarperCollins Publishers *sing*; **einen ~ finden** to find a publisher; **in** *or* **bei welchem ~ ist das erschienen?** who published it?; **der ~ zahlt nicht viel** the publishers do not pay much; **ein Buch in ~ nehmen** to publish a book; **ein Buch in ~ geben** to have a book published **b** *(= Zwischenhandelsgeschäft)* (firm of) distributors *pl*

ver|la|gern *ptp* **verlagert** VT *(lit, fig) Gewicht, Schwerpunkt, Betonung* to shift; *Interessen, Verkehr auch* to transfer; *(lit: an anderen Ort)* to move VR *(lit, fig)* to shift; *(Met: Tief, Hoch etc)* to move; *(fig: Problem, Frage)* to change in emphasis *(auf +acc* to)

Ver|la|ge|rung F shift; *(von Interessen auch)* transfer; *(an anderen Ort)* moving, movement; *(fig: von Problem, Frage)* change in emphasis

Ver|lags-: **Ver|lags|an|stalt** F publishing firm; **Ver|lags|buch|han|del** M publishing trade; **Ver|lags|buch|händ|ler(in)** M(F) publisher; **Ver|lags|buch|hand|lung** F publishing firm, publisher; **Ver|lags|grup|pe** F publishing group; **Ver|lags|haus** NT publishing house; **Ver|lags|kauf|frau** F, **Ver|lags|kauf|mann** M publishing manager; **Ver|lags|lei|ter(in)** M(F) publishing director; **Ver|lags|pro|gramm** NT list; **Ver|lags|recht** NT publishing rights *pl*; **Ver|lags|re|dak|teur(in)** M(F) (publishing) editor; **Ver|lags|we|sen** NT, *no pl* publishing *no art*

ver|lan|den *ptp* **verlandet** VI *aux sein* to silt up; *(durch Austrocknen)* to dry up

Ver|lan|dung F silting up; *(durch Austrocknen)* drying up

ver|lan|gen *ptp* **verlangt** VT **a** *(= fordern)* to demand; *(= wollen)* to want; *Preis* to ask; *Qualifikationen, Erfahrung* to require; **was verlangt der Kunde/das Volk?** what does the customer/do the people want?; **wie viel verlangst du für dein Auto?** how much are you asking for your car?, how much do you want for your car?
b *(= erwarten)* to ask *(von* of); **ich verlange nichts als Offenheit und Ehrlichkeit** I am asking nothing but frankness and honesty; **es wird von jdm verlangt, dass ...** it is required *or* expected of sb that ...; **das ist nicht zu viel verlangt** it's not asking too much; **das ist ein bisschen viel verlangt** that's asking rather a lot, that's rather a tall order
c *(= erfordern)* to require, to call for
d *(= fragen nach)* to ask for; **er verlangte meinen Pass** he asked to see my passport; **Sie werden am Telefon verlangt** you are wanted on the phone; **ich verlange/ich verlangte den Geschäftsführer (zu sprechen)** I want *or* demand/I asked *or* demanded to see the manager
VI **~ nach** to ask for; *(= sich sehnen nach)* to long for; *(stärker)* to crave
VT *impers (liter)* **es verlangt jdn nach jdm/etw** sb craves sth; *(nach der Heimat, Geliebten)* sb yearns for sb/sth

Ver|lan|gen [fɛɐ'laŋən] NT **-s, -** *(nach* for) desire; *(= Sehnsucht)* yearning, longing; *(= Begierde)* craving; *(= Forderung)* request; **kein ~ nach etw haben** to have no desire *or* wish for sth; **auf ~** on demand; **auf ~ des Gerichts** by order of the court; **auf ~ der Eltern** at the request of the parents

ver|lan|gend ADJ longing

ver|län|gern [fɛɐ'lɛŋɐn] *ptp* **verlängert** VT **a** *(= länger machen)* to extend; *(esp räumlich)* to lengthen, to make longer; *(esp zeitlich)* to prolong; *Leben, Schmerzen, Leiden etc* to prolong; *Hosenbein, Ärmel etc* to lengthen; *Pass, Abonnement etc* to renew; **die Suppe/Soße ~** *(fig inf)* to make the soup/gravy go further; **ein verlängertes Wochenende** a long weekend; **verlängerte Werkbank** *(fig inf)* extended production line → **Rücken b** *(Sport) Ball, Pass* to touch *(zu jdm* to sb)
VR to be extended; *(räumlich auch)* to be lengthened; *(zeitlich auch, Leiden etc)* to be prolonged
VI *(Sport)* to play on

Ver|län|ge|rung F **-, -en a** *(= das Verlängern)* extension; *(esp räumlich)* lengthening; *(esp zeitlich)* prolonging, prolongation; *(von Pass, Abonnement etc)* renewal **b** *(Gegenstand)* extension **c** *(Sport) (von Spielzeit)* extra time *(Brit)*, over time *(US)*; *(= nachgespielte Zeit)* injury time *(Brit)*, over time *(US)*; *(von Pass)* play-on *(zu* to); **das Spiel geht in die ~** they're going to play extra time *etc*, they're going into extra time *etc*; **eine ~ von fünf Minuten** five minutes' extra time *etc*

Ver|län|ge|rungs-: **Ver|län|ge|rungs|frist** F *(= Zeitspanne)* extension period; *(= Zeitpunkt)* extension deadline; **Ver|län|ge|rungs|ka|bel** NT, **Ver|län|ge|rungs|schnur** F *(Elec)* extension lead; **Ver|län|ge|rungs|stück** NT extension (piece)

ver|lang|sa|men [fɛɐ'laŋzaːmən] *ptp* **verlangsamt** VT to slow down *or* up; *Geschwindigkeit* to reduce, to decelerate; *Produktion auch* to decelerate; *Entwicklung auch* to retard; **er musste das Tempo/seine Schritte ~** he had to slow down
VR to slow down *or* up; *(Produktion auch)* to decelerate

Ver|lang|sa|mung F **-, -en** slowing down *or* up; *(von Geschwindigkeit, Produktion auch)* deceleration; *(von Entwicklung)* retarding, retardation

ver|läp|pern *ptp* **verläppert** VR to be *or* get lost; *(Geld)* to disappear, to vanish

Ver|lass [fɛɐ'las] M **-es**, *no pl* **auf jdn/etw ist kein ~, es ist kein ~ auf jdn/etw** there is no relying on sb/sth, you can't rely on sb/sth

ver|las|sen ✪ 42.1 *ptp* **verlassen** *irreg* VT to leave, *Ort auch* to quit; *(fig: Mut, Kraft, Hoffnung) jdn* to desert; *(= im Stich lassen)* to desert, to abandon, to forsake *(liter)*; *(Comput) Datei, Programm* to exit; **jdn ~** *(nach Beziehung)* to walk out on sb; **... und da verließen sie mich/ihn** *etc (iro, inf)* ... that's as far as I/he *etc* got → **Geist b**
VR **sich auf jdn/etw ~** to rely *or* depend on sb/sth; **darauf können Sie sich ~** you can be sure of that, you can depend on that, take my word for it; **worauf du dich ~ kannst!** you can depend on that!, you bet!

ver|las|sen [fɛɐ'lasn] ADJ **a** *Gegend, Ort, Straßen* deserted; *(= öd)* desolate; **eine Tanne, einsam und ~** a solitary fir tree **b** *Mensch (= alleingelassen)* deserted; *(= einsam)* lonely, solitary; **einsam und ~** so all alone **c** *(= ohne Besitzer) Haus, Fabrik* deserted; *Auto* abandoned

Ver|las|sen NT **-s**, *no pl* **vor/nach ~ des Gebäudes** before/after leaving the building; **böswilliges ~** *(Jur)* wilful abandonment

Ver|las|sen|heit F **-**, *no pl* **a** *(von Gegend, Ort, Straßen)* desertedness; *(= Ödheit)* desolateness **b** *(von Mensch)* loneliness, solitariness

Ver|las|sen|schaft [fɛɐ'lasnʃaft] F **-, -en** *(Aus, Sw)* estate; *(literarisch)* legacy

Ver|las|sen|schafts|ab|hand|lung F *(Aus, Sw)* negotiation on inheritance

ver|läss|lich ADJ reliable; *Mensch auch* dependable

Ver|läss|lich|keit [fɛɐ'lɛslɪçkait] F **-**, *no pl* reliability; *(von Mensch auch)* dependability

Ver|laub [fɛɐ'laup] M **mit ~** *(geh, iro)* by your leave *(old)*, with your permission; **mit ~ (zu sagen)** if you will pardon *or* forgive my saying so

Ver|lauf M course; *(= Ausgang)* end, issue; *(Comput, Internet)* history; **im ~ der Zeit** in the course of time; **im ~ des Tages** in *or* during the course of the day; **im ~ der Jahre/Monate** over the (course of the) years/months; **im ~ der Verhandlungen/Arbeit** in the course of the negotiations/work; **einen guten/schlechten ~ nehmen** to go well/badly; **den ~ einer Sache verfolgen/beobachten** to follow/observe the course (which) sth takes; **im weiteren ~ der Sache zeichnete sich folgende Tendenz ab** as things developed the following tendency became apparent

ver|lau|fen *ptp* **verlaufen** *irreg* VI *aux sein* **a** *(= ablaufen) (Tag, Prüfung, Entwicklung)* to go; *(Feier, Demonstration)* to go off; *(Kindheit)* to pass; *(Untersuchung)* to proceed; **beschreiben Sie, wie diese Krankheit normalerweise verläuft** describe the course this illness usually takes; **die Verhandlungen verliefen in angespannter Atmosphäre** the negotiations took place in a tense atmosphere
b *(= sich erstrecken)* to run
c *(= auseinanderfließen, dial: = schmelzen)* to run; **die Spur verlief im Sand/Wald** the track disappeared in the sand/forest; **~e Farben** runny colours *(Brit) or* colors *(US)* → **Sand**
VR **a** *(= sich verirren)* to get lost, to lose one's way
b *(= verschwinden) (Menschenmenge)* to disperse; *(Wasser)* to drain away; *(= sich verlieren: Spur, Weg)* to disappear

Ver|laufs|form F *(Gram)* progressive *or* continuous form

ver|laust [fɛɐ'laust] ADJ lice-ridden

ver|laut|ba|ren [fɛɐ'lautbaːrən] *ptp* **verlautbart** *(form)* VTI to announce; **es wird amtlich verlautbart, dass ...** it is officially announced that ..., a statement has been issued to the effect that ...; **etw ~ lassen** to let sth be announced *or* made known

Ver|laut|ba|rung F **-, -en** announcement; *(inoffiziell)* report

ver|lau|ten *ptp* **verlautet** VI **etwas/nichts ~ lassen** to give an/no indication, to say something/nothing; **er hat ~ lassen, dass ...** he indicated that ...; **er hat keinen Ton** *or* **kein Wort ~ lassen** he hasn't said a word VI *impers aux sein or haben* **es verlautet, dass ...** it is reported that ...; **wie aus Bonn verlautet** according to reports from Bonn

ver|le|ben *ptp* **verlebt** VT to spend; **eine schöne Zeit ~** to have a nice time

ver|lebt [fɛɐ'leːpt] ADJ worn-out, dissipated

ver|le|gen *ptp* **verlegt** VT **a** *(an anderen Ort)* to transfer, to move; *Patienten* to move; *Schauplatz* to move, to shift **b** *(= verschieben)* to postpone *(auf +acc* until); *(= vorverlegen)* to bring forward *(auf +acc* to) **c** *(= an falschen Platz legen)* to mislay, to misplace **d** *(= anbringen) Kabel, Fliesen etc* to lay **e** *(= drucken lassen)* to publish VR **sich auf etw** *(acc)* **~** to resort to sth; **er hat sich neuerdings auf Golf verlegt** he has taken to golf recently; **sich aufs Unterrichten ~** to take up teaching

ver|le|gen [fɛɐ'leːgn] ADJ **a** embarrassed *no adv* **b um Worte/eine Antwort ~ sein** to be lost *or* at a loss for words/an answer; **um Geld ~ sein** to be financially embarrassed ADV in embarrassment; **~ sah er zu Boden** he looked at the floor in embarrassment; **das habe ich vergessen, sagte sie ~** I forgot about that, she said, embarrassed

Ver|le|gen|heit F **-, -en a** *no pl (= Betretenheit, Befangenheit)* embarrassment; **jdn in ~ bringen** to embarrass sb; **so ein wunderschöner Strauß, du bringst mich ja ganz in ~** such a lovely bouquet, you really shouldn't have; **in ~ kommen** *or* **geraten** to get *or* become embarrassed **b** *(= unangenehme Lage)* embarrassing *or* awkward situation; **wenn er in finanzieller ~ ist** when he's in financial difficulties, when he's financially embarrassed; **ich bin (finanziell) zurzeit leider etwas in ~** I'm afraid I'm rather short (of funds) at the moment

Ver|le|gen|heits-: **Ver|le|gen|heits|ge|schenk** NT last resort present; **Ver|le|gen|heits|lö|sung** F stopgap; **Ver|le|gen|heits|pau|se** F embarrassed pause *or* silence; **eine ~ machen** to be at a loss for words, to be at a loss as to what to say/how to react

Ver|le|ger [fɛɐ'leːgɐ] M **-s, -**, **Ver|le|ge|rin** [-ərɪn] F **-, -nen** publisher; *(= Händler)* distributor

ver|le|ge|risch [fɛɐ'leːgərɪʃ] ADJ *attr* publishing *attr*

Ver|le|gung [fɛɐ'leːgʊŋ] F **-, -en a** *(räumlich)* transfer, moving; *(von Schauplatz)* transposition, shifting **b** *(zeitlich)* postponement *(auf +acc* until); *(= Vorverlegung)* bringing forward *(auf +acc* to) **c** *(von Kabeln etc)* laying

ver|lei|den *ptp* **verleidet** VT **jdm etw ~** to spoil sth for sb, to put sb off sth; **das ist mir jetzt schon verleidet** you've/he's put me off it

Ver|leih [fɛɐ'lai] M **-(e)s, -e a** *(= Unternehmen)* hire *(Brit) or* rental company; *(= Autoverleih)* car hire *(Brit) or* rental; *(= Filmverleih)* distributor(s *pl*) **b** *(= das Verleihen)* renting (out), hiring (out) *(Brit)*; *(= Filmverleih)* distribution; **der ~ von Büchern** the lending *or* loan of books

ver|lei|hen *ptp* **verliehen** [fɛɐ'liːən] VT *irreg* **a** *(= ausleihen)* to lend, to loan *(an jdn* to sb); *(gegen Gebühr)* to rent (out), to hire (out) *(Brit)* **b** *(= zuerkennen)* to award *(jdm* (to) sb); *Titel, Ehrenbürgerwürde* to confer, to bestow *(jdm* on sb); *Amt* to bestow *(jdm* upon sb) **c** *(= geben, verschaffen)* to give; *Eigenschaft, Klang, Note* to lend, to give; **einer Sache** *(dat)* **Gewicht ~** to lend weight to sth; **ihre Anwesenheit verlieh der Veranstaltung das gewisse Etwas** her presence gave *or* lent a certain something to the occasion

Ver|lei|her [fɛɐ'laiɐ] M **-s, -**, **Ver|lei|he|rin** [-ərɪn] F **-, -nen** hire *(Brit) or* rental firm; *(von Kostümen etc)* renter, hirer *(Brit)*; *(von Filmen)* distributor, (firm of) distributors *pl*; *(von Büchern)* lender

Ver|lei|hung F -, -en **a** (= das Ausleihen) lending, loan(ing); (gegen Gebühr) renting, rental, hire (Brit), hiring (Brit) **b** (von Preis etc) award(ing); (von Titel, Ehrenbürgerwürde) conferment, conferring; (von Amt) bestowal, bestowment; **die ~ des Preises findet am 26. September statt** the prize will be awarded on 26 September

ver|lei|men ptp **verleimt** VT to glue

ver|lei|ten ptp **verleitet** VT **a** (= verlocken) to tempt; (= verführen) to lead astray; **die Sonne hat mich verleitet, schwimmen zu gehen** the sun tempted or enticed me to go swimming; **jdn zur Sünde ~** to lead sb into sin; **jdn zum Stehlen/Lügen ~** to lead or encourage sb to steal/lie; **jdn zu einem Verbrechen ~** to lead or encourage sb to commit a crime; **jdn zum Ungehorsam ~** to encourage sb to be disobedient; **jdn dazu ~, die Schule zu schwänzen** to encourage sb to play truant **b** (= veranlassen) **jdn zu etw ~** to lead sb to sth; **jdn zu einem Irrtum ~** to lead sb to make or into making a mistake

Ver|lei|tung F **a** (= Verführung) leading astray; (zum Lügen, Stehlen) encouragement; **die ~ der Menschen zur Sünde** leading people into sin **b** (= Veranlassung) **die ~ zu einer vorschnellen Äußerung** leading sb to make a hasty comment

ver|ler|nen ptp **verlernt** VT to forget, to unlearn; **das Tanzen ~** to forget how to dance

ver|le|sen ptp **verlesen** irreg VT **a** (= vorlesen) to read (out); Namen to read out, to call out **b** Gemüse, Linsen, Früchte etc to sort; Feldsalat to clean VR (beim Vorlesen) to make a slip; **ich habe mich wohl ~** I must have read it wrong(ly), I must have misread it

Ver|le|sung F reading (out); (von Namen) calling out

ver|letz|bar ADJ (lit, fig) vulnerable

Ver|letz|bar|keit [fɛɐ̯ˈlɛtsbaːɐ̯kait] F -, no pl (lit, fig) vulnerability

ver|let|zen [fɛɐ̯ˈlɛtsn] ptp **verletzt** VT **a** (= verwunden) to injure; (in Kampf etc, mit Kugel, Messer) to wound; (fig) jdn to hurt, to wound; jds Stolz, Gefühle to hurt, to wound, to injure; jds Ehrgefühl to injure, to offend; jds Schönheitssinn, zarte Ohren to offend; **das verletzt den guten Geschmack** it offends against good taste **b** Gesetz to break; Pflicht, Rechte, Intimsphäre to violate VR to injure oneself

ver|let|zend ADJ Bemerkung hurtful

ver|letz|lich [fɛɐ̯ˈlɛtslɪç] ADJ vulnerable

Ver|letz|lich|keit F -, no pl vulnerability

Ver|letz|te(r) [fɛɐ̯ˈlɛtstə] MF decl as adj injured person; (= Unfallverletzter auch) casualty; (bei Kampf) wounded man; **die ~n** the injured/wounded; **es gab drei ~** three people were injured or hurt/wounded

Ver|let|zung F -, -en **a** (= Wunde) injury **b** (= das Verletzen) injuring; (in Kampf, mit Waffe) wounding; (fig) hurting, wounding; (von Ehrgefühl, Schönheitssinn) offending; **zur ~ des Knies führen** to cause a knee injury

Ver|let|zungs-: **ver|let|zungs|an|fäl|lig** ADJ injury-prone attr; **ver|let|zungs|be|dingt** ADJ Ausfall etc due to injury pred ADV pausieren due to injury; **Ver|let|zungs|ge|fahr** F risk of injury; **Ver|let|zungs|pau|se** F injury lay-off

ver|leug|nen ✪ 53.6 ptp **verleugnet** VT to deny; Kind auch to disown; **ich kann es nicht ~, dass ...** I cannot deny that ...; **es lässt sich nicht ~, dass ...** there is no denying that ...; **er lässt sich immer (vor ihr) ~** he always pretends not to be there (when she calls); **sich (selbst) ~** to deny one's own self

Ver|leug|nung F denial; (von Kind auch) disownment

ver|leum|den [fɛɐ̯ˈlɔymdn] ptp **verleumdet** VT to slander, to calumniate (form); (schriftlich) to libel

Ver|leum|der [fɛɐ̯ˈlɔymdɐ] M -s, -, **Ver|leum|de|rin** [-ərɪn] F -, -nen slanderer; (durch Geschriebenes) libeller (esp Brit), libeler (US)

ver|leum|de|risch [fɛɐ̯ˈlɔymdərɪʃ] ADJ slanderous; (in Schriftform) libellous (esp Brit), libelous (US)

Ver|leum|dung F -, -en slandering; (schriftlich) libelling (esp Brit), libeling (US); (= Bemerkung) slander, calumny; (= Bericht) libel

Ver|leum|dungs-: **Ver|leum|dungs|kam|pag|ne** F smear campaign; **Ver|leum|dungs|kla|ge** F libel action or suit; **eine ~ einreichen** to sue for libel

ver|lie|ben ptp **verliebt** VR to fall in love (in +acc with); **das Kleid ist zum Verlieben (schön)** I love that dress

ver|liebt [fɛɐ̯ˈliːpt] ADJ Benehmen, Blicke, Worte amorous; **(in jdn/etw) ~ sein** to be in love (with sb/sth); **die Verliebten** the courting couple/couples, the lovers → Ohr ADV ansehen lovingly, adoringly; **sie sah ihn ~ an** she looked at him lovingly

Ver|liebt|heit F -, no pl **seine ~ dauert nie lange** he is never in love for very long; **in einem Moment großer ~** feeling (all at once) tremendously in love

ver|lie|ren [fɛɐ̯ˈliːrən] pret **verlor** [fɛɐ̯ˈloːɐ̯], ptp **verloren** [fɛɐ̯ˈloːrən] VT to lose; Blätter auch to shed; **jdn/etw aus dem Gedächtnis ~** to lose all memory of sb/sth, to forget sb/sth; **kein Wort über jdn/etw ~** not to say a word about sb/sth; **wir brauchen kein Wort darüber zu ~** we don't need to waste any words on it; **an ihm hast du nichts verloren** he's no (great) loss; **das/er hat hier nichts verloren** (inf) that/he has no business to be here; **diese Bemerkung hat hier nichts verloren** (inf) that remark is out of place; **nichts (mehr) zu ~ haben** to have nothing (more) to lose

VI to lose; **sie hat an Schönheit/Charme verloren** she has lost some of her beauty/charm; **sie/die Altstadt** etc **hat sehr verloren** she/the old town etc is not what she/it etc used to be; **durch etw ~** to lose (something) by sth; **bei jdm ~** to go down in sb's eyes or estimation

VR **a** (Menschen) to lose each other; (Mensch: = sich verirren) to get lost, to lose one's way **b** (= verschwinden) to disappear; (= verhallen) to fade away, to die; **der Klang verlor sich in dem riesigen Saal/in den Bergen** the sound was lost in the enormous room/faded away or died among the mountains **c** (fig) (= geistesabwesend sein) to become lost to the world; (= abschweifen) to lose one's train of thought; **sich in etw** (acc) **~** to become absorbed in sth; **sich in etw** (dat) **~** to get or become lost in sth → auch **verloren**

Ver|lie|rer [fɛɐ̯ˈliːrɐ] M -s, -, **Ver|lie|re|rin** [-ərɪn] F -, -nen loser

Ver|lie|rer-: **Ver|lie|rer|sei|te** F **auf der ~ sein** (inf) to be on the losing side; **Ver|lie|rer|stra|ße** F **auf der ~ sein** (inf) to be on the downward slope

Ver|lies [fɛɐ̯ˈliːs] NT -es, -e [-zə] dungeon

ver|lin|ken [fɛɐ̯ˈlɪŋkən] ptp **verlinkt** VT (Comput, Internet) to link (up) (mit to/with)

ver|lo|ben ✪ 51.2 ptp **verlobt** VR (mit to) to become or get engaged, to become betrothed (old) VT **jdn mit jdm ~** to betroth sb to sb (old); **verlobt sein** to be engaged or betrothed (old) (mit to)

Ver|löb|nis [fɛɐ̯ˈløːpnɪs] NT -ses, -se (old) engagement, betrothal (old)

Ver|lob|te(r) [fɛɐ̯ˈloːptə] MF decl as adj **mein ~r** my fiancé; **meine ~** my fiancée; **die ~n** the engaged couple

Ver|lo|bung [fɛɐ̯ˈloːbʊŋ] ✪ 51.2, 52.2 F -, -en engagement

Ver|lo|bungs- in cpds engagement; **Ver|lo|bungs|an|zei|ge** F engagement announcement; **Ver|lo|bungs|ring** M engagement ring; **Ver|lo|bungs|zeit** F engagement

ver|lo|cken ptp **verlockt** VTI to entice, to tempt

ver|lo|ckend ADJ enticing, tempting

Ver|lo|ckung F enticement, temptation; (= Reiz) allure

ver|lo|dern ptp **verlodert** VI aux sein (geh) to flare up and die

ver|lo|gen [fɛɐ̯ˈloːgn] ADJ Mensch lying, mendacious (form); Komplimente, Versprechungen false; Moral, Freundlichkeit, Gesellschaft hypocritical

Ver|lo|gen|heit F -, -en (von Mensch) mendacity (form); (von Versprechungen) falseness; (von Moral, Gesellschaft) hypocrisy

ver|loh|nen ptp **verlohnt** VIR impers (rare) to be worthwhile

ver|lor pret von **verlieren**

ver|lo|ren [fɛɐ̯ˈloːrən] ptp von **verlieren** ADJ lost; (= einsam auch) forlorn; Mühe vain, wasted; (Cook) Eier poached; **in den Anblick ~ sein** to be lost in contemplation; **~e Generation** lost generation; **der ~e Sohn** (Bibl) the prodigal son; **jdn/etw ~ geben** to give sb/sth up for lost; **auf ~em Posten kämpfen** or **stehen** to be fighting a losing battle or a lost cause → auch **verlieren**

ver|lo|ren+ge|ben VT sep irreg → **verloren**

ver|lo|ren ge|hen irreg aux sein, **ver|lo|ren+ge|hen** sep irreg aux sein VI to get or be lost; (Zeit, Geld) to be lost or wasted; **an ihm ist ein Sänger verloren gegangen** he would have made a (good) singer, he ought to have been a singer

Ver|lo|ren|heit F -, no pl forlornness

ver|lö|schen [fɛɐ̯ˈlœʃn] pret **verlosch** [fɛɐ̯ˈlɔʃ], ptp **verloschen** [fɛɐ̯ˈlɔʃn] VI aux sein to go out; (Inschrift, Farbe, Tinte) to fade; (Mond, Sterne) to set; (Erinnerung, Ruhm) to fade (away); **sein Leben(slicht) ist verloschen** (liter) he has departed this life (liter) ptp **verlöscht** [fɛɐ̯ˈlœʃt] VT reg (geh) = **auslöschen**

ver|lo|sen ptp **verlost** VT to raffle (off); **wir ~ das letzte Stück Kuchen** we'll draw lots or straws for the last piece of cake

Ver|lo|sung F (= das Verlosen) raffling; (= Lotterie) raffle, draw; (= Ziehung) draw

ver|lö|ten ptp **verlötet** VT to solder

ver|lot|tern ptp **verlottert** aux sein (inf) VI (Stadt, Restaurant) to get or become run down; (Garten) to run wild; (Mensch) to go to the dogs; (moralisch) to go downhill; **er verlottert immer mehr** he is sliding further and further downhill; **das Haus ist ganz verlottert** the house is a complete shambles VT Geld to squander, to fritter away

ver|lot|tert [fɛɐ̯ˈlɔtɐt] ADJ (inf) Stadt run-down; Garten wild; Mensch, Aussehen scruffy; (moralisch) dissolute

ver|lu|dern [fɛɐ̯ˈluːdɐn] ptp **verludert** VTI (inf) = **verlottern**

ver|lum|pen ptp **verlumpt** (inf) VT Geld to chuck away (inf) VI aux sein to go to the dogs; (moralisch) to go downhill

ver|lumpt [fɛɐ̯ˈlʊmpt] (dial) ADJ down and out; Kleider worn-out ADV in rags; **~ herumlaufen** to go about in rags; **~ aussehen** to look like a down-and-out

Ver|lust [fɛɐ̯ˈlʊst] M -(e)s, -e **a** loss; **~ bringend** lossmaking; **~ bringend arbeiten** to work at a loss; **mit ~ verkaufen** to sell at a loss; **in ~ geraten** (form) to be lost **b Verluste** PL losses pl; (= Tote auch) casualties pl; (bei Glücksspiel) losses pl; **schwere ~e haben/machen** to sustain/make heavy losses → **Rücksicht**

Ver|lust-: **Ver|lust|an|zei|ge** F "lost" notice; **Ver|lust|aus|gleich** M loss compensation; **Ver|lust|be|trieb** M (inf) lossmaking business (Brit), lossmaker (Brit), lame duck (inf); **ver|lust|brin|gend** ADJ → **Verlust a**; **Ver|lust|brin|ger** [-brɪŋɐ] M -s, - lossmaker (Brit), business operating in the red; **Ver|lust|ge|schäft** NT (= Firma) lossmaking business (Brit), lossmaker (Brit), business operating in the red; **ich habe es schließlich verkauft, aber das war ein ~** I sold it eventually, but I made a loss or but at a loss

ver|lus|tie|ren [fɛɐ̯lʊsˈtiːrən] ptp **verlustiert** VR (hum) to amuse oneself

ver|lus|tig ADJ *(form)* **einer Sache** *(gen)* **~ gehen** *or* **werden** to forfeit *or* lose sth; **jdn seiner Rechte für ~ erklären** to declare sb's rights forfeit

Ver|lust-: **Ver|lust|kon|to** NT *(Econ)* deficit account; **Ver|lust|leis|tung** F *(Elec)* dissipation; **Ver|lust|lis|te** F *(Mil)* casualty list, list of casualties; **Ver|lust|mel|dung** F **a** report of the loss; **der Absender muss eine ~ machen** the sender must report the loss **b** *(Mil)* casualty report, casualty figures *pl*; **Ver|lust|rech|nung** F *(Econ)* loss account *or* statement; **ver|lust|reich** ADJ **a** *(Comm) Firma* heavily loss-making; **ein ~es Jahr** a year in which heavy losses were made, a year of heavy losses; **ein ~es Geschäft** a deal on which heavy losses were made **b** *(Mil) Schlacht* involving heavy losses *or* casualties; **Ver|lust|zo|ne** F **die ~** the red; **in die ~ geraten** to go into the red; **die ~ verlassen** to return to credit; **Ver|lust|zu|wei|sung** F *(Econ)* allocation of losses

Verm. *abbr von* **Vermerk**

ver|ma|chen *ptp* **vermacht** VT **jdm etw ~** to leave *or* bequeath sth to sb; *(inf: geben)* to bequeath sth to sb; **jdm etw als Schenkung ~** to bequeath sth to sb

Ver|mächt|nis [fɛɐ'mɛçtnɪs] NT **-ses, -se** bequest, legacy; *(fig)* legacy

Ver|mächt|nis- *(Jur)*: **Ver|mächt|nis|ge|ber(in)** M(F) legator; **Ver|mächt|nis|neh|mer(in)** M(F) legatee

ver|mah|len *ptp* **vermahlen** VT *irreg* to grind

ver|mäh|len [fɛɐ'mɛːlən] *ptp* **vermählt** *(form)* VT to marry, to wed; **frisch vermählt sein** to be newly married *or* wed(ded) VR **sich (mit jdm) ~** to marry *or* wed (sb); **„wir haben uns vermählt …"** "the marriage is announced of …"

Ver|mähl|te(r) [fɛɐ'mɛːltə] MF *decl as adj (form)* **die beiden ~n** the newly-married couple; **die soeben ~** the bride; **der soeben ~** the (bride)-groom

Ver|mäh|lung ✪ 51.3 F **-, -en** *(form)* marriage

Ver|mäh|lungs|an|zei|ge F marriage announcement

ver|mah|nen *ptp* **vermahnt** VT *(dated)* to warn

ver|ma|le|deit [fɛɐmale'dait] ADJ *(old)* (ac)cursed *(old)*, damned *(inf)*

ver|ma|len *ptp* **vermalt** VT *Farben* to use up

ver|männ|li|chen [fɛɐ'mɛnlɪçn] *ptp* **vermännlicht** VT to masculinize, to make masculine VI *aux sein (Frauen)* to become masculine, to become like men; *(Gesellschaft)* to become male-dominated

Ver|männ|li|chung F **-, -en** masculinization

ver|man|schen *ptp* **vermanscht** VT *(inf)* to mash up

ver|mark|ten [fɛɐ'marktn] *ptp* **vermarktet** VT to market; *(fig)* to commercialize

Ver|mark|ter M **-s, -** *(= Vermarktungsgesellschaft)* marketing company

Ver|mark|ter M **-s, -**, **Ver|mark|te|rin** F **-, -nen** marketer; **sie ist ~in** she works in marketing

Ver|mark|tung F **-, -en** marketing; *(fig)* commercialization

Ver|mark|tungs|stra|te|gie F marketing strategy

ver|mas|seln [fɛɐ'masln] *ptp* **vermasselt** VT *(inf)* to ruin, to mess up *(inf)*; *Prüfung, Klassenarbeit* to make a mess *or* cockup *(Brit inf)* of → **Tour**

ver|mas|sen [fɛɐ'masn] *ptp* **vermasst** VI *aux sein* to lose one's identity *or* individuality, to become stereotyped; **die Gesellschaft vermasst immer mehr** society is becoming more and more uniform VT *die Gesellschaft* to make uniform

Ver|mas|sung F **-, -en** loss of identity *or* individuality, stereotyping, de-individualization; **die ~ der Gesellschaft** the stereotyping of society

ver|matscht [fɛɐ'matʃt] ADJ *(dial)* squashy

ver|mau|ern *ptp* **vermauert** VT to wall *or* brick up

ver|meh|ren *ptp* **vermehrt** VT to increase; *(= fortpflanzen)* to breed; *Bakterien* to multiply; **vermehrt** increased; **diese Fälle treten vermehrt auf** these cases are occurring with increased *or* increasing frequency *or* are happening increasingly often VR to increase; *(= sich fortpflanzen)* to reproduce, to breed; *(Bakterien, Zellen)* to multiply; *(Pflanzen)* to propagate

Ver|meh|rung F increase; *(= Fortpflanzung)* reproduction, breeding; *(von Bakterien)* multiplying; *(von Pflanzen)* propagation

ver|meid|bar ADJ avoidable

ver|mei|den ✪ 29.2, 42.1 *ptp* **vermieden** VT [fɛɐ'miːdn] *irreg* to avoid; *Frage auch* to evade; **~, dass eine Sache an die Öffentlichkeit dringt** to avoid letting a matter become public; **es lässt sich nicht ~** it cannot be avoided *or* helped, it is inevitable *or* unavoidable; **es lässt sich nicht ~, dass …** it is inevitable *or* unavoidable that …; **nicht, wenn ich es ~ kann** not if I can avoid *or* help it; **er vermeidet keinen Streit** he's not one to avoid an argument

Ver|mei|dung [fɛɐ'maidʊŋ] F **-, -en** avoidance; **die ~ eines Skandals ist nur dann möglich, wenn …** a scandal can only be avoided if …; **zur ~** *+gen or* **von …** to avoid …

ver|meil [vɛr'mɛːj] ADJ vermilion

Ver|meil [vɛr'mɛːj] NT **-s**, *no pl* gilded silver

ver|mei|nen *ptp* **vermeint** VT *(geh)* to think; **ich vermeinte, eine Stimme zu hören** I thought I heard a voice

ver|meint|lich [fɛɐ'maintlɪç] ADJ *attr* putative, supposed; *Täter, Vater eines Kindes* putative ADV supposedly

ver|mel|den *ptp* **vermeldet** VT **a** *(liter: = mitteilen)* to announce; **was hast du Neues zu ~?** *(hum)* what news do you have to announce *or* report? **b** *Erfolg, Verluste* to report

ver|men|gen *ptp* **vermengt** VT to mix; *(fig inf: = durcheinanderbringen) Begriffe etc* to mix up, to confuse

Ver|men|gung [fɛɐ'mɛŋʊŋ] F **-, -en** mixing

ver|mensch|li|chen [fɛɐ'mɛnʃlɪçn] *ptp* **vermenschlicht** VT to humanize; *(= als Menschen darstellen auch)* to anthropomorphize

Ver|mensch|li|chung F **-, -en** humanization

Ver|merk [fɛɐ'mɛrk] M **-(e)s, -e** note, remark; *(im Kalender auch)* entry; *(in Pass)* observation; *(postalisch)* remark; *(= Stempel)* stamp

ver|mer|ken *ptp* **vermerkt** VT **a** *(= aufschreiben)* to make a note of, to note (down), to write down; *(in Pass, Karte) Namen, Datum etc* to record; **alle Verkehrssünder werden in Flensburg vermerkt** a record of (the names of) all traffic offenders is kept in Flensburg; **sich** *(dat)* **etw ~** to make a note of sth, to note *or* write sth down; **etw positiv/negativ ~** to note sth on the plus/negative side **b** *(zur Kenntnis nehmen)* to note, to make a (mental) note of

ver|mes|sen *ptp* **vermessen** *irreg* VT to measure; *Land, Gelände* to survey VR **a** *(geh: = sich anmaßen)* to presume, to dare; **wie kann er sich ~, …?** how dare he …? **b** *(= falsch messen)* to measure wrongly

ver|mes|sen [fɛɐ'mɛsn] ADJ *(= anmaßend)* presumptuous; *Diener* impudent; *(= kühn) Unterfangen* bold

Ver|mes|sen|heit F **-, -en** *(= Anmaßung)* presumption, presumptuousness; *(= Kühnheit)* boldness; **es wäre eine ~, das zu tun** that would be a presumptuous thing to do

Ve|rmes|sung F measurement; *(von Land, Gelände)* survey

Ver|mes|sungs-: **Ver|mes|sungs|amt** NT, **Ver|mes|sungs|bü|ro** NT land survey(ing) office; **Ver|mes|sungs|in|ge|ni|eur(in)** M(F) land surveyor; **Ver|mes|sungs|schiff** NT survey ship; **Ver|mes|sungs|tech|nik** F, *no pl* surveying (technology)

ver|mie|sen [fɛɐ'miːzn] *ptp* **vermiest** VT *(inf)* **jdm etw ~** to spoil sth for sb; **das hat mir die ganze Sache vermiest** that spoiled everything for me

ver|miet|bar ADJ rentable; **schlecht ~** difficult to rent (out) *or* let (out) *(esp Brit)*; **es ist nur als Büroraum ~** it can only be rented (out) *or* let (out) *(esp Brit)* as office premises

ver|mie|ten *ptp* **vermietet** VT to rent (out), to let (out) *(esp Brit)*, to lease *(Jur)*; *Boot, Auto* to rent (out), to hire (out) *(Brit)*, to lease *(Jur)*; **Zimmer zu ~** room to let *(esp Brit)*, room for rent VI to rent (out) *or* let (out) *(esp Brit)* a room/rooms; **„zu ~"** "to let" *(esp Brit)*, "for rent"

Ver|mie|ter M lessor; *(von Wohnung etc)* landlord, lessor *(Jur)*

Ver|mie|te|rin F lessor; *(von Wohnung etc)* landlady, lessor *(Jur)*

Ver|mie|tung [fɛɐ'miːtʊŋ] F **-, -en** renting (out), letting (out) *(esp Brit)*; *(von Auto, Boot)* rental, hiring (out) *(Brit)*

ver|min|dern *ptp* **vermindert** VT to reduce, to decrease; *Gefahr, Anfälligkeit, Einfluss etc auch, Ärger, Zorn* to lessen; *Widerstandsfähigkeit, Reaktionsfähigkeit* to diminish, to reduce; *Schmerzen* to ease, to lessen, to reduce; *(Mus)* to diminish; **verminderte Zurechnungsfähigkeit** *(Jur)* diminished responsibility VR to decrease; *(Gefahr, Anfälligkeit, Einfluss auch, Ärger, Zorn)* to lessen; *(Widerstandsfähigkeit, Reaktionsfähigkeit)* to diminish; *(Schmerzen)* to ease off, to lessen, to decrease

Ver|min|de|rung F reduction (*+gen* of), decrease (*+gen* in); *(von Gefahr, Anfälligkeit, Einfluss auch, von Ärger, Zorn)* lessening; *(von Widerstandsfähigkeit, Reaktionsfähigkeit)* diminishing; *(von Schmerzen)* easing

ver|mi|nen [fɛɐ'miːnən] *ptp* **vermint** VT to mine

Ver|mi|nung F **-, -en** mining

ver|mi|schen *ptp* **vermischt** VT to mix; *Tabaksorten, Teesorten etc* to blend; **vermischte Schriften** miscellaneous writings; **„Vermischtes"** "miscellaneous" VR to mix; *(Rassen auch)* to interbreed; *(Elemente, Klänge, Farben)* to blend, to mingle; **Freude vermischt sich mit Leid** joy mingles *or* is mingled with sorrow; **wo sich Tradition und Fortschritt ~** where tradition and progress are blended (together) *or* combined

Ver|mi|schung F mixing, mixture; *(von Tabaksorten, Teesorten)* blending; *(von Rassen)* interbreeding; *(von Elementen, Klängen, Farben)* blending, mingling; *(von Gefühlen, Stilebenen, Metaphern)* mixture

ver|mis|sen *ptp* **vermisst** VT to miss; **vermisst werden** to be missing; **vermisst sein, als vermisst gemeldet sein** to be reported missing; **ich vermisse zwei silberne Teelöffel** two (of my) silver teaspoons are missing, I'm missing two silver teaspoons; **ich vermisse die Blumen auf den Tischen** I see you don't have the flowers on the tables; **etw an jdm/etw ~** to find sb/sth lacking in sth; **was ich bei dieser Beschreibung vermisse, ist …** what I miss in this description is …; **wir haben dich bei der Party vermisst** we didn't see you at the party; **entschuldige, dass ich zu spät komme – wir hatten dich noch gar nicht vermisst** sorry I'm late – we hadn't even noticed you weren't here; **etw ~ lassen** to lack sth, to be lacking in sth

ver|mis|sen+las|sen VT *sep irreg ptp* **vermissenlassen** *or (rare)* **vermissengelassen** → **vermissen**

Ver|miss|ten|an|zei|ge F missing persons report; **eine ~ aufgeben** to report someone (as) missing

Ver|miss|te(r) [fɛɐ'mɪstə] MF *decl as adj* missing person

ver|mit|tel|bar ADJ *Idee, Gefühl* communicable; *Arbeitsloser* placeable; **der Sachverhalt ist ihm nur schwer ~** it is very difficult to get the facts across to him

Ver|mit|tel|bar|keit [fɛɐ'mɪtlbaːɐkait] F **-**, *no pl* **die hohe/niedrige ~ eines Arbeitslosen** the ease/difficulty of placing an unemployed person

ver|mit|teln [fɛɐ'mɪtln] *ptp* **vermittelt** VT to arrange (*jdm* for sb); *Stelle, Partner, Privatschüler,*

Kontakte to find (*jdm* for sb); *Aushilfskräfte, Lehrer etc* to find jobs *or* positions for, to place; *(Telec) Gespräch* to put through, to connect; *Hypotheken, Kredite, Geschäfte* to arrange, to negotiate (*jdm* for sb); *Lösung, Kompromiss, Waffenstillstand* to arrange, to negotiate, to mediate; *Gefühl, Bild, Idee, Einblick* to convey, to give (*jdm* to sb); *Verständnis* to give (*jdm* (to) sb); *Wissen* to impart (*jdm* to sb); **jdm etw ~** to get sth for sb; **eine Stelle, die Hotelunterkunft vermittelt** an office which finds hotel accommodation; **wir ~ Geschäftsräume** we are agents for business premises; **ich kann dir eine billige Ferienwohnung ~** I can get you a cheap holiday flat *(Brit) or* vacation apartment *(US)*
VI to mediate, to act as mediator *or* a go-between; **~d eingreifen** to intervene; **~de Worte** conciliatory words

ver|mit|tels(t) [fɛɐ'mɪtls(t)] PREP *+gen (form)* by means of

Ver|mitt|ler(in) M(F) **a** mediator, go-between **b** *(Comm)* agent; *(Fin) (= Heiratsvermittler)* broker; *(von Anleihe)* negotiator

Ver|mitt|ler|ge|bühr F commission; *(Fin auch)* brokerage

Ver|mitt|ler|rol|le F role of mediator

Ver|mitt|lung [fɛɐ'mɪtlʊŋ] F -, -en **a** *(= das Vermitteln)* arranging, arrangement; *(von Stelle, Briefpartner, Privatschüler)* finding; *(von Arbeitskräften)* finding of jobs *or* positions (*+gen* for), placing; *(Telec: von Gespräch)* connection; *(von Hypothek, Kredit, Geschäft, Wertpapier)* negotiation; *(in Streitigkeiten)* mediation; *(von Gefühl, Bild, Idee, Einblick)* conveying; *(von Verständnis)* giving; *(von Wissen)* imparting; **sie haben sich durch die ~ einer Agentur kennengelernt** they met through an agency; **ich habe das Zimmer/die Stelle durch ~ eines Freundes bekommen** I got the room/job through *or* via a friend; **durch seine freundliche ~** with his kind help; **zur ~ eines besseren Verständnisses** to give a better understanding; **zur ~ eines besseren Eindrucks** to give *or* convey a better impression; **heute geht die telefonische ~ automatisch vor sich** nowadays telephone calls are put through *or* connected automatically
b *(= Schlichtung)* mediation; **eine ~ zwischen den beiden ist mir leider nicht gelungen** unfortunately I was unable to reconcile them *or* to bring about a reconciliation between them
c *(= Stelle, Agentur)* agency; *(= Heiratsvermittlung)* marriage bureau *or* agency; *(= Wohnungsvermittlung)* estate agent's *or* agency *(Brit)*, realtor *(US)*, real estate agent's *or* agency *(esp US)*; *(= Arbeitsvermittlung)* employment agency
d *(Telec) (= Amt)* exchange; *(in Firma etc)* switchboard; *(= Mensch)* operator; **~, bitte geben Sie mir Göhren 487** give me Göhren 487 please, operator

Ver|mitt|lungs-: **Ver|mitt|lungs|amt** NT *(Telec)* telephone exchange; **Ver|mitt|lungs|aus|schuss** M *(Econ, Pol)* mediation committee; **Ver|mitt|lungs|be|mü|hun|gen** PL efforts *pl* to mediate; **Ver|mitt|lungs|chan|ce** F *usu pl* chance of being placed in a job; **Ver|mitt|lungs|ge|bühr** F, **Ver|mitt|lungs|pro|vi|si|on** F commission; **Ver|mitt|lungs|stel|le** F agency; *(Telec)* (telephone) exchange; *(in Firma etc)* switchboard; **Ver|mitt|lungs|ver|fah|ren** NT *(Pol)* joint committee procedure; **Ver|mitt|lungs|ver|such** M attempt at mediation

ver|mö|beln [fɛɐ'mø:bln] *ptp* **vermöbelt** VT *(inf)* to beat up; *(als Strafe)* to thrash

ver|mo|dern [fɛɐ'mo:dɐn] *ptp* **vermodert** VI *aux sein* to moulder *(Brit)*, to molder *(US)*, to decay

Ver|mo|de|rung [fɛɐ'mo:dərʊŋ] F -, -en, **Ver|mod|rung** [fɛɐ'mo:drʊŋ] F -, -en decay

ver|mö|ge [fɛɐ'mø:gə] PREP *+gen (liter)* by dint of

ver|mö|gen *ptp* **vermocht** [fɛɐ'mɔxt] VT *irreg*, V AUX *(geh)* **etw zu tun ~, (es) ~, etw zu tun** to be able to do sth, to be capable of doing sth; **er vermochte (es) nicht, sich von den Fesseln zu befreien** he was unable *or* was not able to free himself from the chains; **viel ~** to be capable of a lot; **wenig ~** not to be capable of very much; **etwas Verständnis/Geduld vermag viel bei ihm** a little understanding/patience works wonders with him

Ver|mö|gen [fɛɐ'mø:gn] NT -s, - **a** *(= Reichtum, viel Geld)* fortune; **das ist ein ~ wert** it's worth a fortune; **eine Frau, die ~ hat** a woman who has money, a woman of means; **die erste Frage war, ob ich ~ hatte** the first question was whether I had private means **b** *(= Besitz)* property; **mein ganzes ~ besteht aus …** my entire assets consist of … **c** *(= Können)* ability, capacity; *(= Macht)* power

ver|mö|gend ADJ *(= reich)* wealthy, well-off; **ein ~er Mann** a man of means, a wealthy man

Ver|mö|gens-: **Ver|mö|gens|ab|ga|be** F property levy; **Ver|mö|gens|an|la|ge** F capital investment; **Ver|mö|gens|be|ra|ter(in)** M(F) financial consultant *or* adviser; **Ver|mö|gens|be|ra|tung** F financial consulting; **ver|mö|gens|bil|dend** ADJ wealth-creating; **Ver|mö|gens|bil|dung** F creation of wealth; *(durch Prämiensparen)* wealth formation by long-term saving with tax concessions; **Ver|mö|gens|er|klä|rung** F statement of property; *(Wertpapiere)* statement of assets; **Ver|mö|gens|kon|zent|ra|ti|on** F concentration of wealth; **Ver|mö|gens|po|li|tik** F policy on the distribution of wealth; **Ver|mö|gens|steu|er** F wealth tax; **Ver|mö|gens|ver|hält|nis|se** PL financial *or* pecuniary circumstances *pl*; **Ver|mö|gens|ver|tei|lung** F distribution of wealth; **Ver|mö|gens|ver|wal|ter(in)** M(F) property administrator; **Ver|mö|gens|ver|wal|tung** F property administration; **Ver|mö|gens|wer|te** PL assets *pl*; **ver|mö|gens|wirk|sam** ADJ profitable, profit-yielding; **~e Leistungen** employer's contributions to tax-deductible savings scheme ADV **Geld ~ investieren** to invest money profitably; **Ver|mö|gens|zu|wachs** M increase of wealth

ver|mot|tet [fɛɐ'mɔtət] ADJ *(lit, fig)* moth-eaten

ver|mum|men [fɛɐ'mʊmən] *ptp* **vermummt** VT to wrap up (warm) VR **a** *(= sich warm anziehen)* to wrap (oneself) up (warm); **vermummte Gestalten in einer Winterlandschaft** muffled-up figures in a winter landscape **b** *(= sich verkleiden)* to disguise oneself; **eine vermummte Gestalt betrat den Raum** a cloaked figure entered the room; **tief vermummt** heavily disguised; **vermummte Demonstranten** masked demonstrators

Ver|mum|mung F -, -en disguise; *(von Demonstranten)* covering of the face

Ver|mum|mungs|ver|bot NT **das ~ bei Demonstrationen** the law requiring demonstrators to leave their faces uncovered

ver|murk|sen *ptp* **vermurkst** VT *(inf)* **etw/sich** *(dat)* **etw ~** to mess sth up *(inf)*, to make a mess of sth

ver|mu|ten [fɛɐ'mu:tn] *ptp* **vermutet** VT to suspect; **ich vermute es nur** that's only an assumption, I'm only assuming that, that's only what I suspect to be the case; **wir haben ihn dort nicht vermutet** we did not expect him to be there; **ich hatte dich nicht so früh vermutet** I didn't suspect you would be so early; **es ist zu ~, dass …** it may be supposed that …, we may assume *or* presume that …; **Wissenschaftler ~ Leben auf der Venus** scientists suspect that there is life on Venus; **die Entwicklung lässt ~, dass …** developments lead one to assume that…, developments give rise to the suspicion *or* supposition that …

ver|mut|lich [fɛɐ'mu:tlɪç] ADJ *attr* presumable; *Täter* suspected ADV presumably

Ver|mu|tung F -, -en *(= Annahme)* supposition, assumption; *(= Mutmaßung)* conjecture; *(= Verdacht)* hunch, suspicion; **die ~ liegt nahe, dass …** there are grounds for the supposition *or* assumption that …; **das sind alles nur ~en** that is pure conjecture, those are purely suppositions *or* assumptions; **wir sind nur auf ~en angewiesen** we have to rely on suppositions *or* assumptions *or* guesswork; **meine ~en waren doch richtig** my guess *or* suspicion *or* hunch was right

ver|nach|läs|sig|bar [fɛɐ'na:xlɛsɪçba:ɐ] ADJ negligible

ver|nach|läs|si|gen [fɛɐ'na:xlɛsɪgn] *ptp* **vernachlässigt** VT to neglect; *(Schicksal) jdn* to be unkind *or* harsh to; **das können wir ~** *(= nicht berücksichtigen)* we can ignore that VR to neglect oneself *or* one's appearance

Ver|nach|läs|si|gung F -, -en neglect; *(= Nichtberücksichtigung)* ignoring, disregarding

ver|na|geln *ptp* **vernagelt** VT to nail up; **etw mit Brettern ~** to board sth up

ver|na|gelt [fɛɐ'na:glt] ADJ *(fig inf)* thick *no adv (inf)*, wooden-headed *(Brit inf)*; *(= engstirnig)* small-minded; **ich war wie ~** I couldn't think straight

ver|nä|hen *ptp* **vernäht** VT to neaten; *Wunde* to stitch (up); *(= verbrauchen)* to use up

ver|nar|ben [fɛɐ'narbn] *ptp* **vernarbt** VI *aux sein* to heal *or* close (up)

ver|narbt [fɛɐ'narpt] *ptp von* **vernarben** ADJ scarred; **~es Gesicht** *(durch Pocken auch)* pockmarked *or* pitted face

Ver|nar|bung F -, -en healing; **leichte Massagen sorgen für schöne ~en** gentle massages help the skin to scar over nicely; **eine gute ~** a good heal

ver|nar|ren *ptp* **vernarrt** VR *(inf)* **sich in jdn/etw ~** to fall for sb/sth, to be smitten by sb/sth; **in jdn/etw vernarrt sein** to be crazy *(inf) or* nuts *(inf)* about sb/sth, to be infatuated with sb

Ver|narrt|heit [fɛɐ'narthait] F -, -en infatuation (*in +acc* with)

ver|na|schen *ptp* **vernascht** VT *Süßigkeiten* to eat up; *Geld* to spend on sweets; *(inf) Mädchen, Mann* to make it with *(inf)*

ver|ne|beln [fɛɐ'ne:bln] *ptp* **vernebelt** VT *(Mil)* to cover with a smoke screen; *(fig) Tatsachen* to obscure, to obfuscate *(form)*; *(inf) Zimmer* to fug up; **die Dinge ~** to confuse the issue, to muddy the waters; **jdm den Verstand** *or* **den Kopf ~** to cloud sb's mind

Ver|ne|be|lung [fɛɐ'ne:bəlʊŋ] F -, -en, **Ver|neb|lung** [fɛɐ'ne:blʊŋ] F -, -en, *no pl (Mil)* screening; *(fig: von Tatsachen)* obscuring

ver|nehm|bar ADJ **a** *(= hörbar)* audible, perceptible **b** *(= vernehmungsfähig)* able to be questioned ADV *(= hörbar)* audibly; **sie murmelte kaum ~ ein Gebet** she mumbled a prayer, scarcely audible

ver|neh|men *ptp* **vernommen** [fɛɐ'nɔmən] VT *irreg* **a** *(= hören)* to hear; **sich zu etw** *or* **über etw** *(acc)* **~ lassen** to comment on sth **b** *(= erfahren)* to hear, to learn; **das Presseamt hat ~ lassen, dass …** the press agency has given to understand that …; **er hat über seine Pläne nichts ~ lassen** he has let nothing be known about his plans **c** *(Jur) Zeugen, Angeklagte* to examine; *(Polizei)* to question; **zu diesem Fall wurden fünfzig Zeugen vernommen** fifty witnesses were heard in connection with this case

Ver|neh|men [fɛɐ'ne:mən] NT -s, *no pl* **dem ~ nach** from what I/we *etc* hear; **gutem/sicherem ~ nach** according to well-informed/reliable sources

Ver|nehm|las|sung [fɛɐ'ne:mlasʊŋ] F -, -en *(Sw)* **a** *(Admin: = Bekanntmachung)* notice, announcement **b** *(Parl: = Beratung)* discussion stage **c** *(= Meinung, Stellungnahme)* opinion

ver|nehm|lich [fɛɐ'ne:mlɪç] ADJ clear, audible ADV **a** audibly; **es tönte laut und ~ …** it sounded loud and clear …, we heard loud and clear … **b** *(= dem Vernehmen nach)* from what I/we *etc* hear

Ver|neh|mung [fɛɐ̯'neːmʊŋ] F -, -en *(Jur: von Zeugen, Angeklagten)* examination; *(durch Polizei)* questioning

Ver|neh|mungs-: **Ver|neh|mungs|be|am|te(r)** M *decl as adj*, **Ver|neh|mungs|be|am|tin** F police interrogator; **ver|neh|mungs|fä|hig** ADJ able to be examined; *(durch Polizei)* able to be questioned; **Ver|neh|mungs|rich|ter(in)** M(F) ≈ examining judge; **ver|neh|mungs|un|fä|hig** ADJ unfit to be examined; *(durch Polizei)* unfit to be questioned

ver|nei|gen *ptp* **verneigt** VR to bow; **sich vor jdm/etw ~** *(lit)* to bow to sb/sth; *(fig)* to bow down before sb/sth

Ver|nei|gung F bow, obeisance *(form)* *(vor +dat* before); **eine ~ machen** to bow

ver|nei|nen [fɛɐ̯'naɪnən] *ptp* **verneint** VTI *Frage* to answer in the negative; *(= leugnen) Tatsache, Existenz Gottes etc* to deny; *These, Argument* to dispute; *(Gram, Logik)* to negate; **die verneinte Form** the negative (form); **eine Seite seines Wesens, die stets verneint** a side of his nature that always denies *(liter)* or that is always negative

ver|nei|nend ADJ *(auch Gram)* negative ADV *antworten* in the negative; **er schüttelte ~ den Kopf** he shook his head

Ver|nei|nung F -, -en *(= Leugnung)* denial; *(von These etc)* disputing; *(Gram, Philos)* negation; *(= verneinte Form)* negative; **die ~ meiner Frage** the negative answer to my question

ver|net|zen *ptp* **vernetzt** VT *(esp Mot)* to link up, to integrate; *(Comput)* to network; **vernetzt sein** *(Comput) (= im Netzwerk arbeiten)* to be networked; *(= Internetanschluss haben)* to have Internet access

Ver|net|zung [fɛɐ̯'nɛtsʊŋ] F -, -en *(esp Mot)* linking-up, integration; *(Comput)* networking

Ver|net|zungs|kon|zept NT *(Mot)* integration concept; *(Comput)* networking concept

ver|nich|ten [fɛɐ̯'nɪçtn] *ptp* **vernichtet** VT *(lit, fig)* to destroy; *Schädlinge, Menschheit auch* to exterminate; *Feind auch* to annihilate

ver|nich|tend ADJ *Kritik, Urteil* devastating; *Blick auch* withering; *Niederlage* crushing ADV **~ über jdn urteilen** to make a devastating appraisal of sb; **jdn ~ schlagen** *(Mil, Sport)* to annihilate sb

Ver|nich|tung F -, -en destruction; *(von Schädlingen, der Menschheit auch)* extermination; *(von Feinden, der Menschheit auch)* annihilation

Ver|nich|tungs-: **Ver|nich|tungs|krieg** M war of extermination; **Ver|nich|tungs|la|ger** NT extermination camp; **Ver|nich|tungs|mit|tel** NT insecticide; *(gegen Unkraut)* weedkiller; **Ver|nich|tungs|schlag** M devastating blow; **das war der ~ für die Regierung** that was the final blow for the government; **zum ~ ausholen** *(Mil, fig)* to prepare to deliver the final blow; **Ver|nich|tungs|waf|fe** F destructive or doomsday weapon

ver|ni|ckeln [fɛɐ̯'nɪkln] *ptp* **vernickelt** VT to nickel-plate

Ver|ni|cke|lung F -, -en nickel plating *no pl*

ver|nied|li|chen [fɛɐ̯'niːtlɪçn] *ptp* **verniedlicht** VT to trivialize, to play down

Ver|nied|li|chung [fɛɐ̯'niːtlɪçʊŋ] F minimization; *(eines Fehlers, Problems etc)* playing down

ver|nie|ten *ptp* **vernietet** VT to rivet

Ver|nie|tung [fɛɐ̯'niːtʊŋ] F -, -en riveting

Ver|nis|sa|ge [vɛrnɪ'saːʒə] F -, -n opening, preview *(at art gallery)*

Ver|nunft [fɛɐ̯'nʊnft] F -, *no pl* reason *(auch Philos)*, good sense; **zur ~ kommen** to come to one's senses; **~ annehmen** to see reason; **nimm doch ~ an!** why don't you see sense or reason?; **jdm ~ predigen** to reason with sb; **gegen alle (Regeln der) ~** against all (the laws of) reason; **~ walten lassen** *(geh)* to let reason prevail; **~ beweisen** to show (good) sense or common sense; **etw mit/ohne ~ tun** to do sth sensibly/foolishly; **etw mit ~ essen/trinken** to eat/drink sth appreciatively; **Kinder zur ~ erziehen** to bring children up to be sensible; **jdn zur ~ bringen** to make sb see sense or reason

Ver|nunft-: **ver|nunft|be|gabt** ADJ rational, endowed with reason; **Ver|nunft|be|griff** M concept of reason; **Ver|nunft|ehe** F *(lit, fig)* marriage of convenience; **ver|nunft|ge|lei|tet** [-gəlaitət] ADJ rational; **ver|nunft|ge|mäß** ADJ rational ADV rationally, from a rational point of view; **Ver|nunft|glau|be(n)** M rationalism; **Ver|nunft|grün|de** PL rational grounds *pl*; **Ver|nunft|hei|rat** F marriage of convenience

ver|nünf|tig [fɛɐ̯'nʏnftɪç] ADJ sensible; *(= logisch denkend)* rational; *(inf) (= ordentlich, anständig)* decent; *(= annehmbar)* reasonable; **sei doch ~!** be sensible or reasonable!; **ich kann keinen ~en Gedanken fassen** I can't think properly ADV sensibly; *(= logisch)* rationally; *(inf) (= anständig, ordentlich)* decently; *(= annehmbar)* reasonably; *(= tüchtig)* properly *(inf)*; **~ reden** *(inf)* to speak properly; **er kann ganz ~ kochen** *(inf)* he can cook reasonably well

ver|nünf|ti|ger|wei|se [fɛɐ̯'nʏnftɪgɐ'vaizə] ADV **etw ~ tun** to have the (good) sense to do sth; **du solltest dich ~ ins Bett legen** you should be sensible and go to bed

Ver|nünf|tig|keit F -, *no pl* good sense

Ver|nunft-: **Ver|nunft|mensch** M rational person; **ver|nunft|wid|rig** ADJ irrational

ver|öden [fɛɐ̯'løːdn] *ptp* **verödet** VT *(Med) Krampfadern* to sclerose VI *aux sein* to become desolate; *(= sich entvölkern auch)* to become deserted; *(fig: = geistig veröden)* to become stultified

Ver|ödung F -, -en **a** desolation; *(= Entvölkerung)* depopulation; *(fig)* stultification **b** *(Med: von Krampfadern)* sclerosis

ver|öf|fent|li|chen [fɛɐ̯'lœfntlɪçn] *ptp* **veröffentlicht** VTI to publish

Ver|öf|fent|li|chung F -, -en publication

ver|ord|nen *ptp* **verordnet** VT **a** *(= anordnen)* to prescribe, to order; *Medikament* to prescribe *(jdm etw* sth for sb) **b** *(old: = verfügen)* to decree, to ordain

Ver|ord|nung F **a** *(Med)* prescription; **nach ~ des Arztes einzunehmen** to be taken as directed by the doctor **b** *(form: = Verfügung)* decree, ordinance

ver|pach|ten *ptp* **verpachtet** VT to lease, to rent out *(an +acc* to)

Ver|päch|ter(in) M(F) lessor

Ver|pach|tung F lease

ver|pa|cken *ptp* **verpackt** VT to pack; *(verbrauchergerecht)* to package; *(= einwickeln)* to wrap

Ver|pa|ckung F **a** *(= Material)* packaging *no pl* **b** *no pl (= das Verpacken)* packing; *(verbrauchergerecht)* packaging; *(= das Einwickeln)* wrapping

Ver|pa|ckungs-: **Ver|pa|ckungs|ab|fall** M packaging waste; **Ver|pa|ckungs|ge|wicht** NT weight of packaging, tare (weight); **Ver|pa|ckungs|in|dust|rie** F packaging industry; **Ver|pa|ckungs|kos|ten** PL packaging charges *pl*; **Ver|pa|ckungs|ma|te|ri|al** NT packaging material; *(= Papier)* wrapping; **Ver|pa|ckungs|müll** M packaging waste

ver|päp|peln *ptp* **verpäppelt** VT *(inf)* to mollycoddle *(esp Brit inf)*, to pamper *(inf)*

ver|pa|schen [fɛɐ̯'paʃn] *ptp* **verpascht** VT *(Aus)* to sell (off), to flog *(Brit inf)*

ver|pas|sen *ptp* **verpasst** VT **a** *(= versäumen)* to miss; *(= zu kurz kommen bei)* to miss out on → **Anschluss** **b** *(inf: = zuteilen)* **jdm etw ~** to give sb sth; *(= aufzwingen)* to make sb have sth; **jdm eins** or **eine** or **eine Ohrfeige ~** to clout *(Brit)* or smack sb one *(inf)*; **jdm eine Tracht Prügel ~** to give sb a good hiding *(inf)*; **jdm einen Denkzettel ~** to give sb something to think about *(inf)*

ver|pat|zen *ptp* **verpatzt** VT *(inf)* to spoil; *Vortrag, Auftritt auch, Examen* to make a mess of; **sich** *(dat)* **etw ~** to spoil sth/make a mess of sth

ver|pen|nen *ptp* **verpennt** *(inf)* VT *(= verschlafen) Termin, Zeit* to miss by oversleeping; *(= schlafend verbringen) Tag, Morgen etc* to sleep through; *(= verpassen) Einsatz* to miss; *Leben* to waste away; *(fig: = nicht bemerken)* to sleep through VIR to oversleep

ver|pennt [fɛɐ̯'pɛnt] ADJ *(inf)* sleepy; *(= trottelig) Mensch* dozy; **ein ~er Typ** *(= Vielschläfer)* a sleepyhead *(inf)*; *(= Trottel)* a dummy *(inf)*

ver|pes|ten [fɛɐ̯'pɛstn] *ptp* **verpestet** VT to pollute, to contaminate; **die Luft im Büro ~** *(inf)* to stink out *(Brit)* or up *(US)* the office *(inf)*

Ver|pes|tung F -, *(rare)* -en pollution, contamination

ver|pet|zen *ptp* **verpetzt** VT *(inf)* to tell or sneak *(Brit)* or narc *(US)* on *(inf)* *(bei* to)

ver|pfän|den *ptp* **verpfändet** VT to pawn, to (put in) hock *(inf)*; *(Jur)* to mortgage; **(jdm) sein Wort ~** *(obs)* to pledge one's word (to sb)

Ver|pfän|dung F pawning; *(Jur)* mortgage; **etw zur ~ ins Leihhaus bringen** to take sth to be pawned (in a pawnshop), to put sth in pawn or hock *(inf)*

ver|pfei|fen *ptp* **verpfiffen** [fɛɐ̯'pfɪfn] VT *irreg* *(inf)* to grass on *(bei* to) *(inf)*

ver|pflan|zen *ptp* **verpflanzt** VT *(Bot, Med, fig)* to transplant; *Haut* to graft

Ver|pflan|zung F *(Med)* transplant; *(von Haut)* grafting

ver|pfle|gen *ptp* **verpflegt** VT to feed; *(Mil) Heer auch* to ration VR **sich (selbst) ~** to feed oneself; *(= selbst kochen)* to cater for oneself

Ver|pfle|gung [fɛɐ̯'pfleːgʊŋ] F -, -en **a** *(= das Verpflegen)* catering; *(Mil)* rationing; **die ~ von 4 Leuten** feeding 4 people, catering for 4 people **b** *(= Essen)* food; *(Mil)* rations *pl*, provisions *pl*; **mit voller ~** including food; *(= mit Vollpension)* with full board

Ver|pfle|gungs-: **Ver|pfle|gungs|kos|ten** PL cost *sing* of food; **Ver|pfle|gungs|mehr|auf|wand** M additional meal allowance

ver|pflich|ten [fɛɐ̯'pflɪçtn] ✪ 37.1, 37.3 *ptp* **verpflichtet** VT **a** *(= moralische Pflicht auferlegen)* to oblige, to place under an obligation; **verpflichtet sein, etw zu tun, zu etw verpflichtet sein** to be obliged to do sth; **sich verpflichtet fühlen, etw zu tun, sich zu etw verpflichtet fühlen** to feel obliged to do sth; **der Tradition verpflichtet** bound by tradition; **jdm verpflichtet sein** to be under an obligation to sb; **sich jdm verpflichtet fühlen** to feel under an obligation to sb

b *(= binden)* to commit; *(vertraglich, durch Eid, durch Handschlag etc)* to bind; *(durch Gesetz)* to oblige; **verpflichtet sein, etw zu tun** to be committed to doing sth; *(durch Gesetz)* to be obliged to do sth; **jdn auf die Verfassung ~** to make sb swear to uphold the constitution; **auf die Verfassung verpflichtet werden** to be sworn to uphold the constitution; **~d** *(Zusage, Unterschrift, Versprechen)* binding

c *(= einstellen)* to engage; *Sportler* to sign on; *(Mil)* to enlist

VI *(= moralische Pflicht darstellen)* to carry an obligation *(zu etw* to do sth); *(= bindend sein)* to be binding; **das verpflichtet zu nichts** there is no obligation involved → **Adel a**

VR *(moralisch)* to make a commitment; *(eidlich, vertraglich)* to commit oneself; *(Mil)* to enlist, to sign up; **sich zu etw ~** to undertake to do sth; *(vertraglich, eidlich)* to commit oneself to doing sth

Ver|pflich|tung F -, -en **a** obligation *(zu etw* to do sth); *(finanziell)* commitment *(zu etw* to do sth); *(= Aufgabe)* duty; **dienstliche ~en** official duties; **~en gegen jdn haben** to be in sb's debt *(auch finanziell)*, to be indebted to sb; **seinen ~en nachkommen** to fulfil *(Brit)* or fulfill *(US)* one's obligations **b** *(= Einstellung)* engaging; *(von Sportlern)* signing on; *(Mil)* enlistment **c** *(= das Sich-Verpflichten)* *(für, auf +acc* for) signing on; *(Mil)* signing up; **ich habe meine ~ auf**

sechs Monate bereut I regret having signed on *or* committed myself/signed up for six months

Ver|pflich|tungs|er|klä|rung F *(Jur, Econ)* formal obligation

ver|pfu|schen *ptp* **verpfuscht** VT *(inf) Arbeit etc* to bungle; *Leben, Erziehung, Urlaub etc* to muck up *(Brit inf)*, to screw up *(sl)*, to ruin; *Mensch* to ruin; *Kind* to spoil; **jdm/sich den Abend** *etc* ~ to ruin sb's/one's evening *etc*

ver|pie|pelt [fɛɐ'pi:plt], **ver|pim|pelt** [fɛɐ'pɪmplt] ADJ *(dial)* soft *(inf)*; **tu nicht so ~** don't act *or* be so soft *(inf)*

ver|pis|sen *ptp* **verpisst** VR *(sl)* to piss off *(esp Brit sl)*, to clear out *(inf)*

ver|pla|nen *ptp* **verplant** VT *Zeit* to book up; *Geld* to budget; **jdn ~** *(inf)* to fill up all sb's spare time (for him/her) VR to plan badly *or* wrongly; *(= falsch berechnen)* to miscalculate

ver|plap|pern *ptp* **verplappert** VR *(inf)* to open one's mouth too wide *(inf)*

ver|plau|dern *ptp* **verplaudert** VT *Zeit* to talk *or* chat away VR *(inf)* to forget the time talking *or* chatting

ver|plau|schen *ptp* **verplauscht** VR *(Aus)* to forget the time chatting *or* talking

ver|plem|pern *ptp* **verplempert** VT *(inf) Zeit* to waste, to fritter away; *Geld auch* to squander VR to waste oneself

ver|plom|ben [fɛɐ'plɔmbn] *ptp* **verplombt** VT to seal

ver|pönt [fɛɐ'pø:nt] ADJ frowned (up)on *(bei* by)

ver|pop|pen [fɛɐ'pɔpn] *ptp* **verpoppt** VT to jazz up, to make a pop version of

ver|pras|sen *ptp* **verprasst** VT to blow *(inf)* *(für* on); **etw sinnlos ~** to fritter sth away, to squander sth

ver|prel|len *ptp* **verprellt** VT to put off, to intimidate

ver|pro|vi|an|tie|ren [fɛɐproviаn'ti:rən] *ptp* **verproviantiert** VT to supply with food VR to get a food supply

ver|prü|geln *ptp* **verprügelt** VT to thrash, to beat up

ver|puf|fen *ptp* **verpufft** VI *aux sein* to (go) pop; *(fig)* to fall flat

Ver|puf|fung [fɛɐ'pʊfʊŋ] F -, -en *(= Explosion)* muffled explosion

ver|pul|vern [fɛɐ'pʊlvɐn, -fɐn] *ptp* **verpulvert** VT *(inf)* to fritter away, to squander

ver|pum|pen *ptp* **verpumpt** VT *(inf)* to lend out, to loan *(an +acc* to)

ver|pup|pen [fɛɐ'pʊpn] *ptp* **verpuppt** VR to pupate

ver|pus|ten *ptp* **verpustet** VIR *(inf)* to get one's breath back

Ver|putz M plaster, plasterwork; *(= Rauputz)* roughcast; **über/unter ~** on top of/under plaster

ver|put|zen *ptp* **verputzt** VT **a** *Gebäude, Wand* to plaster; *(mit Rauputz)* to roughcast **b** *(inf: = aufessen)* to polish off *(inf)*, to demolish *(inf)*; **ich kann ihn/das nicht ~** *(inf)* I can't stomach him/it

ver|qual|men *ptp* **verqualmt** VT *Zimmer, Luft* to fill with smoke; *(inf) Zigaretten etc* to smoke; *Geld* to spend on smoking; **ein verqualmtes Zimmer** a room full of smoke

ver|quast [fɛɐ'kva:st] ADJ *(inf: = verworren)* mixed-up; *Sprache, Text* garbled; *Ideen* half-baked

ver|quat|schen [fɛɐ'kvatʃn] *ptp* **verquatscht** *(inf)* VT to chat away VR **a** *(= lange plaudern)* to forget the time chatting **b** *(= Geheimnis ausplaudern)* to open one's mouth too wide *(inf)*

ver|quel|len *ptp* **verquollen** [fɛɐ'kvɔlən] VI *irreg aux sein* to swell; *(Holz auch)* to warp; **verquollene Augen** puffy *or* swollen eyes

ver|quer [fɛɐ'kve:ɐ] ADJ squint, skewwhiff *(Brit inf)*; **das ist eine ~e Optik** that's a twisted way of looking at things ADV **das kommt mir jetzt etwas ~** that could have come at a better time → **verquergehen**

ver|quer+ge|hen VI *sep irreg aux sein (inf)* **(jdm) ~** *(= schiefgehen)* to go wrong (for sb); **so etwas geht mir verquer** that goes against the grain

ver|qui|cken [fɛɐ'kvɪkn] *ptp* **verquickt** VT **a** *(Chem)* to amalgamate **b** *(fig)* to bring together, to combine; *(= vermischen)* to mix; **eng miteinander verquickt** closely related VR **sich (miteinander) ~** to combine

Ver|qui|ckung F -, -en **a** amalgamation **b** *(fig)* combination

ver|quir|len *ptp* **verquirlt** VT to whisk

ver|ram|meln *ptp* **verrammelt** VT to barricade

ver|ram|schen [fɛɐ'ramʃn] *ptp* **verramscht** VT *(Comm)* to sell off cheap; *(inf auch)* to flog *(Brit inf)*

Ver|rat M, *no pl* betrayal *(an +dat* of); *(Jur)* treason *(an +dat* against); **~ an jdm üben** to betray sb

ver|ra|ten *ptp* **verraten** *irreg* VT **a** *Geheimnis, Absicht, jdn* to betray, to give away; *(= bekannt geben, ausplaudern)* to tell; *(fig: = erkennen lassen)* to reveal, to show; **nichts ~!** don't say a word!; **er hat es ~** he let it out **b** *Freunde, Vaterland, gute Sache etc* to betray *(an +acc* to); **~ und verkauft** *(inf)* well and truly sunk *(inf)* VR to give oneself away, to betray oneself

Ver|rä|ter [fɛɐ'rɛ:tɐ] M -s, -, **Ver|rä|te|rin** [-ərɪn] F -, -nen traitor *(+gen* to)

ver|rä|te|risch [fɛɐ'rɛ:tərɪʃ] ADJ treacherous, perfidious *(liter)*; *(Jur)* treasonable; *(= verdächtig) Hinweis, Blick, Lächeln etc* telltale *attr* ADV *(= etwas erkennen lassend)* revealingly, in a telltale way; **ihre Augen zwinkerten ~** her eyes twinkled conspiratorially

ver|rau|chen *ptp* **verraucht** VI *aux sein (fig: Zorn, Enttäuschung)* to subside VT *Tabak, Zigarren etc* to smoke; *Geld* to spend on smoking

ver|räu|chern *ptp* **verräuchert** VT to fill with smoke

ver|raucht [fɛɐ'rauxt] ADJ smoky, filled with smoke

ver|räu|men *ptp* **verräumt** VT *(S Ger, Aus, Sw)* to put away somewhere

ver|rau|schen *ptp* **verrauscht** VI *aux sein (fig)* to die *or* fade away

ver|rech|nen *ptp* **verrechnet** VT *(= begleichen)* to settle; *Scheck* to clear; *Lieferung, Leistungen, Guthaben (= gutschreiben)* to credit to an account; *(= belasten)* to debit to an account; *Gutschein* to redeem; **die Spesen von der Firma ~ lassen** to have one's expenses paid by the firm; **etw mit etw ~** *(= zusammen abrechnen)* to settle sth (together) with sth; *(= gegeneinander aufrechnen)* to balance sth with sth, to offset sth against sth VR to miscalculate; *(= Rechenfehler machen)* to make a mistake/mistakes; *(inf: = sich täuschen)* to be mistaken; **sich um einen Euro ~** to be out by one euro

Ver|rech|nung F settlement; *(von Scheck)* clearing; *(= Gutschrift)* crediting to an account; *(= Belastung)* debiting to an account; **„nur zur ~"** "A/C payee only"

Ver|rech|nungs-: **Ver|rech|nungs|ein|heit** F clearing unit; **Ver|rech|nungs|kon|to** NT offset account; **Ver|rech|nungs|prei|se** PL *(Comm)* internal prices *pl*; **Ver|rech|nungs|scheck** M crossed *or* non-negotiable cheque *(Brit)*, voucher check *(US)*; **Ver|rech|nungs|stel|le** F clearing house

ver|re|cken *ptp* **verreckt** VI *aux sein (vulg)* to croak *(inf)*; *(sl: = kaputtgehen)* to give up the ghost *(inf)*; **er ist elend(ig)** *or* **elendiglich verreckt** he died like a dog *(inf)*; **soll er doch ~!** let him bloody well *(Brit sl)* *or* damn well *(inf)* die!; **jetzt ist der Alte endlich verreckt** he's finally kicked the bucket *(inf)* *or* snuffed it *(Brit inf)*; **zu tausenden** *or* **Tausenden ~** to perish in their thousands; **es ist zum Verrecken** *(sl)* it's damn awful *(inf)*, it's bloody terrible *(Brit inf)*; **etw nicht ums Verrecken tun** *(sl)* **etw ums Verrecken nicht tun** *(sl)* to damn well *(inf)* *or* bloody well *(Brit inf)* refuse to do sth

ver|reg|nen *ptp* **verregnet** VI *aux sein* to be spoiled *or* ruined by rain

ver|reg|net [fɛɐ're:gnət] ADJ rainy, wet

ver|rei|ben *ptp* **verrieben** [fɛɐ'ri:bn] VT *irreg* to rub *(auf +dat* into); *Salbe* to massage *(auf +dat* into)

ver|rei|sen *ptp* **verreist** VI *aux sein* to go away (on a trip *or* journey); **er ist verreist** he's away; **er ist geschäftlich verreist** he's away on business; **wohin ~ Sie in diesem Jahr?** where are you going (on holiday *(esp Brit)* *or* vacation *(US)*) this year?; **mit dem Auto/der Bahn ~** to go on a car/train journey; *(in Urlaub)* to go on holiday *(esp Brit)* *or* vacation *(US)* by car/train

ver|rei|ßen *ptp* **verrissen** [fɛɐ'rɪsn] VT *irreg* **a** *(= kritisieren)* to tear to pieces **b** *(dial)* = **zerreißen** **c** *(dial) Schuss, Lenkrad* to jerk; *Wagen* to make swerve

ver|ren|ken [fɛɐ'rɛŋkn] *ptp* **verrenkt** VT to dislocate, to put out of joint; *Gelenk* to dislocate; *Hals* to crick; **sich** *(dat)* **die Zunge ~** to twist one's tongue; **lieber sich den Bauch** *or* **Magen ~, als dem Wirt was schenken** *(prov)* waste not, want not *(prov)* → **Hals a** VR to contort oneself

Ver|ren|kung F -, -en **a** contortion; **~en machen** to contort oneself **b** *(Med: = das Verrenken)* dislocation

ver|ren|nen *ptp* **verrannt** [fɛɐ'rant] VR *irreg* to get carried away; **sich in etw** *(acc)* **~** to get stuck on sth

Ver|ren|tung [fɛɐ'rɛntʊŋ] F -, -en retirement; **frühe ~** early retirement

ver|rich|ten *ptp* **verrichtet** VT *Arbeit* to perform, to carry out; *Andacht* to perform; *Gebet* to say → **Geschäft d, Notdurft**

Ver|rich|tung F performing, carrying out; **alltägliche/häusliche ~en** routine *or* daily/domestic *or* household tasks

ver|rie|geln [fɛɐ'ri:gln] *ptp* **verriegelt** VT to bolt; *(Comput) Tastatur* to lock; *Laufwek* to close

Ver|rie|ge|lung F -, -en *(= Vorrichtung)* bolt

ver|rin|gern [fɛɐ'rɪŋɐn] *ptp* **verringert** VT to reduce VR to decrease; *(Abstand, Vorsprung auch)* to lessen, to diminish; *(Qualität auch, Leistung)* to deteriorate

Ver|rin|ge|rung F -, -en *(= das Verringern)* reduction; *(= Abnahme)* decrease; *(von Qualität, Leistung)* deterioration; *(von Abstand, Vorsprung)* lessening, diminution

ver|rin|nen *ptp* **verronnen** [fɛɐ'rɔnən] VI *irreg aux sein (Wasser)* to trickle away *(in +dat* into); *(Zeit)* to elapse

Ver|riss M slating review

ver|ro|hen [fɛɐ'ro:ən] *ptp* **verroht** VT to brutalize VI *aux sein (Mensch, Gesellschaft)* to become brutalized; *(Sitten)* to coarsen

Ver|ro|hung F -, -en brutalization

ver|ros|ten *ptp* **verrostet** VI *aux sein* to rust; *(fig: = steif werden)* to get rusty; **verrostet** rusty; *(fig: = steif)* stiff, rusty

ver|rot|ten [fɛɐ'rɔtn] *ptp* **verrottet** VI *aux sein* to rot; *(= sich organisch zersetzen)* to decompose

ver|rucht [fɛɐ'ru:xt] ADJ despicable, loathsome; *Tat auch* heinous; *(= lasterhaft)* disreputable

Ver|rucht|heit F -, *no pl (von Lokal etc)* disreputable air

ver|rü|cken *ptp* **verrückt** VT to move, to disarrange

ver|rückt [fɛɐ'rʏkt] ADJ **a** *(= geisteskrank)* mad, insane **b** *(inf)* crazy, mad; **~ auf** *(+acc)* *or* **nach** crazy *or* mad about *(inf)*; **wie ~** like mad *or* crazy *(inf)*; **die Leute kamen wie ~** loads of people came *(inf)*; **so etwas Verrücktes!** what a crazy idea!; **jdn ~ machen** to drive sb crazy *or* mad *or* wild *(inf)*; **~ werden** to go crazy; **bei dem Lärm kann man ja ~ werden** this noise is enough to drive you round the bend *(Brit)* *or* crazy *(inf)*; **ich werd ~!** *(inf)* (well,) I'll be blowed *(Brit)* *or* damned! *(inf)*; **du bist wohl ~!** you must be crazy *or* mad!; **~ spielen** → **verrücktspielen**

Ver|rück|te(r) [fɛɐ̯'rʏktə] MF decl as adj (inf) lunatic

Ver|rückt|heit F -, -en (inf) madness, craziness; (Handlung) mad or crazy thing

ver|rückt+spie|len VI sep (inf) to play up

Ver|rückt|wer|den NT zum ~ enough to drive one mad or crazy or round the bend (Brit) or up the wall (all inf)

Ver|ruf M, no pl in ~ kommen or geraten to fall into disrepute; jdn/etw in ~ bringen to bring sb/sth into disrepute

ver|ru|fen [fɛɐ̯'ru:fn] ADJ disreputable

ver|rüh|ren ptp verrührt VT to mix, to stir

ver|ru|ßen ptp verrußt VI aux sein to get or become sooty

ver|rut|schen ptp verrutscht VI aux sein to slip

Vers [fɛrs] M -es, -e [-zə] verse (auch Bibl); (= Zeile) line; etw in ~e bringen or setzen to put sth into verse; ~e machen or schmieden (inf) to make up poems; ich kann mir keinen ~ darauf machen (fig) there's no rhyme or reason to it

ver|sach|li|chen [fɛɐ̯'zaxlɪçn] ptp versachlicht VT to objectify

Ver|sach|li|chung F -, no pl objectification

ver|sa|cken ptp versackt VI aux sein a (lit) to sink, to become submerged b (fig inf) (= lange zechen) to get involved in a booze-up (inf); (= nicht wegkommen) to stay on; (= herunterkommen) to go downhill

ver|sa|gen ptp versagt VT jdm/sich etw ~ to deny sb/oneself sth; (= verweigern) to refuse sb/oneself sth; ich kann es mir nicht ~, eine Bemerkung zu machen I can't refrain from making a comment; sich jdm ~ (geh) to refuse to give oneself to sb; etw bleibt or ist jdm versagt sth is denied sb, sb is denied sth → Dienst c VI to fail; (Mensch: im Leben auch) to be a failure; (Maschine) to break down; (Gewehr) to fail to function; die Beine/Nerven etc versagten ihm his legs/nerves etc gave way; da versagt diese Methode this method doesn't work there

Ver|sa|gen [fɛɐ̯'za:gn] NT -s, no pl failure; (von Maschine) breakdown; menschliches ~ human error

Ver|sa|gens|angst F usu pl fear of failure

Ver|sa|ger [fɛɐ̯'za:gɐ] M -s, -, **Ver|sa|ge|rin** [-ərɪn] F -, -nen failure, flop (inf)

Ver|sa|gung [fɛɐ̯'za:gʊŋ] F -, -en denial; (= Entbehrung) privation

Ver|sail|ler Ver|trag [vɛr'zaiɐ-] M Treaty of Versailles

Ver|sal [vɛr'za:l] M -s, Versalien [-liən] usu pl (Typ) capital letter, cap (Typ inf)

ver|sal|zen ptp versalzen VT irreg to put too much salt in/on, to oversalt; (inf: = verderben) to spoil; ~ sein to be too salty; ~es Essen oversalty food → Suppe

ver|sam|meln ptp versammelt VT to assemble (auch Mil), to gather together; Truppen auch to rally, to muster; Leute um sich ~ to gather people about (Brit) or around one; vor versammelter Mannschaft (inf) in front of or before the assembled company VR to assemble; (Parlament) to sit; (Ausschuss, Verein, Mitglieder) to meet; (Tagung) to convene

ver|sam|melt [fɛɐ̯'zamlt] ADJ (Reitsport) collected

Ver|samm|lung F a (= Veranstaltung) meeting; (= versammelte Menschen) assembly; verfassunggebende ~ legislative assembly b (= das Versammeln) assembly, gathering (together); (von Truppen) rallying, mustering; (von Ausschuss, Verein, Mitgliedern) meeting c (Reitsport) collection

Ver|samm|lungs-: **Ver|samm|lungs|frei|heit** F freedom of assembly; **Ver|samm|lungs|lo|kal** NT meeting place; **Ver|samm|lungs|raum** M (in Hotel etc) conference room; (form: allgemein) assembly room; **Ver|samm|lungs|recht** NT right of assembly; **Ver|samm|lungs|ver|bot** NT prohibition of assembly

Ver|sand [fɛɐ̯'zant] M -(e)s [-dəs], no pl a (= das Versenden) dispatch (esp Brit), shipment; (= das Vertreiben) distribution; der ~ per Land/Schiene shipment by land/rail b (Abteilung) dispatch (esp Brit) or shipping department c (inf: = Versandkaufhaus) mail-order firm

Ver|sand-: **Ver|sand|ab|tei|lung** F dispatch (esp Brit) or shipping department; **Ver|sand|an|zei|ge** F dispatch (esp Brit) or shipping advice; **Ver|sand|ar|ti|kel** M article for dispatch (esp Brit) or shipping; **Ver|sand|bahn|hof** M dispatch (esp Brit) or shipping station; **ver|sand|be|reit** ADJ ready for dispatch (esp Brit) or shipment; **Ver|sand|buch|han|del** M mail-order book business; **Ver|sand|do|ku|ment** NT usu pl shipping document

ver|san|den [fɛɐ̯'zandn] ptp versandet VI aux sein to silt (up); (fig) to peter out, to fizzle out (inf)

Ver|sand-: **ver|sand|fer|tig** ADJ = versandbereit; **Ver|sand|ge|schäft** NT a (Firma) mail-order firm b (Handel) mail-order business; **Ver|sand|gut** NT goods pl for dispatch (esp Brit) or shipment; **Ver|sand|han|del** M mail-order business; **Ver|sand|haus** NT mail-order firm or house; **Ver|sand|haus|ka|ta|log** M mail-order catalogue (Brit) or catalog (US); **Ver|sand|kos|ten** PL transport(ation) costs pl; **ver|sand|ko|sten|frei** ADJ postage-free; (Comm) free of forwarding costs; **Ver|sand|pa|pie|re** PL transport(ation) documents pl; **Ver|sand|ta|sche** F padded envelope, Jiffy bag® (Brit)

Ver|san|dung F -, -en silting (up); (fig) petering out, fizzling out (inf)**Ver|sand-**: **Ver|sand|un|ter|neh|men** NT mail-order business; **Ver|sand|weg** M auf dem ~ by mail order

Ver|satz M, no pl a (= das Versetzen) pawning b (Min) packing, stowing

Ver|satz-: **Ver|satz|amt** NT (dial) pawnshop; **Ver|satz|stück** NT a (Theat) set piece b (fig) setting, background c (Aus: = Pfandstück) pledge

ver|sau|beu|teln [fɛɐ̯'zaubɔytln] ptp versaubeutelt VT (inf) a (= verschlampen) to go and lose (inf) b (= verderben) to mess up (inf)

ver|sau|en ptp versaut VT (inf) a (= verschmutzen) to make a mess of; Umwelt to mess up b (= verderben, ruinieren) to ruin; Kinder, Moral, Mensch to screw up (inf); (= schlecht machen) Arbeit to make a mess of; der Chirurg hat ihn versaut the surgeon made a mess of him

ver|sau|ern [fɛɐ̯'zauɐn] ptp versauert (inf) VI aux sein to stagnate; eine versauerte alte Jungfer an embittered old spinster VT jdm etw ~ to mess sth up for sb (inf), to ruin sth for sb

Ver|saue|rung [fɛɐ̯'zauərʊŋ] F -, -en, **Ver|säu|e|rung** [fɛɐ̯'zɔyərʊŋ] F -, -en (von Gewässer, Boden) acidification

ver|sau|fen ptp versoffen [fɛɐ̯'zɔfn] irreg (inf) VT Geld to spend on booze (inf); seinen Verstand ~ to drink oneself silly VI aux sein (dial) a (= ertrinken) to drown b (Motor) to flood

ver|säu|men ptp versäumt VT to miss; Zeit to lose; Pflicht to neglect; (Sw: = aufhalten) jdn to delay, to hold up; (es) ~, etw zu tun to fail to do sth; nichts ~, um jdn glücklich zu machen to do everything to make sb happy; das Versäumte what one has missed; die versäumte Zeit aufholen to make up for lost time

Ver|säum|nis [fɛɐ̯'zɔymnɪs] NT -ses, -se (= Fehler, Nachlässigkeit) failing; (= Unterlassung) omission; (= versäumte Zeit, Sch) absence (+gen from); (Jur) default (+gen in); bei ~ rechtzeitiger Bezahlung in the event that payment is not made punctually

Ver|säum|nis|ur|teil NT (Jur) judgement by default

ver|saut ADJ (sl: = schweinisch) filthy

Vers|bau M, no pl versification, metrical structure

ver|scha|chern ptp verschachert VT to sell off

ver|schach|telt [fɛɐ̯'ʃaxtlt] ADJ Satz encapsulated, complex; (Comput) Menü, Befehle nested; ineinander ~ interlocking

ver|schaf|fen ptp verschafft VT a jdm etw ~ (Geld, Kapital, Alibi) to provide or supply sb with sth or sth for sb; Arbeit, Stelle auch to find sth for sb; Erleichterung, Genugtuung, Vergnügen to give sb sth; Ansehen, Respekt to earn sb sth → Ehre b sich (dat) etw ~ to obtain sth; Kenntnisse to acquire sth; Ansehen, Vorteil to gain sth; Ruhe, Respekt to get sth; sich mit Gewalt Zutritt ~ to force an entry, to force one's way in; ich muss mir darüber Gewissheit ~ I must be certain about it; ich muss mir darüber Klarheit ~ I must clarify the matter

ver|scha|len [fɛɐ̯'ʃa:lən] ptp verschalt VT Wand to panel; Heizung etc to box in, to encase; (für Beton) to build a framework or mould (Brit) or mold (US) for VI (für Beton) to build a framework or mould (Brit) or mold (US)

Ver|scha|lung F a no pl (= das Verschalen) (mit Holz) panelling (Brit), paneling (US); (von Heizung etc) casing; (für Beton) building a framework or mould (Brit) or mold (US) b (= Bretter etc) framework, mould (Brit), mold (US)

ver|schämt [fɛɐ̯'ʃɛ:mt] ADJ coy ADV coyly

Ver|schämt|heit F -, no pl coyness

ver|schan|deln [fɛɐ̯'ʃandln] ptp verschandelt VT to ruin

Ver|schan|de|lung [fɛɐ̯'ʃandəlʊŋ] F -, -en, **Ver|schand|lung** [fɛɐ̯'ʃandlʊŋ] F -, -en ruining

ver|schan|zen ptp verschanzt VT (Mil) to fortify VR (Mil, fig) to entrench oneself (hinter +dat behind); (= sich verbarrikadieren) to barricade oneself in (in etw (dat) sth); (= Deckung suchen) to take cover (hinter +dat behind)

Ver|schan|zung [fɛɐ̯'ʃantsʊŋ] F -, -en (Mil) a fortification; (von Truppen) entrenchment; (= Verbarrikadierung) barricading b (= Befestigung) fortification

ver|schär|fen ptp verschärft VT (= erhöhen) Tempo, Aufmerksamkeit to increase; Gegensätze to intensify; (= verschlimmern) Lage to aggravate; Spannungen to heighten; (= strenger machen) Kontrollen, Strafe, Gesetze, Maßnahmen, Prüfungen, Grenzwerte to tighten VR (Tempo, Aufmerksamkeit) to increase; (Wettbewerb, Gegensätze) to intensify; (Lage) to become aggravated; (Spannungen) to heighten, to mount; (Kontrollen, Gesetze, Maßnahmen, Prüfungen) to become tighter

ver|schärft [fɛɐ̯'ʃɛrft] ADJ a (= erhöht) Tempo, Aufmerksamkeit, Wettbewerb increased; Gegensätze intensified; (= verschlimmert) Lage aggravated; Spannungen heightened; (= strenger) Kontrollen, Strafe, Maßnahmen tightened; Arrest close b (inf: = gut) brilliant (inf), wicked (sl) ADV (= intensiver) more intensively; (= strenger) more severely; prüfen more closely; ~ aufpassen to keep a closer watch; ~ kontrollieren to keep a tighter control; ~ vorgehen to take more stringent measures

Ver|schär|fung F increase; (von Gegensätzen) intensification; (= Verschlimmerung) aggravation; (von Spannung) heightening, mounting; (von Regeln, Gesetzen) tightening

ver|schar|ren ptp verscharrt VT to bury

ver|schät|zen ptp verschätzt VR to misjudge, to miscalculate (in etw (dat) sth); sich um zwei Monate ~ to be out by two months

ver|schau|en ptp verschaut VR (Aus) a (= nicht richtig sehen) to make a mistake b (= sich verlieben) sich in jdn ~ to fall for sb

ver|schau|keln ptp verschaukelt VT (inf) to take for a ride (inf)

ver|schei|den ptp verschieden [fɛɐ̯'ʃi:dn] VI irreg aux sein (geh) to pass away, to expire

ver|schei|ßen ptp verschissen [fɛɐ̯'ʃɪsn] VT irreg (vulg) to cover with shit (vulg) → auch verschissen

ver|schei|ßern [fɛɐ̯'ʃaisɐn] ptp verscheißert VT (inf) jdn ~ to take the piss out of sb (Brit sl), to make fun of sb

ver|schen|ken ptp verschenkt VT (lit, fig) to give away; sein Herz an jdn ~ (liter) to give sb one's heart VR sich an jdn ~ to throw oneself away on sb

ver|scher|beln [fɛɐ̯ˈʃɛrbln] *ptp* **verscherbelt** VT *(inf)* to flog *(Brit inf)*, to sell

ver|scher|zen *ptp* **verscherzt** VT **sich** *(dat)* **etw ~** to lose *or* forfeit sth; **sich** *(dat)* **seine Chancen ~** to throw away one's chances; **sich** *(dat)* **jds Gunst** *or* **Wohlwollen ~** to lose *or* forfeit sb's favour *(Brit) or* favor *(US)*; **es sich** *(dat)* **mit jdm ~** to spoil things (for oneself) with sb

ver|scheu|chen *ptp* **verscheucht** VT to scare *or* frighten off *or* away; *Fliegen* to chase away; *(fig) Sorgen, Gedanken etc* to drive away

ver|scheu|ern *ptp* **verscheuert** VT *(inf)* to sell off, to flog off *(Brit inf)*

ver|schi|cken *ptp* **verschickt** VT **a** *(= versenden)* to send out *or* off **b** *(zur Kur etc)* to send away **c** *(= deportieren)* to deport

ver|schieb|bar ADJ *Möbel etc* movable; *Regler, Spange, Teil* sliding; **leicht ~e Gegenstände** objects which are easy to move; **der Termin ist ~** this appointment can be changed

Ver|schie|be- *(Rail)*: **Ver|schie|be|bahn|hof** M shunting yard; **Ver|schie|be|gleis** NT shunting track; **Ver|schie|be|lo|ko|mo|ti|ve** F shunter

ver|schie|ben *ptp* **verschoben** [fɛɐ̯ˈʃoːbn] *irreg* VT **a** *(= verrücken)* to move *(auch Comput)*, to shift; *Truppen* to displace; *(Rail) Eisenbahnwagen* to shunt; *Perspektive* to alter, to shift **b** *(= aufschieben)* to change; *(auf später)* to postpone, to put off, to defer (*um* for) **c** *(inf) Waren, Devisen* to traffic in VR **a** *(= verrutschen)* to move out of place; *(fig: Perspektive, Schwerpunkt)* to alter, to shift **b** *(zeitlich)* to be postponed, to be put off *or* deferred **c** *(Med) (bei Knochenbruch)* to become displaced; *(Kniescheibe, Bandscheibe)* to slip **d** *(Ling: Laute)* to shift

Ver|schie|bung F **a** *(= das Verschieben)* moving, shifting; *(von Truppen)* displacement; *(fig: von Perspektiven)* alteration **b** *(von Termin)* postponement, deferment **c** *(inf: von Waren, Devisen)* trafficking **d** *(Geol)* displacement, heave **e** *(Ling: von Lauten)* shift **f** *(Med) (bei Knochenbruch)* displacement; *(von Kniescheibe)* slip **g** *(Psych)* displacement

ver|schie|den [fɛɐ̯ˈʃiːdn] ADJ **a** *(= unterschiedlich)* different; *(= unähnlich)* dissimilar; *Meinungen etc* differing, different; **die ~sten Sorten** many different kinds, all sorts; **das ist ganz ~** *(= wird verschieden gehandhabt)* that varies, that just depends **b** *attr (= mehrere, einige)* various, several; **~e Mal** several times **c** *(substantivisch)* **Verschiedene** various *or* several people; **Verschiedenes** different things; *(in Zeitungen, Listen)* miscellaneous ADV differently; **die Häuser sind ~ lang/breit/hoch** the houses vary *or* are different in length/breadth/height

ver|schie|den|ar|tig ADJ different; *(= mannigfaltig)* various, diverse; **die ~sten Dinge** all sorts *or* manner of things

Ver|schie|den|ar|tig|keit F, *no pl* different nature; *(= Mannigfaltigkeit)* variety, diversity

ver|schie|de|ne|mal △ [fɛɐ̯ˈʃiːdənəmaːl] ADV → **verschieden ADJ b**

ver|schie|de|ner|lei [fɛɐ̯ˈʃiːdənɐˈlai] ADJ *inv* **a** *attr* many different, various **b** *(substantivisch)* many different things, various things

ver|schie|den|far|big, *(Aus)* **ver|schie|den|fär|big** ADJ different-coloured *(Brit)*, different-colored *(US)*; **die Kostüme waren ~** the costumes were many different colours *(Brit) or* colors *(US)*

Ver|schie|den|heit F **-, -en** difference (*+gen* of, in); *(= Unähnlichkeit)* dissimilarity; *(= Vielfalt)* variety

ver|schie|dent|lich [fɛɐ̯ˈʃiːdntlɪç] ADV *(= mehrmals)* on several occasions, several times; *(= vereinzelt)* occasionally

ver|schie|ßen *ptp* **verschossen** [fɛɐ̯ˈʃɔsn] *irreg* VT **a** *Munition* to use up; *Pfeile* to shoot off; *(inf) Fotos, Film* to take, to use up → **Pulver b** *(Sport)* to miss VR *(inf)* **sich in jdn ~** to fall for sb *(inf)*; **in jdn verschossen sein** to be crazy about sb *(inf)* VI *aux sein (Stoff, Farbe)* to fade

ver|schif|fen *ptp* **verschifft** VT to ship; *Sträfling* to transport

Ver|schif|fung [fɛɐ̯ˈʃɪfʊŋ] F **-, -en** shipment; *(von Sträflingen)* transportation

ver|schil|fen [fɛɐ̯ˈʃɪlfn] *ptp* **verschilft** VI *aux sein* to become overgrown with reeds

ver|schim|meln *ptp* **verschimmelt** VI *aux sein (Nahrungsmittel)* to go mouldy *(Brit) or* moldy *(US)*; *(Leder, Papier etc)* to become mildewed, to go mildewy; *(Wand)* to become mildewed; **verschimmelt** *(lit)* mouldy *(Brit)*, moldy *(US)*; mildewed, mildewy; *(fig) Ansichten etc* fusty

ver|schis|sen [fɛɐ̯ˈʃɪsn] ADJ *(vulg) Unterhose* shitty *(sl)*; **du hast bei mir ~** *(sl)* I'm through with you *(inf)* → *auch* **verscheißen**

ver|schla|cken [fɛɐ̯ˈʃlakn] *ptp* **verschlackt** VI *aux sein (Ofen)* to become clogged (up) with slag; *(Med: Gewebe)* to become clogged

ver|schla|fen *ptp* **verschlafen** *irreg* VIR to oversleep VT *Termin* to miss by oversleeping; *(= schlafend verbringen) Tag, Morgen* to sleep through; *Leben* to sleep away; *(= verpassen) Einsatz* to miss

ver|schla|fen ADJ sleepy; *(= trottelig) Mensch* dozy *(inf)*; **~ sein** *(= Vielschläfer sein)* to like one's sleep

Ver|schla|fen|heit F **-**, *no pl* sleepiness; *(= Trotteligkeit)* doziness *(inf)*

Ver|schlag M *(= abgetrennter Raum)* partitioned area; *(= Schuppen)* shed; *(grob gezimmert)* shack; *(esp für Kaninchen)* hutch; *(ans Haus angebaut)* lean-to; *(unter der Treppe)* glory hole; *(= elende Behausung)* hovel; *(= Verpackung)* crate

ver|schla|gen *ptp* **verschlagen** VT *irreg* **a etw mit Brettern ~** to board sth up **b** *(= nehmen) Atem* to take away; **das hat mir die Sprache ~** it left me speechless **c** *(= geraten lassen)* to bring; **auf eine einsame Insel ~ werden** to be cast up on a lonely island; **an einen Ort ~ werden** to end up somewhere **d** *(Sport) Ball* to mishit **e** *(= verblättern) Seite, Stelle* to lose **f** *(dial: = verprügeln)* to wallop *(inf)*, to thrash

ver|schla|gen ADJ **a** *Mensch, Blick, Tier etc* sly, artful **b** *(dial: = lauwarm)* tepid, lukewarm

Ver|schla|gen|heit F **-**, *no pl* slyness, artfulness

ver|schlam|men [fɛɐ̯ˈʃlamən] *ptp* **verschlammt** VI *aux sein* to silt up

ver|schlam|pen *ptp* **verschlampt** *(inf)* VT **a** *(= verlieren)* to go and lose *(inf)* **b** *(= verkommen lassen)* to spoil VI *aux sein (Mensch)* to go to seed *(inf)*

ver|schlan|ken [fɛɐ̯ˈʃlaŋkn] *ptp* **verschlankt** VT *(inf) Produktion* to cut back, to trim; *Personal* to cut, to trim

Ver|schlan|kung [fɛɐ̯ˈʃlaŋkʊŋ] F **-, -en** *(inf, von Produktion)* cutting-back (*gen* on), trimming; *(von Personal)* cutting, trimming

ver|schlech|tern [fɛɐ̯ˈʃlɛçtɐn] *ptp* **verschlechtert** VT to make worse, to worsen; *Zustand, Lage auch* to aggravate; *Qualität* to impair; *Aussicht* to diminish, to decrease VR to get worse, to worsen, to deteriorate; *(Leistungen auch)* to decline; **sich (notenmäßig) ~** *(Sch)* to downgrade; **sich finanziell ~** to be worse off financially; **sich beruflich ~** to take a worse job

Ver|schlech|te|rung F **-, -en** worsening, deterioration; *(von Leistung)* decline; **eine finanzielle ~** a financial setback; **eine berufliche ~** a retrograde step professionally

ver|schlei|ern [fɛɐ̯ˈʃlaiɐn] *ptp* **verschleiert** VT to veil; *(fig auch)* to disguise, to cover up; *Blick* to blur; **Nebel verschleiert die Aussicht/die Berge** the view is/the mountains are hidden by *or* under a veil of mist VR *(Frau)* to veil oneself; *(Himmel)* to become hazy; *(Blick)* to become blurred; *(= träumerisch werden)* to become hazy; *(Stimme)* to become husky

ver|schlei|ert [fɛɐ̯ˈʃlaiɐt] ADJ *Frau* veiled; *Augen, Aussicht* misty; *Berge* misty, veiled in mist; *Stimme* husky; *Blick* blurred; *(fig) Behauptungen* veiled; *Werbung* indirect; *(= träumerisch)* hazy; *(Phot)* foggy; **etw nur ~ sehen** to see sth only hazily

Ver|schlei|e|rung F **-, -en** veiling; *(fig auch)* disguising, covering up; *(von Blick)* blurring

Ver|schlei|e|rungs-: **Ver|schlei|e|rungs|tak|tik** F cover-up (*+gen* by); **Ver|schlei|e|rungs|ver|such** M attempt at covering up

ver|schlei|fen *ptp* **verschliffen** [fɛɐ̯ˈʃlɪfn] VT *irreg* to slur

ver|schlei|men *ptp* **verschleimt** VT to block *or* congest with phlegm; **verschleimt sein** *(Patient)* to be congested with phlegm VI *aux sein* to become blocked *or* congested with phlegm

Ver|schlei|mung [fɛɐ̯ˈʃlaimʊŋ] F **-, -en** mucous congestion

Ver|schleiß [fɛɐ̯ˈʃlais] M **-es, -e a** *(lit, fig)* wear and tear; *(= Verbrauch)* consumption; *(= Verluste)* loss; **ein ~ deiner Kräfte** a drain on your strength; **eingeplanter ~** built-in obsolescence; **sein ~ an Frauen** *(hum)* the rate he goes through women **b** *(Aus: = Kleinverkauf)* retail trade

ver|schlei|ßen [fɛɐ̯ˈʃlaisn] *pret* **verschliss** [fɛɐ̯ˈʃlɪs], *ptp* **verschlissen** [fɛɐ̯ˈʃlɪsn] VT **a** *(= kaputtmachen)* to wear out; *(= verbrauchen)* to use up; **der Verein hat dieses Jahr schon drei Trainer verschlissen** the club has already gone through three managers this year **b** *(Aus)* to retail VI *aux sein* to wear out → *auch* **verschlissen** VR to wear out; *(Menschen)* to wear oneself out

Ver|schlei|ßer [fɛɐ̯ˈʃlaisɐ] M **-s, -**, **Ver|schlei|ße|rin** [-ərɪn] F **-, -nen** *(Aus)* retailer

Ver|schleiß-: **Ver|schleiß|er|schei|nung** F sign of wear; **Ver|schleiß|krieg** M war of attrition; **Ver|schleiß|prü|fung** F wear test; **Ver|schleiß|teil** NT part subject to wear and tear

ver|schlep|pen *ptp* **verschleppt** VT **a** *(= entführen) jdn* to abduct; *Gefangene, Kriegsopfer* to displace; *Kunstschätze etc* to carry off; *(inf) etw* to go off with **b** *(= verbreiten) Seuche* to spread, to carry **c** *(= hinauszögern) Prozess, Verhandlung, Ermittlungen* to draw out, to protract; *(Pol) Gesetzesänderung etc* to delay; *Krankheit* to protract

Ver|schlepp|te(r) [fɛɐ̯ˈʃlɛptə] MF *decl as adj* displaced person; **die ~n** the displaced *pl*

Ver|schlep|pung [fɛɐ̯ˈʃlɛpʊŋ] F **-, -en a** *(von Menschen)* abduction; *(von Kunstschätzen)* carrying off **b** *(= Verbreitung)* spreading, carrying **c** *(= Verzögerung)* protraction; *(von Gesetzesänderung)* delay; *(von Krankheit)* protraction

Ver|schlep|pungs|tak|tik F delaying tactics *pl*

ver|schleu|dern *ptp* **verschleudert** VT *(Comm)* to dump; *(= vergeuden) Vermögen, Geld, Energie, Ressourcen* to squander

ver|schließ|bar ADJ *Dosen, Gläser etc* closeable, sealable; *Tür, Schublade, Zimmer etc* lockable

ver|schlie|ßen *ptp* **verschlossen** [fɛɐ̯ˈʃlɔsn] *irreg* VT **a** *(= abschließen)* to lock (up); *(fig)* to close, to shut; *(= versperren)* to bar; *(mit Riegel)* to bolt; **jdm etw ~** *(fig)* to deny sb sth → *auch* **verschlossen**

b *(= wegschließen)* to lock up *or* away

c *(= zumachen)* to close; *(dauerhaft) Einmachglas, Karton, Brief* to seal; *(mit Pfropfen) Flasche* to cork; **die Augen/Ohren/sein Herz (vor etw** *dat***) ~** to shut one's eyes/ears/heart (to sth); **seine Gedanken/seinen Kummer in sich** *(dat)* **~** to keep one's thoughts/one's worries to oneself

VR *(Reize, Sprache, Möglichkeit)* to be closed (*+dat* to); *(Mensch: = reserviert sein)* to shut oneself off (*+dat* from); **sich vor jdm ~** to shut oneself off from sb; **sich einer Sache** *(dat)* *or* **gegen etw ~** to close one's mind to sth; **ich kann mich der Tatsache nicht ~, dass …** I can't close my eyes to the fact that …

ver|schlimm|bes|sern [fɛɐ̯ˈʃlɪmbɛsɐn] *ptp* **verschlimmbessert** VT *insep (hum)* to make worse, to disimprove

Ver|schlimm|bes|se|rung F *(hum)* worsening, disimprovement

ver|schlim|mern [fɛɐ'ʃlɪmɐn] *ptp* **verschlimmert** VT to make worse, to aggravate; *Schmerzen auch* to increase VR to get worse, to worsen

Ver|schlim|me|rung F -, -en worsening; *(von Schmerzen auch)* increase

ver|schlin|gen *ptp* **verschlungen** [fɛɐ'ʃlʊŋən] *irreg* VT **a** *(= verflechten)* to entwine, to intertwine; **er stand mit verschlungenen Armen da** he stood there with his arms folded; **ein verschlungener Pfad** a winding path **b** *(= fressen, gierig essen)* to devour; *(fig) (Welle, Dunkelheit)* to engulf; *(= verbrauchen) Geld, Strom etc* to eat up, to consume; *(inf) Buch, jds Worte* to devour; **jdn mit Blicken** *or* **den Augen ~** to devour sb with one's eyes VR to become entwined *or* intertwined; *(zu einem Knoten etc)* to become entangled; *(Därme)* to become twisted

Ver|schlin|gung [fɛɐ'ʃlɪŋʊŋ] F -, -en **a** *(von Fäden etc)* tangle; *(von Muster, Arabeske)* interlacing **b** *(von Darm)* twisting

ver|schliss *pret von* **verschleißen**

ver|schlis|sen [fɛɐ'ʃlɪsn] *ptp von* **verschleißen** ADJ worn (out); *Kleidung, Teppich, Material auch* threadbare; *(fig) Arbeiter, Politiker etc* burned-out *(inf)*

ver|schlos|sen [fɛɐ'ʃlɔsn] ADJ closed; *(mit Schlüssel) Tür, Fach etc* locked; *(mit Riegel)* bolted; *Dose* closed, sealed; *Briefumschlag* sealed; *(fig: = unzugänglich)* reserved; **gut ~ aufbewahren** keep tightly closed; **etw bleibt jdm ~** sth is (a) closed (book) to sb; **hinter ~en Türen** behind closed doors; **wir standen vor ~er Tür** we were left standing on the doorstep → *auch* **verschließen**

Ver|schlos|sen|heit F -, *no pl (von Mensch)* reserve, reticence

ver|schlu|cken *ptp* **verschluckt** VT to swallow; *(fig auch) Wörter, Silben, Buchstaben* to slur; *Geld* to consume; *Schall* to deaden → **Erdboden** VR to swallow the wrong way; *(fig)* to splutter

ver|schlu|dern *ptp* **verschludert** *(inf)* VT to go and lose *(inf)* VI *aux sein* to let oneself go

Ver|schluss M **a** *(= Schloss)* lock; *(luft-, wasserdicht, für Zoll)* seal; *(= Deckel, Klappe)* top, lid; *(= Pfropfen, Stöpsel)* stopper; *(an Kleidung)* fastener; *(an Schmuck)* catch; *(an Tasche, Buch, Schuh)* clasp; **etw unter ~ halten** to keep sth under lock and key **b** *(Phot)* shutter; *(an Waffe)* breechblock **c** *(Med, Phon)* occlusion

ver|schlüs|seln [fɛɐ'ʃlʏsln] *ptp* **verschlüsselt** VT to (put into) code, to encode; *E-Mail, Daten* to encrypt

Ver|schlüs|se|lung [fɛɐ'ʃlʏsəlʊŋ] F -, -en coding; *(von E-Mail, Daten)* encryption

Ver|schluss|kap|pe F (screw) cap

Ver|schluss|laut M *(Phon)* plosive

Ver|schlüss|lung [fɛɐ'ʃlʏslʊŋ] F -, -en coding

Ver|schluss|sa|che F (piece of) classified information; **~n** *pl* classified information *sing*

ver|schmach|ten *ptp* **verschmachtet** VI *aux sein* to languish *(vor +dat* for); **vor Durst/Hitze ~** *(inf)* to be dying of thirst/heat *(inf)*

ver|schmä|hen *ptp* **verschmäht** VT to spurn, to scorn; *Liebhaber* to spurn, to reject; **verschmähte Liebe** unrequited love; **einen Whisky verschmähe ich nie** I never say no to a whisky

ver|schmä|lern *ptp* **verschmälert** VT to make narrower VR to become narrower, to narrow

ver|schmau|sen *ptp* **verschmaust** VT *(inf)* to feast on

ver|schmel|zen *ptp* **verschmolzen** [fɛɐ'ʃmɔltsn] *irreg* VI *aux sein* to melt together; *(Metalle)* to fuse; *(Farben)* to blend; *(Betriebe etc)* to merge; *(fig)* to blend *(zu* into); **zu einer Einheit ~** to blend into one VT **a** *(= verbinden) Metalle* to fuse; *Farben* to blend; *Betriebe, Firmen* to merge **b** *Bruchflächen* to smooth, to round off **c** *(fig)* to unify *(zu* into)

Ver|schmel|zung [fɛɐ'ʃmɛltsʊŋ] F -, -en **a** *(= Verbindung)* fusion; *(von Reizen, Eindrücken, Farben)* blending **b** *(von Bruchflächen)* smoothing, rounding off **c** *(fig: von Völkern, Begriffen etc)* fusion **d** *(Comm)* merger

ver|schmer|zen *ptp* **verschmerzt** VT to get over

ver|schmie|ren *ptp* **verschmiert** VT **a** *(= verstreichen) Salbe, Schmiere, Creme, Fett* to spread *(in +dat* over) **b** *(= verputzen) Löcher* to fill in **c** *(= verwischen) Fenster, Gesicht* to smear; *Geschriebenes, Lippenstift, Schminke* to smudge VI to smudge

ver|schmiert [fɛɐ'ʃmiːɐt] ADJ *Hände, Gesicht* smeary; *Schminke* smudged

ver|schmitzt [fɛɐ'ʃmɪtst] ADJ mischievous ADV mischievously

ver|schmort [fɛɐ'ʃmoːɐt] ADJ *Braten* charred

ver|schmust [fɛɐ'ʃmuːst] ADJ *(inf)* cuddly; **~ sein** to like cuddling, to be cuddly

ver|schmut|zen *ptp* **verschmutzt** VT to dirty, to soil; *Luft, Wasser, Umwelt* to pollute; *Zündkerze* to foul; *Fahrbahn* to make muddy; *Straße, Bürgersteig* to dirty; *(Hund)* to foul VI *aux sein* to get dirty; *(Luft, Wasser, Umwelt)* to become polluted

ver|schmutzt [fɛɐ'ʃmʊtst] ADJ dirty, soiled; *Luft etc* polluted; **stark ~** very dirty, badly soiled; **„verschmutzte Fahrbahn"** "mud on road"

Ver|schmut|zung [fɛɐ'ʃmʊtsʊŋ] F -, -en **a** *no pl (= das Verschmutzen)* dirtying, soiling; *(von Luft, Wasser, Umwelt)* pollution; *(von Fahrbahn)* muddying **b** *(= das Verschmutztsein)* dirtiness *no pl*; *(von Luft etc)* pollution; **starke ~en auf der Straße** a great deal of mud on the road

ver|schnau|fen *ptp* **verschnauft** VIR *(inf)* to have a breather, to have a rest

Ver|schnauf|pau|se F breather

ver|schnei|den *ptp* **verschnitten** [fɛɐ'ʃnɪtn] VT *irreg* **a** *Wein, Rum, Essigsorten* to blend **b** *(= stutzen) Flügel, Hecke* to clip **c** *(= falsch schneiden) Kleid, Stoff* to cut wrongly; *Haar* to cut badly **d** *Tiere* to geld, to castrate

ver|schneit [fɛɐ'ʃnait] ADJ snow-covered; **tief ~** thick with snow

Ver|schnitt M **a** *(von Rum, Wein, Essig)* blend **b** *(= Abfall)* waste material, clippings *pl*

ver|schnör|keln [fɛɐ'ʃnœrkln] *ptp* **verschnörkelt** VT to adorn with flourishes

ver|schnör|kelt [fɛɐ'ʃnœrklt] ADJ ornate

Ver|schnör|ke|lung [fɛɐ'ʃnœrkəlʊŋ] F -, -en **a** *(= das Verschnörkeln)* embellishing (with flourishes) **b** *(= Schnörkel)* flourish

ver|schnupft [fɛɐ'ʃnʊpft] ADJ *(inf)* **a** *(= erkältet) Mensch* with a cold; *Nase* bunged up *(inf)* **b** *(usu pred: = beleidigt)* peeved *(inf)*

ver|schnü|ren *ptp* **verschnürt** VT to tie up; *Schuhe auch* to lace

Ver|schnü|rung [fɛɐ'ʃnyːrʊŋ] F -, -en **a** *(= das Verschnüren)* tying (up); *(von Schuhen)* lacing **b** *(= Schnur)* string; *(= Schnürband)* lace

ver|schol|len [fɛɐ'ʃɔlən] ADJ *Schiff, Flugzeug, Gemälde, Mensch etc* missing, lost without trace; *Literaturwerk* forgotten; **ein lange ~er Freund** a long-lost friend; **er ist ~** *(im Krieg)* he is missing, presumed dead

Ver|schol|le|ne(r) [fɛɐ'ʃɔlənə] MF *decl as adj* missing person; *(Jur)* person presumed (to be) dead

ver|scho|nen *ptp* **verschont** VT to spare *(jdn von etw* sb sth); *(von Steuern auch)* to exempt; **verschone mich mit deinen Reden!** spare me your speeches; **verschone mich damit!** spare me that!; **von etw verschont bleiben** to escape sth

ver|schö|nen *ptp* **verschönt**, **ver|schö|nern** [fɛɐ'ʃøːnɐn] *ptp* **verschönert** VT to improve (the appearance of); *Wohnung, Haus, Zimmer* to brighten (up)

Ver|schö|ne|rung [fɛɐ'ʃøːnərʊŋ] F -, -en, **Ver|schö|nung** [fɛɐ'ʃøːnʊŋ] F -, -en improvement; *(von Wohnung, Zimmer)* brightening up

Ver|scho|nung F sparing; *(von Steuern)* exemption

ver|schor|fen [fɛɐ'ʃɔrfn] *ptp* **verschorft** VI *aux sein* to (form a) scab; **die verschorfte Wunde** the encrusted wound

Ver|schor|fung F -, -en encrustation, scabbing

ver|schos|sen [fɛɐ'ʃɔsn] *ptp* → **verschießen** ADJ **a** *Farbe* faded **b** *(fig inf)* **in jdn ~ sein** to be crazy about sb *(inf)* **c** *(Ftbl)* **~er Elfmeter** missed penalty

ver|schram|men *ptp* **verschrammt** VT to scratch VI *aux sein* to become *or* get scratched

ver|schrän|ken [fɛɐ'ʃrɛŋkn] *ptp* **verschränkt** VT to cross over; *Arme* to fold; *Beine* to cross; *Hände* to clasp; **verschränkter Reim** embracing rhyme

Ver|schrän|kung F -, -en **a** *(= das Verschränktsein)* fold **b** *(= das Verschränken)* crossing over; *(von Armen)* folding; *(von Beinen)* crossing; *(von Händen)* clasping

ver|schrau|ben *ptp* **verschraubt** VT to screw together

ver|schre|cken *ptp* **verschreckt** VT to frighten *or* scare off *or* away

ver|schreckt [fɛɐ'ʃrɛkt] ADJ frightened, scared

ver|schrei|ben *ptp* **verschrieben** [fɛɐ'ʃriːbn] *irreg* VT **a** *(= verordnen)* to prescribe **b** *(old: = übereignen)* to make over, to transfer; **seine Seele dem Teufel ~** to sign away one's soul to the devil **c** *Papier* to use up; *(rare) Wort* to write incorrectly VR **a** *(= falsch schreiben)* to make a slip (of the pen) **b** **sich einer Sache** *(dat)* **~** to devote *or* dedicate oneself to sth; **sich dem Teufel ~** to sell oneself to the devil

Ver|schrei|bung F **a** *(= Verordnung)* prescription **b** *(old: = Übertragung)* making over, transference **c** *(= Schreibfehler)* mistake, error

ver|schrei|bungs|pflich|tig [-pflɪçtɪç] ADJ only available on prescription, ethical

ver|schrei|en [fɛɐ'ʃraiən] *ptp* **verschrien** [-'ʃriːən, -'ʃriːn] VT *irreg* **a** *(= herbeireden)* **verschrei's nicht!** don't speak too soon, don't put the kiss of death on it **b** *(= öffentlich schlechtmachen)* to denounce, to slam *(inf)*, trash *(inf)*

ver|schrien [fɛɐ'ʃriːən, fɛɐ'ʃriːn] ADJ notorious; **als etw ~** notorious for being sth

ver|schro|ben [fɛɐ'ʃroːbn] ADJ eccentric, odd

Ver|schro|ben|heit F -, -en **a** *no pl* eccentricity **b** **Verschrobenheiten** *pl (= Handlungen)* eccentricities *pl*

ver|schro|ten *ptp* **verschrotet** VT to grind coarsely

ver|schrot|ten [fɛɐ'ʃrɔtn] *ptp* **verschrottet** VT to scrap

Ver|schrot|tung F -, -en scrapping; **etw zur ~ geben** to send sth to be scrapped

ver|schrum|peln *ptp* **verschrumpelt** VI *aux sein* to shrivel

ver|schüch|tern [fɛɐ'ʃʏçtɐn] *ptp* **verschüchtert** VT to intimidate

ver|schul|den *ptp* **verschuldet** VT *(= schuldhaft verursachen)* to be to blame for, to be responsible for; *Unfall, Unglück* to cause VI *aux sein (= in Schulden geraten)* to get into debt; **immer mehr ~** to get deeper and deeper into debt; **verschuldet sein** to be in debt VR to get into debt

Ver|schul|den [fɛɐ'ʃʊldn] NT -s, *no pl* fault; **durch eigenes ~** through one's own fault; **ohne sein/mein ~** through no fault of his (own)/of my own *or* of mine

Ver|schul|dung [fɛɐ'ʃʊldʊŋ] F -, -en **a** *(= Schulden)* indebtedness **b** *(= schuldhafte Verursachung)* blame *(+gen* for); **bei eigener ~ eines Schadens** if one is (oneself) to blame for damage caused

ver|schus|seln *ptp* **verschusselt** VT *(inf) (= vermasseln)* to mess *or* muck *(Brit)* up *(inf)*; *(= vergessen)* to forget; *(= verlegen)* to mislay, to lose

ver|schus|selt [fɛɐ'ʃʊslt] ADJ = **schusselig**

ver|schütt [fɛɐ'ʃʏt] ADJ **~ gehen** *(inf) (= verschwinden)* to disappear; *(= abhandenkommen)* to get lost; *(= umkommen)* to buy it *(inf)*, to snuff it *(inf)*; *(sl: = ins Gefängnis kommen)* to get banged up *(inf)*

ver|schüt|ten *ptp* **verschüttet** VT **a** *Flüssigkeit* to spill **b** *(= zuschütten) Brunnen, Flussarm* to fill in **c** *(= begraben)* **verschüttet werden** *(Mensch)* to be buried (alive); *(fig)* to be submerged **d** *(= blockieren) Weg* to block

ver|schüt|tet [fɛɐ̯ˈʃʏtət] ADJ buried (alive); *(fig)* submerged

Ver|schüt|te|te(r) [fɛɐ̯ˈʃʏtətə] MF *decl as adj* person buried in the disaster/accident

ver|schütt+ge|hen *sep irreg aux sein*, **ver|schütt ge|hen** △ *irreg aux sein* VI *(inf)* to get lost

ver|schwä|gert [fɛɐ̯ˈʃvɛːgɐt] ADJ related (by marriage) *(mit* to)

Ver|schwä|ge|rung [fɛɐ̯ˈʃvɛːgərʊŋ] F -, -en relationship by marriage *(mit* to)

ver|schwei|gen *ptp* **verschwiegen** [fɛɐ̯ˈʃviːgn] VT *irreg Tatsachen, Wahrheit etc* to hide, to conceal, to withhold *(jdm etw* sth from sb); **ich habe nichts zu ~** I've nothing to hide → *auch* **verschwiegen**

Ver|schwei|gen NT concealment, hiding, withholding; **das ~ der Wahrheit** concealing *or* withholding the truth

ver|schwei|ßen *ptp* **verschweißt** VT to weld (together)

ver|schwe|len *ptp* **verschwelt** VTI *Holz* to burn; *(Tech) Kohle* to carbonize

ver|schwen|den [fɛɐ̯ˈʃvɛndn] *ptp* **verschwendet** VT to waste *(auf +acc, an +acc, für* on); *(= leichtsinnig vertun) Geld* to squander

Ver|schwen|der [fɛɐ̯ˈʃvɛndɐ] M -s, -, **Ver|schwen|de|rin** [-ərɪn] F -, -nen spendthrift, squanderer

ver|schwen|de|risch [fɛɐ̯ˈʃvɛndərɪʃ] ADJ wasteful; *Leben* extravagant; *(= üppig)* lavish, sumptuous; *Fülle* lavish ADV wastefully, extravagantly; *(= üppig)* lavishly, sumptuously; **mit etw ~ umgehen** to be lavish with sth

Ver|schwen|dung F -, -en wastefulness; **~ von Geld/Zeit** waste of money/time

Ver|schwen|dungs-: **Ver|schwen|dungs|sucht** F, *no pl* extravagance; **ver|schwen|dungs|süch|tig** ADJ (wildly) extravagant

ver|schwie|gen [fɛɐ̯ˈʃviːgn] ADJ *Mensch* discreet; *Ort* secluded → *auch* **verschweigen, Grab**

Ver|schwie|gen|heit F -, *no pl (von Mensch)* discretion; *(von Ort)* seclusion; **zur ~ verpflichtet** bound to secrecy → **Siegel**

ver|schwie|melt [fɛɐ̯ˈʃviːmlt] ADJ *(N Ger inf)* swollen

ver|schwim|men *ptp* **verschwommen** [fɛɐ̯ˈʃvɔmən] VI *irreg aux sein* to become blurred *or* indistinct; **es verschwamm ihr alles vor den Augen** everything went fuzzy *or* hazy; **ineinander ~** to melt into one another, to merge (into one another) → *auch* **verschwommen**

ver|schwin|den *ptp* **verschwunden** [fɛɐ̯ˈʃvʊndn] VI *irreg aux sein* to disappear, to vanish; **verschwinde!** clear off *(Brit) or* out! *(inf)*, away! *(liter)*; **etw ~ lassen** *(Zauberer)* to make sth disappear *or* vanish; *(= verstecken)* to dispose of sth; *(= stehlen)* to steal *or* filch *(inf)* sth; **von der Landkarte ~** to disappear off the map; **etw in etw** *(dat)* **~ lassen** to slip sth into sth; **neben jdm/etw ~** to pale into insignificance beside sb/sth, to be eclipsed by sb/sth; *(in Bezug auf Größe)* to look minute beside sb/sth; **(mal) ~ müssen** *(euph inf)* to have to spend a penny *(Brit inf)*, to have to go to the bathroom → *auch* **verschwunden**

Ver|schwin|den [fɛɐ̯ˈʃvɪndn] NT -s, *no pl* disappearance

ver|schwin|dend ADJ *Anzahl, Menge* insignificant; *Minderheit* tiny ADV **~ wenig** very, very few; **~ klein** *or* **gering** minute

ver|schwis|tern [fɛɐ̯ˈʃvɪstɐn] *ptp* **verschwistert** VR *(fig)* to form a close union; *(Städte)* to become twinned *(Brit) or* sister cities *(US)*; *(liter. Seelen)* to become closely united

ver|schwis|tert [fɛɐ̯ˈʃvɪstɐt] ADJ **(miteinander) ~ sein** to be brother and sister, to be siblings *(Sociol, Med etc)*; *(Brüder)* to be brothers; *(Schwestern)* to be sisters; *(fig)* to be close; *(Städte)* to be twinned *(Brit) or* sisters *(US)*, to be twin towns *(Brit) or* sister cities *(US)*; **~e Seelen** *(liter)* kindred spirits

ver|schwit|zen *ptp* **verschwitzt** VT **a** *Kleidung* to make sweaty **b** *(fig inf)* to forget

ver|schwitzt [fɛɐ̯ˈʃvɪtst] ADJ *Kleidungsstück* sweat-stained; *(= feucht)* sweaty; *Mensch* sweaty

ver|schwol|len [fɛɐ̯ˈʃvɔlən] ADJ swollen

ver|schwom|men [fɛɐ̯ˈʃvɔmən] ADJ *Foto, Umrisse* blurred, fuzzy; *Berge* hazy, indistinct; *Erinnerung, Vorstellung* vague, hazy; *Argumente, Begriffe* woolly *(esp Brit)*, vague ADV *wahrnehmen, sehen* blurred, hazy; *sich erinnern, sich vorstellen* vaguely, hazily; *sprechen, reden* vaguely; **ich sehe alles ~** everything looks hazy to me → *auch* **verschwimmen**

Ver|schwom|men|heit F -, *no pl (von Foto, Umrissen)* fuzziness; *(von Anblick)* haziness, indistinctness; *(von Erinnerung, Vorstellung)* vagueness; *(von Argumenten, Begriffen)* woolliness *(esp Brit)*, vagueness

ver|schwo|ren [fɛɐ̯ˈʃvoːrən] ADJ **a** *Gesellschaft* sworn **b einer Sache** *(dat)* **~ sein** to have given oneself over to sth

ver|schwö|ren *ptp* **verschworen** [fɛɐ̯ˈʃvoːrən] VR *irreg* **a** *(= ein Komplott schmieden)* to conspire, to plot *(mit* with, *gegen* against); **sich zu etw ~** to plot sth, to conspire to do sth; **sie haben sich zu einem Attentat gegen den Diktator verschworen** they are conspiring *or* plotting to assassinate the dictator; **alles hat sich gegen mich verschworen** *(fig)* there's a conspiracy against me **b** *(= sich verschreiben)* **sich einer Sache** *(dat)* **~** to give oneself over to sth

Ver|schwo|re|ne(r) [fɛɐ̯ˈʃvoːrənə] MF *decl as adj* conspirator, plotter; *(fig)* ally, accomplice

Ver|schwö|rer [fɛɐ̯ˈʃvøːrɐ] M -s, -, **Ver|schwö|re|rin** [-ərɪn] F -, -nen conspirator

Ver|schwö|rung [fɛɐ̯ˈʃvøːrʊŋ] F -, -en conspiracy, plot

ver|schwun|den [fɛɐ̯ˈʃvʊndn] ADJ missing, who/that has/had disappeared; **das ~e Mädchen/Auto** the missing girl/car → *auch* **verschwinden**

Vers|dich|tung F *(Liter)* poetry

ver|sechs|fa|chen [fɛɐ̯ˈzɛksfaxn] *ptp* **versechsfacht** VT to multiply by six VR to increase sixfold

ver|se|hen *ptp* **versehen** *irreg* VT **a** *(= ausüben) Amt, Stelle etc* to occupy, to hold; *Dienst* to perform, to discharge *(form)*; *(= sich kümmern um)* to look after, to take care of; *Küche* to see to, to do; *(Bus, Schiff etc) Route* to provide the/a service on; *Dienst* to provide; **den Dienst eines Kollegen ~** to take a colleague's place, to perform a colleague's duties **b** *(= ausstatten)* **jdn mit etw ~** to provide *or* supply sb with sth; *(= ausrüsten auch)* to equip sb with sth; **etw mit etw ~** to put sth on/in sth; *(= montieren)* to fit sth with sth; **ein Buch mit einem Umschlag ~** to provide a book with a dust jacket; **mit etw ~ sein** to have sth; **mit Blättern/Wurzeln/Haaren** *etc* **~ sein** to have leaves/roots/hairs *etc*; **mit Etiketten/Wegweisern ~ sein** to be labelled *(Brit) or* labeled *(US)*/signposted; **mit allem reichlich** *or* **wohl ~ sein** to be well provided for; **die Bücherei ist gut (mit Fachliteratur) ~** the library is well stocked (with specialist literature) **c** *(Eccl)* **jdn (mit den Sterbesakramenten) ~** to administer the last rites *or* sacraments to sb **d** *(= geben)* to give; **jdn mit einer Vollmacht ~** to invest sb with full powers; **etw mit seiner Unterschrift ~** to affix one's signature to sth *(form)*, to sign sth; **etw mit einem Stempel ~** to stamp sth; **etw mit einem Siegel ~** to affix a seal to sth; **etw mit Akzept ~** *(Fin)* to accept sth
VR **a** *(= sich irren)* to be mistaken, to make a mistake **b sich mit etw ~** *(= sich versorgen)* to provide oneself with sth; *(= sich ausstatten)* to equip oneself with sth **c ehe man sichs versieht** before you could turn (a)round, before you could say Jack Robinson *(esp Brit inf)*, lickety-split *(US inf)*

Ver|se|hen [fɛɐ̯ˈzeːən] ✪ 45.4 NT -s, - *(= Irrtum)* mistake, error; *(= Unachtsamkeit)* inadvertence, oversight; **aus ~** by mistake, inadvertently

ver|se|hent|lich [fɛɐ̯ˈzeːəntlɪç] ADJ *attr* inadvertent; *(= irrtümlich)* erroneous ADV inadvertently, by mistake

Ver|seh|gang M *pl* **-gänge** *(Eccl)* visit to a/the dying man/woman

ver|seh|ren *ptp* **versehrt** VT *(geh) (= verletzen)* to injure, to hurt; *(= zum Invaliden machen)* to disable; *(= beschädigen)* to damage

Ver|sehr|ten-: **Ver|sehr|ten|ren|te** F disability *or* invalidity pension; **Ver|sehr|ten|sport** M sport for the disabled

Ver|sehr|te(r) [fɛɐ̯ˈzeːɐtə] MF *decl as adj* disabled person/man/woman *etc*; **Platz für ~** seat for the disabled, seat for disabled persons

ver|sei|fen *ptp* **verseift** VT *(Chem)* to saponify

ver|selbst|stän|di|gen *ptp* **verselbstständigt**, **ver|selb|stän|di|gen** *ptp* **verselbständigt** VR to become independent; *(beruflich auch)* to become self-employed

Ver|selbst|stän|di|gung F -, -en, **Ver|selb|stän|di|gung** F -, -en **die ~ der Kinder fördern** to help the children to become independent

ver|sen|den *ptp* **versendet** *(rare) or* **versandt** [fɛɐ̯ˈzant] VT *irreg or reg* to send; *(Comm auch)* to forward; *(= verfrachten auch)* to ship; *Kataloge, Heiratsanzeige etc* to send (out)

Ver|sen|dung F sending; *(Comm auch)* forwarding; *(= das Verfrachten auch)* shipment; *(von Heiratsanzeige)* sending out; **die ~ der Kataloge** sending (out) the catalogues *(Brit) or* catalogs *(US)*

ver|sen|gen *ptp* **versengt** VT **a** *(Sonne, mit Bügeleisen)* to scorch; *(Feuer)* to singe **b** *(inf: = verprügeln)* to thrash, to wallop *(inf)*

ver|senk|bar ADJ that can be lowered; *Scheinwerfer* retractable; *Nähmaschine, Tischplatte* foldaway *attr*; **nicht ~** *(Schiff)* unsinkable

ver|sen|ken *ptp* **versenkt** VT **a** *Schatz, Behälter, Bohrinsel* to sink; *Leiche, Sarg* to lower; *Schiff* to sink, to send to the bottom; *das eigene Schiff* to scuttle; **die Hände in die Taschen ~** to thrust one's hands into one's pockets; **den Kopf in ein Buch ~** to bury one's head in a book, to immerse oneself in a book **b** *Schraube* to countersink; *Tischplatte* to fold away; *(Theat)* to lower; **eine Nähmaschine, die man ~ kann** a foldaway sewing machine VR **sich in etw** *(acc)* **~** to become immersed in sth; *in Gedanken auch, in Anblick* to lose oneself in sth

Ver|sen|kung F **a** *(= das Versenken)* sinking; *(von Leiche, Sarg)* lowering; *(von eigenem Schiff)* scuttling **b** *(Theat)* trap(door) **c** *(= das Sichversenken)* immersion; **jdn aus seiner ~ reißen** to tear sb from (his absorption *or* immersion in) his book/work *etc*; **seine ~ in diesen Anblick** his rapt contemplation of this sight; **innere/mystische ~** inner/mystic contemplation **d** *(inf)* **in der ~ verschwinden** to vanish; *(berühmter Mensch, Buch etc)* to vanish *or* disappear from the scene, to sink into oblivion; **aus der ~ auftauchen** to reappear; *(Mensch auch)* to re-emerge (on the scene)

Vers|epos NT *(Liter)* epic poem

Vers|schmied(in) M(F) *(pej)* rhymester *(pej)*, versifier *(pej)*

ver|ses|sen [fɛɐ̯ˈzɛsn] ADJ *(fig)* **auf etw** *(acc)* **~ sein** to be very keen on sth, to be mad *or* crazy about sth *(inf)*

Ver|ses|sen|heit F -, -en keenness *(auf +acc* on)

ver|set|zen *ptp* **versetzt** VT **a** *(= an andere Stelle setzen) Gegenstände, Möbel, Schüler* to move, to shift; *Pflanzen* to transplant, to move; *(= nicht geradlinig anordnen)* to stagger **b** *(beruflich)* to transfer, to move; **jdn in einen höheren Rang ~** to promote sb, to move sb up → **Ruhestand** **c** *(Typ, Mus)* to transpose **d** *(Sch: in höhere Klasse)* to move *or* put up **e** *(inf) (= verkaufen)* to flog *(Brit inf)*, to sell; *(=*

verpfänden) to pawn, to hock *(inf)*
f *(inf: = nicht erscheinen)* **jdn ~** to stand sb up *(inf)*
g *(= in bestimmten Zustand bringen)* **etw in Bewegung ~** to set sth in motion; **etw in Schwingung ~** to set sth swinging; **jdn in Wut ~** to send sb into a rage; **jdn in fröhliche Stimmung ~** to put sb in a cheerful mood; **jdn in Sorge/Unruhe ~** to worry/disturb sb; **jdn in Angst (und Schrecken) ~** to frighten sb, to make sb afraid; **jdn in die Lage ~, etw zu tun** to put sb in a position to do sth
h *(= geben) Stoß, Schlag, Tritt etc* to give; **jdm eins ~** *(inf)* to belt sb *(inf)*, to land sb one *(Brit inf)*; **jdm einen Stich ~** *(fig)* to cut sb to the quick *(Brit)*, to wound sb (deeply)
i *(= mischen)* to mix
j *(= antworten)* to retort
VR **a** *(= sich an andere Stelle setzen)* to move (to another place), to change places
b **sich in jdn/in jds Lage/Gefühle ~** to put oneself in sb's place *or* position
c **sich in eine frühere Zeit/seine Jugend** *etc* **~** to take oneself back to an earlier period/one's youth *etc*, to imagine oneself back in an earlier period/one's youth *etc*

Ver|set|zung [fɛɐ̯ˈzɛtsʊŋ] **F -, -en** **a** *(beruflich)* transfer; **seine ~ in einen höheren Rang** his promotion (to a higher rank) **b** *(Sch)* moving up, being put up; **bei nicht erfolgter ~** when the pupil isn't moved *or* put up **c** *(Mus, Typ)* transposition **d** *(= nicht geradlinige Anordnung)* staggering **e** *(= Vermischung)* mixing

Ver|set|zungs-: **Ver|set|zungs|kon|fe|renz F** end of year staff meeting *(to decide whether pupils should be put up to next class)*; **Ver|set|zungs|zei|chen NT** *(Mus)* accidental; **Ver|set|zungs|zeug|nis NT** end-of-year report

ver|seu|chen [fɛɐ̯ˈzɔyçn] *ptp* **verseucht VT** *(mit Bakterien)* to infect; *(mit Gas, Giftstoffen)* to contaminate; *(fig)* to contaminate, to poison; *(Comput)* to infect with a virus

ver|seucht ADJ *(mit Bakterien, Viren)* infected; *(mit Gas, Giftstoffen)* contaminated, poisoned; **radioaktiv ~** contaminated by radiation *or* radioactivity

Ver|seu|chung F -, -en *(mit Bakterien, Viren)* infection; *(mit Gas, Giftstoffen)* contamination *no pl*; *(fig)* poisoning *no pl*

Ver|seu|chungs|grad M contamination level

Vers-: **Vers|form F** *(Poet)* verse form; **Vers|fuß M** *(Poet)* (metrical) foot

Ver|si|che|rer [fɛɐ̯ˈzɪçərɐ] **M -s, -**, **Ver|si|che|rin** [-ərɪn] **F -, -nen** insurer; *(bei Lebensversicherung)* assurer *(Brit)*, insurer; *(bei Schiffen)* underwriter

ver|si|chern ✪ 42.1 *ptp* **versichert VT** **a** *(= bestätigen)* to assure; *(= beteuern)* to affirm, to protest; **jdm ~, dass ...** to assure sb that ...; **jdm etw ~** to assure sb of sth; *seine Unschuld* to affirm *or* protest sth to sb
b *(geh)* **jdn einer Sache** *(gen)* **~** to assure sb of sth; **seien Sie versichert, dass ...** (you can *or* may) rest assured that ...
c *(Insur, gegen Betrag)* to insure; *Leben* to assure *(Brit)*, to insure; **gegen etw versichert sein** to be insured against sth
VR **a** *(= Versicherung abschließen)* to insure oneself *(mit* for); *(Lebensversicherung)* to take out a life assurance *(Brit) or* insurance policy; **sich gegen Unfall ~** to take out accident insurance
b *(= sich vergewissern)* to make sure *or* certain
c **sich jds/einer Sache ~** *(geh)* to secure sb/sth

Ver|si|cher|ten|kar|te F health insurance card

Ver|si|cher|te(r) [fɛɐ̯ˈzɪçɐtə] **MF** *decl as adj* insured (party); *(bei Lebensversicherung)* assured *(Brit) or* insured (party)

Ver|si|che|rung F **a** *(= Bestätigung)* assurance; *(= Beteuerung)* affirmation, protestation **b** *(= Feuerversicherung etc)* insurance; *(= Lebensversicherung)* assurance *(Brit)*, insurance **c** *(= Gesellschaft)* insurance company; *(für Lebensversicherung)* assurance *(Brit) or* insurance company

Ver|si|che|rungs-: **Ver|si|che|rungs|agent(in) M(F)** *(Aus)* insurance agent; **Ver|si|che|rungs|an|spruch M** insurance claim; **Ver|si|che|rungs|an|stalt F** insurance company; **Ver|si|che|rungs|aus|weis M** insurance certificate; **Ver|si|che|rungs|bei|trag M** **a** *(bei staatlicher Versicherung etc)* insurance contribution **b** *(bei Haftpflichtversicherung etc)* insurance premium; **Ver|si|che|rungs|be|trug M** insurance fraud; **Ver|si|che|rungs|dau|er F** period of insurance; **Ver|si|che|rungs|fall M** *(= Verlust)* event of loss; *(= Schaden)* event of damage; **ver|si|che|rungs|fremd ADJ ~e Leistungen** payments unrelated to insurance; **Ver|si|che|rungs|ge|sell|schaft F** insurance company; *(für Lebensversicherung)* assurance *(Brit) or* insurance company; **Ver|si|che|rungs|kar|te F** insurance card; **die grüne ~** *(Mot)* the green card *(Brit), insurance document for driving abroad*; **Ver|si|che|rungs|kauf|frau F**, **Ver|si|che|rungs|kauf|mann M** insurance broker; **Ver|si|che|rungs|leis|tung F** insurance benefit; **Ver|si|che|rungs|ma|the|ma|tik F** actuarial theory; **Ver|si|che|rungs|neh|mer(in) M(F)** *(form)* policy holder, insurant *(form)*; **Ver|si|che|rungs|num|mer F** ≈ National Insurance number, ≈ Social Security number *(US)*; *(von Versicherungspolice)* policy number; **Ver|si|che|rungs|pflicht F** compulsory insurance; **jeder Autofahrer unterliegt der ~** insurance is compulsory for every driver; **ver|si|che|rungs|pflich|tig** [-pflɪçtɪç] **ADJ** subject to compulsory insurance; **Ver|si|che|rungs|po|li|ce F** insurance policy; *(von Lebensversicherung)* assurance *(Brit) or* insurance policy; **Ver|si|che|rungs|prä|mie F** insurance premium; **Ver|si|che|rungs|satz M** rate of insurance; **Ver|si|che|rungs|schein M** insurance policy; **Ver|si|che|rungs|schutz M** insurance cover; **Ver|si|che|rungs|sum|me F** sum insured; *(bei Lebensversicherung auch)* sum assured; **Ver|si|che|rungs|trä|ger(in) M(F)** = **Versicherer**; **Ver|si|che|rungs|ver|tre|ter(in) M(F)** insurance agent; **Ver|si|che|rungs|wert M** insurance value; **Ver|si|che|rungs|we|sen NT**, *no pl* insurance (business); **Ver|si|che|rungs|zwang M** compulsory insurance

ver|si|ckern *ptp* **versickert VI** *aux sein* to seep away; *(fig) (Gespräch, Unterstützung)* to dry up; *(Interesse, Teilnahme)* to peter out; *(Geld)* to trickle away

ver|sie|ben *ptp* **versiebt VT** *(inf)* *(= vergessen)* to forget; *(= verlieren)* to lose; *(= verpfuschen)* to make a mess of *(inf)*

ver|sie|ben|fa|chen [fɛɐ̯ˈziːbnfaxn] *ptp* **versiebenfacht VT** to multiply by seven **VR** to increase sevenfold

ver|sie|geln *ptp* **versiegelt VT** *Brief, Tür* to seal (up); *Parkett etc* to seal

Ver|sie|ge|lung [fɛɐ̯ˈziːgəlʊŋ] **F -, -en** *(Vorgang)* sealing; *(= Siegel)* seal

ver|sie|gen *ptp* **versiegt VI** *aux sein (Fluss, Quelle)* to dry up, to run dry; *(fig) (Gespräch, Unterstützung)* to dry up; *(Interesse)* to peter out; *(Tränen)* to dry up; *(gute Laune, Humor, Kräfte)* to fail; **nie ~de Hoffnung** never-failing *or* undying hope

ver|siert [vɛrˈziːɐ̯t] **ADJ** experienced, practised *(Brit)*, practiced *(US)*; **in etw** *(dat)* **~ sein** to be experienced *or (in Bezug auf Wissen)* (well) versed in sth

Ver|siert|heit F -, *no pl* experience *(in +dat* in); *(in Bezug auf Wissen)* knowledge *(in +dat* of)

ver|sifft [fɛɐ̯ˈzɪft] **ADJ** *(sl)* grotty *(Brit inf)*, yucky *(inf)*

ver|sil|bern [fɛɐ̯ˈzɪlbɐn] *ptp* **versilbert VT** *(= silbern bemalen)* to paint silver; *(= mit Silber überziehen)* to silver(-plate); *(fig inf: = verkaufen)* to flog *(Brit inf)*, to sell; *(fig liter: Mond)* to silver

Ver|sil|be|rung F -, -en *(Vorgang)* silvering, (silver-)plating; *(= Silberschicht)* silver plate

ver|sim|peln [fɛɐ̯ˈzɪmpln] *ptp* **versimpelt** *(inf)* **VT** *(= vereinfachen)* to make easier *or* simpler **VI** *aux sein (= einfältig werden)* **sie ist völlig versimpelt** her mind has completely gone to seed

ver|sin|ken *ptp* **versunken** [fɛɐ̯ˈzʊŋkn] **VI** *irreg aux sein (= untergehen)* to sink; *(Schiff auch)* to founder; **ich hätte im Boden** *or* **in der Erde/vor Scham ~ mögen** I wished the ground would (open and) swallow me up; **im Laster ~** to sink into a life of vice; **in etw** *(acc)* **~** *(fig, in Trauer, Melancholie, Chaos)* to sink into sth; *in Anblick* to lose oneself in sth; *in Gedanken, Musik* to become immersed in sth, to lose oneself in sth; **alles versinkt um ihn (herum)** *(fig)* he becomes totally oblivious to everything (around him) → *auch* **versunken**

ver|sinn|bild|li|chen [fɛɐ̯ˈzɪnbɪltlɪçn] *ptp* **versinnbildlicht VT** to symbolize, to represent

Ver|sinn|bild|li|chung F -, -en symbolization, representation

Ver|si|on [vɛrˈzioːn] **F -, -en** version

ver|sippt [fɛɐ̯ˈzɪpt] **ADJ** *(pej)* interrelated

ver|sit|zen *ptp* **versessen** [fɛɐ̯ˈsɛsn] **VT** *irreg (inf) Kleidung* to crease, to crush; **ich habe heute Morgen meine ganze Zeit beim Arzt versessen** I sat about (waiting) the whole morning at the doctor's

ver|skla|ven [fɛɐ̯ˈsklaːvn, -aːfn] *ptp* **versklavt VT** *(lit, fig)* to enslave

Ver|skla|vung F -, -en enslavement

Vers|kunst F versification

Vers|leh|re F study of verse

ver|slu|men [fɛɐ̯ˈslamən] **VI** *Stadtzentrum, Stadtteil* to turn into *or* to become a slum

Ver|slu|mung [fɛɐ̯ˈslamʊŋ] **F die ~ ganzer Stadtteile** the deterioration of whole parts of a/the city into slums

Vers|maß NT metre *(Brit)*, meter *(US)*

ver|sno|ben [fɛɐ̯ˈsnɔbn] *ptp* **versnobt VI** *aux sein (pej)* to become snobbish *or* a snob; **versnobt** snobbish, snobby *(inf)*

ver|sof|fen [fɛɐ̯ˈzɔfn] **ADJ** *(inf)* boozy *(inf)*; **ein ~es Genie** a drunken genius → *auch* **versaufen**

ver|soh|len *ptp* **versohlt VT** *(inf)* to belt *(inf)*; *(zur Strafe auch)* to leather

ver|söh|nen [fɛɐ̯ˈzøːnən] *ptp* **versöhnt VT** to reconcile; *(= besänftigen) jdn, Götter* to placate, to appease; *(fig) Unterschiede, jdn* to reconcile; **~de Worte** conciliatory words; *(besänftigend)* placatory words; **das versöhnt einen dann wieder** it almost makes up for it **VR** to be(come) reconciled; *(Streitende)* to make it up; **sich mit Gott ~** to make one's peace with God; **sich mit etw ~** to reconcile oneself to sth

ver|söhn|lich [fɛɐ̯ˈzøːnlɪç] **ADJ** *Mensch* conciliatory; *Laune, Ton, Geste auch* placatory; *Schluss (von Film, Roman)* upbeat; *(= nicht nachtragend)* forgiving; **die Götter ~ stimmen** to placate *or* appease the gods

Ver|söh|nung F -, -en reconciliation; *(= Beschwichtigung)* appeasement; **zur ~ opferte er den Göttern ...** to appease *or* placate the gods he sacrificed ...

Ver|söh|nungs-: **Ver|söh|nungs|fest NT** *(Rel)* Day of Atonement, Yom Kippur *no def art*; **Ver|söh|nungs|po|li|tik F** policy of reconciliation; **Ver|söh|nungs|tag M** *(Rel)* = **Versöhnungsfest**

ver|son|nen [fɛɐ̯ˈzɔnən] **ADJ** *(= in Gedanken verloren) Gesichtsausdruck* pensive, thoughtful; *Mensch auch* lost in thought; *(= träumerisch) Blick* dreamy **ADV** *blicken* pensively; *(= träumerisch)* dreamily

ver|sor|gen *ptp* **versorgt VT** **a** *Kinder, Tiere, Pflanzen, Haushalt, finanzielle Angelegenheiten* to look after, to take care of; *(= bedienen) Maschine, Lift, Heizung* to look after; **jdn medizinisch ~** to give sb medical attention *or* treatment
b *(= beliefern)* to supply; **jdn mit etw ~** *(= versehen)* to provide *or* supply sb with sth; **das Gehirn mit Sauerstoff ~** to supply oxygen to the brain
c *(= unterhalten) Familie* to provide for, to support; **versorgt sein** to be provided for, to be

taken care of
d *(dial: = wegräumen)* to put away
VR a sich mit etw ~ to provide oneself with sth
b sich selbst ~ to look after oneself, to take care of oneself

Ver|sor|ger [fɛɐ'zɔrgɐ] **M -s, -, Ver|sor|ge|rin** [-ərɪn] **F -, -nen a** *(= Ernährer)* provider, bread-winner **b** *(= Belieferer)* supplier

Ver|sor|gung [fɛɐ'zɔrgʊŋ] **F -, -en a** *(= Pflege)* care; **die ~ des Haushalts** looking after the house; **medizinische ~** medical care; **vielen Dank für die gute ~ meiner Katze/Pflanzen** many thanks for taking such good care of my cat/plants
b *(= Belieferung)* supply; **die ~ mit Strom/Gas/Wasser** the supply of electricity/gas/water; **die ~ dieses Gebiets mit Bussen** the supply of buses to *or* the provision of buses for this district; **die ~ der Truppen (mit Munition)** supplying the troops (with ammunition); **Probleme mit der ~ haben** to have supply problems; **auf Grund der schlechten ~ der Truppen** because the troops were being poorly supplied
c *(= Unterhalt)* **die ~ im Alter/einer sechsköpfigen Familie** providing for one's old age/a family of six; **der Staat übernimmt die ~ von Witwen und Waisen** the state undertakes to provide for widows and orphans

Ver|sor|gungs-: **Ver|sor|gungs|an|spruch M** claim to maintenance *(Brit) or* alimony; **Ver|sor|gungs|an|stalt F ~ des Bundes und der Länder** *institution that provides additional pension benefits for public employees and their dependents*; **Ver|sor|gungs|aus|gleich M** *(bei Ehescheidung)* maintenance *(Brit)*, alimony; **ver|sor|gungs|be|rech|tigt ADJ** entitled to maintenance *(Brit) or* alimony; *(durch Staat)* entitled to (state) benefit; **Ver|sor|gungs|be|trieb M** public utility; **Ver|sor|gungs|emp|fän|ger(in) M(F)** recipient of state benefit; **Ver|sor|gungs|eng|pass M** supply shortage *or* bottleneck; **Ver|sor|gungs|fahr|zeug NT** *(Mil)* supply vehicle; **Ver|sor|gungs|flug|zeug NT** supply plane; **Ver|sor|gungs|gü|ter PL** supplies *pl*; **Ver|sor|gungs|kri|se F** supply crisis; **Ver|sor|gungs|la|ge F** supply situation; **Ver|sor|gungs|lü|cke F** *(bei Vorräten etc)* supply gap; *(bei Rente)* ≈ pension gap; **Ver|sor|gungs|netz NT** *(= Wasserversorgung, Gasversorgung etc)* (supply) grid; *(von Waren)* supply network; **Ver|sor|gungs|schwie|rig|kei|ten PL** supply problems *pl*; **Ver|sor|gungs|staat M** all-providing state; **Ver|sor|gungs|trup|pen PL** supply troops *pl*; **Ver|sor|gungs|weg M** supply channel

ver|spach|teln *ptp* **verspachtelt VT a** *Loch, Ritze, Fuge* to fill in **b** *(fig inf: = aufessen)* to put *or* tuck away *(inf)*

ver|span|nen *ptp* **verspannt VT** to brace, to stay, to guy **VR** *(Muskeln)* to tense up

ver|spannt [fɛɐ'ʃpant] **ADJ** *Muskeln* tense, tensed up *pred*

Ver|span|nung F a *(Seile etc)* bracing, stays *pl* **b** *(von Muskeln)* tenseness *no pl*

ver|spä|ten [fɛɐ'ʃpɛːtn] *ptp* **verspätet VR a** *(= zu spät kommen)* to be late; **der Frühling hat sich verspätet** spring is late **b** *(= nicht rechtzeitig wegkommen)* to be late leaving; *(= aufgehalten werden)* to be delayed, to be held up

ver|spä|tet [fɛɐ'ʃpɛːtət] **ADJ** *Zug, Flugzeug* delayed, late *pred*; *Ankunft, Eintreten, Frühling, Entwicklung* late; *Glückwunsch* belated; *Bewerbung* late, belated **ADV** late; *sich bewerben, gratulieren* belatedly

Ver|spä|tung F -, -en *(von Verkehrsmitteln)* delay; *(von Mensch)* late arrival; *(von Glückwunsch etc)* belatedness; **(10 Minuten) ~ haben** to be (10 minutes) late; **der Flug hat ~** the flight is delayed; **eine zweistündige ~** a delay of two hours, a two-hour delay; **die ~ aufholen** to catch up lost time; **mit ~ abfahren/ankommen** to leave/arrive late; **ohne ~ ankommen** to arrive on time; **mit zwanzig Minuten ~** twenty minutes late *or (von Verkehrsmitteln auch)* behind schedule; **mit sechsmonatiger** *etc* **~** six months *etc* late; *(nach Ablauf der Frist auch)* six months *etc* too late

ver|spei|sen *ptp* **verspeist VT** *(geh)* to consume

ver|spe|ku|lie|ren *ptp* **verspekuliert VT** to lose through speculation **VR** to ruin oneself by speculation; *(fig)* to miscalculate, to be out in one's speculations

ver|sper|ren *ptp* **versperrt VT a** *Weg, Durchgang* to block; *Aussicht* to obstruct, to block **b** *(dial: = verschließen)* to lock *or* close up

ver|spie|geln *ptp* **verspiegelt VT** *Wand, Decke* to cover with mirrors; **verspiegelte Sonnenbrille** mirror(ed) *or* reflecting sunglasses *pl*

ver|spie|len *ptp* **verspielt VT** *(lit, fig) Geld, Chancen, Zukunft* to gamble away; *Vorteile* to bargain away; *Vertrauen, Glaubwürdigkeit* to lose; **den ganzen Abend ~** to spend the whole evening playing; **allen Kredit ~** *(fig)* to lose all credibility **VI** *(fig)* **jetzt hast du verspielt** it's all up with you now *(esp Brit inf)*, you've had it now *(inf)*; **er hatte bei ihr verspielt** he was finished *or* he had had it *(inf)* as far as she was concerned

ver|spielt [fɛɐ'ʃpiːlt] **ADJ** *Kind, Katze etc* playful; *Frisur* pretty; *Muster, Kleid* pretty, dainty; *Verzierung* dainty

ver|spin|nen *ptp* **versponnen** [fɛɐ'ʃpɔnən] *irreg* **VT** *(zu Faden)* to spin; *(= verbrauchen)* to use **VR die Larve verspinnt sich (zur Puppe)** the larva spins itself into a cocoon, the larva forms a cocoon; **sich in etw** *(dat)* **~** *(fig, in Ideen)* to become immersed in sth; *in Lügen* to become embroiled *or* enmeshed in sth

ver|spon|nen [fɛɐ'ʃpɔnən] **ADJ** airy-fairy *(Brit inf)*, ivory-towered *(US)*; *Ideen auch* wild *attr*; *Mensch* head-in-the-clouds *pred*

ver|spot|ten *ptp* **verspottet VT** to mock; *(höhnisch)* to jeer at, to deride

Ver|spot|tung [fɛɐ'ʃpɔtʊŋ] **F -, -en a** *no pl (= das Verspotten)* mocking *no indef art*; *(höhnisch)* jeering *no indef art*, derision *no indef art* **b** *(= spöttische Rede)* mockery *no indef art, no pl*; *(= höhnische Rede)* jeer, derision *no indef art, no pl*

ver|spre|chen *ptp* **versprochen** [fɛɐ'ʃprɔxn] *irreg* **VT a** *(= zusagen)* to promise *(jdm etw* sb sth*)*; **aber er hat es doch versprochen!** but he promised!; **jdm versprochen sein** *(obs)* to be betrothed *(old) or* promised to sb; **einander versprochen sein** *(obs)* to be betrothed *(old)* → **hoch 2 f, Blaue(s)**
b *(= erwarten lassen)* to promise; **das verspricht interessant zu werden** it promises to be interesting; **das Wetter verspricht schön zu werden** the weather looks promising, the weather promises to be good; **nichts Gutes ~** to be ominous, to bode ill *(liter)*
c *(= erwarten)* **sich** *(dat)* **viel/wenig von jdm/etw ~** to have high hopes/no great hopes of sb/sth; **was versprichst du dir davon?** what do you expect to achieve *or* gain (by that)?
VR *(= falsch sagen, aussprechen)* to pronounce a word/words wrong(ly); *(= etwas Nichtgemeintes sagen)* to make a slip (of the tongue), to make a mistake; **bei dem Wort verspreche ich mich noch immer** I still can't pronounce that word properly

Ver|spre|chen [fɛɐ'ʃprɛçn] **NT -s, -** promise

Ver|spre|cher M *(inf)* slip (of the tongue); **ein freudscher ~** a Freudian slip

Ver|spre|chung [fɛɐ'ʃprɛçʊŋ] **F -, -en** promise

ver|spren|gen *ptp* **versprengt VT a** *Flüchtlinge, Soldaten* to disperse, to scatter; **versprengte Soldaten** scattered soldiers **b** *Wasser* to sprinkle

ver|sprit|zen *ptp* **verspritzt VT a** *(= versprühen, verteilen)* to spray; *(= versprengen)* to sprinkle; *Farbe* to spray on; *(= zuspritzen) Fugen* to seal by injection moulding *(Brit) or* molding *(US)*; *(fig) Tinte* to use up → **Gift b** *(beim Planschen) Wasser* to splash, to sp(l)atter; *(= verkleckern) Farbe, Boden, Heft, Kleidung* to sp(l)atter **c** *(= verbrauchen) Wasser, Farbe etc* to use **VI** *aux sein (Wasser)* to spray; *(Fett)* to sp(l)atter

ver|spro|che|ner|ma|ßen [fɛɐ'ʃprɔxənɐ'maːsn] **ADV** as promised

ver|sprö|den [fɛɐ'ʃprøːdn] *ptp* **versprödet VI** *aux sein* to go brittle

ver|sprü|hen *ptp* **versprüht VT** to spray; *Funken auch* to send up *or* out; *Charme* to exude; *(= verbrauchen)* to use; **Witz/Geist ~** to scintillate

ver|spü|ren *ptp* **verspürt VT** to feel, to be conscious of; **er verspürte keine Lust, zur Arbeit zu gehen** he felt no desire to go to work

ver|staat|li|chen [fɛɐ'ʃtaːtlɪçn] *ptp* **verstaatlicht VT** to nationalize; *Schulen* to put under state control; *Kirchen* to secularize

Ver|staat|li|chung F -, -en nationalization; *(von Schulen)* putting under state control; *(von Kirchen)* secularization

ver|städ|tern [fɛɐ'ʃtɛːtɐn, fɛɐ'ʃtɛtɐn] *ptp* **verstädtert VT** to urbanize **VI** *aux sein* to become urbanized

Ver|städ|te|rung [fɛɐ'ʃtɛːtərʊŋ, fɛɐ'ʃtɛt-] **F** urbanization

Ver|stand [fɛɐ'ʃtant] **M -(e)s** [-dəs], *no pl (= Fähigkeit zu denken)* reason; *(= Intellekt)* mind, intellect; *(= Vernunft)* (common) sense; *(= Urteilskraft)* (powers *pl* of) judgement; **das müsste dir dein ~ sagen** your common sense should tell you that; **den ~ verlieren** to lose one's mind; **hast du denn den ~ verloren?, bist du denn noch bei ~?** have you taken leave of your senses? *(esp Brit)*, are you out of your mind?; **jdn um den ~ bringen** to drive sb out of his mind; **nicht recht** *or* **ganz bei ~ sein** not to be in one's right mind; **zu ~ kommen** to come to one's senses; **mit seinem ~ am Ende sein** to be at one's wits' end; **das geht über meinen ~** it's beyond me, it beats me *(inf)*; **da steht einem der ~ still** *(fig inf)*, **da bleibt einem der ~ stehen** *(fig inf)* the mind boggles *(inf)*; **etw ohne ~ tun** to do sth mindlessly; **etw ohne ~ essen/trinken** to eat/drink sth without paying attention; **etw mit ~ genießen/essen/trinken** to savour *(Brit) or* savor *(US)* sth, to relish sth → **klar**

Ver|stan|des-: **Ver|stan|des|ehe F** marriage of convenience; **Ver|stan|des|kraft F** mental *or* intellectual faculties *pl or* powers *pl*; **ver|stan|des|mä|ßig ADJ** rational **ADV** rationally; **~ leuchtet mir das ein** it makes (rational) sense to me; **Ver|stan|des|mensch M** rational person; **Ver|stan|des|schär|fe F** acuteness *or* sharpness of mind *or* intellect

ver|stän|dig [fɛɐ'ʃtɛndɪç] **ADJ** *(= vernünftig)* sensible; *(= einsichtig)* understanding

ver|stän|di|gen [fɛɐ'ʃtɛndɪgn] *ptp* **verständigt VT** to notify, to advise *(von* of, about*)* **VR** to communicate (with each other); *(= sich einigen)* to come to an understanding *or* agreement; **sich mit jdm ~** to communicate with sb

Ver|stän|di|gung F -, *(rare)* **-en a** *(= Benachrichtigung)* notification, advising **b** *(= das Sichverständigen)* communication *no indef art*; **die ~ am Telefon war schlecht** the (telephone) line was bad **c** *(= Einigung)* understanding, agreement

Ver|stän|di|gungs-: **Ver|stän|di|gungs|be|reit|schaft F** willingness *or* readiness to negotiate; **Ver|stän|di|gungs|mög|lich|keit F** *(= Gelegenheit)* opportunity *or* chance to communicate; *(= Verständigungsmittel)* means *sing* of communication; **Ver|stän|di|gungs|schwie|rig|kei|ten PL** communication difficulties *pl*; **Ver|stän|di|gungs|ver|such M** attempt at rapprochement

ver|ständ|lich [fɛɐ'ʃtɛntlɪç] **ADJ** *(= begreiflich) Reaktion etc* understandable; *(= intellektuell erfassbar)* comprehensible; *(= hörbar)* audible; *(= klar) Erklärung, Ausdruck* intelligible; **allgemein ~** readily comprehensible; **eine schwer ~e Unterscheidung** a distinction that is difficult to grasp *or* understand; **jdm etw ~ machen** to make sb understand sth; **sich ~ machen** to make oneself understood; *(= sich klar ausdrücken)* to make oneself clear, to express oneself intelligibly; *(gegen Lärm)* to make oneself heard; **nicht ~** incomprehensible; inaudible; unintelligible **ADV** *(= hörbar)* clearly, audibly; *(= begreifbar)* clearly, comprehensibly

ver|stạ̈nd|li|cher|wei|se [fɛɐ̯ˈʃtɛntlɪçɐˈvaizə] ADV understandably (enough)

Ver|stạ̈nd|lich|keit F -, *no pl* comprehensibility; *(= Hörbarkeit)* audibility; *(= Klarheit: von Erklärung, Ausdruck)* intelligibility

Ver|stạ̈nd|nis [fɛɐ̯ˈʃtɛntnɪs] NT **-ses,** *no pl* **a** *(= das Begreifen)* understanding *(für* of), comprehension *(für* of); *(= Einfühlungsvermögen, Einsicht)* understanding *(für* for); *(= Mitgefühl)* sympathy *(für* for); **solche Grausamkeiten gehen über menschliches/mein ~** such cruelty is beyond human/my comprehension; **für etw ~ aufbringen** to show understanding *or* sympathy for sth; **für etw kein ~ haben** to have no understanding/sympathy for sth; *(für Probleme, Lage auch)* to have no feeling for sth; **für so was habe ich kein ~** I have no time for that kind of thing; **dafür hast du mein vollstes ~** you have my fullest sympathy; **wir bitten um Ihr ~** we apologize for any inconvenience **b** *(= intellektuelles Erfassen) (für* of) understanding, comprehension; **mit ~ lesen/zuhören** to read/listen with understanding **c** *(= Kunstverständnis etc)* appreciation *(für* of) **d** *(= Verständigung)* understanding

Ver|stạ̈nd|nis-: ver|stạ̈nd|nis|in|nig ADJ *(liter)* knowing *attr*, meaningful; **ver|stạ̈nd|nis|los** **ADJ** uncomprehending; *Gesicht, Blick auch* blank; *(= ohne Mitgefühl)* unsympathetic *(für* towards); *(für Kunst)* unappreciative *(für* of) **ADV** uncomprehendingly; *(= ohne Mitgefühl)* unsympathetically; *(gegenüber Kunst)* unappreciatively; **Ver|stạ̈nd|nis|lo|sig|keit** F -, *no pl* lack of understanding; *(in Gesichtsausdruck, Blick)* blankness; *(= Mangel an Mitgefühl)* lack of sympathy; *(gegenüber Kunst)* lack of appreciation; **ver|stạ̈nd|nis|voll** **ADJ** understanding; *(= mitfühlend auch)* sympathetic *(für* towards); *Blick* knowing *no pred* **ADV** understandingly; *(= mitfühlend auch)* sympathetically; **sie nickte ~ mit dem Kopf** she nodded her head understandingly; **sie gibt sich gern ~** she likes to seem sympathetic

ver|stạ̈n|kern *ptp* **verstạ̈nkert** VT *(inf) Zimmer* to stink out *(Brit inf) or* up *(US inf)*; *Stadt* to pollute

ver|stạ̈r|ken *ptp* **verstạ̈rkt** **VT** *Eindruck, Truppen, Mannschaft, Präsenz* to reinforce; *Argumente, Mauer auch* to strengthen; *Spannung, Zweifel, Zusammenarbeit* to intensify, to increase; *(Chem)* to concentrate; *(Phot)* to intensify; *(Elec) Signal, Strom, Spannung* to boost, to amplify; *Stimme, Musik, Musikinstrument* to amplify **VR** *(fig)* to intensify; *(= sich vermehren)* to increase

Ver|stạ̈r|ker [fɛɐ̯ˈʃtɛrkɐ] M **-s, -** *(Rad, Elec)* amplifier; *(Telec)* repeater; *(von Signalen etc)* booster; *(Phot)* intensifier

Ver|stạ̈r|ker|röh|re F *(Elec)* amplifier valve

Ver|stạ̈r|kung F reinforcement; *(von Argumenten, Mauer auch)* strengthening; *(von Spannung, Zweifel)* intensification, increase; *(Chem)* concentration; *(Elec)* boosting, amplification; *(Mus)* amplification

ver|stau|ben *ptp* **verstaubt** VI *aux sein* to get dusty, to get covered in dust; *(Möbel, Bücher auch, fig)* to gather dust; **verstaubt** dusty, covered in dust; *(fig) Ideen, Ansichten* fuddy-duddy *(inf)*

ver|stau|chen *ptp* **verstaucht** VT to sprain; **sich** *(dat)* **die Hand/den Fuß** *etc* **~** to sprain one's hand/foot *etc*

Ver|stau|chung [fɛɐ̯ˈʃtauxʊŋ] F **-, -en** sprain; *(= das Verstauchen)* spraining

ver|stau|en *ptp* **verstaut** VT *(in +dat* in(to)) *Gepäck* to load, to pack; *(Naut)* to stow; *(hum) Menschen* to pile, to pack; **etw im Kofferraum ~** to load sth into the boot *(Brit) or* trunk *(US)*

Ver|stẹck [fɛɐ̯ˈʃtɛk] NT **-(e)s, -e** hiding place; *(von Verbrechern)* hide-out; **~ spielen** to play hide-and-seek *(Brit) or* hide-and-go-seek *(US)*

ver|stẹ|cken *ptp* **verstẹckt** **VT** to hide, to conceal *(vor* from) **VR** to hide, to conceal oneself; **sich vor jdm ~** to hide from sb; **sich vor** *or* **neben jdm ~ können/müssen** *(fig)* to be no match for sb; **sich (vor** *or* **neben jdm) nicht zu ~ brauchen** *(fig)* not to need to fear comparison (with sb); **sich hinter etw** *(dat)* **~** *(fig, hinter Pseudonym)* to write under sth; *hinter falschem Namen, Maske* to hide behind sth; *hinter Andeutungen* to be behind sth; **Verstecken spielen** to play hide-and--seek *(Brit) or* hide-and-go-seek *(US)*

Ver|stẹck|spiel NT *(lit, fig)* hide-and-seek *(Brit)*, hide-and-go-seek *(US)*

ver|stẹckt [fɛɐ̯ˈʃtɛkt] ADJ **a** *(lit: = verborgen)* hidden; *(= nicht leicht sichtbar) Eingang, Tür, Winkel* concealed; *(= abgelegen) Ort* secret, hidden **b** *(fig) Lächeln, Blick* furtive; *Bemerkung, Andeutung* veiled; *Bedeutung* hidden, concealed

ver|ste|hen ✪ 33.3, 53.1, 53.5 *ptp* **verstạnden** *irreg* [fɛɐ̯ˈʃtandn] **VTI** **a** *(= begreifen)* to understand; *(= einsehen)* to see, to understand; **jdn/etw falsch** *or* **nicht recht ~** to misunderstand sb/sth; **versteh mich recht** don't misunderstand me, don't get me wrong; **wenn ich recht verstehe ...** if I understand correctly ...; **jdm zu ~ geben, dass ...** to give sb to understand that ...; **ich gab ihm meinen Standpunkt zu ~** I intimated my point of view to him; **ein ~der Blick** a knowing look; **(ist das) verstanden?** (is that) understood? → **Bahnhof, Spaß** **b** *(= hören)* to hear, to understand → **Wort b** **VT** **a** *(= können, beherrschen)* to know; *Sprache* to understand, to know; **es ~, etw zu tun** to know how to do sth; **es mit Kindern ~** to be good with children, to have a way with children; **es mit seinen Kollegen ~** to know how to get on *(Brit) or* along with one's colleagues; **etwas/nichts von etw ~** to know something/nothing about sth; **etw machen, so gut man es versteht** to do sth to the best of one's ability, to do sth as well as one can → **Handwerk a** **b** *(= auslegen)* to understand, to interpret, to see; **etw unter etw** *(dat)* **~** to understand sth by sth; **wie soll ich das ~?** how am I supposed to take that?; **das ist bildlich** *or* **nicht wörtlich zu ~** that isn't to be taken literally **VR** **a** *(= kommunizieren können)* to understand each other **b** *(= miteinander auskommen)* to get on *(Brit) or* along (with each other *or* together); **sich mit jdm ~** to get on *(Brit) or* along with sb; **wir ~ uns (schon)** *(= sind einer Meinung)* we understand each other **c** *(= klar sein)* to go without saying; **versteht sich!** *(inf)* of course!, naturally!; **das versteht sich von selbst** that goes without saying **d** *(= auffassen)* **sich als etw ~** *(Mensch)* to think of *or* see oneself as sth **e** *(= können)* **sich auf etw** *(acc)* **~** to be (an) expert at sth, to be a dab hand at sth *(Brit inf)*, to be very good at sth **f** *(= einverstanden sein)* **sich zu etw ~** *(form)* to agree to sth **g** *(Comm)* to be; **die Preise ~ sich einschließlich Lieferung** prices are inclusive of delivery

ver|stei|fen *ptp* **versteift** **VT** to strengthen, to reinforce; *(Tech)* to strut; *(Comm)* to tighten; *(Sew)* to stiffen **VR** to stiffen up; *(fig) (Haltung, Gegensätze)* to harden; *(Maßnahmen)* to tighten (up); **sich auf etw** *(acc)* **~** *(fig)* to become set on sth; **er hat sich darauf versteift** he is set on it

Ver|stei|fung [fɛɐ̯ˈʃtaifʊŋ] F **-, -en** **a** *no pl* strengthening, reinforcement; *(Tech)* strutting; *(Sew)* stiffening **b** *(= Verstärkung)* stiffener **c** *(Med)* stiffening *no pl* **d** *(fig) (von Haltung)* hardening; *(von Maßnahmen)* tightening (up); *(von Gegensätzen)* increasing intractability

ver|stei|gen *ptp* **verstiegen** [fɛɐ̯ˈʃtiːgn] VR *irreg (lit)* to get into difficulties (while climbing); **er hat sich zu der Behauptung verstiegen, dass ...** he presumed to claim that ...; **er verstieg sich zu völlig übertriebenen Forderungen** he had the presumption to make quite excessive demands → *auch* **verstiegen**

ver|stei|gern *ptp* **versteigert** VT to auction (off); **etw ~ lassen** to put sth up for auction

Ver|stei|ge|rung F (sale by) auction; **zur ~ kommen** to be put up for auction

ver|stei|nern [fɛɐ̯ˈʃtainɐn] *ptp* **versteinert** **VI** *aux sein (Geol) (Pflanzen, Tiere)* to fossilize; *(Holz)* to petrify; *(fig: Miene)* to harden; **versteinerte Pflanzen/Tiere** fossilized plants/animals; **wie versteinert (da)stehen** to stand there petrified **VR** *(fig) (Miene, Gesicht)* to harden; *(Lächeln)* to become fixed *or* set

Ver|stei|ne|rung F **-, -en** *(Vorgang)* fossilization; *(von Holz)* petrifaction, petrification; *(= versteinertes Tier etc)* fossil; *(fig: von Miene)* hardening

ver|stẹll|bar ADJ adjustable; **in der Höhe ~** adjustable for height

Ver|stẹll|bar|keit [fɛɐ̯ˈʃtɛlbaːɐ̯kait] F -, *no pl* adjustability

ver|stẹl|len *ptp* **verstẹllt** **VT** **a** *(= anders einstellen, regulieren)* to adjust; *Signal, Zahlen* to alter, to change; *Möbel, Gegenstände* to move *or* shift (out of position *or* place); *(= in Unordnung bringen)* to put in the wrong place, to misplace; *(= falsch einstellen)* to adjust wrongly; *Radio* to alter the tuning of; *Uhr* to put *(Brit) or* set wrong **b** *Stimme* to disguise **c** *(= versperren)* to block, to obstruct; *(= vollstellen) Zimmer* to clutter up; **das verstellt den Blick auf das Wesentliche** that obscures one's view of the essential **VR** to move (out of position); *(fig)* to act *or* play a part; *(= Gefühle verbergen)* to hide one's (true) feelings; **er kann sich gut ~** he's good at playing *or* acting a part

Ver|stẹl|lung F **a** *(= Regulierung)* adjustment; *(von Signal, Zahlen)* alteration; *(von Möbeln, Gegenständen)* moving *or* shifting (out of position) *no indef art* **b** *(von Stimme)* disguise **c** *(Versperrung)* blockage, obstruction **d** *(= Vortäuschung)* pretending, feigning

ver|stẹp|pen [fɛɐ̯ˈʃtɛpn] *ptp* **verstẹppt** VTI to turn into desert

Ver|stẹp|pung F **-, -en** desertification

ver|stẹr|ben ✪ 51.4 *ptp* **verstọrben** VI [fɛɐ̯ˈʃtɔrbn] *irreg aux sein* to die, to pass away *or* on → *auch* **verstorben**

ver|steu|er|bar ADJ taxable

ver|steu|ern *ptp* **versteuert** VT to pay tax on; **versteuerte Waren** taxed goods; **das versteuerte Einkommen** taxed income; **das zu ~de Einkommen** taxable income

Ver|steu|e|rung F taxation

ver|stie|gen [fɛɐ̯ˈʃtiːgn] ADJ *(fig: = überspannt)* extravagant, fantastic; *Pläne, Ideen auch* highflown

Ver|stie|gen|heit F **-, -en** extravagance

ver|stịm|men *ptp* **verstịmmt** VT *(lit)* to put out of tune; *(fig)* to put out, to disgruntle

ver|stịmmt [fɛɐ̯ˈʃtɪmt] ADJ *Klavier etc* out of tune; *(fig) (= verdorben) Magen* upset; *(= verärgert)* put out, disgruntled

Ver|stịm|mung F disgruntlement; *(zwischen Parteien)* ill feeling, ill will

ver|stọckt [fɛɐ̯ˈʃtɔkt] ADJ *Kind, Wesen* obstinate, stubborn; *Sünder* unrepentant, unrepenting

Ver|stọckt|heit F -, *no pl (von Kind, Wesen)* obstinacy, stubbornness

ver|stoh|len [fɛɐ̯ˈʃtoːlən] **ADJ** furtive, surreptitious **ADV** furtively, surreptitiously

ver|stọp|fen *ptp* **verstọpft** VT to stop up; *Ohren auch* to plug; *Ausguss auch* to block (up); *Straße* to block, to jam; *Blutgefäß* to block

ver|stọpft [fɛɐ̯ˈʃtɔpft] ADJ blocked; *Straßen auch* jammed; *Nase* stuffed up, blocked (up); *Mensch* constipated

Ver|stọp|fung [fɛɐ̯ˈʃtɔpfʊŋ] F **-, -en** blockage; *(= Verkehrsstauung)* jam; *(Med)* constipation

verstorben [fɛɐ'ʃtɔrbn] ADJ deceased; **mein ~er Mann** my late husband; **eine 1995 ~e Frau** a woman who died in 1995 → *auch* **versterben**

Ver|stor|be|ne(r) [fɛɐ'ʃtɔrbənə] MF *decl as adj* deceased

ver|stö|ren *ptp* **verstört** VT to disturb

ver|stört [fɛɐ'ʃtøːɐt] ADJ disturbed; *(vor Angst)* distraught ADV in a disturbed way; *(vor Angst)* in a distraught way

Ver|stört|heit F -, *no pl* disturbed state; *(vor Angst)* distraction; *(= Verwirrung)* confusion

Ver|stoß M violation *(gegen* of); *(gegen Gesetz auch)* offence *(Brit)*, offense *(US)*

ver|sto|ßen *ptp* **verstoßen** *irreg* VT *jdn* to disown, to repudiate; **jdn aus einem Verein/einer Gruppe ~** to expel sb from a club/group, to throw sb out of a club/group VI **gegen etw ~** to offend against sth; *gegen Gesetz, Regel auch* to contravene sth

Ver|sto|ße|ne(r) [fɛɐ'ʃtoːsənə] MF *decl as adj* outcast

ver|strah|len *ptp* **verstrahlt** VT **a** *Licht, Wärme* to give off **b** *(radioaktiv)* to expose to radiation; *Gebäude, Gebiet* to make (highly) radioactive

ver|strahlt [fɛɐ'ʃtraːlt] ADJ contaminated (by radiation); **lebensgefährlich ~ sein** to have had a potentially lethal dose of radiation

Ver|strah|lung F radiation

ver|stre|ben *ptp* **verstrebt** VT to brace, to strut

Ver|stre|bung F supporting *no pl*; *(= Strebebalken)* support(ing beam)

ver|strei|chen *ptp* **verstrichen** [fɛɐ'ʃtrɪçn] *irreg* VT *Salbe, Farbe* to put on, to apply *(auf +dat* to); *Butter etc* to spread *(auf +dat* on); *Riss* to fill (in); *(= verbrauchen)* to use VI *aux sein (Zeit)* to pass (by), to elapse; *(Frist, Ultimatum)* to expire

ver|streu|en *ptp* **verstreut** VT to scatter; *(versehentlich)* to spill; **seine Kleider/Spielsachen im ganzen Zimmer ~** to scatter *or* strew one's clothes/toys over the (whole) room

ver|stri|cken *ptp* **verstrickt** VT **a** *Wolle* to use **b** *(fig)* to involve, to embroil, to mix up; **in eine Angelegenheit verstrickt sein** to be mixed up *or* involved *or* embroiled in an affair VR **a** *(Wolle)* to knit (up) **b** *(fig)* to become entangled, to get tangled up

Ver|stri|ckung [fɛɐ'ʃtrɪkʊŋ] F -, -en *(fig)* entanglement

ver|stro|men [fɛɐ'ʃtroːmən] *ptp* **verstromt** VT *Kohle* to convert into electricity

ver|strö|men *ptp* **verströmt** VT *(lit, fig)* to exude; *(liter) sein Blut* to shed

Ver|stro|mung -, -en F *(von Kohle)* conversion into electricity

ver|strub|beln [fɛɐ'ʃtrʊbln] *ptp* **verstrubbelt** VT **jdm die Haare ~** to muss up *or* tousle sb's hair; *(beim Fönen)* to ruffle sb's hair

ver|stüm|meln [fɛɐ'ʃtʏmln] *ptp* **verstümmelt** VT to mutilate, to maim; *(fig) Nachricht, Bericht* to garble, to distort; *Namen* to mutilate; **sich selbst ~** to mutilate oneself

Ver|stüm|me|lung F -, -en mutilation; *(von Nachricht, Bericht)* garbling *no pl*, distortion

ver|stum|men [fɛɐ'ʃtʊmən] *ptp* **verstummt** VI *aux sein (Mensch)* to go *or* fall silent, to stop talking; *(Geräusch, Gespräch, Musik, Beifall)* to cease, to stop; *(Wind, Glocken, Instrumente)* to become silent *or* still *(liter)*; *(= langsam verklingen)* to die away; *(fig) (Kritik, Stimmen der Opposition)* to become silent *or* still; *(= sich langsam legen)* to subside; *(Gerüchte)* to subside; **jdn/etw ~ lassen** *or* **zum Verstummen bringen** to silence sb/sth; **vor Entsetzen ~** to be struck dumb with terror, to be speechless with terror

Ver|such [fɛɐ'zuːx] M -(e)s, -e attempt *(zu tun* at doing, to do); *(wissenschaftlich)* experiment, test; *(= Test)* trial, test; *(= Essay)* essay; *(Rugby)* try; **einen ~ machen** to make an attempt; to do *or* carry out an experiment/a trial; **mit jdm/etw einen ~ machen** to give sb/sth a try *or* trial; *(Forscher)* to do a trial/an experiment with sb/sth; **das käme auf einen ~ an** we'll have to (have a) try; **sie unternahm den ~, ihn umzustimmen** she made an attempt at changing *or* to change his mind, she had a try at changing his mind *(esp Brit)*; **wir sollten es auf einen ~ ankommen lassen** we should give it a try; **das wollen wir doch auf einen ~ ankommen lassen!** we'll see about that!

ver|su|chen ✪ 27.3, 27.4, 45.4 *ptp* **versucht** VT **a** *auch vi (= probieren, kosten)* to try; *(= sich bemühen)* to attempt, to try; **es mit etw ~** to try sth; **versuchs doch!** try, have a try *(esp Brit)*; **es mit jdm ~** to give sb a try; **versuchter Mord/Diebstahl** attempted murder/theft **b** *(= in Versuchung führen)* to tempt; **sich versucht fühlen** to feel tempted; **versucht sein** to be tempted VR **sich an** *or* **in etw** *(dat)* **~** to try one's hand at sth

Ver|su|cher M tempter; **der ~** *(Rel)* the Tempter

Ver|su|che|rin F temptress

Ver|suchs-: **Ver|suchs|ab|tei|lung** F experimental department; **Ver|suchs|an|la|ge** F experimental plant; **Ver|suchs|an|ord|nung** F test arrangement; **Ver|suchs|an|stalt** F research institute; **Ver|suchs|bal|lon** M sounding balloon; **einen ~ steigen lassen, es mit einem ~ probieren** *(fig)* to fly a kite; **Ver|suchs|be|din|gun|gen** PL test conditions *pl*; **Ver|suchs|boh|rung** F experimental drilling; **Ver|suchs|ge|län|de** NT test *or* testing site; **Ver|suchs|ka|nin|chen** NT *(lit)* laboratory rabbit; *(fig)* guinea pig; **Ver|suchs|la|bor** NT experimental lab(oratory); **Ver|suchs|ob|jekt** NT test object; *(fig: Mensch)* guinea pig; **Ver|suchs|per|son** F test *or* experimental subject; **Ver|suchs|rei|he** F series *sing* of experiments; **Ver|suchs|sta|di|um** NT experimental stage; **Ver|suchs|stre|cke** F test track; **Ver|suchs|tier** NT laboratory animal; **ver|suchs|wei|se** ADV as a trial, on a trial basis; *einstellen, engagieren* on probation, on trial; **Ver|suchs|zweck** M **zu ~en** *pl* for experimental purposes *pl*

Ver|su|chung [fɛɐ'zuːxʊŋ] F -, -en temptation *(auch Rel)*; **jdn in ~ führen** to lead sb into temptation; **und führe uns nicht in ~** *(Bibl)* and lead us not into temptation *(Bibl)*; **in ~ geraten** *or* **kommen** to be tempted

ver|su|deln *ptp* **versudelt** VT to scribble on

ver|sump|fen *ptp* **versumpft** VI *aux sein* **a** *(Gebiet)* to become marshy *or* boggy **b** *(fig inf)* *(= verwahrlosen)* to go to pot *(inf)*; *(= lange zechen)* to get involved in a booze-up *(inf)*

Ver|sump|fung [fɛɐ'zʊmpfʊŋ] F -, -en *(lit)* increasing marshiness

ver|sün|di|gen *ptp* **versündigt** VR *(geh)* **sich an jdm/etw ~** to sin against sb/sth; **sich an seiner Gesundheit ~** to abuse one's health

Ver|sün|di|gung [fɛɐ'zʏndɪgʊŋ] F -, -en sin *(an +dat* against); **eine ~ an der Gesundheit** an abuse of one's health

ver|sun|ken [fɛɐ'zʊŋkn] ADJ sunken, submerged; *Kultur* submerged; *(fig)* engrossed, absorbed; **in Gedanken ~** lost *or* immersed in thought; **völlig in diesen Anblick ~** completely lost in *or* caught up in this sight → *auch* **versinken**

Ver|sun|ken|heit F -, *no pl (fig)* **jdn aus seiner ~ reißen** to tear sb from his (immersion in his) book/thoughts *etc*; **seine ~ in diesen Anblick** his rapt contemplation of this sight

ver|sü|ßen *ptp* **versüßt** VT *(fig)* to sweeten; **jdm etw ~** to sweeten sth for sb → **Pille**

ver|tä|feln *ptp* **vertäfelt** VT to panel

Ver|tä|fe|lung F panelling *no pl, no indef art*

ver|ta|gen *ptp* **vertagt** VTI to adjourn; *(= verschieben)* to postpone, to defer *(auf +acc* until, till); *(Parl)* to adjourn, to prorogue *(form)* VR to be adjourned, to adjourn

Ver|ta|gung F adjournment; *(= Verschiebung auf später)* postponement; *(Parl)* prorogation *(form)*

ver|tän|deln *ptp* **vertändelt** VT *(geh)* to fritter away, to squander

ver|täu|en [fɛɐ'tɔyən] *ptp* **vertäut** VT *(Naut)* to moor

ver|tausch|bar ADJ exchangeable *(gegen* for); *(miteinander)* interchangeable

ver|tau|schen *ptp* **vertauscht** VT **a** *(= austauschen)* to exchange *(gegen, mit* for); *(miteinander)* to interchange; *Auto, Plätze* to change *(gegen, mit* for); *(Elec) Pole* to transpose; **vertauschte Rollen** reversed roles **b** *(= verwechseln)* to mix up; **seinen Mantel mit einem anderen ~** to mistake another coat for one's own, to mix one's coat up with another

Ver|tau|schung [fɛɐ'taufʊŋ] F -, -en **a** *(= Austausch)* exchange; *(von Auto, von Plätzen)* changing *no pl*; *(Elec: von Polen)* transposition **b** *(= Verwechslung)* mix-up; *(= das Vertauschen)* mixing up

Ver|täu|ung F -, -en *(= das Vertäuen)* mooring; *(= die Taue)* moorings *pl*

ver|tei|di|gen [fɛɐ'taidɪgn] *ptp* **verteidigt** VT to defend VR to defend oneself *(auch Sport)*; **sich selbst ~** *(vor Gericht)* to conduct one's own defence *(Brit) or* defense *(US)* VI *(Sport)* to defend; *(= als Verteidiger spielen)* to be a defender, to play as a defender; *(= defensiv spielen)* to play a defensive game, to play defensively

Ver|tei|di|ger [fɛɐ'taidɪgɐ] M -s, -, **Ver|tei|di|ge|rin** [-ərɪn] F -, -nen defender *(auch Sport)*; *(= Fürsprecher auch)* advocate; *(= Anwalt)* defence *(Brit) or* defense *(US)* lawyer; **der ~ des Angeklagten** the counsel for the defence *(Brit) or* defense *(US)*, the defence *(Brit) or* defense *(US)* counsel

Ver|tei|di|gung F -, -en *(alle Bedeutungen)* defence *(Brit)*, defense *(US)*; **zur ~ von** *or gen* in defence *(Brit) or* defense *(US)* of; **zu ihrer/seiner eigenen ~** in her/one's own defence *(Brit) or* defense *(US)*; **er ist immer zur ~ seiner Meinung bereit** he is always ready to defend his opinion

Ver|tei|di|gungs- *in cpds* defence *(Brit)*, defense *(US)*; **Ver|tei|di|gungs|bei|trag** M defence contribution; **Ver|tei|di|gungs|bünd|nis** NT defence alliance; **ver|tei|di|gungs|fä|hig** ADJ able to defend itself/oneself; **Ver|tei|di|gungs|fä|hig|keit** F defensive capability; **Ver|tei|di|gungs|fall** M **wenn der ~ eintritt** if defence should be necessary; **Ver|tei|di|gungs|ge|mein|schaft** F defence community; **Ver|tei|di|gungs|ini|ti|a|ti|ve** F defence initiative; **Ver|tei|di|gungs|krieg** M defensive war; **Ver|tei|di|gungs|li|nie** F line of defence *(Brit) or* defense *(US)*; *(Sport)* defence *(Brit) or* defense *(US)* line; **Ver|tei|di|gungs|mi|nis|ter(in)** M(F) Minister of Defence *(Brit)*, Secretary of Defense *(US)*; **Ver|tei|di|gungs|mi|nis|te|ri|um** NT Ministry of Defence *(Brit)*, Department of Defense *(US)*; **Ver|tei|di|gungs|re|de** F *(Jur)* speech for the defence; *(fig)* apologia; **Ver|tei|di|gungs|schlacht** F defensive battle; **Ver|tei|di|gungs|schrift** F *(Jur)* (written) defence statement; *(fig)* apologia; **Ver|tei|di|gungs|spie|ler(in)** M(F) defender; **Ver|tei|di|gungs|stel|lung** F defensive position; **in ~ gehen** to adopt a defensive position; **Ver|tei|di|gungs|sys|tem** NT defence system, defences *pl*; **das ~ der Nato** the Nato defence system; **ver|tei|di|gungs|un|fä|hig** ADJ defenceless *(Brit)*, defenseless *(US)*; **Ver|tei|di|gungs|waf|fe** F defensive weapon; **Ver|tei|di|gungs|wil|le** M spirit of resistance; **Ver|tei|di|gungs|zu|stand** M defence alert; **im ~** in a defence alert; **im ~ sein** on the defence alert; **Ver|tei|di|gungs|zweck** M **für ~e, zu ~en** for defence purposes, for purposes of defence

ver|tei|len *ptp* **verteilt** VT **a** *(= austeilen) (an +acc* to) *(unter +acc* among) to distribute; *Flugblätter* to hand out, to distribute; *Süßigkeiten etc* to share out; *Preise auch* to give out; *Essen* to dish out; *(Theat) Rollen* to allot, to allocate **b** *(= anordnen, aufteilen)* to distribute; *Investitio-*

nen, soziale Lasten to spread (*über +acc* over); *(Mil)* to deploy; *(= verstreuen)* to spread out; *(= streichen) Aufstrich, Farbe etc* to spread; *(= streuen) Sand, Zucker, Puder* to sprinkle; **Blumen im Zimmer/auf verschiedene Vasen ~** to arrange flowers around the room/in different vases; **verteilte Datenbank** *(Comput)* distributed database **VR** *(Zuschauer, Polizisten etc)* to spread (themselves) out; *(Bevölkerung)* to spread (itself) out; *(Farbe, Wasser)* to spread (itself) out; *(Med: Bakterien, Metastasen)* to spread; *(Reichtum etc)* to be spread *or* distributed; *(zeitlich)* to be spread (*über +acc* over); **auf dem ganzen Platz verteilt** spread out over the square; **übers ganze Land verteilt** spread throughout the country

Ver|tei|ler [fɛɐ'tailɐ] M **-s, - a** *(Tech)* distributor **b** *(= Verteilerschlüssel)* distribution list; **„Verteiler:"** *(= Auflistung weiterer Empfänger)* cc:, carbon copy for

Ver|tei|ler [fɛɐ'tailɐ] M **-s, -**, **Ver|tei|le|rin** [-ərɪn] F **-, -nen** *(Comm)* distributor

Ver|tei|ler-: **Ver|tei|ler|de|ckel** M distributor cap; **Ver|tei|ler|do|se** F *(Elec)* junction box; **Ver|tei|ler|kas|ten** M *(Elec)* distribution box; **Ver|tei|ler|kopf** M *(Aut)* distributor head; **Ver|tei|ler|lis|te** F distribution list; *(für E-Mails, Briefe)* mailing list; **Ver|tei|ler|netz** NT *(Elec)* distribution system; *(Comm)* distribution network; **Ver|tei|ler|schlüs|sel** M distribution list

Ver|tei|lung F distribution; *(= Zuteilung)* allocation; *(Mil)* deployment; *(Theat)* casting

Ver|tei|lungs|kampf M struggle over distribution; **einen ~ um etw führen** to battle for a share of sth

ver|te|le|fo|nie|ren *ptp* **vertelefoniert** VT *(inf) Geld, Zeit* to spend on the phone

ver|tel|len [fɛɐ'tɛlən] *ptp* **vertellt** VT *(N Ger inf)* to tell; *Unsinn* to talk

ver|teu|ern [fɛɐ'tɔyɐn] *ptp* **verteuert** **VT** to make more expensive, to increase *or* raise the price of **VR** to become more expensive, to increase in price, to go up in price

Ver|teu|e|rung F rise *or* increase in price

ver|teu|feln [fɛɐ'tɔyfln] *ptp* **verteufelt** VT to condemn

ver|teu|felt [fɛɐ'tɔyflt] *(inf)* **ADJ** *Lage, Angelegenheit* devilish *(dated inf)*, tricky, awkward; **~es Glück haben** to be damned *or* darned *or* deuced *(dated)* lucky *(inf)* **ADV** *(mit adj)* damned *(inf)*, darned *(inf)*, deuced *(dated inf)*, devilish *(dated inf)*; *(mit vb)* a lot

Ver|teu|fe|lung F **-, -en** condemnation

ver|tie|fen [fɛɐ'ti:fn] *ptp* **vertieft** **VT** *Graben, Loch etc* to deepen; *(fig) Eindruck auch* to heighten; *Kenntnis, Wissen auch* to extend; *Zusammenarbeit* to intensify; *Kontakte* to strengthen; *(Sch) Unterrichtsstoff* to consolidate, to reinforce; *(Mus)* to flatten **VR** *(lit, fig)* to deepen; *(fig: Lehrstoff)* to be consolidated *or* reinforced; **sich in etw** *(acc)* **~** *(fig)* to become engrossed *or* absorbed in sth; **in etw** *(acc)* **vertieft sein** *(fig)* to be engrossed *or* absorbed in sth → **Gedanke**

Ver|tie|fung F **-, -en a** *(= das Vertiefen)* deepening; *(von Eindruck)* heightening, deepening; *(von Kenntnissen, Wissen)* extension, deepening; *(von Unterrichtsstoff)* consolidation, reinforcement; *(Mus)* flattening **b** *(in Oberfläche)* depression **c** *(= Vertieftsein)* engrossment, absorption

ver|ti|kal [vɛrti'ka:l] **ADJ** vertical **ADV** vertically

Ver|ti|ka|le [vɛrti'ka:lə] F **-, -n** vertical line; **in der ~n** vertically, in a vertical plane

Ver|ti|ko ['vɛrtiko] NT **-s, -s** *small two-door chest with a drawer and display shelf at the top*, ≈ hutch *(US)*

Ver|ti|ku|tie|rer [vɛrtiku'ti:rɐ] M **-s, -** aerator

ver|til|gen *ptp* **vertilgt** VT **a** *Unkraut etc* to destroy, to eradicate, to kill off; *Ungeziefer* to exterminate, to destroy **b** *(inf: = aufessen)* to demolish *(inf)*, to polish off *(inf)*

Ver|til|gung F *(von Unkraut)* destruction, eradication; *(von Ungeziefer)* extermination

Ver|til|gungs|mit|tel NT weedkiller; *(= Insektenvertilgungsmittel)* pesticide

ver|tip|pen *ptp* **vertippt** *(inf)* **VR a** *(beim Schreiben)* to make a typo *(inf) or* a typing error **b** *(beim Lotto, Toto etc)* to slip up *(inf)* **VT** to mistype, to type wrongly

ver|to|nen *ptp* **vertont** VT to set to music; *Theaterstück auch* to make a musical version of; *Film etc* to add a soundtrack to

ver|tö|nen *ptp* **vertönt** VI *aux sein* to fade *or* die away

Ver|to|nung [fɛɐ'to:nʊŋ] F **-, -en** *(= das Vertonen)* setting (to music); *(von Film)* adding a soundtrack (*+gen* to); *(= vertonte Fassung)* musical version

ver|tor|fen [fɛɐ'tɔrfn] *ptp* **vertorft** VI *aux sein* to turn into peat

Ver|tor|fung F **-, -en** conversion into peat

ver|trackt [fɛɐ'trakt] ADJ *(inf)* awkward, tricky; *(= verwickelt)* complicated, complex; **sich in einer ~en Situation befinden** to be in a tricky position

Ver|trackt|heit F **-**, *(rare)* **-en** *(inf)* awkwardness, trickiness; *(= Verwickeltheit)* complexity

Ver|trag [fɛɐ'tra:k] M **-(e)s, =e** [-'trɛ:gə] contract; *(= Abkommen)* agreement; *(Pol: = Friedensvertrag)* treaty; **mündlicher ~** verbal *or* oral agreement; **laut ~** under the terms of the contract; **jdn unter ~ nehmen** to contract sb; **(bei jdm) unter ~ stehen** to be under contract (to sb)

ver|tra|gen *ptp* **vertragen** *irreg* **VT a** to take; *(= aushalten)* to stand, to take; *(viel)* to tolerate, to endure, to stand for; **Eier vertrage ich nicht** *or* **kann ich nicht ~** I can't take eggs, eggs don't agree with me; **ein Automotor, der viel verträgt** an engine that can stand (up to) a lot *or* can take a lot; **Kontaktlinsen/synthetische Stoffe vertrage ich nicht** *or* **kann ich nicht ~** I can't wear contact lenses/synthetics; **Patienten, die kein Penizillin ~** patients who are allergic to penicillin; **so etwas kann ich nicht ~** I can't stand that kind of thing; **er verträgt keinen Spaß** he can't take a joke; **viel ~ können** *(inf: Alkohol)* to be able to hold one's drink *(Brit) or* liquor *(US)*; **er verträgt nichts** *(inf: Alkohol)* he can't take his drink *(Brit) or* liquor *(US)*; **jd/etw könnte etw ~** *(inf)* sb/sth could do with sth **b** *(dial) Kleider* to wear out; **~ sein** to be (well) worn

c *(Sw)* to deliver

VR sich (mit jdm) ~ to get on *or* along (with sb); **sich wieder ~** to be friends again; **sich mit etw ~** *(Nahrungsmittel, Farbe)* to go with sth; *(Aussage, Verhalten)* to be consistent with sth; **diese Farben ~ sich nicht** these colours *(Brit) or* colors *(US)* don't go together; **diese Aussagen ~ sich nicht** these statements are inconsistent *or* not consistent

Ver|trä|ger(in) M(F) *(Sw)* delivery man/woman; *(= Zeitungsverträger)* paper boy/girl/man/woman

ver|trag|lich [fɛɐ'tra:klɪç] **ADJ** contractual **ADV** by contract; *festgelegt* in the/a contract; **ein ~ zugesichertes Recht** a contractual right

ver|träg|lich [fɛɐ'trɛ:klɪç] ADJ *(= friedlich, umgänglich)* good-natured; *Speise* digestible; *(= bekömmlich)* wholesome; *(Med)* well tolerated *(für* by); **gut ~** easily digestible; *(Med)* well tolerated; **ökologisch/sozial ~** ecologically/socially acceptable

Ver|träg|lich|keit F **-**, *no pl (= Friedlichkeit, Umgänglichkeit)* good nature; *(von Speise)* digestibility; *(= Bekömmlichkeit)* wholesomeness; **die ~ dieses Medikaments** the fact that this medicine is well tolerated; **ökologische/soziale ~** ecological/social acceptability

Ver|trags-: **Ver|trags|ab|schluss** M conclusion of a/the contract; **Ver|trags|ar|bei|ter(in)** M(F) *(im ehemaligen Ostblock)* contract worker; **Ver|trags|be|din|gung** F condition of a/the contract; **~en** *pl (auch)* terms *pl* of a/the contract; **Ver|trags|bruch** M → **Vertrag** breach of contract; breaking of an/the agreement; breaking of a/the treaty; **ver|trags|brü|chig** ADJ → **Vertrag** who is in breach of contract; who has broken an/the agreement; who has broken a/the treaty; **~ werden** to be in breach of contract; to break an/the agreement; to break a/the treaty; **Ver|trags|dau|er** F term of a/the contract; **Ver|trags|ent|wurf** M → **Vertrag** draft contract/agreement/treaty; **Ver|trags|gast|stät|te** F tied house; **Ver|trags|ge|gen|stand** M → **Vertrag** object of the contract/agreement/treaty; **ver|trags|ge|mäß** → **Vertrag** **ADJ** (as) stipulated in the contract/agreement/treaty **ADV** as stipulated in the contract/agreement/treaty; **Ver|trags|ha|fen** M treaty port; **Ver|trags|händ|ler(in)** M(F) concessionary, appointed retailer; **Ver|trags|klau|sel** F contract clause; **Ver|trags|part|ner(in)** M(F) → **Vertrag** party to a/the contract/agreement/treaty; **ver|trags|schlie|ßend** ADJ contracting; **Ver|trags|spie|ler(in)** M(F) player under contract; **Ver|trags|stra|fe** F penalty for breach of contract; **Ver|trags|ur|kun|de** F deed, indenture; **Ver|trags|ver|län|ge|rung** F extension *or* renewal of a/the contract; **Ver|trags|ver|let|zung** F → **Vertrag** breach of contract; infringement of the agreement/treaty; **Ver|trags|werk** NT contract; *(Pol)* treaty; **Ver|trags|werk|stät|te** F authorized repair shop; **ver|trags|wid|rig** → **Vertrag** **ADJ** contrary to (the terms of) the contract/agreement/treaty **ADV** in breach of contract/the agreement/the treaty

ver|trau|en *ptp* **vertraut** VI **jdm/einer Sache ~** to trust sb/sth, to have trust in sb/sth; **auf jdn/etw ~** to trust in sb/sth; **auf sein Glück ~** to trust to luck; **sich** *(dat)* **selbst ~** to have confidence in oneself → *auch* **vertraut**

Ver|trau|en [fɛɐ'trauən] NT **-s**, *no pl* trust, confidence *(zu, in +acc, auf +acc* in); *(Pol)* confidence; **voll ~** full of confidence; **im ~ (gesagt)** strictly in confidence; **ich habe dir das im ~ gesagt** that's strictly in confidence, that's strictly between you and me; **im ~ auf etw** *(acc)* trusting in sth; **im ~ darauf, dass ...** confident that ..., in the confidence that ...; **~ erweckend = vertrauenerweckend**; **~ zu jdm fassen** to gain confidence in sb; **jdn ins ~ ziehen** to take sb into one's confidence; **jdm das ~ aussprechen/entziehen** *(Parl)* to pass a vote of confidence/no confidence in sb

ver|trau|en|er|we|ckend ADJ **ein ~er Mensch/Arzt** *etc* a person/doctor *etc* who inspires confidence; **einen ~en Eindruck machen, ~ aussehen** to inspire confidence

Ver|trau|ens-: **Ver|trau|ens|an|trag** M *(Pol)* motion of no confidence, no-confidence motion; **Ver|trau|ens|arzt** M, **Ver|trau|ens|ärz|tin** F *doctor who examines patients signed off sick for a lengthy period by their private doctor*; **Ver|trau|ens|be|weis** M vote of confidence; **ver|trau|ens|bil|dend** ADJ confidence-building; **Ver|trau|ens|bil|dung** F confidence building; **Ver|trau|ens|bruch** M breach of confidence *or* trust; **Ver|trau|ens|fra|ge** F question *or* matter of trust; **die ~ stellen** *(Parl)* to ask for a vote of confidence; **Ver|trau|ens|frau** F → **Vertrauensmann**; **Ver|trau|ens|leh|rer(in)** M(F) liaison teacher *(between pupils and staff)*; **Ver|trau|ens|mann** M *pl* **-leute** *or* **-männer** intermediary agent; *(in Gewerkschaft)* (union) negotiator *or* representative; **Ver|trau|ens|per|son** F someone to confide in, confidant(e); **Ver|trau|ens|pos|ten** M position of trust; **Ver|trau|ens|sa|che** F *(= vertrauliche Angelegenheit)* confidential matter; *(= Frage des Vertrauens)* question *or* matter of trust; **Ver|trau|ens|schwund** M loss of confidence; **ver|trau|ens|se|lig** ADJ trusting; *(= leichtgläubig auch)* credulous; **Ver|trau|ens|se|lig|keit** F trustfulness; *(= Leichtgläubigkeit auch)* credulity; **Ver|-**

trau|ens|stel|lung F position of trust; **Ver|trau|ens|ver|hält|nis** NT mutual trust *no indef art*; **persönliches ~** relationship of personal trust; **Ver|trau|ens|ver|lust** M loss of confidence; **ver|trau|ens|voll** ADJ trusting ADV trustingly, confidently; **wende dich ~ an mich** you know you can always turn to me (for help); **Ver|trau|ens|vor|schuss** M trust; **Ver|trau|ens|vo|tum** NT *(Parl)* vote of confidence; **ver|trau|ens|wür|dig** ADJ trustworthy; **Ver|trau|ens|wür|dig|keit** F trustworthiness

ver|trau|ern *ptp* **vertrauert** VT to spend (in) moping, to mope away

ver|trau|lich [fɛɐˈtraulɪç] ADJ **a** *(= geheim) Angelegenheit, Ton, Gespräch, Schriftstück, Daten* confidential **b** *(= freundschaftlich)* friendly, matey *(Brit inf)*, pally *(Brit inf)*, buddy-buddy *(esp US inf)*; *(= plumpvertraulich)* familiar; **~ werden** to take liberties ADV **a** confidentially, in confidence **b** in a friendly/familiar way

Ver|trau|lich|keit F **-, -en** confidentiality; *(= vertrauliche Mitteilung)* confidence; *(= Aufdringlichkeit)* familiarity; **mit aller ~** in strict(est) confidence; **plumpe/dreiste ~** familiarity

ver|träu|men *ptp* **verträumt** VT to dream away

ver|träumt [fɛɐˈtrɔymt] ADJ dreamy; *(= idyllisch) Städtchen etc auch* sleepy

ver|traut [fɛɐˈtraut] ✪ 46.2 ADJ intimate; *Freund auch* close; *(= bekannt) Gesicht, Umgebung* familiar, well-known; **ein ~er Freund** a close friend, an intimate friend; **sich mit etw ~ machen** to familiarize *or* acquaint oneself with sth; **sich mit dem Gedanken ~ machen, dass …** to get used to the idea that …; **mit etw ~ sein** to be familiar *or* well acquainted with sth; **mit jdm ~ werden** to become friendly with sb; **mit jdm sehr ~ werden** to get on intimate terms with sb, to become close friends with sb → *auch* **vertrauen**

Ver|trau|te(r) [fɛɐˈtrautə] MF *decl as adj* close *or* intimate friend; *(Mann auch)* confidant; *(Frau auch)* confidante

Ver|traut|heit F **-,** *(rare)* **-en** intimacy; *(von Freund)* closeness; *(von Gesicht, Umgebung)* familiarity

ver|trei|ben *ptp* **vertrieben** [fɛɐˈtriːbn] VT *irreg Tiere, Wolken, Einbrecher, Geister* to drive away; *(aus Haus etc)* to drive *or* turn out *(aus* of); *(aus Land, Gebiet)* to drive out *(aus* of), to expel *(aus* from); *(aus Amt, von Stellung)* to oust; *Feind* to drive off, to repulse; *(fig) Sorgen, Schmerzen* to drive away, to banish; *(Comm) Waren, Produkte* to sell; **ich wollte Sie nicht ~, bleiben Sie doch noch ein wenig** I didn't mean to chase *or* drive you away – do stay a bit longer; **ich wollte Sie nicht von Ihrem Stuhl/Platz ~** I didn't mean to take your chair/seat; **jdn vom Thron/aus seinem Amt ~** to oust sb from the throne/his office; **jdm die Zeit mit etw ~** to help sb pass the time with sth; **sich** *(dat)* **die Zeit mit etw ~** to pass (away) *or* while away the time with sth → *auch* **vertrieben**

Ver|trei|bung [fɛɐˈtraibʊŋ] F **-, -en** *(aus* from) expulsion; *(aus Amt etc)* ousting; *(von Feind)* repelling

ver|tret|bar ADJ justifiable; *Theorie, Argument* defensible, tenable; **nicht ~** unjustifiable; indefensible, untenable

ver|tre|ten *ptp* **vertreten** VT *irreg* **a** *(= jds Stelle, Dienst übernehmen) Kollegen, Arzt etc* to replace, to stand in for, to deputize for; *Schauspieler* to replace, to stand in for; *(fig: = Funktion einer Sache übernehmen)* to replace, to take the place of **b** *jds Interessen, Firma, Land, Wahlkreis* to represent; *Sache* to look after, to attend to; *(Rechtsanwalt) Klienten* to represent, to appear for; *Fall* to plead **c** *(Comm: = Waren vertreiben für) (Firma)* to be the agent for; *(Angestellter)* to represent **d** *(= verfechten, angehören) Standpunkt, Doktrin, Theorie* to support; *Meinung* to hold, to be of; *Ansicht* to take, to hold; *Kunstrichtung* to represent; *(= rechtfertigen)* to justify *(vor* to) **e ~ sein** to be represented **f jdm den Weg ~** to bar sb's way **g sich** *(dat)* **den Fuß ~** to twist *or* strain one's ankle; **sich** *(dat)* **die Beine** *or* **Füße ~** *(inf)* to stretch one's legs

Ver|tre|ter [fɛɐˈtreːtɐ] M **-s, -, Ver|tre|te|rin** [-ərɪn] F **-, -nen a** *(von Land, Firma etc)* representative; *(Comm) (Firma)* agent; *(Angestellter)* (sales) representative, rep *(inf)*; **~ für Damenkleider** (sales) representative *or* rep *(inf)* for ladies' wear; **~ einer Versicherung** insurance representative *or* rep *(inf)*; **ein übler ~** *(fig inf)* a nasty piece of work *(inf)* **b** *(= Ersatz)* replacement; *(im Amt)* deputy; *(von Arzt)* locum **c** *(= Verfechter) (von Doktrin)* supporter, advocate; *(von Meinung)* holder; *(von Kunstrichtung)* representative

Ver|tre|tung [fɛɐˈtreːtʊŋ] F **-, -en a** *(von Menschen)* replacement; **die ~ (für jdn) übernehmen** to replace sb, to stand in (for sb); **die ~ (für jdn) haben** to stand in (for sb), to deputize (for sb); **X spielt in ~** X is appearing in his/her place; **in ~** *(in Briefen)* on behalf of **b** *(von Interessen, Firma, Land, Wahlkreis)* representation; **~ vor Gericht** court representation; **X übernimmt die ~ des Klienten/Falles** X is appearing for the client/pleading the case; **die ~ meiner Interessen** representing my interests **c** *(= das Verfechten)* supporting; *(von Meinung)* holding; *(von Kunstrichtung)* representation **d** *(Comm: = Firma)* agency **e** *(= Botschaft)* **diplomatische ~** diplomatic mission, embassy **f** = **Vertreter a, b**

Ver|tre|tungs-: **Ver|tre|tungs|stun|de** F *(Sch) class where one teacher stands in for another*, stand-in class; **~n geben** to stand in for another teacher; **ver|tre|tungs|wei|se** ADV as a replacement; *(bei Amtsperson)* as a deputy; **er übernimmt heute ~ meine Deutschstunde** he's taking my German lesson for me today

Ver|trieb [fɛɐˈtriːp] M **-(e)s, -e** [-bə] **a** *no pl* sales *pl*; **der ~ eines Produktes** the sale of a product; **den ~ für eine Firma haben** to have the (selling) agency for a firm **b** *(= Abteilung einer Firma)* sales department

ver|trie|ben [fɛɐˈtriːbn] ADJ *(aus Land)* expelled; **die nach dem Krieg ~en Deutschen** the Germans who were driven out of their homeland after the war → *auch* **vertreiben**

Ver|trie|be|nen-: **Ver|trie|be|nen|tref|fen** NT reunion of exiles; **Ver|trie|be|nen|ver|band** M association of exiles

Ver|trie|be|ne(r) [fɛɐˈtriːbənə] MF *decl as adj* exile

Ver|triebs-: **Ver|triebs|ab|tei|lung** F sales department; **Ver|triebs|be|auf|trag|te(r)** MF sales representative; **Ver|triebs|er|lös** M sales revenue; **Ver|triebs|ge|sell|schaft** F marketing company; **Ver|triebs|ka|nal** M distribution channel; **Ver|triebs|kos|ten** PL marketing costs *pl*; **Ver|triebs|lei|ter(in)** M(F) sales manager; **Ver|triebs|sys|tem** NT distribution system; **Ver|triebs|weg** M channel of distribution

ver|trim|men *ptp* **vertrimmt** VT *(inf)* to belt *(inf)*, to wallop *(inf)*

ver|trin|ken *ptp* **vertrunken** [fɛɐˈtrʊŋkn] VT *irreg* to drink away, to spend on drink *(Brit)*

ver|trock|nen *ptp* **vertrocknet** VI *aux sein* to dry out; *(Esswaren)* to go dry; *(Pflanzen)* to wither, to shrivel; *(Quelle)* to dry up; **er ist ein vertrockneter Mensch** he's a dry old stick *(Brit inf) or* an old bat *(US inf)*

ver|trö|deln *ptp* **vertrödelt** VT *(inf)* to fritter away, to squander

ver|trös|ten *ptp* **vertröstet** VT to put off; **jdn auf ein andermal/auf später ~** to put sb off VR to be content to wait *(auf +acc* for)

ver|trot|teln [fɛɐˈtrɔtln] *ptp* **vertrottelt** VI *(inf) aux sein* to vegetate

ver|trot|telt ADJ *(inf)* goofy *(inf)*; *älterer Mensch (auch)* senile

ver|trus|ten [fɛɐˈtrastn] *ptp* **vertrustet** VT *(Comm)* to form into a trust

ver|tü|dern [fɛɐˈtyːdɐn] *ptp* **vertüdert** *(N Ger)* VR to get tangled up VT to tangle up

ver|tun *ptp* **vertan** [fɛɐˈtaːn] *irreg* VT to waste VR *(inf)* to make a mistake *or* slip, to slip up *(inf)*

ver|tu|schen *ptp* **vertuscht** VT to hush up; **~, dass …** to hush up the fact that …; **etw vor jdm ~** to keep sth from sb

Ver|tu|schung [fɛɐˈtʊʃʊŋ] F **-, -en** cover-up

Ver|tu|schungs|ver|such M attempt to hush things up

ver|übeln [fɛɐˈlyːbln] *ptp* **verübelt** VT **jdm etw ~** not to be at all pleased with sb for doing sth; **ich hoffe, Sie werden mir die Frage nicht ~** I hope you won't mind my asking (this); **das kann ich dir nicht ~** I can't blame you for that

ver|üben *ptp* **verübt** VT to commit, to perpetrate *(form)*

ver|ul|ken *ptp* **verulkt** VT *(inf)* to make fun of, to take the mickey out of *(Brit inf)*

ver|un|fal|len [fɛɐˈlʊnfalən] *ptp* **verunfallt** VI *aux sein (Sw)* to have an accident

Ver|un|fall|te(r) [fɛɐˈlʊnfaltə] MF *decl as adj (form)* accident casualty *or* victim

ver|un|glimp|fen [fɛɐˈlʊnglɪmpfn] *ptp* **verunglimpft** VT *jdn* to disparage; *Ruf, Ehre, Worte auch* to decry

Ver|un|glimp|fung F **-, -en** disparagement

ver|un|glü|cken [fɛɐˈlʊnglʏkn] *ptp* **verunglückt** VI *aux sein (Mensch)* to have an accident; *(Fahrzeug, Flugzeug)* to crash; *(fig inf: = misslingen)* to go wrong; **mit dem Flugzeug ~** to be in a plane crash; **mit dem Auto ~** to be in a car crash, to have a car accident → **tödlich**

ver|un|glückt [fɛɐˈlʊnglʏkt] ADJ *(fig) Versuch, Aufführung etc* unsuccessful

Ver|un|glück|te(r) [fɛɐˈlʊnglʏktə] MF *decl as adj* casualty, victim; **10 Tote, 20 ~** 10 dead, 20 injured

ver|un|mög|li|chen [fɛɐˈlʊnmøːklɪçn] *ptp* **verunmöglicht** VT *(esp Sw)* to make impossible; **jdm ~, etw zu tun** to make it impossible for sb to do sth

ver|un|rei|ni|gen [fɛɐˈlʊnrainɪgn] *ptp* **verunreinigt** VT *Fluss, Luft, Wasser* to pollute; *(= beschmutzen)* to dirty, to soil; *(euph: Hund etc)* to foul

Ver|un|rei|ni|gung F *(von Fluss, Luft, Wasser)* pollution; *(= Beschmutzung)* dirtying, soiling; *(euph: durch Hund)* fouling; **~en in der Luft/im Wasser** pollutants in the atmosphere/in the water

ver|un|si|chern [fɛɐˈlʊnzɪçɐn] *ptp* **verunsichert** VT to make unsure *or* uncertain *(in +dat* of); **jetzt hast du mich völlig verunsichert** I just don't know at all any more; **sie versuchten, ihn zu ~** they tried to throw him; **verunsichert sein** to be uncertain; **verunsicherte Kunden/Patienten** confused customers/patients

Ver|un|si|che|rung F *(= mangelnde Gewissheit)* uncertainty; **das führte zur ~ der Wähler/Schüler** it put the electors/pupils into a state of uncertainty

ver|un|stal|ten [fɛɐˈlʊnʃtaltn] *ptp* **verunstaltet** VT to disfigure; *Landschaft auch* to scar; **jdn ~, jds Gesicht ~** to spoil *or* mar sb's looks

Ver|un|stal|tung F **-, -en** disfigurement

ver|un|treu|en [fɛɐˈlʊntrɔyən] *ptp* **veruntreut** VT to embezzle, to misappropriate

Ver|un|treu|ung F **-, -en** embezzlement, misappropriation

ver|un|zie|ren [fɛɐˈlʊntsiːrən] *ptp* **verunziert** VT *Landschaft, Kunstwerk, Zimmer* to spoil; **jdn ~, jds Gesicht ~** to spoil sb's looks

ver|ur|sa|chen [fɛɐˈluːɐzaxn] *ptp* **verursacht** VT to cause; *Schwierigkeiten auch* to create *(+dat* for), to give rise to *(+dat* for); *Entrüstung, Zorn auch* to provoke; **jdm große Kosten ~** to cause sb a lot of expense; **jdm Umstände ~** to put sb to trouble, to cause sb trouble

Ver|ur|sa|cher [fɛɐ'luːɐzaxɐ] M **-s, -**, **Ver|ur|sa|che|rin** [-ərɪn] F **-, -nen** cause; **der ~ kommt für den Schaden auf** the party responsible is liable for the damage

Ver|ur|sa|cher|prin|zip NT originator principle; *(bei Umweltschäden auch)* polluter pays principle

Ver|ur|sa|chung F **-,** *no pl* causing; *(von Schwierigkeiten auch)* creation; *(von Entrüstung, Zorn auch)* provocation

ver|ur|tei|len ✪ 41 *ptp* **verurteilt** VT to condemn; *(Jur) (= für schuldig befinden)* to convict *(für* of); *(zu Strafe)* to sentence; **jdn zu einer Geldstrafe von 1.000 Euro ~** to fine sb 1,000 euros, to impose a fine of 1,000 euros on sb; **jdn zum Tode ~** to condemn *or* sentence *(Jur)* sb to death; **jdn zu einer Gefängnisstrafe ~** to give sb a prison sentence

ver|ur|teilt [fɛɐ'lurtailt] ADJ **zu etw ~ sein** *(Jur)* to be sentenced to sth; *(fig)* to be condemned to sth; **zum Tode ~** condemned *or* sentenced *(Jur)* to death → **Scheitern**

Ver|ur|teil|te(r) [fɛɐ'lurtailtə] MF *decl as adj* convicted man/woman, convict *(Jur)*; **der zum Tode ~** the condemned man

Ver|ur|tei|lung F condemnation; *(= das Schuldigsprechen)* conviction; *(zu einer Strafe)* sentencing; **seine ~ zu 5 Jahren** his being sentenced to 5 years; **seine ~ zum Tode** his being condemned/sentenced to death

Ver|ve ['vɛrvə] F **-,** *no pl (geh)* verve, spirit

ver|viel|fa|chen [fɛɐ'fiːlfaxn] *ptp* **vervielfacht** VTR to multiply

Ver|viel|fa|chung F **-, -en** multiplication

ver|viel|fäl|ti|gen *ptp* **vervielfältigt** VT to duplicate; *(= fotokopieren)* to photocopy

Ver|viel|fäl|ti|gung F **-, -en** **a** *(= das Vervielfältigen)* duplication; *(= Fotokopieren)* photocopying **b** *(= Abzug)* copy; *(= Fotokopie)* photocopy

Ver|viel|fäl|ti|gungs-: **Ver|viel|fäl|ti|gungs|ap|pa|rat** M duplicating *or* copying machine, duplicator; *(= Fotokopierer)* photocopier; **Ver|viel|fäl|ti|gungs|recht** NT right of reproduction, copyright; **Ver|viel|fäl|ti|gungs|ver|fah|ren** NT duplicating process, copying process

ver|vier|fa|chen [fɛɐ'fiːɐfaxn] *ptp* **vervierfacht** VTR to quadruple

ver|voll|komm|nen [fɛɐ'fɔlkɔmnən] *ptp* **vervollkommnet** VT to perfect VR to perfect oneself

Ver|voll|komm|nung F **-, -en** perfection

ver|voll|stän|di|gen [fɛɐ'fɔlʃtɛndɪgn] *ptp* **vervollständigt** VT to complete; *Kenntnisse, gutes Essen auch* to round off; *Erlebnis* to make complete VR to be completed

Ver|voll|stän|di|gung F **-, -en** completion; *(von Kenntnissen auch)* rounding off

ver|wach|sen *ptp* **verwachsen** VI *irreg aux sein* **a** *(= zusammenwachsen)* to grow (in) together, to grow into one; *(Narbe)* to heal over; *(Knochen)* to knit; *(Wunde)* to heal, to close (over); **mit etw ~** to grow into sth **b** *(fig: Menschen, Gemeinschaft)* to grow closer (together); **zu etw ~** to grow into sth; **mit etw ~** *(mit Arbeit, Aufgabe, Traditionen)* to become caught up in sth; **mit etw ~ sein** to have very close ties with sth; **ein Volk, das mit seinen Traditionen/seiner Kultur ~ ist** a nation whose traditions are/culture is deeply rooted within it; **mit jdm ~ sein** to have become very close to sb

ver|wach|sen ADJ **a** *Mensch, Tier, Glied* deformed; *Pflanze* malformed; *(= verkümmert)* stunted **b** *(= überwuchert)* overgrown

Ver|wach|sung [fɛɐ'vaksʊŋ] F **-, -en** *(Med)* deformation; *(= verwachsenes Glied auch)* deformity; *(Biol, Min)* adhesion

ver|wa|ckeln *ptp* **verwackelt** VT to blur

ver|wäh|len ✪ 27.7 *ptp* **verwählt** VR to misdial, to dial the wrong number

ver|wah|ren *ptp* **verwahrt** VT *(= aufbewahren)* to keep (safe); **jdm etw zu ~ geben** to give sth to sb for safekeeping VR **sich gegen etw ~** to protest against sth

ver|wahr|lo|sen [fɛɐ'vaːɐloːzn] *ptp* **verwahrlost** VI *aux sein* to go to seed, to go to pot *(inf)*; *(Gebäude auch)* to fall into disrepair, to become dilapidated; *(Park)* to become neglected; *(Mensch)* to let oneself go, to neglect oneself; *(= verwildern)* to run wild; *(= auf die schiefe Bahn geraten)* to get into bad habits

ver|wahr|lost [fɛɐ'vaːɐloːst] ADJ neglected; *Mensch, Äußeres auch* unkempt; **sittlich ~** decadent

Ver|wahr|lo|sung F **-,** *no pl* neglect; *(von Gebäude auch)* dilapidation; *(von Mensch)* neglect (of oneself); *(= Verwilderung)* wildness; *(moralisch)* waywardness

Ver|wahr|sam [fɛɐ'vaːɐzaːm] M **-s,** *no pl* **etw in jds ~ geben** to give sth to sb for safekeeping; **etw in ~ haben** to keep sth safe; **etw in ~ nehmen** to take sth into safekeeping

Ver|wah|rung F **a** *no pl (von Geld etc)* keeping; *(von Täter)* custody, detention; **die ~ eines Menschen in einem Heim** keeping a person in a home; **jdm etw in ~ geben, etw bei jdm in ~ geben** to give sth to sb for safekeeping; **etw in ~ nehmen** to take sth into safekeeping; *(Behörde)* to take possession of sth; **jdn in ~ nehmen** to take sb into custody **b** *(= Einspruch)* protest; **gegen etw ~ einlegen** to make *or* lodge a protest against sth

ver|wai|sen [fɛɐ'vaizn] *ptp* **verwaist** VI *aux sein* to become an orphan, to be orphaned, to be made an orphan; *(fig)* to be deserted *or* abandoned; **verwaist** orphaned; *(fig)* deserted, abandoned

ver|wal|ken *ptp* **verwalkt** VT *(inf)* to wallop *(inf)*, to belt *(inf)*

ver|wal|ten *ptp* **verwaltet** VT to manage; *Firma auch* to run; *Angelegenheiten auch* to conduct; *Erbe, Vermögen auch* to administer; *Treuhandsgut* to hold in trust; *Amt* to hold; *(Pol) Provinz etc* to govern; *(Beamter)* to administer; *(Rel)* to administer; **sich selbst ~** *(Pol)* to be self-governing

Ver|wal|ter [fɛɐ'valtɐ] M **-s, -**, **Ver|wal|te|rin** [-ərɪn] F **-, -nen** administrator; *(= Treuhänder)* trustee, custodian; **der Papst als ~ Gottes** the Pope as God's steward

Ver|wal|tung [fɛɐ'valtʊŋ] F **-, -en** **a** *(= das Verwalten)* management; *(von Firma)* running, management; *(von Erbe, Vermögen)* administration, management; *(von Treuhandgut)* holding in trust; *(von Amt)* holding; *(von Provinz)* government; **jdm etw zur ~ übergeben** to put sb in charge of (the management/running *etc* of) sth **b** *(= Behörde, Abteilung)* administration; *(= Hausverwaltung)* management; **städtische ~** municipal authorities *pl*

Ver|wal|tungs-: **Ver|wal|tungs|akt** M administrative act; **Ver|wal|tungs|an|ge|stell|te(r)** MF *decl as adj* admin(istration) employee; **Ver|wal|tungs|ap|pa|rat** M administrative machinery; **Ver|wal|tungs|auf|wand** M administrative costs *pl*; **Ver|wal|tungs|be|am|te(r)** M *decl as adj*, **Ver|wal|tungs|be|am|tin** F government (administration) official; **Ver|wal|tungs|be|hör|de** F administration; **Ver|wal|tungs|be|reich** M *(= Bezirk)* administrative district; *(= Aufgabenbereich)* area or field of administration; **Ver|wal|tungs|be|zirk** M administrative district; **Ver|wal|tungs|dienst** M admin(istration); **Ver|wal|tungs|ge|bäu|de** NT admin(istration) building *or* block; **Ver|wal|tungs|ge|bühr** F administrative charge; **Ver|wal|tungs|ge|richt** NT Administrative Court; **Ver|wal|tungs|kos|ten** PL administrative expenses *pl*; **Ver|wal|tungs|kram** M *(inf) (Admin)* paperwork *no pl*, administrativia *pl (hum)*; *(= Bürokratie)* red tape *(inf)*; **Ver|wal|tungs|rat** M board; **Ver|wal|tungs|rich|ter(in)** M(F) administrative court judge; **Ver|wal|tungs|weg** M administrative channels *pl*; **auf dem ~e** through (the) administrative channels

ver|wam|sen [fɛɐ'vamzn] *ptp* **verwamst** VT *(inf)* to belt *(inf)*, to clobber *(inf)*

ver|wan|del|bar ADJ *(Math, Econ)* convertible

ver|wan|deln *ptp* **verwandelt** VT *(= umformen)* to change, to transform; *Bett, Zimmer* to convert; *(Math, Econ, Chem)* to convert; *(Theat) Szene* to change; *(Jur) Strafe* to commute; **jdn/etw in etw** *(acc)* **~** to turn sb/sth into sth; *(= verzaubern auch)* to change *or* transform sb/sth into sth; **die Vorlage ~** *(Ftbl)* to score from the pass; **einen Strafstoß ~** to score (from) a penalty; **Müller verwandelte den Pass zum 2:0** Müller put the pass away to make it 2-0; **den Matchball ~** *(Tennis)* to convert the match point; **ein Gebäude in einen Trümmerhaufen ~** to reduce a building to a pile of rubble; **er ist wie verwandelt** he's a changed man
VI *(Sport sl)* **zum 1:0 ~** to make it 1-0
VR to change; *(Zool)* to metamorphose; **sich in etw** *(acc) or* **zu etw ~** to change *or* turn into sth; **Zeus hat sich in einen Stier verwandelt** Zeus turned *or* transformed himself into a bull

Ver|wand|lung F **a** *(= das Verwandeln)* transformation; *(von Bett, Zimmer, Math, Econ, Chem)* conversion; *(Theat)* change, changing; *(von Strafe)* commuting **b** *(= das Sichverwandeln)* change; *(Zool)* metamorphosis; *(von Göttern, von der Natur)* transformation; **eine ~ durchmachen** to undergo a change *or* transformation; **seine erstaunliche ~** the remarkable change in him; **„die ~"** *(Liter)* "the Metamorphosis"

Ver|wand|lungs-: **Ver|wand|lungs|künst|ler(in)** M(F) quick-change artist; **Ver|wand|lungs|sze|ne** F *(Theat)* transformation scene

ver|wandt [fɛɐ'vant] *ptp von* **verwenden** ADJ *(lit, fig)* related *(mit* to); *Probleme, Methoden, Fragen, Wissenschaften auch* allied; *Philosophien, Kultur, Gefühle auch, Denker, Geister* kindred *attr*; **~e Seelen** *(fig)* kindred spirits; **~e Themen** *(fig)* related topics; **geistig ~ sein** *(fig)* to be kindred spirits; **wir sind uns darin ~, dass ...** we're akin to each other in that ... → **Ecke**

ver|wand|te *pret von* **verwenden**

Ver|wand|te(r) [fɛɐ'vantə] MF *decl as adj* relation, relative

Ver|wand|ten|kreis M (circle of) relatives *pl*; **im ~** among my/your *etc* relatives

Ver|wandt|schaft [fɛɐ'vantʃaft] F **-, -en** relationship; *(= die Verwandten)* relations *pl*, relatives *pl*; *(fig)* affinity, kinship; **er leugnete die ~ zu mir** he denied being related to me, he denied any relationship with me

ver|wandt|schaft|lich [fɛɐ'vantʃaftlɪç] ADJ family *attr*

Ver|wandt|schafts|grad M degree of relationship; **wir kennen ihren ~ nicht** we don't know how closely they are related

ver|wanzt [fɛɐ'vantst] ADJ *Betten, Kleider* bug-ridden, bug-infested; *(inf: = mit Abhörgeräten)* bugged

ver|war|nen *ptp* **verwarnt** VT to caution, to warn

Ver|war|nung F caution, warning → **gebührenpflichtig**

Ver|war|nungs|geld NT exemplary fine

ver|wa|schen [fɛɐ'vaʃn] ADJ faded *(in the wash)*; *(= verwässert) Farbe* watery; *Sprache* slurred; *(fig)* wishy-washy *(inf)*, woolly *(esp Brit inf)*

ver|wäs|sern *ptp* **verwässert** VT to water down; *(fig auch)* to dilute

Ver|wäs|se|rung F watering down; *(fig auch)* dilution

ver|we|ben *ptp* **verwebt** *or* **verwoben** [fɛɐ'voːbn] VT *irreg* **a** *auch reg Garne* to weave; *(= verbrauchen)* to use **b** *(lit, fig: = verflechten)* to interweave *(mit, in +acc* with)

ver|wech|seln *ptp* **verwechselt** VT *Gegenstände* to mix up, to get muddled *or* mixed up; *Begriffe, Menschen auch* to confuse; **jdn (mit jdm) ~** to confuse sb with sb; *(= für jdn halten auch)* to mistake sb for sb; **entschuldigen Sie, ich habe Sie verwechselt** sorry - I thought you were someone else *or* I (mis)took you for someone else; **zum Verwechseln ähnlich sein** to be the spitting image of each other, to be as like as two peas in a pod; **ich habe meinen Schirm verwechselt** I took somebody else's umbrella by mistake; **sie verwechselt mir und mich** *(lit)* she mixes up *or* confuses "mir" and "mich"; *(fig)* she doesn't know her grammar

Ver|wechs|lung [fɛɐ'vɛksluŋ] F -, -en confusion; *(= Irrtum)* mistake; **die Polizei ist sicher, dass eine ~ (des Täters) völlig ausgeschlossen ist** the police are certain that there can be absolutely no mistake (about the culprit); **es kam deshalb zu einer ~, weil ...** there was a mix-up *or* confusion because ...; **das muss eine ~ sein, da muss es sich um eine ~ handeln** there must be some mistake

Ver|wechs|lungs|ko|mö|die F comedy of mistaken identity

ver|we|gen [fɛɐ've:gn] ADJ daring, bold; *(= tollkühn)* foolhardy, rash; *(= keck)* cheeky *(Brit)*, saucy; **den Hut ~ aufsetzen** to set one's hat at a jaunty *or* rakish angle

Ver|we|gen|heit F -, -en daring, boldness; *(= Tollkühnheit)* foolhardiness, rashness; *(= Keckheit)* cheek(iness) *(Brit)*, sauciness

ver|we|hen *ptp* **verweht** VT *Blätter* to blow away, to scatter; *Spur, Pfad* to cover over, to obliterate; **vom Winde verweht** gone with the wind VI *aux sein (geh) (Worte, Musik)* to be carried away, to drift away; *(Spur, Pfad)* to be obliterated, to be covered over

ver|weh|ren *ptp* **verwehrt** VT *(geh)* **jdm etw ~** to refuse *or* deny sb sth; **die neu gebauten Häuser ~ ihnen jetzt den Blick auf ...** the newly built houses now obstruct their view of ...; **jdm ~, etw zu tun** to bar sb from doing sth

Ver|we|hung [fɛɐ've:ʊŋ] F -, -en *(= Schneeverwehung)* (snow)drift; *(= Sandverwehung)* (sand)drift

ver|weich|li|chen [fɛɐ'vaiçlıçn] *ptp* **verweichlicht** VT **jdn ~** to make sb soft; **ein verweichlichter Mensch** a weakling; **ein verweichlichtes Muttersöhnchen** a mollycoddled mummy's boy *(Brit)*, a pampered momma's boy *(US)* VI *aux sein* to get *or* grow soft

Ver|weich|li|chung F -, *no pl* softness; **Zentralheizung führt zur ~** central heating makes you soft

Ver|wei|ge|rer [fɛɐ'vaigərɐ] M -s, -, **Ver|wei|ge|rin** [-ərın] F -, -nen refusenik *(inf)*; *(= Kriegsdienstverweigerer)* conscientious objector

ver|wei|gern *ptp* **verweigert** VT to refuse; *Befehl* to refuse to obey; *Kriegsdienst* to refuse to do; **jdm etw ~** to refuse *or* deny sb sth; **die Zustimmung zu etw ~** to refuse to give approval to sth; **er kann ihr keinen Wunsch ~** he can refuse *or* deny her nothing; **es war ihr verweigert, ihren Sohn wiederzusehen** she was denied seeing her son; **die Annahme eines Briefes ~** to refuse (to accept *or* to take delivery of) a letter; **er verweigerte die Unterschrift** he refused to sign; **das Pferd hat (das Hindernis) verweigert** the horse refused (at the fence *or* jump); **sich jdm ~** *(euph)* to refuse to be intimate with sb → **Aussage**

Ver|wei|ge|rung F refusal; *(von Hilfe, Auskunft etc auch)* denial; **~ der Aussage** *(Jur)* refusal to make a statement; *(von Zeuge)* refusal to testify *or* give evidence; **~ des Kriegsdienstes** refusal to do (one's) military service; **~ des Gehorsams** disobedience

Ver|wei|ge|rungs|fall M *(Jur)* **im ~** in case of refusal to make a statement

Ver|weil|dau|er F length of stay

ver|wei|len *ptp* **verweilt** VI *(geh) (Mensch)* to stay; *(Blick)* to rest; *(Gedanken)* to dwell, to linger; **bei einer Sache ~** to dwell on sth; **hier lasst uns ~** let us linger *or* tarry *(liter)* here VR to linger, to tarry *(liter)*

Ver|wei|len [fɛɐ'vailən] NT -s, *no pl (geh)* stay; **sein ~ bei dem Gedanken/Thema** his dwelling on the thought/theme; **hier ist meines ~s nicht mehr** *(liter)* I can no longer tarry here *(liter)*

ver|weint [fɛɐ'vaint] ADJ *Augen* tear-swollen; *Gesicht* tear-stained; *Mensch* with (a) tear-stained face; **~ aussehen** to look as though one has (just) been crying

Ver|weis [fɛɐ'vais] M -es, -e [-zə] **a** *(= Rüge)* reprimand, rebuke, admonishment; **jdm einen ~ erteilen** *or* **aussprechen** to reprimand *or* rebuke *or* admonish sb **b** *(= Hinweis)* reference *(auf +acc* to); *(Internet)* link *(auf +acc* to)

ver|wei|sen *ptp* **verwiesen** [fɛɐ'vi:zn] *irreg* VT **a** *(= hinweisen)* **jdn auf etw** *(acc)***/an jdn ~** to refer sb to sth/sb **b** *(von der Schule)* to expel; **jdn des Landes** *or* **aus dem Lande ~** to expel sb (from the country); **jdn vom Platz** *or* **des Spielfeldes ~** to send sb off; **jdn auf den zweiten Platz ~** *(Sport)* to relegate sb to second place **c** *(Jur)* to refer *(an +acc* to) **d** *(dated: = rügen)* **jdn ~** to rebuke *or* reprove *or* admonish sb VI **auf etw** *(acc)* **~** to refer to sth

Ver|wei|sung F **a** *(= Ausschluss, Ausweisung)* expulsion **b** *(= Hinweis)* reference *(auf +acc* to) **c** *(Jur)* referral *(an +acc* to)

Ver|weis|zei|chen NT *(Typ)* reference sign *or* mark

ver|wel|ken *ptp* **verwelkt** VI *aux sein (Blumen)* to wilt; *(fig)* to fade; **ein verwelktes Gesicht** a worn face; **eine verwelkte Schönheit** a faded beauty

ver|welt|li|chen [fɛɐ'vɛltlıçn] *ptp* **verweltlicht** VT to secularize

Ver|welt|li|chung F -, *no pl* secularization

ver|wend|bar ADJ usable *(zu* for); **das ist nur einmal ~** it can be used once only; **ein vielseitig ~es Gerät** a device with many uses

Ver|wend|bar|keit [fɛɐ'vɛntba:ɐkait] F -, *no pl* usability

ver|wen|den [fɛɐ'vɛndn] *pret* **verwendete** *or* **verwandte** [fɛɐ'vɛndətə, fɛɐ'vantə], *ptp* **verwendet** *or* **verwandt** [fɛɐ'vɛndət, fɛɐ'vant] VT to use; *Methode, Mittel auch* to employ; *(= verwerten auch)* to make use of, to utilize; **Mühe/Fleiß auf etw** *(acc)* **~** to put effort/hard work into sth; **Zeit auf etw** *(acc)* **~** to spend time on sth, to put time into sth VR **sich (bei jdm) für jdn ~** to intercede (with sb) *or* to approach sb on sb's behalf

Ver|wen|dung F **a** use; *(von Mitteln etc)* use, employment; *(von Zeit, Geld)* expenditure *(auf +acc* on); **keine ~ für etw haben** to have no use for sth; **für alles ~ haben** *(inf)* to have a use for everything; **~ finden** to have a use, to come in handy *or* useful; **für jdn/etw ~ finden** to find a use for sb/sth; **in ~ stehen** *(Aus)* to be in use; **etw in ~ nehmen** *(Aus)* to put sth into service **b** *(old: = Fürsprache)* intercession *(bei* with)

Ver|wen|dungs-: **ver|wen|dungs|fä|hig** ADJ usable; **für etw ~ sein** to be suitable for sth; **Ver|wen|dungs|mög|lich|keit** F (possible) use; **Ver|wen|dungs|wei|se** F manner of use; **die ~ von etw** the way in which sth is used; **Ver|wen|dungs|zweck** M use, purpose

ver|wer|fen *ptp* **verworfen** [fɛɐ'vɔrfn] *irreg* VT **a** *(= ablehnen)* to reject; *eigene Meinung, Ansicht, Gedanken* to discard; *(Jur) Klage, Antrag, Revision* to dismiss; *Urteil* to quash; *(= kritisieren) Handlungsweise, Methode* to condemn; *(Comput) Änderungen* to discard **b** *Ball* to lose → *auch* **verworfen** VR **a** *(Holz)* to warp; *(Geol)* to fault **b** *(Cards)* to misdeal VI *(Tier)* to abort

ver|werf|lich [fɛɐ'vɛrflıç] ADJ reprehensible

Ver|werf|lich|keit F -, *no pl* reprehensibleness

Ver|wer|fung [fɛɐ'vɛrfʊŋ] F -, -en **a** *(= Ablehnung)* rejection; *(Jur)* dismissal; *(von Urteil)* quashing **b** *(Geol)* fault; *(von Holz)* warping

Ver|wer|fungs|li|nie F *(Geol)* fault line

ver|wert|bar ADJ usable

Ver|wert|bar|keit [fɛɐ've:ɐtba:ɐkait] F -, *no pl* usability

ver|wer|ten *ptp* **verwertet** VT *(= verwenden)* to make use of, to utilize; *Reste* to use, to make use of; *Kenntnisse, Erfahrungen* to utilize, to put to good use; *(kommerziell) Erfindung, Material etc* to exploit; *(Körper) Nahrung* to process; **dieser Stoff wird sich gut für ein Kleid ~ lassen** this material will make a nice dress

Ver|wer|tung F utilization; *(von Resten)* using; *(kommerziell)* exploitation

ver|we|sen [fɛɐ've:zn] *ptp* **verwest** VI *aux sein* to decay; *(Fleisch)* to rot VT *(obs)* to administer; **jds Amt ~** to deputize for sb

Ver|we|ser [fɛɐ've:zɐ] M -s, -, **Ver|we|se|rin** [-ərın] F -, -nen administrator; *(= Amtsverweser)* deputy; *(= Pfarrverweser)* locum (tenens) *(Brit)*, administrator *(US)*

ver|west|li|chen [fɛɐ'vɛstlıçn] *ptp* **verwestlicht** VI to become westernized

Ver|west|li|chung [fɛɐ'vɛstlıçʊŋ] F westernization

Ver|we|sung F -, *no pl* decay; **in ~ übergehen** to start to decay

ver|wet|ten *ptp* **verwettet** VT to gamble away

ver|wich|sen *ptp* **verwichst** VT *(inf)* **a** *(= schlagen)* to belt *(inf)*, to clobber *(inf)* **b** *Geld* to blow *(inf)*

ver|wi|ckeln *ptp* **verwickelt** VT *Fäden etc* to tangle (up), to get tangled up; **jdn in etw** *(acc)* **~** to involve sb in sth; *in Kampf, in dunkle Geschäfte auch* to get sb mixed up in sth; *in Skandal auch* to get sb mixed up in sth, to embroil sb in sth; **in etw verwickelt sein** to be involved/mixed up/embroiled in sth VR *(Fäden etc)* to tangle (up), to become tangled; **sich in etw ~** *(lit)* to become entangled in sth, to get caught up in sth; *(fig) in Widersprüche* to get oneself tangled up in sth; *in Skandal* to get mixed up *or* involved *or* embroiled in sth

ver|wi|ckelt [fɛɐ'vıklt] ADJ *(fig inf) (= schwierig)* involved, complicated, intricate; *(= verwirrt) Mensch* fuddled *(Brit)*, confused

Ver|wi|cke|lung [fɛɐ'vıkəlʊŋ] F -, -en, **Ver|wick|lung** [fɛɐ'vıklʊŋ] F -, -en involvement *(in +acc* in); *(in Skandal auch)* embroilment; *(= Komplikation)* complication; *(= Verwirrung)* confusion; *(Theat, Liter)* intrigue, intricacy (of plot)

ver|wil|dern *ptp* **verwildert** VI *aux sein (Garten)* to become overgrown, to overgrow; *(Pflanzen)* to grow wild; *(Haustier)* to become wild; *(hum inf: Mensch)* to run wild

ver|wil|dert [fɛɐ'vıldɐt] ADJ wild; *Garten* overgrown; *Aussehen* unkempt

Ver|wil|de|rung [fɛɐ'vıldərʊŋ] F -, -en *(von Garten)* overgrowing; **Zustand der ~** state of neglect; **mangelnde Sorge führte zur ~ des Tieres/der Kinder** as a result of negligence the animal became wild/the children ran wild

ver|win|den *ptp* **verwunden** [fɛɐ'vʊndn] VT *irreg* to get over

ver|win|kelt [fɛɐ'vıŋklt] ADJ *Straße, Gasse* winding; *Gebäude, Raum* full of nooks and crannies

ver|wir|beln *ptp* **verwirbelt** VT to swirl

ver|wir|ken *ptp* **verwirkt** VT *(geh)* to forfeit

ver|wirk|li|chen [fɛɐ'vırklıçn] *ptp* **verwirklicht** VT to realize; *Hoffnung auch* to fulfil *(Brit)*, to fulfill *(US)*; *Idee, Plan auch* to put into effect, to translate into action; *Wunsch, Traum auch* to make come true, to turn into a reality VR to be realized; *(Hoffnung auch)* to be fulfilled; *(Idee auch)* to be put into effect, to be translated into action; *(Wunsch, Traum auch)* to come true, to become a reality; *(Mensch)* to fulfil *(Brit) or* fulfill *(US)* oneself

Ver|wirk|li|chung F -, -en realization; *(von Hoffnung, Selbstverwirklichung)* fulfilment *(Brit)*, fulfillment *(US)*

Ver|wir|kung F, *no pl* forfeit(ure); **~ einer Strafe** *(Jur)* incurrence of a penalty

ver|wir|ren [fɛɐ'vırən] *ptp* **verwirrt** VT **a** *Haar* to tousle, to ruffle (up); *Fäden etc* to tangle (up), to get tangled up **b** *(= durcheinanderbringen)* to confuse; *(= konfus machen)* to bewilder; *Sinne, Verstand* to confuse, to (be)fuddle VR *(Fäden etc)* to become tangled (up) *or* snarled up; *(Haare)* to become tousled *or* dishevelled; *(fig)* to become confused

Ver|wirr|spiel NT *(fig)* confusion; **ein ~ mit jdm treiben** to try to confuse sb

Ver|wir|rung F *(= Durcheinander, Verlegenheit)* confusion; *(= Fassungslosigkeit auch)* bewilderment; **jdn in ~ bringen** to confuse/bewilder sb; *(= verlegen machen)* to fluster sb

ver|wirt|schaf|ten *ptp* **verwirtschaftet** VT to squander (away)

ver|wi|schen *ptp* **verwischt** VT *(= verschmieren)* to smudge, to blur; *(lit, fig) Spuren* to cover over; *(fig) Eindrücke, Erinnerungen* to blur VR *(lit, fig)* to become blurred; *(Schrift etc auch)* to become smudged; *(Erinnerung auch)* to fade

ver|wit|tern *ptp* **verwittert** VI *aux sein* to weather

ver|wit|tert [fɛɐ'vɪtɐt] ADJ *Gestein* weathered; *Gesicht auch* weather-beaten

Ver|wit|te|rung F weathering

ver|wit|wet [fɛɐ'vɪtvət] ADJ widowed; **Frau Meier, ~e Schulz** Mrs Meier, the widow of Mr Schulz

ver|woh|nen *ptp* **verwohnt** VT *Wohnung* to run down; *Möbel* to wear out

ver|wöh|nen [fɛɐ'vø:nən] *ptp* **verwöhnt** VT to spoil; *(Schicksal)* to smile upon, to be good to VR to spoil oneself

ver|wohnt [fɛɐ'vo:nt] ADJ *Wohnung* run-down; *Möbel* battered

ver|wöhnt [fɛɐ'vø:nt] ADJ spoiled; *Kunde, Geschmack* discriminating; **vom Schicksal/von den Göttern ~** smiled upon by fate/the gods

Ver|wöh|nung F -, *no pl* spoiling

ver|wor|fen [fɛɐ'vɔrfn] ADJ *(geh)* depraved, degenerate; *Blick* depraved → *auch* **verwerfen**

Ver|wor|fen|heit F -, *no pl* depravity

ver|wor|ren [fɛɐ'vɔrən] ADJ confused, muddled; *(= verwickelt)* complicated, involved, intricate

Ver|wor|ren|heit F -, *no pl* confusion; *(= Verwickeltheit)* intricacy

ver|wund|bar ADJ *(lit, fig)* vulnerable

Ver|wund|bar|keit [fɛɐ'vʊntba:ɐkait] F -, *no pl (lit, fig)* vulnerability

ver|wun|den [fɛɐ'vʊndn] *ptp* **verwundet** VT to wound; *(lit auch)* to injure → *auch* **verwundet**

ver|wun|der|lich ADJ surprising; *(stärker)* astonishing, amazing; *(= sonderbar)* strange, odd; **es ist sehr ~, dass ...** it's most amazing *or* surprising that ...; **es ist nicht ~, dass ...** it is no wonder *or* not surprising that ...

ver|wun|dern *ptp* **verwundert** VT to astonish, to amaze VR *(über +acc* at) to be amazed *or* astonished, to wonder; **sich über etw** *(acc)* **sehr ~ müssen** to be most amazed at sth

ver|wun|dert ADJ amazed, astonished ADV in amazement, in astonishment

Ver|wun|de|rung [fɛɐ'vʊndərʊŋ] F -, *no pl* astonishment, amazement; **zu meiner größten ~** to my great astonishment *or* amazement

ver|wun|det [fɛɐ'vʊndət] ADJ *(lit, fig)* wounded → *auch* **verwunden**

Ver|wun|de|te(r) [fɛɐ'vʊndətə] MF *decl as adj* casualty; **die ~n** *(Mil)* the wounded

Ver|wun|dung F -, **-en** wound

ver|wun|schen [fɛɐ'vʊnʃn] ADJ enchanted

ver|wün|schen *ptp* **verwünscht** VT **a** *(= verfluchen)* to curse; **verwünscht** cursed, confounded **b** *(in Märchen) (= verzaubern)* to enchant, to put *or* cast a spell on *or* over; *(= verhexen)* to bewitch

Ver|wün|schung [fɛɐ'vʏnʃʊŋ] F -, **-en a** *(= Fluch)* curse, oath **b** *no pl (= Verzauberung)* enchantment; *(= Verhexung)* bewitchment

ver|wurs|teln *ptp* **verwurstelt** VT *(inf)* to mess up *(inf)*, to make a mess of

ver|wur|zelt [fɛɐ'vʊrtslt] ADJ **~ sein** *(Pflanze)* to be rooted; **(fest) in** *or* **mit etw** *(dat)* **~ sein** *(fig)* to be deeply rooted in sth

Ver|wur|ze|lung [fɛɐ'vʊrtsəlʊŋ] F -, **-en** *(lit)* rooting; *(fig)* rootedness

ver|wu|scheln *ptp* **verwuschelt** VT *(inf) Haare* to tousle, to ruffle

ver|wüs|ten [fɛɐ'vy:stn] *ptp* **verwüstet** VT to devastate, to ravage; *(fig) Gesicht* to ravage

Ver|wüs|tung F -, **-en** devastation *no pl*, ravaging *no pl*; *(von Gesicht)* ravages *pl*; **die ~en durch den Sturm** the devastation caused by the storm, the ravages of the storm; **~en anrichten** to inflict devastation

ver|za|gen *ptp* **verzagt** VI *(geh)* to become disheartened, to lose heart; **an etw** *(dat)* **~** to despair of sth; **nicht ~!** don't despair

ver|zagt [fɛɐ'tsa:kt] ADJ disheartened, despondent ADV disheartened, despondently

Ver|zagt|heit F -, *no pl* despondency

ver|zäh|len *ptp* **verzählt** VR to miscount, to count wrongly VTI *(dial inf)* = **erzählen**

ver|zah|nen *ptp* **verzahnt** VT *Bretter* to dovetail; *Zahnräder* to cut teeth *or* cogs in, to gear *(Brit)*; *(fig)* to (inter)link, to dovetail; **ineinander verzahnt sein** to mesh

Ver|zah|nung [fɛɐ'tsa:nʊŋ] F -, **-en** *(von Brettern) (= das Verzahnen)* dovetailing; *(= das Verzahntsein)* dovetail; *(von Zahnrädern)* (toothed) gearing; *(fig)* dovetailing

ver|zan|ken *ptp* **verzankt** VR *(inf)* to quarrel, to fall out

ver|zap|fen *ptp* **verzapft** VT **a** *Getränke* to serve *or* sell on draught *(Brit) or* draft *(US)* **b** *Holzstücke* to mortice and tenon; *(mit Dübel)* to dowel **c** *(inf) Unsinn* to come out with; *(pej) Gedichte, Artikel* to concoct

ver|zär|teln [fɛɐ'tsɛrtln] *ptp* **verzärtelt** VT *(pej)* to mollycoddle *(esp Brit)*, to pamper

Ver|zär|te|lung [fɛɐ'tsɛrtəlʊŋ] F -, *no pl (pej)* mollycoddling *(esp Brit)*, pampering

ver|zau|bern *ptp* **verzaubert** VT *(lit)* to cast a spell on *or* over, to put a spell on; *(fig) jdn auch* to enchant; **jdn in etw** *(acc)* **~** to turn sb into sth; **eine verzauberte Prinzessin** an enchanted princess

Ver|zau|be|rung [fɛɐ'tsaubərʊŋ] F -, **-en** *(lit, fig)* enchantment; *(= Verhexung)* bewitchment; **die ~ des Prinzen in einen Frosch** turning the prince into a frog

ver|zehn|fa|chen [fɛɐ'tse:nfaxn] *ptp* **verzehnfacht** VTR to increase tenfold

Ver|zehr [fɛɐ'tse:ɐ] M **-(e)s**, *no pl* consumption

Ver|zehr|bon M *(für Essen)* food voucher; *(für Getränke)* drinks *or* beverage *(US)* voucher

ver|zeh|ren *ptp* **verzehrt** VT *(form: lit, fig)* to consume VR *(geh)* to languish *(liter)*, to eat one's heart out; **sich vor Gram/Sorgen ~** to be consumed by *or* with grief/worries; **sich nach jdm ~** to pine *(esp Brit) or* yearn for sb

ver|zeich|nen *ptp* **verzeichnet** VT **a** *(= notieren, aufweisen)* to record; *(esp in Liste)* to enter; **gewaltige Änderungen sind zu ~** enormous changes are to be noted; **Todesfälle waren nicht zu ~** there were no fatalities; **einen Erfolg zu ~ haben** to have scored a success; **das kann die Regierung als (einen) Erfolg ~** the government can mark this up as a success; **in einer Liste ~** to list **b** *(= falsch zeichnen)* to draw wrong(ly); *(fig)* to misrepresent, to distort VR to make mistakes/a mistake in one's drawing VTI *(Opt)* to distort

Ver|zeich|nis [fɛɐ'tsaiçnɪs] NT **-ses, -se** index; *(= Tabelle)* table; *(= Namensverzeichnis: esp amtlich)* register; *(= Aufstellung)* list; *(Comput)* directory

ver|zei|gen *ptp* **verzeigt** VT *(Sw)* **jdn ~** to report sb to the police

Ver|zei|gung [fɛɐ'tsaigʊŋ] F -, **-en** *(Sw)* reporting

ver|zei|hen ✪ 45.1 *ptp* **verziehen** VTI [fɛɐ'tsi:ən] *irreg (= vergeben)* to forgive; *(Gott, Gebieter)* to pardon; *(= entschuldigen)* to excuse, to pardon; **jdm (etw) ~** to forgive sb (for sth); **ich kann es mir nicht ~, dass ich sie geschlagen habe** I'll never forgive myself for hitting her; **das ist nicht zu ~** that's unforgivable; *(= nicht zu entschuldigen auch)* that's inexcusable *or* unpardonable; **es sei dir noch einmal verziehen** you're forgiven *or* excused!, we'll forgive you!; **~ Sie!** excuse me!; *(als Entschuldigung)* I beg your pardon! *(Brit)*, excuse me!; **~ Sie die Störung, ~ Sie, dass ich stören muss** excuse me for disturbing you

ver|zeih|lich [fɛɐ'tsailɪç] ADJ forgivable; *(= zu entschuldigen)* excusable, pardonable

Ver|zei|hung [fɛɐ'tsaiʊŋ] F -, *no pl* forgiveness; *(= Entschuldigung)* pardon; **~!** excuse me!; *(als Entschuldigung auch)* sorry!; **(jdn) um ~ bitten** *(= sich entschuldigen)* to apologize (to sb); **ich bitte vielmals um ~** I do apologize *(für* for), I'm terribly sorry *(für* about)

ver|zer|ren *ptp* **verzerrt** VT *(lit, fig)* to distort; *Gesicht etc* to contort; *Sehne, Muskel* to strain, to pull; **etw verzerrt darstellen** *(fig)* to present a distorted picture of sth; **verzerrte Gitarren** distorted guitars VI *(Lautsprecher, Spiegel etc)* to distort VR to become distorted; *(Gesicht etc)* to become contorted *(zu* in)

Ver|zer|rung F *(lit, fig)* distortion; *(von Gesicht etc)* contortion; *(von Muskel, Sehne)* straining, pulling; *(Statistik)* bias

ver|zet|teln [fɛɐ'tsɛtln] *ptp* **verzettelt** VR to waste a lot of time; *(bei Aufgabe, Diskussion)* to get bogged down VT *(= verschwenden)* to waste; *Zeit etc* to waste, to fritter away

Ver|zicht [fɛɐ'tsɪçt] M **-(e)s, -e** renunciation *(auf +acc* of); *(auf Anspruch)* abandonment *(auf +acc* of); *(= Opfer)* sacrifice; *(auf Recht, Eigentum, Amt)* relinquishment *(auf +acc* of); *(auf Thron)* abdication *(auf +acc* of); **der ~ auf Zigaretten fällt ihm schwer** he finds it hard to give up cigarettes; **ein ~, der mir nicht schwerfällt** that's something I can easily do without; **~ ist ein Fremdwort für sie** doing *(Brit) or* going without is foreign to her; **~ leisten** *or* **üben** *(form)* = **verzichten**

ver|zicht|bar [fɛɐ'tsɪçtba:ɐ] ADJ dispensable; **nicht ~** indispensable

ver|zich|ten [fɛɐ'tsɪçtn] *ptp* **verzichtet** VI to do *(Brit) or* go without; *(= Opfer bringen)* to make sacrifices; **einer muss leider ~** somebody has to do *(Brit) or* go without, I'm afraid; **sie verzichtete zugunsten ihrer Schwester auf das Auto** she let her sister have the car; **der Kandidat hat zugunsten eines Jüngeren verzichtet** the candidate stepped down in favour *(Brit) or* favor *(US)* of a younger man; **dankend ~** *(iro)* to decline politely; **danke, ich verzichte** *(iro)* not for me, thanks; **auf jdn/etw ~** *(= ohne auskommen müssen)* to do *(Brit) or* go without sb/sth; *auf Alkohol, Süßigkeiten etc auch* to abstain from sth; *(= aufgeben)* to give up sb/sth; *auf Erbschaft, Eigentum* to renounce sth; *auf Anspruch* to waive sth; *auf Recht* to relinquish sth; *(von etw absehen) auf Kommentar, Anzeige etc* to abstain from sth; *auf Kandidatur, Wiederwahl, Amt* to refuse sth; **auf jdn/etw ~ können** to be able to do *(Brit) or* go without sb/sth; **auf den Thron ~** to abdicate; **auf Einzelheiten/eine förmliche Vorstellung ~ können** to be able to dispense with details/a formal introduction

Ver|zicht-: **Ver|zicht|er|klä|rung** F *(auf +acc* of) renunciation; *(auf finanzielle Leistungen)* disclaimer; *(auf Rechte)* waiver; **Ver|zicht|leis|tung** F *(Jur)* renunciation; **Ver|zicht|po|li|tik** F *(pej)* policy of surrender; **Ver|zicht|po|li|ti|ker(in)** M(F) *(pej)* politician supporting a policy of surrender

ver|zie|hen *ptp* **verzogen** [fɛɐ'tso:gn] *irreg* VT **a** *Mund, Züge etc* to twist *(zu* into); **das Gesicht ~** to pull *(Brit) or* make a face, to grimace; **den Mund ~** to turn up one's mouth; **keine Miene ~** not to turn a hair *(Brit) or* bat an eyelash
b *Stoff* to pull out of shape, to stretch; *Chassis, Gestell* to bend out of shape; *Holz* to warp
c *Kinder* to bring up badly; *(= verwöhnen)* to spoil; *Tiere* to train badly → *auch* **verzogen**
d *Pflanzen* to thin out
VR **a** *(Stoff)* to go out of shape, to stretch; *(Chassis)* to be bent out of shape; *(Holz)* to warp
b *(Mund, Gesicht etc)* to twist *(zu* into), to contort
c *(= verschwinden)* to disappear *(auch inf)*; *(Gewitter)* to pass; *(Nebel, Wolken)* to disperse; *(inf: = schlafen gehen)* to go to bed

VI *aux sein* to move (*nach* to); **„verzogen"** (*= unbekannt*) "no longer at this address"

ver|zie|ren *ptp* **verziert** VT to decorate; (*= verschönern*) to embellish; (*Mus*) to ornament

Ver|zie|rung [fɛɐ'tsi:rʊŋ] F -, -en decoration; (*= Verschönerung*) embellishment; (*Mus: = verzierende Noten*) ornament

ver|zin|ken *ptp* **verzinkt** VT *Metalle* to galvanize

ver|zins|bar ADJ = **verzinslich**

ver|zin|sen *ptp* **verzinst** VT to pay interest on; **jdm sein Kapital (mit** *or* **zu 5%) ~** to pay sb (5%) interest on his/her capital; **das Geld wird mit 3% verzinst** 3% interest is paid on the money, the money yields *or* bears 3% interest VR **sich (mit 6%) ~** to yield *or* bear (6%) interest

ver|zins|lich [fɛɐ'tsɪnslɪç] ADJ interest-bearing *attr*, yielding *or* bearing interest; **~ sein** to yield *or* bear interest; **zu 3%/einem hohen Satz ~** yielding *or* bearing 3% interest/a high rate of interest; **nicht ~** free of interest; **das ist ~ vom ersten Mai** the interest on that is payable from the 1st of May ADV **Kapital ~ anlegen** to put capital out at interest

Ver|zin|sung [fɛɐ'tsɪnzʊŋ] F -, -en (*= das Verzinsen*) payment of interest (*+gen, von* on); (*= Zinsertrag*) interest (yield *or* return) (*+gen, von* on); (*= Zinssatz*) interest rate

ver|zo|cken *ptp* **verzockt** VT (*inf*) to gamble away

ver|zo|gen [fɛɐ'tso:gn] ADJ *Kind* badly brought up; (*= verwöhnt*) spoiled; *Tier* badly trained → *auch* **verziehen**

ver|zö|gern *ptp* **verzögert** VT to delay; (*= verlangsamen*) to slow down VR to be delayed

Ver|zö|ge|rung [fɛɐ'tsø:gərʊŋ] F -, -en **a** delay, hold-up **b** *no pl* (*= das Verzögern*) delaying; (*= Verlangsamung*) slowing down; (*Phys*) deceleration; (*Mil*) holding action

Ver|zö|ge|rungs|tak|tik F delaying tactics *pl*

ver|zol|len *ptp* **verzollt** VT to pay duty on; **diese Waren müssen verzollt werden** you must pay duty on these articles; **haben Sie etwas zu ~?** have you anything to declare?; **verzollt** duty-paid

Ver|zol|lung [fɛɐ'tsɔlʊŋ] F -, -en payment of duty (*+gen* on)

ver|zopft [fɛɐ'tsɔpft] ADJ (*inf: = veraltet*) outdated

ver|zü|cken *ptp* **verzückt** VT to enrapture, to send into raptures *or* ecstasies

ver|zu|ckern *ptp* **verzuckert** VI *aux sein* (*Honig etc*) to crystallize VT (*fig*) to sweeten; **jdm etw ~** to sweeten sth for sb → **Pille**

ver|zückt [fɛɐ'tsʏkt] ADJ enraptured, ecstatic ADV *ansehen* adoringly; **~ lauschte er der Musik** he listened enraptured to the music

Ver|zü|ckung [fɛɐ'tsʏkʊŋ] F -, -en rapture, ecstasy; **in ~ geraten** to go into raptures *or* ecstasies (*wegen* over)

Ver|zug M, *no pl* **a** delay; (*= Rückstand von Zahlung*) arrears *pl*; **ohne ~** without delay, forthwith; **bei ~ (der Zahlungen)** on default of payment; **im ~** in arrears *pl* (*esp Brit*), behind; **mit etw in ~ geraten** to fall behind with sth; *mit Zahlungen* to fall into arrears (*esp Brit*) *or* behind with sth **b es ist Gefahr im ~** there's danger ahead **c** (*form: aus Stadt*) moving away

Ver|zugs|zin|sen PL interest *sing* payable (on arrears (*esp Brit*))

ver|zup|fen *ptp* **verzupft** VR (*Aus inf*) to be off (*inf*)

ver|zwackt [fɛɐ'tsvakt] ADJ (*inf*) tricky

ver|zwei|feln *ptp* **verzweifelt** VI *aux sein* to despair (*an +dat* of); **am Leben ~** to despair of life; **nur nicht ~!** don't despair!, don't give up!; **es ist zum Verzweifeln!** it makes you despair!, it drives you to despair!

ver|zwei|felt [fɛɐ'tsvaiflt] ADJ *Blick, Stimme etc* despairing *attr*, full of despair; *Mensch auch, Lage, Versuch, Kampf etc* desperate; **ich bin (völlig) ~** I'm in (the depths of) despair; (*= ratlos*) I just don't know what to do, I'm at my wits' end ADV desperately; *fragen, ringen um auch* despairingly; **..., sagte er ~** ... he said despairingly; **schau nicht so ~** don't look so desperate

Ver|zweif|lung [fɛɐ'tsvaiflʊŋ] F -, -en (*Gemütszustand*) despair; (*= Ratlosigkeit*) desperation; **etw in seiner ~ tun, etw aus ~ tun** to do sth in desperation; **in ~ geraten** to despair; **jdn zur** *or* **in die ~ treiben** to drive sb to despair → **bringen e**

Ver|zweif|lungs|tat F act of desperation

ver|zwei|gen [fɛɐ'tsvaign] *ptp* **verzweigt** VR (*Bäume*) to branch (out); (*Straße*) to branch (off); (*Leitung*) to branch; (*Firma*) to establish branches; (*Anat, fig*) to ramify

ver|zweigt [fɛɐ'tsvaikt] ADJ *Baum, Familie, Firma, Straßennetz* branched; (*Anat, fig*) ramified

Ver|zwei|gung F -, -en (*von Baum*) branching (out); (*von Straße*) branching (off); (*von Leitung*) branching; (*Anat, fig*) ramification

ver|zwickt [fɛɐ'tsvɪkt] ADJ (*inf*) tricky

Ves|per[1] ['fɛspɐ] F -, -n (*Eccl*) vespers *pl*

Ves|per[2] NT -s, - (*dial*) (*auch* **Vesperpause, Vesperzeit**) break; (*auch* **Vesperbrot**) sandwiches *pl*

ves|pern ['fɛspɐn] (*dial*) VT to guzzle (*inf*) VI (*= essen*) to guzzle things (*inf*); (*= Pause machen*) to have a break; **er vespert gerade** he's just having his break

Ves|ti|bül [vɛsti'by:l] NT -s, -e (*dated, geh*) vestibule

Ve|te|ran[1] [vete'ra:n] M -en, -en (*Aut*) vintage car

Ve|te|ran[2] [vete'ra:n] M -en, -en, **Ve|te|ra|nin** [-'ra:nɪn] F -, -nen (*Mil, fig*) veteran

Ve|te|ri|när [veteri'nɛ:ɐ] M -s, -e, **Ve|te|ri|nä|rin** [-'nɛ:rɪn] F -, -nen (*old, form*) veterinary surgeon

Ve|te|ri|när|me|di|zin F veterinary medicine

Ve|to ['ve:to] NT -s, -s veto → **einlegen**

Ve|to|recht NT right of veto

Vet|tel ['fɛtl] F -, -n (*old pej*) hag

Vet|ter ['fɛtɐ] M -s, -n cousin; (*in Märchen*) Brother, Brer

Vet|tern|wirt|schaft F (*inf*) nepotism

Ve|xier|bild [vɛ'ksi:ɐ-] NT picture puzzle

ve|xie|ren [vɛ'ksi:rən] *ptp* **vexiert** VT (*old*) to vex

Ve|xier|spiel [vɛ'ksi:ɐ-] NT game of deception

V-Form ['fau-] F V-shape; **in ~** in a V-shape, in (the shape of) a V

v-för|mig ['fau-], **V-för|mig** ADJ V-shaped, in (the shape of) a V ADV in the shape of a V; **~ aussehen** to look like a V, to be V-shaped; **der Pullover ist ~ ausgeschnitten** this sweater has a V-neck

V-Frau ['fau-] F *abbr von* **Verbindungsfrau**

VGA-Kar|te [fauge:'la:-] F (*Comput*) VGA card

vgl. *abbr von* **vergleiche** cf

v. H. *abbr von* **vom Hundert** per cent (*Brit*), percent (*US*)

VHS[1] [fauha:'lɛs] F -, *no pl abbr von* **Volkshochschule**

VHS[2] [fauha:'lɛs] NT -, *no pl abbr von* **Video-Home-System** VHS

via ['vi:a] ADV via

Via|dukt [via'dʊkt] M -(e)s, -e viaduct

Vi|ag|ra® [vi'a:gra] NT -s Viagra®

Vib|ra|fon [vibra'fo:n] NT -s, -e, **Vib|ra|phon** [vibra'fo:n] NT -s, -e vibraphone, vibraharp (*US*)

Vib|ra|ti|on [vibra'tsio:n] F -, -en vibration

vib|ra|to [vi'bra:to:] ADV (*Mus*) vibrato

Vib|ra|to [vi'bra:to:] NT -s, -s *or* **Vibrati** (*Mus*) vibrato

Vib|ra|tor [vi'bra:to:ɐ] M -s, **Vibratoren** [-'to:rən] vibrator (*auch Telec*)

vib|rie|ren [vi'bri:rən] *ptp* **vibriert** VI to vibrate; (*Stimme*) to quiver, to tremble; (*= schwanken: Ton*) to vary, to fluctuate

Vi|deo ['vi:deo] NT -s, -s video; **etw auf ~ aufnehmen** to video sth, to record sth on video

Vi|deo- *in cpds* video; **Vi|deo|auf|nah|me** F video recording; **Vi|deo|band** [-bant] NT *pl* **-bänder** video tape; **Vi|deo|bot|schaft** F video message; **eine ~ ausstrahlen** to broadcast a video message; **Vi|deo|clip** M video clip; **Vi|deo|film** M video (film); **Vi|deo|ge|rät** NT video (recorder); **Vi|deo|in|ter|view** NT video interview; **Vi|deo|ka|me|ra** F video camera; **Vi|deo|kar|te** F (*Comput*) video card; **Vi|deo|kon|fe|renz** F video conference; **Vi|deo|pi|rat(in)** M(F) video pirate; **Vi|deo|print** [-prɪnt] NT -s, -s video print; **Vi|deo|prin|ter** [-prɪntɐ] M -s, - video printer; **Vi|deo|re|cor|der** = **Videorekorder**; **Vi|deo|re|kor|der** M video recorder; **Vi|deo|spiel** NT video game; **Vi|deo|tech|nik** F video technology; **Vi|deo|te|le|fo|nie** F video conferencing; **Vi|deo|text** M Teletext®; **Vi|deo|thek** [video'te:k] F -, -en video (tape) library; **vi|deo|über|wacht** ADJ under video surveillance *pred*; **der Tunnel ist nicht ~** the tunnel has no closed-circuit TV cameras (installed)

Vi|deo|über|wa|chung F closed-circuit TV, CCTV, video surveillance

Vi|deo|über|wa|chungs|ka|me|ra F CCTV camera

Vi|deo|ver|fah|ren NT video *no art*

Viech [fi:ç] NT -(e)s, -er (*inf*) creature

Vie|che|rei [fi:çə'rai] F -, -en (*inf*) **a** (*= Quälerei*) torture *no indef art* (*inf*) **b** (*= grober Scherz*) rotten trick

Vieh [fi:] NT -(e)s, *no pl* **a** (*= Nutztiere*) livestock; (*= esp Rinder*) cattle *pl*; **10 Stück ~** 10 head of livestock/cattle **b** (*inf: = Tier*) animal, beast (*usu hum*) **c** (*pej inf: Mensch*) swine

Vieh-: **Vieh|ab|trieb** M **der ~ findet jetzt statt** the livestock are being brought down from the mountain pastures now; **Vieh|auf|trieb** M **wir brauchen Leute für den ~** we need people to drive the livestock up into the mountain pastures; **Vieh|be|stand** M livestock; **Vieh|fut|ter** NT (animal) fodder *or* feed; **Vieh|hal|tung** F keeping of livestock; (*von Rindern*) keeping of cattle; **Vieh|han|del** M livestock trade; (*esp mit Rindern*) cattle trade; **Vieh|händ|ler(in)** M(F) livestock dealer; (*esp mit Rindern*) cattle dealer

vie|hisch ['fi:ɪʃ] ADJ brutish; *Schmerzen* beastly; (*= unzivilisiert*) *Benehmen* swinish ADV **a** *jucken, brennen* unbearably; **~ wehtun** to be unbearably painful **b** *sich benehmen* like an animal/animals; **~ essen** to eat like a pig; **~ hausen** to live like animals/an animal

Vieh-: **Vieh|markt** M livestock market; (*esp für Rinder*) cattle market; **Vieh|salz** NT (*für Tiere*) cattle salt; (*zum Streuen*) road salt; **Vieh|seu|che** F livestock disease; **Vieh|stall** M cattle shed; **Vieh|trei|ber(in)** M(F) drover; **Vieh|wa|gen** M cattle truck; **Vieh|wei|de** F pasture; **Vieh|wirt|schaft** F (live)stock farming, animal husbandry; **Vieh|zeug** NT, *no pl* (*inf*) animals *pl*, creatures *pl*; **Vieh|zucht** F (live)stock breeding; (*= Rinderzucht auch*) cattle breeding

viel [fi:l] INDEF PRON, ADJ *comp* **mehr** [me:ɐ], *superl* **meiste(r, s)** *or adv* **am meisten** ['maistə] **a** *sing* (*adjektivisch*) a lot of, a great deal of; (*substantivisch*) a lot, a great deal; (*esp fragend, verneint*) much; **~es** a lot of things; **~(es), was ...**, **~(es) von dem, was ...** a lot *or* great deal of what ...; **in ~em, in ~er Hinsicht** *or* **Beziehung** in many respects; **mit ~em** with a lot of things; **um ~es besser** *etc* a lot *or* much *or* a great deal better *etc*; **sehr ~ (Geld** *etc*) a lot *or* a great deal (of money *etc*); **nicht sehr ~ (Geld** *etc*) not very much (money *etc*); **so ~** so much; **halb/doppelt so ~** half/twice as much; **so ~ als** *or* **wie ...** as much as ...; **nimm dir so ~ du willst** take as much as you like; **noch einmal so ~** the same again; (*= doppelt so viel*) twice as much; **das ist so ~ wie eine Zusage** that is tantamount to a promise, that amounts to a promise; **so ~ für heute!** that's all for today; **so ~, was ihn betrifft** so much for him; **so ~ (Arbeit** *etc*) so much *or* such a lot (of work *etc*); **noch (ein)mal so ~ (Zeit** *etc*) as much (time *etc*) again; **zweimal so**

~ **(Arbeit** *etc*) twice as much (work *etc*); **gleich ~ (Gewinn** *etc*) the same amount (of profit *etc*); **wie ~** how much; *(bei Mehrzahl)* how many; **(um) wie ~ größer** how much bigger; **ziemlich ~ (Schmutz** *etc*) rather a lot (of dirt *etc*); **zu ~** too much; (*inf:* = *zu viele*) too many; **~ zu ~** much *or* far too much; **besser zu ~ als zu wenig** better too much than too little; **wenns dir zu ~ wird, sag Bescheid** say if it gets too much for you; **ihm ist alles zu ~** (*inf*) it's all too much for him; **da krieg ich zu ~** (*inf*) I blow my top (*inf*); **einer/zwei** *etc* **zu ~** one/two *etc* too many; **einen/ein paar zu ~ trinken** (*inf*) to drink *or* have (*inf*) one/a few too many; **was zu ~ ist, ist zu ~** that's just too much, there's a limit to everything; **ein bisschen ~ (Regen** *etc*) a bit too much (rain *etc*); **furchtbar ~ (Regen** *etc*) an awful lot (of rain *etc*); **~ Erfolg!** good luck!, I wish you every success!; **~ Spaß!** have fun!, enjoy yourself/yourselves!; **~ Neues/Schönes** *etc* a lot of *or* many new/beautiful *etc* things; **~ Volk** a lot of people; **das ~e Geld** all that money; **sein ~es Geld** all his money; **das ~e Geld/Lesen** *etc* all this money/reading *etc*; **~ zu tun haben** to have a lot to do; **er hält ~ von ihm/davon** he thinks a lot *or* a great deal of him/it; **er hält nicht ~ von ihm/davon** he doesn't think much of him/it; **das will ~/nicht ~ heißen** *or* **sagen** that's saying a lot *or* a great deal/not saying much

b **~e** *pl (adjektivisch)* many, a lot of, a great number of; *(substantivisch)* many, a lot; **es waren nicht ~e auf der Party** there weren't many (people) *or* a lot (of people) at the party; **es waren nicht ~e in der Schule** there weren't many (children) *or* a lot (of children) at school; **da wir so ~e sind** since there are so many *or* such a lot of us; **davon gibt es nicht ~e** there aren't many *or* a lot about; **davon gibt es nicht mehr ~e** there aren't many *or* a lot left; **furchtbar ~e (Kinder/Bewerbungen** *etc*) a tremendous number *or* an awful lot (of children/applications *etc*); **gleich ~e (Angestellte/Anteile** *etc*) the same number (of employees/shares *etc*); **so/zu ~e (Menschen/Fehler** *etc*) so/too many (people/mistakes *etc*); **er hat ~(e) Sorgen/Probleme** *etc* he has a lot of worries/problems *etc*; **~e hundert** *or* **Hundert Menschen** many hundreds of people; **die/seine ~en Fehler** *etc* the/his many mistakes *etc*; **die ~en Leute/Bücher!** all these people/books!; **~e glauben, ...** many (people) *or* a lot of people believe ...; **und ~e andere** and many others; **es waren deren** *or* **ihrer ~e** (*liter*) there were many of them

c *(adverbial: mit vb)* a lot, a great deal; *(esp fragend, verneint)* much; **er arbeitet ~** he works a lot; **er arbeitet nicht ~** he doesn't work much; **er arbeitet zu ~** he works too much; **er arbeitet so ~** he works so much *or* such a lot; **sie ist ~ krank/von zu Hause weg** she's ill/away a lot; **die Straße wird (sehr/nicht) ~ befahren** this street is (very/not very) busy; **dieses Thema wird ~ diskutiert** this subject is much debated; **sich ~ einbilden** to think a lot of oneself

d *(adverbial: mit adj, adv)* much, a lot; **~ größer** *etc* much *or* a lot bigger *etc*; **~ beschäftigt** very busy; **~ diskutiert** much discussed; **~ erörtert** much discussed; **~ gehasst** much-hated; **~ gekauft** frequently bought, much-purchased; **~ geliebt** much-loved; **~ genannt** much-cited, frequently mentioned; **~ geprüft** (*hum*) sorely tried; **~ gereist** much-travelled (*Brit*), much-traveled (*US*); **~ geschmäht** much-maligned; **~ sagend** = **vielsagend**; **~ umworben** much-sought-after; *Frau* much-courted; **~ verheißend** promising, full of promise; *anfangen* promisingly; **sich ~ verheißend anhören** to sound promising; **~ versprechend** = **vielversprechend**; **nicht ~ anders** not very *or* much *or* a lot different; **~ zu ...** much too ...; **~ zu ~** much *or* far too much; **~ zu ~e** far too many; **ich würde ~ lieber auf eine Party gehen** I'd much rather go to a party, I'd much prefer to go to a party

Viel-: **viel|bän|dig** ADJ multivolumed, in many volumes; **viel|be|schäf|tigt** ADJ → **viel d**; **viel|deu|tig** [-dɔytɪç] ADJ ambiguous; **Viel|deu|tig|keit** F -, *no pl* ambiguity; **viel|dis|ku|tiert** [-dɪskuti:ɐt] ADJ → **viel d**; **Viel|eck** NT polygon; **viel|eckig** ADJ polygonal (*Math*), many-sided; **Viel|ehe** F polygamy

vie|len|orts ['fi:lən'ɔrts] ADV = **vielerorts**

vie|ler|lei ['fi:lɐ'lai] ADJ *inv* **a** various, all sorts of, many different **b** *(substantivisch)* all kinds *or* sorts of things

vie|ler|ör|tert ['fi:lɐɐlœrtɐt] ADJ → **viel d**

vie|ler|orts ['fi:lɐ'ɔrts] ADV in many places

viel|fach ['fi:lfax] ADJ multiple *attr*, manifold; **ein ~er Millionär** a multimillionaire; **auf ~e Weise** in many ways; **auf ~en Wunsch** at the request of many people ADV many times; (= *in vielen Fällen*) in many cases; (= *auf vielfache Weise*) in many ways; (*inf:* = *häufig*) frequently; **~ bewährt** tried and tested many times

Viel|fa|che(s) ['fi:lfaxə] NT *decl as adj (Math)* multiple; **das kleinste gemeinsame ~** (*Math*) the least *or* lowest common multiple; **um ein ~s** many times over; **um ein ~s besser/teurer** *etc* many times better/more expensive *etc*; **der Gewinn hat sich um ein ~s vermehrt** *or* **ist um ein ~s gestiegen** the profit has been multiplied several times; **er verdient ein ~s von dem, was ich verdiene** his salary is many times larger than mine

Viel|fah|rer(in) M(F) *(mit öffentlichen Verkehrsmitteln)* frequent traveller (*Brit*) *or* traveler (*US*) (*on public transport*); *(mit Auto)* frequent car user

Viel|falt ['fi:lfalt] F -, *no pl* (great) variety

viel|fäl|tig ['fi:lfɛltɪç] ADJ varied, diverse

Viel|fäl|tig|keit F -, *no pl* variety, diversity

Viel-: **viel|far|big**, (*Aus*) **viel|fär|big** ADJ multicoloured (*Brit*), multicolored (*US*); (*Tech*) polychrome *attr*, polychromatic; **viel|flä|chig** ADJ many-faced, polyhedral (*Math*); **Viel|fläch|ner** [-flɛçnɐ] M **-s, -** (*Math*) polyhedron; **Viel|flie|ger(in)** M(F) frequent flier; **Viel|fraß** M **a** (*fig*) glutton **b** (*Zool*) wolverine, glutton; **viel|ge|hasst** [-gəhast] ADJ → **viel d**; **viel|ge|kauft** [-gəkauft] ADJ → **viel d**; **viel|ge|liebt** ADJ → **viel d**; **viel|ge|nannt** ADJ → **viel d**; **viel|ge|prüft** [-gəpry:ft] ADJ → **viel d**; **viel|ge|reist** [-gəraist] ADJ → **viel d**; **viel|ge|schmäht** [-gəʃmɛ:t] ADJ → **viel d**; **viel|ge|stal|tig** [-gɛʃtaltɪç] ADJ variously shaped, varied in shape and form, multiform (*form*); (*fig:* = *mannigfaltig*) varied; **in ~er Weise** in multifarious ways; **Viel|ge|stal|tig|keit** F -, *no pl* (*Sci*) polymorphism; (*fig*) variety; **viel|glie|de|rig** [-gli:dərɪç], **viel|glied|rig** [-gli:drɪç] ADJ having many parts, with many parts; (*Math*) polynomial; **Viel|göt|te|rei** [-gœtə'rai] F -, *no pl* polytheism; **viel|hun|dert|mal** [fi:l'hʊndɐtma:l] ADV (*liter*) hundreds upon hundreds of times, many hundreds of times; **viel|köp|fig** ADJ many-headed, polycephalous (*Sci, form*); (*inf*) *Familie, Schar* large

viel|leicht [fi'laiçt] ADV **a** perhaps; *(esp in Bitten)* by any chance; **ja, ~** yes, perhaps *or* maybe; **haben Sie ~ meinen Hund gesehen?** have you seen my dog by any chance?; **könnten Sie mir ~ sagen, wie spät es ist?** could you possibly tell me the time?; **~ könnten Sie so freundlich sein und ...?** perhaps you'd be so kind as to ...?; **~ sagst du mir mal, warum** you'd better tell me why; **~ hältst du mal den Mund!** keep your mouth shut; **hat er sich ~ verirrt/wehgetan?** maybe he has got lost/has hurt himself; **hast du ihm das ~ erzählt?** did you perhaps tell him that?; (*entsetzt:* = *denn etwa*) you didn't tell him that, did you?; **~ hast du recht** perhaps you're right, you may be right, maybe you're right; **~, dass ...** it could be that ...

b (= *wirklich, tatsächlich, inf: verstärkend*) really; **soll ich ~ 24 Stunden arbeiten?!** am I supposed to work 24 hours then?; **willst du mir ~ erzählen, dass ...?!** do you really mean to tell me that ...?; **du bist ~ ein Idiot!** you really are an idiot!; **ich war ~ nervös!** I wasn't half nervous! (*Brit inf*), was I nervous!, I was as nervous as anything (*inf*); **das ist ~ ein Haus!** that's what I call a house! (*inf*), that's some house! (*inf*)

c (= *ungefähr*) perhaps, about

viel|mal ['fi:lma:l] ADV (*Sw*) = **vielmals**

viel|ma|lig ['fi:lma:lɪç] ADJ *attr* repeated

viel|mals ['fi:lma:ls] ADV **a** *(in bestimmten Wendungen)* **danke ~!** thank you very much!, many thanks!; **ich bitte ~ um Entschuldigung!** I do apologize!; **er lässt ~ grüßen** he sends his best regards **b** (*liter:* = *häufig*) many times, ofttimes (*liter*)

Viel|män|ne|rei [-mɛnə'rai] F -, *no pl* polygamy, polyandry

viel|mehr [fi:l'me:ɐ, 'fi:l-] ADV rather; (= *sondern, nur*) just; **ich glaube ~, dass ...** rather I *or* I rather think that ...; **nicht dumm, ~ faul** lazy rather than stupid, not stupid just lazy

Viel-: **viel|sa|gend** [-za:gnt] ADJ meaningful, significant ADV meaningfully; **jdn ~ ansehen** to give sb a meaningful look; **sie schwiegen ~** there was a meaningful silence; **~ lächeln** to give a meaningful smile; **viel|schich|tig** [-ʃɪçtɪç] ADJ (*lit rare*) multilayered; (*fig*) complex; **Viel|schich|tig|keit** F -, *no pl (fig)* complexity; **Viel|schrei|ber(in)** M(F) prolific writer; **er ist ein richtiger ~** (*pej*) he really churns out the stuff (*inf*); **viel|sei|tig** [-zaitɪç] ADJ (*lit*) many-sided; *Mensch, Gerät, Verwendung* versatile; *Interessen* varied; *Ausbildung* broad, all-round *attr* (*Brit*), all-around *attr* (*US*); **dieser Beruf ist sehr ~** there are many different sides to this job; **auf ~en Wunsch** by popular request ADV **~ interessiert/anwendbar** *etc* to have varied interests/many uses *etc*; **~ ausgebildet sein** to have an all-round (*Brit*) *or* all-around (*US*) education; **~ gebildet sein** to be well-educated; **~ informiert sein** to be well-informed; **~ anwendbar/einsetzbar sein** to be versatile; **Kompost ist ~ verwendbar** compost can be used for many purposes; **Viel|sei|tig|keit** F -, *no pl (von Mensch, Gerät, Verwendung)* versatility; *(von Interessen)* multiplicity; *(von Ausbildung)* broadness, all-round nature (*Brit*); **viel|spra|chig** ADJ multilingual, polyglot; **er ist ~** he is multilingual *or* a polyglot; **Viel|staa|te|rei** [-ʃta:tə'rai] F -, *no pl* particularism; **viel|stim|mig** ADJ *Chor, Gesang, Schreie* many-voiced; **viel|tau|send|mal** [fi:l'tauzntma:l] ADV (*liter*) thousands upon thousands of times, many thousands of times; **viel|um|wor|ben** [-lʊmvɔrbn] ADJ → **viel d**; **viel|ver|hei|ßend** [-fɛɐhaisnt] ADJ → **viel d**; **viel|ver|spre|chend** [-fɛɐʃprɛçnt] ADJ promising, encouraging; **~ klingen** to sound promising ADV *anfangen* promisingly; **Viel|völ|ker|staat** [fi:l'fœlkɐ-] M multiracial state; **Viel|wei|be|rei** [-vaibə'rai] F -, *no pl* polygamy, polygyny; **Viel|zahl** F multitude; **eine ~ von Abbildungen** a wealth of illustrations

Viel|zweck- *in cpds* multipurpose; **Viel|zweck|rei|ni|ger** M multipurpose cleaner

vier [vi:ɐ] NUM **a** four; **die ersten/nächsten/letzten ~** the first/next/last four; **sie ist ~ (Jahre)** she's four (years old); **mit ~ (Jahren)** at the age of four; **~ Millionen** four million; **es ist ~ (Uhr)** it's four (o'clock); **um/gegen ~ (Uhr)** *or* **~e** (*inf*) at/around four (o'clock); **~ Uhr ~** four minutes past four; **~/fünf Minuten vor/nach ~** four minutes/five (minutes) to/past four; **halb ~** half past three; **~ Minuten vor halb ~** twenty-six minutes past three; **~ Minuten nach halb ~** twenty-six minutes to four; **für** *or* **auf ~ Tage** for four days; **in ~ Tagen** in four days, in four days' time; **~ zu drei** (*geschrieben 4:3*) four-three, four to three, 4-3; **wir waren ~** *or* **zu ~t** *or* **zu ~en** *or* **unser ~** (*geh*) there were four of us, we were four in number (*form*); **wir fahren zu ~t** *or* **mit ~en in Urlaub** there are four of us going on holiday (*esp Brit*) *or* vacation (*US*) together, we are going on holiday (*esp Brit*) *or* vacation (*US*) as a foursome; **sie kamen zu ~t** *or* **zu ~en**

four of them came; **stellt euch ~ und ~** *or* **zu je ~** *or* **zu ~t** *or* **zu ~en auf** line up in fours; **eine Familie von ~en** *(inf)* a family of four; **Vater ~er Töchter, Vater von ~ Töchtern** father of four daughters

b jdn unter ~ Augen sprechen to speak to sb privately *or* in private; **ein Gespräch unter ~ Augen** a private conversation *or* talk, a tête-à-tête; **jdn um ein Gespräch unter ~ Augen bitten** to ask to speak to sb privately *or* in private; **~ Augen sehen mehr als zwei** *(prov)* two heads are better than one *(prov)*; **alle ~e von sich strecken** *(inf) (= ausgestreckt liegen)* to stretch out; *(= tot sein)* to have given up the ghost; **auf allen ~en** *(inf)* on all fours; **sich auf seine ~ Buchstaben setzen** *(hum inf)* to sit oneself down → **Wind b, Wand, Hand b**

Vier [viːɐ] **F -, -en** four; *(Buslinie etc)* (number) four

Vier-: **Vier|ach|ser** [-laksɐ] **M -s, -** *(Aut)* four-axle vehicle; **vier|ar|mig ADJ** with four arms; *Leuchter* with four branches; **Vier|au|gen|ge|spräch NT** personal *or* private discussion; **vier|bän|dig ADJ** four-volume *attr*, in four volumes; **Vier|bei|ner** [-bainɐ] **M -s, -** *(hum)* four-legged friend *(hum)*; **vier|bei|nig ADJ** four-legged; **vier|blät|te|rig, vier|blätt|rig ADJ** four-leaf *attr*, four-leaved; **vier|di|men|si|o|nal ADJ** four-dimensional; **Vier|eck NT** four-sided figure, quadrilateral *(Math)*; *(= Rechteck)* rectangle; **vier|eckig ADJ** square; *(esp Math)* four-sided, quadrangular, quadrilateral; *(= rechteckig)* rectangular; **vier|ein|halb** [ˈfiːɐlainˈhalp] **NUM** four and a half

Vie|rer [ˈfiːrɐ] **M -s, -** *(Rudern, Sch)* four; *(Golf)* foursome; *(inf: = Linie)* (number) four; *(Aus, S Ger: Ziffer)* four; **einen ~ im Lotto haben** to have four numbers in the lottery

Vie|rer-: **Vie|rer|ban|de F** Gang of Four; **Vie|rer|bob M** four-man bob *(Brit)* *or* bobsled *(US)*; **Vie|rer|grup|pe F** group of four; **vie|rer|lei** [ˈfiːrɐˈlai] **ADJ** *inv* **a** *attr Brot, Käse, Wein* four kinds *or* sorts of; *Möglichkeiten, Fälle, Größen* four different **b** *(substantivisch)* four different things; *(= vier Sorten)* four different kinds; **Vie|rer|pasch M** (all) fours *no indef art*; **Vie|rer|rei|he F** row of four; **Vie|rer|tref|fen NT** *(Pol) (der vier Mächte)* four-power conference, meeting of the four powers; *(von Politikern)* meeting of four politicians

vier|fach [ˈfiːɐfax] **ADJ** fourfold, quadruple *(esp Math)*; **die ~e Größe/Menge/Anzahl** four times the size/amount/number; **in ~er Ausfertigung** in quadruplicate; **in ~er Vergrößerung** enlarged four times **ADV** four times, fourfold; **das Papier ~ legen** *or* **nehmen** to fold the paper in four; **den Faden ~ nehmen** to take four threads together; **er hat den Band ~** he has four copies of the book

Vier|fa|che(s) [ˈfiːɐfaxə] **NT** *decl as adj* four times the amount, quadruple *(Math)*; **das ~ von 3 ist 12** four times 3 is 12; **um das ~ zunehmen** to quadruple; **das ~ von jdm verdienen** to earn four times as much as sb

Vier-: **Vier|fach|steck|do|se F** *(Elec)* 4-socket plug; **vier|fäl|tig ADJ = vierfach**; **Vier|far|ben|druck M** *pl* **-drucke** *(Verfahren)* four-colour *(Brit)* *or* four-color *(US)* printing; *(Erzeugnis)* four-colo(u)r print; **Vier|far|ben|stift M, Vier|farb|stift M** four-colour *(Brit)* *or* four-color *(US)* pen; **vier|far|big ADJ** four-colour *attr (Brit)*, four-color *attr (US)* **ADV** in four colo(u)rs; **Vier|fel|der|wirt|schaft F** four-course rotation; **Vier|flach** [-flax] **NT -(e)s, -e** *(Math)* tetrahedron; **vier|flä|chig ADJ** *Körper, Gebilde* tetrahedral; **Vier|frucht|mar|me|la|de F** four-fruit jam; **Vier|fü|ßer** [-fyːsɐ] **M -s, -** *(Zool)* quadruped, tetrapod *(spec)*; **vier|fü|ßig ADJ** four-legged, quadruped(al) *(spec)*; *(Poet)* tetrameter *attr*, with four feet; **Vier|füß|ler** [-fyːslɐ] **M -s, -** *(Zool)* quadruped, tetrapod *(spec)*; **Vier|gang|ge|trie|be NT** four-speed gearbox; **vier|ge|schos|sig**, *(Aus, S Ger)* **vier|ge|scho|ßig ADJ, ADV** four-storey *attr (Brit)*, four-story *attr (US)*, four-storeyed *(Brit)*, four-storied *(US)*; **~ bauen** to build houses with four storeys *(Brit)* *or* stories *(US)*; **Vier|ge|spann NT** *(= vier Tiere, Wagen mit vier Tieren)* four-in-hand; *(Hist: = Quadriga)* quadriga; *(= vier Menschen)* foursome; **vier|glied|rig** [-gliːdrɪç] **ADJ** *(Math)* quadrinomial; **vier|hän|dig ADJ** *(Mus)* four-handed **ADV ~ spielen** to play something for four hands; **vier|he|big ADJ** *(Poet)* tetrameter; **~ sein** to be a tetrameter

vier|hun|dert [ˈfiːɐˈhʊndɐt] **NUM** four hundred

Vier|hun|dert|jahr|fei|er F quatercentenary *(Brit)*, quadricentennial *(US)*

vier|hun|derts|te(r, s) [ˈfiːɐˈhʊndɐtstə] **ADJ** four hundredth

vier|hun|dert|tau|send NUM four hundred thousand

Vier-: **Vier|jah|res|plan M** *(Econ)* four-year plan; **vier|jäh|rig, 4-jäh|rig ADJ** *(= 4 Jahre alt)* four-year-old *attr*; *(= 4 Jahre dauernd)* four-year *attr*, quadrennial; **ein ~es Kind** a four-year-old child, a child of four; **Vier|jäh|ri|ge(r)** [-jɛːrɪgə] **MF** *decl as adj* four-year-old; **Vier|kampf M** *(Sport)* four-part competition; **vier|kant** [-kant] **ADJ, ADV** *(Naut)* square; **Vier|kant** [-kant] **M OR NT -(e)s, -e** *(Tech)* square; *(Math)* tetrahedron; **Vier|kant|ei|sen NT** square steel bar; **Vier|kant|holz NT** squared timber; **vier|kan|tig ADJ** square(-headed) → **achtkantig**; **Vier|kant|schlüs|sel M** square box spanner *(Brit)* *or* wrench *(US)*; **vier|köp|fig ADJ** *Ungeheuer* four-headed; **eine ~e Familie** a family of four

Vier|ling [ˈfiːɐlɪŋ] **M -s, -e** quadruplet, quad *(inf)*

Vier|mäch|te|ab|kom|men NT *(esp Hist: über Berlin)* quadripartite *or* four-power agreement

vier|mal [ˈfiːɐmaːl] **ADV** four times; **~ so viele** four times as many

vier|ma|lig [ˈfiːɐmaːlɪç] **ADJ** done *or* repeated four times; *Weltmeister, Olympiasieger etc* four-times *attr*; **~es Klingeln** four rings; **~e Vorstellungen** four performances; **nach ~em Versuch** after the fourth attempt; **nach ~er Aufforderung** after the fourth time of asking, after four repeated requests

Vier-: **Vier|mas|ter** [-mastɐ] **M -s, -** *(Naut)* four-master; **vier|mo|na|tig ADJ** *attr Säugling* four-month-old; *Abstände* four-monthly; *Lieferungsfrist, Aufenthalt, Waffenstillstand* four-month; **vier|mo|nat|lich ADJ** *attr Erscheinen* four-monthly **ADV** *erscheinen, sich wiederholen* every four months; **vier|mo|to|rig ADJ** four-engined; **Vier|pfün|der M** four-pounder; **vier|pha|sig ADJ** *(Elec)* four-phase

Vier|rad- *(Aut)*: **Vier|rad|an|trieb M** four-wheel drive; **Vier|rad|brem|se F** four-wheel braking system

Vier-: **vier|rä|de|rig, vier|räd|rig ADJ** four-wheel *attr*, four-wheeled; **das Auto ist ~** that car is a four-wheeler; **vier|sai|tig ADJ** four-stringed; **~ sein** to have four strings; **Vier|schan|zen|tour|nee F** *(Ski)* Four Hills Tournament; **vier|schrö|tig** [-ʃrøːtɪç] **ADJ** burly; **vier|sei|tig** [-zaitɪç] **ADJ** four-sided; *Abkommen, Verhandlungen etc* quadripartite; *Brief, Broschüre* four-page *attr*; **Vier|sil|ber** [-zɪlbɐ] **M -s, -** *(Poet)* tetrasyllable; **vier|sil|big ADJ** four-syllable *attr*, quadrisyllabic, tetrasyllabic; **Vier|sit|zer M** four-seater; **vier|sit|zig** [-zɪtsɪç] **ADJ** four-seater *attr*, with four seats; **~ sein** to be a four-seater, to have four seats; **vier|spal|tig** [-ʃpaltɪç] **ADJ** four-column *attr*; **~ sein** to have four columns **ADV** in four columns; **Vier|spän|ner M** four-in-hand; **vier|spän|nig ADJ** *Wagen* four-horse *attr* **ADV ~ fahren** to drive a team of four horses, to drive a four-in-hand; **vier|spra|chig ADJ** *Mensch, Wörterbuch* quadrilingual; *Speisekarte* in four languages; **das Buch wird ~ angeboten** the book is available in four languages; **vier|spu|rig** [-ʃpuːrɪç] **ADJ** four-lane *attr*; **~ sein** to have four lanes **ADV eine Straße ~ bauen/planen** to build/plan a four-lane road; **etw vielspurig ausbauen** to expand sth to four lanes; **vier|stel|lig ADJ** four-figure *attr*; *(Math) Funktion, Dezimalbruch* four-place *attr*; **~ sein** to have four figures/places; **Rechnungen in ~er Höhe** four-figure bills; **Vier|ster|ne|ho|tel NT** 4-star hotel; **vier|stim|mig ADJ** four-part *attr*, for four voices **ADV ~ singen** to sing a song for four voices; **vier|stö|ckig ADJ** *Haus* four-storey *attr (Brit)*, four-story *attr (US)*, four-storeyed *(Brit)*, four-storied *(US)*, four storeys *(Brit)* *or* stories *(US)* high **ADV ~ bauen** to build houses with four storeys *(Brit)* *or* stories *(US)*; **vier|strah|lig ADJ** *Flugzeug* four-jet *attr*, four-engined; **vier|stro|phig ADJ** *Gedicht* four-verse *attr*, four-stanza *attr*; **~ sein** to have four verses *or* stanzas; **Vier|stu|fen|ra|ke|te F** four-stage rocket; **vier|stu|fig ADJ** four-stage *attr*; **~ sein** to have four stages; **vier|stün|dig ADJ** *attr Reise, Vortrag* four-hour; **vier|stünd|lich ADJ** *attr* four-hourly **ADV** every four hours

viert [fiːɐt] **ADJ a zu ~** → **vier b** → **vierte(r, s)**

Vier-: **Vier|ta|ge|wo|che F** four-day week; **vier|tä|gig ADJ** *attr (= 4 Tage dauernd)* four-day; *(= 4 Tage alt)* four-day-old; **vier|täg|lich ADJ, ADV** every four days; **Vier|tak|ter** [-taktɐ] **M -s, -** *(inf)*, **Vier|takt|mo|tor M** four-stroke (engine); **vier|tau|send** [ˈfiːɐˈtauznt] **NUM** four thousand; **Vier|tau|sen|der** [ˈfiːɐˈtauzndɐ] **M -s, -** *(Berg)* four-thousand-metre *(Brit)* *or* four-thousand-meter *(US)* mountain

vier|te ADJ → **vierte(r, s)**

vier-: **vier|tei|len** [ˈfiːɐtailən] **VT a** *insep (Hist)* to quarter **b** *sep* = **vierteln**; **vier|tei|lig ADJ** *(= mit vier einzelnen Teilen)* four-piece *attr*; *Roman, Fernsehserie* four-part *attr*, in four parts; **~ sein** to have four pieces/parts; **ich habe dieses Service nur ~** I only have four settings of this dinner service

vier|tel [ˈfɪrtl] **ADJ** *inv* quarter; **ein ~ Liter/Pfund** a quarter (of a) litre *(Brit)* *or* liter *(US)*/pound; **drei ~ Liter** three quarters of a litre *(Brit)* *or* liter *(US)*; **drei ~ voll** three-quarters full → *auch* **Viertel**

Vier|tel [ˈfɪrtl] **NT (SW AUCH M) -s, - a** *(Bruchteil)* quarter; *(inf) (= Viertelpfund)* ≈ quarter; *(= Viertelliter)* quarter litre *(Brit)* *or* liter *(US)*; **drei ~ der Bevölkerung** three quarters of the population; **der Mond ist im ersten/letzten ~** the moon is in the first/last quarter; **ein ~ Wein** a quarter litre *(Brit)* *or* liter *(US)* of wine; **ein ~ Butter** a quarter of butter

b *(Uhrzeit)* **(ein) ~ nach/vor sechs** (a) quarter past/to six; **(ein) ~ sechs** (a) quarter past five; **drei viertel sechs** *(dial)* (a) quarter to six; **um viertel/drei viertel sechs** *(dial)* at (a) quarter past five/(a) quarter to six; **fünf Minuten vor ~/drei ~** ten past/twenty to; **es ist ~** it's (a) quarter past; **die Uhr schlug ~** the clock struck (a) quarter past *or* the quarter → **akademisch**

Vier|tel [ˈfɪrtl] **NT -s, -** *(= Stadtbezirk)* quarter, district

Vier|tel-: **Vier|tel|dre|hung F** quarter turn; **Vier|tel|fi|na|le NT** quarterfinals *pl*; **Vier|tel|fi|nal|spiel NT** quarterfinal

Vier|tel|jahr NT three months *pl*, quarter *(Comm, Fin)*

Vier|tel|jah|res- *in cpds* quarterly; **Vier|tel|jah|res|er|geb|nis NT** *(Comm)* quarterly results *pl*; **Vier|tel|jah|res|schrift F** quarterly

Vier|tel-: **Vier|tel|jahr|hun|dert NT** quarter of a century; **vier|tel|jäh|rig ADJ** *attr Kind etc* three-month-old; *Aufenthalt, Frist* three months'; **vier|tel|jähr|lich ADJ** quarterly; *Kündigungsfrist* three months' *attr* **ADV** quarterly, every three months; **~ kündigen** to give three months' notice; **Vier|tel|kreis M** quadrant; **Vier|tel|li|ter M OR NT** quarter of a litre *(Brit)* *or* liter *(US)*, quarter litre *(Brit)* *or* liter *(US)*

vier|teln [ˈfɪrtln] **VT** *(= in vier Teile teilen)* to divide into four; *Kuchen, Apfel etc auch* to divide into quarters; *(= durch vier teilen)* to divide by four; *Summe, Gewinn* to quarter, to divide by four

Vier|tel-: **Vier|tel|no|te** F crotchet *(Brit)*, quarter note *(US)*; **Vier|tel|pau|se** F crotchet rest *(Brit)*, quarter-note rest *(US)*; **Vier|tel|pfund** NT ≈ quarter of a pound, ≈ quarter (pound); **Vier|tel|stun|de** F quarter of an hour; **vier|tel|stün|dig** ADJ *attr Abstand* quarter-hour, of a quarter of an hour; *Vortrag* lasting *or* of a quarter of an hour; **vier|tel|stünd|lich** ADJ *attr Abstand* quarter-hour, of a quarter of an hour ADV every quarter of an hour, quarter-hourly; **Vier|tel|ton** M *pl* **-töne** quarter tone

vier|tens ['fi:ɐtns] ADV fourth(ly), in the fourth place

Vier|te(r) ['fi:ɐtə] MF *decl as adj* fourth; **~r werden** to be *or* come fourth; **am ~n (des Monats)** on the fourth (of the month); **Karl IV.** *or* **der ~** Charles IV *or* the Fourth; **er war ~r im Rennen** he was *or* came fourth in the race; **als ~r durchs Ziel gehen** to be fourth at the finish; **du bist der ~, der mich das fragt** you're the fourth person to ask me that; **jeder ~ muss ...** every fourth person/boy *etc* has to ...

vier|te(r, s) ['fi:ɐtə] ADJ fourth; **der ~ Oktober** the fourth of October; **den 4. Oktober** October 4th, October the fourth; **am ~n Oktober** on the fourth of October; **der ~ Stock** the fourth *(Brit) or* fifth *(US)* floor; **der ~ Stand** the Fourth Estate; **im ~n Kapitel/Akt** in the fourth chapter/act, in chapter/act four → *auch* **Vierte(r)**

viert|letz|te(r, s) ['fi:ɐt'lɛtstə] ADJ fourth (from) last

Vier-: **Vier|ton|ner** [-tɔnɐ] M **-s, -** ≈ four-ton truck, four-tonner; **Vier|tü|rer** [-ty:rɐ] M **-s, -** *(Aut)* four-door model; **vier|tü|rig** ADJ four-door *attr*, with four doors; **~ sein** to have four doors; **Vier|uhr|zug** M, **4-Uhr-Zug** M four o'clock (train); **vier|und|ein|halb** NUM four and a half; **Vier|und|sech|zigs|tel|no|te** F hemidemisemiquaver *(Brit)*, sixty-fourth note *(US)*; **Vier|und|sech|zigs|tel|pau|se** F hemidemisemiquaver rest *(Brit)*, sixty-fourth note rest *(US)*; **vier|und|zwan|zig** NUM twenty-four

Vie|rung ['fi:rʊŋ] F **-, -en** *(Archit)* crossing

Vie|rungs-: **Vie|rungs|kup|pel** F *(Archit)* crossing cupola; **Vie|rungs|turm** M *(Archit)* crossing tower

Vier|vier|tel|takt [-'fɪrtl-] M four-four *or* common time

Vier|wald|stät|ter See [fi:ɐ'valtʃtɛtɐ] M Lake Lucerne

vier-: **vier|wer|tig** ADJ *(Chem)* quadrivalent, tetravalent; *(Ling)* four-place; **vier|wö|chent|lich** ADJ *adv* every four weeks; **vier|wö|chig** [-vœçɪç] ADJ four-week *attr*, four weeks long

vier|zehn ['fɪrtse:n] NUM fourteen; **~ Uhr** 2 pm; *(auf Fahrplan, Mil)* fourteen hundred hours, 1400; **~ Tage** two weeks, a fortnight *sing (Brit)*; **die Vierzehn Punkte** *(Hist)* the Fourteen Points

Vier|zehn-: **Vier|zehn|en|der** M *(Hunt)* fourteen-pointer; **vier|zehn|tä|gig** ADJ two-week *attr*, lasting a fortnight *(Brit) or* two weeks; **nach ~er Dauer** after two weeks, after a fortnight *(Brit)*; **vier|zehn|täg|lich** ADJ, ADV fortnightly *(Brit)*, every two weeks

vier|zehn|te(r, s) ['fɪrtse:ntə] ADJ fourteenth → **vierte(r, s), Vierte(r)**

Vier-: **Vier|zei|ler** [-tsailɐ] M **-s, -** four-line poem; *(= Strophe)* four-line stanza, quatrain; **vier|zei|lig** ADJ four-line *attr*, of four lines; **~ sein** to have four lines

vier|zig ['fɪrtsɪç] NUM forty; **(mit) ~ (km/h) fahren** to drive at forty kilometres *(Brit) or* kilometers *(US)* an hour; **etwa ~ (Jahre alt)** about forty (years old); *(Mensch auch)* fortyish *(inf)*; **mit ~ (Jahren)** at forty (years of age); **Mitte ~** in one's mid-forties; **über ~** over forty; **der Mensch über ~** people *pl* over forty; **im Jahre ~** in forty; *(= vierzig nach/vor Christi Geburt)* in (the year) forty (AD)/BC

Vier|zig ['fɪrtsɪç] F **-, -en** forty

vier|zi|ger, 40er ['fɪrtsɪgɐ] ADJ *attr inv* **die ~ Jahre** the forties; **ein ~ Jahrgang** *(Mensch)* a person born in nineteen forty; *(Wein)* a vintage forty

Vier|zi|ger ['fɪrtsɪgɐ] M **-s, -** **a** *(Wein)* wine of vintage forty **b** *(Aus, S Ger: Geburtstag)* fortieth (birthday) **c** **die ~** *pl (= Vierzigerjahre)* one's forties; **er ist in den ~n** he is in his forties; **er ist Mitte der ~** he is in his mid-forties; **in die ~ kommen** to be getting on for forty

Vier|zi|ger ['fɪrtsɪgɐ] M **-s, -**, **Vier|zi|ge|rin** [-ərɪn] F **-, -nen** forty-year-old; **die ~** *pl* people in their forties

Vier|zi|ger|jah|re PL **die ~** one's forties

Vier|zig-: **vier|zig|fach** ['fɪrtsɪçfax] ADJ forty-fold ADV forty times → **vierfach**; **vier|zig|jäh|rig** ['fɪrtsɪç-] ADJ *attr (= 40 Jahre alt)* forty-year-old; *(= 40 Jahre dauernd)* forty-year; **das ~e Jubiläum** the 40th anniversary; **ein Vierzigjähriger** a forty-year-old; **vier|zig|mal** ['fɪrtsɪçma:l] ADV forty times

vier|zigs|tel ['fɪrtsɪçstl] ADJ *inv* fortieth; **eine ~ Minute** a *or* one fortieth of a minute

Vier|zigs|tel ['fɪrtsɪçstl] NT **-s, -** fortieth; **ein ~ des Kuchens/der Summe** a fortieth (part) of the cake/the amount

vier|zigs|te(r, s) ['fɪrtsɪçstə] ADJ fortieth

Vier|zig|stun|den|wo|che F forty-hour week

Vier-: **Vier|zim|mer|woh|nung** F four-room *or* three-bedroom(ed) flat *(Brit) or* apartment; **Vier|zy|lin|der|mo|tor** M four-cylinder engine; **vier|zy|lind|rig** ADJ four-cylinder *attr*

Vi|et|cong [viet'kɔŋ] M **-, -(s)**, **Vi|et|kong** [viet-'kɔŋ] M **-, -(s)** Vietcong

Vi|et|nam [viet'nam] NT **-s** Vietnam

Vi|et|na|me|se [vietna'me:zə] M **-n, -n**, **Vi|et|na|me|sin** [-'me:zɪn] F **-, -nen** Vietnamese; **zum ~n gehen** to go to a *or* the Vietnamese restaurant

vi|et|na|me|sisch [vietna'me:zɪʃ] ADJ Vietnamese

Vi|et|na|me|sisch(e) NT *(Ling)* Vietnamese → *auch* **Deutsch(e)**

vif [vi:f] ADJ *(old, dial)* bright

Vi|gil [vi'gi:l] F **-, -ien** [-liən] vigil

Vig|net|te [vɪn'jɛtə] F **-, -n** vignette; *(Aut)* permit *(for motorway driving)*

> **VIGNETTE**
>
> A **Vignette** is a car windscreen sticker which must be purchased for use on motorways in Austria and Switzerland. The aim is to cover the cost of maintaining motorways worn out by the high volume of through traffic. In Switzerland a **Vignette** is valid for one year. In Austria, where it is also jocularly known as a **Pickerl**, one can buy a **Vignette** that is valid for one week or two months. On certain motorways in Austria, a toll, the **Maut**, is also payable.

Vi|kar [vi'ka:ɐ] M **-s, -e**, **Vi|ka|rin** [-'ka:rɪn] F **-, -nen** curate; *(Sw Sch)* supply teacher *(Brit)*, substitute teacher *(US)*

Vi|ka|ri|at [vika'ria:t] NT **-(e)s, -e** curacy

vik|to|ri|a|nisch [vɪkto'ria:nɪʃ] ADJ Victorian; **das ~e Zeitalter** the Victorian Age

Vik|tu|a|li|en [vɪk'tua:liən] PL *(obs)* victuals *pl (old, form)*

Vik|tu|a|li|en|markt M food market

Vil|la ['vɪla] F **-, Vil|len** [-lən] villa

Vil|len|vier|tel NT exclusive residential area

Vi|naig|ret|te [vinɛ'grɛtə] F **-, -n** *(Cook)* vinaigrette (sauce); *(= Salatdressing auch)* vinaigrette dressing

vin|ku|lie|ren [vɪŋku'li:rən] *ptp* **vinkuliert** VT *(Fin)* to restrict transferability of

Vi|nyl [vi'ny:l] NT **-s**, *no pl (Chem)* vinyl

Vi|o|la ['vi:ola] F **-, Vi|o|len** ['vio:lən] **a** *(Mus)* viola **b** *(Bot)* violet

Vi|o|la da Gam|ba ['vio:la da 'gamba] F **- - -, Vi|o|le - -** ['vio:lə] viola da gamba

Vi|o|le ['vio:lə] F **-, -n** F *(Bot)* violet

vi|o|lett [vio'lɛt] ADJ purple, violet; *(im Spektrum, Regenbogen)* violet

Vi|o|lett [vio'lɛt] NT **-s, -** purple, violet; *(im Spektrum, Regenbogen)* violet

Vi|o|li|ne [vio'li:nə] F **-, -n** violin; **die erste/zweite ~ spielen** to play first/second violin

Vi|o|li|nist [violi'nɪst] M **-en, -en**, **Vi|o|li|nis|tin** [-'nɪstɪn] F **-, -nen** violinist

Vi|o|lin-: **Vi|o|lin|kon|zert** NT violin concerto; *(Darbietung)* violin concert; **Vi|o|lin|schlüs|sel** M treble clef

Vi|o|lon|cell [violɔn'tʃɛl] NT **-s, -e**, **Vi|o|lon|cel|lo** [violɔn'tʃɛlo] NT violoncello

VIP [vɪp] M **-, -s** *(inf)*, **V. I. P.** [vi:lai'pi:] M **-, -s** *(inf) abbr von* **Very Important Person** VIP

Vi|per ['vi:pɐ] F **-, -n** viper, adder

Vi|ren *pl von* **Virus**

Vi|ren|such|pro|gramm NT *(Comput)* virus checker *(Brit) or* scanner

vi|ren|ver|seucht ADJ *(Comput)* infected *or* contaminated with a virus, corrupted by a virus

Vir|gel ['vɪrgl] F **-, -n** *(Typ)* virgule *(spec)*, slash

Vir|gi|nia|ta|bak [vɪr'gi:nia-, vɪr'dʒi:nia-] M Virginia tobacco

vi|ril [vi'ri:l] ADJ virile

Vi|ri|li|tät [virili'tɛ:t] F **-**, *no pl* virility

Vi|ro|lo|ge [viro'lo:gə] M **-n, -n**, **Vi|ro|lo|gin** [-'lo:gɪn] F **-, -nen** virologist

Vi|ro|lo|gie [virolo'gi:] F **-**, *no pl* virology

vi|ro|lo|gisch [viro'lo:gɪʃ] ADJ virological

vir|tu|ell [vɪr'tuɛl] ADJ *Realität etc* virtual; **~er Arbeitsspeicher** virtual memory; **~er Einkaufskorb** virtual shopping basket ADV in virtual reality

vir|tu|os [vɪr'tuo:s] ADJ virtuoso *attr* ADV *beherrschen* expertly, like a virtuoso; **~ spielen** to give a virtuoso performance, to play like a virtuoso

Vir|tu|o|se [vɪr'tuo:zə] M **-n, -n**, **Vir|tu|o|sin** [-'tuo:zɪn] F **-, -nen** virtuoso

Vir|tu|o|si|tät [vɪrtuozi'tɛ:t] F **-**, *no pl* virtuosity

vi|ru|lent [viru'lɛnt] ADJ *(Med, fig)* virulent

Vi|ru|lenz [viru'lɛnts] F **-, -en** *(Med, fig)* virulence, virulency

Vi|rus ['vi:rʊs] NT OR M **-, Vi|ren** [-rən] *(auch Comput)* virus

Vi|rus-: **Vi|rus|er|ken|nung** F *(Comput)* virus detection; **Vi|rus|er|kran|kung** F viral *or* virus disease; **Vi|rus|in|fek|ti|on** F viral *or* virus infection; **Vi|rus|krank|heit** F viral disease; **Vi|rus|pro|gramm** NT *(Comput)* virus (program)

Vi|sa *pl von* **Visum**

Vi|sa|ge [vi'za:ʒə] F **-, -n** *(inf)* face

Vi|sa|ge|bühr F visa fee *or* charge

Vi|sa|gist [viza:'ʒɪst] M **-en, -en**, **Vi|sa|gis|tin** [-'ʒɪstɪn] F **-, -nen** make-up artist

Vi|sa|vis [viza'vi:] NT **-, -** *(dated)* person (sitting) opposite, vis-à-vis *(form)*; **mein ~** the person opposite me

vis-à-vis [viza'vi:], **vis-a-vis** *(dated)* ADV opposite (*von* to) PREP *+dat* opposite (to)

Vi|sen *pl von* **Visum**

Vi|sier [vi'zi:ɐ] NT **-s, -e** **a** *(am Helm)* visor; **mit offenem ~ kämpfen** to fight with an open visor; *(fig)* to be open and above board (in one's dealings) **b** *(an Gewehren)* sight; **jdn/etw ins ~ bekommen** to get sb/sth in one's sights; **jdn/etw ins ~ nehmen** *or* **fassen** to train one's sights on sb/sth; **jdn/etw im ~ haben** *(fig)* to have sb/sth in one's sights; **in jds ~ geraten** *(fig)* to become a target for sb

vi|sie|ren [vi'zi:rən] *ptp* **visiert** VI **~ auf** *(+acc)* to take aim at

Vi|si|on [vi'zio:n] F **-, -en** vision

vi|si|o|när [vizio'nɛ:ɐ] ADJ visionary

Vi|si|o|när [vizio'nɛ:ɐ] M **-s, -e**, **Vi|si|o|nä|rin** [-'nɛ:rɪn] F **-, -nen** visionary

Vi|si|ta|ti|on [vizita'tsio:n] F **-, -en** *(form)* **a** *(= Besuch)* visitation *(auch Eccl)*, inspection **b** *(= Durchsuchung)* search, inspection

Vi|si|te [vi'zi:tə] F -, -n **a** *(Med) (im Krankenhaus)* round; *(zu Hause)* visit, house call; **um 9 Uhr ist ~** the doctors do their rounds at 9 o'clock; **~ machen** to do one's round/to do visits *or* house calls; *(dated inf)* to visit *(bei jdm* sb), to pay a visit *(bei* to); **zur ~ kommen** to come on one's round/on a visit *or* house call **b** *(= Staatsbesuch)* visit

Vi|si|ten|kar|te [vi'zi:tn-] F *(lit, fig)* visiting *or* calling *(US)* card

vi|si|tie|ren [vizi'ti:rən] *ptp* **visitiert** VT **a** *(form) Amtsbezirk etc* to visit, to inspect **b** *(old) Gepäck* to search, to inspect

Vi|sit|kar|te [vi'zi:t-] F *(Aus)* visiting or calling *(US)* card

vis|kos [vɪs'ko:s], **vis|kös** [vɪs'kø:s] ADJ viscous

Vis|ko|se [vɪs'ko:zə] F -, *no pl* viscose

Vis|ko|si|tät [vɪskozi'tɛ:t] F -, *no pl* viscosity

vi|su|ell [vi'zuɛl] ADJ visual

Vi|sum ['vi:zʊm] NT -s, **Vi|sa** *or* **Vi|sen** [-za, -zn] visa

Vi|sum(s)-: **Vi|sum(s)|an|trag** M visa application; **Vi|sum(s)|pflicht** F visa requirement

Vi|sum|zwang M obligation to hold a visa; **für San Lucia besteht ~** it is necessary to obtain a visa for San Lucia

Vi|ta ['vi:ta] F -, **Vi|ten** *or* **Vi|tae** [-tn, -tɛ:] *(geh)* life

vi|tal [vi'ta:l] ADJ vigorous, energetic; *(= lebenswichtig)* vital

Vi|ta|li|tät [vitali'tɛ:t] F -, *no pl* vitality, vigour *(Brit)*, vigor *(US)*

Vi|ta|min [vita'mi:n] NT -s, -e vitamin; **~ B** *(lit)* vitamin B; *(fig inf)* contacts *pl*

Vi|ta|min-: **vi|ta|min|arm** ADJ poor in vitamins; **eine ~e Zeit** a time when there are/were few vitamins available ADV **~ leben/essen** to live on/have a vitamin-deficient diet; **Vi|ta|min|be|darf** M vitamin requirement; **Vi|ta|min-C-hal|tig** [-'tse:-] ADJ containing vitamin C; **~ sein** to contain vitamin C; **Vi|ta|min|ge|halt** M vitamin content; **vi|ta|min|hal|tig**, *(Aus)* **vi|ta|min|häl|tig** ADJ containing vitamins; **~ sein** to contain vitamins

vi|ta|mi|nie|ren [vitami'ni:rən] *ptp* **vitaminiert** VT to add vitamins to**Vi|ta|min-**: **Vi|ta|min|man|gel** M vitamin deficiency; **Vi|ta|min|man|gel|krank|heit** F disease due to a vitamin deficiency; **vi|ta|min|reich** ADJ rich in vitamins; **Vi|ta|min|sprit|ze** F vitamin injection; *(fig)* shot in the arm *(fig inf)*; **Vi|ta|min|stoß** M (massive) dose of vitamins; **Vi|ta|min|ta|blet|te** F vitamin pill *or* tablet

Vit|ri|ne [vi'tri:nə] F -, -n *(= Schrank)* glass cabinet; *(= Schaukasten)* showcase, display case

Vit|ri|ol [vitri'o:l] NT -s, -e vitriol

Vi|va|ri|um [vi'va:riʊm] NT -s, **Vivarien** [-riən] vivarium

vi|vat ['vi:vat] INTERJ *(geh)* vivat *(form)*

Vi|vi|sek|ti|on [vivizɛk'tsio:n] F vivisection

vi|vi|se|zie|ren [vivize'tsi:rən] *ptp* **viviseziert** VTI to vivisect

Vi|ze ['fi:tsə] M -s, - *(inf)* number two *(inf)*, second-in-command; *(= Vizemeister)* runner-up

Vi|ze- *in cpds* vice-; **Vi|ze|kanz|ler(in)** M(F) vice chancellor; **Vi|ze|kö|nig** M viceroy; **Vi|ze|meis|ter(in)** M(F) runner-up; **Vi|ze|meis|ter|schaft** F second place; **die ~ gewinnen** to come second in the championship, to finish as runners-up; **Vi|ze|prä|si|dent(in)** M(F) vice president; **Vi|ze|rek|tor(in)** M(F) *(von Schule)* deputy headmaster/-mistress, vice principal *(esp US)*; *(von Universität)* deputy vice chancellor *or* rector *(US)*

Vlies [fli:s] NT -es, -e [-zə] fleece

Vlie|se|li|ne® [flizə'li:nə] F -, *no pl* interfacing

VL *abbr von* **vermögenswirksame Leistung(en)**

Vlies|ja|cke F fleece (jacket)

VLS *abbr von* **Verkehrsleitsystem** TMS

V-Mann ['fau-] M *pl* **-Männer** *or* **-Leute** *abbr von* **Verbindungsmann**

VN [fau'lɛn] PL *abbr von* **Vereinte Nationen** UN *sing*

Vo|gel ['fo:gl] M -s, ⸚ ['fø:gl] *(lit, fig)* bird; **ein seltener ~** *(lit, fig)* a rare bird; **ein seltsamer ~** *(inf)* a strange bird *(inf) or* customer *(inf)*; **ein lustiger ~** *(inf)* a lively character *(inf)*; **~ friss oder stirb** *(prov)* do or die! *(prov)*; **den ~ abschießen** *(inf)* to surpass everyone *(iro)*; **einen ~ haben** *(inf)* to be crazy *(inf)*, to have a screw loose *(inf)*; **jdm den ~ zeigen** *(inf)* to tap one's forehead *(to indicate to sb that he's not quite right in the head)* → **ausfliegen**

Vo|gel-: **Vo|gel|art** F type *or* species of bird, bird species; **Vo|gel|bau|er** NT *pl* **-bauer** birdcage; **Vo|gel|bee|re** F *(auch* **Vogelbeerbaum)** rowan (tree), mountain ash; *(= Frucht)* rowan(berry)

Vö|gel|chen ['fø:glçən] NT -s, - little bird; **gleich kommts ~ raus** *(inf)* watch the birdie *(inf)*

Vo|gel-: **Vo|gel|dreck** M bird droppings *pl*; **Vo|gel|ei** ['fo:glai] NT bird's egg; **~er** *(verschiedene Arten)* birds' eggs *pl*

Vö|ge|lei [fø:gə'lai] F -, -en *(inf)* screwing *(sl)*

Vö|ge|lein ['fø:gəlain] NT -s, - *(liter)* little bird

Vo|gel-: **Vo|gel|fän|ger(in)** M(F) bird-catcher, fowler; **Vo|gel|flug** M flight of birds; **Vo|gel|flug|li|nie** F **in der ~** as the crow flies; **vo|gel|frei** ADJ *(Hist)* outlawed; **für ~ erklärt werden** to be outlawed, to be declared an outlaw/outlaws; **Vo|gel|fut|ter** NT bird food; *(= Samen)* birdseed; **Vo|gel|grip|pe** F bird flu, avian influenza *or* flu; **Vo|gel|haus** NT *(im Zoo)* aviary; **Vo|gel|häus|chen** [-hɔysçən] NT *(= Futterhäuschen)* birdhouse; **Vo|gel|kä|fig** M birdcage; **Vo|gel|kun|de** F ornithology; **Vo|gel|männ|chen** NT cock (bird), male bird

vö|geln ['fø:gln] VTI *(inf)* to screw *(sl)*

Vo|gel-: **Vo|gel|nest** NT bird's nest; **Vo|gel|per|spek|ti|ve** F, **Vo|gel|schau** F bird's-eye view; **(ein Bild von) Ulan Bator aus der ~** a bird's-eye view of Ulan Bator; **Vo|gel|scheu|che** [-ʃɔyçə] F -, -n *(lit, fig inf)* scarecrow; **Vo|gel|schutz** M protection of birds; **Vo|gel|schwarm** M flock of birds; **Vo|gel|spin|ne** F *(Zool)* bird-eating spider; **Vo|gel|stim|me** F birdcall; **Vo|gel-Strauß-Po|li|tik** F head-in-the-sand *or* ostrich-like policy; **~ treiben** to bury one's head in the sand; **Vo|gel|trän|ke** F birdbath; **Vo|gel|war|te** F ornithological station; **Vo|gel|weib|chen** NT hen (bird), female bird; **Vo|gel|zug** M *(Wanderung)* bird migration

Vo|gerl|sa|lat ['fo:gel-] M *(Aus)* corn salad, lamb's lettuce

Vo|ge|sen [vo'ge:zn] PL Vosges *pl*

Vög|lein ['fø:glain] NT -s, - *(liter)* little bird

Vogt [fo:kt] M -(e)s, ⸚e ['fø:ktə] *(Hist) (= Kirchenvogt)* church advocate; *(= Reichsvogt)* protector; *(= Landvogt)* landvogt, governor; *(von Burg, Gut)* steward, bailiff

Vog|tei [fo:k'tai] F -, -en → **Vogt** office of church advocate; protectorate; governorship; *(= Gebiet)* area administered by a/the church advocate; protectorate; province; *(= Residenz)* church advocate's/protector's/landvogt's *or* governor's residence

Voice|mail ['vɔisme:l] F - *(Telec)* voice mail

Voice|re|cor|der ['vɔisrekɔrdɐ] M -s, - = **Voicerekorder**

Voice|re|kor|der ['vɔisrekɔrdɐ] M -s, - *(Aviat)* (cockpit) voice recorder

Vo|ka|bel [vo'ka:bl] F -, -n *or (Aus) nt* -s, - word; **~n** *pl* vocabulary *sing*, vocab *sing (Sch inf)*

Vo|ka|bel-: **Vo|ka|bel|heft** NT vocabulary book; **Vo|ka|bel|schatz** M vocabulary

Vo|ka|bu|lar [vokabu'la:ɐ] NT -s, -e vocabulary

vo|kal [vo'ka:l] *(Mus)* ADJ vocal ADV vocally

Vo|kal [vo'ka:l] M -s, -e vowel

Vo|ka|li|sa|ti|on [vokaliza'tsio:n] F -, -en vocalization

vo|ka|lisch [vo'ka:lɪʃ] ADJ *(Ling)* vocalic; **~e Anlaute/Auslaute** initial/final vowels

Vo|ka|lis|mus [voka'lɪsmʊs] M -, *no pl (Ling)* vocalism

Vo|ka|list [voka'lɪst] M -en, -en, **Vo|ka|lis|tin** [-'lɪstɪn] F -, -nen *(Mus, geh)* vocalist

Vo|kal|mu|sik F vocal music

Vo|ka|tiv ['vo:kati:f, voka'ti:f] M -s, -e [-və] vocative

vol. *abbr von* **Volumen**

Vol.-% *abbr von* **Volumprozent**

Vo|lant [vo'lã:] M -s, -s **a** *(= Stoffbesatz)* valance; *(am Rock, Kleid)* flounce **b** AUCH NT *(Aus, Sw old: = Lenkrad)* steering wheel

Vo|li|e|re [vo'lie:rə, -'liɛ:rə] F -, -n aviary

Volk [fɔlk] NT -(e)s, ⸚er ['fœlkɐ] **a** *no pl* people *pl*; *(= Nation)* nation; *(= Volksmasse)* masses *pl*, people *pl*; *(inf: = Gruppe)* crowd *pl*; *(pej: = Pack)* rabble *pl*; **alles ~** everybody; **viel ~** lots of people *pl*, crowds *pl*; **etw unters ~ bringen** *(Nachricht)* to spread sth; *Geld* to spend sth; **die sind ein lustiges ~** *(inf)* they are a lively lot *(Brit inf) or* bunch *(inf) or* crowd; **da verkehrt ein ~!** there's a really strange crowd there! → **Mann a, fahrend b** *(= ethnische Gemeinschaft)* people *sing*; **die Völker Afrikas** the peoples of Africa; **ein ~ für sich sein** to be a race apart **c** *(Zool)* colony

Völk|chen ['fœlkçən] NT -s, - **a** *(= kleine Nation)* small nation **b** *(inf: = Gruppe)* lot *(inf)*, crowd; **ein ~ für sich sein** to be a race apart

Völ|ker-: **Völ|ker|ball** M *game for two teams where the object is to hit an opponent with a ball and thus put him out of the game*, ≈ dodgeball *(Brit)*, ≈ warball *(US)*; **Völ|ker|bund** M, *no pl (Hist)* League of Nations; **Völ|ker|freund|schaft** F friendship among nations; **Völ|ker|ge|mein|schaft** F international community, community of nations; **Völ|ker|kun|de** F ethnology; **Völ|ker|kun|de|mu|se|um** NT museum of ethnology; **Völ|ker|kund|ler** [-kʊntlɐ] M -s, -, **Völ|ker|kund|le|rin** [-ərɪn] F -, -nen ethnologist; **völ|ker|kund|lich** [-kʊntlɪç] ADJ ethnological; **Völ|ker|mord** M genocide; **Völ|ker|recht** NT international law, law of nations; **völ|ker|recht|lich** ADJ *Vertrag, Entscheidung, Anerkennung, Status, Verpflichtungen* under international law; *Frage, Thema, Hinsicht, Standpunkt* of international law; *Anspruch, Haftung* international; **vom ~en Standpunkt** according to *or* under international law; **~e Anerkennung eines Staates** recognition of a state ADV *regeln, entscheiden* by international law; *klären* according to international law; *bindend sein* under international law; **Völ|ker|schlacht** F *(Hist)* Battle of the Nations; **Völ|ker|ver|stän|di|gung** F international understanding; **Völ|ker|wan|de|rung** F *(Hist)* migration of the peoples; *(hum)* mass migration *or* exodus

völ|kisch ['fœlkɪʃ] ADJ *(NS)* national

volk|reich ADJ populous

Volks- *in cpds* popular; *(= auf ein Land bezogen)* national; *(Pol)* people's; **Volks|ab|stim|mung** F plebiscite; **Volks|ar|mee** F *(DDR)* People's Army; **Volks|ar|mist** [-armɪst] M -en, -en, **Volks|ar|mis|tin** [-mɪstɪn] F -, -nen *(DDR)* soldier in the People's Army; **Volks|auf|stand** M national uprising; **Volks|aus|ga|be** F popular edition; **Volks|be|auf|trag|te(r)** MF *decl as adj* people's representative *or* delegate; **Volks|be|fra|gung** F public opinion poll; **Volks|be|frei|ungs|ar|mee** F people's liberation army; **Volks|be|geh|ren** NT petition for a referendum; **Volks|be|lus|ti|gung** F public entertainment; **Volks|be|we|gung** F popular movement; **Volks|bil|dung** F national education; *(= Erwachsenenbildung)* adult education; **Volks|brauch** M national custom; **Volks|bü|che|rei** F public library; **Volks|büh|ne** F people's theatre *(Brit) or* theater *(US)*; **Volks|cha|rak|ter** M national character; **Volks|de|mo|kra|tie** F people's democracy; **Volks|deut|sche(r)** MF *decl as adj* ethnic German; **Volks|dich|ter(in)** M(F) people's poet; **Volks|dich|tung** F folk literature; *(= Gedichte)* folk poetry; **volks|ei|gen** ADJ *(DDR)* nationally-owned; *(in Namen)* People's Own; **Volks|ei|gen|tum** NT *(DDR)* national property, property of the people; **im ~** nationally-owned, owned by the people; **Volks|ein|kom|men** NT national income; **Volks|emp|fin|den** NT public feeling; **das gesunde ~** popular sentiment; **Volks|ent|scheid** M referendum; **Volks|er|he|bung** F popular *or* national uprising; **Volks|ety|mo|lo|gie** F folk etymology; **Volks|feind(in)** M(F) enemy of the people; **volks|feind|lich** ADJ hostile to the people; **Volks|fest** NT public festival; *(= Jahrmarkt)* funfair; **Volks|front** F *(Pol)* popular front; **Volks|ge|nos|se** M, **Volks|ge|nos|sin** F *(NS)* national comrade; **Volks|ge|richts|hof** M *(NS)* People's Court; **Volks|ge|sund|heit** F public health; **Volks|glau|be(n)** M popular belief; **Volks|grup|pe** F ethnic group; *(= Minderheit)* ethnic minority; **Volks|held(in)** M(F) popular hero/heroine; *(= Held des Landes)* national hero/heroine; **Volks|herr|schaft** F popular rule, rule of the people; **Volks|hoch|schu|le** F adult education centre *(Brit)* *or* center *(US)*; **einen Kurs an der ~ machen** to do an adult education class; *(am Abend auch)* to do an evening class

VOLKSHOCHSCHULE

Volkshochschulen, or **VHS** for short, play an important part in German life. They offer evening and morning courses and lectures for all age groups in a wide range of subjects. For example, school students can take courses to catch up in particular subjects, adults can learn languages or crafts and foreigners can improve their knowledge of German. There are also **VHS** courses leading to **zweiter Bildungsweg** qualifications such as the **Abitur**. → ABITUR, ZWEITER BILDUNGWEG, MITTLERE REIFE

Volks-: **Volks|ini|ti|a|ti|ve** F *(Pol) (Ger) petition for a matter to be debated in the state parliament (Sw)* petition for a referendum; **Volks|jus|tiz** F popular justice; **Volks|kam|mer** F *(DDR)* East German Parliament; **Volks|krank|heit** F widespread disease; **Volks|kü|che** F soup kitchen; **Volks|kun|de** F folklore; **Volks|kund|ler** [-kʊntlɐ] M **-s, -**, **Volks|kund|le|rin** [-ərɪn] F **-, -nen** folklorist; **volks|kund|lich** [-kʊntlɪç] ADJ folkloristic; **ein ~es Institut** an institute of folklore; **Volks|lauf** M *(Sport)* open cross-country race; **Volks|lied** NT folk song; **Volks|mär|chen** NT folk tale; **Volks|mei|nung** F public *or* popular opinion; **Volks|men|ge** F crowd, mob *(pej)*; **Volks|mund** M, *no pl* vernacular; **im ~ nennt man das ...** this is popularly called ..., in the vernacular this is called ...; **Volks|mu|sik** F folk music; **volks|nah** ADJ popular, in touch with the people; *(Pol)* grass-roots *attr*; **Volks|nä|he** F **sie ist bekannt für ihre ~** she is renowned for her popular touch; **Volks|par|tei** F people's party; **Volks|po|e|sie** F folk poetry; **Volks|po|li|zei** F *(DDR)* People's Police; **Volks|po|li|zist(in)** M(F) *(DDR)* member of the People's Police; **Volks|re|de** F *(rare: lit)* public speech; *(inf)* (long) speech; **du sollst keine ~ halten!** *(inf)* I/we don't want any speeches!; **Volks|re|pub|lik** F people's republic; **Volks|sa|ge** F folk legend, folk tale; **Volks|schicht** F level of society, social stratum; **Volks|schul|ab|schluss** M *(dated)* elementary school-leaving certificate; **Volks|schu|le** F *(dated)* ≈ elementary school *(Hist), school providing basic primary and secondary education*; **Volks|schü|ler(in)** M(F) *(dated)* ≈ pupil at elementary school *(Hist)*; **Volks|schul|leh|rer(in)** M(F) *(dated)* ≈ elementary school teacher *(Hist)*; **Volks|see|le** F soul of the people; **die kochende ~** the seething *or* angry populace; **Volks|seu|che** F epidemic; **Volks|sou|ve|rä|ni|tät** F *(Pol)* sovereignty of the people; **Volks|sport** M national sport; **Volks|spra|che** F everyday language, vernacular; **Volks|staat** M *(Pol)* people's state; **Volks|stamm** M tribe; **Volks|stim|me** F voice of the people; **Volks|stück** NT dialect folk play; **Volks|sturm** M *(Hist)* Volkssturm, German territorial army; **Volks|tanz** M folk dance; **Volks|the|a|ter** NT folk theatre *(Brit)* *or* theater *(US)*; *(Gattung auch)* folk drama; **Volks|tracht** F traditional costume; *(eines Landes)* national costume; **Volks|trau|er|tag** M national day of mourning, ≈ Remembrance Day *(Brit)*, ≈ Veterans' Day *(US)*; **Volks|tri|bun** M *(Hist)* tribune (of the people); **Volks|tum** ['fɔlkstu:m] NT **-s**, *no pl* national traditions *pl*, folklore; **Volks|tü|me|lei** [fɔlksty:mə'lai] F **-, -en** *(inf)* folksiness *(inf)*; **volks|tüm|lich** ['fɔlksty:mlɪç] ADJ folk *attr*, folksy *(inf)*; *(= traditionell, überliefert)* traditional; *(= beliebt)* popular; **ein ~er König** a king with the common touch ADV **etw ~ darstellen** to popularize sth; **etw ~ ausdrücken** to express oneself in plain language; **Volks|tüm|lich|keit** F **-**, *no pl* folksiness *(inf)*; *(= traditionelle, überlieferte Art)* tradition; *(= Beliebtheit)* popularity; *(von Darstellungs-, Ausdrucksweise)* popular appeal; *(von König)* common touch; **volks|ver|bun|den** ADJ close to the people; **Volks|ver|füh|rer(in)** M(F) demagogue; **Volks|ver|het|zung** F incitement (of the people *or* masses); **Volks|ver|mö|gen** NT national wealth; **Volks|ver|samm|lung** F people's assembly; *(= Kundgebung)* public gathering; **Volks|ver|tre|ter(in)** M(F) representative *or* delegate of the people; **Volks|ver|tre|tung** F representative body (of the people); **Volks|wirt(in)** M(F) economist; **Volks|wirt|schaft** F national economy; *(Fach)* economics *sing*, political economy; **Volks- und Betriebswirtschaft** economics and business studies; **Volks|wirt|schaft|ler(in)** M(F) economist; **volks|wirt|schaft|lich** ADJ *Schaden, Nutzen* economic; **Volks|wirt|schafts|leh|re** F economics *sing*, political economy; **Volks|wohl** NT good *or* welfare of the people, public weal; **Volks|zäh|lung** F (national) census; **Volks|zorn** M public anger; **Volks|zu|ge|hö|rig|keit** F ethnic origin

voll [fɔl] ADJ **a** *(= gefüllt)* full; **~er ...** full of ...; **~ (von** *or* **mit) etw** full of sth; *(= bedeckt mit)* covered with sth; **~ des Lobes** full of praise; **~er Widersprüche sein** to be full of contradictions; **mit ~em Mund** with one's mouth full; **aus dem Vollen leben** to live a life of luxury, to live in the lap of luxury; **aus dem Vollen schöpfen** to draw on unlimited resources
b *(= ganz)* full; *Satz, Service, Erfolg* complete; *Woche, Jahr* full, whole; *Wahrheit* whole; **ein ~es Dutzend** a full *or* whole dozen; **~e drei Jahre/Tage** three whole years/days, fully three years/days; **~e neuneinhalb Stunden schlafen** to sleep a solid nine and a half hours; **die Uhr schlägt nur die ~e Stunde** the clock only strikes the full hour; **mehr Nachrichten zur ~en Stunde** more news at the top of the hour; **die Zahl ist ~** the numbers are complete; **die ~e Summe bezahlen** to pay the full sum, to pay the sum in full; **in ~er Fahrt/~em Galopp/~em Lauf** at full speed/gallop/speed; **in ~er Größe** *(Bild)* life-size; *(bei plötzlicher Erscheinung etc)* large as life; **sich zu ~er Größe aufrichten** to draw oneself up to one's full height; **im ~en Tageslicht** in full daylight; **in ~er Uniform** in full dress *or* uniform; **jdn nicht für ~ nehmen** not to take sb seriously; **aus ~em Halse** *or* **~er Kehle** *or* **Brust singen** to sing at the top of one's voice; **etw mit ~em Recht tun** to be perfectly right to do sth; **mit dem ~en Namen unterschreiben** to sign one's full name, to sign one's name in full
c **~ sein** *(inf)* *(= satt)* to be full, to be full up *(Brit)*; *(= betrunken)* to be plastered *(inf)* *or* tight *(Brit inf)*; **~ wie ein Sack** *or* **eine Strandhaubitze** *or* **tausend Mann** absolutely plastered *(inf)*, roaring drunk *(Brit inf)*
d *(= üppig) Gesicht, Busen etc* full; *Wangen* chubby; *Haar* thick; **~er werden** to fill out
e *Stimme, Ton* full, rich; *Farbton* rich
ADV fully; *(= vollkommen auch)* completely; *(sl: = total)* dead *(Brit inf)*, real *(US inf)*; **~ und ganz** completely, wholly; **die Straße ist ~ gesperrt** the road is completely closed; **die Straße ist wieder ~ befahrbar** the road is completely free again; **jdn ~ ansehen** to look sb straight in the face; **eine Rechnung ~ bezahlen** to pay a bill in full; **~ hinter jdm/etw stehen** to be *or* stand fully behind sb/sth; **den Mund recht** *or* **ganz schön ~ nehmen** *(fig)* to exaggerate greatly, to overdo it; **jdn/etw ~ treffen** *(mit Stein, Bombe etc)* to score a direct hit on sb/sth; *(ins Gesicht)* to hit sb full in the face; **etw ~ ausnützen** to take full advantage of sth; **~ zuschlagen** *(inf)* to lam out *(Brit inf)*, to hit out; **~ durcharbeiten** *(inf)* to work solidly (throughout); **~ drinstecken** *(inf)* *(bei Arbeit)* to be in the middle of it; *(in unangenehmer Situation)* to be right in it; **~ (Stoff) gegen etw fahren** *(inf)* to run full tilt *or* slap-bang *(inf)* into sth; **nicht ~ da sein** *(inf)* to be not quite with it *(inf)*; **~ dabei sein** *(inf)* to be totally involved → **vollnehmen**

volladen △ VT → **vollladen**

Voll|aka|de|mi|ker(in) M(F) honours *(Brit)* *or* honors *(US)* graduate

Vollast △ F → **Volllast**

Vollastbetrieb △ F → **Volllastbetrieb**

voll|auf ['fɔllauf, fɔl'lauf] ADV fully, completely; **~ genug** quite enough; **das genügt ~** that's quite enough; **~ zu tun haben** to have quite enough to do *(mit* with)

vollaufen △ VI → **volllaufen**

Voll-: **Voll|aus|schlag** M *(Tech: eines Instruments)* full swing; **voll|au|to|ma|tisch** ADJ fully automatic ADV (completely) automatically; **voll|au|to|ma|ti|siert** [-lautomatizi:ɐt] ADJ fully automated; **Voll|bad** NT (proper) bath; **Voll|bart** M (full) beard; **voll+be|kom|men** *sep irreg*, **voll be|kom|men** △ *irreg* VT to (manage to) fill; **voll|be|rech|tigt** ADJ *attr* with full rights; *Unterhändler* fully authorized; *Mitglied* full; **voll|be|schäf|tigt** ADJ *Arbeiter* employed full time; *(attr: = sehr beschäftigt)* fully occupied; **Voll|be|schäf|ti|gung** F full employment; **Voll|be|sitz** M **im ~** *+gen* in full possession of; **Voll|bier** NT *beer with 11-14% original wort*; **Voll|bild** NT *(Med: von Krankheit)* full-blown form; **Voll|bild-Aids** NT full-blown Aids

Voll|blut NT, *no pl* thoroughbred

Voll|blut- *in cpds (lit: Tier)* thoroughbred; *(fig)* full-blooded

Voll-: **Voll|blü|ter** [-bly:tɐ] M **-s, -** thoroughbred; **voll|blü|tig** ADJ thoroughbred; *(fig)* full-blooded

Voll|blut-: **Voll|blut|op|por|tu|nist(in)** M(F) full-blooded opportunist; **Voll|blut|po|li|ti|ker(in)** M(F) thoroughbred politician

Voll-: **Voll|brem|sung** F emergency stop; **eine ~ machen** to slam on the brakes *(inf)*, to do an emergency stop; **voll|brin|gen** [fɔl'brɪŋən] *ptp* **vollbracht** [fɔl'braxt] VT *insep irreg (= ausführen)* to accomplish, to achieve; *Wunder* to work, to perform; **eine große Leistung ~** to achieve a lot; **es ist vollbracht** *(Bibl)* it is done *(Bibl)*; **Voll|brin|gung** [fɔl'brɪŋʊŋ] F **-, -en** accomplishment, achievement; **voll|bu|sig** [-bu:zɪç] ADJ full-bosomed, bosomy *(inf)*

Voll|dampf M *(Naut)* full steam; **mit ~** at full steam *or* speed; *(inf)* flat out *(esp Brit)*; **mit ~ voraus** full steam *or* speed ahead; *(inf)* full tilt

voll+dröh|nen *sep*, **voll dröh|nen** △ VTR = **zudröhnen**

Völ|le|ge|fühl ['fœlə-] NT (unpleasant) feeling of fullness

voll|elekt|ro|nisch ADJ fully electronic

voll|en|den [fɔl'ɛndn] *ptp* **vollendet** *insep* VT *(= abschließen)* to complete; *(liter) Leben* to bring to an end; *(= vervollkommnen)* to make complete; *Geschmack* to round off VR *(= zum Abschluss* *kommen)* to come to an end; *(= vollkommen werden)* to be completed; *(Liebe)* to be fulfilled

vol|len|det [fɔl'ɛndət] ADJ *(= vollkommen)* completed; *Tugend, Schönheit* perfect; *Mensch* accomplished; *(Jur) Straftat* completed; **nach ~em 18. Lebensjahr** upon completion of one's 18th year; **bis zum ~en 6. Lebensjahr** until one's 6th birthday, until one turns 6 → **Tatsache** ADV perfectly; **~ Klavier spielen** to be an accomplished pianist

vol|lends ['fɔlɛnts] ADV **a** *(= völlig)* completely, altogether **b** *(= besonders)* especially, particularly

Vol|len|dung F completion; *(= Vervollkommnung, Vollkommenheit)* perfection; *(von Liebe)* fulfilment

vol|ler ['fɔlɐ] ADJ → **voll**

Völ|le|rei [fœlə'rai] F -, -en gluttony

voll+es|sen *sep irreg,* **voll es|sen** △ *irreg* VR *(inf)* to gorge oneself

Vol|ley ['vɔli] M -s, -s volley

Vol|ley|ball M volleyball

Vol|ley|bal|ler ['vɔlibalɐ] -s, - M, **Vol|ley|bal|le|rin** [-balərɪn] -, -nen F volleyball player

voll|fett ADJ full fat

Voll|fett|kä|se M full fat cheese

voll+fres|sen *sep irreg,* **voll fres|sen** △ *irreg* VR *(Tier)* to gorge itself; *(pej inf: Mensch)* to stuff oneself *or* one's face *(inf)*

voll|füh|ren [fɔl'fyːrən] *ptp* **vollführt** VT *insep* to execute, to perform; *Tanz, Kunststück* to perform; *Lärm, Theater* to create

Voll-: **voll+fül|len** *sep,* **voll fül|len** △ VT to fill (up); **Voll|gas** NT, *no pl* full speed *or* throttle; **~ geben** to open it right up; *(mit Auto auch)* to put one's foot hard down; **mit ~ fahren** to drive at full throttle; **mit ~** *(fig inf)* full tilt; **mit ~ arbeiten** to work flat out *(esp Brit) or* as hard as possible; **Voll|ge|fühl** NT **im ~** *+gen* fully aware of; **im ~ der Jugend** in the full bloom of youth; **im ~ der Lebensfreude** full of the joys of life; **Voll|ge|nuss** M **im ~** *+gen* in full enjoyment of; **voll+gie|ßen** *sep irreg,* **voll gie|ßen** △ *irreg* VT *(= auffüllen)* to fill (up); **sie hat sich** *(dat)* **den Rock vollgegossen/mit Kaffee vollgegossen** *(inf)* she spilled it/coffee all over her skirt; **voll|gül|tig** ADJ *attr Pass* fully valid; *Berufsabschluss* fully recognized; *Ersatz* completely satisfactory; *Beweis* conclusive; **Voll|gum|mi** NT OR M solid rubber; **Voll|gum|mi|rei|fen** M solid rubber tyre *(Brit) or* tire *(US)*; **Voll|idi|ot(in)** M(F) *(inf)* complete idiot

völ|lig ['fœlɪç] ✪ 38.1, 39.1, 39.2 ADJ complete; **das ist mein ~er Ernst** I'm completely *or* absolutely serious ADV completely; **es genügt ~** that's quite enough; **er hat ~ recht** he's absolutely right

Voll-: **voll|in|halt|lich** ADJ *attr* full, complete; **Voll|in|va|li|de** M, **Voll|in|va|li|din** F complete *or* total invalid; **voll|jäh|rig** ADJ of age; **~ werden/sein** to come/be of age; **sie hat drei ~e Kinder** she has three children who are of age; **Voll|jäh|ri|ge(r)** [-jɛːrɪgə] MF *decl as adj* major; **Voll|jäh|rig|keit** [-jɛːrɪçkait] F -, *no pl* majority *no art*; **bei (Erreichen der) ~** on attaining one's majority; **Voll|ju|rist(in)** M(F) fully qualified lawyer; **Voll|kas|ko** NT -, *no pl* fully comprehensive insurance; **voll|kas|ko|ver|si|chert** [-fɛɐzɪçɐt] ADJ comprehensively insured; **~ sein** to have fully comprehensive insurance; **Voll|kas|ko|ver|si|che|rung** F -, *no pl* fully comprehensive insurance; **voll|kli|ma|ti|siert** [-klimatiziːɐt] ADJ fully air-conditioned

voll|kom|men [fɔl'kɔmən, 'fɔl-] ✪ 34.5, 38.1, 40.1, 53.6 ADJ perfect; *(= völlig)* complete, absolute; *(Math) Zahl* perfect; **sein Glück war ~** his happiness was complete ADV completely

Voll|kom|men|heit F -, *no pl* perfection; *(= Vollständigkeit)* completeness, absoluteness; **die ~ ihrer Schönheit** her perfect beauty

Voll-: **Voll|korn|brot** NT coarse wholemeal *(Brit) or* wholegrain bread; **voll+kot|zen** *sep,* **voll kot|zen** △ VT *(sl)* to puke (up) over *(inf)*; **Voll|kraft** F *(geh)* **in der ~ seiner Jahre/seines Schaffens** in his prime; **voll+la|bern** *sep,* **voll la|bern** △ VT *(inf)* to chatter (on) to; **voll+la|den** *sep irreg,* **voll la|den** △ *irreg* VT to load up; **vollgeladen** fully-laden; **Voll|last** F, *no pl (Tech)* full load; **Voll|last|be|trieb** M, *no pl (Tech)* **im ~** at full load; **voll+lau|fen** *sep irreg aux sein,* **voll lau|fen** △ *irreg aux sein* VI to fill up; **etw ~ lassen** to fill sth (up); **sich ~ lassen** *(inf)* to get tanked up *(inf)*; **voll+ma|chen** *sep,* **voll ma|chen** △ VT **a** *Gefäß* to fill (up); *Zahl, Dutzend* to make up; *Sammlung, Set* to complete → **Maß a b** *(inf) Hosen* to make a mess in; *Windeln* to fill *(Brit),* to dirty *(US)*; **sich** *(dat)* **die Hosen ~** *(fig inf)* to wet oneself *(inf)* VR *(inf)* to get messed up, to get dirty; *(= in die Hosen machen)* to make a mess in one's pants; *(Baby)* to fill one's nappy *(Brit),* to dirty one's diaper *(US)*

Voll|macht F -, -en (legal) power *or* authority *no pl, no indef art*; *(Urkunde)* power of attorney; **jdm eine ~ erteilen** *or* **ausstellen** to give *or* grant sb power of attorney

Voll|macht|ge|ber(in) M(F) principal; **~ und Vollmachtnehmer** principal and agent

Voll|machts|ur|kun|de F power of attorney

Voll-: **voll|mast** ['fɔlmast] ADV full mast; **auf ~** at full mast; **Voll|mat|ro|se** M, **Voll|mat|ro|sin** F able-bodied seaman; **Voll|milch** F full-cream milk; **Voll|milch|scho|ko|la|de** F full-cream milk chocolate; **Voll|mit|glied** NT full member; **Voll|mond** M full moon; **heute ist ~** there's a full moon today; **Voll|mond|ge|sicht** NT *(inf)* moon face; **Voll|mond|nacht** F night of a full moon; **voll|mun|dig** ADJ *Wein* full-bodied; *Unterstützung, Versprechen* wholehearted; *Ankündigung, Erklärung* grandiose ADV **a ~ schmecken** to taste full-bodied **b** *(= großsprecherisch)* grandiosely; **etw ~ gutheißen** to support sth wholeheartedly; **etw ~ bestreiten** to dispute sth vehemently; **Voll|nar|ko|se** F general anaesthetic *(Brit) or* anesthetic *(US)*; **voll+neh|men** *sep irreg* **den Mund ~** *(inf, fig)* to exaggerate, to overdo it; → *auch* **voll** ADV; **voll+pa|cken** *sep,* **voll pa|cken** △ VT *(lit, fig)* to pack full; *jdn* to load up; **Voll|pen|si|on** F full board; **voll+pis|sen** *sep,* **voll pis|sen** △ VT *(vulg)* to piss on *(sl)*; *Hose* to piss in *(sl)*; **voll+pfrop|fen** *sep,* **voll pfrop|fen** △ VT *(inf)* to cram full; **voll+pum|pen** *sep,* **voll pum|pen** △ VT to fill (up); **Voll|rausch** M drunken stupor; **einen ~ haben** to be in a drunken stupor; **voll|reif** ADJ fully ripe; **voll+sau|gen** *sep reg or irreg,* **voll sau|gen** △ *reg or irreg* VR to become saturated; **voll+schen|ken** *sep,* **voll schen|ken** △ VT to fill; **voll+schla|gen** *sep irreg,* **voll schla|gen** △ *irreg* VT *(inf)* **sich** *(dat)* **den Bauch ~** to stuff oneself (with food) *(inf)*; **voll|schlank** ADJ plump, stout; **Mode für ~e Damen** fashion for the fuller figure, fashion for ladies with a fuller figure; **voll+schmie|ren** *sep,* **voll schmie|ren** △ VT to mess up VR to mess oneself up; **voll+schrei|ben** *sep irreg,* **voll schrei|ben** △ *irreg* VT *Heft, Seite* to fill (with writing); *Tafel* to cover (with writing); **Voll|sper|rung** F *(Mot)* complete closure; **Voll|spur** F *(Rail)* standard gauge, standard-gauge track; **voll|spu|rig** [-ʃpuːrɪç] *(Rail)* ADJ standard-gauge ADV on standard-gauge track

voll|stän|dig ADJ complete; *Sammlung, Satz auch* entire *attr*; *Adresse* full *attr*; **nicht ~** incomplete; **etw ~ machen** to complete sth; **etw ~ haben** to have sth complete ADV completely, entirely

Voll|stän|dig|keit [-ʃtɛndɪçkait] F -, *no pl* completeness; **der ~ halber** to complete the picture; **keinen Anspruch auf ~ erheben** to make no claim to be exhaustive

voll+stop|fen *sep,* **voll stop|fen** △ VT to cram full

voll|streck|bar ADJ enforceable, able to be carried out *or* executed; *(Jur)* **~e Urkunde** executory deed

voll|stre|cken [fɔl'ʃtrɛkn] *ptp* **vollstreckt** VT *insep* to execute; *Urteil, Haftbefehl* to carry out; *Pfändung* to enforce; **~de Gewalt** executive (power); **ein Todesurteil an jdm ~** to execute sb

Voll|stre|cker [fɔl'ʃtrɛkɐ] M -s, -, **Voll|stre|cke|rin** [-ərɪn] F -, -nen executor; *(Frau auch)* executrix; **~ des Todesurteils** executioner

Voll|stre|ckung F -, -en execution; *(von Todesurteil)* carrying out; *(von Pfändung)* enforcement

Voll|stre|ckungs-: **Voll|stre|ckungs|be|am|te(r)** M *decl as adj,* **Voll|stre|ckungs|be|am|tin** F enforcement officer; **Widerstand gegen ~** obstructing an officer in the performance of his duties; **Voll|stre|ckungs|be|fehl** M enforcement order, writ of execution; **Voll|stre|ckungs|ge|richt** NT court of execution *or* enforcement; *(bei Konkursverfahren)* bankruptcy court

Voll-: **Voll|stu|di|um** NT complete course of study; **voll|syn|chro|ni|siert** [-zynkroniziːɐt] ADJ fully synchronized; **voll+tan|ken** *sep,* **voll tan|ken** △ VTI to fill up; **bitte ~** fill her up, please

Voll|text M *(Comput)* full text

Voll|text- *(Comput)*: **Voll|text|da|ten|bank** F full text database; **Voll|text|su|che** F full text search

Voll-: **voll|tö|nend** [-tøːnənt] ADJ resonant, sonorous; **Voll|tref|fer** M *(lit, fig)* bull's eye; **voll+trin|ken** *sep irreg,* **voll trin|ken** △ *irreg* VR to drink one's fill; **voll|trun|ken** ADJ completely *or* totally drunk; **in ~em Zustand Auto fahren** to drive when drunk, to drive in a drunken state; **Voll|trun|ken|heit** F total inebriation; **Voll|ver|samm|lung** F general assembly; *(von Stadtrat etc)* full meeting *or* assembly; **Voll|ver|si|on** F *(von Software)* full version; **Voll|wai|se** F orphan; **Voll|wasch|mit|tel** NT detergent; **voll|wer|tig** ADJ *Mitglied, Partner* full *attr*; *Stellung* equal; *Ersatz, Kost* (fully) adequate; **jdn als ~ behandeln/betrachten** to treat/regard sb as an equal; **Voll|wert|kost** F wholefoods *pl*; **Voll|wert|kü|che** F wholefood cuisine; **Voll|zah|ler(in)** M(F) *(für Fahrkarte etc)* person paying full fare; **voll|zäh|lig** [-tsɛːlɪç] ADJ *usu pred Satz, Anzahl, Mannschaft* complete; *(= ausnahmslos anwesend)* all present *pred*; **um ~es Erscheinen wird gebeten** everyone is requested to attend ADV **sie sind ~ erschienen** everyone came; **~ versammelt sein** to be assembled in full force *or* strength; **Voll|zäh|lig|keit** F -, *no pl* full number; *(= ausnahmslose Anwesenheit)* full attendance

Voll|zeit- *in cpds* full-time; **Voll|zeit|be|schäf|tig|te(r)** MF *decl as adj* full-time employee *or* worker; **Voll|zeit|stel|le** F full-time position

voll|zieh|bar ADJ *Strafe, Urteil* enforceable, executable

Voll|zieh|bar|keit [fɔl'tsiːbaːɐkait] F -, *no pl* enforceability

voll|zie|hen [fɔl'tsiːən] *ptp* **vollzogen** [fɔl'tsoːgn] *insep irreg* VT to carry out; *Befehl auch* to execute; *Strafe, Urteil auch* to execute, to enforce; *Opferung, Trauung* to perform; *Bruch* to make; *(form) Ehe* to consummate; **einen Gedankengang ~ können** to be capable of a train of thought; **die ~de Gewalt** the executive (power) VR to take place; *(Trauung)* to be performed; *(jds Schicksal)* to be fulfilled

Voll|zie|hung F *(= Ausführung)* carrying out; *(von Befehl auch)* execution; *(von Strafe, Urteil auch)* execution, enforcement; *(von Opferung, Trauung)* performance; *(von Bruch)* making; *(von Ehe)* consummation

Voll|zug [fɔl'tsuːk] M, *no pl* **a** *(= Strafvollzug)* penal system; **offener ~** *daytime release for prisoners pending parole* **b** = **Vollziehung**

Voll|zugs-: **Voll|zugs|an|stalt** F *(form)* penal institution; **Voll|zugs|be|am|te(r)** M *decl as adj,* **Voll|zugs|be|am|tin** F *(form)* warder

Vo|lon|tär [volɔn'tɛːɐ] M **-s, -e**, **Vo|lon|tä|rin** [-'tɛːrɪn] F **-, -nen** trainee

Vo|lon|ta|ri|at [volɔnta'riaːt] NT **-(e)s, -e** **a** *(Zeit)* practical training **b** *(Stelle)* position as a trainee

VOLONTARIAT

A **Volontariat** is a period of voluntary training within a profession. The term is used principally in connection with journalism, since there were formerly no specific training opportunities in this field. Trainees (**Volontäre**) gain practical experience across a range of areas and also receive some tuition.

vo|lon|tie|ren [volɔn'tiːrən] *ptp* **volontiert** VI to be training *(bei* with)

Volt [vɔlt] NT **-(e)s, -** volt

Vol|te ['vɔltə] F **-, -n** **a** *(Fechten, Reiten)* volte **b** *(Cards)* sleight of hand

vol|ti|gie|ren [vɔlti'ʒiːrən] *ptp* **voltigiert** VI to perform exercises on horseback; *(im Zirkus)* to do trick riding

Volt-: **Volt|me|ter** NT voltmeter; **Volt|zahl** F voltage

Vo|lu|men [vo'luːmən] NT **-s, -** *or* **Volumina** [-na] **a** *(lit, fig: = Inhalt)* volume **b** *(obs: = Schriftrolle, Band)* volume

Vo|lu|men|pro|zent NT per cent *no pl (Brit) or* percent *no pl (US)* by volume

Vo|lum|ge|wicht [vo'luːm-] NT *(Phys)* volumetric weight

vo|lu|mi|nös [volumi'nøːs] ADJ *(geh)* voluminous

Vo|lu|te [vo'luːtə] F **-, -n** *(Archit)* scroll

vom [fɔm] *contr von* **von dem**; **~ 10. September an** from the 10th September *(Brit)*, from September 10th; **das kommt ~ Rauchen/Trinken** that comes from smoking/drinking; **ich kenne ihn nur ~ Sehen** I know him only by sight; **~ Kochen hat er keine Ahnung** he has no idea about cooking

von [fɔn] PREP *+dat* **a** *(einen Ausgangspunkt angebend, räumlich, zeitlich)* from; **der Wind kommt ~ Norden** the wind comes from the North; **nördlich ~** to the North of; **~ München nach Hamburg** from Munich to Hamburg; **~ weit her** from a long way away; **~ … an** from …; **~ Jugend an** from early on; **vom 10. Lebensjahr an** since he/she was ten years old; **~ diesem Tag/Punkt an** *or* **ab** from this day/point on(wards); **~ heute ab** *or* **an** from today; **Waren ~ 5 Euro an** *or* **ab** goods from 5 euros *(Brit)*, goods from 5 euros on *(US)*; **~ … aus** from …; **~ dort aus** from there; **etw ~ sich aus wissen** to know sth by oneself; **etw ~ sich aus tun** to do sth of one's own accord; **~ … bis** from … to; **~ morgens bis abends** from morning till night; **Ihr Brief ~ vor 2 Wochen** your letter of two weeks ago; **~ … zu** from … to
b *(von … weg)* from; **etw ~ etw nehmen/abreißen** to take/tear sth off sth; **vom Zug abspringen** to jump off the train; **alles ~ sich werfen** to throw everything down *or* aside; **~ der Stelle weichen** to move from the spot
c *(in Verbindung mit adj, vb siehe auch dort) (Ursache, Urheberschaft ausdrückend, im Passiv)* by; **das Gedicht ist ~ Schiller** the poem is by Schiller; **ein Kleid ~ Dior** a Dior dress; **ein Kind ~ jdm kriegen** to have a child by sb; **das Kind ist ~ ihm** the child is his; **~ etw müde** tired from sth; **~ etw begeistert** enthusiastic about sth; **~ etw satt** full up with sth; **~ etw beeindruckt/überrascht** impressed/surprised by sth
d *(partitiv, anstelle von Genitiv)* of; **jeweils zwei ~ zehn** two out of every ten; **ein Riese ~ einem Mann** *(inf)* a giant of a man; **ein Prachtstück ~ einem Hund** *(inf)* a magnificent (specimen of a) dog; **dieser Dummkopf ~ Gärtner …!** *(inf)* that idiot of a gardener …!
e *(in Verbindung mit n, adj, vb siehe auch dort) (Beschaffenheit, Eigenschaft etc ausdrückend, bestehend aus)* of; **~ 50 m Länge** 50 m in length; **im Alter ~ 50 Jahren** at the age of 50; **Kinder ~ 10 Jahren** ten-year-old children; **~ Bedeutung sein** to be of significance; **~ Dauer sein** to be lasting; **das ist sehr freundlich ~ Ihnen** that's very kind of you; **frei ~ etw sein** to be free of sth
f *(in Titel)* of; *(bei deutschem Adelstitel)* von; **die Königin ~ England** the Queen of England; **Otto ~ Bismarck** Otto von Bismarck; **~ und zu Falkenburg** von Falkenburg; **ein „von (und zu)" sein** to have a handle to one's name; **sich „von" schreiben** *(lit)* to have a "von" before one's name; **da kannst du dich aber „von" schreiben** *(fig)* you can be really proud yourself (there)
g *(= über)* about; **er erzählte ~ seiner Kindheit** he talked about his childhood; **Geschichten vom Weihnachtsmann/~ Feen** stories about Santa Claus/fairies
h *(mit Fragepronomen)* from; **~ wo/wann/was** where/when/what … from, from where/when/what *(form)*
i *(inf: in aufgelösten Kontraktionen)* **~ dem halte ich gar nichts** I don't think much of him; **da weiß ich nichts ~** I don't know anything about it
j *(inf)* **~ wegen** no way! *(inf)*; **~ wegen der Karte/dem Buch** *(incorrect)* about the map/the book

von|ei|nan|der [fɔnlai'nandɐ] ADV of each other, of one another; **etwas/nichts ~ haben** to see something/nothing of each other *or* one another; *(= Zusammensein genießen)* to be able/not to be able to enjoy each other's company; *(= ähnlich aussehen)* to look/not to look like each other; *(= sich im Wesen ähnlich sein)* to have a lot/nothing in common; **sie konnten die Augen nicht ~ wenden** they couldn't take their eyes off *or* away from each other *or* one another; **sich ~ trennen** to part *or* separate (from each other *or* one another); **sie hatten ~ die Nase voll** *(inf)* they were fed up with each other *or* one another

von|nö|ten [fɔn'nøːtn] ADJ **~ sein** to be necessary

von|sei|ten , **von Sei|ten** [fɔn'zaitn] PREP *+gen* on the part of

von|stat|ten+ge|hen [fɔn'ʃtatn-] VI *sep irreg aux sein (= stattfinden)* to take place; **wie geht so etwas vonstatten?** what is the procedure for that?; **es ging alles gut vonstatten** everything went well

Voo|doo ['vuːdu, vu'duː] M **-**, *no pl* voodoo

Voo|doo-: **Voo|doo|kult** M, *no pl* voodooism; **Voo|doo|pries|ter(in)** M(F) voodoo priest/priestess

Vo|po ['foːpo] M **-s, -s** *(DDR) abbr von* **Volkspolizist(in)**

vor [foːɐ] PREP *+acc or dat* **a** *+dat (räumlich)* in front of; *(= außerhalb von)* outside; *(= vor Hintergrund)* against; *(= in Gegenwart von)* in front of; *(= in jds Achtung)* in the eyes of; *(bei Reihenfolge)* before; *(bei Rangordnung)* before, ahead of; **der See/die Stadt lag ~ uns** the lake/town lay before us; **~ jdm herfahren/hergehen** to drive/walk in front of *or* ahead of sb; **~ der Kirche rechts abbiegen** turn right before the church; **~ der Stadt** outside the town; **~ einer Kommission/allen Leuten** before *or* in front of a commission/everyone; **~ Gott sind alle Menschen gleich** all people are equal before God *or* in God's sight; **sich ~ jdm/etw verneigen** *(lit, fig)* to bow before *or* to sb/sth; **~ allen Dingen, ~ allem** above all; **~ dem Fernseher sitzen** *or* **hocken** *(inf)* to sit in front of the TV
b *+acc (Richtung angebend)* in front of; *(= außerhalb von)* outside; **ein Schlag ~ den Oberkörper** a blow on the chest
c *+dat (zeitlich)* before; **~ Christi Geburt** before Christ, BC; **zwanzig (Minuten) ~ drei** twenty (minutes) to three; **heute ~ acht Tagen** a week ago today; **das ist** *or* **liegt noch ~ uns** this is still to come; **ich war ~ ihm an der Reihe** I was in front of him; **ich war ~ ihm da** I was there before him; **~ einigen Tagen/langer Zeit/fünf Jahren** a few days/a long time/five years ago; **am Tage ~ der Prüfung** the day before the examination
d *+acc* **~ sich hin summen/lachen/sprechen** *etc* to hum/laugh/talk *etc* to oneself; **~ sich hin schreiben/arbeiten** to write/work away; **~ sich hin wandern** to wander on
e *+dat* **~ sich her** before one, in front of one; **er ließ die Schüler ~ sich her gehen** he let the pupils go in front (of him)
f *+dat (Ursache angebend)* with; **~ Hunger sterben** to die of hunger; **~ Kälte zittern** to tremble with *or* from cold; **~ Schmerz laut schreien** to cry out with *or* in pain; **~ lauter Arbeit** for *or* because of work; **alles strahlt ~ Sauberkeit** everything is shining clean
g *(in fester Verbindung mit n, vb, adj siehe auch dort)* **Schutz ~ jdm/etw suchen** to seek protection from sb/sth; **~ jdm/etw sicher sein** to be safe from sb/sth; **Achtung ~ jdm/etw haben** to have respect for sb/sth; **sich ~ jdm verstecken** to hide from sb; **wie ist das ~ sich gegangen?** how did it happen?
ADV **a ~ und zurück** backwards and forwards; **alle kleinen Kinder ~!** all small children to the front!; **wer Karten will, ~!** come up and get your tickets!; **Borussia ~, noch ein Tor!** come on Borussia, let's have another!
b → **nach**
c *(N Ger inf: = davor)* **da sei Gott ~** God forbid; **das wird nicht passieren, da bin ich ~** that won't happen, I'll see to it

vor|ab [foːɐ'lap] ADV to begin *or* start with; **lassen Sie mich ~ erwähnen …** first let me mention …

Vor-: **Vor|ab|druck** M *pl* **-drucke** preprint; **Vor|abend** M evening before; *(mit nachfolgendem Genitiv auch)* eve *(auch fig)*; **das war am ~** that was the evening before; **am ~ von Weihnachten** (on) the evening before Christmas, on Christmas Eve; **am ~ der Revolution** *(fig)* on the eve of revolution; **Vor|a|bend|pro|gramm** NT *(TV)* early evening schedule; **Vor|ab|ex|emp|lar** NT advance copy; **Vor|ab|in|for|ma|ti|on** F advance information; **Vor|ab|ver|si|on** F *(von Software)* pre-release (version); **Vor|ah|nung** F presentiment, premonition; **Vor|al|pen** PL foothills *pl* of the Alps

vo|ran [fo'ran] ADV **a** *(= vorn, an der Spitze)* first; **ihm/ihr ~** in front of him/her; **der Festzug mit der Kapelle ~** the parade, led by the band; **mit dem Kopf ~ fallen** to fall head first **b** *(= vorwärts)* forwards; **nur** *or* **immer ~** keep going; **immer langsam ~!** gently *(Brit) or* easy does it!

vo|ran-: **vo|ran+brin|gen** VT *sep irreg* to make progress with; **vo|ran+ge|hen** VI *sep irreg aux sein* **a** *(= an der Spitze gehen)* to go first *or* in front; *(= anführen)* to lead the way; *(fig: Einleitung etc)* to precede (*+dat* sth); **jdm ~** to go ahead of sb **b** *(= zeitlich vor jdm gehen)* to go on ahead; **sie war ihm vorangegangen** *(euph: = gestorben)* she had passed on before him; **jdn ~ lassen** to let sb go first; **wie im Vorangehenden berichtet** as reported (in the) above → **Beispiel**
c *(zeitlich)* **einer Sache** *(dat)* **~** to precede sth; **das Vorangegangene** what has gone before **d** *auch vi impers (= Fortschritte machen)* to come on *(Brit) or* along, to make progress *or* headway; **es will mit der Arbeit nicht so richtig ~** the work's not coming on *(Brit) or* along very well; **vo|ran|ge|stellt** [-gəʃtɛlt] ADJ *(Gram)* preceding *attr*; **~ sein** to precede; **vo|ran+kom|men** VI *sep irreg aux sein* to get on *or* along, to make progress *or* headway; **im Leben/beruflich ~** to get on in life/in one's job; **nur langsam ~** to make slow progress, to make little headway

Vor|an|kün|di|gung F anouncement; **ohne jede ~** without prior notice

vo|ran+ma|chen VI *sep (inf)* to hurry up, to get a move on *(inf)*

Vor-: **Vor|an|mel|dung** F appointment; *(von Telefongespräch)* booking; **ohne ~** without an appointment/without booking; **Vor|an|schlag** M estimate

vo|ran-: **vo|ran+schrei|ten** VI *sep irreg aux sein (geh) (lit)* to stride ahead *or* in front *(jdm* of sb); *(Zeit)* to march on; *(Entwicklung)* to progress; *(= Fortschritte machen)* to progress; **vo|ran+stel|len** VT *sep* to put *or* place in front *(+dat* of); *(fig)* to give precedence *(+dat* over); **vo|ran+trei|ben** VT *sep irreg* to drive forward *or* on; *(fig auch)* to hurry along

Vor-: **Vor|an|zei|ge** F *(für Theaterstück)* advance notice; *(für Film)* trailer, preview *(US)*; **Vor|ar|beit** F preparatory *or* preliminary work, groundwork; **gute ~ leisten** to do good groundwork, to prepare the ground well; **vor+ar|bei|ten** *sep* VI *(inf)* to (do) work in advance VT to work in advance VR to work one's way forward; **Vor|ar|bei|ter** M foreman; **Vor|ar|bei|te|rin** F forewoman

Vor|arl|berg ['fo:ɐarlbɛrk, fo:ɐ'arl-] NT **-s** Vorarlberg

vo|rauf [fo'rauf] ADV *(rare)* = **voran, voraus**

vo|raus [fo'raus] ADV **a** *(= voran)* in front *(+dat* of); *(Naut, fig)* ahead *(+dat* of); **er ist den anderen Schülern/seiner Zeit ~** he is ahead of the other pupils/his time **b** *(= vorher)* **im Voraus** in advance

Vo|raus-: **Vo|raus|ab|tei|lung** F *(Mil)* advance party; **vo|raus+ah|nen** VT *sep* to anticipate; **vo|raus|be|re|chen|bar** ADJ predictable; **vo|raus+be|rech|nen** *ptp* **vorausberechnet** VT *sep* to predict; *Wahlergebnis auch* to forecast; *Kosten* to estimate; **vo|raus+be|stim|men** *ptp* **vorausbestimmt** VT *sep* to predict, to forecast; **Vo|raus|be|zah|lung** F payment in advance, advance payment; **vo|raus+bli|cken** VI *sep* to look ahead; **vo|raus|bli|ckend** ADJ foresighted ADV with regard to the future; **vo|raus+ei|len** VI *sep aux sein (geh) (lit, fig)* to hurry on ahead, to rush (on) ahead *(+dat* of); **einer Sache** *(dat)* **~** to be ahead of *or* in advance of sth; **vo|raus+fah|ren** VI *sep irreg aux sein* to go in front *(+dat* of); *(Fahrer)* to drive in front *(+dat* of); *(= früher fahren)* to go on ahead; *(Fahrer)* to drive on ahead; **vo|raus+ge|hen** VI *sep irreg aux sein* = **vorangehen**; **vo|raus|ge|setzt** ADJ **~, (dass) ...** provided (that) ...; **vo|raus+ha|ben** VT *sep irreg* **jdm etw ~** to have the advantage of sth over sb; **jdm viel ~** to have a great advantage over sb; **Vo|raus|kas|se** F *(Comm)* prepayment, advance payment; **vo|raus+lau|fen** VI *sep irreg aux sein* to run (on) ahead *(+dat* of); **vo|raus+pla|nen** VTI *sep* to plan ahead; **vo|raus+rei|ten** VI *sep irreg aux sein (an der Spitze)* to ride in front *(+dat* of); *(früher)* to ride on ahead; **Vo|raus|sa|ge** F prediction; *(= Wettervoraussage)* forecast; **vo|raus+sa|gen** VT *sep* to predict *(jdm* for sb); *(= prophezeien auch)* to prophesy; *Wahlergebnisse auch, Wetter* to forecast; **jdm die Zukunft ~** to foretell sb's future; **vo|raus|schau|end** ADJ *adv* = **vorausblickend**; **vo|raus+schi|cken** VT *sep* to send on ahead *or* in advance *(+dat* of); *(fig: = vorher sagen)* to say in advance *(+dat* of); **vo|raus+se|hen** VT *sep irreg* to foresee; **ich habe es ja vorausgesehen, dass ...** I knew that ...; **das war vorauszusehen!** that was (only) to be expected!

vo|raus+set|zen VT *sep* to presuppose; *(= als selbstverständlich, sicher annehmen) Interesse, Zustimmung, jds Liebe, Verständnis* to take for granted; *(= erfordern) Qualifikation, Kenntnisse, Geduld etc* to require, to demand; **wenn wir einmal ~, dass ...** let us *or* if we assume that ...; **etw als selbstverständlich ~** to take sth for granted; **etw als bekannt ~** to assume that everyone knows sth

Vo|raus|set|zung [-zɛtsʊŋ] F **-, -en** prerequisite, condition, precondition; *(= Qualifikation)* qualification; *(= Erfordernis)* requirement; *(= Annahme)* assumption, premise; **unter der ~, dass ...** on condition that ...; **eine Mitarbeit hat zur ~, dass ...** a requirement of cooperation is that ...

Vo|raus-: **Vo|raus|sicht** F foresight; *(= Erwartung)* anticipation; **aller ~ nach** in all probability; **in der ~, dass ...** anticipating that ...; **in kluger** *or* **weiser ~** with great foresight *or* forethought; **nach menschlicher ~** as far as we can foresee; **vo|raus|sicht|lich** ADJ expected; **~e Ankunftszeit** estimated time of arrival ADV probably; **er wird ~ gewinnen** he is expected to win; **~ wird es keine Schwierigkeiten geben** we don't anticipate *or* expect any difficulties

Vor|aus|wahl F, *no pl* preliminary selection *or* round of selections; **eine ~ treffen** to narrow down the choice, to draw up a shortlist

Vo|raus|zah|lung F payment in advance, advance payment

Vor|bau M *ptp* **-bauten** porch; *(= Balkon)* balcony; *(Min)* advancing working; **sie hat einen ganz schönen ~** *(hum: = vollbusig)* she's well-stacked *(inf)*

vor+bau|en *sep* VT *(= anbauen)* to build on (in front); **Häuser bis an die Straße ~** to build houses right on the road; **ein weit vorgebauter Erker** a deep oriel window VI *(= Vorkehrungen treffen)* to take precautions; **einer Sache** *(dat)* **~** to provide against sth → **klug**

Vor|be|dacht M **mit/ohne ~** *(= Überlegung)* with/without due care *or* consideration; *(= Absicht)* intentionally/unintentionally; *(Jur)* with/without intent

Vor|be|deu|tung F portent, presage, prognostic

Vor|be|din|gung F precondition

Vor|be|halt [-bəhalt] ✪ 53.6 M **-(e)s, -e** reservation; **unter dem ~, dass ...** with the reservation that ...

vor+be|hal|ten *ptp* **vorbehalten** VT *sep irreg* **sich** *(dat)* **etw ~** to reserve sth (for oneself); *Recht* to reserve sth; **jdm etw ~** to leave sth (up) to sb; **diese Entscheidung ist** *or* **bleibt ihm ~** this decision is left (up) to him; **alle Rechte ~** all rights reserved; **Änderungen (sind) ~** subject to alterations; **Irrtümer ~** errors excepted

vor|be|halt|lich [-bəhaltlɪç], **vor|be|hält|lich** [-bəhɛltlɪç] PREP *+gen (form)* subject to; **~ anderer Bestimmungen** unless otherwise provided *(form)*; **~ Artikel 3** save as provided in paragraph 3 *(form)*

vor|be|halt|los [-bəhaltlo:s] ADJ unconditional, unreserved ADV without reservations; *lieben* unconditionally

vor|bei [fo:ɐ'bai] ADV **a** *(räumlich)* past, by; **er möchte hier ~** he wants to go past *or* by; **~ an** *(+dat)* past; **~!** *(= nicht getroffen)* missed! **b** *(zeitlich)* **~ sein** to be past; *(= vergangen auch, beendet)* to be over *or* finished; *(Sorgen)* to be over; *(Schmerzen)* to be gone; **es ist schon 8 Uhr ~** it's already past *or* after *or* gone 8 o'clock; **damit ist es nun ~** that's all over now; **~ die schöne Zeit!** gone are the days!; **es war schon ~ mit ihm** it was all up with him; **aus und ~** over and done; **~ ist ~** what's past is past; *(= reden wir nicht mehr davon)* let bygones be bygones

vor|bei- PREF *(= vorüber)* past; **vor|bei+be|neh|men** *ptp* **vorbeibenommen** VR *sep irreg (inf)* to make an exhibition of oneself; **vor|bei+brin|gen** VT *sep irreg (inf)* to drop off *or* by *or* in; **vor|bei+drü|cken** VR *sep (inf) (an jdm/etw* sb/sth) to squeeze past; *(fig)* to slip past; **vor|bei+dür|fen** VI *sep irreg (inf)* to be allowed past; **dürfte ich bitte vorbei?** could I come *or* get past *or* by, please?; **vor|bei+fah|ren** *sep irreg* VI *aux sein (an jdm/etw* sb/sth) to go/drive/sail past, to pass; **im Vorbeifahren** in passing; **bei jdm ~** *(inf)* to drop *or* call in on sb, to stop *or* drop by sb's house *(inf)* VT **jdn an etw** *(dat)* **~** to drive sb past sth; **ich kann dich ja schnell dort/bei ihnen ~** *(inf)* I can run *or* drive you over there/to their place; **vor|bei+ge|hen** VI *sep irreg aux sein* **a** *(lit, fig) (an jdm/etw* sb/sth) to go past *or* by, to pass; **an etw** *(dat)* **~** *(fig: = nicht beachten)* to overlook sth; **bei jdm ~** *(inf)* to drop *or* call in on sb, to stop *or* drop by sb's house *(inf)*; **eine Gelegenheit ~ lassen** to let an opportunity pass by *or* slip by; **das Leben geht an ihm vorbei** life is passing him by; **an der Wirklichkeit ~** *(Bericht etc)* to miss the truth; *(Mensch)* to be unrealistic; **im Vorbeigehen** *(lit, fig)* in passing **b** *(= vergehen)* to pass; *(Laune, Zorn)* to blow over, to pass **c** *(= danebengehen)* to miss *(an etw (dat)* sth); **vor|bei+kom|men** VI *sep irreg aux sein* **a** *(an jdm/etw* sb/sth) to pass, to go past; *(an einem Hindernis)* to get past *or* by; **an einer Sache/Aufgabe nicht ~** to be unable to avoid a thing/task; **wir kommen nicht an der Tatsache vorbei, dass ...** there's no escaping the fact that ... **b bei jdm ~** *(inf)* to drop *or* call in on sb, to stop *or* drop by sb's house *(inf)*; **komm doch mal wieder vorbei!** *(inf)* drop *or* call in again sometime!, stop *or* drop by again sometime! *(inf)*; **vor|bei+kön|nen** VI *sep irreg* to be able to get past *or* by *(an etw (dat)* sth); **vor|bei+las|sen** VT *sep irreg* to let past *(an jdm/etw* sb/sth); **vor|bei+lau|fen** VI *sep irreg aux sein (an jdm/etw* sb/sth) to run past; *(inf: = vorbeigehen)* to go *or* walk past; *(fig)* to miss; **vor|bei+le|ben** VI *sep* **aneinander ~** to live *or* lead separate lives (within a partnership); **Vor|bei|marsch** M march past; **vor|bei+mar|schie|ren** *ptp* **vorbeimarschiert** VI *sep aux sein* to march past; **vor|bei+mo|geln** *sep* VT **jdn/etw an jdm ~** to smuggle sb/sth past sb VR **sich an jdm ~** to sneak past sb; **vor|bei+müs|sen** VI *sep irreg (an jdm/etw* sb/sth) to have to go past, to have to pass; **vor|bei+rau|schen** VI *sep aux sein Bach* to rush past; *Auto* to streak *or* whizz *(US)* past; *(fig: = vorbeigehen) hochnäsig* to sweep past *(an jdm* sb); **das ist alles an mir vorbeigerauscht** *(inf)* it all passed me by; **vor|bei+re|den** VI *sep* **an etw** *(dat)* **~** to talk round sth; *(absichtlich)* to skirt sth; **aneinander ~** to talk at cross purposes; **vor|bei+schau|en** VI *sep (esp dial inf)* = **vorbeikommen b**; **vor|bei+schie|ßen** VI *sep irreg* **a** *aux sein (an jdm/etw* sb/sth) to shoot past *or* by; *(an Kurve)* to overshoot **b** *(am Ziel etc)* to shoot wide *(an +dat* of), to miss *(an etw (dat)* sth); **vor|bei+schram|men** VI to scrape past *(an +dat* sth); **am Konkurs/an der Niederlage ~** to escape bankruptcy/defeat by the skin of one's teeth; **haarscharf am Bankrott ~** to come within an inch of bankruptcy

vor|bei+zie|hen *sep irreg* VI *aux sein (an jdm/etw* sb/sth) to file past; *(Truppen, Festzug etc)* to march past; *(Wolken, Rauch, Duft)* to drift past *or* by; *(Sportler)* to draw ahead of; **an jdm ~, vor jds innerem Auge ~** to go through sb's mind VT to pull past *(an jdm* sb)

vor|be|las|tet [-bəlastət] ADJ handicapped; **von den Eltern/vom Milieu her ~ sein** to be at a disadvantage because of one's parents/background; **dazu will ich mich nicht äußern, da bin ich ~** I don't want to comment on that, I'm biased → **erblich**

Vor|be|mer|kung F introductory *or* preliminary remark; *(= kurzes Vorwort)* (short) preface *or* foreword

vor+be|rei|ten *ptp* **vorbereitet** *sep* VT to prepare; **auf etw** *(acc)* **vorbereitet sein** to be prepared for sth; **jdn (schonend) auf etw** *(acc)* **~** to prepare sb for sth VR *(Mensch)* to prepare (oneself) *(auf +acc* for); *(Ereignisse)* to be in the offing *(inf)*

vor|be|rei|tend ADJ *attr* preparatory, preliminary

Vor|be|rei|tung F preparation; **~en (für** *or* **zu etw) treffen** to make preparations (for sth)

Vor|be|rei|tungs- *in cpds* preparatory; **Vor|be|rei|tungs|dienst** M teaching practice; **Vor|be|rei|tungs|kurs** M preparatory course; **Vor|be|rei|tungs|tref|fen** NT preparatory meeting; **Vor|be|rei|tungs|zeit** F preparation time

Vor-: **Vor|be|richt** M preliminary report; **Vor|be|scheid** M preliminary notice; **Vor|be|sit|-**

zer(in) M(F) previous owner; **Vor|be|spre|chung** F preliminary meeting *or* discussion; **vor+be|stel|len** *ptp* **vorbestellt** VT *sep* to order in advance; *Platz, Tisch, Zimmer, Karten auch* to reserve; **Vor|be|stel|lung** F advance order; *(von Platz, Tisch, Zimmer)* (advance) booking; **bei ~** when ordering/booking in advance; **vor|be|stimmt** [-bəʃtɪmt] ADJ *Schicksal* predetermined, preordained; **vor|be|straft** [-bəʃtra:ft] ADJ previously convicted; **er ist schon einmal/dreimal ~** he (already) has a previous conviction/three previous convictions; **wegen Körperverletzung ~ sein** to have a previous conviction for bodily harm; **Vor|be|straf|te(r)** [-bəʃtra:ftə] MF *decl as adj* person/man/woman with a previous conviction *or* a record; **vor+be|ten** *sep* VI to lead the prayer/prayers VT **jdm etw ~** *(lit)* to lead sb in sth; *(fig inf)* to keep spelling sth out for sb *(inf)*; **Vor|be|ter(in)** M(F) prayer leader

Vor|beu|ge|haft F preventive custody

vor+beu|gen *sep* VI to prevent *(einer Sache dat* sth); *einer Möglichkeit, einem Fehler auch* to preclude; **~ ist besser als heilen** *(prov)* prevention is better than cure *(prov)* VT *Kopf, Oberkörper* to bend forward VR to lean *or* bend forward

vor|beu|gend ADJ preventive ADV as a preventive measure

Vor|beu|gung F prevention *(gegen, von* of); **zur ~** *(Med)* as a prophylactic

Vor|beu|gungs-: **Vor|beu|gungs|haft** F preventive custody; **Vor|beu|gungs|maß|nah|me** F preventive measure

Vor|bild NT model; *(= Beispiel)* example; **nach dem ~** *+gen* based on the model of; **nach amerikanischem ~** following the American example; **das diente ihm als ~ für seine Skulptur** his sculpture was modelled *(Brit)* or modeled *(US)* on this; **er/sein Engagement kann uns zum ~ dienen** he/his commitment is an example to us; **sich** *(dat)* **jdn zum ~ nehmen** to model oneself on sb; *(= sich ein Beispiel nehmen an)* to take sb as an example; **jdn/etw als ~/leuchtendes ~ hinstellen** to hold sb/sth up as an example/a shining example

vor|bild|lich ADJ exemplary ADV exemplarily; **sich ~ benehmen** to be on one's best behaviour *(Brit)* or behavior *(US)*; **sich ~ verhalten** to act in an exemplary fashion

Vor|bild|lich|keit F exemplary nature

Vor-: **Vor|bil|dung** F previous experience; *(schulisch)* educational background; **vor+bin|den** VT *sep irreg (inf)* to put *or* tie on; **jdm/sich etw ~** to put *or* tie sth on sb/one; **Vor|bör|se** F before-hours market; **vor|börs|lich** [-bœrzlɪç] ADJ before official hours; **~er Handel** IPO-trading; **Vor|bo|te** M, **Vor|bo|tin** F *(fig)* harbinger, herald

vor+brin|gen VT *sep irreg* **a** *(inf: = nach vorn bringen)* to take up *or* forward; *(Mil)* to take up to the front **b** *(= äußern)* to say; *Plan* to propose; *Meinung, Wunsch, Anliegen, Forderung* to express, to state; *Klage, Beschwerde* to make, to lodge; *Entschuldigung* to make, to offer; *Kritik, Einwand* to make, to raise; *Bedenken* to express; *Argument, Beweis* to produce, to bring forward; *Grund* to put forward; **können Sie dagegen etwas ~?** have you anything to say against it?; **was hast du zu deiner Entschuldigung vorzubringen?** what have you to say in your defence *(Brit)* or defense *(US)*?; **er brachte vor, er hätte ...** *(= sagte)* he said that he ...; *(= behauptete)* he claimed *or* alleged that he ... **c** *(inf: = hervorbekommen)* to get out *(hinter +dat* from behind); **die Katze war nicht hinter dem Ofen vorzubringen** the cat couldn't be got out from behind the stove

Vor-: **Vor|büh|ne** F apron; **vor|christ|lich** ADJ pre-Christian; **das zweite ~e Jahrhundert** the second century before Christ; **Vor|dach** NT canopy; **vor+da|tie|ren** *ptp* **vordatiert** VT *sep* to postdate; *Ereignis* to predate, to antedate, to foredate; **Vor|da|tie|rung** [-dati:rʊŋ] F **-, -en** postdating; *(von Ereignis)* predating, antedating, foredating

vor|dem [fo:ɐ'de:m, 'fo:ɐ-] ADV **a** *(= zuvor)* before **b** *(old: = früher)* in days of yore *(old, liter)*, in (the) olden days

Vor|den|ker(in) M(F) mentor; *(= Prophet)* prophet

Vor|der-: **Vor|der|ach|se** F front axle; **Vor|der|an|sicht** F front view; **vor|der|asi|a|tisch** ADJ Near Eastern; **Vor|der|asi|en** NT Near East; **in ~** in the Near East; **Vor|der|bein** NT foreleg; **Vor|der|deck** NT foredeck

Vor|de|re(r) ['fɔrdərə] MF *decl as adj* person/man/woman *etc* in front

vor|de|re(r, s) ['fɔrdərə] ADJ front; **die ~ Seite des Hauses** the front of the house; **der Vordere Orient** the Near East; **einen ~n Platz einnehmen** *(Sport)* to occupy one of the top places; *(fig)* to occupy an important place → **vorderste(r, s)**

Vor|der-: **Vor|der|front** F frontage; **Vor|der|fuß** M forefoot; **Vor|der|gau|men|laut** M palatal (sound); **Vor|der|grund** M foreground *(auch Comput)*; *(fig auch)* fore(front); **im ~ stehen** *(fig)* to be to the fore; **sich in den ~ schieben** *or* **drängen** *(fig)* to push oneself to the fore(front); **etw in den ~ rücken** *or* **stellen** *(fig)* to give priority to sth, to place special emphasis on sth; **in den ~ rücken/treten** *(fig)* to come to the fore; *(Mensch auch)* to step into the limelight; **sich in den ~ spielen** *(fig)* to push oneself forward; **immer im ~** *(= Comput)* always on top; **vor|der|grün|dig** [-grʏndɪç] ADJ *(fig) (= oberflächlich)* superficial ADV *behandeln* superficially; **~ geht es darum, dass sie mehr Geld wollen** it appears at first that they want more money; **vor|der|hand** ADV for the time being, for the present; **Vor|der|hand** F *(von Tier)* forehand; *(Cards)* lead; **Vor|der|haus** NT front-facing house, front building; **Vor|der|la|der** [-la:dɐ] M **-s, -** muzzle-loader; **vor|der|las|tig** [-lastɪç] ADJ *Schiff, Flugzeug* front-heavy; **Vor|der|lauf** M *(Hunt)* foreleg; **Vor|der|mann** M *pl* **-männer** person in front; *(Auto)* car in front; **sein ~** the person/car in front of him; **jdn auf ~ bringen** *(fig inf)* to get sb to shape up; *(gesundheitlich)* to get sb fighting fit *(inf)*; **etw auf ~ bringen** *(fig inf, Haushalt, Auto etc)* to get sth shipshape; *Kenntnisse, Wissen* to brush sth up; *Finanzen* to get sth straightened out; *(= auf neuesten Stand bringen) Listen, Garderobe* to bring sth up-to-date; **Vor|der|pfo|te** F front paw; **Vor|der|rad** NT front wheel; **Vor|der|rad|an|trieb** M front-wheel drive; **Vor|der|rei|fen** M front tyre *(Brit)* or tire *(US)*; **Vor|der|rei|he** F front row; **Vor|der|schin|ken** M shoulder of ham; **Vor|der|sei|te** F front; *(von Münze)* head, obverse; **Vor|der|sitz** M front seat

vor|ders|te(r, s) ['fɔrdɛstə] ADJ *superl von* **vordere(r, s)** front(most); **der/die Vorderste in der Schlange** the first man/woman in the queue *(Brit)* or line *(US)*; **an ~r Front stehen** *(fig)* to be in the front line; **an ~r Stelle stehen** *(fig: Thema, Aufgabe etc)* to have top priority

Vor|der-: **Vor|der|ste|ven** M *(Naut)* stem; **Vor|der|teil** M OR NT front; **Vor|der|tür** F front door; **Vor|der|zahn** M front tooth; **Vor|der|zim|mer** NT front room

Vor|dip|lom NT first diploma

vor+drän|geln VR *sep*, **vor+drän|gen** VR *sep* to push to the front; **sich in einer Schlange vordrängen** to jump a queue *(Brit)*, to push to the front of a line *(US)*; *(= in den Mittelpunkt stellen)* to try to be the centre *(Brit)* or center *(US)* of attention, to try to be the centre *(Brit)* or center *(US)* stage

vor+drin|gen VI *sep irreg aux sein* to advance; *(Mil, in den Weltraum auch)* to penetrate *(in +acc* into); **bis zu jdm/etw ~** to reach sb/sth, to get as far as sb/sth

vor|dring|lich ADJ urgent, pressing ADV **Dinge, die ich ~ erledigen muss** things that I must take care of first; **~ zu besprechende Punkte** points that are most urgent, points that have to be discussed first

Vor|druck M *pl* **-drucke** form

vor|ehe|lich ADJ *attr* premarital

vor|ei|lig ADJ rash; **~e Schlüsse ziehen** to jump to conclusions ADV rashly; **~ urteilen** to be rash in one's judgement

vor|ei|nan|der [fo:ɐlai'nandɐ] ADV *(räumlich)* in front of *or* before one another *or* each other; *(= einander gegenüber)* face to face; **wir haben keine Geheimnisse ~** we have no secrets from each other; **Angst ~ haben** to be afraid of each other; **sie schämten sich ~** they were embarrassed with each other

vor|ein|ge|nom|men ADJ prejudiced, biased

Vor|ein|ge|nom|men|heit F **a** *no pl* prejudice, bias **b** *usu pl (= Vorurteil)* prejudice *no pl*

vor|ein|ge|stellt ADJ preset; *(Comput)* default

Vor|ein|stel|lung F presetting; *(Comput)* default

vor+ent|hal|ten *ptp* **vorenthalten** VT *sep irreg* **jdm etw ~** to withhold sth from sb; *Nachricht auch* to keep sth from sb

Vor|ent|schei|dung F preliminary decision; *(Sport: auch* **Vorentscheidungskampf, Vorentscheidungsrunde***)* preliminary round *or* heat

vor|erst ['fo:ɐle:ɐst, fo:ɐ'le:ɐst] ADV for the time being, for the moment *or* present

vor|er|wähnt ['fo:ɐlɛɐvɛ:nt] ADJ *attr (form)* aforementioned, aforesaid

Vor|fahr ['fo:ɐfa:ɐ] M **-en, -en** forefather, ancestor

vor+fah|ren *sep irreg* VI *aux sein* **a** *(= nach vorn fahren)* to go *or* move forward, to move up; *(in Auto)* to drive *or* move forward **b** *(= ankommen)* to drive up; **den Wagen ~ lassen** to have the car brought (up), to send for *or* order the car **c** *(= früher fahren)* to go on ahead; **wir fahren schon mal vor** we'll go on ahead **d** *(= an der Spitze fahren)* to drive in front VT **a** *(= weiter nach vorn fahren)* to move up *or* forward **b** *(= vor den Eingang fahren)* to drive up

Vor|fah|rin ['fo:ɐfa:rɪn] F **-, -nen** ancestor

Vor|fahrt F, *no pl* right of way; **~ haben** to have (the) right of way; **die ~ beachten/nicht beachten** to observe/ignore the right of way; **„Vorfahrt (be)achten** *or* **gewähren"** "give way" *(Brit)*, "yield" *(US)*; **(sich** *dat)* **die ~ erzwingen** to insist on one's right of way; **jdm die ~ nehmen** to ignore sb's right of way

Vor|fahrts-: **vor|fahrts|be|rech|tigt** ADJ having (the) right of way; **~ sein** to have (the) right of way; **der/die Vorfahrtsberechtigte** the driver with (the) right of way; **Vor|fahrts|recht** NT right of way; **Vor|fahrts|re|gel** F rule on (the) right of way; **Vor|fahrts|schild** NT *pl* **-schilder** give way *(Brit)* or yield *(US)* sign; **Vor|fahrts|stra|ße** F major road; **Vor|fahrts|zei|chen** NT give way *(Brit)* or yield *(US)* sign

Vor|fall M **a** incident, occurrence **b** *(Med)* prolapse

vor+fal|len VI *sep irreg aux sein* **a** *(= sich ereignen)* to occur, to happen; **was ist während meiner Abwesenheit vorgefallen?** what's been happening while I've been away? **b** *(inf: = nach vorn fallen)* to fall forward

Vor-: **vor+fa|seln** VT *sep* **jdm etw ~** *(pej inf)* to prattle on about sth to sb; **vor|fei|ern** VTI *sep* to celebrate early; **Vor|feld** NT *(Mil)* territory situated in front of the main battle line; *(Aviat)* apron; *(fig)* run-up (+*gen* to); **im ~ der Wahlen** in the run-up to the elections; **im ~ der Verhandlungen** in the preliminary stages of the negotiations; **etw im ~ klären** to clear sth up beforehand; **vor+fer|ti|gen** VT *sep* to prefabricate; **Vor|film** M supporting film *or* programme *(Brit)* or program *(US)*, short; **vor+fi|nan|zie|ren** *ptp* **vorfinanziert** VT *sep* to finance in advance, to pre-finance; **Vor|fi|nan|zie|rung** F prefinancing; **vor+fin|den** VT *sep* *irreg* to find, to discover; **vor+flun|kern** VT *sep (inf)* **jdm etwas ~** to tell sb a fib/fibs; **vor+for|mu|lie|ren** *ptp* **vorformuliert** VT *sep* to pre-formulate; *Fragen* to formulate in advance; **Vor|freu|de** F anticipation; **Vor|früh|ling** M early spring, foretaste of spring

vor+füh|len VI *sep (fig)* to put *or* send out (a few) feelers; **bei jdm ~** to sound *or* feel (*US*) sb out

Vor|führ|ef|fekt M Sod's law; **der ~ trat ein** it was a case of Sod's law

vor+füh|ren VT *sep* **a** *Angeklagten etc* to bring forward; **den Gefangenen dem Haftrichter ~** to bring the prisoner up before the magistrate; **den Patienten einem Spezialisten ~** to have the patient seen by a specialist **b** (*= zeigen*) to present; *Theaterstück auch, Kunststücke* to perform (*dat* to *or* in front of); *Film* to show; *Mode* to model; *Übung* to demonstrate (*dat* to); (*Vertreter*) *Modell, Gerät* to demonstrate (*dat* to) **c** (*= bloßstellen*) **jdn ~** to make sb look silly *or* ridiculous; **er wurde vom Direktor regelrecht vorgeführt** the director really made him look small *or* silly

Vor|füh|rer(in) M(F) projectionist

Vor|führ|mo|dell NT demonstration model

Vor|führ|raum M projection room

Vor|füh|rung F presentation; (*von Angeklagten, Zeugen etc*) production *no pl*; (*von Filmen*) showing; (*von Mode*) modelling (*esp Brit*), modeling (*US*); (*von Geräten, Modellen, Übungen*) demonstration; (*von Theaterstück, Kunststücken*) performance

Vor|führ|wa|gen M demonstration model *or* car

Vor|ga|be F handicap

Vor|gang M *pl* **-gänge** **a** (*= Ereignis*) event, occurrence; (*= Ablauf, Hergang*) series *or* course of events; **jdm den genauen ~ eines Unfalls schildern** to tell sb exactly what happened in an accident **b** (*Biol, Chem, Tech, Comput*) process **c** (*form: = Akten*) file, dossier

Vor|gän|ger [-gɛŋɐ] M **-s, -**, **Vor|gän|ge|rin** [-ərɪn] F **-, -nen** predecessor, precursor (*form*)

Vor|gän|ger|mo|dell NT previous model

Vor|gän|ger|ver|si|on F (*also Comput*) previous version

Vor|gangs|be|ar|bei|tung F (*Comput*) transaction processing

Vor|gar|ten M front garden

vor+gau|keln VT *sep* **jdm etw ~** to lead sb to believe in sth; **jdm ~, dass ...** to lead sb to believe that ...; **er hat ihr ein Leben im Luxus vorgegaukelt** he led her to believe that he lived in luxury

vor+ge|ben VT *sep irreg* **a** (*= vortäuschen*) to pretend; (*= fälschlich beteuern*) to profess; **sie gab Zeitmangel vor, um ...** she pretended to be pressed for time in order to ... **b** (*Sport*) to give (a start of) **c** (*inf: = nach vorn geben*) to pass forward

Vor|ge|bir|ge NT foothills *pl*

vor|geb|lich [-ge:plɪç] ADJ, ADV = **angeblich**

vor|ge|burt|lich [-gəbu:ɐtlɪç] ADJ *attr* prenatal

vor|ge|druckt ADJ pre-printed

vor|ge|fasst ADJ *Meinung* preconceived

Vor|ge|fühl NT anticipation; (*= böse Ahnung*) presentiment, foreboding

vor+ge|hen VI *sep irreg aux sein* **a** (*= handeln*) to act, to proceed; **gerichtlich/energisch gegen jdn ~** to take legal proceedings *or* legal action/assertive action against sb; **die Polizei ging gegen die Demonstranten vor** the police took action against the demonstrators

b (*= geschehen, vor sich gehen*) to go on, to happen

c (*Uhr*) (*= spätere Zeit anzeigen*) to be fast; (*= zu schnell gehen*) to gain; **meine Uhr geht (zwei Minuten) vor** my watch is (two minutes) fast; **meine Uhr geht pro Tag zwei Minuten vor** my watch gains two minutes a day

d (*= nach vorn gehen*) to go forward, to go to the front; (*Mil*) to advance

e (*= als Erster gehen*) to go first; (*= früher gehen*) to go on ahead

f (*= den Vorrang haben*) to come first, to take precedence, to have priority

Vor|ge|hen NT action

Vor|ge|hens|wei|se F procedure

Vor-: **vor|ge|la|gert** [-gəla:gɐt] ADJ *Insel* offshore; **es ist dem Kap ~** it lies off the Cape; **vor|ge|nannt** ADJ (*form*) aforementioned, aforesaid; **Vor|ge|plän|kel** NT preliminary skirmish; **Vor|ge|richt** NT hors d'oeuvre, starter (*Brit*); **Vor|ge|schich|te** F **a** (*eines Falles*) past history **b** (*= Urgeschichte*) prehistory, prehistoric times *pl*; **aus der ~** from prehistoric times; **vor|ge|schicht|lich** ADJ prehistoric; **Vor|ge|schmack** M (*fig*) foretaste; **vor|ge|schrit|ten** ADJ advanced; **im ~en Alter** at an advanced age; **zu ~er Stunde** at a late hour

Vor|ge|setz|te(r) ['fo:ɐgezɛtstə] MF *decl as adj* superior

vor|ges|tern ADV the day before yesterday; **von ~** (*fig*) antiquated; *Methoden, Ansichten auch, Kleidung* old-fashioned; **~ Abend/Morgen** the evening/morning before last; **~ Mittag** midday the day before yesterday

vor|gest|rig ADJ *attr* of the day before yesterday

vor+glü|hen VI *sep Motor* to preheat

vor+grei|fen VI *sep irreg* to anticipate; (*= verfrüht handeln*) to act prematurely; **jdm ~** to forestall sb; **einer Sache** (*dat*) **~** to anticipate sth

Vor|griff M anticipation (*auf +acc* of); (*in Erzählung*) leap ahead; **im ~ auf** (*+acc*) in anticipation of; **verzeihen Sie mir den ~ auf** (*+acc*) **...** excuse me for leaping ahead to ...

vor+ha|ben ✪ 29.2, 35.1, 35.2, 35.3 VT *sep irreg* to intend; (*= geplant haben*) to have planned; **was haben Sie heute vor?** what are your plans for today?, what do you intend doing today?; **ich habe morgen nichts vor** I've nothing planned *or* no plans for tomorrow; **hast du heute Abend schon etwas vor?** have you already got something planned this evening?, are you already doing something this evening?; **wenn du nichts Besseres vorhast ...** if you've nothing better *or* else to do ...; **etw mit jdm/etw ~** to intend doing sth with sb/sth; (*= etw geplant haben*) to have sth planned for sb/sth; **die ehrgeizigen Eltern haben viel mit dem Kind vor** the ambitious parents have great plans for the child; **was hast du jetzt wieder vor?** what are you up to now?

Vor|ha|ben ['fo:ɐhabn] NT **-s, -** plan; (*= Absicht*) intention

Vor|hal|le F (*von Tempel*) portico; (*= Diele*) entrance hall, vestibule; (*= Foyer*) foyer; (*von Parlament*) lobby

vor+hal|ten *sep irreg* VT **a** = **vorwerfen a b** (*als Beispiel*) **jdm jdn/etw ~** to hold sb/sth up to sb; **man hält ihm den älteren Bruder als Vorbild vor** his elder brother is held up to him as an example; **jdm die Qualen der Hölle ~** to hold up the torments of hell before sb's eyes **c** (*= vor den Körper halten*) to hold up; (*beim Niesen etc*) *Hand, Taschentuch* to put in front of one's mouth; **mit vorgehaltener Pistole** at gunpoint; **sich** (*dat*) **ein Handtuch ~** to hold up a towel in front of oneself → **Spiegel a** VI (*= anhalten*) to last

Vor|hal|tung F *usu pl* reproach; **jdm/sich (wegen etw) ~en machen** to reproach sb/oneself (with *or* for sth)

Vor|hand F (*Sport*) forehand; (*von Pferd*) forehand; (*Cards*) lead

vor|han|den [fo:ɐ'handn] ADJ (*= verfügbar*) available; (*= existierend*) in existence, existing; (*Comput*) existing; **eine Dusche ist hier leider nicht ~** I'm afraid there isn't a shower here; **davon ist genügend/nichts mehr ~** there's plenty/no more of that

Vor|hang M curtain; **die Schauspieler bekamen 10 Vorhänge** the actors got *or* took 10 curtain calls, the actors took 10 curtains

Vor|hän|ge|schloss ['fo:ɐhɛŋə-] NT padlock

Vor|hang-: **Vor|hang|stan|ge** F (*zum Aufhängen*) curtain pole; (*zum Ziehen*) curtain rod; **Vor|hang|stoff** M curtaining *no pl*, curtain (-ing) material *or* fabric

Vor-: **Vor|haus** NT (*Aus*) hall; **Vor|haut** F foreskin, prepuce (*spec*)

vor|her [fo:ɐ'he:ɐ, 'fo:ɐ-] ADV before(hand); (*= früher*) before; **am Tag(e) ~** the day before, the previous day; **man weiß ~ nie, wie die Sache ausgeht** one never knows beforehand *or* in advance how things will turn out; **konntest du das nicht ~ sagen?** couldn't you have said that earlier?

Vor|her-: **vor|her+be|stim|men** *ptp* **vorherbestimmt** VT *sep* to determine *or* ascertain in advance; *Schicksal, Zukunft* to predetermine; (*Gott*) to preordain; **es war ihm vorherbestimmt ...** he was predestined ...; **vor|her+ge|hen** VI *sep irreg aux sein* to go first *or* in front, to lead the way; (*fig*) to precede; **vor|her|ge|hend** ADJ *Tag, Ereignisse* preceding, previous

vor|he|rig [fo:ɐ'he:rɪç, 'fo:ɐ-] ADJ *attr* previous; (*= ehemalig*) former; (*= vorhergehend*) *Anmeldung, Genehmigung, Vereinbarung* prior

Vor|herr|schaft F predominance, supremacy; (*= Hegemonie*) hegemony

vor+herr|schen VI *sep* to predominate, to prevail; **Rot herrscht in diesem Winter vor** red is predominant this winter

vor|herr|schend ADJ predominant; *Ansicht, Meinung auch* prevailing, prevalent; (*= weitverbreitet*) prevalent

Vor|her-: **Vor|her|sa|ge** F forecast; **vor|her+sa|gen** VT *sep* = **voraussagen**; **vor|her+se|hen** VT *sep irreg* to foresee

vor+heu|cheln VT *sep* to feign, to pretend; **jdm etw ~** to feign *or* pretend sth to sb; **jdm ~, dass ...** to pretend to sb that ...; **er heuchelt dir doch bloß was vor!** (*inf*) he's just putting on an act

vor+heu|len VT *sep (inf)* **jdm etwas ~** to give sb a sob story (*inf*)

Vor|him|mel M first heaven

vor|hin [fo:ɐ'hɪn, 'fo:ɐ-] ADV just now, a little while ago

Vor|hi|nein ['fo:ɐhɪnain] ADV **im ~** in advance

Vor-: **Vor|hof** M forecourt; (*Anat: von Herz, Ohr*) vestibule; **Vor|hof|flim|mern** NT (*Med*) auricular fibrillation (*spec*); **Vor|höl|le** F limbo; **in der ~** in limbo; **Vor|hut** F **-, -en** (*Mil*) vanguard, advance guard

vo|rig [fo:rɪç] ADJ *attr* (*= früher*) *Besitzer, Wohnsitz* previous; (*= vergangen*) *Jahr, Woche etc* last; **im Vorigen** (in the) above, earlier; **der/die/das Vorige** the above(-mentioned); **die Vorigen** (*Theat*) the same

vor|ins|tal|liert ADJ (*Comput*) *Programm* preinstalled, preloaded

Vor|jahr NT previous year, year before

Vor|jah|res-: **Vor|jah|res|er|geb|nis** NT previous year's result; **Vor|jah|res|ni|veau** NT previous year's level; **Vor|jah|res|um|satz** M previous year's turnover; **Vor|jah|res|wert** M previous year's value; **Vor|jah|res|zeit|raum** M same period the previous year; (*im letzten Jahr*) same period last year

Vor-: **vor|jäh|rig** ADJ of the previous year, of the year before; **vor+jam|mern** VTI *sep* **jdm (etwas) ~** to moan to sb (*von* about); **Vor|kal|ku|la|ti|on** F preliminary costing *or* calculation; **Vor|kam|mer** F (*Anat: von Herz*) vestibule; (*Tech*) precombustion chamber; **Vor|kämp|fer(in)** M(F) (*für* of) pioneer, champion; **Vor|kas|se** F advance payment; **per ~ zahlen** to pay in advance; **„Zahlung nur gegen ~"** "advance payment only"; **vor+kau|en** VT *sep Nahrung* to chew; **jdm etw** (*acc*) **~** (*fig inf*) to spoon-feed sth to sb (*inf*); **Vor|kaufs|recht** NT option of purchase *or* to buy

Vor|keh|rung ['fo:ɐke:rʊŋ] F **-, -en** precaution; **~en treffen** to take precautions

Vor|kennt|nis F previous knowledge *no pl*; *(= Erfahrung)* previous experience *no pl*; **sprachliche ~se** previous knowledge of languages/the language

vor+knöp|fen VT *sep (fig inf)* **sich** *(dat)* **jdn ~** to take sb to task; **den hat sich die Mafia vorgeknöpft** the Mafia got him

vor+ko|chen VI *sep Mahlzeit, (= ankochen)* to precook; **für morgen ~** to cook ahead for tomorrow

vor+kom|men VI *sep irreg aux sein* **a** *auch vi impers (= sich ereignen)* to happen; **so etwas ist mir noch nie vorgekommen** such a thing has never happened to me before; **dass mir das nicht noch einmal vorkommt!** don't let it happen again!; **das soll nicht wieder ~** it won't happen again; **das kann schon mal ~** it can happen, it has been known to happen; *(= das ist nicht ungewöhnlich)* that happens; **so was soll ~!** that's life!
b *(= vorhanden sein, auftreten)* to occur; *(Pflanzen, Tiere)* to be found; **in dem Aufsatz dürfen keine Fehler ~** there mustn't be any mistakes in the essay
c *(= erscheinen)* to seem; **das kommt mir bekannt/merkwürdig vor** that seems familiar/strange to me; **sich** *(dat)* **überflüssig/dumm ~** to feel superfluous/silly; **sich** *(dat)* **klug ~** to think one is clever; **das kommt dir nur so vor** it just seems that way *or* like that to you; **wie kommst du mir denn vor?** *(inf)* who do you think you are?
d *(= nach vorn kommen)* to come forward *or* to the front
e *(= herauskommen)* to come out

Vor|kom|men ['fo:ɐkɔmən] NT **-s, -** *(no pl: = das Auftreten)* occurrence, incidence; *(Min)* deposit

Vor|komm|nis ['fo:ɐkɔmnɪs] NT **-ses, -se** incident, event, occurrence

Vor|kos|ter [-kɔstɐ] M **-s, -**, **Vor|kos|te|rin** [-ərɪn] F **-, -nen** taster; *(fig)* guinea pig

Vor|kriegs- *in cpds* prewar; **Vor|kriegs|zeit** F prewar period

vor+la|den VT *sep irreg (Jur)* to summons; *Zeugen auch* to subpoena

Vor|la|dung F summons; *(von Zeuge auch)* subpoena

Vor|la|ge F **a** *no pl (= das Vorlegen) (von Dokument)* presentation, production; *(von Scheck, Schuldschein)* presentation; *(von Beweismaterial)* submission; **gegen ~ einer Sache** *(gen)* (up)on production *or* presentation of sth; **zahlbar bei ~** payable on demand
b *(= Muster) (zum Stricken, Nähen)* pattern; *(Liter)* model; *(Comput: = Dokumentvorlage)* template; **etw von einer ~ abzeichnen/nach einer ~ machen** to copy sth; **hattest du dafür eine ~?** did you have a pattern for it?; did you copy it from something?
c *(= Entwurf)* draft; *(Parl: = Gesetzesvorlage)* bill
d *(Ftbl)* through-ball; **jdm eine ~ machen** to set the ball up for sb; **das war eine tolle ~** the ball was beautifully set up
e *(Ski)* vorlage, forward lean (position)
f *(Comm: = geliehene Summe)* advance; **mit 500 Euro in ~ treten** to pay 500 euros in advance
g *(= Vorleger)* mat; *(= Bettvorlage)* (bedside) rug

Vor|land NT *(der Alpen etc)* foothills *pl*; *(vor Deich)* foreshore

vor+las|sen VT *sep irreg* **a** *(inf)* **jdn ~** *(= nach vorn gehen lassen)* to let sb go in front; *(in der Schlange auch)* to let sb go first; *(= vorbeigehen lassen)* to let sb (go) past, to let sb pass; **ein Auto ~** *(= einbiegen lassen)* to let a car in; *(= überholen lassen)* to let a car pass, to let a car (go) past **b** *(= Empfang gewähren)* to allow in, to admit

Vor|lauf M **a** *(Sport)* qualifying *or* preliminary heat **b** *(Chem: bei Destillation)* forerun **c** *(Tech: von Rad)* offset **d** *(von Film, Band)* leader; *(von Tonbandgerät)* fast-forward

vor+lau|fen VI *sep irreg aux sein (inf) (= vorauslaufen)* to run on ahead *or* in front; *(= nach vorne laufen)* to run to the front

Vor|läu|fer(in) M(F) forerunner *(auch Ski)*, precursor

vor|läu|fig ADJ temporary; *Regelung auch, Schätzungen, Berechnungen* provisional; *Urteil* preliminary; *Verfügung des Gerichts* interim, provisional ADV *(= einstweilig)* temporarily; *(= fürs Erste)* for the time being, for the present, provisionally → **festnehmen**

Vor|lauf|zeit F *(Sport)* qualifying time; *(Ind: = Entwicklungszeit)* lead time

vor|laut ADJ cheeky *(Brit)*, impertinent

vor+le|ben VT *sep* **jdm etw ~** to set an example of sth to sb

Vor|le|ben NT past (life)

Vor|le|ge-: **Vor|le|ge|be|steck** NT serving cutlery, serving spoons *pl*; *(= Tranchierbesteck)* carvers *pl*; **Vor|le|ge|ga|bel** F serving fork; *(von Tranchierbesteck)* carving fork; **Vor|le|ge|löf|fel** M serving spoon, tablespoon; **Vor|le|ge|mes|ser** NT carving knife

vor+le|gen *sep* VT **a** *(= präsentieren)* to present; *Entwurf, Doktorarbeit auch* to submit; *Pass* to show, to produce; *Beweismaterial* to submit; *Zeugnisse, Bewerbungsunterlagen* to produce; *Schulzeugnis* to show; *Schularbeit* to hand in; *(Pol) Entwurf* to table *(Brit)*, to introduce; **jdm etw zur Unterschrift ~** to give *or* present sth to sb for signature *or* signing; **etw dem Parlament ~** to lay sth before the house, to table sth *(Brit)*; **jdm eine Frage ~** to put a question to sb; **ein schnelles Tempo ~** to go at a fast pace; **ein schnelleres Tempo ~** to speed up, to quicken the pace
b *Speisen* to serve; *(= hinlegen) Futter* to put down (+*dat* for); **jdm etw ~** to serve sth to sb, to serve sb with sth
c *Riegel* to put across, to shoot (across); *Schloss, Kette* to put on; *(inf: = davorlegen)* to put in front
d *(Ftbl)* **jdm den Ball ~** to set the ball up for sb
e *(= vorstrecken) Geld* to advance
VI *(Kellner)* to serve

Vor|le|ger ['fo:ɐle:gɐ] M **-s, -** mat; *(= Bettvorleger auch)* (bedside) rug

Vor|le|ge|schloss NT padlock

vor+leh|nen VR *sep* to lean forward

Vor|leis|tung F *(Econ) (= Vorausbezahlung)* advance (payment); *(= finanzielle Aufwendung)* outlay *no pl* (*an* +*dat* on); *(= vorausgehende Arbeit)* preliminary work; *(Pol)* prior concession

vor+le|sen VTI *sep irreg* to read aloud *or* out loud; **jdm (etw) ~** to read (sth) to sb

Vor|le|ser(in) M(F) reader

Vor|le|sung F *(Univ)* lecture; *(= Vorlesungsreihe)* course (of lectures), lectures *pl*; **über etw** *(acc)* **~en halten** to give (a course of) lectures on sth; **~en hören** to go to lectures

Vor|le|sungs-: **Vor|le|sungs|be|ginn** M ≈ start *or* beginning of term; **~ ist am …** term starts on …; **Vor|le|sungs|be|trieb** M lectures *pl*; **vor|le|sungs|frei** ADJ **~e Zeit** free period(s *pl*); **Vor|le|sungs|rei|he** F series of lectures, lecture series; **Vor|le|sungs|ver|zeich|nis** NT lecture timetable

vor|letz|te(r, s) ['fo:ɐlɛtstə] ADJ last but one *(Brit)*, next to last, penultimate; **im ~n Jahr** the year before last

Vor|lie|be ✪ 34.5 F predilection, special liking, preference; **etw mit ~ tun** to particularly like doing sth

vor|lieb+neh|men *sep irreg*, **vor|lieb neh|men** △ [fo:ɐ'li:p-] *irreg* VI **mit jdm/etw ~** to make do with sb/sth, to put up with sb/sth

vor+lie|gen *sep irreg* VI *(= zur Verfügung stehen: Beweise, Katalog, Erkenntnisse)* to be available; *(Urteil)* to be known; *(= eingereicht, vorgelegt sein: Unterlagen, wissenschaftliche Arbeit)* to be in, to have come in; *(Pol) (Gesetzesvorlage)* to be before the house; *(Haushalt)* to be published, to be out; *(= vorhanden sein) (Irrtum, Schuld etc)* to be; *(Symptome)* to be present; *(Gründe, Voraussetzungen)* to exist; **jdm ~** *(Unterlagen, Akten etc)* to be with sb; **die Ergebnisse liegen der Kommission vor** the commission has the results; **das Beweismaterial liegt dem Gericht vor** the evidence is before the court; **mir liegt ein Brief vor** I have (here) a letter; **etw liegt gegen jdn vor** sth is against sb; *(gegen Angeklagten)* sb is charged with sth
VI *impers* to be; **es liegen fünf Bewerbungen vor** there are *or* we have five applications; **es muss ein Irrtum ~** there must be some mistake

vor|lie|gend ADJ *attr Gründe* existing; *Akten, Unterlagen* on hand; *(Typ) Auflage* on hand; *Frage* at issue; *Angelegenheit, Probleme* in hand; *Ergebnisse, Erkenntnisse, Zahlen* available; *Bericht* submitted; **im ~en Fall** in this case, in the present case; **die uns ~en Ergebnisse** the results we have to hand; **sein jetzt ~er dritter Film** his third and current film

vor+lü|gen VT *sep irreg* **jdm etwas ~** to lie to sb

vorm. *abbr von* **vormittags**

vor+ma|chen VT *sep* **a (jdm) etw ~** *(= zeigen)* to show (sb) how to do sth, to demonstrate sth (to sb); *(fig: = als Beispiel dienen)* to show sb sth **b jdm etwas ~** *(fig: = täuschen)* to fool *or* kid *(inf)* sb; **ich lasse mir so leicht nichts ~** you/he *etc* can't fool *or* kid *(inf)* me so easily; **er lässt sich** *(dat)* **von niemandem etwas ~** nobody can fool him, he's nobody's fool; **mach mir doch nichts vor** don't try and fool *or* kid *(inf)* me; **sich** *(dat)* **(selbst) etwas ~** to fool *or* kid *(inf)* oneself → **Dunst c** *(inf: = davorlegen, -stellen etc) Kette, Schürze, Riegel* to put on; *Brett* to put across

Vor|macht(stel|lung) F supremacy *(gegenüber* over); **eine Vormachtstellung haben** to have supremacy

Vor|ma|gen M *(von Rind)* rumen; *(von Vogel)* crop

vor|ma|lig ['fo:ɐma:lɪç] ADJ *attr* former

vor|mals ['fo:ɐma:ls] ADV formerly

Vor|marsch M *(Mil)* advance; **im ~ sein** to be on the advance, to be advancing; *(fig)* to be gaining ground

Vor|märz M *(Hist) period from 1815 to March revolution of 1848*

Vor|mast M foremast

vor+mer|ken VT *sep* to note down, to make a note of; *(bei Bestellung auch)* to take an order for; *Plätze* to reserve, to book; **ich werde Sie für Mittwoch ~** I'll put you *or* your name down for Wednesday; **können Sie für mich 5 Exemplare ~?** can you put me down for 5 copies?, can you reserve 5 copies for me?; **sich beim Friseur ~ lassen** to make an appointment at the hairdresser's; **sich für einen Kursus ~ lassen** to put one's name *or* oneself down for a course

Vor|mie|ter(in) M(F) previous tenant

Vor|mit|tag M morning; **am ~** in the morning; **heute/gestern/morgen ~** this/yesterday/tomorrow morning

vor|mit|tä|gig ADJ morning

vor|mit|tags ADV in the morning; *(= jeden Morgen)* in the morning(s)

Vor|mit|tags|fi|xing NT *(Fin)* morning fixing

Vor|mit|tags|markt M *(Comm)* morning market

Vor|mo|nat M previous month

Vor|mund M **-(e)s, -e** *or* **Vormünder** guardian; **ich brauche keinen ~** *(fig)* I don't need anyone to tell me what to do

Vor|mund|schaft ['fo:ɐmʊntʃaft] F **-, -en** guardianship, tutelage; **jdn unter ~ stellen** to place sb under the care of a guardian

Vor|mund|schafts|ge|richt NT *court dealing with matters relating to guardianship*

vorn [fɔrn] ADV **a** in front; **von ~** from the front; **nach ~** *(= ganz nach vorn)* to the front; *(= weiter nach vorn)* forwards; **von weit ~** from the very front; **~ im Buch/in der Schlange** at the front of the book/queue *(Brit) or* line *(US)*; **~ auf der Liste** at the top of the list; **sich ~ anstel-**

len to join the front of the queue *(Brit) or* line *(US)*; **~ im Bild** in the front of the picture; **nach ~ abgehen** *(Theat)* to exit at the front of the stage; **nach ~ laufen** to run to the front; **~ bleiben** *(lit)* to stay in front; *(fig)* not to lag behind; **wenn es etwas umsonst gibt, ist er immer ganz ~(e)** when something's free he's always (the) first on the scene
b *(= am Anfang)* **von ~** from the beginning; **wie schon ~ erklärt** as explained above; **von ~ anfangen** to begin at the beginning, to start from the beginning; *(= von Neuem)* to start (all) over again, to start again from scratch; *(neues Leben)* to start afresh, to make a fresh start; **etw ~ anfügen** to add sth at the beginning; **das Auto kam von ~ auf ihn zugefahren** the car came at him head on
c *(= am vorderen Ende)* at the front; *(Naut)* fore; **von ~** from the front; **jdn von ~ sehen** to see sb's face; **~ im Auto/Bus** in the front of the car/bus; **der Blinker ~** the front indicator *(esp Brit) or* blinker *(US)*; **nach ~** to the front; *fallen, ziehen* forwards; **ganz ~ mitmischen** *(inf)* to be (at) the cutting edge
d *(= auf der Vorderseite)* at the front; **das Buch ist ~ schmutzig** the front of the book is dirty; **~ auf der Medaille** on the face of the medal; **ein nach ~ gelegenes Zimmer** a room facing the front
e *(= weit entfernt)* **das Auto da ~** the car in front *or* ahead there; **sie waren ziemlich weit ~** they were quite far ahead *or* quite a long way ahead; *(Läufer auch)* they were quite a long way (out) in front *or* quite a long way in the lead
f ich kann doch nicht ~ und hinten gleichzeitig sein I can't be everywhere at once; **sich von ~(e) bis** *or* **und hinten bedienen lassen** to be waited on hand and foot; **er betrügt sie von ~ bis hinten** he deceives her right, left and centre *(Brit) or* center *(US)* → *auch* **hinten**

Vor|nah|me [-na:mə] F **-, -n** *(form)* undertaking; **die ~ von Änderungen am Text bleibt dem Autor überlassen** it is left to the author to undertake changes to the text

Vor|na|me M Christian name, first name

vor|ne ['fɔrnə] ADV = **vorn**

vor|nehm ['fo:ɐne:m] ADJ **a** *(von hohem Rang) Familie, Kreise* distinguished, high-ranking; *(von adliger Herkunft)* aristocratic, noble; *(= kultiviert) Herr, Dame* distinguished, posh *(inf)*; *Manieren, Art, Benehmen* genteel, refined; *(= edel) Gesinnung, Charakter, Handeln* noble; **die ~e Gesellschaft** high society; **ihr seid mir eine ~e Gesellschaft** *(iro)* you're a fine lot! *(inf)*; **die ~e Welt, die Vornehmen** fashionable society; **so was sagt/tut man nicht in ~en Kreisen** one doesn't say/do that in polite society; **ein ~er Besuch** a distinguished visitor; **~er Anstrich** *(fig)* distinguished air
b *(= elegant, luxuriös) Wohngegend* fashionable, smart, posh *(inf)*; *Haus* smart, posh *(inf)*; *Geschäft* exclusive, posh *(inf)*; *Kleid, Äußeres* elegant, stylish; *Auto* smart, posh *(inf)*; *Geschmack* refined, exclusive
c *(dated)* **die ~ste Pflicht/Aufgabe** the first *or* foremost duty/task
ADV *wohnen* grandly; *schweigen, sich zurückhalten* grandly; **~ heiraten** to marry into high society; **~ tun** *(pej inf)* to act posh *(inf)*; **~ geht die Welt zugrunde** *(iro)* aren't we going up in the world! *(iro)*

vor+neh|men ✪ 35.2 VT *sep irreg* **a** *(= ausführen)* to carry out; *Umfrage, Änderungen* to carry out, to do; *Messungen* to take; *Einsparungen* to make
b *(= in Angriff nehmen)* (**sich** *dat*) **etw ~** to get to work on sth
c sich *(dat)* **etw ~** *(= planen, vorhaben)* to intend *or* mean to do sth; *(= Vorsatz fassen)* to have resolved to do sth; **ich habe mir vorgenommen, das nächste Woche zu tun** I intend *or* mean to do that next week; **ich habe mir zu viel vorgenommen** I've taken on too much
d sich *(dat)* **jdn ~** *(inf)* to have a word with sb
e *(= früher drannehmen) Kunden, Patienten* to attend to *or* see first
f *(inf: = vorhalten) Schürze, Serviette* to put on; *Hand* to put in front of one's mouth; *(= vorbeugen) Schultern* to hunch

Vor|nehm|heit F **-,** *no pl* **a** *(= hoher Rang: von Familie etc)* high rank; *(= Kultiviertheit) (von Mensch)* distinguished ways *pl*; *(von Art, Benehmen)* refinement **b** *(= Eleganz) (von Wohngegend, Haus)* smartness, poshness *(inf)*; *(von Kleid, Äußerem)* elegance, stylishness; *(von Geschmack)* refinement

vor|nehm|lich ['fo:ɐne:mlɪç] ADV *(= hauptsächlich, vor allem)* principally, especially, above all; *(= vorzugsweise)* first and foremost ADJ principal, main, chief

vor+nei|gen VTR *sep* to lean forward

Vor|ne|ver|tei|di|gung F *(Mil)* forward defence *(Brit) or* defense *(US)*

vor|ne|weg ['fɔrnəvɛk, fɔrnə'vɛk] ADV ahead, in front, first; *(= als Erstes)* first; **er geht immer ~** he always walks on ahead *or* in front; **mit dem Kopf ~** head first; **gleich ~** straight away; **mit dem Mund ~ sein** *(inf)* to have a big mouth

vorn|he|rein ['fɔrnhɛrain, fɔrnhɛ'rain] ADV **von ~** from the start *or* outset

Vor|nie|re F pronephros *(spec)*

vorn-: **vorn|über** [fɔrn'ly:bɐ] ADV forwards; **vorn|über+fal|len** VI *sep* to fall (over) forwards; **vorn|weg** ['fɔrnvɛk, fɔrn'vɛk] ADV = **vorneweg**

Vor|ort ['fo:ɐlɔrt] M *pl* **-orte** *(= Vorstadt)* suburb

Vor-Ort- [fo:ɐ'lɔrt] *in cpds* on-site

Vor|ort-: **Vor|ort|bahn** ['fo:ɐlɔrt-] F suburban line; *(für Berufsverkehr)* commuter line; **Vor|ort|ver|kehr** M suburban traffic; *(von öffentlichen Verkehrsmitteln)* suburban service; **Vor|ort|zug** M suburban train; *(im Berufsverkehr)* commuter train

Vor-Ort-Kon|trol|le [fo:ɐ'lɔrt-] F on-site supervision

Vor-: **vor|ös|ter|lich** ADJ immediately before Easter; **Vor|platz** M forecourt; **Vor|pom|mern** ['fo:ɐpɔmɐn] NT West Pomerania; **Vor|pos|ten** M *(Mil)* outpost; **Vor|prä|mie** F *(St Ex)* call option; **vor+pre|schen** VI *sep aux sein (lit, fig)* to press ahead; **Vor|pro|gramm** NT supporting bill *or* programme *(Brit)*, warm-up act *(US)*; **im ~** on the supporting bill *(Brit)*, as the warm-up act *(US)*; **vor|pro|gram|mier|bar** ADJ (pre)programmable *(Brit)*, (pre)programable *(US)*; **vor+pro|gram|mie|ren** *ptp* **vorprogrammiert** VT *sep* to preprogram; *(fig auch)* to precondition; **vor|pro|gram|miert** [-programi:ɐt] ADJ *Erfolg, Antwort* automatic; *Verhaltensweise* preprogrammed; *Weg* predetermined, preordained; **die nächste Krise ist ~** the seeds of the next crisis have been sown; **Vor|prü|fung** F preliminary examination; **vor+quel|len** VI *sep irreg* **a** *(Erbsen, Linsen)* to soak **b** *aux sein (Augen)* to bulge → **hervorquellen**

Vor|rang M, *no pl* **a ~ haben** to have priority, to take precedence; **den ~ vor etw** *(dat)* **haben** to take precedence over sth; **jdm/einer Sache den ~ geben** *or* **einräumen** to give sb/a matter priority; **jdm/einer Sache den ~ streitig machen** to challenge sb's/sth's pre-eminence; **mit ~** *(= vorrangig)* as a matter of priority **b** *(Aus: = Vorfahrt)* right of way

vor|ran|gig ['fo:ɐraŋɪç] ADJ priority *attr*; **~ sein** to have (top) priority ADV as a matter of priority; **eine Angelegenheit ~ erledigen/behandeln** to give a matter priority treatment

Vor|rang|stel|lung F pre-eminence *no indef art*; **er hat in der Firma eine ~** he has a position of prime importance in the firm

Vor|rat ['fo:ɐra:t] M **-(e)s, Vorräte** [-rɛ:tə] *(an +dat* of) stock, supply; *(esp Comm)* stocks *pl*; *(= Geldvorrat)* reserves *pl*; *(an Atomwaffen)* stockpile; *(an Geschichten, Ideen)* stock; **heimlicher ~** (secret) hoard; **etw auf ~ kaufen** to stock up with sth; **Vorräte anlegen** *or* **ansammeln** to build up reserves; *(= Geldvorräte)* to build up financial *or* monetary reserves; **solange der ~ reicht** *(Comm)* while stocks last; **etw auf ~ haben** to have sth in reserve; *(Comm)* to have sth in stock

vor|rä|tig ['fo:ɐrɛ:tɪç] ADJ in stock; *(= verfügbar)* available; **etw nicht mehr ~ haben** to be out (of stock) of sth

Vor|rats-: **Vor|rats|hal|tung** F stockpiling; *(bei Tieren)* storage habit; **Vor|rats|kam|mer** F store *(Brit) or* storage *(esp US)* cupboard; *(für Lebensmittel)* larder *(Brit)*, pantry; **Vor|rats|raum** M storeroom; *(in Geschäft)* stockroom

Vor|raum M anteroom; *(Büro)* outer office; *(von Gericht)* lobby; *(von Kino, Theater)* foyer

vor+rech|nen VT *sep* **jdm etw ~** to work out *or* reckon up *or* calculate sth for sb; **er rechnet mir dauernd vor, wie viel alles kostet** he's always pointing out to me how much everything costs; **jdm seine Fehler ~** *(fig)* to enumerate sb's mistakes

Vor|recht NT prerogative; *(= Vergünstigung)* privilege

Vor|re|de F *(= Vorwort)* preface; *(Theat)* prologue *(Brit)*, prolog *(US)*; *(= einleitende Rede)* introductory speech

vor+re|den VT *sep (inf)* **jdm etwas ~** to tell sb a tale; **red mir doch nichts vor** don't give me that *(inf)*

Vor|red|ner(in) M(F) *(= vorheriger Redner)* previous speaker; *(= einleitender Redner)* introductory speaker; **mein ~ hat gesagt ...** the previous speaker said ...

vor+rei|ten *sep irreg* VI **a** *aux sein (= vorausreiten)* to ride on ahead **b** *(zur Demonstration)* to demonstrate *(a riding exercise)* VT *(= demonstrieren) Übung* to demonstrate

Vor|rei|ter(in) M(F) **a** forerunner; **den ~ für etw machen** to be the first to do sth **b** *(beim Reiten)* demonstrator

Vor|rei|ter|rol|le F **eine ~ für andere einnehmen** to make the running for others

vor+ren|nen VI *sep irreg aux sein (inf) (voraus)* to run *or* race (on) ahead; *(nach vorn)* to run forward

vor+rich|ten VT *sep* to prepare; *Zutaten, Gegenstände* to get ready

Vor|rich|tung F device, gadget

vor+rü|cken *sep* VT to move forward; *Schachfigur* to advance, to move on VI *aux sein* to move *or* go forward; *(Mil)* to advance; *(Sport, im Beruf etc)* to move up; *(Uhrzeiger)* to move on; **mit dem Stuhl ~** to move one's chair forward; **in vorgerücktem Alter** in later life; **zu vorgerückter Stunde** at a late hour

Vor|ru|he|stand M early retirement

Vor|ru|he|ständ|ler(in) M(F) person taking early retirement

Vor|ru|he|stands|re|ge|lung F early retirement scheme

Vor|ru|he|stands|leis|tun|gen PL early retirement benefits *pl*

Vor|run|de F *(Sport)* preliminary *or* qualifying round; *(von Saison)* first part (of the season)

Vor|run|den|grup|pe F *(Sport)* qualifying group

Vor|run|den|spiel NT *(Sport)* qualifying game

vor+sa|gen *sep* VT **jdm etw ~** *(Gedicht)* to recite sth to sb; *Antwort, Lösung* to tell sb sth VI *(Sch)* **jdm ~** to tell sb the answer

Vor|sai|son F low season, early (part of the) season

Vor|sän|ger(in) M(F) *(Eccl)* precentor; *(in Chor)* choir leader; *(fig)* leading voice

Vor|satz M **a** (firm) intention; **mit ~** *(Jur)* with intent; **den ~ haben, etw zu tun** to (firmly) intend to do sth; **den ~ fassen, etw zu tun** to make up one's mind to do sth, to resolve to do sth; *(zum neuen Jahr)* to make a resolution to do sth; **bei seinen Vorsätzen bleiben, seinen Vorsätzen treu bleiben** to keep to one's resolve *or* resolution → **Weg b** *(von Buch)* endpaper

Vor|satz|blatt NT *(Typ)* endpaper

vor|sätz|lich [-zɛtslɪç] ADJ deliberate, intentional; *Lüge* deliberate; *(Jur) Mord, Brandstiftung etc* wilful ADV deliberately, intentionally; **jdn ~ töten** to kill sb intentionally

Vor|satz|lin|se F *(Phot)* ancillary lens

Vor|schalt|ge|setz NT *(Pol)* interim law *(preparing the way for a subsequent law)*

Vor|schau F preview; *(für Film)* trailer, preview *(US)*; *(= Wettervorschau)* forecast

Vor|schein M **zum ~ bringen** *(lit: = zeigen)* to produce; *Fleck* to show up; *(fig: = deutlich machen)* to bring to light; **zum ~ kommen** *(lit: = sichtbar werden)* to appear; *(fig: = entdeckt werden)* to turn up, to come to light; *(Tatsachen)* to come to light, to come out

vor+schie|ben *sep irreg* VT **a** *(= davorschieben)* to push in front; *Riegel* to put across, to shoot (across); *(= nach vorn schieben)* to push forward; *Kopf* to stick forward; *Unterlippe, Kinn* to stick out → **Riegel a b** *(Mil) Truppen* to move forward; **vorgeschobener Posten** advance guard, advance party **c** *(fig: = vorschützen)* to put forward as a pretext *or* excuse; **vorgeschobene Gründe** pretexts *pl*, excuses *pl* **d jdn ~** to put sb forward as a front man VR *(Wolken, Erdmassen)* to advance, to move forward; *(Menschen)* to push *or* press forward

vor+schie|ßen *sep irreg* VT **jdm Geld ~** to advance sb money VI *aux sein* to shoot forward; *(Schlange, Läufer auch)* to dart forward

Vor|schiff NT forecastle, fo'c's'le

vor+schla|fen *sep irreg* VI **ein bisschen ~** to stock up on a bit of sleep, to stockpile some Zs *(US)*

Vor|schlag ✪ 28.1, 28.2 M **a** suggestion, proposal; *(= Rat)* recommendation, advice; *(= Angebot)* offer, proposition; *(Pol: von Kandidaten)* proposal; **auf ~ von** *or +gen* at *or* on the suggestion of, on the recommendation of; **das ist ein ~!** that's an idea!; **wäre das nicht ein ~?** how's that for an idea? → **Güte a b** *(Mus)* appoggiatura **c** *(Typ)* sink **d** *(Sw: = Gewinn)* profit

vor+schla|gen ✪ 28.1, 28.2 VT *sep irreg* **a** *(= als Vorschlag unterbreiten)* to suggest, to propose; **jdn für ein Amt ~** to propose *or* nominate sb for a post *(esp Brit) or* position; **jdm ~, dass er etw tut** to suggest that sb do(es) sth, to suggest to sb that he do(es) sth **b den Takt ~** to beat time

Vor|schlag|ham|mer M sledgehammer

Vor|schluss|run|de F *(Sport)* semifinal(s *pl*)

vor|schnell ADJ, ADV = **voreilig**

Vor|scho|ter [-ʃoːtɐ] M **-s, -**, **Vor|scho|te|rin** [-ərɪn] F **-, -nen** *(Naut)* sheethand

vor+schrei|ben VT *sep irreg* **a** *(= befehlen)* to stipulate; *(Med) Dosis* to prescribe; **jdm ~, wie/was ...** to dictate to sb how/what ...; **ich lasse mir nichts ~** I won't be dictated to; **vorgeschriebene Lektüre** *(Sch, Univ)* prescribed texts; **gesetzlich vorgeschrieben** stipulated by law **b** *(lit)* to write out (*+dat* for)

vor+schrei|ten VI *sep irreg aux sein* to progress, to make progress → **vorgeschritten**

Vor|schrift F *(= gesetzliche etc Bestimmung)* regulation, rule; *(= Anweisung)* instruction, order, direction; **nach ~ des Arztes** according to doctor's orders *or* the doctor's instructions; **~en für den Verkehr** traffic regulations; **jdm ~en machen** to give sb orders, to dictate to sb; **ich lasse mir (von dir) keine ~en machen lassen** I won't be dictated to (by you), I won't take orders (from you); **sich an die ~en halten** to observe the regulations, to follow the instructions; **Arbeit nach ~** work to rule; **das ist ~** that's the regulation

vor|schrifts-: **vor|schrifts|ge|mäß, vor|schrifts|mä|ßig** ADJ regulation *attr*; *Signal, Parken, Verhalten* correct, proper *attr*; *(Med) Dosis* prescribed ADV *(= laut Anordnung)* as instructed *or* directed, according to (the) regulations; *(Med)* as directed; **~ gekleidet sein** to be in regulation dress; **vor|schrifts|wid|rig** ADJ ADV contrary to (the) regulations; *(Med) Dosis* contrary to the prescription

Vor|schub M **jdm ~ leisten** to encourage sb; **einer Sache** *(dat)* **~ leisten** to encourage *or* foster sth

Vor|schul|al|ter NT preschool age

Vor|schu|le F nursery school; *(= Vorschuljahre)* preschool years *pl*

Vor|schul|er|zie|hung F preschool education

vor|schu|lisch ADJ preschool *attr*

Vor|schuss M advance; **jdm einen ~ leisten** to give sb an advance

Vor|schuss-: **Vor|schuss|lor|bee|ren** PL premature praise *sing*; **Vor|schuss|zin|sen** PL *(Fin)* penalty interest on early settlement

vor+schüt|zen VT *sep* to plead as an excuse, to put forward as a pretext; *Krankheit auch* to feign; *Unwissenheit* to plead; **er schützte vor, dass ...** he pretended that ... → **Müdigkeit**

vor+schwär|men VTI *sep* **jdm von jdm/etw ~** to go into raptures over sb/sth; **jdm ~, wie schön etw ist** to go into raptures over how beautiful sth is

vor+schwat|zen VT *sep (inf)* **jdm etwas ~** to tell sb a lot of rubbish *(Brit inf) or* crap *(inf)*; **schwatz mir doch nichts vor** don't give me that rubbish *(Brit inf) or* crap *(inf)*

vor+schwe|ben VI *sep* **jdm schwebt etw vor** sb has sth in mind

vor+schwin|deln VT *sep* **jdm etwas ~** to lie to sb; **jdm ~, dass ...** to lie to sb that ...; **ich lasse mir doch von dir nichts ~** I won't have any of your lies

vor+se|hen *sep irreg* VT *(= planen)* to plan; *(zeitlich auch)* to schedule; *(= einplanen) Kosten, Anschaffungen* to provide *or* allow for; *Zeit* to allow; *Fall* to provide *or* cater for; *(im Gesetz, Vertrag)* to provide for; **etw für etw ~** *(= bestimmen)* to intend sth for sth; *Geld* to earmark *or* destine sth for sth; **jdn für etw ~** *(= beabsichtigen)* to have sb in mind for sth; *(= bestimmen)* to designate sb for sth; **er ist für dieses Amt vorgesehen** we have him in mind/he has been designated for this post *(esp Brit) or* position; **was haben wir für heute vorgesehen?** what is on the agenda today?, what have we planned for today?; **der Plan sieht vor, dass das Projekt bis September abgeschlossen ist** the project is scheduled to be finished by September VR *(= sich in Acht nehmen)* to be careful, to watch out, to take care; **sich vor jdm/etw ~** to beware of sb/sth, to be wary of sb/sth; *vor Hund auch* to mind sth VI *(= sichtbar sein)* to appear; **hinter/unter etw** *(dat)* **~** to peep out from behind/under sth

Vor|se|hung [ˈfoːɐzeːʊŋ] F **-,** *no pl* **die (göttliche) ~** (divine) Providence

vor+set|zen *sep* VT **a** *(nach vorn)* to move forward; *Fuß* to put forward; *Schüler* to move (up) to the front **b** *(= davorsetzen)* to put in front; **etw vor etw** *(acc)* **~** to put sth in front of sth *or* before sth **c jdm etw ~** *(= geben)* to give sb sth, to put sth in front of sb; *(= anbieten)* to offer sb sth; *(fig inf) Lügen, Geschichte, Erklärung* to serve *or* dish sth up to sb *(inf)* **d** *(dated)* **jdn jdm/einer Sache ~** *(als Vorgesetzten)* to put sb in charge of sb/sth VR to sit in (the) front; **sich in die erste Reihe ~** to move to the front row

Vor|sicht [ˈfoːɐzɪçt] F **-,** *no pl* care; *(bei Gefahr)* caution; *(= Überlegtheit)* circumspection, prudence; *(= Behutsamkeit)* guardedness, wariness; **~ walten lassen** *or* **üben** to be careful; *(bei Gefahr)* to exercise caution, to be cautious; *(= überlegt handeln)* to be circumspect *or* prudent; *(= behutsam vorgehen)* to be wary; **jdn zur ~ (er)mahnen** to advise sb to be careful/cautious/circumspect; **zur ~ raten/mahnen** to advise caution; **~!** watch *or* look *or* mind *(Brit)* out!; **„Vorsicht bei Einfahrt des Zuges"** "stand back when the train approaches the platform"; **„Vorsicht Bahnübergang"** "Level crossing" *(Brit)*, "Grade crossing" *(US)*; **„Vorsicht Gift"** "Poison"; **„Vorsicht Kurve"** "Bend"; **„Vorsicht feuergefährlich"** "danger - inflammable"; **„Vorsicht zerbrechlich"** "fragile - with care"; **„Vorsicht Glas"** "glass - with care"; **„Vorsicht nicht knicken"** "do not bend"; **„Vorsicht Stufe"** "mind the step"; **mit ~** carefully; *(bei Gefahr)* cautiously; *(= überlegt)* prudently; *(= behutsam)* guardedly, warily; **etw zur ~ tun** to do sth as a precaution, to do sth to be on the safe side; **was er sagt/dieser Artikel ist mit ~ zu genießen** *(hum inf)* you have to take what he says/this article with a pinch of salt *(inf)*; **sie ist mit ~ zu genießen** *(hum inf)* she has to be handled with kid gloves; **~ ist besser als Nachsicht** *(Prov)* better safe than sorry; **~ ist die Mutter der Porzellankiste** *(inf)* better safe than sorry

vor|sich|tig [ˈfoːɐzɪçtɪç] ADJ careful; *(= besonnen)* cautious; *(= überlegt)* prudent; *(= misstrauisch)* wary; *Äußerung* cautious, guarded; *Schätzung* cautious, conservative ADV **a** *(umsichtig)* carefully **b** *(zurückhaltend)* **sich ~ äußern** to be very careful what one says; **ich schätze die Kosten ~ auf 35.000 Euro** to give you a conservative estimate of the costs I would say 35,000 euros

Vor|sich|tig|keit F **-,** *no pl* carefulness; *(= Besonnenheit)* caution, cautiousness

Vor|sichts-: **vor|sichts|hal|ber** ADV as a precaution, to be on the safe side; **Vor|sichts|maß|nah|me** F precaution, precautionary measure; **~n treffen** to take precautions, to take precautionary measures; **Vor|sichts|maß|re|gel** F = **Vorsichtsmaßnahme**

Vor-: **Vor|sig|nal** NT *(Rail)* warning signal; **Vor|sil|be** F prefix; **vor+sin|gen** *sep irreg* VTI **a** *(vor Zuhörern)* **jdm (etw) ~** to sing (sth) to sb; **ich singe nicht gern vor** I don't like singing to people *or* in front of people **b** *(= als Erster singen)* to sing first VI *(zur Prüfung)* to have a singing test; *(esp Theat: vor Einstellung)* to audition; **vor|sint|flut|lich** [-zɪntfluːtlɪç] ADJ *(inf)* antiquated, prehistoric *(hum)*, antediluvian

Vor|sitz M chairmanship; *(= Amt eines Präsidenten)* presidency; **unter dem ~ von** under the chairmanship of; **(bei etw) den ~ haben** *or* **innehaben** *or* **führen** to be chairman (of sth); **bei einer Sitzung den ~ haben** *or* **führen** to chair a meeting; **den ~ übernehmen** to take the chair

vor+sit|zen VI *sep irreg* **einer Versammlung/Diskussion** *(dat)* **~** to chair a meeting/discussion

Vor|sit|zen|de(r) [ˈfoːɐzɪtsndə] MF *decl as adj* chairperson; *(Mann auch)* chairman; *(Frau auch)* chairman, chairwoman; *(von Firma)* chairperson, president *(US)*; *(von Verein)* president; *(von Partei, Gewerkschaft etc)* leader; **der ~ Richter** the presiding judge; **der ~ Mao** Chairman Mao

Vor|sor|ge F, *no pl (= Vorsichtsmaßnahme)* precaution; *(= vorherplanende Fürsorge)* provision(s *pl*) *no def art*; **zur ~** as a precaution; **~ tragen** to make provision; **~ treffen** to take precautions; *(fürs Alter)* to make provision

vor+sor|gen VI *sep* to make provision *(dass* so that); **für etw ~** to provide for sth, to make provision for sth

Vor|sor|ge|un|ter|su|chung F *(Med)* medical checkup

vor|sorg|lich [-zɔrklɪç] ADJ precautionary; *Mensch* cautious ADV as a precaution, to be on the safe side

Vor|spann [ˈfoːɐʃpan] M **-(e)s, -e a** *(= Vordergespann)* extra team (of horses) **b** *(= Vorlauf: von Film, Tonband)* leader; *(Film, TV: Titel und Namen)* opening credits *pl*; *(Press)* introductory *or* opening paragraph

vor+span|nen VT *sep Pferde* to harness; *(Elec)* to bias; *(Tech) Waffe* to pre-cock; **jdn ~** *(fig)* to enlist sb's help, to rope sb in *(inf)*

Vor|span|nung F *(Elec)* bias (voltage)

Vor|spei|se F hors d'"oe)uvre, starter *(Brit)*

vor+spie|geln VT *sep* to feign, to sham; *Krankheit, Bedürftigkeit auch* to plead; **jdm ~, dass ...** to pretend to sb that ...

Vor|spie|ge|lung F pretence *(Brit)*, pretense *(US)*; **unter ~ von etw** under the pretence

(Brit) or pretense *(US)* of sth; **das ist nur (eine) ~ falscher Tatsachen** *(hum)* it's all sham → **Tatsache**

Vor|spiel NT *(= Einleitung)* prelude; *(= Ouvertüre)* overture; *(Theat)* prologue *(Brit)*, prolog *(US)*; *(Sport)* preliminary match; *(bei Geschlechtsverkehr)* foreplay; *(von Musiker)* performance; *(bei Prüfung)* practical (exam); *(bei Einstellung)* audition; **das ist erst das ~** *(hum)* that is just for starters *(inf)*

vor+spie|len *sep* VT **a** **jdm etw ~** *(Mus)* to play sth to *or* for sb; *(Theat)* to act sth to *or* for sb; *(fig)* to act out a sham of sth in front of sb; **jdm eine Szene ~** *(lit)* to play a scene to *or* for sb; **jdm eine Komödie ~** *(fig)* to play *or* act out a farce in front of sb; **jdm ~, dass ...** to pretend to sb that ...; **spiel mir doch nichts vor** don't try and put on an act for me, don't try and pretend to me
b *(= zuerst spielen)* to play first
VI *(vor Zuhörern)* to play; *(Mus, Theat) (zur Prüfung)* to do one's practical (exam); *(bei Einstellung)* to audition; **jdm ~** *(Mus)* to play for sb; *(Theat)* to act (a role) for *or* in front of sb; **jdn ~ lassen** *(bei Einstellung)* to audition sb

Vor|spra|che F *(form: Besuch)* visit *(bei, auf +dat* to)

vor+spre|chen *sep irreg* VT to say first; *(= vortragen)* to recite; **jdm etw ~** to pronounce sth for sb, to say sth for sb; **wiederholt, was ich euch vorspreche** repeat after me VI **a** *(form: = jdn aufsuchen)* to call *(bei jdm* on sb); **bei** *or* **auf einem Amt ~** to call at an office **b** *(Theat)* to audition; **jdn ~ lassen** to audition sb

vor+sprin|gen VI *sep irreg aux sein* to jump *or* leap out; *(vorwärts)* to jump *or* leap forward; *(= herausragen)* to jut out, to project; *(Nase)* to be prominent; *(Kinn)* to be prominent, to protrude; **vor etw** *(dat)* **~** to jump *or* leap (out) in front of sth

vor|sprin|gend ADJ projecting; *Nase* prominent; *Kinn, Backenknochen* prominent, protruding

Vor|sprung M **a** *(Archit)* projection; *(= Felsvorsprung)* ledge; *(von Küste)* promontory **b** *(Sport, fig: = Abstand)* lead *(vor +dat* over); *(= Vorgabe)* start; **jdm 2 Meter/10 Minuten ~ geben** to give sb a 2-metre *(Brit) or* 2-meter *(US)*/a 10-minute start, to give sb 2 metres' *(Brit) or* meters' *(US)*/10 minutes' start; **einen ~ vor jdm haben** to be ahead of sb; *(Sport auch)* to be leading sb, to be in the lead; **einen ~ vor jdm gewinnen** to gain a lead over sb, to get ahead of sb

Vor-: **Vor|stadt** F suburb; **vor|städ|tisch** ADJ suburban

Vor|stand M **a** *(= leitendes Gremium)* board; *(von Firma)* board (of directors); *(von Verein)* committee; *(von Partei)* executive; *(von Akademie)* board (of governors) **b** *(= Leiter)* chairman, managing director **c** *(Aus)* = **Vorsteher**

Vor|stands-: **Vor|stands|eta|ge** F boardroom; **Vor|stands|mit|glied** NT member of the board; *(von Verein)* committee member; *(von Partei)* member of the executive; **Vor|stands|sit|zung** F *(von Firma)* board meeting; *(von Partei)* executive meeting; **Vor|stands|vor|sit|zen|de(r)** MF *decl as adj* chair(man) *or* chairperson of the board of directors; **Vor|stands|wahl** F *(in Firma)* elections *pl* to the board; *(in Partei)* elections *pl* to the executive

vor+ste|cken VT *sep (= anstecken)* to put on; *Brosche auch* to pin on

Vor|steck|na|del F *(= Brosche)* brooch; *(= Krawattennadel)* tiepin

vor+ste|hen VI *sep irreg aux haben or sein* **a** *(= hervorragen)* to project, to jut out; *(Zähne)* to stick out, to protrude; *(Backenknochen, Kinn)* to be prominent, to protrude; *(Nase)* to be prominent; **~de Zähne** protruding teeth, buck teeth
b **einer Sache ~** *(dem Haushalt)* to preside over sth; *einer Firma, einer Partei, einem Gremium* to be the chairman *or* chairperson of sth; *der Regierung* to be the head of sth; *einer Schule* to be the head(master/mistress) *or* principal *(US)* of sth; *einem Geschäft* to manage sth; *einer Abteilung, einer Behörde* to be in charge of sth
c *(form)* **wie im Vorstehenden** as above; **die ~den Erläuterungen** the above explanations
d *(Hunt: Hund)* to set, to point

Vor|ste|her M *(= Klostervorsteher)* abbot; *(= Bürovorsteher)* manager; *(= Gefängnisvorsteher)* governor; *(= Gemeindevorsteher)* chairman of parish council; *(dated Sch)* head(master), principal *(US)* → *auch* **Vorsteherin**

Vor|ste|her|drü|se F prostate (gland)

Vor|ste|he|rin F *(= Klostervorsteherin)* abbess; *(= Bürovorsteherin)* manager; *(= Gefängnisvorsteherin)* governor; *(= Gemeindevorsteherin)* chairman of parish council; *(dated Sch)* head(mistress), principal *(US)*

Vor|steh|hund M pointer; *(langhaariger)* setter

vor|stell|bar ADJ conceivable, imaginable; **das ist nicht ~** that is inconceivable *or* unimaginable

vor+stel|len *sep* ✪ 33.2, 34.3, 35.1 VT **a** *(nach vorn) Tisch, Stuhl, Auto* to move forward; *Bein* to put out; *Uhr* to put forward *or* on *(um* by)
b *(inf: = davorstellen)* **etw (vor etw** *acc)* **~** to put sth in front of sth; *Auto auch* to park sth in front of sth
c *(= darstellen)* to represent; *(= bedeuten)* to mean, to signify; **was soll das ~?** *(inf)* what is that supposed to be?; **etwas ~** *(fig) (= gut aussehen)* to look good; *(= Ansehen haben)* to count for something
d *(= bekannt machen)* **jdn jdm ~** to introduce sb to sb
e *(= bekannt machen, vorführen)* to present *(jdm* to sb); **jdm etw ~** to show sb sth
f *(= sich ausmalen)* **sich** *(dat)* **etw ~** to imagine sth; **stell dir mal vor** just imagine; **das kann ich mir gut ~** I can imagine that (well); **das muss man sich** *(dat)* **mal (bildlich** *or* **plastisch) ~** just imagine *or* picture it!; **sich** *(dat)* **etw unter etw** *(dat)* **~** *(Begriff, Wort)* to understand sth by sth; **darunter kann ich mir nichts ~** it doesn't mean anything to me; **das Kleid ist genau, was ich mir vorgestellt hatte** the dress is just what I had in mind; **was haben Sie sich (als Gehalt) vorgestellt?** what (salary) did you have in mind?; **ich kann sie mir gut als Lehrerin ~** I can just imagine *or* see her as a teacher; **stell dir das nicht so einfach vor** don't think it's so easy
VR **a** *(= sich nach vorn stellen)* to move *or* go forward; *(in Schlange)* to stand at the front
b *(= sich bekannt machen)* to introduce oneself *(jdm* to sb); *(bei Bewerbung)* to come/go for an interview; *(= Antrittsbesuch machen)* to present oneself *(+dat, bei* to)

vor|stel|lig ADJ **bei jdm ~ werden** to go to sb; *(wegen Beschwerde)* to complain to sb, to lodge a complaint with sb

Vor|stel|lung ✪ 28.2, 53.1, 53.3 F **a** *(= Gedanke)* idea; *(bildlich)* picture; *(= Einbildung)* illusion; *(= Vorstellungskraft)* imagination; **in meiner ~ sah das größer aus** I imagined it bigger; **in meiner ~ ist Gott kein alter Mann** I don't picture God as an old man; **du hast falsche ~en** you are wrong (in your ideas); **es übertrifft alle ~en** it's incredible *or* unbelievable; **das entspricht ganz meiner ~** that is just how I imagined *or* saw it; **sich** *(dat)* **eine ~ von etw machen** to form an idea *or (Bild)* picture of sth; **du machst dir keine ~, wie schwierig das ist** you have no idea how difficult that is
b *(Theat etc)* performance; *(Film)* showing, performance
c *(= das Bekanntmachen) (zwischen Leuten)* introduction; *(bei Hofe)* presentation *(bei* at); *(= Vorführung: von Geräten, neuem Artikel etc)* presentation; *(bei Bewerbung, Antrittsbesuch)* interview *(bei* with)
d *(= Einwand)* objection, protest

Vor|stel|lungs-: **Vor|stel|lungs|be|ginn** M start of a/the performance; **vor ~** before the start of a/the performance; **~ um 20 Uhr** performance starts at 8 pm *or* P.M. *(US)*; **Vor|stel|lungs|en|de** NT end of a/the performance; **nach ~** after a/the performance; **Vor|stel|lungs|ge|spräch** ✪ 46.4, 46.6 NT *(job)* interview; **Vor|stel|lungs|kraft** F imagination; **Vor|stel|lungs|ter|min** M appointment for an/the interview, interview appointment; **Vor|stel|lungs|ver|mö|gen** NT powers *pl* of imagination; **Vor|stel|lungs|welt** F imagination

Vor|stop|per(in) M(F) *(Ftbl)* centre half *(Brit)*, center half *(US)*

Vor|stoß M **a** *(= Vordringen)* venture; *(Mil)* advance, push; *(fig: = Versuch)* attempt **b** *(Tech: an Rädern)* wheel rim; *(Sew)* edging; *(= Litze)* braiding

vor+sto|ßen *sep irreg* VT to push forward VI *aux sein* to venture; *(Sport)* to attack; *(Mil)* to advance; **ins All ~** *(Rakete, Mensch)* to venture into space; **ins Viertelfinale ~** to advance into the quarterfinal

Vor|stra|fe F previous conviction

Vor|stra|fen|re|gis|ter NT criminal *or* police record; *(= Kartei)* criminal *or* police records *pl*

vor+stre|cken VT *sep* to stretch forward; *Arme* to stretch out; *Hand* to stretch *or* put out; *Bauch* to stick out; *Krallen* to put out; *(fig) Geld* to advance *(jdm* sb)

Vor|stu|fe F preliminary stage; *(von Entwicklung)* early stage

vor+stür|men VI *sep aux sein* to charge *or* rush forward *(hinter +dat* from behind)

Vor|tag M day before, eve; **am ~ der Konferenz** (on) the day before the conference, on the eve of the conference

Vor|ta|ges|schluss M *(St Ex)* close of trading on the previous day

vor+tan|zen *sep* VT **jdm einen Tanz/die Schritte ~** to dance a dance/the steps for sb; *(zur Demonstration)* to demonstrate a dance/the steps for sb VI *(zur Demonstration)* to demonstrate a dance/step *etc (jdm* to sb); *(als Prüfung)* to dance *(jdm* in front of sb)

Vor|tän|zer(in) M(F) leading dancer; *(= Anführer eines Tanzes)* leader of the dance

vor+täu|schen VT *sep Krankheit, Armut* to feign; *Schlag, Straftat, Orgasmus* to fake; **sie hat mir eine glückliche Ehe vorgetäuscht** she pretended to me that her marriage was happy

Vor|täu|schung F pretence *(Brit)*, pretense *(US)*, fake; **die ~ einer Krankheit** feigning an illness; **die ~ eines Schlags** faking a blow; **~ von Tatsachen** *(Jur)* misrepresentation of the facts; **unter ~ falscher Tatsachen** under false pretences *(Brit) or* pretenses *(US)*

Vor|teil ['foːɐtail] ✪ 40.2, 53.4 M **-s, -e** advantage *(auch Tennis)*; **den ~ haben, dass ...** to have the advantage that ...; **die Vor- und Nachteile** the pros and cons; **auf den eigenen ~ bedacht sein** to have an eye to one's own interests; **jdm gegenüber im ~ sein** to have an advantage over sb; **sich zu seinem ~ ändern** to change for the better; **ein ~ sein** to be an advantage, to be advantageous; **von ~ sein** to be advantageous; **das kann für dich nur von ~ sein** it can only be to your advantage; **ich habe dabei an deinen ~ gedacht** I was thinking of your interests; **im ~ sein** to have the advantage *(jdm gegenüber* over sb); **~e aus etw ziehen** to benefit from sth, to gain advantage from sth; **„Vorteil Sampras"** *(Tennis)* "advantage Sampras"

vor|teil|haft ADJ advantageous; *Kleid, Frisur* flattering; *Geschäft* lucrative, profitable; **ein ~er Kauf** a good buy, a bargain ADV **~ aussehen** to look one's best; **der helle Teppich wirkt ~** the light carpet looks good; **sie war nicht sehr ~ geschminkt** her make-up wasn't very flattering; **du solltest dich ~er kleiden** you should wear more flattering clothes; **etw ~ verkaufen** *(finanziell)* to sell sth for a profit; **etw ~ kaufen** to get sth at a good price

Vor|teils|an|nah|me F *(Jur)* accepting an advantage

Vor|trag ['fo:ɐtra:k] M -(e)s, **Vorträge** [-trɛ:gə] **a** *(= Vorlesung)* lecture; *(= Bericht, Beschreibung)* talk; **einen ~ halten** to give a lecture/talk; **halt keine Vorträge** *(inf)* don't give a whole lecture **b** *(= Darbietung)* performance; *(eines Gedichtes)* reading, recitation; *(Mus: = Solovortrag)* recital **c** *(= Art des Vortragens)* performance **d** *(Fin)* balance carried forward

vor+tra|gen VT *sep irreg* **a** *(lit)* to carry forward **b** *(= berichten)* to report; *(= förmlich mitteilen) Fall, Angelegenheit* to present; *Forderungen* to present, to convey; *Beschwerde* to lodge; *Meinung, Bedenken* to express, to convey; *Wunsch* to express **c** *(= vorsprechen) Gedicht* to recite; *Rede* to give; *(Mus)* to perform, to play; *Lied* to sing, to perform **d** *(Fin)* to carry forward

Vor|tra|gen|de(r) ['fo:ɐtra:gndə] MF *decl as adj* lecturer; *(von Rede, Bericht)* speaker; *(von Musikstück, Lied etc)* performer

Vor|trags-: **Vor|trags|abend** M lecture evening; *(mit Gedichten)* poetry evening; *(mit Musik)* recital; **Vor|trags|fol|ge** F series of lectures; *(einzelne Sendung)* lecture in a series; **Vor|trags|kunst** F skill as a performer; *(von Redner)* skill as a speaker; **Vor|trags|rei|he** F series of lectures

vor|treff|lich [fo:ɐ'trɛflɪç] ADJ excellent, splendid, superb ADV excellently, splendidly, superbly; **~ schmecken** to taste excellent; **sich ~ amüsieren** to have a splendid time

Vor|treff|lich|keit F -, *no pl* excellence

vor+tre|ten VI *sep irreg aux sein* **a** *(lit)* to step forward, to come forward **b** *(= hervorragen)* to project, to jut out; *(Augen)* to protrude; **~de Backenknochen** prominent cheekbones

Vor|tritt M, *no pl* precedence, priority; *(Sw: = Vorfahrt)* right of way; **in etw** *(dat)* **den ~ haben** *(fig)* to have precedence in sth *(vor +dat* over); **jdm den ~ lassen** *(lit)* to let sb go first; *(fig auch)* to let sb go ahead

vor+trock|nen VT *sep* to dry partially

Vor|trupp M advance guard, advance party

vor+tun VT *sep irreg (inf) Schürze, Riegel, Kette etc* to put on

vor+tur|nen *sep* VT **jdm eine Übung ~** *(= vormachen)* to demonstrate an exercise to sb; *(= öffentlich zeigen)* to perform an exercise in front of sb VI **jdm ~** *(= vormachen)* to demonstrate to sb; *(öffentlich)* to perform in front of sb

Vor|tur|ner(in) M(F) demonstrator (of gymnastic exercises); *(fig sl)* front man/woman

vo|rü|ber [fo'ry:bɐ] ADV **~ sein** *(räumlich, Jugend)* to be past; *(zeitlich auch, Gewitter, Winter, Kummer)* to be over; *(Schmerz)* to have gone

vo|rü|ber- PREF → *auch* **vorbei-**: **vo|rü|ber+ge|hen** VI *sep irreg aux sein* **a** *(räumlich) (an etw (dat)* sth) to go past, to pass (by); **im Vorübergehen** in passing; **an jdm/etw ~** *(fig: = ignorieren)* to ignore sb/sth **b** *(zeitlich)* to pass; *(Gewitter)* to blow over; **eine Gelegenheit ~ lassen** to let an opportunity slip **c an jdm ~** *(= sich nicht bemerkbar machen)* to pass sb by; **an jdm nicht ~** *(Erlebnis etc)* to leave its/their mark on sb; **vo|rü|ber|ge|hend** ADJ *(= flüchtig)* momentary, passing *attr*; *Krankheit* short; *(= zeitweilig)* temporary ADV temporarily, for a while; **sich ~ im Ausland aufhalten** to stay abroad for a short time; **jdn ~ festnehmen** to detain sb temporarily

Vor|über|le|gung F initial *or* preliminary consideration

Vor-: **Vor|übung** F preliminary exercise; **Vor|un|ter|su|chung** F preliminary examination; *(Jur)* preliminary *or* initial investigation

Vor|ur|teil NT prejudice *(gegenüber* against); **das ist ein ~** it's prejudice; **~e haben** *or* **hegen, in ~en befangen sein** to be prejudiced

Vor|ur|teils-: **vor|ur|teils|frei, vor|ur|teils|los** ADJ unprejudiced; *Entscheidung, Verhalten auch* unbiased ADV without prejudice, without bias; **Vor|ur|teils|lo|sig|keit** F -, *no pl* freedom from prejudice

Vor-: **Vor|vä|ter** PL forefathers *pl*, ancestors *pl*, forebears *pl*; **Vor|ver|gan|gen|heit** F *(Gram)* pluperfect; **Vor|ver|hand|lung** F preliminary negotiations *or* talks *pl*; *(Jur)* preliminary hearing; **Vor|ver|kauf** M *(Theat, Sport)* advance booking; **sich** *(dat)* **Karten im ~ besorgen** to buy tickets in advance; **Vor|ver|kaufs|ge|bühr** F advance booking fee; **Vor|ver|kaufs|kas|se** F, **Vor|ver|kaufs|stel|le** F advance booking office

vor+ver|le|gen *ptp* **vorverlegt** VT *sep* **a** *Termin* to bring forward **b** *(Mil) Front, Gefechtslinie* to push forward; **das Feuer ~** to increase the range

Vor-: **Vor|ver|ständ|nis** NT preconception; **Vor|ver|stär|ker** M preamplifier; **Vor|ver|trag** M preliminary contract; *(Pol)* preliminary treaty; **Vor|ver|ur|tei|lung** F prejudgement; **vor|vor|ges|tern** ADV *(inf)* three days ago; **vor|vo|rig** ADJ *(inf)* **~e Woche** the week before last; **~es Jahr** the year before last; **vor|vor|letz|te(r, s)** ADJ last but two

vor+wa|gen VR *sep (lit)* to venture forward; *(fig auch)* to venture

Vor|wahl F **a** preliminary election; *(US)* primary **b** *(Telec)* dialling *(Brit) or* area *(US)* code

vor+wäh|len VT *sep (Telec)* to dial first

Vor|wahl|num|mer F, **Vor|wähl|num|mer** F dialling *(Brit) or* area *(US)* code

vor+wal|ten VI *sep (geh)* to prevail

Vor|wand ['fo:ɐvant] M -(e)s, **Vorwände** [-vɛndə] pretext, excuse; **unter dem ~, dass …** under the pretext that …

vor+wär|men VT *sep* to preheat; *Teller* to heat; *Bett* to warm up

vor+war|nen VT *sep* **jdn ~** to tell *or* warn sb in advance, to give sb advance notice *or* warning

Vor|war|nung F (prior *or* advance) warning; *(Mil: vor Angriff)* early warning

vor|wärts ['fo:ɐvɛrts] ADV forwards, forward; **~!** *(inf)* let's go *(inf)*; *(Mil)* forward march!; **weiter ~** further ahead *or* on; **~ und rückwärts** backwards and forwards; **etw ~ und rückwärts kennen** *(fig inf)* to know sth backwards *(Brit)*, to know sth backwards and forwards *(US)*, to know sth inside out; **Rolle/Salto ~** forward roll/somersault

Vor|wärts-: **Vor|wärts|be|we|gung** F forward movement; **vor|wärts+brin|gen** *sep irreg*, **vor|wärts brin|gen** △ *irreg* VT *(fig)* to advance; **jdn ~** to help sb to get on; **Vor|wärts|gang** M *pl* **-gänge** forward gear; **vor|wärts+ge|hen** *sep irreg aux sein*, **vor|wärts ge|hen** △ *irreg aux sein (fig)* VI to progress, to come on VI *impers* **es geht wieder vorwärts** things are looking up; **mit etw geht es vorwärts** sth is progressing *or* going well; **vor|wärts+kom|men** *sep irreg aux sein*, **vor|wärts kom|men** △ *irreg aux sein* VI **a wir kamen nur langsam vorwärts** we made slow progress **b** *(fig)* to make progress, to get on *(in, mit* with); *(beruflich, gesellschaftlich)* to get on; **im Leben/Beruf ~** to get on in life/one's job; **Vor|wärts|kom|men** NT -s, *no pl (= Fortschritt)* progress; *(= Erfolg)* success; **da ist kein ~** *(auch fig)* there's no progress *or* headway to be made; **Vor|wärts|ver|tei|di|gung** F *(Mil)* forward defence *(Brit) or* defense *(US)*

Vor|wä|sche F, **Vor|wasch|gang** M prewash

vor+wa|schen VT *sep irreg* to prewash

vor|weg [fo:ɐ'vɛk] ADV *(= voraus, an der Spitze)* at the front; *(= vorher)* before(hand); *(= als Erstes, von vornherein)* at the outset

Vor|weg-: **Vor|weg|leis|tung** F *(Sw: = Vorauszahlung)* advance (payment); **Vor|weg|nah|me** [-na:mə] F -, -n anticipation; **vor|weg+neh|men** VT *sep irreg* to anticipate; **um das Wichtigste vorwegzunehmen** to come to the most important point first

vor|weih|nacht|lich ADJ pre-Christmas *attr* ADV **vorweihnachlich geschmückt** decorated for Christmas

Vor|weih|nachts|zeit F pre-Christmas period

vor+wei|sen VT *sep irreg* to show, to produce; *Zeugnisse* to produce; **etw ~ können** *(fig)* to have *or* possess sth

vor+wer|fen VT *sep irreg* **a** *(fig)* **jdm etw/Unpünktlichkeit ~** *(= anklagen)* to reproach sb for sth/for being unpunctual; *(= beschuldigen)* to accuse sb of sth/of being unpunctual; **jdm ~, dass er etw getan hat** to reproach sb for having done sth; **jdm ~, dass er etw nicht getan hat** to accuse sb of not having done sth; **das wirft er mir heute noch vor** he still holds it against me; **ich habe mir nichts vorzuwerfen** my conscience is clear; **muss ich mir das ~ lassen?** do I have to listen to these accusations? **b** *(lit)* **Tieren/Gefangenen etw ~** to throw sth down for the animals/prisoners

Vor|werk NT *(von Gut)* outlying estate; *(von Burg)* outwork

vor|wie|gend ['fo:ɐvi:gnt] ADJ *attr* predominant ADV predominantly, mainly, chiefly

Vor|wis|sen NT previous knowledge; *(= Vorherwissen)* foreknowledge; **ohne mein ~** without my previous knowledge

Vor|witz M, *no pl (= Keckheit)* cheek(iness) *(Brit)*, freshness *(US)*; *(= Vorlautheit)* forwardness, pertness; *(dial: = Neugier)* inquisitiveness, curiosity

vor|wit|zig ADJ *(= keck)* cheeky *(Brit)*, fresh *(US)*; *(= vorlaut)* forward, pert; *(dial: = neugierig)* inquisitive, curious

Vor|wo|chen|schluss M *(St Ex)* close of trading the previous week

Vor|wort NT **a** *pl* **-worte** foreword; *(esp von Autor)* preface **b** *pl* **-wörter** *(Aus: = Präposition)* preposition

Vor|wurf M **a** reproach; *(= Beschuldigung)* accusation; **man machte ihm den ~ der Bestechlichkeit** he was accused of being open to bribery; **jdm/sich große Vorwürfe machen, dass …** to reproach sb/oneself for …; **ich habe mir keine Vorwürfe zu machen** my conscience is clear; **jdm etw zum ~ machen** to reproach sb with sth; **jdm (wegen etw) Vorwürfe machen** to reproach sb (for sth) **b** *(= Vorlage)* subject

vor|wurfs|voll ADJ reproachful ADV reproachfully

vor+zäh|len VT *sep* **jdm etw ~** to count sth out to sb; *(fig: = auflisten)* to enumerate sth to sb

vor+zau|bern VT *sep* **jdm Kunststücke ~** to perform conjuring *or* magic tricks for sb; **jdm etw ~** *(fig)* to conjure sth up for sb

Vor|zei|chen NT *(= Omen)* omen, sign; *(Med)* early symptom; *(Math)* sign; *(Mus) (Kreuz/b)* sharp/flat (sign); *(vor einzelner Note)* accidental; *(von Tonart)* key signature; **positives/negatives ~** *(Math)* plus/minus (sign); **unter umgekehrtem/dem gleichen ~** *(fig)* under different/the same circumstances; **dadurch haben die Verhandlungen ein negatives ~ erhalten** that put the negotiations under a cloud

vor+zeich|nen VT *sep Linien etc* to sketch *or* draw (out); **jdm etw ~** *(zum Nachmalen)* to sketch *or* draw sth out for sb; *(fig)* to map *or* mark sth out for sb; **diese Entwicklung ist vorgezeichnet** this development has been marked out

vor|zeig|bar ADJ presentable

Vor|zei|ge- *in cpds (= vorbildlich)* model, exemplary; *(= führend)* leading; **Vor|zei|ge|fir|ma** F model company; **Vor|zei|ge|frau** F *(= Vorbild)* female role model; *(= Alibifrau)* token woman

vor+zei|gen VT *sep* to show, to produce; *Zeugnisse* to produce; **jdm die Hände ~** to show sb one's hands

Vor|zei|ge|ob|jekt NT, **Vor|zei|ge|stück** NT showpiece

Vor|zeit F prehistoric times *pl*; **in der ~** in prehistoric times; *(= vor Langem)* in the dim and distant past → **grau**

vor|zei|ten [fo:ɐ'tsaitn] ADV *(liter)* in days gone by, in olden times

vor|zei|tig ADJ early; *Geburt, Altern etc* premature ADV early, prematurely

Vor|zei|tig|keit F -, *no pl (Gram)* anteriority
vor|zeit|lich ADJ prehistoric; *(fig)* archaic
Vor|zelt NT awning
vor+zie|hen VT *sep irreg* **a** *(= hervorziehen)* to pull out; *(= nach vorne ziehen) Stuhl etc* to pull up; *Truppen* to move up; *(= zuziehen) Vorhänge* to draw, to close; **etw hinter/unter etw** *(dat)* ~ to pull sth out from behind/under sth **b** *(fig) (= lieber mögen)* to prefer; *(= bevorzugen) jdn* to favour *(Brit)*, to favor *(US)*; **etw einer anderen Sache ~** to prefer sth to sth else; **es ~, etw zu tun** to prefer to do sth; *(allgemein gesehen)* to prefer doing sth **c** *(= zuerst behandeln, abfertigen)* to give priority to **d** *Wahlen, Termin* to bring forward; **vorgezogener Ruhestand** early retirement
Vor|zim|mer NT anteroom; *(= Büro)* outer office; *(Aus: = Diele)* hall
Vor|zim|mer-: **Vor|zim|mer|da|me** F receptionist; **Vor|zim|mer|wand** F *(Aus)* hall stand
Vor|zug M **a** preference; *(= Vorteil)* advantage; *(= gute Eigenschaft)* merit, asset; **einer Sache** *(dat)* **den ~ geben** *(form)* to prefer sth, to give sth preference; *(= Vorrang geben)* to give sth precedence; **den ~ vor etw** *(dat)* **haben** to be preferable to sth; **den ~ haben, dass ...** to have the advantage that ... **b** *(Aus Sch)* distinction
Vor|zug M *(Rail)* train in front; *(= früher fahrend)* train before; *(= Entlastungszug)* relief train
vor|züg|lich [foːɐ'tsyːklɪç, *(esp Aus)* 'foːɐ-] ADJ excellent, superb; *Qualität, Arbeit auch* exquisite → **Hochachtung** ADV excellently, superbly; *(= vornehmlich)* especially, particularly; **der Wein schmeckt ~** the wine tastes excellent *or* superb
Vor|züg|lich|keit F -, *no pl* excellence
Vor|zugs-: **Vor|zugs|ak|tie** F *(St Ex)* preference share; **Vor|zugs|be|hand|lung** F preferential treatment *no indef art*; **Vor|zugs|milch** F *milk with high fat content*, ≈ gold-top milk *(Brit)*, ≈ full milk *(US)*; **Vor|zugs|preis** M special discount price; **Vor|zugs|schü|ler(in)** M(F) *(Aus)* star pupil; **vor|zugs|wei|se** ADV preferably, by preference; *(= hauptsächlich)* mainly, chiefly; **etw ~ trinken** to prefer to drink *or* drinking sth
Vor|zün|dung F *(Aut)* pre-ignition
Vo|ten, **Vo|ta** *(geh) pl von* **Votum**
vo|tie|ren [vo'tiːrən] *ptp* **votiert** VI *(geh)* to vote
Vo|tiv- [vo'tiːf-]: **Vo|tiv|bild** NT votive picture; **Vo|tiv|ka|pel|le** F votive chapel; **Vo|tiv|ta|fel** F votive tablet
Vo|tum ['voːtʊm] NT **-s, Voten** *or* **Vota** [-tn, -ta] *(geh)* vote
Vo|yeur [voa'jøːɐ] M **-s, -e**, **Vo|yeu|rin** [-'jøːrɪn] F **-, -nen** voyeur
Vo|yeu|ris|mus [voajø'rɪsmʊs] M -, *no pl* voyeurism
vo|yeu|ris|tisch [voajø'rɪstɪʃ] ADJ voyeuristic
VP [fau'peː] F - *(DDR) abbr von* **Volkspolizei**
VPS [faupeː'lɛs] *abbr von* **Videoprogrammsystem** VPS
V-Pul|lo|ver ['fau-] M V-neck pullover
VR [fau'lɛr] **a** *abbr von* **Volksrepublik** VR **b** *abbr von* **virtuelle Realität**
v. R. w. *abbr von* **von Rechts wegen**
V-Shirt NT **-s, -s** V-neck shirt
v. T. *abbr von* **vom Tausend**
vul|gär [vʊl'gɛːɐ] ADJ vulgar ADV vulgarly; **~ aussehen** to look vulgar; **drück dich nicht so ~ aus** don't be so vulgar
Vul|gär|aus|druck M *pl* **-ausdrücke** vulgar expression, vulgarity
Vul|ga|ri|tät [vʊlgari'tɛːt] F **-, -en** vulgarity
Vul|gär|la|tein NT vulgar Latin
vul|go ['vʊlgo] ADV in plain language
Vul|kan [vʊl'kaːn] M **-(e)s, -e** volcano; **auf einem ~ leben** *(fig)* to be living on the edge of a volcano → **Tanz b**
Vul|kan-: **Vul|kan|aus|bruch** M volcanic eruption; **Vul|kan|fi|ber** F vulcanized fibre *(Brit) or* fiber *(US)*
Vul|ka|ni|sa|ti|on [vʊlkaniza'tsioːn] F **-, -en** *(Tech)* vulcanization
vul|ka|nisch [vʊl'kaːnɪʃ] ADJ volcanic
Vul|ka|ni|sier|an|stalt [vʊlkani'ziːr-] F vulcanization plant
vul|ka|ni|sie|ren [vʊlkani'ziːrən] *ptp* **vulkanisiert** VT to vulcanize
Vul|ka|no|lo|ge [vʊlkano'loːgə] M **-n, -n**, **Vul|ka|no|lo|gin** [-'loːgɪn] F **-, -nen** volcanologist
Vul|ka|no|lo|gie [vʊlkanolo'giː] F -, *no pl* volcanology
Vul|va ['vʊlva] M **-, Vulven** *(Anat)* vulva
v. u. Z. *abbr von* **vor unserer Zeitrechnung** BC
V-Waf|fen ['fau-] PL *abbr von* **Vergeltungswaffen**

W, w [ve:] NT **-, -** W, w

W *abbr von* **Westen**

WAA [ve:la:'la:] F *abbr von* **Wiederaufbereitungsanlage**

Waadt [va(:)t] F **-** Vaud

Waa|ge ['va:gə] F **-, -n** **a** *(Gerät)* scales *pl*; *(= Federwaage, Apothekerwaage)* balance; *(für Lastwagen, Autos)* weighbridge *(Brit)*, weigh station; **eine ~** a pair of scales; **sich** *(dat)* **die ~ halten** *(fig)* to balance one another *or* each other; **einer Sache** *(dat)* **die ~ halten** to balance sth (out) → **Zünglein b** *(Astron, Astrol)* Libra; **er ist (eine) ~** he's (a) Libra **c** *(Sport: = Standwaage)* horizontal single leg stand

Waa|ge-: **Waa|ge|bal|ken** M (balance *or* scale) beam; **waa|ge|recht** ADJ horizontal, level; *Linie, Ebene* horizontal; *(im Kreuzworträtsel)* across ADV levelly; **Waa|ge|rech|te** F *decl as adj* horizontal; **etw in die ~ bringen** to make sth horizontal *or* level; **etw in der ~n transportieren** to transport sth horizontally

Waag-: **waag|recht** ADJ, ADV = **waagerecht**; **Waag|rech|te** F *decl as adj* = **Waagerechte**; **Waag|scha|le** F (scale) pan, scale; **(schwer) in die ~ fallen** *(fig)* to carry weight; **jedes Wort auf die ~ legen** to weigh every word (carefully); **seinen Einfluss/seine Autorität/sein ganzes Gewicht in die ~ werfen** *(fig)* to bring one's influence/one's authority/one's full weight to bear

wab|be|lig ['vabəlɪç] ADJ *Pudding, Gelee* wobbly; *Mensch* flabby

wab|beln ['vabln] VI to wobble

wabb|lig ADJ = **wabbelig**

Wa|be ['va:bə] F **-, -n** honeycomb

Wa|ben-: **wa|ben|för|mig** ADJ honeycombed; **Wa|ben|ho|nig** M comb honey

wa|bern ['va:bɐn] VI *(geh)* to undulate; *(Nebel, Gerüche)* to drift, to waft; *(Gerücht)* to float; *(obs, dial: = flackern)* to flicker

wach [vax] ADJ awake *pred*; *(fig: = aufgeweckt)* alert, wide-awake; *Nacht* sleepless, wakeful; **in ~em Zustand** in the waking state; **sich ~ halten** to keep *or* stay awake, to keep oneself awake; **~ werden** to wake up; **~ liegen** to lie awake; **jdn ~ schütteln** to shake sb awake; **jdn ~ küssen** to wake sb with a kiss → *auch* **wachhalten**

Wach-: **Wach|ab|lö|sung** F changing of the guard; *(fig: = Regierungswechsel)* change of government; *(Mensch)* relief guard; **Wach|ba|tail|lon** NT guard battalion, guards *pl*; **Wach|boot** NT patrol boat; **Wach|dienst** M lookout, guard (duty); *(Mil)* guard (duty); *(Naut)* watch; **~ haben/machen** to be on guard (duty); *(Naut)* to have the watch

Wa|che ['vaxə] F **-, -n** **a** *(= Wachdienst)* guard (duty); **auf ~** on guard (duty); **(bei jdm) ~ halten** to keep guard *or* watch (over sb); *(= Krankenwache)* to keep watch (at sb's bedside), to watch over sb; *(= Totenwache)* to watch over sb; **~ stehen** *or* **schieben** *(inf)* to be on guard (duty); *(Dieb, Schüler etc)* to keep a lookout **b** *(Mil)* *(= Wachposten)* guard, sentry; *(Gebäude)* guardhouse; *(Raum)* guardroom **c** *(Naut: Personen, Dauer)* watch; **~ haben** to be on watch **d** *(= Polizeiwache)* (police) station

wa|chen ['vaxn] VI **a** *(= wach sein)* to be awake; *(= nicht schlafen können)* to lie awake **b** *(= Wache halten)* to keep watch; **bei jdm ~** to sit up with sb, to keep watch by sb's bedside; **das Wachen am Krankenbett** sitting up with a/the patient *or* at a/the sickbed; **über etw** *(acc)* **~** to (keep) watch over sth; *über Verkehr* to supervise sth; **der Polizist wachte darüber, dass niemand ...** the policeman watched that no-one ...

Wach-: **wach|ha|bend** ADJ *attr* duty; **Wach|ha|ben|de(r)** ['vaxha:bndə] MF *decl as adj* *(= Offizier)* duty officer; *(Naut)* watch; **wach+hal|ten** *sep irreg*, **wach hal|ten** △ *irreg* VT *(fig) Erinnerung* to keep alive; *Interesse auch* to keep up → *auch* **wach**; **Wach|heit** F **-**, *no pl (fig)* alertness; **(die) ~ des Geistes** alertness of mind, an alert *or* wide-awake mind; **Wach|hund** M *(lit, fig)* watchdog; *(lit auch)* guard dog; **wach+küs|sen** VT *sep* → **wach**; **Wach|leu|te** *pl von* **Wachmann**; **wach+lie|gen** VI *sep irreg* → **wach**; **Wach|lo|kal** NT guardroom; **Wach|ma|cher** M *(Med inf)* stimulant; **Wach|mann** M *pl* **-leute** watchman; *(Aus)* policeman; **Wach|mann|schaft** F men *or* squad on guard; *(Naut)* watch; **Wach|of|fi|zier(in)** M(F) *(Naut)* officer of the watch

Wa|chol|der [va'xɔldɐ] M **-s, -** **a** *(Bot)* juniper (tree) **b** = **Wacholderschnaps**

Wa|chol|der-: **Wa|chol|der|bee|re** F juniper berry; **Wa|chol|der|brannt|wein** M *(form)*, **Wa|chol|der|schnaps** M spirit *(Brit)* *or* alcohol made from juniper berries, ≈ gin; **Wa|chol|der|strauch** M juniper (tree)

Wach-: **Wach|pos|ten** M sentry, guard; *(= Schüler, Dieb etc)* lookout; **wach+ru|fen** VT *sep irreg (fig) Erinnerung etc* to call to mind, to evoke; **wach+rüt|teln** VT *sep (fig)* to shake up, to (a)rouse; *Gewissen* to stir, to (a)rouse; **jdn aus seiner Apathie ~** to shake sb out of his apathy

Wachs [vaks] NT **-es, -e** wax; **weich wie ~** as soft as butter; **meine Knie wurden weich wie ~** my knees turned to jelly; **~ in jds Händen sein** *(fig)* to be putty in sb's hands

wach|sam ['vaxza:m] ADJ watchful, vigilant; *(= vorsichtig)* on one's guard; **ein ~es Auge auf jdn/etw haben** to keep a watchful *or* sharp eye on sb/sth → **Holzauge** ADV watchfully, vigilantly

Wach|sam|keit F **-**, *no pl* watchfulness, vigilance; *(= Vorsichtigkeit)* guardedness

Wachs-: **Wachs|bild** NT waxen image; **wachs|bleich** ADJ waxen; **Wachs|boh|ne** F wax bean; **Wachs|bunt|stift** M wax crayon

Wach|schiff NT patrol ship

wach+schüt|teln VT *sep* → **wach**

wach|seln ['vaksln] VT *(Aus: = mit Wachs behandeln)* to wax

wach|sen ['vaksn] *pret* **wuchs** [vu:ks], *ptp* **gewachsen** VI *aux sein* to grow; *(Spannung, Begeisterung auch)* to mount; **in die Breite ~** to broaden (out), to get *or* grow broader; **in die Länge ~** to lengthen, to get *or* grow longer; **in die Höhe ~** to grow taller; *(Kind)* to shoot up *(inf)*; **sich** *(dat)* **einen Bart ~ lassen** to grow a beard; **sich** *(dat)* **die Haare ~ lassen** to let one's hair grow, to grow one's hair; **ich lese dieses Buch mit ~der Begeisterung** I'm really getting into this book; **gut gewachsen** *(Baum)* well-grown; *Mensch* with *or* having a good figure; **wie gewachsen** with fat and gristle not removed; **er wächst mit** *or* **an seiner Verantwortung** *(fig)* he grows with his responsibility → *auch* **gewachsen**

wach|sen VT to wax

wäch|sern ['vɛksɐn] ADJ *(lit, fig)* waxen

Wachs-: **Wachs|far|be** F **a** *(= Farbstift)* wax crayon; **mit ~(n) gemalt** drawn with wax crayons *or* in wax crayon **b** *(= Farbstoff)* wax dye; **Wachs|farb|stift** M wax crayon; **Wachs|fi|gur** F wax figure; **Wachs|fi|gu|ren|ka|bi|nett** NT waxworks *pl*; **Wachs|ker|ze** F wax candle; **Wachs|licht** NT night-light; **Wachs|ma|le|rei** F **a** *no pl (Technik)* encaustic painting **b** *(Bild)* encaustic; **Wachs|mal|stift** M, **Wachs|mal|krei|de** F wax crayon; **Wachs|mas|ke** F wax mask; **Wachs|mat|ri|ze** F stencil; **Wachs|pa|pier** NT waxed paper; **Wachs|stift** M wax crayon; **Wachs|stock** M wax taper

wächst [vɛkst] *3. pers sing pres von* **wachsen**

Wach|stu|be ['vaxʃtu:bə] F guardroom; *(von Polizei)* duty room

Wachs|tuch ['vaks-] NT *pl* **-tücher** oilcloth

Wachs|tum ['vakstu:m] NT **-s**, *no pl* growth; **im ~ zurückgeblieben** stunted; **eigenes ~ (des Winzers)** from *or* grown in our own vineyards

Wachs|tums-: **Wachs|tums|ak|tie** F growth stock; **Wachs|tums|bran|che** F growth industry; **Wachs|tums|fonds** M growth fund; **wachs|tums|för|dernd** ADJ *(Econ, Biol)* growth-promoting; **wachs|tums|hem|mend** ADJ *(Econ, Biol)* growth-inhibiting; **Wachs|tums|hem|mung** F inhibition of growth *no pl*; **Wachs|tums|hor|mon** NT growth hormone; **Wachs|tums|po|li|tik** F growth policy; **Wachs|tums|ra|te** F *(Biol, Econ)* growth rate; **Wachs|tums|schmer|zen** PL growing pains *pl*; **wachs|tums|stark** ADJ *(Econ) Markt, Branche* booming; **Wachs|tums|stö|rung** F disturbance of growth

Wachs-: **wachs|weich** ADJ (as) soft as butter; *Ausrede* lame; *Erklärung, Formulierung* woolly *(esp Brit)*, vague; **~ werden** *(Mensch)* to melt; *(Knie)* to turn to jelly; **Wachs|zie|her** [-tsi:ɐ] M **-s, -**, **Wachs|zie|he|rin** [-ərın] F **-, -nen** chandler

Wacht [vaxt] F **-, -en** *(obs, liter)* = **Wache a**

Wach|tel ['vaxtl] F **-, -n** quail; *(fig inf: Frau)* silly goose *(inf)*; **alte ~** *(inf)* *(unfreundlich)* old hen *(inf)*; *(dumm)* silly old goose *(inf)*

Wäch|ter ['vɛçtɐ] M **-s, -** guard dog, watchdog

Wäch|ter ['vɛçtɐ] M **-s, -**, **Wäch|te|rin** [-ərın] F **-, -nen** guardian; *(= Nachtwächter)* watchman; *(= Turmwächter)* watch; *(= Museumswächter, Parkplatzwächter)* attendant

Wacht-: **Wacht|meis|ter(in)** M(F) **a** *(old Mil)* sergeant **b** *(= Polizist)* (police) constable *(Brit)*, patrolman/-woman *(US)*; **Herr ~** officer, constable *(Brit)*; **Wacht|pos|ten** M sentry, guard; *(= Schüler, Dieb etc)* lookout

Wach|traum M daydream

Wach(t)|turm M watchtower

Wach-: **Wach- und Schließ|ge|sell|schaft** F security corps; **Wach|wech|sel** M *(lit, fig)* changing of the guard; **Wach|zim|mer** NT

(Aus) guardroom; **Wạch|zu|stand** M **im ~** in the waking state

Wạ|ckel|da|ckel M nodding dog *(Brit)*, bobblehead *(US)*

Wạ|cke|lei [vakəˈlai] F **-, -en** *(inf)* wobbling

wạ|cke|lig [ˈvakəlɪç] **ADJ** wobbly; *Möbelstück auch* rickety; *Zahn, Schraube auch* loose; *(fig) Firma, Unternehmen, Kompromiss* shaky; *Mehrheit* flimsy; **~ auf den Beinen sein** *(inf) (Patient)* to be wobbly on one's legs, to be shaky; *(alter Mensch)* to be doddery *(esp Brit) or* shaky; **auf ~en Füßen stehen** *(fig)* to have no sound *or* firm basis **ADV ~ stehen** *(lit)* to be unsteady *or* wobbly; *(fig: Unternehmen, Schüler)* to be shaky

Wạ|ckel|kon|takt M loose connection

wạ|ckeln [ˈvakln] VI **a** *(= sich bewegen)* to wobble; *(= zittern)* to shake; *(Zahn, Schraube)* to be loose; *(fig) (Thron)* to totter; *(Position)* to be shaky; **du hast gewackelt** you wobbled/shook; *(beim Fotografieren)* you moved; **mit den Ohren ~** to waggle *(Brit) or* wiggle one's ears; **mit den Hüften/dem Hintern ~** to wiggle one's hips/bottom; **mit dem Kopf/Schwanz ~** to wag one's head/its tail **b** *aux sein (= langsam, unsicher gehen)* to totter; *(kleines Kind)* to toddle

Wạ|ckel|pud|ding M, **Wạ|ckel|pe|ter** [-peːtɐ] M **-s, -** *(inf)* jelly *(Brit)*, Jell-O® *(US)*

wạ|cker [ˈvakɐ] **ADJ a** *(= tapfer)* brave, valiant **b** *(old: = tüchtig)* upright, honest **ADV** *(= tapfer)* bravely; **sich ~ halten** *(inf)* to stand *or* hold one's ground; **sich ~ schlagen** *(inf)* to put up a brave fight

Wạ|cker|stein M boulder

wạck|lig [ˈvaklɪç] ADJ, ADV = **wackelig**

Wa|de [ˈvaːdə] F **-, -n** calf

Wa|den-: **Wa|den|bein** NT fibula; **Wa|den|krampf** M cramp in the/one's calf; **Wa|den|strumpf** M half stocking; **Wa|den|wi|ckel** M *(Med)* compress around the leg

Wạf|fe [ˈvafə] F **-, -n** *(lit, fig)* weapon; *(= Schusswaffe)* gun; *(Mil: = Waffengattung)* arm; **~n** *(Mil)* arms; **~n tragen** to carry arms; **zu den ~n rufen** to call to arms; **zu den ~n greifen** to take up arms; **unter ~n (stehen)** (to be) under arms; **die ~n strecken** *(lit, fig)* to lay down one's arms, to surrender; **jdn mit seinen eigenen ~n schlagen** *(fig)* to beat sb at his own game, to beat sb with his own weapons

Wạf|fel [ˈvafl] F **-, -n** waffle; *(= Keks, Eiswaffel)* wafer; *(= Eistüte)* cornet; **einen** *or* **was an der ~ haben** *(sl: = verrückt sein)* to have a screw loose *(inf)*, to be (a)round the bend *or* off one's nut *(inf)*

Wạf|fel-: **Wạf|fel|ei|sen** NT waffle iron; **Wạf|fel|stoff** M honeycomb cloth

Wạf|fen- *in cpds* arms; **Wạf|fen|ar|se|nal** NT arsenal; *(von Staat)* stockpile; **Wạf|fen|be|sitz** M possession of firearms; **Wạf|fen|bru|der** M *(old)* comrade in arms *(old)*; **Wạf|fen|dienst** M *(old)* military service; **Wạf|fen|em|bar|go** NT arms embargo; **wạf|fen|fä|hig** ADJ **a** *Uran, Plutonium* weapons-grade **b** = **wehrfähig**; **Wạf|fen|gang** M *pl* **-gänge** *(old Mil)* passage at arms, armed encounter; *(Univ)* round; **Wạf|fen|gat|tung** F *(Mil)* arm of the service; **Wạf|fen|ge|brauch** M use of firearms; **Wạf|fen|ge|setz** NT *usu pl* gun control law; **Wạf|fen|ge|walt** F force of arms; **mit ~** by force of arms; **Wạf|fen|han|del** M arms trade *or* traffic; *(illegal auch)* gunrunning; **der ~ ist ...** arms trade *or* traffic/gunrunning is ...; **Wạf|fen|händ|ler(in)** M(F) arms dealer; *(illegal auch)* gunrunner; **Wạf|fen|hil|fe** F military assistance; **Wạf|fen|kam|mer** F armoury *(Brit)*, armory *(US)*; **Wạf|fen|la|ger** NT *(von Armee)* ordnance depot; *(von Terroristen)* cache; **Wạf|fen|lie|fe|rung** F supply of arms; **wạf|fen|los** ADJ unarmed; **Wạf|fen|rock** M *(old)* uniform; **Wạf|fen|ru|he** F ceasefire; **Wạf|fen|schein** M firearms *or* gun licence *(Brit) or* license *(US)*; **Wạf|fen|schie|ber(in)** M(F) arms broker *or* dealer; **Wạf|fen|schie|be|rei** F arms broking *or* dealing; **Wạf|fen|schmied** M *(Hist)* armourer *(Brit)*, armorer *(US)*; **Wạf|fen|schmug|gel** M gunrunning, arms smuggling; **Wạf|fen-SS** [-lɛslɛs] F *(NS)* Waffen-SS; **wạf|fen|star|rend** ADJ bristling with weapons

Wạf|fen|still|stand M armistice

Wạf|fen|still|stands-: **Wạf|fen|still|stands|ab|kom|men** NT armistice agreement; **Wạf|fen|still|stands|li|nie** F ceasefire *or* armistice line

Wạf|fen-: **Wạf|fen|sys|tem** NT weapon system; **Wạf|fen|trä|ger** M *(Fahrzeug)* weapon carrier; **Wạf|fen|trä|ger(in)** M(F) **~(in) sein** to carry arms

wạff|nen [ˈvafnən] VR = **wappnen**

wäg|bar ADJ *(geh)* ponderable; **ein nicht ~es Risiko** an imponderable risk

Wa|ge-: **Wa|ge|hals** M daredevil; **wa|ge|hal|sig** ADJ = **waghalsig**

Wä|gel|chen [ˈvɛːglçən] NT **-s, -** *dim von* **Wagen**

Wa|ge-: **Wa|ge|mut** M, *no pl (geh)* (heroic) daring *or* boldness; **wa|ge|mu|tig** ADJ daring, bold

wa|gen [ˈvaːgn] ✪ 42.3, 53.6 **VT** to venture; *(= riskieren) hohen Einsatz, sein Leben* to risk; *(= sich getrauen)* to dare; **es ~, etw zu tun** to venture to do sth; to risk doing sth; to dare (to) do sth; **wage nicht, mir zu widersprechen!** don't you dare (to) contradict me!; **ich wags** I'll risk it, I'll take the risk *or* plunge; **davon hätte ich nicht zu träumen gewagt** I would never even have dreamed it; **wer wagt, gewinnt** *(Prov)* **wer nicht wagt, der nicht gewinnt** *(Prov)* nothing ventured, nothing gained *(Prov)* → **Tänzchen, frisch ADV**

VR to dare; **sich ~, etw zu tun** to dare (to) do sth; **sich an etw** *(acc)* **~** to venture to do sth; **ich wage mich nicht daran** I dare not do it; **sich auf ein Gebiet ~** to venture into an area; **bei dem schönen Wetter kann ich mich aus dem Haus/ins Wasser ~** in this lovely weather I can venture out of doors/into the water; **er wagt sich nicht mehr aus dem Haus** he doesn't venture out (of the house) any more, he doesn't dare leave the house any more → *auch* **gewagt**

Wa|gen [ˈvaːgn] M **-s, -** *or (S Ger, Aus)* = [ˈvɛːgn] **a** *(= Personenwagen)* car; *(= Lieferwagen)* van; *(= Planwagen)* (covered) wagon; *(= Zirkuswagen, Zigeunerwagen)* caravan, wagon; *(von Pferden gezogen)* wagon, cart; *(= Kutsche)* coach; *(= Puppenwagen, Kinderwagen)* pram *(Brit)*, baby carriage *(US)*; *(= Handwagen)* (hand)cart; *(= Kofferkuli, Einkaufswagen)* trolley; *(= Schreibmaschinenwagen)* carriage; *(= Straßenbahnwagen, Seilbahnwagen)* car; *(= Eisenbahnwagen)* coach *(Brit)*, car, carriage *(Brit)*; *(= Omnibus)* bus; **jdm an den ~ fahren** *(fig)* to pick holes in sb; **sich nicht vor jds ~ spannen lassen** *(fig)* not to allow oneself to be used *or* made use of by sb → **Rad a**

b *(Astron)* **der Große ~** the Plough *(Brit)*, the Big Dipper; **der Kleine ~** the Little Dipper

wä|gen [ˈvɛːgn] *pret* **wog** *or* **wägte** [voːk, ˈvɛːktə], *ptp* **gewogen** *or* **gewägt** [gəˈvoːgn, gəˈvɛːkt] VT *(old, form)* to weigh; *(geh: = bedenken auch)* to ponder; **erst ~, dann wagen** *(Prov)* look before you leap *(Prov)*

Wa|gen-: **Wa|gen|ab|teil** NT *(Rail)* compartment; **Wa|gen|bau|er(in)** M(F) *pl* **-bauer(innen)** coach-builder; **Wa|gen|burg** F barricade (of wagons); **Wa|gen|deich|sel** F shaft; **Wa|gen|fol|ge** F → **Wagen a** order of cars/coaches *or* carriages *etc*; **Wa|gen|füh|rer(in)** M(F) driver; **Wa|gen|he|ber** M jack; **Wa|gen|la|dung** F *(von Lastwagen)* lorryload *(Brit)*, truckload; *(von Eisenbahn)* wagonload; **Wa|gen|len|ker** M *(Hist)* charioteer; **Wa|gen|pa|pie|re** PL car *or* vehicle documents *pl*; **Wa|gen|park** M fleet of cars; *(= Lieferwagen)* fleet of vans; **Wa|gen|pfle|ge** F care of the/one's car; **Wa|gen|rad** NT cartwheel; *(hum: = Hut)* picture hat; **Wa|gen|ren|nen** NT *(Hist)* chariot racing; *(einzelner Wettkampf)* chariot race; **Wa|gen|rück|lauf** M *(an Schreibmaschine)* carriage return; **Wa|gen|schlag** M *(von Kutsche)* carriage door; *(von Auto)* car door; **Wa|gen|schmie|re** F cart grease; **Wa|gen|typ** M type of car; **Wa|gen|wä|sche** F car wash; *(= das Waschen)* car washing

Wa|ge|stück NT daring deed, deed of daring

Wag|gon [vaˈgõː, vaˈgɔŋ] M **-s, -s** (goods) wagon, freight car *(US)*; *(= Ladung)* wagonload/carload

wag|gon|wei|se [vaˈgõː-, vaˈgɔŋ-] ADV by the wagonload *or* carload *(US)*

Wag-: **Wag|hals** M daredevil; **wag|hal|sig** ADJ foolhardy, daredevil *attr*; **Wag|hal|sig|keit** [ˈvaːkhalzɪçkait] F **-, -en** foolhardiness

Wag|ner [ˈvaːgnɐ] M **-s, -**, **Wag|ne|rin** [-ərɪn] F **-, -nen** *(dial)* coach-builder

Wag|ne|ri|a|ner [vaːgnəˈriaːnɐ] M **-s, -**, **Wag|ne|ri|a|ne|rin** [-ərɪn] F **-, -nen** Wagnerian

Wag|nis [ˈvaːknɪs] NT **-ses, -se** hazardous business; *(= Risiko)* risk

Wag|nis|ka|pi|tal NT *(Fin)* venture capital

Wa|gon [vaˈgoːn] [vaˈgoːn] M **-s, -s** → **Waggon**

wa|gon|wei|se [vaˈgoːn-] ADV → **waggonweise**

Wä|he [ˈvɛːə] F **-, -n** *(esp Sw) flan with a sweet or salty topping*

Wahl [vaːl] ✪ 45.4, 53.2 F **-, -en a** *(= Auswahl)* choice; **die ~ fiel auf ihn/dieses Buch** he/this book was chosen; **aus freier ~** of one's own free choice; **wir hatten keine (andere) ~(, als)** we had no alternative *or* choice (but); **es gab** *or* **blieb keine andere ~(, als)** there was no alternative (but); **das ließ mir keine (andere) ~** it left me no (other) choice; **jdm die ~ lassen** to leave (it up to) sb to choose; **jdm etw zur ~ stellen** to give sb the choice of sth; **drei Kandidaten stehen zur ~** there is a choice of three candidates; **seine/eine ~ treffen** to make one's/a choice *or* selection; **du hast die ~** take your choice *or* pick; **sie hat die ~, ob sie ...** the choice is hers whether she ..., it's up to her whether she ...; **wer die ~ hat, hat die Qual** *(Prov)* he is/you are *etc* spoiled for choice → **eng ADJ a**

b *(Pol etc)* election; *(= Abstimmung)* vote; *(geheim)* ballot; **geheime ~** secret ballot; **freie ~** free elections; **~ durch Handerheben** vote by (a) show of hands; **(die) ~en** (the) elections; **~ eines Präsidenten** election of a president; **seine ~ in den Vorstand/zum Präsidenten** his election to the board/as president; **die ~ gewinnen** to win the election; **zur ~ gehen** to go to vote, to go to the polls; **jdn zur ~ aufstellen** *or* **vorschlagen** to propose sb *or* put sb up as a candidate (for election); **sich zur ~ stellen** to stand (as a candidate), to stand (at the/an election), to run (for parliament/president *etc*); **zur ~ schreiten** to take a vote *or (geheim)* ballot; **die ~ annehmen** to accept the *or* one's election

c *(= Qualität)* quality; **erste ~** top quality; *Gemüse, Eier* class *or* grade one; **zweite/dritte ~** second/third quality; *Gemüse, Eier* class *or* grade two/three; **Waren erster ~** top-quality goods; **Eier erster ~** class-one *or* grade-one eggs; **Fleisch erster ~** prime meat; **Waren zweiter ~** seconds *pl*; **Gemüse zweiter ~** class-two *or* grade-two vegetables; **der Teller war zweite ~** the plate was a second

Wahl-: **Wahl|akt** M polling; **Wahl|al|ter** NT voting age; **Wahl|ana|ly|ti|ker(in)** M(F) election analyst; **Wahl|auf|ruf** M election announcement; **Wahl|auf|trag** M election brief; **Wahl|aus|gang** M outcome of an/the election, election results *pl*; **Wahl|aus|schuss** M election committee

Wähl|au|to|ma|tik F *(Telec)* automatic dialling *(Brit) or* dialing *(US)*

wähl|bar ADJ **a** eligible (for office), able to stand at an/the election **b** *(= auswählbar)* **frei ~** of one's choice

Wähl|bar|keit [ˈvɛːlbaːɐkait] F **-**, *no pl* eligibility (for office)

Wahl-: **Wahl|be|nach|rich|ti|gung** F, **Wahl|be|nach|rich|ti|gungs|kar|te** F polling card; **wahl|be|rech|tigt** ADJ entitled to vote;

Wahl|be|rech|tig|te(r) [-bərɛçtɪçtə] MF *decl as adj* person entitled to vote; **Wahl|be|rech|ti|gung** F (right to) vote; **Wahl|be|tei|li|gung** F poll; **eine hohe ~** a heavy poll, a high *or* good turnout (at an/the election); **Wahl|be|trug** M electoral fraud; (= *Manipulation des Wahlergebnisses*) ballot- *or* vote-rigging *(inf)*; **Wahl|be|zirk** M ward; **Wahl|brief** M *letter containing completed postal vote*; **Wahl|bünd|nis** NT electoral pact; **Wahl|bür|ger(in)** M(F) *(form)* voter; **Wahl|bü|ro** NT election office

Wahl|de|ba|kel F *(Pol)* election debacle

wäh|len [ˈvɛːlən] ✪ 27.3 VT **a** *(von* from, out of) to choose; (= *auswählen*) to select, to pick; **seine Worte ~** to choose one's words, to select *or* pick one's words carefully → *auch* **gewählt**
b *(Telec) Nummer* to dial
c (= *durch Wahl ermitteln) Regierung, Sprecher etc* to elect; (= *sich entscheiden für) Partei, Kandidaten* to vote for; **jdn ins Parlament ~** to elect *or* return sb to Parliament; **jdn in den Vorstand ~** to elect *or* vote sb onto the board; **jdn zum Präsidenten ~** to elect sb president
VI **a** (= *auswählen*) to choose
b *(Telec)* to dial
c (= *Wahlen abhalten*) to hold elections; (= *Stimme abgeben*) to vote; **wann wird gewählt?** when are the elections?; **man darf ab 18 ~** you can vote at 18; **durch Handerheben ~** to vote by (a) show of hands; **~ gehen** to go to the polls, to go to vote

Wahl|ent|schei|dung F choice (in an election), decision who *or* what to vote for; **wovon machst du deine ~ abhängig?** what will decide your vote (in the elections)?

Wäh|ler [ˈvɛːlɐ] M **-s, -** *(Tech)* selector

Wäh|ler [ˈvɛːlɐ] M **-s, -**, **Wäh|le|rin** [-ərɪn] F **-, -nen** *(Pol)* elector, voter; **der** *or* **die ~** the electorate *sing or pl*, the electors *pl*

Wäh|ler|auf|trag M mandate

Wahl|er|geb|nis NT election result; (= *Stimmenverteilung auch*) election returns *pl*

Wäh|ler|ge|mein|schaft F electorate; **Freie ~** Association of Independent Voters

Wäh|ler|ini|ti|a|ti|ve F pressure from the electorate

wäh|le|risch [ˈvɛːlərɪʃ] ADJ particular; *Geschmack, Kunde* discriminating; **sei nicht so ~!** don't be so choosy *(inf) or* fussy

Wäh|ler|re|ser|voir NT source of votes

Wäh|ler|schaft [ˈvɛːlɐʃaft] F **-, -en** electorate *sing or pl*; *(eines Wahlkreises)* constituents *pl*

Wäh|ler-: **Wäh|ler|schicht** F section of the electorate; **Wäh|ler|schwund** M loss of voters; **Wäh|ler|stim|me** F vote; **10% der ~n** 10% of the vote(s) *or* poll; **Wäh|ler|ver|zeich|nis** NT electoral roll *or* register; **Wäh|ler|wan|de|rung** F shift of votes; **wäh|ler|wirk|sam** ADJ *Politik, Parole* vote-winning, popular with the voters

Wahl-: **Wahl|fach** NT *(Sch)* option, optional subject, elective *(US)*; **Wahl|fäl|schung** F vote-rigging, electoral fraud; **Wahl|feld|zug** M election(eering) campaign; **Wahl|fie|ber** NT election fever; **Wahl|for|scher(in)** M(F) electoral researcher, psephologist; **Wahl|frau** F delegate; **wahl|frei** ADJ *(Sch)* optional; **~er Zugriff** *(Comput)* random access; **Wahl|frei|heit** F *(Pol)* electoral freedom; *(Sch)* freedom of choice; **Wahl|gang** M *pl* **-gänge** ballot; **Wahl|ge|heim|nis** NT secrecy of the ballot; **Wahl|ge|schenk** NT pre-election promise; **Wahl|ge|setz** NT electoral law; **Wahl|hei|mat** F country of adoption *or* of (one's) choice, adopted country; **Wahl|hel|fer(in)** M(F) *(im Wahlkampf)* electoral *or* election assistant; *(bei der Wahl)* polling officer; **Wahl|ka|bi|ne** F polling booth; **Wahl|kampf** M election(eering) campaign; **einen ~ führen** to conduct an election campaign; **Wahl|kampf|ma|nö|ver** NT campaign move; **Wahl|kampf|schla|ger** M *(inf)* major campaign issue, vote winner; **Wahl|kreis** M constituency; **Wahl|lei|ter(in)** M(F) returning officer *(Brit)*, chief election official *(US)*; **Wahl|lo|kal** NT polling station; **Wahl|lo|ko|mo|ti|ve** F *(inf)* vote-puller; **wahl|los** ADJ indiscriminate ADV at random, haphazardly; (= *nicht wählerisch*) indiscriminately; **Wahl|mann** M *pl* **-männer** delegate; **Wahl|ma|ra|thon** NT *(Pol inf)* election marathon; **Wahl|mög|lich|keit** F choice, option; **Wahl|nacht** F election night; **Wahl|nie|der|la|ge** F election defeat; **Wahl|pe|ri|o|de** F lifetime of a/the parliament; **Wahl|pflicht** F electoral duty; **seine ~ erfüllen** to use one's vote; **Wahl|pflicht|fach** NT *(Sch)* (compulsory) optional subject; **ich muss zwei Wahlpflichtfächer belegen** I have to take two optional subjects; **Wahl|pla|kat** NT election poster; **Wahl|pro|pa|gan|da** F election propaganda; **Wahl|recht** NT **a** (right to) vote; **allgemeines ~** universal franchise *(esp Brit) or* suffrage; **das kommunale ~ haben** to have the right to vote in local elections; **das aktive ~** the right to vote; **das passive ~** eligibility (for political office); **mit 21/18 bekommt man das passive ~** at 21/18 one becomes eligible for political office) **b** (= *Gesetze*) electoral law *no def art*; **Wahl|re|de** F election speech; **Wahl|re|form** F electoral reform

Wähl|schei|be F *(Telec)* dial

Wahl-: **Wahl|schein** M polling card; **Wahl|schlap|pe** F election setback; **Wahl|sieg** M electoral *or* election victory; **Wahl|slo|gan** M election slogan; **Wahl|sonn|tag** M polling Sunday; **Wahl|spruch** M **a** (= *Motto*) motto, watchword **b** (= *Wahlslogan*) election slogan; **Wahl|sys|tem** NT electoral system; **Wahl|tag** M election *or* polling day; **Wahl|un|ter|la|gen** PL election papers *pl*; **Wahl|ur|ne** F ballot box; **Wahl|ver|an|stal|tung** F election rally; **Wahl|ver|fah|ren** NT electoral procedure; **Wahl|ver|ge|hen** NT electoral misdemeanour *(Brit) or* misdemeanor *(US)*; **Wahl|ver|hal|ten** NT behaviour *(Brit) or* behavior *(US)* at the polls; **Wahl|ver|samm|lung** F election meeting; **Wahl|ver|spre|chun|gen** PL election promises *pl*; **Wahl|ver|wandt|schaft** F *(Chem)* elective attraction; *(fig)* affinity *(von* between); **„die ~en"** *(Liter)* "The Elective Affinities"; **Wahl|volk** NT, *no pl* **das ~** the electorate; **wahl|wei|se** ADV alternatively; **~ Kartoffeln oder Reis** (a) choice of potatoes or rice; **Sie können ~ Wasserski fahren oder reiten** you have a choice between water-skiing and riding; **die Modelle sind ~ mit Sechs- oder Zwölfzylindermotor ausgestattet** the models have the option of a six- or a twelve-cylinder engine; **Wahl|wie|der|ho|lung** F *(Telec)* **(automatische) ~** (automatic) redial

Wähl|zei|chen NT *(Telec)* dialling *(Brit) or* dial *(US)* tone

Wahl|zel|le F polling booth

Wahl|zet|tel M ballot paper

Wahn [vaːn] M **- (e)s**, *no pl* **a** illusion, delusion; **in dem ~ leben, dass ...** to labour *(Brit) or* labor *(US)* under the delusion that ... **b** (= *Manie*) mania

Wahn|bild NT delusion, illusion

wäh|nen [ˈvɛːnən] *(geh)* VT to imagine (wrongly), to believe (wrongly); **wir wähnten ihn glücklich** we (wrongly) imagined *or* believed him (to be) happy VR **sich sicher/von allen verlassen ~** to imagine *or* believe oneself (to be) safe/abandoned by all

Wahn|idee F delusion; (= *verrückte Idee*) mad *or* crazy notion

Wahn|sinn M, *no pl* **a** *(old Psych)* insanity, lunacy, madness; **in ~ verfallen** to go mad *or* insane **b** (= *Verrücktheit, Unvernunft*) madness, insanity; **jdn in den ~ treiben** to drive sb mad; **des ~s fette Beute sein** *(inf)* to be off one's rocker *(inf)*; **das ist doch (heller) ~, so ein ~!** that's sheer madness *or* idiocy!; **Mensch, ~** *or* **einfach ~!** *(inf:* = *prima)* wicked! *(Brit sl)* **c religiöser ~** religious mania

wahn|sin|nig ADJ **a** *(old Psych)* insane, mad **b** *(inf)* (= *verrückt*) mad, crazy; (= *toll, super*) brilliant *(inf)*, great *(inf)*; *(attr:* = *sehr groß, viel)* terrible, awful, dreadful; **eine ~e Arbeit** a crazy *or* an incredible amount of work; **ein ~es Geld** a crazy *or* an incredible amount of money; **wie ~** *(inf)* like mad; **das macht mich ~** *(inf)* it's driving me mad *or* crazy *(inf)*, it's driving me round *(Brit) or* around *(US)* the bend *(inf)*; **~ werden** to go mad *or* crazy *(inf)*, to go round *(Brit) or* around *(US)* the bend *(inf)*; **ich werde ~!** it's mind-blowing! *(inf)*
ADV *(inf)* incredibly *(inf)*; **~ verliebt** madly in love; **~ viele/viel** an incredible number/amount *(inf)*

Wahn|sin|ni|ge(r) [-zɪnɪgə] MF *decl as adj* madman/madwoman, lunatic

Wahn|sin|nig|wer|den NT **zum ~** enough to drive you round *(Brit) or* around *(US)* the bend *(inf) or* up the wall *(inf)*

Wahn|sinns- *in cpds (inf)* (= *verrückt*) crazy; (= *prima*) fantastic *(inf)*, incredible *(inf)*; **Wahn|sinns|ar|beit** F **eine ~** a crazy *or* an incredible amount of work *(inf)*

Wahn-: **Wahn|vor|stel|lung** F delusion; **Wahn|witz** M, *no pl* utter *or* sheer foolishness; **wahn|wit|zig** ADJ mad, crazy, lunatic *attr* ADV terribly, awfully

wahr [vaːɐ] ADJ *Geschichte, Liebe, Glaube etc* true; (= *echt*) *Kunst, Glück etc auch* real, genuine; *Freund, Freundschaft auch* real; *(attr:* = *wirklich)* real, veritable; **im ~sten Sinne des Wortes** in the true sense of the word; **daran ist kein ~es Wort, davon ist kein Wort ~** there's not a word of truth in it; **da ist etwas Wahres daran** there's some truth in that; **da hast du ein ~es Wort gesprochen** *(inf)* that's very true, there's a lot of truth in that; **etw ~ machen** *(Pläne)* to make sth a reality; *Versprechung, Drohung* to carry sth out; **~ werden** to come true; *(Hoffnung, Pläne auch)* to become a reality; **so ~ mir Gott helfe!** so help me God!; **so ~ ich lebe/hier stehe** as sure as I'm alive/standing here, as sure as eggs is eggs *(Brit inf)*; **das darf** *or* **kann doch nicht ~ sein!** *(inf)* it can't be true!; **das ist schon gar nicht mehr ~** *(inf) (verstärkend)* it's not true! *(inf)*; (= *schon lange her*) that was ages ago; **das ist nicht der ~e Jakob** *or* **Otto** *(inf)* **das ist nicht das Wahre** *(inf)* it's no great shakes *(inf)*; **die Stelle ist nicht gerade der ~e Jakob** *or* **Otto** *or* **das Wahre** *(inf)* it's not exactly the greatest job (on earth) → **nicht, einzig**

wah|ren [ˈvaːrən] VT **a** (= *wahrnehmen) Interessen, Rechte* to look after, to protect, to safeguard **b** (= *erhalten) Autorität, Ruf, Würde* to preserve, to keep; *Geheimnis* to keep; *Chancen* to keep alive; *gute Manieren* to adhere to, to observe; **die Form ~** to adhere to correct form; **den Anstand ~** to observe the proprieties → **Schein b, Gesicht a**

wäh|ren [ˈvɛːrən] VI *(geh)* to last; **es währte nicht lange, da geschah ein Unglück** it was not long before misfortune struck; **was lange währt, wird endlich gut** *(Prov)* a happy outcome is worth waiting for → **ehrlich ADJ**

wäh|rend [ˈvɛːrənt] PREP *+gen or dat* during; **~ eines Zeitraums** over a period of time; **~ der ganzen Nacht** all night long, all during the night, throughout the night CONJ while; (= *wohingegen auch*) whereas

wäh|rend|dem [vɛːrəntˈdeːm] *(inf)*, **wäh|rend|des|sen** [vɛːrəntˈdɛsn] ADV meanwhile, in the meantime

Wahr-: **wahr+ha|ben** VT *sep irreg* **etw nicht ~ wollen** not to want to admit sth; **wahr|haft** ADJ (= *ehrlich*) truthful; (= *echt*) *Freund* true, real; *Enttäuschung* real; *(attr:* = *wirklich)* real, veritable ADV really, truly; **wahr|haf|tig** [vaːɐˈhaftɪç, ˈvaːɐ-] ADJ *(geh)* (= *aufrichtig*) truthful; *Gemüt* honest; *Worte etc* true; **der ~e Gott** the true God; **~er Gott!** *(inf)* strewth! *(inf)* ADV really;

(= tatsächlich) actually; **Wahr|haf|tig|keit** F -, *no pl (geh)* truthfulness; *(von Aussage auch)* veracity

Wahr|heit ✪ 53.4, 53.6 F -, **-en** truth; **in ~** in reality; **die ~ sagen** to tell the truth; **um die ~ zu sagen** to tell the truth; **das ist nur die halbe ~** that's only half (of) the truth; **das schlägt der ~ ins Gesicht** that's patently untrue; **er nimmt es mit der ~ nicht so genau** *(inf)* you have to take what he says with a pinch *(esp Brit)* or grain *(US)* of salt → **Ehre**

Wahr|heits-: **Wahr|heits|be|weis** M *(Jur)* **den ~ bringen** or **antreten** to supply proof of the truth of a/one's statement; **Wahr|heits|fin|dung** [-fɪndʊŋ] F -, *no pl* establishment of the truth; **Wahr|heits|ge|halt** M substance; **wahr|heits|ge|mäß** ADJ true, truthful ADV truthfully, in accordance with the facts; **wahr|heits|ge|treu** ADJ *Bericht* truthful; *Darstellung* faithful; **ein ~es Bild** *(fig)* a factual or true picture ADV truthfully; **Wahr|heits|lie|be** F love of truth; **wahr|heits|lie|bend** ADJ truth-loving; *(= ehrlich)* truthful; **wahr|heits|wid|rig** ADJ false ADV falsely

wahr|lich ['va:ɐlɪç] ADV really, indeed, verily *(Bibl)*; *(= garantiert)* certainly, definitely

Wahr-: **wahr+ma|chen** VT *sep* → **wahr**; **wahr|nehm|bar** ADJ perceptible, noticeable; **nicht ~** imperceptible, not noticeable; **mit bloßem Auge ~/nicht ~** visible/invisible to the naked eye; **wahr+neh|men** VT *sep irreg* **a** *(= mit den Sinnen erfassen)* to perceive; *(= bemerken) Vorgänge, Veränderungen etc* to be aware of; *(= entdecken, erkennen) Geräusch* to hear; *Licht* to see; *Geruch* to detect; *(= heraushören) Unterton, Stimmung* to detect, to discern; **nichts mehr/alles um sich herum ~** to be no longer aware of anything/to be aware of everything around one **b** *(= nutzen, vertreten) Frist, Termin* to observe; *Gelegenheit* to take; *Interessen, Angelegenheiten* to look after; *Verantwortung* to exercise; **sein Recht auf etw** *(acc)* **~** to exercise one's right to sth; **Wahr|neh|mung** [-ne:mʊŋ] F -, **-en** **a** *(mit den Sinnen)* perception; *(von Vorgängen etc)* awareness; *(von Geruch, Stimmung)* detection **b** *(von Interessen, Angelegenheiten)* looking after; **Wahr|neh|mungs|ver|mö|gen** NT perceptive faculty; **wahr|sa|gen** *sep or insep* VI to tell fortunes, to predict the future; **aus dem Kaffeesatz/aus den Teeblättern/aus den Karten ~** to read coffee grounds/tea leaves/cards; **jdm ~** to tell sb's fortune, to predict the future (to sb); **sich** *(dat)* **~ lassen** to have one's fortune told VT **(jdm) die Zukunft ~** to tell sb's fortune, to predict the future (to sb); **er hat mir wahrgesagt** or **gewahrsagt, dass ...** he predicted (to me) that ...; **Wahr|sa|ger** [-za:gɐ] M -s, -, **Wahr|sa|ge|rin** [-ərɪn] F -, **-nen** fortune-teller, soothsayer *(old)*; **Wahr|sa|ge|rei** [-za:gə'rai] F -, **-en** **a** *no pl* fortune-telling **b** prediction; **wahr|sa|ge|risch** [-za:gərɪʃ] ADJ prophetic; **Wahr|sa|gung** [-za:gʊŋ] F -, **-en** prediction

währ|schaft ['vɛ:ɐʃaft] ADJ *(Sw) (= gediegen) Ware, Arbeit* reliable; *(= reichhaltig) Essen* wholesome; *(= kernig) Mensch* down to earth

Wahr|schau F **~!** *(Naut)* attention!

wahr|schein|lich [va:ɐ'ʃainlɪç, 'va:ɐ-] ✪ 42.2, 43.2, 53.2, 53.6 ADJ probable, likely; *(= glaubhaft)* plausible; **es liegt im Bereich des Wahrscheinlichen** it is quite within the bounds of probability ADV probably; **er kommt ~ erst später** he probably won't come till later, he won't come till later most likely

Wahr|schein|lich|keit ✪ 42.2 F -, **-en** probability, likelihood *no pl*; *(= Glaubhaftigkeit)* plausibility; **mit großer ~, aller ~ nach, in aller ~** in all probability or likelihood

Wahr|schein|lich|keits|rech|nung F probability calculus, theory of probabilities

Wah|rung ['va:rʊŋ] F -, *no pl* **a** *(= Wahrnehmung)* protection, safeguarding **b** *(= Erhaltung)* preservation; *(von Geheimnis)* keeping; **~ der guten Manieren** adherence to or observance of good manners

Wäh|rung ['vɛ:rʊŋ] F -, **-en** currency

Wäh|rungs- *in cpds* currency, monetary; **Wäh|rungs|aus|gleich** M currency conversion compensation; **Wäh|rungs|block** M *pl* **-blöcke** monetary bloc; **Wäh|rungs|ein|heit** F monetary unit; **Wäh|rungs|fonds** M Monetary Fund; **Wäh|rungs|ge|biet** NT currency area; **Wäh|rungs|hü|ter(in)** M(F) *(inf)* monetary regulator; **Wäh|rungs|in|sti|tut** NT monetary institute; **Europäisches ~** European Monetary Institute; **Wäh|rungs|kri|se** F monetary or currency crisis; **Wäh|rungs|kurs** M value of a currency; **Wäh|rungs|pa|ri|tät** F mint par of exchange; **Wäh|rungs|re|form** F monetary or currency reform; **Wäh|rungs|re|ser|ve** F monetary or currency reserve; **Wäh|rungs|schlan|ge** F (currency) snake; **Wäh|rungs|sys|tem** NT monetary system; **Wäh|rungs|um|stel|lung** F currency changeover or switch, changeover or switch to a new currency; **Wäh|rungs|uni|on** F monetary union; **europäische ~** European monetary union

Wahr|zei|chen NT *(von Stadt, Verein)* emblem; *(= Gebäude, Turm etc)* symbol

Waid- ['vait] *in cpds* = **Weid-**

Wai|se ['vaizə] F -, **-n** orphan

Wai|sen-: **Wai|sen|haus** NT orphanage; **Wai|sen|kind** NT orphan; **Wai|sen|kna|be** M *(liter)* orphan (boy); **gegen dich ist er ein ~** or **Waisenknabe** *(inf)* he's no match for you, you would run rings round him *(inf)*; **Wai|sen|ren|te** F orphan's allowance

Wal [va:l] M -(e)s, -e whale

Wald [valt] M -(e)s, ⸚er ['vɛldɐ] wood(s *pl*); *(großer)* forest; *(no pl: = Waldland)* woodland(s *pl*), wooded country; **~ und Wiese/Feld** or **Flur** *(liter)* woods and meadows/fields; **ich glaub, ich steh im ~** *(inf)* I must be seeing/hearing things! *(inf)*; **er sieht den ~ vor lauter Bäumen nicht** he can't see the wood *(Brit)* or forest *(US)* for the trees *(Prov)*; **wie es in den ~ hineinschallt** or **wie man in den ~ hineinruft, so schallt es wieder heraus** *(Prov)* you get as much as you give; **der Thüringer ~** the Thuringian Forest, the Thüringer Wald

Wald-: **Wald|amei|se** F red ant; **Wald|ar|bei|ter** M forestry worker; *(= Holzfäller)* lumberjack, woodman; **Wald|ar|bei|te|rin** F forestry worker; **Wald|be|stand** M forest land; **Wald|blu|me** F woodland flower; **Wald|bo|den** M forest soil; **Wald|brand** M forest fire

Wäld|chen ['vɛltçən] NT -s, - *dim von* **Wald** little wood

Wald|erd|bee|re F wild strawberry

Wal|des- *(liter)*: **Wal|des|dun|kel** NT gloom of the forest; **Wal|des|rau|schen** NT -s, *no pl* → **Wald** rustling or whispering of the woods/forest; **Wal|des|saum** M → **Wald** edge of the wood(s)/forest

Wald-: **Wald|flä|che** F wooded area, woodland(s *pl*); **Wald|fre|vel** M offence *(Brit)* or offense *(US)* against the forest laws; **Wald|ge|biet** NT woodland area; **weite ~e** *pl* huge tracts *pl* of forest; **Wald|geist** M sylvan *(poet)* or silvan *(poet)* or forest spirit; **Wald|hei|ni** M *(inf)* nitwit *(inf)*; **Wald|horn** NT *(Mus)* French horn

wal|dig ['valdɪç] ADJ wooded, woody

Wald-: **Wald|kauz** M *(Orn)* tawny owl; **Wald|land** NT woodland(s *pl*); **Wald|land|schaft** F → **Wald** woodland/forest landscape; **Wald|lauf** M cross-country running; *(einzelner Lauf)* cross-country run; **Wald|lehr|pfad** M nature trail; **Wald|meis|ter** M *(Bot)* woodruff

Wal|dorf-: **Wal|dorf|sa|lat** M *(Cook)* Waldorf salad; **Wal|dorf|schu|le** F Rudolf Steiner School

Wald-: **Wald|rand** M **am ~** at or on the edge of the forest; **wald|reich** ADJ densely wooded; **Wald|reich|tum** M → **Wald** abundance of woods/forests; **Wald|scha|den** M → **Wald** damage to woods/forests; **Wald|schnei|se** F lane; **Wald|schrat** M wood gnome; **Wald|ster|ben** NT dying of the forests *(due to pollution)*; **Wald|tier** NT → **Wald** woodland/forest creature

Wald-und-Wie|sen- *in cpds (inf)* common-or--garden *(Brit inf)*, garden-variety *(US inf)*; **ein ~Politiker** a common-or-garden *(Brit)* or garden-variety *(US)* politician *(inf)*

Wal|dung ['valdʊŋ] F -, **-en** *(geh)* woodland(s *pl*)

Wald-: **Wald|vo|gel** M woodland bird; **Wald|weg** M → **Wald** woodland/forest path; **Wald|wie|se** F glade; **Wald|wirt|schaft** F forestry

Wales [we:ls, we:lz] NT -' Wales

Wal-: **Wal|fang** M whaling; **Wal|fang|boot** NT whaler, whaling boat; **Wal|fän|ger** M *(= Schiff)* whaler; **Wal|fän|ger(in)** M(F) whaler; **Wal|fang|ver|bot** NT whaling ban; **Wal|fisch** M *(inf)* whale; **Wal|fisch|speck** M blubber; **Wal|fisch|tran** M sperm oil

wal|gen ['valgn], **wäl|gern** ['vɛlgɐn] VT *(dial) Teig* to roll out

Wal|hall ['valhal, val'hal] F -, *no pl*, **Wal|hal|la** [val'hala] F -, *no pl (Myth)* Valhalla

Wa|li|ser [va'li:zɐ] M -s, - Welshman

Wa|li|se|rin [va'li:zərɪn] F -, **-nen** Welshwoman

wa|li|sisch [va'li:zɪʃ] ADJ Welsh

Wa|li|sisch(e) NT *(Ling)* Welsh → *auch* **Deutsch(e)**

Wal|ke ['valkə] F -, **-n** fulling machine

wal|ken ['valkn] VT *Felle, Leder* to drum, to tumble; *Wollgewebe* to full, to mill; *Blech* to flex; **jdn ~** *(inf)* to give sb a belting *(inf)*

wal|ken ['wɔ:kn] VI *aux sein (Sport)* to speed--walk, to go speed walking

Wal|kie-Tal|kie ['wɔ:ki'tɔ:ki] NT -(s), -s walkie-talkie

Wal|king ['wɔ:kɪŋ] NT -s, *no pl* speed walking

Walk|man® ['wɔ:kmən] M -s, -s or **Walkmen** *(Rad)* Walkman®

Wal|kü|re [val'ky:rə, 'valky:rə] F -, **-n** *(Myth, fig)* Valkyrie

Wall [val] M -(e)s, ⸚e ['vɛlə] embankment; *(Mil)* rampart; *(fig)* bulwark, rampart

Wal|lach ['valax] M -(e)s, -e gelding

wal|len ['valən] VI **a** *(liter) (Meer) (= brodeln)* to surge, to seethe; *(= fließen)* to flow; *(Dämpfe, Nebel)* to surge; *(fig) (Blut)* to boil; *(hum: Busen)* to heave **b** *(obs) aux sein (= wallfahren)* to go on a pilgrimage

wall|fah|ren ['valfa:rən] VI *insep reg aux sein* to go on a pilgrimage

Wall|fah|rer(in) M(F) pilgrim

Wall|fahrt F pilgrimage

Wall|fahrts-: **Wall|fahrts|kir|che** F pilgrimage church; **Wall|fahrts|ort** M *pl* **-orte** place of pilgrimage; **Wall|fahrts|stät|te** F place of pilgrimage; *(Grab, Kirche etc auch)* shrine

Wall|gra|ben M moat

Wal|lis ['valɪs] NT -' Valais

Wal|li|ser ['valizɐ] M -s, -, **Wal|li|se|rin** [-ərɪn] F -, **-nen** inhabitant of the Valais

Wal|li|ser Al|pen PL **die ~** the Valais Alps *pl*

wal|li|se|risch ['valizərɪʃ] ADJ Valaisan

Wal|lo|ne [va'lo:nə] M -n, -n, **Wal|lo|nin** [-'lo:nɪn] F -, **-nen** Walloon

Wal|lung ['valʊŋ] F -, **-en** **a** *(geh)* **das Meer war in ~** the sea was surging or seething; **in ~ geraten** *(See, Meer)* to begin to surge or seethe; *(Mensch) (vor Leidenschaft)* to be in a turmoil; *(vor Wut)* to fly into a rage or passion; **sein Blut geriet in ~** his blood began to surge through his veins; **jds Blut** or **jdn in ~ bringen** to make sb's blood surge through his/her veins **b** *(Med)* (hot) flush *(Brit)* or flash *(US) usu pl*

Walm|dach ['valm-] NT *(Archit)* hipped roof

Wal|nuss ['val-] F walnut

Wal|nuss|baum M walnut (tree)

Wal|pur|gis|nacht [val'pʊrgɪs-] F Walpurgis Night, Walpurgisnacht

Wal|ross ['val-] NT walrus; *(pej: Mensch)* baby elephant *(inf)*; **schnaufen wie ein ~** *(pej)* to puff like a grampus

Wal|statt ['va:l-, 'val-] F **-, -stätten** [-ʃtɛtn] *(obs)* battlefield

wal|ten ['valtn] VI *(geh)* to prevail, to reign *(in +dat* over); *(= wirken: Mensch, Naturkräfte)* to be at work; **über jdm/etw ~** to rule (over) sb/sth; **Vernunft ~ lassen** to let reason prevail; **Vorsicht/Milde ~ lassen** to exercise caution/leniency; **Gnade ~ lassen** to show mercy; **das Walten der Naturgewalten/Gottes** the workings of the forces of nature/of God; **jdn ~ lassen** to let sb have a free rein, to let sb do as he pleases; **das walte Gott** *or (inf)* **Hugo** amen (to that)! → **Amt b, schalten VI b**

Wal|tran ['va:l-] M sperm oil

Walz [valts] F *(dated)* **auf die ~ gehen** to go off on one's travels; **auf der ~ sein** to be on the road

Walz|blech NT sheet metal

Wal|ze ['valtsə] F **-, -n** roller; *(von Schreibmaschine auch)* platen; *(= Drehorgelwalze)* barrel; *(von Spieluhr)* cylinder, drum

wal|zen ['valtsn] VT to roll VI **a** *aux sein or haben (dated: = tanzen)* to waltz **b** *aux sein (old inf: = wandern)* to tramp, to hike

wäl|zen ['vɛltsn] VT **a** *(= rollen)* to roll; *(Cook) (in Ei, Mehl)* to coat *(in +dat* with); *(in Butter, Petersilie)* to toss **b** *(inf) Akten, Bücher* to pore over; *Probleme, Gedanken, Pläne* to turn over in one's mind; **die Schuld/Verantwortung auf jdn ~** to shift *or* shove *(inf)* the blame/responsibility onto sb VR to roll; *(vor Schmerzen)* to writhe *(vor +dat* with); *(schlaflos im Bett)* to toss and turn; *(fig: Menschenmenge, Wassermassen)* to surge; *(im Schlamm)* to wallow

wal|zen|för|mig ADJ cylindrical

Wal|zer ['valtsɐ] M **-s, -** waltz; **Wiener ~** Viennese waltz; **~ tanzen** to (dance the/a) waltz; **sich im ~ drehen** *(liter)* to waltz around and around

Wäl|zer ['vɛltsɐ] M **-s, -** *(inf)* heavy *or* weighty tome *(hum)*

Wal|zer-: **Wal|zer|mu|sik** F waltz music; **Wal|zer|schritt** M waltz step; **Wal|zer|takt** M waltz time

Walz-: **Walz|stra|ße** F rolling train; **Walz|werk** NT rolling mill

Wam|me ['vamə] F **-, -n a** *(= Hautfalte)* dewlap **b** *(von Pelz)* belly part **c** *(dial: = Bauch)* paunch

Wam|pe ['vampə] F **-, -n** *(inf)* paunch

Wams [vams] NT **-es, =er** ['vɛmzɐ] *(old, dial: = Jacke)* jerkin; *(unter Rüstung)* gambeson; *(dial: = Weste)* waistcoat *(Brit)*, vest *(US)*

WAN [wɛn] NT **-(s), -s** *abbr von* **wide area network** *(Comput)* WAN

wand *pret von* **winden**

Wand [vant] F **-, =e** ['vɛndə] wall *(auch Anat)*; *(= nicht gemauerte Trennwand)* partition (wall); *(von Gefäß, Behälter, Schiff)* side; *(= Felswand)* (rock) face; *(= Wolkenwand)* bank of clouds; *(Biol)* septum *(spec)*; *(fig)* barrier, wall; **spanische ~** (folding) screen; **etw an die ~ werfen** *or* **schmeißen** *or* **schleudern** *(inf) (lit)* to throw sth against *or* at the wall; *(fig: aus Wut, Verzweiflung)* to throw sth out of the window; **~ an ~** wall to wall; **in seinen vier Wänden** *(fig)* within one's own four walls; **weiß wie die ~** as white as a sheet; **wenn die Wände reden könnten** if walls could speak; **man rennt bei denen gegen eine ~** with them you come up against a brick wall; **mit dem Kopf gegen die ~ rennen** *(fig)* to bang one's head against a brick wall; **jdn an die ~ drücken** *(fig)* to push *or* drive sb to the wall; **jdn an die ~ spielen** *(fig)* to outdo *or* outshine sb; *(Theat)* to steal the show from sb, to upstage sb; **jdn an die ~ stellen** *(fig)* to shoot sb, to send sb before the firing squad; **er lachte/tobte** *etc*, **dass die Wände wackelten** *(inf) or* **zitterten** *(inf)* he raised the roof (with his laughter/ranting and raving *etc*) *(inf)*; **die ~** *or* **Wände hochgehen** *(inf)* to go up the wall *(inf)*; **das ist, um an den Wänden hochzugehen** *(inf)* **es ist zum Die-Wände-Hochgehen** *(inf)* it's enough to drive you up the wall *(inf)*

Wan|da|le [van'da:lə] M **-n, -n**, **Wan|da|lin** [-'da:lɪn] F **-, -nen** *(Hist)* = **Vandale**

Wan|da|lis|mus [vanda'lɪsmʊs] M **-**, *no pl* = **Vandalismus**

Wand-: **Wand|be|hang** M wall hanging; **Wand|be|klei|dung** F wall covering; *(aus Holz)* panelling *(esp Brit)*, paneling *(US)*; **Wand|be|wurf** M plaster(ing); *(= Rauhputz)* roughcast; **Wand|bild** NT wall painting, mural; *(= Fresko)* fresco; **Wand|bord** NT, **Wand|brett** NT (wall) shelf

Wan|del ['vandl] M **-s**, *no pl* **a** change; **im ~ der Zeiten** throughout the ages, throughout the changing times; **im ~ der Jahrhunderte** down the centuries **b** *(= Lebenswandel)* way *or* mode of life → **Handel b**

Wan|del-: **Wan|del|al|tar** M polyptych; **Wan|del|an|lei|he** F convertible loan; **wan|del|bar** ADJ changeable; **Wan|del|bar|keit** ['vandlba:ɐkait] F **-**, *no pl* changeability; **Wan|del|gang** M *pl* **-gänge** covered walk; **Wan|del|hal|le** F foyer; *(im Parlament)* lobby; *(im Kurhaus)* pump room

wan|deln ['vandln] VTR *(= ändern)* to change

wan|deln VI *aux sein (geh: = gehen)* to walk, to stroll; **ein ~des Wörterbuch** *(hum)* a walking dictionary; **er ist die ~de Güte** he is goodness *or* kindness itself *or* personified → **Leiche**

Wan|del|ob|li|ga|ti|on F, **Wan|del|schuld|ver|schrei|bung** F *(Fin)* convertible bond

Wan|del|stern M *(old)* planet

Wan|de|lung F **-, -en** *(Jur)* cancellation of sale

Wan|der-: **Wan|der|amei|se** F army ant; **Wan|der|ar|bei|ter(in)** M(F) migrant worker; **Wan|der|aus|stel|lung** F travelling *(esp Brit) or* traveling *(US)* exhibition, touring exhibition; **Wan|der|büh|ne** F touring company; *(Hist)* strolling players *pl*; **Wan|der|bur|sche** M *(obs)* journeyman; **Wan|der|dü|ne** F shifting *or* drifting (sand) dune

Wan|de|rer ['vandərɐ] M **-s, -**, **Wan|de|rin** [-ərɪn] F **-, -nen** hiker; *(= esp Angehöriger eines Wandervereins)* rambler *(esp Brit)*, hiker; *(old: = Reisender)* traveller *(esp Brit)*, traveler *(US)*, wayfarer *(old)*

Wan|der-: **Wan|der|fahrt** F hiking trip; *(old: = Reise)* journey; **Wan|der|fal|ke** M peregrine (falcon); **Wan|der|freund(in)** M(F) hiker; **Wan|der|heu|schre|cke** F migratory locust

Wan|de|rin [-ərɪn] F → **Wanderer**

Wan|der-: **Wan|der|jah|re** PL years *pl* of travel; **Wan|der|kar|te** F map of walks *or* trails; **Wan|der|klei|dung** F hiking outfit; **Wan|der|le|ben** NT roving *or* wandering life; *(fig)* unsettled life; **Wan|der|le|ber** F floating liver; **Wan|der|lied** NT hiking song; **Wan|der|lust** F wanderlust; **wan|der|lus|tig** ADJ filled with wanderlust, with a passion for travel

wan|dern ['vandɐn] VI *aux sein* **a** *(= gehen)* to wander, to roam; *(old: = reisen)* to travel, to journey; *(Wanderbühne, Sinti und Roma)* to travel; **durchs Leben ~** *(liter)* to journey through life **b** *(= sich bewegen)* to move, to travel; *(Wolken, Gletscher)* to drift; *(Düne)* to shift, to drift; *(Med: Leber, Niere)* to float; *(Blick)* to rove, to roam, to wander; *(Gedanken)* to roam, to wander, to stray; *(= weitergegeben werden)* to be passed (on) **c** *(Vögel, Tiere, Völker)* to migrate **d** *(zur Freizeitgestaltung)* to hike; *(esp in Verein)* to ramble *(esp Brit)*, to hike **e** *(inf: ins Bett, in den Papierkorb, ins Feuer)* to go; **hinter Schloss und Riegel ~** to be put behind bars; **ins Krankenhaus/ins Leihhaus ~** to end *or* land up in hospital/at the pawnbroker's

Wan|der-: **Wan|der|nie|re** F floating kidney; **Wan|der|po|kal** M challenge cup; **Wan|der|pre|di|ger(in)** M(F) itinerant preacher; **Wan|der|preis** M challenge trophy; **Wan|der|rat|te** F brown rat

Wan|der|schaft ['vandɐʃaft] F **-**, *no pl* travels *pl*; **auf (der) ~ sein** to be on one's travels; *(Handwerksgeselle)* to travel around; *(Tier)* to be on the move; **auf ~ gehen** to go off on one's travels; *(Tier)* to set off on the move

Wan|der-: **Wan|der|schau|spie|ler(in)** M(F) travelling *(esp Brit) or* traveling *(US)* actor/actress; *(Hist)* strolling player; **Wan|der|schu|he** PL walking shoes *pl*

Wan|ders|mann M *pl* **-leute** *(liter)* = **Wanderer**

Wan|der-: **Wan|der|stab** M staff; **den ~ ergreifen** *(fig)* to take to the road; **Wan|der|stock** M hiking *or* trekking pole, hiking stick; **Wan|der|tag** M *day in German schools on which pupils go hiking*; **Wan|der|trieb** M *(von Tier)* migratory instinct; *(Psych)* urge to travel, dromomania *(spec)*; *(fig)* wanderlust, passion for travel; **Wan|der|trup|pe** F touring company; *(Hist)* strolling players *pl*

Wan|de|rung ['vandərʊŋ] F **-, -en a** *(= Ausflug)* walk; **eine ~ machen** to go on a walk *or* hike *or* ramble *(esp Brit)* **b** *(old: = Reise, von Handwerksgesellen, fig liter: durchs Leben)* journey **c** *(von Vögeln, Tieren, Völkern)* migration; *(Sociol: = Wohnortwechsel)* shift (in the population), population shift

Wan|de|rungs|ge|winn M *(Sociol)* increase in population (through population shifts)

Wan|der-: **Wan|der|ver|ein** M rambling *(esp Brit) or* hiking club; **Wan|der|vo|gel** M *(Hist)* member of the Wandervogel youth movement; *(= begeisterter Wanderer)* hiker; *(fig inf)* bird of passage, rolling stone *(inf)*; **Wan|der|weg** M walk, trail, (foot)path; **Wan|der|zir|kus** M travelling *(esp Brit) or* traveling *(US)* circus

Wand-: **Wand|flä|che** F wall area; **Wand|ge|mäl|de** NT mural, wall painting; **Wand|hal|ter** M, **Wand|hal|te|rung** F *(für PC, Fernseher etc)* wall bracket; **Wand|hal|te|rung** F *(für PC, Fernseher etc)* wall bracket

-wan|dig [vandɪç] ADJ *suf* -walled; **dünnwandig** *(Gebäude)* thin-walled; **eine dünnwandige/dickwandige Mauer** a thin/thick wall

Wand-: **Wand|ka|len|der** M wall calendar; **Wand|kar|te** F wall map; **Wand|lam|pe** F wall lamp; **Wand|leuch|ter** M wall bracket, sconce; **Wand|schmuck** M wall decoration

Wand|lung ['vandlʊŋ] F **-, -en a** *(= Wechsel, Wandel)* change; *(= völlige Umwandlung)* transformation; **~ zum Guten** change for the better; **eine ~ durchmachen** to undergo a change **b** *(Eccl)* transubstantiation; *(= Teil der Messe)* consecration **c** *(Jur)* cancellation of sale contract

wand|lungs|fä|hig ADJ adaptable; *Schauspieler etc* versatile

Wand|lungs|fä|hig|keit F adaptability; *(von Schauspieler etc)* versatility

Wand-: **Wand|ma|le|rei** F mural painting; *(Bild)* mural, wall painting; **Wand|pfei|ler** M *(Archit)* pilaster

Wand|rer ['vandrɐ] M **-s, -**, **Wand|re|rin** [-ərɪn] F **-, -nen** → **Wanderer**

Wand-: **Wand|schirm** M screen; **Wand|schrank** M wall cupboard; **Wand|ta|fel** F (black)board

wand|te *pret von* **wenden**

Wand-: **Wand|tel|ler** M wall plate; **Wand|tep|pich** M tapestry, wall hanging; **Wand|uhr** F wall clock; **Wand|ver|klei|dung** F wall covering; *(aus Holz)* panelling *(esp Brit)*, paneling *(US)*; **Wand|zei|tung** F wall newssheet

Wan|ge ['vaŋə] F **-, -n a** *(geh)* cheek; **~ an ~** cheek to cheek **b** *(von Treppe)* stringboard

Wank [vaŋk] M *(Sw)* **keinen ~ tun** not to lift a finger

Wan|kel|mo|tor ['vaŋkl-] M Wankel engine

Wan|kel|mut M, **Wan|kel|mü|tig|keit** F **-**, *no pl* fickleness, inconstancy

wan|kel|mü|tig ['vaŋklmy:tɪç] ADJ fickle, inconstant

wan|ken ['vaŋkn] VI **a** *(= schwanken) (Mensch, Gebäude)* to sway; *(Knie)* to shake, to wobble; *(Boden)* to rock; *(fig: Thron, Regierung)* to totter;

(= unsicher sein/werden) to waver, to falter; **nicht ~ und nicht weichen** not to move *or* budge an inch; **ihm wankt der Boden unter den Füßen** *(fig)* he is on shaky ground; **ins Wanken geraten** *(lit)* to begin to sway/rock; *(fig)* to begin to totter/waver *or* falter/vacillate; **etw ins Wanken bringen** *(lit)* to cause sth to sway/rock; *(fig) Thron, Regierung* to cause sth to totter; *Glauben, Mut* to shake sth; *Moral* to throw doubt upon sth; *Weltbild* to shake sth; **jds Entschluss ins Wanken bringen** to make sb waver in his decision

b *aux sein (= gehen)* to stagger; *(alter Mensch)* to totter

wann [van] INTERROG ADV when; **~ ist er angekommen?** when did he arrive?; **~ kommt ihr?** when *or* (at) what time are you coming?; **~ (auch) immer** whenever; **bis ~ ist das fertig?** when will that be ready (by)?; **bis ~ gilt der Ausweis?** until when is the pass valid?, when is the pass valid until?; **seit ~ bist/hast du …?** *(zeitlich)* how long have you been/had …?; *(bezweifelnd, entrüstet etc)* since when are you/do you have …?; **von ~ an bist du in Deutschland?** from when will you be in Germany?; **von ~ bis ~?** when?, during what times?

Wan|ne ['vanə] F **-, -n** bath; *(= Badewanne auch)* (bath)tub; *(= Ölwanne)* reservoir; *(im Auto)* sump *(Brit)*, oil pan *(US)*

wan|nen ['vanən] ADV *(obs)* **von ~** whence *(liter)*

Wan|nen|bad NT bath

Wanst [vanst] M **-(e)s, ⸚e** ['vɛnstə] *(Zool: = Pansen)* rumen; *(inf: = dicker Bauch)* paunch *(inf)*, belly *(inf)*; **sich** *(dat)* **den ~ vollschlagen** *(inf)* to stuff oneself *(inf)*

Want [vant] F **-, -en** *(Naut)* shroud

Wan|ze ['vantsə] F **-, -n** *(Zool, inf: = Abhörgerät)* bug

Wap|pen ['vapn] NT **-s, -** coat of arms; *(auf Münze)* heads *no art*; **etw im ~ führen** to have *or* bear sth on one's coat of arms; *(fig)* to have sth as one's trademark

Wap|pen-: **Wap|pen|kun|de** F heraldry; **Wap|pen|schild** M OR NT *pl* **-schilder** *or* **-schilde** shield; **Wap|pen|sei|te** F heads side; **Wap|pen|tier** NT heraldic animal

wapp|nen ['vapnən] VR *(fig)* **sich (gegen etw) ~** to prepare (oneself) (for sth); **gewappnet sein** to be prepared *or* forearmed

war *pret von* **sein**

warb *pret von* **werben**

ward *(old, liter) pret von* **werden 1 c 2 d**

Wa|re ['va:rə] ✪ 47 F **-, -n** **a** product; *(einzelne Ware)* article; *(als Sammelbegriff)* goods *pl*, merchandise; **gute ~ hält sich** *(prov)* good quality goods last longer **b Waren** PL goods *pl*; *(zum Verkauf auch)* merchandise *sing*, wares *pl (esp old, hum)*

wä|re ['vɛ:rə] *pret subjunc von* **sein**

Wa|ren-: **Wa|ren|an|ge|bot** NT range of goods for sale; **Wa|ren|an|nah|me** F *(= das Annehmen)* acceptance of goods; *(= Annahmestelle)* (goods) reception, deliveries *pl (US)*; **Wa|ren|auf|zug** M goods hoist; **Wa|ren|aus|fuhr** F export of goods *or* merchandise; **Wa|ren|aus|ga|be** F *(= das Ausgeben)* distribution of goods; *(= Ausgabestelle)* collection point; **Wa|ren|aus|gang** M outgoing goods *pl*; **Wa|ren|aus|tausch** M exchange *or (bei Tauschgeschäft)* barter of goods; **Wa|ren|be|gleit|pa|pie|re** PL shipping documents *pl*; **Wa|ren|be|lei|hung** F loan against goods; **Wa|ren|be|stand** M stocks *pl* of goods *or* merchandise; **Wa|ren|bör|se** F commodity exchange; **Wa|ren|ein|fuhr** F import of goods *or* merchandise; **Wa|ren|ein|gang** M stock receipt, incoming goods *pl*; **Wa|ren|ex|port** M export of goods *or* merchandise; **Wa|ren|haus** NT (department) store, emporium *(old)*; **Wa|ren|im|port** M import of goods *or* merchandise; **Wa|ren|korb** M *(Econ)* basket of goods; **Wa|ren|la|ger** NT warehouse; *(= Bestand)* stocks *pl*; **Wa|ren|mus|ter** NT, **Wa|ren|pro|be** F trade sample; **Wa|ren|sen|dung** F trade sample *(sent by post)*; **Wa|ren|sor|ti|ment** NT line of goods; **Wa|ren|ter|min|bör|se** F *(St Ex)* commodity futures exchange; **Wa|ren|ter|min|ge|schäft** NT *(St Ex)* commodity futures transaction; *(= Branche)* commodity futures *pl* (trading); **Wa|ren|test** M test of goods; **Wa|ren|um|satz** M turnover of goods *or* merchandise; **Wa|ren|um|satz|steu|er** F *(Sw)* value added tax, VAT; **Wa|ren|ver|kehr** M goods traffic; **Wa|ren|wirt|schafts|sys|tem** NT materials management system; **Wa|ren|zei|chen** NT trademark

warf *pret von* **werfen**

warm [varm] **ADJ** *comp* **⸚er** ['vɛrmɐ], *superl* **⸚ste(r, s)** ['vɛrmstə] *(lit, fig)* warm; *Wetter auch, Getränk, Speise (auf Wasserhahn)* hot; *(dated inf: = homosexuell)* queer *(pej inf)*; **mir ist ~** I'm warm; **aus dem Warmen in die Kälte kommen** to come out of the warm(th) into the cold; **das hält ~** it keeps you warm; **das macht ~** it warms you up; **das Essen ~ machen** to warm *or* heat up the food; **das Essen ~ stellen** to keep the food hot *or* warm; **~e Miete** rent including heating; **nur einen ~en Händedruck bekommen** *(fig inf)* to get nothing for one's pains; **wie ~e Semmeln weggehen** *(inf)* to sell *or* go like hot cakes; **weder ~ noch kalt sein** *(fig)* to be indifferent; **~ werden** *(fig inf)* to thaw out *(inf)*; **mit jdm ~ werden** *(inf)* to get close to sb; **mit etw ~ werden** *(mit Stelle)* to get used to sth; *mit Stadt auch* to get to know sth → **Bruder, laufen, spielen**

ADV *comp* **⸚er**, *superl* **am ⸚sten** *sitzen* in a warm place; *schlafen* in a warm room; **am Kamin sitzen wir wärmer** we'll be warmer by the fireplace; **liegt das Baby ~ genug?** is the baby warm enough?; **~ duschen** to take a warm shower; **die Milch ~ trinken** to drink warm milk; **sich ~ anziehen** to dress up warmly; *(fig inf: bei Schwierigkeiten)* to prepare oneself for a rough ride; **jdn/etw wärmstens empfehlen** to recommend sb/sth warmly

Warm-: **Warm|blut** NT *pl* **-blüter** crossbreed; **Warm|blü|ter** [-bly:tɐ] M **-s, -** *(Zool)* warm-blooded animal; **warm|blü|tig** ADJ warm-blooded; **Warm|du|scher** [-du:ʃɐ] M **-s, -** *(sl: = Weichling)* wimp *(inf)*, wet *(inf)*

Wär|me ['vɛrmə] F **-,** *(rare)* **-n** *(lit, fig)* warmth; *(von Wetter etc, Phys)* heat; *(Wetterlage)* warm weather; **10 Grad ~** 10 degrees above zero *or* above freezing; **an dem Gerät kann man verschiedene ~n einstellen** you can adjust the appliance to different heat settings; **ist das eine ~!** isn't it warm!; **komm in die ~** come into the warm(th); **mit ~** *(fig)* warmly

Wär|me-: **Wär|me|be|hand|lung** F *(Med)* heat treatment; **wär|me|be|stän|dig** ADJ heat-resistant; **Wär|me|bild|ka|me|ra** F thermal imaging camera; **Wär|me|dä|mmung** F (heat) insulation; **Wär|me|ein|heit** F thermal unit, unit of heat; **Wär|me|ener|gie** F thermal energy; **Wär|me|ge|wit|ter** NT heat thunderstorm; **Wär|me|grad** M degree of heat; **Wär|me|iso|la|ti|on** F, **Wär|me|iso|lie|rung** F heat *or* thermal insulation; **Wär|me|kraft|werk** NT thermal power station; **Wär|me|leh|re** F theory of heat; **Wär|me|lei|ter** M heat conductor; **Wär|me|mes|ser** M **-s, -** thermometer

wär|men ['vɛrmən] **VT** to warm; *Essen, Kaffee etc* to warm *or* heat up; **das wärmt einem das Herz** it's heartwarming **VI** *(Kleidung, Sonne)* to be warm; *(Ofen auch)* to provide warmth; **Schnaps wärmt** schnapps warms you up **VR** to warm oneself (up), to warm up; **sich gegenseitig ~** to keep each other warm

Wär|me|pum|pe F heat pump

War|me(r) ['varmə] M *decl as adj (dated inf)* queer *(pej inf)*, poof *(Brit pej inf)*, fag *(US inf)*

Wär|me-: **Wär|me|reg|ler** M thermostat; **Wär|me|rück|ge|win|nung** F heat recovery; **Wär|me|schutz** M heat shield; **Wär|me|spei|cher** M storer of heat; *(Gerät)* heat storer *or* accumulator; **Wär|me|stau** M build-up of heat; *(Met)* greenhouse effect; **Wär|me|strah|lung** F thermal radiation, radiant heat; **Wär|me|stu|be** F *(für Obdachlose etc)* warm room; **Wär|me|tau|scher** [-tauʃɐ] M **-s, -** heat exchanger; **Wär|me|tech|nik** F heat technology; **Wär|me|ver|lust** M heat loss

Wärm|fla|sche F hot-water bottle

Warm-: **Warm|front** F *(Met)* warm front; **warm|ge|mä|ßigt** ADJ *(Geog)* temperate; **warm+hal|ten** *sep irreg*, **warm hal|ten** △ *irreg* VT **sich** *(dat)* **jdn ~** *(fig inf)* to keep in with sb *(inf)*; **Warm|hal|te|plat|te** F hot plate; **warm|her|zig** ADJ warm-hearted; **Warm|her|zig|keit** ['varmhɛrtsɪçkait] F **-,** *no pl* warm-heartedness; **warm lau|fen** VI *irreg aux sein* to warm up; **Warm|luft** F warm air; **Warm|luft|zu|fuhr** F inflow *or* influx of warm air; *(von Heizung)* warm air supply; **warm+ma|chen** VT *sep* → **warm ADJ**; **Warm|mie|te** F rent including heating; **Warm|start** M *(Aut, Comput)* warm start; *(Comput auch)* warm boot; **warm+stel|len** VT *sep* → **warm ADJ**

Warm|was|ser-: **Warm|was|ser|be|rei|ter** [varm'vasɐbəraitɐ] M **-s, -** water heater; **Warm|was|ser|hei|zung** F hot-water central heating; **Warm|was|ser|lei|tung** F hot-water pipe; **Warm|was|ser|spei|cher** M hot-water tank; **Warm|was|ser|ver|sor|gung** F hot-water supply

warm+wer|den VI *sep irreg aux sein (fig)* → **warm ADJ**

Warn-: **Warn|an|la|ge** F warning system; **Warn|blink|an|la|ge** F flashing warning lights *pl*; *(an Auto)* hazard (warning) lights *pl*; **Warn|blink|leuch|te** F flashing warning light; **Warn|blink|licht** NT flashing warning light; *(an Auto)* hazard warning light; **Warn|drei|eck** NT warning triangle

war|nen ['varnən] ✪ 29.3 VTI to warn *(vor +dat* of); **die Polizei warnt vor Schneeglätte** the police have issued a warning of snow and ice on the roads; **jdn (davor) ~, etw zu tun** to warn sb against doing sth, to warn sb not to do sth; **vor Taschendieben wird gewarnt!** beware of pickpockets!; **ich warne dich!** I'm warning you!

Warn-: **Warn|hin|weis** M *(= Aufdruck)* warning; **Warn|kreuz** NT warning cross (before level crossing *(Brit) or* grade crossing *(US)*); **Warn|mel|dung** F warning (announcement); *(Comput)* warning message; **Warn|ruf** M warning cry; **Warn|schild** NT *pl* **-schilder** warning sign; **Warn|schuss** M warning shot; **Warn|sig|nal** NT warning signal; **Warn|streik** M token strike

War|nung ['varnʊŋ] F **-, en** warning; **~ vor etw** *(dat)* warning about sth; *vor Gefahr* warning of sth

Warn-: **Warn|vor|rich|tung** F warning system; **Warn|zei|chen** NT warning sign; *(hörbar)* warning signal

War|rant ['vɔrənt] M **-s, -s** warrant

War|schau ['varʃau] NT **-s** Warsaw

War|schau|er ['varʃauɐ] ADJ *attr* Warsaw

War|schau|er ['varʃauɐ] M **-s, -**, **War|schau|e|rin** [-ərɪn] F **-, -nen** native of Warsaw; *(Einwohner)* inhabitant of Warsaw

War|schau|er Pakt M *(Hist)* Warsaw Pact

War|schau|er-Pakt-Staa|ten PL *(Hist)* Warsaw Pact states *pl*

War|te ['vartə] F **-, -n** observation point; *(fig)* standpoint, viewpoint; **von jds ~ (aus)** *(fig)* from sb's point of view, from sb's standpoint; **von seiner hohen ~ aus** *(fig iro)* from his lofty standpoint *(iro)*

War|te-: **War|te|frist** F waiting period; *(für Lieferung)* delivery time; **War|te|hal|le** F waiting room; *(im Flughafen)* departure lounge; **War|te|lis|te** F waiting list

war|ten ['vartn] VI to wait *(auf +acc* for); **warte mal!** hold on, wait a minute; *(überlegend)* let me see; **na warte!** *(inf)* just you wait!; **warte, wenn**

ich das noch mal sehe! just let me see that again; **bitte ~** *(Telec)* hold the line please; *(Zeichen)* please wait; **du wirst ~ können** you'll have to wait; **da kannst du ~, bis du schwarz wirst** *(inf)* **da(rauf) kannst du lange ~** *(iro)* you can wait till the cows come home; **auf Antwort/Einlass ~** to wait for an answer/to be let in; **mit dem Essen auf jdn ~** to wait for sb (to come) before eating; to wait with lunch/dinner *etc* for sb; **ich bin gespannt, was da auf mich wartet** I wonder what's waiting for me *or* what awaits me *or* what's in store for me there; **auf sie/darauf habe ich gerade noch gewartet!** *(iro)* she/that was all I needed!; **lange auf sich ~ lassen** *(Sache)* to be a long time (in) coming; *(Mensch)* to take one's time; **nicht lange auf sich ~ lassen** *(Sache)* to be not long in coming; *(Mensch)* to not take long; **das lange Warten hatte ihn müde gemacht** the long wait had made him tired

war|ten VT **a** *Auto* to service; *Maschine* to maintain, to service **b** *(dated liter: = pflegen) Kinder etc* to look after; *Tiere* to tend

Wär|ter [ˈvɛrtɐ] **M -s, -, Wär|te|rin** [-ərɪn] **F -, -nen** attendant; *(= Leuchtturmwärter, Tierwärter)* keeper; *(= Krankenwärter)* nurse, orderly; *(= Gefängniswärter)* warder *(Brit)*, guard

War|te-: War|te|raum M waiting room; **War|te|saal** M waiting room; **War|te|schlan|ge** F queue *(Brit)*, line *(US)*; **War|te|schlei|fe** F *(Aviat)* holding pattern, stack; **~n ziehen** *or* **drehen** to circle; **War|te|stel|lung** F **in ~** on hold, waiting; **War|te|zeit** F waiting period; *(an Grenze etc)* wait; **War|te|zim|mer** NT waiting room; **War|te|zo|ne** F waiting area; **War|te|zyk|lus** M *(Comput)* wait state

-wärts [vɛrts] ADV *suf* -wards; **südwärts** southwards

War|tung [ˈvartʊŋ] **F -, -en** *(von Auto)* servicing; *(von Maschine auch, von EDV-Geräten etc)* maintenance

War|tungs-: War|tungs|ar|bei|ten PL maintenance work *no pl*; **war|tungs|arm** ADJ low-maintenance; **der Motor ist sehr ~** the engine needs very little maintenance; **war|tungs|frei** ADJ maintenance-free; **War|tungs|kos|ten** PL maintenance costs *pl*; **War|tungs|ver|trag** M service contract

wa|rum [vaˈrʊm] INTERROG ADV why; **~ nicht?** why not?; **~ nicht gleich so!** that's better; **nach dem Warum fragen** to ask why; **das Warum und Weshalb** the whys and wherefores

War|ze [ˈvartsə] **F -, -n** wart; *(= Brustwarze)* nipple

War|zen-: War|zen|hof M *(Anat)* areola *(spec)*; **War|zen|schwein** NT warthog

was [vas] INTERROG PRON **a** what; *(= wie viel)* how much, what; **~ kostet das?** how much is that?, what does *or* how much does that cost?; **~ ist** *or* **gibts?** what is it?, what's up?; **~ ist, kommst du mit?** well, are you coming?; **sie kommt nicht – ~?** she's not coming – what?; **~ hast du denn?, ~ ist denn los?** what's the matter (with you)?, what's wrong?; **~ willst** *or* **hast du denn?** what are you talking about?; **~ denn?** *(ungehalten)* what (is it)?; *(um Vorschlag bittend)* but what?; **~ denn, bist du schon fertig?** what, are you finished already?; **das ist gut, ~?** *(inf)* that's good, isn't it?; **~ haben wir gelacht!** *(inf)* how we laughed!; **~ ist das doch schwierig** *(inf)* it's really difficult

b *(inf: = warum)* why, what … for; **~ lachst du denn so?** what are you laughing for?, why are you laughing?

c ~ für … what sort *or* kind of …; **~ für ein Haus hat er?** what sort *or* kind of (a) house does he have?; **~ für ein schönes Haus!** what a lovely house!; **und ~ für ein Haus!** and what a house!; **~ für ein Wahnsinn!** what madness!

REL PRON *(auf ganzen Satz bezogen)* which; **das, ~ …** that which …, what …; **ich weiß, ~ ich/er tun soll** I know what I should do *or* what to do/what he should do; **~ auch (immer)** whatever; **das ist etwas, ~ ich nicht verstehe** that is something (which) I don't understand; **alles, ~ …** everything *or* all (that) …; **das Beste/Schönste/wenige/Einzige, ~ ich …** the best/prettiest/little/only thing (that) I …; **schreib/iss etc ~ du kannst** *(inf)* write/eat *etc* what you can; **lauf, ~ du kannst!** *(inf)* run as fast as you can!; **~ du immer hast!** you do go on!

INDEF PRON *(inf) abbr von* **etwas** something; *(fragend, bedingend auch, verneint)* anything; *(unbestimmter Teil einer Menge)* some, any; **(na,) so ~!** well I never!; **so ~ von Blödheit** such stupidity; **er ist so ~ von doof** he's so incredibly stupid; **kann ich dir ~ helfen?** *(inf)* can I give you a hand?; **ist (mit dir) ~?** is something the matter (with you)? → *auch* **etwas, sehen**

Wasch-: wasch|ak|tiv ADJ active detergent *attr*; **Wasch|an|la|ge** F *(für Autos)* car wash; *(= Scheibenwaschanlage)* wipers *pl*; *(fig inf: für Geld)* laundering facility; **Wasch|an|lei|tung** F washing instructions *pl*; **Wasch|an|wei|sung** F washing instructions *pl*; **Wasch|au|to|mat** M automatic washing machine; **wasch|bar** ADJ washable; **Wasch|bär** M raccoon; **Wasch|be|cken** NT washbasin; *(= Schüssel)* washbowl; **Wasch|ben|zin** NT benzine; **Wasch|be|ton** M washed concrete; **Wasch|beu|tel** M sponge bag; **Wasch|brett** NT **a** washboard **b** *(sl: = flachbusige Frau)* **ein ~ sein** to be as flat as a pancake *(Brit inf) or* a board *(US inf)*; **Wasch|brett|bauch** M washboard stomach, washboard abs *pl (inf)*, sixpack *(inf)*; **Wasch|büt|te** F washtub

Wä|sche [ˈvɛʃə] **F -, *no pl*** **a** washing; *(= Schmutzwäsche, bei Wäscherei)* laundry; **große/kleine ~ haben** *(in Bezug auf Menge)* to have a large/small amount of washing (to do); *(in Bezug auf Größe der Teile)* to wash the big/small things; **bei** *or* **in der ~** in the wash; **in der ~ sein** to be in the wash; *(= in der Wäscherei)* to be at the laundry; **etw in die ~ geben** to put sth in the wash; *(= in die Wäscherei)* to send sth to the laundry; **jdm an die ~ gehen** *(sl)* to touch sb up *(inf)* → **schmutzig**

b *(= Stoffzeug) (= Bettwäsche, Tischwäsche, Küchenwäsche)* linen; *(= Unterwäsche)* underwear; **dumm aus der ~ gucken** *(inf)* to look stupid

Wä|sche|beu|tel M dirty clothes bag; *(für Wäscherei)* laundry bag

wasch|echt ADJ *Farbe* fast; *Stoff auch* colourfast *(Brit)*, colorfast *(US)*; *(fig)* genuine, real, pukka *(Brit inf)*

Wä|sche-: Wä|sche|ge|schäft NT draper's (shop); **Wä|sche|klam|mer** F clothes peg *(Brit)*, clothes pin *(US)*; **Wä|sche|knopf** M linen-covered button; **Wä|sche|korb** M dirty clothes basket; **Wä|sche|lei|ne** F (clothes)-line; **Wä|sche|man|gel** F mangle

wa|schen [ˈvaʃn] *pret* **wusch** [vuːʃ], *ptp* **gewa|schen** [gəˈvaʃn] VT to wash; *Gold etc* to pan; *(fig inf) Geld, Spenden* to launder; **(Wäsche) ~** to do the washing; **etw** *(acc)* **warm/kalt ~** to wash sth in hot/cold water; **sich** *(dat)* **die Hände/Haare** *etc* **~** to wash one's hands/hair *etc*; **Waschen und Legen** *(beim Friseur)* shampoo and set

VR *(Mensch/Tier)* to wash (oneself/itself); *(Stoff)* to wash; **das hat sich gewaschen** *(inf)* that really made itself felt, that really had an effect; **eine Geldbuße, die sich gewaschen hat** *(inf)* a really heavy fine; **eine Ohrfeige, die sich gewaschen hat** *(inf)* a hard slap on *(Brit) or* in the face; **eine Klassenarbeit, die sich gewaschen hat** *(inf)* a real stinker of a test *(inf)*

Wä|sche|puff M *pl* **-puffe** dirty clothes basket

Wä|scher [ˈvɛʃɐ] **M -s, -** launderer

Wä|sche|rei [vɛʃəˈrai] **F -, -en** laundry

Wä|sche|rin [ˈvɛʃərɪn] **F -, -nen** washerwoman *(Brit)*, washwoman *(US)*; *(Berufsbezeichnung)* laundress

Wä|sche-: Wä|sche|rol|le F *(esp Aus)* mangle; **Wä|sche|sack** M laundry bag; **Wä|sche|schleu|der** F spin-drier; **Wä|sche|schrank** M linen cupboard; **Wä|sche|spin|ne** F revolving *or* rotary clothes dryer; **Wä|sche|stän|der** M clotheshorse; **Wä|sche|stär|ke** F starch; **Wä|sche|stück** NT piece of laundry; **Wä|sche|tin|te** F marking ink; **Wä|sche|trock|ner** M **-s, -** *(= Ständer)* clotheshorse; *(= Trockenautomat)* drier; **Wä|sche|zei|chen** NT name tape

Wasch-: Wasch|fass NT washtub; **Wasch|frau** F washerwoman *(Brit)*, washwoman *(US)*; **Wasch|gang** M *pl* **-gänge** stage of the washing programme *(Brit) or* program *(US)*; **Wasch|gel** NT (facial) wash gel; **Wasch|ge|le|gen|heit** F washing facilities *pl*; **Wasch|hand|schuh** M flannel mitt; **Wasch|haus** NT wash house, laundry; **Wasch|kes|sel** M (wash) boiler, copper; **Wasch|kü|che** F washroom, laundry; *(inf: = Nebel)* peasouper *(Brit inf)*, dense fog; **Wasch|lap|pen** M flannel; *(fürs Gesicht auch)* face cloth *(Brit)*, washcloth *(US)*; *(inf: = Feigling)* sissy *(inf)*, softy *(inf)*; **Wasch|lau|ge** F suds *pl*; **Wasch|le|der** NT chamois leather; **Wasch|ma|schi|ne** F washing machine; **wasch|ma|schi|nen|fest** ADJ machine-washable; **Wasch|mit|tel** NT detergent; **Wasch|pul|ver** NT washing powder; **Wasch|raum** M washroom; **Wasch|rum|pel** [-rʊmpl] **F -, -n** *(Aus: = Waschbrett)* washboard; **Wasch|sa|lon** M laundry; *(zum Selbstwaschen)* laundrette *(Brit)*, Launderette® *(Brit)*, Laundromat® *(US)*; **Wasch|schüs|sel** F washbowl, washbasin; **Wasch|sei|de** F washable silk; **Wasch|stra|ße** F *(zur Autowäsche)* car wash; **Wasch|stück** NT cleansing bar

wäscht [vɛʃt] *3. pers sing pres von* **waschen**

Wasch-: Wasch|tag M washday; **~ haben** to have one's washday; **Wasch|tisch** M washstand; **Wasch|toi|let|te** F = **Waschtisch**; **Wasch|trog** M washing trough

Wa|schung [ˈvaʃʊŋ] **F -, -en** *(Rel, Med)* ablution

Wasch-: Wasch|was|ser NT, *no pl* washing water; **Wasch|weib** NT *(fig pej)* washerwoman; **Wasch|zet|tel** M *(Typ)* blurb; **Wasch|zeug** NT, *no pl* toilet *or* washing things *pl*; **Wasch|zu|ber** M washtub; **Wasch|zwang** M *(Psych)* obsession with washing oneself

Wa|serl [ˈvaːzɐl] **NT -s, -(n)** *(Aus inf)* **armes ~** poor thing

Was|ser [ˈvasɐ] **NT -s, -** *or* **=** [ˈvɛsɐ] **a** *no pl* water; **~ abstoßend, ~ abweisend** water-repellent; **bei ~ und Brot** *(euph)* behind bars, in prison; **das ist ~ auf seine Mühle** *(fig)* this is all grist to *(Brit) or* for his mill; **bis dahin fließt noch viel ~ den Bach** *or* **den Rhein** *or* **die Donau** *etc* **hinunter** a lot of water will have flowed under the bridge by then; **dort wird auch nur mit ~ gekocht** *(fig)* they're no different from anybody else (there); **ihr kann er nicht das ~ reichen** *(fig)* he can't hold a candle to her, he's not a patch on her *(Brit)*; **~ lassen** *(Med)* to pass water → **Blut, Rotz, abgraben, rein ADJ a**

b *pl* **Wässer** *(= Flüssigkeit, Abwaschwasser etc)* water; *(medizinisch)* lotion; *(= Parfüm)* cologne, scent; *(= Mineralwasser)* mineral water; *(= Schnaps)* schnapps; *(= Tränen)* tears *pl*; *(= Speichel)* saliva; *(= Schweiß)* sweat; *(= Urin)* water, urine; *(Med: in Beinen etc)* fluid; *(= Abwasser)* sewage *no pl*; **~ mit Geschmack** *(inf)* fizzy pop *(inf)*; **dabei läuft mir das ~ im Mund(e) zusammen** it makes my mouth water

c *(= Wassermasse, im Gegensatz zu Land)* water; **die ~** *pl (geh)* the waters *pl*; **etw unter ~ setzen** to flood sth; **unter ~ stehen** to be flooded, to be under water; **~ treten** *(beim Schwimmen)* to tread water; *(Med)* to paddle *(in cold water as a therapy)*; **zu ~** on the water *or (Meer)* sea; *(= auf dem Wasserweg)* by water/sea; **ein Boot zu ~ lassen** to launch a boat; **einen Ort zu ~ erreichen** to reach a place by water; **ins ~ fallen, zu ~ werden** *(fig)* to fall through; **nahe ans** *or* **am ~ gebaut haben** *(inf)* to be inclined to tears, to be weepy; **ins ~ gehen** *(euph)* to drown oneself; **sich über ~ halten** *(fig)* to keep one's head above water; **er ist mit allen ~n gewaschen** he is a shrewd customer, he knows all the tricks → **Schlag a, Hals a, abgraben** **d** *(= Gezeiten)* tide; **das ~ läuft ab/kommt** the tide is going out/coming in → **auflaufen c**

Was|ser-: **was|ser|ab|sto|ßend**, **was|ser|ab|wei|send** ADJ → **Wasser a**; **Was|ser|an|schluss** M mains water supply; *(auf Zeltplatz)* water point; **was|ser|arm** ADJ *Gegend, Zeitraum* arid; **Was|ser|ar|mut** F aridity; **Was|ser|auf|be|rei|tung** F treatment of water; **Was|ser|auf|be|rei|tungs|an|la|ge** F (waste) water treatment plant; **Was|ser|bad** NT water bath; *(Cook)* double boiler, bain-marie; **im ~** *(Cook)* in a double boiler, in a bain-marie; **Was|ser|ball** M **a** *no pl (Spiel)* water polo **b** *(Ball)* beach ball; *(fürs Wasserballspiel)* water polo ball; **Was|ser|bau** M, *no pl* hydraulic engineering; **Was|ser|be|darf** M water requirements *pl*; **Was|ser|be|häl|ter** M water storage tank; *(kleiner)* cistern; **was|ser|be|stän|dig** ADJ water-resistant; **Was|ser|bett** NT water bed; **Was|ser|bla|se** F (water) blister; **Was|ser|bob** M jet ski; **~ fahren** to ride on a jet ski; **Was|ser|bom|be** F *(Mil)* depth charge; *(inf)* water bomb; **Was|ser|bruch** M *(Med)* hydrocele; **Was|ser|burg** F castle built in water

Wäs|ser|chen ['vɛsɐçən] NT **-s, -** little stream *or* brook; *(= Parfüm)* scent, perfume; *(kosmetisch)* lotion, potion; **ein ~ machen** *(baby-talk)* to do a wee-wee *(baby-talk)*; **er sieht aus, als ob er kein ~ trüben könnte** he looks as if butter wouldn't melt in his mouth

Was|ser-: **Was|ser|dampf** M steam; **was|ser|dicht** ADJ *(lit, fig)* watertight; *Uhr, Stoff etc* waterproof; **Was|ser|druck** M water pressure; **was|ser|durch|läs|sig** ADJ permeable; **Was|ser|ei|mer** M bucket, pail; **Was|ser|ent|här|ter** M water softener; **Was|ser|er|hit|zer** [-lɛɐhɪtsɐ] M **-s, -** water heater; **Was|ser|fahr|zeug** NT watercraft; **Was|ser|fall** M waterfall; **wie ein ~ reden** *(inf)* to talk nineteen to the dozen *(Brit inf)*, to talk a blue streak *(US inf)*; **Was|ser|far|be** F watercolour *(Brit)*, watercolor *(US)*; **was|ser|fest** ADJ waterproof; **Was|ser|floh** M water flea; **Was|ser|flug|zeug** NT seaplane; **Was|ser|frosch** M aquatic frog; **Was|ser|gas** NT water gas; **Was|ser|ge|halt** M water content; **Was|ser|geist** M water sprite; **was|ser|ge|kühlt** ADJ water-cooled; **Was|ser|glas** NT **a** *(= Trinkglas)* water glass, tumbler → **Sturm a** **b** *no pl (Chem)* water glass; **Was|ser|glät|te** F slippery roads *pl* due to surface water; **Was|ser|gra|ben** M *(Sport)* water jump; *(um Burg)* moat; **Was|ser|gym|nas|tik** F aqua aerobics, aquarobics *sing*; **Was|ser|hahn** M water tap *(esp Brit)*, faucet *(US)*; *(= Haupthahn)* stopcock; **was|ser|hal|tig** ADJ *(Chem)* aqueous; **~ sein** to contain water; **Was|ser|här|te** F hardness of water; **Was|ser|haus|halt** M *(Biol etc)* water balance; **Was|ser|ho|se** F *(Met)* waterspout; **Was|ser|huhn** NT coot

wäs|se|rig ['vɛsərɪç] ADJ *(lit, fig)* watery; *Augen* pale-coloured *(Brit)*, pale-colored *(US)*; *(Chem)* aqueous; **jdm den Mund ~ machen** *(inf)* to make sb's mouth water

Was|ser-: **Was|ser|jung|fer** F *(Zool)* dragonfly; **Was|ser|jung|frau** F *(Myth)* naiad; **Was|ser|kan|te** F = **Waterkant**; **Was|ser|kes|sel** M kettle; *(Tech)* boiler; **Was|ser|kis|sen** NT *(Med)* water cushion; **Was|ser|klo|sett** NT water closet *(dated)*; **Was|ser|knapp|heit** F water shortage; **Was|ser|ko|cher** M electric kettle; **Was|ser|kopf** M water on the brain *no indef art*, hydrocephalus *no indef art (spec)*; *(inf)* big head; **bürokratischer ~** *(fig)* top-heavy bureaucracy; **Was|ser|kraft** F water power; **Was|ser|kraft|werk** NT hydroelectric power station; **Was|ser|kreis|lauf** M water cycle; **Was|ser|kres|se** F watercress; **Was|ser|küh|lung** F *(Aut)* water-cooling; **mit ~** water-cooled; **~ haben** to be water-cooled; **Was|ser|la|che** F pool of water, puddle (of water); **Was|ser|las|sen** NT **-s**, *no pl (Med)* passing water, urination; **Was|ser|lauf** M watercourse; **Was|ser|läu|fer** M *(Vogel)* shank, sandpiper; *(Insekt)* water measurer, water skater; **dunkler ~** spotted redshank; **Was|ser|lei|che** F drowned body; **Was|ser|lei|tung** F *(= Rohr)* water pipe; *(= Anlagen)* plumbing *no pl*; *(inf: = Hahn)* tap, faucet *(US)*; **Was|ser|li|lie** F water lily; **Was|ser|li|nie** F *(Naut)* water line; **Was|ser|loch** NT water hole; **was|ser|lös|lich** ADJ water-soluble, soluble in water; **Was|ser|man|gel** M water shortage; **Was|ser|mann** M *pl* **-männer** **a** *(Myth)* water sprite **b** *(Astrol)* Aquarius *no art*, Water Carrier; **~ sein** to be (an) Aquarius; **Was|ser|mas|sen** PL mass *no pl* of water, deluge *no pl* of water; **Was|ser|me|lo|ne** F watermelon; **Was|ser|mes|ser** M **-s, -** water meter; **Was|ser|müh|le** F water mill

was|sern ['vasɐn] VI *(Aviat)* to land on water *or* *(im Meer auch)* in the sea; *(Space)* to splash down

wäs|sern ['vɛsɐn] VT *Heringe, Erbsen etc* to soak; *(Phot)* to rinse; *(= bewässern) Pflanzen, Felder, Rasen* to water VI to water; **mir ~ die Augen** my eyes are watering

Was|ser-: **Was|ser|ni|xe** F *(Myth)* water nymph; **Was|ser|nu|del** F *(Sport)* aqua *or* water *or* swim noodle; **Was|ser|ober|flä|che** F surface of the water/lake/sea *etc*; **Was|ser|or|gel** F hydraulic organ; **Was|ser|pfei|fe** F hookah *(Brit)*, hubble-bubble *(Brit)*, (water) bong *(US)*; **Was|ser|pfen|nig** M *(fig)* water surcharge *(to help finance water supply measures)*; **Was|ser|pflan|ze** F aquatic plant; **Was|ser|pis|to|le** F water pistol; **Was|ser|po|cken** PL *(Med)* chickenpox *sing*; **Was|ser|po|li|zei** F = **Wasserschutzpolizei**; **Was|ser|qua|li|tät** F water quality; **Was|ser|rad** NT water wheel; **Was|ser|rat|te** F water rat, water vole; *(inf: Kind)* water baby; **Was|ser|recht** NT *laws pertaining to water and waterways*; **was|ser|reich** ADJ *Gebiet* with plenty of water, abounding in water; *Fluss* containing a lot of water; *Zeitraum* when water is/was plentiful; **Was|ser|re|ser|voir** NT reservoir; **Was|ser|rohr** NT water pipe; **Was|ser|rut|sche** F water slide *or* chute; **Was|ser|säu|le** F water column; **Was|ser|scha|den** M water damage; **Was|ser|schaff** [-ʃaf] NT **-(e)s, -e** *(Aus)* water tub; **Was|ser|schei|de** F watershed; **was|ser|scheu** ADJ scared of water; **Was|ser|scheu** F fear of water; *(Psych)* water phobia; **Was|ser|schi** M NT = **Wasserski**; **Was|ser|schild|krö|te** F turtle; **Was|ser|schlan|ge** F **a** *(Zool)* water snake; *(Myth)* (sea)serpent **b** *(Astron)* Hydra; **Was|ser|schlauch** M **a** (water) hose; *(= Behälter)* skin **b** *(Bot)* bladderwort; **Was|ser|schloss** NT castle surrounded by water; **Was|ser|schutz|ge|biet** NT water reserve; **Was|ser|schutz|po|li|zei** F *(auf Flüssen, Wasserwegen)* river police; *(im Hafen)* harbour *(Brit)* *or* harbor *(US)* police; *(auf der See)* coastguard service; **Was|ser|ski** M water-ski NT water-skiing; **Was|ser|spei|er** [-ʃpaiɐ] M **-s, -** gargoyle; **Was|ser|spen|der** M *(= Trinkgerät)* water cooler; **Was|ser|spie|gel** M *(= Oberfläche)* surface of the water; *(= Wasserstand)* water level; **Was|ser|sport** M **der ~** water sports *pl*; **Was|ser|sport|fahr|zeug** NT water sport craft; **Was|ser|sport|ler(in)** M(F) water sportsman/-woman; **Was|ser|spü|lung** F flush; **Klosett mit ~** flush toilet, water closet *(dated)*; **Was|ser|stand** M water level; **niedriger/hoher ~** low/high water; **Was|ser|stands|an|zei|ger** M water level indicator; **Was|ser|stands|mel|dun|gen** PL water level *or* *(für Gezeiten)* tide report; **Was|ser|stel|le** F watering place *or* hole

Was|ser|stoff M hydrogen

Was|ser|stoff-: **was|ser|stoff|blond** ADJ *attr Haar* peroxide blonde; **ein ~es Mädchen** a peroxide blonde *(inf)*; **Was|ser|stoff|bom|be** F hydrogen bomb, H-bomb; **Was|ser|stoff|su|per|oxid**, **Was|ser|stoff|su|per|oxyd** NT hydrogen peroxide

Was|ser-: **Was|ser|strahl** M jet of water; **Was|ser|stra|ße** F waterway; **Was|ser|sucht** F dropsy; **was|ser|süch|tig** ADJ suffering from dropsy, dropsical; **Was|ser|tank** M water tank; *(für WC)* cistern; **Was|ser|tier** NT aquatic animal; **Was|ser|trä|ger(in)** M(F) water carrier; **Was|ser|tre|ten** NT **-s**, *no pl (Sport)* treading water; *(Med)* paddling *(in cold water as therapy)*; **Was|ser|trop|fen** M water drop, drop of water; **Was|ser|turm** M water tower; **Was|ser|uhr** F *(= Wasserzähler)* water meter; *(Hist)* water clock

Was|se|rung ['vasərʊŋ] F **-, -en** water landing; *(im Meer)* sea landing; *(Space)* splashdown

Wäs|se|rung ['vɛsərʊŋ] F **-, -en** *(von Fisch, Gemüse etc)* soaking; *(Phot)* rinsing; *(= Bewässerung)* watering

Was|ser-: **Was|ser|ver|brauch** M water consumption *no def art*; **Was|ser|ver|sor|gung** F water supply; **Maßnahmen zur ~** measures to ensure the supply of water; **Was|ser|ver|un|rei|ni|gung** F water pollution; **Was|ser|vo|gel** M waterfowl; **Was|ser|waa|ge** F spirit level *(Brit)*, water level gauge *(US)*; **Was|ser|wacht** F water rescue service; **Was|ser|weg** M waterway; **auf dem ~** by water *or* *(Meer)* sea; **Was|ser|wel|le** F water wave; **Was|ser|wer|fer** M water cannon; **Was|ser|werk** NT waterworks *sing or pl*; **Was|ser|wirt|schaft** F water supply (and distribution); **Was|ser|zäh|ler** M water meter; **Was|ser|zei|chen** NT watermark

wäss|rig ['vɛsrɪç] ADJ = **wässerig**

wa|ten ['va:tn] VI *aux sein* to wade

Wa|ter|kant ['va:tɐkant] F **-**, *no pl* coast *(esp North Sea coast of Germany)*

Wat|sche ['va:tʃə] F **-n, -n** *(S Ger inf)* slap (on *or* round *(Brit)* the face); *(als Strafe)* clip round the ear *(Brit)*, smack on the ear

wat|sche|lig ['va:tʃəlɪç, 'vat-] ADJ waddling *attr* ADV **~ laufen** to waddle

wat|scheln ['va:tʃln, 'vat-] VI *aux sein* to waddle

wat|schen ['va:tʃn, 'vat-] VT *(S Ger inf)* **jdm eine ~** *(auf Backe)* to slap sb's face; *(ans Ohr)* to give sb a clip round *(Brit)* *or* smack on the ear; **eine gewatscht kriegen** to get a slap in the face/clip round *(Brit)* *or* smack on the ear

Wat|schen ['va:tʃn, 'vat-] F **-, -** *(Aus, S Ger. inf)* = **Ohrfeige**

Wat|schen|mann M *pl* **-männer** *(Aus) (lit)* fairground dummy *(fig)* Aunt Sally *(Brit fig)*, punching bag *(US fig)*

Wat|stie|fel ['va:t-] M wader

Watt [vat] NT **-s, -** *(Elec)* watt

Watt NT **-(e)s, -en** *(Geog)* mud flats *pl*

Wat|te ['vatə] F **-, -n** cotton wool *(Brit)*, cotton *(US)*; *(zur Polsterung)* padding, wadding; **jdn in ~ packen** *(fig inf)* to wrap sb in cotton wool *(Brit)*, to molly-coddle sb; **lass dich doch in ~ packen!** you're far too over-sensitive!

Wat|te|bausch M cotton-wool *(Brit)* *or* cotton *(US)* ball

Wat|ten|meer NT mud flats *pl*

Wat|te-: **Wat|te|pad** [-pɛd] M **-s, -s** cotton (-wool *(Brit)*) pad; **Wat|te|stäb|chen** NT cotton bud

wat|tie|ren [va'ti:rən] *ptp* **wattiert** VT to pad; *(= füttern)* to line with padding; *(und absteppen) Stoff, Steppdecke* to quilt; **wattierte Umschläge** padded envelopes; **wattierte Jacken** quilted jackets

Wat|tie|rung F **-, -en** padding

Watt-: **Watt|me|ter** NT wattmeter; **Watt|se|kun|de** F watt-second; **Watt|stun|de** F watt-hour; **Watt|zahl** F wattage

Wat|vo|gel ['va:t-] M wader *(Brit)*, wading bird

wau wau ['vau 'vau, vau 'vau, 'vau vau] INTERJ bow-wow, woof-woof

Wau|wau ['vauvau, vau'vau] M **-s, -s** *(baby-talk)* bow-wow *(baby-talk)*

WC [ve:'tse:] NT **-s, -s** WC

WC-: **WC-Bürs|te** [veː'tseː-] F toilet brush, loo brush *(inf)*; **WC-Rei|ni|ger** [veː'tseː-] M *(= Reinigungsmittel)* toilet cleaner

WDR [veːdeː'ɛr] M - *abbr von* **Westdeutscher Rundfunk**

Web [wɛb] NT **-(s)**, *no pl* Web; **im ~** on the Web

Web- ['wɛb-]: **web|ba|siert** ADJ *(Internet)* Web-based; **Web|brow|ser** M Web browser; **Web|de|sig|ner(in)** M(F) Web designer

We|be ['veːbə] F **-, -n** *(Aus)* linen

We|be|kan|te F selvage, selvedge

we|ben ['veːbn] *pret* **webte** *or (liter, fig)* **wob** ['veːptə, voːp], *ptp* **gewebt** *or (liter, fig)* **gewoben** [gə'veːpt, gə'voːbn] VTI *(lit, fig)* to weave; *Spinnennetz, Lügennetz* to spin

We|ber ['veːbɐ] M **-s, -**, **We|be|rin** [-ərɪn] F **-, -nen** weaver

We|be|rei [veːbə'rai] F **-, -en** **a** *no pl (= das Weben)* weaving **b** *(= Betrieb)* weaving mill **c** *(= Zeug)* woven article

We|ber-: **We|ber|kamm** M weaver's reed; **We|ber|knecht** M *(Zool)* daddy-longlegs *(Brit)*, crane fly; **We|ber|kno|ten** M reef knot; **We|ber|schiff|chen** NT shuttle

Web-: **Web|feh|ler** M weaving flaw; **einen ~ haben** *(fig inf)* to have a screw loose *(inf)*; **Web|garn** NT weaving yarn

We|bi|nar ['wɛbinaːɐ] NT **-s, -e** *(Internet)* webinar

Web|kan|te F selvage, selvedge *(Brit)*

Web- ['wɛb-]: **Web|mail** ['wɛbmeːl] F **-**, *no pl (Internet)* webmail; **Web|mas|ter** ['wɛbˌmaːstɐ] F *(Internet)* webmaster; **Web|pub|li|sher** ['wɛbˌpablɪʃɐ] M *(Internet)* Web publisher; **Web|sei|te** F *(Internet)* Web page; **Web|ser|ver** F *(Internet)* Web server; **Web|site** F *(Internet)* Web site

Web|stuhl M loom

Web|wa|ren PL woven goods *pl*

Wech|sel ['vɛksl] M **-s, -** **a** *(= Änderung)* change; *(abwechselnd)* alternation; *(= Geldwechsel)* exchange; *(der Jahreszeiten, Agr: = Fruchtwechsel)* rotation; **ein ~ der Wohnung/Schule** *etc* a change of address/school *etc*; **der ~ von Tag und Nacht** the alternation of day and night; **im ~ der Zeiten** through the ages; **in buntem ~** in motley succession; **im ~** *(= abwechselnd)* in turn, alternately **b** *(Sport) (= Staffelwechsel)* (baton) change, changeover; *(Ftbl etc)* substitution **c** *(Fin)* bill (of exchange); *(inf: = Geldzuwendung)* allowance **d** *(Hunt)* trail used by game *or* by wild animals

Wech|sel-: **Wech|sel|bad** NT alternating hot and cold baths *pl*; **~ der Gefühle** *(fig)* emotional roller coaster; **jdn einem ~ aussetzen** *(fig)* to blow hot and cold with sb; **Wech|sel|balg** M changeling (child); *(inf)* little monster *(inf)*; **Wech|sel|bank** F *pl* **-banken** *(Fin)* discount house; **Wech|sel|be|zie|hung** F correlation, interrelation; **in ~ miteinander** *or* **zueinander stehen** to be correlated *or* interrelated; **Wech|sel|bürg|schaft** F guarantee (on a bill); **Wech|sel|fäl|le** PL vicissitudes *pl*; **Wech|sel|fie|ber** NT *(old)* malaria; **Wech|sel|frist** F *(Fin)* usance; **Wech|sel|geld** NT change; **Wech|sel|ge|sang** M antiphonal singing; **Wech|sel|ge|spräch** NT dialogue *(Brit)*, dialog *(US)*; **Wech|sel|ge|trie|be** NT *(Tech)* variable gears *pl*; **wech|sel|haft** ADJ changeable; *Schicksal, Mensch auch* fickle, capricious ADV **~ verlaufen** to be changeable; **Wech|sel|haf|tig|keit** F changeability; *(von Schicksal, Mensch auch)* fickleness, capriciousness; **Wech|sel|jah|re** PL menopause *sing*, change of life *sing*; **in die ~ kommen** to start the menopause, to reach menopause; **in den ~n sein** to be going through the menopause; **Frauen/Männer in den ~n** women/men going through the menopause; **Wech|sel|kurs** M rate of exchange

wech|seln ['vɛksln] VT to change *(in +acc* into); *(= austauschen)* to exchange; *(Ftbl etc)* to substitute *(gegen* for); **den Arzt ~** to change doctors *or* one's doctor; **den Tisch/die Schule/das Hemd ~** to change tables/schools/one's shirt; **die Farbe ~** to change colour *(Brit) or* color *(US)*; **den Platz mit jdm ~** to exchange one's seat with sb; **Briefe ~** to correspond *or* be in correspondence *(mit* with); **die Wohnung ~** to move house *(Brit)*, to move; **den Wohnsitz ~** to move to another place; **können Sie (mir) 10 Euro ~?** can you change 10 euros (for me)?; **Wäsche zum Wechseln** a change of underwear

VI **a** to change; *(Sport)* to change (over); *(= einander ablösen)* to alternate; **ich kann Ihnen leider nicht ~** I'm sorry, I don't have any change **b** *(Hunt)* to pass by; **über die Grenze ~** *(Mensch)* to cross the border

wech|selnd ['vɛkslnt] ADJ changing; *(= einander ablösend, abwechselnd)* alternating; *Launen, Stimmungen* changeable; *Winde* variable; *Bewölkung* variable, intermittent; **mit ~em Erfolg** with varying (degrees of) success; **~e Mehrheiten** *(Parl) majorities formed by parties voting together according to particular issues* ADV alternately; **~ bewölkt** cloudy with sunny intervals

Wech|sel-: **Wech|sel|neh|mer(in)** M(F) payee of a bill; **Wech|sel|plat|te** F *(Comput)* removable disk; **Wech|sel|pro|test** M protest of a bill; **Wech|sel|rah|men** M clip-on picture frame; **Wech|sel|recht** NT law relating to bills of exchange; **Wech|sel|schal|ter** M **a** *(Elec)* changeover switch **b** *(in Bank)* counter for foreign currency exchange; **Wech|sel|schuld|ner(in)** M(F) payer of a bill; **wech|sel|sei|tig** [-zaitɪç] ADJ reciprocal; *(= gegenseitig auch)* mutual ADV reciprocally; *sich beschimpfen, sich hassen* one another; **Wech|sel|spiel** NT interplay; **wech|sel|stän|dig** ADJ *(Bot)* alternate; **Wech|sel|strom** M alternating current; **Wech|sel|stu|be** F bureau de change *(Brit)*, exchange; **Wech|sel|tier|chen** NT amoeba; **wech|sel|voll** ADJ varied; **Wech|sel|wäh|ler(in)** M(F) floating voter; **wech|sel|wei|se** ADV in turn, alternately; **Wech|sel|wir|kung** F interaction; **in ~ stehen** to interact

Wechs|ler[1] ['vɛkslɐ] M **-s, -** *(= Automat)* change machine, change dispenser

Wechs|ler[2] ['vɛkslɐ] M **-s, -**, **Wechs|le|rin** [-ərɪn] F **-, -nen** *(= Geldwechsler)* moneychanger

Weck [vɛk] M **-(e)s, -e** *(dial)* (bread) roll; *(Aus: = Brot)* loaf

Weck-: **Weck|ap|pa|rat** M preserving and bottling equipment; **Weck|dienst** M *(Telec)* alarm call service, wake-up service; *(Mil)* reveille; **~ machen** to do reveille

We|cke ['vɛkə] F **-, -n** *(dial)* (bread) roll

we|cken ['vɛkn] VT to wake (up), to waken; *(fig)* to arouse; *Bedarf* to create; *Erinnerungen* to bring back, to revive; **sich ~ lassen** to have sb wake one up; *(telefonisch)* to get an alarm call

We|cken[1] ['vɛkn] NT **-s**, *no pl* waking-up time; *(Mil)* reveille; **Ausgang bis zum ~** overnight leave (until reveille)

We|cken[2] M **-s, -** *(dial)* (bread) roll

We|cker ['vɛkɐ] M **-s, -** alarm clock; **jdm auf den ~ fallen** *or* **gehen** *(inf)* to get on sb's nerves, to drive sb up the wall *(inf)*

Weck-: **Weck|glas®** NT ≈ preserving *or* Kilner® *(Brit)* jar; **Weck|ring®** M rubber ring *(for preserving jars)*; **Weck|ruf** M *(Telec)* wake-up call; *(Mil)* reveille; **Weck|uhr** F alarm clock

We|del ['veːdl] M **-s, -** fly whisk; *(= Fächer)* fan; *(= Staubwedel aus Federn)* feather duster; *(= Zweig)* twig; *(zum Besprengen)* sprinkler; *(= Zweig)* twig; *(Eccl)* ≈ palm leaf; *(Bot: = Blatt)* frond; *(Hunt)* tail

we|deln ['veːdln] VI **a** **(mit dem Schwanz) ~** *(Hund)* to wag its tail; **mit etw ~** *(= winken)* to wave sth; **mit dem Fächer ~** to wave the fan **b** *(Ski)* to wedel; **das Wedeln** wedel(l)ing VT to waft

we|der ['veːdɐ] CONJ **~ ... noch ...** neither ... nor ...; **er ist ~ gekommen, noch hat er angerufen** he neither came nor phoned (up); **~ das eine noch das andere** *(als Antwort)* neither

weg [vɛk] ADV *(= fort)* **~ sein** *(= fortgegangen, abgefahren, verschwunden)* to have *or* be gone; *(= nicht hier, entfernt)* to be away; *(inf) (= geistesabwesend)* to be not quite with it *(inf)*; *(= eingeschlafen)* to have dozed off; *(= tot)* to be dead; *(= begeistert)* to be really taken, to be bowled over *(von* by); **von zu Hause ~ sein** to be away from home; *(erwachsene Kinder)* to have left home; **über etw** *(acc)* **~ sein** *(inf)* to have got over sth; **er ist schon lange darüber ~** *(inf)* he got over it a long while ago; **über den Tisch ~** across the table; **über meinen Kopf ~** over my head; **weit ~ von hier** far (away) from here; **~ (von hier)!** get away from here!; let's get away from here; **~ mit euch!** away with you!, scram! *(inf)*; **nichts wie** *or* **nur ~ von hier!** let's scram *(inf)*; **~ da!** (get) out of the way!; **~ damit!** *(mit Schere etc)* put it away!; **immer ~ damit** throw *or* chuck *(inf)* it all out; **~ mit den alten Traditionen!** away with these old traditions!; **Hände ~!** hands off!; **in einem ~** *(inf)* non-stop

Weg [veːk] M **-(e)s, -e** [-gə] **a** *(= Pfad, Gehweg, fig)* path; *(= Waldweg, Wanderweg etc)* track, path; *(= Straße)* road; **am ~e** by the wayside; **woher des ~(e)s?** *(old)* where have you come from?, whence comest thou? *(obs)*; **wohin des ~(e)s?** *(old)* where are you going to?, whither goest thou? *(obs)*; **des ~(e)s kommen** *(old)* to come walking/riding *etc* up; **in einer Gegend ~ und Steg kennen** to know an area like the back of one's hand; **jdm in den ~ treten, jdm den ~ versperren** *or* **verstellen** to block *or* bar sb's way; **jdm/einer Sache im ~ stehen** *(fig)* to stand in the way of sb/sth; **sich selbst im ~ stehen** *(fig)* to be one's own worst enemy; **jdm Hindernisse** *or* **Steine in den ~ legen** *(fig)* to put obstructions in sb's way; **jdm nicht über den ~ trauen** *(fig)* not to trust sb an inch; **jdn aus dem ~ räumen** *(fig)* to get rid of sb; **etw aus dem ~ räumen** *(fig)* to remove sth; *Missverständnisse* to clear sth up; **neue ~e beschreiten** *(fig)* to tread new paths; **den ~ der Sünde/Tugend gehen** to follow the path of sin/virtue; **die ~e Gottes** the ways of the Lord; **den ~ des geringsten Widerstandes gehen** to follow the line of least resistance; **der ~ zur Hölle ist mit guten Vorsätzen gepflastert** *(Prov)* the road to Hell is paved with good intentions *(prov)* → **irdisch**

b *(lit, fig: = Route)* way; *(= Entfernung)* distance; *(= Reise)* journey; *(zu Fuß)* walk; *(fig: zum Erfolg)* way, road; *(= Bildungsweg)* road; **ich muss diesen ~ jeden Tag zweimal gehen/fahren** I have to walk/drive this stretch twice a day; **auf dem ~ nach London/zur Arbeit** on the way to London/work; **auf dem ~ zu jdm/nach einem Ort sein** to be on the *or* one's way to sb's/a place; **sich auf den ~ machen** to set off; **6 km ~** 6 kms away; **noch zwei Stunden/ein Stück ~ vor sich haben** to still have two hours/some distance to travel; **jdn ein Stück ~(es) begleiten** *(geh)* to accompany sb part of the way; **mein erster ~ war zur Bank** the first thing I did was go to the bank; **jdn auf seinem letzten ~ begleiten** *(euph)* to pay one's last respects to sb; **seiner ~e gehen** *(geh) (lit)* to go on one's way; *(fig)* to go one's own way; **welchen ~ haben sie eingeschlagen?** *(lit)* what road did they take?; **einen neuen ~ einschlagen** *(fig)* to follow a new avenue; *(beruflich)* to follow a new career; **den falschen/richtigen ~ einschlagen** to follow the wrong/right path *or* road *or (fig)* avenue; **jdm etw mit auf den ~ geben** *(lit)* to give sb sth to take with him/her *etc*; **jdm einen guten Rat mit auf den ~ geben** to give sb good advice to follow in life; **jdm/einer Sache aus dem ~ gehen** *(lit)* to get out of sb's way/the way of sth; *(fig)* to avoid sb/sth; **jdm über den ~ laufen** *(fig)* to run into sb; **seinen ~ (im Leben/Beruf) machen** *(fig)* to make one's way in life/one's career; **seinen ~ nehmen** *(fig)* to take its course; **etw in die ~e leiten** to arrange sth; **etw auf den ~ bringen** to get sth under way; **jdm/sich den ~ verbauen** to ruin sb's/one's chances *or* pros-

pects (*für* of); **auf dem besten ~ sein, etw zu tun** to be well on the way to doing sth; **der gerade ~ ist der kürzeste** *or* **beste** *(Prov)* honesty is the best policy
c *(= Mittel, Art und Weise)* way; *(= Methode)* method; **auf welchem ~ kommt man am schnellsten zu Geld?** what's the fastest way of making *or* to make money?; **auf welchem ~ sind Sie zu erreichen?** how can I get in touch with you?; **auf diesem ~e** this way; **auf diplomatischem ~e** through diplomatic channels; **auf gesetzlichem** *or* **legalem ~e** legally, by legal means; **auf künstlichem ~e** artificially, by artificial means; **zu ~e** = **zuwege**
d *(inf: = Besorgung)* errand

weg+ar|bei|ten ['vɛk-] VT *sep (inf)* **alles ~** to get through all one's work; **nicht viel ~** not to get much work done

Weg|be|glei|ter(in) ['ve:k-] M(F) *(fig)* companion

weg+be|kom|men ['vɛk-] *ptp* **wegbekommen** VT *sep irreg* **a** *(= entfernen, loswerden)* to get rid of (*von* from); *Klebstoff, Fleck etc* to remove (*von* from), to get off; *(von bestimmtem Ort) jdn, Hund* to get away (*von* from) **b** *(inf: = erhalten)* to get; *Grippe* to catch → **Fett**

Weg-: **Weg|be|rei|ter** ['ve:kbəraitɐ] M **-s, -**, **Weg|be|rei|te|rin** [-ərɪn] F **-, -nen** precursor, forerunner; **~ einer Sache** *(gen)* *or* **für etw sein** to pave the way for sth; **~ für jdn sein** to prepare the way for sb; **Weg|be|schrei|bung** F (written) directions *pl*; **Weg|bie|gung** F turn, bend

weg+bla|sen VT *sep irreg* to blow away; **wie weggeblasen sein** *(fig)* to have vanished

weg+blei|ben VI *sep irreg aux sein* to stay away; *(= nicht mehr kommen)* to stop coming; *(Satz, Wort etc)* to be left out *or* omitted; **mir blieb die Luft** *or* **Puste** *(inf)* **weg** *(lit)* I couldn't breathe; **mir bleibt die Spucke** *or* **Luft weg!** *(inf)* I'm absolutely speechless *or* flabbergasted!; **sein Wegbleiben** his absence

weg+brin|gen VT *sep irreg* to take away; *(zur Reparatur)* to take in; *(inf: = wegbekommen)* to get rid of

weg+den|ken VT *sep irreg* **sich** *(dat)* **etw ~** to imagine *or* picture things *etc* without sth; **die Elektrizität ist aus unserem modernen Leben nicht mehr wegzudenken** we cannot imagine life today without electricity

weg+dis|ku|tie|ren *ptp* **wegdiskutiert** VT *sep* to explain away; **dieses Problem lässt sich nicht ~** talking about it won't make the problem go away

weg+dür|fen VI *sep irreg* to be allowed to go *or* leave; *(inf: = ausgehen dürfen)* to be allowed to go out

We|ge|geld ['ve:gə-] NT *(Hist)* (road) toll

weg+ekeln ['vɛk-] VT *sep (inf)* to drive away

We|ge|la|ge|rer ['ve:gəla:gərɐ] M **-s, -** highwayman; *(zu Fuß)* footpad *(old Brit)*, highwayman

we|gen ['ve:gn] ✪ 44.1 PREP *+gen or (inf) +dat* because of, on account of; *(= infolge auch)* due to; **jdn ~ einer Sache bestrafen/verurteilen/entlassen** *etc* to punish/sentence/dismiss *etc* sb for sth; **von ~!** *(inf)* you've got to be kidding! *(inf)*; *(Verbot auch)* no way! *(inf)*, no chance! *(inf)*; **... aber von ~!** *(inf)* ... but not a bit of it! *(inf)*; **er ist krank – von ~ krank!** *(inf)* he's ill – since when? *(iro)* or what do you mean "ill"? *(iro)*; **~ mir** *(inf)* *or* **meiner** *(obs)* = **meinetwegen**, → **Amt a**, **Recht a**

We|ge|rich ['ve:gərɪç] M **-s, -e** *(Bot)* plantain

weg+es|sen ['vɛk-] VT *sep irreg* **jdm den Kuchen** *etc* **~** to eat sb's cake *etc*; **er hat (mir) alles weggegessen** he's eaten all my food

weg+fah|ren ['vɛk-] *sep irreg* VI *aux sein (= abfahren)* to leave; *(Auto, Bus, Fahrer)* to drive off *or* away; *(im Boot)* to sail away; *(zum Einkaufen, als Ausflug)* to go out; *(= verreisen)* to go away VT *Menschen, Gegenstände* to take away; *Fahrzeug* to drive away; *(= umstellen)* to move

Weg|fahr|sper|re ['vɛk-] F *(Aut)* **(elektronische) ~** (electronic) immobilizer

Weg|fall ['vɛk-] M, *no pl (= Einstellung)* discontinuation; *(von Kontrollen)* removal; *(= Aufhören)* cessation *(form)*; *(= Streichung)* cancellation; *(= Unterbleiben)* loss; *(= Auslassung)* omission; **in ~ kommen** *(form)* to be discontinued; *(Bestimmung)* to cease to apply

weg+fal|len ['vɛk-] VI *sep irreg aux sein* to be discontinued; *(Arbeitsplätze)* to be lost; *(Kontrollen)* to be removed; *(Bestimmung, Regelung)* to cease to apply; *(= unterbleiben)* to be lost; *(= überflüssig werden)* to become no longer necessary; *(= ausgelassen werden)* to be omitted; **~ lassen** to discontinue; *(= auslassen)* to omit; **wir haben den Nachtisch ~ lassen** we did without dessert, we dispensed with dessert

weg-: **weg+fe|gen** VT *sep (lit, fig)* to sweep away; **weg+fi|schen** VT *sep* to catch; *(fig inf)* to snap up; **er hat uns alle Forellen weggefischt** he's caught all our trout; **weg+flie|gen** VI *sep irreg aux sein* to fly away *or* off; *(Hut)* to fly off; *(mit Flugzeug)* to fly out; **wann bist du denn in Frankfurt weggeflogen?** when did you fly out of Frankfurt?; **weg+fres|sen** VT *sep (inf)* → **wegessen**; **weg+füh|ren** *sep* VT to lead away VI **das führt zu weit (vom Thema) weg** that will lead *or* take us too far off the subject

Weg|ga|be|lung ['ve:k-] F fork (in the road), bifurcation *(form)*

Weg|gang ['vɛkgaŋ] M, *no pl* departure, leaving

weg+ge|ben ['vɛk-] VT *sep irreg (= verschenken)* to give away; *(= in Pflege geben)* to have looked after; **eine kaputte Uhr ~** to take in a broken watch; **seine Wäsche (zum Waschen) ~** to have one's washing done

Weg|ge|fähr|te ['ve:k-] M, **Weg|ge|fähr|tin** F *(fig)* companion

weg+ge|hen ['vɛk-] VI *sep irreg aux sein* to go, to leave; *(= verreisen, umziehen etc)* to go away; *(= ausgehen)* to go out; *(inf) (Fleck)* to come off; *(Ware)* to sell; **über etw** *(acc)* **~** *(inf)* to ignore sth, to pass over sth; **aus Heidelberg/aus dem Büro/von der Firma/von zu Hause ~** to leave Heidelberg/the office/the firm/home; **geh mir damit weg!** *(inf)* don't give me that! *(inf)*; **geh mir mit dem weg!** *(inf)* don't talk to me about him!

Weg|ge|nos|se ['ve:k-] M, **Weg|ge|nos|sin** F *(lit, fig)* companion

Weg|gli ['vɛkli] NT **-s, -** *(Sw)* (bread) roll

weg+gu|cken ['vɛk-] *sep* VI to look away VT **es wird dir schon niemand was ~!** *(hum)* we/they *etc* won't be seeing anything we/they *etc* haven't seen before *(hum)*

weg+ha|ben ['vɛk-] VT *sep irreg (inf) (= erledigt haben)* to have got done; *(= bekommen, verstanden haben)* to have got; *(= entfernt haben) Fleck etc* to have got rid of *(inf)*; *(= umstellen, umhängen) Tisch, Gegenstand* to have moved; **jdn/etw ~ wollen** *(inf)* to want to get rid of sb/sth; **der hat was weg** *(inf)* he's really clever; **darin hat er was weg** *(inf)* he's pretty good at that; **du hast deine Strafe/deinen Denkzettel weg** you have had your punishment; **einen ~** *(inf) (= verrückt sein)* to be off one's head *(inf)*, to have a screw loose *(inf)* → **Fett, Ruhe d, Teil c**

weg-: **weg+hel|fen** VI *sep irreg* **jdm von irgendwo ~** to help sb get away from *or* out of *(inf)* a place; **jdm über etw** *(acc)* **~** *(fig)* to help sb (to) get over sth; **weg+hol|len** VT *sep* to take away; *(= abholen)* to fetch; **sich** *(dat)* **was/eine Krankheit ~** *(inf)* to catch something/a disease; **weg+hö|ren** VI *sep* not to listen; **weg+ja|gen** VT *sep* to chase away, to drive away *or* off; *Menschen auch* to send packing *(inf)*; *(aus Land)* to drive out; **weg+kna|cken** VI *sep (sl: = einschlafen)* to crash (out) *(inf)*

weg+kom|men ['vɛk-] VI *sep irreg aux sein* **a** *(inf) (= entfernt werden)* to go; *(= abhandenkommen)* to disappear; *(= weggehen können)* to get away; *(aus dem Haus)* to get out; **was ich nicht brauche, kommt weg** what I don't want can go; **das Buch ist mir weggekommen** the book has disappeared, I've lost the book; **mach, dass du wegkommst!** make yourself scarce! *(inf)*, hop it! *(inf)*; **gut/schlecht (bei etw) ~** to come off well/badly (with sth); **über etw** *(acc)* **~/nicht ~** to get over/be unable to get over sth; **ich komme nicht darüber weg, dass ...** *(inf)* I can't get over the fact that ...
b *(dial: = herkommen)* to come from

Weg-: **Weg|kreuz** NT **a** *(= Kruzifix)* wayside cross **b** *(= Kreuzung)* crossroads; **Weg|kreu|zung** F crossroads

weg+krie|gen ['vɛk-] VT *sep (inf)* = **wegbekommen a**

Weg|krüm|mung ['ve:k-] F bend in the road

weg-: **weg+las|sen** VT *sep irreg (= auslassen)* to leave out; *(= nicht benutzen)* not to use; *(inf: = gehen lassen)* to let go; **ich lasse heute den Zucker im Kaffee weg** I won't have *(Brit)* *or* take any sugar in my coffee today; **weg+lau|fen** VI *sep irreg aux sein* to run away (*vor +dat* from); **seine Frau ist ihm weggelaufen** his wife has run away (from him), his wife has run off (and left him); **das läuft (dir) nicht weg!** *(fig hum)* that can wait; **weg+le|gen** VT *sep (in Schublade etc)* to put away; *(zur Seite, zum späteren Verbrauch)* to put aside; **weg+leug|nen** VT *sep* to deny; **weg+lo|ben** VT *sep* = **fortloben**; **weg+ma|chen** ['vɛk-] *sep* VT *(inf)* to get rid of; **sie ließ sich** *(dat)* **das Kind ~** *(sl)* she got rid of the baby *(inf)* VI *aux sein or haben (dial, inf)* to get away (*aus* from), to get out (*aus* of)

weg+müs|sen ['vɛk-] VI *sep irreg* to have to go; *(= weggehen müssen auch)* to have to leave *or* to be off *(inf)*; *(= entfernt werden)* to have to be removed; **ich muss eine Zeit lang von/aus New York weg** I must get away from/get out of New York for a while; **du musst da weg, du behinderst ja den ganzen Verkehr** you'll have to move (from there), you're blocking all the traffic; **die paar Reste müssen weg** we/you *etc* can't leave those little bits; **wenn wir die Wand streichen wollen, muss das Sofa weg** if we're going to paint the wall, we'll have to move the sofa (out of the way)

Weg|nah|me ['vɛkna:mə] F **-,** *no pl* taking; *(= Entziehung)* taking away; *(von Sicht)* blocking

weg+neh|men ['vɛk-] VT *sep irreg* to take *(auch Chess)*; *(= fortnehmen, entfernen, entziehen)* to take away; *(= absorbieren) Strahlen, Licht, Lärm* to absorb; *(= verdecken) Licht, Sonne* to block out; *Aussicht, Sicht* to block; *(= beanspruchen) Zeit, Platz* to take up; **Gas ~** *(Aut)* to ease off the accelerator *or* gas *(US)*; **fünf Tage vom Urlaub ~** to take five days off the holiday *(esp Brit)* *or* vacation *(US)*; **die Bässe ~** to turn down *or* reduce the bass; **jdm seine Kinder ~** to take sb's children away (from him/her); **jdm seine Frau ~** to steal sb's wife

weg-: **weg+pa|cken** VT *sep* to pack *or* put away; *(inf: = essen)* to put away *(inf)*; **weg+put|zen** VT *sep* to wipe away *or* off; *(inf: = essen)* to polish off; **er putzt ganz schön was weg** *(inf)* he doesn't half eat a lot *or* stow a lot away *(Brit inf)*, he can put a lot away *(inf)*; **weg+raf|fen** VT *sep* to snatch away; *(liter: durch Tod)* to carry off

Weg|rand ['ve:k-] M wayside, side of the path *or (von Straße)* road

weg-: **weg+ra|sie|ren** *ptp* **wegrasiert** VT *sep* to shave off; **er hat mir den vorderen Kotflügel wegrasiert** *(fig inf)* he took my front mudguard with him *(hum)*; **weg+ra|ti|o|na|li|sie|ren** *ptp* **wegrationalisiert** VT *sep Arbeitsplätze* to rationalize away; **weg+räu|men** VT *sep* to clear away; *(in Schrank)* to put away; **weg+rei|ßen** VT *sep irreg* to tear away (*jdm* from sb); *Zweige* to break off; *(inf) Häuser etc* to tear *or* pull down; **der Fluss hat die Brücke weggerissen** the river swept away the bridge; **weg+ren|nen** VI *sep irreg aux sein (inf)* to run away; **weg+re|tu|schie|ren** *ptp* **wegretuschiert** VT *sep* to spot out; **weg+rü|cken** VTI *sep (vi: aux sein)* to move away; **weg+ru|fen** VT *sep irreg* to call away; **weg+rut|schen** VI *sep aux sein (aus der Hand etc)* to slip away; *(auf Eis etc)* to slide away; **mein Wagen ist mir weggerutscht** my car went into a skid; **weg+sa|cken** VI *sep aux sein (inf)* **a** *(Schiff)* to sink; *(Flugzeug)* to (suddenly) drop, to lose height **b** *(= zusammenbrechen)* to give way

weg|sam ['veːkzaːm] ADJ *(obs)* passable

weg-: **weg+schaf|fen** VT *sep (= beseitigen, loswerden)* to get rid of; *(= wegräumen)* to clear away; *(= wegtragen, wegfahren)* to remove, to cart away *(inf)*; *(= erledigen) Arbeit* to get done; **weg+schau|en** VI *sep (esp dial)* = **wegsehen**

Weg|schei|de ['veːk-] F parting of the ways *(liter)*

weg-: **weg+schen|ken** VT *sep (inf)* to give away; **weg+sche|ren** VR *sep (inf)* to clear out *(inf)*, to shove off *(inf)*; **weg+schi|cken** VT *sep Brief etc* to send off *or* away; *jdn* to send away; *(um etwas zu holen etc)* to send off; **weg+schie|ben** VT *sep irreg* to push away; *(= beiseiteschieben: Teller etc)* to push aside; **weg+schie|ßen** VT *sep irreg* **jdm den Arm** *etc* ~ to shoot sb's arm *etc* off; **weg+schlaf|fen** VI *sep aux sein (sl)* to peg *or* poop out *(inf)*; **er schlaffte ihm immer wieder weg** it kept on going limp on him *(inf)*; **weg+schlei|chen** VIR *sep irreg (vi: aux sein)* to creep *or* steal away; **weg+schlep|pen** *sep* VT to drag *or* lug *(inf) or* haul away *or* off; *(= tragen)* to carry off VR to drag *or* haul oneself away; **weg+schlie|ßen** VT *sep irreg* to lock away; **weg+schmei|ßen** VT *sep irreg (inf)* to chuck away *(inf)*; **weg+schnap|pen** VT *sep (inf)* **jdm etw** ~ to snatch sth (away) from sb; **die andere Kundin hat mir das Kleid weggeschnappt** the other customer snapped up the dress before I could; **jdm die Freundin/den Job** ~ to pinch *(Brit) or* snatch *(US)* sb's girlfriend/job *(inf)*

Weg|schne|cke ['veːk-] F slug *(of the genus Arionidae)*

weg-: **weg+schüt|ten** VT *sep* to tip away; **weg+schwem|men** VT *sep* to wash away; **weg+se|hen** VI *sep irreg* to look away; **über etw** *(acc)* ~ *(lit)* to look over sth; *(fig inf)* to overlook sth, to turn a blind eye to sth; **weg+set|zen** ['vɛk-] *sep* VT to move (away); *(= wegstellen)* to put away VR to move away; **sich über etw** *(acc)* ~ *(inf)* to ignore sth, to pay no attention to sth VI *aux sein or haben* **über etw** *(acc)* ~ to leap *or* jump over sth, to clear sth; **weg+sol|len** VI *sep irreg (inf)* **das soll weg** that is to go; **ich soll von London weg** I should leave London; **warum soll ich/mein Auto da weg?** why should I move/my car be moved?; **weg+spü|len** VT *sep* to wash away; *(in der Toilette)* to flush away; **weg+ste|cken** VT *sep (lit)* to put away; *(inf) Niederlage, Kritik* to take; *Enttäuschung, Verlust* to get over; **weg+steh|len** VR *sep irreg* to steal away; **weg+stel|len** VT *sep* to put away; *(= abstellen)* to put down; **weg+ster|ben** VI *sep irreg aux sein (inf)* to die off; **jdm** ~ to die on sb *(inf)*; **weg+sto|ßen** VT *sep irreg* to push *or* shove away; *(mit Fuß)* to kick away

Weg-: **Weg|stre|cke** F *(rare)* stretch of road; **schlechte** ~ poor road surface; **Weg|stun|de** F *(old)* hour

weg-: **weg+tau|chen** VI *sep aux sein* to disappear; *(inf: aus unangenehmer Situation)* to duck out *(inf)*; **weg+tra|gen** VT *sep irreg* to carry away *or* off; **weg+trei|ben** *sep irreg* VT *Boot etc* to carry away *or* off; *(= vertreiben) Vieh etc* to drive away *or* off VI *aux sein* to drift away; **weg+tre|ten** VI *sep irreg aux sein (rare)* to step away *or* aside; *(Mil)* to fall out; **(lassen Sie)** ~! *(Mil)* dismiss!, dismissed!; **er ist (geistig) weggetreten** *(inf) (= geistesabwesend)* he's miles away *(inf)*; *(= schwachsinnig)* he's soft in the head *(inf)*, he's not all there *(inf)*; **weg+tun** VT *sep irreg* to put away; *(= sparen) Geld etc auch* to put by *or* aside; *(= wegwerfen)* to throw away; *(= verstecken)* to hide away; **tu die Hände weg!** take your hands off!

Weg|war|te ['veːk-] F *(Bot)* chicory

weg-: **weg+wa|schen** VT *sep irreg Fleck* to wash off; *(= wegspülen) Erde etc* to wash away; **weg+we|hen** VTI *sep (vi: aux sein)* to blow away

Weg-: **weg|wei|send** ADJ pioneering *attr*, revolutionary, pathbreaking *(US)*; **Weg|wei|ser** ['veːkvaizɐ] M **-s, -** sign; *(an einem Pfosten)* signpost; *(fig: Buch etc)* guide

Weg|werf- ['vɛkvərf] *in cpds* disposable, throwaway

weg-: **weg+wer|fen** *sep irreg* VT to throw away; **weggeworfenes Geld** money down the drain VR **sich (an jdn)** ~ to waste oneself (on sb), to throw oneself away (on sb); **weg|wer|fend** ADJ dismissive, disdainful

Weg|werf-: **Weg|werf|ge|sell|schaft** F throwaway society; **Weg|werf|ver|pa|ckung** F disposable *or* throwaway packaging

weg+wi|schen ['vɛk-] VT *sep* to wipe off; *(fig)* to dismiss

weg+wol|len ['vɛk-] VI *sep irreg (= verreisen)* to want to go away; *(= weggehen von Haus, Party etc)* to want to leave *or* go; *(= hinausgehen)* to want to go out

weg+wün|schen ['vɛk-] VT *sep* **jdn** ~ to wish sb would go away

weg+zäh|len ['vɛk-] VT *sep (Aus)* to take away, to subtract

weg|zap|pen VT *sep (TV inf)* to zap off *(inf)*

weg+zau|bern ['vɛk-] VT *sep* to make disappear *(lit)* by magic *or (fig)* as if by magic

Weg|zeh|rung ['veːk-] F *(liter)* provisions *pl* for the journey; *(Eccl)* viaticum

weg+zie|hen ['vɛk-] *sep irreg* VT to pull away *(jdm* from sb); *Vorhang* to draw back VI *aux sein* to move away; *(Vögel)* to migrate

Weg|zug ['vɛk-] M move *(aus, von* (away) from)

weh [veː] ADJ **a** *(= wund)* sore; *(geh: = schmerzlich)* aching *attr*; **sie verspürte ein ~es Gefühl** *(geh)* her heart ached; **mir ist so ~ zumute** *or* **ums Herz** *(old, liter)* my heart is sore *(liter)*, I am sore of heart *(old)* **b** ~ **tun** = **wehtun** INTERJ *(geh, liter)* woe *(old)*; *(bedauernd)* alas *(liter)*, alack *(old)*; **o ~!** oh dear!, oh my goodness!;; **(über jdn) ~ schreien** *(old)* to lament (sb); **~ mir!** woe is me! *(liter)*; **~ mir, wenn …** woe betide me if … → **ach**

Weh [veː] NT **-(e)s, -e** *(old, liter)* woe; *(= dumpfes Gefühl)* ache; *(= Leid, Gram)* grief; **ein tiefes ~ erfüllte ihn** his heart ached

we|he ['veːə] INTERJ ~ **(dir), wenn du das tust** you'll be sorry *or* you'll regret it if you do that; **darf ich das anfassen? – ~ (dir)!** can I touch? – you dare! *(inf)*; **~ dem, der …!** woe betide anyone who …!

We|he ['veːə] F **-, -n a** *(= Schneewehe etc)* drift **b** **Wehen** PL *(lit: = Geburtswehen)* (labour *(Brit) or* labor *(US))* pains *pl*, contractions *pl*; *(fig)* birth pangs *pl*; **in den ~n liegen** to be in labour *(Brit) or* labor *(US)*; **die ~n setzten ein** labour *(Brit) or* labor *(US) or* the contractions started, she went into labour *(Brit) or* labor *(US)*

we|hen ['veːən] VI **a** *(Wind)* to blow; *(Fahne)* to wave, to flutter; *(Haare)* to blow about; **der Geist der Aufklärung wehte durch Deutschland** *(geh)* the spirit of enlightenment was abroad *or* reigned in Germany; **es weht ein warmer Wind** there's a warm wind (blowing), a warm wind is blowing; **kein Lüftchen wehte** there wasn't even a breeze → **Fahne a**, **Wind a** **b** *aux sein (Geruch, Klang)* to drift; *(Duft)* to waft VT to blow *(von* off); *(sanft)* to waft

We|hen|schrei|ber M tocograph *(spec)*

Weh-: **Weh|ge|fühl** NT *(geh)* ache; **ein ~ befiel ihn** his heart ached; **Weh|ge|schrei** NT wailing, cries *pl* of woe *(liter)*; **in ~ ausbrechen, ein ~ anstimmen** to start to wail, to give vent to one's woe *(liter)*; **Weh|kla|ge** F *(liter)* lament (-ation); **weh|kla|gen** VI *insep (liter)* to lament, to wail; **über etw** *(acc)* ~ to lament (over) sth, to bewail sth; **um jdn** ~ to lament the loss of sb; **Weh|laut** M *(liter)* cry of pain; *(bei Kummer)* cry of woe; *(leise)* whimper; **weh|lei|dig** ADJ over-sensitive to pain; *(= jammernd)* whining *attr*, snivelling *attr (esp Brit)*, sniveling *attr (US)*; *(= voller Selbstmitleid)* sorry for oneself, self-pitying; **er ist ja so ~** he whines at the least little thing; he's always feeling sorry for himself; **Weh|lei|dig|keit** F self-pity; **Weh|mut** ['veːmuːt] F **-,** *no pl (geh)* melancholy; *(= Sehnsucht)* wistfulness; *(nach Vergangenem)* nostalgia; **weh|mü|tig** ['veːmyːtɪç], **weh|muts|voll** *(geh)* ADJ melancholy; *(= sehnsuchtsvoll)* wistful; *(= nostalgisch)* nostalgic ADV *(= traurig)* sadly; *(= sehnsuchtsvoll)* wistfully; *(= nostalgisch)* nostalgically; **seine Stimme klang ~** his voice sounded melancholy; **du wirst dich noch ~ nach mir zurücksehnen** you'll miss me terribly

Wehr [veːɐ] F **-, -en a** *(= Feuerwehr)* fire brigade *(Brit)*, fire department *(US)* **b** *(old) (= Bollwerk)* defences *pl (Brit)*, defenses *pl (US)*; *(no pl: = Widerstand)* defence *(Brit)*, defense *(US)*; **mit ~ und Waffen** *(old)* in full panoply *(old)*; **sich zur ~ setzen** to defend oneself

Wehr NT **-(e)s, -e** weir

Wehr- *in cpds* defence *(Brit)*, defense *(US)*; **Wehr|be|auf|trag|te(r)** MF *decl as adj* commissioner for the armed forces; **Wehr|be|reich** M military district; **Wehr|dienst** M military service; **seinen ~ (ab)leisten** to do one's military service; **jdn zum ~ einberufen** to call sb up *(Brit)*, to draft sb *(US)*; **wehr|dienst|pflich|tig** [-pflɪçtɪç] ADJ liable for military service; **Wehr|dienst|pflich|ti|ge(r)** [-pflɪçtɪgə] MF *decl as adj* person liable for military service; *(der schon eingezogen ist)* conscript *(Brit)*, draftee *(US)*; **Wehr|dienst|ver|wei|ge|rer** M, **Wehr|dienst|ver|wei|ge|rin** F conscientious objector

> **WEHRDIENST**
>
> **Wehrdienst** is compulsory military service for all male nationals. The training lasts nine months in Germany, six months in Austria and 18 to 21 weeks in Switzerland. This is generally followed by refresher courses taking place every two years. If a man refuses to do military service as a matter of principle, he may do **Zivildienst** instead (although not in Switzerland). → ZIVILDIENST

weh|ren ['veːrən] VT *(obs)* = **verwehren** VR to defend oneself; *(= sich aktiv widersetzen)* to (put up a) fight; **sich gegen einen Plan** *etc* ~ to fight (against) a plan *etc*; **dagegen weiß ich mich zu ~** I know how to deal with that VI *+dat (geh)* to fight; *(= Einhalt gebieten)* to check; **wehret den Anfängen!** these things must be nipped in the bud, these things must be stopped before they get out of hand

Wehr-: **Wehr|er|fas|sung** F *compilation of the call-up list for military service*; **Wehr|er|satz|be|hör|de** F military recruitment board *or* agency; **Wehr|er|satz|dienst** M alternative national service; **Wehr|etat** M defence *(Brit) or* defense *(US)* budget; **Wehr|ex|per|te** M, **Wehr|ex|per|tin** F defence *(Brit) or* defense *(US)* expert; **wehr|fä|hig** ADJ fit for military service, able-bodied; **Männer im ~en Alter** men of the right age for military service; **Wehr|gang** M *pl* **-gänge** walk along the battlements; **wehr|haft** ADJ *(geh)* able to put up a fight; *Stadt etc* well-fortified; **Wehr|haf|tig|keit** F *(geh)* ability to put up a fight; **Wehr|ho|heit** F military sovereignty; **Wehr|kir|che** F fortified church; **Wehr|kraft** F military strength; **Wehr|kraft|zer|set|zung** F undermining of military morale; **wehr|los** ADJ defenceless *(Brit)*, defenseless *(US)*; *(fig: gegenüber Gemeinheiten etc)* helpless ADV defencelessly *(Brit)*, defenselessly *(US)*, helplessly; **jdm ~ ausgeliefert sein** to be at sb's mercy; **Wehr|lo|sig|keit**

F -, *no pl* defencelessness *(Brit)*, defenselessness *(US)*; *(fig: gegenüber Gemeinheiten etc)* helplessness; **Wehr|macht** F armed forces *pl*; *(Hist)* Wehrmacht; **Wehr|mann** M *pl* **-männer** *(Sw)* soldier; **Wehr|pass** M service record (book); **Wehr|pflicht** F **(allgemeine) ~** (universal) conscription, compulsory military service; **wehr|pflich|tig** [-pflıçtıç] ADJ = **wehrdienstpflichtig**; **Wehr|pflich|ti|ge(r)** [-pflıçtıgə] MF *decl as adj* = **Wehrdienstpflichtige(r)**; **Wehr|sold** M (military) pay; **Wehr|sport|grup|pe** F paramilitary group; **Wehr|turm** M fortified tower; **Wehr|übung** F reserve duty training exercise

weh+tun *sep irreg*, **weh tun** *irreg* VI *(lit, fig)* to hurt; **mir tut der Rücken weh** my back hurts *or* is aching; **mir tut mein verbrannter Finger weh** my finger hurts *or* is sore where I burned it; **sich/jdm ~** *(lit, fig)* to hurt oneself/sb; **was tut dir denn nun schon wieder weh?** what's the matter now?; **wo tut es denn weh?** *(fig inf)* what's your problem?, what's up? *(inf)*

Weh|weh ['ve:ve:, ve:'ve:] NT **-s, -s** *(baby-talk)* hurt (place)

Weh|weh|chen [ve:'ve:çən, 've:-] NT **-s, -** *(inf)* (minor) complaint; **seine tausend ~** all his little aches and pains

Weib [vaip] NT **-(e)s, -er** [-bɐ] woman, female *(pej)*, broad *(US pej inf)*; *(old, Bibl: = Ehefrau)* wife; *(pej inf: Mann)* old woman *(neg!)*; **~ und Kind** *(old)* wife and children; **eine Frau zu seinem ~(e) nehmen** *(old)* to take a woman to wife *(old Brit)* or as one's wife; **sie ist ein tolles ~** *(inf)* she's quite a woman, she's quite a dame *(US pej inf)*

Weib|chen ['vaipçən] NT **-s, -** *(Zool)* female; *(hum: = Ehefrau)* little woman *(hum)*; *(pej: = nicht emanzipierte Frau)* dumb female

Wei|ber-: **Wei|ber|art** F *(old, pej)* woman's way; **Wei|ber|fast|nacht** F *day during the carnival period when women assume control*; **Wei|ber|feind** M woman hater, misogynist; **Wei|ber|ge|schich|ten** PL sexploits *pl* *(hum)*; *(= Affären auch)* womanizing *sing*; **Wei|ber|ge|schwätz** NT *(pej)* women's talk; **Wei|ber|hass** M *(inf)* misogyny; **Wei|ber|held** M *(pej)* lady-killer, womanizer; **Wei|ber|herr|schaft** F *(pej)* petticoat government *(inf)*; **Wei|ber|kram** M *(pej)* women's stuff *(inf)*; **Wei|ber|volk** NT *(obs)* womenfolk *pl*; *(pej)* females *pl (pej)*; **Wei|ber|wirt|schaft** F *(pej)* henhouse *(inf)*

wei|bisch ['vaibıʃ] ADJ effeminate

Weib|lein ['vaiplain] NT **-s, -** little woman; **ein altes ~** a little old woman, an old dear *(inf)*

weib|lich ['vaiplıç] ADJ *(Zool, Bot: = von Frauen)* female; *(Gram, Poet: = fraulich, wie Frauen)* feminine

Weib|lich|keit F -, *no pl* femininity; *(= Frauen)* women *pl*; **die holde ~** *(hum)* the fair sex

Weibs|bild NT *(old)* woman; *(junge Frau auch)* wench *(old)*; *(pej auch)* female

Weib|sen ['vaipsn] NT **-s, -** *usu pl (hum inf)* woman, female

Weibs|per|son F *(old)* woman

Weib(s)|stück NT *(pej)* bitch *(inf)*, cow *(inf)*

weibs|toll ['vaips-] ADJ woman-mad

weich [vaiç] ADJ soft *(auch fig, Ling, Phot)*; *Ei* soft-boiled; *Fleisch, Gemüse* tender; *Energietechnik* non-nuclear; *Währung* soft; *(Comput) Trennung, Zeilenumbruch* soft; *(= geschmeidig) Bewegungen* smooth; *Mensch (= nachgiebig)* soft; *(= mitleidig)* soft-hearted; **~e Drogen** soft drugs; **~er Boykott** civil disobedience; **~ werden** *(lit, fig)* to soften; **die Knie wurden mir ~** my knees turned to jelly, I went weak at *(Brit)* or in *(US)* the knees; **~ machen** to soften → *auch* **weichmachen**; **ein ~es Herz haben** to be soft-hearted, to have a soft heart; **eine ~e Birne** or **einen ~en Keks haben** *(inf)* to be soft in the head *(inf)*

ADV softly, gently; *landen* softly; **~ geklopft** *(Fleisch)* hammered tender; **~ gekocht** *(Ei)* soft-boiled; *Fleisch, Gemüse* boiled until tender; *Nudeln* cooked until soft; **die Kupplung ~ kommen lassen** to let out the clutch smoothly; **~ landen** to land softly; *(= auf weichem Untergrund)* to have a soft landing → **betten VT, VR**

Weich|bild NT **im ~ der Stadt** within the town or *(größere Stadt)* city precincts

Wei|che ['vaiçə] F **-, -n** **a** *no pl* = **Weichheit** **b** *(= Seite)* side, flank

Wei|che F **-, -n** **a** *(Rail)* points *pl (Brit)*, switch *(US)*; **die ~n stellen** *(lit)* to switch the points *(Brit)*, to change the switch *(US)*; *(fig)* to set the course **b** *(= Ausweichstelle)* passing place

Weich|ei NT *(pej sl: = Weichling, Feigling)* wimp *(inf)*

wei|chen VTI *(vi: aux haben or sein)* to soak

wei|chen ['vaiçn] *pret* **wich** [vıç], *ptp* **gewichen** [gə'vıçn] VI *aux sein* **a** *(Mensch, Tier, Fahrzeug: = weggehen, verlassen)* to move; *(Armee, Mensch, Tier: = zurückweichen)* to retreat (+*dat*, *vor* +*dat* from); *(= Platz machen, fig: = nachgeben)* to give way (+*dat* to); **(nicht) von jdm** or **jds Seite ~** (not) to leave sb's side; **er wich nicht** or **keinen Schritt vom Wege** he did not deviate an inch; **sie wich nicht von der Stelle** she refused to or wouldn't budge (an inch); **alles** or **das Blut/die Farbe wich aus ihren Wangen** *(liter)* the blood/colour *(Brit)* or color *(US)* drained from her cheeks; **die Begeisterung ist der Ernüchterung gewichen** enthusiasm has given way to disillusionment; **die Angst ist von ihr gewichen** her fear has left her or has disappeared; **weiche, böser Geist!** *(liter)* begone evil spirit! *(liter)* **b** *(Gefühl, Druck, Schmerz) (= nachlassen)* to ease, to abate; *(= verschwinden)* to go

Wei|chen-: **Wei|chen|stel|ler** [-ʃtɛlɐ] M **-s, -**, **Wei|chen|stel|le|rin** [-ərın] F **-, -nen** pointsman *(Brit)*, switchman *(US)*; *(fig)* guiding spirit, moving force (+*gen* behind); **Wei|chen|stel|lung** F *(lit)* changing the points *(Brit)* or switch *(US)*; *(fig)* setting the course

weich-: **weich|ge|klopft** [-gəklɔpft] ADJ → **weich ADV**; **weich|ge|kocht** [-gəkɔxt] ADJ → **weich ADV**

Weich|heit F -, *no pl* softness *(auch fig, Ling, Phot)*; *(von Fleisch, Gemüse)* tenderness; *(= Geschmeidigkeit: von Bewegungen)* smoothness

Weich-: **weich|her|zig** ADJ soft-hearted; **Weich|her|zig|keit** ['vaiçhɛrtsıçkait] F -, *no pl* soft-heartedness; **Weich|holz** NT softwood; **Weich|kä|se** M soft cheese; **weich+klop|fen** *sep*, **weich klop|fen** △, **weich+krie|gen** *sep*, **weich krie|gen** △ VT *(fig inf)* to soften up

weich|lich ['vaiçlıç] ADJ *(lit)* soft; *(fig)* weak; *(= weibisch)* effeminate; *(= verhätschelt)* soft ADV **ein Kind zu ~ erziehen** to mollycoddle *(Brit)* or pamper a child

Weich|ling ['vaiçlıŋ] M **-s, -e** *(pej)* weakling, softy *(inf)*

Weich-: **weich+ma|chen** *sep*, **weich ma|chen** △ VT *(fig)* to soften up → *auch* **weich**; **Weich|ma|cher** M *(Chem)* softener, softening agent; **weich|scha|lig** [-ʃa:lıç] ADJ soft-shelled; *Apfel* soft-skinned

Weich|sel ['vaiksl] F - Vistula

Weich|sel|kir|sche ['vaiksl-] F St Lucie cherry

Weich-: **weich+spü|len** VT *sep* to condition; *Wäsche* to use (fabric) conditioner or softener on; **Weich|spü|ler** M conditioner; *(für Wäsche auch)* (fabric) softener; **Weich|tei|le** PL soft parts *pl*; *(inf: = Geschlechtsteile)* privates *pl*, private parts *pl*; **Weich|tier** NT mollusc; **weich+wer|den** VI *sep irreg aux sein (fig)* → **weich**; **Weich|zeich|ner** M *(Phot)* soft-focus lens

Wei|de ['vaidə] F **-, -n** *(Bot)* willow

Wei|de F **-, -n** *(Agr)* pasture; *(= Wiese)* meadow; **auf die** or **zur ~ treiben** to put out to pasture or to graze or to grass; **auf der ~ sein** to be grazing, to be out at pasture

Wei|de-: **Wei|de|flä|che** F, **Wei|de|land** NT *(Agr)* pasture(land), grazing land, pasturage; **Wei|de|mo|nat** M *(old)* month of May

wei|den ['vaidn] VI to graze VT to (put out to) graze, to put out to pasture; **seine Blicke** or **Augen an etw** *(dat)* **~** to feast one's eyes on sth VR **sich an etw** *(dat)* **~** *(fig)* to revel in sth; *(sadistisch auch)* to gloat over sth

Wei|den-: **Wei|den|baum** M willow tree; **Wei|den|busch** M willow bush; **Wei|den|ger|te** F willow rod or switch; *(zum Korbflechten)* osier, wicker; **Wei|den|kätz|chen** NT pussy willow, catkin *(Brit)*; **Wei|den|korb** M wicker basket; **Wei|den|laub|sän|ger** M *(Orn)* chiffchaff; **Wei|den|rös|chen** NT *(Bot)* willowherb; **schmalblättriges ~** rosebay willowherb; **Wei|den|rost** M cattle grid

Wei|de-: **Wei|de|platz** M pasture; **Wei|de|wirt|schaft** F *(Econ)* pastural agriculture

weid|ge|recht ADJ in accordance with hunting principles ADV correctly; **ein Tier ~ erlegen** to kill an animal with a well placed shot

weid|lich ['vaitlıç] ADV *(mit adj)* pretty; **sich über etw** *(acc)* **~ amüsieren** to be highly amused at sth; **etw ~ ausnutzen** to make full use of sth; **er hat sich ~ bemüht** he tried pretty hard ADJ *(rare)* = **weidmännisch**

Weid-: **Weid|mann** M *pl* **-männer** *(liter)* huntsman, hunter; **weid|män|nisch** [-mɛnıʃ] ADJ huntsman's *attr*; **das ist nicht ~** that's not done in hunting ADV in a huntsman's manner; *ausgebildet* as a huntsman; **Weid|manns|dank** INTERJ *(Hunt)* thank you *(as answer to Weidmannsheil)*; **Weid|manns|heil** INTERJ *(Hunt)* good hunting; **Weid|werk** NT, *no pl* art of hunting; **weid|wund** ADJ *(Hunt)* wounded in the belly

Wei|gand ['vaigant] M **-(e)s, -e** [-də] *(obs)* warrior

wei|gern ['vaigɐn] ✪ 39.3 VR to refuse VT *(old)* **jdm etw ~** to deny sb sth

Wei|ge|rung ['vaigərʊŋ] F **-, -en** refusal

Wei|ge|rungs|fall M *(form)* **im ~** in case of refusal *(form)*

Weih [vai] M **-(e)s, -e** *(Orn)* harrier

Weih|bi|schof M suffragan bishop

Wei|he ['vaiə] F **-, -n** *(Orn)* harrier

Wei|he F **-, -n** **a** *(Eccl)* consecration; *(= Priesterweihe)* ordination; **die niederen/höheren ~n** minor/major orders **b** *(= Einweihung) (eines Gebäudes)* inauguration; *(einer Brücke)* (ceremonial) opening; *(eines Denkmals)* unveiling **c** *(= Feierlichkeit)* solemnity **d** *(= Ehre)* **höhere ~n** *(fig)* greater glory, greater things

wei|hen ['vaiən] VT **a** *(Eccl) Altar, Glocke, Kirche, Bischof* to consecrate; *Priester* to ordain; **jdn zum Bischof ~** to consecrate sb (as a) bishop; **jdn zum Priester ~** to ordain sb (as a) priest **b** *Gebäude* to inaugurate; *Brücke* to open; *Denkmal* to unveil **c** *(= widmen)* **etw jdm/einer Sache ~** to dedicate sth to sb/sth; *(Eccl auch, sehr feierlich)* to consecrate sth to sb/sth; **dem Tod(e)/Untergang geweiht** doomed (to die/fall) VR +*dat (liter)* to devote or dedicate oneself to

Wei|her ['vaiɐ] M **-s, -** pond

Wei|he-: **Wei|he|stät|te** F holy place; **wei|he|voll** ADJ *(liter)* solemn

Weih-: **Weih|ga|be** F *(Rel)* (votive) offering, oblation *(form)*; **Weih|ge|fäß** NT *(Rel)* votive vessel

Weih|nacht ['vainaxt] F -, *no pl* = **Weihnachten**

weih|nach|ten ['vainaxtn] VI *impers (poet, iro)* **es weihnachtet sehr** Christmas is very much in evidence

Weih|nach|ten ['vainaxtn] ✪ 50.2 NT **-, -** Christmas; *(geschrieben auch)* Xmas *(inf)*; **fröhliche** or **gesegnete** or **schöne** or **frohe(s)** or **ein fröhliches ~!** happy *(esp Brit)* or merry Christmas!; **(zu** or **an) ~** at Christmas; **(zu** or **an) ~ nach Hause fahren** to go home for Christmas; **etw zu ~ bekommen** to get sth for Christmas; **etw zu ~ schenken** to give sth as a Christmas present; **weiße ~** (a) white Christmas; **grüne ~**

(a) Christmas without snow; **das ist ein Gefühl wie ~(, nur nicht so feierlich)** *(iro inf)* it's an odd feeling

weih|nacht|lich ['vainaxtlɪç] ADJ Christmassy *(inf)*, festive ADV *geschmückt* for Christmas, festively; **~ gestimmt sein** to be feeling Christmassy *(inf)*; **~ anmutende Lieder** Christmassy sounding songs *(inf)*

Weih|nachts- *in cpds* Christmas; **Weih|nachts|abend** M Christmas Eve; **Weih|nachts|bä|cke|rei** F Christmas baking; **Weih|nachts|baum** M Christmas tree; **Weih|nachts|but|ter** F *reduced-price butter at Christmas time*; **Weih|nachts|ein|käu|fe** PL Christmas shopping *sing*; **Weih|nachts|fei|er** F Christmas celebrations(s *pl*); **Weih|nachts|fei|er|tag** M *(erster)* Christmas Day; *(zweiter)* Boxing Day; **Weih|nachts|fe|ri|en** PL Christmas holidays *pl (Brit)*, Christmas vacation *sing (US)*; **Weih|nachts|fest** NT Christmas; **Weih|nachts|gans** F Christmas goose; **jdn ausnehmen wie eine ~** *(inf)* to fleece sb *(inf)*, to take sb to the cleaners *(inf)*; **Weih|nachts|ge|bäck** NT Christmas biscuits *pl (Brit)*, Christmas cookies *pl (US)*; **Weih|nachts|geld** NT Christmas money; *(= Weihnachtsgratifikation)* Christmas bonus; *(für Briefträger etc)* Christmas box; **Weih|nachts|ge|schenk** NT Christmas present *or* gift; **Weih|nachts|ge|schich|te** F Christmas story; **Weih|nachts|gruß** M Christmas greeting; **Weih|nachts|in|sel** F Christmas Island; **Weih|nachts|kak|tus** M *(Bot)* Christmas cactus; **Weih|nachts|kar|te** F Christmas card; **Weih|nachts|lied** NT (Christmas) carol; **Weih|nachts|mann** M *pl* **-männer** Father Christmas *(Brit)*, Santa Claus; *(pej inf)* clown *(pej inf)*; **Weih|nachts|mär|chen** NT (Christmas) pantomime; **Weih|nachts|markt** M Christmas fair

> **WEIHNACHTSMARKT**
>
> Many towns have a **Weihnachtsmarkt** (also called **Christkindlmarkt**) during Advent. The largest is in Nuremberg, where there has been a market since the middle of the 16th century. Among the things you can buy at a **Weihnachtsmarkt** are tree decorations, baking utensils for traditional biscuits and cakes, carved wooden nativity scenes and **Weihnachtspyramiden** – miniature carousels turned by a wheel which catches the warm air from candles below.

Weih|nachts-: **Weih|nachts|plätz|chen** NT Christmas biscuit *(Brit) or* cookie *(US)*; **Weih|nachts|spiel** NT nativity play; **Weih|nachts|stern** M **a** *(Bot)* poinsettia **b** *(Rel)* star of Bethlehem; **Weih|nachts|tag** M = **Weihnachtsfeiertag**; **Weih|nachts|tel|ler** M *plate of biscuits, chocolates etc*; **Weih|nachts|tisch** M table for Christmas presents; **Weih|nachts|wunsch** M Christmas wish; **Weih|nachts|zeit** F Christmas (time), Yuletide *(old, liter)*, Christmas season *(esp Comm)*

Weih-: **Weih|rauch** M incense; **jdm ~ streuen** *(fig)* to praise *or* laud sb to the skies; **Weih|rauch|fass** NT censer, thurible *(form)*; **Weih|rauch|schiff|chen** NT incense boat; **Weih|was|ser** NT, *no pl* holy water; **Weih|was|ser|be|cken** NT stoup, holy water font

weil [vail] CONJ because

weil|land ['vailant] ADV *(obs, hum)* formerly; **Botho von Schmettwitz, ~ Leutnant der Kürassiere** Botho von Schmettwitz, formerly *or* erstwhile *or* one-time lieutenant of the cuirassiers; **er hat eine Frisur wie ~ Napoleon** he has a haircut like Napoleon's in former times

Weil|chen ['vailçən] NT **-s, - ein ~** a (little) while, a bit

Wei|le ['vailə] F **-,** *no pl* while; **wir können eine ~ Karten spielen** we could play cards for a while; **vor einer (ganzen) ~, eine (ganze) ~ her** quite a while ago; **damit hat es noch (gute) ~, das hat noch (gute) ~** there's no hurry

wei|len ['vailən] VI *(geh)* to be; *(= bleiben)* to stay, to tarry *(poet)*; **er weilt nicht mehr unter uns** he is no longer with *or* among us

Wei|ler ['vailɐ] M **-s, -** hamlet

Wei|ma|rer Re|pub|lik ['vaimaːrɐ] F Weimar Republic

Wein [vain] M **-(e)s, -e** wine; *(no pl: = Weinstöcke)* vines *pl*; *(no pl: = Weintrauben)* grapes *pl*; **in Frankreich wächst viel ~** there is a lot of wine growing in France; **offener ~** draught *(Brit) or* draft *(US)* wine; **wilder ~** Virginia creeper; **neuen ~ in alte Schläuche füllen** *(Prov)* to pour new wine into old bottles *(Brit) or* wine skins *(US) (Prov)*; **das ist doch nur alter ~ in neuen Schläuchen** that's just old wine in new bottles, that's just the same old thing in a new guise; **jdm reinen** *or* **klaren ~ einschenken** to tell sb the truth, to come clean with sb *(inf)*; **im ~ ist Wahrheit** *(Prov)* in vino veritas *(Prov)*; **heimlich ~ trinken und öffentlich Wasser predigen** *(geh)* not to practise *(Brit) or* practice *(US)* what one preaches; **voll des süßen ~es sein** *(liter, hum)* to be heavy with wine

> **WEIN**
>
> High-quality wines are produced in areas of Germany where the climate is suitable, especially in the Southwest along the Rhine and its tributaries. These wines generally have a low alcohol content and a fruity acidity. The most important types of white grape are the **Müller-Thurgau** and **Riesling**, which together account for almost 50% of the total wine-growing area. The main types of grape for red wine, which is becoming increasingly popular, are the **Spätburgunder** and **Portugieser**.
>
> German wine is divided into three grades. The lowest grade is **Tafelwein**, next is **Qualitätswein bestimmter Anbaugebiete** – indicated on the bottle by **QbA-** and the best is **Qualitätswein mit Prädikat**, eg **Kabinett** or **Auslese**. Whether a wine is dry, medium-dry or sweet is shown by the seal on the bottle.
>
> In Austria the most important type of grape is the **Grüner Veltliner**. → EISWEIN, FEDERWEISSER, HEURIGER

Wein- *in cpds (auf Getränk bezogen)* wine; *(auf Pflanze bezogen)* vine; **Wein|bau** M, *no pl* wine growing, viniculture *(form)*; **Wein|bau|er** M *pl* **-bauern**, **Wein|bäu|e|rin** F wine grower; **Wein|bau|land** NT wine-growing country; **Wein|bee|re** F grape; *(= Rosine)* raisin; **Wein|bei|ßer** [-baisɐ] M **-s, -** *(Aus: Lebkuchenart)* sugar-coated ginger biscuit *(Brit) or* cookie *(US)*; **Wein|bei|ßer** [-baisɐ] M **-s, -**, **Wein|bei|ße|rin** [-ərɪn] F **-, -nen** *(Aus: = Weinkenner)* wine connoisseur; **Wein|berg** M vineyard; **Wein|berg|schne|cke** F snail; *(auf Speisekarte)* escargot; **Wein|blatt** NT vineleaf; **gefüllte Weinblätter** *(Cook)* stuffed vineleaves; **Wein|brand** M brandy; **Wein|bren|ne|rei** F brandy distillery

Wein|chen ['vainçən] NT **-s, -** *dim von* **Wein** *(inf)* **ein ~** *(= etwas Wein)* a little wine; **das ist vielleicht ein ~!** that's a really beautiful wine!

wei|nen ['vainən] VTI to cry; *(aus Trauer, Kummer auch)* to weep *(um* for, *über +acc* over, *aus, vor +dat* with); **etw nass ~** to make sth wet with one's tears; **sich** *(dat)* **die Augen rot ~, sich** *(dat)* **die Augen aus dem Kopf ~** to cry one's eyes *or* heart out; **sich in den Schlaf ~** to cry oneself to sleep; **sich müde ~** to tire oneself out crying; **es ist zum Weinen!, man könnte ~!** it's enough to make you weep! *(esp Brit)*, it makes you want to cry!; **es ist zum Weinen mit dieser Frau** that woman is enough to make you want to cry; **leise ~d** weeping *or* crying softly; *(inf: = kleinlaut)* rather crestfallen *or* subdued; *(inf: = resigniert)* resignedly; *(iro inf: = mir nichts, dir nichts)* with a shrug of the shoulders

Wei|ne|rei [vainə'rai] F **-,** *no pl (inf)* crying, howling

wei|ner|lich ['vainɐlɪç] ADJ whining, whiny *(inf)* ADV whinily; **~ reden/sagen** to whine

Wei|ner|lich|keit F whininess *(inf)*

Wein-: **Wein|ern|te** F grape harvest; **Wein|es|sig** M wine vinegar; **Wein|fass** NT wine cask; **Wein|fest** NT wine festival; **Wein|fla|sche** F wine bottle; **Wein|gar|ten** M vineyard; **Wein|gärt|ner(in)** M(F) wine grower; **Wein|ge|gend** F wine-growing area; **Wein|geist** M spirits of wine *(old)*, (ethyl) alcohol; **Wein|glas** NT wine glass; **Wein|gum|mi** NT OR M wine gum; **Wein|gut** NT wine-growing estate; **Wein|händ|ler(in)** M(F) wine dealer; *(für Großhandel auch)* vintner; **Wein|hand|lung** F wine shop *(esp Brit) or* store; **Wein|hau|er(in)** M(F) *(esp Aus)* wine grower; **Wein|haus** NT wine tavern, wine bar; *(Geschäft)* wine shop; **Wein|he|ber** M wine cradle *or* basket

wei|nig ['vainɪç] ADJ winy, vinous *(form)*

Wein-: **Wein|jahr** NT **ein gutes/schlechtes ~** a good/bad year for wine; **Wein|kar|te** F wine list; **Wein|kel|ler** M wine cellar; *(= Lokal)* wine bar *or* tavern; **Wein|kel|le|rei** F winery; **Wein|kel|ter** F wine press; **Wein|ken|ner(in)** M(F) connoisseur of wine, wine connoisseur

Wein|krampf M crying fit; *(Med)* uncontrollable fit of crying

Wein-: **Wein|kraut** NT sauerkraut; **Wein|kü|fer(in)** M(F) cellarman; **Wein|kul|tur** F wine culture; *(= Weinbau)* wine growing, viniculture *(form)*; **Wein|la|ge** F vineyard location; **Wein|land** NT wine-growing *or* wine-producing country; **Wein|laub** NT vine leaves *pl*; **Wein|lau|be** F vine arbour *(Brit) or* arbor *(US)*, vine bower; **Wein|lau|ne** F **in einer ~ beschlossen sie ...** after a few glasses of wine they decided ...; **Wein|le|se** F grape harvest, vintage; **Wein|lo|kal** NT wine bar; **Wein|mo|nat M**, **Wein|mond** M *(old)* grape-harvesting month; *(= Oktober)* (month of) October; **Wein|pan|scher(in)** M(F) wine-adulterator, wine-doctorer *(inf)*; **Wein|pan|sche|rei** F wine-adulterating, wine-doctoring *(inf)*; **Wein|pro|be** F wine tasting; **Wein|prü|fer(in)** M(F) wine taster; **Wein|re|be** F (grape)vine; **wein|rot** ADJ wine-red, claret; **Wein|säu|re** F *(Chem)* tartaric acid; **Wein|schlauch** M wineskin; **Wein|schor|le** F spritzer; **wein|se|lig** ADJ merry *(Brit inf) or* tipsy with wine; **Wein|sor|te** F sort *or* type of wine; **Wein|stein** M tartar; **Wein|stock** M vine; **Wein|stra|ße** F wine trail *or* route; **Wein|stu|be** F wine tavern; **Wein|trau|be** F grape; **Wein|trin|ker(in)** M(F) wine drinker; **Wein|zierl** [-tsiːɐl] M **-s, -(n)** *(Aus)* wine grower **Wein|zwang** M obligation to order wine; **in diesem Restaurant ist ~** you have to order wine in this restaurant

> **WEINSTUBE**
>
> A **Weinstube** is a place where mainly wine is served with meals. It may be a normal restaurant or pub with an extensive wine list, but it may also - in wine-growing areas - specialize in wine-tasting, allowing the various wines of a region to be sampled.

wei|se ['vaizə] ADJ *(geh)* wise; **die ~ Frau** *(old)* the midwife

Wei|se ['vaizə] F **-, -n** **a** *(= Verfahren etc)* way, manner, fashion; **auf diese ~** in this way; **auf geheimnisvolle** *etc* **~** in a mysterious *etc* way *or* manner *or* fashion, mysteriously *etc*; **auf jede (erdenkliche) ~** in every conceivable way; **in gewisser/keiner** *or* **keinster** *(inf)* **~** in a/no way; **in der ~, dass ...** in such a way that ...; **jeder nach seiner ~** each in his own way, each after his own fashion → **Art c b** *(liter: = Melodie)* tune, melody

-wei|se [vaizə] ADV *suf (an Substantiv)* as a …; *(bei Maßangabe)* by the …; *(an Adjektiv)* -ly; **ausnahmsweise** as an exception; **meterweise** by the metre *(Brit) or* meter *(US)*; **bedauerlicherweise** regrettably; **er hat mir netterweise …** it was kind of him to …

Wei|sel [ˈvaizl] M **-s, -** queen bee

wei|sen [ˈvaizn] *pret* **wies** [viːs], *ptp* **gewiesen** [gəˈviːzn] *(geh)* VT **jdm etw ~** *(lit, fig)* to show sb sth; **jdn aus dem Lande ~** to expel sb; **jdn aus dem Saal ~** to eject sb (from the hall); **jdn vom Feld** *or* **Platz ~** *(Sport)* to order sb off (the field); *(als Strafe auch)* to send sb off; **jdn von der Schule ~** to expel sb (from school); **etw (weit) von sich ~** *(fig)* to reject sth (emphatically); **jdn zur Ruhe/Ordnung ~** *(form)* to order sb to be quiet/to behave himself → **Hand d** VI to point *(nach* towards, *auf +acc* at) → **Finger**

Wei|se(r) [ˈvaizə] MF *decl as adj* wise man/woman; *(= Denker auch)* sage; **die drei ~n aus dem Morgenland** the three Wise Men from the East; **die Fünf ~n** *(Ger Pol) panel of five experts advising government on economic policy*

> **DIE FÜNF WEISEN**
>
> **Die Fünf Weisen** is the popular name of the **Sachverständigenrat zur Begutachtung der gesamtwirtschaftlichen Entwicklung.** The five wise men are distinguished economists appointed as an independent body by the **Bundespräsident** for a period of five years. They present a report on the economy every year and forecast how it will develop. → BUNDESPRÄSIDENT

Wei|ser [ˈvaizɐ] M **-s, -** *(= Biene)* queen bee

Weis|heit [ˈvaishait] F **-, -en a** *no pl* wisdom; **das war der ~ letzter Schluss** that was all they/we *etc* came up with; **das ist auch nicht der ~ letzter Schluss** that's not exactly the ideal solution; **er glaubt, er hat die ~ gepachtet** *or* **mit Löffeln gegessen** *or* **gefressen** he thinks he knows it all; **er hat die ~ nicht gepachtet** *or* **mit Löffeln gegessen** *or* **gefressen** he's not so bright → **Ende b** *(= weiser Spruch)* wise saying, pearl of wisdom *(usu iro)*; **eine alte ~** a wise old saying; **deine ~en kannst du für dich behalten!** keep your pearls of wisdom to yourself!

Weis|heits|zahn M wisdom tooth

weis+ma|chen [ˈvais-] VT *sep* **jdm etw ~** to make sb believe sth; **er wollte uns ~, dass …** he would have us believe that …; **wie konnten sie ihm ~, dass …?** how could they fool him into believing that …?; **das kannst du mir nicht ~!** you can't expect me to believe that; **das kannst du (einem) andern ~!** (go) tell that to the marines *(Brit) or* judge! *(inf)*, pull the other one(, it's got bells on)! *(Brit hum inf)*, and pigs fly *(esp US inf)*

weiß [vais] ADJ white; **ein ~es (Blatt) Papier** a blank *or* clean sheet of paper; **ein ~er Fleck (auf der Landkarte)** a blank area (on the map); **das Weiße Haus** the White House; **das Weiße Meer** the White Sea; **der Weiße Nil** the White Nile; **Weißer Sonntag** Low Sunday; **der Weiße Sport** *(= Tennis)* tennis; **der Weiße Tod** death in the snow; **~ werden** to go *or* turn white; *(Sachen auch)* to whiten; **~ wie Kreide** *or* **die Wand** white as chalk *or* a sheet *or* a ghost; **das Weiße des Eis** *or* **vom Ei** egg white; **das Weiße von drei Eiern** the white(s) of three eggs; **das Weiße im Auge** the whites of the eyes → **Weste, Maus a** ADV *(mit weißer Farbe) anstreichen, lackieren* white; *tapezieren auch, einrichten, sich kleiden, umranden* in white; **~ glühend** white-hot, incandescent

weiß [vais] *3. pers sing pres von* **wissen**

Weiß [vais] NT **-(es), -** white

Weiß|af|ri|ka NT White Africa

Weis-: **weis|sa|gen** [ˈvais-] VT *insep* to prophesy, to foretell; **Weis|sa|ger** [ˈvaisaːgɐ] M **-s, -**, **Weis|sa|ge|rin** [-ərɪn] F **-, -nen** *(liter)* seer, prophet; **Weis|sa|gung** [ˈvaisaːgʊŋ] F **-, -en** prophecy

Weiß-: **Weiß|bier** NT weissbier, *light, fizzy beer made using top-fermentation yeast*; **Weiß|bin|der(in)** M(F) *(dial) (= Böttcher)* cooper; *(= Anstreicher)* house painter; **weiß|blau** ADJ *(inf: = bayrisch)* Bavarian; *(farblich)* in the Bavarian colours *(Brit) or* colors *(US)*; **Weiß|blech** NT tinplate; **weiß|blond** ADJ ash blond(e); **Weiß|blu|ten** NT **jdn bis zum ~ ausbeuten** to bleed sb white; **bis zum ~ zahlen müssen** to be bled white; **Weiß|brot** NT white bread; *(= Laib)* loaf of white bread, white loaf; **Weiß|buch** NT *(Pol)* white paper; **Weiß|bu|che** F *(Bot)* hornbeam; **Weiß|dorn** M *pl* **-dorne** *(Bot)* whitethorn

Wei|ße [ˈvaisə] F **-, -n a** *(= Weißheit)* whiteness **b** → **Berliner**

wei|ßeln [ˈvaisln] VTI *(S Ger, Aus)* to whitewash

wei|ßen [ˈvaisn] VT to whiten; *(= weiß tünchen)* to whitewash

Wei|ße(r) [ˈvaisə] MF *decl as adj* white, white man/woman; **die ~n** the whites, white people

Weiß-: **Weiß|fisch** M whitefish; **Weiß|fuchs** M white fox; **Weiß|gar|dist** M *(Hist)* member of the White Guard; **weiß|glü|hend** ADJ → **weiß ADV**; **Weiß|glut** F white heat, incandescence; **jdn zur ~ bringen, jdn bis zur ~ reizen** to make sb livid (with rage), to make sb see red *(inf)*; **Weiß|gold** NT white gold; **weiß|haa|rig** ADJ white-haired

Weiß|heit [ˈvaishait] F **-**, *no pl* whiteness

Weiß-: **Weiß|herbst** M ≈ rosé; **Weiß|ka|bis** M *(Sw)* white cabbage; **Weiß|kä|se** M *(dial)* quark; **Weiß|kohl** M, *(S Ger, Aus)* **Weiß|kraut** NT white cabbage

weiß|lich [ˈvaislɪç] ADJ whitish

Weiß-: **Weiß|ma|cher** M *(in Waschmittel)* brightening agent; *(in Papier)* whitener; **Weiß|me|tall** NT white metal; **Weiß|nä|he|rin** F (plain) seamstress; **Weiß|rus|se** M, **Weiß|rus|sin** F White Russian; **weiß|rus|sisch(e)** ADJ White Russian; **Weiß|rus|sisch(e)** NT *(Ling)* White Russian → *auch* **Deutsch(e)**; **Weiß|russ|land** NT White Russia; **Weiß|sucht** F albinism; **Weiß|tan|ne** F *(Bot)* silver fir; **Weiß|wal** M white whale; **Weiß|wand|rei|fen** M *(Aut)* whitewall (tyre *(Brit) or* tire *(US)*); **Weiß|wa|ren** PL linen *sing*; **weiß+wa|schen** VTR *sep irreg (fig, usu pej)* **sich/jdn ~** to whitewash one's/sb's reputation; **Weiß|wein** M white wine; **Weiß|wurst** F veal sausage; **Weiß|zeug** NT, *no pl* linen

Wei|sung [ˈvaizʊŋ] F **-, -en** directive, instruction, direction; *(Jur)* ruling; **auf ~** on instructions; **ich habe ~, keine Auskünfte zu geben** I have instructions not to give any details

Wei|sungs-: **Wei|sungs|be|fug|nis** F authority to issue directives; **wei|sungs|be|rech|tigt** ADJ *(Jur)* authorized to issue directives; **wei|sungs|ge|bun|den** ADJ subject to directives; **wei|sungs|ge|mäß** ADJ, ADV according to instructions, as per instructions, as instructed *or* directed; **Wei|sungs|recht** NT authority to issue directives

weit [vait]

1 ADJEKTIV	2 ADVERB

1 – ADJEKTIV

> Siehe auch Einträge *weitere, weitgehend, weitgreifend, weitreichend, weittragend, weitverbreitet, weitverzweigt.*

a [= breit] wide; *Pupille* dilated; *Meer* open; *Begriff* broad; *Unterschied, Herz* big; **das Herz wurde mir weit** *(liter)* my heart swelled (with emotion); **weite Kreise** *or* **Teile der Bevölkerung** large sections of the population; **im weiteren Sinne** in the broader *or* wider sense; **das ist ein weites Feld** *(fig)* that is a big subject

b [= lang] *Weg, Reise, Wurf etc* long; **in weiten Abständen** widely spaced; *(zeitlich)* at long intervals; **man hat hier einen weiten Blick** *or* **eine weite Sicht** you can see a long way from here; **in weiter Ferne** far in the distance, a long way away; **das liegt (noch) in weiter Ferne** it's still a long way away; *(zeitlich auch)* it's still in the distant future, it's still a long way off

♦ **so weit sein** *(= bereit)* to be ready; **seid ihr schon so weit, dass ihr anfangen könnt?** are you ready to start?; **es ist/war bald so weit** the time has/had nearly come; **wie lange dauert es noch, bis der Film anfängt? – es ist gleich so weit** how long will it be till the film starts? – not long, it'll start any minute now

2 – ADVERB

a [Entfernung] far; **weiter** further, farther; **am weitesten** (the) furthest, (the) farthest; **wie weit ist Bremen?** how far is (it to) Bremen?; **Bremen ist 10 km weit** Bremen is 10 kms away, it's 10 kms to Bremen; **es ist noch weit bis Bremen** it's still a long way to Bremen; **hast du es noch weit (nach Hause)?** have you got a long way *or* far to go (to get home)?; **3,60 m weit springen** to jump 3m 60; **wie weit bist du gesprungen?** how far did you jump?; **(sehr) weit springen/fahren** to jump/drive a (very) long way; **weit gereist** widely travelled *(Brit) or* traveled *(US)*; **weit hergeholt** far-fetched; **weit und breit** for miles around; **weit ab** *or* **weg (von)** far away (from); **weit am Anfang/Ende/Rand** right at the beginning/end/edge; **ziemlich weit am Ende** fairly near the end; **weit vom Thema** well off the subject; **wir kommen immer weiter vom Thema ab** we're getting further and further away from the subject; **von Weitem** from a long way away; **von weit her** from a long way away; **weit blickend** = **weitblickend**; **weit gesteckt** ambitious

♦ **weit entfernt** far away, a long way away; **weiter entfernt** further *or* farther away; **ich bin weit davon entfernt, das zu tun** I have no intention of doing that; **der Prototyp ist weit davon entfernt, in Serie gebaut zu werden** the prototype is a long way from being ready for mass-production; **weit entfernt** *or* **gefehlt!** far from it!

b [= breit] *offen, öffnen* wide; *verzweigt, herumkommen* widely; **10 cm weit** 10cm wide; **weit verbreitet** = **weitverbreitet**; **weit bekannt** widely known; **weit ausholend** *(Geste etc)* expansive; *(fig) Erzählung etc* long-drawn-out, long-winded; **etw weit ausholend erzählen** to tell sth at great length

c [in Entwicklung] **weit fortgeschritten** far *or* well advanced; **die Krankheit ist schon ziemlich weit** the disease is already quite far advanced; **wie weit bist du?** how far have you got?; **wie weit ist das Essen?** how far have you/they *etc* got with the food?; **so weit, so gut** so far so good; **sie sind nicht weit gekommen** they didn't get far; **jdn so weit bringen, dass …** to bring sb to the point where …

♦ **es weit bringen er wird es weit bringen** he will go far; **er hat es weit gebracht** he has achieved a lot; **es so weit bringen, dass …** to bring it about that …; **sie hat es so weit gebracht, dass man sie entließ** she drove them to dismiss her

d [zeitlich] **es ist noch weit (hin) bis Ostern** Easter is still a long way off; **(bis) weit in die Nacht** (till) far into the night; **weit nach Mitternacht** well *or* long after midnight; **weit zurückliegen** to be a long way back

e [= erheblich] far; **das hat unsere Erwartungen weit übertroffen** it far exceeded our expectations; **weit über 60** well over 60

f [andere Wendungen]

♦ **zu weit zu weit gehen** to go too far; **das geht zu weit!** that's going too far!; **etw zu weit treiben** to carry sth too far; **das würde zu weit führen** that would be taking things too far

♦ **so weit** *(= im Großen und Ganzen)* by and large, on the whole; *(= bis jetzt)* up to now; *(= bis zu diesem Punkt)* thus far; **so weit ganz gut** *(inf)* not too bad; **so weit wie** *or* **als möglich** as far as possible; **ich bin so weit fertig** I'm more or less ready

♦ **bei Weitem bei Weitem besser** *etc* **als** far better *etc* than; **bei Weitem der Beste** by far the best; **bei Weitem nicht so gut** *etc* **(wie…)** not nearly as good *etc* (as …); **bei Weitem nicht!** not by a long way! *(inf)*

♦ **nicht weit her das ist nicht weit her** *(inf)* that's not up to much (*Brit inf*), that's nothing to write home about *(inf)*; **damit ist es nicht weit her** *(inf)* this isn't up to much (*Brit inf*), this isn't much use

♦ **weit reichen sein Einfluss reicht sehr weit** his influence is far-reaching; **das Geld reicht nicht weit** the money won't go far

Weit-: **weit|ab** ['vait'lap] ADV ~ **von** far (away) from; **weit|aus** ['vait'laus] ADV *(vor comp)* far; *(vor superl)* (by) far, far and away; **weit|aus|ho|lend** ADJ → **weit 2 b**; **weit|be|kannt** ADJ → **weit 2 b**; **Weit|blick** M, *no pl (fig)* vision, far-sightedness; **weit|bli|ckend** *comp* **weitblickender**, *superl* **weitblickendste(r,s)**, **weit bli|ckend** *comp* **weiter blickend**, *superl* **am weitesten blickend** ADJ *(fig)* far-sighted

Wei|te ['vaitə] F -, -n *(= Entfernung, Ferne)* distance; *(= Länge)* length; *(= Größe)* expanse; *(= Durchmesser, Breite)* width; **in die ~ blicken** to look into the distance; **etw in der ~ ändern** to alter the width of sth; **in der ~ passt das Hemd** the shirt fits as regards width; **etw in die ~ ziehen** to pull sth out; *Pullover* to stretch sth out

Wei|te NT -n, *no pl* distance; **ins ~ gehen** to go out into the distance; **das ~ suchen** to take to one's heels; **das ~ gewinnen** *(liter)* to reach freedom

wei|ten ['vaitn] VT to widen; *(durch Ziehen auch)* to stretch VR to widen, to broaden *(auch fig)*; *(Pupille, Gefäße)* to dilate; *(fig liter: Herz)* to swell

wei|ter ['vaitɐ] *comp von* **weit** ADJ *(fig)* further; *(= zusätzlich auch)* additional; *(= andere)* other; **~e Auskünfte** further information

ADV *(= noch hinzu)* further; *(= außerdem)* furthermore; *(= sonst)* otherwise; *(= nachher)* afterwards; **nichts ~, ~ nichts** *(= darüber hinaus nichts)* nothing further *or* more *or* else; **~ nichts?** is that all?; **nichts ~ als …, ~ nichts als …** nothing more than …, nothing but …; **ich brauche ~ nichts** that's all I need, I don't need anything else; **ich brauche nichts ~ als …** all I need is …; **er wollte ~ nichts, als nach Hause gehen** all he wanted was to go home; **wenn es ~ nichts ist, …** well, if that's all (it is), …; **außer uns war ~ niemand** *or* **niemand ~ da** there was nobody else there besides us; **nicht ~, ~ nicht** *(= eigentlich)* not really; **das stört ~ keinen** that doesn't really bother anybody; **das hat ~ nichts** *or* **nichts ~ zu sagen** that doesn't really matter, that's neither here nor there; **das macht ~ nichts** it's not that *or* really important; **etw ~ tun** to continue to do sth, to continue doing sth, to go *or* carry on doing sth; **immer ~** on and on; *(Anweisung)* keep on (going); **er hat sich immer ~ verbessert** he kept on improving; **nur immer ~!** keep at it!; **und ~?** and then?; **was geschah (dann) ~?** what happened then *or* next?; **und so ~** and so on *or* forth, et cetera; **und so ~ und so fort** and so on and so forth, et cetera et cetera; **kein Wort ~!** not another word! → **Weitere(s)**

wei|ter- PREF *(= weitermachen mit)* to carry on *or* go on *or* continue +*prp*, to continue to +*infin*; *(= nicht aufhören mit)* to keep on *or* go on +*prp*; *(bei Bewegung, Beförderung, Reise etc) vb* + on

Wei|ter-: **wei|ter be|we|gen**, **wei|ter+be|we|gen** *sep* VR *(weiterhin)* to carry on moving; **wei|ter+ar|bei|ten** VI *sep* → **weiter-** to carry on *etc* working, to work on; **an einer Sache** *(dat)* **~** to do some more work on sth; **wei|ter+be|för|dern** *ptp* **weiterbefördert** VT *sep* to send on; *Passagiere* to transport; *jdn (in Firma etc)* to promote further; **wei|ter+be|han|deln** *ptp* **weiterbehandelt** VT *sep* → **weiter-** to carry on *etc* treating; **Wei|ter|be|hand|lung** F further treatment; **Wei|ter|be|schäf|ti|gung** F continued employment; **wei|ter be|ste|hen** *irreg*, **wei|ter+be|ste|hen** *sep irreg* VI to continue to exist, to survive; **Wei|ter|be|ste|hen** NT continued existence; **wei|ter|be|we|gen** *ptp* **weiterbewegt** *sep* VT to move further VR to move further; **wei|ter+bil|den** *sep* VT **jdn ~** to give sb further education, to educate sb further VR to continue one's education; **Wei|ter|bil|dung** F continuation of one's education; *(an Hochschule)* further education; **Wei|ter|bil|dungs|an|ge|bot** NT opportunities *pl* for further education; **wei|ter+brin|gen** VT *sep irreg* to take further, to advance; **das bringt uns auch nicht weiter** that's not much help (to us), that doesn't get us any further; **wei|ter+den|ken** *sep irreg* VT to think out (further) VI **a** to think it out **b** *(an Zukünftiges)* to think ahead; **wei|ter den|ken** △ VI *irreg* → **weiterdenken VI b**; **wei|ter+emp|feh|len** *ptp* **weiterempfohlen** VT *sep irreg* to recommend (to one's friends *etc*); **wei|ter+ent|wi|ckeln** *ptp* **weiterentwickelt** *sep* VT to develop; *Idee* to develop (further) VR to develop (*zu* into); **Wei|ter|ent|wick|lung** F development; **wei|ter+er|zäh|len** *ptp* **weitererzählt** VT *sep* → **weiter-** to carry on *etc* telling; *Geheimnis etc* to repeat, to pass on; **das hat er der ganzen Klasse weitererzählt** he told the whole class

Wei|te|re(s) ['vaitərə] NT *decl as adj* further details *pl*; **ich habe nichts ~s zu sagen** I have nothing further to say; **das ~** the rest; **alles ~** everything else, all the rest; **des ~n** in addition, furthermore; **bis auf ~s** for the time being; *(amtlich, auf Schildern etc)* until further notice; **im ~n** subsequently, afterwards; **zum ~n** furthermore, in addition, on top of that → **ohne PREP b**

Wei|ter-: **wei|ter+fah|ren** *sep irreg* VT → **weiter-** to carry on *etc* driving, to keep on driving VI *aux sein* **a** *(= Fahrt fortsetzen)* to go on, to continue; *(= durchfahren)* to drive on; *(= weiterreisen)* to travel on **b** *(dial)* = **fortfahren VI b**; **Wei|ter|fahrt** F continuation of the/one's journey; **vor der ~ sahen wir …** before continuing our journey we saw …; **wei|ter+flie|gen** VI *sep irreg aux sein* to fly on; **die Maschine fliegt in 10 Minuten weiter** the plane will take off again in 10 minutes; **Wei|ter|flug** M continuation of the/one's flight; **auf dem ~** after we'd taken off again; **Passagiere zum ~ nach …** passengers continuing their flight to …; **wei|ter+füh|ren** *sep* VT to continue; *Gespräch auch* to carry on (with) VI to continue, to lead on; **das führt nicht weiter** *(fig)* that doesn't lead *or* get us anywhere; **wei|ter|füh|rend** ADJ *Schule* secondary; *Bildungsgang, Qualifikation* higher; *Entwicklung, Lektüre* further; **Wei|ter|ga|be** F passing on; *(von Informationen, Erbfaktoren auch)* transmission; **wei|ter+ge|ben** VT *sep irreg* to pass on; to transmit; **wei|ter+ge|hen** VI *sep irreg aux sein* to go on; **bitte ~!** *(Polizist etc)* move along *or* on (there), please!; **so kann es nicht ~** *(fig)* things can't go on like this; **wie soll es nun ~?** *(fig)* what's going to happen now?; **wei|ter+hel|fen** VI *sep irreg* to help (along) *(jdm* sb); **wei|ter|hin** ['vaitɐ'hɪn] ADV *(= außerdem)* furthermore, on top of that; **etw ~ tun** to carry on *etc* doing sth; **wei|ter+kämp|fen** VI *sep* to fight on; **wei|ter+kom|men** VI *sep irreg aux sein* to get further; *(fig auch)* to make progress *or* headway; **nicht ~** *(fig)* to be stuck, to be bogged down; **wir kommen einfach nicht weiter** we're just not getting anywhere; **Wei|ter|kom|men** NT advancement; **wei|ter+kön|nen** VI *sep irreg* to be able to carry on *or* go on *or* continue; **ich kann nicht weiter** I can't go on; *(bei Rätsel, Prüfung etc)* I'm stuck; **wei|ter+lau|fen** VI *sep irreg aux sein* to run on; *(= gehen)* to walk on; *(Film)* to go on; *(Betrieb, Produktion)* to go on, to continue; *(Gehalt)* to continue to be paid; *(Motor)* to keep on running; **ich kann nicht ~** I can't walk any further; **den Motor ~ lassen** to leave the engine running; **wei|ter+le|ben** VI *sep* to live on, to continue to live; **wei|ter+lei|ten** VT *sep* to pass on (*an* +*acc* to); *(= weiterbefördern, -senden)* to forward; **wei|ter+ma|chen** VTI *sep* to carry on (*etw* with sth), to continue; **~!** *(Mil)* carry on!; **Wei|ter|marsch** M **zum ~ bereit** ready to march on; **auf dem ~ waren sie …** as they marched on they were …; **wei|ter+rei|chen** VT *sep* to pass on; **Wei|ter|rei|se** F continuation of the/one's journey; **ich wünsche Ihnen eine gute ~** I hope the rest of the journey goes well; **auf der ~ nach …** when I *etc* was travelling *(Brit) or* traveling *(US)* on to …; **wei|ter+rü|cken** *sep* VT to move further along VI *aux sein* to move up, to move further along

wei|ters ['vaitɐs] ADV *(Aus)* = **ferner**

wei|ter-: **wei|ter+sa|gen** VT *sep* to repeat, to pass on; **~!** pass it on!; **nicht ~!** don't tell anyone!; **wei|ter+schen|ken** VT *sep* to give away (to somebody else); **wei|ter+schla|fen** VI *sep irreg* to sleep on, to go on sleeping; *(= wieder einschlafen)* to go back to sleep; **wei|ter+schlep|pen** *sep* VT to haul *or* drag further VR to drag *or* haul oneself on; **wei|ter+sen|den** *sep irreg* VTI *(Rad, TV)* → **weiter-** to carry on *etc* broadcasting VT *(form)* to forward; **wei|ter+spin|nen** VT *sep irreg (fig) Gedanken etc* to develop further; **wei|ter+su|chen** VI *sep* to go on searching (*nach* for); **„weitersuchen"** *(Comput: Befehl)* "find next"

Wei|te|run|gen ['vaitərʊŋən] PL *(old, form)* complications *pl*, difficulties *pl*; **unangenehme ~ zur Folge haben** to have unpleasant consequences**wei|ter-**: **wei|ter+ver|ar|bei|ten** *ptp* **weiterverarbeitet** VT *sep* to process; **Wei|ter|ver|ar|bei|tung** F (further) processing; **wei|ter+ver|bin|den** *ptp* **weiterverbunden** VT *sep irreg (am Telefon)* to put through (*an* +*acc* to); **wei|ter+ver|brei|ten** *ptp* **weiterverbreitet** *sep* VT to spread (further), to repeat, to propagate *(form)* VR to spread (further); **wei|ter+ver|fol|gen** *ptp* **weiterverfolgt** VT *sep* → **weiter-** *Entwicklung, Straße* to carry on *etc* following; *Verbrecher* to continue to pursue; *Idee, Pläne* to pursue further; **Wei|ter|ver|kauf** M resale; **nicht zum ~ bestimmt** not for resale; **wei|ter+ver|kau|fen** *ptp* **weiterverkauft** VTI *sep* to resell; **wei|ter+ver|mie|ten** *ptp* **weitervermietet** VT *sep* to sublet; **Wei|ter|ver|sand** M redispatch; **wei|ter+ver|wen|den** *ptp* **weiterverwendet** VT *sep* to continue to use; *(Ecology: Glas etc)* to reuse; **wei|ter+wis|sen** VI *sep irreg* **nicht (mehr) ~** not to know how to go on; *(bei Rätsel, Prüfung)* to be stuck; *(= verzweifelt sein)* to be at one's wits' end; **wei|ter+wol|len** VI *sep irreg* to want to go on; **der Esel wollte einfach nicht weiter** the donkey simply wouldn't go any further; **wei|ter+zah|len** VTI *sep* to continue paying *or* to pay

wei|test|ge|hend ['vaitəst-] ADV to the greatest possible extent

weit-: **weit|ge|hend** *comp* **weitgehender**, *superl* **weitgehendste(r,s)**, **weit ge|hend** *comp* **weiter gehend**, *superl* **am weitesten gehend** ADJ *Vollmachten etc* far-reaching, extensive, wide; *Übereinstimmung etc* a large degree of; **er hatte viel ~ere** *or* **weiter gehende Befürchtungen** his fears went a lot further than that; **weit|ge|hend** *comp* **weitgehender**, *superl* **weitgehendst** ADV to a great *or* large extent, largely → *auch* **weitestgehend**; **weit|ge|reist** [-gəraist] ADJ *attr* → **weit 2 a**; **weit|ge|steckt** [-gəʃtɛkt] ADJ → **weit 2 f**; **weit|grei|fend** *comp* **weitgreifender**, *superl* **weitgreifendste(r,s)**, **weit grei|fend** *comp* **weiter greifend**, *superl* **am weitesten greifend** ADJ *attr* far-reaching; **weit|her** ['vait'heːɐ, vait'heːɐ] ADV (*auch* **von weit her**) from a long way away, from far away, from afar *(liter)*; **weit|her|ge|holt** ['vaitheːɐgəhoːlt] ADJ *attr* → **weit 2 a**; **weit|her|zig** ADJ understanding, charitable; **weit|hin** ['vait'hɪn] ADV over a long distance, for a long way; *(fig) bekannt, beliebt* widely; *unbekannt* largely; *(= weitgehend)* to a large *or* great extent

weit|läu|fig ADJ **a** *Park, Gebäude* spacious; *(= verzweigt)* rambling; *Dorf* covering a wide area, sprawling *attr*; *(fig) Erzählung* lengthy, long-drawn-out, long-winded **b** *Verwandte* distant ADV **etw ~ erzählen** to tell sth at (great) length; **sie sind ~ verwandt** they are distant relatives; **ich bin mit ihm ~ verwandt** I am distantly related to him

Weit|läu|fig|keit ['vaitlɔyfɪçkait] F -, -en *(von Park, Gebäude)* spaciousness; *(fig: von Erzählung)* length, long-windedness

Weit-: **weit|ma|schig** [-maʃɪç] ADJ *Netz* coarse-meshed, wide-meshed, broad-meshed; *Gestricktes* loosely knitted, loose-knit; **weit|räu|mig** [-rɔymɪç] ADJ wide-ranging ADV **ein Gelände ~ absperren** to cordon off a wide area around a site; **die Unfallstelle ~ umfahren** to keep well away from the scene of the accident; **der Verkehr am Stuttgarter Kreuz ist zum Erliegen gekommen und wird ~ umgeleitet** traffic has come to a complete stop at the Stuttgart intersection and is being diverted well away from the obstruction; **~er spielen** *(Ftbl)* to cover more of the field; **weit|rei|chend** *comp* **weitreichender**, *superl* **weitreichendste(r, s)**, **weit rei|chend** *comp* **weiter reichend**, *superl* **am weitesten reichend** ADJ *(fig)* far-reaching; *(Mil)* long-range *attr*; **weiter reichend** further reaching; **weit|schau|end** ADJ = **weitblickend**; **weit|schwei|fig** [-ʃvaifɪç] ADJ long-winded, circumlocutory, prolix *(form)* ADV long-windedly, lengthily; **Weit|sicht** F *(fig)* far-sightedness; **weit|sich|tig** [-zɪçtɪç] ADJ *(Med)* long-sighted *(Brit)*, far-sighted *(esp US)*; *(fig)* far-sighted; **Weit|sich|tig|keit** F -, *no pl (Med)* long-sightedness *(Brit)*, far-sightedness *(esp US)*; **weit+sprin|gen** VI *sep (infin only) (Sport)* to do the long jump; **Weit|sprin|gen** NT *(Sport)* long jump; **Weit|sprin|ger(in)** M(F) *(Sport)* long jumper; **Weit|sprung** M *(Sport)* long jump; **weit|tra|gend** *comp* **weittragender**, *superl* **weittragendste(r, s)**, **weit tra|gend** *comp* **weiter tragend**, *superl* **am weitesten tragend** *(Mil)* long-range *attr*; *(fig)* far-reaching, far-ranging; **weiter tragend** *(Mil)* longer-range *attr*; *(fig)* further-reaching; **weit|um** ['vait'lʊm] ADV for miles around

Wei|tung ['vaitʊŋ] F -, -en *(geh)* widening

Weit-: **weit|ver|brei|tet** [-fɛɐbraitət] *comp* **weitverbreiteter**, *superl* **weitverbreiteteste(r, s)**, **weit ver|brei|tet** *comp* **weiter verbreitet**, *superl* **am weitesten verbreitet** ADJ widespread, common; *Ansicht auch* widely held; *Zeitung* with a wide circulation; **weit|ver|zweigt** *comp* **weitverzweigter**, *superl* **weitverzweigteste(r,s)**, **weit ver|zweigt** *comp* **weiter verzweigt**, *superl* **am weitesten verzweigt** ADJ *Straßensystem* branching out in all directions; *Konzern, Familie, Stammbaum* with many branches; *Computersystem* extensive; **Weit|win|kel|ob|jek|tiv** NT wide-angle lens

Wei|zen ['vaitsn] M -s, *no pl* wheat → **Spreu**

Wei|zen-: **Wei|zen|bier** NT *light, very fizzy beer made by using wheat, malt and top-fermentation yeast*; **Wei|zen|brot** NT wheat *or* wheaten *(Brit)* bread; **Wei|zen|kei|me** PL *(Cook)* wheat germ *sing*; **Wei|zen|keim|öl** NT *(Cook)* wheat germ oil; **Wei|zen|kleie** F *(Cook)* wheat bran; **Wei|zen|mehl** NT wheat *or* wheaten *(Brit)* flour; **Wei|zen|schrot** M OR NT wheatmeal

welch [vɛlç] INTERROG PRON *inv* **a** *(geh: in Ausrufen)* what; **~ friedliches Bild!** what a peaceful scene! **b** *(in indirekten Fragesätzen)* **~ (ein)** what REL PRON *inv* **X, Y und Z, ~ letztere(r, s) ...** *(obs, form)* X, Y and Z, the last of which/whom ...

wel|che(r, s) ['vɛlçə] INTERROG PRON **a** *(adjektivisch)* what; *(bei Wahl aus einer begrenzten Menge)* which; **~r Mensch könnte behaupten ...?** what person could claim ...?; **~s Kleid soll ich anziehen, das rote oder das grüne?** which dress shall I wear, the red one or the green one? **b** *(substantivisch)* which (one); **~r von den beiden?** which (one) of the two?; **~s sind die Symptome dieser Krankheit?** what are the symptoms of this illness?; **es gibt viele schöne Frauen, aber ~ könnte sich mit Isabella vergleichen?** there are many beautiful women, but which of them could compare with Isabella? **c** *(in Ausrufen)* **~ Schande!** what a disgrace!; **~ Freude!** what joy!
INDEF PRON some; *(in Fragen, konditional auch, verneint)* any; **es gibt ~, die glauben ...** there are some (people) who think ...; **ich habe keine Tinte/Äpfel, haben Sie ~?** I don't have any ink/apples, do you have some *or* any?
REL PRON *(rare) (Mensch)* who; *(Sache)* which, that; **~(r, s) auch immer** whoever/whichever/whatever

wel|cher|art ['vɛlçɐ'laːɐt] INTERROG ADJ *inv (geh) (attributiv)* what kind of; *(substantivisch)* of what kind; **sagen Sie mir, ~ Ihre Erfahrungen sind** tell me what sort of experiences you (have) had; **~ Ihre Erfahrungen auch sein mögen** whatever your experiences may have been like INTERROG ADV in what way

wel|cher|lei ['vɛlçɐ'lai] INTERROG ADJ *inv (geh)* what kind *or* sort of

wel|ches ['vɛlçəs] PRON → **welche(r, s)**

Wel|fe ['vɛlfə] M -n, -n, **Wel|fin** ['vɛlfɪn] F -, -nen *(Hist)* Guelph

wel|fisch ['vɛlfɪʃ] ADJ *(Hist)* Guelphic

welk [vɛlk] ADJ *Blume, Pflanze* wilted, faded; *Blatt* dead; *(fig) Schönheit* fading, wilting; *Haut, Gesicht* tired-looking; *(= schlaff)* flaccid; *Hände* withered; **wie ein ~es Pflänzchen** *(inf)* like a wet rag *(inf)*

wel|ken ['vɛlkn] VI *aux sein (lit, fig)* to fade, to wilt; *(Haut, Gesicht)* to grow tired-looking; *(= schlaff werden)* to sag

Welk|heit F -, *no pl* wilted state; *(von Haut, Gesicht)* tired look

Well|blech ['vɛl-] NT corrugated iron

Well|blech|hüt|te ['vɛl-] F corrugated-iron hut; *(halbrund)* Nissen hut *(esp Brit)*, Quonset hut *(US)*

Wel|le ['vɛlə] F -, -n **a** wave *(auch fig, Phys, im Haar etc)*; *(Rad: = Frequenz)* wavelength; **sein Grab in den ~n finden** *(geh)* to go to a watery grave; **weiche ~** *(inf)* soft line; **mach keine ~n!** *(inf)* don't make such a fuss; **(hohe) ~n schlagen** *(fig)* to create (quite) a stir **b** *(fig: = Mode)* craze; **die Neue ~** *(Film)* the nouvelle vague, the New Wave; *(Mus)* the New Wave **c** *(Tech)* shaft **d** *(Sport)* circle

wel|len ['vɛlən] VT *Haar* to wave; *Blech etc* to corrugate VR *(= gewellt sein)* to be wavy; *(= Wellen bekommen)* to become wavy; **gewelltes Haar** wavy hair

Wel|len-: **wel|len|ar|tig** ADJ wave-like; *Linie etc* wavy ADV like a wave; **Wel|len|bad** NT *swimming pool with wave machine*; **Wel|len|be|reich** M *(Phys, Telec)* frequency range; *(Rad)* waveband; **Wel|len|berg** M mountainous *or* giant wave; **Wel|len|be|we|gung** F undulation, wave motion; **Wel|len|bre|cher** M breakwater, groyne *(Brit)*, groin *(esp US)*; **wel|len|för|mig** ADJ wave-like; *Linie* wavy ADV in the form of waves; **Wel|len|gang** [-gaŋ] M, *no pl* waves *pl*, swell; **starker ~** heavy sea(s) *or* swell; **leichter ~** light swell; **Wel|len|kamm** M crest (of a wave); **Wel|len|kraft|werk** NT wave-power generator; **Wel|len|län|ge** F *(Phys, Telec)* wavelength; **sich auf jds ~ (acc) einstellen** *(inf)* to get on sb's wavelength *(inf)*; **auf der gleichen ~ sein** *or* **liegen, die gleiche ~ haben** *(inf)* to be on the same wavelength *(inf)*; **Wel|len|li|nie** F wavy line; **Wel|len|me|cha|nik** F *(Phys)* wave mechanics *sing*; **Wel|len|rei|ten** NT -s, *no pl (Sport)* surfing; *(auf Fluss) sport of balancing on a board attached by a rope to the riverbank*; **Wel|len|sa|lat** M *(Rad inf)* jumble of frequencies; **Wel|len|schlag** M breaking of the waves; *(sanft auch)* lapping of the waves; *(heftig auch)* pounding of the waves; **Wel|len|schliff** M *(am Messer)* serrated edge; **Wel|len|sit|tich** M budgerigar, budgie *(inf)*; **Wel|len|tal** NT (wave) trough

Well-: **Well|fleisch** NT boiled pork; **Well|horn|schne|cke** F whelk

wel|lig ['vɛlɪç] ADJ *Haar etc* wavy; *Oberfläche, Fahrbahn* uneven; *Hügelland* rolling, undulating

Well|ness ['wɛlnɛs] F -, *no pl* wellness

Well|ness|wo|chen|en|de NT wellness weekend

Well|pap|pe ['vɛl-] F corrugated cardboard

Wel|pe ['vɛlpə] M -n, -n pup, whelp; *(von Wolf, Fuchs)* cub, whelp

Wels [vɛls] M -es, -e [-zə] catfish

welsch [vɛlʃ] ADJ **a** *(old)* Latin, Southern European; *(= welschsprachig)* Romance-speaking; **~e Sitten und Gebräuche** dubious morals and practices **b** *(Aus pej: = italienisch)* Eyetie *(Brit pej sl)*, wop *(pej sl)*; **die Welschen** the Eyeties *(Brit pej sl)*, the wops *(pej sl)* **c** *(Sw)* (Swiss) French; **die ~e Schweiz** French Switzerland

Welsch-: **Welsch|land** NT -s *(Sw)* French Switzerland; **Welsch|schwei|zer(in)** M(F) *(Sw)* French Swiss; **welsch|schwei|ze|risch** ADJ *(Sw)* Swiss-French

Welt [vɛlt] F -, -en *(lit, fig)* world; **die ~ im Kleinen** the microcosm; **die ~ im Großen** the macrocosm; **die (große) weite ~** the big wide world; **der höchste Berg der ~** the highest mountain in the world, the world's highest mountain; **die ~ von heute/morgen** the world of today/tomorrow, today's/tomorrow's world; **die ~ der Oper/des Kindes** the world of opera/the child, the operatic/child's world; **die Alte/Neue/freie/Dritte ~** the Old/New/Free/Third World; **die große** *or* **vornehme ~** high society; **alle ~, Gott und die ~** everybody, the whole world, the world and his wife *(hum)*; **eine ~ brach für ihn zusammen** his whole world collapsed about *(Brit) or* around him *or* his ears, the bottom fell out of his world; **das ist doch nicht die ~** it isn't as important as all that; **davon** *or* **deswegen geht die ~ nicht unter** *(inf)* it isn't the end of the world; **das kostet doch nicht die ~** it won't cost the earth *(Brit) or* a fortune; **uns/sie trennen ~en** *(fig)* **zwischen uns/ihnen liegen ~en** *(fig)* we/they are worlds apart; **auf der ~** in the world; **davon gibt es noch mehr auf der ~** there are plenty of those around; **etw mit auf die ~ bringen** to be born with sth; **aus aller ~** from all over the world; **aus der ~ schaffen** to eliminate; **aus der ~ scheiden** *(geh)* to depart this life *(liter)*; *(= Selbstmord begehen)* to put an end to one's life; **in aller ~** all over the world; **in alle ~ zerstreut** scattered all over the world *or* globe; **warum/wer in aller ~ ...?** why/who on earth ...?, why/who in the world ...?; **so geht es nun mal in der ~** that's the way of the world, that's the way things go; **in einer anderen ~ leben** to live in a different world; **in seiner eigenen ~ leben** to live in a world of one's own; **um nichts in der ~, nicht um alles in der ~, um keinen Preis der ~** not for love (n)or money, not at any price, not for all the tea in China *(inf)*; **ein Kind in die ~ setzen** to bring a child into the world; **ein Gerücht in die ~ setzen** to put about *or* spread a rumour *(Brit) or* rumor *(US)*; **ein Mann/eine Frau von ~** a man/woman of the world; **die beste Frau** *etc* **(von) der ~** the best woman *etc* in the world; **vor aller ~** publicly, in front of everybody, openly; **zur ~ bringen** to give birth to, to bring into the world; **auf die** *or* **zur ~ kommen** to come into the world, to be born → **Brett, Ende**

Welt- *in cpds* world; **welt|ab|ge|wandt** [-lapgəvant] ADJ withdrawn; **Welt|all** NT universe, cosmos; **Welt|al|ter** NT age, epoch; **welt|an|schau|lich** ADJ ideological; **Welt|an|schau|ung** F philosophy of life; *(Philos, Pol)* world view, weltanschauung; **Welt|aus|stel|lung** F world exhibition, world's fair; **Welt|bank** F, *no pl* World Bank; **welt|be|kannt** ADJ world-famous; **welt|be|rühmt** ADJ world-famous; *Schriftsteller, Künstler etc auch* world-renowned; **Welt|bes|te(r)** [-bɛstə] MF *decl as adj* world's best; **welt|bes|te(r, s)** ADJ *attr* world's best; **Welt|best|leis|tung** F world's best performance, world best *(inf)*; **Welt|be|völ|ke|rung** F world population; **welt|be|we|gend** ADJ world-shattering; **Welt|bild** NT conception of the world; *(= jds Ansichten)* philosophy, view of life; **Welt|blatt** NT *(Press)* international (news)paper; **Welt|brand** M global conflagration; **Welt|bür|ger(in)** M(F) citizen of the world, cosmopolitan; **Welt|bür|ger|tum** NT cosmopolitanism; **Welt|chro|nik** F world chronicle; **Welt|cup** M *(Sport)* World Cup; **Welt|cup|sieg** M victory in the World Cup; **Welt|cup|sie|ger(in)** M(F) winner of the World Cup; **Welt|emp|fän|ger** M world receiver *or* radio

Wel|ten-: **Wel|ten|bumm|ler(in)** M(F) globetrotter; **Wel|ten|raum** M *(liter)* space

welt|ent|rückt [-lɛntrʏkt] ADJ remote, isolated

Welt|er|folg M global *or* worldwide success *or* hit *(inf)*

Wel|ter|ge|wicht NT *(Boxen)* welterweight

Welt-: **Welt|er|näh|rungs|or|ga|ni|sa|ti|on** F Food and Agriculture Organization; **welt|er|schüt|ternd** ADJ world-shattering; **welt|fern** ADJ unrealistic, naïve; **Welt|flucht** F flight from reality, escapism; **welt|fremd** ADJ unworldly; **Welt|fremd|heit** F unworldliness; **Welt|frie|de(n)** M world peace; **Welt|frie|dens|tag** M World Peace Day; **Welt|ge|fü|ge** NT universe, world system, scheme of things; **Welt|geist** M, *no pl (Philos)* world spirit; **Welt|geist|li|che(r)** MF *decl as adj* secular priest; **Welt|gel|tung** F international standing, worldwide recognition; **Welt|ge|mein|schaft** F international community; **Welt|ge|richt** NT Last Judgement; **Welt|ge|richts|hof** M International Court; **Welt|ge|schich|te** F world history; **in der ~ herumfahren** *(inf)* to travel around all over the place; **welt|ge|schicht|lich** ADJ **ein ~e Ereignis** an important event in the history of the world; **von ~er Bedeutung** of great significance in world history; **~ gesehen, aus ~er Sicht** looked at from the point of view of world history; **Welt|ge|sund|heits|or|ga|ni|sa|ti|on** F World Health Organization; **Welt|ge|trie|be** NT *(liter)* (hustle and) bustle of the world; **welt|ge|wandt** ADJ sophisticated, well-versed in the ways of the world; **Welt|ge|wandt|heit** F sophistication, experience in the ways of the world; **Welt|han|del** M world trade; **Welt|han|dels|or|ga|ni|sa|ti|on** F World Trade Organization; **Welt|herr|schaft** F world domination; **Welt|hilfs|spra|che** F international auxiliary language; **Welt|hun|ger|hil|fe** F world famine relief; **Welt|kar|te** F map of the world; **Welt|kir|chen|rat** M World Council of Churches; **Welt|klas|se** F **ein Hochspringer der ~** a world-class high jumper; **~ sein** to be world class; *(inf)* to be great *(inf) or* fantastic *(inf)*; **welt|klug** ADJ worldly-wise; **Welt|kör|per** M *(old: = Himmelskörper)* heavenly *or* celestial body; **Welt|krieg** M world war; **der Erste/Zweite ~** World War One/Two, the First/Second World War; **Welt|ku|gel** F globe; **Welt|kul|tur** F world culture; **Welt|kul|tur|er|be** NT world cultural heritage; *(= einzelnes Kulturgut)* World Heritage Site; **Welt|lauf** M way of the world; **welt|läu|fig** ADJ cosmopolitan; **Welt|läu|fig|keit** F cosmopolitanism; **welt|lich** [ˈvɛltlɪç] ADJ worldly, mundane; *(= nicht kirchlich, geistlich)* secular; *Macht* temporal; **Welt|li|ga** F *(Sport)* world league; **Welt|li|te|ra|tur** F world literature; **Welt|macht** F world power; **Welt|mann** M *pl* **-männer** man of the world; **welt|män|nisch** [-mɛnɪʃ] ADJ urbane, sophisticated; **Welt|mar|ke** F name known all over the world; **Welt|markt** M world market; **Welt|markt|füh|rer** M global market leader; **Welt|markt|preis** M world (market) price; **Welt|meer** NT ocean; **die sieben ~e** the seven seas; **Welt|meis|ter(in)** M(F) world *or* world's *(US)* champion; **England/die englische Mannschaft ist ~** England/the English team are (the) world *or* world's *(US)* champions; **Welt|meis|ter|schaft** F world *or* world's *(US)* championship; *(Ftbl)* World Cup; **Welt|meis|ter|ti|tel** M world title (*in +dat* in); **Welt|na|tur|er|be** NT World Heritage Sites *pl*; *(= einzelne Landschsft etc)* World Heritage Site; **Welt|neu|heit** F world first; **„schweizerische Forscher präsentieren technologische ~"** "Swiss researchers unveil technological first"; **welt|of|fen** ADJ liberal-minded, cosmopolitan; **Welt|of|fen|heit** F cosmopolitan attitudes *pl*; **Welt|öf|fent|lich|keit** F general public; **was meint die ~ dazu?** what is world opinion on this?, what does the world think about this?; **etw der ~ zugänglich machen** to make sth accessible to the world at large; **Welt|ord|nung** F world order; **Welt|po|li|tik** F world politics *pl*; **welt|po|li|tisch** ADJ **eine/die ~e Entwicklung** a development in/the development of world politics; **eine ~e Entscheidung** a decision affecting world politics; **die ~e Rolle Deutschlands** Germany's role in world politics; **von ~er Bedeutung** of importance in world politics; **aus ~er Sicht** seen from the standpoint of world politics ADV *gesehen* from the standpoint of world politics; **eine ~ wichtige Situation** an important international political situation; **~ nicht von Interesse** *or* **nicht bedeutsam** unimportant in the realm of world politics; **Welt|po|li|zist** M *(Pol fig)* world policeman; **Welt|rang** M **von ~** world-famous; **~ genießen** to have world status; **Welt|rang|lis|te** F world rankings *pl*

Welt|raum M (outer) space

Welt|raum- *in cpds* space → *auch* **Raum-**; **Welt|raum|ab|wehr** F space defence *(Brit) or* defense *(US)*; **Welt|raum|bahn|hof** M *(inf)* space mission launch centre; **Welt|raum|be|hör|de** F space agency; **Welt|raum|fah|rer(in)** M(F) space traveller *(Brit) or* traveler *(US)*; **Welt|raum|fahrt** F space travel; **Welt|raum|fahr|zeug** NT spacecraft, spaceship; **Welt|raum|for|schung** F space research; **welt|raum|ge|stützt** [-gəʃtʏtst] ADJ space-based; **Welt|raum|la|bor** NT space laboratory; **Welt|raum|rüs|tung** F space weaponry; **Welt|raum|schrott** M space junk; **Welt|raum|spa|zier|gang** M space walk; **Welt|raum|sta|ti|on** F space station; **Welt|raum|te|le|skop** NT space telescope; **Welt|raum|waf|fe** F space weapon

Welt-: **Welt|reich** NT empire; **Welt|rei|se** F world tour, journey (a)round the world; **eine ~ machen** to go (a)round the world; **das ist doch schließlich keine ~** *(inf)* it's not the other end of the world; **Welt|rei|sen|de(r)** MF *decl as adj* globetrotter; **Welt|re|kord** M world *or* world's *(US)* record; **Welt|re|kord|in|ha|ber(in)** M(F), **Welt|re|kord|ler** [-rekɔrtlɐ] M **-s, -**, **Welt|re|kord|le|rin** [-ərɪn] F **-, -nen** world *or* world's *(US)* record holder; **Welt|re|li|gi|on** F world religion; **Welt|re|vo|lu|ti|on** F world revolution; **Welt|ruf** M world(wide) reputation; **~ haben** to have a world(wide) reputation; **Welt|ruhm** M world fame; **Welt|schmerz** M world-weariness, weltschmerz *(liter)*; **Welt|si|cher|heits|rat** M *(Pol)* (United Nations) Security Council; **Welt|sicht** F view of the world; **Welt|spit|ze** F world leadership; *(Sport)* number one position in the world; **~ sein** to be number one *or* the best in the world, to be the world leader *or* the world's number one; **Welt|spra|che** F world language; **Welt|stadt** F international *or* cosmopolitan city, metropolis; **welt|städ|tisch** ADJ cosmopolitan; **Welt|um|run|dung** [-lʊmrʊndʊŋ] F **-, -en** *(Space)* orbit of the earth; *(Naut)* circumnavigation of the earth; **Welt|um|seg|ler(in)** M(F) circumnavigator (of the globe); *(Sport)* round-the-world *(Brit) or* around-the-world *(US)* yachtsman/-woman; **welt|um|span|nend** ADJ worldwide, global; **Welt|un|ter|gang** M *(lit, fig)* end of the world; **Welt|un|ter|gangs|stim|mung** F apocalyptic mood; **Welt|ver|bes|se|rer** M, **Welt|ver|bes|se|rin** F starry-eyed idealist; **welt|weit** ADJ worldwide, global ADV worldwide; **Welt|wirt|schaft** F world economy; **Welt|wirt|schafts|gip|fel** M World Economic Summit; **Welt|wirt|schafts|kri|se** F world economic crisis; **Welt|wun|der** NT **die Sieben ~** the Seven Wonders of the World; **er starrte mich an wie ein ~** *(fig)* he stared at me as if I were from another planet *or* as if I were some kind of freak; **Welt|zeit** F Greenwich Mean Time, GMT; **Welt|zeit|uhr** F world clock

wem [veːm] *dat von* **wer** INTERROG PRON who ... to, to whom; **mit/von** *etc* **~ ...** who ... with/from *etc*, with/from *etc* whom; **~ von euch soll ich den Schlüssel geben?** which (one) of you should I give the key to?, to which (one) of you should I give the key? REL PRON *(= derjenige, dem)* the person (who ...) to, the person to whom ...; *(= jeder, dem)* anyone to whom ..., anyone ... to; **~ ... auch (immer)** whoever ... to, no matter who ... to INDEF PRON *(inf: = jemandem)* to somebody; *(in Fragen auch)* (to) anybody

Wem|fall M dative (case)

wen [veːn] *acc von* **wer** INTERROG PRON who, whom; **an ~ hast du geschrieben?** who did you write to?, to whom did you write?; **~ von den Schülern kennst du?** which (one) of these pupils do you know?; **für ~ arbeitet er?** who does he work for?, for whom does he work? REL PRON *(= derjenige, den)* the person (who *or* whom); *(= jeder, den)* anybody (who *or* whom); **~ ... auch immer** whoever ... INDEF PRON *(inf: = jemanden)* somebody; *(in Fragen auch)* anybody

Wen|de [ˈvɛndə] F **-, -n** turn; *(= Veränderung)* change; *(= Wendepunkt)* turning point; *(Turnen: am Pferd)* face *or* front vault; *(Pol)* (political) watershed; **die ~ vom 19. zum 20. Jahrhundert** the transition from the 19th to the 20th century; **nach dem Tod seines Vaters nahm seine Entwicklung eine ~** after the death of his father his development changed direction *or* started to take a different direction

> **WENDE**
>
> When a significant political or social change takes place in Germany, the term **Wende** is often used. Nowadays it generally refers to the collapse of the Communist system which lead to the dissolution of East Germany in 1989.

Wen|de [ˈvɛndə] M **-n, -n**, **Wen|din** [ˈvɛndɪn] F **-, -nen** Wend

Wen|de-: **Wen|de|flä|che** F *(Mot)* turning area; **Wen|de|hals** M *(Orn)* wryneck; *(fig inf)* turncoat *(pej)*; **er ist einer der Wendehälse** he's one of those who have done a (complete) U-turn; **Wen|de|ham|mer** M *(Mot)* turning bay; **Wen|de|ja|cke** F reversible jacket

Wen|de|kreis M **a** tropic; **der nördliche ~** *(Geog)* **der ~ des Krebses** *(Astrol)* the Tropic of Cancer; **der südliche ~** *(Geog)* **der ~ des Steinbocks** *(Astrol)* the Tropic of Capricorn **b** *(Aut)* turning circle

Wen|del [ˈvɛndl] F **-, -n** spiral, helix; *(in Glühbirne etc)* coil

Wen|del-: **Wen|del|boh|rer** M twist drill; **Wen|del|rut|sche** F spiral chute; **Wen|del|trep|pe** F spiral staircase

Wen|de-: **Wen|de|ma|nö|ver** NT **a** *(Mot)* turning manoeuvre *(Brit)* or maneuver *(US)*; *(auf engem Raum)* three-point turn **b** *(fig)* U-turn *(fig)*; **Wen|de|man|tel** M reversible coat; **Wen|de|mar|ke** F *(Sport)* turning mark

wen|den ['vɛndn] *pret* **wendete** *or (liter)* **wandte** ['vɛndətə, 'vantə], *ptp* **gewendet** *or (liter)* **gewandt** [gə'vɛndət, gə'vant] VT **a** *(= umdrehen)* to turn *(auch Sew)*; *(auf die andere Seite)* to turn (over); *(in die entgegengesetzte Richtung)* to turn ((a)round); *(Cook) Eierpfannkuchen* to toss; *Schnitzel etc* to turn (over); **bitte ~!** please turn over; **seinen Blick nach Norden ~** *(geh)* to turn *or* bend one's eyes to(wards) the north, to look to(wards) the north; **seinen Schritt gen Süden ~** *(liter)* to turn *or* bend one's steps southwards *(liter)*; **sie wandte kein Auge von ihm** *(geh)* she did not take her eyes off him; **wie man es auch wendet ..., man kann die Sache** *or* **es drehen und ~, wie man will ...** *(fig)* whichever way you (care to) look at it ...
b *(= aufbringen)* **Geld/Zeit auf etw** *(acc)* **~** *(geh)* to spend money/time on sth; **viel Mühe/Sorgfalt** *etc* **an etw** *(acc)* **~** *(geh)* to devote a lot of effort/care *etc* to sth
VR **a** *(= sich umdrehen)* to turn ((a)round); *(Wetter, Glück)* to change, to turn; **sich nach links/zum Gehen/zur Tür ~** to turn to the left/to go/to the door; **sich ins Gegenteil ~** to become the opposite; **seine Liebe wendete sich ins Gegenteil** his love turned to hate; **seine Freude wendete sich ins Gegenteil** his joy turned to despair; **das Gespräch wendete sich** the conversation took another turn; **sich von jdm ~** *(esp Bibl)* to turn from sb *(liter)*; **sich zu jdm/etw ~** to turn to face sb/sth, to turn toward(s) sb/sth; **sich zum Guten** *or* **Besseren/Schlimmeren ~** to take a turn for the better/worse; **sich zum Besten ~** to turn out for the best
b sich an jdn ~ *(um Auskunft)* to consult sb; *(um Hilfe)* to turn to sb; *(Buch, Fernsehserie etc)* to be directed at sb, to be (intended) for sb; **sich gegen jdn/etw ~** to come out against sb/sth, to oppose sb/sth
VI to turn *(auch Sport)*; *(= umkehren)* to turn (a)round; **„wenden verboten"** "no U-turns"

Wen|de-: **Wen|de|platz** M turning area *or* place; **Wen|de|punkt** M turning point; *(Math)* point of inflection; **Wen|de|schlei|fe** F *(Mot)* turning loop

wen|dig ['vɛndɪç] ADJ agile, nimble; *Auto* manoeuvrable *(Brit)*, maneuverable *(US)*; *(fig) Politiker etc* agile

Wen|dig|keit F -, *no pl* agility, nimbleness; *(von Auto etc)* manoeuvrability *(Brit)*, maneuverability *(US)*; *(fig: von Politiker etc)* agility

Wen|din F -, -nen Wendish woman, Wend

wen|disch ['vɛndɪʃ] ADJ Wendish

Wen|dung ['vɛndʊŋ] F -, -en **a** turn *(auch Mil)*; *(= Veränderung)* change; **eine interessante/unerwartete ~ nehmen** *(fig)* to take an interesting/unexpected turn; **eine ~ zum Besseren** *or* **Guten/Schlechten nehmen** to take a turn for the better/worse, to change for the better/worse; **einer Sache** *(dat)* **eine unerwartete/neue ~ geben** to give sth an unexpected/new turn; **das gab seinem Leben eine neue ~** that changed the direction of his life; **eine interessante** *etc* **~ trat ein** there was an interesting *etc* turn of events **b** *(= Redewendung)* expression, phrase; **eine feste** *or* **feststehende ~** a set *or* fixed expression

Wen|fall M accusative (case)

we|nig ['veːnɪç] → *auch* **weniger, wenigste(r, s)**
ADJ INDEF PRON **a** *sing* little; **ich habe ~** I have only a little; **(nur) ~ Geld** (only a) little money; **ich besitze nur ~** I only own a few things, I don't own much, I own little; **hast du Zeit? – ~!** have you got time? – not much; **das ist ~** that isn't much; **so ~ wie** *or* **als möglich** as little as possible; **sie ist mir so ~ sympathisch wie dir** I don't like her any more than you do; **du sagst so ~** you're not saying much; **darüber weiß ich ~** I don't know much about that, I know little about that; **mein ~es Geld** what little money I have; **das ~e, was er übrig hatte** the little he had left; **das ~e Geld muss ausreichen** we'll have to make do with this small amount of money; **um ein ~es jünger (als)** *(geh)* a little younger (than); **es fehlte (nur) ~, und er wäre überfahren worden** he was very nearly run over; **wir haben nicht ~ Mühe damit gehabt** we had more than a little *or* we had no little difficulty with that; **er gibt sich mit ~(em) zufrieden** *(= verlangt nicht viel)* he is satisfied with a little; *(= ist selten zufrieden)* he isn't satisfied with much; **sie hat zu ~ Geld** *etc* she doesn't have enough money *etc*; **ein Exemplar zu ~ haben** to have one copy too few; **ich habe ihm £20 zu ~ geboten** I offered him £20 too little
b ~e *pl (= ein paar)* a few; *(einschränkend: = nicht viele)* few; **da wir nur ~e sind** as there are only a few of us, as we are only a few; **er ist ein Freund, wie es nur ~e gibt** there are few friends like him; **in ~en Tagen** in (just) a few days; **es sind nur noch ~e Stunden, bis ...** there are only a few hours to go until ...; **nicht ~e (waren da)** quite a few people (were there); **einige ~e Leute** a few people
c *(auch adv)* **ein ~** a little; **ein ~ Salz/besser** a little salt/better
ADV little; **sie kommt (nur) ~ raus** she doesn't get out very often; **er hat sich nicht ~ geärgert** he was not a little annoyed; **das überraschte ihn nicht ~** he was more than a little surprised; **~ besser** little better; **~ bekannt** little-known *attr*, little known *pred*; **~ mehr** little more, not much more; **~ erfreulich** not very pleasant; **zu ~** too little, not enough; *(inf: = zu wenige)* too few, not enough; **du schläfst zu ~** you don't get enough sleep; **einer/zwei** *etc* **zu ~** one/two *etc* too few

We|nig ['veːnɪç] NT **viele ~ machen ein Viel** *(Prov)* it all adds up, many a mickle makes a muckle *(Scot Prov)*

we|ni|ger ['veːnɪgɐ] *comp von* **wenig** ADJ INDEF PRON less; *(+pl)* fewer; **~ werden** to get less and less; **mein Geld wird immer ~** my money is dwindling away; **er wird immer ~** *(inf)* he's getting thinner and thinner; **~ wäre mehr gewesen** it's quality not quantity that counts; **~ Geld** less money; **~ Unfälle** fewer accidents
ADV less; **ihr kommt es ~ auf die Liebe als (vielmehr) auf das Geld an** she's less interested in love than in money; **die Vorlesung war ~ lehrreich als belustigend** the lecture was not so much instructive as amusing; **das finde ich ~ schön!** that's not so nice!; **ich kann seinen Brief kaum lesen, noch viel ~ verstehen** I can hardly read his letter much less understand it *or* let alone understand it; **je mehr ... desto** *or* **umso ~ ...** the more ... the less ...; **ich glaube ihm umso ~, weil ...** I believe him all the less because ...; **ich möchte nichts ~, als ihn (zu) beleidigen** the last thing I'd want to do is insult him → **mehr ADV**
CONJ PREP *+acc or gen* less; **sieben ~ drei ist vier** seven less three is four

We|nig|keit F -, *no pl (dated: = Kleinigkeit)* little, small amount; **meine ~** *(hum inf)* yours truly *(inf)*; **und meine ~ hat er vergessen** and he forgot little me *(hum inf)*

we|nigs|tens ['veːnɪçstns] ADV at least

we|nigs|te(r, s) ['veːnɪçstə] *superl von* **wenig** ADJ INDEF PRON ADV **am ~n** least; *(pl)* fewest; **er hat von uns allen das ~** *or* **am ~n Geld** he has the least money of any of us; **sie hat von uns allen die ~n** *or* **am ~n Sorgen** she has the fewest worries of any of us; **von den vier Bildern finde ich diese am ~n schön** of the four pictures I think this one is the least attractive; **das konnte er am ~n vertragen** he could tolerate that least of all; **die ~n (Leute) glauben das** very few (people) believe that; **das ist (doch) das ~, was du tun könntest** that's the (very) least you could do; **das ist noch das ~!** *(inf)* that's the least of it!; **das am ~n!** that least of all!

wenn [vɛn] ✪ 28.1, 29, 30, 31, 33.2, 34.1, 34.4, 36, 38.1, 39.1, 42.2, 45.2 CONJ **a** *(konditional, konzessiv bei Wünschen)* if; **~ er nicht gewesen wäre, hätte ich meine Stelle verloren** if it had not been for him *or* had it not been for him, I'd have lost my job; **selbst** *or* **und ~** even if; **~ das Wörtchen ~ nicht wär(, wär mein Vater Millionär)** *(Prov)* if ifs and ans were pots and pans (there'd be no need for tinkers) *(Prov)*; **~ ... auch ...** even though *or* if ...; **~ ... gleich ...** *(geh)* although ..., even though ...; **~ er auch noch so dumm sein mag, ...** however stupid he may be, ...; **~ auch!** *(inf)* even so!, all the same!; **~ es denn gar nicht anders geht** well, if there's no other way; **~ es schon sein muss** well, if that's the way it's got to be; **es ist nicht gut, ~ man mit vollem Magen schwimmt** it's not good to swim on a full stomach; **~ man bedenkt, dass ...** when you consider that ..., considering ...; **~ wir erst das neue Haus haben** once we get the new house; **~ ich doch** *or* **nur** *or* **bloß ...** if only I ...; **~ er nur da wäre!** if only he were *or* was here!; **es ist, als** *or* **wie** *(inf)* **~ ...** it's as if ...; **außer ~** except if, unless; **~ du das schon machen willst, (dann) mache es wenigstens richtig** if you want to do it at least do it properly → **wennschon**
b *(zeitlich)* when; **jedes Mal** *or* **immer ~** whenever; **außer ~** except when, unless

Wenn [vɛn] NT **-s, - (die** *pl or* **das) ~ und Aber** (the) ifs and buts; **ohne ~ und Aber** without any ifs and buts

wenn|gleich [vɛn'glaiç] CONJ *(geh)* although, even though; *(mit adj auch)* albeit *(form)*

wenn|schon ['vɛnʃoːn] ADV *(inf)* **(na** *or* **und) ~!** what of it?, so what? *(inf)*; **~, dennschon!** in for a penny, in for a pound! *(esp Brit prov)*, if you're going to do something at all, you might as well do it properly!

Wen|zel ['vɛntsl] M **-s, -** *(Cards)* jack, knave *(form, dated)*

wer [veːɐ] INTERROG PRON who; **~ von ...** which (one) of ...; **~ da?** *(Mil)* who goes there?; **~ ist da?** *(an Tür)* who's there? REL PRON *(= derjenige, der)* the person who; *(= jeder, der)* anyone *or* anybody who; *(esp in Sprichwörtern)* he who; **~ ... auch (immer)** whoever ... INDEF PRON *(inf: = jemand)* somebody, someone; *(in Fragen auch)* anybody, anyone; **ist da ~?** is somebody *or* anybody there?; **~ sein** to be somebody *(inf)*

Wer|be- *in cpds* advertising; **Wer|be|ab|tei|lung** F publicity department; **Wer|be|agen|tur** F advertising agency; **Wer|be|ak|ti|on** F advertising campaign; **Wer|be|ant|wort** F business reply card; **Wer|be|ar|ti|kel** M promotional article; **Wer|be|auf|wand** M advertising costs *pl*, expenditure on advertising; **Wer|be|ban|ner** NT *(Internet)* banner ad; **Wer|be|block** M *pl* **-blocks** *or* **-blöcke** *(TV)* commercial break; **Wer|be|bot|schaft** F advertising message; **Wer|be|bran|che** F advertising industry; **Wer|be|chef(in)** M(F) advertising *or* publicity manager; **Wer|be|ein|nah|men** PL advertising revenue *sing*; **Wer|be|etat** M advertising budget; **Wer|be|fach|frau** F advertising woman; **Wer|be|fach|mann** M advertising man; **Wer|be|feld|zug** M advertising campaign; **Wer|be|fern|se|hen** NT commercial television; *(Sendung)* TV advertisements *pl or* commercials *pl*; **Wer|be|film** M advertising *or* promotional film; *(= Spot)* (filmed) commercial; **Wer|be|flä|che** F advertising space; **Wer|be|frit|ze** M *(inf)* PR man; **Wer|be|funk** M radio commercials *pl*; **Wer|be|gag** M publicity stunt *or* gimmick; **Wer|be|ge|mein|schaft** F joint advertising arrangement; **Wer|be|ge|schenk** NT gift *(from company)*; *(zu Gekauftem)* free gift; **Wer|be|-**

gra|fi|ker(in) M(F) commercial artist; **Wer|be|kam|pag|ne** F publicity campaign; *(für Verbrauchsgüter)* advertising campaign; **wer|be|kräf|tig** ADJ *Aufmachung etc* catchy; **ein ~er Slogan** an effective publicity slogan; **ein ~er Faktor** a good advertising point; **Wer|be|lei|ter(in)** M(F) advertising *or* publicity manager, head of advertising *or* promotions; **Wer|be|ma|te|ri|al** NT advertising material; **Wer|be|me|di|en** PL advertising media *pl*; **Wer|be|mit|tel** NT means *sing* of advertising; **Wer|be|mus|ter** NT advertising sample

wer|ben ['vɛrbn] *pret* **warb** [varp], *ptp* **geworben** [gə'vɔrbn] VT *Mitglieder, Mitarbeiter* to recruit; *Kunden, Abonnenten, Stimmen* to attract, to win; *Soldaten* to recruit, to enlist

VI to advertise; **für etw ~** to advertise sth, to promote sth; **für eine Partei ~** to try to get support for a party; **Plakate, die für den linken Kandidaten ~** placards supporting the left-wing candidate; **um etw ~** to solicit sth, to court sth; **um Unterstützung/Verständnis ~** to try to enlist support/understanding; **um junge Wähler/neue Kunden ~** to try to attract *or* woo young voters/new customers; **um ein Mädchen ~** to court *or* woo *(old)* a girl; **er hat bei ihren Eltern um sie geworben** he asked her parents for permission to marry her

Wer|be-: **Wer|be|of|fi|zier(in)** M(F) recruiting officer; **Wer|be|pla|kat** NT advertisement, advertising poster, billboard *(US)*; **Wer|be|pros|pekt** M advertising *or* publicity brochure

Wer|ber ['vɛrbɐ] M **-s, -** *(um Kunden, Wähler)* canvasser; *(um Mädchen)* suitor; *(für Mitglieder etc, Mil Hist)* recruiter, recruiting officer; *(inf: = Werbefachmann)* adman *(inf)*

Wer|be|rin ['vɛrbərɪn] F **-, -nen** *(um Kunden, Wähler)* canvasser; *(für Mitglieder)* recruiter; *(inf: = Werbefachfrau)* adwoman *(inf)*

wer|be|risch ['vɛrbərɪʃ] ADJ advertising *attr*, promotional ADV publicity-wise

Wer|be-: **Wer|be|rum|mel** M *(inf)* hype *(inf)*; **Wer|be|schrift** F publicity leaflet; *(für Verbrauchsgüter)* advertising leaflet; **~en** promotional literature *sing*; **Wer|be|slo|gan** M publicity slogan; *(für Verbrauchsgüter)* advertising slogan; **Wer|be|spot** M commercial; **Wer|be|spruch** M = **Werbeslogan**; **Wer|be|stu|dio** NT advertising agency; **Wer|be|text** M advertising copy *no pl*; **zwei ~e** two pieces of advertising copy; **~e verfassen** to write (advertising) copy; **Wer|be|tex|ter(in)** M(F) (advertising) copywriter; **Wer|be|tour** F publicity tour; **auf ~ sein** to be on a publicity tour; **Wer|be|trä|ger** M advertising medium; **Wer|be|trom|mel** F **die ~ (für etw) rühren** *(inf)* to beat the big drum (for sth) *(inf)*, to push sth *(inf)*; **Wer|be|un|ter|bre|chung** F commercial break; **Wer|be|ver|an|stal|tung** F publicity event; **wer|be|wirk|sam** ADJ effective (for advertising purposes); **der Skandal erwies sich als äußerst ~** the scandal proved to be excellent publicity *or* proved to have excellent publicity value; **Wer|be|wirk|sam|keit** F publicity value

werb|lich ['vɛrplɪç] ADJ advertising *attr*, promotional ADV in advertising *or* promotional terms; **~ gesehen** from an advertising point of view

Wer|bung ['vɛrbʊŋ] F **-, -en** *(esp Comm)* advertising; *(= Werbeabteilung)* publicity department; *(Pol: = Propaganda)* pre-election publicity; *(von Kunden, Stimmen)* winning, attracting; *(von Mitgliedern, Soldaten etc)* recruitment, recruiting; *(um Mädchen)* courting *(um* of); **~ für etw machen** to advertise sth

Wer|bungs|kos|ten PL *(von Mensch)* professional outlay *sing or* expenses *pl*; *(von Firma)* business expenses *pl*

Wer|da|ruf ['ve:ɐda-, ve:ɐ'da:-] M *(Mil)* call of "who goes there?", challenge

Wer|de|gang M *pl* **-gänge** development; *(beruflich)* career

wer|den ['ve:ɐdn]

pret **wurde** ['vʊrdə], *ptp* **geworden** [gə'vɔrdn] *aux sein*

1 HILFSVERB	2 INTRANSITIVES VERB

1 – HILFSVERB

a zur Bildung des Futurs

> Die Kurzform *'ll* (für *will*) ist im gesprochenen Englisch sehr gebräuchlich, ebenfalls *won't* (= *will not*). Die unveränderliche Vollform *will* wird in der Schriftsprache sowie zur Betonung verwendet.

ich werde es tun I'll do it; **wir werden es tun** we'll do it; **ich werde das nicht tun** I won't do that; **er wird es tun, das verspreche ich euch** he will do it, I promise you; **ich bin sicher, dass er das nicht freiwillig tun wird** he won't do it voluntarily, I'm sure

> *going to* drückt Sicherheit aus. Es wird ebenfalls für Voraussagen verwendet.

es wird gleich regnen it's going to rain; **du wirst heute schön zu Hause bleiben!** you're going to stay at home today!; **wer wird denn gleich weinen!** you're not going to cry now, are you?; **wer wird denn gleich!** *(inf)* come on, now!

♦ **es wird … werden es wird schon werden** *(inf)* it's going to be okay *(inf)*; **es wird schon wieder (gut) werden** it'll turn out all right; **es wird sicher ein Junge werden** it's bound to be a boy

♦ **es will … werden es will einfach nicht werden** it's simply not working

b zur Bildung des Konjunktivs

> Die Kurzformen *'d* (für *would*) und *wouldn't* (für *would not*) sind sehr gebräuchlich; zur Betonung wird jedoch die Vollform *would* verwendet.

das würde ich gerne tun I'd like to do that; **das würde ich nicht gerne tun** I wouldn't like to do that; **ich glaube, das würde dir nicht gefallen – doch, das würde mir sogar sehr gefallen** I suppose you wouldn't like that? – yes, I would like it very much; **er würde kommen, wenn es nicht regnete** he would come if it wasn't raining; **er hat gesagt, er werde** *or* **würde kommen** he said he would *or* he'd come; **würden Sie mir bitte das Buch geben?** would you give me the book, please?

c zur Bildung des Passivs *pret auch* **ward** *(old, liter) ptp* **worden geschlagen werden** to be beaten; **was ist mit ihm? – er ist erschossen worden** [vart] what happened to him? – he has been shot dead; **er ist gestern erschossen worden** ['vɔrdn] he was shot dead yesterday; **das Haus wird (gerade) renoviert** the house is being redecorated; **mir wurde gesagt, dass …** I was told that …; **es wurde gesungen** there was singing; **hier wird nicht geraucht!** there's no smoking here; **in England wird links gefahren** in England you drive on the left

d bei Vermutung **sie wird wohl in der Küche sein** she'll probably be in the kitchen; **er wird (wohl) ausgegangen sein** he will *or* he'll (probably) have gone out; **er wird sicher gerade auf dem Heimweg sein** he will definitely be on his way home; **das wird etwa 20 Euro kosten** it will cost roughly 20 euros

2 – INTRANSITIVES VERB

pret auch **ward** [vart] *(old, liter) ptp* **geworden** [gə'vɔrdn]

a mit Adjektiv to get; **mir wird kalt/warm** I'm getting cold/warm; **verrückt/blind werden** to go crazy/blind; **rot/sauer/blass/kalt werden** to go red/sour/pale/cold; **mir wird schlecht/besser** I feel bad/better; **anders werden** to change; **die Fotos sind gut geworden** the photos have come out well

b mit Substantiv, Pronomen to become; *(= sich verwandeln in)* to turn into; **Lehrer werden** to become a teacher; **was willst du einmal werden?** what do you want to be when you grow up?; **ich will Lehrer werden** I want to be a teacher; **Erster werden** to come *or* be first; **er ist nichts (Rechtes) geworden** he hasn't got anywhere in life; **er ist etwas geworden** he's got somewhere in life; **das ist nichts geworden** it came to nothing; **das Eis wird Wasser** the ice is turning into water; **das wird bestimmt ein guter Eintopf** the stew is going to be good; **das wird ein guter Urlaub werden** it's going to be a good holiday *(esp Brit) or* vacation *(US)*; **was soll das werden? – das wird ein Pullover** what's that going to be? – it's going to be a pullover; **wie soll der neue Swimmingpool werden?** what is the new swimming pool going to be like?

c bei Altersangaben **er wird am 8. Mai 36 (Jahre alt)** he will be 36 on the 8th of May; **er ist gerade 40 geworden** he has just turned 40

d in festen Wendungen

♦ **es wird … es wird bald ein Jahr, dass …** it's almost a year since …; **es wird jetzt 13 Uhr** in a moment it will be 1 o'clock; **es wurde 10 Uhr, und …** 10 o'clock came, and …; **es wird Zeit, dass er kommt** it's time (that) he came; **es wird kalt/dunkel/spät** it's getting cold/dark/late; **es wird Nacht** it's getting dark; **es wird Tag** it's getting light; **… es werde Licht! und es ward Licht** *(Bibl)* … let there be light, and there was light *(Bibl)*; **es wird Winter** winter is coming

♦ **werden + aus was ist aus ihm geworden?** what has become of him?; **aus ihm ist ein großer Komponist geworden** he has become a great composer; **aus ihm ist nichts (Rechtes) geworden** he hasn't got *(Brit) or* gotten *(US)* anywhere in life; **aus ihm ist etwas geworden** he has got *(Brit) or* gotten *(US)* somewhere in life; **aus ihm wird noch einmal was!** he'll make something of himself yet!; **aus dir wird nie etwas!** you'll never be anything!; **daraus wird nichts** that won't come to anything, nothing will come of that; *(= das kommt nicht infrage)* that's out of the question; **was soll nur aus ihm werden?** what will become of him?; **daraus wird bestimmt nichts Gutes/kann nichts Gutes werden** no good will/can come of it; **was wird daraus (werden)?** what will come of it? → **nichts**

♦ **werden + zu zu etw werden** to turn into sth; **nachts wird er zum Vampir** at night he turns into a vampire; **zu Staub werden** to turn to dust

♦ **werden + wie er wird mal wie sein Vater** he's going to be like his father

e andere Wendungen **alles Leben wird und vergeht** *(liter)* life comes into being and then passes away *(liter)*; **ihm ist ein großes Glück geworden** *(old, liter)* he has been favoured *(Brit) or* favored *(US)* with great fortune *(liter)*; **was nicht ist, kann (ja) noch werden** *(prov inf)* my/your *etc* day will come; **was soll nun werden?** so what's going to happen now?; **ich dachte, ich werd nicht wieder** *or* **mehr!** *(inf)* I was flabbergasted *(inf)*

Wer|den ['ve:ɐdn] NT **-s**, *no pl* **a** *(= Entstehung)* development; **im ~ sein** to be in the making; **die lebenden Sprachen sind immer im ~ begriffen** living languages are in a state of continual development **b** *(Philos)* Becoming

wer|dend ADJ nascent, emergent; **~e Mutter** expectant mother, mother-to-be; **~er Vater** father-to-be

Wer|fall M nominative (case)

wer|fen ['vɛrfn] *pret* **warf** [varf], *ptp* **geworfen** [gə'vɔrfn] VT **a** *(in Verbindung mit n siehe auch dort)* to throw *(auch beim Ringkampf)* *(nach* at), to cast *(liter, Bibl)*; *Tor, Korb* to score; **Bomben ~** *(von Flugzeug)* to drop bombs; **eine Münze ~** to toss a coin; **„nicht ~"** "handle with care"; **Bilder an die Wand ~** to project pictures onto the wall; **etw auf jdn/etw ~** to throw sth at sb/sth;

etw auf den Boden ~ to throw sth to the ground, to throw sth on(to) the ground; **etw auf das Dach ~** to throw sth on(to) the roof; **die Sonne warf ihre Strahlen auf den See** the sun cast its rays on the lake; **die Tischlampe wirft ihr Licht auf …** the table lamp throws its light on …; **die Laterne wirft ein helles Licht** the lantern gives off a bright light; **billige Waren auf den Markt ~** to dump cheap goods on the market; **jdn aus der Firma/dem Haus** *etc* **~** to throw *or* kick sb out (of the firm/house *etc*); **jdn ins Gefängnis** *etc* **~** to throw sb into prison *etc*; **alle Sorgen von sich ~** *(fig)* to cast aside all one's worries; **Geld in den Automaten ~** to put money in the machine; **etw ins Gespräch/in die Debatte ~** to throw sth into the conversation/debate; **etw aufs Papier ~** *(geh)* to jot sth down; **die Kleider von sich ~** to throw *or* cast off one's clothes → **Blick a**, **Licht b**

b *(= Junge kriegen)* to have, to throw *(spec)*

VI **a** *(= schleudern)* to throw; **mit etw (auf jdn/etw) ~** to throw sth (at sb/sth); **mit Geld (nur so) um sich ~** *(inf)* to throw *or* chuck *(inf)* one's money around; **mit Komplimenten (nur so) um sich ~** to be free and easy *or* to be lavish with one's compliments; **mit Fremdwörtern (nur so) um sich ~** to bandy foreign words about *(Brit)*, to toss foreign words around *(esp US)*

b *(Tier)* to have its young; *(esp Katze, Hund etc)* to have a litter, to litter; *(bei einzelnen Jungen)* to have a pup *etc*

VR to throw oneself (*auf +acc* (up)on, at); *(Holz)* to warp; *(Metall, Asphalt etc)* to buckle; **sich auf eine Aufgabe** *etc* **~** to throw oneself into a task *etc*; **sich in die Kleider ~** to throw on one's clothes → **Brust a**, **Hals a**

Wer|fer ['vɛrfɐ] M **-s, -**, **Wer|fe|rin** [-ərɪn] F **-, -nen** thrower; *(Kricket)* bowler; *(Baseball)* pitcher

Werft [vɛrft] F **-, -en** shipyard; *(für Flugzeuge)* hangar

Werft|ar|bei|ter(in) M(F) shipyard worker

Werg [vɛrk] NT **-(e)s** [-gəs] *no pl* tow

Wer|geld ['veːɐgɛlt] NT *(Hist Jur)* wer(e)gild

Werk [vɛrk] NT **-(e)s, -e** **a** *(= Arbeit, Tätigkeit)* work *no indef art*; (*geh*: *= Tat*) deed, act; *(= Schöpfung, Kunstwerk, Buch)* work; *(= Gesamtwerk)* works *pl*; **Schweitzer hat in Afrika ein bedeutendes ~ vollbracht** Schweitzer has done (some) important work in Africa; **ein ~ wie das verdient unsere Förderung** work such as that deserves our support; **das ~ eines Augenblicks** the work of a moment; **das ist sein ~** this is his doing; **das ~ vieler Jahrzehnte** the work of many decades; **das ~ jahrelanger Arbeit/seines Fleißes** the product of many years of work/of his industry; **die ~e Gottes** the works of God; **gute ~e tun** to do good works; **ein gutes ~ (an jdm) tun** to do a good deed (for sb); **du tätest ein gutes ~, wenn …** *(auch hum)* you'd be doing me/him *etc* a favour *(Brit)* or favor *(US)* if …, you'd be doing your good deed for the day if … *(hum)*; **ein ~ der Nächstenliebe** an act of charity; **ans ~ gehen, sich ans ~ machen, zu ~e gehen** *(geh)* to set to work, to go to work; **(frisch) ans ~!** *(old, liter)* to work!; **am ~ sein** to be at work; **etw ins ~ setzen** *(geh)* to set sth in motion; **wir müssen vorsichtig zu ~e gehen** we must proceed cautiously

b *(= Betrieb, Fabrik)* works *sing or pl (Brit)*, factory, plant; **ab ~** *(Comm)* ex works *(Brit)*, ex factory

c *(= Triebwerk)* works *pl*, mechanism

d *usu pl (= Festungswerke)* works *pl*

Werk- *in cpds* works *(Brit)*, factory → *auch* **Werk(s)-**; **Werk|bank** F *pl* **-bänke** workbench

Wer|kel ['vɛrkl] NT **-s, -(n)** *(Aus)* hurdy-gurdy, street organ

Wer|kel|mann M *pl* **-männer** *(Aus)* organ grinder

wer|keln ['vɛrkln] VI *(dated inf)* to potter about *or* around *(Brit)*, to putter around *(US)*; **daran ist noch einiges zu ~** it still needs a bit of fixing

wer|ken ['vɛrkn] **VI** to work, to be busy; *(handwerklich)* to do handicrafts; **Werken** *(Sch)* handicrafts **VT** to make

Werk-: **werk|ge|treu** ADJ true *or* faithful to the original; **Werk|hal|le** F factory building; **werk|im|ma|nent** **ADJ** *(Liter)* text-based **ADV** **etw ~ interpretieren** to make a text-based interpretation of sth; **Werk|kunst|schu|le** F arts and crafts school; **Werk|leh|rer(in)** M(F) woodwork/metalwork *etc* teacher, handicrafts teacher; **Werk|leu|te** PL *(old, liter)* craftsmen *pl*, artisans *pl*; **Werk|meis|ter** M foreman; **Werk|meis|te|rin** F forewoman

Werk(s)-: **Werk(s)|an|ge|hö|ri|ge(r)** MF *decl as adj* works *(Brit)* or factory employee; **Werk(s)|arzt** M, **Werk(s)|ärz|tin** F works *(Brit) or* company doctor

Werk|schau F exhibition *(of sb's work)*, retrospective

Werk|schutz M works *(Brit) or* factory security service

Werks-: **werks|ei|gen** ADJ company *attr*; **~ sein** to be company-owned, to belong to the company; **Werks|ein|stel|lun|gen** PL *(Comput)* factory defaults; **Werks|fah|rer(in)** M(F) company *or* factory driver; **Werks|feu|er|wehr** F works *(Brit) or* factory fire service; **Werks|ge|län|de** NT works *(Brit) or* factory premises *pl*; **Werks|hal|le** F workshop; **Werks|kan|ti|ne** F works *(Brit) or* factory canteen; **Werks|kü|che** F works *(Brit) or* factory kitchen; **Werks|lei|ter(in)** M(F) works *(Brit) or* factory director *or* manager; **Werks|lei|tung** F works *(Brit) or* factory management; **Werks|schlie|ßung** F plant closure; **Werks|spi|o|na|ge** F industrial espionage

Werk|statt F *pl* **-stätten** [-ʃtɛtn], **Werk|stät|te** F workshop *(auch fig)*; *(für Autoreparaturen)* garage; *(von Künstler)* studio; **geschützte** *or* **beschützende ~** *(für Behinderte)* sheltered workshop

Werk|statt|wa|gen M breakdown *(Brit) or* tow *(US)* truck, wrecker *(US)*

Werk-: **Werk|stoff** M material; **Werk|stück** NT *(Tech)* workpiece; **Werk|stu|dent(in)** M(F) working student; **~ sein** to work one's way through college

Werk|stoff-: **Werk|stoff|prü|fer(in)** M(F) materials tester; **Werk|stoff|prü|fung** F testing of materials

Werk(s)-: **Werk(s)|ver|kehr** M company transport; **Werk(s)|ver|trag** M contract of manufacture; **Werk(s)|woh|nung** F company flat *(Brit) or* apartment

Werk|tag M working day, workday

werk|täg|lich **ADJ** *attr* weekday; *Kleidung etc* workaday; **~e Öffnung** weekday opening **ADV** *(= werktags)* on weekdays

werk|tags ['vɛrktaːks] ADV on weekdays

werk|tä|tig ADJ working

Werk|tä|ti|ge(r) [-tɛːtɪgə] MF *decl as adj* working man/woman; **die ~n** the working people *pl*

Werk-: **Werk|tisch** M worktable; **werk|treu** ADJ true *or* faithful to the original; **Werk|treue** F faithfulness to the original; **Werk|un|ter|richt** M handicraft lessons *pl*, woodwork/metalwork *etc* instruction

Werk|zeug NT *pl* **-zeuge** *(lit, fig, Comput)* tool

Werk|zeug-: **Werk|zeug|kas|ten** M toolbox; **Werk|zeug|leis|te** F *(Comput)* toolbar; **Werk|zeug|ma|cher(in)** M(F) toolmaker; **Werk|zeug|ma|schi|ne** F machine tool; **Werk|zeug|stahl** M *(Tech)* tool steel

Wer|mut ['veːɐmuːt] M **-(e)s**, *no pl* **a** *(Bot)* wormwood; **ein Tropfen ~** *(fig geh)* a drop of bitterness **b** *(= Wermutwein)* vermouth

Wer|muts|trop|fen M *(fig geh)* drop of bitterness

Werst [vɛrst] F **-, -e** *(Maß)* verst

wert [veːɐt] ADJ **a** (*old, form*: *Anrede*) dear; **Ihr ~es Schreiben** *(form)* your esteemed letter *(form)*; **wie war doch gleich Ihr ~er Name?** *(form)* what was the name, sir/madam?

b **etw ~ sein** to be worth sth; **nichts ~ sein** to be worthless, to be worth nothing; *(= untauglich)* to be no good; **sie war ihm offenbar nicht viel ~** she obviously didn't mean all that much to him; **er ist £ 100.000 ~** *(Press sl)* he is worth £100,000; **Glasgow ist eine Reise ~** Glasgow is worth a visit; **einer Sache** *(gen)* **~ sein** *(geh)* to be worthy of sth; **es ist der Mühe ~** it's worth the trouble, it's worth it; **es ist nicht der Rede ~** it's not worth mentioning; **er ist es nicht ~, dass man ihm vertraut** he doesn't deserve to be trusted; **er ist (es) nicht ~, dass wir ihn unterstützen** he is not worthy of our support, he does not deserve our support; **dieser Film ist es durchaus ~, dass man sich ihn ansieht** this film is definitely worth seeing

c *(= nützlich)* useful; **ein Auto ist viel ~** a car is very useful; **das ist schon viel ~** *(= erfreulich)* that's very encouraging

Wert [veːɐt] M **-(e)s, -e** **a** value; *(esp menschlicher)* worth; *(von Banknoten, Briefmarken)* denomination; *(= Wertsache)* article of value, valuable object; **einen ~ von 5 Euro haben** to be worth 5 euros, to have a value of 5 euros; **im ~(e) von** to the value of, worth; **an ~ verlieren/zunehmen, im ~ sinken/steigen** to decrease/increase in value, to depreciate/appreciate *(esp Econ)*; **eine Sache unter/über (ihrem wirklichen) ~ verkaufen** to sell sth for less/more than its true value; **sie hat innere ~e** she has certain inner qualities; **~ auf etw** *(acc)* **legen** *(fig)* to set great store by sth *(esp Brit)*, to attach importance to sth; **ich lege ~ darauf, festzustellen, dass …** I think it important to establish that …; **das hat keinen ~** *(inf)* there's no point

b *usu pl (von Test, Analyse)* result

Wert-: **Wert|an|ga|be** F declaration of value; **Wert|ar|beit** F craftsmanship, workmanship; **Wert|be|rich|ti|gung** F *(Comm)* valuation adjustment; **wert|be|stän|dig** ADJ stable in value; **Wert|be|stän|dig|keit** F stability of value; **Wert|brief** M registered letter *(containing sth of value)*

Wer|te|be|wusst|sein NT sense of right and wrong

wer|ten ['veːɐtn] VTI *(= einstufen)* to rate (*als* as); *Klassenarbeit etc* to grade; *(= beurteilen)* to judge (*als* to be); *(Sport) (= als gültig werten)* to allow; *(= Punkte geben)* to give a score; **ein Tor nicht ~** *(Ftbl etc)* to disallow a goal; **der Punktrichter aus Polen wertete besonders hoch** the Polish judge gave particularly high marks; **je nachdem, wie gewertet wird** according to how the scoring is done; **ohne (es) ~ zu wollen …** without wanting to make any judgement (on it) …

Wert|er|hal|tung F value preservation; **die ~ von Immobilien** preserving the value of property

Wer|te-: **Wer|te|sys|tem** NT system of values; **Wer|te|wan|del** M change in values

wert|frei **ADJ** neutral **ADV** in a neutral way; *sagen auch* neutrally

Wert|ge|gen|stand M object of value; **Wertgegenstände** *pl* valuables *pl*

Wer|tig|keit ['veːɐtɪçkait] F **-, -en** **a** *(Chem, Ling)* valency **b** *(= Wert)* importance, value

Wert-: **Wert|kar|te** F *(Aus Telec)* phonecard; **Wert|kar|ten|te|le|fon** NT *(Aus)* card telephone; **wert|kon|ser|va|tiv** ADJ espousing conservative values, conservative; **wert|los** ADJ worthless, valueless; **Wert|lo|sig|keit** F **-**, *no pl* worthlessness; **Wert|mar|ke** F ticket; *(zum Aufkleben)* stamp; **Wert|maß** NT, **Wert|maß|stab** M, **Wert|mes|ser** M **-s, -** standard, yardstick; **Wert|min|de|rung** F reduction in value; **wert|neut|ral** **ADJ** value-free **ADV** avoiding (making) value judgements; **Wert|ob|jekt** NT object of value; **Wert|ord|nung** F system of values; **Wert|pa|ket** NT registered parcel *(esp Brit) or* package *(containing sth of value)*; **Wert|pa|pier** NT security, bond; **~e** *pl* stocks and shares *pl*

Wert|pa|pier-: Wert|pa|pier|bör|se F stock exchange; **Wert|pa|pier|ge|schäft** NT securities trading; *(einzelne Transaktion)* securities transaction; **Wert|pa|pier|han|del** M securities trading; **Wert|pa|pier|markt** M securities market

Wert|phi|lo|so|phie F *(= analytische Wertphilosophie)* axiology; *(= allgemeine Ethik)* moral philosophy

Wert|sa|che F object of value

wert+schät|zen VT *sep (liter)* to (hold in high) esteem

Wert|schät|zung F *(liter)* esteem, high regard

Wert|schöp|fung F *(Econ)* net product

Wert|schrift F *(Sw)* = **Wertpapier**

Wert|sen|dung F registered consignment

Wert|set|zung [-zɛtsʊŋ] F **-, -en** scale of values; *(= das Festsetzen)* fixing of values

Wert|stei|ge|rung F increase in value

Wert|stel|lung F *(Fin)* value

Wert|stoff M reusable material; **das Recyceln von ~en** the recycling of reusable materials

Wert|stoff|hof M recycling depot

Wert|stoff|ton|ne F bin for reusable materials

Wert|sys|tem NT system of values, value system

Wer|tung [ˈveːɐtʊŋ] F **-, -en** **a** *(= Bewertung)* evaluation, assessment; *(von Jury etc)* judging, scoring; *(= Punkte)* score; **aus der ~ fallen** to be disqualified **b** *(= das Werten)* rating; *(von Klassenarbeit)* grading; *(= das Beurteilen)* judging; *(Sport: = Punktvergabe)* scoring

Wer|tungs- *(Sport etc)*: **Wer|tungs|ge|richt** NT jury; **Wer|tungs|rich|ter(in)** M(F) judge

Wert|ur|teil NT value judgement

Wert|ur|teils-: wert|ur|teils|frei ADJ free from value judgements; **Wert|ur|teils|frei|heit** F avoidance of (making) value judgements

Wert|ver|lust M depreciation

wert|voll ADJ valuable; *(moralisch) Mensch* worthy, estimable

Wert-: Wert|vor|stel|lung F moral concept; **Wert|zei|chen** NT *(form)* postage stamp; **Wert|zu|wachs** M appreciation; *(von Geldsumme)* capital gain; **Wert|zu|wachs|steu|er** F capital gains tax

wer|wei|ßen [ˈveːɐvaisn] VI *insep (Sw)* to guess

Wer|wolf [ˈveːɐvɔlf] M werewolf

wes [vɛs] PRON *(old) gen von* **wer** whose *gen von* **was** of which

We|sen [ˈveːzn] NT **-s, -** **a** *no pl* nature; *(= Wesentliches)* essence; **am ~ unserer Beziehung hat sich nichts geändert** the basic nature of our relationship remains unchanged; **es liegt im ~ einer Sache ...** it's in the nature of a thing ...; **das gehört zum ~ der Demokratie** it is of the essence of democracy
b *no pl* **sein ~ treiben** *(geh) (Dieb etc)* to be at work; *(Schalk etc)* to be up to one's tricks; *(Gespenst)* to be abroad; **viel ~s machen (um** *or* **von)** to make a lot of fuss (about)
c *(= Geschöpf)* being; *(= tierisches Wesen)* creature; *(= Mensch)* person, creature; **armes ~** poor thing *or* creature; **das höchste ~** the Supreme Being; **ein menschliches ~** a human being; **ein weibliches ~** a female; **ein männliches ~** a male

we|sen [ˈveːzn] VI *(liter)* to be present

We|sen-: we|sen|haft ADJ intrinsic, essential; **We|sen|heit** F **-, -en** *(Philos)* being; **we|sen|los** ADJ insubstantial, unreal

We|sens-: we|sens|ähn|lich ADJ similar in nature; **We|sens|art** F nature, character; **es ist griechische ~, zu ...** it's a Greek characteristic to ...; **we|sens|ei|gen** ADJ intrinsic; **we|sens|fremd** ADJ *(= im Wesen verschieden)* different *or* dissimilar in nature; **das Lügen ist ihm völlig ~** lying is completely foreign *or* alien to his nature; **we|sens|ge|mäß** ADJ **das ist ihm nicht ~** it's not in accordance with his nature; **we|sens|gleich** ADJ essentially alike, identical in character *or* nature; **We|sens|gleich|heit** F essential similarity; **We|sens|merk|mal** NT (basic *or* essential) trait; **We|sens|un|ter|schied** M difference in nature *or* character; **we|sens|ver|wandt** ADJ related in character; **We|sens|ver|wandt|schaft** F relatedness of character; **We|sens|zug** M characteristic, trait

we|sent|lich [ˈveːzntlɪç] ADJ *(= den Kern der Sache betreffend, sehr wichtig)* essential; *(= grundlegend)* fundamental; *(= erheblich)* substantial, considerable, appreciable; *(= wichtig)* important; **das Wesentliche** the essential part *or* thing; *(von dem, was gesagt wurde)* the gist; **im Wesentlichen** in essence, basically, essentially; *(= im Großen und Ganzen)* in the main ADV *(= grundlegend)* fundamentally; *(= erheblich)* considerably; **es ist mir ~ lieber, wenn wir ...** I would much rather we ...; **sie hat sich nicht ~ verändert** she hasn't changed much

Wes|fall M genitive case

wes|halb [vɛsˈhalp, ˈvɛs-] INTERROG ADV why REL ADV which is why, for which reason; **der Grund, ~ ...** the reason why ...; **das ist es ja, ~ ...** that is why ...

We|sir [veˈziːɐ] M **-s, -e** vizi(e)r

Wes|pe [ˈvɛspə] F **-, -n** wasp

Wes|pen-: Wes|pen|nest NT wasp's nest; **in ein ~ stechen** *(fig)* to stir up a hornets' nest; **das war ein Stich ins ~** *(fig)* that stirred up a hornets' nest; **Wes|pen|stich** M wasp sting; **Wes|pen|tail|le** F *(fig)* wasp waist

wes|sen [ˈvɛsn] PRON *gen von* **wer** **a** *interrog* whose **b** *rel, indef* **~ Handschrift das auch (immer) sein mag, ...** no matter whose handwriting it may be, ... *gen von* **was** *(liter)* **c** *interrog* **~ hat man dich angeklagt?** of what have you been accused? **d** *rel, indef* **~ man dich auch (immer) anklagt, ...** whatever they *or* no matter what they accuse you of ...

wes|sent|we|gen [ˈvɛsntˈveːgn] INTERROG ADV *(geh)* why

wes|sent|wil|len [ˈvɛsntˈvɪlən] INTERROG ADV *(geh)* **um ~** for whose sake

Wes|si [ˈvɛsi] M **-s, -s** *(inf)* Westerner, West German

> **WESSI**
>
> **Wessi** is used in a similar way to **Ossi** and refers to a person from the former West Germany. After the **Wende** many West Germans went to the new **Länder** with an arrogant sense of superiority. This led to the term **Besserwessi,** a combination of **Besserwisser** (smart aleck) and **Wessi.** → OSSI, WENDE

West [vɛst] M **-s,** *no pl* **a** *(Naut, Met, liter)* west **b** *(liter: = Westwind)* west wind

West- *in cpds (in Ländernamen) (politisch)* West; *(geografisch auch)* the West of ..., Western; **West|af|ri|ka** NT West Africa; **West|aus|tra|li|en** NT Western Australia; **West|ber|lin** NT *(Hist)* West Berlin; **west|deutsch** ADJ *(Geog)* Western German; *(Pol Hist)* West German; **West|deut|sche(r)** MF *decl as adj* West German; **West|deutsch|land** NT *(Geog)* the West of Germany; *(Pol Hist)* West Germany, Western Germany

Wes|te [ˈvɛstə] F **-, -n** waistcoat *(Brit)*, vest *(US)*; **eine reine** *or* **saubere** *or* **weiße ~ haben** *(fig)* to have a clean slate

Wes|ten [ˈvɛstn] M **-s,** *no pl* west; *(von Land)* West; **der ~** *(Pol)* the West; *(im Gegensatz zum Orient auch)* the Occident; **aus dem ~, von ~ (her)** from the west; **gegen** *or* **gen** *(liter) or* **nach ~** west(wards), to the west; **nach ~ (hin)** to the west; **im ~ der Stadt/des Landes** in the west of the town/country; **weiter im ~** further west; **im ~ Frankreichs** in the west of France, in Western France → **wild**

Wes|ten|ta|sche F waistcoat *(Brit) or* vest *(US)* pocket; **etw wie seine ~ kennen** *(inf)* to know sth like the back of one's hand *(inf)*

Wes|ten|ta|schen|for|mat NT *(hum)* **ein X im ~** a miniature X

Wes|tern [ˈvɛstɐn] M **-(s), -** western

West-: West|eu|ro|pa NT Western Europe; **west|eu|ro|pä|isch** ADJ West(ern) European; **~e Zeit** Greenwich Mean Time, Western European Time *(rare)*; **die Westeuropäische Union** the Western European Union

West|fa|le [vɛstˈfaːlə] M **-n, -n**, **West|fä|lin** [-ˈfɛːlɪn] F **-, -nen** Westphalian

West|fa|len [vɛstˈfaːlən] NT **-s** Westphalia

West|fä|lin [-ˈfɛːlɪn] F **-, -nen** Westphalian (woman)

west|fä|lisch [vɛstˈfɛːlɪʃ] ADJ Westphalian; **der Westfälische Friede** *(Hist)* The Treaty of Westphalia

West|frie|si|sche In|seln PL West Frisians *pl*, West Frisian Islands *pl*

West-: West|geld NT Western currency; **West|ger|ma|nen** PL *(Hist)* West Germanic peoples *pl or* tribes *pl*; **west|ger|ma|nisch** ADJ *(Hist, Ling)* West Germanic; **West|go|ten** PL *(Hist)* Visigoths *pl*, West Goths *pl*; **west|grie|chisch** ADJ Western Greek; **West|in|di|en** NT the West Indies *pl*; **west|in|disch** ADJ West Indian; **die Westindischen Inseln** the West Indies *pl*; **West|in|teg|ra|ti|on** F *(Pol)* integration with the West; **West|jor|dan|land** [vɛstˈjɔrdan-] NT **das ~** the West Bank; **West|küs|te** F west coast

west|lich [ˈvɛstlɪç] ADJ western; *Kurs, Wind, Richtung* westerly; *(Pol)* Western; **der ~ste Ort** the westernmost place ADV (to the) west; **~ von ...** (to the) west of ...; **es liegt ~er** *or* **weiter ~** it is further (to the) west PREP *+gen* (to the) west of

West-: West|mäch|te PL *(Pol)* **die ~** the western powers *pl*; **West|mark** F *(Hist inf)* West German mark; **west|mit|tel|deutsch** ADJ West Middle German; **West|nord|west** M **a** *(Naut, Met, liter)* west-north-west **b** *(liter: Wind)* west-north-west wind; **west|öst|lich** ADJ west-to-east; **in ~er Richtung** from west to east; **West|po|li|tik** F policy toward(s) the west, western policy; **West|preu|ßen** NT West Prussia; **West|rom** NT *(Hist)* Western Roman Empire; **west|rö|misch** ADJ *(Hist)* Western Roman; **West|rus|sen** PL White Russians *pl*; **West|schweiz** F **die ~** Western Switzerland; **West|sek|tor** M western sector; **West|süd|west** M **a** *(Naut, Met, liter)* west-south-west **b** *(liter: Wind)* west-south-west wind; **West|wall** M *(Hist)* Siegfried Line; **west|wärts** [ˈvɛstvɛrts] ADV westward(s), (to the) west; **West|wind** M west wind

wes|we|gen [vɛsˈveːgn, ˈvɛs-] INTERROG ADV why

wett [vɛt] ADJ *pred* **~ sein** to be quits

Wett|an|nah|me(|stel|le) F betting office

Wett|be|werb M competition; **mit jdm in ~ stehen/treten** to be in/enter into competition with sb, to be competing/to compete with sb; **außer ~ teilnehmen** *or* **laufen** to take part hors concours *(Brit)*, to take part as a noncompetitor

Wett|be|wer|ber(in) M(F) competitor

Wett|be|werbs-: Wett|be|werbs|be|din|gun|gen PL terms *pl* of a/the competition; **Wett|be|werbs|be|schrän|kung** F restraint of trade; **wett|be|werbs|fä|hig** ADJ competitive; **Wett|be|werbs|fä|hig|keit** F competitiveness; **Wett|be|werbs|klau|sel** F non-competition clause; **Wett|be|werbs|nach|teil** M competitive disadvantage; **Wett|be|werbs|recht** NT competition law *(Brit)*, antitrust law *(US)*; **wett|be|werbs|recht|lich** ADJ, ADV with regard to competition law *(Brit) or* antitrust law *(US)*; **Wett|be|werbs|teil|neh|mer(in)** M(F) competitor; **Wett|be|werbs|ver|zer|rung** F distortion of competition; **Wett|be|werbs|vor|teil** M competitive advantage *or* edge; **wett|be|werbs|wid|rig** ADJ *Verhalten, Absprache, Werbung* anticompetitive ADV **~ handeln** *(unlauter)* to violate fair trade practices; *(ungesetzlich)* to violate competition law *(Brit) or* antitrust law *(US)*; **Wẹtt|be|werbs|wirt|schaft** F competitive economy

Wẹtt|bü|ro NT betting office

Wẹt|te ['vɛtə] F **-, -n** bet *(auch Sport)*; wager; **eine ~ machen** *or* **abschließen/annehmen** to make/take up *or* accept a bet; **eine ~ auf ein Pferd abschließen** to place a bet on a horse; **darauf gehe ich jede ~ ein** I'll bet you anything you like; **was gilt die ~?** what will you bet me?, what are you betting?; **die ~ gilt!** done!, you're on! *(inf)*; **um die ~ laufen/schwimmen** to run/swim a race (with each other); **mit jdm um die ~ laufen** *or* **rennen** to race sb; **sie arbeiten um die ~** they're working as hard as they can; **sie singen um die ~** they're singing at the tops of their voices; **sie schreien um die ~** they're having a screaming competition

Wẹtt|ei|fer M competitive zeal, competitiveness

wẹtt|ei|fern VI *insep* **mit jdm um etw ~** to compete *or* contend *or* vie with sb for sth

wẹt|ten ['vɛtn] VTI to bet *(auch Sport)*, to wager; **(wollen wir) ~?** (do you) want to bet?; **~, dass ich recht habe?** (I) bet you I'm right!; **so haben wir nicht gewettet!** that's not part of the deal *or* bargain!; **auf etw** *(acc)* **~** to bet on sth; **mit jdm ~** to bet with sb; **(mit jdm) (darauf) ~, dass ...** to bet (sb) that ...; **(mit jdm) um 5 Euro/eine Flasche Bier** *etc* **~** to bet (sb) 5 euros/a bottle of beer *etc*; **wir wetteten um einen Kasten Sekt** we bet each other a case of champagne; **ich habe mit ihm um 10 Euro auf den Sieg der Brasilianer gewettet** I bet him 10 euros that the Brazilians would win; **gegen etw ~** to bet against sth; **da wette ich gegen** *(inf)* I bet you that isn't so/won't happen *etc*; **ich wette 100 gegen 1(, dass ...)** I'll bet *or* lay *(Brit)* (you) 100 to 1 (that ...); **ich wette meinen Kopf (darauf)(, dass ...)** I'll bet you anything (you like) (that ...)

Wẹt|ter ['vɛtɐ] NT **-s, -** a weather *no indef art*; **bei jedem ~** in all weathers; **bei so einem ~** in weather like that, in such weather; **das ist vielleicht ein ~!** *(inf)* what weather!; **was haben wir heute für ~?** what's the weather like today?; **wir haben herrliches ~** the weather's marvellous *(Brit) or* marvelous *(US)*; **ein ~ zum Eierlegen** *(inf) or* **Heldenzeugen** *(inf)* fantastic weather *(inf)*; **übers** *or* **vom ~ sprechen** to talk about the weather; **(bei jdm) gut ~ machen** *(inf)* to make up to sb; **(jdn) um gutes ~ bitten** *(inf)* to try to smooth things over (with sb); **alle ~!** *(inf)* my goodness!, by Jove! *(dated)*
b *(= Unwetter)* storm
c *usu pl (Min)* air; **matte ~** *pl* chokedamp *sing (Brit)*, blackdamp *sing*; **giftige** *or* **böse ~** *pl* whitedamp *sing*; **schlagende ~** *pl* firedamp *sing*

Wẹt|ter ['vɛtɐ] M **-s, -**, **Wẹt|te|rin** [-ərɪn] F **-, -nen** better

Wẹt|ter-: **Wẹt|ter|amt** NT weather *or* met(eorological) office *(Brit)*, weather bureau; **Wẹt|ter|aus|sich|ten** PL weather outlook *sing or* prospects *pl*; **Wẹt|ter|bal|lon** M weather *or* meteorological balloon; **wẹt|ter|be|dingt** ADJ *Störung* weather-related, caused by the weather *pred* ADV *ausfallen* due to *or* because of the weather; **Wẹt|ter|be|din|gun|gen** PL weather conditions *pl*; **Wẹt|ter|be|ob|ach|tung** F meteorological observation; **Wẹt|ter|be|richt** M weather report; **Wẹt|ter|bes|se|rung** F improvement in the weather; **wẹt|ter|be|stän|dig** ADJ weatherproof; **wẹt|ter|be|stim|mend** ADJ weather-determining; **~ sein** to determine the weather

Wẹt|ter|chen ['vɛtɐçən] NT **-s, -** *(inf)* **das ist ja heute ein ~!** the weather's really great *or* fantastic today! *(inf)*

Wẹt|ter-: **Wẹt|ter|dienst** M weather *or* meteorological service; **wẹt|ter|emp|find|lich** ADJ sensitive to (changes in) the weather; **Wẹt|ter|fah|ne** F weather vane; **wẹt|ter|fest** ADJ weatherproof, weather-resistant; *(fig: = krisensicher)* crisis-proof; **Wẹt|ter|fleck** M *(Aus)* weatherproof cape; **Wẹt|ter|frau** F weatherwoman; **Wẹt|ter|front** F front; **Wẹt|ter|frosch** M a *type of barometer using a frog* b *(hum inf)* weatherman *(inf)*; **wẹt|ter|füh|lig** [-fy:lɪç] ADJ sensitive to (changes in) the weather; **Wẹt|ter|füh|lig|keit** F sensitivity to (changes in) the weather; **Wẹt|ter|füh|rung** F *(Min)* ventilation; **wẹt|ter|ge|schützt** ADJ sheltered; **Wẹt|ter|glas** NT *(old)* weatherglass; **Wẹt|ter|gott** M weather god; **der ~** *(hum)* the person up there who controls the weather *(hum)*; **Wẹt|ter|hahn** M weathercock *(esp Brit)*, weather vane; **Wẹt|ter|häus|chen** [-hɔysçən] NT weather house *or* box

Wẹt|te|rin [-ərɪn] F **-, -nen** better

Wẹt|ter-: **Wẹt|ter|ka|nal** M *(Min)* fan drift; **Wẹt|ter|kar|te** F weather map *or* chart; **Wẹt|ter|kun|de** F meteorology; **wẹt|ter|kund|lich** [-kʊntlɪç] ADJ meteorological; **Wẹt|ter|la|ge** F weather situation, state of the weather; **Wẹt|ter|lam|pe** F *(Min)* safety lamp; **Wẹt|ter|lei|den** NT ailment *or* complaint caused by the weather; **wẹt|ter|leuch|ten** VI *impers insep* **es wetterleuchtet** there's sheet lightning; *(fig)* there's a storm brewing; **Wẹt|ter|leuch|ten** NT **-s,** *no pl* sheet lightning; *(fig)* storm clouds *pl*; **Wẹt|ter|mann** M *pl* **-männer** weatherman; **Wẹt|ter|mel|dung** F weather *or* meteorological report

wẹt|tern ['vɛtɐn] VI *impers* **es wettert** it's thundering and lightening, there's a thunderstorm VI to curse and swear; **gegen** *or* **auf etw** *(acc)* **~** to rail against sth

Wẹt|ter-: **Wẹt|ter|prog|no|se** F *(Aus)* weather forecast; **Wẹt|ter|pro|phet** M *(hum)* weatherman *(inf)*;; **Wẹt|ter|pro|phe|tin** F *(hum)* weather girl *(inf)*; **Wẹt|ter|re|gel** F weather maxim *or* saying; **Wẹt|ter|sa|tel|lit** M weather satellite; **Wẹt|ter|schacht** M *(Min)* ventilation shaft; **Wẹt|ter|schei|de** F weather *or* meteorological divide; **Wẹt|ter|schiff** NT weather ship; **Wẹt|ter|sei|te** F windward side, side exposed to the weather; **Wẹt|ter|sta|ti|on** F weather *or* meteorological station; **Wẹt|ter|stö|rung** F weather *or* meteorological disturbance; **Wẹt|ter|sturz** M sudden fall in temperature and atmospheric pressure; **Wẹt|ter|um|bruch** M *(esp Sw)*, **Wẹt|ter|um|schlag** M, **Wẹt|ter|um|schwung** M sudden change in the weather; **Wẹt|ter|ver|hält|nis|se** PL weather conditions *pl*; **Wẹt|ter|ver|schlech|te|rung** F deterioration in *or* worsening of the weather; **Wẹt|ter|vo|raus|sa|ge** F, **Wẹt|ter|vor|her|sa|ge** F weather forecast; **Wẹt|ter|war|te** F weather station; **Wẹt|ter|wech|sel** M change in the weather; **wẹt|ter|wen|disch** ADJ *(fig)* changeable, moody; **Wẹt|ter|wol|ke** F storm cloud

Wetteufel △ M → **Wettteufel**

Wẹtt-: **Wẹtt|fahrt** F race; **Wẹtt|kampf** M competition; **Wẹtt|kämp|fer(in)** M(F) competitor; **Wẹtt|kampf|sport** M competitive sport; **Wẹtt|lauf** M race; **einen ~ machen** to run a race; **ein ~ mit der Zeit** *or* **gegen die Zeit** a race against time; **wẹtt|lau|fen** VI *(infin only)* to run a race/races; **Wẹtt|läu|fer(in)** M(F) runner (in a/the race)

wẹtt+ma|chen VT *sep* to make up for; *Verlust etc* to make good; *Rückstand, Vorsprung* to make up

Wẹtt-: **wẹtt|ren|nen** VI *(infin only)* to run a race; **Wẹtt|ren|nen** NT *(lit, fig)* race; **ein ~ machen** to run a race; **Wẹtt|ru|dern** NT **-s, -** boat race; **Wẹtt|rüs|ten** NT **-s,** *no pl* arms race; **Wẹtt|schein** M betting slip; **Wẹtt|schie|ßen** NT **-s, -** shooting competition *or* contest; **Wẹtt|schuld** F betting debt; **Wẹtt|schwim|men** NT swimming competition *or* contest; **Wẹtt|sin|gen** NT *pl* **-** singing competition *or* contest; **Wẹtt|streit** M competition *(auch fig)*, contest; **mit jdm im ~ liegen** to compete with sb; **mit jdm in ~ treten** to enter into competition with sb; **Wẹtt|teu|fel** M *(inf)* betting bug *(inf)*; **ihn hat der ~ gepackt** he's got the betting bug *(inf)*; **Wẹtt|tur|nen** NT *pl* **-** gymnastics competition; **Wẹtt|zet|tel** M betting slip *or* ticket

wẹt|zen ['vɛtsn] VT to whet VI *aux sein (inf)* to scoot *(inf)*

Wẹtz-: **Wẹtz|stahl** M steel; **Wẹtz|stein** M whetstone

WEU [ve:le:'lu:] F **-** *abbr von* **Westeuropäische Union** WEU

WEZ [ve:le:'tsɛt] *abbr von* **Westeuropäische Zeit** GMT

WG [ve:'ge:] F **-, -s** *abbr von* **Wohngemeinschaft**

WGB [ve:ge:'be:] M **-** *abbr von* **Weltgewerkschaftsbund** WFTU

WG-: **WG-Be|woh|ner(in)** M(F) flat *(Brit) or* apartment *or* house sharer; **WG-Zim|mer** NT room in a shared flat *etc*

Whirl|pool ['wœrlpu:l, 'wø:ɐl-] M **-s, -s** ≈ Jacuzzi®

Whis|ky ['wɪski] M **-s, -s** whisky, whiskey *(US)*; *(schottischer auch)* Scotch; *(irischer)* whiskey; *(amerikanischer Maiswhisky)* bourbon (whiskey); *(amerikanischer Roggenwhisky)* rye (whiskey); **~ mit Eis** whisk(e)y and ice, whisk(e)y on the rocks; **~ (mit) Soda** whisk(e)y and soda

Whist [wɪst] NT **-(e)s,** *no pl* whist

wịch *pret von* **weichen**

Wịchs [vɪks] M **-es, -e** *(Aus)* F **-, -en in vollem** *or (Aus)* **voller ~** *(Univ)* in full dress, in full regalia; **sich in ~ werfen** *(Univ, fig)* to dress up

Wịchs|bir|ne ['vɪks-] F *(sl)* wanker *(Brit sl)*, jerk-off *(US sl)*

Wịch|se ['vɪksə] F **-, -n** a *(dated: = Schuhwichse)* shoe polish; **schwarze ~** blacking *(dated)*, black shoe polish b *no pl (inf: = Prügel)* **~ bekommen** to get a hiding *(inf)*

wịch|sen ['vɪksn] VT a *auch vi (dated) Schuhe* to polish; *(mit schwarzer Wichse)* to black *(dated)*; *Schnurrbart, Boden etc* to wax → *auch* **gewichst** b *(inf: = prügeln)* **jdn (ganz schön) ~** to give sb a (good) hiding *(inf)* VI *(sl: = onanieren)* to jerk *or* toss off *(sl)*, to (have a) wank *(Brit vulg)*

Wịch|ser ['vɪksɐ] M **-s, -** *(sl)* wanker *(Brit sl)*, jerk-off *(US sl)*

Wịchs|lein|wand ['vɪks-] F *(Aus: = Wachstuch)* oilcloth

Wịcht [vɪçt] M **-(e)s, -e** *(= Kobold)* goblin, wight *(obs)*; *(= kleiner Mensch)* titch *(inf)*; *(= Kind)* (little) creature; *(fig: = verachtenswerter Mensch)* scoundrel; **ein armer ~** a poor devil *(inf) or* wretch; *(= Kind)* a poor little thing *or* creature

Wịch|te ['vɪçtə] F **-, -n** *(Phys)* density

Wịch|tel ['vɪçtl] M **-s, -** a *(auch* **Wichtelmännchen)** gnome; *(= Kobold)* goblin, imp; *(= Heinzelmännchen)* brownie b *(bei Pfadfinderinnen)* Brownie

wịch|tig ['vɪçtɪç] ✪ 28.1, 53.1, 53.2, 53.6 ADJ important; **eine ~e Miene machen** to put on an air of importance; **alles Wichtige** everything of importance; **Wichtigeres zu tun haben** to have more important things to do, to have better things to do; **nichts Wichtigeres zu tun haben** to have nothing better to do; **das Wichtigste** *(= die wichtigste Sache)* the most important thing; *(= die wichtigsten Einzelheiten)* the most important details
ADV **sich selbst/etw (zu) ~ nehmen** to take oneself/sth (too) seriously; **es mit etw ~ haben** *(inf)* to take sth (very) seriously; **du hasts aber ~!** *(inf)* what's all the fuss about?; **sich** *(dat)* **~ vorkommen** to be full of oneself → **wichtigmachen, wichtigtun**

Wịch|tig|keit F **-, -en** importance; **einer Sache** *(dat)* **große** *etc* **~ beimessen** *or* **beilegen** to place great *etc* importance on sth

Wịch|tig-: **wịch|tig+ma|chen** VR *sep* to be full of one's own importance, to be self-important *or* pompous; **er will sich nur ~** he just wants to get attention, he's trying to make himself seem important; **sich mit etw ~** to go on and on about sth; **Wịch|tig|ma|cher(in)** *(Aus)* M(F) = **Wichtigtuer(in)**; **Wịch|tig|tu|er**

[-tu:ɐ] M **-s, -**, **Wich|tig|tu|e|rin** [-tu:ərɪn] F **-, -nen** *(pej)* pompous ass *or* idiot; **Wich|tig|tu|e|rei** [-tu:əˈrai] F *(pej)* pomposity, pompousness; **wich|tig|tu|e|risch** [-tu:ərɪʃ] ADJ pompous; **wich|tig+tun** *sep irreg* VI *(inf: sich aufspielen)* to be full of one's own importance VR = **wichtigmachen**

Wi|cke [ˈvɪkə] F **-, -n** *(Bot)* vetch; *(= Gartenwicke)* sweet pea

Wi|ckel [ˈvɪkl] M **-s, -** **a** *(Med)* compress **b** *(= Rolle)* reel, spool; *(= Lockenwickel)* roller, curler **c** *(inf)* **jdn am** *or* **beim ~ packen** *or* **nehmen** *or* **kriegen/haben** to grab/have sb by the scruff of the neck; *(fig)* to give sb a good talking to *(inf)*; *(stärker)* to have sb's guts for garters *(Brit inf)*, to have sb for dinner *(inf)*

Wi|ckel-: **Wi|ckel|auf|la|ge** F changing mat; **Wi|ckel|blu|se** F wraparound blouse; **Wi|ckel|ga|ma|sche** F puttee; **Wi|ckel|kind** NT babe in arms; **Wi|ckel|kleid** NT wraparound dress; **Wi|ckel|kom|mo|de** F baby's changing unit *or* station

wi|ckeln [ˈvɪkln] VT **a** *(= schlingen)* to wind *(um* round); *(Tech) Spule, Transformator etc* to coil, to wind; *Verband etc* to bind; *Haare, Locken* to put in rollers *or* curlers; *Zigarren* to roll; *(= umschlagen)* to wrap; **sich** *(dat)* **eine Decke um die Beine ~** to wrap a blanket around one's legs → **Finger, schiefgewickelt**

b *(= einwickeln)* to wrap *(in +acc* in); *(mit Verband)* to dress, to bandage; **einen Säugling ~** to put on a baby's nappy *(Brit) or* diaper *(US)*; *(= frisch wickeln)* to change a baby's nappy *(Brit) or* diaper *(US)*

VR to wrap oneself *(in +acc* in); **sich um etw ~** to wrap itself around sth; *(Schlange, Pflanze)* to wind itself around sth

Wi|ckel-: **Wi|ckel|raum** M *(in Kaufhaus etc)* mothers' (and babies') room *(Brit)*, nursing room *(Brit)*, (baby) changing room; **Wi|ckel|rock** M wraparound skirt; **Wi|ckel|tisch** M baby's changing table

Wid|der [ˈvɪdɐ] M **-s, -** *(Zool)* ram; *(Astrol)* Aries; *(Mil, Hist)* battering ram; **er/sie ist (ein) ~** *(Astrol)* he's/she's an Arian *or* (an) Aries; **der ~** *(Astron, Astrol)* Aries, the Ram

Wid|der-: **Wid|der|frau** F *(Astrol inf)* (female) Arian, Aries (woman); **Wid|der|mann** M *pl* **-männer** *(Astrol inf)* (male) Arian, Aries (man)

wi|der [ˈvi:dɐ] PREP *+acc (geh)* against; *(= entgegen auch)* contrary to; **~ Erwarten** contrary to expectations; **~ alles Erwarten** against all expectations, contrary to all expectations → **Für, löcken, Wille**

Wi|der-: **wi|der|bors|tig** ADJ contrary, perverse; **Wi|der|bors|tig|keit** [ˈvi:dɐbɔrstɪçkait] F **-,** *no pl* contrariness, perversity; **Wi|der|druck** M *pl* **-drucke** *(Typ)* perfecting

wi|der|fah|ren [vi:dɐˈfa:rən] *ptp* **widerfahren** VI IMPERS *insep irreg aux sein +dat (geh)* to happen *(jdm* to sb); *(Unglück etc)* to befall *(jdm* sb) *(liter)*; **ihr ist eine Ungerechtigkeit ~** she has met with an injustice; **mir ist in meinem Leben schon viel Gutes ~** life has given me many good things

Wi|der-: **Wi|der|ha|ken** M barb; *(an größerer Harpune)* fluke; **Wi|der|hall** M echo, reverberation; **(bei jdm) keinen ~ finden** *(Interesse)* to meet with no response (from sb); *(Gegenliebe etc)* not to be reciprocated (by sb); **wi|der+hal|len** VI *sep or (rare) insep* to echo *or* reverberate *(von* with); **Wi|der|hand|lung** F *(Sw)* contravention, violation; **Wi|der|kla|ge** F counterclaim; **wi|der+klin|gen** VI *sep irreg* to resound *or* ring *(von* with)

wi|der|leg|bar ADJ refutable, disprovable; **nicht ~** irrefutable

wi|der|le|gen [vi:dɐˈle:gn] *ptp* **widerlegt** VT *insep Behauptung etc* to refute, to disprove; *jdn* to prove wrong

Wi|der|le|gung F **-, -en** refutation, disproving

wi|der|lich [ˈvi:dɐlɪç] ADJ disgusting, revolting; *Mensch* repulsive; *Kopfschmerzen* nasty ADV *sich benehmen* disgustingly; **~ riechen/schmecken** to smell/taste disgusting

Wi|der|lich|keit F **-, -en** *(= widerliche Sache)* disgusting *or* revolting thing; *(von Mensch)* repulsiveness; *(von Kopfschmerzen)* nastiness; **die ~ des Anblicks** the disgusting *or* revolting sight; **die ~ seines Benehmens** his disgusting *or* revolting behaviour *(Brit) or* behavior *(US)*

Wi|der|ling [ˈvi:dɐlɪŋ] M **-s, -e** *(pej inf)* repulsive creep *(inf)*

wi|dern [ˈvi:dɐn] VT, VT IMPERS **es/etw widert jdn** sb finds it/sth disgusting *or* revolting

Wi|der-: **wi|der|na|tür|lich** ADJ unnatural; *(= pervers auch)* perverted; **Wi|der|na|tür|lich|keit** F unnaturalness; *(= Perversität auch)* perversion; **Wi|der|part** M *(old, geh: = Gegner)* adversary, opponent; **jdm ~ bieten** *or* **geben** *(geh)* to oppose sb

wi|der|ra|ten [vi:dɐˈra:tn] *ptp* **widerraten** VI *insep irreg (old)* **jdm ~, etw zu tun** to advise *or* counsel sb against doing sth

wi|der|recht|lich ADJ unlawful, illegal ADV illegally; **etw ~ betreten** *(Gelände)* to trespass (up)on sth; *Gebäude* to enter sth unlawfully *or* illegally; **sich** *(dat)* **etw ~ aneignen** to misappropriate sth

Wi|der|re|de F **a** *(= Widerspruch)* contradiction, argument; **keine ~!** no arguing!, don't argue!; **er duldet keine ~** he will not have any arguments about it; **ohne ~** without protest *or* demur **b** *(= Antwort)* reply; **Rede und ~** dialogue *(Brit)*, dialog *(US)*

Wi|der|ruf M revocation *(auch Jur)*, withdrawal, cancellation; *(von Aussage, Geständnis, Behauptung)* retraction *(auch Jur)*, withdrawal; *(von Befehl)* cancellation, countermand; *(von ketzerischen Behauptungen)* recantation; **~ leisten** to recant; **bis auf ~** until revoked *or* withdrawn, until cancelled *(Brit) or* canceled *(US)*

wi|der|ru|fen [vi:dɐˈru:fn] *ptp* **widerrufen** *insep irreg* VT *Erlaubnis, Anordnung etc* to revoke *(auch Jur)*, to withdraw, to cancel; *Aussage, Geständnis, Behauptung* to retract *(auch Jur)*, to withdraw; *Befehl* to cancel, to countermand VI *(bei Verleumdung etc)* to withdraw; *(esp bei ketzerischen Behauptungen)* to recant

wi|der|ruf|lich [ˈvi:dɐru:flɪç, vi:dɐˈru:flɪç] *(form)* ADJ revocable, revokable ADV until revoked *or* withdrawn

Wi|der-: **Wi|der|sa|cher** [ˈvi:dɐzaxɐ] M **-s, -**, **Wi|der|sa|che|rin** [-ərɪn] F **-, -nen** adversary, antagonist, opponent; **wi|der+schal|len** VI *sep (old)* to echo *or* reverberate *(von* with); **Wi|der|schein** M *(liter)* reflection; **wi|der|set|zen** [vi:dɐˈzɛtsn] *ptp* **widersetzt** VR *insep* **sich jdm/einer Sache ~** to oppose sb/sth; *einem Polizisten, der Festnahme* to resist sb/sth; *einem Befehl, einer Aufforderung* to refuse to comply with sth; **wi|der|setz|lich** [vi:dɐˈzɛtslɪç, ˈvi:dɐ-] ADJ contrary, obstreperous; *Befehlsempfänger* insubordinate; **Wi|der|sinn** M, *no pl* absurdity, illogicality; **wi|der|sin|nig** ADJ absurd, nonsensical; **wi|der|spens|tig** ADJ stubborn; *Kind* unruly, wilful; *Material, Plastik* difficult to work with; *Haar* unruly, unmanageable; **„Der Widerspenstigen Zähmung"** "The Taming of the Shrew"; **Wi|der|spens|tig|keit** [ˈvi:dɐʃpɛnstɪkkait] F **-, -en** stubbornness; *(von Kind)* unruliness, wilfulness; *(von Haar)* unruliness; **ein Material von einer gewissen ~** a material that is somewhat difficult to work with; **wi|der+spie|geln** *sep* VT *(lit, fig)* to reflect; *Gegenstand auch* to mirror VR *(lit, fig)* to be reflected/mirrored; **Wi|der|spie|ge|lung** F, **Wi|der|spieg|lung** [-ʃpi:glʊŋ] F **-, -en** reflection; **Wi|der|spiel** NT **das ~ der Kräfte** the play of forces

wi|der|spre|chen [vi:dɐˈʃprɛçn] ✪ 53.6 *ptp* **widersprochen** *insep irreg* [vi:dɐˈʃprɔxn] VI **jdm/einer Sache ~** to contradict sb/sth; *(= nicht übereinstimmen mit) den Tatsachen etc auch* to be inconsistent with sth; **da muss ich aber ~** I've got to *(Brit) or* I have to contradict you there; **das widerspricht meinen Grundsätzen** that goes *or* is against my principles VR *(einander)* to contradict each other *or* one another; *(= nicht übereinstimmen: Aussagen etc auch)* to be inconsistent, to conflict; **sich (selbst) ~** to contradict oneself

wi|der|spre|chend ADJ **(sich** *or* **einander) ~** contradictory, conflicting, inconsistent

Wi|der|spruch M **a** *(= Gegensätzlichkeit)* contradiction *(auch Philos)*; *(= Unvereinbarkeit)* inconsistency; **ein ~ in sich selbst** a contradiction in terms; **in** *or* **im ~ zu** contrary to; **in ~ zu** *or* **mit etw geraten** to come into conflict with sth, to contradict sth; **sich in ~ zu jdm/etw setzen** to go against sb/sth; **in** *or* **im ~ zu** *or* **mit etw stehen** to conflict with sth, to stand in contradiction to sth, to be contrary to sth

b *(= Widerrede)* contradiction, dissent; *(= Protest)* protest; *(= Ablehnung)* opposition; *(Jur)* appeal; **kein ~!** don't argue!; **er duldet keinen ~** he won't have any argument *(Brit)*, he won't stand for any back talk *(US)*; **es erhob sich ~** there was opposition *(gegen* to), there were protests *(gegen* against); **~ erheben** to protest; **~ einlegen** to lodge a protest; *(Jur)* to appeal; **~ gegen etw einlegen** to protest against sth; **~ erfahren, auf ~ stoßen** to meet with opposition *(bei* from)

wi|der|sprüch|lich [-ʃprʏçlɪç] ADJ contradictory; *Erzählung, Theorie auch, Verhalten* inconsistent ADV contradictorily; *sich verhalten auch* inconsistently

Wi|der|sprüch|lich|keit F **-, -en** contradiction, contradictoriness; *(von Erzählung, Theorie auch, von Verhalten)* inconsistency

Wi|der|spruchs-: **wi|der|spruchs|frei** ADJ *Theorie* consistent; **Wi|der|spruchs|geist** M, *no pl* spirit of opposition; **Wi|der|spruchs|kla|ge** F *(Jur)* interference proceedings *pl*; **wi|der|s|pruchs|los** ADJ *(= unangefochten) Zustimmung, Annahme* unopposed; *(= ohne Einwände) Zuhören, Befolgen von Anordnung* without contradiction; *(= folgsam) Kind, Gehorchen* unprotesting; *(= nicht widersprüchlich) Theorie, Mensch, Verhalten* consistent ADV *(= unangefochten)* without opposition; *(= ohne Einwände)* without contradiction; *(= folgsam)* without protest; **wi|der|spruchs|voll** ADJ full of contradictions; *(= voller Unvereinbarkeiten)* full of inconsistencies

Wi|der|stand M resistance *(auch Pol, Elec etc)*; *(im 2. Weltkrieg)* Resistance; *(= Ablehnung)* opposition; *(Elec: Bauelement)* resistor; **zum ~ aufrufen** to call upon people to resist; **es erhebt sich ~** there is resistance; **jdm/einer Sache** *or* **gegen jdn/etw ~ leisten** to resist sb/sth, to put up *or* offer *(form)* resistance to sb/sth; **seine inneren Widerstände überwinden** to overcome one's inhibitions; **~ gegen die Staatsgewalt** obstructing an officer in the performance of his duties *(Brit) or* in the line of duty → **Weg a**

Wi|der|stands-: **Wi|der|stands|bei|wert** M drag factor; **Wi|der|stands|be|we|gung** F resistance movement; *(im 2. Weltkrieg)* Resistance movement; **wi|der|stands|fä|hig** ADJ robust; *Pflanze* hardy; *(Med, Tech etc)* resistant *(gegen* to); **Wi|der|stands|fä|hig|keit** F robustness; *(von Pflanze)* hardiness; *(Med, Tech etc)* resistance *(gegen* to); **Wi|der|stands|kämp|fer(in)** M(F) member of the resistance; *(im 2. Weltkrieg)* member of the Resistance, Resistance fighter; **Wi|der|stands|kraft** F (power of) resistance; **wi|der|stands|los** ADJ ADV without resistance; *(Phys)* non-resistant; **Wi|der|stands|mes|ser** M **-s, -** *(Elec)* ohmmeter; **Wi|der|stands|nest** NT *(Mil)* pocket of resistance

wi|der|ste|hen [vi:dɐˈʃte:ən] *ptp* **widerstanden** [vi:dɐˈʃtandn] VI *insep irreg +dat* **a** *(= nicht nachgeben)* to resist; *(= standhalten)* to withstand; **einer Versuchung/einem Erdbeben ~ können** to be able to resist a temptation/withstand an earthquake **b** *(= anekeln)* **etw widersteht jdm** sb loathes sth

wi|der|stre|ben [vi:dɐˈʃtre:bn] *ptp* **widerstrebt** VI *insep +dat* **jdm/einer Sache ~** *(Mensch)* to oppose sb/sth; **etw widerstrebt einer Sache** sth conflicts with sth; **jds sittlichem Empfinden/jds Interessen** *etc* **~** to go against sb's moral sense/sb's interests *etc;* **das widerstrebt mir** *(= das möchte ich nicht tun)* I can't do things like that, I can't be like that; **es widerstrebt mir, so etwas zu tun** *(= lehne ich ab)* it goes against the grain *(Brit) or* my grain *(US)* to do anything like that; *(= möchte ich nicht)* I am reluctant to do anything like that

Wi|der|stre|ben NT reluctance; **nach anfänglichem ~** after some initial reluctance

wi|der|stre|bend ADJ *(= gegensätzlich) Interessen* conflicting; *(= widerwillig, zögernd)* reluctant; **mit ~en Gefühlen** with (some) reluctance ADV *(widerwillig)* unwillingly, reluctantly

Wi|der|streit M *(geh)* conflict; **im** *or* **in ~ zu etw stehen** to be in conflict with sth

wi|der|strei|tend ADJ *(geh)* **(einander) ~** conflicting

wi|der+tö|nen VI *sep* to echo; **seine Worte tönten ihr noch im Ohr wider** his words were still ringing in her ears

wi|der|wär|tig [-vɛrtɪç] ADJ *Verhalten* offensive, objectionable; *(= ekelhaft)* disgusting; *Aufgabe, Arbeit, Verhalten* objectionable; **etw ist jdm ~** sb finds sth offensive/disgusting/objectionable ADV **~ schmecken/stinken** to taste/smell disgusting

Wi|der|wär|tig|keit F **-, -en** **a** *no pl* offensiveness; *(von Arbeit)* objectionable nature; **die ~ dieses Essens** this disgusting food **b** *(= widerwärtige Tat)* unpleasantness

Wi|der|wil|le M *(= Abscheu, Ekel)* disgust *(gegen* for), revulsion; *(= Abneigung)* distaste *(gegen* for), aversion *(gegen* to); *(= Widerstreben)* reluctance; **etw mit größtem ~n tun** to do sth with the greatest reluctance; **etw mit größtem ~n trinken** to drink sth with intense distaste

wi|der|wil|lig ADJ reluctant, unwilling ADV reluctantly, unwillingly

Wi|der|wor|te PL answering *or* talking back *sing;* **~ geben** *or* **machen** to answer *or* talk back; **er tat es ohne ~** he did it without protest

wid|men [ˈvɪtmən] VT **jdm etw ~** to dedicate sth to sb; *(= schenken, verwenden auf)* to devote sth to sb VR *+dat* to devote oneself to; *(= sich kümmern um) den Gästen etc* to attend to; *einem Problem, einer Aufgabe* to apply oneself to, to attend to; **nun kann ich mich dir/dieser Aufgabe ganz ~** I can now give you/this task my undivided attention

Wid|mung [ˈvɪtmʊŋ] F **-, -en** *(in Buch etc)* dedication *(an +acc* to)

wid|rig [ˈvi:drɪç] ADJ adverse; *Winde, Umstände auch* unfavourable *(Brit),* unfavorable *(US)*

wid|ri|gen|falls ADV *(form)* if this is not the case, otherwise; *(Nebensatz einleitend)* failing which

Wid|rig|keit F **-, -en** adversity; **wegen der ~ des Wetters** because of the unfavourable *(Brit) or* unfavorable *(US)* weather; **allen ~en zum Trotz** in the face of great adversity

wie [vi:] INTERROG ADV **a** how; **~ anders ...?** how else ...?; **~ schwer/oft** *etc***?** how heavy/often *etc*?; **~ viele?** how many?; **~ das?** how come?; **~ ist dir (zumute** *or* **zu Mute)?** how do you feel?; **aber frag (mich) nicht ~!** but don't ask me how!; **~ wärs (mit uns beiden** *etc***)** *(inf)* how about it? *(inf)*; **~ wärs mit einem Whisky?** *(inf)* how about a whisky?; **~ wäre es, wenn du mir ein Bier bezahlen würdest?** how *or* how's *(inf)* about (you) buying me a beer?

b *(= welcher Art)* **~ wars auf der Party/in Italien?** what was it like at the party/in Italy?, what was the party/Italy like?, how was the party/Italy?; **~ ist er (denn)?** what's he like?; **~ war das Wetter?** what was the weather like?, how was the weather?; **~ ist es eigentlich, wenn ...?** what's the situation if ...?, what happens if ...?; **~ war das (noch mal genau) mit dem Unfall?** what (exactly) happened in the accident?; **und ~ ist es mit deinem Job?** and what about your job?; **Sie wissen ja, ~ das so ist** well, you know how it is

c *(= was)* **~ heißt er/das?** what's he/it called?; **~ nennt man das?** what is that called?; **~?** what?; **~ bitte?, ~ war das?** *(inf)* **~ meinen** *or* **belieben?** *(inf)* sorry?, pardon?, come again? *(inf)*; **~ bitte?!** *(entrüstet)* I beg your pardon!

d *(in Ausrufen)* how; **und ~!, aber ~!** and how! *(inf)*; **~ groß er ist!** how big he is!, isn't he big!; **~ schrecklich!** how terrible!; **~ haben wir gelacht, als ...** how we laughed when ...

e *(= nicht wahr?)* eh; **das macht dir Spaß, ~?** you like that, don't you?; **das macht dir keinen Spaß, ~?** you don't like that, do you?

ADV **a** *(relativ)* **die Art, ~ sie geht** the way (in which) she walks; **in dem Maße, ~ ...** to the same extent that ...; **in dem Stil, ~ er jetzt Mode ist** in the style which *or* that is now fashionable; **es war ein Sonnenuntergang, ~ er noch nie einen gesehen hatte** it was a sunset the like of which he had never seen before

b *(in Verbindung mit auch)* **~ stark du auch sein magst** however strong you may be; **~ auch immer du das machen wirst** however you are going to do it, whatever way you are going to do it; **~ sehr ... auch** however much; **~ sie auch alle heißen** whatever they're called

CONJ **a** *(vergleichend) (wenn sich Vergleich auf adj, adv bezieht)* as; *(wenn sich Vergleich auf n bezieht, bei Apposition)* like; **so ... ~** as ... as; **so lang ~ breit** the same length and width, as long as it *etc* is wide; **weiß ~ Schnee** (as) white as snow; **mutig ~ ein Löwe** as brave as a lion; **eine Nase ~ eine Kartoffel** a nose like a potato; **ein Mann ~ er** a man like him, a man such as he *(form)*; **in einer Lage ~ dieser** in a situation like this *or* such as this; **er ist Lehrer, ~ sein Vater es war** he is a teacher like his father was *(inf) or* as was his father; **T ~ Theodor** "t" as in "Tommy"; *(bei Rundfunk etc)* t for Tommy; **er ist intelligent, ~ wir** he is intelligent like us; **~ gewöhnlich/immer** as usual/always *or* ever; **ich fühlte mich ~ betrunken** I felt (as if I were *or* was) drunk; **ich fühlte mich ~ im Traum** I felt as if I were *or* was *or* like I was *(inf)* dreaming; **~ sie nun (ein)mal ist, musste sie ...** the way she is she just had to ...; **~ du weißt/man sagt** as you know/they say; **~ noch nie** as never before

b *(= zum Beispiel)* **~ (zum Beispiel** *or* **etwa)** such as (for example)

c *(incorrect: = als)* **größer/schöner ~** bigger/more beautiful than; **nichts ~ Ärger** *etc* nothing but trouble *etc*

d *(= und)* as well as; **Alte ~ Junge** old and young alike

e *(inf)* **~ wenn** as if *or* though

f *(bei Verben der Gefühlsempfindung)* **er sah, ~ es geschah** he saw it happen; **sie spürte, ~ es kalt wurde** she felt it getting cold; **er hörte, ~ der Regen fiel** he heard the rain falling

g *(zeitlich: = als)* **~ ich mich umdrehte, sah ich ...** as I turned around, I saw ..., turning around, I saw ...; **~ ich mit der Schule fertig war, ...** *(inf)* when I was finished with school, ...

Wie [vi:] NT **-s,** *no pl* **das ~ spielt dabei keine Rolle** how (it'll happen/it'll be done *etc*) is unimportant; **dass es geschehen muss, ist klar, nur das ~ ist noch ein Problem** it's clear that it has to happen, the only problem is how; **das ~ und Wann werden wir später besprechen** we'll talk about how and when later

Wie|de|hopf [ˈvi:dəhɔpf] M **-(e)s, -e** hoopoe

wie|der [ˈvi:dɐ] ADV **a** again; **~ nüchtern/glücklich** *etc* sober/happy *etc* again; **immer ~, ~ und ~** again and again; **~ mal, (ein)mal ~** (once) again; **komm doch ~ mal vorbei** come and see me/us again; **~ ist ein Jahr vorbei** another year has passed; **~ was anderes** *or* **Neues** something else again, something quite different; **wie, schon ~?** what, again?; **~ da** back (again); **da bin ich ~!** I'm back!, here I am again!; **das ist auch ~ wahr** that's true; **da sieht man mal ~, ...** it just shows ...

b *(in Verbindung mit vb)* again; **das fällt mir schon ~ ein** I'll remember it again; **das Boot tauchte ~ auf** the boat resurfaced; **wenn die Wunde ~ aufbricht** if the wound reopens → **wiedergeboren, wiederverwendbar, wiederverwertbar**

Wie|der-, wie|der- PREF re; *(bei Verben) (= erneut, noch einmal)* again; *(= zurück)* back; **Wie|der|ab|druck** M reprint; **wie|der+auf|ar|bei|ten** *sep,* **wie|der auf|ar|bei|ten** VT to recycle; *Atommüll* to reprocess; **Wie|der|auf|ar|bei|tung** F **-, -en** recycling; *(von Atommüll)* reprocessing; **Wie|der|auf|ar|bei|tungs|an|la|ge** F recycling plant; *(für Atommüll)* reprocessing plant; **Wie|der|auf|bau** M *no pl (lit, fig)* reconstruction, rebuilding; **der ~ nach dem Krieg** post-war reconstruction; **der ~ des Hauses** the rebuilding of the house; **wie|der+auf|bau|en** *sep,* **wie|der auf|bau|en** VTI to reconstruct, to rebuild; **Wie|der|auf|bau|hil|fe** F *no pl* reconstruction aid; **wie|der+auf|be|rei|ten** *sep,* **wie|der auf|be|rei|ten** △ VT to recycle; *Atommüll, Abwasser* to reprocess → **wiederaufarbeiten**; **Wie|der|auf|be|rei|tung** F recycling; *(von Atommüll)* reprocessing; **Wie|der|auf|be|rei|tungs|an|la|ge** F recycling plant; *(für Atommüll)* reprocessing plant; **wie|der+auf|er|ste|hen** *sep irreg aux sein,* **wie|der auf|er|ste|hen** △ *irreg aux sein* VI to rise from the dead, to be resurrected; **Wie|der|auf|er|ste|hung** F resurrection; **wie|der+auf|fors|ten** *sep,* **wie|der auf|fors|ten** VTI to reforest; **wie|der+auf|füh|ren** *sep,* **wie|der auf|füh|ren** VT *Theaterstück* to revive; *Film* to reshow, to rerun; *Musikwerk* to reperform; **wie|der+auf|la|den** *sep irreg,* **wie|der auf|la|den** *irreg* VT to recharge; **wie|der+auf|le|ben** *sep aux sein,* **wie|der auf|le|ben** *aux sein* VI to revive; **Erinnerungen ~ lassen** to revive memories → *auch* **aufleben**; **Wie|der|auf|le|ben** NT, *no pl* revival; *(von Nationalismus etc auch)* resurgence; **wie|der+auf|le|gen** *sep,* **wie|der auf|le|gen** VT to republish; **Wie|der|auf|nah|me** [vi:dɐˈlaufna:mə] F **a** *(von Tätigkeit, Gespräch etc)* resumption; *(von Beziehungen)* re-establishment, resumption; *(von Gedanken, Idee)* readoption; *(von Thema)* reversion *(+gen* to); **die ~ des Verfahrens** *(Jur)* the reopening of proceedings **b** *(von verstoßenem Menschen)* taking back; *(im Verein etc)* readmittance, reacceptance; *(von Patienten)* readmission; **Wie|der|auf|nah|me|ver|fah|ren** NT *(Jur) (im Zivilrecht)* rehearing; *(im Strafrecht)* retrial; **wie|der+auf|neh|men** *sep irreg,* **wie|der auf|neh|men** *irreg* VT **a** *(= wieder beginnen)* to resume; *Beziehungen* to re-establish, to resume; *Gedanken, Idee, Hobby* to take up again; *Thema* to revert to; *(Jur) Verfahren* to reopen **b** *verstoßenen Menschen* to take back; *(in Verein etc)* to readmit, to reaccept; *Patienten* to readmit; **wie|der+auf|rich|ten** *sep,* **wie|der auf|rich|ten** VT *(fig) jdn* to give new heart to; **wie|der+auf|rüs|ten** *sep irreg,* **wie|der auf|rüs|ten** to rearm; **jdn moralisch ~** to raise sb's morale → *auch* **aufrüsten**; **Wie|der|auf|rüs|tung** F rearmament; **jds moralische ~** the raising of sb's morale; **Wie|der|aus|fuhr** [vi:dɐˈlausfu:ɐ] F re-export; **wie|der+aus|füh|ren** *sep,* **wie|der aus|füh|ren** VT to re-export; **Wie|der|be|ginn** M recommencement, restart; *(von Schule)* reopening; **wie|der+be|kom|men** *ptp* **wiederbekommen** VT *sep irreg* to get back; **das bekommst du wieder, du gemeines Stück** I'll get my own back, you bastard! *(Brit sl)*, I'll get back at you, you dirty skunk! *(US sl)*; **wie|der+be|le|ben** VT *sep Bewusstlosen* to revive, to resuscitate; **wie|der be|le|ben** VT *(fig) Brauch etc* to revive, to resurrect; *Wirtschaft* to revive; **Wie|der|be|le|bung** F resuscitation, revival; *(fig)* revival, resurrection; **Wie|der|be|-**

le|bungs|ver|such M attempt at resuscitation; *(fig)* attempt at revival; **~e bei jdm anstellen** to attempt to revive *or* resuscitate sb

wie|der+be|schaf|fen *ptp* **wiederbeschafft** VT *sep* to replace; *(= zurückbekommen)* to recover

Wie|der|be|schaf|fung F replacement; *(= Zurückbekommen)* recovery

Wie|der|be|schaf|fungs- *(Comm)*: **Wie|der|be|schaf|fungs|kos|ten** PL replacement cost *sing*; **Wie|der|be|schaf|fungs|wert** M replacement value

Wie|der-: **wie|der+be|set|zen** *sep*, **wie|der be|set|zen** VT **eine Stelle ~** to fill a vacancy; **wie|der+be|waff|nen** *sep*, **wie|der be|waff|nen** VR to rearm; **Wie|der|be|waff|nung** F rearmament; **wie|der+brin|gen** VT *sep irreg* to bring back; **wie|der+ein|bür|gern** *sep*, **wie|der ein|bür|gern** VT to renaturalize; **wie|der+ein|fin|den** *sep irreg*, **wie|der ein|fin|den** *irreg* VR to turn up again; **Wie|der|ein|fuhr** [vi:dɐˈlainfuːɐ] F reimport(ation); **wie|der+ein|füh|ren** *sep*, **wie|der ein|füh|ren** VT to reintroduce; *Todesstrafe auch* to bring back; *(Comm) Waren* to reimport; **Wie|der|ein|füh|rung** F reintroduction; **wie|der+ein|glie|dern** *sep*, **wie|der ein|glie|dern** VT to reintegrate (*in +acc* into); **einen Straftäter in die Gesellschaft ~** to rehabilitate a criminal offender; **Wie|der|ein|glie|de|rung** F reintegration; **die ~ eines Straftäters in die Gesellschaft** the rehabilitation of a criminal offender; **wie|der+ein|lie|fern** *sep*, **wie|der ein|lie|fern** VT *Kranken* to readmit (*in +acc* to); *Häftling* to reimprison; **Wie|der|ein|nah|me** [vi:dɐˈlainna:mə] F *(Mil)* recapture, retaking; **wie|der+ein|neh|men** *sep irreg*, **wie|der ein|neh|men** *irreg* VT *(Mil)* to retake, to recapture; **Wie|der|ein|rei|se** F *(in ein Land)* re-entry; **wie|der+ein|set|zen** *sep*, **wie|der ein|set|zen** VT to reinstate (*in +acc* to); **jdn als König ~** to restore sb to the throne VI *(Regen)* to start up again; *(Med: Fieber, Schmerzen, Wehen)* to recur; **Wie|der|ein|set|zung** F reinstatement; *(von König)* restoration; **Wie|der|ein|stei|ger(in)** M(F) *(in Beruf)* returnee, labour market returner *(Brit spec)*; **wie|der+ein|stel|len** *sep*, **wie|der ein|stel|len** VT to re-employ, to re-engage; *(nach ungerechtfertigter Entlassung)* to reinstate; **Wie|der|ein|stel|lung** F re-employment, re-engagement; *(nach ungerechtfertigter Entlassung)* reinstatement; **Wie|der|ein|stel|lungs|klau|sel** F reinstatement clause; **Wie|der|ein|stieg** F *(beruflich)* return (in *+acc* to); **Wie|der|ein|tritt** M reentry *(auch Space)* (*in +acc* into); **wie|der+ent|de|cken** *sep*, **wie|der ent|de|cken** △ VT *(lit, fig)* to rediscover; **Wie|der|ent|de|ckung** F rediscovery; **wie|der+er|grei|fen** *sep irreg*, **wie|der er|grei|fen** *irreg* VT to recapture; **Wie|der|er|grei|fung** [-lɛɐgraifʊŋ] F **-, -en** recapture; **wie|der+er|hal|ten** *ptp* **wiedererhalten** VT *sep irreg* to recover; **wie|der+er|ken|nen** *sep irreg*, **wie|der er|ken|nen** △ *irreg* VT to recognize; **das/er war nicht wiederzuerkennen** it/he was unrecognizable; **wie|der+er|lan|gen** *ptp* **wiedererlangt** VT *sep* to regain; *Eigentum* to recover; **Wie|der|er|lan|gung** F regaining; *(von Eigentum)* recovery; **wie|der+er|nen|nen** *sep irreg*, **wie|der er|nen|nen** *irreg* VT to reappoint (*zu etw* (as) sth); **Wie|der|er|nen|nung** F reappointment (*zu* as); **wie|der+er|öff|nen** *sep*, **wie|der er|öff|nen** VTI to reopen; **Wie|der|er|öff|nung** F reopening; **wie|der+er|schei|nen** *sep irreg aux sein*, **wie|der er|schei|nen** *irreg aux sein* VI to reappear; *(Buch etc)* to be republished; **wie|der+er|stat|ten** *ptp* **wiedererstattet** VT *sep Unkosten etc* to refund, to reimburse (*jdm etw* sb for sth); **Wie|der|er|stat|tung** F refund(ing), reimbursement; **wie|der+er|ste|hen** *sep irreg aux sein*, **wie|der er|ste|hen** *irreg aux sein* VI to rise again; **wie|der+er|wa|chen** *sep aux sein*, **wie|der er|wa|chen** *aux sein* VI to reawake(n); **wie|der+er|we|cken** *sep*, **wie|der er|we|cken** △ VT to bring back to life, to revive *(auch fig)*; **wie|der+fin|den** *sep irreg*, **wie|der fin|den** △ *irreg* VT to find again; *(fig) Selbstachtung, Mut etc* to regain; **die Sprache ~** *(fig)* to find one's tongue again *(Brit)*, to regain one's speech *(US)* VR *(nach Schock)* to recover; **sich irgendwo ~** to find oneself somewhere; **sich** *or* **einander ~** to find each other again

Wie|der|ga|be F **a** *(von Rede, Ereignis, Vorgang)* account, report; *(= Beschreibung)* description; *(= Wiederholung: von Äußerung etc)* repetition; *(als Taste, Schaltfläche)* play **b** *(= Darbietung: von Stück etc)* rendering, rendition **c** *(= Übersetzung)* translation **d** *(= Darstellung)* representation **e** *(= Reproduktion) (von Gemälde, Farben, akustisch)* reproduction; **bei der ~** in reproduction **f** *(= Rückgabe)* return; *(von Rechten, Freiheit etc)* restitution

Wie|der|ga|be-: **Wie|der|ga|be|ge|rät** NT playback unit; **Wie|der|ga|be|treue** F fidelity of sound reproduction; **hohe ~** high fidelity

wie|der+ge|ben VT *sep irreg* **a** *Gegenstand, Geld* to give back; *(fig) Rechte, Mut etc* to restore, to give back; **jdm ein Buch ~** to give a book back to sb, to give sb his/her book back; **jdm die Freiheit ~** to restore sb's freedom, to give sb back his freedom **b** *(= erzählen)* to give an account of; *(= beschreiben)* to describe; *(= wiederholen)* to repeat; **seine Worte sind nicht wiederzugeben** his words are unrepeatable **c** *Gedicht* to recite; *Theaterstück, Musik* to perform **d** *(= übersetzen)* to translate **e** *(= darstellen, porträtieren)* to represent **f** *(= reproduzieren) Gemälde, Farbe, Ton* to reproduce **g** *(= vermitteln) Bedeutung, Gefühl, Erlebnis* to convey

Wie|der-: **wie|der|ge|bo|ren** ADJ *(lit, fig)* reborn; **~ werden** to be reborn; **Wie|der|ge|burt** F *(lit, fig)* rebirth; **Wie|der|ge|ne|sung** F recovery; **wie|der+ge|win|nen** *ptp* **wiedergewonnen** VT *sep irreg (lit, fig)* to regain; *jdn* to win back; *Land, Rohstoffe etc* to reclaim; *Geld, Selbstvertrauen* to recover; **wie|der+grü|ßen** VTI *sep* **(jdn) ~** to return sb's greeting; *(= einen ausgerichteten Gruß erwidern)* to send sb one's regards in return; *(Mil)* to return the/sb's salute; **wie|der+gut|ma|chen** *sep*, **wie|der gut|ma|chen** △ VT *Schaden* to compensate for; *Fehler* to rectify; *Beleidigung* to put right; *(= sühnen)* to atone for; *(Pol)* to make reparations for; *(Jur)* to redress; **das ist nie wiedergutzumachen** that can never be put right; **das kann ich ja gar nicht ~!** *(fig)* how on earth can I ever repay you!; **Wie|der|gut|ma|chung** F **-, -en** compensation; *(= Sühne)* atonement; *(Pol)* reparations *pl*; *(Jur)* redress; **als ~ für mein Benehmen** to make up for my behaviour *(Brit) or* behavior *(US)*; **als ~ für den Schaden** to compensate for the damage; **als ~ für den Fehler** to rectify the fault; **als ~ für die Beleidigung** to put right the insult; **wie|der+ha|ben** VT *sep irreg (inf)* to have (got) back *(Brit)*, to get back; **etw ~ wollen** to want sth back; **wie|der+her|rich|ten** *sep*, **wie|der her|rich|ten** △ VT to repair; *Zimmer* to redecorate; **wie|der+her|stel|len** *sep*, **wie|der her|stel|len** △ VT *Gebäude, Ordnung, Frieden, Demokratie, Gesundheit* to restore; *Vertrauen, Glaubwürdigkeit auch, Beziehungen* to re-establish; *Patienten* to restore to health; *(Comput) Datei, Daten* to recover; *minimiertes Fenster* to restore; *(beim Bearbeiten) rückgängig gemachte Aktion* to redo; **von einer Krankheit wiederhergestellt sein** to have recovered from an illness; **Wie|der|her|stel|lung** F *(von Gebäude, Ordnung, Frieden, Gesundheit)* restoration; *(von Beziehungen)* re-establishment; **Wie|der|her|stel|lungs|kos|ten** PL restoration costs *pl*

wie|der|hol|bar [vi:dɐˈho:lba:ɐ] ADJ repeatable; **leicht/schwer ~** easy/hard to repeat; **das ist nicht ~** that can't be repeated

wie|der|ho|len [vi:dɐˈho:lən] *ptp* **wiederholt** *insep* VTI to repeat; *(= zum zweiten Mal, mehrmals) Forderung etc* to reiterate; *(Comput: = erneut ausführen)* to retry, to try again; *(zusammenfassend)* to recapitulate; *Lernstoff* to revise, to review *(US)*; *Prüfung* to retake, to resit *(Brit)*; *(Film) Szene* to retake; *(Sport) Elfmeter etc* to retake, to take again; *Spiel* to replay; **wiederholt, was ich euch vorsage** repeat after me; **(eine Klasse** *or* **ein Jahr) ~** *(Sch)* to repeat a year VR *(Mensch)* to repeat oneself; *(Thema, Ereignis)* to recur, to be repeated; *(Dezimalstelle)* to recur; **es wiederholt sich doch alles im Leben** life has a habit of repeating itself

wie|der+ho|len [ˈvi:dɐho:lən] VT *sep (= zurückholen)* to get back

wie|der|holt [vi:dɐˈho:lt] ADJ repeated; **zu ~en Malen** repeatedly, on repeated occasions; **zum ~en Male** once again ADV repeatedly

Wie|der|ho|lung [vi:dɐˈho:lʊŋ] F **-, -en** repetition; *(von Prüfung, Filmszene)* retaking; *(von Aufführung)* repeat performance; *(von Sendung)* repeat; *(in Zeitlupe)* replay; *(von Lernstoff)* revision; *(zum zweiten Mal, mehrmals: von Forderung etc)* reiteration; *(zusammenfassend)* recapitulation; *(Sport) (von Elfmeter)* retaking, retake; *(von Spiel)* replay; **trotz zweimaliger ~ derselben Klasse** in spite of repeating the year twice

Wie|der|ho|lungs-: **Wie|der|ho|lungs|kurs** M refresher course; **Wie|der|ho|lungs|prü|fung** F *(Sch)* repeat examination; **Wie|der|ho|lungs|spiel** NT *(Sport)* replay; **Wie|der|ho|lungs|tas|te** F repeat key; **Wie|der|ho|lungs|tä|ter(in)** M(F) *(Jur) (bei erster Wiederholung)* second offender; *(bei ständiger Wiederholung)* persistent offender, recidivist *(form)*; **Wie|der|ho|lungs|zei|chen** NT *(Mus)* repeat (mark); *(Typ)* ditto mark *or* sign; *(= Tilde)* tilde; **Wie|der|ho|lungs|zwang** M *(Psych)* recidivism; *(Sprachfehler)* palilalia *(spec)*

Wie|der-: **Wie|der|hö|ren** NT **(auf) ~!** *(am Telefon)* goodbye!; *(im Hörfunk)* goodbye for now!; **Wie|der|imp|fung** F revaccination; **Wie|der|in|be|sitz|nah|me** [vi:dɐlɪnbəˈzɪtsna:mə] F *(form)* resumption of possession; **Wie|der|in|be|trieb|nah|me** [vi:dɐlɪnbəˈtri:pna:mə] F *(form)* putting into operation again; *(von U-Bahnlinie)* reopening; **Wie|der|in|stand|set|zung** [vi:dɐlɪnˈʃtantzɛtsʊŋ] F *(form)* repair, repairs *pl* (*+gen* to); **wie|der+käu|en** *sep* VT to ruminate, to chew again; *(fig inf)* to go over again and again VI to ruminate, to chew the cud; *(fig inf)* to harp on; **Wie|der|käu|er** [-kɔyɐ] M **-s, -** ruminant

Wie|der|kehr [ˈvi:dɐke:ɐ] F **-,** *no pl (geh) (= Rückkehr)* return; *(= zweites, ständiges Vorkommen)* recurrence; *(esp langweilig)* repetition; *(von Datum, Ereignis)* anniversary; **die ewige ~** the eternal recurrence

wie|der+keh|ren VI *sep aux sein (= zurückkehren)* to return; *(= sich wiederholen, wieder vorkommen)* to recur, to be repeated

wie|der|keh|rend ADJ recurring; **regelmäßig/oft ~** recurrent; **immer ~** ever-recurring; **ein jährlich ~es Fest** an annual festival

Wie|der-: **wie|der+ken|nen** *sep irreg*, **wie|der ken|nen** △ *irreg* VT *(inf)* to recognize; **wie|der+kom|men** VI *sep irreg aux sein (lit, fig)* to come back, to return; **komm doch mal wieder!** you must come again!; **wie|der+krie|gen** VT *sep (inf)* to get back; **warte nur, das kriegst du (von mir) wieder!** just you wait, I'll get my own back (on you)! *(Brit)*, just you wait, I'll get back at you! *(US)*; **Wie|der|kunft** [ˈvi:dɐkʊnft] F **-,** *no pl (liter)* return; **die ~ Christi** the Second Coming; **wie|der+lie|ben** VT *sep* to love back; **Wie|der|schau|en** NT **(auf) ~!** *(geh, S Ger, Aus, Sw)* goodbye!, good day! *(form)*; **wie|der+schen|ken** VT *sep* **jdm etw ~** to give sth back to sb; **er wurde dem Leben wiederge-**

schenkt he was restored to life; **wie|der+se|hen** VT *sep irreg* to see again; *(= wieder zusammentreffen mit auch)* to meet again; **wann sehen wir uns wieder?** when will we see each other *or* meet again?; **Wie|der|se|hen** ['vi:dɐze:ən] NT **-s, -** *(nach kürzerer Zeit)* (another) meeting; *(nach längerer Zeit)* reunion; **ich freue mich auf das ~ mit meinen Freunden/mit der Heimat** I'm looking forward to seeing my friends/to being back home again; **sie hofften auf ein baldiges ~** they hoped to see each other *or* meet again soon; **irgendwo, irgendwann gibt es ein ~** we'll meet again, don't know where, don't know when; **(auf) ~!** goodbye!; **(Auf *or* auf) ~ sagen** to say goodbye; **~ macht Freude!** *(hum)* I hope that's not the last I see of it!, I wouldn't mind having it back again!; **Wie|der|se|hens|freu|de** F **unsere ~ war groß** we were very pleased *(esp Brit)* *or* happy to see each other again; **meine ~ war groß** I was very pleased *(esp Brit)* *or* happy to see him/her *etc* again; **wie|der tun** VT *irreg* to do again; **Wie|der|tau|fe** F *(Rel)* rebaptism; **Wie|der|täu|fer(in)** M(F) *(Rel, Hist)* Anabaptist

wie|de|rum ['vi:dərʊm] ADV **a** *(= andrerseits)* on the other hand; *(= allerdings)* though; **das ist ~ richtig, daran habe ich nicht gedacht** that's quite correct, I didn't think of that **b** *(geh: = nochmals)* again, anew *(liter)* **c** *(= seinerseits etc)* in turn; **er ~ wollte ...** he, for his part, wanted ...

Wie|der-: **wie|der+ver|ei|ni|gen** *sep*, **wie|der ver|ei|ni|gen** △ VT *Menschen, Fraktionen* to reunite; *Kirche auch, Land* to reunify; **wie|der ver|ei|ni|gen** VR to reunite, to come together again; **Wie|der|ver|ei|ni|gung** F reunification; **wie|der+ver|hei|ra|ten** *sep*, **wie|der ver|hei|ra|ten** VR to remarry; **Wie|der|ver|hei|ra|tung** F remarriage; **Wie|der|ver|kauf** M resale; *(durch Einzelhandel)* retail; **wie|der+ver|kau|fen** *sep*, **wie|der ver|kau|fen** VT to resell; *(Einzelhändler)* to retail; **Wie|der|ver|käu|fer(in)** M(F) reseller; *(= Einzelhändler)* retailer; **Wie|der|ver|kaufs|preis** M resale price; **Wie|der|ver|kaufs|wert** M resale value; **wie|der+ver|pflich|ten** *sep*, **wie|der ver|pflich|ten** VR *(Mil)* to re-enlist; **wie|der|ver|wend|bar** ADJ reusable; **Wie|der|ver|wend|bar|keit** F reusability; **wie|der+ver|wen|den** *sep*, **wie|der ver|wen|den** VT to reuse; **Wie|der|ver|wen|dung** F reuse; **wie|der|ver|wert|bar** ADJ recyclable; **Wie|der|ver|wert|bar|keit** F recyclability; **wie|der+ver|wer|ten** *sep*, **wie|der ver|wer|ten** VT to recycle; **Wie|der|ver|wer|tung** F recycling; **Wie|der|vor|la|ge** F, *no pl (form)* resubmission; **zur ~** for resubmission; **Wie|der|wahl** F re-election; **eine ~ ablehnen** to decline to run for re-election; **wenn es zu einer ~ der Partei kommt** if the party is returned (to power) again; **wie|der+wäh|len** *sep*, **wie|der wäh|len** VT to re-elect; **wie|der+zu|las|sen** *sep irreg*, **wie|der zu|las|sen** *irreg* VT *Auto* to relicense; **Wie|der|zu|las|sung** F relicensing

wie|fern [vi'fɛrn] ADV = **inwiefern**

Wie|ge ['vi:gə] F **-, -n** *(lit, fig, Tech)* cradle; **seine ~ stand in Schwaben** *(geh)* his birthplace was Swabia; **es ist mir/ihm auch nicht an der ~ gesungen worden, dass ...** no-one could have foreseen that ...; **das ist ihm (schon *or* gleich) in die ~ gelegt worden** he inherited it; **damals lagst du noch in der ~** at that time you were still a babe in arms; **von der ~ bis zur Bahre** *(geh)* from the cradle to the grave; **die ~ der Demokratie** the cradle of democracy

Wie|ge|mes|ser NT chopper, chopping knife *(Brit)*, cleaver

wie|gen ['vi:gn] VT **a** *(= hin und her bewegen)* to rock; *Kopf* to shake (slowly); *Hüften* to sway; *(Wind) Äste etc* to sway; **~de Bewegung** swaying motion; **einen ~den Gang haben** to sway one's hips when one walks **b** *(= zerkleinern)* to chop up VR *(Boot etc)* to rock (gently); *(Mensch, Äste etc)* to sway; **sich im Tanz ~** to do an undulating dance; **sich in trügerischen Hoffnungen ~** to nurture false hopes

wie|gen *pret* **wog** [vo:k], *ptp* **gewogen** [gə'vo:gn] VTI *(= abwiegen)* to weigh; **ein knapp gewogenes Kilo** something short of a kilo; **wie viel wiegst du?** how heavy are you?, what do you weigh?; **schwer ~** *(fig)* to carry a lot of weight; *(Irrtum)* to be serious; **gewogen und zu leicht befunden** *(Bibl, fig)* weighed and found wanting → *auch* **gewogen**

Wie|gen-: **Wie|gen|druck** M *pl* **-drucke** incunabulum; *(Verfahren)* early printing; **Wie|gen|fest** NT *(geh)* birthday; **Wie|gen|kind** NT *(liter)* infant, babe in arms; **Wie|gen|lied** NT lullaby, cradlesong

wie|hern ['vi:ɐn] VI to neigh; *(leiser)* to whinny; **(vor Lachen) ~** to bray with laughter; **das ist ja zum Wiehern** *(inf)* that's dead funny *(Brit inf)*, that's very funny

Wien [vi:n] NT **-s** Vienna

Wie|ner ['vi:nɐ] ADJ *attr* Viennese; **~ Würstchen** frankfurter, wiener (sausage) *(esp US)*; **~ Schnitzel** Wiener schnitzel

Wie|ner ['vi:nɐ] M **-s, -**, **Wie|ne|rin** [-ərɪn] F **-, -nen** Viennese

wie|ne|risch ['vi:nərɪʃ] ADJ Viennese; **das Wienerische** Viennese, the Viennese dialect

Wie|ner|le ['vi:nɐlə] NT **-s, -** *(S Ger)*, **Wie|ner|li** ['vi:nɐli] NT **-s, -** *(Sw)* frankfurter, wiener (sausage) *(esp US)*

wie|nerln ['vi:nɐln] ['vi:nɐln], **wie|nern** ['vi:nɐn] VI *(inf)* to speak Viennese

wie|nern VT *(usu pej)* to polish, to shine

wies *pret von* **weisen**

Wie|se ['vi:zə] F **-, -n** meadow; *(inf: = Rasen)* grass, lawn; **auf der grünen ~** *(fig)* in the open countryside

wie|sehr △ [vi'ze:ɐ] CONJ → **wie ADV b**

Wie|sel ['vi:zl] NT **-s, -** weasel; **schnell *or* flink wie ein ~** quick as a flash; **laufen *or* rennen wie ein ~** to run like a hare *(Brit)* *or* rabbit *(US)*

wie|sel|flink ADJ quick, quicksilver *attr* ADV quick as a flash

wie|seln ['vi:zln] VI *aux sein* to scurry, to scuttle

Wie|sen-: **Wie|sen|blu|me** F meadow flower; **Wie|sen|grund** M *(poet)* meadow, mead *(poet)*; **Wie|sen|rain** M *(liter)* meadow's edge; **Wie|sen|schaum|kraut** NT lady's smock

Wiesn ['vi:zn] F **-, -** *(dial)* fair

wie|so [vi'zo:] INTERROG ADV why; *(= aus welchem Grund auch)* how come *(inf)*; **~ gehst du nicht?** how come you're not going? *(inf)*, why aren't you going?; **~ nicht** why not; **~ sagst du das?** why do you say that?; **~ weißt du das?** how do you know that?

wie|viel △ [vi'fi:l, 'vi:-] INTERROG ADV → **viel a**

wie|vie|ler|lei [vi'fi:lɐ'lai, 'vi:-] INTERROG ADJ *inv* how many sorts *or* kinds of; **~ verschiedene (Whiskys *etc*)?** how many different sorts *or* kinds (of whisky *etc*)?

wie|viel|mal [vi'fi:lma:l, 'vi:-] INTERROG ADV how many times

Wie|viel|te(r) [vi'fi:ltə, 'vi:-] M *decl as adj (bei Datum)* **den ~n haben wir heute?, der ~ ist heute?** what's the date today?; **am ~n (des Monats)?** what date?, what day of the month?; **der ~ ist Donnerstag?** what's the date on Thursday?

wie|viel|te(r, s) [vi'fi:ltə, 'vi:-] INTERROG ADJ **das ~ Kind ist das jetzt?** how many children is that now?; **das ~ Kind bist du? – das zweite** which child are you? – the second; **der ~ Band fehlt?** which volume is missing?; **den ~n Platz hat er im Wettkampf belegt?** where did he come in the competition?; **als Wievielter ging er durchs Ziel?** what place did he come?; **das ~ Mal *or* zum ~n Mal bist du schon in England?** how often *or* how many times have you been to England?; **am ~n September hast du Geburtstag?** what date *or* when in September is your birthday?; **das ~ Jahr bist du jetzt in Schottland?** how many years have you lived in Scotland now?; **ich habe morgen Geburtstag! – der ~ ist es denn?** it's my birthday tomorrow! – how old will you be?

wie|weit [vi'vait] CONJ to what extent, how far

wie|wohl [vi'vo:l] CONJ *(old)* **a** *(= obwohl)* although, (even) though **b** *(= dafür aber auch)* and at the same time, as well as

Wig|wam ['vɪkvam] M OR NT **-s, -s** wigwam

Wi|kin|ger ['vi:kɪŋɐ, 'vɪkɪŋɐ] M **-s, -**, **Wi|kin|ge|rin** [-ərɪn] F **-, -nen** Viking

Wi|kin|ger-: **Wi|kin|ger|schiff** NT longboat, Viking ship; **Wi|kin|ger|zeit** F age of the Vikings, Viking age

wi|kin|gisch ['vi:kɪŋɪʃ, 'vɪkɪŋɪʃ] ADJ Viking *attr*

wild [vɪlt] ADJ wild; *Schönheit auch* rugged; *Kind auch, Haar* unruly; *Stamm* savage; *(= laut, ausgelassen)* boisterous; *(= heftig) Kampf* fierce; *(= zornig) Blick* fierce, furious; *(= ungesetzlich) Parken, Zelten etc* illegal; *Streik* wildcat *attr*, unofficial; **~es Fleisch** proud flesh; **der Wilde Jäger** the Wild Huntsman; **den ~en Mann spielen** *(inf)* *or* **machen** *(inf)* to come the heavy *(Brit inf)*, to play all that *(US sl)*; **der Wilde Westen** the Wild West; **seid nicht so ~!** calm down a bit!; **jdn ~ machen** to make sb mad *(Brit inf)* *or* furious, to drive sb crazy; *(esp vor Vergnügen etc)* to drive sb wild; **~ werden** to go wild *(auch inf)*, to go nuts *or* crazy; *(Kinder: = ausgelassen werden)* to run wild; **der Bulle wurde ~** *(inf)* the bull was enraged; **ich könnte ~ werden** *(inf)* I could scream *(inf)*; **~ auf jdn/etw sein** *(inf)* to be wild *or* crazy *or* mad about sb/sth *(inf)*; **das ist nicht so *or* halb so ~** *(inf)* never mind → **Ehe, Wein**
ADV **a** *(= unordentlich)* **~ ins Gesicht hängende Haare** wild, tousled hair hanging over one's face; **~ durcheinanderliegen *or* herumliegen** to be strewn all over the place; **dann ging alles ~ durcheinander** there was chaos then **b** *(= hemmungslos)* like mad *or* crazy; *brüllen, auf jdn einschlagen, um sich schlagen* wildly; **wie ~ rennen/arbeiten** *etc* to run/work *etc* like mad; **~ drauflosreden** to talk nineteen to the dozen *(Brit)*, to talk like crazy *(US)*; **~ drauflosschreiben** to write furiously; **~ entschlossen** *(inf)* really *or* dead *(inf)* determined **c** *(= in der freien Natur)* **~ leben** to live in the wild; **~ lebend** wild, living in the wild; **~ wachsen** to grow wild; **~ wachsend** wild(-growing)

Wild [vɪlt] NT **-(e)s** [-dəs], *no pl (= Tiere, Fleisch)* game; *(= Rotwild)* deer; *(= Fleisch von Rotwild)* venison; **ein Stück ~** a head of game

Wild-: **Wild|bach** M torrent; **Wild|bahn** F hunting ground *or* preserve; **auf *or* in freier ~** in the wild; **Wild|be|stand** M game population, stock of game; **Wild|bra|ten** M roast venison; **ein ~** a roast of venison; **Wild|bret** [-brɛt] NT **-s**, *no pl* game; *(von Rotwild)* venison

Wild|card ['waildka:d] F **-, -s** *(Comput)* wildcard (character)

Wild-: **Wild|dieb(in)** M(F) poacher; **Wild|dieb|stahl** M poaching

Wil|de(r) ['vɪldə] MF *decl as adj* savage, wild man/woman; *(fig)* madman, maniac; **die ~n** the savages

Wild|en|te F wild duck

Wil|de|rei [vɪldə'rai] F **-, -en** poaching

Wil|de|rer ['vɪldərɐ] M **-s, -**, **Wil|de|rin** [-ərɪn] F **-, -nen** poacher

wil|dern ['vɪldɐn] VI *(Mensch)* to poach; *(Hund etc)* to kill game; **~der Hund** dog which kills game

Wil|dern NT **-s**, *no pl* poaching; *(von Hund etc)* killing game

Wild-: **Wild|esel** M wild ass; **Wild|fal|le** F trap set for game; **Wild|fang** M **a** *(Hunt) (Falke)* passage *or* wild-caught hawk; *(Tier)* animal captured in the wild **b** *(dated inf)* little rascal *or* devil, scamp; *(Mädchen)* tomboy; **Wild|fleisch** NT game; *(von Rotwild)* venison; **Wild|fraß** M damage caused by game; **wild|fremd** ['vɪlt'frɛmt] ADJ *(inf)* completely strange; **~e Leute/Menschen** complete strangers; **ein Wildfremder, ein ~er Mensch** a complete stranger;

Wild|füt|te|rung F feeding of game animals; **Wild|gans** F wild goose; **Wild|gat|ter** NT game grid; *(= Zaun)* game fence; **Wild|ge|he|ge** NT game enclosure *or* preserve; **Wild|ge|schmack** M gam(e)y taste

Wild|heit F -, -en wildness; *(von Kind auch, von Haar)* unruliness; *(von Stamm etc)* savagery; *(von Kampf, Blick)* fierceness; *(= Leidenschaft)* wild passion

Wild-: **Wild|hü|ter(in)** M(F) gamekeeper; **Wild|ka|nin|chen** NT wild rabbit; **Wild|kat|ze** F wildcat; **wild|le|bend** ADJ *attr* → **wild** ADV c; **Wild|le|der** NT suede; **wild|le|dern** ADJ suede; **wild+ma|chen** VT *sep* → **wild**

Wild|nis ['vɪltnɪs] F -, -se *(lit, fig)* wilderness; **Tiere der ~** wild animals; **in der ~ leben/geboren werden** to live/be born in the wild

Wild-: **Wild|park** M game park; *(für Rotwild)* deer park; **Wild|reich|tum** M abundance of game; **Wild|re|ser|vat** NT game reserve; **wild|ro|man|tisch** [vɪltro'mantɪʃ] ADJ *(iro)* terribly romantic; **Wild|sau** F wild sow; *(fig sl)* pig *(inf)*; **Wild|scha|den** M damage caused by game; **Wild|schütz** [-ʃʏts] M -en, -en, **Wild|schüt|ze** M *(obs)* poacher; **Wild|schutz|ge|biet** NT game preserve; **Wild|schwein** NT wild boar *or* pig; **wild|wach|send** ADJ *attr* → **wild** ADV c; **Wild|was|ser** NT *pl* -wasser white water; **Wild|was|ser|boot** NT white-water canoe; **Wild|was|ser|fah|ren** NT white-water canoeing *or* rafting; **Wild|was|ser|ren|nen** NT fast-water canoe race; **Wild|wech|sel** M path used by game *or* by wild animals; *(bei Rotwild)* deer path; **„Wildwechsel"** "wild animals"; **Wild|west** *no art* the Wild West; **Wild|west|film** M western; **Wild|west|me|tho|den** PL *(pej inf)* Mafia methods; **Wild|west|ro|man** M western; **Wild|wuchs** M *(geh)* rank growth; *(fig)* proliferation; **Wild|zaun** M game fence

Wil|helm ['vɪlhɛlm] M -s William; **falscher ~** *(inf)* toupee; **seinen (Friedrich) ~ unter etw** *(dat)* **setzen** *(inf)* to put one's signature *or* moniker *(inf)* to sth, to John Hancock sth *(US inf)*

Wil|hel|mi|nisch [vɪlhɛl'mi:nɪʃ] ADJ *(Hist)* Wilhelminian *(pertaining to the reign of William II of Germany 1888 - 1918)*

will *1. and 3. pers pres von* **wollen**

Wil|le ['vɪlə] M -ns, *no pl* will; *(= Absicht, Entschluss)* intention; **nach jds ~n** as sb wanted/wants; *(von Architekt etc)* as sb intended/intends; **der ~ zur Macht** the will to power; **der ~ zur Zusammenarbeit** the will to cooperate; **keinen ~n (zu etw) haben** *or* **zeigen** to have *or* show no will (for sth); **wenn es nach ihrem ~n ginge** if she had her way; **etw mit ~n tun** to do sth on purpose *or* deliberately; **das geschah gegen** *or* **wider meinen ~n** *(= gegen meinen Wunsch)* that was done against my will; *(= unabsichtlich)* I didn't intend that to happen; **er musste wider ~n** *or* **gegen seinen ~n lachen** he couldn't help laughing; **jds ~n tun** to do sb's will; **es steht (nicht) in unserem ~n, das zu tun** *(geh)* it is (not) our intention to do that; **seinen ~n durchsetzen** to get one's (own) way; **auf seinem ~n bestehen** to insist on having one's way; **jdm seinen ~n lassen** to let sb have his own way; **er soll seinen ~n haben** let him have his (own) way; **seinen eigenen ~n haben** to be self-willed, to have a mind of one's own; **beim besten ~n nicht** not with all the will *or* with the best will in the world; **ich hätte das beim besten ~n nicht machen können** I couldn't have done that for the life of me; **es war kein** *or* **nicht böser ~** there was no ill will intended; **etw aus freiem ~n tun** to do sth of one's own free will; **der gute ~** good will; **guten ~ns sein** to be full of good intentions; **alle Menschen, die guten ~ns sind** all people of good will; **den guten ~n für die Tat nehmen** to take the thought for the deed; **jdm zu ~n sein** to comply with sb's wishes; *(Mädchen: = sich hingeben)* to yield to sb, to let sb have his way with one; **sich** *(dat)* **jdn zu ~n machen** to bend sb to one's will, to force sb to do one's will; *Mädchen* to have one's way with sb; **wo ein ~ ist, ist auch ein Weg** *(Prov)* where there's a will there's a way *(Prov)* → **letzte(r, s) a**

wil|len ['vɪlən] PREP → **um** PREP *+gen*

Wil|len-: **wil|len|los** ADJ weak-willed, spineless; **völlig ~ sein** to have no will of one's own; **jds ~es Werkzeug sein** to be sb's mere tool ADV **jdm ~ ergeben sein** to be totally submissive to sb; **sich jdm ~ unterwerfen** to submissively obey sb; **Wil|len|lo|sig|keit** F -, *no pl* spinelessness

wil|lens ['vɪləns] ADJ *(geh)* **~ sein** to be willing *or* prepared

Wil|lens-: **Wil|lens|akt** M act of will; **Wil|lens|an|stren|gung** F effort of will; **Wil|lens|äu|ße|rung** F expression of will; **Wil|lens|bil|dung** F development of an informed opinion; **Wil|lens|er|klä|rung** F professed intention; **Wil|lens|frei|heit** F freedom of (the) will; **aufgrund seiner ~** on the basis of his freedom of will; **Wil|lens|kraft** F willpower, strength of mind; **Wil|lens|mensch** M *(inf)* very determined person; **wil|lens|schwach** ADJ weak-willed; **Wil|lens|schwä|che** F weak will; **wil|lens|stark** ADJ strong-willed, determined; **Wil|lens|stär|ke** F willpower; **Wil|lens|voll|stre|cker(in)** M(F) *(Sw)* executor; *(Frau auch)* executrix

wil|lent|lich ['vɪləntlɪç] ADJ wilful, deliberate ADV deliberately

will|fah|ren [vɪl'fa:rən, 'vɪl-] *pret* **willfahrte** [vɪl'fa:ɐtə, 'vɪl-], *ptp* **willfahrt** [vɪl'fa:ɐt, 'vɪl-] VI *+dat (old, liter)* to please, to satisfy, to obey *(jdm* sb)

will|fäh|rig ['vɪlfɛ:rɪç, vɪl'fɛ:rɪç] ADJ *(old, liter)* submissive, compliant; **jdm ~ sein** to submit to sb

Will|fäh|rig|keit F -, *(rare)* -en *(old, liter)* submissiveness, compliance

wil|lig ['vɪlɪç] ADJ willing ADV willingly

wil|li|gen ['vɪlɪgn] VI *(old, liter)* **in etw** *(acc)* **~** to agree to sth

Wil|lig|keit F -, *no pl* willingness

Will|komm ['vɪlkɔm] M -s, -e *(old, liter)* **a** welcome **b** *(auch* **Willkommbecher**) cup of welcome *(old)*

will|kom|men [vɪl'kɔmən] ADJ welcome; **du bist (mir) immer ~** you are always welcome; **jdn ~ heißen** to welcome *or* greet sb; **seid (herzlich) ~!** welcome, welcome!; **herzlich ~** welcome *(in +dat* to); **es ist mir ganz ~, dass ...** I quite welcome the fact that ...; **die Gelegenheit, das zu sagen/zu tun, ist mir ~** I welcome the opportunity of saying/doing this

Will|kom|men [vɪl'kɔmən] NT -s, - welcome; **jdm ein ~ bieten** *(liter)* to bid sb welcome; **ein herzliches ~!** welcome indeed!

Will|kom|mens-: **Will|kom|mens|gruß** M greeting, welcome; **Will|kom|mens|trunk** M welcoming drink, cup of welcome *(old)*

Will|kür ['vɪlky:ɐ] F -, *no pl* capriciousness; *(politisch)* despotism; *(bei Entscheidungen, Handlungen)* arbitrariness; **sie sind seiner ~ schutzlos preisgegeben** *or* **ausgeliefert** they are completely at his mercy; **das ist reinste ~** that is purely arbitrary; **ein Akt der ~** an act of caprice/a despotic act/an arbitrary act

Will|kür-: **Will|kür|akt** M → **Willkür** act of caprice; despotic act; arbitrary act; **Will|kür|herr|schaft** F tyranny, despotic rule

will|kür|lich ['vɪlky:ɐlɪç] ADJ **a** arbitrary; *Herrscher* autocratic **b** *Muskulatur, Kontraktion* voluntary ADV *(= nach eigenem Belieben) anordnen, handeln, vorgehen* arbitrarily; **sie kann ~ Tränen produzieren** she can produce tears at will; **einen Muskel ~ betätigen** to make a voluntary move of a muscle

Will|kür|lich|keit F -, -en arbitrariness; *(von Herrscher)* autocracy

Will|kür|maß|nah|me F arbitrary measure

Wil|ly ['vili] M -s, -s *(sl: = Penis)* willy *(Brit inf)*, weenie *(US inf)*

wim|meln ['vɪmln] VI **a** *auch vi impers (= in Mengen vorhanden sein)* **der See wimmelt von Fischen, in dem See wimmelt es von Fischen** the lake is teeming with fish; **hier wimmelt es von Fliegen/Pilzen/Menschen** this place is swarming with flies/overrun with mushrooms/teeming with people; **der Käse wimmelt von Maden** the cheese is crawling with maggots; **dieses Buch wimmelt von Fehlern** this book is riddled with mistakes **b** *aux sein (= sich bewegen)* to teem; *(Mücken, Ameisen)* to swarm

wim|men ['vɪmən] *(Sw)* VT to harvest, to gather VI to harvest *or* gather (the) grapes

Wim|merl ['vɪmɐl] NT -(s), -n *(Aus)* **a** *(= Pickel)* spot *(Brit)*, pimple **b** *(= Skiläufertasche)* pouch

wim|mern ['vɪmɐn] VI to whimper

Wim|met ['vɪmət] M OR F -, *no pl (esp Sw, Aus)* grape harvest

Wim|pel ['vɪmpl] M -s, - pennant

Wim|per ['vɪmpɐ] F -, -n **a** (eye)lash; **ohne mit der ~ zu zucken** *(fig)* without batting an eyelid *(Brit) or* eyelash *(US)* **b** *(Bot, Zool)* cilium

Wim|pern|tu|sche F mascara

Wim|per|tier|chen NT ciliate

wind [vɪnt] ADJ *(S Ger, Sw)* **jdm wird es ~ und weh** *(= übel)* sb feels really ill; *(= traurig)* sb feels really sad; *(= angst)* sb feels really afraid

Wind [vɪnt] M -(e)s, -e [-də] **a** wind; **bei** *or* **in ~ und Wetter** in all weathers; **~ und Wetter ausgesetzt sein** to be exposed to the elements; **laufen wie der ~** to run like the wind; **sich verbreiten wie der ~** to spread like wildfire; **der ~ dreht sich** the wind is changing direction; *(fig)* the climate is changing; **wissen/merken, woher der ~ weht** *or* **bläst** *(fig)* to know/notice the way the wind is blowing; **daher weht der ~!** *(fig)* so that's the way the wind is blowing; **seither weht** *or* **bläst ein anderer/frischer ~** *(fig)* things have changed since then; **ihm weht** *or* **bläst der ~ ins Gesicht** *(fig)* he's having a hard *or* tough time; **ein neuer ~ weht durch das Land** *(fig)* the wind of change is blowing in the country; **frischen** *or* **neuen ~ in etw** *(acc)* **bringen** *(fig)* to breathe new life into sth; **mach doch nicht so einen ~** *(inf)* don't make such a to-do *(inf)*; **viel ~ um etw machen** *(inf)* to make a lot of fuss *or* to-do *(inf)* about sth; **vor dem ~ segeln** *(lit)* to sail with the wind (behind one); **gegen den ~ segeln** *(lit)* to sail into the wind; *(fig)* to swim against the stream, to run against the wind *(US)*; **mit dem ~ zu segeln verstehen** *(fig)* to know how to bend with the wind; **den Mantel** *or* **das Mäntelchen** *or* **die Fahne** *or* **das Fähnchen nach dem ~ hängen** *or* **drehen** *or* **richten** to trim one's sails to the wind, to swim with the tide; **jdm den ~ aus den Segeln nehmen** *(fig)* to take the wind out of sb's sails; **sich** *(dat)* **den ~ um die Nase** *or* **Ohren wehen lassen** to see a bit of the world; **etw in den ~ schlagen** *(Warnungen, Rat)* to turn a deaf ear to sth; *Vorsicht, Vernunft* to throw *or* cast sth to the winds; **in den ~ reden** to waste one's breath; **wer ~ sät, wird Sturm ernten** *(Prov)* sow the wind and reap the whirlwind *(prov)*

b *(Himmelsrichtung)* wind (direction); **in alle (vier) ~e** to the four winds; **in alle (vier) ~e zerstreut sein** *(fig)* to be scattered to the four corners of the earth *or* to the four winds

c *(Med: = Blähung)* wind; **einen ~ fahren** *or* **streichen lassen** to break wind, to fart *(inf)*

d *(Hunt)* wind; **von jdm/etw ~ nehmen** *or* **bekommen** to take *or* get the wind of sb/sth; **von etw ~ bekommen** *or* **kriegen/haben** *(fig inf)* to get/have wind of sth

Wind-: **Wind|beu|tel** M **a** cream puff **b** *(inf: Mensch)* rake; **Wind|blu|se** F windcheater; **Wind|bö(e)** F gust of wind; **Wind|büch|se** F *(inf)* air rifle

Win|de ['vɪndə] F -, -n *(Tech)* winch, windlass

Win|de F -, -n *(Bot)* bindweed, convolvulus

Wind|ei ['vɪntlai] NT *(fig)* nonstarter

Win|del ['vɪndl] F -, -n nappy *(Brit)*, diaper *(US)*; **damals lagst du noch in den ~n** you were still in nappies *(Brit) or* diapers *(US)* then; **noch in den ~n stecken** *or* **liegen** *(fig)* to be still in its infancy

Win|del-: **Win|del|ein|la|ge** F, **Win|del|fo|lie** F nappy *(Brit) or* diaper *(US)* liner; **Win|del|hös|chen** [-hø:sçən] NT plastic pants *pl*

win|deln ['vɪndln] VT **ein Baby ~** to put a baby's nappy *(Brit) or* diaper *(US)* on; *(= neu windeln)* to change a baby, to change a baby's nappy *(Brit) or* diaper *(US)* VI to put on nappies/a nappy *(Brit) or* diapers/a diaper *(US)*

win|del|weich ['vɪndl'vaiç] ADV **jdn ~ schlagen** *or* **hauen** *(inf)* to beat sb black and blue, to beat the living daylights out of sb ADJ *(= nachgiebig)* softly-softly

win|den[1] ['vɪndn] *pret* **wand** [vant], *ptp* **gewun|den** [gə'vʊndn] VT to wind; *Kranz* to bind; *(= hochwinden) Eimer, Last* to winch; **jdm etw aus der Hand ~** to wrest sth out of sb's hand VR *(Pflanze, Schlange)* to wind (itself); *(Bach)* to wind, to meander; *(Mensch) (durch Menge, Gestrüpp etc)* to wind (one's way); *(vor Schmerzen)* to writhe (*vor* with, in); *(vor Scham, Verlegenheit)* to squirm (*vor* with, in); *(fig: = ausweichen)* to try to wriggle out; **sich ~ wie ein (getretener) Wurm** to squirm → *auch* **gewunden**

win|den[2] VI *impers* **es windet (sehr)** the wind is blowing (hard)

win|den[3] VTI *(Hunt)* = **wittern**

Wind|ener|gie F wind energy

Wind|ener|gie|an|la|ge F wind energy plant

Win|des-: **Win|des|ei|le** F **etw in** *or* **mit ~ tun** to do sth in no time (at all); **sich in** *or* **mit ~ verbreiten** to spread like wildfire; **Win|des|flü|gel** PL *(liter)* **auf ~n** like the wind

Wind-: **Wind|fah|ne** F *(Met)* wind vane; **Wind|fang** M draught excluder *(Brit)*, draft guard *(US)*; *(Raum)* porch; **Wind|fang|tür** F porch *(Brit) or* screen *(US)* door; **Wind|farm** F wind farm; **Wind|ge|ne|ra|tor** M wind generator; **wind|ge|schützt** ADJ sheltered (from the wind) ADV in a sheltered place; **Wind|ge|schwin|dig|keit** F wind speed; **Wind|ha|fer** M wild oat; **Wind|har|fe** F wind harp; **Wind|hauch** M breath of wind; **Wind|ho|se** F vortex

Wind|huk ['vɪnthʊk, 'vɪnthu:k] NT **-s** Windhoek

Wind|hund M **a** *(Hund)* greyhound; *(= Afghanischer Windhund)* Afghan (hound) **b** *(fig pej)* rake

win|dig ['vɪndɪç] ADJ windy; *(fig) Bursche, Sache* dubious, dodgy *(inf)*

win|disch ['vɪndɪʃ] ADJ *(Aus usu pej)* Slovene

Wind-: **Wind|ja|cke** F windcheater *(Brit)*, windproof jacket; **Wind|jam|mer** [-jamɐ] M **-s, -** *(Naut)* windjammer; **Wind|ka|nal** M wind tunnel; *(an Orgel)* wind trunk; **Wind|kraft** F wind power; **Wind|kraft|an|la|ge** F, **Wind|kraft|werk** NT wind power station; **Wind|licht** NT lantern; **Wind|loch** NT *(Aviat)* air pocket; **Wind|mes|ser** [-mɛsɐ] M **-s, -** wind meter, anemometer *(spec)*; **Wind|müh|le** F windmill; **gegen ~n (an)kämpfen** *(fig)* to tilt at windmills; **Wind|müh|len|flü|gel** M windmill sail *or* vane; **Wind|(müh|len)|park** M wind farm; **Wind|po|cken** PL chickenpox *sing*; **Wind|rad** NT *(Tech)* wind turbine; **Wind|räd|chen** NT *(= Spielzeug)* windmill, pinwheel *(US)*; **Wind|rich|tung** F wind direction; **Wind|rös|chen** [-rø:sçən] NT anemone; **Wind|ro|se** F *(Naut)* compass card; *(Met)* wind rose; **Wind|sack** M *(Aviat)* windsock, air sock; *(an Dudelsack etc)* (pipe) bag

Winds|braut F *(old, liter)* storm, tempest *(liter)*; *(= Wirbelwind)* whirlwind; **wie eine** *or* **die ~** *(fig geh)* like a whirlwind

Wind-: **Wind|schat|ten** M lee; *(von Fahrzeugen)* slipstream; **Wind|schei|be** F *(Sw Aut)* windscreen *(Brit)*, windshield *(US)*; **wind|schief** ADJ crooked; *Dach auch* askew *pred*; *Haus* crooked; **Wind|schirm** M windbreak; **wind|schlüp|fig** [-ʃlʏpfɪç] ADJ streamlined; **wind|schlüpf|rig**, **wind|schnit|tig** ADJ streamlined; **Wind|schutz** M protection from wind; *(= Vorrichtung)* windbreak; **Wind|schutz|schei|be** F windscreen *(Brit)*, windshield *(US)*; **Wind|sei|te** F windward side; **Wind|ska|la** F wind scale; **Wind|spiel** NT greyhound; **Wind|stär|ke** F strength of the wind; *(Met)* wind force; **wind|still** ADJ still, windless; *Platz, Ecke etc* sheltered; **wenn es völlig ~ ist** when there is no wind at all; **Wind|stil|le** F calm; **Wind|stoß** M gust of wind; **Wind|surf|brett** NT sailboard, windsurfer; **wind|sur|fen** VI *insep* to sailboard, to windsurf; **~ gehen** to go sailboarding *or* windsurfing; **Wind|sur|fen** NT **-s**, *no pl* sailboarding, windsurfing; **Wind|sur|fer(in)** M(F) sailboarder, windsurfer; **Wind|tur|bi|ne** F wind turbine

Win|dung ['vɪndʊŋ] F **-, -en** *(von Weg, Fluss etc)* meander; *(von Schlange)* coil; *(Anat: von Darm)* convolution; *(Tech: von Schraube)* thread; *(= eine Umdrehung)* revolution; *(Elec: von Spule)* coil

Win|gert ['vɪŋɐt] M **-s, -e** *(dial, Sw)* vineyard

Wink [vɪŋk] M **-(e)s, -e** *(= Zeichen)* sign; *(mit der Hand)* wave (*mit* of); *(mit dem Kopf)* nod (*mit* of); *(= Hinweis, Tip)* hint, tip; **er gab mir einen ~, dass ich still sein sollte** he gave me a sign to be quiet

Win|kel ['vɪŋkl] M **-s, - a** *(Math)* angle → **tot b b** *(Tech)* square **c** *(Mil: = Rangabzeichen)* stripe **d** *(fig) (= Stelle, Ecke)* corner; *(= Plätzchen: esp von Land, Wald etc)* place, spot; **jdn/etw in allen (Ecken und) ~n suchen** to look high and low for sb/sth; **in einem verborgenen ~ seines Herzens** in a hidden corner of his heart

Win|kel-: **Win|kel|ad|vo|kat(in)** M(F) *(pej)* incompetent lawyer; **Win|kel|ei|sen** NT angle iron; **win|kel|för|mig** ADJ angled ADV **~ gebogen** bent at an angle; **Win|kel|funk|ti|on** F *(Math)* trigonometrical function; **Win|kel|hal|bie|ren|de** [-halbi:rəndə] F *decl as adj* bisector of an/the angle

win|ke|lig ['vɪŋkəlɪç] ADJ = **winklig**

Win|kel-: **Win|kel|maß** NT **a** *(Astron)* Norma, the Level **b** *(= Winkel)* square; **Win|kel|mes|ser** M **-s, -** protractor; **Win|kel|schlei|fer** M angle grinder; **Win|kel|zug** M *(= Trick)* dodge, trick; *(= Ausflucht)* evasion; **mach keine Winkelzüge** stop evading the issue

win|ken ['vɪŋkn] *ptp* **gewinkt** *or (dial)* **gewunken** [gə'vɪŋkt, gə'vʊŋkn] VI to wave (*jdm* to sb); **jdm ~, etw zu tun** to signal sb to do sth; **sie winkte mit einem Fähnchen/den Armen** she waved a flag/her arms; **einem Taxi ~** to hail a taxi; **dem Kellner ~** to signal to the waiter; **jdm winkt etw** *(fig: = steht in Aussicht)* sb can expect sth; **bei der Verlosung ~ wertvolle Preise** valuable prizes are being offered in the draw; **dem Sieger winkt eine Reise nach Italien** the winner will receive (the attractive prize of) a trip to Italy; **ihm winkt das Glück** fortune *or* luck is smiling on him, luck is on his side VT to wave; *(esp Sport: = anzeigen)* to signal; *Taxi* to hail; *Kellner* to call; **jdn zu sich ~** to beckon sb over to one

Win|ker ['vɪŋkɐ] M **-s, -** *(old Aut)* indicator *(Brit)*, blinker *(US)*, trafficator

Win|ker|al|pha|bet NT semaphore alphabet

win|ke, win|ke ma|chen ['vɪŋkə 'vɪŋkə] VI *(baby-talk)* to wave

wink|lig ['vɪŋklɪç] ADJ *Haus, Altstadt* full of nooks and crannies; *Gasse* twisty, windy

Wink|zei|chen NT signal; *(Mot)* hand signal; *(mit Fahne)* semaphore signal

Winsch [vɪnʃ] F **-, -en** *(Naut)* windlass, winch

win|seln ['vɪnzln] VTI to whimper; *(pej: um Gnade etc)* to grovel

Win|ter ['vɪntɐ] M **-s, -** winter; **es ist/wird ~** winter is here *or* has come/is coming; **im/über den ~** in (the)/over the winter; **über den ~ kommen** to get through the winter; **der nächste ~ kommt bestimmt** *(inf)* you never know how long the good times are going to last; **der nukleare ~** nuclear winter

Win|ter- *in cpds* winter; **Win|ter|an|fang** M beginning of winter; **vor/seit ~** before/since the beginning of winter; **Win|ter|dienst** M *(Mot)* winter road treatment; **Win|ter|ein|bruch** M onset of winter; **Win|ter|fahr|plan** M winter timetable; **Win|ter|fell** NT winter coat; **win|ter|fest** ADJ *Kleidung* winterproof; *Pflanzen* hardy; *Saat* winter *attr*; **dieses Haus ist nicht ~** this house won't withstand winter conditions; **~ machen** *(Auto, Gebäude)* to get ready for winter, to winterize *(US)*; **Win|ter|flug|plan** M winter flight schedule; **Win|ter|gar|ten** M winter garden; **Win|ter|ge|trei|de** NT winter crop; **Win|ter|halb|jahr** NT winter; **im ~** from September to March; **im ~ 1998/99** in the winter of 1998/99; **win|ter|hart** ADJ *Pflanzen* hardy; **Win|ter|käl|te** F cold winter weather; **in der größten ~** in the depths of winter; **Win|ter|kar|tof|feln** PL (old) potatoes *pl*; **Win|ter|kleid** NT winter dress; *(Zool)* winter coat; *(liter: von Landschaft etc)* winter covering (of snow); **Win|ter|klei|der** PL winter clothes *pl*; **Win|ter|klei|dung** F winter clothing; **Win|ter|land|schaft** F winter landscape

win|ter|lich ['vɪntɐlɪç] ADJ wintry; *Wetter auch, Kleidung, Beschäftigung* winter *attr* ADV **es ist ~ kalt** it's as cold as it is in winter; **~ kalte Temperaturen** cold winter temperatures; **~ gekleidet** dressed for winter

Win|ter-: **Win|ter|man|tel** M winter coat; **Win|ter|mo|nat** M winter month

win|tern ['vɪntɐn] VI *impers (liter)* **es winterte schon** winter was coming

Win|ter-: **Win|ter|nacht** F winter night; **Win|ter|obst** NT winter fruit; **Win|ter|olym|pi|a|de** F Winter Olympics *pl*; **Win|ter|pau|se** F winter break; **Win|ter|quar|tier** NT *(Mil)* winter quarters *pl*; **Win|ter|rei|fen** M winter tyre *(Brit) or* tire *(US)*

win|ters ['vɪntɐs] ADV in winter, in the wintertime

Win|ter-: **Win|ter|saat** F winter seed; **Win|ter|sa|chen** PL winter clothes *pl*; **Win|ter|schlaf** M *(Zool)* hibernation; **(den) ~ halten** to hibernate; **Win|ter|schluss|ver|kauf** M winter (clearance) sale; **Win|ter|se|mes|ter** NT winter semester; **Win|ter|son|nen|wen|de** F winter solstice; **Win|ter|speck** M *(inf)* winter flab *(inf)*; **Win|ter|spie|le** PL **(Olympische) ~** Winter Olympic Games *pl*, Winter Olympics *pl*; **Win|ter|sport** M winter sports *pl*; *(= Wintersportart)* winter sport; **in den ~ fahren** to go on a winter sports holiday *(esp Brit) or* vacation *(US)*; **Win|ter|star|re** F *(Zool)* (winter) torpor

Win|ters-: **win|ters|über** ['vɪntɐsly:bɐ] ADV in winter; **Win|ters|zeit** F *(liter)* wintertime

Win|ter-: **Win|ter|tag** M winter('s) day; **Win|ter|wet|ter** NT winter weather; **Win|ter|zeit** F winter time; *(Jahreszeit)* wintertime

Win|zer ['vɪntsɐ] M **-s, -**, **Win|ze|rin** [-ərɪn] F **-, -nen** wine grower; *(= Weinleser)* grape picker

Win|zer|ge|nos|sen|schaft F wine growers' organization

win|zig ['vɪntsɪç] ADJ tiny; **ein ~es bisschen** a tiny little bit; **~ klein** minute, tiny little *attr*

Win|zig|keit F **-, -en a** *no pl* tiny size **b** *(= winzige Menge)* tiny drop/bit/quantity *etc*; *(= Geschenk)* little thing

Winz|ling ['vɪntslɪŋ] M **-s, -e** *(inf)* mite

Wip|fel ['vɪpfl] M **-s, -** treetop; **in den ~n der Bäume** in the treetops, in the tops of the trees

Wip|pe ['vɪpə] F **-, -n** *(zum Schaukeln)* seesaw; *(= Babywippe)* bouncy chair

wip|pen ['vɪpn] VI *(auf und ab)* to bob up and down; *(hin und her)* to teeter; *(Schwanz)* to wag; *(= mit Wippe schaukeln)* to seesaw; **mit dem Schwanz ~** to wag its tail; **mit dem Fuß ~** to jiggle one's foot; **in den Knien ~** to buckle at the knees; **den Fuß/Kopf im Takt** *or* **Rhythmus ~** to move one's foot/head in time to the music *or* rhythm; **~der Gang** bouncing gait *or* stride

wir [viːɐ] PERS PRON *gen* **unser** ['ʊnzɐ], *dat* **uns** [ʊns], *acc* **uns** [ʊns] we; **~ alle** all of us; **~ beide** both *or* the two of us; **~ drei** the three of us; **~ als Betroffene/Kollegen ...** as those affected/as colleagues, we ...; **~ Armen** we poor people; **~ Kommunisten** we Communists; **~, die ~ ...** we who ...; **~ (selbst) sind/waren es, die ...** we are/were the ones who ..., it is/was we *(form) or* us who ...; **nicht nur ~ sind der Ansicht ...** it is not only we who are of the opinion ...; **immer sollen ~s gewesen sein** everyone always blames us; **wer war das? – ~ nicht** who was that? – it wasn't us; **wer kommt noch mit? – ~/~ nicht** who's coming along? – we are/not us; **wer ist da? – ~ (sinds)** who's there? – (it's) us; **trinken ~ erst mal einen** let's have a drink first; **da haben ~ wohl nicht aufgepasst?** *(iro)* we weren't paying attention, were we?; **~, Wilhelm, Kaiser von ...** we, William, Emperor of ...

wirb [vɪrp] IMPER *sing von* **werben**

Wir|bel ['vɪrbl] M **-s, -** a *(lit, fig)* whirl; *(von Wind auch)* eddy; *(in Fluss etc)* whirlpool, eddy; *(= Drehung beim Tanz etc)* pirouette; *(der Gefühle, Ereignisse)* turmoil; *(= Aufsehen)* to-do; **im ~ des Festes** in the whirl *or* hurly-burly *(Brit) or* hoopla *(US)* of the party; **(viel/großen) ~ machen/verursachen** to make/cause (a lot of/a big) commotion b *(= Haarwirbel)* crown; *(nicht am Hinterkopf)* cowlick; *(auf Fingerkuppe, in Stein)* whorl c *(= Trommelwirbel)* (drum) roll d *(Anat)* vertebra e *(an Saiteninstrument)* peg; *(an Fenster)* catch

Wir|bel|dü|se F water nozzle *or* jet

Wir|bel|fort|satz M *(Anat)* spinous process

wir|be|lig ['vɪrbəlɪç] ADJ *(= temperamentvoll)* vivacious, lively; *(= wirr)* dizzy

wir|bel|los ADJ *(Zool)* invertebrate; **die Wirbellosen** the invertebrates

wir|beln ['vɪrbln] VI a *aux sein (Mensch, Wasser etc)* to whirl; *(Laub)* to swirl; *(Rauch)* to whirl, to swirl b **mir wirbelt der Kopf** *(inf)* my head is spinning *or* reeling c *(Trommeln etc)* to roll VT *jdn, Wasser* to whirl; *Staub, Laub etc auch* to swirl

Wir|bel-: **Wir|bel|säu|le** F *(Anat)* spinal column; **Wir|bel|sturm** M whirlwind, tornado, cyclone; **Wir|bel|tier** NT vertebrate; **Wir|bel|wind** M whirlwind; **wie der** *or* **ein ~** like a whirlwind

wirb|lig ['vɪrblɪç] ADJ = **wirbelig**

wirbt [vɪrpt] *3. pers sing pres von* **werben**

wird [vɪrt] *3. pers sing pres von* **werden**

wirf [vɪrf] *imper sing von* **werfen**

Wir|form F first person plural

wirft [vɪrft] *3. pers sing pres von* **werfen**

Wir|ge|fühl NT feeling of belonging together, community feeling

wir|ken ['vɪrkn] VI a *(geh: = tätig sein) (Mensch)* to work; *(Einflüsse, Kräfte etc)* to be at work; **ich werde dahin ~, dass man ihn befördert** I will work for his promotion

b *(= Wirkung haben)* to have an effect; *(= erfolgreich sein)* to work; **als Gegengift ~** to work as an antidote; **als Katalysator ~** to act as a catalyst; **schalldämpfend/abführend ~** to have a soundproofing/laxative effect; **die Pillen ~ gut gegen Bauchschmerzen** the pills are good for stomachache; **eine stark ~de Droge** a strong drug

c *(= einwirken)* **auf etw** *(acc)* **~** *(esp Chem)* to act on sth; **etw auf sich** *(acc)* **~ lassen** to take sth in

d *(= erscheinen)* to seem, to appear; **nervös/ruhig (auf jdn) ~** to give (sb) the impression of being nervous/calm, to seem nervous/calm (to sb); **das wirkt auf viele als Provokation** many people see that as a provocation; **diese Bemerkung wirkt abstoßend auf mich** I find this remark repulsive

e *(= zur Geltung kommen)* to be effective; **neben diesen Gardinen wirkt das Muster nicht (richtig)** the pattern loses its effect next to those curtains; **ich finde, das Bild wirkt** I think the picture has something; **die Musik wirkt erst bei einer gewissen Lautstärke** you only get the full effect of the music when it's played loud

VT *(geh: = tun) Gutes* to do; *Wunder* to work → **Wunder a**

wir|ken VT a *(liter) Teppiche, Stoffe* to weave b *(spec) Maschinentextilien* to knit; **Goldfäden durch etw ~** to work gold threads into sth

wir|ken VT *(dial: = kneten) Teig* to knead, to work

Wir|ken NT **-s**, *no pl* work

Wir|ker ['vɪrkɐ] M **-s, -**, **Wir|ke|rin** [-ərɪn] F **-, -nen** knitter

Wir|ke|rei [vɪrkə'rai] F **-, -en** a knitting b *(Fabrik)* knitwear factory

Wirk|kraft F effect

wirk|lich ['vɪrklɪç] ADJ a *(= zur Wirklichkeit gehörig)* real; *(= tatsächlich) Sachverhalt, Aussage, Meinung etc* actual, real; **im ~en Leben** in real life b *(= echt)* real; *Freund* real, true ADV really; **ich wüsste gern, wie es ~ war** I would like to know what really happened; **nicht ~** not really; **das meinst du doch nicht ~** you don't really mean that; **ich war das ~ nicht** it really was not me; **~?** *(als Antwort)* really?; **nein, ~?** *(als Antwort)* what, really?; **er ist es ~** it really is him; **~ und wahrhaftig** really and truly

Wirk|lich|keit ✪ 53.4, 53.6 F **-, -en** reality; **~ werden** to come true; **die Literatur spiegelt die ~ wider** literature reflects reality; **in ~** in reality; **in ~ heißt er anders** his real name is different → **Boden d**

Wirk|lich|keits-: **Wirk|lich|keits|form** F *(Gram)* indicative; **wirk|lich|keits|fremd** ADJ unrealistic; **wirk|lich|keits|ge|treu**, **wirk|lich|keits|nah** ADJ realistic ADV realistically; **etw ~ abbilden** to paint a realistic picture of sth; **etw wirklichkeitsnah erzählen** to give a realistic account of sth; **Wirk|lich|keits|sinn** M, *no pl* realism

Wirk|ma|schi|ne F knitting machine

wirk|sam ['vɪrkzaːm] ADJ effective; **~ bleiben** to remain in effect; **mit (dem)** *or* **am 1. Januar ~ werden** *(form: Gesetz)* to take effect on *or* from January 1st ADV effectively; *verbessern* significantly

Wirk|sam|keit F **-**, *no pl* effectiveness

Wirk|stoff M *(esp Physiol)* active substance

Wir|kung ['vɪrkʊŋ] F **-, -en** effect *(bei* on); *(von Tabletten etc)* effects *pl*; **seine ~ tun** to have an effect; *(Droge)* to take effect; **ohne ~ bleiben** to have no effect; **an ~ verlieren** to lose its effect; **seine ~ verfehlen** not to have the desired effect; **zur ~ kommen** *(Medikament)* to take effect; *(fig: = zur Geltung kommen)* to show to advantage; *(durch Kontrast)* to be set off, to stand out; **mit ~ vom 1. Januar** *(form)* with effect from January 1st

Wir|kungs-: **Wir|kungs|be|reich** M *(eines Menschen)* domain; *(einer Tageszeitung)* area of influence; *(von Atombombe, Golfstrom)* affected area; **der ~ des atlantischen Tiefs** the area affected by the Atlantic depression; **Wir|kungs|dau|er** F period over which sth is effective; **Wir|kungs|feld** NT field (of activity); **Wir|kungs|grad** M (degree of) effectiveness; **Wir|kungs|kreis** M sphere of activity; **wir|kungs|los** ADJ ineffective; **Wir|kungs|lo|sig|keit** F **-**, *no pl* ineffectiveness; **Wir|kungs|stät|te** F *(geh)* domain; **wir|kungs|voll** ADJ effective ADV effectively; **Wir|kungs|wei|se** F *(von Medikament)* action; **die ~ eines Kondensators** the way a condenser works

Wirk|wa|ren PL knitwear *sing*; *(= Strümpfe etc auch)* hosiery *sing*

wirr [vɪr] ADJ confused; *Blick* crazed; *(= unordentlich) Haare, Fäden* tangled; *Gedanken, Vorstellungen, Träume* weird; *(= unrealistisch, verstiegen)* wild; **er ist ~ im Kopf** *(= geistig gestört)* he is confused in his mind; *(= konfus)* he is confused *or* muddled; *(= benommen: esp von Lärm)* his head is reeling *or* swimming; **mach mich nicht ~** don't confuse me; **er ist ein ~er Kopf** he has crazy ideas; **~es Zeug reden** to talk gibberish ADV **alles lag ~ durcheinander** everything was in chaos *(Brit) or* a mess; **das Haar hängt ihm ~ ins Gesicht** his hair is hanging in tangles in his face; **sich ~ ausdrücken** to express oneself in a confused way

Wir|ren ['vɪrən] PL confusion *sing*, turmoil *sing*

Wirr|kopf M *(pej)* muddle-head, ditz *(US inf)*; **das sind alles Wirrköpfe** they've all got crazy ideas

Wirr|nis ['vɪrnɪs] F **-, -se**, **Wirr|sal** ['vɪrzaːl] NT **-(e)s, -e** *(liter)* confusion

Wir|rung ['vɪrʊŋ] F **-, -en** *(liter)* confusion

Wirr|warr ['vɪrvar] M **-s**, *no pl* confusion; *(von Stimmen)* hubbub; *(von Verkehr)* chaos *no indef art*; *(von Fäden, Haaren etc)* tangle

Wir|sing ['vɪrzɪŋ] M **-s**, *no pl*, **Wir|sing|kohl** M savoy cabbage

Wirt [vɪrt] M **-(e)s, -e** *(= Gastwirt, Untervermieter)* landlord; *(Biol, rare: = Gastgeber)* host; **den ~ machen** to play the host, to do the honours *(Brit) or* honors *(US)* → **Rechnung b**, **Wirtin**

wir|ten ['vɪrtn] VI *(Sw)* to be a/the landlord

Wir|tin ['vɪrtɪn] F **-, -nen** landlady; *(= Gastgeberin)* hostess; *(= Frau des Wirts)* landlord's wife

Wirt|schaft ['vɪrtʃaft] F **-, -en** a *(= Volkswirtschaft)* economy; *(= Handel, Geschäftsleben)* industry and commerce; *(= Finanzwelt)* business world; **freie ~** free market economy; **er ist in der ~ tätig** he works in industry; he's a businessman; **ein Mann der ~** a man of industry and commerce; **seitens der ~ können wir keine Unterstützung erwarten** we can expect no support from the business world

b *(= Gastwirtschaft)* ≈ pub *(Brit)*, ≈ public house *(Brit form)*, ≈ bar *(US)*, ≈ saloon *(dated US)*; **~!** *(inf neg!)* waiter!; **Frau ~!** *(hum inf neg!)* waitress!

c *(dated: = Haushalt)* household; **jdm die ~ führen** to keep house for sb; **er gründete eine eigene ~** he set up house on his own

d *(dated: = landwirtschaftlicher Betrieb)* farm; **in einer ~ arbeiten** to work on a farm

e *(inf: = Zustände)* state of affairs; **du hast vielleicht eine ~ in deinem Haus/auf deinem Schreibtisch** a fine mess *or* state your house/desk is in; **eine schöne** *or* **saubere ~** *(iro)* a fine state of affairs; **jetzt werden wir hier erst mal reine ~ machen** *(dial)* first of all we'll put this house in order

f *(inf: = Umstände)* trouble, bother; **sich** *(dat)* **eine ~ machen** to go to a lot of trouble *or* bother

wirt|schaf|ten ['vɪrtʃaftn] VI a *(= sparsam sein)* to economize; **gut ~ können** to be economical; **sparsam ~** to economize, to budget carefully; **ins Blaue hinein ~** not to budget at all → **Tasche b** b *(= den Haushalt führen)* to keep house c *(inf: = sich betätigen)* to busy oneself; *(gemütlich)* to potter about *(Brit)*, to putter around *(US)*; *(= herumfummeln)* to rummage about VT **jdn/etw zugrunde ~** to ruin sb/sth financially

Wirt|schaf|ter ['vɪrtʃaftɐ] M **-s, -**, **Wirt|schaf|te|rin** [-ərɪn] F **-, -nen** a *(= Verwalter)* manager b *(im Haushalt, Heim etc)* housekeeper c *(= Unternehmer)* businessman/-woman

Wirt|schaft|ler ['vɪrtʃaftlɐ] M **-s, -**, **Wirt|schaft|le|rin** [-ərɪn] F **-, -nen** a *(= Wissenschaftler)* economist b *(= Unternehmer)* businessman/-woman

wirt|schaft|lich ['vɪrtʃaftlɪç] ADJ a *(= die Wirtschaft betreffend)* economic b *(= sparsam)* economical; *Hausfrau* careful, thrifty ADV a *(= finanziell)* financially; **jdm geht es ~ gut/schlecht** sb is in a good/bad financial *or* economic position b *(= ökonomisch)* economically; **nicht ~ handeln** to be uneconomical

Wirt|schaft|lich|keit F **-**, *no pl* a *(= Rentabilität)* profitability b *(= ökonomischer Betrieb)* economy

Wirt|schaft|lich|keits|be|rech|nung F evaluation of economic efficiency

Wirt|schafts- *in cpds* economic; **Wirt|schafts|auf|schwung** M economic upswing *or* upturn;

Wịrt|schafts|aus|künf|te PL financial information *sing*; **Wịrt|schafts|aus|kunf|tei** F credit investigation agency *(Brit)*, credit bureau *(US)*; **Wịrt|schafts|aus|schuss** M economic committee; **Wirtschafts- und Sozialausschuss** *(der EU)* Economic and Social Committee; **Wịrt|schafts|be|ra|ter(in)** M(F) business consultant; **Wịrt|schafts|be|zie|hun|gen** PL business relations *pl*; **Wịrt|schafts|block** M *pl* **-blöcke** *or (rare)* **-blocks** *(Pol)* economic bloc; **Wịrt|schafts|boss** M *(inf)* business leader, (business) tycoon; **Wịrt|schafts|de|mo|kra|tie** F industrial democracy; **Wịrt|schafts|fak|tor** M economic factor; **Wịrt|schafts|flücht|ling** *(oft neg!)* M economic refugee; **Wịrt|schafts|form** F economic system; **gemischte ~** mixed economy; **Wịrt|schafts|füh|rer(in)** M(F) leading industrialist; **Wịrt|schafts|füh|rung** F management; **Wịrt|schafts|ge|bäu|de** NT working quarters *pl*; **Wịrt|schafts|ge|fü|ge** NT economic framework; **Wịrt|schafts|geld** NT housekeeping (money) *(Brit)*, household allowance *(US)*; **Wịrt|schafts|ge|mein|schaft** F economic community; **Wịrt|schafts|geo|gra|fie**, **Wịrt|schafts|geo|gra|phie** F economic geography; **Wịrt|schafts|gip|fel** M economic summit; **Wịrt|schafts|gü|ter** PL economic goods *pl*; **Wịrt|schafts|gym|na|si|um** NT *grammar school or high school which places emphasis on economics, law, management studies etc*; **Wịrt|schafts|hil|fe** F economic aid; **Wịrt|schafts|hoch|schu|le** F business school; **Wịrt|schafts|in|ge|ni|eur(in)** M(F) ≈ industrial engineer; **Wịrt|schafts|ka|pi|tän(in)** M(F) *(inf)* captain of industry; **Wịrt|schafts|kraft** F economic power; **Wịrt|schafts|krieg** M economic war; **Wịrt|schafts|kri|mi|na|li|tät** F white collar crime; **Wịrt|schafts|kri|se** F economic crisis; **Wịrt|schafts|la|ge** F economic situation; **Wịrt|schafts|le|ben** NT business life; **er ist im ~ zu Hause** he is at home in the business world; **Persönlichkeiten des ~s** business personalities; **Wịrt|schafts|macht** F economic power; **Wịrt|schafts|mi|nis|ter(in)** M(F) minister of trade and industry *(Brit)*, secretary of commerce *(US)*; **Wịrt|schafts|mi|nis|te|ri|um** NT ministry of trade and industry *(Brit)*, department of commerce *(US)*; **Wịrt|schafts|ord|nung** F economic order *or* system; **Wịrt|schafts|plan** M economic plan; **Wịrt|schafts|po|li|tik** F economic policy; **wịrt|schafts|po|li|tisch** ADJ *Maßnahmen etc* economic policy *attr*; **~er Sprecher** spokesman on economic policy ADV *geboten, sinnvoll* for the economy; *unerlässlich* to the economy; **~ verfehlt** bad for the economy; **~ ist es unmöglich …** in terms of economic policy it is impossible …; **Wịrt|schafts|prü|fer(in)** M(F) accountant; *(zum Überprüfen der Bücher)* auditor; **Wịrt|schafts|prü|fung** F *(= Einzelprüfung)* audit; **Wịrt|schafts|raum** M **a** *(Agr)* working area **b** *(Econ)* economic area; **Europäischer ~** European Economic Area; **Wịrt|schafts|recht** NT commercial *or* business law; **Wịrt|schafts|sank|ti|on** F *usu pl* economic sanction *(gegen* against); **~en gegen ein Land verhängen** to impose economic sanctions against a country; **Wịrt|schafts|sek|tor** M business sector; **Wịrt|schafts|spi|o|na|ge** F industrial espionage; **Wịrt|schafts|stand|ort** M business location; **der ~ Deutschland** Germany as a business location; **Wịrt|schafts|sys|tem** NT economic system; **Wịrt|schafts|teil** M business *or* financial section; **Wịrt|schafts|the|o|rie** F economic theory; **Wịrt|schafts|trei|ben|de(r)** [-traibndə] MF *decl as adj (Aus)* trader; **Wịrt|schafts|uni|on** F economic union; **Wirtschafts- und Währungsunion** *(der EU)* Economic and Monetary Union; **Wịrt|schafts|un|ter|neh|men** NT business (enterprise); **Wịrt|schafts|ver|band** M business *or* commercial association; **Wịrt|schafts|ver|bre|chen** NT business *or* white-collar crime; **Wịrt|schafts|wachs|tum** NT economic growth; **Wịrt|schafts|wis|sen|schaft** F economics *sing*; **Wịrt|schafts|wis|sen|schaft|ler(in)** M(F) economist; **Wịrt|schafts|wun|der** NT economic miracle; **Wịrt|schafts|zei|tung** F financial *or* business (news)paper; **Wịrt|schafts|zo|ne** F economic zone; **Wịrt|schafts|zweig** M branch of industry

Wịrts-: **Wịrts|haus** NT ≈ pub *(Brit)*, ≈ bar *(US)*, ≈ saloon *(dated US)*; *(esp auf dem Land)* inn; **Wịrts|haus|schlä|ge|rei** F pub *(Brit) or* bar *(US)* brawl; **Wịrts|leu|te** PL landlord and landlady; **Wịrts|pflan|ze** F host (plant); **Wịrts|pro|gramm** NT *(Comput)* host program; **Wịrts|stu|be** F lounge; **Wịrts|tier** NT host (animal)

Wịsch [vɪʃ] M **-(e)s, -e** *(pej inf)* piece of paper; *(mit Gedrucktem, = Dokument)* piece of bumph *(Brit inf)*, piece of stuff for reading *(inf)*; *(= Zettel mit Notiz)* note

wi|schen [ˈvɪʃn] VTI to wipe; *(= mit Lappen reinigen)* to wipe clean; *(Sw: = fegen)* to sweep; **mit einem Tuch über eine Schallplatte ~** to wipe a record with a cloth; **jdm über den Ärmel ~** to wipe sb's sleeve; **sie wischte ihm/sich den Schweiß mit einem Handtuch von der Stirn** she wiped the sweat from his/her brow with a towel; **Bedenken/Einwände (einfach) vom Tisch ~** *(fig)* to sweep aside thoughts/objections
VI *aux sein (= sich schnell bewegen)* to whisk
VT *(inf)* **jdm eine ~** to clout sb one *(Brit inf)*, to clobber sb *(inf)*; **einen gewischt bekommen** *(Elec)* to get a shock

Wi|scher [ˈvɪʃɐ] M **-s, -** *(Aut)* (windscreen *(Brit) or* windshield *(US)*) wiper

Wi|scher|blatt NT *(Aut)* wiper blade

wisch|fest [ˈvɪʃ-] ADJ *Farbe etc* smearproof, non-smear *attr*

Wi|schi|wa|schi [vɪʃiˈvaʃi] NT **-s**, *no pl (pej inf)* drivel *(inf)*

Wisch-: **Wisch|lap|pen** M cloth; *(für Fußboden)* floorcloth; *(dial: für Geschirr)* dishcloth; **Wisch|tuch** NT *pl* **-tücher** cloth; *(dial: für Geschirr)* dishcloth; **Wisch-Wasch-Au|to|ma|tik** F *(Aut)* wash-wipe *(Brit)*, wash-n-wipe *(US)*

Wi|sent [ˈviːzɛnt] M **-s, -e** bison

Wis|mut [ˈvɪsmuːt] NT OR (AUS) M **-(e)s**, *no pl (abbr* **Bi***)* bismuth

wis|pern [ˈvɪspɐn] VTI to whisper; *(unverständlich auch)* to mumble

Wiss|be|gier|(de) F thirst for knowledge

wiss|be|gie|rig ADJ *Kind* eager to learn

wis|se [ˈvɪsə] IMPER *sing von* **wissen**

wis|sen [ˈvɪsn] ✪ 28.2, 30, 33.1, 43.1, 43.4, 49, 52.5, 53.6 *pret* **wusste**, [ˈvʊstə] *ptp* **gewusst** VTI [gəˈvʊst] **a** *(= informiert sein)* to know *(über +acc, von* about); **ich weiß (es) (schon)** I know; **ich weiß (es) nicht** I don't know; **weißt du schon das Neuste?** have you heard the latest?; **das weiß alle Welt/jedes Kind** (absolutely) everybody/any fool knows that; **was ich alles ~ soll!, als ob ich das wüsste!** how should I know?; **ich weiß von ihr** *or* **über sie nur, dass sie …** all I know about her is that she …, I only know that she …; **von ihr weiß ich das Alter** I know her age, I know how old she is; **von jdm/etw nichts ~ wollen** not to be interested in sb/sth; **er weiß es nicht anders/besser** he doesn't know any different/better; **er weiß zu genießen** he knows how to enjoy himself; **jdn/etw zu schätzen ~** to appreciate sb/sth; **das musst du (selbst) ~** it's your decision; **das solltest du selber ~** you ought to know; **das hättest du ja ~ müssen!** you ought to have realized that; **man kann nie ~** you never know; **man weiß nie, wozu das (noch mal) gut ist** you never know when it will come in handy; **das ~ die Götter** *(inf)* **das weiß der Henker** *(inf)* God only knows; **weiß Gott** *(inf)* God knows *(inf)*; **sich für weiß Gott was halten** *(inf)* to think one is somebody really special; **sie hält sich für wer weiß wie klug** *(inf)* she doesn't half think she's clever *(Brit inf)*, she thinks she's pretty clever; **… oder was weiß ich** *(inf)* … or something; **… und was weiß ich noch alles** *(inf)* … and whatever *(inf)*; **er ist wieder wer weiß wo** *(inf)* goodness knows where he's got to *(Brit) or* gone to *(US)* again *(inf)*; **(ja) wenn ich das wüsste!** goodness knows!; **wenn ich nur wüsste …** if only I knew …; **nicht, dass ich wüsste** not to my knowledge, not as far as I know; **gewusst wie/wo!** *etc* sheer brilliance!; **weißt du was?** (do) you know what?; **weißt du, …** you know …; **ja, weißt du** well, you see; **dass du es (nur) (gleich) weißt** just so you know; **ich weiß sie in Sicherheit/glücklich** I know that she is safe/happy; **was ich/er nicht weiß, macht mich/ihn nicht heiß** *(Prov)* what I don't/he doesn't know won't hurt me/him, what the eye does not see the heart cannot grieve over *(Prov)*
b *(= sich erinnern)* to remember; *(= sich vor Augen führen)* to realize; **ich weiß seine Adresse nicht mehr** I can't remember his address; **weißt du noch, wie schön es damals war?** do you remember how great things were then?; **weißt du noch, damals im Mai/in Stone?** do you remember that May/the times in Stone?; **du musst ~, dass …** you must realize that …
VT **a** *(= kennen)* to know; **ich weiß keinen größeren Genuss, als …** I know (of) no greater delight than …
b *(= erfahren)* **jdn etw ~ lassen** to let sb know sth, to tell sb sth
VI **um etw** *(acc)* **~** *(geh)* **von etw ~** to know of *or* about sth; **ich/er weiß von nichts** I don't/he doesn't know anything about it; **… als ob er von nichts wüsste** … as if he didn't know a thing → **helfen a**

Wis|sen [ˈvɪsn] NT **-s**, *no pl* knowledge; **meines ~s** to my knowledge; **etw ohne jds ~ tun** to do sth without sb's knowledge; **etw gegen** *or* **wider** *(geh)* **(sein) besseres ~ tun** to do sth against one's better judgement; **nach bestem ~ und Gewissen** to the best of one's knowledge and belief; **mit jds ~ und Willen** with sb's knowledge and consent; **~ ist Macht** knowledge is power

wis|send ADJ *Blick etc* knowing ADV knowingly

Wis|sen|de(r) [ˈvɪsndə] MF *decl as adj (= Eingeweihter)* initiate; **die ~n schwiegen** those who knew kept silent

wis|sen+las|sen VT → **wissen VT b**

Wis|sen|schaft [ˈvɪsnʃaft] F **-, -en** science

Wis|sen|schaf|ter [ˈvɪsnʃaftɐ] M **-s, -**, **Wis|sen|schaf|te|rin** [-ərɪn] F **-, -nen** *(old, Sw, Aus)* scientist; *(= Geisteswissenschafter)* academic

Wis|sen|schaft|ler [ˈvɪsnʃaftlɐ] M **-s, -**, **Wis|sen|schaft|le|rin** [-ərɪn] F **-, -nen** scientist; *(= Geisteswissenschaftler)* academic

wis|sen|schaft|lich [ˈvɪsnʃaftlɪç] ADJ scientific; *(= geisteswissenschaftlich)* academic; **Wissenschaftlicher Assistent** assistant lecturer; **Wissenschaftlicher Rat** lecturer, assistant professor *(US)* ADV *arbeiten, etw untersuchen* scientifically

Wis|sen|schaft|lich|keit F -, *no pl* scientific nature; *(in Bezug auf Geisteswissenschaften)* academic nature; **der Arbeit mangelt es an ~** this thesis lacks a scientific approach

wis|sen|schaft|lich-tech|nisch ADJ *Fortschritt, Problem* technological

Wis|sen|schafts-: **Wis|sen|schafts|be|trieb** M academic life; **Wis|sen|schafts|leh|re** F epistemology; **Wis|sen|schafts|zweig** F discipline, branch of learning

Wis|sens-: **Wis|sens|drang** M, **Wis|sens|durst** M *(geh)* urge *or* thirst for knowledge; **Wis|sens|ge|biet** NT field (of knowledge); **Wis|sens|lü|cke** F gap in one's knowledge, knowledge gap; **~n bei jdm schließen** to fill (in) gaps in sb's knowledge; **Wis|sens|schatz** M *(geh)* store of knowledge; **Wis|sens|stand** M state of knowledge; **nach dem gegenwärtigen ~** according to current knowledge; **Wis|sens|stoff** M material; **das ist ~ der 3. Klasse** that's material learned in the 3rd form *(Brit) or*

7th grade *(US)*; **ein enormer ~** an enormous amount of material; **Wis|sens|vor|sprung** M knowledge lead; **wis|sens|wert** ADJ worth knowing; *Information auch* valuable; **das Buch enthält viel Wissenswertes** the book contains much valuable information

wis|sent|lich ['vɪsntlɪç] ADJ deliberate, intentional ADV knowingly, deliberately, intentionally

wis|set ['vɪsət], **wisst** [vɪst] *imper pl von* **wissen**

Wit|frau ['vɪtfrau] F *(old)*, **Wi|tib** ['vi:tɪp, 'vɪtɪp] F **-, -e** [-bə] *(obs)* widow

Wit|mann ['vɪtman] M *pl* **-männer** *(old)* widower

wit|tern ['vɪtɐn] VI *(Wild)* to sniff the air VT *(Wild)* to scent, to get wind of; *(Riese, Teufel)* to smell; *(fig: = ahnen) Geschäft, Chance* to sense; *Gefahr etc* to sense, to scent; **wenn er eine Klassenarbeit witterte ...** whenever he suspected that a test was in the offing *(Brit)* or in the air *(US)* ...

Wit|te|rung F **-, -en** **a** *(= Wetter)* weather; **bei günstiger** *or* **guter ~** if the weather is good **b** *(Hunt) (= Geruch)* scent *(von* of); *(= Geruchssinn)* sense of smell

Wit|te|rungs-: **wit|te|rungs|be|stän|dig** ADJ weatherproof; **Wit|te|rungs|ein|flüs|se** PL effects *pl* of the weather; **Wit|te|rungs|la|ge** F weather; **Wit|te|rungs|um|schlag** M change in the weather; **Wit|te|rungs|ver|hält|nis|se** PL weather conditions *pl*

Wit|tib ['vɪtɪp] F **-, -e** [-bə] *(Aus)* = **Witwe**

Wit|ti|ber ['vɪtɪbɐ] M **-s, -** *(Aus)* = **Witwer**

Wit|we ['vɪtvə] F **-, -n** widow; **~ werden** to be widowed

Wit|wen-: **Wit|wen|geld** NT widow's allowance; **Wit|wen|jahr** NT year of mourning; **Wit|wen|ren|te** F widow's pension; **Wit|wen|schaft** ['vɪtvənʃaft] F **-, -en** widowhood; **Wit|wen|schlei|er** M widow's veil; **Wit|wen|stand** M widowhood; **Wit|wen|trös|ter** M *(pej inf)* widow chaser *(inf)*; **Wit|wen|ver|bren|nung** F suttee

Wit|wer ['vɪtvɐ] M **-s, -** widower

Witz [vɪts] M **-es, -e** **a** *(= Geist)* wit **b** *(Äußerung)* joke *(über +acc* about); **einen ~ machen** *or* **reißen** *(inf)* to make *or* crack a joke; **mach keine ~e!** don't be funny; **ich mach keine ~e** I'm not being funny; **das soll doch wohl ein ~ sein, das ist doch wohl ein ~** that must be a joke, he/you *etc* must be joking; **die Prüfung/der Preis war ein ~** *(inf)* the exam/price was a joke **c der ~ an der Sache ist, dass ...** the great thing about it is that ...; **das ist der ganze ~** that's the thing

Witz-: **Witz|blatt** NT joke book; **Witz|blatt|fi|gur** F *(fig inf)* joke figure; **sich** *(dat)* **wie eine ~ vorkommen** to feel ridiculous; **Witz|bold** ['vɪtsbɔlt] M **-(e)s, -e** [-də] joker; *(= unterhaltsamer Mensch)* comic; **du bist vielleicht ein ~!** *(iro)* you're a great one! *(iro)*

Wit|ze|lei [vɪtsə'lai] F **-, -en** teasing *no pl*; **lass doch diese blöde ~** stop teasing

wit|zeln ['vɪtsln] VI to joke *(über +acc* about)

Witz|fi|gur F *(lit)* joke character; *(fig inf)* figure of fun

wit|zig ['vɪtsɪç] ADJ funny

Wit|zig|keit F **-,** *no pl* humour *(Brit)*, humor *(US)*

witz|los ADJ *(inf: = unsinnig)* pointless, futile

w. L. *abbr von* **westlicher Länge**

Wla|di|wos|tok [vladivɔs'tɔk] NT **-s** Vladivostok

WLAN [ˌwaiɐlɛs'lɛn] NT **-(s), -s** *abbr von* **wireless local area network** *(Comput)* WLAN, wireless LAN

WM [ve:'lɛm] F **-, -s** *abbr von* **Weltmeisterschaft**

WNW *abbr von* **Westnordwest** WNW

wo [vo:] INTERROG, REL ADV **a** where; *(= irgendwo)* somewhere; **überall, wo** wherever; **wo könnte er anders** *or* **wo anders könnte er sein als auf der Arbeit?** where else could he be but at work?; **wo immer ...** wherever ...; **der Tag/eine Zeit wo ...** *(inf)* the day/a time when ...; **ach** *or* **i wo!** *(inf)* nonsense!

b *(inf: = der/die/das)* that; **der Mann/die Frau/das Auto, wo ...** the man/woman/car that ...

CONJ **wo möglich** where *or* if possible; **wo er doch wusste, dass ich nicht kommen konnte** when he knew I couldn't come; **wo du doch in die Stadt gehst, könntest du ...?** *(inf)* seeing that you're going into town, could you ...?; **wo ich gerade daran denke** *(inf)* while I'm thinking about it; **und das jetzt, wo ich doch dazu keine Lust habe** *(inf)* and that now when I'm just not in the mood

w. o. *abbr von* **wie oben**

wo-: **wo|an|ders** [vo'landɐs] ADV somewhere else, elsewhere; **wo|an|ders|her** [vo'landɐs'he:ɐ] ADV from somewhere else, from elsewhere; **wo|an|ders|hin** [vo'landɐshɪn] ADV somewhere else, elsewhere

wob *pret von* **weben**

wo|bei [vo'bai] ADV → *auch* **bei** **a** *interrog* **~ ist das passiert?** how did that happen?; **~ hast du ihn erwischt?** what did you catch him at *or* doing?; **~ seid ihr gerade?** what are you doing just now?; *(im Buch)* where are you at just now?

b *rel* in which; **ich erzähle mal, was passiert ist, ~ ich allerdings das Unwichtige auslasse** I will tell you what happened but I will leave out all the unimportant details; **~ man sehr aufpassen muss, dass man nicht betrogen wird/keinen Sonnenstich bekommt** and you have to be very careful that you don't get cheated/don't get sunburnt; **~ mir gerade einfällt** which reminds me; **das Auto prallte gegen einen Baum, ~ der Fahrer schwer verletzt wurde** the car hit a tree severely injuring the driver

Wo|che ['vɔxə] F **-, -n** week; **zweimal in der ~** twice a week; **in dieser ~** this week; **in die ~n kommen** *(old)* to be near one's time *(old)*

Wo|chen-: **Wo|chen|ar|beits|zeit** F working week; **welche ~ haben Sie?** what is your working week?, how many hours a week do you work?; **Wo|chen|be|ginn** M beginning *or* start of the week; **Wo|chen|be|richt** M weekly report; **Wo|chen|bett** NT **im ~ liegen** to be lying in *(esp Brit old)*, to be confined; **im ~ sterben** to die in the weeks following childbirth; **Wo|chen|bett|de|pres|si|on** F postnatal depression, baby blues *(inf)*; **Wo|chen|bett|fie|ber** NT puerperal fever

Wo|chen|end- *in cpds* weekend; **Wo|chen|end|aus|flug** M weekend trip; **Wo|chen|end|aus|ga|be** F weekend edition; **Wo|chen|end|bei|la|ge** F weekend supplement

Wo|chen|end|be|zie|hung F long-distance relationship

Wo|chen|en|de NT weekend; **schönes ~!** have a nice weekend; **langes** *or* **verlängertes ~** long weekend

Wo|chen|end|haus NT *(meist)* weekend cottage

Wo|chen|end|ler [-lɛndlɐ] M **-s, -**, **Wo|chen|end|le|rin** [-ərɪn] F **-, -nen** *(inf)* weekender

Wo|chen|end-: **Wo|chen|end|se|mi|nar** NT weekend seminar; **Wo|chen|end|ta|rif** M *(Telec)* weekend rate; **Wo|chen|end|ver|kehr** M weekend traffic

Wo|chen-: **Wo|chen|fluss** M *(Med)* lochia *(spec)*; **Wo|chen|ka|len|der** M week-by-week calendar; **Wo|chen|kar|te** F weekly season ticket; **wo|chen|lang** ADJ ADV for weeks; **nach ~em Warten** after waiting for weeks, after weeks of waiting; **Wo|chen|lohn** M weekly wage; **Wo|chen|markt** M weekly market

> **WOCHENMARKT**
>
> Fruit and vegetables can be bought at a German **Wochenmarkt**, where local farmers sell their produce one or two mornings a week. You can also buy cheese, sausage, meat, poultry and fish, as well as other groceries and cut flowers.

Wo|chen-: **Wo|chen|schau** F newsreel; **Wo|chen|schrift** F weekly (periodical); **Wo|chen|stun|den** PL **wie viele ~ arbeitest du?** how many hours a week do you work?; **wie viele ~ habt ihr (in) Mathe?** how many math(s) lessons a week do you have?; **Wo|chen|tag** M weekday *(including Saturday)*; **was ist heute für ein ~?** what day (of the week) is it today?; **wo|chen|tags** ['vɔxnta:ks] ADV on weekdays

wö|chent|lich ['vœçntlɪç] ADJ weekly ADV weekly; *(= einmal pro Woche)* once a week; **zwei Vormittage ~ kommen** to come two mornings a week; **~ zweimal** twice a week; **sich ~ abwechseln** to take turns every week

Wo|chen-: **wo|chen|wei|se** ADV week by week; *(= einmal pro Woche)* once a week; *(= für eine Woche)* by the week; **Wo|chen|zeit|schrift** F weekly (magazine *or* periodical); **Wo|chen|zei|tung** F weekly (paper)

Wöch|ne|rin ['vœçnərɪn] F **-, -nen** *woman who has recently given birth*, woman in childbed *(old)*, puerpera *(spec)*

Wöch|ne|rin|nen|sta|ti|on F maternity ward

Wo|dan ['vo:dan] M **-s** *(Myth)* Wotan

Wod|ka ['vɔtka] M **-s, -s** vodka

wo|durch [vo'dʊrç] ADV → *auch* **durch** **a** *interrog* how **b** *rel* which; **alles, ~ sie glücklich geworden war ...** everything which had made her happy ...

wo|fern [vo'fɛrn] CONJ *(old)* if

wo|für [vo'fy:ɐ] ADV → *auch* **für** **a** *interrog* for what, what ... for; *(= warum)* why **b** *rel* for which, which ... for

wog *pret von* **wiegen**

Wo|ge ['vo:gə] F **-, -n** wave; *(fig auch)* surge; **wenn sich die ~n geglättet haben** *(fig)* when things have calmed down

wo|ge|gen [vo'ge:gn] ADV → *auch* **gegen** **a** *interrog* against what, what ... against; **~ ist dieses Mittel?** what's this medicine for? **b** *rel* against which, which ... against

wo|gen ['vo:gn] VI *(liter)* to surge *(auch fig)*; *(Kornfeld)* to wave, to undulate; *(fig: Kampf)* to rage; *(Busen)* to heave

Wo|gen|schlag M pounding (of the waves)

wo|her [vo'he:ɐ] ADV **a** *interrog* where ... from; **~ weißt du das?** how do you (come to) know that?; **~ kommt es eigentlich, dass ...** how is it that ...?, how come ... *(inf)*; **ach ~!** *(dial inf)* nonsense! **b** *rel* from which, where ... from

wo|hin [vo'hɪn] ADV **a** *interrog* where; **~, bitte?, ~ solls gehen?** where to?, where do you want to go?; **~ so eilig?** where are you off to so fast, where are you rushing off to?; **~ damit?** where shall I/we put it?; **ich muss mal ~** *(euph inf)* I've got to go somewhere *(euph inf)* **b** *rel* where; **~ man auch schaut** wherever you look

wo|hi|nein [vohɪ'nain] ADV = **worein**

wo|hin|ge|gen [vohɪn'ge:gn] CONJ whereas, while

wo|hin|ter [vo'hɪntɐ] ADV → *auch* **hinter** **a** *interrog* what *or* where ... behind; **~ kann ich in Deckung gehen?** what can I take cover behind?, behind what can I take cover? **b** *rel* behind which; **~ man sich auch versteckt** whatever you hide behind

wohl [vo:l] ADV **a** *comp* **-er**, *superl* **am -sten** *(= angenehm zumute)* happy; *(= gesund)* well; **sich ~er fühlen** to feel happier; *(= wie zu Hause)* to feel more at home; *(gesundheitlich)* to feel better → *auch* **wohlfühlen**; **bei dem Gedanken ist mir nicht ~** I'm not very happy at the thought; **am ~sten wäre mir, wenn ...** I'd feel happier if ...; **jdm ist ~ ums Herz** sb feels light of heart; **~ oder übel** whether one likes it or not, willy-nilly; **~ dem, der ...** happy the man who ...; **~ ihm, dass ...** it's a good thing for him that ...; **es sich** *(dat)* **~ gehen** *or* **sein** *or* **ergehen lassen** to enjoy oneself

b *(= gut) comp* **besser**, *superl* **bestens** *or* **am besten** well; **nun ~!** now then!; **ich wünsche ~ gespeist/geruht zu haben** *(dated)* I do hope you have enjoyed your meal/have had a pleasant sleep; **lasst es euch ~ schmecken!** I hope you like *or* enjoy it; **~ ausgewogen** = **wohlausgewogen**; **~ bedacht** = **wohlbedacht**; **~ begründet** = **wohlbegründet**; **~ bekannt** well-known; **sie ist mir ~ bekannt** I know her well; **~ beraten** = **wohlberaten**; **~ durchdacht** = **wohldurchdacht**; **~ erprobt** = **wohlerprobt**; **~ erwogen** = **wohlerwogen**; **~ erzogen** = **wohlerzogen**; **~ geformt** = **wohlgeformt**; **~ gemeint** = **wohlgemeint**; **~ genährt** = **wohlgenährt**; **~ geordnet** = **wohlgeordnet**; **~ geraten** = **wohlgeraten**; **~ klingend** = **wohlklingend**; **~ proportioniert** = **wohlproportioniert**; **~ riechend** = **wohlriechend**; **~ schmeckend** = **wohlschmeckend**; **~ temperiert** = **wohltemperiert**; **~ überlegt** = **wohlüberlegt**; **~ unterrichtet** = **wohlunterrichtet**; **~ versorgt** = **wohlversorgt**; **~ verstanden** = **wohlverstanden** → **bekommen**

c *(= wahrscheinlich)* probably, no doubt; *(iro: = bestimmt)* surely; **er ist ~ schon zu Hause** he's probably at home by now, no doubt he's at home by now; **das ist ~ nicht gut möglich** I should think it's unlikely; **es ist ~ anzunehmen, dass ...** it is to be expected that ...; **du bist ~ verrückt** you must be crazy!; **das ist doch ~ nicht dein Ernst!** surely you're not serious!, you can't be serious!

d *(= vielleicht)* perhaps, possibly; *(= etwa)* about; **ob ~ noch jemand kommt?** I wonder if anybody else is coming?; **das kann man sich ~ vorstellen, nicht wahr?** you can just imagine something like that, can't you?; **das mag ~ sein** that may well be; **willst du das ~ lassen!** I wish you'd stop (doing) that

e *(= durchaus)* well; **das kann ~ mal vorkommen** that might well happen; **ich denke, ich verstehe dich sehr ~!** I think I understand you very *or* perfectly well; **doch, das glaube ich ~** I certainly do believe it; **sehr ~ (der Herr)!** *(old)* very good (sir); **~!** *(= doch)* yes!; *(S Ger, Sw: = selbstverständlich)* of course!

CONJ *(= zwar)* **er hat es ~ versprochen, aber ...** he may have promised, but ...; **~, aber ...** that may well be, but ...

Wohl [vo:l] NT **-(e)s**, *no pl* welfare, wellbeing; **das öffentliche ~ und das ~ des Individuums** the public good *or* common weal and the welfare of the individual; **der Menschheit zum ~e** for the benefit of mankind; **das ~ und Weh(e)** the weal and woe; **zu eurem ~** for your benefit *or* good; **zum ~!** cheers!; **auf dein ~!** your health!; **auf jds ~ trinken** to drink sb's health

Wohl-: **wohl|an** [vo'lan, vo:l'lan] INTERJ *(old, poet)* come *or* well now; **wohl|an|stän|dig** ADJ respectable; *Benehmen* proper, correct; **wohl|auf** [vo:l'lauf, vo'lauf] ADJ *pred* well, in good health INTERJ = **wohlan**; **wohl|aus|ge|wo|gen** ADJ (well) balanced; **wohl|be|dacht** ADJ well considered; **Wohl|be|fin|den** NT wellbeing; **wohl|be|grün|det** ADJ well-founded; *Maßnahme, Strafe* well-justified; **Wohl|be|ha|gen** NT feeling of wellbeing; **wohl|be|hal|ten** ADV *ankommen* safe and sound, intact; **wohl|be|kannt** ADJ well-known → *auch* **wohl ADV b**; **wohl|be|leibt** ADJ *(hum)* stout, portly *(form)*; **wohl|be|ra|ten** ADJ well-advised; **wohl|be|stallt** [-bəʃtalt] ADJ *attr (form)* well-established; **wohl|durch|dacht** ADJ well *or* carefully thought out; **wohl+er|ge|hen** *sep irreg impers aux sein*, **wohl er|ge|hen** *irreg impers aux sein* VI **es ist ihm wohlergangen** he fared well; **es sich** *(dat)* **~ lassen** to enjoy oneself; **Wohl|er|ge|hen** [-lɛɐge:ən] NT **-s**, *no pl* welfare; **wohl|er|probt** [-lɛɐpro:pt] ADJ well-tested, well-tried; *Mitarbeiter* experienced; **wohl|er|wo|gen** [-lɛɐvo:gn] ADJ *comp* **besser erwogen**, *superl* **besterwogen** well *or* carefully considered; **wohl|er|zo|gen** [-lɛɐtso:gn] ADJ *comp* **besser erzogen**, *superl* **besterzogen** *(geh)* well-bred; *Kind* well-mannered; **~ sein** to be well-bred ADV **sich ~ benehmen** to be well-mannered

Wohl|fahrt F **-**, *no pl* **a** *(old geh: = Wohlergehen)* welfare **b** *(= Fürsorge)* welfare; **bei der ~ arbeiten** to do welfare work

Wohl|fahrts-: **Wohl|fahrts|amt** NT *(dated, inf)* social security office; **Wohl|fahrts|aus|schuss** M *(Hist)* Committee of Public Safety *(Brit)*, Public Welfare Committee *(US)*; **Wohl|fahrts|ein|rich|tung** F social service; **Wohl|fahrts|mar|ke** F charity stamp; **Wohl|fahrts|or|ga|ni|sa|ti|on** F charity, charitable institution *or* organization; **Wohl|fahrts|pfle|ge** F social *or* welfare work; **freie ~** voluntary social *or* welfare work; **Wohl|fahrts|ren|te** F benefit pension; **Wohl|fahrts|staat** M welfare state; **Wohl|fahrts|un|ter|stüt|zung** F *(dated)* income support, welfare (aid) *(US)*

Wohl-: **wohl|feil** ADJ **a** *(old, liter)* inexpensive **b** *(fig) (= abgedroschen) Ratschlag, Worte, Reden* hackneyed, cheapened *(US)*; *(= bequem) Ausrede* convenient; **wohl+füh|len** *sep*, **wohl füh|len** VR to feel happy; *(= wie zu Hause)* to feel at home → *auch* **wohl ADV a**; **Wohl|füh|len** NT **-s**, *no pl* (sense of) well-being; **Möbel** *etc* **zum ~** furniture *etc* for feeling at home; **Wohl|fühl|fak|tor** M feel-good factor; **wohl|ge|bo|ren** ADJ *(obs)* **Eure** *or* **Euer ~** Sir; **Seiner ~ Herr XY** XY Esq; **Wohl|ge|fal|len** NT satisfaction, pleasure; **sein ~ an etw** *(dat)* **haben** to take pleasure in sth; **sich in ~ auflösen** *(hum) (Freundschaft, Argument)* to peter out; *(Plan, Problem)* to vanish into thin air; *(Auto, Kleidung)* to fall apart; **wohl|ge|fäl|lig** ADJ *(= gefallend)* pleasing; *(= zufrieden, erfreut)* well-pleased; **Gott ~** well-pleasing to God; **wohl|ge|formt** [-gəfɔrmt] ADJ *comp* **wohlgeformter**, *superl* **bestgeformt** well-shaped; *Körperteil* shapely; *Satz* well-formed; **Wohl|ge|fühl** NT feeling *or* sense of wellbeing; **wohl|ge|lit|ten** ADJ *comp* **wohlgelittener**, *superl* **wohlgelittenste(r, s)** *(geh)* well-liked; **wohl|ge|meint** [-gəmaint] ADJ well-meant, well-intentioned; **wohl|ge|merkt** [-gəmɛrkt] ADV mark you *(esp Brit)*, mind (you); **das waren ~ englische Pfund** that was English pounds, mark you *(esp Brit) or* mind you; **wohl|ge|mut** [-gəmu:t] ADJ *comp* **wohlgemuter**, *superl* **wohlgemuteste(r, s)** *(old, liter)* cheerful; **wohl|ge|nährt** [-gənɛ:ɐt] ADJ *comp* **wohlgenährter**, *superl* **wohlgenährteste(r, s)** well-fed; **wohl|ge|ord|net** ADJ *(geh)* well-ordered; *Leben auch* well-regulated, well-organized; **wohl|ge|ra|ten** ADJ *comp* **wohlgeratener**, *superl* **wohlgeratenste(r, s)** *(geh) Kind* fine; *Werk* successful; **Wohl|ge|ruch** M *(geh)* pleasant smell; *(von Garten, Blumen etc auch)* fragrance; **Wohl|ge|schmack** M *(geh)* flavour *(Brit)*, flavor *(US)*, pleasant taste; **wohl|ge|sinnt** ADJ *comp* **wohlgesinnter**, *superl* **wohlgesinnteste(r, s)** *(geh)* well-disposed (*+dat* towards); *Worte* well-meaning; **wohl|ge|stalt** [-gəʃtalt] ADJ *(geh) Gegenstand* well-shaped; *Körperteil, Frau* shapely; *Mann* well-proportioned; **wohl|ge|stal|tet** [-gəʃtaltət] ADJ *comp* **wohlgestalteter**, *superl* **wohlgestaltetste(r, s)** well-shaped, well-proportioned; **wohl|ge|tan** ADJ *(old, liter)* well done *pred*; **wohl|ha|bend** ADJ *comp* **wohlhabender**, *superl* **wohlhabendste(r, s)** well-to-do, prosperous; **Wohl|ha|ben|heit** ['vo:lha:bnhait] F **-**, *no pl* prosperity, affluence

woh|lig ['vo:lɪç] ADJ pleasant; *(= gemütlich)* cosy; *Ruhe* blissful ADV *warm* comfortably; **~ rekelte er sich in der Sonne** he stretched luxuriously in the sun

Wohl-: **Wohl|klang** M *(geh)* melodious sound; **wohl|klin|gend** ADJ *comp* **wohlklingender**, *superl* **wohlklingendste(r, s)** pleasant(-sounding), melodious; **Wohl|le|ben** NT *(geh)* life of luxury; **wohl|mei|nend** ADJ *comp* **wohlmeinender**, *superl* **wohlmeinendste(r, s)** well-meaning; **wohl|pro|por|ti|o|niert** ADJ *comp* **besser proportioniert** *or* **wohlproportionierter**, *superl* **bestproportioniert** well-proportioned; **wohl|rie|chend** ADJ *comp* **wohlriechender**, *superl* **wohlriechendste(r, s)** *(geh)* fragrant; **wohl|schme|ckend** ADJ *comp* **wohlschmeckender**, *superl* **wohlschmeckendste(r, s)** *(geh)* palatable; **Wohl|sein** NT **zum ~!, auf Ihr ~!** your health!

Wohl|stand M, *no pl* affluence, prosperity → **ausbrechen VI c**

Wohl|stands-: **Wohl|stands|bür|ger(in)** M(F) *(pej)* member of the affluent society; **Wohl|stands|ge|sell|schaft** F affluent society; **Wohl|stands|kri|mi|na|li|tät** F *crimes typical of the affluent society*; **Wohl|stands|müll** M refuse of the affluent society

Wohl|tat F **a** *(= Genuss)* relief **b** *(= Dienst, Gefallen)* favour *(Brit)*, favor *(US)*; *(= gute Tat)* good deed; **jdm eine ~ erweisen** to do sb a favour *(Brit) or* favor *(US) or* a good turn

Wohl|tä|ter M benefactor

Wohl|tä|te|rin F benefactress

wohl|tä|tig ADJ **a** charitable **b** *(dial)* = **wohltuend**

Wohl|tä|tig|keit F charity, charitableness

Wohl|tä|tig|keits-: **Wohl|tä|tig|keits|ba|sar** M charity bazaar; **Wohl|tä|tig|keits|kon|zert** NT charity concert; **Wohl|tä|tig|keits|ver|an|stal|tung** F charity event; *(Sport auch)* charity fixture; **Wohl|tä|tig|keits|ver|ein** M charitable organization, charity; **Wohl|tä|tig|keits|zweck** M charitable cause, good cause

Wohl-: **wohl|tem|pe|riert** [-tɛmpəri:ɐt] ADJ *(Wein, Bad, Zimmer)* at the right temperature *no comp*; *Zimmer (auch)* at a pleasant temperature; *Wein (auch)* at the correct temperature; **das „Wohltemperierte Klavier"** "The Well-Tempered Clavier"; **wohl|tu|end** ADJ *comp* **wohltuender**, *superl* **wohltuendste(r, s)** (most) agreeable; **wohl+tun** *sep irreg*, **wohl tun** △ *irreg* VI **a** *(= angenehm sein)* to do good (*jdm* sb), to be beneficial (*jdm* to sb); **das tut wohl** that's good **b** *(old, liter: = Gutes tun)* to benefit (*jdm* sb); **wohl|über|legt** ADJ well thought out ADV **etw ~ machen** to do sth after careful consideration; **wohl|un|ter|rich|tet** ADJ well-informed; **wohl|ver|dient** ADJ *Strafe* well-deserved; *Belohnung, Ruhe etc auch* well-earned; **Wohl|ver|hal|ten** NT *(usu iro)* good conduct *or* behaviour *(Brit) or* behavior *(US)*; **wohl|ver|sorgt** [-fɛɐzɔrkt] ADJ well-provided-for; **wohl|ver|stan|den** [-vɛɐʃtandn] ADJ *attr (geh)* well-understood ADV mark *(esp Brit) or* mind you; **wohl|weis|lich** ['vo:lvaislɪç, 'vo:l'vaislɪç] ADV very wisely; **ich habe das ~ nicht gemacht** I was careful not to do that; **wohl+wol|len** *sep irreg*, **wohl wol|len** △ *irreg* VI *(geh)* **jdm ~** to wish sb well; **Wohl|wol|len** NT **-s**, *no pl* goodwill; **selbst bei dem größten** *or* **mit größtem ~** with the best will in the world; **jdn mit ~ betrachten** to regard sb benevolently; **sich** *(dat)* **jds ~ erwerben** to win sb's favour *(Brit) or* favor *(US)*; **wohl|wol|lend** ADJ *comp* **wohlwollender**, *superl* **wohlwollendste(r, s)** benevolent; **jdm gegenüber ~ sein** to be kindly disposed toward(s) sb ADV favourably *(Brit)*, favorably *(US)*; **jdm ~ geneigt** *or* **gesonnen sein** to be kindly disposed toward(s) sb; **einer Sache** *(dat)* **~ gegenüberstehen** to approve of sth

Wohn-: **Wohn|an|hän|ger** M caravan *(Brit)*, trailer *(US)*; **Wohn|an|la|ge** F housing area; **Wohn|bau** M *pl* **-bauten** residential building; **Wohn|be|völ|ke|rung** F residential population; **Wohn|block** M *pl* **-blocks** block of flats *(Brit)*, apartment house *(US)*; **Wohn|con|tai|ner** M Portakabin® *(Brit)*, trailer *(US)*; **Wohn|dich|te** F *(Sociol)* occupant density; **Wohn|die|le** F hall-cum-living-room; **Wohn|ei|gen|tum** NT property ownership; **Wohn|ein|heit** F accommodation *or* residential unit

woh|nen ['vo:nən] VI **a** *(= Behausung haben)* to live; *(vorübergehend)* to stay; **wo ~ Sie?** where do you live/are you staying?; **er wohnt (in der) Friedrichstraße 11** he lives at (number) 11 Friedrichstraße; **wir ~ sehr schön** we have a very nice flat *(Brit) or* apartment/house *etc*; **wir ~ da sehr schön** it's very nice where we live;

hier wohnt es sich gut, hier lässt es sich gut ~ it's a nice place to live/stay **b** *(fig liter)* to dwell *(liter)*, to live

Wohn-: **Wohn|flä|che** F living space; **50 Quadratmeter ~** living room(, dining room) and bedroom(s) totalling 50 square metres *(Brit) or* totaling 50 square meters *(US)*; **Wohn|ge|bäu|de** NT residential building; **Wohn|ge|biet** NT residential area; **Wohn|ge|gend** F residential area; **Wohn|geld** NT housing benefit *(Brit)*, housing *or* rent subsidy *(US)*; **Wohn|ge|mein|schaft** F *(Menschen)* people sharing a flat *(Brit) or* apartment/house; **unsere ~** the people I share a flat *etc* with; **in einer ~ leben** to share a flat *etc*; **Wohn|gift** NT poisonous substance found in the home; **wohn|haft** ADJ *(form)* resident; **Wohn|haus** NT residential building; **Wohn|heim** NT *(esp für Arbeiter)* hostel; *(für Studenten)* hall (of residence), dormitory *(US)*; *(für alte Menschen)* home; **Wohn|klo** NT *(hum inf)* **~ (mit Kochnische)** tiny flat *(Brit) or* apartment, shoebox *(inf)*; **Wohn|kom|fort** M comfort of one's home; **ein Appartement mit sämtlichem ~** an apartment with every modern convenience, an apartment with all mod cons *(Brit) or* all amenities *(US)*; **Wohn|kom|plex** M housing estate *(Brit) or* development, subdivision *(US)*; **Wohn|kü|che** F kitchen-cum-living-room; **Wohn|kul|tur** F style of home décor; **keine ~ haben** to have no taste in home décor; **Wohn|la|ge** F residential area; **unsere ~ ist schön/ungünstig** our house/apartment is nicely/awkwardly situated; **Wohn|land|schaft** F landscaped interior; **wohn|lich** [ˈvoːnlɪç] ADJ homely, cosy; **es sich** *(dat)* **~ machen** to make oneself comfortable; **Wohn|lich|keit** F -, *no pl* homeliness, cosiness; **Wohn|mo|bil** [-mobiːl] NT **-s, -e** Dormobile®, camper *(US)*, motor caravan, RV *(US)*; **Wohn|ob|jekt** NT *(Aus form)* accommodation *or* residential unit; **Wohn|ort** M *pl* **-orte** place of residence; **Wohn|par|tei** F *(esp Aus)* tenant; *(mehrere Personen)* tenants *pl*; **Wohn|qua|li|tät** F quality of housing; **Wohn|raum** M living room; *(no pl: = Wohnfläche)* living space; **Wohn-Schlaf|zim|mer** NT bedsitting room; **Wohn|sied|lung** F housing estate *(Brit) or* scheme *or* development, subdivision *(US)*; **Wohn|si|lo** M *(pej)* concrete block; **Wohn|sitz** M domicile; **ohne festen ~** of no fixed abode; **wohn|sitz|los** ADJ homeless; **Wohn|stadt** F residential town; **Wohn|stu|be** F living room; **Wohn|turm** M tower block *(Brit)*, high rise *(esp US)*

Woh|nung [ˈvoːnʊŋ] F **-, -en** flat *(Brit)*, apartment; *(liter: von Tieren etc)* habitation; *(= Wohneinheit)* dwelling *(form)*; *(= Unterkunft)* lodging, accommodations *pl (US)*; **1.000 neue ~en** 1,000 new homes; **~ nehmen** *(form)* to take up residence *(form)*; **freie ~ haben** to have free lodging

Woh|nungs-: **Woh|nungs|amt** NT (public) housing office; **Woh|nungs|auf|lö|sung** F flat *(Brit) or* apartment clearance; **wegen ~ abzugeben** *(in Annonce)* house clearance sale *(Brit)*, moving sale *(US)*; **Woh|nungs|bau** M, *no pl* house building *no def art*; **Woh|nungs|bau|pro|gramm** NT housing programme *(Brit) or* program *(US)*; **Woh|nungs|be|darf** M housing requirements *pl*; **Woh|nungs|be|set|zer(in)** M(F) squatter; **Woh|nungs|ein|rich|tung** F furnishings *pl*; *(Innenarchitektur)* interior design; **Woh|nungs|in|ha|ber(in)** M(F) householder, occupant; *(= Eigentümer auch)* owner-occupier, owner-occupant; **woh|nungs|los** ADJ homeless; **Woh|nungs|lo|se(r)** MF *decl as adj* homeless person; **für ~** for the homeless; **Woh|nungs|lo|sig|keit** F homelessness; **Woh|nungs|mak|ler(in)** M(F) estate agent *(esp Brit)*, real estate agent *(US)*; **Woh|nungs|man|gel** M housing shortage; **Woh|nungs|markt** M housing market; **Woh|nungs|nach|weis** M accommodation registry; **Woh|nungs|not** F serious housing shortage, serious lack of housing; **Woh|nungs|schlüs|sel** M key (to the flat *(Brit) or* apartment); **Woh|nungs|su|che** F flat-hunting *(Brit)*, apartment-hunting *(esp US)*; **auf ~ sein** to be looking for a flat *(Brit) or* apartment, to be flat-hunting *(Brit) or* apartment-hunting *(esp US)*; **woh|nungs|su|chend** ADJ *attr* looking for accommodation; **Woh|nungs|su|chen|de(r)** MF *decl as adj* person seeking accommodation; **Hilfe für ~** help for those seeking accommodation; **Woh|nungs|tausch** M exchange (of flats *(Brit) or* apartments/houses); **Woh|nungs|tür** F door (to the flat *(Brit) or* apartment); **Woh|nungs|wech|sel** M change of address; **Woh|nungs|we|sen** NT housing

Wohn-: **Wohn|ver|hält|nis|se** PL *(von Familie)* living conditions *pl*; *(in Stadt)* housing conditions *pl*; **Wohn|vier|tel** NT residential area *or* district; **Wohn|wa|gen** M caravan *(Brit)*, trailer *(US)*; **Wohn|wert** M **einen hohen ~ haben** to be an attractive place to live in; **Wohn|zim|mer** NT living room; **Wohn|zwe|cke** PL residential purposes *pl*

Wok [vɔk] M **-s, -s** *(Cook)* wok

wöl|ben [ˈvœlbn] VT to curve; *Blech etc* to bend; *Dach etc* to vault VR to curve; *(Asphalt)* to bend, to buckle; *(Tapete)* to bulge out; *(Brust)* to swell; *(Stirn)* to be domed; *(Decke, Brücke)* to arch; **ein klarer Sternenhimmel wölbte sich über uns** the clear sky formed a star-studded dome above us *(liter)* → *auch* **gewölbt**

Wöl|bung F **-, -en** curvature; *(kuppelförmig)* dome; *(bogenförmig)* arch; *(von Körperteil)* curve; *(von Straße)* camber; *(von Tapete)* bulge

Wolf [vɔlf] M **-(e)s, =e** [ˈvœlfə] **a** wolf; **ein ~ im Schafspelz** a wolf in sheep's clothing; **mit den Wölfen heulen** *(fig)* to run with the pack **b** *(Tech)* shredder; *(= Fleischwolf)* mincer *(Brit)*, grinder *(US)*; **Fleisch durch den ~ drehen** to mince meat *(Brit)*, to grind meat *(US)*; **jdn durch den ~ drehen** *(fig)* to give sb a hard time of it; **ich fühle mich wie durch den ~ gedreht** I feel as if I've been on the rack **c** *(Med)* intertrigo *no art (spec), inflammation of the skin caused by chafing between skin surfaces*

Wölf|chen [ˈvœlfçən] NT **-s, -** *dim von* **Wolf** wolf cub

Wöl|fin [ˈvœlfɪn] F **-, -nen** she-wolf

wöl|fisch [ˈvœlfɪʃ] ADJ wolfish

Wölf|ling [ˈvœlflɪŋ] M **-s, -e** *(= Pfadfinder)* cub (scout)

Wolf|ram [ˈvɔlfram] NT **-s**, *no pl (abbr* **W**) tungsten, wolfram

Wolfs-: **Wolfs|hund** M Alsatian *(Brit)*, German shepherd; **Irischer ~** Irish wolfhound; **Wolfs|hun|ger** M *(fig inf)* ravenous hunger; **ich hatte einen ~** I was ravenous; **Wolfs|mensch** M **a** wolf child; **er war ein ~** he had been reared by wolves **b** *(= Werwolf)* werewolf; **Wolfs|milch** F *(Bot)* spurge; **Wolfs|ra|chen** M *(Med)* cleft palate; **Wolfs|ru|del** NT pack of wolves; **Wolfs|spin|ne** F wolf spider

Wol|ga [ˈvɔlga] F **-** Volga

Wölk|chen [ˈvœlkçən] NT **-s, -** *dim von* **Wolke**

Wol|ke [ˈvɔlkə] F **-, -n** *(lit, fig)* cloud; *(in Edelstein)* flaw; **aus allen ~n fallen** *(fig)* to be flabbergasted *(inf)*; **das ist 'ne ~** *(inf)* it's fantastic *(inf)* → **schweben a**

Wol|ken-: **Wol|ken|band** NT band of cloud; **Wol|ken|bank** F *pl* **-bänke** cloud bank; **Wol|ken|bil|dung** F cloud formation; **es kann zu ~ kommen** it may become cloudy *or* overcast; **Wol|ken|bruch** M cloudburst; **wol|ken|bruch|ar|tig** ADJ torrential; **Wol|ken|de|cke** F cloud cover; **die Stadt liegt unter einer dichten ~** the town lies under a heavy layer of cloud; **Wol|ken|him|mel** M cloudy *or* overcast sky; **Wol|ken|krat|zer** M skyscraper; **Wol|ken|ku|ckucks|heim** NT cloud-cuckoo-land; **in einem ~ leben** to live in cloud-cuckoo-land; **Wol|ken|land|schaft** F *(liter)* clouds *pl*; **wol|ken|los** ADJ cloudless; **Wol|ken|meer** NT *(liter)* sea of clouds; **Wol|ken|schicht** F layer of cloud, cloud layer; **Wol|ken|schlei|er** M *(liter)* veil of cloud *(liter)*; **von einem ~ eingehüllt** veiled in cloud; **Wol|ken|strei|fen** M streak of cloud; **wol|ken|ver|han|gen** [-fɛɐhaŋən] ADJ overcast; **Wol|ken|wand** F cloud bank

wol|kig [ˈvɔlkɪç] ADJ cloudy; *(fig)* obscure

Woll|de|cke F (woollen *(Brit) or* woolen *(US)*) blanket

Wol|le [ˈvɔlə] F **-, -n** wool; **in der ~ gefärbt** *(fig)* dyed-in-the-wool; **mit jdm in die ~ kommen** *or* **geraten** *(fig inf)* **sich mit jdm in die ~ kriegen** *(fig inf)* to start squabbling with sb; **sich mit jdm in der ~ haben** *(fig inf)* to be at loggerheads with sb

wol|len¹ [ˈvɔlən] ADJ *attr* woollen *(Brit)*, woolen *(US)*

wol|len² [ˈvɔlən]
pret **wollte** [ˈvɔltə], *ptp* **gewollt** [gəˈvɔlt]
✪ 35.1, 52.2, 53.5

1 HILFSVERB	3 INTRANSITIVES VERB
2 TRANSITIVES VERB	

wollen wird normalerweise mit *to want* übersetzt.

1 – HILFSVERB *ptp* wollen

a [= Willen haben] **sie will nach Hause gehen** she wants to go home; **sie will nicht nach Hause gehen** she doesn't want to go home; *(= weigert sich)* she won't go home; **etw haben wollen** to want (to have) sth; **ich will lieber ins Kino gehen** I'd prefer to go to the cinema; **er wollte unbedingt nach Frankreich ziehen** he was desperate to move to France; **ich will so einen Fehler nie wieder machen** I won't make that mistake again; **er will immer alles besser wissen** he thinks he knows it all; **wenn man darauf noch Rücksicht nehmen wollte** if you are going to take that into account as well; **das wollen wir doch erst mal sehen!** we'll see about that!; **er will und will sich nicht ändern** he just will not change; **was will man da schon machen/sagen?** what can you do/say?

b [= beabsichtigen] **etw gerade tun wollen** to be going to do sth; **wolltest du gerade weggehen?** were you just leaving?; **ich wollte schon gehen/gerade aufhören, als …** I was just going to leave/just about to stop when …; **es sieht aus, als wollte es regnen** it looks as if it's going to rain; **es will nicht besser/wärmer werden** it just won't get better/won't warm up; **es will und will nicht aufhören** it just goes on and on

c [= müssen] **das will alles genauestens überlegt sein** *or* **werden** it all has to be most carefully considered; **die Pflanzen wollen oft gegossen werden** the plants need to be watered frequently

d [= zugeben, behaupten] **keiner wollte etwas gehört/gesehen haben** nobody would admit to hearing/seeing anything; **keiner will es gewesen sein** nobody will admit to it; **der Zeuge will den Dieb beobachtet haben** the witness claims to have seen the thief; **und so jemand will Lehrer sein!** and he calls himself a teacher

e [Wunsch] **das wolle Gott verhüten** heaven forbid; **wenn er mir das doch ersparen wollte!** if only he would spare me that!

f [Aufforderung] **wollen wir uns nicht setzen?** why don't we sit down?; **wenn Sie bitte Platz nehmen wollen** if you would please take a seat; **man wolle bitte …** would you kindly …; **na, wollen wir gehen?** well, shall we go?; **darauf wollen wir mal anstoßen!** let's drink to that; **wir wollen beten!** let us pray; **wir wollen mal nicht übertreiben** let's not exaggerate; **wir wollen mal in Ruhe überlegen** let's think about it calmly

g [andere Wendungen] **komme, was da wolle** come what may; **sei er, wer er wolle** whoever he may be

♦ **es will ...** *(unpersönlich)* **es will mir nicht einleuchten, warum** I really can't see why; **es will mir scheinen, dass ...** it seems to me that ...

2 – TRANSITIVES VERB

a [= wünschen] to want; **er will doch nur dein Bestes** he only wants the best for you; **was wollen sie?** what do they want?; **was wollten sie denn von dir?** what did they want then?; **sie wollten nur mein Geld** all they wanted was my money; **ohne es zu wollen** without wanting to; **das wollte ich nicht** *(= war unbeabsichtigt)* I didn't mean to (do that); **was willst du (noch) mehr!** what more do you want!; **ich weiß nicht, was du willst, das ist doch ausgezeichnet** I don't know what you're on about, it's excellent; **er hat gar nichts zu wollen** he has no say at all

b [= bezwecken] **was willst du mit dem Messer?** what are you doing with that knife?; **was willst du mit der Frage?** why are you asking that?; **was wollen die Leute mit solchen Filmen?** what do people hope to achieve with films like that? → *auch* **gewollt**

c [= brauchen] to want, to need; **diese Pflanzen wollen viel Sonne** these plants need a lot of sun

3 – INTRANSITIVES VERB

a [= Willen haben] **er kann schon, wenn er nur will** he can (do it) if he really wants (to); **man muss nur wollen** you just have to want to; **man muss sich nur sagen: ich will** you only have to say: I will do it; **da ist nichts zu wollen** there is nothing we/you can do (about it)

b [= bereit sein] **wenn er will** if he wants to; **er will nicht so recht** he seems rather unwilling; **so Gott will** God willing

c [= mögen] to want to; **wollen, dass jd etw tut** to want sb to do sth; **ich wollte, ich wäre ...** I wish I were ...; **ob du willst oder nicht** whether you like it or not, whether you want to or not

> Nach *wenn, wer* und *wie* wird *wollen* mit *to like* übersetzt.

wenn du willst if you like; **wenn man so will** as it were; **ganz wie du willst** just as you like; **wenn du willst, machen wir das so** if you want to *or* if you like, we'll do it that way; **wer nicht will, der hat schon** if you don't/he doesn't like it, you/he can lump it *(inf)*

d [= gehen wollen] to want to go; **er will ins Kino** he wants to go to the cinema; **ich will nach Hause/hier raus/weg** I want to go home/to get out of here/to get away; **wo willst du hin?** where do you want to go?; **zu wem wollen Sie?** whom do you want to see?

Woll-: **Woll|fa|ser** F wool fibre; **Woll|fett** NT wool fat, lanolin; **Woll|garn** NT woollen *(Brit)* or woolen *(US)* yarn; **Woll|gras** NT *(Bot)* cotton grass

wol|lig ['vɔlɪç] ADJ woolly

Woll-: **Woll|ja|cke** F cardigan; **Woll|käm|me|rei** F **a** *(Fabrik)* wool-carding shop **b** *(Tätigkeit)* wool-carding; **Woll|knäu|el** NT ball of wool; **Woll|maus** F *(inf) (big) ball of fluff,* dust bunny *(US inf)*; **Woll|milch|sau** F **Eier legende ~** all-providing genetically engineered animal; **Woll|sa|chen** PL woollens *pl (Brit),* woolens *pl (US)*; **Woll|sie|gel** NT Woolmark®; **Woll|spin|ne|rei** F **a** *(Fabrik)* woollen *(Brit) or* woolen *(US)* mill **b** *(Tätigkeit)* wool-spinning; **Woll|stoff** M woollen *(Brit) or* woolen *(US)* material; **Woll|strumpf** M woollen *(Brit) or* woolen *(US)* stocking

Wol|lust F *(liter) (= Sinnlichkeit)* sensuality, voluptuousness; *(= Lüsternheit)* lust, lewdness, lasciviousness; **~ empfinden** to be in ecstasy; **etw mit wahrer ~ tun** *(fig)* to delight in doing sth

wol|lüs|tig ['vɔlʏstɪç] *(geh)* ADJ *(= sinnlich)* sensual; *Frau auch* voluptuous; *(= lüstern)* lascivious, lusty; *(= verzückt, ekstatisch)* ecstatic; **seine ~e Freude an etw** *(dat)* **haben** *(fig)* to go into ecstasies over sth ADV *streicheln, sich winden* sensually; *stöhnen* ecstatically; *etw ansehen* lustily; **jdn ~ anblicken** to give sb a lascivious look; **sich ~ im warmen Bad rekeln** to luxuriate in a warm bath

Wol|lüst|ling M *(hum inf)* sensualist

Woll-: **Woll|wa|ren** PL woollen *(Brit) or* woolen *(US)* goods *pl,* woollens *pl (Brit),* woolens *pl (US)*; **Woll|wä|sche** F washing woollens *(Brit) or* woolens *(US) no art*; *(= Wollartikel)* woollens *pl (Brit),* woolens *pl (US)*; **Woll|wasch|gang** M wool wash (cycle); **Woll|wasch|mit|tel** NT detergent for woollens *(Brit) or* woolens *(US)*

wo|mit [vo'mɪt] ADV → *auch* **mit a** *interrog* with what, what ... with; **~ kann ich dienen?** what can I do for you? **b** *rel* with which; *(auf ganzen Satz bezüglich)* by which; **ein Gerät, ~ man auch bohren kann** an appliance you can drill with too; **das ist es, ~ ich nicht einverstanden bin** that's what I don't agree with; **~ ich nicht sagen will, dass ...** by which I don't mean (to say) that ..., which doesn't mean to say that ...; **~ man es auch versuchte ...** whatever they tried to do it with ...

wo|mög|lich [vo'mø:klɪç] ADV possibly → **wo**

wo|nach [vo'na:x] ADV → *auch* **nach a** *interrog* after what, what ... after; **~ sehnst du dich?** what do you long for?; **~ riecht das?** what does it smell of?; **~ sollen wir uns richten?** what should we go by? **b** *rel* **das Land, ~ du dich sehnst** the land for which you are longing, the land (which) you are longing for; **das war es, ~ ich mich erkundigen wollte** that was what I wanted to ask about; **die Nachricht, ~ er ...** the news that he ...

Won|ne ['vɔnə] F **-, -n** *(geh) (= Glückseligkeit)* bliss *no pl*; *(= Vergnügen)* joy, delight; **mit ~** with great delight; **(aber) mit ~!** with great pleasure!; **das ist ihre ganze ~** that's all her joy; **in eitel ~ schwimmen** to be lost in rapture; **die ~n der Liebe** the joys *or* delights of love; **die ~(n) des Paradieses** the delights of paradise; **es ist eine wahre ~** it's a sheer delight

Won|ne-: **Won|ne|ge|fühl** NT blissful feeling; **Won|ne|mo|nat** M, **Won|ne|mond** M *(poet)* May; **im ~ Mai** in the merry month of May; **Won|ne|prop|pen** [-prɔpn] M **-s, - a** *(hum inf: = Baby)* bundle of joy **b** *pl (sl: = Busen)* boobs *pl (inf)*; **Won|ne|schau|er** M thrill of joy; **Won|ne|schrei** M cry of delight; **won|ne|voll** ADJ *Gefühl* blissful; *Kind, Anblick* delightful; *Gesichtsausdruck* delighted

won|nig ['vɔnɪç] ADJ delightful; *Gefühl, Ruhe* blissful

won|nig|lich ['vɔnɪklɪç] ADJ *(poet) Gefühl, Stunden* blissful; *Kind, Anblick* delightful

wo|ran [vo'ran] ADV → *auch* **an a** *interrog* **~ soll ich den Kleiderbügel hängen?** what shall I hang the coat hanger on?; **~ denkst du?** what are you thinking about?; **man weiß bei ihm nie, ~ man ist** you never know where you are with him; **~ liegt das?** what's the reason for it?; **~ ist er gestorben?** what did he die of? **b** *rel (auf vorausgehenden Satz bezogen)* by which; **das, ~ ich mich gerne erinnere** what I like to recall; **die Wand, ~ sie immer die Plakate kleben** the wall on which they are always sticking posters, the wall they're always sticking posters on; **..., ~ ich schon gedacht hatte ...** which I'd already thought of; **~ ich merkte, dass ...** which made me realize that ...; **~ er auch immer gestorben ist ...** whatever he died of ...

wo|rauf [vo'rauf] ADV → *auch* **auf a** *interrog (räumlich)* on what, what ... on; **~ wartest du?** what are you waiting for?; **~ sollte ich mich freuen?** what do I have to look forward to? **b** *rel (zeitlich)* whereupon; **~ du dich verlassen kannst** of that you can be sure; **das ist etwas, ~ ich mich freue** that's something I'm looking forward to; **das, ~ er sich vorbereitet hatte** what he was prepared for; **~ er einen Wutanfall bekam** whereupon he flew into a rage; **~ er sich auch beruft ...** whatever his arguments are ...

wo|rauf|hin [vorauf'hɪn] REL ADV whereupon

wo|raus [vo'raus] ADV → *auch* **aus a** *interrog* out of what, what ... out of; **~ ist der Pullover?** what is the pullover made (out) of?; **~ schließt du das?** from what do you deduce that? **b** *rel* out of which, which ... out of; **das Buch, ~ ich gestern vorgelesen habe** the book I was reading from yesterday; **~ ich schließe/gelernt habe, dass ...** from which I conclude/have learned that ...; **~ man das Öl auch gewinnt ...** whatever oil is obtained from ...

wor|den *ptp von* **werden 1 c**

wo|rein [vo'rain] ADV → *auch* **hinein a** *interrog* in what, what ... in; **~ soll ich den Salat tun?** what shall I put the salad in? **b** *rel* in which, which ... in; **das ist etwas, ~ ich mich nie fügen werde** that's something I shall never submit to *or* put up with

wor|feln ['vɔrfln] VTI *(Agr)* to winnow

wo|rin [vo'rɪn] ADV → *auch* **in a** *interrog* in what, what ... in; **~ war das eingewickelt?** what was it wrapped in?; **~ liegt der Unterschied/Vorteil?** what is the difference/advantage? **b** *rel* in which, which ... in, wherein *(form)*; **das ist etwas, ~ wir nicht übereinstimmen** that's something we don't agree on; **dann sagte er ..., ~ ich mit ihm übereinstimme** then he said ..., which is where I agree with him; **~ du es auch einwickelst ...** whatever you wrap it in ...

Wor|ka|ho|lic M **-s, -s** workaholic

Work|flow-Ma|nage|ment ['wø:ɐkflo:-, 'wœrkflo:-] NT, **Work|flow|ma|nage|ment** NT workflow management

Work|shop ['wø:ɐkʃɔp, 'wœrk-] M **-s, -s** workshop

Work|sta|tion ['wø:ɐkste:ʃn, 'wœrk-] F **-, -s** *(Comput)* work station

World Wide Web [wø:ɐld 'waid 'wɛb] NT **-,** *no pl (Comput)* World Wide Web

Wort [vɔrt] NT **-(e)s, -e** *or* **⁼er** ['vœrtɐ] **a** *pl usu* **⁼er** *(= Vokabel)* word; **ein ~ mit sechs Buchstaben** a word with six letters, a six-letter word; **~ für ~** word for word → **wahr**

b *pl* **-e** *(= Äußerung)* word; **nichts als ~e** nothing but words *or* talk; **genug der ~e!** enough talk!; **das ist ein ~!** wonderful!; **in ~ und Schrift** in speech and writing; **er beherrscht die Sprache in ~ und Schrift** he has a command of the written and spoken language; **in ~ und Tat** in word and deed; **in ~en und Werken sündigen** to sin in words and deeds; **~en Taten folgen lassen** to suit the action to the word(s); **mit einem ~** in a word; **mit anderen/wenigen ~en** in other/a few words; **hast du** *or* **hat der Mensch (da noch) ~e!** it leaves you speechless; **kein ~ mehr** not another word; **kein ~ von etw sagen** *or* **erwähnen** *or* **fallen lassen** not to say one word *or* a thing about sth; **keine ~e für etw finden** to find no words for sth; *(sprachlos sein auch)* to be speechless at sth; **kein ~ von etw wissen/verstehen** not to know/understand a thing about sth; **ich verstehe kein ~!** I don't understand a word (of it); *(= kann nichts hören)* I can't hear a word (that's being said); **er sagte** *or* **sprach kein einziges ~** he didn't say a single word; **ein ~ mit jdm sprechen** *or* **reden** to have a word with sb; **mit dir habe ich noch ein ~ zu reden!** I want a word with you!; **ein ernstes ~ mit jdm reden** to have a serious talk with sb; **kein ~ miteinander/mit jdm sprechen** *or* **reden** not to say a word to each other/to sb; **hättest du doch ein ~ gesagt** if only you had said something; **davon hat man mir kein ~ gesagt** they didn't tell me anything about it; **man kann sein eigenes ~ nicht (mehr) verstehen** *or* **hören**

you can't hear yourself speak; **um nicht viel(e) ~e zu machen** to make it brief; **ich konnte kein ~ anbringen** I couldn't get a word in edgeways; **ein ~ gab das andere** one thing led to another; **jdm das ~** *or* **die ~e im Mund (her)umdrehen** to twist sb's words; **du sprichst ein großes** *or* **wahres ~ gelassen aus** how true, too true; **die passenden/keine ~e für etw finden** to find the right/no words for sth; **das rechte ~ zur rechten Zeit** the right word at the right time; **jdn mit schönen ~en abspeisen** to fob sb off *(Brit)*, to put sb off; **er hat nur schöne ~e gemacht** it was just talk; **auf ein ~!** a word!; **jdm aufs ~ glauben** to believe sb implicitly; **das glaub ich dir aufs ~** I can well believe it; **ohne ein ~ (zu sagen)** without (saying) a word; **dein ~ in Gottes Ohr** let us hope so; **seine ~e galten dir** he meant you, he was talking about you → **verlieren VT, Mund**

c *no pl (= Rede, Recht zu sprechen)* **das ~ nehmen** to speak; *(bei Debatte auch)* to take the floor; **das große ~ haben** *or* **führen** *(inf)* to shoot one's mouth off *(inf)*; **einer Sache** *(dat)* **das ~ reden** to put the case for sth; **das ~ an jdn richten** to address (oneself to) sb; **jdm ins ~ fallen** to interrupt sb; **jdm das ~ abschneiden** to cut sb short; **zu ~ kommen** to get a chance to speak; **ums ~ bitten, sich zu ~ melden** to ask to speak; **er hat das ~** it's his turn to speak; *(bei Debatte auch)* he has the floor; **jdm das ~ erteilen** *or* **geben** to allow sb to speak; *(bei Debatte auch)* to allow sb to take the floor; **er hat mir das ~ verboten** he forbade me to speak

d *pl* **-e** *(= Ausspruch)* saying; *(= Zitat)* quotation; *(Rel)* Word; **ein ~, das er immer im Munde führt** one of his favourite *(Brit)* *or* favorite *(US)* sayings; **ein ~ Goethes/aus der Bibel** a quotation from Goethe/the Bible; **das ~ zum Sonntag** *short religious broadcast on Saturday night,* ≈ late call *(dated Brit)*; **nach dem ~ des Evangeliums** according to the Gospel

e *pl* **-e** *(= Text, Sprache)* words *pl*; **in ~en** in words; **in ~ und Bild** in words and pictures; **etw in ~e fassen** to put sth into words; **das geschriebene/gedruckte/gesprochene ~** the written/printed/spoken word; **das ~ als Kommunikationsmittel** language as a means of communication

f *pl* **-e** *(= Befehl, Entschluss)* **das ~ des Vaters ist ausschlaggebend** the father's word is law; **das ~ des Königs** the king's command; **jdm aufs ~ gehorchen** *or* **folgen** to obey sb's every word; **dabei habe ich auch (noch) ein ~ mitzureden** *or* **mitzusprechen** I (still) have something to say about that too; **das letzte ~ ist noch nicht gesprochen** the final decision hasn't been taken yet; **das letzte ~ haben** to have the last word; **musst du immer das letzte ~ haben?** do you always have to have the last word?

g *no pl (= Versprechen)* word; **auf mein ~** I give (you) my word; **jdn beim ~ nehmen** to take sb at his word; **ich gebe mein ~ darauf** I give you my word on it; **sein ~ halten** to keep one's word; **(bei jdm) im ~ stehen** *or* **sein** to have given one's word (to sb), to have made a commitment (to sb)

Wort-: **Wort|ak|zent** M word stress; **Wort|art** F *(Gram)* part of speech; **Wort|auf|wand** M verbosity; **Wort|aus|wahl** F choice of words; **Wort|be|deu|tung** F meaning of a/the word; **Wort|bei|trag** M (verbal) contribution; **einen ~ leisten** to make a verbal contribution, to say a few words; **Wort|bil|dung** F *(Ling)* morphology; **Wort|bruch** M **das wäre ein ~** that would be breaking your/my *etc* promise; **wort|brü|chig** ADJ false; **~ werden** to break one's word

Wört|chen ['vœrtçən] NT **-s, -** *dim von* **Wort** little word; **da habe ich wohl ein ~ mitzureden** *(inf)* I think I have some say in that; **mit ihm habe ich noch ein ~ zu reden** *(inf)* I want a word with him

Wort|ent|spre|chung F equivalent (word); **~en** *pl* matching words

Wör|ter-: **Wör|ter|buch** NT dictionary; **Wör|ter|ver|zeich|nis** NT vocabulary; *(von Spezialbegriffen)* glossary

Wort-: **Wort|fa|mi|lie** F word family; **Wort|feld** NT semantic field; **Wort|fet|zen** M scrap of conversation; **Wort|fol|ge** F *(Gram)* word order; **Wort|form** F word form; **Wort|füh|rer** M spokesman; **Wort|füh|re|rin** F spokeswoman; **Wort|ge|bühr** F *(Telec)* rate per word; **Wort|ge|fecht** NT battle of words; **Wort|ge|klin|gel** NT *(pej)* verbiage; **Wort|ge|o|gra|fie**, **Wort|ge|o|gra|phie** F word geography; **Wort|ge|plän|kel** NT banter; **wort|ge|treu** ADJ ADV verbatim; **wort|ge|wal|tig** ADJ *Redner, Text* powerful, powerfully eloquent; **wort|ge|wandt** ADJ eloquent; **Wort|ge|wandt|heit** F eloquence; **Wort|gut** NT, *no pl* vocabulary; **Wort|hül|se** F *(pej)* hollow word; **wort|karg** ADJ taciturn; **Wort|karg|heit** F taciturnity; **Wort|klau|ber** [-klaubɐ] M **-s, -**, **Wort|klau|be|rin** [-ərɪn] F **-, -nen** caviller *(Brit)*, caviler *(US)*, quibbler; **Wort|klau|be|rei** [-klaubə'rai] F **-, -en** cavilling *(Brit)*, caviling *(US)*, quibbling; **Wort|kun|de** F lexicology; *(= Vokabelsammlung)* vocabulary; **Wort|laut** M wording; **im ~** verbatim; **folgenden ~ haben** to read as follows

Wört|lein ['vœrtlain] NT **-s, -** = **Wörtchen**

wört|lich ['vœrtlɪç] ADJ *Bedeutung* literal; *Übersetzung, Wiedergabe etc auch* word-for-word; *Rede* direct ADV *wiedergeben, zitieren, abschreiben* verbatim, word for word; *übersetzen* literally, word for word; **das darf man nicht so ~ nehmen** you mustn't take it literally; **darf ich das ~ nehmen?** do you really mean that?; **das hat er ~ gesagt** those were his very *or* actual words

Wort-: **wort|los** ADJ silent ADV without saying a word; **Wort|mel|dung** F request to speak; **wenn es keine weiteren ~en gibt** if nobody else wishes to speak; **Wort|prä|gung** F, **Wort|neu|bil|dung** F neologism; **ein Meister der ~** a master at coining words; **Wort|rät|sel** NT word puzzle; **wort|reich** ADJ *Rede, Erklärung etc* verbose, wordy; *Sprache* rich in vocabulary *or* words ADV profusely; **Wort|reich|tum** M *(von Rede, Erklärung etc)* verbosity, wordiness; *(von Sprache)* richness in vocabulary; **Wort|schatz** M vocabulary; **Wort|schöp|fung** F neologism; **Wort|schwall** M torrent of words; **Wort|sinn** M meaning of a/the word; **Wort|spiel** NT pun, play on words; **Wort|stamm** M *(Ling)* root (of a/the word); **Wort|stel|lung** F *(Gram)* word order; **Wort|ver|bin|dung** F *(Ling)* word combination; *(= Kollokation)* collocation; *(= Kompositum)* compound; **Wort|ver|dre|hung** F twisting of words; **Wort|wahl** F choice of words; **Wort|wech|sel** M exchange (of words), verbal exchange; **wort|wei|se** ADJ, ADV word for word; **Wort|witz** M pun; **wort|wört|lich** ADJ word-for-word ADV word for word, quite literally; **Wort|zu|sam|men|set|zung** F compound (word)

wo|rü|ber [vo'ry:bɐ] ADV → *auch* **über** **a** *interrog* about what, what … about; *(örtlich)* over what, what … over **b** *rel* about which, which … about; *(örtlich)* over which, which … over; *(auf vorausgehenden Satz bezogen)* which; **das Thema, ~ ich gerade einen Artikel gelesen habe** the subject I have just read an article about; **~ sie sich auch unterhalten, sie …** whatever they talk about they …

wo|rum [vo'rʊm] ADV → *auch* **um** **a** *interrog* about what, what … about; **~ handelt es sich?** what's it about? **b** *rel* about which, which … about; **der Ast, ~ ich die Schnur gebunden hatte** the branch I tied the rope (a)round; **~ die Diskussion auch geht, …** whatever the discussion is about …

wo|run|ter [vo'rʊntɐ] ADV → *auch* **unter** **a** *interrog* under what, what … under; **ich weiß nicht, ~ er leidet** I don't know what he is suffering from **b** *rel* under which, which … under

wo|selbst [vo'zɛlpst] REL ADV *(obs)* where

Wo|tan ['vo:tan] M **-s** *(Myth)* Wotan

wo|von [vo'fɔn] ADV → *auch* **von** **a** *interrog* from what, what … from; **~ hat er das abgeleitet?** what did he derive that from? **b** *rel* from which, which … from; *(auf vorausgehenden Satz bezogen)* about which, which … about; **das ist ein Gebiet, ~ er viel versteht** that is a subject he knows a lot about; **~ du dich auch ernährst, …** whatever you eat …

wo|vor [vo'fo:ɐ] ADV → *auch* **vor** **a** *interrog (örtlich)* before what, what … before; **~ fürchtest du dich?** what are you afraid of? **b** *rel* before which, which … before; **das Ereignis, ~ ich schon immer gewarnt habe** the event I have always warned you about; **~ du dich auch fürchtest, …** whatever you're afraid of …

wo|zu [vo'tsu:] ADV → *auch* **zu** **a** *interrog* to what, what … to; *(= warum)* why; **~ soll ich das legen?** where shall I put it?; **~ hast du dich entschlossen?** what have you decided on?; **~ soll das gut sein?** what's the point of that?; **~ denn das?** what for?; **~ denn?** why should I/you? *etc*

b *rel* to which, which … to; **das, ~ ich am meisten neige** what I'm most inclined to do; **das Verfahren, ~ ich raten würde** the procedure I would advise; **…, ~ ich mich jetzt auch entschlossen habe** … which I have now decided to do; **sie haben geheiratet, ~ ich nichts weiter sagen möchte** they have got married, and I shall say no more about that; **~ du dich auch entschließt, …** whatever you decide (on) …

Wrack [vrak] NT **-s, -s** *or (rare)* **-e** wreck; *(fig)* (physical) wreck

Wrack|bo|je F, **Wrack|ton|ne** F *(Naut)* wreck buoy

wrang *pret von* **wringen**

Wra|sen ['vra:zn] M **-s, -** *(esp N Ger)* vapour *(Brit)*, vapor *(US)*

wrin|gen ['vrɪŋən] *pret* **wrang** [vraŋ], *ptp* **gewrungen** [gə'vrʊŋən] VTI to wring

WS [ve:'ʔɛs] NT *(Univ) abbr von* **Wintersemester**

WSV [ve:ʔɛs'fau] M *abbr von* **Winterschlussverkauf**

WSW *abbr von* **Westsüdwest** WSW

Wu|cher ['vu:xɐ] M **-s**, *no pl* profiteering; *(bei Geldverleih)* usury; **das ist doch ~!** that's daylight *(Brit)* *or* highway *(US)* robbery!

Wu|che|rer ['vu:xərɐ] M **-s, -**, **Wu|che|rin** [-ərɪn] F **-, -nen** profiteer; *(= Geldverleiher)* usurer

Wu|cher|ge|schäft NT profiteering *no pl*; *(= Geldverleih)* usury *no pl*

wu|che|risch ['vu:xərɪʃ] ADJ profiteering; *Geldverleih, Zinsen* usurious; *Bedingungen, Preis, Miete etc* exorbitant, extortionate

Wu|cher|mie|te F exorbitant *or* extortionate rent

wu|chern ['vu:xɐn] VI **a** *aux sein or haben (Pflanzen)* to grow rampant, to proliferate; *(Geschwür)* to grow rapidly; *(wildes Fleisch)* to proliferate; *(Bart, Haare)* to grow profusely; **in die Höhe ~** to shoot up(wards) **b** *(fig: = sich verbreiten)* to be rampant; **sein Hass wuchert im Verborgenen** his hatred is quietly intensifying **c** *(Kaufmann etc)* to profiteer; *(Geldverleiher)* to practise *(Brit)* *or* practice *(US)* usury; **mit seinen Talenten ~** *(fig)* to make the most of one's talents

wu|chernd ADJ *Pflanzen* rampant, proliferous; *wildes Fleisch* proliferous; *Bart* straggly; *(fig)* proliferating; *Bürokratie, Kriminalität, Korruption* rampant

Wu|cher|preis M exorbitant price; **~e bezahlen** to pay through the nose

Wu|che|rung F **-, -en** rank growth, proliferation; *(Med)* growth; *(= wildes Fleisch)* proud flesh

Wu|cher|zins M exorbitant *or* usurious interest

wuchs *pret von* **wachsen**

Wuchs [vu:ks] M **-es**, *no pl (= Wachstum)* growth; *(= Gestalt, Form)* stature; *(von Mensch)* build, stature

Wucht [vʊxt] F **-**, *no pl* **a** force; *(= Stoßkraft)* momentum, force; *(fig)* force, power; **mit aller ~** with all one's force *or* might; **mit voller ~** with full force **b** *(inf: = Menge)* load *(inf)*; **eine**

~ (Prügel) a good hiding **c** (inf) **er/das ist die** or **eine ~!** he's/that's smashing! (Brit inf), he's/ that's a hit (US inf)

wuch|ten ['vʊxtn] VT *Koffer, Karton, Paket* to heave, to drag, to haul; *Gewicht* to heave; **er wuchtete den Ball ins Tor** he belted the ball into the goal VR **er wuchtete sich aus dem Auto** he heaved or hauled himself out of the car; **Ikarus wuchtete sich in die Lüfte** Ikarus launched himself into the air

Wucht|ge|schoss NT stun bullet

wuch|tig ['vʊxtɪç] ADJ massive; *Schlag* heavy, powerful; *Klänge* powerful; *Wein (fig)* heavy

Wühl|ar|beit F (fig pej) subversive activities pl

wüh|len ['vy:lən] VI **a** (nach for) to dig; (Maulwurf etc) to burrow; (Schwein, Vogel) to root; **im Bett ~** to toss and turn; **im Schmutz** or **Dreck ~** (fig) to wallow in the mire or mud **b** (= suchen) to rummage, to root (nach etw for sth); **in den Schubladen ~** to rummage through the drawers **c** (fig) to gnaw (in +dat at) **d** (inf: = schwer arbeiten) to slog (inf) **e** (= Untergrundarbeit leisten) to stir things up VT to dig, to burrow; **er wühlte seinen Kopf in die Kissen** he buried his face in the pillows VR **sich durch die Menge/das Gestrüpp/die Akten ~** to burrow one's way through the crowd/ the undergrowth/the files

Wüh|ler ['vy:lɐ] M **-s, -, Wüh|le|rin** [-ərɪn] F **-, -nen** **a** (pej: = Aufrührer) agitator, subversive **b** (inf: = schwer Arbeitender) slogger (Brit inf), toiler (US inf) **c** (inf: = unruhig Schlafender) wriggler

Wüh|le|rei [vy:lə'rai] F **-, -en** **a** digging; (von Maulwurf) burrowing **b** (= Sucherei) rummaging or rooting (about) **c** (inf: = Arbeiten) slogging **d** (Pol inf) agitation

Wühl-: **Wühl|maus** F vole; (fig pej) subversive; **Wühl|tisch** M (inf) bargain counter

Wulst [vʊlst] M **-es, =e** or f **-, =e** ['vʏlstə] bulge; (an Reifen) bead; (an Flasche, Glas) lip; (Archit) torus; (Her) wreath; (Naut) bulb; **ein ~ von Fett** a roll of fat; **die dicken Wülste seiner Lippen** his thick lips

wuls|tig ['vʊlstɪç] ADJ bulging; *Rand, Lippen* thick

Wulst-: **Wulst|lip|pen** PL thick lips pl; **Wulst|rei|fen** M bead tyre (Brit) or tire (US)

wum|mern ['vʊmɐn] VI (inf) **a** (= dröhnen) to rumble; (= pochen) to drum; **an** or **gegen die Tür ~** to hammer at the door **b** aux sein (= dröhnend fahren) to rumble along

wund [vʊnt] ADJ sore; **ein ~er Punkt, eine ~e Stelle** a sore point; **ein ~es Herz** (liter) a wounded heart ADV **etw ~ kratzen/scheuern/reiben** to scratch/ chafe/rub sth until it's raw; **das Pferd/ich war vom Reiten ~ gescheuert** the horse/I was saddle-sore; **ein Tier ~ schießen** to wound an animal; **sich (dat) die Füße/Fersen ~ laufen** (lit) to walk until one's feet/heels are raw; (fig) to walk one's legs off; **sich (dat) die Finger ~ nähen/schreiben** to sew/write one's fingers to the bone; **sich (dat) den Mund ~ reden** (fig) to talk till one is blue in the face; **ein ~ gelegener Patient** a patient with bedsores; **eine ~ gelegene Stelle** a bedsore; **~ gelegen sein** to have bedsores → **wund liegen**

Wund-: **Wund|arzt** M, **Wund|ärz|tin** F (old) surgeon; **Wund|auf|la|ge** F wound dressing; **Wund|ben|zin** NT surgical spirit (Brit), rubbing alcohol (US); **Wund|brand** M gangrene

Wun|de ['vʊndə] F **-, -n** (lit, fig) wound; **alte ~n/ eine alte ~ wieder aufreißen** (fig) to open up old sores; **an eine alte ~ rühren** (fig geh) to touch on a sore point; **(bei jdm) tiefe ~n schlagen** (fig) to scar sb; **den Finger auf die (brennende) ~ legen** (fig) to bring up a painful subject; **Salz in eine/jds ~ streuen** (fig) to turn the knife in the wound; **Balsam** or **Öl in eine/jds ~ gießen** or **träufeln** (fig geh) to comfort sb

wun|der △ ['vʊndɐ] ADV inv → **Wunder b**

Wun|der ['vʊndɐ] NT **-s, -** **a** (= übernatürliches Ereignis, auch Rel) miracle; (= wunderbare Erscheinung) wonder; (= Leistung) marvel, miracle; (= erstaunlicher Mensch) marvel; **~ tun** or **wirken** (Rel) to work miracles; **das grenzt an ein ~** it verges on the miraculous, it's almost a miracle; **durch ein ~** by a miracle; **wie durch ein ~** as if by a miracle; **nur durch ein ~ können sie noch gerettet werden** only a miracle can save them now; **die ~ der Natur/dieser Welt** the wonders of nature/this world; **ein architektonisches ~** an architectural miracle **b** **meine Eltern denken ~ was passiert ist/~ was über mein Privatleben** my parents think goodness knows what has happened/goodness knows what about my private life; **das hat er sich ~ wie einfach vorgestellt** he imagined it would be ever so easy; **er glaubt, ~ wer zu sein/~ was geleistet zu haben** he thinks he's marvellous (Brit) or marvelous (US)/done something marvel(l)ous; **er meint, ~ wie schön das sei** he thinks it's fantastic; **er bildet sich ~ was ein** he thinks he's too wonderful for words **c** (= überraschendes Ereignis) **~ tun** or **wirken** to do wonders; **diese Medizin wirkt ~** this medicine works wonders; **es ist ein/kein ~, dass …** it's a wonder/no wonder or small wonder that …; **ist es ein ~, dass er dick ist?** is it any wonder that he's fat?; **kein ~** no wonder; **was ~, wenn …** it's no wonder or surprise if … → **blau a**

wun|der|bar ADJ **a** (= schön) wonderful, marvellous (Brit), marvelous (US) **b** (= übernatürlich, wie durch ein Wunder) miraculous ADV (= herrlich) wonderfully

wun|der|ba|rer|wei|se ['vʊndɐba:rɐ'vaizə] ADV miraculously

Wun|der-: **Wun|der|ding** NT marvellous (Brit) or marvelous (US) thing; **dass er überlebt hat, ist ein ~** that he survived is a miracle; **Wun|der|dok|tor(in)** M(F) wonder doctor; (pej: = Quacksalber) quack; **Wun|der|dro|ge** F (von Zauberer, Fee etc) miracle drug; (fig auch) wonder drug; **Wun|der|glau|be** M belief in miracles; **wun|der|gläu|big** ADJ **~ sein** to believe in miracles; **ein ~er Mensch** a person who believes in miracles; **Wun|der|hei|ler(in)** M(F) wonder doctor; (pej) faith healer; **Wun|der|horn** NT (liter, Myth) magic horn; **wun|der|hübsch** ADJ wonderfully pretty, wondrously beautiful (liter); **Wun|der|ker|ze** F sparkler; **Wun|der|kind** NT child prodigy; **Wun|der|kna|be** M (usu iro) wonder boy or child; **Wun|der|kur** F (iro) miracle cure; **Wun|der|lam|pe** F magic lamp or lantern; **Wun|der|land** NT wonderland; **wun|der|lich** ['vʊndɐlɪç] ADJ **a** (= merkwürdig) strange, odd **b** (= wundersam) wondrous (liter); **Wun|der|lich|keit** F **-, -en** (= Merkwürdigkeit) strangeness, oddness; **Wun|der|mit|tel** NT miracle cure; (von Fee etc) magic potion

wun|dern ['vʊndɐn] VT impers to surprise; **es wundert mich** or **mich wundert, dass er noch nicht hier ist** I'm surprised or it surprises me that he is not here yet; **das wundert mich nicht** I'm not surprised, that doesn't surprise me; **das würde mich nicht ~** I shouldn't be surprised; **es sollte mich (nicht) ~, wenn …** it would (not) surprise me if …; **mich wundert gar nichts mehr** nothing surprises me any more VR to be surprised (über +acc at); **du wirst dich ~!** you'll be amazed!; **ich wunderte mich über seine schnelle Rückkehr** I was surprised at or about his quick return; **du wirst dich noch einmal ~!** you're in for a shock or surprise!; **da wirst du dich aber ~!** you're in for a surprise; **ich muss mich doch sehr ~!** well, I am surprised (at you/him etc); **ich wundere mich über gar nichts mehr** nothing surprises me any more; **dann darfst** or **brauchst du dich nicht ~, wenn …** then don't be surprised if …

Wun|der-: **wun|der+neh|men** sep irreg VI impers (geh) to be surprising VT impers to surprise; **es nimmt mich wunder, ob …** (Sw: = ich frage mich) I wonder if …; **wun|der|sam** ['vʊndɐza:m] ADJ (liter) wondrous (liter); **wun|der|schön** ADJ beautiful, lovely; (= herrlich auch) wonderful; **einen ~en guten Morgen/Tag** etc a very good morning/day etc to you; **Wun|der|tat** F miracle; **Wun|der|tä|ter(in)** M(F) miracle worker; **wun|der|tä|tig** ADJ magic, miraculous; *Leben, Heilige* miracle-working; **~ wirken** to perform miracles; **Wun|der|tier** NT (hum) weird and wonderful animal (hum); **Wun|der|tü|te** F surprise packet; **wun|der|voll** ADJ wonderful, marvellous (Brit), marvelous (US) ADV wonderfully; **Wun|der|waf|fe** F wonder weapon; **Wun|der|welt** F (im Märchen etc) magic world; (= zauberhafte Umgebung) world of wonders; **die ~ der Mineralien** the wonderful world of minerals; **Wun|der|werk** NT miracle, marvel; **Wun|der|zei|chen** NT miraculous sign

Wund-: **Wund|fie|ber** NT traumatic fever; **wund|ge|le|gen** ADJ → **wund ADV**; **Wund|heit** F **-**, no pl soreness; **Wund|in|fek|ti|on** F wound infection; **wund+krat|zen** VT sep → **wund**; **wund+lau|fen** VT sep irreg → **wund**; **wund lie|gen** irreg, **wund+lie|gen** sep irreg VR to get bedsores; **Wund|mal** NT pl **-male** **a** (Rel) stigma **b** (liter) scar; **Wund|pflas|ter** NT adhesive plaster; **Wund|rand** M edge (of a/ the wound); **wund+re|den** VT sep → **wund**; **wund+rei|ben** VT sep irreg → **wund**; **Wund|ro|se** F (Med) erysipelas (spec), St Anthony's fire; **Wund|sal|be** F ointment; **wund+scheu|ern** VT sep → **wund**; **wund+schie|ßen** VT sep irreg → **wund**; **wund+schrei|ben** VT sep irreg → **wund**; **Wund|sein** NT soreness; **Wund|sek|ret** NT secretion of a/the wound; **Wund|starr|krampf** M tetanus, lockjaw; **Wund|ver|sor|gung** F dressing a/the wound/ wounds; **Wund|wat|te** F surgical wool

Wunsch [vʊnʃ] ✪ 50 M **-(e)s, =e** **a** ['vʏnʃə] wish; (= sehnliches Verlangen) desire; (= Bitte) request; **ein Pferd war schon immer mein ~** I've always wanted a horse; **nach ~** just as he/she etc wants/wanted; (= wie geplant) according to plan, as planned; (= nach Bedarf) as required; **auf** or **nach ~ der Eltern** as his/her etc parents wish/wished; **alles geht nach ~** everything is going smoothly; **von dem ~ beseelt sein, …** to be filled with the desire …; **hier ist der ~ der Vater des Gedankens** (prov) the wish is father to the thought (prov); **ich habe einen ~ an dich** I've a request to make of you; **was haben Sie für einen ~?** what can I do for you?; **haben Sie (sonst) noch einen ~?** (beim Einkauf etc) is there anything else you would like?, is there anything else I can do for you?; **sonst noch Wünsche?** (iro) any other requests?; **auf ~** by or on request; **auf jds (besonderen/ausdrücklichen) ~ hin** at sb's (special/express) request; **auf allgemeinen/vielfachen ~ hin** by popular request or demand → **ablesen, fromm b** **b** usu pl (= Glückwunsch) wish; **beste Wünsche zum Fest** the compliments of the season

wünsch|bar ADJ (Sw) = **wünschenswert**

Wunsch-: **Wunsch|bild** NT ideal; **Wunsch|den|ken** NT wishful thinking

Wün|schel|ru|te ['vʏnʃl-] F divining or dowsing rod

Wün|schel|ru|ten|gän|ger [-gɛŋɐ] M **-s, -**, **Wün|schel|ru|ten|gän|ge|rin** [-ərɪn] F **-, -nen** diviner, dowser

wün|schen ['vʏnʃn] ✪ 27.3, 50.1, 50.5, 52.4 VT **a** **sich (dat) etw ~** to want sth; (= den Wunsch äußern) to ask for sth; (im Stillen: bei Sternschnuppe etc) to wish for sth; **ich wünsche mir das** I would like that, I want that; **ich wünsche mir, dass du …** I would like you to …; **… wie ich mir das gewünscht habe** … as I wanted; **das habe ich mir von meinen Eltern zu Weihnachten gewünscht** I asked my parents to give me that for Christmas, I asked for that for Christmas from my parents; **ich wünsche mir einen Mantel**

von dir I'd like a coat from you; **er wünscht sich** *(dat)*, **dass das Projekt erfolgreich sein wird** he wants the project to be successful, he hopes the project will be successful; **er wünscht sich** *(dat)* **ein glückliches Leben für seine Kinder** he would like his children to have a happy life; **er wünscht sich** *(dat)* **diesen Mann als Lehrer/Vater/als** *or* **zum Freund** he wishes that this man was his teacher/father/friend; **was wünschst du dir?** what do you want?, what would you like?; *(im Märchen)* what is your wish?; **du darfst dir was (zum Essen) ~** you can say what you'd like (to eat); **du darfst dir etwas ~** *(= Wunsch frei haben)* you can make a wish; *(im Märchen auch)* I'll give you a wish; **sie haben alles, was man sich** *(dat)* **nur ~ kann** they have everything you could possibly wish for; **man hätte es sich** *(dat)* **nicht besser ~ können** you couldn't have wished for anything better **b** **jdm etw ~** to wish sb sth; **jdm einen guten Morgen ~** to wish sb good morning; **wir ~ dir gute Besserung/eine gute Reise** we hope you get well soon/have a pleasant journey; **wir ~ gute Fahrt** we hope you have a good journey, we wish you a good journey; **jdm den Tod/die Pest an den Hals ~** *(fig inf)* to wish sb would die/drop dead *(inf)*; **das würde ich meinem schlimmsten Feind nicht ~** I wouldn't wish that on my worst enemy **c** *(= ersehnen, hoffen)* to wish; **jdn fort/weit weg ~** to wish sb would go away/were far away; **es bleibt/wäre zu ~, dass ...** it is to be hoped that ...; **ich wünschte, ich hätte dich nie gesehen** I wish I'd never seen you **d** *(= begehren, verlangen)* to want; **was ~ Sie?** *(Diener)* yes, Sir/Madam?; *(in Geschäft)* what can I do for you?, can I help you?; *(in Restaurant)* what would you like?; **wen ~ Sie zu sprechen?** to whom would you like to speak?; **ich wünsche, dass du das machst** I want you to do that

VI *(= begehren)* to wish; **Sie ~?** what can I do for you?; *(in Restaurant)* what would you like?; **ganz wie Sie ~** (just) as you wish *or* please *or* like; **zu ~/viel zu ~ übrig lassen** to leave something/a great deal to be desired

VR **sich in eine andere Lage/weit weg ~** to wish one were in a different situation/far away

wün|schens|wert ADJ desirable

Wunsch-: **Wunsch|form** F *(Gram)* optative (mood); **wunsch|ge|mäß** ADJ desired; *(= erbeten)* requested; *(= geplant)* planned ADV as desired; *(= wie erbeten)* as requested; *(= wie geplant)* as planned; **Wunsch|kan|di|dat(in)** M(F) ideal candidate; **Wunsch|kind** NT planned child; **unser Töchterchen war ein ~** our little daughter was planned; **Wunsch|kon|zert** NT *(Rad)* musical request programme *(Brit) or* program *(US)*; **Wunsch|lis|te** F = **Wunschzettel**; **wunsch|los** ADJ *Mensch* content(ed); *Glück* perfect ADV **~ glücklich** perfectly happy; **Wunsch|part|ner(in)** M(F) ideal partner; **Wunsch|satz** M *(Gram)* optative clause; **Wunsch|sen|dung** F *(Rad)* request programme *(Brit) or* program *(US)*; **Wunsch|traum** M dream; *(= Illusion)* illusion; **das ist doch bloß ein ~** that's just a pipe dream; **Wunsch|vor|stel|lung** F ideal; **Wunsch|zet|tel** M wish list; **das steht schon lange auf meinem ~** *(fig)* I've wanted that for a long time

wupp (dich) [vʊp], **wupps** [vʊps] INTERJ whoomph

Wupp|(dich) ['vʊp(dɪç)] M **-s**, *no pl (inf)* **mit einem ~** in a flash

wur|de *pret von* **werden**

Wür|de ['vʏrdə] F **-, -n** **a** *no pl* dignity; **(seine) ~ bewahren** to preserve one's dignity; **unter aller ~ sein** to be beneath contempt; **unter jds ~ sein** to be beneath sb *or* sb's dignity; **etw mit ~ tragen** to bear sth with dignity **b** *(= Auszeichnung)* honour *(Brit)*, honor *(US)*; *(= Titel)* title; *(= Amt)* rank; **~ bringt Bürde** *(Prov)* the burdens of office

wür|de|los ADJ undignified ADV *sich benehmen* undignified; **jdn ~ behandeln** to treat sb contemptuously; **~ um Gnade flehen** to beg pitifully for mercy; **sich ~ verhalten** to demean oneself

Wür|de|lo|sig|keit F **-**, *no pl* lack of dignity

Wür|den|trä|ger(in) M(F) dignitary

wür|de|voll ADJ dignified ADV *sich verhalten* with dignity

wür|dig ['vʏrdɪç] ADJ **a** *(= würdevoll)* dignified **b** *(= wert)* worthy; **jds/einer Sache ~/nicht ~ sein** to be worthy/unworthy of sb/sth; **eine ihm ~e Verabschiedung** a farewell worthy of him; **sich jds/einer Sache ~ erweisen** *or* **zeigen** to prove oneself to be worthy of sb/sth; **jdn einer Sache** *(gen)* **für ~ halten** *or* **befinden** *(geh)* to find sb worthy of sth ADV *sich verhalten* with dignity; *beerdigen* respectfully; *jdn behandeln* with respect; *begrüßen, empfangen* with great respect; *vertreten* worthily

wür|di|gen ['vʏrdɪgn] VT **a** *(= anerkennen)* to appreciate; *(= lobend erwähnen)* to acknowledge; *(= respektieren)* to respect; *(= ehren)* to pay tribute to; **etw gebührend** *or* **nach Gebühr/richtig ~** to appreciate sth properly/fully; **etw zu ~ wissen** to appreciate sth **b** *(geh: = für würdig befinden)* **jdn einer Sache** *(gen)* **~** to deem sb worthy of sth; **jdn eines/keines Blickes/Grußes** *etc* **~** to deign/not to deign to look at/greet *etc* sb

Wür|dig|keit F **-**, *no pl* **a** *(= Würde)* dignity **b** *(= Wert)* merit

Wür|di|gung ['vʏrdɪgʊŋ] F **-, -en** **a** *no pl (= das Würdigen)* appreciation; *(= lobende Erwähnung)* acknowledgement; *(= Respektierung)* respect **b** *(= lobende Worte, Artikel)* appreciation **c** *(= Ehrung)* honour *(Brit)*, honor *(US)*; **die zahlreichen ~en der Gäste** the numerous tributes paid to the guests

Wurf [vʊrf] M **-(e)s, ¨-e** ['vʏrfə] **a** throw; *(beim Kegeln etc)* bowl; *(beim Baseball)* pitch; **drei ~ or Würfe zwei Euro** three goes *or* throws for two euros **b** *no pl (= das Werfen)* throwing; **beim ~** when throwing; **zum ~ ansetzen/ausholen** to get ready to throw; **sich auf den ~ konzentrieren** to concentrate on throwing **c** *(fig: = Erfolg)* success, hit *(inf)*; **mit dem Film ist ihm ein großer ~ gelungen** this film is a great success *or* a big hit *(inf)* for him; **einen großen** *or* **glücklichen ~ tun** *(= Erfolg haben)* to be very successful *or* have great success; *(= Glück haben)* to have a stroke of luck **d** *(Zool)* litter; *(= das Gebären)* birth **e** *(= Faltenwurf)* fall; **einen eleganten ~ haben** to hang elegantly **f** *(Mil: von Bomben)* dropping

Wurf-: **Wurf|an|ker** M grappling hook; **Wurf|arm** M *(Sport)* throwing arm; **Wurf|bahn** F trajectory; **Wurf|dis|zip|lin** F *(Sport)* throwing discipline *or* event

Wür|fel ['vʏrfl] M **-s, -** **a** *(auch Math)* cube; **etw in ~ schneiden** to dice sth, to cut sth into cubes **b** *(= Spielwürfel)* dice, die *(form)*; **die ~ sind gefallen** *(fig)* the die is cast; **~ spielen** to play at dice

Wür|fel-: **Wür|fel|be|cher** M shaker; **Wür|fel|brett** NT dice board; **Wür|fel|form** F cube shape; **~ haben** to be cube-shaped; **wür|fel|för|mig** ADJ cube-shaped, cubic *(esp Math)*

wür|fe|lig ['vʏrfəlɪç] ADJ cubic ADV **etw ~ schneiden** to cut sth into cubes

wür|feln ['vʏrfln] VI to throw, to have a throw; *(= Würfel spielen)* to play at dice; **hast du schon gewürfelt?** have you had your throw *or* go?; **um etw ~** to throw dice for sth VT **a** *Zahl* to throw **b** *(= in Würfel schneiden)* to dice, to cut into cubes

Wür|fel-: **Wür|fel|spiel** NT *(= Partie)* game of dice; *(= Spielart)* dice; **beim ~** at dice; **Wür|fel|spie|ler(in)** M(F) dice player; **Wür|fel|zu|cker** M cube sugar

Wurf-: **Wurf|ge|schoss** NT projectile, missile; **Wurf|ham|mer** M *(Sport)* hammer; **Wurf|hand** F *(Sport)* throwing hand; **Wurf|kör|per** M *(Phys)* projectile; **Wurf|kraft** F *(Phys)* projectile force; *(Sport)* throwing strength; **wurf|kräf|tig** ADJ *(Sport)* strong-armed

würf|lig ['vʏrflɪç] ADJ, ADV = **würfelig**

Wurf-: **Wurf|mal** NT *pl* **-male** *(Baseball)* pitcher's mound; **Wurf|ma|schi|ne** F *(Mil Hist)* catapult; *(beim Tontaubenschießen)* trap; **Wurf|mes|ser** NT throwing knife; **Wurf|pa|ra|bel** F *(Phys)* trajectory (parabola); **Wurf|pfeil** M dart; **Wurf|ring** M quoit; **Wurf|schei|be** F *(Leichtathletik)* discus; **Wurf|sen|dung** F circular; **Reklame durch ~en** direct advertising; **Wurf|speer** M, **Wurf|spieß** M javelin; **Wurf|stern** M *spiked metal disc thrown as a weapon*; **Wurf|tau|be** F *(Sport)* clay pigeon; **Wurf|tau|ben|schie|ßen** NT *(Sport)* clay pigeon shooting; **Wurf|waf|fe** F missile; *(= Speer)* throwing spear; **Wurf|wei|te** F throwing range; *(von Geschütz)* mortar range; **Wurf|win|kel** M *(Sport)* throwing angle

Wür|ge-: **Wür|ge|en|gel** M Angel of Death; **Wür|ge|griff** M *(lit, fig)* stranglehold; **Wür|ge|mal** NT *pl* **-male** strangulation mark

wür|gen ['vʏrgn] VT *jdn* to strangle, to throttle; *(fig: Angst)* to choke VI **a** *(= mühsam schlucken)* to choke; *(Schlange)* to gulp; **an etw** *(dat)* **~** *(lit)* to choke on sth; *(fig) (an Kritik)* to find sth hard to swallow; *(an Arbeit)* to struggle over sth **b** *(beim Erbrechen)* to retch; **ein Würgen im Hals spüren** to feel one is going to be sick VT *impers* **es würgte sie (im Hals** *etc***)** she felt she was going to be sick; **mit Hängen und Würgen** by the skin of one's teeth

Würg|en|gel M Angel of Death

Wür|ger ['vʏrgɐ] M **-s, -** **a** *(poet: = der Tod)* death *no art* **b** *(Orn)* shrike

Wür|ger ['vʏrgɐ] M **-s, -**, **Wür|ge|rin** [-ərɪn] F **-, -nen** strangler

Würg|schrau|be F garrotte

Wurm [vʊrm] M **-(e)s, ¨-er** ['vʏrmɐ] **a** worm; *(= Made)* maggot; *(poet: = Schlange)* snake; *(Myth: = Lindwurm)* dragon; **der (nagende) ~ des schlechten Gewissens** the (gnawing) pangs of a guilty conscience; **da ist** *or* **steckt** *or* **sitzt der ~ drin** *(fig inf)* there's something wrong somewhere; *(= seltsam)* there's something odd about it; *(= verdächtig)* there's something fishy about it *(inf)* → **winden VR** **b** AUCH NT *(inf: = Kind)* (little) mite **c** *(Comput: = Computerwurm)* (computer) worm

Würm|chen ['vʏrmçən] NT **-s, -** *dim von* **Wurm** little worm; *(inf: = Kind)* (poor) little mite *or* thing

wur|men ['vʊrmən] VT *impers (inf)* to rankle with

Wurm-: **Wurm|fort|satz** M *(Anat)* vermiform appendix; **Wurm|fraß** M, *no pl* worm damage

wur|mig ['vʊrmɪç] ADJ worm-eaten; *(= madig) Obst* maggoty

Wurm-: **Wurm|krank|heit** F worm disorder, helminthiasis *(spec)*; **Wurm|kur** F worming treatment; **die Katze braucht eine ~** the cat needs to be wormed; **eine ~ machen** to have worm treatment; **Wurm|loch** NT wormhole; **Wurm|mit|tel** NT vermicide, vermifuge; **wurm|sti|chig** [-ʃtɪçɪç] ADJ *Holz* full of wormholes; *(= madig auch) Obst* maggoty

Wurscht *etc* [vʊrʃt] *(inf)* = **Wurst** *etc*

Wurst [vʊrst] F **-, ¨-e** ['vʏrstə] sausage; *(= Salami)* salami; *(= wurstförmiges Gebilde)* roll, sausage; *(inf: = Kot von Hund)* dog's mess *(inf)*; **jetzt geht es um die ~** *(fig inf)* the moment of truth has come *(inf)*; **mit der ~ nach der Speckseite** *or* **nach dem Schinken werfen** *(prov)* to cast a sprat to catch a mackerel; **es ist jdm (vollkommen) ~** *or* **Wurscht** *(inf)* it's all the same to sb

> **WURST**
>
> German-speaking countries are famous for their wide variety of **Wurst**. Some, such as **Zervelatwurst**, are salami-type sausages.

Others, such as **Wiener Würstchen**, **Frankfurter Würstchen** or **Bratwurst**, are cooked. Less well known abroad are various kinds of **Streichwurst** (eg **Teewurst** and **Leberwurst**): they are made from sausage that has been smoked and then chopped up so finely that it can be spread on bread.

Wurst-: **Wurst|auf|schnitt** M → **Wurst** assortment of sliced sausage/salami; **Wurst|brot** NT → **Wurst** open sausage/salami sandwich; *(zusammengeklappt)* sausage/salami sandwich; **Wurst|brü|he** F sausage stock

Würst|chen ['vʏrstçən] NT **-s, -** a *dim von* **Wurst** small sausage; **heiße** *or* **warme** ~ hot sausages; *(in Brötchen)* ≈ hot dogs; **Frankfurter/Wiener** ~ frankfurters/wienies b *(pej: Mensch)* squirt *(inf)*, nobody; **ein armes** ~ *(fig)* a poor soul

Würst|chen|bu|de F, **Würst|chen|stand** M sausage stand, ≈ hot-dog stand

wurst|egal ADJ *(inf)* **das ist mir** ~ I couldn't care less (about that)

Wurs|tel ['vʊrstl] M **-s, -** *(Aus)* = **Hanswurst**

Würs|tel ['vʏrstl] NT **-s, -** *(dial)* = **Würstchen**

Wurs|te|lei [vʊrstə'lai] F **-, -en** *(inf)* muddle

wurs|teln ['vʊrstln] VI *(inf)* to muddle along; **sich durchs Leben/die Schule** ~ to muddle (one's way) through life/school

wurs|ten ['vʊrstn] VI to make sausages

Wurs|ter ['vʊrstɐ] M **-s, -**, **Wurs|te|rin** [-ərɪn] F **-, -nen** *(S Ger)* butcher

Wurs|te|rei [vʊrstə'rai] F **-, -en** *(S Ger)* butcher('s shop)

Wurst|fin|ger PL *(pej inf)* podgy *(Brit)* or pudgy fingers *pl*

wurs|tig ['vʊrstɪç] ADJ *(inf)* devil-may-care *attr*, couldn't-care-less *attr (inf)*; **sei doch nicht so ~!** don't be such a wet blanket! *(inf)*

Wurs|tig|keit F **-,** *no pl (inf)* devil-may-care *or* couldn't-care-less *(inf)* attitude

Wurst-: **Wurst|kon|ser|ve** F tinned *(Brit) or* canned sausages; **Wurst|ma|xe** [-maksə] M **-n, -n** *(inf)* man who sells sausages, ≈ hot-dog man *(inf)*; **Wurst|plat|te** F platter of cold cuts; **Wurst|ring** M sausage ring; **Wurst|sa|lat** M sausage salad; **Wurst|schei|be** F slice of sausage; **Wurst|ver|gif|tung** F sausage poisoning; **Wurst|wa|ren** PL sausages *pl*; **Wurst|zip|fel** M sausage end

Würt|tem|berg ['vʏrtəmbɛrk] NT **-s** Württemberg

Würt|tem|ber|ger ['vʏrtəmbɛrgɐ] M **-s, -** *(= Wein)* Württemberg wine

Würt|tem|ber|ger ['vʏrtəmbɛrgɐ] M **-s, -**, **Würt|tem|ber|ge|rin** [-ərɪn] F **-, -nen** native of Württemberg; *(Einwohner)* inhabitant of Württemberg

würt|tem|ber|gisch ['vʏrtəmbɛrgɪʃ] ADJ Württembergian

Wür|ze ['vʏrtsə] F **-, -n** a *(= Gewürz)* seasoning, spice; *(= Aroma)* aroma; *(fig: = Reiz)* spice; **das gibt dem Leben die** ~ that adds spice to life → **Kürze** b *(von Bier)* wort

Wur|zel ['vʊrtsl] F **-, -n** a *(lit, fig)* root; *(= Handwurzel)* wrist; *(= Fußwurzel)* ankle; **etw mit der ~ ausreißen** to pull sth out by the root; **etw mit der ~ ausrotten** *(fig)* to eradicate sth; **das Übel an der ~ packen** to tackle the root of the problem; **~n schlagen** *(lit)* to root; *(fig) (= sich einleben)* to put down roots; *(= an einem Ort hängen bleiben)* to grow roots; **die ~ Jesse** *(Bibl)* the stem of Jesse b *(Math)* root; **~n ziehen** to find the roots; **die ~ aus einer Zahl ziehen** to find the root of a number; **(die) ~ aus 4 ist 2** the square root of 4 is 2; **die vierte ~ aus 16 ist 2** the fourth root of 16 is 2; **unter/außerhalb der ~ stehen** to be inside/outside the radical sign c *(N Ger: = Möhre)* carrot

Wur|zel-: **Wur|zel|bal|len** M *(Hort)* rootball; **Wur|zel|be|hand|lung** F *(von Zahn)* root treatment; **Wur|zel|bil|dung** F rooting; **Wur|zel|bürs|te** F (coarse) scrubbing brush

Wür|zel|chen ['vʏrtslçən] NT **-s, -** *dim von* **Wurzel** little root, rootlet**Wur|zel-**: **Wur|zel|ent|zün|dung** F *(an Zahn)* inflammation of the root/roots; **Wur|zel|ex|po|nent** M *(Math)* radical index; **Wur|zel|ge|mü|se** NT root vegetables *pl*; **Wur|zel|knol|le** F *(Bot)* root tuber; **wur|zel|los** ADJ *Pflanze* without roots; *(fig auch)* rootless; **Wur|zel|mann** M *pl* **-männer**, **Wur|zel|männ|chen** NT *(= Alraune)* mandrake

wur|zeln ['vʊrtsln] VI a *(lit, fig)* to be rooted; **in etw** *(dat)* ~ *(fig)* to be rooted in sth; *(= verursacht sein)* to have its/their roots in sth b *(rare: = Wurzeln schlagen)* to (take) root

Wur|zel-: **Wur|zel|re|sek|ti|on** [-rezɛktsio:n] F **-, -en** *(Zahnmedizin)* root resection; **Wur|zel|sepp** M *(inf)* country bumpkin *(inf)*; **Wur|zel|sil|be** F *(Ling)* root syllable; **Wur|zel|stock** M *(Bot)* rhizome; **Wur|zel|ver|zeich|nis** NT *(Comput)* root directory; **Wur|zel|werk** NT, *no pl* a root system, roots *pl* b *(Cook)* flavouring *(Brit) or* flavoring *(US)* greens *pl*; **Wur|zel|zei|chen** NT *(Math)* radical sign; **Wur|zel|zie|hen** NT **-s**, *no pl (Math)* root extraction

wur|zen ['vʊrtsn] VTI *(Aus inf)* to get everything one can *(jdn* out of sb)

wür|zen ['vʏrtsn] VT to season; *(fig)* to add spice to; **eine Geschichte mit etw** ~ to season a story with sth

Wur|ze|rei [vʊrtsə'rai] F **-, -en** *(Aus inf)* robbery *(inf)*

wür|zig ['vʏrtsɪç] ADJ *Speise* tasty; *(= scharf)* spicy; *Zigaretten, Tabak, Geruch etc* aromatic; *Luft* fragrant, tangy; *Wein, Bier* full-bodied ADV ~ **schmecken** to be spicy; *(Käse)* to have a sharp taste; *(Wein)* to have a full-bodied taste; ~ **riechen** to smell spicy

Würz-: **Würz|mi|schung** F mixed spices *pl*; **Würz|nel|ke** F clove; **Würz|stoff** M flavouring *(Brit)*, flavoring *(US)*

wusch *pret von* **waschen**

wusch [vu:ʃ] INTERJ *(Aus) (= erstaunt)* whoops; *(= schnell)* zoom

Wu|schel|haar NT *(inf)* mop of curly hair

wu|sche|lig ['vʊʃəlɪç] ADJ *(inf) Tier* shaggy; *Haare* fuzzy *(inf)*

Wu|schel|kopf M a *(= Haare)* mop of curly hair, fuzz *(inf)* b *(= Mensch)* fuzzy head *(inf)*

wusch|lig ['vʊʃlɪç] ADJ = **wuschelig**

wu|se|lig ['vu:zəlɪç] ADJ *(dial) (= lebhaft)* lively; *(= unruhig)* fidgety; *(= bewegt)* busy, bustling; *Ameisenhaufen* teeming; **das ~e Treiben** the hustle and bustle

wu|seln ['vu:zln] VI *(dial)* a *(= belebt sein)* to be teeming b *aux sein (= sich schnell bewegen)* to scurry

wuss|te *pret von* **wissen**

Wust [vu:st] M **-(e)s,** *no pl (inf) (= Durcheinander)* jumble; *(= Menge)* pile; *(= unordentlicher Haufen)* heap; *(= Kram, Gerümpel)* junk *(inf)*; **dieser ~ von Kleidern** this pile of clothes

wüst [vy:st] ADJ a *(= öde)* desert *attr*, waste, desolate; **die Erde war ~ und leer** *(Bibl)* the earth was without form, and void *(Bibl)* b *(= unordentlich)* wild, chaotic; *Aussehen, Haar* wild c *(= ausschweifend)* wild d *(= rüde) Beschimpfung, Beleidigung etc* vile e *(= arg)* terrible, awful; *Übertreibung* terrible, wild ADV ~ **aussehen** to look a real mess; ~ **feiern** to have a wild party; **jdn ~ beschimpfen** to use vile language to sb; ~ **fluchen** to swear vilely; **jdn ~ zurichten** to beat sb to a pulp

Wüs|te ['vy:stə] F **-, -n** *(Geog)* desert; *(= Ödland)* waste, wilderness *(liter)*; *(fig)* waste(land), wilderness, desert; **die ~ Gobi** the Gobi Desert; **jdn in die ~ schicken** *(fig)* to send sb packing *(inf)*

wüs|ten ['vy:stn] VI *(inf)* **mit etw ~** to squander *or* waste sth; **mit seiner Gesundheit/seinen Kräften ~** to ruin one's health/strength

Wüs|te|nei [vy:stə'nai] F **-, -en** a *(= öde Gegend)* wasteland, desert b *(fig: = wildes Durcheinander)* chaos

Wüs|ten-: **Wüs|ten|fuchs** M desert fox; **Wüs|ten|kli|ma** NT desert climate; **Wüs|ten|kö|nig** M *(poet)* king of the desert *(poet)*; **Wüs|ten|land|schaft** F desert landscape; **Wüs|ten|sand** M desert sand; **Wüs|ten|schiff** NT *(poet)* ship of the desert *(poet)*, camel; **Wüs|ten|staat** M desert state; **Wüs|ten|step|pe** F steppe

Wüst|ling ['vy:stlɪŋ] M **-s, -e** *(dated, iro)* lecher

Wüs|tung ['vy:stʊŋ] F **-, -en** deserted settlement

Wut [vu:t] F **-,** *no pl* a *(= Zorn, Raserei)* rage, fury; *(fig: der Elemente)* fury; **vor ~ heulen** to yell with rage; **(auf jdn/etw) eine ~ haben** to be furious (with sb/sth), to be mad (at sb/sth); **eine ~ im Bauch haben** *(inf)* to be seething, to be hopping mad *(inf)*; **eine ~ haben/kriegen** *or* **bekommen** to be in/get into a rage; **in ~ geraten, von der ~ gepackt werden** to fly into a rage; **jdn in ~ bringen** *or* **versetzen** to infuriate sb → **schäumen VI, kochen VI a** b *(= Verbissenheit)* frenzy; **mit einer wahren ~** as if possessed, like crazy *(inf)*

Wut-: **Wut|an|fall** M fit of rage; *(esp von Kind)* tantrum; **Wut|aus|bruch** M outburst of rage or fury; *(esp von Kind)* tantrum

wü|ten ['vy:tn] VI *(lit, fig) (= toben)* to rage; *(= zerstörerisch hausen)* to cause havoc; *(verbal)* to storm *(gegen* at); *(Menge)* to riot

wü|tend ['vy:tnt] ADJ furious, enraged; *Tier* enraged; *Menge* angry; *Kampf, Elemente* raging; *(fig) Schmerz, Hass* fierce; *Proteste* fierce, angry; **auf jdn/etw** *(acc)* **~ sein** to be mad at sb/sth; **über jdn/etw** *(acc)* **~ sein** to be furious about sb/sth ADV in (a) rage, angrily; **~ raste der Stier auf ihn zu** the enraged bull raced toward(s) him

wut-: **wut|ent|brannt** [-lɛntbrant] ADJ furious, enraged ADV in a fury *or* rage; **wut|er|füllt** [-lɛɐfʏlt] ADJ filled *or* seething with rage, furious ADV in a blind rage

Wü|te|rich ['vy:tərɪç] M **-s, -e** brute

Wut-: **Wut|ge|heul** NT howl of fury; **Wut|ge|schrei** NT cries *pl* of rage

wutsch [vʊtʃ] INTERJ whoosh

wut|schäu|mend ADJ, ADV foaming with rage

wut|schen ['vʊtʃn] VI *aux sein (inf)* to whoosh *(inf)*; *(= schnell verschwinden)* to whiz *(inf)*, to zoom *(inf)*

Wut-: **wut|schnau|bend** ADJ, ADV snorting with rage; **Wut|schrei** M yell of rage; **wut|ver|zerrt** [-fɛɐtsɛrt] ADJ distorted with rage

Wutz [vʊts] F **-, -en** *(pej dial)* pig *(inf)*

Wu|zerl ['vu:tsɐl] NT **-s, -(n)** *(Aus)* a *(= Kind)* porker *(inf)* b *(= Fussel)* piece of fluff

wu|zerl|dick ADJ *(Aus)* porky *(inf)*

Wwe. *abbr von* **Witwe**

WWF M **-s** *abbr von* **World Wide Fund for Nature** WWF

WWU F **-** *abbr von* **Wirtschafts- und Währungsunion** EMU

WWW [ve:ve:'ve:] NT **-,** *no pl (Comput) abbr von* **World Wide Web** WWW

WWW-Sei|te F *(Comput)* WWW page

Wz *abbr von* **Warenzeichen**

X, **x** [ɪks] NT **-, -** X, x; **Herr X** Mr X; **jdm ein X für ein U vormachen** to put one over on sb *(inf)*; **er lässt sich kein X für ein U vormachen** he's not easily fooled

x-Ach|se ['ɪks-] F x-axis

Xan|thip|pe [ksan'tɪpə] F **-, -n** *(fig inf)* shrew

X-Bei|ne ['ɪks-] PL knock-knees *pl*; **~ haben** to be knock-kneed

x-bei|nig ['ɪks-], **X-bei|nig** ADJ knock-kneed

x-be|lie|big [ɪks-] ADJ any old *(inf)*; **wir können uns an einem ~en Ort treffen** we can meet anywhere you like ADV as you like

X-Chro|mo|som ['ɪks-] NT X-chromosome

Xe|non ['kse:nɔn] NT **-s**, *no pl* (*abbr* **Xe**) xenon

xe|no|phil [kseno'fi:l] ADJ *(geh)* xenophile *(form)*

Xe|no|phi|lie [ksenofi'li:] F **-**, *no pl (geh)* xenophilia *(form)*

xe|no|phob [kseno'fo:p] ADJ *(geh)* xenophobic

Xe|no|pho|bie [ksenofo'bi:] F, *no pl (geh)* xenophobia

Xe|ro|gra|fie, **Xe|ro|gra|phie** [kserogra'fi:] F **-, -n** [-'fi:ən] Xerox® (copy)

Xe|ro|ko|pie [kseroko'pi:] F Xerox® (copy)

xe|ro|ko|pie|ren [kseroko'pi:rən] *ptp* **xerokopiert** VTI *insep* to Xerox®

x-fach ['ɪks-] ADJ **die ~e Menge** *(Math)* n times the amount; **trotz ~er Ermahnungen** *(inf)* in spite of umpteen *or* n warnings *(inf)* ADV so many times

x-för|mig ['ɪks-], **X-för|mig** ADJ X-shaped ADV *angeordnet* in an X; **die Fäden ~ verkreuzen** to cross the threads to form an X

x-mal ['ɪksma:l] ADV *(inf)* n (number of) times *(inf)*, umpteen times *(inf)*

x-ma|lig ['ɪksma:lɪç] ADJ *(inf)* n number of *(inf)*, umpteen *(inf)*; **wenn ein ~er Weltmeister ...** when somebody who has been world champion n (number of) times *or* umpteen times ...

XML [ɪksɛm'lɛl] NT **-**, *no pl abbr von* **extensible markup language** *(Comput)* XML

XSL [ɪksɛs'lɛl] NT **-**, *no pl abbr von* **extensible stylesheet language** *(Comput)* XSL

X-Strah|len ['ɪks-] PL *(dated)* X-rays *pl*

x-te(r, s) ['ɪkstə] ADJ *(Math)* nth; *(inf)* nth *(inf)*, umpteenth *(inf)*; **zum ~n Mal(e)** for the nth *or* umpteenth time *(inf)*

Xy|lo|fon [ksylo'fo:n] NT **-s, -e**, **Xy|lo|phon** NT **-s, -e** xylophone

Y, y ['ʏpsilɔn] NT **-, -** Y, y
y-Ach|se ['ʏpsilɔn-] F y-axis
Yacht [jaxt] F **-, -en** yacht
Yak [jak] M **-s, -s** yak
Ya|ku|za [ja'ku:za] F **-**, *no pl* Yakuza, Japanese mafia
Yams|wur|zel ['jams-] F yam
Yan|kee ['jɛŋki] M **-s, -s** *(pej)* Yankee, Yank
Yard [ja:ɐt] NT **-s, -s** yard
Y-Chro|mo|som ['ʏpsilɔn-] NT Y-chromosome
Yen [jɛn] M **-(s), -(s)** yen
Ye|ti ['je:ti] M **-s, -s** Yeti, abominable snowman
Yo|ga ['jo:ga] M OR NT **-(s)** yoga
Yo|gi ['jo:gi] M **-s, -s** yogi
Yp|si|lon ['ʏpsilɔn] NT **-(s), -s** y; *(= griechischer Buchstabe)* upsilon
Ysop ['i:zɔp] M **-s, -e** *(Bot)* hyssop
Ytong® ['y:tɔŋ] M **-s, -s** ≈ breeze block *(Brit)*, ≈ cinder block *(US)*
Yt|ter|bi|um [ʏ'tɛrbiʊm] NT **-s**, *no pl* (*abbr* **Yb**) ytterbium
Ytt|ri|um ['ʏtrium] NT **-s**, *no pl* (*abbr* **Y**) yttrium
Yuc|ca ['jʊka] F **-, -s** yucca
Yup|pie ['jʊpi:, 'japi:] M **-s,-s** yuppie

Z

Z, z [tsɛt] NT -, - Z, z

z. A. *abbr von* **zur Ansicht** on approval *von* **zur Anstellung** on probation

zack [tsak] INTERJ *(inf)* pow, zap *(inf)*; **~, ~!** chop-chop! *(inf)*; **sei nicht so langsam, mach mal ein bisschen ~, ~** don't be so slow, get a move on *(inf)*; **bei uns muss alles ~, ~ gehen** we have to do everything chop-chop *(inf)*; **die Leute waren so gut gedrillt, die ganze Sache lief ~, ~** the people were drilled so well that the whole thing went off just like that *(inf)*

Zack [tsak] M **-s,** *no pl (inf)* **auf ~ bringen** to knock into shape *(inf)*; **auf ~ sein** to be on the ball *(inf)*

Za|cke ['tsakə] F **-, -n** point; *(von Gabel)* prong; *(von Kamm)* tooth; *(= Bergzacke)* jagged peak; *(= Auszackung)* indentation; *(von Fieberkurve etc)* peak; *(inf: = Nase)* conk *(inf)*, beak *(inf)* → **Krone b**

za|cken ['tsakn] VT to serrate; *Kleid, Saum, Papier* to pink → *auch* **gezackt**

Za|cken ['tsakn] M **-s, -** = **Zacke**

Za|cken-: **Za|cken|li|nie** F jagged line; *(= Zickzack)* zigzag (line); **Za|cken|lit|ze** F ricrac braid

za|ckig ['tsakɪç] ADJ **a** *(= gezackt)* jagged; *Stern* pointed **b** *(inf) Soldat, Bursche* smart; *Tempo, Musik* brisk; *Team, Manager etc* dynamic, zippy *(inf)* ADV **a** *(= gezackt)* **~ schreiben** to write a very angular hand **b** *(inf: = schnell) laufen* briskly; *fahren, bedienen* quickly; **bring mir meine Hausschuhe, aber ein bisschen ~!** fetch me my slippers, and make it snappy! *(inf)*

zag [tsa:k] ADJ *(liter)* = **zaghaft**

za|gen ['tsa:gn] VI *(liter)* to be apprehensive, to hesitate → **Zittern a**

zag|haft ADJ timid ADV timidly

Zag|haf|tig|keit ['tsa:khaftɪçkait] F -, *no pl* timidity

zäh [tsɛ:] ADJ *Fleisch, Mensch, Verhandlungen* tough; *(= dickflüssig)* glutinous; *(= schleppend) Verkehr etc* slow-moving; *(= ausdauernd)* dogged, tenacious; **ein ~es Leben haben** *(lit: Mensch, Tier)* to have a tenacious hold on life; *(fig)* to die hard; **mit ~em Fleiß** doggedly, with dogged application ADV *verhandeln* tenaciously; *sich widersetzen* doggedly; *fließen* slowly

Zä|heit △ ['tsɛ:hait] F -, *no pl* → **Zähheit**

zäh|flüs|sig ADJ thick, viscous; *Verkehr, Verhandlung* slow-moving

Zäh|flüs|sig|keit F thickness, viscosity; **die ~ des Verkehrs** the slow-moving traffic

Zäh|heit ['tsɛ:hait] F -, *no pl* toughness

Zä|hig|keit ['tsɛ:ɪçkait] F -, *no pl* toughness; *(= Dickflüssigkeit)* glutinous nature; *(= Ausdauer)* doggedness, tenacity

Zahl [tsa:l] F **-, -en** *(Math, Gram)* number; *(= Verkaufszahl, Maßangabe, bei Geldmengen etc auch)* figure; *(= Ziffer auch)* numeral, figure; **~en nennen** to give figures; **wie waren die ~en im letzten Jahr?** what did the figures look like last year?; **sie hat ein gutes Gedächtnis für ~en** she has a good memory for figures *or* numbers; **eine fünfstellige ~** a five-figure number; **der ~ nach** numerically; **gut mit ~en umgehen können** to be good with figures, to be numerate; **die ~en stimmen nicht** the figures don't add up *or* tally; **~ oder Wappen** heads or tails; **100 an der ~** *(old)* 100 in number; **in großer ~** in large *or* great numbers; **die ~ ist voll** the numbers are complete; **in voller ~** in full number; **der Aufsichtsrat war in voller ~ versammelt** there was a full turnout for the meeting of the board; **ohne ~** *(geh)* without number; **Leiden/Wonnen ohne ~** *(poet)* countless tribulations/joys

zahl|bar ADJ payable *(an +acc* to); **~ bei Lieferung** *or* **nach Erhalt** payable on delivery *or* receipt, to be paid for on delivery *or* receipt

zähl|bar ADJ countable

Zahl|brett NT, **Zähl|brett** NT money tray

zäh|le|big [-le:bɪç] ADJ hardy, tough; *(fig) Gerücht, Vorurteil* persistent

Zah|le|mann ['tsa:ləman] M, *no pl* **~ und Söhne** *(inf hum)* (it's) paying-up time

zah|len ['tsa:lən] VI to pay; **Herr Ober, (bitte) ~!** waiter, the bill *(esp Brit) or* check *(US)* please; **dort zahlt man gut/schlecht** the pay there is good/bad, they pay well/badly; **wenn er nicht bald zahlt, dann ...** if he doesn't pay up soon, then ... VT *(= bezahlen)* to pay; **was habe ich (Ihnen) zu ~?** what do I owe you?; **einen hohen Preis ~** *(lit, fig)* to pay a high price; **ich zahle dir ein Bier** I'll buy you a beer; **ich zahle dir den Flug** I'll pay for your flight; **ich zahle dir das Kino** I'll pay for you to go to the cinema; **lass mal, ich zahls** no no, I'll pay *or* it's on me *or* it's my treat *(inf)*

zäh|len ['tsɛ:lən] VI **a** *(= zahlenmäßig erfassen)* to count; **bis hundert ~** to count (up) to a hundred
b *(= gehören)* **zu einer Gruppe/Menge ~** to be one of a group/set; **er zählt zu den besten Schriftstellern unserer Zeit** he ranks as one of the best authors of our time; **zu welcher Sprachengruppe zählt Gälisch?** to which language group does Gaelic belong?
c *(= wichtig sein)* to matter; **es zählt nicht, ob/dass ...** it doesn't matter if *or* whether/that ...
d *(= rechnen mit)* **auf jdn/etw ~** to count *or* rely on sb/sth
e *(= gelten)* to count; **schon eine Stunde pro Woche zählt als Teilzeitjob** working just one hour per week counts as a part-time job
VT **a** *(= zahlenmäßig erfassen)* to count; **seine Tage sind gezählt** his days are numbered
b *(= zahlenmäßig betragen)* to have; **die Stadt zählt 2 Millionen Einwohner** the town has two million inhabitants; **Stanford zählt 12.000 Studenten** Stanford numbers *or* has 12,000 students
c *(= dazurechnen)* **jdn/sich zu einer Gruppe ~** to regard sb/oneself as part of a group, to number *or* count sb/oneself among a group
d *(geh)* **sie zählt 27 Jahre** she is 27 years old
e *(= wert sein)* to count; **bei diesem Spiel zählt der König 5 Punkte** in this game the king counts as 5 points

Zah|len-: **Zah|len|ak|ro|ba|tik** F *(inf)* juggling with statistics *or* figures, statistical sleight of hand; **Zah|len|an|ga|be** F figure; **ich kann keine genauen ~n machen** I can't give *or* quote any precise figures; **Zah|len|bei|spiel** NT numerical example; **Zah|len|dre|her** M transposed figures *pl*; **Zah|len|fol|ge** F order of numbers; **Zah|len|ge|dächt|nis** NT memory for numbers; **Zah|len|kom|bi|na|ti|on** F number combination, combination (of numbers); **Zah|len|leh|re** F arithmetic; **Zah|len|lot|te|rie** F, **Zah|len|lot|to** NT National Lottery; **(im) Zahlenlotto spielen** to do the National Lottery; **zah|len|mä|ßig** ADJ numerical ADV **a** *(= der Anzahl nach)* **~ überlegen sein** to be greater in number; **~ schwach/unbedeutend** small in number; **~ stark** large in number; **Frauen sind ~ stärker vertreten** there's a greater number of women **b** *(= in Zahlen)* in figures, numerically; **etw ~ ausdrücken** to express sth in figures; **Zah|len|ma|te|ri|al** NT figures *pl*; **Zah|len|mys|tik** F number mysticism; *(Astrol)* numerology; **Zah|len|rät|sel** NT number *or* numerical puzzle; **Zah|len|rei|he** F sequence of numbers; **Zah|len|schloss** NT combination lock; **Zah|len|sinn** M, *no pl* head for figures; **Zah|len|sym|bo|lik** F number symbolism; **Zah|len|sys|tem** NT numerical system; **Zah|len|the|o|rie** F *(Math)* theory of numbers, number theory; **Zah|len|to|to** M = **Toto**; **Zah|len|ver|hält|nis** NT (numerical) ratio; **Zah|len|ver|rie|ge|lung** [-fɛɐri:gəlʊŋ] F **-, -en** *(Comput)* numbers lock; **Zah|len|wert** M numerical value; *(auf Messgeräten)* (numerical) reading; **welche ~e hat die Analyse ergeben?** what figures did the analysis give?; **die ~e der beiden Versuche** the figures yielded by the two experiments

Zah|ler ['tsa:lɐ] M **-s, -**, **Zah|le|rin** [-ərɪn] F **-, -nen** payer

Zäh|ler ['tsɛ:lɐ] M **-s, -** **a** *(Math)* numerator **b** *(= Messgerät)* meter **c** *(Comput etc)* counter

Zäh|ler|ab|le|sung F meter reading

Zäh|ler|stand M meter reading

Zahl-: **Zahl|gren|ze** F fare stage; **Zahl|kar|te** F giro transfer form; **Zahl|kell|ner(in)** M(F) *waiter/waitress who presents the bill and collects payment*; **zahl|los** ADJ countless, innumerable

Zähl|maß NT numerical measure, unit of measurement**Zahl-**: **Zahl|meis|ter(in)** M(F) *(Naut)* purser; *(Mil)* paymaster; **Zahl|mut|ter** F *pl* **-mütter** mother supporting a child; **zahl|reich** ADJ numerous; **wir hatten mit einer ~eren Beteiligung gerechnet** we had expected more participants ADV numerously; **die Veranstaltung war ~ besucht** the event was (very) well attended; **Zahl|stel|le** F payments office; **Zahl|tag** M payday

Zah|lung ['tsa:lʊŋ] F **-, -en** payment; **eine einmalige ~ leisten** to make a lump-sum payment; **in ~ nehmen** to take in part exchange, to take as a trade-in; **in ~ geben** to trade in, to give in part exchange; **gegen eine ~ von 500 Dollar erhalten Sie ...** on payment of 500 dollars you will receive ...

Zäh|lung ['tsɛ:lʊŋ] F **-, -en** count; *(= Volkszählung)* census

Zah|lungs-: **Zah|lungs|ab|kom|men** NT payments agreement; **Zah|lungs|an|wei|sung** F giro transfer order *(Brit)*, money transfer order *(US)*; **Zah|lungs|art** F method *or* mode of payment; **Zah|lungs|auf|for|de|rung** F request for payment; **Zah|lungs|auf|schub** M extension (of credit), moratorium *(Jur)*; **Zah|lungs|auf|trag** M payment order; **Zah|lungs|be|din|gun|gen** PL terms *pl* (of payment); **erleichterte ~** easy terms; **Zah|lungs|be|fehl** M order to pay; **Zah|lungs|bi|lanz** F balance of payments; **Zah|lungs|emp|fän|ger(in)** M(F) payee; **Zah|lungs|er|leich|te|rung** F more convenient method of payment; **~en** easy terms; **zah|lungs|fä|hig** ADJ able to pay; *Firma* solvent; **Zah|lungs|fä|hig|keit** F ability to pay; *(von Firma)* solvency; **Zah|lungs|frist** F time *or* period allowed for payment; **Zah|lungs|kraft** F, *no pl* **a** *(Econ)* solvency, financial resources *pl*; *(= Wohlstand)* wealth **b** *(einer Währung)* **~ haben** to be legal tender; **zah|lungs|kräf|tig** ADJ wealthy; **Zah|lungs|mit|tel** NT means *sing* of payment; *(= Münzen, Banknoten)* currency; **gesetzliches ~** legal tender; **Zah|lungs|mo|dus** M method of payment; **Zah|lungs|mo|ral** F payment practice; **eine gute/schlechte ~ haben** to be a good/bad payer; **zah|lungs|pflich|tig** [-pflɪçtɪç] ADJ obliged to pay; **Zah|lungs|rück|stand** M arrears *pl*, backlog of payments; **Zah|lungs|schwie|rig|kei|ten** PL financial difficulties *pl*; **Zah|lungs|sys|tem** NT method of payment; **Zah|lungs|ter|min** M date for payment; **zah|lungs|un|fä|hig** ADJ unable to pay; *Firma* insolvent; **Zah|lungs|un|fä|hig|keit** F inability to pay; *(von Firma)* insolvency; **zah|lungs|un|wil|lig** ADJ unwilling to pay; **Zah|lungs|ver|kehr** M payments *pl*, payment transactions *pl*; **Zah|lungs|ver|pflich|tung** F obligation *or* liability to pay; **Zah|lungs|ver|zug** M default, arrears *pl*; **Zah|lungs|wei|se** F mode *or* method of payment; **Zah|lungs|ziel** NT *(Comm)* period allowed for payment

Zahl|va|ter M father supporting a child

Zähl|wei|se F **a** *(= Art zu zählen)* way of counting; **nach meiner ~** by my reckoning **b** *(= Zahlensystem)* numbering *or* enumeration system

Zähl|werk NT counter

Zahl-: **Zahl|wort** NT *pl* **-wörter** numeral; **Zahl|zei|chen** NT numerical symbol

zahm [tsaːm] ADJ *(lit, fig)* tame; **er ist schon ~er geworden** *(inf)* he has calmed down a bit *(inf)*, he's a bit tamer now *(inf)*

zähm|bar ADJ tam(e)able

zäh|men ['tsɛːmən] VT to tame; *(fig) Leidenschaft, Bedürfnisse* to control

Zäh|mung F **-,** *(rare)* **-en** taming

Zahn [tsaːn] M **-(e)s, ¨-e** ['tsɛːnə] **a** *(Anat: = Zacke)* tooth; *(von Briefmarke)* perforation; *(= Radzahn)* cog, tooth; **künstliche** *or* **falsche Zähne** false teeth *pl*; **Zähne bekommen** *or* **kriegen** *(inf)* to cut one's teeth; **die ersten Zähne** one's milk teeth; **die zweiten Zähne** one's second set of teeth; **die dritten Zähne** *(hum)* false teeth; **diese Portion reicht** *or* **ist für den hohlen ~** *(inf)* that's hardly enough to satisfy a mouse *(inf)*; **der ~ der Zeit** the ravages *pl* of time; **ihm tut kein ~ mehr weh** *(inf)* he's gone to join his ancestors; **die Zähne zeigen** *(Tier)* to bare its teeth; *(fig inf)* to show one's teeth; **jdm einen ~ ziehen** *(lit)* to pull a tooth out, to extract a tooth; *(fig)* to put an idea out of sb's head; **ich muss mir einen ~ ziehen lassen** I've got to have a tooth out *or* extracted; **den ~ kannst du dir ruhig ziehen lassen!** *(fig inf)* you can put that idea right out of your head!; **jdm auf den ~ fühlen** *(= aushorchen)* to sound sb out; *(= streng befragen)* to grill sb, to give sb a grilling; **etw mit Zähnen und Klauen verteidigen** to defend sth tooth and nail → **bewaffnet, ausbeißen**

b *(inf: = Geschwindigkeit)* **einen ~ draufhaben** to be going like the clappers *(inf)*; **mit einem unheimlichen ~** at an incredible lick *(inf)* → **zulegen VT c**

Zahn-: **Zahn|arzt** M, **Zahn|ärz|tin** F dentist; **Zahn|arzt|hel|fer(in)** M(F) dental nurse; **zahn|ärzt|lich** ADJ dental; **sich in ~e Behandlung begeben** *(form)* to have dental treatment; **~er Helfer, ~e Helferin** *(form)* dental nurse ADV by a dentist; **sich ~ behandeln lassen** to go to the dentist; **Zahn|arzt|pra|xis** F dental practice *or* surgery; **Zahn|be|hand|lung** F dental treatment; **Zahn|be|lag** M film on the teeth; **Zahn|bett** NT socket (of a/the tooth); **Zahn|bürs|te** F toothbrush; **Zahn|creme** F toothpaste

Zäh|ne-: **Zäh|ne|flet|schen** NT **-s,** *no pl* baring of teeth, snarling; **zäh|ne|flet|schend** ADJ *attr* ADV snarling; **Zäh|ne|klap|pern** NT **-s,** *no pl* chattering of teeth → **Heulen a**; **zäh|ne|klap|pernd** ADJ *attr* ADV with teeth chattering; **Zäh|ne|knir|schen** NT **-s,** *no pl* grinding one's teeth; *(fig)* gnashing of teeth; **zäh|ne|knir|schend** ADJ *attr* ADV grinding one's teeth; *(fig)* gnashing one's teeth; **er fand sich ~ damit ab** he agreed with (a) bad grace

zah|nen ['tsaːnən] VI to teethe, to cut one's teeth/a tooth; **das Zahnen** teething

zäh|nen ['tsɛːnən] VT to tooth; *Briefmarken* to perforate → *auch* **gezähnt**

Zäh|ne|put|zen NT **-s,** *no pl* tooth-brushing; **~ nicht vergessen!** don't forget to brush your teeth

Zahn-: **Zahn|er|satz** M dentures *pl*, set of dentures; **Zahn|fäu|le** F tooth decay, caries *sing*; **Zahn|fleisch** NT gum(s *pl*); **(nur noch) auf dem ~ gehen** *or* **kriechen** *(inf)* to be all in *(inf)*, to be on one's last legs *(inf)*; **Zahn|fleisch|blu|ten** NT **-s,** *no pl* bleeding of the gums; **Zahn|fleisch|ent|zün|dung** F inflammation of the gum(s *pl*), gingivitis *(spec)*; **Zahn|fül|lung** F filling; **Zahn|hals** M neck of a tooth; **Zahn|heil|kun|de** F dentistry; **Zahn|höh|le** F pulp cavity; **Zahn|im|plan|tat** NT dental implant; **Zahn|klam|mer** F brace; **Zahn|klemp|ner(in)** M(F) *(hum)* dentist; **Zahn|kli|nik** F dental clinic *or* hospital; **Zahn|kranz** M *(Tech)* gear rim; **Zahn|kro|ne** F crown; **Zahn|laut** M *(Ling)* dental (consonant); **zahn|los** ADJ *(lit, fig)* toothless; **~er Tiger** *(fig)* toothless tiger; **Zahn|lo|sig|keit** F **-,** *no pl* toothlessness; **Zahn|lü|cke** F gap between one's teeth; **Zahn|mark** NT dental pulp; **Zahn|me|di|zin** F dentistry; **zahn|me|di|zi|nisch** ADJ *Untersuchung* dental; *Gutachten* dentist's; **aus ~er Sicht** from a dental point of view; **Zahn|pas|ta** F, **Zahn|pas|te** F toothpaste; **Zahn|pfle|ge** F dental hygiene; **Zahn|pro|the|se** F set of dentures; **Zahn|pul|ver** NT tooth powder; **Zahn|putz|glas** NT toothbrush glass; **Zahn|rad** NT cogwheel, gear (wheel); **Zahn|rad|bahn** F rack railway *(Brit)*, rack railroad *(US)*; **Zahn|rad|ge|trie|be** NT gear mechanism; **Zahn|rei|he** F row of teeth; **Zahn|schei|be** F *(Tech)* cog; **Zahn|schein** M *(inf) form for free dental treatment*; **Zahn|schmelz** M (tooth) enamel; **Zahn|schmer|zen** PL toothache *no pl*; **Zahn|sei|de** F dental floss; **Zahn|span|ge** F brace; **Zahn|stein** M tartar; **Zahn|sto|cher** [-ʃtɔxɐ] M **-s, -** toothpick; **Zahn|stum|mel** M stump; **Zahn|tech|ni|ker(in)** M(F) dental technician

Zäh|nung ['tsɛːnʊŋ] F **-, -en a** *(= Zähne, Gezahntsein)* teeth *pl*; *(von Briefmarken)* perforations *pl* **b** *(= das Zähnen)* toothing; *(von Briefmarken)* perforation**Zahn-**: **Zahn|wal** M toothed whale; **Zahn|wech|sel** M second dentition *(form)*; **Zahn|weh** NT toothache; **Zahn|wur|zel** F root (of a/the tooth); **Zahn|ze|ment** M (dental) cement

Zäh|re ['tsɛːrə] F **-, -n** *(old, poet)* tear

Za|ire [za'iːr(ə)] NT *(Hist)* **-s** Zaire

Za|i|rer [za'iːrɐ] M **-s, -, Za|i|re|rin** [za'iːrərɪn] F **-, -nen** *(Hist)* Zairean

za|i|risch [za'iːrɪʃ] ADJ *(Hist)* Zairean

Zam|pa|no ['tsampano] M **-s, -s** *(inf)* **der große ~** the big cheese *(inf)*

Zan|der ['tsandɐ] M **-s, -** *(Zool)* pikeperch

Zan|ge ['tsaŋə] F **-, -n** *(= Flachzange, Rundzange)* (pair of) pliers *pl*; *(= Beißzange)* (pair of) pincers *pl*; *(= Greifzange, Kohlenzange, Zuckerzange)* (pair of) tongs *pl*; *(von Tier)* pincers *pl*; *(Med)* forceps *pl*; *(inf: Ringen)* double lock; **jdn in die ~ nehmen** *(Ringen)* to put a double lock on sb; *(Ftbl etc)* to sandwich sb; *(fig)* to put the screws on sb *(inf)*; **jetzt haben wir ihn in der ~** *(fig)* we've got him now; **ihn/das möchte ich nicht mit der ~ anfassen** *(inf)* I wouldn't touch him/it with a bargepole *(Brit inf)* or a ten-foot pole *(US inf)*

Zan|gen-: **Zan|gen|be|we|gung** F *(Mil)* pincer movement; **zan|gen|för|mig** ADJ pincer-shaped; **Zan|gen|ge|burt** F forceps delivery; **Zan|gen|griff** M *(Ringen)* double lock

Zank [tsaŋk] M **-(e)s,** *no pl* squabble, quarrel; **zwischen ihnen gab es dauernd ~** they were continually squabbling *or* quarrelling *(Brit)* or quarreling *(US)*; **~ und Streit** trouble and strife

Zank|ap|fel M *(fig)* bone of contention

zan|ken ['tsaŋkn] VIR to quarrel, to squabble; **wir haben uns gezankt** we've had a row, we've quarrelled *(Brit)* or quarreled *(US)*; **(sich) um etw ~** to quarrel over sth

Zän|ker ['tsɛŋkɐ] M **-s, -, Zän|ke|rin** [-ərɪn] F **-, -nen** quarreller *(Brit)*, quarreler *(US)*, squabbler

Zan|ke|rei [tsaŋkə'rai] F **-, -en** quarrelling *(Brit)*, quarreling *(US)*, squabbling

zän|kisch ['tsɛŋkɪʃ] ADJ *(= streitsüchtig)* quarrelsome; *(= tadelsüchtig) Frau* nagging *attr*, shrewish

Zank|sucht F, *no pl* quarrelsomeness; *(= Tadelsucht: von Frau)* nagging, shrewishness

zank|süch|tig ADJ = **zänkisch**

Zäpf|chen ['tsɛpfçən] NT **-s, -** *dim von* **Zapfen** small plug *etc*; *(= Gaumenzäpfchen)* uvula; *(= Suppositorium)* suppository; **~-r, ~-R** *(Ling)* uvular "r"

zap|fen ['tsapfn] VT to tap, to draw; **dort wird das Pils frisch gezapft** they have draught *(Brit)* or draft *(US)* Pilsener there, they have Pilsener on draught *(Brit)* or draft *(US)* or tap there

Zap|fen ['tsapfn] M **-s, -** *(= Spund)* bung, spigot; *(= Pfropfen)* stopper, bung; *(= Tannenzapfen etc, von Auge)* cone; *(= Eiszapfen)* icicle; *(Mech: von Welle, Lager etc)* journal; *(= Holzverbindung)* tenon

zap|fen|för|mig ADJ cone-shaped, conical

Zap|fen|streich M *(Mil)* tattoo, last post *(Brit)*, taps *sing (US)*; **den ~ blasen** to sound the tattoo; **der Große ~** the Ceremonial Tattoo; **um 12 Uhr ist ~** *(fig inf)* lights out is at 12 o'clock

Zap|fer ['tsapfɐ] M **-s, -** *(dial)* barman, tapster *(old)*

Zap|fe|rin ['tsapfərɪn] F **-, -nen** *(dial)* barmaid

Zapf-: **Zapf|hahn** M tap; **Zapf|pis|to|le** F (petrol *(Brit)* or gas *(US)* pump) nozzle; **Zapf|säu|le** F petrol pump *(Brit)*, gas pump *(US)*; **Zapf|stel|le** F tap; *(Elec)* (power) point; *(= Tankstelle)* petrol *(Brit)* or gas *(US)* station

Za|pon|lack [tsa'poːnlak] M cellulose lacquer

zap|pe|lig ['tsapəlɪç] ADJ wriggly; *(= unruhig)* fidgety

zap|peln ['tsapln] VI to wriggle; *(Hampelmann)* to jiggle; *(= unruhig sein)* to fidget; **er zappelte mit Armen und Beinen** he was all of a fidget *(Brit)*, he couldn't sit still; **jdn ~ lassen** *(fig inf)* to keep sb in suspense; **in der Schlinge ~** *(fig)* to be caught in the net

Zap|pel|phi|lipp [-fɪlɪp] M **-s, -e** *or* **-s** fidget(er)

zap|pen ['zɛpn] VI *(TV inf)* to zap *(inf)*; **in den Konkurrenzkanal ~** to zap over to the other channel *(inf)*; **Zappen macht Spaß** zapping is fun *(inf)*

zap|pen|dus|ter ['tsapn'duːstɐ] ADJ *(inf)* pitch-black, pitch-dark; **wie sieht es denn mit euren Plänen aus? – ~** how are your plans working out? – grim; **dann ist es ~** you'll/we'll *etc* be in trouble *or* (dead) shtuck *(Brit inf)*

Zap|per ['zɛpɐ] M **-s, -, Zap|pe|rin** [-ərɪn] F **-, -nen** *(inf)* zapper *(inf)*; **er ist ein leidenschaftlicher ~** he just loves zapping *(inf)*

zapp|lig ['tsaplɪç] ADJ = **zappelig**

Zar [tsaːɐ] M **-en, -en** tsar, czar

Za|re|witsch [tsaˈreːvɪtʃ] M **-(e)s, -e** tsarevitch

Zar|ge [ˈtsargə] F **-, -n** frame; *(von Geige etc)* rib; *(von Plattenspieler)* plinth

Za|rin [ˈtsaːrɪn] F **-, -nen** tsarina, czarina

Za|ris|mus [tsaˈrɪsmʊs] M **-,** *no pl* tsarism, czarism

za|ris|tisch [tsaˈrɪstɪʃ] ADJ tsarist, czarist *no adv*

zart [tsaːɐt] **ADJ** *(= weich) Haut, Flaum* soft; *(= leise) Töne, Stimme* soft; *Braten, Gemüse* tender; *Geschmack, Porzellan, Blüte, Gebäck, Farben, Teint* delicate; *(= schwächlich) Gesundheit, Kind* delicate; *(= feinfühlig) Gemüt, Gefühle* sensitive, tender, delicate; *(= sanft) Wind, Berührung* gentle, soft; **nichts für ~e Ohren** not for tender *or* sensitive ears; **im ~en Alter von …** at the tender age of …; **das ~e Geschlecht** the gentle sex **ADV** *umgehen, berühren, andeuten* gently; **~ schmecken** to have a delicate taste; **~ besaitet** = **zartbesaitet**; **~ fühlend** = **zartfühlend**

Zart-: **zart|be|sai|tet** [-bəzaitət] ADJ highly sensitive; **~ sein** to be very sensitive; **zart|bit|ter** ADJ *Schokolade* plain; **zart|blau** ADJ pale blue; **zart|füh|lend** ADJ sensitive; **Zart|ge|fühl** NT delicacy of feeling, sensitivity; **zart|glied|rig** [-gliːdrɪç] ADJ dainty; **zart|grün** ADJ pale green

Zart|heit F **-, -en** *(von Haut, Stimme)* softness; *(von Gemüse, Braten)* tenderness; *(von Farben, Teint)* delicacy, delicateness; *(von Gemüt)* sensitivity; *(von Wind, Berührung)* gentleness

zärt|lich [ˈtsɛːɐtlɪç] **ADJ** tender, affectionate, loving **ADV** tenderly

Zärt|lich|keit F **-,-en** **a** *no pl* affection, tenderness **b** *(= Liebkosung)* caress; **~en** *(= Worte)* tender *or* loving words, words of love; **jdm ~en ins Ohr flüstern** to whisper sweet nothings in sb's ear

zart|ro|sa ADJ pale *or* delicate pink

Zä|si|um [ˈtsɛːziʊm] NT **-s,** *no pl* caesium *(Brit)*, cesium *(US)*

Zast, ZAST [tsast] F **a** *abbr von* **Zinsabschlagsteuer b** *abbr von* **Zentrale Anlaufstelle für Asylbewerber** *central refuge for asylum seekers*

Zas|ter [ˈtsastɐ] M **-s,** *no pl (inf: = Geld)* dosh *(inf)*, brass *(inf)*, readies *pl (inf)*

Zä|sur [tsɛˈzuːɐ] F **-, -en** caesura *(Brit)*, cesura *(US)*; *(fig)* break

Zau|ber [ˈtsaubɐ] M **-s, -** *(= Magie)* magic; *(= Zauberbann)* (magic) spell; *(fig: = Reiz)* magic, charm; **den ~ lösen** to break the spell; **fauler ~** *(inf)* humbug *no indef art*; **der ganze ~** *(inf)* the whole lot *(inf)*; **warum der ganze ~?** *(inf: = Getue)* why all the fuss?

Zau|ber-: **Zau|ber|bann** M (magic) spell; **unter einem ~ stehen** to be under a spell; **Zau|ber|buch** NT book of spells; *(für Zauberkunststücke)* conjuring book

Zau|be|rei [tsaubəˈrai] F **-, -en** **a** *no pl (= das Zaubern)* magic **b** *(= Zauberkunststück)* conjuring trick

Zau|be|rer [ˈtsaubərɐ] M **-s, -** magician; *(in Märchen etc auch)* sorcerer, wizard; *(= Zauberkünstler auch)* conjurer → *auch* **Zauberin**

Zau|ber-: **Zau|ber|flö|te** F magic flute; **Zau|ber|for|mel** F magic formula; **zau|ber|haft** **ADJ** enchanting **ADV** fantastically; **Zau|ber|hand** F **wie von** *or* **durch ~** as if by magic

Zau|be|rin [ˈtsaubərɪn] F **-, -nen** (female) magician; *(in Märchen etc auch)* enchantress, sorceress; *(= Zauberkünstlerin auch)* (female) conjurer

zau|be|risch [ˈtsaubərɪʃ] ADJ = **zauberhaft**

Zau|ber-: **Zau|ber|kas|ten** M magic set; **Zau|ber|kraft** F magic power; **Zau|ber|kunst** F magic, conjuring; **Zau|ber|künst|ler(in)** M(F) conjurer, magician; **Zau|ber|kunst|stück** NT conjuring trick; **Zau|ber|land|schaft** F fairy-tale scene; **Zau|ber|macht** F magical powers *pl*; **Zau|ber|mit|tel** NT magical cure; *(= Trank)* magic potion, philtre *(Brit)*, philter *(US)*

zau|bern [ˈtsaubɐn] **VI** to do *or* perform magic; *(= Kunststücke vorführen)* to do conjuring tricks; **ich kann doch nicht ~!** *(inf)* I'm not a magician!, I can't perform miracles! **VT** **a** **etw ~** to conjure sth out of sth **b** *(fig) Lösung, Essen* to produce as if by magic, to conjure up

Zau|ber-: **Zau|ber|nuss** F wych-hazel, witch hazel; **Zau|ber|reich** NT enchanted *or* magic realm; **Zau|ber|schloss** NT enchanted castle; **Zau|ber|spruch** M (magic) spell; **Zau|ber|stab** M (magic) wand; **Zau|ber|trank** M magic potion, philtre *(Brit)*, philter *(US)*; **Zau|ber|trick** M conjuring trick; **Zau|ber|werk** NT sorcery, wizardry; **Zau|ber|we|sen** NT magical being; **Zau|ber|wort** NT *pl* **-worte** magic word; **Zau|ber|wür|fel** M Rubik's cube®; **Zau|ber|wur|zel** F mandrake root

Zau|de|rer [ˈtsaudərɐ] M **-s, -**, **Zau|de|rin** [-ərɪn] F **-, -nen** vacillator, irresolute person

zau|dern [ˈtsaudɐn] VI to hesitate, to vacillate; **etw ohne zu ~ tun** to do sth without hesitating *or* any hesitation

Zaum [tsaum] M **-(e)s, Zäume** [ˈtsɔymə] bridle; **einem Pferd den ~ anlegen** to put a bridle on a horse; **jdn/etw im ~(e) halten** *(fig)* to keep a tight rein on sb/sth, to keep sb/sth in check; **sich im ~(e) halten** *(fig)* to control oneself, to keep oneself in check; **seine Ungeduld/seinen Zorn im ~e halten** *(fig)* to control *or* curb one's impatience/anger

zäu|men [ˈtsɔymən] VT to bridle

Zaum|zeug NT *pl* **-zeuge** bridle

Zaun [tsaun] M **-(e)s, Zäune** [ˈtsɔynə] fence; **einen Streit vom ~(e) brechen** to pick a quarrel, to start a fight

Zaun-: **Zaun|ei|dech|se** F sand lizard; **Zaun|gast** M *sb who manages to get a free view of an event*; **Zaun|kö|nig** M *(Orn)* wren; **Zaun|lat|te** F picket; **Zaun|lü|cke** F gap in the fence; **Zaun|pfahl** M (fencing) post; **jdm einen Wink mit dem ~ geben** to give *or* drop sb a broad hint; **Zaun|pfos|ten** M → **Zaunpfahl**; **Zaun|re|be** F climbing plant; **Zaun|win|de** F *(Bot)* great bindweed

Zau|sel [ˈtsauzl] M **-s, -s** *(inf)* codger *(inf)*

zau|sen [ˈtsauzn] **VT** to ruffle; *Haare* to ruffle, to tousle; *(fig inf: = in Mitleidenschaft ziehen) Finanzen etc* to run down **VI** **in etw** *(dat)* **~** *(Wind)* to ruffle sth

z. B. [tsɛtˈbeː] *abbr von* **zum Beispiel** eg

z. b. V. *abbr von* **zur besonderen Verwendung**

ZDF [tsɛtdeːˈʔɛf] NT **-(s)** *abbr von* **Zweites Deutsches Fernsehen**

> **ZDF**
>
> **ZDF** – short for **Zweites Deutsches Fernsehen** – is the second public service television station in Germany and the largest in Europe. In contrast to **ARD**, it broadcasts exclusively on television. It was established in 1961 and has its headquarters in Mainz. Since 1984 **ZDF** – together with **ORF** and **SRG** – has been running the international channel **3sat**, and since 1994 it has also been involved in the European television channel **ARTE**. Both these channels focus on cultural programming. **ZDF** is financed through licence fees and strictly controlled advertising. → ARD, ORF, SRG

ZDLer [tsɛtdeːˈʔɛlɐ] M **-s, -** *(inf) abbr von* **Zivildienstleistende(r)**

Ze|ba|oth [ˈtseːbaɔt] M **-s der Herr ~** *(Bibl)* Jehovah

Ze|bra [ˈtseːbra] NT **-s, -s** zebra

Ze|bra|strei|fen M zebra crossing *(Brit)*, pedestrian crossing *or* crosswalk *(US)*

Ze|bu [ˈtseːbu] NT **-s, -s** zebu

Zech|bru|der M boozer *(inf)*; *(= Kumpan)* drinking mate *(Brit inf)*, drinking buddy *(inf)*

Ze|che [ˈtsɛçə] F **-, -n** **a** *(= Rechnung)* bill *(esp Brit)*, check *(US)*; **die (ganze) ~ (be)zahlen** *(lit, fig)* to foot the bill *etc*; **(den Wirt um) die ~ prellen** to leave without paying (the bill *etc*); **eine (hohe) ~ machen** to run up a (large) bill *etc* **b** *(= Bergwerk)* (coal) mine, pit, colliery

ze|chen [ˈtsɛçn] VI to booze *(inf)*; *(= Zechgelage abhalten)* to carouse

Ze|cher [ˈtsɛçɐ] M **-s, -**, **Ze|che|rin** [-ərɪn] F **-, -nen** boozer *(inf)*; *(bei einem Zechgelage)* carouser, reveller *(Brit)*, reveler *(US)*

Ze|che|rei [tsɛçəˈrai] F **-, -en** booze-up *(inf)*; *(= Zechgelage)* carousal; *(= das Zechen)* boozing/carousing

Zech-: **Zech|ge|la|ge** NT carousal *(old, hum)*; **Zech|kum|pan(in)** M(F) drinking mate *(Brit inf)*, drinking buddy *(inf)*; **Zech|prel|ler** [-prɛlɐ] M **-s, -**, **Zech|prel|le|rin** [-ərɪn] F **-, -nen** *person who leaves without paying the bill at a restaurant etc*, Dine-n-Dasher *(US sl)*; **Zech|prel|le|rei** F *leaving without paying the bill at a restaurant etc*, Dine-n-Dash *(US sl)*; **Zech|schwes|ter** F drinking mate *(Brit inf)*, drinking buddy *(inf)*; **Zech|stein** M *(Geol)* Zechstein (period), Upper Permian; **Zech|tour** F *(inf)* pub-crawl *(esp Brit inf)*, bar hop *(US inf)*

Zeck [tsɛk] NT OR M **-(e)s, -e** *(dial: = Fangspiel)* tag

Ze|cke [ˈtsɛkə] [ˈtsɛka] **F** **-, -n**, **Zeck** *(Aus)* **M** **-(e)s, -en** tick

Ze|cken|biss M tick bite; **ich habe einen ~** I've been bitten by a tick

Ze|dent [tseˈdɛnt] M **-en, -en**, **Ze|den|tin** [-ˈdɛntɪn] F **-, -nen** *(Jur)* assignor

Ze|der [ˈtseːdɐ] F **-, -n** cedar

ze|dern [ˈtseːdɐn] ADJ cedar

Ze|dern|holz NT cedar, cedarwood

Ze|dern|öl NT cedarwood oil

ze|die|ren [tseˈdiːrən] *ptp* **zediert** VT *(Jur)* to cede, to assign, to transfer

Zeh [tseː] M **-s, -en**, **Ze|he** [ˈtseːə] F **-, -n** toe; *(= Knoblauchzehe)* clove; **großer/kleiner ~, große/kleine ~e** big/little toe; **auf (den) ~en gehen/schleichen** to tiptoe, to walk/creep on tiptoe; **sich auf die ~en stellen** to stand on tiptoe; **jdm auf die ~en treten** *(fig inf)* to tread on sb's toes

Ze|hen-: **Ze|hen|na|gel** M toenail; **Ze|hen|san|da|le** F flip-flop *(Brit)*, thong *(US)*; **Ze|hen|spit|ze** F tip of the toe; **auf (den) ~n** on tiptoe, on tippy-toes *(US inf)*; **sich auf die ~n stellen** to stand on tiptoe; **auf (den) ~n gehen** to tiptoe, to walk on tiptoe; **auf den ~n tanzen** to dance on one's toes

zehn [tseːn] NUM ten; **(ich wette) ~ zu** *or* **gegen eins** (I bet) ten to one → *auch* **vier**

Zehn [tseːn] F **-, -en** ten → *auch* **Vier**

Zehn-: **Zehn|cent|mün|ze** F, **Zehn|cent|stück** NT ten-cent piece; **Zehn|eck** NT decagon; **zehn|eckig** ADJ ten-sided, decagonal

Zeh|ner [ˈtseːnɐ] M **-s, -** **a** *(Math)* ten → *auch* **Vierer b** *(inf) (= Zehncentstück)* ten-cent piece, ten; *(= Zehneuroschein)* tenner *(inf)*

Zeh|ner-: **Zeh|ner|bruch** M decimal (fraction); **Zeh|ner|kar|te** F *(für Bus etc)* 10-journey ticket; *(für Schwimmbad etc)* 10-visit ticket; **Zeh|ner|pa|ckung** F packet of ten; **Zeh|ner|stel|le** F ten's (place); **Zeh|ner|sys|tem** NT decimal system; **Zeh|ner|tas|ta|tur** F *(Comput)* numeric keypad, number pad

Zehn-: **Zehn|eu|ro|schein** M [tseːnˈɔyro-] ten-euro note *(Brit)* or bill *(US)*; **Zehn|fin|ger|sys|tem** NT touch-typing method; **Zehn|kampf** M *(Sport)* decathlon; **Zehn|kämp|fer** M decathlete; **zehn|mal** [ˈtseːnmaːl] ADV ten times → *auch* **viermal**; **Zehn|mark|schein** M *(Hist)* ten-mark note; **Zehn|me|ter|brett** NT ten-metre *(Brit)* or ten-meter *(US)* board; **Zehn|mi|nu|ten|takt** M **im ~** every ten minutes, at ten-minute intervals

Zehnt [tseːnt] M **-en, -en** *(Hist)* tithe

zehn|tau|send [ˈtseːnˈtauznt] NUM ten thousand; **~e** *or* **Zehntausende von Menschen** tens of thousands of people → **obere(r, s)**

zehn|tel [ˈtseːntl] ADJ tenth

Zehn|tel [ˈtseːntl] NT **-s, -** tenth

Zehn|tel|se|kun|de F tenth of a second; **um zwei ~n** *(Sport)* by two tenths *or* point two of a second

zehn|tens ['tse:ntns] ADV tenth(ly), in the tenth place

zehn|te(r, s) ['tse:ntə] ADJ tenth → *auch* **vierte(r, s)**

Zehn|te(r) ['tse:ntə] M *decl as adj (Hist)* tithe

zeh|ren ['tse:rən] VI **a** **von etw ~** *(lit)* to live off *or* on sth; *(fig)* to feed on sth **b** **an jdm/etw ~** to wear sb/sth out; *an Kraft auch* to sap sth; *an Nerven* to ruin sth; *(Anstrengung) am Herzen* to weaken sth; *(Kummer)* to gnaw at sth; *an Gesundheit* to undermine sth

Zehr|geld NT, **Zehr|pfen|nig** M *(obs)* travelling *(Brit) or* traveling *(US)* monies *pl (old)*

Zeh|rung ['tse:rʊŋ] F -, *no pl (old)* provisions *pl*

Zei|chen ['tsaiçn] NT **-s, -** sign; *(Sci, algebraisch, auf Landkarte)* symbol; *(= Schriftzeichen, auch Comput)* character; *(= Anzeichen: von Krankheit, Winter, = Beweis: von Friedfertigkeit)* sign, indication; *(= Hinweis, Signal)* signal; *(= Erkennungszeichen)* identification; *(= Lesezeichen)* bookmark, marker; *(= Vermerk)* mark; *(auf Briefköpfen)* reference; *(= Satzzeichen)* punctuation mark; *(= Warenzeichen)* trademark; **wenn nicht alle ~ trügen** if I'm/we're *etc* not completely mistaken; **es ist ein ~ unserer Zeit, dass ...** it is a sign of the times that ...; **ein ~ setzen** to set an example; **die ~ erkennen** to see the writing on the wall; **die ~ der Zeit erkennen** to recognize the mood of the times; **es geschehen noch ~ und Wunder!** *(hum)* wonders will never cease! *(hum)*; **als** *or* **zum ~** as a sign; **ein ~ des Himmels** a sign from heaven; **als ~ von etw** as a sign *or* indication of sth; **zum ~, dass ...** as a sign that ..., to show that ...; **als ~ der Verehrung** as a mark *or* token of respect; **jdm ein ~ geben** *or* **machen** to give sb a signal *or* sign, to signal to sb; **etw zum ~ tun** to do sth as a signal, to signal by doing sth; **das ~ zum Aufbruch geben** to give the signal to leave; **unser/Ihr ~** *(form)* our/your reference; **seines ~s** *(old, hum)* by trade; **er ist im ~** *or* **unter dem ~ des Widders geboren** he was born under the sign of Aries; **unter dem ~ von etw stehen** *(fig: Konferenz etc)* to take place against a background of sth; **das Jahr 1979 stand unter dem ~ des Kindes** 1979 was the year of the child; **die ~ stehen auf Sturm** *(fig)* there's a storm brewing

Zei|chen-: **Zei|chen|be|le|gung** F *(Comput)* character mapping; **Zei|chen|block** M *pl* **-blöcke** *or* **-blocks** drawing *or* sketch pad; **Zei|chen|brett** NT drawing board; **Zei|chen|drei|eck** NT set square; **Zei|chen|er|ken|nung** F *(Comput)* character recognition; **optische ~** optical character recognition; **Zei|chen|er|klä|rung** F *(auf Fahrplänen etc)* key (to the symbols); *(auf Landkarte)* legend; **Zei|chen|fe|der** F drawing pen; **Zei|chen|fol|ge** F character string *or* sequence; **zei|chen|haft** ADJ symbolic; **Zei|chen|heft** NT drawing book; **Zei|chen|kar|te** F *(Comput)* graphics card; **Zei|chen|ket|te** F *(Comput)* character string; **Zei|chen|koh|le** F charcoal; **Zei|chen|kunst** F (art of) drawing; **Zei|chen|leh|rer(in)** M(F) art teacher; **Zei|chen|pa|pier** NT drawing paper; **Zei|chen|saal** M art room; **Zei|chen|satz** M *(Comput)* character set, font; **Zei|chen|schutz** M protection of registered trademarks; **Zei|chen|set|zung** [-zɛtsʊŋ] F **-, -en** punctuation; **Zei|chen|spra|che** F sign language; **Zei|chen|stift** M drawing pencil; **Zei|chen|stun|de** F art *or* drawing lesson; **Zei|chen|sys|tem** NT notation; *(Ling)* system of signs; **Zei|chen|ta|bel|le** F *(Comput)* character map; **Zei|chen|tisch** M drawing table; **Zei|chen|trick|film** M (animated) cartoon; **Zei|chen|un|ter|richt** M art; *(= Unterrichtsstunde)* drawing *or* art lesson; **Zei|chen|vor|la|ge** F original, model *(for a drawing or trademark)*

zeich|nen ['tsaiçnən] VI to draw; *(form: = unterzeichnen)* to sign; **an dem Entwurf hat er lange gezeichnet** he has spent a long time drawing the blueprint; **gezeichnet XY** signed, XY → **verantwortlich** VT **a** *(= abzeichnen)* to draw; *(= entwerfen) Plan, Grundriss* to draw up, to draft; *(fig: = porträtieren)* to portray, to depict **b** *(= kennzeichnen)* to mark; **das Gefieder des Vogels ist hübsch gezeichnet** the bird's plumage has attractive markings → *auch* **gezeichnet** **c** *(Fin) Betrag* to subscribe; *Aktien* to subscribe (for); *Anleihe* to subscribe to; **gezeichnet** *(Kapital)* subscribed

Zeich|ner ['tsaiçnɐ] M **-s, -**, **Zeich|ne|rin** [-ərɪn] F **-, -nen** **a** artist; **muss ein Maler auch immer ein guter ~ sein?** must a painter always be a good draughtsman *(Brit) or* draftsman *(US)* too? → **technisch ADJ b** **b** *(Fin)* subscriber *(von* to)

zeich|ne|risch ['tsaiçnərɪʃ] ADJ *Darstellung, Gestaltung, Werk* graphic; **sein ~es Können** his drawing ability ADV **~ begabt sein** to have a talent for drawing; **etw ~ erklären** to explain sth with a drawing; **etw ~ festhalten** to draw sth; *(Polizei)* to make a diagram of sth; **etw ~ darstellen** to represent sth in a drawing

Zeich|nung ['tsaiçnʊŋ] F **-, -en** **a** *(= Darstellung)* drawing; *(= Entwurf)* draft, drawing; *(fig: = Schilderung)* portrayal, depiction **b** *(= Muster)* patterning; *(von Gefieder, Fell)* markings *pl* **c** *(Fin)* subscription; **eine Anleihe zur ~ auflegen** to invite subscriptions for a loan

Zeich|nungs-: **zeich|nungs|be|rech|tigt** ADJ authorized to sign; **Zeich|nungs|frist** F *(Fin)* subscription period; **Zeich|nungs|voll|macht** F authority to sign

Zei|ge|fin|ger M index finger, forefinger

Zei|ge|ge|rät NT *(Tech, Comput)* pointing device

zei|gen ['tsaign] VI to point; **nach Norden/rechts ~** to point north *or* to the north/to the right; **auf jdn/etw ~** to point at sb/sth; *(= hinweisen auch)* to point to sb/sth; **mit der Maus auf etw ~** *(Comput)* to point the mouse at sth VT to show; *(Thermometer, Messgerät auch)* to be at *or* on, to indicate; **jdm etw ~** to show sb sth *or* sth to sb; **ich muss mir mal von jemandem ~ lassen, wie man das macht** I'll have to get someone to show me how to do it; **die Uhr zeigte fünf nach zwölf** the clock showed five past twelve; **dem werd ichs (aber) ~!** *(inf)* I'll show him!; **zeig mal, was du kannst!** let's see what you can do!, show us what you can do! VR to appear; *(Gefühle)* to show; **sich mit jdm ~** to let oneself be seen with sb; **in dem Kleid kann ich mich doch nicht ~** I can't be seen in a dress like that; **er zeigt sich nicht gern in der Öffentlichkeit** he doesn't like showing himself *or* being seen in public; **sich ~ als ...** to show *or* prove oneself to be ...; **er zeigte sich befriedigt** he was satisfied; **es zeigt sich, dass ...** it turns out that ...; **es zeigt sich (doch) wieder einmal, dass ...** it just goes to show ...; **es wird sich ~, wer recht hat** time will tell who is right, we shall see who's right; **daran zeigt sich, dass ...** that shows (that) ...; **das zeigt sich jetzt** it's beginning to show

Zei|ger ['tsaigɐ] M **-s, -** indicator, pointer; *(= Uhrzeiger)* hand; *(= Mauszeiger)* pointer; **der große/kleine ~** the big/little hand; **jdm auf den ~ gehen** *(inf)* to get on sb's wick *(Brit inf) or* nerves

Zei|ger|aus|schlag M pointer *or* indicator deflection

Zei|ger|ge|schwin|dig|keit F *(von Computermaus)* pointer speed

Zei|ge|stab M, **Zei|ge|stock** M pointer

zei|hen ['tsaiən] *pret* **zieh** [tsi:], *ptp* **geziehen** [gə'tsi:ən] VT *(old)* **jdn einer Sache** *(gen)* **~** to accuse sb of sth

Zei|le ['tsailə] F **-, -n** line; *(= Häuserzeile, Baumzeile etc auch)* row; *(von Tabelle)* row; **davon habe ich keine ~ gelesen** I haven't read a single word of it; **zwischen den ~n lesen** to read between the lines; **vielen Dank für deine ~n** many thanks for your letter; **jdm ein paar ~n schreiben** to write sb a few lines; *(= Brief schreiben auch)* to drop sb a line

Zei|len-: **Zei|len|ab|stand** M line spacing; **Zei|len|ab|tas|tung** F *(TV)* line scan(ning); **Zei|len|bau|wei|se** F ribbon development; **Zei|len|be|fehl** M *(Comput)* line command; **Zei|len|end|schal|tung** F *(Comput)* carriage return; **Zei|len|fang** M *(TV)* horizontal hold; **Zei|len|ho|no|rar** NT payment per line; **~ bekommen** to be paid by the line; **Zei|len|län|ge** F length (of a/the line); **Zei|len|norm** F *(TV)* line standard; **Zei|len|schal|ter** M line spacer; **Zei|len|schal|tung** F line spacing; **Zei|len|setz|ma|schi|ne** F Linotype® machine; **Zei|len|sprung** M *(Liter)* enjambement; *(Comput)* line skip; **Zei|len|um|bruch** F line break; **automatischer ~** *(Comput)* wordwrap; **Zei|len|vor|schub** M *(Comput)* line feed; **zei|len|wei|se** ADV in lines; *(= nach Zeilen)* by the line; **etw ~ vorlesen** to read sth out line by line

-zei|lig [tsailɪç] ADJ *suf* with ... lines; **es ist vierzeilig** it has four lines

Zei|sig ['tsaizɪç] M **-s, -e** [-gə] *(Orn)* siskin → **locker**

zeit [tsait] PREP *+gen* **~ meines/seines Lebens** in my/his lifetime

Zeit [tsait] F **-, -en** **a** time; *(= Epoche)* age; **die gute alte ~** the good old days; **es erinnerte ihn an alte ~en** it reminded him of the old days; **das waren noch ~en!** those were the days; **die ~en sind schlecht** times are bad; **die ~en haben sich geändert** times have changed; **die ~ Goethes** the age of Goethe; **die damalige ~ machte die Einführung neuer Methoden erforderlich** the situation at the time required the introduction of new methods; **wenn ~ und Umstände es erfordern** if circumstances demand it, if the situation requires it; **die jetzigen ~en erfordern, ...** the present situation requires ...; **für alle ~en** for ever, for all time *(liter)*; **etw für alle ~en entscheiden** to decide sth once and for all; **in seiner/ihrer besten ~** at his/her peak; **mit der ~ gehen** to move with the times; **vor der ~ alt werden** to get old before one's time; **vor jds** *(dat)* **~** before sb's time; **die ~ ist knapp bemessen** time is short; **die ~ verging wie im Flug** time flew by; **die ~ wurde mir lang** time hung heavy on my hands; **eine lange ~ her sein** *or* **zurückliegen, dass ...** to be a long time (ago *or* back) since ...; **eine Stunde ~ haben** to have an hour (to spare); **Fräulein Glück, haben Sie vielleicht einen Augenblick ~?** Miss Glück, do you have a moment?; **~ raubend** = **zeitraubend**; **~ sparend** = **zeitsparend**; **sich** *(dat)* **für jdn/etw ~ nehmen** to devote time to sb/sth; **sich ~ füreinander nehmen** to make time for one another; **dafür muss ich mir mehr ~ nehmen** I need more time for that; **sich** *(dat)* **die ~ nehmen, etw zu tun** to take the time to do sth; **du hast dir aber reichlich ~ gelassen** you certainly took your time; **hier bin ich die längste ~ gewesen** it's about time *or* it's high time I was going; **keine ~ verlieren** to lose no time; **damit hat es noch ~** there's no rush *or* hurry, there's plenty of time; **das hat ~ bis morgen** that can wait until tomorrow; **lass dir ~** take your time; **... aller ~en** ... of all time, ... ever; **auf bestimmte ~** for a certain length of time; **auf unbestimmte ~** for an indefinite period; **in letzter ~** recently; **die ganze ~ über** the whole time; **eine ~ lang** a while, a time; **wir sind eine ~ lang dortgeblieben** we stayed there (for) a while *or* for a time; **eine ~ lang ist das ganz schön** for a while *or* time it's quite nice; **mit der ~** gradually, in time; **nach ~ bezahlt werden** to be paid by the hour; **die ~ heilt alle Wunden** *(Prov)* time is a great healer *(prov)*; **auf ~ spielen** *(Sport, fig)* to play for time; **es wird langsam ~, dass ...** it's about time that ...; **für dich wird es langsam ~, dass ...** it's about time that you …; **seine ~ ist gekommen** his time has come; **hast du (die) genaue ~?** do you have the exact time?; **in der ~ von 10 bis 12** between 10 and 12 (o'clock); **es ist an der ~, dass …** it is about time *or* it's high time (that) …; **Vertrag auf ~** fixed-term contract; **Beamter auf ~** ≈ non-permanent civil servant; **Soldat auf ~** soldier serving for a set time; **seit dieser ~** since then; **zur ~** *or* **zu ~en Königin Viktorias** in Queen Victoria's time; **zu der ~, als …** (at the time) when …; **alles zu seiner ~** *(prov)* all in good time; **von ~ zu ~** from time to time → **kommen 1 a, zurzeit**

b *(Ling)* tense; **in welcher ~ steht das Verb?** what tense is the verb in?

Zeit-: **Zeit|ab|schnitt** M period (of time); **Zeit|ab|stand** M interval; **in regelmäßigen Zeitabständen** at regular intervals, periodically; **Zeit|al|ter** NT age; **das goldene ~** the golden age; **in unserem ~** nowadays, in this day and age; **Zeit|an|ga|be** F *(= Datum)* date; *(= Uhrzeit)* time (of day); **die ~ kommt vor der Ortsangabe** *(Gram)* time is given before place; **Zeit|an|sa|ge** F *(Rad)* time check; *(Telec)* speaking clock; **Zeit|an|zei|ge** F time display; **Zeit|ar|beit** F temporary work; **Zeit|ar|bei|ter(in)** M(F) temporary worker, temp; **Zeit|ar|beits|fir|ma** F temping agency, agency for temporary work; **Zeit|ar|beitskraft** F temporary worker, temp; **Zeit|auf|nah|me** F *(Phot)* time exposure; **Zeit|auf|wand** M time *(needed to complete a task)*; **mit möglichst wenig ~** taking as little time as possible; **dieses Dokument wurde unter großen ~ erstellt** it took an enormous amount of time to produce this document; **mit großem ~ verbunden sein** to be extremely time-consuming; **zeit|auf|wän|dig** ADJ time-consuming; **Zeit|be|griff** M conception of time; **Zeit|be|stim|mung** F *(Gram)* designation of the tense of a verb; **Zeit|bom|be** F *(lit, fig)* time bomb; **Zeit|do|ku|ment** NT contemporary document; **Zeit|druck** M, *no pl* pressure of time; **unter ~** under pressure; **Zeit|ein|heit** F time unit; **Zeit|ein|tei|lung** F division of time; *(= Zeitplan)* timetable, schedule *(esp US)*

Zei|ten-: **Zei|ten|fol|ge** F *(Gram)* sequence of tenses; **Zei|ten|wen|de** F **nach der ~** anno Domini; **vor der ~** before Christ

Zeit-: **Zeit|er|fas|sung** F *(Ind)* recording of time worked; **Zeit|er|fas|sungs|ge|rät** NT *(Ind)* time recorder, time-recording device; **Zeit|er|spar|nis** F saving of time; **Zeit|fah|ren** NT **-s**, *no pl (Sport)* time trial; **Zeit|fens|ter** NT time slot; **Zeit|fol|ge** F sequence, chronological order; **Zeit|form** F *(Gram)* tense; **Zeit|fra|ge** F question of time; **zeit|ge|bun|den** ADJ tied to *or* dependent on a particular time; *Mode* temporary; **Zeit|ge|fühl** NT, *no pl* sense of time; **Zeit|geist** M, *no pl* Zeitgeist, spirit of the times; **zeit|ge|mäß** ADJ up-to-date; **~ sein** to be in keeping with the times ADV in keeping with the times; **Zeit|ge|nos|se** M, **Zeit|ge|nos|sin** F contemporary; **ein seltsamer ~** *(iro)* an odd bod *(inf)*, an oddball *(esp US inf)*; **zeit|ge|nös|sisch** [-gənœsɪʃ] ADJ contemporary; **Zeit|ge|sche|hen** NT events *pl* of the day; **Zeit|ge|schich|te** F, *no pl* contemporary history; **Zeit|ge|schmack** M prevailing taste; **Zeit|ge|winn** M gain in time; **sich um einen ~ bemühen** to try to gain time; **zeit|gleich** ADJ *Erscheinungen* contemporaneous; *Läufer* with the same time; *(Film)* synchronized, in sync(h) *(inf)* ADV at the same time *(mit* as); **~ den ersten Platz belegen** to tie for first place; **Zeit|his|to|ri|ker(in)** M(F) contemporary historian

zei|tig ['tsaitɪç] ADJ ADV early

zei|ti|gen ['tsaitɪgn] VT *(geh) Ergebnis, Wirkung* to bring about; *Erfolg auch* to lead to; **Früchte ~** to bear fruit

Zeit-: **Zeit|kar|te** F season ticket; *(= Wochenkarte)* weekly ticket; **Zeit|kar|ten|in|ha|ber(in)** M(F) season ticket holder; *(von Wochenkarte)* weekly ticket holder; **Zeit|kon|to** NT record of hours worked; **Zeit|kon|trol|le** F time study; **zeit|kri|tisch** ADJ **a** *Aufsatz, Artikel* full of comment on contemporary issues; **seine ~en Bemerkungen** his thoughtful remarks on contemporary issues; **seine ~e Haltung** his awareness of contemporary issues **b** *(Comput) Anwendung, Prozess* time-critical; **Zeit|lang** ['tsaitlaŋ] F → **Zeit a**; **Zeit|läuf|te** PL *(geh)* course *no pl* of time; **zeit|le|bens** [tsait-'le:bns] ADV all one's life

zeit|lich ['tsaitlɪç] ADJ temporal; *Verzögerungen* time-related; *(= chronologisch) Reihenfolge* chronological; **aus ~en Gründen** for reasons of time; **in kurzem/großem ~em Abstand** at short/long intervals (of time); **einen hohen ~en Aufwand erfordern** to require a great deal of time; **das Zeitliche segnen** *(euph: Mensch)* to depart this life; *(inf: Sache)* to bite the dust *(inf)*

ADV timewise *(inf)*, from the point of view of time; *(= chronologisch)* chronologically; **das kann sie ~ nicht einrichten** she can't fit that in (timewise *(inf)*), she can't find (the) time for that; **das passt ihr ~ nicht** the time isn't convenient for her; **~ befristet sein** to have a time limit; **~ zusammenfallen** to coincide; **die Uhren/Pläne ~ aufeinander abstimmen** to synchronize one's watches/plans

Zeit-: **Zeit|li|mit** NT time limit; **Zeit|lohn** M hourly rate; **~ bekommen** to be paid by the hour; **zeit|los** ADJ timeless; *Stil auch* which doesn't date; *Kleidung auch* classic; **Zeit|lo|sig|keit** F -, *no pl* timelessness; **Zeit|lu|pe** F slow motion *no art*; **etw in (der) ~ zeigen** to show sth in slow motion; **Wiederholung in (der) ~** slow-motion replay; **Zeit|lu|pen|auf|nah|me** F slow-motion shot; **Zeit|lu|pen|tem|po** NT slow speed; **im ~** *(lit)* in slow motion; *(fig)* at a snail's pace; **Zeit|ma|nage|ment** NT time management; **Zeit|man|gel** M lack of time; **aus ~** for lack of time; **Zeit|ma|schi|ne** F time machine; **Zeit|maß** NT tempo; **Zeit|mes|ser** M **-s, -** timekeeper; **Zeit|mes|sung** F timekeeping *(auch Sport)*, measurement of time; **zeit|nah** ADJ contemporary; *Problem auch* of our age; *Gottesdienst, Übersetzung auch* modern; *Bücher, Unterricht* relevant to present times ADV in a contemporary way; **Zeit|nah|me** [-na:mə] F **-, -n** *(Sport)* timekeeping *no pl*; **Zeit|neh|mer(in)** M(F) *(Sport, Ind)* timekeeper; **Zeit|not** F shortage of time; **in ~ sein** to be pressed for time, to be short of time; **Zeit|plan** M schedule, timetable; **Zeit|punkt** M *(= Termin)* time; *(= Augenblick auch)* moment; **zu diesem ~** at that time; **den ~ für etw festlegen** to set a time for sth; **Zeit|raf|fer** [-rafɐ] M **-s**, *no pl* time-lapse photography; **einen Film im ~ zeigen** to show a time-lapse film; **zeit|rau|bend** ADJ time-consuming; **Zeit|raum** M period of time; **in einem ~ von …** over a period of …; **Zeit|rech|nung** F calendar; **nach christlicher/jüdischer ~** according to the Christian/Jewish calendar; **vor unserer ~** before Christ, BC; **nach unserer ~** anno Domini, AD; **Zeit|schalt|uhr** F timer, time switch; **Zeit|schrift** F *(= Illustrierte)* magazine; *(wissenschaftlich)* periodical, journal; **Zeit|schrif|ten|ka|ta|log** M periodicals catalogue *(Brit) or* catalog *(US)*; **Zeit|sinn** M sense of time; **Zeit|sol|dat(in)** M(F) regular soldier *(who has signed up for a fixed period of time)*; **Zeit|span|ne** F period of time; **zeit|spa|rend** ADJ time-saving ADV expeditiously; **möglichst ~ vorgehen** to save as much time as possible; **Zeit|stu|die** F *(Ind)* time (and motion) study; **zeit|syn|chron** ADJ synchronized *no adv*, at the same time; **Zeit|ta|fel** F chronological table; **Zeit|takt** M **a** *(Telec)* unit length **b** timing; **im 10-minütigen ~** every 10 minutes; **Zeit|um|stän|de** PL prevailing circumstances *pl*, circumstances *pl* of the time; **Zeit|um|stel|lung** F **a** *(= Zeitänderung)* changing the clocks, putting the clocks back/forward **b** *(= Zeitunterschied)* time difference

Zei|tung ['tsaitʊŋ] F **-, -en** (news)paper; **er hat bei der ~ gearbeitet** he worked for a newspaper

Zei|tungs- *in cpds* newspaper; **Zei|tungs|abon|ne|ment** NT subscription to a newspaper; **Zei|tungs|an|zei|ge** F newspaper advertisement; *(= Familienanzeige)* announcement in the (news)paper; **Zei|tungs|ar|ti|kel** M newspaper article; *(= aktueller Bericht)* news report; **Zei|tungs|aus|schnitt** M newspaper cutting; **Zei|tungs|aus|trä|ger** M paperboy; **Zei|tungs|aus|trä|ge|rin** F papergirl; **Zei|tungs|bei|la|ge** F newspaper supplement; **Zei|tungs|druck|pa|pier** NT newsprint; **Zei|tungs|en|te** F *(inf)* canard, false newspaper report; **Zei|tungs|frau** F *(inf)* **a** *(= Journalistin)* newspaper woman **b** *(= Austrägerin)* paperwoman; **Zei|tungs|händ|ler(in)** M(F) newsagent, newsdealer *(US)*; **Zei|tungs|in|se|rat** NT newspaper advertisement; **Zei|tungs|jar|gon** M journalese; **Zei|tungs|jun|ge** M paperboy; **Zei|tungs|ki|osk** M newspaper kiosk; **Zei|tungs|kor|res|pon|dent(in)** M(F) newspaper correspondent; **Zei|tungs|la|den** M paper shop; **Zei|tungs|le|sen** NT **-s**, *no pl* reading the (news)paper *no art*; **er war gerade beim ~** he was just reading the paper/papers; **Zei|tungs|le|ser(in)** M(F) newspaper reader; **Zei|tungs|mäd|chen** NT papergirl; **Zei|tungs|mann** M *(inf)* **a** *pl* **-leute** *(= Journalist)* newspaper man **b** *(= Austräger)* paperman; **Zei|tungs|no|tiz** F press item; **Zei|tungs|pa|pier** NT newsprint; *(als Altpapier)* newspaper; **Zei|tungs|re|dak|teur(in)** M(F) newspaper editor; **Zei|tungs|stän|der** M magazine *or* newspaper rack; **Zei|tungs|ver|le|ger(in)** M(F) newspaper publisher; **Zei|tungs|we|sen** NT, *no pl* press, newspaper world; **das ~ in Deutschland** the German press; **im ~ tätig sein** to be in the newspaper business; *(Journalist)* to be in journalism; **Zei|tungs|wis|sen|schaft** F journalism; **Zei|tungs|zar** M press baron

Zeit-: **Zeit|un|ter|schied** M time difference; **Zeit|ver|geu|dung** F waste of time; **Zeit|ver|lust** M loss of time; **das bedeutet mehrere Stunden ~** this will mean wasting several hours; **ohne ~** without losing any time; **Zeit|ver|schie|bung** F **a** *(= Zeitunterschied)* time difference **b** *(von Termin etc)* rescheduling, change in timing; **Zeit|ver|schwen|dung** F waste of time; **das wäre ~** that would be a waste of time; **zeit|ver|setzt** ADJ staggered; **Zeit|ver|trag** M temporary contract; **Zeit|ver|treib** [-fɛɐtraip] M **-(e)s, -e** [-bə] way of passing the time; *(= Hobby)* pastime; **zum ~** to pass the time, as a way of passing the time; **Zeit|vor|ga|be** F **a** *(= Zeitbestimmung)* time setting **b** *(= Vorsprung)* head start; **zeit|wei|lig** [-vailɪç] ADJ temporary ADV for a while; *(= kurzzeitig)* temporarily; **zeit|wei|se** ADV at times; **und ~ Regen** with rain at times; **Zeit|wen|de** F = **Zeitenwende**; **Zeit|wert** M *(Fin)* current value; *(= Marktwert)* market value; *(= Messergebnis)* time; **Zeit|wort** NT *pl* **-wörter** verb; **Zeit|zei|chen** NT time signal; **Zeit|zeu|ge** M, **Zeit|zeu|gin** F contemporary witness; **Zeit|zo|ne** F time zone; **Zeit|zün|der** M time fuse

ze|leb|rie|ren [tseleˈbri:rən] *ptp* **zelebriert** VT to celebrate

Ze|leb|ri|tät [tselebriˈtɛ:t] F **-, -en** *(rare)* celebrity

Zell|at|mung F cellular respiration

Zel|le ['tsɛlə] F **-, -n** cell *(auch Sci, Pol, Comput)*; *(= Kabine)* cabin; *(= Telefonzelle)* (phone) box *(Brit) or* booth; *(bei Flugzeug)* airframe

Zell-: **Zell|ge|we|be** NT cell tissue; **Zell|gift** NT cytotoxin; **Zell|kern** M nucleus (of a/the cell); **Zell|kern|tei|lung** F cell division, mitosis; **Zell|kul|tur** F cell culture; **Zell|memb|ran** F cell membrane

Zel|lo|phan [tsɛloˈfa:n] NT **-s,** *no pl* cellophane®

Zell-: **Zell|plas|ma** NT cytoplasm; **Zell|prä|pa|rat** NT cell culture; **Zell|stoff** M cellulose; **Zell|stoff|win|del** F disposable nappy *(Brit) or* diaper *(US)*; **Zell|tei|lung** F cell division

zel|lu|lar [tsɛluˈla:ɐ] ADJ cellular

Zel|lu|lar|the|ra|pie F cell therapy

Zel|lu|li|tis [tsɛluˈli:tɪs] F -, *no pl (Med)* cellulite

Zel|lu|loid [tsɛluˈlɔyt, tsɛluloˈi:t] NT **-s,** *no pl* celluloid

Zel|lu|lo|se [tsɛluˈlo:zə] F **-, -n** cellulose

Zell-: **Zell|ver|schmel|zung** F cell fusion; **Zell|wand** F cell wall; **Zell|wol|le** F spun rayon

Ze|lot [tseˈlo:t] M **-en, -en** *(fig geh: = Eiferer)* zealot, fanatic

Ze|lot M, **Ze|lo|tin** [tseˈlo:tɪn] F **-, -nen** *(Hist)* Zealot

Zelt [tsɛlt] NT **-(e)s, -e** tent; *(= Bierzelt, Festzelt etc auch)* marquee; *(= Indianerzelt)* wigwam, te(e)pee; *(= Zirkuszelt)* big top; *(liter: des Himmels)* canopy; **seine ~e aufschlagen** *(fig)* to settle down; **seine ~e abbrechen** *(fig)* to pack one's bags

Zelt-: **Zelt|bahn** F strip of canvas; **Zelt|dach** NT tent roof; *(Dachform)* pyramid roof

zel|ten [ˈtsɛltn] VI to camp; **Zelten verboten** no camping

Zel|ter [ˈtsɛltɐ] M **-s, -** *(Hist: = Pferd)* palfrey

Zel|ter [ˈtsɛltɐ] M **-s, -, Zel|te|rin** [-ərɪn] F **-, -nen** camper

Zelt-: **Zelt|he|ring** M tent peg; **Zelt|la|ger** NT camp; **wann fahrt ihr ins ~?** when are you going to camp?; **Zelt|lein|wand** F, *no pl* canvas; **Zelt|mast** M tent pole; **Zelt|mis|si|on** F *evangelistic mission with a tent as its base*; **Zelt|pflock** M tent peg; **Zelt|pla|ne** F tarpaulin; **Zelt|platz** M camp site; **Zelt|stan|ge** F tent pole

Ze|ment [tseˈmɛnt] M **-(e)s, -e** cement

ze|men|tie|ren [tsemɛnˈti:rən] *ptp* **zementiert** VT to cement; *(= verputzen)* to cement over; *Stahl* to carburize *(spec)*; *(fig)* to reinforce; *Freundschaft* to cement

Ze|men|tie|rung F **-, -en** *(fig)* reinforcement; *(von Freundschaft)* cementing

Ze|ment(misch)|ma|schi|ne F cement mixer

Zen [zɛn, tsɛn] NT **-s,** *no pl* Zen (Buddhism)

Ze|nit [tseˈni:t] M **-(e)s,** *no pl (lit, fig)* zenith; **die Sonne steht im ~** the sun is at its zenith; **im ~ des Lebens stehen** *(liter)* to be at one's peak

Ze|no|taph [tsenoˈta:f] M **-s, -e** cenotaph

zen|sie|ren [tsɛnˈzi:rən] *ptp* **zensiert** VT **a** *auch vi (= benoten)* to mark; **einen Aufsatz mit einer Drei ~** to give an essay a three **b** *Bücher etc* to censor

Zen|sor [ˈtsɛnzo:ɐ] M **-s, Zensoren** [-ˈzo:rən], **Zen|so|rin** [-ˈzo:rɪn] F **-, -nen** censor

Zen|sur [tsɛnˈzu:ɐ] F **-, -en a** *no pl (= Kontrolle)* censorship *no indef art*; *(= Prüfstelle)* censors *pl*; *(esp bei Film)* board of censors; **eine ~ findet nicht statt** there is no censorship; **durch die ~ gehen** to be censored; **der ~ unterliegen** to be subject to censorship **b** *(= Note)* mark; **der Plan erhielt von der Presse schlechte ~en** the plan got the thumbs down from the press *(inf)* **c Zensuren** PL *(= Zeugnis)* report *sing*; **wenn es auf die ~en zugeht** when report time approaches

zen|su|rie|ren [tsɛnzuˈri:rən] *ptp* **zensuriert** VT *(Aus, Sw)* to censor

Zen|sus [ˈtsɛnzʊs] M **-, -** [-zu:s] *(= Volkszählung)* census

Zen|taur [tsɛnˈtaur] M **-en, -en** centaur

Zen|ti-: **Zen|ti|grad** [tsɛntiˈgra:t, ˈtsɛnti-] M hundredth of a degree; **Zen|ti|gramm** [tsɛntiˈgram, ˈtsɛnti-] NT centigram(me); **Zen|ti|li|ter** [tsɛntiˈli:tɐ, -ˈlɪtɐ, ˈtsɛnti-] M OR NT centilitre *(Brit)*, centileter *(US)*; **Zen|ti|me|ter** [tsɛntiˈme:tɐ, ˈtsɛnti-] M OR NT centimetre *(Brit)*, centimeter *(US)*; **Zen|ti|me|ter|maß** [tsɛntiˈme:tɐ-] NT (metric) tape measure

Zent|ner [ˈtsɛntnɐ] M **-s, -** (metric) hundredweight, 50 kg; *(Aus, Sw)* 100 kg

Zent|ner-: **Zent|ner|last** F *(fig)* heavy burden; **mir fiel eine ~ vom Herzen** it was a great weight *or* load off my mind; **zent|ner|schwer** ADJ weighing over a hundredweight; *(fig)* heavy ADV *im Magen liegen* like a ton (of lead); **~ auf jdm** *or* **jds Seele lasten** to weigh sb down; **zent|ner|wei|se** ADV by the hundredweight

zent|ral [tsɛnˈtra:l] *(lit, fig)* ADJ central ADV centrally

Zent|ral- *in cpds* central; **Zent|ral|abi|tur** NT nationwide uniform A-level *(Brit) or* high-school *(US)* school-leaving examinations, centrally standardized final exam; **Zent|ral|bank** F *pl* **-banken** central bank; **Zen|tral|bank|prä|si|dent(in)** M(F) president of the Central Bank; **Zent|ral|bank|rat** M *council of the German central bank*

Zent|ra|le [tsɛnˈtra:lə] F **-, -n** *(von Firma etc)* head office; *(für Taxis, Mil)* headquarters *sing or pl*; *(für Busse etc)* depot; *(= Schaltzentrale)* central control (office); *(= Telefonzentrale)* exchange; *(von Firma etc, Mil)* switchboard

Zent|ral-: **Zent|ral|ein|heit** F *(Comput)* CPU, central processing unit; **Zent|ral|ge|walt** F central(ized) power; **Zent|ral|hei|zung** F central heating

Zent|ra|li|sa|ti|on [tsɛntralizaˈtsio:n] F **-, -en** centralization

zent|ra|li|sie|ren [tsɛntraliˈzi:rən] *ptp* **zentralisiert** VT to centralize

Zent|ra|li|sie|rung F **-, -en** centralization

Zent|ra|lis|mus [tsɛntraˈlɪsmʊs] M **-,** *no pl* centralism

zent|ra|lis|tisch [tsɛntraˈlɪstɪʃ] ADJ centralist ADV from a centralist perspective

Zent|ral-: **Zent|ral|ko|mi|tee** NT central committee; **Zent|ral|ner|ven|sys|tem** NT central nervous system; **Zent|ral|or|gan** NT *(= Zeitung einer Partei oder Organisation)* main *or* official organ; **Zent|ral|rat** M central council; **~ der Juden in Deutschland** Central Council of Jews in Germany; **Zent|ral|rech|ner** M *(Comput)* mainframe; **Zent|ral|spei|cher** M *(Comput)* central memory; **Zent|ral|stel|le** F **~ für Arbeitsvermittlung** Central Employment Office *(Brit)*, Employment and Training Administration *(US)*; **~ für die Vergabe von Studienplätzen** ≈ Universities and Colleges Admissions Service *(Brit)*, ≈ Scholastic Aptitude Test Center *(US)*; **Zent|ral|ver|rie|ge|lung** [-fɛɐri:gəlʊŋ] F **-, -en** *(Aut)* central (door) locking; **Zent|ral|ver|schluss** M leaf shutter; **Zent|ral|ver|wal|tung** F central administration

Zent|ren *pl von* **Zentrum**

Zent|rier|au|to|ma|tik F *(Comput)* automatic centering

zent|rie|ren [tsɛnˈtri:rən] *ptp* **zentriert** VT *(auch Comput)* to centre *(Brit)*, to center *(US)*

zent|ri|fu|gal [tsɛntrifuˈga:l] ADJ centrifugal

Zent|ri|fu|gal|kraft F centrifugal force

Zent|ri|fu|ge [tsɛntriˈfu:gə] F **-, -n** centrifuge

zent|ri|pe|tal [tsɛntripeˈta:l] ADJ centripetal

Zent|ri|pe|tal|kraft F centripetal force

zent|risch [ˈtsɛntrɪʃ] ADJ concentric; *Anziehung* centric

Zent|rum [ˈtsɛntrʊm] NT **-s, Zentren** [-trən] *(lit, fig)* centre *(Brit)*, center *(US)*; *(= Innenstadt)* (town) centre *(Brit) or* center *(US)*; *(von Großstadt)* (city) centre *(Brit) or* center *(US)*; **sie wohnt im ~ (der Stadt)/von Chicago** she lives in the (town/city) centre *(Brit) or* center *(US)*/in the centre *(Brit) or* center *(US)* of Chicago, she lives downtown/in downtown Chicago *(US)*; **im ~ des Interesses stehen** to be the centre *(Brit) or* center *(US)* of attention

Zent|rums|par|tei F *(Hist)* Centre *(Brit) or* Center *(US)* party *(German Catholic party representing the centre politically)*

Ze|phir [ˈtse:fi:ɐ] M **-s, -e** *(esp Aus)*, **Ze|phyr** [ˈtse:fy:ɐ] M **-s, -e** *(liter)* zephyr

Zep|pe|lin [ˈtsɛpəli:n] M **-s, -e** zeppelin

Zep|ter [ˈtsɛptɐ] NT **-s, -** sceptre *(Brit)*, scepter *(US)*; **das ~ führen** *or* **schwingen** *(inf)* to wield the sceptre *(Brit) or* scepter *(US)*; *(esp Ehefrau)* to rule the roost

Zer [tse:ɐ] NT **-s,** *no pl (abbr* **Ce**) cerium

zer|bei|ßen *ptp* **zerbissen** [tsɛɐˈbɪsn] VT *irreg* to chew; *Knochen, Bonbon, Keks etc* to crunch; *(= beschädigen) Pantoffel etc* to chew to pieces; *(= auseinanderbeißen) Kette, Leine* to chew through

zer|bers|ten *ptp* **zerborsten** [tsɛɐˈbɔrstn] VI *irreg aux sein* to burst; *(Glas)* to shatter

Zer|be|rus [ˈtsɛrberʊs] M **-, -se a** *no pl (Myth)* Cerberus **b** *(fig hum)* watchdog

zer|beu|len *ptp* **zerbeult** VT to dent; **zerbeult** battered

zer|bom|ben *ptp* **zerbombt** VT to flatten with bombs, to bomb to smithereens *(inf)*; *Gebäude auch* to bomb out; **zerbombt** *(Stadt, Gebäude)* bombed out; **zerbombt werden** to be flattened by bombs

zer|bre|chen *ptp* **zerbrochen** [tsɛɐˈbrɔxn] *irreg* VT *(lit)* to break into pieces; *Glas, Porzellan etc* to smash, to shatter; *Ketten (lit, fig)* to break, to sever; *(fig) Widerstand* to break down; *Lebenswille* to destroy → **Kopf c** VI *aux sein* to break into pieces; *(Glas, Porzellan etc)* to smash, to shatter; *(fig)* to be destroyed *(an +dat* by); *(Ehe)* to fall apart; *(Widerstand)* to collapse *(an +dat* in the face of); **er ist am Leben zerbrochen** he has been broken *or* destroyed by life

zer|brech|lich [tsɛɐˈbrɛçlɪç] ADJ fragile; *alter Mensch* frail; **„Vorsicht ~!"** "fragile, handle with care"

Zer|brech|lich|keit F **-,** *no pl* fragility; *(von altem Menschen)* frailness

zer|brö|ckeln *ptp* **zerbröckelt** VTI *(vi: aux sein)* to crumble

zer|dät|schen [tsɛɐˈdɛtʃn] *ptp* **zerdätscht** VT *(inf)* to squash, to crush

zer|dep|pern [tsɛɐˈdɛpɐn] *ptp* **zerdeppert** VT *(inf)* to smash

zer|drü|cken *ptp* **zerdrückt** VT to squash, to crush; *Gemüse* to mash; *(= zerknittern)* to crush, to crease, to crumple; *(inf) Träne* to squeeze out

Ze|re|a|li|en [tsereˈa:liən] PL cereals *pl*

Ze|re|mo|nie [tseremoˈni:, tsereˈmo:niə] F **-, -n** [-ˈni:ən, -niən] ceremony

ze|re|mo|ni|ell [tseremoˈniɛl] ADJ ceremonial ADV ceremonially

Ze|re|mo|ni|ell [tseremoˈniɛl] NT **-s, -e** ceremonial

Ze|re|mo|ni|en|meis|ter(in) [tsereˈmo:niən-] M(F) master of ceremonies

zer|fah|ren [tsɛɐˈfa:rən] ADJ scatty *(esp Brit inf)*, scatterbrained; *(= unkonzentriert)* distracted

Zer|fall M, *no pl* disintegration; *(von Gebäude auch, von Atom)* decay; *(von Leiche, Holz etc)* decomposition; *(von Land, Kultur)* decline, decay, fall; *(von Gesundheit)* decline

zer|fal|len *ptp* **zerfallen** VI *irreg aux sein* **a** *(= sich auflösen)* to disintegrate; *(Gebäude)* to decay, to fall into ruin; *(Atomkern)* to decay; *(= auseinanderfallen)* to fall apart, to disintegrate; *(Leiche, Holz etc)* to decompose; *(Reich, Kultur, Moral)* to decay, to decline; *(Gesundheit)* to decline; **zu Staub ~** to crumble (in)to dust **b** *(= sich gliedern)* to fall *(in +acc* into)

zer|fal|len ADJ **a** *Haus* tumbledown; *Gemäuer* crumbling **b** *(= verfeindet)* **mit jdm ~ sein** to have fallen out with sb; **mit sich** *(dat)* **und der Welt/mit sich** *(dat)* **selbst ~ sein** to be at odds with the world/oneself

Zer|falls-: **Zer|falls|er|schei|nung** F sign of decay; **Zer|falls|ge|schwin|dig|keit** F rate of decay; **Zer|falls|pro|dukt** NT daughter product

zer|fa|sern *ptp* **zerfasert** VT *aux haben* to fray VI *aux sein* to fray

zer|fet|zen *ptp* **zerfetzt** VT to tear *or* rip to pieces *or* shreds; *Brief etc* to rip up, to tear up (into little pieces); *(Geschoss) Arm etc* to mangle, to tear to pieces; *(fig)* to pull *or* tear to pieces

zer|fẹtzt [tsɛɐ'fɛtst] ADJ *Hose* ragged, tattered; *Körper, Arm* lacerated

zer|flẹd|dern [tsɛɐ'flɛdɐn] *ptp* **zerflẹddert**, **zer|-fle|dern** [tsɛɐ'fle:dɐn] *ptp* **zerflẹdert** VT *(inf)* to tatter, to get tatty *(esp Brit inf)*

zer|flei|schen [tsɛɐ'flaiʃn] *ptp* **zerfleischt** VT to tear to pieces; **einander ~** *(fig)* to tear each other apart VR *(fig)* **er zerfleischt sich in (Selbst)-vorwürfen** he torments *or* tortures himself with self-reproaches; **sich gegenseitig ~** to tear each other apart

zer|flie|ßen *ptp* **zerflọssen** [tsɛɐ'flɔsn] VI *irreg aux sein (Tinte, Make-up etc)* to run; *(Eis etc, fig: Reichtum etc)* to melt away; **in Tränen ~** to dissolve into tears; **seine Hoffnungen zerflossen in nichts** his hopes melted away; **vor Mitleid ~** to be overcome with pity

zer|frạnst [tsɛɐ'franst] ADJ frayed

zer|frẹs|sen *ptp* **zerfrẹssen** VT *irreg* to eat away; *(Säure, Rost auch)* to corrode; *(Motten, Mäuse etc)* to eat; *(fig)* to consume; **die Säure hat ihr das Gesicht ~** the acid burned into her face; **(von Motten/Würmern) ~ sein** to be moth-eaten/worm-eaten

zer|fur|chen *ptp* **zerfụrcht** VT to furrow

zer|gẹ|hen *ptp* **zergạngen** [tsɛɐ'gaŋən] VI *irreg aux sein* to dissolve; *(= schmelzen)* to melt; **auf der Zunge ~** *(Gebäck etc)* to melt in the mouth; *(Fleisch)* to fall apart; **vor Mitleid ~** to be overcome with pity

zer|glie|dern *ptp* **zergliedert** VT *(Biol)* to dissect; *Satz* to parse; *(fig)* to analyse *(Brit)*, to analyze *(US)*

Zer|glie|de|rung F *(Biol)* dissection; *(von Satz)* parsing; *(fig)* analysis

zer|hạ|cken *ptp* **zerhạckt** VT to chop up

Zer|hạ|cker M *(Telec)* scrambler

zer|hau|en *ptp* **zerhauen** VT *irreg* to chop in two; *(in viele Stücke)* to chop up; *Knoten (lit, fig)* to cut; *(inf: = kaputtschlagen)* to smash

zer|kau|en *ptp* **zerkaut** VT to chew; *(Hund) Leine* to chew up

zer|klei|nern [tsɛɐ'klainɐn] *ptp* **zerkleinert** VT to cut up; *(= zerhacken)* to chop (up); *(= zerbrechen)* to break up; *(= zermahlen)* to crush

zer|klüf|tet [tsɛɐ'klʏftət] ADJ *Tal etc* rugged; *Ufer* indented; *(Med) Mandeln* fissured; **tief ~es Gestein** rock with deep fissures, deeply fissured rock

zer|knaut|schen *ptp* **zerknautscht** VT *(inf)* to crease, to crumple

zer|knautscht [tsɛɐ'knautʃt] ADJ *(inf) Kleidung* creased, crumpled; *Gesicht (= faltig)* wizened; **du siehst heute fürchterlich ~ aus** you're looking somewhat the worse for wear today

zer|knị|cken *ptp* **zerknịckt** VT *aux haben (= verbiegen)* to bend; *(= zerbrechen)* to snap VI *aux sein Zweig, Baum* to be bent; *(= abbrechen)* to snap

zer|knịrscht [tsɛɐ'knɪrʃt] ADJ remorseful, overcome with remorse; *Gesicht* remorse-filled

Zer|knirscht|heit F -, *no pl*, **Zer|knịr|schung** [tsɛɐ'knɪrʃʊŋ] F -, *no pl* remorse

zer|knịt|tern *ptp* **zerknịttert** VT to crease, to crumple

zer|knịt|tert [tsɛɐ'knɪtɐt] ADJ **a** *Kleid, Stoff* creased **b** *(inf) (= schuldbewusst)* overcome with remorse; *(= unausgeschlafen)* washed-out *(inf)*

zer|knül|len *ptp* **zerknüllt** VT to crumple up, to scrunch up *(inf)*

zer|kọ|chen *ptp* **zerkọcht** VTI *(vi: aux sein)* to cook to a pulp; *(= zu lange kochen auch)* to overcook

zer|krạt|zen *ptp* **zerkrạtzt** VT to scratch

zer|krü|meln *ptp* **zerkrümelt** VT to crumble; *Boden* to loosen

zer|lạs|sen *ptp* **zerlạssen** VT *irreg* to melt

zer|lau|fen *ptp* **zerlaufen** VI *irreg aux sein* to melt

zer|lẹg|bar ADJ able to be taken apart; *Maschine, Gerüst auch* able to be dismantled; *(Gram)* analysable *(Brit)*, analyzable *(US)*; *(Math)* reducible; **die Möbel waren leicht ~** the furniture could easily be taken apart, the furniture was easily taken apart

zer|le|gen *ptp* **zerlẹgt** VT *(= auseinandernehmen)* to take apart *or* to pieces; *Gerüst, Maschine auch* to dismantle; *Motor, Getriebe auch* to strip down; *Theorie, Argumente* to break down; *(Gram)* to analyse *(Brit)*, to analyze *(US)*; *(Chem)* to break down; *(= zerschneiden)* to cut up; *Geflügel, Wild* to carve up; *(Biol)* to dissect; **etw in seine Einzelteile ~** to take sth to pieces; to dismantle sth completely; to strip sth down; to break sth down into its (individual) constituents; *Satz* to parse sth; **eine Zahl in ihre Faktoren ~** to factorize a number

Zer|le|gung [tsɛɐ'le:gʊŋ] F -, -en taking apart; *(von Gerüst, Maschine auch)* dismantling; *(von Motor, Getriebe auch)* stripping down; *(Gram)* analysis; *(Math)* reduction; *(Biol)* dissection

zer|le|sen [tsɛɐ'le:zn] ADJ *Buch* well-thumbed

zer|lumpt [tsɛɐ'lʊmpt] ADJ *Kleidung* ragged, tattered *no adv*; *Kind, Gestalt etc* ragged

zer|mah|len *ptp* **zermahlen** VT to grind; *(in Mörser)* to crush

zer|mal|men [tsɛɐ'malmən] *ptp* **zermạlmt** VT *(lit, fig)* to crush; *(mit den Zähnen)* to crunch, to grind

zer|man|schen *ptp* **zermạnscht** VT *(inf)* to squash; *(mit Gabel)* to mash

zer|mar|tern *ptp* **zermạrtert** VT **sich** *(dat)* **den Kopf** *or* **das Hirn ~** to rack *or* cudgel *(Brit)* one's brains

zer|mat|schen *ptp* **zermạtscht** VT *(inf)* to squash; *(mit Gabel)* to mash

zer|mür|ben [tsɛɐ'mʏrbn] *ptp* **zermürbt** VT **a** *(fig)* **jdn ~** to wear sb down; **~d** wearing, trying **b** *(rare: = brüchig machen)* to make brittle

Zer|mür|bung F -, -en *(eines Gegners etc)* wearing down *no pl*, attrition

Zer|mür|bungs-: **Zer|mür|bungs|krieg** M war of attrition; **Zer|mür|bungs|tak|tik** F tactics *pl* of attrition

zer|na|gen *ptp* **zernagt** VT to chew to pieces; *(Nagetiere)* to gnaw to pieces

Ze|ro ['ze:ro] F -, -s *or nt* -s, -s zero

Ze|ro|bond ['ze:robɔnt] M -s, -s *(St Ex)* zero-coupon bond

zer|pflü|cken *ptp* **zerpflụ̈ckt** VT *(lit, fig)* to pick to pieces

zer|plat|zen *ptp* **zerplạtzt** VI *aux sein* to burst; *(Glas)* to shatter

zer|quält [tsɛɐ'kvɛ:lt] ADJ tortured

zer|quet|schen *ptp* **zerquetscht** VT to squash, to crush; *(mit Gabel) Kartoffeln etc* to mash; *(inf) Träne* to squeeze out

Zer|quetsch|te [tsɛɐ'kvɛtʃtə] PL *decl as adj (inf)* **10 Euro und ein paar ~** 10 euros something (or other), 10 euros odd; **hundert** *or* **Hundert und ein paar ~** a hundred odd; **elf Uhr und ein paar ~** eleven something (or other)

zer|rau|fen *ptp* **zerrauft** VT to ruffle; **zerrauft** dishevelled

Zerr|bild NT *(lit: in Spiegel)* distorted picture *or* image; *(fig auch)* caricature; *(von Verhältnissen, System, Gesellschaft etc auch)* travesty

zer|re|den *ptp* **zerredet** VT to beat to death *(inf)*

zer|rei|ben *ptp* **zerrieben** [tsɛɐ'ri:bn] VT *irreg* to crumble, to crush; *(in Mörser etc)* to grind; *(fig)* to crush

zer|rei|ßen *ptp* **zerrịssen** [tsɛɐ'rɪsn] *irreg* VT **a** *(aus Versehen)* to tear; *(in Stücke)* to tear to pieces *or* shreds; *Faden, Seil etc* to break; *(absichtlich) Brief etc* to tear up; *(= zerfleischen)* to tear apart; *(= plötzlich aufreißen, durchbrechen) Wolkendecke, Stille etc* to rend *(liter)*; *(fig) Land* to tear apart *or* in two; *Bindungen* to break; **es zerreißt mir das Herz** *(liter)* it is heart-rending *or* heartbreaking, it breaks my heart → *auch* **zerrissen**

b *(= kritisieren) Autor, Stück, Film* to tear apart, to tear to pieces → **Luft a**, **Maul**

VI *aux sein (Stoff)* to tear; *(Band, Seil etc)* to break

VR *(fig)* **ich könnte mich vor Wut ~** I'm hopping (mad) *(esp Brit inf)*, I'm totally pissed *(US inf)*; **ich kann mich doch nicht ~!** I can't be in two places at once; **sich ~, (um) etw zu tun** to go to no end of trouble to do sth

Zer|reiß-: **zer|reiß|fest** ADJ tear-resistant; **Zer|reiß|pro|be** F *(lit)* pull test; *(fig)* real test; **eine ~ für ihre Ehe** *etc* a crucial test of their marriage *etc*; **eine ~ für meine Geduld** a real test of my patience

zer|ren ['tsɛrən] VT to drag; *Sehne* to pull, to strain; **sich** *(dat)* **einen Muskel ~** to pull a muscle; **jdm die Kleider vom Leib ~** to tear the clothes from sb's body; **sich** *(dat)* **die Kleider vom Leib ~** to tear one's clothes off; **etw an die Öffentlichkeit ~** to drag sth into the public eye VI **an etw** *(dat)* **~** to tug *or* pull at sth; **an den Nerven ~** to be nerve-racking

zer|rin|nen *ptp* **zerrọnnen** [tsɛɐ'rɔnən] VI *irreg aux sein* to melt (away); *(fig) (Träume, Pläne)* to melt *or* fade away; *(Geld, Vermögen)* to disappear; **jdm unter den Händen** *or* **zwischen den Fingern ~** *(Geld)* to run through sb's hands like water; **die Zeit zerrinnt mir unter den Händen** the time just goes without me knowing where

zer|ris|sen [tsɛɐ'rɪsn] ADJ *(fig) Volk, Partei* strife-torn, disunited; *Mensch* (inwardly) torn → *auch* **zerreißen**

Zer|ris|sen|heit F -, *no pl (fig) (von Volk, Partei)* disunity *no pl*; *(von Mensch)* (inner) conflict

Zerr|spie|gel M *(lit)* distorting mirror; *(fig)* travesty

Zer|rung ['tsɛrʊŋ] F -, -en *(= das Zerren: von Sehne, Muskel)* pulling; **eine ~** *(von Sehne)* a pulled ligament; *(von Muskel)* a pulled muscle

zer|rup|fen *ptp* **zerrupft** VT to pick *or* pull to pieces

zer|rüt|ten [tsɛɐ'rʏtn] *ptp* **zerrüttet** VT to destroy, to ruin, to wreck; *Ehe* to break up, to destroy; *Geist* to destroy; *Nerven* to shatter; **eine zerrüttete Ehe/Familie** a broken marriage/home; **ein zerrüttetes Verhältnis zu jdm haben** to have a disturbed *or* troubled relationship with sb; **sich in einem zerrütteten Zustand befinden** to be in a very bad way *or* in terrible shape

Zer|rüt|tung F -, -en destruction; *(von Ehe)* breakdown; *(von Nerven)* shattering; *(Zustand)* shattered state; **der Staat befindet sich im Zustand der ~** the state is in a bad way *or* in terrible shape; **ihre Ehe befindet sich im Zustand der ~** their marriage is breaking down

Zer|rüt|tungs|prin|zip NT principle of irretrievable breakdown

zer|sä|gen *ptp* **zersägt** VT to saw up

zer|schel|len *ptp* **zerschẹllt** VI *aux sein (Schiff, Flugzeug)* to be dashed *or* smashed to pieces; *(Vase etc)* to smash (to pieces *or* smithereens); **das zerschellte Schiff** the wrecked ship

zer|schie|ßen *ptp* **zerschọssen** [tsɛɐ'ʃɔsn] VT *irreg* to shoot to pieces; *(= durchlöchern)* to riddle with bullets; **er hatte ein zerschossenes Bein** his leg had been shot to pieces/was riddled with bullets

zer|schla|gen *ptp* **zerschlagen** *irreg* VT **a** *(Mensch)* to smash (to pieces); *Stein, Porzellan, Glas etc* to shatter, to smash; *(Hagel) Ernte, Wein* to crush; *(= auseinanderschlagen)* to break up **b** *(fig) Angriff, Widerstand, Opposition* to crush; *Hoffnungen, Pläne* to shatter; *Verbrecherring etc, Vereinigung* to break; *Großunternehmen* to break up; *Staat* to smash VR *(= nicht zustande kommen)* to fall through; *(Hoffnung, Aussichten)* to be shattered

zer|schla|gen ADJ *pred* washed out *(inf)*; *(nach Anstrengung, langer Reise etc)* shattered *(Brit inf)*, worn out; *Gesicht* drawn, haggard; **ich wachte wie ~ auf** I woke up feeling washed out *(inf)*

Zer|schla|gen|heit F -, *no pl* exhaustion

Zer|schla|gung [tsɛɐ'ʃlaːgʊŋ] F -, -en *(fig)* suppression; *(von Hoffnungen, Plänen)* shattering

zer|schlei|ßen [tsɛɐ'ʃlaisn] *pret* **zerschliss** [tsɛɐ'ʃlɪs], *ptp* **zerschlissen** [tsɛɐ'ʃlɪsn] VTI *(vi: aux sein)* to wear out; **zerschlissene Kleider** worn-out *or* threadbare clothes

zer|schmei|ßen *ptp* **zerschmissen** [tsɛɐ'ʃmɪsn] VT *(inf) irreg* to shatter, to smash (to pieces)

zer|schmel|zen *ptp* **zerschmolzen** [tsɛɐ'ʃmɔltsn] VI *irreg aux sein (lit, fig)* to melt; **vor Rührung/Mitleid** *(dat)* ~ *(iro)* to brim (over) with emotion/pity

zer|schmet|tern *ptp* **zerschmettert** VT *(lit, fig)* to shatter; *Feind* to crush; *(Sport) Gegner* to smash VI *aux sein* to shatter

zer|schnei|den *ptp* **zerschnitten** [tsɛɐ'ʃnɪtn] VT *irreg* to cut; *(in zwei Teile)* to cut in two; *(in Stücke)* to cut up; *(= verschneiden) Stoff* to cut wrongly; *(fig) Stille* to pierce; **jdm das Herz** ~ to cut sb to the heart *(US) or* quick

zer|schnip|peln *ptp* **zerschnippelt** VT *(inf)* to snip to pieces

zer|schram|men *ptp* **zerschrammt** VT *Haut, Möbel* to scratch to pieces; *Lack* to scratch

zer|set|zen *ptp* **zersetzt** VT to decompose; *(Säure)* to corrode; *(fig)* to undermine, to subvert VR to decompose; *(durch Säure)* to corrode; *(fig)* to become undermined *or* subverted

zer|set|zend ADJ *(fig)* subversive

Zer|set|zung [tsɛɐ'zɛtsʊŋ] F -, -en *(Chem)* decomposition; *(durch Säure)* corrosion; *(fig) (= Untergrabung)* undermining, subversion; *(von Gesellschaft)* decline *(von* in), decay

Zer|set|zungs-: **Zer|set|zungs|er|schei|nung** F *(fig)* sign of decline *or* decay; **Zer|set|zungs|pro|dukt** NT *substance produced by decomposition*; **Zer|set|zungs|pro|zess** M → **Zersetzung** (process of) decomposition/corrosion/subversion; decline *(von* in), decay

zer|sie|deln *ptp* **zersiedelt** VT to spoil (by development)

Zer|sie|de|lung [tsɛɐ'ziːdəlʊŋ] F -, -en, **Zer|sied|lung** F overdevelopment

zer|spal|ten *ptp* **zerspalten** VT to split; *Gemeinschaft* to split up

zer|split|tern *ptp* **zersplittert** VT to shatter; *Holz* to splinter; *(fig) Kräfte, Zeit* to dissipate, to squander; *Gruppe, Partei* to fragment VI *aux sein* to shatter; *(Holz, Knochen)* to splinter; *(fig)* to split up VR to shatter; *(Holz)* to splinter; *(fig)* to dissipate *or* squander one's energies; *(Gruppe, Partei)* to fragment, to become fragmented; **der Widerstand ist zu zersplittert** the opposition is too fragmented

Zer|split|te|rung [tsɛɐ'ʃplɪtərʊŋ] F -, -en shattering; *(von Holz)* splintering; *(fig)* dissipation, squandering; *(von Gruppe, Partei)* fragmentation

zer|spren|gen *ptp* **zersprengt** VT to burst; *(fig) Volksmenge* to disperse, to scatter; *Heer* to scatter

zer|sprin|gen *ptp* **zersprungen** [tsɛɐ'ʃprʊŋən] VI *irreg aux sein* to shatter; *(Saite)* to break; *(= einen Sprung bekommen)* to crack; **in tausend Stücke** ~ to shatter in(to) a thousand pieces; **das Herz wollte ihr vor Freude/Ungeduld fast** ~ *(liter)* her heart was bursting with joy/impatience

zer|stamp|fen *ptp* **zerstampft** VT *(= zertreten)* to stamp *or* trample on; *(= zerkleinern)* to crush; *(im Mörser)* to grind, to pound; *Kartoffeln etc* to mash

zer|stäu|ben *ptp* **zerstäubt** VT to spray

Zer|stäu|ber [tsɛɐ'ʃtɔybɐ] M -s, - spray; *(= Parfümzerstäuber auch)* atomizer

zer|ste|chen [tsɛɐ'ʃtɔxn] VT *irreg* **a** *(Mücken)* to bite (all over); *(Bienen etc)* to sting (all over); **wir sind ganz zerstochen worden** we've been bitten/stung all over; **von Injektionen zerstochene Venen** veins scarred by injections **b** *Material, Haut, Reifen* to puncture; *Finger* to prick

zer|stie|ben *ptp* **zerstoben** [tsɛɐ'ʃtoːbn] VI *irreg aux sein* to scatter; *(Wasser)* to spray

zer|stör|bar ADJ destructible; **nicht** ~ indestructible

zer|stö|ren *ptp* **zerstört** VT *(lit, fig)* to destroy; *Gebäude, Ehe, Glück auch* to wreck; *(= verwüsten auch)* to ruin; *(Rowdys)* to vandalize; *Gesundheit* to wreck, to ruin VI to destroy → **Boden a**

Zer|stö|rer [tsɛɐ'ʃtøːrɐ] M -s, - *(old Aviat)* fighter; *(Naut)* destroyer

Zer|stö|rer [tsɛɐ'ʃtøːrɐ] M -s, -, **Zer|stö|re|rin** [-ərɪn] F -, -nen destroyer

zer|stö|re|risch [tsɛɐ'ʃtøːrərɪʃ] ADJ destructive ADV destructively; ~ **wirken** to wreak destruction

Zer|stö|rung F **a** *no pl (= das Zerstören)* destruction *no pl*; *(von Gebäude, Ehe, Glück auch)* wrecking; *(durch Rowdys)* vandalizing **b** *(durch Krieg, Katastrophe etc)* destruction *no pl*, devastation *no pl*; *(von Daten)* corruption *no pl*

Zer|stö|rungs-: **Zer|stö|rungs|drang** M destructive urge *or* impulse; **Zer|stö|rungs|lust** F delight in destruction; **Zer|stö|rungs|trieb** M destructive urge *or* impulse; **Zer|stö|rungs|werk** NT work of destruction; **Zer|stö|rungs|wut** F destructive mania

zer|sto|ßen *ptp* **zerstoßen** VT *irreg* **a** *(= zerkleinern)* to crush; *(im Mörser)* to pound, to grind; **~es Eis** crushed ice **b** *(= durch Stoßen beschädigen)* to damage; *Leder, Schuh* to scuff

zer|strei|ten *ptp* **zerstritten** [tsɛɐ'ʃtrɪtn] VR *irreg* to quarrel, to fall out → *auch* **zerstritten**

zer|streu|en *ptp* **zerstreut** VT **a** *(= verstreuen)* to scatter *(in +dat* over); *Volksmenge etc* to disperse; *Licht* to diffuse; *(fig)* to dispel, to allay **b** *(= ablenken)* **jdn** ~ to take sb's mind off things, to divert sb VR **a** *(= sich verteilen)* to scatter; *(Menge)* to scatter, to disperse; *(fig)* to be dispelled *or* allayed **b** *(= sich ablenken)* to take one's mind off things; *(= sich amüsieren)* to amuse oneself

zer|streut [tsɛɐ'ʃtrɔyt] ADJ *(fig) Mensch* absent-minded; **sie ist heute sehr** ~ her mind is elsewhere today

Zer|streut|heit F -, *no pl* absent-mindedness

Zer|streu|ung F **a** *no pl (= das Zerstreuen)* scattering; *(von Menge)* dispersal; *(von Licht)* diffusion; *(fig)* dispelling, allaying **b** *(= Ablenkung)* diversion; **zur** ~ as a diversion **c** *(= Zerstreutheit)* absent-mindedness

zer|strit|ten [tsɛɐ'ʃtrɪtn] ADJ ~ **sein** *(Paar, Geschäftspartner)* to have fallen out; *(Partei)* to be disunited; **mit jdm** ~ **sein** to have fallen out with sb; **sie sind seit Langem** ~ they fell out a long time ago → *auch* **zerstreiten**

Zer|strit|ten|heit F *(von Paar, Geschäftspartnern)* bad blood *(+gen* between); *(von Partei)* disunity

zer|stü|ckeln *ptp* **zerstückelt** VT *(lit)* to cut up; *Leiche* to dismember; *Land* to divide *or* carve up; *(fig) Tag, Semester etc* to break up

zer|tei|len *ptp* **zerteilt** VT to split up; *(in zwei Teile auch)* to divide; *(= zerschneiden)* to cut up; *Wogen, Wolken* to part; **ich kann mich nicht ~!** I can't be in two places at once

Zer|ti|fi|kat [tsɛrtifi'kaːt] NT -(e)s, -e certificate

zer|ti|fi|zie|ren [tsɛrtifi'tsiːrən] VT *ptp* **zertifiziert** to certify

Zer|ti|fi|zie|rung [tsɛrtifi'tsiːrʊŋ] F -, -en certification; ~ **nach DIN EN 9002** certification in accordance with DIN EN 9002, DIN EN 9002 certification

zer|tram|peln *ptp* **zertrampelt** VT to trample on

zer|tren|nen *ptp* **zertrennt** VT to sever, to cut through; *(= auftrennen) Nähte* to undo; *Kleid* to undo the seams of

zer|tre|ten *ptp* **zertreten** VT *irreg* to crush (underfoot); *Rasen* to ruin; **jdn wie einen Wurm** ~ to grind sb into the ground

zer|trüm|mern [tsɛɐ'trʏmɐn] *ptp* **zertrümmert** VT to smash; *Gebäude auch* to wreck, to destroy; *Einrichtung* to smash up; *Hoffnungen, Ordnung* to wreck, to destroy

Zer|trüm|me|rung F -, -en smashing; *(von Einrichtung)* smashing up; *(von Hoffnungen, Ordnung)* wrecking, destruction; *(dated: von Atom)* splitting

Zer|ve|lat|wurst [tsɛrvə'laːt-] F cervelat, German salami

zer|vi|kal [tsɛrvi'kaːl] ADJ *(spec)* cervical

zer|wer|fen *ptp* **zerworfen** [tsɛɐ'vɔrfn] VR *irreg (fig)* to fall out *(mit jdm* with sb)

zer|wüh|len *ptp* **zerwühlt** VT to ruffle up, to tousle; *Bett, Kopfkissen* to rumple (up); *(= aufwühlen) Erdboden* to churn up; *(Wildschwein etc)* to churn *or* root up

Zer|würf|nis [tsɛɐ'vʏrfnɪs] NT -ses, -se row, disagreement

zer|zau|sen *ptp* **zerzaust** VT to ruffle; *Haar* to tousle

zer|zaust [tsɛɐ'tsaust] ADJ windswept; *Haare auch* dishevelled, tousled

Ze|ter ['tseːtɐ] NT ~ **und Mord(io) schreien** *(lit)* to scream blue *(Brit) or* bloody murder *(inf)*; *(fig)* to raise a hue and cry

Ze|ter-: **Ze|ter|ge|schrei** NT *(lit)* hullabaloo; *(fig)* hue and cry; **ze|ter|mor|dio** [tseːtɐ'mɔrdio] ADV ~ **schreien** to scream blue *(Brit) or* bloody murder *(inf)*

ze|tern ['tseːtɐn] VI *(pej)* to clamour *(Brit)*, to clamor *(US)*; *(= keifen)* to scold, to nag; *(= jammern)* to moan

Zet|tel ['tsɛtl] M -s, - piece of paper; *(= Notizzettel)* note; *(= Karteizettel)* card; *(= Anhängezettel)* label; *(mit Angabe über Inhalt, Anschrift etc)* chit *(inf)*, ticket; *(= Bekanntmachung)* notice; *(= Handzettel)* leaflet, handbill *(esp US)*, flyer; *(= Formular)* form; *(= Stimmzettel)* ballot paper; *(= Bestellzettel)* coupon; *(= Kassenzettel, Beleg)* receipt; **„Zettel ankleben verboten"** "stick no bills" *(Brit)*, "no posters allowed"

Zet|tel-: **Zet|tel|kar|tei** F card index; **Zet|tel|kas|ten** M file-card box; *(= Zettelkartei)* card index; **Zet|tel|ka|ta|log** M card index; **Zet|tel|ver|tei|ler(in)** M(F) person who hands out leaflets; **Zet|tel|wirt|schaft** F, *no pl (pej)* **eine ~ haben** to have bits of paper everywhere; **du mit deiner** ~ you and all your bits of paper

Zeug [tsɔyk] NT -(e)s [-gəs], *no pl* **a** *(inf)* stuff *no indef art, no pl*; *(= Ausrüstung)* gear *(inf)*; *(= Kleidung)* clothes *pl*, things *pl (inf)*; *(= Getier)* things *pl*; **altes** ~ junk, trash; **... und solches** ~ ... and such things **b** *(inf: = Unsinn)* nonsense, rubbish *(esp Brit)*; **ein/dieses** ~ a/this load of nonsense *or* rubbish *(esp Brit)*; **dummes** *or* **ungereimtes ~ reden** to talk a lot of nonsense *or* drivel *(inf) or* twaddle *(inf)*; **rede kein dummes** ~ don't talk nonsense **c** *(= Fähigkeit, Können)* **das ~ zu etw haben** to have (got) what it takes to be sth *(inf)*; **er hat nicht das ~ dazu** he hasn't got what it takes *(inf)* **d** *(old) (= Stoff)* material; *(= Wäsche)* linen; **jdm etwas am ~ flicken** *(inf)* to tell sb what to do; **was das ~ hält** *(inf)* for all one is worth; *laufen, fahren* like mad; **lügen, was das ~ hält** *(inf)* to lie one's head off *(inf)*; **sich für jdn ins ~ legen** *(inf)* to stand up for sb; **sich ins ~ legen** to go flat out *(esp Brit) or* all out *(US)*; *(bei Arbeit auch)* to work flat out *(esp Brit) or* all out *(US)*

Zeug|amt NT *(obs Mil)* arsenal

Zeu|ge ['tsɔygə] M -n, -n, **Zeu|gin** ['tsɔygɪn] F -, -nen *(Jur, fig)* witness *(+gen* to); ~ **eines Unfalls/Gesprächs sein** to be a witness to an accident/a conversation; **sich als ~ zur Verfügung stellen** to come forward as a witness; **vor** *or* **unter ~n** in front of witnesses; **Gott ist mein** ~ as God is my witness; **die ~n Jehovas** Jehovah's Witnesses

zeu|gen ['tsɔygn] VT *Kind* to father; *(Bibl)* to beget; *(fig geh)* to generate, to give rise to

zeu|gen VI **a** *(vor +dat* to) *(= aussagen)* to testify; *(esp vor Gericht)* to give evidence; **für/gegen jdn** ~ to testify for/against sb (;), to give evidence for/against sb **b von etw** ~ to show sth

Zeu|gen-: **Zeu|gen|aus|sa|ge** F testimony; **Zeu|gen|bank** F *pl* **-bänke** witness box *(Brit)*, witness stand *(US)*; **er sitzt auf der ~** he's in the witness box *(Brit) or* witness stand *(US)*; **Zeu|gen|be|ein|flus|sung** F subornation of a witness/witnesses; **Zeu|gen|be|weis** M evidence (of a witness); **Zeu|gen|la|dung** F summoning of a witness/witnesses; **Zeu|gen|schutz** M witness protection; **unter ~** *(dat)* **stehen** to be under witness protection; **jdn unter ~** *(dat)* **stellen** to place sb under witness protection; **Zeu|gen|schutz|pro|gramm** NT witness protection programme *(Brit) or* program *(US)*; **Zeu|gen|stand** M witness box *(Brit)*, witness stand *(US)*; **in den ~ treten** to go into the witness box *(Brit)*, to take the (witness) stand *(US)*; **Zeu|gen|ver|ei|di|gung** F swearing in of a witness/witnesses; **Zeu|gen|ver|neh|mung** F examination of the witness (-es)

Zeug|haus NT *(obs Mil)* arsenal, armoury *(Brit)*, armory *(US)*

Zeu|gin ['tsɔygɪn] F **-, -nen** witness → *auch* **Zeuge**

Zeug|nis ['tsɔyknɪs] NT **-ses, -se** **a** *(esp liter: = Zeugenaussage)* evidence; **für/gegen jdn ~ ablegen** to give evidence for/against sb, to testify for/against sb; **für jds Ehrlichkeit** *etc* **~ ablegen** to bear witness to sb's honesty *etc*; **falsches ~ ablegen** *(Bibl)*, **falsch ~ reden** *(Bibl)* to bear false witness **b** *(fig: = Beweis)* evidence **c** *(= Schulzeugnis)* report; *(= Note)* mark, grade *(esp US)* **d** *(= Bescheinigung)* certificate; *(von Arbeitgeber)* testimonial, reference; **gute ~se haben** to have good qualifications; *(von Arbeitgeber)* to have good references; **jdm ein ~ ausstellen** to give sb a reference *or* testimonial; **ich kann ihm nur das beste ~ ausstellen** *(fig)* I cannot speak too highly of him

Zeug|nis-: **Zeug|nis|ab|schrift** F → **Zeugnis c, d** copy of one's report/certificate/testimonial; **Zeug|nis|heft** NT *(Sch)* report book *(Brit)*, report card; **Zeug|nis|kon|fe|renz** F *(Sch) staff meeting to decide on marks etc*; **Zeug|nis|pa|pie|re** PL certificates *pl*; *(von Arbeitgeber)* testimonials *pl*; **Zeug|nis|pflicht** F *(Jur)* obligation to give evidence; **Zeug|nis|ver|wei|ge|rung** F *(Jur)* refusal to give evidence; **Zeug|nis|ver|wei|ge|rungs|recht** NT right of a witness to refuse to give evidence

Zeugs [tsɔyks] NT **-**, *no pl (pej inf)* = **Zeug a, b**

Zeu|gung ['tsɔygʊŋ] F **-, -en** fathering; *(Bibl)* begetting; *(fig geh)* generating

Zeu|gungs-: **Zeu|gungs|akt** M act of procreation; *(fig)* creative act; **zeu|gungs|fä|hig** ADJ fertile; **Zeu|gungs|fä|hig|keit** F, **Zeu|gungs|kraft** *(geh)* F fertility; **Zeu|gungs|or|gan** NT *(spec)* male reproductive organ; **zeu|gungs|un|fä|hig** ADJ sterile; **Zeu|gungs|un|fä|hig|keit** F sterility

Zeus [tsɔys] M -' *(Myth)* Zeus

zeu|seln ['tsɔyzln] VI *(Sw: = zündeln)* to play with matches

ZEVIS ['tse:vɪs] NT *abbr von* **Zentrales Verkehrsinformationssystem**

ZH *(in Annoncen) abbr von* **Zentralheizung** CH

z. H(d). *abbr von* **zu Händen** attn

Zi|be|be [tsi'be:bə] F **-, -n** *(S Ger, Aus)* sultana

Zi|cho|rie [tsɪ'ço:riə] F **-, -n** chicory

Zi|cke ['tsɪkə] F **-, -n** **a** nanny goat **b** *(pej inf: = Frau)* silly cow *(inf)*

Zi|ckel ['tsɪkl] NT **-s, -(n)** *(= junge Ziege)* kid; *(= junges Reh)* fawn

Zi|cken ['tsɪkn] PL *(inf)* nonsense *no pl*; **mach bloß keine ~!** no nonsense now!; **~ machen** to make trouble

Zi|cken-: **Zi|cken|alarm** M *(inf, hum)* bitch alert *(inf)*; **Vorsicht! ~!** Warning! Bitch approaching!; **Zi|cken|krieg** M *(inf, hum)* battle of the divas *(inf)*; **da herrscht ~** it's handbags at dawn (time) *(Brit)*

zi|ckig ['tsɪkɪç] ADJ *(inf: = prüde)* awkward

Zick|lein ['tsɪklain] NT **-s, -** *(= junge Ziege)* kid; *(= junges Reh)* fawn

Zick|zack ['tsɪktsak] M **-(e)s, -e** zigzag; **zickzack** *or* **im ~ laufen** to zigzag; **~ nähen** to zigzag

Zick|zack-: **zick|zack|för|mig** ADJ zigzag ADV **~ verlaufen** to zigzag; **eine ~ genähte Naht** a zigzag stitch seam; **Zick|zack|kurs** M zigzag course; *(von Hase etc)* zigzag path; **im ~ fahren/laufen** to zigzag; **Zick|zack|li|nie** F zigzag; **Zick|zack|sche|re** F pinking shears *pl*; **Zick|zack|stich** M zigzag stitch

Zie|ge ['tsi:gə] F **-, -n** **a** goat; *(weiblich)* (nanny) goat **b** *(pej inf: = Frau)* cow *(inf)*

Zie|gel ['tsi:gl] M **-s, -** *(= Backstein)* brick; *(= Dachziegel)* tile; **ein Dach mit ~n decken** to tile a roof

Zie|gel-: **Zie|gel|bau** M *pl* **-bauten** brick building; **Zie|gel|bren|ner(in)** M(F) brickmaker; *(von Dachziegeln)* tilemaker; **Zie|gel|bren|ne|rei** F = **Ziegelei**; **Zie|gel|dach** NT tiled roof

Zie|ge|lei [tsi:gə'lai] F **-, -en** brickworks *sing or pl*; *(für Dachziegel)* tilemaking works *sing or pl*

Zie|gel-: **zie|gel|rot** ADJ brick-red; **Zie|gel|stein** M brick

Zie|gen-: **Zie|gen|bart** M **a** *(an Hut)* shaving brush *(hum)*; *(hum: = Bart)* goatee (beard) **b** *(Bot)* goat's-beard mushroom; **Zie|gen|bock** M billy goat; **Zie|gen|fell** NT goatskin; **Zie|gen|her|de** F herd of goats; **Zie|gen|hirt** M, **Zie|gen|hir|tin** F goatherd; **Zie|gen|kä|se** M goat's milk cheese; **Zie|gen|le|der** NT kid (leather), kidskin; **Zie|gen|milch** F goat's milk; **Zie|gen|pe|ter** [-pe:tɐ] M **-s, -** mumps *sing*

zieh [tsi:] *pret von* **zeihen**

Zieh-: **Zieh|brü|cke** F drawbridge; **Zieh|brun|nen** M well; **Zieh|el|tern** PL *(old, fig)* foster parents *pl*

zie|hen ['tsi:ən]

pret **zog** [tso:k], *ptp* **gezogen** [gə'tso:gn]

1 TRANSITIVES VERB	3 UNPERSÖNLICHES VERB
2 INTRANSITIVES VERB	4 REFLEXIVES VERB

In Verbindungen mit Substantiv siehe auch Eintrag für das jeweilige Substantiv.

1 – TRANSITIVES VERB

a [allgemein] to pull; *Handbremse* to put on; *Choke, Starter* to pull out; *Hut* to raise; *(Comput: mit gedrückter Maustaste) Symbol, Element* to drag; **etw durch etw ziehen** to pull sth through sth; **jdn nach unten ziehen** to pull *or (fig)* drag sb down; **der Hund zog die Tischdecke vom Tisch** the dog pulled the cloth off the table; **den Ring vom Finger ziehen** to pull one's ring off (one's finger); **die Mütze tiefer ins Gesicht ziehen** to pull one's hat further down over one's face; **den Mantel fest um sich ziehen** to pull one's coat tight around one; **den Mantel übers Kleid ziehen** *(= anziehen)* to put one's coat on over one's dress; **die Vorhänge vors Fenster ziehen** to pull *or* draw the curtains; **die Schultern in die Höhe ziehen** to raise one's shoulders; **das Flugzeug nach oben/unten ziehen** to put the plane into a climb/descent; **die Stirn in Falten ziehen** to knit one's brow;; **(neue) Saiten auf ein Instrument ziehen** to (re)string an instrument **etw an die gewünschte Stelle ziehen** *(Comput)* to drag sth to the desired position → **krausziehen**

b [= hinziehen] *fig* **was zieht dich denn nach Hause?** what is drawing you home?; **meine Liebe zu den Bergen hat mich in die Schweiz gezogen** my love of the mountains drew me to Switzerland; **es zog ihn in die weite Welt** he felt drawn toward(s) the big wide world; **etw ins Komische ziehen** to ridicule sth; **musst du immer alles ins Lächerliche ziehen?** must you always make fun of everything?; **unangenehme Folgen nach sich ziehen** to have unpleasant consequences; **die Aufmerksamkeit** *or* **die Blicke auf sich** *(acc)* **ziehen** to attract attention; **jds Hass auf sich** *(acc)* **ziehen** to incur sb's hatred; **jdn ins Gespräch** *or* **in die Unterhaltung ziehen** to bring sb into the conversation

c [= herausziehen] to pull out *(aus* of); *Zahn* to take out, to extract; *Fäden* to take out, to remove; *Korken, Schwert, Revolver* to draw, to pull out; *Wasserproben* to take; *(Math) Wurzel* to work out; *Los, Spielkarte, Schlussfolgerungen* to draw; *Vergleich* to draw, to make; **Wein auf Flaschen ziehen** to bottle wine; **die Pflanze zieht ihre Nahrung aus dem Boden** the plant takes its nourishment from the soil; **Zigaretten/Kaugummi (aus dem Automaten) ziehen** to get cigarettes/chewing gum from the machine

d [= zeichnen] *Kreis, Linie* to draw

e [= verlegen, anlegen] *Kabel, Leitung etc* to lay; *Graben, Furchen* to dig; *Mauer* to build; *Zaun* to put up; *Grenze* to draw; **Perlen auf eine Schnur ziehen** to thread pearls

f [= herstellen] *Draht, Kerzen, Kopien* to make; **Kopien von etw ziehen** to copy sth, to make a copy of sth

g [= züchten] *Blumen* to grow; *Tiere* to breed; **sie haben die Kinder gut gezogen** *(inf)* they brought the children up well

2 – INTRANSITIVES VERB

a [= zerren] to pull; **an etw** *(dat)* **ziehen** to pull (on *or* at) sth; **ein ziehender Schmerz** an ache

b [= umziehen] *aux sein* to move; **nach Bayern/München ziehen** to move to Bavaria/Munich; **zu jdm ziehen** to move in with sb

c [= sich bewegen] *aux sein* to move, to go; *(Soldaten, Volksmassen)* to march; *(= durchstreifen)* to wander, to roam; *(Wolken, Rauch)* to drift; *(Gewitter)* to move; *(Vögel)* to fly; *(während des Vogelzugs)* to migrate; **durch die Welt ziehen** to roam the world; **durch die Stadt ziehen** to wander about the town; **in den Krieg/die Schlacht ziehen** to go to war/battle; **heimwärts ziehen** to make one's way home; **lass mich ziehen** *(old, liter)* let me go; **die Jahre zogen ins Land** *(liter)* the years passed

d [= eindringen] *aux sein* to penetrate *(in etw (acc)* sth); *(Rauch, Nebel)* to drift *(in etw (acc)* into sth)

e [= rücken] *mit Spielfigur* to move; *(= abheben)* to draw; **mit dem Turm ziehen** to move the rook; **wer zieht?** whose move is it?

f [= Zug haben] *Feuer, Ofen, Pfeife* to draw; **an der Pfeife/Zigarette ziehen** to take a drag on one's pipe/cigarette

g [= Eindruck machen] *inf* **so was zieht beim Publikum/bei mir nicht** the public/I don't like that sort of thing; **der Film zieht immer noch** the film is still popular; **so was zieht immer** that sort of thing always goes down well

h [= sieden] *Tee* to draw; *(in Kochwasser)* to simmer; *(in Marinade)* to marinade

3 – UNPERSÖNLICHES VERB

♦ **es zieht** there's a draught *(Brit) or* draft *(US)*; **wenn es dir zieht** if you're in a draught *(Brit) or* draft *(US)*; **mir ziehts im Nacken** there is *or* I can feel a draught *(Brit) or* draft *(US)* round my neck; **in diesem Haus zieht es aus allen Ritzen** there are draughts *(Brit) or* drafts *(US)* everywhere in this house; **mir ziehts im Rücken** *(= tut der Rücken weh)* my back hurts

4 – REFLEXIVES VERB

♦ **sich ziehen**

a [= sich erstrecken] to extend; **das Industriegebiet zieht sich bis weit in die Tiefebene (hinein)** the industrial area extends far across the plain; **dieses Treffen zieht sich!** this meeting is dragging on!; **sich zickzackförmig durchs Land ziehen** to zigzag through the countryside; **sich in Schlingen/Serpentinen durch etw ziehen** to

twist *or* wind its way through sth; **dieses Thema zieht sich durch das ganze Buch** this theme runs throughout the whole book
b (= sich dehnen) to stretch; *(Klebstoff)* to be tacky; *(Käse)* to form strings; *(Holz)* to warp; *(Metall)* to bend
c (= sich befreien) **sich an etw** *(dat)* **aus dem Schlamm/in die Höhe ziehen** to pull oneself out of the mud/up on sth → **Affäre, Patsche**

Zie|hen NT **-s**, *no pl (= Schmerz)* ache; *(im Unterleib)* abdominal pain

Zieh-: **Zieh|har|mo|ni|ka** F concertina; *(mit Tastatur)* accordion; **Zieh|kind** NT *(old, fig)* foster child; **Zieh|mut|ter** F *pl* **-mütter** *(old, fig)* foster mother; **Zieh|sohn** M *(lit old)* foster son; *(fig)* foster child

Zie|hung [ˈtsiːʊŋ] F **-, -en** draw

Zieh|va|ter M *(old, fig)* foster father

Ziel [tsiːl] NT **-(e)s, -e** **a** *(= Reiseziel)* destination; *(= Absicht, Zweck)* goal, aim, objective; *(von Wünschen, Spott)* object; **mit dem ~ ...** with the aim *or* intention ...; **etw zum ~ haben** to have sth as one's goal *or* aim; **jdm/sich ein ~ stecken** *or* **setzen** to set sb/oneself a goal; **er hatte sich sein ~ zu hoch gesteckt** he had set his sights too high; **sich** *(dat)* **etw zum ~ setzen** to set sth as one's goal *etc*; **einer Sache** *(dat)* **ein ~ setzen** to put a limit on sth; *(= eindämmen)* to limit sth; **zum ~ kommen** *or* **gelangen** *(fig)* to reach *or* attain one's goal *etc*; **am ~ sein** to be at one's destination, to have reached one's destination; *(fig)* to have reached *or* achieved one's goal; **dieser Weg führte ihn nicht zum ~** *(fig)* this avenue did not lead him to his goal
b *(Sport)* finish; *(bei Pferderennen)* finish(ing post), winning post; *(bei Rennen)* finish(ing line); **durchs ~ gehen** to pass the winning post *or* finishing post/to cross the finishing line
c *(Mil, Schießsport, fig)* target; **ins ~ treffen** to hit the target; **über das ~ hinausschießen** *(fig)* to overshoot the mark
d *(Comm: = Frist)* credit period; **mit drei Monaten ~** with a three-month credit period

Ziel-: **Ziel|bahn|hof** M destination; **Ziel|band** [-bant] NT *pl* **-bänder** finishing tape; **ziel|be|wusst** ADJ purposeful, decisive; **Ziel|be|wusst|sein** NT purposefulness, decisiveness; **mangelndes ~** lack of purpose; **Ziel|da|tei** F target *or* destination file

zie|len [ˈtsiːlən] VI **a** *(Mensch)* to aim *(auf +acc, nach* at); *(Waffe, Schuss)* to be aimed *(auf +acc* at) **b** *(fig: Bemerkung, Kritik, Tat)* to be aimed *or* directed *(auf +acc* at); **ich weiß, worauf deine Bemerkungen ~** I know what you're driving at; **das zielt auf uns** that's aimed at *or* meant for us, that's for our benefit → *auch* **gezielt**

zie|lend ADJ *(Gram) Zeitwort* transitive

Ziel-: **Ziel|fern|rohr** NT telescopic sight; **Ziel|flug|ge|rät** NT homing indicator; **Ziel|fo|to** NT, **Ziel|fo|to|gra|fie** F photograph of the finish; **Ermittlung des Siegers durch ~** photo finish; **ziel|füh|rend** ADJ *Maßnahme etc* carefully targeted; *(= Erfolg versprechend)* successful; *(= sinnvoll, zweckmäßig)* practical, suitable ADV with clear goals in mind, suitably; **ziel|ge|nau** ADJ accurate; *Maßnahme, Politik* carefully targeted; **Ziel|ge|nau|ig|keit** F accuracy; *(von Maßnahme, Politik)* careful targeting; **Ziel|ge|ra|de** F home *or* finishing straight; **Ziel|ge|rät** NT *(Mil)* bombsight; **ziel|ge|rich|tet** ADJ goal-directed; *(= gezielt)* purposeful; **Ziel|grup|pe** F target group; **Ziel|ha|fen** M port of destination; **Ziel|kauf** M *(Comm)* credit purchase; **Ziel|kon|flikt** M conflict of aims; **Ziel|kur|ve** F final bend; **Ziel|lauf|werk** NT *(Comput)* target *or* destination drive; **Ziel|li|nie** F *(Sport)* finishing line; **ziel|los** ADJ aimless, purposeless ADV aimlessly; **Ziel|lo|sig|keit** F **-**, *no pl* lack of purpose, purposelessness; **ziel|ori|en|tiert** ADJ goal-directed; *Handeln, Planen* purposeful ADV with clear goals in mind, purposefully; **Ziel|ort** M *pl* **-orte** destination; **Ziel|pho|to|gra|phie** F = **Zielfotografie**; **Ziel|rich|ter(in)** M(F) *(Sport)* finishing-line judge; **Ziel|schei|be** F target; *(von Spott auch)* object; **Ziel|set|zung** [-zɛtsʊŋ] F **-, -en** target, objective; **ziel|si|cher** ADJ unerring; *Handeln, Planen* purposeful ADV unerringly; **~ auf jdn/etw zugehen** to go straight up to sb/sth; **Ziel|si|cher|heit** F (unerring) accuracy; **Ziel|spra|che** F target language; **ziel|stre|big** [ˈtsiːlʃtreːbɪç] ADJ *Mensch, Handlungsweise* determined, single-minded ADV full of determination; **Ziel|stre|big|keit** F **-**, *no pl* determination, single-mindedness; **ziel|su|chend** ADJ target-seeking; **Ziel|vor|ga|be** F **a** *(= zu erreichendes Ziel)* set target; **es gibt klare ~n** clear targets have been set **b** *(= Zielfestlegung)* target-setting; **Ziel|vor|stel|lung** F objective; **Ziel|was|ser** NT *pl* **-wässer** *(hum inf)* schnapps *(drunk at a shooting match)*

zie|men [ˈtsiːmən] VR *impers (geh)* **es ziemt sich nicht** it is not proper *or* seemly; **das ziemt sich nicht (für dich)** it is not proper (for you) VI *(old)* **jdm ~** to become sb

Zie|mer [ˈtsiːmɐ] M **-s, -** **a** *(= Wildrücken)* saddle **b** *(= Peitsche)* whip

ziem|lich [ˈtsiːmlɪç] ADJ **a** *(old: = geziemend)* proper, fitting
b *attr (= beträchtlich) Anzahl, Strecke* considerable, fair; *Vermögen* sizable; *Genugtuung* reasonable; **das ist eine ~e Frechheit** that's a real cheek *(Brit)*, that's really fresh *(US)*; **eine ~e Zeit/Anstrengung/Arbeit** quite a time/an effort/a lot of work; **sie unterhielten sich mit ~er Lautstärke** they were talking quite loudly; **mit ~er Sicherheit** pretty *(inf) or* fairly certainly; *sagen, behaupten* with a reasonable *or* fair degree of certainty, with reasonable certainty
ADV **a** *(= beträchtlich)* rather, quite, pretty *(inf)*; *sicher, genau* reasonably; **sie hat sich ~ anstrengen müssen** she had to make quite an effort; **wir haben uns ~ beeilt** we've hurried quite a bit; **~ lange** quite a long time, a fair time; **~ viel** quite a lot
b *(inf: = beinahe)* almost, nearly; **so ~** more or less; **so ~ alles** just about everything, more or less everything; **so ~ dasselbe** pretty well *(inf) or* much the same; **sie ist so ~ in meinem Alter** she is about the same age as me

zie|pen [ˈtsiːpn] VI to chirp, to tweet, to cheep VI *impers (inf: = wehtun)* **es ziept** it hurts VT *(inf: = ziehen)* to pull, to tweak; **jdn an den Haaren ~** to pull *or* tug sb's hair

Zier [tsiːɐ] F **-**, *no pl (old, poet)* = **Zierde**

Zie|rat △ [ˈtsiːraːt] M **-(e)s, -e** *(geh)* → **Zierrat**

Zier|de [ˈtsiːɐdə] F **-, -n** ornament, decoration; *(= Schmuckstück)* adornment; *(fig: = Tugend)* virtue; **zur ~** for decoration; **das alte Haus ist eine ~ der Stadt** the old house is one of the beauties of the town; **eine Eins im Betragen war die einzige ~ seines Zeugnisses** a one for behaviour *(Brit) or* behavior *(US)* was the only bright spot on his report; **eine ~ des männlichen Geschlechts** a fine specimen of the male sex; **eine ~ des weiblichen Geschlechts** a flower of the female sex; **die ~ der Familie** *(fig)* a credit to the family

zie|ren [ˈtsiːrən] VT to adorn; *Speisen* to garnish; *Kuchen* to decorate; *(fig: = auszeichnen)* to grace; **deine Eifersucht ziert dich nicht gerade** your envy does not exactly do you credit
VR *(= sich bitten lassen)* to make a fuss, to need a lot of pressing; *(Mädchen)* to act coyly; *(= sich gekünstelt benehmen)* to be affected; **du brauchst dich nicht zu ~, es ist genügend da** there's no need to be polite, there's plenty there; **er zierte sich nicht lange und sagte Ja** he didn't need much pressing before he agreed; **ohne sich zu ~** without having to be pressed; **zier dich nicht!** don't be shy *or* silly *(inf)* → *auch* **geziert**

Zie|re|rei [tsiːrəˈrai] F **-, -en** *(= gekünsteltes Benehmen)* affectedness

Zier-: **Zier|farn** M decorative fern; **Zier|fisch** M ornamental fish; **Zier|gar|ten** M ornamental garden; **Zier|ge|wächs** NT ornamental plant; **Zier|gras** NT ornamental grass; **Zier|leis|te** F border; *(an Auto)* trim; *(an Möbelstück)* edging; *(an Wand)* moulding *(Brit)*, molding *(US)*

zier|lich [ˈtsiːɐlɪç] ADJ dainty; *Frau auch* petite; *Porzellanfigur, Möbel etc* delicate

Zier|lich|keit F **-**, *no pl* daintiness; *(von Porzellanfigur, Möbel etc)* delicateness

Zier-: **Zier|naht** F decorative seam; **Zier|pflan|ze** F ornamental plant; **Zier|rat** [ˈtsiːɐraːt] M **-(e)s, -e** *(geh)* decoration; **Zier|schrift** F ornamental lettering; **Zier|stich** M embroidery stitch; **Zier|strauch** M ornamental shrub

Zie|sel [ˈtsiːzl] M **-s, -** ground squirrel, suslik

Zif|fer [ˈtsɪfɐ] F **-, -n** **a** *(abbr* **Ziff.**) *(= Zahlzeichen)* digit; *(= Zahl)* figure, number; **römische/arabische ~n** roman/arabic numerals; **eine Zahl mit drei ~n** a three-figure number; **etw in ~n schreiben** to write sth in figures *or* numbers **b** *(eines Paragrafen)* clause

Zif|fer|blatt NT *(an Uhr)* dial, (clock) face; *(von Armbanduhr)* (watch) face

Zif|fern|block M *(auf Tastatur)* number pad, numeric keypad

zig [tsɪç] ADJ *(inf)* umpteen *(inf)*

zig- [ˈtsɪç] PREF *(inf)* umpteen *(inf)*; **zighundert** umpteen hundred *(inf)*

Zi|ga|ret|te [tsigaˈrɛtə] F **-, -n** cigarette; **~ mit Filter** filter cigarette

Zi|ga|ret|ten- *in cpds* cigarette; **Zi|ga|ret|ten|an|zün|der** M *(in Auto)* cigar lighter; **Zi|ga|ret|ten|au|to|mat** M cigarette machine; **Zi|ga|ret|ten|do|se** F cigarette box; **Zi|ga|ret|ten|etui** NT cigarette case; **Zi|ga|ret|ten|kip|pe** F cigarette end *or* butt, fag end *(Brit inf)*; **Zi|ga|ret|ten|län|ge** F **auf** *or* **für eine ~ hinausgehen** to go out for a cigarette *or* smoke; **Zi|ga|ret|ten|pa|pier** NT cigarette paper; **Zi|ga|ret|ten|pau|se** F break for a cigarette *or* a smoke, cigarette break; **Zi|ga|ret|ten|qualm** M *(pej)*, **Zi|ga|ret|ten|rauch** M cigarette smoke, fug *(inf)*; **Zi|ga|ret|ten|rau|cher(in)** M(F) cigarette smoker; **Zi|ga|ret|ten|schach|tel** F cigarette packet *(Brit) or* pack *(US)*; **Zi|ga|ret|ten|spit|ze** F cigarette holder; **Zi|ga|ret|ten|stum|mel** M cigarette end *or* butt, fag end *(Brit inf)*

Zi|ga|ril|lo [tsigaˈrɪlo, -ˈrɪljo] M OR NT **-s, -s** cigarillo

Zi|gar|re [tsiˈgarə] F **-, -n** **a** cigar **b** *(inf: = Verweis)* dressing-down; **jdm eine ~ verpassen** to give sb a dressing-down

Zi|gar|ren- *in cpds* cigar; **Zi|gar|ren|ab|schnei|der** M cigar cutter; **Zi|gar|ren|kis|te** F cigar box; **Zi|gar|ren|rau|cher(in)** M(F) cigar smoker; **Zi|gar|ren|spit|ze** F cigar holder; **Zi|gar|ren|stum|mel** M cigar butt

Zi|geu|ner [tsiˈgɔynɐ] M **-s, -** *(neg!)*, **Zi|geu|ne|rin** [-ərɪn] F **-, -nen** *(neg!)* gypsy, gipsy; *(Rasse auch)* Romany; *(pej inf)* vagabond; *(= Streuner)* gypsy, gipsy

zi|geu|ner|haft ADJ gypsylike, gipsylike

zi|geu|ne|risch [tsiˈgɔynərɪʃ] ADJ gypsylike, gipsylike

Zi|geu|ner-: **Zi|geu|ner|la|ger** NT *(neg!)* gypsy camp *or* encampment; **Zi|geu|ner|le|ben** NT *(neg!)* gypsy life; *(fig)* vagabond *or* rootless life

zi|geu|nern [tsiˈgɔynɐn] *ptp* **zigeunert** *(neg!)* VI *aux haben or (bei Richtungsangabe) sein (inf)* to rove, to roam

Zi|geu|ner-: **Zi|geu|ner|pri|mas** M *(neg!)* leader of a gypsy band; **Zi|geu|ner|schnit|zel** NT *(Cook) cutlet served in a spicy sauce with green and red peppers*; **Zi|geu|ner|spra|che** F *(neg!)* Romany, Romany *or* Gypsy language; **Zi|geu|ner|steak** NT *(Cook) steak served in a spicy sauce with green and red peppers*; **Zi|geu|ner|wa|gen** M *(neg!)* gypsy caravan

zig|fach ['tsɪçfax] ADJ *(inf)* umpteen times *(inf)*; **die ~e Menge** umpteen times the amount; **das Zigfache** umpteen times (the amount); **das Zigfache ihres eigenen Körpergewichts** umpteen times her/their own bodyweight
zig|mal ['tsɪçma:l] ADV *(inf)* umpteen times *(inf)*
Zi|ka|de [tsi'ka:də] F -, -n cicada
zi|li|ar [tsi'lia:ɐ] ADJ *(Anat)* ciliary
Zil|le ['tsɪlə] F -, -n barge
Zim|bab|we [zɪm'babvə] NT -s Zimbabwe
Zim|bab|wer [zɪm'babvɐ] M -s, -, **Zim|bab|we|rin** [-ərɪn] F -, -nen Zimbabwean
zim|bab|wisch [zɪm'babvɪʃ] ADJ Zimbabwean
Zim|bal ['tsɪmbal] NT -s, -e *or* -s cymbals *pl*
Zim|bel ['tsɪmbl] F -, -n *(Mus)* cymbal; *(= Hackbrett)* cymbalon
zimb|risch ['tsɪmbrɪʃ] ADJ Cimbrian
Zim|mer ['tsɪmɐ] NT -s, - room; **„Zimmer frei"** "vacancies"
Zim|mer-: **Zim|mer|an|ten|ne** F indoor aerial *(Brit)* or antenna *(US)*; **Zim|mer|ar|beit** F carpentry job, piece of carpentry; **Zim|mer|ar|rest** M confinement to one's room; **~ haben** to be confined to one's room; **Zim|mer|brand** M fire in a/the room; **Zim|mer|de|cke** F ceiling
Zim|me|rei [tsɪmə'rai] F -, -en **a** *(= Handwerk)* carpentry **b** *(= Werkstatt)* carpenter's shop
Zim|mer|ein|rich|tung F furniture
Zim|me|rer ['tsɪmərɐ] M -s, -, **Zim|me|rin** [-ərɪn] F -, -nen carpenter
Zim|mer-: **Zim|mer|flucht** F suite of rooms; **Zim|mer|ge|nos|se** M, **Zim|mer|ge|nos|sin** F roommate; **Zim|mer|ge|sel|le** M, **Zim|mer|ge|sel|lin** F journeyman carpenter; **Zim|mer|hand|werk** NT carpentry, carpenter's trade; **Zim|mer|herr** M (gentleman) lodger
-zim|me|rig [tsɪmərɪç] ADJ *suf* -roomed, with ... rooms; **ein fünfzimmeriges Haus** a five-roomed house, a house with five rooms
Zim|me|rin [-ərɪn] F -, -nen carpenter
Zim|mer-: **Zim|mer|kell|ner** M room waiter; **Zim|mer|kell|ne|rin** F room waitress; **Zim|mer|laut|stär|ke** F low volume; **Zim|mer|leh|re** F apprenticeship in carpentry; **Zim|mer|lehr|ling** M carpenter's apprentice, apprentice carpenter; **Zim|mer|lin|de** F African hemp; **Zim|mer|mäd|chen** NT chambermaid
Zim|mer|mann M *pl* **-leute** carpenter; **jdm zeigen, wo der ~ das Loch gelassen hat** *(inf)* to show sb the door
Zim|mer|manns-: **Zim|mer|manns|beil** NT carpenter's hatchet; **Zim|mer|manns|kno|ten** M, **Zim|mer|manns|stek** [-ste:k, -ʃt-] M -s, -s timber hitch
Zim|mer|meis|ter(in) M(F) master carpenter
zim|mern ['tsɪmɐn] VT to make *or* build *or* construct from wood; *(fig) Alibi, Lösung* to construct; *Ausrede* to make up VI to do woodwork *or* carpentry; **an etw** *(dat)* **~** *(lit)* to make sth from wood; *(fig)* to work on sth
Zim|mer-: **Zim|mer|nach|weis** M accommodation service; **Zim|mer|num|mer** F room number; **Zim|mer|pflan|ze** F house plant; **Zim|mer|ser|vice** [-zø:ɐvɪs, -zœrvɪs] M room service; **Zim|mer|su|che** F room hunting, hunting for rooms/a room; **auf ~ sein** to be looking for rooms/a room; **Zim|mer|tem|pe|ra|tur** F room temperature; **Zim|mer|the|a|ter** NT small theatre *(Brit)* or theater *(US)*; **Zim|mer|tür** F door (to the room); **Zim|mer|ver|mitt|lung** F accommodation service
Zim|met ['tsɪmət] M -s, *no pl (obs)* cinnamon
-zimm|rig [tsɪmrɪç] ADJ *suf* = **-zimmerig**
zim|per|lich ['tsɪmpɐlɪç] ADJ *(= überempfindlich)* nervous *(gegen* about*)*; *(beim Anblick von Blut etc)* squeamish; *(= prüde)* prissy; *(= wehleidig)* soft; **sei doch nicht so ~** don't be so silly; **da ist er gar nicht (so) ~** he doesn't have any qualms about that; **da darf man nicht so ~ sein** you can't afford to be soft; **mit Vorwürfen ist sie nicht ~** she doesn't hold back when it comes to reproaching people ADV oversensitively; **du behandelst ihn viel zu ~** you're much too soft with him
Zim|per|lie|se ['tsɪmpɐli:zə] F -, -n *(pej inf)* cissy *(inf)*
Zimt [tsɪmt] M -(e)s, -e **a** *(= Gewürz)* cinnamon **b** *(fig inf) (= Kram)* rubbish *(esp Brit)*, garbage; *(= Unsinn)* rubbish *(esp Brit)*, nonsense
Zimt-: **zimt|far|ben** [-farbn], **zimt|far|big** ADJ cinnamon-coloured *(Brit)*, cinnamon-colored *(US)*; **Zimt|stan|ge** F stick of cinnamon; **Zimt|stern** M *(Cook) cinnamon-flavoured star-shaped biscuit*; **Zimt|zi|cke** F *(inf)* stupid cow *(inf)*, silly old bat *(inf)*
Zink [tsɪŋk] NT -(e)s, *no pl (abbr* **Zn***)* zinc
Zink M -(e)s, -e(n) *(Mus)* cornet
Zink-: **Zink|blech** NT sheet zinc; **Zink|blen|de** F zinc blende; **Zink|dach** NT zinc roof
Zin|ke ['tsɪŋkə] F -, -n *(von Gabel)* prong; *(von Kamm, Rechen)* tooth; *(= Holzzapfen)* tenon
Zin|ken ['tsɪŋkn] M -s, - **a** *(sl: = Gaunerzeichen)* secret mark **b** *(inf: = Nase)* hooter *(Brit inf)*, shnaz *(US inf)* **c** = **Zinke d** *(Mus)* cornet
zin|ken ['tsɪŋkn] VT **a** *Karten* to mark **b** *Holz etc* to tenon
zin|ken ADJ zinc *attr*, made of zinc
Zink-: **Zink|far|be** F zinc(-based) paint; **zink|hal|tig** ADJ containing zinc; **~ sein** to contain zinc; **Zink|leim** M Unna's paste; **Zink|sal|be** F zinc ointment; **Zink|weiß** NT Chinese white
Zinn [tsɪn] NT -(e)s, *no pl* **a** *(abbr* **Sn***)* tin **b** *(= Legierung)* pewter **c** *(= Zinnprodukte)* pewter, pewter ware
Zinn|be|cher M pewter tankard
Zin|ne ['tsɪnə] F -, -n *(Hist)* merlon; **~n** *(von Burg)* battlements; *(von Stadt)* towers; *(von Gebirgsmassiv)* peaks, pinnacles
zin|nen ['tsɪnən], **zin|nern** ['tsɪnɐn] ADJ pewter
Zinn-: **Zinn|fi|gur** F pewter figure *or* statuette; **Zinn|ge|schirr** NT pewter ware; **Zinn|gie|ßer(in)** M(F) pewterer
Zin|nie ['tsɪniə] F -, -n zinnia
Zinn|kraut NT horsetail
Zin|no|ber [tsɪ'no:bɐ] M -s, *no pl* **a** *(Farbe)* vermilion, cinnabar **b** *(inf) (= Getue)* fuss, commotion; *(= Kram)* stuff *(inf)*; *(= Unsinn)* nonsense *no indef art*, rubbish *no indef art (esp Brit)*; **macht keinen (solchen) ~** stop making such a fuss *or* commotion
Zin|no|ber-: **zin|no|ber|rot** ADJ vermilion; **Zin|no|ber|rot** NT vermilion
Zinn-: **Zinn|pest** F tin disease; **Zinn|sol|dat** M tin soldier; **Zinn|tel|ler** M pewter plate; **Zinn|ver|bin|dung** F tin compound
Zins [tsɪns] M -es, -e [-zə] *(Hist: = Abgabe)* tax; *(S Ger, Aus, Sw) (= Pachtzins, Mietzins)* rent; *(= Wasserzins)* water rates *pl*
Zins M -es, -en *usu pl (= Geldzins)* interest *no pl*; **~en bringen** to earn interest; **~en tragen** *(lit)* to earn interest; *(fig)* to pay dividends; **Darlehen zu 10% ~en** loan at 10% interest; **Kapital auf ~en legen** to invest capital at interest; **jdm etw mit ~en** *or* **mit ~ und ~eszins heimzahlen** *or* **zurückgeben** *(fig)* to pay sb back for sth with interest
Zins-: **Zins|ab|schlag** M deduction for tax *(on interest earned that is not subject to capital gains tax)*; **Zins|ab|schlag|steuer** F tax on interest payments; **Zins|aus|fall** M loss of interest; **Zins|bau|er** M -n, -n *(Hist)* tenant farmer; **Zins|be|las|tung** F interest load; **Zins|bin|dung** F pegging of interest rates; **Zins|bo|gen** M *(Fin)* interest sheet; **zins|brin|gend** ADJ interest-bearing *attr*
zin|sen ['tsɪnzn] VI *(Hist: = Abgaben zahlen)* to pay one's tax; *(Sw: = Pacht zahlen)* to pay one's rent
Zin|sen|kon|to NT interest account
Zins-: **Zins|er|hö|hung** F increase *or* rise in interest rates; **Zins|er|trä|ge** PL interest earnings *pl*; **~ aus ...** *(auch)* interest yield on ...
Zin|ses|zins M compound interest → **Zins**
Zin|ses|zins|rech|nung F calculation of compound interest
Zins-: **zins|frei** ADJ **a** *(= frei von Abgaben)* tax-free; *(S Ger, Aus, Sw) (= pachtfrei, mietfrei)* rent-free; *Wasser* rate-free **b** *Darlehen* interest-free ADV *Geld leihen* interest-free; **Zins|fuß** M interest rate, rate of interest; **Zins|ge|fäl|le** NT difference between interest levels; **zins|güns|tig** ADJ ADV at a favourable *(Brit)* or favorable *(US)* rate of interest; **Zins|gut** NT *pl* **-güter** *(Hist)* tenant farm; **Zins|herr** M *(Hist)* landlord, lord of the manor; **Zins|knecht|schaft** F *(Hist) system of holding land in tenancy to a landlord*; **zins|los** ADJ ADV interest-free; **Zins|ni|veau** NT level of interest rates; **Zins|pflicht** F *(Hist)* obligation to pay tax; **zins|pflich|tig** [-pflɪçtɪç] ADJ *(Hist)* tax-paying; **~ sein** to be obliged to pay tax; **Zins|po|li|tik** F interest policies *pl*; **Zins|rech|nung** F calculation of interest; **Zins|satz** M interest rate, rate of interest; *(bei Darlehen)* lending rate; **Zins|schein** M *(Fin)* interest sheet; **Zins|schritt** M *(Fin)* change in the interest rate *or* in interest rates; **Zins|schwan|kun|gen** PL fluctuations *pl* in the interest rate *or* in interest rates; **Zins|sen|kung** F reduction in the interest rate; **Zins|span|ne** F margin between interest rates paid by borrowers and to investors; **Zins|ter|min** M interest due date; **Zins|ver|bil|li|gung** F reduction in the interest rate; **Zins|ver|lust** M loss on interest; **Zins|wu|cher** M usury; **Zins|zah|lung** F interest payment, payment of interest
Zi|o|nis|mus [tsio'nɪsmʊs] M -, *no pl* Zionism
Zi|o|nist [tsio'nɪst] M -en, -en, **Zi|o|nis|tin** [-'nɪstɪn] F -, -nen Zionist
zi|o|nis|tisch [tsio'nɪstɪʃ] ADJ Zionist
Zip|fel ['tsɪpfl] M -s, - **a** *(von Tuch, Decke, Stoff)* corner; *(von Mütze)* point; *(von Hemd, Jacke)* tail; *(am Saum)* dip *(an +dat* in*)*; *(von Wurst)* end; *(von Land)* tip; **jdn (gerade noch) am (letzten) ~ erwischen** *(fig inf)* to catch sb (just) at the last minute **b** *(inf: = Mensch)* silly *(inf)*
zip|fe|lig ['tsɪpfəlɪç] ADJ **a** *Saum* uneven; *Pullover, Rock etc* with an uneven hem **b** *(inf: = nervös)* fidgety *(inf)*
Zip|fel|müt|ze F pointed cap *or* hat
zip|feln ['tsɪpfln] VI *(Rock)* to be uneven
zipf|lig ['tsɪpflɪç] ADJ = **zipfelig**
zip|pen VT *(Comput) Datei* to zip
Zip|per|lein ['tsɪpɐlain] NT -s, - *(old, hum)* gout
Zipp|(ver|schluss)® M *(Aus)* zip (fastener)
Zir|bel|drü|se ['tsɪrbl-] F pineal body
Zir|bel|kie|fer F Swiss *or* stone pine
zir|ka ['tsɪrka] ADV about, approximately; *(bei Datumsangaben)* circa, about
Zir|kel ['tsɪrkl] M -s, - **a** *(= Gerät)* pair of compasses, compasses *pl*; *(= Stechzirkel)* pair of dividers, dividers *pl* **b** *(lit, fig: = Kreis)* circle **c** *(= studentischer Zirkel) monogram of a student organization*
Zir|kel-: **Zir|kel|de|fi|ni|ti|on** F circular definition; **Zir|kel|kas|ten** M compasses case
zir|keln ['tsɪrkln] VI *(= genau abmessen)* to measure exactly
Zir|kel-: **Zir|kel|schluss** M circular argument; **Zir|kel|trai|ning** NT *(Sport)* circuit training
Zir|kon [tsɪr'ko:n] M -s, *no pl* zircon
Zir|ko|ni|um [tsɪr'ko:niʊm] NT -s, *no pl (abbr* **Zr***)* zirconium
Zir|ku|lar [tsɪrku'la:ɐ] NT -s, -e *(old)* circular
Zir|ku|la|ti|on ['tsɪrkula'tsio:n] F -, -en circulation
Zir|ku|la|ti|ons-: **Zir|ku|la|ti|ons|pum|pe** F circulation pump; **Zir|ku|la|ti|ons|stö|rung** F circulation *or* circulatory problem
zir|ku|lie|ren [tsɪrku'li:rən] *ptp* **zirkuliert** VI to circulate
Zir|kum|flex ['tsɪrkʊmflɛks, tsɪrkʊm'flɛks] M -es, -e *(Ling)* circumflex
Zir|kum|po|lar|stern [tsɪrkʊmpo'la:ɐ-] M circumpolar star

Zir|kus ['tsɪrkʊs] M **-, -se** **a** circus; **in den ~ gehen** to go to the circus **b** *(inf) (= Skizirkus, Tenniszirkus etc)* circus; *(= Getue, Theater)* fuss, to-do *(inf)*

Zir|kus- *in cpds* circus; **Zir|kus|ar|tist(in)** M(F) circus performer *or* artiste; **Zir|kus|wa|gen** M circus caravan *(Brit) or* trailer *(US)*; **Zir|kus|zelt** NT big top

Zir|pe ['tsɪrpə] F **-, -n** cicada

zir|pen ['tsɪrpn] VI to chirp, to cheep

Zir|rho|se [tsɪ'ro:zə] F **-, -n** cirrhosis

Zir|rus ['tsɪrʊs] M **-, -** *or* **Zirren** [-rən], **Zir|rus|wol|ke** F cirrus (cloud)

zir|zen|sisch [tsɪr'tsɛnzɪʃ] ADJ circus *attr*

zis|al|pin [tsɪsal'pi:n], **zis|al|pi|nisch** [tsɪsal'pi:nɪʃ] ADJ cisalpine

zisch [tsɪʃ] INTERJ hiss; *(Rakete, Schnellzug etc)* whoosh

zi|scheln ['tsɪʃln] VI to whisper

zi|schen ['tsɪʃn] **VI** **a** *(= zischendes Geräusch machen)* to hiss; *(Limonade)* to fizz; *(Fett, Wasser)* to sizzle **b** *aux sein (inf: = abzischen)* to whizz **VT** **a** *(= zischend sagen)* to hiss **b** *(inf: = trinken)* **einen ~** to have a quick one *(inf)* **c** *(inf: = ohrfeigen)* **jdm eine ~** to belt *or* clout sb one *(inf)*; **eine gezischt bekommen** to get belted *or* clouted *(inf)*

Zisch|laut M *(Ling)* sibilant

zi|se|lie|ren [tsizə'li:rən] *ptp* **ziseliert** VTI to chase

Zi|se|lie|rer [tsizə'li:rɐ] M **-s, -**, **Zi|se|lie|re|rin** [-ərɪn] F **-, -nen** engraver

Zis|ter|ne [tsɪs'tɛrnə] F **-, -n** well

Zis|ter|zi|en|ser [tsɪstɛr'tsiɛnzɐ] M **-s, -**, **Zis|ter|zi|en|se|rin** [-ərɪn] F **-, -nen** Cistercian; *(Mönch auch)* Cistercian monk; *(Nonne auch)* Cistercian nun

Zis|ter|zi|en|ser|or|den M Cistercian order

Zi|ta|del|le [tsita'dɛlə] F **-, -n** citadel

Zi|tat [tsi'ta:t] NT **-(e)s, -e** quotation; **ein falsches ~** a misquotation; **~ ... Ende des ~s** quote ... unquote

Zi|ta|ten-: **Zi|ta|ten|le|xi|kon** NT dictionary of quotations; **Zi|ta|ten|samm|lung** F collection of quotations; **Zi|ta|ten|schatz** M store of quotations; *(= Buch)* treasury of quotations

Zi|ther ['tsɪtɐ] F **-, -n** zither

Zi|ther-: **Zi|ther|spiel** NT zither-playing; **Zi|ther|spie|ler(in)** M(F) zither player

zi|tie|ren [tsi'ti:rən] *ptp* **zitiert** VT **a** *jdn, Ausspruch, Textstelle* to quote; *Beispiel* to cite, to quote **b** *(= vorladen, rufen)* to summon *(vor +acc* before, *an +acc, zu* to)

Zit|ro|nat [tsitro'na:t] NT **-(e)s, -e** candied lemon peel

Zit|ro|ne [tsi'tro:nə] F **-, -n** lemon; *(= Getränk)* lemon drink; *(= Baum)* lemon tree; **jdn wie eine ~ auspressen** *or* **ausquetschen** to squeeze sb dry

Zit|ro|nen-: **Zit|ro|nen|fal|ter** M brimstone (butterfly); **zit|ro|nen|gelb** ADJ lemon yellow; **Zi|tro|nen|gras** NT *(Bot, Cook)* lemon grass; **Zit|ro|nen|li|mo|na|de** F lemonade; **Zit|ro|nen|me|lis|se** F (lemon) balm; **Zit|ro|nen|pres|se** F lemon squeezer; **Zit|ro|nen|saft** M lemon juice; **Zit|ro|nen|säu|re** F citric acid; **Zit|ro|nen|scha|le** F lemon peel; **Zit|ro|nen|schei|be** F lemon slice, slice of lemon; **Zit|ro|nen|was|ser** NT, *no pl* fresh lemon squash

Zit|rus|frucht F citrus fruit

Zit|ter-: **Zit|ter|aal** M electric eel; **Zit|ter|gras** NT quaking grass; **Zit|ter|greis(in)** M(F) *(inf)* old dodderer *(inf)*, doddering old man/woman

zit|te|rig ['tsɪtərɪç] ADJ *Hand, Körper, Stimme* shaky

zit|tern ['tsɪtɐn] VI **a** *(vor +dat* with) to shake, to tremble; *(vor Kälte)* to shiver, to tremble; *(Stimme)* to tremble, to quaver; *(Lippen, Blätter, Gräser)* to tremble, to quiver; *(Pfeil)* to quiver; **an allen Gliedern ~, am ganzen Körper ~** to shake *or* tremble all over; **mir ~ die Knie** my knees are shaking *or* trembling **b** *(= erschüttert werden)* to shake **c** *(inf: = Angst haben)* to tremble *or* shake with fear; **vor jdm ~** to be terrified of sb; **sie zittert jetzt schon vor der nächsten Englischarbeit** she's already trembling *or* terrified at the thought of the next English test

Zit|tern NT **-s**, *no pl* **a** *(= Beben)* shaking, trembling; *(vor Kälte)* shivering; *(von Stimme)* quavering; **ein ~ ging durch seinen Körper** a shiver ran through his body; **mit ~ und Zagen** in fear and trembling; **da hilft kein ~ und Zagen** it's no use being afraid **b** *(= Erschütterung)* shaking; **ein ~** a tremor

Zit|ter-: **Zit|ter|pap|pel** F aspen (tree); **Zit|ter|par|tie** F *(fig)* nail-biting event, nail-biter *(inf)*; **Zit|ter|ro|chen** M electric ray

zitt|rig ['tsɪtrɪç] ADJ *Hand, Körper, Stimme* shaky

Zit|ze ['tsɪtsə] F **-, -n** teat, dug

Zi|vi ['tsi:vi] M **-(s), -s** *(inf) abbr von* **Zivildienstleistende(r)**

zi|vil [tsi'vi:l] ADJ **a** *(= nicht militärisch)* civilian; *Schaden* nonmilitary; **im ~en Leben** in civilian life, in *(Brit) or* on civvy street *(inf)*; **~er Ersatzdienst** community service *(as alternative to military service)*; **~er Bevölkerungsschutz** civil defence *(Brit) or* defense *(US)* **b** *(inf: = angemessen, anständig)* civil, friendly; *Bedingungen, Forderungen, Preise* reasonable

Zi|vil [tsi'vi:l] NT **-s**, *no pl* **a** *(nicht Uniform)* civilian clothes *pl*, civvies *pl (inf)*; **in ~** *(Soldat)* in civilian clothes, in civvies; *(inf) Arzt etc* in mufti *(inf)*; **Polizist in ~** plain-clothes policeman **b** *(old: = Bürgerstand)* civilian populace *no pl*

Zi|vil-: **Zi|vil|be|ruf** M civilian profession; **Zi|vil|be|schäf|tig|te(r)** MF *decl as adj* civilian employee; **Zi|vil|be|völ|ke|rung** F civilian population; **Zi|vil|cou|ra|ge** F courage *(to stand up for one's beliefs)*; **der Mann hat ~** that man has the courage to stand up for his beliefs; **Zi|vil|dienst** M community service *(as alternative to military service)*; **Zi|vil|dienst|leis|ten|de(r)** [-laistndə] MF *decl as adj* person doing community service *or* work *(instead of military service)*; **zi|vil|dienst|pflich|tig** [-pflɪçtɪç] ADJ liable for community work *(instead of military service)*; **Zi|vil|ehe** F civil marriage

> **ZIVILDIENST**
>
> **Zivildienst** is community service done as an alternative to compulsory military service or **Wehrdienst**. Anyone seeking exemption from military service must present his case at a special hearing. **Zivildienst** is mainly carried out in the social services sector, where Zivis - as those doing community work are known - are generally welcomed, since they are an inexpensive and well-motivated workforce.
> In Switzerland there is no way of avoiding compulsory military service. → WEHRDIENST

Zi|vi|le(r) [tsi'vi:lə] MF *decl as adj (inf)* plain-clothes policeman/-woman

Zi|vil-: **Zi|vil|fahn|der(in)** M(F) plain-clothes policeman/-woman; **Zi|vil|flug|ha|fen** M civil airport; **Zi|vil|ge|richt** NT civil court; **Zi|vil|ge|setz|buch** NT *(Sw)* code of civil law

Zi|vi|li|sa|ti|on [tsiviliza'tsio:n] F **-, -en** civilization *(especially its technological aspects)*

Zi|vi|li|sa|ti|ons-: **zi|vi|li|sa|ti|ons|krank** ADJ **~ sein** to suffer from an illness caused by today's lifestyle; **Zi|vi|li|sa|ti|ons|krank|heit** F illness caused by today's lifestyle; **Zi|vi|li|sa|ti|ons|schä|den** PL *(am Menschen)* ills *pl* of civilization; *(an der Natur)* ravages *pl* of civilization

zi|vi|li|sa|to|risch [tsiviliza'to:rɪʃ] **ADJ** of civilization **ADV** in terms of civilization

zi|vi|li|sier|bar ADJ civilizable

zi|vi|li|sie|ren [tsivili'zi:rən] *ptp* **zivilisiert** VT to civilize

zi|vi|li|siert [tsivili'zi:ɐt] **ADJ** civilized **ADV** **sich ~ benehmen** to behave civilly *or* in a civilized manner

Zi|vi|list [tsivi'lɪst] M **-en, -en**, **Zi|vi|lis|tin** [-'lɪstɪn] F **-, -nen** civilian

Zi|vil-: **Zi|vil|kam|mer** F civil division; **Zi|vil|kla|ge** F civil action; **Zi|vil|klei|dung** F = **Zivil a**; **Zi|vil|le|ben** NT civilian life, civvy street *(inf)*; **Zi|vil|lis|te** F civil list; **Zi|vil|per|son** F civilian; **Zi|vil|pro|zess** M civil action; **Zi|vil|pro|zess|ord|nung** F *(Jur)* code of civil procedure; **Zi|vil|recht** NT civil law; **zi|vil|recht|lich** **ADJ** civil law *attr*, of civil law; *Prozess, Auseinandersetzung, Anspruch* civil *attr* **ADV** **etw ~ klären** to settle sth in a civil court; **jdn ~ verfolgen/belangen** to bring a civil action against sb; **~ relevant sein** to be a matter for civil law *or* a civil court; **Zi|vil|rich|ter(in)** M(F) civil court judge; **Zi|vil|sa|che** F matter for a civil court

Zi|vil|schutz M civil defence *(Brit) or* defense *(US)*

Zi|vil|schutz-: **Zi|vil|schutz|be|hör|de** F Federal Emergency Agency, Civil Defence Corps *(Brit)*, FEMA *(US)*; **Zi|vil|schutz|raum** M civilian air-raid shelter

Zi|vil-: **Zi|vil|se|nat** M *(Jur)* civil court of appeal; **Zi|vil|stand** M civilian status; **Zi|vil|stands|amt** NT *(Sw)* registry office; **Zi|vil|strei|fe** F plainclothes policemen *pl* (on the beat); **Zi|vil|trau|ung** F civil marriage; **Zi|vil|ver|fah|ren** NT civil proceedings *pl*

ZK [tsɛt'ka:] NT **-s, -s** *abbr von* **Zentralkomitee**

Zmit|tag ['tsmɪta:k] M **-, -** *(Sw)* lunch

Zmor|ge ['tsmɔrgə] M **-, -** *(Sw)* breakfast

Znacht [tsnaxt] M **-s, -** *(Sw)* supper

Znü|ni ['tsny:ni] M **-, -** *(Sw)* morning break, ≈ elevenses *(Brit)*

Zo|bel ['tso:bl] M **-s, -** **a** *(Zool)* sable **b** *(auch* **Zobelpelz)** sable (fur)

zo|ckeln ['tsɔkln] VI *aux sein (inf)* = **zuckeln**

zo|cken ['tsɔkn] VI *(inf)* to gamble

Zo|cker ['tsɔkɐ] M **-s, -**, **Zo|cke|rin** [-ərɪn] F **-, -nen** *(inf)* gambler

Zo|fe ['tso:fə] F **-, -n** lady's maid; *(von Königin)* lady-in-waiting

Zoff [tsɔf] M **-s**, *no pl (inf: = Ärger)* trouble; **dann gibts ~** then there'll be trouble

zog *pret von* **ziehen**

zö|ger|lich ['tsø:gelɪç] **ADJ** hesitant **ADV** hesitantly

Zö|ger|lich|keit F **-**, *no pl* hesitancy

zö|gern ['tsø:gɐn] VI to hesitate; **er tat es ohne zu ~** he did it without hesitating *or* hesitation; **er zögerte lange mit der Antwort** he hesitated (for) a long time before replying; **sie zögerte nicht lange mit ihrer Zustimmung** she lost little time in agreeing

Zö|gern NT **-s**, *no pl* hesitation; **ohne ~** without hesitation, unhesitatingly; **nach langem ~** after hesitating a long time

zö|gernd **ADJ** hesitant, hesitating **ADV** hesitantly, hesitatingly

Zög|ling ['tsø:klɪŋ] M **-s, -e** *(old, hum)* pupil

Zö|li|bat [tsøli'ba:t] NT OR M **-(e)s**, *no pl* celibacy; *(= Gelübde)* vow of celibacy; **im ~ leben** to be celibate, to practise *(Brit) or* practice *(US)* celibacy

zö|li|ba|tär [tsøliba'tɛ:ɐ] ADJ celibate

Zoll [tsɔl] M **-(e)s, -** *(= Längenmaß)* inch; **jeder ~ ein König, ~ für ~ ein König** every inch a king; **~ breit** = **Zollbreit**

Zoll M **-(e)s, ⸗e** ['tsœlə] **a** *(= Warenzoll)* customs duty; *(= Brückenzoll, Straßenzoll)* toll; **für etw ~ bezahlen** to pay (customs) duty on sth; **einem ~ unterliegen** to carry duty; **darauf liegt (ein) ~, darauf wird ~ erhoben** there is duty to pay on that **b** *(= Stelle)* **der ~** customs *pl*; **durch den ~ gehen/kommen** to go/get through customs

Zoll-: **Zoll|ab|fer|ti|gung** F **a** *(= Vorgang)* customs clearance **b** *(= Dienststelle)* customs post *or* checkpoint; **Zoll|ab|kom|men** NT customs *or* tariff agreement

Zollager △ NT → **Zolllager**

Zoll-: **Zoll|amt** NT customs house *or* office; **zoll|amt|lich** ADJ customs *attr* ADV ~ **geöffnet** opened by customs; ~ **abgefertigt werden** to go through customs, to be cleared by customs; **Zoll|aus|land** NT *foreign country which one has to go through customs to enter*; **Zoll|be|am|te(r)** M *decl as adj*, **Zoll|be|am|tin** F customs officer *or* official; **Zoll|be|gleit|pa|pie|re** PL customs documents *pl*; **Zoll|be|hör|de** F customs authorities *pl*, customs *pl*; **Zoll|be|stim|mung** F *usu pl* customs regulation; **zoll|breit** ['tsɔlbrait] ADJ one inch wide, inch-wide *attr*; **Zoll|breit** ['tsɔlbrait] M -, - inch; **keinen ~ zurückweichen** not to give *or* yield an inch; **Zoll|dek|la|ra|ti|on** F *(form)* customs declaration; **Zoll|ein|nah|men** PL customs revenue *sing*; **Zoll|ein|neh|mer(in)** M(F) *(old)* tax collector

zol|len ['tsɔlən] VT **jdm Anerkennung/Achtung/Bewunderung** ~ to acknowledge/respect/admire sb; **jdm Beifall** ~ to applaud sb, to give sb applause; **jdm Dank** ~ to extend *or* offer one's thanks to sb; **jdm seinen Tribut** ~ to pay tribute to sb

Zol|ler ['tsɔlɐ] M **-s, -**, **Zol|le|rin** [-ərın] F **-, -nen** *(Sw)* customs officer *or* official

Zoll-: **Zoll|er|klä|rung** F customs declaration; **Zoll|fahn|der(in)** M(F) customs investigator; **Zoll|fahn|dung** F customs investigation department; **zoll|frei** ADJ duty-free, exempt from duty ADV duty-free; **etw ~ einführen** to import sth free of duty; **Zoll|frei|heit** F exemption from duty; **Zoll|ge|biet** NT customs area *or* territory; **Zoll|ge|bühr** F (customs) duty, excise; **Zoll|grenz|be|zirk** M customs and border district; **Zoll|gren|ze** F customs border *or* frontier; **Zoll|ha|fen** M port of entry; **Zoll|in|halts|er|klä|rung** F customs declaration; **Zoll|in|spek|ti|on** F customs inspection; **Zoll|kon|trol|le** F customs check; **Zoll|lager** NT bonded warehouse

Zöll|ner ['tsœlnɐ] M **-s, -**, **Zöll|ne|rin** [-ərın] F **-, -nen** *(old, Bibl)* tax collector; *(inf: = Zollbeamter)* customs officer *or* official

Zoll-: **Zoll|pa|pie|re** PL customs documents *pl*; **zoll|pflich|tig** [-pflıçtıç] ADJ dutiable; **Zoll|recht** NT **a** *(Hist)* right to levy tolls **b** *(Jur)* customs law; **Zoll|schran|ke** F customs barrier; **Zoll|stock** M ruler, inch rule; **Zoll|ta|rif** M customs tariff; **Zoll|uni|on** F customs union; **Zoll|ver|ein** M *(Hist)* **Deutscher ~** German Customs Union (of 1844)

Zom|bie ['tsɔmbi] M **-(s), -s** *(lit, fig)* zombie

Zo|ne ['tso:nə] F **-, -n** zone; *(von Fahrkarte)* fare stage; *(fig: von Misstrauen etc)* area; **blaue ~** *(in Straßenverkehr)* restricted parking area; **die ~** *(old inf: = DDR)* the Eastern Zone, East Germany

Zo|nen-: **Zo|nen|gren|ze** F zonal border; **die ehemalige ~** *(zur DDR)* the former border (with East Germany); **Zo|nen|rand|ge|biet** NT *(Hist)* border area (with East Germany); **Zo|nen|ta|rif** M *(= Fahrgeld) fare for a journey within a fare stage (Post, Telec)* zonal charge; **Zo|nen|zeit** F zonal time

Zoo [tso:] M **-s, -s** zoo; **gestern waren wir im ~** we went to the zoo yesterday

Zoo|hand|lung F pet shop

Zoo|lo|ge [tsoo'lo:gə] M **-n, -n**, **Zoo|lo|gin** [-'lo:gın] F **-, -nen** zoologist

Zoo|lo|gie [tsoolo'gi:] F **-**, *no pl* zoology

zoo|lo|gisch [tsoo'lo:gıʃ] ADJ zoological ADV zoologically

Zoom [zu:m] NT **-s, -s** zoom shot; *(= Objektiv)* zoom lens

zoo|men ['zu:mən] VT to zoom in on VI to zoom (in)

Zoom|ob|jek|tiv ['zu:m-] NT zoom lens

Zo|on po|li|ti|kon ['tso:ɔn politi'kɔn] NT **-**, *no pl* political animal

Zoo|wär|ter(in) M(F) zoo keeper

Zopf [tsɔpf] M **-(e)s, =e** ['tsœpfə] **a** *(= Haartracht)* pigtail, plait, braid *(esp US)*; **Zöpfe tragen** to wear one's hair in pigtails; **das Haar in Zöpfe flechten** to plait *or* braid *(esp US)* one's hair; **ein alter ~(, der abgeschnitten werden müsste)** *(fig)* an antiquated custom (that should be done away with) **b** *(= Gebäck)* plait, plaited loaf **c** *(= Baumwipfel)* tree top

Zopf-: **Zopf|band** [-bant] NT *pl* **-bänder** hair ribbon; **Zopf|mus|ter** NT cable stitch; **Zopf|span|ge** F clip

Zo|res ['tso:rəs] M **-**, *no pl (dial)* **a** *(= Ärger, Streit)* trouble, argy-bargy *(Brit inf)*, a ruckus *(US inf)* **b** *(= Gesindel)* rabble

Zorn [tsɔrn] M **-(e)s**, *no pl* anger, rage, wrath *(liter)*; **der ~ Gottes** the wrath of God; **jds ~ fürchten** to fear sb's anger *or* wrath; **jds ~ heraufbeschwören** to incur sb's wrath; **jdn in ~ bringen** to anger *or* enrage sb; **wenn ihn der ~ überkommt** when he becomes angry, when he loses his temper; **in ~ geraten** *or* **ausbrechen** to fly into a rage, to lose one's temper; **der ~ packte ihn** he became angry, he flew into a rage; **im ~** in a rage, in anger; **in gerechtem ~** in righteous anger; **einen ~ auf jdn haben** to be furious with sb

Zorn-: **Zorn|ader** F = **Zornesader**

Zorn|aus|bruch M fit of anger *or* rage

Zor|nes-: **Zor|nes|ader** F **auf seiner Stirn schwoll eine ~** he was so angry you could see the veins standing out on his forehead; **Zor|nes|aus|bruch** M fit of anger *or* rage; **Zor|nes|fal|te** F angry furrow *(on one's forehead)*; **Zor|nes|rö|te** F flush of anger; **Zor|nes|trä|nen** PL tears *pl* of rage

zor|nig ['tsɔrnıç] ADJ angry, furious; **(leicht) ~ werden** to lose one's temper (easily); **auf jdn ~ sein** to be angry *or* furious with sb; **ein ~er junger Mann** *(fig)* an angry young man ADV angrily, furiously

zo|ro|ast|risch [tsoro'astrıʃ] ADJ zoroastrian

Zo|te ['tso:tə] F **-, -n** dirty joke

zo|tig ['tso:tıç] ADJ dirty, filthy, smutty

Zot|te ['tsɔtə] F **-, -n** **a** *(Anat)* villus **b** *(= Haarsträhne)* rat's tail *(inf)*

Zot|tel ['tsɔtl] F **-, -n** *(inf)* rat's tail *(inf)*; *(an Mütze)* pompom

Zot|tel|haar NT *(inf)* shaggy hair

zot|te|lig ['tsɔtəlıç] ADJ *(inf) Haar, Fell* shaggy

zot|teln ['tsɔtln] VI *aux sein (inf)* to amble

Zot|tel|trab M gentle trot

zot|tig ['tsɔtıç] ADJ **a** *Fell, Tier* shaggy **b** *(Anat)* villous, villose

ZPO [tsetpe:'lo:] *abbr von* **Zivilprozessordnung**

z. T. *abbr von* **zum Teil**

Ztr. *abbr von* **Zentner**

zu [tsu:]

1 PRÄPOSITION	3 ADJEKTIV
2 ADVERB	4 BINDEWORT

1 – PRÄPOSITION *(+dat)*

a [örtlich: Richtung, Ziel] to; **zum Bahnhof** to the station; **zur Stadt gehen** to go to town; **zur Stadtmitte gehen** to go to the town centre *(Brit) or* center *(US)*; **zum Bäcker/Arzt gehen** to go to the baker's/doctor's; **zum Theater gehen** *(beruflich)* to go on the stage; **zum Militär gehen, zu den Soldaten gehen** to join the army, to join up; **bis zu** as far as; **(bis) zum Bahnhof sind es 5 km** it's 5 kms to the station; **zum Meer hin** toward(s) the sea; **zum Himmel weisen** to point heavenwards; **zur Decke sehen** to look up at the ceiling; **zu jdm/etw hinaufsehen** to look up at sb/sth; **zu jdm herübersehen/hinübersehen** to look across at sb; **sie wandte sich zu ihm hin** she turned to him; **sie sah zu ihm hin** she looked toward(s) him; **die Tür zum Keller** the door to the cellar; **sich zu Tisch setzen** *(geh)* to sit down at the table; **sich zu jdm setzen** to sit down next to *or* beside sb; **setz dich doch zu uns** come and sit with us; **etw zu sich stecken** to take sth; **zum Fenster herein/hinaus** in (at)/out of the window; **zur Tür hinaus/herein** out of/in the door; **das Zimmer liegt zur Straße hin** the room looks out onto the street

b [örtlich: Lage] *bei Stadt* in; **zu Frankfurt** *(old)* in Frankfurt; **der Dom zu Köln** the cathedral in Cologne, Cologne cathedral; **der Reichstag zu Worms** *(Hist)* the Diet of Worms; **zu Hause** at home; **zu seiner Linken saß ...** *(geh)* on his left sat ...; **zu beiden Seiten (des Hauses)** on both sides (of the house); **zu Lande und zu Wasser** on land and sea; **jdm zur Seite stehen** to stand beside sb; **jdm zur Seite sitzen** *(geh)* to sit at sb's side

c [zeitlich] at; **zu früher/später Stunde** at an early/late hour; **zu Mittag** *(= am Mittag)* at midday *or* noon; *(= bis Mittag)* by midday *or* noon; **zu Ostern** at Easter; **letztes Jahr zu Weihnachten** last Christmas; **(bis) zum 15. April/Donnerstag/Abend** until 15th April/Thursday/(this) evening; *(= nicht später als)* by 15th April/Thursday/(this) evening; **zum Wochenende hat sich Besuch angesagt** we're having visitors at the weekend; **die Zahlung ist zum 15. April fällig** the payment is due on 15th April; **zum 31. Mai kündigen** to give in *(Brit) or* turn in *(US)* one's notice for 31st May → **Anfang, Schluss, Zeit**

d [Zusammengehörigkeit, Begleitung, Zusatz] **Wein zum Essen trinken** to drink wine with one's meal; **der Deckel zu diesem Topf** the lid for this pan; **nehmen Sie Milch zum Kaffee?** do you take milk in your coffee?; **zur Gitarre singen** to sing to *(Brit) or* with *(US)* a/the guitar; **Lieder zur Laute** songs accompanied by the lute; **die Melodie zu dem Lied** the tune of the song; **Vorwort/Anmerkungen zu etw** preface/notes to sth; **zu dem kommt noch, dass ich ...** on top of that I ...; **etw zu etw tragen** *(Kleidung)* to wear sth with sth; **etw zu etw legen** to put sth with sth

e [Zweck, Bestimmung] for; **Wasser zum Waschen** water for washing; **Papier zum Schreiben** paper to write on, writing paper; **ein Bett zum Schlafen** a bed to sleep in; **der Knopf zum Abstellen** the off button; **Stoff zu einem Kleid** material for a dress; **die Luke zum Einsteigen** the entrance hatch; **das Zeichen zum Aufbruch** the signal to leave; **etw zur Antwort geben** to say sth in reply; **zur Einführung ...** by way of (an) introduction ...; **zu seiner Entschuldigung muss man sagen ...** in his defence *(Brit) or* defense *(US)* one must say ...; **zu seiner Entschuldigung sagte er ...** by way of apology he said ...; **zur Erklärung** by way of explanation; **er sagte das nur zu ihrer Beruhigung** he said that just to set her mind at rest; **zu nichts taugen, zu nichts zu gebrauchen sein** to be no use to anyone *(inf)*

f [Anlass] **etw zum Geburtstag/zu Weihnachten bekommen** to get sth for one's birthday/for Christmas; **ein Geschenk zum Hochzeitstag** a wedding anniversary present; **zu Ihrem 60. Geburtstag** on your 60th birthday; **jdm zu etw gratulieren** to congratulate sb on sth; **jdn zum Essen einladen** to invite sb for a meal; **zu Ihrem schweren Verlust** on your sad loss; **Ausstellung zum Jahrestag der Revolution** exhibition to mark the anniversary of the revolution; **zu dieser Frage möchte ich Folgendes sagen** my reply to this question is as follows, on this I would like to say the following; **was sagen Sie zu diesen Preisen?** what do you think of these prices?; **zum Thema Gleichberechtigung** on the subject of equal rights; **eine Rede zu Schillers Todestag** a speech on the anniversary of Schiller's death; **„Zum Realismusbegriff"** "On the Concept of Realism"; **jdn zu etw vernehmen** to question sb about sth

g [Folge, Umstand] **zu seinem Besten** for his own good; **zum Glück** luckily; **zu meiner Schande/Freude** *etc* to my shame/joy *etc*; **es ist zum Lachen** it's really funny; **es ist zum Weinen** it's enough to make you cry, it makes you want to cry

h Mittel, Art und Weise **zu Fuß/Pferd** on foot/horseback; **zu Schiff** by ship; **zu Deutsch** in German; **etw zu einem hohen Preis verkaufen** to sell sth at a high price; **etw zu einem hohen Preis versteigern** to bid up the price of sth

i Veränderung into; **zu etw werden** to turn into sth; *(Mensch auch)* to become sth; **Leder zu Handtaschen verarbeiten** to make handbags out of leather; **jdn/etw zu etw machen** to make sb/sth (into) sth; **jdn zum Mann machen** to make a man of sb; **zu Asche verbrennen** to burn to ashes; **wieder zu Staub werden** to return to dust; **etw zu Pulver zermahlen** to grind sth into powder; **sie ist zu einer wahren Schönheit herangewachsen** she has grown up into a real beauty; **jdn zum Major befördern** to promote sb to (the rank of) major

j = als as; **jdn zum König wählen** to choose sb as king; **jdn zu etw ernennen** to nominate sb sth; **er machte mich zu seinem Stellvertreter** he made me his deputy; **jdn zum Freund haben** to have sb as a friend; **er machte sie zu seiner Frau, er nahm sie zur Frau** he made her his wife; **zum Künstler geboren sein** to be born to be an artist → **Vorbild**

k Verhältnis, Beziehung **Liebe zu jdm** love for sb; **aus Freundschaft zu jdm** because of one's friendship with sb; **Vertrauen zu jdm/etw** trust in sb/sth; **meine Beziehung zu ihm** my relationship with him

l in Vergleichen **im Vergleich zu** in comparison with, compared with; **im Verhältnis drei zu zwei** *(Math)* in the ratio (of) three to two; **Wasser und Saft im Verhältnis drei zu eins mischen** take three parts water to one of juice; **drei zu zwei** *(Sport)* three-two; **das Spiel steht 3 zu 2** *or* *(geschrieben)* **3:2** the score is 3-2 *or* *(gesprochen)* three-two; **wir haben 4 zu 3 gewonnen** we won 4-3 → **Verhältnis**

m bei Zahlenangaben **zu zwei Prozent** at two per cent *(Brit)* *or* percent *(US)*; **wir verkaufen die Gläser jetzt das Stück zu 99 Cent** we're selling the glasses now at *or* for 99 cents each; **fünf (Stück) zu 80 Cent** five for 80 cents; **zu zwei Dritteln (gefüllt)** two-thirds (full); **zum halben Preis** at half price; **die Arbeit ist schon zur Hälfte getan** the work is already half done; **zum ersten Mal(e)** for the first time; **zum Ersten ..., zum Zweiten ...** *(Aufzählung)* first ..., second ...; **zum Ersten, zum Zweiten, zum Dritten** *(bei Auktion)* for the first time, for the second time, for the third time → **vier, bis**

n mit Fragepronomen **zu wem wollen Sie?** who do you want?; **zu wem gehen Sie?** who are you going to see?; **zu wem sprechen Sie morgen bei der Konferenz?** who will you be speaking to *or* who will you be addressing at the conference tomorrow?; **zu was** *(inf)* *(Zweck)* for what; *(= warum)* why

o bei Namen **der Graf zu Ehrenstein** the Count of Ehrenstein; **Gasthof zum goldenen Löwen** the Golden Lion (Inn)

p getrenntes „dazu" *inf* **da komme ich nicht zu** I can't get (a)round to it → **dazu**

q andere Wendungen **zum Beispiel** for example; **zu Hilfe!** help!; **jdm zu Hilfe kommen** to come to sb's aid; **zu jds Gedächtnis** in memory of sb; **zum Gedächtnis von jdm** in sb's memory; **zum Lobe von jdm/etw** in praise of sb/sth; **zur Strafe** as a punishment; **zur Belohnung** as a reward; **zur Warnung** as a warning; **zur Beurteilung/Einsicht** for inspection; **zur Probe/Ansicht** on trial/approval; **zur Unterschrift** for signature

2 – ADVERB

a = allzu too; **zu sehr** too much; **sie liebte ihn zu sehr, als dass sie ihn verraten hätte** she loved him too much to betray him; **zu verliebt** too much in love; **das war einfach zu dumm!** *(inf)* it was so stupid!; **ich wäre zu gern mitgekommen** I'd have loved to come

b = geschlossen shut, closed; **auf/zu** *(an Hähnen etc)* on/off; **Tür zu!** *(inf)* shut the door; **die Geschäfte haben jetzt zu** the shops are shut *or* closed now

c = los, weiter *inf* **dann mal zu!** right, off we go!; **du wolltest mir was vorsingen, dann mal zu** you wanted to sing me something? OK, go ahead; **immer** *or* **nur zu!** just keep on!; **ihr seid auf dem richtigen Wege, nur zu!** you're on the right track, just keep going; **schreie nur zu, es hilft doch nichts!** scream then, but it won't do any good!; **mach zu!** get a move on!; **lauft schon zu, ich komme nach** you go on, I'll catch you up

d örtlich toward(s); **nach hinten zu** toward(s) the back; **auf den Wald zu** toward(s) the forest; **dem Ausgang zu** toward(s) the exit → **ab**

3 – ADJEKTIV

(= geschlossen, inf) Tür, Geschäft, Kiste etc shut; *Kleid, Verschluss* done up; **die zue** *or* **zune Tür** *(strictly incorrect)* the shut door → **zu sein**

4 – BINDEWORT

a mit Infinitiv to; **etw zu essen** sth to eat; **der Fußboden ist noch zu fegen** the floor still has to be swept; **er hat zu gehorchen** he has to do as he's told; **jdm befehlen** *or* **den Auftrag erteilen, etw zu tun** to order sb to do sth; **das Material ist noch/nicht mehr zu gebrauchen** the material is still/is no longer usable; **diese Rechnung ist bis Montag zu bezahlen** this bill has to be paid by Monday; **zu stehen kommen** to come to a stop; **zu liegen kommen** to come to rest; **ich habe noch zu arbeiten** I have still got *(esp Brit)* *or* I still have some work to do; **ohne es zu wissen** without knowing it; **um besser sehen zu können** in order to see better; **ich komme, um mich zu verabschieden** I've come to say goodbye

b mit Partizip **noch zu bezahlende Rechnungen** outstanding bills; **nicht zu unterschätzende Probleme** problems (that are) not to be underestimated; **das sind alles nur winzige, leicht zu übersehende Punkte** these are just small points that can easily be overlooked; **der zu prüfende Kandidat, der zu Prüfende** the candidate to be examined

---

zu|al|ler-: **zu|al|ler|al|ler|letzt** [tsu'alɐ'lalɐ'lɛtst] ADV *(inf)* very last of all; **zu|al|ler|erst** [tsu'lalɐ'le:ɐst] ADV first of all; **zu|al|ler|letzt** [tsu'lalɐ'lɛtst] ADV last of all

zu+ar|bei|ten VI *sep* **jdm ~** to do sb's groundwork

zu+bau|en VT *sep Lücke* to fill in; *Platz, Gelände* to build up; *Blick* to block with buildings/a building

Zu|be|hör ['tsu:bəhø:ɐ] NT OR M **-(e)s,** *(rare)* **-e** equipment *no pl*; *(= Zusatzgeräte, Autozubehör)* accessories *pl*; *(= Zubehörteil)* attachments *pl*, accessories *pl*; *(zur Kleidung; in Windows®)* accessories *pl*; **Küche mit allem ~** fully equipped kitchen

Zu|be|hör-: **Zu|be|hör|han|del** M accessories trade; **Zu|be|hör|teil** NT accessory, attachment

zu+bei|ßen VI *sep irreg* to bite; *(beim Zahnarzt)* to bite (one's teeth) together; **der Hund fasste mich am Bein und biss zu** the dog got hold of my leg and sank his teeth into it

zu+be|kom|men *ptp* **zubekommen** VT *sep irreg* *(inf) Kleidung* to get done up; *Koffer auch, Tür, Fenster* to get shut *or* closed

zu|be|nannt ['tsu:bənant] ADJ *(liter)* also called

Zu|ber ['tsu:bɐ] M **-s, -** (wash)tub

zu+be|rei|ten *ptp* **zubereitet** VT *sep Essen* to prepare; *Arznei auch* to make up; *Cocktail* to mix

Zu|be|rei|tung F **a** *no pl* preparation; *(von Cocktail)* mixing; **eine neue ~ für Blumenkohl** a new way of preparing cauliflower **b** *(= Präparat)* preparation

Zu|be|rei|tungs|zeit F preparation time

zu+be|to|nie|ren *ptp* **zubetoniert** VT *sep Loch, Spalt etc* to concrete over, to cement over; *(pej) Landschaft* to concrete over

Zu|bett|ge|hen [tsu'bɛtge:ən] NT **vor dem ~** before (going to) bed; **beim ~** on going to bed; **nach dem ~** after going to bed

zu+bie|gen VT *sep irreg* to bend shut

zu+bil|li|gen VT *sep* **jdm etw ~** to grant sb sth, to allow sb sth; **jdm mildernde Umstände ~** to recognize that there are/were mitigating circumstances for sb; **ich will ihm gerne ~, dass er sich bemüht hat** he certainly made an effort, I'll grant *or* allow him that

zu+bin|den VT *sep irreg* to tie up, to do up; *Schuhe auch* to lace up; **jdm die Augen ~** to blindfold sb

zu+blei|ben VI *sep irreg aux sein (inf)* to stay shut

zu+blin|zeln VI *sep* **jdm ~** to wink at sb

zu+brin|gen VT *sep irreg* **a** *(= verbringen)* to spend **b** *(= herbeibringen)* to bring to, to take to; **jdm ~, dass ...** *(fig)* to inform sb that ...; **es ist mir zugebracht worden** *(fig)* it has been brought to my notice *or* attention, I have been informed **c** *(inf: = zumachen können) Kiste, Koffer, Tür, Fenster* to get shut *or* closed; *Knöpfe, Reißverschluss, Kleidung* to get done up

Zu|brin|ger ['tsu:brɪŋɐ] M **-s, - a** *(Tech)* conveyor **b** *(= Straße)* feeder road **c** *(auch* **Zubringerbus**) shuttle (bus); *(zum Flughafen)* airport bus; *(auch* **Zubringerflugzeug**) feeder plane

Zu|brin|ger-: **Zu|brin|ger|dienst** M shuttle service; **Zu|brin|ger|flug** M feeder flight; **Zu|brin|ger|li|nie** F feeder route; **Zu|brin|ger|stra|ße** F feeder road

Zu|brot NT, *no pl (= zusätzlicher Verdienst)* extra income; **ein kleines ~ verdienen** to earn *or* make a bit on the side *(inf)*

zu+but|tern VT *sep (inf) (= zuschießen)* to contribute, to add on; *(= zuzüglich bezahlen)* to pay out (on top); *(= dazuverdienen)* to add on; **zu seinem Gehalt etwas ~** to boost *or* to up *(inf)* one's salary a bit

Zuc|chi|ni [tsʊ'ki:ni] F **-, -** courgette *(Brit)*, zucchini *(US)*

Zucht [tsʊxt] F **-, -en a** *(= Disziplin)* discipline; **~ und Ordnung** discipline; **jdn in strenge ~ nehmen** *(liter)* to take sb firmly in hand; **jdn in ~ halten** to keep a tight rein on sb **b** *no pl (= Aufzucht, das Züchten) (von Tieren)* breeding; *(von Pflanzen)* growing, cultivation; *(von Bakterien, Perlen)* culture; *(von Bienen)* keeping; **Tiere zur ~ halten** to keep animals for breeding; **die ~ von Pferden** horse breeding; **die ~ von Bienen** beekeeping **c** *(= Zuchtgeneration) (von Tieren)* breed, stock; *(von Pflanzen)* stock, variety; *(von Bakterien, Perlen)* culture

Zucht-: **Zucht|buch** NT studbook; **Zucht|bul|le** M breeding bull; **Zucht|eber** M breeding boar

züch|ten ['tsʏçtn] VT *Tiere, Menschen* to breed; *Bienen* to keep; *Pflanzen* to grow, to cultivate; *Perlen, Bakterien* to cultivate; *Kristalle* to grow, to synthesize; *(fig) Hass* to breed

Züch|ter ['tsʏçtɐ] M **-s, -**, **Züch|te|rin** [-ərɪn] F **-, -nen** *(von Tieren)* breeder; *(von Pflanzen)* grower, cultivator; *(von Bienen)* keeper; *(von Perlen, Bakterien)* culturist

Zucht|haus NT *(= Gebäude)* prison *(for serious offenders)*, penitentiary *(US)*; **zu 7 Jahren ~ verurteilt werden** to be sentenced to 7 years' in prison *or* 7 years' imprisonment; **dafür bekommt man ~, darauf steht ~** you'll go to prison for that

Zucht|häus|ler [-hɔyslɐ] M **-s, -**, **Zucht|häus|le|rin** [-ərɪn] F **-, -nen** *(inf)* convict, con *(inf)*

Zucht|haus|stra|fe F prison sentence

Zucht|hengst M stud horse, breeding stallion

züch|tig ['tsʏçtɪç] *(liter)* ADJ *(= keusch, anständig) Mädchen* modest, chaste; *Wangen* innocent; *Augen, Benehmen, Kleidung* modest; *(= tugendhaft)* virtuous ADV modestly; *(= tugendhaft)* virtuously
züch|ti|gen ['tsʏçtɪgn] VT *(geh)* to beat; *(stärker, Jur)* to flog; *Schüler* to use corporal punishment on *(form)*, ≈ to cane
Züch|tig|keit F -, *no pl (liter)* modesty, chasteness
Züch|ti|gung F -, -en beating; *(stärker, Jur)* flogging; *(von Schüler)* ≈ caning; **körperliche ~** corporal punishment
Züch|ti|gungs|recht NT right to use corporal punishment
Zucht-: **zucht|los** ADJ *(dated)* undisciplined; **Zucht|meis|ter(in)** M(F) *(liter)* disciplinarian; **Zucht|mit|tel** NT *(old)* disciplinary measure; **Zucht|per|le** F cultured pearl; **Zucht|ru|te** F *(fig)* rod; **unter jds ~** *(dat)* **stehen** to be under sb's rod; **Zucht|stier** M breeding bull; **Zucht|stu|te** F brood mare, breeding mare; **Zucht|tier** NT breeding animal, animal for breeding
Züch|tung ['tsʏçtʊŋ] F -, -en **a** *(von Tieren)* breeding; *(von Bienen)* keeping; *(von Pflanzen)* growing; *(von Kristallen)* synthesis **b** *(= Zuchtart) (Pflanzen)* strain, variety; *(Tiere)* breed
Zucht-: **Zucht|vieh** NT breeding cattle; **Zucht|wahl** F selective breeding; **natürliche ~** natural selection
zuck [tsʊk] INTERJ → **ruck, zuck**
Zuck [tsʊk] M -s, *no pl (= Körperbewegung)* sudden movement; *(mit Augenlidern)* flutter; *(beim Reißen)* jerk, tug, yank; *(beim Ziehen)* jerk, tug
zu|ckeln ['tsʊkln] VI *aux sein (inf)* to jog; **er zuckelte müde hinter den anderen drein** he trotted wearily along behind the others
Zu|ckel|trab M jog trot; **im ~** at a jog trot
zu|cken ['tsʊkn] VI **a** *(nervös, krampfhaft)* to twitch; *(vor Schreck)* to start; *(vor Schmerzen)* to flinch; *(Fisch, verwundetes Tier)* to thrash about; **er zuckte ständig mit dem Mund** his mouth kept twitching; **mit den Schultern** *or* **Achseln ~** to shrug (one's shoulders); **es zuckte um ihre Mundwinkel** the corner of her mouth twitched; **ein Lächeln zuckte um ihren Mund** a smile played around her lips; **es zuckte mir in den Fingern, das zu tun** *(fig)* I was itching to do that; **es zuckte mir in der Hand** *(fig)* I was itching to hit him/her → **Wimper a**
b *(= aufleuchten) (Blitz)* to flash; *(Flammen)* to flare up; **die ~den Flammen** the flames flaring up
c *(= wehtun)* **der Schmerz zuckte (mir) durch den ganzen Körper** the pain shot right through my body *or* through me; **es zuckte mir im Knie** *(inf)* I had a twinge in my knee
VT **die Achseln** *or* **Schultern ~** to shrug (one's shoulders)
zü|cken ['tsʏkn] VT *Messer, Pistole* to pull out; *Schwert* to draw; *(inf: = hervorziehen) Notizbuch, Bleistift, Brieftasche* to pull *or* take out
Zu|cker ['tsʊkɐ] M -s, *no pl* **a** sugar; **ein Stück ~** a lump of sugar, a sugar lump *(esp Brit) or* cube; **du bist doch nicht aus** *or* **von ~!** *(inf)* don't be such a softie! *(inf)* **b** *(Med) (= Zuckergehalt)* sugar; *(= Krankheit)* diabetes *sing*; **~ haben** *(inf)* to be a diabetic; **bei ~ muss Insulin gespritzt werden** diabetics need insulin injections
Zu|cker-: **Zu|cker|bä|cker(in)** M(F) *(old, S Ger, Aus)* confectioner; **Zu|cker|bä|cke|rei** F *(old, S Ger, Aus)* confectioner's (shop); **Zu|cker|bä|cker|stil** M wedding-cake style; **Zu|cker|brot** NT *(obs)* sweetmeat *(old)*; **mit ~ und Peitsche** *(prov)* with a stick and a carrot
Zu|cker|chen ['tsʊkɐçən] NT -s, -, **Zü|cker|chen** ['tsʏkɐçən] NT -s, - *(dial: = Bonbon)* sweet *(esp Brit)*, candy *(US)***Zu|cker-**: **Zu|cker|cou|leur** F, *no pl (Cook)* caramel; **Zu|cker|do|se** F sugar basin *or* bowl; **Zu|cker|erb|se** F mangetout (pea) *(Brit)*, sweet pea *(US)*; **zu|cker|frei** ADJ sugar-free; **Zu|cker|früch|te** PL crystallized fruits *pl*; **Zu|cker|ge|halt** M sugar content; **Zu|cker|gla|sur** F → **Zuckerguss**; **Zu|cker|guss** M icing, frosting *(esp US)*; **mit ~ überziehen** to ice, to frost; **ein Kuchen mit ~** an iced *or* a frosted cake; **zu|cker|hal|tig** ADJ containing sugar; **diese Hustenbonbons sind ~** these cough sweets contain sugar; **Zu|cker|hut** M sugarloaf; **der ~ in Rio** the Sugar Loaf Mountain in Rio
zu|cke|rig ['tsʊkərɪç] ADJ sugary
Zu|cker-: **Zu|cker|kand** [-kant] M -(e)s [-dəs], *no pl*, **Zu|cker|kan|dis** M rock *(Brit)*, rock candy *(esp US)*; **zu|cker|krank** ADJ diabetic; **Zu|cker|kran|ke(r)** MF *decl as adj* diabetic; **Zu|cker|krank|heit** F diabetes *sing*
Zu|ckerl ['tsʊkɐl] NT -s, -(n) *(S Ger, Aus)* sweet *(esp Brit)*, candy *(US)*
Zu|cker-: **Zu|cker|le|cken** NT **das ist kein ~** *(inf)* it's no picnic *(inf)*; **Zu|cker|lö|sung** F sugar solution; **Zu|cker|mais** M sweetcorn; **Zu|cker|me|lo|ne** F muskmelon
zu|ckern ['tsʊkɐn] VT to sugar, to put sugar in; **zu stark gezuckert sein** to have too much sugar in it
Zu|cker-: **Zu|cker|plan|ta|ge** F sugar plantation; **Zu|cker|plätz|chen** NT *(= Bonbon)* sweet *(Brit)*, candy *(US)*; *(= Keks)* sugar-coated biscuit *(Brit) or* cookie *(US)*; **Zu|cker|pup|pe** F *(dated inf)* sweetie *(inf)*; *(als Anrede auch)* sugar *(inf)*, sweetie-pie *(inf)*; **Zu|cker|raf|fi|na|de** F refined sugar; **Zu|cker|raf|fi|ne|rie** F sugar refinery; **Zu|cker|rohr** NT sugar cane; **Zu|cker|rü|be** F sugar beet; **Zu|cker|schle|cken** NT **das ist kein ~** *(inf)* it's no picnic *(inf)*; **Zu|cker|spie|gel** M *(Med)* (blood) sugar level; **Zu|cker|stan|ge** F stick of rock *(Brit) or* candy *(US)*; **Zu|cker|streu|er** M sugar sprinkler; **zu|cker|süß** ADJ *(lit, fig)* sugar-sweet, as sweet as sugar; **Zu|cker|was|ser** NT, *no pl* sugar(ed) water; **Zu|cker|wat|te** F candy floss; **Zu|cker|werk** NT sweets *pl (esp Brit)*, candies *pl (US)*; **Zu|cker|wür|fel** M sugar cube; **Zu|cker|zan|ge** F sugar tongs *pl*; **Zu|cker|zeug** NT *(pej)* sweet stuff; **Zu|cker|zu|satz** M **ohne ~** without *or* with no added sugar; *(auf Verpackung)* no added sugar
zuck|rig ['tsʊkrɪç] ADJ = **zuckerig**
Zu|ckung ['tsʊkʊŋ] F -, -en *(= nervöse Zuckung)* twitch; *(von Muskeln auch)* spasm; *(von Augenlidern auch)* flutter; *(stärker: krampfhaft)* convulsion; *(von sterbendem Tier)* convulsive movement; **die letzten ~en** *(lit, fig)* the death throes
Zu|de|cke F *(dial)* cover *(on bed)*
zu+de|cken VT *sep* to cover; *jdn, Beine auch* to cover up; *(im Bett)* to tuck up *or* in; *Gestorbenen, Grube, Fleck* to cover (up *or* over); **jdn/sich (mit etw) ~** to cover sb/oneself up (with sth); to tuck sb/oneself up (in sth)
zu|dem [tsu'deːm] ADV *(geh)* moreover, furthermore, in addition
zu+den|ken VT *sep irreg (geh)* **jdm etw ~** to intend *or* destine sth for sb; **das Schicksal hatte mir schwere Schläge zugedacht** Fate had some cruel blows in store for me; **jdm zugedacht sein** to be intended *or* destined *or* earmarked for sb; *(Geschenk)* to be intended *or* meant for sb; **dieses Glück war uns aber offenbar nicht zugedacht** but we were evidently not destined to be so lucky
zu+dik|tie|ren *ptp* **zudiktiert** VT *sep (inf) Strafe* to hand out
Zu|drang M, *no pl (rare)* = **Andrang a**
zu+dre|hen *sep* VT *Wasserhahn etc* to turn off; *(= zuwenden)* to turn (+*dat* to) VR to turn (+*dat* to)
zu|dring|lich ADJ *Art* pushing, pushy *(inf)*; *Nachbarn* intrusive; **dieser ~e Kerl** this guy who's always forcing himself upon her/me *etc*; **~ werden** *(zu einer Frau)* to make advances *(zu* to)
Zu|dring|lich|keit F **seine ~ (gegenüber jdm)** his way of forcing himself upon sb
zu+dröh|nen *(sl)* VT **jdn (voll) ~** *(mit Drogen)* to dose *or* dope sb up *(inf)*; *(mit Alkohol)* to get sb tanked up *(inf)*; **er war total zugedröhnt** *(mit Drogen)* he was doped up to the eyeballs *(inf)*; *(mit Alkohol)* he was completely tanked up *(inf)* *or* loaded *(inf)* VR *(mit Drogen)* to dose *or* dope oneself up *(inf)*; *(mit Alkohol)* to get tanked up *(inf)*; *(inf: mit Musik)* to blow *(Brit) or* blast one's head off *(inf)*
zu+drü|cken VT *sep* to press shut; *Tür auch* to push shut; **jdm die Kehle ~** to throttle sb; **einem Toten die Augen ~** to close a dead person's eyes → **Auge a**
zu+eig|nen VT *sep (geh) Buch, Gedicht* to dedicate (*jdm* to sb)
Zu|eig|nung F *(geh: von Gedicht, Buch)* dedication
zu+ei|len VI *sep aux sein (geh)* **auf jdn ~** to rush *or* hurry toward(s) sb *or (bis zu jdm)* up to sb; **auf etw** *(acc)* **~** to hurry *or* rush toward(s)/up to sth
zu|ei|nan|der [tsuˈlaiˈnandɐ] ADV *(= gegenseitig)* to each other, to one another; *Vertrauen haben* in each other, in one another; *(= zusammen)* together; **~ passen** = **zueinanderpassen**
zu|ei|nan|der-: **zu|ei|nan|der+fin|den** *sep irreg*, **zu|ei|nan|der fin|den** △ *irreg* VI to find common ground; *(= sich versöhnen)* to be reconciled; **zu|ei|nan|der+ge|sel|len** , **zu|ei|nan|der ge|sel|len** △ VR *(geh)* to join each other; *(fig)* to be combined; **zu|ei|nan|der+pas|sen** *sep*, **zu|ei|nan|der pas|sen** *irreg* VI to go together; *(Menschen)* to suit each other *or* one another, to be suited, to be well matched; **Braun und Grün passen gut zueinander** brown and green go together well *or* go well together; **zu|ei|nan|der+ste|hen** *sep irreg*, **zu|ei|nan|der ste|hen** △ VI *irreg (geh)* to stick *or* stay together
zu+er|ken|nen *ptp* **zuerkannt** VT *sep irreg Preis* to award (*jdm* to sb); *Würde, Auszeichnung, Orden auch* to confer, to bestow (*jdm* on sb); *Sieg auch, Recht* to grant, to accord (*jdm etw* sb sth); *(vor Gericht) Entschädigung, Rente etc* to award (*jdm etw* sb sth); *Strafe* to impose, to inflict (*jdm* (up)on sb); **das Gemälde wurde dem höchsten Bieter zuerkannt** the painting went to the highest bidder; **ihm wurde der Preis zuerkannt** he was awarded the prize; **jdm eine Rolle ~** to award *or* grant sb a role
Zu|er|ken|nung F *(von Preis, Entschädigung, Rente)* awarding; *(von Würde, Orden auch)* conferring, bestowing; *(von Sieg auch, von Recht)* granting, accordance; *(von Strafe)* imposition
zu|erst [tsu'leːɐst] ADV **a** *(= als Erster)* first; **ich kam ~ an** I was (the) first to arrive, I arrived first; **wollen wir ~ essen?** shall we eat first?; **~ an die Reihe kommen** to be first; **~ bin ich Geschäftsmann, dann Privatmann** I am first and foremost a businessman, and only then a private individual; **das muss ich morgen früh ~ machen** I must do that first thing tomorrow (morning), I must do that first thing in the morning → **kommen a**
b *(= zum ersten Mal)* first, for the first time
c *(= anfangs)* at first; **er sprach ~ gar nicht** at first he didn't speak at all; **~ muss man ...** to begin *or* start with you have to ..., first (of all) you have to ...
zu+er|tei|len *ptp* **zuerteilt** VT *sep* = **zuerkennen**
zu+fä|cheln VT *sep (geh)* to fan; **sich/jdm Kühlung ~** to fan oneself/sb
zu+fah|ren VI *sep irreg aux sein* **a** **auf jdn ~** *(mit Kfz)* to drive toward(s) sb; *(mit Fahrrad)* to ride toward(s) sb; *(direkt)* to drive/ride up to sb; **auf etw** *(acc)* **~** to drive/ride toward(s) sth, to head for sth; **er kam genau auf mich zugefahren** he drove/rode straight at *or* for me **b** *(= weiterfahren, losfahren)* **fahren Sie doch zu!** go on then!, get a move on then! *(inf)* **c** *(Tür: = plötzlich schließen)* to slide shut

Zu|fahrt F approach (road); *(= Einfahrt)* entrance; *(zu einem Haus)* drive(way); **„keine ~ zum Krankenhaus"** "no access to hospital"

Zu|fahrts|stra|ße F access road; *(zur Autobahn)* approach road

Zu|fall M chance, accident; *(= Zusammentreffen)* coincidence; **das ist ~** it's pure chance; **durch ~** (quite) by chance *or* accident; **ich habe durch ~ gesehen, wie er das Geld in die Tasche gesteckt hat** I happened to see him putting the money in his pocket; **per ~** *(inf)* by a (pure) fluke *(inf)*; **per ~ trafen wir uns im Bus** we happened to meet on the bus; **ein merkwürdiger ~** a remarkable *or* strange coincidence; **es war reiner** *or* **purer ~, dass ...** it was pure chance that ...; **es ist kein ~, dass ...** it's no accident that ...; **es war ein glücklicher ~, dass ...** it was lucky that ..., it was a stroke *or* bit of luck that ...; **welch ein ~!** what a coincidence!; **wie es der ~ so will** as chance would have it; **der ~ wollte es, dass er ...** by a stroke of luck he ..., as chance would have it he ...; **etw dem ~ überlassen** to leave sth to chance; **etw dem ~ verdanken** to owe sth to chance; **es hängt vom ~ ab, ob ...** it's a matter of chance whether ...

zu+fal|len VI *sep irreg aux sein* **a** *(= sich schließen) (Fenster etc)* to close, to shut; **die Tür fiel laut zu** the door slammed *or* banged shut; **ihm fielen beinahe die Augen zu** he could hardly *or* scarcely keep his eyes open **b jdm ~** *(= zuteilwerden) (Erbe)* to pass to sb, to devolve upon sb *(Jur)*; *(Preis, Geldsumme etc)* to go to sb, to be awarded to sb; *(Aufgabe, Rolle)* to fall to *or* upon sb **c** *(= zukommen)* **diesem Treffen fällt große Bedeutung zu** this meeting is of the utmost importance

zu|fäl|lig ADJ chance *attr*; *Ergebnis auch* accidental; *Zusammentreffen auch* coincidental, accidental; **das war rein ~** it was pure chance, it was purely by chance; **es ist nicht ~, dass er ...** it's no accident that he ...; **das kann doch nicht ~ gewesen sein** that can't have happened by chance; **„Ähnlichkeiten mit lebenden Personen sind rein ~"** ≈ "any similarities with persons living or dead are purely coincidental"

ADV **a** by chance; *(esp bei Zusammentreffen von Ereignissen)* coincidentally; **er ging ~ vorüber** he happened to be passing; **ich traf ihn ~ im Bus** I happened to meet him on the bus, I bumped *or* ran into him on the bus; **das habe ich ganz ~ gesehen** I just happened to see it, I saw it quite by chance *or* accident; **wir haben gestern darüber gesprochen, und heute habe ich ~ einen Artikel darüber gefunden** we were talking about it yesterday, and quite coincidentally I found an article on it today; **wenn Sie das ~ wissen sollten** if you (should) happen to know; **~ auf ein Zitat stoßen** to chance upon a quotation, to happen to find a quotation

b *(in Fragen)* by any chance; **kannst du mir ~ 10 Euro leihen?** can you lend me 10 euros by any chance?

zu|fäl|li|ger|wei|se ['tsu:fɛlɪgɐ'vaizə] ADV = **zufällig ADV**

Zu|fäl|lig|keit F **a** chance nature; *(von Zusammentreffen)* coincidence; **~en** chance happenings **b** *(Statistik)* chance; *(Philos)* contingency

Zu|falls- *in cpds* chance; **Zu|falls|aus|wahl** F random selection; **Zu|falls|be|kannt|schaft** F chance acquaintance; **Zu|falls|fund** M lucky find; **Zu|falls|ge|ne|ra|tor** M random generator; *(für Zahlen)* random-number generator; **Zu|falls|glau|be** M fortuitism; **Zu|falls|prin|zip** NT randomness; **nach dem ~** at random, randomly; **Zu|falls|tor** NT *(Sport)* lucky *or* fluke *(inf)* goal; **Zu|falls|tref|fer** M fluke; **einen ~ machen** to make a lucky choice

zu+fas|sen VI *sep* **a** *(= zugreifen)* to take hold of it/them; *(Hund)* to make a grab; *(fig: = schnell handeln)* to seize *or* grab an/the opportunity **b** *(= helfen)* to lend a hand, to muck in *(Brit inf)*

zu+fa|xen VT *sep* **jdm etw ~** to fax sb sth, to fax sth (through) to sb, to send sb sth by fax

zu+flie|gen VI *sep irreg aux sein* **a auf etw** *(acc)* **~** to fly toward(s) *or (direkt)* into sth; **auf etw** *(acc)* **zugeflogen kommen** to come flying toward(s) sth **b** *+dat* to fly to; **der Vogel ist uns zugeflogen** the bird flew into our house; **„grüner Wellensittich zugeflogen"** "green budgerigar found"; **alle Herzen flogen ihr zu** she won the heart(s) of everyone; **ihm fliegt alles nur so zu** *(fig)* everything comes so easily to him **c** *(inf: Fenster, Tür)* to bang *or* slam shut

zu+flie|ßen VI *sep irreg aux sein +dat* to flow to(wards); *(Süßwasser etc, fig: Geld)* to flow into; **das Wasser wird nie warm, weil immer kaltes zufließt** the water never gets warm because cold water is constantly flowing into it; **jdm Geld ~ lassen** to pour money into sb's coffers

Zu|flucht F refuge *(auch fig)*, shelter *(vor +dat* from); **~ suchen** *(lit, fig)* to seek refuge; **zu etw ~ nehmen** *(fig)* to resort to sth; **zu Lügen ~ nehmen** to take refuge in lying; **du bist meine letzte ~** *(fig)* you are my last hope *or* resort; **er findet ~ in seiner Musik** *(liter)* he finds refuge in his music

Zu|fluchts|ort M *pl* **-orte**, **Zu|fluchts|stät|te** F place of refuge; *(fig auch)* sanctuary

Zu|fluss M **a** *no pl (lit, fig: = Zufließen)* influx, inflow; *(Mech: = Zufuhr)* supply; **~ kalter Meeresluft** a stream of cold air from the sea **b** *(= Nebenfluss)* affluent, tributary; *(zu Binnensee)* inlet

zu+flüs|tern VTI *sep* **jdm (etw) ~** to whisper (sth) to sb; *(Theat)* to prompt sb (with sth)

zu|fol|ge [tsu'fɔlgə] PREP *+dat or gen (form) (= gemäß)* according to; *(= auf Grund)* as a consequence *or* result of; **dem Bericht ~, ~ des Berichtes** according to the report

zu|frie|den [tsu'fri:dn] ADJ contented, content *pred*; **ein ~es Gesicht machen** to look pleased; **mit jdm/etw ~ sein** to be satisfied *or* happy with sb/sth; **wie gehts? – man ist ~** *(inf)* how are things? – can't complain *or* mustn't grumble *(inf)*; **er ist nie ~** he's never content *or* satisfied; **er ist mit nichts ~** nothing pleases him, there's no pleasing him *(inf)*; **es ~ sein** *(old)* to be well pleased ADV contentedly; **~ lächeln** to smile contentedly

Zu|frie|den-: **zu|frie|den+ge|ben** *sep irreg*, **zu|frie|den ge|ben** △ *irreg* VR **sich mit etw ~** to be content *or* satisfied with sth; **gib dich endlich zufrieden!** can't you be content with what you have?; **Zu|frie|den|heit** F -, *no pl* contentedness; *(= Befriedigtsein)* satisfaction; **zu meiner ~** to my satisfaction; **zur allgemeinen ~** to everyone's satisfaction; **zu|frie|den+las|sen** *sep irreg*, **zu|frie|den las|sen** △ *irreg* VT to leave alone *or* in peace; **lass mich damit zufrieden!** *(inf)* shut up about it! *(inf)*; **zu|frie|den+stel|len** *sep*, **zu|frie|den stel|len** VT to satisfy; *Wünsche, Ehrgeiz auch* to gratify; *Kunden etc auch* to give satisfaction to; **schwer zufriedenzustellen sein** to be hard *or* difficult to please; **eine ~de Note** a satisfactory mark *(Brit) or* grade *(US)*; **eine wenig ~de Antwort** a less than satisfactory answer

zu+frie|ren VI *sep irreg aux sein* to freeze (over)

zu+fü|gen VT *sep* **a** *Kummer, Leid, Schmerz* to cause; *Verlust, Niederlage* to inflict; **jdm/einer Sache Schaden ~** to harm sb/sth; **jdm etw ~** to cause sb sth/inflict sth on sb; **jdm eine Verletzung (mit einem Messer** *etc***) ~** to injure sb (with a knife *etc*); **was du nicht willst, dass man dir tu, das füg auch keinem andern zu** *(Prov)* do as you would be done by *(Prov)* **b** *(= hinzufügen)* to add; *(= beilegen)* to enclose

Zu|fuhr ['tsu:fu:ɐ] F **-, -en** *(= Versorgung)* supply *(in +acc, nach* to); *(Mil: = Nachschub, von Stadt)* supplies *pl*; *(Met: von Luftstrom)* influx; **die ~ von Lebensmitteln** the supply of provisions; **jdm die ~ abschneiden** to cut off sb's supplies, to cut off supplies to sb

zu+füh|ren *sep* VT *+dat* **a** *(= versorgen mit, beliefern)* to supply; *(Comput) Papier* to feed *(+dat* to); **jdm etw ~** to supply sb with sth; **einem Gerät Elektrizität ~** to supply an appliance with electricity; **etw seiner Bestimmung** *(dat)* **~** to put sth to its intended use

b *(= bringen, zur Verfügung stellen)* to bring; **etw gemeinnützigen Zwecken** *(dat)* **~** to give sth to a charitable cause; **die Abfälle der Wiederverwertung** *(dat)* **~** to supply refuse for recycling; **einem Geschäft Kunden ~** to bring customers to a business; **er führte ihm junge Mädchen zu** he supplied him with young girls; **dem Magen Nahrung ~** to supply food to the stomach; **jdn dem Richter ~** to bring sb before the court; **jdn der gerechten Strafe ~** to give sb the punishment he/she deserves; **jdn dem Verderben ~** to lead sb on the road to ruin

VI *sep* **auf etw** *(acc)* **~** *(lit, fig)* to lead to sth

Zu|füh|rung F **a** *no pl (= Versorgen, Beliefern)* supplying; *(= Versorgung)* supply; *(Comput: von Papier)* feed **b** *(= Leitung)* feed pipe; *(Comput: = Einzelblattzuführung)* sheetfeed

Zu|fuß|ge|hen [tsu'fu:sge:ən] NT walking *no art*

Zug [tsu:k] M **-(e)s, =e** ['tsy:gə] **a** *no pl (= Ziehen) (an +dat* on, at) pull, tug; *(= Zugkraft, Spannung)* tension

b *no pl (= Fortziehen: von Zugvögeln, Menschen)* migration; *(der Wolken)* drifting; **im ~e** *(= im Verlauf)* in the course *(gen* of); **einen ~ durch die Kneipen machen** to do the rounds of the pubs *(esp Brit) or* bars; **das ist der ~ der Zeit, das liegt im ~ der Zeit** it's a sign of the times, that's the way things are today; **dem ~ seines Herzens folgen** to follow the dictates of one's heart

c *(= Luftzug)* draught *(Brit)*, draft *(US)*; *(= Atemzug)* breath; *(an Zigarette, Pfeife)* puff, drag; *(= Schluck)* gulp, mouthful, swig *(inf)*; **einen ~ machen** *(an Zigarette etc)* to take a drag; **das Glas in einem ~ leeren** to empty the glass with one gulp *or* in one go, to down the glass in one *(inf)*; **etw in vollen Zügen genießen** to enjoy sth to the full *or* max *(inf)*; **er genoss sein Leben in vollen Zügen** he enjoyed life to the full; **in den letzten Zügen liegen** *(inf)* to be at one's last gasp *(inf)*, to be on one's last legs *(inf)*; **er hat einen guten ~** *(inf)* he can really put it away *(inf)*; **er hat ~ abbekommen** *or* **gekriegt** *(inf)* he got a stiff neck *etc* from sitting in a draught *(Brit) or* draft *(US)*

d *(beim Schwimmen)* stroke; *(beim Rudern)* pull *(mit* at); *(= Federzug)* stroke (of the pen); *(bei Brettspiel)* move; **einen ~ machen** *(beim Schwimmen)* to do a stroke; *(bei Brettspiel)* to make a move; **~ um ~** *(fig)* step by step, stage by stage; **(nicht) zum ~e kommen** *(inf)* (not) to get a look-in *(inf)*; **du bist am ~** *(bei Brettspiel, fig)* it's your move *or* turn; **etw in großen Zügen darstellen/umreißen** to outline sth, to describe/outline sth in broad *or* general terms; **das war kein schöner ~ von dir** that wasn't nice of you

e *(= Zugvorrichtung) (= Klingelzug)* bell pull; *(bei Feuerwaffen)* groove; *(= Orgelzug)* stop

f *(= Gruppe) (von Fischen)* shoal; *(= Gespann von Ochsen etc)* team; *(von Vögeln)* flock, flight; *(von Menschen)* procession; *(Mil)* platoon; *(= Abteilung)* section

g *(= Feldzug)* expedition, campaign; *(= Fischzug)* catch, haul

Zug M **-(e)s, =e** *(= Eisenbahnzug)* train; *(= Lastzug)* truck and trailer; **mit dem ~ fahren** to go by train; **jdn zum ~ bringen** to take sb to the station *or* train, to see sb off at the station; **im falschen ~ sitzen** *(fig inf)* to be on the wrong track, to be barking up the wrong tree *(inf)*; **auf den fahrenden ~ aufspringen** *(fig)* to jump on the bandwagon *(inf)* → **abfahren VI a**

Zug M **-(e)s, =e** *(= Gesichtszug)* feature; *(= Charakterzug auch)* characteristic, trait; *(sadistisch, brutal etc)* streak; *(= Anflug)* touch; **das ist ein schöner ~ von ihm** that's one of the nice things about him; **das ist kein schöner ~ von ihm** that's not one of his nicer characteristics; **die Sache hat einen ~ ins Lächerliche** *(fig)* the affair has something (of the) ridiculous about it, the affair verges on the ridiculous

Zug NT **-s** *(Kanton)* Zug

Zu|ga|be F extra, bonus; *(Comm: = Werbegeschenk etc)* free gift; *(Mus, Theat)* encore; **~! ~!** encore! encore!, more! more!

Zug-: **Zug|ab|stand** M interval between trains; **Zug|ab|teil** NT railway *(Brit)* or train compartment

Zu|gang M *pl* **-gänge** **a** *(= Eingang, Einfahrt)* entrance; *(= Zutritt)* admittance, access; *(zu Internet etc)* access; *(fig)* access; **~ zu einem Tresor/Informationen** *etc* **haben** to have access to a safe/information *etc*; **das Tal gab freien ~ zum Meer** the valley gave direct access to the sea; **er hat** *or* **findet keinen ~ zur Musik/Kunst** *etc* music/art *etc* doesn't mean anything to him; **„kein ~"** "no admittance *or* entry" **b** *(von Patienten)* admission; *(von Schülern)* intake; *(von Soldaten)* recruitment; *(von Waren)* receipt; *(von Büchern)* acquisition; *(von Abonnement)* new subscription; **in dieser Schule haben wir die meisten Zugänge im Frühling** our largest intake at this school is in spring

zu|gan|ge [tsu'gaŋə] ADJ *pred (esp N Ger)* **~ sein** *(= beschäftigt)* to be busy; *(= aufgestanden)* to be up and about; *(euph: in Nebenzimmer etc)* to be carrying on *(inf)*

zu|gäng|lich ['tsu:gɛŋlɪç] ADJ *(+dat, für* to) *(= erreichbar) Gelände, Ort* accessible; *(= verfügbar auch) Bücher, Dokumente* available; *öffentliche Einrichtungen* open; *(fig: = umgänglich) Mensch, Vorgesetzter* approachable; **eine private Sammlung der Allgemeinheit ~ machen** to open a private collection to the public; **der Allgemeinheit/Öffentlichkeit ~** open to the public; **sein Charakter ist mir nur wenig ~** his character is more or less a closed book to me; **er ist nur schwer ~** *(fig)* **er ist ein schwer ~er Mensch** *(fig)* he's not very approachable; **für etw leicht/nicht ~ sein** to respond/not to respond to sth; *für Komplimente, Annäherungsversuche, guten Rat etc auch* to be/not to be amenable to sth

Zu|gäng|lich|keit F **-**, *no pl (= Erreichbarkeit)* accessibility; *(= Verfügbarkeit)* availability; *(= Umgänglichkeit)* approachability; **die leichte ~ dieser Dokumente** the availability of these documents

Zu|gangs-: **Zu|gangs|be|rech|ti|gung** F *(Comput)* access (authorization); **Zu|gangs|code, Zu|gangs|kode** M *(Comput)* access code; **Zu|gangs|soft|ware** F access software

Zu|gangs|vo|raus|set|zung F condition of entry

Zug-: **Zug|an|schluss** M *(Rail)* (train) connection; **Zug|aus|kunft** F *(Rail)* **a** *(= Information)* (information on) train times *pl*, train timetables *pl* **b** *(= Schalter)* information office *or* desk, enquiries *pl (Brit)*, inquiry office *or* desk *(esp US)*; **Zug|be|glei|ter** M *(Rail: = Zugfahrplan)* train timetable; **Zug|be|glei|ter(in)** M(F) *(Rail)* guard *(Brit)*, conductor *(US)*; **Zug|be|gleit|per|so|nal** NT *(Rail)* train crew; **Zug|brü|cke** F drawbridge

zu+ge|ben VT *sep irreg* **a** *(= zusätzlich geben)* to give as an extra *or* a bonus; **jdm etw ~** to give sb sth extra *or* as a bonus; *(bei Verkauf auch)* to throw sth in for sb *(inf)* **b** *(= hinzufügen) (Cook)* to add; *(Mus, Theat)* to do *or* perform as an encore **c** *(= zugestehen, einräumen)* to admit, to acknowledge; *(= eingestehen)* to admit (to), to own up to; **er gab zu, es getan zu haben** he admitted (to) having done it, he owned up *or* confessed to having done it; **jdm gegenüber etw ~** to confess sth to sb; **zugegeben** admittedly, granted; **gibs zu!** admit it!

zu|ge|ge|be|ner|ma|ßen ['tsu:gəge:bnɐ'ma:sn] ADV admittedly

zu|ge|gen [tsu'ge:gn] ADV *(geh)* **~ sein** to be present; *(bei Versammlung, Konferenz etc auch)* to be in attendance *(form)*

zu+ge|hen *sep irreg aux sein* VI **a** *(Tür, Deckel)* to shut, to close; **der Koffer geht nicht zu** the case won't shut *or* close **b** **auf jdn/etw ~** to approach sb/sth, to go toward(s) sb/sth; **direkt auf jdn/etw ~** to go straight *or* right up to sb/sth; **geradewegs auf etw** *(acc)* **~** *(fig)* to get straight *or* right down to sth; **aufeinander ~** to approach one another; *(fig auch)* to compromise; **es geht nun auf den Winter zu** winter is drawing in *or* near; **er geht schon auf die siebzig zu** he's getting on for *or* nearing *or* approaching seventy; **dem Ende ~** to draw to a close, to near its end; *(Vorräte)* to be running out **c** *+dat (Nachricht, Brief etc)* to reach; **der Brief ist uns noch nicht zugegangen** the letter hasn't reached us yet, we haven't received the letter yet; **mir ist gestern ein Brief zugegangen** I received a letter yesterday; **die Nachricht, die ich Ihnen gestern habe ~ lassen** the message I sent you yesterday; **der Polizei sind schon mehrere Hinweise zugegangen** the police have already received several clues **d** *(inf: = weiter-, losgehen)* to get a move on *(inf)*

VI *impers* **a** **dort geht es ... zu** things are ... there; **es ging sehr lustig/fröhlich** *etc* **zu** *(inf)* we/they *etc* had a great time *(inf)*; **du kannst dir nicht vorstellen, wie es dort zugeht** you can't imagine what goes on there *(inf)*; **hier gehts ja zu wie in einem Affenhaus!** it's like a zoo here! **b** *(= geschehen)* to happen; **hier geht es nicht mit rechten Dingen zu** there's something odd going on here; **so geht es nun einmal zu in der Welt** that's the way of the world → **Teufel b**

Zu|ge|he|rin F, **Zu|geh|frau** F, **Zu|geh|hil|fe** F *(S Ger, Aus)* char(woman) *(Brit)*, cleaning woman

Zu|ge|hör ['tsu:gəhø:ɐ] NT **-(e)s**, *no pl (Sw)* = **Zubehör**

zu+ge|hö|ren *ptp* **zugehört** VI *sep irreg +dat (liter)* to belong to

zu|ge|hö|rig ADJ *attr* **a** *(geh) (= dazugehörend)* accompanying; *(= verbunden)* affiliated *(+dat* to) **b** *(old: = gehörend)* belonging to; **die einst dem britischen Weltreich ~e Insel** the island that once belonged to the British Empire

Zu|ge|hö|rig|keit F **-, -en** **a** *(zu Land, Glauben)* affiliation; *(= Mitgliedschaft)* membership *(zu* of) **b** *(= Zugehörigkeitsgefühl)* sense of belonging

zu|ge|knöpft ['tsu:gəknœpft] ADJ *(fig inf) Mensch* close, reserved → *auch* **zuknöpfen**

Zü|gel ['tsy:gl] M **-s, -** rein *(auch fig)*; **einem Pferd in die ~ fallen** to seize a horse by the reins, to seize a horse's reins; **die ~ anziehen** *(lit)* to draw in the reins; *(fig)* to keep a tighter rein *(bei* on); **die ~ fest in der Hand haben/behalten** *(fig)* to have/keep things firmly in hand *or* under control; **die ~ locker lassen** *(lit)* to slacken one's hold on the reins; *(fig)* to give free rein *(bei* to); **die ~ an sich** *(acc)* **reißen** *(fig)* to seize the reins; **seiner Wut/seinen Gefühlen** *etc* **die ~ schießen lassen** *(fig)* to give full vent *or* free rein to one's rage/feelings *etc*; **jdm ~ anlegen** to take sb in hand; **einer Sache** *(dat)* **~ anlegen** to contain *or* control sth; **jds Übermut ~ anlegen** *(liter)* to curb sb's overexuberance; **seinen Begierden ~ anlegen** *(liter)* to curb *or* bridle one's desires → **schleifen VI b**

zu|ge|las|sen ADJ authorized; *Heilpraktiker* licensed, registered; *Kfz* licensed; *Arzneimittel* approved; **amtlich ~ sein** to be authorized; **staatlich ~ sein** to be state-registered; **er ist an allen** *or* **für alle Gerichte ~** he is authorized to practise *(Brit) or* practice *(US)* in any court; **eine nicht ~e Partei** an illegal party; **als Kassenarzt ~ sein** ≈ to be registered as a GP; **als Heilpraktiker ~ sein** to be a licensed *or* registered non-medical practitioner; **für Personenbeförderung nicht ~** not licensed to carry passengers → *auch* **zulassen**

Zü|gel-: **zü|gel|los** ADJ *(fig)* unbridled *no adv*, unrestrained; **Zü|gel|lo|sig|keit** F **-, -en** *(fig)* lack of restraint, unrestraint; *(esp Pol)* anarchy

zü|geln ['tsy:gln] VT *Pferd* to rein in; *(fig)* to curb, to check VR to restrain oneself VI *aux sein (Sw: = umziehen)* to move (house)

Zü|ge|lung F **-**, *no pl* **a** *(von Pferd)* reining in; *(fig)* curbing, checking **b** *(= Selbstbeschränkung)* self-restraint

zu|ge|näht ['tsu:gənɛ:t] ADJ **verflixt** *or* **verflucht und ~!** *(inf)* damn and blast! *(inf)* → *auch* **zunähen**

Zü|gen|glöck|lein ['tsy:gnglœklain] NT **-s, -** *(S Ger, Aus)* = **Sterbeglocke**

Zu|ge|reis|te(r) ['tsu:gəraistə] MF *decl as adj (S Ger)* newcomer

zu+ge|sel|len *ptp* **zugesellt** *sep* VT *(rare)* to give as a companion VR *(geh)* **sich jdm ~** *(Mensch)* to join sb; **seinem Bankrott gesellten sich dann noch familiäre Probleme zu** on top of his bankruptcy he had family problems

zu|ge|stan|de|ner|ma|ßen ['tsu:gəʃtandnɐ'ma:sn] ADV admittedly, granted

Zu|ge|ständ|nis NT concession *(+dat, an +acc* to); **er war zu keinem ~ bereit** he would make no concession(s)

zu+ge|ste|hen *ptp* **zugestanden** VT *sep irreg (= einräumen) Recht, Erlass etc* to concede, to grant; *(= zugeben)* to admit, to acknowledge; **jdm etw ~** *(= einräumen)* to grant sb sth; **man gestand ihm zu, dass ...** it was admitted *or* acknowledged that he ...; **man gestand ihm zu, nicht aus Habgier gehandelt zu haben** it was acknowledged that he had not acted out of greed; **zugestanden, Sie haben recht** you're right, I grant you (that), I admit you're right

zu|ge|tan ['tsu:gəta:n] ADJ **jdm/einer Sache ~ sein** to be fond of sb/sth; **der dem Alkohol sehr ~e Major X** Major X who was very fond of alcohol; **der Hund war seinem Herrn sehr ~** the dog was very attached *or* devoted to his master

Zu|ge|wan|der|te(r) ['tsu:gəvandɐtə] MF *decl as adj (Admin)* newcomer

zu|ge|wandt ['tsu:gəvant] ADJ facing, overlooking; **der Zukunft** *(dat)* **~ sein** to be turned toward(s) the future

Zu|ge|winn M *(Jur) increase in value of a married couple's property during the years of joint ownership through marriage*

Zu|ge|winn|aus|gleich M *(Jur)* equitable division of community property, property acquired in the course of a marriage

Zu|ge|winn|ge|mein|schaft F *(Jur)* community of property

Zu|ge|zo|ge|ne(r) ['tsu:gətso:gənə] MF *decl as adj* newcomer

Zug-: **Zug|fe|der** F *(Tech)* tension spring; *(bei Uhr)* mainspring; **zug|fest** ADJ *(Mech)* tension-proof; *Stahl* high-tensile; **Zug|fes|tig|keit** F *(Mech)* tensile strength; **Zug|fol|ge** F *(Rail)* succession of trains; **zug|frei** ADJ *Raum* draught-free *(Brit)*, draft-free *(US)*; **Zug|füh|rer(in)** M(F) **a** *(Rail)* chief guard *(Brit) or* conductor *(US)* **b** *(Aus Mil)* platoon leader; **Zug|funk** M *(Rail)* train radio

zu+gie|ßen VT *sep irreg* **a** *(= hinzugießen)* to add; **darf ich Ihnen noch (etwas Kaffee) ~?** may I pour you a little more (coffee)?; **er goss sich** *(dat)* **ständig wieder zu** he kept topping up his glass/cup **b** *(mit Beton etc)* to fill (in)

zu|gig ['tsu:gɪç] ADJ draughty *(Brit)*, drafty *(US)*

zü|gig ['tsy:gɪç] ADJ swift, speedy; *Tempo, Bedienung auch* brisk, rapid, smart; *Handschrift* smooth; *Studium* quickly completed ADV quickly

zu+gip|sen VT *sep Loch* to plaster up, to fill (in)

Zug-: **Zug|kraft** F *(Mech)* tractive power; *(fig)* attraction, appeal; **zug|kräf|tig** ADJ *(fig) Werbetext, Titel, Plakat* catchy, eye-catching; *Schauspieler* crowd-pulling *attr*, of wide appeal

zu|gleich [tsu'glaiç] ADV *(= zur gleichen Zeit)* at the same time; *(= ebenso auch)* both; **er ist ~ Gitarrist und Komponist** he is both a guitarist and a composer; **die älteste und ~ modernste Stadt des Landes** the country's oldest and at the same time most modern town

Zug|lei|ne F pull cord

Züg|le|te ['tsy:glətə] F -, -n (*Sw:* = *Umzug*) move

Zug-: **Zug|loch** NT (*bei Ofen*) air hole, air vent; **Zug|luft** F draught (*Brit*), draft (*US*); **zu viel ~ bekommen** to be in too much of a draught (*Brit*) *or* draft (*US*); **Zug|ma|schi|ne** F towing vehicle; (*von Sattelschlepper*) traction engine, tractor; **Zug|mit|tel** NT (*fig:* = *Köder*) draw, attraction; **Zug|num|mer** F **a** (*Rail*) train number **b** (*fig*) crowd puller, drawing card (*US*); **Zug|och|se** M draught (*Brit*) *or* draft (*US*) ox; **Zug|per|so|nal** NT (*Rail*) train personnel; **Zug|pferd** NT carthorse, draught (*Brit*) *or* draft (*US*) horse; (*fig*) crowd puller; **Zug|pflas|ter** NT (*Med*) poultice; **Zug|reg|ler** M (*bei Ofen*) damper, draught (*Brit*) *or* draft (*US*) regulator

zu+grei|fen VI *sep irreg* **a** (= *schnell nehmen*) to grab it/them; (*fig*) to act fast *or* quickly, to get in quickly (*inf*); (*bei Tisch*) to help oneself; **greifen Sie bitte zu!** please help yourself! **b** (*fig:* = *einschreiten*) to step in quickly, to act fast *or* quickly **c** (= *schwer arbeiten*) to put one's back into it *or* into one's work, to get down to it *or* to work **d** (*Comput*) **auf etw** (*acc*) **~** to access sth

Zug|res|tau|rant NT dining car

Zu|griff M **a** **durch raschen ~** by stepping in quickly, by acting quickly *or* fast; **sich dem ~ der Polizei/Gerichte entziehen** to evade justice **b** (*Fin, Comput, Internet*) access (*auf* to) **c** (*Internet: auf Internetseite, Homepage*) hit; **meine Homepage hat schon 1000 ~e** I've already had 1000 visits to my home page

Zu|griffs-: **Zu|griffs|be|rech|ti|gung** F, **Zu|griffs|er|laub|nis** F access permission *or* rights *pl*; **Zu|griffs|rech|te** PL (*Comput*) access rights *pl* *or* permission *sing*; **Zu|griffs|schlüs|sel** M (*Comput*) access key; **Zu|griffs|steu|e|rung** F (*Comput*) access control; **Zu|griffs|tas|te** F (*Comput*) access key, accelerator key; **Zu|griffs|ver|let|zung** F (*Comput*) access violation; (*im Netz*) sharing violation; **Zu|griffs|zeit** F access time

zu|grun|de, zu Grun|de [tsu'grʊndə] ADV **a** **~ gehen** to perish; **jdn/etw ~ richten** to destroy sb/sth; (*finanziell*) to ruin sb/sth; **er wird daran nicht ~ gehen** he'll survive; (*finanziell*) it won't ruin him **b** **einer Sache** (*dat*) **~ liegen** to form the basis of sth, to underlie sth; **diesem Lied liegt ein Gedicht von Heine ~** this song is based on a poem by Heine; **~ liegend** underlying; **etw einer Sache** (*dat*) **~ legen** to take sth as a basis for sth, to base sth on sth; **und welche Überlegungen haben Sie diesen Ihren Behauptungen ~ gelegt?** and on what considerations do you base these claims of yours?

Zu|grun|de-: **Zu|grun|de|le|gung** [-le:gʊŋ] F -, *no pl* **unter/bei ~ dieser Daten** taking this data as a basis; **zu|grun|de|lie|gend** ADJ *attr* → **zugrunde b**

Zugs- *in cpds (Aus)* = **Zug-**

Zug-: **Zug|sal|be** F (*Med*) poultice; **Zug|seil** NT tow(ing) rope; **Zug|span|nung** F (*Mech*) tensile stress; **Zug|tier** NT draught animal (*Brit*), draft animal (*US*)

zu+gu|cken VI *sep* = **zusehen a**

Zug|un|glück NT train accident

zu|guns|ten, zu Guns|ten [tsu'gʊnstn] PREP +*gen* (*bei Voranstellung*) *or dat* (*bei Nachstellung*) in favour (*Brit*) *or* favor (*US*) of; **~ von** in favour (*Brit*) *or* favor (*US*) of; **~ seines Bruders, seinem Bruder ~** in favour (*Brit*) *or* favor (*US*) of his brother

zu|gu|te- [tsu'gu:tə]: **zu|gu|te+hal|ten** VT *sep irreg* **a** **jdm etw ~** to grant sb sth; (= *Verständnis haben*) to make allowances for sth; **Sie waren monatelang krank, das haben wir Ihnen zugutegehalten** you were ill for some months and we've made allowances for that **b** **sich** (*dat*) **auf etw** (*acc*) **etwas ~** (*geh*) to pride *or* preen oneself on sth; **zu|gu|te+kom|men** VI *sep irreg aux sein* **einer Sache/jdm ~** to come in useful for sth/to sb, to be of benefit to sth/sb; (*Geld, Erlös*) to benefit sth/sb; **das ist seiner Gesundheit zugutegekommen** his health benefited by *or* from it; **zu|gu|te+tun** VI *sep irreg* = **zugutehalten b**

Zug-: **Zug|ver|bin|dung** F train connection; **Zug|ver|kehr** M (*Rail*) rail *or* train services *pl*; **starker ~** heavy rail traffic; **Zug|vieh** NT, *no pl* draught (*Brit*) *or* draft (*US*) cattle; **Zug|vo|gel** M migratory bird; (*fig*) bird of passage; **Zug|wa|gen** M towing vehicle; **Zug|wind** M draught (*Brit*), draft (*US*); **zu viel ~ bekommen** to be in too much of a draught (*Brit*) *or* draft (*US*); **Zug|zwang** M (*Chess*) zugzwang; (*fig*) tight spot; **jdn in ~ bringen** to put sb in zugzwang/on the spot; **in ~ geraten** to get into zugzwang/be put on the spot; **unter ~ stehen** to be in zugzwang/in a tight spot; **die Gegenseite steht jetzt unter ~** the other side is now forced to move

zu+ha|ben *sep irreg* (*inf*) VI (*Geschäft, Museum, Behörde etc*) to be closed *or* shut VT *Geschäft, Tür etc* to keep closed *or* shut; *Kleid, Mantel etc* to have done up; **jetzt habe ich den Koffer endlich zu** I've finally got the case shut

zu+ha|ken VT *sep* to hook up

zu+hal|ten *sep irreg* VT to hold closed *or* shut *or* to; **sich** (*dat*) **die Nase ~** to hold one's nose; **sich** (*dat*) **die Augen/Ohren/den Mund ~** to put one's hands over one's eyes/ears/mouth, to cover one's eyes/ears/mouth with one's hands; **er hielt ihr beide Augen zu** he put his hands over her eyes VI **auf etw** (*acc*) **~** to head *or* make straight for sth

Zu|häl|ter ['tsu:hɛltɐ] M -s, - pimp, procurer

Zu|häl|te|rei [tsu:hɛltə'rai] F -, *no pl* procuring, pimping

Zu|häl|te|rin ['tsu:hɛltərɪn] F -, -nen procuress

Zu|häl|ter-: **Zu|häl|ter|typ** M (*pej*) **mit so einem ~** with someone who looks like a pimp; **Zu|häl|ter|un|we|sen** NT (*pej*) procuring

zu|han|den [tsu'handn] ADV (*form: Sw, Aus*) **a** (*auch old*) to hand → **zuhandenkommen** **b** for the attention of; **~ (von) Herrn Braun** *or* **des Herrn Braun** (*rare*) for the attention of Mr Braun, attention Mr Braun

zu|han|den+kom|men VI *sep irreg aux sein* (*form: Sw, Aus*) **es ist mir zuhandengekommen** it came to hand, it came into my hands

zu+hän|gen VT *sep* to cover up *or* over; **etw mit einem Tuch ~** to cover sth (up *or* over) with a cloth, to hang a cloth over sth

zu+hau|en *sep irreg* VT **a** *Baumstamm* to hew; *Stein* to trim, to pare **b** (*inf*) *Tür etc* to slam *or* bang (shut) VI **a** (*mit Axt*) to strike; (*mit Fäusten, Schwert*) to strike out; **hau zu!** let him *etc* have it! **b** (*inf: Tür, Fenster*) to slam *or* bang (shut)

zu|hauf [tsu'hauf] ADV (*old*) in throngs, in droves; **~ liegen** to lie in a heap *or* pile, to be piled up; **etw ~ legen** to put sth in a heap *or* pile, to pile sth up; **Beispiele dafür gibt es ~** there are numerous examples of it

zu|hau|se [tsu'hauzə], **zu Hau|se** ADV → **Haus**

Zu|hau|se [tsu'hauzə] NT -s, *no pl* home

Zu|hau|se|ge|blie|be|ne(r) [-gəbli:bənə] MF *decl as adj* he/she *or* him/her who stayed at home; **die ~n waren …** those who stayed at home were …

zu+hei|len VI *sep aux sein* to heal up *or* over

Zu|hil|fe|nah|me [tsu'hɪlfəna:mə] F **unter ~ von** *or* +*gen* with the aid *or* help of

zu|hin|terst [tsu'hɪntɐst] ADV right at the back, at the very back

zu|höchst [tsu'hø:çst] ADV **a** (= *ganz oben*) right at the top, at the very top **b** (= *sehr*) highly, extremely

zu+hö|ren VI *sep* to listen (+*dat* to); (= *lauschen, abhören auch*) to listen in (+*dat* on *or* to), to eavesdrop (+*dat* on); **hör mal zu!** (*drohend*) now (just) listen (to me)!; **gut ~ können** to be a good listener; **hör mir mal genau zu!** now listen carefully to me

Zu|hö|rer(in) M(F) listener; **die ~** (= *das Publikum*) the audience *sing*; (*Rad auch*) the listeners

Zu|hö|rer|schaft F audience; (*Rad auch*) listeners *pl*

zu|in|nerst [tsu'ɪnɐst] ADV deeply; **tief ~** in his/her *etc* heart of hearts, deep down

zu+ju|beln VI *sep* **jdm ~** to cheer sb

Zu|kauf M additional purchase

zu+kau|fen VT *sep* **etw ~** to buy more (of) sth; **Einzelstücke ~** to buy extra separate parts

zu+keh|ren VT *sep* (= *zuwenden*) to turn; **jdm das Gesicht ~** to turn to face sb, to turn one's face to *or* toward(s) sb; **jdm den Rücken ~** (*lit, fig*) to turn one's back on sb

zu+kif|fen VR *sep* (*sl*) to get spaced out (*sl*); **zugekifft** spaced out (*sl*)

zu+klap|pen VTI *sep* (*vi: aux sein*) to snap shut; (*Tür, Fenster*) to click shut

zu+kle|ben VT *sep Loch etc* to stick over *or* up; *Briefumschlag* to stick down (*esp Brit*), to seal; *Brief* to seal (up); (*mit Klebstoff, Klebeband*) to stick up

zu+kleis|tern VT *sep* (*inf: lit, fig*) to patch up

zu+klin|ken ['tsu:klɪŋkn] *sep* VT *Tür* to latch VI *aux sein* **die Tür klinkte zu** the latch fell shut

zu+knal|len VTI *sep* (*vi: aux sein*) (*inf*) to slam *or* bang (shut)

zu+knei|fen VT *sep irreg* to pinch hard; *Augen* to screw up; *Mund* to shut tight(ly)

zu+knöp|fen VT *sep* to button (up); **sich** (*dat*) **die Jacke/das Hemd ~** to button (up) one's jacket/shirt → *auch* **zugeknöpft**

zu+kno|ten VT *sep* to knot up

zu+kom|men VI *sep irreg aux sein* **a** **auf jdn/etw ~** to come toward(s) *or* (*direkt*) up to sb/sth; **das Gewitter kam genau auf uns zu** the storm was heading straight for us, the storm was coming right at us; **die Aufgabe, die nun auf uns zukommt** the task which is now in store for us, the task which now stands before us *or* confronts us; **die Dinge auf sich** (*acc*) **~ lassen** to take things as they come; **alles auf sich** (*acc*) **~ lassen** to let everything take its course **b** **jdm etw ~ lassen** (*Brief etc*) to send sb sth; (= *schenken*) *Hilfe* to give sb sth **c** +*dat* (= *geziemen, gebühren*) to befit, to become; **ein solches Verhalten kommt dir nicht zu** such behaviour (*Brit*) *or* behavior (*US*) doesn't become *or* befit you, such behaviour (*Brit*) *or* behavior (*US*) ill becomes you; **es kommt Ihnen nicht zu, darüber zu entscheiden** it isn't up to you to decide this; **dieser Titel kommt ihm nicht zu** he has no right to this title; **diesem Treffen kommt große Bedeutung zu** this meeting is of (the) utmost importance

zu+kor|ken ['tsu:kɔrkn] VT *sep* to cork (up)

zu+krie|gen VT *sep* (*inf*) = **zubekommen**

Zu|kunft ['tsu:kʊnft] F -, *no pl* **a** **die ~** the future; **in ~** in future; **in ferner/naher/nächster ~** in the remote *or* distant/near/immediate future; **ein Beruf mit/ohne ~** a career with/without prospects; **das hat keine ~** it has no future, there's no future in it; **unsere gemeinsame ~** our future together; **in die ~ blicken** *or* **sehen** to look *or* see into the future; **wir müssen abwarten, was die ~ bringt** we must wait and see what the future has in store *or* holds; **das gilt für alle ~** that applies without exception from now on; **das bleibt der ~** (*dat*) **überlassen** *or* **vorbehalten** that remains to be seen; **viel Glück für Ihre ~!** best wishes for the future! **b** (*Gram*) future (tense)

zu|künf|tig ADJ future; **der ~e Präsident/Bischof** the president/bishop elect *or* designate; **meine Zukünftige** (*inf*)/**mein Zukünftiger** (*inf*) my future wife/husband, my wife-to-be/husband-to-be, my intended (*hum*) ADV in future, from now on

Zu|kunfts-: **Zu|kunfts|angst** F *(vor der Zukunft)* fear of the future; *(um die Zukunft)* fear for the future; **Zu|kunfts|aus|sich|ten** PL future prospects *pl*; **Zu|kunfts|be|ruf** M job for the future; **Zu|kunfts|bran|che** F new *or* sunrise *(inf)* industry; **Zu|kunfts|chan|cen** PL chances *pl* for the future, future chances *pl*; **Zu|kunfts|fach** NT *(Univ)* new science; **zu|kunfts|fä|hig** ADJ *Branche, Lösung* with a future *(nachgestellt)*; *Entwicklung, Technologie, Wirtschaft* sustainable; **~ sein** to have a future; **Zu|kunfts|for|scher(in)** M(F) futurologist; **Zu|kunfts|for|schung** F futurology; **Zu|kunfts|fra|ge** F question about the future; **zu|kunfts|froh** ADJ optimistic (about the future); **Zu|kunfts|ge|stal|tung** F planning for the future; **Zu|kunfts|glau|be** M belief in the future; **zu|kunfts|gläu|big** ADJ believing in the future; **Zu|kunfts|kon|zept** NT plans *pl* for the future; **Zu|kunfts|mu|sik** F *(fig inf)* pie in the sky *(inf)*, Zukunftsmusik; **Zu|kunfts|op|ti|mis|mus** M optimism about the future; **zu|kunfts|ori|en|tiert** [-lorienti:ɐt] ADJ forward-looking, looking to the future, future-oriented; **Zu|kunfts|per|spek|ti|ve** F future prospects *pl*; **Zu|kunfts|plä|ne** PL plans *pl* for the future; **Zu|kunfts|prog|no|se** F forecast; **zu|kunfts|reich** ADJ *(geh)* = **zukunftsträchtig**; **Zu|kunfts|ro|man** M *(naturwissenschaftlich)* science fiction novel; *(gesellschaftspolitisch)* utopian novel; **zu|kunfts|si|cher** ADJ with a guaranteed future, future-proof; **Zu|kunfts|si|che|rung** F safeguarding the future; **Zu|kunfts|sze|na|rio** NT vision of the future; **Zu|kunfts|tech|nik** F, **Zu|kunfts|tech|no|lo|gie** F new *or* sunrise *(inf)* technology; **zu|kunfts|träch|tig** ADJ with a promising future, promising; **Zu|kunfts|vi|si|on** F future vision, vision for the future; **zu|kunfts|wei|send** ADJ forward-looking

Zu|kurz|ge|kom|me|ne(r) [tsu-'kʊrtsgəkɔmənə] MF *decl as adj* loser

zu+la|bern VT *sep (inf)* **jdn ~** to rattle on at sb *(inf)*, to rabbit on at sb *(Brit inf)*; **sie hat mich total zugelabert** she went on and on at me

zu+lä|cheln VI *sep* **jdm ~** to smile at sb

zu+la|chen VI *sep* **jdm ~** to give sb a friendly laugh

zu+la|den VTI *sep irreg* to load more on/in

Zu|la|dung F *(bei Kfz)* useful load; *(Naut)* deadweight

Zu|la|ge F **a** *(= Geldzulage)* extra *or* additional pay *no indef art*; *(= Sonderzulage)* bonus (payment); *(= Gefahrenzulage)* danger money *no indef art*; **eine ~ von 100 Euro** an extra 100 euros pay; a bonus (payment) of 100 euros; 100 euros danger money **b** *(= Gehaltserhöhung)* rise *(Brit)*, raise *(US)*; *(regelmäßig)* increment

zu|lan|de △ [tsu'landə] ADV → **Land a**

zu+lan|gen VI *sep* **a** *(inf: Dieb, Fiskus, beim Essen)* to help oneself; **kräftig ~** *(beim Essen)* to tuck in *(inf)* **b** *(inf: = zuschlagen)* to hit *(esp Brit)* or strike out **c** *(dial: = reichen)* to do *(inf)*; **es langt nicht zu** there's not enough

zu|läng|lich ['tsu:lɛŋlɪç] ADJ *(geh)* adequate

Zu|läng|lich|keit F **-, -en** *(geh)* adequacy

zu+las|sen VT *sep irreg* **a** *(= Zugang gewähren)* to admit; **eine Partei zur Wahl ~** to permit a party to enter the/an election
b *(amtlich)* to authorize; *Arzt* to register; *Heilpraktiker* to register, to license; *Kraftfahrzeug* to license; *Rechtsanwalt* to call (to the bar), to admit (as a barrister *or* to the bar); *Prüfling* to admit; **etw als Beweismittel ~** to allow sth as evidence; **zugelassene Aktien** listed securities → *auch* **zugelassen**
c *(= dulden, gestatten)* to allow, to permit; **das lässt nur den Schluss zu, dass ...** that leaves *or* allows only one conclusion that ...; **eine Ausnahme ~** *(Vorschriften)* to allow (of) *or* admit (of) *or* permit an exception; *(Mensch)* to allow *or* permit an exception; **sein Schweigen lässt keine andere Erklärung zu(, als dass ...)** there is no other explanation for his silence (but that ...); **ich lasse nicht zu, dass mein Bruder benachteiligt wird** I won't allow *or* permit my brother to be discriminated against; **das lässt mein Pflichtbewusstsein nicht zu** my sense of duty won't allow *or* permit *or* countenance that
d *(= geschlossen lassen)* to leave *or* keep shut *or* closed

zu|läs|sig ['tsu:lɛsɪç] ADJ permissible; *Beweis, Klage, Vorgehen* admissible; *Fangquote* allowable; **~e Abweichung** *(Tech)* tolerance, permissible variation; **die Berufung ist ~** *(Jur)* there is a right of appeal; **eine Berufung für ~ erklären** *(Jur)* to grant leave for an appeal; **~es Gesamtgewicht** *(Mot)* maximum laden weight; **~e Höchstgeschwindigkeit** (upper) speed limit; **~e Höchstbelastung** weight limit; **es ist nicht ~, hier zu parken** parking is prohibited *or* not permitted here

Zu|läs|sig|keit F **-**, *no pl* admissibility

Zu|las|sung ['tsu:lasʊŋ] F **-, -en** **a** *no pl (= Gewährung von Zugang)* admittance, admission **b** *no pl (amtlich)* authorization; *(von Kfz)* licensing; *(als Rechtsanwalt)* call to the bar; *(von Prüfling)* admittance *(form)*; *(als praktizierender Arzt)* registration; **Antrag auf ~ zu einer Prüfung** application to enter an examination; **seine ~ als Rechtsanwalt bekommen** to be called to the bar; **~ (von Aktien) zur Börse** listing on the Stock Exchange **c** *(Dokument)* papers *pl*; *(esp von Kfz)* vehicle registration document, logbook; *(= Lizenz)* licence *(Brit)*, license *(US)*

Zu|las|sungs-: **Zu|las|sungs|be|schrän|kung** F *(esp Univ)* restriction on admissions; **Zu|las|sungs|num|mer** F *(Mot)* registration number; **Zu|las|sungs|pa|pie|re** PL *(Mot)* registration papers *pl*; **Zu|las|sungs|sper|re** F *(esp Univ)* bar on admissions; **Zu|las|sungs|stel|le** F registration office; **Zu|las|sungs|stopp** M *(esp Univ)* block on admissions; **Zu|las|sungs|ver|fah|ren** NT *(esp Univ)* admissions procedure

zu|las|ten, **zu Las|ten** [tsu'lastn] ADV **der neuerliche Überfall geht ~ der Rebellen** the rebels are being held responsible for the recent attack; **das geht ~ der Sicherheit im Lande** that is detrimental to national security → *auch* **Last c**

Zu|lauf M, *no pl* **großen ~ haben** *(Geschäft, Restaurant)* to be very popular; *(Arzt etc auch)* to be much sought-after, to be in great demand; **die Aufführung hat sehr großen ~ gehabt** the performance drew large crowds

zu+lau|fen VI *sep irreg aux sein* **a auf jdn/etw ~, auf jdn/etw zugelaufen kommen** to run toward(s) sb/sth, to come running toward(s) sb/sth; *(direkt)* to run up to sb/sth, to come running up to sb/sth **b** → **spitz c** *(Wasser etc)* to run in, to add; **lass noch etwas kaltes Wasser ~** run in *or* add some more cold water **d** *(inf: = sich beeilen)* to hurry (up); **lauf zu!** hurry up! **e** *(Hund etc)* **jdm ~** to stray into sb's house; **eine zugelaufene Katze** a stray (cat)

zu+le|gen *sep* VT **a** *(= dazulegen)* to put on; **legen Sie noch zwei Scheiben zu, bitte** please put on another two slices
b *Geld* to add; *(bei Verlustgeschäft)* to lose; **der Chef hat mir 200 Euro im Monat zugelegt** the boss has given me 200 euros a month extra, the boss has given me an extra 200 euros a month; **die fehlenden 20 Euro legte meine Mutter zu** my mother made up the remaining 20 euros
c etwas Tempo *(inf) or* **einen Zahn** *(inf)* **~** to get a move on *(inf)*, to step on it *(inf)*
d *(inf: an Gewicht)* to put on; **er hat schon wieder 5 kg zugelegt** he's put on *(esp Brit) or* gained another 5 kg; **die SPD konnte 5% ~** the SPD managed to gain 5%
e *(= anschaffen)* **sich** *(dat)* **etw ~** *(inf)* to get oneself sth; **er hat sich** *(dat)* **eine teure Pfeife zugelegt** he has treated himself to an expensive pipe; **er hat sich eine Braut/Freundin zugelegt** *(hum)* he has got himself *or* has acquired a fiancée/girlfriend
VI *(inf)* **a** *(an Gewicht)* to put on weight; *(Wirtschaftswachstum, Umsatz)* to increase; **die SPD hat in den Umfragen zugelegt** the SPD has gained support in the opinion polls
b *(= sich mehr anstrengen)* to pull one's *or* the finger out *(Brit inf)*, to make an effort; *(= sich steigern)* to do better; *(Sport)* to step up the pace *(inf)*

zu|lei|de, **zu Lei|de** [tsu'laidə] ADV **jdm etwas ~ tun** to do sb harm, to harm sb; **was hat er dir ~ getan?** what (harm) has he done to you?; **wer hat dir etwas ~ getan?** who has harmed you? → **Fliege**

zu+lei|ten VT *sep Wasser, Strom* to supply; *Schreiben, Waren* to send on, to forward

Zu|lei|tung F *(Tech)* supply

zu|letzt [tsu'lɛtst] ADV **a** *(= schließlich, endlich, zum Schluss)* in the end; **~ kam sie doch** she came in the end; **~ kam auch Gaston** in the end *or* finally Gaston came too; **wir blieben bis ~** we stayed to the very *or* bitter end; **ganz ~** right at the last moment, at the very last moment **b** *(= als Letzte(r, s), an letzter Stelle, zum letzten Mal)* last; **ich kam ~** I came last, I was last to come; **wann haben Sie ihn ~ gesehen?** when did you last see him?; **ganz ~** last of all; **nicht ~ dank/wegen** not least thanks to/because of

zu|lie|be [tsu'li:bə] ADV **etw jdm ~ tun** to do sth for sb's sake *or* for sb; **das geschah nur ihr ~** it was done just for her

Zu|lie|fer|be|trieb M *(Econ)* supplier

Zu|lie|fe|rer ['tsu:li:fərɐ] M **-s, -**, **Zu|lie|fe|rin** [-ərɪn] F **-, -nen** *(Econ)* supplier

Zu|lie|fer|in|dust|rie F *(Econ)* supply industry

zu+lie|fern VT *sep* to supply

Zu|lie|fe|rung F supply

zu+lö|ten VT *sep* to solder

Zu|lu ['tsu:lu] M **-(s), -(s)** *or f* **-, -s** Zulu

Zu|lu NT **-(s)** *(Sprache)* Zulu

zum [tsʊm] *contr von* **zu dem a** *(räumlich)* **geht es hier ~ Bahnhof?** is this the way to the station?; **„Gasthof Zum Löwen"** "The Lion Inn" **b** *(mit Infinitiv)* **~ Schwimmen gehen** to go swimming; **~ Essen gehen** to go and eat **c** *(Folge)* **es ist ~ Verrücktwerden/Weinen** it's enough to drive you mad *(esp Brit) or* crazy *(inf)*/make you cry **d** *(Zweck)* **dieses Gerät ist ~ Messen des Blutdrucks** this apparatus is for measuring (the) blood pressure **e** *(in Verbindung mit vb siehe auch dort)* **~ Spießbürger/Verräter werden** to become bourgeois/a traitor

zu+ma|chen *sep* VT *(= schließen)* to shut, to close; *Flasche* to close; *Brief* to seal; *(inf: = auflösen) Laden etc* to close (down); **die Augen ~** *(lit, fig)* to close *or* shut one's eyes *(fig: bei etw* to sth) VI *(inf)* **a** *(= den Laden zumachen)* to close (down), to shut up shop; *(fig)* to pack *or* jack *(Brit)* it in *(inf)*, to call it a day **b** *(inf: = sich beeilen)* to get a move on *(inf)*, to step on it *(inf)*

zu|mal [tsu'ma:l] CONJ **~ (da)** especially *or* particularly as *or* since ADV **a** *(= besonders)* especially, particularly **b** *(obs: = zugleich)* at the same time

zu+mau|ern VT *sep* to brick up, to wall up

zu|meist [tsu'maist] ADV mostly, in the main, for the most part

zu+mes|sen VT *sep irreg (geh)* to measure out *(jdm* for sb), to apportion *(jdm* to sb); *Essen* to dish out *(jdm* to sb); *Zeit* to allocate (+*dat* for); *Schuld* to attribute *(jdm* to sb); *Bedeutung* to attribute *(einer Sache (dat)* to sth); **ihm wurde eine hohe Strafe zugemessen** he was dealt a stiff punishment; **dem darf man keine große Bedeutung ~** one can't attach too much importance to that

zu|min|dest [tsu'mɪndəst] ADV at least; **er hätte mich ~ anrufen können** he could at least have phoned me, he could have phoned me at least, at least he could have phoned me

zu+müll|len ['tsu:mylən] VT *sep* **a** *(inf. = mit Müll zuschütten)* to cover over with rubbish *(Brit) or* garbage **b** *(inf. mit Werbesendungen)* to bombard *(inf)*; *(Internet: mit Werbe-E-Mails etc)* to spam **c** *(sl)* = **zulabern**

zu|mut|bar ADJ reasonable; **jdm** *or* **für jdn ~ sein** to be reasonable for sb; **es ist ihm (durchaus) ~, dass er das tut** he can reasonably be expected to do that; **nicht ~ sein** to be unreasonable

Zu|mut|bar|keit ['tsu:mu:tba:ɐkait] F -, *no pl* reasonableness

zu|mu|te, zu Mu|te [tsu'mu:tə] ADV **wie ist Ihnen ~?** how do you feel?; **mir ist traurig/seltsam** *etc* ~ I feel sad/strange *etc*; **mir ist lächerlich ~** I'm in a silly mood; **mir ist gar nicht lächerlich ~** I'm not in a laughing mood; **ihm war recht wohl ~** he felt wonderful *or* good; **mir war dabei gar nicht wohl ~** I didn't feel right about it, I felt uneasy about it

zu+mu|ten VT *sep* **jdm etw ~** to expect *or* ask sth of sb; **Sie wollen mir doch wohl nicht ~, diesen Unsinn zu lesen** you surely don't expect me to *or* aren't asking me to read this nonsense; **das können Sie niemandem ~** you can't ask *or* expect that of anyone; **Sie muten mir doch wohl nicht zu, das zu glauben!** you surely don't expect me to *or* aren't asking me to believe that; **sich** *(dat)* **zu viel ~** to take on too much, to overdo things, to overtax oneself; **seinem Körper zu viel ~** to overtax oneself

Zu|mu|tung ['tsu:mu:tʊŋ] F -, -en unreasonable demand; *(= Unverschämtheit)* cheek *(esp Brit)*, nerve *(inf)*; **das ist eine ~!** that's a bit much!

zu|nächst [tsu'nɛ:çst] ADV **a** *(= zuerst)* first (of all); **~ einmal** first of all **b** *(= vorläufig)* for the time being, for the moment PREP +*dat (rare) (= neben)* next to

zu+na|geln VT *sep Fenster etc* to nail up; *(mit Brettern, Pappe etc)* to board up; *Sarg, Kiste etc* to nail down

zu+nä|hen VT *sep* to sew up → *auch* **zugenäht**

Zu|nah|me ['tsu:na:mə] F -, -n (+*gen, an +dat* in) increase; *(= Anstieg auch)* rise

Zu|na|me M surname, last name

Zünd|an|lass- *(Aut)*: **Zünd|an|lass|schal|ter** M ignition switch; **Zünd|an|lass|schloss** NT ignition lock

Zünd|blätt|chen NT *(für Spielzeugpistole)* cap

zün|deln ['tsʏndln] VI to play (about) with fire; **mit Streichhölzern ~** to play (about) with matches

zün|den ['tsʏndn] VI to catch light *or* fire, to ignite; *(Pulver)* to ignite; *(Streichholz)* to light; *(Motor)* to fire; *(Sprengkörper)* to go off; *(fig)* to kindle enthusiasm; **dieses Streichholz zündet nicht** this match won't light; **hat es endlich bei dir gezündet?** *(inf)* has the penny finally dropped?, have you finally cottoned on? *(Brit inf)* VT to ignite, to set alight; *Rakete* to fire; *Sprengkörper* to set off, to detonate; *Feuerwerkskörper* to let off

zün|dend ADJ *(fig)* stirring, rousing; *Vorschlag* exciting

Zun|der ['tsʊndɐ] M -s, - tinder; *(= Schicht auf Metall)* scale (oxide); *(inf. = Prügel)* good hiding *(inf)*, thrashing; **wie ~ brennen** to burn like tinder; **~ kriegen** *(inf)* to get a good hiding *(inf) or* thrashing; **jdm ~ geben** *(inf)* to give sb a good hiding *(inf) or* thrashing

Zün|der ['tsʏndɐ] M -s, - **a** igniter; *(für Sprengstoff, Bombe, Torpedo etc)* fuse; *(für Mine)* detonator **b** *(Aus inf. = Zündholz)* match

Zun|der|schwamm M *(Bot)* touchwood

Zünd-: **Zünd|flam|me** F pilot light; **Zünd|fol|ge** F *(Tech)* ignition sequence, firing order; **Zünd|fun|ke** M *(Aut)* ignition spark; **Zünd|holz** NT match(stick); **ein ~ anreißen** to strike a match; **Zünd|hüt|chen** NT percussion cap; **Zünd|ka|bel** NT *(Aut)* plug lead; **Zünd|kap|sel** F detonator; **Zünd|ker|ze** F *(Aut)* spark(-ing) plug; **Zünd|plätt|chen** NT *(für Spielzeugpistole)* cap; **Zünd|schloss** NT *(Aut)* ignition lock; **Zünd|schlüs|sel** M *(Aut)* ignition key; **Zünd|schnur** F fuse; **Zünd|spu|le** F ignition *or* spark coil; **Zünd|stoff** M inflammable *or* flammable *(esp US)* matter; *(= Sprengstoff)* explosives *pl*, explosive material; *(fig)* inflammatory *or* explosive stuff

Zün|dung ['tsʏndʊŋ] F -, -en ignition; *(= Zündvorrichtung bei Sprengkörpern)* detonator, detonating device; **die ~ ist nicht richtig eingestellt** *(Aut)* the timing is out, the timing is wrongly set; **die ~ einstellen** *(Aut)* to adjust the timing

Zünd-: **Zünd|ver|tei|ler** M *(Aut)* distributor; **Zünd|vor|rich|tung** F igniting device, detonator; **Zünd|wa|ren|steu|er** F tax on matches; **Zünd|wil|lig|keit** F -, *no pl (Tech)* combustibility; **Zünd|zeit|punkt** M moment of ignition

zu+neh|men *vi sep irreg* VI *(an Zahl etc, beim Stricken)* to increase; *(= anwachsen auch)* to grow; *(Tage)* to draw out; *(an Weisheit, Erfahrung etc)* to gain (*an +dat* in); *(Mensch: an Gewicht)* to put on *or* gain weight; *(Mond)* to wax; **im Zunehmen sein** to be on the increase; *(Mond)* to be waxing; **der Wind nimmt (an Stärke) zu** the wind is getting up *or* increasing VT *(Mensch: an Gewicht)* to gain, to put on; **ich habe 2 kg/viel zugenommen** I've gained *or* put on 2 kg/a lot of weight

zu|neh|mend ADJ increasing, growing; *Mond* crescent; **mit ~en Jahren glaubte er …** as he advanced in years he believed …; **bei** *or* **mit ~em Alter** with advancing age; **wir haben ~en Mond** there is a crescent moon; **in ~em Maße** to an increasing degree ADV increasingly; **~ an Einfluss gewinnen** to gain increasing influence

zu+nei|gen *sep +dat* VI to be inclined toward(s); **ich neige der Auffassung zu, dass …** I am inclined to think that …; **jdm zugeneigt sein** *(geh)* to be well disposed toward(s) sb VR to lean towards; *(fig: Glück etc)* to favour *(Brit)*, to favor *(US)*; **sich dem Ende ~** *(geh) (Tag etc)* to be drawing to a close; *(= knapp werden: Vorräte etc)* to be running out

Zu|nei|gung F affection; **eine starke ~ zu jdm empfinden** to feel strong affection toward(s) *or* for sb; **~ zu jdm fassen** to take a liking to sb, to grow fond of sb

Zunft [tsʊnft] F -, **=e** ['tsʏnftə] *(Hist)* guild; *(hum inf)* brotherhood; **die ~ der Bäcker/Fleischer** *etc* the bakers'/butchers' *etc* guild

Zunft-: **Zunft|brief** M *(Hist)* guild charter; **Zunft|ge|nos|se** M guildsman; *(fig pej)* crony *(pej)*; **Zunft|ge|nos|sin** F guildswoman; *(fig pej)* crony *(pej)*

zünf|tig ['tsʏnftɪç] ADJ **a** *(Hist)* belonging to a guild **b** *(= fachmännisch) Arbeit etc* expert, professional; *Kleidung* professional(-looking); *(inf) (= ordentlich, regelrecht)* proper; *(= gut, prima)* great; **eine ~e Ohrfeige** a hefty box on the ears *(esp Brit)*, a hefty slap across the face

Zunft- *(Hist)*: **Zunft|meis|ter(in)** M(F) master of a/the guild, guild master; **Zunft|we|sen** NT, *no pl* guild system, system of guilds; **Zunft|zwang** M compulsory membership of a guild

Zun|ge ['tsʊŋə] F -, -n tongue; *(Mus: von Fagott, Akkordeon)* reed; *(von Waage)* pointer; *(geh: = Sprache)* tongue; *(Zool: = Seezunge)* sole; **mit der ~ anstoßen** to lisp; **das brennt auf der ~** that burns the tongue; **jdm die ~ herausstrecken** to stick one's tongue out at sb; **die ~ herausstrecken** *(beim Arzt)* to stick out one's tongue; **mit schwerer ~ sprechen** to speak in a slurred voice; **eine böse** *or* **giftige/scharfe** *or* **spitze/lose ~ haben** to have an evil/a sharp/a loose tongue; **lose ~n behaupten, …** rumour *(Brit) or* rumor *(US)* has it …; **böse ~n behaupten, …** malicious gossip has it …; **eine feine ~ haben** to be a gourmet, to have a discriminating palate; **sich** *(dat)* **die ~ abbrechen** *(fig)* to tie one's tongue in knots; **eher beißt er sich** *(dat)* **die ~ ab, als …** he'd do anything rather than …; **das Wort liegt** *or* **schwebt mir auf der ~, ich habe das Wort auf der ~** the word is on the tip of my tongue; **der Wein löste ihm die ~** the wine loosened his tongue; **mir hängt die ~ zum Hals heraus** *(inf)* my tongue is hanging out; **ein Lyriker polnischer** *(gen)* **~** a poet of the Polish tongue; **alle Länder arabischer** *(gen)* **~** all Arabic-speaking countries; **in fremden ~n reden** to speak in tongues

zün|geln ['tsʏŋln] VI *(Schlange)* to dart its tongue in and out; *(Flamme, Feuer)* to lick

Zun|gen-: **Zun|gen|bein** NT tongue bone, hyoid bone; **Zun|gen|be|lag** M coating of the tongue; **Zun|gen|bre|cher** M tongue twister; **zun|gen|fer|tig** ADJ *(geh)* eloquent; *(pej)* glib; **Zun|gen|fer|tig|keit** F *(geh)* eloquence; *(pej)* glibness; **Zun|gen|kuss** M French kiss; **Zun|gen|laut** M *(Ling)* lingual (sound); **Zun|gen|pfei|fe** F *(Mus)* reed pipe; **Zun|gen-R** [-lɛr] NT, **Zun|gen-r** NT *(Ling)* trilled *or* rolled "r"; **Zun|gen|rü|cken** M back of the tongue; **Zun|gen|schlag** M *(durch Alkohol)* slur; *(Mus)* tonguing; **ein falscher ~** an unfortunate turn of phrase; **zwei Töne mit ~ spielen** to tongue two notes; **Zun|gen|spit|ze** F tip of the tongue; **Zun|gen|wurst** F *(Cook)* tongue sausage; **Zun|gen|wur|zel** F root of the tongue

Züng|lein ['tsʏŋlain] NT -s, - *dim von* **Zunge** tongue; *(rare: der Waage)* pointer; **das ~ an der Waage sein** *(fig)* to tip the scales; *(Pol)* to hold the balance of power

zu|nich|te- [tsu'nɪçtə]: **zu|nich|te+ma|chen** VT *sep (geh)* to wreck, to ruin; *Hoffnungen auch* to shatter, to destroy; **zu|nich|te+wer|den** VI *sep irreg aux sein (geh)* to be wrecked *or* ruined; *(Hoffnungen auch)* to be shattered *or* destroyed

zu+ni|cken VI *sep* **jdm ~** to nod to *or* at sb; **jdm freundlich/aufmunternd ~** to give sb a friendly/encouraging nod

zu|nut|ze, zu Nut|ze [tsu'nʊtsə] ADV **sich** *(dat)* **etw ~ machen** *(= verwenden)* to make use of sth, to utilize sth; *(= ausnutzen)* to capitalize on sth, to take advantage of sth

zu|oberst [tsu'lo:bɐst] ADV on *or* at the (very) top, right on *or* at the top → **unterste(r, s)**

zu+ord|nen VT *sep +dat* to assign to; **ein Tier einer Gattung ~** to assign an animal to a genus; **jdn/etw jdm ~** to assign sb/sth to sb; **diesen Dichter ordnet man der Romantik zu** this poet is classified as a Romantic(ist); **wie sind diese Begriffe einander zugeordnet?** how are these concepts related (to each other)?

Zu|ord|nung F assignment *(zu einer Periode)*, classification; *(= Beziehung zueinander)* relation

zu+pa|cken VI *sep (inf)* **a** *(= zugreifen)* to make a grab for it *etc* **b** *(bei der Arbeit)* to knuckle down (to it), to get down to it **c** *(= helfen)* **mit ~** to give me/them *etc* a hand

zu|pa|ckend ADJ *Film, Theaterstück, Steuersystem* hard-hitting; *(= forsch)* straightforward, direct; *(= aggressiv)* vigorous ADV purposefully

zu+par|ken VT *sep* to block, to obstruct; **zugeparkt** blocked (with parked cars); *Auto* blocked in (by parked cars); *Straße* full of *or* chock-a-block with *(inf)* parked cars; **die Straße ist zugeparkt** there's not a single parking space in *or* on *(esp US)* the street

zu|pass+kom|men [tsu'pas-], **zu|pas|se+kom|men** [tsu'pasə-] VI *sep irreg aux sein* **jdm ~** *(Mensch, Hilfe)* to have come at the right time for sb; **dieser Holzblock kommt mir zupass(e)** this block of wood is just what I needed

zu|pass kom|men △ [tsu'pas-], **zu|pas|se kom|men** △ [tsu'pasə-] VI *irreg aux sein* → **zupasskommen**

zup|fen ['tsʊpfn] VT to pick; *Saite auch, Gitarre, Cello* to pluck; *Unkraut* to pull (up); **jdn am Ärmel ~** to tug at sb's sleeve; **sich** *(dat or acc)* **am Bart/Ohr** *etc* **~** to pull at one's beard/ear *etc* VI **an etw** *(dat)* **~** *(an Haaren, Ohrläppchen, Kleidung)* to pull at sth; *an Instrument* to pluck at sth

Zupf-: **Zupf|gei|ge** F *(dated)* guitar; **Zupf|in|stru|ment** NT *(Mus)* plucked string instrument

zu+pfrop|fen VT *sep* to cork, to stopper

zu+pres|sen VT *sep Tür etc* to press shut; **ein Loch/Leck (mit der Hand** *etc*) ~ to press one's hand *etc* over a hole/leak

zu+pros|ten VI *sep* **jdm** ~ to raise one's glass to sb, to drink sb's health

zur [tsuːɐ, tsʊr] *contr von* **zu der**; ~ **Schule gehen** to go to school; **jdn** ~ **Tür bringen** to see sb to the door; ~ **See fahren** to go to sea; **„Gasthof Zur Post\(** "The Post Inn\); ~ **Zeit** at the moment; ~ **Weihnachtszeit** at Christmas time; ~ **Orientierung** for orientation; ~ **Abschreckung** as a deterrent

zu|ran|de , **zu Ran|de** [tsu'randə] ADV **mit etw/jdm** ~ **kommen** (to be able) to cope with sth/sb

zu|ra|te , **zu Ra|te** [tsu'raːtə] ADV **mit jdm** ~ **gehen** *(liter)* to seek sb's advice, to consult sb; **ich muss erst mit mir** ~ **gehen** I'll have to consider it first; **jdn/etw** ~ **ziehen** to consult sb/sth; **einen Anwalt/Arzt** ~ **ziehen** to take legal/medical advice, to consult a lawyer/doctor; **einen Kollegen** ~ **ziehen** to get a second opinion, to consult a colleague

zu+ra|ten VI *sep irreg* **jdm** ~, **etw zu tun** to advise sb to do sth; **er hat mich gefragt, ob er ins Ausland gehen soll, und ich habe ihm zugeraten** he asked me whether he should go abroad and I said he should; **ich will weder** ~ **noch abraten** I won't advise you one way or the other; **auf sein Zuraten (hin)** on his advice

zu+rau|nen VT *sep (liter)* **jdm etw** ~ to whisper sth to sb

Zür|cher ['tsʏrçɐ] M **-s, -**, **Zür|che|rin** [-ərɪn] F **-, -nen** native of Zurich

zür|che|risch ['tsʏrçərɪʃ] ADJ of Zurich

zu+rech|nen VT *sep* a *(inf: = dazurechnen)* to add to b *(fig: = zuordnen)* (+*dat* with) to class, to include; *Kunstwerk etc (dat* to) to attribute, to ascribe; **sie wird dem linken Flügel der Partei zugerechnet** she is seen as belonging to the left wing of the party

Zu|rech|nung F a **unter** ~ **aller Kosten** inclusive of all charges b *(= Zuordnung)* assignment (to), inclusion (with)

Zu|rech|nungs-: **zu|rech|nungs|fä|hig** ADJ of sound mind, compos mentis *pred (esp Jur, inf)*; **Zu|rech|nungs|fä|hig|keit** F soundness of mind; **verminderte** ~ diminished responsibility; **auf verminderte** ~ **plädieren** to plead diminished responsibility; **ich muss doch schon manchmal an seiner** ~ **zweifeln!** *(inf)* I sometimes wonder if he's quite right in the head *(inf)*

zu|recht-: **zu|recht+bas|teln** VT *sep* **sich** *(dat)* **etw** ~ *(auch fig, iro)* to construct sth; **zu|recht+bie|gen** VT *sep irreg* to bend into shape; *(fig)* to twist; **er hat alles wieder zurechtgebogen** *(inf)* he has straightened *or* smoothed everything out again; **zu|recht+fei|len** VT *sep* to file into shape; **zu|recht+fin|den** VR *sep irreg* to find one's way *(in +dat* around); **sich in der Welt nicht mehr** ~ not to be able to cope with the world any longer; **ich finde mich in dieser Tabelle nicht zurecht** I can't make head nor tail of this table; **sich mit etw** ~ to get the hang of sth *(inf)*; *(durch Gewöhnung)* to get used to sth; **zu|recht+kom|men** VI *sep irreg aux sein* a *(= rechtzeitig kommen)* to come in time b *(fig)* to get on; *(= schaffen, bewältigen)* to cope; *(= genug haben)* to have enough; **kommen Sie ohne das zurecht?** *(inf)* can you manage without it?; **er kam nie zurecht im Leben** he was never able to cope with life c *(finanziell)* to manage; **mit 50 Euro am Tag kann man gut** ~ you can manage easily on 50 euros a day; **zu|recht+le|gen** VT *sep irreg* to lay *or* get out ready; **sich** *(dat)* **etw** ~ to lay *or* get sth out ready; *(fig)* to work sth out; **sich** *(dat)* **alle Argumente** ~ to marshal all one's arguments; **das hast du dir (bloß) zurechtgelegt!** *(gedeutet)* that's just your interpretation; *(erfunden)* you just made that up!; **zu|recht+ma|chen** *sep (inf)* VT a *Zimmer, Essen etc* to prepare, to get ready; *Bett* to make up b *(= anziehen)* to dress; *(= schminken)* to make up VR to get dressed *or* ready; *(= sich schminken)* to put on one's make-up; **auf etw** *(acc)* **zurechtgemacht sein** *(inf)* to be done up as sth *(inf)*; **zu|recht+rü|cken** VT *sep Brille, Hut etc* to adjust; *Stühle etc* to straighten (up), to put straight; *(fig)* to straighten out, to put straight → **Kopf a**; **zu|recht+schnei|den** VT *sep irreg* to cut to shape; *Haar, Nagel, Hecke* to trim, to cut; **zu|recht+schus|tern** VT *sep (inf)* to throw together; **zu|recht+set|zen** *sep* VT **sich** *(dat)* **den Hut/die Brille** ~ to adjust *or* straighten one's hat/glasses → **Kopf a** VR to settle oneself; **zu|recht+stau|chen** *sep (inf)* **jdn** ~ to haul *(Brit) or* rake *(US)* sb over the coals *(inf)*; **zu|recht+stel|len** *sep* VT to set out ready VR to pose, to arrange oneself; **zu|recht+stut|zen** VT *sep* to trim, to cut; *Hecke auch* to clip; *(fig)* to lick *(esp Brit) or* whip into shape; **zu|recht+wei|sen** VT *sep irreg* to rebuke; *Schüler etc* to reprimand; **Zu|recht|wei|sung** F rebuke; *(von Schüler)* reprimand; **zu|recht+zim|mern** VT *sep* to throw together; *(fig)* to construct

zu+re|den VI *sep* **jdm** ~ *(= ermutigen)* to encourage sb; *(= überreden)* to persuade sb; **wenn du ihm gut zuredest, hilft er dir** if you talk to him nicely, he'll help you; **sie hat ihrem Vater so lange zugeredet, bis er ihr das Auto kaufte** she kept on at her father till he bought her the car; **auf mein Zureden (hin)** with my encouragement; *(Überreden)* with my persuasion; **gutes** *or* **freundliches Zureden** friendly persuasion

zu+rei|chen *sep* VT **jdm etw** ~ to hand *or* pass sth to sb VI to be enough *or* sufficient; **ein ~der Grund** a sufficient *or* adequate reason

zu+rei|ten *sep irreg* VT *Pferd* to break in VI *aux sein (= weiterreiten)* to ride on; *(schneller)* to ride faster; **auf jdn/etw** ~, **auf jdn/etw zugeritten kommen** to ride toward(s) *or (direkt)* up to sb/sth

Zu|rei|ter(in) M(F) roughrider; *(für Wildpferde auch)* broncobuster

Zü|rich ['tsyːrɪç] NT **-s** Zurich

Zü|ri|cher ['tsyːrɪçɐ] M **-s, -**, **Zü|ri|che|rin** [-ərɪn] F **-, -nen** → **Zürcher**

Zü|rich|see M Lake Zurich

zu+rich|ten VT *sep* a *Essen etc* to prepare; *Stein, Holz* to square; *Leder, Pelz, Stoff* to finish, to dress; *(Typ)* to justify b *(= beschädigen, verunstalten)* to make a mess of; *(= verletzen)* to injure; **jdn übel** ~ to knock sb about *(Brit inf)*, to beat sb up

Zu|rich|ter(in) M(F) *(Typ)* justifier; *(von Stoffen, Pelzen)* dresser, finisher

Zu|rich|tung F *(Typ)* justifying, justification; *(von Geweben, Pelzen)* dressing, finishing

zu+rie|geln ['tsuːriːgln] VT *sep* to bolt (shut)

zür|nen ['tsʏrnən] VI *(geh)* **jdm** ~ to be angry with sb; **dem Schicksal** ~ to rage against fate

zu+rol|len VTI *sep (vi: aux sein)* to roll; **auf jdn/etw** ~, **auf jdn/etw zugerollt kommen** to roll toward(s) *or (direkt)* up to sb/sth

zur|ren ['tsʊrən] VT *(Naut)* to lash; *Deckladung, Beiboot etc* to lash down

Zur|schau|stel|lung [tsʊr'ʃau-] F display, exhibition

zu|rück [tsu'rʏk] ADV back; *(mit Zahlungen)* behind; *(fig: = zurückgeblieben) (von Kind)* backward; **in Französisch (sehr)** ~ **sein** *(fig)* to be (really) behind in French; **fünf Punkte** ~ *(Sport)* five points behind; ~ **nach** *etc* back to *etc*; ~**!** get back!; ~ **an Absender** return to sender; **einmal München und** ~ a return *(esp Brit) or* round-trip ticket *(US)* to Munich; **seit wann ist Trevor ~?** when did Trevor get back?; **ich bin in zehn Minuten wieder** ~ I will be back (again) in 10 minutes; **ein paar Jahre** ~ a few years back *or* ago; **hinter jdm** ~ **sein** *(fig)* to lie behind sb; **es gibt kein Zurück (mehr)** there's no going back

Zu|rück-: **zu|rück+be|ge|ben** *ptp* **zurückbegeben** VR *irreg (geh)* to return, to go back; **zu|rück+be|hal|ten** *ptp* **zurückbehalten** VT *sep irreg* to keep (back); **er hat Schäden/einen Schock** ~ he suffered lasting damage/lasting shock; **Zu|rück|be|hal|tungs|recht** NT *(Jur)* right of retention; **zu|rück+be|kom|men** *ptp* **zurückbekommen** VT *sep irreg* a *(= zurückerhalten)* to get back *(Brit)*, to get back at b *(inf: = heimgezahlt bekommen)* **das wirst du (von mir) ~!** I'll get my own back on you for that! *(Brit)*, I'll get back at you for that!; **zu|rück+be|or|dern** *ptp* **zurückbeordert** VT *sep* to recall, to order back; **zu|rück+be|ru|fen** *ptp* **zurückberufen** VT *sep irreg* to recall; **zu|rück+beu|gen** *sep* VT to bend back VR to lean *or* bend back; **zu|rück+be|we|gen** *ptp* **zurückbewegt** VTR *sep* to move back(wards); *(drehend)* to turn backwards; **zu|rück+bil|den** VR *sep (Geschwür)* to recede; *(Muskel)* to become wasted, to atrophy; *(Biol)* to regress; *(esp Sw: = abnehmen)* to decrease; **zu|rück+bin|den** VT *sep irreg Haare* to tie back

zu|rück+blei|ben VI *sep irreg aux sein* a *(an einem Ort)* to stay *or* remain behind; *(= weiter hinten gehen)* to stay (back) behind
b *(= übrig bleiben: Rest, Rückstand)* to be left; *(als Folge von Krankheit etc: Schaden, Behinderung)* to remain; **er blieb als Waise/Witwer zurück** he was left an orphan/a widower
c *(= nicht Schritt halten, auch fig: mit Arbeitsleistung etc)* to fall behind; *(Uhr)* to lose; *(in Entwicklung)* to be retarded *or* backward; *(Sport)* to be behind; **20 Meter** ~ to be 20 metres *(Brit) or* meters *(US)* behind; **die Einnahmen blieben hinter den Erwartungen zurück** the takings didn't come up to expectations → *auch* **zurückgeblieben**

zu|rück-: **zu|rück+blen|den** VI *sep (lit, fig)* to flash back *(auf +acc* to); **zu|rück+bli|cken** VI *sep* to look back *(auf +acc* at); *(fig)* to look back *(auf +acc* on); **zu|rück+brin|gen** VT *sep irreg (= wieder herbringen)* to bring back *(lit, fig)*; *(= wieder wegbringen)* to take back; **jdn ins Leben** ~ to bring sb back to life, to revive sb; **zu|rück+da|tie|ren** *ptp* **zurückdatiert** VT *sep* to backdate; **zu|rück+den|ken** VI *sep irreg* to think back *(an +acc* to); **so weit ich** ~ **kann** as far as I can recall *or* remember; **wenn man so zurückdenkt** when I think back; **zu|rück+drän|gen** VT *sep* to force *or* push back; *(Mil)* to drive back, to repel; *(fig: = eindämmen)* to repress, to restrain; **zu|rück+dre|hen** VT *sep* to turn back; *Uhr* to put *(Brit) or* turn *(US)* back; **die Uhr** *or* **Zeit** ~ to put *(Brit) or* turn *(US)* back the clock; **das Rad (der Geschichte)** ~ to turn back the hands of time; **zu|rück+dür|fen** VI *sep irreg (inf)* to be allowed back; **zu|rück+ei|len** VI *sep aux sein (geh)* to hurry back; **zu|rück+er|hal|ten** *ptp* **zurückerhalten** VT *sep irreg* to have returned; **zu|rück+er|in|nern** *ptp* **zurückerinnert** VR *sep* to remember, to recall *(an +acc* sth); **sich bis zu seinem 5. Lebensjahr/bis 1945** ~ **können** to be able to remember being 5 years old/as far back as 1945; **zu|rück+er|obern** *ptp* **zurückerobert** VT *sep (Mil)* to recapture, to retake, to reconquer; *(fig) Position, Marktanteil* to recapture, to regain; *Freund etc* to win back; **zu|rück+er|stat|ten** *ptp* **zurückerstattet** VT *sep* to refund; *Ausgaben* to reimburse; **zu|rück+er|war|ten** *ptp* **zurückerwartet** VT *sep* **jdn** ~ to expect sb back; **zu|rück+fah|ren** *sep irreg* VI *aux sein* a *(an einen Ort)* to go back, to return; *(esp als Fahrer)* to drive back b *(= zurückweichen)* to start back VT a *(mit Fahrzeug)* to drive back b *(= drosseln) Produktion, Investitionen* to cut back

zu|rück+fal|len VI *sep irreg aux sein* to fall back; *(Sport)* to drop back; *(fig) (Umsätze etc)* to fall, to drop (back); *(an Besitzer)* to revert *(an +acc* to); *(in Leistungen)* to fall behind; *(Schande, Vor-*

wurf etc) to reflect *(auf +acc* on); **in alte Gewohnheiten ~** to fall back into old habits; **er fällt immer wieder in seine alten Gewohnheiten zurück** he always lapses back into his old ways; **das würde bloß auf deine armen Eltern ~** that would only reflect (badly) on your poor parents

zu|rück-: zu|rück+fin|den VI *sep irreg* to find the *or* one's way back; **findest du allein zurück?** can you find your own way back?; **er fand zu sich selbst zurück** he found himself again; **er fand zu Gott/zum Sozialismus zurück** he found his way back to God/to Socialism; **zu|rück+flie|gen** VTI *sep irreg (vi: aux sein)* to fly back; **zu|rück+flie|ßen** VI *sep irreg aux sein (lit, fig)* to flow back; **zu|rück+flu|ten** VI *sep aux sein (Wellen)* to flow back; *(fig)* to stream back; **zu|rück+for|dern** VT *sep* **etw ~** to ask for sth back; *(stärker)* to demand sth back; **zu|rück+fra|gen** *sep* VT **etw ~** to ask sth back *or* in return VI to ask something *or* a question back; *(wegen einer Auskunft)* to check back; **zu|rück|führ|bar** ADJ traceable *(auf +acc* to); **auf eine Formel ~** reducible to a formula

zu|rück+füh|ren *sep* VT **a** *(= zurückbringen)* to lead back **b** *(= ableiten aus)* to put down to; **etw auf seine Ursache ~** to put sth down to its cause; **etw auf eine Formel/Regel ~** to reduce sth to a formula/rule; **das ist darauf zurückzuführen, dass ...** that can be put down to the fact that ... **c** *(= bis zum Ursprung zurückverfolgen)* to trace back VI to lead back; **es führt kein Weg zurück** there's no way back; *(fig)* there's no going back

zu|rück+ge|ben VT *sep irreg* to give back, to return; *Wechselgeld* to give back; *Ball, Kompliment, Beleidigung* to return; *(= erwidern)* to retort, to rejoin; **er gab mir das Buch zurück** he gave the book back to me, he returned the book to me; **das Geld kannst du dir von der Firma ~ lassen** you can ask the firm to give you the money back; **dieser Erfolg gab ihm seine Zuversicht wieder zurück** this success gave him back *or* restored his confidence; **jdm sein Wort ~** to release sb from his/her *etc* word; *(= sich entloben)* to break off one's engagement

zu|rück|ge|blie|ben ADJ **geistig/körperlich ~** mentally/physically retarded → *auch* **zurückbleiben**

zu|rück+ge|hen VI *sep irreg aux sein* **a** *(= zurückkehren)* to go back, to return *(nach, in +acc* to); *(fig: in der Geschichte etc)* to go back *(auf +acc, in +acc* to); *(= seinen Ursprung haben)* to go back to *(auf +acc* to); **er ging zwei Schritte zurück** he stepped back two paces, he took two steps back; **Waren/Essen** *etc* **~ lassen** to send back goods/food *etc*; **der Brief ging ungeöffnet zurück** the letter was returned unopened

b *(= zurückweichen)* to retreat, to fall back; *(fig: = abnehmen) (Hochwasser, Schwellung, Vorräte, Preise etc)* to go down; *(Geschäft, Umsatz, Produktion)* to fall off; *(Seuche, Schmerz, Sturm)* to die down; **im Preis ~** to fall *or* drop in price

zu|rück+ge|win|nen *ptp* **zurückgewonnen** VT *sep irreg* **a** *(beim Spiel)* to win back **b** *(Mil) Land* to reconquer, to regain **c** *(= wiederbekommen) Selbstvertrauen* to regain **d** *(Tech) Rohstoff* to recover

Zu|rück-: zu|rück|ge|zo|gen ADJ *Mensch* withdrawn, retiring; *Lebensweise* secluded ADV in seclusion; **er lebt sehr ~** he lives a very secluded life → *auch* **zurückziehen**; **Zu|rück|ge|zo|gen|heit** F -, *no pl* seclusion; **zu|rück+grei|fen** VI *sep irreg (fig)* to fall back *(auf +acc* upon); *(zeitlich)* to go back *(auf +acc* to); **da müsste ich weit ~** I would have to go back a long way; **zu|rück+ha|ben** VT *sep irreg (inf)* to have (got *(Brit) or* gotten *(US))* back; **ich will mein Geld ~** I want my money back; **hast du das Buch schon zurück?** have you got *(Brit) or* gotten *(US)* the book back yet?

zu|rück+hal|ten *sep irreg* VT *(= daran hindern, sich zu entfernen)* to hold back; *(= nicht durchlassen, aufhalten) jdn* to hold up, to detain; *(= nicht freigeben) Manuskript, Film, Informationen* to withhold; *(= eindämmen) Gefühle, Ärger etc* to restrain, to suppress; *(= unterdrücken) Tränen, Orgasmus* to keep *or* hold back; **jdn von etw** *(dat)* ~ to keep sb from sth

VR *(= sich beherrschen)* to contain *or* restrain oneself, to control oneself; *(= reserviert sein)* to be retiring *or* withdrawn; *(= im Hintergrund bleiben)* to keep in the background; *(bei Verhandlung, Demonstration etc)* to keep a low profile; *(bei Investitionen)* to be restrained; **sich mit seiner Kritik ~** to be restrained in one's criticism; **ich musste mich schwer ~** I had to take a firm grip on myself; **Sie müssen sich beim Essen sehr ~** you must cut down a lot on what you eat

VI **mit etw ~** *(= verheimlichen)* to hold sth back

zu|rück|hal|tend ADJ **a** *(= beherrscht, kühl)* restrained; *(= reserviert)* reserved; *(= vorsichtig)* cautious, guarded; *Börse* dull **b** *(= nicht großzügig)* sparing; **mit Tadel** *or* **Kritik nicht ~ sein** to be unsparing in one's criticism ADV with restraint; **sich ~ über etw** *(acc)* **äußern** to be restrained in one's comments about sth; **das Publikum reagierte ~** the audience's response was restrained

Zu|rück-: Zu|rück|hal|tung F, *no pl (= Beherrschtheit)* restraint; *(= Reserviertheit)* reserve; *(= Vorsicht)* caution; **sich** *(dat)* **~ auferlegen, ~ üben** to exercise restraint; **zu|rück+ho|len** VT *sep* to fetch back; *Geld* to get back; **jdn ~** *(fig)* to ask sb to come back; **zu|rück+ja|gen** *sep* VT to chase back VI *aux sein* to chase *or* dash back; **zu|rück+käm|men** VT *sep* to comb back; **zu|rück+kau|fen** VT *sep* to buy back, to repurchase; **zu|rück+keh|ren** VI *sep aux sein* to return *or* come back *(von, aus* from); to return *or* go back *(nach, zu* to); **zu|rück+kom|men** VI *sep irreg aux sein (lit, fig)* to come back, to return; *(= Bezug nehmen)* to refer *(auf +acc* to); **der Brief kam zurück** the letter was returned, the letter came back; **ich werde später auf deinen Vorschlag/dieses Angebot ~** I'll come back to your suggestion/this offer later; **zu|rück+kön|nen** VI *sep irreg (inf)* to be able to go back; **ich kann nicht mehr zurück** *(fig)* there's no going back!; **zu|rück+krie|gen** VT *sep (inf)* = **zurückbekommen**; **zu|rück+las|sen** VT *sep irreg* **a** *(= hinterlassen)* to leave; *(= liegen lassen)* to leave behind; *(fig: = übertreffen)* to leave behind, to outstrip; *(Leichtathletik)* to leave behind, to outdistance **b** *(inf: = zurückkehren lassen)* to allow back, to allow to return; **Zu|rück|las|sung** [-lasʊŋ] F -, *no pl* **unter ~ all seiner Habseligkeiten** *etc* leaving behind all one's possessions *etc*; **zu|rück+lau|fen** VI *sep irreg aux sein* to run back; *(= zurückgehen)* to walk *or* go back

zu|rück+le|gen *sep* VT **a** *(an seinen Platz)* to put back **b** *Kopf* to lay *or* lean back **c** *(= aufbewahren, reservieren)* to put aside *or* to one side; *(= sparen)* to put away, to lay aside; **jdm etw ~** to keep sth for sb **d** *Strecke* to cover, to do; **er hat schon ein ganzes Stück auf seinem Weg zum Diplomaten zurückgelegt** he has already gone a long way toward(s) becoming a diplomat VR to lie back

Zu|rück-: zu|rück+lehnen VTR *sep* to lean back; **zu|rück+lei|ten** VT *sep* to lead back; *Postsendung* to return; *Wasser etc* to feed back, to run back; **zu|rück+lie|gen** VI *sep irreg (örtlich)* to be behind; **der Unfall liegt etwa eine Woche zurück** the accident was about a week ago, it is about a week since the accident; **das liegt schon so weit zurück, dass ...** that is so long ago now that ...; **es liegt zwanzig Jahre zurück, dass ...** it is twenty years since ...; **zu|rück+mel|den** *sep* VTR to report back VR *(Univ)* to matriculate for the new term; **zu|rück+müs|sen** VI *sep irreg (inf)* to have to go back; **Zu|rück|nah|me** [-na:mə] F -, -n withdrawal *(auch Jur, Mil)*; *(von Aussage auch)* retraction; *(von Entscheidung)* reversal; **wir bitten um ~ dieser Sendung** we ask you to accept the return of this consignment

zu|rück+neh|men VT *sep irreg* to take back; *(Mil)* to withdraw; *Verordnung etc* to revoke; *Entscheidung* to reverse; *Angebot* to withdraw; *Auftrag, Bestellung* to cancel; *(Sport) Spieler* to bring *or* call back; *Schachzug* to go back on; **sein Wort/Versprechen ~** to go back on *or* break one's word/promise; **ich nehme alles zurück (und behaupte das Gegenteil)** I take it all back

zu|rück-: zu|rück+pfei|fen VT *sep irreg Hund etc* to whistle back; **jdn ~** *(fig inf)* to bring sb back into line; **zu|rück+pral|len** VI *sep aux sein* to rebound, to bounce back; *(Geschoss)* to ricochet; *(Strahlen, Hitze)* to be reflected; **von etw ~** to bounce/ricochet/be reflected off sth; **vor Schreck ~** to recoil in horror; **zu|rück+rech|nen** VTI *sep* to count back; **zu|rück+rei|chen** *sep* VT *Gegenstand* to hand *or* pass back VI *(Erinnerung, Tradition etc)* to go back *(in +acc* to); **zu|rück+rei|sen** VI *sep aux sein* to travel back, to return; **zu|rück+rei|ßen** VT *sep irreg* to pull back; **zu|rück+rol|len** VTI *sep (vi: aux sein)* to roll back; **zu|rück+ru|fen** *sep irreg* VT to call back; *(am Telefon auch)* to ring back *(Brit)*; *Botschafter, fehlerhafte Produkte* to recall; **jdn ins Leben ~** to bring sb back to life; **jdm etw in die Erinnerung** *or* **ins Gedächtnis ~** to conjure sth up for sb; **sich** *(dat)* **etw in die Erinnerung** *or* **ins Gedächtnis ~** to recall sth, to call sth to mind VI to call back; *(am Telefon auch)* to ring back *(Brit)*; **zu|rück+schal|len** VI *sep* to re-echo, to resound; **zu|rück+schal|ten** VI *sep* to change back; **zu|rück+schau|dern** VI *sep aux sein* to shrink back *(vor +acc* from), to recoil *(vor +acc* from); **zu|rück+schau|en** VI *sep (lit, fig)* to look back *(auf +acc (lit)* at, *(fig)* on); **zu|rück+scheu|chen** VT *sep* to chase back; **zu|rück+scheu|en** VI *sep aux sein* to shy away *(vor +dat* from); **vor nichts ~** to stop at nothing; **zu|rück+schi|cken** VT *sep* to send back; **jdm etw ~** to send sth back to sb, to send sb sth back; **zu|rück+schie|ben** VT *sep irreg* to push back

zu|rück+schla|gen *sep irreg* VT **a** *Ball* to knock away; *(mit Schläger)* to return, to hit back; *Feind, Angriff, Truppen etc* to beat back, to beat off *(Brit)*, to repulse **b** *(= umschlagen) Gardinen* to pull back; *Decke* to fold back; *Kragen* to turn down; *Schleier* to lift; *Buchseiten* to leaf back VI *(lit, fig)* to hit back; *(Mil, fig)* to retaliate, to strike back; *(Flamme)* to flare back; *(Pendel)* to swing back; **auf jdn/etw ~** to have repercussions for sb/sth

zu|rück-: zu|rück+schnei|den VT *sep irreg Hecke, Pflanze* to cut back; *Krallen* to trim; **zu|rück+schnel|len** VI *sep aux sein* to spring back; **zu|rück+schrau|ben** VT *sep* to screw back; *(fig inf) Erwartungen* to lower; *Subventionen* to cut back; **seine Ansprüche ~** to lower one's sights; **zu|rück+schre|cken** VI *sep irreg aux sein or haben* to shrink back, to start back, to recoil; *(fig)* to shy away *(vor +dat* from); **vor nichts ~** to stop at nothing; **zu|rück+se|hen** VI *sep irreg* to look back; **auf etw** *(acc)* **~** *(fig)* to look back on sth; **zu|rück+seh|nen** *sep* VR to long to return *(nach* to); **sich nach der guten alten Zeit ~** to long for the good old days VT *(liter)* **jdn/etw ~** to long for the return of sb/sth; **zu|rück+sen|den** VT *sep irreg* to send back, to return

zu|rück+set|zen *sep* VT **a** *(nach hinten)* to move back; *Auto* to reverse, to back **b** *(an früheren Platz)* to put back **c** *(dial) Preis, Waren* to reduce, to mark down; **zurückgesetzt** reduced, marked down **d** *(fig: = benachteiligen)* to neglect VR to sit back; **er setzte sich zwei Reihen zurück** he went to sit *or* he sat two rows back VI *(mit Fahrzeug)* to reverse, to back

Zu|rück-: **Zu|rück|set|zung** [-zɛtsʊŋ] F -, *no pl* (*fig*: = *Benachteiligung*) neglect; **von ~ der Mädchen kann keine Rede sein** there's no question of the girls being neglected; **zu|rück+sin|ken** VI *sep irreg aux sein* (*lit, fig*) to sink back (*in +acc* into); **zu|rück+spie|len** *sep* VT (*Sport*) to play back; (*Ftbl auch*) to pass back VI to play the ball *etc* back; (*Ftbl auch*) to pass back; **zu|rück+sprin|gen** VI *sep irreg aux sein* to leap *or* jump back; (*fig*: *Häuserfront*) to be set back; **zu|rück+ste|cken** *sep* VT to put back VI **a** (= *weniger Ansprüche stellen*) to lower one's expectations; (= *weniger ausgeben*) to cut back **b** (= *nachgeben, einlenken*) to backtrack

zu|rück+ste|hen VI *sep irreg* **a** (*Haus etc*) to stand back **b** (*an Leistung etc*) to be behind (*hinter jdm* sb) **c** (= *verzichten*) to miss out; (= *ausgelassen werden*) to be left out **d** (= *hintangesetzt werden*) to take second place; **hinter etw** (*dat*) **~** to take second place to sth; **sie muss immer hinter ihm ~** she always comes off worse than he does

zu|rück+stel|len VT *sep* **a** (*an seinen Platz*) *Uhr* to put back; (*nach hinten*) to move back **b** *Waren* to put aside *or* by **c** (*Aus*: = *zurücksenden*) to send back, to return **d** (*fig*) *Schüler* to keep down; **jdn vom Wehrdienst ~** to defer sb's military service **e** (*fig*: = *verschieben*) to defer; *Investitionen, Pläne* to postpone; *Bedenken, Forderungen etc* to put aside; *Sport, Privatleben, Hobbys etc* to spend less time on; **persönliche Interessen hinter etw** (*dat*) **~** to put one's personal interests after sth, to subordinate one's personal interests to sth; **persönliche Interessen ~** to put one's own interests last

Zu|rück-: **Zu|rück|stel|lung** F **a** (*Aus*: = *Zurücksendung*) return **b** (= *Aufschub, Mil*) deferment **c** (= *Hintanstellung*) **unter ~ seiner eigenen Interessen** putting his own interests last *or* aside; **zu|rück+sto|ßen** *sep irreg* VT **a** (= *wegstoßen*) to push back; (*fig*) to reject **b** (*fig*: = *abstoßen*) to put off VTI (*vi*: *aux sein*) (*Aut*: = *zurücksetzen*) to reverse, to back; **zu|rück+strah|len** *sep* VT to reflect VI to be reflected; **zu|rück+strei|chen** VT *sep irreg Haar* to smooth back; **sich** (*dat*) **das Haar ~** to smooth one's hair back; **zu|rück+strei|fen** VT *sep Ärmel etc* to pull up; **zu|rück+strö|men** VI *sep aux sein* to flow back; (*geh*: *Menschen*) to stream back; **zu|rück+stu|fen** VT *sep* to downgrade; **zu|rück+tau|meln** VI *sep aux sein* to reel back; **zu|rück+tra|gen** VT *sep irreg* to carry *or* take back; **zu|rück+trei|ben** VT *sep irreg* to drive back; (*Mil auch*) to repel, to repulse

zu|rück+tre|ten *sep irreg* VI *aux sein* **a** (= *zurückgehen*) to step back; (*fig*: *Fluss, Hochwasser etc*) to go down, to subside; **bitte ~!** stand back, please!; **einen Schritt ~** to take a step back **b** (*Regierung*) to resign; (*von einem Amt*) to step down, to resign **c** (*von einem Vertrag etc*) to withdraw (*von* from), to back out (*von* of); **von einem Anspruch/einem Recht ~** to renounce a claim/a right **d** (*fig*: = *geringer werden*) to decline, to diminish; (*Wald*) to recede; (= *an Wichtigkeit verlieren*) to fade (in importance); (= *im Hintergrund bleiben*) to come second (*hinter jdm/etw* to sb/sth) VTI (*mit Fuß*) to kick back

Zu|rück-: **zu|rück+tun** VT *sep irreg* (*inf*) to put back; **zu|rück+über|set|zen** *ptp* **zurückübersetzt** VT *sep* to translate back; **zu|rück+ver|fol|gen** *ptp* **zurückverfolgt** VT *sep* (*fig*) to trace back, to retrace; **zu|rück+ver|lan|gen** *ptp* **zurückverlangt** *sep* VT to demand back VI **nach etw ~** (*geh*) to yearn for the return of sth; **zu|rück+ver|le|gen** *ptp* **zurückverlegt** VT *sep* **a** (*zeitlich*) to set back **b** (*Mil*) *Front etc* to move back, to withdraw; *Deich* to move back **c** *Wohn-, Firmensitz* to move back; **zu|rück+ver|set|zen** *ptp* **zurückversetzt** *sep* VT **a** (*in seinen alten Zustand*) to restore (*in +acc* to); (*in eine andere Zeit*) to take back (*in +acc* to); **wir fühlten uns ins 18. Jahrhundert zurückversetzt** we felt as if we had been taken back *or* transported to the 18th century **b** *Beamte etc* to transfer back; *Schüler* to move down (*in +acc* into) VR to think oneself back (*in +acc* to); **zu|rück+ver|wan|deln** *ptp* **zurückverwandelt** VTR *sep* to turn *or* change back (*in +acc, zu* to); **zu|rück+ver|wei|sen** *ptp* **zurückverwiesen** VT *sep irreg* (*auch Jur*) to refer back; *jdn auch* to direct back; (*Parl*) *Gesetzentwurf* to recommit; **zu|rück+wei|chen** VI *sep irreg aux sein* (*vor +dat* from) (*erschrocken*) to shrink back; (*ehrfürchtig*) to stand back; (*nachgeben*) to retreat; (*vor Verantwortung, Hindernis*) to shy away; (*Mil*) to withdraw, to fall back; (*Hochwasser*) to recede, to subside; **zu|rück+wei|sen** VT *sep irreg* to reject; *Angebot auch, Geschenk* to refuse; *Gäste, Bittsteller* to turn away; *Berichte, Vorwurf* to dismiss; *Angriff* to repel, to repulse; (*Jur*) *Klage, Berufung* to dismiss, to reject; (*an der Grenze*) to turn back; **Zu|rück|wei|sung** F rejection; (*von Geschenk*) refusal; (*von Angriff*) repulsion; (*Jur*: *von Klage, Berufung*) dismissal; (*an der Grenze*) turning back; **er protestierte gegen seine ~ an der Grenze** he protested against being turned away at the border; **zu|rück+wen|den** VTR *sep irreg* to turn back; **zu|rück+wer|fen** VT *sep irreg Ball, Kopf* to throw back; *Feind* to repulse, to repel; *Strahlen, Schall* to reflect; (*fig*: *wirtschaftlich, gesundheitlich*) to set back (*um* by); **zu|rück+wir|ken** VI *sep* to react (*auf +acc* upon); **zu|rück+wol|len** VI *sep* (*inf*) to want to go back; **zu|rück+wün|schen** VT *sep* **sich** (*dat*) **jdn/etw ~** to wish sb/sth back, to wish that sb/sth were back

zu|rück+zah|len VT *sep* to repay, to pay back; *Schulden auch* to pay off; *Spesen etc* to refund; **das werde ich ihm noch ~!** (*fig*) I'll pay him back for that!

zu|rück+zie|hen *sep irreg* VT to pull *or* draw back; *Hand, Fuß* to pull *or* draw away *or* back; *Truppen* to pull back; (= *rückgängig machen*) *Antrag, Bemerkung, Klage etc* to withdraw VR to retire, to withdraw; (= *sich zur Ruhe begeben*) to retire; (*Mil*) to withdraw, to retreat; (*vom Geschäft, von der Politik etc*) to retire (*von, aus* from); **sich von jdm ~** to withdraw from sb; **sich von der Welt/in sich** (*acc*) **~** to retire from the world/into oneself → *auch* **zurückgezogen** VI *aux sein* to move back; (*Truppen*) to march back; (*Vögel*) to fly back

Zu|rück-: **Zu|rück|zie|hung** F withdrawal, retraction; **zu|rück+zu|cken** VI *sep aux sein* to recoil, to start back; (*Hand, Fuß*) to jerk back

Zu|ruf M shout, call; (*aufmunternd*) cheer; **durch ~ abstimmen** *or* **wählen** to vote by acclamation; **~e** shouts; (= *Zwischenrufe*) heckling

zu+ru|fen VTI *sep irreg* **jdm etw ~** to shout sth to *or* at sb; (*feierlich*) to call sth out to sb; **jdm anfeuernd ~** to cheer sb

zu+rüs|ten *sep* VT to set up, to get ready, to prepare VI to get everything set up *or* ready

Zu|rüs|tung F setting-up, preparation

zur|zeit [tsʊr'tsait] ADV at present, at the moment

Zu|sa|ge F **a** (= *Zustimmung*) assent, consent **b** (= *Verpflichtung*) undertaking, commitment **c** (= *Annahme*) acceptance; (= *Bestätigung*) confirmation **d** (= *Versprechen*) promise, pledge; **ich kann Ihnen keine ~n machen** I can't make you any promises

zu+sa|gen *sep* VT **a** (= *versprechen*) to promise; (= *bestätigen*) to confirm; **er hat sein Kommen fest zugesagt** he has promised firmly that he will come **b jdm etw auf den Kopf ~** (*inf*) to tell sb sth outright; **ich kann ihm auf den Kopf ~, wenn er mich belügt** I can tell straight away when he's lying VI **a** (= *annehmen*) **(jdm) ~** to accept; **eine ~de Antwort** a favourable (*Brit*) *or* favorable (*US*) reply **b** (= *gefallen*) **jdm ~** to appeal to sb; **das will mir gar nicht ~** I don't like it one little bit

zu|sam|men [tsu'zamən] ADV together; **alle/alles ~** all together; **wir hatten ~ 100 Euro zum Ausgeben** between us we had 100 euros to spend; **wir bestellten uns ~ eine Portion** we ordered one portion between us; **~ mit** together *or* along with; **das macht ~ 50 Euro** that comes to *or* makes 50 euros all together *or* in all; **er zahlt mehr als wir alle ~** he pays more than all of us *or* the rest of us put together; **David und Sarah sind ~** (= *sind ein Paar*) David und Sarah are an item (*inf*)

Zu|sam|men-: **Zu|sam|men|ar|beit** F co-operation; (*mit dem Feind*) collaboration; **in ~ mit** in co-operation with; **zu|sam|men+ar|bei|ten** VI *sep* to co-operate, to work together; (*mit dem Feind*) to collaborate; **zu|sam|men+ba|cken** VI *sep aux sein* (*inf*: = *kleben*) to stick together

zu|sam|men+bal|len *sep* VT *Schnee, Lehm* to make into a ball; *Papier* to screw (*Brit*) *or* crumple up into a ball VR (= *sich ansammeln*) to accumulate; (*Menge*) to mass (together); (*Mil*) to be concentrated *or* massed; **das Unheil ballte sich über seinem Haupt zusammen** (*liter*) disaster loomed over him

Zu|sam|men-: **Zu|sam|men|bal|lung** F accumulation; **Zu|sam|men|bau** M, *no pl* assembly; **zu|sam|men+bau|en** VT *sep* to assemble, to put together; **etw wieder ~** to reassemble sth; **zu|sam|men+bei|ßen** VT *sep irreg* **die Zähne ~** (*lit*) to clench one's teeth; (*fig*) to grit one's teeth; **zu|sam|men+be|kom|men** *ptp* **zusammenbekommen** VT *sep irreg* to get together; *Geld, Spenden* to collect; *Wortlaut* to remember; **zu|sam|men+bet|teln** VT *sep* **sich** (*dat*) **etw ~** to raise the money for sth; *Geld* to get sth together; **zu|sam|men+bin|den** VT *sep irreg* to tie *or* bind together; **zu|sam|men+blei|ben** VI *sep irreg aux sein* to stay together; **zu|sam|men+bor|gen** VT *sep* **sich** (*dat*) **Geld ~** to raise money; **sich** (*dat*) **etw ~** to borrow sth; **zu|sam|men+brau|en** *sep* VT (*inf*) to concoct, to brew (up) VR (*Gewitter, Unheil etc*) to be brewing

zu|sam|men+bre|chen VI *sep irreg aux sein* (*Gebäude*) to cave in; (*Brücke auch*) to give way; (*Wirtschaft, Markt, Imperium*) to collapse; (*Widerstand*) to crumble; (= *zum Stillstand kommen*) (*Verkehr etc*) to come to a standstill *or* halt; (*Verhandlungen, Telefonverbindung, Mil*: *Angriff*) to break down; (*Elec*: *Spannung*) to fail; (*Comput*: *Rechner*) to crash; (*Mensch*) to break down; (*vor Erschöpfung*) to collapse

zu|sam|men+brin|gen VT *sep irreg* **a** (= *sammeln*) to bring together, to collect; *Geld* to raise **b** (*inf*: = *zustande bringen*) to manage; *Gedanken* to collect; *Worte, Sätze* to put together; (= *ins Gedächtnis zurückrufen*) to remember; (= *zusammenkriegen, -bauen*) to get together **c** (= *in Kontakt bringen*) *Stoffe* to bring into contact with each other; (= *bekannt machen*) *Menschen* to bring together; **wieder ~** (= *versöhnen*) to reconcile, to bring back together; **die beiden Katzen darfst du nicht ~** you must not let the two cats get near each other

Zu|sam|men|bruch M (*von Beziehungen, Kommunikation*) breakdown; (*Comput*) crash; (*fig*) collapse; (= *Nervenzusammenbruch*) breakdown

zu|sam|men+drän|gen *sep* VT *Menschen* to crowd *or* herd together; (*fig*) *Ereignisse, Fakten* to condense VR (*Menschen*) to crowd (together); (*Mil*: *Truppen*) to be concentrated *or* massed; **die ganze Handlung des Stücks drängt sich im letzten Akt zusammen** all the action of the play is concentrated into the last act

Zu|sam|men-: **zu|sam|men+drü|cken** *sep* VT to press together; (= *verdichten*) to compress VR to be compressed; **zu|sam|men+fah|ren** *sep irreg* VI *aux sein* **a** (= *zusammenstoßen*) to collide **b** (= *erschrecken*) to start; (*vor Schmerz*) to flinch VT (*inf*) **a** (= *überfahren*) to run over **b** *Fahrzeug* to crash, to wreck; **Zu|sam|men|fall** M (*von Ereignissen*) coincidence

zu|sam|men+fal|len VI *sep irreg aux sein* **a** (= *einstürzen*) to collapse; **in sich** (*acc*) **~** (*lit, fig*) to collapse; (*Lügengebäude auch*) to fall apart; (*Hoff-*

nungen) to be shattered **b** *(= niedriger werden, sich senken)* to go down; **die Glut war (in sich) zusammengefallen** the fire had died down **c** *(durch Krankheit etc)* to waste away; **er sah ganz zusammengefallen aus** he looked very decrepit **d** *(Ereignisse)* to coincide

zu|sam|men+fal|ten VT *sep* to fold up

zu|sam|men+fan|ta|sie|ren *ptp* **zusammenfantasiert** VT *sep* **(sich** *dat***) etw ~** to dream sth up; *(inf: = lügen)* to make sth up

zu|sam|men+fas|sen *sep* VT **a** *(= verbinden)* to combine *(zu* in*)*; *(= vereinigen)* to unite; *(Math)* to sum; *(Mil) Truppen* to concentrate **b** *Bericht etc* to summarize; **etw in einem Satz ~** to sum sth up in one sentence VI *(= das Fazit ziehen)* to summarize, to sum up; **ein ~der Bericht** a summary, a résumé; **~d kann man sagen, ...** to sum up *or* in summary, one can say ...; **wenn ich kurz ~ darf** just to sum up

Zu|sam|men-: Zu|sam|men|fas|sung F **a** *no pl* combination; *(= Vereinigung)* union; *(Math)* summing; *(Mil: von Truppen)* concentration **b** *(= Überblick)* summary, synopsis, résumé; *(von Abhandlung)* abstract; **zu|sam|men+fe|gen** VT *sep* to sweep together; **zu|sam|men+fin|den** VR *sep irreg* to meet; *(= sich versammeln)* to congregate; **zu|sam|men+fli|cken** VT *sep* to patch together; *(inf) Verletzten* to patch up *(inf)*; *(fig) Aufsatz etc* to throw together; **zu|sam|men+flie|ßen** VI *sep irreg aux sein* to flow together, to meet; *(Farben)* to run together; **Zu|sam|men|fluss** M confluence; **zu|sam|men+fü|gen** *sep* VT to join together; *(Tech)* to fit together; **etw zu etw ~** to join/fit sth together to make sth VR to fit together; **sich gut ~** *(fig)* to turn out well; **zu|sam|men+füh|ren** VT *sep* to bring together; *Familie* to reunite; *(Comput) Dokumente* to merge; **zu|sam|men+ge|ben** VT *sep irreg (dial) Zutaten* to mix together; **zu|sam|men+ge|hen** VI *sep irreg aux sein* **a** *(= sich vereinen)* to unite; *(Linien etc)* to meet; *(Unternehmen)* to merge **b** *(= einlaufen: Wäsche)* to shrink **c** *(inf: = sich verbinden lassen)* to go together; **zu|sam|men+ge|hö|ren** *ptp* **zusammengehört** VI *sep (Menschen, Städte, Firmen etc)* to belong together; *(Gegenstände)* to go together, to match; *(als Paar)* to form a pair; *(Themen etc)* to go together; **zu|sam|men|ge|hö|rig** ADJ *Kleidungsstücke etc* matching; *(= verwandt)* related, connected; **~ sein** to match; to be related *or* connected; **Zu|sam|men|ge|hö|rig|keit** F **-,** *no pl* common bond; **Zu|sam|men|ge|hö|rig|keits|ge|fühl** NT *(in Gemeinschaft)* communal spirit; *(esp Pol)* feeling of solidarity; *(in Mannschaft)* team spirit; *(in Familie)* sense of a common bond; **zu|sam|men+ge|ra|ten** *ptp* **zusammengeraten** VI *sep irreg aux sein* **a** *(= zusammenkommen)* **mit jdm ~** to get together with sb **b** *(fig) (= aneinander geraten)* to come to blows *(mit* with*)*; *(= streiten)* to have words *(mit* with*)*

zu|sam|men|ge|setzt ADJ **aus etw ~ sein** to consist of sth, to be composed of sth; **~es Wort/Verb** compound (word)/verb; **~e Zahl** compound *or* complex number; **~er Satz** complex sentence → *auch* **zusammensetzen**

Zu|sam|men-: zu|sam|men|ge|wür|felt [-gəvʏrflt] ADJ oddly assorted, motley; *Mannschaft* scratch *attr*; **ein bunt ~er Haufen** a motley crowd; **zu|sam|men+gie|ßen** VT *sep irreg* to pour together; **zu|sam|men+ha|ben** VT *sep irreg (inf)* **etw ~** to have got *(Brit)* or gotten *(US)* sth together; *Geld auch* to have raised sth; **Zu|sam|men|halt** M, *no pl (Tech)* (cohesive) strength; *(einer Erzählung)* coherence, cohesion; *(fig: in einer Gruppe)* cohesion; *(esp Pol)* solidarity; *(fig: einer Mannschaft)* team spirit

zu|sam|men+hal|ten *sep irreg* VT **a** *(= verbinden)* to hold together; *(inf) Geld etc* to hold on to; **seine fünf Sinne ~** to keep one's wits about one **b** *(= nebeneinanderhalten)* to hold side by side VI to hold together; *(fig: Freunde, Gruppe etc)* to stick *or* stay together → **Pech a**

Zu|sam|men|hang M *(= Beziehung)* connection *(von, zwischen +dat* between*)*; *(= Wechselbeziehung)* correlation *(von, zwischen +dat* between*)*; *(= Verflechtung)* interrelation *(von, zwischen +dat* between*)*; *(von Geschichte)* coherence; *(im Text)* context; **jdn/etw mit jdm/etw in ~ bringen** to connect sb/sth with sb/sth; **im** *or* **in ~ mit etw stehen** to be connected with sth; **etw aus dem ~ reißen** to take sth out of its context; **nicht im ~ mit etw stehen** to have no connection with sth; **ich habe seinen Namen im ~ mit dieser Sache gehört** I've heard his name mentioned in connection with this; **in diesem ~** in this context, in connection with this

zu|sam|men+hän|gen *sep* VT *Kleider in Schrank etc* to hang (up) together VI *irreg* to be joined (together); *(fig)* to be connected; **~d** *(Rede, Erzählung)* coherent; **das hängt damit zusammen, dass ...** that is connected with the fact that ...

Zu|sam|men|hang(s)-: zu|sam|men|hang(s)|los ADJ incoherent, disjointed; *(= weitschweifig auch)* rambling ADV incoherently; **Sachen ~ anordnen** to arrange things haphazardly; **Zu|sam|men|hang(s)|lo|sig|keit** F **-,** *no pl* incoherence, disjointedness

Zu|sam|men-: zu|sam|men+har|ken VT *sep* to rake together; **zu|sam|men+hau|en** VT *sep irreg (inf)* **a** *(= zerstören)* to smash to pieces; **jdn ~** to beat sb up *(inf)* **b** *(fig: = pfuschen)* to knock together; *Geschriebenes* to scribble (down); **zu|sam|men+hef|ten** VT *sep (mit Heftklammern)* to staple together; *(Sew)* to tack together; **zu|sam|men+hei|len** VI *sep aux sein (Wunde)* to heal (up); *(Knochen)* to knit (together); **zu|sam|men+ho|len** VT *sep Sachen* to gather together; *Menschen* to bring together; **zu|sam|men+kau|ern** VR *sep (vor Kälte)* to huddle together; *(vor Angst)* to cower; **zu|sam|men+kau|fen** VT *sep* to buy (up); **zu|sam|men+keh|ren** VT *sep* to sweep together; **zu|sam|men+ket|ten** VT *sep* to chain together; *(fig)* to bind together; **Zu|sam|men|klang** M *(Mus, fig geh)* harmony, accord; **zu|sam|men|klapp|bar** ADJ folding; *Stuhl, Tisch auch* collapsible

zu|sam|men+klap|pen *sep* VT *Messer, Stuhl, Tisch etc* to fold up; *Schirm* to shut; **die Hacken ~** to click one's heels VI *aux sein* **a** *(Stuhl etc)* to collapse **b** *(fig inf)* to flake out *(inf)*; *(nach vorne)* to double up

Zu|sam|men-: zu|sam|men+klau|ben VT *sep* to gather (together), to collect; **zu|sam|men+klau|en** VT *sep (inf)* **sich** *(dat)* **etw ~** to collect sth (by stealing); **zu|sam|men+kle|ben** VTI *sep (vi: aux sein)* to stick together; **zu|sam|men+kleis|tern** VT *sep (inf)* **a** *(= zusammenkleben)* to paste together **b** *(fig)* to patch up *or* together; **zu|sam|men+klin|gen** VI *sep irreg* to sound together; *(fig: Farben etc)* to harmonize; **zu|sam|men+knei|fen** VT *sep irreg Lippen, Pobacken etc* to press together; *Augen* to screw up; **zusammengekniffen** *(Augen)* screwed-up; *Mund* pinched; **zu|sam|men+kno|ten** VT *sep* to knot *or* tie together; **zu|sam|men+knül|len** VT *sep* to screw *(esp Brit)* or crumple up

zu|sam|men+kom|men VI *sep irreg aux sein* to meet (together), to come together; *(Umstände)* to combine; *(fig: = sich einigen)* to agree, to come to an agreement; *(fig) (= sich ansammeln: Schulden etc)* to mount up, to accumulate; *(Geld bei einer Sammlung)* to be collected; **er kommt viel mit Menschen zusammen** he meets a lot of people; **wir kommen zweimal jährlich zusammen** we meet twice a year, we get together twice a year; **heute kommt wieder mal alles zusammen** *(inf)* it's all happening at once today

Zu|sam|men-: zu|sam|men+kop|peln VT *sep Anhänger, Wagen* to couple together; *(Space)* to dock; **zu|sam|men+kra|chen** VI *sep aux sein (inf)* **a** *(= einstürzen)* to crash down; *(fig: Börse, Wirtschaft)* to crash **b** *(= zusammenstoßen: Fahrzeuge)* to crash (into each other); **zu|sam|men+kramp|fen** VR *(Hände)* to clench; *(Muskel, Magen)* to tense up; **da krampfte sich mein Herz zusammen** my heart nearly stopped; **zu|sam|men+krat|zen** VT *sep* to scrape *or* scratch *(esp Brit)* together; *(fig inf) Geld etc* to scrape together; **zu|sam|men+krie|gen** VT *sep (inf)* = **zusammenbekommen**; **Zu|sam|men|kunft** [tsuˈzamənkʊnft] F **-, -künfte** [-kʏnftə] meeting; *(von mehreren auch)* gathering; *(zwanglos)* get-together; **zu|sam|men+läp|pern** VR *sep (inf)* to add *or* mount up; **zu|sam|men+las|sen** VT *sep irreg* to leave together

zu|sam|men+lau|fen VI *sep irreg aux sein* **a** *(= an eine Stelle laufen)* to gather; *(Flüssigkeit)* to collect **b** *(Flüsse etc)* to flow together, to meet; *(Farben)* to run together; *(Math)* to intersect, to meet; *(Straßen)* to converge; *(fig: Fäden etc)* to meet **c** *(Stoff)* to shrink **d** *(Milch)* to curdle, to coagulate

zu|sam|men+le|ben *sep* VI to live together VR to learn to live with each other

Zu|sam|men|le|ben NT living together *no art*; *(von Ländern etc)* coexistence; **das ~ der Menschen** the social life of man; **mein ~ mit ihm war ...** living with him was ...; **das menschliche ~** social existence; **eheliches ~** married life; **außereheliches ~** cohabitation

zu|sam|men+le|gen *sep* VT **a** *(= falten)* to fold (up) **b** *(= stapeln)* to pile *or* heap together **c** *(= vereinigen)* to combine, to merge; *Aktien* to amalgamate, to consolidate; *Grundstücke* to join; *Veranstaltungen* to hold together, to hold at the same time; *Häftlinge, Patienten* to put together; *Termine* to combine; *(= zentralisieren)* to centralize; **sie legten ihr Geld zusammen** they pooled their money, they clubbed *(Brit)* or pitched in *(US)* together VI *(= Geld gemeinsam aufbringen)* to club *(Brit)* or pitch in *(US)* together, to pool one's money; **für ein Geschenk ~** to club *(Brit)* or pitch in *(US)* together for a present

Zu|sam|men-: Zu|sam|men|le|gung [-leːgʊŋ] F **-, -en** *(= Vereinigung)* amalgamation, merging; *(von Aktien)* amalgamation, consolidation; *(von Grundstücken)* joining; *(= Zentralisierung)* centralization; *(von Terminen)* combining; **die ~ aller Patienten auf eine Station** putting all the patients together in one ward; **zu|sam|men+lei|hen** VT *sep irreg* **sich** *(dat)* **etw ~** to borrow sth; **zu|sam|men+lei|men** VT *sep* to glue together; **zu|sam|men+lö|ten** VT *sep* to solder together; **zu|sam|men+lü|gen** VT *sep irreg (inf)* to make up, to concoct; **was der (sich** *dat***) wieder zusammenlügt!** the stories he makes up!; **zu|sam|men+na|geln** VT *sep* to nail together; **zu|sam|men+nä|hen** VT *sep* to sew *or* stitch together

zu|sam|men+neh|men *sep irreg* VT to gather up *or* together; *Mut* to summon up, to muster up; *Gedanken* to collect; **seine ganze Kraft ~** to gather all one's strength; **alles zusammengenommen** all together, all in all; **wenn wir alle Ereignisse ~** if we consider everything that happened VR *(= sich zusammenreißen)* to pull oneself together, to get a grip on oneself *(Brit)*, to take hold of oneself *(US)*; *(= sich beherrschen)* to control oneself, to take a grip on oneself

Zu|sam|men-: zu|sam|men+packen *sep* VT to pack up together; **pack (deine Sachen) zusammen!** get packed! VI *(= einpacken)* to pack, to do one's packing; **zu|sam|men+pas|sen** VI *sep (Menschen)* to suit each other, to be suited to each other; *(Farben, Stile)* to go together; **gut ~** to go well together; **überhaupt nicht ~** not to go together at all; **das passt nicht mit den Tatsachen zusammen** it doesn't fit the facts; **zu|sam|men+pfer|chen** VT *sep* to herd together; *(fig)* to pack together; **zu|sam|men+phan|ta|sie|ren** VT *sep* = **zusammenfantasieren**; **Zu|sam|men|prall** M collision; *(fig)* clash; **zu|sam|men+pral|len** VI *sep aux sein* to collide; *(fig)* to clash; **zu|sam|men+pres|sen** VT *sep* to press *or* squeeze together; *(= verdichten)* to compress; **zu|sạm|men+raf|fen** *sep* VT **a** *Gegenstände, Habseligkeiten* to bundle together; *Röcke* to gather up **b** *(fig) Mut* to summon up, to muster (up) **c** *(fig pej: = anhäufen)* to amass, to pile up VR to pull oneself together; **zu|sạm|men+ras|seln** VI *sep aux sein (inf)* to collide; *(fig)* to have a row; **zu|sạm|men+rau|fen** VR *sep* to get it all together *(inf)*, to achieve a viable working relationship; **zu|sạm|men+rech|nen** VT *sep* to add *or* total up; **alles zusammengerechnet** all together; *(fig)* all in all

zu|sạm|men+rei|men *sep* VT *(inf)* **sich** *(dat)* **etw ~** to figure sth out (for oneself); **das kann ich mir nicht ~** I can't make head or tail of this, I can't figure it out at all; **sich** *(dat)* **den Rest ~** to put two and two together; **das kann ich mir jetzt ~, warum ...** I can see now why ... VR to make sense; **wie soll sich das ~?** it doesn't make sense

Zu|sạm|men-: **zu|sạm|men+rei|ßen** *sep irreg* VR to pull oneself together VT **die Hacken ~** to click one's heels; **zu|sạm|men+rol|len** *sep* VT to roll up VR to curl up; *(Igel)* to roll *or* curl (itself) up (into a ball); *(Schlange)* to coil up; **zu|sạm|men+rot|ten** VR *sep (pej) (esp Jugendliche)* to gang up *(gegen* against); *(esp heimlich)* to band together *(gegen* against); *(in aufrührerischer Absicht)* to form a mob; **Zu|sạm|men|rot|tung** [-rɔtʊŋ] F **-, -en a** *no pl* ganging up; *(esp heimlich)* banding together **b** *(= Gruppe) (esp von Jugendlichen)* gang; *(in aufrührerischer Absicht)* mob; *(Jur)* riotous assembly; **zu|sạm|men+rü|cken** *sep* VT *Möbel etc* to move closer together; *(schreiben) Wörter etc* to close up VI *aux sein* to move up closer, to move closer together; **zu|sạm|men+ru|fen** VT *sep irreg* to call together; **zu|sạm|men+sa|cken** VI *sep aux sein* to slump; *(Gebäude)* to cave in; **in sich** *(acc)* **~** *(lit)* to collapse; *(fig) (bei Nachricht etc)* to seem to crumble; *(= Schwung verlieren)* to have lost all interest; **zu|sạm|men+scha|ren** VR *sep* to gather; *(Menschen auch)* to congregate; **Zu|sạm|men|schau** F overall view; **erst in der ~ ...** only when you view everything as a whole ...; **zu|sạm|men+schei|ßen** VT *sep irreg (inf)* **jdn ~** to give sb a bollocking *(Brit inf)*, to kick sb's ass *(US sl)*; **zu|sạm|men+schie|ßen** VT *sep irreg* to shoot up, to riddle with bullets, to shoot to pieces; *(mit Artillerie)* to pound to pieces

zu|sạm|men+schla|gen *sep irreg* VT **a** *(= aneinanderschlagen)* to knock *or* bang *or* strike together; *Becken* to clash; *Hacken* to click; *Hände* to clap **b** *(= falten)* to fold up **c** *(= verprügeln)* to beat up; *(= zerschlagen) Einrichtung* to smash up, to wreck VI *aux sein* **über jdm/etw ~** *(Wellen etc)* to close over sb/sth; *(stärker)* to engulf sb/sth; *(fig: Unheil etc)* to descend upon sb/sth, to engulf sb/sth

Zu|sạm|men-: **zu|sạm|men+schlie|ßen** VR *sep irreg* to join together, to combine; *(Comm)* to amalgamate, to merge; **sich gegen jdn ~** to band together against sb; **Zu|sạm|men|schluss** M joining together, combining; *(Comm)* amalgamation, merger; *(von politischen Gruppen)* amalgamation; **zu|sạm|men+schmel|zen** *sep irreg* VT *(= verschmelzen)* to fuse VI *aux sein* **a** *(= verschmelzen)* to fuse, to melt together **b** *(= zerschmelzen)* to melt (away); *(Widerstand, Vorsprung)* to melt away; *(Anzahl, Vermögen)* to dwindle; **zu|sạm|men+schnü|ren** VT *sep* to tie up; **dieser traurige Anblick schnürte mir das Herz zusammen** this pitiful sight made my heart bleed; **zu|sạm|men+schnur|ren** VI *sep (inf: = schrumpfen)* to shrink; **zu|sạm|men+schrau|ben** VT *sep* to screw together; *(mit Bolzen)* to bolt together; **zu|sạm|men+schre|cken** VI *sep irreg aux sein* to start

zu|sạm|men+schrei|ben VT *sep irreg* **a** *Wörter (orthographisch)* to write together; *(im Schriftbild)* to join up **b** *(pej: = verfassen)* to scribble down; **was der für einen Mist zusammenschreibt** what a load of rubbish *(esp Brit) or* garbage he writes **c** *(inf: = durch Schreiben verdienen)* **sich** *(dat)* **ein Vermögen ~** to make a fortune with one's writing

Zu|sạm|men-: **zu|sạm|men+schrump|fen** VI *sep aux sein* to shrivel up; *(fig)* to dwindle *(auf +acc* to); **zu|sạm|men+schus|tern** VT *sep* to throw together; **zu|sạm|men+schwei|ßen** VT *sep (lit)* to weld together; **zu|sạm|men sein** VI *sep irreg aux sein* **mit jdm ~** to be with sb; *(inf: = befreundet)* to be going out with sb; *(euph: = mit jdm schlafen)* to sleep with sb

Zu|sạm|men|sein NT being together *no art*; *(von Gruppe)* get-together

zu|sạm|men+set|zen *sep* VT **a** *Schüler, Gäste etc* to put *or* seat together **b** *Gerät, Gewehr etc* to put together, to assemble *(zu* to make) VR **a** *(= sich zueinandersetzen)* to sit together; *(um etwas zu besprechen, zu trinken etc)* to get together; **sich mit jdm (am Tisch) ~** to join sb (at their table); **sich gemütlich ~** to have a cosy get-together; **sich auf ein Glas Wein ~** to get together over a glass of wine **b sich ~ aus** to consist of, to be composed of, to be made up of → *auch* **zusammengesetzt**

Zu|sạm|men-: **Zu|sạm|men|setz|spiel** NT puzzle; *(= Puzzle)* jigsaw (puzzle); **Zu|sạm|men|set|zung** [-zɛtsʊŋ] F **-, -en** putting together; *(von Gerät auch)* assembly; *(= Struktur)* composition, make-up; *(= Mischung)* mixture, combination *(aus* of); *(Gram)* compound; **das Team in dieser ~** the team in this line-up; **zu|sạm|men+sin|ken** VI *sep irreg aux sein* **(in sich) ~** to slump; *(Gebäude)* to cave in; **zusammengesunken** *(vor Kummer etc)* bowed; **zu|sạm|men+sit|zen** VI *sep irreg aux haben or (Aus, S Ger, Sw) sein* to sit next to each other; *(= zusammen sein)* to sit together; **wir saßen gerade gemütlich zusammen, als ...** we were just sitting together having a nice chat when ...; **zu|sạm|men+spa|ren** VT *sep* to save up; **Zu|sạm|men|spiel** NT *(Mus)* ensemble playing; *(Theat)* ensemble acting; *(Sport)* teamwork; *(fig)* co-operation, teamwork; *(von Kräften etc)* interaction; **zu|sạm|men+stau|chen** VT *sep (inf)* to give a dressing-down *(inf)*, to chew out *(US inf)*; **zu|sạm|men+ste|cken** *sep* VT *Einzelteile* to fit together; *(mit Nadeln etc)* to pin together; **sie steckten die Köpfe zusammen** *(inf)* they put their heads together; *(um zu flüstern)* they whispered to each other VI *(inf)* to be together; **immer ~** to be inseparable, to be as thick as thieves *(pej inf) or* blood *(US inf)*; **zu|sạm|men+ste|hen** VI *sep irreg* to stand together, to stand side by side; *(Gegenstände)* to be together, to be side by side; *(fig)* to stand by each other

zu|sạm|men+stel|len VT *sep* to put together; *(nach einem Muster, System)* to arrange; *Bericht, Programm* to compile, to put together; *(= sammeln) Daten* to compile; *Liste, Fahrplan* to draw up; *Rede* to draft; *Sammlung* to assemble, to put together; *Gruppe* to assemble; *(Sport) Mannschaft* to pick; **etw nach Gruppen** *etc* **~** to arrange sth in groups *etc*

Zu|sạm|men|stel|lung F **a** *no pl* putting together; *(nach Muster, System)* arranging; *(von Bericht, Programm, Daten)* compiling; *(von Liste, Fahrplan)* drawing up; *(von Mannschaft)* picking **b** *(= Kombination) (nach Muster, System)* arrangement; *(von Daten, Programm)* compilation; *(= Liste)* list; *(= Zusammensetzung)* composition; *(= Übersicht)* survey; *(= Gruppierung)* assembly, group; *(von Farben)* combination

Zu|sạm|men-: **zu|sạm|men+stim|men** VI *sep (farblich)* to match; *(musikalisch)* to harmonize; *(= übereinstimmen)* to agree, to tally *(mit* with); **zu|sạm|men+stop|peln** [-ʃtɔpln] VT *sep (inf)* to throw together; **sich** *(dat)* **eine Rede** *etc* **~** to throw a speech *etc* together; **Zu|sạm|men|stoß** M collision, crash; *(Mil, fig: = Streit)* clash

zu|sạm|men+sto|ßen *sep irreg* VI *aux sein (= zusammenprallen)* to collide; *(Mil, fig: = sich streiten)* to clash; *(= sich treffen)* to meet; *(= gemeinsame Grenze haben)* to adjoin; **mit jdm ~** to collide with sb, to bump into sb; *(fig)* to clash with sb; **sie stießen mit den Köpfen zusammen** they banged *or* bumped their heads together; **mit der Polizei ~** to clash with the police VT to knock together; **er stieß sie mit den Köpfen zusammen** he banged *or* knocked their heads together

Zu|sạm|men-: **zu|sạm|men+strei|chen** VT *sep irreg* to cut (down) *(auf +acc* to); **zu|sạm|men+strö|men** VI *sep aux sein (Flüsse)* to flow into one another, to flow together; *(geh: Menschen)* to flock *or* swarm together; **zu|sạm|men+stü|ckeln** VT *sep* to patch together; **zu|sạm|men+stür|zen** VI *sep aux sein* **a** *(= einstürzen)* to collapse, to tumble down **b** *(= zusammenlaufen)* to rush to gather round; **zu|sạm|men+su|chen** VT *sep* to collect (together); **sich** *(dat)* **etw ~** to find sth; **zu|sạm|men+tra|gen** VT *sep irreg (lit, fig)* to collect; *(Typ) Bögen* to collate; **zu|sạm|men+tref|fen** VI *sep irreg aux sein (Menschen)* to meet; *(Ereignisse)* to coincide; **mit jdm ~** to meet sb; **Zu|sạm|men|tref|fen** NT meeting; *(esp zufällig)* encounter; *(zeitlich)* coincidence; **zu|sạm|men+trei|ben** VT *sep irreg* to round up; **zu|sạm|men+tre|ten** *sep irreg* VT *(= zertrampeln)* to trample *or* crush underfoot VI *aux sein (Verein etc)* to meet; *(Parlament auch)* to assemble; *(Gericht)* to sit; **Zu|sạm|men|tritt** M meeting; *(von Parlament auch)* assembly; *(von Gericht)* session; **zu|sạm|men+trom|meln** VT *sep (inf)* to round up *(inf)*; **zu|sạm|men+tun** *sep irreg* VT *(inf)* to put together; *(= vermischen)* to mix VR to get together; **zu|sạm|men+wach|sen** VI *sep irreg aux sein* to grow together; *(= zuheilen: Wunde)* to heal (up), to close; *(Knochen)* to knit; *(fig)* to grow close; **zusammengewachsen sein** *(Knochen)* to be joined *or* fused; **zu|sạm|men+wer|fen** VT *sep irreg* **a** *Gegenstände* to throw together; *(fig) (= durcheinanderbringen)* to mix *or* jumble up; *(= in einen Topf werfen)* to lump together **b** *(= umwerfen)* to throw down; **zu|sạm|men+wir|ken** VI *sep* to combine, to act in combination; **zu|sạm|men+wür|feln** VT *sep* to throw together; **zusammengewürfelt** thrown together; **zusammengewürfelte Mannschaft** scratch team; **ein bunt zusammengewürfelter Haufen** a motley crowd; **zu|sạm|men+zäh|len** VT *sep* to add up; **alles zusammengezählt macht es 50 Euro** that makes 50 euros altogether *or* all told *or* in all

zu|sạm|men+zie|hen *sep irreg* VT **a** *Muskel* to draw *or* pull together; *(= verengen)* to narrow; *Knoten, Schlinge* to tighten; *Augenbrauen, Stirn* to knit; **ein Loch in einem Strumpf ~** to mend a hole in a stocking *(by pulling the sides together and sewing it up)*; **der saure Geschmack zog ihm den Mund zusammen** he screwed up his mouth at the bitter taste; **das zieht einem das Herz zusammen** it really pulls at the heartstrings; **~de Mittel** *(Med)* astringents

b *(fig) Truppen, Polizei* to assemble

c *(= kürzen) Wörter etc* to contract, to shorten; *(Math) Zahlen* to add together; *mathematischen Ausdruck* to reduce

VR *(esp Biol, Sci)* to contract; *(= enger werden)* to narrow; *(Wunde)* to close (up); *(Gewitter, Unheil)* to be brewing

VI *aux sein* to move in together; **mit jdm ~** to move in with sb

zu|sạm|men+zu|cken VI *sep aux sein* to start

Zu̲|satz M addition; *(= Bemerkung)* additional remark; *(zu Gesetz, Vertrag etc)* rider; *(zu Testament)* codicil; *(Gram)* expression in opposition; *(= Verbzusatz)* separable element; *(= Beimischung)* addition, additive; **durch/nach ~ von etw** by/after adding sth, with *or* by/after the addition of sth

Zu̲|satz- *in cpds* additional, supplementary; **Zu̲|satz|ab|kom|men** NT supplementary agreement; **Zu̲|satz|ak|tie** F bonus share;

Zu|satz|an|trag M *(Parl etc)* amendment; **Zu|satz|ar|ti|kel** M additional *or* supplementary article; **Zu|satz|be|las|tung** F additional load; **Zu|satz|be|stim|mung** F supplementary provision; **Zu|satz|er|klä|rung** F *(Pol)* supplementary declaration; **Zu|satz|fra|ge** F follow-up question; **Zu|satz|ge|rät** NT attachment; *(Comput)* peripheral (device), add-on; **Zu|satz|in|for|ma|ti|o|nen** PL additional information *no pl*; **Zu|satz|klau|sel** F additional clause; *(Jur)* rider *(Brit)*; **Zu|satz|kos|ten** PL additional costs *pl*

zu|sätz|lich ['tsu:zɛtslɪç] ADJ additional; *(= weiter auch)* added *attr*, further *attr*; *(= ergänzend auch)* supplementary ADV in addition

Zu|satz-: **Zu|satz|mit|tel** NT additive; **Zu|satz|pla|ti|ne** F *(Comput)* daughterboard; **Zu|satz|pro|gramm** NT *(Comput)* applet; **Zu|satz|stoff** M additive; **Zu|satz|ver|si|che|rung** F additional *or* supplementary insurance; **Zu|satz|zahl** F *(Lotto)* additional number, bonus number *(Brit)*

zu+sau|fen VR *sep irreg (sl: = sich betrinken)* to get pissed *(Brit inf) or* plastered *(inf)*

zu|schalt|bar ADJ connectible

zu+schal|ten *sep* VT to switch on (in addition); *Rundfunk-, Fernsehanstalt* to link up with VR to come on; *(Rundfunk-, Fernsehanstalt)* to link into the network

zu|schan|den, zu Schan|den [tsu'ʃandn] ADV *(geh)* ~ **machen** *(fig)* to ruin, to wreck; **ein Auto ~ fahren** to wreck a car; **ein Pferd ~ reiten** to ruin a horse; ~ **werden** *(fig)* to be wrecked *or* ruined

zu+schan|zen VT *sep (inf)* **jdm etw ~** to make sure sb gets sth

zu+schar|ren VT *sep* to cover over *or* up

zu+schau|en VI *sep (esp dial)* = **zusehen**

Zu|schau|er ['tsu:ʃauɐ] M **-s, -**, **Zu|schau|e|rin** [-ərɪn] F **-, -nen** spectator *(auch Sport)*; *(TV)* viewer; *(Theat)* member of the audience; *(= Beistehender)* onlooker; **die ~** *pl* the spectators *pl*; *(esp Ftbl auch)* the crowd *sing*; *(TV)* the (television) audience *sing*, the viewers; *(Theat)* the audience *sing*; **einer der ~** *(Theat)* one of the audience, a member of the audience; **wie viele ~ waren da?** *(Sport)* how many spectators were there?; *(esp Ftbl auch)* how large was the crowd?

Zu|schau|er-: **Zu|schau|er|be|fra|gung** F *(TV)* (television) audience survey; **Zu|schau|er|ku|lis|se** F, **Zu|schau|er|men|ge** F *(Sport)* crowd, gathering of spectators; **Zu|schau|er|rang** M *(Sport)* stand; **Zu|schau|er|raum** M auditorium; **Zu|schau|er|re|ak|ti|on** F audience response; *(TV)* viewer response; *(Sport)* reaction of the crowd; **Zu|schau|er|ter|ras|se** F *(Sport)* (spectators') stand; *(auf Flughafen)* observation deck, spectators' gallery; **Zu|schau|er|tri|bü|ne** F *(esp Sport)* stand; **Zu|schau|er|um|fra|ge** F *(TV)* (television) audience survey; **Zu|schau|er|zahl** F attendance figure; *(Sport auch)* gate

zu+schau|feln VT *sep* to fill up

zu+schi|cken VT *sep* **jdm etw ~** to send sth to sb, to send sb sth; *(mit der Post® auch)* to post *(Brit) or* mail *(esp US)* sth to sb; **sich** *(dat)* **etw ~ lassen** to send for sth; **etw zugeschickt bekommen** to receive sth (by post *(Brit) or* mail), to get sth sent to one

zu+schie|ben VT *sep irreg* **a jdm etw ~** to push sth over to sb; *(heimlich)* to slip sb sth; *(fig: = zuschanzen)* to make sure sb gets sth; **jdm die Verantwortung/Schuld ~** to put the responsibility/blame on sb → **schwarz ADJ a b** *(= schließen) Tür, Fenster* to slide shut; *Schublade* to push shut

zu+schie|ßen *sep irreg* VT **a jdm den Ball ~** to kick the ball (over) to sb; **jdm wütende Blicke ~** to dart angry glances at sb, to look daggers at sb *(Brit)* **b** *Geld etc* to contribute; **Geld für etw ~** to put money toward(s) sth; **jdm 100 Euro ~/zu etw ~** to give sb 100 euros toward(s) it/sth VI *aux sein (inf)* **auf jdn/etw ~** *or* **zugeschossen kommen** to rush *or* shoot up to sb/sth

Zu|schlag M **a** *(= Erhöhung)* extra charge, surcharge *(esp Comm, Econ)*; *(auf Briefmarke)* supplement; *(Rail)* supplement, supplementary charge; **für diese Züge muss man ~ bezahlen** you have to pay a supplement *or* a supplementary charge on these trains
b *(Tech)* addition
c *(bei Versteigerung)* acceptance of a bid; *(= Auftragserteilung)* acceptance of a/the tender; **mit dem ~ des Versteigerers ...** when the auctioneer concluded the bidding; **jdm den ~ erteilen** *(form) or* **geben** to knock down the lot *or* item to sb; *(nach Ausschreibung)* to award the contract to sb; **er erhielt den ~** the lot went to him; *(nach Ausschreibung)* he obtained the contract, he was awarded the contract

zu+schla|gen *sep irreg* VT **a** *Tür, Fenster* to slam (shut), to bang shut; **die Tür hinter sich** *(dat)* **~** to slam the door behind one
b *(Sport: = zuspielen)* **jdm den Ball ~** to hit the ball to sb; *(Ftbl inf)* to kick the ball to sb
c *(rare: = zufügen)* to add (on) (*+dat, zu* to)
d *(bei Versteigerung)* **jdm etw ~** to knock sth down to sb; **einer Firma einen Vertrag ~** to award a contract to a firm
e *(= zuerkennen) Gebiet* to annex (*+dat* to); *Geld, Güter* to award
VI **a** *(= kräftig schlagen)* to strike *(auch fig)*; *(= losschlagen)* to hit out; **schlag zu!** hit me/him/it etc!; **das Schicksal hat entsetzlich zugeschlagen** *(geh)* fate has struck a terrible blow
b *aux sein (Tür)* to slam (shut), to bang shut
c *(fig inf: = zugreifen) (bei Angebot)* to go for it; *(beim Essen)* to get stuck in *(inf)*; *(Polizei)* to pounce, to strike; **die EU-Bürokratie hat wieder zugeschlagen** EU bureaucracy has struck again *(inf)*

Zu|schlag(s)-: **zu|schlag(s)|frei** ADJ *Zug* not subject to a supplement ADV **alle Überstunden sind ~** all overtime is paid at the normal hourly rate; **Zu|schlag(s)|kar|te** F *(Rail)* supplementary ticket *(for trains on which a supplement is payable)*; **zu|schlag(s)|pflich|tig** ADJ *Zug, Service* subject to a supplement

zu+schlie|ßen *sep irreg* VT to lock; *Laden* to lock up VI to lock up

zu+schmei|ßen VT *sep irreg (inf) Tür etc* to slam (shut), to bang shut

zu+schmie|ren VT *sep (inf)* to smear over; *Löcher* to fill in

zu+schnal|len VT *sep* to fasten, to buckle; *Koffer* to strap up

zu+schnap|pen VI *sep* **a** *(= zubeißen)* **der Hund schnappte zu** the dog snapped at me/him *etc* **b** *(fig: Polizei)* to pounce **c** *aux sein (Schloss)* to snap *or* click shut; *(Falle) (lit)* to snap shut; *(fig)* to close

zu+schnei|den VT *sep irreg* to cut to size; *(Sew)* to cut out; **auf etw** *(acc)* **zugeschnitten sein** *(fig)* to be geared to sth; **auf jdn/etw genau zugeschnitten sein** *(lit, fig)* to be tailor-made for sb/sth

Zu|schnei|der(in) M(F) cutter

zu+schnei|en VI *sep aux sein* to snow in *or* up

Zu|schnitt M **a** *no pl (= Zuschneiden)* cutting **b** *(= Form)* cut; *(fig)* calibre *(Brit)*, caliber *(US)*

zu+schnü|ren VT *sep* to tie up; *Schuhe, Mieder* to lace up; **die Angst/innere Bewegung** *etc* **schnürte ihm die Kehle zu** he was choked with fear/emotion *etc*; **der Hals** *or* **die Kehle war ihm (vor Rührung/Trauer) wie zugeschnürt** *(fig)* he felt choked (with emotion/grief); **jdm das Herz ~** to make sb's heart bleed

zu+schrau|ben VT *sep Hahn etc* to screw shut; *Deckel etc* to screw on; **eine Flasche ~** to screw on the top of a bottle

zu+schrei|ben VT *sep irreg* **a** *(inf: = hinzuschreiben)* to add **b** *(= übertragen)* to transfer, to sign over (*+dat* to) **c** *(fig)* to ascribe, to attribute (*+dat* to); **das hast du dir selbst zuzuschreiben** you've only got yourself to blame; **das ist nur seiner Dummheit/ihrem Geiz zuzuschreiben** that can only be put down to his stupidity/her meanness

zu+schrei|ten VI *sep irreg aux sein (geh)* **tüchtig ~** to walk briskly; **auf jdn/etw ~** to stride *or* walk toward(s) *or (bis zu)* up to sb/sth

Zu|schrift F letter; *(amtlich auch)* communication; *(auf Anzeige)* reply

zu|schul|den, zu Schul|den [tsu'ʃʊldn] ADV **sich** *(dat)* **etwas ~ kommen lassen** to do something wrong; **solange man sich nichts ~ kommen lässt** as long as you don't do anything wrong

Zu|schuss M subsidy, grant; *(nicht amtlich)* something toward(s) it, contribution; *(esp regelmäßig von Eltern)* allowance; **einen ~ zu einer Sache gewähren** *or* **geben** to give a subsidy for sth; to make a contribution toward(s) sth; **mit einem kleinen ~ von meinen Eltern kann ich ...** if my parents give me something toward(s) it I can ...

Zu|schuss-: **Zu|schuss|be|trieb** M lossmaking *(Brit) or* losing *(US)* concern; **Zu|schuss|ge|schäft** NT lossmaking *(Brit) or* losing *(US)* deal; *(inf: = Zuschussunternehmen)* lossmaking *(Brit) or* losing *(US)* business

zu+schus|tern VT *sep (inf)* **jdm etw ~** to make sure sb gets sth

zu+schüt|ten *sep* VT to fill in *or* up; *(= hinzuschütten)* to add; *(fig: = verdecken)* to submerge VR *(inf) (mit Alkohol)* to have a skinful *(Brit inf)*, to be two sheets to the wind *(US)*; *(mit Drogen)* to get completely drugged up *(inf)*

zu+schwal|len ['tsu:ʃvalən] VT *sep (sl)* to chatter (on) to

zu+se|hen VI *sep irreg* **a** *(= beobachten, mit ansehen)* to watch; *(= unbeteiligter Zuschauer sein)* to look on; *(= etw dulden)* to sit back *or* stand by (and watch); **jdm/einer Sache ~** to watch sb/sth; **bei etw ~** to watch sth; *(= etw dulden)* to sit back *or* stand by and watch sth; **jdm bei der Arbeit ~** to watch sb working; **er sah zu, wie ich das machte** he watched me doing it; **ich kann doch nicht ~, wie er ...** *(= dulden)* I can't sit back *or* stand by and watch him ...; **ich habe nur zugesehen** I was only a spectator *or* an onlooker; **durch bloßes Zusehen** just by watching; **bei näherem Zusehen** when you watch/I watched *etc* more closely
b *(= dafür sorgen)* **~, dass ...** to see to it that ..., to make sure (that) ...; **sieh mal zu!** *(inf)* see what you can do

zu|se|hends ['tsu:ze:ənts] ADV visibly; *(= merklich auch)* noticeably, appreciably; *(= rasch)* rapidly; **~ im Verfall begriffen sein** to be in rapid decline

Zu|se|her(in) M(F) *(Aus TV)* viewer

zu sein VI *irreg aux sein* to be shut *or* closed; *(inf: = betrunken, high sein)* to be stoned *(inf)*

zu+sen|den VT *sep irreg* to send, to forward; *Geld auch* to remit *(form)*

zu+set|zen *sep* VT *(= hinzufügen)* to add; *(inf: = verlieren) Geld* to shell out *(inf)*, to pay out; **er setzt immer (Geld) zu** *(inf)* he's always having to shell out *(inf) or* pay out; **er hat nichts mehr zuzusetzen** *(inf)* he has nothing in reserve VI **jdm ~** *(= unter Druck setzen)* to lean on sb *(inf)*; *dem Gegner, Feind* to harass sb, to press sb hard; *(= drängen)* to badger *or* pester sb; *(= schwer treffen)* to hit sb hard, to affect sb (badly); *(Kälte, Krankheit etc)* to take a lot out of sb

zu+si|chern VT *sep* **jdm etw ~** to assure sb of sth, to promise sb sth; **mir wurde zugesichert, dass ...** I was assured *or* promised that ...

Zu|si|che|rung F assurance, promise

Zu|spät|kom|men|de(r) [tsu'ʃpɛ:tkɔmәndә] MF *decl as adj* latecomer

zu+sper|ren VT *sep (S Ger, Aus, Sw) (= zuschließen)* to lock; *Haus, Laden* to lock up; *(= verriegeln)* to bolt

Zu|spiel NT *(Sport)* passing

zu+spie|len VT *sep Ball* to pass (*+dat* to); **jdm etw ~** *(fig)* to pass sth on to sb; *(der Presse)* to leak sth to sb

zu+spit|zen *sep* VT *Stock etc* to sharpen; **zugespitzt** sharpened; *Turm, Schuhe etc* pointed; *(fig)* exaggerated VR to be pointed; *(fig: Lage, Konflikt)* to intensify; **die Lage spitzt sich immer mehr zu** the situation is worsening

Zu|spit|zung [ˈtsuːʃpɪtsʊŋ] F **-, -en** *(von Turm, Schuhen etc)* pointing; *(fig: von Lage, Konflikt)* worsening

zu+spre|chen *sep irreg* VT *(Jur)* to award; *Preis, Gewinn etc* to award; *Kind* to award *or* grant custody of; **das Kind wurde dem Vater zugesprochen** the father was granted custody (of the child); **jdm Mut/Trost ~** *(fig)* to encourage/comfort sb VI **a jdm (gut/besänftigend) ~** to talk *or* speak (nicely/gently) to sb **b dem Essen/Wein** *etc* **tüchtig** *or* **kräftig ~** to tuck into *(Brit) or* dig into *(US)* the food/wine *etc (inf)*; **dem Alkohol (kräftig) ~** to indulge (heavily) in alcohol

zu+sprin|gen VI *sep irreg aux sein* **a** *(Schloss, Tür)* to spring *or* snap shut **b auf jdn ~** *or* **zugesprungen kommen** to spring *or* leap toward(s) sb; *(Ball)* to bounce toward(s) sb

Zu|spruch M, *no pl* **a** *(= Worte)* words *pl*; *(= Aufmunterung)* (words *pl* of) encouragement; *(= Rat)* advice; *(tröstlich)* (words *pl* of) comfort **b** *(= Anklang)* **(großen) ~ finden** *or* **haben, sich großen ~s erfreuen** to be (very) popular; *(Stück, Film)* to meet with general acclaim; *(Anwalt, Arzt)* to be (very) much in demand

Zu|stand M state; *(von Haus, Ware, Auto, Med)* condition; *(= Lage)* state of affairs, situation; **in gutem/schlechtem ~** in good/poor condition; *(Mensch auch)* in good/bad shape; *(Haus)* in good/bad repair; **in ungepflegtem/baufälligem ~** in a state of neglect/disrepair; **in angetrunkenem ~** under the influence of alcohol; **Wasser in flüssigem ~** water in its fluid state; **eine Frau in ihrem ~ ...** a woman in her condition ...; **er war wirklich in einem üblen ~** he really was in a bad way; *(seelisch)* he really was in a state; **Zustände bekommen** *or* **kriegen** *(inf)* to have a fit *(inf)*, to hit the roof *(inf)*; **das ist doch kein ~** that's not right; **das sind ja schöne** *or* **nette Zustände!** *(iro)* that's a fine state of affairs! *(iro)*; **das sind ja Zustände!** *(inf)* it's terrible; **das sind doch keine Zustände!** *(inf)* it's just dreadful *or* terrible!

zu|stan|de, zu Stan|de [tsuˈʃtandə] ADV **a ~ bringen** to manage; *Arbeit* to get done; *Ereignis, Frieden etc* to bring about, to achieve; **es ~ bringen, dass jd etw tut** to (manage to) get sb to do sth; **ein Gespräch ~ bringen** *(am Fernsprecher)* to (manage to) put a call through (*nach* to) **b ~ kommen** *(= erreicht werden)* to be achieved; *(= geschehen)* to come about; *(= stattfinden)* to take place; *(Plan etc)* to materialize; *(Gewagtes, Schwieriges)* to come off

Zu|stan|de|kom|men NT **die Chancen für das ~ eines Plans/einer Koalition** the chances of a plan materializing/of a coalition coming about; **die Ostdeutschen hatten einen wesentlichen Anteil am ~ der Wiedervereinigung** the East Germans played a significant part in bringing about reunification

zu|stän|dig [ˈtsuːʃtɛndɪç] ADJ *(= verantwortlich)* responsible; *(= entsprechend) Amt etc* appropriate, relevant; *(= Kompetenz habend)* competent *(form, Jur)*; **dafür ist er ~** that's his responsibility; **der dafür ~e Beamte** the official responsible for *or* in charge of such matters; **~ sein** *(Jur)* to have jurisdiction; **in erster Instanz ~ sein** *(Jur)* to have original jurisdiction; **nach einer Stadt ~ sein** *(Aus form) (= wohnhaft sein)* to be domiciled in a town; *(= Wohnrecht haben)* to have the right of domicile in a town

Zu|stän|dig|keit F **-, -en a** *(= Kompetenz)* competence; *(Jur)* jurisdiction, competence; *(= Verantwortlichkeit)* responsibility **b** = **Zuständigkeitsbereich**

Zu|stän|dig|keits-: **Zu|stän|dig|keits|be|reich** M area of responsibility; *(Jur)* jurisdiction, competence; **das fällt/fällt nicht in unseren ~** that is/isn't our responsibility; *(Jur)* that is within/outside our jurisdiction *(Jur)*; **zu|stän|dig|keits|hal|ber** ADV *(Admin, form)* for reasons of competence

Zu|stands|verb NT *(Ling)* stative verb

zu|stat|ten+kom|men [tsuˈʃtatn-] VI *sep irreg aux sein* **jdm ~** *(geh)* to come in useful for sb

zu+ste|cken VT *sep* **a** *Kleid etc* to pin up *or* together **b jdm etw ~** to slip sb sth

zu+ste|hen VI *sep irreg* **etw steht jdm zu** sb is entitled to sth; **darüber steht mir kein Urteil zu** it's not for me to judge that, it's not up to me to judge that; **es steht ihr nicht zu, das zu tun** it's not for her to do that, it's not up to her to do that

zu+stei|gen VI *sep irreg aux sein* to get on, to board; **noch jemand zugestiegen?** *(in Zug)* tickets please!; *(in Bus)* any more fares, please?

Zu|stell-: **Zu|stell|be|reich** M postal district; **Zu|stell|dienst** M delivery service

zu+stel|len VT *sep* **a** *Brief, Paket etc* to deliver; *(Jur)* to serve (*jdm etw* sb with sth) **b** *Tür etc* to block

Zu|stel|ler [ˈtsuːʃtɛlɐ] M **-s, -** *(= Zustellfirma)* delivery agent

Zu|stel|ler [ˈtsuːʃtɛlɐ] M **-s, -**, **Zu|stel|le|rin** [-ərɪn] F **-, -nen** deliverer; *(Jur)* server; *(= Briefträger)* postman/-woman *(Brit)*, mailman/-woman *(US)*

Zu|stell|ge|bühr F delivery charge

Zu|stel|lung F delivery; *(Jur)* service (of a writ)

Zu|stel|lungs|ur|kun|de F *(Jur)* writ of summons

Zu|stell|ver|merk M reason for non-delivery; **mit einem ~ versehen** with (the) reason for non-delivery attached

zu+steu|ern *sep* VI *aux sein* **auf etw** *(acc)* **~** *(lit, fig)*, **einer Sache** *(dat)* **~** *(geh) (lit, fig)* to head for sth; *(beim Gespräch)* to steer toward(s) sth VT *(= beitragen)* to contribute (*zu* to)

zu+stim|men VI *sep* **(einer Sache** *dat***) ~** to agree (to sth); *(= einwilligen)* to consent (to sth); *(= billigen)* to approve (of sth); **jdm (in einem Punkt) ~** to agree with sb (on a point); **einer Politik ~** to endorse a policy; **dem kann man nur ~** I/we *etc* quite agree with you/him *etc*; **er nickte ~d** he nodded in agreement; **eine ~de Antwort** an affirmative answer

Zu|stim|mung F *(= Einverständnis)* agreement, assent; *(= Einwilligung)* consent; *(= Beifall)* approval; **seine ~ geben/verweigern** *or* **versagen** *(geh)* to give/refuse one's consent *or* assent; **allgemeine ~ finden** to meet with general approval; **das fand meine ~** I agreed with it completely; **mit/ohne ~** *(+gen)* with/without the agreement *or* approval of

zu+stop|fen VT *sep* to stop up, to plug; *(mit Faden)* to darn

zu+stöp|seln VT *sep* to stopper; *Flasche* to put the stopper *or* cork in

zu+sto|ßen *sep irreg* VT *Tür etc* to push shut VI **a** *(mit Messer, Schwert etc)* to plunge a/the knife/sword *etc* in; *(Stier, Schlange)* to strike; **stoß zu!** go on, stab him/her *etc*!; **der Mörder hatte (mit dem Messer) dreimal zugestoßen** the murderer had stabbed him/her *etc* three times **b** *(= passieren) aux sein* **jdm ~** to happen to sb; **wenn mir einmal etwas zustößt ...** *(euph)* if anything should happen to me ...; **ihm muss etwas zugestoßen sein** he must have had an accident, something must have happened to him

zu+stre|ben VI *sep aux sein (geh)* **~ auf** *(+acc)* to make *or* head for; *(fig)* to strive for

Zu|strom M, *no pl (fig: = Menschenmenge) (hineinströmend)* influx; *(herbeiströmend)* stream (of visitors *etc*); *(= Andrang)* crowd, throng; *(Met)* inflow; **großen ~ haben** to be very popular, to have crowds of people coming to it/them *etc*

zu+strö|men VI *sep aux sein +dat (Fluss)* to flow toward(s); *(fig) (geh: Menschen)* to stream toward(s); *(Aufträge etc)* to pour in to

zu+stür|zen VI *sep aux sein* **auf jdn/etw ~** *or* **zugestürzt kommen** to rush up to sb/sth

zu|ta|ge, zu Ta|ge [tsuˈtaːgə] ADV **etw ~ fördern** to unearth sth *(auch hum)*; *(aus Wasser)* to bring sth up; **etw ~ bringen** *(fig)* to bring sth to light, to reveal sth; **(offen) ~ liegen** to be clear *or* evident; **~ kommen** *or* **treten** *(lit, fig)* to come to light, to be revealed

Zu|ta|ten [ˈtsuːtaːtn] PL *(Cook)* ingredients *pl*; *(fig)* accessories *pl*, extras *pl*

zu|teil+wer|den [tsuˈtail-] VI *sep irreg aux sein (geh)* **jdm wird etw zuteil** sb is granted sth, sth is granted to sb; **mir wurde die Ehre zuteil, zu ...** I was given *or* I had the honour *(Brit) or* honor *(US)* of ...; **jdm etw ~ lassen** to give sb sth; **jdm große Ehren ~ lassen** to bestow great honours *(Brit) or* honors *(US)* upon sb; **da ward ihm großes Glück ~** *(old)* he was favoured *(Brit) or* favored *(US)* with great fortune

zu+tei|len VT *sep (jdm* to sb) *(als Anteil) Wohnung, Aktien* to allocate; *Rolle, Aufgabe auch* to allot, to assign; *Arbeitskraft, Leibwächter* to assign; **etw zugeteilt bekommen** to be allocated sth; *Aufgabe etc auch* to be assigned sth; *Lebensmittel* to be apportioned sth

Zu|tei|lung F allocation; *(von Rolle, Aufgabe auch)* assigning; *(von Arbeitskraft)* assignment; *(von Lebensmitteln)* apportionment; **Fleisch gab es nur auf ~** meat was only available on ration

zu+tex|ten VT *sep (sl) (= viel schreiben)* to write at length to; *(= viel reden)* to chatter (on) to

zu|tiefst [tsuˈtiːfst] ADV deeply; **er war ~ betrübt** he was greatly saddened

zu+tra|gen *sep irreg* VT to carry (*jdm* to sb); *(fig: = weitersagen)* to report (*jdm* to sb) VR *(liter)* to take place

Zu|trä|ger(in) M(F) informer

zu|träg|lich [ˈtsuːtrɛːklɪç] ADJ good (*+dat* for), beneficial (*+dat* to); *(= förderlich auch)* conducive (*+dat* to); **ein der Gesundheit ~es Klima** a salubrious climate, a climate conducive to good health

Zu|träg|lich|keit F **-,** *no pl (geh)* beneficial effect; *(von Klima auch)* salubrity *(liter, form)*

zu+trau|en VT *sep* **jdm etw ~** *(Aufgabe, Tat, Sieg)* to believe *or* think sb (is) capable of (doing) sth; **sich** *(dat)* **~, etw zu tun** to think one can do sth, to think one is capable of doing sth; **sich** *(dat)* **zu viel ~** to overrate one's own abilities; *(= sich übernehmen)* to take on too much; **sich** *(dat)* **nichts ~** to have no confidence in oneself; **der traut sich was zu!** *(inf)* he's pretty confident, isn't he?; **den Mut/die Intelligenz (dazu) traue ich ihr nicht zu** I don't credit her with the courage/intelligence to do it, I don't believe she has the courage/intelligence to do it; **das hätte ich ihm nie zugetraut!** I would never have thought him capable of it!; *(bewundernd auch)* I never thought he had it in him!; **jdm viel/wenig ~** to think/not to think a lot of sb, to have/not to have a high opinion of sb; **ich traue ihnen viel** *or* **einiges/alles zu** *(Negatives)* I wouldn't put much/anything past them; **das ist ihm zuzutrauen!** *(iro)* I can well believe it (of him)!; *(esp als Antwort auf Frage)* I wouldn't put it past him!

Zu|trau|en NT **-s,** *no pl* confidence (*zu* in); **zu jdm ~ fassen** to begin to trust sb

zu|trau|lich ADJ *Kind* trusting; *Tier* friendly

Zu|trau|lich|keit F *(von Kind)* trusting nature; *(von Tier)* friendliness

zu+tref|fen VI *sep irreg (= gelten)* to apply (*auf +acc, für* to); *(= richtig sein)* to be accurate *or* correct; *(= wahr sein)* to be true, to be the case; **es trifft nicht immer zu, dass ...** it doesn't always follow that ...; **seine Beschreibung traf überhaupt nicht zu** his description was completely inaccurate; **das trifft zu** that is so

zu|tref|fend ADJ *(= richtig)* accurate; *(= auf etw zutreffend)* applicable; **Zutreffendes bitte unter-**

streichen underline where applicable *or* appropriate ADV accurately, precisely

zu|tref|fen|den|falls ['tsu:trɛfndən'fals] ADV *(form)* if applicable *or* appropriate

zu+tre|ten VI *sep irreg* **a** *(mit Fuß)* to kick him/it *etc* **b** *aux sein* **auf jdn/etw ~** to step up to sb/sth

zu+trin|ken VI *sep irreg* **jdm ~** to drink to sb; *(mit Trinkspruch)* to toast sb

Zu|tritt M, *no pl (= Einlass)* admission, admittance, entry; *(= Zugang)* access; **kein ~, ~ verboten** no admittance *or* entry; **freien ~ zu einer Veranstaltung haben** to be admitted to an event free of charge; **~ bekommen** *or* **erhalten, sich ~ verschaffen** to gain admission *or* admittance *(zu* to); **jdm ~ gewähren** *(geh)* to admit sb; **jdm den ~ verwehren** *or* **verweigern** to refuse sb admission *or* admittance

zu+tun VT *sep irreg* **a ich habe die ganze Nacht kein Auge zugetan** I didn't sleep a wink all night **b** *(inf: = hinzufügen)* to add *(+dat* to)

Zu|tun NT, *no pl* assistance, help; **es geschah ohne mein ~** I did not have a hand in the matter

zu|un|guns|ten, zu Un|guns|ten [tsu-'lʊŋgʊnstn] PREP *(vor n) +gen, (nach n) +dat* to the disadvantage of

zu|un|terst [tsu'lʊntɐst] ADV right at the bottom

zu|ver|läs|sig ['tsu:fɛɐlɛsɪç] ADJ reliable; *(= verlässlich) Mensch auch* dependable; *(= vertrauenswürdig auch)* trustworthy; **aus ~er Quelle** from a reliable source ADV *funktionieren* reliably; **etw ~ wissen** to know sth for sure *or* for certain; **etw ~ beurteilen** to make a reliable judgement about sth; **seinen Pflichten ~ nachkommen** to reliably fulfil one's duties

Zu|ver|läs|sig|keit F -, *no pl* reliability; *(= Verlässlichkeit auch)* dependability; *(= Vertrauenswürdigkeit auch)* trustworthiness

Zu|ver|sicht F, *no pl* confidence; *(religiös)* faith, trust; **die feste ~ haben, dass ...** to be quite confident that ..., to have every confidence that ...; **in der festen ~, dass ...** confident that ...

zu|ver|sicht|lich ADJ confident; **er zeigte sich ~, dass ...** he was confident that ...

Zu|ver|sicht|lich|keit F -, *no pl* confidence

zu|viel △ [tsu'fi:l] ADJ ADV → **viel a**

Zu|viel [tsu'fi:l] NT **ein ~ an etw** *(dat)* an excess of sth

zu|vor [tsu'vo:ɐ] ADV before; *(= zuerst)* beforehand; **im Jahr ~** the year before, in the previous year; **am Tage ~** the day before, on the previous day

zu|vor|derst [tsu'fɔrdɐst] ADV right at the front

zu|vör|derst [tsu'fœrdɐst] ADV *(old)* first and foremost

zu|vor+kom|men VI *sep irreg aux sein +dat* to anticipate; *(= verhindern) einer Gefahr, unangenehmen Fragen etc* to forestall; **jdm ~** to beat sb to it; **jemand ist uns zuvorgekommen** somebody beat us to it

zu|vor|kom|mend ADJ obliging; *(zu* towards) ADV obligingly

Zu|vor|kom|men|heit [tsu'vo:ɐkɔmənhait] F -, *no pl* obliging ways *pl*

Zu|wachs ['tsu:vaks] M **-es, Zuwächse** [-vɛksə] **a** *no pl (= Wachstum)* growth *(an +dat* of) **b** *(= Höhe, Menge des Wachstums)* increase *(an +dat* in); **~ bekommen** *(inf: ein Baby)* to have an addition to the family; **ein Kleid für jdn auf ~ kaufen** *(inf)* to buy a dress for sb to grow into

zu+wach|sen VI *sep irreg aux sein* **a** *(Öffnung, Loch)* to grow over; *(Garten etc, hum: Gesicht)* to become overgrown; *(Aussicht)* to become blocked (by trees *etc*); *(Wunde)* to heal **b** *(esp Econ, Gewinn etc)* to accrue *(jdm* to sb); **jdm wächst Autorität/Macht/Popularität zu** sb gains authority/power/popularity

Zu|wachs|quo|te F, **Zu|wachs|ra|te** F rate of increase

Zu|wachs|si|che|rung F *(Comput)* incremental backup

Zu|wan|de|rer M, **Zu|wan|de|rin** F immigrant

zu+wan|dern VI *sep aux sein* to immigrate

Zu|wan|de|rung F immigration

Zu|wan|de|rungs-: Zu|wan|de|rungs|ge|setz NT immigration law; **Zu|wan|de|rungs|po|li|tik** F immigration policy

zu+war|ten VI *sep* to wait

zu|we|ge, zu We|ge [tsu've:gə] ADV **etw ~ bringen** to manage sth; *(= erreichen)* to achieve *or* accomplish sth; **mit etw ~ kommen** to (be able to) cope with sth; **mit jdm ~ kommen** to get on with sb all right; **es ~ bringen, dass jd etw tut** to (manage to) get sb to do sth; **gut/schlecht ~ sein** *(inf)* to be in good/bad *or* poor health; **er ist ganz schön ~** *(dial)* he's a bit on the heavy side *(inf)*

zu+we|hen *sep* VT **a** *(= zutreiben)* to waft *(+dat* towards, over to); **jdm (kalte** *etc***) Luft ~** to fan sb (with cold *etc* air) **b** *(= zudecken)* to block (up); **mit Schnee zugeweht werden** to become snowed up VI *aux sein* **auf jdn/etw ~** to blow toward(s) sb/sth; *(sachte)* to waft toward(s) sb/sth

zu|wei|len [tsu'vailən] ADV *(geh)* (every) now and then, occasionally, from time to time

zu+wei|sen VT *sep irreg* to assign, to allocate *(jdm etw* sth to sb); *(Comput) Tastenkombination, Speicheradresse etc* to assign

Zu|wei|sung F allocation, assignment

zu+wen|den *sep irreg* VT **a** *(lit, fig)* to turn *(+dat* to, towards); *(fig: = völlig widmen)* to devote *(+dat* to); **jdm das Gesicht ~** to turn to face sb, to turn one's face toward(s) sb; **jdm seine ganze Liebe ~** to bestow all one's affections on sb; **die dem Park zugewandten Fenster** the windows facing the park; **der Zukunft** *(dat)* **zugewandt sein** to be turned toward(s) the future **b jdm Geld** *etc* **~** to give sb money *etc* VR **sich jdm/einer Sache ~** to turn to (face) sb/sth; *(fig)* to turn to sb/sth; *(= sich widmen, liebevoll)* to devote oneself to sb/sth; **wann wird das Glück sich uns wieder ~?** when will luck smile on us again?

Zu|wen|dung F **a** *(fig: = das Sichzuwenden)* turning *(zu* to); *(= Liebe)* care **b** *(= Geldsumme)* sum (of money); *(= Beitrag)* financial contribution; *(= Schenkung)* donation

zu|we|nig △ [tsu've:nɪç] ADJ ADV → **wenig ADV**

Zu|we|nig [tsu've:nɪç] NT **-s,** *no pl* **ein ~ an etw** a lack of sth

zu+wer|fen VT *sep irreg* **a** *(= schließen) Tür* to slam (shut) **b** *(= auffüllen) Graben* to fill up **c** *(= hinwerfen)* **jdm etw ~** to throw sth to sb; **jdm einen Blick ~** to cast a glance at sb; **jdm einen bösen** *or* **giftigen Blick ~** to look daggers at sb *(Brit)*, to give sb the evil eye; **jdm einen feurigen Blick ~** to flash a fiery glance at sb; **jdm Blicke ~** to make eyes at sb; **jdm eine Kusshand ~** to blow sb a kiss

zu|wi|der [tsu'vi:dɐ] ADV **a er/das ist mir ~** I find him/that unpleasant; *(stärker)* I detest *or* loathe him/that; *(= ekelerregend)* I find him/that revolting **b** *(old: = ungünstig)* **das Glück war ihm ~** luck was against him PREP *+dat* **a** *(liter: = entgegen)* **dem Gesetz ~** contrary to *or* against the law; **etw einem Befehl ~ tun** to do sth in defiance of an order **b** *(old: = ungünstig)* **unseren Plänen** *etc* **~** unfavourable *(Brit) or* unfavorable *(US)* to our plans *etc*

Zu|wi|der-: zu|wi|der+han|deln VI *sep +dat (geh)* to go against; *einem Verbot, Befehl auch* to defy; *einem Prinzip auch* to violate; *dem Gesetz* to contravene, to violate; **Zu|wi|der|han|deln|de(r)** [tsu'vi:dɐhandlndə] MF *decl as adj (form)* offender, transgressor, violator *(esp US)*; **Zu|wi|der|hand|lung** F *(form)* contravention, violation; **zu|wi|der+lau|fen** VI *sep irreg aux sein +dat* to run counter to, to go directly against

zu+win|ken VI *sep* **jdm ~** to wave to sb; *(= Zeichen geben)* to signal to sb

zu+zah|len *sep* VT **10 Euro ~** to pay another 10 euros VI to pay extra

zu+zäh|len VT *sep (inf) (= addieren)* to add; *(= einbeziehen)* to include *(zu* in)

Zu|zah|lung F **-, -en** additional payment; *(Insur)* supplementary charge

zu|zei|ten [tsu'tsaitn] ADV *(old)* at times

zu+zie|hen *sep irreg* VT **a** *Vorhang* to draw; *Tür* to pull shut; *Knoten, Schlinge* to pull tight, to tighten; *Arzt etc* to call in, to consult; **einen weiteren Fachmann ~** to get a second opinion **b sich** *(dat)* **jds Zorn/Hass** *etc* **~** to incur sb's anger/hatred *etc*; **sich** *(dat)* **eine Krankheit ~** *(form)* to contract an illness; **sich** *(dat)* **eine Verletzung ~** *(form)* to sustain an injury VR *(Schlinge etc)* to tighten, to pull tight; **es hat sich zugezogen** *(Wetter)* it has clouded over VI *aux sein* to move in, to move into the area; **er ist kürzlich aus Berlin zugezogen** he has recently moved here from Berlin; **auf die Stadt** *etc* **~** to move toward(s) the town *etc*

Zu|zug M *(= Zustrom)* influx; *(von Familie etc)* arrival *(nach* in), move *(nach* to)

Zu|zü|ger ['tsu:tsy:gɐ] M **-s, -, Zu|zü|ge|rin** ['tsu:tsy:gərɪn] F **-, -nen** *(Sw)* **a** → **Zuzügler, Zuzüglerin b** *(= neues Mitglied)* newcomer

Zu|züg|ler ['tsu:tsy:glɐ] M **-s, -, Zu|züg|le|rin** ['tsu:tsy:glərɪn] F **-, -nen** *(in Ortschaft)* incomer, newcomer

zu|züg|lich ['tsu:tsy:klɪç] PREP *+gen* plus

zu+zwin|kern VI *sep* **jdm ~** to wink at sb, to give sb a wink

Zvie|ri ['tsfi:ri] M OR NT **-s,** *no pl (Sw)* afternoon snack

ZVS [tsɛtfau'lɛs] F - *abbr von* **Zentralstelle für die Vergabe von Studienplätzen** ≈ UCAS *(Brit)*, ≈ SAT center *(US)*

zw. *abbr von* **zwischen**

zwang *pret von* **zwingen**

Zwang [tsvaŋ] M **-(e)s, =e** ['tsvɛŋə] *(= Notwendigkeit)* compulsion; *(= Gewalt)* force; *(= Verpflichtung)* obligation; *(= hemmender Zwang)* constraint; **einem inneren ~ folgen** to follow an inner compulsion; **das ist ~** that is compulsory; **der ~ der Ereignisse** the pressure of events; **gesellschaftliche Zwänge** social constraints; **unter ~** *(dat)* **stehen/handeln** to be/act under duress; **etw aus ~ tun** to do sth under duress, to be forced to do sth; **etw ohne ~ tun** to do sth without being forced to; **auf jdn ~ ausüben** to exert pressure on sb; **sich** *(dat)* **~ antun** to force oneself to be something one isn't; *(= sich zurückhalten)* to restrain oneself *(etw nicht zu tun* from doing sth); **tu dir keinen ~ an** don't feel you have to be polite; *(iro)* don't force yourself; **darf ich rauchen? – ja, tu dir keinen ~ an** may I smoke? – feel free; **seinen Gefühlen ~ antun** to force oneself to ignore one's true feelings; **sie tut ihren Gefühlen keinen ~ an** she doesn't hide her feelings; **dem Gesetz ~ antun** to stretch the law; **der ~ des Gesetzes/der Verhältnisse/Konvention** the force of the law/of circumstances/of convention; **allen ~ ablegen** to dispense with all formalities; **er brauchte sich** *(dat)* **keinen ~ aufzuerlegen** he didn't need to make a big effort

zwän|gen ['tsvɛŋən] VT to force; *mehrere Sachen (in Koffer etc)* to cram; **sich in/durch etw** *(acc)* **~** to squeeze into/through sth

Zwang-: zwang|haft *(Psych)* ADJ compulsive ADV compulsively; **zwang|los** ADJ *(= ohne Förmlichkeit)* informal; *(= locker, unbekümmert)* casual, free and easy; *(= frei)* free; **in ~er Folge, ~** at irregular intervals ADV informally, casually; **da geht es recht ~ zu** *(im Hotel, Club)* things are very informal there; *(bei der Arbeit auch)* things are very relaxed there; **Zwang|lo|sig|keit** F **-,** *no pl* informality; *(= Lockerheit)* casualness

Zwangs-: Zwangs|ab|ga|be F *(Econ)* compulsory levy *or* charge; **Zwangs|ab|lie|fe|rung** F compulsory delivery; **Zwangs|ab|tre|tung** F compulsory cession; **Zwangs|an|lei|he** F compulsory *or* forced loan; **Zwangs|ar|beit** F hard labour *(Brit) or* labor *(US)*; *(von Kriegsgefangenen)* forced labo(u)r; **zwangs|be|wirt|schaf|tet** [-bəvɪrtʃaftət] ADJ controlled; *Wohnraum* rent-controlled; **Zwangs|be|wirt|schaf|tung** F (economic) control; *(von Wohnraum)* rent control; **die ~ aufheben** to decontrol the economy/rents; **Zwangs|ein|wei|sung** F compulsory hospitalization; **Zwangs|ent|eig|nung** F compulsory expropriation; **zwangs|er|näh|ren** *ptp* **zwangsernährt** VT *insep* to force-feed; **Zwangs|er|näh|rung** F force-feeding; **Zwangs|er|schei|nung** F *(Psych)* compulsion; **Zwangs|geld** NT *(Jur)* coercive fine *or* penalty; **Zwangs|hand|lung** F *(Psych)* compulsive act; **Zwangs|hy|po|thek** F *compulsory mortgage to enforce payment of debt(s)*; **Zwangs|idee** F *(Psych)* obsession; **Zwangs|ja|cke** F *(lit, fig)* straitjacket; **jdn in eine ~ stecken** to put sb in a straitjacket, to straitjacket sb; **Zwangs|kurs** M *(Fin)* compulsory rate; **Zwangs|la|ge** F predicament, dilemma; **zwangs|läu|fig** ADJ inevitable, unavoidable ADV inevitably, unavoidably; **das musste ja ~ so kommen** that had to happen, it was inevitable that that would happen; **Zwangs|läu|fig|keit** [-lɔyfɪçkait] F **-, -en** inevitability; **zwangs|mä|ßig** ADJ *(form)* compulsory; **Zwangs|maß|nah|me** F compulsory measure; *(Pol)* sanction; **Zwangs|mit|tel** NT means *sing* of coercion; *(Pol)* sanction; **Zwangs|neu|ro|se** F obsessional neurosis; **Zwangs|pau|se** F *(beruflich)* **eine ~ machen** *or* **einlegen müssen** to have to stop work temporarily; **Zwangs|pen|si|o|nie|rung** F compulsory retirement; **Zwangs|räu|mung** F compulsory evacuation; **zwangs|um|sie|deln** *ptp* **zwangsumgesiedelt** VT *infin, ptp only* to displace (by force); **Zwangs|um|tausch** M compulsory exchange; **Zwangs|ur|laub** M *(inf)* temporary lay-off; **einen ~ antreten müssen** to have to be laid off temporarily; **jdn in den ~ schicken** to lay sb off temporarily; **Zwangs|ver|kauf** M (en)forced sale; **zwangs|ver|pflich|tet** [-fɛɐpflɪçtət] ADJ drafted (*zu* into); **Zwangs|ver|schi|ckung** [-fɛɐʃɪkʊŋ] F **-, -en** deportation; **Zwangs|ver|si|che|rung** F compulsory insurance; **zwangs|ver|stei|gern** *ptp* **zwangsversteigert** VT *infin, ptp only* to put (sth) up for compulsory auction; **Zwangs|ver|stei|ge|rung** F compulsory auction; **Zwangs|voll|stre|ckung** F execution; **Zwangs|vor|füh|rung** F *(Jur)* enforced appearance in court; **Zwangs|vor|stel|lung** F *(Psych)* obsession, obsessive idea; **zwangs|wei|se** ADV compulsorily ADJ compulsory; **Zwangs|wirt|schaft** F Government *or* State control

zwan|zig ['tsvantsɪç] NUM twenty → *auch* **vierzig, vier**

Zwan|zig ['tsvantsɪç] F **-, -en** [-gn] twenty → *auch* **Vierzig, Vier**

Zwan|zi|ger ['tsvantsɪgɐ] M **-s, -** *(inf: = Geldschein)* twenty-euro *etc* note *(Brit) or* bill *(US)*

Zwan|zi|ger ['tsvantsɪgɐ] M **-s, -**, **Zwan|zi|ge|rin** [-ərɪn] F **-, -nen** twenty-year-old; *(zwischen 20 und 30)* man in his/woman in her twenties → *auch* **Vierziger**

Zwan|zig-: **Zwan|zig|euro|schein** M twenty-euro note *(Brit) or* bill *(US)*; **Zwan|zig|mark|schein** M *(Hist)* twenty-mark note *(Brit) or* bill *(US)*

zwan|zigs|te(r, s) ['tsvantsɪçstə] ADJ twentieth → *auch* **vierzigste(r, s)**

zwar [tsvaːɐ] ADV **a** *(= wohl)* **er war ~ Zeuge des Unfalls, kann sich aber nicht mehr so genau erinnern** he did witness the accident *or* it's true he witnessed the accident but he can't remember much about it any more; **sie ist ~ sehr schön/krank, aber ...** it's true she's very beautiful/ill but ..., she may be very beautiful/ill but ...; **ich weiß ~, dass es schädlich ist, aber ...** I do know it's harmful but ...

b *(erklärend, betont)* **und ~** in fact, actually; **er ist tatsächlich gekommen, und ~ um 4 Uhr** he really did come, at 4 o'clock actually *or* in fact; **er hat mir das anders erklärt, und ~ so ...** he explained it differently to me(, like this) ...; **ich mache das, und ~ so, wie ich es für richtig halte** I'll do it and I'll do it just as I see fit; **und ~ einschließlich ...** inclusive of ...; **die Schulen, und ~ vor allem die Grundschulen** the schools, (and more) especially the primary schools; **das hat er gemacht, und ~ so gründlich, dass ...** he did it and (he did it) so thoroughly that ...; **ich werde ihm schreiben, und ~ noch heute** I'll write to him and I'll do it today *or* this very day

Zweck [tsvɛk] M **-(e)s, -e** **a** *(= Ziel, Verwendung)* purpose; **einem ~ dienen** to serve a purpose; **einem guten ~ dienen** to be for *or* in a good cause; **Spenden für wohltätige ~e** donations to charity; **seinen ~ erfüllen** to serve its/one's purpose; **seinem ~ entsprechen** to serve its purpose; **das entspricht nicht meinen ~en** that won't serve my purpose → **heiligen**

b *(= Sinn)* point; **was soll das für einen ~ haben?** what's the point of that?; **das hat keinen ~** there is no point in it, it's pointless; **es hat keinen ~, darüber zu reden** there is no point (in) talking about it, it's pointless talking about it; **es hat ja doch alles keinen ~ mehr** there is no point (in) *or* it's pointless going on any more; **das ist ja der ~ der Übung** that's the point of the exercise, that's what it's all about *(inf)*

c *(= Absicht)* aim; **zum ~ der Völkerverständigung** (in order) to promote understanding between nations; **zu welchem ~?** for what purpose?, to what end?; **zu diesem ~** to this end, with this aim in view; **einen ~ verfolgen** to have a specific aim

Zweck-: **Zweck|bau** M *pl* **-bauten** functional building; **zweck|be|dingt** ADJ determined by its function; **zweck|be|stimmt** ADJ *Gebäude* functional; *Gelder* earmarked; *(Tech)* dedicated; **Zweck|bünd|nis** NT alliance *or* marriage of convenience; **zweck|dien|lich** ADJ *(= zweckentsprechend)* appropriate; *(= nützlich)* useful; **~e Hinweise** (any) relevant information; **es wäre ~, das zu tun** it would be expedient to do that; **Zweck|dien|lich|keit** F **-**, *no pl (= Nützlichkeit)* usefulness; *(Pol)* expediency

Zwe|cke ['tsvɛkə] F **-, -n** tack; *(= Schuhzwecke)* nail; *(= Reißzwecke)* drawing pin *(Brit)*, thumbtack *(US)*

Zweck-: **zweck|ent|frem|den** *ptp* **zweckentfremdet** VT *insep* **etw ~** to use sth in a way in which it wasn't intended to be used; **etw als etw ~** to use sth as sth; **Zweck|ent|frem|dung** F misuse; **zweck|ent|spre|chend** ADJ appropriate ADV **etw ~ benutzen** to use sth properly *or* correctly, to put sth to its proper *or* correct use; **zweck|frei** ADJ *Forschung etc* pure; **zweck|ge|bun|den** ADJ *Geldmittel, Steuern etc* for a specific purpose, appropriated *(spec) no adv*; **zweck|ge|mäß** ADJ ADV = **zweckentsprechend**; **Zweck|ge|mein|schaft** F partnership of convenience; **zweck|los** ADJ pointless; *Versuch, Anstrengungen* useless, futile; **es ist ~, hierzubleiben** it's pointless staying here, there's no point (in) staying here; **Zweck|lo|sig|keit** F **-**, *no pl* pointlessness; *(von Versuch, Anstrengungen)* uselessness, futility; **zweck|mä|ßig** ADJ *(= nützlich)* useful; *(= wirksam)* effective; *(= ratsam)* advisable, expedient *(form)*; *(= zweckentsprechend) Kleidung etc* suitable; **Zweck|mä|ßig|keit** ['tsvɛkmɛːsɪçkait] F **-**, *no pl (= Nützlichkeit)* usefulness; *(= Wirksamkeit)* effectiveness, efficacy; *(von Kleidung etc)* suitability; **Zweck|mä|ßig|keits|er|wä|gung** F consideration of expediency; **Zweck|op|ti|mis|mus** M calculated optimism; **Zweck|pes|si|mis|mus** M calculated pessimism; **Zweck|pro|pa|gan|da** F calculated propaganda

zwecks [tsvɛks] PREP *+gen (form)* for the purpose of; **~ Wiederverwendung** for re-use

Zweck-: **Zweck|satz** M *(Gram)* final clause; **Zweck|steu|er** F regulatory tax; **Zweck|ver|band** M *association of local authorities for the joint management of a particular service*, joint board; **Zweck|ver|mö|gen** NT *(Jur)* special-purpose fund; **zweck|voll** ADJ **a** = **zweckmäßig** **b** *(Psych) Handlung* purposive; **zweck|wid|rig** ADJ inappropriate ADV inappropriately, improperly, incorrectly

zween [tsveːn] NUM *(obs)* twain *(obs)*

zwei [tsvai] NUM two; **wir ~** (**beiden** *(inf)*) the two of us, we two, us two *(inf)*; **das ist so sicher wie ~ mal ~ vier ist** *(inf)* you can bet on that *(inf)*; **dazu gehören ~** *(inf)* it takes two; **~ Gesichter haben** *(fig)* to be two-faced → **Dritte(r)**, → *auch* **vier**

Zwei [tsvai] F **-, -en** two → *auch* **Vier**

Zwei- *in cpds* → *auch* **Vier-**: **Zwei|ach|ser** [-laksɐ] M **-s, -** two-axle vehicle; **zwei|ach|sig** [-laksɪç] ADJ two-axled; **Zwei|ak|ter** [-laktɐ] M **-s, -** *(Theat)* two-act play *or* piece; **zwei|ar|mig** ADJ *(Physiol)* with two arms; *(Tech)* with two branches; **zwei|ato|mig** [-latoːmɪç] ADJ *(Phys)* diatomic; **Zwei|bei|ner** [-bainɐ] M **-s, -**, **Zwei|bei|ne|rin** [-ərɪn] F **-, -nen** *(hum inf)* human being; **die ~** human beings, the bipeds *(hum)*; **zwei|bei|nig** ADJ two-legged, biped(-al) *(spec)*; **Zwei|bett|zim|mer** NT twin room; **Zwei|bund** M *pl* **-bünde** *(Hist)* dual alliance; **Zwei|cent|stück** [tsvai'(t)sɛnt-] NT two-cent piece; **Zwei|de|cker** [-dɛkɐ] M **-s, -** *(Aviat)* biplane; **zwei|deu|tig** [-dɔytɪç] ADJ ambiguous, equivocal; *(= schlüpfrig)* suggestive, risqué; **~e Reden führen** to use a lot of doubles entendres *(esp Brit) or* words with double meanings ADV ambiguously; **Zwei|deu|tig|keit** F **-, -en** **a** *no pl* ambiguity; *(= Schlüpfrigkeit)* suggestiveness **b** *(= Bemerkung)* ambiguous *or* equivocal remark, double entendre *(esp Brit)*; *(= Witz)* risqué joke; **zwei|di|men|si|o|nal** ADJ two-dimensional ADV two-dimensionally; **Zwei|drit|tel|mehr|heit** F *(Parl)* two-thirds majority; **der Streikbeschluss wurde mit ~ gefasst** the decision to strike was taken with a two-thirds majority; **zwei|ei|ig** [-laiɪç] ADJ *Zwillinge* nonidentical, fraternal *(spec)*

Zwei|er ['tsvaiɐ] M **-s, -** two; *(dial: Sch)* good; *(= Zweicentstück)* two-cent piece → *auch* **Vierer**

Zwei|er-: **Zwei|er|be|zie|hung** F relationship; **Zwei|er|bob** M two-man bob; **Zwei|er|ka|jak** M OR NT *(= Kanu)* double kayak; *(= Disziplin)* kayak pairs; **Zwei|er|ka|na|di|er** M Canadian pair; *(Disziplin)* Canadian pairs

zwei|er|lei ['tsvaiɐ'lai] ADJ *inv* **a** *attr Brot, Käse, Wein* two kinds *or* sorts of; *Möglichkeiten, Größen, Fälle* two different; **auf ~ Art** in two different ways; **~ Handschuhe/Strümpfe** *etc* odd gloves/socks *etc*; **~ Meinung sein** to be of (two) different opinions → **Maß** **b** *(substantivisch)* two different things; *(= zwei Sorten)* two different kinds

Zwei|er|rei|he F two rows *pl*; **~n** rows of twos; **in ~n marschieren** to march two abreast, to march in twos

Zwei|eu|ro|stück [tsvai'ɔyro-] NT two-euro piece

zwei|fach ['tsvaifax] ADJ double; *(= zweimal)* twice; **in ~er Ausfertigung** in duplicate ADV **diesen Satz Briefmarken besitze ich ~** I have two sets of these stamps; **diese Titel sind ~ vorhanden** there are two copies of this book; **eine Urkunde ~ ausfertigen** to make up a document in duplicate; **~ gesichert** doubly secure; **ein Tuch ~ legen** to lay a cloth double

Zwei-: **Zwei|fa|mi|li|en|haus** NT two-family house; **Zwei|far|ben|druck** M *pl* **-drucke** *(Typ)* two-colour *(Brit) or* two-color *(US)* print; *(Verfahren)* two-colo(u)r printing; **zwei|far|big** ADJ two-colour *(Brit)*, two-color *(US)*, two-tone ADV **etw ~ anstreichen** to paint sth in two (different) colours *(Brit) or* colors *(US)*; **es**

ist ~ gemustert it has a two-colour *(Brit)* or two-color *(US)* pattern

Zwei|fel ['tsvaifl] M **-s, -** doubt; **außer ~** beyond doubt; **im ~** in doubt; **ohne ~** without doubt, doubtless; **kein ~, er ist der Sieger** there's no doubt about it, he's the winner; **außer ~ stehen** to be beyond doubt; **über allen ~ erhaben** beyond all (shadow of a) doubt; **da kann es gar keinen ~ geben** there can be no doubt about it; **es besteht kein ~, dass ...** there is no doubt that ...; **~ an etw** *(dat)* **haben** to have one's doubts about sth; **da habe ich meine ~** I have my doubts, I'm doubtful; **etw in ~ ziehen** to call sth into question, to challenge sth; **ich bin mir im ~, ob ich das tun soll** I'm in two minds *(Brit)* or double-minded *(US)* or I'm doubtful whether I should do that

zwei|fel|haft ADJ doubtful; *(= verdächtig auch)* dubious; **von ~em Wert** of doubtful *or* debatable value; **es ist ~, ob ...** it is doubtful *or* questionable *or* debatable whether ...

zwei|fel|los ADV without (a) doubt, undoubtedly, unquestionably; *(als Antwort)* undoubtedly; **er hat ~ recht** he is undoubtedly *or* unquestionably right, without (a) doubt he is right ADJ *Sieger etc* undisputed

zwei|feln ['tsvaifln] VI to doubt; **an etw/jdm ~** to doubt sth/sb; *(= skeptisch sein auch)* to be sceptical *(esp Brit)* or skeptical *(US)* about sth/sb; **daran ist nicht zu ~** there's no doubt about it; **ich zweifle nicht, dass ...** I do not doubt that ..., I have no doubt that ...; **ich zweifle noch, wie ich mich entscheiden soll** I am still in two minds *(esp Brit)* or double-minded *(US)* about it

Zwei|fels-: **Zwei|fels|fall** M doubtful *or* borderline case; **im ~** in case of doubt, when in doubt; *(inf: = gegebenenfalls)* if need be, if necessary; **zwei|fels|frei** ADJ unequivocal ADV beyond (all) doubt; **zwei|fels|oh|ne** [tsvaifls'lo:nə] ADV undoubtedly, without (a) doubt

Zwei|fin|ger|such|sys|tem [tsvaifɪŋɐ-] NT *(hum)* peer *(Brit)* or hunt *(US)* and peck method *(hum)*; **ich tippe im ~** I use two fingers, I type with two fingers

Zweif|ler ['tsvaiflɐ] M **-s, -**, **Zweif|le|rin** [-ərɪn] F **-, -nen** sceptic *(esp Brit)*, skeptic *(US)*

zweif|le|risch ['tsvaiflərɪʃ] ADJ sceptical *(esp Brit)*, skeptical *(US)*

Zwei-: **zwei|flü|ge|lig** [-fly:gəlɪç] ADJ *Tür, Tor, Fenster* double; *Insekt* two-winged, dipterous *(spec)*; **Zwei|flüg|ler** [-fly:glɐ] M **-s, -** *(Zool)* dipteran *(spec)*; **zwei|flüg|lig** [-fly:glɪç] ADJ = **zweiflügelig**; **Zwei|fron|ten|krieg** [tsvai'frɔntn-] M war on two fronts

Zweig [tsvaik] M **-(e)s, -e** [-gə] **a** *(= Ast)* branch, bough *(liter)*; *(dünner, kleiner)* twig **b** *(fig)* *(von Wissenschaft, Familie etc, Rail, Comput)* branch; *(= Abteilung)* department → **grün**

Zweig-: **Zweig|bahn** F branch line; **Zweig|be|trieb** M branch

Zwei-: **zwei|ge|schlech|tig** [-gəʃlɛçtɪç] ADJ *(Biol)* hermaphroditic; **Zwei|ge|schlech|tig|keit** F **-,** *no pl (Biol)* hermaphroditism; **zwei|ge|schlecht|lich** ADJ *Berufsstand, Besatzung* male and female; **Zwei|ge|spann** NT carriage and pair; *(fig inf)* duo, two-man band *(hum inf)*; **zwei|ge|stri|chen** ADJ *(Mus)* **das ~e C** the C (an octave) above middle C; **das ~e A** the A an octave above middle C

Zweig-: **Zweig|ge|schäft** NT branch; **Zweig|ge|sell|schaft** F subsidiary (company)

zwei-: **zwei|glei|sig** ADJ double-tracked, double-track *attr* ADV **~ fahren** *(lit)* to be double-tracked; *(fig inf)* to have two strings to one's bow; **~ argumentieren** to argue along two different lines; **zwei|glied|rig** [-gli:drɪç] ADJ *(fig)* bipartite; *(Admin) System* two-tier; *(Math)* binominal

Zweig-: **Zweig|li|nie** F branch line; **Zweig|nie|der|las|sung** F subsidiary; **Zweig|post|amt** NT sub-post office; **Zweig|stel|le** F branch (office); **Zweig|stel|len|lei|ter(in)** M(F) (branch) manager; *(Frau auch)* (branch) manageress; **Zweig|werk** NT *(Fabrik)* branch; **Zweig|werk** NT *(von Baum, Gesträuch)* branches *pl*

Zwei-: **Zwei|hän|der** [-hɛndɐ] M **-s, - a** *(= Schwert)* two-handed sword **b** *(Zool)* two-handed *or* bimanous *(spec)* animal; **zwei|hän|dig** ADJ with two hands, two-handed; *(Mus)* for two hands ADV *(Mus) spielen* two-handed; **die Rückhand ~ schlagen** *(Sport)* to use two hands for one's backhand; **zwei|häu|sig** [-hɔyzɪç] ADJ *(Bot)* dioecian; **Zwei|heit** F **-,** *no pl (Philos, Liter etc)* duality; **zwei|hö|cke|rig, zwei|höck|rig** ADJ *Kamel* two-humped

zwei|hun|dert ['tsvai'hʊndɐt] NUM two hundred

Zwei|hun|dert-: **Zwei|hun|dert|jahr|fei|er** F bicentenary, bicentennial; **zwei|hun|dert|jäh|rig** ADJ *Dauer* two-hundred-year *attr*; *Tradition, Geschichte* two-hundred-year-old *attr*; **nach über ~er Knechtschaft** after more than two hundred years of servitude

zwei|jäh|rig ADJ **a** *attr Kind etc* two-year-old *attr*, two years old; *Dauer* two-year *attr*, of two years; **mit ~er Verspätung** two years late **b** *(Bot) Pflanze* biennial

zwei|jähr|lich ADJ two-yearly *attr*, biennial, every two years ADV biennially, every two years

Zwei-: **Zwei|kam|mer|sys|tem** [tsvai'kamɐ-] NT *(Pol)* two-chamber system; **Zwei|kampf** M single combat; *(= Duell)* duel; **jdn zum ~ (her-aus)fordern** to challenge sb to a duel; **zwei|kampf|stark** ADJ *(Sport) Spieler(in)* strong in the challenge *pred*; **Zwei|ka|nal|ton** M dual channel sound; **mit ~** *(TV)* with bilingual facility, with two language channels; **Zwei|keim|blät|te|ri|ge** [-blɛtərɪgə] PL, **Zwei|keim|blätt|ri|ge** [-blɛtrɪgə] PL *decl as adj (Bot)* dicotyledons *pl*; **Zwei|klang|horn** NT, **Zwei|klang|hu|pe** F two-tone horn; **Zwei|klas|sen|ge|sell|schaft** F two-tier society; **Zwei|klas|sen|me|di|zin** F two-tier health service, two-tier medical system; **Zwei|kom|po|nen|ten|kleb|stoff** [tsvaikɔmpo'nɛntn-] M two-part adhesive; **zwei|köp|fig** ADJ two-headed; **Zwei|kreis|brem|se** F dual-circuit brake; **Zwei|li|ter|fla|sche** F two-litre *(Brit)* or two-liter *(US)* bottle

zwei|mal ['tsvaima:l] ADV twice; **~ jährlich** *or* **im Jahr/täglich** *or* **am Tag** twice yearly *or* a year/twice daily *or* a day; **sich** *(dat)* **etw ~ überlegen** to think twice about sth; **das lasse ich mir nicht ~ sagen** I don't have to be told twice; **das mache ich bestimmt nicht ~** I certainly won't do that/it again

zwei|ma|lig ['tsvaima:lɪç] ADJ *attr* twice repeated; *Weltmeister etc* two-times *attr*; **nach ~er Aufforderung** after being told twice; **nach ~er Wiederholung konnte er den Text auswendig** after twice repeating the text he knew it (off) by heart

Zwei-: **Zwei|mann|boot** NT two-man boat; **Zwei|mark|stück** [tsvai'mark-] NT *(Hist)* two-mark piece; **Zwei|mas|ter** [-mastɐ] M **-s, -** two-master; **zwei|mo|na|tig** ADJ *attr* **a** *Dauer* two-month *attr*, of two months **b** *Säugling etc* two-month-old *attr*, two months old; **zwei|mo|nat|lich** ADJ every two months, bimonthly *(esp Comm, Admin)* ADV every two months, bimonthly *(esp Comm, Admin)*, every other month; **Zwei|mo|nats|schrift** [tsvai'mo:nats-] F bimonthly; **zwei|mo|to|rig** ADJ twin-engined; **Zwei|par|tei|en|sys|tem** [tsvaipar'taiən-] NT two-party system; **Zwei|pfen|nig|stück** [tsvai'pfɛnɪç-] NT *(Hist)* two-pfennig piece; **Zwei|pha|sen|strom** [tsvai'fa:zn-] M two-phase current; **zwei|po|lig** [-po:lɪç] ADJ *(Elec)* double-pole, bipolar; **Zwei|rad** NT *(form)* two-wheeled vehicle, two-wheeler; *(= Fahrrad)* (bi)cycle; *(für Kinder)* two-wheeler, bicycle; **zwei|rä|de|rig, zwei|räd|rig** ADJ two-wheeled; **Zwei|rei|her** [-raiɐ] M **-s, -** double-breasted suit *etc*; **zwei|rei|hig** ADJ double-row *attr*, in two rows; *Anzug* double-breasted ADV in two rows; **das Jackett wird ~ geknöpft** the jacket is double-breasted; **Zwei|sam|keit** ['tsvaiza:mkait] F **-, -en** *(liter, hum)* togetherness; **zwei|schlä|fig** [-ʃlɛ:fɪç], **zwei|schlä|fe|rig, zwei|schläf|rig** ADJ double; **zwei|schnei|dig** ADJ two-edged, double-edged *(auch fig)*; **das ist ein ~es Schwert** *(fig)* it cuts both ways; **zwei|sei|tig** [-zaitɪç] ADJ *Brief, Erklärung etc* two-page *attr*; *Kleidungsstück* reversible; *Vertrag etc* bilateral, bipartite; *(Comput) Diskette* double-sided ADV on two sides; **ein ~ tragbarer Anorak** a reversible anorak; **zwei|sil|big** ADJ disyllabic; **ein ~es Wort** a disyllable *(spec)*, a disyllabic word; **Zwei|sit|zer** M *(Aut, Aviat)* two-seater; **zwei|sit|zig** [-zɪtsɪç] ADJ *Sportwagen, Sofa* two-seater *attr*; **zwei|spal|tig** [-ʃpaltɪç] ADJ double-columned, in two columns ADV **der Artikel ist ~ (abgedruckt)** the article is printed in two columns; **Zwei|spän|ner** M carriage and pair; **zwei|spän|nig** ADJ drawn by two horses ADV **~ fahren** to drive (in) a carriage and pair; **zwei|spra|chig** ADJ *Mensch, Wörterbuch* bilingual; *Land auch* two-language *attr*; *Dokument* in two languages ADV in two languages; **~ aufwachsen** to grow up bilingual *or* speaking two languages; **Zwei|spra|chig|keit** F **-,** *no pl* bilingualism; **zwei|spu|rig** [-ʃpu:rɪç] ADJ double-tracked, double-track *attr*; *Autobahn* two-laned, two-lane *attr*; **zwei|stel|lig** ADJ *Zahl* two-digit *attr*, with two digits; **~er Dezimalbruch** number with two decimal places; **~e Millionenbeträge** sums over ten million ADV *steigen, zunehmen* by more than ten per cent *(Brit)* or percent *(US)*; **~ gewinnen** to win by more than ten; **der Umsatz ist ~ gewachsen** the increase in turnover has reached double figures; **zwei|stim|mig** *(Mus)* ADJ for two voices, two-part *attr* ADV **~ singen/spielen** to sing/play in two parts; **zwei|stö|ckig** ADJ two-storey *attr (Brit)*, two-story *attr (US)*, two-storeyed *(Brit)*, two-storied *(US)*; **ein ~es Bett** bunk beds *pl* → *auch* **doppelstöckig** ADV **~ bauen** to build buildings with two storeys *(Brit)* or stories *(US)*; **zwei|strah|lig** ADJ *Flugzeug* twin-jet *attr*; **Zwei|strom|land** [tsvai'ʃtro:m-] NT **das ~** Mesopotamia; **Zwei|stu|fen|schei|ben|wi|scher** [tsvai'ʃtu:fn-] M *(Aut)* two-speed windscreen *(Brit)* or windshield *(US)* wiper; **zwei|stu|fig** ADJ two-stage; *System auch* two-tier; *Plan auch* two-phase; *Scheibenwischer, Schaltgetriebe* two-speed; **zwei|stün|dig** ADJ two-hour *attr*, of two hours; **zwei|stünd|lich** ADJ ADV every two hours, two-hourly

zweit [tsvait] ADV **zu ~** *(= in Paaren)* in twos; **wir gingen zu ~ spazieren** the two of us went for a walk; **ich gehe lieber zu ~ auf Partys** I prefer going to parties with somebody; **das Leben zu ~ ist billiger** it's cheaper for two people to live together; **das Leben zu ~** living with someone → *auch* **vier**

Zwei-: **zwei|tä|gig** ADJ two-day *attr*, of two days; **Zwei|tak|ter** [-taktɐ] M **-s, -** *(inf)* two-stroke *(inf)*; **Zwei|tak|ter|ge|misch** NT two-stroke mixture; **Zwei|takt|mo|tor** M two-stroke engine

zweit|äl|tes|te(r, s) ['tsvait'ɛltəstə] ADJ second eldest *or* oldest; **unser Zweitältester** our second (child *or* son)

Zwei-: **zwei|tau|send** ['tsvai'tauznt] NUM two thousand; **das Jahr ~** the year two thousand; **Zwei|tau|sen|der** ['tsvai'tauzndɐ] M **-s, -** *(= Berg)* two thousand metre *(Brit)* or meter *(US)* peak; **Zwei|tau|send|jahr|fei|er** F bimillenary

Zweit-: **Zweit|aus|fer|ti|gung** F *(form)* copy, duplicate; **es liegt nur in ~ vor** we/I have only a copy *or* duplicate; **Zweit|au|to** NT second car; **Zweit|be|set|zung** F *(Theat)* understudy; **sie ist die ~ für die (Rolle der) Desdemona/für A. Kirchschlager** she's the understudy for Desdemona/to A. Kirchschlager; **zweit|bes|te(r, s)** ['tsvait'bɛstə] ADJ second best; **er ist der Zweitbeste** he is the second best; **Zweit|druck** M *pl* **-drucke** reprint

Zwei-: **zwei+tei|len** VT *sep, infin, ptp only* to divide (into two); **zweigeteilt** bipartite; *(= gespalten)* divided, split; **Zwei|tei|ler** M *(Fashion)* two-piece; **zwei|tei|lig** ADJ *Roman* two-part *attr*, in two parts; *Plan* two-stage; *Kleidungsstück* two-piece; *Formular etc* two-part *attr*, in two sections; **Zwei|tei|lung** F division; *(Math: von Winkel)* bisection

zwei|tens ['tsvaitns] ADV secondly; *(bei Aufzählungen auch)* second

Zwei|te(r) ['tsvaitə] MF *decl as adj* second; *(Sport etc)* runner-up; **wie kein ~r** as no-one else can, like nobody else

zwei|te(r, s) ['tsvaitə] ADJ second; ~ **Klasse** *(Rail etc)* second class; **~r Klasse fahren** to travel second (class); **Bürger ~r Klasse** second-class citizen(s); **jeden ~n Tag** every other *or* second day; **jeder Zweite** *(lit, inf: = sehr viele)* every other; **zum Zweiten** secondly, second; **ein ~r Caruso** another Caruso; **in ~r Linie** secondly, second → **Garnitur, Hand, Ich, Wahl** *etc*, → *auch* **erste(r, s), vierte(r, s)**

Zweit-: **Zweit|er|kran|kung** F secondary illness; *(von Organ, Pflanze, Tier)* secondary disease; **Zweit|fri|sur** F wig; **zweit|ge|bo|ren** ADJ *attr* second-born; **Zweit|ge|rät** NT *(TV etc)* second set; **zweit|größ|te(r, s)** ['tsvait-'grø:stə] ADJ second largest; *Zimmer auch, Mensch* second biggest; **der/die Zweitgrößte** the second biggest; **zweit|höchs|te(r, s)** ['tsvait-'hø:çstə] ADJ second highest; *Baum auch* second tallest; *(fig: im Rang)* second most senior; **zweit|klas|sig** ADJ *(fig)* second-class, second-rate *(esp pej)*; **Zweit|kor|rek|tor(in)** M(F) second marker; **zweit|letz|te(r, s)** ['tsvait-'lɛtstə] ADJ last but one *attr, pred*; *(in Reihenfolge auch)* penultimate; **der/die Zweitletzte** the last but one, the penultimate; **Zweit|li|gist** M second-division team; **Zweit|plat|zier|te(r)** ['tsvaitplatsi:ɐtə] MF *decl as adj (Sport)* runner-up, second-placed finisher; **zweit|ran|gig** [-raŋɪç] ADJ = **zweitklassig**; **Zweit|schlag|ka|pa|zi|tät** F second-strike capability; **Zweit|schlüs|sel** M duplicate key; **Zweit|schrift** F copy; **Zweit|stim|me** F second vote → *auch* **Erststimme**; **Zweit|stu|di|um** NT second degree; **ein ~ machen** to take another degree

Zwei|tü|rer [-ty:rɐ] M *(Aut)* **-s, -** two-door

zwei|tü|rig ADJ *(Aut)* two-door

Zweit-: **Zweit|wa|gen** M second car; **Zweit|wohn|sitz** M second home; **Zweit|woh|nung** F second home

Zwei|und|drei|ßigs|tel ['tsvailʊnt'draisɪçstl] NT, **Zwei|und|drei|ßigs|tel|no|te** F *(Mus)* demisemiquaver *(Brit)*, thirty-second note *(US)*

Zwei|und|drei|ßigs|tel|pau|se F *(Mus)* demisemiquaver rest *(Brit)*, thirty-second note rest *(US)*

Zwei-: **Zwei|vier|tel|takt** [tsvai'vɪrtl-] M *(Mus)* two-four time; **zwei|wer|tig** ADJ *(Chem)* bivalent, divalent; *(Ling)* two-place; **zwei|wö|chent|lich** ADJ two-weekly, fortnightly *(esp Brit)*, biweekly *(US)* ADV every two weeks, fortnightly *(esp Brit)*, biweekly *(US)*; **zwei|wö|chig** [-vœçɪç] ADJ two-week *attr*, of two weeks; **zwei|za|ckig** ADJ two-pronged; **Zwei|zei|ler** [-'tsailɐ] M **-s, -** *(Liter)* couplet; **zwei|zei|lig** ADJ two-line *attr*; *(Typ) Abstand* double-spaced ADV ~ **schreiben** to double-space; **Zwei|zim|mer|woh|nung** [tsvai'tsɪmɐ-] F two-room(ed) flat *(Brit)* or apartment; **zwei|zü|gig** ADJ *Schule* with two classes in each year; *(mit zwei Abteilungen)* with two alternative subject areas; **Zwei|zy|lin|der** M two-cylinder; **Zwei|zy|lin|der|mo|tor** M two-cylinder engine; **zwei|zy|lind|rig** ADJ two-cylinder *attr*

Zwerch|fell ['tsvɛrçfɛl] NT *(Anat)* diaphragm; **jdm das ~ massieren** *(hum inf)* to make sb split his/her sides (laughing) *(inf)*

Zwerch|fell-: **Zwerch|fell|at|mung** F abdominal *or* diaphragmatic breathing; **zwerch|fell|er|schüt|ternd** ADJ side-splitting *(inf)*; **Zwerch|fell|mas|sa|ge** F *(hum inf)* **es war die reinste ~** it was an absolute scream *(inf)* or hoot *(inf)*

Zwerg [tsvɛrk] M **-(e)s, -e** [-gə], **Zwer|gin** ['tsvɛrgɪn] F **-, -nen** dwarf; *(= Gartenzwerg)* gnome; *(fig: = Knirps)* midget; *(pej: = unbedeutender Mensch)* squirt *(inf)*

Zwerg|en|auf|stand M *(inf, hum)* to-do *(inf)*, unnecessary fuss

zwer|gen|haft ADJ dwarfish; *(fig)* diminutive, minute; *(pej: = minderwertig)* insignificant

Zwerg-: **Zwerg|huhn** NT bantam; **Zwerg|ka|nin|chen** NT pygmy rabbit; **Zwerg|pin|scher** M pet terrier; **Zwerg|pu|del** M toy poodle; **Zwerg|schu|le** F *(Sch inf)* village school; **Zwerg|staat** M miniature state; **Zwerg|stamm** M, **Zwerg|volk** NT pygmy tribe; **Zwerg|wuchs** M stunted growth, dwarfism; **zwerg|wüch|sig** [-vy:ksɪç] ADJ *attr Mensch* dwarfish; *Baum* dwarf *attr*

Zwetsch|ge ['tsvɛtʃgə] F **-, -n** plum; **seine** *or* **die sieben ~n (ein)packen** *(inf)* to pack one's bags (and go)

Zwetsch|gen-: **Zwetsch|gen|dat|schi** [-da:t-ʃi] M **-s, -s** *(S Ger)* (type of) plum cake; **Zwetsch|gen|knö|del** M *(S Ger)* plum dumpling; **Zwetsch|gen|schnaps** M, **Zwetsch|gen|was|ser** NT *pl* **-wässer** plum brandy

Zwetsch|ke ['tsvɛtʃkə] F **-, -n** *(Aus)* = **Zwetschge**

Zwi|ckel ['tsvɪkl] M **-s, -** *(Sew)* gusset; *(am Segel)* gore; *(Archit)* spandrel

zwi|cken ['tsvɪkn] VT *(inf, Aus) (= kneifen)* to pinch; *(= leicht schmerzen)* to hurt; *(esp S Ger: = ärgern)* to bother VI to pinch; *(= leicht schmerzen)* to hurt

Zwi|cker ['tsvɪkɐ] M **-s, -** pince-nez

Zwick|müh|le ['tsvɪk-] F *(beim Mühlespiel)* double mill; **in der ~ sitzen** *(fig)* to be in a catch-22 situation *(inf)*, to be in a dilemma

Zwie|back ['tsvi:bak] M **-(e)s, -e** *or* **=e** [-bɛkə] rusk

Zwie|bel ['tsvi:bl] F **-, -n** **a** onion; **~n hacken** *or* **schneiden** to chop onions **b** *(= Blumenzwiebel)* bulb **c** *(hum inf: = Uhr)* watch **d** *(= Haarknoten)* tight bun

Zwie|bel-: **Zwie|bel|fisch** M *(Typ)* literal *(character typed in wrong face)*; **zwie|bel|för|mig** ADJ onion-shaped; **Zwie|bel|ku|chen** M onion tart; **Zwie|bel|kup|pel** F *(Archit)* imperial roof; **Zwie|bel|mus|ter** NT onion pattern

zwie|beln ['tsvi:bln] VT *(inf)* **jdn ~** to drive *or* push sb hard; *(= schikanieren)* to harass sb; **er hat uns so lange gezwiebelt, bis wir das Gedicht konnten** he kept (on) at us until we knew the poem

Zwie|bel-: **Zwie|bel|ring** M onion ring; **Zwie|bel|scha|le** F onion skin; **Zwie|bel|sup|pe** F onion soup; **Zwie|bel|turm** M onion dome

Zwie-: **zwie|fach** ['tsvi:fax], **zwie|fäl|tig** ADJ ADV *(old)* = **zweifach**; **Zwie|ge|spräch** NT dialogue; **ein ~ mit sich selbst** an internal dialogue; *(laut)* a soliloquy; **Zwie|laut** M *(Ling)* diphthong; **Zwie|licht** NT, *no pl* twilight; *(abends auch)* dusk; *(morgens)* half-light; **ins ~ geraten sein** *(fig)* to appear in an unfavourable *(Brit)* or unfavorable *(US)* light; **zwie|lich|tig** ['tsvi:lɪçtɪç] ADJ *(fig)* shady; **Zwie|spalt** M *pl rare (der Natur, der Gefühle etc)* conflict; *(zwischen Menschen, Parteien etc)* rift, gulf; **ich bin im ~ mit mir, ob ich ...** I'm in conflict with myself whether to ...; **in ~ mit jdm geraten** to come into conflict with sb; **in einen fürchterlichen ~ geraten** to get into a terrible conflict; **zwie|späl|tig** ['tsvi:ʃpɛltɪç] ADJ *Gefühle* mixed, conflicting *attr*; **mein Eindruck war ~** my impressions were very mixed; **ein ~er Mensch** a man/woman of contradictions; **Zwie|späl|tig|keit** F *(von Gefühlen)* conflicting nature; *(in jds Verhalten)* contradiction; **Zwie|spra|che** F dialogue; **~ mit jdm/etw halten** to commune with sb/sth; **Zwie|tracht** F, *no pl* discord; **~ säen** to sow (the seeds of) discord

Zwil|le ['tsvɪlə] F **-, -n** *(N Ger)* catapult *(Brit)*, slingshot *(US)*

Zwil|lich ['tsvɪlɪç] M **-s, -e** *(Tex)* drill

Zwil|ling ['tsvɪlɪŋ] M **-s, -e** twin; *(= Gewehr)* double-barrelled *(Brit)* or double-barreled *(US)* gun; *(Chem: = Doppelkristall)* twin crystal; **die ~e** *(Astrol)* Gemini, the Twins; *(Astron)* Gemini; **~ sein** *(Astrol)* to be (a) Gemini

Zwil|lings-: **Zwil|lings|bru|der** M twin brother; **Zwil|lings|for|mel** F *(Ling)* dual expression, set phrase with two elements; **Zwil|lings|ge|burt** F twin birth; **Zwil|lings|paar** NT twins *pl*; **Zwil|lings|rei|fen** M *(Aut)* double *or* twin tyres *pl (Brit)* or tires *pl (US)*; **Zwil|lings|schwes|ter** F twin sister

Zwing|burg F *(Hist, fig)* stronghold, fortress

Zwin|ge ['tsvɪŋə] F **-, -n** *(Tech)* (screw) clamp; *(am Stock)* tip, ferrule; *(an Schirm)* tip; *(an Werkzeuggriff)* ferrule

zwin|gen ['tsvɪŋən] *pret* **zwang** [tsvaŋ], *ptp* **gezwungen** [gə'tsvʊŋən] VT **a** *(= nötigen)* to force, to compel; **jdn ~, etw zu tun** to force *or* compel sb to do sth; **er hat mich gezwungen, das zu tun** he forced *or* compelled me to do it, he made me do it; **jdn zu etw ~** to force sb to do sth; **sie ist dazu gezwungen worden** she was forced *or* compelled *or* made to do it; **ich lasse mich nicht (dazu) ~** I won't be forced (to do it *or* into it), I won't respond to force; **jdn an den Verhandlungstisch ~** to force sb to the bargaining table; **jdn zum Handeln ~** to force sb into action *or* to act; **jdn zum Gehorsam ~** to force *or* compel sb to obey, to make sb obey; **jdn zur Prostitution ~** to force sb into prostitution; **die Regierung wurde zum Rücktritt gezwungen** the government was forced *or* compelled to step down; **man kann niemanden zu seinem Glück ~** you can't force people → *auch* **gezwungen, Knie, sehen 2**

b *(dial inf: = bewältigen) Essen, Arbeit* to manage

VR to force oneself; **sich ~, etw zu tun** to force oneself to do sth, to make oneself do sth; **sich zur Ruhe ~** to force oneself to be calm

VI **zum Handeln/Umdenken ~** to force *or* compel us/them *etc* to act/rethink; **diese Tatsachen ~ zu der Annahme, dass ...** these facts force *or* compel one to assume that ...

zwin|gend ADJ *Notwendigkeit* urgent; *(= logisch notwendig)* necessary; *Schluss, Beweis, Argumente* conclusive; *Argument* cogent; *Gründe* compelling; **dass B aus A resultiert, ist nicht ~** it isn't necessarily so *or* the case that B results from A ADV **etwas ~ darlegen** to present sth conclusively; **etw ist ~ vorgeschrieben** sth is mandatory; **daraus folgert ~** the logical conclusion is; **diese Schlussfolgerung ergab sich ~ aus den Beweisen** this conclusion was inevitable due to the evidence

Zwin|ger ['tsvɪŋɐ] M **-s, -** *(= Käfig)* cage; *(= Bärenzwinger)* bear pit; *(= Hundezwinger)* kennels *pl*; *(von Burg)* (outer) ward

Zwing-: **Zwing|herr** M *(Hist, fig)* oppressor, tyrant; **Zwing|herr|schaft** F *(Hist, fig)* oppression, tyranny

Zwing|li|a|ner [tsvɪŋ'lia:nɐ] M **-s, -**, **Zwing|li|a|ne|rin** [-ərɪn] F **-, -nen** *(Hist, Rel)* Zwinglian

zwin|kern ['tsvɪŋkɐn] VI to blink; *(um jdm etw zu bedeuten)* to wink; *(lustig)* to twinkle; **mit den Augen ~** to blink (one's eyes) (;), to wink (;), to twinkle

Zwir|bel|bart M handlebar moustache *(Brit)* or mustache *(US)*

zwir|beln ['tsvɪrbln] VT *Bart* to twirl; *Schnur* to twist

Zwirn [tsvɪrn] M **-s, -e** (strong) thread, yarn → **Himmel b**

zwir|nen ['tsvɪrnən] VTI to twist; **dieses Handtuch ist gezwirnt** this towel is made of strong thread

Zwir|ne|rei [tsvɪrnə'rai] F -, -en (cotton-spinning) mill

Zwirns|fa|den M thread

zwi|schen ['tsvɪʃn] PREP +*dat or (mit Bewegungsverben)* +*acc* between; *(in Bezug auf mehrere auch)* among; **mitten ~** right in the middle *or* midst of; **die Liebe ~ den beiden** the love between the two of them; **die Kirche stand ~ Bäumen** the church stood among(st) trees → **Stuhl a, Tür, Zeile** *etc*

Zwi|schen-: **Zwi|schen|ab|la|ge** F *(Comput)* clipboard; **Zwi|schen|ab|rech|nung** F interim invoice; **Zwi|schen|akt** M *(Theat)* interval, intermission; **im ~** during the interval *or* intermission; **Zwi|schen|akt(s)|mu|sik** F interlude; **Zwi|schen|an|sa|ge** F *(Rad etc)* announcement *(interrupting a programme)*; *(= Kurznachricht)* newsflash; **Zwi|schen|ap|plaus** M *(Theat)* spontaneous applause *(during the performance)*; **Zwi|schen|auf|ent|halt** M stopover, layover *(US)*; **Zwi|schen|be|mer|kung** F interjection; *(= Unterbrechung)* interruption; **wenn Sie mir eine kurze ~ erlauben** if I may just interrupt; **Zwi|schen|be|richt** M interim report; **Zwi|schen|be|scheid** M provisional notification *no indef art*; **Zwi|schen|bi|lanz** F *(Comm)* interim balance; *(fig)* provisional appraisal; **eine ~/~en ziehen** *(fig)* to take stock provisionally; **Zwi|schen|blatt** NT interleaf; **zwi|schen+blen|den** VT *sep* to blend in; *(Film, Rad etc)* to insert; *(nachträglich) Musik etc* to dub on *(Brit) or* in; **Zwi|schen|blu|tung** F *(Med)* breakthrough *or* intermenstrual *(spec)* bleeding; **Zwi|schen|bo|den** M false floor; **Zwi|schen|buch|han|del** M intermediate book trade; **Zwi|schen|deck** NT *(Naut)* 'tween deck; **im ~** 'tween decks *(Brit)*, between (the) decks; **Zwi|schen|de|cke** F false ceiling; **Zwi|schen|ding** NT cross (between the two), hybrid; **was er schreibt, ist ein ~ zwischen Lyrik und Prosa** his writing is a cross between *or* is halfway between poetry and prose; **zwi|schen|drin** ['tsvɪʃn'drɪn] ADV *(dial)* **a** = **zwischendurch b** = **dazwischen**; **zwi|schen|durch** ['tsvɪʃn'dʊrç] ADV **a** *(zeitlich)* in between times; *(= inzwischen)* (in the) meantime; *(= nebenbei)* on the side; **er macht ~ mal Pausen** he keeps stopping for a break in between times; **das mache ich so ~** I'll do that on the side; **Schokolade für ~** chocolate for between meals **b** *(örtlich)* in between; **Zwi|schen|eis|zeit** F *(Geol)* interglacial period; **Zwi|schen|er|geb|nis** NT interim result; *(von Untersuchung auch)* interim findings; *(Sport)* latest score; **Zwi|schen|fall** M incident; **ohne ~** without incident, smoothly; **es kam zu schweren Zwischenfällen** there were serious incidents, there were clashes; **zwi|schen+fi|nan|zie|ren** *ptp* **zwischenfinanziert** VT *sep usu infinitive and ptp (Fin)* **etw ~** to provide interim finance for sth; **Zwi|schen|fi|nan|zie|rung** F bridging *or* interim finance; **Zwi|schen|fra|ge** F question; **Zwi|schen|fre|quenz** F *(Rad)* intermediate frequency; **Zwi|schen|frucht|bau** M, *no pl (Agr)* intercropping; **Zwi|schen|fut|ter** NT *(Sew)* interlining; **Zwi|schen|gang** M *pl* **-gänge** *(Cook)* entrée; **Zwi|schen|gas** NT, *no pl (old Aut)* **~ geben** to double-declutch *(Brit)*, to double-clutch *(US)*; **Zwi|schen|ge|richt** NT *(Cook)* entrée; **zwi|schen|ge|schlecht|lich** ADJ between the sexes; **Zwi|schen|ge|schoss** NT mezzanine (floor); **Zwi|schen|glied** NT *(lit, fig)* link; **Zwi|schen|grö|ße** F in-between size; **Zwi|schen|halt** M *(Sw)* stopover, layover *(US)*; **Zwi|schen|han|del** M intermediate trade; **Zwi|schen|händ|ler(in)** M(F) middleman; **zwi|schen|hi|nein** ADV *(Sw)* = **zwischendurch**; **Zwi|schen|hirn** NT *(Anat)* interbrain, diencephalon *(spec)*; **Zwi|schen|hoch** NT *(Met)* ridge of high pressure; **Zwi|schen|kie|fer|(kno|chen)** M *(Anat)* intermaxillary (bone); **Zwi|schen|la|ger** NT temporary store; **zwi|schen|la|gern** VT *insep inf and ptp only* to store (temporarily); **Zwi|schen|la|ge|rung** F temporary storage; **zwi|schen+lan|den** VI *sep aux sein (Aviat)* to stop over *or* off, to lay over *(US)*; **Zwi|schen|lan|dung** F *(Aviat)* stopover, layover *(US)*; **ohne ~** without a stopover *or* layover *(US)*; **Zwi|schen|lauf** M *(Sport)* intermediate heat; **Zwi|schen|lö|sung** F temporary *or* interim *or* provisional solution; **Zwi|schen|mahl|zeit** F snack (between meals); **zwi|schen|mensch|lich** ADJ *attr* interpersonal; **~e Beziehungen** interpersonal relations; **Zwi|schen|mu|sik** F interlude; **Zwi|schen|pau|se** F break; *(Theat)* interval, intermission *(US)*; **Zwi|schen|pro|dukt** NT intermediate product; **Zwi|schen|prü|fung** F intermediate examination; **Zwi|schen|raum** M gap, space; *(= Wort-, Zeilenabstand)* space; *(zeitlich)* interval; **ein ~ von 5 m, 5 m ~** a gap/space of 5m, a 5m gap/space; **Zwi|schen|ring** M *(Phot)* adapter; **Zwi|schen|ruf** M interruption; **~e** heckling; **einen Redner durch ~e stören** to heckle a speaker; **Zwi|schen|ru|fer** [-ru:fɐ] M -s, -, **Zwi|schen|ru|fe|rin** [-ərɪn] F -, -nen heckler; **Zwi|schen|run|de** F *(esp Sport)* intermediate round; **Zwi|schen|sai|son** F low season; **Zwi|schen|satz** M *(Gram)* inserted *or* parenthetic clause, parenthesis; **zwi|schen+schal|ten** VT *sep (Elec)* to insert; *(fig)* to interpose, to put in between; **Zwi|schen|schal|ter** M *(Elec)* interruptor; **Zwi|schen|schal|tung** F *(Elec)* insertion; *(fig)* interposition; **zwi|schen+schie|ben** VT *sep irreg Termin etc* to fit *or* squeeze in; **Zwi|schen|schritt** M **a** *(fig: = Arbeitsgang)* intermediate stage **b** *(= Schritt beim Tanzen)* linking step; **Zwi|schen|soh|le** F midsole; **Zwi|schen|spei|cher** M *(Comput)* cache (memory); **zwi|schen+spei|chern** VT *sep (Comput)* to store in a/the cache (memory); **Zwi|schen|spiel** NT *(Mus)* intermezzo; *(Theat, fig)* interlude; **Zwi|schen|spurt** M *(Sport)* short burst (of speed); **einen ~ einlegen** to put in a burst of speed; **zwi|schen|staat|lich** ADJ *attr* international; *(zwischen Bundesstaaten)* interstate; **Zwi|schen|sta|di|um** NT intermediate stage; **Zwi|schen|stand** M *(Sport)* current score; *(in Tabelle)* current position; *(der Teilnehmer)* current rankings *pl*; **Zwi|schen|sta|ti|on** F (intermediate) stop; **in London machten wir ~** we stopped off in London; **Zwi|schen|ste|cker** M *(Elec)* adapter (plug); **Zwi|schen|stel|lung** F intermediate position; **Zwi|schen|stock** M, **Zwi|schen|stock|werk** NT mezzanine (floor); **Zwi|schen|stopp** M stop (on the way); *(beim Flug)* stopover → *auch* **Zwischenstation**; **Zwi|schen|stück** NT connection, connecting piece; **Zwi|schen|stu|fe** F *(fig)* intermediate stage; **Zwi|schen|stun|de** F *(Sch)* hour's break, break of an hour; **Zwi|schen|sum|me** F subtotal; **Zwi|schen|text** M inserted text; **Zwi|schen|ti|tel** M *(Film etc)* title link; **Zwi|schen|ton** M *pl* **-töne** *(Farbe)* shade; **Zwischentöne** *(fig)* nuances; **Zwi|schen|trä|ger(in)** M(F) informer, telltale, tattletale *(US)*; **Zwi|schen|ur|teil** NT *(Jur)* interlocutory decree; **Zwi|schen|vor|hang** M *(Theat)* drop scene; **Zwi|schen|wahl** F intermediary elections *pl*; **Zwi|schen|wand** F dividing wall; *(= Stellwand)* partition; **Zwi|schen|wirt** M *(Biol)* intermediate host; **Zwi|schen|zäh|ler** M *(Elec)* intermediate meter; **Zwi|schen|zeit** F **a** *(= Zeitraum)* interval; **in der ~** (in the) meantime, in the interim **b** *(Sport)* intermediate time; **zwi|schen|zeit|lich** ADV *(rare)* in between; *(= inzwischen)* (in the) meantime; **Zwi|schen|zeug|nis** NT *(Sch)* interim *or* end of term report; *(von Chef)* interim appraisal, intermediate reference; **Zwi|schen|zins** M *(Fin)* interim interest

Zwist [tsvɪst] M **-es,** *(rare)* **-e** *(geh)* discord, discordance; *(= Fehde, Streit)* dispute, strife *no indef art*; **den alten ~ begraben** to bury the hatchet; **mit jdm über etw** *(acc)* **in ~** *(acc)* **geraten** to become involved in a dispute with sb about *or* over sth

Zwis|tig|keit ['tsvɪstɪçkait] F -, -en *usu pl* dispute

zwit|schern ['tsvɪtʃɐn] VTI to twitter, to chir(ru)p; *(Lerche)* to warble; **~d sprechen** to twitter; **Zwitschern** twittering, chir(ru)ping, warbling; **einen ~** *(inf)* to have a drink

Zwit|ter ['tsvɪtɐ] M -s, - hermaphrodite; *(fig)* cross *(aus* between)

Zwit|ter-: **Zwit|ter|bil|dung** F hermaphroditism; **Zwit|ter|blü|te** F *(Bot)* hermaphrodite; **Zwit|ter|ding** NT *(fig)* hybrid, crossbreed; **Zwit|ter|form** F *(Biol)* hermaphroditic stage; *(fig)* hybrid form; **zwit|ter|haft** ADJ hermaphroditic

zwit|te|rig ['tsvɪtərɪç], **zwitt|rig** ['tsvɪtrɪç] ['tsvɪtrɪç] ADJ hermaphroditic; *(Bot auch)* androgynous

Zwit|ter-: **Zwit|ter|stel|lung** F **eine ~ einnehmen zwischen** *(+dat)* **... und ...** to be a halfway house between ... and ...; **Zwit|ter|tum** ['tsvɪtɐtu:m] NT -s, *no pl* hermaphroditism; *(Bot auch)* androgyny; **Zwit|ter|we|sen** NT hermaphrodite

zwitt|rig ['tsvɪtrɪç] ['tsvɪtrɪç] ADJ = **zwitterig**

zwo [tsvo:] NUM *(Telec, inf)* two

zwölf [tsvœlf] NUM twelve; **die ~ Apostel** the twelve apostles; **die Zwölf Nächte** the Twelve Days of Christmas; **~ Uhr mittags/nachts** (12 o'clock) noon *or* midday/midnight; **fünf Minuten vor ~** *(fig)* at the eleventh hour; **davon gehen ~ aufs Dutzend** they're ten a penny *(Brit inf)*, they're a dime a dozen *(US inf)* → *auch* **vier**

Zwölf- *in cpds* → *auch* **Vier-**: **Zwölf|eck** NT *(Math)* dodecagon; **zwölf|eckig** ADJ dodecagonal; **Zwölf|en|der** M *(Hunt)* royal; **zwölf|fach** ['tsvœlffax] ADJ ADV twelve-fold → *auch* **vierfach**; **Zwölf|fin|ger|darm** [tsvœlf'fɪŋɐ-] M duodenum; **ein Geschwür am ~** a duodenal ulcer; **Zwölf|flach** [-flax] NT -(e)s, -e, **Zwölf|fläch|ner** [-flɛçnɐ] M -s, - *(Math)* dodecahedron; **Zwölf|kampf** M *(Sport)* twelve-exercise event; **Zwölf|mei|len|zo|ne** [tsvœlf'mailən-] F twelve-mile zone

Zwölf|tel ['tsvœlftl] NT -s, - twelfth → *auch* **Viertel**

zwölf|tens ['tsvœlftns] ADV twelfth(ly), in twelfth place

zwölf|te(r, s) ['tsvœlftə] ADJ twelfth → *auch* **vierte(r, s)**

Zwölf|tö|ner [-tø:nɐ] M -s, -, **Zwölf|tö|ne|rin** [-ərɪn] F -, -nen *(Mus)* twelve-tone composer

Zwölf|ton-: **Zwölf|ton|leh|re** F twelve-tone system; **Zwölf|ton|mu|sik** F twelve-tone music; **Zwölf|ton|rei|he** F twelve-tone row *or* series

zwo|te(r, s) ['tsvo:tə] ADJ *(Telec, inf)* = **zweite(r, s)**

Zy|an [tsy'a:n] NT -s, *no pl (Chem)* cyanogen

Zy|a|nid [tsya'ni:t] NT -s, -e [-də] cyanide

Zy|an|ka|li [tsya:n'ka:li] NT -s, *no pl (Chem)* potassium cyanide

Zy|go|te [tsy'go:tə] F -, -n *(Biol)* zygote

Zyk|la|den [tsy'kla:dn] PL *(Geog)* Cyclades *pl*

Zyk|la|me [tsy'kla:mə] F -, -n *(Aus)*, **Zyk|la|men** [tsy'kla:mən] NT -s, - *(spec)* cyclamen

zyk|lisch ['tsy:klɪʃ] ADJ cyclic(al) ADV cyclically

Zyk|lon [tsy'klo:n] M -s, -e cyclone

Zyk|lon NT -s, *no pl (Chem)* cyanide-based poison, cyanide

Zyk|lo|ne [tsy'klo:nə] F -, -n *(Met)* depression, low(-pressure area)

Zyk|lop [tsy'klo:p] M -en, -en *(Myth)* Cyclops

Zyk|lo|pen|mau|er F *(Archeol)* cyclopean wall

zyk|lo|pisch [tsy'klo:pɪʃ] ADJ *(Myth)* Cyclopean; *(liter: = gewaltig)* gigantic

Zyk|lot|ron ['tsy:kloτro:n, 'tsyk-] NT -s, -e *(Phys)* cyclotron

Zyk|lus ['tsy:klʊs] M -, **Zyklen** [-lən] cycle *(auch Physiol)*

Zyk|lus|stö|rung ['tsy:klʊs-] F *(Med)* menstrual disorder

Zyk|lus|zeit ['tsy:klʊs-] F *(Comput)* cycle time

Zy|lin|der [tsi'lɪndɐ, tsy-] M -s, - **a** *(Math, Tech)* cylinder; *(= Lampenzylinder)* chimney **b** *(= Hut)* top hat, topper *(inf)*

Zy|lin|der-: **Zy|lin|der|block** M *pl* **-blöcke** *(Aut)* engine *or* cylinder block; **Zy|lin|der|dich|tungs|ring** M *(Aut)* cylinder ring; **zy|lin|der|för|mig** ADJ = **zylindrisch**; **Zy|lin|der|hut** M top hat, topper *(inf)*; **Zy|lin|der|kopf** M *(Aut)* cylinder head; **Zy|lin|der|kopf|dich|tung** F cylinder head gasket; **Zy|lin|der|man|tel** M *(Tech)* cylinder jacket; **Zy|lin|der|schloss** NT cylinder lock

-zy|lind|rig [tsilɪndrɪç, tsy-] ADJ *suf* -cylinder; **zweizylindrig** two-cylinder *attr*

zy|lind|risch [tsi'lɪndrɪʃ, tsy-] ADJ cylindrical ADV cylindrically

Zym|bal ['tsʏmbal] NT -s, -e *(Mus)* cymbal

Zy|ni|ker ['tsy:nikɐ] M -s, -, **Zy|ni|ke|rin** [-ərɪn] F -, -nen cynic

zy|nisch ['tsy:nɪʃ] ADJ cynical ADV cynically

Zy|nis|mus [tsy'nɪsmʊs] M -, **Zynismen** [-mən] cynicism

Zy|pern ['tsy:pɐn] NT -s Cyprus

Zyp|res|se [tsy'prɛsə] F -, -n *(Bot)* cypress

Zyp|ri|er ['tsy:priɐ] M -s, -, **Zyp|ri|e|rin** [-iərɪn] F -, -nen *(rare)*, **Zyp|ri|ot** [tsypri'o:t] M -en, -en, **Zyp|ri|o|tin** [-'o:tɪn] F -, -nen Cypriot

zyp|ri|o|tisch [tsypri'o:tɪʃ], **zyp|risch** ['tsy:prɪʃ] ADJ Cypriot, Cyprian

Zys|te ['tsʏstə] F -, -n cyst

zys|tisch ['tsʏstɪʃ] ADJ cystic; ~e **Fibrose** cystic fibrosis

Zy|to|lo|gie [tsytolo'gi:] F -, *no pl (Biol)* cytology

Zy|to-: **Zy|to|plas|ma** [tsyto'plasma] NT *(Biol)* cytoplasm; **Zy|to|sta|ti|kum** [tsyto'sta:tikʊm] NT -s, **Zytostatika** [-ka] cytostatic drug

zz(t). *abbr von* **zurzeit**

z. Z(t). *abbr von* **zur Zeit, zu Zeiten**

German Verbs

REGULAR VERBS

1. The present tense is formed by adding

-e, -st, -t, -en, -t, -en

to the stem of the verb (infinitive minus *-en* or, with verbs in *-ln, -rn,* minus *-n*).

Verbs ending in *-s, -ß, -z, -tz* form the second person singular by adding *-t*

heißen – du heißt

except in literary usage when the ending *-est* may be added

preisen – du preisest (*liter*)

2. The preterite, or past tense, is formed by adding

-te, -test, -te, -ten, -tet, -ten

to the stem of the verb.

3. The past participle is formed by adding the prefix *ge-* and the ending *-t* to the stem of the verb.

4. The present participle is formed by adding *-d* to the infinitive.

5. The *Sie* form imperative of both regular and irregular verbs is formed with the infinitive

machen Sie schnell!
kommen Sie her!

IRREGULAR VERBS

1. The forms of compound verbs (beginning with the prefixes *auf-, ab-, be-, er-, zer-, etc*) are the same as for the simplex verb.

2. The past participle of modal auxiliary verbs (dürfen, müssen *etc*) is replaced by the infinitive form when following another infinitive form, eg ich habe gehen dürfen; non-modal use: ich habe gedurft.

3. The formation of the present subjunctive is regular, requiring the following endings to be added to the verb stem:

sehen		**sein**	
ich seh-e	wir seh-en	ich sei	wir sei-en
du seh-est	ihr seh-et	du seist, du seiest (*liter*)	ihr sei-et
er seh-e	sie seh-en	er sei	sie sei-en

INFINITIVE	PRESENT INDICATIVE *2nd pers singular* *♦3rd pers singular*	IMPERFECT INDICATIVE	IMPERFECT SUBJUNCTIVE	IMPERATIVE *Singular* *♦Plural*	PAST PARTICIPLE
backen	bäckst, backst ♦ bäckt, backt	backte, buk (*old*)	backte, büke (*old*)	back(e) ♦ backt	gebacken
befehlen	befiehlst ♦ befiehlt	befahl	beföhle, befähle	befiehl ♦ befehlt	befohlen
befleißen (*old*)	befleißt ♦ befleißt	befliss	beflisse	befleiß(e) ♦ befleißt	beflissen
beginnen	beginnst ♦ beginnt	begann	begänne, begönne (*rare*)	beginn(e) ♦ beginnt	begonnen
beißen	beißt ♦ beißt	biss	bisse	beiß(e) ♦ beißt	gebissen
bergen	birgst ♦ birgt	barg	bärge	birg ♦ bergt	geborgen
bersten	birst ♦ birst	barst	bärste	birst ♦ berstet	geborsten
bewegen (= *veranlassen*)	bewegst ♦ bewegt	bewog	bewöge	beweg(e) ♦ bewegt	bewogen
biegen	biegst ♦ biegt	bog	böge	bieg(e) ♦ biegt	gebogen
bieten	bietest ♦ bietet	bot	böte	biet(e) ♦ bietet	geboten
binden	bindest ♦ bindet	band	bände	bind(e) ♦ bindet	gebunden
bitten	bittest ♦ bittet	bat	bäte	bitt(e) ♦ bittet	gebeten
blasen	bläst ♦ bläst	blies	bliese	blas(e) ♦ blast	geblasen
bleiben	bleibst ♦ bleibt	blieb	bliebe	bleib(e) ♦ bleibt	geblieben
bleichen (*vi, old*)	bleichst ♦ bleicht	blich (*old*)	bliche	bleich(e) ♦ bleicht	geblichen
braten	brätst ♦ brät	briet	briete	brat(e) ♦ bratet	gebraten
brechen	brichst ♦ bricht	brach	bräche	brich ♦ brecht	gebrochen
brennen	brennst ♦ brennt	brannte	brennte (*rare*)	brenn(e) ♦ brennt	gebrannt
bringen	bringst ♦ bringt	brachte	brächte	bring(e) ♦ bringt	gebracht
denken	denkst ♦ denkt	dachte	dächte	denk(e) ♦ denkt	gedacht
dingen	dingst ♦ dingt	dang	dingte	dingt ♦ dingt	gedungen
dreschen	drischst ♦ drischt	drosch	drösche, dräsche (*old*)	drisch ♦ drescht	gedroschen
dringen	dringst ♦ dringt	drang	dränge	dring(e) ♦ dringt	gedrungen
dünken	*3rd only* dünkt, deucht (*old*)	dünkte, deuchte (*old*)	dünkte, deuchte (*old*)		gedünkt, gedeucht (*old*)
dürfen	*1st* darf *2nd* darfst *3rd* darf	durfte	dürfte		gedurft; (*after infin*) dürfen

INFINITIVE	PRESENT INDICATIVE	IMPERFECT INDICATIVE	IMPERFECT SUBJUNCTIVE	IMPERATIVE	PAST PARTICIPLE
	2nd pers singular ♦ *3rd pers singular*			*Singular* ♦ *Plural*	
empfangen	empfängst ♦ empfängt	empfing	empfinge	empfang(e) ♦ empfangt	empfangen
empfehlen	empfiehlst ♦ empfiehlt	empfahl	empföhle, empfähle (*rare*)	empfiehl ♦ empfehlt	empfohlen
empfinden	empfindest ♦ empfindet	empfand	empfände	empfind(e) ♦ empfindet	empfunden
essen	isst ♦ isst	aß	äße	iss ♦ esst	gegessen
fahren	fährst ♦ fährt	fuhr	führe	fahr(e) ♦ fahrt	gefahren
fallen	fällst ♦ fällt	fiel	fiele	fall(e) ♦ fallt	gefallen
fangen	fängst ♦ fängt	fing	finge	fang(e) ♦ fangt	gefangen
fechten	fichtst ♦ ficht	focht	föchte	ficht ♦ fechtet	gefochten
finden	findest ♦ findet	fand	fände	find(e) ♦ findet	gefunden
flechten	flichtst ♦ flicht	flocht	flöchte	flicht ♦ flechtet	geflochten
fliegen	fliegst ♦ fliegt	flog	flöge	flieg(e) ♦ fliegt	geflogen
fliehen	fliehst ♦ flieht	floh	flöhe	flieh(e) ♦ flieht	geflohen
fließen	fließt ♦ fließt	floss	flösse	fließ(e) ♦ fließt	geflossen
fressen	frisst ♦ frisst	fraß	fräße	friss ♦ fresst	gefressen
frieren	frierst ♦ friert	fror	fröre	frier(e) ♦ friert	gefroren
gären	gärst ♦ gärt	gor, gärte (*esp fig*)	göre, gärte (*esp fig*)	gär(e) ♦ gärt	gegoren, gegärt (*esp fig*)
gebären	gebierst ♦ gebiert	gebar	gebäre	gebier ♦ gebärt	geboren
geben	gibst ♦ gibt	gab	gäbe	gib ♦ gebt	gegeben
gedeihen	gedeihst ♦ gedeiht	gedieh	gediehe	gedeih(e) ♦ gedeiht	gediehen
gehen	gehst ♦ geht	ging	ginge	geh(e) ♦ geht	gegangen
gelingen	gelingt	gelang	gelänge	geling(e) (*rare*) ♦ gelingt (*rare*)	gelungen
gelten	giltst ♦ gilt	galt	gölte, gälte	gilt (*rare*) ♦ geltet (*rare*)	gegolten
genesen	genest ♦ genest	genas	genäse	genese ♦ genest	genesen
genießen	genießt ♦ genießt	genoss	genösse	genieß(e) ♦ genießt	genossen
geschehen	geschieht	geschah	geschähe	geschieh ♦ gescheht	geschehen
gewinnen	gewinnst ♦ gewinnt	gewann	gewönne, gewänne	gewinn(e) ♦ gewinnt	gewonnen
gießen	gießt ♦ gießt	goss	gösse	gieß(e) ♦ gießt	gegossen
gleichen	gleichst ♦ gleicht	glich	gliche	gleich(e) ♦ gleicht	geglichen
gleiten	gleitest ♦ gleitet	glitt	glitte	gleit(e) ♦ gleitet	geglitten
glimmen	glimmst ♦ glimmt	glomm	glömme, glimmte (*rare*)	glimm(e) ♦ glimmt	geglommen
graben	gräbst ♦ gräbt	grub	grübe	grab(e) ♦ grabt	gegraben
greifen	greifst ♦ greift	griff	griffe	greif(e) ♦ greift	gegriffen
haben	hast ♦ hat	hatte	hätte	hab(e) ♦ habt	gehabt
halten	hältst ♦ hält	hielt	hielte	halt(e) ♦ haltet	gehalten
hängen	hängst ♦ hängt	hing	hinge	häng(e) ♦ hängt	gehangen
hauen	haust ♦ haut	haute	haute, hiebe	hau(e) ♦ haut	gehauen
heben	hebst ♦ hebt	hob	höbe, hübe (*old*)	heb(e) ♦ hebt	gehoben
heißen	heißt ♦ heißt	hieß	hieße	heiß(e) ♦ heißt	geheißen
helfen	hilfst ♦ hilft	half	hülfe, hälfe (*rare*)	hilf ♦ helft	geholfen
kennen	kennst ♦ kennt	kannte	kennte	kenn(e) ♦ kennt	gekannt
klimmen	klimmst ♦ klimmt	klomm, klimmte	klömme, klimmte	klimm(e) ♦ klimmt	geklimmt, geklommen
klingen	klingst ♦ klingt	klang	klänge	kling(e) ♦ klingt	geklungen
kneifen	kneifst ♦ kneift	kniff	kniffe	kneif(e) ♦ kneift	gekniffen
kommen	kommst ♦ kommt	kam	käme	komm(e) ♦ kommt	gekommen
können	*1st* kann *2nd* kannst *3rd* kann	konnte	könnte		gekonnt; (*after infin*) können
kreischen	kreischst ♦ kreischt	kreischte, krisch (*old, hum*)	kreischte, krische (*old, hum*)	kreisch(e) ♦ kreischt	gekreischt, gekrischen (*old, hum*)
kriechen	kriechst ♦ kriecht	kroch	kröche	kriech(e) ♦ kriecht	gekrochen
küren	kürst ♦ kürt	kürte, kor (*rare*)	kürte, köre (*rare*)	kür(e) ♦ kürt	gekürt, gekoren (*rare*)
laden[1]	lädst ♦ lädt	lud	lüde	lad(e) ♦ ladet	geladen

INFINITIVE	PRESENT INDICATIVE	IMPERFECT INDICATIVE	IMPERFECT SUBJUNCTIVE	IMPERATIVE	PAST PARTICIPLE
	2nd pers singular ♦*3rd pers singular*			*Singular* ♦*Plural*	
laden[2]	lädst ♦ lädest (*dated, dial*)	lud	lüde	lad(e) ♦ ladet	geladen
lassen	lässt ♦ lässt	ließ	ließe	lass ♦ lasst	gelassen; (*after infin*) lassen
laufen	läufst ♦ läuft	lief	liefe	lauf(e) ♦ lauft	gelaufen
leiden	leidest ♦ leidet	litt	litte	leid(e) ♦ leidet	gelitten
leihen	leihst ♦ leiht	lieh	liehe	leih(e) ♦ leiht	geliehen
lesen	liest ♦ liest	las	läse	lies ♦ lest	gelesen
liegen	liegst ♦ liegt	lag	läge	lieg(e) ♦ liegt	gelegen
löschen	lischst ♦ lischt	losch	lösche	lisch ♦ löscht	geloschen
lügen	lügst ♦ lügt	log	löge	lüg(e) ♦ lügt	gelogen
mahlen	mahlst ♦ mahlt	mahlte	mahlte	mahl(e) ♦ mahlt	gemahlen
meiden	meidest ♦ meidet	mied	miede	meid(e) ♦ meidet	gemieden
melken	melkst ♦ melkt	melkte	mölke	melk(e), milk ♦ melkt	gemolken
messen	misst ♦ misst	maß	mäße	miss ♦ messt	gemessen
misslingen	misslingt	misslang	misslänge		misslungen
mögen	*1st* mag *2nd* magst *3rd* mag	mochte	möchte		gemocht; (*after infin*) mögen
müssen	*1st* muss *2nd* musst *3rd* muss	musste	müsste		müssen; (*vi*) gemusst
nehmen	nimmst ♦ nimmt	nahm	nähme	nimm ♦ nehmt	genommen
nennen	nennst ♦ nennt	nannte	nennte (*rare*)	nenn(e) ♦ nennt	genannt
pfeifen	pfeifst ♦ pfeift	pfiff	pfiffe	pfeif(e) ♦ pfeift	gepfiffen
pflegen	pflegst ♦ pflegt	pflegt, pflog (*old*)	pflegte, pflöge (*old*)	pfleg(e) ♦ pflegt	gepflegt, gepflogen (*old*)
preisen	preist ♦ preist	pries	priese	preis(e) ♦ preis(e)t	gepriesen
quellen	quillst ♦ quillt	quoll	quölle	quill (*rare*) ♦ quellt	gequollen
raten	rätst ♦ rät	riet	riete	rat(e) ♦ ratet	geraten
reiben	reibst ♦ reibt	rieb	riebe	reib(e) ♦ reibt	gerieben
reißen	reißt ♦ reißt	riss	risse	reiß(e) ♦ reißt	gerissen
reiten	reitest ♦ reitet	ritt	ritte	reit(e) ♦ reitet	geritten
rennen	rennst ♦ rennt	rannte	rennte (*rare*)	renn(e) ♦ rennt	gerannt
riechen	riechst ♦ riecht	roch	röche	riech(e) ♦ riecht	gerochen
ringen	ringst ♦ ringt	rang	ränge	ring(e) ♦ ringt	gerungen
rinnen	rinnst ♦ rinnt	rann	ränne	rinn(e) ♦ rinnt	geronnen
rufen	rufst ♦ ruft	rief	riefe	ruf(e) ♦ ruft	gerufen
salzen	salzt ♦ salzt	salzte	salzte	salz(e) ♦ salzt	gesalzen
saufen	säufst ♦ säuft	soff	söffe	sauf(e) ♦ sauft	gesoffen
saugen	saugst ♦ saugt	sog	söge, saugte	saug(e) ♦ saugt	gesogen, gesaugt
schaffen	schaffst ♦ schafft	schuf	schüfe	schaff(e) ♦ schafft	geschaffen
schallen	schallst ♦ schallt	schallte, scholl (*rare*)	schallte, schölle (*rare*)	schall(e) ♦ schallt	geschallt
scheiden	scheidest ♦ scheidet	schied	schiede	scheid(e) ♦ scheidet	geschieden
scheinen	scheinst ♦ scheint	schien	schiene	schein(e) ♦ scheint	geschienen
scheißen	scheißt ♦ scheißt	schiss	schisse	scheiß(e) ♦ scheißt	geschissen
schelten	schiltst ♦ schilt	schalt	schölte	schilt ♦ scheltet	gescholten
scheren	scherst ♦ schert	schor	schöre	scher(e) ♦ schert	geschoren
schieben	schiebst ♦ schiebt	schob	schöbe	schieb(e) ♦ schiebt	geschoben
schießen	schießt ♦ schießt	schoss	schösse	schieß(e) ♦ schießt	geschossen
schinden	schindest ♦ schindet	schindete	schünde	schind(e)	geschunden
schlafen	schläfst ♦ schläft	schlief	schliefe	schlaf(e) ♦ schlaft	geschlafen
schlagen	schlägst ♦ schlägt	schlug	schlüge	schlag(e) ♦ schlagt	geschlagen
schleichen	schleichst ♦ schleicht	schlich	schliche	schleich(e) ♦ schleicht	geschlichen
schleifen	schleifst ♦ schleift	schliff	schliffe	schleif(e) ♦ schleift	geschliffen
schleißen	schleißt ♦ schleißt	schliss; (*vt auch*) schleißte	schlisse; schleißte	schleiß(e) ♦ schleißt	geschlissen; (*vt auch*) geschleißt
schließen	schließt ♦ schließt	schloss	schlösse	schließ(e) ♦ schließt	geschlossen
schlingen	schlingst ♦ schlingt	schlang	schlänge	schling(e) ♦ schlingt	geschlungen

INFINITIVE	PRESENT INDICATIVE	IMPERFECT INDICATIVE	IMPERFECT SUBJUNCTIVE	IMPERATIVE	PAST PARTICIPLE
	2nd pers singular ♦ *3rd pers singular*			*Singular* ♦ *Plural*	
schmeißen	schmeißt ♦ schmeißt	schmiss	schmisse	schmeiß(e) ♦ schmeißt	geschmissen
schmelzen	schmilzt ♦ schmilzt	schmolz	schmölze	schmilz ♦ schmelzt	geschmolzen
schnauben	schnaubst ♦ schnaubt	schnaubte, schnob (*old*)	schnaubte, schnöbe (*old*)	schnaub(e) ♦ schnaubt	geschnaubt, geschnoben (*old*)
schneiden	schneid(e)st ♦ schneidet	schnitt	schnitte	schneid(e) ♦ schneidet	geschnitten
schrecken	schrickst ♦ schrickt	schreckte, schrak	schreckte, schräke	schrick ♦ schreckt	geschreckt, geschrocken (*old*)
schreiben	schreibst ♦ schreibt	schrieb	schriebe	schreib(e) ♦ schreibt	geschrieben
schreien	schreist ♦ schreit	schrie	schriee	schrei(e) ♦ schreit	geschrie(e)n
schreiten	schreitest ♦ schreitet	schritt	schritte	schreit(e) ♦ schreitet	geschritten
schweigen	schweigst ♦ schweigt	schwieg	schwiege	schweig(e) ♦ schweigt	geschwiegen
schwellen	schwillst ♦ schwillt	schwoll	schwölle	schwill ♦ schwellt	geschwollen
schwimmen	schwimmst ♦ schwimmt	schwamm	schwämme, schwamme (*rare*)	schwimm(e) ♦ schwimmt	geschwommen
schwinden	schwindest ♦ schwindet	schwand	schwände	schwind(e) ♦ schwindet	geschwunden
schwingen	schwingst ♦ schwingt	schwang	schwänge	schwing(e) ♦ schwingt	geschwungen
schwören	schwörst ♦ schwört	schwor	schwüre, schwöre (*rare*)	schwör(e) ♦ schwört	geschworen
sehen	siehst ♦ sieht	sah	sähe	sieh(e) ♦ seht	gesehen; (*after infin*) sehen
sein	*1st* bin *2nd* bist *3rd* ist *1st pl* sind *2nd pl* seid *3rd pl* sind	war	wäre	sei ♦ seid	gewesen
senden (= *schicken*)	sendest ♦ sendet	sandte	sendete	send(e) ♦ sendet	gesandt
sieden	siedest ♦ siedet	siedete, sott	siedete, sötte	sied(e) ♦ siedet	gesiedet, gesotten
singen	singst ♦ singt	sang	sänge	sing(e) ♦ singt	gesungen
sinken	sinkst ♦ sinkt	sank	sänke	sink(e) ♦ sinkt	gesunken
sinnen	sinnst ♦ sinnt	sann	sänne	sinn(e) ♦ sinnt	gesonnen
sitzen	sitzt ♦ sitzt	saß	säße	sitz(e) ♦ sitzt	gesessen
sollen	*1st* soll *2nd* sollst *3rd* soll	sollte	sollte		gesollt; (*after infin*) sollen
spalten	spaltest ♦ spaltet	spaltete	spalte	spalt(e) ♦ spaltet	gespalten
speien	speist ♦ speit	spie	spiee	spei(e) ♦ speit	gespie(e)n
spinnen	spinnst ♦ spinnt	spann	spönne, spänne	spinn(e) ♦ spinnt	gesponnen
spleißen	spleißt ♦ spleißt	spliss	splisse	spleiß(e) ♦ spleißt	gesplissen
sprechen	sprichst ♦ spricht	sprach	spräche	sprich ♦ sprecht	gesprochen
sprießen	sprießt ♦ sprießt	spross, sprießte	sprösse	sprieß(e) ♦ sprießt	gesprossen
springen	springst ♦ springt	sprang	spränge	spring(e) ♦ springt	gesprungen
stechen	stichst ♦ sticht	stach	stäche	stich ♦ stecht	gestochen
stecken (*vi*)	steckst ♦ steckt	steckte, stak	steckte, stäke (*rare*)	steck(e) ♦ steckt	gesteckt
stehen	stehst ♦ steht	stand	stünde, stände	steh ♦ steht	gestanden
stehlen	stiehlst ♦ stiehlt	stahl	stähle, stöhle (*obs*)	stiehl ♦ stehlt	gestohlen
steigen	steigst ♦ steigt	stieg	stiege	steig ♦ steigt	gestiegen
sterben	stirbst ♦ stirbt	starb	stürbe	stirb ♦ sterbt	gestorben
stieben	stiebst ♦ stiebt	stob, stiebte	stöbe, stiebte	stieb(e) ♦ stiebt	gestoben, gestiebt
stinken	stinkst ♦ stinkt	stank	stänke	stink(e) ♦ stinkt	gestunken
stoßen	stößt ♦ stößt	stieß	stieße	stoß(e) ♦ stoßt	gestoßen
streichen	streichst ♦ streicht	strich	striche	streich(e) ♦ streicht	gestrichen
streiten	streitest ♦ streitet	stritt	stritte	streit(e) ♦ streitet	gestritten
tragen	trägst ♦ trägt	trug	trüge	trag(e) ♦ tragt	getragen
treffen	triffst ♦ trifft	traf	träfe	triff ♦ trefft	getroffen
treiben	treibst ♦ treibt	trieb	triebe	treib ♦ treibt	getrieben
treten	trittst ♦ tritt	trat	träte	tritt ♦ tretet	getreten

INFINITIVE	PRESENT INDICATIVE	IMPERFECT INDICATIVE	IMPERFECT SUBJUNCTIVE	IMPERATIVE	PAST PARTICIPLE
	2nd pers singular ♦*3rd pers singular*			*Singular* ♦*Plural*	
triefen	triefst ♦ trieft	trieft(e), troff (*geh*)	triefte, tröffe (*geh*)	trief(e) ♦ trieft	getrieft, getroffen (*rare*)
trinken	trinkst ♦ trinkt	trank	tränke	trink ♦ trinkt	getrunken
trügen	trügst ♦ trügt	trog	tröge	trüg(e) ♦ trügt	getrogen
tun	*1st* tue *2nd* tust *3rd* tut	tat	täte	tu(e) ♦ tut	getan
verderben	verdirbst ♦ verdirbt	verdarb	verdärbe	verdirb ♦ verderbt	verdorben
verdrießen	verdrießt ♦ verdrießt	verdross	verdrösse	verdrieß(e) ♦ verdrießt	verdrossen
vergessen	vergisst ♦ vergisst	vergaß	vergäße	vergiss ♦ vergesst	vergessen
verlieren	verlierst ♦ verliert	verlor	verlöre	verlier(e) ♦ verliert	verloren
verzeihen	verzeihst ♦ verzeiht	verzieh	verziehe	verzeih(e) ♦ verzeiht	verziehen
wachsen	wächst ♦ wächst	wuchs	wüchse	wachs(e) ♦ wachst	gewachsen
wägen	wägst ♦ wägt	wog	wöge, wägte (*rare*)	wäg(e) ♦ wägt	gewogen
waschen	wäschst ♦ wäscht	wusch	wüsche	wasch(e) ♦ wascht	gewaschen
weben	webst ♦ webt	webte, wob (*liter, fig*)	webte, wöbe (*liter, fig*)	web(e) ♦ webt	gewebt, gewoben (*liter, fig*)
weichen	weichst ♦ weicht	wich	wiche	weich(e) ♦ weicht	gewichen
weisen	weist ♦ weist	wies	wiese	weis(e) ♦ weist	gewiesen
wenden	wendest ♦ wendet	wendete	wendete	wend(e) ♦ wendet	gewendet, gewandt
werben	wirbst ♦ wirbt	warb	würbe	wirb ♦ werbt	geworben
werden	wirst ♦ wird	wurde	würde	werde ♦ werdet	geworden; (*after ptp*) worden
werfen	wirfst ♦ wirft	warf	würfe	wirf ♦ werft	geworfen
wiegen	wiegst ♦ wiegt	wog	wöge	wieg(e) ♦ wiegt	gewogen
winden	windest ♦ windet	wand	wände	wind(e) ♦ windet	gewunden
winken	winkst ♦ winkt	winkte	winkte	wink(e) ♦ winkt	gewinkt, gewunken
wissen	*1st* weiß *2nd* weißt *3rd* weiß	wusste	wüsste	wisse (*liter*) ♦ wisset (*liter*)	gewusst
wollen	*1st* will *2nd* willst *3rd* will	wollte	wollte	wolle (*liter*) ♦ wollt	gewollt; (*after infin*) wollen
wringen	wringst ♦ wringt	wrang	wränge	wring(e) ♦ wringt	gewrungen
zeihen	zeihst ♦ zeiht	zieh	ziehe	zeih(e) ♦ zeiht	geziehen
ziehen	ziehst ♦ zieht	zog	zöge	zieh(e) ♦ zieht	gezogen
zwingen	zwingst ♦ zwingt	zwang	zwänge	zwing(e) ♦ zwingt	gezwungen

Englische Verben

REGELMÄSSIGE VERBEN IM ENGLISCHEN

1. **Bildung des Präteritums und des 2. Partizips**

1.1 In den meisten Fällen wird *-ed* an die Infinitivform angehängt.

remain *pret, ptp* **remained**

1.2 Verben mit Konsonant +*y* im Auslaut werden zu *-ied.*

try *pret, ptp* **tried**

1.3 Verben mit stummen *-e* oder mit *-ee, -ye, -oe, -ge* im Auslaut verlieren das zweite *-e.*

abate *pret, ptp* **abated**
agree *pret, ptp* **agreed**
dye *pret, ptp* **dyed**
hoe *pret, ptp* **hoed**
singe *pret, ptp* **singed**

1.4 Verben, die auf Konsonant nach einfachem, betontem Vokal enden, verdoppeln diesen Endkonsonanten.

bar *pret, ptp* **barred**
permit *pret, ptp* **permitted**

Nach Doppelvokal wird der Konsonant im Auslaut nicht verdoppelt

dread *pret, ptp* **dreaded**

ebenso wenig nach unbetontem Vokal

visit *pret, ptp* **visited**

mit Ausnahme von auslautendem *-l* und *-p* im britischen Englisch.

level *pret, ptp* **levelled** *or* (*US*) **leveled**
worship *pret, ptp* **worshipped** *or* (*US*) **worshiped**

Verben mit Vokal +*c* im Auslaut werden zu *-cked.*

panic *pret, ptp* **panicked**

2. **Bildung des 1. Partizips**

2.1 Die meisten Verben bilden das 1. Partizip durch Anhängen von *-ing.*

2.2 Für Verben, die auf Vokal + Konsonant enden, gelten die gleichen Regeln wie für die Bildung des Präteritums; siehe **1.4**.

2.3 Verben, die auf *-ie* enden, werden zu *-ying.*

die *prp* **dying**

2.4 Verben mit stummem *-e* im Auslaut verlieren diesen Vokal

like *prp* **liking**

außer wenn sie in der Kombination *-ye, -oe* auftreten.

dye *prp* **dyeing**
hoe *prp* **hoeing**

UNREGELMÄSSIGE ENGLISCHE VERBEN

INFINITIV	PRÄTERITUM	PARTIZIP PERFEKT
abide	abode, abided	abode, abided
arise	arose	arisen
awake	awoke	awaked
be (am, is, are; being)	was (*sing*), were (*pl*)	been
bear	bore	born(e)
beat	beat	beaten
become	became	become
befall	befell	befallen
beget	begot, begat (*obs*)	begotten
begin	began	begun
behold	beheld	beheld
bend	bent	bent
beseech	besought	besought
beset	beset	beset
bet	bet, betted	bet, betted
bid (*at auction, cards*)	bid	bid
bid (*= say*)	bade	bidden
bind	bound	bound
bite	bit	bitten
bleed	bled	bled
blow	blew	blown
break	broke	broken
breed	bred	bred
bring	brought	brought
build	built	built
burn	burnt, burned	burnt, burned
burst	burst	burst
buy	bought	bought
can	could	(been able)
cast	cast	cast
catch	caught	caught
chide	chid	chidden, chid
choose	chose	chosen
cleave[1] (*= cut*)	clove, cleft	cloven, cleft
cleave[2] (*= adhere*)	cleaved, clave	cleaved
cling	clung	clung
come	came	come
cost	cost	cost
cost (*= work out price of*)	costed	costed
creep	crept	crept
cut	cut	cut
deal	dealt	dealt
dig	dug	dug
do (*3rd person:* he/she/it does)	did	done
draw	drew	drawn
dream	dreamed, dreamt	dreamed, dreamt
drink	drank	drunk
drive	drove	driven
dwell	dwelt	dwelt
eat	ate	eaten
fall	fell	fallen
feed	fed	fed
feel	felt	felt
fight	fought	fought
find	found	found
flee	fled	fled
fling	flung	flung
fly	flew	flown
forbid	forbad(e)	forbidden
forecast	forecast	forecast
forget	forgot	forgotten

INFINITIV	PRÄTERITUM	PARTIZIP PERFEKT
forgive	forgave	forgiven
forsake	forsook	forsaken
freeze	froze	frozen
get	got	got, (*US*) gotten
gild	gilded	gilded, gilt
gird	girded, girt	girded, girt
give	gave	given
go (**goes**)	went	gone
grind	ground	ground
grow	grew	grown
hang	hung	hung
hang (= *execute*)	hanged	hanged
have	had	had
hear	heard	heard
heave	heaved, (*Naut*) hove	heaved, (*Naut*) hove
hew	hewed	hewed, hewn
hide	hid	hidden
hit	hit	hit
hold	held	held
hurt	hurt	hurt
keep	kept	kept
kneel	knelt, kneeled	knelt, kneeled
know	knew	known
lade	laded	laden
lay	laid	laid
lead	led	led
lean	leant, leaned	leant, leaned
leap	leapt, leaped	leapt, leaped
learn	learnt, learned	learnt, learned
leave	left	left
lend	lent	lent
let	let	let
lie (**lying**)	lay	lain
light	lit, lighted	lit, lighted
lose	lost	lost
make	made	made
may	might	—
mean	meant	meant
meet	met	met
mistake	mistook	mistaken
mow	mowed	mown, mowed
must	(had to)	(had to)
pay	paid	paid
put	put	put
quit	quit, quitted	quit, quitted
read [ri:d]	read [red]	read [red]
rend	rent	rent
rid	rid	rid
ride	rode	ridden
ring[2]	rang	rung
rise	rose	risen
run	ran	run
saw	sawed	sawed, sawn
say	said	said
see	saw	seen
seek	sought	sought
sell	sold	sold
send	sent	sent
set	set	set
sew	sewed	sewn
shake	shook	shaken
shave	shaved	shaved, shaven
shear	sheared	shorn, sheared
shed	shed	shed
shine	shone	shone
shoe	shod	shod
shoot	shot	shot
show	showed	shown
shrink	shrank	shrunk
shut	shut	shut
sing	sang	sung
sink	sank	sunk
sit	sat	sat
slay	slew	slain
sleep	slept	slept
slide	slid	slid
sling	slung	slung
slink	slunk	slunk
slit	slit	slit
smell	smelt, smelled	smelt, smelled
smite	smote	smitten
sow	sowed	sown, sowed
speak	spoke	spoken
speed	sped, speeded	sped, speeded
spell	spelt, spelled	spelt, spelled
spend	spent	spent
spill	spilt, spilled	spilt, spilled
spin	spun	spun
spit	spat	spat
split	split	split
spoil	spoiled, spoilt	spoiled, spoilt
spread	spread	spread
spring	sprang	sprung
stand	stood	stood
stave	stove, staved	stove, staved
steal	stole	stolen
stick	stuck	stuck
sting	stung	stung
stink	stank	stunk
strew	strewed	strewed, strewn
stride	strode	stridden
strike	struck	struck
string	strung	strung
strive	strove	striven
swear	swore	sworn
sweep	swept	swept
swell	swelled	swollen, swelled
swim	swam	swum
swing	swung	swung
take	took	taken
teach	taught	taught
tear	tore	torn
tell	told	told
think	thought	thought
thrive	throve, thrived	thriven, thrived
throw	threw	thrown
thrust	thrust	thrust
tread	trod	trodden
wake	woke, waked	woken, waked
wear	wore	worn
weave	wove	woven
weave (= *wind*)	weaved	weaved
wed	wedded, wed	wedded, wed
weep	wept	wept
win	won	won
wind[2]	wound	wound
wring	wrung	wrung
write	wrote	written

Numerals, Weights and Measures, Time and Dates

Zahlen, Masse und Gewichte, Zeit und Datum

NUMERALS

ZAHLEN

CARDINAL NUMBERS / KARDINALZAHLEN

nought, zero	**0**	null
one	**1**	eins*; (*m, nt*) ein, (*f*) eine
two	**2**	zwei
three	**3**	drei
four	**4**	vier
five	**5**	fünf
six	**6**	sechs
seven	**7**	sieben
eight	**8**	acht
nine	**9**	neun
ten	**10**	zehn
eleven	**11**	elf
twelve	**12**	zwölf
thirteen	**13**	dreizehn
fourteen	**14**	vierzehn
fifteen	**15**	fünfzehn
sixteen	**16**	sechzehn
seventeen	**17**	siebzehn
eighteen	**18**	achtzehn
nineteen	**19**	neunzehn
twenty	**20**	zwanzig
twenty-one	**21**	einundzwanzig
twenty-two	**22**	zweiundzwanzig
twenty-three	**23**	dreiundzwanzig
thirty	**30**	dreißig
thirty-one	**31**	einunddreißig
thirty-two	**32**	dreiunddreißig
forty	**40**	vierzig
fifty	**50**	fünfzig
sixty	**60**	sechzig
seventy	**70**	siebzig
eighty	**80**	achtzig
ninety	**90**	neunzig
ninety-nine	**99**	neunundneunzig
a (*or* one) hundred	**100**	(ein)hundert
a hundred and one	**101**	(ein)hundert(und)eins; -eine(r, s)
a hundred and two	**102**	(ein)hundert(und)zwei
a hundred and ten	**110**	(ein)hundert(und)zehn
a hundred and eighty-two	**182**	(ein)hundert(und)-zweiundachtzig
two hundred	**200**	zweihundert
two hundred and one	**201**	zweihundert(und)eins; -eine(r, s)
two hundred and two	**202**	zweihundert(und)zwei
three hundred	**300**	dreihundert
four hundred	**400**	vierhundert
five hundred	**500**	fünfhundert
six hundred	**600**	sechshundert
seven hundred	**700**	siebenhundert
eight hundred	**800**	achthundert
nine hundred	**900**	neunhundert
a (*or* one) thousand	**1000**	(ein)tausend
a thousand and one	**1001**	(ein)tausend(und)eins, -eine(r, s)
a thousand and two	**1002**	(ein)tausend(und)zwei
two thousand	**2000**	zweitausend
ten thousand	**10,000**	zehntausend
a (*or* one) hundred thousand	**100,000**	(ein)hunderttausend
a (*or* one) million	**1,000,000**	eine Million
two million	**2,000,000**	zwei Millionen

Notes on the use of cardinal numbers

(a) ***eins** is used in counting or in listing; when 'one' directly replaces a noun, use the declined form.

(b) **one**, and the other numbers ending in one, agree in German with the noun (stated or implied): *ein Mann, eine Frau, (ein)hundert(und)ein Haus.*

(c) To divide thousands and above clearly, a point may be used in German where English places a comma: English 1,000 / German 1.000; English 2,304,770 / German 2.304.770.

Anstelle des im Deutschen zuweilen verwendeten Punktes zur Unterteilung von Zahlen über 1000 verwendet man in Englischen ein Komma: 1,000 statt 1.000 oder 1000, 2,304,770 statt 2.304.770.

ORDINAL NUMBERS / ORDINALZAHLEN

first	**1**	erste(r, s)
second	**2**	zweite(r, s)
third	**3**	dritte(r, s)
fourth	**4**	vierte(r, s)
fifth	**5**	fünfte(r, s)
sixth	**6**	sechste(r, s)
seventh	**7**	siebte(r, s)
eighth	**8**	achte(r, s)
ninth	**9**	neunte(r, s)
tenth	**10**	zehnte(r, s)
eleventh	**11**	elfte(r, s)
twelfth	**12**	zwölfte(r, s)
thirteenth	**13**	dreizehnte(r, s)
fourteenth	**14**	vierzehnte(r, s)
fifteenth	**15**	fünfzehnte(r, s)
sixteenth	**16**	sechzehnte(r, s)
seventeenth	**17**	siebzehnte(r, s)
eighteenth	**18**	achtzehnte(r, s)
nineteenth	**19**	neunzehnte(r, s)
twentieth	**20**	zwanzigste(r, s)
twenty-first	**21**	einundzwanzigste(r, s)
twenty-second	**22**	zweiundzwanzigs-te(r, s)
thirtieth	**30**	dreißigste(r, s)
thirty-first	**31**	einunddreißigste(r, s)
fortieth	**40**	vierzigste(r, s)
fiftieth	**50**	fünfzigste(r, s)
sixtieth	**60**	sechzigste(r, s)
seventieth	**70**	siebzigste(r, s)
eightieth	**80**	achtzigste(r, s)
ninetieth	**90**	neunzigste(r, s)
hundredth	**100**	(ein)hundertste(r, s)
hundred and first	**101**	(ein)hundert(und)-erste(r, s)
hundred and tenth	**110**	(ein)hundert(und)-zehnte(r, s)
two hundredth	**200**	zweihundertste(r, s)
three hundredth	**300**	dreihundertste(r, s)
four hundredth	**400**	vierhundertste(r, s)
five hundredth	**500**	fünfhundertste(r, s)
six hundredth	**600**	sechshundertste(r, s)
seven hundredth	**700**	siebenhundertste(r, s)
eight hundredth	**800**	achthundertste(r, s)
nine hundredth	**900**	neunhundertste(r, s)
thousandth	**1000**	(ein)tausendste(r, s)
two thousandth	**2000**	zweitausendste(r, s)
millionth	**1,000,000**	(ein)millionste(r, s)
two millionth	**2,000,000**	zweimillionste(r, s)

Notes on the use of the ordinal numbers

(a) All ordinal numbers agree in German with the noun (stated or implied): *ihr erster Mann, die fünfte Frau, ein zweites Haus.*

(b) Abbreviations: English 1st, 2nd, 3rd, 4th etc = German 1., 2., 3., 4. and so on.

(c) See also notes on dates below.

Siehe ebenfalls die Anmerkungen bezüglich Datum.

FRACTIONS — BRÜCHE

one half, a half	$\frac{1}{2}$	ein halb
one and a half helpings	$1\frac{1}{2}$	eineinhalb *oder* anderthalb Portionen
two and a half kilos	$2\frac{1}{2}$	zweieinhalb Kilo
one third, a third	$\frac{1}{3}$	ein Drittel
two thirds	$\frac{2}{3}$	zwei Drittel
one quarter, a quarter	$\frac{1}{4}$	ein Viertel
three quarters	$\frac{3}{4}$	drei Viertel
one sixth, a sixth	$\frac{1}{6}$	ein Sechstel
five and five sixths	$5\frac{5}{6}$	fünf fünf Sechstel
one twelfth, a twelfth	$\frac{1}{12}$	ein Zwölftel
seven twelfths	$\frac{7}{12}$	sieben Zwölftel
one hundredth, a hundredth	$\frac{1}{100}$	ein Hundertstel
one thousandth, a thousandth	$\frac{1}{1000}$	ein Tausendstel

DECIMALS — DEZIMALZAHLEN

In German, a comma is written where English uses a point: English 3.56 (three point five six) = German 3,56 (drei Komma fünf sechs); English .07 (point nought seven) = German 0,07 (null Komma null sieben). Note that a German number cannot start with *Komma* — *null* must precede it.

Im Englischen wird anstelle des im Deutschen gebräuchlichen Kommas ein Punkt verwendet: 3.56 (three point five six). Bei Zahlen unter 1 kann die Null vor dem Punkt entfallen: 0.07 (nought point nought seven) oder .07 (point nought seven).

UNITS — EINHEITEN

3,684 is a four digit number	*3684 ist eine vierstellige Zahl.*
It contains 4 units, 8 tens, 6 hundreds and 3 thousands	*Sie enthält 4 Einer, 8 Zehner, 6 Hunderter und 3 Tausender.*
The decimal .234 contains 2 tenths, 3 hundredths and 4 thousandths	*Die Dezimalzahl 0,234 enthält 2 Zehntel, 3 Hundertstel und 4 Tausendstel.*

PERCENTAGES — PROZENTZAHLEN

$2\frac{1}{2}$% two and a half per cent	*zweieinhalb Prozent*
18% of the people here are over 65	*18% der Leute hier sind über 65*
Production has risen by 8%	*die Produktion ist um 8% gestiegen*
(See also the main text of the dictionary)	(*Siehe ebenfalls die entsprechenden Einträge des Wörterbuchs*)

SIGNS — ZEICHEN

English

$+$	addition sign, plus sign (*eg* +7 = plus seven)
$-$	subtraction sign, minus sign (*eg* −3 = minus three)
$\times$	multiplication sign
$\div$	division sign
$\sqrt{\ }$	square root sign
∞	infinity
$\equiv$	sign of identity, is equal to
$=$	equals sign
$\approx$	is approximately equal to
$\neq$	sign of inequality, is not equal to
$>$	is greater than
$<$	is less than

Deutsch

$+$	Additions-Zeichen, Plus-Zeichen (*z. B.* +7 = *plus sieben*)
$-$	Subtraktions-Zeichen, Minus-Zeichen (*z. B.* −3 = *minus drei*)
$\times$	Multiplikations-Zeichen
$:$	Divisions-Zeichen
$\sqrt{\ }$	Quadratwurzel-Zeichen
∞	Unendlichkeits-Symbol
$\equiv$	Identitäts-Zeichen
$=$	Gleichheitszeichen, ist gleich
$\approx$	ist ungefähr gleich
$\neq$	Ungleichheitszeichen, ist nicht gleich
$>$	ist größer als
$<$	ist kleiner als

CALCULATIONS — RECHNEN

8+6 = 14 eight and (*or* plus) six are (*or* make) fourteen	*acht und* (oder *plus*) *sechs ist* (oder *macht* oder *gleich*) *vierzehn*
15-3 = 12 fifteen take away (*or* minus) three equals twelve, three from fifteen leaves twelve	*fünfzehn weniger drei ist* (oder *macht*) *zwölf, fünfzehn minus drei gleich zwölf*
3×3 = 9 three threes are nine, three times three is nine	*drei mal drei ist* (oder *macht* oder *gleich*) *neun*
32÷8 = 4 thirty-two divided by (*or* over) eight is (*or* equals) four	*zweiunddreißig geteilt durch acht ist* (oder *macht* oder *gleich*) *vier*
$3^2 = 9$ three squared is nine	*drei hoch zwei ist neun, drei zum Quadrat gleich neun*
$2^5 = 32$ two to the fifth (*or* to the power of five) is (*or* equals) thirty-two	*zwei hoch fünf ist* (oder *gleich*) *zweiunddreißig*
$\sqrt{16} = 4$ the square root of sixteen is 4	*die* (*Quadrat*)*wurzel aus sechzehn ist vier*

WEIGHTS AND MEASURES — MASSE UND GEWICHTE

METRIC SYSTEM — METRISCHES SYSTEM

deca-	10 times	10-mal	*Deka-*
hecto-	100 times	100-mal	*Hekto-*
kilo-	1000 times	1000-mal	*Kilo-*
deci-	one tenth	ein Zehntel	*Dezi-*
centi-	one hundredth	ein Hundertstel	*Zenti-*
mil(l)i-	one thousandth	ein Tausendstel	*Milli-*

Linear measures — Längenmaße

1 millimetre (Millimeter)	=	0.03937 inch
1 centimetre (Zentimeter)	=	0.3937 inch
1 metre (Meter)	=	39.37 inches
	=	1.094 yards
1 kilometre (Kilometer)	=	0.6214 mile ($\frac{5}{8}$ mile)

Square measures — Flächenmaße

1 square centimetre (Quadratzentimeter)	=	0.155 square inch
1 square metre (Quadratmeter)	=	10.764 square feet
	=	1.196 square yards
1 square kilometre (Quadratkilometer)	=	0.3861 square mile
	=	247.1 acres
1 are (Ar) = 100 square metres	=	119.6 square yards
1 hectare (Hektar) = 100 ares	=	2.471 acres

Cubic measures — Raummaße

1 cubic centimetre (Kubikzentimeter)	=	0.061 cubic inch
1 cubic metre (Kubikmeter)	=	35.315 cubic feet
	=	1.308 cubic yards

Measures of capacity — Hohlmaße

1 litre (Liter) = 1000 cubic centimetres	=	1.76 pints
	=	0.22 gallon

Weights — Gewichte

1 gram (Gramm)	=	15.4 grains
1 kilogram (Kilogramm)	=	2.2046 pounds
1 metric ton (Tonne) = 1000 kilograms	=	0.9842 ton

BRITISH SYSTEM — BRITISCHES SYSTEM

Linear measures — Längenmaße

1 inch (Zoll)	=	2,54 Zentimeter
1 foot (Fuß) = 12 inches	=	30,48 Zentimeter
1 yard (Yard) = 3 feet	=	91,44 Zentimeter
1 furlong = 220 yards	=	201,17 Meter
1 mile (Meile) = 1760 yards	=	1,609 Kilometer

Surveyor's measures — Feldmaße

1 link = 7.92 inches	=	20,12 Zentimeter
1 rod (*or* pole, perch) = 25 links	=	5,029 Meter
1 chain = 22 yards = 4 rods	=	20,12 Meter

Square measures — Flächenmaße

1 square inch (Quadratzoll)	=	6,45 cm^2
1 square foot (Quadratfuß) = 144 square inches	=	929,03 cm^2
1 square yard (Quadratyard) = 9 square feet	=	0.836 m^2
1 square rod - 30.25 square yards	=	25,29 m^2
1 acre - 4840 square yards	=	40.47 Ar
1 square mile (Quadratmeile) = 640 acres	=	2,59 km^2

Cubic measures — Raummaße

1 cubic inch (Kubikzoll)	=	16,387 cm³
1 cubic foot (Kubikfuß) = 1728 cubic inches	=	0,028 m³
1 cubic yard (Kubikyard) = 27 cubic feet	=	0,765 m³
1 register ton (Registertonne) = 100 cubic feet	=	2,832 m³

Measures of capacity — Hohlmaße

(a) Liquid — Flüssigkeitsmaße

1 gill	=	0,142 Liter
1 pint (Pint) = 4 gills	=	0,57 Liter
1 quart = 2 pints	=	1,136 Liter
1 gallon (Gallone) = 4 quarts	=	4,546 Liter

(b) Dry — Trockenmaße

1 peck = 2 gallons	=	9,087 Liter
1 bushel = 4 pecks	=	36,36 Liter
1 quarter = 8 bushels	=	290,94 Liter

Weights — Avoirdupois system — Handelsgewichte

1 grain (Gran)	=	0,0648 Gramm
1 drachm *or* dram = 27.34 grains	=	1,77 Gramm
1 ounce (Unze) = 16 drachms	=	28,35 Gramm
1 pound (britisches Pfund) = 16 ounces	=	453,6 Gramm
	=	0,453 Kilogramm
1 stone = 14 pounds	=	6,348 Kilogramm
1 quarter = 28 pounds	=	12,7 Kilogramm
1 hundredweight = 112 pounds	=	50,8 Kilogramm
1 ton (Tonne) = 2240 pounds = 20 hundredweight	=	1.016 Kilogramm

US MEASURES — AMERIKANISCHE MASSE

In the US, the same system as that which applies in Great Britain is used for the most part; the main differences are mentioned below:

In den Vereinigten Staaten gilt großenteils dasselbe System wie in Großbritannien; die Hauptunterschiede sind im Folgenden aufgeführt:

Measures of Capacity — Hohlmaße

(a) Liquid — Flüssigkeitsmaße

1 US liquid gill	=	0,118 Liter
1 US liquid pint = 4 gills	=	0,473 Liter
1 US liquid quart = 2 pints	=	0,946 Liter
1 US gallon = 4 quarts	=	3,785 Liter

(b) Dry — Trockenmaße

1 US dry pint	=	0,550 Liter
1 US dry quart = 2 dry pints	=	1,1 Liter
1 US peck = 8 dry quarts	=	8,81 Liter
1 US bushel = 4 pecks	=	35,24 Liter

Weights — Gewichte

1 hundredweight (*or* short hundredweight) = 100 pounds	=	45,36 Kilogramm
1 ton (*or* short ton) = 2000 pounds = 20 short hundredweights	=	907,18 Kilogramm

TEMPERATURE CONVERSION — TEMPERATURUMRECHNUNG

Fahrenheit — Celsius

Subtract 32 and multiply by 5/9
32 abziehen und mit 5/9 multiplizieren

°F		°C
0		-17.8
32		0
50		10
70		21.1
90		32.2
98.4	≈	37
212		100

Celsius — Fahrenheit

Multiply by 9/5 and add 32
Mit 9/5 multiplizieren und 32 addieren

°C		°F
–10		14
0		32
10		50
20		68
30		86
37	≈	98.4
100		212

TIME | ZEIT

TIME	ZEIT
2 hours 33 minutes and 14 seconds	*zwei Stunden, dreiunddreißig Minuten und vierzehn Sekunden*
half an hour	*eine halbe Stunde*
a quarter of an hour	*eine Viertelstunde, eine viertel Stunde*
three quarters of an hour	*eine Dreiviertelstunde*
what's the time?	*wie spät ist es?*
what time do you make it?	*wie spät haben Sie es?*
have you the right time?	*haben Sie die richtige Zeit?*
I make it 2.20	*nach meiner Uhr ist es 2 Uhr 20*
my watch says 3.37	*auf meiner Uhr ist es 3 Uhr 37*
it's 1 o'clock	*es ist ein Uhr*
it's 2 o'clock	*es ist zwei Uhr*
it's 5 past 4	*es ist fünf (Minuten) nach vier*
it's 10 past 6	*es ist zehn (Minuten) nach sechs*
it's half past 8	*es ist halb neun**
it's (a) quarter past 9	*es ist Viertel nach neun*
it's (a) quarter to 2	*es ist Viertel vor zwei*
at 10 a.m.	*um 10 Uhr (morgens)*
at 4 p.m.	*um 4 Uhr nachmittags, um 16 Uhr*
at 11 p.m.	*um 11 Uhr abends, um 23 Uhr*
at exactly 3 o'clock, at 3 sharp, at 3 on the dot	*um Punkt drei Uhr*
the train leaves at 19.32	*der Zug fährt um 19 Uhr 32 ab*
(at) what time does it start?	*um wie viel Uhr fängt es an?*
it is just after 3	*es ist gerade drei (Uhr) vorbei*
it is nearly 9	*es ist fast neun (Uhr)*
about 8 o'clock	*etwa acht Uhr, ungefähr acht Uhr*
at (*or* by) 6 o'clock at the latest	*spätestens um sechs Uhr*
have it ready for 5 o'clock	*es muss bis fünf Uhr fertig sein*
it is full each night from 7 to 9	*es ist jeden Abend von 7 bis 9 Uhr voll*
"closed from 1.30 to 4.30"	*„geschlossen von ein Uhr dreißig bis vier Uhr dreißig"*
until 8 o'clock	*bis acht Uhr*
it would be about 11	*es wäre etwa 11 (Uhr)*
it would have been about 10	*es wäre etwa um zehn (Uhr) gewesen*
at midnight	*um Mitternacht*
before midday, before noon	*vormittags, am Vormittag*

*In German, the half hour is expressed by referring forwards to the next full hour as opposed to backwards to the last full hour as in English.

DATES | DAS DATUM

N.B. The days of the week and the months are written with capitals as in English.

DATES	DAS DATUM
the 1st of July, July 1st	*der 1. Juli*
the 2nd of May, May 2nd	*der 2. Mai*
on June 21st, on the 21st (of) June	*am 21. Juni*
on Monday	*am Montag*
he comes on Mondays	*er kommt montags*
"closed on Fridays"	*„freitags geschlossen"*
he lends it to me from Monday to Friday	*er leiht es mir von Montag bis Freitag*
from the 14th to the 18th	*vom 14. bis (zum) 18.*
what's the date?, what date is it today?	*welches Datum haben wir (heute)?*
today's the 12th	*heute ist der 12.*
one Thursday in October	*an einem Donnerstag im Oktober*
about the 4th of July	*etwa am 4. Juli*
Heading of letters:	*Im Briefkopf:*
19th May 2009	*19. Mai 2009*
1978 nineteen (hundred and) seventy-eight	*neunzehnhundert(und)achtundsiebzig*
4 B.C., B.C. 4	*4 v. Chr.*
70 A.D., A.D. 70	*70 n. Chr.*
in the 13th century	*im 13. Jahrhundert*
in (*or* during) the 1930s	*in den 30er-Jahren, während der 30e-Jahre*
in 1940 something	*irgendwann in den vierziger Jahren or Vierzigerjahren*
(See also the main text of the dictionary)	*(Siehe ebenfalls die entsprechenden Einträge des Wörterbuchs)*

Business & Finance Supplement
Wirtschafts- & Ergänzungsbeilage

This brand-new glossary covers essential business and finance vocabulary in German and English

Dieses brandneue Glossar enthält alle wichtigen Wirtschafts- und Finanzbegriffe in Deutsch und Englisch

Englisch-Deutsch

Aa

ABA [ˌeɪ biː ˈeɪ] ABBR ABA *abbr (= Verband amerikanischer Banken und Bankiers)*

abandon [əˈbændən] VT aufgeben *vt*

ability to work [əˌbɪlɪtɪ tə ˈwɜːk] N Arbeitsfähigkeit *f*

above par [əˌbʌv ˈpɑːʳ] ADJ über pari *adj*

above the line [əˌbʌv ðə ˈlaɪn] ADJ über dem Strich *adj*

accept a risk [əˌksɛpt ə ˈrɪsk] PHRS Risiko akzeptieren

accident-free discount [ˌæksɪdənt friː ˈdɪskaʊnt] N Schadenfreiheitsrabatt *m*

accident insurance [ˈæksɪdənt ɪnˌʃʊərəns] N Unfallversicherung *f*

account [əˈkaʊnt] N Konto *nt*

accounting [əˈkaʊntɪŋ] N Buchhaltung *f*

accounts payable [əˌkaʊnts ˈpeɪəbəl] N Verbindlichkeiten *fpl*

accounts receivable [əˌkaʊnts rɪˈsiːvəbəl] N Forderungen *fpl*

accredited investor [əˌkrɛdɪtɪd ɪnˈvɛstəʳ] N zugelassener Anleger *m*

accrual [əˈkruːəl] N Rechnungsabgrenzungsposten *m*

accrual basis [əˈkruːəl ˌbeɪsɪs] N periodengerechte Erfassung *f*

accrue [əˈkruː] VI antizipativ abgrenzen *vt/vi*

ACH [ˌeɪ siː ˈeɪtʃ] ABBR ACH *abbr (= automatisierte Verrechnungsstelle in den USA)*

acquisition [ˌækwɪˈzɪʃən] N Akquisition *f*

acquisition costs [ˌækwɪˈzɪʃən ˌkɒsts] N Akquisitionskosten *fpl*

act of God [ˌækt əv ˈgɒd] N höhere Gewalt *f*

actual cash value basis [ˌæktjʊəl ˌkæʃ ˈvælyuː ˌbeɪsɪs] N Versicherungswertberechnung *f*

actuarial science [ˌæktjʊɛərɪəl ˈsaɪəns] N Versicherungswissenschaft *f*

actuary [ˈæktjʊərɪ] N Versicherungsmathematiker(in) *m(f)*

AD&D [ˌeɪ diː ən ˈdiː] ABBR AD&D *abbr (= Unfallversicherung im Todes-oder Invaliditätsfall)*

adjust [əˈdʒʌst] VT anpassen *vt*, festsetzen *vt*

adjusted [əˈdʒʌstɪd] ADJ festgesetzt *adj*

adjusting journal entry [əˌdʒʌstɪŋ ˈdʒɜːnəl ˌɛntrɪ] N Berichtigungsbuchung *f* im Journal

ADL [ˌeɪ diː ˈɛl] ABBR *Verrichtungen des täglichen Lebens*

administrative expenses [ədˌmɪnɪstrətɪv ɪksˈpɛnsɪz] NPL Verwaltungsaufwendungen *mpl*

ad valorem [ˌæd vəˈlɔːrɛm] ADJ Wertsteuer *f*

advance [ədˈvɑːns] VT Vorauszahlung leisten

advance payment [ədˈvɑːns ˈpeɪmənt] N Vorauszahlung *f*

adverse action [ˌædvɜːs ˈækʃən] N Ablehnungsbescheid *m*

adverse selection [ˌædvɜːs sɪˈlɛkʃən] N Ausscheiden *nt* der besseren Risiken

afloat [əˈfləʊt] ADV zahlungsfähig *adv*

aftermarket [ˈɑːftəˌmɑːkɪt] N Sekundärmarkt *m*

agency [ˈeɪdʒənsɪ] N Versicherungsagentur *f*

agree [əˈgriː] VI übereinstimmen *vt/vi*, abstimmen *vt*

agreement [əˈgriːmənt] N Vereinbarung *f*

all-cash deal [ˌɔːlˈkæʃ ˌdiːl] N Bargeschäft *nt*

allocate [ˈæləʊkeɪt] VT zuteilen *vt*

allocation [æləʊˈkeɪʃən] N Allokation *f*

allowance for bad debts [əˌlaʊəns fə ˌbæd ˈdɛts] N Wertberichtigung *f* auf uneinbringliche Forderungen

all-risk policy [ɔːlˈrɪsk ˌpɒlɪsɪ] N Allgefahren-Versicherungspolice *f*

ambulance insurance [ˈæmbjʊləns ɪnˌʃʊərəns] N Ambulantversicherung *f*

Amex [ˈæmɛks] N AMEX *f*

amortization [əˌmɔːtaɪˈzeɪʃən] N Amortisation *f*

amortize [əˈmɔːtaɪz] VT amortisieren *vt*

amount [əˈmaʊnt] N Betrag *m*

angel [ˈeɪndʒəl] N Risikokapitalgeber(in) *m(f)*

annual report [ˌænjʊəl rɪˈpɔːt] N Jahresbericht *m*

annuitant [əˈnjuːɪtənt] N Rentenempfänger(in) *m(f)*

annuitize [əˈnjuːɪtaɪz] VT verrenten *vt*

annuity [əˈnjuːɪtɪ] N Rentenversicherung *f*, Zeitrente *f*

annuity rate [əˈnjuːɪtɪ ˌreɪt] N Rentensatz *m*

antitrust [ˈæntɪˈtrʌst] ADJ kartellrechtlich *adj*

any occupation [ˌɛnɪ ɒkjəˈpeɪʃən] PHRS Erwerbsunfähigkeit *f*

appointed actuary [əˌpɔɪntɪd ˈæktjʊərɪ] N Ernannter Versicherungsmathematiker *m*

appraisal [əˈpreɪzəl] N Schätzung *f*

appraiser [əˈpreɪzəʳ] N Schätzer(in) *m(f)*

APR [ˌeɪ piː ˈɑːʳ] ABBR effektiver Jahreszins

APY [ˌeɪ piː ˈwaɪ] ABBR jährliche Kapitalrendite

arbitrage [ˈɑːbɪtrɪdʒ] N Arbitrage *f*

arbitration [ˌɑːbɪˈtreɪʃən] N Schiedsverfahren *nt*

ARM [ˌeɪ ɑːr ˈɛm] ABBR variabel verzinsliche Hypothek

arrears [əˈrɪəz] NPL Rückstände *pl*

arson [ˈɑːsn] N Brandstiftung *f*

arsonist [ˈɑːsənɪst] N Brandstifter(in) *m(f)*

ask [ɑːsk] N Angebotspreis *m*

asset account [ˈæsɛt əˌkaʊnt] N Bestandskonto *nt*

assets [ˈæsɛts] NPL Vermögenswerte *mpl*

asset-stripping [ˈæsɛtˌstrɪpɪŋ] N Anlagenausschlachtung *f*

asset turnover ratio [ˌæsɛt ˈtɜːnəʊvə ˌreɪʃɪəʊ] N Kapitalumschlagsratio *f*

assign a policy [əˌsaɪn ə ˈpɒlɪsɪ] PHRS Abtretung *f* einer Versicherungspolice

assumption of risk [əˌsʌmpʃən əv ˈrɪsk] N Risikoübernahme *f*

at par [æt ˈpɑːʳ] ADJ zum Nennwert *m*

audit [ˈɔːdɪt] N Buchprüfung *f*; VT Bücher *pl* prüfen

auditor [ˈɔːdɪtəʳ] N Buchprüfer(in) *m(f)*

audit trail [ˈɔːdɪt ˌtreɪl] N Prüfungspfad *m*

automobile insurance [ˈɔːtəməbiːl ɪnˌʃʊərəns] N Kraftfahrzeugversicherung *f*

average adjuster [ˈævərɪdʒ əˌdʒʌstəʳ] N Havariekommissar(in) *m(f)*

aviation insurance [eɪvɪˈeɪʃən ɪnˌʃʊərəns] N Luftfahrtversicherung *f*

Bb

backdate [ˌbækˈdeɪt] VT rückdatieren *vt*

back-end load [ˌbæk ɛnd ˈləʊd] N Rücknahmekommission *f*

backer [ˈbækəʳ] N Sponsor(in) *m(f)*

backing [ˈbækɪŋ] N Unterstützung *f*

backwardation [ˌbækwəˈdeɪʃən] N Deport *m*

bad debt [ˌbæd ˈdɛt] N uneinbringliche Forderung *f*

bailout [ˈbeɪlaʊt] N Rettungspaket *nt*

balance [ˈbæləns] N Kontostand *m*; VI ausgleichen *vt*

balance an account [ˌbæləns ən əˈkaʊnt] PHRS ausgleichen *vt*

balanced scorecard [ˌbælənst ˈskɔː kɑːd] N Balanced Scorecard *f*

balance of payments [ˌbæləns əv ˈpeɪmənts] N Zahlungsbilanz *f*

balance sheet ['bæləns ʃiːt] N Bilanz *f*

balance sheet account ['bæləns ʃiːt əˌkaʊnt] N Bestandskonto *nt*

balance sheet equation ['bæləns ʃiːt ɪˌkweɪʒən] N Bilanzgleichung *f*

balance transfer [ˌbæləns 'trænsfɜːʳ] N Saldenübertrag *m*

balloon mortgage [bə'luːn ˌmɔːgɪdʒ] N endfällige Hypothek *f*

balloon payment [bə'lun ˌpeɪmənt] N Ballonzahlung *f*

bank [bæŋk] N Bank *f*

bank account ['bæŋk əˌkaʊnt] N Bankkonto *nt*

bank draft ['bæŋk ˌdrɑːft] N Bankscheck *m*

banker's acceptance [ˌbæŋkəz ək'sɛptəns] N Bankakzept *nt*

bank reconciliation [ˌbæŋk ˌrɛkənsɪlɪ'eɪʃən] N Kontoabstimmung *f*

bankruptcy ['bæŋkrəptsɪ] N Insolvenz *f*, Konkurs *m*

bank statement ['bæŋk ˌsteɪtmənt] N Kontoauszug *m*

basis point ['beɪsɪs ˌpɔɪnt] N Basispunkt *m*

bear [bɛəʳ] N Baisse-Spekulant(in) *m(f)*

bear market ['bɛə ˌmɑːkɪt] N Baissemarkt *m*

bear raid ['bɛə ˌreɪd] N Baissemanöver *nt*

beginning inventory [bəˌgɪnɪŋ 'ɪnvəntrɪ] N Anfangsbestand *m*

below par [bɪˌləʊ 'pɑːʳ] ADJ unter pari *adj*

below the line [bɪˌləʊ ðə 'laɪn] ADJ unter dem Strich

beneficiary [ˌbɛnɪ'fɪʃərɪ] N Anspruchsberechtigte(r) *mf*

benefit ['bɛnɪfɪt] VI leistungsberechtigt sein *vi*

benefits ['bɛnɪfɪts] N Leistungen *fpl*

BIC [ˌbiː aɪ 'siː] ABBR BIC-Code *m*

bid [bɪd] N Kaufangebot *nt*

Big Board [ˌbɪg 'bɔːd] N Big Board *nt*

bill [bɪl] N Rechnung *f*; VI Rechnung *f* ausstellen

billable ['bɪləbəl] ADJ abrechenbar *adj*

bill of exchange [ˌbɪl əv ɪks'tʃeɪndʒ] N Wechsel *m*

bill of lading [ˌbɪl əv 'leɪdɪŋ] N Frachtbrief *m*

bill of sale [ˌbɪl əv 'seɪl] N Verkaufsurkunde *f*

binder ['baɪndəʳ] N vorläufige Versicherungspolice *f*

biometric risk [ˌbaɪəmɛtrɪk 'rɪsk] N biometrische Risiken *fpl*

BIS [ˌbiː aɪ 'ɛs] ABBR BIS *(= Bank for international Settlements)*

black knight [ˌblæk 'naɪt] N Schwarzer Ritter *m*

blind trust [ˌblaɪnd 'trʌst] N verdeckte Treuhand *f*

blue-chip ['blutʃɪp] ADJ Bluechip-

board of directors [ˌbɔːd əv dɪ'rɛktəz] N Verwaltungsrat *m*

bodily injury [ˌbɒdɪlɪ 'ɪndʒərɪ] N Körperverletzung *f*

bolt-on ['bəʊltɒn] ADJ branchennah *adj*

bond [bɒnd] N Anleihe *f*

bonded ['bɒndɪd] ADJ *durch eine Vertrauensschadenversicherung abgedeckt*

bondholder ['bɒndˌhəʊldəʳ] N Anleiheninhaber(in) *m(f)*

bonding ['bɒndɪŋ] N Vertrauensschadenversicherung *f*

bonus ['bəʊnəs] N Extradividende *f*, Bonus *m*

bonus issue ['bəʊnəs ˌɪʃuː] N Gratisaktie *f*

book [bʊk] VT verbuchen *vt*

book depreciation [ˌbʊk dɪˌpriːʃɪ'eɪʃən] N Buchwertabschreibung *f*

bookkeeping ['bʊkˌkiːpɪŋ] N Buchhaltung *f*

book of business [ˌbʊk əv 'bɪznɪs] N Geschäftsportfolio *nt*

books [bʊks] NPL Bücher *npl*

book-to-tax reconciliation [ˌbʊktətæks ˌrɛkənsɪlɪ'eɪʃən] N steuerliche Überleitungsrechnung *f*

book value ['bʊk ˌvæljuː] N Buchwert *m*, Nettowert *m*

boom [buːm] N Boom *m*

boom-bust cycle [ˌbuːm'bʌst ˌsaɪkəl] N Boom-Bust-Zyklus *m*

bootstrap ['buːtˌstræp] ADJ fremdfinanziert *adj*; VT aus eigener Kraft finanzieren *vt*

bordereau ['bɔːdərəʊ] N Versicherungsverzeichnis *nt*

bottom fishing ['bɒtəm ˌfɪʃɪŋ] N Wertpapierkauf *m* zu Tiefstkursen

bottom line [ˌbɒtəm 'laɪn] N Endergebnis *nt*

break even [ˌbreɪk 'iːvn] VI ausgeglichen abschließen *vi*

breakeven [ˌbreɪk'iːvən] N Gewinnschwelle *f* erreichen

breakeven point [ˌbreɪk'iːvənˌpɔɪnt] N Gewinnschwelle *f*

break-up value ['breɪkʌp ˌvæljuː] N Liquidationswert *m*

bridging loan ['brɪdʒɪŋ ˌləʊn] N Überbrückungskredit *m*

bring forward [ˌbrɪŋ 'fɔːwəd] VT übertragen *vt*

bring over [ˌbrɪŋ 'əʊvəʳ] VT vortragen *vt*

broker ['brəʊkəʳ] N Broker(in) *m(f)*

brokerage ['brəʊkərɪdʒ] N Courtage *f*

brokerage account ['brəʊkərɪdʒ əˌkaʊnt] N Courtagekonto *nt*

bubble ['bʌbl] N Blase *f*

budget ['bʌdʒɪt] N Budget *nt*, Etat *m*; VT etatisieren *vt/vi*, budgetieren *vt/vi*

budget for ['bʌdʒɪt ˌfɔː] VT veranschlagen *vt*

bull [bʊl] N Haussespekulant(in) *m(f)*

bull market ['bʊl ˌmɑːkɪt] N Haussemarkt *m*

burn rate ['bɜːn ˌreɪt] N Kapitalvernichtungsrate *f*

business interruption insurance [ˌbɪznɪs ɪntə'rʌpʃən ɪnˌʃʊərəns] N Betriebsunterbrechungsversicherung *f*

business overhead expense insurance [ˌbɪznɪs ˌəʊvəhɛd ɪks'pɛns ɪnˌʃʊərəns] N *Versicherung für Allgemeinkosten des Unternehmens bei Arbeitsunfähigkeit des Unternehmers*

bust [bʌst] N Zusammenbruch *m*

buy forward [ˌbaɪ 'fɔːwəd] VT per Termin kaufen *vt*

buy out [ˌbaɪ 'aʊt] VT aufkaufen *vt*, abfinden *vt*

calculate a premium [ˌkælkjʊleɪt ə 'priːmɪəm] PHRS Beitragsberechnung *f*

calculate a risk [ˌkælkjʊleɪt ə 'rɪsk] PHRS Risiko kalkulieren

calendar year [ˌkælɪndə 'jɪəʳ] N Kalenderjahr *nt*

call [kɔːl] N Kaufoption *f*

cancel a policy [ˌkænsəl ə 'pɒlɪslɪ] PHRS einen Versicherungsvertrag kündigen

C & F [ˌsiː ənd 'ɛf] ABBR C&F *abbr (= Kosten und Fracht)*

capital ['kæpɪtl] N Kapital *nt*

capital account [ˌkæpɪtl ə'kaʊnt] N Kapitalkonto *nt*

capital employed [ˌkæpɪtl ɪm'plɔɪd] N eingesetztes Kapital *nt*

capital expenditure [ˌkæpɪtl ɪks'pɛndɪtʃəʳ] N Investitionsaufwand *m*

capital expense [ˌkæpɪtl ɪks'pɛns] N Investitionsaufwendungen *fpl*

capital gain [ˌkæpɪtl 'geɪn] N Kapitalzuwachs *m*, Wertzuwachs *m*

capital gains [ˌkæpɪtl 'geɪnz] NPL Kapitalertrag *m*

capitalization [ˌkæpɪtəlaɪ'zeɪʃən] N Kapitalisierung *f*

capitalize ['kæpɪtə,laɪz] VT kapitalisieren *vt*

capital lease [,kæpɪtl 'li:s] N Finanzierungsleasing *nt*

capital loss [,kæpɪtl 'lɒs] N Kapitalverlust *m*

capital stock [,kæpɪtl 'stɒk] N Stammkapital *nt*

captive ['kæptɪv] N Selbstversicherungsgesellschaft *f*

carry back [,kærɪ 'bæk] VT rücktragen *vt*

carry forward [,kærɪ 'fɔ:wəd] VT übertragen *vt*, vortragen *vt*

carrying charge ['kærɪɪŋ ,tʃɑ:dʒ] N Lagerhaltungskosten *fpl*

carry over [,kærɪ 'əʊvə^r] VT vortragen *vt*

cash [kæʃ] N Bargeld *nt*

cash basis ['kæʃ ,beɪsɪs] N Buchführung *f* auf Einnahmen- und Ausgabenbasis

cash book ['kæʃ ,bʊk] N Kassenbuch *nt*

cash discount [,kæʃ 'dɪskaʊnt] N Barzahlungsrabatt *m*

cash flow ['kæʃ ,fləʊ] N Cashflow *m*

cashier's cheque [,kæʃɪəz 'tʃɛk] N Bankscheck *m*

cash-in-lieu [,kæʃɪn'lu:] N Barausgleich *m*

cash plan ['kæʃ ,plæn] N medizinische Kostenerstattung *f*

casualty ['kæʒjʊltɪ] N Unfallopfer *nt*

catastrophe excess of loss [kə,tæstrəfɪ ,ɛksɛs əv 'lɒs] PHRS Katastrophenexzedent *m*

catastrophic illness [kætə,strɒfɪk 'ɪlnɪs] N schwere Krankheit *f*

C corporation ['si: kɔ:pə,reɪʃən] N C-Corporation *f*

CD [,si: 'di:] ABBR Einlagenzertifikat *nt*

CDO [,si: d:i 'əʊ] ABBR verbriefte Schuldverschreibung

cedant ['si:dənt] N Zedent *m*

cede [si:d] VT zedieren *vt*

certified cheque [,sɜ:tɪfaɪd 'tʃɛk] N bestätigter Scheck *m*

certified public accountant [,sɜ:tɪfaɪd ,pʌblɪk ə'kaʊntənt] N Wirtschaftsprüfer(in) *m(f)*

charge [tʃɑ:dʒ] N Tarif *f*, Belastung *f*; VI berechnen *vt/vi*

chargeback ['tʃɑ:dʒ,bæk] N Rückbelastung *f*

chart of accounts [,tʃɑ:t əv ə'kaʊnts] N Kontenplan *m*

check [tʃɛk] N Scheck *m*; VT prüfen *vt*

check stub ['tʃɛk ,stʌb] N Scheck-Kontrollabschnitt *m*

cheque register ['tʃɛk ,rɛdʒɪstə^r] N Scheckausgangsbuch *nt*

CHIPS [tʃɪps] ABBR CHIPS *abbr (= Internes Abrechnungsszstem der New Yorker Banken)*

churn [tʃɜ:n] VT häufig umschichten *vt*

CIF [,si: aɪ 'ɛf] ABBR cif *abbr*

civil unrest [,sɪvl ʌn'rɛst] N Bürgerunruhen *fpl*

claim [kleɪm] N Forderung *f*; VT fordern *vt*

claimant ['kleɪmənt] N Antragsteller(in) *m(f)*

claim form ['kleɪm ,fɔ:m] N Schadenmeldeformular *nt*

claims investigator ['kleɪmz ɪn,vɛstɪgeɪtə^r] N Schadensermittler(in) *m(f)*

claims notification [,kleɪmz ,nəʊtɪfɪ'keɪʃən] N Schadensmeldung *f*

claims ratio ['kleɪmz ,reɪʃɪəʊ] N Schadensquote *f*

classify ['klæsɪ,faɪ] VT klassifizieren *vt*

clear [klɪə^r] ADJ rein *adj*

clearing ['klɪərɪŋ] N Clearing *nt*

clearing house ['klɪərɪŋ ,haʊs] N Clearinghaus *nt*

closed-end fund ['kləʊzdɛnd ,fʌnd] N geschlossener Fonds *m*

closed-end loan ['kləʊzdɛnd ,ləʊn] N geschlossenes Darlehen *nt*

close out [,kləʊz 'aʊt] VT abwickeln *vt*

close the books [,kləʊz ðə 'bʊks] PHRS Bücher abschließen

COBRA ['kəʊbrə] ABBR COBRA *abbr*

COD [,si:əʊ'di:] ABBR COD *abbr (= Zahlung bei Lieferung)*

coinsurance [,kəʊɪn'ʃʊərəns] N Mitversicherung *f*

coinsure [,kəʊɪn'ʃʊə^r] VT mitversichern *vt*

coinsurer [,kəʊɪn'ʃʊərə^r] N Mitversicherer *m*

collateral [kɒ'lætərəl] N Sicherungsgegenstand *m*

collect [kə'lɛkt] VT einziehen *vt*

collide with [kə'laɪd ,wɪθ] VT kollidieren *vt*

collision coverage [kə'lɪʒən ,kʌvərɪdʒ] N Kaskoversicherung *f*

collision damage waiver [kə,lɪʒən 'dæmɪdʒ ,weɪvə^r] N Versicherung *f* mit Haftungsreduzierung

combined ratio [kəm,baɪnd 'reɪʃɪəʊ] N *Addition von Schadens- und Kostenquote*

commercial bank [kə,mɜ:ʃəl 'bæŋk] N Geschäftsbank *f*

commercial paper [kə,mɜ:ʃəl 'peɪpə^r] N Commercial Paper *nt*

commission [kə'mɪʃən] N Provision *f*

commodity [kə'mɒdɪtɪ] N Rohstoff *m*

common stock [,kɒmən 'stɒk] N Stammaktie *f*

commutation [,kɒmjʊ'teɪʃən] N Ablösung *f*

commute [kə'mju:t] VT umwandeln *vt*

compensation [,kɒmpən'seɪʃən] N Schadensersatz *m*

compound interest [,kɒmpaʊnd 'ɪntrɪst] N Zinseszins *m*

comprehensive [,kɒmprɪ'hɛnsɪv] ADJ umfassend *adj*

condominium [,kɒndə'mɪnɪəm] N Eigentumswohnung *f*

condo owner ['kɒndəʊ ,əʊnə^r] N Besitzer *m* einer Eigentumswohnung

consequential loss [kɒnsɪ,kwɛnʃəl 'lɒs] N Folgeschaden *m*

consignment [kən'saɪnmənt] N Konsignation *f*

contango [kən'tæŋgəʊ] N Contango *m*

contingency [kən'tɪndʒənsɪ] N unvorhergesehenes Ereignis *nt*

contra account ['kɒntrə ə,kaʊnt] N Gegenkonto *nt*

contract ['kɒntrækt] N Vertrag *m*

contribution [,kɒntrɪ'bju:ʃən] N Beitrag *m*

contributory [kən'trɪbjʊtərɪ] ADJ beitragsbezogen *adj*

control [kən'trəʊl] VT kontrollieren *vt*, prüfen *vt*

control account [kən'trəʊl ə,kaʊnt] N Sammelkonto *nt*

conventional mortgage [kən'vɛnʃənəl ,mɔ:gɪdʒ] N herkömmlicher Hypothekenkredit *m*

convertible [kən'vɜ:təbl] ADJ wandelbar *adj*

convertible currency [kən,vɜ:təbl 'kʌrənsɪ] N konvertierbare Währung *f*

convertible term insurance [kən,vɜ:təbl ,tɜ:m ɪn'ʃʊərəns] N Risikoumtauschversicherung *f*

cooling-off period [,ku:lɪŋ'ɒf ,pɪərɪəd] N Überdenkungszeit *f*

copay [,kəʊ'peɪ] N Eigenbeteiligung *f*

corporate ['kɔ:pərɪt] ADJ Unternehmens- *adj*

corporate venturing [,kɔ:pərɪt 'vɛntʃərɪŋ] N Corporate Venturing *nt*

corporation [,kɔ:pə'reɪʃən] N Gesellschaft *f*

correspondent bank [,kɒrɪs,pɒndənt 'bæŋk] N Korrespondenzbank *f*

cost [kɒst] VT kosten *vt/vi*

cost accounting [,kɒst ə'kaʊntɪŋ] N Kostenrechnung *f*

cost centre ['kɒst ,sɛntə^r] N Kostenstelle *f*

cost of capital [,kɒst əv 'kæpɪtl] N Kapitalkosten *pl*

cost of goods available for sale [,kɒst əv ,gʊdz ə,veɪləbəl fə 'seɪl] N Warenkosten *pl*

cost of goods sold [,kɒst əv ,gʊdz 'səʊld] N Umsatzkosten *pl*

cost overrun [,kɒst 'əʊvərrʌn] N Mehrkosten *pl*

counteroffer ['kaʊntər,ɒfə^r] N Gegenofferte *f*

coupon rate ['ku:pɒn ,reɪt] N Anleihezins *m*

cover ['kʌvəʳ] N Deckung *f*; VT decken *vt*, absichern *vt*

coverage ['kʌvərɪdʒ] N Versicherungsdeckung *f*

CPA [ˌsiː piː 'eɪ] ABBR geprüfter Buchhalter *m*, geprüfte Buchhalterin *f*

CPI [ˌsiːpiː'aɪ] ABBR *Verbraucherpreisindexinflation*

crash [kræʃ] N Unfall *m*; VI verunglücken *vi*

credit ['krɛdɪt] N Gutschrift *f*; VT gutschreiben *vt*

credit bureau ['krɛdɪt ˌbjʊərəʊ] N Auskunftei *f*

credit card insurance ['krɛdɪt ˌkɑːd ɪnˌʃʊərəns] N Kreditkartenversicherung *f*

credit memo ['krɛdɪt ˌmɛməʊ] N Gutschriftsanzeige *f*

creditor ['krɛdɪtəʳ] N Gläubiger *m*

credit rating ['krɛdɪt ˌreɪtɪŋ] N Bonität *f*

credit risk ['krɛdɪt ˌrɪsk] N Kreditrisiko *nt*

credit score ['krɛdɪt ˌskɔːʳ] N Kredit-Score *m*

credit side ['krɛdɪt ˌsaɪd] N Habenseite *f*

credit swap ['krɛdɪt ˌswɒp] N Kredit-Swap *m*

credit union ['krɛdɪt ˌjuːnjən] N Kreditgenossenschaft *f*

critical illness insurance [ˌkrɪtɪkəl 'ɪlnɪs ɪnˌʃʊərəns] N Dread-Disease-Versicherung *f*

cross rate ['krɒs ˌreɪt] N Paritätsrate *f*

CSO [ˌsiː ɛs 'əʊ] ABBR CSO *abbr*

cum dividend [kʊm 'dɪvɪdɛnd] ADJ mit Dividende *f*

cumulative ['kjuːmjʊlətɪv] ADJ kumulativ *adj*

current ['kʌrənt] ADJ gegenwärtig *adj*

current account ['kʌrənt əˌkaʊnt] N laufendes Konto *nt*

current assets [ˌkʌrənt 'æsɛts] NPL Umlaufvermögen *nt*

current cost [ˌkʌrənt 'kɒst] N betrieblicher Aufwand *m*

current expenses [ˌkʌrənt ɪks'pɛnsɪz] NPL laufende Aufwendungen *fpl*

current liabilities ['kʌrənt ˌlaɪə'bɪlɪtɪz] NPL kurzfristige Verbindlichkeiten *fpl*

current ratio [ˌkʌrənt 'reɪʃɪəʊ] N Liquidität *f* dritten Grades

current yield [ˌkʌrənt 'jiːld] N laufende Rendite *f*

CUSIP number ['kjuːsɪp ˌnʌmbəʳ] N Wertpapier-Kennnummer *f*

custodian bank [kʌs'təʊdɪən ˌbæŋk] N Depotbank *f*

customer ['kʌstəməʳ] N Kunde *m*, Kundin *f*

customs duty ['kʌstəmz ˌdjuːtɪ] N Zoll *m*

cutoff time ['kʌtɒf ˌtaɪm] N Stichzeit *f*

Dd

damage ['dæmɪdʒ] N Schaden *m*; VT beschädigen/verletzen *vt*

D&O insurance [ˌdiː ənd 'əʊ ɪnˌʃʊərəns] ABBR D&O-Versicherung *abbr*

dealer ['diːləʳ] N Händler(in) *m(f)*

death benefits ['dɛθ ˌbɛnɪfɪts] NPL Todesfallleistung *f*

debenture [dɪ'bɛntʃəʳ] N Schuldverschreibung *f*

debit ['dɛbɪt] N Belastung *f*; VT belasten *vt*, abbuchen *vt*

debit side ['dɛbɪt ˌsaɪd] N Sollseite *f*

debt [dɛt] N Schuld *f*

debt covenant [ˌdɛt 'kʌvənənt] N Kreditklausel *f*

debtor ['dɛtəʳ] N Schuldner(in) *m(f)*

debt relief ['dɛt ˌrɪliːf] N Schuldenerlass *m*

debt restructuring [ˌdɛt riː'strʌktʃərɪŋ] N Umschuldung *f*

debt swap ['dɛt ˌswɒp] N Schuldenswap *m*

debt-to-equity ratio [ˌdɛt tʊ 'ɛkwɪtɪ ˌreɪʃɪəʊ] N Netto-Verschuldung *f* zu Eigenkapital

deceased [dɪ'siːst] N Verstorbene(r) *mf*

decreasing term insurance [dɪˌkriːsɪŋ 'tɜːm ɪˌnʃʊərəns] N *temporäre Todesfallversicherung mit fallender Summe*

deductible [dɪ'dʌktəbl] ADJ abzugsfähig *adj*; N Abzugsfranchise *f*

deduction [dɪ'dʌkʃən] N Abzug *m*

default [dɪ'fɔːlt] N Ausfall *m*; VI in Verzug geraten *vi*

deferral [dɪ'fɜːrəl] N transitorischer Rechnungsabgrenzungsposten *m*

deferred [dɪ'fɜːd] ADJ aktivisch abgegrenzt *adj*

deferred annuity [dɪˌfɜːd ə'njuːɪtɪ] N aufgeschobene Rente *f*

deferred period [dɪ'fɜːd ˌpɪərɪəd] N Übergangsperiode *f*

deficit ['dɛfɪsɪt] N Defizit *nt*

defined benefit plan [dɪˌfaɪnd 'bɛnɪfɪt ˌplæn] N leistungsorientierter Pensionsplan *m*

defined contribution plan [dɪˌfaɪnd kɒntrɪ'bjuːʃən ˌplæn] N beitragsorientierter Pensionsplan *m*

defraud [dɪ'frɔːd] VT betrügen *vt*

demand curve [dɪ'mɑːnd ˌkɜːv] N Nachfragekurve *f*

demand note [dɪ'mɑːnd ˌnəʊt] N Zahlungsaufforderung *f*

demutualization [diːˌmjuːtjʊəlaɪ'zeɪʃən] N Demutualisierung *f*

dental care ['dɛntl ˌkɛəʳ] N Zahnpflege *f*

dental insurance ['dɛntl ɪnˌʃʊərəns] N Zahnversicherung *f*

deny a claim [dɪˌnaɪ ə 'kleɪm] PHRS Forderung ablehnen

dependent [dɪ'pɛndənt] N Abhängige(r) *mf*

deposit [dɪ'pɒzɪt] VT einzahlen *vt/vi*

deposit slip [dɪ'pɒzɪt ˌslɪp] N Einzahlungsschein *m*

depreciable [dɪ'priːʃɪəbəl] ADJ abschreibungsfähig *adj*

depreciate [dɪ'priːʃɪeɪt] VT an Nutzwert verlieren

depreciation [dɪˌpriːʃɪ'eɪʃən] N Wertverlust *m*, Wertminderung *f*

depreciation expense [dɪˌpriːʃɪ'eɪʃən ɪksˌpɛns] N Abschreibungsaufwand *m*

derivative [dɪ'rɪvətɪv] N Derivat *nt*

devaluation [ˌdɪvæljʊ'eɪʃən] N Abwertung *f*

devalue [ˌdiː'væljuː] VT abwerten *vt*

dilution [daɪ'luːʃən] N Verwässerung *f*

diminishing returns [dɪˌmɪnɪʃɪŋ rɪ'tɜːnz] NPL abnehmende Erträge *mpl*

direct [daɪ'rɛkt] ADJ direkt *adj*

direct debit [daɪˌrɛkt 'dɛbɪt] N Lastschrift *f*

direct deposit [daɪˌrɛkt dɪ'pɒzɪt] N Direkttransfer *m*

direct insurer [dɪaˌrɛkt ɪn'ʃʊərəʳ] N Direktversicherer *m*

direct public offering [daɪˌrɛkt ˌpʌblɪk 'ɒfərɪŋ] N direktes öffentliches Zeichnungsangebot *nt*

disability clause [dɪsə'bɪlɪtɪ ˌklɔːz] N Schwerstbehinderungsklausel *f*

disability insurance [dɪsə'bɪlɪtɪ ɪnʃʊərəns] N Invaliditätsversicherung *f*

disabled [dɪs'eɪbld] ADJ behindert *adj*

disclose [dɪs'kləʊz] VT offenlegen *vt*

disclosure [dɪs'kləʊʒəʳ] N Offenlegung *f*

discounted cash flow [dɪsˌkaʊntɪd 'kæʃ ˌfləʊ] N DCF *abbr*, diskontierter Cashflow *m*

discount rate ['dɪskaʊnt ˌreɪt] N Diskontsatz *m*

discretionary trust [dɪsˌkrɛʃənərɪ 'trʌst] N diskretionärer Trust *m*

disinvest [ˌdɪsɪn'vɛst] VT Investment *nt* abziehen, disinvestieren *vt*

disorder [dɪs'ɔːdəʳ] N Störung *f*

distribution [dɪstrɪ'bjuːʃən] N Ausschüttung *f*

distribution channel [dɪstrɪ'bjuːʃən ˌtʃænəl] N Absatzweg *m*

diversification ['daɪˌvɜːsɪfɪ'keɪʃən] N Diversifikation *f*

divest [daɪ'vɛst] VT abstoßen *vt*

dividend ['dɪvɪˌdɛnd] N Dividende *f*

dividend cover ['dɪvɪˌdɛnd 'kʌvəʳ] N Gewinn-Dividenden-Verhältnis *nt*

dividends ['dɪvɪˌdɛndz] NPL Dividenden *fpl*

dollar cost averaging [ˌdɒlə ˌkɒst 'ævərədʒɪŋ] N Kursdurchschnittsverfahren *nt*

double entry [ˌdʌbəl 'ɛntrɪ] N doppelte Buchführung *f*

double indemnity [ˌdʌbəl ɪn'dɛmnɪtɪ] N *Verdopplung der Lebensversicherungssumme im Todesfall*

draw a pension [ˌdrɔː ə 'pɛnʃən] PHRS Pension beziehen

due date ['djuː ˌdeɪt] N Fälligkeitstermin *m*

dynamic insurance [daɪˌnæmɪk ɪn'ʃʊərəns] N dynamische Versicherung *f*

Ee

E&O [ˌiː ənd 'əʊ] ABBR E&O *abbr*

early retirement [ˌɜːlɪ rɪ'taɪəmənt] N Vorruhestand *m*

earnings ['ɜːnɪŋz] NPL Gewinn *m*

earnings per share [ˌɜːnɪŋz pə 'ʃɛəʳ] NPL Ergebnis *nt* je Aktie

earthquake ['ɜːθˌkweɪk] N Erdbeben *nt*

earthquake coverage ['ɜːθˌkweɪk ˌkʌvərɪdʒ] N Erdbebenversicherung *f*

EBIT ['iːbɪt] ABBR EBIT *nt (= Ergebnis vor Zinsen und Steuern)*

EBITDA [iː'bɪtdɑː] ABBR EBITDA *nt (= Ergebnis vor Zinsen, Steuern und Abschreibungen)*

ECB [ˌiː siː 'biː] ABBR EZB *abbr*

efficient frontier [ɪˌfɪʃənt frʌ'ntɪəʳ] N Effizienzlinie *f*

EFT [ˌiː ɛf 'tiː] ABBR elektronischer Zahlungsverkehr *m*

electronic cheque conversion [ɪlɛkˌtrɒnɪk 'tʃɛk kənˌvɜːʃən] N elektronische Scheckkonvertierung *f*

eligibility [ˌɛlɪdʒə'bɪlɪtɪ] N Anspruchsberechtigung *f*

eligible ['ɛlɪdʒəbl] ADJ anspruchsberechtigt *adj*

emergency room [ɪ'mɜːdʒənsɪ ˌrʊm] N Notaufnahme *f*

employer-provided [ɪmˌplɔɪə prə'vaɪdɪd] ADJ arbeitgeberseitig *adj*

ending inventory ['ɛndɪŋ ˌɪnvəntrɪ] N Schlussbestand *m*

endorse [ɪn'dɔːs] VT unterzeichnen *vt*, erweitern *vt*

endorsement [ɪn'dɔːsmənt] N Nachtrag *m*

endowment insurance [ɪn'daʊmənt ɪnˌʃʊərəns] N gemischte Lebensversicherung *f*

endowment mortgage [ɪn'daʊmənt ˌmɔːgɪdz] N Ausstattungshypothek *f*

endowment policy [ɪn'daʊmənt ˌpɒlɪsɪ] N Aussteuerversicherung *f*

entity ['ɛntɪtɪ] N Körperschaft *f*

entry ['ɛntrɪ] N Eintragung *f*

e.o.m. [ˌiː əʊ 'ɛm] ABBR zum Monatsende

equity ['ɛkwɪtɪ] N Eigenkapital *nt*

equity account ['ɛkwɪtɪ əˌkaʊnt] N Eigenkapitalkonto *nt*

equity-linked policy [ˌɛkwɪtlɪlɪŋkt 'pɒlɪslɪ] N aktiengebundene Politik *f*

escalation [ˌɛskə'leɪʃən] N Preisgleitklausel *f*

escheat [ɪs'tʃːit] N Heimfall *m*

escrow ['ɛskrəʊ] N Treuhandverwahrung *f*

ESOP ['iːsɒp] ABBR Belegschaftsaktienfonds *m*

estate [ɪs'teɪt] N Nachlass *m*

estimated maximum loss [ˌɛstɪmeɪtɪd ˌmæksɪməm 'lɒs] N geschätzter Maximalverlust *m*

ETF [ˌiː tiː 'ɛf] ABBR ETF *nt*

Eurodollars ['jʊərəʊˌdɒləz] NPL Eurodollars *mpl*

excess [ɪk'sɛs] N Exzedent *m*

excess of loss reinsurance [ɪkˌsɛs əv ˌlɒs 'riːɪnʃʊərəns] N Schadensexzedenten-Rückversicherung *f*

exchange rate [ɪks'tʃeɪndʒ ˌreɪt] N Wechselkurs *m*

exclude a risk [ɪksˌklud ə 'rɪsk] PHRS Risiko ausschließen

exclusion [ɪks'kluːʒən] N Ausschließung *f*

ex dividend [ˌɛks 'dɪvɪdɛnd] ADJ ohne Dividende *adj*

ex-dividend date [ˌɛks'dɪvɪdɛnd ˌdeɪt] N Ex-Dividendendatum *nt*

exercise price ['ɛksəsaɪz ˌpraɪs] N Ausübungskurs *m*

expense [ɪks'pɛns] N Kosten ; VT als Aufwand *m* erfassen

expense account [ɪks'pɛns əˌkaʊnt] N Spesenkonto *nt*, Aufwandskonto *nt*

expenses [ɪks'pɛnsɪz] NPL Spesen *pl*

experience rating [ɪks'pɪərɪəns ˌreɪtɪŋ] N Prämienfestsetzung *f*

experience table [ɪks'pɪərɪəns ˌteɪbl] N Erfahrungstafel *f*

expiration date [ˌɛkspɪ'reɪʃən ˌdeɪt] N Ablaufdatum *nt*

expire [ɪks'paɪəʳ] VI ablaufen *vi*

exposed to [ɪks'pəʊzd tʊ] ADJ ausgesetzt *adj*

exposure [ɪks'pəʊʒəʳ] N Risiko *nt*, Risiko *nt*

extraordinary [ɪks'trɔːdnrɪ] ADJ außerordentlich *adj*

Ff

face value [ˌfeɪs 'væljuː] N Nennbetrag *m*, Nominalwert *m*

factoring ['fæktərɪŋ] N Forderungsverkauf *m*

facultative ['fækəltətɪv] ADJ fakultativ *adj*

fair market value [ˌfɛə ˌmɑːkɪt 'væljuː] N fairer Marktpreis *m*

Fannie Mae [ˌfænɪ 'meɪ] N Fannie Mae, *weltweit größte staatlich geförderte Hypothekenbank in den USA*

FDIC [ˌɛf diː aɪ 'siː] ABBR FDIC *abbr (= Bundes-Einlagenversicherung)*

Federal Reserve [ˌfɛdərəl rɪ'zɜːv] N Federal Reserve *f*

Fedwire ['fɛdˌwaɪəʳ] N Fed Wire *nt (= elektronisches Clearing- und Kommunikationssystem des Federal Reserve Board)*

fender-bender ['fɛndəˌbɛndəʳ] N *(= Autounfall mit geringem Sachschaden)*

FICO ['faɪkəʊ] ABBR FICO *abbr*

fiduciary [fɪ'duːʃɪərɪ] N Treuhänder(in) *m(f)*

FIFO ['faɪfəʊ] ABBR FIFO-Methode *f*

file a claim [ˌfaɪl ə 'kleɪm] PHRS Forderung anmelden

finance charge ['faɪnæns ˌtʃɑːdʒ] N Finanzierungskosten *pl*

financial adviser [faɪˌnænʃəl əd'vaɪzəʳ] N Finanzberater(in) *m(f)*

financial instrument [faɪˌnænʃəl 'ɪnstrəmənt] N Finanzinstrument *nt*

financial statements [faɪˌnænʃəl 'steɪtmənts] NPL Finanzausweis *m*

financial underwriter [faɪˌnænʃəl 'ʌndəˌraɪtəʳ] N Risikoprüfer(in) *m(f)*

financial underwriting [faɪˌnænʃəl 'ʌndəˌraɪtɪŋ] N Risikoübernahmen *fpl*

financial year [faɪˌnænʃəl 'jɪəʳ] N Bilanzjahr *nt*

finished goods [ˌfɪnɪʃt 'gʊdz] NPL Fertigwaren *fpl*

fire extinguisher ['faɪər ɪksˌtɪŋgwɪʃəʳ] N Feuerlöscher *m*

fire insurance ['faɪər ɪnˌʃʊərəns] N Feuerversicherung *f*

first-loss policy [ˌfɜːst'lɒs ˌpɒlɪsɪ] N Erstrisikoversicherungspolice *f*

first-round financing ['fɜːstˌraʊnd 'faɪnænsɪŋ] N Erstrundenfinanzierung *f*

fiscal year [ˌfɪskəl 'jɪəʳ] N Geschäftsjahr *nt*

fixed assets [ˌfɪkst 'æsɛts] NPL Anlagevermögen *nt*

fixed charge [ˌfɪkst 'tʃɑːdʒ] N feste Belastung *f*

fixed costs ['fɪkst ˌkɒsts] NPL Fixkosten *pl*

fixed exchange rate [ˌfɪkst ɪks'tʃeɪndʒ ˌreɪt] N fester Wechselkurs *m*

fixed rate [ˌfɪkst 'reɪt] N Festzinssatz *m*

fleet insurance ['fli:t ɪnʃʊərəns] N Kfz-Sammelversicherung *f*

fleet rate ['fl:it ˌreɪt] N Sammelversicherungsrabatt *m*

float [fləʊt] VT an die Börse bringen *vt*

floater ['fləʊtəʳ] N Floater-Versicherung *f*

floating rate ['fləʊtɪŋ ˌreɪt] N freier Wechselkurs *m*

flood [flʌd] N Flut *f*

flood coverage ['flʌd ˌkʌvərɪdʒ] N Flutwasserversicherung *f*

FOB destination [ˌɛf əʊ 'bi: ˌdɛstɪ'neɪʃən] PHRS FOB-Bestimmungsort *m*

FOB shipping point [ˌɛf əʊ 'bi: 'ʃɪpɪŋ ˌpɔɪnt] PHRS FOB-Versandort *m*

foot [fʊt] VT addieren *vt*

footing ['fʊtɪŋ] N Summe *f*

footnotes ['fʊtˌnəʊts] NPL Fußnote *f*

forced place insurance [ˌfɔ:st 'pleɪs ɪnʃʊərəns] N *Versicherung gegen Feuer, Überflutung und andere Gefahren für Immobilien, die als hypothekarische Sicherheit dienen*

force majeure [ˌfɔ:s mæ'ʒɜ:ʳ] N höhere Gewalt *f*

forecast ['fɔ:ˌkɑ:st] N Prognose *f*

foreclosure [fɔ:'kləʊʒəʳ] N Zwangsvollstreckung *f*

forex ['fɔ:rɛks] N Devisenmarkt *m*

forward contracts [ˌfɔ:wəd 'kɒntrækts] NPL Terminkontrakt *m*

forward rate [ˌfɔ:wəd 'reɪt] N Terminkurs *m*

401K [ˌfɔ:r əʊ wʌn 'keɪ] N 401 (k) Plan *m*

franchise ['fræntʃaɪz] N Franchise *f*

fraud [frɔ:d] N Betrug *m*

fraudulent ['frɔ:djʊlənt] ADJ betrügerisch *adj*

FRB [ˌɛf ɑ: 'bi:] ABBR FRB *abbr*

Freddie Mac [ˌfrɛdɪ 'mæk] N Freddie Mac, *weltweit zweitgrößte staatlich geförderte Hypothekenbank in den USA*

free cash flow [ˌfri: 'kæʃ ˌfləʊ] N freier Cashflow *m*

freight-in [ˌfreɪt'ɪn] N Eingangsfracht *f*

freight-out [ˌfreɪt'aʊt] N Ausgangsfracht *f*

front-end ['frʌntˌɛnd] ADJ Anfangskosten *pl*

front-end load [ˌfrʌntɛnd 'ləʊd] N Anfangskosten *pl*

frozen account [ˌfrəʊzən ə'kaʊnt] N gesperrtes Konto *nt*

FSA [ˌɛf ɛs 'eɪ] ABBR *Spezialkonto für Angestellte in den USA in Bezug auf medizinische Ausgaben*

functional currency [ˌfʌŋkʃnəl 'kʌrənsɪ] N funktionale Währung *f*

fund [fʌnd] N Fonds *m*

fund manager [ˌfʌnd 'mænɪdʒəʳ] N Fondsmanager(in) *m(f)*

funds [fʌndz] NPL Mittel *pl*

funeral ['fju:nərəl] N Beerdigung *f*

funeral expenses ['fju:nərəl ɪksˌpɛnsɪz] NPL Bestattungskosten *pl*

funeral plan ['fju:nərəl ˌplæn] N Sterbekasse *f*

futures ['fju:tʃəz] NPL Termingeschäft *nt*

Gg

GAAP [gæp] ABBR GAAP *abbr (= Grundsätze ordnungsmäßiger Rechnungslegung)*

gain on sale [ˌgeɪn ɒn 'seɪl] N Verkaufserlös *m*

gain on translation [ˌgeɪn ɒn ˌtrænz'leɪʃən] N Währungskonvertierungserlös *m*

gains [geɪnz] NPL Gewinne *mpl*

GAP insurance ['gæp ɪnʃʊərəns] N GAP-Versicherung *f*

gatekeeper ['geɪtˌki:pəʳ] N Gatekeeper *m*

GDP [ˌdʒi: di: 'pi:] ABBR BIP *abbr*

gender ['dʒɛndəʳ] N Geschlecht *nt*

general average [ˌdʒɛnərəl 'ævərɪdʒ] N gemeinschaftliche Havarie *f*

general insurance ['dʒɛnərəl ɪnʃʊərəns] N Sachversicherung *f*

general journal [ˌdʒɛnərəl 'dʒɜ:nəl] N Sammeljournal *nt*

general ledger [ˌdʒɛnərəl 'lɛdʒəʳ] N Hauptbuch *nt*

general partnership [ˌdʒɛnərəl 'pɑ:tnəʃɪp] N allgemeine Personengesellschaft *f*

Ginnie Mae [ˌdʒɪnɪ 'meɪ] N Ginnie Mae, *bundesstaatliche Hypothekenkreditanstalt*

GNP [ˌdʒi: ɛn 'pi:] ABBR BSP *abbr*

go bust [ˌgəʊ 'bʌst] PHRS bankrottgehen *vi*

going concern [ˌgəʊɪŋ kən'sɜ:n] N arbeitendes Unternehmen *nt*

golden parachute [ˌgəʊldən 'pærəʃu:t] N großzügige Abfindung *f*

go long [ˌgəʊ 'lɒŋ] PHRS Long gehen *vi*

good driver discount [ˌgʊd 'draɪvə ˌdɪskaʊnt] N *Rabatt für sicheres Fahren*

goods [gʊdz] NPL Waren *fpl*

goodwill [ˌgʊd'wɪl] N Goodwill *m*

government deficit [ˌgʌvənmənt 'dɛfɪsɪt] N Haushaltsdefizit *nt*

gross [grəʊs] ADJ brutto *adj*; VT brutto einnehmen *vt*

gross premium [ˌgrəʊs 'pri:mɪəm] N Bruttoprämie *f*

gross profit [ˌgrəʊs 'prɒfɪt] N Bruttogewinn *m*

gross profit margin [ˌgrəʊs 'prɒfɪt ˌmɑ:dʒɪn] N Bruttogewinnmarge *f*

gross up [ˌgrəʊs 'ʌp] VT hochrechnen *vt*

gross written premiums [ˌgrəʊs 'rɪtɜ:n ˌpri:mɪəmz] NPL Bruttoprämien *pl*

group insurance ['gru:p ɪnʃʊərəns] N Kollektivversicherung *f*

Hh

hard copy [ˌhɑ:d 'kɒpɪ] N Papierdokument *nt*

hard currency [ˌhɑ:d 'kʌrənsɪ] N harte Währung *f*

hazard ['hæzəd] N Risiko *nt*

health insurance exchange ['hɛlθ ɪnʃʊərəns ɪksˌtʃeɪndʒ] N *Börse in den USA für Gesundheitsversicherungen*

health maintenance organization ['hɛlθ ˌmeɪntənəns ˌɔ:gənaɪˌzeɪʃən] N *private Krankenversicherungsorganisation in den USA*

health maintenance plan ['hɛlθ ˌmeɪntənəns ˌplæn] N *Kostenplan für medizinische Versorgung in den USA*

health questionnaire ['hɛlθ ˌkwɛstʃəˌnɛəʳ] N Gesundheitsfragebogen *m*

hedge [hɛdʒ] VI sichern *vt/vi*

hedge fund ['hɛdʒ ˌfʌnd] N Hedgefonds *m*

HELOC ['hi:lɒk] ABBR HELOC *abbr*

high-deductible health plan [ˌhaɪdɪˌdʌktɪbəl 'hɛlθ ˌplæn] N *spezielle Form der Gesundheitsversicherung in den USA*

high-risk [ˌhaɪ'rɪsk] ADJ risikoreich *adj*

HIPAA ['hɪpə] ABBR HIPAA *abbr*

historical cost [hɪs'tɒrɪkəl ˌkɒst] N historische Kosten *pl*

hit and run [ˌhɪt ən 'rʌn] N Fahrerflucht *f*

holding company ['həʊldɪŋ ˌkʌmpənɪ] N Holdinggesellschaft *f*

home insurance ['həʊm ɪnʃʊərəns] N Hausratversicherung *f*

homeowner ['həʊm,əʊnə^r] N Hauseigentümer(in) *m(f)*

hostile takeover [,hɒstaɪl 'teɪkəʊvə^r] N feindliche Übernahme *f*

HRA [,eɪtʃ ɑːr 'eɪ] ABBR HRA *abbr*

HSA [,eɪtʃ ɛs 'eɪ] ABBR HSA *abbr*

hurricane ['hʌrɪkən] N Orkan *m*

hybrid basis ['haɪbrɪd ,beɪsɪs] N hybride Rechnungslegung *f*

Ii

IBAN ['aɪbæn] ABBR IBAN *abbr*

IMF [,aɪ ɛm 'ɛf] ABBR IWF *abbr*

immediate annuity [ɪ,miːdɪət ə'njuːɪtɪ] N nachschüssige Rente *f*

impairment [ɪm'pɛəmənt] N Wertminderung *f*, Gesundheitsschädigung *f*

inception [ɪn'sɛpʃən] N Beginn *m*

income ['ɪnkʌm] N Einkommen *nt*

income account ['ɪnkʌm ə,kaʊnt] N Einkommenskonto *nt*

income protection insurance [,ɪnkʌm prə'tɛkʃən ɪn,ʃʊərəns] N Einkommensschutzversicherung *f*

income statement ['ɪnkʌm ,steɪtmənt] N Ertragsbilanz *f*

income tax ['ɪnkʌm ,tæks] N Einkommenssteuer *f*

indemnity [ɪn'dɛmnɪtɪ] N Entschädigung *f*

indemnity plan [ɪn'dɛmnɪtɪ ,plæn] N *Gesundheitsversicherung, die dem Nutzer die Auswahl eines Anbieters ermöglicht*

independent contractor [,ɪndɪ,pɛndənt kən'træktə^r] N selbstständiger Unternehmer *m*

index ['ɪndɛks] N Index *m*

index-linked [,ɪndɛks'lɪŋkt] ADJ indexgebunden *adj*

indirect [,ɪndɪ'rɛkt] ADJ indirekt *adj*

inflation [ɪn'fleɪʃən] N Inflation *f*

inflation rider [ɪn'fleɪʃən ,raɪdə^r] N Inflations-Zusatzbestimmung *f*

initial commission [ɪ,nɪʃəl kə'mɪʃən] N Abschlussprovision *f*

initial public offering [ɪ,nɪʃəl ,pʌblɪk 'ɒfərɪŋ] N Börsengang *m*

inpatient ['ɪn,peɪʃənt] N stationärer Patient *m*

insider trading [,ɪnsaɪdə 'treɪdɪŋ] N Insiderhandel *m*

insolvency [ɪn'sɒlvənsɪ] N Insolvenz *f*

insolvent [ɪn'sɒlvənt] ADJ insolvent *adj*

instalment sales [ɪn'stɔːlmənt ,seɪlz] NPL Teilzahlungsverkauf *m*

institution [,ɪnstɪ'tjuːʃən] N Institution *f*

insurability [ɪn,ʃʊərə'bɪlɪtɪ] N Versicherungsfähigkeit *f*

insurable [ɪn'ʃʊərəbl] ADJ versicherungsfähig *adj*

insurable interest [ɪn,ʃʊərəbl 'ɪntrɪst] N versicherbares Interesse *nt*

insurance [ɪn'ʃʊərəns] N Versicherung *f*

insurance agent [ɪn'ʃʊərəns ,eɪdʒənt] N Versicherungsvertreter(in) *m(f)*

insurance broker [ɪn'ʃʊərəns ,brəʊkə] N Versicherungsmakler(in) *m(f)*

insurance class [ɪn'ʃʊərəns ,klɑːs] N Versicherungszweig *m*

insurance salesman [ɪn'ʃʊərəns ,seɪlzmən] N Versicherungsverkäufer(in) *m(f)*

insure [ɪn'ʃʊə^r] VT versichern *vt*

insured [ɪn'ʃʊəd] ADJ versichert *adj*; N Versicherte(r) *mf*

insurer [ɪn'ʃʊərə^r] N Versicherer *m*

intangible [ɪn'tændʒəbl] ADJ immateriell *adj*

intangible assets [ɪn,tændʒɪbəl 'æsɛts] NPL immaterielle Aktiva *pl*

intellectual property [ɪntɪ,lɛktjʊə'l 'prɒpətɪ] N geistiges Eigentum *nt*

interbank rate ['ɪntə,bæŋk ,reɪt] N Interbankrate *f*

interest ['ɪntrɪst] N Zins *m*

interest rate ['ɪntrɪst ,reɪt] N Zinssatz *m*

interest rate swap ['ɪntrɪst ,reɪt ,swɒp] N Zins-Swap *m*

interim results [,ɪntərɪm rɪ'zʌlts] NPL Zwischenergebnis *nt*

intermediary [,ɪntə'miːdɪərɪ] N Vermittler(in) *m(f)*

internal rate of return [ɪn,tɜːnəl ,reɪt əv rɪ'tɜːn] N interner Zinsfuß *m*

international accounting standards [ɪntə,næʃnəl ə,kaʊntɪŋ 'stændədz] NPL Internationale Standards *mpl* der Rechnungslegung

in the money [ɪn ðə 'mʌnɪ] PHRS im Geld

inventory ['ɪnvəntrɪ] N Inventar *f*; VT Inventur machen *vi*

inventory turnover ['ɪnvəntrɪ ,tɜːnəʊvə^r] N Lagerumschlag *m*

invest [ɪn'vɛst] VT investieren *vt/vi*

investment [ɪn'vɛstmənt] N Investment *nt*

investment bank [ɪn'vɛstmənt ,bæŋk] N Investmentbank *f*

investment bond [ɪn'vɛstmənt ,bɒnd] N festverzinsliches Anlagepapier *nt*

invoice ['ɪnvɔɪs] VT in Rechnung stellen *vt*; N Rechnung *f*

IRA [,aɪ ɑːr 'eɪ] ABBR IRA *abbr (= individueller Pensionsplan in den USA)*

IRS [,aɪ ɑːr 'ɛs] ABBR IRS *abbr (= größte US-Steuerbehörde)*

ISIN [,aɪ ɛs aɪ 'ɛn] ABBR ISIN *abbr*

issue a policy [,ɪʃuː ə 'pɒlɪsɪ] PHRS eine Police ausfertigen

issue price ['ɪʃuː ,praɪs] N Ausgabekurs *m*

item ['aɪtəm] N Posten *m*

Jj

joint account ['dʒɔɪnt ə,kaʊnt] N Gemeinschaftskonto *nt*

joint life annuity [,dʒɔɪnt ,laɪf ə'njuːɪtɪ] N verbundene Rente *f*

joint venture [,dʒɔɪnt 'vɛntʃə^r] N Jointventure *nt*

journal ['dʒɜːnl] N Journal *nt*

journal entry ['dʒɜːnəl ,ɛntrɪ] N Journalbuchung *f*

junk bonds ['dʒʌŋk ,bɒndz] N Ramschanleihe *f*

Kk

keep the books [,kiːp ðə 'bʊks] PHRS Buch führen

key man insurance [,kiː 'mæn ɪn,ʃʊərəns] N Führungskräfteversicherung *f*

Ll

ladder ['lædəʳ] VT *eine Serie von Investments mit aufeinanderfolgenden Fälligkeiten machen*

lagging indicator ['lægɪŋ ˌɪndɪkeɪtəʳ] N Spätindikator *m*

landslide ['lændˌslaɪd] N Erdrutsch *m*

lapse [læps] N Erlöschung *f*

large-cap ['lɑːdʒˌkæp] ADJ Large Cap *m*

LBO [ˌɛl biː 'əʊ] ABBR fremdfinanzierte Übernahme *f*

leading indicator [ˌliːdɪŋ 'ɪndɪkeɪtəʳ] N Frühindikator *m*

leakage ['liːkɪdʒ] N *Kapitalverlust für Versicherungen durch Betrug, mangelhafte Schadensfallbearbeitung oder fehlerhafte Kontrollen*

lease [liːs] N Pacht *f*; VT pachten *vt*

lease-back ['liːsˌbæk] N Verkauf *m* mit gleichzeitiger Rückmiete

lease with option to buy [ˌliːs wɪð ˌɒpʃən tə 'baɪ] N Pacht *f* mit Kaufoption

ledger ['lɛdʒəʳ] N Hauptbuch *nt*

legal expenses insurance ['liːgəl ɪksˌpɛnsɪz ɪnʃʊərəns] N Rechtsschutzversicherung *f*

lessee [lɛ'siː] N Pächter(in) *m(f)*

lessor [lɛ'sɔːʳ] N Leasinggeber(in) *m(f)*

letter of credit [ˌlɛtər əv 'krɛdɪt] N Kreditbrief *m*

level premium term insurance [ˌlɛvl ˌpriːmɪəm 'tɜːm ɪnʃʊərəns] N Lebensversicherung *f* mit gleichbleibender Prämie

leverage ['liːvərɪdʒ] N Leverage *nt*

liabilities [ˌlaɪə'bɪlɪtɪz] NPL Verbindlichkeiten *fpl*

liability [ˌlaɪə'bɪlɪtɪ] N Haftung *f*

liability account [ˌlaɪə'bɪlɪtɪ əˌkaʊnt] N Passivkonto *nt*

liable ['laɪəbl] ADJ haftbar *adj*

LIBOR ['laɪbɔːʳ] ABBR LIBOR *abbr*

licence ['laɪsəns] N Lizenz *f*

licensed ['laɪsənst] ADJ lizenziert *adj*

lien [lːin] N Pfandrecht *nt*

life insurance ['laɪf ɪnʃʊərəns] N Lebensversicherung *f*

life table ['laɪf ˌteɪbl] N Sterblichkeitstafel *f*

lifetime limit [ˌlaɪftaɪm 'lɪmɪt] N *Kostenobergrenze für die gesamte Dauer einer Gesundheitsversicherung*

LIFO ['laɪfəʊ] ABBR LIFO-Methode *f*

lightning ['laɪtnɪŋ] N Blitz *m*

limited partnership [ˌlɪmɪtɪd 'pɑːtnəʃɪp] N Kommanditgesellschaft *f*

line [laɪn] N Linie *f*

line of business [ˌlaɪn əv 'bɪznɪs] N Geschäftszweig *m*

line of credit [ˌlaɪn əv 'krɛdɪt] N Kreditlinie *f*

liquid assets [ˌlɪkwɪd 'æsɛts] NPL liquide Vermögenswerte *mpl*

liquidity [lɪ'kwɪdɪtɪ] N Liquidität *f*

liquidity event [lɪ'kwɪdɪtɪ ˌɪvɛnt] N Liquiditäts-Event *nt*

list price ['lɪst ˌpraɪs] N Listenpreis *m*

LLC [ˌɛl ɛl 'siː] ABBR LLC *abbr*

Lloyd's of London [ˌlɔɪdz əv 'lʌndən] N Lloyd's of London

LLP [ˌɛl ɛl 'piː] ABBR GmbH *abbr*

load [ləʊd] VT zuschlagen *vt*

loading ['əʊdɪŋ] N Zuschlag *m*

loan [ləʊn] N Darlehen *nt*

lockbox ['lɒkˌbɒks] N Lockbox *f*

longevity [lɒŋ'dʒɛvɪtɪ] N Langlebigkeit *f*

longevity risk [lɒn'dʒɛvɪtɪ ˌrɪsk] N Lebensdauerrisiko *f*

long-tail claims ['lɒŋteɪl ˌkleɪmz] NPL Langzeitschäden *mpl*

long-term ['lɒŋ'tɜːm] ADJ langfristig *adj*

long-term care insurance [ˌlɒŋgˌtɜːm 'kɛər ɪnʃʊərəns] N langfristige Pflegeversicherung *f*

long-term liabilities [ˌlɒŋˌtɜːm ˌlaɪə'bɪlɪtɪz] NPL langfristige Verbindlichkeiten *fpl*

loss [lɒs] N Verlust *m*, Schaden *m*, Schadenfall *m*

loss adjuster ['lɒs əˌdʒʌstəʳ] N Schadenregulierer(in) *m(f)*

losses ['lɒsɪz] NPL Verluste *pl*

loss on sale [ˌlɒs ɒn 'seɪl] N Verkaufsverlust *m*

loss on translation [ˌlɒs ɒn ˌtrænz'leɪʃən] N Währungskonvertierungsverlust *m*

loss ratio ['lɒs ˌreɪʃɪəʊ] N Schadenquote *f*

lower of cost or market [ˌləʊər əv ˌkɒst ə 'mɑːkɪt] PHRS Niederstwert *m*

low-risk [ˌləʊ'rɪsk] ADJ risikoarm *adj*

LTV [ˌɛl tiː 'viː] ABBR LTV *abbr*

lump sum payment [ˌlʌmp ˌsʌm 'peɪmənt] N einmaliger Kapitalbetrag *m*

make a market [ˌmeɪk ə 'mɑːkɪt] PHRS Geld- und Briefkurse stellen

make a policy paid up [ˌmeɪk ə ˌpɒlɪsɪ ˌpeɪd'ʌp] PHRS beitragsfreie Police *f*

malicious damage [məˌlɪʃəs 'dæmɪdʒ] N vorsätzliche Beschädigung *f*

manage a risk [ˌmænɪdʒ ə 'rɪsk] PHRS Risiko managen

manufacturing [ˌmænjə'fæktʃərɪŋ] N Produktion *f*

margin ['mɑːdʒɪn] N Gewinnspanne *f*, Kreditfinanzierung *f*

margin call ['mɑːdʒɪn ˌkɔːl] N Nachschussforderung *f*

marine insurance [mə'riːn ɪnʃʊərəns] N Seetransportversicherung *f*

mark down [ˌmɑːk 'daʊn] VT senken *vt*

market ['mɑːkɪt] N Markt *m*

marketable securities [ˌmɑːkɪtəbl sɪ'kjʊərɪtɪz] NPL börsengängige Wertpapiere *pl*

market cap [ˌmɑːkɪt 'kæp] N Marktkapitalisierung *f*

mark-to-market [ˌmɑːktə'mɑːkɪt] PHRS Mark-to-Market-Bewertung *f*

mark-up ['mɑːkˌʌp] N Preisheraufsetzung *f*

material [mə'tɪərɪəl] ADJ wesentlich *adj*

mature [mə'tjʊəʳ] ADJ fällig *adj*; VI fällig werden *vi*

maturity [mə'tjʊərɪtɪ] N Laufzeit *f*, Fälligkeit *f*

maturity value [mə'tjʊərɪtɪ ˌvælyuː] N Fälligkeitswert *m*

maximum lifetime benefit [ˌmæksɪməm ˌlaɪftaɪm 'bɛnɪfɪt] N *Kostenobergrenze für die gesamte Dauer eines Kostenplans einer Gesundheitsversicherung*

Medicaid ['mɛdɪˌkeɪd] N *staatlicher Gesundheitsdienst in den USA (für Einkommensschwache)*

medical procedure ['mɛdɪkəl prəˌsːidʒəʳ] N medizinische Behandlung *f*

medical underwriting [ˌmɛdɪkəl 'ʌndəˌraɪtɪŋ] N medizinische Risikoprüfung *f*

Medicare ['mɛdɪˌkɛəʳ] N *US-Gesundheitsdienst für Rentenempfänger*

Medigap policy ['mɛdɪgæp ˌpɒlɪsɪ] N *Private Zusatzversicherung zu Medicare*

Medivac ['mɛdɪˌvæk] N *Versicherung für den Transport vom Unfallort zum Krankenhaus*

mental impairment [ˌmɛntəl ɪm'pɛəmənt] N geistige Beeinträchtigung *f*

merchandise ['mɜːtʃənˌdaɪz] N Waren *fpl*

merchant account ['mɜːtʃənt əˌkaʊnt] N Handelskonto *nt*

merchant fees ['mɜːtʃənt ˌfiːz] NPL Händlergebühr *f*

merchant service ['mɜːtʃənt ˌsɜːvɪs] N Merchant Service *m*

merger ['mɜːdʒəʳ] N Fusion *f*

MICR encoding ['mɪkər ɪnˌkəʊdɪŋ] N MICR-Kodierung *f*

mid-cap ['mɪd,kæp] ADJ Mid Cap *m*

mitigate a risk [,mɪtɪgeɪt ə 'rɪsk] PHRS Risiko abschwächen

modification [,mɒdɪfɪ'keɪʃən] N Modifikation *f*

money market ['mʌnɪ ,mɑːkɪt] N Geldmarkt *m*

money supply ['mʌnɪ sə,plaɪ] N Geldmenge *f*

moral hazard [,mɒrəl 'hæʒəd] N Risiko *nt* unehrlichen Verhaltens

morbidity table [mɔː'bɪdɪtɪ ,teɪbl] N Morbiditätstafel *f*

mortality rate [mɔː'tælɪtɪ ,reɪt] N Sterblichkeitsrate *f*

mortality table [mɔː'tælɪtɪ ,teɪbl] N Sterbetafel *f*

mortgage insurance ['mɔːgɪdʒ ɪn,ʃʊərəns] N Hypothekenversicherung *f*

muni bonds ['mjuːnɪ ,bɒndz] N Kommunalanleihe *f*

mutual ['mjuːtjʊəl] ADJ gemeinschaftlich *adj*

mutual aid society [,mjuːtjʊəl 'eɪd sə,saɪɪtɪ] N Gesellschaft *f* für gegenseitige Hilfeleistungen

mutual fund ['mjuːtjʊəl ,fʌnd] N Investmentfonds *m*

mutual insurance [,mjuːtjʊəl ɪn'ʃʊərəns] N Versicherung *f* auf Gegenseitigkeit

mutual insurer [,mjuːtjʊəl ɪn'ʃʊərə^r] N Versicherer *m* auf Gegenseitigkeit

MVA [,ɛm viː 'eɪ] ABBR Kraftfahrzeugunfall *m*

Nn

NAFTA ['næftə] ABBR NAFTA *abbr (= Nordamerikanische Freihandelsvereinbarung)*

NAIC [,ɛn eɪ aɪ 'siː] ABBR NAIC *abbr (= US-Bundesverband der Versicherungskommissare)*

NASDAQ ['næzdæk] ABBR NASDAQ *abbr (= automatisierte elektronische Börse in den USA, wo vor allem Technologieunternehmen gehandelt werden)*

national bank [,næʃənl 'bæŋk] N Nationalbank *f*

national debt [,næʃənl 'dɛt] N Staatsschuld *f*

natural catastrophe [,nætʃrəl kə'tæstrəfɪ] N Naturkatastrophe *f*

NCUA [,ɛn siː jʊ 'eɪ] ABBR NCUA *abbr*

negligence ['nɛglɪdʒəns] N Fahrlässigkeit *f*

negligent ['nɛglɪdʒənt] ADJ fahrlässig *adj*

negotiable [nɪ'gəʊʃɪəbl] ADJ übertragbar *adj*

net [nɛt] ADJ netto *adj*; VT aufrechnen *vt*

net assets [,nɛt 'æsɛts] NPL Nettovermögen *nt*

net asset value [,nɛt ,æsɛt 'væljuː] N Nettoinventarwert

net earnings [,nɛt 'ɜːnɪŋz] NPL Nettoverdienst *mpl*

net income [,nɛt 'ɪnkʌm] N Nettogewinn *m*

net loss [,nɛt 'lɒs] N Nettoverlust *m*

net present value [,nɛt ,prɛzənt 'væljuː] N Gegenwartswert *m*

net profit [,nɛt 'prɒfɪt] N Reingewinn *m*

net realizable value [,nɛt rɪə,laɪzəbəl 'væljuː] N Nettorealisationswert *m*

net sales [,nɛt 'seɪlz] NPL Nettoabsatz *m*

new business [,njuː 'bɪznɪs] N Neugeschäft *nt*

new business profit margin [,njuː ,bɪznɪs 'prɒfɪt ,mɑːdʒɪn] N Anfangsgewinnmarge *f*

no-fault insurance [,nəʊfɔːlt ɪn'ʃʊərəns] N *Kfz-Versicherung gegen Personenschäden*

noncontributory [,nɒnkən'trɪbjʊtərɪ] ADJ beitragsunabhängig *adj*

non-disclosure [,nɒndɪs'kləʊʒə^r] N Mitteilungsunterlassung *f*

nonparticipating [,nɒnpɑː'tɪsɪpeɪtɪŋ] ADJ ohne Gewinnbeteiligung *f*

nonproportional cover [,nɒnprə,pɔːʃənl 'kʌvə^r] N nichtproportionaler Versicherungsschutz *m*

normal balance [,nɔːməl 'bæləns] N Sollseite *f*

nostro account ['nɒstrəʊ ə,kaʊnt] N Nostro-Konto *nt*

note payable [,nəʊt 'peɪəbl] N Verbindlichkeitserklärung *f*

NSF [,ɛn ɛs 'ɛf] ABBR *Prüfung auf unzureichende Deckung*

NYSE [,ɛn waɪ ɛs 'iː] ABBR NYSE *abbr*

Oo

OCC [,əʊ siː 'siː] ABBR OCC *abbr*

occupation [,ɒkjʊ'peɪʃən] N berufliche Tätigkeit *f*

occupational group [,ɒkjʊ,peɪʃənl 'gruːp] N Berufsgruppe *f*

occupational hazard [,ɒkjʊ,peɪʃənl 'hæzəd] N Berufsrisiko *nt*

ocean marine insurance [,əʊʃən mə,riːn ɪn'ʃʊərəns] N Seeversicherung *f*

off [ɒf] ADJ falsch *adj*

offer ['ɒfə^r] N Angebot *nt*

on account [,ɒn ə'kaʊnt] PHRS auf Kredit

on-the-job injury [,ɒnðədʒɒb 'ɪndʒərɪ] N Arbeitsunfall *m*

open-ended loan ['əʊpən,ɛndɪd ,ləʊn] N unbefristete Leihgabe *f*

open policy [,əʊpən 'pɒlɪsɪ] N Police *f* ohne Wertangabe

operating budget ['ɒpəreɪtɪŋ ,bʌdʒɪt] N operativer Rahmenplan *m*

operating cost ['ɒpəreɪtɪŋ ,kɒst] N Betriebsbudget *nt*

operating expenses ['ɒpəreɪtɪŋ ɪks,pɛnsɪz] NPL Betriebsaufwand *m*

operating income ['ɒpəreɪtɪŋ ,ɪnkʌm] N Betriebsertrag *m*

operating margin ['ɒpəreɪtɪŋ ,mɑːdʒɪn] N Gewinnmarge *f*

operating profit ['ɒpəreɪtɪŋ ,prɒfɪt] N Betriebsgewinn *m*

operation [,ɒpə'reɪʃən] N Operation *f*

opportunity cost [,ɒpə'tjuːnɪtɪ ,kɒst] N Opportunitätskosten *pl*

option ['ɒpʃən] N Option *f*

order ['ɔːdə^r] N Bestellung *f*; VT bestellen *vt*

ordinary gain [,ɔːdnrɪ 'geɪn] N ordentliches Einkommen *nt*

ordinary loss [,ɔːdnrɪ 'lɒs] N *Verluste außer denen aus Kapitalvermögen*

other expenses [,ʌðər ɪks'pɛnsɪz] NPL sonstige Aufwendungen *fpl*

other income [,ʌðər 'ɪnkʌm] N betriebsfremde Erträge *mpl*

out of the money [,aʊt əv ðə 'mʌnɪ] PHRS aus dem Geld

outpatient ['aʊt,peɪʃənt] N ambulanter Patient *m*

outstanding [,aʊt'stændɪŋ] ADJ ausstehend *adj*

overheads ['əʊvə,hɛdz] NPL Gemeinkosten *pl*

overinsured [,əʊvərɪn'ʃʊəd] ADJ überversichert *adj*

overlimit [,əʊvə'lɪmɪt] ADJ überzogen *adj*

overstated [,əʊvə'steɪtɪd] ADJ überhöht *adj*

over-the-counter [,əʊvə ðə 'kaʊntə^r] ADJ außerbörslich *adj*

own occupation coverage [,əʊn ɒkyə'peɪʃən ,kʌvərɪdʒ] N *Versicherung, falls die Berufsausübung im eigentlichen Beruf in Folge eines Unfalls etc. unmöglich ist*

own or similar occupation [,əʊn ə ,sɪmɪlər ,ɒkjə'peɪʃən] PHRS *ehemalige Hauptberufstätigkeit*

Pp

packing slip ['pækɪŋ ˌslɪp] N Packzettel *m*

paid-in capital [ˌpeɪdɪn 'kæpɪtl] N eingezahltes Kapital *nt*

paid-up ['peɪdˌʌp] ADJ beitragsfreie Police *f*

par [pɑːʳ] N Parikurs *m*

partial ['pɑːʃəl] ADJ teilweise *adj*

participating [ˌpɑː'tɪsɪpeɪtɪŋ] ADJ partizipierend *adj*

participating insurance [ˌpɑː'tɪsɪpeɪtɪŋ ɪnʃʊərəns] N Versicherung *f* mit Gewinnbeteiligung

particular average [pəˌtɪkjʊlər 'ævərɪdʒ] N besondere Havarie *f*

partnership ['pɑːtnəʃɪp] N Personengesellschaft *f*

par value ['pɑː ˌvæljuː] N Nennbetrag *m*

past due [ˌpɑːst 'djuː] ADJ überfällig *adj*

pay a claim [ˌpeɪ ə 'kleɪm] PHRS Schaden bezahlen

pay a pension [ˌpeɪ ə 'pɛnʃən] PHRS Pension zahlen

payday loan [ˌpeɪdeɪ 'ləʊn] N Zahltag-Darlehen *nt*

payee [peɪ'iː] N Zahlungsempfänger(in) *m(f)*

payment in advance [ˌpeɪmənt ɪn əd'vɑːns] N Vorauszahlung *f*

payor [peɪ'ɔːʳ] N Zahler(in) *m(f)*

pay out [ˌpeɪ 'aʊt] VT auszahlen *vt/vi*

payout ['peɪaʊt] N Auszahlung *f*

peg [pɛg] VT binden *vt*

peg ratio ['pɛg ˌreɪʃɪəʊ] N Peg-Ratio *f*

penny stocks ['pɛnɪ ˌstɒks] NPL Pfennigaktie *f*

pension fund ['pɛnʃən ˌfʌnd] N Pensionsfonds *m*

peril ['pɛrɪl] N Gefahr *f*

period costs ['pɪərɪəd ˌkɒsts] NPL wiederkehrende Aufwendungen *fpl*

periodic rate [ˌpɪərɪˌɒdɪk 'reɪt] N periodischer Zins *m*

permanent account [ˌpɜːmənənt ə'kaʊnt] N Dauerkonto *nt*

personal injury [ˌpɜːsənəl 'ɪndʒərɪ] N Personenschaden *m*

personal injury insurance [ˌpɜːsənəl 'ɪndʒərɪ ɪnʃʊərəns] N Personenschadenversicherung *f*

personal liability insurance [ˌpɜːsənəl ˌlaɪə'bɪlɪtɪ ɪnʃʊərəns] N Privathaftpflichtversicherung *f*

personal property [ˌpɜːsənəl 'prɒpətɪ] N bewegliches Vermögen *nt*

petty cash [ˌpɛtɪ 'kæʃ] N Portokasse *f*

physical impairment [ˌfɪzɪkəl ɪm'pɛəmənt] N Körperbehinderung *f*

piggyback investing [ˌpɪgɪbæk ɪn'vɛstɪŋ] N Huckepackinvestment *nt*

PIN [pɪn] ABBR PIN *abbr*

PITI ['pɪtɪ] ABBR PITI *abbr*

plan [plæn] N Plan *m*

plant [plɑːnt] N Fabrik *f*

plate glass insurance [ˌpleɪt glɑːs ɪn'ʃʊərəns] N Glasversicherung *f*

PMI [ˌpiː ɛm 'aɪ] ABBR Kreditversicherung *f*, private Krankenversicherung *f*

poison pill ['pɔɪzn ˌpɪl] N Anti-Übernahme-Strategie *f*

policy ['pɒlɪsɪ] N Police *f*

policyholder ['pɒlɪsɪˌhəʊldəʳ] N Versicherungsnehmer(in) *m(f)*

policy issuance ['pɒlɪsɪ ˌɪʃʊəns] N Ausfertigung *f* einer Police

policy loan ['pɒlɪsɪ ˌləʊn] N Beleihung *f* einer Versicherungspolice

policy term ['pɒlɪsɪ ˌtɜːm] N Vertragsdauer *f*

policy wording ['pɒlɪsɪ ˌwɜːdɪŋ] N Wortlaut *m* der Versicherungspolice

pool a risk [ˌpuːl ə 'rɪsk] PHRS Risikopoolung *f*

portability [ˌpɔːtə'bɪlɪtɪ] N Übertragbarkeit *f*

portfolio [ˌpɔːt'fəʊlɪəʊ] N Portfolio *nt*, Versicherungsbestand *m*, Portfolio *nt*

possessions [pə'zɛʃənz] NPL Besitztümer *pl*

post [pəʊst] VT eintragen *vt*

postdate [ˌpəʊst'deɪt] VT nachdatieren *vt*

PPACA [ˌpiː piː ˌeɪ siː 'eɪ] ABBR PPACA *abbr* (*= US-Gesetz zur Regelung des Zugangs zur Krankenversicherung*)

PPE [ˌpiː piː 'iː] ABBR Sachanlagen *fpl*

preexisting condition [ˌpriːɪgˌzɪstɪŋ kən'dɪʃən] N präexistenter Zustand *m*

preferred provider organization [prɪˌfɜːd prəˌvaɪdər ˌɔːgən'aɪzeɪʃən] N bevorzugter Anbieter *m*

preferred provider plan [prɪˌfɜːd pr'əvaɪdə ˌplæn] N *Spezielle Gesundheitsversicherung in den USA*

preferred stock [prɪˌfɜːd 'stɒk] N Vorzugsaktie *f*

premium ['priːmɪəm] N Agio *nt*, Beitrag *m*

premium income [ˌpriːmɪəm 'ɪnkʌm] N Prämienbeiträge *mpl*

prepaid expense [ˌpriːpeɪd ɪks'pɛns] N Rechnungsabgrenzungsposten *m*

prepayment [ˌpriː'peɪmənt] N Vorauszahlung *f*

present value of future cash flows [ˌprɛzənt 'væljuː əv ˌfjuːtʃə 'kæʃ ˌfləʊz] N diskontierter künftiger Cashflow *m*

price [praɪs] N Preis *m*

price earnings ratio [ˌpraɪs 'ɜːnɪŋz ˌreɪʃɪəʊ] N Kursgewinnverhältnis *nt*

primary insurer [ˌpraɪmərɪ ɪn'ʃʊərəʳ] N Erstversicherer *m*

prime [praɪm] ADJ erstklassig *adj*

prime cost [ˌpraɪm 'kɒst] N Anschaffungskosten *pl*

prime rate [ˌpraɪm 'reɪt] N Bankzinssatz *m*

principal ['prɪnsɪpəl] N Kapitalsumme *f*

private health insurance [ˌpraɪvɪt 'hɛlθ ɪnʃʊərəns] N private Krankenversicherung *f*

private placement [ˌpraɪvɪt 'pleɪsmənt] N Privatplatzierung *f*

probable maximum loss [ˌprɒbəbl ˌmæksɪməm 'lɒs] N wahrscheinlicher Höchstschaden *m*

proceeds ['prəʊsiːdz] NPL Erlös *m*

product ['prɒdʌkt] N Produkt *nt*

product costs ['prɒdʌkt ˌkɒsts] NPL Produktkosten *pl*

production [prə'dʌkʃən] N Produktion *f*

product liability insurance [ˌprɒdʌkt laɪə'bɪlɪtɪ ɪnʃʊərəns] N Produkthaftpflichtversicherung *f*

professional liability insurance [prəˌfɛʃənl laɪə'bɪlɪtɪ ɪnʃʊərəns] N Berufshaftpflichtversicherung *f*

profit ['prɒfɪt] N Gewinn *m*

profitability [ˌprɒfɪtə'bɪlɪtɪ] N Rentabilität *f*

profit and loss statement [ˌprɒfɪt ənd 'lɒs ˌsteɪtmənt] N Gewinn- und Verlustrechnung *f*

profit centre ['prɒfɪt ˌsɛntəʳ] N Profitcenter *nt*

profit margin ['prɒfɪt ˌmɑːdʒɪn] N Gewinnspanne *f*

profit warning ['prɒfɪt ˌwɔːnɪŋ] N Gewinnwarnung *f*

pro forma [ˌprəʊ 'fɔːmə] ADJ pro forma *adj*

promissory ['prɒmɪsərɪ] ADJ versprechend *adj*

promissory note ['prɒmɪsərɪ ˌnəʊt] N Schuldschein *m*

proof of coverage [ˌpruːf əv 'kʌvərɪdʒ] N Nachweis *m* über Versicherungsschutz

property ['prɒpətɪ] N Eigentum *nt*

property and casualty insurance [ˌprɒpətɪ ən 'kæʒjʊltɪ ɪnʃʊərəns] N Vermögens- und Schadenversicherung *f*

proportional reinsurance coverage [prəˌpɔːʃənl riːɪn'ʃʊərəns ˌkʌvərɪdʒ] N proportionale Rückversicherung *f*

proposal [prə'pəʊzl] N Antrag *m*

proposal form [prə'pəʊzl ˌfɔːm] N Antragsformular *nt*

proposer [prə'pəʊzəʳ] N Antragsteller(in) *m(f)*

pro rata [ˌprəʊ 'rɑːtə] ADJ anteilig *adj*

prospectus [prəs'pɛktəs] N Emissionsprospekt *m*

provision [prə'vɪʒən] N Rückstellung *f*, Vorsorge *f*, Bestimmung *f*

proxy ['prɒksɪ] N Vollmachtsaktionär(in) *m(f)*

public company [,pʌblɪk 'kʌmpənɪ] N Aktiengesellschaft *f*

purchase ledger [,pɜ:tʃɪs 'lɛdʒəʳ] N Kaufhauptbuch *nt*

purchase order ['pɜ:tʃɪs ,ɔ:dəʳ] N Auftrag *m*

put [pʊt] N Verkaufsoption *f*

Qq

quick ratio ['kwɪk ,reɪʃɪəʊ] N Liquidität *f* zweiten Grades

quota share reinsurance [,kwʊətə ʃɛə ,ri:ɪn'ʃʊərəns] N Quotenrückversicherung *f*

quote [kwəʊt] N Kostenvoranschlag *m*, Notierung *f*, Preisangebot *nt*; VT angeben *vt*

Rr

ramen profitable [,rɑ:mən 'prɒfɪtəbl] ADJ nur kostendeckend *adj*

rate of return [,reɪt əv rɪ'tɜ:n] N Rendite *f*

raw materials [,rɔ: mə'tɪərɪəlz] NPL Rohmaterialien *pl*

real estate ['rɪ:l ɪs,teɪt] N Immobilie *f*

real estate insurance ['ri:l ɪs,teɪt ɪn,ʃʊərəns] N Immobilienversicherung *f*

real estate liability ['ri:l ɪs,teɪt ,laɪə'bɪlɪtɪ] N Immobilienverbindlichkeiten *fpl*

realized gains [,rɪəlaɪzd 'geɪnz] NPL realisierte Gewinne *mpl*

realized losses [,rɪəlaɪzd 'lɒsɪz] NPL realisierte Verluste *mpl*

real property ['ri:l ,prɒpətɪ] N Liegenschaften *fpl*

rebate ['ri:beɪt] N Rückzahlung *f*

receipt [rɪ'si:t] N Quittung *f*

receipts [rɪ'si:ts] NPL Einnahmen *fpl*

receivables [rɪ'si:vəblz] NPL Außenstände *mpl*

receivables collection period [rɪ,si:vəblz kə'lɛkʃən ,pɪərɪəd] N Forderungseinzugsperiode *f*

receivables turnover [rɪ,si:vəblz 'tɜ:nəʊvəʳ] N Forderungsumschlag *m*

receiver [rɪ'si:vəʳ] N Empfangsbestätigung *f*

recession [rɪ'sɛʃən] N Rezession *f*

reclassify [,ri:'klæsɪfaɪ] VT umbuchen *vt*

recognize ['rɛkəg,naɪz] VT verbuchen *vt*

reconcile an account [,rɛkənsaɪl ən ə'kaʊnt] PHRS Konto abstimmen

recovery [rɪ'kʌvərɪ] N Einnahmen *fpl* aus Rückgriffen

recurring [rɪ'kʌrɪŋ] ADJ wiederkehrend *adj*

redeem [rɪ'di:m] VT einlösen *vt*

reduce a risk [rɪ,dju:s ə' rɪsk] PHRS Risiko reduzieren

refinance [,ri:faɪ'næns] VT refinanzieren *vt/vi*

refund ['ri:,fʌnd] VT erstatten *vt*

refuse a proposal [rɪ,fju:z ə prə'pəʊzəl] PHRS Antrag ablehnen

register ['rɛdʒɪstəʳ] N Register *nt*

regular premium [,rɛgjʊlə 'pri:mɪəm] N laufende Prämie *f*

reimburse [,ri:ɪm'bɜ:s] VT erstatten *vt*

reimbursement [,ri:ɪm'bɜ:smənt] N Erstattung *f*

reinsurance [,ri:ɪn'ʃʊərəns] N Rückversicherung *f*

reinsurance treaty [,ri:ɪn'ʃʊərəns ,tr:ɪtɪ] N Rückversicherungsvertrag *f*

reinsure [,ri:ɪn'ʃʊəʳ] VT rückversichern *vt*

reinsurer [,ri:ɪn'ʃʊərəʳ] N Rückversicherer *m*

remit [rɪ'mɪt] VT überweisen *vt*

remittance advice [rɪ'mɪtəns əd,vaɪs] N Überweisungsanzeige *f*

renew [rɪ'nju:] VT verlängern *vt*

renewable term insurance [rɪ,nju:əbəl 'tɜ:m ɪn,ʃʊərəns] N erneuerbare Risikoversicherung *f*

renewal [rɪ'nju:əl] N Verlängerung *f*

renewal date [rɪ'nju:əl ,deɪt] N Verlängerungsdatum *nt*

renter [,rɛntəʳ] N Mieter(in) *m(f)*

renter's insurance ['rɛntəz ɪn,ʃʊərəns] N Hausratversicherung *f*

repatriate [ri:'pætrɪ,eɪt] VT rückführen *vt/vi*

repatriation [ri:,pætrɪ'eɪʃən] N Rückführung *f*

repatriation expenses [ri:,pætrɪ'eɪʃən ɪks,pɛnsɪz] NPL Rückführungskosten *pl*

replacement cost basis [rɪ,pleɪsmənt 'kɒst ,beɪsɪs] N Wiederbeschaffungskostenbasis *f*

replacement cost insurance [rɪ,pleɪsmənt 'kɒst ɪn,ʃʊərəns] N Neuwertversicherung *f*

report [rɪ'pɔ:t] VT berichten *vt/vi*

report a claim [rɪ,pɔ:t ə 'kleɪm] PHRS Anspruch anmelden

report an accident [rɪ,pɔ:t ən 'æksɪdənt] PHRS Unfall anzeigen

reporting [rɪ'pɔ:tɪŋ] N Berichterstattung *f*

rescind a contract [rɪ,sɪnd ə 'kɒntrækt] PHRS Vertrag aufheben

rescission [rɪ,sɪʃən] N Aufhebung *f*

reserve [rɪ'zɜ:v] N Reserven *fpl*

reserves [rɪzɜ:vz] NPL Rücklagen *fpl*

residence insurance ['rɛzɪdəns ɪn,ʃʊərəns] N Gebäudeversicherung *f*

residual [rɪ'zɪdjʊəl] ADJ zurückbleibend *adj*

residual debt insurance [rɪ,zɪdjʊəl 'dɛt ɪn,ʃʊərəns] N Restschuldenversicherung *f*

restricted [rɪ'strɪktɪd] ADJ eingeschränkt *adj*

retail ['ri:,teɪl] ADJ Einzelhandels-

retain [rɪ'teɪn] VT zurückbehalten *vt*

retained earnings [rɪ,teɪnd 'ɜ:nɪŋz] NPL thesaurierte Erträge *mpl*

retention [rɪ'tɛnʃən] N Bindung *f*

retention of risk [rɪ,tɛnʃən əv 'rɪsk] N Risikoselbstbehalt *m*

retire [rɪ'taɪəʳ] VI in den Ruhestand treten *vi*

retiree [rɪ,taɪə'ri:] N Ruheständler(in) *m(f)*

retirement [rɪ'taɪəmənt] N Ruhestand *m*

retirement age [rɪ'taɪəmənt ,eɪdʒ] N Rentenalter *nt*

retroactive [,rɛtrəʊ'æktɪv] ADJ rückwirkend *adj*

retrocession [,rɛtrə'sɛʃən] N Retrozession *f*

return [rɪ'tɜ:n] N Rendite *f*

return of capital [rɪ,tɜ:n əv 'kæpɪtl] N Kapitalerstattung *f*

return on assets [rɪ,tɜ:n ɒn 'æsɛts] N Vermögensrendite *f*

return on capital [rɪ,tɜ:n ɒn 'kæpɪtl] N Kapitalertrag *m*

return on equity [rɪ,tɜ:n ɒn 'ɛkwɪtɪ] N Eigenkapitalrendite *f*

return on investment [rɪ,tɜ:n ɒn ɪn'vɛstmənt] N Investitionsrendite *f*

revenue ['rɛvənju:] N Einkommen *nt*

revenue stream ['rɛvənju: ,str:ɪm] N Einkommensstrom *m*

reverse mortgage [rɪ,vɜ:s 'mɔ:gɪdʒ] N Umkehrhypothek *f*

reversion [rɪ'vɜ:ʃən] N Immobilienverrentung *f*

reversionary bonus [rɪ,vɜːʃnərɪ 'bəʊnəs] N Summenzuwachs *m*

reviewable [rɪ'vjuːəbl] ADJ überprüfbar *adj*

rider ['raɪdəʳ] N Zusatzbestimmung *f*

riot ['raɪət] N Aufruhr *m*

risk [rɪsk] N Risiko *nt*

risk excess of loss [,rɪsk ,ɛksɛs əv 'lɒs] N Schadensexzedent *m* pro Risiko

risk management [,rɪsk 'mænɪdʒmənt] N Risikomanagement *nt*

risk manager [,rɪsk 'mænɪdʒəʳ] N Risikomanager(in) *m(f)*

risk pooling ['rɪsk ,puːlɪŋ] N Risikopoolung *f*

Roth IRA [,rɒθ ,aɪ ɑːr 'eɪ] N Roth IRA *f* *(= Alterversorgungsplan in den USA)*

RSU [,ɑːr ɛs 'juː] ABBR RSU *abbr*

RTGS [,ɑː ti dʒiː 'ɛs] ABBR RTGS *abbr*

RTN [,ɑː tiː ,ɛn] ABBR RTN *abbr*

run-off ['rʌn,ɒf] N Abwicklung *f*

run on a bank [,rʌn ɒn ə 'bæŋk] PHRS Bankpanik *f*

Ss

safe deposit box [,seɪf dɪ'pɒzɪt ,bɒks] N Bankschließfach *nt*

safety belt ['seɪftɪ ,bɛlt] N Sicherheitsgurt *m*

safety device ['seɪftɪ dɪ,vaɪs] N Schutzvorrichtung *f*

salary ['sælərɪ] N Lohn *m*

sales [seɪlz] N Absatz *m*

sales ledger ['seɪlz ,lɛdʒəʳ] N Verkaufsjournal *nt*

sales revenue ['seɪlz ,rɛvənjuː] N Umsatzergebnis *nt*

sales slip ['seɪlz ,slɪp] N Verkaufsbeleg *m*

Sallie Mae [,sælɪ 'meɪ] N Sallie Mae, *In den USA die größte Bank für die Vergabe von Studentenkrediten*

salvage ['sælvɪdʒ] N Bergung *f*, Bergungswert *m*

savings account ['seɪvɪŋz ə,kaʊnt] N Sparkonto *nt*

savings and loan [,seɪvɪŋz ən 'ləʊn] N Spar- und Darlehenskasse *f*

schedule ['ʃɛdjuːl] N Versicherungsverzeichnis *nt*

S corporation ['ɛs ,kɔːpə,reɪʃən] N S-Corporation *f*

SEC [,ɛs iː 'siː] ABBR SEC *abbr* *(= US-Wertpapier- und Börsenaufsichtsbehörde)*

second-hand endowment [,sɛkənd,hænd ɪn'daʊmənt] N Zweitmarkt-Police *f*

secured [sɪ'kjʊəd] ADJ gesichert *adj*

securities [sɪ'kjʊərɪtɪz] NPL Wertpapier *nt*

seed capital ['siːd ,kæpɪtl] N Startkapital *nt*

seed money ['siːd ,mʌnɪ] N Gründungskapital *nt*

seigniorage ['seɪnjərɪdʒ] N Geldschöpfungsgewinn *m*

self-insurance [,sɛlfɪn'ʃʊərəns] N Selbstversicherung *f*

selling expenses ['sɛlɪŋ ɪks,pɛnsɪz] NPL Verkaufsspesen *pl*

selloff ['sɛlɒf] N Ausverkauf *m*

sell short [,sɛl 'ʃɔːt] PHRS leer verkaufen

serial bonds ['sɪərɪəl ,bɒndz] NPL Serienanleihe *f*

service industry ['sɜːvɪs ,ɪndəstrɪ] N Dienstleistungsindustrie *f*

services ['sɜːvɪsɪz] NPL Dienstleistung *f*

set off [,sɛt 'ɒf] VT aufrechnen *vt*

settle ['sɛtl] VT ausführen *vt*

settle a claim [,sɛtl ə 'kleɪm] PHRS Forderung befriedigen

settlement agent ['sɛtlmənt ,eɪdʒənt] N ausführender Agent *m*

settlement date ['sɛtlmənt ,deɪt] N Ausführungsdatum *nt*

settlement price ['sɛtlmənt ,praɪs] N Liquidationskurs *m*

severe [sɪ'vɪəʳ] ADJ schwer *adj*

severity [sɪ'vɛrɪtɪ] N Schwere *f*

share [ʃɛəʳ] N Anteil *m*

share capital ['ʃɛə ,kæpɪtl] N Aktienkapital *nt*

share certificate ['ʃɛə sə:,tɪfɪkɪt] N Aktienzertifikat *nt*

shareholder ['ʃɛə,həʊldəʳ] N Anteilseigner(in) *m(f)*

shareholders' equity [ʃɛəhəʊldəz 'ɛkwɪtɪ] N Anteilskapital *nt*

share repurchase [ʃɛə riː'pɜːtʃɪs] N Aktienrückkauf *m*

shipment ['ʃɪpmənt] N Verschiffung *f*

shipping documents ['ʃɪpɪŋ ,dɒkjʊmənts] NPL Transportdokumente *pl*

shop around [ʃɒp ə'raʊnd] VI Preise vergleichen *vt*

short-tail business [ʃɔːtteɪl 'bɪznɪs] N kurz abwickelndes Geschäft *nt*

short-term ['ʃɔːt,tɜːm] ADJ kurzfristig *adj*

single entry [,sɪŋgl 'ɛntrɪ] N Einfachbuchführung *f*

single life annuity [,sɪŋgl ,laɪf ə'njuːɪtɪ] N Rente *f* auf ein Leben

single premium [,sɪŋgl 'priːmɪəm] N Einzelprämie *f*

single premium insurance [,sɪŋgl ,priːmɪəm ɪn'ʃʊərəns] N Einmalbeitragsversicherung *f*

sinking fund ['sɪŋkɪŋ ,fʌnd] N Tilgungsfonds *m*

small-cap ['smɔːl,kæp] ADJ Small Cap *f* *(= Kleines Unternehmen an der Börse)*

soft currency [,sɒft 'kʌrənsɪ] N Weichwährung *f*

sovereign debt [,sɒvrɪn 'dɛt] N Staatsanleihe *f*

SOX [sɒks] ABBR SOX *abbr*

speculation [,spɛkjʊ'leɪʃən] N Spekulation *f*

spin off [,spɪn 'ɒf] VT ausgliedern *vt*

spot market ['spɒt ,mɑːkɪt] N Kassamarkt *m*

spot price ['spɒt ,praɪs] N Kassapreis *m*

spot rate ['spɒt ,reɪt] N Kassakurs *m*

spouse [spaʊs] N Ehegatte *m*, Ehegattin *f*

spread [sprɛd] N Spread *m*

stalking horse ['stɔːkɪŋ ,hɔːs] N Mindestangebot *nt*

standard annuity [,stændəd ə'njuːɪtɪ] N *f* *(= Altersrente auf Pauschalzahlung)*

standard cost [,stændəd 'kɒst] N Normalkosten *pl*

standing settlement instructions [,stændɪŋ 'sɛtlmənt ɪn,strʌkʃənz] NPL *festgelegte, wiederholbare Zahlungsanweisungen*

startup ['stɑːtʌp] N Neugründung *f*

statement ['steɪtmənt] N Kontoauszug *m*

statement of cash flows [,steɪtmənt əv 'kæʃ ,fləʊz] N Cashflow-Bilanz *f*

statement of earnings and comprehensive income [,steɪtmənt əv 'ɜːnɪŋz ən kɒmprɪ,hɛnsɪv 'ɪnkʌm] N Ertrags- und Einkommenserklärung *f*

stock [stɒk] N Anteil *m*, Lagerbestand *m*, Anteile *pl*

stock dividend [,stɒk 'dɪvɪdɛnd] N Aktiendividende *f*

stock options [,stɒk 'ɒpʃənz] NPL Aktienoptionen *pl*

stock split ['stɒk ,splɪt] N Aktiensplit *m*

stock symbol ['stɒk ,sɪmbəl] N Aktienzeichen *nt*

stock warrant ['stɒk ,wɒrənt] N Aktienbezugsrechtsschein *m*

stop loss reinsurance [,stɒp 'lɒs riːɪnʃʊərəns] N Gesamtschadenexzedentenversicherung *f*

stop payment [,stɒp 'peɪmənt] PHRS Zahlungssperre *f*

straddle ['strædl] N *Optionsstrategie, bei der man auf sich stark ändernde oder gleich bleibende Kurse spekuliert*

straight-line depreciation [ˌstreɪtlaɪn dɪˌpriːʃɪ'eɪʃən] N lineare Abschreibung *f*

strike price ['straɪk ˌpraɪs] N Zuschlagspreis *m*

subcontract [ˌsʌbkən'trækt] VT untervergeben *vt*

sublease [sʌb'liːs] N Untermietvertrag *m*

subordinated [sə'bɔːdɪˌneɪtɪd] ADJ nachrangig *adj*

subprime loan [ˌsʌbpraɪm 'ləʊn] N Subprime-Hypothekendarlehen *nt*

subrogation [ˌsʌbrə'geɪʃən] N Regress *m*

subsidence [səb'saɪdəns] N Bodensenkung *f*

subsidiary [səb'sɪdɪərɪ] N Tochtergesellschaft *f*

sum assured [ˌsʌm ə'ʃʊəd] N Versicherungssumme *f*

sum insured [ˌsʌm ɪn'ʃʊəd] N Deckungssumme *f*

sunk cost ['sʌŋk ˌkɒst] N geleistete Kosten *pl*

supplementary insurance [ˌsʌplɪ'mɛntərɪ ɪnˌʃʊərəns] N Ergänzungsversicherung *f*

supplier [sə'plaɪə^r] N Lieferant *m*

supply chain [sə'plaɪ ˌtʃeɪn] N Versorgungskette *f*

surplus ['sɜːpləs] N Überschuss *m*

surplus reinsurance [ˌsɜːplʌs ˌriːɪn'ʃʊərəns] N Summenexzedenten *pl*

surrender [sə'rɛndə^r] N Verkauf *m (einer Lebensversicherung durch Rückkauf)*; VT verkaufen *vt*

surrender value [sə'rɛndə ˌvæljuː] N Rückkaufwert *m*

survive [sə'vaɪv] VI überleben *vt/vi*

surviving [sə'vaɪvɪŋ] ADJ überlebend *adj*

suspense account [sə'spɛns əˌkaʊnt] N Zwischenkonto *nt*

swap [swɒp] N Swap *m*

swaption ['swɒpʃən] N Swaption *m*

sweat equity [ˌswɛt 'ɛkwɪtɪ] N Sweat-Equity-Beteiligung *f*

SWIFT [swɪft] ABBR SWIFT *abbr*

syndicate ['sɪndɪkɪt] N Syndikat *nt*

Tt

T account ['tiː əˌkaʊnt] N T-Konto *nt*

take out insurance [ˌteɪk aʊt ɪn'ʃʊərəns] PHRS Versicherung abschließen

tangible ['tændʒəbl] ADJ materiell *adj*

tax [tæks] N Steuer *f*

taxable ['tæksəbl] ADJ steuerpflichtig *adj*

taxation [tæk'seɪʃən] N Besteuerung *f*

tax avoidance ['tæks əˌvɔɪdəns] N Steuervermeidung *f*

tax deductible [ˌtæks dɪ'dʌktɪbl] ADJ steuerlich abzugsfähig *adj*

tax deduction ['tæks dɪˌdʌkʃən] N Steuerabzug *m*

tax-deferred [ˌtæksdɪ'fɜːd] ADJ = *latente Steuern fpl*

tax depreciation [ˌtæks dɪˌpriːʃɪ'eɪʃən] N steuerliche Abschreibung *f*

tax evasion ['tæks ɪˌveɪʒən] N Steuerhinterziehung *f*

tax exempt [ˌtæks ɪg'zɛmpt] ADJ steuerfrei *adj*

tax haven ['tæks ˌheɪvən] N Steueroase *f*

tax holiday ['tæks ˌhɒlɪdeɪ] N Steuerferien *pl*

tax loss ['tæks ˌlɒs] N Steuerverlustabzug *m*

tax rate ['tæks ˌreɪt] N Steuersatz *m*

tax refund ['tæks ˌriːfʌnd] N Steuerrückzahlung *f*

tax relief ['tæks rɪˌliːf] N Steuererleichterung *f*

tax return ['tæks rɪˌtɜːn] N Steuererklärung *f*

tax shelter ['tæks ʃɛltə^r] N Steuerbegünstigung *f*

tax year ['tæks ˌjɪə^r] N Steuerjahr *nt*

T-bill ['tiːˌbɪl] N T-Bill *f*

T-bond ['tiːˌbɒnd] N T-Bond *m*

teaser rate ['tiːzə ˌreɪt] N Anreizrate *f*

technical reserves [ˌtɛknɪkəl rɪ'zɜːvz] NPL versicherungstechnische Rückstellung *f*

temporary account [ˌtɛmpərərɪ ə'kaʊnt] N vorläufiges Konto *nt*

tenant ['tɛnənt] N Mieter(in) *m(f)*

tender offer ['tɛndər ˌɒfə^r] N Übernahmeangebot *nt*

terminal illness [ˌtɜːmɪnəl 'ɪlnɪs] N unheilbare Krankheit *f*

term insurance ['tɜːm ɪnˌʃʊərəns] N Risikolebensversicherung *f*

terms and conditions [ˌtɜːmz ən kən'dɪʃənz] NPL Versicherungsbedingungen *fpl*

term sheet ['tɜːm ʃiːt] N Konditionsvereinbarung *f*

terms of payment [ˌtɜːmz əv 'peɪmənt] NPL Zahlungsbedingungen *fpl*

theft [θɛft] N Diebstahl

third party [ˌθɜːd 'pɑːtɪ] N Dritte(r) *mf*

third party liability [ˌθɜːd ˌpɑːtɪ ˌlaɪə'bɪlɪtɪ] N gesetzliche Haftpflicht *f*

ticker ['tɪkə^r] N Kursanzeiger *m*

time deposit ['taɪm dɪˌpɒzɪt] N Termineinlage *f*

title ['taɪtl] N Besitzurkunde *f*

tontine ['tɒntiːn] N Tontine *f*

tornado [tɔː'neɪdəʊ] N Tornado *m*

total loss [ˌtəʊtl 'lɒs] N Totalschaden *m*

total probable loss [ˌtəʊtl 'prɒbəbl ˌlɒs] N größtmöglicher Schaden *m*

tracker ['trækə^r] N Tracker *m*

tracker fund ['trækə ˌfʌnd] N Tracker-Fonds *m*

traded endowment [ˌtreɪdɪd ɪn'daʊmənt] N gehandelte Kapitallebensversicherungspolice *f*

trade discount [ˌtreɪd 'dɪskaʊnt] N Warenskonto *m*

traditional policy [trəˌdɪʃənl 'pɒlɪsɪ] N traditionelle Police *f*

trail commission ['treɪl kəˌmɪʃən] N laufende Vertriebsprovision *f*

tranche [trɑːnʃ] N Tranche *f*

transaction [træn'zækʃən] N Transaktion *f*

transfer pricing [ˌtrænsfɜ 'praɪsɪŋ] N Verrechnungspreise *pl*

translation [trænz'leɪʃən] N Konvertierung *f*

transpose [træns'pəʊz] VT vertauschen *vt*

travel insurance ['trævl ɪnˌʃʊərəns] N Reiseversicherung *f*

Treasury ['trɛʒərɪ] N Schatzamt *nt*

treasury stock ['trɛʒərɪ ˌstɒk] N eigene Anteile *mpl*

treaty ['triːtɪ] N Vertrag *m*

trial balance [ˌtraɪəl 'bæləns] N Probebilanz *f*

trust [trʌst] N Treuhand *f*

trust account ['trʌst əˌkaʊnt] N Treuhandkonto *nt*

trustee [trʌs'tiː] N Treuhänder(in) *m(f)*

tsunami [tsʊ'nɑːmɪ] N Tsunami *m*

turnover ['tɜːnˌəʊvə^r] N Umsatz *m*

Uu

umbrella policy [ʌm'brɛlə ˌpɒlɪsɪ] N Dachpolice *f*

unallocated [ˌʌn'æləkeɪtɪd] ADJ nicht zugeteilt *adj*

unappropriated [ˌʌnə'prəʊprɪetɪd] ADJ nicht verwendet *adj*

unbalanced [ˌʌnˈbælənst] ADJ unausgeglichen *adj*

underinsured [ˌʌndərɪnˈʃʊəd] ADJ unterversichert *adj*

understated [ˌʌndəˈsteɪtɪd] ADJ unterbewertet *adj*

underwater [ˌʌndəˈwɔːtəʳ] ADJ *Darlehen, dessen Sicherheit weniger wert ist als die ausstehende Kapitalsumme*

underwrite [ˈʌndəˌraɪt] VT übernehmen *vt*, zeichnen *vt*

underwriter [ˈʌndəˌraɪtəʳ] N Versichungsgeber(in) *m(f)*

underwriting [ˈʌndəˌraɪtɪŋ] N Zeichnung *f*

unearned income [ˌʌnɜːnd ˈɪnkʌm] N nicht arbeitsbezogenes Einkommen *nt*

unemployment insurance [ˌʌnɪmˈplɔɪmənt ɪnʃʊərəns] N Arbeitslosenversicherung *f*

uninsurable [ˌʌnɪnˈʃʊərəbl] ADJ unversicherbar *adj*

uninsured [ˌʌnɪnˈʃʊəd] ADJ unversichert *adj*

unit trust [ˌjuːnɪt ˈtrʌst] N Investmentfonds *m*

unload [ʌnˈləʊd] VT abstoßen *vt*

unrealized gains [ʌnˌrɪəlaɪzd ˈgeɪnz] NPL nicht realisierte Gewinne *mpl*

unrealized losses [ʌnˌrɪəlaɪzd ˈlɒsɪz] NPL nicht realisierte Verluste *mpl*

unrestricted [ˌʌnrɪˈstrɪktɪd] ADJ uneingeschränkt *adj*

unsecured [ˌʌnsɪˈkjʊəd] ADJ ungesichert *adj*

upfront [ˌʌpˈfrʌnt] ADJ im Voraus *adj*

US Savings bond [ˌjuː ɛs ˈseɪvɪŋz ˌbɒnd] N US-Sparbrief *m*

usury [ˈjuːʒʊrɪ] N Wucher *m*

utmost good faith [ˌʌtməʊst ˌgʊd ˈfeɪθ] N höchste Gutgläubigkeit *f*

Vv

valuation [ˌvæljʊˈeɪʃən] N Bewertung *f*

value [ˈvæljuː] N Wert *m*

value added [ˌvæljuː ˈædɪd] N Mehrwert *m*

valued policy [ˌvæljuːd ˈpɒlɪsɪ] N Police *f* mit vereinbarter Wertangabe

variable costs [ˌvɛərɪəbəl ˈkɒsts] NPL variable Kosten *pl*

variable universal life insurance [ˌvɛərɪəbl juːnɪˌvɜːsl ˌlaɪf ɪnʃʊərəns] N fondsgebundene Lebensversicherung *f*

variance [ˈvɛərɪəns] N Abweichung *f*

vehicle [ˈviːɪkl] N Fahrzeug *nt*

vehicle insurance [ˈviːɪkl ɪnʃʊərəns] N Fahrzeugversicherung *f*

vendor [ˈvɛndɔːʳ] N Verkäufer(in) *mf*

venture capital [ˌvɛntʃə ˈkæpɪtl] N Risikokapital *nt*

venture capitalist [ˌvɛntʃə ˈkæpɪtəlɪst] N Risikokapitalgeber(in) *m(f)*

vesting [ˈvɛstɪŋ] N Anwartsschaftszeit *f*

viatical settlement [vaɪˌætɪkl ˈsɛtlmənt] N Viatical-Settlement *nt*

vision care [ˈvɪʒən ˌkeəʳ] N Augenheilkunde *f*

void [vɔɪd] ADJ ungültig *adj*; VT ungültig erklären *vt*

vostro account [ˈvɒstrəʊ əˌkaʊnt] N Lorokonto *nt*

voucher [ˈvaʊtʃəʳ] N Gutschein *m*

Ww

wages [ˈweɪdʒɪz] NPL Arbeitslohn *m*

waiting period [ˈweɪtɪŋ ˌpɪərɪəd] N Karenzzeit *f*

waiver of premium [ˌweɪvər əv ˈpriːmɪəm] N Beitragsbefreiung *f*

warehouse [ˈwɛəˌhaʊs] N Lagerhaus *nt*

warehouse receipt [ˌwɛəhaʊs rɪˈsiːt] N Einlagerungsschein *m*

wash sale [ˈwɒʃ ˌseɪl] N Scheingeschäft *nt*

weighted average cost of capital [ˌweɪtɪd ˌævərɪdʒ ˌkɒst əv ˈkæpɪtl] N gewichtete durchschnittliche Kapitalkosten *pl*

white knight [ˌwaɪt ˈnaɪt] N Weißer Ritter *m*

whole life insurance [ˌhəʊl ˈlaɪf ɪnʃʊərəns] N lebenslängliche Kapitalversicherung *f*

wholesale [ˈhəʊlseɪl] ADJ Großhandels-

widow [ˈwɪdəʊ] N Witwe *f*

widower [ˈwɪdəʊəʳ] N Witwer *m*

will [wɪl] N Testament *nt*

windfall profits [ˈwɪndfɔːl ˌprɒfɪts] NPL Zufallsgewinn *m*

wire transfer [ˌwaɪə ˈtrænsfəʳ] N elektronischer Zahlungsverkehr *m*

withdraw [wɪθˈdrɔː] VT abheben *vt*

workers' compensation [ˌwɜːkəz ˌkɒmpənˈseɪʃən] N Entschädigung *f* bei Betriebsunfall

working capital [ˌwɜːkɪŋ ˈkæpɪtl] N Betriebskapital *nt*

work-in-progress [ˌwɜːkɪnˈprəʊgrɛs] N laufende Arbeit *f*

write cover [ˌraɪt ˈkʌvəʳ] PHRS Versicherung übernehmen

write down [ˌraɪt ˈdaʊn] VT im Wert verringern *vt*

write off [ˌraɪt ˈɒf] VT abschreiben *vt*

write-off [ˈraɪtˌɒf] N Abschreibung *f*, Totalschaden *m*

write-up [ˈraɪtˌʌp] N Zuschreibung *f*

Yy

year end [ˌjɪər ˈɛnd] N Jahresende *nt*

yield [jiːld] N Rendite *f*

yield curve [ˈjiːld ˌkɜːv] N Zinsstrukturkurve *f*

yield to maturity [ˌjiːld tə məˈtjʊərɪtɪ] N Rendite *f* auf Endfälligkeit

Zz

zero-coupon bonds [ˌzɪərəʊˌkuːpɒn ˈbɒndz] NPL Nullkuponanleihe *f*

German-English

Aa

abbuchen ['apbu:xn] VT debit
abfinden [apfɪndn] VT buy out
Abhängige(r) ['aphɛŋɪgɐ, 'aphɛŋɪgə] MF dependent
abheben ['aphe:bn] VT withdraw
Ablaufdatum ['aplauf,da:tʊm] NT expiration date
ablaufen ['aplaufn] VI expire
Ablösung ['aplø:zʊŋ] F commutation
abrechenbar ['aprɛçnba:ɐ] ADJ billable
Absatz ['apzats] M sales
Absatzweg ['apzatsve:k] M distribution channel
Abschlussprovision ['apʃlʊsprovi,zio:n] F initial commission
abschreiben ['apʃraibn] VT write off
Abschreibungsaufwand ['apʃraibʊŋs,|aufvant] M depreciation expense
abschreibungsfähig ['apʃraibʊŋsfɛ:ɪç] ADJ depreciable
absichern ['apzɪçɐn] VT cover
abstimmen ['apʃtɪmən] VT agree
abstoßen ['apʃto:sn] VT divest, unload
Abweichung ['apvaɪçʊŋ] F variance
abwerten ['apve:ɐtn] VT devalue
Abwertung ['apve:ɐtʊŋ] F devaluation
abwickeln ['apvɪkln] VT close out
Abzug ['aptsu:k] M deduction
abzugsfähig ['aptsu:ksfɛ:ɪç] ADJ deductible
Abzugsfranchise ['abtsu:ksfrɛntʃaiz] F deductible
addieren [a'di:rən] VT foot
Agio ['a:ʒio] NT premium
Akquisition [akvizi'tsio:n] F acquisition
Akquisitionskosten [akvizi'tsio:nskɔstn] PL acquisition costs
Aktienbezugsrechtsschein [,aktsiənbə'tsu:ksrɛçtsʃain] M stock warrant
Aktiendividende ['aktsiəndivi,dɛndə] F stock dividend
Aktiengesellschaft ['aktsiəngə,zɛlʃaft] F public company
Aktienkapital ['aktsiənkapi,ta:l] NT share capital
Aktienoptionen ['aktsiən|op,tsio:nən] FPL stock options
Aktienrückkauf ['aktsiən'rʏkkauf] M share repurchase
Aktiensplit ['aktsiənʃplɪt] M stock split
Aktienzeichen ['aktsiən,tsaiçn] NT stock symbol
Aktienzertifikat ['aktsiəntsɛrtifi,ka:t] NT share certificate
Allokation [aloka'tsi:on] F allocation
Ambulantversicherung [ambu'lantfɛɐ,zɪçərʊŋ] F ambulance insurance
AMEX ['a:mɛks] F Amex
Amortisation [amɔrtiza'tsio:n] F amortization
amortisieren [amɔrti'zi:rən] VT amortize
Anfangsbestand ['anfaŋsbəʃtant] M beginning inventory
Anfangsgewinnmarge ['anfaŋsgə,vɪnmarʒə] F new business profit margin
angeben ['ange:bn] VT quote
Angebot ['angəbo:t] NT offer
Angebotspreis ['angəbo:tsprais] M ask
Anlagevermögen ['anla:gəfɐmø:gn] NT fixed assets
Anleihe ['anlaiə] F bond
Anleiheninhaber(in) ['anlaiən,|ɪnha:bɐ, 'anlaiən,|ɪnha:bərɪn] M(F) bondholder
Anleihezins ['anlaiətsɪns] M coupon rate
anpassen ['anpasn] VT adjust
Anreizrate ['anraits,ra:tə] F teaser rate
Anschaffungskosten ['anʃafʊŋskɔstn] PL prime cost
anspruchsberechtigt ['anʃprʊxsbə,rɛçtɪçt] ADJ eligible
Anspruchsberechtigte(r) ['anʃprʊxsbə,rɛçtɪçtɐ, 'anʃprʊxsbə,rɛçtɪçtə] MF beneficiary
Anspruchsberechtigung ['anʃprʊxsbə,rɛçtɪgʊŋ] F eligibility
Anteil ['antail] M share, stock
Anteile ['antailə] PL stock
anteilig ['antailɪç] ADJ pro rata
Anteilseigner(in) ['antails|aignɐ, 'antails|aignərɪn] M(F) shareholder
Anteilskapital ['antailskapi,ta:l] NT shareholders' equity
Antrag ['antra:k] M proposal
Antragsformular ['antra:ksfɔrmula:ɐ] NT proposal form
Antragsteller(in) ['antra:kʃtɛlɐ, 'antra:kʃtɛlərɪn] M(F) claimant, proposer
Anwartsschaftszeit ['anvartʃafts,tsait] F vesting
Arbeitsfähigkeit ['arbaitsfɛ:ɪçkait] F ability to work
Arbeitslohn ['arbaitslo:n] M wages
Arbeitslosenversicherung ['arbaitslo:znfɛɐ,zɪçərʊŋ] F unemployment insurance
Arbitrage [arbi'tra:ʒə] F arbitrage
Aufhebung ['aufhe:bʊŋ] F rescission
aufkaufen ['aufkaufn] VT buy out
aufrechnen ['aufrɛçnən] VT net, set off
Aufruhr ['aufru:ɐ] M riot
Auftrag ['auftra:k] M purchase order
Aufwandskonto ['aufvants,kɔnto] NT expense account
Augenheilkunde ['augnhailkʊndə] F vision care
Ausfall ['ausfal] M default
ausführen ['ausfy:rən] VT settle
Ausführungsdatum ['ausfy:rʊŋs,da:tʊm] NT settlement date
Ausgabekurs ['ausga:bekʊrs] M issue price
ausgesetzt ['ausgəzɛtst] ADJ exposed to
ausgleichen ['ausglaiçn] VT balance, balance an account
ausgliedern ['ausgli:dɐn] VT spin off
Auskunftei [auskʊnf'tai] F credit bureau
Ausschließung ['ausʃli:sʊŋ] F exclusion
Ausschüttung ['ausʃʏtʊŋ] F distribution
Außenstände ['ausnʃtɛndə] MPL receivables
außerordentlich [ausɐ'ɔrdntlɪç] ADJ extraordinary
ausstehend ['ausʃte:ənd] ADJ outstanding
Aussteuerversicherung ['ausʃtɔyɐfɛɐ,zɪçərʊŋ] F endowment policy
Ausübungskurs ['aus|y:bʊŋskʊrs] M exercise price
Ausverkauf ['ausfɛɐkauf] M selloff
auszahlen ['austsa:lən] VT/VI pay out
Auszahlung ['austsa:lʊŋ] F payout

Bb

Baissemanöver ['bɛ:səmanø:vɐ] NT bear raid
Baissemarkt ['bɛ:səmarkt] M bear market
Baisse-Spekulant(in) ['bɛ:səʃpeku,lant, 'bɛ:səʃpeku,lantɪn] M(F) bear
Ballonzahlung [ba'lõtsa:lʊŋ] F balloon payment
Bank [baŋk] F bank
Bankakzept ['baŋkak,tsɛpt] NT banker's acceptance
Bankkonto ['baŋkkɔnto] NT bank account
Bankpanik ['baŋkpa:nɪk] F run on a bank
bankrottgehen [baŋ'krɔtge:ən] VI go bust

Bankscheck ['baŋkʃɛk] M bank draft, cashier's cheque

Bankschließfach ['baŋkʃli:sfax] NT safe deposit box

Bankzinssatz ['baŋktsınszats] M prime rate

Bargeld ['ba:ɐgɛlt] NT cash

Barzahlungsrabatt ['ba:ɐtsa:lʊŋsra,bat] M cash discount

Basispunkt ['ba:zispʊŋkt] M basis point

Beerdigung [bə'|e:ɐdɪgʊŋ] F funeral

Beginn [bə'gɪn] M inception

behindert [bə'hɪndɐt] ADJ disabled

Beitrag ['baitra:k] M contribution, premium

Beitragsbefreiung ['baitra:ksbə,fraiʊŋ] F waiver of premium

beitragsbezogen ['baitra:ksbə,tso:gn] ADJ contributory

beitragsunabhängig [,baitra:ks'ʊnaphɛŋɪç] ADJ noncontributory

belasten [bə'lastn] VT debit

Belastung [bə'lastʊŋ] F charge, debit

Belegschaftsaktienfonds [bə'le:ktʃafts,|aktsiənfõ] M ESOP

berechnen [bə'rɛçnən] VT/VI charge

Bergung ['bɛrgʊŋ] F salvage

Bergungswert ['bɛrgʊŋsve:ɐt] M salvage

berichten [bə'rɪçtn] VT/VI report

Berichterstattung [bə'rɪçt|ɛɐʃtatʊŋ] F reporting

Berufsgruppe [bə'ru:fsgrʊpə] F occupational group

Berufshaftpflichtversicherung [bəru:fs'haftpflɪçtfɛɐ,zɪçərʊŋ] F professional liability insurance

Berufsrisiko [bə'rʊ:fsri:ziko] NT occupational hazard

Besitztümer [bə'zɪtsty:mɐ] NTPL possessions

Besitzurkunde [bə'zɪts|u:ɐkʊndə] F title

Bestandskonto [bə'ʃtantskɔnto] NT asset account, balance sheet account

Bestattungskosten [bə'ʃtatʊŋskɔstn] PL funeral expenses

bestellen [bə'ʃtɛlən] VT order

Bestellung [bə'ʃtɛlʊŋ] F order

Besteuerung [bə'ʃtɔyərʊŋ] F taxation

Bestimmung [bə'ʃtɪmʊŋ] F provision

Betrag [bə'tra:k] M amount

Betriebsaufwand [bə'tri:ps|aufvant] M operating expenses

Betriebsbudget [bə'tri:psb'dʒe:] NT operating cost

Betriebsertrag [bə'tri:ps|ɛɐtra:k] M operating income

Betriebsgewinn [bə'tri:psgəvɪn] M operating profit

Betriebskapital [bə'tri:pskapita:l] NT working capital

Betriebsunterbrechungsversicherung [bətri:ps|ʊntɐ'brɛçʊŋs-fɛɐzɪçərʊŋ] F business interruption insurance

Betrug [bə'tru:k] M fraud

betrügen [bə'try:gn] VT defraud

betrügerisch [bə'try:gərɪʃ] ADJ fraudulent

Bewertung [bə've:ɐtʊŋ] F valuation

BIC-Code [be:|i:'tse:ko:t] M BIC

Bilanz [bi'lants] F balance sheet

Bilanzgleichung [bi'lantsglaiçʊŋ] F balance sheet equation

Bilanzjahr [bi:lantsja:ɐ] NT financial year

binden ['bɪndn] VT peg

Bindung ['bɪndʊŋ] F retention

BIP ABK GDP

Blase ['bla:zə] F bubble

Blitz [blits] M lightning

Bodensenkung ['bo:dnzɛŋkʊŋ] F subsidence

Bonität [boni'tɛ:t] F credit rating

Bonus ['bo:nʊs] M bonus

Boom [bu:m] M boom

Börsengang ['bœrzngaŋ] M initial public offering

Brandstifter(in) ['brantʃtɪftɐ, 'brantʃtɪftərɪn] M(F) arsonist

Brandstiftung ['brantʃtɪftʊŋ] F arson

Broker(in) ['bro:kɐ, 'bro:kərɪn] M(F) broker

brutto ['brʊto] ADJ gross

brutto einnehmen VT gross

Bruttogewinn ['brʊtogəvin] M gross profit

Bruttogewinnmarge ['brʊtogə,vinmarʒə] F gross profit margin

Bruttoprämie ['brʊtoprɛ:miə] F gross premium

Bruttoprämien ['brʊtoprɛ:miən] FPL gross written premiums

BSP ABK GNP

Bücher ['by:çɐ] PL books

Bücher prüfen PHRS audit

Buchhaltung ['bu:xhaltʊŋ] F accounting, bookkeeping

Buchprüfer(in) ['bu:xpry:fɐ, 'bu:xpry:fərɪn] M(F) auditor

Buchprüfung ['bu:xpry:fʊŋ] F audit

Buchwert ['bu:xve:ɐt] M book value

Buchwertabschreibung ['bu:xve:ɐt,|apʃraibʊŋ] F book depreciation

Budget [bʏ'dʒe:] NT budget

budgetieren [bʏ'dʒe'ti:rən] VT/VI budget

Bürgerunruhen ['bʏrgɐ|ʊnru:ən] PL civil unrest

Cashflow ['kɛʃflo:] M cash flow

Cashflow-Bilanz ['kɛʃflo:bi,lants] F statement of cash flows

CHIPS [tʃɪps] ABK (= **Internes Abrechnungsszstem der New Yorker Banken**) CHIPS

cif [tsɪf] ABK CIF

Clearing ['kli:rɪŋ] NT clearing

Clearinghaus ['kli:rɪŋhaus] NT clearing house

COD ABK (= **Zahlung bei Lieferung**) COD

Contango [kɔn'taŋgo] M contango

Courtage [kʊr'ta:ʒə] F brokerage

Courtagekonto [kʊr'ta:ʒəkɔnto] NT brokerage account

CSO ABK CSO

Dachpolice ['daxpoli:sə] F umbrella policy

Darlehen ['da:ɐle:ən] NT loan

Dauerkonto ['dauɐkɔnto] NT permanent account

DCF ABK discounted cash flow

decken [dɛkn] VT cover

Deckung ['dɛkʊŋ] F cover

Deckungssumme ['dɛkʊŋszʊmə] F sum insured

Defizit ['de:fitsɪt] NT deficit

Demutualisierung [,demutuali'zi:rʊŋ] F demutualization

Deport [de'pɔrt] M backwardation

Depotbank [de'po:baŋk] F custodian bank

Derivat [deri'va:t] NT derivative

Devisenmarkt [de'vi:znmarkt] M forex

Diebstahl ['di:pʃta:l] M theft

Dienstleistung ['di:nstlaistʊŋ] F services

Dienstleistungsindustrie ['di:nstlaistʊŋs|ɪndʊs,tri:] F service industry

direkt [di'rɛkt] ADJ direct

Direkttransfer [di'rɛkttrans,fe:ɐ] M direct deposit

Direktversicherer [di'rɛktfɛɐ'zɪçərɐ] M direct insurer

disinvestieren ['dɪs|ɪnves'ti:rən] VT disinvest

Diskontsatz [dɪs'kɔntzats] M discount rate

Diversifikation [divɛrzifika'tsio:n] F diversification

Dividende [divi'dɛndə] F dividend

Dividenden [divi'dɛndən] PL dividends

Dread-Disease-Versicherung [drɛddɪ'zi:zfɛɐ,zɪçərʊŋ] F critical illness insurance

Dritte(r) ['drɪtɐ, 'drɪtə] MF third party

Ee

EBIT ['e:bɪt] NT (= **Ergebnis vor Zinsen und Steuern**) EBIT

EBITDA ['e:bɪtda] NT (= **Ergebnis vor Zinsen, Steuern und Abschreibungen**) EBITDA

Effizienzlinie [ɛfi'tsiɛntsli:niə] F efficient frontier

Ehegatte, Ehegattin ['e:əgatə, 'e:əgatɪn] M(F) spouse

Eigenbeteiligung ['aignbətailɪgʊŋ] F copay

Eigenkapital ['aignkapita:l] NT equity

Eigenkapitalkonto ['aignkapita:l,kɔnto] NT equity account

Eigenkapitalrendite ['aignkapita:lrɛn,di:tə] F return on equity

Eigentum ['aigntu:m] NT property

Eigentumswohnung ['aigntu:ms,vo:nʊŋ] F condominium

Einfachbuchführung ['ainfax,bu:xfy:rʊŋ] F single entry

eingeschränkt ['aingəʃrɛŋkt] ADJ restricted

Einkommen ['ainkɔmən] NT income, revenue

Einkommenskonto ['ainkɔməns,kɔnto] NT income account

Einkommensschutzversicherung ['ainkɔmənsʃʊtzfɛɐ,zɪçərʊŋ] F income protection insurance

Einkommenssteuer ['ainkɔmənsʃtɔyɐ] F income tax

Einkommensstrom ['ainkɔmənsʃtro:m] M revenue stream

Einlagenzertifikat ['ainla:gntsɛrtɪfɪ,ka:t] NT CD

Einlagerungsschein ['ainla:gərʊŋsʃain] M warehouse receipt

einlösen ['ainlø:zn] VT redeem

Einmalbeitragsversicherung ['ainma:l,baitra:ksfɛɐzɪçərʊŋ] F single premium insurance

Einnahmen ['ainna:mən] FPL receipts

eintragen ['aintra:gn] VT post

Eintragung ['aintra:gʊŋ] F entry

einzahlen ['aintsa:lən] VT/VI deposit

Einzahlungsschein ['aintsa:lʊŋsʃain] M deposit slip

Einzelhandels- ['aintsəlhandəls-] ADJ retail

Einzelprämie ['aintsəlprɛ:miə] F single premium

einziehen ['aintsi:ən] VT collect

Emissionsprospekt [emi'sio:nspros'pɛkt] M prospectus

Empfangsbestätigung [em'pfaŋsbəʃtɛ:tɪgʊŋ] F receiver

Entschädigung [ɛnt'ʃɛ:dɪgʊŋ] F indemnity

Erdbeben ['e:ɐtbe:bn] NT earthquake

Erdbebenversicherung ['e:ɐtbe:bnfɛɐ,zɪçərʊŋ] F earthquake coverage

Erdrutsch [e:ɐtrʊtʃ] M landslide

Erfahrungstafel [ɛɐ'fa:rʊŋsta:fl] F experience table

Ergänzungsversicherung [ɛɐ'gɛntsʊŋsfɛɐ,zɪçərʊŋ] F supplementary insurance

Erlös [ɛɐ'lø:s] M proceeds

Erlöschung [ɛɐ'lœʃʊŋ] F lapse

erstatten [ɛɐ'ʃtatn] VT refund, reimburse

Erstattung [ɛɐ'ʃtatʊŋ] F reimbursement

erstklassig ['e:ɐstklasɪç] ADJ prime

Erstversicherer ['e:ɐstfɛɐzɪçərɐ] M primary insurer

Ertragsbilanz [ɛɐ'tra:ksbi,lants] F income statement

erweitern [ɛɐ'vaitɐn] VT endorse

Etat [e'ta:] M budget

etatisieren [eta:i'zi:rən] VT/VI budget

ETF NT ETF

Eurodollars ['ɔyrodɔlars] MPL Eurodollars

Extradividende ['ekstradivi,dɛndə] F bonus

Exzedent [ekstse'dɛnt] M excess

EZB ABK ECB

Ff

Fabrik [fa'bri:k] F plant

Fahrerflucht ['fa:rɐflʊxt] F hit and run

fahrlässig ['fa:ɐlɛsɪç] ADJ negligent

Fahrlässigkeit ['fa:ɐlɛsɪçkait] F negligence

Fahrzeug ['fa:ɐtsɔyk] NT vehicle

Fahrzeugversicherung ['fa:ɐtsɔykfɛɐ,zɪçərʊŋ] F vehicle insurance

fakultativ ['fakʊltati:f] ADJ facultative

fällig ['fɛliç] ADJ mature

Fälligkeit ['fɛliçkait] F maturity

Fälligkeitstermin ['fɛliçkaitstɛɐmi:n] M due date

Fälligkeitswert ['fɛliçkaitsve:ɐt] M maturity value

falsch [falʃ] ADJ off

Fertigwaren ['fɛrtiçva:rən] FPL finished goods

festgesetzt ['fɛstgəzɛtst] ADJ adjusted

festsetzen ['fɛstzɛtsn] VT adjust

Festzinssatz ['fɛsttsɪntszats] M fixed rate

Feuerlöscher ['fɔyɐlœʃɐ] M fire extinguisher

Feuerversicherung ['fɔyɐfɛɐ,zɪçərʊŋ] F fire insurance

FICO ABK FICO

FIFO-Methode ['fi:fometo:də] F FIFO

Finanzausweis [fi'nants|ausvais] M financial statements

Finanzberater(in) [fi'nantsbəra:tɐ, fi'nantsbəra:tərɪn] M(F) financial adviser

Finanzierungskosten [finan'tsi:rʊŋskɔstn] PL finance charge

Finanzierungsleasing [finan'tsi:rʊŋs,li:zɪŋ] NT capital lease

Finanzinstrument [fi'nants|ɪnstru,mɛnt] NT financial instrument

Fixkosten ['fɪkskɔstn] PL fixed costs

Floater-Versicherung ['flo:tɐfɛɐ,zɪçərʊŋ] F floater

Flut [flu:t] F flood

Flutwasserversicherung ['flu:tvasɐfɛɐ,zɪçərʊŋ] F flood coverage

FOB-Bestimmungsort [,fɔbbə'ʃtɪmʊŋs|ɔrt] M FOB destination

FOB-Versandort [fɔbfɛɐ'zant|ɔrt] M FOB shipping point

Folgeschaden ['fɔlgəʃa:dn] M consequential loss

Fonds ['fõ] M fund

Fondsmanager(in) ['fõmɛnɛdʒɐ, 'fõmɛnɛdʒərɪn] M(F) fund manager

fordern ['fɔrdɐn] VT claim

Forderung ['fɔrdərʊŋ] F claim

Forderung ablehnen deny a claim

Forderungen ['fɔrdərʊŋən] FPL accounts receivable

Forderungseinzugsperiode [,fɔrdərʊŋs'|aintsu:ksperio:də] F receivables collection period

Forderungsumschlag ['fɔrdərʊŋs|ʊmʃla:k] M receivables turnover

Forderungsverkauf ['fɔrdərʊŋsfɛɐkauf] M factoring

Frachtbrief ['fraxtbri:f] M bill of lading

Franchise ['frɛntʃaiz] F franchise

FRB ABK FRB

fremdfinanzierte Übernahme LBO

Frühindikator ['fry:|ɪndi,ka:to:ɐ] M leading indicator

Führungskräfteversicherung ['fy:rʊŋskrɛftəfɛɐ,zɪçərʊŋ] F key man insurance

Fusion [fu:'zio:n] F merger

Fußnote ['fu:sno:tə] F footnotes

Gg

GAP-Versicherung ['gɛpfɛɐ,zɪçərʊŋ] F GAP insurance

Gatekeeper ['ge:tki:pɐ] M gatekeeper

Gebäudeversicherung [gə'bɔydəfɐ,zɪçərʊŋ] F residence insurance

Gefahr [gə'fa:ɐ] F peril

Gegenkonto ['ge:gnkɔnto] NT contra account

Gegenofferte ['ge:gn|ɔfɛrtə] F counteroffer

gegenwärtig ['ge:gnvɛrtɪç] ADJ current

Gegenwartswert ['ge:gnvartsve:ɐt] M net present value

Geldmarkt ['gɛltmarkt] M money market

Geldmenge ['gɛltmɛŋə] F money supply

Geldschöpfungsgewinn ['gɛltʃœpfʊŋsgəvɪn] M seigniorage

Gemeinkosten [gə'mainkɔstn] PL overhead

gemeinschaftlich [gə'mainʃaftlɪç] ADJ mutual

Gemeinschaftskonto [gə'mainʃafts,kɔnto] NT joint account

gemischte Lebensversicherung F endowment insurance

geprüfte Buchhalterin F CPA

geprüfter Buchhalter M CPA

Geschäftsbank [gə'ʃɛftsbaŋk] F commercial bank

Geschäftsjahr [gə'ʃɛftsja:ɐ] NT fiscal year

Geschäftsportfolio [gə'ʃɛftspɔrt,fo:lio] NT book of business

Geschäftszweig [gə'ʃɛftstsvaik] M line of business

Geschlecht [gə'ʃlɛçt] NT gender

Gesellschaft [gə'zɛlʃaft] F corporation

gesichert [gə'zɪçət] ADJ secured

Gesundheitsfragebogen [gə'zʊnthaits,fra:gəbo:gn] M health questionnaire

Gesundheitsschädigung [gə'zʊnthaitsʃɛ:digʊŋ] F impairment

Gewinn [gə'vɪn] M earnings, profit

Gewinne [gə'vɪnə] MPL gains

Gewinnmarge [gə'vinmarʒə] F operating margin

Gewinnschwelle [gə'vɪnʃvɛlə] F breakeven point

Gewinnspanne [gə'vinʃpanə] F margin, profit margin

Gewinnwarnung [gə'vinvarnʊŋ] F profit warning

Glasversicherung ['gla:sfɛɐ,zɪçərʊŋ] F plate glass insurance

Gläubiger ['glɔybɪgɐ] M creditor

GmbH ABK LLP

Goodwill [gʊd'vɪl] M goodwill

Gratisaktie ['gra:tɪs,|aktsiə] F bonus issue

Großhandels- ['gro:shandls] ADJ wholesale

Gründungskapital ['gr'ndʊŋskapita:l] NT seed money

Gutschein ['gu:tʃain] M voucher

gutschreiben ['gu:tʃraibn] VT credit

Gutschrift ['gu:tʃrɪft] F credit

Gutschriftsanzeige ['gu:tʃrɪfts,|antsaigə] F credit memo

Habenseite ['ha:bnzaitə] F credit side

haftbar ['haftba:ɐ] ADJ liable

Haftung ['haftʊŋ] F liability

Handelskonto ['handlskɔnto] NT merchant account

Händlergebühr ['hɛntlɐgəby:ɐ] F merchant fees

Händler(in) [hɛntlɐ, 'hɛntlərɪn] M(F) dealer

Hauptbuch ['hauptbu:x] NT general ledger, ledger

Hauseigentümer(in) ['haus,|aignty:mɐ, 'haus,|aignty:mərɪn] M(F) homeowner

Haushaltsdefizit ['haushaltsde:fitsɪt] NT government deficit

Hausratversicherung ['hausra:tfɛɐ,zɪçərʊŋ] F home insurance, renter's insurance

Haussemarkt ['ho:səmarkt] M bull market

Haussespekulant(in) ['ho:səʃpeku,lant, 'ho:səʃpeku,lantɪn] M(F) bull

Havariekommissar(in) [hava'ri:kɔmɪ'sa:ɐ, hava'ri:kɔmɪ'sa:rɪn] M(F) average adjuster

Hedgefonds ['hɛdʒfõ] M hedge fund

Heimfall ['haimfal] M escheat

hochrechnen ['ho:xrɛçnən] VT gross up

Holdinggesellschaft ['ho:ldɪŋgə,zɛlʃaft] F holding company

Huckepackinvestment ['hʊkəpak|ɪn,vɛstmənt] NT piggyback investing

Hypothekenversicherung [hypo'te:knfɛɐ,zɪçərʊŋ] F mortgage insurance

IBAN ABK IBAN

immateriell ['immate,riɛl] ADJ intangible

Immobilie [ɪmo'bi:liə] F real estate

Immobilienverbindlichkeiten [ɪmo'bi:liənfɛɐ,bɪntlɪçkaitn] FPL real estate liability

Immobilienverrentung [ɪmo'bi:liənfɛɐ,rɛntʊŋ] F reversion

Immobilienversicherung [ɪmo'bi:liənfɛɐ,zɪçərʊŋ] F real estate insurance

Index ['ɪndeks] M index

indexgebunden ['ɪndeksgə,bʊndn] ADJ index-linked

indirekt ['ɪndirɛkt] ADJ indirect

Inflation [infla'tsio:n] F inflation

Insiderhandel ['ɪnsaidɐhandl] M insider trading

insolvent ['ɪnzɔlvɛnt] ADJ insolvent

Insolvenz ['ɪnzɔlvɛnts] F bankruptcy, insolvency

Institution [ɪnstitu'tsio:n] F institution

Interbankrate ['ɪntɐbaŋkra:tə] F interbank rate

Invaliditätsversicherung [ɪnvalidi'tɛ:tsfɛɐ,zɪçərʊŋ] F disability insurance

Inventar [ɪnvɛn'ta:ɐ] F inventory

investieren [ɪnvɛs'ti:rən] VT/VI invest

Investitionsaufwand [ɪnvɛsti'tsio:ns|aufvant] M capital expenditure

Investitionsaufwendungen [ɪnvɛsti'tsio:ns,|aufvɛndʊŋən] PL capital expense

Investitionsrendite [ɪnvɛsti'tsio:nsrɛndi:tə] F return on investment

Investment [ɪn'vɛstmənt] NT investment

Investmentbank [ɪn'vɛstməntbaŋk] F investment bank

Investmentfonds [ɪn'vɛstməntfõ] M mutual fund, unit trust

IRA ABK (= **individueller Pensionsplan in den USA**) IRA

IRS ABK (= **größte US-Steuerbehörde**) IRS

ISIN ABK ISIN

IWF ABK IMF

Jj

Jahresbericht ['ja:rəsbərɪçt] M annual report

Jahresende [,ja:rəs'|ɛndə] NT year end

Jointventure [dʒɔynt'vɛntʃɐ] NT joint venture

Journal [ʒʊr'na:l] NT journal

Journalbuchung [ʒʊr'na:lbu:xʊŋ] F journal entry

Kk

Kalenderjahr [ka'lɛndɐja:ɐ] NT calendar year

Kapital [kapi'ta:l] NT capital

Kapitalerstattung [kapi'ta:l|ɛɐ,ʃtatʊŋ] F return of capital

Kapitalertrag [kapita:l|ɛɐ,tra:k] FPL capital gains; M return on capital

kapitalisieren [kapitalɪ'zi:rən] VT capitalize

Kapitalisierung [kapitalɪ'zi:rʊŋ] F capitalization

Kapitalkonto [kapi'ta:lkɔnto] NT capital account

Kapitalkosten [kapi'ta:lkɔstn] PL cost of capital

Kapitalsumme [kapi'ta:lzʊmə] F principal

Kapitalumschlagsratio [kapita:l'|ʊmʃla:ks,ra:tsio] F asset turnover ratio

Kapitalverlust [kapita:lfɐlʊst] M capital loss

Kapitalzuwachs [kapi'ta:ltsu:vaks] M capital gain

Karenzzeit [ka'rɛntstsait] F waiting period

kartellrechtlich [kar'tɛlrɛçtlɪç] ADJ antitrust

Kaskoversicherung [kaskofɛɐ,zɪçərʊŋ] F collision coverage

Kassakurs ['kasakʊrs] M spot rate

Kassamarkt ['kasamarkt] M spot market

Kassapreis ['kasaprais] M spot price

Kassenbuch ['kasnbu:x] NT cash book

Katastrophenexzedent [katas'tro:fn|ɛkstse,dɛnt] M catastrophe excess of loss

Kaufangebot ['kauf,|angəbo:t] NT bid

Kaufhauptbuch [kauf'hauptbu:x] NT purchase ledger

Kaufoption ['kauf|ɔptsio:n] F call

klassifizieren [klasifitsi:rən] VT classify

Kollektivversicherung [kɔlɛk'ti:ffɛɐ,zɪçərʊŋ] F group insurance

kollidieren [kɔli'di:rən] VT collide with

Kommanditgesellschaft [kɔman'di:tgə,zɛlʃaft] F limited partnership

Kommunalanleihe [kɔmʊ'na:l|anlaiə] F muni bonds

Konditionsvereinbarung [kɔndɪ'tsio:nsfɛɐ,|ainba:rʊŋ] F term sheet

Konkurs [kɔŋ'kʊrs] M bankruptcy

Konsignation [kɔnzigna'tsio:n] F consignment

Kontenplan ['kɔntnpla:n] NT chart of accounts

Konto ['kɔnto] NT account

Kontoabstimmung ['kɔnto,|apʃtɪmʊŋ] F bank reconciliation

Kontoauszug ['kɔnto,|austsu:k] M bank statement, statement

Kontostand ['kɔntoʃtant] M balance

kontrollieren [kɔntrɔ'li:rən] VT control

Konvertierung [kɔnvɛr'ti:rʊŋ] F translation

Körperbehinderung ['kœrpɐbə,hɪndərʊŋ] F physical impairment

Körperschaft ['kœrpɐʃaft] F entity

Körperverletzung ['kœrpɐfɛɐ,lɛtsʊŋ] F bodily injury

Korrespondenzbank [kɔrɛspɔn'dɛntsbaŋk] F correspondent bank

Kosten ['kɔstn] NT expense

kosten ['kɔstn] VT/VI cost

Kostenrechnung ['kɔstnrɛçnʊŋ] F cost accounting

Kostenstelle ['kɔstnʃtɛlə] F cost centre

Kostenvoranschlag [,kɔstn'fo:ɐ|anʃla:k] M quote

Kraftfahrzeugunfall ['kraftfa:ɐtsɔyk,|ʊnfal] M MVA

Kraftfahrzeugversicherung ['kraftfa:ɐtsɔykfɛɐ,zɪçərʊŋ] F automobile insurance

Kreditbrief [kre'di:tbri:f] M letter of credit

Kreditfinanzierung [kre'di:tfinantsi:rʊŋ] F margin

Kreditgenossenschaft [kre'di:tgənɔsnʃaft] F credit union

Kreditkartenversicherung [kre'di:tkartnfɛɐ,zɪçərʊŋ] F credit card insurance

Kreditklausel [kre'di:tklauzl] F debt covenant

Kreditlinie [kre'di:tli:niə] F line of credit

Kreditrisiko [kre'di:tri:ziko] NT credit risk

Kredit-Score [kre'di:tsko:ɐ] M credit score

Kredit-Swap [kre'di:tsvɔp] M credit swap

Kreditversicherung [kre'di:tfɛɐzɪçərʊŋ] F PMI

kumulativ [kumula'ti:f] ADJ cumulative

Kunde, Kundin ['kʊndə, 'kʊndɪn] M(F) customer

Kursanzeiger ['kʊrs,|antsaigɐ] M ticker

Kursgewinnverhältnis [kʊrsgə'vɪnfɐhɛltnɪs] NT price earnings ratio

Ll

Lagerbestand ['la:gɐbəʃtant] M stock

Lagerhaltungskosten ['la:gɐhaltʊŋs,kɔstn] PL carrying charge

Lagerhaus ['la:gɐhaus] NT warehouse

Lagerumschlag ['la:gɐ,|ʊmʃla:k] M inventory turnover

Langlebigkeit ['laŋle:bɪçkait] F longevity

Lastschrift ['lastʃrift] F direct debit

Laufzeit ['lauftsait] F maturity

Leasinggeber(in) ['li:zɪŋge:bɐ, 'li:zɪŋge:bərin] M(F) lessor

Lebensdauerrisiko ['le:bnsdauɐ,ri:ziko] F longevity risk

Lebensversicherung ['le:bnsfɛɐ,zɪçərʊŋ] F life insurance

Leistungen ['laistʊŋən] FPL benefits

Leverage ['li:vərɪdʒ] NT leverage

LIBOR ['li:bo:ɐ] ABK LIBOR

Lieferant [lifə'rant] M supplier

Liegenschaften ['li:gnʃaftn] FPL real property

LIFO-Methode ['li:fome,to:də] F LIFO

Linie ['li:niə] F line

Liquidationskurs [likvida'tsio:nskʊrs] M settlement price

Liquidität [likvidi'tɛ:t] F liquidity

Listenpreis ['lɪstnprais] M list price

Lizenz [li'tsɛnts] F licence

lizenziert [litsɛn'tsi:ɐt] ADJ licensed

LLC ABK LLC

Lockbox ['lɔkbɔks] F lockbox

Lohn [lo:n] M salary

Lorokonto ['lo:rokɔnto] NT vostro account

LTV ABK LTV

Luftfahrtversicherung ['lʊftfa:ɐtfɛɐ,zɪçərʊŋ] F aviation insurance

Mm

Markt [markt] M market

Marktkapitalisierung ['marktkapitali,zi:rʊŋ] F market cap

materiell [mate'riɛl] ADJ tangible

Mehrkosten ['me:ɐkɔstn] PL cost overrun

Mehrwert ['me:ɐve:ɐt] M value added

Mieter(in) ['mi:tɐ, 'mi:tərɪn] M(F) renter, tenant

Mindestangebot ['mɪndəst,|angəbo:t] NT stalking horse

Mittel ['mɪtl] PL funds

Mitversicherer ['mɪtfɛɐ,zɪçərɐ] M coinsurer

mitversichern [mɪtfɛɐ,zɪçɐn] VT coinsure

Mitversicherung ['mɪtfɛɐ,zɪçərʊŋ] F coinsurance

Modifikation [modifika'tsio:n] F modification

Morbiditätstafel [mɔrbidi'tɛ:tsta:fl] F morbidity table

Nn

nachdatieren ['na:xdati:rən] VT postdate

Nachfragekurve [na:xfra:gə,kʊrvə] F demand curve

Nachlass ['na:xlas] M estate

nachrangig ['na:xraŋɪç] ADJ subordinated

Nachschussforderung ['na:xʃʊs,fɔrdərʊŋ] F margin call

Nachtrag ['na:xtra:k] M endorsement

NAFTA ['nafta] ABK (= **Nordamerikanische Freihandelsvereinbarung**) NAFTA

NASDAQ ['nasdak] ABK (= **automatisierte elektronische Börse in den USA, wo vor allem Technologieunternehmen gehandelt werden**) NASDAQ

Nationalbank [natsio'na:lbaŋk] F national bank

Naturkatastrophe [na'tu:ɐkatastro:fə] F natural catastrophe

Nennbetrag ['nɛnbətra:k] M face value, par value

netto ['nɛto] ADJ net

Nettoabsatz ['nɛto,|apzats] M net sales

Nettogewinn ['nɛtogə,vɪn] M net income

Nettoinventarwert [,nɛto|ɪnvɛn'ta:ɐve:ɐt] M net asset value

Nettorealisationswert [,nɛtorealiza'tsio:nsve:ɐt] M net realizable value

Nettoverdienst ['nɛtofɛɐdi:nst] M net earnings

Nettoverlust ['nɛtofɛɐlʊst] M net loss

Nettovermögen ['nɛtofɛɐmø:gn] NT net assets

Nettowert ['nɛtove:ɐt] M book value

Neugeschäft ['nɔygəʃɛft] NT new business

Neugründung ['nɔygrʏndʊŋ] F startup

Neuwertversicherung ['nɔyve:ɐtfɛɐ,zɪçərʊŋ] F replacement cost insurance

Niederstwert ['ni:dɐstve:ɐt] M lower of cost or market

Nominalwert [nomi'na:lve:ɐt] M face value

Normalkosten [nɔr'ma:lkɔstn] PL standard cost

Nostro-Konto ['nɔstro,kɔnto] NT nostro account

Notaufnahme ['no:t|aufna:mə] F emergency room

Notierung [no'ti:rʊŋ] F quote

Oo

offenlegen ['ɔfnle:gn] VT disclose

Offenlegung ['ɔfnle:gʊŋ] F disclosure

Operation [opəra'tsio:n] F operation

Opportunitätskosten [ɔpɔrtuni'tɛ:tskɔstn] PL opportunity cost

Option [ɔp'tsio:n] F option

Orkan [ɔr'ka:n] M hurricane

Pp

Pacht [paxt] F lease

pachten [paxtn] VT lease

Pächter(in) ['pɛçtɐ, 'pɛçtərɪn] M(F) lessee

Packzettel ['paktsɛtl] M packing slip

Papierdokument [pa'pi:ɐdoku,mɛnt] NT hard copy

Parikurs ['pa:rikʊrs] M par

Paritätsrate [pari'tɛ:tsra:tə] F cross rate

partizipierend [partitsi'pi:rənt] ADJ participating

Passivkonto ['pasi:fkɔnto] NT liability account

Peg-Ratio ['pɛkra:tsio] F peg ratio

Pensionsfonds [pã'zio:nsfõ] M pension fund

Personengesellschaft [pɛr'zo:nəngə,zɛlʃaft] F partnership

Personenschaden [pɛr'zo:nənʃa:dn] M personal injury

Personenschadenversicherung [pɛr'zo:nənʃa:dnfɛɐ,zɪçərʊŋ] F personal injury insurance

Pfandrecht ['pfantrɛçt] NT lien

Pfennigaktie ['pfɛnɪç,|aktsiə] F penny stocks

PIN [pɪn] ABK PIN

PITI ABK PITI

Plan [pla:n] M plan

Police [po'li:sə] F policy

Portfolio [pɔrt'fo:lio] NT portfolio

Portokasse ['pɔrtokasə] F petty cash

Posten ['pɔstn] M item

PPACA ABK (= **US-Gesetz zur Regelung des Zugangs zur Krankenversicherung**) PPACA

Prämienbeiträge ['prɛ:miən,baitrɛ:gə] MPL premium income

Prämienfestsetzung ['prɛ:miən,fɛstzɛtsʊŋ] F experience rating

Preis [prais] M price

Preisangebot ['prais|angəbo:t] NT quote

Preisgleitklausel ['praisglait,klauzl] F escalation

private Krankenversicherung F PMI

Privathaftpflichtversicherung [pri'va:thaftpflɪçtfɛɐ,zɪçərʊŋ] F personal liability insurance

Privatplatzierung [pri'va:tplatsi:rʊng] F private placement

Probebilanz ['pro:bəbi,lants] F trial balance

Produkt [pro'dʊkt] NT product

Produkthaftpflichtversicherung [pro'dʊkthaftpflɪçtfɛɐ,zɪçərʊŋ] F product liability insurance

Produktion [prodʊk'tsio:n] F manufacturing, production

Produktkosten [pro'dʊktkɔstn] PL product costs

Profitcenter ['prɔfitsentɐ] NT profit centre

pro forma ADJ pro forma

Prognose [pro'gno:zə] F forecast

Provision [provi'zio:n] F commission

prüfen ['pry:fn] VT check, control

Prüfungspfad ['pry:fʊŋspfa:t] M audit trail

Quittung ['kvɪtʊŋ] F receipt

Quotenrückversicherung [kvo:tn'rʏkfɛɐzɪçərʊŋ] F quota share reinsurance

Ramschanleihe ['ramʃ|anlaiə] F junk bonds

Rechnung ['rɛçnʊŋ] F bill, invoice

Rechnung ausstellen PHRS bill

Rechnungsabgrenzungsposten [,rɛçnʊŋs'|apgrɛntsʊŋspɔstn] M prepaid expense

Rechtsschutzversicherung ['rɛçtsʃʊtsfɛɐ,zɪçərʊŋ] F legal expenses insurance

refinanzieren [re:finan'tsi:rən] VT/VI refinance

Register [re'gɪstɐ] NT register

Regress [re'grɛs] M subrogation

Reingewinn ['raingəvɪn] M net profit

Reiseversicherung ['raizəfɛɐ,zɪçərʊŋ] F travel insurance

Rendite [rɛn'di:tə] F rate of return, return, yield

Rentabilität [rɛntabili'tɛ:t] F profitability

Rentenalter ['rɛntn|altɐ] NT retirement age

Rentenempfänger(in) ['rɛntnɛm,pfɛŋɐ, 'rɛntnɛm,pfɛŋərɪn] M(F) annuitant

Rentensatz ['rɛntnzats] M annuity rate

Rentenversicherung ['rɛntnfɛɐ,zɪçərʊŋ] F annuity

Reserven [re'zɛrvn] FPL reserve

Restschuldenversicherung ['rɛstʃʊldnfɛɐ,zɪçərʊŋ] F residual debt insurance

Retrozession [retrotse'sio:n] F retrocession

Rettungspaket ['rɛtʊŋspake:t] NT bailout

Rezession [retsɛ'sio:n] F recession

Risiko ['ri:ziko] NT exposure, hazard, risk

Risiko ausschließen PHRS exclude a risk

Risikokapital ['ri:zikokapita:l] NT venture capital

Risikokapitalgeber(in) ['ri:zikokapita:lge:bɐ, 'ri:zikokapita:lge:bərɪn] M(F) angel, venture capitalist

Risikolebensversicherung ['ri:zikole:bnsfɛɐ,zɪçərʊŋ] F term insurance

Risikomanagement ['ri:ziko,mɛnɛdʒmənt] NT risk management

Risiko managen PHRS manage a risk

Risikomanager(in) ['ri:ziko,mɛnɛdʒɐ, 'ri:ziko,mɛnɛdʒərɪn] M(F) risk manager

Risikopoolung ['ri:zikopu:lʊŋ] F pool a risk, risk pooling

Risikoprüfer(in) ['ri:zikopry:fɐ, 'ri:zikopry:fərɪn] M(F) financial underwriter

Risikoselbstbehalt [,ri:ziko'zɛlpstbəhalt] M retention of risk

Risikoübernahme ['ri:ziko,|y:bɐna:mə] F assumption of risk

Risikoübernahmen [ri:ziko,|y:bɐna:mən] PL financial underwriting

Risikoumtauschversicherung [,ri:ziko'|ʊmtauʃfɛɐzɪçərʊŋ] F convertible term insurance

Rohmaterialien ['ro: mate,ria:liən] PL raw materials

Rohstoff ['ro:ʃtɔf] M commodity

RSU ABK RSU

RTGS ABK RTGS

RTN ABK RTN

Rückbelastung ['rʏkbəlastʊŋ] F chargeback

rückdatieren ['rʏkdati:rən] VT backdate

rückführen ['rʏkfy:rən] VT/VI repatriate

Rückführung ['rʏkfy:rʊŋ] F repatriation

Rückführungskosten ['rʏkfy:rʊŋs,kɔstn] PL repatriation expenses

Rückkaufwert ['rʏkkaufve:ɐt] M surrender value

Rücklagen ['rʏkla:gn] FPL reserves

Rückstände ['rʏkʃtɛndə] MPL arrears

Rückstellung ['rʏkʃtɛlʊŋ] F provision

rücktragen ['rʏktra:gn] VT carry back

Rückversicherer ['rʏkfɛɐzɪçərɐ] M reinsurer

rückversichern ['rʏkfɛɐzɪçən] VT reinsure

Rückversicherung ['rʏkfɛɐzɪçərʊŋ] F reinsurance

Rückversicherungsvertrag ['rʏkfɛɐzɪçərʊŋsfɛɐˌtra:k] F reinsurance treaty

rückwirkend ['rʏkvɪrknt] ADJ retroactive

Rückzahlung ['rʏktsa:lʊŋ] F rebate

Ruhestand ['ru:əʃtant] M retirement

Ruheständler(in) ['ru:əʃtɛntlɐ, 'ru:əʃtɛntlərɪn] M(F) retiree

Ss

Sachanlagen ['zax|anla:gn] FPL PPE

Sachversicherung ['zaxfɛɐzɪçərʊŋ] F general insurance

Saldenübertrag ['zaldn,|y:bɐtra:k] M balance transfer

Sammeljournal ['zamlʒʊrˌna:l] NT general journal

Sammelkonto ['zamlkɔnto] NT control account

Sammelversicherungsrabatt ['zamlfɛɐzɪçərʊŋsraˌbat] M fleet rate

Schaden ['ʃa:dn] M damage, loss

Schadenfall ['ʃa:dnfal] M loss

Schadenmeldeformular ['ʃa:dnmɛldəfɔrmuˌla:ɐ] NT claim form

Schadenquote ['ʃa:dnkvo:tə] F loss ratio

Schadenregulierer(in) ['ʃa:dnreguli:rɐ, 'ʃa:dnreguli:rərɪn] M(F) loss adjuster

Schadensermittler(in) ['ʃa:dns|ɛɐˌmɪtlɐ, 'ʃa:dns|ɛɐˌmɪtlərɪn] M(F) claims investigator

Schadensersatz ['ʃa:dns|ɛɐˌzats] M compensation

Schadensmeldung ['ʃa:dnsmɛldʊŋ] F claims notification

Schadensquote ['ʃa:dnskvo:tə] F claims ratio

Schatzamt ['ʃats|amt] NT Treasury

Schätzer(in) ['ʃɛtsɐ, 'ʃɛtsərɪn] M(F) appraiser

Schätzung ['ʃɛtsʊŋ] F appraisal

Scheck [ʃɛk] M check

Scheckausgangsbuch [ʃɛk'ausgaŋsbu:x] NT cheque register

Scheck-Kontrollabschnitt [ʃɛkkɔn'trɔl|apʃnɪt] M check stub

Scheingeschäft ['ʃaingəʃɛft] NT wash sale

Schiedsverfahren ['ʃi:tsfɛɐfa:rən] NT arbitration

Schlussbestand ['ʃlʊsbəʃtant] M ending inventory

Schuld [ʃʊlt] F debt

Schuldenerlass ['ʃʊldn|ɛɐˌlas] M debt relief

Schuldenswap ['ʃʊldnsvɔp] M debt swap

Schuldner(in) ['Suldnɐ, 'ʃʊldnərɪn] M(F) debtor

Schuldschein ['ʃʊltʃain] M promissory note

Schuldverschreibung ['ʃʊltfɛɐʃraibʊŋ] F debenture

Schutzvorrichtung ['ʃʊtsfo:ɐˌrɪçtʊŋ] F safety device

schwer [ʃve:ɐ] ADJ severe

Schwere ['ʃve:rə] F severity

Schwerstbehinderungsklausel ['ʃve:ɐstbəhɪndərʊŋsˌklauzl] F disability clause

SEC ABK (= **US-Wertpapier- und Börsenaufsichtsbehörde**) SEC

Seetransportversicherung ['ze:transpɔrtfɛɐˌzɪçərʊŋ] F marine insurance

Seeversicherung ['ze:fɛɐˌzɪçərʊŋ] F ocean marine insurance

Sekundärmarkt [zekʊn'dɛ:ɐmarkt] M aftermarket

Selbstversicherungsgesellschaft ['zɛlpstfɛɐˌzɪçərʊŋsgəzɛlʃaft] F captive

senken ['zɛŋkn] VT mark down

Serienanleihe ['ze:riən,|anlaiə] F serial bonds

Sicherheitsgurt ['zɪçɐhaitsgʊrt] M safety belt

sichern ['zɪçɐn] VT/VI hedge

Sicherungsgegenstand ['zɪçərʊŋsˌge:gnʃtant] M collateral

Sollseite ['zɔlzaitə] F debit side, normal balance

SOX ABK SOX

Sparkonto ['ʃpa:ɐkɔnto] NT savings account

Spätindikator ['ʃpɛ:t|ɪndika:to:ɐ] M lagging indicator

Spekulation [ʃpekula'tsio:n] F speculation

Spesen ['ʃpe:zn] PL expenses

Spesenkonto ['ʃpe:znkɔnto] NT expense account

Sponsor(in) ['ʃpɔnzɐ, ʃpɔn'zo:rɪn] M(F) backer

Spread [sprɛd] M spread

Staatsanleihe ['ʃta:tsˌ|anlaiə] F sovereign debt

Staatsschuld ['ʃta:tsʃʊlt] F national debt

Stammaktie ['ʃtam|aktsiə] F common stock

Stammkapital ['ʃtamkapita:l] NT capital stock

Startkapital ['ʃtartkapita:l] NT seed capital

Sterbekasse ['ʃtɛrbəkasə] F funeral plan

Sterbetafel ['ʃtɛrbəta:fl] F mortality table

Sterblichkeitsrate ['ʃtɛrplɪçkaitsˌra:tə] F mortality rate

Sterblichkeitstafel ['ʃtɛrplɪçkaitsˌta:fl] F life table

Steuer ['ʃtɔyɐ] F tax

Steuerabzug ['ʃtɔyɐˌ|aptsu:k] M tax deduction

Steuerbegünstigung ['ʃtɔyɐbəˌgynstɪgʊŋ] F tax shelter

Steuererklärung ['ʃtɔyɐ|ɛrklɛ:rʊŋ] F tax return

Steuererleichterung ['ʃtɔyɐ|ɛɐˌlaiçtərʊŋ] F tax relief

Steuerferien ['ʃtɔyɐfe:riən] PL tax holiday

steuerfrei ['ʃtɔyɐfrai] ADJ tax exempt

Steuerhinterziehung ['ʃtɔyɐhɪntɐˌtsi:ʊŋ] F tax evasion

Steuerjahr ['ʃtɔyɐja:ɐ] NT tax year

Steueroase ['ʃtɔyɐ|o,a:zə] F tax haven

steuerpflichtig ['ʃtɔyɐpflɪçtɪç] ADJ taxable

Steuerrückzahlung ['ʃtɔyɐrʏktsa:lʊŋ] F tax refund

Steuersatz ['ʃtɔyɐzats] M tax rate

Steuerverlustabzug [ʃtɔyɐfɛɐ'lʊst|aptsu:k] M tax loss

Steuervermeidung ['ʃtɔyɐfɛɐˌmaidʊŋ] F tax avoidance

Stichzeit ['ʃtɪçtsait] F cutoff time

Störung ['ʃtø:rʊŋ] F disorder

Summe ['zʊmə] F footing

Summenexzedenten ['zʊmən|ɛkstseˌdɛntn] PL surplus reinsurance

Summenzuwachs ['zʊməntsu:vaks] M reversionary bonus

Swap [svɔp] M swap

Swaption ['svɔpʃn] M swaption

SWIFT [svɪft] ABK SWIFT

Syndikat [s'ndi'ka:t] NT syndicate

Tt

Tarif [ta'ri:f] F charge

teilweise ['tailvaizə] ADJ partial

Teilzahlungsverkauf ['tai;tsa:lʊŋsfɛɐ,kauf] M instalment sales

Termineinlage [tɛɐ'mi:n|ainla:gə] F time deposit

Termingeschäft [tɛɐ'mi:ngəʃɛft] NT futures

Terminkontrakt [tɛɐ'mi:nkɔn,trakt] M forward contracts

Terminkurs [tɛɐ'mi:nkʊrs] M forward rate

Testament [tɛsta'mɛnt] NT will

Tilgungsfonds ['tɪlgʊŋsfõ] M sinking fund

T-Konto ['te:kɔnto] NT T account

Tochtergesellschaft ['tɔxtɐgə,zɛlʃaft] F subsidiary

Todesfallleistung ['to:dəsfal,laistʊŋ] F death benefits

Tontine [tɔnti:nə] F tontine

Tornado [tɔr'na:do] M tornado

Totalschaden [to'ta:lʃa:dn] M total loss

Tracker ['trɛkɐ] M tracker

Tracker-Fonds ['trɛkɐfõ] M tracker fund

Tranche ['trãʃə] F tranche

Transaktion [trans|ak'tsio:n] F transaction

Transportdokumente [trans'pɔrtdoku,mɛntə] PL shipping documents

Treuhand ['trɔyhant] F trust

Treuhänder(in) ['trɔyhɛndɐ, 'trɔyhɛndərɪn] M(F) fiduciary, trustee

Treuhandkonto ['trɔyhant,kɔnto] NT trust account

Treuhandverwahrung ['trɔyhantfɛɐva:rʊŋ] F escrow

Tsunami [tsu'na:mi] M tsunami

Uu

Überbrückungskredit [y:bɐ'brʏkʊŋskredi:t] M bridging loan

übereinstimmen [y:bɐ'|ainʃtɪmən] VT/VI agree

überfällig ['y:bɐfɛlɪç] ADJ past due

Übergangsperiode ['y:bɐgaŋspe'rio:də] F deferred period

überhöht [y:bɐ'hø:t] ADJ overstated

überleben [y:bɐ'le:bn] VT/VI survive

überlebend [y:bɐ'le:bnt] ADJ surviving

Übernahmeangebot ['y:bɐna:mə,|angəbo:t] NT tender offer

übernehmen [y:bɐ'ne:mən] VT underwrite

überprüfbar [y:bɐ'pry:fba:ɐ] ADJ reviewable

Überschuss ['y:bɐʃʊs] M surplus

übertragbar [y:bɐ'tra:kba:ɐ] ADJ negotiable

Übertragbarkeit [y:bɐ'tra:kba:ɐkait] F portability

übertragen [y:bɐ'tra:gn] VT bring forward, carry forward

überversichert ['y:bɐfɛɐ,zɪçɐt] ADJ overinsured

überweisen [y:bɐ'vaizn] VT remit

Überweisungsanzeige [y:bɐ'vaizʊŋs,|antsaigə] F remittance advice

überzogen [y:bɐ'tso:gn] ADJ overlimit

umbuchen ['ʊmbu:xn] VT reclassify

umfassend [ʊm'fasnt] ADJ comprehensive

Umkehrhypothek ['ʊmke:ɐhypote:k] F reverse mortgage

Umlaufvermögen ['ʊmlauffɐmø:gn] NT current assets

Umsatz ['ʊmzats] M turnover

Umsatzergebnis ['ʊmzats|ɛɐge:pnɪs] NT sales revenue

Umsatzkosten ['ʊmzatskɔstn] PL cost of goods sold

Umschuldung ['ʊmʃʊldʊŋ] F debt restructuring

umwandeln ['ʊmvandln] VT commute

unausgeglichen ['ʊn|ausgə,glɪçn] ADJ unbalanced

uneingeschränkt ['ʊn|aingəʃrɛŋt] ADJ unrestricted

Unfall ['ʊnfal] M crash

Unfallopfer ['ʊnfal|ɔpfɐ] NT casualty

Unfallversicherung ['ʊnfalfɛɐ,zɪçərʊŋ] F accident insurance

ungesichert ['ʊngəzɪçɐt] ADJ unsecured

ungültig ['ʊng'ltɪç] ADJ void

unterbewertet ['ʊntɐbə,veɐtət] ADJ understated

Untermietvertrag ['ʊntɐmi:tfɛɐ,tra:k] M sublease

Unternehmens- [ʊntɐ'ne:məns-] ADJ corporate

Unterstützung [ʊntɐ'ʃt'tsʊŋ] F backing

untervergeben ['ʊntɐfɐge:bn] VT subcontract

unterversichert ['ʊntɐfɐ,zɪçət] ADJ underinsured

unterzeichnen [ʊntɐ'tsaiçnən] VT endorse

unversicherbar [ʊnfɐ'zɪçəba:ɐ] ADJ uninsurable

unversichert ['ʊnfɐzɪçɐt] ADJ uninsured

veranschlagen [fɛɐ'|anʃla:gn] VT budget for

Verbindlichkeiten [fɛɐ'bɪntlɪçkaitn] FPL accounts payable; PL liabilities

Verbindlichkeitserklärung [fɛɐ'bɪntlɪçkaits|ɛɐ,klɛ:rʊŋ] F note payable

verbuchen [fɛɐ'bu:xn] VT book, recognize

Vereinbarung [fɛɐ'|ainba:rʊŋ] F agreement

verkaufen [fɛɐ'kaufn] VT surrender

Verkäufer(in) [fɛɐ'kɔyfɐ, fɛɐ'kɔyfərɪn] M(F) vendor

Verkaufsbeleg [fɛɐ'kaufsbəle:k] M sales slip

Verkaufserlös [fɛɐ'kaufs|ɛɐlø:s] M gain on sale

Verkaufsjournal [fɛɐ'kaufsʒʊrna:l] NT sales ledger

Verkaufsoption [fɛɐ'kaufs|ɔp,tsio:n] F put

Verkaufsspesen [fɛɐ'kaufsʃpe:zn] PL selling expenses

Verkaufsurkunde [fɛɐ'kaufs|,u:ɐkʊndə] F bill of sale

Verkaufsverlust [fɛɐ'kaufsfɛɐlʊst] M loss on sale

verlängern [fɛɐ'lɛŋɐn] VT renew

Verlängerung [fɛɐ'lɛŋərʊŋ] F renewal

Verlängerungsdatum [fɛɐ'lɛŋərʊŋs,da:tʊm] NT renewal date

Verlust [fɛɐ'lʊst] M loss

Verluste [fɛɐ'lʊstə] MPL losses

Vermittler(in) [fɛɐ'mɪtlɐ, fɛɐ'mɪtlərɪn] M(F) intermediary

Vermögensrendite [fɛɐ'mø:gnsrɛndi:tə] F return on assets

Vermögenswerte [fɛɐ'mø:gnsve:ɐtə] MPL assets

Verrechnungspreise [fɛɐ'rɛçnʊŋs,praizə] PL transfer pricing

verrenten [fɛɐ'rentn] VT annuitize

Verschiffung [fɛɐ'ʃɪfʊŋ] F shipment

Versicherer [fɛɐ'zɪçərɐ] M insurer

versichern [fɛɐ'zɪçɐn] VT insure

versichert [fɛɐ'zɪçɐt] ADJ insured

Versicherte(r) [fɛɐ'zɪçɐtɐ, vɛɐ'zɪçɐtə] MF insured

Versicherung [fɛɐ'zɪçərʊŋ] F insurance

Versicherungsbedingungen [fɛɐ'zɪçərʊŋsbə,dɪŋʊŋən] FPL terms and conditions

Versicherungsbestand [fɛɐ'zɪçərʊŋsbəʃtant] M portfolio

Versicherungsdeckung [fɛɐ'zɪçərʊŋs,dɛkʊŋ] F coverage

versicherungsfähig [fɛɐ'zɪçərʊŋsfɛ:ɪç] ADJ insurable

Versicherungsfähigkeit [fɛɐ'zɪçərʊŋsfɛ:ɪçkait] F insurability

Versicherungsmakler(in) [fɛɐ'zɪçərʊŋsma:klɐ, fɛɐ'zɪçərʊŋsma:klərɪn] M(F) insurance broker

Versicherungsmathematiker(in) [fɛɐ'zɪçərʊŋsmate,ma:tikɐ, fɛɐ'zɪçərʊŋsmate,ma:tikərɪn] M(F) actuary

Versicherungsnehmer(in) [fɛɐ'zɪçərʊŋsne:mɐ, fɛɐ'zɪçərʊŋsne:mərɪn] M(F) policyholder

Versicherungssumme [fɛɐ'zɪçərʊŋs,zʊmə] F sum assured

Versicherungsverkäufer(in) [fɛɐ'zɪçərʊŋsfɛɐ,kɔyfɐ, fɛɐ'zɪçərʊŋsfɛɐ,kɔyfərɪn] M(F) insurance salesman

Versicherungsvertreter(in) [fɛɐ'zɪçərʊŋsfɛɐtre:tɐ, fɛɐ'zɪçərʊŋsfɛɐtre:tərɪn] M(F) insurance agent

Versicherungsverzeichnis [fɛɐ'zɪçərʊŋsfɛɐ,tsaiçnɪs] NT bordereau, schedule

Versicherungswertberechnung [fɛɐ'zɪçərʊŋsve:ɐtbə,rɛçnʊŋ] F actual cash value basis

Versicherungswissenschaft [fɛɐ'zɪçərʊŋs,vɪsnʃaft] F actuarial science

Versicherungszweig [fɛɐ'zɪçərʊŋstsvaik] M insurance class

Versichungsgeber(in) [fɛɐ'zɪçərʊŋsge:bɐ, fɛɐ'zɪçərʊŋsge:bərɪn] M(F) underwriter

Versorgungskette [fɛɐ'zɔrgʊŋs,kɛtə] F supply chain

versprechend [fɛɐ'ʃprɛçnt] ADJ promissory

Verstorbene(r) [fɛɐ'ʃtɔrbənɐ, fɛɐ'ʃtɔrbənə] M(F) deceased

vertauschen [fɛɐ'tauʃn] VT transpose

Vertrag [fɛɐ'tra:k] M contract, treaty

Vertragsdauer [fɛɐ'tra:ksdauɐ] F policy term

verunglücken [fɛɐ'ʊngl'kn] VI crash

Verwaltungsaufwendungen [ɛɐ'valtʊŋs,|aʊfvɛndʊŋən] FPL administrative expenses

Verwaltungsrat [fɛɐ'valtʊŋsra:t] M board of directors

Verwässerung [fɛɐ'vɛsərʊŋ] F dilution

Vollmachtsaktionär(in) ['fɔlmaxts|aktsionɛ:ɐ, 'fɔlmaxts|aktsionɛ:ɐrɪn] M(F) proxy

Vorauszahlung [fo'raustsa:lʊŋ] F advance payment, payment in advance, prepayment

Vorruhestand ['fo:ɐ,ru:əʃtant] M early retirement

Vorsorge ['fo:ɐzɔrgə] F provision

vortragen ['fo:ɐtra:gn] VT bring over, carry forward, carry over

Vorzugsaktie ['fo:ɐtsu:ks,|aktsiə] F preferred stock

Währungskonvertierungsverlust M loss on translation

wandelbar ['vandlba:ɐ] ADJ convertible

Waren ['va:rən] FPL goods, merchandise

Warenkosten ['va:rənkɔstn] PL cost of goods available for sale

Warenskonto ['va:rənskɔnto] M trade discount

Wechsel ['vɛksl] M bill of exchange

Wechselkurs ['vɛkslkʊrs] M exchange rate

Weichwährung ['vaiçvɛ:rʊŋ] F soft currency

Wert ['ve:ɐt] M value

Wertminderung ['ve:ɐtmɪndərʊŋ] F depreciation, impairment

Wertpapier ['ve:ɐtpa,pi:ɐ] NT securities

Wertsteuer ['ve:ɐtʃtɔyɐ] F ad valorem

Wertverlust ['ve:ɐtfɐlʊst] M depreciation

Wertzuwachs ['ve:ɐttsu:vaks] M capital gain

wesentlich ['ve:zntlɪç] ADJ material

Wiederbeschaffungskostenbasis ['vi:dɐbə,ʃafʊŋs,kɔstnba:zis] F replacement cost basis

wiederkehrend ['vi:dɐke:rənt] ADJ recurring

Wirtschaftsprüfer(in) ['vɪrtʃafts,pry:fɐ, 'vɪrtʃafts,pry:fərɪn] M(F) certified public accountant

Witwe ['vɪtvə] F widow

Witwer ['vɪtvɐ] M widower

Wucher ['vu:xɐ] M usury

Zz

Zahler(in) ['tsa:lɐ, 'tsa:lərɪn] M(F) payor

Zahltag-Darlehen ['tsa:lta:k,da:le:ən] NT payday loan

Zahlungsaufforderung ['tsa:lʊŋs,|auffɔrdərʊŋ] F demand note

Zahlungsbedingungen ['tsa:lʊŋsbə,dɪŋʊŋən] FPL terms of payment

Zahlungsbilanz ['tsa:lʊŋsbi,lants] F balance of payments

Zahlungsempfänger(in) ['tsa:lʊŋs|ɛm,pfɛŋɐ, 'tsa:lʊŋs|ɛm,pfɛŋərɪn] M(F) payee

zahlungsfähig ['tsa:lʊŋsfɛ:ɪç] ADV afloat

Zahlungssperre ['tsa:lʊŋsʃpɛrə] F stop payment

Zahnpflege ['tsa:npfle:gə] F dental care

Zahnversicherung ['tsa:nfɛɐ,zɪçərʊŋ] F dental insurance

Zedent [tse'dɛnt] M cedant

zedieren [tse'di:rən] VT cede

zeichnen ['tsaiçnən] VT underwrite

Zeichnung ['tsaiçnʊŋ] F underwriting

Zeitrente ['tsaitrɛntə] F annuity

Zins ['tsɪns] M interest

Zinseszins ['tsɪnzəstzɪns] M compound interest

Zinssatz ['tsɪnszats] M interest rate

Zinsstrukturkurve [tsɪns'ʃtrʊktu:ɐ,kʊrvə] F yield curve

Zins-Swap ['tsɪnssvɔp] M interest rate swap

Zoll [tsɔl] M customs duty

Zufallsgewinn ['tsu:falsgə,vɪn] M windfall profits

zurückbehalten [tsu'rʏkbəhaltn] VT retain

zurückbleibend [tsu'rʏkblaibnt] ADJ residual

Zusammenbruch [tsu'zamənbrʊx] M bust

Zusatzbestimmung ['tsu:zatsbəʃtɪmʊŋ] F rider

Zuschlag ['tsu:ʃla:k] M loading

zuschlagen ['tsu:ʃla:gn] VT load

Zuschlagspreis ['tsu:ʃla:kprais] M strike price

zuteilen ['tsu:tailən] VT allocate

Zwangsvollstreckung ['tsvaŋsfɔl,ʃtrekʊŋ] F foreclosure

Zwischenergebnis ['tsvɪʃn|ɛɐge:pnɪs] NT interim results

Zwischenkonto ['tsvɪʃnkɔnto] NT suspense account

Abkürzungen, Sachbereichs- und Stilangaben

Abbreviations, field labels and style labels

Abkürzung	*abbr*	abbreviation
Akkusativ	*acc*	accusative
Adjektiv	ADJ, *adj*	adjective
attributives Adjektiv, Adjektiv in attributiver Stellung	ADJ ATTR	attributive adjective
prädikatives Adjektiv, Adjektiv in prädikativer Stellung	ADJ PRED	predicative adjective
Verwaltung	*Admin*	administration
Adverb	ADV, *adv*	adverb
Landwirtschaft	*Agr*	agriculture
Anatomie	*Anat*	anatomy
Archäologie	*Archeol*	arch(a)eology
Architektur	*Archit*	architecture
Artikel	*ART, art*	article
Kunst	*Art*	art
Astrologie	*Astrol*	astrology
Astronomie	*Astron*	astronomy
attributiv	ATTR, *attr*	attributive
österreichisch	*Aus*	Austrian
australisch	*Austral*	Australian
Kraftfahrzeuge	*Aut*	automobiles
Hilfsverb	AUX VB, *aux vb*	auxiliary verb
Luftfahrt	*Aviat*	aviation
Kindersprache	*baby-talk*	
biblisch	*Bibl*	biblical
Biologie	*Biol*	biology
Botanik	*Bot*	botany
britisch	*Brit*	British
Hoch- und Tiefbau	*Build*	building
Kartenspiel	*Cards*	
Chemie	*Chem*	chemistry
Schach	*Chess*	
Handel	*Comm*	commerce
Komparativ	*comp*	comparative
Computer	*Comput*	computers
Konjunktion	CONJ, *conj*	conjunction
Zusammenziehung	*contr*	contraction
Kochen	*Cook*	cooking
Kompositum, zusammengesetztes Wort	*cpd*	compound
zusammengesetzte Verben	*cpd vbs*	compound verbs
Dativ	*dat*	dative
altmodisch	*dated*	
Deutsche Demokratische Republik (1949–90)	*DDR*	German Democratic Republic (1949–90)
dekliniert	*decl*	declined
bestimmt	*def*	definite
bestimmter Artikel	DEF ART, *def art*	definite article
demonstrativ, hinweisend	*dem*	demonstrative
demonstratives Adjektiv	DEM ADJ	demonstrative adjective
demonstratives Adverb	DEM ADV	demonstrative adverb
Demonstrativpronomen, hinweisendes Fürwort	DEM PRON, *dem pron*	demonstrative pronoun
Dialekt	*dial*	dialect
Verkleinerung	*dim*	diminutive
Akkusativobjekt	*dir obj*	direct object
kirchlich	*Eccl*	ecclesiastical
Volkswirtschaft	*Econ*	economics
ostdeutsch	*E Ger*	East German
Elektrizität	*Elec*	electricity
betont	*emph*	emphatic
besonders	*esp*	especially
et cetera, und so weiter	*etc*	et cetera
etwas	*etw*	something
Euphemismus, Hüllwort	*euph*	euphemism
Femininum	*F, f*	feminine
Mode	*Fashion*	
figurativ, übertragen	*fig*	figurative
Finanzen	*Fin*	finance
Angeln/Fischen	*Fishing*	
Forstwirtschaft	*Forest*	forestry
förmlich	*form*	formal
Fußball	*Ftbl*	football
gehoben	*geh*	elevated
Genitiv	*gen*	genitive
Geografie	*Geog*	geography
Geologie	*Geol*	geology
Deutschland	*Ger*	Germany
Grammatik	*Gram*	grammar
Heraldik, Wappenkunde	*Her*	heraldry
Geschichte	*Hist*	history
Gartenbau	*Hort*	horticulture
scherzhaft	*hum*	humorous
Jagd	*Hunt*	hunting
Imperativ, Befehlsform	IMPER, *imper*	imperative
unpersönlich	IMPERS, *impers*	impersonal
Industrie	*Ind*	industry
unbestimmt	*indef*	indefinite
unbestimmter Artikel	INDEF ART, *indef art*	indefinite article
Indefinitpronomen, unbestimmtes Fürwort	INDEF PRON, *indef pron*	indefinite pronoun
Dativobjekt	*indir obj*	indirect object
umgangssprachlich	*inf*	informal
Infinitiv	*infin*	infinitive
nicht trennbar(es Verb)	INSEP, *insep*	inseparable
Versicherungen	*Insur*	insurance
Interjektion, Ausruf	*interj*	interjection
interrogativ, fragend	*interrog*	interrogative
interrogatives Adjektiv, Frageadjektiv	INTERROG ADJ	interrogative adjective
interrogatives Adverb, Frageadverb	INTERROG ADV	interrogative adverb
Interrogativpronomen, Fragepronomen	INTERROG PRON, *interrog pron*	interrogative pronoun
unveränderlich	*inv*	invariable
irisch	*Ir*	Irish
ironisch	*iro*	ironical
unregelmäßig	*irreg*	irregular
jemand, jemandes,	*jd, jds*	somebody, somebody's
jemandem, jemanden	*jdm, jdn*	somebody
Rechtspflege, Juristerei	*Jur*	law
Sprachwissenschaft	*Ling*	linguistics
wörtlich	*lit*	literal
literarisch	*liter*	literary